LONGMAN Pronunciation Dictionary

LONGMAN Pronunciation Dictionary

J C Wells

PEARSON
Longman

Pearson Education Limited
Edinburgh Gate
Harlow
Essex CM20 2JE
England
and Associated Companies throughout the World

Visit our website: http://www.longman.com/dictionaries

First edition 1990
Second edition 2000
Third edition 2008
Second impression 2008

ISBN 9781405881173 (cased edition + CD)
ISBN 9781405881180 (paperback edition + CD)

British Library Cataloguing-in-Publication Data
A catalogue record for this book is available from the British Library.

Designed by Richard Jervis
Illustrations by Tony Wilkins

Set in Times and Frutiger by Letterpart, UK
Printed in China
GCC/02

John Wells is Emeritus Professor of Phonetics at UCL in the University of London. He was born in Lancashire in 1939. Both at school and as an undergraduate at Cambridge he specialized in Classics, but switched to phonetics as a postgraduate at UCL, where he became a member of the academic staff (faculty) in 1962. He was elected a Fellow of the British Academy in 1996. Throughout his career he taught English phonetics, both to native speakers and to EFL learners, as well as general phonetics and phonology and the phonetics of various other languages.

Among the books he has written are the three-volume *Accents of English* and *English Intonation: an Introduction*. His first published work was an Esperanto dictionary.

Visit his website at **www.phon.ucl.ac.uk/home/wells**

CONTENTS

Spelling-to-sound guidelines (grapheme-to-phoneme rules) for each letter of the alphabet are distributed throughout LPD, each at the head of the entries beginning with that letter. (See also DOUBLE CONSONANT LETTERS; SHORT VOWEL, LONG VOWEL.)

Index to notes on pronunciation and phonetics

Type in blue indicates a Language Panel on that topic.

Acknowledgements

I am fortunate in the many people who have been ready to help me as I planned and prepared this dictionary. My colleagues in Phonetics and Linguistics at University College London, including several now retired, have patiently tolerated my obsessive questioning: among them I would mention especially the late Prof. A.C. Gimson, with whom I held many discussions on the problems of compiling and maintaining a pronouncing dictionary and on the changing nature of RP (Received Pronunciation).

For detailed advice on American English, I am grateful to Linda Shockey; for checking the Russian transcriptions, to John Baldwin and Sue Barry; for the Arabic, to Janaan Dawood; for the Hindi, to Neil and Saras Smith; and the Japanese, to Kazuhiko Matsuno and Noriko Hattori. Thanks, too, to Graham Pointon of the BBC Pronunciation Unit. Jill House and Dinah Jackson made various helpful suggestions in the course of proof-reading. Any remaining errors are naturally my own responsibility.

I am, of course, greatly indebted to successive editions of Daniel Jones's *English Pronouncing Dictionary* (Dent, 12th edn, 1963; 13th edn revised by A.C. Gimson, 1967; 14th edn, 1977; reprinted with revisions and supplement by S.M. Ramsaran 1988). EPD has set the standard against which other dictionaries must inevitably be judged. Other pronouncing dictionaries I have frequently consulted include *BBC Pronouncing Dictionary of British Names*, 2nd edn by G.E. Pointon (Oxford University Press, 1983); *NBC Handbook of Pronunciation*, 4th edn by Eugene Ehrlich and Raymond Hand, Jr. (Harper and Row, 1984); and *A Pronouncing Dictionary of American English* by J.S. Kenyon and T.A. Knott (Merriam, 1953). For American pronunciation I have also regularly explored *Webster's Ninth New Collegiate Dictionary* (Merriam-Webster, 1983), the *American Heritage Dictionary* (Houghton Mifflin, 1981), and *The Random House Dictionary*, 2nd edn (Random House, 1987). For Australian pronunciation I have used *The Macquarie Dictionary* (Macquarie Library, 1981), and for Indian words *Common Indian Words in English* by R.E. Hawkins (Delhi: Oxford University Press, 1984). I have taken certain medical terms from *Butterworths Medical Dictionary* (2nd edn Butterworth & Co, 1978). Not only for German, but also for information about proper names from a variety of foreign languages, *Duden Aussprachewörterbuch* by Max Mangold (2nd edn, Bibliographisches Institut Mannheim, 1974) has proved invaluable. For French I have drawn particularly on *Dictionnaire de la prononciation* by Alain Lerond (Larousse, 1980); for Italian on *Dizionario d'ortografia e di pronunzia* by Migliorini, Tagliavini & Fiorelli (ERI–Edizioni RAI, 1969). For the entries on affixes and the spelling-to-sound boxes I have taken advantage of ideas contained in *The Groundwork of English Stress* by Roger Kingdon (Longman, 1958), *English Word-Stress* by Erik Fudge (Allen & Unwin, 1984), *Rules of Pronunciation for the English Language* by Axel Wijk (Oxford University Press, 1966), and a number of works by Lionel Guierre, including *Drills in English Stress-Patterns* (4th edn Paris: Armand Colin–Longman, 1984).

Nearly three hundred native speakers of British English took the time and trouble to answer a detailed questionnaire about preferences in the pronunciation of particular words (see 1.7 below, Opinion polls). Thanks to all of them: their chief reward is to have their views recorded in the polling figures presented in this book.

My particular thanks go to Susan Maingay and Stephen Crowdy of Longman Dictionaries, who have been consistently supportive and cooperative, everything a publisher should be; and to Clare Fletcher, who made numerous suggestions for clearer or more felicitous wording and presentation.

John Wells

Note to the second edition

My thanks for helpful suggestions go to the many reviewers and friendly critics of the first edition of the *Longman Pronunciation Dictionary* (LPD), and in particular to Jack Windsor Lewis.

Since the first appearance of LPD there have been new editions of many of the works of reference listed above. I have made particular use of the invaluable Duden *Aussprachewörterbuch* (3rd edn, 1990) and – for Australian names – of *The Macquarie Dictionary* (2nd edn, Macquarie University NSW, 1991).

A much fuller treatment of English spelling-to-sound rules is now available in *A Survey of English Spelling* by Edward Carney (Routledge, 1994).

I have been stimulated by the radical revisions made in the 15th edition of the Daniel Jones *English Pronouncing Dictionary*, now edited by Peter Roach and James Hartman (Cambridge University Press, 1997).

For advice on Chinese names I am indebted to Siew-Yue Killingley and John Maidment, for Cantonese to Cheung Kwan-Hin, for Arabic to Bruce Ingham, and for further information on Japanese to Mitsuhiro Nakamura.

I am grateful to Rebecca Dauer for checking the 5000 new entries from the point of view of American English. Particular thanks also to my graduate student Yuko Shitara for allowing me to include the findings of her 1993 AmE pronunciation preference survey.

Thanks are due to the volunteers who participated in the 1998 pronunciation preference poll – not 275 this time, but over 1900 – to Jonathan Wadman for turning questionnaire responses into computer files, and to my colleague Andy Faulkner for help with processing the data.

Longman have continued to be supportive in every way. Thanks particularly to Adam Gadsby, Emma Campbell, Emma Williams, Dinah Jackson and Sheila Dallas; and to Della Summers who commissioned both the first edition of this dictionary and this current revision.

John Wells
London, March 1999

Note to the third edition

Renewed thanks to Jack Windsor Lewis for helpful comments. Thanks also to Tommaso Francesco Borri for a large number of suggestions concerning pronunciations in Italian and other foreign languages; to Cheung Kwan-hin for help with the transcription of Chinese (Mandarin) and Cantonese words; to Kayoko Yanagisawa for help with new Japanese entries; to Ho-young Lee and Joe-Eun Kim for Korean; for other languages to the BBC Pronunciation Unit and to other colleagues and correspondents too many to name; and to Dinah Jackson for help with proof reading.

Bert Vaux kindly allowed me to use the results of his 2002 polling figures for AmE. Thanks also to all who took part in the new 2007 BrE poll, and to Longman for organizing it.

As my publishers, Pearson Education have given every support. Thanks particularly to Michael Mayor, Editorial Director of the Dictionaries Section, and to my editors, Paola Rocchetti (who also organized the recording sessions) and Nicky Thompson. Allan Ørsnes converted everything to XML/Unicode, and Denise McKeough helped me in the early stages of using the XML editor. Susan Maingay wrote the exercises for the CD-ROM.

John Wells
London, October 2007

Foreword to the third edition

In this edition over 3000 new headwords have been added. They include:

- terms relating to the internet: **Bebo**, **blogging**, **chatroom**, **digicam**, **eBay**, **Google**, **iPod**, **phish**, **podcast**, **unsubscribe**, **Wi-Fi**, **Wikipedia**
- other words that have come into use, or into wider use, since the previous edition: **Asbo**, **Asperger's**, **Botox**, **burqa**, **chav**, **fashionista**, **hijab**, **latte**, **qi**
- proper names previously missing: **al-Qaeda**, **Benfica**, **Beyoncé**, **Condoleezza**, **Federer**, **Lidl**, **Merkel**, **Rowling**, **Sentamu**, **Titchmarsh**
- and many other assorted categories.

This edition is the first to have an accompanying CD-ROM: the Longman Pronunciation Coach. On it you will find hundreds of interactive practice exercises, with help and feedback from me, in addition to the complete text of the *Longman Pronunciation Dictionary* with all words and phrases spoken aloud in both British and American English. Learners whose own language is a tone language are reminded that although the headwords are all spoken here with a falling nuclear tone, stress in English words may, depending on intonation, alternatively involve a rising or falling-rising tone or, if not nuclear, a level high or low tone.

Entries for words containing **be-**, **de-**, **e-**, **pre-**, **re-** and **se-** (also **rede-**, **unre-** etc.) have been simplified. When unstressed, these prefixes are now shown with i. This reflects the fact that, like words ending in i, such as **happy**, they may be pronounced indifferently with ɪ or iː. (These prefixes also have variants with ə, shown explicitly.)

Following research into contemporary RP by Bente Hannisdal, I have removed the § sign from forms with tʃuː and dʒuː deriving from traditional tjuː and djuː.

In view of the declining use in AmE of hw in words with the spelling **wh-**, I have changed the relevant recommendation for those learning AmE and made the corresponding change in the alphabetic entries.

As in previous editions, tone numbers in transcriptions of tone languages are put at the *beginning* of the relevant syllable (contrary to practice in some other circles). This preserves the analogy with stress marks in non-tone languages.

It is sometimes difficult to decide on stress-marking for compound adjectives such as **God-given**, **hard-drinking**, **long-term**. In general I have shown them as having end-stress, with a stress-shift mark. But since they usually precede a noun, itself likely to be stressed, in practice they undergo stress shift much more often than not. There is also a problem in deciding whether to show words such as **one-size-fits-all**, **MRSA** with four stresses or (as they are usually pronounced) just with two; and likewise whether to show three or two stresses in words such as **nondenominational**.

John Wells

London, October 2007

A quick guide to the dictionary

British and American pronunciations

Where only one pronunciation is given this means that the word has a similar pronunciation in both British and American English.

The symbol ‖ is used to introduce American English (AmE) pronunciations when these are different from British English (BrE) forms. Sometimes, when the AmE pronunciation is different in only one part of a word, the dictionary shows only this part.

bad bæd
pronunciation used in both BrE and AmE

batter ˈbæt ə ‖ ˈbæţ ᵊr
BrE AmE

bender ˈbend ə ‖ -ᵊr **~s** z
the AmE pronunciation is ˈbend ᵊr

Main pronunciations and alternatives

All main pronunciations (recommended as models for learners of English) are shown in bold type. If there are alternative pronunciations, these are shown in ordinary black type.

Where only one pronunciation is given for the main pronunciation and for the alternative, this means that both have a similar pronunciation in BrE and AmE.

Sometimes when an alternative pronunciation is different only in one part of a word, the *Longman Pronunciation Dictionary* (LPD) shows only this part.

Pronunciations which are widespread among educated speakers of BrE but which are not, however, considered to belong to RP (Received Pronunciation) are marked with the symbol §.

LPD also includes pronunciations which are generally considered to be incorrect.

main BrE — main AmE
baroque bə ˈrɒk bæ-, -ˈrəʊk ‖ -ˈroʊk -ˈrɑːk
alternative BrE — alternative AmE

bankrupt ˈbæŋk rʌpt -rəpt
pronunciation and alternative both used in BrE and AmE

ballroom ˈbɔːl ruːm -rʊm ‖ ˈbɑːl-
alternative used only in AmE

bases *pl of* **basis** ˈbeɪs iːz
an alternative pronunciation is ˈbeɪs əz

bath *n* bɑːθ §bæθ ‖ bæθ **baths** bɑːðz §bɑːθs,
the RP form is bɑːθ; in England bæθ is a localized northern form, though it is standard in AmE

grievous ˈgriːv əs ⚠ˈgriːv i̯əs **~ly** li **~ness** nəs nɪs
be careful not to use this pronunciation

Pronunciations of foreign words

For words belonging to foreign languages, which are in use in English, LPD shows both their anglicized pronunciations and their pronunciations in the language of origin.

pronunciation in BrE and AmE
Benz benz —*Ger* [bɛnts]
original German pronunciation

Inflected and derived forms

Entries include information about the pronunciation of the different forms of headword (plurals, past tense forms, etc.). Sometimes the different forms are shown in full.

Sometimes just the endings are shown.

Sometimes an ending is added not to the complete word but to just part of it. The symbol | is used to show exactly which part is concerned.

blub blʌb **blubbed** blʌbd **blubbing** 'blʌb ɪŋ **blubs** blʌbz

building 'bɪld ɪŋ **~s** z **'building block**; **'building so,ciety**

the plural form **buildings** is pronounced 'bɪld ɪŋz

beef|y 'bi:f |i **~ier** i‿ə ‖ i‿ᵊr **~iest** i‿ɪst i‿əst

beef + ier = 'bi:fi‿ə   beef + iest = 'bi:fi‿ɪst

Stress marks

Words of more than one syllable are marked for stress. LPD recognizes two types of stress. (See the panel on 'Stress', p.783.)

When alternative pronunciations are different only in the way in which they are stressed, the full pronunciation is not repeated but small blocks (• •) are used to represent the syllables of the word.

secondary stress   primary stress

interchangeability ,ɪnt ə ,tʃeɪndʒ ə 'bɪl ət i -ɪt i ‖ ,ɪnṭ ᵊr ,tʃeɪndʒ ə 'bɪl əṭ i

backslid|e 'bæk slaɪd ,·'· **~er/s** ə/z ‖ ᵊr/z **~ing** ɪŋ

an alternative stress pattern is ,bæk 'slaɪd

Stress shift

Some words have different stress patterns according to whether they are being used alone or directly before a noun. (See the panel on 'Stress shift', p.784.) The symbol ◀ is used to show words which can behave in this way.

academic ,æk ə 'dem ɪk ◀ **~al/s** ᵊl/z **~ally** ᵊl‿i **~s** s

Stress in compounds

The pronunciation of compound words can often be derived from their component parts. Stress patterns, however, are not always easy to predict and so important compounds and their patterns are listed after the main entry.

bee bi: **bees, bee's** bi:z **,bee's 'knees**; **'bee sting**

compounds showing stress pattern

Continued ►

Special notes

The dictionary makes use of some special symbols to help you to arrive at the right pronunciation.

! This symbol is a warning that the pronunciation is quite different from what the spelling might lead you to expect!

bury 'ber i *(! = berry)* **buried** 'ber id **buries** 'ber iz **burying** 'ber i‿ɪŋ

* This symbol is a warning that the British and American pronunciations are different in an important and unpredictable way.

baton 'bæt ɒn -ᵊn ‖ bə 'tɑːn *(*)—See also phrases with this word* **~s** z

= This symbol draws attention to another word which has exactly the same pronunciation as the word looked up.

blew bluː *(= blue)*

→ This symbol shows that an alternative pronunciation is the result of a general rule which affects not just this word but a whole range of words and phrases in the language.

bridegroom 'braɪd gruːm →'braɪg-, -grʊm **~s** z

(See the panel on 'Assimilation', p.51.)

For more detailed information see 'Index to notes on pronunciation and phonetics', p.vii, and 'Symbols', p.xxxi.

1 Introduction

This is a specialist dictionary of **pronunciation**. It offers the user three kinds of information about English pronunciation that are not available in a general dictionary: information on **variants**, on **inflected** and **derived** forms, and on **proper names**. It covers both British and American English.

1.1 Variants Many English words have a number of different possible pronunciations. Some of the users of LPD will be teachers and learners of EFL/ESL (English as a foreign or second language), and will look for advice on how to pronounce a given word. For them one **main pronunciation**, printed in bold, is given at each entry. This is the form recommended for EFL purposes. (See the CITATION FORM panel for how to unpack the abbreviatory conventions.) If the British English (BrE) and American English (AmE) recommended forms are different from one another, then both are given in bold. Other users of LPD, especially those who are native speakers of English, will be interested not only to see what form is recommended but also what **variants** are recognized. Where pronunciations other than the main one are in common educated use, they too are included, but as **secondary pronunciations**, printed in ordinary black type. Some pronunciations are controversial, and so as evidence for the selection of a main pronunciation, between 200 and 300 entries include a report of one or more **opinion polls** of pronunciation preferences (see 1.7 below).

The wide coverage of variants makes LPD suitable for use not only in speech production but also in speech recognition: not only for human speakers of English but also for computer applications.

1.2 Inflected and derived forms As well as the uninflected forms of words, LPD systematically includes the plurals of nouns (and possessives if they are pronounced differently from plurals), the third person singular present tense (*s*-forms), present participles (*ing*-forms), past tenses and past participles (*ed*-forms) of verbs, the comparatives and superlatives of adjectives, and derivatives such as those in *-ly, -able, -er, -less, -ness, -ship*. Where the base form has only one syllable, pronunciations for inflected forms are given in full; otherwise they are usually cut back.

1.3 Proper names LPD includes all the more commonly encountered proper names – **personal** names (first names, Christian names), **family** names (surnames, last names), names of **mythical** and **literary** characters, **place** names, and **commercial** names (particularly names of products). British names are covered as thoroughly as possible within the space available, while American, Irish and Australian ones have not been neglected. Many names from other languages are also included, in most cases with their pronunciation in the language of origin as well as in an anglicized form.

1.4 Compounds and phrases As well as all the above, LPD also includes a good selection of **compounds and phrases**, showing their stress patterns. Some of these illustrate the effect of the highly productive principle of STRESS SHIFT which affects many longer English words. The effects of affixes on word stress are discussed in the special entries devoted to affixes and word endings.

1.5 Spelling **English spelling** is notorious for its shortcomings. Knowing the orthography of a word does not enable one to predict its pronunciation with any confidence. Nevertheless, certain general principles do govern the relationship between spelling and sound (grapheme and phoneme), even though they may be subject to exceptions and uncertainties. Although many handbooks of English pronunciation ignore them entirely, on the implicit grounds that these rules are so chaotic that it is better to learn the pronunciation of each new word separately, it nevertheless seemed helpful for LPD to offer the user something rather than nothing. Accordingly, guidelines designed to be useful particularly to the EFL learner are given at each letter of the alphabet.

1.6 Homophones Learners and native speakers alike can reinforce their grasp of the distinction between sound and spelling by noting **homophones** (= words distinct in spelling but pronounced identically). LPD points them out in notes such as

bear (= *bare*) **write** (= *right*)

1.7 Opinion polls For many words of uncertain pronunciation, LPD reports the preferences expressed in five opinion polls:

- a postal opinion poll carried out by the author in 1988 among a panel of 275 native speakers of BrE from throughout Britain;
- a postal opinion poll carried out by Yuko Shitara in 1993 among a panel of 400 native speakers of AmE from throughout the United States;
- an opinion poll carried out by the author in 1998 among a panel of 1932 native speakers of BrE from throughout Britain, some of whom answered by postal questionnaire but others by e-mail or interactively online.
- an on-line dialect survey conducted by Prof. Bert Vaux, then of Harvard University, among a panel of self-selected respondents from the United States in 1999-2002; most questions received about 11,000 answers. Details of the respondents' ages are not available.
- an online poll of BrE conducted by Pearson Education and myself in April-June 2007.

Polling figures in the text are no longer identified by year. Further details of the polls, and of which words were in which poll, can be found on my UCL website. **www.phon.ucl.ac.uk/home/wells**

2 Types of pronunciation recorded

2.1 British pronunciation The model of British English pronunciation recorded in LPD is a modernized version of the type known as **Received Pronunciation**, or **RP**.

In England and Wales, RP is widely regarded as a model for correct pronunciation, particularly for educated formal speech. It is what was traditionally used by BBC news readers – hence the alternative name **BBC pronunciation**, although now that the BBC admits regional accents among its announcers this name has become less appropriate. It is the usual standard in teaching English as a foreign language, in all countries where the model is BrE rather than AmE.

RP itself inevitably changes as the years pass. There is also a measure of diversity within it. Furthermore, the democratization undergone by English society during the second half of the twentieth century means that it is nowadays necessary to define RP in a rather broader way than was once customary. LPD includes a number of pronunciations that diverge from traditional, 'classical' RP. The 'RP' transcriptions shown in LPD in fact cover very much more than a narrowly defined RP.

2.2 Other varieties of British English British Received Pronunciation (RP) is not **localized** (= not associated with any particular city or region). It is to be heard in all parts of the country from those with the appropriate social or educational background. On the other hand, most people do have some degree of local colouring in their speech.

To a large extent, this is manifested in details of phonetic realization (use of particular allophones, for example a glottal rather than an alveolar plosive for t in certain positions – see PHONEME AND ALLOPHONE and GLOTTAL STOP) rather than in any substantial deviation from the RP system (= the inventory of vowel and consonant phonemes). Hence it is automatically covered by the transcription used in LPD.

Pronunciations widespread in England among educated speakers, but which are nevertheless judged to fall outside RP, are marked with the special sign §. Since LPD aims to portray the current state of the English language, we think it important not to ignore them, as other dictionaries do.

one	wʌn §wɒn	The general form is wʌn; wɒn is a localized northern form.
last	lɑːst §læst	The RP form is lɑːst. In England læst is a localized northern form (though it is standard in AmE).

Many other BrE 'educated non-RP' forms are not mentioned explicitly.

Speech with local features of the southeast of England is often referred to as **Estuary English**. This involves, in particular,

- frequent use of ʔ for syllable-final t (see GLOTTAL STOP).
- vocalization of l, i.e. the use of a vowel or semivowel of the o type in place of a dark l, thus **milk** mɪok, **table** ˈteɪb o.
- use of tʃ and dʒ in place of tj and dj, thus **tune** tʃuːn, **reduce** rɪ ˈdʒuːs (=yod coalescence, see ASSIMILATION).

Other widespread but local pronunciation characteristics from various parts of the British Isles include the following:

- ŋg for ŋ at the end of a stem: for example, **sing** sɪŋ is also regionally sɪŋg, and **singer** ˈsɪŋ ə is also regionally ˈsɪŋ gə.
- ɔə for ɔː in certain words: for example, **four** fɔː (also regionally, and formerly in RP, fɔə).
- use of vowel qualities closer to iː, uː than to ɪə, ʊə in words such as **periodic**, **purity**.
- ʌ and ə not distinguished in quality, both being like RP ə.
- r corresponding to spelling *r* before a consonant sound or at the end of a word: for example, **cart** kɑːt, regionally also kɑːrt (as in AmE).
- many other forms characteristic of Scottish or Irish pronunciation.

These and other pronunciation features associated with regional accents may often be inferred from LPD transcriptions. For example, broad local accents of the north of England have ʊ wherever LPD writes ʌ – for example **love** lʌv, regionally also lʊv. In London and increasingly elsewhere, some people replace θ and ð with f and v respectively, at least in casual speech.

For a few words, LPD includes a pronunciation variant that is not considered correct. These variants are included because of the fact that they are in widespread use. They are marked with the special sign ⚠.

grievous ˈgriːv əs ⚠ ˈgriːv i‿əs

Australian pronunciation is phonemically similar to RP, though with certain important differences. See AUSTRALIAN ENGLISH. For detailed descriptions of many varieties of native English pronunciation throughout the world, see the author's *Accents of English* (three volumes and cassette, Cambridge University Press, 1982).

2.3 American pronunciation The AmE pronunciations shown in LPD are those appropriate to the variety (accent) known as **General American**. This is what is spoken by the majority of Americans, namely those who do not have a noticeable eastern or southern accent. It is the appropriate model for EFL learners who wish to speak AmE rather than BrE.

American pronunciation is shown in LPD entries after the mark ‖. If an entry contains no ‖, then the American pronunciation is the same as the British. If the pronunciation after ‖ is *not* in colour, then the main AmE pronunciation is the same as in BrE.

docile	ˈdəʊs aɪᵊl ‖ ˈdɑːsᵊl	The AmE pronunciation is ˈdɑːsᵊl.
crown	kraʊn	The AmE pronunciation is kraʊn, the same as in BrE.
tomato	tə ˈmɑːt əʊ ‖ -meɪṭ oʊ	The AmE pronunciation is tə ˈmeɪṭ oʊ.
ability	ə ˈbɪl ət i ‖ -əṭ i	The AmE pronunciation is ə ˈbɪl əṭ i.
tritium	ˈtrɪt i‿əm ‖ ˈtrɪṭ- ˈtrɪʃ-	The AmE pronunciation is usually ˈtrɪṭ i‿əm, less commonly ˈtrɪʃ i‿əm
thorax	ˈθɔːr æks ‖ ˈθoʊr-	The AmE pronunciation is usually ˈθɔːr æks, as in BrE. Less commonly it is ˈθoʊr æks.

The mark (*), sparingly used, draws attention to cases where the BrE (RP) and AmE pronunciations differ in unpredictable or unexpected ways.

GenAm is not as tightly codified for EFL purposes as RP. Accordingly, some of the conventions followed in LPD need to be discussed.

There is considerable variability in GenAm vowels in the open back area. LPD follows tradition in continuing to distinguish the vowel of **lot** lɑːt from that of **thought** θɔːt. (Note, though, that books by American scholars generally do not use length marks.) However, fewer and fewer Americans distinguish these two vowel sounds from one another; so a secondary AmE pronunciation with ɑː is given for all words having ɔː (except before r).

LPD distinguishes between the vowels ʌ and ə, although in AmE they can generally be regarded as allophones of the same phoneme, and for some speakers are more or less identical phonetically too. Thus where LPD writes **above** ə ˈbʌv some speakers pronounce ə ˈbəv. Similarly LPD distinguishes between ɜ˞ː and ᵊr, as in **further** ˈfɜ˞ːð ᵊr, although many speakers have a similar syllabic [r] in both syllables. All these qualities arguably represent the same phoneme ə, with or without a following r.

Where RP has ɜː followed by a vowel sound, most Americans use ɜ˞ː, and that is what is shown in LPD entries: **courage** ˈkʌr ɪdʒ ‖ ˈkɜ˞ː-. It should be noted, however, that there are other Americans who use ʌr, as in RP.

AmE pronunciations not explicitly shown in LPD include the use of ɪ rather than e before a nasal, as when **ten** is pronounced tɪn. Although this is typically a 'southern' variant, it can also be heard elsewhere, for example in California. Another southwestern pronunciation not shown is the use of iː rather than ɪ before the velar nasal, as when **thing** is pronounced θiːŋ.

For most Americans ə and ɪ are not distinct as weak vowels (so that **rabbit** rhymes with **abbot**). For AmE LPD follows the rule of showing ɪ before palato-alveolar and velar consonants (ʃ, tʃ, dʒ, k, g, ŋ), but ə elsewhere. Where no separate indication is given for AmE, but both ɪ and ə variants are shown for an entry, it may be assumed that AmE prefers ɪ or ə according to this rule. The actual quality used by Americans for ə varies considerably, being typically more ɪ-like when followed by a consonant but more ʌ-like when at the end of a word.

3 The English phonemic system and its notation

3.1 Vowels and diphthongs The English vowels and diphthongs are conveniently considered in five groups (A, B, C, D, E below). There are certain differences between RP and GenAm, both in realization (vowel quality) and in the system (vowel inventory).

The **short** vowels are:

A

ɪ kit, bid
e dress, bed
æ trap, bad
ɒ (RP) lot, odd
ʌ strut, bud
ʊ foot, good

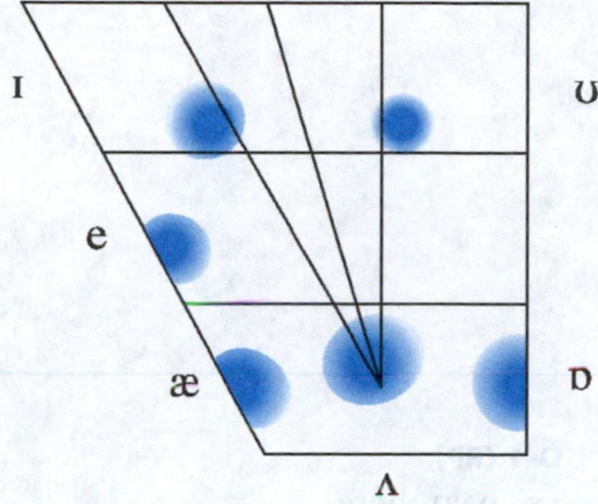

The **long vowels** and **diphthongs** are:

B

iː fleece, see
eɪ face, day
aɪ price, high
ɔɪ choice, boy

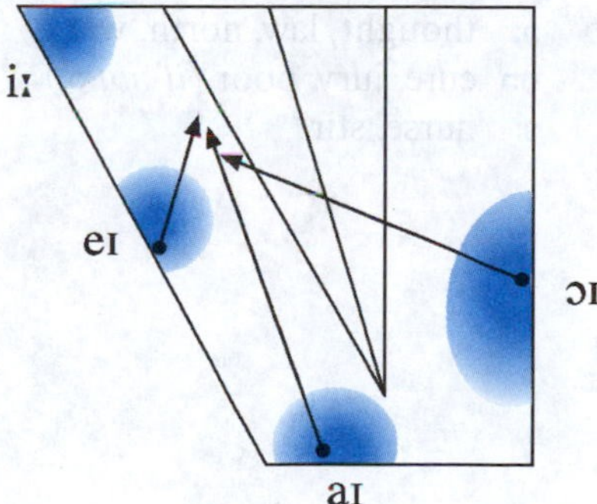

C-1 (RP)

uː goose, two
əʊ goat, show
aʊ mouth, now
ɒʊ *near-RP variant in* cold *(see 3.6)*

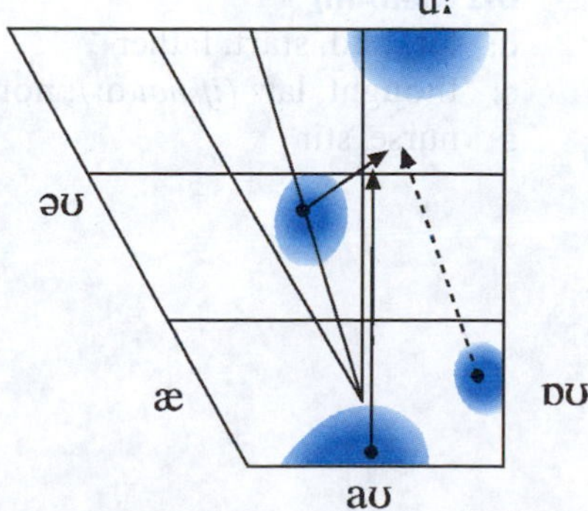

C-2 (GenAm)

uː goose, two

oʊ goat, show

aʊ mouth, now

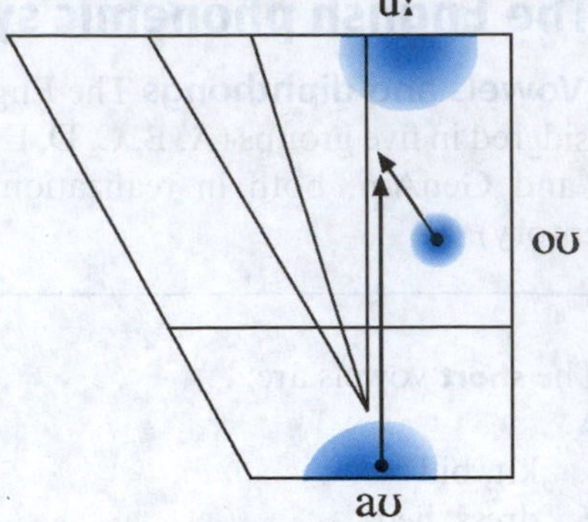

D-1 (RP)

ɪə near, here

eə square, fair

ɑː start, father

ɔː thought, law, north, war

ʊə cure, jury, poor *(if not* ɔː*)*

ɜː nurse, stir

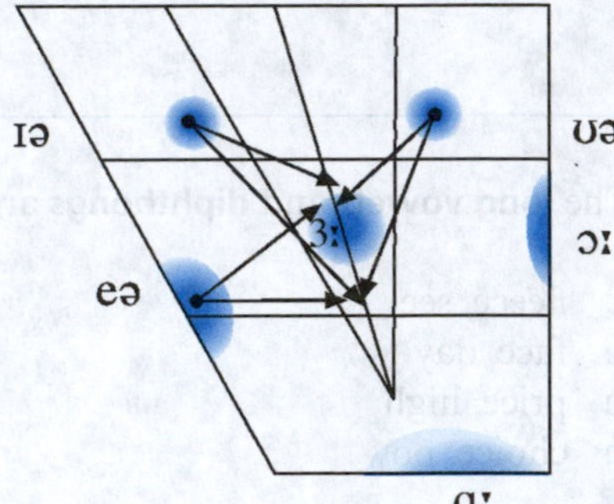

D-2 (GenAm)

ɑː lot, odd, start, father

ɔː thought, law *(if not* ɑː*)*, north, war

ɜ˞ː nurse, stir

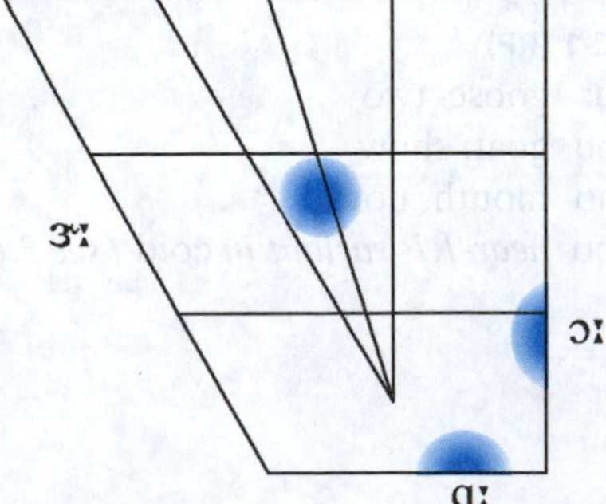

The **weak** vowels are:

E

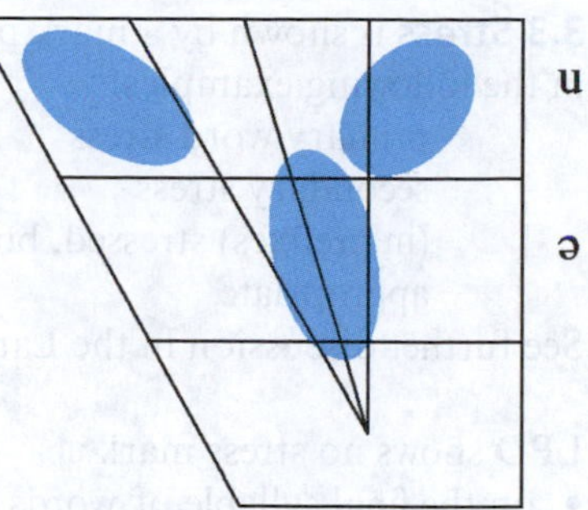

i (happ)y, (rad)i(ation), (glor)i(ous)
ə a(bout), (comm)a, (comm)o(n)
u (infl)u(ence), (sit)u(ation), (biv)ou(ac)

– although the weak vowel system also includes

ɪ i(ntend), (rabb)i(t) *(if not* ə*)*
ʊ (stim)u(lus), (ed)u(cate) *(if not* ə *or* u*)*

and the syllabic consonants (see below).
See WEAK VOWELS.

3.2 Consonants The English consonants are p, b, t, d, k, g, tʃ, dʒ, f, v, θ, ð, s, z, ʃ, ʒ, h, r, l, j, w, m, n, ŋ. For their classification by voicing, place, and manner, see the articles on VOICED AND VOICELESS and ARTICULATION.

The symbols p, b, t, d, k, f, v, h, r, l, w, m, n stand for the English consonant sounds usually so spelled. Keywords for the remaining consonant sounds are as follows:

tʃ	church	dʒ	judge
θ	thin, author, path	ð	this, other, smooth
s	cease, sister	z	zone, roses
ʃ	ship, ocean	ʒ	vision
j	yet	ŋ	sing, long, thanks
g	go, give, gag		

The GenAm transcriptions also make use of the symbol ţ, representing the often voiced alveolar tap used for t in certain positions, as in **atom, better**: see T-VOICING.

In words and names from foreign languages some speakers also use x (Scots *ch*, voiceless velar fricative) and ɬ (Welsh *ll*, voiceless alveolar lateral fricative), which can thus to some extent be considered marginal members of the English consonant system.

As explained at OPTIONAL SOUNDS, symbols written raised denote sounds that are sometimes optionally inserted. Likely syllabic consonants are shown in this way, since a syllabic consonant always has an optional variant involving ə and a non-syllabic consonant:

ᵊl (midd)le, (tot)al
ᵊn (sudd)en(ly), (serv)an(t)
ᵊr *AmE* (fath)er, (stand)ar(d).

Symbols written in *italics* denote sounds sometimes omitted. See OPTIONAL SOUNDS.

hɪn*d*ʒ hinge

3.3 Stress is shown by a mark placed at the beginning of the syllable in question, as in the following examples:

ˈ	primary word stress	reˈMEMber
ˌ	secondary stress	ˌACaˈDEMic; ˈBUTter ˌFINgers
¦	(in prefixes) stressed, but level undefined: primary or secondary as appropriate.	

See further discussion in the Language Panel on STRESS.

LPD shows no stress mark

- on the final syllable of words such as **celebrate** ˈsel ə breɪt
- on the monosyllabic second element of an early-stressed compound or phrase, for example **selling price** ˈsel ɪŋ praɪs
- on entries that are words of one syllable, for example **time** taɪm.

Stress is always relative; LPD marks it only in branching structures.

3.4 Transcription systems There are various systems of transcription in use for English, including several which conform to the principles of the International Phonetic Alphabet (IPA). The differences between them are in many cases trivial. The system used in LPD conforms to the current de facto standard.

The user's attention is drawn to the abbreviatory conventions explained in the panel on CITATION FORM. Other dictionaries use other abbreviatory conventions and may differ, for example, in how (if at all) syllable divisions are shown. Early editions of Jones's *English Pronouncing Dictionary* (before 1977) used a typographically simpler, 'broad' transcription system for RP. In some parts of the world this system still persists. It involves

- i, ɔ, u for the short vowels LPD writes as ɪ, ɒ, ʊ;
- ei, ou, ai, au, ɔi, iə, ɛə, uə for the diphthongs LPD writes as eɪ, əʊ, aɪ, aʊ, ɔɪ, ɪə, eə, ʊə;
- əː for the long vowel LPD writes as ɜː.

The current, 17th edition of EPD (CUP, 2006) writes

- ɚ corresponding to LPD's ᵊr.

For AmE, authors in the IPA tradition often use the Kenyon and Knott system, which involves

- no length marks
- ɛ for the vowel which LPD writes as e
- e, o for the normally diphthongal vowels LPD writes as eɪ, oʊ
- ɚ corresponding to LPD's ᵊr.

A different AmE tradition, that of Trager and Smith, involves

- š, ž, č, ǰ for the IPA ʃ, ʒ, tʃ, dʒ
- the representation of long vowels and diphthongs as sequences such as iy, ow, ɔh (= LPD iː, oʊ, ɔː)
- acute and grave marks over vowels (é, è) to show stress, corresponding to the IPA marks ˈ, ˌ before the syllable.

3.5 Syllabification Syllable divisions are shown in LPD by spacing. This makes the transcriptions of long words easier to read and makes certain details of pronunciation more explicit.

The rhythm of a word or phrase is determined by the number and nature of the syllables it contains. Thus syllables 'carry' stress and intonation. (This is obviously particularly important for poetry and singing.) The division of a word into syllables is its **syllabification**.

The question of syllabification in English is controversial: different phoneticians hold very different views about it. The syllabification principles adopted in LPD are those which most helpfully predict the **distribution of allophones** (see PHONEME AND ALLOPHONE).

LPD assumes that there is a syllable boundary wherever there is a boundary between the elements of a compound: thus **playtime** is ˈpleɪ taɪm. It is also assumed that every word consists of whole syllables, and that a consonant cannot belong to two syllables at once. Thus **city** must be either ˈsɪt i or ˈsɪ ti – the t cannot be in both syllables. (In fact it must be the first, ˈsɪt i, because the t is pronounced in a way typical of final t: not aspirated like initial plosives, but on the contrary potentially subject to T-VOICING and glottalling, see GLOTTAL STOP.)

It is generally agreed that phonetic syllable divisions must as far as possible avoid creating consonant clusters which are not found at the edges of words. This is the **phonotactic** constraint. Thus **windy** might be ˈwɪn di or ˈwɪnd i, but it could not be ˈwɪ ndi (because English words cannot begin with nd). LPD takes the view that the syllabification of this word actually parallels its morphology: **wind+y**, ˈwɪnd i. For the same reason, **language** must be ˈlæŋ gwɪdʒ, not ˈlæŋg wɪdʒ or ˈlæ ŋgwɪdʒ.

The principle that LPD adopts is that **consonants are syllabified with whichever of the two adjacent vowels is more strongly stressed**. If they are both unstressed, it goes with the leftward one. A **weak** vowel counts as 'less stressed' than an unstressed strong one.

In general, this principle is subject to the phonotactic constraint. However, there are some cases where correct prediction of allophones requires us to override it.

(i) Certain unstressed syllables end in a strong short vowel, even though words cannot. In **nostalgia** the t is unaspirated (as in **stack** stæk, not as in **tack** tæk), so the syllabification is (BrE) nɒ ˈstældʒ ə.

(ii) r can end a syllable, even though in BrE it cannot end a word pronounced in isolation. The r in **starry** ˈstɑːr i is like the r in **star is**, and different from the more forceful r in **star runner**. Likewise, ʒ can end a syllable: **vision** ˈvɪʒ ᵊn.

(iii) Within a morpheme, tr and dr are not split. If **petrol** were ˈpet rəl, as the phonotactic constraint leads us to expect (since English words do not end in tr), its t would likely be glottal and its r voiced (as in **rat-race** ˈræt reɪs). In fact, the tr in this word is pronounced as a voiceless affricate; so LPD syllabifies it ˈpetr əl.

For further discussion, please see the author's article 'Syllabification and allophony' in Ramsaran, S. (ed.), 1990, *Studies in the pronunciation of English*, London: Edward Arnold.

3.6 Phonological processes in speech The mark → precedes secondary pronunciations that can be regarded as derived by automatic rule from the main pronunciation. Examples of processes covered by such a rule include ASSIMILATION and the use of the special allophone ɒʊ before l in some varieties of (near-)RP:

include ɪn ˈkluːd →ɪŋ ˈkluːd
cold kəʊld → kɒʊld

For some speakers, a form shown with → may correspond to the way a word is stored in the mental lexicon, whereas for others the same form may be derived by phonological rule.

The mark → is not applied to phrases exemplifying STRESS SHIFT, since stress shift is shown by the symbol ◂.

In general, LPD shows results only of processes operating within the word, independently of the phonetic context afforded by surrounding words. Hence, for example, it does not show the optional variant of **ribbon** derived by perseverative ASSIMILATION (ˈrɪb m), since this form is restricted to cases where the following word does not begin with a vowel. But the corresponding variant of **vacant** (ˈveɪk ŋt) is included, since its occurrence is context-free.

4 Foreign languages

4.1 Names from foreign languages can either be pronounced in a way that imitates the foreign language or be integrated into the English sound system. Although this applies mainly to personal and geographical names, to some extent it applies to ordinary words too. Accordingly, for many such words LPD shows their pronunciation in the language of origin as well as their anglicized pronunciation. There are two reasons for this: the obvious one of giving the user information about the foreign-language pronunciation, and the less obvious one that those speakers of English who have some knowledge of the foreign language may well pronounce such words or names in a way that imitates the phonetics of the foreign language, or occupies some half-way stage between the foreign-language pronunciation and the anglicization.

Educated speakers of BrE usually know some French. So do Canadians. They will therefore try to pronounce French names in a French way. They may well use nasalized vowels (or attempts at them) and other characteristics of French pronunciation when they pronounce words they perceive as French. The sounds represented as ɒ̃, æ̃, ɜ̃ː (as in **bon, vingt-et-un**) may for this reason be regarded as marginal members of the RP vowel system. On the whole, though, it is only those whose knowledge of French goes beyond the average who succeed in differentiating the real-French vowels ɔ̃ and ɑ̃ (as in **bon** and **banc** respectively), or y and u (as in **rue** and **roue**) or in producing œ̃ rather than ɜ̃.

Educated speakers of AmE usually know some Spanish, and may incorporate some characteristics of Spanish phonetics when pronouncing Spanish words or names. Apart from Hispanics, though, most Americans would not distinguish between ɾ (**puro**) and ɾɾ (**burro**) in the way native speakers of Spanish do.

People living in Wales, whether or not they speak Welsh, can often pronounce the ɬ appropriate for many Welsh names; so can some other speakers of BrE, but usually not of AmE.

Ignorance may lead to surprising results. The German city of **München** (*Ger* ˈmʏn çən) has an English name **Munich** ˈmjuːn ɪk. But British people sometimes think that this is its German name, and attempt to pronounce it as German, producing the quite inappropriate ˈmjuːn ɪx.

Seeing the Pinyin spelling **Beijing** for the city whose traditional English name is **Peking** (Chinese ³pei ¹tɕiŋ), English speakers suppose that the letter **j** should have the same value as in French, ʒ, and say ˌbeɪ ˈʒɪŋ – whereas ˌbeɪ ˈdʒɪŋ would be much closer to the Chinese.

4.2 Transcriptions of foreign languages call for a number of phonetic symbols not included in the list of those used for English. More subtly, they call for certain differences of interpretation in some of the symbols that are also used for English. Thus the symbol t is used not only for the typically alveolar and often aspirated sound of English, but also for the typically dental and unaspirated sound of French. IPA symbols must be always allowed a certain leeway in their interpretation if the transcription is not to be intolerably burdened with diacritic details.

In transcriptions of German, Danish, Swedish, Norwegian, Icelandic, Welsh, Irish, Scottish Gaelic, and Japanese, voiceless plosives may be assumed to be aspirated, at least when at the beginning of a stressed syllable, much as in English. Voiced obstruents in these languages, as in English, may be susceptible to devoicing. In all other foreign languages both plosives and affricates should be assumed to be unaspirated unless explicitly marked as aspirated. Thus both syllables in the Chinese pronunciation of **Beijing** [^{3}pei ^{1}tɕiŋ] start with voiceless unaspirated consonants, which sound similar to the devoiced b, dʒ of English. In certain cases, including notably Hindi, Chinese, and Korean, aspiration is distinctive in both plosives and affricates.

In general, the transcription LPD uses for foreign languages is a phonemic one for the language in question, sometimes modified in the direction of greater phonetic explicitness. Thus the French vowel of **vin** is shown as æ̃, rather than the more customary ɛ̃, because of the phonetic similarity to the vowel quality of English æ. In Spanish, LPD distinguishes between the plosive and the fricative/approximant allophones of b, d, g, since they sound so different to the English ear. Because LPD uses r for the English consonant as in **red**, it transcribes ɾ or rr in languages that typically have a tongue-tip tapped or rolled r-sound, and ʁ for those that typically have a uvular r-sound.

No stress-marks are used in the transcription of French and Hindi, since these languages have no lexical stress. Nevertheless, there may often appear to be stress on the final syllable of French words and on long vowels in Hindi words.

Japanese pitch-accent is shown in accordance with IPA principles, although this differs from notation that is customary among Japanese scholars. Namely, the accent, if there is one in the word, is shown by the mark [ˈ] **before** the accented mora; this is the mora after which the pitch is typically lower. The pitch upstep that occurs automatically on the second mora of words not bearing an accent on the first two moras is shown as [ˌ]. This mark is not used before a moraic obstruent.

In transcriptions of Swedish and other languages with two types of word-stress, the mark ˈˈ denotes tone 2. In Chinese (Putonghua), the tones are as follows:

1 high level [^{1}ma] mā *mother*
2 rising [^{2}ma] má *hemp*
3 low fall-rise [^{3}ma] mǎ *horse*
4 falling [^{4}ma] mà *to scold*

In Cantonese, they are:

1 high level/ high fall [^{1}fan] *to separate*
2 high rise [^{2}fan] *powder*
3 mid level [^{3}fan] *to sleep*
4 low fall [^{4}fan] *tomb*
5 low rise [^{5}fan] *to work hard*
6 lowish level [^{6}fan] *participation*

In Burmese, they are:

1 low [^{1}kʰà] *shake*
2 high [^{2}kʰá] *be bitter*
3 creaky [^{3}kʰa̰] *fee*
4 checked [^{4}kʰaʔ] *draw off*

5 Symbols

5.1 Phonetic symbols This list includes both the symbols used for English and other symbols of the International Phonetic Alphabet that appear in LPD. These general-phonetic symbols are used for transcribing words in foreign languages and occasionally also for allophonic transcription of English. Their meaning is in most cases somewhat flexible: for example, the symbol e stands for a range of similar but not identical vowel qualities in Danish, German, French, Spanish, Japanese, and English.

For the meaning of the terms used in the definitions, see note at ARTICULATION. 'Chinese' means the Pinyin romanization.

a open front unrounded vowel; also for open vowel between front and back; French/German/Italian/Spanish *a*; first element of English diphthongs in *price, high* (aɪ), and *mouth, how* (aʊ)

ɑ open back unrounded vowel; English *father* (ɑː)

ɑ̃ nasalized open back unrounded vowel, French *an*

æ raised open front unrounded vowel; English *trap, bad*

æ̃ nasalized raised open front unrounded vowel, French *in*

ɐ open variety of [ə], German *-er*

ɐ̯ non-syllabic ɐ, German *r* in *Uhr*

b voiced bilabial plosive, English *b*

β voiced bilabial fricative, Spanish *b*/*v* between vowels

ɓ voiced bilabial implosive (glottalic ingressive plosive), Zulu *b*

c voiceless palatal plosive, like [kj]

ç voiceless palatal fricative, German *ich*

d voiced alveolar (sometimes: dental) plosive, English *d*

dʒ voiced palato-alveolar affricate, English *j*

dr voiced post-alveolar affricate, English *dr*

dʑ voiced alveolo-palatal affricate, Japanese *j*

ð voiced dental fricative, in English *father*

d̪ voiced dental plosive (where dentality is distinctive)

ɖ voiced retroflex plosive

ðˤ pharyngealized ('emphatic') [ð]

e close-mid front unrounded vowel, French *é*; also for vowel between close-mid and open-mid, English *dress*; first element of English diphthongs in *face* (eɪ) and (RP) *square* (eə)

ɛ open-mid front unrounded vowel, French *è*

ə mid central unrounded vowel; English vowel at beginning of *about* and at end of *comma*; first element of RP diphthong in *goat, blow* (əʊ); second element of RP diphthongs in *near, square, cure*

ɚ rhotacized [ə], in GenAm *better* (= syllabic [r])

ɜ mid central unrounded vowel, RP *nurse, stir* (ɜː)

ɝ rhotacized [ɜ], GenAm *nurse, stir* (ɝː)

f voiceless labiodental fricative, English *f*

g voiced velar plosive, English 'hard' *g*

ɣ voiced velar fricative (= voiced [x])

h voiceless glottal fricative, English *h*

ħ voiceless pharyngeal fricative
ʰ aspiration
ɦ breathy-voiced glottal fricative, Afrikaans *h*
ʱ breathy-voiced aspiration
i close front unrounded vowel, French *i*; English *fleece, key* (iː); English neutralization of iː-ɪ, *happy*
i̯ non-syllabic i, German *i* in *Studie*
ɪ lax (lowered-centralized) [i], English *kit*; second element of English diphthongs in *face, price, choice*
ɨ close central unrounded vowel, Polish *y*, Russian ы, north Welsh *u*
i̥ voiceless [i]
j voiced palatal approximant (semivowel), English *y* in *yet*
ɟ voiced palatal plosive, like [gj]
ʲ palatalized, [i]-coloured (e.g. tʲ = palatalized t)
k voiceless velar plosive, English *k*
l voiced alveolar lateral, English *l*
ɫ velarized voiced alveolar lateral, English 'dark' l
ɬ voiceless alveolar lateral fricative, Welsh *ll*
ʎ voiced palatal lateral, Italian *gl*
m voiced bilabial nasal, English *m*
m̥ voiceless bilabial nasal
n voiced alveolar (sometimes: dental) nasal, English *n*
n̪ voiced dental nasal (where dentality is distinctive)
ŋ voiced velar nasal, English *ng*
ɲ voiced palatal nasal, Spanish *ñ*
ɳ voiced retroflex nasal
ɴ voiced uvular nasal; Japanese *-n*, alternatively pronounced as a nasalized close back vowel; in Burmese either nasalization of the preceding vowel or a nasal consonant homorganic with the following consonant
o close-mid back rounded vowel, French *o*; also for back rounded vowel between close-mid and open-mid, Spanish *o*; first element of AmE diphthong in *goat, blow* (oʊ)
ɔ open-mid back rounded vowel; English *north, thought*; first element of English diphthong in *choice*; French o in *pomme*
ɔ̃ nasalized open-mid back rounded vowel, French *on*
ɒ open back rounded vowel; RP *lot*; first element of BrE diphthong variant in *cold* (ɒʊ)
ø close-mid front rounded vowel, in French *deux*, German *schön*
œ open-mid front rounded vowel, in French *neuf*, German *plötzlich*
œ̃ nasalized open-mid front rounded vowel, French *un*
p voiceless bilabial plosive, English *p*
ɸ voiceless bilabial fricative, Japanese *f*
q voiceless uvular plosive, Arabic *q*
r voiced post-alveolar approximant, English *red* (this differs from the usual IPA value, which is a trill, LPD's ɾɾ)
r̝ voiced alveolar fricative trill, Czech *ř*
ɾ voiced alveolar tap, Spanish single *r*

ɾɾ	voiced alveolar trill, Spanish initial *r* or double *rr*
ɽ	voiced retroflex flap
ʁ	voiced uvular fricative/approximant, French *r*
s	voiceless alveolar fricative, English *s*
ʃ	voiceless palato-alveolar fricative, English *sh*
ɕ	voiceless alveolo-palatal fricative, Japanese *sh*, Chinese *x*
ʂ	voiceless retroflex fricative, Chinese *sh*
sˤ	pharyngealized ('emphatic') [s]
t	voiceless alveolar (sometimes: dental) plosive, English *t*
t̬	alveolar tap, usually voiced, AmE *t* in *city*
tʃ	voiceless palato-alveolar affricate, English *ch*
tr	voiceless post-alveolar affricate, English *tr*
tɕ	voiceless alveolopalatal affricate, Japanese *ch*, Chinese *q*
t̪	voiceless dental plosive (where dentality is distinctive)
θ	voiceless dental fricative, English *th*
ʈ	voiceless retroflex plosive
tˤ	pharyngealized ('emphatic') [t]
u	close back rounded vowel, French *ou*; English *goose* (uː); English neutralization of uː-ʊ, *thank you*
ʊ	lax (lowered-centralized) [u], English *foot*; second element in English diphthongs in *mouth, goat*
ʉ	close central rounded vowel, Swedish *u*
ɯ	close back unrounded vowel, Japanese *u*
ɯ̥	voiceless [ɯ]
ɰ	voiced velar approximant (semivowel), Japanese *w*
v	voiced labiodental fricative, English v
ʋ	voiced labiodental approximant, Dutch *w*
ʌ	open-mid back unrounded vowel; also for open-mid unrounded vowel between back and front, English *strut, love*
w	voiced labial-velar approximant (semivowel), English *w*
ʍ	voiceless labial-velar fricative/approximant, Scottish *wh*
x	voiceless velar fricative, German *ach*, Spanish *jota*
χ	voiceless uvular fricative, Welsh *ch*
y	close front rounded vowel, in French *lune,* German *über*
ʏ	lax (lowered-centralized) [y], in German *hübsch*
ɥ	voiced labial-palatal approximant (semivowel), in French *huit*
z	voiced alveolar fricative, English *z*
ʒ	voiced palato-alveolar fricative, in English *measure*
ʑ	voiced alveopalatal fricative, second element of Japanese *j*
ʔ	glottal plosive, glottal stop
ʕ	voiced pharyngeal fricative/approximant, Arabic *'ayn*
ǀ	voiceless dental click, Zulu *c*
ǁ	voiceless lateral click, Zulu *x*
ˈ	primary word stress (re ˈMEMber)
ˌ	secondary stress (ˌACa ˈDEMic)
ˈˌ	stress (= ˈ or ˌ as appropriate)
ː	length

5.2 Key to phonetic symbols for English

RP	Gen Am	Consonants	
•	•	p	**p**en, co**p**y, ha**pp**en
•	•	b	**b**ack, **b**u**bb**le, jo**b**
•	•	t	**t**ea, **t**igh**t**, bu**tt**on
	•	ţ	ci**t**y, be**tt**er
•	•	d	**d**ay, la**dd**er, o**dd**
•	•	k	**c**up, **k**i**ck**, s**ch**ool
•	•	g	**g**et, **g**i**gg**le, **gh**ost
•	•	tʃ	**ch**ur**ch**, ma**tch**, na**t**ure
•	•	dʒ	**j**u**dge**, a**ge**, sol**di**er
•	•	f	**f**at, co**ff**ee, rou**gh**
•	•	v	**v**iew, hea**v**y, mo**ve**
•	•	θ	**th**ing, au**th**or, pa**th**
•	•	ð	**th**is, o**th**er, smoo**th**
•	•	s	**s**oon, **c**ea**s**e, **s**i**s**ter
•	•	z	**z**ero, **z**one, ro**s**e**s**, bu**zz**
•	•	ʃ	**sh**ip, **s**ure, sta**ti**on
•	•	ʒ	plea**s**ure, vi**si**on
•	•	h	**h**ot, **wh**ole, be**h**ind
•	•	m	**m**ore, ha**mm**er, su**m**
•	•	n	**n**ice, **kn**ow, fu**nn**y, su**n**
•	•	ŋ	ri**ng**, lo**ng**, tha**n**ks, su**ng**
•	•	l	**l**ight, va**ll**ey, fee**l**
•	•	r	**r**ight, so**rr**y, a**rr**ange
•	•	j	**y**et, **u**se, b**eau**ty
•	•	w	**w**et, **o**ne, **wh**en, q**u**een

In foreign words only:

RP	Gen Am		
•	•	x	lo**ch**, **ch**utzpah
•		ɬ	**Ll**anelli, **Hl**uh**l**uwe

RP	Gen Am	Vowels	
•	•	ɪ	k**i**t, b**i**d, h**y**mn
•	•	e	dr**e**ss, b**e**d
•	•	æ	tr**a**p, b**a**d
•		ɒ	l**o**t, **o**dd, w**a**sh
•	•	ʌ	str**u**t, b**u**d, l**o**ve
•	•	ʊ	f**oo**t, g**oo**d, p**u**t
•	•	iː	fl**ee**ce, s**ea**, mach**i**ne
•	•	eɪ	f**a**ce, d**ay**, st**ea**k
•	•	aɪ	pr**i**ce, h**igh**, tr**y**
•	•	ɔɪ	ch**oi**ce, b**oy**
•	•	uː	g**oo**se, tw**o**, bl**ue**
•		əʊ	g**oa**t, sh**ow**, n**o**
	•	oʊ	g**oa**t, sh**ow**, n**o**
•		ɒʊ	*variant in* c**o**ld
•	•	aʊ	m**ou**th, n**ow**
•		ɪə	n**ear**, h**ere**, s**er**ious
•		eə	squ**are**, f**air**, v**ar**ious
•	•	ɑː	st**ar**t, f**a**ther
	•	ɑː	l**o**t, **o**dd
•	•	ɔː	th**ou**ght, l**aw**, n**or**th, w**ar**
•		ʊə	c**ure**, p**oor**, j**u**ry
•		ɜː	n**ur**se, st**ir**
	•	ɝː	n**ur**se, st**ir**, c**our**age
•	•	i	happ**y**, rad**i**ation, glor**i**ous
•	•	ə	**a**bout, comm**a**, comm**o**n
•			fath**er**, stand**ar**d
•	•	u	infl**u**ence, sit**u**ation, thank y**ou**
•	•	ɪ	**i**ntend, bas**i**c
•		ʊ	stim**u**lus, comm**u**nist

In foreign words only:

RP	Gen Am		
•		ɒ̃	gr**an**d prix, ch**an**son
	•	ɑ̃ː	gr**an**d prix, ch**an**son
•	•	æ̃	v**in**gt-et-un
•		ɜ̃ː	vingt-et-**un**

5.3 Other symbols

‖ GenAm pronunciation follows (see p.xx)

§ BrE non-RP (see p.xix)

⚠ pronunciation considered incorrect (see p.xx)

◀ stress shift possible (see p.784)

→ variant derived by rule (see p.xxviii)

‿ possible compression (see p.173)

(!) pronunciation unexpected for this spelling

(*) RP and GenAm differ in an unpredictable and striking way

= is pronounced the same as

≠ is pronounced differently from

+ (in prefix) attracts consonant from next syllable

~ recapitulates headword up to |, otherwise all of headword

| end of part to be recapitulated

- recapitulates as many syllables from the main or preceding pronunciation as it contains, minus the number of syllables preceding/following this mark (count syllables by counting spaces plus ‿ and • symbols

6 Abbreviations

adj	adjective
adv	adverb
AK	Alaska
AL	Alabama
AmE	American English
AmSp	American Spanish
AR	Arkansas
AZ	Arizona
BBC	British Broadcasting Corporation
Berks	Berkshire
BrE	British English
BrazPort	Brazilian Portuguese
Bucks	Buckinghamshire
CA	California
Chi	Chinese
Co.	County
comb.	combining
conj	conjunction
CT	Connecticut
DE	Delaware
E	East
EFL	English as a foreign language
e.g.	for example
esp.	especially
etc.	et cetera (and the rest)
Fr	French
GA	Georgia; General American
GenAm	General American
Glam	Glamorgan
Gloucs	Gloucestershire
H&W	Hereford & Worcester
Hung	Hungarian
IA	Iowa
IL	Illinois
IN	Indiana
interj	interjection
IPA	International Phonetic Alphabet
It	Italian
Jp	Japanese
KS	Kansas
Lancs	Lancashire
Leics	Leicestershire
LI	Long Island
LPD	*Longman Pronunciation Dictionary*
MA	Massachusetts
MD	Maryland
ME	Maine
med	medical(ly)
MI	Michigan
MN	Minnesota
MO	Missouri
ModGk	Modern Greek
MT	Montana
mus	musically, in music
n	noun
N	North
naut	nautical
NB	Nebraska; nota bene, note well
NC	North Carolina
Nfk	Norfolk
NH	New Hampshire
NJ	New Jersey
NM	New Mexico
Norw	Norwegian
Notts	Nottinghamshire
NSW	New South Wales
N. Terr	Northern Territories
NY	New York
NYC	New York City
NYks	North Yorkshire
NZ	New Zealand
OH	Ohio
OR	Oregon
PA	Pennsylvania
part	participle
pl	plural
Port	Portuguese
pp	past participle
PR	Puerto Rico
prep	preposition
pres	present
ptcp	participle

RI	Rhode Island	*Sx*	Sussex
RP	Received Pronunciation	*SYks*	South Yorkshire
Russ	Russian	*tdmk*	trademark, trade name, proprietary name*
S	South	*TX*	Texas
SC	South Carolina	*UK*	United Kingdom
ScG	Scottish Gaelic	*US*	United States
S-Cr	Serbo-Croat	*v*	verb
SD	South Dakota	*VA*	Virginia
sing.	singular	*VT*	Vermont
Skt	Sanskrit	*W*	West
Sp	Spanish	*Warks*	Warwickshire
Staffs	Staffordshire	*WYks*	West Yorkshire
StdEng	Standard English		
Swed	Swedish		

* Dictionary entries that we believe to constitute trademarks have been designated *tdmk*. However, neither the presence nor the absence of this designation should be regarded as affecting the legal status of any trademark.

A

a Spelling-to-sound

1 Where the spelling is **a**, the pronunciation differs according to whether the vowel is short or long, followed or not by **r**, and strong or weak.

2 The 'strong' pronunciation is regularly
æ as in **cat** kæt ('short A') or
eɪ as in **face** feɪs ('long A').

3 Where **a** is followed by **r**, the 'strong' pronunciation is
ɑː as in **start** stɑːt ‖ stɑːrt or
eə ‖ e as in **square** skweə ‖ skwer
or, indeed, there may be the regular 'short' pronunciation
æ as in **carol** ˈkær əl (although in this position many speakers of GenAm use e, thus ˈker əl).

4 Less frequently, the 'strong' pronunciation is
ɑː as in **father** ˈfɑːð ə ‖ ˈfɑːð ᵊr
ɑː ‖ æ as in **bath** bɑːθ ‖ bæθ
ɒ ‖ ɑː as in **watch** wɒtʃ ‖ wɑːtʃ (especially after the sound w)
ɔː ‖ ɔː as in **talk** tɔːk ‖ tɔːk (especially before the letter **l**) or
ɔː ‖ ɔː as in **warm** wɔːm ‖ wɔːrm.

5 The 'weak' pronunciation is
ə as in **about** ə ˈbaʊt or
ɪ as in **village** ˈvɪl ɪdʒ.

6 Because of COMPRESSION, **a** is usually silent in the ending **-ally** as in **basically** ˈbeɪs ɪk li.

7 Note that where the spelling is **a** the pronunciation is not ʌ (except in a few words from foreign languages).

8 **a** also forms part of the digraphs **ai, au, aw, ay**.

ai, ay Spelling-to-sound

1 Where the spelling is one of the digraphs **ai**, **ay**, the pronunciation is regularly
eɪ as in **rain** reɪn, **day** deɪ or before **r**
eə ‖ e as in **fair** feə ‖ fer.

2 Occasionally with these digraphs the pronunciation is 'weak':
ə as in **curtain** ˈkɜːt ᵊn ‖ ˈkɝːt ᵊn (for a few speakers ɪ, thus ˈkɜːt ɪn) or
i as in **Murray** ˈmʌr i ‖ ˈmɝː i, when at the end of a word. (For **Monday** etc., see note at **-day**.)

3 Note also the exceptional words **says, said, again, against**, usually pronounced with e.

au, aw Spelling-to-sound

1 Where the spelling is one of the digraphs **au** and **aw**, the pronunciation is regularly
ɔː as in **author** ˈɔːθ ə ‖ ˈɔːθ ᵊr, **law** lɔː.

2 In a few words, the pronunciation is
ɑː ‖ æ as in **laugh** lɑːf ‖ læf
or, in loanwords from foreign languages,
əʊ ‖ oʊ as in **gauche** gəʊʃ ‖ goʊʃ or aʊ as in **sauerkraut** ˈsaʊ-
or, in BrE only,
ɒ as in **sausage** ˈsɒs ɪdʒ.

A, a *name of letter* eɪ **A's, As, a's** eɪz *—Communications code name:* Alfa **ˌA'1◂, ˌA-'1**; **ˌA1('M)**; **ˌA,30'3** *—These patterns apply to all British road numbers.* **ˌA'4◂**; **ˌA4 'paper**

a *indef article, before a consonant sound, strong form* eɪ, *weak form* ə *—See also* **an**

a *Latin prep* eɪ ɑː *—See also phrases with this word*

a, à *French prep* æ ɑː *—See also phrases with this word*

a- *comb. form* ¦eɪ, eɪ, ¦æ, æ, ə *—When it has a negative meaning, this prefix is usually* eɪ (ˌathe'istic), *though in some words there are alternative pronunciations with* æ *or* ə (ˌa'moral, a'moral), *and sometimes* ə *is the only form* (a'morphous). *With other meanings, the pronunciation is regularly* ə (a'way, a'spire), *unless stressed because of a suffix, in which case it is* ¦æ (ˌaspi'ration).

Aachen ˈɑːk ən *—Ger* [ˈʔaː xən]

aah ɑː **aah'd, aahed** ɑːd **aahing, aah'ing** ˈɑːʳ ɪŋ ‖ ˈɑː ɪŋ **aahs, aah's** ɑːz

Aalborg ˈɔːl bɔːg ˈɑːl- ‖ -bɔːrg *—Danish* Ålborg [ˈʌl bɔːʔ]

Aaliyah *singer* ɑː ˈliː ə

Aalto ˈɑːlt əʊ ‖ -oʊ *—Finnish* [ˈɑːl to]

aardvark ˈɑːd vɑːk ‖ ˈɑːrd vɑːrk **~s** s

aard|wolf ˈɑːd |wʊlf ‖ ˈɑːrd- **~wolves** wʊlvz

aargh ɑːx ɑː, ɑːg, ɑːɣ ‖ ɑːrg ɜː *—and various non-speech exclamations involving a mid or open vowel and perhaps a velar component*

Aarhus ˈɔː huːs ˈɑː-, -hʊs ‖ ˈɔːr- ˈɑːr- *—Danish* Århus [ˈɔː huːʔs]

Aaron *(i)* ˈeər ən ‖ ˈer ən, *(ii)* ˈær ən ‖ ˈer- *—In BrE traditionally (i), and still usually so for the biblical character; but the personal name may nowadays be either (i) or (ii)*

Aaronic ₍ˌ₎eə ˈrɒn ɪk ◂ ‖ æ ˈrɑːn ɪk e-

ab æb *—See also phrases with this word* **abs** æbz

AB ˌeɪ ˈbiː **~s, ~'s** z

ab- (¦)æb, əb *—As a true prefix meaning 'away', ab- is usually* æb, *though with unstressed and reduced-vowel variants* (ab'duct). *It is always* ¦æb *when it means 'cgs unit'* ('abvolt, ˌab'coulomb). *With a vaguer meaning, it is mostly* əb (ab'stain) *unless stressed* ('abdicate, 'abstract).

aback ə ˈbæk

Abaco ˈæb ə kəʊ ‖ -koʊ

abacus ˈæb ək əs **~es** ɪz əz

Abadan ˌæb ə ˈdɑːn -ˈdæn

Abaddon ə ˈbæd ᵊn

abaft ə ˈbɑːft §-ˈbæft ‖ ə ˈbæft

abalone ˌæb ə ˈləʊn i ‖ -ˈloʊn- **~s** z

abandon ə ˈbænd ən **~ed** d **~ing** ɪŋ **~s** z

abandonment ə ˈbænd ən mənt →-əm-

abase ə ˈbeɪs **abased** ə ˈbeɪst **abases** ə ˈbeɪs ɪz -əz **abasing** ə ˈbeɪs ɪŋ

abasement ə ˈbeɪs mənt

abash ə ˈbæʃ **abashed** ə ˈbæʃt **abashes** ə ˈbæʃ ɪz -əz **abashing** ə ˈbæʃ ɪŋ

abashment ə ˈbæʃ mənt

abate ə ˈbeɪt **abated** ə ˈbeɪt ɪd -əd **abates** ə ˈbeɪts **abating** ə ˈbeɪt ɪŋ

abatement ə ˈbeɪt mənt **~s** s

abatis, abattis ˈæb ət ɪs §-əs; ˌæb ə ˈtiː, ˈ· · · ‖ -əţ əs -ə tiː **~es** *pl after* s *forms* ɪz əz; *for those who pronounce* -ˈtiː, *the pl is written as the sing. but pronounced with added* **z**

abattoir ˈæb ə twɑː ‖ -twɑːr -twɔːr **~s** z

Abba ˈæb ə

abbac|y ˈæb əs |i **~ies** iz

Abbado ə ˈbɑːd əʊ ‖ -oʊ —*It* [ab ˈbaː do]

Abbas *(i)* ˈæb əs, *(ii)* ə ˈbɑːs

Abbasid ə ˈbæs ɪd ˈæb əs-, §-əd **~s** z

abbatial ə ˈbeɪʃ ᵊl

abbe, abbé, A~ ˈæb eɪ ‖ æ ˈbeɪ ˈæb eɪ —*Fr* [a be] **~s** z

Abberton ˈæb ət ən ‖ -ᵊrt ᵊn

abbess ˈæb es -ɪs, §-əs; æ ˈbes ‖ -əs **~es** ɪz əz

Abbeville ˈæb vɪl ˈæb ɪ vɪl, -ə- ‖ æb ˈviːᵊl ˈæb i vɪl —*Fr* [ab vil]

Abbevillian ˌæb ˈvɪl i̯ ən ◂ ˌæb ɪ ˈvɪl-, §ˌæb ə-

abbey, Abbey ˈæb i **~s** z

Abbie ˈæb i

abbot, Abbot ˈæb ət **~s** s

Abbotsbury ˈæb əts bər‿i ‖ -ˌber i

abbotship ˈæb ət ʃɪp **~s** s

Abbott ˈæb ət

abbrevi|ate ə ˈbriːv i |eɪt **~ated** eɪt ɪd -əd ‖ eɪţ əd **~ates** eɪts **~ating** eɪt ɪŋ ‖ eɪţ ɪŋ

abbreviation ə ˌbriːv i ˈeɪʃ ᵊn **~s** z

abbreviator ə ˈbriːv i eɪt ə ‖ -eɪţ ᵊr **~s** z

abbreviatory ə ˈbriːv i̯ ət̬ ər i ə ˌbriːv i ˈeɪt ər i ◂ ‖ -i̯ ə tɔːr i -toʊr i

Abbs æbz

Abby ˈæb i

ABC ˌeɪ biː ˈsiː **ABCs** ˌeɪ biː ˈsiːz

abdabs ˈæb dæbz

Abdela æb ˈdel ə

abdi|cate ˈæbd ɪ |keɪt -ə- **~cated** keɪt ɪd -əd ‖ keɪţ əd **~cates** keɪts **~cating** keɪt ɪŋ ‖ keɪţ ɪŋ

abdication ˌæbd ɪ ˈkeɪʃ ᵊn -ə- **~s** z

abdomen ˈæbd əm ən -ɪn, -ə men; æb ˈdəʊm- **~s** z

abdominal æb ˈdɒm ɪn ᵊl əb-, -ən ᵊl ‖ -ˈdɑːm- **~ly** i **~s** z

abduct ₍ₗ₎æb ˈdʌkt əb- **~ed** ɪd əd **~ing** ɪŋ **~s** s

abduction ₍ₗ₎æb ˈdʌk ʃᵊn əb- **~s** z

abductor ₍ₗ₎æb ˈdʌkt ə əb- ‖ -ᵊr **~s** z

Abdul ˈæbd ʊl -ᵊl

Abdulla, Abdullah æb ˈdʌl ə əb-, -ˈdʊl- —*Arabic* [ʕab ˈduɫ ɫɑh]

Abe *short for* Abraham eɪb

Abe *Jp name* ˈɑːb eɪ

à Becket ə ˈbek ɪt §-ət

abed ə ˈbed

Abednego ˌæb ed ˈniːg əʊ ə ˈbed nɪ gəʊ, -nə- ‖ ə ˈbed nɪ goʊ

Abel ˈeɪb ᵊl

Abelard ˈæb ə lɑːd -ɪ- ‖ -lɑːrd —*Fr* [a be laːʁ]

abele ə ˈbiːᵊl ˈeɪb ᵊl

Abelian ə ˈbiːl i̯ ən

abelmosk ˈeɪb ᵊl mɒsk ‖ -mɑːsk

Aber ˈæb ə ‖ -ᵊr

Aberaeron, Aberayron ˌæb ər ˈaɪᵊr ən ‖ -ər- —*Welsh* [a ber ˈəi ron]

Aberavon ˌæb ər ˈæv ᵊn ‖ -ər- —*Welsh* Aberafan [a ber ˈa van]

Abercon|way ˌæb ə ˈkɒn |weɪ ‖ -ᵊr ˈkɑːn- **~wy** wi

Abercorn ˈæb ə kɔːn ‖ ᵊr kɔːrn

Abercrombie, Abercromby *(i)* ˈæb ə ˌkrʌm bi ˌ· ·ˈ· · ‖ ˈæb ᵊr-, *(ii)* -ˌkrɒm bi ˌ· ·ˈ· · ‖ ˌkrɑːm-

Aberdare ˌæb ə ˈdeə ‖ -ᵊr ˈdeᵊr -ˈdæᵊr

Aberdaron ˌæb ə ˈdær ən ‖ -ᵊr- -ˈder-

Aberdeen *place in Scotland* ˌæb ə ˈdiːn ‖ -ᵊr- —*but places in the US are* ˈ· · · **~shire** ʃə -ʃɪə, §-ʃaɪ‿ə ‖ ʃɪr -ʃᵊr

Aberdonian ˌæb ə ˈdəʊn i̯ ən ◂ ‖ -ᵊr ˈdoʊn- **~s** z

Aberdour ˌæb ə ˈdaʊ‿ə ‖ -ᵊr ˈdaʊ‿ᵊr

Aberdovey ˌæb ə ˈdʌv i ‖ -ᵊr-

Aberfan ˌæb ə ˈvæn ‖ -ᵊr- —*also, inappropriately,* -ˈfæn —*Welsh* [a ber ˈvan]

Aberfeldy ˌæb ə ˈfeld i ‖ -ᵊr-

Aberffraw ə ˈbeə fraʊ ‖ -ˈber-

Aberfoyle ˌæb ə ˈfɔɪᵊl ‖ -ᵊr-

Abergavenny ˌæb ə gə ˈven i ‖ ˌæb ᵊr- —*as a family name also* ˌæb ə ˈgen i ‖ -ᵊr-

Abergele ˌæb ə ˈgel i -eɪ ‖ -ᵊr- —*Welsh* [a ber ˈge le]

Abermule ˌæb ə ˈmjuːl ‖ -ᵊr-

Abernethy, a~ ˌæb ə ˈneθ i -ˈniːθ- ‖ -ᵊr- ˈ· · · ·

Aberporth ˌæb ə ˈpɔːθ ‖ -ᵊr ˈpɔːrθ

aberranc|e æ ˈber ənᵗs ə-, ˈæb ər- **~es** ɪz əz **~y** i

aberrant æ ˈber ənt ə-, ˈæb ər- **~ly** li

aberration ˌæb ə ˈreɪʃ ᵊn **~s** z

Abersoch ˌæb ə ˈsəʊk -ˈsɒk ‖ -ᵊr ˈsoʊk —*Welsh* [a ber ˈsoːχ]

Abersychan ˌæb ə ˈsɪk ən -ˈsʌk- ‖ -ᵊr- —*Welsh* [a ber ˈsə χan]

Abertawe ˌæb ə ˈtaʊ i -eɪ —*Welsh* [a ber ˈta we]

Abertillery ˌæb ə tɪ ˈleər i -tə'- ‖ -ᵊr tə ˈler i

Aberystwyth ˌæb ə ˈrɪst wɪθ —*Welsh* [a ber ˈə sduiθ]

abet ə ˈbet **abets** ə ˈbets **abetted** ə ˈbet ɪd -əd ‖ ə ˈbeţ əd **abetting** ə ˈbet ɪŋ ‖ ə ˈbeţ ɪŋ

abetment ə ˈbet mənt

abetter, abettor ə ˈbet ə ‖ ə ˈbeţ ᵊr **~s** z

abey|ance ə ˈbeɪ |ənᵗs **~ant** ənt

Ab Fab ˌæb ˈfæb

abhor əb ˈhɔː æb-, ə ˈbɔː ‖ æb ˈhɔːr əb- **abhorred** əb ˈhɔːd æb-, ə ˈbɔːd ‖ æb ˈhɔːrd əb- **abhorring** əb ˈhɔːr ɪŋ æb-, ə ˈbɔːr- ‖ æb- əb- **abhors** əb ˈhɔːz æb-, ə ˈbɔːz ‖ æb ˈhɔːrz əb-

abhorrence əb ˈhɒr ənᵗs æb-, ə ˈbɒr- ‖ æb ˈhɔːr ənᵗs əb-, -ˈhɑːr-

abhorrent əb ˈhɒr ənt æb-, ə ˈbɒr- ‖ æb ˈhɔːr ənt əb-, -ˈhɑːr- **~ly** li

abide ə ˈbaɪd **abided** ə ˈbaɪd ɪd -əd **abides** ə ˈbaɪdz **abiding/ly** ə ˈbaɪd ɪŋ /li **abode** ə ˈbəʊd ‖ ə ˈboʊd

A

Abidjan ˌæb i ˈdʒɑːn -ˈdʒæn —*Fr* [a bid ʒɑ̃]
Abigail, a~ ˈæb ɪ geɪᵊl §-ə-
Abilene *places in TX, KS* ˈæb ə liːn -ɪ-
abilit|y ə ˈbɪl ət |i -ɪt- ‖ -əṭ |i **~ies** iz
-ability ə ˈbɪl ət i -ɪt- ‖ -əṭ i —*A word with this suffix has a secondary stress in the same place as the primary stress in the corresponding word with* -able (ˌcookaˈbility, ˌpreferaˈbility).
Abingdon ˈæb ɪŋ dən
Abinger ˈæb ɪndʒ ə ‖ -ᵊr
ab initio ˌæb ɪ ˈnɪʃ i əʊ ˌ·ə-, -ˈnɪs- ‖ -oʊ
abiotic ˌeɪ baɪ ˈɒt ɪk ◂ ‖ -ˈɑːṭ ɪk
abject ˈæb dʒekt **-ly** li ·ˈ· ·
abjection æb ˈdʒek ʃᵊn
abjuration ˌæb dʒuᵊ ˈreɪʃ ᵊn -dʒɔː-, -dʒə- ‖ -dʒə-
abjure əb ˈdʒʊə æb-, -ˈdʒɔː ‖ æb ˈdʒʊᵊr **~d** d **~s** z **abjuring** əb ˈdʒʊər ɪŋ æb-, -ˈdʒɔːr- ‖ æb ˈdʒʊr ɪŋ
Abkhazi|a æb ˈkɑːz i ə |ə -ˈkeɪz- **~an/s** ən/z
ab|late ⁽ˌ⁾æb |ˈleɪt **~lated** ˈleɪt ɪd -əd ‖ ˈleɪṭ əd **~lates** ˈleɪts **~lating** ˈleɪt ɪŋ ‖ ˈleɪṭ ɪŋ
ablation ⁽ˌ⁾æb ˈleɪʃ ᵊn
ablatival ˌæb lə ˈtaɪv ᵊl ◂
ablative *'ablating'* ⁽ˌ⁾æb ˈleɪt ɪv ‖ -leɪṭ ɪv
ablative *case* ˈæb lət ɪv ‖ -ləṭ- **~s** z
ˌ**ablative ˈabsolute**
ablaut ˈæb laʊt —*Ger* [ˈʔap laut]
ablaze ə ˈbleɪz
able ˈeɪb ᵊl **abler** ˈeɪb lə ‖ -lᵊr **ablest** ˈeɪb lɪst -ləst
-able əb ᵊl —*In general, this suffix is stress-neutral* (inˈterpretable, deˈsirable, comˈmunicable). *There are, however, some important exceptions* (ˈadmirable, ˈpreferable, ˈreputable)*, and speakers disagree for some words* (applicable, comparable, formidable, hospitable, irrevocable, lamentable, transferable) *— see individual entries.*
able-bodied ˌeɪb ᵊl ˈbɒd id ◂ ‖ -ˈbɑːd-
ablution ə ˈbluːʃ ᵊn æ- **~s** z
ably ˈeɪb li
-ably əb li —*The stress is always as in the corresponding* -able *form.*
abne|gate ˈæb nɪ |geɪt -nə-, -ne- **~gated** geɪt ɪd -əd ‖ geɪṭ əd **~gates** geɪts **~gating** geɪt ɪŋ ‖ geɪṭ ɪŋ
abnegation ˌæb nɪ ˈgeɪʃ ᵊn -nə-, -ne-
Abner ˈæb nə ‖ -nᵊr
Abney ˈæb ni
abnormal ⁽ˌ⁾æb ˈnɔːm ᵊl əb- ‖ -ˈnɔːrm- **~ly** i
abnormalit|y ˌæb nɔː ˈmæl ət |i ˌ·nə-, -ɪt i ‖ -nɔːr ˈmæl əṭ |i **~ies** iz
Abo, abo *'aboriginal'* ˈæb əʊ ‖ -oʊ **~s** z
ABO *blood type classification* ˌeɪ biː ˈəʊ ‖ -ˈoʊ
aboard ə ˈbɔːd ‖ ə ˈbɔːrd -ˈboʊrd
abode ə ˈbəʊd ‖ ə ˈboʊd **~s** z
abolish ə ˈbɒl ɪʃ ‖ ə ˈbɑːl- **~ed** t **~es** ɪz əz **~ing** ɪŋ
abolition ˌæb ə ˈlɪʃ ᵊn **~ism** ˌɪz əm **~ist/s** ˌɪst/s əst/s
abomas|um ˌæb əʊ ˈmeɪs |əm ‖ -oʊ- **~a** ə
A-bomb ˈeɪ bɒm ‖ -bɑːm **~s** z
abominab|le ə ˈbɒm ɪn əb |ᵊl -ən əb- ‖ ə ˈbɑːm- **~ly** li
aˌ**bominable ˈsnowman,** ·ˌ·· · ˈ· ·
abomi|nate ə ˈbɒm ɪ |neɪt -ə- ‖ ə ˈbɑːm- **~nated** neɪt ɪd -əd ‖ neɪṭ əd **~nates** neɪts **~nating** neɪt ɪŋ ‖ neɪṭ ɪŋ
abomination ə ˌbɒm ɪ ˈneɪʃ ᵊn -ə- ‖ ə ˌbɑːm- **~s** z
aboriginal, A~ ˌæb ə ˈrɪdʒ ᵊn əl ◂ -ɪn ᵊl **~ly** i
aboriginalit|y, A~ ˌæb ə ˌrɪdʒ ə ˈnæl ət |i -ɪˈ·-, -ɪt |i ‖ -əṭ |i **~ies** iz
aborigine, A~ ˌæb ə ˈrɪdʒ ən i -ɪn i **~s** z
aborning ə ˈbɔːn ɪŋ ‖ ə ˈbɔːrn ɪŋ
abort ə ˈbɔːt ‖ ə ˈbɔːrt **aborted** ə ˈbɔːt ɪd -əd ‖ ə ˈbɔːrṭ əd **aborting** ə ˈbɔːt ɪŋ ‖ ə ˈbɔːrṭ ɪŋ **aborts** ə ˈbɔːts ‖ ə ˈbɔːrts
abortifacient ə ˌbɔːt ɪ ˈfeɪʃ ᵊnt §-ə-, -ˈfeɪʃ i ənt ‖ ə ˌbɔːrṭ ə- **~s** s
abortion ə ˈbɔːʃ ᵊn ‖ ə ˈbɔːrʃ- **~s** z
abortionist ə ˈbɔːʃ ᵊn ɪst §əst ‖ ə ˈbɔːrʃ- **~s** s
abortive ə ˈbɔːt ɪv ‖ ə ˈbɔːrṭ ɪv **~ly** li
Aboukir ˌæb u ˈkɪə ‖ -kɪr —*Arabic* [ʔa buː ˈqiːr, -ˈʔiːr]
abound ə ˈbaʊnd **abounded** ə ˈbaʊnd ɪd -əd **abounding/ly** ə ˈbaʊnd ɪŋ /li **abounds** ə ˈbaʊndz
about ə ˈbaʊt
about-fac|e ə ˌbaʊt ˈfeɪs ·ˈ· · **~ed** t **~es** ɪz əz **~ing** ɪŋ
about-turn ə ˌbaʊt ˈtɜːn ‖ -ˈtɜːn **~ed** d **~ing** ɪŋ **~s** z
above ə ˈbʌv
aboveboard ə ˌbʌv ˈbɔːd ◂ ·ˈ· · ‖ ə ˈbʌv bɔːrd -boʊrd
above-mentioned ə ˌbʌv ˈmenᵗʃ ᵊnd ◂
the aˌ**bove-ˌmentioned ˈfacts**
Aboyne ə ˈbɔɪn
abracadabra ˌæb rə kə ˈdæb rə
abrad|e ə ˈbreɪd **~ed** ɪd əd **~es** z **~ing** ɪŋ
Abraham ˈeɪb rə hæm -həm **~s** z
Abram *place in Greater Manchester* ˈæb rəm ˈɑːb-, -ræm
Abramovich ˌæb rə ˈməʊv ɪtʃ ‖ -ˈmoʊv- —*popularly also* ə ˈbræm ə vɪtʃ —*Russian* [ə brɐ ˈmo vʲitʃ]
Abrams ˈeɪb rəmz
Abramson ˈeɪb rəm sən
abrasion ə ˈbreɪʒ ᵊn **~s** z
abrasive ə ˈbreɪs ɪv -ˈbreɪz- **~ly** li **~ness** nəs nɪs **~s** z
abraxas, A~ ə ˈbræks əs
abreact ˌæb ri ˈækt **~ed** ɪd əd **~ing** ɪŋ **~s** s
abreaction ˌæb ri ˈæk ʃᵊn **~s** z
abreast ə ˈbrest
abridg|e ə ˈbrɪdʒ **~ed** d **~es** ɪz əz **~ing** ɪŋ
Abridge ˈeɪ brɪdʒ
abridgement, abridgment ə ˈbrɪdʒ mənt **~s** s
abroad ə ˈbrɔːd ‖ -ˈbrɑːd *(!)*
abro|gate ˈæb rə |geɪt **~gated** geɪt ɪd -əd ‖ geɪṭ əd **~gates** geɪts **~gating** geɪt ɪŋ ‖ geɪṭ ɪŋ
abrogation ˌæb rə ˈgeɪʃ ᵊn

A

abrupt ə ˈbrʌpt **~ly** li **~ness** nəs nɪs
Abruzzi ə ˈbrʊts i —*It* [a ˈbrut tsi]
ABS ˌeɪ biː ˈes
Absalom ˈæb səl əm
abscess ˈæb ses -sɪs, §-səs **~ed** t **~es** ɪz əz
absciss|a æb ˈsɪs |ə əb- **~ae** iː **~as** əz
abscission æb ˈsɪʃ ən -ˈsɪʒ-
abscond əb ˈskɒnd æb- ‖ -ˈskɑːnd **~ed** ɪd əd **~er/s** ə/z ‖ ər/z **~ing** ɪŋ **~s** z
Abse ˈæbz i
abseil ˈæb seɪəl ˈæp-, -saɪəl **~ed** d **~ing** ɪŋ **~s** z
absenc|e ˈæb sənts **~es** ɪz əz
absent *adj* ˈæb sənt **~ly** li
ab|sent *v* æb |ˈsent əb- **~sented** ˈsent ɪd -əd ‖ˈsenṭ əd **~senting** ˈsent ɪŋ ‖ ˈsenṭ ɪŋ **~sents** ˈsents
absentee ˌæb sən ˈtiː ◂ **~s** z
absenteeism ˌæb sən ˈtiː ˌɪz əm
absentia æb ˈsent i ə əb-, -ˈsentʃ-
absently ˈæb sənt li
absent-minded ˌæb sənt ˈmaɪnd ɪd ◂ -əd **~ly** li **~ness** nəs nɪs
ˌabsentˌminded proˈfessor
absinth, absinthe ˈæb sɪntθ -sæ̃θ
absit omen ˌæb sɪt ˈəʊm en ‖ -sɪţ ˈoʊm-
absolute ˈæb sə luːt -ljuːt, ˌ·ˈ·◂ **~ness** nəs nɪs
absolutely ˈæb sə luːt li -ljuːt li, ˌ··ˈ··◂ —*There are also casual rapid-speech forms* ˈæbs i, ˈæbs li
absolution ˌæb sə ˈluːʃ ən -ˈljuːʃ- **~s** z
absolutism ˈæb sə luːt ˌɪz əm -sə ljuːt-, ˌ·ˈ·· ‖ -luːţ ˌɪz əm
absolutist ˌæb sə ˈluːt ɪst -ˈljuːt-, §-əst; ˈ···· ‖ -ˈluːţ- **~s** s
absolutive ˌæb sə ˈluːt ɪv ◂ -ˈljuːt- ‖ -ˈluːţ- **~s** z
absolv|e əb ˈzɒlv §æb-, §-ˈzəʊlv ‖ -ˈzɑːlv -ˈsɑːlv, -ˈzɔːlv, -ˈsɔːlv **~ed** d **~es** z **~ing** ɪŋ

ABSORB

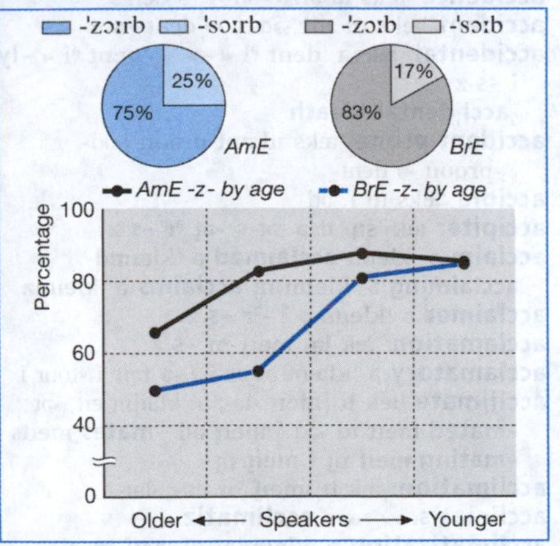

absorb əb ˈzɔːb æb-, -ˈsɔːb ‖ -ˈzɔːrb -ˈsɔːrb **~ed** d **~ing/ly** ɪŋ /li **~s** z — *Preference polls, AmE:* -ˈzɔːrb *75%,* -ˈsɔːrb *25%; BrE,* -ˈzɔːb *83%,* -ˈsɔːb *17%.*
absorbedly əb ˈzɔːb ɪd li æb-, -ˈsɔːb-, -əd-; -ˈzɔːbd li, -ˈsɔːbd li ‖ -ˈzɔːrb- -ˈsɔːrb-
absorbency əb ˈzɔːb ənts i æb-, -ˈsɔːb- ‖ -ˈzɔːrb- -ˈsɔːrb-
absorbent əb ˈzɔːb ənt æb-, -ˈsɔːb- ‖ -ˈzɔːrb- -ˈsɔːrb-
absorber əb ˈzɔːb ə æb-, -ˈsɔːb- ‖ -ˈzɔːrb ər -ˈsɔːrb- **~s** z
absorption əb ˈzɔːp ʃən æb-, -ˈsɔːp- ‖ -ˈzɔːrp- -ˈsɔːrp-
absorptive əb ˈzɔːpt ɪv æb-, -ˈsɔːpt- ‖ -ˈzɔːrpt- -ˈsɔːrpt-
absorptivity ˌæb zɔːp ˈtɪv ət i ˌ·sɔːp-, -ɪt i ‖ -zɔːrp ˈtɪv əţ i ˌ·sɔːrp-
abstain əb ˈsteɪn æb- **~ed** d **~er/s** ə/z ‖ ər/z **~ing** ɪŋ **~s** z
abstemious əb ˈstiːm i əs æb- **~ly** li **~ness** nəs nɪs
abstention əb ˈstentʃ ən æb- **~s** z
abstinence ˈæb stɪn ənts
abstinent ˈæb stɪn ənt **~ly** li
abstract *n* ˈæb strækt **~s** s
abstract *v 'summarize'* ˈæb strækt **~ed** ɪd əd **~er/s** ə/z ‖ ər/z **~ing** ɪŋ **~s** s
abstract *adj* ˈæb strækt ‖ ₍ˌ₎ˈ·
abstract *v 'remove'* ₍ˌ₎æb ˈstrækt əb-, ˈ·· **~ed/ly** ɪd /li əd /li **~ing** ɪŋ **~s** s
abstraction ₍ˌ₎æb ˈstræk ʃən əb- **~ism** ˌɪz əm **~ist/s** ɪst/s §əst/s **~s** z
abstractive ₍ˌ₎æb ˈstrækt ɪv əb-
abstract|ly ˈæb strækt| li ‖ ₍ˌ₎ˈ·· **~ness** nəs nɪs
abstruse ₍ˌ₎æb ˈstruːs əb- **~ly** li **~ness** nəs nɪs
abstrusity ₍ˌ₎æb ˈstruːs ət i -ɪt- ‖ əţ i

ABSURD

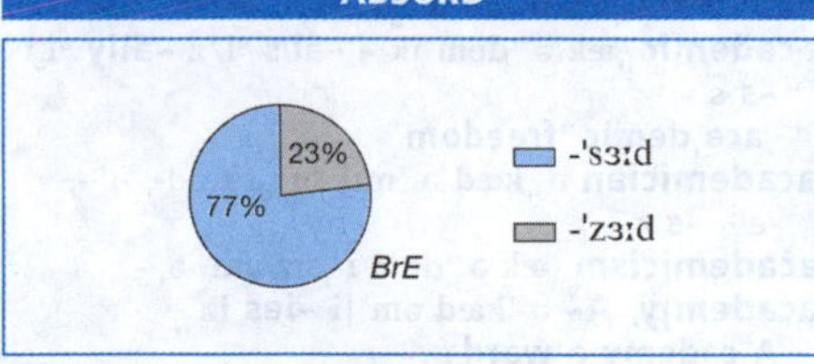

absurd, A~ əb ˈsɜːd §æb-, -ˈzɜːd ‖ -ˈsɜːd -zɜːd **~ism** ˌɪz əm **~ist/s** ɪst/s §əst/s **~ly** li — *Preference poll, BrE:* -ˈsɜːd *77%,* -ˈzɜːd *23%.*
absurdit|y əb ˈsɜːd ət |i §æb-, -ˈzɜːd-, -ɪt- ‖ -ˈsɜːd əţ |i -ˈzɜːd- **~ies** iz
ABTA ˈæb tə
Abu Dhabi ˌæb u ˈdɑːb i ˌɑːb-, -ˈdæb- ‖ ˌɑːb- —*Arabic* [ʔa buː ˈðˤɑ bi]
Abu Ghraib ˌæb u ˈɡreɪb ‖ ˌɑːb-—*Arabic* [ʔa buː ɣʊ ˈrɛib]
Abuja ə ˈbuːdʒ ə ɑː-
abulia ə ˈbuːl i ə eɪ-, -ˈbjuːl-
abundance ə ˈbʌnd ənts
abundant ə ˈbʌnd ənt **~ly** li
Abu Nidal ˌæb uː niː ˈdɑːl ˌɑːb-, -ˈdæl ‖ ˌɑːb- ˌæb- —*Arabic* [ʔa buː ni ˈdˤɑːl]
abuse *v* ə ˈbjuːz **abused** ə ˈbjuːzd **abuses** ə ˈbjuːz ɪz -əz **abusing** ə ˈbjuːz ɪŋ

A

abuse *n* ə ˈbjuːs **abuses** ə ˈbjuːs ɪz -əz *(NB verb ≠ noun)*

abuser ə ˈbjuːz ə ‖ -ᵊr **~s** z

Abu Simbel ˌæb uː ˈsɪm bᵊl ˌɑːb-, -bel ‖ ˌɑːb-, ˌæb-

abusive ə ˈbjuːs ɪv -ˈbjuːz- **~ly** li **~ness** nəs nɪs

abut ə ˈbʌt **abuts** ə ˈbʌts **abutted** ə ˈbʌt ɪd -əd ‖ ə ˈbʌţ əd **abutting** ə ˈbʌt ɪŋ ‖ ə ˈbʌţ ɪŋ

abutilon ə ˈbjuːt ɪl ən §-əl-, -ɪ lɒn, -ə lɒn, -ᵊl ɒn ‖ ə ˈbjuːţ ᵊl ɑːn -ən **~s** z

abutment ə ˈbʌt mənt **~s** s

abutt... —*see* **abut**

abuttal ə ˈbʌt ᵊl ‖ ə ˈbʌţ ᵊl **~s** z

abuzz ə ˈbʌz

Abydos ə ˈbaɪd ɒs -əs ‖ -ɑːs -ɔːs

abysm ə ˈbɪz əm

abysmal ə ˈbɪz mᵊl æ- **~ly** i

abyss ə ˈbɪs æ-, ˈæb ɪs **~es** ɪz əz

abyssal ə ˈbɪs ᵊl æ-

Abyssini|a ˌæb ɪ ˈsɪn i‿|ə ˌæb ə- **~an/s** ən/z

-ac *This suffix and word-ending is mostly* **æk** (ˈcardiac, ˈmaniac); *but note* ˌeleˈgiac *usually with* **ək**.

a/c —*see* **account**

ac- *This prefix is a variant of* **ad-**. *Its pronunciation varies according to context. (1) When followed in spelling by* ce, ci, *it is usually* **ək** (acˈcelerate), *but* ¦**æk** *if stressed because of a suffix* (ˌacciˈdental) *and in a few two-syllable nouns* (ˈaccess). *(2) Otherwise, it is* ə, *but* ¦æ *if stressed because of a suffix* (acˈclaim; ˌacclaˈmation).

AC ˌeɪ ˈsiː

acacia ə ˈkeɪʃ ə -ˈkeɪs i‿ə **~s** z

academe, A~ ˈæk ə diːm ,·ˈ·

academia ˌæk ə ˈdiːm i‿ə

academic ˌæk ə ˈdem ɪk ◂ **~al/s** ᵊl/z **~ally** ᵊl‿i **~s** s

ˌ**acaˌdemic ˈfreedom**

academician ə ˌkæd ə ˈmɪʃ ᵊn ˌæk əd-, -ɪˈ--, -eˈ-- **~s** z

academicism ˌæk ə ˈdem ɪ ˌsɪz əm -əˌ--

academ|y, A~ ə ˈkæd əm |i **~ies** iz

Aˌcademy aˈward

Acadi|a ə ˈkeɪd i‿|ə **~an/s** ən/z

acai, açaí əˈsaɪ —*BrazPort* [asaˈi]

acanth|us ə ˈkænᵗθ |əs **~i** aɪ **~uses** əs ɪz -əz

a cappella ˌæk ə ˈpel ə ˌɑːk-, -æ- ‖ ˌɑː kə- —*It* [ak kap ˈpɛl la]

Acapulco ˌæk ə ˈpʊlk əʊ ‖ ˌɑːk ə ˈpuːlk oʊ -ˈpʊlk- —*Sp* [a ka ˈpul ko]

acarid ˈæk ər ɪd §-əd **~s** z

ACAS ˈeɪk æs

acatalectic ˌeɪ ˌkæt ə ˈlekt ɪk ◂ ·ˌ·-, æˌ·-, əˌ·-

acced|e ək ˈsiːd æk-, ɪk- **~ed** ɪd əd **~es** z **~ing** ɪŋ

accelerando æk ˌsel ə ˈrænd əʊ ək-, ɪk-; ə ˌtʃel- ‖ -ˈrɑːnd oʊ ɑː ˌtʃel- —*It* [at tʃe le ˈran do]

accelerant ək ˈsel ər ənt æk-, ɪk- **~s** s

accele|rate ək ˈsel ə |reɪt æk-, ɪk- **~rated** reɪt ɪd -əd ‖ reɪţ əd **~rates** reɪts **~rating** reɪt ɪŋ ‖ reɪţ ɪŋ

acceleration ək ˌsel ə ˈreɪʃ ᵊn æk-, ɪk- **~s** z

accelerator ək ˈsel ə reɪt ə æk-, ɪk- ‖ -reɪţ ᵊr **~s** z

accelerometer ək ˌsel ə ˈrɒm ɪt ə æk-, ɪk-, -ət ə ‖ -ˈrɑːm əţ ᵊr **~s** z

accent *n* ˈæks ᵊnt ˈæk sent ‖ ˈæk sent **~s** s

ac|cent *v* æk ˈ|sent ək-, ɪk-, ˈæk |sent; ˈæk |sᵊnt ‖ ˈæk |sent ·ˈ· **~cented** sent ɪd sᵊnt-, -əd ‖ senţ əd **~centing** sent ɪŋ sᵊnt- ‖ senţ ɪŋ **~cents** sents sᵊnts ‖ sents

accentor æk ˈsent ə ək-, ɪk- ‖ -ˈsenţ ᵊr **~s** z

accentual ək ˈsentʃ u‿əl æk-, ɪk-, -ˈsent ju‿ **~ly** i

accentu|ate ək ˈsentʃ u |eɪt æk-, ɪk-, -ˈsent ju- **~ated** eɪt ɪd -əd ‖ eɪţ əd **~ates** eɪts **~ating** eɪt ɪŋ ‖ eɪţ ɪŋ

accentuation ək ˌsentʃ u ˈeɪʃ ᵊn æk-, ɪk-, -ˌsent ju-

accept ək ˈsept æk-, ɪk- **~ed** ɪd əd **~ing** ɪŋ **~s** s

acceptability ək ˌsept ə ˈbɪl ət i æk-, ɪk-, -ɪt i ‖ -əţ i

acceptab|le ək ˈsept əb |ᵊl æk-, ɪk- **~ly** li

acceptanc|e ək ˈsept ənᵗs æk-, ɪk- **~es** ɪz əz

acceptation ˌæks ep ˈteɪʃ ᵊn

acceptor ək ˈsept ə æk-, ɪk- ‖ -ᵊr **~s** z

access *v, n* ˈæk ses —*as a v, occasionally also* ·ˈ· **~ed** t **~es** ɪz əz **~ing** ɪŋ

ˈaccess time

accessibility ək ˌses ə ˈbɪl ət i æk-, ɪk-, -ˌ·ɪ-, -ɪt i ‖ -əţ i

accessib|le ək ˈses əb |ᵊl æk-, ɪk-, -ɪb- **~leness** ᵊl nəs -nɪs **~ly** li

accession ək ˈseʃ ᵊn æk-, ɪk- **~ed** d **~ing** ‿ɪŋ **~s** z

accessoris|e, accessoriz|e ək ˈses ə raɪz æk-, ɪk- **~ed** d **~es** ɪz əz **~ing** ɪŋ

accessor|y ək ˈses ər‿|i æk-, ɪk-, ⚠ə- **~ies** iz

acciaccatura ə ˌtʃæk ə ˈtʊər ə ⚠-ˌkætʃ- ‖ ɑː ˌtʃɑːk ə ˈtʊr ə —*It* [at tʃak ka ˈtuː ra]

accidence ˈæks ɪd ənᵗs -əd- ‖ -ə denᵗs

accident ˈæks ɪd ənt -əd- ‖ -ə dent **~s** s

accidental ˌæks ɪ ˈdent ᵊl ◂ -ə- ‖ -ˈdenţ ᵊl ◂ **~ly** i **~s** z

ˌ**acciˌdental ˈdeath**

accident-prone ˈæks ɪd ənt prəʊn ˈ·əd- ‖ -proʊn -ə dent-

accidie ˈæks ɪd i -əd-

accipiter æk ˈsɪp ɪt ə -ət- ‖ -əţ ᵊr **~s** z

acclaim ə ˈkleɪm **acclaimed** ə ˈkleɪmd **acclaiming** ə ˈkleɪm ɪŋ **acclaims** ə ˈkleɪmz

acclaimer ə ˈkleɪm ə ‖ -ᵊr **~s** z

acclamation ˌæk lə ˈmeɪʃ ᵊn **~s** z

acclamatory ə ˈklæm ət‿ər i ‖ -ə tɔːr i -toʊr i

accli|mate ˈæk lɪ |meɪt -lə-; ə ˈklaɪ|m eɪt, -ət **~mated** meɪt ɪd -əd ‖ meɪţ əd **~mates** meɪts **~mating** meɪt ɪŋ ‖ meɪţ ɪŋ

acclimation ˌæk lɪ ˈmeɪʃ ᵊn -lə-, -laɪ-

acclimatis... —*see* **acclimatiz...**

acclimatization ə ˌklaɪm ət aɪ ˈzeɪʃ ᵊn -ɪˈ-- ‖ -əţ ə-

acclimatiz|e ə ˈklaɪm ə taɪz **~ed** d **~es** ɪz əz **~ing** ɪŋ

acclivit|y ə ˈklɪv ət |i æ-, -ɪt- ‖ -əţ |i **~ies** iz

accolade 'æk ə leɪd -lɑːd, ˌ· ·'· **~s** z
accommo|date ə 'kɒm ə |deɪt ‖ ə 'kɑːm- **~dated** deɪt ɪd -əd ‖ deɪţ əd **~dates** deɪts **~dating/ly** deɪt ɪŋ /li ‖ deɪţ ɪŋ /li
accommodation ə ˌkɒm ə 'deɪʃ ᵊn ‖ ə ˌkɑːm- *(not* ˌæk ɒm-*)* **~s** z
accompaniment ə 'kʌmp ən‿i mənt **~s** s
accompanist ə 'kʌmp ən‿ɪst §‿əst **~s** s
accompan|y ə 'kʌmp ən‿|i **~ied** id **~ies** iz **~ying** i ɪŋ
accomplic|e ə 'kʌmp lɪs ə 'kɒmp-, -ləs ‖ ə 'kɑːmp ləs ə 'kʌmp- **~es** ɪz əz

ACCOMPLISH

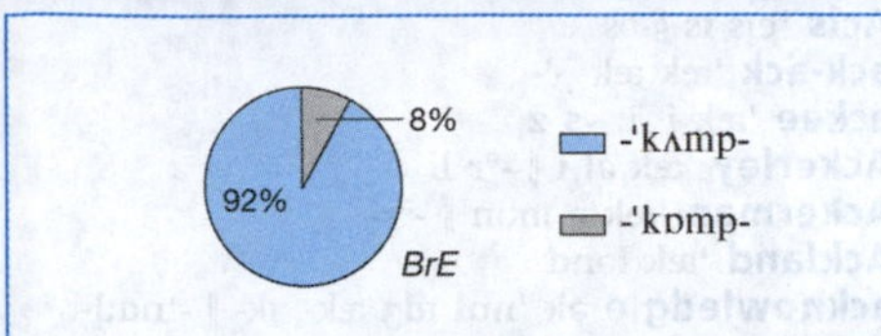

accomplish ə 'kʌmp lɪʃ ə 'kɒmp- ‖ ə 'kɑːmp- ə 'kʌmp- — *Preference poll, BrE:* -'kʌmp- *92%,* -'kɒmp- *8%. In AmE, however,* -'kɑːmp- *clearly predominates.* **~ed** t **~er/s** ə/z ‖ ᵊr/z **~es** ɪz əz **~ing** ɪŋ **~ment/s** mənt/s
accord ə 'kɔːd ‖ ə 'kɔːrd **~ed** ɪd əd **~ing** ɪŋ **~s** z
accordance ə 'kɔːd ᵊnᵗs ‖ ə 'kɔːrd ᵊnᵗs
accordant ə 'kɔːd ᵊnt ‖ ə 'kɔːrd ᵊnt **~ly** li
according ə 'kɔːd ɪŋ ‖ ə 'kɔːrd ɪŋ **~ly** li
accordion ə 'kɔːd i‿ən ‖ ə 'kɔːrd- **~ist/s** ɪst/s §əst/s **~s** z
accost ə 'kɒst ‖ ə 'kɔːst ə 'kɑːst **~ed** ɪd əd **~ing** ɪŋ **~s** s
accouchement ə 'kuːʃ mɒ̃ -mɑ̃ː ‖ -mɑːnt ˌæk uːʃ 'mɑ̃ː
accoucheur ˌæk uː 'ʃɜː ‖ -'ʃɜ˞ː **~s** z
account ə 'kaʊnt **accounted** ə 'kaʊnt ɪd -əd ‖ ə 'kaʊnţ əd **accounting** ə 'kaʊnt ɪŋ ‖ ə 'kaʊnţ ɪŋ
accountability ə ˌkaʊnt ə 'bɪl ət i -ɪt i ‖ ə ˌkaʊnţ ə 'bɪl əţ i
accountable ə 'kaʊnt əb ᵊl ‖ ə 'kaʊnţ- **~ness** nəs nɪs
accountancy ə 'kaʊnt ənᵗs i ‖ -ᵊnᵗs i
accountant ə 'kaʊnt ənt ‖ -ᵊnt **~s** s
accoutered, accoutred ə 'kuːt əd ‖ ə 'kuːţ ᵊrd
accouterment, accoutrement ə 'kuːtr ə mənt ə 'kuːt- ‖ ə 'kuːţ ᵊr- ə 'kuːtr ə- **~s** s
Accra ə 'krɑː æ-
accred|it ə 'kred |ɪt §-ət ‖ -|ət **~ited** ɪt ɪd §ət-, -əd ‖ əţ əd **~iting** ɪt ɪŋ §ət- ‖ əţ ɪŋ **~its** ɪts §əts ‖ əts
accreditation ə ˌkred ɪ 'teɪʃ ᵊn -ə-
ac|crete ə |'kriːt æ- **~creted** 'kriːt ɪd -əd ‖ 'kriːţ əd **~cretes** 'kriːts **~creting** 'kriːt ɪŋ ‖ 'kriːţ ɪŋ
accretion ə 'kriːʃ ᵊn æ- **~s** z
Accrington 'æk rɪŋ tən

accrual ə 'kruː‿əl §ə 'kruːl **~s** z
accrue ə 'kruː **accrued** ə 'kruːd **accrues** ə 'kruːz **accruing** ə 'kruː‿ɪŋ
accultu|rate ə 'kʌltʃ ə |reɪt æ- **~rated** reɪt ɪd -əd ‖ reɪţ əd **~rates** reɪts **~rating** reɪt ɪŋ ‖ reɪţ ɪŋ
acculturation ə ˌkʌltʃ ə 'reɪʃ ᵊn æ-
accumulable ə 'kjuːm jəl əb ᵊl -'·jʊl-
accumu|late ə 'kjuːm jə |leɪt -ju-, ⚠-ə- **~lated** leɪt ɪd -əd ‖ leɪţ əd **~lates** leɪts **~lating** leɪt ɪŋ ‖ leɪţ ɪŋ
accumulation ə ˌkjuːm jə 'leɪʃ ᵊn -ju'·-, ⚠-ə'·- **~s** z
accumulative ə 'kjuːm jəl ət ɪv -'·jʊl-, ⚠-'·əl-; -'·jə leɪt ɪv, -'·ju-, ⚠-'·ə- ‖ -jə leɪţ ɪv -jəl əţ- **~ly** li **~ness** nəs nɪs
accumulator ə 'kjuːm jə leɪt ə -'·ju-, ⚠-'·ə- ‖ -leɪţ ᵊr **~s** z
accurac|y 'æk jər əs |i '·jʊr-, -ɪs i **~ies** iz
accurate 'æk jər ət -jʊr-, -ɪt **~ly** li **~ness** nəs nɪs
Accurist *tdmk* 'æk jʊr ɪst -jər-, §-əst
accursed ə 'kɜːs ɪd ə 'kɜːst ‖ ə 'kɜ˞ːst ə 'kɜ˞ːs əd **~ly** li **~ness** nəs nɪs
accurst ə 'kɜːst ‖ ə 'kɜ˞ːst
accusal ə 'kjuːz ᵊl **~s** z
accusation ˌæk ju 'zeɪʃ ᵊn ‖ -jə- **~s** z
accusatival ə ˌkjuːz ə 'taɪv ᵊl ◂
accusative ə 'kjuːz ət ɪv ‖ -əţ- **~ly** li **~s** z
accusatorial ə ˌkjuːz ə 'tɔːr i‿əl ◂ ‖ -'toʊr-
accusatory ə 'kjuːz ə‿tər i ˌæk ju 'zeɪt ər i ‖ -tɔːr i -toʊr i
accus|e ə 'kjuːz **~ed** d **~es** ɪz əz **~ing/ly** ɪŋ /li
accuser ə 'kjuːz ə ‖ -ᵊr **~s** z
accustom ə 'kʌst əm **~ed** d **~ing** ɪŋ **~s** z
AC/DC, ac-dc ˌeɪ siː 'diː siː ◂
ace eɪs **aced** eɪst **aces** 'eɪs ɪz -əz **acing** 'eɪs ɪŋ
-acea 'eɪs i‿ə 'eɪʃ ə — **Crustacea** krʌ 'steɪs i‿ə -'steɪʃ ə
-aceae 'eɪs i iː 'eɪʃ- — **Rosaceae** rəʊ 'zeɪs i iː -'zeɪʃ- ‖ roʊ-
Aceh 'ætʃ eɪ 'ɑːtʃ- ‖ 'ɑːtʃ eɪ —*Indonesian* [ʔa 'tçɛh]
Aceldama ə 'keld əm ə ə 'seld-; ˌæk el 'dɑːm ə ‖ ə 'seld-
-aceous 'eɪʃ əs — **rosaceous** rəʊ 'zeɪʃ əs ‖ roʊ-
acephalous ˌeɪ 'sef əl əs ə-
acequia ə 'seɪk i‿ə ɑː- **~s** z
Acer *tdmk* 'eɪs ə ‖ -ᵊr
acerbic ə 'sɜːb ɪk æ- ‖ -'sɜ˞ːb ɪk **~ally** ᵊl‿i
acerbit|y ə 'sɜːb ət |i æ-, -ɪt- ‖ -'sɜ˞ːb əţ |i **~ies** iz
acetabul|um ˌæs ɪ 'tæb jʊl |əm ˌ·ə-, -jəl əm ‖ -jəl |əm **~a** ə
acetaldehyde ˌæs ɪ 'tæld ɪ haɪd ˌ·ə-, -'·ə-
acetaminophen ə ˌsiːt ə 'mɪn ə fen -ˌset-, -əf ən; ˌæs ɪt- ‖ ə ˌsiːţ- ˌæs əţ-
acetanilide ˌæs ɪ 'tæn ə laɪd ˌ·ə-, -'·ɪ-, -ᵊl aɪd ‖ -ᵊl aɪd -əd
acetate 'æs ə teɪt -ɪ- **~s** s
acetic ə 'siːt ɪk ə 'set- ‖ ə 'siːţ ɪk
aˌcetic 'acid

acetification ə ˌset ɪf ɪ ˈkeɪʃ ən -ˌsiːt-, -ˌəf-, §-əˈ-- ‖ ə ˌset̬- ə ˌsiːt̬-
aceti|fy ə ˈset ɪ |faɪ ə ˈsiːt-, -ə- ‖ -ˈset̬- -ˈsiːt̬- **~fied** faɪd **~fier/s** faɪ‿ə/z ‖ faɪ‿ər/z **~fies** faɪz **~fying** faɪ ɪŋ
acetone ˈæs ə təʊn -ɪ- ‖ -toʊn
acetyl ˈæs ɪ taɪəl -ə-; -ɪt ɪl, -ət-, -əl; ə ˈsiːt aɪəl, -ɪl, -əl ‖ ˈæs ət̬ əl ə ˈsiːt̬ əl, ˈæs ə tiːəl
acetylcholine ˌæs ɪ taɪəl ˈkəʊl iːn ˌ-ə-; ˌæs ɪt ɪl-, ˌæs ət-, -əlˈ--; ə ˌsiːt aɪəl-, -ˌ·ɪl-, -ˌ·əl-; -ɪn ‖ ə ˌsiːt̬ əl ˈkoʊl- ə ˌset̬-; ˌæs ət̬-, ˌæs ə tiːəl-
acetylene ə ˈset ə liːn -ɪ-; -əl iːn; -əl ɪn, §-ən ‖ ə ˈset̬ əl iːn -ən
acetylsalicylic ˌæs ɪ taɪəl ˌsæl ə ˈsɪl ɪk ◂ ˌ·ə-, ˌæs ɪt ɪl-, ˌæs ət-, -əl,ˈ--; ə ˌsiːt aɪəl-, ·ˌ·ɪl-, ·ˌ·əl-; -ɪˈ-- ‖ ə ˌsiːt̬ əl- ˌæs ət̬-
ach ɑːx æx —*Ger* [ʔax]
Achae|a ə ˈkiː‿|ə **~an/s** ən/z
Achaemenid ə ˈkiːm ən ɪd -ˈkem-, -ɪn-, §-əd **~s** z
Achai|a ə ˈkaɪ‿|ə **~an/s** ən/z
Achates ə ˈkeɪt iːz -ˈkɑːt- ‖ ə ˈkeɪt̬ iːz
ache eɪk *(!)* **ached** eɪkt **aches** eɪks **aching/ly** ˈeɪk ɪŋ /li
Achebe ə ˈtʃeɪb i -eɪ
Achelous ˌæk ə ˈləʊ əs -ɪ- ‖ -ˈloʊ-
achene ə ˈkiːn eɪ- **~s** z
Acheron ˈæk ər ən -ə rɒn ‖ -ə rɑːn
Acheson ˈætʃ ɪs ən -əs-
Acheulian ə ˈʃuːl i‿ən -ˈtʃuːl-
achievable ə ˈtʃiːv əb əl
achieve ə ˈtʃiːv **achieved** ə ˈtʃiːvd **achieves** ə ˈtʃiːvz **achieving** ə ˈtʃiːv ɪŋ
achievement ə ˈtʃiːv mənt **~s** s
a'chievement test
achiever ə ˈtʃiːv ə ‖ -ər **~s** z
Achill ˈæk ɪl -əl
achillea ˌæk ɪ ˈliː‿ə -ə- **~s** z
Achilles, ~' ə ˈkɪl iːz
Aˌchilles' 'heel; **Aˌchilles' 'tendon**
Achitophel ə ˈkɪt ə fel ‖ ə ˈkɪt̬-
ach-laut ˈæx laʊt ˈæk- ‖ ˈɑːx- —*Ger* Achlaut [ˈʔax laut] **~s** s
Achnasheen ˌæk nə ˈʃiːn ˌæx-
achondroplasia ˌeɪ ˌkɒndr əʊ ˈpleɪz i‿ə ə ˌkɒndr- ‖ ˌeɪ ˌkɑːndr ə ˈpleɪʒ i‿ə -ˈpleɪʒ ə
achondroplastic ˌeɪ ˌkɒndr əʊ ˈplæst ɪk ə ˌkɒndr-, -ˈplɑːst- ‖ ˌeɪ ˌkɑːndr ə-
achoo ə ˈtʃuː
achromatic ˌæk rəʊ ˈmæt ɪk ◂ ˌeɪ krəʊ- ‖ ˌæk rə ˈmæt̬ ɪk ◂ **~ally** əl‿i
achromatism ə ˈkrəʊm ə ˌtɪz əm $_{(ˌ)}$æ-, $_{(ˌ)}$eɪ- ‖ $_{(ˌ)}$eɪ ˈkroʊm-
achtung ˌæx ˈtʊŋ ˌɑːx-, ˈ· · ‖ ˌɑːx- —*Ger* A~ [ˈʔax tʊŋ]
achy ˈeɪk i
ach-y-fi ˌæx ə ˈviː ˌʌx-, ˌæk-, ˌʌk- —*Welsh* [aːχ ə ˈviː]
acicul|a ə ˈsɪk jʊl |ə -jəl- ‖ -jəl |ə **~ae** iː **~ar** ə ‖ ər
acid ˈæs ɪd §-əd **~ly** li **~ness** nəs nɪs **~s** z
ˌacid 'rain; **ˌacid 'rock**; **ˌacid 'test**

acidhead ˈæs ɪd hed §-əd- **~s** z
acidic ə ˈsɪd ɪk æ-
acidification ə ˌsɪd ɪf ɪ ˈkeɪʃ ən -ˌ·əf-, §-əˈ--
acidi|fy ə ˈsɪd ɪ |faɪ æ-, -ə- **~fied** faɪd **~fier/s** faɪ‿ə/z ‖ faɪ‿ər/z **~fies** faɪz **~fying** faɪ ɪŋ
acidity ə ˈsɪd ət i æ-, -ɪt- ‖ -ət̬ i
acidophilus ˌæs ɪ ˈdɒf ɪl əs ˌ·ə-, -əl‿əs ‖ -ˈdɑːf-
acidu|late ə ˈsɪd ju |leɪt æ-, -jə-; -ˈsɪdʒ u-, -ə- ‖ ə ˈsɪdʒ ə- **~lated** leɪt ɪd -əd ‖ leɪt̬ əd **~lates** leɪts **~lating** leɪt ɪŋ ‖ leɪt̬ ɪŋ
acidulous ə ˈsɪd jʊl əs æ-, -ˈsɪdʒ ʊl- ‖ ə ˈsɪdʒ əl əs
acing ˈeɪs ɪŋ
ac|inus ˈæs |ɪn əs -ən- **~ini** ɪ naɪ ə-
Acis ˈeɪs ɪs §-əs
ack-ack ˈæk æk ˌ·ˈ·
ackee ˈæk i -iː **~s** z
Ackerley ˈæk əl i ‖ -ər li
Ackerman ˈæk ə mən ‖ -ər-
Ackland ˈæk lənd
acknowledg|e ək ˈnɒl ɪdʒ æk-, ɪk- ‖ -ˈnɑːl- **~ed** d **~es** ɪz əz **~ing** ɪŋ
acknowledgement, acknowledgment ək ˈnɒl ɪdʒ mənt æk-, ɪk- ‖ -ˈnɑːl- **~s** s
Ackroyd ˈæk rɔɪd
Acland ˈæk lənd
Acle ˈeɪk əl
acme ˈæk mi **~s** z
acne ˈæk ni **~d** d
Acol, acol *(i)* ˈæk əl, *(ii)* ˈeɪk ɒl ‖ -ɑːl —*The place in Kent is* ˈeɪk ɒl
acolyte ˈæk ə laɪt -əl aɪt **~s** s
Acomb ˈeɪk əm
Aconcagua ˌæk ən ˈkæg wə →-əŋ-, -ɒn- ‖ -ˈkɑːg- ˌɑːk- —*Sp* [a koŋ ˈka ɣwa]
aconite ˈæk ə naɪt **~s** s
acorn ˈeɪk ɔːn ‖ ˈeɪk ɔːrn *(!)* **~s** z
acotyledon ˌeɪ ˌkɒt ɪ ˈliːd ən ə ˌkɒt-, æ-, -əˈ--, -əl ˈiːd- ‖ ˌeɪ ˌkɑːt̬ əl ˈiːd ən **~s** z
A'Court ˈeɪ kɔːt ‖ ˈeɪ kɔːrt -koʊrt
acoustic ə ˈkuːst ɪk -ˈkʊst- —*formerly also* -ˈkaʊst- **~s** s
acoustical ə ˈkuːst ɪk əl **~ly** ‿i
acoustician ˌæk u ˈstɪʃ ən **~s** z
acquaint ə ˈkweɪnt **acquainted** ə ˈkweɪnt ɪd -əd ‖ ə ˈkweɪnt̬ əd **acquainting** ə ˈkweɪnt ɪŋ ‖ ə ˈkweɪnt̬ ɪŋ **acquaints** ə ˈkweɪnts
acquaintanc|e ə ˈkweɪnt ənts ‖ -ənts **~es** ɪz əz
acquaintanceship ə ˈkweɪnt ən ʃɪp -ənts-, →-əntʃ- ‖ ənts- **~s** s
acquiesc|e ˌæk wi ˈes **~ed** t **~es** ɪz əz **~ing** ɪŋ
acquiescence ˌæk wi ˈes ənts
acquiescent ˌæk wi ˈes ənt ◂ **~ly** li
acquire ə ˈkwaɪ‿ə ‖ ə ˈkwaɪ‿ər **~d** d **~ment/s** mənt/s **~s** z **acquiring** ə ˈkwaɪ‿ər ɪŋ ‖ ə ˈkwaɪ ər ɪŋ
acquisition ˌæk wɪ ˈzɪʃ ən -wə- **~s** z
acquisitive ə ˈkwɪz ət ɪv æ-, -ɪt- ‖ -ət̬ ɪv **~ly** li **~ness** nəs nɪs
acquit ə ˈkwɪt **acquits** ə ˈkwɪts **acquitted** ə ˈkwɪt ɪd -əd ‖ ə ˈkwɪt̬ əd **acquitting** ə ˈkwɪt ɪŋ ‖ ə ˈkwɪt̬ ɪŋ
acquittal ə ˈkwɪt əl ‖ ə ˈkwɪt̬ əl **~s** z

acre, Acre ˈeɪk ə ‖ ˈeɪk ər **~d** d **~s** z
ˌ**Acre ˈLane**
Acre *place in Israel* ˈeɪk ə ˈɑːk- ‖ -ər
acreag|e ˈeɪk ər‿ɪdʒ **~es** ɪz əz
acrid ˈæk rɪd §-rəd **~ly** li **~ness** nəs nɪs
acridity æ ˈkrɪd ət i ə-, -ɪt- ‖ -əţ i
acriflavine ˌæk rɪ ˈfleɪv iːn -rə-, -ɪn, §-ən
Acrilan *tdmk* ˈæk rɪ læn -rə-, -lən
acrimonious ˌæk rɪ ˈməʊn i‿əs ◂ ˌ·rə- ‖ -ˈmoʊn- **~ly** li **~ness** nəs nɪs
acrimony ˈæk rɪm ən i ˈ·rəm- ‖ -ə moʊn i
acro- *comb. form*
with stress-neutral suffix ¦æk rəʊ ‖ ¦æk rə -roʊ — **acrophobia** ˌæk rəʊ ˈfəʊb i‿ə ‖ -rə ˈfoʊb-
with stress-imposing suffix ə ˈkrɒ+ ‖ ə ˈkrɑː+ — **acropetal** ə ˈkrɒp ɪt əl §-ət- ‖ ə ˈkrɑːp əţ əl
acrobat ˈæk rə bæt **~s** s
acrobatic ˌæk rə ˈbæt ɪk ◂ ‖ -ˈbæţ ɪk **~ally** əl‿i **~s** s
acrolect ˈæk rəʊ lekt ‖ -roʊ- -rə- **~s** s
acrolectal ˌæk rəʊ ˈlekt əl ‖ -roʊ- -rə-
acromegalic ˌæk rəʊ mə ˈgæl ɪk ◂ -mɪˈ-- ‖ ˌæk roʊ-
acromegaly ˌæk rəʊ ˈmeg əl i ‖ ˌæk roʊ-
acronym ˈæk rə nɪm **~s** z
acrophob|ia ˌæk rəʊ ˈfəʊb |i‿ə ‖ -rə ˈfoʊb- **~ic** ɪk ◂
acropolis ə ˈkrɒp əl ɪs §-əs ‖ -ˈkrɑːp-
across ə ˈkrɒs ‖ ə ˈkrɔːs -ˈkrɑːs
across-the-board ə ˌkrɒs ðə ˈbɔːd ◂ ‖ ə ˌkrɔːs ðə ˈbɔːrd ◂ ə ˌkrɑːs-, -ˈboʊrd
an aˌcross-the-ˌboard ˈincrease
acrostic ə ˈkrɒst ɪk ‖ ə ˈkrɔːst ɪk -ˈkrɑːst- **~ally** əl‿i **~s** s
acrylic ə ˈkrɪl ɪk æ- **~s** s
act ækt **acted** ˈækt ɪd -əd **acting** ˈækt ɪŋ **acts, Acts** ækts
ˌ**act of ˈGod**
Actaeon æk ˈtiː‿ən
ACTH ˌeɪ siː tiː ˈeɪtʃ ækθ
actinic æk ˈtɪn ɪk
actinide ˈækt ɪ naɪd §-ə- **~s** z
actinism ˈækt ɪ ˌnɪz əm §-ə-
actinium æk ˈtɪn i‿əm
actinometer ˌækt ɪ ˈnɒm ɪt ə §ˌ·ə-, -ət ə ‖ -ˈnɑːm əţ ər **~s** z
action ˈæk ʃən **~ed** d **~ing** ɪŋ **~s** z
ˈ**action man**; ˌ**action ˈreplay**; ˈ**action ˌstations**, ˌ· · ˈ· ·
actionab|le ˈæk ʃən‿əb |əl **~ly** li
action-packed ˈæk ʃən pækt →-ʃəm-
Actium ˈækt i‿əm
acti|vate ˈækt ɪ |veɪt -ə- **~vated** veɪt ɪd -əd ‖ veɪţ əd **~vates** veɪts **~vating** veɪt ɪŋ ‖ veɪţ ɪŋ
activation ˌækt ɪ ˈveɪʃ ən -ə- **~s** z
activator ˈækt ɪ veɪt ə ‖ -veɪţ ər **~s** z
active ˈækt ɪv **~ly** li **~ness** nəs nɪs **~s** z
Activex, ActiveX *tdmk* ˈækt ɪ veks -ə-
activism ˈækt ɪv ˌɪz əm §-əv-
activist ˈækt ɪv ɪst §-əv-, §-əst **~s** s

activit|y æk ˈtɪv ət |i -ɪt- ‖ -əţ |i **~ies** iz
Acton ˈækt ən
actor ˈækt ə ‖ -ər —*There is also a mannered pronunciation* -ɔː ‖ -ɔːr **~s** z
actress ˈæk trəs -trɪs, -tres **~es** ɪz əz
actressy ˈæk trəs i -trɪs-
actual ˈæk tʃu‿əl ˈæk tʃəl, ˈæk ʃu‿əl, ˈæk ʃəl, ˈækt ju‿əl
actualis... —*see* **actualiz...**
actualité ˌækt ju ˈæl ɪ teɪ ˌæk tʃu-, -ə- ‖ ˌɑːk tʃu ɑːl ə ˈteɪ ˌæk- —*Fr* [ak ty al i te]
actualit|y ˌæk tʃu ˈæl ət |i ˌ·tju-, ˌ·ʃu-, -ɪt i ‖ -əţ |i **~ies** iz
actualization ˌæk tʃu‿əl aɪ ˈzeɪʃ ən ˌ·tju‿, ˌ·ʃu‿, -ɪˈ-- ‖ -əˈ--
actualiz|e ˈæk tʃu‿ə laɪz ˈækt ju‿, ˈæk ʃu‿ **~ed** d **~es** ɪz əz **~ing** ɪŋ
actually ˈæk tʃu‿əl i ˈæk tʃəl i, ˈæk ʃu‿əl i, ˈæk ʃəl‿i, ˈækt ju‿əl i —*There is also a very casual form* ˈæk ʃi
actuarial ˌæk tʃu ˈeər i‿əl ◂ ˌækt ju-, ˌæk ʃu- ‖ -ˈer- **~ly** i
actuar|y ˈæk tʃu‿ər |i ˈækt ju‿, ˈæk ʃu‿ ‖ -er |i **~ies** iz
actu|ate ˈæk tʃu |eɪt ˈækt ju-, ˈæk ʃu- **~ated** eɪt ɪd -əd ‖ eɪţ əd **~ates** eɪts **~ating** eɪt ɪŋ ‖ eɪţ ɪŋ
actuation ˌæk tʃu ˈeɪʃ ən ˌækt ju-, ˌæk ʃu-
actuator ˈæk tʃu eɪt ə ˈækt ju-, ˈæk ʃu- ‖ -eɪţ ər
acuity ə ˈkjuː‿ət i ɪt- ‖ -əţ i
acumen ˈæk jʊm ən -jəm-; -ju men, -jə-; ə ˈkjuːm en, -ən ‖ ə ˈkjuːm ən ˈæk jəm-
acuminate ə ˈkjuːm ɪn ət -ən-, -ɪt; -ɪ neɪt, -ə-
acupuncture ˈæk ju ˌpʌŋk tʃə -jə-, §-ə-, ⚠-wə-, -ʃə ‖ -jə ˌpʌŋk tʃər
acupuncturist ˈæk ju ˌpʌŋk tʃər ɪst ˈ·jə-, §ˈ·ə-, ⚠ˈ·wə-, ˌ· ·ˈ--, -ʃər ɪst, §-əst ‖ ˈæk jə- **~s** s
acute ə ˈkjuːt **~ly** li **~ness** nəs nɪs
aˌcute ˈaccent
-acy əs i —*Words with this suffix are stressed in the same way as the corresponding form with* -ate, *if there is one* (leˈgitimacy). *Otherwise, the stem keeps its usual stress, though sometimes with a vowel change* (suˈpreme — suˈpremacy). *See also* -cracy.
acyclic (ˌ)eɪ ˈsaɪk lɪk -ˈsɪk-
acyclovir eɪ ˈsaɪk ləʊ vɪə ‖ -oʊ vɪr
AD ˌeɪ ˈdiː
ad æd *(= add)* **ads** ædz —*See also phrases with this word*
ad- əd, (¦)æd —*This prefix is strong* ¦æd *when stressed, (1) because of a suffix* (ˌadapˈtation), *and (2) in some two-syllable nouns* (ˈadverb). *Otherwise, in RP and GenAm, it is usually unstressed and weak* (aˈdapt), *although some speakers use a strong vowel if the following stem begins with a consonant* (adˈmit). *Before a stem with initial* **d** *or* **dʒ** *the prefix regularly loses its* **d** (adˈdiction). *Note the irregularly stressed word* ˈadjective.
-ad æd, əd — **octad** ˈɒkt æd -əd ‖ ˈɑːkt-
Ada ˈeɪd ə
adag|e ˈæd ɪdʒ **~es** ɪz əz

adagio ə 'dɑːdʒ i̯əʊ -'dɑːʒ-, -'dɑːdʒ əʊ ‖ ə 'dɑːdʒ oʊ -'dɑːdʒ i̯oʊ **~s** z
Adair ə 'deə ‖ ə 'deᵊr -'dæᵊr
Adam 'æd əm **~'s** z —*but for the French composer,* æ 'dɒ̃ ‖ ɑː 'dɑːm —*Fr* [a dɑ̃]
ˌAdam's 'apple ‖ '. . . .
adamancy 'æd əm ənᵗs i
adamant 'æd əm ənt **~ly** li
adamantine ˌæd ə 'mænt aɪn ◂ ‖ -iːn -aɪn, -ᵊn
Adamawa ˌæd ə 'mɑː wə
Adamic ə 'dæm ɪk æ-
Adams 'æd əmz
Adamsez 'æd əmz ɪz -əz; -əm sez
Adamson 'æd əm sən
adapt ə 'dæpt **adapted** ə 'dæpt ɪd -əd **adapting** ə 'dæpt ɪŋ **adapts** ə 'dæpts
adaptability ə ˌdæpt ə 'bɪl ət i -ɪt i ‖ -əṭ i
adaptab|le ə 'dæpt əb |ᵊl **~ly** li
adaptation ˌæd æp 'teɪʃ ᵊn -əp- **~s** z
adapter ə 'dæpt ə ‖ -ᵊr **~s** z
adaptive ə 'dæpt ɪv **~ly** li **~ness** nəs nɪs
adaptor ə 'dæpt ə ‖ -ᵊr **~s** z
Adare ə 'deə ‖ ə 'deᵊr -'dæᵊr
ADC ˌeɪ diː 'siː **~s, ~'s** z
Adcock 'æd kɒk →'æg- ‖ -kɑːk
add æd **added** 'æd ɪd -əd **adding** 'æd ɪŋ **adds** ædz
ADD *'attention deficit disorder'* ˌeɪ diː 'diː
Addams 'æd əmz
addax 'æd æks
addend|um ə 'dend |əm **~a** ə
adder 'æd ə ‖ 'æd ᵊr **~s** z
addict *n* 'æd ɪkt **addicts** 'æd ɪkts
addict *v* ə 'dɪkt **addicted** ə 'dɪkt ɪd -əd **addicting** ə 'dɪkt ɪŋ **addicts** ə 'dɪkts
addiction ə 'dɪk ʃᵊn **~s** z
addictive ə 'dɪkt ɪv **~ly** li **~ness** nəs nɪs
Addie 'æd i
Addington 'æd ɪŋ tən
Addis 'æd ɪs §-əs
ˌAddis 'Ababa 'æb əb ə
Addiscombe 'æd ɪs kəm §-əs-
Addison 'æd ɪs ən §-əs- **~'s** z
'Addison's diˌsease
addition ə 'dɪʃ ᵊn **~s** z
additional ə 'dɪʃ ᵊn‿əl **~ly** i
additive 'æd ət ɪv -ɪt- ‖ -əṭ ɪv **~s** z
addle 'æd ᵊl **addled** 'æd ᵊld **addles** 'æd ᵊlz **addling** 'æd ᵊl‿ɪŋ
Addlebrough 'æd ᵊl bər‿ə ‖ -ˌbɜː oʊ
Addlestone 'æd ᵊl stəʊn ‖ -stoʊn
add-on 'æd ɒn ‖ -ɑːn -ɔːn **~s** z
address *v* ə 'dres æ- **~ed** t **~es** ɪz əz **~ing** ɪŋ

ADDRESS

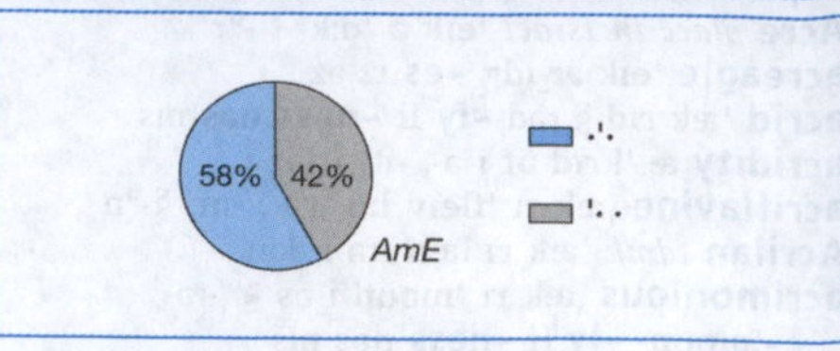

address *n* ə 'dres ‖ 'ædr es **~es** ɪz əz — *Preference poll, AmE:* ·'· *58%,* '·· *42%.*
addressable ə 'dres əb ᵊl
addressee ˌædr es 'iː ə ˌdres 'iː **~s** z
Addressograph *tdmk* ə 'dres əʊ grɑːf -græf ‖ -ə græf
adduc|e ə 'djuːs æ-, →-'dʒuːs ‖ ə 'duːs -'djuːs **~ed** t **~es** ɪz əz **~ing** ɪŋ
adduct ə 'dʌkt æ- **~ed** ɪd əd **~ing** ɪŋ **~s** s
adduction ə 'dʌk ʃᵊn
adductor ə 'dʌkt ə ‖ -ᵊr **~s** z
Addy 'æd i
-ade 'eɪd —*This suffix is usually stressed* (ˌlemo'nade, ˌharlequi'nade). *When* -ade *is not a true suffix it may be stressed or unstressed, taking one of the forms* eɪd, 'eɪd, ɑːd, 'ɑːd, *depending on the particular word* ('marmelade; ˌprome'nade, '· · ·) —*see individual entries.*
Adel 'æd ᵊl
Adela 'æd ɪl ə -əl-; ə 'deɪl ə
Adelaide 'æd ə leɪd -ɪ-, →-ᵊl eɪd
Adele, Adèle ə 'del
Adelie, Adélie ə 'deɪl i ə 'diːl-, 'æd ɪl i, -əl i
Adelina ˌæd ə 'liːn ə -ɪ-; -ᵊl 'iːn-
Adeline 'æd ə laɪn -ɪ-, -liːn; -ᵊl aɪn, -iːn
Adelphi ə 'delf i
Aden 'eɪd ᵊn *Arabic* ['ʔa dan]
Adenauer 'æd ə naʊ‿ə 'ɑːd-, →-ᵊn aʊ‿ə ‖ -naʊ‿ᵊr —*Ger* ['ʔaː də naʊ ɐ]
Adeney 'eɪd ən‿i
adenine 'æd ə niːn -naɪn, -nɪn ‖ -ᵊn iːn
adenoid 'æd ɪ nɔɪd -ə-, →-ᵊn ɔɪd ‖ -ᵊn ɔɪd **~s** z
adenoidal ˌæd ɪ 'nɔɪd ᵊl ◂ -ə-, →-ᵊn 'ɔɪd- ‖ ˌæd ᵊn 'ɔɪd ᵊl ◂ **~ly** i
adenom|a ˌæd ɪ 'nəʊm |ə -ə-, →-ᵊn 'əʊm- ‖ ˌæd ᵊn 'oʊm |ə **~as** əz **~ata** ət ə ‖ əṭ ə
adenopathy ˌæd ɪ 'nɒp əθ i ˌ-ə-, →-ᵊn 'ɒp- ‖ ˌæd ᵊn 'ɑːp-
adenosine ə 'den əʊ siːn æ-; ˌæd ɪ 'nəʊs iːn, -ə- ‖ -ə siːn -əs ən
adept *n* 'æd ept ə 'dept, æ 'dept **~s** s
adept *adj* ə 'dept æ-, 'æd ept **~ly** li **~ness** nəs nɪs
adequacy 'æd ɪk wəs i '-ək-, -wɪs i
adequate 'æd ɪk wət -ək-, -wɪt **~ly** li **~ness** nəs nɪs
adessive æ 'des ɪv ə- **~s** z
adeste fideles æd ˌest i fɪ 'deɪl eɪz əd-, -eɪs
à deux æ 'dɜː ɑː- ‖ -'dʌ —*Fr* [a dø]
Adger 'ædʒ ə ‖ -ᵊr
adhere əd 'hɪə (ˌ)æd- ‖ -'hɪᵊr **~d** d **~s** z
adhering əd 'hɪər ɪŋ (ˌ)æd- ‖ -'hɪr ɪŋ

adherence əd 'hɪər ənᵗs (ˌ)æd-, -'her- ‖ -'hɪr-
adherent əd 'hɪər ənt (ˌ)æd-, -'her- ‖ -'hɪr- **~ly** li **~s** s
adhesion əd 'hiːʒ ᵊn (ˌ)æd-
adhesive əd 'hiːs ɪv (ˌ)æd-, -'hiːz- **~ly** li **~ness** nəs nɪs **~s** z
ad hoc (ˌ)æd 'hɒk ◂ -'həʊk ‖ -'hɑːk ˌɑːd-, -'hoʊk
adhoc-ery, adhockery ˌæd 'hɒk ər i -'həʊk- ‖ -'hɑːk- ˌɑːd-, -'hoʊk-
ad hominem (ˌ)æd 'hɒm ɪ nem -ə- ‖ -'hɑːm- ˌɑːd-, -ən əm
adiabatic ˌæd i‿ə 'bæt ɪk ◂ ˌeɪ ˌdaɪ‿ə- ‖ -'bæṭ ɪk **~ally** ᵊl‿i
Adidas *tdmk* 'æd ɪ dæs -ə-, ə 'diːd æs, -əz ‖ 'ɑːd ə- ə 'diːd əz, -əs
Adie 'eɪd i
Adiemus ˌæd i 'eɪm əs
adieu ə 'djuː æ-, →-'dʒuː, -'djɜː ‖ -'duː -'djuː —*Fr* [a djø] **~s** z **~x** z —*or as sing.*
Adi Granth ˌɑːd i 'grʌnt
ad infinitum ˌæd ˌɪn fɪ 'naɪt əm ·ˌ-·-, -fə'-- ‖ -'naɪṭ əm ˌɑːd-
adios ˌæd i 'ɒs ‖ -'oʊs ˌɑːd- —*Sp* [a 'ðjos]
adipocere 'æd ɪ pəʊ sɪə -ə-, -pə-, ˌ· · ·'· ‖ -ə poʊ sɪr
adipose 'æd ɪ pəʊs -ə-, -pəʊz ‖ -poʊs **~ness** nəs nɪs
adiposity ˌæd ɪ 'pɒs ət i ˌ-ə-, -ɪt i ‖ -'pɑːs əṭ i
Adirondack ˌæd ə 'rɒnd æk -ɪ- ‖ -'rɑːnd- **~s** s
adit 'æd ɪt §-ət **~s** s
adjacency ə 'dʒeɪs ᵊnᵗs i
adjacent ə 'dʒeɪs ᵊnt **~ly** li
adjectival ˌædʒ ɪk 'taɪv ᵊl ◂ -ek-, -ək- **~ly** i **~s** z
adjective 'ædʒ ɪkt ɪv -ekt-, -əkt- ‖ ⚠-əṭ- **~s** z
adjoin ə'dʒɔɪn æ- **~ed** d **~ing** ɪŋ **~s** z
adjourn ə 'dʒɜːn ‖ ə 'dʒɝːn **~ed** d **~ing** ɪŋ **~s** z
adjournment ə 'dʒɜːn mənt →-'dʒɜːm- ‖ -'dʒɝːn- **~s** s
adjudg|e ə 'dʒʌdʒ æ- **~ed** d **~es** ɪz əz **~ing** ɪŋ
adjudi|cate ə 'dʒuːd ɪ |keɪt -ə- **~cated** keɪt ɪd -əd ‖ keɪṭ əd **~cates** keɪts **~cating** keɪt ɪŋ ‖ keɪṭ ɪŋ
adjudication ə ˌdʒuːd ɪ 'keɪʃ ᵊn -ə'-- **~s** z
adjudicator ə 'dʒuːd ɪ keɪt ə -'ə- ‖ -keɪṭ ᵊr **~s** z
adjunct 'ædʒ ʌŋ*k*t **~s** s
adjunction ə 'dʒʌŋ*k* ʃᵊn æ-, ˌæd-
adjunctive ə 'dʒʌŋ*k*t ɪv æ-, ˌæd-
adjuration ˌædʒ uᵊ 'reɪʃ ᵊn -ə- **~s** z
adjure ə 'dʒʊə -'dʒɔː ‖ ə 'dʒʊᵊr **~d** d **~s** z **adjuring** ə 'dʒʊər ɪŋ -'dʒɔːr- ‖ ə 'dʒʊᵊr ɪŋ
adjust ə 'dʒʌst **~ed** ɪd əd **~ing** ɪŋ **~s** s
adjustab|le ə 'dʒʌst əb |ᵊl **~ly** li
adjuster ə 'dʒʌst ə ‖ -ᵊr **~s** z
adjustment ə 'dʒʌ*s*t mənt **~s** s
adjutancy 'ædʒ ʊt ənᵗs i
adjutant 'ædʒ ʊt ənt -ət- **~s** s
Adkins 'æd kɪnz →'æg-
Adlai 'æd leɪ -laɪ
adland 'æd lænd
Adlard 'æd lɑːd -ləd ‖ -lɑːrd
Adler *(i)* 'æd lə ‖ -lᵊr, *(ii)* 'ɑːd- —*Ger* ['ʔaːd lɐ]
Adlerian æd 'lɪər i‿ən ‖ -'ler- **~s** z
Adlestrop 'æd ᵊl strɒp ‖ -strɑːp
ad lib ˌæd 'lɪb
ad-lib ˌæd 'lɪb ◂ **~bed** d **~bing** ɪŋ **~s** z
ad|man 'æd |mæn -mən **~men** men mən
admass 'æd mæs
admeasure æd 'meʒ ə əd- ‖ -ᵊr -'meɪʒ- **~s** z
admen 'æd men -mən
Admetus æd 'miːt əs ‖ -'miːṭ-
admin 'æd mɪn ˌ·'·
administer əd 'mɪn ɪst ə æd-, →əb-, -əst- ‖ -ᵊr **~ed** d **administering** əd 'mɪn ɪst ər ɪŋ -'·əst-; →-'ɪs trɪŋ, →-'·əs trɪŋ **~s** z
admini|strate əd 'mɪn ɪ |streɪt æd-, →əb-, -ə- **~strated** streɪt ɪd -əd ‖ streɪṭ əd **~strates** streɪts **~strating** streɪt ɪŋ ‖ streɪṭ ɪŋ
administration əd ˌmɪn ɪ 'streɪʃ ᵊn æd-, →əb-, -ə- **~s** z
administrative əd 'mɪn ɪs trət ɪv æd-, →əb-, -'·əs-; -ɪ streɪt-, -'·ə- ‖ -ə streɪṭ ɪv -əs trəṭ ɪv **~ly** li
administrator əd 'mɪn ɪ streɪt ə æd-, →əb-, -'·ə- ‖ -streɪṭ ᵊr **~s** z
admirable 'æd mər‿əb ᵊl →'æb- **~ness** nəs nɪs
admirably 'æd mər‿əb li →'æb-
admiral 'æd mᵊr‿əl →'æb- **~s** z
admiral|ty 'æd mᵊr‿əl |ti →'æb- **~ties** tiz
ˌAdmiralty 'Arch
admiration ˌæd mə 'reɪʃ ᵊn →ˌæb-, -mɪ-
admire əd 'maɪ‿ə §æd-, →əb- ‖ əd 'maɪ‿ᵊr **~d** d **~s** z **admiring/ly** əd 'maɪ‿ər ɪŋ /li §æd- ‖ əd 'maɪ‿ᵊr ɪŋ /li
admirer əd 'maɪ‿ər ə §æd-, →əb- ‖ əd 'maɪ‿ᵊr ər **~s** z
admissibility əd ˌmɪs ə 'bɪl ət i æd-, →əb-, -ˌɪ-, -ɪt i ‖ -əṭ i
admissib|le əd 'mɪs əb |ᵊl æd-, →əb-, -ɪb- **~ly** li
admission əd 'mɪʃ ᵊn æd-, →əb- **~s** z
ad|mit əd |'mɪt æd-, →əb- **~mits** 'mɪts **~mitted** 'mɪt ɪd -əd ‖ 'mɪṭ əd **~mitting** 'mɪt ɪŋ ‖ 'mɪṭ ɪŋ
admittance əd 'mɪt ᵊnᵗs æd-, →əb-
admitted əd 'mɪt ɪd æd-, →əb-, -əd ‖ -'mɪṭ əd **~ly** li
admixture əd 'mɪks tʃə æd-, →əb- ‖ -tʃᵊr **~s** z
admonish əd 'mɒn ɪʃ æd-, →əb- ‖ -'mɑːn- **~ed** t **~es** ɪz əz **~ing** ɪŋ **~ment/s** mənt/s
admonition ˌæd mə 'nɪʃ ᵊn →ˌæb- **~s** z
admonitory əd 'mɒn ɪt ər i æd-, →əb-, -'·ə- ‖ -'mɑːn ə tɔːr i -toʊr i
ad nauseam ˌæd 'nɔːz i æm -'nɔːs-, -əm ‖ -'nɑːz-
adnominal (ˌ)æd 'nɒm ɪn ᵊl -ən-, -ᵊn‿əl ‖ -'nɑːm- **~s** z
ado ə 'duː
adobe ə 'dəʊb i ‖ ə 'doʊb i
adolescence ˌæd ə 'les ᵊnᵗs -ᵊl 'es-
adolescent ˌæd ə 'les ᵊnt ◂ -ᵊl 'es- **~s** s
Adolf 'æd ɒlf ‖ 'eɪd ɑːlf 'æd-
Adolfo ə 'dɒlf əʊ ‖ ə 'dɑːlf oʊ

A

Adolph ˈæd ɒlf ‖ ˈeɪd ɑːlf ˈæd-
Adolphus ə ˈdɒlf əs ‖ ə ˈdɑːlf əs
Adonai ˌæd əʊ ˈnaɪ ˌ· · ·, -ɒ-, ˌ· ·ˈneɪ aɪ; ə ˈdəʊn i ˌaɪ ‖ ˌɑːd ə ˈnaɪ ˈnɔɪ
Adonis ə ˈdəʊn ɪs -ˈdɒn-, -əs ‖ -ˈdoʊn- ˈdɑːn-
adopt ə ˈdɒpt ‖ ə ˈdɑːpt **~ed** ɪd əd **~er/s** ə/z ‖ ᵊr/z **~ing** ɪŋ **~s** s
adoptee ə ˌdɒp ˈtiː ‖ ə ˌdɑːp ˈtiː **~s** z
adoption ə ˈdɒp ʃᵊn ‖ ə ˈdɑːp- **~s** z
adoptive ə ˈdɒpt ɪv ‖ ə ˈdɑːpt- **~ly** li
adorab|le ə ˈdɔːr əb |ᵊl ‖ -ˈdoʊr- **~leness** ᵊl nəs -nɪs **~ly** li
adoration ˌæd ə ˈreɪʃ ᵊn -ɔː-
adore ə ˈdɔː ‖ ə ˈdɔːr -ˈdoʊr **adored** ə ˈdɔːd ‖ ə ˈdɔːrd -ˈdoʊrd **adores** ə ˈdɔːz ‖ ə ˈdɔːrz -ˈdoʊrz **adoring/ly** ə ˈdɔːr ɪŋ /li ‖ -ˈdoʊr-
adorer ə ˈdɔːr ə ‖ ᵊr -ˈdoʊr- **~s** z
adorn ə ˈdɔːn ‖ ə ˈdɔːrn **~ed** d **~ing** ɪŋ **~s** z
adornment ə ˈdɔːn mənt →-ˈdɔːm- ‖ -ˈdɔːrn- **~s** s
adrenal ə ˈdriːn ᵊl
adrenalin, A~ *tdmk,* **adrenaline** ə ˈdren əl ɪn -ˈdriːn-, §-ən
adrenocorticotrophic ə ˌdriːn əʊ ˌkɔːt ɪk əʊ ˈtrɒf ɪk ◂ ‖ -oʊ ˌkɔːrṭ ɪk oʊ ˈtroʊf ɪk ◂ -ˈtrɑːf-
Adrian ˈeɪdr i ˌən
Adriana ˌeɪdr i ˈɑːn ə
Adriatic ˌeɪdr i ˈæt ɪk ◂ ‖ -ˈæṭ- ˌ**Adri**ˌ**atic** ˈ**Sea**
Adrienne ˈeɪdr i ˌən ˌ· ·ˈen
adrift ə ˈdrɪft
adroit ə ˈdrɔɪt **~ly** li **~ness** nəs nɪs
adsorb ₍ˌ₎æd ˈsɔːb əd-, -ˈzɔːb ‖ -ˈsɔːrb -ˈzɔːrb **~ed** d **~ing** ɪŋ **~s** z
adsorption ₍ˌ₎æd ˈsɔːp ʃᵊn əd-, -ˈzɔːp- ‖ -ˈsɔːrp- -ˈzɔːrp-
adstrate ˈæd streɪt
adsum ˈæd sʊm -sʌm
aduki ə ˈduːk i
adu|late ˈæd ju |leɪt ˈædʒ u-, ˈædʒ ə- ‖ ˈædʒ ə- ˈæd jə-, ˈæd ə- **~lated** leɪt ɪd -əd ‖ leɪṭ əd **~lates** leɪts **~lating** leɪt ɪŋ ‖ leɪṭ ɪŋ
adulation ˌæd ju ˈleɪʃ ᵊn ˌædʒ u-, ˌædʒ ə- ‖ ˌædʒ ə- ˌæd jə-, ˌæd ə-
adulator ˈæd ju leɪt ə ˈædʒ u-, ˈædʒ ə- ‖ ˈædʒ ə leɪṭ ᵊr ˈæd jə-, ˈæd ə- **~s** z
adulatory ˌæd ju ˈleɪt ər i ◂ ˌædʒ u-, ˌædʒ ə-, ˈ· · · ·; ˈædʒ ʊl ət ər i ‖ ˈædʒ əl ə tɔːr i ˈæd jəl-, ˈæd ᵊl-, -toʊr i
Adullam ə ˈdʌl əm
Adullamite ə ˈdʌl ə maɪt **~s** s
adult *adj, n* ˈæd ʌlt ə ˈdʌlt ‖ ə ˈdʌlt ˈæd ʌlt **~s** s — *Preference polls (noun), AmE:* *ˈ· · 88%, ·ˈ· 12%; BrE: ˈ· · 84%, ·ˈ· 16%.*
adulterant ə ˈdʌlt ər ənt **~s** s
adulte|rate ə ˈdʌlt ə |reɪt **~rated** reɪt ɪd -əd ‖ reɪṭ əd **~rates** reɪts **~rating** reɪt ɪŋ ‖ reɪṭ ɪŋ
adulteration ə ˌdʌlt ə ˈreɪʃ ᵊn **~s** z
adulterator ə ˈdʌlt ə reɪt ə ‖ -reɪṭ ᵊr **~s** z
adulterer ə ˈdʌlt ər ə ‖ ˌᵊr ər **~s** z
adulteress ə ˈdʌlt ər es -ɪs, -əs ‖ -əs **~es** ɪz əz
adulterous ə ˈdʌlt ər əs **~ly** li

ADULT

ˈ· · ·ˈ·

16% 84% BrE

88% 12% AmE

adulter|y ə ˈdʌlt ər |i **~ies** iz
adulthood ˈæd ʌlt hʊd ə ˈdʌlt- ‖ ə ˈdʌlt- ˈæd ʌlt-
adum|brate ˈæd ʌm |breɪt -əm-; ə ˈdʌm- **~brated** breɪt ɪd -əd ‖ breɪṭ əd **~brates** breɪts **~brating** breɪt ɪŋ ‖ breɪṭ ɪŋ
adumbration ˌæd ʌm ˈbreɪʃ ᵊn -əm-
Adur ˈeɪd ə ‖ -ᵊr
ad valorem ˌæd və ˈlɔːr em -væ-, -əm ‖ -əm -ˈloʊr-
advanc|e əd ˈvɑːnᵗs §₍ˌ₎æd-, §-ˈvænᵗs ‖ -ˈvænᵗs **~ed** t **~ement/s** mənt/s **~es** ɪz əz **~ing** ɪŋ
advantag|e əd ˈvɑːnt ɪdʒ §æd-, §-ˈvænt- ‖ -ˈvænṭ- —*When explicitly opposed to* disadvantage, *sometimes contrastively stressed* ˈ· · ·. *In public tennis scoring often* æd ˈvɑːnt eɪdʒ ‖ -ˈvænt- **~ed** d **~es** ɪz əz
advantageous ˌæd vən ˈteɪdʒ əs ◂ -væn-, -vɑːn- **~ly** li **~ness** nəs nɪs
advent, Advent ˈæd vent -vᵊnt
Advent|ism ˈæd vənt |ˌɪz əm -vent-; əd ˈvent ˌ· ·, æd- ‖ ˈæd venṭ|- əd ˈvent|ˌ· ·, æd- **~ist/s** ɪst/s §-əst/s
adventitious ˌæd vən ˈtɪʃ əs ◂ -ven- **~ly** li **~ness** nəs nɪs
adventive əd ˈvent ɪv æd- ‖ -ˈvenṭ- **~ly** li
adventure əd ˈventʃ ə §æd- ‖ -ᵊr **~d** d **~s** z **adventuring** əd ˈventʃ ər ɪŋ §æd-
adventurer əd ˈventʃ ᵊr ə §æd- ‖ ər **~s** z
adventuress əd ˈventʃ ər əs §æd-, -ɪs, -ə res **~es** ɪz əz
adventur|ism əd ˈventʃ ər ˌɪz əm §æd- **~ist/s** ɪst/s §əst/s
adventurous əd ˈventʃ ər əs §æd- **~ly** li **~ness** nəs nɪs
adverb ˈæd vɜːb ‖ -vɜːb **~s** z
adverbial əd ˈvɜːb i əl æd- ‖ -ˈvɜːb- **~ly** i **~s** z
adversarial ˌæd vɜː ˈseər i əl ◂ ˌ·və- ‖ -vᵊr ˈser- ˌ·və- **~ly** i
adversar|y ˈæd vəs ər |i -er i; §əd ˈvɜːs ər |i, §æd- ‖ ˈæd vᵊr ser |i ˈ·və- **~ies** iz
adversative əd ˈvɜːs ət ɪv æd- ‖ -ˈvɜːs əṭ- **~ly** li **~s** z
adverse ˈæd vɜːs əd ˈvɜːs, ˌæd- ‖ æd ˈvɜːs ˈ· · **~ly** li **~ness** nəs nɪs
adversit|y əd ˈvɜːs ət |i æd-, -ɪt- ‖ æd ˈvɜːs əṭ |i **~ies** iz
ad|vert *v* əd |ˈvɜːt æd- ‖ æd |ˈvɜːt **~verted** ˈvɜːt ɪd -əd ‖ ˈvɜːṭ əd **~verting** ˈvɜːt ɪŋ ‖ ˈvɜːṭ ɪŋ **~verts** ˈvɜːts ‖ ˈvɜːts
advert *n* ˈæd vɜːt ‖ -vɜːt **~s** s
advertis|e ˈæd və taɪz ‖ -vᵊr- **~ed** d **~er/s** ə/z ‖ ᵊr/z **~es** ɪz əz **~ing** ɪŋ

advertisement əd ˈvɜːt ɪs mənt -ɪz-, -əs-, -əz-; §ˈæd və taɪz mənt, §ˌ·ˈ·ˈ·· ‖ ˌæd vᵊr ˈtaɪz mənt əd ˈvɜːt̬ əs-, -əz- *(*)* **~s** s

advertorial ˌæd və ˈtɔːr i‿əl -vɜː- ‖ -vᵊr- -ˈtoʊr- **~s** z

advice əd ˈvaɪs §æd-

Advil *tdmk* ˈæd vɪl -vᵊl

advisability əd ˌvaɪz ə ˈbɪl ət i §æd- ‖ -ət̬ i

advisab|le əd ˈvaɪz əb |ᵊl §æd- **~ly** li

advis|e əd ˈvaɪz §æd- **~ed** d **~es** ɪz əz **~ing** ɪŋ

advisedly əd ˈvaɪz ɪd li §æd-, -əd-

adviser, advisor əd ˈvaɪz ə §æd- ‖ -ᵊr **~s** z

advisor|y əd ˈvaɪz ər‿|i §æd- **~ies** iz

advocaat ˈæd vəʊ kɑː -kɑːt ‖ -voʊ-

advocacy ˈæd vək əs i

advo|cate *v* ˈæd və |keɪt **~cated** keɪt ɪd -əd ‖ keɪt̬ əd **~cates** keɪts **~cating** keɪt ɪŋ ‖ keɪt̬ ɪŋ

advocate *n* ˈæd vək ət -ɪt; -və keɪt **~s** s

advokaat ˈæd vəʊ kɑː -kɑːt ‖ -voʊ-

advowson əd ˈvaʊz ᵊn æd- **~s** z

Adwick-le-Street ˌæd wɪk li ˈstriːt

adz, adze ædz **adzed** ædzd **adzes** ˈædz ɪz -əz **adzing** ˈædz ɪŋ

adzuki æd ˈzuːk i —*Jp* [a ˌdzɯ ˈki] **ad'zuki bean**

aedes, Aedes, Aëdes eɪ ˈiːd iːz

aedile ˈiːd aɪᵊl ‖ -ᵊl **~s** z **~ship/s** ʃɪp/s

Aegean ɪ ˈdʒiː‿ən iː- **Aeˌgean 'Sea**

Aegina i ˈdʒaɪn ə -ˈgiːn- —*ModGk* [ˈe ji na]

aegis ˈiːdʒ ɪs §-əs

Aegisthus i ˈdʒɪs θəs

aegrotat ˈaɪg rəʊ tæt ˈiːg-; i ˈgrəʊt æt ‖ -roʊ- **~s** s

Aelfric, Ælfric ˈælf rɪtʃ -rɪk

-aemia *comb. form* ˈiːm i‿ə — **septicaemia** ˌsept ɪ ˈsiːm i‿ə ˌ·ə-

Aeneas i ˈniː‿əs -ˈneɪ-, -æs

Aeneid ˈiːn i‿ɪd i ˈniː ɪd

Aeolian i ˈəʊl i‿ən eɪ- ‖ i ˈoʊl- **~s** z

Aeolic i ˈɒl ɪk -ˈəʊl- ‖ i ˈɑːl-

Aeolus ˈiː‿əl əs i ˈəʊl-

aeon ˈiː‿ən ˈiː ɒn ‖ -ɑːn **~s** z

aepyornis ˌiːp i ˈɔːn ɪs §-əs ‖ -ˈɔːrn-

aer|ate ˈeər |eɪt ⚠ˈeər i |eɪt ‖ ˈer- ˈær- **~ated** eɪt ɪd -əd ‖ eɪt̬ əd **~ates** eɪts **~ating** eɪt ɪŋ ‖ eɪt̬ ɪŋ

aeration (ı)eə ˈreɪʃ ᵊn ‖ (ı)e- (ı)æ-

aerator ˈeər eɪt ə ⚠ˈeər i· · ‖ ˈer eɪt̬ ᵊr ˈær- **~s** z

aerial ˈeər i‿əl ‖ ˈer- ˈær-; eɪ ˈɪr- —*in RP formerly also* eɪ ˈɪər i‿əl **~s** z

aerialist ˈeər i‿əl ɪst §-əst ‖ ˈer- ˈær- **~s** s

aerie ˈɪər i ˈeər-, ˈaɪᵊr- ‖ ˈer i ˈær-, ˈɪr-; ˈeɪ ri **~s** z

Aer Lingus *tdmk* ˌeə ˈlɪŋ gəs ‖ ˌer- ˌær-

aero, Aero ˈeər əʊ ‖ ˈer oʊ ˈær- **~s** z

aero- *comb. form*
with stress-neutral suffix ˌeər əʊ ‖ ˌer oʊ ˌær-, -ə — **aerobiosis** ˌeər əʊ baɪ ˈəʊs ɪs §-əs ‖ ˌer oʊ baɪ ˈoʊs əs ˌær-
with stress-imposing suffix (ı)eə ˈrɒ+ ‖ (ı)e ˈrɑː+ (ı)æ- — **aerography** (ı)eə ˈrɒg rəf i ‖ (ı)e ˈrɑːg- (ı)æ-

aerobatic ˌeər əʊ ˈbæt ɪk ◂ ‖ ˌer ə ˈbæt̬ ɪk ◂ ˌær- **~ally** ᵊl‿i **~s** s

aerobic (ı)eə ˈrəʊb ɪk ‖ (ı)e ˈroʊb ɪk (ı)æ- **~ally** ᵊl‿i **~s** s

aerodrome ˈeər ə drəʊm ‖ ˈer ə droʊm ˈær- **~s** z

aerodynamic ˌeər əʊ daɪ ˈnæm ɪk ◂ -dɪˈ- ‖ ˌer oʊ- ˌær- **~ally** ᵊl‿i **~s** s

aerodyne ˈeər əʊ daɪn ‖ ˈer ə- ˈær- **~s** z

Aeroflot *tdmk* ˈeər əʊ flɒt ‖ ˈer ə floʊt ˈær-, -flɑːt —*Russ* [ʌ ɪ rʌ ˈfɫot]

aerofoil ˈeər əʊ fɔɪᵊl ‖ ˈer oʊ- ˈær- **~s** z

aerogram, aerogramme ˈeər əʊ græm ‖ ˈer ə- ˈær- **~s** z

aerolite ˈeər əʊ laɪt ‖ ˈer ə- ˈær- **~s** s

aerolith ˈeər əʊ lɪθ ‖ ˈer ə- ˈær- **~s** s

aeronaut ˈeər əʊ nɔːt ‖ ˈer ə- ˈær-, -nɑːt **~s** s

aeronautic ˌeər əʊ ˈnɔːt ɪk ◂ ‖ ˌer ə ˈnɔːt̬ ɪk ◂ ˌær-, -ˈnɑːt̬- **~al** ᵊl **~ally** ᵊl‿i **~s** s

Aeronwy aɪᵊ ˈrɒn wi ‖ -ˈrɑːn- —*Welsh* [əi ˈron ui, -wi]

aeroplane ˈeər ə pleɪn ‖ ˈer- ˈær- **~s** z

aerosol ˈeər əʊ sɒl ‖ ˈer ə sɑːl ˈær-, -sɔːl **~s** z

aerospace ˈeər əʊ speɪs ‖ ˈer oʊ- ˈær-

aerostatic ˌeər əʊ ˈstæt ɪk ◂ ‖ ˌer oʊ ˈstæt̬ ɪk ◂ ˌær- **~ally** ᵊl‿i **~s** s

aertex, A~ *tdmk* ˈeə teks ‖ ˈer- ˈær-

aer|y *'nest, high place'* ˈɪər |i ˈeər-, ˈaɪᵊr- ‖ ˈer |i ˈær-, ˈɪr-; ˈeɪ r|i **~ies** iz

aery *'ethereal'* ˈeər i ‖ ˈer i ˈær-; ˈeɪ ər i

Aeschines ˈiːsk ɪ niːz -ə- ‖ ˈesk- ˈiːsk-

Aeschylus ˈiːsk əl əs -ɪl- ‖ ˈesk- ˈiːsk-

Aesculapi|an ˌiːsk ju ˈleɪp i‿|ən ˌ-jə- ‖ ˌesk jə- ˌ·ə- **~us** əs

Aesop ˈiːs ɒp ‖ -ɑːp -əp

Aesopian iː ˈsəʊp i‿ən -ˈsɒp- ‖ -ˈsoʊp- -ˈsɑːp-

aesthete ˈiːs θiːt ‖ ˈes- *(*)* **~s** s

aesthetic iːs ˈθet ɪk ɪs-, eɪs- ‖ es ˈθet̬ ɪk ɪs- **~ally** ᵊl‿i **~s** s

aestheticism iːs ˈθet ɪ ˌsɪz əm -ə- ‖ es ˈθet̬ ə- ɪs-

aestival i ˈstaɪv ᵊl ‖ ˈest əv ᵊl

aesti|vate ˈiːst ɪ |veɪt ˈest-, -ə- ‖ ˈest- **~vated** veɪt ɪd -əd ‖ veɪt̬ əd **~vates** veɪts **~vating** veɪt ɪŋ ‖ veɪt̬ ɪŋ

aestivation ˌiːst ɪ ˈveɪʃ ᵊn ˌest-, -ə- ‖ ˌest- **~s** z

Æthelbert ˈeθ ᵊl bɜːt ‖ -bɜːt

Æthelred ˈeθ ᵊl red

aether, Aether ˈiːθ ə ‖ -ᵊr *(= ether)*

Aetherius iː ˈθɪər i‿əs ɪ- ‖ ɪ ˈθɪr-

aetiological ˌiːt i‿ə ˈlɒdʒ ɪk ᵊl ◂ ‖ ˌiːt̬ i‿ə ˈlɑːdʒ- **~ly** ‿i

aetiolog|y ˌiːt i ˈɒl ədʒ |i ‖ ˌiːt̬ i ˈɑːl- **~ies** iz

Aetna ˈet nə

Aetoli|a i ˈtəʊl i‿|ə ‖ -ˈtoʊl- **~an/s** ən/z

af- ə, æ —*This variant of* ad- *is usually* ə (afˈfirm); *but if stressed because of a suffix it is* ˌæ (ˌaffirˈmation).

afar ə ˈfɑː ‖ ə ˈfɑːr

Afar *African people* ˈæf ɑː æ ˈfɑː, ə- ‖ ˈɑːf ɑːr **~s** z

A

AFASIC eɪ 'feɪz ɪk
affability ˌæf ə 'bɪl ət i -ɪt i ‖ -əţ i
affab|le 'æf əb |ᵊl **~ly** li
affair ə 'feə ‖ ə 'feᵊr ə 'fæᵊr **~s** z
affaire ə 'feə ‖ ə 'feᵊr ə 'fæᵊr —*Fr* [a fɛːʁ] **~s** z
affect *v* ə 'fekt —*Also, to highlight the contrast with* effect, *sometimes* ₍ᵢ₎æ- **~ed** ɪd əd **~ing** ɪŋ **~s** s
affect *n* 'æf ekt ə 'fekt **~s** s
affectation ˌæf ek 'teɪʃ ᵊn -ɪk- **~s** z
affected ə 'fekt ɪd -əd **~ly** li **~ness** nəs nɪs
affection ə 'fek ʃᵊn **~s** z
affectionate ə 'fek ʃᵊn‿ət ‿ɪt **~ly** li **~ness** nəs nɪs
affective æ 'fekt ɪv
affenpinscher 'æf ᵊn ˌpɪnᵗʃ ə ‖ -ᵊr **~s** z
afferent 'æf ər ənt
affianc|e ə 'faɪ‿ənᵗs æ- **~ed** t **~es** ɪz əz **~ing** ɪŋ
affidavit ˌæf ɪ 'deɪv ɪt -ə-, §-ət **~s** s
affiliate *n, adj* ə 'fɪl i‿ət ‿ɪt, -eɪt **~s** s
affili|ate *v* ə 'fɪl i |eɪt **~ated** eɪt ɪd -əd ‖ eɪţ əd **~ates** eɪts **~ating** eɪt ɪŋ ‖ eɪţ ɪŋ
affiliation ə ˌfɪl i 'eɪʃ ᵊn **~s** z
afˌfili'ation ˌorder
affinit|y ə 'fɪn ət |i -ɪt- ‖ -əţ |i **~ies** iz
affirm ə 'fɜːm ‖ ə 'fɝːm **~ed** d **~ing** ɪŋ **~s** z
affirmation ˌæf ə 'meɪʃ ᵊn ‖ -ᵊr- **~s** z
affirmative ə 'fɜːm ət ɪv ‖ ə 'fɝːm əţ ɪv **~ly** li
affix *v* ə 'fɪks æ- **~ed** t **~es** ɪz əz **~ing** ɪŋ
affix *n* 'æf ɪks **~es** ɪz əz
affixation ˌæf ɪk 'seɪʃ ᵊn
afflatus ə 'fleɪt əs æ- ‖ -'fleɪţ-
Affleck 'æf lek
afflict ə 'flɪkt **~ed** ɪd əd **~ing** ɪŋ **~s** s
affliction ə 'flɪk ʃᵊn **~s** z
afflictive ə 'flɪkt ɪv **~ly** li
affluence 'æf lu‿ənᵗs
affluent 'æf lu‿ənt **~ly** li
afflux 'æf lʌks **~es** ɪz əz
afford ə 'fɔːd ‖ ə 'fɔːrd -'fourd **~ed** ɪd əd **~ing** ɪŋ **~s** z
affordability ə ˌfɔːd ə 'bɪl ət i -ɪt- ‖ ə ˌfɔːrd ə 'bɪl əţ i -ˌfourd-
affordab|le ə 'fɔːd əb| ᵊl ‖ -'fɔːrd- 'fourd- **~ly** li
afforest ə 'fɒr ɪst æ-, -əst ‖ -'fɔːr əst -'fɑːr- **~ed** ɪd əd **~ing** ɪŋ **~s** s
afforestation ə ˌfɒr ɪ 'steɪʃ ᵊn æ-, -ə- ‖ ˌfɔːr ə- -ˌfɑːr-; ˌæˌ·ˈ··
affray ə 'freɪ **~s** z
Affric 'æf rɪk
affricate *n* 'æf rɪk ət -rək-, -ɪt; -rɪ keɪt, -rə- **~s** s
affri|cate *v* 'æf rɪ |keɪt -rə- **~cated** keɪt ɪd -əd ‖ keɪţ əd **~cates** keɪts **~cating** keɪt ɪŋ ‖ keɪţ ɪŋ
affrication ˌæf rɪ 'keɪʃ ᵊn -rə-
affricative æ 'frɪk ət ɪv ə-; 'æf rɪ keɪt-, '·rə- ‖ -əţ- **~ly** li
affright ə 'fraɪt
affront *n, v* ə 'frʌnt **affronted** ə 'frʌnt ɪd -əd ‖ ə 'frʌnţ əd **affronting** ə 'frʌnt ɪŋ ‖ ə 'frʌnţ ɪŋ **affronts** ə 'frʌnts

Afghan, a~ 'æf gæn -gɑːn, -gən **~s** z
afghani æf 'gɑːn i -'gæn- **~s** z
Afghanistan æf 'gæn ɪ stɑːn -ə-, -stæn, ·ˌ· ·'·, ˌ· · ·'· ‖ -ə stæn
aficionado ə ˌfɪʃ i‿ə 'nɑːd əʊ ə ˌfɪs-, ə ˌfɪʃ ə'·- ‖ -'nɑːd oʊ —*Sp* [a fi θjo 'na ðo, -sjo'·-] **~s** z
afield ə 'fiːᵊld
afire ə 'faɪ‿ə ‖ ə 'faɪ‿ᵊr
aflame ə 'fleɪm
aflatoxin ˌæf lə 'tɒks ɪn §-ən ‖ -'tɑːks ən **~s** z
AFL-CIO ˌeɪ ef 'el ˌsiː aɪ 'əʊ ‖ -'oʊ
afloat ə 'fləʊt ‖ ə 'floʊt
aflutter ə 'flʌt ə ‖ ə 'flʌţ ᵊr
Afon 'æv ᵊn -ɒn ‖ -ɑːn —*Welsh* ['a von]
afoot ə 'fʊt
afore ə 'fɔː ‖ ə 'fɔːr -'foʊr
aforementioned ə ˌfɔː 'menᵗʃ ᵊnd ◂ ·'·ˌ·· ‖ ə ˌfɔːr- -ˌfoʊr-
aforesaid ə 'fɔː sed ‖ ə 'fɔːr- -'foʊr-
aforethought ə 'fɔː θɔːt ‖ ə 'fɔːr- -'foʊr-, -θɑːt
aforetime ə 'fɔː taɪm ‖ ə 'fɔːr- -'foʊr-
a fortiori ˌeɪ ˌfɔːt i 'ɔːr aɪ ˌɑː-, -i ‖ ˌeɪ ˌfɔːrʃ i 'ɔːr i ˌfɔːrţ-, -'oʊr-, -aɪ
afoul ə 'faʊl
afraid ə 'freɪd
A-frame 'eɪ freɪm **~s** z
afresh ə 'freʃ
Africa 'æf rɪk ə
African 'æf rɪk ən **~s** z
African-American ˌæf rɪk ən ə 'mer ɪk ən ◂ **~s** z
Africanis... —*see* **Africaniz...**
Africanist 'æf rɪk ən ɪst §-əst **~s** s
Africanization ˌæf rɪk ən aɪ 'zeɪʃ ᵊn ˌ·rək-, ·ɪ'-- ‖ -ə'-- **~s** z
Africaniz|e 'æf rɪk ə naɪz '·rək- **~ed** d **~es** ɪz əz **~ing** ɪŋ
Afrikaans ˌæf rɪ 'kɑːnᵗs ◂ -rə-, -'kɑːnz ‖ ˌɑːf-
Afrikaner ˌæf rɪ 'kɑːn ə ◂ -rə- ‖ -ᵊr ˌɑːf- **~dom** dəm **~s** z
Afro, afro 'æf rəʊ ‖ -roʊ **~s** z
Afro- *comb. form* ¦æf rəʊ ‖ -roʊ — **Afro-Cuban** ˌæf rəʊ 'kjuːb ən ◂ ‖ -roʊ-
Afro-American ˌæf rəʊ ə 'mer ɪk ən ◂ ‖ ˌæf roʊ- **~s** z
Afro-Asiatic ˌæf rəʊ ˌeɪʃ i 'æt ɪk ◂ -ˌeɪz-, -ˌeɪʒ-, -ˌeɪs- ‖ -roʊ ˌeɪʒ i 'æţ ɪk ◂
Afro-Caribbean ˌæf rəʊ ˌkær ə 'biː‿ən ◂ -ˌ·ɪ-; -kə 'rɪb i‿ən ‖ -ˌker-; -kə 'rɪb i‿ən **~s** z
Afrocentric ˌæf rəʊ 'sentr ɪk ◂ ‖ -roʊ-
afrormosia ˌæf rɔː 'məʊz i‿ə ‖ ˌæf rɔːr 'moʊʒ ə
aft ɑːft §æft ‖ æft
after 'ɑːft ə §'æft- ‖ 'æft ᵊr **~s** z
after- ¦ɑːft ə §¦æft ə ‖ ¦æft ᵊr —*Compounds with this prefix are almost always early-stressed* ('afterˌburner). *There is one important exception:* ˌafter'noon.
afterbirth 'ɑːft ə bɜːθ §'æft- ‖ 'æft ᵊr bɝːθ **~s** s
afterburner 'ɑːft ə ˌbɜːn ə §'æft- ‖ 'æft ᵊr ˌbɝːn ᵊr **~s** z
aftercare 'ɑːft ə keə §'æft- ‖ 'æft ᵊr ker -kær

A

Affricates

1 An **affricate** is a complex consonant sound consisting of a plosive that is immediately followed by a fricative (see ARTICULATION) made at the same place of articulation. It can therefore also be described as a plosive that has a slow release.

2 English has two affricate phonemes: tʃ as in **church** tʃɜːtʃ ‖ tʃɝːtʃ and dʒ as in **judge** dʒʌdʒ. Their place of articulation is palato-alveolar. In addition to this pair, the clusters tr and dr are pronounced as affricates in RP and GenAm as in **try** traɪ and **dream** driːm. Their place of articulation is post-alveolar.

3 Affricates always belong together in the same syllable: **achieve** ə ˈtʃiːv, **address** ə ˈdres, **natural** ˈnætʃ rəl.

4 Other affricate-like sequences of consonants are found in words such as **obvious** ˈɒb vi‿əs ‖ ˈɑːb vi‿əs, **eighth** eɪtθ, **cats** kæts, **rides** raɪdz; but we do not usually list bv, tθ, ts, dz among the English affricates. Notice also that the t followed by ʃ in **nutshell** ˈnʌt ʃel is not an affricate.

aftereffect ˈɑːft ər ɪ ˌfekt §ˈæft-, ˈ‿ər-, ˌə‚ ‖ ˈæft ər- **~s** s
afterglow ˈɑːft ə gləʊ §ˈæft- ‖ ˈæft ᵊr gloʊ
after-hours ˌɑːft ərˈaʊ‿əz ◂ §ˌæft- ‖ ˌæft ᵊr ˈaʊ‿ᵊrz
afterlife ˈɑːft ə laɪf §ˈæft- ‖ ˈæft ᵊr-
aftermath ˈɑːft ə mæθ §æft-, -mɑːθ ‖ ˈæft ᵊr-
afternoon ˌɑːft ə ˈnuːn ◂ §ˌæft-, §-ˈnʊn, -ᵊn ˈuːn ‖ ˌæft ᵊr- **~s** z
ˌafternoon ˈtea
after-sales ˌɑːft ə ˈseɪᵊlz ◂ §ˌæft- ‖ ˌæft ᵊr-
after-school ˌɑːft ə ˈskuːl ◂ §ˌæft- ‖ ˌæft ᵊr-
aftershave ˈɑːft ə ʃeɪv §ˈæft-, ˌ·ˈ· ‖ ˈæft ᵊr- **~s** z
ˈaftershave ˌlotion, ˌ··ˈ·ˌ··
aftershock ˈɑːft ə ʃɒk §ˈæft- ‖ ˈæft ᵊr ʃɑːk **~s** s
aftertaste ˈɑːft ə teɪst §ˈæft- ‖ ˈæft ᵊr- **~s** s
afterthought ˈɑːft ə θɔːt §ˈæft- ‖ ˈæft ᵊr- -θɑːt **~s** s
afterward ˈɑːft ə wəd §ˈæft- ‖ ˈæft ᵊr wᵊrd **~s** z
afterword ˈɑːft ə wɜːd §ˈæft- ‖ ˈæft ᵊr wɝːd **~s** z
Afton ˈæft ən
ag- ə, æ —*This variant of* ad- *is usually* ə (agˈgression), *but* ¦æ *if stressed because of a suffix* (ˈaggravate).
Aga, aga ˈɑːg ə
ˌAga ˈKhan
Agadir ˌæg ə ˈdɪə ‖ ˌɑːg ə ˈdɪᵊr ˌæg-
Agag ˈeɪg æg

AGAIN

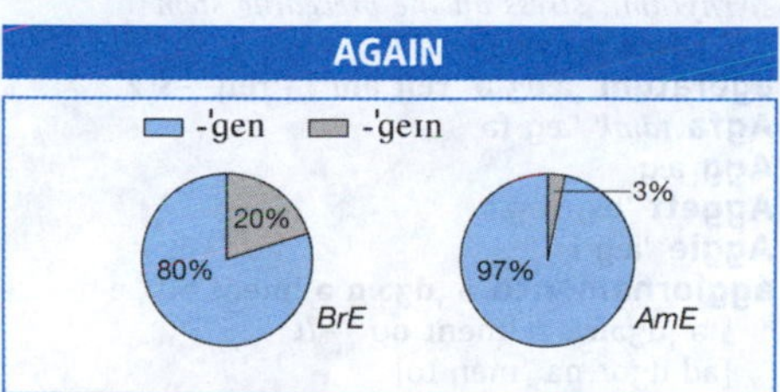

again ə ˈgen ə ˈgeɪn — *Preference polls, BrE:* -ˈgen *80%,* -ˈgeɪn *20%. Many BrE speakers use both pronunciations. AmE:* -ˈgen *97%,* -ˈgeɪn *3%.*
against ə ˈgenᵗst ə ˈgeɪnᵗst
agama ˈæg əm ə ə ˈgɑːm ə **~s** z
Agamemnon ˌæg ə ˈmem nən -nɒn ‖ -nɑːn
agapanthus ˌæg ə ˈpænᵗθ əs **~es** ɪz əz
agape *n 'love, love feast'* ˈæg əp i -eɪ; ə ˈgɑːp i ‖ ɑː ˈgɑːp eɪ ˈɑːg ə peɪ
agape *adv, adj 'wide open'* ə ˈgeɪp
agar ˈeɪg ə -ɑː ‖ ˈɑːg ᵊr ˈeɪg-, -ɑːr
Agar *family name (i)* ˈeɪg ə ‖ -ᵊr, *(ii)* -ɑː ‖ -ɑːr
agar-agar ˌeɪg ər ˈeɪg ə ‖ ˌɑːg ər ˈɑːg ᵊr
agaric ˈæg ər ɪk ə ˈgær- **~s** s
Agassi, Agassiz ˈæg əs i
agate ˈæg ət -ɪt
Agate *family name (i)* ˈæg ət, *(ii)* ˈeɪg ət
Agatha ˈæg əθ ə
agave ə ˈgeɪv i əˈgɑːv i, ˈæg eɪv ‖ ə ˈgɑːv i **~s** z
-age ɪdʒ, (¦)ɑːʒ —*In most words* -age *is pronounced* ɪdʒ (perˈcentage), *although some recent French borrowings are pronounced with*

ɑːʒ, *stressed in AmE and sometimes in BrE* (ˌentouˈrage). *Some words have two or more competing variants* (garage), *and there are exceptions* (outrage).

age eɪdʒ **aged** *past, pp* eɪdʒd **ageing, aging** ˈeɪdʒ ɪŋ **ages** ˈeɪdʒ ɪz -əz
ˌage of conˈsent

aged *'having a specified age'; past and pp of* **age** eɪdʒd

aged *'very old'* ˈeɪdʒ ɪd -əd; §eɪdʒd

Agee ˈeɪdʒ iː

ageing ˈeɪdʒ ɪŋ

ageism ˈeɪdʒ ˌɪz əm

ageist ˈeɪdʒ ɪst §-əst **~s** s

ageless ˈeɪdʒ ləs -lɪs **~ly** li **~ness** nəs nɪs

age-long ˌeɪdʒ ˈlɒŋ ◂ ‖ ˈeɪdʒ lɔːŋ -lɑːŋ

agenc|y ˈeɪdʒ ənᵗs |i **~ies** iz

agenda ə ˈdʒend ə **~s** z

agene ˈeɪdʒ iːn

agent ˈeɪdʒ ənt **~s** s —*See also phrases with this word*

agentive ˈeɪdʒ ənt ɪv

agent provocateur ˌæʒ ɒ̃ prə ˌvɒk ə ˈtɜː ˌeɪdʒ ənt- ‖ ˌɑːʒ ɑ̃ː proʊ ˌvɑːk ə ˈtɜː -ˈtʊᵊr —*Fr* [a ʒɑ̃ pʁɔ vɔ ka tœːʁ] **agents provocateurs** *same pronunciation, or* -z

age-old ˌeɪdʒ ˈəʊld ◂ →-ˈɒʊld ‖ -ˈoʊld ◂

-ageous ˈeɪdʒ əs —*This suffix may impose rhythmic stress on the preceding stem* (ˌadvanˈtageous).

ageratum ˌædʒ ə ˈreɪt əm ‖ -ˈreɪt̬- **~s** z

Agfa *tdmk* ˈæg fə

Agg æg

Aggett ˈæg ɪt -ət

Aggie ˈæg i

aggiornamento ə ˌdʒɔːn ə ˈment əʊ ˌæ- ‖ ə ˌdʒɔːrn ə ˈment oʊ —*It* [ad dʒor na ˈmen to]

agglome|rate *v* ə ˈglɒm ə |reɪt ‖ ə ˈglɑːm- **~rated** reɪt ɪd -əd ‖ reɪt̬ əd **~rates** reɪts **~rating** reɪt ɪŋ ‖ reɪt̬ ɪŋ

agglomerate *adj, n* ə ˈglɒm ər ət -ɪt, -ə reɪt ‖ ə ˈglɑːm- **~s** s

agglomeration ə ˌglɒm ə ˈreɪʃ ᵊn ‖ ə ˌglɑːm- **~s** z

agglutinate *adj, n* ə ˈgluːt ɪn ət -ən-, -ɪt; -ɪ neɪt, -ə- ‖ -ᵊn- **~s** s

aggluti|nate *v* ə ˈgluːt ɪ |neɪt -ə- ‖ -ᵊ|n eɪt **~nated** neɪt ɪd -əd ‖ neɪt̬ əd **~nates** neɪts **~nating** neɪt ɪŋ ‖ neɪt̬ ɪŋ

agglutination ə ˌgluːt ɪ ˈneɪʃ ᵊn -ə- ‖ -ᵊn ˈeɪʃ-

agglutinative ə ˈgluːt ɪn ət ɪv -ˈən-; -ɪ neɪt-, -ə neɪt-, -ᵊn eɪt- ‖ -ᵊn eɪt̬ ɪv -ᵊn ət̬ ɪv **~ly** li

aggrandis... —*see* **aggrandiz...**

aggrandiz|e ə ˈgrænd aɪz ˈæg rən daɪz **~ed** d **~es** ɪz əz **~ing** ɪŋ

aggrandizement ə ˈgrænd ɪz mənt -əz-, -aɪz-

aggra|vate ˈæg rə |veɪt **~vated** veɪt ɪd -əd ‖ veɪt̬ əd **~vates** veɪts **~vating/ly** veɪt ɪŋ /li ‖ veɪt̬ ɪŋ /li

aggravation ˌæg rə ˈveɪʃ ᵊn **~s** z

aggregate *adj, n* ˈæg rɪg ət -rəg-, -ɪt; -rɪ geɪt, -rə- **~s** s

aggre|gate *v* ˈæg rɪ |geɪt -rə- **~gated** geɪt ɪd -əd ‖ geɪt̬ əd **~gates** geɪts **~gating** geɪt ɪŋ ‖ geɪt̬ ɪŋ

aggregation ˌæg rɪ ˈgeɪʃ ᵊn -rə- **~s** z

aggression ə ˈgreʃ ᵊn

aggressive ə ˈgres ɪv **~ly** li **~ness** nəs nɪs

aggressor ə ˈgres ə ‖ -ᵊr **~s** z

aggrieved ə ˈgriːvd

aggro ˈæg rəʊ ‖ -roʊ

Agha- *comb. form in Irish place names* ¦æx ə — **Aghacully** ˌæx ə ˈkʌl i

aghast ə ˈgɑːst §-ˈgæst ‖ ə ˈgæst

agile ˈædʒ aɪᵊl ‖ -ᵊl -aɪᵊl **~ly** li **~ness** nəs nɪs

agility ə ˈdʒɪl ət i -ɪt i ‖ -ət̬ i

agin ə ˈgɪn

Agincourt ˈædʒ ɪn kɔː ˈæʒ-, §-ən-, -kɔːt ‖ -kɔːrt -kourt

agio ˈædʒ i‿əʊ ‖ -oʊ **~s** z

agiotage ˈædʒ ət ɪdʒ ˈædʒ i‿ət ɪdʒ, ə tɑːʒ ‖ ˈædʒ i‿ət̬ ɪdʒ ˌæʒ ə ˈtɑːʒ

agist *v* ə ˈdʒɪst **~ed** ɪd əd **~ing** ɪŋ **~ment/s** mənt/s **~s** s

agi|tate ˈædʒ ɪ |teɪt -ə- **~tated/ly** teɪt ɪd /li -əd /li ‖ teɪt̬ əd /li **~tates** teɪts **~tating** teɪt ɪŋ ‖ teɪt̬ ɪŋ

agitation ˌædʒ ɪ ˈteɪʃ ᵊn -ə- **~s** z

agitato ˌædʒ ɪ ˈtɑːt əʊ -ə- ‖ -oʊ

agitator ˈædʒ ɪ teɪt ə ˌ-ə- ‖ -teɪt̬ ᵊr **~s** z

agitprop ˈædʒ ɪt prɒp §-ət-, ˌ·ˈ· ‖ -prɑːp

Aglaia ə ˈglaɪ‿ə -ˈgleɪ ə

agleam ə ˈgliːm

aglet ˈæg lət -lɪt **~s** s

agley ə ˈgleɪ -ˈglaɪ, -ˈgliː

aglimmer ə ˈglɪm ə ‖ -ᵊr

aglitter ə ˈglɪt ə ‖ ə ˈglɪt̬ ᵊr

aglow ə ˈgləʊ ‖ ə ˈgloʊ

AGM ˌeɪ dʒiː ˈem **~s, ~'s** z

agma ˈæg mə ˈæŋ- **~s** z

agnail ˈæg neɪᵊl **~s** z

agnate ˈæg neɪt **~s** s

Agnes ˈæg nɪs -nəs

Agnew ˈæg njuː ‖ -nuː

Agni ˈæg ni ˈʌg- —*Hindi* [əg n̪i]

agnomen æg ˈnəʊm en ‖ -ˈnoʊm ən

agnosia æg ˈnəʊz i‿ə ‖ -ˈnoʊʒ ə -ˈnoʊʃ-

agnostic (ı)æg ˈnɒst ɪk əg- ‖ -ˈnɑːst- **~ally** ᵊl‿i **~s** s

agnosticism (ı)æg ˈnɒst ɪ ˌsɪz əm əg-, -ə- ‖ -ˈnɑːst-

Agnus Dei ˌæg nəs ˈdeɪ‿iː ˌɑːg-, -nʊs-, ˌɑːn jʊs-, -ˈdiː aɪ

ago ə ˈgəʊ ‖ ə ˈgoʊ

agog ə ˈgɒg ‖ ə ˈgɑːg

-agogic ə ˈgɒdʒ ɪk -ˈgəʊdʒ- ‖ -ˈgɑːdʒ- -ˈgoʊdʒ- — **hypnagogic** ˌhɪp nə ˈgɒdʒ ɪk ◂ -ˈgəʊdʒ- ‖ -ˈgɑːdʒ- -ˈgoʊdʒ-

a-go-go, à gogo ə ˈgəʊ gəʊ ‖ ɑː ˈgoʊ goʊ —*Fr* [a go go]

-agogue *stress-imposing* ə gɒg ‖ ə gɑːg — **galactogogue** gə ˈlækt ə gɒg ‖ -gɑːg

-agogy ə gɒdʒ i -gɒg-, -gəʊg- ‖ ə gɑːdʒ i -gɑːg-, -goʊg- — **pedagogy** ˈped ə gɒdʒ i -gɒg i ‖ -gɑːdʒ i -gɑːg i

agoni... —*see* **agony**
agonis... —*see* **agonize**
agonist 'æg ən ɪst §-əst **~s** s
Agonistes ˌæg əʊ 'nɪst iːz ‖ -ə-
agoniz|e 'æg ə naɪz **~ed** d **~es** ɪz əz **~ing/ly** ɪŋ /li
agon|y 'æg ən |i **~ies** iz
'agony aunt; **''agony ˌcolumn**
agora, Agora 'æg ər ə **~s** z
agoraphobia ˌæg ər‿ə 'fəʊb i‿ə ‖ -'foʊb-
agoraphobic ˌæg ər‿ə 'fəʊb ɪk ◂ ‖ -'foʊb- **~s** s
agouti ə 'guːt i ‖ ə 'guːṭ i **~es, ~s** z
Agra 'ɑːg rə 'æg-
agranulocytosis ə ˌgræn jʊl əʊ saɪ 'təʊs ɪs ˌeɪˌ-, -jəl ··'··, §-əs ‖ ˌeɪ ˌgræn jə loʊ saɪ 'toʊs əs
agrapha 'æg rəf ə
agraphia ₍ˌ₎eɪ 'græf i‿ə æ-
agrarian ə 'greər i‿ən æ- ‖ ə 'grer- ə 'grær-
~ism ˌɪz əm **~s** z
agree ə 'griː **agreed** ə 'griːd **agrees** ə 'griːz
agreeing ə 'griː‿ɪŋ
agreeab|le ə 'griː‿əb |əl **~leness** əl nəs -nɪs
~ly li
agreement ə 'griː mənt **~s** s
agribusiness 'æg ri ˌbɪz nəs -nɪs
Agricola ə 'grɪk əl ə æ-
agricultural ˌæg rɪ 'kʌltʃ ər‿əl ◂ ˌ·rə- **~ly** i
agriculturalist ˌæg rɪ 'kʌltʃ ər‿əl ɪst ˌ·rə-, §-əst
~s s
agriculture 'æg rɪ ˌkʌltʃ ə -rə-, ˌ··'·· ◂‖ -ər
agriculturist ˌæg rɪ 'kʌltʃ ər ɪst ˌ·rə-, §-əst **~s** s
Agrigento ˌæg rɪ 'dʒent əʊ -rə- ‖ -oʊ —*It* [a gri 'dʒɛn to]
agrimony 'æg rɪm ən i '·rəm- ‖ -ə moʊn i
Agrippa ə 'grɪp ə
Agrippina ˌæg rɪ 'piːn ə -rə-
agro- *comb. form*
with stress-neutral suffix ˈæg rəʊ ‖ -roʊ — **agrobiology** ˌæg rəʊ baɪ 'ɒl ədʒ i ‖ -roʊ baɪ 'ɑːl-
with stress-imposing suffix ə 'grɒ æ- ‖ə'grɑː+ — **agrology** ə 'grɒl ədʒ i æ- ‖ -'grɑːl-
agronomic ˌæg rəʊ 'nɒm ɪk ◂ ‖ -rə 'nɑːm-
~al/ly əl /ˌi **~s** s
agronomist ə 'grɒn əm ɪst §-əst ‖ ə 'grɑːn- **~s** s
agronomy ə 'grɒn əm i ‖ ə 'grɑːn-
aground ə 'graʊnd
aguardiente ˌæg wɑːd i 'ent i ‖ ˌɑːg wɑːrd i 'enṭ i -'ent eɪ —*Sp* [a ɣwar 'ðjen te]
ague 'eɪg juː **~s** z
Aguecheek 'eɪg juː tʃiːk
Aguilera ˌæg ɪ 'leər ə -jɪ- ‖ ˌɑːg ə 'ler ə —*Sp* [a ɣi 'le ra]
aguish 'eɪg ju ɪʃ **~ly** li **~ness** nəs nɪs
Agulhas ə 'gʌl əs
Agutter *(i)* 'æg ət ə ‖ -əṭ ər, *(ii)* ə 'gʌt ə ‖ ə 'gʌṭ ər
ah ɑː
aha ɑː 'hɑː ə-

Ahab 'eɪ hæb
Ahasuerus ˌeɪ hæz ju 'ɪər əs ə ˌhæz-, -'eər- ‖ -'ɪr-
ahead ə 'hed
ahem [ʔm ʔmː] *said with tense voice; also* [m 'm̥m]*; also spelling pronunciation* ə 'hem
Ahenobarbus ə ˌhiːn əʊ 'bɑːb əs -ˌhen- ‖ -oʊ 'bɑːrb-
Ahern, Aherne *(i)* ə 'hɜːn ‖ ə 'hɝːn, *(ii)* 'eɪ hɜːn ‖ -hɝːn
ahimsa ə 'hɪm sɑː
ahistorical ˌeɪ hɪ 'stɒr ɪk əl ‖ -'stɔːr- -'stɑːr-
~ly i
Ahithophel ə 'hɪθ ə fel
Ahmadabad 'ɑːm əd ə bæd '·ɪd-, -bɑːd
Ahmadinejad ˌɑː mə 'diːn ə dʒæd -dʒɑːd —*Persian (Farsi)* [æh mæ di ne 'ʒɒd]
Ahmed 'ɑːm ed
Ahmedabad 'ɑːm əd ə bæd '·ɪd-, '·ed-, -bɑːd
ahoy ə 'hɔɪ
Ahura Mazda ə ˌhʊər ə 'mæz də ‖ ə ˌhʊr- ɑː-, -'mɑːz-
ai *'three-toed sloth'* 'ɑː i 'ɑː i, aɪ **ais** 'aɪ iz 'ɑː iz, aɪz
Al ˌeɪ 'aɪ
aid eɪd **aided** 'eɪd ɪd -əd **aiding** 'eɪd ɪŋ **aids** eɪdz
AID ˌeɪ aɪ 'diː
Aida, Aïda aɪ 'iːd ə ɑː- —*It* [a 'iː da]
Aidan 'eɪd ən
aide eɪd *(= aid)* **aides** eɪdz
aide|-de-camp ˌeɪd| də 'kɑːmp -'kɒ̃, -'kɑ̃ː ‖ -'kæmp —*Fr* [ɛd də kɑ̃] **aides~** ˌeɪd- ˌeɪdz- —*Fr* [ɛd də kɑ̃]
aide-memoire, aide-mémoire ˌeɪd mem 'wɑː ˌ·'·· ‖ -'wɑːr —*Fr* [ɛd me mwaːʁ]
AIDS, Aids eɪdz
'AIDS ˌpatient
aigrette 'eɪg ret eɪ 'gret **~s** s
aiguille 'eɪg wiːl -wɪl ‖ ˌeɪ 'gwiːəl —*Fr* [e gɥij]
~s z *or as sing.*
aiguillette ˌeɪg wɪ 'let -wə- **~s** s
Aiken 'eɪk ən
aikido aɪ 'kiːd əʊ 'aɪk ɪ dəʊ ‖ aɪ 'kiːd oʊ ˌaɪk ɪ 'doʊ —*Jp* [aˌi 'ki doo]
ail eɪəl *(= ale)* **ailed** eɪəld **ailing** 'eɪəl ɪŋ **ails** eɪəlz
ailanthus eɪ 'lænᵗθ əs **~es** ɪz əz
Ailbhe 'ælv ə
Aileen *(i)* 'eɪl iːn ‖ eɪ 'liːn, *(ii)* 'aɪl iːn ‖ aɪ 'liːn
aileron 'eɪl ə rɒn ‖ -rɑːn **~s** z
ailment 'eɪəl mənt **~s** s
Ailsa 'eɪəls ə 'eɪəlz ə
ˌAilsa 'Craig
ailuro- *comb. form* aɪ ¦lʊər əʊ eɪ-, -¦ljʊər-; ¦eɪl juər əʊ ‖ aɪ ¦lʊr ə — **ailurophobia** aɪ ˌlʊər əʊ 'fəʊb i‿ə eɪ-, -ˌljʊər-; ˌeɪl juər- ‖ aɪ ˌlʊr ə 'foʊb-
aim eɪm **aimed** eɪmd **aiming** 'eɪm ɪŋ **aims** eɪmz
Aimee, Aimée 'eɪm eɪ -i ‖ e 'meɪ eɪ- —*Fr* [ɛ me]

aimless ˈeɪm ləs -lɪs **~ly** li **~ness** nəs nɪs
ain eɪn
Ainscough, Ainscow ˈeɪnz kəʊ ‖ -koʊ
Ainsdale ˈeɪnz deɪᵊl
Ainsley, Ainslie ˈeɪnz li
Ainsworth ˈeɪnz wɜːθ -wəθ ‖ -wᵊrθ
ain't eɪnt
Aintree ˈeɪn triː ˈeɪntr i
Ainu ˈaɪn uː **~s** z
aioli, aïoli aɪ ˈəʊl i eɪ- ‖ -ˈoʊl i —*It* [a ˈjɔ li]
air eə ‖ eᵊr æᵊr **aired** eəd ‖ eᵊrd æᵊrd **airing** ˈeər ɪŋ ‖ ˈer ɪŋ ˈær- **airs** eəz ‖ eᵊrz æᵊrz
ˈair ˌchamber; **ˌair chief ˈmarshal◂**; **ˌair ˈcommodore◂**; **ˈair freight**; **ˌair ˈmarshal◂**; **ˈair raid**; **ˈair ˌrifle**; **ˈair ˌterminal**; **ˌair ˌtraffic conˈtrol,** ˌ ˌˈ · · ·ˌ ˌˈ ·ˌ · ·ˌ ·ˌ ˌ **ˌair vice-ˈmarshal◂**
airbag ˈeə bæg ‖ ˈer- ˈær- **~s** z
airbas|e ˈeə beɪs ‖ ˈer- ˈær- **~es** ɪz əz
airbed ˈeə bed ‖ ˈer- ˈær- **~s** z
airbladder ˈeə ˌblæd ə ‖ ˈer ˌblæd ᵊr ˈær- **~s** z
airborne ˈeə bɔːn ‖ ˈer bɔːrn ˈær-, -boʊrn
airbrake ˈeə breɪk ‖ ˈer- ˈær- **~s** s
airbrick ˈeə brɪk ‖ ˈer- ˈær- **~s** s
airbrush ˈeə brʌʃ ‖ ˈer- ˈær- **~ed** t **~es** ɪz əz **~ing** ɪŋ
airburst ˈeə bɜːst ‖ ˈer bɜːst ˈær- **~s** s
airbus, A~ *tdmk* ˈeə bʌs ‖ ˈer- ˈær- **~es** ɪz əz
air-condition ˈeə kən ˌdɪʃ ᵊn ˌ· ·ˈ· · ‖ ˈer- ˈær- **~ed** d **~ing** ˌɪŋ **~s** z
air-cool ˈeə kuːl ‖ ˈer- ˈær- **~ed** d **~ing** ɪŋ **~s** z
aircraft ˈeə krɑːft §-kræft ‖ ˈer kræft ˈær-
ˈaircraft ˌcarrier
aircraft|man ˈeə krɑːft |mən §-kræft- ‖ ˈer kræft- ˈær- **~men** mən **~woman** ˌwʊm ən **~women** ˌwɪm ɪn §-ən
aircrafts|man ˈeə krɑːfts |mən §-kræfts- ‖ ˈer kræfts- ˈær- **~men** mən **~woman** ˌwʊm ən **~women** ˌwɪm ɪn §-ən
aircrew ˈeə kruː ‖ ˈer- ˈær- **~s** z
aircushion ˈeə ˌkʊʃ ᵊn ‖ ˈer- ˈær- **~s** z
Airdrie ˈeədr i ‖ ˈerdr i
air-drie... —*see* **air-dry**
Airdrieonian ˌeədr i ˈəʊn i‿ən ◂ ‖ ˌerdr i ˈoʊn- **~s** z
airdrop ˈeə drɒp ‖ ˈer drɑːp ˈær- **~ped** t **~ping** ɪŋ **~s** s
air-|dry ˈeə |draɪ ‖ ˈer- ˈær- **~dries** draɪz **~dried** draɪd **~drying** draɪ ɪŋ
Aire eə ‖ eᵊr æᵊr
Airedale ˈeə deɪᵊl ‖ ˈer- ˈær- **~s** z
airer ˈeər ə ‖ ˈer ᵊr ˈær- **~s** z
Airey ˈeər i ‖ ˈer i ˈær i
airfare ˈeə feə ‖ ˈer fer ˈær fær **~s** z
airfield ˈeə fiːᵊld ‖ ˈer- ˈær- **~s** z
airflow ˈeə fləʊ ‖ ˈer floʊ ˈær- **~s** z
airfoil ˈeə fɔɪl ‖ ˈer- ˈær- **~s** z
airforc|e ˈeə fɔːs ‖ ˈer fɔːrs ˈær-, -foʊrs **~es** ɪz əz
airframe ˈeə freɪm ‖ ˈer- ˈær- **~s** z
airgun ˈeə gʌn ‖ ˈer- ˈær- **~s** z
airhead ˈeə hed ‖ ˈer- ˈær- **~s** z
airhole ˈeə həʊl →-hɒʊl ‖ ˈer hoʊl ˈær- **~s** z
airhostess ˈeə ˌhəʊst es -ɪs, -əs ‖ ˈer ˌhoʊst əs ˈær- **~es** ɪz əz
airi... —*see* **airy**
airily ˈeər əl i -ɪ li ‖ ˈer- ˈær-
airiness ˈeər i nəs -nɪs ‖ ˈer- ˈær-
airing ˈeər ɪŋ ‖ ˈer ɪŋ ˈær- **~s** z
ˈairing ˌcupboard
air-intake ˈeər ˌɪn teɪk ‖ ˈer- ˈær- **~s** s
airlane ˈeə leɪn ‖ ˈer- ˈær- **~s** z
airless ˈeə ləs -lɪs ‖ ˈer- ˈær- **~ness** nəs nɪs
airletter ˈeə ˌlet ə ‖ ˈer ˌleţ ᵊr ˈær- **~s** z
airlift ˈeə lɪft ‖ ˈer- ˈær- **~ed** ɪd əd **~ing** ɪŋ **~s** s
airline ˈeə laɪn ‖ ˈer- ˈær- **~s** z
airliner ˈeə ˌlaɪn ə ‖ ˈer ˌlaɪn ᵊr ˈær- **~s** z
airlock ˈeə lɒk ‖ ˈer lɑːk ˈær- **~s** s
airmail ˈeə meɪᵊl ‖ ˈer- ˈær- **~ed** d **~ing** ɪŋ **~s** z
air|man ˈeə |mən -mæn ‖ ˈer- ˈær- **~men** mən men
airmobile ˌeə ˈməʊb aɪᵊl ◂ ˈ·ˌ· · ‖ ˌer ˌmoʊb ᵊl ˈær-, -iːᵊl, -aɪᵊl; -moʊ ˌbiːᵊl
airplane ˈeə pleɪn ‖ ˈer- ˈær- **~s** z
airplay ˈeə pleɪ ‖ ˈer- ˈær-
airpocket ˈeə ˌpɒk ɪt §-ət ‖ ˈer ˌpɑːk ət ˈær- **~s** s
airport ˈeə pɔːt ‖ ˈer pɔːrt ˈær-, -poʊrt **~s** s
airscrew ˈeə skruː ‖ ˈer- ˈær- **~s** z
air-sea ˌeə ˈsiː ◂ ‖ ˌer-, ˌær-
ˌair-sea ˈrescue
airshaft ˈeə ʃɑːft §-ʃæft ‖ ˈer ʃæft ˈær- **~s** s
airship ˈeə ʃɪp ‖ ˈer- ˈær- **~s** s
airsick ˈeə sɪk ‖ ˈer- ˈær- **~ness** nəs nɪs
airside ˈeə saɪd ‖ ˈer- ˈær-
airspace ˈeə speɪs ‖ ˈer- ˈær-
airspeed ˈeə spiːd ‖ ˈer- ˈær- **~s** z
airstream ˈeə striːm ‖ ˈer- ˈær- **~s** z
ˈairstream ˌmechanism
airstrike ˈeə straɪk ‖ ˈer- ˈær- **~s** s
airstrip ˈeə strɪp ‖ ˈer- ˈær- **~s** s
airtight ˈeə taɪt ‖ ˈer- ˈær-
airtime ˈeə taɪm ‖ ˈer- ˈær-
air-to-air ˌeə tu ˈeə ◂ -tə- ‖ ˌer tə ˈer ◂ ˌær tə ˈær, -tu-
airwaves ˈeə weɪvz ‖ ˈer- ˈær-
airway ˈeə weɪ ‖ ˈer- ˈær- **~s** z
air|woman ˈeə |ˌwʊm ən ‖ ˈer- ˈær- **~women** ˌwɪm ɪn §-ən
airworth|y ˈeə ˌwɜːð |i ‖ ˈer ˌwɜːð |i ˈær- **~iness** i nəs i nɪs
air|y, Air|y ˈeər |i ‖ ˈer |i ˈær i **~ier** i‿ə ‖ i‿ᵊr **~iest** i‿ɪst i‿əst
airy-fairy ˌeər i ˈfeər i ◂ ‖ ˌer i ˈfer i ◂ ˌær i ˈfær i
Aisha *(i)* aɪ ˈiːʃ ə ɑː-, eɪ-, *(ii)* ˈeɪʃ ə ˈaɪʃ ə
aisle aɪᵊl *(= isle)* **aisles** aɪᵊlz
Aisling ˈæʃ lɪŋ
Aisne eɪn —*Fr* [ɛn]
ait eɪt *(= eight)* **aits** eɪts
aitch eɪtʃ **aitches** ˈeɪtʃ ɪz -əz
aitch-bone ˈeɪtʃ bəʊn ‖ -boʊn **~s** z
Aitchison ˈeɪtʃ ɪs ən -əs-
Aithne ˈeθ nə -ni
Aitken, Aitkin *(i)* ˈeɪt kɪn, *(ii)* ˈeɪk ɪn
Aiwa ˈaɪ wə —*Jp* [a ˌi wa]

Aix eɪks eks —*Fr* [ɛks]
Aix-en-Provence ˌeɪks ɒn prə ˈvɒnᵗs ˌeks-, →ˌ·ɒm- ‖ -ɑːn proʊ ˈvɑ̃ːs —*Fr* [ɛk sɑ̃ pʁɔ vɑ̃ːs]
Aix-la-Chapelle ˌeɪks lɑː ʃæ ˈpel ˌeks-, ˌ·læ-, ˌ·lə- ‖ -ʃɑː ˈpel —*Fr* [ɛks la ʃa pɛl]
Aix-les-Bains ˌeɪks leɪ ˈbæ̃ ˌeks-, -ˈbæn —*Fr* [ɛks le bɛ̃]
Ajaccio æ ˈdʒæs i əʊ -ˈʒæks- ‖ ɑː ˈjɑːtʃ oʊ -i oʊ —*Fr* [a ʒak sjo]
ajar ə ˈdʒɑː ‖ ə ˈdʒɑːr
Ajax *(i)* ˈeɪdʒ æks, *(ii)* ˈaɪ æks —*The Greek hero is (i), as is the scouring powder (tdmk); the Dutch football team is (ii)*
Ajman ædʒ ˈmɑːn —*Arabic* [ʕɑ ˈdʒmaːn]
aka —*see* **also known as**; *sometimes said aloud as* ˈæk ə *or* ˌeɪ keɪ ˈeɪ
Akabusi ˌæk ə ˈbuːs i
Akai *tdmk* ˈæk aɪ ‖ ə ˈkaɪ
Akan ə ˈkæn ‖ ˈɑːk ɑːn —*Akan* [a kã]
Akbar ˈæk bɑː ‖ -bɑːr
Akela ɑː ˈkeɪl ə
Akerman *(i)* ˈæk ə mən ‖ -ᵊr-, *(ii)* ˈeɪk-
Akhenaten, Akhenaton ˌæk ə ˈnɑːt ᵊn
Akihito ˌæk i ˈhiːt əʊ ‖ ˌɑːk i ˈhiːt oʊ —*Jp* [a ˈki çi̥ to]
akimbo ə ˈkɪm bəʊ ‖ -boʊ
akin ə ˈkɪn
Akins ˈeɪk ɪnz §-ənz
Akita, akita ə ˈkiːt ə ‖ ə ˈkiːt̬ ə —*Jp* [ˈa ki̥ ta] **~s** z
Akkad ˈæk æd ‖ ˈɑːk ɑːd
Akkadian ə ˈkeɪd iˌən æ-, -ˈkæd-
Akron ˈæk rɒn -rən ‖ -rən
Akrotiri ˌæk rəʊ ˈtɪər i ‖ ˌɑːk roʊ ˈtɪr i
Al æl
al æl —*It, Arabic* [al] —*See also phrases with this word*
al- ə, æ —*This variant of* ad- *is usually* ə (alˈlot), *but* æ *if stressed because of a suffix* (ˌalloˈcation).
-al ᵊl, əl —*When forming an adjective, this suffix imposes stress one or two syllables back* (ˌuniˈversal, ˈpersonal). *When forming a noun, it is stress-neutral* (ˌdisapˈproval).
a la, à la ˌæl ɑː -ə, ˌɑː lɑː ‖ ˌɑː lɑː ˌɑːl ə, ˌæl ə —*Fr* [a la]
ˌa la ˈcarte, ˌà la ˈcarte kɑːt ‖ kɑːrt —*Fr* [kaʁt]; **ˌa la ˈgrecque, ˌà la ˈgrecque** grek —*Fr* [ɡʁɛk]; **ˌa la ˈmode, ˌà la ˈmode** məʊd ‖ moʊd —*Fr* [mɔd]
al|a ˈeɪl |ə **~ae** iː
Alabam|a ˌæl ə ˈbæm |ə ◂ -ˈbɑːm- **~an/s** ən/z **~ian/s** iˌən/z
alabaster ˈæl ə bɑːst ə -bæst ə, ˌ· · ˈ· · ‖ -bæst ᵊr
alack ə ˈlæk
alackaday ə ˌlæk ə ˈdeɪ ·ˈ· ·
alacrity ə ˈlæk rət i -rɪt- ‖ -rət̬ i
Aladdin ə ˈlæd ɪn §-ᵊn
Alagiah ˌæl ə ˈɡaɪˌə
Alaister ˈæl ɪst ə -əst- ‖ -ᵊr
alameda, A~ ˌæl ə ˈmiːd ə -ˈmeɪd- —*Sp* [a la ˈme ða] **~s** z
Alamein ˈæl ə meɪn ˌ· ·ˈ·
Alamo ˈæl ə məʊ ‖ -moʊ
Alamogordo ˌæl əm ə ˈɡɔːd əʊ ‖ -ˈɡɔːrd oʊ
Alan ˈæl ən
Alana ə ˈlæn ə -ˈlɑːn-
Alanbrooke ˈæl ən brʊk →-əm-
Aland, Åland ˈɔː lənd ˈɑː- —*Swed* [ˈoː land]
alanine ˈæl ə niːn -naɪn
Al-Anon ˌæl ə ˈnɒn ‖ -ˈnɑːn
alar ˈeɪl ə -ɑː ‖ -ᵊr
Alaric ˈæl ər ɪk
alarm ə ˈlɑːm ‖ ə ˈlɑːrm **~ed** d **~ing/ly** ɪŋ /li **~s** z
aˈlarm clock
alarm|ism ə ˈlɑːm |ˌɪz əm ‖ ə ˈlɑːrm- **~ist/s** ɪst/s §əst/s
alarum ə ˈlær əm -ˈlɑːr-, -ˈleər- ‖ -ˈler- **~s** z
alas ə ˈlæs -ˈlɑːs
Alasdair ˈæl əst ə -ə steə ‖ -ᵊr
Alask|a, a~ ə ˈlæsk |ə **~an/s** ən/z
Alastair ˈæl əst ə -ə steə ‖ -ᵊr
alate ˈeɪl eɪt **~s** s
alb ælb **albs** ælbz
Alba, alba ˈælb ə
Albacete ˌælb ə ˈθeɪt i -eɪ —*Spanish* [al βa ˈθe te]
albacore ˈælb ə kɔː ‖ -kɔːr -koʊr **~s** z
Alban ˈɔːlb ən ˈɒlb- ‖ ˈɑːlb-
Albani|a æl ˈbeɪn iˌ|ə ɔːl- **~an/s** ən/z
Albany ˈɔːlb ən i ˈɒlb-, §ˈælb- ‖ ˈɑːlb-
Albarn ˈɔːl bɑːn ‖ -bɑːrn ˈɑːl-
albatross ˈælb ə trɒs ‖ -trɑːs -trɔːs **~es** ɪz əz
albedo æl ˈbiːd əʊ ‖ -oʊ **~s** z
Albee *(i)* ˈɔːlb iː ‖ ˈɔːlb i ˈɑːlb-, *(ii)* ˈælb iː
albeit ₍ˌ₎ɔːl ˈbiːˌɪt §₍ˌ₎æl-, ət ‖ ₍ˌ₎ɑːl-, ₍ˌ₎æl-
Albemarle ˈælb ə mɑːl ‖ -mɑːrl
ˌAlbemarle ˈSound
Albéniz æl ˈbeɪn ɪθ ‖ ɑːl ˈbeɪn iːs —*Sp* [al ˈβe niθ]
Alberich ˈælb ə rɪk -rɪx —*Ger* [ˈal bə ʁɪç]
Albert, a~ ˈælb ət ‖ -ᵊrt —*but as a French name,* æl ˈbeə ‖ ɑːl ˈbeᵊr —*Fr* [al bɛːʁ] **~s, ~'s** s
Alberta æl ˈbɜːt ə ‖ -ˈbɜːt̬ ə
Albertina ˌælb ə ˈtiːn ə ‖ -ᵊr-
Albertine ˈælb ə tiːn ˌ· ·ˈ· ‖ -ᵊr-
albescence æl ˈbes ᵊnᵗs
albescent æl ˈbes ᵊnt
Albigenses ˌælb ɪ ˈdʒenᵗs iːz -ə-, -ˈɡenᵗs-
Albigensian ˌælb ɪ ˈdʒenᵗs iˌən ◂ ˌ·ə-, -ˈɡenᵗs- ‖ -ˈdʒenᵗʃ ən ◂ **~s** z
albinism ˈælb ɪ ˌnɪz əm -ə-
albino æl ˈbiːn əʊ ‖ -ˈbaɪn oʊ *(*)* **~s** z
Albinoni ˌælb ɪ ˈnəʊn i §-ə- ‖ -ˈnoʊn i —*It* [al bi ˈnoː ni]
Albion ˈælb iˌən
albite ˈælb aɪt
Alborg ˈɔːl bɔːɡ ˈɑːl- ‖ -bɔːrɡ —*Danish* Ålborg [ˈʌl bɔːʔ]
Albright ˈɔːl braɪt ˈɒl- ‖ ˈɑːl-
Albrow ˈɔːl braʊ ‖ ˈɑːl-
Albufeira ˌælb u ˈfeər ə ‖ -ˈfer- —*Port* [ɐl βu ˈfei ɾɐ]

A

album 'ælb əm **~s** z
albumen 'ælb jum ɪn -jəm-, -ən; -ju men, -jə- ‖ æl 'bjuːm ən
albumin 'ælb jum ɪn -jəm-, -ən ‖ æl 'bjuːm ən
albuminous æl 'bjuːm ɪn əs -ən-
albuminuria æl ˌbjuːm ɪ 'njʊər i‿ə -ˌə- ‖ -'nʊr- -'njʊr-
Albuquerque 'ælb ə kɜːk i ˌ· ·'· · ‖ -kɝːk i
Albury 'ɔːl bər‿i 'ɒl-, 'ɔː- ‖ 'ɔːl ˌber i 'ɑːl-
Alcaeus æl 'siː‿əs
Alcaic, a~ æl 'keɪ ɪk **~s** s
alcalde æl 'kæld i ‖ -'kɑːld-, -eɪ **~s** z
Alcan *tdmk* 'æl kæn
Alcatraz 'ælk ə træz ˌ· ·'·
Alcazar, a~ ˌælk ə 'zɑː æl 'kæz ə ‖ 'ælk ə zɑːr æl 'kæz ᵊr, -'kɑːz- —*Sp* Alcázar [al 'ka θar] **~s** z
Alceste æl 'sest
Alcester 'ɔːlst ə ‖ -ᵊr 'ɑːlst-
Alcestis æl 'sest ɪs §-əs
alchemist 'ælk əm ɪst -ɪm-, §-əst **~s** s
alchemy 'ælk əm i -ɪm-
alcheringa ˌæltʃ ə 'rɪŋ gə
Alcibiades ˌæls ɪ 'baɪ‿ə diːz ˌ·ə-
Alcinous æl 'sɪn əʊ əs ‖ -oʊ-
Alcmene ælk 'miːn i
Alcoa *tdmk* æl 'kəʊ ə ‖ -'koʊ-
Alcock *(i)* 'æl kɒk ‖ -kɑːk, *(ii)* 'ɔːl- 'ɒl- ‖ 'ɑːl-
alcohol 'ælk ə hɒl ‖ -hɔːl -hɑːl **~s** z
alcohol-free ˌælk ə hɒl 'friː ◂ ‖ -ə hɔːl- -ə hɑːl-
alcoholic ˌælk ə 'hɒl ɪk ◂ ‖ -'hɑːl- -'hɔːl- **~s** s
alcoholism 'ælk ə hɒl ˌɪz əm -həl ˌ-- ‖ -hɑːl ˌɪz əm -hɔːl ˌ--
Alconbury 'ɔːlk ən bər‿i 'ɔːk-, 'ɒlk-, →'·əm- ‖ 'ɔːlk ən ˌber i 'ɑːlk-
alcopop 'ælk əʊ pɒp ‖ -oʊ pɑːp **~s** s
Alcott *(i)* 'ɔːlk ət 'ɒlk-, -ɒt ‖ 'ɔːlk ɑːt 'ɑːlk-, *(ii)* 'ælk-
alcove 'ælk əʊv ‖ -oʊv **~s** z
Alcuin 'ælk wɪn §-wən
Alcyone æl 'saɪ‿ən i -'siː‿
Alda 'ɔːld ə
Aldabra ₍ₗ₎æl 'dæbr ə
Aldebaran æl 'deb ᵊr‿ən -ə ræn
Aldeburgh 'ɔːl*d* bər‿ə 'ɒl*d*- ‖ 'ɔːl*d* ˌbɝː oʊ 'ɑːl*d*-
aldehyde 'æld ɪ haɪd -ə- **~s** z
Alden 'ɔːld ən 'ɒld- ‖ 'ɑːld-
Aldenham 'ɔːld ən‿əm 'ɒld- ‖ 'ɑːld-
al dente ₍ₗ₎æl 'dent i -eɪ ‖ ₍ₗ₎ɑːl- —*It* [al 'dɛn te]
alder, Alder 'ɔːld ə 'ɒld- ‖ 'ɔːld ᵊr 'ɑːld- **~s** z
Aldergrove 'ɔːld ə grəʊv 'ɒld- ‖ 'ɔːld ᵊr groʊv 'ɑːld-
Alderley 'ɔːld ə li 'ɒld-, -ᵊl i ‖ -ᵊr- 'ɑːld-
alder|man 'ɔːld ə |mən 'ɒld- ‖ -ᵊr- 'ɑːld- **~men** mən
aldermanic ˌɔːld ə 'mæn ɪk ◂ ˌɒld- ‖ -ᵊr- ˌɑːld-
Aldermaston 'ɔːld ə ˌmɑːst ən 'ɒld-, §-ˌmæst- ‖ -ᵊr ˌmæst- 'ɑːld-
Alderney 'ɔːld ən i 'ɒld- ‖ -ᵊrn i 'ɑːld-
Aldersgate 'ɔːld əz geɪt 'ɒld-, -gɪt, -gət ‖ -ᵊrz- 'ɑːld-
Aldershot 'ɔːld ə ʃɒt 'ɒld- ‖ 'ɔːld ᵊr ʃɑːt 'ɑːld-
Alderson 'ɔːld əs ən 'ɒld- ‖ -ᵊrs- 'ɑːld-
Alderton 'ɔːld ət ən 'ɒld- ‖ 'ɔːld ᵊrt ᵊn 'ɑːld-
Aldgate 'ɔːl*d* gɪt 'ɒl*d*-, -geɪt, -gət ‖ 'ɔːl*d* geɪt 'ɑːl*d*-
Aldhelm 'ɔːld helm 'ɒld- ‖ 'ɑːld-
Aldi *tdmk* 'æld i
Aldine 'ɔːld aɪn 'ɒld-, -iːn ‖ 'ɑːld-
Aldington 'ɔːld ɪŋ tən 'ɒld- ‖ 'ɑːld-
Aldis, Aldiss 'ɔːld ɪs 'ɒld-, §-əs ‖ 'ɑːld-
aldol 'æld ɒl ‖ -ɑːl -ɔːl, -oʊl
aldosterone æl 'dɒst ə rəʊn ˌæld əʊ 'stɪər əʊn ‖ -'dɑːst ə roʊn ˌæld oʊ stə 'roʊn
Aldous 'ɔːld əs 'ɒld- ‖ 'ɑːld-
Aldrich 'ɔːld rɪtʃ 'ɒld-, -rɪdʒ ‖ 'ɑːld-
Aldridge 'ɔːld rɪdʒ 'ɒld- ‖ 'ɑːld-
Aldrin, a~ 'ɔːldr ɪn 'ɒldr-, §-ən ‖ 'ɑːldr-
Aldus 'ɔːld əs 'ɒld-, 'æld- ‖ 'ɑːld-
Aldwych 'ɔːld wɪtʃ 'ɒld- ‖ 'ɑːld-
ale eɪᵊl **ales** eɪᵊlz
aleatoric ˌæl i‿ə 'tɒr ɪk ◂ ˌeɪl- ‖ -'tɔːr- -'tɑːr- **~ally** ᵊl‿i
aleatory ˌæl i 'eɪt ər i 'eɪl i‿ət‿ər i ‖ 'eɪl i‿ə tɔːr i -toʊr i
Alec, Aleck, a~ 'æl ɪk -ek
Alecto ə 'lekt əʊ æ- ‖ -oʊ
Aled 'æl ed -ɪd —*Welsh* ['a led]
ale|house 'eɪᵊl |haʊs **~houses** haʊz ɪz -əz
aleikum ə 'leɪk ʊm æ- —*Arabic* [ʔæ 'lɐik um]
Alemannic ˌæl ə 'mæn ɪk ◂ -ɪ-
alembic ə 'lem bɪk **~s** s
Alencon, Alençon 'æl ən sɒ̃ ‖ ˌæl ɑːn 'soʊn —*Fr* [a lɑ̃ sɔ̃]
aleph 'æl ef 'ɑːl-, -ɪf, §-əf ‖ 'ɑːl əf -ef **~s** s
Aleppo ə 'lep əʊ ‖ -oʊ
alert ə 'lɜːt ‖ ə 'lɝːt **alerted** ə 'lɜːt ɪd -əd ‖ ə 'lɝːţ əd **alerting** ə 'lɜːt ɪŋ ‖ ə 'lɝːţ ɪŋ **alerts** ə 'lɜːts ‖ ə 'lɝːts
alert|ly ə 'lɜːt| li ‖ ə 'lɝːt| li **~ness** nəs nɪs
Aleut 'æl i uːt ˌ· ·'·; æ 'luːt, ə-, -'ljuːt ‖ ə 'luːt **~s** s
Aleutian ə 'luːʃ ᵊn -'ljuːʃ-, -'i‿ən **~s** z
A-level 'eɪ ˌlev ᵊl **~s** z
ale|wife 'eɪᵊl |waɪf **~wives** waɪvz
Alex 'æl ɪks -eks
Alexander ˌæl ɪg 'zɑːnd ə -eg-, -ɪk-, -'zænd- ‖ -'zænd ᵊr —*There is also a Scottish form* 'elʃ ɪnd ə ‖ -ᵊr
alexanders ˌæl ɪg 'zɑːnd əz -eg-, -ɪk-, -'zænd- ‖ -'zænd ᵊrz
Alexandra ˌæl ɪg 'zɑːndr ə -eg-, -ɪk-, -'zændr- ‖ -'zændr ə
Alexandretta ˌæl ɪg zɑːn 'dret ə ˌ·eg-, ˌ·ɪk-, -zæn'-- ‖ -zæn 'dreţ ə
Alexandria ˌæl ɪg 'zɑːndr i‿ə ˌ·eg-, ˌ·ɪk-, -'zændr- ‖ -'zændr-
Alexandrian, a~ ˌæl ɪg 'zɑːndr i‿ən ◂ ˌ·eg-, ˌ·ɪk-, -'zændr- ‖ -'zændr- **~s** z
alexandrine ˌæl ɪg 'zændr aɪn -eg-, -ɪk-, -'zɑːndr-, -iːn, -ɪn **~s** z

alexia ˌeɪ ˈleks i̯ə əˈ-
Alexis ə ˈleks ɪs §-əs
Alf ælf
alfa, Alfa ˈælf ə **~s** z
Alfa-Laval ˌælf ə lə ˈvæl ‖ -ˈvɑːl
alfalfa æl ˈfælf ə
Alfa-Romeo *tdmk* ˌælf ə rəʊ ˈmeɪ əʊ -ˈrəʊm i əʊ ‖ -roʊ ˈmeɪ oʊ **~s** z
Al-Fayed æl ˈfaɪ ed
Alfie ˈælf i
Alfonso æl ˈfɒnz əʊ -ˈfɒnᵗs- ‖ -ˈfɑːnᵗs oʊ *—Sp* [al ˈfon so]
Alford *(i)* ˈɔːl fəd ˈɒl- ‖ ˈɔːl fᵊrd ˈɑːl-, *(ii)* ˈæl-
Alfred ˈælf rɪd -rəd
Alfreda æl ˈfriːd ə
alfresco æl ˈfresk əʊ ‖ -oʊ
Alfreton ˈɔːlf rɪt ən ˈɒlf-, ˈælf-, -rət- ‖ ˈɔːlf rət ᵊn ˈɑːlf-, ˈælf-
alga ˈælg ə **algae** ˈældʒ iː ˈælg-, -aɪ
Algarve æl ˈgɑːv ˈ· · ‖ ɑːl ˈgɑːrv ə *—Port* [aɫ ˈgarv]
algebra ˈældʒ ɪb rə -əb- **~s** z
algebraic ˌældʒ ɪ ˈbreɪ ɪk ◂ -ə- **~al** ᵊl **~ally** ᵊl i
algebraist ˌældʒ ɪ ˈbreɪ ɪst -ə-, §-əst **~s** s
Algeciras ˌældʒ ɪ ˈsɪər əs -ə-, -e-, -ˈsɪr- ‖ -ˈsɪr- *—Sp* [al xe ˈθi ɾas]
Algeo ˈældʒ i əʊ ‖ -oʊ
Alger ˈældʒ ə ‖ -ᵊr
Algeri|a æl ˈdʒɪər i̯|ə ‖ -ˈdʒɪr- **~an/z** ən/z
Algernon ˈældʒ ən ən ‖ -ᵊrn-
Algie ˈældʒ i
Algiers ₍ˌ₎æl ˈdʒɪəz ˈ· · ‖ -ˈdʒɪᵊrz
alginate ˈældʒ ɪ neɪt -ə- **~s** s
Algipan *tdmk* ˈældʒ ɪ pæn -ə-
Algoa æl ˈgəʊ ə ‖ -ˈgoʊ-
Algol, ALGOL ˈælg ɒl ‖ -ɑːl -ɔːl
algolagnia ˌælg əʊ ˈlæg ni̯ə ‖ ˌælg oʊ-
Algonkian æl ˈgɒŋk i̯ən -wi̯ən ‖ -ˈgɑːŋk- **~s** z
Algonquian æl ˈgɒŋk wi̯ən -i̯ən ‖ -ˈgɑːŋk- **~s** z
Algonquin æl ˈgɒŋk wɪn -ɪn, §-wən, §-ən ‖ -ˈgɑːŋk- **~s** z
algorithm ˈælg ə ˌrɪð əm **~s** z
algorithmic ˌælg ə ˈrɪð mɪk ◂ **~ally** ᵊl i
Algy ˈældʒ i
alhaji æl ˈhædʒ i -ˈhɑːdʒ- *—Arabic* [ʔal ˈħaːd dʒi]
Alhambra æl ˈhæm brə əl-; ə ˈlæm- *—Sp* [a ˈlam bɾa]
Ali ˈæl i ˈɑːl- ‖ ˈɑːl i *—but the former boxer* Muhammad Ali *pronounces* ɑː ˈliː *—Arabic* [ˈʕa li]
ˌ**Ali ˈBaba** ˈbɑːb ɑː
alias ˈeɪl i̯əs -æs **~es** ɪz əz **~ing** ɪŋ
alibi ˈæl ə baɪ -ɪ- **~ed** d **~ing** ɪŋ **~s** z
Alicante ˌæl ɪ ˈkænt i -ə-, -eɪ ‖ -ˈkænt̬ i ˌɑːl ə ˈkɑːnt̬- *—Sp* [a li ˈkan te]
Alice ˈæl ɪs §-əs **~'s** ɪz əz
ˌ**Alice ˈSprings**
Alicia ə ˈlɪʃ ə ə ˈlɪs i̯ə, -ˈlɪʃ i̯ə
Alick ˈæl ɪk
lidade ˈæl ɪ deɪd -ə- **~s** z
ien ˈeɪl i̯ən **~s** z

alienable ˈeɪl i̯ən əb ᵊl
alie|nate ˈeɪl i̯ə |neɪt **~nated** neɪt ɪd -əd ‖ neɪt̬ əd **~nates** neɪts **~nating** neɪt ɪŋ ‖ neɪt̬ ɪŋ
alienation ˌeɪl i̯ə ˈneɪʃ ᵊn **~s** z
alienist ˈeɪl i̯ən ɪst §-əst **~s** s
alight ə ˈlaɪt **alighted** ə ˈlaɪt ɪd -əd ‖ ə ˈlaɪt̬ əd **alighting** ə ˈlaɪt ɪŋ ‖ ə ˈlaɪt̬ ɪŋ **alights** ə ˈlaɪts **alit** ə ˈlɪt
align ə ˈlaɪn **aligned** ə ˈlaɪnd **aligning** ə ˈlaɪn ɪŋ **aligns** ə ˈlaɪnz
alignment ə ˈlaɪn mənt **~s** s
alike ə ˈlaɪk
alimentary ˌæl ɪ ˈment̬ər i ◂ ˌ·ə-
alimentation ˌæl ɪ men ˈteɪʃ ᵊn ˌ·ə-, -mən ˈ-
alimon|y ˈæl ɪ mən |i ˈ·ə- ‖ -moʊn |i **~ies** iz
aliphatic ˌæl ɪ ˈfæt ɪk ◂ -ə- ‖ -ˈfæt̬-
aliquot ˈæl ɪ kwɒt -ə- ‖ -kwɑːt -kwət
Alisha ə ˈlɪʃ ə
Alison, a~ ˈæl ɪs ən -əs-
A-list ˈeɪ lɪst
Alistair ˈæl ɪst ə -əst-; -ɪ steə, -ə- ‖ -ə ster -əst ᵊr
alit ə ˈlɪt
Alitalia *tdmk* ˌæl ɪ ˈtæl i̯ə -ˈtɑːl- ‖ ˌɑːl ɪ ˈtɑːl- *—It* [a li ˈtaː lja]
alive ə ˈlaɪv
aliyah ə ˈliː ə -jə *—Hebrew* [(ʕ)a ˈlij jah]
alizarin ə ˈlɪz ər ɪn §-ən
al-Jazeera ˌæl dʒə ˈzɪər ə ‖ ˌɑːl dʒə ˈzɪr ə *—Arabic* [al dʒa ˈziː ɾaː]
alkali ˈælk ə laɪ **~s** z
alkaline ˈælk ə laɪn
alkalinity ˌælk ə ˈlɪn ət i -ɪt i ‖ -ət̬ i
alkaloid ˈælk ə lɔɪd **~s** z
alkane ˈælk eɪn **~s** z
alkanet ˈælk ə net **~s** s
Alka-Seltzer *tdmk* ˌælk ə ˈselts ə ˈ· · ˌ· · ‖ ˈælk ə ˌselts ᵊr **~s** z
alkene ˈælk iːn **~s** z
alkyd ˈælk ɪd §-əd
alkyl ˈælk ɪl -aɪᵊl, §-ᵊl ‖ -ᵊl **~s** z
alkyne ˈælk aɪn **~s** z
all ɔːl ‖ ɑːl
ˌ**all ˈclear**; ˌ**All ˈSaints**; ˌ**All ˈSaints' Day**; ˌ**All ˈSouls'**; ˌ**all the ˈsame**
all- ¦ɔːl ‖ ¦ɑːl — **all-important** ˌɔːl ɪm ˈpɔːt ᵊnt ◂ ‖ -ˈpɔːrt ᵊnt ◂ ˌɑːl-
alla ˈæl ə ˈɑːl-, -ɑː ‖ ˈɑːl ə ˈæl ə *—It* [ˈal la]
ˌ**alla ˈbreve** ˈbreɪv i -ˈbrev-, -eɪ; ˈbrev *—It* [ˈbreː ve]
Allah ˈæl ə ə ˈlɑː; æ ˈlɑː, ə- *—Arabic* [aɫ ˈɫaːh]
Allahabad ˌæl ə hə ˈbɑːd -ˈbæd *—Hindi/Urdu* [ɪ laː haː baːd̪]
allamanda ˌæl ə ˈmænd ə **~s** z
all-American ˌɔːl ə ˈmer ɪk ən ◂ ‖ ˌɑːl-
ˌ**all-Aˌmerican ˈathlete**
Allan ˈæl ən
Allan-a-Dale ˌæl ən ə ˈdeɪᵊl
Allandale ˈæl ən deɪᵊl
allanto|in ə ˈlænt əʊ| ɪn ˌæl ən ˈtəʊ|-, §-ən ‖ -oʊ|- **~is** ɪs §əs
Allardice ˈæl ə daɪs ‖ -ᵊr-

all-around ˌɔːl ə ˈraʊnd ◂ ‖ ˌɑːl-

Allason ˈæl əs ən

allative ˈæl ət ɪv ‖ -əṭ- **~s** z

Allaun ə ˈlɔːn ‖ -ˈlɑːn

allay ə ˈleɪ **~ed** d **~ing** ɪŋ **~s** z

Allbeury ɔːl ˈbjʊər i ɔːl ˈbjʊr i ɑːl-

All-Black ˈɔːl blæk ‖ ˈɑːl- **~s** s

All-Bran *tdmk* ˈɔːl bræn ‖ ˈɑːl-

all-day ˌɔːl ˈdeɪ ◂ ‖ ˌɑːl-
ˌall-day ˈmeeting

Allder ˈɔːld ə ˈɒld- ‖ ˈɔːld ᵊr ˈɑːld- **~'s** z

allegation ˌæl ə ˈgeɪʃ ᵊn -ɪ- **~s** z

alleg|e ə ˈledʒ (ˌ)æ- **~ed** d **~es** ɪz əz **~ing** ɪŋ

allegedly ə ˈledʒ ɪd li -əd-

Alleghany, Allegheny ˌæl ɪ ˈgeɪn i -ə-, -ˈgen-

allegianc|e ə ˈliːdʒ ənᵗs **~es** ɪz əz

allegorical ˌæl ə ˈgɒr ɪk ᵊl ◂ ˌ-ɪ- ‖ -ˈgɔːr- -ˈgɑːr- **~ly** i

allegor|y ˈæl əg ər‿|i ˈ-ɪg- ‖ -ə gɔːr |i -goʊr i **~ies** iz **~ist/s** ɪst/s §əst/s

allegretto ˌæl ə ˈgret əʊ -ɪ- ‖ -ˈgreṭ oʊ **~s** z

Allegri ə ˈleɪg riː -ˈleg-, -ri

allegro ə ˈleg rəʊ -ˈleɪg- ‖ -roʊ **~s** z

allele ə ˈliːᵊl **~s** z

all-electric ˌɔːl ə ˈlek trɪk ◂ -ɪ- ‖ ˌɑːl-

allelic ə ˈliːl ɪk

allelomorph ə ˈliːl əʊ mɔːf ‖ -ə mɔːrf **~s** s

alleluia ˌæl ə ˈluː jə ◂ -ɪ-, -eɪ- —*In hymns also occasionally* æ ˌleɪ luː ˈjɑː *(where final stress is called for)* **~s** z

allemande ˈæl ə mænd -ɪ-, -mɑːnd ‖ -mæn, -mɑːnd, ˌ· · ˈ· —*Fr* [al mɑ̃ːd] **~s** z

all-embracing ˌɔːl ɪm ˈbreɪs ɪŋ ◂ -əm-, -em- ‖ ˌɑːl-

Allen ˈæl ən -ɪn

Allenby ˈæl ən bi →-əm-

Allendale ˈæl ən deɪᵊl -ɪn-

Allende aɪ ˈend i -ˈjend-, -eɪ ‖ ɑː ˈjend- ˌɑːl- —*Sp* [a ˈʎen de, -ˈjen-]

Allentown ˈæl ən taʊn

allergen ˈæl ə dʒen -ɜː-, -ədʒ ən ‖ -ᵊr- **~s** z

allergenic ˌæl ə ˈdʒen ɪk ◂ -ɜː- ‖ -ᵊr-

allergic ə ˈlɜːdʒ ɪk ‖ ə ˈlɜːdʒ ɪk

allerg|y ˈæl ədʒ |i ‖ -ᵊrdʒ |i **~ies** iz **~ist/s** ɪst/s §əst/s

Allerton ˈæl ət ən ‖ -ᵊrt ᵊn —*but some places of this name in Yks are* ˈɒl-

allevi|ate ə ˈliːv i |eɪt **~ated** eɪt ɪd -əd ‖ eɪṭ əd **~ates** eɪts **~ating** eɪt ɪŋ ‖ eɪṭ ɪŋ

alleviation ə ˌliːv i ˈeɪʃ ᵊn

alley ˈæl i **~s** z

Alleyn ˈæl ɪn -ən

Alleyne *(i)* æ ˈleɪn, *(ii)* -ˈliːn, *(iii)* ˈæl ən -ɪn

alleyway ˈæl i weɪ **~s** z

Allhallows (ˌ)ɔːl ˈhæl əʊz ‖ -oʊz (ˌ)ɑːl-

allheal ˈɔːl hiːᵊl ‖ ˈɑːl-

allianc|e ə ˈlaɪ‿ənᵗs **~es** ɪz əz

Allie ˈæl i

allied *adj* ˈæl aɪd ə ˈlaɪd

allies *n* ˈæl aɪz ə ˈlaɪz, *v* ə ˈlaɪz ˈæl aɪz

alligator ˈæl ɪ geɪt ə ˌ-ə- ‖ -geɪṭ ᵊr **~s** z

all-important ˌɔːl ɪm ˈpɔːt ᵊnt ◂ ‖ -ˈpɔːrt- ˌɑːl-

all-in ˌɔːl ˈɪn ◂ ‖ ˌɑːl-
ˌall-in ˈwrestling

all-inclusive ˌɔːl ɪn ˈklus ɪv ◂ →-ɪŋ-, §-ˈkluːz- ‖ ˌɑːl-

All-India ˌɔːl ˈɪnd i‿ə ◂ ‖ ˌɑːl-
ˌAll-ˌIndia ˈRadio

Allingham ˈæl ɪŋ əm

all-in-one ˌɔːl ɪn ˈwʌn ◂ -ən-, §-ˈwɒn ‖ ˌɑːl-

Allinson ˈæl ɪn sən §-ən-

Allison ˈæl ɪs ən -əs-

allite|rate ə ˈlɪt ə |reɪt ‖ ə ˈlɪṭ ə- **~rated** reɪt ɪd -əd ‖ reɪṭ əd **~rates** reɪts **~rating** reɪt ɪŋ ‖ reɪṭ ɪŋ

alliteration ə ˌlɪt ə ˈreɪʃ ᵊn ‖ ə ˌlɪṭ- **~s** z

alliterative ə ˈlɪt‿ər ət ɪv -ə reɪt ɪv ‖ ə ˈlɪṭ ər əṭ ɪv -ə reɪṭ ɪv **~ly** li **~ness** nəs nɪs

allium ˈæl i‿əm

all-night ˌɔːl ˈnaɪt ◂ ‖ ˌɑːl-
ˌall-night ˈparty

all-nighter ˌɔːl ˈnaɪt ə ◂ ‖ ˌɔːl ˈnaɪṭ ᵊr ˌɑːl- **~s** z

allo- *comb. form*
with stress-neutral suffix ¦æl əʊ ‖ ¦æl ə -oʊ
— **allotrope** ˈæl əʊ trəʊp ‖ -ə troʊp
with stress-imposing suffix ə ˈlɒ+ æ ˈlɒ+ ‖ -ˈlɑː+ — **allotropy** ə ˈlɒtr əp i æ- ‖ ə ˈlɑːtr-

'allo *non-standard interjection* ə ˈləʊ æ- ‖ -ˈloʊ

Alloa ˈæl əʊ ə ‖ -oʊ ə

allo|cate ˈæl ə |keɪt **~cated** keɪt ɪd -əd ‖ keɪṭ əd **~cates** keɪts **~cating** keɪt ɪŋ ‖ keɪṭ ɪŋ

allocation ˌæl ə ˈkeɪʃ ᵊn **~s** z

allochthonous æ ˈlɒk θən əs ə- ‖ -ˈlɑːk- **~ly** li

allocution ˌæl ə ˈkjuːʃ ᵊn **~s** z

allograph ˈæl əʊ grɑːf -græf ‖ -ə græf **~s** s

allographic ˌæl əʊ ˈgræf ɪk ◂ ‖ -ə- **~ally** ᵊl‿i

allomorph ˈæl əʊ mɔːf ‖ -ə mɔːrf **~s** s

allomorphic ˌæl əʊ ˈmɔːf ɪk ◂ ‖ -ə ˈmɔːrf- **~ally** ᵊl‿i

allomorph|ism ˈæl əʊ mɔːf |ˌɪz əm ‖ -ə mɔːrf- **~y** i

allopathic ˌæl ə ˈpæθ ɪk ◂ **~ally** ᵊl‿i

allopathy ə ˈlɒp əθ i æ- ‖ ə ˈlɑːp-

allophone ˈæl ə fəʊn ‖ -foʊn **~s** z

allophonic ˌæl ə ˈfɒn ɪk ◂ ‖ -ˈfɑːn- **~ally** ᵊl‿i

allophony æ ˈlɒf ən i ə-; ˈæl ə fəʊn i ‖ ə ˈlɑːf ən i ˈæl ə foʊn i

all-or-nothing ˌɔːl ɔː ˈnʌθ ɪŋ ◂ ‖ ˌɔːl ᵊr- ˌɑːl-, -ɔːr-

allot ə ˈlɒt ‖ ə ˈlɑːt **allots** ə ˈlɒts ‖ ə ˈlɑːts **allotted** ə ˈlɒt ɪd -əd ‖ ə ˈlɑːṭ əd **allotting** ə ˈlɒt ɪŋ ‖ ə ˈlɑːṭ ɪŋ

allotment ə ˈlɒt mənt ‖ ə ˈlɑːt- **~s** s

allotone ˈæl əʊ təʊn ‖ -ə toʊn **~s** z

allotrope ˈæl ə trəʊp ‖ -troʊp **~s** s

Allott ˈæl ət

allott... —*see* **allot**

all-out ˌɔːl ˈaʊt ◂ ‖ ˌɑːl-
ˌall-out ˈeffort

all-over ˈɔːl ˌəʊv ə ‖ -oʊv ᵊr ˈɑːl-

allow ə ˈlaʊ **allowed** ə ˈlaʊd *(= aloud)* **allowing** ə ˈlaʊ‿ɪŋ **allows** ə ˈlaʊz

allowable ə ˈlaʊ‿əb ᵊl

A

allowanc|e ə ˈlaʊ˽ənts **~es** ɪz əz
Alloway ˈæl ə weɪ
allowedly ə ˈlaʊ ɪd li -əd-
alloy *n* ˈæl ɔɪ ə ˈlɔɪ **~s** z
alloy *v* ə ˈlɔɪ ˈæl ɔɪ **~ed** d **~ing** ɪŋ **~s** z
all-party ˌɔːl ˈpɑːt i ◂ ‖ -ˈpɑːrt̬ i ◂ ˌɑːl-
all-points ˌɔːl ˈpɔɪnts ◂ ‖ ˌɑːl-
all-powerful ˌɔːl ˈpaʊ˽ə fəl ◂ -fʊl ‖ -ˈpaʊ˽ər- ˌɑːl-
all-purpose ˌɔːl ˈpɜːp əs ◂ ‖ -ˈpɜːp- ˌɑːl-
all-round ˌɔːl ˈraʊnd ◂ ‖ ˌɑːl-
ˌall-round ˈathlete
all-rounder ˌɔːl ˈraʊnd ə ‖ -ər ˌɑːl- **~s** z
all-seater ˌɔːl ˈsiːt ə ◂ ‖ -ˈsiːt̬ ər ˌɑːl-
Allsop, Allsopp ˈɔːl sɒp ˈɒl- ‖ ˈɔːl sɑːp ˈɑːl-
allsort ˈɔːl sɔːt ‖ ˈɔːl sɔːrt ˈɑːl- **~s** s
allspice ˈɔːl spaɪs ‖ ˈɑːl-
all-star *adj* ˌɔːl ˈstɑː ◂ ˈ·· ‖ -ˈstɑːr ˌɑːl-
ˌall-star ˈcast
all-star *n* ˈɔːl stɑː ‖ -stɑːr ˈɑːl- **~s** z
Allston ˈɔːlst ən ˈɒlst- ‖ ˈɑːlst-
all-terrain ˌɔːl tə ˈreɪn ◂ -te-, -tɪ- ‖ ˌɑːl-
all-time ˌɔːl ˈtaɪm ◂ ‖ ˌɑːl-
ˌall-time ˈgreats
allud|e ə ˈluːd ə ˈljuːd **~ed** ɪd əd **~es** z **~ing** ɪŋ
allure ə ˈlʊə -ˈljʊə, -ˈljɔː ‖ ə ˈlʊər **~d** d **~ment/s** mənt/s **~s** z **alluring/ly** ə ˈlʊər ɪŋ /li -ˈljʊər-, -ˈljɔːr- ‖ ə ˈlʊr ɪŋ /li
allusion ə ˈluːʒ ən -ˈljuːʒ- **~s** z
allusive ə ˈluːs ɪv -ˈljuːs- ‖ -ˈluːz- **~ly** li **~ness** nəs nɪs
alluvi|al ə ˈluːv i˽|əl -ˈljuːv- **~a** ə **~on** ən **~um** əm
all-weather ˌɔːl ˈweð ə ◂ ‖ -ər ◂ ˌɑːl-
ˌall-ˌweather ˈgarments
Allworthy ˈɔːl ˌwɜːð i ‖ ˈɔːl ˌwɜːð i ˈɑːl-
Ally *personal name* ˈæl i

ALLY

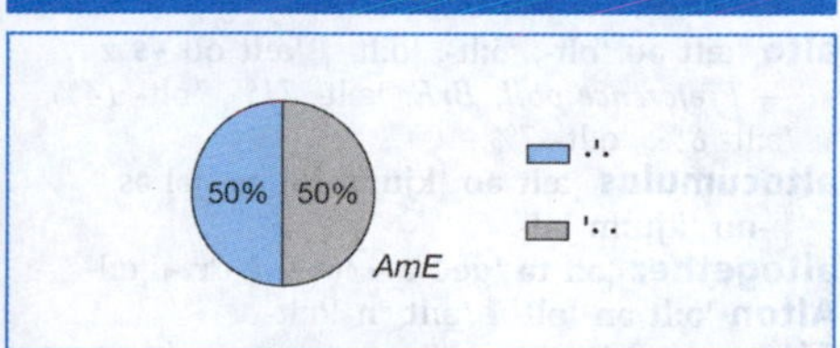

ally *v* ə ˈlaɪ ˈæl aɪ **allied** ə ˈlaɪd ˈæl aɪd —*but in* allied forces *usually* ˈæl aɪd **allies** ə ˈlaɪz ˈæl aɪz **allying** ə ˈlaɪ ɪŋ ˈæl aɪ- — *Preference poll, AmE:* ·ˈ· *50%,* ˈ·· *50%.*
ally *n* ˈæl aɪ ə ˈlaɪ **allies** ˈæl aɪz ə ˈlaɪz
-ally əl i —*but* -ically *is usually reduced by* COMPRESSION *to* ɪk li
allyl ˈæl aɪəl -ɪl, §-əl ‖ -əl
Alma ˈælm ə —*See also phrases with this word*
Alma Ata æl ˌmɑː ə ˈtɑː
almagest, A~ ˈælm ə dʒest
alma mater ˌælm ə ˈmɑːt ə -ˈmeɪt- ‖ -ˈmɑːt̬ ər
almanac, almanack ˈɔːlm ə næk ˈɒlm-, ˈælm- ‖ ˈɑːlm-, ˈælm- **~s** s
almandine ˈælm ən diːn ˈɑːm-, ˈɑːlm-, -dɪn, -daɪn; ˌ··ˈ· **~s** z
Alma-Tadema ˌælm ə ˈtæd ɪm ə §-əm ə
Almaty æl ˈmɑːt i -ə —*Russ* [al ˈma tɨ]
Almeida æl ˈmiːd ə
Almeria ˌælm ə ˈriː˽ə —*Sp* Almería [al me ˈri a]
almight|y ⁽ˌ⁾ɔːl ˈmaɪt |i ‖ ɔːl ˈmaɪt̬ |i ɑːl- **~ily** ɪ li əl i ‖ əl i
Almodóvar ˌælm ə ˈdəʊv ɑː -ɒ- ‖ -ˈdoʊv ɑːr —*Sp* [al mo ˈðo βar]

ALMOND

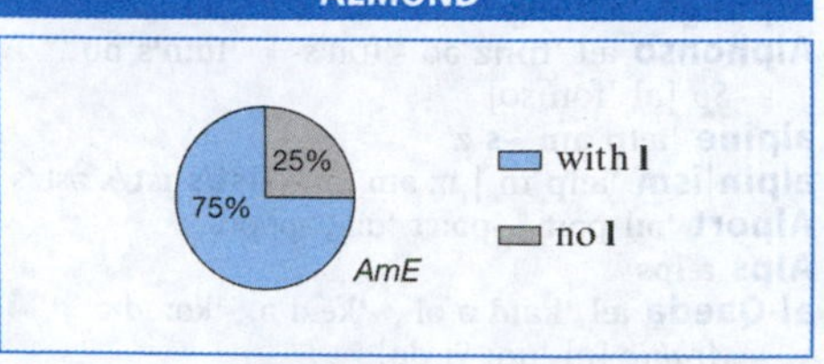

almond, A~ ˈɑːm ənd §ˈɑːlm-, §ˈælm-, §ˈɒlm- ‖ ˌɑːlm-, ˌælm-, ˌɑːm-, ˌæm- **~s** z *Preference poll, AmE: with* l *75%, no* l *25%.*
almond-eyed ˌɑːm ənd ˈaɪd ◂ §ˌɑːlm-, ˌælm-, ˌɒlm- ‖ ˈɑːlm- ˈælm-, ˈɑːm-, ˈæm-
Almondsbury ˈɑːm əndz bər˽i §ˈɑːlm-, §ˈælm-, §ˈɒlm- ‖ -ˌber i —*in Avon locally also* ˈeɪmz bər˽i
almoner ˈɑːm ən ə ˈælm-, §ˈɒlm- ‖ ˈælm ən ər ˈɑːm- **~s** z
almon|ry ˈɑːm ən| ri **~ries** riz
almost ˈɔːl məʊst ˈɒl-, ·ˈ·◂ ‖ ˈɔːl moʊst ɑːl-
alms ɑːmz §ɑːlmz, §ɒlmz ‖ ɔːlmz
alms-|house ˈɑːmz |haʊs §ˈɑːlmz-, §ˈɒlmz- ‖ ˈɔːlmz- **~houses** haʊz ɪz -əz
Alne *(i)* ɔːn ‖ ɑːn, *(ii)* ɔːln ‖ ɑːln, *(iii)* æln
Alnmouth ˈæln maʊθ →ˈælm-, ˈeɪəl-
Alnwick ˈæn ɪk
aloe ˈæl əʊ ‖ -oʊ **~s** z
aloft ə ˈlɒft ‖ ə ˈlɑːft -ˈlɔːft
aloha ə ˈləʊ hə -hɑː ‖ ə ˈloʊ hɑː ɑː-
alone ə ˈləʊn ‖ ə ˈloʊn
along ə ˈlɒŋ ‖ ə ˈlɔːŋ -ˈlɑːŋ
alongside ə ˌlɒŋ ˈsaɪd ◂ ·ˈ·· ‖ ə ˈlɔːŋ saɪd -ˈlɑːŋ-, ·ˌ·ˈ·
Alonso ə ˈlɒnz əʊ -ˈlɒnts- ‖ ə ˈlɑːnz oʊ -ˈlɑːnts- —*Sp* [a ˈlon so]
Alonzo ə ˈlɒnz əʊ ‖ ə ˈlɑːnz oʊ —*Sp* [a ˈlon θo, -so]
aloof ə ˈluːf **~ness** nəs nɪs
alopecia ˌæl ə ˈpiːʃ ə -ˈpiːʃ i˽ə
aloud ə ˈlaʊd
Aloysius ˌæl əʊ ˈɪʃ əs -ˈɪs i˽əs ‖ ˌæl ə ˈwɪʃ əs
alp ælp **alps, Alps** ælps
alpaca æl ˈpæk ə **~s** z
Alpen *tdmk* ˈælp ən
alpenglow ˈælp ən gləʊ →-əŋ- ‖ -gloʊ
alpenhorn ˈælp ən hɔːn ‖ -hɔːrn **~s** z
alpenstock ˈælp ən stɒk ‖ -stɑːk **~s** s
Alperton ˈælp ət ən ‖ -ərt ən
Alph ælf
alpha, Alpha ˈælf ə **~s** z
ˌAlpha Cenˈtauri sen ˈtɔːr i ken-, -ˈtaʊər-; **ˈalpha ˌparticle**; **ˈalpha ˌrhythm**

alphabet 'ælf ə bet -bɪt, §-bət **~s** s
alphabetic ˌælf ə 'bet ɪk ◂ ‖ -'beţ- **~al** ᵊl **~ally** ᵊl‿i
alphabetis... —*see* **alphabetiz...**
alphabetization ˌælf ə bet aɪ 'zeɪʃ ᵊn ˌ·bɪt-, -ɪ'·- ‖ -beţ ə 'zeɪʃ-
alphabetiz|e 'ælf ə bet aɪz -bə taɪz, -bɪ taɪz ‖ -bə taɪz **~ed** d **~es** ɪz əz **~ing** ɪŋ
alphanumeric ˌælf ə nju 'mer ɪk ◂ §-nu'·- ‖ -nu 'mer- -nju'·- **~al** ᵊl
Alphege 'ælf ɪdʒ
Alphonso æl 'fɒnz əʊ -'fɒnᵗs- ‖ -'fɑːnᵗs oʊ —*Sp* [al 'fon so]
alpine 'ælp aɪn **~s** z
alpin|ism 'ælp ɪn |ˌɪz əm -ən- **~ist/s** ɪst/s əst/s
Alport 'ɔːl pɔːt ‖ -pɔːrt 'ɑːl-, -pourt
Alps ælps
al-Qaeda æl 'kaɪd ə əl-, -'keɪd ə, -'kɑː ɪd ə —*Arabic* [al 'qɑː ʕi da]
al-Qaradawi əl ˌkær ə 'dɑː wi æl- ‖ ɑːl-, -ˈker- —*Arabic* [al qa ɾa 'dˤɑː wi]
already ɔːl 'red i ɒl-, ˌ·'·- ‖ ɑːl-
Alresford 'ɔːlz fəd ‖ -fᵊrd ɑːlz- —*but places of this name are locally also* 'ɑːlz-, 'ɑːls-, 'eᵊls-
alright ˌɔːl 'raɪt ◂ ‖ ˌɔːl- ˌɑːl-
Alsace æl 'sæs -'zæs; 'ælz æs —*Fr* [al zas]
Alsager *(i)* ɔːl 'seɪdʒ ə ‖ -ᵊr ɑːl-, *(ii)* 'ɔːls ədʒ ə -ɪdʒ- ‖ -ᵊr 'ɑːls-
Alsatian æl 'seɪʃ ᵊn ˌ·-, -'ˈi‿ən **~s** z
alsike 'æls ɪk -aɪk
also 'ɔːls əʊ 'ɒls- ‖ 'ɔːls oʊ 'ɑːls-
Alsop 'ɔːl sɒp 'ɒl- ‖ 'ɔːl sɑːp 'ɑːl-
also-ran 'ɔːls əʊ ræn 'ɒls-, ˌ·-'· ‖ -oʊ- 'ɑːls-
Alstom 'ælst ɒm ‖ -ɑːm
Alston 'ɔːlst ən 'ɒlst- ‖ 'ɑːlst-
alt *musical term* ælt ‖ ɑːlt
Alt *name of river; key on computer keyboard* ɔːlt ɒlt ‖ ɑːlt
Altai ⁽ˌ⁾ɑːl 'taɪ
Altaic æl 'teɪ ɪk
Altair 'ælt eə æl 'teə ‖ æl 'teᵊr -'tæᵊr, -'taɪᵊr, '· ·; -'tɑː ᵊr
Altamira ˌælt ə 'mɪər ə ‖ ˌɑːlt ə 'mɪr ə —*Sp* [al ta 'mi ɾa]
altar 'ɔːlt ə 'ɒlt- ‖ 'ɔːlt ᵊr 'ɑːlt- *(= alter)* **~s** z
'**altar boy**
Altarnun ˌɔːlt ə 'nʌn ˌɒlt- ‖ -ᵊr- ˌɑːlt-
altarpiec|e 'ɔːlt ə piːs 'ɒlt- ‖ -ᵊr- 'ɑːlt- **~es** ɪz əz
Altavista *tdmk* ˌælt ə 'vɪst ə
altazimuth ælt 'æz ɪm əθ §-əm-
Altdorfer 'ælt dɔːf ə ‖ -dɔːrf ᵊr 'ɑːlt- —*Ger* ['ʔalt dɔʁf ɐ]
alter *v* 'ɔːlt ə 'ɒlt- ‖ 'ɔːlt ᵊr 'ɑːlt- **~ed** d
altering 'ɔːlt‿ər ɪŋ 'ɒlt‿ ‖ 'ɑːlt‿ **~s** z —*See also phrases with this word*
alteration ˌɔːlt ə 'reɪʃ ᵊn ˌɒlt- ‖ ˌɑːlt- **~s** z
altercation ˌɔːlt ə 'keɪʃ ᵊn ˌɒlt- ‖ -ᵊr- ˌɑːlt- **~s** z
alter ego ˌælt ər 'iːg əʊ ˌɔːlt-, ˌɒlt-, -'eg- ‖ ˌɑːlt ᵊr 'iːg oʊ ˌɔːlt- **~s** z
alternant ɔːl 'tɜːn ənt ɒl- ‖ 'ɔːlt ᵊrn ənt 'ɑːlt- **~s** s
alternate *adj, n* ɔːl 'tɜːn ət ɒl-, -ɪt ‖ 'ɔːlt ᵊrn ət 'ɑːlt- *(*)* **~ly** li **~s** s
alter|nate *v* 'ɔːlt ə |neɪt 'ɒlt- ‖ -ᵊr- 'ɑːlt- **~nated** neɪt ɪd -əd ‖ neɪţ əd **~nates** neɪts **~nating** neɪt ɪŋ ‖ neɪţ ɪŋ
ˌ**alternating 'current**
alternation ˌɔːlt ə 'neɪʃ ᵊn ˌɒlt- ‖ -ᵊr- ˌɑːlt- **~s** z
alternative ɔːl 'tɜːn ət ɪv ɒl- ‖ ɔːl 'tɜːn əţ ɪv ɑːl-, æl- **~ly** li **~s** z
alternator 'ɔːlt ə neɪt ə 'ɒlt- ‖ 'ɔːlt ᵊr neɪţ ᵊr 'ɑːlt-, 'ælt- **~s** z
althaea, althea *'hollyhock'* æl 'θiː‿ə **~s** z
Althea *personal name* 'ælᵗθ i‿ə
Althorp *(i)* 'ɔːl θɔːp ‖ -θɔːrp 'ɑːl-, *(ii)* 'æl- —*but the place in Northants is locally also* 'ɔːltr əp, *as is Viscount A~*
although ɔːl 'ðəʊ ɒl-, ˌ·-, §-'θəʊ ‖ ɔːl 'ðoʊ ɑːl-
Althusser ˌælt u 'seə ‖ ˌɑːlt uː 'seᵊr —*Fr* [al ty sɛːʁ]
altimeter 'ælt ɪ ˌmiːt ə 'ɔːlt-, 'ɒlt-, -ə-; æl 'tɪm ɪt ə, -ət- ‖ æl 'tɪm əţ ᵊr 'ælt ə ˌmiːţ ᵊr **~s** z
Altiplano ˌælt ɪ 'plɑːn əʊ ‖ -oʊ ˌɑːlt- —*Sp* [al ti 'pla no]
altissimo æl 'tɪs ɪ məʊ -ə- ‖ -moʊ ɑːl-
altitude 'ælt ɪ tjuːd 'ɔːlt-, 'ɒlt-, -ə-, →-tʃuːd ‖ -tuːd -tjuːd **~s** z
Altman 'ɔːlt mən ‖ 'ɑːlt-

ALTO

7% 8% 71% 14% BrE
'ælt-
'ɒlt-
'ɔːlt-
'ɑːlt-

alto 'ælt əʊ 'ɒlt-, 'ɔːlt-, 'ɑːlt- ‖ 'ælt oʊ **~s** z — *Preference poll, BrE:* 'ælt- *71%,* 'ɒlt- *14%,* 'ɔːlt- *8%,* 'ɑːlt- *7%.*
altocumulus ˌælt əʊ 'kjuːm jʊl əs -jəl əs ‖ -oʊ 'kjuːm jəl-
altogether ˌɔːl tə 'geð ə ◂ '· · · · ‖ -ᵊr ◂ ˌɑːl-
Alton 'ɔːlt ən 'ɒlt- ‖ 'ɔːlt ᵊn 'ɑːlt-
Altoona æl 'tuːn ə
alto-relievo ˌælt əʊ rɪ 'liː vəʊ -rə'·- ‖ -oʊ rɪ 'liːv oʊ ˌɑːlt-
altostratus ˌælt əʊ 'streɪt əs -'strɑːt- ‖ -oʊ 'streɪţ əs -'stræţ-
altricial æl 'trɪʃ ᵊl
Altrincham 'ɔːltr ɪŋ əm 'ɒltr- ‖ 'ɑːltr-
altruism 'æltr u ˌɪz əm
altruist 'æltr u ɪst §-əst **~s** s
altruistic ˌæltr u 'ɪst ɪk ◂ **~ally** ᵊl‿i
alum 'æl əm
alumina ə 'luːm ɪn ə -'ljuːm-
aluminium ˌæl ə 'mɪn i‿əm ◂ ˌ-u-, ˌju-, ˌjə-
aluminous ə 'luːm ɪn əs -'ljuːm-, -ən-
aluminum ə 'luːm ɪn əm -'ljuːm-, -ən-
alum|na ə 'lʌm |nə **~nae** niː **~ni** naɪ **~nus** nəs
Alun 'æl ɪn —*Welsh* ['a lɪn, -lin]

Alva 'ælv ə

Alvar 'ælv ɑː -ə ‖ -ɑːr -ᵊr

Alvarez *(i)* æl 'vɑːr ez, *(ii)* 'ælv ə rez —*Sp* Álvarez ['al βa ɾeθ]

alveolar ˌælv i 'əʊl ə ◂ æl 'viː̮əl ə, 'ælv i̮əl ə ‖ æl 'viː əl ᵊr **~s** z

alveolaris... —*see* **alveolariz...**

alveolarity ˌælv i̮ə 'lær ət i æl ˌviː̮ə-, -ɪt i ‖ æl ˌviː ə 'lær əţ i -'ler-

alveolarization ˌælv i ˌəʊl ər aɪ 'zeɪʃ ᵊn æl ˌviː̮əl-, ˌælv i̮əl-, -ɪ'-- ‖ æl ˌviː əl ər ə-

alveolariz|e ˌælv i 'əʊl ə raɪz æl 'viː̮əl-, 'ælv i̮əl- ‖ æl 'viː əl ə raɪz **~ed** d **~es** ɪz əz **~ing** ɪŋ

alveole 'ælv i əʊl →-ɒʊl ‖ -oʊl **~s** z

alveol|us ˌælv i 'əʊl |əs æl 'viː̮əl |əs, 'ælv i̮əl |əs ‖ æl 'viː əl- **~i** aɪ iː

Alvey 'ælv i

Alvin 'ælv ɪn §-ən

Alvis 'ælv ɪs §-əs

always 'ɔːl weɪz §'ɒl-, -wɪz, -wəz ‖ 'ɑːl-

Alwyn *(i)* 'ɔːl wɪn ‖ 'ɑːl-, *(ii)* 'æl-

Alyn 'æl ɪn -ən

Alyson 'æl ɪs ən -əs-

alyssum 'æl ɪs əm -əs- ‖ ə 'lɪs əm

Alzheimer 'ælts haɪm ə 'ælz- ‖ 'ɑːlts haɪm ᵊr —*Ger* ['ʔalts haim ɐ] **~'s** z

'Alzheimer's diˌsease

am *from* **be**, *strong form* æm, *weak form* əm —*see* I'm, 'm

AM, am, a.m. *'amplitude modulation'*; *'ante meridiem'* ˌeɪ 'em ◂

AMA ˌeɪ em 'eɪ

Amadeus ˌæm ə 'deɪ əs ‖ ˌɑːm ə 'deɪ ʊs -əs

amadou 'æm ə duː

amah 'ɑːm ə 'æm-, -ɑː **~s** z

Amahl 'æm ɑːl ‖ ə 'mɑːl

Amalekite ə 'mæl ə kaɪt ‖ 'æm ə lek aɪt, ˌ·'·· **~s** s

Amalfi ə 'mælf i ‖ ə 'mɑːlf i —*It* [a 'mal fi]

amalgam ə 'mælg əm **~s** z

amalga|mate ə 'mælg ə |meɪt **~mated** meɪt ɪd -əd ‖ meɪţ əd **~mates** meɪts **~mating** meɪt ɪŋ ‖ meɪţ ɪŋ

amalgamation ə ˌmælg ə 'meɪʃ ᵊn **~s** z

Amalthea ˌæm ᵊl 'θiː̮ə

Amanda ə 'mænd ə

amanita ˌæm ə 'naɪt ə -'niːt- ‖ -'naɪţ ə -'niːţ ə **~s** z

Amanpour ˌæm ən 'pʊə ‖ -pʊᵊr

amanuens|is ə ˌmæn ju 'enᵗs |ɪs §-əs **~es** iːz

amaranth 'æm ə rænᵗθ **~s** s

amaranthine ˌæm ə 'rænᵗθ aɪn ◂ ‖ -ᵊn ◂ -aɪn

amarett|o ˌæm ə 'ret| əʊ ‖ -'reţ| oʊ **~i** iː

Amarillo ˌæm ə 'rɪl əʊ ‖ -oʊ

amaryllis, A~ ˌæm ə 'rɪl ɪs §-əs **~es** ɪz əz

amass ə 'mæs **amassed** ə 'mæst **amasses** ə 'mæs ɪz -əz **amassing** ə 'mæs ɪŋ

amassment ə 'mæs mənt

amateur 'æm ət ə 'æm ə tʃʊə, -tʃə, -tjʊə; ˌæm ə 'tɜː ◂ ‖ 'æm ə tʃʊr -əţ ᵊr, -ə tjʊr **~s** z

amateurish 'æm ət ər ɪʃ -ətʃ ər-, -ə tʊər-; ˌæm ə 'tjʊər ɪʃ ◂, -'tɜːr- ‖ ˌæm ə 'tʊr ɪʃ ◂ -'tʃʊr-, -'tɜː-, -'tjʊr- **~ly** li **~ness** nəs nɪs

amateurism 'æm ət ər ˌɪz əm '-ətʃ-, -ə tɜːr-, -ə tʃʊər-, -ə tjʊər- ‖ 'æm ə tʃʊr- -əţ ᵊr-, -ə tjʊr-

Amati ə 'mɑːt i æ- —*It* [a 'maː ti]

amatol 'æm ə tɒl ‖ -tɑːl -tɔːl, -toʊl

amatory 'æm ət ər i ‖ -ə tɔːr i -toʊr i

amaurosis æm ɔː 'rəʊs ɪs §-əs ‖ -'roʊs əs -ɑː-

amaze ə 'meɪz **amazed** ə 'meɪzd **amazes** ə 'meɪz ɪz -əz **amazing** ə 'meɪz ɪŋ

amazed|ly ə 'meɪz ɪd| li -'-əd- **~ness** nəs nɪs

amazement ə 'meɪz mənt

amazing ə 'meɪz ɪŋ **~ly** li

amazon, Amazon 'æm əz ən ‖ -ə zɑːn -əz ən **~s** z

Amazonia ˌæm ə 'zəʊn i̮ə ‖ -'zoʊn-

amazonian, A~ ˌæm ə 'zəʊn i̮ən ◂ ‖ -'zoʊn- **~s** z

Amazulu ˌæm ə 'zuːl uː

ambassador æm 'bæs əd ə -ɪd- ‖ -ᵊr **~s** z

ambassadorial æm ˌbæs ə 'dɔːr i əl ◂, ˌ·,··'··, -ɪ'- ‖ -'doʊr-

ambassadorship æm 'bæs əd ə ʃɪp -'·ɪd- ‖ -ᵊr ʃɪp **~s** s

ambassadress æm 'bæs ə dres -ədr ɪs, -əs; ·ˌ·ə 'dres ‖ -ədr əs **~es** ɪz əz

amber, Amber 'æm bə ‖ -bᵊr

ambergris 'æm bə griːs -griː, -grɪs ‖ -grɪs -griːs

ambi- *comb. form* ¦æm bi-

Ambi *tdmk* 'æm bi

ambiance 'æm bi̮ənᵗs 'ɒm-, -ɒnᵗs, -õs ‖ ˌɑːm bi 'ɑːnᵗs —*Fr* [ɑ̃ bjɑ̃ːs]

ambidexterity ˌæm bi dek 'ster ət i -ɪt i ‖ -əţ i

ambidextrous ˌæm bi 'deks trəs ◂ **~ly** li

ambience 'æm bi̮ənᵗs 'ɒm-, -ɒnᵗs, -õs ‖ ˌɑːm bi 'ɑːnᵗs —*Fr* ambiance [ɑ̃ bjɑ̃ːs]

ambient 'æm bi̮ənt

ambiguit|y ˌæm bɪ 'gjuː̮ət |i ˌ·bə-, -ɪt i ‖ əţ |i **~ies** iz

ambiguous æm 'bɪg ju̮əs **~ly** li **~ness** nəs nɪs

ambisyllabic ˌæm bi sɪ 'læb ɪk ◂ -sə-

ambisyllabicity ˌæm bi ˌsɪl ə 'bɪs ət i -ɪt i ‖ -əţ i

ambit 'æm bɪt -bət **~s** s

ambition æm 'bɪʃ ᵊn **~s** z

ambitious æm 'bɪʃ əs **~ly** li **~ness** nəs nɪs

ambivalence æm 'bɪv əl ənᵗs ˌæm bi 'veɪl ənᵗs

ambivalent æm 'bɪv əl ənt ˌæm bi 'veɪl ənt ◂ **~ly** li

amble 'æm bᵊl **ambled** 'æm bᵊld **ambles** 'æm bᵊlz **ambling** 'æm bᵊl̮ɪŋ

Ambler 'æm blə ‖ 'æm blᵊr

Ambleside 'æm bᵊl saɪd

amblyopia ˌæm bli 'əʊp i̮ə ‖ -'oʊp-

ambo, Ambo 'æm bəʊ ‖ -boʊ

Amboina, a~ æm 'bɔɪn ə

Amboinese ˌæm bɔɪ 'niːz ◂ ‖ -'niːs ◂

amboyna æm 'bɔɪn ə

Ambridge 'æm brɪdʒ

Ambrose 'æm brəʊz -brəʊs ‖ -broʊz

A

ambrosi|a æm ˈbrəʊz i‿ə ·ˈbrəʊʒ |ə ‖ æm ˈbroʊʒ |ə **~al** əl **~an** ən
ambsace ˈeɪmz eɪs ˈæmz-
ambulac|rum ˌæm bju ˈleɪk |rəm -ˈlæk- ‖ -bjə- **~ra** rə
ambulanc|e ˈæm bjəl ənᵗs -bjʊl-, §-bəl- **~es** ɪz əz
ambulance|man ˈæm bjəl ənᵗs |mæn ˈ·bjʊl-, §ˈ·bəl- **~men** men **~woman** ˌwʊm ən **~women** ˌwɪm ɪn §-ən
ambulant ˈæm bjəl ənt -bjʊl-
ambu|late æm bju |leɪt -bjə- ‖ -bjə- **~lated** leɪt ɪd -əd ‖ leɪţ əd **~lates** leɪts **~lating** leɪt ɪŋ ‖ leɪţ ɪŋ
ambulation ˌæm bju ˈleɪʃ ən -bjə- ‖ -bjə- **~s** z
ambulator|y ˌæm bju ˈleɪt ər |i ◂ ˌ·bjə-, ˈ· ·lət‿ər i ‖ ˈæm bjəl ə tɔːr |i -toʊr i **~ies** iz
ambuscad|e ˌæm bə ˈskeɪd ‖ ˈæm bə skeɪd **~ed** ɪd əd **~es** z **~ing** ɪŋ
ambush ˈæm bʊʃ **~ed** t **~es** ɪz əz **~ing** ɪŋ
ambystoma æm ˈbɪst əm ə **~s** z
Amdahl *tdmk* ˈæm dɑːl
ameb|a ə ˈmiːb |ə **~ae** iː **~as** əz
amebiasis ˌæm iː ˈbaɪ‿əs ɪs §-əs
amebic ə ˈmiːb ɪk
ameboid ə ˈmiːb ɔɪd
AMEC ˈæm ek
Ameche ə ˈmiːtʃ i
Amelia ə ˈmiːl i‿ə
amelio|rate ə ˈmiːl i‿ə |reɪt **~rated** reɪt ɪd -əd ‖ reɪţ əd **~rates** reɪts **~rating** reɪt ɪŋ ‖ reɪţ ɪŋ
amelioration ə ˌmiːl i‿ə ˈreɪʃ ən **~s** z
ameliorative ə ˈmiːl i‿ə reɪt ɪv -rət ɪv ‖ -reɪţ ɪv
ameliorator ə ˈmiːl i‿ə reɪt ə ‖ -reɪţ ər **~s** z
amen ˌɑː ˈmen ◂ ˌeɪ- —*Although* ˌɑː- *is the usual form among Protestants in Britain,* ˌeɪ- *is preferred by Roman Catholics and also in non-religious contexts, as in* ˌAmen ˈCorner. *In AmE,* ˌeɪ- *predominates in speech, but* ˌɑː- *is preferred in singing.* **~s** z
amenability ə ˌmiːn ə ˈbɪl ət i -ˌmen-, -ɪt i ‖ -əţ i
amenab|le ə ˈmiːn əb |əl -ˈmen- **~ly** li
amend ə ˈmend **amended** ə ˈmend ɪd -əd **amending** ə ˈmend ɪŋ **amends** ə ˈmendz
amendment ə ˈmend mənt →-ˈmem- **~s** s
Amenhotep ˌɑːm ən ˈhəʊt ep ‖ -ˈhoʊt-
amenit|y ə ˈmiːn ət |i -ˈmen-, -ɪt- ‖ -əţ |i **~ies** iz
amenorrhea, amenorrhoea ₍ˌ₎eɪ ˌmen ə ˈriː‿ə ˌæ- ‖ ˌɑː-
ament *'mentally deficient person'* ˈeɪ ment -mənt; æ ˈment **~s** s
ament *'catkin'* ˈæm ənt ˈeɪm- **~s** s
amentia ₍ˌ₎eɪ ˈmenᵗʃ ə ₍ˌ₎æ-, -ˈmenᵗʃ i‿ə
America ə ˈmer ɪk ə -ək—*also sometimes* ⚠-ˈmər-; *so also in derivatives* **~s, ~'s** z
American ə ˈmer ɪk ən -ək- **~s** z
AˌmericanˈEnglish; **AˌmericanExˈpress** *tdmk*; **AˌmericanˈIndian**
Americana ə ˌmer ɪ ˈkɑːn ə -ˌə- ‖ -ˈkæn-
americanis... —*see* **americaniz...**
Americanism ə ˈmer ɪk ən ˌɪz əm -ˈ·ək- **~s** z
americanization ə ˌmer ɪk ən aɪ ˈzeɪʃ ən -ˌək-, -ɪˈ·- ‖ -ə ˈzeɪʃ-
americaniz|e ə ˈmer ɪk ə naɪz -ˈ·ək- **~ed** d **~es** ɪz əz **~ing** ɪŋ
americium ˌæm ə ˈrɪs i‿əm -ˈrɪʃ-
Amerind ˈæm ə rɪnd **~s** z
Amerindian ˌæm ə ˈrɪnd i‿ən ◂ **~s** z
Amersham ˈæm əʃ əm ‖ -ərʃ-
Amery ˈeɪm ər i
Ames eɪmz
Amesbury ˈeɪmz bər‿i ‖ -ˌber i
Ameslan ˈæm ə slæn ˈæm slæn
amethyst ˈæm əθ ɪst -ɪθ-, §-əst **~s** s
amethystine ˌæm ə ˈθɪst aɪn ◂ -ɪ- ‖ -ən -aɪn
Amex *tdmk* ˈæm eks
Amharic æm ˈhær ɪk əm- ‖ ɑːm ˈhɑːr-
Amherst *(i)* ˈæm əst ‖ -ərst, *(ii)* -hɜːst ‖ -hɜːst — *(i) is the traditional form in both BrE and AmE, and hence appropriate for Baron A~, the 18th-century general, and for the place in MA.*
Amhrán na bhFiann ˌær ɔːn næ ˈviːn —*Irish* [ˌəu ɾˠaːn̪ˠ nˠə ˈvʲiːn̪ˠ]
amiability ˌeɪm i‿ə ˈbɪl ət i -ɪt i ‖ -əţ i
amiab|le ˈeɪm i‿əb |əl **~leness** əl nəs nɪs **~ly** li
amicability ˌæm ɪk ə ˈbɪl ət i ˌ·ək-, -ɪt i ‖ -əţ i
amicab|le ˈæm ɪk əb |əl ˈ·ək-; ə ˈmɪk- **~leness** əl nəs nɪs **~ly** li
amic|e ˈæm ɪs §-əs **~es** ɪz əz
Amice ˈeɪm ɪs §-əs
amicus, A~ ə ˈmaɪk əs æ-, -ˈmiːk-, -ʊs; ˈæm ɪk- —*The trade union is* ˈ· ·.
aˌmicus ˈcuriae ˈkjʊər i iː -aɪ ‖ ˈkjʊr- ˈkʊr-
amid ə ˈmɪd
amide ˈæm aɪd ˈeɪm- ‖ -əd **~s** z
Amidol *tdmk* ˈæm ɪ dɒl §-ə- ‖ -dɑːl -dɔːl, -doʊl
amidships ə ˈmɪd ʃɪps
amidst ə ˈmɪdst -ˈmɪtst
Amiens ˈæm i‿ɒ̃ -æ̃, -ənz —*formerly, and as an English-language name, and for the Dublin street,* ˈeɪm i‿ənz; *in Shakespeare* ˈæm i‿ənz —*Fr* [a mjæ̃]
Amies ˈeɪm iz
Amiga *tdmk* ə ˈmiːg ə
amigo ə ˈmiːg əʊ æ- ‖ -oʊ ɑː- —*Sp* [a ˈmi ɣo]
Amin ₍ˌ₎ɑː ˈmiːn ₍ˌ₎æ-
amine ˈæm iːn -ɪn, §-ən; ə ˈmiːn ‖ ə ˈmiːn ˈæm iːn, -ən **~s** z
amino ə ˈmiːn əʊ -ˈmaɪn-; ˈæm ɪn əʊ, -ən- ‖ -oʊ
aˌmino ˈacid
amir ə ˈmɪə ‖ ə ˈmɪər **~s** z
Amis ˈeɪm ɪs §-əs
Amish ˈɑːm ɪʃ ˈæm-
amiss ə ˈmɪs
Amistad ˈæm ɪ stæd -ə- ‖ ˈɑːm ə stɑːd
amit|y ˈæm ət |i -ɪt i ‖ -əţ |i **~ies** iz
Amlwch ˈæm lʊk -lʊx —*Welsh* [ˈam luχ]
Amman *place in Jordan* ə ˈmɑːn æ-, -ˈmæn, ‖ ˈɑːm ɑːn —*Arabic* [ʕam ˈmaːn]
Amman *river in Wales* ˈæm ən
ammeter ˈæm iːt ə -ɪt-, -ˌmiːt- ‖ -iːţ ər **~s** z
ammo ˈæm əʊ ‖ -oʊ
Ammon ˈæm ən

ammonia ə 'məʊn i‿ə ‖ ə 'moʊn-
ammoniac ə 'məʊn i æk ‖ ə 'moʊn-
ammoniated ə 'məʊn i eɪt ɪd -əd ‖ ə 'moʊn i eɪţ əd
ammonite, A~ 'æm ə naɪt **~s** s
ammonium ə 'məʊn i‿əm ‖ ə 'moʊn-
ammunition ˌæm ju 'nɪʃ ᵊn -jə- ‖ -jə-
amnesia æm 'niːz i‿ə -'niːʒ ə ‖ -'niːʒ ə
amnesiac æm 'niːz i æk ‖ -'niːʒ- **~s** s
amnesic æm 'niːz ɪk -'niːs- **~s** s
amnest|y, A~ 'æm nəst |i -nɪst- **~ies** iz
  ˌ**Amnesty** ˌ**Inter'national**
amniocentesis ˌæm ni‿əʊ sen 'tiːs ɪs §-əs ‖ ˌæm ni oʊ-
amnion 'æm ni‿ən -ɒn ‖ -ɑːn ən **~s** z
amniote 'æm ni əʊt ‖ -oʊt **~s** s
amniotic ˌæm ni 'ɒt ɪk ◂ ‖ -'ɑːţ ɪk
Amoco *tdmk* 'æm ə kəʊ ‖ -koʊ
amoeb|a ə 'miːb |ə **~ae** iː **~as** əz
amoebiasis ˌæm iː 'baɪ‿əs ɪs §-əs
amoebic ə 'miːb ɪk
amoeboid ə 'miːb ɔɪd
amok ə 'mɒk ə 'mʌk, 'ɑːm əʊ ‖ ə 'mʌk -'mɑːk
among ə 'mʌŋ §-'mɒŋ
amongst ə 'mʌŋᵏst §-'mɒŋᵏst
amontillado ˌæm ɒnt ɪ 'lɑːd əʊ əˌmɒnt-, -ə'- ‖ əˌmɑːnt ə 'lɑːd oʊ —*Sp* [a mon ti 'ʎa ðo, -'ja-] **~s** z
amoral ˌeɪ 'mɒr əl ◂ ₍ₗ₎æ- ‖ -'mɔːr- -'mɑːr- **~ly** i
amorality ˌeɪ mɒ 'ræl ət i ˌæ-, -ˌmə-, -ɪt i ‖ ˌeɪ mə 'ræl əţ i ˌ-mɔː-
amorett|o, A~ ˌæm ə 'ret |əʊ ‖ -'reţ |oʊ ˌɑːm- **~i** iː
Amorite 'æm ə raɪt **~s** s
amoroso ˌæm ə 'rəʊs əʊ ‖ ˌɑːm ə 'roʊs oʊ
amorous 'æm ər‿əs **~ly** li **~ness** nəs nɪs
amorphous ə 'mɔːf əs ‖ ə 'mɔːrf- **~ly** li **~ness** nəs nɪs
amortis... —*see* **amortiz...**
amortizable ə 'mɔːt aɪz əb ᵊl ‖ 'æm ᵊr taɪz- ə 'mɔːr-
amortization ə ˌmɔːt aɪ 'zeɪʃ ᵊn -ɪ- ‖ ˌæm ᵊrţ ə- ə ˌmɔːrţ ə-
amortiz|e ə 'mɔːt aɪz ‖ 'æm ᵊr taɪz ə 'mɔːr- **~ed** d **~ement/s** mənt/s **~es** ɪz əz **~ing** ɪŋ
Amory 'eɪm ər i
Amos 'eɪm ɒs ‖ -əs
amount ə 'maʊnt **amounted** ə 'maʊnt ɪd -əd ‖ ə 'maʊnţəd **amounting** ə 'maʊnt ɪŋ ‖ ə 'maʊnţ ɪŋ **amounts** ə 'maʊnts
amour ə 'mʊə ˌæ- ‖ ə 'mʊᵊr ɑː- **~s** z
amour-propre ˌæm ʊə 'prɒp‿rə ‖ ˌɑːm ʊr 'proʊp‿rə ˌæm- —*Fr* [a muʀ pʀɔpχ]
amoxicillin ə ˌmɒks ɪ 'sɪl ɪn æ- ‖ -ˌmɑːks-
Amoy ə 'mɔɪ ɑː-, æ- —*Chinese* Xiàmén [^{4}ɕja ^{2}mən]
amp æmp **amps** æmps
ampelopsis ˌæmp ɪ 'lɒps ɪs -ə-, §-əs ‖ -'lɑːps-
amperag|e 'æmp ər‿ɪdʒ -ɪər- ‖ -ɪr- **~es** ɪz əz
ampere, ampère, A~ 'æmp eə ‖ -ɪr -er —*Fr* [ɑ̃ pɛːʁ] **~s** z
ampersand 'æmp ə sænd ‖ -ᵊr- **~s** z

Ampex *tdmk* 'æmp eks
amphetamine æm 'fet ə miːn -mɪn, §-mən ‖ -'feţ- **~s** z
amphi- *comb. form*
  with stress-neutral suffix ¦æmᵖf i —
  amphipathic ˌæmᵖf i 'pæθ ɪk ◂
  with stress-imposing suffix æm 'fɪ+ —
  amphitropous æm 'fɪtr əp əs
amphibian ₍ₗ₎æm 'fɪb i‿ən **~s** z
amphibious ₍ₗ₎æm 'fɪb i‿əs **~ly** li **~ness** nəs nɪs
amphibole *mineral* 'æmᵖf ɪ bəʊl §-ə-, →-bɒʊl ‖ -boʊl **~s** z
amphibolite æm 'fɪb ə laɪt **~s** s
amphibolog|y ˌæmᵖf i 'bɒl ədʒ| i ‖ -'bɑːl- **~ies** iz
amphibrach 'æmᵖf i bræk **~s** s
amphictyonic, A~ æm ˌfɪkt i 'ɒn ɪk ◂ ‖ -'ɑːn-
amphimacer æm 'fɪm əs ə ‖ -ᵊr **~s** z
amphisbaena ˌæmᵖf ɪs 'biːn ə §-əs- **~s** z

AMPHITHEATER

57% 43%
'æmp-
'æmᵖf-
AmE

amphitheater, amphitheatre 'æmᵖf i ˌθɪət ə §'· ·θi ˌet ə ‖ 'æmp ə ˌθiː əţ ᵊr 'æmᵖf- **~s** z — *Preference poll, AmE:* 'æmp- *57%,* 'æmᵖf- *43%.*
Amphitrite ˌæmᵖf i 'traɪt i '· ·ˌ· · ‖ -ə 'traɪţ i
Amphitryon æm 'fɪtr i‿ən
amph|ora 'æmᵖf |ər ə **~orae** ə riː **~oras** ər əz
ampicillin ˌæmp ɪ 'sɪl ɪn -ə-, §-ən
ample 'æmp ᵊl **ampler** 'æm plə ‖ -plᵊr
  amplest 'æm plɪst -pləst
Ampleforth 'æmp ᵊl fɔːθ ‖ -fɔːrθ -foʊrθ
Amplex *tdmk* 'æmp leks
amplexicaul æm 'pleks ɪ kɔːl §-ə- ‖ -kɑːl
amplification ˌæmp lɪf ɪ 'keɪʃ ᵊn ˌ·ləf-, §-ə'·- **~s** z
ampli|fy 'æmp lɪ |faɪ -lə- **~fied** faɪd **~fier/s** faɪ‿ə/z ‖ faɪ‿ᵊr/z **~fies** faɪz **~fying** faɪ ɪŋ
amplitude 'æmp lɪ tjuːd -lə-, →-tʃuːd ‖ -tuːd -tjuːd **~s** z
amply 'æmp li
Ampney *(i)* 'æmp ni, *(ii)* 'æm ni
ampoule 'æmp uːl -juːl **~s** z
Ampthill 'æmᵖt hɪl -ɪl
ampule 'æmp juːl **~s** z
ampull|a æm 'pʊl |ə -'pʌl- **~ae** iː **~as** əz
ampu|tate 'æmp ju |teɪt §-jə- ‖ -jə- **~tated** teɪt ɪd -əd ‖ teɪţ əd **~tates** teɪts **~tating** teɪt ɪŋ ‖ teɪţ ɪŋ
amputation ˌæmp ju 'teɪʃ ᵊn §-jə- ‖ -jə- **~s** z
amputee ˌæmp ju 'tiː §-jə- ‖ -jə- **~s** z
Amritsar æm 'rɪts ə əm-, -ɑː ‖ -ᵊr —*Hindi* [əm rɪţ sər]
Amstel 'æm stəl —*Dutch* ['ɑm stəl]

A

Amsterdam 'æm^p st ə dæm ˌ·ˈ·◂ ‖ -ᵊr- —*Dutch* [ˌɑm stər ˈdɑm]
Amstrad *tdmk* ˈæm stræd **~s, ~'s** z
Amtrak *tdmk* ˈæm træk
amuck ə ˈmʌk
Amu Darya ˌɑːm uː ˈdɑːr i‿ə ə ˌmuː-
amulet ˈæm jʊl ət §-jəl-, -ɪt, -ju let ‖ -jəl- **~s** s
Amundsen ˈɑːm ənd sən ˈæm-, -ʊnd- —*Norw* [ˈaː mun sən]
Amur əˈmʊə ˈæm ʊə ‖ ɑː ˈmʊᵊr —*Russ* [ʌ ˈmur]
amuse ə ˈmjuːz **amused** ə ˈmjuːzd **amuses** ə ˈmjuːz ɪz -əz **amusing** ə ˈmjuːz ɪŋ
amusement ə ˈmjuːz mənt **~s** s
  a'musement arˌcade; **a'musement park**
amusing ə ˈmjuːz ɪŋ **~ly** li **~ness** nəs nɪs
Amway *tdmk* ˈæm weɪ
Amy ˈeɪm i
Amyas ˈeɪm i‿əs
amyg|dala ə ˈmɪg |dəl ə **~dalae** də liː **~daloid** də lɔɪd
amygdaloid ə ˈmɪgd ə lɔɪd
amyl ˈæm ᵊl ˈeɪm-, -aɪᵊl, -ɪl
  ˌamyl ˈnitrite
amylase ˈæm ɪ leɪz -ə-
amytal, A~ *tdmk* ˈæm ɪ tæl -ə- ‖ -tɑːl -tɔːl
an *strong form* æn, *weak form* ən —*see also* **a**
an- (¦) æn, ən —*When it is a variant of* ad-, *this prefix is usually* ə (an'nul), *but* æ *if stressed because of a suffix* ('annotate). *As a negative prefix, it is usually* æn (ˌan'oxia), *undergoing reduction to* ən *only in a few better-known words* (a'nonymous).
A.N.Other ˌeɪ ˌen ˈʌð ə ‖ -ᵊr
ana ˈɑːn ə
ana- *comb. form*
  before stress-neutral suffix ¦æn ə — **Anabaptist** ˌæn ə ˈbæpt ɪst §-əst
  before stress-imposing suffix ə ˈnæ+ — **anadromous** ə ˈnædr əm əs
Anabaptist ˌæn ə ˈbæpt ɪst ◂ §-əst **~s** s
anabasis ə ˈnæb əs ɪs §-əs
anabatic ˌæn ə ˈbæt ɪk ◂ ‖ -ˈbæṭ-
anabolic ˌæn ə ˈbɒl ɪk ◂ ‖ -ˈbɑːl-
  ˌanaˌbolic ˈsteroid
anachronism ə ˈnæk rə ˌnɪz əm **~s** z
anachronistic ə ˌnæk rə ˈnɪst ɪk ◂ **~ally** ᵊl‿i
Anacin *tdmk* ˈæn ə sɪn
anacoluth|on ˌæn ək ə ˈluːθ |ᵊn -ˈljuːθ-, -|ɒn ‖ -|ɑːn **~a** ə **~ons** ᵊnz ɒnz ‖ ɑːnz
anaconda, A~ ˌæn ə ˈkɒnd ə ‖ -ˈkɑːnd ə **~s** z
Anacreon ə ˈnæk ri‿ən -ɒn ‖ -ɑːn
anacrus|is ˌæn ə ˈkruːs |ɪs §-əs **~es** iːz
anacrustic ˌæn ə ˈkrʌst ɪk ◂
Anadin *tdmk* ˈæn ə dɪn
anaemia ə ˈniːm i‿ə
anaemic ə ˈniːm ɪk **~ally** ᵊl‿i
anaerobic ˌæn ə ˈrəʊb ɪk ◂ -eə- ‖ -ˈroʊb- -e- **~ally** ᵊl‿i **~s** s
anaesthesia ˌæn əs ˈθiːz i‿ə ˌ·iːs-, ˌ·ɪs-, -ˈθiːʒ ə ‖ -ˈθiːʒ ə
anaesthesiologist ˌæn əs ˌθiːz i ˈɒl ədʒ ɪst §-əst ‖ -ˈɑːl- **~s** s
anaesthesiology ˌæn əs ˌθiːz i ˈɒl ədʒ i ‖ -ˈɑːl-
anaesthetic ˌæn əs ˈθet ɪk ◂ -iːs-, -ɪs- ‖ -ˈθeṭ- **~s** s
anaesthetis... —*see* **anaesthetiz...**
anaesthetist ə ˈniːs θət ɪst æ-, -θɪt-, §-əst ‖ ə ˈnes θəṭ əst *(*)* **~s** s
anaesthetization ə ˌniːs θət aɪ ˈzeɪʃ ᵊn -ɪ'-- ‖ ə ˌnes θəṭ ə-
anaesthetiz|e ə ˈniːs θə taɪz -θɪ- ‖ ə ˈnes- *(*)* **~ed** d **~es** ɪz əz **~ing** ɪŋ
anaglyph ˈæn ə glɪf **~s** s
anaglypta, A~ *tdmk* ˌæn ə ˈglɪpt ə
anagram ˈæn ə græm **~med** d **~ming** ɪŋ **~s** z
anagrammatic ˌæn ə grə ˈmæt ɪk ◂ ‖ -ˈmæṭ- **~ally** ᵊl‿i
Anaheim ˈæn ə haɪm
Anais, Anaïs ˌæn aɪ ˈiːs ◂ ə ˈnaɪ‿əs
anal ˈeɪn ᵊl **~ly** i
analect ˈæn ə lekt -ᵊl ekt **~s** s
analecta ˌæn ə ˈlekt ə
analemma ˌæn ə ˈlem ə
analemmatic ˌæn ə le ˈmæt ɪk ◂ ‖ -ˈmæṭ-
analeptic ˌæn ə ˈlept ɪk ◂
analgesia ˌæn ᵊl ˈdʒiːz i‿ə ˌ·æl-, -ˈdʒiːs- ‖ -ˈdʒiːʒ ə
analgesic ˌæn ᵊl ˈdʒiːz ɪk ◂ -æl-, -ˈdʒiːs- **~s** s
analog ˈæn ə lɒg -ᵊl ɒg ‖ ˈæn ᵊl ɔːg -ɑːg **~s** z
analogical ˌæn ə ˈlɒdʒ ɪk ᵊl ◂ -ᵊl ˈɒdʒ- ‖ -ᵊl ˈɑːdʒ- **~ly** i
analogis|e, analogiz|e ə ˈnæl ə dʒaɪz **~ed** d **~es** ɪz əz **~ing** ɪŋ
analogous ə ˈnæl əg əs -ədʒ- **~ly** li
analogue ˈæn ə lɒg -ᵊl ɒg ‖ ˈæn ᵊl ɔːg -ɑːg **~s** z
analog|y ə ˈnæl ədʒ |i **~ies** iz
analphabetic ˌæn ælf ə ˈbet ɪk ◂ ˌ·ˌ·ˈ·· ‖ -ˈbeṭ-
anal-retentive ˌeɪn ᵊl rɪ ˈtent ɪv -rə'--, §-riː'· ‖ -ˈtenṭ-
analysable ˈæn ə laɪz əb ᵊl →ˈæn ᵊl aɪz-; ˌ·ˈ··
analysand ə ˈnæl ɪ sænd -ə- **~s** z
analys|e ˈæn ə laɪz -ᵊl aɪz **~ed** d **~er/s** ə/z ‖ ᵊr/z **~es** *v* ɪz əz **~ing** ɪŋ
analysis ə ˈnæl əs ɪs -ɪs ɪs, §-əs **analyses** *n* ə ˈnæl ə siːz -ɪ-
analyst ˈæn əl ɪst §-əst **~s** s
analytic ˌæn ə ˈlɪt ɪk ◂ -ᵊl ˈɪt- ‖ -ᵊl ˈɪṭ ɪk ◂ **~al** ᵊl **~ally** ᵊl‿i
analyzable ˈæn ə laɪz əb ᵊl →ˈæn ᵊl aɪz-; ˌ·ˈ··
analyz|e ˈæn ə laɪz -ᵊl aɪz **~ed** d **~er/s** ə/z ‖ ᵊr/z **~es** ɪz əz **~ing** ɪŋ
anamnesis ˌæn æm ˈniːs ɪs §-əs
Anancy ə ˈnænᵗs i
Ananda ə ˈnænd ə -ˈnʌnd-
Ananias ˌæn ə ˈnaɪ‿əs
anapaest, anapest ˈæn ə piːst -pest ‖ -pest **~s** s
anapaestic, anapestic ˌæn ə ˈpiːst ɪk ◂ -ˈpest- ‖ -ˈpest-
anaphor ˈæn ə fɔː -əf ə ‖ -fɔːr **~s** z
anaphora ə ˈnæf ər ə

anaphoric ˌæn ə ˈfɒr ɪk ◂ ‖ -ˈfɔːr- -ˈfɑːr- **~ally** ᵊl‿i
anaphylactic ˌæn ə fɪ ˈlækt ɪk -ə fə- **~ally** ᵊl‿i
anaphylaxis ˌæn ə fɪ ˈlæks ɪs -ə fə-, §-əs
anaptyctic ˌæn əp ˈtɪkt ɪk ◂ -æp-
anaptyxis ˌæn əp ˈtɪks ɪs -æp-, §-əs
anarch ˈæn ɑːk ‖ -ɑːrk **~s** s
anarchic æ ˈnɑːk ɪk ə- ‖ -ˈnɑːrk- **~al** ᵊl **~ally** ᵊl‿i
anarchism ˈæn ə ˌkɪz əm -ɑː- ‖ -ᵊr- -ɑːr-
anarchist ˈæn ək ɪst -ɑːk-, §-əst ‖ -ᵊrk- -ɑːrk- **~s** s
anarchistic ˌæn ə ˈkɪst ɪk ◂ -ɑː- ‖ -ᵊr- -ɑːr-
anarchy ˈæn ək i -ɑːk- ‖ -ᵊrk i -ɑːrk-
anarthria æn ˈɑːθ ri‿ə ‖ -ˈɑːrθ-
anarthric æn ˈɑːθ rɪk ‖ -ˈɑːrθ-
Anastasia ˌæn ə ˈsteɪz i‿ə -ˈstɑːz- ‖ -ˈsteɪʒ ə -ˈstɑːʒ ə
anastigmat æn ˈæst ɪg mæt ən-; ˌæn ə ˈstɪg- **~s** s
anastigmatic ˌæn ə stɪg ˈmæt ɪk ◂ æn ˌæst ɪg-, ən- ‖ -ˈmæt̬-
anastomos|e ə ˈnæst ə məʊz æ- ‖ -moʊz -moʊs **~ed** d **~es** ɪz əz **~ing** ɪŋ
anastomos|is ə ˌnæst ə ˈməʊs |ɪs æ-, ˌæn əst-, §-əs ‖ -ˈmoʊs- **~es** iːz
anastrozole ə ˈnæs trə zəʊl →-zɒʊl ‖ -zoʊl
anathema ə ˈnæθ əm ə -ɪm- **~s** z
anathematis|e, anathematiz|e ə ˈnæθ əm ə taɪz -ˈ·ɪm- **~ed** d **~es** ɪz əz **~ing** ɪŋ
Anatole ˈæn ə təʊl →-tɒʊl ‖ -toʊl —*Fr* [a na tɔl]
Anatoli|a ˌæn ə ˈtəʊl i‿|ə ‖ -ˈtoʊl- **~an/s** ən/z
anatomical ˌæn ə ˈtɒm ɪk ᵊl ◂ ‖ -ˈtɑːm- **~ly** i
anatomis|e ə ˈnæt ə maɪz ‖ ə ˈnæt̬- **~ed** d **~es** ɪz əz **~ing** ɪŋ
anatomist ə ˈnæt əm ɪst §-əst ‖ ə ˈnæt̬- **~s** s
anatomiz|e ə ˈnæt ə maɪz ‖ ə ˈnæt̬- **~ed** d **~es** ɪz əz **~ing** ɪŋ
anatom|y ə ˈnæt əm |i ‖ ə ˈnæt̬- **~ies** iz
Anaxagoras ˌæn æk ˈsæg ər əs -ə ræs
Anaximander æ ˌnæks ɪ ˈmænd ə ə-; ˌæn æks- ‖ -ᵊr
ANC ˌeɪ en ˈsiː
-ance əntˢ —*Words with this suffix are stressed like words in* -ant. *Examples:* conˈtrive, conˈtrivance; reˈluctant, reˈluctance. *Exception:* reˈconnaissance.
ancestor ˈæntˢ est ə -ɪst-, -əst- ‖ -ᵊr **~s** z
ancestral æn ˈses trəl **~ly** i
ancestress ˈæntˢ es tres -ɪs-, -əs-, -trəs, -trɪs ‖ -trəs **~es** ɪz əz
ances|try ˈæntˢ es |tri -ɪs-, -əs- **~tries** triz
Anchises æn ˈkaɪs iːz →æŋ-
anchor ˈæŋk ə ‖ ˈæŋk ᵊr **~ed** d **anchoring** ˈæŋk ər ɪŋ **~s** z
anchorag|e, A~ ˈæŋk ər ɪdʒ **~es** ɪz əz
anchoress ˈæŋk ər ɪs -əs, -ə res **~es** ɪz əz
anchorite ˈæŋk ə raɪt **~s** s
anchor|man ˈæŋk ə |mæn ‖ -ᵊr- **~men** men **~person** ˌpɜːs ᵊn ‖ ˌpɜ˞ːs ᵊn **~woman** ˌwʊm ən **~women** ˌwɪm ɪn §-ən
anchov|y ˈæntʃ əv |i æn ˈtʃəʊv |i ‖ ˈæn tʃoʊv |i ·ˈ·· **~ies** iz
ancien regime, ancien régime ˌɒnˢ i æn reɪ ˈʒiːm ˌɑːnˢs-, ˌ·ɒn-; ɑːn ˌsjæn·ˈ· ‖ ˌɑːnˢ jæn ·ˈ· —*Fr* [ɑ̃ sjæ̃ ʁe ʒim]
ancient ˈeɪnˢtʃ ənt **~ness** nəs nɪs
ˌAncient ˈGreek; **ˌancient ˈmonument**
ancillar|y æn ˈsɪl ər |i ⚠ˈsɪl i‿ər |i ‖ ˈænˢ ə ler |i *(*)* **~ies** iz
Ancoats ˈæŋ kəʊts ‖ -koʊts
Ancona æŋ ˈkəʊn ə ‖ -ˈkoʊn ə —*It* [aŋ ˈkoː na]
Ancram ˈæŋk rəm
Ancren Riwle ˌæŋk ren ˈriː ʊl i ˌ·rɪn-, ˌ·rən-, -ə
-ancy ənˢs i —*Words with this suffix are stressed like words in* -ant. *Example:* ˈhesitant, ˈhesitancy
and *strong form* ænd, *weak forms* ənd, ən —*The presence or absence of* d *in the weak form is not sensitive to phonetic context: the choice depends on the fact that the weak form* ənd *is slightly more formal than* ən. *From* ən, *regular processes of SYLLABIC CONSONANT formation and ASSIMILATION produce the phonetic variants* m, n, ŋ *(all syllabic, though they can lose their syllabicity by COMPRESSION before a weak vowel) and* əm, əŋ.
and ˈso on
Andalusi|a ˌænd ə ˈluːs i‿|ə -ˈluːz-, -lu ˈsiː‿ə ‖ -ˈluːʒ |ə —*Sp* Andalucía [an da lu ˈθi a] **~an/s** ən/z ‖ ᵊn/z
Andaman ˈænd əm ən -ə mæn **~s** z
Andamanese ˌænd əm ə ˈniːz ◂ ‖ -ˈniːs ◂
andante æn ˈdænt i -eɪ ‖ ɑːn ˈdɑːnt eɪ æn ˈdænt̬ i —*It* [an ˈdan te]
andantino ˌænd æn ˈtiːn əʊ ‖ ˌɑːnd ɑːn ˈtiːn oʊ —*It* [an dan ˈtiː no]
Andean æn ˈdiː‿ən ˈænd i‿ən **~s** z
Andersen, Anderson ˈænd əs ən ‖ -ᵊrs-
Andersonstown ˈænd əs ənz taʊn ‖ ˈ·ᵊrs-
Andes ˈænd iːz
andesite ˈænd ɪ zaɪt -ə-, -saɪt
Andhra Pradesh ˌændr ə prɑː ˈdeʃ ˌɑːndr-, -ˈdeɪʃ —*Hindi* [aːn̪d̪ʱr prə d̪eːʃ]
andiron ˈænd ˌaɪ‿ən ‖ -ˌaɪ‿ᵊrn **~s** z
and/or ˌænd ˈɔː ◂ ‖ -ˈɔːr
ˌapples ˌand/or ˈpears
Andorr|a æn ˈdɔːr |ə -ˈdɒr- ‖ -ˈdɑːr ə —*Catalan* [ən ˈdɔr rə] **~an/s** ən/z
andouille ɒn ˈdwiː —*Fr* [ɑ̃ duj]
Andover ˈænd əʊv ə ‖ -oʊv ᵊr
Andre, André ˈɒndr eɪ ˈændr-, ˈɑːndr- ‖ ˈɑːndr- —*Fr* [ɑ̃ dʁe]
Andrea ˈændr i‿ə —*but as an Italian name,* æn ˈdreɪ ə —*It* [an ˈdrɛː a]
Anˌdrea del ˈSarto del ˈsɑːt əʊ ‖ -ˈsɑːrt oʊ —*It* [del ˈsar to]
Andreas ˈændr i‿əs, -æs —*but the place in the Isle of Man is* ˈændr əs; *as a Spanish name,* æn ˈdreɪ əs —*Sp* [an ˈdre as]

Andrei 'ɒndr eɪ 'ændr-, 'ɑːndr- ‖ 'ɑːndr- —*Russ* [ʌn 'drʲej]
Andrew 'ændr uː
Andrewes, Andrews 'ændr uːz
Andrex *tdmk* 'ændr eks
Andria 'ændr i‿ə
andro- *comb. form*
with stress-neutral suffix ¦ændr əʊ ‖ -ə — **androcentric** ˌændr əʊ 'sentr ɪk ◂ ‖ -ə-
with stress-imposing suffix æn 'drɒ+ ‖ -'drɑː+ — **androgyny** æn 'drɒdʒ ən i -ɪn- ‖ -'drɑːdʒ-
Androcles 'ændr ə kliːz
androgen 'ændr ədʒ ən -ə dʒen **~s** z
androgynous æn 'drɒdʒ ən əs -ɪn- ‖ -'drɑːdʒ-
androgyny æn 'drɒdʒ ən i -ɪn- ‖ -'drɑːdʒ-
android 'ændr ɔɪd **~s** z
Andromache æn 'drɒm ək i ‖ -'drɑːm-
Andromeda æn 'drɒm ɪd ə -əd- ‖ -'drɑːm-
Andronicus *(i)* æn 'drɒn ɪk əs ‖ -'drɑːn-, *(ii)* ˌændr ə 'naɪk əs —*in Shakespeare's* Titus A~, *(i)*
Andropov æn 'drɒp ɒf 'ændr ə pɒf ‖ ɑːn 'droʊp ɔːf -'drɑːp-, -ɑːf —*Russ* [ʌn 'dro pəf]
Andros 'ændr ɒs ‖ -əs -ɑːs
-androus 'ændr əs — **polyandrous** ˌpɒl i 'ændr əs ◂ ‖ ˌpɑːl-
-andry 'ændr i — **polyandry** ˌpɒl i 'ændr i ‖ ˌpɑːl-
Andy 'ænd i
-ane eɪn — **pentane** 'pent eɪn
anecdotage 'æn ɪk dəʊt ɪdʒ 'ek-, 'ək- ‖ -doʊt̬ ɪdʒ
anecdotal ˌæn ɪk 'dəʊt ᵊl ◂ -ek-, -ək- ‖ -'doʊt̬-
anecdote 'æn ɪk dəʊt -ek-, -ək- ‖ -doʊt **~s** s
anecdotist 'æn ɪk dəʊt ɪst -ek-, -ək-, §-əst ‖ -doʊt̬ əst **~s** s
anechoic ˌæn ɪ 'kəʊ ɪk ◂ -e-, -ə- ‖ -'koʊ-
Aneirin ə 'naɪᵊr ɪn -ən —*Welsh* [a 'nəi rin]
anemia ə 'niːm i‿ə
anemic ə 'niːm ɪk **~ally** ᵊl‿i
anemometer ˌæn ɪ 'mɒm ɪt ə ˌ·ə-, -ət ə ‖ -'mɑːm ət̬ ᵊr **~s** z
anemone ə 'nem ən i ⚠ə 'nen əm i **~s** z
anencephalic ˌæn en ke 'fæl ɪk ◂ →ˌ·eŋ-, ˌ·en sɪ-, ˌ·en sə-
anencephaly ˌæn en 'kef əl i →ˌ·eŋ-, -en 'sef-
anent ə 'nent
aneroid 'æn ə rɔɪd
anesthesia ˌæn əs 'θiːz i‿ə ˌ·iːs-, ˌ·ɪs-, -'θiːʒ ə ‖ -'θiːʒ ə
anesthesiologist ˌæn əs ˌθiːz i 'ɒl ədʒ ɪst §-əst ‖ -'ɑːl- **~s** s
anesthesiology ˌæn əs ˌθiːz i 'ɒl ədʒ i ‖ -'ɑːl-
anesthetic ˌæn əs 'θet ɪk ◂ -iːs-, -ɪs- ‖ -'θet̬- **~s** s
anesthetist ə 'niːs θət ɪst æ-, -θɪt-, §-əst ‖ ə 'nes θət əst *(*)* **~s** s
anesthetization ə ˌniːs θət aɪ 'zeɪʃ ᵊn -ɪ'-- ‖ ə ˌnes θət̬ ə-
anesthetiz|e ə 'niːs θə taɪz -θɪ- ‖ ə 'nes- *(*)* **~ed** d **~es** ɪz əz **~ing** ɪŋ
aneurin *'thiamine'* ə 'njʊər ɪn §-'nʊər-; 'æn jʊr-, -ən ‖ 'æn jər ən
Aneurin ə 'naɪᵊr ɪn -ən —*Welsh* [a 'nəi rin, -'nəi-]
aneurism, aneurysm 'æn jə ˌrɪz əm -juᵊ- **~s** z
aneurismal, aneurysmal ˌæn jə 'rɪz məl ◂ -juᵊ-
anew ə 'njuː ‖ ə 'nuː -'njuː
Anfield 'æn fiːᵊld
anfractuosit|y ˌæn frækt ju 'ɒs ət |i -fræk tʃu-, ·ˌ·-, -ɪt i ‖ æn ˌfræk tʃu 'ɑːs ət̬ |i **~ies** iz
anfractuous ⁽ˌ⁾æn 'frækt ju‿əs -'fræk tʃu‿ ‖ -'fræk tʃu‿əs
angary 'æŋ gər i
angel, Angel 'eɪndʒ ᵊl —*but as a Spanish name,* 'ɑːn hel —*Sp* Ángel ['aŋ xel] **~s** z
Angela 'ændʒ əl ə -ɪl-
Angeleno ˌændʒ ə 'liːn əʊ ‖ -oʊ —*Sp* Angeleño [aŋ xe 'le ɲo] **~s** z
angelfish 'eɪndʒ ᵊl fɪʃ
angelic æn 'dʒel ɪk **~ally** ᵊl‿i
angelica, A~ æn 'dʒel ɪk ə
Angelico æn 'dʒel ɪ kəʊ ‖ -koʊ ɑːn-,-'dʒeɪl- —*It* [an 'dʒɛː li ko]
Angelina ˌændʒ ə 'liːn ə -e-, -ɪ-
Angell 'eɪndʒ ᵊl
Angelo 'ændʒ ə ləʊ -ɪ- ‖ -loʊ
Angelou 'ændʒ ə luː
angelus, A~ 'ændʒ əl əs -ɪl- **~es** ɪz əz
anger 'æŋ gə ‖ 'æŋ gᵊr **angered** 'æŋ gəd ‖ -gᵊrd **angering** 'æŋ gər‿ɪŋ **angers** 'æŋ gəz ‖ -gᵊrz
Angers *place in France* ˌɑːn 'ʒeɪ ˌɒ̃- —*Fr* [ɑ̃ ʒe]
Angevin 'ændʒ əv ɪn -ɪv-, §-ən
Angharad æŋ 'hær əd æn- ‖ -'her- —*Welsh* [aŋ 'ha rad]
angi- *comb. form before vowel* ¦ændʒ i — **angioma** ˌændʒ i 'əʊm ə ‖ -'oʊm-
Angie 'ændʒ i
angina æn 'dʒaɪn ə
anˌgina 'pectoris 'pekt ər ɪs §-əs
angio- *comb. form*
with stress-neutral suffix ¦ændʒ i‿əʊ ‖ ə — **angiogram** 'ændʒ i‿əʊ græm ‖ ə græm
with stress-imposing suffix ˌændʒ i 'ɒ+ ‖ -'ɑː+ — **angiography** ˌændʒ i 'ɒg rəf i ‖ -'ɑːg-
angioplasty 'ændʒi‿əʊ ˌplæst i ‖ -i‿ə-
angiosperm 'ændʒ i‿əʊ spɜːm ‖ -ə spɜːm **~s** z
Angkor 'æŋ kɔː ‖ -kɔːr
ˌAngkor 'Wat
angle, Angle 'æŋ gᵊl **angled** 'æŋ gᵊld **angles, Angles** 'æŋ gᵊlz **angling** 'æŋ glɪŋ 'æŋ gᵊl‿ɪŋ
'angle ˌbracket
Anglepoise *tdmk* 'æŋ gᵊl pɔɪz
angler 'æŋ glə ‖ -glᵊr **~s** z
Anglesey 'æŋ gᵊls i -iː
anglesite 'æŋ gᵊl saɪt
Angli|a 'æŋ gli‿|ə **~an/s** ən/z
Anglican 'æŋ glɪk ən **~ism** ˌɪz əm **~s** z

anglice, A~ ˈæŋ glɪs i -gləs-
anglicis... —*see* **angliciz...**
anglicism, A~ ˈæŋ glɪ ˌsɪz əm -glə-
anglicization, A~ ˌæŋ glɪs aɪ ˈzeɪʃ ən ˌgləs-, -ɪˈ-- ‖ -ə ˈzeɪʃ- **~s** z
angliciz|e, A~ ˈæŋ glɪ saɪz -glə- **~ed** d **~es** ɪz əz **~ing** ɪŋ
angling ˈæŋ glɪŋ
Anglo ˈæŋ gləʊ ‖ -gloʊ **~s** z
Anglo- ¦æŋ gləʊ ‖ -gloʊ — **Anglo-Spanish** ˌæŋ gləʊ ˈspæn ɪʃ ◂ ‖ -gloʊ-
Anglo-American ˌæŋ gləʊ ə ˈmer ɪk ən ◂ -ək ən ‖ ˌ·gloʊ- **~s** z
Anglo-Catholic ˌæŋ gləʊ ˈkæθ lɪk ◂ -ˈkæθ əl ɪk, -ˈkɑːθ- ‖ -gloʊ- **~s** s
Anglo-Catholicism ˌæŋ gləʊ kə ˈθɒl ə ˌsɪz əm -ɪ,-- ‖ -gloʊ kə ˈθɑːl-
Anglo-French ˌæŋ gləʊ ˈfrentʃ ◂ ‖ -gloʊ-
Anglo-Indian ˌæŋ gləʊ ˈɪnd i‿ən ◂ ‖ ˌ·gloʊ- **~s** z
Anglo-Irish ˌæŋ gləʊ ˈaɪər ɪʃ ◂ ‖ -gloʊ-
the ˌAnglo-ˌIrish Aˈgreement
Anglo-Norman ˌæŋ gləʊ ˈnɔːm ən ◂ ‖ -gloʊ ˈnɔːrm-
anglophile ˈæŋ gləʊ faɪəl ‖ -glə- **~s** z
anglophilia ˌæŋ gləʊ ˈfɪl i‿ə ‖ ˌ·glə-
anglophobe ˈæŋ gləʊ fəʊb ‖ -glə foʊb **~s** z
anglophobia ˌæŋ gləʊ ˈfəʊb i‿ə ‖ -glə ˈfoʊb-
Anglophone, a~ ˈæŋ glə fəʊn ‖ -foʊn
Anglo-Saxon ˌæŋ gləʊ ˈsæks ən ◂ ‖ -gloʊ- **~s** z
Angmering ˈæŋ mər ɪŋ
Angol|a æŋ ˈgəʊl |ə ‖ -ˈgoʊl |ə **~an/s** ən/z
angora, A~ æŋ ˈgɔːr ə ‖ -ˈgoʊr-
angostura, A~ ˌæŋ gə ˈstjʊər ə ◂ -gɒ-, -ˈstʊər-, -ˈstjɔːr- ‖ -ˈstʊr ə ◂ —*Sp* [aŋ gos ˈtu ɾa]
ˌAngoˌstura ˈbitters
Angouleme, Angoulême ˌɒŋ gu ˈlem ‖ ˌɑːŋ- —*Fr* [ɑ̃ gu lɛm]
angry ˈæŋ gri **angrier** ˈæŋ gri‿ə ‖ ər **angriest** ˈæŋ gri‿ɪst əst **angrily** ˈæŋ grəl i -grɪ li
angst æŋkst ‖ ɑːŋkst —*Ger* [ʔaŋst]
angstrom, A~ ˈæŋks trəm -trʌm —*Swedish* Ångström [ˈˈɔŋ strœm] **~s** z
ˈangstrom ˌunit
Anguill|a æŋ ˈgwɪl |ə -ˈgwiːl- **~an/s** ən/z
anguish ˈæŋ gwɪʃ **~ed** t **~es** ɪz əz **~ing** ɪŋ
angular ˈæŋ gjʊl ə -gjəl- ‖ -gjəl ər **~ly** li **~ness** nəs nɪs
angularit|y ˌæŋ gju ˈlær ət |i ˌ·gjə-, -ɪt i ‖ -gjə ˈlær əṭ |i -ˈler- **~ies** iz
Angus ˈæŋ gəs
anharmonic ˌæn hɑː ˈmɒn ɪk ◂ ‖ -hɑːr ˈmɑːn-
anhinga æn ˈhɪŋ gə **~s** z
Anhui ˌæn ˈhweɪ ‖ ˌɑːn- —*Chinese* Ānhuī [¹an ¹xwei]
anhydride ₍ˌ₎æn ˈhaɪdr aɪd **~s** z
anhydrite ₍ˌ₎æn ˈhaɪdr aɪt **~s** z
anhydrous ₍ˌ₎æn ˈhaɪdr əs
ani *bird* ˈɑːn i **anis** ˈɑːn iz
aniconic ˌæn aɪ ˈkɒn ɪk ◂ ‖ -ˈkɑːn-
anil ˈæn ɪl -əl
Anil ə ˈniːəl
aniline ˈæn əl ɪn -ɪl-, -iːn, §-ən
anilingus ˌeɪn i ˈlɪŋ gəs
anima ˈæn ɪm ə §-əm-
animadversion ˌæn ɪm æd ˈvɜːʃ ən §ˌ·əm-, -ədˈ--, -ˈvɜːʒ- ‖ -ˈvɜːʒ- -ˈvɜːʃ- **~s** z
animad|vert ˌæn ɪm æd |ˈvɜːt §ˌ·əm-, -ədˈ· ‖ -|ˈvɜːt **~verted** ˈvɜːt ɪd -əd ‖ ˈvɜːṭ əd **~verting** ˈvɜːt ɪŋ ‖ ˈvɜːṭ ɪŋ **~verts** ˈvɜːts ‖ ˈvɜːts
animal ˈæn ɪm əl -əm- **~s** z
ˌanimal ˈhusbandry
animalcule ˌæn ɪ ˈmæl kjuːl -ə- **~s** z
animalia ˌæn ɪ ˈmeɪl i‿ə ˌ·ə-
animalism ˈæn ɪm əl ˌɪz əm
animalistic ˌæn ɪm ə ˈlɪst ɪk ◂ ·əl ˈɪst-
animality ˌæn ɪ ˈmæl ət i ˌ·ə-, -ɪt i ‖ -əṭ i
animate *adj* ˈæn ɪm ət -əm-, ɪt; -ɪ meɪt, -ə- **~ness** nəs nɪs
ani|mate *v* ˈæn ɪ |meɪt -ə- **~mated/ly** meɪt ɪd /li -əd ‖ meɪṭ əd /li **~mates** meɪts **~mating** meɪt ɪŋ ‖ meɪṭ ɪŋ
animation ˌæn ɪ ˈmeɪʃ ən -ə- **~s** z
animator ˈæn ɪ meɪt ə ˈ·ə- ‖ -meɪṭ ər **~s** z
animatronic ˌæn ɪm ə ˈtrɒn ɪk ◂ ˌ·əm- ‖ -ˈtrɑːn- **~s** s
anime, animé ˈæn ɪ meɪ -ə- **~s** z
animism ˈæn ɪ ˌmɪz əm -ə-
animist ˈæn ɪm ɪst -əm-, §-əst **~s** s
animosit|y ˌæn ɪ ˈmɒs ət |i ˌ·ə-, -ɪt i ‖ -ˈmɑːs əṭ |i **~ies** iz
animus ˈæn ɪm əs -əm-
anion ˈæn ˌaɪ‿ən **~s** z
anionic ˌæn aɪ ˈɒn ɪk ◂ ‖ -ˈɑːn-
anis ˈæn iː -iːs; æ ˈniːs ‖ ɑː ˈniːs -ˈniː —*Fr* [a ni, -nis], *Sp* anís [a ˈnis]
anise ˈæn ɪs §-əs
aniseed ˈæn ɪ siːd -ə-
anisette ˌæn ɪ ˈzet §-ə-, -ˈset **~s** s
anisogamy ˌæn aɪ ˈsɒg əm i ‖ -ˈsɑːg-
anisomorphic æn ˌaɪs əʊ ˈmɔːf ɪk ◂ ˌ·ˌ·-- ‖ -ə ˈmɔːrf- **~ally** əl‿i
anisotropic æn ˌaɪs əʊ ˈtrɒp ɪk ◂ ˌ·ˌ·-, -ˈtrəʊp- ‖ -ə ˈtrɑːp- -ə ˈtroʊp-
Aniston ˈæn ɪst ən §-əst-
Anita ə ˈniːt ə ‖ ə ˈniːṭ ə
Anjou ˌɑːn ˈʒuː ˌɒ̃- ‖ ˈɑːndʒ uː —*Fr* [ɑ̃ ʒu]
Ankara ˈæŋk ər ə ‖ ˈɑːŋk- —*Turkish* [ˈaŋ ka ɾa]
ankh æŋk ɑːŋk **ankhs** æŋks ɑːŋks
ankle ˈæŋk əl **~s** z
ˈankle sock
anklebone ˈæŋk əl bəʊn ‖ -boʊn **~s** z
anklet ˈæŋk lət -lɪt **~s** s
ankylos|e ˈæŋk ɪ ləʊz -ə-, -ləʊs ‖ -loʊs -loʊz **~ed** d ‖ t **~es** ɪz əz **~ing** ɪŋ
ankylosis ˌæŋk ɪ ˈləʊs ɪs -ə-, §-əs ‖ -ˈloʊs-
Anlaby ˈæn ləb i
Ann æn
₍ˌ₎Ann ˈArbor
Anna, anna ˈæn ə **~'s, ~s** z
Annabel ˈæn ə bel
Annabella ˌæn ə ˈbel ə

Annalisa ˌæn ə ˈliːz ə -ˈliːs-
annalist ˈæn əl ɪst §-əst *(= analyst)* **~s** s
annals ˈæn ᵊlz
Annam (ˌ)æ ˈnæm ˈæn æm
Annamarie, Anna-Marie ˌæn ə mə ˈriː
Annamese ˌæn ə ˈmiːz ◂ -ˈmiːs ◂
Annan ˈæn ən *—but the former Secretary-General of the UN is* -æn, ə ˈnɑːn, ə ˈnæn
Annapolis ə ˈnæp əl ɪs §-əs
Annapurna ˌæn ə ˈpɜːn ə -ˈpʊən- ‖ -ˈpʊrn ə -ˈpɜːn-
annatto, A~ ə ˈnæt əʊ ‖ ə ˈnɑːt̬ oʊ
Anne æn
anneal ə ˈniːᵊl **annealed** ə ˈniːᵊld **annealing** ə ˈniːᵊl ɪŋ **anneals** ə ˈniːᵊlz
Anneka ˈæn ɪk ə -ək-
annelid ˈæn ə lɪd §-əl əd **~s** z
Annemarie, Anne-Marie ˌæn mə ˈriː →ˌæm-
Annesley *(i)* ˈænz li, *(ii)* ˈæn ɪz li -əz-
Annet, Annett ˈæn ɪt -ət
Annette ə ˈnet æ-
annex *v* ə ˈneks æ- **~ed** t **~es** ɪz əz **~ing** ɪŋ
annex *n* ˈæn eks **~es** ɪz əz
annexation ˌæn ek ˈseɪʃ ᵊn -ɪk- **~s** z
annex|e ˈæn eks **~es** ɪz əz
annexure ˈæn ek ʃʊə ‖ -ʃʊr **~s** z
Annie ˈæn i
Annigoni ˌæn i ˈgəʊn i ‖ -ˈgoʊn i *—It* [an ni ˈgoː ni]
annihi|late ə ˈnaɪ‿ə |leɪt ɪ- **~lated** leɪt ɪd -əd ‖ leɪt̬ əd **~lates** leɪts **~lating** leɪt ɪŋ ‖ leɪt̬ ɪŋ
annihilation ə ˌnaɪ‿ə ˈleɪʃ ᵊn ɪ-
Annika ˈæn ɪk ə
Annis ˈæn ɪs §-əs
Anniston ˈæn ɪst ən §-əst-
anniversar|y ˌæn ɪ ˈvɜːs ər‿|i ◂ ˌ·ə-, →-ˈvɜːʃ ri ‖ -ˈvɜːs- **~ies** iz
Anno Domini ˌæn əʊ ˈdɒm ɪ naɪ -ə-, -niː ‖ ˌæn oʊ ˈdɑːm ə niː -ˈdoʊm-, -naɪ
anno|tate ˈæn əʊ |teɪt ‖ -ə- **~tated** teɪt ɪd -əd ‖ teɪt̬ əd **~tates** teɪts **~tating** teɪt ɪŋ ‖ teɪt̬ ɪŋ
annotation ˌæn əʊ ˈteɪʃ ᵊn ‖ -ə- **~s** z
annotative ˈæn əʊ teɪt ɪv ‖ -ə teɪt̬-
annotator ˈæn əʊ teɪt ə ‖ -ə teɪt̬ ᵊr **~s** z
announc|e ə ˈnaʊnᵗs **~ed** t **~es** ɪz əz **~ing** ɪŋ
announcement ə ˈnaʊnᵗs mənt **~s** s
announcer ə ˈnaʊnᵗs ə ‖ -ᵊr **~s** z
annoy ə ˈnɔɪ **annoyed** ə ˈnɔɪd **annoying/ly** ə ˈnɔɪ ɪŋ /li **annoys** ə ˈnɔɪz
annoyanc|e ə ˈnɔɪ ənᵗs **~es** ɪz əz
annual ˈæn ju‿əl **~ly** i **~s** z
annualis|e, annualiz|e ˈæn ju‿ə laɪz ˈ·ju · **~ed** d **~es** ɪz əz **~ing** ɪŋ
annuitant ə ˈnjuː‿ɪt ənt ət- ‖ ə ˈnuː ət ᵊnt -ˈnjuː- **~s** s
annuit|y ə ˈnjuː‿ət |i ɪt- ‖ ə ˈnuː ət̬ |i -ˈnjuː- **~ies** iz
annul ə ˈnʌl **~led** d **~ling** ɪŋ **~s** z
annular ˈæn jʊl ə -jəl- ‖ -jəl ᵊr
annu|late ˈæn ju |leɪt -jə- ‖ -jə- **~lated** leɪt ɪd -əd ‖ leɪt̬ əd
annuli ˈæn ju laɪ ‖ -jə-
annull... *—see* **annul**
annulment ə ˈnʌl mənt **~s** s
annulus ˈæn jʊl əs -jəl- ‖ -jəl- **annuli** ˈæn ju laɪ ‖ -jə-
annum ˈæn əm
annunci|ate ə ˈnʌnᵗs i |eɪt ə ˈnʌnᵗʃ- **~ated** eɪt ɪd -əd ‖ eɪt̬ əd **~ates** eɪts **~ating** eɪt ɪŋ ‖ eɪt̬ ɪŋ
annunciation, A~ ə ˌnʌnᵗs i ˈeɪʃ ᵊn ə ˌnʌnᵗʃ- **~s** z
annunciative ə ˈnʌnᵗs i‿ət ɪv ə ˈnʌnᵗʃ-, -eɪt ɪv; -ˈnʌnᵗʃ ət ɪv ‖ -eɪt̬ ɪv
annunciator ə ˈnʌnᵗs i eɪt ə ə ˈnʌnᵗʃ- ‖ -eɪt̬ ᵊr **~s** z
annunciatory ə ˈnʌnᵗs i‿ət‿ər i ə ˈnʌnᵗʃ-, ·ˌ· ·ˈeɪt ər i; ə ˈnʌnᵗʃ ət‿ər i ‖ -ə tɔːr i -toʊr i
annus ˈæn əs -ʊs ‖ ˈɑːn-
ˌannus miˈrabilis mɪ ˈrɑːb əl ɪs mə-, -ˈræb-, -ɪl-, §-əs
Anny ˈæn i
anoa ə ˈnəʊ ə ‖ ə ˈnoʊ ə **anoas** ə ˈnəʊ əz ‖ -ˈnoʊ-
anode ˈæn əʊd ‖ -oʊd **~s** z
anodic æ ˈnɒd ɪk ‖ ə ˈnɑːd ɪk
anodis|e, anodiz|e ˈæn əʊ daɪz ‖ -ə- **~ed** d **~es** ɪz əz **~ing** ɪŋ
anodyne ˈæn əʊ daɪn ‖ -ə- **~s** z
anoint ə ˈnɔɪnt **anointed** ə ˈnɔɪnt ɪd -əd ‖ ə ˈnɔɪnt̬ əd **anointing** ə ˈnɔɪnt ɪŋ ‖ ə ˈnɔɪnt̬ ɪŋ **anoints** ə ˈnɔɪnts
anointment ə ˈnɔɪnt mənt **~s** s
anole ə ˈnəʊl i ‖ -ˈnoʊl- **~s** z
anomalistic ə ˌnɒm ə ˈlɪst ɪk ◂ ‖ ə ˌnɑːm- **~ally** ᵊl‿i
anomalous ə ˈnɒm əl əs ‖ ə ˈnɑːm- **~ly** li **~ness** nəs nɪs
anomal|y ə ˈnɒm əl |i ‖ ə ˈnɑːm- **~ies** iz
anomic ə ˈnɒm ɪk æ-, -ˈnəʊm- ‖ -ˈnɑːm- -ˈnoʊm-
anomie, anomy ˈæn əʊm i ‖ -əm i
anon ə ˈnɒn ‖ ə ˈnɑːn
Anona ə ˈnəʊn ə ‖ ə ˈnoʊn ə
anonymity ˌæn ə ˈnɪm ət i ˌæn ɒ-, -ɪt i ‖ -ət̬ i
anonymous ə ˈnɒn ɪ məs -ə- ‖ ə ˈnɑːn- **~ly** li
anopheles, A~ ə ˈnɒf ə liːz -ɪ- ‖ ə ˈnɑːf-
anorak ˈæn ə ræk **~s** s
anorectic ˌæn ə ˈrekt ɪk ◂ **~s** s
anorexia ˌæn ə ˈreks i‿ə ◂ ˌæn ɒ- **~s** z
ˌanoˌrexia nerˈvosa nɜː ˈvəʊs ə -ˈvəʊz- ‖ nᵊr ˈvoʊs ə -ˈvoʊz-
anorexic ˌæn ə ˈreks ɪk ◂ **~s** s
anosmia æn ˈɒz mi‿ə -ˈɒs- ‖ -ˈɑːz- -ˈɑːs-
another ə ˈnʌð ə ‖ -ᵊr *—There is also an occasional emphatic form* ˌeɪ- **~'s** z
Anouilh ˈæn u iː ˈɒn-, ˌ· ·ˈ·; æ ˈnuː‿i ‖ ɑː ˈnuː jə æ-, -iː; ˌ· ·ˈiː *—Fr* [a nuj]
ANOVA ˌæn əʊ ˈvɑː ˈ· · · ‖ -oʊ-
anoxia (ˌ)æn ˈɒks i‿ə ‖ -ˈɑːks-
ansaphone *tdmk* ˈɑːnᵗs ə fəʊn §ˈænᵗs- ‖ ˈænᵗs ə foʊn **~s** z
Ansbacher ˈænz bæk ə ‖ -ᵊr
Anschluss, a~ ˈæn ʃlʊs ‖ ˈɑːn- *—Ger* Anschluß [ˈʔan ʃlʊs]

Anscombe ˈæn^t^s kəm
Ansell ˈænᵗs ᵊl
Anselm ˈænᵗs elm
anserine ˈænᵗs ə raɪn -riːn, -rɪn
Ansermet ˈɒnᵗs ə meɪ ˈɑːnᵗs-, ˈɒ̃- ‖ ˌɑːnᵗs ᵊr ˈmeɪ —*Fr* [ɑ̃ sɛʁ mɛ]
Ansett æn set
Anshun ˌæn ˈʃʊn ‖ ˌɑːn ˈʃuːn —*Chinese* Ānshùn [¹an ⁴ʂwən]
ANSI ˈænᵗs i
Anson ˈænᵗs ᵊn
Anstey ˈænᵗst i
Anstruther ˈænᵗs trʌð ə ‖ -ᵊr —*The place in Fife is locally also* ˈeɪnᵗst ə ‖ -ᵊr
Ansty ˈænᵗst i
answer ˈɑːnᵗs ə §ˈænᵗs ə ‖ ˈænᵗs ᵊr *(!)* **~ed** d
answering ˈɑːnᵗs ər‿ɪŋ §ˈænᵗs- ‖ ˈænᵗs- **~s** z
ˈanswering maˌchine; **ˈanswering ˌservice**
answerability ˌɑːnᵗs ər‿ə ˈbɪl ət i §ˌænᵗs-, -ɪt i ‖ ˌænᵗs ər‿ə ˈbɪl əṱ i
answerab|le ˈɑːnᵗs ər‿əb |ᵊl §ˈænᵗs- ‖ ˈænᵗs- **~ly** li
answerphone ˈɑːnᵗs ə fəʊn §ˈænᵗs- ‖ ˈænᵗs ᵊr foʊn **~s** z
ant, Ant ænt **ants** æn*t*s
ant- *comb. form before vowel* ¦ænt, ænt — **antacid** ₍ˌ₎ænt ˈæs ɪd §-əd **, antonym** ˈænt ən ɪm §-əm
-ant ənt —*When attached to an independent stem, this suffix is usually stress-neutral* (acˈcount — acˈcountant; inˈhabit — inˈhabitant). *Otherwise, it imposes stress: on the antepenultimate syllable if the penultimate is weak* (ˈarrogant, ˈapplicant, sigˈnificant), *but on the penultimate itself if it is strong* (flamˈboyant, reˈluctant). *There are several exceptions: note* exˈecutant, ˈignorant, ˈProtestant.
Antabuse *tdmk* ˈænt ə bjuːs -bjuːz ‖ ˈænṱ-
antacid ₍ˌ₎ænt ˈæs ɪd §-əd **~s** z
Antaeus æn ˈtiː‿əs -ˈteɪ-
antagonis... —*see* **antagoniz...**
antagonism æn ˈtæg ə ˌnɪz əm **~s** z
antagonist æn ˈtæg ən ɪst §-əst **~s** s
antagonistic æn ˌtæg ə ˈnɪst ɪk ◂ ˌænt æg- **~ally** ᵊl‿i
antagoniz|e æn ˈtæg ə naɪz **~ed** d **~es** ɪz əz **~ing** ɪŋ
Antalya æn ˈtæl jə ‖ ɑːn ˈtɑːl jə —*Turkish* [an ˈtal ja]
Antananarivo ˌænt ə ˌnæn ə ˈriːv əʊ ‖ -oʊ
antarctic, A~ ₍ˌ₎ænt ˈɑːkt ɪk ⚠-ˈɑːt- ‖ ₍ˌ₎ænṱ ˈɑːrkt- -ˈɑːrt-
Antˌarctic ˈCircle, ˌˌ·-
Antarctica ₍ˌ₎ænt ˈɑːkt ɪk ə ⚠-ˈɑːt- ‖ -ˈɑːrkt- -ˈɑːrṱ-
Antares æn ˈteər iːz ‖ -ˈter- -ˈtær-
ant-bear ˈænt beə ‖ -ber -bær **~s** z
ante ˈænt i ‖ ˈænṱ i **~d, ~ed** d **~ing** ‿ɪŋ **~s** z
ˌante meˈridiem mə ˈrɪd i‿əm -em

ante- *comb. form with stress-neutral suffix* ¦ænt i ‖ ¦ænṱ i *(= anti-)* — **antebellum** ˌænt i ˈbel əm ◂ ‖ ˌænṱ i-
anteater ˈænt ˌiːt ə ‖ ˈænṱ ˌiːṱ ᵊr **~s** z
antecedence ˌænt ɪ ˈsiːd ᵊnᵗs -ə- ‖ ˌænṱ ə-
antecedent ˌænt ɪ ˈsiːd ᵊnt ◂ -ə- ‖ ˌænṱ ə- **~s** s
antechamber ˈænt i ˌtʃeɪm bə ‖ ˈænṱ i ˌtʃeɪm bᵊr **~s** z
ante|date ˌænt i ˈ|deɪt ◂ ˈ· · · ‖ ˈænṱ i |deɪt **~dated** deɪt ɪd -əd ‖ deɪṱ əd **~dates** deɪts **~dating** deɪt ɪŋ ‖ deɪṱ ɪŋ
antediluvian ˌænt i dɪ ˈluːv i‿ən ◂ -dəˈ-, -daɪˈ--, -ˈljuːv- ‖ ˌænṱ i- **~s** z
antelope ˈænt ɪ ləʊp -ə- ‖ ˈænṱ ə loʊp **~s** s
antenatal ˌænt i ˈneɪt ᵊl ◂ ‖ ˌænṱ i ˈneɪṱ ᵊl ◂ **~s** z
antenn|a æn ˈten |ə **~ae** iː **~as** əz
antepenult ˌænt i pɪ ˈnʌlt -pəˈ·, -peˈ· ‖ ˌænṱ i ˈpiːn ʌlt -pɪ ˈnʌlt **~s** s
antepenultimate ˌænt i pɪ ˈnʌlt ɪm ət ◂ -pəˈ--, -peˈ--, -əm ət, -ɪt ‖ ˌænṱ i- **~ly** li **~s** s
anterior æn ˈtɪər i‿ə ‖ -ˈtɪr i‿ᵊr **~ly** li
anteriority æn ˌtɪər i ˈɒr ət i -ɪt i ‖ æn ˌtɪr i ˈɔːr əṱ i
anteroom ˈænt i ruːm -rʊm ‖ ˈænṱ i- **~s** z
Anthea ˈænᵗθ i‿ə
anthelion ænt ˈhiːl i‿ən æn ˈθiːl- **~s** z
anthelminthic ˌænᵗθ el ˈmɪnᵗθ ɪk ◂ ˌænt hel- **~s** s
anthelmintic ˌænᵗθ el ˈmɪnt ɪk ◂ ˌænt hel- ‖ -ˈmɪnṱ- **~s** s
anthem ˈænᵗθ əm **~s** z
anthemic æn ˈθem ɪk -ˈθiːm-
anther ˈænᵗθ ə ‖ -ᵊr **~s** z
anthill ˈænt hɪl **~s** z
anthologis... —*see* **anthologiz...**
anthologist æn ˈθɒl ədʒ ɪst §-əst ‖ -ˈθɑːl- **~s** s
anthologiz|e æn ˈθɒl ə dʒaɪz ‖ -ˈθɑːl- **~ed** d **~es** ɪz əz **~ing** ɪŋ
antholog|y æn ˈθɒl ədʒ |i ‖ -ˈθɑːl- **~ies** iz
Anthony *(i)* ˈænt ən i, *(ii)* ˈænᵗθ- —*in BrE (i) predominates, in AmE (ii).*
anthracite ˈænᵗθ rə saɪt
anthracnose æn ˈθræk nəʊs -nəʊz ‖ -noʊs
anthrax ˈænᵗθ ræks
anthropic æn ˈθrɒp ɪk ‖ -ˈθrɑːp-
anthropo- *comb. form with stress-neutral suffix* ¦ænᵗθ rəʊp əʊ ‖ ¦ænᵗθ rəp ə — **anthropophobia** ˌænᵗθ rəʊp əʊ ˈfəʊb i‿ə ‖ ˌænᵗθ rəp ə ˈfoʊb- *with stress-imposing suffix* ˌænᵗθ rəʊ ˈpɒ+ ‖ ˌænᵗθ rə ˈpɑː+ — **anthroposcopy** ˌænᵗθ rəʊ ˈpɒsk əp i ‖ -rə ˈpɑːsk-
anthropocentric ˌænᵗθ rəʊp əʊ ˈsentr ɪk◂ ‖ -rəp ə- **~ally** ᵊl‿i
anthropoid ˈænᵗθ rəʊ pɔɪd ‖ -rə- **~s** z
anthropological ˌænᵗθ rəʊp ə ˈlɒdʒ ɪk ᵊl◂ ‖ -rəp ə ˈlɑːdʒ- **~ly** ‿i
anthropologist ˌænᵗθ rə ˈpɒl ədʒ ɪst §-əst ‖ -ˈpɑːl- **~s** s
anthropology ˌænᵗθ rə ˈpɒl ədʒ i ‖ -ˈpɑːl-

anthropometry ˌænᵗθ rəʊ ˈpɒm ətr i -ɪtr i ‖ -rə ˈpɑːm-

anthropomorphic ˌænᵗθ rəʊp əʊ ˈmɔːf ɪk ◂ ‖ -rəp ə ˈmɔːrf- **~ally** ᵊl i

anthropomorphism ˌænᵗθ rəʊp əʊ ˈmɔːf ˌɪz əm ‖ -rəp ə ˈmɔːrf-

anthropophagi ˌænᵗθ rəʊ ˈpɒf ə dʒaɪ -gaɪ ‖ -rə ˈpɑːf-

anthropophagous ˌænᵗθ rəʊ ˈpɒf əg əs ‖ -rə ˈpɑːf-

anthropophagy ˌænᵗθ rəʊ ˈpɒf ədʒ i ‖ -rə ˈpɑːf-

anthroposophy ˌænᵗθ rəʊ ˈpɒs əf i ‖ -rə ˈpɑːs-

anthurium æn ˈθjʊər i̯ əm -ˈθʊər- ‖ -ˈθʊr- -ˈθjʊr-

anti ˈænt i ‖ ˈænţ i ˈænt aɪ **~s** z

anti- *comb. form*
with stress-neutral suffix ¦ænt i ‖ ¦ænţ i ¦ænt aɪ — **antibacterial** ˌænt i bæk ˈtɪər i̯ əl ◂ ‖ ˌænţi bæk ˈtɪr- ˌænt aɪ-
with stress-imposing suffix æn ˈtɪ + — **antiphony** æn ˈtɪf ən i

antiabortion ˌænt i ə ˈbɔːʃ ᵊn ‖ ˌænţ i ə ˈbɔːrʃ ᵊn ˌænt aɪ- **~ist/s** ɪst/s §əst/s

antiaircraft, anti-aircraft ˌænt i ˈeə krɑːft ◂ §-kræft ‖ ˌænţ i ˈer kræft ˌænt aɪ-, -ˈær-

antialias ˌænt i ˈeɪl i̯ əs ‖ ˌænţ i- ˌænt aɪ- **~ed** t **~es** ɪz əz **~ing** ɪŋ

antiballistic ˌænt i bə ˈlɪst ɪk ◂ ‖ ˌænţ i- ˌænt aɪ-
ˌantibalˌlistic ˈmissile

Antibes ɒn ˈtiːb ɑːn-, æn- ‖ ɑːn- —*Fr* [ɑ̃ tib]

antibiotic ˌænt i baɪ ˈɒt ɪk ◂ ‖ ˌænţ i baɪ ˈɑːţ ɪk ◂ ˌænt aɪ- **~ally** ᵊl i **~s** s

antibod|y ˈænt i ˌbɒd |i ‖ ˈænţ i ˌbɑːd |i ˈænt aɪ- **~ies** iz

antic ˈænt ɪk ‖ ˈænţ ɪk **~s** s

anticholinergic ˌænt i ˌkəʊl ɪ ˈnɜːdʒ ɪk -ˌkɒl-, -ə'-- ‖ ˌænţ i ˌkoʊl ə ˈnɜːdʒ ɪk ˌænt aɪ-

Antichrist, a~ ˈænt i kraɪst ‖ ˈænţ i- ˈænt aɪ-

antici|pate æn ˈtɪs ɪ |peɪt ◂ -ə- **~pated** peɪt ɪd -əd ‖ peɪţ əd **~pates** peɪts **~pating** peɪt ɪŋ ‖ peɪţ ɪŋ

anticipation æn ˌtɪs ɪ ˈpeɪʃ ᵊn ˌ·ˈ--, -ə'-- **~s** z

anticipatory æn ˈtɪs ɪp ət ər i ˌ·ˈ-əp-; ·ˌ·ɪ ˈpeɪt ər i, ˌ·-·ˈ--, -ə'-- ‖ æn ˈtɪs əp ə tɔːr i -toʊr i

anticlerical ˌænt i ˈkler ɪk ᵊl ◂ ‖ ˌænţ i- ˌænt aɪ- **~ism** ˌɪz əm

anticlimactic ˌænt i klaɪ ˈmækt ɪk ◂ -klɪ'--, -klə'-- ‖ ˌænţ i- ˌænt aɪ- **~ally** ᵊl i

anticlimax ˌænt i ˈklaɪm æks ‖ ˌænţ i- ˌænt aɪ- **~es** ɪz əz

anticline ˈænt i klaɪn ‖ ˈænţ i- ˈænt aɪ- **~s** z

anticlockwise ˌænt i ˈklɒk waɪz ◂ ‖ ˌænţ i ˈklɑːk- ˌænt aɪ-

anticoagulant ˌænt i kəʊ ˈæg jʊl ənt ◂ -jəl ənt ‖ ˌænţ i koʊ ˈæg jəl ənt ˌænt aɪ- **~s** s

anticonvulsant ˌænt i kən ˈvʌls ənt ◂ §-kɒn'-- ‖ ˌænţ i- ˌænt aɪ- **~s** s

Anticosti ˌænt ɪ ˈkɒst i -ə- ‖ ˌænţ ə ˈkɑːst i -ˈkɔːst-

anticyclone ˌænt i ˈsaɪk ləʊn ‖ ˌænţ i ˈsaɪk loʊn ˌænt aɪ- **~s** z

anticyclonic ˌænt i saɪ ˈklɒn ɪk ◂ ‖ ˌænţ i saɪ ˈklɑːn ɪk ◂ ˌænt aɪ-

antidepressant ˌænt i dɪ ˈpres ᵊnt ◂ -də'-, §-diː'-- ‖ ˌænţ i- ˌænt aɪ- **~s** s

antidote ˈænt i dəʊt ‖ ˈænţ i doʊt **~s** s

Antietam æn ˈtiːt əm ‖ -ˈtiːţ-

antiformant ˈænt i ˌfɔːm ənt ‖ ˈænţ i ˌfɔːrm- ˈænt aɪ- **~s** s

antifouling ˌænt i ˈfaʊl ɪŋ ‖ ˌænţ i- ˌænt aɪ-

antifreeze ˈænt i friːz ˌ·ˈ· ‖ ˈænţ i-

anti-fungal ˌænt i ˈfʌŋ gᵊl ◂ ‖ ˌænţ i- ˌænt aɪ-

anti-g ˌænt i ˈdʒiː ‖ ˌænţ i- ˌænt aɪ-

antigen ˈænt ɪdʒ ən -ədʒ-, -i dʒen ‖ ˈænţ- **~s** z

Antigone æn ˈtɪg ən i

Antigonus æn ˈtɪg ən əs

Antigu|a æn ˈtiːg |ə —*there is also an occasional spelling pronunciation* -w|ə **~an/s** ən/z

antihero ˈænt i ˌhɪər əʊ ‖ ˈænţ i ˌhɪr oʊ ˌænt aɪ-, -ˌhiː roʊ **~es** z

antihistamine ˌænt i ˈhɪst ə miːn -mɪn, -mən ‖ ˌænţ i- ˌænţ ə-

anti-inflammatory ˌænt i ɪn ˈflæm ət ər i ◂ ‖ ˌænţ i ɪn ˈflæm ə tɔːr i ◂ ˌænt aɪ-, -toʊr i

antiknock ˌænt i ˈnɒk ‖ ˌænţ i ˈnɑːk ˌænt aɪ-

Antillean æn ˈtɪl i̯ ən **~s** z

Antilles æn ˈtɪl iːz

anti-lock ˌænt i ˈlɒk ◂ ‖ ˌænţ i ˈlɑːk ◂ ˌænt aɪ-

antilog ˈænt i lɒg ‖ ˈænţ i lɔːg ˈænt aɪ-, -lɑːg **~s** z

antilogarithm ˌænt i ˈlɒg ə rɪð əm -rɪθ· ‖ ˌænţ i ˈlɔːg- ˌænt aɪ-, -ˈlɑːg- **~s** z

antimacassar ˌænt i mə ˈkæs ə ‖ ˌænţ i mə ˈkæs ᵊr ˌænt aɪ- **~s** z

antimagnetic ˌænt i mæg ˈnet ɪk ◂ -məg'-- ‖ ˌænţ i mæg ˈneţ ɪk ◂ ˌænt aɪ-

antimalarial ˌænt i mə ˈleər i̯ əl ◂ ‖ ˌænţ i mə ˈler- ˌænt aɪ- **~s** z

antimatter ˈænt i ˌmæt ə ‖ ˈænţ i ˌmæţ ᵊr ˈænt aɪ-

antimissile ˌænt i ˈmɪs aɪᵊl ◂ ‖ ˌænţ i ˈmɪs ᵊl ◂ ˌænt aɪ- **~s** z

antimony ˈænt ɪ mən i ˈ·ə- ‖ ˈænţ ə moʊn i

anting ˈænt ɪŋ ‖ ˈænţ ɪŋ

antinomian ˌænt i ˈnəʊm i̯ ən ◂ ‖ ˌænţ i ˈnoʊm- ˌænt aɪ- **~ism** ˌɪz əm

antinomy æn ˈtɪn əm i

Antinous æn ˈtɪn əʊ əs ‖ -oʊ-

antinovel ˈænt i ˌnɒv ᵊl ‖ ˈænţ i ˌnɑːv ᵊl ˈænt aɪ-

antinuclear ˌænt i ˈnjuːk li̯ ə ◂ §-ˈnuːk-, ⚠-jəl ə ‖ ˌænţ i ˈnuːk li̯ ᵊr ˌænt aɪ-, -ˈnjuːk-, ⚠-jəl ᵊr

Antioch ˈænt i ɒk ‖ ˈænţ i ɑːk

Antiochus æn ˈtaɪ ək əs

antioxidant ˌænt i ˈɒks ɪd ənt -əd ənt ‖ ˌænţ i ˈɑːks- ˌænt aɪ- **~s** s

antiparticle ˈænt i ˌpɑːt ɪk ᵊl ‖ ˈænţ i ˌpɑːrt- ˈænt aɪ- **~s** z

Antipas 'ænt i pæs ‖ 'ænţ i-
antipasto 'ænt i ˌpæst əʊ -ˌpɑːst-, ˌ·ˈ·· ‖ ˌænţ i 'pɑːst oʊ -'pæst-
Antipater æn 'tɪp ət ə ‖ -əţ ᵊr
antipathetic ˌænt i pə 'θet ɪk ◂ æn ˌtɪp ə- ‖ ˌænţ i pə 'θeţ ɪk ◂ **~ally** ᵊl‿i
antipath|y æn 'tɪp əθ |i **~ies** iz
antipersonnel ˌænt i ˌpɜːs ə 'nel ‖ ˌænţ i ˌpɜːs- ˌænt aɪ-
ˌantiˌperson'nel mine
antiperspirant ˌænt i 'pɜːsp ᵊr ənt -ɪr ənt ‖ ˌænţ i 'pɜːsp- ˌænt aɪ- **~s** s
antiphon 'ænt ɪf ən §-əf-; -ɪ fɒn, -ə- ‖ 'ænţ ə fɑːn -əf ən **~s** z
antiphonal æn 'tɪf ᵊn əl **~ly** i
antiphrasis æn 'tɪf rəs ɪs §-əs
antipodal æn 'tɪp əd ᵊl
antipodean, A~ ₍ˌ₎æn ˌtɪp ə 'diː‿ən **~s** z
antipodes, A~ æn 'tɪp ə diːz
antipyretic ˌænt i paɪᵊ 'ret ɪk ‖ ˌænţ i paɪ 'reţ ɪk ◂ ˌænt aɪ- **~s** s
antiquarian ˌænt ɪ 'kweər i‿ən ◂ ˌ·ə- ‖ ˌænţ ə 'kwer- **~ism** ˌɪz əm **~s** z
antiquar|y 'ænt ɪk wər |i '·ək- ‖ 'ænţ ə kwer |i **~ies** iz
antiquated 'ænt ɪ kweɪt ɪd '·ə-, -əd ‖ 'ænţ ə kweɪţ əd **~ness** nəs nɪs
antique ₍ˌ₎æn 'tiːk —*formerly also* 'ænt ɪk **~ly** li **~ness** nəs nɪs
antiquit|y æn 'tɪk wət |i -wɪt- ‖ -wəţ |i **~ies** iz
anti-rac|ism ˌænt i 'reɪs ˌɪz əm ‖ ˌænţ i- ˌænt aɪ- **~ist/s** ɪst/s əst/s
antirrhinum ˌænt ɪ 'raɪn əm -ə- ‖ ˌænţ ə- **~s** z
antiscorbutic ˌænt i skɔː 'bjuːt ɪk ◂ ‖ ˌænţ i skɔːr 'bjuːţ ɪk ◂ ˌænt aɪ- **~s** s
anti-Semite ˌænt i 'siːm aɪt -'sem- ‖ ˌænţ i 'sem- ˌænt aɪ- **~s** s
anti-Semitic ˌænt i sə 'mɪt ɪk ◂ -sɪ'·- ‖ ˌænţ i sə 'mɪţ ɪk ◂ ˌænt aɪ-
anti-Semitism ˌænt i 'sem ə ˌtɪz əm -'·ɪ- ‖ ˌænţ i- ˌænt aɪ-
antisepsis ˌænt i 'seps ɪs ◂ -ə-, §-əs ‖ ˌænţ ə-
antiseptic ˌænt i 'sept ɪk ◂ -ə- ‖ ˌænţ ə- **~ally** ᵊl‿i **~s** s
antisocial ˌænt i 'səʊʃ ᵊl ◂ ‖ ˌænţ i 'soʊʃ ᵊl ◂ ˌænt aɪ- **~ly** i
anti-spam ˌænt i 'spæm ‖ ˌænţ i- ˌænt aɪ-
antispasmodic ˌænt i spæz 'mɒd ɪk ◂ ‖ ˌænţ i spæz 'mɑːd- ˌænt aɪ-
antistatic ˌænt i 'stæt ɪk ◂ ‖ ˌænţ i 'stæţ ɪk ◂ ˌænt aɪ-
Antisthenes æn 'tɪs θə niːz -ɪ-
antistrophe æn 'tɪs trəf i
antitank ˌænt i 'tæŋk ‖ ˌænţ i- ˌænt aɪ-
antith|esis æn 'tɪθ |əs ɪs -ɪs-, §-əs **~eses** ə siːz -ɪ-
antithetic ˌænt i 'θet ɪk ◂ -ə- ‖ ˌænţi 'θeţ ɪk ◂ **~al** ᵊl **~ally** ᵊl‿i
antitoxin ˌænt i 'tɒks ɪn §-ᵊn ‖ ˌænţ i 'tɑːks ᵊn ˌænt aɪ- **~s** z
antitrust ˌænt i 'trʌst ‖ ˌænţ i- ˌænt aɪ-
antitussive ˌænt i 'tʌs ɪv ‖ ˌænţ i- ˌænt aɪ- **~s** z
antivir|al ˌænt i 'vaɪᵊr |əl ‖ ˌænţ i- ˌænt aɪ- **~us** əs
antivivisection|ism ˌænt i ˌvɪv ɪ 'sek ʃᵊn| ˌɪz əm §-ˌ·ə- ‖ ˌænţ i- ˌænt aɪ- **~ist/s** ɪst/s ˌəst/s
antler 'ænt lə ‖ -lᵊr **~ed** d **~s** z
antlike 'ænt laɪk
antlion 'ænt ˌlaɪ‿ən **~s** z
Antofagasta ˌænt əf ə 'gæst ə —*Sp* [an to fa 'ɣas ta]
Antoine ɒn 'twɑːn ɑːn-, -'twæn, '·· ‖ ɑːn 'twɑːn —*Fr* [ɑ̃ twan]
Antoinette ˌænt wə 'net ˌɑːnt-, -wɑː- —*Fr* [ɑ̃ twa nɛt]
Anton 'ænt ɒn ‖ -ɑːn
Antonia æn 'təʊn i‿ə ‖ -'toʊn-
Antonian æn 'təʊn i‿ən ‖ -'toʊn- **~s** z
Antonine 'ænt ə naɪn ‖ 'ænţ-
Antoninus ˌænt ə 'naɪn əs ◂ ‖ ˌænţ-
ˌAntoˌninus 'Pius
Antonio æn 'təʊn i‿əʊ ‖ -'toʊn i‿oʊ
Antonioni ˌænt əʊn i 'əʊn i æn ˌtəʊn- ‖ ˌɑːnt oʊn 'joʊn i —*It* [an to 'njoː ni]
Antonius æn 'təʊn i‿əs ‖ -'toʊn-
antonomasia ˌænt ə nəʊ 'meɪz i‿ə æn ˌtɒn əʊ-, -'meɪʒ- ‖ ˌænt ᵊn oʊ 'meɪʒ i‿ə -'meɪʒ ə
Antonov æn 'tɒn ɒf ‖ -'tɔːn ɔːf -'tɑːn ɑːf, -'toʊn- —*Russ* [ʌn 'to nəf]
Antony 'ænt ən i ‖ -ᵊn i
antonym 'ænt ə nɪm ‖ -ᵊn ɪm **~s** z
antonym|ous æn 'tɒn əm |əs -ɪm- ‖ -'tɑːn- **~y** i
Antrim 'æntr ɪm -əm
Antrobus 'æntr əb əs
antr|um 'æntr| əm **~a** ə
antsy 'ænts i
Antwerp 'ænt wɜːp ‖ -wɜːp —*Dutch* Antwerpen ['ɑnt ʋɛrp ən]
Anubis ə 'njuːb ɪs §-əs ‖ ə 'nuːb- ə 'njuːb-
anuresis ˌæn juᵊ 'riːs ɪs §-əs
anuria ₍ˌ₎æn 'jʊər i‿ə ˌæn juᵊ 'riː‿ə ‖ -'jʊr-
anus 'eɪn əs **~es** ɪz əz
anvil 'æn vɪl -vᵊl **~s** z
Anwar 'æn wɑː ‖ 'ɑːn wɑːr
Anwen 'æn wen
Anwyl 'æn wɪl -wəl
anxiet|y æŋ 'zaɪ‿ət |i §æŋg-, -ɪt- ‖ -əţ |i **~ies** iz
anxious 'æŋkʃ əs **~ly** li **~ness** nəs nɪs
any *strong form* 'en i (!); *occasional weak form* ən i → ᵊn‿i —*In Irish English,* any *and its compounds are often* 'æn i
Anyang ˌæn 'jæŋ ‖ ˌɑːn 'jɑːŋ —*Chinese* Ānyáng [¹an ²jaŋ]
anybody 'en i bɒd i 'en ə-, -bəd i ‖ -bɑːd i —*also weak form* ən-
anyhow 'en i haʊ -ə-
anymore ˌen i 'mɔː ‖ -'mɔːr -'moʊr
anyone 'en i wʌn -ə-, §-wɒn, -wən —*also weak form* ən-
anyplace 'en i pleɪs -ə- —*also weak form* ən-
anyroad 'en i rəʊd -ə- ‖ -roʊd

A

anything 'en i θɪŋ -ə-; ⚠-θɪŋk —*also weak form* ən-
anytime 'en i taɪm
anyway 'en i weɪ -ə- **~s** z
anywhere 'en i weə -ə-, -hweə ‖ wer -hwer, -wær, -hwær, -wᵊr, -hwᵊr —*also occasional weak form* ən-
Anzac 'ænz æk
Anzio 'ænz i əʊ ‖ -oʊ 'ɑːnz- —*It* ['an tsio]
ANZUS 'ænz əs -ʊs
AOB ˌeɪ əʊ 'biː ‖ -oʊ-
A-OK, A-Okay ˌeɪ əʊ 'keɪ ‖ -oʊ-
AOL *tdmk* ˌeɪ əʊ 'el ‖ -oʊ-
aorist 'eər ɪst 'eɪ ər ɪst, -əst ‖ 'eɪ ər əst **~s** s
aoristic ₍ˌ₎eə 'rɪst ɪk ◂ ˌeɪ ə'-- ‖ ˌeɪ ə 'rɪst- **~ally** ᵊl‿i
aort|a eɪ 'ɔːt |ə ‖ -'ɔːrt̬ |ə **~al** ᵊl **~as** əz **~ic** ɪk
Aotearoa ˌɑː əʊ tiː‿ə 'rəʊ ə ‖ ˌɑː oʊ tiː ə 'roʊ ə
aoudad 'aʊd æd 'ɑː u dæd **~s** z
ap- ə, æ —*This variant of* **ad-** *is usually* ə (ap'pear), *but* æ *if stressed because of a suffix* (ˌappa'rition).
Ap *in Welsh names* æp
apace ə 'peɪs
Apache ə 'pætʃ i **~s** z —*for the obsolete sense 'ruffian', the pronunciation was* ə 'pæʃ —*Fr* [a paʃ]
Apalachicola ˌæp ə lætʃ ɪ 'kəʊl ə ◂ -ə'-- ‖ -'koʊl-
apanage 'æp ən ɪdʒ
apart ə 'pɑːt ‖ ə 'pɑːrt
apartheid ə 'pɑːt heɪt -haɪt, -eɪt, -aɪt, -aɪd ‖ ə 'pɑːrt eɪt -aɪt —*Afrikaans* [a 'part heit]
apartment ə 'pɑːt mənt ‖ ə 'pɑːrt- **~s** s
a'partment ˌbuilding; **a'partment house**
apathetic ˌæp ə 'θet ɪk ◂ ‖ -'θet̬- **~ally** ᵊl‿i
apathy 'æp əθ i
apatite 'æp ə taɪt
ape eɪp **aped** eɪpt **apes** eɪps **aping** 'eɪp ɪŋ
apelike 'eɪp laɪk
ape|man 'eɪp| mæn **~men** men
Apennines 'æp ə naɪnz -ɪ-, -e-
aperçu ˌæp ɜː 'sjuː -ə-, -'suː ‖ -ᵊr 'suː ˌɑːp- —*Fr* [a pɛʁ sy] **~s** z —*or as singular*
aperient ə 'pɪər i‿ənt ‖ ə 'pɪr- **~s** s
aperiodic ˌeɪ ˌpɪər i 'ɒd ɪk ‖ -ˌpɪr i 'ɑːd- **~ally** ᵊl i
aperiodicity ˌeɪ ˌpɪər i‿ə 'dɪs ət i ˌ'ˌi ɒ-, -ɪt i ‖ -ˌpɪr i‿ə 'dɪs ət̬ i
aperitif, apéritif ə ˌper ə 'tiːf æ-, -ɪ-, ·'· ·tɪf ‖ ɑː- —*Fr* [a pe ʁi tif] **~s** s
aperture 'æp ə tʃə -tjʊə, -tʃʊə ‖ -ᵊr tʃʊr -tʃᵊr, -tjʊr **~s** z
apeshit 'eɪp ʃɪt
apex, Apex, APEX 'eɪp eks **~es** ɪz əz
apfelstrudel 'æp fəl ˌstruːd ᵊl -ˌʃtruːd-, ˌ·'·.· —*Ger* ['apf ᵊl ˌʃtʁuːd ᵊl] **~s** z
aphaeresis æ 'fɪər əs ɪs ə-, -ɪs ɪs, §-əs ‖ ə 'fer-
aphasia ə 'feɪz i‿ə eɪ-, æ-, -'feɪʒ ə, -'feɪʒ i‿ə ‖ ə 'feɪʒ ə
aphasic ə 'feɪz ɪk eɪ-, æ-
aphelion æ 'fiːl i‿ən æp 'hiːl-
apheresis æ 'fɪər əs ɪs ə-, -ɪs ɪs, §-əs ‖ ə 'fer-
aphesis 'æf əs ɪs -ɪs ɪs, §-əs
aphetic ə 'fet ɪk æ- ‖ -'fet̬- **~ally** ᵊl‿i
aphid 'eɪf ɪd 'æf-, §-əd **~s** z
aph|is 'eɪf |ɪs 'æf-, §-əs **~ides** ɪ diːz §ə-
aphonia ₍ˌ₎eɪ 'fəʊn i‿ə ‖ -'foʊn-
aphorism 'æf ə ˌrɪz əm **~s** z
aphorist 'æf ər ɪst §-əst **~s** s
aphoristic ˌæf ə 'rɪst ɪk ◂ **~ally** ᵊl‿i
Aphra 'æf rə
aphrodisiac ˌæf rə 'dɪz i æk ‖ -'diːz- **~s** s
Aphrodite ˌæf rə 'daɪt i ‖ -'daɪt̬ i
aphtha 'æfθ ə
aphthous 'æfθ əs
Apia ɑː 'piː‿ə ə-, -ɑː
apian 'eɪp i‿ən
apiar|y 'eɪp i‿ər |i ‖ -er |i **~ies** iz **~ist/s** ɪst/s §əst/s
apical 'æp ɪk ᵊl 'eɪp-
apices 'eɪp ɪ siːz 'æp-, -ə-
apiculture 'eɪp i ˌkʌltʃ ə §-ə- ‖ -ᵊr
apiece ə 'piːs
aping 'eɪp ɪŋ
Apis *sacred bull* 'æp ɪs 'ɑːp-, 'eɪp-, §-əs
apish 'eɪp ɪʃ **~ly** li **~ness** nəs nɪs
aplastic ₍ˌ₎eɪ 'plæst ɪk -'plɑːst-
aplenty ə 'plent i ‖ ə 'plent̬ i
aplomb ə 'plɒm æ- ‖ -'plɑːm -'plʌm
apnea, apnoea æp 'niː‿ə 'æp ni‿ə
apo- *comb. form*
with stress-neutral suffix ¦æp əʊ ‖ ¦æp ə —**apogamic** ˌæp əʊ 'gæm ɪk ◂ ‖ -ə-
with stress-imposing suffix ə pɒ+ æ 'pɒ+ ‖ ə 'pɑː+ — **apogamous** ə 'pɒg əm əs æ- ‖ -'pɑːg-
apocalyps|e, A~ ə 'pɒk ə lɪps ‖ ə 'pɑːk- **~es** ɪz əz
apocalyptic ə ˌpɒk ə 'lɪpt ɪk ◂ ‖ ə ˌpɑːk- **~ally** ᵊl‿i
apocope ə 'pɒk əp i ‖ ə 'pɑːk- *(!)*
apocrypha, A~ ə 'pɒk rəf ə -rɪf ə ‖ ə 'pɑːk-
apocryphal ə 'pɒk rəf ᵊl -rɪf ᵊl ‖ ə 'pɑːk- **~ly** i
apodosis ə 'pɒd əs ɪs §-əs ‖ ə 'pɑːd-
apogee 'æp əʊ dʒiː ‖ -ə-
apolitical ˌeɪ pə 'lɪt ɪk ᵊl ◂ ‖ -'lɪt̬- **~ly** ˌi
Apollinaire ə ˌpɒl ɪ 'neə -ə- ‖ ə ˌpɑːl ə 'neᵊr -'næᵊr —*Fr* [a pɔ li nɛːʁ]
Apollinaris ə ˌpɒl ɪ 'neər ɪs -ə-, -'nɑːr-, §-əs ‖ ə ˌpɑːl ə 'ner əs
Apollo, a~ ə 'pɒl əʊ ‖ ə 'pɑːl oʊ
Apollodorus ə ˌpɒl ə 'dɔːr əs ‖ ə ˌpɑːl- -'doʊr-
Apollonian ˌæp ə 'ləʊn i‿ən ‖ -'loʊn-
Apollonius ˌæp ə 'ləʊn i‿əs ‖ -'loʊn-
Apollyon ə 'pɒl i‿ən ‖ ə 'pɑːl jən
apologetic ə ˌpɒl ə 'dʒet ɪk ◂ ‖ ə ˌpɑːl ə 'dʒet̬ ɪk ◂ **~ally** ᵊl‿i **~s** s
apologia ˌæp ə 'ləʊdʒ i‿ə -'ləʊdʒ ə ‖ -'loʊdʒ-
apologies ə 'pɒl ədʒ iz ‖ -'pɑːl-
apologis... —*see* **apologiz...**
apologist ə 'pɒl ədʒ ɪst §-əst ‖ ə 'pɑːl- **~s** s
apologiz|e ə 'pɒl ə dʒaɪz ‖ ə 'pɑːl- **~ed** d **~es** ɪz əz **~ing** ɪŋ
apologue 'æp əʊ lɒg ‖ -ə lɔːg -lɑːg **~s** z

apolog|y ə 'pɒl ədʒ |i ‖ ə 'pɑːl- **~ies** iz
apophthegm 'æp ə θem **~s** z
apoph|ysis ə 'pɒf |əs ɪs -ɪs ɪs, §-əs ‖ ə 'pɑːf- **~yses** ə siːz ɪ-
apoplectic ˌæp ə 'plekt ɪk ◂ **~ally** əl‿i
apoplexy 'æp ə pleks i
apoptosis ˌæp əp 'təʊs ɪs ˌeɪ pɒp-, §-əs ‖ -'toʊs- ˌeɪ pɑːp-
aport ə 'pɔːt ‖ ə 'pɔːrt -'poʊrt
aposiopesis ˌæp əʊ ˌsaɪ‿ə 'piːs ɪs §-əs ‖ ˌæp ə-
apostas|y ə 'pɒst əs |i ‖ ə 'pɑːst- **~ies** iz
apostate ə 'pɒst eɪt -ət, -ɪt ‖ ə 'pɑːst- *(!)* **~s** s
apostatis|e, apostatiz|e ə 'pɒst ə taɪz ‖ ə 'pɑːst- **~ed** d **~es** ɪz əz **~ing** ɪŋ
a posteriori ˌeɪ pɒ ˌster i 'ɔːr aɪ ˌɑː-, -ˌstɪər-, -i ‖ ˌɑː poʊ ˌstɪr i 'ɔːr i ˌeɪ-, ˌpɑː-, -'oʊr i
apostle ə 'pɒs əl ‖ ə 'pɑːs əl **~s, ~s'** z **~ship** ʃɪp
Aˌpostles' 'Creed
apostolate ə 'pɒst ə leɪt ‖ ə 'pɑːst-
apostolic ˌæp ə 'stɒl ɪk ◂ -ɒ- ‖ -'stɑːl- **~ally** əl‿i
ˌapoˌstolic suc'cession
apostrophe ə 'pɒs trəf i ‖ ə 'pɑːs- **~s** z
apostrophis|e, apostrophiz|e ə 'pɒs trə faɪz ‖ ə 'pɑːs- **~ed** d **~es** ɪz əz **~ing** ɪŋ
apothecar|y ə 'pɒθ ək ər‿|i -'ɪk- ‖ ə 'pɑːθ ə ker |i **~ies, ~ies'** iz
apothegm 'æp ə θem **~s** z
apotheosis ə ˌpɒθ i 'əʊs ɪs ◂ ˌæp əθ-, §-əs ‖ ə ˌpɑːθ i 'oʊs əs ˌæp əθ-
apotheosis|e, apotheosiz|e ə ˌpɒθ i 'əʊs aɪz ˌæp əθ- ‖ ə ˌpɑːθ i 'oʊs aɪz ˌæp əθ- **~ed** d **~es** ɪz əz **~ing** ɪŋ
app æp apps æps
appal ə 'pɔːl ‖ -'pɑːl **~led** d **~ling/ly** ɪŋ /li **~s** z
Appalach|ia ˌæp ə 'leɪtʃ |i‿ə -'leɪtʃ |ə; -'leɪʃ- **~ian/s** i‿ən/z ən/z
appall ə 'pɔːl ‖ -'pɑːl **~ed** d **~ing/ly** ɪŋ /li **~s** z
Appaloosa, a~ ˌæp ə 'luːs ə **~s** z
appanag|e 'æp ən ɪdʒ **~es** ɪz əz
apparat ˌæp ə 'rɑːt ‖ ˌɑːp- 'æp ə ræt
apparatchik ˌæp ə 'ræt tʃɪk -'rɑːt-, -'rætʃ ɪk, -'rɑːtʃ ɪk ‖ ˌɑːp ə 'rɑːt- -'rɑːtʃ ɪk **~s** s
apparatus *sing., pl* ˌæp ə 'reɪt əs -'rɑːt-, -'ræt- ‖ -'ræṭ əs -'reɪṭ- **~es** ɪz əz
apparel *n, v* ə 'pær əl ‖ -'per- **~ed, ~led** d **~ing, ~ling** ɪŋ **~s** z
apparent ə 'pær ənt -'peər- ‖ -'per- **~ly** li **~ness** nəs nɪs
apparition ˌæp ə 'rɪʃ ən **~s** z
appassionata ə ˌpæs i‿ə 'nɑːt ə ‖ -'nɑːṭ ə -ˌpɑːs-
appeal ə 'piːəl **appealed** ə 'piːəld **appealing/ly** ə 'piːəl ɪŋ li **appeals** ə 'piːəlz
appear ə 'pɪə ‖ ə 'pɪər **appeared** ə 'pɪəd ‖ ə 'pɪərd **appearing** ə 'pɪər ɪŋ ‖ ə 'pɪr ɪŋ **appears** ə 'pɪəz ‖ ə 'pɪərz
appearanc|e ə 'pɪər ənts ‖ ə 'pɪr- **~es** ɪz əz
appeas|e ə 'piːz **~ed** d **~ement** mənt **~er/s** ə/z ‖ ər/z **~es** ɪz əz **~ing** ɪŋ
appellant ə 'pel ənt **~s** s
appellate ə 'pel ət -ɪt, -eɪt
appellation ˌæp ə 'leɪʃ ən -ɪ-, -e- **~s** z
appellation contrôlée ˌæp ə ˌlæs i ɒ̃ kɒn 'trəʊl eɪ ‖ -ˌlɑːs i oʊn ˌkɑːn troʊ 'leɪ —*Fr* [a pe la sjɔ̃ kɔ̃ tʁo le]
appellative ə 'pel ət ɪv æ- ‖ -əṭ ɪv **~ly** li
appellee ˌæp el 'iː -ə 'liː **~s** z
append ə 'pend **~ed** ɪd əd **~ing** ɪŋ **~s** z
appendag|e ə 'pend ɪdʒ **~es** ɪz əz
appendectom|y ˌæp ən 'dekt əm |i →ˌæp m-; ˌæp en- **~ies** iz
appendicectom|y ə ˌpend ɪ 'sekt əm |i -ˌ·ə- **~ies** iz
appendices ə 'pend ɪ siːz -ə-
appendicitis ə ˌpend ə 'saɪt ɪs -ˌ·ɪ-, §-əs ‖ -'saɪṭ əs
append|ix ə 'pend |ɪks **~ices** ɪ siːz ə- **~ixes** ɪks ɪz -əz
apperceiv|e ˌæp ə 'siːv ‖ -ər- **~ed** d **~es** z **~ing** ɪŋ
apperception ˌæp ə 'sep ʃən ‖ -ər- **~s** z
apperceptive ˌæp ə 'sept ɪv ◂ ‖ -ər-
Apperley 'æp əl i ‖ -ər li
appertain ˌæp ə 'teɪn ‖ -ər- **~ed** d **~ing** ɪŋ **~s** z
appestat 'æp ɪ stæt -ə- **~s** s
appetenc|e 'æp ɪt əns -ət- **~y** i
appetent 'æp ɪt ənt -ət-
appetis|e 'æp ɪ taɪz -ə- **~er/s** ə/z ‖ ər/z **~ing/ly** ɪŋ /li
appetite 'æp ɪ taɪt -ə- **~s** s
appetiz|e 'æp ɪ taɪz -ə- **~er/s** ə/z ‖ ər/z **~ing/ly** ɪŋ /li
Appian 'æp i‿ən
ˌAppian 'Way
applaud ə 'plɔːd ‖ -'plɑːd **~ed** ɪd əd **~ing** ɪŋ **~s** z
applause ə 'plɔːz ‖ -'plɑːz
apple 'æp əl **~s** z
'apple ˌblossom; **ˌapple 'green◂**; **ˌapple 'pie**; **ˌapple 'sauce** ‖ '· · ·; **'apple tree**
Appleby 'æp əl bi
applecart 'æp əl kɑːt ‖ -kɑːrt **~s** s
apple-cheeked ˌæp əl 'tʃiːkt ◂
Appledore 'æp əl dɔː ‖ -dɔːr
Applegarth 'æp əl gɑːθ ‖ -gɑːrθ
applejack 'æp əl dʒæk
apple-pie ˌæp əl 'paɪ ◂
ˌapple-pie 'order
Appleseed 'æp əl siːd
applet 'æp lət -lɪt **~s** s
Appleton 'æp əl tən
Appleyard 'æp əl jɑːd ‖ -jɑːrd
applianc|e ə 'plaɪ‿ənts **~es** ɪz əz
applicability ə ˌplɪk ə 'bɪl ət i ˌæp lɪk-, -ɪt i ‖ -əṭ i

APPLICABLE

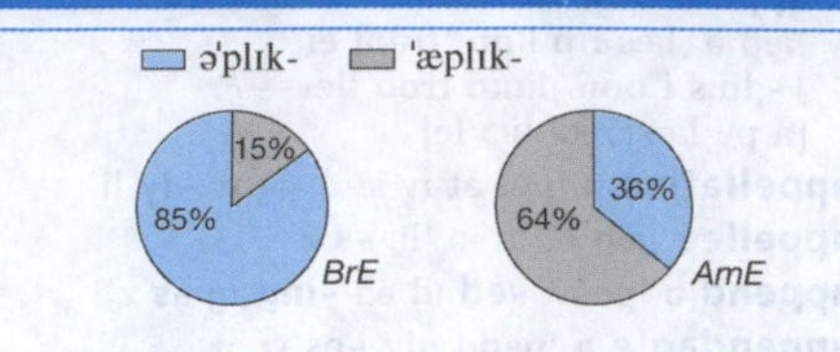

applicab|le ə 'plɪk əb |əl 'æp lɪk əb |əl **~ly** li — *Preference polls, BrE:* ə'plɪk- *85%,* 'æplɪk- *15%; AmE:* 'æplɪk- *64%,* ə'plɪk- *36%.*
applicant 'æp lɪk ənt -lək- **~s** s
application ˌæp lɪ 'keɪʃ ən -lə- **~s** z
applicator 'æp lɪ keɪt ə '·lə- ‖ -keɪţ ər **~s** z
applie... —*see* **apply**
appliqué ə 'pliːk eɪ æ- ‖ ˌæp lə 'keɪ **~d** d **~ing** ɪŋ **~s** z
apply ə 'plaɪ **applied** ə 'plaɪd **applies** ə 'plaɪz **applying** ə 'plaɪ ɪŋ
appoggiatura ə ˌpɒdʒ ə 'tʊər ə -ˌ·i‿ə'·-, -'tjʊər- ‖ ə ˌpɑːdʒ ə 'tʊr ə **~s** z
appoint ə 'pɔɪnt **appointed** ə 'pɔɪnt ɪd -əd ‖ ə 'pɔɪnţ əd **appointing** ə 'pɔɪnt ɪŋ ‖ ə 'pɔɪnţ ɪŋ **appoints** ə 'pɔɪnts
appointee ə ˌpɔɪn 'tiː ˌæp ɔɪn- **~s** z
appointive ə 'pɔɪnt ɪv ‖ ə 'pɔɪnţ ɪv
appointment ə 'pɔɪnt mənt **~s** s
Appomattox ˌæp ə 'mæt əks ‖ -'mæţ-
apport ə 'pɔːt ‖ ə 'pɔːrt -'poʊrt
apportion ə 'pɔːʃ ən ‖ ə 'pɔːrʃ ən -'poʊrʃ- **~ed** d **~ing** ‿ɪŋ **~ment/s** mənt/s **~s** z
appos|e æ 'pəʊz ə- ‖ -'poʊz **~ed** d **~es** ɪz əz **~ing** ɪŋ
apposite 'æp əz ɪt -ət; -ə zaɪt **~ly** li **~ness** nəs nɪs
apposition ˌæp ə 'zɪʃ ən
appositional ˌæp ə 'zɪʃ ən‿əl ◂ **~ly** i
appositive ə 'pɒz ət ɪv æ-, -ɪt- ‖ -'pɑːz əţ- **~ly** li
appraisal ə 'preɪz əl **~s** z
apprais|e ə 'preɪz **~ed** d **~er/s** ə/z ‖ ər/z **~es** ɪz əz **~ing** ɪŋ
appraisement ə 'preɪz mənt **~s** s
appreciab|le ə 'priːʃ əb |əl -'·i‿əb-, ə 'priːs i‿ ‖ ə 'prɪʃ- **~ly** li
appreci|ate ə 'priːʃ i |eɪt ə 'priːs- ‖ ə 'prɪʃ- **~ated** eɪt ɪd -əd ‖ eɪţ əd **~ates** eɪts **~ating** eɪt ɪŋ ‖ eɪţ ɪŋ
appreciation əˌpriːʃ i 'eɪʃ ən -ˌpriːs- ‖ ə ˌprɪʃ-
appreciative ə 'priːʃ i‿ət ɪv -'priːs-, -eɪt-; -'priːʃ ət ɪv ‖ ə 'priːʃ əţ ɪv ə 'prɪʃ-; -'·i eɪţ- **~ly** li **~ness** nəs nɪs
appreciatory ə 'priːʃ i‿ət‿ər i -'priːs-, ·ˌ· ·'eɪt ər i ◂ ‖ ə 'priːʃ ə tɔːr i -'prɪʃ-, -toʊr i
apprehend ˌæp rɪ 'hend ◂ -rə- **~ed** ɪd əd **~ing** ɪŋ **~s** z
apprehensibility ˌæp rɪ ˌhentʃ ə 'bɪl ət i ˌ·rə-, -ˌ·ə-, -ɪt i ‖ -əţ i
apprehensib|le ˌæp rɪ 'hentʃ əb |əl ˌ·rə-, -ɪb əl **~ly** li
apprehension ˌæp rɪ 'hentʃ ən -rə- **~s** z
apprehensive ˌæp rɪ 'hentʃ ɪv -rə- **~ly** li **~ness** nəs nɪs
apprentic|e ə 'prent ɪs -əs ‖ ə 'prenţ- **~ed** t **~es** ɪz əz **~ing** ɪŋ
apprenticeship ə 'prent ɪs ʃɪp →-ɪʃ·, -ɪ ·, §-əs · ‖ ə 'prenţ əs- →-əʃ·, -ə · **~s** s
appris|e, appriz|e ə 'praɪz **~ed** d **~es** ɪz əz **~ing** ɪŋ
appro 'æp rəʊ ‖ -roʊ
approach *v, n* ə 'prəʊtʃ ‖ ə 'proʊtʃ **~ed** t **~es** ɪz əz **~ing** ɪŋ
approachability ə ˌprəʊtʃ ə 'bɪl ət i -ɪt i ‖ ə ˌproʊtʃ ə 'bɪl əţ i
approachab|le ə 'prəʊtʃ əb |əl ‖ ə 'proʊtʃ- **~ly** li
appro|bate 'æp rəʊ |beɪt ‖ -rə- **~bated** beɪt ɪd -əd ‖ beɪţ əd **~bates** beɪts **~bating** beɪt ɪŋ ‖ beɪţ ɪŋ
approbation ˌæp rəʊ 'beɪʃ ən ‖ -rə-
approbative 'æp rəʊ beɪt ɪv ‖ -rə beɪţ ɪv
approbatory ˌæp rəʊ 'beɪt ər i ◂ ‖ ə 'proʊb ə tɔːr i 'æp rəb-, -toʊr i
appropriacy ə 'prəʊp ri‿əs i ‖ ə 'proʊp-
appropri|ate *v* ə 'prəʊp ri |eɪt ‖ ə 'proʊp- **~ated** eɪt ɪd -əd ‖ eɪţ əd **~ates** eɪts **~ating** eɪt ɪŋ ‖ eɪţ ɪŋ
appropriate *adj* ə 'prəʊp ri‿ət ɪt ‖ ə 'proʊp- **~ly** li **~ness** nəs nɪs
appropriation ə ˌprəʊp ri 'eɪʃ ən ‖ ə ˌproʊp- **~s** z
approval ə 'pruːv əl **~s** z
approv|e ə 'pruːv **~ed** d **~es** z **~ing/ly** ɪŋ /li
approx. ə 'prɒks ‖ ə 'prɑːks
approximant ə 'prɒks ɪm ənt -əm- ‖ ə 'prɑːks- **~s** s
approxi|mate *v* ə 'prɒks ɪ |meɪt -ə- ‖ -'prɑːks- **~mated** meɪt ɪd -əd ‖ meɪţ əd **~mates** meɪts **~mating** meɪt ɪŋ ‖ meɪţ ɪŋ
approximate *adj* ə 'prɒks ɪm ət -əm-, -ɪt ‖ ə 'prɑːks- **~ly** li
approximation ə ˌprɒks ɪ 'meɪʃ ən -ə- ‖ -ˌprɑːks- **~s** z
approximative ə 'prɒks ɪm ət ɪv -'·əm-; §-ɪ meɪt ɪv, §-ə · · ‖ ə 'prɑːks ə meɪţ ɪv **~ly** li
Apps æps
appurtenanc|e ə 'pɜːt ɪn əntʃ -ən- ‖ ə 'pɜːt ən‿əntʃ **~es** ɪz əz
appurtenant ə 'pɜːt ɪn ənt -ən- ‖ ə 'pɜːt ən‿ənt
APR ˌeɪ piː 'ɑː ‖ -'ɑːr
Aprahamian ˌæp rə 'heɪm i‿ən
apraxia (ˌ)eɪ 'præks i‿ə ə-, æ-
apres, après 'æp reɪ ‖ ˌɑː 'preɪ ◂ ˌæ- —*Fr* [a pʁɛ]
apres-ski, après-ski ˌæp reɪ 'skiː ◂ ‖ ˌɑːp-ˌæp-
apricot 'eɪp rɪ kɒt -rə- ‖ -kɑːt 'æp- **~s** s
April 'eɪp rəl -rɪl
ˌApril 'fool, ˌApril 'Fools' Day
a priori ˌeɪ praɪ 'ɔːr aɪ ˌɑː-, -pri-, -i ‖ ˌɑː pri 'ɔːr i ˌeɪ-, ˌæp ri-, -'oʊr-
aprioristic ˌeɪ ˌpraɪ‿ə 'rɪst ɪk ˌɑː-, -ˌpriː‿ -ɔː'·- **~ally** əl‿i

apriority ˌeɪ praɪ ˈɒr ət i -ɪt i ‖ ˌɑː pri ˈɔːr əṭ i ˌeɪ-, ˌæp ri-
apron ˈeɪp rən ‖ -ᵊrn **~ed** d **~ing** ɪŋ **~s** z
ˈapron strings
apropos ˌæp rə ˈpəʊ ◂ ˈ· · · ‖ -ˈpoʊ
apse æps **apses** ˈæps ɪz -əz
apsidal ˈæps ɪd ᵊl §-əd-; æp ˈsaɪd ᵊl
Apsley ˈæps li
apt æpt **apter** ˈæpt ə ‖ -ᵊr **aptest** ˈæpt ɪst §-əst
Apted ˈæpt ɪd -əd
apterous ˈæpt ər əs
apteryx ˈæpt ə rɪks
aptitude ˈæpt ɪ tjuːd -ə-, →§-tʃuːd ‖ -tuːd -tjuːd **~s** z
ˈaptitude test
apt|ly ˈæpt |li **~ness** nəs nɪs
Apuleius ˌæp ju ˈliː͜əs -ˈleɪ- ‖ -jə-
Apulia ə ˈpjuːl i͜ə —*It* Puglia [ˈpuʎ ʎa]
Apus ˈeɪp əs
Aqaba, ʻAqaba ˈæk əb ə ‖ ˈɑːk ə bɑː ˈæk-, -əb ə —*Arabic* [ˈʕɑ qɑ bah]
aq|ua ˈæk |wə ‖ ˈɑːk- ˈæk- **~uae** wiː waɪ, weɪ —*see also phrases with this word*
ˌaqua ˈfortis
aquacade ˈæk wə keɪd ‖ ˈɑːk- ˈæk- **~s** z
aquaculture ˈæk wə ˌkʌltʃ ə ‖ ˈɑːk wə ˌkʌltʃ ᵊr ˈæk-
aqualung, Aqua-Lung *tdmk* ˈæk wə lʌŋ ‖ˈɑːk- ˈæk- **~s** z
aquamarine ˌæk wə mə ˈriːn ◂ ‖ ˌɑːk- ˌæk- **~s** z
aquanaut ˈæk wə nɔːt ‖ ˈɑːk- ˈæk-, -nɑːt **~s** s
aquaplan|e ˈæk wə pleɪn ‖ ˈɑːk- ˈæk- **~ed** d **~es** z **~ing** ɪŋ
aqua regia ˌæk wə ˈriːdʒ i͜ə -ˈriːdʒ ə ‖ ˌɑːk- ˌæk-
aquarelle ˌæk wə ˈrel ‖ ˌɑːk- ˌæk- **~s** z
aquarellist ˌæk wə ˈrel ɪst §-əst ‖ ˌɑːk- ˌæk- **~s** s
aquaria ə ˈkweər i͜ə ‖ ə ˈkwer- ə ˈkwær-
Aquarian ə ˈkweər i͜ən ‖ ə ˈkwer- ə ˈkwær- **~s** z
aquarist ˈæk wər ɪst §-əst ‖ ə ˈkwer- ə ˈkwær- (*) **~s** s
aquari|um ə ˈkweər i͜ |əm ‖ ə ˈkwer- ə ˈkwær- **~a** ə **~ums** əmz
Aquarius ə ˈkweər i͜əs ‖ ə ˈkwer- ə ˈkwær-
aquarobics ˌæk wə ˈrəʊb ɪks ‖ -ˈroʊb-
Aquascutum *tdmk* ˌæk wə ˈskjuːt əm ‖ -ˈskjuːṭ-
aquatic ə ˈkwæt ɪk -ˈkwɒt- ‖ ə ˈkwɑːṭ ɪk -ˈkwæṭ- **~ally** ᵊl͜i **~s** s
aquatint ˈæk wə tɪnt ‖ ˈɑːk- ˈæk- **~s** s
aquavit ˈæk wə vɪt -viːt ‖ ˈɑːk wə viːt **~s** s
aqua vitae ˌæk wə ˈvaɪt iː -ˈviːt aɪ ‖ ˌɑːk wə ˈvaɪṭ i ˌæk-
aqueduct ˈæk wɪ dʌkt -wə- **~s** s
aqueous ˈeɪk wi əs ˈæk-
aquifer ˈæk wɪf ə -wəf- ‖ -ᵊr **~s** z
Aquila ˈæk wɪl ə -wəl-; ə ˈkwɪl ə
aquilegia ˌæk wɪ ˈliːdʒ i͜ə ˌ-wə-, -ˈliːdʒ ə **~s** z
aquiline ˈæk wɪ laɪn -wə- ‖ -wəl ən
Aquinas ə ˈkwaɪn əs æ-, -æs
Aquino ə ˈkiːn əʊ ‖ -oʊ —*Sp* [a ˈki no]
Aquitaine ˌæk wɪ ˈteɪn -wə-, ˈ· · · —*Fr* [a ki tɛn]
Aquitania ˌæk wɪ ˈteɪn i͜ə ˌ-wə-
aquiver ə ˈkwɪv ə ‖ -ᵊr
-ar ə, ɑː ‖ ᵊr, ɑːr —*In most words this ending is pronounced weak,* ə ‖ ᵊr (ˈcedar, ˈstellar). *In a few rarer or newer words it is pronounced strong,* ɑː ‖ ɑːr, *either as an alternative or as the only form* (ˈlumbar, ˈradar).
ar- ə, æ —*This variant of* ad- *is usually* ə (arˈrange), *but* æ *if stressed because of a suffix* (ˈarrogant).
Arab ˈær əb **~s** z
Arabella ˌær ə ˈbel ə ‖ ˌer-
arabesque ˌær ə ˈbesk ◂ ‖ ˌer- **~s** s
Arabia ə ˈreɪb i͜ə
Arabian ə ˈreɪb i͜ən **~s** z
AˌrabianˈNights
Arabic ˈær əb ɪk ‖ ˈer-
ˌArabic ˈnumeral
arabica ə ˈræb ɪk ə **~s** z
arabinose ə ˈræb ɪ nəʊz §-ə-, -nəʊs ‖ -noʊs -noʊz
arabis ˈær əb ɪs §-əs ‖ ˈer-
Arabist ˈær əb ɪst §-əst ‖ ˈer- **~s** s
arable ˈær əb ᵊl ‖ ˈer-
Araby ˈær əb i ‖ ˈer-
arachnid ə ˈræk nɪd §-nəd **~s** z
arachnoid ə ˈræk nɔɪd **~s** z
arachnophobia ə ˌræk nəʊ ˈfəʊb i͜ə ‖ -nə ˈfoʊb-
Arafat ˈær ə fæt ‖ ˈer-, -fɑːt —*Arabic* [ʕa ra ˈfaːt]
Arafura ˌær ə ˈfʊər ə -ˈfjʊər- ‖ ˌɑːr ə ˈfʊr ə
Aragon ˈær əg ən ‖ -ə gɑːn -əg ən —*Sp* Aragón [a ra ˈɣon]*but as a Fr family name,* [-əg õ ‖ -ə gɔːn], *Fr* [a ʁa gɔ̃]
aragonite ə ˈræg ə naɪt ˈær əg-
arak ˈær ək -æk ‖ ˈer-; ə ˈræk
Aral ˈær əl ˈɑːr-, ˈeər- ‖ ˈer-
Araldite *tdmk* ˈær əl daɪt ‖ ˈer-
aralia ə ˈreɪl i͜ə **~s** z
Aramaic ˌær ə ˈmeɪ ɪk ◂ ‖ ˌer-
Araminta ˌær ə ˈmɪnt ə ‖ -ˈmɪnṭ ə ˌer-
Aran ˈær ən ‖ ˈer-
Aranda ˈær ənd ə ə ˈrʌnt ə
Arapaho ə ˈræp ə həʊ ‖ -hoʊ
Ararat ˈær ə ræt ‖ ˈer-
Araucania ˌær ɔː ˈkeɪn i͜ə ‖ ˌer-, ˌɑː-; ə ˌrɔː-, ə ˌrɑː-
araucaria ˌær ɔː ˈkeər i͜ə ‖ -ˈker- ˌer-, ˌɑː-, -ˈkær- **~s** z
Arawak ˈær ə wæk ‖ -wɑːk ˈer- **~an** ən **~s** s
arbalest, arbalist ˈɑːb əl ɪst -əst ‖ ˈɑːrb- **~s** s
Arbela ɑː ˈbiːl ə ‖ ɑːr-
arbiter, A~ ˈɑːb ɪt ə -ət- ‖ ˈɑːrb əṭ ᵊr **~s** z
arbitrage ˈɑːb ɪ trɑːʒ -ə-, -trɪdʒ, ˌ· ·ˈtrɑːʒ ‖ ˈɑːrb-
arbitrageur ˌɑːb ɪ trɑː ˈʒɜː ˌ-ə-, -trə-ˈ-, -ˈʒʊə ‖ ˌɑːrb ə trɑː ˈʒɜː **~s** z
arbitral ˈɑːb ɪtr əl -ətr- ‖ ˈɑːrb-
arbitrament ɑː ˈbɪtr ə mənt ‖ ɑːr- **~s** s

arbitrarily ˈɑːb ɪtr ər əl i ˈ·ətr-, -ɪ li; ⚠ˈ· ·ə li; ˌɑːb ə ˈtreər· ·, -ˈtrer-, §-ˈtrær- ‖ ˌɑːr bə ˈtrer əl i
arbitrar|y ˈɑːb ɪtr ər|i ˈ·ətr-; ⚠ˈ· ·|i ‖ ˈɑːrb ə trer| i **~iness** i nəs i nɪs
arbi|trate ˈɑːb ɪ |treɪt -ə- ‖ ˈɑːrb- **~trated** treɪt ɪd -əd ‖ treɪţ əd **~trates** treɪts **~trating** treɪt ɪŋ ‖ treɪţ ɪŋ
arbitration ˌɑːb ɪ ˈtreɪʃ ən -ə- ‖ˌɑːrb- **~s** z
arbitrator ˈɑːb ɪ treɪt ə ˈ·ə-‖ ˈɑːrb ə treɪţ ər **~s** z
Arblaster ˈɑːb lɑːst ə §-læst- ‖ ˈɑːrb læst ər
arbor *'tree'* ˈɑːb ə -ɔː ‖ ˈɑːrb ər **~s** z
 ˌarbor ˈvitae ˈvaɪt iː ˈviːt aɪ ‖ ˈvaɪţ i
arbor *'arbour'; 'shaft'* ˈɑːb ə ‖ ˈɑːrb ər **~s** z
Arbor ˈɑːb ə ‖ ˈɑːrb ər
 ˈArbor Day
arboraceous ˌɑːb ə ˈreɪʃ əs ◂ -ɔː- ‖ ˌɑːrb-
arbore|al ɑː ˈbɔːr i ̮|əl ‖ ɑːr- -ˈboʊr- **~ally** əl ̮i **~ous** əs
arboresc|ence ˌɑːb ə ˈres |ənts ◂ ‖ˌɑːrb- **~ent** ənt
arboret|um ˌɑːb ə ˈriːt |əm ‖ ˌɑːrb ə ˈriːţ |əm **~a** ə
Arborfield ˈɑːb ə fiːəld ‖ ˈɑːrb ər-
arboriculture ˈɑːb ər i ˌkʌltʃ ə ˌ·· ·ˈ· ·; ɑː ˈbɒr-, ·ˌ· ·ˈ· · ‖ ˈɑːrb ər i ˌkʌltʃ ər ɑːr ˈbɔːr-, -ˈboʊr-
arborist ˈɑːb ər ɪst §-əst ‖ ˈɑːrb- **~s** s
Arborite *tdmk* ˈɑːb ə raɪt ‖ ˈɑːrb-
arbour ˈɑːb ə ‖ ˈɑːrb ər **~s** z
arbovirus ˈɑːb əʊ ˌvaɪər əs ‖ ˈɑːrb oʊ- **~es** ɪz əz
Arbroath ɑː ˈbrəʊθ ‖ ɑːr ˈbroʊθ
Arbuckle ˈɑː ˌbʌk əl ˌ·ˈ· · ‖ ˈɑːr-
Arbuthnot ɑː ˈbʌθ nət ə-, -nɒt ‖ ɑːr-
arbutus ɑː ˈbjuːt əs ‖ ɑːr ˈbjuːţ əs **~es** ɪz əz
arc ɑːk ‖ ɑːrk *(= ark)* **arced, arcked** ɑːkt ‖ ɑːrkt **arcing, arcking** ˈɑːk ɪŋ ‖ ˈɑːrk ɪŋ **arcs** ɑːks ‖ ɑːrks —*See also phrases with this word*
arcad|e ₍ı₎ɑː ˈkeɪd ‖ ɑːr- **~ed** ɪd əd **~es** z
Arcadi|a ɑː ˈkeɪd i ̮|ə ‖ ɑːr- **~an/s** ən/z
Arcady ˈɑːk əd i ‖ ˈɑːrk-
arcana ɑː ˈkeɪn ə -ˈkɑːn- ‖ ɑːr-
arcane ₍ı₎ɑː ˈkeɪn ‖ ɑːr-
arcan|um ɑː ˈkeɪn |əm -ˈkɑːn- ‖ ɑːr- **~a** ə
Arc de Triomphe ˌɑːk də ˈtriː ɒmpf -əʊmpf ‖ ˌɑːrk də tri ˈɑːmpf -ˈɔːmpf —*Fr* [aʁk də tʁi ɔ̃ːf]
arced ɑːkt ‖ ɑːrkt
arch, Arch ɑːtʃ ‖ ɑːrtʃ **arched** ɑːtʃt ‖ ɑːrtʃt **arches** ˈɑːtʃ ɪz -əz ‖ ˈɑːrtʃ- **arching** ˈɑːtʃ ɪŋ ‖ ˈɑːrtʃ-
arch- ¦ɑːtʃ ‖ ¦ɑːrtʃ — **arch-rival** ˌɑːtʃ ˈraɪv əl ‖ ˌɑːrtʃ- —*Note however the exception* archangel ¦ɑːk- ‖¦ɑːrk-, *and compare* archi-
-arch ɑːk ‖ ɑːrk — **ecclesiarch** ɪ ˈkliːz i ɑːk ‖ -ɑːrk —*but in* monarch *usually* ək *in RP.*
Archaean ɑː ˈkiː ̮ən ‖ ɑːr-
archaeo- *comb. form*
with stress-neutral suffix ¦ɑːk i əʊ ‖ ¦ɑːrk i oʊ — **archaeoastronomy** ˌɑːk i əʊ ə ˈstrɒn əm i ‖ ˌɑːrk i oʊ ə ˈstrɑːn-
with stress-imposing suffix ˌɑːk i ˈɒ+ ‖ ˌɑːrk i ˈɑː+ — **archaeopteryx** ˌɑːk i ˈɒpt ə rɪks ‖ ˌɑːrk i ˈɑːpt-
archaeological ˌɑːk i ̮ə ˈlɒdʒ ɪk əl ◂ ‖ ˌɑːrk i ̮ə ˈlɑːdʒ- **~ly** ̮i
archaeologist ˌɑːk i ˈɒl ədʒ ɪst §-əst ‖ ˌɑːrk i ˈɑːl- **~s** s
archaeology ˌɑːk i ˈɒl ədʒ i ‖ ˌɑːrk i ˈɑːl-
archaeopteryx ˌɑːk i ˈɒpt ə rɪks ‖ ˌɑːrk i ˈɑːpt-
Archaeozoic, a~ ˌɑːk i ̮ə ˈzəʊ ɪk ◂ ‖ ˌɑːrk i ̮ə ˈzoʊ ɪk ◂
archaic ₍ı₎ɑː ˈkeɪ ɪk ‖ ɑːr- **~ally** əl ̮i
archais... —*see* **archaiz...**
archaism ˈɑːk eɪ ˌɪz əm ‖ ˈɑːrk i- ˈ·eɪ- **~s** z
archaiz|e ˈɑːk eɪ aɪz -i- ‖ ˈɑːrk i- -eɪ- **~ed** d **~es** ɪz əz **~ing** ɪŋ
archangel, A~ ˈɑːk ˌeɪndʒ əl ˌ·ˈ· ·‖ˈɑːrk- **~s** z
archbishop ₍ı₎ɑːtʃ ˈbɪʃ əp ‖ ₍ı₎ɑːrtʃ- **~s** s
archbishopric ₍ı₎ɑːtʃ ˈbɪʃ əp rɪk ‖ ₍ı₎ɑːrtʃ- **~s** s
Archbold ˈɑːtʃ bəʊld →-bɒʊld ‖ ˈɑːrtʃ boʊld
archdeacon, A~ ₍ı₎ɑːtʃ ˈdiːk ən ‖ ₍ı₎ɑːrtʃ- **~s** z
archdeacon|ry ₍ı₎ɑːtʃ ˈdiːk ən |ri ‖ ₍ı₎ɑːrtʃ- **~ries** riz
archdi|ocese ˌɑːtʃ ˈdaɪ ̮|əs ɪs §-əs; ə siːz, -siːs ‖ ˌɑːrtʃ ˈdaɪ |əs əs **~oceses** ə siːz əs ɪs ɪz, -əs-, -əz; ə siːz ɪz, -siːs-, -əz ‖ ə səs əz, -iːz
archducal ˌɑːtʃ ˈdjuːk əl ◂ →§-ˈdʒuːk- ‖ ˌɑːrtʃ ˈduːk əl ˈdjuːk-
archduchess ˌɑːtʃ ˈdʌtʃ ɪs -əs ‖ˌɑːrtʃ- **~es** ɪz əz
archduch|y ˌɑːtʃ ˈdʌtʃ |i ‖ ˌɑːrtʃ- **~ies** iz
archduke ˌɑːtʃ ˈdjuːk ◂ →§-ˈdʒuːk ‖ ˌɑːrtʃ ˈduːk ◂ -ˈdjuːk **~s** s
Archean ɑː ˈkiː ̮ən ‖ ɑːr-
arched ɑːtʃt ‖ ɑːrtʃt
Archelaus ˌɑːk ɪ ˈleɪ əs -ə- ‖ ˌɑːrk-
archenem|y ˌɑːtʃ ˈen əm |i -ɪm- ‖ ˌɑːrtʃ- **~ies** iz
archeo- *comb. form*
with stress-neutral suffix ¦ɑːk i əʊ ‖ ¦ɑːrk i oʊ — **archaeoastronomy** ˌɑːk i əʊ ə ˈstrɒn əm i ‖ ˌɑːrk i oʊ ə ˈstrɑːn-
with stress-imposing suffix ˌɑːk i ˈɒ+ ‖ ˌɑːrk i ˈɑː+ — **archaeopteryx** ˌɑːk i ˈɒpt ə rɪks ‖ ˌɑːrk i ˈɑːpt-
archeological ˌɑːk i ̮ə ˈlɒdʒ ɪk əl ◂ ‖ ˌɑːrk i ̮ə ˈlɑːdʒ- **~ly** ̮i
archeologist ˌɑːk i ˈɒl ədʒ ɪst §-əst ‖ ˌɑːrk i ˈɑːl- **~s** s
archeology ˌɑːk i ˈɒl ədʒ i ‖ ˌɑːrk i ˈɑːl-
archeopteryx ˌɑːk i ˈɒpt ə rɪks ‖ ˌɑːrk i ˈɑːpt-
Archeozoic, a~ ˌɑːk i ̮ə ˈzəʊ ɪk ◂ ‖ ˌɑːrk i ̮ə ˈzoʊ ɪk ◂
archer, A~ ˈɑːtʃ ə ‖ ˈɑːrtʃ ər **~s** z
archery ˈɑːtʃ ər i ‖ ˈɑːrtʃ-
arches, A~ ˈɑːtʃ ɪz -əz ‖ ˈɑːrtʃ-
archetypal ˌɑːk i ˈtaɪp əl ◂ ˈ· ·ˌ· · ‖ ˌɑːrk- **~ly** i
archetype ˈɑːk i taɪp ‖ ˈɑːrk- **~s** s
archetypical ˌɑːk ɪ ˈtɪp ɪk əl ◂ ˌ-ə- ‖ ˌɑːrk- **~ly** ̮i
archi- ¦ɑːk i -ɪ ‖¦ɑːrk i -ə — **archicarp** ˈɑːk i kɑːp ‖ ˈɑːrk i kɑːrp
Archibald ˈɑːtʃ ɪ bɔːld -ə- ‖ ˈɑːrtʃ ə- -bɑːld

-archic *comb. form* 'ɑːk ɪk ‖ 'ɑːrk-
— **heptarchic** hep 'tɑːk ɪk ‖ -'tɑːrk-
Archie 'ɑːtʃ i ‖ 'ɑːrtʃ i
archimandrite ˌɑːk i 'mændr aɪt ◂ ‖ ˌɑːrk ə-
~s s
Archimedean ˌɑːk ɪ 'miːd i‿ən -'meɪd-;
-miː 'diː‿ən ‖ ˌɑːrk-
Archimedes ˌɑːk ɪ 'miːd iːz ◂ -ə-, -'meɪd-
‖ ˌɑːrk-
arching 'ɑːtʃ ɪŋ ‖ 'ɑːrtʃ-
archipelago ˌɑːk ɪ 'pel ə gəʊ ˌ-ə-, -ɪ gəʊ
‖ ˌɑːrk ə 'pel ə goʊ **~es, ~s** z
archiphoneme 'ɑːk i ˌfəʊn iːm ˌ· ·'· ·
‖ 'ɑːrk i ˌfoʊn- **~s** z
archiphonemic ˌɑːk i fəʊ 'niːm ɪk ◂
‖ ˌɑːrk i foʊ- **~ally** əl‿i
architect 'ɑːk ɪ tekt -ə- ‖'ɑːrk- **~s** s
architectonic ˌɑːk ɪ tek 'tɒn ɪk ◂ ˌ-ə-
‖ ˌɑːrk ə tek 'tɑːn- **~ally** əl‿i **~s** s
architectural ˌɑːk ɪ 'tek tʃər‿əl ◂ ˌ-ə- ‖ ˌɑːrk-
~ly i
architecture 'ɑːk ɪ tek tʃə '·ə-
‖ 'ɑːrk ə tek tʃər
architrave 'ɑːk ɪ treɪv -ə- ‖ 'ɑːrk- **~s** z
archival ɑː 'kaɪv əl ‖ ɑːr-
archiv|e 'ɑːk aɪv ‖ 'ɑːrk- **~ed** d **~es** z **~ing** ɪŋ
archivist 'ɑːk ɪv ɪst -əv-, §-əst ‖ 'ɑːrk- -aɪv- **~s** s
archly 'ɑːtʃ li ‖ 'ɑːrtʃ li
archon 'ɑːk ən -ɒn ‖ 'ɑːrk ɑːn **~s** z **~ship** ʃɪp
archway 'ɑːtʃ weɪ ‖ 'ɑːrtʃ- **~s** z
-archy ɑːk i ‖ ɑːrk i — **heptarchy** 'hept ɑːk i
‖ -ɑːrk i —*but in* 'anarchy, 'monarchy *usually*
ək i ‖ ərk i
arcing, arck... —*see* **arc**
arco, Arco *tdmk* 'ɑːk əʊ ‖ 'ɑːrk oʊ
arcsin, arcsine 'ɑːk saɪn ˌ·'· ‖ 'ɑːrk-
arctan 'ɑːk tæn ˌ·'· ‖ 'ɑːrk-
arctic, A~ 'ɑːkt ɪk ⚠ 'ɑːt- ‖ 'ɑːrkt- 'ɑːrt̬- **~ally**
əl‿i
ˌ**Arctic 'Circle**
Arcturus ɑːk 'tjʊər əs ‖ ɑːrk 'tʊr-
arc-weld ˌɑːk 'weld ‖ ˌɑːrk- **~ed** ɪd əd **~ing** ɪŋ
~s z
ard ɑːd ‖ ɑːrd **ards** ɑːdz ‖ ɑːrdz
-ard əd, ɑːd ‖ ərd, ɑːrd —*In well-known words this ending is* əd ‖ ərd ('standard, 'custard, 'wizard, 'Edward). *In less familiar words* ɑːd ‖ ɑːrd *is an alternative or sometimes the only pronunciation, often through the influence of the spelling* ('bollard, 'mansard). *The suffix* -ward(s) *is usually* wəd(z) ‖ wərd(z), *but* -yard *is* jɑːd ‖ jɑːrd *except usually in* 'vineyard.
Ardagh 'ɑːd ə -ɑː ‖ 'ɑːrd ə
Ardeche, Ardèche ɑː 'deʃ ‖ ɑːr- —*Fr* [aʁ dɛʃ]
Ardee ɑː 'diː ‖ ɑːr-
Arden 'ɑːd ən ‖ 'ɑːrd-
ardency 'ɑːd ənts i ‖ 'ɑːrd-
Ardennes ɑː 'den -'denz ‖ ɑːr- —*Fr* [aʁ dɛn]
ardent 'ɑːd ənt ‖ 'ɑːrd- **~ly** li
ard fhéis ˌɑːd 'eɪʃ ˌɔːd- ‖ ˌɑːrd- —*Irish*
[ɔrd̪ 'eːʃ]
rding 'ɑːd ɪŋ ‖ 'ɑːrd-
dingly 'ɑːd ɪŋ laɪ ˌ· ·'· ‖ 'ɑːrd-

Ardizzone ˌɑːd ɪ 'zəʊn i -ə- ‖ ˌɑːrd ə 'zoʊn i
Ardmore ɑːd 'mɔː →ɑːb- ‖ ɑːrd 'mɔːr -'moʊr
Ardnamurchan ˌɑːd nə 'mɜːk ən -'mɜːx-
‖ ˌɑːrd nə 'mɝːk ən
ardor, ardour 'ɑːd ə ‖ 'ɑːrd ər
Ardoyne ɑː 'dɔɪn ‖ ɑːr-
Ardrishaig ɑː 'drɪʃ ɪg -eɪg ‖ ɑːr-
Ardrossan ɑː 'drɒs ən ‖ ɑːr 'drɑːs ən -'drɔːs-
Ards ɑːdz ‖ ɑːrdz
arduous 'ɑːd ju‿əs 'ɑːdʒ u‿ ‖ 'ɑːrdʒ u‿əs **~ly** li
~ness nəs nɪs
Ardwick 'ɑːd wɪk ‖ 'ɑːrd-
are *v from* be, *strong form* ɑː ‖ ɑːr, *weak form* ə
‖ ər
are *n '100 m²'* eə ɑː ‖ eər æər, ɑːr
area 'eər i‿ə ‖ 'er- 'ær- **~s** z
'**area code**
areca ə 'riːk ə 'ær ɪk ə **~s** z
arena ə 'riːn ə **~s** z
Arendt 'ɑːr ənt —*German* ['aːʁ ənt]
Arenig ə 'ren ɪg —*Welsh* [a 're nig]
aren't ɑːnt ‖ ɑːrnt
are|ola ə 'riː‿|əl ə æ- **~olae** ə liː **~olas** əl əz
areometer ˌeər i 'ɒm ɪt ə ˌær-, -ət ə
‖ ˌer i 'ɑːm ət̬ ər ˌær- **~s** z
Areopagite ˌær i 'ɒp ə gaɪt -dʒaɪt ‖ ˌær i 'ɑːp-
ˌer- **~s** s
Areopagitic ˌær i ɒp ə 'dʒɪt ɪk -'gɪt-
‖ ˌær i ɑːp ə 'dʒɪt̬ ɪk ˌer- **~a** ə
Areopagus ˌær i 'ɒp əg əs ‖ -'ɑːp- ˌer-
Ares 'eər iːz ‖ 'er- 'ær-
arete, arête ə 'reɪt æ-, -'ret —*Fr* [a ʁɛt] **~s** s
Aretha ə 'riːθ ə
Arethusa ˌær ɪ 'θjuːz ə -ə-, -e-, -'θuːz-
‖ -'θuːz ə ˌer-
Arfon 'ɑːv ən -ɒn ‖ 'ɑːrv- -ɑːn —*Welsh*
['ar von]
argali 'ɑːg əl i ‖ 'ɑːrg- **~s** z
Argand, a~ 'ɑːg ænd -ənd ‖ ˌɑːr 'gɑːn ◂ -'gæn
—*Fr* [aʁ gɑ̃]
argent, A~ 'ɑːdʒ ənt ‖ 'ɑːrdʒ-
Argentina ˌɑːdʒ ən 'tiːn ə ‖ ˌɑːrdʒ-
Argentine *inhabitant* 'ɑːdʒ ən tiːn -taɪn
‖ 'ɑːrdʒ- **~s** z
Argentine *country* 'ɑːdʒ ən taɪn -tiːn ‖ 'ɑːrdʒ-
Argentinian ˌɑːdʒ ən 'tɪn i‿ən ◂ ‖ ˌɑːrdʒ- **~s** z
Argie 'ɑːdʒ i ‖ 'ɑːrdʒ i **~s** z
argillaceous ˌɑːdʒ ɪ 'leɪʃ əs ◂ -ə- ‖ ˌɑːrdʒ-
arginine 'ɑːdʒ ɪ niːn -ə-, -naɪn ‖ 'ɑːrdʒ-
Argive 'ɑːg aɪv 'ɑːdʒ- ‖ 'ɑːrdʒ- 'ɑːrg- **~s** z
Argo 'ɑːg əʊ ‖ 'ɑːrg oʊ
argol 'ɑːg ɒl -əl ‖ 'ɑːrg ɑːl -ɔːl, -əl
Argolis 'ɑːg ə lɪs ‖ 'ɑːrg-
argon 'ɑːg ɒn -ən ‖ 'ɑːrg ɑːn
Argonaut 'ɑːg ə nɔːt ‖ 'ɑːrg- -nɑːt **~s** s
Argos 'ɑːg ɒs ‖ 'ɑːrg ɑːs -əs
argos|y 'ɑːg əs |i ‖ 'ɑːrg- **~ies** iz
argot 'ɑːg əʊ -ət, -ɒt ‖ 'ɑːrg oʊ -ət
arguab|le 'ɑːg ju‿əb |əl ‖ 'ɑːrg- **~ly** li
argu|e 'ɑːg juː ‖ 'ɑːrg- **~ed** d **~es** z **~ing** ɪŋ
argument 'ɑːg ju mənt -jə- ‖ 'ɑːrg jə- **~s** s
argumentation ˌɑːg ju men 'teɪʃ ən ˌ-jə-,
-mən'-- ‖ ˌɑːrg jə mən- -men'--

argumentative ˌɑːg ju ˈment ət ɪv ◂ ˌ·jə- ‖ ˌɑːrg jə ˈmenṭ əṭ ɪv ◂ **~ly** li **~ness** nəs nɪs
argus, Argus ˈɑːg əs ‖ ˈɑːrg-
argy-bargy ˌɑːdʒ i ˈbɑːdʒ i ‖ ˌɑːrdʒ i ˈbɑːrdʒ i
Argyle, a~, Argyll ₍ˌ₎ɑː ˈgaɪəl ‖ ₍ˌ₎ɑːr-ˈ· ·—*For the name of the type of sock and sock pattern, AmE prefers the stressing* ˈ· ·
Argyrol *tdmk* ˈɑːdʒ ə rɒl -ɪ- ‖ ˈɑːrdʒ ə roʊl -rɑːl, -rɔːl
Arhus ˈɔː huːs ˈɑː-, -hʊs ‖ ˈɑːr- ˈɔːr- —*Danish* Århus [ˈɔː huːʔ s]
aria ˈɑːr i‿ə **~s** z
Ariadne ˌær i ˈæd ni ‖ ˌer-, -ˈɑːd-
Arial ˈeər i‿əl ‖ ˈer- ˈær-
Arian ˈeər i‿ən ‖ ˈer- ˈær- **~s** z
-arian *comb. form* ˈeər i‿ən ‖ ˈer- ˈær- — **libertarian** ˌlɪb ə ˈteər i‿ən ‖ -ər ˈter- -ˈtær-
Ariane ˌær i ˈæn ‖ ˌɑːr i ˈɑːn —*Fr* [a ʁjan]
Arianna ˌær i ˈæn ə ‖ ˌer-
arid ˈær ɪd §-əd ‖ ˈer- **~ly** li **~ness** nəs nɪs
aridit|y ə ˈrɪd ət |i æ-, -ɪt i ‖ -əṭ |i **~ies** iz
Ariel, ariel ˈeər i‿əl ‖ ˈer- ˈær-
Arien ˈeər i‿ən ‖ ˈer- ˈær-
Aries ˈeər iːz ˈeər i iːz ‖ ˈer iːz ˈær-, ˈ·i iːz
arietta ˌær i ˈet ə ‖ ˌɑːr i ˈeṭ ə ˌær-, ˌer- —*It* [a ri ˈet ta] **~s** z
aright ə ˈraɪt
aril ˈær əl -ɪl ‖ ˈer- **~s** z
-arily ər‿əl i ər‿ li; ˈer·-, §ˈær- · ‖ ˈer əl i —*Compare* -ary. *The traditional RP form is now increasingly replaced by* ˈer-, *giving a mismatch between adjective and adverb; see* (necessarily, primarily, voluntarily)
Arimathaea, Arimathea ˌær ɪm ə ˈθiː‿ə ˌ·əm- ‖ ˌer-
arioso ˌɑːr i ˈəʊz əʊ ˌær-, -ˈəʊs- ‖ -ˈoʊs oʊ -ˈoʊz- **~s** z
Ariosto ˌær i ˈɒst əʊ ‖ ˌɑːr i ˈɑːst oʊ -ˈɔːst-, -ˈoʊst- —*It* [a ˈrjɔs to, a ri ˈɔs to]
arise ə ˈraɪz **arisen** ə ˈrɪz ən *(!)* **arises** ə ˈraɪz ɪz -əz **arising** ə ˈraɪz ɪŋ **arose** ə ˈrəʊz ‖ ə ˈroʊz
Aristaeus ˌær ɪ ˈstiː‿əs -ə- ‖ ˌer-
Aristarchus ˌær ɪ ˈstɑːk əs -ə- ‖ -ˈstɑːrk- ˌer-
Aristide ˌær ɪ ˈstiːd ‖ ˌer-, -ə- —*Fr* [a ʁis tid]
Aristides ˌær ɪ ˈstaɪd iːz -ə- ‖ ˌer-
Aristippus ˌær ɪ ˈstɪp əs -ə- ‖ ˌer-
aristo ə ˈrɪst əʊ ‖ -oʊ **~s** z
Aristoc *tdmk* ˈær ɪ stɒk -ə- ‖ -stɑːk ˈer-
aristocrac|y ˌær ɪ ˈstɒk rəs |i ˌ·ə- ‖ -ˈstɑːk- ˌer- **~ies** iz
aristocrat ˈær ɪst ə kræt ˈ·əst-, ə ˈrɪst- ‖ ə ˈrɪst- **~s** s
aristocratic ˌær ɪst ə ˈkræt ɪk ◂ ˌ·əst-, ə ˌrɪst- ‖ ə ˌrɪst ə ˈkræṭ ɪk ◂ **~ally** əl‿i
Aristophanes ˌær ɪ ˈstɒf ə niːz ˌ·ə- ‖ -ˈstɑːf- ˌer-
Aristophanic ˌær ɪst ə ˈfæn ɪk ◂ ˌ·əst-, -ɒˈ·- ‖ ˌer-
Aristotelian ˌær ɪst ə ˈtiːl i‿ən ◂ ˌ·əst-, -ɒˈ·-, -ˈtel- ‖ ˌer- **~s** z
ˌAristoˌtelian ˈlogic
Aristotle ˈær ɪ stɒt əl ˈ·ə- ‖ -stɑːṭ əl ˈer-
arithmetic *n* ə ˈrɪθ mə tɪk
arithmetic *adj* ˌær ɪθ ˈmet ɪk ◂ -əθ- ‖ -ˈmeṭ ɪk ◂ ˌer- **~al** əl **~ally** əl‿i
ˌarithˌmetic proˈgression
arithmetician ə ˌrɪθ mə ˈtɪʃ ən ˌær ɪθ-, ˌær əθ- **~s** z
-arium *comb. form* ˈeər i‿əm ‖ ˈer- ˈær- — **planetarium** ˌplæn ə ˈteər i‿əm ˌ·ɪ- ‖ -ˈter- -ˈtær-
Arizon|a ˌær ɪ ˈzəʊn |ə ◂ -ə- ‖ -ˈzoʊn |ə ˌer- **~an/s** ən/z **~ian/s** i‿ən/z
Arjuna ˈɑːdʒ ʊn ə ‖ ˈɑːrdʒ- —*Hindi* [ər dʒʊn]
ark, Ark ɑːk ‖ ɑːrk **arks** ɑːks ‖ ɑːrks
Arkansan ɑː ˈkænz ən ‖ ɑːr- **~s** z
Arkansas ˈɑːk ən sɔː ‖ ˈɑːrk- -sɑː —*but the* A~ River *is also* ɑː ˈkænz əs ‖ ɑːr-
Arkell *(i)* ˈɑːk əl ‖ ˈɑːrk-, *(ii)* ɑː ˈkel ‖ ɑːr-
Arkhangelsk ˌɑːk æŋ ˈgelsk ɑː ˈkæŋ gelsk ‖ ɑːr ˈkɑːn gelsk —*Russ* [ʌr ˈxan gʲilʲsk]
Arkle ˈɑːk əl ‖ ˈɑːrk-
Arklow ˈɑːk ləʊ ‖ ˈɑːrk loʊ
Arkwright ˈɑːk raɪt ‖ ˈɑːrk-
Arlen ˈɑːl ən ‖ ˈɑːrl-
Arlene ˈɑːl iːn ‖ ɑːr ˈliːn
Arles ɑːlz ɑːl ‖ ɑːrl —*Fr* [aʁl]
Arlette ₍ˌ₎ɑː ˈlet ‖ ɑːr-
Arlington ˈɑːl ɪŋ tən ‖ ˈɑːrl-
Arlott ˈɑːl ət ‖ ˈɑːrl-
arm ɑːm ‖ ɑːrm **armed** ɑːmd ‖ ɑːrmd **arming** ˈɑːm ɪŋ ‖ ˈɑːrm ɪŋ **arms** ɑːmz ‖ ɑːrmz
armada ɑː ˈmɑːd ə ‖ ɑːr- —*formerly* -ˈmeɪd- **~s** z
Armadale ˈɑːm ə deɪəl ‖ ˈɑːrm-
armadillo ˌɑːm ə ˈdɪl əʊ ‖ ˌɑːrm ə ˈdɪl oʊ **~s** z
Armageddon ˌɑːm ə ˈged ən ‖ ˌɑːrm-
Armagh ˌɑː ˈmɑː ◂ ‖ ˌɑːr-
Armagnac, a~ ˈɑːm ən jæk ‖ ˌɑːrm ən ˈjæk -ˈjɑːk —*Fr* [aʁ ma njak]
Armalite, ArmaLite *tdmk* ˈɑːm ə laɪt ‖ ˈɑːrm- **~s** s
armament ˈɑːm ə mənt ‖ ˈɑːrm- **~s** s
armamentarium ˌɑːm ə men ˈteər i‿əm -mənˈ·- ‖ ˌɑːrm ə men ˈter-
Armand ˈɑːm ənd ‖ ɑːr ˈmɑːn —*Fr* [aʁ mɑ̃]
Armani ɑː ˈmɑːn i ‖ ɑːr- —*It* [ar ˈmaː ni]
Armathwaite ˈɑːm ə θweɪt ‖ ˈɑːrm-
Armatrading ˌɑːm ə ˈtreɪd ɪŋ ‖ ˌɑːrm-
armature ˈɑːm ətʃ ə -ə tjʊə, -ə tʃʊə ‖ ˈɑːrm ə tʃʊr -tʊr, -ətʃ ər **~s** z
armband ˈɑːm bænd ‖ ˈɑːrm- **~s** z
armchair ˈɑːm tʃeə ˌ·ˈ· ‖ ˈɑːrm tʃer -tʃær **~s** z
armed ɑːmd ‖ ɑːrmd
ˌarmed ˈforces
Armeni|a ɑː ˈmiːn i‿|ə ‖ ɑːr- **~an/s** ‿ən/z
Armentieres, Armentières ˈɑːm ən tɪəz ˌ·ˈ· ‖ ˌɑːrm ən ˈtjeər —*Fr* [aʁ mɑ̃ tjɛːʁ]
armeria ɑː ˈmɪər i‿ə ‖ ɑːr ˈmɪr-
Armfield ˈɑːm fiːəld ‖ ˈɑːrm-
armful ˈɑːm fʊl ‖ ˈɑːrm- **~s** z
armhole ˈɑːm həʊl →-hɒʊl ‖ ˈɑːrm hoʊl **~s** z
Armidale ˈɑːm ɪ deɪəl -ə- ‖ ˈɑːrm-
armie... —*see* **army**

armiger, A~ ˈɑːm ɪdʒ ə §-ədʒ- ‖ ˈɑːrm ɪdʒ ᵊr **~s** z
armigerous ɑː ˈmɪdʒ ər əs ‖ ɑːr-
armillary ɑː ˈmɪl ər i ˈɑːm ɪl- ‖ ˈɑːrm ə ler i ɑːr ˈmɪl ər i
Arminian ɑː ˈmɪn i‿ən ‖ ɑːr- **~ism** ˌɪz əm **~s** z
Arminius ɑː ˈmɪn i‿əs ‖ ɑːr-
Armistead ˈɑːm ɪ sted -stɪd ‖ ˈɑːrm-
armistic|e ˈɑːm ɪst ɪs -əst-, §-əs; §ɑː ˈmɪst ɪs ‖ ˈɑːrm- **~es** ɪz əz
ˈArmistice Day
Armitage ˈɑːm ɪt ɪdʒ -ət- ‖ ˈɑːrm əṭ-
armlet ˈɑːm lət -lɪt ‖ ˈɑːrm- **~s** s
Armley ˈɑːm li ‖ ˈɑːrm-
armload ˈɑːm ləʊd ‖ ˈɑːrm loʊd **~s** z
armlock ˈɑːm lɒk ‖ ˈɑːrm lɑːk **~s** s
armoire ɑː ˈmwɑː ‖ ɑːr ˈmwɑːr **~s** z
armor, A~ ˈɑːm ə ‖ ˈɑːrm ᵊr **~ed** d **armoring** ˈɑːm ər ɪŋ ‖ ˈɑːrm- **~s** z
ˌarmored ˈcar; ˌarmor ˈplate ‖ ˈ· · ·
armorer ˈɑːm ər ə ‖ ˈɑːrm ər ᵊr **~s** z
armorial ɑː ˈmɔːr i‿əl ‖ ɑːr- -ˈmoʊr- **~s** z
Armoric|a ɑː ˈmɒr ɪk |ə ‖ ɑːr ˈmɔːr- -ˈmɑːr- **~an/s** ən/z
armor|y ˈɑːm ər |i ‖ ˈɑːrm- **~ies** iz
armour, A~ ˈɑːm ə ‖ ˈɑːrm ᵊr **~ed** d **armouring** ˈɑːm ər ɪŋ ‖ ˈɑːrm- **~s** z
ˌarmoured ˈcar; ˌarmour ˈplate ‖ ˈ· · ·
armourer ˈɑːm ər ə ‖ ˈɑːrm ər ᵊr **~s** z
armour|y ˈɑːm ər |i ‖ ˈɑːrm- **~ies** iz
armpit ˈɑːm pɪt ‖ ˈɑːrm- **~s** s
armrest ˈɑːm rest ‖ ˈɑːrm- **~s** s
arms ɑːmz ‖ ɑːrmz
ˈarms race
Armstrong ˈɑːm strɒŋ ‖ ˈɑːrm strɔːŋ -strɑːŋ
arm|y ˈɑːm |i ‖ ˈɑːrm |i **~ies** iz
ˌarmy ˈofficer
Arndale ˈɑːn deɪᵊl ‖ ˈɑːrn-
Arne ɑːn ‖ ɑːrn
Arnhem ˈɑːn əm ‖ ˈɑːrn- —*Dutch* [ˈɑrn hɛm, -əm]
ˈArnhem Land
arnica ˈɑːn ɪk ə ‖ ˈɑːrn-
Arnie ˈɑːn i ‖ ˈɑːrn i
Arno ˈɑːn əʊ ‖ ˈɑːrn oʊ —*It* [ˈar no]
Arnold ˈɑːn ᵊld ‖ ˈɑːrn-
Arnot, Arnott ˈɑːn ət -ɒt ‖ ˈɑːrn- -ɑːt
A-road ˈeɪ rəʊd ‖ -roʊd **~s** z
aroint ə ˈrɔɪnt
aroma ə ˈrəʊm ə ‖ ə ˈroʊm ə **~s** z
aromatherap|y ə ˌrəʊm ə ˈθer əp |i ·ˌ··ˈ··· ‖ -ˌroʊm- **~ist/s** ɪst/s §əst/s
aromatic ˌær ə ˈmæt ɪk ◂ -əʊ- ‖ -ˈmæṭ- ˌer- **~ally** ᵊl i
aromaticity ˌær ə mə ˈtɪs ət i -mæˈ--, ə ˌrəʊm ə-, -ɪt i ‖ -əṭ i ˌer-; ə ˌroʊm ə-
aromatis|e, aromatiz|e ə ˈrəʊm ə taɪz ‖ ə ˈroʊm- **~ed** d **~es** ɪz əz **~ing** ɪŋ
Aronowitz ə ˈrɒn ə wɪts ‖ ə ˈrɑːn-
arose ə ˈrəʊz ‖ ə ˈroʊz
around ə ˈraʊnd
around-the-clock ə ˌraʊnd ðə ˈklɒk ◂ ‖ -ˈklɑːk ◂

arousal ə ˈraʊz ᵊl **~s** z
arous|e ə ˈraʊz **~ed** d **~es** ɪz əz **~ing** ɪŋ
Arp ɑːp ‖ ɑːrp
arpeggio ɑː ˈpedʒ i əʊ -ˈpedʒ əʊ ‖ ɑːr ˈpedʒ i oʊ -ˈpedʒ oʊ **~ed** d **~s** z
arquebus ˈɑːk wɪb əs -wəb- ‖ ˈɑːrk- **~es** ɪz əz
arrack ˈær ək -æk ‖ ˈer-; ə ˈræk
arraign ə ˈreɪn **~ed** d **~ing** ɪŋ **~ment/s** mənt/s **~s** z
Arran ˈær ən ‖ ˈer-
arrange ə ˈreɪndʒ **arranged** ə ˈreɪndʒd **arranges** ə ˈreɪndʒ ɪz -əz **arranging** ə ˈreɪndʒ ɪŋ
arrangement ə ˈreɪndʒ mənt **~s** s
arranger ə ˈreɪndʒ ə ‖ -ᵊr **~s** z
arrant ˈær ənt ‖ ˈer- **~ly** li
arras ˈær əs ‖ ˈer- **~es** ɪz əz
Arras ˈær əs ‖ ˈer- —*Fr* [a ʁɑːs]
Arrau ə ˈraʊ —*Sp* [a ˈrrau]
array ə ˈreɪ **arrayed** ə ˈreɪd **arraying** ə ˈreɪ ɪŋ **arrays** ə ˈreɪz
arrear ə ˈrɪə ‖ ə ˈrɪᵊr **~s** z
arrearag|e ə ˈrɪər ɪdʒ ‖ ə ˈrɪr- **~es** ɪz əz
Arrecife ˌær ə ˈsiːf eɪ -ɪ-, -e- ‖ ˌɑːr- —*Sp* [a rre ˈθi fe, -ˈsi-]
arrest *v, n* ə ˈrest **~ed** ɪd əd **~ing/ly** ɪŋ /li **~s** s
arrestable ə ˈrest əb ᵊl
arrester, arrestor ə ˈrest ə ‖ -ᵊr **~s** z
arrhythmia ə ˈrɪð mi‿ə eɪ-
Arrian ˈær i‿ən ‖ ˈer-
arriere-pensee, arrière-pensée ˌær i eə ˈpɒ̃ᵗs eɪ -pɒn ˈseɪ ‖ -ˌer pɑːn ˈseɪ ˌer- —*Fr* [a ʁjɛʁ pɑ̃ se]
arris ˈær ɪs §-əs ‖ ˈer- **~es** ɪz əz
Arriva *tdmk* ə ˈriːv ə
arrival ə ˈraɪv ᵊl **~s** z
arˈrival time
arrive ə ˈraɪv **arrived** ə ˈraɪvd **arrives** ə ˈraɪvz **arriving** ə ˈraɪv ɪŋ
arrivederci ə ˌriːv ə ˈdɜːtʃ i -ˈdeətʃ- ‖ -ˈdertʃ i —*It* [ar ri ve ˈder tʃi]
arriving ə ˈraɪv ɪŋ
arriviste, ~s ˌær iː ˈviːst -ˈvɪst; ə ˈriːv ɪst ‖ ˌer- —*Fr* [a ʁi vist]
Arrochar ˈær ək ə -əx- ‖ -ᵊr ˈer-
arrogance ˈær əg ənᵗs ‖ ˈer-
arrogant ˈær əg ənt ‖ ˈer- **~ly** li
arro|gate ˈær ə |geɪt ‖ ˈer- **~gated** geɪt ɪd -əd ‖ geɪṭ əd **~gates** geɪts **~gating** geɪt ɪŋ ‖ geɪṭ ɪŋ
arrogation ˌær ə ˈgeɪʃ ᵊn ‖ ˌer- **~s** z
arrondissement ˌær ɒn ˈdiːs mɒ̃ ‖ æ ˌrɑːnd iːs ˈmɑːn ə- —*Fr* [a ʁɔ̃ dis mɑ̃]
arrow ˈær əʊ ‖ -oʊ ˈer- **~ed** d **~ing** ɪŋ **~s** z
arrowhead ˈær əʊ hed ‖ -oʊ- ˈer- **~s** z
arrowroot ˈær əʊ ruːt ‖ -oʊ- ˈer-
Arrowsmith ˈær əʊ smɪθ ‖ -oʊ- ˈer-
arrowwood ˈær əʊ wʊd ‖ -oʊ- ˈer-
arroyo ə ˈrɔɪ əʊ ‖ -oʊ —*Sp* [a ˈrro jo] **~s** z
ars ɑːz ‖ ɑːrs
ˌars poˈetica pəʊ ˈet ɪk ə ‖ poʊ ˈeṭ-

arse ɑːs ‖ æs ɑːrs **arsed** ɑːst ‖ æst ɑːrst **arses** 'ɑːs ɪz -əz ‖ 'æs- 'ɑːrs- **arsing** 'ɑːs ɪŋ ‖ 'æs- 'ɑːrs-
arsehole 'ɑːs həʊl →-hɒʊl ‖ 'æs hoʊl 'ɑːrs- **~d** d **~s** z
arse-lick|er 'ɑːs ˌlɪk ə ‖ 'æs ˌlɪk ᵊr **~ers** əz ‖ ᵊrz **~ing** ɪŋ
arsenal, A~ 'ɑːs ᵊn‿əl ‖ 'ɑːrs- **~s, ~'s** z
arsenate 'ɑːs ə neɪt -ɪ-; -ən ət, -ɪn-, -ɪt ‖ 'ɑːrs- **~s** s
arsenic *adj* ɑː 'sen ɪk ‖ ɑːr- **~al/s** ᵊl/z
arsenic *n* 'ɑːs ᵊn‿ɪk ‖ 'ɑːrs-
arsenide 'ɑːs ə naɪd -ɪ- ‖ 'ɑːrs- **~s** z
arsine 'ɑːs iːn ‖ 'ɑːrs- ɑːr 'siːn
arsis 'ɑːs ɪs §-əs ‖ 'ɑːrs-
arson 'ɑːs ᵊn ‖ 'ɑːrs-
arsonist 'ɑːs ᵊn ɪst §-əst ‖ 'ɑːrs- **~s** s
art *n* ɑːt ‖ ɑːrt *—but in certain French phrases also* ɑː ‖ ɑːr **arts** ɑːts ‖ ɑːrts *—See also phrases with this word*
'art form; **ˌarts and 'crafts**; **'Arts ˌFaculty**
art *v, from* **be**, *usual form* ɑːt ‖ ɑːrt, *occasional weak form* ət ‖ ᵊrt
Art *name* ɑːt ‖ ɑːrt
Artaxerxes ˌɑːt ə 'zɜːks iːz -əg-, -ək-, '·ˌ·ˌ·· ‖ ˌɑːrṱ ə 'zɜ·ːks iːz
art deco, Art Deco ˌɑːt 'dek əʊ ˌɑː-, -'deɪk- ‖ ˌɑːrt deɪ 'koʊ ˌɑːr-, -'deɪk oʊ *—Fr* Art Déco [aʁ de ko]
artefact 'ɑːt ɪ fækt -ə- ‖ 'ɑːrṱ- **~s** s
Artemis 'ɑːt ɪm ɪs -əm-, §-əs ‖ 'ɑːrṱ-
artemisia ˌɑːt ɪ 'mɪz i‿ə ˌ-ə-, -'miːz- ‖ ˌɑːrṱ ə 'mɪʒ ə -'mɪʒ i‿ə, -'mɪz- **~s** z
Artemus 'ɑːt ɪm əs -əm- ‖ 'ɑːrṱ-
arterial ɑː 'tɪər i‿əl ‖ ɑːr 'tɪr- **~ly** i
arteries 'ɑːt ər iz ‖ 'ɑːrṱ-
arteriole ɑː 'tɪər i əʊl →-ɒʊl ‖ ɑːr 'tɪr i oʊl **~s** z
arteriosclerosis ɑː ˌtɪər i əʊ sklə 'rəʊs ɪs -sklɪə'--, -sklɪ'--, §-əs ‖ ɑːr ˌtɪr i oʊ sklə 'roʊs əs
Arterton 'ɑːt ət ən ‖ 'ɑːrṱ ᵊrt ᵊn
arter|y 'ɑːt ər |i ‖ 'ɑːrṱ- **~ies** iz
artesian ɑː 'tiːz i‿ən -'tiːʒ-; -'tiːʒ ᵊn ‖ ɑːr 'tiːʒ ᵊn
arˌtesian 'well
Artex *tdmk* 'ɑːt eks ‖ 'ɑːrt-
artful 'ɑːt fᵊl -fʊl ‖ 'ɑːrt- **~ly** ‿i
ˌArtful 'Dodger
Arthington *(i)* 'ɑːð ɪŋ tən ‖ 'ɑːrð-, *(ii)* 'ɑːθ- ‖ 'ɑːrθ-
arthr- *comb. form before vowel*
with stressed suffix ɑː θr+ ‖ ɑːr θr+ — **arthralgia** ɑː 'θrældʒ i‿ə ‖ ɑːr-
with unstressed suffix ¦ɑːθ r+ ‖ ¦ɑːrθ r+ — **arthrous** 'ɑːθ rəs ‖ 'ɑːrθ-
arthritic ɑː 'θrɪt ɪk ‖ ɑːr 'θrɪṱ ɪk **~ally** ᵊl‿i
arthritis ɑː 'θraɪt ɪs ⚠ˌɑːθ ə 'raɪt-, §-əs ‖ ɑːr 'θraɪṱ əs
arthro- *comb. form*
with stress-neutral suffix ¦ɑːθ rəʊ ‖ ¦ɑːrθ rə — **arthrospore** 'ɑːθ rəʊ spɔː ‖ 'ɑːrθ rə spɔːr -spoʊr
with stress-imposing suffix ɑː 'θrɒ+ ‖ ɑːr 'θrɑː+ — **arthropodous** ɑː 'θrɒp əd əs ‖ ɑːr 'θrɑːp-
arthropod 'ɑːθ rə pɒd ‖ 'ɑːrθ rə pɑːd **~s** z
Arthur 'ɑːθ ə ‖ 'ɑːrθ ᵊr
Arthurian ɑː 'θjʊər i‿ən -'θʊər- ‖ ɑːr 'θʊr-
arti... *—see* **arty**
artic *'articulated vehicle'* ɑː 'tɪk 'ɑːt ɪk ‖ ɑːr- **~s** s
artichoke 'ɑːt ɪ tʃəʊk -ə- ‖ 'ɑːrṱ ə tʃoʊk **~s** s
article 'ɑːt ɪk ᵊl ‖ 'ɑːrṱ- **~d** d **~s** z
articulacy ɑː 'tɪk jʊl əs i -'·jəl- ‖ ɑːr 'tɪk jəl əs i
articulate *adj* ɑː 'tɪk jʊl ət -jəl-, -ɪt ‖ ɑːr 'tɪk jəl ət **~ly** li **~ness** nəs nɪs
articu|late *v* ɑː 'tɪk ju |leɪt -jə- ‖ ɑːr 'tɪk jə- **~lated** leɪt ɪd -əd ‖ leɪṱ əd **~lates** leɪts **~lating** leɪt ɪŋ ‖ leɪṱ ɪŋ
articulation ɑː ˌtɪk ju 'leɪʃ ᵊn -jə- ‖ ɑːr ˌtɪk jə- **~s** z
articulative ɑː 'tɪk jʊl ət ɪv -ju leɪt ɪv ‖ ɑːr 'tɪk jəl əṱ ɪv -jə leɪṱ-
articulator ɑː 'tɪk ju leɪt ə -'·jə- ‖ ɑːr 'tɪk jə leɪṱ ᵊr
articulator|y ɑː 'tɪk jʊl ət‿ər |i -'·jəl-; ɑː ˌtɪk ju 'leɪt ər |i, -ˌ·jə-, ·'·····‖ ɑːr 'tɪk jəl ə tɔːr |i -toʊr i **~ily** əl i ɪ li
Artie 'ɑːt i ‖ 'ɑːrṱ i
artifact 'ɑːt ɪ fækt -ə- ‖ 'ɑːrṱ- **~s** s
artific|e 'ɑːt ɪf ɪs -əf-, §-əs ‖ 'ɑːrṱ- **~es** ɪz əz
artificer ɑː 'tɪf ɪs ə -əs- ‖ ɑːr 'tɪf əs ᵊr **~s** z
artificial ˌɑːt ɪ 'fɪʃ ᵊl ◂ -ə- ‖ ˌɑːrṱ- **~ly** i
ˌartiˌficial in'telligence; **ˌartiˌficial 'kidney**; **ˌartiˌficial ˌrespi'ration**
artificiality ˌɑːt ɪ ˌfɪʃ i 'æl ət i ˌ-ə-, -ɪt i ‖ ˌɑːrṱ ə ˌfɪʃ i 'æl əṱ i
artillery ɑː 'tɪl ər‿i ‖ ɑːr-
artillery|man ɑː 'tɪl ər‿i |mən -mæn ‖ ɑːr- **~men** mən men
artisan ˌɑːt ɪ 'zæn -ə-, '·ˌ·· ‖ 'ɑːrṱ əz ən -əs- *(*)* **~s** z
artisanal ɑː 'tɪz ᵊn‿əl ˌɑːt ɪ 'zæn ᵊl ◂ ‖ 'ɑːrṱ əz-
artisanate ˌɑːt ɪ 'zæn eɪt -ə- ‖ 'ɑːrṱ əz ə neɪt '·əs-
artist 'ɑːt ɪst §-əst ‖ 'ɑːrṱ əst **~s** s
artiste ɑː 'tiːst ‖ ɑːr- *—Fr* [aʁ tist] **~s** s
artistic ɑː 'tɪst ɪk ‖ ɑːr- **~ally** ᵊl‿i
artistry 'ɑːt ɪst ri §-əst- ‖ 'ɑːrṱ-
artless 'ɑːt ləs -lɪs ‖ 'ɑːrt- **~ly** li **~ness** nəs nɪs
art nouveau, Art Nouveau ˌɑːt nuː 'vəʊ ˌɑː- ‖ ˌɑːrt nuː 'voʊ ˌɑːr- *—Fr* [aʁ nu vo]
Artois ɑː 'twɑː ‖ ɑːr- *—Fr* [aʁ twa]
artsy 'ɑːts i ‖ 'ɑːrts i
artsy-craftsy ˌɑːts i 'krɑːfts i ◂ §-'kræfts- ‖ ˌɑːrts i 'kræfts i ◂
artsy-fartsy ˌɑːts i 'fɑːts i ◂ ‖ ˌɑːrts i 'fɑːrts i ◂
Arturo ɑː 'tʊər əʊ ‖ ɑːr 'tʊr oʊ *—It* [ar 'tuː ro]
artwork 'ɑːt wɜːk ‖ 'ɑːrt wɜ·ːk
art|y 'ɑːt |i ‖ 'ɑːrṱ |i **~ier** i‿ə ‖ i‿ᵊr **~iest** i‿ɪst i‿əst **~ily** ɪ li əl i **~iness** i nəs i nɪs

Articulation

1 **Articulation** is the production of speech sounds by using the speech organs to modify the air stream set in motion by the lungs. (Regularly in some languages, and very occasionally in English, the air may be set in motion in a way not involving the lungs. This applies, for example, in CLICKS.) Consonants are classified according to their **place** and **manner** of articulation.

2 English consonant sounds have the following **places of articulation**:

p, b, m	are **bilabials**	articulated by the lower lip against the upper lip
f, v	are **labiodentals**	articulated by the lower lip against the upper teeth
θ, ð	are **dentals**	articulated by the tongue tip against the upper teeth
t, d, n, l, s, z	are **alveolars**	articulated by the tongue tip or blade against the alveolar ridge
r, tr, dr	are **post-alveolars**	articulated by raising the tongue tip towards the rear of the alveolar ridge
ʃ, ʒ, tʃ, dʒ	are **palato-alveolars**	articulated by the retracted blade of the tongue against the alveolar ridge and hard palate (usually accompanied by some lip-rounding)
j	is a **palatal**	articulated by raising the front of the body of the tongue towards the hard palate
k, g, ŋ	are **velars**	articulated by the back of the tongue against the soft palate
w	is a **labial-velar**	articulated by raising the back of the tongue towards the soft palate and rounding the lips
ʔ	is a **glottal**	(see GLOTTAL STOP)

3 Note that in some other languages there are also:

- **alveolo-palatals** articulated by the front of the body of the tongue against the hard palate, together with raising the blade of the tongue towards the alveolar ridge (e.g. the Japanese *sh* ɕ)
- **labial-palatals** articulated like palatals but with rounding of the lips (e.g. the French ɥ in *juin* ʒɥæ̃)
- **retroflexes** articulated by curling the tongue tip back against the alveolar ridge or hard palate (e.g. the Hindi *ṭ* ʈ)

Articulation ►

Articulation continued

- **uvulars** articulated by the extreme back of the tongue against the uvula (e.g. the French *r* ʁ)
- **pharyngals** articulated by squeezing the pharynx (e.g. the Arabic ʕ)

4 English consonants have the following typical **manners of articulation**:

p, t, k, b, d, g	are **plosives**	articulated with a complete obstruction of the mouth passage, entirely blocking the air-flow for a moment
f, v, θ, ð, s, z, ʃ, ʒ	are **fricatives**	articulated by narrowing the mouth passage so as to make the air-flow turbulent, while allowing it to pass through continuously
tʃ, dʒ (and also usually tr, dr)	are **affricates**	articulated with first a complete obstruction and then a narrowing of the mouth passage (see AFFRICATES)
m, n, ŋ	are **nasals**	articulated by completely obstructing the mouth passage but allowing the air to pass out through the nose
r, l	are **liquids**	articulated by diverting or modifying the air-flow through the mouth
j, w	are **semivowels**	articulatorily like vowels, but functioning as consonants because they are not syllabic

Plosives, fricatives, and affricates are all **obstruents**; nasals, liquids, and semivowels are **sonorants**. Liquids and semivowels are usually **approximants** (= the air escapes freely through the mouth with no turbulence).

arty-crafty ˌɑːt i ˈkrɑːft i ◂ §-ˈkræft- ‖ ˌɑːrţ i ˈkræft i ◂

arty-farty ˌɑːt i ˈfɑːt i ◂ ‖ ˌɑːrţ i ˈfɑːrţ i ◂

Arub|a ə ˈruːb |ə —*Dutch* [ɑ ˈryː baː] **~an/s** ən/z

arugula ə ˈruːg əl ə -jʊl-, -jəl-

arum ˈeər əm ‖ ˈer- ˈær-

Arun ˈær ən ‖ ˈer-

Arunachal ˌær u ˈnɑːtʃ ᵊl ‖ ˌer- —*Hindi* [ə rʊ ŋaː tʃəl]

Arundel *(i)* ˈær ənd ᵊl ‖ ˈer-, *(ii)* ə ˈrʌnd ᵊl —*The place in Sussex is (i), that in MD (ii).*

arvo ˈɑːv əʊ ‖ -oʊ **~s** z

Arwel ˈɑː wel ‖ ˈɑːr- —*Welsh* [ˈar wel]

Arwyn ˈɑː wɪn ‖ ˈɑːr- —*Welsh* [ˈar win, -wɨn]

-ary əri, eri —*In words of three syllables this suffix is usually weak,* ər i (ˈbinary, ˈglossary). *In longer words it is usually weak in BrE,* ər i *(frequently reduced to* ri*); but strong in AmE,* er i*: thus* ˈarbitrary ˈɑːb ɪtr ər i ‖ ˈɑːrb ə trer i, ˈcustomary ˈkʌst əm ər i ‖ ˈkʌst ə mer i. *The stress may fall either one or two syllables further back* (exˈemplary, ˌanniˈversary; ˈmercenary, ˌinterˈplanetary). *A few words differ in stress as between BrE and AmE* (coˈrollary ‖ ˈcorollary).

Aryan ˈeər i ən ˈɑːr- ‖ ˈer- ˈær-, ˈɑːr- **~s** z

aryl ˈær ɪl -əl ‖ ˈer-

arytenoid ˌær ɪ ˈtiːn ɔɪd ◂ -ə- ‖ ə ˈrɪt ᵊn ɔɪd ˌær ə ˈtiːn ɔɪd, ˌer- *(*)* **~s** z
ˌaryˌtenoid ˈcartilage ‖ ·ˌ· · ··

as *strong form* æz, *weak form* əz

as- *This variant of* ad- *is usually* ə, *but* æ *if stressed because of a suffix* (asˈsign; ˌassigˈnation).

Asa *(i)* ˈeɪs ə, *(ii)* ˈeɪz ə, *(iii)* ˈɑːs ə

asafetida, asafoetida ˌæs ə ˈfet ɪd ə -ˈfiːt-, §-əd- ‖ -ˈfeţ əd ə

asap *'as soon as possible'* ˌeɪ es eɪ 'piː —*sometimes spoken as* 'eɪs æp, 'æs-

Asaph 'æs əf

asarabacca ˌæs ər ə 'bæk ə

asbestos æs 'best əs æz-, -ɒs

asbestosis ˌæs be 'stəʊs ɪs ˌæz-, §-əs ‖ -'stoʊs-

Asbo 'æz bəʊ ‖ -boʊ **~s** z

Asbury 'æz bər‿i ‖ 'æz ˌber i -bər‿i

ˌAsbury 'Park

Ascalon 'æsk ə lɒn -əl ən ‖ -lɑːn

ascarid 'æsk ə rɪd **~s** z

ascend ə 'send —*also, when in contrast with* descend, ˌæ- **~ed** ɪd əd **~ing** ɪŋ **~s** z

ascendanc|e ə 'send ənᵗs **~y** i

ascendant ə 'send ənt

ascendenc|e ə 'send ənᵗs **~y** i

ascendent ə 'send ənt

ascender ə 'send ə ‖ -ᵊr **~s** z

ascension, A~ ə 'senᵗʃ ᵊn

As'cension Day

Ascensiontide ə 'senᵗʃ ᵊn taɪd

ascent ə 'sent —*also, when in contrast with* descent, ˌæ- *(= assent)* **~s** s

ascertain ˌæs ə 'teɪn ‖ -ᵊr- **~ed** d **~ing** ɪŋ **~s** z

ascertainable ˌæs ə 'teɪn əb ᵊl ◂ ‖ -ᵊr-

ascertainment ˌæs ə 'teɪn mənt →-'teɪm- ‖ -ᵊr-

ascetic ə 'set ɪk æ- ‖ -'set̬ ɪk **~ally** ᵊl‿i **~s** s

asceticism ə 'set ɪ ˌsɪz əm æ-, -ə‚- ‖ -'set̬-

Asch æʃ

Ascham 'æsk əm

Ascherson 'æʃ əs ən ‖ -ᵊrs-

asci 'æsk aɪ 'æs-, -iː

ascidian ə 'sɪd i‿ən **~s** z

ASCII 'æsk i

ASCIIzation ˌæsk i aɪ 'zeɪʃ ᵊn -i ɪ- ‖ -i‿ə- **~s** z

Asclepius ə 'skliːp i‿əs æ-

Ascomycetes, a~ ˌæsk əʊ maɪ 'siːt iːz ‖ -oʊ maɪ 'siːt̬ iːz

Ascona æ 'skəʊn ə ‖ -'skoʊn- —*It* [as 'koː na]

ascorbic ə 'skɔːb ɪk æ- ‖ -'skɔːrb-

Ascot, ascot 'æsk ət §-ɒt ‖ -ɑːt **~'s, ~s** s

ascribable ə 'skraɪb əb ᵊl

ascrib|e ə 'skraɪb **~ed** d **~es** z **~ing** ɪŋ

ascription ə 'skrɪp ʃᵊn æ- **~s** z

ascus 'æsk əs **asci** 'æsk aɪ 'æs-, -iː

Asda *tdmk* 'æz də

asdic 'æz dɪk **~s** s

-ase eɪz eɪs — **oxidase** 'ɒks ɪ deɪz -ə-, -deɪs ‖ 'ɑːks-

ASEAN 'æz i‿ən 'æs-

asepsis ₍ˌ₎eɪ 'seps ɪs ə-, æ-

aseptic ₍ˌ₎eɪ 'sept ɪk ə-, æ-

asexual ₍ˌ₎eɪ 'sek ʃu‿əl æ-, -'seks ju‿əl, -'sek ʃᵊl **~ly** i

Asfordby 'æs fəd bi 'æz-, →-fəb- ‖ -fᵊrd-

Asgarby 'æz gə bi ‖ -gᵊr-

Asgard 'æs gɑːd 'æz- ‖ -gɑːrd

ash, Ash æʃ **ashes** 'æʃ ɪz -əz

ˌAsh 'Wednesday

ashamed ə 'ʃeɪmd

Ashanti ə 'ʃænt i ‖ -'ʃɑːnt-

Ashbee 'æʃ bi -biː

ashbin 'æʃ bɪn **~s** z

Ashbourne 'æʃ bɔːn ‖ -bɔːrn -boʊrn

Ashburton æʃ 'bɜːt ᵊn 'æʃ ˌbɜːt-, -bət- ‖ 'æʃ ˌbɝːt ᵊn

Ashby 'æʃ bi

Ashby-de-la-Zouch ˌæʃ bi də lə 'zuːʃ ˌ· ·ˌde·'·, -lɑː'·

ashcan 'æʃ kæn **~s** z

Ashcombe 'æʃ kəm

Ashcroft 'æʃ krɒft ‖ -krɔːft -krɑːft

Ashdod 'æʃ dɒd ‖ -dɑːd

Ashdown 'æʃ daʊn

Ashe æʃ

ashen 'æʃ ᵊn

Asher 'æʃ ə ‖ -ᵊr

ashes, Ashes 'æʃ ɪz -əz

Asheville 'æʃ vɪl

Ashfield 'æʃ fiːᵊld

Ashford 'æʃ fəd ‖ -fᵊrd

Ashgabat ˌæʃ kə 'bæt -xə- ‖ ˌɑːʃ kə 'bɑːt —*Turkmen* Aşgabat [aʃ χa 'bat]

ashi... —*see* **ashy**

Ashington 'æʃ ɪŋ tən

Ashkenaz|i, ~y ˌæʃ kə 'nɑːz |i -kɪ- ‖ ˌɑːʃ- **~im** ɪm §-əm

Ashkhabad 'æʃ kə bæd -bɑːd; ˌ· ·'·, ˌɑːʃ- ‖ ˌɑːʃ kə 'bɑːd '· · · —*Russ* [əʃ xʌ 'bat]

ashlar 'æʃ lə ‖ -lᵊr **~s** z

Ashleigh, Ashley, Ashlie 'æʃ li

Ashman 'æʃ mən

Ashmole 'æʃ məʊl →-mɒʊl ‖ -moʊl

Ashmolean æʃ 'məʊl i‿ən ‖ -'moʊl-

Ashmore 'æʃ mɔː ‖ -mɔːr -moʊr

ashore ə 'ʃɔː ‖ ə 'ʃɔːr -'ʃoʊr

ashplant 'æʃ plɑːnt §-plænt ‖ -plænt **~s** s

ashram 'æʃ rəm 'ɑːʃ-, -ræm **~s** z

Ashton 'æʃt ən

Ashton-in-Makerfield ˌæʃt ən ɪn 'meɪk ə fiːᵊld →-ɪm'-- ‖ -ᵊr fiːᵊld

Ashton-under-Lyne ˌæʃt ən ˌʌnd ə 'laɪn ˌ·'·· · ‖ -ˌʌnd ᵊr-

Ashtoreth 'æʃt ə reθ

ashtray 'æʃ treɪ **~s** z

Ashurst 'æʃ hɜːst -ɜːst ‖ -hɝːst

Ashwell 'æʃ wel -wᵊl

Ashworth 'æʃ wɜːθ ‖ -wɝːθ

ash|y 'æʃ |i **~ier** i‿ə ‖ i‿ᵊr **~iest** i‿ɪst i‿əst

Asia 'eɪʒ ə 'eɪʃ ə — *Preference polls, AmE:* 'eɪʒ ə *91%,* 'eɪʃ ə *9%; BrE:* 'eɪʒ ə *64%,* 'eɪʃ ə *36%; those born before 1942,* 'eɪʒ ə *32%,* 'eɪʃ ə *68%. See chart on p. 48.*

ˌAsia 'Minor

Asiago ˌæz i 'ɑːg əʊ ‖ ˌɑːs i 'ɑːg oʊ ˌɑːz-, ˌɑːʃ-, ˌɑːʒ- —*It* [a 'zjaː go]

Asian 'eɪʒ ᵊn 'eɪʃ- **~s** z *See preference polls at* Asia

Asiana *tdmk* ˌæs i 'ɑːn ə

Asian-American ˌeɪʒ ᵊn‿ə'mer ɪk ən ◂ ˌeɪʃ-

Asiatic ˌeɪʒ i 'æt ɪk ◂ ˌeɪz-, ˌeɪʃ-, ˌeɪs- ‖ -'æt̬ ɪk ◂ **~s** s

Asics *tdmk* 'æz ɪks 'æs-

aside ə 'saɪd **~s** z

Asimov 'æs ɪ mɒv 'æz-, -ə- ‖ 'æz ə mɑːf -mɔːf

A

ASIA

ˈeɪʒə ˈeɪʃə

9% 91% AmE

36% 64% BrE

BrE ˈeɪʒə by age

Percentage 80 70 60 50 40 30 0

Older ◄— Speakers —► Younger

asinine ˈæs ɪ naɪn -ə- **~ly** li
asininity ˌæs ɪ ˈnɪn ət i ˌ-ə-, -ɪt i ‖ -əṭ i
ask ɑːsk §æsk, ⚠ɑːks ‖ æsk **asked** ˈɑːs*k*t §æs*k*t, ⚠ɑːkst ‖ æs*k*t **asking** ˈɑːsk ɪŋ §ˈæsk-, ⚠ˈɑːks- ‖ ˈæsk ɪŋ **asks** ɑːsks §æsks, ⚠ˈɑːks ɪz ‖ æsks
  ˈasking price
askance ə ˈskænᵗs -ˈskɑːnᵗs ‖ ə ˈskænᵗs
askari æ ˈskɑːr i ə- **~s** z
Aske æsk
Askelon ˈæsk əl ən -ɪl-, -ə lɒn, -ɪ- ‖ -ə lɑːn
askew *adv* ə ˈskjuː
Askew *family name* ˈæsk juː
Askey ˈæsk i
Askham ˈæsk əm
Askrigg ˈæsk rɪg
aslant ə ˈslɑːnt §-ˈslænt ‖ ə ˈslænt
asleep ə ˈsliːp
ASLEF ˈæz lef
A/S level ˌeɪ ˈes ˌlev ᵊl **~s** z
ASLIB ˈæz lɪb
Asmara æs ˈmɑːr ə æz- ‖ -ˈmær-, -ˈmer-
Asmodeus æs ˈməʊd i‿əs ˌæs məʊ ˈdiː‿əs ‖ ˌæz mə ˈdiː‿əs
asocial (ˌ)eɪ ˈsəʊʃ ᵊl ‖ -ˈsoʊʃ-
Asoka ə ˈsəʊk ə -ˈʃəʊk- ‖ ə ˈsoʊk ə —*Hindi* [ə ʃoːk]
asp æsp **asps** æsps
asparagus ə ˈspær əg əs -ˈsper-
aspartame ˈæsp ə teɪm ə ˈspɑːt eɪm ‖ -ᵊr-
aspartic ə ˈspɑːt ɪk ‖ ə ˈspɑːrṭ-
Aspasia æ ˈspeɪz i‿ə ə-, -ˈspeɪʒ- ‖ æ ˈspeɪʒ ə
Aspatria ə ˈspeɪtr i‿ə æ-
aspect ˈæsp ekt **~s** s
  ˈaspect ˌratio
aspectual æ ˈspek tʃu‿əl ə-, -tju‿ **~ly** i
Aspel, Aspell ˈæsp ᵊl
aspen, Aspen ˈæsp ən **~s** z
Asperger's ˈæsp ɜːg əz ‖ -ɝːg ᵊrz
Asperges, a~ æ ˈspɜːdʒ iːz ə- ‖ -ˈspɝːdʒ-
asperit|y æ ˈsper ət |i ə-, -ɪt- ‖ -əṭ |i **~ies** iz
aspersion ə ˈspɜːʃ ᵊn æ-, §-ˈspɜːʒ- ‖ -ˈspɝːʒ- -ˈspɝːʃ- **~s** z
asphalt ˈæs fælt ˈæʃ-, -fɔːlt, ⚠-felt ‖ -fɔːlt -fɑːlt **~ed** ɪd əd **~ing** ɪŋ **~s** s
asphodel ˈæs fə del ˈæʃ- **~s** z
asphyxia æs ˈfɪks i‿ə əs-
asphyxiant æs ˈfɪks i‿ənt əs-
asphyxi|ate æs ˈfɪks i |eɪt əs- **~ated** eɪt ɪd -əd ‖ eɪṭ əd **~ates** eɪts **~ating** eɪt ɪŋ ‖ eɪṭ ɪŋ
asphyxiation æs ˌfɪks i ˈeɪʃ ᵊn əs- **~s** z
aspic ˈæsp ɪk
aspidistra ˌæsp ɪ ˈdɪs trə -ə- **~s** z
Aspinall ˈæsp ɪn ᵊl -ən-; -ɪ nɔːl, -ə-
aspirant ˈæsp ər ənt -ɪr-; ə ˈspaɪᵊr- **~s** s
aspirate *n* ˈæsp ər‿ət -ɪr-, ɪt **~s** s
aspi|rate *v* ˈæsp ə |reɪt -ɪ- **~rated** reɪt ɪd -əd ‖ reɪṭ əd **~rates** reɪts **~rating** reɪt ɪŋ ‖ reɪṭ ɪŋ
aspiration ˌæsp ə ˈreɪʃ ᵊn -ɪ- **~al** ‿əl **~s** z
aspirator ˈæsp ə reɪt ə ˈ-ɪ- ‖ -reɪṭ ᵊr **~s** z
aspire ə ˈspaɪ‿ə ‖ ə ˈspaɪ‿ᵊr **~d** d **~s** z **aspiring** ə ˈspaɪ‿ər ɪŋ ‖ ə ˈspaɪ‿ᵊr ɪŋ
aspirin ˈæsp rɪn -rən; ˈæsp ər ən, -ɪn **~s** z
aspiring ə ˈspaɪ‿ər ɪŋ ‖ ə ˈspaɪ‿ᵊr ɪŋ **~ly** li
asplenium æ ˈspliːn i‿əm ə- **~s** z
Aspley ˈæsp li
Asprey ˈæsp ri
Aspro *tdmk* ˈæsp rəʊ ‖ -roʊ **~s** z
Asquith ˈæsk wɪθ
ass æs —*As a term of abuse, in BrE also* ɑːs *(which may however be taken as a pronunciation rather of* arse) **asses** ˈæs ɪz -əz
Assad ˈæs æd ‖ ˈɑːs ɑːd —*Arabic* [ˈas ad]
assagai ˈæs ə gaɪ **~s** z
assai æ ˈsaɪ —*It* [as ˈsai]
assail ə ˈseɪᵊl **~ed** d **~ing** ɪŋ **~s** z
assailant ə ˈseɪl ənt **~s** s
Assam æ ˈsæm ˈæs æm
Assamese ˌæs ə ˈmiːz ◂ -æ- ‖ -ˈmiːs
assassin ə ˈsæs ɪn -ᵊn **~s** z
assassi|nate ə ˈsæs ɪ |neɪt -ə- **~nated** neɪt ɪd -əd ‖ neɪṭ əd **~nates** neɪts **~nating** neɪt ɪŋ ‖ neɪṭ ɪŋ
assassination ə ˌsæs ɪ ˈneɪʃ ᵊn -ə- **~s** z
assault ə ˈsɔːlt -ˈsɒlt ‖ -ˈsɑːlt **~ed** ɪd əd **~ing** ɪŋ **~s** s
  asˈsault course
assay *n* ə ˈseɪ æ-; ˈæs eɪ ‖ ˈæs eɪ æ ˈseɪ **~s** z
assay *v* ə ˈseɪ æ- **~ed** d **~er/s** ə/z ‖ ᵊr/z **~ing** ɪŋ **~s** z
assegai ˈæs ɪ gaɪ -ə- **~s** z
assemblag|e ə ˈsem blɪdʒ —*but with reference to wine blending,* ˌæs ɒm ˈblɑːʒ ‖ ˌɑːs ɑːm- —*Fr* [a sɑ̃ blaːʒ] **~es** ɪz əz
assembl|e ə ˈsem bᵊl **~ed** d **~er/s** ‿ə/z ‖ ᵊr/z **~es** z **~ing** ‿ɪŋ
assem|bly ə ˈsem |bli **~blies** bliz
  asˈsembly ˌlanguage; asˈsembly line

Aspiration

An **aspirated** consonant is one that is accompanied by a brief h-sound.

In certain environments the English plosives p, t, k are aspirated. That is to say, there is a delay between the release of the primary closure of the articulators and the beginning of voicing for the sound that follows. In the word **pan** pæn, for example, the voicing for æ does not begin immediately after the lips separate for the end of the p. There is a moment's delay, during which the air escapes freely through the mouth, impeded neither by the lips nor by the vocal folds. This constitutes the aspiration of the p. It is one of the ways we recognize the plosive as being a p rather than a b.

We can distinguish three possibilities for the aspiration of English p, t, k, depending on their position.

1 They are **aspirated**

when they occur at the **beginning of a syllable** in which the vowel is strong as in

pin pɪn (like pʰɪn)
tail teɪᵊl
come kʌm
appeal ə ˈpiːᵊl
retain ri ˈteɪn
maritime ˈmær ɪ taɪm.

If one of l, r, w, j comes between the plosive and the vowel, then aspiration takes the form of making this consonant voiceless as in

play pleɪ (here the l is voiceless)
approve ə ˈpruːv (the r is voiceless)
twin twɪn (the w is voiceless)
accuse ə ˈkjuːz (the j is voiceless).

2 They are **unaspirated**

- when preceded by s at the beginning of a syllable as in **spin** spɪn (the ɪ starts immediately upon the release of the p), **stack** stæk, **school** skuːl, **screen** skriːn (the r may be voiced)
- when followed by any FRICATIVE as in **lapse** læps, **depth** depθ, **sets** sets, **fix** fɪks
- if immediately followed by another plosive as with the k in **doctor** ˈdɒktə ‖ ˈdɑːkt ᵊr. The release stage of the first plosive is then usually inaudible ('masked').

3 Otherwise, they are **unaspirated** or just **slightly aspirated.** For example:

ripe raɪp, **shut** ʃʌt, **lake** leɪk
happy ˈhæp i, **writer** ˈraɪt ə (BrE), **lucky** ˈlʌk i
wasp wɒsp ‖ wɑːsp, **resting** ˈrest ɪŋ, **Oscar** ˈɒsk ə ‖ ˈɑːsk ᵊr, **lifted** ˈlɪft ɪd
today tə ˈdeɪ (note that the t, although at the beginning of a syllable, is followed by a WEAK vowel).

assembly|man ə 'sem bli |mən **~men** mən men **~woman** ˌwʊm ən **~women** ˌwɪm ɪn §-ən
assent *n, v* ə 'sent (= *ascent*) **assented** ə 'sent ɪd -əd ‖ ə 'senţ əd **assenting** ə 'sent ɪŋ ‖ ə 'senţ ɪŋ **assents** ə 'sents
Asser 'æs ə ‖ -ᵊr
assert ə 'sɜːt ‖ ə 'sɜˑːt **asserted** ə 'sɜːt ɪd -əd ‖ ə 'sɜˑːţ əd **asserting** ə 'sɜːt ɪŋ ‖ ə 'sɜˑːţ ɪŋ **asserts** ə 'sɜːts ‖ ə 'sɜˑːts
assertion ə 'sɜːʃ ᵊn ‖ ə 'sɜˑːʃ ᵊn **~s** z
assertive ə 'sɜːt ɪv ‖ ə 'sɜˑːţ ɪv **~ly** li **~ness** nəs nɪs
assess ə 'ses **~ed** t **~es** ɪz əz **~ing** ɪŋ
assessment ə 'ses mənt **~s** s
assessor ə 'ses ə ‖ -ᵊr **~s** z
asset 'æs et -ɪt **~s** s
asset-strip|per 'æs et ˌstrɪp| ə -ɪt- ‖ -ᵊr **~pers** əz ‖ ᵊrz **~ping** ɪŋ
asseve|rate ə 'sev ə |reɪt æ- **~rated** reɪt ɪd -əd ‖ reɪţ əd **~rates** reɪts **~rating** reɪt ɪŋ ‖ reɪţ ɪŋ
asseveration ə ˌsev ə 'reɪʃ ᵊn æ- **~s** z
assez 'æs eɪ ‖ ɑː 'seɪ —*Fr* [a se]
asshole 'ɑːs həʊl 'æs-, →-hɒʊl ‖ 'æs hoʊl **~s** z
assibi|late ə 'sɪb ə |leɪt æ-, -ɪ- **~lated** leɪt ɪd -əd ‖ leɪţ əd **~lates** leɪts **~lating** leɪt ɪŋ ‖ leɪţ ɪŋ
assibilation ə ˌsɪb ə 'leɪʃ ᵊn æ-, -ɪ- **~s** z
assiduit|y ˌæs ɪ 'djuː‿ət |i ˌ-ə-, →-'dʒuː‿, ɪt i ‖ -'duː əţ |i -'djuː- **~ies** iz
assiduous ə 'sɪd ju‿əs §-'sɪdʒ u‿ ‖ ə 'sɪdʒ u‿əs **~ly** li **~ness** nəs nɪs
assign ə 'saɪn **~ed** d **~ing** ɪŋ **~s** z
assignab|le ə 'saɪn əb |ᵊl **~ly** li
assig|nat 'æs ɪg |næt ˌæs iː |'njɑː **~nats** næts 'njɑːz —*Fr* [a si nja]
assignation ˌæs ɪg 'neɪʃ ᵊn **~s** z
assignee ˌæs aɪ 'niː -ɪ-, §-ə- ‖ ə ˌsaɪ 'niː ˌæs ə 'niː **~s** z
assignment ə 'saɪn mənt →-'saɪm- **~s** s
assimilable ə 'sɪm əl əb ᵊl -'ɪl-
assimi|late ə 'sɪm ə |leɪt -ɪ- **~lated** leɪt ɪd -əd ‖ leɪţ əd **~lates** leɪts **~lating** leɪt ɪŋ ‖ leɪţ ɪŋ
assimilation ə ˌsɪm ə 'leɪʃ ᵊn -ɪ- **~s** z
assimilative ə 'sɪm əl ət ɪv -ə leɪt ɪv ‖ -ə leɪţ ɪv -əl əţ- **~ly** li
assimilatory ə 'sɪm əl ət‿ər i -'·ɪl-; ·ˌ·ə 'leɪt ər i, -ˌ·ɪ- ‖ -ə tɔːr i -toʊr i
Assiniboin, Assiniboine ə 'sɪn ɪ bɔɪn -ə- **~s** z
Assisi ə 'siːs i æ-, -'siːz- ‖ -'sɪs- —*It* [as 'siː zi]
assist ə 'sɪst **~ed** ɪd əd **~ing** ɪŋ **~s** s
assistance ə 'sɪst ənᵗs
assistant ə 'sɪst ənt **~s** s
As͵sistant Pro'fessor; **As͵sistant 'Secretary**
assiz|e ə 'saɪz **~es** ɪz əz
associ|ate *v* ə 'səʊs i‿eɪt -'səʊʃ- ‖ ə 'soʊʃ- ə 'soʊs- **~ated** eɪt ɪd -əd ‖ eɪţ əd **~ates** eɪts **~ating** eɪt ɪŋ ‖ eɪţ ɪŋ — *Preference poll, BrE:* -'səʊs- *69%*, -'səʊʃ- *31%*.

ASSOCIATE (verb)

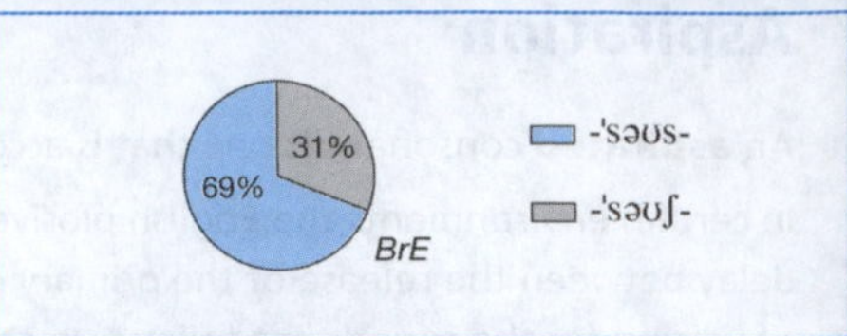

associate *n, adj* ə 'səʊs i‿ət -'səʊʃ-, -ɪt, -eɪt ‖ ə 'soʊʃ- ə 'soʊs- **~s** s

ASSOCIATION

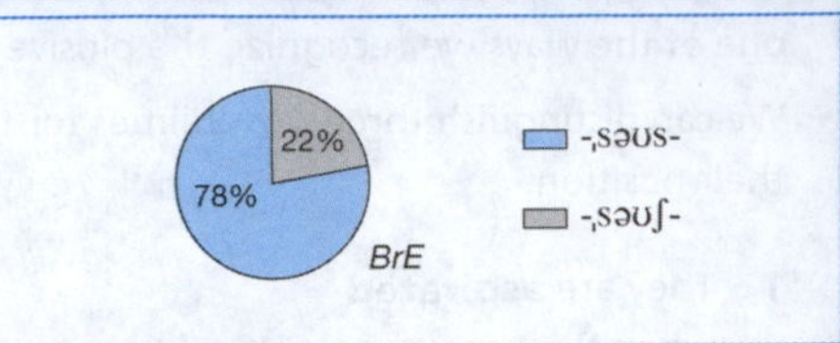

association ə ˌsəʊs i 'eɪʃ ᵊn ◂ -ˌsəʊʃ- ‖ ə ˌsoʊs- ə ˌsoʊʃ- **~s** z — *Preference poll, BrE:* -ˌsəʊs- *78%*, ˌsəʊʃ- *22%*.
As͵soci͵ation 'football
associative ə 'səʊs i‿ət ɪv -'səʊʃ-, -eɪt ɪv ‖ ə 'soʊʃ i eɪţ ɪv -'soʊs-, əţ ɪv **~ly** li
associativity ə ˌsəʊs i‿ə 'tɪv ət i -ˌsəʊʃ-, -ɪt i ‖ ə ˌsoʊʃ i‿ə 'tɪv əţ i -ˌsoʊs-
assonanc|e 'æs ən ənᵗs **~es** ɪz əz
assonant 'æs ən ənt **~s** s
assort ə 'sɔːt ‖ ə 'sɔːrt **assorted** ə 'sɔːt ɪd -əd ‖ ə 'sɔːrţ əd **assorting** ə 'sɔːt ɪŋ ‖ ə 'sɔːrţ ɪŋ **assorts** ə 'sɔːts ‖ ə 'sɔːrts
assortment ə 'sɔːt mənt ‖ ə 'sɔːrt- **~s** s
Assouan, Assuan ˌæs 'wɑːn ◂ ˌɑːs-, -'wæn, '· · —*Arabic* [ʔɑ 'sˤwɑːn]
assuag|e ə 'sweɪdʒ **~ed** d **~er/s** ə/z ‖ ᵊr/z **~es** ɪz əz **~ement** mənt **~ing** ɪŋ
assuasive ə 'sweɪs ɪv -'sweɪz-

ASSUME

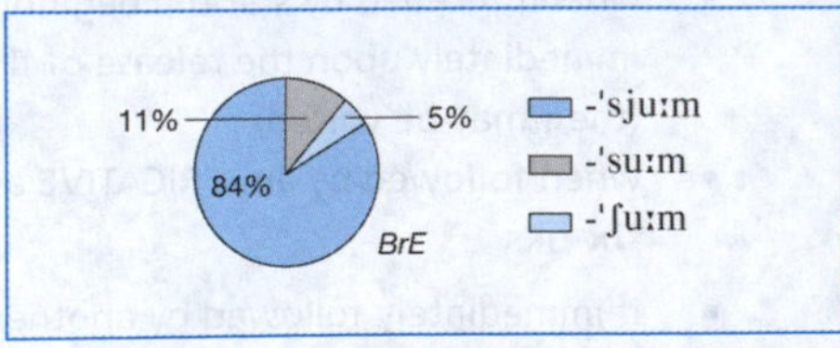

assum|e ə 'sjuːm -'suːm, §-'ʃuːm ‖ ə 'suːm — *Preference poll, BrE:* -'sjuːm *84%*, -'suːm *11%*, -'ʃuːm *5%*. **~ed** d **~es** z **~ing/ly** ɪŋ /li
assumption, A~ ə 'sʌmp ʃᵊn **~s** z
assumptive ə 'sʌmpt ɪv
assuranc|e ə 'ʃɔːr ənᵗs -'ʃʊər- ‖ ə 'ʃʊr- -'ʃɜː- **~es** ɪz əz
assur|e ə 'ʃɔː -'ʃʊə ‖ ə 'ʃʊᵊr -'ʃɜː **~ed** d **~es** z **assuring** ə 'ʃɔːr ɪŋ -'ʃʊər- ‖ ə 'ʃʊr ɪŋ -'ʃɜː-
assuredly ə 'ʃɔːr ɪd li -'ʃʊər-, -əd- ‖ ə 'ʃʊr- -'ʃɜː-
assurer ə 'ʃɔːr ə ə 'ʃʊər ə ‖ ə 'ʃʊr ᵊr -'ɜː- **~s** z

Assimilation

1 **Assimilation** is a type of COARTICULATION. It is the alteration of a speech sound to make it more similar to its neighbours. In English it mainly affects PLACE OF ARTICULATION.

2 The alveolar consonants t, d, n, when they occur at the end of a word or syllable, can optionally assimilate to the place of articulation of the next syllable ('regressive' assimilation).

Thus n can become m before p, b, m as in the examples

ten men ˌten ˈmen → ˌtem ˈmen

downbeat ˈdaʊn biːt → ˈdaʊm biːt.

Similarly, n can become ŋ before k, g as in

fine grade ˌfaɪn ˈɡreɪd → ˌfaɪŋ ˈɡreɪd

incredible ɪn ˈkred əb ᵊl → ɪŋ ˈkred əb ᵊl.

In the same way d can change to b and g respectively as in

red paint ˌred ˈpeɪnt → ˌreb ˈpeɪnt

admit əd ˈmɪt → əb ˈmɪt

bad guys ˈbæd ɡaɪz → ˈbæɡ ɡaɪz.

It is also possible for t to change to p and k, though a more frequent possibility is for t, when followed by another consonant, to be realized as a GLOTTAL STOP.

eight boys ˌeɪt ˈbɔɪz → ˌeɪp ˈbɔɪz

or, more usually, → ˌeɪʔ ˈbɔɪz.

3 In the same way s and z can change to ʃ and ʒ respectively, but only before ʃ or j at the beginning of the next syllable. In **you, your** the j may then disappear.

this shape ˌðɪs ˈʃeɪp → ˌðɪʃ ˈʃeɪp

these shoes ˌðiːz ˈʃuːz → ˌðiːʒ ˈʃuːz

this unit ˌðɪs ˈjuːn ɪt → ˌðɪʃ ˈjuːn ɪt

unless you... ən ˈles ju → ən ˈleʃ (j)u

as you see ˌæz ju ˈsiː → ˌæʒ (j)u ˈsiː

4 Assimilation can also sometimes operate in the other direction: that is, a consonant can assimilate to the place of articulation of the consonant at the end of the preceding syllable ('progressive' assimilation). In English this applies only to SYLLABIC n, changing it to syllabic m or ŋ as appropriate.

ribbon (ˈrɪb ən →) ˈrɪb n → ˈrɪb m

bacon (ˈbeɪk ən →) ˈbeɪk n → ˈbeɪk ŋ

up and down (ˌʌp ən ˈdaʊn →) ˌʌp n ˈdaʊn → ˌʌp m ˈdaʊn

Assimilation ▸

Assimilation continued

This assimilation can operate only if the words are said without a phonetic ə between the plosive and the nasal. Furthermore, it cannot apply if the sound after the nasal is a vowel.

happens (ˈhæp ənz →) ˈhæp nz → ˈhæp mz

happened (ˈhæp ənd →) ˈhæp nd → ˈhæp md

happening (ˈhæp ən ɪŋ →) ˈhæp n ɪŋ (cannot assimilate further).

5 **Yod coalescence** (or 'coalescent' assimilation) is the process which changes t or d plus j into tʃ or dʒ respectively. Across word boundaries it mainly affects phrases involving **you** or **your**.

let you out ˌlet ju ˈaʊt → ˌletʃ u ˈaʊt

would you try ˌwʊd ju ˈtraɪ → ˌwʊdʒ u ˈtraɪ

get your bags ˌget jɔː ˈbægz → ˌgetʃ ɔː ˈbægz ‖ ˌget jᵊr ˈbægz → ˌgetʃ ᵊr ˈbægz

6 Within a word, the status of yod coalescence depends on whether the following vowel is STRONG or WEAK.

- Where the vowel is strong, i.e. uː or ʊə, yod coalescence can frequently be heard in BrE, although not in careful RP. (In AmE there is usually no j, so the possibility does not arise.)

  tune tjuːn → tʃuːn

  endure ɪn ˈdjʊə → ɪn ˈdʒʊə

- Where the vowel is weak, i.e. u or ə, assimilation is often variable in BrE, but obligatory in AmE.

  factual ˈfækt ju‿əl → ˈfæk tʃu‿əl

  educate ˈed ju keɪt → ˈedʒ u keɪt

7 Historically, a process of yod coalescence is the origin of the tʃ used by all speakers in words such as **nature**, and of the dʒ in words such as **soldier**. Similarly, yod coalescence involving fricatives (sj → ʃ, zj → ʒ) explains the ʃ in words such as **pressure**, **delicious**, **patient**, **Russian**, and the ʒ in words such as **measure**. For example, **delicious** came to English from Latin via the French **délicieux** de li sjø, but in English the sj coalesced into ʃ several centuries ago.

8 Some speakers of BrE assimilate s to ʃ before tr and tʃ, thus **strong** strɒŋ → ʃtrɒŋ, **student** ˈstjuːd ᵊnt → ˈstʃuːd- → ˈʃtʃuːd-. This is not shown in this dictionary.

Assyri|a ə ˈsɪr i‿|ə **~an/s** ən/z

Assyriologist, a~ ə ˌsɪr i ˈɒl ədʒ ɪst §-əst ‖ -ˈɑːl- **~s** s

Assyriology ə ˌsɪr i ˈɒl ədʒ i ‖ -ˈɑːl-

Asta ˈæst ə

astable ₍ˌ₎eɪ ˈsteɪb ᵊl

Astaire ə ˈsteə ‖ ə ˈsteᵊr -ˈstæᵊr

Astarte æ ˈstɑːt i ə- ‖ -ˈstɑːrt̬-

astatine ˈæst ə tiːn -tɪn

Astbury ˈæst bər‿i ‖ -ˌber i

aster ˈæst ə ‖ -ᵊr **~s** z

ASTERISK

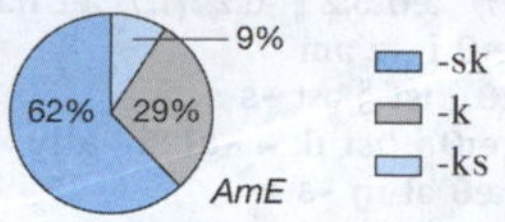

asterisk *n, v* ˈæst ə rɪsk ⚠-rɪks ‖ ⚠-rɪk — *Preference poll, AmE:* -sk *62%,* -k *29%,* -ks *9%.* **~ed** t **~ing** ɪŋ **~s** s
asterism ˈæst ə ˌrɪz əm **~s** z
Asterix ˈæst ə rɪks
astern ə ˈstɜːn ‖ ə ˈstɝːn
asteroid ˈæst ə rɔɪd **~s** z
asthenia æs ˈθiːn i‿ə
asthenic æs ˈθen ɪk **~al** ᵊl
asthma ˈæs mə ˈæsθ- ‖ ˈæz- *(*)*
asthmatic æs ˈmæt ɪk æsθ- ‖ æz ˈmæţ ɪk **~ally** ᵊl‿i **~s** s
Asti ˈæst i -iː ‖ ˈɑːst i —*It* [ˈas ti]
ˌ**Asti spuˈmante** spu ˈmænt i ‖ spu ˈmɑːnt i —*It* [spu ˈman te]
astigmatic ˌæst ɪg ˈmæt ɪk ◂ ‖ -ˈmæţ- **~ally** ᵊl‿i
astigmatism ə ˈstɪg mə ˌtɪz əm æ- **~s** z
astilbe ə ˈstɪlb i **~s** z
astir ə ˈstɜː ‖ ə ˈstɝː
Astle *(i)* ˈæst ᵊl, *(ii)* ˈæs ᵊl
Astley ˈæst li
Aston ˈæst ən
ˌ**Aston ˈMartin** *tdmk*; ˌ**Aston ˈVilla**
astonish ə ˈstɒn ɪʃ ‖ ə ˈstɑːn ɪʃ **~ed** t **~es** ɪz əz **~ing/ly** ɪŋ /li
astonishment ə ˈstɒn ɪʃ mənt ‖ -ˈstɑːn-
Astor ˈæst ə ‖ -ᵊr
Astoria ə ˈstɔːr i‿ə æ-
astound ə ˈstaʊnd **~ed** ɪd əd **~ing/ly** ɪŋ /li **~s** z
astra, Astra ˈæs trə
astragal ˈæs trəg ᵊl -trɪg- **~s** z
astrag|alus ə ˈstræg |əl əs **~ali** ə laɪ
astrakhan, A~ ˌæs trə ˈkæn ◂ -ˈkɑːn —*Russ* [ˈas trə xənʲ]
astral ˈæs trəl **~ly** i
astray ə ˈstreɪ
Astrid ˈæs trɪd
astride ə ˈstraɪd
astringency ə ˈstrɪndʒ ənᵗs i
astringent ə ˈstrɪndʒ ənt **~ly** li **~s** s
astro- *comb. form*
with stress-neutral suffix ˌæs trəʊ ‖ -trə — **astrosphere** ˈæs trəʊ sfɪə ‖ -trə sfɪr
with stress-imposing suffix ə ˈstrɒ+ æ ˈstrɒ+ ‖ ə ˈstrɑː+ — **astrophorous** ə ˈstrɒf ər əs æ- ‖ -ˈstrɑːf-
astrodome, A~ ˈæs trəʊ dəʊm ‖ -trə doʊm
astrolabe ˈæs trəʊ leɪb ‖ -trə- **~s** z
astrologer ə ˈstrɒl ədʒ ə æ- ‖ ə ˈstrɑːl ədʒ ᵊr **~s** z
astrological ˌæs trə ˈlɒdʒ ɪk ᵊl ◂ ‖ -ˈlɑːdʒ- **~ly** i
astrology ə ˈstrɒl ədʒ i æ- ‖ -ˈstrɑːl-
astronaut ˈæs trə nɔːt ‖ -nɑːt **~s** s
astronautical ˌæs trə ˈnɔːt ɪk ᵊl ◂ ‖ -ˈnɔːţ- -ˈnɑːţ- **~ly** i
astronautics ˌæs trə ˈnɔːt ɪks ‖ -ˈnɔːţ- -ˈnɑːţ-
astronomer ə ˈstrɒn əm ə ‖ ə ˈstrɑːn əm ᵊr **~s** z
astronomic ˌæs trə ˈnɒm ɪk ◂ ‖ -ˈnɑːm- **~al** ᵊl **~ally** ᵊl‿i
astronomy ə ˈstrɒn əm i ‖ -ˈstrɑːn-
astrophys|ical ˌæs trəʊ ˈfɪz |ɪk ᵊl ◂ ‖ ˌæs trə-, ˌtroʊ- **~icist/s** ɪs ɪst/s -əs-, §-əst/s **~ics** ɪks
astroturf, AstroTurf *tdmk* ˈæs trəʊ tɜːf ‖ -troʊ tɝːf **~ed** t
Asturias æ ˈstʊər i æs ə-, -ˈstjʊər-, -əs ‖ -ˈstʊr- —*Sp* [as ˈtur jas]
astute ə ˈstjuːt æ-, →-ˈstʃuːt ‖ ə ˈstuːt ə ˈstjuːt **~ly** li **~ness** nəs nɪs
Astyanax æ ˈstaɪ‿ə næks ə-
Asunción æ ˌsʊnᵗs i ˈɒn -ˈəʊn, ˌ· · ˈ· ‖ ɑː ˌsuːnᵗs i ˈoʊn ˌ· · ˈ· —*AmSp* [a sun ˈsjon]
asunder ə ˈsʌnd ə ‖ -ᵊr
Aswad ˈæz wɒd ‖ -wɑːd
Aswan ˌæs ˈwɑːn ◂ ˌɑːs-, -ˈwæn, ˈ· · —*Arabic* [ʔa ˈsˤwaːn]
asyl|um ə ˈsaɪl |əm **~a** ə **~ums** əmz
asymmetric ˌeɪ sɪ ˈmetr ɪk ◂ ˌeɪ sə-; ˌæs ɪ-, ˌæs ə- **~al** ᵊl **~ally** ᵊl‿i
asymmetry ₍ˌ₎æ ˈsɪm ətr i ˌeɪ-, -ɪtr- ‖ ˌeɪ-
asymptote ˈæs ɪmp təʊt -əmp- ‖ -toʊt **~s** s
asymptotic ˌæs ɪmp ˈtɒt ɪk ◂ -əmp- ‖ -ˈtɑːţ ɪk ◂ **~ally** ᵊl‿i
asynchronous ₍ˌ₎eɪ ˈsɪŋk rən əs -ˈsɪn krən- **~ly** li
asyndetic ˌæs ɪn ˈdet ɪk ◂ §-ᵊn-; ˌeɪ sɪn- ‖ -ˈdeţ ɪk ◂
asyndeton æ ˈsɪnd ɪt ən ə-, §-ət-; -ɪ tɒn, -ə- ‖ ə ˈsɪnd ə tɑːn ˌeɪ-
at *strong form* æt, *weak form* ət —*The phrase* at all *'in any degree, ever' is usually syllabified irregularly as* ə ˈtɔːl *in BrE and sometimes as* ə ˈtɔːl, ə ˈtɑːl *in AmE.*
at- *This variant of* ad- *is usually* ə (atˈtach), *but* ˌæ *if stressed because of a suffix* (ˌattriˈbution).
AT&T *tdmk* ˌeɪ tiː ən ˈtiː
atabrin, atabrine, A~ *tdmk* ˈæt əb rɪn §-rən, -ə briːn ‖ ˈæţ-
Atacama ˌæt ə ˈkɑːm ə ◂ ‖ ˌɑːt ɑː- —*Sp* [a ta ˈka ma]
Atack ˈeɪt æk
Atahualpa ˌæt ə ˈwɑːlp ə -ˈwælp- ‖ ˌæţ-
Atalanta ˌæt ə ˈlænt ə ‖ ˌæţ ə ˈlænţ ə
Atari *tdmk* ə ˈtɑːr i æ-
Ataturk, Atatürk ˈæt ə tɜːk ‖ ˈæţ ə tɝːk —*Turkish* [ɑ tɑ ˈtyrk]
atavism ˈæt ə ˌvɪz əm ‖ ˈæţ-
atavistic ˌæt ə ˈvɪst ɪk ◂ ‖ ˌæţ- **~ally** ᵊl‿i
ataxia ə ˈtæks i‿ə ₍ˌ₎eɪ-, æ-
ataxic ə ˈtæks ɪk **~s** s
ataxy ə ˈtæks i

Atchison 'ætʃ ɪs ən -əs-
atchoo ə 'tʃuː
Atco *tdmk* 'æt kəʊ ‖ -koʊ
Ate *Greek goddess* 'ɑːt i 'eɪt-, -iː ‖ 'eɪţ i

ATE

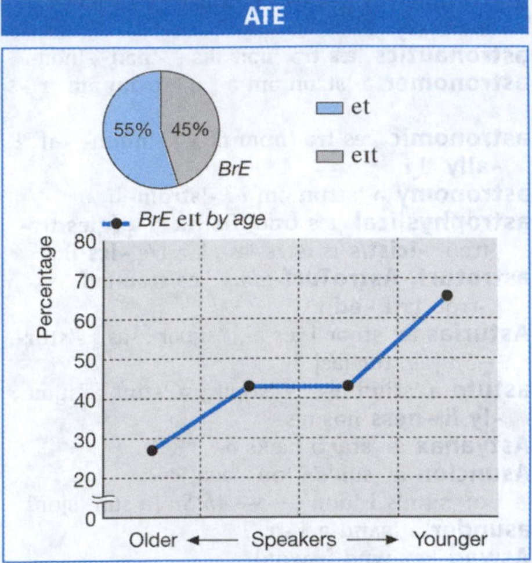

ate *past of* **eat** et eɪt ‖ eɪt ⚠et — *Preference poll, BrE:* et *55%,* eɪt *45%. In AmE, however,* et *is considered non-standard.*
-ate eɪt, ət ɪt, ¦eɪt —*This suffix is regularly strong,* **eɪt**, *in verbs, but often weakened to* **ət**, **ɪt** *in nouns and adjectives. Its influence on stress depends on the length of the word. (1) In two-syllable verbs stress usually falls on the suffix in BrE* (vi'brate, cre'ate), *but on the stem in AmE* ('vibrate, 'create). *(2) In longer verbs, the stress generally falls on the antepenultimate* ('demonstrate, dis'criminate, as'sociate). *There are a few exceptions and cases where speakers disagree* ('sequestrate *or* se'questrate). *(3) In nouns and adjectives the suffix is unstressed* ('private, 'climate), *and in longer words the primary stress generally falls two syllables back from the suffix* ('delegate, 'vertebrate, ap'propriate; *important exceptions are* in'nate, or'nate, se'date). *The suffix vowel is generally weak in familiar words* ('climate, 'private), *though in some words speakers vary* ('candidate, 'magistrate). *In more technical words a strong vowel is retained* ('sulphate, 'caudate). *(4) Note the distinction between verb and noun/adj in cases such as* 'separate, as'sociate, 'moderate, 'delegate.
A-team 'eɪ tiːm
atebrin *tdmk* 'æt əb rɪn §-rən, -ə briːn ‖ 'æţ-
atelier ə 'tel i‿eɪ æ-; 'æt ᵊl jeɪ ‖ ˌæţ ᵊl 'jeɪ —*Fr* [a tə lje] **~s** z
a tempo ₍ₗ₎ɑː 'temp əʊ ‖ -oʊ
atenolol ə 'ten ə lɒl æ- ‖ -lɑːl -lɔːl
Athabasc|a, Athabask|a ˌæθ ə 'bæsk |ə **~an** ən
Athanasian ˌæθ ə 'neɪʃ ᵊn ◂ -'neɪʒ-; -'neɪʃ i‿ən, -'neɪs-, -'neɪz- ‖ -'neɪʒ-
the ˌAthaˌnasian 'creed
Athanasius ˌæθ ə 'neɪʃ əs ◂ -'neɪʒ-; -'neɪʃ i‿əs, -'neɪs-, -'neɪz- ‖ -'neɪʒ-
Athapascan, Athapaskan ˌæθ ə 'pæsk ən ◂
Athawes *(i)* 'æθ ɔːz ‖ -ɑːz, *(ii)* 'æt hɔːz ‖ -hɑːz
atheism 'eɪθ i ˌɪz əm
atheist 'eɪθ i ɪst §-əst **~s** s
atheistic ˌeɪθ i 'ɪst ɪk ◂ **~al** ᵊl **~ally** ᵊl‿i
atheling 'æθ əl ɪŋ **~s** z
Athelstan 'æθ ᵊl stən -stæn —*in Old English was* 'æð ᵊl stɑːn
athematic ˌæθ iː 'mæt ɪk ◂ -ɪ-, -ə-; ˌeɪ θiː-, -θɪ-, -θə- ‖ -'mæţ-
Athena ə 'θiːn ə
Athenaeum ˌæθ ɪ 'niː‿əm -ə-
Athene ə 'θiːn i -iː
Athenian ə 'θiːn i‿ən **~s** z
Athenry ˌæθ ᵊn 'raɪ -ɪn-
Athens 'æθ ɪnz -ᵊnz
atherom|a ˌæθ ə 'rəʊm |ə ‖ -'roʊm |ə **~as** əz **~ata** ət ə ‖ əţ ə
atheroscle|rosis ˌæθ ə rəʊ sklə |'rəʊs ɪs -skle'--, -sklɪ'--, §-əs ‖ -roʊ sklə |'roʊs əs **~rotic** 'rɒt ɪk ◂ ‖ 'rɑːţ ɪk ◂
Atherstone 'æθ ə stəʊn ‖ -ᵊr stoʊn
Atherton *(i)* 'æθ ət ən ‖ -ᵊrt ᵊn, *(ii)* 'æð- —*the place near Manchester is (ii).*
athetoid 'æθ ə tɔɪd -ɪ-
athetosis ˌæθ ə 'təʊs ɪs -ɪ-, §-əs ‖ -'toʊs-
Athey 'æθ i
athirst ə 'θɜːst ‖ ə 'θɜːst
athlete 'æθ liːt ⚠'æθ ə liːt **~s, ~'s** s
ˌathlete's 'foot
athletic æθ 'let ɪk əθ-; ⚠ˌæθ ə 'let- ‖ -'leţ- **~ally** ᵊl‿i
athleticism æθ 'let ɪ ˌsɪz əm əθ-, -'·ə-; ⚠ˌæθ ə 'let- ‖ -'leţ-
Athlone ₍ₗ₎æθ 'ləʊn ‖ -'loʊn
Athol *place in MA* 'æθ ɒl ‖ -ɑːl -ɔːl, -ᵊl
Atholl *place in Scotland* 'æθ ᵊl
at-home ət 'həʊm æt-; ə 'təʊm ‖ -'hoʊm **~s** z
Athos 'æθ ɒs 'eɪθ- ‖ -ɑːs —*ModGk* ['a θɔs]
athwart ə 'θwɔːt ‖ ə 'θwɔːrt
Athy ə 'θaɪ
-ation 'eɪʃ ᵊn —*This suffix bears the primary word stress. In words of four or more syllables, a further rhythmic (secondary) stress falls two syllables further back* (ˌconso'lation, conˌside'ration, neˌgoti'ation, asˌsoci'ation). *Words in* -isation/-ization, *however, have the secondary stress earlier if possible, namely in the same place as the primary stress of the corresponding* -ise/-ize *word* (ˌorgani'zation, ˌatomi'zation, ˌdramati'zation, ˌactuali'zation).
atishoo ə 'tɪʃ uː
Ativan *tdmk* 'æt ɪ væn §-ə- ‖ 'æţ ə-
-ative ət ɪv, eɪt ɪv ‖ əţ ɪv, eɪţ ɪv *In words of three syllables, the first receives the stress, and the suffix vowel is weak* ('fricative, 'vocative, 'laxative, 'narrative; *exception* cre'ative). *In longer words, the stress usually falls on the same syllable as in the underlying stem:* ac'cusative, con'sultative, pre'servative; 'operative, 'qualitative, ag'glutinative,

ˌargu'mentative; ad'ministrative. *There is sometimes a vowel change* (de'rive - de'rivative), *and there are several exceptional cases* (com'bine —'combinative, 'alternate — al'ternative, in'terrogate —ˌinter'rogative, 'demonstrate — de'monstrative). *Where the primary stress is on the last syllable of the stem, the suffix has a reduced vowel* (ˌinter'rogative); *but otherwise in these longer words* ('cumulative, 'legislative) *the choice between weak-vowelled* **ət ɪv ‖ ət̬ ɪv** *and strong-vowelled* **eɪt ɪv ‖ eɪt̬ ɪv** *depends partly on social or regional factors, with BrE RP tending to prefer* **ət ɪv**, *AmE* **eɪt̬ ɪv**: *see individual entries.*

Atka 'æt kə ‖ 'ɑːt-

Atkins 'æt kɪnz

Atkinson 'æt kɪnᵗs ən

Atlanta ət 'lænt ə æt- ‖ æt 'lænt̬ ə ət-

Atlantean ˌæt læn 'tiː‿ən ◂ æt 'lænt i‿ən, ət-

atlantes ət 'lænt iːz æt-

Atlantic, a~ ət 'lænt ɪk §₍ₗ₎æt- ‖ -'lænt̬- **Atˌlantic 'City**; **Atˌlantic 'Ocean**

Atlantis ət 'lænt ɪs ₍ₗ₎æt-, §-əs ‖ -'lænt̬-

atlas, Atlas 'æt ləs **~es** ɪz əz

Atletico æt 'let ɪ kəʊ ‖ ɑːt 'let ɪ koʊ —*Sp* Atlético [at 'le ti ko]

ATM ˌeɪ tiː 'em **~s** z

atman 'ɑːt mən

atmosphere 'æt məs fɪə ‖ -fɪr **~s** z

atmospheric ˌæt məs 'fer ɪk ◂ ‖ -'fɪr- **~al** ᵊl **~ally** ᵊl‿i **~s** s

ˌatmosˌpheric 'pressure

atoll 'æt ɒl ə 'tɒl ‖ 'æt ɔːl -ɑːl **~s** z

atom 'æt əm ‖ 'æt̬ əm **~s** z

'atom bomb

atomic ə 'tɒm ɪk ‖ ə 'tɑːm- **~ally** ᵊl‿i

aˌtomic 'bomb; **aˌtomic 'energy**

atomis... —*see* **atomiz...**

atomism 'æt ə ˌmɪz əm ‖ 'æt̬-

atomistic ˌæt ə 'mɪst ɪk ◂ ‖ ˌæt̬- **~ally** ᵊl‿i

atomiz|e 'æt ə maɪz ‖ 'æt̬ ə- **~ed** d **~er/s** ə/z ‖ ᵊr/z **~es** ɪz əz **~ing** ɪŋ

atonal ₍ₗ₎eɪ 'təʊn ᵊl æ-, ə- ‖ -'toʊn- **~ism** ˌɪz əm **~ly** i

atonality ˌeɪ təʊ 'næl ət i ˌæ-, ˌ-tə-, -ɪt i ‖ -toʊ 'næl ət̬ i

aton|e ə 'təʊn ‖ ə 'toʊn **~ed** d **~es** z **~ing** ɪŋ

atonement ə 'təʊn mənt ‖ ə 'toʊn- **~s** s

atoneness ₍ₗ₎æt 'wʌn nəs -nɪs

atonic ₍ₗ₎eɪ 'tɒn ɪk ₍ₗ₎æ-, ə- ‖ -'tɑːn-

atoning ə 'təʊn ɪŋ ‖ ə 'toʊn ɪŋ

atony 'æt ən i ‖ 'æt ᵊn i

atop ə 'tɒp ‖ ə 'tɑːp

atopic ˌeɪ 'tɒp ɪk ◂ ‖ -'tɑːp- -'toʊp- **~ally** ᵊl‿i

atopy 'æt əp i ‖ 'æt̬-

-ator eɪt ə ‖ eɪt̬ ᵊr —*Stress falls on the same syllable(s) as for the corresponding verb in* -ate — **radiator** 'reɪd i eɪt ə ‖ -eɪt̬ ᵊr

Atora *tdmk* ə 'tɔːr ə

atorvastatin ə ˌtɔːv ə 'stæt ɪn -ᵊn, ·ˈ··ˌ·· ‖ -ˌtɔːrv-

-atory *The BrE and AmE pronunciations of this suffix differ. In BrE the vowel of the penultimate syllable is always weak: the suffix is either* **ət‿ər i** *or* **eɪt ər i** *and, if the latter, may be stressed. Different speakers often pronounce differently. Thus* ar'ticulatory *may have* **-jʊl ət‿ər i** *or* **-ju leɪt ər i**, *or alternatively may be stressed* arˌticu'latory ◂. *In AmE the suffix always has a strong vowel,* ə tɔːr i ə toʊr i, *stress remaining as for the corresponding verb in* -ate: ar'ticulatory, 'mandatory.

ATP ˌeɪ tiː 'piː

atrabilious ˌætr ə 'bɪl i‿əs ◂ **~ness** nəs nɪs

atresia ə 'triːz i‿ə æ-, -'triːʒ-, -'triːʒ ə ‖ ə 'triːʒ ə

Atreus 'eɪtr i əs -uːs; 'eɪtr uːs

at-risk ₍ₗ₎æt 'rɪsk ət-

atri|um 'eɪtr i |əm 'ætr- **~a** ə **~al** əl

atrocious ə 'trəʊʃ əs ‖ ə 'troʊʃ əs **~ly** li **~ness** nəs nɪs

atrocit|y ə 'trɒs ət |i -ɪt i ‖ ə 'trɑːs ət̬ |i **~ies** iz

atrophic æ 'trɒf ɪk ₍ₗ₎eɪ-, ə- ‖ -'trɑːf-

atr|ophy *n, v* 'ætr |əf i ⚠-ə faɪ **~ophied** əf id ⚠ə faɪd **~ophies** əf iz ⚠ə faɪz **~ophying** əf i ɪŋ ⚠ə faɪ ɪŋ

atropine 'ætr ə piːn -əp ɪn, §-əp ən

Atropos 'ætr ə pɒs -əp əs ‖ -pɑːs

attaboy 'æt ə bɔɪ ‖ 'æt̬-

attach ə 'tætʃ **attached** ə 'tætʃt **attaches** ə 'tætʃ ɪz əz **attaching** ə 'tætʃ ɪŋ

attaché ə 'tæʃ eɪ -i ‖ ˌæt̬ ə 'ʃeɪ æt æ- *(*)* **~s** z **at'taché case** ! **ˌatta'ché case**

attachment ə 'tætʃ mənt **~s** s

attack ə 'tæk **attacked** ə 'tækt **attacking** ə 'tæk ɪŋ **attacks** ə 'tæks

attacker ə 'tæk ə ‖ -ᵊr **~s** z

attain ə 'teɪn **~ed** d **~ing** ɪŋ **~s** z

attainability ə ˌteɪn ə 'bɪl ət i -ɪt i ‖ -ət̬ i

attainable ə 'teɪn əb ᵊl

attainder ə 'teɪnd ə ‖ -ᵊr

attainment ə 'teɪn mənt →-'teɪm- **~s** s

attar 'æt ə -ɑː ‖ 'æt̬ ᵊr 'æt ɑːr **~s** z

attempt ə 'tempt **~ed** ɪd əd **~ing** ɪŋ **~s** s

Attenborough 'æt ᵊn bər‿ə →'·əm-, §-ˌbʌr ə ‖ -ˌbɜː oʊ

attend ə 'tend **~ed** ɪd əd **~ing** ɪŋ **~s** z

attendanc|e ə 'tend ənᵗs **~es** ɪz əz

attendant ə 'tend ənt **~s** s

attendee ə ˌten 'diː ˌæt en- **~s** z

attention ə 'tenᵗʃ ᵊn **~s** z

attentive ə 'tent ɪv ‖ ə 'tent̬ ɪv **~ly** li **~ness** nəs nɪs

attenuate *adj* ə 'ten ju‿ət ɪt, -eɪt

attenu|ate *v* ə 'ten ju |eɪt **~ated** eɪt ɪd -əd ‖ eɪt̬ əd **~ates** eɪts **~ating** eɪt ɪŋ ‖ eɪt̬ ɪŋ

attenuation ə ˌten ju 'eɪʃ ᵊn **~s** z

attenuator ə 'ten ju eɪt ə ‖ -eɪt̬ ᵊr **~s** z

Attercliffe 'æt ə klɪf ‖ 'æt̬ ᵊr-

attest ə 'test **~ed** ɪd əd **~ing** ɪŋ **~s** s

attestation ˌæt e 'steɪʃ ᵊn -ə- **~s** z

attestor ə 'test ə ‖ -ᵊr **~s** z

A

attic, Attic ˈæt ɪk ‖ ˈæṭ- **~s** s
Attica ˈæt ɪk ə ‖ ˈæṭ-
Atticism ˈæt ɪ ˌsɪz əm §-ə- ‖ ˈæṭ-
Attila ə ˈtɪl ə ˈæt ɪl-
attire ə ˈtaɪ‿ə ‖ ə ˈtaɪ‿ᵊr **~d** d **~s** z **attiring** ə ˈtaɪ‿ər ɪŋ ‖ ə ˈtaɪ‿ᵊr ɪŋ

ATTITUDE

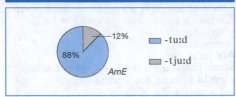

88% -tuːd
12% -tjuːd
AmE

attitude ˈæt ɪ tjuːd -ə-, →-tʃuːd ‖ ˈæṭ ə tuːd -tjuːd **~s** z — *Preference poll, AmE:* -tuːd *88%,* -tjuːd *12%.*
attitudinal ˌæt ɪ ˈtjuːd ɪn ᵊl ◂ ˌ·ə-, →-ˈtʃuːd-, -ᵊn‿əl ‖ ˌæṭ ə ˈtuːd ᵊn‿əl ◂ ˈtjuːd- **~ly** i
attitudinis|e, attitudiniz|e ˌæt ɪ ˈtjuːd ɪ naɪz ˌ·ə-, →-ˈtʃuːd-, -ə naɪz, -ᵊn aɪz ‖ ˌæṭ ə ˈtuːd ᵊn aɪz -ˈtjuːd- **~ed** d **~es** ɪz əz **~ing** ɪŋ
Attleborough ˈæt ᵊl bər‿ə ‖ ˈæṭ ᵊl ˌbɜː oʊ
Attlee ˈæt li
atto- ¦æt əʊ ‖ ¦æṭ oʊ — **attogram** ˈæt əʊ græm ‖ ˈæṭ oʊ-
attorney ə ˈtɜːn i ‖ ə ˈtɜːn i *(!)* **~ship/s** ʃɪp/s **~s** z
atˌtorney ˈgeneral
attract ə ˈtrækt **~ed** ɪd əd **~ing** ɪŋ **~s** s
attractant ə ˈtrækt ənt **~s** s
attraction ə ˈtræk ʃᵊn **~s** z
attractive ə ˈtrækt ɪv **~ly** li **~ness** nəs nɪs
attractor ə ˈtrækt ə ‖ -ᵊr **~s** z
attributab|le ə ˈtrɪb jʊt əb |ᵊl -ˈjət-, -ˈjuːt- ‖ -ˈtrɪb jəṭ- **~ly** li
attribute *v* ə ˈtrɪb juːt §ˈætr ɪ bjuːt, §-ə- ‖ ə ˈtrɪb jət -juːt **attributed** ə ˈtrɪb jʊt ɪd ˈætr ɪ bjuːt-, ˈ·ə-, -əd ‖ ə ˈtrɪb jəṭ əd -juːṭ əd **attributes** *v* ə ˈtrɪb juːts §ˈætr ɪ bjuːts, §-ə- ‖ ə ˈtrɪb jəts -juːts **attributing** ə ˈtrɪb jʊt ɪŋ ˈætr ɪ bjuːt-, ˈ·ə- ‖ ə ˈtrɪb jəṭ ɪŋ -juːṭ ɪŋ
attribute *n* ˈætr ɪ bjuːt -ə- **~s** s
attribution ˌætr ɪ ˈbjuːʃ ᵊn -ə- **~s** z
attributive ə ˈtrɪb jʊt ɪv -jət ɪv, -juːt ɪv; §ˈætr ɪ bjuːt ɪv, §ˈ·ə- ‖ -jəṭ ɪv **~ly** li **~ness** nəs nɪs
attrition ə ˈtrɪʃ ᵊn æ-
Attu ˈæt uː
Attucks ˈæt əks ‖ ˈæṭ-
attun|e ə ˈtjuːn æ-, →-ˈtʃuːn ‖ ə ˈtuːn ə ˈtjuːn **~ed** d **~es** z **~ing** ɪŋ
Attw... — *see* **Atw...**
ATV ˌeɪ tiː ˈviː **~s** z
Atwater ˈæt ˌwɔːt ə ‖ -ˌwɔːṭ ᵊr -ˌwɑːṭ ᵊr
Atwell ˈæt wel
atwitter ə ˈtwɪt ə ‖ ə ˈtwɪṭ ᵊr
Atwood ˈæt wʊd
atypical (ˌ)eɪ ˈtɪp ɪk ᵊl **~ly** i

au əʊ ‖ oʊ —*Fr* [o] —*See also phrases with this word*
aubade əʊ ˈbɑːd ‖ oʊ- —*Fr* [o bad] **~s** z
auberge, ~s əʊ ˈbeəʒ ‖ ˌoʊ ˈbeᵊrʒ —*Fr* [o bɛʁʒ]
aubergine ˈəʊb ə ʒiːn -dʒiːn ‖ ˈoʊb ᵊr- **~s** z
Auberon ˈɔːb ᵊr‿ən ˈəʊb-, -ə rɒn, ˈ·rɒn ‖ ˈɑːb-, -ə rɑːn —*The writer* A~ Waugh *pronounced* ˈɔːb-
Aubrey ˈɔːb ri ‖ ˈɑːb-
aubrietia ɔː ˈbriːʃ ə -ˈbriːʃ i‿ə ‖ ɑː-, oʊ- **~s** z
auburn, A~ ˈɔːb ən ˈɔː bɜːn ‖ ˈɔːb ᵊrn ˈɑːb-
Aubusson ˈəʊb ju sɒn ‖ ˌoʊb ə ˈsɑːn -ˈsoʊn —*Fr* [o by sɔ̃]
Auchinleck ˈɔːk ɪn lek ˈɒx-, -ən-, ˌ·ˈ· ‖ ˈɑːk-
Auchterarder ˌɒkt ər ˈɑːd ə ˌɒxt- ‖ ˌɔːkt ər ˈɑːrd ᵊr ˌɑːkt-
Auchtermuchty ˌɔːkt ə ˈmʌkt i ˌɒkt-; ˌɒxt ə ˈmʌxt i ‖ -ᵊr- ˌɑːkt-
Auckland ˈɔːk lənd ‖ ˈɑːk-
au contraire ˌəʊ kɒn ˈtreə ‖ ˌoʊ kɑːn ˈtreᵊr -ˈtræᵊr —*Fr* [o kɔ̃ tʁɛːʁ]
au courant əʊ ˈkʊr ɒ̃ ‖ ˌoʊ ku ˈrɑːn —*Fr* [o ku ʁɑ̃]

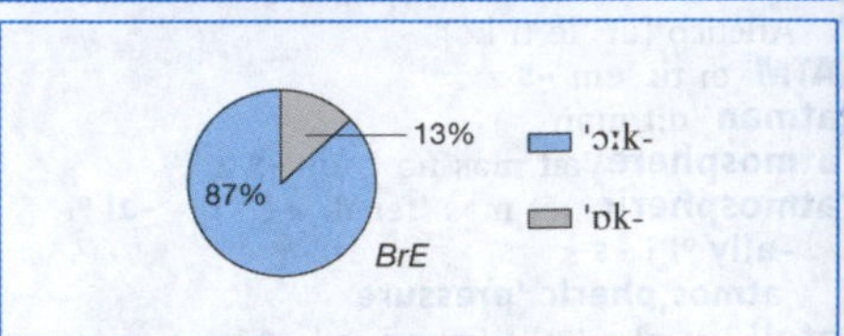

auction ˈɔːk ʃᵊn ˈɒk- ‖ ˈɑːk- — *Preference poll, BrE:* ˈɔːk- *87%,* ˈɒk- *13%.* **~ed** d **~ing** ‿ɪŋ **~s** z
auctioneer ˌɔːk ʃə ˈnɪə ◂ ˌɒk- ‖ -ˈnɪᵊr ˌɑːk- **~s** z
auctorial ɔːk ˈtɔːr i‿əl ‖ ɑːk-, -ˈtoʊr-
audacious ɔː ˈdeɪʃ əs ‖ ɑː- **~ly** li **~ness** nəs nɪs
audacit|y (ˌ)ɔː ˈdæs ət |i -ɪt i ‖ -əṭ |i (ˌ)ɑː- **~ies** iz
Auden ˈɔːd ᵊn ‖ ˈɑːd-
Audenshaw ˈɔːd ᵊn ʃɔː ‖ ˈɑːd ᵊn ʃɑː
Audi *tdmk* ˈaʊd i ˈɔːd- ‖ ˈɔːd-, ˈɑːd-
audibility ˌɔːd ə ˈbɪl ət i ˌ·ɪ-, -ɪt i ‖ -əṭ i ˌɑːd-
audib|le ˈɔːd əb |ᵊl -ɪb- ‖ ˈɑːd- **~ly** li
Audie ˈɔːd i ‖ ˈɑːd-
audienc|e ˈɔːd i‿ənᵗs ‖ ˈɑːd- **~es** ɪz əz
audile ˈɔːd aɪᵊl -ɪl ‖ ˈɑːd-
audio ˈɔːd i‿əʊ ‖ ‿oʊ ˈɑːd- **~s** z
ˌaudio casˈsette
audiolingual ˌɔːd i‿əʊ ˈlɪŋ gwəl ◂ -ˈlɪŋ gju‿əl ‖ ‿oʊ- ˌɑːd- **~ly** i
audiological ˌɔːd i‿ə ˈlɒdʒ ɪk ᵊl ◂ ‖ -ˈlɑːdʒ- ˌɑːd- **~ly** ‿i
audiologist ˌɔː di ˈɒl ədʒ ɪst §-əst ‖ -ˈɑːl- ˌɑːd- **~s** s
audiology ˌɔːd i ˈɒl ədʒ i ‖ -ˈɑːl- ˌɑːd-
audiometer ˌɔːd i ˈɒm ɪt ə -ət ə ‖ -ˈɑːm əṭ ᵊr ˌɑːd- **~s** z
audiometry ˌɔːd i ˈɒm ətr i -ɪtr i ‖ -ˈɑːm- ˌɑːd-
audiophile ˈɔːd i‿əʊ faɪl ‖ ‿oʊ- ˈɑːd- **~s** z
audiotape ˈɔːd i‿əʊ teɪp ‖ ‿oʊ- ˈɑːd- **~s** s

audiotyp|ing ˈɔːd i‿əʊ ˌtaɪp |ɪŋ ‖ ˈ‿oʊ- ˈɑːd-
~ist/s ɪst/s əst/s
audiovisual ˌɔːd i‿əʊ ˈvɪʒ u‿əl ◂ -ˈvɪz ju‿əl, -ˈvɪʒ ᵊl ‖ ‿oʊ- ˌɑːd-, -ˈvɪʒ ᵊl **~ly** i
ˌaudioˌvisual ˈaids
aud|it ˈɔːd |ɪt §-ət ‖ ˈɔːd |ət ˈɑːd- **~ited** ɪt ɪd §ət-, -əd ‖ əţ əd **~iting** ɪt ɪŋ §ət- ‖ əţ ɪŋ **~its** ɪts §əts ‖ əts
audition ɔː ˈdɪʃ ᵊn ‖ ɑː- **~ed** d **~ing** ‿ɪŋ **~s** z
auditor ˈɔːd ɪt ə -ət- ‖ -əţ ᵊr ˈɑːd- **~s** z
auditori|um ˌɔːd ɪ ˈtɔːr i‿|əm ˌ·ə- ‖ ˌɑːd-, -ˈtoʊr- **~a** ə **~ums** əmz
auditor|y ˈɔːd ɪt‿ər |i ˌ·ət‿ ‖ ˈɔːd ə tɔːr |i ˈɑːd-, -toʊr i **~ily** əl i ɪ li
Audlab *tdmk* ˈɔːd læb ‖ ˈɑːd-
Audlem ˈɔːd ləm ‖ ˈɑːd-
Audley ˈɔːd li ‖ ˈɑːd-
Audrey ˈɔːdr i ‖ ˈɑːdr-
Audubon ˈɔːd ə bɒn -əb ən ‖ -bɑːn ˈɑːd-, -əb ən
AUEW ˌeɪ juː ˌiː ˈdʌb ᵊl ju
auf *German prepn* aʊf —*Ger* [auf] —*See also phrases with this word*
au fait ₍ᵢ₎əʊ ˈfeɪ ‖ ₍ᵢ₎oʊ- —*Fr* [o fɛ]
au fond ₍ᵢ₎əʊ ˈfɒ̃ ‖ ₍ᵢ₎oʊ ˈfoʊn -ˈfɔ̃ː —*Fr* [o fɔ̃]
auf Wiedersehen ₍ᵢ₎aʊf ˈviːd ə zeɪn -ˈwiːd-, -ˈ· ·ˌzeɪ ən ‖ -ᵊr- —*Ger* [auf ˈviː dɐ ˌzeː ən]
Augean ɔː ˈdʒiː‿ən ‖ ɑː-
auger, Auger ˈɔːg ə ‖ -ᵊr ˈɑːg- **~s** z
aught ɔːt ‖ ɑːt *(= ought)*
Aughton ˈɔːt ᵊn ‖ ˈɑːt- —*but there is one village of this name, near Lancaster, which is* ˈæft ən
augite ˈɔːdʒ aɪt ‖ ˈɑːdʒ-
aug|ment *v* ₍ᵢ₎ɔːg |ˈment ‖ ₍ᵢ₎ɑːg- **~mented** ˈment ɪd -əd ‖ ˈmenţ əd **~menting** ˈment ɪŋ ‖ ˈmenţ ɪŋ **~ments** ˈments
augment *n* ˈɔːg ment -mənt ‖ ˈɑːg- **~s** s
augmentation ˌɔːg men ˈteɪʃ ᵊn -mən- ‖ ˌɑːg- **~s** z
augmentative ɔːg ˈment ət ɪv ‖ -ˈmenţ əţ ɪv ɑːg- **~s** z
Augrabies ə ˈgrɑːb iːz
au gratin əʊ ˈgræt æn ‖ oʊ ˈgrɑːt ᵊn —*Fr* [o gʁa tɛ̃]
Augsburg ˈaʊgz bɜːg ˈaʊks-, -bʊəg ‖ -bɜːg ˈɑːgz-, -bʊrg —*Ger* [ˈauks bʊʁk]
augur *n, v* ˈɔːg ə -jə ‖ -ᵊr ˈɑːg- **~ed** d **auguring** ˈɔːg ər ɪŋ -jər- ‖ ˈɑːg- **~s** z
augur|y ˈɔːg jʊr |i -jər-, -ər- ‖ -jər |i ˈɑːg-, -ər- **~ies** iz
august *adj* ₍ᵢ₎ɔː ˈgʌst ‖ ₍ᵢ₎ɑː-; ˈ· · **~ly** li **~ness** nəs nɪs
August *n, name of month* ˈɔːg əst ‖ ˈɑːg-
August *personal name,* **august** *n 'clown'* ˈaʊg ʊst **~s** s
Augusta ɔː ˈgʌst ə ə- ‖ ɑː-
Augustan ɔː ˈgʌst ən ə- ‖ ɑː- **~s** z
Augustine ɔː ˈgʌst ɪn ə-, §-ən ‖ ˈɔːg ə stiːn ˈɑːg- *(*)*
Augustinian ˌɔːg ə ˈstɪn i‿ən ◂ ˌ·ʌ- ‖ ˌɑːg- **~s** z
Augustus ɔː ˈgʌst əs ə- ‖ ɑː-
au jus əʊ ˈʒuː -ˈʒuːs ‖ oʊ- —*Fr* [o ʒy]
auk ɔːk ‖ ɑːk **auks** ɔːks ‖ ɑːks
auklet ˈɔːk lət -lɪt ‖ ˈɑːk- **~s** s
aul|a ˈɔːl |ə ˈaʊl- ‖ ˈɑːl- **~ae** iː
au lait əʊ ˈleɪ ‖ oʊ- —*Fr* [o lɛ]
auld, Auld ɔːld ‖ ɑːld
ˌauld ˌlang ˈsyne zaɪn saɪn; **ˌAuld ˈReekie** ˈriːk i
Aulis ˈɔːl ɪs ˈaʊl-, §-əs ‖ ˈɑːl-
Aum ɔːm ‖ ɑːm
au naturel əʊ ˌnæt ju ˈrel -ˌnætʃ ə-, -ˌnæt jə-, ˌ·ˌ·- ‖ oʊ ˌnɑːtʃ ə ˈrel —*Fr* [o na ty ʁɛl]
Aung San Suu Kyi aʊŋ ˌsæn suː ˈtʃiː ‖ -ˌsɑːn-

AUNT

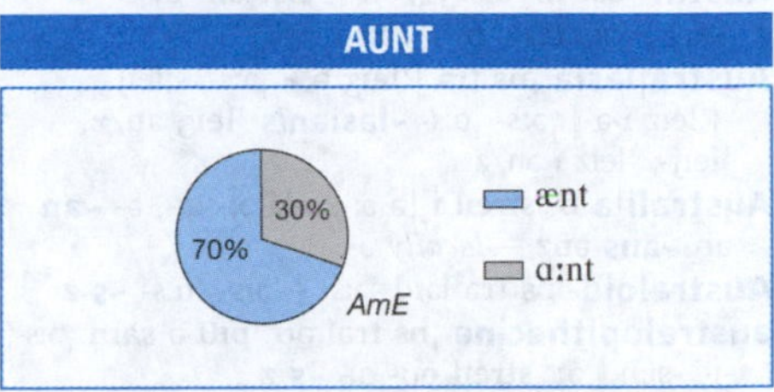

aunt ɑːnt §ænt ‖ ænt ɑːnt **aunts** ɑːnts §ænts ‖ ænts ɑːnts — *Preference poll, AmE:* ænt *70%,* ɑːnt *30%.*
ˌAunt ˈSally
aunt|ie, aunt|y, Auntly ˈɑːnt |i §ˈænt- ‖ ˈænţ |i ˈɑːnt- **~ies** iz
au pair ₍ᵢ₎əʊ ˈpeə ‖ ₍ᵢ₎oʊ ˈpeᵊr -ˈpæᵊr —*Fr* [o pɛʁ] **~s** z
au poivre əʊ ˈpwɑːv -ˈ·rə ‖ oʊ- —*Fr* [o pwaːvʁ]
aur|a ˈɔːr |ə **~ae** iː
aural ˈɔːr əl —*Sometimes* ˈaʊᵊr əl, *to avoid confusion with* oral **~ly** i
Aurangzeb ˈɔːr əŋ zeb
aureate ˈɔːr i eɪt ət, ɪt **~ly** li **~ness** nəs nɪs
Aurelian ɔː ˈriːl i‿ən
Aurelius ɔː ˈriːl i‿əs
aureola ɔː ˈriː‿əl ə ˌɔːr i ˈəʊl ə, ˌɒr- ‖ ˌɔːr i ˈoʊl ə **~s** z
aureole ˈɔːr i əʊl ‖ -oʊl **~s** z
aureomycin, A~ *tdmk* ˌɔːr i əʊ ˈmaɪs ɪn §-ᵊn ‖ -oʊˈ--
au revoir ˌəʊ rə ˈvwɑː -rɪ-, §-riː- ‖ ˌoʊ rə ˈvwɑːr —*Fr* [oʁ vwaːʁ]
auricle ˈɔːr ɪk ᵊl ˈɒr- **~s** z
auricul|a ɔː ˈrɪk jʊl |ə ɒ-, -jəl- ‖ -jəl |ə **~ar** ə ‖ ᵊr **~as** əz
Auriel ˈɔːr i‿əl
auriferous ɔː ˈrɪf ər‿əs
Auriga ɔː ˈraɪg ə ‖ ɑː-
Aurignacian ˌɔːr ɪg ˈneɪʃ ᵊn ◂ -iːn ˈjeɪʃ-
aurochs ˈɔːr ɒks ˈaʊᵊr- ‖ -ɑːks **~es** ɪz əz
auror|a, A~ ə ˈrɔːr |ə ɔː- **~ae** iː **~as** əz
auˌrora auˈstralis ɒ ˈstreɪl ɪs ɔː-, ə-, -ˈstrɑːl-, §-əs ‖ ɔː ˈstreɪl əs ɑː-; **auˌrora ˌboreˈalis**
Auschwitz ˈaʊʃ wɪts -vɪts —*Ger* [ˈauʃ vɪts]
auscultation ˌɔːsk ᵊl ˈteɪʃ ᵊn ˌɒsk-, -ʌl- ‖ ˌɑːsk-
auslese, A~ ˈaʊs leɪz ə —*Ger* [ˈaus leː zə]
auspices ˈɔːsp ɪs ɪz ˈɒsp-, -əs-, -əz, -iːz ‖ ˈɑːsp-
auspicious ɔː ˈspɪʃ əs ɒ- ‖ ɑː- **~ly** li **~ness** nəs nɪs
Aussie ˈɒz i ‖ ˈɔːs i ˈɑːs-, ˈɔːz-, ˈɑːz- **~s** z

A

Aust ɔːst ‖ ɑːst
Austell 'ɒst ᵊl 'ɔːst- ‖ 'ɑːst- — St A~'s *in Cornwall is locally also* -'ɔːs ᵊlz
Austen 'ɒst ɪn 'ɔːst-, §-ən ‖ 'ɔːst- 'ɑːst-
Auster 'ɔːst ə ‖ -ᵊr 'ɑːst-
austere ɔː 'stɪə ɒ- ‖ ɔː 'stɪᵊr ɑː-, -'steᵊr **~ly** li
austerit|y ɔː 'ster ət |i ɒ-, -ɪt i ‖ ɔː 'ster əṭ |i ɑː-, -'stɪr- **~ies** iz
Austerlitz 'ɔːst ə lɪts 'aʊst- ‖ -ᵊr- 'ɑːst-
Austick 'ɔːst ɪk ‖ 'ɑːst-
Austin 'ɒst ɪn 'ɔːst-, §-ən ‖ 'ɔːst ən 'ɑːst-
austral 'ɔːs trəl 'ɒs- ‖ 'ɑːs-
Austra|lasia ˌɒs trə |'leɪʒ ə ◂ ˌɔːs-, -'leɪʃ-, -|'leɪz i‿ə ‖ ˌɔːs- ˌɑːs- **~lasian/s** 'leɪʒ ən/z 'leɪʃ-, 'leɪz i‿ən/z
Australi|a ɒ 'streɪl i‿|ə ɔː-, ə- ‖ ɔː- ɑː-, ə- **~an** ən **~ans** ənz —*locally* ə-
Australoid 'ɒs trə lɔɪd 'ɔːs- ‖ 'ɔːs- 'ɑːs- **~s** z
australopithecine ˌɒs trəl əʊ 'pɪθ ə saɪn ˌɔːs-, -ɪ-, -siːn ‖ ɔː ˌstreɪl oʊ- ɑː- **~s** z
australopithecus ˌɒs trəl əʊ 'pɪθ ɪk əs -ək əs ‖ ɔː ˌstreɪl oʊ ˈ- ɑː-
Austri|a 'ɒs tri‿|ə 'ɔːs- ‖ 'ɔːs- 'ɑːs- **~an/s** ən/z
Austro- *comb. form* ¦ɒs trəʊ ¦ɔːs trəʊ ‖ ¦ɔːs troʊ ¦ɑːs troʊ — **Austro-Hungarian** ˌɒs trəʊ hʌŋ 'geər i‿ən ◂ ˌɔːs- ‖ ˌɔːs troʊ hʌŋ 'ger- ˌɑːs-, -'gær-
Austronesi|a ˌɒs trəʊ 'niːz i‿|ə ◂ ˌɔːs-, -'niːʒ |ə, -'niːs i‿|ə, -'niːʃ |ə ‖ ˌɔːs troʊ 'niːʒ |ə ˌɑːs-, -'niːʃ- **~an/s** ən/z
Austyn 'ɒst ɪn 'ɔːst-, §-ən ‖ 'ɔːst- ɑːst-
AUT ˌeɪ juː 'tiː
autarchic ɔː 'tɑːk ɪk ‖ -'tɑːrk- ɑː- **~al** ᵊl
autarchy 'ɔːt ɑːk i ‖ -ɑːrk i 'ɑːt-
autarkic ɔː 'tɑːk ɪk ‖ -'tɑːrk- ɑː- **~al** ᵊl
autarky 'ɔːt ɑːk i ‖ -ɑːrk i 'ɑːt-
auteur ɔː 'tɜː ₍ₗ₎əʊ- ‖ oʊ 'tɜː —*Fr* [o tœːʁ]
authentic ɔː 'θent ɪk ‖ -'θenṭ ɪk ɑː- **~ally** ᵊl‿i
authenti|cate ɔː 'θent ɪ |keɪt §-ə- ‖ -'θenṭ- ɑː- **~cated** keɪt ɪd -əd ‖ keɪṭ əd **~cates** keɪts **~cating** keɪt ɪŋ ‖ keɪṭ ɪŋ **~cator/s** keɪt ə/z ‖ keɪṭ ᵊr/z
authentication ɔː ˌθent ɪ 'keɪʃ ᵊn §-ə- ‖ -ˌθenṭ- ɑː- **~s** z
authenticity ˌɔːθ en 'tɪs ət i ˌ·ᵊn-, -ɪt i ‖ -əṭ i ˌɑːθ-, ˌ·ᵊn-
author 'ɔːθ ə ‖ 'ɔːθ ᵊr 'ɑːθ- **~ed** d **authoring** 'ɔːθ ər‿ɪŋ ‖ 'ɑːθ- **~s** z
authoress 'ɔːθ ə res -ər ɪs, -ər əs, ˌɔːθ ə 'res ‖ 'ɔːθ ər əs 'ɑːθ- **~es** ɪz əz
authorial ɔː 'θɔːr i‿əl ‖ ɑː- **~ly** i
authoris... —*see* **authoriz...**
authoritarian ɔː ˌθɒr ɪ 'teər i‿ən ◂ -ə'-- ‖ -ˌθɔːr ə 'ter- ɑː-, ə- **~ism** ˌɪz əm **~s** z
authoritative ɔː 'θɒr ɪt ət ɪv -ˌət-; -ɪ teɪt ɪv, -ə · · ‖ ə 'θɔːr ə teɪṭ ɪv ɔː-, ɑː- **~ly** li **~ness** nəs nɪs
authorit|y ɔː 'θɒr ət |i ə-, -ɪt i ‖ ə 'θɔːr əṭ |i ɔː-, ɑː- **~ies** iz
authorization ˌɔːθ ər‿aɪ 'zeɪʃ ᵊn -ər‿ɪ- ‖ ‿ə- ˌɑːθ- **~s** z
authoriz|e 'ɔːθ ə raɪz ‖ 'ɑːθ- **~ed** d **~es** ɪz əz **~ing** ɪŋ
ˌ**Authorized 'Version**
authorship 'ɔːθ ə ʃɪp ‖ -ᵊr- 'ɑːθ-
autism 'ɔːt ˌɪz əm ‖ 'ɑːt-
autistic ɔː 'tɪst ɪk ‖ ɑː- **~ally** ᵊl‿i
auto 'ɔːt əʊ ‖ 'ɔːṭ oʊ 'ɑːṭ- **~s** z
auto- *comb. form*
with stress-neutral suffix ¦ɔːt əʊ ‖ ¦ɔːṭ oʊ ¦ɑːṭ- — **autoimmune** ˌɔːt əʊ ɪ 'mjuːn ‖ ˌɔːṭ oʊ- ˌɑːṭ-
with stress-imposing suffix ɔː 'tɒ+ ‖ ɔː 'tɑː+ ɑː- — **autolysis** ɔː 'tɒl əs ɪs -ɪs-, §-əs ‖ ɔː 'tɑːl- ɑː-
autobahn 'ɔːt əʊ bɑːn 'aʊt- ‖ 'ɔːṭ oʊ- 'ɑːṭ- —*Ger* ['aʊ to baːn] **~s** z
autobiographer ˌɔːt əʊ baɪ 'ɒg rəf ə ‖ ˌɔːṭ ə baɪ 'ɑːg rəf ᵊr ˌɑːṭ- **~s** z
autobiographic ˌɔːt əʊ ˌbaɪ‿ə 'græf ɪk ◂ -ˌbaɪ əʊ- ‖ ˌɔːṭ ə ˌbaɪ ə- ˌɑːṭ- **~al** ᵊl **~ally** ᵊl‿i
autobiograph|y ˌɔːt əʊ baɪ 'ɒg rəf |i ‖ ˌɔːṭ ə baɪ 'ɑːg- ˌɑːṭ- **~ies** iz
autocar, A~ 'ɔːt əʊ kɑː ‖ 'ɔːṭ oʊ kɑːr 'ɑːṭ- **~s** z
autochang|e 'ɔːt əʊ tʃeɪndʒ ‖ 'ɔːṭ oʊ- 'ɑːṭ- **~es** ɪz əz
autochanger 'ɔːt əʊ ˌtʃeɪndʒ ə ‖ 'ɔːṭ oʊ ˌtʃeɪndʒ ᵊr 'ɑːṭ- **~s** z
autochthon ɔː 'tɒk θᵊn -θɒn ‖ -'tɑːk- ɑː-, -θɑːn **~s** z
autochthonous ɔː 'tɒk θən əs ‖ -'tɑːk- ɑː- **~ly** li
autoclav|e 'ɔːt əʊ kleɪv ‖ 'ɔːṭ oʊ- 'ɑːṭ- **~ed** d **~es** z **~ing** ɪŋ
autocorrelation ˌɔːt əʊ ˌkɒr ə 'leɪʃ ᵊn -ɪ'-- ‖ ˌɔːṭ oʊ ˌkɔːr- ˌɑːṭ-, -ˌkɑːr-
autocrac|y ɔː 'tɒk rəs |i ‖ -'tɑːk- ɑː- **~ies** iz
autocrat 'ɔːt ə kræt ‖ 'ɔːṭ ə- 'ɑːṭ- **~s** s
autocratic ˌɔːt ə 'kræt ɪk ◂ ‖ ˌɔːṭ ə 'kræṭ ɪk ◂ ˌɑːṭ- **~al** ᵊl **~ally** ᵊl‿i
autocross 'ɔːt əʊ krɒs ‖ 'ɔːṭ oʊ krɔːs 'ɑːṭ-, -krɑːs
autocue, A~ *tdmk* 'ɔːt əʊ kjuː ‖ 'ɔːṭ oʊ- 'ɑːṭ- **~s** z
autocycle 'ɔːt əʊ ˌsaɪk ᵊl ‖ 'ɔːṭ oʊ- 'ɑːṭ- **~s** z
auto-da-fé ˌɔːt əʊ də 'feɪ ˌaʊt-, -dɑː'· ‖ ˌɔːṭ oʊ- ˌɑːṭ- —*Port* [au tu da 'fɛ]
autodestruct ˌɔːt əʊ di 'strʌkt -də'· ‖ ˌɔːṭ oʊ- ˌɑːṭ- **~ed** ɪd əd **~ing** ɪŋ **~s** s
autodidact 'ɔːt əʊ dɪ ˌdækt -ˌdaɪd ækt, ˌ· ·'· · ‖ ˌɔːṭ oʊ 'daɪd ækt ˌɑːṭ-, -də 'dækt **~s** s
autodidactic ˌɔːt əʊ dɪ 'dækt ɪk ◂ -daɪ'-- ‖ ˌɔːṭ oʊ daɪ- ˌɑːṭ-, · ·də- **~ally** ᵊl‿i
autoerotic ˌɔːt əʊ ɪ 'rɒt ɪk ◂ -ə'-- ‖ ˌɔːṭ oʊ ɪ 'rɑːṭ ɪk ◂ ˌɑːṭ-
autoeroticism ˌɔːt əʊ ɪ 'rɒt ɪ ˌsɪz əm -ə'--, -əˌ- ‖ ˌɔːṭ oʊ ɪ 'rɑːṭ ə- ˌɑːṭ-
autoerotism ˌɔːt əʊ 'er ə ˌtɪz əm ‖ ˌɔːṭ oʊ- ˌɑːṭ-
autogiro ˌɔːt əʊ 'dʒaɪᵊr əʊ ‖ ˌɔːṭ oʊ 'dʒaɪᵊr oʊ ˌɑːṭ- **~s** z
autograph 'ɔːt ə grɑːf -græf ‖ 'ɔːṭ ə græf 'ɑːṭ- **~ed** t **~ing** ɪŋ **~s** s

A

Australian English

The pronunciation of English in Australia is generally similar to BrE rather than AmE. Some of the points of difference are as follows:

- If there is a choice between ɪ and ə as a weak vowel, Australian English prefers ə.

  valid ˈvæl əd (rhymes with **salad** ˈsæl əd)

  boxes ˈbɒks əz (sounds just like **boxers**).

- Australian English uses fewer GLOTTAL STOPs than BrE. When t is between vowels it is often voiced as in AmE; and, as in AmE, it may be elided after n (see T-VOICING).

  better ˈbeţ ə

  entertain ˌenţ ə ˈteɪn.

- The vowels ɪ, e and æ tend to be closer than in BrE RP; ɑː tends to be fronter; ɪə and eə are monophthongal (like ɪː, eː); and the diphthongs eɪ and əʊ tend to be wider (almost like aɪ and aʊ), while aɪ and aʊ sound more like ɑɪ, æʊ.

autogyro ˌɔːt əʊ ˈdʒaɪᵊr əʊ ‖ ˌɔːţ oʊ ˈdʒaɪᵊr oʊ ˌɑːţ- **~s** z

autoharp, A~ *tdmk* ˈɔːt əʊ hɑːp ‖ ˈɔːţ oʊ hɑːrp ˈɑːţ- **~s** s

autoimmun|e ˌɔːt əʊ ɪ ˈmjuːn ◂ ‖ ˌɔːţ oʊ- ˌɑːţ- **~ity** ət i ɪt i ‖ əţ i

autoload ˌɔːt əʊ ˈləʊd ˈ· · · ‖ ˌɔːţ oʊ ˈloʊd ˌɑːţ- **~ed** ɪd əd **~ing** ɪŋ ◂ **~s** z

autologous ɔː ˈtɒl əg əs ‖ -ˈtɑːl- ɑː- **~ly** li

Autolycus ɔː ˈtɒl ɪk əs ‖ -ˈtɑːl- ɑː-

automaker ˈɔːt əʊ ˌmeɪk ə ‖ ˈɔːţ oʊ ˌmeɪk ᵊr **~s** z

automat, A~ *tdmk* ˈɔːt ə mæt ‖ ˈɔːţ- ˈɑːţ- **~s** s

automata ɔː ˈtɒm ət ə ‖ ɔː ˈtɑːm əţ ə ɑː-

auto|mate ˈɔːt ə |meɪt ‖ ˈɔːţ- ˈɑːţ- **~mated** meɪt ɪd -əd ‖ meɪţ əd **~mates** meɪts **~mating** meɪt ɪŋ ‖ meɪţ ɪŋ

automatic ˌɔːt ə ˈmæt ɪk ◂ ‖ ˌɔːţ ə ˈmæţ ɪk ◂ ˌɑːţ- **~ally** ᵊl‿i

ˌautoˌmatic ˈpilot

automation ˌɔːt ə ˈmeɪʃ ᵊn ‖ ˌɔːţ- ˌɑːţ-

automatism ɔː ˈtɒm ə ˌtɪz əm ‖ ɔː ˈtɑːm- ɑː-

autom|aton ɔː ˈtɒm |ət ən ‖ ɔː ˈtɑːm |ət ᵊn ɑː-, -|ə tɑːn **~ata** ət ə ‖ əţ ə **~atons** ət ənz ‖ ət ᵊnz

automobile ˈɔːt ə məʊ ˌbiːᵊl ˌ· · ˈ· ‖ ˈɔːţ ə moʊ ˌbiːᵊl ˈɑːţ-; ˌ· · ˈ·; ˌ· · ˈ· **~s** z

automotive ˌɔːt əʊ ˈməʊt ɪv ◂ ‖ ˌɔːţ ə ˈmoʊţ ɪv ◂ ˌɑːţ-

autonomic ˌɔːt ə ˈnɒm ɪk ◂ ‖ ˌɔːţ ə ˈnɑːm ɪk ◂ ˌɑː- **~ally** ᵊl‿i

ˌautonomic ˈnervous ˌsystem

autonomous ɔː ˈtɒn əm əs ‖ ɔː ˈtɑːn- ɑː- **~ly** li

autonom|y ɔː ˈtɒn əm |i ‖ ɔː ˈtɑːn- ɑː- **~ies** iz

autopilot ˈɔːt əʊ ˌpaɪl ət ‖ ˈɔːţ oʊ- ˈɑːţ- **~s** s

autopista ˌaʊt əʊ ˈpiːst ə ‖ -oʊ- —*Sp* [au to ˈpis ta]

autops|y ˈɔːt ɒps |i -əps-; ɔː ˈtɒps |i ‖ ˈɔːt ɑːps |i ˈɑːt-; ˈɔːţ əps i, ˈɑːţ- **~ies** iz

autoreverse ˌɔːt əʊ ri ˈvɜːs -rə·- ‖ ˌɔːţ oʊ ri ˈvɜːs ˌɑːţ-

autoroute ˈɔːt əʊ ruːt ‖ ˈɔːţ oʊ- ˈɑːţ- —*Fr* [o to ʁut] **~s** s

autosegmental ˌɔːt əʊ seg ˈment ᵊl ◂ -səg'-, -sɪg'- ‖ ˌɔːţ oʊ seg ˈmenţ ᵊl ◂ ˌɑːţ- **~ly** i

autostrada ˈɔːt əʊ ˌstrɑːd ə ˈaʊt- ‖ ˈaʊţ oʊ- ˈɔːţ-, ˈɑːţ- —*It* [au to ˈstraː da] **~s** z

autosuggestion ˌɔːt əʊ sə ˈdʒes tʃən -ˈdʒeʃ- ‖ ˌɔːţ oʊ səg ˈdʒes tʃən ˌɑːţ-

Autrey ˈɔːtr i ‖ ˈɑːtr-

autumn, A~ ˈɔːt əm ‖ ˈɔːţ əm ˈɑːţ- **~s** z

autumnal ɔː ˈtʌm nəl ‖ ɑː- **~ly** i

Auty ˈɔːt i ‖ ˈɔːţ i ˈɑːţ i

Auvergne əʊ ˈveən -ˈvɜːn ‖ oʊ ˈveᵊrn -ˈvɜːn —*Fr* [o vɛʁnj, ɔ-]

au vin əʊ ˈvæ̃ -ˈvæn ‖ oʊ- —*Fr* [o væ̃]

AUX ɔːks ‖ ɑːks

ˈAUX node

Auxerre əʊ ˈseə ‖ oʊ ˈseᵊr —*Fr* [o sɛːʁ]

auxiliar|y ɔːg ˈzɪl i‿ər |i ɔːk-, ɔːk ˈsɪl-, ⚠-ˈər |i ‖ ɑːg-, -ˈzɪl ər |i **~ies** iz

auxin ˈɔːks ɪn §-ən ‖ ˈɑːks- **~s** z

Ava *(i)* ˈɑːv ə, *(ii)* ˈeɪv ə

avail ə ˈveᵊl **~ed** d **~ing** ɪŋ **~s** z

availabilit|y ə ˌveɪl ə ˈbɪl ət |i -ɪt i ‖ -əţ |i **~ies** iz

availab|le ə ˈveɪl əb |ᵊl **~ly** li

avalanch|e ˈæv ə lɑːntʃ §-læntʃ ‖ -læntʃ **~es** ɪz əz

Avalon ˈæv ə lɒn ‖ -lɑːn

avant-garde ˌæv ɒŋ ˈgɑːd ◂ -ᵊnt-, -ɒ̃- ‖ ˌɑːv ɑːn ˈgɑːrd ◂ ˌæv-; ə ˈvɑːnt gɑːrd —*Fr* [a vɑ̃ gaʁd]

Avar ˈæv ɑː ˈeɪv- ‖ -ɑːr

avarice ˈæv ər‿ɪs §‿əs

avaricious ˌæv ə ˈrɪʃ əs ◂ **~ly** li **~ness** nəs nɪs
avast ə ˈvɑːst §-ˈvæst ‖ ə ˈvæst
Avastin *tdmk* eɪ ˈvæst ɪn
avatar ˈæv ə tɑː ˌ· ·ˈ· ‖ -tɑːr **~s** z
avaunt ə ˈvɔːnt ‖ -ˈvɑːnt
ave, Ave *'hail'; 'prayer'* ˈɑːv eɪ -i
  ˌAve Maˈria; **ˌAve Maˌria ˈLane**
Ave. *—see* **Avenue**; *sometimes spoken as* æv
Avebury ˈeɪv bər‿i ‖ -ˌber i *—locally also* ˈeɪb ər‿i
avenge ə ˈvendʒ **avenged** ə ˈvendʒd **avenges** ə ˈvendʒ ɪz -əz **avenging/ly** ə ˈvendʒ ɪŋ /li
avenger ə ˈvendʒ ə ‖ -ər **~s** z
avens ˈeɪv ənz ˈæv-, -ɪnz ‖ ˈæv-
Aventine ˈæv ən taɪn
aventurine ə ˈventʃ ə riːn -ər ɪn, -ər ən
avenue ˈæv ə njuː -ɪ- ‖ -nuː -njuː **~s** z
aver ə ˈvɜː ‖ ə ˈvɝː **averred** ə ˈvɜːd ‖ ə ˈvɝːd **averring** ə ˈvɜːr ɪŋ ‖ ə ˈvɝː ɪŋ **avers** ə ˈvɜːz ‖ ə ˈvɝːz
averag|e ˈæv ər‿ɪdʒ **~ed** d **~es** ɪz əz **~ing** ɪŋ
Averil, Averill ˈæv ər‿ɪl ər‿əl
Avernus ə ˈvɜːn əs ‖ ə ˈvɝːn əs
averr... *—see* **aver**
Averroes, Averroës ə ˈver əʊ iːz ˌæv ə ˈrəʊ- ‖ -oʊ-
averse ə ˈvɜːs ‖ ə ˈvɝːs **~ly** li **~ness** nəs nɪs
aversion ə ˈvɜːʃ ən §-ˈvɜːʒ- ‖ ə ˈvɝːʒ ən -ˈvɝːʃ- **~s** z
  aˈversion ˌtherapy
aversive ə ˈvɜːs ɪv §-ˈvɜːz- ‖ ə ˈvɝːs ɪv -ˈvɝːz-
avert ə ˈvɜːt ‖ ə ˈvɝːt **averted** ə ˈvɜːt ɪd -əd ‖ ə ˈvɝːţ əd **averting** ə ˈvɜːt ɪŋ ‖ ə ˈvɝːţ ɪŋ **averts** ə ˈvɜːts ‖ ə ˈvɝːts
Avery ˈeɪv ər‿i
Aves, aves ˈeɪv iːz
Avesta ə ˈvest ə
Avestan ə ˈvest ən
avgolemono ˌæv gəʊ ˈlem ə nəʊ ‖ ˌɑːv goʊ ˈlem ə noʊ *—Gk* [av ɣɔ ˈlɛ mɔ nɔ]
Avia *tdmk* ˈeɪv i‿ə
avian ˈeɪv i‿ən
aviar|y ˈeɪv i‿ər |i ‖ -er |i **~ies** iz
aviation ˌeɪv i ˈeɪʃ ən
aviator ˈeɪv i eɪt ə ‖ -eɪţ ər **~s** z
Avicenna ˌæv ɪ ˈsen ə §-ə-
avid ˈæv ɪd §-əd **~ly** li
avidity ə ˈvɪd ət i æ-, -ɪt- ‖ -əţ i
Aviemore ˌæv i ˈmɔː ‖ -ˈmɔːr -ˈmoʊr
avifauna ˈeɪv ɪ ˌfɔːn ə ˈæv-, §-ə- ‖ -ˌfɑːn-
Avignon ˈæv iːn jɔ̃ ‖ ˌæv iːn ˈjoʊn -ˈjɑːn, -ˈjɔːn *—Fr* [a vi ɲɔ̃]
Avila ˈæv ɪl ə -əl- ‖ ˈɑːv- *—Sp* [ˈa βi la]
avionic ˌeɪv i ˈɒn ɪk ◂ ‖ -ˈɑːn- **~s** s
avirulent ˌeɪ ˈvɪr ʊl ənt ◂ ə'--, jʊl-, -jəl-, -əl- ‖ -əl- -jəl-
Avis ˈeɪv ɪs §-əs
Avoca ə ˈvəʊk ə ‖ ə ˈvoʊk ə
avocado ˌæv ə ˈkɑːd əʊ ◂ ‖ -oʊ ˌɑːv- **~s** z
  ˌavoˌcado ˈpear
avocation ˌæv əʊ ˈkeɪʃ ən ‖ -ə- **~al** əl **~s** z
avocet ˈæv ə set **~s** s
Avogadro ˌæv əʊ ˈgɑːdr əʊ -ˈgædr- ‖ -ə ˈgɑːdr oʊ ˌɑːv-, -ˈgædr- *—It* [a vo ˈgaː dro] **~'s** z
  ˌAvoˌgadro('s) ˈnumber
avoid ə ˈvɔɪd **avoided** ə ˈvɔɪd ɪd -əd **avoiding** ə ˈvɔɪd ɪŋ **avoids** ə ˈvɔɪdz
avoidab|le ə ˈvɔɪd əb| əl **~ly** li
avoidance ə ˈvɔɪd ənts
avoirdupois ˌæv wɑː dju ˈpwɑː ◂ -ˈ· ·, ˌæv ə də ˈpɔɪz ◂ ‖ ˌæv ər də ˈpɔɪz ˈ· · ˌ·
Avon *(i)* ˈeɪv ən -ɒn ‖ -ɑːn, *(ii)* ˈæv ən, *(iii)* ɑːn *—In most senses, (i), though the brand of cosmetics is usually* -ɒn ‖ -ɑːn; *the river in England is (ii), while the river and loch in Grampian are (iii).*
Avonmouth ˈeɪv ən maʊθ
Avory ˈeɪv ər‿i
avow ə ˈvaʊ **avowed** ə ˈvaʊd **avowing** ə ˈvaʊ‿ɪŋ **avows** ə ˈvaʊz
avowal ə ˈvaʊ‿əl ə ˈvaʊl **~s** z
avowedly ə ˈvaʊ ɪd li -əd-
Avril ˈæv rəl -rɪl
avuncular ə ˈvʌŋk jʊl ə -jəl- ‖ -jəl ər
aw ɔː ‖ ɑː
AWACS, Awacs ˈeɪ wæks
await ə ˈweɪt **awaited** ə ˈweɪt ɪd -əd ‖ ə ˈweɪţ əd **awaiting** ə ˈweɪt ɪŋ ‖ ə ˈweɪţ ɪŋ **awaits** ə ˈweɪts
awake ə ˈweɪk **awaked** ə ˈweɪkt **awakes** ə ˈweɪks **awaking** ə ˈweɪk ɪŋ **awoke** ə ˈwəʊk ‖ ə ˈwoʊk **awoken** ə ˈwəʊk ən ‖ ə ˈwoʊk ən
awaken ə ˈweɪk ən **~ed** d **~ing/s** ‿ɪŋ/z **~s** z
award ə ˈwɔːd ‖ ə ˈwɔːrd **~ed** ɪd əd **~er/s** ə/z ‖ ər/z **~ing** ɪŋ **~s** z
awardable ə ˈwɔːd əb əl ‖ ə ˈwɔːrd-
aware ə ˈweə ‖ ə ˈweər
awareness ə ˈweə nəs -nɪs ‖ -ˈwer-
awash ə ˈwɒʃ ‖ ə ˈwɔːʃ -ˈwɑːʃ
away ə ˈweɪ
Awbery ˈɔː bər‿i ‖ ˈɔː ˌber i ˈɑː-
awe, Awe ɔː ‖ ɑː **awed** ɔːd ‖ ɑːd
aweigh ə ˈweɪ *(= away)*
awe-inspiring ˈɔːr ɪn ˌspaɪ‿ər ɪŋ ‖ ˈɔː ɪn ˌspaɪ‿ər ɪŋ ˈɑː- **~ly** li
awesome ˈɔː səm ‖ ˈɑː- **~ly** li **~ness** nəs nɪs
awestricken ˈɔː ˌstrɪk ən ‖ ˈɑː-
awestruck ˈɔː strʌk ‖ ˈɑː-
awful ˈɔːf əl -ʊl ‖ ˈɑːf- *—but in the literal meaning 'awe-inspiring',* ˈɔː fʊl ‖ ˈɔː-, ˈɑː- **~ness** nəs nɪs
awfully ˈɔːf li ˈɔːf əl‿i, -ʊl i ‖ ˈɑːf-
awhile ə ˈwaɪəl -ˈhwaɪəl ‖ ə ˈ*h*waɪəl
awkward ˈɔːk wəd ‖ -wərd ˈɑːk- **~ly** li **~ness** nəs nɪs
awl ɔːl ‖ ɑːl *(= all)* **awls** ɔːlz ‖ ɑːlz
awn ɔːn ‖ ɑːn **awns** ɔːnz ‖ ɑːnz
awning ˈɔːn ɪŋ ‖ ˈɑːn- **~s** z
awoke ə ˈwəʊk ‖ ə ˈwoʊk
awoken ə ˈwəʊk ən ‖ ə ˈwoʊk ən
AWOL ˈeɪ wɒl ‖ -wɑːl -wɔːl *—or as letters* ˌeɪ ˌdʌb əl ju ˌəʊ ˈel ‖ -ˌoʊˈ·

awry ə 'raɪ —*jocularly, or by confusion, also* 'ɔːr i
ax, axe æks **axes** 'æks ɪz -əz
axel, Axel 'æks ᵊl *(= axle)* **~s** z
axe|man 'æks |mən -mæn **~men** mən men
axes *pl of* **axis** 'æks iːz
axes *from* **ax, axe** 'æks ɪz -əz
Axholme 'æks həʊm ‖ -hoʊm
axial 'æks i‿əl **~ly** i
axil 'æks ɪl -ᵊl **~s** z
axill|a æk 'sɪl |ə **~ae** iː
axiom 'æks i‿əm **~s** z
axiomatic ˌæks i‿ə 'mæt ɪk ◂ ‖ -'mæţ- **~al** ᵊl **~ally** ᵊl‿i
axis 'æks ɪs §-əs **axes** 'æks iːz
axle 'æks ᵊl **~s** z
ax|man 'æks |mən -mæn **~men** mən men
Axminster 'æks ˌmɪnᵗst ə ‖ -ᵊr **~s** z
axolotl ˌæks ə 'lɒt ᵊl '· · · · ‖ 'æks ə lɑːt ᵊl **~s** z
axon 'æks ɒn ‖ -ɑːn **~s** z
axonometric ˌæks ᵊn əʊ 'metr ɪk ◂ ‖ -ᵊn oʊ- **~ally** ᵊl‿i
ay *'always'* eɪ aɪ
ay *'yes'* aɪ *(= I, eye)*
ayah 'aɪ ə **~s** z
ayatollah ˌaɪ‿ə 'tɒl ə ‖ -'toʊl ə ˌɑː jə- **~s** z
Ayckbourn 'eɪk bɔːn ‖ -bɔːrn -boʊrn
Aycliffe 'eɪ klɪf
aye *'always'* eɪ aɪ
aye *'yes'* aɪ *(= I, eye)* **ayes** aɪz
aye-aye *n* 'aɪ aɪ **~s** z
Ayenbite of Inwyt ˌeɪ ən baɪt əv 'ɪn wɪt ‖ ˌ· ·baɪţ-
Ayer eə ‖ eᵊr æᵊr
Ayers eəz ‖ eᵊrz æᵊrz
ˌ**Ayers 'Rock**
Ayesha aɪ 'iːʃ ə ɑː-; 'aɪʃ ə
Ayia Napa ˌaɪ‿ə 'næp ə —*ModGk* [ˌa ja 'na pa]
Aylesbury 'eɪᵊlz bər‿i ‖ -ˌber i
Aylesford 'eɪᵊlz fəd 'eɪᵊls- ‖ -fᵊrd
Aylesham *place in Kent* 'eɪᵊl ʃəm
Ayling 'eɪl ɪŋ
Aylmer 'eɪᵊl mə ‖ -mᵊr
Aylsham *place in Nfk* 'eɪᵊl ʃəm —*locally also* -səm; 'ɑːl ʃəm
Aylward 'eɪᵊl wəd -wɔːd ‖ -wᵊrd -wɔːrd
Aymara ˌaɪm ə 'rɑː ◂ '· · ·; aɪ 'mɑːr ə —*Sp* Aymará [ai ma 'ɾa] **~s** z
Aynho 'eɪn həʊ ‖ -hoʊ
Ayot 'eɪ ət
Ayr eə ‖ eᵊr æᵊr
Ayrshire 'eə ʃə -ʃɪə, §'eə ˌʃaɪ‿ə ‖ 'er ʃᵊr 'ær-, -ʃɪr, -ˌʃaɪ‿ᵊr
Ayrton 'eət ᵊn ‖ 'ert ᵊn 'ært-
Aysgarth 'eɪz gɑːθ ‖ -gɑːrθ
Ayto 'eɪt əʊ ‖ -oʊ
Ayton, Aytoun 'eɪt ᵊn
ayurved|a, A~ ˌaɪ‿ə 'veɪd ə -ʊə-, ˌɑː jʊə-, -'viːd- ‖ ˌɑː jʊr- **~ic** ɪk ◂
A-Z ˌeɪ tə 'zed ‖ ˌeɪţ ə 'ziː
azalea ə 'zeɪl i‿ə **~s** z
Azani|a ə 'zeɪn i |ə **~an/s** ən/z
Azariah ˌæz ə 'raɪ‿ə
azathioprine ˌæz ə 'θaɪ əʊ priːn ‖ -ə priːn
Azerbaijan ˌæz ə baɪ 'dʒɑːn -'ʒɑːn ‖ ˌɑːz ᵊr- —*Russ* [ʌ zʲɪr bʌj 'dʒan]
Azerbaijani ˌæz ə baɪ 'dʒɑːn i ◂ -'ʒɑːn- ‖ ˌɑːz ᵊr- **~s** z
Azeri æ 'zeər i ə- ‖ ɑː 'zer i ˌæ- **~s** z
azide 'eɪz aɪd **~s** z
azimuth 'æz ɪm əθ -əm- **~s** s
azimuthal ˌæz ɪ 'mʌθ ᵊl ◂ -ə-, -'mjuːθ- **~ly** i
Aziz ə 'ziːz -'zɪz
Aznavour 'æz nə vʊə -vɔː ‖ ˌɑːz nə 'vʊᵊr -'vɔːr —*Fr* [az na vuːʁ]
azo 'eɪz əʊ 'æz- ‖ -oʊ
azo- *comb. form* ¦eɪz əʊ ¦æz əʊ ‖ -oʊ — **azobenzene** ˌeɪz əʊ 'benz iːn ˌæz- ‖ -oʊ-
azoic (ˌ)eɪ 'zəʊ ɪk ‖ -'zoʊ-
Azores ə 'zɔːz ‖ 'eɪz ɔːrz -oʊrz *(*)*
Azov 'eɪz ɒv 'ɑːz-, 'æz- ‖ -ɑːv -ɔːv —*Russ* [ʌ 'zɔf]
AZT *tdmk* ˌeɪ zed 'tiː ‖ -ziː-
Aztec 'æz tek **~s** s
Aztecan 'æz tek ən ·'·
azure 'æʒ ə 'eɪʒ-, -ʊə, -jʊə; 'æz jʊə, 'eɪz-; ə 'zjʊə ‖ 'æʒ ᵊr
azygous 'æz ɪg əs (ˌ)eɪ 'zaɪg əs, ə-

B

b Spelling-to-sound

1 Where the spelling is **b**, the pronunciation is regularly b as in **baby** ˈbeɪb i.

2 Where the spelling is double **bb** the pronunciation is again b as in **shabby** ˈʃæb i.

3 **b** is silent in two groups of words:

- before **t** in **debt** det, **doubt** daʊt, **subtle** ˈsʌt ᵊl ‖ ˈsʌṭ ᵊl
- after **m** at the end of a word or stem as in **climb** klaɪm, **lamb** læm, **thumb** θʌm, **bomber** ˈbɒm ə ‖ ˈbɑːm ᵊr.

B, b biː **Bs, B's, b's** biːz —*Communications code name:* Bravo
ˌB and 'B, ˌb and 'b
BA ˌbiː ˈeɪ
baa bɑː ‖ bæ bɑː **baaed** bɑːd ‖ bæd bɑːd **baaing** ˈbɑːʳ ɪŋ ‖ ˈbæ ɪŋ ˈbɑː ɪŋ **baas** bɑːz ‖ bæz bɑːz
Baader-Meinhof ˌbɑːd ə ˈmaɪn hɒf ‖ -ᵊr ˈmaɪn hoʊf —*Ger* [ˌbaː də ˈmain hɔf, -hoːf]
Baal ˈbeɪ əl beɪᵊl, bɑːl
baa-lamb ˈbɑː læm ‖ ˈbæ- **~s** z
Baalbek, Ba'albek ˈbɑːl bek —*Arabic* [bɑ ˈʕal bak]
baas *from* **baa** bɑːz ‖ bæz bɑːz
baas *'master'* bɑːs
Ba'ath bɑːθ —*Arabic* [bɑʕθ]
Bab *religious leader* bɑːb
baba ˈbɑːb ɑː -ə **~s** z
ˌbaba ga'nush gə ˈnʊʃ
babaco bə ˈbɑːk əʊ ‖ -oʊ **~s** z
Babar ˈbɑːb ɑː ‖ bɑː ˈbɑːr
Babbage ˈbæb ɪdʒ
Babbitt, b~ ˈbæb ɪt §-ət
Babbittry ˈbæb ɪtr i §-ətr-
babbl|e ˈbæb ᵊl **~ed** d **~er/s** ‿ə/z ‖ ‿ᵊr/z **~es** z **~ing** ‿ɪŋ
Babcock ˈbæb kɒk ‖ -kɑːk
babe beɪb **babes** beɪbz
Babel, babel ˈbeɪb ᵊl ‖ ˈbæb-
babi... —*see* **baby**
Babington ˈbæb ɪŋ tən
Babinski bə ˈbɪn ski
babiroussa, babirussa ˌbæb ɪ ˈruːs ə ˌbɑːb-, -ə- **~s** z
Babi Yar ˌbɑːb i ˈjɑː ‖ -ˈjɑːr —*Russ* [ˌba bʲi ˈjar]
baboon bə ˈbuːn ‖ bæ- **~s** z
Babs bæbz
babu, Babu ˈbɑːb uː —*Hindi* [baː buː]
babushka bə ˈbuːʃ kə bæ-, -ˈbʊʃ- —*Russ* [ˈba buʃ kə]
baby, Baby ˈbeɪb i **babied** ˈbeɪb id **babies** ˈbeɪb iz **babying** ˈbeɪb i‿ɪŋ
ˌbaby 'blue◂; **'baby ˌboomer**; **ˌbaby 'boy**; **'baby ˌbuggy**; **'baby ˌcarriage**; **ˌbaby 'girl**; **ˌbaby 'grand**; **'baby talk**; **'baby tooth**
baby-bouncer, B~ *tdmk* ˈbeɪb i ˌbaʊntˢ ə ‖ -ᵊr **~s** z
Babycham *tdmk* ˈbeɪb i ʃæm
baby-faced ˈbeɪb i feɪst
Babygro *tdmk* ˈbeɪb i grəʊ ‖ -groʊ **~s** z
babyhood ˈbeɪb i hʊd
babyish ˈbeɪb i‿ɪʃ **~ly** li **~ness** nəs nɪs
Babylon ˈbæb ɪl ən -əl-; -ɪ lɒn, -ə- ‖ -ə lɑːn -əl ən
Babyloni|a ˌbæb ɪ ˈləʊn i‿|ə ˌ-ə- ‖ -ˈloʊn- **~an/s** ən/z
baby-mind|er ˈbeɪb i ˌmaɪnd |ə ‖ -|ᵊr **~ers** əz ‖ ᵊrz **~ing** ɪŋ
Babyshambles ˈbeɪb i ˌʃæm bᵊlz
baby-|sit ˈbeɪb i |sɪt **~sitter/s** sɪt ə/z ‖ sɪṭ ᵊr/z **~sitting** sɪt ɪŋ ‖ sɪṭ ɪŋ
baby-walker ˈbeɪb i ˌwɔːk ə ‖ -ᵊr **~s** z
BAC ˌbiː eɪ ˈsiː
Bacall bə ˈkɔːl ‖ -ˈkɑːl
Bacardi *tdmk* bə ˈkɑːd i ‖ -ˈkɑːrd- —*Sp* Bacardí [ba kar ˈði] **~s** z
baccalaureate ˌbæk ə ˈlɔːr i‿ət ɪt ‖ -ˈlɑːr- **~s** z
baccara, baccarat ˈbæk ə rɑː ˌ· ·ˈ· ‖ ˈbɑːk- ˌbæk- —*Fr* [ba ka ʁa]
baccate ˈbæk eɪt
Bacchae ˈbæk iː -aɪ
bacchanal ˌbæk ə ˈnæl ˈ· · ·; ˈbæk ən ᵊl ‖ ˌbɑːk- **~s** z
bacchanalia, B~ ˌbæk ə ˈneɪl i‿ə

bacchanalian ˌbæk ə ˈneɪl i‿ən ◂
bacchant ˈbæk ənt →-ŋt ‖ bə ˈkænt -ˈkɑːnt; ˈbæk ənt **~s** s
bacchante bə ˈkænt i bə ˈkænt ‖ -ˈkænt̬ i -ˈkɑːnt̬-; bə ˈkɑːnt **bacchantes** bə ˈkænt iz bə ˈkænts ‖ bə ˈkænt̬ iz -ˈkɑːnt̬-; bə ˈkɑːnts
Bacchic, b~ ˈbæk ɪk
Bacchus ˈbæk əs
bacciferous bæk ˈsɪf ər‿əs
baccy ˈbæk i
Bach, bach bɑːk bɑːx —*Ger* [bax]; *Welsh* [baːχ]
Bacharach ˈbæk ə ræk
bachelor, B~ ˈbætʃ əl‿ə -ɪl ə ‖ -ᵊl‿ər **~hood** hʊd **~ship** ʃɪp **~s** z
ˈ**bachelor girl**; ˌ**Bachelor of ˈArts**; ˈ**bachelor's deˌgree**
bacillar bə ˈsɪl ə ˈbæs ɪl ə, -əl- ‖ -ᵊr
bacillary bə ˈsɪl ər i ˈbæs ɪl-, ˈ·əl- ‖ ˈbæs ə ler i bə ˈsɪl ər i
bacilliform bə ˈsɪl ɪ fɔːm bæ-, -ə- ‖ -fɔːrm
bacill|us bə ˈsɪl |əs **~i** aɪ iː
bacitracin ˌbæs ɪ ˈtreɪs ɪn -ə-, §-ᵊn
back bæk **backed** bækt **backing** ˈbæk ɪŋ **backs** bæks
ˈ**back ˌcountry**; ˌ**back ˈdoor**◂; ˈ**back forˌmation**; ˌ**back ˈgarden**; ˌ**back ˈnumber**; ˌ**back ˈpassage**; ˌ**back ˈseat**; ˈ**back street**; ˈ**back talk**; ˌ**back ˈup**; ˌ**back ˈyard**
backache ˈbæk eɪk **~s** s
backbench ˌbæk ˈbentʃ ◂ ˈ· · **~es** ɪz əz
backbencher ˌbæk ˈbentʃ ə ◂ ˈ· · · ‖ -ᵊr **~s** z
backbit|er ˈbæk baɪt |ə ‖ -baɪt̬ ᵊr **~ers** əz ‖ ᵊrz **~ing** ɪŋ
backblocks ˈbæk blɒks ‖ -blɑːks
backboard ˈbæk bɔːd ‖ -bɔːrd -bourd **~s** z
backbone ˈbæk bəʊn ‖ -boun **~d** d **~s** z
backbreak|er ˈbæk ˌbreɪk |ə ‖ -|ᵊr **~ers** əz ‖ ᵊrz **~ing** ɪŋ
backchat ˈbæk tʃæt
backcloth ˈbæk klɒθ ‖ -klɔːθ -klɑːθ
backcomb ˈbæk kəʊm ‖ -koum **~ed** d **~ing** ɪŋ **~s** z
back|date ˌbæk ˈ|deɪt ◂ ˈ· · ‖ ˈbæk |deɪt **~dated** deɪt ɪd əd ‖ deɪt̬ əd **~dates** deɪts **~dating** deɪt ɪŋ ‖ deɪt̬ ɪŋ
backdrop ˈbæk drɒp ‖ -drɑːp **~s** s
backer, B~ ˈbæk ə ‖ -ᵊr **~s** z
backfield ˈbæk fiːᵊld
backfill ˈbæk fɪl **~ed** d **~ing** ɪŋ **~s** z
backfire *n* ˈbæk ˌfaɪ‿ə ‖ -ˌfaɪ‿ᵊr **~s** z
backfire *v* ˌbæk ˈfaɪ‿ə ◂ ˈ·ˌ· · ‖ ˈbæk ˌfaɪ‿ᵊr **~d** d **~s** z **backfiring** ˌbæk ˈfaɪ‿ər ɪŋ ˈ·ˌ·- ‖ ˈbæk ˌfaɪ‿ᵊr ɪŋ
backflip ˈbæk flɪp **~s** s
back-formation ˈbæk fɔː ˌmeɪʃ ᵊn ‖ -fɔːr- **~s** z
backgammon ˈbæk ˌgæm ən ˌ·ˈ· ·
background ˈbæk graʊnd **~ed** ɪd əd **~ing** ɪŋ **~s** z
backhand ˈbæk hænd **~ed** *v* ɪd əd **~ing** ɪŋ **~s** z
backhanded *adj* ˌbæk ˈhænd ɪd ◂ -əd ‖ ˈbæk hænd əd **~ly** li **~ness** nəs nɪs
backhander ˈbæk hænd ə ˌ·ˈ· · ‖ -ᵊr **~s** z
backhoe ˈbæk həʊ ‖ -hou **~s** z
Backhouse, b~ ˈbæk haʊs -əs
backing ˈbæk ɪŋ
ˈ**backing store**
backlash ˈbæk læʃ
backless ˈbæk ləs -lɪs
backlighting ˌbæk ˈlaɪt ɪŋ ˈ·ˌ· · ‖ ˈbæk ˌlaɪt̬ ɪŋ ˌ·ˈ· ·
backlist ˈbæk lɪst **~s** s
backlit ˌbæk ˈlɪt ◂ ˈ· ·
backlog ˈbæk lɒg ‖ -lɔːg -lɑːg **~s** z
backlot ˈbæk lɒt ‖ -lɑːt **~s** s
backmost ˈbæk məʊst ‖ -moust
backpack ˈbæk pæk **~ed** t **~er/s** ə/z ‖ -ᵊr/z **~ing** ɪŋ **~s** s
backpedal, back-pedal ˌbæk ˈped ᵊl ◂ ˈ·ˌ· · ‖ ˈbæk ˌped ᵊl **~ed, ~led** d **~ing, ~ling** ˌɪŋ **~s** z
backra ˈbʌk rə ˈbæk- ‖ ˈbæk- ˈbʊk-
backrest ˈbæk rest **~s** s
backroom ˈbæk ruːm -rʊm **~s** z
ˈ**backroom boys**
Backs bæks
backscratcher ˈbæk ˌskrætʃ ə ‖ -ᵊr **~s** z
back-seat ˌbæk ˈsiːt ◂
ˌ**back-seat ˈdriver**
backsheesh ˌbæk ˈʃiːʃ ˈ· ·
backside ˈbæk saɪd ˌ·ˈ· **~s** z
backsight ˈbæk saɪt **~s** s
backslapping ˈbæk ˌslæp ɪŋ **~s** z
backslash ˈbæk slæʃ **~es** ɪz əz
backslid|e ˈbæk slaɪd ˌ·ˈ· **~er/s** ə/z ‖ ᵊr/z **~ing** ɪŋ
backspac|e *n* ˈbæk speɪs **~es** ɪz əz
backspac|e *v* ˌbæk ˈspeɪs ◂ ˈ· · **~ed** t **~es** ɪz əz **~ing** ɪŋ
backspin ˈbæk spɪn
backstage ˌbæk ˈsteɪdʒ ◂
ˌ**backstage ˈworkers**
backstair ˌbæk ˈsteə ◂ ‖ ˈbæk ster **~s** z
ˌ**backstairs ˈinfluence**
backstay ˈbæk steɪ **~s** z
backstitch ˈbæk stɪtʃ **~ed** t **~es** ɪz əz **~ing** ɪŋ
backstop ˈbæk stɒp ‖ -stɑːp **~s** s
backstreet ˈbæk striːt
backstroke ˈbæk strəʊk ‖ -strouk **~s** s
backswing ˈbæk swɪŋ **~s** z
back-to-back ˌbæk tə ˈbæk ◂
ˌ**back-to-back ˈhousing**
backtrack ˈbæk træk ˌ·ˈ· **~ed** t **~ing** ɪŋ **~s** s
backup ˈbæk ʌp **~s** s
Backus ˈbæk əs
backward ˈbæk wəd ‖ -wᵊrd **~ly** li **~ness** nəs nɪs
backwardation ˌbæk wə ˈdeɪʃ ᵊn ‖ -wᵊr-
backward-looking ˌbæk wəd ˈlʊk ɪŋ ◂ §-ˈluːk- ‖ -wᵊrd-
backwards ˈbæk wədz ‖ -wᵊrdz
backwash ˈbæk wɒʃ ‖ -wɔːʃ -wɑːʃ **~es** ɪz əz
backwater ˈbæk ˌwɔːt ə ‖ -ˌwɔːt̬ ᵊr -ˌwɑːt̬ ᵊr **~s** z
backwoods ˈbæk wʊdz

B

backwoods|man 'bæk wʊdz |mən ˌ·'·- **~men** mən men
backyard ˌbæk 'jɑːd ◂ ‖ -'jɑːrd ◂ **~s** z
Bacofoil *tdmk* 'beɪk əʊ fɔɪᵊl ‖ -oʊ-
bacon, Bacon 'beɪk ən **~s** z
 ˌbacon 'sandwich
Baconian beɪ 'kəʊn i̯ən bə- ‖ -'koʊn- **~s** z
bacteria bæk 'tɪər i̯ə ‖ -'tɪr-
bacterial bæk 'tɪər i̯əl ‖ -'tɪr- **~ly** i
bactericidal bæk ˌtɪər ɪ 'saɪd ᵊl ◂ -ə- ‖ -ˌtɪr ə- **~ly** i
bactericide bæk 'tɪər ɪ saɪd -ə- ‖ -'tɪr ə- **~s** z
bacteriological bæk ˌtɪər i̯ə 'lɒdʒ ɪk ᵊl ◂ ‖ -ˌtɪr i̯ə 'lɑːdʒ- **~ly** ˌi
bacteriologist bæk ˌtɪər i 'ɒl ədʒ ɪst §-əst ‖ -ˌtɪr i 'ɑːl- **~s** s
bacteriology bæk ˌtɪər i 'ɒl ədʒ i ‖ -ˌtɪr i 'ɑːl-
bacteriophage bæk 'tɪər i̯əʊ feɪdʒ ‖ -'tɪr i̯ə- **~s** z
bacterium bæk 'tɪər i̯əm ‖ -'tɪr-
Bactria 'bæk tri̯ə
Bactrian 'bæk tri̯ən **~s** z
Bacup 'beɪk əp -ʌp
bad bæd
 ˌbad 'blood; **ˌbad 'debt**; **ˌbad 'faith**; **ˌbad 'feeling**; **ˌbad 'form**; **ˌbad 'news**
Bad *in German place names* bæd bɑːd ‖ bɑːd —*Ger* [baːt] —*See also phrases with this word*
Badajoz ˌbæd ə 'hɒz -həʊz, '· · · ‖ ˌbɑːd ə 'hoʊs —*Sp* [ba ða 'xoθ]
badass 'bæd æs **~es** ɪz əz
Badawi bə 'dɑː wi
Badcock 'bæd kɒk →'bæg- ‖ -kɑːk
Baddeley 'bæd ᵊl ˌi
Baddesley *(i)* 'bæd ɪz li -əz-, *(ii)* 'bædz li
baddie, baddy 'bæd i **baddies** 'bæd iz
Baddiel bə 'diːᵊl
baddish 'bæd ɪʃ
bade bæd beɪd
Badedas *tdmk* 'bɑːd ə dæs -ɪ-; bə 'deɪd æs, -əs
Badel bə 'del
Baden *British or American name* 'beɪd ᵊn
Baden *places in German-speaking countries* 'bɑːd ᵊn —*Ger* ['baː dᵊn]
Baden-Baden ˌbɑːd ᵊn 'bɑːd ᵊn —*Ger* [ˌbaː dᵊn 'baː dᵊn]
Baden-Powell ˌbeɪd ᵊn 'pəʊ əl -'paʊ̯əl, -el, -ɪl, -'paʊl ‖ -'poʊ əl
Bader 'bɑːd ə ‖ -ᵊr
badge bædʒ **badges** 'bædʒ ɪz -əz
badger 'bædʒ ə ‖ -ᵊr **~ed** d **badgering** 'bædʒ ər ˌɪŋ **~s** z
Bad Godesberg ˌbæd 'gəʊd əz bɜːg -beəg; -'gəʊdz· ‖ ˌbɑːt 'goʊd əz bɜːg -berg —*Ger* [ˌbaːt 'goː dəs bɛʁk]
badinage 'bæd ɪ nɑːʒ -ə-, -nɑːdʒ, ˌ ·'· —*Fr* [ba di naːʒ]
badlands 'bæd lændz
badly 'bæd li
badly-behaved ˌbæd li bi 'heɪvd ◂ -li bə-
badly-off ˌbæd li 'ɒf ◂ -'ɔːf ‖ -'ɔːf -'ɑːf
badminton, B~ 'bæd mɪn tən →'bæb-, ⚠-mɪŋ-
bad-|mouth 'bæd |maʊθ →'bæb-, -maʊð **~mouthed** maʊθt maʊðd **~mouthing** maʊθ ɪŋ maʊð ɪŋ **~mouths** *v* maʊθs maʊðz
badness 'bæd nəs -nɪs
Badoit *tdmk* 'bæd wɑː ‖ bɑː 'dwɑː —*Fr* [ba dwa]
bad-tempered ˌbæd 'temp əd ◂ ‖ -ᵊrd '· · · **~ly** li
Baedeker 'beɪd ɪk ə -ək-, -ek- ‖ -ᵊr **~s** z —*Ger* ['bɛː də kɐ]
Baer beə ‖ beᵊr
Baerlein 'beə laɪn ‖ 'ber-
Baez 'baɪ ez ·'· —*but the singer* Joan Baez *prefers* baɪz
Baffin 'bæf ɪn §-ᵊn
baffl|e 'bæf ᵊl **~ed** d **~es** z **~ing** ˌɪŋ
bafflement 'bæf ᵊl mənt
BAFTA 'bæft ə
bag bæg **bagged** bægd **bagging** 'bæg ɪŋ **bags** bægz
 'bag ˌlady
Baganda bə 'gænd ə -'gɑːnd-
bagasse bə 'gæs bæ-, -'gɑːs
bagatelle ˌbæg ə 'tel **~s** z
Bagdad ˌbæg 'dæd '· · ‖ 'bæg dæd —*Arabic* [baɣ 'daːd]
Bagehot *(i)* 'bædʒ ət, *(ii)* 'bæg ət —*The economist* Walter B~ *was (i).*
bagel 'beɪg ᵊl **~s** z
bagful 'bæg fʊl **~s** z **bagsful** 'bægz fʊl
bagg... —*see* **bag**
baggag|e 'bæg ɪdʒ **~es** ɪz əz
 'baggage car; **'baggage room**; **'baggage tag**
Baggally 'bæg əl i
Baggie *tdmk* 'bæg i **~s** z
Baggins 'bæg ɪnz §-ənz
bagg|y 'bæg |i **~ier** i̯ə ‖ i̯ᵊr **~iest** i̯ɪst i̯əst **~ily** ɪ li əl i **~iness** i nəs -nɪs
Baghdad ˌbæg 'dæd '· · ‖ 'bæg dæd —*Arabic* [baɣ 'daːd]
Bagley 'bæg li
bag|man 'bæg |mən **~men** mən men
Bagnall, Bagnell 'bæg nᵊl
bagnio 'bæn jəʊ 'bɑːn- ‖ 'bɑːn joʊ **~s** z
Bagnold 'bæg nəʊld →-nɒʊld ‖ -noʊld
bagpip|e 'bæg paɪp **~er/s** ə/z ‖ ᵊr/z **~es** s **~ing** ɪŋ
bagsful 'bægz fʊl
Bagshaw 'bæg ʃɔː ‖ -ʃɑː
Bagshot 'bæg ʃɒt ‖ -ʃɑːt
baguette bæ 'get bə- **~s** s —*Fr* [ba gɛt]
Baguley 'bæg əl ˌi -jʊl-
bagwash 'bæg wɒʃ ‖ -wɔːʃ -wɑːʃ **~s** ɪz əz
bah bɑː ‖ bæ *(= baa)*
bahadur bə 'hɑːd ə -ʊə ‖ -ᵊr -ʊr **~s** z
Bahai, Baha'i, Bahá'í bə 'haɪ bɑː-, -'hɑː i, -'haɪ i **~s** z —*Persian* [ba hɑː ʔiː]
Baha|ism bə 'haɪ |ˌɪz əm bɑː-, -'hɑː- **~ist/s** ɪst/s əst/s
Bahama bə 'hɑːm ə **~s** z
Bahamian bə 'heɪm i̯ən -'hɑːm- **~s** z
Bahasa bə 'hɑːs ə bɑː-

Baha'ullah, Bahá'-u'lláh ˌbɑː hɑː ˈʊl ə bə ˌhɑː ʊ ˈlɑː
Bahia bə ˈhiː ə bɑː ˈiː ə —*Port* [bɐ ˈi ɐ]
Bahrain, Bahrein ˌbɑː ˈreɪn ˌbɑːx-; ˌbɑː hə ˈreɪn —*Arabic* [baħ ˈreːn] **~i/s** i/z
baht bɑːt **bahts** bɑːts
bahuvrihi ˌbɑː huː ˈvriː hi
Baikal baɪ ˈkæl -ˈkɑːl, ˈ· · —*Russ* [bʌj ˈkaɫ]
Baikonur ˌbaɪk ə ˈnʊə ‖ -ˈnʊᵊr —*Russ* [bəj kʌ ˈnur]
bail beɪᵊl **bailed** beɪᵊld **bailing** ˈbeɪᵊl ɪŋ **bails** beɪᵊlz
bailable ˈbeɪᵊl əb ᵊl
Baildon ˈbeɪᵊld ən
Baile Atha Cliath, Baile Átha Cliath ˌblɑː ˈklɪə ˌblɔː- ‖ -ˈkliː ə ˌblɔː- —*Irish* [bɫaː ˈkliə]
bailee ˌbeɪ ˈliː ˌbeɪᵊl ˈiː **~s** z
bailey, B~ ˈbeɪl i **~s, ~'s** z
ˌBailey ˈbridge, ˈ· · ·
bailie ˈbeɪl i **~s** z
bailiff ˈbeɪl ɪf §-əf **~s** s
bailiwick ˈbeɪl i wɪk §-ə- **~s** s
Baillie ˈbeɪl i
Baillieu ˈbeɪl juː
Bailly ˈbeɪl i
bailment ˈbeɪᵊl mənt
bailor ˌbeɪ ˈlɔː ˈbeɪᵊl ə, ˌbeɪᵊl ˈɔː ‖ -ˈlɔːr **~s** z
bailout ˈbeɪᵊl aʊt **~s** s
bails|man ˈbeɪᵊlz |mən **~men** mən men
Baily ˈbeɪl i **~'s** z
Bain beɪn
Bainbridge ˈbeɪn brɪdʒ →ˈbeɪm-
Baines beɪnz
bain-marie ˌbæn mə ˈriː →ˌbæm-, -mə- **~s** z —*Fr* [bɛ̃ ma ʁi]
Bairam baɪ ˈrɑːm -ˈræm; ˈbaɪᵊr əm **~s** z
Baird beəd ‖ beᵊrd
bairn beən ‖ beᵊrn **bairns** beənz ‖ beᵊrnz
Bairnsfather ˈbeənz ˌfɑːð ə ‖ ˈbernz ˌfɑːð ᵊr
Bairstow ˈbeə stəʊ ‖ ˈber stoʊ
bait beɪt **baited** ˈbeɪt ɪd -əd ‖ ˈbeɪt̬ əd **baiting** ˈbeɪt ɪŋ ‖ ˈbeɪt̬ ɪŋ **baits** beɪts
baize beɪz *(= bays)*
Baja ˈbɑː hɑː —*Sp* [ˈba xa]
ˌBaja ˌCaliˈfornia
Bajan ˈbeɪdʒ ən **~s** z
bajra ˈbɑːdʒ rə
bake beɪk **baked** beɪkt **bakes** beɪks **baking** ˈbeɪk ɪŋ
ˌbaked ˈbeans
bake|house ˈbeɪk| haʊs **~houses** haʊz ɪz -əz
bakelite, B~ *tdmk* ˈbeɪk ə laɪt ˈbeɪk laɪt
baker, Baker ˈbeɪk ə ‖ -ᵊr **~s** z
ˌbaker's ˈdozen; **ˈBaker Street**
bakeries ˈbeɪk ər‿iz
Bakerloo ˌbeɪk ə ˈluː ‖ -ᵊr-
ˌBakerˈloo line
Bakersfield ˈbeɪk əz fiːᵊld ‖ -ᵊrz-
baker|y ˈbeɪk ər‿|i **~ies** iz
Bakewell ˈbeɪk wel -wəl
ˌBakewell ˈtart

baking ˈbeɪk ɪŋ
ˈbaking ˌpowder
baklava ˈbɑːk lə vɑː ˈbæk-; ˌ· ·ˈ· **~s** z
baksheesh ˌbæk ˈʃiːʃ ˈ· ·
Bakst bækst ‖ bɑːkst —*Russ* [bakst]
Baku ₍ˌ₎bɑː ˈkuː bæ-
Bakunin bə ˈkuːn ɪn bɑː-, §-ən —*Russ* [bʌ ˈku nʲin]
Bala ˈbæl ə ˈbɑːl ə
Balaam ˈbeɪl əm -æm
balaclava, B~ ˌbæl ə ˈklɑːv ə ◂ —*Russ* [bə ɫʌ ˈkɫa və] **~s** z
balalaika ˌbæl ə ˈlaɪk ə —*Russ* [bə ɫʌ ˈɫaj kə] **~s** z
balanc|e ˈbæl ənᵗs **~ed** t **~es** ɪz əz **~ing** ɪŋ
ˌbalanced ˈdiet; **ˌbalance of ˈpower**; **ˈbalance sheet**; **ˈbalance wheel**; **ˈbalancing act**
Balanchine ˈbæl ən tʃiːn -ʃiːn
balas ˈbæl əs ˈbeɪl-
balata ˈbæl ət ə bə ˈlɑːt ə ‖ bə ˈlɑːt̬ ə **~s** z
Balaton ˈbæl ə tɒn ˈbɒl- ‖ ˈbɑːl ə tɑːn ˈbæl-, -toʊn —*Hung* [ˈbɒ lɒ ton]
Balboa, b~ bæl ˈbəʊ ə ‖ -ˈboʊ- **~s** z *Sp* [bal ˈβo a]
Balbriggan, b~ bæl ˈbrɪɡ ən
Balbus ˈbælb əs
Balchin ˈbɔːltʃ ɪn ˈbɒltʃ-, §-ən ‖ ˈbɑːltʃ-
Balcomb, Balcombe ˈbɔːlk əm ˈbɒlk- ‖ ˈbɑːlk-
Balcon ˈbɔːlk ən ˈbɒlk- ‖ ˈbɑːlk-
balcon|y ˈbælk ən |i **~ies** iz
bald bɔːld ‖ bɑːld *(= bawled)* **balder** ˈbɔːld ə §ˈbɒld- ‖ ˈbɔːld ᵊr ˈbɑːld- **baldest** ˈbɔːld ɪst §ˈbɒld-, əst ‖ ˈbɑːld-
ˈbald ˌeagle
baldachin, baldaquin ˈbɔːld ək ɪn §ˈbɒld-, §-ən ‖ ˈbɑːld-
Balder *name* ˈbɔːld ə ˈbɒld- ‖ ˈbɔːld ᵊr ˈbɑːld-
balderdash ˈbɔːld ə dæʃ §ˈbɒld- ‖ -ᵊr- ˈbɑːld-
bald-faced ˌbɔːld ˈfeɪst ◂ §ˌbɒld- ‖ ˌbɑːld-
baldhead ˈbɔːld hed ‖ ˈbɑːld- **~s** z
baldheaded ˌbɔːld ˈhed ɪd ◂ §ˌbɒld-, -əd ‖ ˌbɑːld-
baldie ˈbɔːld i §ˈbɒld i ‖ ˈbɑːld i **~s** z
baldish ˈbɔːld ɪʃ §ˈbɒld- ‖ ˈbɑːld-
bald|ly ˈbɔːld |li §ˈbɒld- ‖ ˈbɑːld- **~ness** nəs nɪs
Baldock ˈbɔːld ɒk ˈbɒld- ‖ -ɑːk ˈbɑːld-
baldric ˈbɔːldr ɪk §ˈbɒldr- ‖ ˈbɑːldr-
Baldry ˈbɔːldr i ˈbɒldr i ‖ ˈbɑːldr i
Baldwin ˈbɔːld wɪn §ˈbɒld-, §-wən ‖ ˈbɑːld-
bald|y ˈbɔːld |i ‖ ˈbɑːld |i **~ies** iz
bale beɪᵊl *(= bail)* **baled** beɪᵊld **bales** beɪᵊlz **baling** ˈbeɪᵊl ɪŋ
Bale, Bâle *place in Switzerland* bɑːl —*Fr* [bɑːl]
Bale *family name* beɪᵊl
Balearic ˌbæl i ˈær ɪk ◂ bə ˈlɪər ɪk ‖ -ˈer- **~s** s
baleen bə ˈliːn bæ-, beɪ-
baleful ˈbeɪᵊl fᵊl -fʊl **~ly** i **~ness** nəs nɪs
Balenciaga bə ˌlenᵗs i ˈɑːɡ ə bæ- —*Sp* [ba len ˈθja ɣa]
baler ˈbeɪᵊl ə ‖ -ᵊr **~s** z
Balfe bælf

B

Balfour *(i)* ˈbælf ə ‖ -ər, *(ii)* ˈbæl fɔː ‖ -fɔːr -foʊr
the ˌBalfour ˌdeclaˈration
Balham ˈbæl əm
Bali ˈbɑːl i
Balinese ˌbɑːl ɪ ˈniːz ◂ -ə- ‖ -ˈniːs
Baliol ˈbeɪl i‿əl
balk bɔːk bɔːlk ‖ bɑːk **balked** bɔːkt bɔːlkt ‖ bɑːkt **balking** ˈbɔːk ɪŋ ˈbɔːlk- ‖ ˈbɑːk- **balks** bɔːks bɔːlks ‖ bɑːks
Balkan ˈbɔːlk ən ˈbɒlk- ‖ ˈbɑːlk- **~s** z
Balkanis..., b~ *—see* **Balkaniz...**
Balkanization, b~ ˌbɔːlk ən aɪ ˈzeɪʃ ən ˌbɒlk-, -ɪˈ-- ‖ -ə ˈ· · ˌbɑːlk-
Balkaniz|e, b~ ˈbɔːlk ə naɪz ˈbɒlk- ‖ ˈbɑːlk- **~ed** d **~es** ɪz əz **~ing** ɪŋ
balk|y ˈbɔːk |i ‖ ˈbɑːk- **~ier** i‿ə ‖ i‿ər **~iest** i‿ɪst i‿əst
ball, Ball bɔːl ‖ bɑːl **balled** bɔːld ‖ bɑːld *(= bald)* **balling** ˈbɔːl ɪŋ ‖ ˈbɑːl- **balls** bɔːlz ‖ bɑːlz
ˈball boy; **ˈball games**; **ˈball park**
Ballachulish ˌbæl ə ˈhuːl ɪʃ
ballad ˈbæl əd **~s** z
ballade bæ ˈlɑːd bə- **~s** z *—Fr* [ba lad]
balladeer ˌbæl ə ˈdɪə ‖ -ˈdɪər **~s** z
Ballance ˈbæl ənᵗs
ball-and-socket ˌbɔːl ən ˈsɒk ɪt -ənd-, §-ət ‖ -ˈsɑːk ət ˌbɑːl-
Ballantine ˈbæl ən taɪn
Ballantrae ˌbæl ən ˈtreɪ
Ballantyne ˈbæl ən taɪn
Ballarat ˈbæl ə ræt ˌ· ·ˈ·
Ballard ˈbæl ɑːd -əd ‖ -ɑːrd -ərd
ballast ˈbæl əst **~ed** ɪd əd **~ing** ɪŋ **~s** s
Ballater ˈbæl ət ə ‖ -əţ ər
ballbearing ˌbɔːl ˈbeər ɪŋ ‖ -ˈber- ˌbɑːl-, -ˈbær- **~s** z
ballcock ˈbɔːl kɒk ‖ -kɑːk ˈbɑːl- **~s** s
ballerina ˌbæl ə ˈriːn ə **~s** z
Ballesteros ˌbæl ɪ ˈstɪər ɒs -ə-, -e-, -ˈsteər-, -ˈster- ‖ ˌbaɪ ə ˈster oʊs ˌbæl- *—Sp* [ba ʎe ˈste ɾos, ba je-]
ballet ˈbæl eɪ ‖ bæ ˈleɪ ˈbæl eɪ **~s** z
ˈballet ˌdancer ‖ ·ˈ· ˌ· ·
balletic bæ ˈlet ɪk bə- ‖ -ˈleţ-
balletomane ˈbæl ɪt əʊ meɪn ˈ-ət-, ˈ-et-; bə ˈlet· ·, bæ- ‖ bə ˈleţ ə meɪn
balletomania ˌbæl ɪt əʊ ˈmeɪn i‿ə ˌ·ət-, ˌ·et- ‖ bə ˌleţ ə ˈmeɪn i‿ə *(*)*
Balliol ˈbeɪl i‿əl
ballist|a bə ˈlɪst |ə **~ae** iː **~as** əz
ballistic bə ˈlɪst ɪk **~ally** əl‿i **~s** s
Balloch ˈbæl ək -əx *—but the place in Highland region is* bæ ˈlɒx
ballock ˈbɒl ək ‖ ˈbɔːl- ˈbɑːl- **~s** s
balloon bə ˈluːn **~ed** d **~ing** ɪŋ **~s** z
balloonist bə ˈluːn ɪst §-əst **~s** s
ballot ˈbæl ət **balloted** ˈbæl ət ɪd -əd ‖ ˈbæl əţ əd **balloting** ˈbæl ət ɪŋ ‖ ˈbæl əţ ɪŋ **ballots** ˈbæl əts
ˈballot box; **ˈballot ˌpaper**
ballpark ˈbɔːl pɑːk ‖ -pɑːrk ˈbɑːl- **~s** s
ball-peen, ball-pein ˈbɔːl piːn ‖ ˈbɑːl- **~s** z
ballplayer ˈbɔːl ˌpleɪ ə ‖ -ər ˈbɑːl- **~s** z
ballpoint ˈbɔːl pɔɪnt ‖ ˈbɑːl- **~s** s
ballroom ˈbɔːl ruːm -rʊm ‖ ˈbɑːl- **~s** z
ˌballroom ˈdancing
balls, Balls bɔːlz ‖ bɑːlz **ballsed** bɔːlzd ‖ bɑːlzd **ballses** ˈbɔːlz ɪz -əz ‖ ˈbɑːlz- **ballsing** ˈbɔːlz ɪŋ ‖ ˈbɑːlz- *—These are parts of the slang verb* to balls up
balls-up *n* ˈbɔːlz ʌp ‖ ˈbɑːlz- **~s** s
balls|y ˈbɔːlz |i ‖ ˈbɑːlz- **~ier** i‿ə ‖ i‿ər **~iest** i‿ɪst i‿əst **~iness** i nəs i nɪs
bally, Bally ˈbæl i *—but the tdmk for shoes is properly Fr* [ba ji]
Ballycastle ˌbæl i ˈkɑːs əl §-ˈkæs- ‖ -ˈkæs-
ballyhoo ˌbæl i ˈhuː ‖ ˈbæl i huː **~ed** d **~ing** ɪŋ **~s** z
Ballymacarrett ˌbæl i mə ˈkær ət -ɪt ‖ -ˈker-
Ballymena ˌbæl i ˈmiːn ə
Ballymoney ˌbæl i ˈmʌn i
balm bɑːm §bɑːlm, §bɒlm **balms** bɑːmz §bɑːlmz, §bɒlmz
Balmain *(i)* ˌbæl ˈmeɪn, *(ii)* ˈbæl mæ̃ -mæn ‖ -meɪn ·ˈ· *—Fr* [bal mɛ̃] *—as an English or Scottish name, and for the place in Australia, (i); as a French name, (ii)*
Balmoral, b~ bæl ˈmɒr əl ˌ-ˈ-‖ -ˈmɔːr- -ˈmɑːr-
balm|y ˈbɑːm |i §ˈbɑːlm-, §ˈbɒlm- **~ier** i‿ə ‖ i‿ər **~iest** i‿ɪst i‿əst **~ily** ɪ li əl i **~iness** i nəs -nɪs
balneal ˈbæln i‿əl
balneology ˌbæln i ˈɒl ədʒ i ‖ -ˈɑːl-
Balniel bæl ˈniːəl
Balogh ˈbæl ɒg ‖ -ɑːg
baloney bə ˈləʊn i ‖ -ˈloʊn-
Baloo bə ˈluː ˈbɑːl uː
BALPA ˈbælp ə
Balquhidder bæl ˈwɪd ə -ˈhwɪd-, -ˈkwɪd- ‖ -ˈhwɪd ər
balsa ˈbɔːls ə ˈbɒls- ‖ ˈbɑːls- **~s** z
Balsall ˈbɔːls əl ˈbɒls- ‖ -ɔːl ˈbɑːls ɑːl
balsam ˈbɔːls əm ˈbɒls- ‖ ˈbɑːls- **~s** z
balsamic bɔːl ˈsæm ɪk bɒl- ‖ bɑːl-
Balt bɔːlt bɒlt ‖ bɑːlt **Balts** bɔːlts bɒlts ‖ bɑːlts
Balthazar bæl ˈθæz ə ˈbælθ ə zɑː, ˌ·ˈ· ‖ bæl ˈθeɪz ər *—in Shakespeare* ˌbælθ ə ˈzɑː, ˈ· · · ‖ -ˈzɑːr
balti ˈbɔːlt i ˈbɒlt-, ˈbælt- ‖ ˈbɑːlt i ˈbɔːlt-
Baltic ˈbɔːlt ɪk ‖ ˈbɑːlt-
ˌBaltic ˈSea
Baltimore ˈbɔːlt ɪ mɔː ˈbɒlt-, -ə- ‖ -ə mɔːr ˈbɑːlt-, -moʊr; -əm ər
Balto-Slavic ˌbɔːlt əʊ ˈslɑːv ɪk ◂ ˌbɒlt- ‖ -oʊ ˈslæv- ˌbɑːlt-, -ˈslɑːv-
Balto-Slavonic ˌbɔːlt əʊ slə ˈvɒn ɪk ◂ ˌbɒlt- ‖ -oʊ slə ˈvɑːn- ˌbɑːlt-
Baluchi bə ˈluːtʃ i **~s** z
Baluchistan bə ˌluːtʃ ɪ ˈstɑːn -ə-, -ˈstæn, ˈ· · · · ‖ -ə ˈstæn
baluster ˈbæl əst ə ‖ -ər **~s** z
balustrade ˌbæl ə ˈstreɪd ‖ ˈbæl ə streɪd **~s** z
Balzac ˈbælz æk ⚠ˈbɔːlz-, ⚠ˈbɒlz-; bæl ˈzæk ‖ ˈbɔːlz- ˈbɑːlz-, -ɑːk *—Fr* [bal zak]
Bamako ˌbæm ə ˈkəʊ ˈ· · · ‖ -ˈkoʊ ˌbɑːm-

B

Bamber ˈbæm bə ‖ -bᵊr
Bamberg ˈbæm bɜːg ‖ -bɜ˞ːg ˈbɑːm-, -berg —*Ger* [ˈbam bɛʁk]
Bambi ˈbæm bi
bambin|o bæm ˈbiːn |əʊ ‖ -|oʊ bɑːm- **~i** i **~os** əʊz ‖ oʊz —*It* [bam ˈbiː no]
bamboo ˌbæm ˈbuː ◂ **~s** z
ˌbamboo ˈfurniture
bamboozl|e ₍ˌ₎bæm ˈbuːz ᵊl **~ed** d **~es** z **~ing** ˌɪŋ
Bamburgh ˈbæm bər‿ə
Bamford ˈbæm fəd ‖ -fᵊrd
Bamforth ˈbæm fɔːθ ‖ -fɔːrθ -foʊrθ
Bamian ₍ˌ₎bɑːm ˈjɑːn
ban bæn **banned** bænd *(= band)* **banning** ˈbæn ɪŋ **bans** bænz
banal bə ˈnɑːl bæ-, -ˈnæl, §ˈbeɪn ᵊl **~ly** li
banalit|y bə ˈnæl ət |i bæ-, beɪ-, -ɪt i ‖ -əţ |i **~ies** iz
banana bə ˈnɑːn ə ‖ -ˈnæn- **~s** z
baˈnana oil; **baˈnana skin**; **baˌnana ˈsplit**
Bananarama bə ˌnɑːn ə ˈrɑːm ə ‖ bə ˌnæn ə ˈræm ə
Banaras bə ˈnɑːr əs
banausic bə ˈnɔːz ɪk -ˈnɔːs- ‖ -ˈnɔːs- -ˈnɑːs-, -ˈnɔːz-, -ˈnɑːz-
Banbridge bæn ˈbrɪdʒ →bæm-, ˈ· ·
Banbury ˈbæn bər‿i →ˈbæm- ‖ -ˌber i
ˌBanbury ˈCross
Banchory ˈbæŋk ər i ˈbæŋx-
banco ˈbæŋk əʊ ‖ -oʊ **~s** z
Bancroft ˈbæn krɒft →ˈbæŋ- ‖ -krɔːft -krɑːft
band bænd **banded** ˈbænd ɪd -əd **banding** ˈbænd ɪŋ **bands** bændz
ˈband saw
Banda ˈbænd ə ‖ ˈbɑːnd-
bandag|e ˈbænd ɪdʒ **~ed** d **~es** ɪz əz **~ing** ɪŋ
Band-Aid *tdmk,* **band-aid** ˈbænd eɪd **~s** z
bandana, bandanna ₍ˌ₎bæn ˈdæn ə **~s** z
Bandaranaike ˌbænd‿ər ə ˈnaɪ ɪk ə -ˈnaɪk ə ‖ ˌbɑːnd-
Bandar Seri Begawan ˌbænd ə ˌser i bə ˈgɑː wən ˌ·ɑː-, -beˈ·-, -bɪˈ·-, -ˈgaʊ ən ‖ ˌbɑːnd ᵊr-
bandbox ˈbænd bɒks →ˈbæm- ‖ -bɑːks **~es** ɪz əz
bandeau ˈbænd əʊ ‖ bæn ˈdoʊ **~s, ~x** z —*Fr* [bɑ̃ do]
banderol, banderole ˈbænd ə rəʊl →-rɒʊl ‖ -roʊl **~s** z
bandersnatch ˈbænd ə snætʃ ‖ -ᵊr-
bandicoot ˈbænd i kuːt **~s** s
bandie... —*see* **bandy**
bandit ˈbænd ɪt §-ət **~s** s
banditry ˈbænd ɪtr i -ətr-
banditti bæn ˈdɪt i ‖ -ˈdɪţ-
bandleader ˈbænd ˌliːd ə ‖ -ᵊr **~s** z
bandmaster ˈbænd ˌmɑːst ə §-ˌmæst ə ‖ -ˌmæst ᵊr **~s** z
bandoleer, bandolier ˌbænd ə ˈlɪə ‖ -ˈlɪᵊr **~s** z
bandore bæn ˈdɔː ˈbænd ɔː ‖ ˈbænd ɔːr -oʊr **~s** z
band-pass ˈbænd pɑːs §-pæs ‖ -pæs **~es** ɪz əz
bandsaw ˈbænd sɔː **~s** z
bands|man ˈbændz |mən **~men** mən men
bandstand ˈbænd stænd **~s** z
Bandung ˈbæn dʊŋ ˌ·ˈ· ‖ ˈbɑːn-
bandwagon ˈbænd ˌwæg ən **~s** z
bandwidth ˈbænd wɪdθ -wɪtθ **~s** s
band|y ˈbænd |i **~ied** id **~ies** iz **~ying** i‿ɪŋ
bandy-legged ˌbænd i ˈlegd ◂ -ˈleg ɪd, -ˈleg əd
bane beɪn **banes** beɪnz
baneful ˈbeɪn fᵊl -fʊl **~ly** i
Banff bænᵗf →bæmᵖf
Banfield ˈbæn fiːᵊld
bang bæŋ **banged** bæŋd **banging** ˈbæŋ ɪŋ **bangs** bæŋz
Bangalore ˌbæŋ gə ˈlɔː ‖ -ˈlɔːr -ˈloʊr, ˈ· · ·
banger ˈbæŋ ə ‖ -ᵊr **~s** z
Bangkok, b~ ˌbæŋ ˈkɒk ˈ· · ‖ ˈbæŋ kɑːk **~'s, ~s** s
Bangladesh ˌbæŋ glə ˈdeʃ ◂ -ˈdeɪʃ ‖ ˌbɑːŋ-
Bangladeshi ˌbæŋ glə ˈdeʃ i ◂ -ˈdeɪʃ- ‖ ˌbɑːŋ- **~s** z
bangle ˈbæŋ gᵊl **~s** z
bang-on ˌbæŋ ˈɒn ‖ -ˈɔːn -ˈɑːn
Bangor *(i)* ˈbæŋ gə ⚠ˈbæŋ ə ‖ -gᵊr, *(ii)* -gɔː ‖ -gɔːr —*Welsh* [ˈbaŋ gɔr] —*The places in the UK are usually (i), but the place in ME (ii).*
Bangui ˌbɒŋ ˈgiː ˌbɑːŋ- ‖ ˌbɑːŋ- —*Fr* [bɑ̃ gi]
bang-up ˌbæŋ ˈʌp ◂
Banham ˈbæn əm
banian ˈbæn i‿ən ˈbæn jæn **~s** z
banish ˈbæn ɪʃ **~ed** t **~es** ɪz əz **~ing** ɪŋ **~ment** mənt
banister ˈbæn ɪst ə -əst ə ‖ -ᵊr **~s** z
Banja Luka ˌbæn jə ˈluːk ə ˌbɑːn- ‖ ˌbɑːn- —*Serbian* [ˈbaː ɲaː ˈluː ka]
banjax ˈbæn dʒæks **~ed** t
banjo ˈbæn dʒəʊ ˌ·ˈ· ‖ -dʒoʊ **~es, ~s** z
banjoist ˈbæn dʒəʊ ɪst ˌ·ˈ·, §-əst ‖ -dʒoʊ- **~s** s
Banjul bæn ˈdʒuːl ‖ ˈbɑːn dʒuːl
bank bæŋk **banked** bæŋkt **banking** ˈbæŋk ɪŋ **banks** bæŋks
ˈbank acˌcount; **ˈbank ˌbalance**; **ˈbank draft**; **ˌbank ˈholiday**; **ˈbank loan**; **ˈbank ˌmanager**; **ˈbank rate**; **ˈbank ˌstatement**
bankable ˈbæŋk əb ᵊl
bankbill ˈbæŋk bɪl **~s** z
bankbook ˈbæŋk bʊk **~s** s
banker ˈbæŋk ə ‖ -ᵊr **~s** z
ˈbanker's card; **ˌbanker's ˈorder**
Bankes bæŋks
Bankhead ˈbæŋk hed
Ban Ki-Moon ˌbæn ˌkiː ˈmuːn →ˌbæŋ- ‖ ˌbɑːn- —*Korean* [b̥an ĝi mun]
banknote ˈbæŋk nəʊt ‖ -noʊt **~s** s
bankroll ˈbæŋk rəʊl →-rɒʊl ‖ -roʊl **~ed** d **~ing** ɪŋ **~s** z
bankrupt ˈbæŋk rʌpt -rəpt **~ed** ɪd əd **~ing** ɪŋ **~s** s
bankrupt|cy ˈbæŋk rʌpt |si -rəpt- **~cies** siz
Banks bæŋks **Banks's** ˈbæŋks ɪz -əz
banksia ˈbæŋks i‿ə **~s** z
Banksy ˈbæŋks i

Ban-Lon *tdmk* 'bæn lɒn ‖ -lɑːn
Bann bæn
bann... —*see* **ban**
banner, B~ 'bæn ə ‖ -ᵊr **~s** z
ˌbanner 'headline
Bannerman 'bæn ə mən ‖ -ᵊr-
Banning 'bæn ɪŋ
Bannister 'bæn ɪst ə §-əst- ‖ -ᵊr
bannock 'bæn ək **~s** s
Bannockburn 'bæn ək bɜːn ‖ -bɜːn
banns bænz *(= bans)*
banq|uet 'bæŋk |wɪt §-wət ‖ -|wət -wet **~ueted** wɪt ɪd wət əd ‖ wəţ əd weţ əd **~ueter/s** wɪt ə/z wət- ‖ wəţ ᵊr/z weţ- **~ueting** wɪt ɪŋ wət- ‖ wəţ ɪŋ weţ- **~uets** wɪts wəts ‖ wəts wets
banquette (ˌ)bæŋ 'ket **~s** s
Banquo 'bæŋk wəʊ ‖ -woʊ **~'s** z
banshee, banshie 'bæn ʃiː ·'· **~s** z
Banstead 'bæn'st ɪd §-əd, 'bæn sted
bantam, B~ 'bænt əm ‖ 'bænţ- **~s** z
bantamweight 'bænt əm weɪt ‖ 'bænţ- **~s** s
banter 'bænt ə ‖ 'bænţ ᵊr **~ed** d **bantering/ly** 'bænt ər ɪŋ /li ‖ 'bænţ ər ɪŋ /li **~s** z
banterer 'bænt ər ə ‖ 'bænţ ər ᵊr **~s** z
Banting, b~ 'bænt ɪŋ ‖ 'bænţ ɪŋ
Bantoid 'bænt ɔɪd 'bɑːnt-
Bantry 'bæntr i
ˌBantry 'Bay
Bantu ˌbæn 'tuː ◂ ˌbɑːn-, '· · **~s** z
ˌBantu 'languages
bantustan, B~ ˌbæn tuː 'stɑːn ˌbɑːn-, -'stæn, '· · · **~s** z
banyan 'bæn jən -i‿ən, -jæn **~s** z
'banyan tree
banzai (ˌ)bæn 'zaɪ ◂ (ˌ)bɑːn-, '· · ‖ (ˌ)bɑːn- **~s** z —*Jp* [baˌn 'dzai]
baobab 'beɪ əʊ bæb 'baʊ bæb ‖ -ə- **~s** z
'baobab tree
BAOR ˌbiː eɪ əʊ 'ɑː ‖ -oʊ 'ɑːr **~'s** z
bap bæp **baps** bæps
baptis... —*see* **baptiz...**
baptism 'bæpt ˌɪz əm **~s** z
baptismal (ˌ)bæp 'tɪz məl **~ly** i
Baptist 'bæpt ɪst §-əst **~s** s
baptister|y 'bæpt ɪst ər‿i §'-əst- **~ies** iz
baptis|try 'bæpt ɪs |tri §-əs- **~tries** triz

BAPTIZE

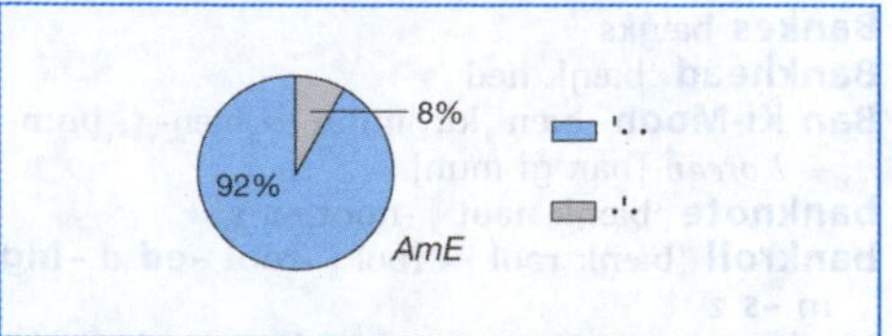

baptiz|e bæp 'taɪz ˌbæp- ‖ 'bæpt aɪz bæp 'taɪz **~ed** d **~er/s** ə/z ‖ ᵊr/z **~es** ɪz əz **~ing** ɪŋ — *Preference poll, AmE:* '·· 92%, ·'· 8%.
Baquba, Baqubah bɑː'kuːb ə —*Arabic* [baʕ 'quː bah]

bar, Bar bɑː ‖ bɑːr **barred** bɑːd ‖ bɑːrd *(= bard)* **barring** 'bɑːr ɪŋ **bars** bɑːz ‖ bɑːrz **ˌbar 'billiards**; **'bar chart**; **'bar graph**; **ˌbar 'none**; **ˌbar 'sinister**
Barabbas bə 'ræb əs
Barack 'bær æk -ək ‖ bə 'rɑːk -'ræk
barathea ˌbær ə 'θiː‿ə ‖ ˌber-
barb bɑːb ‖ bɑːrb **barbed** bɑːbd ‖ bɑːrbd **barbing** 'bɑːb ɪŋ ‖ 'bɑːrb ɪŋ **barbs** bɑːbz ‖ bɑːrbz
ˌbarbed 'wire
Barbadian bɑː 'beɪd i‿ən -'beɪdʒ ən ‖ bɑːr- **~s** z
Barbados bɑː 'beɪd ɒs -əʊz, -əs, -əʊs ‖ bɑːr 'beɪd oʊs **~'s** ɪz əz
Barbara 'bɑːb rə 'bɑːb ər ə ‖ 'bɑːrb- **~'s** z
barbarian bɑː 'beər i‿ən ‖ bɑːr 'ber i‿ən -'bær- **~s** z
barbaric bɑː 'bær ɪk ‖ bɑːr- -'ber- **~ally** ᵊl‿i
barbaris... —*see* **barbariz...**
barbarism 'bɑːb ə ˌrɪz əm ‖ 'bɑːrb- **~s** z
barbarit|y bɑː 'bær ət |i -ɪt- ‖ bɑːr 'bær əţ |i -'ber- **~ies** iz
barbariz|e 'bɑːb ə raɪz ‖ 'bɑːrb- **~ed** d **~es** ɪz əz **~ing** ɪŋ
Barbarossa ˌbɑːb ə 'rɒs ə ‖ ˌbɑːrb ə 'rɔːs ə -'rɑːs-
barbarous 'bɑːb ər‿əs ‖ 'bɑːrb- **~ly** li **~ness** nəs nɪs
Barbary 'bɑːb ər‿i ‖ 'bɑːrb-
ˌBarbary 'ape
barbate 'bɑːb eɪt ‖ 'bɑːrb-
barbecu|e 'bɑːb ɪ kjuː -ə- ‖ 'bɑːrb- **~ed** d **~es** z **~ing** ɪŋ
barbel 'bɑːb ᵊl ‖ 'bɑːrb- **~s** z
barbell 'bɑː bel ‖ 'bɑːr- **~s** z
barbequ|e 'bɑːb i kjuː -ə- ‖ 'bɑːrb- **~ed** d **~es** z **~ing** ɪŋ
barber, B~ 'bɑːb ə ‖ 'bɑːrb ᵊr **~ed** d **barbering** 'bɑːb ər ɪŋ ‖ 'bɑːrb ər ɪŋ **~s** z
barberr|y 'bɑːb ər‿i ‖ 'bɑːr ˌber |i **~ies** iz
barbershop 'bɑːb ə ʃɒp ‖ 'bɑːrb ᵊr ʃɑːp **~s** s
barbet 'bɑːb ɪt §-ət ‖ 'bɑːrb ət **~s** s
barbette bɑː 'bet ‖ bɑːr- **~s** s
barbican, B~ 'bɑːb ɪk ən -ək- ‖ 'bɑːrb- **~s** z
Barbie, b~ 'bɑːb i ‖ 'bɑːrb i
'Barbie doll
Barbirolli ˌbɑːb ɪ 'rɒl i -ə- ‖ ˌbɑːrb ə 'rɑːl i -'rɔːl-
barbital 'bɑːb ɪt ᵊl -ət- ‖ 'bɑːrb ə tɑːl -tɔːl
barbitone 'bɑːb ɪ təʊn -ə- ‖ 'bɑːrb ə toʊn
barbiturate bɑː 'bɪtʃ ʊr ət -'bɪtʃ ər‿ət, -'bɪt jʊr-, -ɪt, -jə reɪt, -juᵊ- ‖ bɑːr 'bɪtʃ ər‿ət -u‿ət; ˌbɑːrb ə 'tjʊr ət, -eɪt **~s** s
Barbizon 'bɑːb ɪ zɒn §-ə- ‖ ˌbɑːrb ə 'zoʊn -'zɑːn —*Fr* [baʁ bi zɔ̃]
Barbour 'bɑːb ə ‖ 'bɑːrb ᵊr
bar-b-que 'bɑːb i kjuː -ə- ‖ 'bɑːrb- **~s** z
Barbra 'bɑːb rə ‖ 'bɑːrb-
Barbuda bɑː 'bjuːd ə ‖ bɑːr-'buːd-
barbule 'bɑːb juːl ‖ 'bɑːrb juᵊl
barbwire ˌbɑːb 'waɪ‿ə ◂ ‖ ˌbɑːrb 'waɪ‿ᵊr ◂ '· ·
Barça 'bɑːs ə ‖ 'bɑːrs ə —*Catalan* ['bar sə]

barcarole, barcarolle ˌbɑːk ə ˈrəʊl →-ˈrɒl, ˈ· · ·‖ ˈbɑːrk ə roʊl **~s** z

Barcelona ˌbɑːs ə ˈləʊn ə ◂ -ə- ‖ ˌbɑːrs ə ˈloʊn ə ◂ —*Sp* [bar θe ˈlo na], *Catalan* [bər sə ˈlo nə]

Barchester ˈbɑː tʃɪst ə -tʃəst-, ˌtʃest ə ‖ ˈbɑːr ˌtʃest ər -tʃəst-

Barclay ˈbɑːk li -leɪ ‖ ˈbɑːrk- **~'s** z

Barclaycard *tdmk* ˈbɑːk li kɑːd -leɪ- ‖ ˈbɑːrk li kɑːrd -leɪ- **~s** z

barcod|e ˈbɑː kəʊd ‖ ˈbɑːr koʊd **~ed** ɪd əd **~es** z **~ing** ɪŋ

Barcoo ˌbɑː ˈkuː ◂ ‖ ˌbɑːr-
ˌBarcoo ˈdog

bard bɑːd ‖ bɑːrd **barded** ˈbɑːd ɪd -əd ‖ ˈbɑːrd əd **barding** ˈbɑːd ɪŋ ‖ ˈbɑːrd ɪŋ **bards** bɑːdz ‖ bɑːrdz

Bardell *(i)* bɑː ˈdel ‖ bɑːr-, *(ii)* ˈbɑːd əl -el ‖ ˈbɑːrd-

bardic ˈbɑːd ɪk ‖ ˈbɑːrd ɪk

bardolater bɑː ˈdɒl ət ə ‖ bɑːr ˈdɑːl əṭ ər **~s** z

bardolatry bɑː ˈdɒl ətr i ‖ bɑːr ˈdɑːl-

Bardolph ˈbɑːd ɒlf ‖ ˈbɑːrd ɑːlf

Bardon ˈbɑːd ən ‖ ˈbɑːrd ən

Bardot bɑː ˈdəʊ ‖ bɑːr ˈdoʊ —*Fr* [baʁ do]

Bardsey ˈbɑːd si ‖ ˈbɑːrd-

Bardsley ˈbɑːdz li ‖ ˈbɑːrdz-

bard|y ˈbɑːd| i ‖ ˈbɑːrd| i **~ies** iz

bare beə ‖ beər bæər *(= bear)* **bared** beəd ‖ beərd bæərd **barer** ˈbeər ə ‖ ˈber ər ˈbær- **bares** beəz ‖ beərz bæərz **barest** ˈbeər ɪst -əst ‖ ˈber əst ˈbær- **baring** ˈbeər ɪŋ ‖ ˈber ɪŋ ˈbær-

bare-arsed, bare-assed ˈbeər ɑːst ‖ ˈber æst ˈbær-

bareback ˈbeə bæk ‖ ˈber- ˈbær-

barebacked ˌbeə ˈbækt ◂ ‖ ˈber bækt ˈbær-

Barebones ˈbeə bəʊnz ‖ ˈber boʊnz ˈbær-

barefaced ˌbeə ˈfeɪst ◂ ‖ ˌber- ˌbær-

barefacedly ˌbeə ˈfeɪst li ◂ -ˈfeɪs ɪd-, -əd-; ˈ· ˌ· · ‖ ˌber- ˌbær-

bare|foot ˈbeə |fʊt ˌ·ˈ· ‖ ˈber- ˈbær- **~footed** fʊt ɪd -əd ‖ fʊṭ əd

bare-handed ˌbeə ˈhænd ɪd ◂ -əd ◂ ‖ ˌber- ˌbær-

bareheaded ˌbeə ˈhed ɪd ◂ -əd ‖ ˌber- ˌbær-

barelegged ˌbeə ˈlegd ◂ -ˈleg ɪd, -əd ‖ ˌber- ˌbær-

barely ˈbeə li ‖ ˈber li ˈbær-

Barenboim ˈbær ən bɔɪm ˈbeər-, →-əm- ‖ ˈber- ˈbær-

bareness ˈbeə nəs -nɪs ‖ ˈber- ˈbær-

Barents ˈbær ənts ‖ ˈber- ˈbær-, ˈbɑːr-

barf bɑːf ‖ bɑːrf **barfed** bɑːft ‖ bɑːrft **barfing** ˈbɑːf ɪŋ ‖ ˈbɑːrf ɪŋ **barfs** bɑːfs ‖ bɑːrfs

bar|fly ˈbɑː |flaɪ ‖ ˈbɑːr- **~flies** flaɪz

Barford ˈbɑː fəd ‖ ˈbɑːr fərd

bargain ˈbɑːg ɪn -ən ‖ ˈbɑːrg- **~ed** d **~er/s** ə/z ‖ ər/z **~ing** ɪŋ **~s** z
ˈbargaining ˌcounter

barge bɑːdʒ ‖ bɑːrdʒ **barged** bɑːdʒd ‖ bɑːrdʒd **barges** ˈbɑːdʒ ɪz -əz ‖ ˈbɑːrdʒ əz **barging** ˈbɑːdʒ ɪŋ ‖ ˈbɑːrdʒ ɪŋ

bargeboard ˈbɑːdʒ bɔːd ‖ ˈbɑːrdʒ bɔːrd -boʊrd **~s** z

bargee ₍ˌ₎bɑː ˈdʒiː ‖ ₍ˌ₎bɑːr- **~s** z

barge|man ˈbɑːdʒ |mən -mæn ‖ ˈbɑːrdʒ- **~men** mən men

bargepole ˈbɑːdʒ pəʊl →-pɒʊl ‖ ˈbɑːrdʒ poʊl **~s** z

barging ˈbɑːdʒ ɪŋ ‖ ˈbɑːrdʒ ɪŋ

Bargoed ˈbɑː gɔɪd ‖ ˈbɑːr-

Barham *(i)* ˈbɑːr əm, *(ii)* ˈbær əm ‖ ˈber-

Barhaugh ˈbɑː hʌf ‖ ˈbɑːr-

barhop ˈbɑː hɒp ‖ ˈbɑːr hɑːp **~ped** t **~ping** ɪŋ **~s** s

Bari ˈbɑːr i —*It* [ˈbaː ri]

baric ˈbeər ɪk ˈbær- ‖ ˈber ɪk

baring ˈbeər ɪŋ ‖ ˈber ɪŋ ˈbær-

Baring *(i)* ˈbeər ɪŋ ‖ ˈber-, *(ii)* ˈbær ɪŋ ‖ ˈber-

Baring-Gould ˌbeər ɪŋ ˈguːld ‖ ˌber- ˌbær-

barista bɑː ˈriːst ə bə-, -ˈrɪst-, -ɑː- **~s** z

baritone ˈbær ɪ təʊn -ə- ‖ ˈbær ə toʊn ˈber- **~s** z

barium ˈbeər i‿əm ‖ ˈber- ˈbær-
ˌbarium ˈmeal

bark bɑːk ‖ bɑːrk **barked** bɑːkt ‖ bɑːrkt **barking** ˈbɑːk ɪŋ ‖ ˈbɑːrk ɪŋ **barks** bɑːks ‖ bɑːrks

barkeep ˈbɑː kiːp ‖ ˈbɑːr- **~ing** ɪŋ **~s** s

barkeeper ˈbɑː ˌkiːp ə ‖ ˈbɑːr ˌkiːp ər **~s** z

barker, B~ ˈbɑːk ə ‖ ˈbɑːrk ər **~s** z

Barking ˈbɑːk ɪŋ ‖ ˈbɑːrk ɪŋ **~'s** z

Barkley, Barkly ˈbɑːk li ‖ ˈbɑːrk-

Barkston ˈbɑːkst ən ‖ ˈbɑːrkst-

Barlaston ˈbɑːl əst ən ‖ ˈbɑːrl-

barley ˈbɑːl i ‖ ˈbɑːrl i
ˈbarley ˌsugar, ˈbarley ˌwater, ˌbarley ˈwine

barleycorn, B~ ˈbɑːl i kɔːn ‖ ˈbɑːrl i kɔːrn

Barlinnie bɑː ˈlɪn i ‖ bɑːr-

Barlow, Barlowe ˈbɑːl əʊ ‖ ˈbɑːrl oʊ

barm bɑːm ‖ bɑːrm
ˈbarm cake

barmaid ˈbɑː meɪd ‖ ˈbɑːr-

bar|man ˈbɑː |mən -mæn ‖ ˈbɑːr- **~men** mən men

barmecidal, B~ ˌbɑːm ɪ ˈsaɪd əl ◂ -ə- ‖ ˌbɑːrm-

Barmecide ˈbɑːm ɪ saɪd -ə- ‖ ˈbɑːrm-

barmi... —*see* **barmy**

bar mitz|vah, bar miz|vah ₍ˌ₎bɑː ˈmɪts |və ‖ ₍ˌ₎bɑːr- **~vahed** vəd **~vahing** vər ɪŋ ‖ və ɪŋ **~vahs** vəz

Barmouth ˈbɑː məθ ‖ ˈbɑːr-

barm|y ˈbɑːm |i ‖ ˈbɑːrm |i **~ier** i‿ə ‖ i‿ər **~iest** i‿ɪst i‿əst **~iness** i nəs -nɪs

barn bɑːn ‖ bɑːrn **barns** bɑːnz ‖ bɑːrnz
ˈbarn dance; ˌbarn ˈdoor; ˈbarn owl

Barnabas ˈbɑːn əb əs -ə bæs ‖ ˈbɑːrn-

Barnaby ˈbɑːn əb i ‖ ˈbɑːrn-

barnacle ˈbɑːn ək əl -ɪk- ‖ ˈbɑːrn- **~d** d **~s** z
ˈbarnacle goose

Barnard *(i)* ˈbɑːn əd ‖ ˈbɑːrn ərd, *(ii)* -ɑːd ‖ -ɑːrd, *(iii)* bə ˈnɑːd ‖ bər ˈnɑːrd

Barnardo bə ˈnɑːd əʊ bɑː- ‖ bər ˈnɑːrd oʊ **~'s** z

B

Barnehurst ˈbɑːn hɜːst ‖ ˈbɑːrn hɜːst
Barnes bɑːnz ‖ bɑːrnz
Barnet ˈbɑːn ɪt §-ət ‖ ˈbɑːrn-
Barnett *(i)* ˈbɑːn ɪt §-ət ‖ ˈbɑːrn ət, *(ii)* bɑː ˈnet ‖ bɑːr-
barney, B~ ˈbɑːn i ‖ ˈbɑːrn i **~ed** d **~ing** ɪŋ **~s** z
Barnoldswick bɑː ˈnəʊldz wɪk →-ˈnɒʊldz- ‖ bɑːr ˈnoʊldz- *—locally also* ˈbɑːl ɪk
Barnsley ˈbɑːnz li ‖ ˈbɑːrnz-
Barnstable ˈbɑːnᵗst əb ᵊl ‖ ˈbɑːrnᵗst-
Barnstaple ˈbɑːnᵗst əp ᵊl ‖ ˈbɑːrnᵗst-
barnstorm ˈbɑːn stɔːm ‖ ˈbɑːrn stɔːrm **~ed** d **~er/s** ə/z ‖ ᵊr/z **~ing** ɪŋ **~s** z
Barnum ˈbɑːn əm ‖ ˈbɑːrn-
barnyard ˈbɑːn jɑːd ‖ ˈbɑːrn jɑːrd **~s** z
baro- *comb. form*
with stress-neutral suffix ˌbær ə ‖ ˌber- — **barogram** ˈbær ə græm ‖ ˈber-
with stress-imposing suffix bə ˈrɒ+ ‖ bə ˈrɑː+ — **barometry** bə ˈrɒm ətr i -ɪtr- ‖ bə ˈrɑːm-
Baroda bə ˈrəʊd ə ‖ -ˈroʊd-
barograph ˈbær ə grɑːf -græf ‖ -græf ˈber- **~s** s
barographic ˌbær ə ˈgræf ɪk ◂ ‖ ˌber- **~al** ᵊl **~ally** ᵊl‿i
barometer bə ˈrɒm ɪt ə -ət- ‖ -ˈrɑːm əṱ ᵊr
barometric ˌbær ə ˈmetr ɪk ◂ ‖ ˌber- **~al** ᵊl **~ally** ᵊl‿i
baron ˈbær ən ‖ ˈber- *(= barren)* **~s** z
Baron *(i)* ˈbær ən ‖ ˈber-, *(ii)* ˈbeər ən ‖ ˈber-
baronag|e ˈbær ən ɪdʒ ‖ ˈber- **~es** ɪz əz
baroness ˈbær ə nes ˌ· · ˈ·◂; ˈbær ən ɪs, -əs ‖ ˈber- **~es** ɪz əz
baronet ˈbær ən ɪt -ət; -ə net, ˌbær ə ˈnet ‖ ˈber- **~s** s
baronetag|e ˈbær ən ɪt ɪdʒ -ət ɪdʒ; -ə net-, ˌbær ə ˈnet- ‖ -əṱ ɪdʒ ˈber- **~es** ɪz əz
baronet|cy ˈbær ən ɪt |si -ət si; -ə net- ‖ ˈber- **~cies** siz
baronial bə ˈrəʊn i‿əl ‖ -ˈroʊn- **~ly** i
baron|y ˈbær ən |i ‖ ˈber- **~ies** iz
baroque bə ˈrɒk bæ-, -ˈrəʊk ‖ -ˈroʊk -ˈrɑːk
Barossa bə ˈrɒs ə ‖ -ˈrɑːs- -ˈrɔːs-
Barotse bə ˈrɒts i ‖ -ˈrɑːts- **~land** lænd
barouch|e bə ˈruːʃ bæ- **~es** ɪz əz
barque bɑːk ‖ bɑːrk *(= bark)* **barques** bɑːks ‖ bɑːrks
barquentine ˈbɑːk ən tiːn →-ŋ- ‖ ˈbɑːrk-
Barr bɑː ‖ bɑːr
Barra ˈbær ə ‖ ˈber-
barrack ˈbær ək ‖ ˈber- **~s** s
Barraclough ˈbær ə klʌf ‖ ˈber-
barracoon ˌbær ə ˈkuːn ‖ ˌber- **~s** z
barracouta ˌbær ə ˈkuːt ə ‖ -ˈkuːṱ ə ˌber- **~s** z
barracuda ˌbær ə ˈkjuːd ə -ˈkuːd- ‖ -ˈkuːd ə ˌber- **~s** z
barrag|e *'dam'* ˈbær ɑːʒ -ɑːdʒ ‖ ˈbɑːr ɪdʒ *(*)* **~es** ɪz əz
barrag|e *'artillery fire'* ˈbær ɑːʒ -ɑːdʒ ‖ bə ˈrɑːʒ -ˈrɑːdʒ **~es** ɪz əz
'barrage bal,loon ‖ ·ˈ· ·ˌ·
barramunda ˌbær ə ˈmʌnd ə ‖ ˌber- **~s** z
barramundi ˌbær ə ˈmʌnd i ‖ ˌber- **~s** z
Barranquilla ˌbær ən ˈkiːl jə ‖ ˌbɑːr ən ˈkiː jə ˌbær-, ˌber- *—AmSp* [ba ɾraŋ ˈki ja]
Barrat, Barratt ˈbær ət ‖ ˈber-
barratry ˈbær ətr i ‖ ˈber-
barre bɑː ‖ bɑːr *—Fr* [baːʁ] **~s** z
barré ˈbær eɪ ‖ bɑː ˈreɪ *—Fr* [ba ʁe]
barred bɑːd ‖ bɑːrd
barrel ˈbær əl ‖ ˈber- **~ed, ~led** d **~ing, ~ling** ɪŋ **~s** z
'barrel ˌorgan
barrel-chested ˌbær əl ˈtʃest ɪd ◂ -əd, ˈ· ·ˌ· · ‖ ˌber-
barrelhouse ˈbær əl haʊs ‖ ˈber-
Barrell ˈbær əl ‖ ˈber-
barren ˈbær ən ‖ ˈber- **~ly** li **~ness** nəs nɪs
Barrett ˈbær ət -ɪt ‖ ˈber-
barrette bə ˈret bɑː- **~s** s
Barri ˈbær i ‖ ˈber-
barricad|e ˌbær ɪ ˈkeɪd -ə-, ˈ· · · ‖ ˈbær ə keɪd ˈber-, ˌ· ·ˈ· **~ed** ɪd əd **~es** z **~ing** ɪŋ
Barrie ˈbær i ‖ ˈber-
barrier ˈbær i‿ə ‖ ᵊr ˈber- **~s** z
'barrier cream; **ˌbarrier 'reef**, ˈ· · · ·
barring ˈbɑːr ɪŋ
Barrington ˈbær ɪŋ tən ‖ ˈber-
barrio ˈbær i‿əʊ ‖ ˈbɑːr i oʊ ˈbær-, ˈber- *—Sp* [ˈba ɾrjo] **~s** z *—Sp* [s]
barrister ˈbær ɪst ə -əst- ‖ -ᵊr ˈber- **~s** z
Barron ˈbær ən ‖ ˈber-
barroom ˈbɑː ruːm -rʊm ‖ ˈbɑːr- **~s** z
barrow, B~ ˈbær əʊ ‖ -oʊ ˈber- **~s** z
'barrow boy
Barrow-in-Furness ˌbær əʊ ɪn ˈfɜːn ɪs §-ən ˈ·-, -əs ‖ ˌbær oʊ ən ˈfɜːn əs ˌber-
Barry ˈbær i ‖ ˈber-
Barrymore ˈbær i mɔː ‖ -mɔːr ˈber-, -moʊr
Barsac, b~ ˈbɑːs æk ‖ bɑːr ˈsæk *—Fr* [baʁ sak]
Barset ˈbɑːs ɪt -ət, -et ‖ ˈbɑːrs- **~shire** ʃə ʃɪə ‖ ʃᵊr ʃɪr
Barsham ˈbɑːʃ əm ‖ ˈbɑːrʃ-
Barstow ˈbɑːst əʊ ‖ ˈbɑːr stoʊ
Bart, bart, BART bɑːt ‖ bɑːrt *—see also* **baronet**
bartender ˈbɑː ˌtend ə ‖ ˈbɑːr ˌtend ᵊr **~s** z
barter ˈbɑːt ə ‖ ˈbɑːrṱ ᵊr **~ed** d **bartering** ˈbɑːt ər ɪŋ ‖ ˈbɑːrṱ ər ɪŋ **~s** z
Barth bɑːt ‖ bɑːrt *—Ger* [baʁt, baːɐt]
Barthes bɑːt ‖ bɑːrt *—Fr* [baʁt]
Bartholdi bɑː ˈtɒld i -ˈθɒld- ‖ bɑːr ˈθɑːld i -ˈtɑːld-, -ˈθɔːld-, -ˈtɔːld- *—Fr* [baʁ tɔl di]
Bartholin ˈbɑːθ əl ɪn ˈbɑːt-, §-ən ‖ ˈbɑːrθ- ˈbɑːrṱ-
Bartholomew bɑː ˈθɒl ə mjuː bə- ‖ bɑːr ˈθɑːl- bᵊr-
Bartle ˈbɑːt ᵊl ‖ ˈbɑːrṱ ᵊl
Bartlett ˈbɑːt lət -lɪt ‖ ˈbɑːrt-
Bartok, Bartók ˈbɑːt ɒk ‖ ˈbɑːrt ɑːk -ɔːk *—Hungarian* [ˈbɒr toːk]
Bartoli ˈbɑːt əl i ‖ ˈbɑːrt- *—It* [ˈbar to li]

B

Bartolommeo bɑː ˌtɒl ə ˈmeɪ əʊ ˌ· · ·ˈ· · ‖ bɑːr ˌtɑːl ə ˈmeɪ oʊ -ˌtɔːl- —*It* [bar to lom ˈmɛː o]
Barton ˈbɑːt ən ‖ ˈbɑːrt ən
Barts, Bart's bɑːts ‖ bɑːrts
bartsia ˈbɑːts i‿ə ‖ ˈbɑːrts- **~s** z
Baruch *name in the Bible (Apocrypha)* ˈbɑːr ʊk ˈbeər-, -ək ‖ bə ˈruːk ˈbɑːr uːk, ˈber-, -ək
Baruch *family name* bə ˈruːk
Barugh bɑːf ‖ bɑːrf
Barwick ˈbær ɪk ˈbɑː wɪk ‖ ˈbɑːr wɪk
baryon ˈbær i ɒn ‖ -ɑːn ˈber- **~s** z
Baryshnikov bə ˈrɪʃ nɪ kɒf -nə- ‖ -kɑːf -kɔːf —*Russ* [bʌ ˈrʲiʃ nʲɪ kəf]
barysphere ˈbær ɪ sfɪə -ə- ‖ -sfɪr ˈber-
baryta bə ˈraɪt ə ‖ -ˈraɪţ-
barytes bə ˈraɪt iːz ‖ -ˈraɪţ iz
barytone ˈbær ɪ təʊn -ə- ‖ -toʊn ˈber- **~s** z
basal ˈbeɪs əl §ˈbeɪz- **ˌbasal ˈganglia**; **ˌbasal meˈtaboˌlism**
basalt ˈbæs ɔːlt -əlt; bə ˈsɔːlt, -ˈsɒlt ‖ bə ˈsɔːlt -ˈsɑːlt; ˈbeɪs ɔːlt, -ɑːlt **~s** s
basaltic bə ˈsɔːlt ɪk -ˈsɒlt- ‖ -ˈsɑːlt-
Basan ˈbeɪs æn
bascule ˈbæsk juːl **~s** z
base beɪs **based** beɪst **bases** ˈbeɪs ɪz -əz **basing** ˈbeɪs ɪŋ **ˌbase ˈmetal**; **ˈbase rate**
baseball ˈbeɪs bɔːl ‖ -bɑːl **~s** z **ˈbaseball bat**; **ˈbaseball cap**
baseboard ˈbeɪs bɔːd ‖ -bɔːrd -boʊrd **~s** z
base-born ˈbeɪs bɔːn ˌ·ˈ· ‖ ˌbeɪs ˈbɔːrn ◂
Basel ˈbɑːz əl —*Ger* [ˈbaː zəl]
baseless ˈbeɪs ləs -lɪs **~ly** li **~ness** nəs nɪs
baseline ˈbeɪs laɪn **~s** z
base|man ˈbeɪs mən **~men** mən
basement ˈbeɪs mənt **~s** s
basenji bə ˈsendʒ i **~s** z
baseplate ˈbeɪs pleɪt **~s** s
baser ˈbeɪs ə ‖ -ər
bases *pl of* **basis** ˈbeɪs iːz
bases *pl of* **base** ˈbeɪs ɪz -əz
basest ˈbeɪs ɪst -əst
Basford *(i)* ˈbeɪs fəd ‖ -fərd, *(ii)* ˈbæs- —*The place in Notts is (i); those in Cheshire and Staffs are (ii)*
bash bæʃ **bashed** bæʃt **bashes** ˈbæʃ ɪz -əz **bashing/s** ˈbæʃ ɪŋ/z
Bashan ˈbeɪʃ æn
-basher ˌbæʃ ə ‖ -ər **~s** z — **gay-basher/s** ˈgeɪ ˌbæʃə/z ‖ ər/z
bashful ˈbæʃ fəl -fʊl **~ly** ‿i **~ness** nəs nɪs
-bashing ˌbæʃ ɪŋ — **square-bashing** ˈskweə ˌbæʃ ɪŋ ‖ ˈskwer-
Bashir bə ˈʃɪə ‖ -ˈʃɪər
Bashkir ₍ı₎bæʃ ˈkɪə ‖ bɑːʃ ˈkɪər **~s** z
Bashkiria ₍ı₎bæʃ ˈkɪər i‿ə -ˈkɪr- ‖ bɑːʃ ˈkɪr-
basho ˈbæʃ əʊ ‖ bɑː ˈʃoʊ **~s** z —*Jp* [ba ˌɕo]
basic, BASIC ˈbeɪs ɪk **~s** s **ˌBasic ˈEnglish**
basically ˈbeɪs ɪk li -ɪk əl‿i
basidiomycete bə ˌsɪd i‿əʊ maɪ ˈsiːt ·ˌ· · ·ˈmaɪs iːt ‖ -oʊ ˈmaɪs iːt ·ˌ· · ·maɪ ˈsiːt
basidi|um bə ˈsɪd i‿əm bæ- **~a** ə **~al** ‿əl
Basie ˈbeɪs i
basil, Basil ˈbæz əl -ɪl ‖ ˈbeɪz əl ˈbeɪs-, ˈbæs-
basilar ˈbæz ɪl ə ˈbæs-, -əl- ‖ -ər
Basildon ˈbæz əl dən
basilect ˈbæz ɪ lekt ˈbeɪs-, -ə- **~s** s
basilectal ˌbæz ɪ ˈlekt əl ◂ ˌbeɪs-, -ə- **~ly** i
basilica bə ˈzɪl ɪk ə -ˈsɪl- ‖ -ˈsɪl- **~s** z
basilisk ˈbæz ə lɪsk ˈbæs-, -ɪ- **~s** s
basin ˈbeɪs ən **~s** z
basinet ˈbæs ɪ net -ə-, -nɪt, ˌ·ˈnet
basinful ˈbeɪs ən fʊl **~s** z
basing *pres part of* **base** ˈbeɪs ɪŋ
Basing *name* ˈbeɪz ɪŋ
Basinger ˈbeɪs ɪndʒ ə ˈbæs-, -əndʒ- ‖ -ər
Basingstoke ˈbeɪz ɪŋ stəʊk ‖ -stoʊk
-basis *stress-imposing* bəs ɪs §-əs — **anabasis** ə ˈnæb əs ɪs §-əs
basis ˈbeɪs ɪs §-əs **bases** ˈbeɪs iːz
bask bɑːsk §bæsk ‖ bæsk **basked** bɑːskt §bæskt ‖ bæskt **basking** ˈbɑːsk ɪŋ §ˈbæsk- ‖ ˈbæsk ɪŋ **basks** bɑːsks §bæsks ‖ bæsks
Baskerville ˈbæsk ə vɪl ‖ -ər- **~s** z
basket ˈbɑːsk ɪt §ˈbæsk-, -ət ‖ ˈbæsk ət **~s** s **ˈbasket case**
basketball ˈbɑːsk ɪt bɔːl §ˈbæsk-, -ət- ‖ ˈbæsk ət bɔːl -bɑːl
basketful ˈbɑːsk ɪt fʊl §ˈbæsk-, -ət- ‖ ˈbæsk-
basketry ˈbɑːsk ɪtr i §ˈbæsk-, -ətr- ‖ ˈbæsk-
basketwork ˈbɑːsk ɪt wɜːk §ˈbæsk-, §-ət- ‖ ˈbæsk ət wɜːk
Baskin ˈbæsk ɪn §-ən
Baskin-Robbins *tdmk* ˌbæsk ɪn ˈrɒb ɪnz §-ən-, §-ənz ‖ -ˈrɑːb-
Basle bɑːl —*Ger* Basel [ˈbaː zəl]
Baslow ˈbæz ləʊ ‖ -loʊ
basmati, B~ bæz ˈmɑːt i bæs-, bəz-, bəs- ‖ bɑːz ˈmɑːţ i —*Hindi* [baː smə ṭiː]
Basnett ˈbæz nɪt -nət, -net
basophil ˈbeɪs əʊ fɪl ˈbeɪz- ‖ -ə-
basophilic ˌbeɪs əʊ ˈfɪl ɪk ◂ ˌbeɪz- ‖ -ə-
Basotho bə ˈsuːt uː -ˈsəʊt əʊ ‖ -ˈsoʊt oʊ
Basque, basque bæsk bɑːsk **Basques, basques** bæsks bɑːsks
Basra, Basrah ˈbæz rə ˈbɑːz- ‖ ˈbɑːs rə ˈbæs-, ˈbɑːz-, ˈbæz- —*Arabic* [ˈbasˤ ra]
bas-relief ˌbɑː ri ˈliːf ◂ ˌbæs-, -rə- **~s** s
bass *in music* beɪs *(= base)* **basses** ˈbeɪs ɪz -əz **ˌbass ˈclef**; **ˌbass ˈfiddle**; **ˌbass guiˈtar**
bass *'fish'; 'bast'* bæs **basses** ˈbæs ɪz -əz
Bass *family name; place name element; beer tdmk* bæs **Basses, Bass's** ˈbæs ɪz -əz **ˌBass ˈRock**
Bassanio bə ˈsɑːn i‿əʊ bæ- ‖ -oʊ
Bassenthwaite ˈbæs ən θweɪt
basset, B~ ˈbæs ɪt -ət **~s** s **ˈbasset horn**; **ˈbasset hound**
Basseterre ˌbæs ˈteə ‖ -ˈteər
Bassetlaw ˌbæs ɪt ˈlɔː -ət- ‖ -ˈlɑː
Bassett ˈbæs ɪt -ət
Bassey ˈbæs i
bassinet, bassinette ˌbæs ɪ ˈnet -ə- **~s** s
Bassingbourn ˈbæs ɪŋ bɔːn ‖ -bɔːrn -boʊrn

B

bassist ˈbeɪs ɪst §-əst **~s** s
basso ˈbæs əʊ ˈbɑːs- ‖ -oʊ —*It* [ˈbas so] **~s** z
ˌbasso proˈfundo prəʊ ˈfʌnd əʊ -ˈfʊnd- ‖ -proʊ ˈfʌnd oʊ —*as if It* [pro ˈfun do]
bassoon bə ˈsuːn bæ- **~ist/s** ɪst/s §əst/s **~s** z
basswood ˈbæs wʊd
bast bæst
Bastable ˈbæst əb ᵊl
bastard ˈbɑːst əd ˈbæst- ‖ ˈbæst ᵊrd **~s** z
bastardis... —*see* **bastardiz...**
bastardization ˌbɑːst əd aɪ ˈzeɪʃ ᵊn ˌbæst-, -ɪˈ-- ‖ ˌbæst ᵊrd ə-
bastardiz|e ˈbɑːst ə daɪz ˈbæst- ‖ ˈbæst ᵊr- **~ed** d **~es** ɪz əz **~ing** ɪŋ
bastard|y ˈbɑːst əd |i ˈbæst- ‖ ˈbæst ᵊrd |i **~ies** iz
baste beɪst *(= based)* **basted** ˈbeɪst ɪd -əd **bastes** beɪsts **basting** ˈbeɪst ɪŋ
Bastedo bə ˈstiːd əʊ ‖ -oʊ
Basten ˈbæst ən -ɪn
Bastille, b~ ₍ₗ₎bæ ˈstiːᵊl —*Fr* [bas tij]
Bastin ˈbæst ɪn §-ən
bastinado ˌbæst ɪ ˈneɪd əʊ -ə-, -ˈnɑːd- ‖ -oʊ
bastion ˈbæst i‿ən ‖ ˈbæs tʃən **~s** z
Basuto bə ˈsuːt əʊ ‖ -ˈsuːṭ oʊ
Basutoland bə ˈsuːt əʊ lænd ‖ -ˈsuːṭ oʊ-
bat bæt **bats** bæts **batted** ˈbæt ɪd -əd ‖ ˈbæṭ əd **batting** ˈbæt ɪŋ ‖ ˈbæṭ ɪŋ
Bata *tdmk* ˈbɑːt ə ‖ ˈbɑːṭ ə
Batavia bə ˈteɪv i‿ə
batboy ˈbæt bɔɪ **~s** z
batch bætʃ **batches** ˈbætʃ ɪz -əz
ˌbatch ˈprocessing
Batchelor ˈbætʃ əl‿ə -ɪl- ‖ -ᵊl‿ər
bate, Bate beɪt **bated** ˈbeɪt ɪd -əd ‖ ˈbeɪṭ əd **bates** beɪts **bating** ˈbeɪt ɪŋ ‖ ˈbeɪṭ ɪŋ
ˌbated ˈbreath
bateleur ˌbæt ə ˈlɜː →-ᵊl ˈɜː; ˈ· · · ‖ ˌbæṭ ᵊl ˈɜː ˈ· · · **~s** z
Bately ˈbeɪt li
Bateman ˈbeɪt mən
Bates beɪts
Batesian ˈbeɪts i‿ən
Bateson ˈbeɪt sən
Batey ˈbeɪt i ‖ ˈbeɪṭ i

BATHS

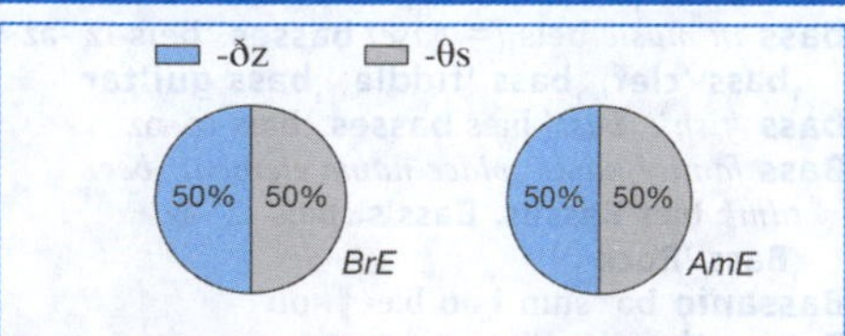

bath *n* bɑːθ §bæθ ‖ bæθ **baths** bɑːðz §bɑːθs, §bæθs, §bæðz ‖ bæðz bæθs — *Preference polls, BrE: -ðz 50%, -θs 50%; AmE, -ðz 50%, -θs 50%. Surprisingly, exactly half of each panel preferred the -θs form, traditionally considered non-standard. Some people differentiate between 'acts of bathing', with -θs, and 'bathtubs, bathhouses', with -ðz.* **bath's** bɑːθs §bæθs ‖ bæθs
ˈbath mat; **ˈbath night**; **ˈbath salts**
bath *v* bɑːθ §bæθ ‖ bæθ **bathed** bɑːθt §bæθt ‖ bæθt **bathing** ˈbɑːθ ɪŋ §ˈbæθ- ‖ ˈbæθ ɪŋ **baths** bɑːθs §bæθs ‖ bæθs —*This verb is not current in AmE.*
Bath *place name* bɑːθ §bæθ ‖ bæθ
ˌBath ˈbun; **ˌBath ˈchair**, ˈ· ·
bathe beɪð **bathed** beɪðd **bathes** beɪðz
bathing ˈbeɪð ɪŋ
bathed *past & pp of* **bath** bɑːθt §bæθt ‖ bæθt
bathed *past & pp of* **bathe** beɪðd
bather ˈbeɪð ə ‖ -ᵊr **~s** z
bathetic bə ˈθet ɪk bæ- ‖ -ˈθeṭ ɪk
bath|house ˈbɑːθ| haʊs §ˈbæθ|- ‖ ˈbæθ|- **~houses** haʊz ɪz -əz
bathing *from* **bathe** ˈbeɪð ɪŋ
ˈbathing ˌbeauty; **ˈbathing ˌcostume**; **ˈbathing maˌchine**; **ˈbathing suit**
bathing *from* **bath** ˈbɑːθ ɪŋ §ˈbæθ- ‖ ˈbæθ ɪŋ
Batho *(i)* ˈbæθ əʊ ‖ -oʊ, *(ii)* ˈbeɪθ-
bathos ˈbeɪθ ɒs ‖ -ɑːs -ɔːs, -oʊs
bathrobe ˈbɑːθ rəʊb §ˈbæθ- ‖ ˈbæθ roʊb **~s** z
bathroom ˈbɑːθ ruːm §ˈbæθ-, -rʊm ‖ ˈbæθ- **~s** z
Bathsheba bæθ ˈʃiːb ə ˈbæθ ʃɪb ə
bathtub ˈbɑːθ tʌb §ˈbæθ- ‖ ˈbæθ- **~s** z
Bathurst ˈbæθ ɜːst ˈbɑːθ-, -əst, -hɜːst ‖ -ɜːst
bathy- *comb. form*
with stress-neutral suffix |bæθ ɪ — **bathymetric** ˌbæθ ɪ ˈmetr ɪk ◂
with stress-imposing suffix bə ˈθɪ+ bæ- — **bathymetry** bə ˈθɪm ətr i bæ-, -ɪtr i
bathyal ˈbæθ i‿əl
bathypelagic ˌbæθ i pə ˈlædʒ ɪk ◂
bathyscaphe ˈbæθ i skeɪf §-ə- **~s** s
bathysphere ˈbæθ i sfɪə -ə- ‖ -sfɪr **~s** z
batik bə ˈtiːk bæ-; ˈbæt ɪk, ˈbɑːt ɪk **~s** s
bating ˈbeɪt ɪŋ ‖ ˈbeɪṭ ɪŋ
Batista bə ˈtiːst ə bæ-, bɑː- —*Sp* [ba ˈtis ta]
batiste bæ ˈtiːst bə- **~s** s
Batley ˈbæt li
batman *'army servant'* ˈbæt mən **batmen** ˈbæt mən -men
Batman *cartoon character* ˈbæt mæn
bat mitzvah ˌbɑːt ˈmɪts və
baton ˈbæt ɒn -ᵊn ‖ bə ˈtɑːn *(*)* —*See also phrases with this word* **~s** z
Baton Rouge ˌbæt ᵊn ˈruːʒ
bats bæts
Batsford ˈbæts fəd ‖ -fᵊrd
bats|man ˈbæts| mən **~men** mən
Batson ˈbæts ən
batt, Batt bæt
batt... —*see* **bat**
battalion bə ˈtæl jən -ˈtæl i‿ən **~s** z
battels ˈbæt ᵊlz ‖ ˈbæṭ-
batten, B~ ˈbæt ᵊn **~ed** d **~ing** ‿ɪŋ **~s** z
Battenberg ˈbæt ᵊn bɜːg ‖ -bɜːg —*Ger* [ˈbat ᵊn bɛʁk]
ˌBattenberg ˈcake

batter ˈbæt ə ‖ ˈbæţ ər **~ed** d **battering/s** ˈbæt‿ər ɪŋ/z ‖ ˈbæţ ər ɪŋ/z **~s** z
'**battering ram**
batteries —*see* **battery**
Battersby ˈbæt əz bi ‖ ˈbæţ ərz-
Battersea ˈbæt əs i -ə siː ‖ ˈbæţ ər siː
batter|y ˈbætr |i ˈbæt ər |i ‖ ˈbæţ ər |i →ˈbætr |i **~ies** iz
batti... —*see* **batty**
batting ˈbæt ɪŋ ‖ ˈbæţ ɪŋ
'**batting ˌaverage**
Battisford ˈbæt ɪs fəd §-əs- ‖ ˈbæţ əs fərd
battl|e, B~ ˈbæt əl ‖ ˈbæţ əl **~ed** d **~es** z **~ing** ‿ɪŋ
'**battle ˌcruiser**; '**battle cry**; '**battle faˌtigue**; ˌ**battle 'royal**
battleax, battleax|e ˈbæt əl æks ‖ ˈbæţ- **~es** ɪz əz
battledore ˈbæt əl dɔː ‖ ˈbæţ əl dɔːr -dour **~s** z
battledress ˈbæt əl dres ‖ ˈbæţ-
battlefield, B~ ˈbæt əl fiːəld ‖ ˈbæţ- **~s** z
battlefront ˈbæt əl frʌnt ‖ ˈbæţ- **~s** s
battleground ˈbæt əl graʊnd ‖ ˈbæţ- **~s** z
battlement ˈbæt əl mənt ‖ ˈbæţ- **~ed** ɪd əd **~s** s
battleship ˈbæt əl ʃɪp ‖ ˈbæţ- **~s** s
ˌ**battleship 'grey**
battue bæ ˈtuː -ˈtjuː —*Fr* [ba ty]
batt|y ˈbæt |i ‖ ˈbæţ |i **~ier** i‿ə ‖ i‿ər **~iest** i‿ɪst i‿əst **~iness** i nəs -nɪs
Batty, Battye ˈbæt i ‖ ˈbæţ i
batwing ˈbæt wɪŋ **~s** z
bauble ˈbɔːb əl ‖ ˈbɑːb- **~s** z
Baucis ˈbɔːs ɪs §-əs ‖ ˈbɑːs-
baud bɔːd bəʊd ‖ bɑːd
Baudelaire ˈbəʊd ə leə -əl eə, ˌ· ·ˈ· ‖ ˌboud əl ˈeər —*Fr* [bod lɛːʁ]
Bauer ˈbaʊ‿ə ‖ ˈbaʊ‿ər —*Ger* [ˈbau ɐ]
Baugh bɔː ‖ bɑː
Baughan *(i)* bɔːn ‖ bɑːn, *(ii)* ˈbɒf ən ‖ ˈbɑːf- ˈbɔːf-
Bauhaus ˈbaʊ haʊs —*Ger* [ˈbau haus]
bauhinia bəʊ ˈhɪn i‿ə bɔː- ‖ bɔː- bɑː-
Baulch bɒlʃ ‖ bɑːlʃ bɔːlʃ
baulk bɔːk bɔːlk ‖ bɑːk **baulked** bɔːkt bɔːlkt ‖ bɑːkt **baulking** ˈbɔːk ɪŋ ˈbɔːlk- ‖ ˈbɑːk- **baulks** bɔːks bɔːlks ‖ bɑːks
Baum baʊm —*as an American family name, also* bɑːm, bɔːm
Baumé ˈbəʊm eɪ ‖ boʊ ˈmeɪ —*Fr* [bo me]
bauxite ˈbɔːks aɪt ‖ ˈbɑːks-
Bavari|a bə ˈveər i‿|ə ‖ -ˈver- -ˈvær- **~an/s** ən/z
bavarois|e ˌbæv ə ˈwɑːz -ɑː- ‖ -ɑːr- **~es** ɪz əz —*Fr* [ba va ʁwaːz]
Baverstock ˈbæv ə stɒk ‖ -ər stɑːk
Baw Baw ˈbɔː bɔː ‖ ˈbɑː bɑː
bawbee ˌbɔː ˈbiː ˈbɔːb i ‖ ˈbɔːb i ˈbɑːb-; ˌbɔː ˈbi;, ˌbɑː- **~s** z
bawd bɔːd ‖ bɑːd **bawds** bɔːdz ‖ bɑːdz
Bawden ˈbɔːd ən ‖ ˈbɑːd-
bawd|y ˈbɔːd |i ‖ ˈbɑːd- **~ier** i‿ə ‖ i‿ər **~iest** i‿ɪst i‿əst **~ily** ɪ li əl i **~iness** i nəs i nɪs
bawdyhouse ˈbɔːd i haʊs ‖ ˈbɑːd-
bawl bɔːl ‖ bɑːl *(= ball)* **bawled** bɔːld ‖ bɑːld **bawling** ˈbɔːl ɪŋ ‖ ˈbɑːl- **bawls** bɔːlz ‖ bɑːlz
Bawtree, Bawtry ˈbɔːtr i ‖ ˈbɑːtr-
Bax bæks
Baxendale ˈbæks ən deɪəl
Baxter ˈbækst ə ‖ -ər
bay beɪ **bays** beɪz *(= baize)*
'**bay leaf**; ˌ**bay 'rum**; '**Bay Stater**; '**Bay Street**; '**bay tree**; ˌ**bay 'window**
bayadere ˌbaɪ‿ə ˈdɪə -ˈdeə ‖ ˈbaɪ ə dɪr
Bayard, b~ ˈbeɪ ɑːd -əd ‖ -ərd -ɑːrd
bayberry ˈbeɪ ˌber i
Bayer *tdmk* ˈbeɪ ə ‖ -ər
Bayes beɪz
Bayesian ˈbeɪz i‿ən ‖ ˈbeɪʒ ən
Bayeux ₍ˌ₎baɪ ˈɜː ₍ˌ₎beɪ-, -ˈjɜː ‖ ˈbeɪ u ˈbaɪ- —*Fr* [ba jø]
Bayh baɪ
Bayley ˈbeɪl i
Baylis, Bayliss ˈbeɪl ɪs §-əs
Bayne beɪn
Baynes beɪnz
bay|onet ˈbeɪ |ən ɪt -ət; -ə net, ˌ· ·ˈ· ‖ -|ən ət -ə net, ˌ· ·ˈnet **~oneted, ~onetted** ən ɪt ɪd -ət-, -əd; ə net-, ˌ· ·ˈ· · ‖ ən əţ əd ə neţ-, ˌ· ·ˈ· · **~oneting, ~onetting** ən ɪt ɪŋ -ət-; ə net-, ˌ· ·ˈ· · ‖ ən əţ ɪŋ ə neţ-, ˌ· ·ˈ· · **~onets** ən ɪts -əts; ə nets, ˌ· ·ˈ· ‖ ən əts ə nets, ˌ·ə ˈnets
Bayonne *place in France* baɪ ˈɒn ‖ -ˈɔːn ˈoʊn, -ˈɑːn —*Fr* [ba jɔn]
Bayonne *place in NJ* beɪ ˈəʊn ‖ -ˈoʊn
bayou ˈbaɪ uː -juː ‖ -oʊ -uː **~s** z
Bayreuth ˌbaɪə ˈrɔɪt ˈbaɪər ɔɪt —*Ger* [bai ˈʁɔyt]
Bayswater ˈbeɪz ˌwɔːt ə ‖ -ˌwɔːţ ər -ˌwɑːţ-
Baywatch ˈbeɪ wɒtʃ ‖ -wɑːtʃ
Baz bæz
bazaar, bazar bə ˈzɑː ‖ -ˈzɑːr **~s** z
Bazalgette ˈbæz əl dʒet
Bazell bə ˈzel
bazooka bə ˈzuːk ə **~s** z
B-ball ˈbiː bɔːl ‖ -bɑːl
BBC ˌbiː biː ˈsiː◂ ˌbiːb i-
ˌ**BBC-'2**; ˌ**BBC ˌWorld 'Service**, ˌ· · · ˈ· ˌ· ·
BB gun ˈbiːb i gʌn **~s** z
BBQ, bbq ˈbɑːb ɪ kjuː -ə- ‖ ˈbɑːrb-
bdellium ˈdel i‿əm bə ˈdel-
be *strong form* biː, *weak form* bi —*For* am, are, aren't, art, been, being, is, isn't, was, wasn't, wast, were, weren't, *see separate entries*
be- bi bə *This prefix is always unstressed:* beˈneath, beˈfriend.
Bea biː
beach biːtʃ **beached** biːtʃt **beaches** ˈbiːtʃ ɪz -əz **beaching** ˈbiːtʃ ɪŋ
'**beach ball**; '**beach ˌbuggy**
beachchair ˈbiːtʃ tʃeə ‖ -tʃer **~s** z
beachcomber ˈbiːtʃ ˌkəʊm ə ‖ -ˌkoʊm ər **~s** z
beachfront ˈbiːtʃ frʌnt
beachhead ˈbiːtʃ hed **~s** z
Beach-la-Mar, beach-la-mar ˌbiːtʃ lə ˈmɑː ‖ -ˈmɑːr
beachwear ˈbiːtʃ weə ‖ -wer

B

Beachy ˈbiːtʃ i
ˌBeachy ˈHead
beacon, B~ ˈbiːk ən **~s** z
Beaconsfield *(i)* ˈbek ənz fiːəld *(ii)* ˈbiːk- *—The place in Bucks is (i); Disraeli's title and the places in Tasmania and Canada are (ii)*
bead biːd **beaded** ˈbiːd ɪd -əd **beading/s** ˈbiːd ɪŋ/z **beads** biːdz
beadi... *—see* **beady**
beadle, B~ ˈbiːd əl **~s** z
beadwork ˈbiːd wɜːk ‖ -wɜːk
bead|y ˈbiːd |i **~ier** i‿ə ‖ i‿ər **~iest** i‿ɪst i‿əst **~ily** ɪ li əl i **~iness** i nəs -nɪs
beady-eyed ˌbiːd i ˈaɪd ◂
beagle ˈbiːg əl **~s** z **beagling** ˈbiːg əl‿ɪŋ
beak biːk **beaked** biːkt **beaks** biːks
Beaken ˈbiːk ən
beaker ˈbiːk ə ‖ -ər **~s** z
ˈBeaker Folk
beakerful ˈbiːk ə fʊl ‖ -ər-
beaklike ˈbiːk laɪk
Beal, Beale biːəl
be-all and end-all ˌbiː ɔːl ən ˈend ɔːl -ənd'- ‖ -ɑːl ən ˈend ɑːl
beam biːm **beamed** biːmd **beaming** ˈbiːm ɪŋ **beams** biːmz
beam-ends ˌbiːm ˈendz
Beamer ˈbiːm ə ‖ -ər **~s** z
Beaminster ˈbem ɪnˈst ə ‖ -ər *—There is also a spelling pronunciation* ˈbiːm-
Beamish ˈbiːm ɪʃ
bean, Bean biːn **beans** biːnz
ˈbean curd
beanbag ˈbiːn bæg →ˈbiːm- **~s** z
beanfeast ˈbiːn fiːst **~s** s
beanie ˈbiːn i **~s** z
ˈbeanie ˌbaby
beano, Beano ˈbiːn əʊ ‖ -oʊ **~s** z
beanpole ˈbiːn pəʊl →ˈbiːm-, →-pɒʊl ‖ -poʊl **~s** z
beanshoot ˈbiːn ʃuːt **~s** s
beansprout ˈbiːn spraʊt **~s** s
beanstalk ˈbiːn stɔːk ‖ -stɑːk **~s** s
bear *n, v* beə ‖ beər bæər *(= bare)* **bearing** ˈbeər ɪŋ ‖ ˈber ɪŋ ˈbær- **bears** beəz ‖ beərz bæərz **bore** bɔː ‖ bɔːr boʊr **borne** bɔːn ‖ bɔːrn boʊrn
ˈbear ˌgarden; **ˈbear hug**; **ˈbear ˌmarket**; **ˌbear ˈup**
bearab|le ˈbeər əb |əl ‖ ˈber- ˈbær- **~ly** li
bear-baiting ˈbeə ˌbeɪt ɪŋ ‖ ˈber ˌbeɪṭ ɪŋ ˈbær-
beard, Beard bɪəd ‖ bɪərd **bearded** ˈbɪəd ɪd -əd ‖ ˈbɪrd əd **bearding** ˈbɪəd ɪŋ ‖ ˈbɪrd ɪŋ **beards** bɪədz ‖ bɪərdz
beardless ˈbɪəd ləs -lɪs ‖ ˈbɪrd ləs **~ness** nəs nɪs
Beardsall, Beardsell ˈbɪəd səl ‖ ˈbɪrd-
Beardsley ˈbɪədz li ‖ ˈbɪrdz-
Beare bɪə ‖ bɪr *—but* ˌBeare ˈGreen *in Surrey is* beə
bearer ˈbeər ə ‖ ˈber ər **~s** z
bearhug ˈbeə hʌg ‖ ˈber- **~s** z
bearing ˈbeər ɪŋ ‖ ˈber ɪŋ ˈbær- **~s** z
bearish ˈbeər ɪʃ ‖ ˈber ɪʃ ˈbær- **~ly** li **~ness** nəs nɪs
bearnaise, béarnaise, B~ ˌbeɪ ə ˈneɪz ◂ -ɑː-, -ˈnez ‖ ˈbeɪ ər neɪz -ɑːr- *—Fr* [be aʁ nɛːz]
Bearsden ˌ₍ˌ₎beəz ˈden ‖ ₍ˌ₎berz-
bearskin ˈbeə skɪn ‖ ˈber- **~s** z
Bearsted *(i)* ˈbɜː sted ‖ ˈbɜː-, *(ii)* ˈbeə- ‖ ˈber-
Beasant ˈbez ənt
beast biːst **beasts** biːsts
ˌbeast of ˈburden
beastie ˈbiːst i **~s** z
beast|ly ˈbiːst |li **~liness** li nəs -nɪs
beat biːt **beaten** ˈbiːt ən **beating** ˈbiːt ɪŋ ‖ ˈbiːṭ ɪŋ **beats** biːts
beatbox ˈbiːt bɒks ‖ -bɑːks **~er/s** ə/z ‖ ər/z **~ing** ɪŋ
beater ˈbiːt ə ‖ ˈbiːṭ ər **~s** z
beatific ˌbiː‿ə ˈtɪf ɪk ◂ **~ally** əl‿i
beatification bi ˌæt ɪ fɪ ˈkeɪʃ ən -ˌ·ə-, §-fə'- ‖ -ˌæṭ-
beati|fy bi ˈæt ɪ |faɪ -ə- ‖ -ˈæṭ- **~fied** faɪd **~fies** faɪz **~fying** faɪ ɪŋ
beating ˈbiːt ɪŋ ‖ ˈbiːṭ ɪŋ **~s** z
beatitude, B~ bi ˈæt ɪ tjuːd -ə-, →-tʃuːd ‖ -ˈæṭ ə tuːd -tjuːd **~s** z
Beatle ˈbiːt əl ‖ ˈbiːṭ əl *(= beetle)* **~s** z
beatnik ˈbiːt nɪk **~s** s
Beaton ˈbiːt ən
Beatrice ˈbɪətr ɪs -əs ‖ ˈbiː ətr əs *—also, in imitated Italian,* ˌbeɪ ə ˈtriːtʃ eɪ, -ɑː-, -i *—Italian* [be a ˈtriː tʃe]
Beatrix ˈbɪətr ɪks ‖ ˈbiː ə trɪks
Beattie ˈbiːt i ‖ ˈbiːṭ i
Beattock ˈbiːt ək ‖ ˈbiːṭ ək
Beatty *(i)* ˈbiːt i ‖ ˈbiːṭ i, *(ii)* ˈbeɪt i ‖ ˈbeɪṭ i *—The film actor Warren B~ is (ii)*
beat-up ˈbiːt ʌp ‖ ˈbiːṭ-
beau bəʊ ‖ boʊ *—Fr* [bo] **beaus, beaux** bəʊz bəʊ ‖ boʊz *—See also phrases with this word*
Beaucaire ˌbəʊ ˈkeə ‖ ˌboʊ ˈkeər
Beauchamp ˈbiːtʃ əm
Beauclerk ˈbəʊ kleə ·ˈ· ‖ ˈboʊ klɜːk
beaucoup ˈbəʊ kuː ˌ·ˈ· ◂ ‖ ˈboʊ- *—Fr* [bo ku]
Beaufort *(i)* ˈbəʊ fət -fɔːt ‖ ˈboʊ fərt, *(ii)* ˈbjuː- *—The British dukedom, the personal and family name, the places in NC and Australia, the Arctic sea, and the wind scale are (i); the place in SC is (ii).*
ˈBeaufort scale; **ˌBeaufort ˈSea**
beau geste ˌbəʊ ˈʒest ‖ ˌboʊ- *—Fr* [bo ʒɛst]
Beaujolais ˈbəʊʒ ə leɪ -ɒ- ‖ ˌboʊʒ ə ˈleɪ *—Fr* [bo ʒɔ lɛ]
ˌBeaujolais nouˈveau nu ˈvəʊ ‖ -ˈvoʊ *—Fr* [nu vo]
Beaulieu ˈbjuːl i *(!)*
Beauly ˈbjuːl i
Beaumaris bəʊ ˈmær ɪs bjuː-, §-əs ‖ boʊ- -ˈmer-
beau monde ˌbəʊ ˈmɒnd ‖ ˌboʊ ˈmɔːnd -ˈmɑːnd *—Fr* [bo mɔ̃ːd]
Beaumont ˈbəʊ mənt -mɒnt ‖ ˈboʊ mɑːnt ˌ·ˈ· *—but the place in Cumbria is* ˈbiː-
Beaune bəʊn ‖ boʊn *—Fr* [boːn]

B

beaut bjuːt **beauts** bjuːts
beauteous 'bjuːt iˌəs ‖ 'bjuːt̬- **~ly** li
beautician bjuː 'tɪʃ ən **~s** z
beauties 'bjuːt iz ‖ 'bjuːt̬ iz
beautifi... —*see* **beautify**
beautification ˌbjuːt ɪf ɪ 'keɪʃ ən ˌ·əf-, §-ə'·- ‖ ˌbjuːt̬-
beautiful 'bjuːt əf əl -ɪf-; -ɪ fʊl, -ə- ‖ 'bjuːt̬-
beautifully 'bjuːt əf li -ɪf-; -ɪ fʊl i, -ə fʊl i ‖ 'bjuːt̬-
beauti|fy 'bjuːt ɪ |faɪ -ə- ‖'bjuːt̬- **~fied** faɪd **~fies** faɪz **~fying** faɪ ɪŋ
beauty 'bjuːt i ‖ 'bjuːt̬ i **beauties** 'bjuːt iz ‖ 'bjuːt̬ iz
'**beauty ˌcontest**; '**beauty ˌparlour**; '**beauty queen**; '**beauty ˌsalon** ‖ -·ˌ·; '**beauty sleep**; '**beauty spot**
Beauvais ₍ˌ₎bəʊ 'veɪ ‖ ₍ˌ₎boʊ- —*Fr* [bo vɛ]
Beauvoir 'bəʊv wɑː ‖ boʊv 'wɑːr —*Fr* [bo vwaːʁ]
beaux bəʊz bəʊ ‖ boʊz
beaux-arts ₍ˌ₎bəʊ 'zɑː ‖ ₍ˌ₎boʊ 'zɑːr —*Fr* [bo zaːʁ]
Beavan 'bev ən
beaver, B~ 'biːv ə ‖ -ər **~ed** d **beavering** 'biːv ər‿ɪŋ **~s** z
Beaverbrook 'biːv ə brʊk ‖ -ər-
Beavis 'biːv ɪs §-əs
Beazley 'biːz li
Bebb beb
Bebbington, Bebington 'beb ɪŋ tən
Bebo 'biː bəʊ ‖ -boʊ
bebop 'biː bɒp ‖-bɑːp
bebopper 'biː bɒp ə ‖ -bɑːp ər **~s** z
becalm bi 'kɑːm bə-, -'kɑːlm, §-'kɒlm **~ed** d **~ing** ɪŋ **~s** z
became bi 'keɪm bə-

BECAUSE

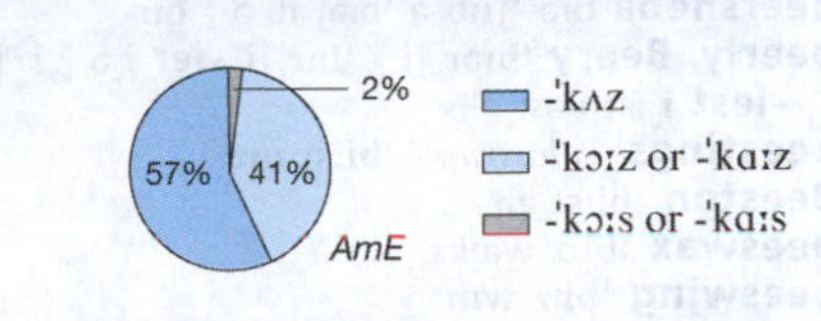

because bi 'kɒz bə-, -'kəz, -kəz, §-'kɔːz, §-'kɒs, §-'kɔːs ‖ -'kʌz -'kɔːz, -'kɑːz, -'kəz, -kəz —*Many speakers use* **bi kəz** *(or* **bə kəz***) as the weak form,* **bi 'kɒz** ‖ **-'kɔːz** *(etc.) as the strong form. Some, though, also use an irregular strong form* **bi 'kəz, bə 'kəz**. *There are also casual variants* **kɒz, kəz** *(etc.)* —*see* **cos.**
—*Preference poll, AmE:* -'kʌz *57%,* -'kɔːz *or* -'kɑːz *41%,* -'kɔːs *or* -'kɑːs *2%.*
Beccles 'bek əlz
bechamel, béchamel ˌbeɪʃ ə 'mel ◂ —*Fr* [be ʃa mɛl]
beche-de-mer, bêche-de-mer ˌbeʃ də 'meə ˌbeɪʃ- ‖ -'meər —*This is not a true French expression.*
Becher's 'biːtʃ əz ‖ -ərz
Bechet 'beʃ eɪ
Bechstein 'bek staɪn
Bechtel 'bekt el
Bechuana ˌbetʃ u 'ɑːn ə ⚠ˌbek ju- **~land** lænd
beck, Beck bek **becks** beks
Beckenbauer 'bek ən baʊ‿ə ‖ -baʊ‿ər —*Ger* ['bɛk ən bau ɐ]
Beckenham 'bek ən‿əm
Becker 'bek ə ‖ -ər —*Ger* ['bɛk ɐ]
Becket, Beckett 'bek ɪt §-ət
Beckford 'bek fəd ‖ -fərd
Beckham 'bek əm
Beckinsale 'bek ɪn seɪəl §-ən-
Beckmann 'bek mən —*Ger* ['bɛk man]
beckon 'bek ən **~ed** d **~ing/ly** ‿ɪŋ /li **~s** z
Beckton 'bekt ən
Beckwith 'bek wɪθ
Becky 'bek i
becloud bi 'klaʊd bə- **~ed** ɪd əd **~ing** ɪŋ **~s** z
be|come bi |'kʌm bə- **~came** 'keɪm **~comes** 'kʌmz **~coming** 'kʌm ɪŋ
becoming bi 'kʌm ɪŋ bə- **~ly** li
Becontree 'bek ən triː 'biːk-
Becquerel, b~ 'bek ər‿əl ˌbek ə 'rel —*Fr* [bɛ kʁɛl] **~s** z
Becton 'bekt ən
bed bed **bedded** 'bed ɪd -əd **bedding** 'bed ɪŋ **beds** bedz
ˌ**bed and 'breakfast**; '**bed ˌlinen**
BEd ˌbiː 'ed
bedad bi 'dæd bə-
Bedale *place in NYks* 'biːd əl 'biː deɪəl
Bedales 'biː deɪəlz
bedaub bi 'dɔːb bə- ‖ -'dɑːb **~ed** d **~ing** ɪŋ **~s** z
bedazzl|e bi 'dæz əl bə- **~ed** d **~es** z **~ing** ɪŋ
bedblock|er 'bed ˌblɒk ə ‖-ˌblɑːk ər **~ers** əz ‖ ərz **~ing** ɪŋ
bedbug 'bed bʌg →'beb- **~s** z
bedchamber 'bed ˌtʃeɪm bə ‖ -bər **~s** z
bedclothes 'bed kləʊðz -kləʊz ‖ -kloʊz -kloʊðz
bedd... —*see* **bed**
beddable 'bed əb əl
Beddau 'beð aɪ —*Welsh* ['be ðai, -ðe]
bedder 'bed ə ‖ -ər **~s** z
Beddgelert beð 'gel ət bed-, beɪð- ‖ -ərt —*Welsh* [ˌbeːð 'ge lert]
bedding, B~ 'bed ɪŋ
'**bedding plant**
Beddoes, Beddowes, Beddows 'bed əʊz ‖ -oʊz
beddy-bye 'bed i baɪ **~s** z
Bede biːd
bedeck bi 'dek bə- **~ed** t **~ing** ɪŋ **~s** s
bedel, bedell 'biːd əl **~s** z
Bedevere 'bed ə vɪə -ɪ- ‖ -vɪr
bedevil bi 'dev əl bə- **~ed, ~led** d **~ing, ~ling** ‿ɪŋ **~ment** mənt **~s** z
bedew bi 'djuː bə-, →-'dʒuː ‖ -'duː -'djuː **~ed** d **~ing** ɪŋ **~s** z
bedfellow 'bed ˌfel əʊ ‖ -oʊ **~s** z
Bedford 'bed fəd ‖ -fərd

B

Bedfordshire 'bed fəd ʃə -ʃɪə ‖ -fᵊrd ʃᵊr -ʃɪr
bedhead 'bed hed **~s** z
bedim bi 'dɪm bə- **~med** d **~ming** ɪŋ **~s** z
Bedivere 'bed ə vɪə -ɪ- ‖ -vɪr
bedizen bi 'daɪz ᵊn bə-, -'dɪz- **~ed** d **~ing** ˌɪŋ **~s** z
bedjacket 'bed ˌdʒæk ɪt §-ət **~s** s
bedlam 'bed ləm
bedlinen 'bed ˌlɪn ɪn §-ən
Bedlington 'bed lɪŋ tən
bedmaker 'bed ˌmeɪk ə →'beb- ‖ -ᵊr **~s** z
bedouin, B~ 'bed u ɪn -æ̃, -ən **~s** z
bedpan 'bed pæn →'beb- **~s** z
bedpost 'bed pəʊst →'beb- ‖ -poʊst **~s** s
bedraggl|e bi 'dræg ᵊl bə- **~ed** d **~es** z **~ing** ˌɪŋ
bedridden 'bed ˌrɪd ᵊn
bedrock 'bed rɒk ‖ -rɑːk
bedroll 'bed rəʊl →-rɒʊl ‖ -roʊl **~s** z

BEDROOM

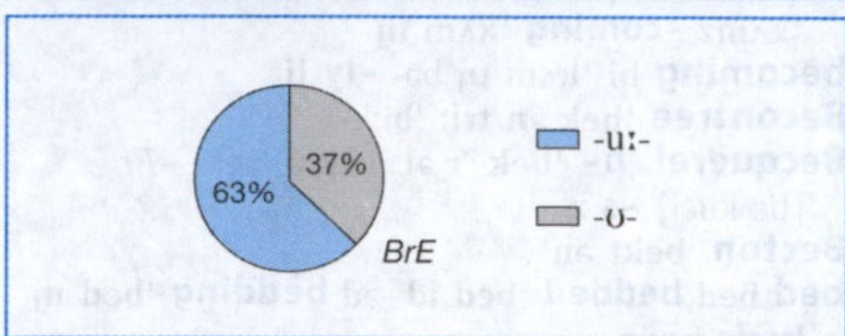

bedroom 'bedr uːm 'bedr ʊm, 'bed ruːm, -rʊm — *Preference poll, BrE:* -uː- *63%,* -ʊ- *37%.* **~s** z
ˌbedroom 'slippers
Bedruthan bi 'drʌð ᵊn bə-
Beds bedz —*see also* **Bedfordshire**
bedside 'bed saɪd
ˌbedside 'manner
bedsit, bed-sit ˌbed 'sɪt ◂ **~s** s
bedsitter, bed-sitter ˌbed 'sɪt ə ‖ -'sɪţ ᵊr **~s** z
bed-sitting room ˌbed 'sɪt ɪŋ ruːm -rʊm ‖ -'sɪţ- **~s** z
bedsock 'bed sɒk ‖ -sɑːk **~s** s
bedsore 'bed sɔː ‖ -sɔːr -soʊr **~s** z
bedspread 'bed spred **~s** z
bedspring 'bed sprɪŋ **~s** z
bedstead 'bed sted **~s** z
bedstraw 'bed strɔː ‖ -strɑː **~s** z
bedtime 'bed taɪm **~s** z
ˌbedtime 'story
Bedwell 'bed wəl -wel
Bedwellty bed 'welt i -'weɬt- —*Welsh* [bed 'weɬ ti]
bed-wett|er 'bed ˌwet| ə ‖ -ˌweţ| ᵊr **~ers** əz ‖ ᵊrz **~ing** ɪŋ
bee biː **bees, bee's** biːz
ˌbee's 'knees; **'bee sting**
Beeb biːb
beech, Beech biːtʃ *(= beach)* **beeches** 'biːtʃ ɪz -əz
Beecham 'biːtʃ əm
Beecher 'biːtʃ ə ‖ -ᵊr
Beeching 'biːtʃ ɪŋ
beechnut 'biːtʃ nʌt **~s** s
beechwood 'biːtʃ wʊd
bee-eater 'biː ˌiːt ə ‖ -ˌiːţ ᵊr **~s** z
beef biːf **beefed** biːft **beefing** 'biːf ɪŋ **beefs** biːfs **beeves** biːvz
ˌbeef 'tea
beefburger 'biːf ˌbɜːg ə ‖ -ˌbɜːg ᵊr **~s** z
beefcake 'biːf keɪk
beefeater 'biːf ˌiːt ə ‖ -ˌiːţ ᵊr **~s** z
beefi... —*see* **beefy**
beefsteak 'biːf steɪk **~s** s
beefwood 'biːf wʊd
beef|y 'biːf |i **~ier** i ə ‖ i ᵊr **~iest** i ɪst i əst
Bee Gee 'biː dʒiː **~s** z
beehive 'biː haɪv **~s** z
beekeep|er 'biː ˌkiːp ə ‖ -ᵊr **~ers** əz ‖ ᵊrz **~ing** ɪŋ
beeline 'biː laɪn
Beelzebub bi 'elz ɪ bʌb -ə-

BEEN

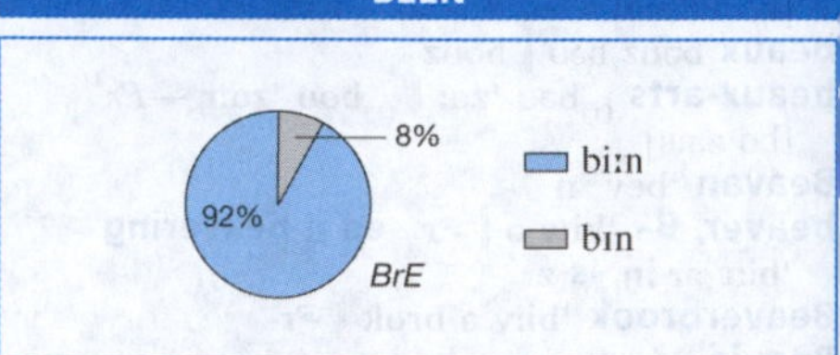

been biːn bɪn ‖ bɪn —*Some BrE speakers have* biːn *as strong form,* bɪn *as weak form. — Preference poll, BrE (for strong form):* biːn *92%,* bɪn *8%.*
beep biːp **beeped** biːpt **beeping** 'biːp ɪŋ **beeps** biːps
beeper 'biːp ə ‖ -ᵊr **~s** z
beer, Beer bɪə ‖ bɪᵊr **~ed** bɪəd ‖ bɪᵊrd **beers** bɪəz ‖ bɪᵊrz
Beerbohm 'bɪə bəʊm ‖ 'bɪr boʊm
beeri... —*see* **beery**
Beersheba bɪə 'ʃiːb ə 'bɪəʃ ɪb ə ‖ bɪr-
beer|y, Beery 'bɪər |i ‖ 'bɪr |i **~ier** i ə ‖ i ᵊr **~iest** i ɪst i əst
beestings *'colostrum'* 'biːst ɪŋz
Beeston 'biːst ən
beeswax 'biːz wæks
beeswing 'biːz wɪŋ
beet biːt *(= beat)* **beets** biːts
Beethoven 'beɪt həʊv ᵊn -əʊv- ‖ 'beɪt oʊv ᵊn —*Ger* ['beːt hoː fᵊn] **~'s** z
beetl|e 'biːt ᵊl ‖ 'biːţ ᵊl **~ed** d **~es** z **~ing** ˌɪŋ
Beeton 'biːt ᵊn
beetroot 'biːtr uːt 'biːt ruːt **~s** s
beeves biːvz
beezer 'biːz ə ‖ -ᵊr
befall bi 'fɔːl bə- ‖ -'fɑːl **~en** ən **~ing** ɪŋ **~s** z
befell bi 'fel bə-
be|fit bi |'fɪt bə- **~fits** 'fɪts **~fitted** 'fɪt ɪd -əd ‖ 'fɪţ əd **~fitting/ly** 'fɪt ɪŋ /li ‖ fɪţ ɪŋ /li
befog bi 'fɒg bə- ‖ -'fɔːg -'fɑːg **~ged** d **~ging** ɪŋ **~s** z
before bi 'fɔː bə- ‖ -'fɔːr -'foʊr
beforehand bi 'fɔː hænd bə- ‖ -'fɔːr- -'foʊr-
befoul bi 'faʊl bə- **~ed** d **~ing** ɪŋ **~s** z

befriend bi ˈfrend bə- **~ed** ɪd əd **~ing** ɪŋ **~s** z
befuddl|e bi ˈfʌd ᵊl bə- **~ed** d **~ement** mənt **~es** z **~ing** ‿ɪŋ
beg beg **begged** begd **begging** ˈbeg ɪŋ **begs** begz
begad bi ˈgæd bə-
began bi ˈgæn bə-
be|get bi |ˈget bə- **~gat/s** ˈgæt/s **~gets** ˈgets **~getting** ˈget ɪŋ ‖ ˈgeţ ɪŋ **~got** ˈgɒt ‖ ˈgɑːt **~gotten** ˈgɒt ᵊn ‖ ˈgɑːt ᵊn
begetter bi ˈget ə bə- ‖ -ˈgeţ ᵊr **~s** z
beggar ˈbeg ə ‖ -ᵊr **~ed** d **beggaring** ˈbeg ər‿ɪŋ **~s** z
beggar|ly ˈbeg ə |li -ᵊl i ‖ -ᵊr- **~liness** li nəs -nɪs
beggar-my-neighb|our, ~or ˌbeg ə mi ˈneɪb ə -maɪˈ-- ‖ ˌbeg ᵊr maɪ ˈneɪb ᵊr
beggary ˈbeg ər i
be|gin bi |ˈgɪn bə- **~gan** ˈgæn **~ginning** ˈgɪn ɪŋ **~gins** ˈgɪnz **~gun** ˈgʌn
Begin *Israeli name* ˈbeɪg ɪn ˈbeg-
beginner bi ˈgɪn ə bə- ‖ -ᵊr **~s** z
beˌginner's ˈluck
beginning bi ˈgɪn ɪŋ bə- **~s** z
begone bi ˈgɒn bə-, §-ˈgɑːn, §-ˈgɔːn ‖ -ˈgɔːn -ˈgɑːn
begonia bi ˈgəʊn i‿ə bə- ‖ -ˈgoʊn jə **~s** z
begorra bi ˈgɒr ə bə- ‖ -ˈgɔːr- -ˈgɑːr-
begot bi ˈgɒt bə- ‖ -ˈgɑːt **~ten** ᵊn
begrim|e bi ˈgraɪm bə- **~ed** d **~es** z **~ing** ɪŋ
begrudg|e bi ˈgrʌdʒ bə- **~ed** d **~es** ɪz əz **~ing/ly** ɪŋ /li
beguil|e bi ˈgaɪᵊl bə- **~ed** d **~es** z **~ing/ly** ɪŋ /li
beguine *'dance', 'music'* bi ˈgiːn bə- **~s** z
Beguine *'member of sisterhood'* ˈbeg iːn ˈbeɪg-; bi ˈgiːn, bə-, ˌbeɪ- **~s** z
begum, Begum ˈbeɪg əm ˈbiːg- **~s** z
begun bi ˈgʌn bə-
behalf bi ˈhɑːf bə- ‖ -ˈhæf
Behan ˈbiː ən
behav|e bi ˈheɪv bə- **~ed** d **~es** z **~ing** ɪŋ
behavior, behaviour bi ˈheɪv jə bə- ‖ -jᵊr **~s** z
beˈhavio(u)r ˌpattern; **beˈhavio(u)r ˌtherapy**
behavior|al, behaviour~ bɪ ˈheɪv jər əl **~ism** ˌɪz əm **~ist/s** ɪst/s §əst/s **~ly** i
behavio|ristic, behaviou~ bi ˌheɪv jə ˈrɪst ɪk ◂ bə-
behead bi ˈhed bə- **~ed** ɪd əd **~ing** ɪŋ **~s** z
beheld bi ˈheld bə-
behemoth, B~ bi ˈhiːm ɒθ bə-, -əθ ‖ -ɑːθ -əθ
behest bi ˈhest bə-
behind bi ˈhaɪnd bə- **~s** z
behindhand bi ˈhaɪnd hænd bə-
Behn ben
behold bi ˈhəʊld bə-, →-ˈhɒʊld ‖ -ˈhoʊld **~ing** ɪŋ **~s** z
beholden bɪ ˈhəʊld ən bə-, §biː-, →-ˈhɒʊld- ‖ -ˈhoʊld-
beholder bi ˈhəʊld ə bə-, →ˈhɒʊld- ‖ -ˈhoʊld ᵊr **~s** z
behoov|e bi ˈhuːv bə- **~ed** d **~es** z **~ing** ɪŋ
behov|e bi ˈhəʊv bə- ‖ -ˈhoʊv **~ed** d **~es** z **~ing** ɪŋ
Behrens ˈbeər ənz ‖ ˈber- —*Ger* [ˈbeːʁ əns]
Beiderbecke ˈbaɪd ə bek ‖ -ᵊr-
beige beɪʒ beɪdʒ
Beighton *(i)* ˈbeɪt ᵊn, *(ii)* ˈbaɪt ᵊn
beignet ˈbeɪn jeɪ ‖ ˌ·ˈ· —*Fr* [bɛ njɛ] **~s** z
Beijing ˌbeɪ ˈdʒɪŋ -ˈʒɪŋ —*Note: there is no justification in Chinese for the -ˈʒɪŋ pronunciation frequently heard in English.* —*Chi* Běijīng [³pei ¹tɕiŋ]
being ˈbiː ɪŋ **~s** z
Beinn *in ScGaelic names* ben
Beira ˈbaɪᵊr ə ‖ ˈbeɪ rə —*Port* [ˈbɐi ɾɐ]
Beirut ˌbeɪ ˈruːt ◂ ˌbeə- —*Arabic* [bej ˈruːt]
Beit baɪt
Beith biːθ —*but the place in Strathclyde is* biːð
bejeweled, bejewelled bi ˈdʒuː‿əld bə-, -ˈdʒuːld
Bekaa, Beqaa be ˈkɑː —*Arabic* [bɛ ˈqɑːʕ]
Bekonscot ˈbek ənz kɒt ‖ -kɑːt
bel, Bel bel *(= bell)* —*It* [bɛl] **bels** belz
ˌbel ˈcanto ˈkænt əʊ ‖ ˈkɑːnt oʊ —*It* [ˈkan to]; **ˌBel Paˈese** paɪ ˈeɪz i pɑː—*It* [pa ˈeː ze]
belabor, belabour bi ˈleɪb ə bə- ‖ -ᵊr **~ed** d **belaboring, belabouring** bɪ ˈleɪb ər‿ɪŋ **~s** z
Belafonte ˌbel ə ˈfɒnt i ‖ -ˈfɑːnţ i -eɪ
Belarius bi ˈleər i‿əs bə-, -ˈlɑːr- ‖ -ˈler- -ˈlær-
Belarus ˌbel ə ˈruːs —*Belorussian* [ˌbʲe ɫa ˈrus], *Russian* [ˌbʲe ɫə ˈrus] **~ian/s** i‿ən/z
belated bi ˈleɪt ɪd bə-, -əd ‖ -ˈleɪţ- **~ly** li **~ness** nəs nɪs
Belau bə ˈlaʊ bi-, be-; ˈbel aʊ
belay bi ˈleɪ bə- **~ed** d **~ing** ɪŋ **~s** z
beˈlaying pin
belch, Belch beltʃ **belched** beltʃt **belching** ˈbeltʃ ɪŋ **belches** ˈbeltʃ ɪz -əz
Belcher ˈbeltʃ ə ˈbelʃ- ‖ -ᵊr
beldam, beldame ˈbeld əm ˈbel dæm, -dɑːm
beleagu|er bi ˈliːg |ə bə- ‖ -|ᵊr **~ered** əd ‖ ᵊrd **~ering** ər ɪŋ **~ers** əz ‖ ᵊrz
Belem be ˈlem bə- —*Port* [bə ˈlẽi, be ˈlẽi]
belemnite ˈbel əm naɪt **~s** z
Belfast ˌbel ˈfɑːst ◂ ˈ·, §-ˈfæst ‖ ˈbel fæst ˌ·ˈ·
belf|ry ˈbelf |ri **~ries** riz
Belgae ˈbelg aɪ ˈbeldʒ iː
Belgian ˈbeldʒ ən **~s** z
Belgic ˈbeldʒ ɪk
Belgium ˈbeldʒ əm
Belgrade ˌbel ˈgreɪd ‖ ˈ· ·
Belgrano bel ˈgrɑːn əʊ ‖ -oʊ —*Sp* [bel ˈɣra no]
Belgrave ˈbel greɪv
ˌBelgrave ˈSquare
Belgravia bel ˈgreɪv i‿ə
Belial ˈbiːl i‿əl
be|lie bi |ˈlaɪ bə- **~lied** ˈlaɪd **~lies** ˈlaɪz **~lying** ˈlaɪ ɪŋ

B

belief bi 'liːf bə- **~s** s
believab|le bi 'liːv əb |əl bə- **~ly** li
believ|e bi 'liːv bə- **~er/s** ə/z ‖ ər/z **~ed** d **~es** z **~ing** ɪŋ
Belinda bə 'lɪnd ə bi-
Belisarius ˌbel ɪ 'sɑːr i‿əs ˌ·ə-, -'seər- ‖ -'ser-
Belisha bə 'liːʃ ə bi-
Beˌlisha 'beacon
belittl|e bi 'lɪt əl bə- ‖ -'lɪţ- **~ed** d **~es** z **~ing** ˌɪŋ
Belize bi 'liːz bə-, be-
Belizean bɪ 'liːz i‿ən bə-, be-, -'lɪz- **~s** z
bell, Bell bel **belled** beld **belling** 'bel ɪŋ **bells** belz
'bell jar; **ˌBell 'Rock**; **'bell tent**
Bella 'bel ə
ˌBella 'Coola 'kuːl ə
belladonna ˌbel ə 'dɒn ə ‖ -'dɑːn-
Bellamy 'bel əm i
bellbird, B~ 'bel bɜːd ‖ -bɜ˞ːd **~s** z
bell-bottom 'bel ˌbɒt əm ‖ -ˌbɑːţ əm **~s** z
bellboy 'bel bɔɪ **~s** z
belle, Belle bel *(= bell)* **belles** belz
ˌbelle é'poque eɪ 'pɒk ‖ -'pɔːk -'pɑːk —*Fr* [bɛ le pɔk]; **ˌBelle 'Fourche** *river in US* fuːʃ
Belleek bə 'liːk bɪ-
Bellenden Ker ˌbel ənd ən 'kɜː ‖ -'kɜ˞ː
Bellerophon bə 'ler əf ən bɪ-
belles-lettres ˌbel 'letr‿ə —*Fr* [bɛl lɛtχ]
Belleville 'bel vɪl ‖ 'bel vɪl
Bellevue ˌbel 'vjuː ‖ 'bel vjuː
Bellew 'bel juː
bellflower, B~ 'bel ˌflaʊ‿ə ‖ -ˌflaʊ‿ər **~s** z
bellhop 'bel hɒp ‖ -hɑːp **~s** s
bellicose 'bel ɪ kəʊs -ə-, -kəʊz ‖ -koʊs **~ly** li **~ness** nəs nɪs
bellicosity ˌbel ɪ 'kɒs ət i ˌ·ə-, -ɪt i ‖ -'kɑːs əţ i
bellie... —*see* **belly**
belligerenc|e bə 'lɪdʒ ər‿ən*t*s bɪ- **~y** i
belligerent bə 'lɪdʒ ər‿ənt bɪ-
Belling 'bel ɪŋ
Bellingham *(i)* 'bel ɪŋ əm -həm, *(ii)* -ɪndʒ əm, *(iii)* -ɪŋ hæm —*The place in Greater London is (i), that in Northumberland (ii), and that in Washington State (iii). The family name may be any of the three.*
Bellingshausen 'bel ɪŋz ˌhaʊz ən
Bellini be 'liːn i bə-—*It* [bel 'liː ni]
bell|man 'bel |mən **~men** mən men
Bellmawr ₍ˌ₎bel 'mɔː ‖ ₍ˌ₎bel 'mɑːr -'mɔːr
Belloc 'bel ɒk -ək ‖ -ɑːk
Bellona be 'ləʊn ə ‖ -'loʊn-
bellow, B~ 'bel əʊ ‖ -oʊ **~ed** d **~ing** ɪŋ **~s** z
Bellows 'bel əʊz ‖ -oʊz
bellpull 'bel pʊl **~s** z
bellring|er 'bel ˌrɪŋ ə ‖ -ər **~ers** əz ‖ ərz **~ing** ɪŋ
bellwether 'bel ˌweð ə ˌ·'·· ‖ -ər **~s** z
bell|y 'bel |i **~ied** id **~ies** iz **~ying** i‿ɪŋ
'belly ˌbutton; **'belly flop**; **'belly laugh**
bellyach|e 'bel i eɪk **~ed** t **~es** s **~ing** ɪŋ
belly-danc|e 'bel i dɑːn*t*s §-dæn*t*s ‖ -dæn*t*s **~er/s** ə/z ‖ ər/z **~ing** ɪŋ
bellyful 'bel i fʊl
belly-landing 'bel i ˌlænd ɪŋ **~s** z
Belmondo bel 'mɒnd əʊ ‖ -'mɑːnd oʊ —*Fr* [bɛl mɔ̃ do]
Belmont 'bel mɒnt -mənt ‖ -mɑːnt
Belmopan ˌbelm əʊ 'pæn ‖ -oʊ-
Belmore 'bel mɔː ‖ -mɔːr -moʊr
Beloff 'bel ɒf ‖ -ɑːf
Belo Horizonte ˌbel əʊ ˌhɒr ɪ 'zɒnt i ˌbeɪl-, -ə'--, -eɪ ‖ -oʊ ˌhɔːr ə 'zɑːnt i —*Port* [ˌbɛ lo ɾi 'zon ti]
belong bi 'lɒŋ bə- ‖ -'lɔːŋ -'lɑːŋ **~ed** d **~ing/s** ɪŋ/z **~s** z
Belorussia ˌbel əʊ 'rʌʃ ə bi ˌel-, -'ruːs i‿ə
Belorussian ˌbel əʊ 'rʌʃ ən bi ˌel-, -'ruːs i‿ən **~s** z
beloved bi 'lʌv ɪd bə-, -əd, -'lʌvd —*but predicatively always* -'lʌvd
below bi 'ləʊ bə- ‖ -'loʊ
Belper 'belp ə ‖ -ər
Belsen 'bels ən —*Ger* ['bɛl zən]
Belshazzar bel 'ʃæz ə ‖ -ər
Belsize 'bel saɪz
ˌBelsize 'Park
Belstead 'bel stɪd -sted, §-stəd
belt belt **belted** 'belt ɪd -əd **belting** 'belt ɪŋ **belts** belts
'belt drive
Beltane 'belt eɪn -ən
beltway 'belt weɪ **~s** z
beluga bə 'luːg ə bi-, be- **~s** z
Belushi bə 'luːʃ i
belvedere, B~ 'belv ə dɪə -ɪ-, ˌ·· '· ‖ -dɪr **~s** z
Belvoir *place in Leics; family name* 'biːv ə ‖ -ər *(!)*
bem|a 'biːm |ə **~as** əz **~ata** ət ə ‖ əţ ə
Bemba 'bem bə **~s** z
Bembo 'bem bəʊ ‖ -boʊ
Bembridge 'bem brɪdʒ
bemoan bi 'məʊn bə- ‖ -'moʊn **~ed** d **~ing** ɪŋ **~s** z
bemus|e bi 'mjuːz bə- **~ed** d **~edly** ɪd li əd li **~ement** mənt **~es** ɪz əz **~ing** ɪŋ
Ben, ben ben **bens** benz —*See also phrases with this word*
benadryl, B~ *tdmk* 'ben ə drɪl **~s** z
Benares bɪ 'nɑːr ɪz bə-, be-, -əz
Benaud 'ben əʊ ‖ -oʊ
Benbecula ben 'bek jʊl ə →bem-
Benbow 'ben bəʊ →'bem- ‖ -boʊ
Bence ben*t*s
bench ben*t*ʃ **benched** ben*t*ʃt **benches** 'ben*t*ʃ ɪz -əz **benching** 'ben*t*ʃ ɪŋ
bencher 'ben*t*ʃ ə ‖ -ər **~s** z
Benchley 'ben*t*ʃ li
benchmark 'ben*t*ʃ mɑːk ‖ -mɑːrk **~ed** t **~ing** ɪŋ **~s** s
benchwarmer 'ben*t*ʃ ˌwɔːm ə ‖ -ˌwɔːrm ər **~s** z
bend bend **bended** 'bend ɪd -əd **bending** 'bend ɪŋ **bends** bendz **bent** bent
ˌbend 'over; **ˌbend 'sinister**
bendable 'bend əb əl

bender 'bend ə ‖ -ᵊr **~s** z
Bendigo 'bend ɪ gəʊ -ə- ‖ -goʊ
Bendix 'bend ɪks
bend|y 'bend |i **~ier** i‿ə ‖ i‿ᵊr **~iest** i‿ɪst i‿əst **~iness** i nəs -nɪs
beneath bi 'niːθ bə-
Benecol *tdmk* 'ben ɪ kɒl -ə- ‖ -kɑːl
Benedicite, b~ ˌben ɪ 'daɪs ət i ˌ-ə-, -'diːtʃ-, -ɪt i; -ɪ teɪ, -ə teɪ ‖ -əţ i **~s** z
Benedick, b~ 'ben ɪ dɪk -ə-
Benedict 'ben ɪ dɪkt -ə- —*The former pronunciation* 'ben ɪt *is nowadays spelt correspondingly as* Bene't *or* Benet.
benedictine, B~ *'liqueur'* ˌben ɪ 'dɪkt iːn ◂ -ə- ‖ -dɪk 'tiːn **~s** z
Benedictine *'monk'* ˌben ɪ 'dɪkt ɪn ◂ -ə-, -iːn, -aɪn **~s** z
benediction ˌben ɪ 'dɪkʃ ᵊn -ə- **~s** z
Benedictus ˌben ɪ 'dɪkt əs -ə-, -ʊs
benefaction ˌben ɪ 'fæk ʃᵊn -ə- **~s** z
benefactive ˌben ɪ 'fækt ɪv -ə-, '· · · · **~s** z
benefactor 'ben ɪ fækt ə '·ə- ‖ -ᵊr **~s** z
benefactress 'ben ɪ fæk trəs '·ə-, -trəs, ˌ·'· **~es** ɪz əz
benefice 'ben ɪf ɪs -əf-, §-əs **~ed** t **~s** ɪz əz
beneficence bə 'nef ɪs əntˢ bɪ-, -əs-
beneficent bə 'nef ɪs ənt bɪ-, -əs- **~ly** li
beneficial ˌben ɪ 'fɪʃ ᵊl ◂ -ə- **~ly** ‿i **~ness** nəs nɪs
beneficiar|y ˌben ɪ 'fɪʃ ər‿|i ˌ-ə-, -'fɪʃ i‿ər |i ‖ -'fɪʃ i er |i -'ər‿|i **~ies** iz
bene|fit 'ben ɪ |fɪt -ə-, §-fət **~fited, ~fitted** fɪt ɪd §fət-, -əd ‖ fɪţ əd **~fiting, ~fitting** fɪt ɪŋ §fət- ‖ fɪţ ɪŋ **~fits** fɪts §fəts
Benelux 'ben ɪ lʌks -ə- **the'Benelux ˌcountries**
Benenden 'ben ənd ən —*formerly also* ˌben ən 'den
Benet, Bene't 'ben ɪt §-ət
Benét *American family name* bə 'neɪ be-
Benetton *tdmk* 'ben ɪt ən -ət-; -ɪ tɒn, -ə- ‖ -ə tɑːn
benevolence bə 'nev əl‿əntˢ bi-
benevolent bə 'nev əl‿ənt bi- **~ly** li
Benfica ben 'fiːk ə —*Port* [bẽ 'fi kɐ]
Benfleet 'ben fliːt
BEng ˌbiː 'endʒ
Bengal ˌben 'gɔːl ◂ →ˌbeŋ-, -'gɑːl
Bengali ben 'gɔːl i →beŋ-, -'gɑːl-, ˌ·'·◂ **~s** z
Benghazi ben 'gɑːz i →beŋ- —*Arabic* [ˌba ni 'ɣaː zi]
Benguela ben 'gwel ə →beŋ-, -'gweɪl-, -'gel-, -'geɪl- —*Port* [beŋ 'gwɛ lɐ]
Ben Gurion, Ben-Gurion ben 'gʊər i‿ən →beŋ- ‖ -'gʊr- ˌben gʊr 'jɑːn, -'jɔːn
Ben Hur, Ben-Hur ˌben 'hɜː ‖ -'hɜː
Benidorm 'ben ɪ dɔːm -ə- ‖ -dɔːrm
benighted bi 'naɪt ɪd bə-, -əd ‖ -'naɪţ- **~ly** li **~ness** nəs nɪs
benign bə 'naɪn bi- **~ly** li
benignanc|y bə 'nɪg nən‿ˢ |i bi- **~ies** iz
benignant bə 'nɪg nənt bi- **~ly** li
benignit|y bə 'nɪg nət |i bi-, -nɪt i ‖ -nəţ |i **~ies** iz
Benin be 'niːn bɪ-, bə-, -'nɪn
Beninese ˌben ɪ 'niːz ◂ be ˌniː-, bɪ-, bə-, -ˌnɪ-
benison 'ben ɪz ən -ɪs-, -əz-, -əs- **~s** z
Benita be 'niːt ə bi-, bə- ‖ -'niːţ-
Benito be 'niːt əʊ bi-, bə- ‖ -'niːţ oʊ
Benjamin, b~ 'bendʒ əm‿ɪn ən
Ben Macdhui ˌben mək 'duː i
Benn ben
benne 'ben i
Bennelong 'ben ə lɒŋ -ɪ- ‖ -lɔːŋ -lɑːŋ
Bennet, Bennett 'ben ɪt §-ət
Ben Nevis ˌben 'nev ɪs §-əs
Bennie, b~ 'ben i **~s** z
Bennington 'ben ɪŋ tən
Benn|y, benn|y 'ben |i **~ies, ~y's** iz
Benoni bə 'nəʊn i bɪ-, be- ‖ -'noʊn-
Ben Rhydding ˌben 'rɪd ɪŋ
Benson 'benᵗs ᵊn
bent bent **bents** bents
Bentall 'bent ᵊl -ɔːl ‖ -ɔːl -ɑːl **~'s** z
Bentham 'benᵗθ əm 'bent-
Benthamism 'benᵗθ ə ˌmɪz əm 'bent-
Benthamite 'benᵗθ ə maɪt 'bent-
benthic 'benᵗθ ɪk
benthos 'benᵗθ ɒs ‖ 'ben θɑːs
Bentinck 'bent ɪŋk
Bentine ben 'tiːn '··
Bentley 'bent li **~s** z
Benton 'bent ən ‖ -ᵊn
bentonite 'bent ə naɪt ‖ -ᵊn aɪt
ben trovato ˌben trəʊ 'vɑːt əʊ ‖ -troʊ 'vɑːţ oʊ —*It* [ˌbɛn tro 'vaː to]
Bentsen 'bents ən
bentwood 'bent wʊd
Benue 'ben u eɪ ‖ 'beɪn weɪ
Benue-Congo ˌben u eɪ 'kɒŋ gəʊ ‖ ˌbeɪn weɪ 'kɑːŋ goʊ
benumb bi 'nʌm bə- **~ed** d **~ing** ɪŋ **~s** z
Benylin *tdmk* 'ben ə lɪn -ɪ-, -ᵊl ɪn
Benyon 'ben jən
Benz benz —*Ger* [bɛnts]
benzedrine, B~ *tdmk* 'benz ə driːn -ɪ-, -drɪn **~s** z
benzene 'benz iːn ben 'ziːn **ˌbenzene 'ring**
benzidine 'benz ɪ diːn -ə-, -dɪn
benzine 'benz iːn ben 'ziːn
benzo- *comb. form with stress-neutral suffix* ¦benz əʊ ‖ -oʊ — **benzosulfate, benzosulphate** ˌbenz əʊ 'sʌlf eɪt ‖ -oʊ-
benzocaine 'benz əʊ keɪn ‖ -ə-
benzodiazepine ˌbenz əʊ daɪ 'æz ə piːn -'eɪz- ‖ ˌbenz oʊ-
benzoic ben 'zəʊ ɪk ‖ -'zoʊ-
benzoin 'benz əʊ ɪn ben 'zəʊ-, §-ən; 'benz ɔɪn ‖ -oʊ- —*Some people claim to distinguish* 'benz əʊ ɪn *etc. 'phenyl benzoyl carbinol' from* 'benz ɔɪn *'gum benjamin'*
benzol 'benz ɒl ‖ -oʊl -ɑːl, -ɔːl
benzole 'benz əʊl →-ɒʊl ‖ -oʊl

benzoyl ˈbenz əʊ ɪl §-əl ‖ -oʊ-
benzpyrene ˌbenz ˈpaɪ^{ə}r iːn
benzyl ˈbenz ɪl -^{ə}l ‖ -iː^{ə}l -^{ə}l
Beowulf ˈbeɪ əʊ wʊlf ‖ -ə-

BEQUEATH

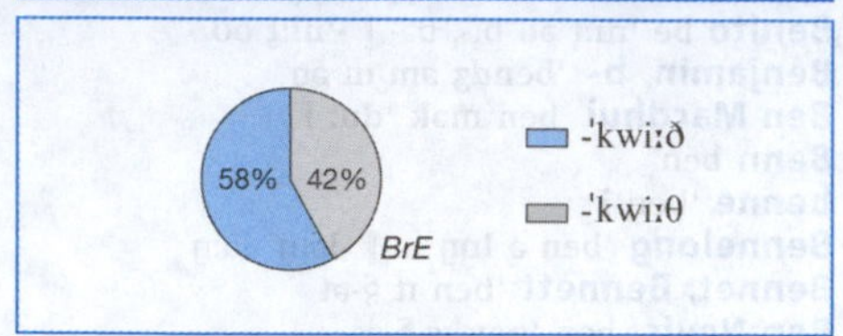

be|queath bi |ˈkwiːð bə-, -ˈkwiːθ — *Preference poll, BrE:* -ˈkwiːð *58%,* -ˈkwiːθ *42%.* **~queathed** ˈkwiːðd ˈkwiːθt **~queathes** ˈkwiːðz ˈkwiːθs **~queathing** ˈkwiːð ɪŋ ˈkwiːθ ɪŋ
bequest bi ˈkwest bə- **~s** s
Bequia *Caribbean island* ˈbek wi -weɪ *(!)*
be|rate bi |ˈreɪt bə- **~rated** ˈreɪt ɪd -əd ‖ ˈreɪţ əd **~rates** ˈreɪts **~rating** ˈreɪt ɪŋ ‖ ˈreɪţ ɪŋ
Berber ˈbɜːb ə ‖ ˈbɝːb ^{ə}r **~s** z
Berbera ˈbɜːb ər ə ‖ ˈbɝːb-
berberis ˈbɜːb ər ɪs §-əs ‖ ˈbɝːb- **~es** ɪz əz
Berbice bɜː ˈbiːs ˈbɜːb ɪs ‖ bɝː-
berceuse beə ˈsɜːz ‖ ber ˈsʊz -ˈsɝːz —*Fr* [bɛʁ søːz]
Berchtesgaden ˈbeəkt əz ɡɑːd ^{ə}n ˈbeəxt- ‖ ˈberkt- —*Ger* [bɛʁç təs ˈɡaːd ^{ə}n]
Bere bɪə ‖ b^{ə}r
bereav|e bi ˈriːv bə- **~ed** d **~ement/s** mənt/s **~es** z **~ing** ɪŋ
bereft bi ˈreft bə-
Berengaria ˌber əŋ ˈɡeər i‿ə ,-ɪŋ-, ,-eŋ- ‖ -ˈɡer-
Berenger ˈber ɪndʒ ə -əndʒ ə ‖ -^{ə}r
Berenice ˌber ɪ ˈnaɪs i -ə-, ˈnaɪk-, -iː; -ˈniːtʃ eɪ, -iː; -ˈniːs
Berenson ˈber ən^{t}s ən
Beresford ˈber ɪs fəd -əs-, -ɪz-, -əz- ‖ -f^{ə}rd
beret ˈber eɪ -i; bə ˈreɪ ‖ bə ˈreɪ —*Formerly also* ˈber ɪt. **~s** z
berg, Berg bɜːɡ ‖ bɝːɡ —*Ger* [bɛʁk] **bergs** bɜːɡz ‖ bɝːɡz
Bergamo ˈbɜːɡ ə məʊ ‖ ˈbɝːɡ ə moʊ —*It* [ˈbɛr ɡa mo]
bergamot ˈbɜːɡ ə mɒt ‖ ˈbɝːɡ ə mɑːt **~s** s
ˈbergamot oil
Bergen ˈbɜːɡ ən ˈbeəɡ- ‖ ˈbɝːɡ- —*Norw* [ˈbær ɡən, ˈbæʁ-]
Berger *(i)* ˈbɜːdʒ ə ‖ ˈbɝːdʒ ^{ə}r, *(ii)* ˈbɜːɡ ə ‖ ˈbɝːɡ ^{ə}r —*as a British name, (i); as an American name, (ii)*
Bergerac ˈbɜːʒ ə ræk ‖ ˌberʒ ə ˈræk -ˈrɑːk
Bergman ˈbɜːɡ mən ‖ ˈbɝːɡ-
bergschrund ˈbɜːɡ ʃrʊnd ‖ ˈbɝːɡ- **~s** z —*Ger* B~ [ˈbɛʁk ʃʁʊnt]
Bergson ˈbɜːɡ s^{ə}n ‖ ˈbɝːɡ- —*Fr* [bɛʁk sɔn]
Bergsonian bɜːɡ ˈsəʊn i‿ən ‖ bɝːɡ ˈsoʊn- berg- **~s** z
beribboned bi ˈrɪb ənd bə-
beriberi ˌber i ˈber i ˈ· ˌ· ·
Bering ˈbeər ɪŋ ˈber- ‖ ˈbɪr ɪŋ ˈber- —*Danish* [ˈbeː ʁeŋ]
ˌBering ˈSea, ˌBering ˈStrait
Berisford ˈber ɪs fəd -əs-, -ɪz-, -əz- ‖ -f^{ə}rd
berk bɜːk ‖ bɝːk **berks** bɜːks ‖ bɝːks
Berkeley *(i)* ˈbɑːk li ‖ ˈbɑːrk-, *(ii)* ˈbɜːk li ‖ ˈbɝːk- —*British and Irish places and names are (i), American places and names are (ii).*
berkelium bɜː ˈkiːl i‿əm bə-, ˈbɜːk li‿əm ‖ ˈbɝːk li‿əm
Berkhamsted ˈbɜːk əm sted ˈbɑːk-, -əm^{p}st ɪd, -əd ‖ ˈbɝːk-
Berkley *place in Michigan* ˈbɜːk li ‖ ˈbɝːk-
Berkoff ˈbɜːk ɒf ‖ ˈbɝːk ɑːf
Berkowitz ˈbɜːk ə wɪts ‖ ˈbɝːk-
Berks *name of county* bɑːks §bɜːks ‖ bɝːks bɑːrks —*see also* **Berkshire**
Berkshire *(i)* ˈbɑːk ʃə -ʃɪə ‖ ˈbɑːrk ʃ^{ə}r -ʃɪr, *(ii)* ˈbɜːk- ‖ ˈbɝːk- —*The English county is (i), though with a non-standard variant (ii). The hills in MA are (ii).* **~s** z
Berlei *tdmk* ˈbɜːl i -aɪ ‖ ˈbɝːl-
Berlin (ˌ)bɜː ˈlɪn ‖ (ˌ)bɝː- —*Ger* [bɛʁ ˈliːn] —*but the town in New Hampshire is* ˈbɜːl ən
Berliner (ˌ)bɜː ˈlɪn ə ‖ b^{ə}r ˈlɪn ^{ə}r **~s** z
Berlioz ˈbeəl i əʊz ˈbɜːl- ‖ ˈberl i oʊz —*Fr* [bɛʁ ljoːz]
Berlitz ˈbɜːl ɪts §-əts ‖ ˈbɝːl ɪts bɝː ˈlɪts
Berlusconi ˌbɜːl ə ˈskəʊn i ˌbeəl-, -u- ‖ ˌbɝːl ə ˈskoʊn i —*It* [ber lu ˈskoː ni]
berm, berme bɜːm ‖ bɝːm **bermes, berms** bɜːmz ‖ bɝːmz
Bermondsey ˈbɜːm əndz i ‖ ˈbɝːm-
Bermuda bə ˈmjuːd ə ‖ b^{ə}r- **~s** z
Berˌmuda ˈshorts; Berˌmuda ˈTriangle
Bermudan bə ˈmjuːd ^{ə}n ‖ b^{ə}r- **~s** z
Bern bɜːn beən ‖ bɝːn bern —*Ger* [bɛʁn]
Bernadette ˌbɜːn ə ˈdet ‖ ˌbɝːn-
Bernadotte ˌbɜːn ə ˈdɒt ˈ· · · ‖ ˈbɝːn ə dɑːt
Bernal *(i)* bə ˈnæl ‖ b^{ə}r-, *(ii)* ˈbɜːn ^{ə}l ‖ ˈbɝːn-
Bernanke bə ˈnæŋk i ‖ b^{ə}r-
Bernard *(i)* ˈbɜːn əd ‖ ˈbɝːn ^{ə}rd, *(ii)* bə ˈnɑːd ‖ b^{ə}r ˈnɑːrd —*As a British name usually (i), as an American name usually (ii).*
Bernardette ˌbɜːn ə ˈdet ‖ ˌbɝːn ^{ə}r- -ə-
Bernardine ˈbɜːn ə dɪn -diːn ‖ ˈbɝːn ^{ə}r-
Berne bɜːn beən ‖ bɝːn bern —*Fr* [bɛʁn]
Berners ˈbɜːn əz ‖ ˈbɝːn ^{ə}rz
Berners-Lee ˌbɜːn əz ˈliː ‖ ˌbɝːn ^{ə}rz ˈli
Bernese ˌbɜː ˈniːz ◂ ‖ ˌbɝː- -ˈniːs
Bernhardt ˈbɜːn hɑːt ‖ ˈbɝːn hɑːrt —*Fr* [bɛʁ naːʁ]
Bernice *(i)* ˈbɜːn ɪs -əs ‖ ˈbɝːn-, *(ii)* bə ˈniːs bɜː- ‖ b^{ə}r-, *(iii)* bɜː ˈnaɪs i ‖ b^{ə}r- —*In AmE usually (ii).*
Bernini bɜː ˈniːn i bə- ‖ b^{ə}r- —*It* [ber ˈniː ni]
Bernoulli bɜː ˈnuːl i bə- ‖ b^{ə}r- —*Fr* [bɛʁ nu ji], *Ger* [bɛʁ ˈnʊl i]
Berˈnouilli efˌfect
Bernstein *(i)* ˈbɜːn staɪn ‖ ˈbɝːn-, *(ii)* -stiːn
Be-Ro *tdmk* ˈbiː rəʊ ‖ -roʊ
Berol *tdmk* ˈbiː rɒl -rəʊl ‖ -rɑːl -rɔːl, -roʊl

Berridge ˈber ɪdʒ
Berriew ˈber i uː
berr|y ˈber |i **~ied** id **~ies** iz **~ying** i ɪŋ
Berry ˈber i
Berryman ˈber i mən
berserk bə ˈzɜːk bɜː-, -ˈsɜːk; ˈbɜːs ɜːk, ˈbɜːz- ‖ bᵊr ˈsɜːk -ˈzɜːk **~er/s** ə/z ‖ ᵊr/z
Bert bɜːt ‖ bɜːt
Bertelsmann *tdmk* ˈbɜːt ᵊlz mæn -mən ‖ ˈbɜːţ- —*Ger* [ˈbɛʁ tᵊls man]
berth bɜːθ ‖ bɜːθ *(= birth)* **berthed** bɜːθt ‖ bɜːθt **berthing** ˈbɜːθ ɪŋ ‖ ˈbɜːθ ɪŋ **berths** bɜːθs bɜːðz ‖ bɜːθs
Bertha ˈbɜːθ ə ‖ ˈbɜːθ ə
Bertie ˈbɜːt i ‖ ˈbɜːţ i *—but as a family name in BrE,* ˈbɑːt i
Bertolucci ˌbɜːt ə ˈlʊtʃ i -ˈluːtʃ- ‖ ˌbɜːţ ə ˈluːtʃ i —*It* [ber to ˈlut tʃi]
Bertram ˈbɜːtr əm ‖ ˈbɜːtr-
Bertrand ˈbɜːtr ənd ‖ ˈbɜːtr-
Berwick ˈber ɪk
Berwick-on-Tweed ˌber ɪk ɒn ˈtwiːd ‖ -ɑːn ˈ- -ɔːn ˈ-
Berwickshire ˈber ɪk ʃə -ʃɪə; ˈ· · ˌʃaɪ‿ə ‖ -ʃɪr -ʃᵊr; ˈ· · ˌʃaɪ‿ᵊr
Berwyn ˈbeə wɪn ˈbɜː- ‖ ˈbɜː-
beryl, Beryl ˈber əl -ɪl **~s** z
beryllium bə ˈrɪl i‿əm be-
Berzelius bə ˈziːl i‿əs -ˈzeɪl- ‖ bᵊr- —*Swed* [bær ˈseː li ʊs]
Besançon bə ˈzɒ̃s ɒ̃ ‖ -ˈzɑːn soʊn -ˈzænᵗs ᵊn —*Fr* [bə zɑ̃ sɔ̃]
Besant *(i)* ˈbes ᵊnt ˈbez-, *(ii)* bɪ ˈzænt bə-
beseech bi ˈsiːtʃ bə- **~ed** t **~es** ɪz əz **~ing/ly** ɪŋ /li **besought** bi ˈsɔːt bə- ‖ ˈsɑːt
beseem bi ˈsiːm bə- **~ed** d **~ing** ɪŋ **~s** z
be|set bi |ˈset bə- **~sets** ˈsets **~setting** ˈset ɪŋ ‖ ˈseţ ɪŋ
beside bi ˈsaɪd bə- **~s** z
besieg|e bi ˈsiːdʒ bə-, -ˈsiːʒ **~ed** d **~ement** mənt **~er/s** ə/z ‖ ᵊr/z **~es** ɪz əz **~ing** ɪŋ
be|smear bi |ˈsmɪə bə- ‖ -|ˈsmɪᵊr **~smeared** smɪəd ‖ ˈsmɪᵊrd **~smearing** ˈsmɪər ɪŋ ‖ ˈsmɪr ɪŋ **~smears** ˈsmɪəz ‖ ˈsmɪᵊrz
besmirch bi ˈsmɜːtʃ bə- ‖ -ˈsmɜːtʃ **~ed** t **~ment** mənt **~es** ɪz əz **~ing** ɪŋ
besom ˈbiːz əm **~ed** d **~ing** ɪŋ **~s** z
besotted bi ˈsɒt ɪd bə-, -ˈzɒt-, -əd ‖ -ˈsɑːţ əd
besought bi ˈsɔːt bə- ‖ -ˈsɑːt
bespangl|e bi ˈspæŋ gᵊl bə- **~ed** d **~es** z **~ing** ‿ɪŋ
bespatt|er bi ˈspæt |ə bə- ‖ -ˈspæţ |ᵊr **~ered** əd ‖ ᵊrd **~ering** ‿ər ɪŋ ‖ ər ɪŋ **~ers** əz ‖ ᵊrz
be|speak bi |ˈspiːk bə- **~speaking** ˈspiːk ɪŋ **~speaks** ˈspiːks **~spoke** ˈspəʊk ‖ ˈspoʊk **~spoken** ˈspəʊk ən ‖ ˈspoʊk ən
bespectacled bi ˈspekt ək ᵊld bə-, -ɪk-
bespok|e bi ˈspəʊk bə- ‖ -ˈspoʊk **~en** ən
besprinkl|e bi ˈsprɪŋk ᵊl bə- **~ed** d **~es** z **~ing** ‿ɪŋ
Bess bes **Bess's** ˈbes ɪz -əz
Bessarabi|a ˌbes ə ˈreɪb i‿|ə **~an/s** ən/z◂
Bessborough ˈbez bər‿ə ‖ -ˌbɜː oʊ
Bessbrook ˈbes brʊk
Bessel, Bessell ˈbes ᵊl
ˈ**Bessel** ˌ**function**
Bessemer ˈbes ɪm ə -əm- ‖ ᵊr
ˌ**Bessemer con**ˈ**verter**
Besses o' th' Barn ˌbes ɪz əð ˈbɑːn ˌ-əz- ‖ -ˈbɑːrn
Bessey, Bessie, Bessy ˈbes i
best, Best best **bested** ˈbest ɪd -əd **besting** ˈbest ɪŋ **bests** bests
ˌ**best** ˈ**man**
bestial ˈbest i‿əl ‖ ˈbes tʃəl →ˈbeʃ-, ˈbiːs- **~ly** i *(*)*
bestialit|y ˌbest i ˈæl ət |i -ɪt i ‖ ˌbes tʃi ˈæl əţ |i →ˌbeʃ-, ˌbiːs- *(*)* **~ies** iz
bestiar|y ˈbest i‿ər |i ‖ ˈbes tʃi er |i →ˈbeʃ-, ˈbiːs- *(*)* **~ies** iz
be|stir bi |ˈstɜː bə- ‖ -|ˈstɜː **~stirred** ˈstɜːd ‖ ˈstɜːd **~stirring** ˈstɜːr ɪŋ ‖ ˈstɜː ɪŋ **~stirs** ˈstɜːz ‖ ˈstɜːz
bestow bi ˈstəʊ bə- ‖ -ˈstoʊ **~ed** d **~ing** ɪŋ **~s** z
bestowal bi ˈstəʊ əl bə- ‖ -ˈstoʊ-
bestrew bi ˈstruː bə-
bestrewn bi ˈstruːn bə-
be|stride bi |ˈstraɪd bə- **~strides** ˈstraɪdz **~stridden** ˈstrɪd ᵊn **~strode** ˈstrəʊd ‖ ˈstroʊd
bestseller, best-seller ˌbest ˈsel ə◂ ‖ -ᵊr **~dom** dəm **~s** z
bestselling, best-selling ˌbest ˈsel ɪŋ◂
Beswick ˈbez ɪk
bet, Bet bet **betted** ˈbet ɪd -əd ‖ ˈbeţ- **betting** ˈbet ɪŋ ‖ ˈbeţ- **bets** bets
beta, Beta ˈbiːt ə ‖ ˈbeɪţ ə *(*)* **~s** z
ˈ**beta** ˌ**particle**; ˈ**beta** ˌ**rhythm**
beta-blocker ˈbiːt ə ˌblɒk ə ‖ ˈbeɪţ ə ˌblɑːk ᵊr **~s** z
betaine ˈbiːt ə iːn -ɪn; bɪ ˈteɪ-, bə- ‖ ˈbiːţ-
be|take bi |ˈteɪk bə- **~taken** ˈteɪk ən **~takes** ˈteɪks **~taking** ˈteɪk ɪŋ **~took** ˈtʊk
Betamax *tdmk* ˈbiːt ə mæks ‖ ˈbeɪţ-
betatron ˈbiːt ə trɒn ‖ ˈbeɪţ ə trɑːn **~s** z
betcha ˈbetʃ ə
betel ˈbiːt ᵊl ‖ ˈbiːţ ᵊl *(= beetle)*
ˈ**betel nut**
Betelgeuse ˈbiːt ᵊl dʒɜːz -ʒɜːz, -dʒuːz, ˌ· · ˈ· ‖ ˈbiːţ ᵊl dʒuːs ˈbeţ-, -dʒuːz
bete noire, bête noire ˌbeɪt ˈnwɑː ˌbet- ‖ ˌbet nə ˈwɑːr ˌbeɪt- —*Fr* [bɛt nwaːʁ] **betes noires, bêtes noires** ˌbeɪt ˈnwɑːz ˌbet-, ˈnwɑː ‖ ˌbet nə ˈwɑːrz ˌbeɪt-, -ˈnwɑːr —*Fr* [bɛt nwaːʁ]
beth *Hebrew letter* bet beθ ‖ beɪt beɪθ, beɪs
Beth *personal name* beθ
Beth-Ann, Bethanne, Beth-Anne ˌbeθ ˈæn
Bethany ˈbeθ ən i
Bethel, bethel ˈbeθ ᵊl **~'s, ~s** z
Bethell *(i)* ˈbeθ ᵊl, *(ii)* be ˈθel
Bethesda be ˈθezd ə bɪ-, bə-
be|think bi |ˈθɪŋk bə- **~thinking** ˈθɪŋk ɪŋ **~thinks** ˈθɪŋks **~thought** ˈθɔːt ‖ ˈθɑːt
Bethlehem ˈbeθ lɪ hem -lə-, -li‿əm

B

Bethnal 'beθ nᵊl
 ˌBethnal 'Green
bethought bi 'θɔːt bə- ‖ -'θɑːt
Bethune, Béthune be 'θjuːn bi-, bə-, -'tjuːn, -'tuːn ‖ -'θuːn —*Fr* [be tyn] —*As a family name, also* 'biːt ᵊn
betid|e bi 'taɪd bə- **~ed** ɪd əd **~es** z **~ing** ɪŋ
betimes bi 'taɪmz bə-
betise, bêtise be 'tiːz ₍ₗ₎beɪ- —*Fr* [bɛ tiːz] **~s** *same pronunciation*
Betjeman 'betʃ ə mən -ɪ-
betoken bi 'təʊk ən bə- ‖ -'toʊk- **~ed** d **~er/s** ˌə/z ‖ ˌᵊr/z **~ing** ˌɪŋ **~s** z
beton|y 'bet ən |i ‖ -ᵊn i **~ies** iz
betook bi 'tʊk bə-
betray bi 'treɪ bə- **~ed** d **~er/s** ə/z ‖ ᵊr/z **~ing** ɪŋ **~s** z
betrayal bi 'treɪ əl bə- **~s** z
betrayment bi 'treɪ mənt bə- **~s** s
be|troth bi |'trəʊð bə-, -'trəʊθ ‖ -|'troʊð -'trɑːθ **~trothed** 'trəʊðd 'trəʊθt ‖ -'troʊðd -'trɑːθt **~trothing** 'trəʊð ɪŋ 'trəʊθ- ‖ -'troʊð ɪŋ -'trɑːθ- **~troths** 'trəʊðz 'trəʊθs ‖ -'troʊðz -'trɑːθs
betrothal bi 'trəʊð ᵊl bə-, -'trəʊθ- ‖ -'troʊð- -'trɑːθ- **~s** z
Betsy 'bets i
bett... —*see* **bet**
Bettany 'bet ən i ‖ -ᵊn i
Bette 'bet i bet
Bettelheim 'bet ᵊl haɪm ‖ 'beţ-
better 'bet ə ‖ 'beţ ᵊr **~ed** d **bettering** 'bet ˌər ɪŋ ‖ 'beţ ər ɪŋ **~s** z
betterment 'bet ə mənt ‖ 'bet ᵊr-
better-off ˌbet ər 'ɒf -'ɔːf ‖ ˌbeţ ər 'ɔːf -'ɑːf
Betterton 'bet ət ən ‖ 'beţ ᵊrt ᵊn
Betteshanger 'bets ˌhæŋ ə ‖ -ᵊr
Bettina be 'tiːn ə bə, bɪ-
betting 'bet ɪŋ ‖ 'beţ ɪŋ
 'betting shop
Betton 'bet ᵊn
bettor 'bet ə ‖ 'beţ ᵊr **~s** z
Bettws 'bet əs -ʊs ‖ 'beţ- —*Welsh* ['bet us]
Bettws... —*see* **Betws...**
Betty 'bet i ‖ 'beţ i **~'s** z
between bi 'twiːn bə-
betweentimes bi 'twiːn taɪmz bə-
betwixt bi 'twɪkst bə-
Betws-y-Coed ˌbet əs i 'kɔɪd ˌ·ʊs-, -'kəʊ ɪd, -ed ‖ ˌbeţ- —*Welsh* [ˌbet us ə 'koːid]
Betws-yn-Rhos ˌbet əs ɪn 'rəʊs ˌ·ʊs-, -ən'· ‖ ˌbeţ əs ən 'roʊs —*Welsh* [ˌbet us ən 'hroːs]
Beulah 'bjuːl ə
Bevan 'bev ᵊn
bevatron 'bev ə trɒn ‖ -trɑːn **~s** z
bevel 'bev ᵊl **~ed, ~led** d **~ing, ~ling** ɪŋ **~s** z
 'bevel gear
beverag|e 'bev ər ˌɪdʒ **~es** ɪz əz
Beveridge 'bev ər ˌɪdʒ
Beverley, Beverly 'bev əl i ‖ -ᵊr li
 ˌBeverly 'Hills
Bevin 'bev ɪn §-ᵊn
Bevis *(i)* 'bev ɪs §-əs, *(ii)* 'biːv-
bevv|y 'bev |i **~ied** id **~ies** iz
bev|y 'bev |i *(= bevvy)* **~ies** iz
bewail bi 'weɪᵊl bə- **~ed** d **~ing** ɪŋ **~s** z
beware bi 'weə bə- ‖ -'weᵊr -'wæᵊr
Bewdley 'bjuːd li
Bewes bjuːz
bewhiskered bi 'wɪsk əd bə-, -'hwɪsk- ‖ -ᵊrd
Bewick, Bewicke 'bjuː ˌɪk
bewigged bi 'wɪgd bə-
bewild|er bi 'wɪld |ə bə- ‖ -|ᵊr **~ered** əd ‖ ᵊrd **~ering/ly** ˌər ɪŋ /li **~erment** ə mənt ‖ ᵊr mənt **~ers** əz ‖ ᵊrz
bewitch bi 'wɪtʃ bə- **~ed** t **~er/s** ə/z ‖ ᵊr/z **~es** ɪz əz **~ing/ly** ɪŋ /li **~ment/s** mənt/s
Bewley 'bjuːl i
Bexar *county in TX* beə ‖ beᵊr
Bexhill ˌbeks 'hɪl ◂
 ˌBexhill-on-'Sea
Bexley 'beks li
Bexleyheath ˌbeks li 'hiːθ
bey, Bey beɪ *(= bay)* **beys, Beys** beɪz
Beyfus 'beɪf əs 'baɪf-
Beynon 'baɪn ən 'beɪn-
Beyoncé bi 'jɒnᵗs eɪ ‖ -'jɑːnᵗs-
beyond bi 'jɒnd bə- bi 'ɒnd ‖ bi 'ɑːnd
bezant, B~ 'bez ᵊnt **~s** s
bezel 'bez ᵊl **~s** z
Beziers, Béziers 'bez i eɪ —*Fr* [be zje]
bezique bɪ 'ziːk bə- **~s** s
bezoar 'biːz ɔː ‖ -ɔːr -oʊr **~s** z
Bhagavad-Gita ˌbʌg əv əd 'giːt ə ˌbæg-, -ə væd- ‖ ˌbɑːg ə ˌvɑːd-
bhagwan, B~ 'bæg wɑːn bʌ 'gwɑːn —*Hindi* [bʱəg ʋaːn]
bhaji, bhajee 'bɑːdʒ i **~s** z —*Hindi* [bʱaː dʒi]
bhang bæŋ —*Hindi* [bʱaːŋ]
bhangra 'bæŋ grə 'bɑːŋ- —*Hindi* [bʱaːŋgr]
bharal 'bʌr əl ‖ 'bɜː ˌəl **~s** z —*Hindi* [bʱərəl]
bhikku 'bɪk uː
bhindi 'bɪnd i —*Hindi* [bʱɪ̃ ɖi]
Bhojpuri bəʊdʒ 'pʊər i ‖ boʊdʒ 'pʊr i —*Hindi* [bʱoːdʒ pʊ riː]
Bhopal ₍ₗ₎bəʊ 'pɑːl ‖ ₍ₗ₎boʊ- —*Hindi* [bʱoː paːl]
Bhreathnach 'vræn ɒk ‖ -ɑːk
Bhumibol 'buːm i bɒn -bɒl ‖ -boʊn -boʊl —*Thai* [pʰuː mi pʰon]
bhuna 'buːn ə
Bhutan ˌbuː 'tɑːn -'tæn
Bhutanese ˌbuːt ə 'niːz ◂ ‖ -'niːs
Bhutto 'buːt əʊ 'bʊt- ‖ 'buːţ oʊ
bi baɪ
bi- *comb. form* ₍ₗ₎baɪ — **biaxial** ₍ₗ₎baɪ 'æks i ˌəl
Biaf|ra bi 'æf |rə baɪ- **~ran/s** rən/z
Bialystok bi 'æl ɪ stɒk -'·ə-; ˌbiː ˌə 'lɪst ɒk ‖ bi 'ɑːl ə stɑːk —*Polish* Białystok [bja 'wɨ stɔk]
Bianca bi 'æŋk ə
biannual ˌbaɪ 'æn ju ˌəl **~ly** i **~s** z
Biarritz ˌbɪə 'rɪts '. . ‖ ˌbiː ə 'rɪts '. . . —*Fr* [bja ʁits]

bias, Bias ˈbaɪ‿əs **~ed, ~sed** t **~es, ~ses** ɪz əz **~ing, ~sing** ɪŋ
ˌbias ˈbinding
biathlete baɪ ˈæθ liːt **~s** z
biathlon baɪ ˈæθ lən -lɒn ‖ -lɑːn **~s** z
bib bɪb **bibbed** bɪbd **bibbing** ˈbɪb ɪŋ **bibs** bɪbz
Bibb bɪb
bibb... —*see* **bib**
Bibby ˈbɪb i **~'s** z
bibelot ˈbɪb ləʊ ‖ ˈbiːb ə loʊ **~s** z —*or as sing.*
bible, Bible ˈbaɪb ᵊl **~s** z
ˈBible belt; **ˈBible ˌstudy**
biblical, B~ ˈbɪb lɪk ᵊl **~ly** ‿i
biblio- *comb. form*
with stress-neutral suffix ¦bɪb li əʊ ‖ -ə
— **bibliomania** ˌbɪb li əʊ ˈmeɪn i‿ə ‖ -ə-
with stress-imposing suffix ˌbɪb li ˈɒ+ ‖ -ˈɑː+
— **bibliolatry** ˌbɪb li ˈɒl ətr i ‖ -ˈɑːl-
bibliographer ˌbɪb li ˈɒg rəf ə ‖ -ˈɑːg rəf ᵊr **~s** z
bibliographic ˌbɪb li‿ə ˈgræf ɪk ◂ **~al** ᵊl **~ally** ᵊl‿i
bibliograph|y ˌbɪb li ˈɒg rəf |i ‖ -ˈɑːg- **~ies** iz
bibliophile ˈbɪb li‿ə faɪᵊl **~s** z
bibulous ˈbɪb jʊl əs -jəl- ‖ -jəl- **~ly** li **~ness** nəs nɪs
Bic, BiC *tdmk* bɪk **Bics, BiCs** bɪks
bicameral ₍ˌ₎baɪ ˈkæm ᵊr‿əl
bicameralism ₍ˌ₎baɪ ˈkæm ər‿ə ˌlɪz əm
bicarb ˈbaɪ kɑːb ˌ·ˈ· ‖ -kɑːrb
bicarbonate ₍ˌ₎baɪ ˈkɑːb ən‿ət -ɪt, -eɪt ‖ -ˈkɑːrb-
biˌcarbonate of ˈsoda
bice baɪs
ˌbice ˈgreen
bicentenar|y ˌbaɪ sen ˈtiːn ər‿|i -ˈten-; ₍ˌ₎baɪ ˈsent ɪn ər‿|i, -ˈsent ən- ‖ -ˈten- ₍ˌ₎-ˈsent ᵊn er |i **~ies** iz
bicentennial ˌbaɪ sen ˈten i‿əl **~s** z
biceps ˈbaɪ seps **~es** ɪz əz
Bicester ˈbɪst ə ‖ -ᵊr *(!)*
Biche-la-mar ˌbiːtʃ lə ˈmɑː ˌbiːʃ-, -læ- ‖ -ˈmɑːr
bichon frise ˌbiːʃ ᵊn ˈfriːz -ɒn- —*Fr* bichon frisé [bi ʃɔ̃ fʁi ze] **~s** ɪz əz
bichromate ₍ˌ₎baɪ ˈkrəʊm eɪt -ət, -ɪt ‖ -ˈkroʊm-
bicker ˈbɪk ə ‖ -ᵊr **~ed** d **~ing** ˈbɪk ər ɪŋ **~s** s
Bickerstaff, Bickerstaffe ˈbɪk ə stɑːf §-stæf ‖ -ᵊr stæf
Bickersteth ˈbɪk ə steθ -stɪθ ‖ -ᵊr-
Bickerton ˈbɪk ət ən ‖ -ᵊrt ᵊn
Bickford ˈbɪk fəd ‖ -fᵊrd
bickie ˈbɪk i **~s** z
Bickley ˈbɪk li
Bicknell ˈbɪk nᵊl
bicoastal ₍ˌ₎baɪ ˈkəʊst ᵊl ‖ -ˈkoʊst-
bicolor, bicolour ˈbaɪ ˌkʌl ə ‖ -ᵊr
biconcave ₍ˌ₎baɪ ˈkɒŋ keɪv -ˈkɒn-, ˌbaɪ kɒn ˈkeɪv ‖ ₍ˌ₎baɪ ˈkɑːn-
biconcavity ˌbaɪ kɒn ˈkæv ət i -ɪt i ‖ ˌbaɪ kɑːn ˈkæv əţ i
biconvex ₍ˌ₎baɪ ˈkɒn veks ˌbaɪ kɒn ˈveks ‖ ₍ˌ₎baɪ ˈkɑːn-
biconvexity ˌbaɪ kɒn ˈveks ət i -ɪt i ‖ ˌbaɪ kɑːn ˈveks əţ i
bicuspid ˌbaɪ ˈkʌsp ɪd §-əd **~s** z
bicuspidate ˌbaɪ ˈkʌsp ɪ deɪt §-ə-
bicycl|e ˈbaɪs ɪk ᵊl -ək- **~ed** d **~es** z **~ing** ‿ɪŋ
ˈbicycle clip; **ˈbicycle pump**
bicyclist ˈbaɪs ɪk lɪst -ək-, §-ləst **~s** s
bid bɪd **bade** bæd beɪd **bidden** ˈbɪd ᵊn **bidding** ˈbɪd ɪŋ **bids** bɪdz
ˈbid price
biddable ˈbɪd əb ᵊl
Biddell *(i)* ˈbɪd ᵊl, *(ii)* bɪ ˈdel
bidden ˈbɪd ᵊn
bidder, B~ ˈbɪd ə ‖ -ᵊr **~s** z
Biddie ˈbɪd i
bidding ˈbɪd ɪŋ
Biddle ˈbɪd ᵊl
Biddulph ˈbɪd ʌlf
Biddy, bidd|y ˈbɪd |i **~ies** iz
bide, Bide baɪd **bided** ˈbaɪd ɪd -əd **biding** ˈbaɪd ɪŋ **bides** baɪdz **bode** bəʊd ‖ boʊd
Bideford ˈbɪd ɪ fəd -ə- ‖ -fᵊrd *(!)*
Biden ˈbaɪd ᵊn
bidet ˈbiːd eɪ ‖ bɪ ˈdeɪ —*Fr* [bi dɛ] *(*)* **~s** z
bidialectal ˌbaɪ ˌdaɪ‿ə ˈlekt ᵊl
bidialectalism ˌbaɪ ˌdaɪ‿ə ˈlekt ə ˌlɪz əm -ᵊl ˌɪz-
bidirectional ˌbaɪ daɪᵊ ˈrek ʃᵊn‿əl ◂ ˌ·də-, ˌ·dɪ- **~ly** i
Bidwell ˈbɪd wel
Bieber ˈbiːb ə ‖ -ᵊr
Biedermeier ˈbiːd ə ˌmaɪ‿ə ‖ -ᵊr ˌmaɪ ᵊr —*Ger* [ˈbiː dɐ ˌmai ɐ]
Bielefeld ˈbiːl ə feld -felt —*Ger* [ˈbiː lə fɛlt]
biennale ˌbiː e ˈnɑːl eɪ **~s** z
biennial baɪ ˈen i‿əl **~ly** i
bien-pensant ˌbjæ̃ ˈpɒ̃s ɒ̃ ‖ -pɑː ˈsɑ̃ː —*Fr* [bjɛ̃ pɑ̃ sɑ̃]
bier bɪə ‖ bɪᵊr *(= beer)* **biers** bɪəz ‖ bɪᵊrz
Bierce bɪəs ‖ bɪᵊrs
bierkeller ˈbɪə ˌkel ə ‖ ˈbɪr ˌkel ᵊr —*Ger* B~ [ˈbiːɐ ˌkɛl ɐ] **~s** z
biff bɪf **biffed** bɪft **biffing** ˈbɪf ɪŋ **biffs** bɪfs
Biffen ˈbɪf ɪn §-ᵊn
Biffo ˈbɪf əʊ ‖ -oʊ
bifid ˈbaɪ fɪd **~ly** li
bifocal ˌbaɪ ˈfəʊk ᵊl ◂ ‖ -ˈfoʊk- **~s** z
bifoliate ˌbaɪ ˈfəʊl i eɪt -i‿ət, ɪt ‖ -ˈfoʊl-
bifurcate *adj* ˌbaɪ ˈfɜːk eɪt -ət, -ɪt; ˈbaɪ fə keɪt, -kət, -kɪt ‖ -ˈfɜːk- **~ly** li
bifur|cate *v* ˈbaɪ fə |keɪt -fɜː- ‖ -fᵊr- **~cated** keɪt ɪd əd ‖ keɪţ əd **~cates** keɪts **~cating** keɪt ɪŋ ‖ keɪţ ɪŋ
bifurcation ˌbaɪ fə ˈkeɪʃ ᵊn -fɜː- ‖ -fᵊr- **~s** z
big bɪg **bigger** ˈbɪg ə ‖ -ᵊr **biggest** ˈbɪg ɪst -əst
ˌBig ˈApple; **ˌbig ˈbang ˌtheory**; **ˌBig ˈBen**; **ˌBig ˈBrother**; **ˌbig ˈbusiness**; **ˌbig ˈdeal**; **ˌbig ˈgame**; **ˌbig ˈstick**; **ˌBig ˈSur** sɜː ‖ sɜː; **ˈbig time**, ˌ·ˈ·; **ˌbig ˈtop**; **ˌbig ˈwheel**
bigami... —*see* **bigamy**
bigamist ˈbɪg əm ɪst §-əst **~s** s
bigamous ˈbɪg əm əs **~ly** li
bigam|y ˈbɪg əm |i **~ies** iz

Bigbury ˈbɪg bər‿i ‖ -ˌber i
Bigelow ˈbɪg ə ləʊ -ɪ- ‖ -loʊ
Bigfoot ˈbɪg fʊt
bigg... —*see* **big**
Biggar ˈbɪg ə ‖ -ᵊr
biggie ˈbɪg i **~s** z
Biggin ˈbɪg ɪn §-ən
biggish ˈbɪg ɪʃ
Biggles ˈbɪg ᵊlz
Biggleswade ˈbɪg ᵊlz weɪd
Biggs bɪgz
bigg|y ˈbɪg| i **~ies** iz
bighead ˈbɪg hed **~s** z
bigheaded ˌbɪg ˈhed ɪd ◂ -əd **~ly** li **~ness** nəs nɪs
big-hearted ˌbɪg ˈhɑːt ɪd ◂ -əd ‖ -ˈhɑːrţ- **~ly** li **~ness** nəs nɪs
bighorn ˈbɪg hɔːn ‖ -hɔːrn **~s** z
bight baɪt *(= bite, byte)* **bighted** ˈbaɪt ɪd -əd ‖ ˈbaɪţ- **bighting** ˈbaɪt ɪŋ ‖ ˈbaɪţ- **bights** baɪts
bigmouth ˈbɪg maʊθ **~s** s
bigmouthed ˌbɪg ˈmaʊðd ◂ -ˈmaʊθt, ˈ· ·
Bignell ˈbɪg nᵊl
bigness ˈbɪg nəs -nɪs
bignonia bɪg ˈnəʊn i‿ə ‖ -ˈnoʊn- **~s** z
bigot ˈbɪg ət **~s** s
bigoted ˈbɪg ət ɪd -əd ‖ -əţ əd **~ly** li **~ness** nəs nɪs
bigotr|y ˈbɪg ətr |i **~ies** iz
big-time ˈbɪg taɪm
bigwig ˈbɪg wɪg **~s** z
Bihar bɪ ˈhɑː ‖ -ˈhɑːr —*Hindi* [bɪ hɑːr]
Bihari bɪ ˈhɑːr i **~s** z
bijou ˈbiːʒ uː biː ˈʒuː **~s, ~x** z
bijouterie bi ˈʒuːt ər i ‖ -ˈʒuːţ- —*Fr* [bi ʒu tʁi]
bike baɪk **biked** baɪkt **bikes** baɪks **biking** ˈbaɪk ɪŋ
biker, Biker ˈbaɪk ə ‖ -ᵊr **~s** z
bikeshed ˈbaɪk ʃed **~s** z
bikini, B~ bɪ ˈkiːn i bə- **~s** z
Biko ˈbiːk əʊ ‖ -oʊ
bilabial ⁽ˌ⁾baɪ ˈleɪb i‿əl **~ly** i **~s** z
bilateral ⁽ˌ⁾baɪ ˈlæt‿ᵊr əl ‖ -ˈlæţ ər əl →-ˈlætr əl **~ly** i **~ness** nəs nɪs
Bilbao bɪl ˈbaʊ -ˈbɑː əʊ ‖ -ˈbɑː oʊ —*Sp* [bil ˈβa o]
bilberr|y ˈbɪl bər‿|i ‖ -ˌber |i **~ies** iz
bilbo, Bilbo ˈbɪlb əʊ ‖ -oʊ **~es, ~s** z
Bildungsroman ˈbɪld ʊŋz rəʊ ˌmɑːn ‖ -roʊˌ· —*Ger* [ˈbɪl dʊŋs ʁo ˌmaːn]
bile baɪᵊl
  ˈbile duct
bilge bɪldʒ **bilged** bɪldʒd **bilges** ˈbɪldʒ ɪz -əz
  bilging ˈbɪldʒ ɪŋ
bilgy ˈbɪldʒ i
bilharzia bɪl ˈhɑːz i‿ə -ˈhɑːts- ‖ -ˈhɑːrz-
biliary ˈbɪl i‿ər i ‖ -er i
bilingual ⁽ˌ⁾baɪ ˈlɪŋ gwəl -ˈlɪŋ gju‿əl **~ism** ˌɪz əm **~ly** i **~s** z
bilious ˈbɪl i‿əs **~ly** li **~ness** nəs nɪs
bilirubin ˌbɪl i ˈruːb ɪn ˌbaɪl-, §-ən

-bility ˈbɪl ət i -ɪt- ‖ -əţ-
bilk bɪlk **bilked** bɪlkt **bilker/s** ˈbɪlk ə/z ‖ -ᵊr/z
  bilking ˈbɪlk ɪŋ **bilks** bɪlks
Bilko ˈbɪlk əʊ ‖ -oʊ
bill, Bill bɪl **billed** bɪld **billing** ˈbɪl ɪŋ **bills** bɪlz
  ˌbill of ˈfare; **ˌbill of ˈrights**; **ˌbill of ˈsale**
billable ˈbɪl əb ᵊl
billabong ˈbɪl ə bɒŋ ‖ -bɔːŋ -bɑːŋ **~s** z
billboard ˈbɪl bɔːd ‖ -bɔːrd -boʊrd **~s** z
Billerica ˌbɪl ˈrɪk ə ˌbel ə ˈ· ·
Billericay ˌbɪl ə ˈrɪk i
bill|et ˈbɪl |ɪt -ət ‖ -|ət **~eted** ɪt ɪd ət-, -əd ‖ əţ əd **~eting** ɪt ɪŋ ət- ‖ əţ ɪŋ **~ets** ɪts əts
billet-doux ˌbɪl eɪ ˈduː -i- —*Fr* [bi jɛ du]
  billets-doux ˌbɪl eɪ ˈduːz -i-, -ˈduː *Fr* [bi jɛ du]
billeter ˈbɪl ɪt ə -ət- ‖ -əţ ᵊr **~s** z
Billett ˈbɪl ɪt §-ət
billettee ˌbɪl ɪ ˈtiː -ə- **~s** z
billfold ˈbɪl fəʊld →-fɒʊld ‖ -foʊld **~s** z
billhook ˈbɪl hʊk §-huːk **~s** s
billiard ˈbɪl i‿əd ‖ ˈbɪl jᵊrd **~s** z
  ˈbilliard ball; **ˈbilliard ˌtable**
Billie ˈbɪl i
Billie-Jean ˌbɪl i ˈdʒiːn ◂
billies —*see* **billy**
Billinge ˈbɪl ɪndʒ
Billingham ˈbɪl ɪŋ əm -hæm
Billings ˈbɪl ɪŋz
Billingsgate ˈbɪl ɪŋz geɪt
Billingshurst ˈbɪl ɪŋz hɜːst ‖ -hɜːst
Billingsley ˈbɪl ɪŋz li
billion ˈbɪl jən ˈbɪl i‿ən **~s** z
billionaire ˌbɪl jə ˈneə ◂ ‖ -ˈneᵊr ◂ **~s** z
billionth ˈbɪl jənᵗθ ˈbɪl i‿ənᵗθ **~s** s
billow ˈbɪl əʊ ‖ -oʊ **~ed** d **~ing** ɪŋ **~s** z
billowy ˈbɪl əʊ i ‖ -oʊ-
billposter ˈbɪl ˌpəʊst ə ‖ -ˌpoʊst ᵊr **~s** z
billposting ˈbɪl ˌpəʊst ɪŋ ‖ -ˌpoʊst-
billsticker ˈbɪl ˌstɪk ə ‖ -ᵊr **~s** z
Billy, billy ˈbɪl i **Billy's, billies** ˈbɪl iz
  ˈbilly goat
billy-can ˈbɪl i kæn **~s** z
billycock ˈbɪl i kɒk ‖ -kɑːk **~s** s
billy-o, billy-oh ˈbɪl i əʊ ‖ -oʊ
Biloxi bɪ ˈlʌks i bə-, -ˈlɒks- ‖ -ˈlɑːks- —*In MS, locally* -ˈlʌks-
Bilston ˈbɪlst ən
Biltmore ˈbɪlt mɔː ‖ -mɔːr -moʊr
biltong ˈbɪl tɒŋ ‖ -tɔːŋ -tɑːŋ
Bim bɪm
bimbo ˈbɪm bəʊ ‖ -boʊ **~s** z
bimetallic ˌbaɪ me ˈtæl ɪk ◂ -mə-, -mɪ-
  ˌbimeˌtallic ˈstrip
bimetallism ˌbaɪ ˈmet ᵊl ˌɪz əm -əl ˌɪz- ‖ -ˈmeţ-
bimillenni|al ˌbaɪ mɪ ˈlen i‿|əl ˌmə- **~um** əm
Bimini, b~ ˈbɪm ən i -ɪn- **~s** z
bimodal ⁽ˌ⁾baɪ ˈməʊd ᵊl ‖ -ˈmoʊd-
bimodality ˌbaɪ məʊ ˈdæl ət i -ɪt i ‖ -moʊ ˈdæl əţ i
bimonth|ly ˌbaɪ ˈmʌnᵗθ |li **~lies** liz
bin bɪn **bins** bɪnz

Bina *(i)* 'baɪn ə, *(ii)* 'biːn ə
binar|y 'baɪn ər |i **~ies** iz
binaural ₍ₗ₎baɪ 'nɔːr əl bɪ-
Binchy 'bɪntʃ i
bind baɪnd **binding** 'baɪnd ɪŋ **binds** baɪndz **bound** baʊnd
binder, B~ 'baɪnd ə ‖ -ᵊr **~s** z
binder|y 'baɪnd‿ər |i **~ies** iz
bindi 'bɪn di —*Hindi* [bɪn̪ d̪iː] **~s** z
binding 'baɪnd ɪŋ **~ly** li **~ness** nəs nɪs **~s** z
bindweed 'baɪnd wiːd
bine baɪn **bines** baɪnz
Binet 'biːn eɪ ‖ bi 'neɪ —*Fr* [bi nɛ]
Binet-Simon ˌbiːn eɪ 'saɪm ən ‖ bi ˌneɪ siː 'moʊn
bing, Bing bɪŋ **bings, Bing's** bɪŋz
binge, Binge bɪndʒ **binged** bɪndʒd **bingeing, binging** 'bɪndʒ ɪŋ **binges** 'bɪndʒ ɪz -əz
Bingen 'bɪŋ ən —*Ger* ['bɪŋ ən]
Bingham 'bɪŋ əm
Binghamton 'bɪŋ əm tən
Bingley 'bɪŋ li
bingo, Bingo 'bɪŋ gəʊ ‖ -goʊ
'bingo hall
Binks bɪŋks
bin Laden ˌbɪn 'lɑːd ᵊn —*Arabic* [bɪn 'laː dɪn]
bin-liner 'bɪn ˌlaɪn ə ‖ -ᵊr **~s** z
bin|man 'bɪn |mæn →'bɪm-, -mən **~men** men -mən
binnacle 'bɪn ək ᵊl -ɪk- **~s** z
Binney, Binnie 'bɪn i
Binns bɪnz
Binoche bɪ 'nɒʃ bə- ‖ -'noʊʃ —*Fr* [bi nɔʃ]
binocular *n* bɪ 'nɒk jʊl ə bə-, baɪ-, -jəl- ‖ -'nɑːk jəl ᵊr **~s** z
binocular *adj* baɪ 'nɒk jʊl ə bɪ-, bə- ‖ -'nɑːk jəl ᵊr **~ly** li
biˌnocular 'vision
binocularity baɪ ˌnɒk ju 'lær ət i bɪ-, bə-, -ˌ·jə-, -ɪt i ‖ -ˌnɑːk jə 'lær əţ i -'ler-
binomial ₍ₗ₎baɪ 'nəʊm i‿əl ‖ -'noʊm- **~ly** i **~s** z
bi'nomial ˌtheorem
bint bɪnt **bints** bɪnts
binturong 'bɪnt ju rɒŋ -jə- ‖ bɪn 'tʊr ɔːŋ -ɑːŋ **~s** z
Binyon 'bɪn jən
bio, Bio 'baɪ əʊ ‖ -oʊ
bio- *comb. form*
with stress-neutral suffix ¦baɪ əʊ ‖ -oʊ —*In some well-known words, the weakening of the second diphthong to* ə *has become thoroughly established, with the consequence in RP that* SMOOTHING *from* ¦baɪ‿ə *to* ¦baə *is also heard. But in some other cases, where the separateness of the prefix is strongly felt,* əʊ ‖ oʊ *remains strong.* —**biolytic** ˌbaɪ əʊ 'lɪt ɪk ◂ ‖ ˌbaɪ oʊ 'lɪţ ɪk ◂
with stress-imposing suffix baɪ 'ɒ+ ‖ -'ɑː+ —**biolysis** baɪ 'ɒl əs ɪs -ɪs-, §-əs ‖ -'ɑːl-
biochemical ˌbaɪ əʊ 'kem ɪk ᵊl ◂ ‖ ˌ·oʊ- **~ly** ‿i **~s** z
biochemist ˌbaɪ əʊ 'kem ɪst §-əst ‖ -oʊ- **~s** s
biochemistry ˌbaɪ əʊ 'kem ɪs tri -əs tri ‖ ˌ·oʊ-
biodata 'baɪ əʊ ˌdeɪt ə -ˌdɑːt- ‖ -oʊ ˌdæţ ə
biodegradability ˌbaɪ əʊdi ˌgreɪd ə 'bɪl ət i -də,-,-, -ɪt i ‖ ˌbaɪ oʊ di ˌgreɪd ə 'bɪl əţ i
biodegradab|le ˌbaɪ əʊ di 'greɪd əb |ᵊl ◂ -də'·- ‖ ˌ·oʊ- **~ly** li
biodegradation ˌbaɪ əʊ ˌdeg rə 'deɪʃ ᵊn ‖ ˌ·oʊ-
biodegrad|e ˌbaɪ əʊdi 'greɪd -də'· ‖ ˌbaɪ oʊ- **~ed** ɪd əd **~es** z **~ing** ɪŋ
biodiversity ˌbaɪ əʊ daɪ 'vɜːs ət i -dɪ'-, -ɪt i ‖ ˌbaɪ oʊ də 'vɜːs əţ i -daɪ'-
bioengineering ˌbaɪ əʊ ˌendʒ ɪ 'nɪər ɪŋ -ˌə- ‖ -oʊ ˌendʒ ə 'nɪr-
biofeedback ˌbaɪ əʊ 'fiːd bæk →-'fiːb- ‖ -oʊ-
biogas 'baɪ əʊ gæs ‖ -oʊ-
biographer baɪ 'ɒg rəf ə ‖ -'ɑːg rəf ᵊr **~s** z
biographic ˌbaɪ‿ə 'græf ɪk ◂ **~al** ᵊl **~ally** ᵊl‿i
biograph|y baɪ 'ɒg rəf |i ‖ -'ɑːg- **~ies** iz
biohazard 'baɪ əʊ ˌhæz əd ‖ -oʊ ˌhæz ᵊrd **~s** z
Bioko bi 'əʊk əʊ ‖ -'oʊk oʊ
biological ˌbaɪ‿ə 'lɒdʒ ɪk ᵊl ◂ ‖ -'lɑːdʒ- **~ly** ‿li
ˌbioˌlogical 'clock
biologist baɪ 'ɒl ədʒ ɪst §-əst ‖ -'ɑːl- **~s** s
biology baɪ 'ɒl ədʒ i ‖ -'ɑːl-
biomass 'baɪ əʊ mæs ‖ -oʊ-
biome 'baɪ əʊm ‖ -oʊm **~s** z
biometric ˌbaɪ əʊ 'metr ɪk ◂ ‖ -oʊ- **~al** ᵊl **~s** s
Bion 'baɪ‿ən -ɒn ‖ 'baɪ ɑːn
bionic ₍ₗ₎baɪ 'ɒn ɪk ‖ -'ɑːn- **~s** s
biopharmaceutic ˌbaɪ əʊ ˌfɑːm ə 'suːt ɪk ◂ -'sjuːt- ‖ ˌbaɪ oʊ ˌfɑːrm ə 'suːţ ɪk ◂ **~al/s** ᵊl/z
biophysical ˌbaɪ əʊ 'fɪz ɪk ᵊl ‖ ˌ·oʊ- **~ly** ‿i
biophysicist ˌbaɪ əʊ 'fɪz ɪs ɪst -əs ɪst, §-əst ‖ ˌ·oʊ- **~s** s
biophysics ˌbaɪ əʊ 'fɪz ɪks ‖ -oʊ-
biopic 'baɪ əʊ pɪk ‖ -oʊ- **~s** s
bioprogram 'baɪ əʊ ˌprəʊ græm ˌ·-'·· ‖ -oʊ ˌproʊ- **~s** z
biops|y 'baɪ ɒps |i ·'·· ‖ -ɑːps- **~ies** iz
biorhythm 'baɪ əʊ ˌrɪð əm ‖ -oʊ- **~s** z
biorhythmic ˌbaɪ əʊ 'rɪð mɪk ◂ ‖ -oʊ-
BIOS 'baɪ ɒs ‖ -ɑːs
bioscope 'baɪ‿ə skəʊp ‖ -skoʊp **~s** s
biosphere 'baɪ əʊ sfɪə ‖ -ə sfɪr **~s** z
Bio-Strath *tdmk* 'baɪ əʊ stræθ ‖ -oʊ-
biota baɪ 'əʊt ə ‖ -'oʊţ-
biotech 'baɪ əʊ tek ‖ -oʊ-
biotechnology ˌbaɪ əʊ tek 'nɒl ədʒ i ‖ -oʊ tek 'nɑːl-
biotic baɪ 'ɒt ɪk ‖ -'ɑːţ-
bipartisan ˌbaɪ ˌpɑːt ɪ 'zæn -ə-; ₍ₗ₎·'··, -ɪz ən, -əz- ‖ ₍ₗ₎baɪ 'pɑːrţ əz ən -əs- **~ship** ʃɪp
bipartite ₍ₗ₎baɪ 'pɑːt aɪt '··· ‖ -'pɑːrt- **~ly** li
bipartition ˌbaɪ pɑː 'tɪʃ ᵊn -pə- ‖ -pɑːr-
biped 'baɪ ped **~s** z
bipedal ˌbaɪ 'piːd ᵊl ◂ -'ped- **~ly** i
biplane 'baɪ pleɪn **~s** z
bipod 'baɪ pɒd ‖ -pɑːd **~s** z
bipolar ˌbaɪ 'pəʊl ə ◂ ‖ -'poʊl ᵊr ◂
bipolarity ˌbaɪ pəʊ 'lær ət i -ɪt i ‖ -poʊ 'lær əţ i -'ler-
biquadratic ˌbaɪ kwɒ 'dræt ɪk ◂ ‖ -kwɑː 'dræţ-

B

biracial ˌbaɪ ˈreɪʃ ᵊl ◂
birch, Birch bɜːtʃ ‖ bɜˑːtʃ **birches, Birch's** ˈbɜːtʃ ɪz -əz ‖ ˈbɜˑːtʃ-
Birchall *(i)* ˈbɜːtʃ ɔːl ‖ ˈbɜˑːtʃ- -ɑːl, *(ii)* -ᵊl
Bircher ˈbɜːtʃ ə ‖ ˈbɜˑːtʃ ᵊr
Birchington ˈbɜːtʃ ɪŋ tən ‖ ˈbɜˑːtʃ-
bird, Bird bɜːd ‖ bɜˑːd **birding** ˈbɜːd ɪŋ ‖ ˈbɜˑːd ɪŋ **birds** bɜːdz ‖ bɜˑːdz
ˈbird ˌfancier; **ˈbird flu**; **ˌbird of ˈpassage**; **ˌbird of ˈprey**; **ˈbird ˌtable**
birdbath ˈbɜːd bɑːθ →ˈbɜːb-, §-bæθ ‖ ˈbɜˑːd bæθ
bird-brained ˈbɜːd breɪnd →ˈbɜːb- ‖ ˈbɜˑːd-
birdcag|e ˈbɜːd keɪdʒ →ˈbɜːg- ‖ ˈbɜˑːd- **~es** ɪz əz
birder ˈbɜːd ə ‖ ˈbɜˑːd ᵊr **~s** z
birdie, B~ ˈbɜːd i ‖ ˈbɜˑːd i **~s** z
birdlike ˈbɜːd laɪk ‖ ˈbɜˑːd-
birdlim|e ˈbɜːd laɪm ‖ ˈbɜˑːd- **~ed** d **~ing** ɪŋ **~s** z
bird|man ˈbɜːd |mæn →ˈbɜːb-, -mən ‖ ˈbɜˑːd- **~men** men -mən
Birdsall *(i)* ˈbɜːd sɔːl ‖ ˈbɜˑːd- -sɑːl, *(ii)* -sᵊl
birdseed ˈbɜːd siːd ‖ ˈbɜˑːd-
bird's-eye, Birdseye ˈbɜːdz aɪ ‖ ˈbɜˑːdz-
bird's-foot ˈbɜːdz fʊt ‖ ˈbɜˑːdz- **~s** s
birdshot ˈbɜːd ʃɒt ‖ ˈbɜˑːd-
bird's-nest ˈbɜːdz nest ‖ ˈbɜˑːdz- **~s** s
birdsong ˈbɜːd sɒŋ ‖ ˈbɜˑːd sɔːŋ -sɑːŋ **~s** z
bird-watch|er ˈbɜːd ˌwɒtʃ |ə ‖ ˈbɜˑːd ˌwɑːtʃ |ᵊr -ˌwɔːtʃ- **~ers** əz ‖ ᵊrz **~ing** ɪŋ
birefring|ence ˌbaɪ ri ˈfrɪndʒ |ən^t s -rə- **~ent** ənt
bireme ˈbaɪ riːm **~s** z
biretta bə ˈret ə bɪ- ‖ -ˈreṭ- **~s** z
Birgit ˈbɪəg ɪt ˈbɜːg-, §-ət ‖ ˈbɪrg-
Birgitta bɪə ˈgɪt ə ‖ bɪr ˈgɪṭ ə —*Swedish* [bir ˈˈgit a]
biriani ˌbɪr i ˈɑːn i **~s** z
Birkbeck ˈbɜːk bek ‖ ˈbɜˑːk- —*but as a family name sometimes* ˈbɜː bek ‖ ˈbɜː-
Birkenhead ˌbɜːk ən ˈhed ˈ· · · ‖ ˌbɜˑːk-
Birkenshaw ˈbɜːk ən ʃɔː ‖ ˈbɜˑːk- -ʃɑː
Birkenstock ˈbɜːk ən stɒk ‖ ˈbɜˑːk ən stɑːk **~s** s
Birkett ˈbɜːk ɪt §-ət ‖ ˈbɜˑːk-
birl bɜːl ‖ bɜˑːl **birled** bɜːld ‖ bɜˑːld **birling** ˈbɜːl ɪŋ ‖ ˈbɜˑːl- **birls** bɜːlz ‖ bɜˑːlz
Birley ˈbɜːl i ‖ ˈbɜˑːl i
Birling ˈbɜːl ɪŋ ‖ ˈbɜˑːl ɪŋ
Birmingham *(i)* ˈbɜːm ɪŋ əm -həm ‖ˈbɜˑːm-, *(ii)* -hæm —*The place in England is (i), but places in the US are (ii).*
Birnam ˈbɜːn əm ‖ ˈbɜˑːn-
Birney, Birnie ˈbɜːn i ‖ ˈbɜˑːn i
biro, Biro *tdmk* ˈbaɪᵊr əʊ ‖ -oʊ —*Hungarian* Biró [ˈbi roː] **~s** z
Birobidzhan ˌbɪr əʊ bɪ ˈdʒɑːn ‖ ˌ·oʊ- —*Russ* [bʲɪ rə bʲɪ ˈdʒan]
birr bɜː ‖ bɜˑː **birred** bɜːd ‖ bɜˑːd **birring** ˈbɜːr ɪŋ ‖ ˈbɜˑː- **birrs** bɜːz ‖ bɜˑːz
Birrane bɪ ˈreɪn bə-
Birrell ˈbɪr əl

Birt bɜːt ‖ bɜˑːt
birth bɜːθ ‖ bɜˑːθ **birthed** bɜːθt ‖ bɜˑːθt **birthing** ˈbɜːθ ɪŋ ‖ ˈbɜˑːθ- **births** bɜːθs ‖ bɜˑːθs
ˈbirth cerˌtificate; **ˈbirth conˌtrol**
birthday ˈbɜːθ deɪ -di ‖ ˈbɜˑːθ- —*See note at* -day **~s** z
ˈbirthday cake; **ˈbirthday card**; **ˌBirthday ˈhonours**; **ˈbirthday ˌparty**; **ˈbirthday ˌpresent**; **ˌbirthday suit**
birthmark ˈbɜːθ mɑːk ‖ ˈbɜˑːθ mɑːrk **~s** s
birthplace ˈbɜːθ pleɪs ‖ ˈbɜˑːθ- **~s** ɪz əz
birthrate ˈbɜːθ reɪt ‖ ˈbɜˑːθ- **~s** s
birthright ˈbɜːθ raɪt ‖ ˈbɜˑːθ- **~s** s
birthroot ˈbɜːθ ruːt ‖ ˈbɜˑːθ-
birthstone ˈbɜːθ stəʊn ‖ ˈbɜˑːθ stoʊn **~s** z
birthwort ˈbɜːθ wɜːt §-wɔːt ‖ ˈbɜˑːθ wɜˑːt -wɔːrt **~s** s
Birtles ˈbɜːt ᵊlz ‖ ˈbɜˑːṭ-
Birtwhistle, Birtwistle ˈbɜːt ˌwɪs ᵊl -ˌhwɪs- ‖ ˈbɜˑːt ˌ*h*wɪs-
biryani ˌbɪr i ˈɑːn i **~s** z
bis bɪs
Biscay ˈbɪsk eɪ -i
Biscayne ˌbɪs ˈkeɪn ◂
ˌBiscayne ˈBoulevard
biscotti bɪ ˈskɒt i ‖ -ˈskɑːṭ- —*It* [bi ˈskɔt ti]
biscuit ˈbɪsk ɪt §-ət **~s** s
bisect ₍ˌ₎baɪ ˈsekt ˈ· · ‖ ˈ· · **~ed** ɪd əd **~ing** ɪŋ **~s** s
bisection ₍ˌ₎baɪ ˈsek ʃᵊn ˈ·ˌ· · ‖ ˈ·ˌ· · **~al** ‿əl **~ally** ‿əl i
bisector ₍ˌ₎baɪ ˈsekt ə ‖ ˈbaɪ ˌsekt ᵊr **~s** z
bisexual ˌbaɪ ˈsek ʃu‿əl ◂ -ˈseks ju‿əl, -ˈsekʃ ᵊl **~ly** i **~s** z
bisexuality ˌbaɪ ˌsek ʃu ˈæl ət i -ˌseks ju-, -ɪt i ‖ -əṭ i
bish bɪʃ **bishes** ˈbɪʃ ɪz -əz
Bishkek ˌbɪʃ ˈkek
bishop, B~ ˈbɪʃ əp **~s** s
ˌBishop's ˈStortford
bishophood ˈbɪʃ əp hʊd
bishopric ˈbɪʃ əp rɪk **~s** s
Bishopsgate ˈbɪʃ əps geɪt
Bishopston ˈbɪʃ əps tən
Bislama ˈbɪʃ lə mɑː
Bisley ˈbɪz li
Bismag *tdmk* ˈbɪz mæg
Bismarck ˈbɪz mɑːk ‖ -mɑːrk —*Ger* [ˈbɪs maʁk]
bismuth ˈbɪz məθ
bismuthic bɪz ˈmjuːθ ɪk -ˈmʌθ-; ˈbɪz məθ-
BiSoDol *tdmk* ˈbaɪ səʊ dɒl ‖ -soʊ dɑːl -dɔːl
bison ˈbaɪs ᵊn ‖ ˈbaɪz- **~s** z
Bispham ˈbɪsp əm —*but as a family name sometimes* ˈbɪs fəm
bisque bɪsk —*Fr* [bisk] **bisques** bɪsks
Bissau bɪ ˈsaʊ ˈbɪs aʊ —*Port* [bi ˈsau]
Bissell ˈbɪs ᵊl
Bisset, Bissett *(i)* ˈbɪs ɪt §-ət, *(ii)* ˈbɪz-
bissextile bɪ ˈsekst aɪᵊl ‖ -ᵊl
bistable ˌbaɪ ˈsteɪb ᵊl
bister ˈbɪst ə ‖ -ᵊr **~ed** d

Bisto *tdmk* 'bɪst əʊ ‖ -oʊ
bistort 'bɪst ɔːt ‖ -ɔːrt **~s** s
bistour|y 'bɪst ər |i **~ies** iz
bistre 'bɪst ə ‖ -ᵊr **~d** d
bistro 'biːs trəʊ 'bɪs- ‖ -troʊ —*Fr (usually* bistrot) [bis tʁo] **~s** z
bit bɪt **bits** bɪts
'bit part
bitch bɪtʃ **bitched** bɪtʃt **bitches** 'bɪtʃ ɪz -əz **bitching** 'bɪtʃ ɪŋ
bitchin 'bɪtʃ ɪn -ən
bitch|y 'bɪtʃ |i **~ier** i‿ə ‖ i‿ᵊr **~iest** i‿ɪst i‿əst **~ily** ɪ li əl i **~iness** i nəs i nɪs
bite baɪt **bit** bɪt **bites** baɪts **biting** 'baɪt ɪŋ ‖ 'baɪţ ɪŋ **bitten** 'bɪt ᵊn
biter 'baɪt ə ‖ 'baɪţ ᵊr **~s** z
bite-size 'baɪt saɪz **~d** d
Bithell *(i)* 'bɪθ ᵊl, *(ii)* bɪ 'θel
Bithynia baɪ 'θɪn i‿ə bɪ-
biting 'baɪt ɪŋ ‖ 'baɪţ ɪŋ **~ly** li
bitmap 'bɪt mæp **~ped** t **~ping** ɪŋ **~s** s
bitsy 'bɪts i
bitt bɪt *(= bit)* **bitts** bɪts
bitten 'bɪt ᵊn
bitt|er 'bɪt |ə ‖ 'bɪţ |ᵊr **~erer** ər ə ‖ ᵊr ər **~erest** ər ɪst -əst **~ers** əz ‖ ᵊrz
ˌbitter 'end; **ˌbitter 'lemon**
bittercress 'bɪt ə kres ‖ 'bɪţ ᵊr-
bitterly 'bɪt ə li -ᵊl i ‖ 'bɪţ ᵊr li
bittern 'bɪt ᵊn -ɜːn ‖ 'bɪţ ᵊrn **~s** z
bitterness 'bɪt ə nəs -nɪs; -ᵊn əs, -ɪs ‖ 'bɪţ ᵊr-
bitternut 'bɪt ə nʌt ‖ 'bɪţ ᵊr- **~s** s
bittersweet 'bɪt ə swiːt ˌ· ·'· ‖ 'bɪţ ᵊr-
bitt|y 'bɪt |i ‖ 'bɪţ |i **~iness** i nəs i nɪs
bitumen 'bɪtʃ ʊm ɪn -əm-, -ən; -u men, -ə-; 'bɪt jʊm ɪn ‖ bə 'tuːm ən bɪ-, baɪ-, -'tjuːm- *(*)*
bituminiz|e bɪ 'tjuːm ɪ naɪz bə-, →-'tʃuːm-, -ə-; 'bɪtʃ ʊm ɪ-, '·əm-, '· ·ə- ‖ bə 'tuːm- bɪ-, baɪ-, -'tjuːm- **~ed** d **~es** ɪz əz **~ing** ɪŋ
bituminous bɪ 'tjuːm ɪn əs bə-, →-'tʃuːm-, -ən əs ‖ -'tuːm- 'tjuːm-
biunique ˌbaɪ ju 'niːk ◂ **~ly** li **~ness** nəs nɪs
bivalenc|e ₍ˌ₎baɪ 'veɪl ənᵗs ◂ 'bɪv əl ənᵗs **~y** i
bivalent ₍ˌ₎baɪ 'veɪl ənt ◂ 'bɪv əl ənt
bivalve 'baɪ vælv **~s** z
bivariate ˌbaɪ 'veər i‿ət ◂ ‿ɪt ‖ -'ver- -'vær-
bivouac 'bɪv u æk **~ked** t **~king** ɪŋ **~s** s
bivv|y 'bɪv |i **~ies** iz
biweek|ly ₍ˌ₎baɪ 'wiːk |li **~lies** liz
biz bɪz
bizarre bɪ 'zɑː bə- ‖ -'zɑːr **~ly** li **~ness** nəs nɪs
Bizet 'biːz eɪ ‖ biː 'zeɪ —*Fr* [bi zɛ] **~'s** z
Bjelke-Petersen ˌbjelk i 'piːt əs ən ‖ -'piːţ ᵊr-
Björk bjɔːk bjɜːk, bi 'ɔːk ‖ bjɔːrk bjɜːk —*Icelandic* [bjœr̥k]
Bjorn, Björn bi 'ɔːn bjɜːn ‖ bi 'ɔːrn bjɜːn —*Swedish* [bjœːn]
blab blæb **blabbed** blæbd **blabbing** 'blæb ɪŋ **blabs** blæbz
blabb|er 'blæb |ə ‖ -|ᵊr **~ered** əd ‖ ᵊrd **~ering** ər‿ɪŋ **~ers** əz ‖ ᵊrz
blabber|mouth 'blæb ə |maʊθ ‖ -ᵊr- **~mouths** maʊðz maʊθs

blabby 'blæb i
Blaby 'bleɪb i
black, Black blæk **blacked** blækt **blacker** 'blæk ə ‖ -ᵊr **blackest** 'blæk ɪst -əst **blacking** 'blæk ɪŋ **blacks, Blacks** blæks
ˌblack and 'blue◂; **ˌblack and 'white◂**; **'Black ˌCountry**; **ˌBlack 'Death**; **ˌblack 'eye**; **ˌBlack 'Forest**; **ˌblack 'hole**; **ˌblack 'ice**; **ˌblack 'magic**; **ˌBlack Ma'ria**; **ˌblack 'market**; **ˌblack ˌmarke'teer**; **ˌBlack 'Mass**; **'black ˌpeople**; **ˌblack 'power**; **ˌblack 'pudding**; **ˌBlack 'Sea**; **'black spot**
Blackadder 'blæk ˌæd ə ˌ·'· ·; 'blæk əd ə ‖ -ᵊr
Blackall 'blæk ɔːl ‖ -ɑːl
blackamoor 'blæk ə mɔː -mʊə ‖ -mʊr **~s** z
black-and-white ˌblæk ən 'waɪt ◂ -ənd-, →-ŋ-, -'hwaɪt
blackball 'blæk bɔːl ‖ -bɑːl **~ed** d **~ing** ɪŋ **~s** z
blackberr|y, BlackBerr|y *tdmk* 'blæk bər‿|i ‖ -ˌber |i **~ied** id **~ies** iz **~ying** i ɪŋ
blackbird 'blæk bɜːd ‖ -bɜ˞ːd **~s** z
blackboard 'blæk bɔːd ‖ -bɔːrd -boʊrd **~s** z
ˌblackboard 'jungle
Blackburn 'blæk bɜːn -bən ‖ -bɜ˞ːn —*locally also* 'blæg-
blackcap 'blæk kæp **~s** s
blackcock 'blæk kɒk ‖ -kɑːk
blackcurrant ˌblæk 'kʌr ənt ◂ ·'· ·, '·ˌ· · ‖ 'blæk ˌkɜː ənt **~s** s
blacken 'blæk ən **~ed** d **~ing** ‿ɪŋ **~s** z
Blacket, Blackett 'blæk ɪt §-ət
black-eyed ˌblæk 'aɪd ◂
ˌblack-eyed 'Susan
blackface 'blæk feɪs
black|fly 'blæk |flaɪ **~flies** flaɪz
Blackfoot 'blæk fʊt
Blackford 'blæk fəd ‖ -fᵊrd
Blackfriars ˌblæk 'fraɪ‿əz ◂ '·ˌ· · ‖ -'fraɪ‿ᵊrz
ˌBlackˌfriars 'Bridge
blackguard 'blæg ɑːd -əd ‖ -ɑːrd -ᵊrd **~ly** li **~s** z
blackhead 'blæk hed **~s** z
Blackheath ˌblæk 'hiːθ ◂
Blackie *(i)* 'blæk i, *(ii)* 'bleɪk i
blacking 'blæk ɪŋ **~s** z
blackish 'blæk ɪʃ **~ly** li
blackjack 'blæk dʒæk **~ed** t **~ing** ɪŋ **~s** s
blacklead 'blæk led ˌ·'· **~ed** ɪd əd **~ing** ɪŋ **~s** z
blackleg 'blæk leg **~ged** d **~ging** ɪŋ **~s** z
Blackley 'blæk li —*but the place in Manchester is* 'bleɪk-
blacklist 'blæk lɪst **~ed** ɪd əd **~ing** ɪŋ **~s** s
Blacklock 'blæk lɒk ‖ -lɑːk
blackly 'blæk li
blackmail 'blæk meɪᵊl **~ed** d **~er** ə ‖ -ᵊr **~ers** əz ‖ ᵊrz **~ing** ɪŋ **~s** z
Blackman 'blæk mən
Blackmore 'blæk mɔː ‖ -mɔːr -moʊr
blackness 'blæk nəs -nɪs
blackout 'blæk aʊt **~s** s
Blackpool 'blæk puːl
Blackshirt 'blæk ʃɜːt ‖ -ʃɜ˞ːt **~s** s
blacksmith 'blæk smɪθ **~ing** ɪŋ **~s** s

Blackstone 'blæk stəʊn -stən ‖ -stoʊn -stən
blackthorn 'blæk θɔːn ‖ -θɔːrn **~s** z
black-tie ˌblæk 'taɪ ◂
blacktop 'blæk tɒp ‖ -tɑːp
Blacktown 'blæk taʊn
Blackwall 'blæk wɔːl ‖ -wɑːl
 ˌBlackwall 'Tunnel
blackwater, B~ 'blæk ˌwɔːt ə ‖ -ˌwɔːṭ ᵊr -ˌwɑːṭ-
Blackwell 'blæk wᵊl -wel
Blackwood, b~ 'blæk wʊd —*but the place in Gwent is* ˌ-'-
bladder 'blæd ə ‖ -ᵊr **~ed** d **~s** z
bladderwort 'blæd ə wɜːt -wɔːt ‖ -ᵊr wɜᵊːt -wɔːrt **~s** s
bladderwrack 'blæd ə ræk ‖ -ᵊr-
blade bleɪd **bladed** 'bleɪd ɪd -əd **blades** bleɪdz
blader 'bleɪd ə ‖ -ᵊr **~s** z
Bladon 'bleɪd ᵊn
blaeberry 'bleɪ bər‿i ‖ -ˌber i
Blaenau 'blaɪn aɪ ⚠ -aʊ; 'bleɪn i —*Welsh* ['bləɨ nai, 'bləi-, -na, -ne]
 ˌBlaenau 'Gwent
blag blæg **blagged** blægd **blagging** 'blæg ɪŋ **blags** blægz
Blagden, Blagdon 'blæg dən
blagger 'blæg ə ‖ -ᵊr **~s** z
blah blɑː **blahs** blɑːz
Blahnik 'blɑːn ɪk
blain, Blain, Blaine bleɪn **blains, Blaine's** bleɪnz
Blair bleə ‖ bleᵊr
Blairgowrie ˌbleə 'gaʊᵊr i ‖ ˌbler-
Blairism 'bleər ˌɪz əm ‖ 'bler-
Blairite 'bleər aɪt ‖ 'bler- **~s** s
Blaise bleɪz
Blake bleɪk **Blake's** bleɪks
Blakemore 'bleɪk mɔː ‖ -mɔːr -moʊr
Blakeney 'bleɪk ni
Blakenham 'bleɪk ən‿əm
blame bleɪm **blamed** bleɪmd **blames** bleɪmz **blaming** 'bleɪm ɪŋ
blameless 'bleɪm ləs -lɪs **~ly** li **~ness** nəs nɪs
blameworth|y 'bleɪm ˌwɜːð |i ‖ -ˌwɜːð |i **~iness** i nəs i nɪs
Blanc blɒ̃ ‖ blɑ̃ː —*Fr* [blɑ̃]
blanch, B~ blɑːntʃ §blæntʃ ‖ blæntʃ **blanched** blɑːntʃt §blæntʃt ‖ blæntʃt **blanches** 'blɑːntʃ ɪz §'blæntʃ-, -əz ‖ 'blæntʃ əz **blanching** 'blɑːntʃ ɪŋ §'blæntʃ- ‖ 'blæntʃ ɪŋ
Blanchard 'blæntʃ əd -ɑːd ‖ -ᵊrd -ɑːrd
Blanche blɑːnᵗʃ ‖ blænᵗʃ
Blanchett 'blɑːntʃ ət 'blæntʃ-, -ɪt ‖ 'blæntʃ-
Blanchflower 'blɑːntʃ ˌflaʊ‿ə §'blæntʃ- ‖ 'blæntʃ ˌflaʊ‿ᵊr
blancmang|e blə 'mɒndʒ ‖ -'mɑːndʒ *(!)* **~es** ɪz əz
blanco, B~ *tdmk* 'blæŋk əʊ ‖ -oʊ **~ed** d **~s** z **~ing** ɪŋ
bland, Bland blænd **blander** 'blænd ə ‖ -ᵊr **blandest** 'blænd ɪst -əst
Blandford 'blænd fəd ‖ -fᵊrd
blandish 'blænd ɪʃ **~ed** t **~es** ɪz əz **~ing** ɪŋ **~ment/s** mənt/s
bland|ly 'blænd |li **~ness** nəs nɪs
blank blæŋk **blanked** blæŋkt **blanking** 'blæŋk ɪŋ **blanks** blæŋks
 ˌblank 'cartridge; **ˌblank 'cheque** *or* **'check**; **ˌblank 'verse**
blank|et 'blæŋk |ɪt §-ət ‖ -|ət **~eted** ɪt ɪd §ət-, əd ‖ əṭ əd **~eting** ɪt ɪŋ ‖ əṭ ɪŋ **~ets** ɪts §əts ‖ əts
blankety-blank ˌblæŋk ət i 'blæŋk ◂ ‖ -əṭ i-
blank|ly 'blæŋk| li **~ness** nəs nɪs
blanquette ₍ₗ₎blɒŋ 'ket ₍ₗ₎blæŋ- ‖ ₍ₗ₎blɑːŋ- —*Fr* [blɑ̃ kɛt]
 blanˌquette de 'veau vəʊ ‖ voʊ —*Fr* [vo]
Blantyre 'blæn ˌtaɪ‿ə ˌblæn 'taɪ‿ə ‖ ˌblæn 'taɪᵊr
blare bleə ‖ bleᵊr **blared** bleəd ‖ bleᵊrd **blares** bleəz ‖ bleᵊrz **blaring** 'bleər ɪŋ ‖ 'bler ɪŋ
blarney, B~ 'blɑːn i ‖ 'blɑːrn i **~ed** d **~s** z **~ing** ɪŋ
blase, blasé 'blɑːz eɪ ‖ blɑː 'zeɪ —*Fr* [bla ze]
blasphem|e ₍ₗ₎blæs 'fiːm ₍ₗ₎blɑːs- ‖ '·· **~ed** d **~er** ə ‖ ᵊr **~ers** əz ‖ ᵊrz **~es** z **~ing** ɪŋ
blasphemi... —*see* **blasphemy**
blasphemous 'blæs fəm əs 'blɑːs-, -fɪm- **~ly** li
blasphem|y 'blæs fəm |i 'blɑːs-, -fɪm- **~ies** iz
blast blɑːst §blæst ‖ blæst **blasted** 'blɑːst ɪd §'blæst-, -əd ‖ 'blæst əd **blasting** 'blɑːst ɪŋ §'blæst- ‖ 'blæst ɪŋ **blasts** blɑːsts §blæsts ‖ blæsts
 'blast ˌfurnace
blasto- *comb. form*
with stress-neutral suffix ˈblæst əʊ ‖ ə — **blastopore** 'blæst əʊ pɔː ‖ -ə pɔːr -poʊr
with stress-imposing suffix blæ 'stɒ+ ‖ -'stɑː+ — **blastolysis** blæ 'stɒl əs ɪs -ɪs-, §-əs ‖ -'stɑːl-
blast-off 'blɑːst ɒf §'blæst-, -ɔːf ‖ 'blæst ɔːf -ɑːf
blastula 'blæst jʊl ə →'blæs tʃʊl ə ‖ 'blæs tʃəl ə
blastulation ˌblæst ju 'leɪʃ ᵊn →ˌblæs tʃə- ‖ ˌblæs tʃə-
blat blæt **blats** blæts **blatted** 'blæt ɪd -əd ‖ 'blæṭ- **blatting** 'blæt ɪŋ ‖ 'blæṭ-
blatancy 'bleɪt ᵊnᵗs i
blatant 'bleɪt ᵊnt **~ly** li
Blatchford 'blætʃ fəd ‖ -fᵊrd
blath|er 'blæð |ə ‖ -|ᵊr **~ered** əd ‖ ᵊrd **~ering** ər‿ɪŋ **~ers** əz ‖ ᵊrz
Blavatsky blə 'væt ski ‖ -'vɑːt-
Blawith *(i)* blɑːð, *(ii)* 'bleɪ wɪθ —*The places in Cumbria are (i).*
Blaydes bleɪdz
Blaydon 'bleɪd ᵊn
blaze bleɪz **blazed** bleɪzd **blazes** 'bleɪz ɪz -əz **blazing/ly** 'bleɪz ɪŋ /li
blazer 'bleɪz ə ‖ -ᵊr **~s** z
blazon 'bleɪz ᵊn **~ed** d **~ing** ‿ɪŋ **~ment/s** mənt/s **~s** z
blazon|ry 'bleɪz ᵊn |ri **~ries** riz
Blea bliː
bleach bliːtʃ **bleached** bliːtʃt **bleaches** 'bliːtʃ ɪz -əz **bleaching** 'bliːtʃ ɪŋ

bleacher 'bliːtʃ ə ‖ -ᵊr **~s** z
bleak bliːk **bleaker** 'bliːk ə ‖ -ᵊr **bleakest** 'bliːk ɪst -əst
bleak|ly 'bliːk |li **~ness** nəs nɪs
blear blɪə ‖ blɪᵊr **bleared** blɪəd ‖ blɪᵊrd **blearing** 'blɪər ɪŋ ‖ 'blɪr ɪŋ **blears** blɪəz ‖ blɪᵊrz
blear|y 'blɪər |i ‖ 'blɪr |i **~ier** i‿ə ‖ i‿ᵊr **~iest** i‿ɪst i‿əst **~ily** əl i ɪ li **~iness** i nəs i nɪs
bleary-eyed ˌblɪər i 'aɪd ◂ ‖ ˌblɪr-
Bleasdale 'bliːz deɪᵊl
bleat bliːt **bleated** 'bliːt ɪd -əd ‖ 'bliːṱ əd **bleats** bliːts **bleating** 'bliːt ɪŋ ‖ 'bliːṱ ɪŋ
bleb bleb **blebs** blebz
bled, Bled bled
Bleddyn 'bleð ɪn
Bledisloe 'bled ɪs ləʊ -əs-, -ɪz- ‖ -loʊ
bleed bliːd **bled** bled **bleeding** 'bliːd ɪŋ **bleeds** bliːdz
bleeder 'bliːd ə ‖ -ᵊr **~s** z
bleep bliːp **bleeped** bliːpt **bleeping** 'bliːp ɪŋ **bleeps** bliːps
bleeper 'bliːp ə ‖ -ᵊr **~s** z
blemish 'blem ɪʃ **~ed** t **~es** ɪz əz **~ing** ɪŋ
Blencathra blen 'kæθ rə
blench blentʃ **blenched** blentʃt **blenches** 'blentʃ ɪz -əz **blenching** 'blentʃ ɪŋ
blend blend **blended** 'blend ɪd -əd **blending** 'blend ɪŋ **blends** blendz
blende blend *(= blend)*
blender 'blend ə ‖ -ᵊr **~s** z
Blenheim 'blen ɪm -əm
Blenkinsop 'bleŋk ɪn sɒp -ən- ‖ -sɑːp
Blennerhassett ˌblen ə 'hæs ɪt §-ət, '· · · · ‖ -ᵊr-
blenn|y 'blen |i **~ies** iz
blent blent
blepharitis ˌblef ə 'raɪt ɪs §-əs ‖ -'raɪṱ əs
blepharo- *comb. form*
with stress-neutral suffix |blef ə rəʊ ‖ -ər ə — **blepharoplasty** 'blef ə rəʊ ˌplæst i ‖ -'blef ər ə-
with stress-imposing suffix ˌblef ə 'rɒ+ ‖ -'rɑː+ — **blepharotomy** ˌblef ə 'rɒt əm i ‖ -'rɑːṱ-
Bleriot, Blériot 'bler i əʊ ‖ ˌbler i 'oʊ '· · · —*Fr* [ble ʁjo]
Bles bles
blesbok 'bles bɒk -bʌk ‖ -bɑːk **~s** s
blesbuck 'bles bʌk **~s** s
bless bles **blesses** 'bles ɪz -əz **blessing** 'bles ɪŋ **blest** blest
blessed *past & pp of* **bless** blest
blessed *adj,* **B~** 'bles ɪd -əd **~ly** li **~ness** nəs nɪs
blessing 'bles ɪŋ **~s** z
Blessington 'bles ɪŋ tən
blest blest
blet blet
Bletchingley 'bletʃ ɪŋ li
Bletchley 'bletʃ li
bleth|er 'bleð |ə ‖ -|ᵊr **~ered** əd ‖ ᵊrd **~ering** ər‿ɪŋ **~ers** əz ‖ ᵊrz
Blethyn 'bleθ ɪn -ᵊn
blew bluː *(= blue)*
Blewett 'bluː‿ɪt §‿ət
blewits 'bluː‿ɪts §‿əts
Blewitt 'bluː‿ɪt §‿ət
Blige blaɪdʒ
Bligh blaɪ
blight blaɪt **blighted** 'blaɪt ɪd -əd ‖ 'blaɪṱ əd **blighting** 'blaɪt ɪŋ ‖ 'blaɪṱ ɪŋ **blights** blaɪts
blighter 'blaɪt ə ‖ 'blaɪṱ ᵊr **~s** z
Blighty 'blaɪt i ‖ 'blaɪṱ i
blimey 'blaɪm i
blimp, Blimp blɪmp **blimps** blɪmps
blimpish 'blɪmp ɪʃ
blind blaɪnd **blinded** 'blaɪnd ɪd -əd **blinder** 'blaɪnd ə ‖ -ᵊr **blindest** 'blaɪnd ɪst -əst **blinding/ly** 'blaɪnd ɪŋ /li **blinds** blaɪndz
ˌ**blind 'alley**; ˌ**blind 'date**; ˌ**blind 'drunk**; ˌ**blind man's 'buff**; '**blind spot**
blinder 'blaɪnd ə ‖ -ᵊr **~s** z
blindfold 'blaɪnd fəʊld →-fɒʊld ‖ -foʊld **~ed** ɪd əd **~ing** ɪŋ **~s** z
Blindley 'blaɪnd li
blindly 'blaɪnd li
blindness 'blaɪnd nəs -nɪs
blindworm 'blaɪnd wɜːm ‖ -wɜːm **~s** z
bling blɪŋ
ˌ**bling'bling**
blini 'blɪn i 'bliːn- **~s** z
blink blɪŋk **blinked** blɪŋkt **blinking** 'blɪŋk ɪŋ **blinks** blɪŋks
blinker 'blɪŋk ə ‖ -ᵊr **~ed** d **~s** z
blinks blɪŋks
blintz blɪnts **blintzes** 'blɪnts ɪz -əz
blintze 'blɪnts ə **~s** z
blip blɪp **blipped** blɪpt **blipping** 'blɪp ɪŋ **blips** blɪps
bliss, Bliss blɪs
Blissett 'blɪs ɪt §-ət
blissful 'blɪs fᵊl -fʊl **~ly** ‿i **~ness** nəs nɪs
B-list 'biː lɪst
blist|er 'blɪst |ə ‖ -|ᵊr **~ered** əd ‖ ᵊrd **~ering/ly** ər‿ɪŋ /li **~ers** əz ‖ ᵊrz
'**blister pack**
BLit ˌbiː 'lɪt
blithe blaɪð ‖ blaɪθ
blithe|ly 'blaɪð |li ‖ 'blaɪθ- **~ness** nəs nɪs
blithering 'blɪð ər‿ɪŋ
blithesome 'blaɪð səm §'blaɪθ- **~ly** li **~ness** nəs nɪs
Blithfield 'blɪθ fiːᵊld —*locally also* 'blɪf iːᵊld
BLitt ˌbiː 'lɪt
blitz blɪts **blitzed** blɪtst **blitzes** 'blɪts ɪz -əz **blitzing** 'blɪts ɪŋ
Blitzer 'blɪts ə ‖ ᵊr
blitzkrieg 'blɪts kriːg —*Ger* B~ ['blɪts kʁiːk] **~s** z
Blix blɪks —*Norw* [bliks]
Blixen 'blɪks ᵊn
blizzard 'blɪz əd ‖ ᵊrd **~s** z
bloat bləʊt ‖ bloʊt **bloated** 'bləʊt ɪd -əd ‖ 'bloʊṱ əd **bloating** 'bləʊt ɪŋ ‖ 'bloʊṱ ɪŋ **bloats** bləʊts ‖ bloʊts
bloater 'bləʊt ə ‖ 'bloʊṱ ᵊr **~s** z

B

blob blɒb ‖ blɑːb **blobs** blɒbz ‖ blɑːbz
bloc blɒk ‖ blɑːk *(= block)* **blocs** blɒks ‖ blɑːks
Bloch blɒk blɒx ‖ blɑːk
block blɒk ‖ blɑːk **blocked** blɒkt ‖ blɑːkt **blocking** ˈblɒk ɪŋ ‖ ˈblɑːk ɪŋ **blocks** blɒks ‖ blɑːks
ˌblock and ˈtackle; **ˌblock ˈletters**; **ˌblock reˈlease**; **ˌblock ˈvote**
blockad|e blɒ ˈkeɪd ‖ blɑː- **~ed** ɪd əd **~er** ə ‖ ᵊr **~ers** əz ‖ ᵊrz **~es** z **~ing** ɪŋ
blockag|e ˈblɒk ɪdʒ ‖ ˈblɑːk- **~es** ɪz əz
blockboard ˈblɒk bɔːd ‖ ˈblɑːk bɔːrd -boʊrd
blockbuster ˈblɒk ˌbʌst ə ‖ ˈblɑːk ˌbʌst ᵊr **~s** z
blockhead ˈblɒk hed ‖ ˈblɑːk- **~s** z
block|house ˈblɒk |haʊs ‖ ˈblɑːk- **~houses** haʊz ɪz -əz
Blodwen ˈblɒd wɪn -wen ‖ ˈblɑːd- —*Welsh* [ˈblod wen]
Bloemfontein ˈbluːm fən ˌteɪn -fɒn- ‖ -fɑːn-
Blofeld ˈbləʊ feld ‖ ˈbloʊ-
blog blɒg ‖ blɔːg blɑːg **blogged** blɒgd ‖ blɔːgd blɑːgd **blogging** ˈblɒg ɪŋ ‖ ˈblɔːg ɪŋ ˈblɑːg ɪŋ **blogs** blɒgz ‖ blɔːgz blɑːgz
blogger ˈblɒg ə ‖ ˈblɑːg ᵊr **~s** z
blogosphere ˈblɒg əʊ sfɪə ‖ ˈblɑːg ə sfɪr
bloke bləʊk ‖ bloʊk **blokes** bləʊks ‖ bloʊks
blokeish, blokish ˈbləʊk ɪʃ ‖ ˈbloʊk- **~ness** nəs nɪs
Blom blɒm ‖ blɑːm
Blomefield ˈbluːm fiːᵊld
Blomfield ˈblɒm fiːᵊld ˈblʌm-, ˈblʊm-, ˈbluːm- ‖ ˈblɑːm-
blond, blonde blɒnd ‖ blɑːnd **blondes, blonds** blɒndz ‖ blɑːndz
Blondel ˌblɒn ˈdel ‖ ˌblɑːn- —*Fr* [blɔ̃ dɛl]
blondie, B~ ˈblɒnd i ‖ ˈblɑːnd i
Blondin ˈblɒnd ɪn ‖ blɑːn ˈdæn —*Fr* [blɔ̃ dɛ̃]
blondish ˈblɒnd ɪʃ ‖ ˈblɑːnd-
blood, Blood blʌd **blooded** ˈblʌd ɪd -əd **blooding** ˈblʌd ɪŋ **bloods** blʌdz
ˈblood bank; **ˌblood ˈbrother**; **ˈblood count**; **ˈblood ˌdonor**; **ˈblood group**; **ˈblood lust**; **ˈblood ˌmoney**; **ˈblood ˌplasma**; **ˈblood ˌpoisoning**; **ˈblood ˌpressure**; **ˌblood ˈred◂**; **ˈblood reˌlation, ˌ· ˈ· ·**; **ˈblood sports**; **ˈblood transˌfusion**; **ˈblood type**; **ˈblood ˌvessel**
blood-and-thunder ˌblʌd ᵊn ˈθʌnd ə ‖ -ᵊr
blood|bath ˈblʌd| bɑːθ →ˈblʌb-, §-bæθ ‖ -bæθ **~baths** bɑːðz §bɑːθs, §bæθs, §bæðz ‖ bæðz bæθs
-blooded ˈblʌd ɪd ◂ -əd — **hot-blooded** ˌhɒt ˈblʌd ɪd ◂ -əd ‖ ˌhɑːt-
bloodhound ˈblʌd haʊnd **~s** z
bloodi... —*see* **bloody**
bloodless ˈblʌd ləs -lɪs **~ly** li **~ness** nəs nɪs
bloodletting ˈblʌd ˌlet ɪŋ ‖ -ˌleţ-
bloodline ˈblʌd laɪn
bloodmobile ˈblʌd mə ˌbiːᵊl **~s** z
bloodshed ˈblʌd ʃed
bloodshot ˈblʌd ʃɒt ‖ -ʃɑːt
bloodstain ˈblʌd steɪn **~ed** d **~s** z
bloodstock ˈblʌd stɒk ‖ -stɑːk
bloodstream ˈblʌd striːm
bloodsucker ˈblʌd ˌsʌk ə ‖ -ᵊr **~s** z
bloodsucking ˈblʌd ˌsʌk ɪŋ
bloodthirst|y ˈblʌd ˌθɜːst |i ‖ -ˌθɜːst |i **~ily** ɪ li əl i **~iness** i nəs i nɪs
blood|y ˈblʌd |i **~ied** id **~ier** i‿ə ‖ i‿ᵊr **~ies** iz **~iest** i‿ɪst i‿əst **~ily** ɪ li əl i **~iness** i nəs i nɪs
ˌBloody ˈMary
bloody-minded ˌblʌd i ˈmaɪnd ɪd ◂ -əd **~ly** li **~ness** nəs nɪs
bloom, Bloom bluːm **bloomed** bluːmd **blooming** ˈbluːm ɪŋ **blooms** bluːmz
Bloomberg ˈbluːm bɜːg ‖ -bɜʳːg
bloomer, B~ ˈbluːm ə ‖ -ᵊr **~s** z
Bloomfield ˈbluːm fiːᵊld
blooming *euphemistic intensifier* ˈbluːm ɪŋ ˈblʊm-, -ɪn, -ən **~ly** li **~ness** nəs nɪs —*The forms with final* **n**, *although non-standard, are sometimes used in RP for jocular effect*
Bloomingdale ˈbluːm ɪŋ deɪᵊl **~'s** z
Bloomington ˈbluːm ɪŋ tən
Bloomsbury ˈbluːmz bər‿i ‖ -ˌber i
ˈBloomsbury Group
bloop bluːp **blooped** bluːpt **blooping** ˈbluːp ɪŋ **bloops** bluːps
blooper ˈbluːp ə ‖ -ᵊr **~s** z
Bloor, Blore blɔː ‖ blɔːr bloʊr
Blorenge ˈblɒr ɪndʒ ‖ ˈblɔːr-
blossom, B~ ˈblɒs əm ‖ ˈblɑːs- **~ed** d **~ing** ɪŋ **~s** z
blot blɒt ‖ blɑːt **blots** blɒts ‖ blɑːts **blotted** ˈblɒt ɪd -əd ‖ ˈblɑːţ əd **blotting** ˈblɒt ɪŋ ‖ ˈblɑːţ ɪŋ
ˈblotting ˌpaper
blotch blɒtʃ ‖ blɑːtʃ **blotched** blɒtʃt ‖ blɑːtʃt
blotch|y ˈblɒtʃ |i ‖ ˈblɑːtʃ |i **~ier** i‿ə ‖ i‿ᵊr **~iest** i‿ɪst i‿əst **~ily** ɪ li əl i **~iness** i nəs i nɪs
blott... —*see* **blot**
blotter ˈblɒt ə ‖ ˈblɑːţ ᵊr **~s** z
blotto ˈblɒt əʊ ‖ ˈblɑːţ oʊ
Blount *(i)* blʌnt, *(ii)* blaʊnt
blouse blaʊz ‖ blaʊs *(*)—in RP formerly also* bluːz **blouses** ˈblaʊz ɪz -əz ‖ ˈblaʊs-
blouson ˈbluːz ɒn ‖ ˈblaʊs ɑːn ˈbluːs-, ˈblaʊz-, ˈbluːz-, -oʊn —*Fr* [blu zɔ̃] **~s** z
blovi|ate ˈbləʊv i |eɪt ‖ ˈbloʊv i |eɪt **~ated** eɪt ɪd -əd ‖ eɪţ əd **~ates** eɪts **~ating** eɪt ɪŋ ‖ eɪţ ɪŋ
bloviation ˌbləʊv i ˈeɪʃ ᵊn ‖ ˌbloʊv-
blow bləʊ ‖ bloʊ **blew** bluː **blowed** bləʊd ‖ bloʊd **blowing** ˈbləʊ ɪŋ ‖ ˈbloʊ ɪŋ **blown** bləʊn §ˈbləʊ ən ‖ bloʊn **blows** bləʊz ‖ bloʊz
blowback ˈbləʊ bæk ‖ ˈbloʊ- **~s** s
blow-by-blow ˌbləʊ baɪ ˈbləʊ ◂ ‖ ˌbloʊ baɪ ˈbloʊ ◂
ˌblow-by-ˌblow acˈcount
blow-drier ˈbləʊ draɪ‿ə ˌ·ˈ· · ‖ ˈbloʊ draɪ‿ᵊr
blow-dry ˈbləʊ draɪ ˌ·ˈ· ‖ ˈbloʊ-
blower ˈbləʊ ə ‖ ˈbloʊ ᵊr **~s** z
blowfish ˈbləʊ fɪʃ ‖ ˈbloʊ- **~es** ɪz əz
blow|fly ˈbləʊ |flaɪ ‖ ˈbloʊ- **~flies** flaɪz

blowgun 'bləʊ gʌn ‖ 'bloʊ- **~s** z
blowhard 'bləʊ hɑːd ‖ 'bloʊ hɑːrd **~s** z
blowhole 'bləʊ həʊl →-hɒʊl ‖ 'bloʊ hoʊl **~s** z
blowlamp 'bləʊ læmp ‖ 'bloʊ- **~s** s
blown bləʊn §'bləʊ ən ‖ bloʊn
blowout 'bləʊ aʊt ‖ 'bloʊ- **~s** s
blowpipe 'bləʊ paɪp ‖ 'bloʊ- **~s** s
blows|y 'blaʊz |i **~ier** i‿ə ‖ i‿ᵊr **~iest** i‿ɪst i‿əst **~ily** ɪ li əl i
blowtorch 'bləʊ tɔːtʃ ‖ 'bloʊ tɔːrtʃ **~es** ɪz əz
blow-up 'bləʊ ʌp ‖ 'bloʊ- **~s** s
blow|y 'bləʊ |i ‖ 'bloʊ |i **~ier** i‿ə ‖ i‿ᵊr **~iest** i‿ɪst əst
blowz|y 'blaʊz |i **~ier** i‿ə ‖ i‿ᵊr **~iest** i‿ɪst i‿əst **~ily** ɪ li əl i
Bloxham 'blɒks əm ‖ 'blɑːks-
BLT, blt ˌbiː el 'tiː
blub blʌb **blubbed** blʌbd **blubbing** 'blʌb ɪŋ **blubs** blʌbz
blubb|er 'blʌb |ə ‖ -|ᵊr **~ered** əd ‖ ᵊrd **~ering** ər‿ɪŋ **~ers** əz ‖ ᵊrz
Blucher, Blücher, b~ 'bluːk ə 'bluːtʃ- ‖ -ᵊr —*Ger* ['blyː çɐ]
bludge blʌdʒ **bludged** blʌdʒd **bludges** 'blʌdʒ ɪz -əz **bludging** 'blʌdʒ ɪŋ
bludgeon 'blʌdʒ ən **~ed** d **~ing** ɪŋ **~s** z
bludger 'blʌdʒ ə ‖ -ᵊr **~s** z
blue, Blue bluː **blued** bluːd **blueing, bluing** 'bluː‿ɪŋ **bluer** 'bluː‿ə ‖ ᵊr **blues** bluːz **bluest** 'bluː‿ɪst əst
ˌ**blue 'blood**; ˌ**blue 'moon**; ˌ**blue 'peter**
bluebag 'bluː bæg
bluebeard, B~ 'bluː bɪəd ‖ -bɪrd
bluebell, B~ 'bluː bel **~s** z
blueberr|y 'bluː bər‿|i -ˌber i ‖ -ˌber |i **~ies** iz
ˌ**blueberry 'pie**
bluebird 'bluː bɜːd ‖ -bɜːd **~s** z
blue-black ˌbluː 'blæk ◂
ˌ**blue-black 'ink**
blue-blooded ˌbluː 'blʌd ɪd ◂ -əd
bluebook 'bluː bʊk §-buːk **~s** s
bluebottle 'bluː ˌbɒt ᵊl ‖ -ˌbɑːt̬- **~s** z
bluecoat 'bluː kəʊt ‖ -koʊt **~s** s
Bluecol *tdmk* 'bluː kɒl ‖ -kɑːl
blue-collar ˌbluː 'kɒl ə ◂ ‖ -'kɑːl ᵊr
blue-eyed ˌbluː 'aɪd ◂
ˌ**blue-eyed 'boy**
Bluefields 'bluː fiːᵊldz
bluefish 'bluː fɪʃ
bluegrass 'bluː grɑːs §-græs ‖ -græs
blue-green ˌbluː 'griːn ◂
ˌ**blue-green 'algae**
blueish 'bluː‿ɪʃ **~ness** nəs nɪs
bluejacket 'bluː ˌdʒæk ɪt §-ət **~s** s
bluejay 'bluː dʒeɪ **~s** z
blueness 'bluː nəs -nɪs
bluenose 'bluː nəʊz ‖ -noʊz
blue-pencil ˌbluː 'penᵗs ᵊl -ɪl **~ed, ~led** d **~ing, ~ling** ‿ɪŋ **~s** z
blue|print 'bluː |prɪnt **~printed** prɪnt ɪd -əd ‖ prɪnt̬ əd **~printing** prɪnt ɪŋ ‖ prɪnt̬ ɪŋ **~prints** prɪnts
blue-ribbon ˌbluː 'rɪb ən ◂
blues bluːz
blue-sky ˌbluː 'skaɪ ◂
bluestocking 'bluː ˌstɒk ɪŋ ‖ -ˌstɑːk- **~s** z
bluesy 'bluːz i
bluet 'bluː‿ɪt §-ət
bluethroat 'bluː θrəʊt ‖ -θroʊt **~s** s
bluetit 'bluː tɪt **~s** s
Bluetooth 'bluː tuːθ §-tʊθ
Bluett 'bluː‿ɪt §‿ət
bluey 'bluː‿i **~s** z
bluff blʌf **bluffed** blʌft **bluffer** 'blʌf ə ‖ -ᵊr **bluffest** 'blʌf ɪst -əst **bluffing** 'blʌf ɪŋ **bluffs** blʌfs
bluffer 'blʌf ə ‖ -ᵊr **~s** z
bluff|ly 'blʌf |li **~ness** nəs nɪs
Bluford 'bluː fəd ‖ -fᵊrd
bluing 'bluː‿ɪŋ
bluish 'bluː‿ɪʃ **~ness** nəs nɪs
Blum bluːm
Blume bluːm
Blundell 'blʌnd ᵊl
Blundellsands ˌblʌnd ᵊl 'sændz
Blunden 'blʌnd ən
blund|er 'blʌnd |ə ‖ -|ᵊr **~ered** əd ‖ ᵊrd **~ering/ly** ‿ər ɪŋ /li **~ers** əz ‖ ᵊrz
blunderbuss 'blʌnd ə bʌs ‖ -ᵊr- **~s** ɪz əz
blunderer 'blʌnd‿ər ə ‖ ᵊr ər **~s** z
blunge blʌndʒ **blunged** blʌndʒd **blunges** 'blʌndʒ ɪz -əz **blunging** 'blʌndʒ ɪŋ
Blunkett 'blʌŋk ɪt -ət
blunt, Blunt blʌnt **blunted** 'blʌnt ɪd əd ‖ 'blʌnt̬ əd **blunter** 'blʌnt ə ‖ 'blʌnt̬ ᵊr **bluntest** 'blʌnt ɪst əst ‖ 'blʌnt̬ əst **blunting** 'blʌnt ɪŋ ‖ 'blʌnt̬ ɪŋ **blunts** blʌnts
blunt|ly 'blʌnt |li **~ness** nəs nɪs
blur, Blur blɜː ‖ blɜː **blurred** blɜːd ‖ blɜːd **blurring** 'blɜːr ɪŋ ‖ 'blɜː ɪŋ **blurs** blɜːz ‖ blɜːz
blurb blɜːb ‖ blɜːb **blurbs** blɜːbz ‖ blɜːbz
blurr... —*see* **blur**
blurry 'blɜːr i ‖ 'blɜː i
blurt blɜːt ‖ blɜːt **blurted** 'blɜːt ɪd -əd ‖ 'blɜːt̬ əd **blurting** 'blɜːt ɪŋ ‖ 'blɜːt̬ ɪŋ **blurts** blɜːts ‖ blɜːts
blush blʌʃ **blushed** blʌʃt **blushes** 'blʌʃ ɪz -əz **blushing/ly** 'blʌʃ ɪŋ /li
blusher 'blʌʃ ə ‖ -ᵊr **~s** z
blust|er 'blʌst |ə ‖ -|ᵊr **~ered** əd ‖ ᵊrd **~ering/ly** ər‿ɪŋ /li **~ers** əz ‖ ᵊrz
blusterous 'blʌst ər‿əs **~ly** li
blustery 'blʌst ər‿i
Blu-Tack *tdmk* 'bluː tæk
Bly blaɪ
Blyth *(i)* blaɪð, *(ii)* blaɪθ, *(iii)* blaɪ —*The place in Northumberland is (i).*
Blythe blaɪð
Blyton 'blaɪt ᵊn
B-movie 'biː ˌmuːv i
BMus ˌbiː 'mʌz
BMW *tdmk* ˌbiː em 'dʌb ᵊl ju **~s, ~'s** z
BMX ˌbiː em 'eks
B'nai B'rith bə ˌneɪ bə 'riːθ -ˌ-'brɪθ
BNOC 'biː nɒk ‖ -nɑːk

B

bo, Bo bəʊ ‖ boʊ
BO ˌbiː ˈəʊ ‖ -ˈoʊ
boa ˈbəʊ ə ‖ ˈboʊ ə —*in RP formerly also* bɔː **boas** ˈbəʊ əz ‖ ˈboʊ əz
Boadicea ˌbəʊ əd ɪ ˈsiː‿ə -əˈ-- ‖ ˌboʊ-
Boakes, Boaks bəʊks ‖ boʊks
Boanerges ˌbəʊ ə ˈnɜːdʒ iːz ‖ ˌboʊ ə ˈnɝːdʒ-
boar bɔː ‖ bɔːr boʊr *(= bore)* **boars** bɔːz ‖ bɔːrz boʊrz
board bɔːd ‖ bɔːrd boʊrd **boarded** ˈbɔːd ɪd -əd ‖ ˈbɔːrd əd ˈboʊrd- **boarding** ˈbɔːd ɪŋ ‖ ˈbɔːrd ɪŋ ˈboʊrd- **boards** bɔːdz ‖ bɔːrdz boʊrdz
ˈboarding card; **ˈboarding school**
boarder ˈbɔːd ə ‖ ˈbɔːrd ᵊr ˈboʊrd- **~s** z
boarding|house ˈbɔːd ɪŋ |haʊs ‖ ˈbɔːrd- ˈboʊrd- **~houses** haʊz ɪz -əz
Boardman ˈbɔːd mən →ˈbɔːb- ‖ ˈbɔːrd- ˈboʊrd-
boardroom ˈbɔːd ruːm -rʊm ‖ ˈbɔːrd- ˈboʊrd- **~s** z
boardwalk ˈbɔːd wɔːk ‖ ˈbɔːrd- ˈboʊrd-, -wɑːk **~s** s
Boas ˈbəʊ æz -æs, -əz, -əs ‖ ˈboʊ-
boast bəʊst ‖ boʊst **boasted** ˈbəʊst ɪd -əd ‖ ˈboʊst- **boasting/ly** ˈbəʊst ɪŋ /li ‖ ˈboʊst- **boasts** bəʊsts ‖ boʊsts
boaster ˈbəʊst ə ‖ ˈboʊst ᵊr **~s** z
boastful ˈbəʊst fᵊl -fʊl ‖ ˈboʊst- **~ly** i **~ness** nəs nɪs
boat bəʊt ‖ boʊt **boated** ˈbəʊt ɪd -əd ‖ ˈboʊt̬ əd **boating** ˈbəʊt ɪŋ ‖ ˈboʊt̬ ɪŋ **boats** bəʊts ‖ boʊts
ˈboat ˌpeople; **ˈboat race**; **ˈboat train**
boatel (ˌ)bəʊ ˈtel ‖ (ˌ)boʊ- **~s** z
Boateng ˈbwɑːt eŋ —*but popularly usually* ˈbəʊt- ‖ ˈboʊt-
boater ˈbəʊt ə ‖ ˈboʊt̬ ᵊr **~s** z
boathook ˈbəʊt hʊk §-huːk ‖ ˈboʊt- **~s** s
boat|house ˈbəʊt |haʊs ‖ ˈboʊt- **~houses** haʊz ɪz -əz
boatload ˈbəʊt ləʊd ‖ ˈboʊt loʊd **~s** z
boat|man ˈbəʊt |mən ‖ ˈboʊt- **~men** mən men
boatshed ˈbəʊt ʃed ‖ ˈboʊt- **~s** z
boatswain ˈbəʊs ᵊn ‖ ˈboʊs ᵊn —*There is also a spelling pronunciation* ˈbəʊt sweɪn ‖ ˈboʊt- **~s** z
boatyard ˈbəʊt jɑːd ‖ ˈboʊt jɑːrd **~s** z
Boaz ˈbəʊ æz ‖ ˈboʊ-
bob, Bob bɒb ‖ bɑːb **bobbed** bɒbd ‖ bɑːbd **bobbing** ˈbɒb ɪŋ ‖ ˈbɑːb ɪŋ **bobs, Bob's** bɒbz ‖ bɑːbz
bobbi... —*see* **bobby**
Bobbie ˈbɒb i ‖ ˈbɑːb i
bobbin ˈbɒb ɪn §-ən ‖ ˈbɑːb ən **~s** z
Bobbitt ˈbɒb ɪt §-ət ‖ ˈbɑːb ət
bobble ˈbɒb ᵊl ‖ ˈbɑːb ᵊl **~s** z
bobbly ˈbɒb ᵊl‿i ‖ ˈbɑːb-
bobby, Bobby ˈbɒb i ‖ ˈbɑːb i **bobbies, Bobby's** ˈbɒb iz ‖ ˈbɑːb-
ˈbobby pin; **ˈbobby socks**
bobby-soxer ˈbɒb i sɒks ə ‖ ˈbɑːbi sɑːks ᵊr
bobcat ˈbɒb kæt ‖ ˈbɑːb- **~s** s
bobolink ˈbɒb ə lɪŋk ‖ ˈbɑːb- **~s** s
bobsled ˈbɒb sled ‖ ˈbɑːb- **~der/s** ə/z ‖ ᵊr/z **~ding** ɪŋ **~s** z
bobsleigh ˈbɒb sleɪ ‖ ˈbɑːb- **~s** z
bobstay ˈbɒb steɪ ‖ ˈbɑːb- **~s** z
bobtail ˈbɒb teɪᵊl ‖ ˈbɑːb- **~ed** d **~ing** ɪŋ **~s** z
bobwhite ˌbɒb ˈwaɪt -ˈhwaɪt ‖ ˌbɑːb ˈ*h*waɪt **~s** s
Boca Raton ˌbəʊk ə rə ˈtəʊn ‖ ˌboʊk ə rə ˈtoʊn
Boccaccio bɒ ˈkɑːtʃ i‿əʊ bə-, -ˈkætʃ- ‖ boʊ ˈkɑːtʃ i‿oʊ —*It* [bok ˈkat tʃo]
Boccherini ˌbɒk ə ˈriːn i ‖ ˌbɑːk- ˌboʊk- —*It* [bok ke ˈriː ni]
Bocelli bɒ ˈtʃel i ‖ boʊ- —*It* [bo ˈtʃɛl li]
Boche, boche bɒʃ ‖ bɑːʃ boʊʃ
Bochum ˈbəʊk əm ‖ ˈboʊk- —*Ger* [ˈboːx ʊm]
bock, Bock bɒk ‖ bɑːk **bocks** bɒks ‖ bɑːks
ˌbock ˈbeer
bod bɒd ‖ bɑːd **bods** bɒdz ‖ bɑːdz
bodacious bəʊ ˈdeɪʃ əs ‖ boʊ- **~ly** li
Boddington ˈbɒd ɪŋ tən ‖ ˈbɑːd-
bode bəʊd ‖ boʊd **boded** ˈbəʊd ɪd -əd ‖ ˈboʊd əd **bodes** bəʊdz ‖ boʊdz **boding** ˈbəʊd ɪŋ ‖ ˈboʊd ɪŋ
bodega bəʊ ˈdiːɡ ə -ˈdeɪɡ- ‖ boʊ ˈdeɪɡ ə —*Sp* [bo ˈðe ɣa] **~s** z
Boˌdega ˈBay
bodge bɒdʒ ‖ bɑːdʒ **bodged** bɒdʒd ‖ bɑːdʒd **bodges** ˈbɒdʒ ɪz -əz ‖ ˈbɑːdʒ əz **bodging** ˈbɒdʒ ɪŋ ‖ ˈbɑːdʒ ɪŋ
bodger ˈbɒdʒ ə ‖ ˈbɑːdʒ ᵊr **~s** z
bodgie ˈbɒdʒ i ‖ ˈbɑːdʒ i **~s** z
Bodhisattva ˌbɒd ɪ ˈsæt və ˌbəʊd-, §-ə-, -ˈsʌt-, -ˈsɑːt-, -wə ‖ ˌboʊd ə ˈsʌt və
bodhrán ˈbɔːr ɑːn baʊ ˈrɑːn
Bodiam *(i)* ˈbəʊd i‿əm ‖ ˈboʊd-, *(ii)* ˈbɒd- ‖ ˈbɑːd-
bodic|e ˈbɒd ɪs -əs ‖ ˈbɑːd- **~es** ɪz əz
bodice-ripper ˈbɒd ɪs ˌrɪp ə -əs- ‖ ˈbɑːd əs ˌrɪp ᵊr **~s** z
Bodie ˈbəʊd i ‖ ˈboʊd i
bodie... —*see* **body**
-bodied ˈbɒd id ◂ ‖ -ˈbɑːd id ◂ — **full-bodied** ˌfʊl ˈbɒd id ◂ ‖ -ˈbɑːd-
bodily ˈbɒd ɪ li -əl i ‖ ˈbɑːd ᵊl i
bodkin, B~ ˈbɒd kɪn ‖ ˈbɑːd- **~s** z
Bodleian bɒd ˈliː‿ən ˈbɒd li‿ən ‖ bɑːd-
Bodley ˈbɒd li ‖ ˈbɑːd-
Bodmer ˈbɒd mə ‖ ˈbɑːd mᵊr
Bodmin ˈbɒd mɪn →ˈbɒb-, §-mən ‖ ˈbɑːd-
Bodnant ˈbɒd nænt ‖ ˈbɑːd-
Bodoni bə ˈdəʊn i ‖ -ˈdoʊn- —*It* [bo ˈdoː ni]
Bodrum ˈbɒdr əm -ʊm ‖ ˈboʊdr əm
body, Body ˈbɒd i ‖ ˈbɑːd i **bodies** ˈbɒd iz ‖ ˈbɑːd iz
ˈbody blow; **ˈbody ˌbuilding**; **ˈbody count**; **ˈbody ˌdouble**; **ˈbody ˌlanguage**; **ˈbody ˌpopping**; **ˈbody ˌsnatcher**; **ˈbody ˌstocking**; **ˈbody ˌwarmer**
bodycheck ˈbɒd i tʃek ‖ ˈbɑːd- **~s** s
bodyguard ˈbɒd i ɡɑːd ‖ ˈbɑːd i ɡɑːrd **~s** z
bodyline ˈbɒd i laɪn ‖ ˈbɑːd- **~s** z
bodywork ˈbɒd i wɜːk ‖ ˈbɑːd i wɝːk

Boehm *(i)* bəʊm ˈbəʊ əm ‖ boʊm, *(ii)* biːm, *(iii)* bɜːm ‖ bɝːm *(iv)* beɪm —*Ger* [bøːm]
boehmite ˈbɜːm aɪt ‖ ˈbeɪm- ˈboʊm- *(*)*
Boeing *tdmk* ˈbəʊ ɪŋ ‖ ˈboʊ ɪŋ
Boeotia bi ˈəʊʃ ə -i‿ə ‖ -ˈoʊʃ ə
Boeotian bi ˈəʊʃ ən -i‿ən ‖ -ˈoʊʃ ən **~s** z
Boer bɔː ˈbəʊ ə, bʊə ‖ bɔːr boʊr, bʊər **Boers** bɔːz ˈbəʊ əz, bʊəz ‖ bɔːrz boʊrz, bʊərz
Boethius bəʊ ˈiːθ i‿əs ‖ boʊ-
boeuf bɜːf ‖ bʊf bʌf, boʊf —*Fr* [bœf]
ˌboeuf ˌbourguiˈgnon ˌbɜːf ˌbɔːg iːn ˈjɒn ˌbɔːg-, -ɪn-, -ən- ‖ ˌbʊrg iːn ˈjɑːn -ˈjɔːn, -ˈjoʊn —*Fr* [buʁ gi ɲɔ̃]
boff bɒf ‖ bɑːf **boffed** bɒft ‖ bɑːft **boffing** ˈbɒf ɪŋ ‖ ˈbɑːf ɪŋ **boffs** bɒfs ‖ bɑːfs
boffin ˈbɒf ɪn §-ən ‖ ˈbɑːf- **~s** z
boffo ˈbɒf əʊ ‖ ˈbɑːf oʊ
Bofors ˈbəʊf əz ‖ ˈboʊ fɔːrz -fɔːrs —*Swed* [buː ˈfɔʂ]
bog bɒg ‖ bɑːg bɔːg **bogged** bɒgd ‖ bɑːgd bɔːgd **bogging** ˈbɒg ɪŋ ‖ ˈbɑːg ɪŋ ˈbɔːg- **bogs** bɒgz ‖ bɑːgz bɔːgz
Bogalusa *place in LA* ˌbəʊg ə ˈluːs ə ‖ ˌboʊg-
Bogarde ˈbəʊg ɑːd ‖ ˈboʊg ɑːrd
Bogart ˈbəʊg ɑːt ‖ ˈboʊg ɑːrt
bogbean ˈbɒg biːn ‖ ˈbɑːg- ˈbɔːg-
Bogdanov bɒg ˈdɑːn ɒv ‖ bɑːg-
bogey, Bogey ˈbəʊg i ‖ ˈboʊg i **~s** z
bogey|man ˈbəʊg i |mæn ‖ ˈboʊg- **~men** men
boggie... —*see* **boggy**
bogginess ˈbɒg i nəs -nɪs ‖ ˈbɑːg- ˈbɔːg-‿
Boggis ˈbɒg ɪs §-əs ‖ ˈbɑːg-
boggl|e ˈbɒg əl ‖ ˈbɑːg əl **~ed** d **~es** z **~ing** ‿ɪŋ
bogg|y ˈbɒg |i ‖ ˈbɑːg |i ˈbɔːg- **~ier** i‿ə ‖ i‿ər **~iest** i‿ɪst i‿əst
bogie ˈbəʊg i ‖ ˈboʊg i *(= bogey)* **~s** z
Bognor ˈbɒg nə ‖ ˈbɑːg nər
BOGOF, bogof ˈbɒg ɒf ‖ ˈbɑːg ɔːf -ɑːf
Bogota, Bogotá ˌbɒg ə ˈtɑː ˌbəʊg- ‖ ˌboʊg ə ˈtɑː ˈ· · · —*Sp* [bo ɣo ˈta] —*but the place in NJ is* bə ˈgoʊṭ ə
bog-standard ˌbɒg ˈstænd əd ◂ ‖ ˌbɑːg ˈstænd ərd ◂ ˌbɔːg-
bogus ˈbəʊg əs ‖ ˈboʊg-
bogy ˈbəʊg i ‖ ˈboʊg i *(= bogey)*
bohea bəʊ ˈhiː ‖ boʊ-
Boheme, Bohème, b~ bəʊ ˈem -ˈeɪm ‖ boʊ-
Bohemia bəʊ ˈhiːm i‿ə ‖ boʊ-
bohemian, B~ bəʊ ˈhiːm i‿ən ‖ boʊ- **~s** z
Böhm bɜːm ‖ boʊm —*Ger* [bøːm]
boho ˈbəʊ həʊ ‖ ˈboʊ hoʊ
Bohr bɔː ‖ bɔːr boʊr —*Danish* [boːʁ]
bohrium ˈbɔːr i‿əm ‖ ˈboʊr-
Bohun *(i)* buːn, *(ii)* ˈbəʊ ən ‖ ˈboʊ-
bohunk ˈbəʊ hʌŋk ‖ ˈboʊ- **~s** s
boil bɔɪəl **boiled** bɔɪəld **boiling** ˈbɔɪl ɪŋ **boils** bɔɪəlz
Boileau ˈbɔɪl əʊ bwæ ˈləʊ ‖ bwɑː ˈloʊ —*Fr* [bwa lo]
boiler ˈbɔɪl ə ‖ -ər **~s** z
ˈ**boiler suit**
boilermak|er ˈbɔɪl ə ˌmeɪk |ə ‖ -ər ˌmeɪk |ər **~ers** əz ‖ ərz **~ing** ɪŋ
boilerplate ˈbɔɪl ə pleɪt ‖ -ər- **~s** s
boiling ˈbɔɪəl ɪŋ
ˈ**boiling point**; ˌ**boiling ˈwater**
boil-in-the-bag ˌbɔɪəl ɪn ðə ˈbæg ◂
boing bɔɪŋ
boink bɔɪŋk
Bois bɔɪz —*but in French place names* bwɑː
Boise *place in ID* ˈbɔɪz i ˈbɔɪs i
boisterous ˈbɔɪst ər əs →ˈbɔɪs trəs **~ly** li **~ness** nəs nɪs
bok choy ˌbɒk ˈtʃɔɪ ‖ ˌbɑːk-
Bokhara bɒ ˈkɑːr ə bəʊ- ‖ boʊ- —*Russ* [bu ˈxa rə]
Bokmål ˈbʊk mɔːl ˈbuːk- ‖ -mɑːl —*Norw* [ˈbuːk moːl]
bola ˈbəʊl ə ‖ ˈboʊl ə —*Sp* [ˈbo la] **~s** z
Bolam ˈbəʊl əm ‖ ˈboʊl-
Bolan ˈbəʊl ən ‖ ˈboʊl-
bolas ˈbəʊl əs ‖ ˈboʊl- —*Sp* [ˈbo las]
bold, Bold bəʊld →bɒʊld ‖ boʊld **bolder** ˈbəʊld ə →ˈbɒʊld ə ‖ ˈboʊld ər **boldest** ˈbəʊld ɪst →ˈbɒʊld-, -əst ‖ ˈboʊld-
boldface ˈbəʊld feɪs →ˈbɒʊld-, ˌ·ˈ· ‖ ˈboʊld- **~d** t
bold|ly ˈbəʊld |li →ˈbɒʊld- ‖ ˈboʊld- **~ness** nəs nɪs
Boldre ˈbəʊld ə →ˈbɒʊld- ‖ ˈboʊld ər
bole bəʊl →bɒʊl ‖ boʊl *(= bowl)* **boles** bəʊlz ‖ boʊlz
Boleat, Boléat ˈbəʊl i‿ət -i ɑː ‖ ˈboʊl-
bolero *'garment'* ˈbɒl ə rəʊ bə ˈleər əʊ ‖ bə ˈler oʊ **~s** z
bolero *'dance'* bə ˈleər əʊ ‖ -ˈler oʊ **~s** z
bo|letus bəʊ |ˈliːt əs ‖ boʊ |ˈliːṭ əs **~leti** ˈliːt aɪ -iː **~letuses** ˈliːt əs ɪz -əz ‖ ˈliːṭ-
Boleyn *(i)* bə ˈlɪn ‖ boʊ-, *(ii)* ˈbʊl ɪn, *(iii)* bʊ ˈliːn
Bolger ˈbɒldʒ ə ˈbɒlʒ- ‖ ˈboʊldʒ ər ˈbɑːldʒ-
bolide ˈbəʊl aɪd -ɪd, §-əd ‖ ˈboʊl- **~s** z
Bolingbroke ˈbɒl ɪŋ brʊk ˈbʊl- ‖ ˈbɑːl-
Bolinger ˈbɒl ɪndʒ ə -əndʒ- ‖ ˈbɑːl əndʒ ər
Bolitho bə ˈlaɪθ əʊ ‖ -oʊ
Bolivar, b~ ˈbɒl ɪ vɑː -ə-; bɒ ˈliːv ɑː ‖ ˈbɑːl əv ər bə ˈliːv ɑːr —*Sp* Bolívar [bo ˈli βar]
Bolivia bə ˈlɪv i‿ə
Bolivian bə ˈlɪv i‿ən **~s** z
boliviano bə ˌlɪv i ˈɑːn əʊ bɒ- ‖ -oʊ **~s** z
boll bəʊl →bɒʊl. bɒl ‖ boʊl *(= bowl)* **bolls** bəʊlz →bɒʊlz. bɒlz ‖ boʊlz
ˌ**boll ˈweevil**
bollard ˈbɒl ɑːd -əd ‖ ˈbɑːl ərd **~s** z
Bollin ˈbɒl ɪn §-ən ‖ ˈbɑːl-
Bollinger ˈbɒl ɪndʒ ə -əndʒ- ‖ ˈbɑːl əndʒ ər
bollix ˈbɒl ɪks **~ed** t **~es** ɪz əz **~ing** ɪŋ
bollock ˈbɒl ək ‖ ˈbɑːl- **~ed** t **~ing/s** ɪŋ/z **~s** s
bollocks-up ˈbɒl əks ʌp ‖ ˈbɑːl-
Bollywood ˈbɒl i wʊd ‖ ˈbɑːl-
bologna *'sausage'* bə ˈləʊn i ‖ bə ˈloʊn i
Bologna bə ˈləʊn jə -ˈlɒn- ‖ -ˈloʊn- —*It* [bo ˈloɲ ɲa]

B

bolognaise, bolognese ˌbɒl ə ˈneɪz ◂ ⚠-əg-, -ˈnez ‖ ˌboʊl ən ˈjeɪz ◂
ˌ**bolognaise 'sauce**
boloney bə ˈləʊn i ‖ bə ˈloʊn i
bolo tie ˈbəʊl əʊ taɪ ‖ ˈboʊl oʊ taɪ **~s** z
Bolshevik ˈbɒlʃ ə vɪk -ɪ- ‖ ˈboʊlʃ- **~s** s
Bolshevism ˈbɒlʃ ə ˌvɪz əm -ɪ- ‖ ˈboʊlʃ-
Bolshevist ˈbɒlʃ əv ɪst -ɪv-, §-əst ‖ ˈboʊlʃ- **~s** s
Bolshevistic ˌbɒlʃ ə ˈvɪst ɪk ◂ -ɪ- ‖ ˌboʊlʃ-
bolshi|e ˈbɒlʃ i ‖ ˈboʊlʃ i **~es** z **~ness** nəs nɪs
Bolshoi, Bolshoy ˌbɒl ˈʃɔɪ ◂ ‖ ˌboʊl- —*Russ* [bʌlʲ ˈʃɔj]
ˌ**Bolshoi 'Ballet** ‖ ˌ· · ·ˈ·
bolshy ˈbɒlʃ i ‖ ˈboʊlʃ i
Bolsover ˈbɒls ˌəʊv ə ˈbəʊlz- ‖ ˈboʊls ˌoʊv ᵊr —*The place in Derbyshire is locally* ˈbəʊlz-, →ˈbɒʊlz-
bolst|er, B~ ˈbəʊlst |ə →ˈbɒʊlst-; §ˈbɒlst- ‖ ˈboʊlst |ᵊr **~ered** əd ‖ ᵊrd **~ering** ər‿ɪŋ **~ers** əz ‖ ᵊrz
bolt, Bolt bəʊlt →bɒʊlt, §bɒlt ‖ boʊlt **bolted** ˈbəʊlt ɪd →ˈbɒʊlt-, §ˈbɒlt-, -əd ‖ ˈboʊlt əd **bolting** ˈbəʊlt ɪŋ →ˈbɒʊlt-, §ˈbɒlt- ‖ ˈboʊlt ɪŋ **bolts, Bolt's** bəʊlts →bɒʊlts, §bɒlts ‖ boʊlts
bolter ˈbəʊlt ə →ˈbɒʊlt-, §ˈbɒlt- ‖ ˈboʊlt ᵊr **~s** z
bolthole ˈbəʊlt həʊl →ˈbɒʊlt hɒʊl, §ˈbɒlt- ‖ ˈboʊlt hoʊl **~s** z
Bolton ˈbəʊlt ən →ˈbɒʊlt- ‖ ˈboʊlt- **~s** z
Bolton-le-Sands ˌbəʊlt ən li ˈsændz →ˌbɒʊlt-, -lə'· ‖ ˌboʊlt-
Boltzmann ˈbɒlts mən ˈbəʊlts- ‖ ˈboʊlts- —*Ger* [ˈbɔlts man]
bolus ˈbəʊl əs ‖ ˈboʊl- **~es** ɪz əz
bomb bɒm ‖ bɑːm **bombed** bɒmd ‖ bɑːmd **bombing** ˈbɒm ɪŋ ‖ ˈbɑːm ɪŋ **bombs** bɒmz ‖ bɑːmz
ˈ**bomb di**ˌ**sposal**
bombard *v* bɒm ˈbɑːd ‖ bɑːm ˈbɑːrd **~ed** ɪd əd **~ing** ɪŋ **~s** z
bombardier ˌbɒm bə ˈdɪə ◂ ‖ ˌbɑːm bᵊr ˈdɪᵊr -bə- **~s** z
bombardment bɒm ˈbɑːd mənt →-ˈbɑːb- ‖ bɑːm ˈbɑːrd- **~s** s
bombasine ˈbɒm bə ziːn ˌ· ·ˈ· ‖ ˌbɑːm bə ˈziːn
bombast ˈbɒm bæst ‖ ˈbɑːm-
bombastic bɒm ˈbæst ɪk ‖ bɑːm- **~ally** ᵊl‿i
Bombay ˌbɒm ˈbeɪ ◂ ‖ ˌbɑːm-
ˌ**Bombay 'duck**
bombazine ˈbɒm bə ziːn ˌ· ·ˈ· ‖ ˌbɑːm bə ˈziːn
bombe bɒm bɒmb ‖ bɑːm —*Fr* [bɔ̃ːb] **bombes** bɒmz bɒmbz ‖ bɑːmz
bomber ˈbɒm ə ‖ ˈbɑːm ᵊr **~s** z
bomblet ˈbɒm lət -lɪt ‖ ˈbɑːm- **~s** s
bombproof ˈbɒm pruːf §-prʊf ‖ ˈbɑːm- **~ed** t
bombshell ˈbɒm ʃel ‖ ˈbɑːm- **~s** z
bombsight ˈbɒm saɪt ‖ ˈbɑːm- **~s** s
bombsite ˈbɒm saɪt ‖ ˈbɑːm- **~s** s
Bompas ˈbʌmp əs
bon bɒn bɒ̃ ‖ bɑːn —*Fr* [bɔ̃] —*See also phrases with this word*
bona ˈbəʊn ə ‖ ˈboʊn ə
ˌ**bona 'fide** ˈfaɪd i ˈfiːd eɪ; ˌ**bona 'fides** ˈfaɪd iːz ˈfiːd eɪz, -eɪs

Bonaire bɒn ˈeə ‖ bə ˈneᵊr
Bonallack bə ˈnæl ək
bonanza bə ˈnænz ə **~s** z
Bonaparte ˈbəʊn ə pɑːt ‖ ˈboʊn ə pɑːrt —*Fr* [bɔ na paʁt]
Bonapartism ˈbəʊn ə pɑːt ˌɪz əm ‖ ˈboʊn ə pɑːrt-
Bonapartist ˈbəʊn ə pɑːt ɪst §-əst ‖ ˈboʊn ə pɑːrţ əst **~s** s
bon appetit ˌbɒn æp e ˈtiː -ɪ ˈtiː ‖ ˌboʊn æp eɪ ˈtiː ˌbɑːn, -ɑːp ə- —*Fr* [bɔ na pe ti]
Bonar *(i)* ˈbəʊn ə ‖ ˈboʊn ᵊr, *(ii)* ˈbɒn ə ‖ ˈbɑːn ᵊr
Bonaventure ˈbɒn ə ˌventʃ ə ˌ· ·ˈ· · ‖ ˈbɑːn ə ˌventʃ ᵊr ˌ· ·ˈ·
bonbon ˈbɒn bɒn →ˈbɒm- ‖ ˈbɑːn bɑːn **~s** z
bonce bɒnᵗs ‖ bɑːnᵗs **bonces** ˈbɒnᵗs ɪz -əz ‖ ˈbɑːnᵗs-
bond, Bond bɒnd ‖ bɑːnd **bonded** ˈbɒnd ɪd -əd ‖ ˈbɑːnd əd **bonding** ˈbɒnd ɪŋ ‖ ˈbɑːnd ɪŋ **bonds, Bond's** bɒndz ‖ bɑːndz
bondage ˈbɒnd ɪdʒ ‖ ˈbɑːnd-
Bondfield ˈbɒnd fiːᵊld ‖ ˈbɑːnd-
bondholder ˈbɒnd ˌhəʊld ə →-ˌhɒʊld- ‖ ˈbɑːnd ˌhoʊld ᵊr **~s** z
Bondi *place in Australia* ˈbɒnd aɪ ‖ ˈbɑːnd-
bondservant ˈbɒnd ˌsɜːv ᵊnt ‖ ˈbɑːnd ˌsɜːv ᵊnt **~s** s
bonds|man ˈbɒndz mən ‖ ˈbɑːndz- **~men** mən men
bone, Bone bəʊn ‖ boʊn **boned** bəʊnd ‖ boʊnd **boning** ˈbəʊn ɪŋ ‖ ˈboʊn ɪŋ **bones** bəʊnz ‖ boʊnz
ˌ**bone 'china**; ˈ**bone** ˌ**marrow**; ˈ**bone meal**
bone-dry ˌbəʊn ˈdraɪ ◂ ‖ ˌboʊn-
bonehead ˈbəʊn hed ‖ ˈboʊn- **~s** z
bone-idle ˌbəʊn ˈaɪd ᵊl ◂ ‖ ˌboʊn-
bone-lazy ˌbəʊn ˈleɪz i ◂ ‖ ˌboʊn-
boneless ˈbəʊn ləs -lɪs ‖ ˈboʊn-
bonemeal ˈbəʊn miːᵊl →ˈbəʊm- ‖ ˈboʊn-
boner ˈbəʊn ə ‖ ˈboʊn ᵊr **~s** z
bone-setter ˈbəʊn ˌset ə ‖ ˈboʊn ˌseţ ᵊr **~s** z
bone-shaker ˈbəʊn ˌʃeɪk ə ‖ ˈboʊn ˌʃeɪk ᵊr **~s** z
Bo'ness ˌbəʊ ˈnes ‖ ˌboʊ-
bonfire ˈbɒn ˌfaɪ‿ə ‖ ˈbɑːn ˌfaɪ‿ᵊr **~s** z
bong bɒŋ ‖ bɑːŋ bɔːŋ **bonged** bɒŋd ‖ bɑːŋd bɔːŋd **bonging** ˈbɒŋ ɪŋ ‖ ˈbɑːŋ ɪŋ ˈbɔːŋ- **bongs** bɒŋz ‖ bɑːŋz bɔːŋz
bongo ˈbɒŋ gəʊ ‖ ˈbɑːŋ goʊ ˈbɔːŋ- **~s** z
Bonham ˈbɒn əm ‖ ˈbɑːn-
Bonham Carter ˌbɒn əm ˈkɑːt ə ‖ ˌbɑːn əm ˈkɑːrţ ᵊr
Bonhoeffer ˈbɒn ˌhɜːf ə ‖ ˈbɑːn ˌhoʊf ᵊr —*Ger* [ˈboːn hœf ɐ, ˈbɔn-]
bonhomie ˈbɒn əm i -ɒm-, -iː ‖ ˌbɑːn ə ˈmiː ˈ· · ·
boni... —*see* **bony**
Boniface ˈbɒn ɪ feɪs -ə- ‖ ˈbɑːn-
Bonington ˈbɒn ɪŋ tən ‖ ˈbɑːn-
Bonio *tdmk* ˈbəʊn i əʊ ‖ ˈboʊn i oʊ **~s** z
Bonita bə ˈniːt ə ‖ -ˈniːţ-

onito bə ˈniːt əʊ ‖ -ˈniːṭ oʊ -ə **~s** z
on Jovi ˌbɒn ˈdʒəʊv i ‖ ˌbɑːn ˈdʒoʊv i
onk bɒŋk ‖ bɑːŋk **bonked** bɒŋ*k*t ‖ bɑːŋ*k*t **bonking** ˈbɒŋk ɪŋ ‖ ˈbɑːŋk ɪŋ **bonks** bɒŋ*k*s ‖ bɑːŋ*k*s
onkbuster ˈbɒŋk ˌbʌst ə ‖ ˈbɑːŋk ˌbʌst ᵊr **~s** z
onkers ˈbɒŋk əz ‖ ˈbɑːŋk ᵊrz
on mot ˌbɔ̃ ˈməʊ ˌbɒn- ‖ ˌbɑːn ˈmoʊ ˌbɔːn- —*Fr* [bɔ̃ mo] **~s** z
onn bɒn ‖ bɑːn —*Ger* [bɔn]
onne bɒn ‖ bɑːn bɔːn, bʌn —*Fr* [bɔn] ˌ**bonne ˈbouche** buːʃ —*Fr* [buʃ]; ˌ**bonne ˈfemme** fæm —*Fr* [fam]
onnet ˈbɒn ɪt §-ət ‖ ˈbɑːn- **~s** s
Bonneville ˈbɒn ə vɪl ‖ ˈbɑːn-
Bonnie ˈbɒn i ‖ ˈbɑːn i ˌ**Bonnie ˌPrince ˈCharlie**
onn|y, Bonny ˈbɒn |i ‖ ˈbɑːn |i **~ier** i‿ə ‖ i‿ᵊr **~iest** i‿ɪst i‿əst **~ily** ɪ li əl i **~iness** i nəs i nɪs
Bono *(i)* ˈbəʊn əʊ ‖ ˈboʊn oʊ *(ii)* ˈbɒn əʊ ‖ ˈbɑːn oʊ —*The American singer is (i), the Irish singer (ii).*
onobo bə ˈnəʊb əʊ ˈbɒn ə bəʊ ‖ bə ˈnoʊb oʊ **~s** z
onsai ˈbɒn saɪ ˈbəʊn- ‖ ˌbɑːn ˈsaɪ ˌboʊn-, ˈ·· —*Jp* [bo‿n sai] **~s** z
Bonser, Bonsor ˈbɒnᵗs ə ‖ ˈbɑːnᵗs ᵊr
onus ˈbəʊn əs ‖ ˈboʊn- **~es** ɪz əz
on vivant ˌbɔ̃ ˈviːv ɒ̃ -viː ˈvɒ̃ ‖ ˌbɑːn viː ˈvɑːnt —*Fr* [bɔ̃ vi vɑ̃]
on viveur ˌbɔ̃ viː ˈvɜː ‖ ˌbɑːn viː ˈvɜː —*not a true French expression* **~s** z
on voyage ˌbɔ̃ vwaɪ ˈɑːʒ ˌ·ˈ· ‖ ˌbɑːn- ˌbɔːn- —*Fr* [bɔ̃ vwa jaːʒ]
on|y ˈbəʊn |i ‖ ˈboʊn |i **~ier** i‿ə ‖ i‿ᵊr **~iest** i‿ɪst i‿əst **~ily** ɪ li əl i **~iness** i nəs i nɪs
Bonython bə ˈnaɪθ ᵊn
onze bɒnz ‖ bɑːnz **bonzes** ˈbɒnz ɪz -əz ‖ ˈbɑːnz əz
onzer ˈbɒnz ə ‖ ˈbɑːnz ᵊr
Bonzo ˈbɒnz əʊ ‖ ˈbɑːnz oʊ
oo buː **booed** buːd **booing** ˈbuː‿ɪŋ **boos** buːz
oob buːb **boobed** buːbd **boobing** ˈbuːb ɪŋ **boobs** buːbz
boo-boo ˈbuː buː **~s** z
booby ˈbuːb i **boobies** ˈbuːb iz ˈ**booby hatch**; ˈ**booby prize**; ˈ**booby trap**
booby-trap ˈbuːb i træp **~ped** t **~ping** ɪŋ **~s** s
boodl|e, B~ ˈbuːd ᵊl **~ed** d **~es, ~e's** z **~ing** ‿ɪŋ
boogaloo ˈbuːg ə luː
booger ˈbʊg ə ˈbuːg- ‖ ᵊr **~s** z
boogie ˈbuːg i ˈbʊg i ‖ ˈbʊg i ˈbuːg i **~d** d **~ing** ɪŋ **~s** z
boogie-woogie ˌbuːg i ˈwuːg i ˌbʊg i ˈwʊg i ‖ ˌbʊg i ˈwʊg i ˌbuːg i ˈwuːg i
boohoo ˌbuː ˈhuː **~ed** d **~ing** ɪŋ **~s** z
boojum ˈbuːdʒ əm
book bʊk §buːk **booked** bʊkt §buːkt **booking** ˈbʊk ɪŋ §ˈbuːk- **books** bʊks §buːks ˈ**book club**; ˈ**book shelf**; ˈ**book ˌtoken**
bookable ˈbʊk əb ᵊl §ˈbuːk-
bookbinder ˈbʊk ˌbaɪnd ə §ˈbuːk- ‖ -ᵊr **~s** z
bookbinder|y ˈbʊk ˌbaɪnd ər‿|i §ˈbuːk- **~ies** iz
bookbinding ˈbʊk ˌbaɪnd ɪŋ §ˈbuːk-
bookcas|e ˈbʊk keɪs §ˈbuːk- **~es** ɪz əz
bookend ˈbʊk end §ˈbuːk-, ˌ·ˈ· **~s** z
Booker, b~ ˈbʊk ə §ˈbuːk- ‖ -ᵊr
Bookham ˈbʊk əm
bookie ˈbʊk i §ˈbuːk- **~s** z
bookish ˈbʊk ɪʃ §ˈbuːk- **~ly** li **~ness** nəs nɪs
bookkeep|er ˈbʊk ˌkiːp |ə §ˈbuːk- ‖ -|ᵊr **~ers** əz ‖ ᵊrz **~ing** ɪŋ
booklet ˈbʊk lət §ˈbuːk-, -lɪt **~s** s
booklover ˈbʊk ˌlʌv ə §ˈbuːk- ‖ -ᵊr **~s** z
bookmaker ˈbʊk ˌmeɪk ə §ˈbuːk- ‖ -ᵊr **~s** z
book|man ˈbʊk| mən §ˈbuːk|-, -mæn **~men** mən men
bookmark ˈbʊk mɑːk §ˈbuːk- ‖ -mɑːrk **~s** s
bookmobile ˈbʊk məʊ ˌbiːl §ˈbuːk- **~s** z
bookplate ˈbʊk pleɪt §ˈbuːk- **~s** s
bookseller ˈbʊk ˌsel ə §ˈbuːk- ‖ -ᵊr **~s** z
book|shelf ˈbʊk |ʃelf §ˈbuːk- **~shelves** ʃelvz
bookshop ˈbʊk ʃɒp §ˈbuːk- ‖ -ʃɑːp **~s** s
bookstall ˈbʊk stɔːl §ˈbuːk- ‖ -stɑːl **~s** z
bookstore ˈbʊk stɔː §ˈbuːk- ‖ -stɔːr -stoʊr **~s** z
bookwork ˈbʊk wɜːk §ˈbuːk- ‖ -wɜ˞ːk
bookworm ˈbʊk wɜːm §ˈbuːk- ‖ -wɜːm **~s** z
Boole buːl
Boolean, b~ ˈbuːl i‿ən **~s** z
boom buːm **boomed** buːmd **booming** ˈbuːm ɪŋ **booms** buːmz ˈ**boom town**
boomer, B~ ˈbuːm ə ‖ -ᵊr **~s** z
boomerang ˈbuːm ə ræŋ **~ed** d **~ing** ɪŋ **~s** z
boomlet ˈbuːm lət -lɪt **~s** s
boomslang ˈbuːm slæŋ **~s** z
boon, Boon buːn **boons** buːnz ˌ**boon comˈpanion**
boondocks ˈbuːn dɒks ‖ -dɑːks
boondoggl|e ˈbuːn ˌdɒg ᵊl ‖ -ˌdɑːg- -ˌdɔːg- **~ed** d **~es** z **~ing** ‿ɪŋ
Boone buːn
boong bʊŋ **boongs** bʊŋz
boonies ˈbuːn iz
boor bʊə bɔː ‖ bʊᵊr bɔːr **boors** bʊəz bɔːz ‖ bʊᵊrz bɔːrz
boorish ˈbʊər ɪʃ ˈbɔːr- ‖ ˈbʊr- ˈbɔːr- **~ly** li **~ness** nəs nɪs
Boosey ˈbuːz i
boost buːst **boosted** ˈbuːst ɪd -əd **boosting** ˈbuːst ɪŋ **boosts** buːsts
booster ˈbuːst ə ‖ -ᵊr **~s** z
boot, Boot buːt **booted** ˈbuːt ɪd -əd ‖ ˈbuːṭ əd **booting** ˈbuːt ɪŋ ‖ ˈbuːṭ ɪŋ **boots, Boots** buːts ˈ**boot camp**
bootable ˈbuːt əb ᵊl ‖ ˈbuːṭ-
bootblack ˈbuːt blæk **~s** s
bootee ˈbuːt iː ₍ₗ₎buː ˈtiː ‖ ₍ₗ₎buː ˈtiː ˈbuːṭ i **~s** z
Bootes, Boötes bəʊ ˈəʊt iːz ‖ boʊ ˈoʊt iːz

B

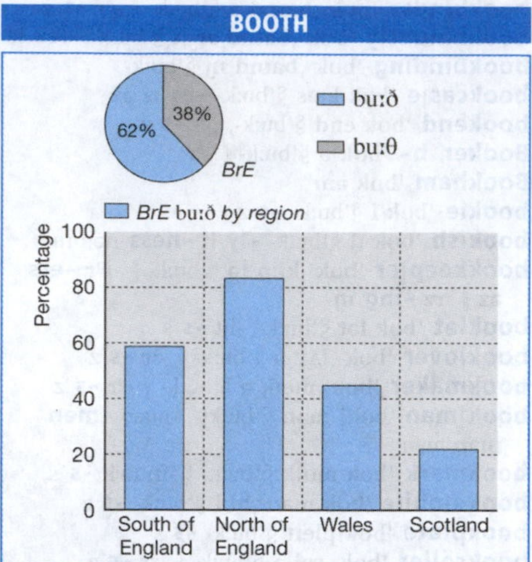

booth, Booth buːð buːθ ‖ buːθ **booths, Booth's** buːðz buːθs ‖ buːθs —*Preference poll, BrE:* buːð *62%,* buːθ *38%*

Bootham 'buːð əm

Boothby 'buːð bi

Boothe buːð buːθ ‖ buːθ

Boothia 'buːθ i‿ə

Boothroyd 'buːθ rɔɪd 'buːð-

bootie 'buːt i ‖ 'buːţ i **~s** z

bootjack 'buːt dʒæk **~s** s

bootlac|e 'buːt leɪs **~es** ɪz əz

Bootle 'buːt ᵊl ‖ 'buːţ ᵊl

bootleg 'buːt leg **~ged** d **~ging** ɪŋ **~s** z

bootlegger 'buːt leg ə ‖ -ᵊr **~s** z

bootless 'buːt ləs -lɪs

Boots *tdmk* buːts

bootstrap 'buːt stræp **~ped** t **~ping** ɪŋ **~s** s

boot|y 'buːt |i ‖ 'buːţ |i **~ies** iz

bootylicious ˌbuːt i 'lɪʃ əs ◂ -ə- ‖ ˌbuːţ-

booze buːz **boozed** buːzd **boozes** 'buːz ɪz -əz **boozing** 'buːz ɪŋ

boozer 'buːz ə ‖ -ᵊr **~s** z

booze-up 'buːz ʌp **~s** z

booz|y 'buːz| i **~ier** i‿ə ‖ i‿ᵊr **~iest** i‿ɪst ‿əst **~ily** ɪ li əl i **~iness** i nəs -nɪs

bop bɒp ‖ bɑːp **bopped** bɒpt ‖ bɑːpt **bopping** 'bɒp ɪŋ ‖ 'bɑːp ɪŋ **bops** bɒps ‖ bɑːps

bo-peep, B~ ₍ˌ₎bəʊ 'piːp ‖ ₍ˌ₎boʊ-

Bophuthatswana ˌbɒp uːt ət 'swɑːn ə ˌu tæt'-; bɒ ˌpuːt ət'-, bəʊ- ‖ ˌboʊ ˌpuːţ ət- -ˌpuːt ɑːt-

bopp... —*see* **bop**

bopper 'bɒp ə ‖ 'bɑːp ᵊr **~s** z

boracic bə 'ræs ɪk bɒ-

borage 'bɒr ɪdʒ 'bʌr- ‖ 'bɔːr- 'bɑːr-

Borat 'bɔːr æt -ɑːt

borate 'bɔːr eɪt -ət, -ɪt ‖ 'boʊr- **~s** s

borax 'bɔːr æks ‖ 'boʊr-

borborygmus ˌbɔːb ə 'rɪg məs ‖ ˌbɔːrb-

Bordeaux ₍ˌ₎bɔː 'dəʊ ◂ ‖ ₍ˌ₎bɔːr 'doʊ —*Fr* [bɔʁ do]
Bor'deaux ˌmixture

Bordelaise, b~ ˌbɔːd ə 'leɪz -ᵊl 'eɪz ‖ ˌbɔːrd- —*Fr* [bɔʁ də lɛːz]

bordello bɔː 'del əʊ ‖ bɔːr 'del oʊ **~s** z

Borden 'bɔːd ᵊn ‖ 'bɔːrd ᵊn

border, B~ 'bɔːd ə ‖ 'bɔːrd ᵊr **~ed** d **bordering** 'bɔːd‿ər ɪŋ ‖ 'bɔːrd‿ər ɪŋ **~s** z
'border ˌterrier

borderer 'bɔːd ər ə ‖ 'bɔːrd ər ᵊr **~s** z

borderland 'bɔːd ə lænd -ᵊl ænd ‖ 'bɔːrd ᵊr- **~s** z

borderline 'bɔːd ə laɪn -ᵊl aɪn ‖ 'bɔːrd ᵊr- **~s** z

bore bɔː ‖ bɔːr boʊr **bored** bɔːd ‖ bɔːrd boʊrd **bores** bɔːz ‖ bɔːrz boʊrz **boring** 'bɔːr ɪŋ ‖ 'boʊr-

boreal 'bɔːr i‿əl ‖ 'boʊr-

borealis ˌbɔːr i 'eɪl ɪs -'ɑːl-, §-əs ‖ -'æl əs ˌboʊr-

Boreas 'bɒr i æs 'bɔːr-, əs ‖ 'bɔːr- 'boʊr-

boredom 'bɔː dəm ‖ 'bɔːr- 'boʊr-

Boreham 'bɔːr əm ‖ 'boʊr-

Borehamwood ˌbɔːr əm 'wʊd ‖ ˌboʊr-

borehole 'bɔː həʊl →-hɒʊl ‖ 'bɔːr hoʊl 'boʊr- **~s** z

borer 'bɔːr ə ‖ -ᵊr 'boʊr- **~s** z

Borg bɔːg ‖ bɔːrg —*Swedish* [bɔrj]

Borges 'bɔːx es 'bɔːg-, -ez ‖ 'bɔːr hes —*Sp* ['boɾ xes]

Borgia 'bɔːdʒ i‿ə 'bɔːʒ-; '-ə ‖ 'bɔːrdʒ- 'bɔːrʒ- —*It* ['bɔr dʒa]

boric 'bɔːr ɪk 'bɒr- ‖ 'boʊr-

Boris 'bɒr ɪs §-əs ‖ 'bɔːr- —*Russ* [bʌ 'rʲis]

Bork bɔːk ‖ bɔːrk

Borland 'bɔː lənd ‖ 'bɔːr-

Borlotti, b~ bɔː 'lɒt i ‖ bɔːr 'lɑːţ i —*It* [bor 'lɔt ti]

Bormann 'bɔː mæn -mən ‖ 'bɔːr- —*Ger* ['boːɐ man]

-born 'bɔːn ◂ ‖ 'bɔːrn ◂ — **free-born** ˌfriː 'bɔːn ◂ ‖ -'bɔːrn ◂

born bɔːn ‖ bɔːrn

born-again ˌbɔːn ə 'gen ◂ -'geɪn ‖ ˌbɔːrn-
ˌborn-aˌgain 'Christian

borne bɔːn ‖ bɔːrn boʊrn

Borneo 'bɔːn i əʊ ‖ 'bɔːrn i oʊ

Bornholm 'bɔːn həʊm -hɒlm ‖ 'bɔːrn hoʊm —*Danish* [bɔʁn 'hɔlʔm]

Borodin 'bɒr ə dɪn ‖ 'bɔːr ə diːn 'bɑːr- —*Russ* [bə rʌ 'dʲin]

Borodino ˌbɒr ə 'diːn əʊ ‖ ˌbɔːr ə 'diːn oʊ ˌbɑːr- —*Russ* [bə rə dʲɪ 'nɔ]

boron 'bɔːr ɒn ‖ -ɑːn 'boʊr-

borough 'bʌr ə ‖ 'bɜː oʊ *(*)* **~s** z

borrow, B~ 'bɒr əʊ ‖ 'bɔːr oʊ 'bɑːr- **~ed** d **~ing** ɪŋ **~s** z

Borrowdale 'bɒr əʊ deɪᵊl ‖ 'bɔːr oʊ- 'bɑːr-

borrower 'bɒr əʊ ə ‖ 'bɔːr oʊ ᵊr 'bɑːr- **~s** z

borsch bɔːʃ ‖ bɔːrʃ

borscht, borshch bɔːʃt bɔːʃtʃ ‖ bɔːrʃt —*Russ* [borɕtɕ]

Borsley 'bɔːz li ‖ 'bɔːrz-

borstal, B~ 'bɔːst ᵊl ‖ 'bɔːrst- **~s** z

bort bɔːt ‖ bɔːrt

Borth bɔːθ ‖ bɔːrθ

orthwick ˈbɔːθ wɪk ‖ ˈbɔːrθ-
orussia bəʊ ˈruːs i‿ə ‖ boʊ- —*Ger* [bo ˈʁʊs i‿a]
orzoi ˈbɔːz ɔɪ ˌbɔː ˈzɔɪ ‖ ˈbɔːrz- **~s** z
osanquet ˈbəʊz ᵊn ket →-ᵊŋ-, -kɪt ‖ ˈboʊz-
oscage ˈbɒsk ɪdʒ ‖ ˈbɑːsk-
oscastle ˈbɒs ˌkɑːs ᵊl -ˌkæs- ‖ ˈbɑːs ˌkæs-
oscawen *(i)* bɒ ˈskəʊ ən bə-, -ˈskɔː- ‖ bɑː ˈskoʊ ən, *(ii)* ˈbɒsk wɪn -§wən, -waɪn, -ə wən ‖ ˈbɑːsk- —*The British family name is usually (i); the place in NH is (ii).*
osch bɒʃ ‖ bɑːʃ bɔːʃ —*Dutch* [bɔs]; *Ger* [bɔʃ]
oscobel ˈbɒsk ə bel ‖ ˈbɑːsk-
ose *(i)* bəʊz ‖ boʊz, *(ii)* bəʊs ‖ boʊs
osh bɒʃ ‖ bɑːʃ
osham ˈbɒz əm ‖ ˈbɑːz- —*There is also a spelling pronunciation* ˈbɒʃ- ‖ ˈbɑːʃ-
osie ˈbəʊz i ‖ ˈboʊz i
oskiness ˈbɒsk i nəs -nɪs ‖ ˈbɑːsk-
osky ˈbɒsk i ‖ ˈbɑːsk i
osley ˈbɒz li ‖ ˈbɑːz-
os'n, bo's'n ˈbəʊs ᵊn ‖ ˈboʊs-
osnia ˈbɒz ni‿ə ‖ ˈbɑːz-
osnian ˈbɒz ni‿ən ‖ ˈbɑːz- **~s** z
osom ˈbʊz əm §ˈbuːz- **~s** z
osomy ˈbʊz əm i ˈbuːz-
oson ˈbəʊs ɒn ˈbəʊz- ‖ ˈboʊs ɑːn ˈboʊz-
Bosphorus ˈbɒsp ər‿əs ˈbɒs fər‿ ‖ ˈbɑːsp- ˈbɑːs fər‿
Bosporus ˈbɒsp ər‿əs ‖ ˈbɑːsp-
oss bɒs ‖ bɔːs bɑːs **bossed** bɒst ‖ bɔːst bɑːst **bosses** ˈbɒs ɪz -əz ‖ ˈbɔːs əz ˈbɑːs- **bossing** ˈbɒs ɪŋ ‖ ˈbɔːs ɪŋ ˈbɑːs-
ˌboss ˈshot
ossa nova ˌbɒs ə ˈnəʊv ə ‖ ˌbɑːs ə ˈnoʊv ə
oss-eyed ˈbɒs aɪd ˌ·ˈ·◂ ‖ ˈbɑːs- ˈbɔːs-
ossi... —*see* **bossy**
Bossom ˈbɒs əm ‖ ˈbɑːs-
boss|y ˈbɒs |i ‖ ˈbɔːs |i ˈbɑːs- **~ier** i‿ə ‖ i‿ᵊr **~iest** i‿ɪst i‿əst **~ily** ɪ li əl i **~iness** i nəs i nɪs
bossy-boots ˈbɒs i buːts ‖ ˈbɔːs- ˈbɑːs-
Bostik *tdmk* ˈbɒst ɪk ‖ ˈbɑːst-
Bostock ˈbɒst ɒk ‖ ˈbɔːst ɑːk ˈbɑːst-
Boston, b~ ˈbɒst ən ‖ ˈbɔːst- ˈbɑːst-
ˌBoston ˈTea ˌParty
bosun ˈbəʊs ᵊn ‖ ˈboʊs- **~s** z
Boswell ˈbɒz wᵊl -wel ‖ ˈbɑːz-
Bosworth ˈbɒz wəθ -wɜːθ ‖ ˈbɑːz wᵊrθ -wɜːθ
ˌBosworth ˈField
bot bɒt ‖ bɑːt **bots** bɒts ‖ bɑːts **botted** ˈbɒt ɪd -əd ‖ ˈbɑːţ- **botting** ˈbɒt ɪŋ ‖ ˈbɑːţ ɪŋ
botanic bə ˈtæn ɪk bɒ- **~al** ᵊl **~ally** ᵊl‿i
botanis... —*see* **botaniz...**
botanist ˈbɒt ən ɪst §-əst ‖ ˈbɑːt ᵊn‿əst **~s** s
botaniz|e ˈbɒt ə naɪz -ᵊn aɪz ‖ ˈbɑːt ᵊn aɪz **~ed** d **~er/s** ə/z ‖ ᵊr/z **~es** ɪz əz **~ing** ɪŋ
botany ˈbɒt ən i ‖ ˈbɑːt ᵊn‿i
ˌBotany ˈBay
botch bɒtʃ ‖ bɑːtʃ **botched** bɒtʃt ‖ bɑːtʃt **botches** ˈbɒtʃ ɪz -əz ‖ ˈbɑːtʃ əz **botching** ˈbɒtʃ ɪŋ ‖ ˈbɑːtʃ ɪŋ
botcher ˈbɒtʃ ə ‖ ˈbɑːtʃ ᵊr **~s** z
botch-up ˈbɒtʃ ʌp ‖ ˈbɑːtʃ- **~s** s
botch|y ˈbɒtʃ |i ‖ ˈbɑːtʃ |i **~ier** i ə ‖ i ᵊr **~iest** i ɪst i əst **~ily** ɪ li əl i
botel ₍ˌ₎bəʊ ˈtel ‖ ₍ˌ₎boʊ- **~s** z
bot|fly ˈbɒt |flaɪ ‖ ˈbɑːt- **~flies** flaɪz
both bəʊθ ‖ boʊθ
Botha ˈbəʊt ə ˈbʊət- ‖ ˈboʊt ə —*Afrikaans* [ˈbʊə ta]
Botham *(i)* ˈbəʊθ əm ‖ ˈboʊθ-, *(ii)* ˈbɒθ əm ‖ ˈbɑːθ- —*The cricketer* Ian B~ *is (i).*
bother ˈbɒð ə ‖ ˈbɑːð ᵊr **~ed** d **bothering** ˈbɒð ər‿ɪŋ ‖ ˈbɑːð ər‿ɪŋ **~s** z
botheration ˌbɒð ə ˈreɪʃ ᵊn ‖ ˌbɑːð-
bothersome ˈbɒð ə səm ‖ ˈbɑːð ᵊr-
bothi... —*see* **bothy**
Bothnia ˈbɒθ ni‿ə ‖ ˈbɑːθ-
Bothwell ˈbɒθ wəl ˈbɒð-, -wel ‖ ˈbɑːθ- ˈbɑːð-
both|y ˈbɒθ |i ‖ ˈbɑːθ |i **~ies** iz
Botley ˈbɒt li ‖ ˈbɑːt-
Botolph ˈbɒt ɒlf ‖ ˈbɑːt ɑːlf
Botox *tdmk* ˈbəʊ tɒks ‖ ˈboʊ tɑːks
botryoid ˈbɒtr i ɔɪd ‖ ˈbɑːtr-
botryoidal ˌbɒtr i ˈɔɪd ᵊl ◂ ‖ ˌbɑːtr-
botrytis bɒ ˈtraɪt ɪs bə-, §-əs ‖ boʊ ˈtraɪţ əs
Botswan|a bɒt ˈswɑːn |ə ‖ bɑːt- —*Tswana* [bʊ ˈtswaː na] **~an/s** ən/z
Bott, bott bɒt ‖ bɑːt
bott... —*see* **bot**
Botticelli ˌbɒt ɪ ˈtʃel i §-ə- ‖ ˌbɑːţ ə- —*It* [bot ti ˈtʃɛl li]
bottl|e ˈbɒt ᵊl ‖ ˈbɑːţ ᵊl **~ed** d **~es** z **~ing** ˌɪŋ
ˈbottle bank; **ˌbottle ˈgreen◂**; **ˈbottle ˌparty**
bottlebrush ˈbɒt ᵊl brʌʃ ‖ ˈbɑːţ- **~es** ɪz əz
bottled-up ˌbɒt ᵊld ˈʌp ◂ ‖ ˌbɑːţ-
bottle-|feed ˈbɒt ᵊl |fiːd ‖ ˈbɑːţ- **~fed** fed **~feeding** fiːd ɪŋ **~feeds** fiːdz
bottleful ˈbɒt ᵊl fʊl ‖ ˈbɑːţ- **~s** z
bottleneck ˈbɒt ᵊl nek ‖ ˈbɑːţ- **~s** s
bottlenose ˈbɒt ᵊl nəʊz ‖ ˈbɑːţ ᵊl noʊz **~d** d
bottler ˈbɒt ᵊl‿ə ‖ ˈbɑːţ ᵊl‿ər **~s** z
bottle-washer ˈbɒt ᵊl ˌwɒʃ ə ‖ ˈbɑːţ ᵊl ˌwɑːʃ ᵊr ˌwɔːʃ- **~s** z
bottom, B~ ˈbɒt əm ‖ ˈbɑːţ- **~ed** d **~ing** ɪŋ **~s** z
ˌbottom ˈdrawer; **ˌbottom ˈline**
Bottome bə ˈtəʊm ‖ -ˈtoʊm
bottomless ˈbɒt əm ləs -lɪs ‖ ˈbɑːţ-
Bottomley ˈbɒt əm li ‖ ˈbɑːţ-
bottommost ˈbɒt əm məʊst ‖ ˈbɑːţ əm moʊst
bottomry ˈbɒt əm ri ‖ ˈbɑːţ-
bottom-up ˌbɒt əm ˈʌp ◂ ‖ ˌbɑːţ-
botulin ˈbɒt jʊl ɪn ˈbɒtʃ əl-, §-ən ‖ ˈbɑːtʃ əl ən
botulinus ˌbɒt ju ˈlaɪn əs ˌbɒtʃ u-, ˌbɒtʃ ə-, -ˈliːn- ‖ ˌbɑːtʃ ə-
botulism ˈbɒt ju ˌlɪz əm ˈbɒtʃ u-, ˈbɒtʃ ə- ‖ ˈbɑːtʃ ə-
bouchee, bouchée ˈbuːʃ eɪ buː ˈʃeɪ ‖ buː ˈʃeɪ —*Fr* [bu ʃe] **~s** z
Boucher *(i)* ˈbaʊtʃ ə ‖ -ᵊr, *(ii)* ˈbuːʃ eɪ ‖ buː ˈʃeɪ
Boucicault ˈbuːs i kəʊ ‖ -kɔːlt -kɑːlt, -koʊ
boucle, bouclé, bouclee, bouclée ˈbuːk leɪ ‖ buː ˈkleɪ
Boudicca ˈbuːd ɪk ə bəʊ ˈdɪk ə ‖ buː ˈdɪk ə

B

Boudin ˈbuːd æ̃ ‖ buː ˈdæn —*Fr* [bu dæ̃]
boudoir ˈbuːd wɑː -wɔː ‖ ˈbuːd wɑːr ˈbʊd- **~s** z
bouffant ˈbuːf ɒ̃ -ɒŋ, -ɒnt ‖ buː ˈfɑːnt ˈbuːf ɑːnt
bougainvillaea, bougainvillea ˌbuːg ən ˈvɪl iˌə ˌbəʊg- ‖ ˌboʊg-, ˌbʊg-, →ˌŋ- **~s** z
Bougainville ˈbuːg ən vɪl →-ŋ- —*in Australian English,* ˈbəʊg- —*Fr* [bu gæ̃ vil]
bough *'branch'* baʊ *(= bow 'bend')* **boughed** baʊd **boughs** baʊz
Bough *name(i)* bɒf ‖ bɔːf bɑːf, *(ii)* baʊ
bought bɔːt ‖ bɑːt
Boughton *(i)* ˈbaʊt ən, *(ii)* ˈbɔːt ən ‖ ˈbɑːt-
bougie ˈbuːʒ iː ˈbuːdʒ-, buː ˈʒiː —*Fr* [bu ʒi] **~s** z
bouillabaisse ˌbuː jə ˈbes -ˈbeɪs, ˈ. . . —*Fr* [bu ja bɛs]
bouillon ˈbuː jɒn ˈbwiː-, -jɒ̃ ‖ ˈbʊl jɑːn —*Fr* [bu jɔ̃]
ˈbouillon cube
Boulby ˈbəʊl bi →ˈbɒʊl- ‖ ˈboʊl-
boulder, B~ ˈbəʊld ə →ˈbɒʊld- ‖ ˈboʊld ər *(= bolder)* **~s** z
ˈboulder clay
boule *'council in ancient Athens'* ˈbuːl eɪ ˈbaʊl-, -iː
boule *'gem'* buːl **boules** *'gems'* buːlz
boules *game* buːl —*Fr* [bul]
boulevard ˈbuːl ə vɑːd ˈbuːl vɑːd, -vɑː ‖ ˈbʊl ə vɑːrd *(*)* **~s** z
boulevardier ₍ˌ₎buːl ˈvɑːd i eɪ ˌbuːl əˈ.- ‖ ˌbʊl ə vɑːr ˈdɪər ˌbuːl-, -ˈdjeɪ **~s** z
Boulez ˈbuːl ez -eɪ ‖ buː ˈlez —*Fr* [bu lɛːz]
Boulogne bu ˈlɔɪn bə- ‖ -ˈloʊn -ˈlɔɪn —*Fr* [bu lɔɲ]
Boult bəʊlt →bɒʊlt ‖ boʊlt
Boulter ˈbəʊlt ə →ˈbɒʊlt- ‖ ˈboʊlt ər
Boulting ˈbəʊlt ɪŋ →ˈbɒʊlt- ‖ ˈboʊlt ɪŋ
Boulton ˈbəʊlt ən →ˈbɒʊlt- ‖ ˈboʊlt ən
bounce baʊnts **bounced** baʊntst **bounces** ˈbaʊnts ɪz -əz **bouncing** ˈbaʊnts ɪŋ
bouncer ˈbaʊnts ə ‖ -ər **~s** z
bounc|y ˈbaʊnts |i **~ier** iˌə ‖ iˌər **~iest** iˌɪst iˌəst **~ily** ɪ li əl i **~iness** i nəs i nɪs
-bound baʊnd — **southbound** ˈsaʊθ baʊnd
bound, Bound baʊnd **bounded** ˈbaʊnd ɪd -əd **bounding** ˈbaʊnd ɪŋ **bounds** baʊndz
ˌbound ˈform
boundar|y ˈbaʊndˌər |i **~ies** iz
ˈboundary ˌlayer
bounden ˈbaʊnd ən
bounder ˈbaʊnd ə ‖ -ər **~s** z
boundless ˈbaʊnd ləs -lɪs **~ly** li **~ness** nəs nɪs
bounteous ˈbaʊnt iˌəs ‖ ˈbaʊnt̬- **~ly** li **~ness** nəs nɪs
bounti... —*see* **bounty**
bountiful ˈbaʊnt ɪf əl -əf-; -ɪ fʊl, -ə- ‖ ˈbaʊnt̬- **~ly** i **~ness** nəs nɪs
bount|y, B~ ˈbaʊnt |i ‖ ˈbaʊnt̬ |i **~ies** iz
ˈbounty ˌhunter

BOUQUET

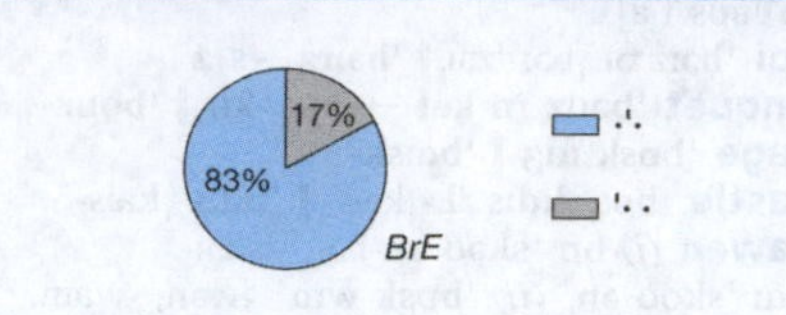

bouquet bu ˈkeɪ bəʊ-, ˈbuːk eɪ ‖ boʊ- — *Preference poll, BrE:* ·ˈ· *83%,* ˈ· · *17%. Some people say* bu- *for the aroma,* bəʊ- ‖ boʊ- *for the flowers.* **~s** z
bouˌquet garˈni gɑː ˈniː ‖ gɑːr-, ˌ· ·-
bourbon *drink* ˈbɜːb ən ˈbʊəb- ‖ ˈbɜːb- **~s** z
Bourbon *dynasty* ˈbʊəb ən ˈbɔːb-, -ɒn ‖ ˈbʊrb ən ˈbɔːrb-, ˈboʊrb- —*Fr* [buʁ bɔ̃] **~s** z —*in French pronounced as the sing.*
bourdon, B~ ˈbʊəd ən ˈbɔːd- ‖ ˈbʊrd- **~s** z
bourgeois, B~ ˈbʊəʒ wɑː ˈbɔːʒ-, ˌ·ˈ· ‖ ˈbʊrʒ-, ˌ·ˈ· —*Fr* [buʁ ʒwa] —*In the noun the plural (spelt identically with the sing.) is pronounced either with* z *or, as in French, identically with the sing. —But the type size is* bɜː ˈdʒɔɪs ‖ bɜː-
bourgeoisie ˌbʊəʒ wɑː ˈziː ˌbɔːʒ- ‖ ˌbʊrʒ- —*Fr* [buʁ ʒwa zi]
Bourke bɜːk ‖ bɜːk
bourn, Bourn, bourne bɔːn bʊən ‖ bɔːrn bʊərn, boʊrn **bourns, bournes** bɔːnz bʊənz ‖ bɔːrnz bʊərnz, boʊrnz
Bourne *(i)* bɔːn ‖ bɔːrn boʊrn, *(ii)* bʊən ‖ bʊərn, *(iii)* bɜːn ‖ bɜːn
Bournemouth ˈbɔːn məθ →ˈbɔːm- ‖ ˈbɔːrn- ˈbʊrn-, ˈboʊrn-
Bournville ˈbɔːn vɪl ‖ ˈbɔːrn- ˈbʊrn-, ˈboʊrn-
Bournvita *tdmk* ˌbɔːn ˈviːt ə ‖ ˌbɔːrn ˈviːt̬ ə ˌbʊrn-, ˌboʊrn-
bourree, bourrée ˈbʊr eɪ ˈbʊər- ‖ bʊ ˈreɪ —*Fr* [bu ʁe] **~s** z
bourse, B~ bʊəs bɔːs ‖ bʊərs **bourses** ˈbʊəs ɪz ˈbɔːs-, -əz ‖ ˈbʊrs əz
Boursin *tdmk* ˈbʊəs æ̃ ˈbɔːs-; bʊə ˈsæ̃, bɔː- ‖ bʊr ˈsæn —*Fr* [buʁ sæ̃]
Bourton ˈbɔːt ən ‖ ˈbɔːrt ən ˈboʊrt-
boustrophedon ˌbuːs trə ˈfiːd ən ˌbaʊs-, -ɒn ‖ -ɑːn
bout baʊt **bouts** baʊts
boutique buː ˈtiːk **~s** s
boutonniere bu ˌtɒn i ˈeə ˌbʊt ɒn ˈjeə, ˌbuːt- ‖ ˌbuːt ən ˈɪər *(*)* **~s** z
Boutros ˈbuːtr ɒs ‖ -oʊs
ˌBoutros ˈGhali ˈgɑːl i
Bouverie ˈbuːv ər i
bouzouki bu ˈzuːk i bə- —*Gk* [bu ˈzu ci] **~s** z
Bovary ˈbəʊv ər i ‖ ˈboʊv- —*Fr* [bo va ʁi]
Bovey *family name (i)* ˈbəʊv i ‖ ˈboʊv i *(ii)* ˈbuːv- *(iii)* ˈbʌv-
Bovey Tracey ˌbʌv i ˈtreɪs i
bovine ˈbəʊv aɪn ‖ ˈboʊv- -iːn **~s** z
Bovingdon ˈbɒv ɪŋ dən ˈbʌv- ‖ ˈbɑːv-
Bovington ˈbɒv ɪŋ tən ‖ ˈbɑːv-
Bovis ˈbəʊv ɪs §-əs ‖ ˈboʊv-

B

ovril *tdmk* 'bɒv rəl -rɪl ‖ 'bɑːv-
ovver 'bɒv ə ‖ 'bɑːv ᵊr **~ed** d
'bovver boots; **'bovver boy**
ow *v 'play a stringed instrument'; 'curve'* bəʊ ‖ boʊ **bowed** bəʊd ‖ boʊd **bowing** 'bəʊ ɪŋ ‖ 'boʊ ɪŋ **bows** bəʊz ‖ boʊz
ow *n ('act of bending'; of boat or ship)* baʊ **bows** baʊz
ow *v 'bend the head/body forward'* baʊ **bowed** baʊd **bowing** 'baʊ ɪŋ **bows** baʊz
ow *n (for arrows, 'knot', for violin)* bəʊ ‖ boʊ **bows** bəʊz ‖ boʊz
ˌbow 'legs
ow *place name* bəʊ ‖ boʊ
owater 'bəʊ ˌwɔːt ə ‖ 'boʊ ˌwɔːt ᵊr -ˌwɑːt-
owden *(i)* 'bəʊd ᵊn ‖ 'boʊd ᵊn, *(ii)* 'baʊd ᵊn
owdler 'baʊd lə ‖ -lᵊr
owdleris... —*see* **bowdleriz...**
owdlerism 'baʊd lər ˌɪz əm ‖ 'boʊd-
owdlerization ˌbaʊd lər aɪ 'zeɪʃ ᵊn -ɪ'-- ‖ -ə 'zeɪʃ- ˌboʊd-
owdleriz|e 'baʊd lə raɪz ‖ 'boʊd- **~ed** d **~er/s** ə/z ‖ ᵊr/z **~es** ɪz əz **~ing** ɪŋ
owdoin, Bowdon 'bəʊd ᵊn ‖ 'boʊd-
owe bəʊ ‖ boʊ
owel 'baʊ‿əl baʊl ‖ 'baʊ‿əl **~s** z
'bowel ˌmovement
owen 'bəʊ ɪn §-ən ‖ 'boʊ-
ower, Bower 'baʊ‿ə ‖ 'baʊ‿ᵊr **~ed** d
bowering 'baʊ‿ər ɪŋ ‖ 'baʊ‿ᵊr ɪŋ **~s** z
owerbird 'baʊ‿ə bɜːd ‖ 'baʊ‿ᵊr bɜːd **~s** z
owers 'baʊ‿əz ‖ 'baʊ‿ᵊrz
owery, b~ 'baʊ‿ər i ‖ 'baʊ‿ᵊr i
owes bəʊz ‖ boʊz
owie *name(i)* 'baʊ i, *(ii)* 'bəʊ i ‖ 'boʊ i, *(iii)* 'buː‿i —*The musician David B~ is (ii). In* **'bowie knife**, *(ii) or (iii)*
owker 'baʊk ə ‖ -ᵊr
owl bəʊl →bɒʊl ‖ boʊl **bowled** bəʊld →bɒʊld ‖ boʊld **bowling** 'bəʊl ɪŋ →'bɒʊl- ‖ 'boʊl ɪŋ **bowls** bəʊlz →bɒʊlz ‖ boʊlz
owland 'bəʊ lənd ‖ 'boʊ-
owlby 'bəʊl bi →'bɒʊl- ‖ 'boʊl-
ow-legged ˌbəʊ 'leg ɪd ◂ -əd, '·ˌ·· ; ˌbəʊ 'legd, '·· ‖ 'boʊ ˌleg əd 'boʊ legd
owler, B~ 'bəʊl ə →'bɒʊl- ‖ 'boʊl ᵊr **~s** z
owles bəʊlz →bɒʊlz ‖ boʊlz
owlful 'bəʊl fʊl →'bɒʊl- ‖ 'boʊl-
owline 'bəʊl ɪn §-ən, §'bəʊ laɪn ‖ 'boʊl- 'boʊ laɪn **~s** z
owling, B~ 'bəʊl ɪŋ →'bɒʊl- ‖ 'boʊl ɪŋ
'bowling ˌalley; **'bowling ˌaverage**; **'bowling green**
bow|man *'archer', B~* 'bəʊ |mən ‖ 'boʊ- **~men** mən men
bow|man *'oarsman'* 'baʊ |mən **~men** mən men
Bown baʊn
Bowness bəʊ 'nes ‖ boʊ-
Bowra 'baʊᵊr ə
Bowring 'baʊᵊr ɪŋ
bowsaw 'bəʊ sɔː ‖ 'boʊ- -sɑː **~s** z
bowser, B~ 'baʊz ə ‖ -ᵊr **~s** z
bowshot 'bəʊ ʃɒt ‖ 'boʊ ʃɑːt
bowsprit 'bəʊ sprɪt ‖ 'boʊ- **~s** s
bowstring 'bəʊ strɪŋ ‖ 'boʊ- **~s** z
bow tie ˌbəʊ 'taɪ ‖ ˌboʊ-
bow window ˌbəʊ 'wɪnd əʊ ‖ ˌboʊ 'wɪnd oʊ
bowwow *interj* ˌbaʊ 'waʊ
bowwow *n* 'baʊ waʊ **~s** z
bowyang 'bəʊ jæŋ ‖ 'boʊ- **~s** z
bowyer, B~ 'bəʊ jə ‖ 'boʊ jᵊr
box, Box bɒks ‖ bɑːks **boxed** bɒkst ‖ bɑːkst **boxes** 'bɒks ɪz -əz ‖ 'bɑːks əz **boxing** 'bɒks ɪŋ ‖ 'bɑːks ɪŋ
ˌBox and 'Cox; **'box ˌcamera**; **ˌbox end 'wrench**; **'box ˌjunction**; **'box ˌnumber**
boxcar 'bɒks kɑː ‖ 'bɑːks kɑːr **~s** z
boxer, Boxer 'bɒks ə ‖ 'bɑːks ᵊr **~s** z
boxercise 'bɒks ə saɪz ‖ 'bɑːks ᵊr-
boxful 'bɒks fʊl ‖ 'bɑːks- **~s** z
boxing 'bɒks ɪŋ ‖ 'bɑːks-
'Boxing Day; **'boxing gloves**; **'boxing ring**
box-offic|e 'bɒks ˌɒf ɪs §-əs ‖ 'bɑːks ˌɑːf əs -ˌɔːf- **~es** ɪz əz
boxroom 'bɒks ruːm -rʊm ‖ 'bɑːks- **~s** z
boxwood 'bɒks wʊd ‖ 'bɑːks-
boxy 'bɒks i ‖ 'bɑːks i
-boy bɔɪ — **schoolboy** 'skuːl bɔɪ
boy, Boy bɔɪ **boys** bɔɪz
ˌboy 'scout ‖ '· ·
boyar 'bɔɪ ə -ɑː; 'bəʊ jɑː, ·'· ‖ boʊ 'jɑːr 'bɔɪ ᵊr **~s** z
Boyce bɔɪs
boy|cott, B~ 'bɔɪ |kɒt -kət ‖ -|kɑːt **~cotted** kɒt ɪd kət-, -əd ‖ kɑːt̬ əd **~cotting** kɒt ɪŋ kət- ‖ kɑːt̬ ɪŋ **~cotts** kɒts kəts ‖ kɑːts
Boyd bɔɪd
boyfriend 'bɔɪ frend **~s** z
boyhood 'bɔɪ hʊd
boyish 'bɔɪ ɪʃ **~ly** li **~ness** nəs nɪs
Boyle bɔɪᵊl
Boyne bɔɪn
boyo 'bɔɪ əʊ ‖ -oʊ **~s** z
boysenberr|y 'bɔɪz ᵊn bər‿|i →'·ᵊm-, -ˌber |i ‖ -ˌber |i **~ies** iz
Boyson 'bɔɪs ᵊn
Boyzone 'bɔɪ zəʊn ‖ -zoʊn
Boz bɒz ‖ bɑːz —*Dickens apparently pronounced* bəʊz
bozo 'bəʊz əʊ ‖ 'boʊz oʊ **~s** z
BP ˌbiː 'piː
BPhil ˌbiː 'fɪl
BR ˌbiː 'ɑː ‖ -'ɑːr
bra brɑː **bras** brɑːz
Brabant brə 'bænt —*Dutch* ['braː bant]*; Fr* [bʁa bɑ̃]
Brabantio brə 'bænt i‿əʊ -'bæntʃ- ‖ oʊ
Brabazon 'bræb əz ən -ə zɒn ‖ -ə zɑːn
Brabham 'bræb əm
Brabin 'breɪb ɪn §-ən
Brabourne 'breɪ bɔːn -bən ‖ -bɔːrn -boʊrn
brace breɪs **braced** breɪst **braces** 'breɪs ɪz -əz **bracing** 'breɪs ɪŋ
ˌbrace and 'bit

Bracegirdle ˈbreɪs ˌɡɜːd əl ‖ -ˌɡɜːd-
bracelet ˈbreɪs lət -lɪt **~s** s
bracer ˈbreɪs ə ‖ -ər **~s** z
bracero, B~ brə ˈseər əʊ braː- ‖ braː ˈser oʊ —*AmSp* [bra ˈse ɾo] **~s** z
brachial ˈbreɪk i‿əl ˈbræk-
brachiate *adj* ˈbreɪk i eɪt ət, ɪt
brachi|ate *v* ˈbreɪk i |eɪt **~ated** eɪt ɪd -əd ‖ eɪţ əd **~ates** eɪts **~ating** eɪt ɪŋ ‖ eɪţ ɪŋ
brachiation ˌbreɪk i ˈeɪʃ ən
brachiopod ˈbreɪk i‿ə pɒd ˈbræk- ‖ -pɑːd **~s** z
brachiosaur|us ˌbreɪk i‿ə ˈsɔːr |əs ˌbræk- **~i** aɪ **~uses** əs ɪz əs əz
brachy- *comb. form*
with stress-neutral suffix ¦bræk i — **brachyglossal** ˌbræk i ˈɡlɒs əl ◂ ‖ -ˈɡlɑːs-
with stress-imposing suffix bræ ˈkɪ+ — **brachylogy** bræ ˈkɪl ədʒ i
brachycephalic ˌbræk i sə ˈfæl ɪk ◂ -sɪˈ-
bracken ˈbræk ən
Brackenbury ˈbræk ən bər‿i →ˈ-əm- ‖ -ˌber i
brack|et ˈbræk |ɪt §-ət ‖ -|ət **~eted** ɪt ɪd §ət-, -əd ‖ əţ əd **~eting** ɪt ɪŋ §ət- ‖ əţ ɪŋ **~ets** ɪts §əts ‖ əts
brackish ˈbræk ɪʃ **~ness** nəs nɪs
Brackley ˈbræk li
Brackman ˈbræk mən
Bracknell ˈbræk nəl
bract brækt **bracts** brækts
bracteole ˈbrækt i əʊl →-ɒʊl ‖ -oʊl **~s** z
brad, Brad bræd **brads** brædz
bradawl ˈbræd ɔːl ‖ -ɑːl **~s** z
Bradbourne ˈbræd bɔːn →ˈbræb- ‖ -bɔːrn -boʊrn
Bradbrook ˈbræd brʊk →ˈbræb-
Bradbury ˈbræd bər‿i →ˈbræb- ‖ -ˌber i
Braddock ˈbræd ək
Braddon ˈbræd ən
Braden ˈbreɪd ən
Bradenton ˈbreɪd ən tən
Bradfield ˈbræd fiːəld
Bradford ˈbræd fəd ‖ -fərd —*in WYks locally also* ˈbræt-
Bradlaugh ˈbræd lɔː ‖ -lɑː
Bradley *(i)* ˈbræd li, *(ii)* ˈbreɪd li
Bradman ˈbræd mən →ˈbræb-
Bradshaw ˈbræd ʃɔː ‖ -ʃɑː
Bradwell ˈbræd wəl -wel
brady- *comb. form* ¦bræd i -ə — **bradycardia** ˌbræd i ˈkɑːd i‿ə ˌ-ə- ‖ -ˈkɑːrd-
Brady ˈbreɪd i
bradykinin ˌbræd ɪ ˈkaɪn ɪn ˌbreɪd-, §-ən
brae breɪ *(= bray)* **braes** breɪz
Braeburn ˈbreɪ bɜːn ‖ -bɜːn
Braemar ˌbreɪ ˈmɑː ◂ ‖ -ˈmɑːr ◂
Braeuisge breɪ ˈwɪsk i
brag bræɡ **bragged** bræɡd **bragging/ly** ˈbræɡ ɪŋ /li **brags** bræɡz
Braganza brə ˈɡænz ə *Port* Bragança [brɐ ˈɣẽ sɐ]
Bragg bræɡ
bragg... —*see* **brag**
braggadocio ˌbræɡ ə ˈdəʊtʃ i‿əʊ -ˈdəʊʃ- ‖ -ˈdoʊʃ i‿oʊ -ˈdoʊs- **~s** z
braggart ˈbræɡ ət -ɑːt ‖ -ərt **~s** s
Brahe ˈbrɑː hə -ə, -hi —*Danish* [ˈbʁaː ə]
Brahma ˈbrɑːm ə —*but as the name of a breed of fowl or cattle, also* ˈbreɪm ə
Brahman ˈbrɑːm ən
Brahmani, Brahmanee brɑː ˈmɑːn i **~s** z
Brahmanic brɑː ˈmæn ɪk
Brahmaputra ˌbrɑːm ə ˈpuːtr ə —*Hindi* [brəhm puʈr]
brahmin, B~ ˈbrɑːm ɪn §-ən **~s** z
Brahminism ˈbrɑːm ɪn ˌɪz əm §-ən-
Brahms brɑːmz —*Ger* [bʁaːms]
Brahui brɑː ˈhuː‿i
braid, Braid breɪd **braided** ˈbreɪd ɪd -əd **braiding** ˈbreɪd ɪŋ **braids** breɪdz
braider ˈbreɪd ə ‖ -ər **~s** z
brail breɪəl **brailed** breɪəld **brailing** ˈbreɪəl ɪŋ **brails** breɪəlz
braille, B~ breɪəl —*Fr* [bʁaj]
brailler ˈbreɪəl ə ‖ -ər **~s** z
brain, Brain breɪn **brained** breɪnd **braining** ˈbreɪn ɪŋ **brains** breɪnz
ˈbrain ˌdamage; **ˈbrain drain**; **ˈbrain(s) trust**
brainbox ˈbreɪn bɒks ‖ -bɑːks **~es** ɪz əz
brain|child ˈbreɪn |tʃaɪəld **~children** tʃɪldr ən
Braine breɪn
brainfart ˈbreɪn fɑːt ‖ -fɑːrt **~s** s
braini... —*see* **brainy**
brainiac, B~ ˈbreɪn i æk **~s** s
brainless ˈbreɪn ləs -lɪs **~ly** li **~ness** nəs nɪs
brainpan ˈbreɪn pæn →ˈbreɪm- **~s** z
brainpower ˈbreɪn ˌpaʊ‿ə ‖ -ˌpaʊ‿ər
brainstem ˈbreɪn stem **~s** z
brainstorm ˈbreɪn stɔːm ‖ -stɔːrm **~ed** d **~ing** ɪŋ **~s** z
brainteaser ˈbreɪn ˌtiːz ə ‖ -ər **~s** z
Braintree ˈbreɪn triː ˈbreɪntr i
brainwash ˈbreɪn wɒʃ ‖ -wɔːʃ -wɑːʃ **~ed** t **~es** ɪz əz **~ing/s** ɪŋ/z
brainwave ˈbreɪn weɪv **~s** z
brain|y ˈbreɪn |i **~ier** i‿ə ‖ i‿ər **~iest** i‿ɪst i‿əst **~ily** ɪ li əl i **~iness** i nəs i nɪs
braise breɪz *(= brays)* **braised** breɪzd **braises** ˈbreɪz ɪz -əz **braising** ˈbreɪz ɪŋ
Braithwaite ˈbreɪθ weɪt
brake, Brake breɪk *(= break)* **braked** breɪkt **brakes** breɪks **braking** ˈbreɪk ɪŋ
ˈbrake ˌfluid; **ˈbrake shoe**
brake|man ˈbreɪk |mən **~men** mən men
braless ˈbrɑː ləs -lɪs
Bram bræm
Bramah *(i)* ˈbrɑːm ə, *(ii)* ˈbræm ə
Bramall ˈbræm ɔːl ‖ -ɑːl
Brambell ˈbræm bəl
bramble, B~ ˈbræm bəl **~s** z
brambling ˈbræm blɪŋ **~s** z
Bramhope ˈbræm həʊp ‖ -hoʊp
Bramley ˈbræm li **~s** z
Brammer ˈbræm ə ‖ -ər
Brampton ˈbræmpt ən

ramwell 'bræm wəl -wel
ran bræn
'bran tub
ranagh 'bræn ə
branch bræŋk — **lamellibranch** lə 'mel ɪ bræŋk §-ə-
ranch brɑːntʃ §bræntʃ ‖ bræntʃ **branched** brɑːntʃt §bræntʃt ‖ bræntʃt **branches** 'brɑːntʃ ɪz §'bræntʃ-, -əz ‖ 'bræntʃ əz
branching 'brɑːntʃ ɪŋ §'bræntʃ- ‖ 'bræntʃ ɪŋ
branchi|a 'bræŋk i‿|ə **~ae** iː **~al** əl
brand, Brand brænd **branded** 'brænd ɪd -əd
branding 'brænd ɪŋ **brands, Brand's** brændz
'brand name
Brandeis 'brænd aɪs
Brandenburg 'brænd ən bɜːg →-əm- ‖ -bɜːg —*Ger* ['bʁan dᵊn bʊʁk] **~s** z
ˌBrandenburg Con'certo; **ˌBrandenburg 'Gate**
Brander 'brænd ə ‖ -ᵊr
Brandi 'brænd i
brandi... —*see* **brandy**
brandish 'brænd ɪʃ **~ed** t **~er/s** ə/z ‖ ᵊr/z **~es** ɪz əz **~ing** ɪŋ
brandling 'brænd lɪŋ **~s** z
brand-new ˌbrænd 'njuː ◂ ‖ -'nuː ◂ -'njuː ◂
ˌbrand-new 'clothes
Brando 'brænd əʊ ‖ -oʊ
Brandon 'brænd ən
Brandreth 'brændr ɪθ -əθ, -eθ
Brandt brænt —*Ger* [bʁant]
brand|y, B~ 'brænd |i **~ied** id **~ies** iz **~ying** i ɪŋ
Brangwyn 'bræŋ gwɪn
Braniff 'bræn ɪf §-əf
Branigan, Brannigan 'bræn ɪg ən §-əg-
branks bræŋks
Branksome 'bræŋk səm
Branson 'brænᵗs ᵊn
Branston 'brænᵗst ən
brant, Brant brænt **brants** brænts
Branwell 'bræn wəl -wel
Braque brɑːk bræk —*Fr* [bʁak]
Brasenose 'breɪz nəʊz ‖ -noʊz
brash bræʃ **brasher** 'bræʃ ə ‖ -ᵊr **brashest** 'bræʃ ɪst -əst
Brasher *family name* 'breɪʃ ə ‖ -ᵊr
brash|ly 'bræʃ |li **~ness** nəs nɪs
Brasilia brə 'zɪl i‿ə —*Port* Brasília [brʌ 'zi ljɐ]
brass, Brass brɑːs §bræs ‖ bræs **brassed** brɑːst §bræst ‖ bræst **brasses** 'brɑːs ɪz §'bræs-, -əz ‖ 'bræs əz
ˌbrass 'band; **ˌbrassed 'off**; **ˌbrass 'hat**; **ˌbrass 'knuckles**; **ˌbrass 'tacks**
brassard 'bræs ɑːd ‖ -ɑːrd brə 'sɑːrd **~s** z
brassbound, B~ 'brɑːs baʊnd §'bræs- ‖ 'bræs-
brasserie 'bræs ər i ˌbræs ə 'riː ‖ ˌbræs ə 'riː **~s** z
brassi- —*see* **brassy**
brassica 'bræs ɪk ə **~s** z
brassie 'brɑːs i 'bræs- ‖ 'bræs i **~s** z
brassiere 'bræz i‿ə 'bræs-, -ɪ eə ‖ brə 'zɪᵊr (*) **~s** z
Brassington 'bræs ɪŋ tən
brass-monkey ˌbrɑːs 'mʌŋk i ◂ §ˌbræs- ‖ ˌbræs-
ˌbrass-'monkey ˌweather
Brasso *tdmk* 'brɑːs əʊ §'bræs- ‖ 'bræs oʊ
brass|y 'brɑːs |i §'bræs- ‖ 'bræs |i **~ier** i‿ə ‖ i‿ᵊr **~iest** i‿ɪst i‿əst **~ily** ɪ li əl i **~iness** i nəs i nɪs
Brasted 'breɪst ed -ɪd, -əd
brat bræt **brats** bræts
Bratby 'bræt bi
Bratislava ˌbræt ɪ 'slɑːv ə -ə-, '• • • • ‖ ˌbrɑːt̬- ˌbræt̬- —*Slovak* ['bra tʲi sla va]
bratpack 'bræt pæk
brattish 'bræt ɪʃ ‖ 'bræt̬-
Brattleboro 'bræt ᵊl bər‿ə ‖ 'bræt̬ ᵊl ˌbɜː oʊ
Bratton 'bræt ᵊn
bratty 'bræt i ‖ 'bræt̬ i
bratwurst 'bræt wɜːst 'brɑːt- ‖ 'brɑːt wɜːst —*Ger* B~ ['bʁaːt vʊʁst]
Bratz *tdmk* bræts
Braun *(i)* brɔːn ‖ brɑːn, *(ii)* braʊn —*As a tdmk, (i)*
Braunton 'brɔːnt ən ‖ 'brɔːnt ᵊn 'brɑːnt-
bravado brə 'vɑːd əʊ ‖ -oʊ **~es, ~s** z
brave breɪv **braved** breɪvd **braver** 'breɪv ə ‖ -ᵊr **braves** breɪvz **bravest** 'breɪv ɪst -əst
braving 'breɪv ɪŋ
brave|ly 'breɪv |li **~ness** nəs nɪs
braver|y 'breɪv ər‿|i **~ies** iz
Bravington 'bræv ɪŋ tən
bravo *name for letter B, b* 'brɑːv əʊ ‖ -oʊ
bravo *n 'assassin'* 'brɑːv əʊ ‖ -oʊ **~es, ~s** z
bravo *interj; n 'shout of approval'* ₍ˌ₎brɑː 'vəʊ 'brɑːv əʊ ‖ 'brɑːv oʊ brɑː 'voʊ **~s** z
Bravo 'brɑːv əʊ ‖ -oʊ
bravura brə 'vjʊər ə -'vʊər- ‖ -'vjʊr- -'vʊr-
braw brɔː ‖ brɑː
Brawdy 'brɔːd i ‖ 'brɑːd-
brawl brɔːl ‖ brɑːl **brawled** brɔːld ‖ brɑːld
brawling/ly 'brɔːl ɪŋ /li ‖ 'brɑːl- **brawls** brɔːlz ‖ brɑːlz
brawler 'brɔːl ə ‖ -ᵊr 'brɑːl- **~s** z
brawn brɔːn ‖ brɑːn
brawn|y 'brɔːn |i ‖ 'brɑːn- **~ier** i‿ə ‖ i‿ᵊr **~iest** i‿ɪst i‿əst **~ily** ɪ li əl i **~iness** i nəs i nɪs
Braxton 'brækst ən
bray, Bray breɪ **brayed** breɪd *(= braid)*
braying 'breɪ ɪŋ **brays** breɪz
braze breɪz *(= braise, brays)* **brazed** breɪzd
brazes 'breɪz ɪz -əz **brazing** 'breɪz ɪŋ
brazen 'breɪz ᵊn **~ed** d **~ing** ˌɪŋ **~ly** li **~ness** nəs nɪs **~s** z
brazer 'breɪz ə ‖ -ᵊr **~s** z
brazier, B~ 'breɪz i‿ə 'breɪʒ ə, 'breɪʒ i‿ə ‖ 'breɪʒ ᵊr **~s** z
Brazil *country,* **b~** *'nut', 'wood', 'dye'* brə 'zɪl
Bra'zil nut
Brazil *family name(i)* 'bræz ᵊl -ɪl, *(ii)* brə 'zɪl
Brazilian brə 'zɪl i‿ən **~s** z

Brazzaville 'bræz ə vɪl 'brɑːz- —*Fr* [bʁa za vil]
Brčko 'bɜːtʃ kəʊ ‖ 'bɝːtʃ koʊ —*S-Cr* ['br̩tʃ kɔː]
breach, B~ briːtʃ *(= breech)* **breached** briːtʃt **breaches** 'briːtʃ ɪz -əz **breaching** 'briːtʃ ɪŋ
bread bred *(= bred)* **breaded** 'bred ɪd -əd **breading** 'bred ɪŋ **breads** bredz **'bread bin**; **'bread box**; **ˌbread 'pudding**; **ˌbread 'sauce**
Breadalbane brə 'dɔːlb ɪn brɪ-, -'dælb-, -ən ‖ -'dɑːlb-
bread-and-butter ˌbred ən 'bʌt ə ◂ →-əm-, →ˌbreb m- ‖ -'bʌţ ər ◂ **ˌbread-and'butter ˌissues**
breadbasket 'bred ˌbɑːsk ɪt →'breb-, §-ˌbæsk-, §-ət ‖ -ˌbæsk ət **~s** s
breadboard 'bred bɔːd →'breb- ‖ -bɔːrd -boʊrd **~s** z
breadcrumb 'bred krʌm →'breg- **~s** z
breadfruit 'bred fruːt **~s** s
bread|knife 'bred| naɪf **~knives** naɪvz
breadline 'bred laɪn **~s** z
breadnut 'bred nʌt **~s** s
breadth bredθ bretθ, §breθ **breadths** bredθs bretθs, §breθs
breadth|ways 'bredθ |weɪz 'bretθ-, §'breθ- **~wise** waɪz
breadwinner 'bred ˌwɪn ə ‖ -ər **~s** z
break breɪk *(= brake)* **breaking** 'breɪk ɪŋ **breaks** breɪks **broke** brəʊk ‖ broʊk **broken** 'brəʊk ən ‖ 'broʊk ən
breakable 'breɪk əb əl **~s** z
breakag|e 'breɪk ɪdʒ **~es** ɪz əz
breakaway 'breɪk ə ˌweɪ **~s** z
breakbeat 'breɪk biːt
breakdanc|e 'breɪk dɑːnts §-dænts ‖ -dænts **~ed** t **~er/s** ə/z ‖ ər/z **~es** ɪz əz **~ing** ɪŋ
breakdown 'breɪk daʊn **~s** z
breaker 'breɪk ə ‖ -ər **~s** z
break-even, breakeven ˌbreɪk 'iːv ən '.ˌ. .
breakfast 'brek fəst §'breɪk- **~ed** ɪd əd **~er/s** ə/z ‖ ər/z **~ing** ɪŋ **~s** s
breakfront 'breɪk frʌnt
break-in 'breɪk ɪn **~s** z
breaking 'breɪk ɪŋ **ˌbreaking and 'entering**; **'breaking point**
breakneck 'breɪk nek
breakout 'breɪk aʊt **~s** s
breakpoint 'breɪk pɔɪnt **~s** s
Breakspear 'breɪk spɪə ‖ -spɪr
breakthrough 'breɪk θruː **~s** z
breakup 'breɪk ʌp **~s** s
breakwater 'breɪk ˌwɔːt ə ‖ -ˌwɔːţ ər ˌwɑːţ- **~s** z
bream, Bream briːm
Brean briːn
Brearley 'brɪə li ‖ 'brɪr-
breast brest **breasted** 'brest ɪd -əd **breasting** 'brest ɪŋ **breasts** brests
breastbone 'brest bəʊn ‖ -boʊn **~s** z
breast-|feed 'brest |fiːd **~fed** fed **~feeding** fiːd ɪŋ **~feeds** fiːdz
breastplate 'brest pleɪt **~s** s
breaststroke 'brest strəʊk ‖ -stroʊk
breastwork 'brest wɜːk ‖ -wɝːk **~s** s
breath breθ **breaths** breθs *(!)* **'breath test**
breathable 'briːð əb əl
breathalys|e, breathalyz|e 'breθ ə laɪz →-əl aɪz **~ed** d **~er/s** *tdmk* ə/z ‖ -ər/z **~es** ɪz əz **~ing** ɪŋ
breathe briːð **breathed** briːðd *(!)* **breathes** briːðz *(!)* **breathing** 'briːð ɪŋ
breathed *past and pp of* **breathe** briːðd
breathed *adj 'having breath; voiceless'* breθt briːðd
breather 'briːð ə ‖ -ər **~s** z
breathi... —*see* **breathy**
breathing 'briːð ɪŋ **'breathing space**
breathless 'breθ ləs lɪs **~ly** li **~ness** nəs nɪs
breathtaking 'breθ ˌteɪk ɪŋ **~ly** li
breath|y 'breθ |i **~ier** i‿ə ‖ i‿ər **~iest** i‿ɪst i‿əst **~ily** ɪ li əl i **~iness** i nəs i nɪs
breathy-voiced ˌbreθ i 'vɔɪst ◂
Brebner 'breb nə ‖ -nər
breccia 'bretʃ i‿ə 'bretʃ ə
brecciated 'bretʃ i eɪt ɪd -əd ‖ -eɪţ-
Brechin 'briːk ɪn 'briːx-, §-ən
Brecht brext brekt ‖ brekt —*Ger* [bʁɛçt]
Brechtian 'brext i‿ən 'brekt- ‖ 'brekt- **~s** z
Breckenridge 'brek ən rɪdʒ →-ŋ-
Breckland 'brek lənd -lænd
Brecknock 'brek nɒk -nək ‖ -nɑːk -nək
Brecon 'brek ən
bred bred *(= bread)*
Breda 'briːd ə 'breɪd ə, breɪ 'dɑː —*Dutch* [bʁe 'daː, bʁə-]
Bredon 'briːd ən
breech briːtʃ **breeches** *pl of* **breech** 'briːtʃ ɪz -əz **'breeches buoy**
breeches *'trousers'* 'brɪtʃ ɪz 'briːtʃ-, -əz
breeching 'brɪtʃ ɪŋ 'briːtʃ-
breech-load|er 'briːtʃ ˌləʊd |ə ˌ.'. . ‖ -ˌloʊd |ər **~ers** əz ‖ ərz **~ing** ɪŋ
breed briːd **bred** bred **breeding** 'briːd ɪŋ **breeds** briːdz
breeder 'briːd ə ‖ -ər **~s** z
breeding-ground 'briːd ɪŋ graʊnd **~s** z
breeks briːks
Breen briːn
breeze, B~ briːz **breezed** briːzd **breezes** 'briːz ɪz -əz **breezing** 'briːz ɪŋ
breezeblock 'briːz blɒk ‖ -blɑːk **~s** s
breezeway 'briːz weɪ **~s** z
breez|y 'briːz |i **~ier** i‿ə ‖ i‿ər **~iest** i‿ɪst i‿əst **~ily** ɪ li əl i **~iness** i nəs i nɪs
Breitling 'braɪt lɪŋ
Brekkies *tdmk* 'brek iz
Bremen 'breɪm ən 'brem- —*Ger* ['bʁeː mən] —*but the places in the US are* 'briːm ən
Bremerhaven 'breɪm ə hɑːv ən 'brem- ‖ '.ər- —*Ger* [breːm ɐ 'haːf ən]
Bremner 'brem nə ‖ -nər

B

Breaking

When a vowel is followed in the same syllable by r or l, a glide sound ə may develop before the liquid. The vowel then becomes a diphthong, and is said to undergo **breaking**.

Two types of breaking are particularly frequent in English, and are shown explicitly in this dictionary:

- **feel** fiːəl Besides the traditional pronunciation fiːl, the form fiːəl (or fɪəl) is often to be heard, especially in BrE. This happens when l follows iː, eɪ, aɪ, ɔɪ, and is termed **pre-l breaking**. (Some speakers of GenAm have pre-l breaking after uː, oʊ, aʊ, thus **rule** ruːəl. This is *not* shown in this dictionary.)
- **fear** fɪə ‖ fɪər In AmE, the usual pronunciation involves the phoneme ɪ. (Unlike BrE, AmE has no phoneme ɪə.) However, this word may actually sound more like fiər or fiər, especially if said slowly. This is due to **pre-r breaking**, which arises in GenAm when r follows ɪ, e, æ.

Both kinds of breaking are particularly common in the last syllable of a stressed word (including words of one syllable).

Bren bren
ˈBren gun
Brend brend
Brenda ˈbrend ə
Brendan ˈbrend ən
Brennan ˈbren ən
Brenner ˈbren ə ‖ -ər —*Ger* [ˈbʁɛn ɐ]
ˌBrenner ˈPass
Brent, brent brent
Brentford ˈbrent fəd ‖ -fərd
Brenton ˈbrent ən
Brentwood ˈbrent wʊd
bre'r, br'er breə brɜː ‖ brɜːr brer
Brereton *(i)* ˈbrɪət ən ‖ ˈbrɪrt ən, *(ii)* ˈbreət ən ‖ ˈbrert ən
bresaola bre ˈsaʊl ə —*It* [bre ˈsa o la]
Brescia ˈbreʃ i‿ə ˈbreʃ ə —*It* [ˈbreʃ ʃa]
Brest brest —*Fr* [bʁɛst]
Brest-Litovsk ˌbrest lɪ ˈtɒfsk -ˈtɒvsk ‖ -ˈtɔːfsk -ˈtɑːfsk, -ˈtoʊfsk —*Russ* [ˌbrʲest lʲɪ ˈtofsk]
brethren ˈbreð rən -rɪn
Breton ˈbret ɒn -ən, -ɒ̃ ‖ -ən —*Fr* [bʁə tɔ̃] **~s** z
Brett bret
Bretton ˈbret ən
Breughel ˈbrɔɪg əl ˈbrɜːg- ‖ ˈbruːg- —*Dutch* [ˈbrøː xəl] **~s, ~'s** z
breve briːv ‖ brev **breves** briːvz ‖ brevz
brevet ˈbrev ɪt §-ət **~s** s
breviar|y ˈbrev i‿ər |i ˈbriːv-, ˈ·ər |i ‖ -er |i **~ies** iz
brevier brə ˈvɪə brɪ- ‖ -ˈvɪər
brevity ˈbrev ət i -ɪt- ‖ -əţ-
brew bruː **brewed** bruːd *(= brood)* **brewing** ˈbruː‿ɪŋ **brews** bruːz *(= bruise)*
brewer, B~ ˈbruː‿ə ‖ ər **~s, ~'s** z
brewer|y ˈbruː‿ər |i **~ies** iz
brewski ˈbruː ski **~s** z
Brewster ˈbruːst ə ‖ -ər
brew-up ˈbruː ʌp
Brezhnev ˈbreʒ nef —*Russ* [ˈbrʲɛʒ nʲɪf]
Brian ˈbraɪ‿ən —*occasionally also* ˈbriː‿ən
ˌBrian Boˈru bə ˈruː
briar ˈbraɪ‿ə ‖ ˈbraɪ‿ər **~s** z
briarroot ˈbraɪ‿ə ruːt ‖ ˈbraɪ‿ər- -rʊt
bribable ˈbraɪb əb əl
bribe braɪb **bribed** braɪbd **bribes** braɪbz **bribing** ˈbraɪb ɪŋ
briber ˈbraɪb ə ‖ ər **~s** z
briber|y ˈbraɪb ər |i **~ies** iz
bric-a-brac, bric-à-brac ˈbrɪk ə bræk
Brice braɪs
bricht brɪxt —*The StdEng equivalent of this Scots dialect word is* **bright** braɪt
brick brɪk **bricked** brɪkt **bricking** ˈbrɪk ɪŋ **bricks** brɪks
brickbat ˈbrɪk bæt **~s** s
brickfield ˈbrɪk fiːəld **~s** z
brickie ˈbrɪk i **~s** z
bricklay|er ˈbrɪk ˌleɪ |ə ‖ -|ər **~ers** əz ‖ ərz **~ing** ɪŋ
brick-red ˌbrɪk ˈred ◂
brickwork ˈbrɪk wɜːk ‖ -wɜːk **~s** s
brickyard ˈbrɪk jɑːd ‖ -jɑːrd **~s** z
bridal ˈbraɪd əl *(= bridle)*
bride, Bride braɪd **brides** braɪdz
ˈbride price
bridegroom ˈbraɪd gruːm →ˈbraɪg-, -grʊm **~s** z

B

Brideshead 'braɪdz hed
bridesmaid 'braɪdz meɪd **~s** z
bride-to-be ˌbraɪd tə 'biː -tu- **brides-to-be** ˌbraɪdz tə 'biː -tu-
Bridewell, b~ 'braɪd wᵊl -wel
bridge, Bridge brɪdʒ **bridged** brɪdʒd **bridges** 'brɪdʒ ɪz -əz **bridging** 'brɪdʒ ɪŋ **'bridge ˌplayer**
bridgeable 'brɪdʒ əb ᵊl
bridgehead 'brɪdʒ hed **~s** z
Bridgeman 'brɪdʒ mən
Bridgend ˌbrɪdʒ 'end '· · —*The town in Mid Glam is locally* brɪ 'dʒend
Bridgeport 'brɪdʒ pɔːt ‖ -pɔːrt -pourt
Bridger 'brɪdʒ ə ‖ -ᵊr
Bridges 'brɪdʒ ɪz -əz
Bridget 'brɪdʒ ɪt -ət
Bridgetown 'brɪdʒ taʊn —*but in Barbados locally* §-tʌŋ
Bridgewater 'brɪdʒ ˌwɔːt ə ‖ -ˌwɔːt̬ ᵊr -ˌwɑːt̬-
bridgework 'brɪdʒ wɜːk ‖ -wɜ˞ːk **~s** s
bridging 'brɪdʒ ɪŋ
'bridging loan
Bridgman 'brɪdʒ mən
Bridgnorth 'brɪdʒ nɔːθ ‖ -nɔːrθ
Bridgwater 'brɪdʒ ˌwɔːt ə ‖ -ˌwɔːt̬ ᵊr -ˌwɑːt̬-
Bridie, b~ 'braɪd i **~s, ~'s** z
bridl|e, B~ 'braɪd ᵊl **~ed** d **~es** z **~ing** ˌɪŋ
'bridle path
bridleway 'braɪd ᵊl weɪ **~s** z
Bridlington 'brɪd lɪŋ tən
bridoon brɪ 'duːn **~s** z
Bridport 'brɪd pɔːt →'brɪb- ‖ -pɔːrt -pourt
Brie, brie briː —*Fr* [bʁi]
brief briːf **briefed** briːft **briefer** 'briːf ə ‖ -ᵊr **briefest** 'briːf ɪst -əst **briefing** 'briːf ɪŋ **briefs** briːfs
briefcas|e 'briːf keɪs **~es** ɪz əz
brief|ly 'briːf |li **~ness** nəs nɪs
brier 'braɪˌə ‖ 'braɪˌᵊr **~s** z
Brierley, Brierly *(i)* 'braɪˌə li ‖ 'braɪˌᵊr-, *(ii)* 'brɪə li ‖ 'brɪr-
Briers 'braɪˌəz ‖ 'braɪˌᵊrz
brig brɪg **brigs** brɪgz
brigade brɪ 'geɪd brə- **~s** z
brigadier ˌbrɪg ə 'dɪə ◂ ‖ -'dɪᵊr ◂ **~s** z
brigadier-general ˌbrɪg ə ˌdɪə 'dʒen ᵊr əl ‖ -ˌdɪr- **~s** z
Brigadoon ˌbrɪg ə 'duːn
brigalow 'brɪg ə ləʊ ‖ -loʊ
brigand 'brɪg ənd **~s** z
brigandage 'brɪg ənd ɪdʒ
brigantine 'brɪg ən tiːn -taɪn **~s** z
Brigg brɪg
Briggs brɪgz
Brigham 'brɪg əm
Brighouse 'brɪg haʊs
bright, Bright braɪt **brighter** 'braɪt ə ‖ 'braɪt̬ ᵊr **brightest** 'braɪt ɪst -əst ‖ 'braɪt̬ əst **brights** braɪts
ˌ**bright 'lights**; **'Bright's diˌsease**; ˌ**bright 'spark**
brighten 'braɪt ᵊn **~ed** d **~ing** ˌɪŋ **~s** z
bright-eyed ˌbraɪt 'aɪd ◂ ‖ ˌbraɪt̬-
Brightlingsea 'braɪt lɪŋ siː
bright|ly 'braɪt |li **~ness** nəs nɪs
Brighton 'braɪt ᵊn *(= brighten)*
brightwork 'braɪt wɜːk ‖ -wɜ˞ːk
Brigid 'brɪdʒ ɪd §-əd
Briginshaw 'brɪg ɪn ʃɔː ‖ -ʃɑː
Brigitte brɪ 'ʒiːt 'brɪʒ ɪt —*Fr* [bʁi ʒit]
brill, Brill brɪl **brills** brɪlz
brillianc|e 'brɪl jənᵗs 'brɪl iˌənᵗs **~y** i
brilliant 'brɪl jənt 'brɪl iˌənt **~ly** li **~ness** nəs nɪs
brilliantine 'brɪl jən tiːn ˌ· ·'· **~d** d
Brillo *tdmk* 'brɪl əʊ ‖ -oʊ
'Brillo pad
brim brɪm **brimmed** brɪmd **brimming** 'brɪm ɪŋ **brims** brɪmz
Brimble 'brɪm bᵊl
brimful, brimfull ˌbrɪm 'fʊl ◂ '· ·
-brimmed 'brɪmd — **wide-brimmed** ˌwaɪd 'brɪmd ◂
brimstone 'brɪm stəʊn -stən ‖ -stoʊn
Brindisi 'brɪnd ɪz i -əz- —*It* ['brin di zi]
brindle 'brɪnd ᵊl **~d** d
Brindley 'brɪnd li
brine braɪn **brined** braɪnd **brines** braɪnz **brining** 'braɪn ɪŋ
Brinell brɪ 'nel brə-
Bri'nell ˌnumber
bring brɪŋ **bringing** 'brɪŋ ɪŋ **brings** brɪŋz **brought** brɔːt ⚠bɔːt ‖ brɑːt
ˌ**bring-and-'buy sale**
bringer 'brɪŋ ə ‖ -ᵊr **~s** z
brini... —*see* **briny**
brinjal 'brɪndʒ əl -ɔːl
brink, Brink brɪŋk **brinks** brɪŋ*k*s
brinkmanship 'brɪŋk mən ʃɪp
brinksmanship 'brɪŋ*k*s mən ʃɪp
Brinks-Mat *tdmk* ˌbrɪŋ*k*s 'mæt
Brinley 'brɪn li
Brinton 'brɪnt ən ‖ -ᵊn
brin|y 'braɪn |i **~ier** iˌə ‖ iˌᵊr **~iest** iˌɪst iˌəst **~iness** i nəs i nɪs
Bri-Nylon *tdmk* ˌbraɪ 'naɪl ɒn ‖ -ɑːn
brio, Brio 'briː əʊ ‖ -oʊ
brioch|e bri 'ɒʃ -'əʊʃ, '· · ‖ -'oʊʃ —*Fr* [bʁi ɔʃ] **~es** ɪz əz
briolette ˌbriː əʊ 'let ‖ -ə- **~s** s
briony, B~ 'braɪˌən i
briquet, briquette brɪ 'ket **~s** s
Brisbane 'brɪz bən -beɪn
Brisco, Briscoe 'brɪsk əʊ ‖ -oʊ
Briseis braɪ 'siː ɪs §-əs
brisk brɪsk **brisker** 'brɪsk ə ‖ -ᵊr **briskest** 'brɪsk ɪst -əst
brisket 'brɪsk ɪt §-ət
brisk|ly 'brɪsk |li **~ness** nɪs nəs
brisling 'brɪz lɪŋ 'brɪs- **~s** z
bristl|e 'brɪs ᵊl **~ed** d **~es** z **~ing** ˌɪŋ
bristlecone 'brɪs ᵊl kəʊn ‖ -koʊn
bristletail 'brɪs ᵊl teɪᵊl **~s** z
bristl|y 'brɪs ᵊlˌi **~iness** i nəs -nɪs

B

Bristol ˈbrɪst ᵊl
ˌBristol ˈChannel; **ˈBristol ˌfashion**
Bristolian brɪs ˈtəʊl iˌən ‖ -ˈtoʊl- **~s** z
Bristow, Bristowe ˈbrɪst əʊ ‖ -oʊ
Brit, brit brɪt **Brits, brits** brɪts
Britain ˈbrɪt ᵊn **~'s** z
Britannia brɪ ˈtæn jə brə-
Britannic brɪ ˈtæn ɪk brə-
Britax *tdmk* ˈbrɪt æks
britches ˈbrɪtʃ ɪz -əz
Briticism ˈbrɪt ɪ ˌsɪz əm -ə- ‖ ˈbrɪţ- **~s** z
British ˈbrɪt ɪʃ ‖ ˈbrɪţ ɪʃ
ˌBritish ˈEnglish; **ˌBritish ˈIsles**; **ˌBritish ˈSummer Time**
Britisher ˈbrɪt ɪʃ ə ‖ ˈbrɪţ ɪʃ ᵊr **~s** z
Britishness ˈbrɪt ɪʃ nəs -nɪs ‖ ˈbrɪţ-
Britoil *tdmk* ˈbrɪt ɔɪᵊl
Briton ˈbrɪt ᵊn *(= Britain)* **~s** z
Britpop ˈbrɪt pɒp ‖ -pɑːp
Britt brɪt
Brittain, Brittan ˈbrɪt ᵊn
Brittany ˈbrɪt ən i ‖ -ᵊn-
Britten ˈbrɪt ᵊn
brittl|e ˈbrɪt ᵊl ‖ ˈbrɪţ ᵊl **~er** ə ‖ ᵊr **~eness** nəs nɪs **~est** ɪst əst
brittle-star ˈbrɪt ᵊl stɑː ‖ ˈbrɪţ ᵊl stɑːr **~s** z
Britvic *tdmk* ˈbrɪt vɪk
Brix brɪks
Brixham ˈbrɪks əm
Brixton ˈbrɪkst ən
Brize Norton ˌbraɪz ˈnɔːt ᵊn ‖ -ˈnɔːrt-
Brno ˈbɜːn əʊ brə ˈnəʊ ‖ ˈbɝːn oʊ —*Czech* [ˈbr̩ no]
bro brəʊ ‖ broʊ
Bro., bro. —*see* **Brother**
broach brəʊtʃ ‖ broʊtʃ **broached** brəʊtʃt ‖ broʊtʃt **broaches** ˈbrəʊtʃ ɪz -əz ‖ ˈbroʊtʃ əz **broaching** ˈbrəʊtʃ ɪŋ ‖ ˈbroʊtʃ ɪŋ
Broackes brəʊks ‖ broʊks
broad, Broad brɔːd ‖ brɑːd *(!)* **broader** ˈbrɔːd ə ‖ -ᵊr ˈbrɑːd- **broadest** ˈbrɔːd ɪst -əst ‖ ˈbrɑːd- **broads, Broads** brɔːdz ‖ brɑːdz
ˌbroad ˈbeans; **ˈbroad jump**
B-road ˈbiː rəʊd ‖ -roʊd
broadband ˈbrɔːd bænd →ˈbrɔːb- ‖ ˈbrɑːd-
broad-based ˌbrɔːd ˈbeɪst ◂ ‖ ˌbrɑːd-
Broadbent ˈbrɔːd bent →ˈbrɔːb- ‖ ˈbrɑːd-
Broadbridge ˈbrɔːd brɪdʒ →ˈbrɔːb- ‖ ˈbrɑːd-
broadbrush ˈbrɔːd brʌʃ ‖ ˈbrɑːd-
broadcast ˈbrɔːd kɑːst →ˈbrɔːg-, §-kæst ‖ -kæst ˈbrɑːd- **~er/s** ə/z ‖ ᵊr/z **~ing** ɪŋ **~s** s
broadcloth ˈbrɔːd klɒθ →ˈbrɔːg-, -klɔːθ ‖ -klɔːθ ˈbrɑːd-, -klɑːθ
broaden ˈbrɔːd ᵊn ‖ ˈbrɑːd- **~ed** d **~ing** ˌɪŋ **~s** z
Broadhead ˈbrɔːd hed ‖ ˈbrɑːd-
Broadhurst ˈbrɔːd hɜːst ‖ -hɝːst ˈbrɑːd-
broad-leaved ˌbrɔːd ˈliːvd ◂ ‖ ˌbrɑːd-
broadloom ˈbrɔːd luːm ‖ ˈbrɑːd-
broadly ˈbrɔːd li ‖ ˈbrɑːd-
broadminded ˌbrɔːd ˈmaɪnd ɪd ◂ →ˌbrɔːb-, -əd ‖ ˌbrɑːd- **~ly** li **~ness** nəs nɪs
Broadmoor ˈbrɔːd mɔː →ˈbrɔːb-, -mʊə ‖ -mʊr ˈbrɑːd-, -mɔːr
broadness ˈbrɔːd nəs -nɪs ‖ ˈbrɑːd-
Broadribb ˈbrɔːd rɪb ‖ ˈbrɑːd-
broadsheet ˈbrɔːd ʃiːt ‖ ˈbrɑːd- **~s** s
broadside ˈbrɔːd saɪd ‖ ˈbrɑːd- **~s** z
broad-spectrum ˌbrɔːd ˈspek trəm ◂ ‖ ˌbrɑːd-
Broadstairs ˈbrɔːd steəz ‖ -sterz ˈbrɑːd-
broadsword ˈbrɔːd sɔːd ‖ -sɔːrd ˈbrɑːd-, -soʊrd **~s** z
Broadwater ˈbrɔːd ˌwɔːt ə ‖ -ˌwɔːţ ᵊr ˈbrɑːd-, -ˌwɑːţ-
broadway, B~ ˈbrɔːd weɪ ‖ ˈbrɑːd- **~s** z
broadwise ˈbrɔːd waɪz ‖ ˈbrɑːd-
Broadwood ˈbrɔːd wʊd ‖ ˈbrɑːd-
Brobat *tdmk* ˈbrəʊb æt ‖ ˈbroʊb-
Brobdingnag ˈbrɒbd ɪŋ næg ‖ ˈbrɑːbd-
Brobdingnagian ˌbrɒbd ɪŋ ˈnæg iˌən ◂ ‖ ˌbrɑːbd-
Broca ˈbrəʊk ə ‖ ˈbroʊk ə —*Fr* [bʁɔ ka] **~'s** z
brocad|e brə ˈkeɪd brəʊ- ‖ broʊ- **~ed** ɪd əd **~es** z **~ing** ɪŋ
brocatel, brocatelle ˌbrɒk ə ˈtel ‖ ˌbrɑːk-
broccoli ˈbrɒk əl i §-ə laɪ ‖ ˈbrɑːk-
broch brɒk brɒx ‖ brɑːx **brochs** brɒks brɒxs ‖ brɑːxs

BROCHURE

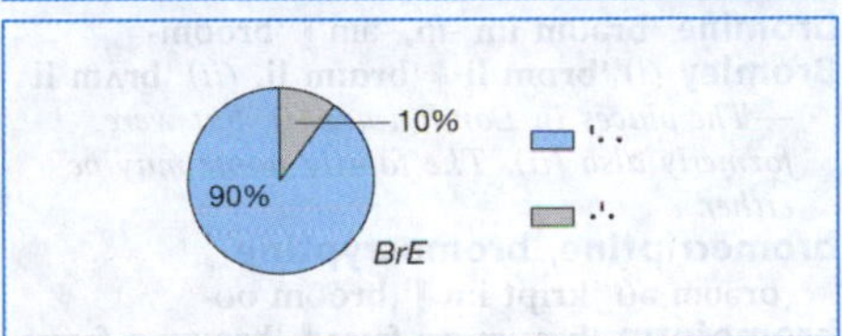

brochure ˈbrəʊʃ ə -ʊə, -jʊə; brɒ ˈʃʊə, brə- ‖ broʊ ˈʃʊᵊr — *Preference poll, BrE:* ˈ· · *90%,* ·ˈ· *10%.* **~s** z
brock, Brock brɒk ‖ brɑːk **brocks, Brock's** brɒks ‖ brɑːks
Brocken ˈbrɒk ən ‖ ˈbrɑːk- —*Ger* [ˈbʁɔk ᵊn]
ˌBrocken ˈspectre
Brockenhurst ˈbrɒk ən hɜːst ‖ ˈbrɑːk ən hɝːst
brocket ˈbrɒk ɪt §-ət ‖ ˈbrɑːk ət **~s** s
Brocklebank ˈbrɒk ᵊl bæŋk ‖ ˈbrɑːk-
Brockley ˈbrɒk li ‖ ˈbrɑːk-
Brockway ˈbrɒk weɪ ‖ ˈbrɑːk-
Brockwell ˈbrɒk wᵊl -wel ‖ ˈbrɑːk-
Broderick ˈbrɒd ˌər ɪk ‖ ˈbrɑːdˌ
broderie anglaise ˌbrəʊd ər i ˈɒŋ gleɪz ˌbrɒd-, -ˈɑːŋ-, -glez, ˌ· · · ˌ(ɪ)ˈ· ‖ ˌbroʊd ə ˌriː ɑːŋ ˈgleɪz —*Fr* [bʁɔd ʁi ɑ̃ glɛːz]
Brodick ˈbrɒd ɪk ‖ ˈbrɑːd-
Brodie, b~ ˈbrəʊd i ‖ ˈbroʊd i
Brodsky ˈbrɒd ski ‖ ˈbrɑːd- —*Russ* [ˈbrɔt skʲɪj]
Broederbond ˈbruːd ə bɒnd ˈbrʊd-, -bɒnt, -bɔːnt ‖ -ᵊr bɑːnt -bɔːnt —*Afrikaans* [ˈbru dər bɔnt]
Brogan, b~ ˈbrəʊg ən ‖ ˈbroʊg-
brogue brəʊg ‖ broʊg **brogues** brəʊgz ‖ broʊgz

broil brɔɪᵊl **broiled** brɔɪᵊld **broiling** ˈbrɔɪᵊl ɪŋ **broils** brɔɪᵊlz

broiler ˈbrɔɪᵊl ə ‖ -ᵊr **~s** z

Brokaw ˈbrəʊk ɔː ‖ ˈbroʊk ɔː -ɑː

broke brəʊk ‖ broʊk

Broke brʊk

broken ˈbrəʊk ən ‖ ˈbroʊk-

ˌBroken ˈHill

broken-down ˌbrəʊk ən ˈdaʊn ◂ ‖ ˌbroʊk-

broken-hearted ˌbrəʊk ən ˈhɑːt ɪd ◂ -əd ‖ ˌbroʊk ən ˈhɑːrt̬ əd ◂

ˌbroken-ˌhearted ˈlover

brokenly ˈbrəʊk ən li ‖ ˈbroʊk-

brok|er ˈbrəʊk |ə ‖ ˈbroʊk |ᵊr **~ering** ər ɪŋ **~ers** əz ‖ ᵊrz

brokerage ˈbrəʊk ər ɪdʒ ‖ ˈbroʊk-

Brolac *tdmk* ˈbrəʊ læk ‖ ˈbroʊ-

broll|y ˈbrɒl |i ‖ ˈbrɑːl |i **~ies** iz

bromate ˈbrəʊm eɪt ‖ ˈbroʊm-

brome brəʊm ‖ broʊm

Brome *(i)* brəʊm ‖ broʊm, *(ii)* bruːm

bromegrass ˈbrəʊm grɑːs §-græs ‖ ˈbroʊm græs

bromeliad brəʊ ˈmiːl i æd ‖ broʊ- **~s** z

Bromfield ˈbrɒm fiːᵊld ‖ ˈbrɑːm-

bromic ˈbrəʊm ɪk ‖ ˈbroʊm-

bromide ˈbrəʊm aɪd ‖ ˈbroʊm- **~s** z

bromidic brəʊ ˈmɪd ɪk ‖ broʊ-

bromine ˈbrəʊm iːn -ɪn, -aɪn ‖ ˈbroʊm-

Bromley *(i)* ˈbrɒm li ‖ ˈbrɑːm li, *(ii)* ˈbrʌm li —*The places in London are (i), but were formerly also (ii). The family name may be either.*

bromocriptine, bromocryptine ˌbrəʊm əʊ ˈkrɪpt iːn ‖ ˌbroʊm oʊ-

bromoform ˈbrəʊm əʊ fɔːm ‖ ˈbroʊm ə fɔːrm

Brompton ˈbrɒmpt ən ˈbrʌmpt- ‖ ˈbrɑːmpt ən

Bromsgrove ˈbrɒmz grəʊv ‖ ˈbrɑːmz groʊv

Bromwich ˈbrɒm ɪtʃ ˈbrʌm-, -ɪdʒ ‖ ˈbrɑːm-

Bromyard ˈbrɒm jɑːd -jəd ‖ ˈbrɑːm jɑːrd

bronc brɒŋk ‖ brɑːŋk **~s** s

bronchi ˈbrɒŋk aɪ -iː ‖ ˈbrɑːŋk-

bronchia ˈbrɒŋk i̯ə ‖ ˈbrɑːŋk-

bronchial ˈbrɒŋk i̯əl ‖ ˈbrɑːŋk-

bronchiole ˈbrɒŋk i əʊl →-ɒʊl ‖ ˈbrɑːŋk i oʊl **~s** z

bronchitic brɒŋ ˈkɪt ɪk brɒn- ‖ brɑːŋ ˈkɪt̬ ɪk brɑːn-

bronchitis (ˌ)brɒŋ ˈkaɪt ɪs (ˌ)brɒn-, §-əs ‖ brɑːŋ ˈkaɪt̬ əs brɑːn-

broncho- *comb. form* *with stress-neutral suffix* ¦brɒŋk əʊ ‖ ¦brɑːŋk ə -oʊ — **bronchogram** ˈbrɒŋk əʊ græm ‖ ˈbrɑːŋk ə- *with stress-imposing suffix* brɒŋ ˈkɒ+ brɒn- ‖ brɑːŋ ˈkɑː+ brɑːn- — **bronchography** brɒŋ ˈkɒg rəf i ‖ brɑːŋ ˈkɑːg-

bronchodilator ˌbrɒŋk əʊ daɪ ˈleɪt ə -dɪˈ--, -dəˈ-- ‖ ˌbrɑːŋk oʊ daɪ ˈleɪt̬ ᵊr -ˈdaɪl eɪt̬ ᵊr **~s** z

bronch|us ˈbrɒŋk |əs ‖ ˈbrɑːŋk- **~i** aɪ iː

bronco ˈbrɒŋk əʊ ‖ ˈbrɑːŋk oʊ **~s** z

Bronski ˈbrɒn ski ‖ ˈbrɑːn-

Bronson ˈbrɒnᵗs ᵊn ‖ ˈbrɑːnᵗs ᵊn

Bronstein ˈbrɒn stiːn ‖ ˈbrɑːn-

Bronte, Brontë ˈbrɒnt i -eɪ ‖ ˈbrɑːnt i -eɪ **~s, ~'s** z

brontosaur ˈbrɒnt ə sɔː ‖ ˈbrɑːnt̬ ə sɔːr

brontosaur|us ˌbrɒnt ə ˈsɔːr |əs ◂ ‖ ˌbrɑːnt̬- **~i** aɪ **~uses** əs ɪz əs əz

Bronwen ˈbrɒn wen -wən, -wɪn ‖ ˈbrɑːn-

Bronx brɒŋks ‖ brɑːŋks

ˌBronx ˈcheer

bronze brɒnz ‖ brɑːnz **bronzed** brɒnzd ‖ brɑːnzd **bronzes** ˈbrɒnz ɪz -əz ‖ ˈbrɑːnz əz **bronzing** ˈbrɒnz ɪŋ ‖ ˈbrɑːnz ɪŋ

ˈBronze Age; ˌbronze ˈmedal

bronzer ˈbrɒnz ə ‖ ˈbrɑːnz ᵊr **~s** z

bronzy ˈbrɒnz i ‖ ˈbrɑːnz i

brooch brəʊtʃ ‖ broʊtʃ bruːtʃ *(!)* **brooches** ˈbrəʊtʃ ɪz -əz ‖ ˈbroʊtʃ əz ˈbruːtʃ-

brood bruːd **brooded** ˈbruːd ɪd -əd **brooding/ly** ˈbruːd ɪŋ /li **broods** bruːdz

brooder ˈbruːd ə ‖ -ᵊr **~s** z

brood|y ˈbruːd |i **~ier** i̯ə ‖ i̯ᵊr **~iest** i̯ɪst i̯əst **~ily** ɪ li əl i **~iness** i nəs i nɪs

brook brʊk §bruːk **brooked** brʊkt §bruːkt **brooking** ˈbrʊk ɪŋ §ˈbruːk- **brooks** brʊks §bruːks

Brook, Brooke brʊk §bruːk

Brookeborough ˈbrʊk bər‿ə

Brookes brʊks §bruːks

Brookfield ˈbrʊk fiːᵊld §ˈbruːk-

Brooking ˈbrʊk ɪŋ §ˈbruːk- **~s** z

Brook|land ˈbrʊk |lənd §ˈbruːk- **~lands** ləndz

brooklime ˈbrʊk laɪm §ˈbruːk- **~s** z

Brookline ˈbrʊk laɪn

Brooklyn ˈbrʊk lɪn -lən

ˌBrooklyn ˈBridge

Brookner ˈbrʊk nə ‖ -nᵊr

Brooks brʊks §bruːks

Brookside ˌbrʊk ˈsaɪd §ˌbruːk-

brookweed ˈbrʊk wiːd

Brookwood ˈbrʊk wʊd

BROOM

8%
92%
bruːm
brʊm
BrE

broom bruːm brʊm — *Preference poll, BrE:* bruːm *92%,* brʊm *8%.* **brooms** bruːmz brʊmz

Broom, Broome bruːm brʊm

Broomfield ˈbrʊm fiːᵊld ˈbruːm-

broomrape ˈbruːm reɪp brʊm- **~s** s

broomstick ˈbruːm stɪk ˈbrʊm- **~s** s

Brophy ˈbrəʊf i ‖ ˈbroʊf i

Bros brɒs brɒz ‖ brɔːs brɑːs *—or see* **Brothers**

brose brəʊz ‖ broʊz

Brosnahan *(i)* ˈbrɒz nə hən ‖ ˈbrɑːz-, *(ii)* ˈbrɒs- ‖ ˈbrɑːs-

Brosnan ˈbrɒz nən ‖ ˈbrɑːz-

B

broth brɒθ brɔːθ ‖ brɔːθ brɑːθ **broths** brɒθs brɔːθs, brɔːðz ‖ brɔːθs brɑːθs

brotha *non-standard variant of* brother 'brʌð ə **~s** z

brothel 'brɒθ ᵊl ‖ 'brɑːθ- 'brɔːθ-, 'brɑːð-, 'brɔːð- **~s** z

brother, B~ 'brʌð ə ‖ -ᵊr **~s** z
 ˌBrother 'Jonathan

brotherhood 'brʌð ə hʊd ‖ -ᵊr- **~s** z

broth|er-in-law 'brʌð |ər_ɪn ˌlɔː 'ə-, ən ˌlɔː ‖ -ˌlɑː **~ers-in-law** əz ɪn ˌlɔː §-ən ˌ· ‖ ᵊrz ən- -ˌlɑː

brother|ly 'brʌð ə |li ‖ -ᵊr- **~liness** li nəs li nɪs

brothers-in-law 'brʌð əz ɪn ˌlɔː §-ən ˌ· ‖ -ᵊrz ən- -ˌlɑː

Brotherton 'brʌð ət ən ‖ -ᵊrt ᵊn

Brough brʌf —*but the place in Highland, Scotland, is* brɒx ‖ brɔːx, brɑːx

brougham 'bruː_əm bruːm **~s** z

Brougham *(i)* brʊm, *(ii)* bruːm, *(iii)* brɔːm ‖ brɑːm, *(iv)* 'bruː_əm, *(v)* 'brəʊ əm ‖ 'broʊ-

brought brɔːt ⚠bɔːt ‖ brɑːt

Broughton *(i)* 'brɔːt ᵊn ‖ 'brɑːt-, *(ii)* 'braʊt ᵊn, *(iii)* 'brʌft ən —*Most places with this name are (i), but the place in Northants is (ii) and places in Wales are (iii).*

brouhaha 'bruː hɑː hɑː ·'·· **~s** z

brow braʊ **brows** braʊz *(= browse)*

brow|beat 'braʊ |biːt **~beaten** biːt ᵊn **~beating** biːt ɪŋ ‖ biːţ ɪŋ **~beats** biːts

brown, Brown braʊn **browned** braʊnd **browner** 'braʊn ə ‖ -ᵊr **brownest** 'braʊn ɪst -əst **browning** 'braʊn ɪŋ **browns** braʊnz
 ˌbrown 'Betty; **ˌbrown 'rat**; **ˌbrown 'rice**; **ˌbrown 'sugar**

brown-bag ˌbraʊn 'bæg **~ging** ɪŋ

Browne braʊn

browned-off ˌbraʊnd 'ɒf ◂ -'ɔːf ◂ ‖ -'ɔːf ◂ -'ɑːf

brownfield 'braʊn fiːᵊld

Brownhills 'braʊn hɪlz

Brownian 'braʊn i_ən

brownie, B~ 'braʊn i **~s** z
 'Brownie Guide; **'brownie point**

Browning, b~ 'braʊn ɪŋ

brownish 'braʊn ɪʃ

Brownjohn 'braʊn dʒɒn ‖ -dʒɑːn

Brownlee, Brownlie 'braʊn li -liː

Brownlow 'braʊn ləʊ ‖ -loʊ

brownness 'braʊn nəs -nɪs

brown-nos|e ˌbraʊn 'nəʊz '·· ‖ -'noʊz **~ed** d **~es** ɪz əz **~ing** ɪŋ

brownout 'braʊn aʊt **~s** s

Brownrigg 'braʊn rɪg

brownshirt, B~ 'braʊn ʃɜːt ‖ -ʃɜ˞ːt **~s** s

brownstone 'braʊn stəʊn ‖ -stoʊn **~s** z

browse braʊz **browsed** braʊzd **browses** 'braʊz ɪz -əz **browsing** 'braʊz ɪŋ

browser 'braʊz ə ‖ -ᵊr **~s** z

Broxbourne 'brɒks bɔːn ‖ 'brɑːks bɔːrn -boʊrn

Broxtowe 'brɒkst əʊ ‖ 'brɑːkst oʊ

brr bə hə hə ‖ bɜ˞ː —*or non-speech sounds, often including the voiced bilabial trill* [ʙ]

Brubeck 'bruː bek

Bruce bruːs

brucellosis ˌbruːs ɪ 'ləʊs ɪs -ə-, §-əs ‖ -'loʊs-

Bruch brʊk —*Ger* [bʁʊx]

Bruckner 'brʊk nə ‖ -nᵊr —*Ger* ['bʁʊk nɐ] —*but as an American name,* 'brʌk-

Bruegel, Brueghel 'brɔɪg ᵊl 'brɜːg-, 'brɜːx- ‖ 'bruːg- —*Dutch* ['brøː xəl]

Bruford 'bruː fəd ‖ -fᵊrd

Bruges bruːʒ bruːdʒ —*Fr* [bʁyːʒ], *Flemish* Brugge ['brʏɣə]

Bruin, bruin 'bruː_ɪn §_ən **~s, ~'s** z

bruise bruːz **bruised** bruːzd **bruises** 'bruːz ɪz -əz **bruising/ly** 'bruːz ɪŋ /li

bruiser 'bruːz ə ‖ -ᵊr **~s** z

bruit bruːt *(= brute)* **bruited** 'bruːt ɪd -əd ‖ 'bruːţ əd **bruiting** 'bruːt ɪŋ ‖ 'bruːţ ɪŋ **bruits** bruːts

Brum brʌm

brumal 'bruːm ᵊl

brum|by, B~ 'brʌm| bi **~bies** biz

Brummagem, b~ 'brʌm ədʒ əm

Brummell 'brʌm ᵊl

Brumm|ie, Brumm|y, b~ 'brʌm |i **~ies** iz

brunch brʌntʃ **brunches** 'brʌntʃ ɪz -əz

Brundisium brʌn 'dɪz i_əm brʊn- ‖ -'dɪʒ-

Brunei 'bruːn aɪ bru 'naɪ

Bruneian bru 'naɪ ən **~s** z

Brunel bru 'nel

brunet, brunette bru 'net **~s** s

Brünnhilde brʊn 'hɪld ə '·,· —*Ger* [bʁʏn 'hɪl də]

Bruno 'bruːn əʊ ‖ -oʊ

Brunson 'brʌnᵗs ᵊn

Brunswick 'brʌnz wɪk

brunt, Brunt brʌnt

Brunton 'brʌnt ən ‖ -ᵊn

bruschetta bru 'sket ə -'ʃet ə —*It* [bru 'sket ta]

brush brʌʃ **brushed** brʌʃt **brushes** 'brʌʃ ɪz -əz **brushing** 'brʌʃ ɪŋ

brushi... —*see* **brushy**

brush-off 'brʌʃ ɒf -ɔːf ‖ -ɔːf -ɑːf

brush-up 'brʌʃ ʌp

brushwood 'brʌʃ wʊd

brushwork 'brʌʃ wɜːk ‖ -wɜ˞ːk

brush|y 'brʌʃ |i **~ier** i_ə ‖ i_ᵊr **~iest** i_ɪst i_əst **~iness** i nəs i nɪs

brusque brʊsk bruːsk, brʌsk ‖ brʌsk

brusque|ly 'brʊsk |li 'bruːsk-, 'brʌsk- ‖ 'brʌsk- **~ness** nəs nɪs

Brussels, b~ 'brʌs ᵊlz —*Fr* Bruxelles [bʁy sɛl], *Dutch* Brussel ['brʏs əl]
 ˌbrussels 'sprouts

brut bruːt —*Fr* [bʁyt]

Brut *tdmk* bruːt

brutal 'bruːt ᵊl ‖ 'bruːţ ᵊl **~ly** i

brutalis... —*see* **brutaliz...**

brutalism 'bruːt ᵊl ˌɪz əm -ə ˌlɪz- ‖ 'bruːţ-

brutalist 'bruːt ᵊl ɪst §-əst ‖ 'bruːţ- **~s** s

brutalit|y bru 'tæl ət |i -ɪt- ‖ -əţ |i **~ies** iz

brutalization ˌbruːt ᵊl aɪ 'zeɪʃ ᵊn -ɪ'-- ‖ ˌbruːţ ᵊl ə-

brutaliz|e ˈbruːt ə laɪz -ᵊl aɪz ‖ ˈbruːt̬ ᵊl aɪz **~ed** d **~es** ɪz əz **~ing** ɪŋ

brute bruːt **brutes** bruːts

brutish ˈbruːt ɪʃ ‖ ˈbruːt̬- **~ly** li **~ness** nəs nɪs

Bruton ˈbruːt ᵊn

Brutus ˈbruːt əs ‖ ˈbruːt̬-

bruxism ˈbrʊks ˌɪz əm ˈbrʌks-

Bryan ˈbraɪ‿ən

Bryant ˈbraɪ‿ənt

Bryce braɪs

Bryden, Brydon ˈbraɪd ᵊn

Brylcreem *tdmk* ˈbrɪl kriːm **~ed** d

Brymon *tdmk* ˈbraɪm ən -ɒn ‖ -ɑːn

Bryn brɪn

Brynley ˈbrɪn li

Bryn Mawr *place in the US* ˌbrɪn ˈmɔː →ˌbrɪm- ‖ -ˈmɑːr

Brynmawr *place in Gwent* brɪn ˈmaʊ‿ə →brɪm- ‖ -ˈmaʊ‿ᵊr —*Welsh* [brin ˈmaur, brɪn-]

Brynmor ˈbrɪn mɔː →ˈbrɪm- ‖ -mɔːr

Brynner ˈbrɪn ə ‖ -ᵊr

bryon|y, B~ ˈbraɪ‿ən |i **~ies** iz

bryophyte ˈbraɪ əʊ faɪt ‖ -ə- **~s** s

bryozoan ˌbraɪ əʊ ˈzəʊ ən ‖ -ə ˈzoʊ- **~s** z

Bryson ˈbraɪs ᵊn

Brythonic brɪ ˈθɒn ɪk brə- ‖ -ˈθɑːn-

Brzezinski brə ˈzɪnˈsk i -ˈʒɪn-

BSc, B.Sc. ˌbiː es ˈsiː

BSE ˌbiː es ˈiː

B-side ˈbiː saɪd **~s** z

BSkyB *tdmk* ˌbiː skaɪ ˈbiː

BST ˌbiː es ˈtiː

BTEC ˌbiː ˈtek ˈ· ·

btw, BTW ₍ˌ₎baɪ ðə ˈweɪ

bub bʌb **bubs** bʌbz

bubal ˈbjuːb ᵊl **~s** z

bubbl|e ˈbʌb ᵊl **~ed** d **~er/s** ‿ə/z ‖ ‿ᵊr/z **~es** z **~ing** ‿ɪŋ

ˌ**bubble and ˈsqueak**; ˈ**bubble bath**; ˈ**bubble ˌchamber**; ˈ**bubble gum**; ˈ**bubble sort**; ˈ**bubble wrap**

bubbl|y ˈbʌb ᵊl|‿i **~ier** ‿i ə ‖ i ᵊr **~iest** ‿i ɪst i əst

Buber ˈbuːb ə ‖ -ᵊr —*Ger* [ˈbuː bɐ]

bubo ˈbjuːb əʊ ˈbuːb- ‖ -oʊ **~s** z

bubonic bju ˈbɒn ɪk bu- ‖ -ˈbɑːn-

buˌ**bonic ˈplague**

buccal ˈbʌk ᵊl *(= buckle)*

buccaneer ˌbʌk ə ˈnɪə ‖ -ˈnɪᵊr **~neered** ˈnɪəd ‖ ˈnɪᵊrd **~neering** ˈnɪər ɪŋ ‖ ˈnɪr ɪŋ **~neers** ˈnɪəz ‖ ˈnɪrz

buccinator ˈbʌks ɪ neɪt ə ˈ·ə- ‖ -neɪt̬ ᵊr **~s** z

Buccleuch bə ˈkluː *(!)*

Bucephalus bju ˈsef əl əs

Buchan ˈbʌk ən ˈbʌx-

Buchanan bju ˈkæn ən bə- —*In Scotland usually* bə-

Bucharest ˌbuːk ə ˈrest ˌbjuːk-, ˌbʊk-, ˌbuːx-, ˈ· · · ‖ ˈbuːk ə rest —*Romanian* București [bu ku reʃ ti]

Buchenwald ˈbuːk ən væld ‖ -wɑːld -wɔːld —*Ger* [ˈbuː xᵊn valt]

Buchman *(i)* ˈbʌk mən, *(ii)* ˈbʊk-

Buchmanism ˈbʌk mən ˌɪz əm ˈbʊk-

buck, Buck bʌk **bucked** bʌkt **bucking** ˈbʌk ɪŋ **bucks** bʌks

buckaroo ˌbʌk ə ˈruː ˈ· · · **~s** z

buckbean ˈbʌk biːn **~s** z

buckboard ˈbʌk bɔːd ‖ -bɔːrd -boʊrd **~s** z

Buckden ˈbʌk dən

bucker ˈbʌk ə ‖ -ᵊr **~s** z

buck|et ˈbʌk |ɪt §-ət ‖ -|ət **~eted** ɪt ɪd §ət-, -əd ‖ ət̬ əd **~eting** ɪt ɪŋ §ət- ‖ ət̬ ɪŋ **~ets** ɪts §əts ‖ əts

ˈ**bucket seat**; ˈ**bucket shop**

bucketful ˈbʌk ɪt fʊl §-ət- **~s** z

buckeye ˈbʌk aɪ **~s** z

Buckfastleigh ˌbʌk fɑːst ˈliː §-fæst- ‖ -fæst-

Buckhurst ˈbʌk hɜːst -ɜːst ‖ -hɜːst

Buckie ˈbʌk i

Buckingham ˈbʌk ɪŋ əm ⚠-ən‿əm, §-hæm **~shire** ʃə ʃɪə ‖ ʃᵊr ʃɪr

ˌ**Buckingham ˈPalace**

buckish ˈbʌk ɪʃ **~ly** li **~ness** nəs nɪs

Buckland ˈbʌk lənd

buckl|e ˈbʌk ᵊl **~ed** d **~es** z **~ing** ‿ɪŋ

buckler, B~ ˈbʌk lə ‖ -lᵊr **~s** z

Buckley ˈbʌk li

buckling ˈbʌk lɪŋ **~s** z

Buckmaster ˈbʌk ˌmɑːst ə §-ˌmæst- ‖ -ˌmæst ᵊr

Buckminster ˈbʌk ˌmɪnˈst ə ‖ ᵊr

Bucknall, Bucknell ˈbʌk nᵊl

buckram ˈbʌk rəm

Bucks, Bucks. bʌks

bucksaw ˈbʌk sɔː ‖ -sɑː **~s** z

buckshee ˌbʌk ˈʃiː ◂ ˈ· · ‖ ˈbʌk ʃiː

buckshot ˈbʌk ʃɒt ‖ -ʃɑːt

buckskin ˈbʌk skɪn

buckteeth ˌbʌk ˈtiːθ

buckthorn ˈbʌk θɔːn ‖ -θɔːrn **~s** z

Buckton ˈbʌkt ən

buck|tooth ˌbʌk |ˈtuːθ §-ˈtʊθ **~teeth** ˈtiːθ

buckwheat ˈbʌk wiːt -hwiːt ‖ -*h*wiːt

buckyball ˈbʌk i bɔːl ‖ -bɑːl **~s** z

bucolic bju ˈkɒl ɪk ‖ -ˈkɑːl- **~ally** ᵊl‿i

Buczacki bu ˈtʃæt ski bju-

bud, Bud bʌd **budded** ˈbʌd ɪd -əd **budding** ˈbʌd ɪŋ **buds** bʌdz

Budapest ˌbjuːd ə ˈpest ◂ ˌbuːd-, ˌbʊd-, ˈ· · · ‖ ˈbuːd ə pest —*Hung* [ˈbu dɒ pɛʃt]

Budd bʌd

budd... —*see* **bud**

Buddha, b~ ˈbʊd ə ‖ ˈbuːd ə —*Hindi* [bʊɖɖʰ] **~s** z

Buddhism ˈbʊd ɪz əm ‖ ˈbuːd-

Buddhist ˈbʊd ɪst §-əst ‖ ˈbuːd-

Buddhistic bu ˈdɪst ɪk

buddi... —*see* **buddy**

Buddig ˈbɪð ɪɡ —*Welsh* [ˈbɨ ðig, ˈbi-]

buddleia ˈbʌd li‿ə bʌd ˈliː‿ə **~s** z

budd|y ˈbʌd |i **~ied** id **~ies** iz **~ying** i‿ɪŋ

buddy-buddy ˌbʌd i ˈbʌd i ˈ· ˌ· ·

Bude bjuːd

budge, Budge bʌdʒ **budged** bʌdʒd **budges** ˈbʌdʒ ɪz -əz **budging** ˈbʌdʒ ɪŋ

budgerigar ˈbʌdʒ ər‿i ɡɑː ‖ -ɡɑːr **~s** z

budg|et, B~ 'bʌdʒ |ɪt §-ət ‖ -|ət **~eted** ɪt ɪd §ət-, -əd ‖ əṭ əd **~eting** ɪt ɪŋ §ət- ‖ əṭ ɪŋ **~ets** ɪts §əts ‖ əts
 'budget acˌcount; **'Budget Day**
budgetary 'bʌdʒ ɪt‿ər i '·ət‿ ‖ -ə ter i
budgie, B~ 'bʌdʒ i **~s** z
Budleigh 'bʌd li
Budweiser *tdmk* 'bʌd waɪz ə ‖ -ᵊr
Buenos Aires ˌbweɪn ɒs 'aɪᵊr iz ˌbwen-, -əs-, -əz-, -'eər-, -iːz, ˌ· ·'eəz ‖ ˌbweɪn əs- —*Spanish* [ˌbwe nos 'ai ɾes], *locally also* [-noh 'ai ɾe]
Buerk bɜːk ‖ bɝːk
buff bʌf **buffed** bʌft **buffing** 'bʌf ɪŋ **buffs** bʌfs
buffalo, B~ 'bʌf ə ləʊ -ᵊl əʊ ‖ -loʊ **~es, ~s** z
 'buffalo grass
buffer 'bʌf ə ‖ -ᵊr **~ed** d **buffering** 'bʌf ər‿ɪŋ **~s** z
 'buffer state; **'buffer stock**; **'buffer zone**
buff|et *v, n 'blow'* 'bʌf |ɪt §-ət ‖ -|ət **~eted** ɪt ɪd ət-, -əd ‖ əṭ əd **~eting/s** ɪt ɪŋ/z ət- ‖ əṭ ɪŋ/z **~ets** ɪts §əts ‖ əts
buffet *n 'meal, sideboard, counter'* 'bʊf eɪ 'bʌf-, -i ‖ bə 'feɪ bu- *(*)*
 'buffet car ‖ ·'· ·
bufflehead 'bʌf ᵊl hed **~ed** ɪd əd **~s** z
buffo 'bʊf əʊ ‖ 'buːf oʊ —*It* ['buf fo]
buffoon bə 'fuːn bʌ- **~s** z
buffooner|y bə 'fuːn ər |i bʌ- **~ies** iz
Buffs bʌfs
bug bʌg **bugged** bʌgd **bugging** 'bʌg ɪŋ **bugs** bʌgz
 ˌBugs 'Bunny
Bug *river* buːg —*Russ, Polish* [buk]
bugaboo 'bʌg ə buː
Buganda bu 'gænd ə
Bugatti bju 'gæt i bu- ‖ -'gɑːṭ-
bugbear 'bʌg beə ‖ -ber **~s** z
bug-eyed ˌbʌg 'aɪd ◂ '· · ‖ '· ·
 ˌbug-eyed 'monster
bugg... —*see* **bug**
bugger 'bʌg ə ‖ -ᵊr **~ed** d **buggering** 'bʌg ər‿ɪŋ **~s** z
bugger-all, bugger all ˌbʌg ər 'ɔːl ◂ ‖ -ər-'ɑːl
buggery 'bʌg ər i
buggi... —*see* **buggy**
Buggins 'bʌg ɪnz §-ənz **~'s** ɪz -əz
 'Buggins'(s) turn
bugg|y 'bʌg |i **~ier** i‿ə ‖ i‿ᵊr **~ies** iz **~iest** i‿ɪst i‿əst **~iness** i nəs i nɪs
bug|house 'bʌg |haʊs **~houses** haʊz ɪz -əz
bugl|e, Bugle 'bjuːg ᵊl **~ed** d **~es** z **~ing** ‿ɪŋ
bugler 'bjuːg lə ‖ -lᵊr **~s** z
bugloss 'bjuː glɒs ‖ -glɑːs -glɔːs **~es** ɪz əz
Bugner *(i)* 'bʌg nə ‖ -nᵊr, *(ii)* 'bʊg-
bugrake 'bʌg reɪk **~s** s
buhl buːl
Buick *tdmk* 'bjuː‿ɪk **~s** s
build bɪld **building** 'bɪld ɪŋ **builds** bɪldz **built** bɪlt
builder 'bɪld ə ‖ -ᵊr **~s** z
building 'bɪld ɪŋ **~s** z
 'building block; **'building soˌciety**
buildup 'bɪld ʌp **~s** s
built bɪlt
Builth bɪlθ
 ˌBuilth 'Wells
built-in ˌbɪlt 'ɪn ◂
 ˌbuilt-in 'cupboards
built-up ˌbɪlt 'ʌp ◂
 ˌbuilt-up 'area
Buist *(i)* bjuːst, *(ii)* 'bjuː‿ɪst
Buitoni *tdmk* bju 'təʊn i ‖ -'toʊn-
Bujumbura ˌbuːdʒ əm 'bʊər ə -ʊm- ‖ -'bʊr-
Bukhara bu 'kɑːr ə -'xɑːr- —*Russ* [bu 'xa rə]
Bukta *tdmk* 'bʌkt ə
Bulawayo ˌbʊl ə 'weɪ əʊ ˌbuːl- ‖ -oʊ —*Ndebele* [ɓu la 'waː jɔ]
bulb bʌlb **bulbs** bʌlbz
bulbar 'bʌlb ə ‖ -ᵊr -ɑːr
bulbil 'bʌlb ɪl §-ᵊl **~s** z
bulbous 'bʌlb əs **~ly** li
bulbul 'bʊl bʊl **~s** z
Bulgar, b~ 'bʌlg ɑː 'bʊlg-, -ə ‖ -ɑːr -ᵊr **~s** z
Bulgari *tdmk* 'bʊlg ər i —*It* ['bul ga ri]
Bulgari|a bʌl 'geər i‿|ə bʊl- ‖ -'ger- -'gær- **~an/s** ən/z
bulge bʌldʒ **bulged** bʌldʒd **bulges** 'bʌldʒ ɪz -əz **bulging** 'bʌldʒ ɪŋ
bulgur 'bʌlg ə ‖ -ᵊr
bulg|y 'bʌldʒ |i **~ier** i‿ə ‖ i‿ᵊr **~iest** i‿ɪst i‿əst **~iness** i nəs i nɪs
bulim|ia bu 'lɪm| i‿ə bju-, bə-, -'liːm|- **~ic** ɪk
bulk bʌlk **bulked** bʌlkt **bulking** 'bʌlk ɪŋ **bulks** bʌlks
bulkhead 'bʌlk hed **~s** z
bulk|y 'bʌlk |i **~ier** i‿ə ‖ i‿ᵊr **~iest** i‿ɪst i‿əst **~ily** ɪ li əl i **~iness** i nəs i nɪs
bull, Bull bʊl **bulls** bʊlz
 ˌbull 'terrier
bull|a 'bʊl |ə 'bʌl- **~ae** iː
bullac|e 'bʊl ɪs -əs **~es** ɪz əz
Bullard *(i)* 'bʊl ɑːd ‖ -ɑːrd, *(ii)* -əd ‖ -ᵊrd
bulldog 'bʊl dɒg ‖ -dɔːg -dɑːg **~s** z
 'bulldog clip
bulldoz|e 'bʊl dəʊz ‖ -doʊz **~ed** d **~es** ɪz əz **~ing** ɪŋ
bulldozer 'bʊl ˌdəʊz ə ‖ -ˌdoʊz ᵊr **~s** z
Bullen 'bʊl ən -ɪn
Buller 'bʊl ə ‖ -ᵊr
bullet 'bʊl ɪt -ət **~s** s
bullet-headed ˌbʊl ɪt 'hed ɪd ◂ -ət-, -əd
bulletin 'bʊl ət ɪn -ɪt-, §-ən ‖ -ᵊn **~s** z
 'bulletin board
bulletproof 'bʊl ɪt pruːf §-ət-, §-prʊf
bullfight 'bʊl faɪt **~s** s
bullfight|er 'bʊl ˌfaɪt |ə ‖ -ˌfaɪṭ |ᵊr **~ers** əz ‖ ᵊrz **~ing** ɪŋ
bullfinch 'bʊl fɪntʃ **~es** ɪz əz
bullfrog 'bʊl frɒg ‖ -frɑːg -frɔːg **~s** z
bullhead 'bʊl hed **~s** z
bullheaded ˌbʊl 'hed ɪd ◂ -əd **~ly** li **~ness** nəs nɪs
bullhorn 'bʊl hɔːn ‖ -hɔːrn **~s** z

B

bulli... —*see* **bully**

bullion 'bʊl i‿ən

bullish 'bʊl ɪʃ **~ly** li **~ness** nəs nɪs

bullnecked ˌbʊl 'nekt ◂

bullnose 'bʊl nəʊz ‖ -noʊz **~d** d

bullock, B~ 'bʊl ək ‖ -ɑːk **~s** s

Bullokar 'bʊl ə kɑː -ək ə ‖ -ə kɑːr -ək ᵊr

Bullough 'bʊl əʊ ‖ -oʊ

bullpen 'bʊl pen **~s** z

bullring 'bʊl rɪŋ **~s** z

bullroarer 'bʊl ˌrɔːr ə ‖ -ᵊr -ˌroʊr- **~s** z

bull's-eye 'bʊlz aɪ **~s** z

bull|shit 'bʊl |ʃɪt **~shitter/s** ʃɪt ə/z ‖ ʃɪt̬ ᵊr/z **~shitting** ʃɪt ɪŋ ‖ ʃɪt̬ ɪŋ **~shits** ʃɪts

bullwhip 'bʊl wɪp -hwɪp ‖ -*h*wɪp **~ped** t **~ping** ɪŋ **~s** s

bull|y 'bʊl |i **~ied** id **~ies** iz **~ying** i‿ɪŋ

ˌbully 'beef, '· · ·

bullyboy 'bʊl i bɔɪ **~s** z

bully-off 'bʊl i ɒf -ɔːf ‖ -ɔːf -ɑːf

bullyrag 'bʊl i ræg **~ged** d **~ging** ɪŋ **~s** z

Bulmer 'bʊlm ə ‖ -ᵊr

Bulow, Bülow 'bjuːl əʊ ‖ -oʊ —*Ger* ['byː lo]

bulrush 'bʊl rʌʃ **~es** ɪz əz

Bulstrode *(i)* 'bʊl strəʊd ‖ -stroʊd, *(ii)* 'bʌl-

Bultitude 'bʌlt ɪ tjuːd -ə-, →-tʃuːd ‖ -tuːd -tjuːd

bulwark 'bʊl wək 'bʌl-, -wɜːk ‖ -wᵊrk **~s** s

Bulwer 'bʊl wə ‖ -wᵊr

bum bʌm **bummed** bʌmd **bumming** 'bʌm ɪŋ **bums** bʌmz

ˌbum's 'rush

bumbag 'bʌm bæg **~s** z

bumbl|e 'bʌm bᵊl **~ed** d **~es** z **~ing/ly** ‿ɪŋ /li

bumblebee 'bʌm bᵊl biː **~s** z

bumbledom 'bʌm bᵊl dəm

bumble-puppy 'bʌm bᵊl ˌpʌp i

bumbler 'bʌm blə ‖ ᵊr **~s** z

bumboat 'bʌm bəʊt ‖ -boʊt **~s** s

bumf bʌmᵖf

bumfuzzled bʌm 'fʌz ᵊld

Bumiputra ˌbuːm ɪ 'puːtr ə

bummalo 'bʌm ə ləʊ ‖ -loʊ

bummaree ˌbʌm ə 'riː '· · · **~s** z

bummer 'bʌm ə ‖ -ᵊr **~s** z

bump bʌmp **bumped** bʌm*p*t **bumping** 'bʌmp ɪŋ **bumps** bʌm*p*s

ˌbump 'start

bumper 'bʌmp ə ‖ -ᵊr **~s** z

bumper-to-bumper ˌbʌmp ə tə 'bʌmp ə ◂ ‖ -ᵊr tə 'bʌmp ᵊr ◂

bumph bʌmᵖf

bumpi... —*see* **bumpy**

bumpkin 'bʌm*p* kɪn **~s** z

bumptious 'bʌm*p* ʃəs **~ly** li **~ness** nəs nɪs

Bumpus 'bʌmp əs

bump|y 'bʌmp |i **~ier** i‿ə ‖ i‿ᵊr **~iest** i‿ɪst i‿əst **~ily** ɪ li əl i **~iness** i nəs i nɪs

bun bʌn **buns** bʌnz

Buna *tdmk* 'buːn ə 'bjuːn-

Bunbury 'bʌn bər‿i →'bʌm- **~ed** d **~ing** ɪŋ **~ish** ɪʃ **~ist/s** ɪst/s §əst/s

bunch, Bunch bʌntʃ **bunched** bʌn*t*ʃt **bunches** 'bʌn*t*ʃ ɪz -əz **bunching** 'bʌn*t*ʃ ɪŋ

Bunche bʌntʃ

bunco 'bʌŋk əʊ ‖ -oʊ **~ed** d **~ing** ɪŋ **~s** z

Buncombe 'bʌŋk əm

bund, Bund bʌnd **bunds** bʌndz

Bundes|bank 'bʊnd əz |bæŋk 'bʌnd- —*Ger* ['bʊn dəs |baŋk] **~rat** rɑːt —*Ger* [ʁaːt] **~tag** tɑːg —*Ger* [taːk] **~wehr** veə ‖ -ver —*Ger* [veːɐ]

bundl|e 'bʌnd ᵊl **~ed** d **~es** z **~ing** ‿ɪŋ

Bundy 'bʌnd i

bunfight 'bʌn faɪt **~s** s

bung bʌŋ **bunged** bʌŋd **bunging** 'bʌŋ ɪŋ **bungs** bʌŋz

bungalow 'bʌŋ gə ləʊ ‖ -loʊ **~s** z

Bungay 'bʌŋ gi

bungee 'bʌndʒ i -iː

'bungee ˌjumping

bunghole 'bʌŋ həʊl →-hɒʊl ‖ -hoʊl **~s** z

bungl|e 'bʌŋ gᵊl **~ed** d **~er/s** ‿ə/z ‖ ᵊr/z **~es** z **~ing/ly** ‿ɪŋ /li

bunion 'bʌn jən **~s** z

bunk bʌŋk **bunked** bʌŋkt **bunking** 'bʌŋk ɪŋ **bunks** bʌŋks

bunker, B~ 'bʌŋk ə ‖ -ᵊr **~ed** d **bunkering** 'bʌŋk ər‿ɪŋ **~s** z

bunk|house 'bʌŋk |haʊs **~houses** haʊz ɪz -əz

bunko 'bʌŋk əʊ ‖ -oʊ **~ed** d **~ing** ɪŋ **~s** z

bunkum 'bʌŋk əm

bunk-up 'bʌŋk ʌp

bunn|y, Bunny 'bʌn |i **~ies** iz

'bunny girl

bunraku bʊn 'rɑːk uː ‖ bɑːn- —*Jp* ['bɯn ɾa kɯ]

bunsen, B~ 'bʌnᵗs ᵊn —*Ger* ['bʊn zᵊn] **~s** z

ˌBunsen 'burner ‖ '· · ˌ· ·

bunt bʌnt **bunted** 'bʌnt ɪd -əd ‖ 'bʌnt̬ əd **bunting** 'bʌnt ɪŋ ‖ 'bʌnt̬ ɪŋ **bunts** bʌnts

Bunter 'bʌnt ə ‖ 'bʌnt̬ ᵊr

bunting, B~ 'bʌnt ɪŋ ‖ 'bʌnt̬ ɪŋ **~s** z

Bunty 'bʌnt i

Buñuel 'buːn ju el ˌ· '· ‖ ˌbuːn 'wel —*Sp* [bu 'ɲwel]

bunya 'bʌn jə **~s** z

Bunyan 'bʌn jən

Bunyanesque ˌbʌn jə 'nesk ◂

bunyip 'bʌn jɪp **~s** s

buoy bɔɪ ‖ 'buː‿i bɔɪ *(in BrE = boy)* **buoyed** bɔɪd ‖ 'buː‿id bɔɪd **buoying** 'bɔɪ ɪŋ ‖ 'buː‿i ɪŋ 'bɔɪ ɪŋ **buoys** bɔɪz ‖ 'buː‿iz bɔɪz

buoyancy 'bɔɪ ənᵗs i ‖ 'buː jənᵗs i

buoyant 'bɔɪ ənt ‖ 'buː jənt **~ly** li

BUPA 'buːp ə 'bjuːp-

bur bɜː ‖ bɜ˞ː **burs** bɜːz ‖ bɜ˞ːz

Burbage 'bɜːb ɪdʒ ‖ 'bɜ˞ːb-

Burbank 'bɜː bæŋk ‖ 'bɜ˞ː-

Burberr|y 'bɜː bər‿|i ‖ 'bɜ˞ː- -ˌber |i **~ies** iz

burbl|e 'bɜːb ᵊl ‖ 'bɜ˞ːb- **~ed** d **~es** z **~ing** ‿ɪŋ

burbot 'bɜːb ət ‖ 'bɜ˞ːb- **~s** s

burbs bɜːbz ‖ bɜ˞ːbz

Burbury 'bɜː bər‿i ‖ 'bɜ˞ː- -ˌber i

Burch bɜːtʃ ‖ bɜ˞ːtʃ

Burchell 'bɜːtʃ əl ‖ 'bɜ˞ːtʃ-

Burcher 'bɜːtʃ ə ‖ 'bɜ˞ːtʃ ᵊr

B

Burchill 'bɜːtʃ əl -ɪl ‖ 'bɜ˞ːtʃ-
Burco *tdmk* 'bɜːk əʊ ‖ 'bɜ˞ːk oʊ
burden, B~ 'bɜːd ən ‖ 'bɜ˞ːd ən **~ed** d **~ing** ɪŋ **~s** z
burdensome 'bɜːd ən səm ‖ 'bɜ˞ːd- **~ly** li **~ness** nəs nɪs
Burdett *(i)* 'bɜːd et ‖ 'bɜ˞ːd-, *(ii)* ˌbɜː 'det bə- ‖ bər 'det
burdock 'bɜː dɒk ‖ 'bɜ˞ː dɑːk **~s** s
Burdon 'bɜːd ən ‖ 'bɜ˞ːd-
bure *'Fijian cottage'* 'bʊr eɪ 'bjʊər- **~s** z
Bure bjʊə ‖ bjʊər
bureau 'bjʊər əʊ 'bjɔːr-; bjuə 'rəʊ ‖ 'bjʊr oʊ —*Fr* [by ʁo] **~s, ~x** z —*or as sing.*
ˌbureau de 'change ʃɒndʒ ʃɒ̃ʒ, ʃɑːndʒ ‖ ʃɑːndʒ —*Fr* [ʃɑ̃ːʒ]
bureaucrac|y bjuə 'rɒk rəs |i bjɔː-, bjə- ‖ -'rɑːk- **~ies** iz
bureaucrat 'bjʊər ə kræt 'bjɔːr- ‖ 'bjʊr- **~s** s
bureaucratic ˌbjʊər ə 'kræt ɪk ◂ ˌbjɔːr- ‖ ˌbjʊr ə 'kræṭ ɪk ◂ **~ally** əl‿i
bureaux 'bjʊər əʊz 'bjɔːr-, -əʊ; bjuə 'rəʊz, -'rəʊ ‖ 'bjʊr oʊz
buret, burette bjuə 'ret **~s** s
Burford 'bɜː fəd ‖ 'bɜ˞ː fərd
burg, Burg bɜːg ‖ bɜ˞ːg **burgs** bɜːgz ‖ bɜ˞ːgz
Burge bɜːdʒ ‖ bɜ˞ːdʒ
burgee 'bɜːdʒ iː ‖ 'bɜ˞ːdʒ iː **~s** z
burgeon 'bɜːdʒ ən ‖ 'bɜ˞ːdʒ- **~ed** d **~ing** ɪŋ **~s** z
burger, B~ 'bɜːg ə ‖ 'bɜ˞ːg ər **~s** z
'Burger ˌKing, ˌ ˌ • '•
burgess, B~ 'bɜːdʒ ɪs -əs, -es ‖ 'bɜ˞ːdʒ- **~es** ɪz əz
burgh 'bʌr ə ‖ 'bɜ˞ː oʊ *(= borough)* **~s** z
Burgh *(i)* 'bʌr ə ‖ 'bɜ˞ː oʊ, *(ii)* bɜːg bɜ˞ːg, *(iii)* bɜː ‖ bɜ˞ː
Burgh-by-Sands *place in Cumbria* ˌbrʌf baɪ 'sændz
Burghclere 'bɜː kleə ‖ 'bɜ˞ː kler
burgher 'bɜːg ə ‖ 'bɜ˞ːg ər **~s** z
Burghfield 'bɜː fiːəld ‖ 'bɜ˞ː-
Burghley 'bɜːl i ‖ 'bɜ˞ːl i
burglar 'bɜːg lə ‖ 'bɜ˞ːg lər **~s** z
'burglar aˌlarm
burglari... —*see* **burglary**
burglaris|e, burglariz|e 'bɜːg lə raɪz ‖ 'bɜ˞ːg- **~ed** d **~es** ɪz əz **~ing** ɪŋ
burglar|y 'bɜːg lər |i ⚠-əl r|i ‖ 'bɜ˞ːg- **~ies** iz
burgl|e 'bɜːg əl ‖ 'bɜ˞ːg əl **~ed** d **~es** z **~ing** ɪŋ
burgomaster 'bɜːg əʊ ˌmɑːst ə § -ˌmæst- ‖ 'bɜ˞ːg ə ˌmæst ər **~s** z
burgoo 'bɜːg uː ‖ 'bɜ˞ːg- bər 'guː
Burgos 'bʊəg ɒs ‖ 'bʊr goʊs -gɑːs —*Sp* ['bur ɣos]
Burgoyne 'bɜːg ɔɪn bɜː 'gɔɪn ‖ bər 'gɔɪn
Burgundian bɜː 'gʌnd i‿ən bə- ‖ bər- **~s** z
Burgund|y, b~ 'bɜːg ənd |i →-ŋd- ‖ 'bɜ˞ːg- **~ies** iz
Burhop 'bʌr əp ‖ 'bɜ˞ː-
buri... —*see* **bury**
burial 'ber i‿əl *(!)* **~s** z

Buriat ˌbʊr i 'ɑːt ◂ ˌbuər-, -'æt; ˌbʊə 'jɑːt ‖ ˌbʊr 'jɑːt ◂ **~s** s
Buridan 'bjʊər ɪd ən -əd- ‖ 'bjʊr-
burin 'bjʊər ɪn -ən ‖ 'bjʊr- 'bɜ˞ː- **~s** z
burk bɜːk ‖ bɜ˞ːk **~s** s
burka 'bɜːk ə ‖ 'bɜ˞ːk ə **~s** z
Burke, burke bɜːk ‖ bɜ˞ːk **burked** bɜːkt ‖ bɜ˞ːkt **burking** 'bɜːk ɪŋ ‖ 'bɜ˞ːk ɪŋ **burkes** bɜːks ‖ bɜ˞ːks
Burkina Faso bɜː ˌkiːn ə 'fæs əʊ ‖ bər ˌkiːn ə 'fɑːs oʊ bʊr-
Burkitt 'bɜːk ɪt §-ət ‖ 'bɜ˞ːk- **~'s** s
burl, Burl bɜːl ‖ bɜ˞ːl **burled** bɜːld ‖ bɜ˞ːld **burling** 'bɜːl ɪŋ ‖ 'bɜ˞ːl ɪŋ **burls** bɜːlz ‖ bɜ˞ːlz
burlap 'bɜː læp ‖ 'bɜ˞ː-
Burleigh 'bɜːl i ‖ 'bɜ˞ːl i
burlesqu|e bɜː 'lesk ‖ bɜ˞ː- **~ed** t **~ely** li **~es** s **~ing** ɪŋ
Burley 'bɜːl i ‖ 'bɜ˞ːl i
burli... —*see* **burly**
Burlington 'bɜːl ɪŋ tən ‖ 'bɜ˞ːl-
burl|y, Burly 'bɜːl |i ‖ 'bɜ˞ːl |i **~ier** i‿ə ‖ i‿ər **~iest** i‿ɪst i‿əst **~ily** ɪ li əl i **~iness** i nəs i nɪs
Burma 'bɜːm ə ‖ 'bɜ˞ːm ə
Burmah 'bɜːm ə ‖ 'bɜ˞ːm ə
Burman 'bɜːm ən ‖ 'bɜ˞ːm ən **~s** z
Burmese ˌbɜː 'miːz ◂ ‖ ˌbɜ˞ː- -'miːs
burn, Burn bɜːn ‖ bɜ˞ːn **burned** bɜːnd ‖ bɜ˞ːnd **burning** 'bɜːn ɪŋ ‖ 'bɜ˞ːn ɪŋ **burns** bɜːnz ‖ bɜ˞ːnz **burnt** bɜːnt ‖ bɜ˞ːnt
Burnaby 'bɜːn əb i ‖ 'bɜ˞ːn-
Burnage 'bɜːn ɪdʒ ‖ 'bɜ˞ːn-
Burnaston 'bɜːn əst ən ‖ 'bɜ˞ːn-
Burne bɜːn ‖ bɜ˞ːn
burned-out ˌbɜːnd 'aʊt ◂ ‖ ˌbɜ˞ːnd-
Burne-Jones ˌbɜːn 'dʒəʊnz ‖ ˌbɜ˞ːn 'dʒoʊnz
Burnell bɜː 'nel ‖ bər-
burner 'bɜːn ə ‖ 'bɜ˞ːn ər **~s** z
burnet 'bɜːn ɪt §-ət ‖ bər 'net 'bɜ˞ːn ət **~s** z
Burnet, Burnett *(i)* bə 'net bɜː- ‖ bər-, *(ii)* 'bɜːn ɪt §-ət ‖ 'bɜ˞ːn-
Burney 'bɜːn i ‖ 'bɜ˞ːn i
Burnham 'bɜːn əm ‖ 'bɜ˞ːn-
Burnham-on-Crouch ˌbɜːn əm ɒn 'kraʊtʃ ‖ ˌbɜ˞ːn əm ɑːn- -ɔːn-
burning 'bɜːn ɪŋ ‖ 'bɜ˞ːn ɪŋ **~ly** li **~s** z
ˌburning 'bush
burnish 'bɜːn ɪʃ ‖ 'bɜ˞ːn ɪʃ **~ed** t **~er/s** ə/z ‖ ər/z **~es** ɪz əz **~ing** ɪŋ
Burnley 'bɜːn li ‖ 'bɜ˞ːn-
burnoos|e, burnous, burnous|e bɜː 'nuːs -'nuːz ‖ bər- **~es** ɪz əz
burnout 'bɜːn aʊt ‖ 'bɜ˞ːn- **~s** s
Burns bɜːnz ‖ bɜ˞ːnz —*In Scottish pronunciation,* bʌrnz
'Burns night
Burnside 'bɜːn saɪd ‖ 'bɜ˞ːn- **b~s** z
burnt bɜːnt ‖ bɜ˞ːnt
ˌburnt 'offering
Burntisland bɜːnt 'aɪl ənd ‖ bɜ˞ːnṭ-
burnt-out ˌbɜːnt 'aʊt ◂ ‖ ˌbɜ˞ːnṭ-
ˌburnt-out 'case
Burntwood 'bɜːnt wʊd ‖ 'bɜ˞ːnt-

B

burn-up ˈbɜːn ʌp ‖ ˈbɜ˞ːn-
buroo bə ˈruː bruː **~s** z
burp bɜːp ‖ bɜ˞ːp **burped** bɜːpt ‖ bɜ˞ːpt **burping** ˈbɜːp ɪŋ ‖ ˈbɜ˞ːp- **burps** bɜːps ‖ bɜ˞ːps
Burpham ˈbɜːf əm ‖ ˈbɜ˞ːf-
burqa ˈbɜːk ə ‖ ˈbɜ˞ːk ə —*Arabic* [ˈbur qʕah] **~s** z
burr, Burr bɜː ‖ bɜ˞ː **burred** bɜːd ‖ bɜ˞ːd *(= bird)* **burring** ˈbɜːr ɪŋ ‖ ˈbɜ˞ː ɪŋ **burrs** bɜːz ‖ bɜ˞ːz
burrawang ˈbʌr ə wæŋ **~s** z
Burrell ˈbʌr əl ‖ ˈbɜ˞ː-
Burren ˈbʌr ən ‖ ˈbɜ˞ː-
burrito bə ˈriːt əʊ bʊ- ‖ bə ˈriːţ oʊ —*Sp* [bu ˈrri to] **~s** z —*Sp* [-s]
burro ˈbʊr əʊ ‖ ˈbɜ˞ː oʊ ˈbʊr- —*Sp* [ˈbu rro] **~s** z
Burrough ˈbʌr əʊ ‖ ˈbɜ˞ː oʊ -ə
Burroughes, Burroughs ˈbʌr əʊz ‖ ˈbɜ˞ː oʊz
burrow, B~ ˈbʌr əʊ ‖ ˈbɜ˞ː oʊ **~ed** d **~ing** ɪŋ **~s** z
Burrows ˈbʌr əʊz ‖ ˈbɜ˞ː oʊz
burry *adj 'prickly'* ˈbɜːr i ‖ ˈbɜ˞ː i
burry *n 'aboriginal'* ˈbʊr i
Burry *family name* ˈbʌr i ‖ ˈbɜ˞ː i
burs|a ˈbɜːs |ə ‖ ˈbɜ˞ːs |ə **~ae** iː **~al** əl **~as** əz
bursar ˈbɜːs ə ‖ ˈbɜ˞ːs ər -ɑːr **~s** z
bursarial bɜː ˈseər i əl ‖ bər ˈser-
bursarship ˈbɜːs ə ʃɪp ‖ ˈbɜ˞ːs ər- **~s** s
bursar|y ˈbɜːs ər‿|i ‖ ˈbɜ˞ːs- **~ies** iz
Burscough ˈbɜːsk əʊ ‖ ˈbɜ˞ːsk oʊ
burse bɜːs ‖ bɜ˞ːs **burses** ˈbɜːs ɪz -əz ‖ ˈbɜ˞ːs əz
bursitis bɜː ˈsaɪt ɪs §-əs ‖ bər ˈsaɪţ-
Burslem ˈbɜːz ləm ‖ ˈbɜ˞ːz-
burst bɜːst ‖ bɜ˞ːst **bursting** ˈbɜːst ɪŋ ‖ ˈbɜ˞ːst ɪŋ **bursts** bɜːsts ‖ bɜ˞ːsts
Burstall ˈbɜːst ɔːl ‖ ˈbɜ˞ːst- ɑːl
Burt bɜːt ‖ bɜ˞ːt
burthen ˈbɜːð ən ‖ ˈbɜ˞ːð- **~ed** d **~ing** ɪŋ **~s** z
Burton, b~ ˈbɜːt ən ‖ ˈbɜ˞ːt- **~s, ~'s** z
Burtonwood ˌbɜːt ən ˈwʊd ‖ ˌbɜ˞ːt-
Burundi bʊ ˈrʊnd i bə- **~an/s** ‿ən/z
Burwash *place in Sussex* ˈbɜː wɒʃ ‖ ˈbɜ˞ː wɑːʃ —*locally also* ˈbʌr əʃ
Burwell ˈbɜː wel -wəl ‖ ˈbɜ˞ː-
bury ˈber i *(! = berry)* **buried** ˈber id **buries** ˈber iz **burying** ˈber i‿ɪŋ
Bury ˈber i —*As a family name, also* ˈbjʊər i ‖ ˈbjʊr i
ˌ**Bury St 'Edmunds**
Buryat ˌbʊr i ˈɑːt◂ ˌbʊər-, -ˈæt; ˌbʊə ˈjɑːt ‖ ˌbʊr ˈjɑːt ◂ **~s** s
bus bʌs **bused, bussed** bʌst *(= bust)* **buses, busses** ˈbʌs ɪz -əz **busing, bussing** ˈbʌs ɪŋ
ˈ**bus bar**; ˈ**bus boy**; ˈ**bus ˌshelter**; ˈ**bus ˌstation**; ˈ**bus stop**
Busan ˌbuː ˈsæn ‖ -ˈsɑːn —*Korean* [b̥u san]
busbar ˈbʌs bɑː ‖ -bɑːr **~s** z
bus|by, Busby ˈbʌz |bi **~bies** biz
Busch bʊʃ
Buse bjuːz
bush, Bush bʊʃ **bushed** bʊʃt **bushes, Bush's** ˈbʊʃ ɪz -əz **bushing** ˈbʊʃ ɪŋ
ˌ**bush 'telegraph**
bushbab|y ˈbʊʃ ˌbeɪb |i **~ies** iz
bushbuck ˈbʊʃ bʌk
bushcraft ˈbʊʃ krɑːft §-kræft ‖ -kræft
bushel ˈbʊʃ əl **~s** z
Bushell *(i)* ˈbʊʃ əl *(ii)* bʊ ˈʃel
Bushey ˈbʊʃ i
bushfire ˈbʊʃ ˌfaɪ‿ə ‖ -ˌfaɪ‿ər **~s** z
bushhammer ˈbʊʃ ˌhæm ə ‖ -ər **~s** z
bushi... —*see* **bushy**
Bushido bu ˈʃiːd əʊ ˌbʊʃ i ˈdəʊ ‖ ˈbuːʃ i doʊ ˈbʊʃ- —*Jp* [bɯ ˈɕi doo]
Bushire bu ˈʃaɪ‿ə bju-, -ˈʃɪə ‖ bu ˈʃɪər
bush|man, B~ ˈbʊʃ |mən **~men** mən men
Bushmills ˈbʊʃ mɪlz
Bushnell ˈbʊʃ nəl
bushranger ˈbʊʃ ˌreɪndʒ ə ‖ -ər **~s** z
bushveld, B~ ˈbʊʃ felt -velt
bushwhack ˈbʊʃ wæk -hwæk **~ed** t **~er/s** ə/z ‖ ər/z **~ing** ɪŋ **~s** s
bush|y ˈbʊʃ |i **~ier** i‿ə ‖ i‿ər **~iest** i‿ɪst i‿əst **~ily** ɪ li əl i **~iness** i nəs i nɪs
bushy-tailed ˌbʊʃ i ˈteɪəld◂
busi... —*see* **busy**
busily ˈbɪz ɪ li -əl i
business ˈbɪz nəs -nɪs **~es** ɪz əz
ˈ**business card**; ˈ**business class**; ˈ**business end**; ˈ**business hours**, ˌ· · ˈ·; ˈ**business suit**
businesslike ˈbɪz nəs laɪk -nɪs-
business|man ˈbɪz nəs |mæn -nɪs-, -mən **~men** men mən **~woman** ˌwʊm ən **~women** ˌwɪm ɪn §-ən
busing ˈbʌs ɪŋ
busk, Busk bʌsk **busked** bʌskt **busking** ˈbʌsk ɪŋ **busks** bʌsks
busker ˈbʌsk ə ‖ -ər **~s** z
buskin ˈbʌsk ɪn §-ən **~ed** d **~s** z
busload ˈbʌs ləʊd ‖ -loʊd **~s** z
bus|man ˈbʌs |mən -mæn **~men** mən men
ˌ**busman's 'holiday**
buss, Buss bʌs **bussed** bʌst **busses** ˈbʌs ɪz -əz **bussing** ˈbʌs ɪŋ
buss... —*see* **bus**
Bussell ˈbʌs əl
bust bʌst **busted** ˈbʌst ɪd -əd **busting** ˈbʌst ɪŋ **busts** bʌsts
bustard ˈbʌst əd ‖ -ərd **~s** z
-buster ˌbʌst ə ‖ -ər — **pricebuster** ˈpraɪs ˌbʌst ə ‖ -ər
buster, B~ ˈbʌst ə ‖ -ər **~s** z
bustier ˈbʌst i eɪ ˈbʊst-, -i‿ə ‖ ˌbuːst i ˈeɪ ˌbʌst- **~s** z
bustl|e ˈbʌs əl **~ed** d **~es** z **~ing/ly** ‿ɪŋ /li
bust-up ˈbʌst ʌp **~s** s
bust|y ˈbʌst |i **~ier** i‿ə ‖ i‿ər **~iest** i‿ɪst i‿əst **~iness** i nəs i nɪs
bus|y ˈbɪz |i **~ier** i‿ə ‖ i‿ər **~iest** i‿ɪst i‿əst **~ily** ɪ li əl i **~yness** i nəs i nɪs
ˌ**busy 'Lizzie**
busybod|y ˈbɪz i ˌbɒd |i ‖ -ˌbɑːd |i **~ies** iz
busywork ˈbɪz i wɜːk ‖ -wɜ˞ːk

but *strong form* bʌt, *weak form* bət
butadlene ˌbjuːt ə ˈdaɪ iːn -ˈ· ‖ ˌbjuːt̬-
butane ˈbjuːt eɪn bjuː ˈteɪn
butanoic ˌbjuːt ə ˈnəʊ ɪk ◂ -ən ˈəʊ- ‖ ˌbjuːt ən ˈoʊ ɪk ◂
butanol ˈbjuːt ə nɒl -ən ɒl ‖ -ən oʊl -ɑːl, -ɔːl
butanone ˈbjuːt ə nəʊn -ən əʊn ‖ -ən oʊn
butch, Butch bʊtʃ
butch|er, B~ ˈbʊtʃ |ə ‖ -|ər **~ered** əd ‖ ərd **~ering** ər ɪŋ **~ers** əz ‖ ərz
butcherbird ˈbʊtʃ ə bɜːd ‖ -ər bɜːd **~s** z
butcher|y ˈbʊtʃ ər |i **~ies** iz
Bute bjuːt
butene ˈbjuːt iːn
Buthelezi ˌbuːt ə ˈleɪz i ‖ ˌbuːt̬- —*Zulu* [bu te ˈleː zi]
butler, B~ ˈbʌt lə ‖ -lər **~s** z
Butlin ˈbʌt lɪn -lən **~'s** z
Butskellite ˈbʌts kə laɪt -kɪ- **~s** s
butt, Butt bʌt **butted** ˈbʌt ɪd -əd ‖ ˈbʌt̬ əd **butting** ˈbʌt ɪŋ ‖ ˈbʌt̬ ɪŋ **butts** bʌts
butte, Butte bjuːt
butter ˈbʌt ə ‖ ˈbʌt̬ ər **~ed** d **buttering** ˈbʌt‿ər ɪŋ ‖ ˈbʌt̬ ər ɪŋ **~s** z
ˈbutter bean; **ˌbutter ˈicing**; **ˈbutter ˌmountain**
butterball ˈbʌt ə bɔːl ‖ ˈbʌt̬ ər- -bɑːl **~s** z
butterbur ˈbʌt ə bɜː ‖ ˈbʌt̬ ər bɜː **~s** z
buttercream ˈbʌt ə kriːm ‖ ˈbʌt̬ ər-
buttercup ˈbʌt ə kʌp ‖ ˈbʌt̬ ər- **~s** s
butterfat ˈbʌt ə fæt ‖ ˈbʌt̬ ər- **~s** s
Butterfield ˈbʌt ə fiːəld ‖ ˈbʌt̬ ər-
butterfingers ˈbʌt ə ˌfɪŋ gəz ‖ ˈbʌt̬ ər ˌfɪŋ gərz
butter|fly ˈbʌt ə |flaɪ ‖ ˈbʌt̬ ər- **~flies** flaɪz
ˈbutterfly bush; **ˈbutterfly stroke**; **ˈbutterfly valve**
butteri... —*see* **buttery**
Butterkist *tdmk* ˈbʌt ə kɪst ‖ ˈbʌt̬ ər-
Buttermere ˈbʌt ə mɪə ‖ ˈbʌt̬ ər mɪr
buttermilk ˈbʌt ə mɪlk ‖ ˈbʌt̬ ər-
butternut ˈbʌt ə nʌt ‖ ˈbʌt̬ ər- **~s** s
Butters ˈbʌt əz ‖ ˈbʌt̬ ərz
butterscotch ˈbʌt ə skɒtʃ ‖ ˈbʌt̬ ər skɑːtʃ
Butterwick ˈbʌt ə wɪk -ər ɪk ‖ ˈbʌt̬ ər wɪk
butterwort ˈbʌt ə wɜːt §-wɔːt ‖ ˈbʌt̬ ər wɜːt -wɔːrt **~s** s
Butterworth ˈbʌt ə wəθ -wɜːθ ‖ ˈbʌt̬ ər wərθ **~'s** s
butter|y ˈbʌt ər |i ‖ ˈbʌt̬- **~ies** iz
Butthead ˈbʌt hed
butthole ˈbʌt həʊl →-hɒʊl ‖ -hoʊl **~s** z
butti... —*see* **butty**
buttinski bʌ ˈtɪn ski ‖ bə ˈdɪn ski **~s** z
buttock ˈbʌt ək ‖ ˈbʌt̬- **~s** s
button, B~ ˈbʌt ən **~ed** d **~ing** ‿ɪŋ **~s** z
button-down ˌbʌt ən ˈdaʊn ◂ **ˌbutton-down ˈcollar**
buttonhol|e ˈbʌt ən həʊl →-hɒʊl ‖ -hoʊl **~ed** d **~es** z **~ing** ɪŋ
buttonhook ˈbʌt ən hʊk §-huːk **~s** s
buttress ˈbʌtr əs -ɪs **~ed** t **~es** ɪz əz **~ing** ɪŋ
butt|y ˈbʌt |i ‖ ˈbʌt̬ |i **~ies** iz
butyl ˈbjuːt aɪəl -ɪl, §-əl ‖ ˈbjuːt̬ əl
butyric bju ˈtɪr ɪk
buxom ˈbʌks əm **~ly** li **~ness** nəs nɪs
Buxted ˈbʌkst ɪd -əd, -ed
Buxtehude ˌbʊkst ə ˈhuːd ə ˈ· · · · —*Ger* [bʊks tə ˈhuː də], *Danish* [buks də ˈhuː ðə]
Buxton ˈbʌkst ən
buy baɪ *(= by)* **bought** bɔːt ‖ bɑːt **buying** ˈbaɪ ɪŋ **buys** baɪz
buyback ˈbaɪ bæk **~s** s
buyer ˈbaɪ‿ə ‖ ˈbaɪ‿ər **~s** z
ˌbuyer's ˈmarket, ˈ· · ˌ· ·
buyout ˈbaɪ aʊt **~s** s
Buys Ballot ˌbaɪs bə ˈlɒt ˌbɔɪs-, ˌbaɪz-, -ˈbæl ət ‖ -ˈlɑːt —*Dutch* [ˌbœys bɑ ˈlɔt]
Buzby ˈbʌz bi
Buzfuz ˈbʌz fʌz
buzz bʌz **buzzed** bʌzd **buzzes** ˈbʌz ɪz -əz **buzzing** ˈbʌz ɪŋ
buzzard, B~ ˈbʌz əd ‖ -ərd **~s** z
buzzcut ˈbʌz kʌt **~s** s
buzzer ˈbʌz ə ‖ -ər **~s** z
buzzword ˈbʌz wɜːd ‖ -wɜːd **~s** z
BVD *tdmk* ˌbiː viː ˈdiː **~'s** z
bwana ˈbwɑːn ə **~s** z
Bwlch bʊlk bʊlx —*Welsh* [bʊlχ]
by baɪ —*This word normally has no weak form. However there is an occasional weak form* **bi**, **bə**, *which is stylistically marked and in RP restricted to set phrases. The EFL learner should always use the pronunciation* **baɪ**.
Byars ˈbaɪ‿əz ‖ ˈbaɪ‿ərz
Byatt ˈbaɪ‿ət
by-blow ˈbaɪ bləʊ ‖ -bloʊ **~s** z
Bydgoszcz ˈbɪd gɒʃ ‖ -gɔːʃ -goʊʃ —*Polish* [ˈbɨd gɔʃtʃ]
bye, Bye baɪ *(= by, buy)* **byes** baɪz
bye- *comb. form* ¦baɪ — **bye-election** ˈbaɪ ɪ ˌlek ʃən -ə-
bye-bye *interj* ₍ˌ₎baɪ ˈbaɪ
bye-byes *n* ˈbaɪ baɪz
byelaw ˈbaɪ lɔː ‖ -lɑː **~s** z
by-election ˈbaɪ ɪ ˌlek ʃən -ə- **~s** z
Byeloruss|ia bi ˌel əʊ ˈrʌʃ |ə ˌbel əʊˈ·-, -ˈruːs |i‿ə ‖ -oʊ ˈrʌʃ |ə —*Also, inappropriately,* ˌbaɪ‿ə ləʊ- **~ian/s** ən/z i‿ən/z
Byers ˈbaɪ‿əz ‖ ˈbaɪ‿ərz
Byfield ˈbaɪ fiːəld
Byfleet ˈbaɪ fliːt
bygone ˈbaɪ gɒn §-gɑːn ‖ -gɔːn -gɑːn **~s** z
Bygraves ˈbaɪ greɪvz
Byker ˈbaɪk ə ‖ -ər
bylaw ˈbaɪ lɔː ‖ -lɑː **~s** z
byline ˈbaɪ laɪn **~s** z
Byng bɪŋ
BYO ˌbiː waɪ ˈəʊ ‖ -ˈoʊ
BYOB ˌbiː waɪ əʊ ˈbiː ‖ -oʊ ˈbiː
bypass ˈbaɪ pɑːs §-pæs ‖ -pæs **~ed** t **~es** ɪz əz **~ing** ɪŋ
ˈbypass ˌsurgery
by|path ˈbaɪ |pɑːθ §-pæθ ‖ -|pæθ **~paths** pɑːðz pɑːθs, §pæθs, §pæðz ‖ -pæðz -pæθs
byplay ˈbaɪ pleɪ

byproduct 'baɪ ˌprɒd ʌkt ‖ -ˌprɑːd əkt **~s** s
Byrd bɜːd ‖ bɝːd
byre 'baɪ‿ə ‖ 'baɪ‿ᵊr **byres** 'baɪ‿əz ‖ 'baɪ‿ᵊrz
Byrne bɜːn ‖ bɝːn
byroad 'baɪ rəʊd ‖ -roʊd **~s** z
Byrom 'barᵊr əm
Byron 'barᵊr ən **~'s** z
Byronic barᵊ 'rɒn ɪk ‖ -'rɑːn- **~ally** ᵊl‿i
Bysshe bɪʃ
byssinosis ˌbɪs ɪ 'nəʊs ɪs -ə-, §-əs ‖ -'noʊs-
byss|us 'bɪs| əs **~i** aɪ **~uses** əs ɪz -əz
bystander 'baɪ ˌstænd ə ‖ -ᵊr **~s** z
byte baɪt *(= bite)* **bytes** baɪts
Byward 'baɪ wəd ‖ -wᵊrd
byway 'baɪ weɪ **~s** z
byword 'baɪ wɜːd ‖ -wɝːd **~s** z
by-your-leave ˌbaɪ jɔː 'liːv -jʊə-, -jə- ‖ -jᵊr-
Byzantian bɪ 'zænt i‿ən bə-, baɪ-, -'zænᵗʃ ᵊn **~s** z
Byzantine, b~ bɪ 'zænt aɪn bə-, baɪ-, -iːn; 'bɪz ᵊn taɪn, -tiːn ‖ 'bɪz ᵊn tiːn -taɪn **~s** z
Byzantium bɪ 'zænt i‿əm bə-, baɪ-, -'zænᵗʃ- ‖ -'zænᵗʃ- -'zænt̬-

Cc

C

c Spelling-to-sound

1 Where the spelling is **c**, the pronunciation is regularly
k as in **cut** kʌt ('hard C') or
s as in **nice** naɪs ('soft C').
Less frequently, it is
ʃ as in **ocean** ˈəʊʃ ən ‖ ˈoʊʃ ən.
c may also form part of the digraphs **ch** and **ck**.

2 The pronunciation is regularly k when **c**

- is at the end of a word, as in **basic** ˈbeɪs ɪk or
- is followed by one of **a**, **o**, **u**, as in **camp** kæmp, **copy** ˈkɒp i ‖ ˈkɑːp i, **curl** kɜːl ‖ kɜ˞ːl or
- is followed by a consonant letter as in **cry** kraɪ.

3 The pronunciation is regularly s when **c**

- is followed by one of **e**, **i**, **y**, as in **central** ˈsentr əl, **city** ˈsɪt i, **cycle** ˈsaɪk əl, **face** feɪs.

Note also **Caesar** ˈsiːz ə ‖ -ər.

4 Where **c** at the end of a stressed syllable is followed by **e** or **i** plus a vowel within a word, the pronunciation is regularly ʃ as in **precious** ˈpreʃ əs, **special** ˈspeʃ əl, **musician** mju ˈzɪʃ ən. In these cases the **e** or **i** is silent, as usually applies when the following vowel is weak; but when the vowel after the **e** or **i** is strong, the pronunciation is i as in **speciality** ˌspeʃ i ˈæl ət i ‖ -əţ i. Sometimes, there is an alternative possibility with s as in **appreciate**, **associate**, **oceanic**; and where there is another ʃ in the same word as in **association**, **pronunciation**, many speakers prefer s.

5 Correspondingly, where the spelling is double **cc**, the pronunciation is k in most positions as in **account** ə ˈkaʊnt, but ks when followed by one of **e**, **i**, **y** as in **accept** ək ˈsept.

6 Correspondingly, too, where the spelling is **sc** the pronunciation is
sk in most positions as in **describe** dɪ ˈskraɪb, but
s when followed by one of **e**, **i**, **y** as in **scent** sent, **disciple** dɪ ˈsaɪp əl
ʃ when at the end of a stressed syllable and followed by **i** plus a vowel within a word as in **luscious** ˈlʌʃ əs.
sc may also form part of the trigraph **sch** (see **ch** 4).

7 **c** is silent in one or two exceptional words, including **muscle** ˈmʌs ᵊl, **indict** ɪn ˈdaɪt, **Connecticut** kə ˈnet ɪk ət ‖ -ˈneṭ-.

C

ch Spelling-to-sound

1 Where the spelling is the digraph **ch**, the pronunciation is regularly

tʃ as in **chip** tʃɪp or

ʃ as in **machine** mə ˈʃiːn or

k as in **chemistry** ˈkem ɪs tri.

ch may also form part of the trigraph **sch** (see 4).

2 Where the spelling is the trigraph **tch**, the pronunciation is regularly tʃ as in **fetch** fetʃ.

3 Otherwise, there is no reliable rule for choosing between the three possibilities for **ch**. In general,

tʃ is the pronunciation in long-established words as in **cheese** tʃiːz, **chain** tʃeɪn, **coach** kəʊtʃ ‖ koʊtʃ

ʃ is the pronunciation in recent loanwords from French as in **champagne** ʃæm ˈpeɪn, **parachute** ˈpær ə ʃuːt

nʃ is also a less usual option in place of ntʃ at the end of a syllable, as in **lunch** lʌntʃ or lʌnʃ

k is the pronunciation in words of Greek origin, as in **chaos** ˈkeɪ-, **monarch** -ək ‖ -ᵊrk. Where **ch** is followed by a consonant letter, the pronunciation is always k as in **Christmas** ˈkrɪs məs, **technical** ˈtek nɪk ᵊl.

4 After **s**, the pronunciation is usually k as in **school** skuːl. Occasionally **sch** is a trigraph, and the pronunciation is ʃ; this applies in words borrowed from German, certain proper names, and the traditional BrE pronunciation of **schedule** ˈʃed-.

5 Occasionally, the pronunciation is

dʒ as in the usual version of **sandwich** ˈsæn wɪdʒ and some other British place-names ending in **-ich** or

x, in certain words from foreign languages, as in **loch** (with k as an anglicizing alternative).

6 **ch** is silent in one or two exceptional words, including **yacht** jɒt ‖ jɑːt.

7 The sound tʃ is also sometimes written **t** as in **question**, **natural**, and **c** as in **cello**.

ck Spelling-to-sound

Where the spelling is the digraph **ck**, the pronunciation is always k as in **back** bæk, **acknowledge** ək ˈnɒl ɪdʒ ‖ ək ˈnɑːl ɪdʒ.

C, c siː **C's, Cs, c's** siːz —*Communications code name:* Charlie
ˌC of ˈE
C++ ˌsiː plʌs ˈplʌs
C3PO ˌsiː ˈθriː piː əʊ ‖ -oʊ
CAA ˌsiː ei ˈeɪ
Caan kɑːn
cab kæb **cabs** kæbz
ˈcab rank
cabal kə ˈbæl ‖ -ˈbɑːl **~s** z
cabala kə ˈbɑːl ə kæ- **~s** z
cabalism ˈkæb ə ˌlɪz əm
cabalistic ˌkæb ə ˈlɪst ɪk ◂
Caballé kə ˈbaɪ eɪ kæ- ‖ ˌkæb ɑː ˈjeɪ -ɑːl- —*Sp* [ka ˈβa ʎe, -je]
caballero ˌkæb ə ˈleər əʊ ‖ -ˈjer oʊ ˌkæb ᵊl- —*Sp* [ka βa ˈʎe ro, -ˈje-]
cabana kə ˈbɑːn ə ‖ kə ˈbæn ə -ˈbɑːn-, -jə —*Sp* cabaña [ka ˈβa ɲa]
cabaret ˈkæb ə reɪ ˌ· ·ˈ· **~s** z
cabbage ˈkæb ɪdʒ **~s** ɪz əz
ˌcabbage ˈwhite
cabbala kə ˈbɑːl ə kæ- **~s** z
cabbalism ˈkæb ə ˌlɪz əm
cabbalistic ˌkæb ə ˈlɪst ɪk ◂
cabbie, cabby ˈkæb i **cabbies** ˈkæb iz
cabdriver ˈkæb ˌdraɪv ə ‖ -ᵊr **~s** z
caber ˈkeɪb ə ‖ -ᵊr ˈkɑːb- **~s** z
cabernet sauvignon, C~ S~ ˌkæb ə neɪ ˌsəʊv iːn ˈjɒn -ˈjɔ̃, -ˈ· · · ‖ ˌkæb ᵊr ˌneɪ ˌsoʊv iːn ˈjoʊn —*Fr* [ka bɛʁ nɛ so vi ɲɔ̃]
Cabildo, c~ kə ˈbɪld əʊ ‖ kə ˈbiːld oʊ —*Sp* [ka ˈbil do] **~s** z
cabin ˈkæb ɪn §-ən **~s** z
ˈcabin boy; **ˈcabin class**; **ˈcabin crew**; **ˈcabin ˌcruiser**; **ˈcabin ˌfever**
Cabinda kə ˈbɪnd ə -ˈbiːnd- —*Port* [kɐ ˈβin dɐ]
cabinet ˈkæb ɪn ət -ən‿ət, -ɪt **~s** s
cabinet-mak|er ˈkæb ɪn ət ˌmeɪk| ə -ən‿ət-, -ɪn ɪt- ‖ -ᵊr **~ers** əz ‖ ᵊrz **~ing** ɪŋ
cabl|e ˈkeɪb ᵊl **~ed** d **~es** z **~ing** ɪŋ
ˈcable car; **ˌcable ˈteleˌvision**, ˌ· · ˌ·ˈ· ·, ˈ· · ˌ· · · ·
cablecast ˈkeɪb ᵊl kɑːst §-kæst ‖ -kæst **~s** s
cablegram ˈkeɪb ᵊl græm **~s** z
cable-knit ˈkeɪb ᵊl nɪt
cableway ˈkeɪb ᵊl weɪ **~s** z
cab|man ˈkæb mən **~men** mən men
cabochon ˈkæb ə ʃɒn ‖ -ʃɑːn —*Fr* [ka bɔ ʃɔ̃]
caboodle kə ˈbuːd ᵊl
caboos|e kə ˈbuːs **~es** ɪz əz
Caborn ˈkeɪ bɔːn ‖ -bɔːrn
Cabot ˈkæb ət **~s** s
cabotage ˈkæb ə tɑːʒ -ət ɪdʒ
Cabrillo kə ˈbrɪl əʊ ‖ -ˈbriː joʊ —*AmSp* [ka ˈβri jo]
Cabrini kə ˈbriːn i
cabriole ˈkæb ri əʊl →-ɒʊl, ˌ· ·ˈ· ‖ -oʊl
cabriolet ˈkæb ri‿ə leɪ -ri əʊ-, ˌ· · ·ˈ· ‖ ˌkæb ri‿ə ˈleɪ **~s** z
cabstand ˈkæb stænd **~s** z
ca'canny ˌkɑː ˈkæn i ‖ ˌkɑː-
cacao kə ˈkaʊ -ˈkɑː əʊ, -ˈkeɪ əʊ ‖ -oʊ
Caccia, c~ ˈkætʃ ə ˈ·i‿ə ‖ ˈkɑːtʃ-
cacciatore ˌkætʃ ə ˈtɔːr i ˌkɑːtʃ-, -eɪ ‖ ˌkɑːtʃ- -ˈtoʊr- —*It* [kat tʃa ˈtoː re]
cachaca, cachaça kə ˈʃæs ə ‖ -ˈʃɑːs- —*BrPort* [ka ˈʃa sa]
cachalot ˈkæʃ ə lɒt ‖ -loʊ -lɑːt
cache kæʃ *(= cash)* **cached** kæʃt **caches** ˈkæʃ ɪz -əz **caching** ˈkæʃ ɪŋ
cachectic kæ ˈkekt ɪk kə-
cachepot ˈkæʃ pəʊ -pɒt, ˌ·ˈ· ‖ ˈkæʃ pɑːt -poʊ
cache-sexe ˌkæʃ ˈseks
cachet ˈkæʃ eɪ kæ ˈʃeɪ ‖ kæ ˈʃeɪ **~s** z
cachexia kæ ˈkeks i‿ə kə-
cachexy kæ ˈkeks i kə-
cachin|nate ˈkæk ɪ |neɪt -ə- **~nated** neɪt ɪd -əd ‖ neɪṭ əd **~nates** neɪts **~nating** neɪt ɪŋ ‖ neɪṭ ɪŋ
cachinnation ˌkæk ɪ ˈneɪʃ ᵊn -ə- **~s** z
cachou kə ˈʃuː kæ-; ˈkæʃ uː **~s** z
cacique kæ ˈsiːk kə- ‖ kə- **~s** s
cack-handed ˌkæk ˈhænd ɪd◂ -əd **~ly** li
cackl|e ˈkæk ᵊl **~ed** d **~er/s** ‿ə/z ‖ ‿ər/z **~es** z **~ing** ‿ɪŋ
caco- *comb. form*
with stress-neutral suffix |kæk əʊ ‖ -ə — **cacographic** ˌkæk əʊ ˈgræf ɪk ◂ ‖ -ə-
with stress-imposing suffix kæ ˈkɒ+ kə- ‖ kæ ˈkɑː+ — **cacography** kæ ˈkɒg rəf i kə- ‖ -ˈkɑːg-
cacoethes ˌkæk əʊ ˈiːθ iːz ‖ -oʊ-
cacophoni... —*see* **cacophony**
cacophonous kə ˈkɒf ən əs kæ- ‖ kæ ˈkɑːf- **~ly** li
cacophon|y kə ˈkɒf ən |i kæ- ‖ kæ ˈkɑːf- **~ies** iz
cact|us ˈkækt |əs **~i** aɪ iː **~uses** əs ɪz əs əz
cacuminal kæ ˈkjuːm ɪn ᵊl kə-, -ən- **~s** z
cad, CAD kæd **cads** kædz
cadastral kə ˈdæs trəl
cadaver kə ˈdæv ə -ˈdɑːv-, -ˈdeɪv- ‖ -ᵊr **~s** z
cadaveric kə ˈdæv ər ɪk
cadaverous kə ˈdæv ər‿əs **~ly** li **~ness** nəs nɪs
Cadbury ˈkæd bər‿i →ˈkæb- ‖ -ˌber i **~'s** z
Cadby ˈkæd bi →ˈkæb-
CAD-CAM, CAD/CAM ˈkæd kæm →ˈkæg-
caddie ˈkæd i **~s** z
caddis ˈkæd ɪs §-əs
ˈcaddis fly
caddish ˈkæd ɪʃ **~ly** li **~ness** nəs nɪs
cadd|y ˈkæd |i **~ies** iz
cade, Cade keɪd
Cadeby ˈkeɪd bi →ˈkeɪb-
Cadell *(i)* kə ˈdel, *(ii)* ˈkæd ᵊl
cadenc|e ˈkeɪd ᵊnᵗs **~ed** t **~es** ɪz əz
cadency ˈkeɪd ᵊnᵗs i
cadent ˈkeɪd ᵊnt
cadenza kə ˈdenz ə **~s** z
Cader Idris ˌkæd ər ˈɪdr ɪs ‖ ˌkɑːd ᵊr- —*Welsh* [ˌka der ˈi dris]
cadet kə ˈdet **~s** s
ca'det corps
cadetship kə ˈdet ʃɪp **~s** s

C

cadge kædʒ **cadged** kædʒd **cadges** 'kædʒ ɪz -əz **cadging** 'kædʒ ɪŋ
cadger 'kædʒ ə ‖ -ᵊr **~s** z
cadi 'kɑːd i 'keɪd i **~s** z
Cadillac *tdmk* 'kæd ɪ læk -ə-, -ᵊl æk **~s** s
Cadiz *place in Spain* kə 'dɪz —*Sp* Cádiz ['ka ðiθ]
Cadmean kæd 'miː‿ən
cadmic 'kæd mɪk →'kæb-
cadmium 'kæd mi‿əm →'kæb-
Cadmus 'kæd məs →'kæb-
Cadogan kə 'dʌg ən
cadre 'kɑːd ə 'keɪd-, -rə ‖ 'kædr i 'kɑːdr-, -eɪ *(*)* **~s** z
caduce|us kə 'djuːs i|‿əs →-'dʒuːs- ‖ -'duːs- -'duːʃ|əs, -'djuːʃ- **~i** aɪ
caducous kə 'djuːk əs →-'dʒuːk- ‖ -'duːk- -'djuːk-
Cadwallader kæd 'wɒl əd ə ‖ -'wɑːl əd ᵊr
caec|um 'siːk |əm **~a** ə **~al** ᵊl
Caedmon 'kæd mən →'kæb-
Caen kɒ̃ kɑːn ‖ kɑːn —*Fr* [kɑ̃]
Caerau 'kar ᵊr aɪ —*Welsh* ['kəi rai, -rai, -re]
Caerleon kɑː 'liː‿ən ˌkaɪ‿ə- ‖ kɑːr-
Caernarfon, Caernarvon kə 'nɑːv ᵊn ‖ kɑːr 'nɑːrv- —*Welsh* [kəir 'nar von] **~shire** ʃə ʃɪə ‖ ʃᵊr ʃɪr
Caerphilly kə 'fɪl i keə-, kɑː- ‖ kɑːr- —*Welsh* [kəir 'fil i, kar-]
Caersws ˌkaɪ‿ə 'suːs ‖ ˌkaɪ‿ᵊr- —*Welsh* [kəir 'suːs]
Caesar 'siːz ə ‖ -ᵊr —*Classical Latin* ['kai sar] **~s, ~'s** z
Caesarea ˌsiːz ə 'riː‿ə
caesarean, caesarian sɪ 'zeər i‿ən sə-, siː- ‖ -'zer- -'zær-
caeˌsarean 'section
caesium 'siːz i‿əm ‖ 'sɪːs-
caesur|a sɪ 'zjʊər |ə sə-, siː-, -'zjɔːr-, -'ʒʊər- ‖ -'zʊr- **~ae** iː aɪ **~as** əz
cafe, café 'kæf eɪ -i; kæ 'feɪ ‖ kæ 'feɪ kə- —*Fr* [ka fe] —*Sometimes also (but in RP only facetiously)* kæf, keɪf **~s** z
ˌcafé au 'lait əʊ 'leɪ ‖ -oʊ- —*Fr* [o lɛ]
cafeteria ˌkæf ə 'tɪər i‿ə -ɪ- ‖ -'tɪr- **~s** z
cafetière ˌkæf ti 'eə ˌ·ə ti'· ‖ ˌkæf ə 'tɪᵊr —*Fr* [kaf tjɛːʁ] **~s** z —*or as sing.*
caff kæf **caffs** kæfs
caffè 'kæf eɪ kæ 'feɪ ‖ kæ 'feɪ **~ latte** 'læt eɪ 'lɑːt- ‖ 'lɑːt- **~ macchiato** ˌmæk i 'ɑːt əʊ ‖ ˌmɑːk i 'ɑːt oʊ —*It* [kaf 'fe, kaf ˌfel 'lat te, kaf ˌfem ma 'kjaː to]
caffeinated 'kæf ɪ neɪt ɪd '·ə-, -əd ‖ -neɪţ-
caffeine 'kæf iːn ‖ kæ 'fiːn *(*)*
Cafferty 'kæf ət i ‖ -ᵊrţ i
Caffin, Caffyn 'kæf ɪn §-ᵊn
Caffrey 'kæf ri
CAFOD, Cafod 'kæf ɒd ‖ -ɑːd
caftan 'kæft æn -ɑːn ‖ 'kæft ən kæf 'tæn **~s** z
cage, Cage keɪdʒ **caged** keɪdʒd **cages** 'keɪdʒ ɪz -əz **caging** 'keɪdʒ ɪŋ
'cage bird

cag|ey 'keɪdʒ |i **~ier** i‿ə ‖ i‿ᵊr **~iest** i‿ɪst i‿əst **~ily** ɪ li -əl i **~iness** i nəs -nɪs
Cagliari ˌkæl i 'ɑːr i 'kæl jər i —*It* ['kaʎ ʎa ri]
Cagliostro ˌkæl i 'ɒs trəʊ ‖ kæl 'jɑːs troʊ kɑːl-, -'jɔːs- —*It* [kaʎ 'ʎɔs tro]
Cagney 'kæg ni
cagoule kə 'guːl kæ- **~s** z
cag|y 'keɪdʒ |i **~ier** i‿ə ‖ i‿ᵊr **~iest** i‿ɪst i‿əst **~ily** ɪ li -əl i **~iness** i nəs -nɪs
Cahill *(i)* 'kɑː hɪl, *(ii)* 'keɪ hɪl
cahoots kə 'huːts
Caiaphas 'kaɪ‿ə fæs
Caicos 'keɪk əs -ɒs
caiman 'keɪm ən keɪ 'mæn, kaɪ- **~s** z
Cain, Caine keɪn *(= cane)* —*but* Cain *as a Welsh female name is* kaɪn
caipirinha ˌkaɪp ɪ 'rɪn jə -'riːn- —*BrPort* [kai pi 'ri ɲɐ]
caique, caïque kaɪ 'iːk kɑː- **~s** s
Caird keəd ‖ keᵊrd
Cairene 'kaɪᵊr iːn
cairn keən ‖ keᵊrn **cairned** keənd ‖ keᵊrnd **cairns** keənz ‖ keᵊrnz
ˌcairn 'terrier
Cairncross 'keən krɒs →'keəŋ-, -krɔːs, ˌ·'· ‖ 'kern krɔːs -krɑːs
Cairngorm, c~ ˌkeən 'gɔːm →ˌkeəŋ-, '· · ‖ 'kern gɔːrm
Cairns keənz ‖ keᵊrnz —*but in Australia the town in Queensland is usually* kænz
Cairo *in Egypt* 'kaɪᵊr əʊ ‖ -oʊ —*but places in the US are* 'ker oʊ, 'keɪ roʊ. —*Arabic* El Qahira [el 'qɑː hi rɑ, il qɑ 'hi ra]
caisson 'keɪs ᵊn -ɒn; kə 'suːn ‖ 'keɪs ɑːn -ᵊn **~s** z
Caister, Caistor 'keɪst ə ‖ -ᵊr
Caithness 'keɪθ nes -nɪs, -nəs, ˌ·'nes
caitiff 'keɪt ɪf §-əf ‖ 'keɪţ əf **~s** s
Caitlin 'keɪt lɪn 'kæt liːn
Caius 'kaɪ‿əs ‖ 'keɪ əs —*but as a family name and for the Cambridge college,* kiːz
cajol|e kə 'dʒəʊl →-'dʒɒʊl ‖ -'dʒoʊl **~ed** d **~es** z **~ing/ly** ɪŋ /li
cajoler|y kə 'dʒəʊl ər| i ‖ -'dʒoʊl- **~ies** iz
Cajun 'keɪdʒ ən **~s** z
cajuput 'kædʒ ə pʊt -pət **~s** s
cake keɪk **caked** keɪkt **cakes** keɪks **caking** 'keɪk ɪŋ
cakewalk 'keɪk wɔːk ‖ -wɑːk **~s** s
CAL kæl ˌsiː eɪ 'el
Calabar ˌkæl ə 'bɑː ◂ '· · · ‖ -'bɑːr ◂
ˌCalabar 'bean
calabash 'kæl ə bæʃ **~es** ɪz əz
calaboos|e 'kæl ə buːs ˌ· ·'· **~es** ɪz əz
calabrese 'kæl ə briːs -briːz, -breɪz; ˌ· ·'·, ˌ·'· i
Calabri|a kə 'læb ri‿|ə -'lɑːb- ‖ -'leɪb- -'lɑːb- —*It* [ka 'laː bria] **~an/s** ən/z
caladium kə 'leɪd i‿əm **~s** z
Calais 'kæl eɪ -i ‖ kæ 'leɪ —*Fr* [ka lɛ]
calaloo, calalu 'kæl ə luː
calamari ˌkæl ə 'mɑːr i ‖ˌkɑːl- —*It* [ka la 'maː ri]
calami 'kæl ə maɪ

calamine 'kæl ə maɪn
'**calamine ˌlotion**, ˌ· · · '· ·
calamint 'kæl ə mɪnt
calamitous kə 'læm ɪt əs -ət- ‖ -əţ əs **~ly** li **~ness** nəs nɪs
calamit|y kə 'læm ət |i -ɪt- ‖ -əţ |i **~ies** iz
Caˌlamity 'Jane
cal|amus 'kæl |əm əs **~ami** ə maɪ
calathea ˌkæl ə 'θiː ə
calcane|us kæl 'keɪn i|‿əs **~a** ‿ə **~al** ‿əl **~i** aɪ **~um** ‿əm
calcareous kæl 'keər i‿əs ‖ -'ker- -'kær-
calceolaria ˌkæls i‿ə 'leər i‿ə ‖ -'ler- **~s** z
calciferol kæl 'sɪf ə rɒl ‖ -roʊl -rɑːl, -rɔːl
calciferous kæl 'sɪf ər‿əs
calcifi... —*see* **calcify**
calcification ˌkæls ɪf ɪ 'keɪʃ ᵊn ˌ·əf-, §-ə'·-
calcifug|e 'kæls ɪ fjuːdʒ §-ə- **~es** ɪz əz
calci|fy 'kæls ɪ |faɪ -ə- **~fied** faɪd **~fies** faɪz **~fying** faɪ ɪŋ
calcination ˌkæls ɪ 'neɪʃ ᵊn -ə-
calcin|e 'kæls aɪn -ɪn **~ed** d **~es** z **~ing** ɪŋ
calcite 'kæls aɪt **~s** s
calcitic kæl 'sɪt ɪk ‖ -'sɪţ-
calcium 'kæls i‿əm
ˌ**calcium 'carbonate**
Calcot, Calcott *(i)* 'kælk ət -ɒt ‖ -ɑːt, *(ii)* 'kɔːlk- 'kɒlk- ‖ 'kɑːlk-
calculability ˌkælk jʊl ə 'bɪl ət i ˌ·jəl-, -ɪt i ‖ -jəl ə 'bɪl əţ i
calculable 'kælk jʊl əb ᵊl '·jəl- ‖ 'kælk jəl-
calcu|late 'kælk ju |leɪt -jə- ‖ -jə- **~lated/ly** leɪt ɪd /li -əd /li ‖ leɪţ əd /li **~lates** leɪts **~lating/ly** leɪt ɪŋ /li ‖ leɪţ ɪŋ /li
calculation ˌkælk ju 'leɪʃ ᵊn -jə- ‖ -jə- **~s** z
calculative 'kælk jʊl ət ɪv '·jəl-, -ju leɪt- ‖ -jə leɪţ-
calculator 'kælk ju leɪt ə '·jə- ‖ -jə leɪţ ᵊr **~s** z
calc|ulus 'kælk |jʊl əs -jəl- ‖ -jəl əs **~uli** ju laɪ jə- ‖ jə laɪ
Calcutta ⁽ˌ⁾kæl 'kʌt ə ‖ -'kʌţ- *Bengali* Kolkata ['kol ka ʈa]
Caldecote 'kɔːld ɪk ət 'kɒld-, -ək- ‖ 'kɔːld ə koʊt 'kɑːld-
Caldecott 'kɔːld ɪ kɒt 'kɒld-, -ə-, -kət ‖ 'kɔːld ə kɑːt 'kɑːld-
Calder 'kɔːld ə 'kɒld- ‖ 'kɔːld ᵊr 'kɑːld-
caldera kæl 'deər ə 'kɔːld ər ə ‖ kæl 'der ə **~s** z
Calderdale 'kɔːld ə deɪᵊl 'kɒld- ‖ -ᵊr- 'kɑːld-
caldron 'kɔːldr ən 'kɒldr- ‖ 'kɑːldr- **~s** z
Caldwell 'kɔːld wel 'kɒld- ‖ 'kɑːld-
Caldy 'kɔːld i 'kɒld- ‖ 'kɑːld-
Cale keɪᵊl
Caleb 'keɪl eb ‖ -əb
Caledon 'kæl ɪd ən -əd-
Caledoni|a ˌkæl ɪ 'dəʊn i‿|ə ˌ·ə- ‖ -'doʊn- **~an/s** ən/z
calefacient ˌkæl ɪ 'feɪʃ i‿ənt -'feɪʃ ᵊnt
calefaction ˌkæl ɪ 'fæk ʃᵊn -ə-
calefactory ˌkæl ɪ 'fæk tər‿i
calendar 'kæl ənd ə -ɪnd- ‖ -ᵊr **~s** z
ˌ**calendar 'month**

calend|er 'kæl ənd |ə -ɪnd- ‖ -|ᵊr *(= calendar)* **~ered** əd ‖ ᵊrd **~ering** ər ɪŋ **~ers** əz ‖ ᵊrz
calendrical kə 'lendr ɪk ᵊl kæ-
calends 'kæl endz 'keɪl-, -ɪndz, -əndz
calendula kæ 'lend jʊl ə kə-, -jəl- ‖ -'lendʒ əl ə **~s** z
calf kɑːf ‖ kæf **calves** kɑːvz ‖ kævz
'**calf love**
calf-length 'kɑːf leŋᵏθ §'kæf-, §-lenᵗθ ‖ 'kæf-
calfskin 'kɑːf skɪn ‖ 'kæf-
Calgary 'kælg ər i
Calhoun *(i)* kæl 'huːn, *(ii)* kə 'huːn
Caliban 'kæl ə bæn -ɪ-
caliber 'kæl əb ə -ɪb-; kə 'liːb ə, -'laɪb- ‖ -ᵊr
cali|brate 'kæl ə |breɪt -ɪ- **~brated** breɪt ɪd -əd ‖ breɪţ əd **~brates** breɪts **~brating** breɪt ɪŋ ‖ breɪţ ɪŋ
calibration ˌkæl ə 'breɪʃ ᵊn -ɪ- **~s** z
calibrator 'kæl ə breɪt ə '·ɪ- ‖ -breɪţ ᵊr **~s** z
calibre 'kæl əb ə -ɪb-; kə 'liːb ə, -'laɪb- ‖ -ᵊr
calico 'kæl ɪ kəʊ -ə- ‖ -koʊ **~es, ~s** z
Calicut 'kæl ɪk ət -ɪ kʌt
California ˌkæl ə 'fɔːn i‿ə ˌ·ɪ- ‖ -'fɔːrn jə
Californian ˌkæl ə 'fɔːn i‿ən ◂ ˌ·ɪ- ‖ -'fɔːrn jən ◂ **~s** z
ˌ**Caliˌfornian 'Desert**
californium ˌkæl ə 'fɔːn i‿əm ˌ·ɪ- ‖ -'fɔːrn-
Caligula kə 'lɪg jʊl ə -jəl-
caliper 'kæl ɪp ə -əp- ‖ -ᵊr **~ed** d **~s** z
caliph 'keɪl ɪf 'kæl-, -əf; kæ 'liːf **~s** s
caliphate 'kæl ɪ feɪt 'keɪl-, -ə- **~s** s
calisthenic ˌkæl ɪs 'θen ɪk ◂ -əs- **~s** s
Calistoga ˌkæl ɪ 'stəʊg ə -ə- ‖ -'stoʊg ə
calk kɔːk ‖ kɑːk **calked** kɔːkt ‖ kɑːkt **calking** 'kɔːk ɪŋ ‖ 'kɑːk- **calks** kɔːks ‖ kɑːks
Calke kɔːk ‖ kɑːk
call, CALL kɔːl ‖ kɑːl **called** kɔːld ‖ kɑːld **calling** 'kɔːl ɪŋ ‖ 'kɑːl- **calls** kɔːlz ‖ kɑːlz
'**call box**; '**call girl**; '**call sign**
calla 'kæl ə **~s** z
Callaghan 'kæl ə hən -hæn
Callander 'kæl ənd ə ‖ -ᵊr
Callanetics *tdmk* ˌkæl ə 'net ɪks ‖ -'neţ-
Callard 'kæl ɑːd ‖ -ɑːrd
Callas 'kæl əs -æs
Callaway 'kæl ə weɪ
callback 'kɔːl bæk ‖ 'kɑːl-
callboy 'kɔːl bɔɪ ‖ 'kɑːl- **~s** z
caller *'one that calls'* 'kɔːl ə ‖ 'kɔːl ᵊr 'kɑːl- **~s** z
calligrapher kə 'lɪg rəf ə kæ- ‖ -ᵊr **~s** z
calligraphic ˌkæl ɪ 'græf ɪk ◂ -ə- **~ally** ᵊl‿i
calligraphist kə 'lɪg rəf ɪst kæ-, §-əst **~s** s
calligraphy kə 'lɪg rəf i kæ-
Callil kə 'lɪl
Callimachus kə 'lɪm ək əs
call-in 'kɔːl ɪn ‖ 'kɑːl-
calling 'kɔːl ɪŋ ‖ 'kɑːl- **~s** z
'**calling card**
Calliope, c~ kə 'laɪ‿əp i kæ- **~s** z
calliper 'kæl ɪp ə -əp- ‖ -ᵊr **~ed** d **~s** z
callipygian ˌkæl ɪ 'pɪdʒ i‿ən ◂ ˌ·ə-
callipygous ˌkæl ɪ 'paɪg əs ◂ -ə-

callisthenic ˌkæl ɪs ˈθen ɪk ◂ -əs- **~s** s
Callisto kə ˈlɪst əʊ kæ- ‖ -oʊ
callosit|y kə ˈlɒs ət |i kæ-, -ɪt- ‖ -ˈlɑːs ət̬ |i **~ies** iz
callous ˈkæl əs **~ed** t **~ly** li **~ness** nəs nɪs
callout ˈkɔːl aʊt ‖ ˈkɑːl- **~s** s
callow, C~ ˈkæl əʊ ‖ -oʊ **~ness** nəs nɪs
Calloway ˈkæl ə weɪ
calltime ˈkɔːl taɪm ‖ ˈkɑːl-
Callum ˈkæl əm
call-up ˈkɔːl ʌp ‖ ˈkɑːl- **~s** s
callus ˈkæl əs *(= callous)* **~es** ɪz əz
calm kɑːm kɑːlm, §kɒlm **calmer** ˈkɑːm ə ˈkɑːlm-, §ˈkɒlm- ‖ -ᵊr **calmest** ˈkɑːm ɪst ˈkɑːlm-, §ˈkɒlm-, -əst
Calman ˈkæl mən
calmative ˈkælm ət ɪv ˈkɑːm- ‖ -ət̬- **~s** z
calm|ly ˈkɑːm |li ˈkɑːlm-, §ˈkɒlm- **~ness** nəs nɪs
Calne kɑːn §kɑːln, §kɒln
calomel ˈkæl ə mel -əm ᵊl
calor, Calor *tdmk* ˈkæl ə ‖ -ᵊr
ˈCalor gas
caloric kə ˈlɒr ɪk kæ-; ˈkæl ər- ‖ -ˈlɔːr- -ˈlɑːr-
calorie, C~ ˈkæl ər i **~s** z
ˈcalorie ˌcounting
calorific ˌkæl ə ˈrɪf ɪk ◂
calorimeter ˌkæl ə ˈrɪm ɪt ə -ət ə ‖ -ət̬ ᵊr **~s** z
calotte kə ˈlɒt ‖ -ˈlɑːt **~s** s
Calpurnia kæl ˈpɜːn i‿ə ‖ -ˈpɜːn-
calque kælk **calqued** kælkt **calques** kælks **calquing** ˈkælk ɪŋ
Calthorpe *(i)* ˈkæl θɔːp ‖ -θɔːrp, *(ii)* ˈkɔːl- ˈkɒl- ‖ ˈkɑːl-
Calton ˈkɔːlt ən ‖ ˈkɑːlt- *—but in Strathclyde locally* ˈkɑːlt-
caltrap, caltrop ˈkæltr əp ˈkɔːltr- **~s** s
Calum ˈkæl əm
calumet ˈkæl ju met -jə-, ˌ··ˈ· **~s** s
calumni|ate kə ˈlʌm ni |eɪt **~ated** eɪt ɪd -əd ‖ eɪt̬ əd **~ates** eɪts **~ating** eɪt ɪŋ ‖ eɪt̬ ɪŋ
calumniation kə ˌlʌm ni ˈeɪʃ ᵊn **~s** z
calumnious kə ˈlʌm ni‿əs **~ly** li
calum|ny ˈkæl əm |ni **~nies** niz
Calvados, c~ ˈkælv ə dɒs ‖ ˌkælv ə ˈdoʊs ˌkɑːlv- *—Fr* [kal va doːs]
Calvar|y, c~ ˈkælv ər |i **~ies** iz
calve kɑːv ‖ kæv *(in RP = carve)* **calved** kɑːvd ‖ kævd **calves** kɑːvz ‖ kævz **calving** ˈkɑːv ɪŋ ‖ ˈkæv-
Calverley ˈkɑːv ə li ˈkælv- ‖ -ᵊr-
Calvert *(i)* ˈkælv ət ‖ -ᵊrt, *(ii)* ˈkɔːlv- ‖ ˈkɑːlv-
Calverton *(i)* ˈkælv ət ən ‖ -ᵊrt ᵊn, *(ii)* ˈkɑːv-
calves *from* **calf, calve** kɑːvz ‖ kævz
Calvin ˈkælv ɪn §-ən
Calvinism ˈkælv ə ˌnɪz əm -ɪ-
Calvinist, c~ ˈkælv ən ɪst §-ɪn-, §-əst **~s** s
Calvinistic ˌkælv ə ˈnɪst ɪk ◂ -ɪ- **~al** ᵊl
Calvocoressi ˌkælv ə kə ˈres i
calx kælks **calxes** ˈkælks ɪz -əz
calyces ˈkeɪl ɪ siːz ˈkæl-, -ə-
Calydon ˈkæl ɪd ən -əd-
calypso, C~ kə ˈlɪps əʊ ‖ -oʊ **~s** z
calypsonian ˌkæl ɪp ˈsəʊn i‿ən ‖ -ˈsoʊn- **~s** z
calyx ˈkeɪl ɪks ˈkæl- **~es** ɪz əz
calzone kæl ˈzəʊn i -eɪ ‖ -ˈzoʊn -ˈzoʊn i; ˌkælt ˈsoʊn i **~s** z *—It* [kal ˈtsoː ne]
cam, Cam kæm **cammed** kæmd **camming** ˈkæm ɪŋ **cams** kæmz
camaraderie ˌkæm ə ˈrɑːd ər i -ˈræd-, -ə riː ‖ ˌkɑːm-
Camargue kæ ˈmɑːg kə- ‖ -ˈmɑːrg *—Fr* [ka maʁg]
camarilla ˌkæm ə ˈrɪl ə -jə ‖ -ˈriː jə *—Sp* [ka ma ˈri ʎa, -ja] **~s** z
Camay *tdmk* kæ ˈmeɪ ˈkæm eɪ
cam|ber, C~ ˈkæm |bə -|bᵊr **~bered** bəd ‖ bᵊrd **~bering** bər ɪŋ **~bers** bəz ‖ bᵊrz
Camberley ˈkæm bə li -bᵊl i ‖ -bᵊr-
Camberwell ˈkæm bə wᵊl -wel ‖ -bᵊr-
ˌCamberwell ˈbeauty
cambium ˈkæm bi‿əm
Cambodi|a kæm ˈbəʊd i‿|ə ‖ -ˈboʊd- **~an/s** ən/z
Camborne ˈkæm bɔːn ‖ -bɔːrn -boʊrn
Cambray ˈkɒm breɪ ˈkɒ̃- ‖ kɑːm ˈbreɪ *—Fr* [kɑ̃ bʁɛ]
Cambri|a ˈkæm bri‿|ə ˈkeɪm- **~an/s** ən/z
cambric ˈkeɪm brɪk **~s** s
Cambridge ˈkeɪm brɪdʒ **~shire** ʃə -ʃɪə ‖ ʃᵊr ʃɪr
Cambuslang ˌkæm bəs ˈlæŋ
Cambyses kæm ˈbaɪs iːz
camcorder ˈkæm ˌkɔːd ə ˌ·ˈ·· ‖ -ˌkɔːrd ᵊr **~s** z
Camden ˈkæm dən
ˌCamden ˈTown
came keɪm
camel ˈkæm ᵊl **~s** z
Camelford ˈkæm ᵊl fəd ‖ -fᵊrd
camelhair ˈkæm ᵊl heə ‖ -her
Camelia kə ˈmiːl i‿ə
camellia kə ˈmiːl i‿ə -ˈmel- **~s** z
Camelot ˈkæm ə lɒt -ɪ- ‖ -lɑːt
Camembert ˈkæm əm beə -bɜːt ‖ -ber -bɜːt *—Fr* [ka mɑ̃ bɛːʁ] **~s** z
cameo ˈkæm i əʊ ‖ -oʊ **~s** z
camera ˈkæm ər‿ə **~s** z
cameral ˈkæm ər əl
camera|man ˈkæm rə |mæn -mən **~men** men mən
camera obscura ˌkæm ər əʳ əb ˈskjʊər ə -ɒbˈ- ‖ -ə əb ˈskjʊr ə
camera-ready ˌkæm rə ˈred i ◂
ˌcamera-ˌready ˈcopy
camera-shy ˈkæm rə ʃaɪ -ər‿ə-
camera|woman ˈkæm rə ˌwʊm ən **~women** ˌwɪm ɪn -ən
Cameron ˈkæm ᵊr‿ən
Cameronian ˌkæm ə ˈrəʊn i‿ən ‖ -ˈroʊn- **~s** z
Cameroon ˌkæm ə ˈruːn ˈ··· **~s** z
Cameroonian ˌkæm ə ˈruːn i‿ən **~s** z
camiknicker ˈkæm i ˌnɪk ə ˌ·ˈ·· ‖ -ᵊr **~s** z
camiknicks ˈkæm i nɪks
Camilla kə ˈmɪl ə
Camille kə ˈmɪl -ˈmiːᵊl
camisole ˈkæm ɪ səʊl -ə-, →-sɒʊl ‖ -soʊl **~s** z
camlet ˈkæm lət -lɪt

C

amoens, Camoëns ˈkæm əʊ enz -enᵗs ‖ -oʊ- —*Port* Camões [kɐ ˈmõiʃ]
amomile ˈkæm ə maɪᵊl **~s** z
ˌ**camomile ˈtea**
amouflag|e ˈkæm ə flɑːʒ -u-, -flɑːdʒ **~ed** d **~es** ɪz əz **~ing** ɪŋ
amoys *(i)* ˈkæm ɔɪz, *(ii)* kə ˈmɔɪz
amp, Camp kæmp **camped** kæmpt **camping** ˈkæmp ɪŋ **camps** kæmps
ˌ**camp ˈbed**; ˌ**Camp ˈDavid**; ˌ**camp ˈfollower**, ˈ· ˌ· · ·
ampaign ₍ₗ₎kæm ˈpeɪn **~ed** d **~er/s** ə/z ‖ ᵊr/z **~ing** ɪŋ **~s** z
Campanella ˌkæmp ə ˈnel ə
ampanile ˌkæmp ə ˈniːl i -eɪ; -ˈniːᵊl ‖ ˌkɑːmp- **~s** z
ampanologist ˌkæmp ə ˈnɒl ədʒ ɪst §-əst ‖ -ˈnɑːl- **~s** s
ampanology ˌkæmp ə ˈnɒl ədʒ i ‖ -ˈnɑːl-
ampanula kæm ˈpæn jʊl ə kəm-, -jəl- **~s** z
Campari kæm ˈpɑːr i ‖ kɑːm- —*It* [kam ˈpaː ri]
Campbell ˈkæm bᵊl **~s, ~'s** z
Campbeltown ˈkæm bᵊl taʊn
Campden ˈkæm dən ˈkæmp-
amper ˈkæmp ə ‖ -ᵊr **~s** z
ampfire ˈkæmp ˌfaɪ‿ə ‖ -ˌfaɪ‿ᵊr **~s** z
ampground ˈkæmp graʊnd **~s** z
amphor ˈkæmᵖf ə ‖ -ᵊr
ampho|rate ˈkæmᵖf ə |reɪt **~rated** reɪt ɪd -əd ‖ reɪt̬ əd
amping ˈkæmp ɪŋ
ampion, C~ ˈkæmp i‿ən **~s** z
Campling ˈkæmp lɪŋ
amp-out ˈkæmp aʊt **~s** s
Campsie ˈkæmps i
ampsite ˈkæmp saɪt **~s** s
ampstool ˈkæmp stuːl **~s** z
ampus ˈkæmp əs **~es** ɪz əz
amp|y ˈkæmp i **~ier** i‿ə ‖ i‿ᵊr **~iest** i‿ɪst ‿əst
ampylobacter ˌkæmp ɪl əʊ ˈbækt ə ˌ·əl-, kæm ˌpɪl-, ˈ· · ·ˌ· · ‖ -oʊ ˈbækt ᵊr
CAMRA ˈkæm rə
amrose ˈkæm rəʊz ‖ -roʊz
amshaft ˈkæm ʃɑːft §-ʃæft ‖ -ʃæft **~s** s
Camus kæ ˈmuː kə-, kɑː- —*Fr* [ka my]
can *n, v 'tin'* kæn **canned** kænd **canning** ˈkæn ɪŋ **cans** kænz
can *v 'be able' strong form* kæn, *weak form* kən
Cana ˈkeɪn ə
Canaan ˈkeɪn ən ˈkeɪn i‿ən
Canaanite ˈkeɪn ə naɪt -i‿ə- **~s** s
Canada ˈkæn əd ə §-ɪd- **~'s** z
Canadian kə ˈneɪd i‿ən **~s** z
canal kə ˈnæl **~s** z
caˈnal boat
Canaletto ˌkæn ə ˈlet əʊ →ᵊl ˈet- ‖ -ᵊl ˈet̬ oʊ —*It* [ka na ˈlet to] **~s, ~'s** z
canalis... —*see* **canaliz...**
canalization ˌkæn əl aɪ ˈzeɪʃ ᵊn -ɪ·- ‖ -ᵊl ə ˈzeɪʃ-
canaliz|e ˈkæn ə laɪz -ᵊl aɪz ‖ ᵊl aɪz **~ed** d **~es** ɪz əz **~ing** ɪŋ

canape, canapé ˈkæn ə peɪ -əp i **~s** z
canard ˈkæn ɑːd kæ ˈnɑːd, kə- ‖ kə ˈnɑːrd —*Fr* [ka naːʁ] **~s** z
canar|y, C~ kə ˈneər |i ‖ -ˈner |i **~ies** iz
canasta kə ˈnæst ə
Canavan ˈkæn əv ən
Canaveral kə ˈnæv ᵊr‿əl
Canberra ˈkæn bər‿ə →ˈkæm- ‖ -ber ə
cancan ˈkæn kæn →ˈkæŋ-
cancel ˈkænᵗs ᵊl **~ed, ~led** d **~ing, ~ling** ‿ɪŋ **~s** z
cancela... —*see* **cancella...**
cancellable ˈkænᵗs ᵊl‿əb ᵊl
canc|ellate ˈkænᵗs| ᵊl ət -ɪt; ˈ· ə leɪt **~ellated** ə leɪt ɪd -əd; →ᵊl eɪt- ‖ ᵊl eɪt̬ əd
cancellation ˌkænᵗs ə ˈleɪʃ ᵊn -ɪ-; -ᵊl ˈeɪʃ- **~s** z
cancellous ˈkænᵗs ᵊl əs
cancer, C~ ˈkænᵗs ə ‖ -ᵊr **~s** z
Cancerian ₍ₗ₎kæn ˈsɪər i‿ən -ˈseər- ‖ -ˈsɪr- **~s** z
cancerous ˈkænᵗs ər‿əs **~ly** li
cancroid ˈkæŋk rɔɪd **~s** z
Cancun, Cancún kæn ˈkuːn ‖ kɑːn- —*Sp* Cancún [kaŋ ˈkun]
Candace ˈkænd ɪs -əs; kæn ˈdeɪs i
candela kæn ˈdiːl ə -ˈdel-, -ˈdeɪl- **~s** z
candelab|ra ˌkænd ə ˈlɑːb |rə -ɪ-, -ˈlæb- **~ras** rəz **~rum/s** rəm/z
Canderel *tdmk* ˈkænd ə rel ˌ· ·ˈ·
Candi ˈkænd i
candi... —*see* **candy**
Candia ˈkænd i‿ə
Candice ˈkænd ɪs -əs
candid ˈkænd ɪd §-əd **~ly** li **~ness** nəs nɪs
Candida, c~ ˈkænd ɪd ə §-əd-
candidac|y ˈkænd ɪd əs |i ˈ·əd- ‖ ˈkæn- **~ies** iz
candidate ˈkænd ɪ deɪt -ə-; -ɪd ət, -əd-, -ɪt ‖ ˈkæn- **~s** s
candidature ˈkænd ɪd ətʃ ə ˈ·əd-, -ɪtʃ-; -ɪ deɪtʃ-, -ə deɪtʃ- ‖ ˈkænd əd ə tʃʊr ˈkæn-, -ətʃ ᵊr **~s** z
Candide ₍ₗ₎kɒn ˈdiːd kõ- ‖ ₍ₗ₎kɑːn- —*Fr* [kɑ̃ did]
candidiasis ˌkænd ɪ ˈdaɪ‿əs ɪs ˌ·ə-, §-əs
candle ˈkænd ᵊl **~s** z
candleholder ˈkænd ᵊl ˌhəʊld ə →-ˌhɒʊld ə ‖ -ˌhoʊld ᵊr **~s** z
candle|light ˈkænd ᵊl| laɪt **~lit** lɪt
Candlemas ˈkænd ᵊl mæs -məs
candlepower ˈkænd ᵊl ˌpaʊ‿ə ‖ -ˌpaʊ‿ᵊr
Candler ˈkænd lə ‖ -lᵊr
candlestick ˈkænd ᵊl stɪk **~s** s
candlewick ˈkænd ᵊl wɪk
Candlin ˈkænd lɪn -lən
can-do ˌkæn ˈduː ◂
candor, candour ˈkænd ə ‖ -ᵊr
cand|y, Candy ˈkænd |i **~ied** id **~ies** iz **~ying** i ɪŋ
ˈ**candy stripe**; ˈ**candy ˌstriper**
candyfloss ˈkænd i flɒs ‖ -flɔːs -flɑːs
candy-striped ˈkænd i straɪpt
candytuft ˈkænd i tʌft
cane, Cane keɪn **caned** keɪnd **canes** keɪnz **caning** ˈkeɪn ɪŋ
canebrake ˈkeɪn breɪk →ˈkeɪm-

C

Canes Venatici ˌkeɪn iːz vɪ ˈnæt ɪ saɪ ˌkɑːn-, ˌ·eɪz-, -və'·-, ve'·-, -ə ·, -kiː
Canewdon kə ˈnjuːd ᵊn
Canfield, C~ ˈkæn fiːᵊld
Canicula kə ˈnɪk jʊl ə -jəl-
canicular kə ˈnɪk jʊl ə -jəl- ‖ -jəl ᵊr
canine ˈkeɪn aɪn ˈkæn- **~s** z
caning ˈkeɪn ɪŋ **~s** z
Canis ˈkeɪn ɪs ˈkæn-, §-əs
canister ˈkæn ɪst ə -əst- ‖ -ᵊr **~s** z
cank|er ˈkæŋk |ə ‖ -|ᵊr **~ered** əd ‖ ᵊrd **~ering** ər ɪŋ **~ers** əz ‖ ᵊrz
cankerous ˈkæŋk ər əs
Cann kæn
cann... —*see* **can**
canna ˈkæn ə **~s** z
cannabis ˈkæn əb ɪs §-əs
Cannae ˈkæn iː
cannel ˈkæn ᵊl
cannelloni, canneloni ˌkæn ə ˈləʊn i -ɪ-; -ᵊl ˈəʊn- ‖ -ᵊl ˈoʊn i —*It* [kan nel ˈloː ni]
canner, C~ ˈkæn ə ‖ -ᵊr
canner|y ˈkæn ər |i **~ies** iz
Cannes kæn kænz —*Fr* [kan]
canni... —*see* **canny**
cannibal ˈkæn ɪb ᵊl -əb- **~s** z
cannibalis... —*see* **cannibaliz...**
cannibalism ˈkæn ɪb ə ˌlɪz əm ˈ·əb-, -ᵊl ˌɪz-
cannibalistic ˌkæn ɪb ə ˈlɪst ɪk ◂ ˌ·əb-, -ᵊl ˈɪst-
cannibalization ˌkæn ɪb ᵊl aɪ ˈzeɪʃ ᵊn ˌ·əb-, -ɪ'·- ‖ -ə ˈzeɪʃ-
cannibaliz|e ˈkæn ɪb ə laɪz ˈ·əb-, -ᵊl aɪz **~ed** d **~es** ɪz əz **~ing** ɪŋ
cannikin ˈkæn ɪk ɪn -ək-, §-ən **~s** z
Canning ˈkæn ɪŋ
Cannizzaro ˌkæn ɪ ˈzɑːr əʊ -ə-, -ˈzeər- ‖ -oʊ —*It* [kan nit ˈtsaː ro]
Cannock ˈkæn ək
cannon, C~ ˈkæn ən **~ed** d **~ing** ɪŋ **~s** z
ˈ**cannon** ˌ**fodder**
cannonad|e ˌkæn ə ˈneɪd **~ed** ɪd əd **~es** z **~ing** ɪŋ
cannonball ˈkæn ən bɔːl →-əm- ‖ -bɑːl **~s** z
cannot ˈkæn ɒt -ət; §kæ ˈnɒt, kə- ‖ ˈkæn ɑːt kə ˈnɑːt, kæ- —*see also* **can't**
cann|ula ˈkæn |jʊl ə -jəl- ‖ -|jəl ə **~ulae** ju liː jə-, -laɪ ‖ jə- **~ulas** jʊl əz jəl- ‖ jəl əz
cann|y ˈkæn |i **~ier** i‿ə ‖ i‿ᵊr **~iest** i‿ɪst i‿əst **~ily** ɪ li əl i **~iness** i nəs i nɪs
canoe kə ˈnuː **~d** d **~ing** ɪŋ **~s** z
canoeist kə ˈnuː ɪst §‿əst **~s** s
canola kə ˈnəʊl ə ‖ -ˈnoʊl-
canon, Canon ˈkæn ən *(= cannon)* **~s** z
ˌ**canon** ˈ**law**
cañon ˈkæn jən —*AmSp* cañón [ka ˈɲon] **~s** z
Canonbury ˈkæn ən bər‿i →ˈ·əm- ‖ -ˌber i
canoness ˌkæn ə ˈnes ˈkæn ən ɪs, §-əs, -ə nes ‖ ˈkæn ən əs **~es** ɪz əz
canonical kə ˈnɒn ɪk ᵊl ‖ -ˈnɑːn- **~ly** ‿i **~s** z
canonicity ˌkæn ə ˈnɪs ət i ˌ·ɒ-, -ɪt i ‖ -əţ i
canonis... —*see* **canoniz...**
canonization ˌkæn ən aɪ ˈzeɪʃ ᵊn -ɪ'·- ‖ -ə ˈzeɪʃ- **~s** z
canoniz|e ˈkæn ə naɪz **~ed** d **~es** ɪz əz **~ing** ɪŋ
canon|ry ˈkæn ən |ri **~ries** riz
canoodl|e kə ˈnuːd ᵊl **~ed** d **~es** z **~ing** ‿ɪŋ
can-opener ˈkæn ˌəʊp ən‿ə ‖ -ˌoʊp ᵊn‿ər **~s** z
canopi... —*see* **canopy**
Canopic kə ˈnəʊp ɪk kæ-, -ˈnɒp- ‖ -ˈnoʊp- -ˈnɑːp-
Canopus kə ˈnəʊp əs kæ- ‖ -ˈnoʊp-
canop|y ˈkæn əp |i **~ied** id **~ies** iz
Canossa kə ˈnɒs ə kæ- ‖ -ˈnɑːs- —*It* [ka ˈnos sa]
canst *strong form* kænˈst, *weak form* kənˈst
cant, Cant kænt **canted** ˈkænt ɪd -əd ‖ ˈkænţ əd **canting/ly** ˈkænt ɪŋ /li ‖ ˈkænţ- **cants** kænts
can't kɑːnt ‖ kænt ⚠keɪnt —*Before a consonant (less frequently before a vowel) also* kɑːn ‖ kæn. *Unlike* can, *this word has no weak form.*
Cantab ˈkænt æb
cantabile kæn ˈtɑːb ɪ leɪ -ə leɪ; -əl i, -ɪl i
Cantabrian kæn ˈteɪb ri‿ən **~s** z
Cantabrigian ˌkænt ə ˈbrɪdʒ i‿ən ◂ **~s** z
cantaloup, cantaloupe ˈkænt ə luːp ‖ ˈkænţ ə loʊp *(*)* **~s** s
cantankerous kæn ˈtæŋk ər‿əs kən- **~ly** li **~ness** nəs nɪs
cantata kæn ˈtɑːt ə kən- ‖ kən ˈtɑːţ ə **~s** z
canteen ₍ˌ₎kæn ˈtiːn **~s** z
canter, C~ ˈkænt ə ‖ ˈkænţ ᵊr **~ed** d **cantering** ˈkænt‿ər ɪŋ ‖ ˈkænţ ər ɪŋ **~s** z
Canterbury, c~ ˈkænt ə bər‿i -ˌber i ‖ ˈkænţ ᵊr ˌber i
cantharides kæn ˈθær ɪ diːz -ə- ‖ -ˈθer-
canth|us ˈkænᵗθ |əs **~i** aɪ
canticle ˈkænt ɪk ᵊl §-ək- ‖ ˈkænţ ək ᵊl **~s** z
cantilena ˌkænt ɪ ˈleɪn ə -ə-, -ˈliːn- ‖ ˌkænţ- **~s** z
cantilev|er ˈkænt ɪ liːv |ə ˈ·ə-; -ᵊl iːv- ‖ ˈkænţ ᵊl iːv |ᵊr -ev ᵊr **~ered** əd ‖ ᵊrd **~ering** ər‿ɪŋ **~ers** əz ‖ ᵊrz
canto ˈkænt əʊ ‖ -oʊ **~s** z
canton *in heraldry; on flag* ˈkænt ən **~ed** d **~ing** ɪŋ **~s** z
canton *v 'quarter (soldiers)'* kæn ˈtuːn kən- ‖ -ˈtɑːn -ˈtoʊn **~ed** d **~ing** ɪŋ **~s** z
canton *'political division, esp. Swiss'* ˈkænt ɒn ₍ˌ₎kæn ˈtɒn ‖ ˈkænt ɑːn -ᵊn; kæn ˈtɑːn **~s** z
Canton *places in the UK, US; family name* ˈkænt ən
Canton *place in China* ˌkæn ˈtɒn ◂ ‖ -ˈtɑːn ◂ —*Chi* Guǎngzhōu [³kwaŋ ¹tʂou]
Cantona ˌkænt ə ˈnɑː —*Fr* [kɑ̃ tɔ na]
cantonal ˈkænt ən ᵊl kæn ˈtəʊn ᵊl, -ˈtɒn- ‖ ˈkænt ᵊn əl kæn ˈtɑːn ᵊl
Cantonese ˌkænt ə ˈniːz ◂ ‖ -ᵊn ˈiːz ◂ -ˈiːs
cantonment kæn ˈtuːn mənt kən-, →-ˈtuːm- ‖ -ˈtɑːn- -ˈtoʊn- **~s** z
cantor, C~ ˈkænt ɔː -ə ‖ -ᵊr
cantorial kæn ˈtɔːr i‿əl ‖ -ˈtoʊr-
cantoris kæn ˈtɔːr ɪs §-əs ‖ -ˈtoʊr-
Cantuar ˈkænt ju ɑː ‖ -ɑːr
Canuck kə ˈnʌk **~s** s

an|ula 'kæn |jʊl ə -jəl- ‖ -|jəl ə **~ulae** ju liː jə-, -laɪ ‖ jə- **~ulas** jʊl əz jəl- ‖ jəl əz
Canute kə 'njuːt -'nuːt ‖ -'nuːt -'njuːt
anvas 'kæn vəs **~es** ɪz əz
anvasback 'kæn vəs bæk **~s** s
anvass 'kæn vəs **~ed** t **~er/s** ə/z ‖ ᵊr/z **~es** ɪz əz **~ing** ɪŋ
Canvey 'kæn vi
anyon 'kæn jən **~ing** ɪŋ **~s** z
ˌ**Canyon de 'Chelly** *place in AZ* də 'ʃeɪ
ap kæp **capped** kæpt **capping** 'kæp ɪŋ **caps** kæps
CAP ˌsiː eɪ 'piː
apabilit|y ˌkeɪp ə 'bɪl ət |i -ɪt i ‖ -əţ |i **~ies** iz
apable 'keɪp əb ᵊl **~ness** nəs nɪs
apably 'keɪp əb li
apacious kə 'peɪʃ əs **~ly** li **~ness** nəs nɪs
apacitanc|e kə 'pæs ɪt ənᵗs -ət- **~es** ɪz əz
apacitor kə 'pæs ɪt ə -ət- ‖ -əţ ᵊr **~s** z
apacit|y kə 'pæs ət |i -ɪt- ‖ -əţ |i **~ies** iz
ap-a-pie ˌkæp ə 'piː -'peɪ
aparison kə 'pær ɪs ən -əs- ‖ -'per- **~ed** d **~ing** ˌɪŋ **~s** z
ape, Cape keɪp **capes** keɪps —*See also phrases with this word*
ˌ**Cape Ca'naveral**; ˌ**Cape 'Horn**; ˌ**Cape of** ˌ**Good 'Hope**; ˌ**Cape 'Province**; '**Cape Town**
Cape Girardeau *place in MO* ˌkeɪp dʒə 'rɑːd əʊ ‖ -'rɑːrd oʊ
Capek 'tʃæp ek ‖ 'tʃɑːp- —*Czech* ['tʃa pek]
Capel 'keɪp ᵊl —*but in Welsh place names* 'kæp- —*Welsh* ['kap el]
ˌ**Capel 'Curig** 'kɪr ɪg -'kjʊər- —*Welsh* ['kɨ rig, 'ke-]
capelin 'keɪp ᵊl ˌɪn §ˌən
Capell 'keɪp ᵊl
Capella kə 'pel ə
capellini ˌkæp ə 'liːn i ˌe- —*It* [ka pel 'liː ni]
Capenhurst 'keɪp ən hɜːst ‖ -hɜːst
cap|er 'keɪp| ə ‖ -ᵊr **~ered** əd ‖ ᵊrd **~ering** ər ˌɪŋ **~ers** əz ‖ ᵊrz
capercaillie, capercailzie ˌkæp ə 'keɪl i -ji ‖ -ᵊr- **~s** z
Capernaum kə 'pɜːn iˌəm -eɪ-; -'əm ‖ -'pɜːn-
Capetian kə 'piːʃ ᵊn **~s** z
Cape Verd|e ˌkeɪp 'vɜːd -'veəd ‖ -'vɜːd **~ean/s** iˌən/z
capful 'kæp fʊl **~s** z
capillarit|y ˌkæp ɪ 'lær ət |i ˌ-ə-, -ɪt i ‖ -əţ |i -'ler- **~ies** iz
capillar|y kə 'pɪl ər |i ‖ 'kæp ə ler |i *(*)* **~ies** iz
Capistrano ˌkæp ɪ 'strɑːn əʊ §-ə- ‖ -oʊ
Capita 'kæp ɪt ə -ət- ‖ -əţ ə
capital 'kæp ɪt ᵊl -ət- ‖ -əţ- **~s** z
ˌ**capital 'gain**; ˌ**capital 'punishment**
capital-intensive ˌkæp ɪt ᵊl ɪn 'tenᵗs ɪv ◂ ˌ-ət-, §-ən'-- ‖ ˌkæp əţ- **~ly** li
capitalis... —*see* **capitaliz...**
capitalism 'kæp ɪt ə ˌlɪz əm '-ət-, -ᵊl ˌɪz-; kæ 'pɪt-, kə- ‖ -əţ ᵊl ˌɪz-
capitalist 'kæp ɪt ᵊl ɪst '-ət-, kæ 'pɪt-, kə 'pɪt-, §-əst ‖ 'kæp əţ ᵊl əst **~s** s
capitalistic ˌkæp ɪt ə 'lɪst ɪk ◂ ˌ-ət-, -ᵊl 'ɪst- ‖ -əţ ᵊl 'ɪst- **~ally** ᵊl ˌi
capitalization ˌkæp ɪt ᵊl aɪ 'zeɪʃ ᵊn ˌ-ət-, -ɪ'--; kæ 'pɪt-, kə- ‖ -ə 'zeɪʃ- **~s** z
capitaliz|e 'kæp ɪt ə laɪz '-ət-, -ᵊl aɪz; kæ 'pɪt-, kə- ‖ -əţ ᵊl aɪz **~ed** d **~es** ɪz əz **~ing** ɪŋ
capitation ˌkæp ɪ 'teɪʃ ᵊn -ə-
capitol, C~ 'kæp ɪt ᵊl -ət-; -ɪ tɒl, -ə- ‖ -əţ ᵊl -ə tɑːl *(usually = capital)* **~s** z
Capitoline kə 'pɪt əʊ laɪn 'kæp ɪt-, '-ət-, -ᵊl aɪn ‖ 'kæp əţ ᵊl aɪn
capitul|a kə 'pɪt jʊl |ə -jəl- ‖ -'pɪtʃ əl |ə **~ar** ə ‖ ᵊr
capitu|late kə 'pɪt ju |leɪt -jə-; -'pɪtʃ u-, -ə- ‖ -'pɪtʃ ə- **~lated** leɪt ɪd əd ‖ leɪţ əd **~lates** leɪts **~lating** leɪt ɪŋ ‖ leɪţ ɪŋ
capitulation kə ˌpɪt ju 'leɪʃ ᵊn -jə-; -ˌpɪtʃ u-, -ə- ‖ -ˌpɪtʃ ə- **~s** z
capitul|um kə 'pɪt jʊl |əm -jəl- ‖ -'pɪtʃ əl- **~a** ə
Caplan 'kæp lən
caplet, C~ *tdmk* 'kæp lət -lɪt
capo *'Mafia leader'* 'kɑːp əʊ 'kæp- ‖ -oʊ **~s** z
capo *for guitar* 'kæp əʊ 'keɪp- ‖ 'keɪp oʊ **~s** z
Capodimonte, Capo-di-Monte ˌkæp əʊ di 'mɒnt eɪ ˌkɑːp-, -i ‖ ˌkɑːp oʊ di 'mɑːnt eɪ —*It* [ka po di 'mon te]
capoeira ˌkæp əʊ 'eər ə -u- ‖ ˌkɑːp oʊ 'er ə —*BrPort* [ka po 'ej ɾa, ka 'pwej ɾa]
capon, Capon 'keɪp ən -ɒn ‖ -ɑːn -ən **~s** z
Capone kə 'pəʊn ‖ -'poʊn
capote kə 'pəʊt ‖ -'poʊt —*Fr* [ka pɔt] **~s** s
Capote kə 'pəʊt i ‖ -'poʊţ i
Capp kæp
capp... —*see* **cap**
Cappa, Cappagh 'kæp ə
Cappadoci|a ˌkæp ə 'dəʊs iˌ|ə -'dəʊʃ-, -'dəʊʃ |ə ‖ -'doʊʃ- **~an/s** ən/z
cappelletti ˌkæp ə 'let i ‖ -'leţ i —*It* [kap pel 'let ti]
capper, C~ 'kæp ə ‖ -ᵊr
cappuccino ˌkæp u 'tʃiːn əʊ -ə- ‖ ˌkɑːp ə 'tʃiːn oʊ -jə- **~s** z
Capra 'kæp rə
Capri kə 'priː kæ-; 'kæp riː —*It* ['kaː pri]
Capriati ˌkæp ri 'ɑːt i
capric 'kæp rɪk
capriccio kə 'priːtʃ iˌəʊ -'prɪtʃ- ‖ oʊ **~s** z
capriccioso kə ˌpriːtʃ i 'əʊs əʊ -ˌprɪtʃ-, -'əʊz- ‖ -'oʊs oʊ
capric|e kə 'priːs **~es** ɪz əz
capricious kə 'prɪʃ əs ‖ -'priːʃ- **~ly** li **~ness** nəs nɪs
Capricorn 'kæp rɪ kɔːn -rə- ‖ -kɔːrn **~s** z
Capricorn|ian ˌkæp rɪ 'kɔːn| iˌən ◂ ˌ-rə- ‖ -'kɔːrn|- **~ians** iˌənz **~us** əs
caprine 'kæp raɪn
capriol|e 'kæp ri əʊl →-ɒʊl ‖ -oʊl **~ed** d **~es** z **~ing** ɪŋ
Caprivi kə 'priːv i kæ-
caproic kə 'prəʊ ɪk kæ- ‖ -'proʊ-
capsicum 'kæps ɪk əm -ək- **~s** z
capsid 'kæps ɪd §-əd **~s** z

CAPSIZE

7%
93%
ˈ· ·
·ˈ·
AmE

capsiz|e ₍ₗ₎kæp ˈsaɪz ‖ ˈkæps aɪz — *Preference poll, AmE:* ˈ· · *93%,* ·ˈ· *7%.* **~ed** d **~es** ɪz əz **~ing** ɪŋ
capstan ˈkæpst ən ‖ -æn **~s** z
ˈcapstan lathe
capstone ˈkæp stəʊn ‖ -stoʊn **~s** z
capsular ˈkæps jʊl ə -jəl- ‖ -ᵊl ər
capsule ˈkæps juːl -ᵊl ‖ -ᵊl -uːl **~s** z
captain ˈkæpt ɪn -ən ‖ -ən —*also, particularly nautical or as a vocative,* ˈkæp ən*; with this pronunciation also spelt* cap'n **~ed** d **~ing** ɪŋ **~s** z
captain|cy ˈkæpt ən |si -ɪn- **~cies** siz
captainship ˈkæpt ɪn ʃɪp -ən-
caption ˈkæp ʃᵊn **~ed** d **~ing** ɪŋ **~s** z
captious ˈkæp ʃəs **~ly** li **~ness** nəs nɪs
capti|vate ˈkæpt ɪ |veɪt -ə- **~vated** veɪt ɪd -əd ‖ veɪţ əd **~vates** veɪts **~vating** veɪt ɪŋ ‖ veɪţ ɪŋ
captivation ˌkæpt ɪ ˈveɪʃ ᵊn -ə-
captivator ˈkæpt ɪ veɪt ə ˈ·ə- ‖ -veɪţ ᵊr **~s** z
captive ˈkæpt ɪv **~s** z
captivit|y kæp ˈtɪv ət |i -ɪt- ‖ -əţ |i **~ies** iz
captor ˈkæpt ə ‖ -ᵊr -ɔːr **~s** z
cap|ture ˈkæp |tʃə -ʃə ‖ -|tʃᵊr -ʃᵊr **~tured** tʃəd ʃəd ‖ tʃᵊrd ʃᵊrd **~tures** tʃəz ʃəz ‖ tʃᵊrz ʃᵊrz **~turing** tʃər ɪŋ ʃər-
Capua ˈkæp ju‿ə —*It* [ˈkaː pu a]
capuch|e kə ˈpuːʃ -ˈpuːtʃ **~es** ɪz əz
capuchin ˈkæp jʊtʃ ɪn -jʊʃ-, §-ən; kə ˈpuːtʃ-, -ˈpuːʃ- ‖ ˈkæp jəʃ ᵊn kə ˈpjuːtʃ ən **~s** z
Capulet ˈkæp ju let -lət, -lɪt ‖ -jəl ət **~s** s
capybara ˌkæp i ˈbɑːr ə ‖ -ˈbær-, -ˈber- **~s** z
car kɑː ‖ kɑːr **cars** kɑːz ‖ kɑːrz
ˌcar ˈboot sale; **ˈcar park**; **ˈcar pool**; **ˈcar wash**
Cara ˈkɑːr ə ‖ ˈkær-, ˈker-
carabiner ˌkær ə ˈbiːn ə ‖ -ᵊr ˌker- **~s** z
carabinieri ˌkær ə bɪn i ˈeər i ‖ ˌkær əb ən ˈjer i ˌker- —*It* [ka ra bi ˈnjɛː ri]
caracal ˈkær ə kæl ‖ ˈker- **~s** z
Caracalla ˌkær ə ˈkæl ə ‖ ˌker-
caracara ˌkær ə ˈkɑːr ə ˌkɑːr- ‖ ˌker-, -kə ˈrɑː **~s** z
Caracas kə ˈræk əs -ˈrɑːk- ‖ -ˈrɑːk- —*Sp* [ka ˈra kas]
caracol|e ˈkær ə kəʊl →-kɒʊl ‖ -koʊl ˈker- **~ed** d **~es** z **~ing** ɪŋ
Caractacus kə ˈrækt ək əs
caracul ˈkær ə kʌl -ək ᵊl ‖ ˈker-
Caradoc kə ˈræd ɒk -ək ‖ -ɑːk
Caradog kə ˈræd ɒg ‖ -ɑːg -ɔːg —*Welsh* [ka ˈra dog]
Caradon ˈkær əd ən ‖ ˈker-
carafe kə ˈræf -ˈrɑːf **~s** s
carambola ˌkær əm ˈbəʊl ə ‖ -ˈboʊl ə ˌker- **~s** z

CARAMEL

50%
50%
3 syllables
2 syllables
AmE

caramel ˈkær ə mel -əm ᵊl ‖ -əm ᵊl ker-, -ə mel; ˈkɑːrm ᵊl — *Preference poll, AmE: three syllables 50%, two syllables 50%.* **~s** z
caramelis|e, carameliz|e ˈkær əm ə laɪz →-ᵊl aɪz; -ə mel aɪz ‖ ˈker-; ˈkɑːrm ə laɪz **~ed** d **~es** ɪz əz **~ing** ɪŋ
Caran d'Ache *tdmk* ˌkær ən ˈdæʃ ‖ ˌkɑːr ən ˈdɑːʃ ˌkær-, ˌker-
carapac|e ˈkær ə peɪs ‖ ˈker- **~es** ɪz əz
carat ˈkær ət ‖ ˈker- *(= carrot)* **~s** s
Caravaggio ˌkær ə ˈvædʒ i əʊ ˌkɑːr-, -ˈvɑːdʒ-, -ˈvæʒ- ‖ ˌkær ə ˈvɑːdʒ oʊ ˌker- —*It* [ka ra ˈvad dʒo]
caravan ˈkær ə væn ˌ· ·ˈ· ‖ ˈker- **~er/s, ~ner/s** ə/z ‖ ᵊr/z **~ing, ~ning** ɪŋ **~s** z
caravansary ˌkær ə ˈvæn sər i ‖ ˌker-
caravanserai ˌkær ə ˈvæn sə raɪ -reɪ, -sər i ‖ ˌker- **~s** z
caravel ˈkær ə vel ˌ· ·ˈ·; ˈkær əv ᵊl ‖ ˈker- **~s** z
caraway ˈkær ə weɪ ‖ ˈker-
carb kɑːb ‖ kɑːrb **carbs** kɑːbz ‖ kɑːrbz
carbamate ˈkɑːb ə meɪt ‖ ˈkɑːrb-
carbazole ˈkɑːb ə zəʊl →-zɒʊl ‖ ˈkɑːrb ə zoʊl
carbide ˈkɑːb aɪd ‖ ˈkɑːrb- **~s** z
carbine ˈkɑːb aɪn ‖ ˈkɑːrb iːn -aɪn **~s** z
carbineer ˌkɑːb ɪ ˈnɪə -ə- ‖ ˌkɑːrb ə ˈnɪᵊr **~s** z
Carbis ˈkɑːb ɪs §-əs ‖ ˈkɑːrb-
carbo ˈkɑːb əʊ ‖ ˈkɑːrb oʊ **~s** z
carbohydrate ˌkɑːb əʊ ˈhaɪdr eɪt ‖ ˌkɑːrb oʊ- -ə- **~s** s
carbolic kɑː ˈbɒl ɪk ‖ kɑːr ˈbɑːl ɪk
carbon ˈkɑːb ən ‖ ˈkɑːrb- **~s** z
ˌcarbon ˈcopy; **ˌcarbon ˈdating**; **ˌcarbon diˈoxide**; **ˈcarbon eˌmission**; **ˈcarbon ˌfootprint**; **ˈcarbon ˌpaper**; **ˈcarbon sink**; **ˈcarbon tax**
carbonade ˌkɑːb ə ˈneɪd -ˈnɑːd, ˈ· · · ‖ ˌkɑːrb- **~s** z
carbonado ˌkɑːb ə ˈneɪd əʊ -ˈnɑːd- ‖ ˌkɑːrb ə ˈneɪd oʊ **~es, ~s** z
carbonara ˌkɑːb ə ˈnɑːr ə ‖ ˌkɑːrb-
carbonate *n* ˈkɑːb ə neɪt -ən ət, -ɪt ‖ ˈkɑːrb- **~s** s
carbo|nate *v* ˈkɑːb ə |neɪt ‖ ˈkɑːrb- **~nated** neɪt ɪd -əd ‖ neɪţ əd **~nates** neɪts **~nating** neɪt ɪŋ ‖ neɪţ ɪŋ
carbonation ˌkɑːb ə ˈneɪʃ ᵊn ‖ ˌkɑːrb-

carbonic kɑː ˈbɒn ɪk ‖ kɑːr ˈbɑːn ɪk
carboniferous, C~ ˌkɑːb ə ˈnɪf ər‿əs ◂ ‖ ˌkɑːrb-
carbonis... —*see* **carboniz...**
carbonization ˌkɑːb ən aɪ ˈzeɪʃ ən -ɪˈ-- ‖ ˌkɑːrb ən ə- **~s** z
carboniz|e ˈkɑːb ə naɪz ‖ ˈkɑːrb- **~ed** d **~es** ɪz əz **~ing** ɪŋ
carbon-neutral ˌkɑːb ən ˈnjuːtrə l ◂ §-ˈnuːtr- ‖ ˌkɑːrb ən ˈnuːtr ə l ◂ -ˈnjuːtr-
carbonyl ˈkɑːb ə naɪəl -nɪl, -ən əl ‖ ˈkɑːrb ə nɪl -niːəl, ˌ· ·ˈ·
carborundum, C~ *tdmk* ˌkɑːb ə ˈrʌnd əm ‖ ˌkɑːrb-
Carbost ˈkɑːb ɒst ‖ ˈkɑːrb ɔːst -ɑːst
carboxyl kɑː ˈbɒks ɪl -aɪəl, §-əl ‖ kɑːr ˈbɑːks əl
carboy ˈkɑːb ɔɪ ‖ ˈkɑːrb- **~s** z
carbuncle ˈkɑːb ʌŋk əl ‖ ˈkɑːrb- **~s** z
carburant ˈkɑːb jʊr ənt -jər-, -ər- ‖ ˈkɑːrb ər- -jər- **~s** s
carburation ˌkɑːb juə ˈreɪʃ ən -jə-, -ə- ‖ ˌkɑːrb ə- -jə-
carburetor, carburetter, carburettor ˌkɑːb ə ˈret ə -juə-, ˈ· · · · ‖ ˈkɑːrb ə reɪt̬ ər *(*)* **~s** z
carcajou ˈkɑːk ə dʒuː -ʒuː ‖ ˈkɑːrk- **~s** z
carcas|e, carcass ˈkɑːk əs ‖ ˈkɑːrk- **~es** ɪz əz
Carcassonne ˌkɑːk ə ˈsɒn ‖ ˌkɑːrk ə ˈsɑːn -ˈsɔːn —*Fr* [kaʁ ka sɔn]
Carchemish ˈkɑːk ə mɪʃ -ɪ-; kɑː ˈkiːm ɪʃ ‖ ˈkɑːrk- kɑːr ˈkiːm ɪʃ
carcinogen kɑː ˈsɪn ədʒ ən ˈkɑːs ɪn-, -ə dʒen ‖ kɑːr- ˈkɑːrs ən ə dʒen **~s** z
carcinogenic ˌkɑːs ɪn ə ˈdʒen ɪk ◂ ˌ-ən-; kɑː ˌsɪn- ‖ ˌkɑːrs ən oʊ- kɑːr ˌsɪn-, -əˈ--
carcinoma ˌkɑːs ɪ ˈnəʊm ə -ə-, -ən ˈəʊm- ‖ ˌkɑːrs ən ˈoʊm ə **~s** z
card kɑːd ‖ kɑːrd **carded** ˈkɑːd ɪd -əd ‖ ˈkɑːrd- **carding** ˈkɑːd ɪŋ ‖ ˈkɑːrd- **cards** kɑːdz ‖ kɑːrdz
ˌ**card ˈindex**, ˈ· ˌ· ·
cardamom, cardamum ˈkɑːd əm əm ‖ ˈkɑːrd- -ə mɑːm
cardan, C~ ˈkɑːd ən -æn ‖ ˈkɑːrd-
cardboard ˈkɑːd bɔːd →ˈkɑːb- ‖ ˈkɑːrd bɔːrd -boʊrd
card-carrying ˈkɑːd ˌkær i‿ɪŋ →ˈkɑːg- ‖ ˈkɑːrd- -ˌker-
Cardew ˈkɑː djuː ‖ ˈkɑːr duː
cardi- *comb. form* ¦kɑːd i ‖ ¦kɑːrd i — **cardialgia** ˌkɑːd i ˈældʒ i‿ə -ˈældʒ ə ‖ ˌkɑːrd-
cardiac ˈkɑːd i æk ‖ ˈkɑːrd-
cardie ˈkɑːd i ‖ ˈkɑːrd i **~s** z
Cardiff ˈkɑːd ɪf §-əf ‖ ˈkɑːrd əf
cardigan, C~ ˈkɑːd ɪg ən ‖ ˈkɑːrd- **~s** z
Cardin ˈkɑːd æ̃ -æn ‖ kɑːr ˈdæn —*Fr* [kaʁ dæ̃]
cardinal ˈkɑːd ɪn əl -ən‿əl ‖ ˈkɑːrd- **~s** z
ˌ**cardinal ˈpoint**; ˌ**cardinal ˈvowel**
cardinality ˌkɑːd ɪ ˈnæl ət i ˌ-ə-, -ən ˈæl-, -ɪt i ‖ ˌkɑːrd ən ˈæl ət̬ i
cardio- *comb. form with stress-neutral suffix* ¦kɑːd i‿əʊ ‖ ¦kɑːrd i‿oʊ ‿ə — **cardiomyopathy** ˌkɑːd i‿əʊ maɪ ˈɒp əθ i ‖ ˌkɑːrd i‿oʊ maɪ ˈɑːp- *with stress-imposing suffix* ˌkɑːd i ˈɒ+ ‖ ˌkɑːrd i ˈɑː+ — **cardiography** ˌkɑːd i ˈɒg rəf i ‖ ˌkɑːrd i ˈɑːg-
cardiogram ˈkɑːd i‿əʊ græm ‖ ˈkɑːrd i‿ə- **~s** z
cardiograph ˈkɑːd i‿əʊ grɑːf -græf ‖ ˈkɑːrd i‿ə græf **~s** s
cardioid ˈkɑːd i ɔɪd ‖ ˈkɑːrd- **~s** z
cardiological ˌkɑːd i‿ə ˈlɒdʒ ɪk əl ◂ ‖ ˌkɑːrd i‿ə ˈlɑːdʒ- **~ly** ‿i
cardiologist ˌkɑːd i ˈɒl ədʒ ɪst §-əst ‖ ˌkɑːrd i ˈɑːl- **~s** s
cardiology ˌkɑːd i ˈɒl ədʒ i ‖ ˌkɑːrd i ˈɑːl-
cardiopulmonary ˌkɑːd i‿əʊ ˈpʌlm ən ər‿i ◂ -ˈpʊlm- ‖ ˌkɑːrd i‿ə ˈpʌlm ə ner i ◂
cardiovascular ˌkɑːd i‿əʊ ˈvæsk jʊl ə ◂ -jəl ə ‖ ˌkɑːrd i oʊ ˈvæsk jəl ər
cardoon ₍ˌ₎kɑː ˈduːn ‖ ₍ˌ₎kɑːr- **~s** z
cardpunch ˈkɑːd pʌntʃ →ˈkɑːb- ‖ ˈkɑːrd- **~es** ɪz əz
cardsharp ˈkɑːd ʃɑːp ‖ ˈkɑːrd ʃɑːrp **~ing** ɪŋ **~s** s
cardsharper ˈkɑːd ˌʃɑːp ə ‖ ˈkɑːrd ˌʃɑːrp ər **~s** z
Cardus ˈkɑːd əs ‖ ˈkɑːrd-
card|y ˈkɑːd| i ‖ ˈkɑːrd| i **~ies** iz
care keə ‖ keər kæər **cared** keəd ‖ keərd kæərd **cares** keəz ‖ keərz kæərz **caring** ˈkeər ɪŋ ‖ ˈker ɪŋ ˈkær-
careen kə ˈriːn **~ed** d **~ing** ɪŋ **~s** z
career kə ˈrɪə ‖ -ˈrɪər **careered** kə ˈrɪəd ‖ -ˈrɪərd **careering** kə ˈrɪər ɪŋ ‖ -ˈrɪr ɪŋ **careers** kə ˈrɪəz ‖ -ˈrɪərz
careerism kə ˈrɪər ˌɪz əm ‖ -ˈrɪr-
careerist kə ˈrɪər ɪst §-əst ‖ -ˈrɪr- **~s** s
carefree ˈkeə friː ˌ·ˈ· ‖ ˈker- ˈkær-
careful ˈkeəf əl -ʊl ‖ ˈkerf- ˈkærf- **~ly** ‿i **~ness** nəs nɪs
caregiver ˈkeə ˌgɪv ə ‖ ˈker ˌgɪv ər ˈkær- **~s** z
careless ˈkeə ləs -lɪs ‖ ˈker- ˈkær- **~ly** li **~ness** nəs nɪs —*See poll figures at* -less
carer ˈkeər ə ‖ ˈker ər ˈkær- **~s** z
caress kə ˈres **~ed** t **~es** ɪz əz **~ing** ɪŋ
caret ˈkær ɪt -ət, -et ‖ ˈker- **~s** s
caretaker ˈkeə ˌteɪk ə ‖ ˈker ˌteɪk ər ˈkær- **~s** z
ˈ**caretaker ˌgovernment**
Carew *place in Dyfed* ˈkeər uː -i ‖ ˈker-
Carew *family name (i)* kə ˈruː, *(ii)* ˈkeər i ‖ ˈker i
careworn ˈkeə wɔːn ‖ ˈker wɔːrn -woʊrn
Carey ˈkeər i ‖ ˈker i
carfare ˈkɑː feə ‖ ˈkɑːr fer
Carfax ˈkɑː fæks ‖ ˈkɑːr-
Cargill *(i)* ˈkɑː gɪl ‖ ˈkɑːr-, *(ii)* kɑː ˈgɪl ‖ kɑːr-
cargo ˈkɑːg əʊ ‖ ˈkɑːrg oʊ **~es, ~s** z
Carholme ˈkɑː həʊm ‖ ˈkɑːr hoʊm
carhop ˈkɑː hɒp ‖ ˈkɑːr hɑːp **~s** s
Caria ˈkeər i‿ə ‖ ˈker- ˈkær-
Carib ˈkær ɪb §-əb ‖ ˈker- **~s** z

CARIBBEAN

9%
91%
BrE
ˌ·ˈ··
·ˈ···

Caribbean ˌkær ə ˈbiː ən ◂ -ɪ-; kə ˈrɪb i ən ‖ ˌker- — *Preference poll, BrE:* ˌ·ˈ·· *91%,* ·ˈ··· *9%.*
ˌCarib ˌbean ˈSea, ·ˌ···ˈ·
caribou ˈkær ə buː -ɪ- ‖ ˈker- **~s** z
caricatur|e ˈkær ɪk ə tʃʊə ˈ·ək-, -tjʊə, -tʃɔː, -tjɔː; ˌ···ˈ· ‖ -tʃʊr ˈker-, -tʊr, -tjʊr; -ətʃ ᵊr **~ed** d **~es** z **caricaturing** ˈkær ɪk ə tʃʊər ɪŋ ˈ·ək-, -tjʊər ɪŋ, -tʃɔːr ɪŋ, -tjɔːr ɪŋ; ˌ···ˈ·· ‖ -tʃʊr ɪŋ ˈker-, -tʊr ɪŋ, -tjʊr ɪŋ; -ətʃ ər ɪŋ
caricaturist ˈkær ɪk ə tʃʊər ɪst ˈ·ək-, -tjʊər ·, -tʃɔːr ·, -tjɔːr ·, §-əst; ˌ···ˈ·· ‖ -tʃʊr əst ˈker-, -tʊr·, -tjʊr ·, -tʃᵊr · **~s** s
CARICOM ˈkær ɪ kɒm -ə- ‖ -kɑːm ˈker-
caries ˈkeər iz -iːz; ˈkeər i iːz ‖ ˈker- ˈkær-
carillon kə ˈrɪl jən -ɒn; ˈkær ɪl-, -əl- ‖ ˈkær ə lɑːn ˈker- **~s** z
carin|a, C~ kə ˈriːn |ə -ˈraɪn- **~ae** iː aɪ **~as** əz
caring ˈkeər ɪŋ ‖ ˈker ɪŋ ˈkær- **~ly** li
Carinthi|a kə ˈrɪnᵗθ i |ə **~an/s** ən/z
carioca, C~ ˌkær i ˈəʊk ə ‖ -ˈoʊk ə ˌker- **~s** z
carious ˈkeər i əs ‖ ˈker- ˈkær-
Carisbrooke ˈkær ɪz brʊk -ɪs-, -əz-, -əs- ‖ ˈker-
carjack ˈkɑː dʒæk ‖ ˈkɑːr- **~ed** t **~er/s** ə/z ‖ ᵊr/z **~ing** ɪŋ **~s** s
Carl kɑːl ‖ kɑːrl
Carla ˈkɑːl ə ‖ ˈkɑːrl ə
Carleen, Carlene ˈkɑːl iːn ‖ ˈkɑːrl-
Carleton ˈkɑːlt ən ‖ ˈkɑːrlt-
carline, C~ ˈkɑːl aɪn -ɪn, §-ən ‖ ˈkɑːrl ən **~s** z
Carling ˈkɑːl ɪŋ ‖ ˈkɑːrl ɪŋ
Carlingford ˈkɑːl ɪŋ fəd ‖ ˈkɑːrl ɪŋ fᵊrd
Carlisle *(i)* ₍ˌ₎kɑː ˈlaᵊl ‖ ₍ˌ₎kɑːr- kᵊr-, *(ii)* ˈkɑː laᵊl ‖ ˈkɑːr- —*In BrE usually (i), although the place in Cumbria is locally (ii); in AmE usually (ii).*
Carlist ˈkɑːl ɪst §-əst ‖ ˈkɑːrl- **~s** s
Carlo ˈkɑːl əʊ ‖ ˈkɑːrl oʊ **~'s** z
carload ˈkɑː ləʊd ‖ ˈkɑːr loʊd **~s** z
Carlos ˈkɑːl ɒs ‖ ˈkɑːrl oʊs -əs —*Sp* [ˈkar los]
Carlotta kɑː ˈlɒt ə ‖ kɑːr ˈlɑːṱ ə
Carlovingian ˌkɑːl əʊ ˈvɪndʒ i ən ◂ -ˈvɪndʒ ən ‖ ˌkɑːrl ə- **~s** z
Carlow ˈkɑːl əʊ ‖ ˈkɑːrl oʊ
Carlsbad ˈkɑːlz bæd ‖ ˈkɑːrlz-
Carlsberg ˈkɑːlz bɜːg ‖ ˈkɑːrlz bɜːg **~s, 's** z
Carlson ˈkɑːls ən ‖ ˈkɑːrls-
Carlton ˈkɑːlt ən ‖ ˈkɑːrlt-
Carly ˈkɑːl i ‖ ˈkɑːrl i
Carlyle ₍ˌ₎kɑː ˈlaᵊl ‖ ₍ˌ₎kɑːr- ˈ· ·
Carman ˈkɑːm ən ‖ ˈkɑːrm-
Carmarthen kə ˈmɑːð ᵊn ‖ kɑːr ˈmɑːrð-
Carmel *(i)* ˈkɑːm el -ᵊl ‖ ˈkɑːrm-, *(ii)* ₍ˌ₎kɑː ˈmel ‖ ₍ˌ₎kɑːr- —*The mountain is usually (i); the place in California is (ii).*
Carmelite ˈkɑːm ə laɪt -ɪ-; -el aɪt ‖ ˈkɑːrm- **~s** s
Carmelle ₍ˌ₎kɑː ˈmel ‖ ₍ˌ₎kɑːr-
Carmen ˈkɑːm en ‖ ˈkɑːrm ən —*Sp* [ˈkar men]
Carmichael kɑː ˈmaɪk ᵊl -ˈmɪx-, ˈ·ˌ·· ‖ ˈkɑːr ˌmaɪk ᵊl
Carmina Burana ˌkɑːm ɪn ə bə ˈrɑːn ə §ˌ·ən-, kɑː ˌmiːn ə-, -bu ˈrɑːn- ‖ ˌkɑːrm ən- kɑːr ˌmiːn-
carminative ˈkɑːm ɪn ət ɪv ˈ·ən- ‖ kɑːr ˈmɪn əṱ ɪv ˈkɑːrm ə neɪṱ- **~s** z
carmine ˈkɑːm aɪn -ɪn, §-ən ‖ ˈkɑːrm- **~s** z
Carmody ˈkɑːm əd i ‖ ˈkɑːrm-
Carnaby ˈkɑːn əb i ‖ ˈkɑːrn-
Carnac ˈkɑːn æk ‖ kɑːr ˈnæk —*Fr* [kaʁ nak]
carnage ˈkɑːn ɪdʒ ‖ ˈkɑːrn-
Carnaghan ˈkɑːn əg ən ‖ ˈkɑːrn- -ə hæn
carnal ˈkɑːn ᵊl ‖ ˈkɑːrn ᵊl **~ly** i
carnality kɑː ˈnæl ət i -ɪt- ‖ kɑːr ˈnæl əṱ i
carnallite ˈkɑːn ə laɪt -ᵊl aɪt ‖ ˈkɑːrn ᵊl aɪt
Carnap ˈkɑːn æp ‖ ˈkɑːrn-
Carnarvon kə ˈnɑːv ᵊn ‖ kᵊr ˈnɑːrv-
carnassial kɑː ˈnæʃ i əl ‖ kɑːr-
Carnatic kɑː ˈnæt ɪk ‖ kɑːr ˈnæṱ ɪk
carnation kɑː ˈneɪʃ ᵊn ‖ kɑːr- **~s** z
carnauba kɑː ˈnɔːb ə -ˈnaʊb- ‖ kɑːr- -ˈnɑːb-
Carnegie *(i)* kɑː ˈneg i ‖ kɑːr-, *(ii)* -ˈneɪg-, *(iii)* -ˈniːg-, *(iv)* ˈkɑːn əg i ‖ ˈkɑːrn- —*Andrew C~ was (ii); but C~ Hall is usually (iv).*
carnelian kɑː ˈniːl i ən kə- ‖ kɑːr- **~s** z
carnet ˈkɑːn eɪ ‖ kɑːr ˈneɪ —*Fr* [kaʁ nɛ] **~s** z
Carney ˈkɑːn i ‖ ˈkɑːrn i
Carnforth ˈkɑːn fɔːθ -fəθ ‖ ˈkɑːrn fɔːrθ -foʊrθ
carnie ˈkɑːn i ‖ ˈkɑːrn i **~s** z
carnival ˈkɑːn ɪv ᵊl -əv- ‖ ˈkɑːrn- **~s** z
carnivore ˈkɑːn ɪ vɔː -ə- ‖ ˈkɑːrn ə vɔːr -voʊr **~s** z
carnivorous kɑː ˈnɪv ər əs ‖ kɑːr- **~ly** li **~ness** nəs nɪs
Carnochan ˈkɑːn ək ən -əx- ‖ ˈkɑːrn-
Carnot ˈkɑːn əʊ ‖ kɑːr ˈnoʊ —*Fr* [kaʁ no]
Carnoustie kɑː ˈnuːst i ‖ kɑːr-
carn|y ˈkɑːn |i ‖ ˈkɑːrn |i **~ies** iz
carob ˈkær əb ‖ ˈker- **~s** z
carol, Carol ˈkær əl ‖ ˈker- **~ed, ~led** d **~ing, ~ling** ɪŋ **~s** z
Carola ˈkær əl ə ‖ ˈker-
Carole ˈkær əl ‖ ˈker-
Carolina ˌkær ə ˈlaɪn ə ◂ ‖ ˌker- **~s, ~'s** z
Caroline *(i)* ˈkær ə laɪn ‖ ˈker-, *(ii)* -əl ɪn §-ən
Carolingian ˌkær ə ˈlɪndʒ i ən ◂ ‖ ˌker- **~s** z
Carolinian ˌkær ə ˈlɪn i ən ◂ ‖ ˌker- **~s** z
Carolyn ˈkær əl ɪn §-ən ‖ ˈker-
carom ˈkær əm ‖ ˈker- **~ed** d **~ing** ɪŋ **~s** z
caron ˈkær ən ‖ ˈker- **~s** z
Caron *(i)* ˈkær ən ‖ ˈker-, *(ii)* kə ˈrɒn ‖ -ˈrɑːn -ˈrɔːn
carotene ˈkær ə tiːn ‖ ˈker-
carotid kə ˈrɒt ɪd §-əd ‖ -ˈrɑːṱ- **~s** z
carousal kə ˈraʊz ᵊl **~s** z
carous|e kə ˈraʊz **~ed** d **~es** ɪz əz **~ing** ɪŋ
carousel ˌkær ə ˈsel -u-, -ˈzel ‖ ˌker-, ˈ··· **~s** z

arp kɑːp ‖ kɑːrp **carped** kɑːpt ‖ kɑːrpt **carping** ˈkɑːp ɪŋ ‖ ˈkɑːrp- **carps** kɑːps ‖ kɑːrps

arpaccio kɑː ˈpætʃ i əʊ -ˈpɑːtʃ-; ·ˈ·əʊ ‖ kɑːr ˈpɑːtʃ oʊ —*It* [kar ˈpat tʃo]

arpal ˈkɑːp ᵊl ‖ ˈkɑːrp- **~s** z

arpathian kɑː ˈpeɪθ i‿ən ‖ kɑːr- **~s** z

arpe diem ˌkɑːp i ˈdiː em ‖ ˌkɑːrp-

arpel ˈkɑːp ᵊl -el ‖ ˈkɑːrp- **~s** z

arpentaria ˌkɑːp ən ˈteər i‿ə →ˌ·m-, ˌ·en- ‖ ˌkɑːrp ən ˈter-

arpenter, C~ ˈkɑːp ənt ə -ɪnt-, →-mt- ‖ ˈkɑːrp ənt̬ ᵊr →-mt̬- **~ed** d **carpentering** ˈkɑːp ənt‿ər ɪŋ -ɪnt‿, →mt‿ ‖ ˈkɑːrp ənt̬ ᵊr ɪŋ →ˈ·əntr ɪŋ, →-mtr- **~s** z

arpentry ˈkɑːp əntr i -ɪntr i, →-m tri ‖ ˈkɑːrp-

arp|et ˈkɑːp |ɪt §-ət ‖ ˈkɑːrp |ət **~eted** ɪt ɪd §ət-, -əd ‖ ət̬ əd **~eting** ɪt ɪŋ §ət- ‖ ət̬ ɪŋ **~ets** ɪts §əts ‖ əts
ˈcarpet ˌbeetle; **ˈcarpet ˌbombing**; **ˈcarpet ˌslippers**

arpetbag ˈkɑːp ɪt bæg §-ət- ‖ ˈkɑːrp- **~ger/s** ə/z ‖ ᵊr/z **~ging** ɪŋ **~s** z

arpet-bomb ˈkɑːp ɪt bɒm §-ət- ‖ ˈkɑːrp ət bɑːm **~ed** d **~ing** ɪŋ **~s** z

arpet-sweeper ˈkɑːp ɪt ˌswiːp ə §-ət- ‖ ˈkɑːrp ət ˌswiːp ᵊr **~s** z

arphone ˈkɑː fəʊn ‖ ˈkɑːr foʊn **~s** z

arpi ˈkɑːp aɪ ‖ ˈkɑːrp-

arping ˈkɑːp ɪŋ ‖ ˈkɑːrp ɪŋ **~ly** li

arpo- *comb. form with stress-neutral suffix* ¦kɑːp əʊ ‖ ¦kɑːrp ə — **carpophore** ˈkɑːp əʊ fɔː ‖ ˈkɑːrp ə fɔːr *with stress-imposing suffix* kɑ ˈpɒ+ ‖ kɑːr ˈpɑː+ — **carpophagous** kɑː ˈpɒf əg əs ‖ kɑːr ˈpɑːf-

arpool ˈkɑː puːl ‖ ˈkɑːr puːl **~ing** ɪŋ **~s** z

arport ˈkɑː pɔːt ‖ ˈkɑːr pɔːrt -poʊrt **~s** s

carpous ˈkɑːp əs ‖ ˈkɑːrp- — **polycarpous** ˌpɒl i ˈkɑːp əs ◂ ‖ ˌpɑːl i ˈkɑːrp-

arp|us ˈkɑːp |əs ‖ ˈkɑːrp- **~i** aɪ iː

arr, Carr kɑː ‖ kɑːr **~s** z

arrageen, carragheen ˈkær ə giːn ˌ· ·ˈ· ‖ ˈker-

arrantuohill, Carrauntoohill ˌkær ən ˈtuː‿əl ‖ ˌker-

arrara kə ˈrɑːr ə —*It* [kar ˈraː ra]

arrbridge ˌkɑː ˈbrɪdʒ ‖ ˌkɑːr-

arrel ˈkær əl ‖ ˈker- *(= carol)* **~s** z

arrhae ˈkær iː ‖ ˈker-

arri... —*see* **carry**

arriacou ˌkær i‿ə ˈkuː ˈ· · · · ‖ ˌker-

arriag|e ˈkær ɪdʒ ‖ ˈker- **~es** ɪz əz

arriageway ˈkær ɪdʒ weɪ ‖ ˈker- **~s** z

arrick, c~ ˈkær ɪk ‖ ˈker-

arrickfergus ˌkær ɪk ˈfɜːg əs ‖ -ˈfɝːg əs ˌker-

arrie ˈkær i ‖ ˈker-

arrier ˈkær i‿ə ‖ ˈkær i‿ᵊr ˈker- **~s** z
ˈcarrier bag, ˌ· · · ˈ·; **ˌcarrier ˈpigeon, ˈ· · ˈ· ·**; **ˈcarrier wave**

arrington ˈkær ɪŋ tən ‖ ˈker-

arrion ˈkær i‿ən ‖ ˈker-
ˌcarrion ˈcrow, ˈ· · · ·

Carrol, Carroll ˈkær əl ‖ ˈker-

Carron ˈkær ən ‖ ˈker-

carrot ˈkær ət ‖ ˈker-

carrot-and-stick ˌkær ət ᵊn ˈstɪk -ət ᵊnd- ‖ ˌker-

carroty ˈkær ət i ‖ -ət̬ i ˈker-

carrousel ˌkær ə ˈsel -u-, -ˈzel ‖ ˌker-, ˈ· · · **~s** z

Carruthers kə ˈrʌð əz ‖ -ᵊrz

carry, Carry ˈkær i ‖ ˈker- **carried** ˈkær id ‖ ˈker- **carries** ˈkær iz ˈker- **carrying** ˈkær i‿ɪŋ ‖ ˈker-

carryall ˈkær i ɔːl ‖ ˈker-, -ɑːl **~s** z

carrycot ˈkær i kɒt ‖ -kɑːt ˈker- **~s** s

carrying ˈkær i‿ɪŋ ‖ ˈker-
ˈcarrying case; **ˈcarrying charge**

carryings-on ˌkær i‿ɪŋz ˈɒn ‖ -ˈɑːn ˌker-, -ˈɔːn

carry-on ˈkær i ɒn ˌ· ·ˈ·◂ ‖ -ɑːn ˈker-, -ɔːn **~s** z

carryout ˈkær i aʊt ‖ ˈker- **~s** s

carry-over ˈkær i ˌəʊv ə ‖ -ˌoʊv ᵊr ˈker- **~s** z

Carse kɑːs ‖ kɑːrs

Carshalton kɑː ˈʃɔːlt ən kə- ‖ kɑːr- -ˈʃɑːlt- —*formerly also* keɪs ˈhɔːt ᵊn

carsick ˈkɑː sɪk ‖ ˈkɑːr-

Carson ˈkɑːs ᵊn ‖ ˈkɑːrs ᵊn
ˌCarson ˈCity

Carstairs ˌkɑː ˈsteəz ˈ· · ‖ ˈkɑːr sterz

cart kɑːt ‖ kɑːrt **carted** ˈkɑːt ɪd -əd ‖ ˈkɑːrt̬ əd **carting** ˈkɑːt ɪŋ ‖ ˈkɑːrt̬ ɪŋ **carts** kɑːts ‖ kɑːrts
ˈcart track

Carta ˈkɑːt ə ‖ ˈkɑːrt̬ ə

cartage ˈkɑːt ɪdʒ ‖ ˈkɑːrt̬-

Cartagena ˌkɑːt ə ˈdʒiːn ə ‖ ˌkɑːrt̬ ə ˈheɪn ə -ˈgeɪn- —*Sp* [kar ta ˈxe na]

carte blanche ˌkɑːt ˈblɑːnᵗʃ -ˈblɒ̃ʃ ‖ ˌkɑːrt- —*Fr* [kaʁ tə blɑ̃ːʃ]

cartel kɑː ˈtel ‖ kɑːr- **~s** z

carter, C~ ˈkɑːt ə ‖ ˈkɑːrt̬ ᵊr **~s** z

Carteret ˈkɑːt ə ret -rɪt, -rət ‖ ˈkɑːrt̬- ˌ· ·ˈret

Cartesian ₍ₗ₎kɑː ˈtiːz i‿ən -ˈtiːʒ ᵊn ‖ kɑːr ˈtiːʒ ᵊn **~s** z

Carthage ˈkɑːθ ɪdʒ ‖ ˈkɑːrθ-

Carthaginian ˌkɑːθ ə ˈdʒɪn i‿ən ◂ ‖ ˌkɑːrθ- **~s** z

Carthew ˈkɑːθ juː ‖ ˈkɑːrθ uː

carthors|e ˈkɑːt hɔːs ‖ ˈkɑːrt hɔːrs **~es** ɪz əz

Carthusian kɑː ˈθjuːz i‿ən -ˈθuːz- ‖ kɑːr ˈθuːʒ ᵊn -ˈθjuːʒ- **~s** z

Cartier ˈkɑːt i eɪ ‖ ˈkɑːrt̬- —*but as a French or French Canadian name,* ˌ· ·ˈ· —*Fr* [kaʁ tje] **~'s** z

cartilage ˈkɑːt əl‿ɪdʒ -ɪl- ‖ ˈkɑːrt̬- **~es** ɪz əz

cartilaginous ˌkɑːt ə ˈlædʒ ɪn əs ◂ -ɪ-, -ᵊl ˈædʒ-, -ən əs ‖ ˌkɑːrt̬ ᵊl ˈædʒ ən əs

Cartland ˈkɑːt lənd ‖ ˈkɑːrt-

cartload ˈkɑːt ləʊd ‖ ˈkɑːrt loʊd **~s** z

Cartmel ˈkɑːt məl -mel ‖ ˈkɑːrt-

cartographer kɑː ˈtɒg rəf ə ‖ kɑːr ˈtɑːg rəf ᵊr **~s** z

cartographic ˌkɑːt ə ˈgræf ɪk ◂ ‖ ˌkɑːrt̬- **~al** ᵊl **~ally** ᵊl‿i

cartography kɑː ˈtɒg rəf i ‖ kɑːr ˈtɑːg-

cartomancy ˈkɑːt əʊ ˌmænᵗs i ‖ ˈkɑːrt̬ ə-

C

carton, C~ 'kɑːt ᵊn ‖ 'kɑːrt ᵊn **~s** z
cartoon kɑː 'tuːn ‖ kɑːr- **~s** z
cartoonish kɑː 'tuːn ɪʃ ‖ kɑːr-
cartoonist kɑː 'tuːn ɪst §-əst ‖ kɑːr- **~s** s
cartophilist kɑː 'tɒf əl ɪst -ɪl-, §-əst ‖ kɑːr 'tɑːf- **~s** s
cartophily kɑː 'tɒf əl i -ɪl- ‖ kɑːr 'tɑːf-
cartouch|e kɑː 'tuːʃ ‖ kɑːr- **~es** ɪz əz
cartridg|e 'kɑːtr ɪdʒ ‖ 'kɑːrtr- §'kætr- **~es** ɪz əz
'cartridge belt; **'cartridge ˌpaper**
cartwheel 'kɑːt wiːᵊl -hwiːᵊl ‖ 'kɑːrt- **~ed** d **~ing** ɪŋ **~s** z
Cartwright, c~ 'kɑːt raɪt ‖ 'kɑːrt-
caruncle kə 'rʌŋk ᵊl kæ-; 'kær əŋk- **~s** z
Caruso kə 'ruːs əʊ -'ruːz- ‖ -oʊ —*It* [ka 'ruː zo]
Caruthers kə 'rʌð əz ‖ -ᵊrz
carve kɑːv ‖ kɑːrv **carved** kɑːvd ‖ kɑːrvd **carves** kɑːvz ‖ kɑːrvz **carving** 'kɑːv ɪŋ ‖ 'kɑːrv ɪŋ
carvel 'kɑːv ᵊl -el ‖ 'kɑːrv- **~s** z
carvel-built 'kɑːv ᵊl bɪlt -el- ‖ 'kɑːrv-
carver, C~ 'kɑːv ə ‖ 'kɑːrv ᵊr **~s** z
carver|y 'kɑːv ər |i ‖ 'kɑːrv- **~ies** iz
carve-up 'kɑːv ʌp ‖ 'kɑːrv-
carving 'kɑːv ɪŋ ‖ kɑːrv ɪŋ **~s** z
'carving knife
Carwardine 'kɑː wə diːn ‖ 'kɑːr wᵊr-
Cary *family name* 'keər i ‖ 'ker i 'kær-
Cary *personal name* 'kær i 'keər- ‖ 'ker-
caryatid ˌkær i 'æt ɪd §-əd; 'kær i‿ə tɪd ‖ -'æţ əd ˌker-; 'kær i‿ə tɪd, 'ker- **~s** z
Caryl 'kær əl -ɪl ‖ 'ker-
Carys 'kær ɪs -əs ‖ 'ker-
Carysfort 'kær ɪs fɔːt -əs- ‖ -fɔːrt 'ker-, -foʊrt
carzey 'kɑːz i ‖ — **~s** z
Casablanca ˌkæs ə 'blæŋk ə ˌkæz- ‖ ˌkɑːs ə 'blɑːŋk ə —*Fr* [ka za blɑ̃ ka]
Casals kə 'sælz ‖ -'sɑːlz kɑː- —*Sp* [ka 'sals], *Catalan* [kə 'zals]
Casanova ˌkæs ə 'nəʊv ə ˌkæz- ‖ ˌkæz ə 'noʊv ə ˌkæs- —*It* [ka sa 'nɔː va]
Casaubon kə 'sɔːb ən 'kæz ə bɒn ‖ -'sɑːb-; 'kæz ə bɑːn —*Fr* [ka zo bɔ̃]
casbah 'kæz bɑː -bə ‖ 'kɑːz-
cascad|e, C~ ˌ₍ˌ₎kæ 'skeɪd **~ed** ɪd əd **~es** z **~ing** ɪŋ
cascara kæ 'skɑːr ə ‖ -'skær- -'sker-
cascarilla ˌkæsk ə 'rɪl ə ‖ -'riː jə, -'rɪl jə
case, Case keɪs **cased** keɪst **cases** 'keɪs ɪz -əz **casing** keɪs ɪŋ
'case ˌending; **ˌcase 'history**; **'case ˌstudy**
casebook 'keɪs bʊk §-buːk **~s** s
casebound 'keɪs baʊnd
case-harden 'keɪs ˌhɑːd ᵊn ‖ -ˌhɑːrd- **~ed** d **~ing** ‿ɪŋ **~s** z
casein 'keɪs i ɪn 'keɪs iːn ‖ keɪ 'siːn
caseload 'keɪs ləʊd ‖ -loʊd **~s** z
casemate 'keɪs meɪt **~s** s
casement, C~ 'keɪs mənt **~ed** ɪd əd **~s** s
ˌcasement 'window
casework 'keɪs wɜːk ‖ -wɜːk
caseworker 'keɪs ˌwɜːk ə ‖ -ˌwɜːk ᵊr **~s** z
Casey 'keɪs i
cash, Cash kæʃ **cashed** kæʃt **cashes** 'kæʃ ɪz -əz **cashing** 'kæʃ ɪŋ
'cash card; **'cash crop**; **ˌcash 'discount**; **'cash diˌspenser**; **'cash flow**; **'cash maˌchine**; **'cash ˌregister**
cashable 'kæʃ əb ᵊl
cash-and-carry ˌkæʃ ᵊn 'kær i →-ᵊŋ- ‖ -'ker-
cashback 'kæʃ bæk
cashbook 'kæʃ bʊk **~s** s
cashew 'kæʃ uː kæ 'ʃuː, kə- **~s** z
ca|shier kæ |'ʃɪə kə- ‖ -'|ʃɪᵊr **~shiered** 'ʃɪəd ‖ 'ʃɪᵊrd **~shiering** 'ʃɪər ɪŋ ‖ 'ʃɪr ɪŋ **~shiers** 'ʃɪəz ‖ 'ʃɪᵊrz
Cashin 'kæʃ ɪn §-ᵊn
cash-in-hand ˌkæʃ ɪn 'hænd §-ᵊn-
cashless 'kæʃ ləs -lɪs
Cashman 'kæʃ mən
cashmere 'kæʃ mɪə ˌ·'· ‖ 'kæʒ mɪr 'kæʃ- **~s** z
cashpoint 'kæʃ pɔɪnt **~s** s
cash-rich ˌkæʃ 'rɪtʃ ◂
cash-starved ˌkæʃ 'stɑːvd ◂ ‖ -'stɑːrvd ◂
cash-strapped ˌkæʃ 'stræpt ◂
casing 'keɪs ɪŋ **~s** z
casino kə 'siːn əʊ ‖ -oʊ **~s** z
Casio *tdmk* 'kæs i‿əʊ ‖ oʊ
cask kɑːsk §kæsk ‖ kæsks **casks** kɑːsks §kæsks ‖ kæsks
casket 'kɑːsk ɪt §'kæsk-, §-ət ‖ 'kæsk ət **~s** s
Caslon 'kæz lɒn -lən ‖ -lɑːn -lən
Caspar 'kæsp ə -ɑː ‖ -ᵊr -ɑːr
Caspian 'kæsp i‿ən
casque kæsk kɑːsk **casques** kæsks kɑːsks
Cass kæs
Cassandra kə 'sændr ə -'sɑːndr- **~s, ~'s** z
cassareep 'kæs ə riːp
cassata kə 'sɑːt ə kæ- ‖ -'sɑːţ ə —*It* [kas 'saː ta]
cassava kə 'sɑːv ə
Cassel, Cassell 'kæs ᵊl —*but as a French name,* kæ 'sel —*Fr* [ka sɛl]
casserol|e 'kæs ə rəʊl →-rɒʊl ‖ -roʊl 'kæz- **~ed** d **~es** z **~ing** ɪŋ
cassette kə 'set kæ- **~s** s
cas'sette reˌcorder
cassia 'kæs i‿ə ‖ 'kæʃ ə *(*)*
Cassidy 'kæs əd i -ɪd-
Cassie 'kæs i
Cassillis 'kæs ᵊlz
Cassio 'kæs i‿əʊ ‖ oʊ
Cassiopeia ˌkæs i əʊ 'piː‿ə -'peɪ ə ‖ ˌkæs i oʊ-
cassis kæ 'siːs kɑː-; 'kæs iːs —*Fr* [ka sis]
cassiterite kə 'sɪt ə raɪt ‖ -'sɪţ-
Cassius 'kæs i‿əs ‖ 'kæʃ əs -i‿əs *(*)*
Cassivelaunus ˌkæs ɪv ə 'lɔːn əs ˌ·əv-, -ɪ'·-, -'laʊn- ‖ -'lɑːn-
cassock 'kæs ək **~s** s
Casson 'kæs ᵊn
cassoulet ˌkæs u 'leɪ -ə-, '· · · ‖ -ə- —*Fr* [ka su lɛ] **~s** z
cassowar|y 'kæs ə weər |i -wər i ‖ -wer |i **~ies** iz

ast kɑːst §kæst ‖ kæst **casting** 'kɑːst ɪŋ §'kæst- ‖ 'kæst ɪŋ **casts** kɑːsts §kæsts ‖ kæsts
astali|a kæ 'steɪl i‿|ə **~an** ən
astanet ˌkæst ə 'net **~s** s
astaway 'kɑːst ə ˌweɪ §'kæst- ‖ 'kæst- **~s** z
aste kɑːst §kæst ‖ kæst *(= cast)* **castes** kɑːsts §kæsts ‖ kæsts
astel Gandolfo ˌkæst el gæn 'dɒlf əʊ ‖ -'dɑːlf oʊ — *It* [kas tɛl gan 'dɔl fo]
astellated 'kæst ə leɪt ɪd '·ɪ-, -ᵊl eɪt-, -əd ‖ -leɪţ əd
aster 'kɑːst ə §'kæst- ‖ 'kæst ᵊr **~s** z
'caster ˌsugar, ˌ·'··
Casterbridge 'kɑːst ə brɪdʒ §'kæst- ‖ 'kæst ᵊr-
asti|gate 'kæst ɪ |geɪt -ə- **~gated** geɪt ɪd -əd ‖ geɪţ- **~gates** geɪts **~gating** geɪt ɪŋ ‖ geɪţ ɪŋ
astigation ˌkæst ɪ 'geɪʃ ᵊn -ə- **~s** z
astigator 'kæst ɪ geɪt ə '·ə- ‖ -geɪţ ᵊr **~s** z
Castile kæ 'stiːᵊl —*but the place in NY is* -'starᵊl
Castilian kæ 'stɪl i‿ən **~s** z
asting 'kɑːst ɪŋ §'kæst- ‖ 'kæst ɪŋ **~s** z
ˌcasting 'vote
ast-iron ˌkɑːst 'aɪ‿ən ◂ §ˌkæst- ‖ ˌkæst 'aɪ ᵊrn ◂
astl|e, C~ 'kɑːs ᵊl §'kæs- ‖ 'kæs ᵊl **~ed** d **~es** z **~ing** ‿ɪŋ
Castlebar ˌkɑːs ᵊl 'bɑː §ˌkæs- ‖ ˌkæs ᵊl 'bɑːr
Castleford 'kɑːs ᵊl fəd §'kæs- ‖ 'kæs ᵊl fᵊrd
Castlemaine 'kɑːs ᵊl meɪn §'kæs- ‖ 'kæs-
Castlenau 'kɑːs ᵊl nɔː §'kæs-, -nəʊ ‖ 'kæs- -nɑː
Castlerea, Castlereagh 'kɑːs ᵊl reɪ §'kæs-, ˌ·'· ‖ 'kæs-
Castleton 'kɑːs ᵊl tən §'kæs- ‖ 'kæs-
Castlewellan ˌkɑːs ᵊl 'wel ən §ˌkæs- ‖ ˌkæs-
castoff, cast-off 'kɑːst ɒf §'kæst-, -ɔːf ‖ 'kæst ɔːf -ɑːf **~s** s
castor, C~ 'kɑːst ə §'kæst- ‖ 'kæst ᵊr *(= caster)* **~s** z
ˌcastor 'oil; 'castor ˌsugar, ˌ·'··
castrate kæ 'streɪt ‖ 'kæs treɪt *(*)* **castrated** kæ 'streɪt ɪd -əd ‖ 'kæs treɪţ əd **castrates** kæ 'streɪts ‖ 'kæs treɪts **castrating** kæ 'streɪt ɪŋ ‖ 'kæs treɪţ ɪŋ
castration kæ 'streɪʃ ᵊn **~s** z
castrat|o kæ 'strɑːt |əʊ kə- ‖ -|oʊ **~i** iː
Castries kæ 'striːz -'striːs
Castro 'kæs trəʊ ‖ -troʊ —*Sp* ['kas tro]
Castrol *tdmk* 'kæs trɒl ‖ -troʊl -trɑːl, -trɔːl

CASUAL

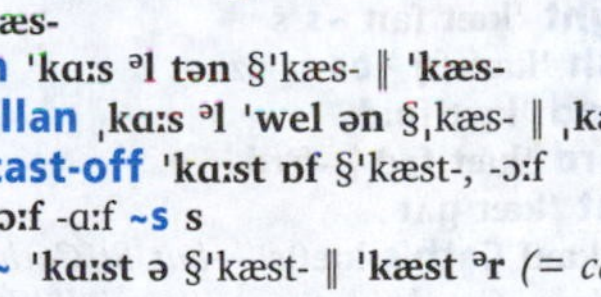

casual 'kæʒ u‿əl -ju‿, 'kæz ju‿; 'kæʒ ᵊl — *Preference poll, BrE:* 'kæʒ- 77%, 'kæz- 23%. **~ly** i **~ness** nəs nɪs **~s** z

casualization, casualisation ˌkæʒ u‿əl aɪ 'zeɪʃ ᵊn ˌ·ju‿, ˌkæz ju‿, ˌkæʒ ᵊl aɪ-; -ɪ'· ‖ -ə'·
casualiz|e, casualis|e 'kæʒ u‿ə laɪz -ju‿, 'kæz ju‿; 'kæʒ ə laɪz **~ed** d **~ing** ɪŋ **~es** ɪz əz
casual|ty 'kæʒ u‿əl |ti 'ju‿, 'kæz ju‿; 'kæʒ ᵊl |ti **~ties** tiz
'casualty ward
casuarina ˌkæz ju‿ə 'riːn ə ˌkæʒ ju‿, ˌkæʒ u‿, ˌkæʒ ə 'riːn ə; -'raɪn- ‖ ˌkæʒ u‿ **~s** z
casuist 'kæz ju‿ɪst 'kæʒ ju‿, 'kæʒ u‿, §‿əst ‖ 'kæʒ u‿əst **~s** s
casuistic ˌkæz ju 'ɪst ɪk ◂ ˌkæʒ ju-, ˌkæʒ u- ‖ ˌkæʒ u- **~ally** ᵊl‿i
casuis|try 'kæz ju‿ɪs |tri 'kæʒ ju‿, 'kæʒ u‿, §‿əs· ‖ 'kæʒ u‿ **~tries** triz
casus belli ˌkɑːs ʊs 'bel iː ·əs-; ˌkeɪs əs 'bel aɪ
cat kæt **cats** kæts
'cat ˌburglar; 'cat ˌcracker; 'cat door; 'cat flap; ˌcat's 'cradle; ˌcat's 'whisker
CAT kæt
'CAT scan, 'CAT ˌscanner
cata- *comb. form with stress-neutral suffix* ¦kæt ə ‖ ¦kæţ ə — **cataclastic** ˌkæt ə 'klæst ɪk ◂ ‖ ˌkæţ- *with stress-imposing suffix* kə 'tæ+ — **catadromous** kə 'tædr əm əs
catabolic ˌkæt ə 'bɒl ɪk ◂ ‖ ˌkæţ ə 'bɑːl- **~ally** ᵊl‿i
catabolism kə 'tæb ə ˌlɪz əm
catachresis ˌkæt ə 'kriːs ɪs §-əs ‖ ˌkæţ-
catachrestic ˌkæt ə 'krest ɪk ◂ ‖ ˌkæţ-
cataclysm 'kæt ə ˌklɪz əm ‖ 'kæţ- **~s** z
cataclysmal ˌkæt ə 'klɪz mᵊl ‖ ˌkæţ- **~ly** i
cataclysmic ˌkæt ə 'klɪz mɪk ◂ ‖ ˌkæţ- **~ally** ᵊl‿i
catacomb 'kæt ə kuːm -kəʊm ‖ 'kæţ ə koʊm **~s** z
catafalque 'kæt ə fælk ‖ 'kæţ ə fɔːk -fɑːk, -fɔːlk, -fælk **~s** s
Catalan 'kæt ə læn -ᵊl ən, ᵊl æn; ˌkæt ə 'læn ‖ 'kæţ ᵊl ən -æn, ˌkɑːt ə 'lɑːn **~s** z
catalectic ˌkæt ə 'lekt ɪk ◂ -ᵊl 'ekt- ‖ ˌkæţ ᵊl 'ekt ɪk ◂
catalepsy 'kæt ə leps i -ᵊl eps- ‖ 'kæţ ᵊl eps i
cataleptic ˌkæt ə 'lept ɪk ◂ -ᵊl 'ept- ‖ ˌkæţ ᵊl 'ept ɪk ◂
Catalina ˌkæt ə 'liːn ə -ᵊl 'iːn- ‖ ˌkæţ ᵊl 'iːn ə
catalog, catalogu|e 'kæt ə lɒg -ᵊl ɒg ‖ 'kæţ ᵊl ɔːg -ɑːg **~ed** d **~ing** ɪŋ **catalogs, catalogues** 'kæt ə lɒgz -ᵊl ɒgz ‖ 'kæţ ᵊl ɔːgz -ɑːgz
Catalonia ˌkæt ə 'ləʊn i‿ə -ᵊl 'əʊn- ‖ ˌkæţ ᵊl 'oʊn-
catalpa kə 'tælp ə ‖ -'tɑːlp-, -'tɔːlp- **~s** z
catalysis kə 'tæl əs ɪs §-əs
catalyst 'kæt əl ɪst §-əst ‖ 'kæţ- **~s** s
catalytic ˌkæt ə 'lɪt ɪk ◂ -ᵊl 'ɪt- ‖ ˌkæţ ᵊl 'ɪţ ɪk ◂ **~ally** ᵊl‿i
catamaran ˌkæt əm ə 'ræn '· · · ‖ ˌkæţ- **~s** z
catamite 'kæt ə maɪt ‖ 'kæţ- **~s** s
catamount 'kæt ə maʊnt ‖ 'kæţ- **~s** s

catamountain ˌkæt ə ˈmaʊnt ɪn -ən ‖ ˌkæţ ə ˈmaʊnt ᵊn **~s** z

cat-and-dog ˌkæt ᵊn ˈdɒg ◂ ‖ -ˈdɔːg -ˈdɑːg

cat-and-mouse ˌkæt ᵊn ˈmaʊs ◂

cataphora kə ˈtæf ər ə

cataphoresis ˌkæt ə fə ˈriːs ɪs -fɒˈ--, §-əs ‖ ˌkæţ-

cataphoretic ˌkæt ə fə ˈret ɪk ◂ -fɒˈ-- ‖ ˌkæţ ə fə ˈreţ ɪk ◂ **~ally** ᵊl‿i

cataphoric ˌkæt ə ˈfɒr ɪk ◂ ‖ ˌkæţ ə ˈfɔːr ɪk ◂ -ˈfɑːr- **~ally** ᵊl‿i

cataplasm ˈkæt ə ˌplæz əm ‖ ˈkæţ- **~s** z

cataplexy ˈkæt ə pleks i ‖ ˈkæţ-

catapult ˈkæt ə pʌlt §-pʊlt ‖ ˈkæţ- **~ed** ɪd -əd **~ing** ɪŋ **~s** s

cataract ˈkæt ə rækt ‖ ˈkæţ- **~s** s

catarrh kə ˈtɑː ‖ -ˈtɑːr

catarrhal kə ˈtɑːr əl

catarrhine ˈkæt ə raɪn ‖ ˈkæţ- **~s** z

catastasis kə ˈtæst əs ɪs §-əs

catastrophe kə ˈtæs trəf i **~s** z

catastrophic ˌkæt ə ˈstrɒf ɪk ◂ ‖ ˌkæţ ə ˈstrɑːf- **~ally** ᵊl‿i

ˌcataˌstrophic ˈfailure

catastrophism kə ˈtæs trə ˌfɪz əm

catatonia ˌkæt ə ˈtəʊn i‿ə ‖ ˌkæţ ə ˈtoʊn-

catatonic ˌkæt ə ˈtɒn ɪk ◂ ‖ ˌkæţ ə ˈtɑːn- **~ally** ᵊl‿i

Catawba, c~ kə ˈtɔːb ə ‖ -ˈtɑːb-

catbird ˈkæt bɜːd ‖ -bɜːd **~s** z

catcall ˈkæt kɔːl ‖ -kɑːl **~s** z

catch kætʃ ⚠ketʃ **catches** ˈkætʃ ɪz ⚠ˈketʃ-, -əz **catching** ˈkætʃ ɪŋ ⚠ˈketʃ- **caught** kɔːt ‖ kɑːt **ˈcatch crop**

catch-22 ˌkætʃ ˌtwent i ˈtuː ⚠ˌketʃ-, ⚠-ˌtwen- ‖ -ˌtwenţ-

catch-all ˈkætʃ ɔːl ⚠ˈketʃ- ‖ -ɑːl

catch-as-catch-can ˌkætʃ əz ˌkætʃ ˈkæn ⚠ˌketʃ əz ˌketʃ-

catcher ˈkætʃ ə ⚠ˈketʃ- ‖ -ᵊr **~s** z

catch|fly ˈkætʃ |flaɪ ⚠ˈketʃ- **~flies** flaɪz

catchi... —*see* **catchy**

catchment ˈkætʃ mənt ⚠ˈketʃ- **ˈcatchment ˌarea**

catchpenny ˈkætʃ ˌpen i ⚠ˈketʃ-

catchphras|e ˈkætʃ freɪz ⚠ˈketʃ- **~es** ɪz əz

Catchpole, c~ ˈkætʃ pəʊl →-pɒʊl ‖ -poʊl **~s** z

catchweight ˈkætʃ weɪt ⚠ˈketʃ- **~s** s

catchword ˈkætʃ wɜːd ⚠ˈketʃ- ‖ -wɜːd **~s** z

catch|y ˈkætʃ |i ⚠ˈketʃ- **~ier** i‿ə ‖ i‿ᵊr **~iest** i‿ɪst i‿əst

cate keɪt **cates** keɪts

catechesis ˌkæt ɪ ˈkiːs ɪs -ə-, §-əs ‖ ˌkæţ-

catechis... —*see* **catechiz...**

catechism ˈkæt ə ˌkɪz əm -ɪ- ‖ ˈkæţ- **~s** z

catechist ˈkæt ək ɪst -ɪk-, §-əst ‖ ˈkæţ- **~s** s

catechiz|e ˈkæt ə kaɪz -ɪ- ‖ ˈkæţ- **~ed** d **~er/s** ə/z ‖ ᵊr/z **~es** ɪz əz **~ing** ɪŋ

catechu ˈkæt ə tʃuː -ɪ-, -ʃuː ‖ ˈkæţ-

catechumen ˌkæt ə ˈkjuːm en -ɪ-, -ɪn, -ən ‖ ˌkæţ- **~s** z

categori... —*see* **category**

categorial ˌkæt ə ˈgɔːr i‿əl ◂ ˌ·ɪ- ‖ ˌkæţ- -ˈgoʊr- **~ly** i

categoric ˌkæt ə ˈgɒr ɪk ◂ -ɪ- ‖ ˌkæţ ə ˈgɔːr ɪk ◂ -ˈgɑːr-

categorical ˌkæt ə ˈgɒr ɪk ᵊl ◂ ˌ·ɪ- ‖ ˌkæţ ə ˈgɔːr ɪk ᵊl ◂ -ˈgɑːr- **~ly** ‿i

ˌcateˌgorical deˈnial

categoris... —*see* **categoriz...**

categorization ˌkæt ɪg ər‿aɪ ˈzeɪʃ ᵊn ɪˈ-- ‖ ˌkæţ ɪg ər ə-

categoriz|e ˈkæt ɪg ə raɪz ˈ-əg- ‖ ˈkæţ- **~ed** d **~es** ɪz əz **~ing** ɪŋ

categor|y ˈkæt əg ər‿|i ˈ·ɪg- ‖ ˈkæţ ə gɔːr |i -goʊr- *(*)* **~ies** iz

catenar|y kə ˈtiːn ər |i ‖ ˈkæt ᵊn er |i *(*)* **~ies** iz

cate|nate *v* ˈkæt ɪ |neɪt -ə-; -ᵊ|n eɪt ‖ ˈkæt ᵊ|n eɪt **~nated** neɪt ɪd -əd ‖ neɪţ əd **~nates** neɪts **~nating** neɪt ɪŋ ‖ neɪţ ɪŋ

catenation ˌkæt ɪ ˈneɪʃ ᵊn -ə-; -ᵊn ˈeɪʃ- ‖ ˌkæt ᵊn ˈeɪʃ ᵊn **~s** z

cater, Cater ˈkeɪt ə ‖ ˈkeɪţ ᵊr **~ed** d **catering** ˈkeɪt‿ər ɪŋ ‖ ˈkeɪţ ər ɪŋ **~s** z

cater-cornered ˌkæt ə ˈkɔːn əd ◂ ‖ ˌkæţ ə ˈkɔːrn ᵊrd ◂ -i-, -ᵊr-, ˈ·ˌ·ˌ· ◂

caterer ˈkeɪt‿ər ə ‖ ˈkeɪţ ər ər **~s** z

Caterham ˈkeɪt‿ər əm ‖ ˈkeɪţ ᵊr hæm

Caterina ˌkæt ə ˈriːn ə ‖ ˌkæţ-

caterpillar ˈkæt ə pɪl ə ‖ ˈkæţ ᵊr pɪl ᵊr **~s** z

caterwaul ˈkæt ə wɔːl ‖ ˈkæţ ᵊr wɔːl -wɑːl **~ed** d **~ing** ɪŋ **~s** z

Catesby ˈkeɪts bi

catfight ˈkæt faɪt **~s** s

catfish ˈkæt fɪʃ **~es** ɪz əz

catfood ˈkæt fuːd

Catford ˈkæt fəd ‖ -fᵊrd

catgut ˈkæt gʌt

Cath kæθ **Cath's** kæθs —*but St Catherine's College, Cambridge, is colloquially known as* kæts

Cathar ˈkæθ ə -ɑː ‖ -ɑːr **~s** z

Catharine ˈkæθ ᵊr‿ɪn ən

Catharism ˈkæθ ə ˌrɪz əm

Catharist ˈkæθ ər ɪst §-əst **~s** s

cathars|is kə ˈθɑːs |ɪs kæ-, §-əs ‖ -ˈθɑːrs- **~es** iːz

cathartic kə ˈθɑːt ɪk kæ- ‖ -ˈθɑːrţ- **~s** s

Cathay *'China'* ˌkæ ˈθeɪ kə-

ˌCathay Paˈcific *tdmk,* ˌ·ˈ· ·ˈ··

Cathays *place in SGlam* kə ˈteɪz

Cathcart ˈkæθ kɑːt ˌ·ˈ· ‖ -kɑːrt *The place in Strathclyde is* ˌ·ˈ·.

cathedra kə ˈθiːdr ə -ˈθedr-, -ˈtedr-

cathedral kə ˈθiːdr əl **~s** z

Cather ˈkæð ə ‖ -ᵊr

Catherine, c~ ˈkæθ ᵊr‿ɪn ən **~'s** z **ˈcatherine wheel**

Catherwood ˈkæθ ə wʊd ˈkæð- ‖ -ᵊr-

catheter ˈkæθ ɪt ə -ət- ‖ ˈkæθ əţ ᵊr ˈkæθt ᵊr **~s** z

catheteris... —*see* **catheteriz...**

catheterization ˌkæθ ɪt‿ər aɪ ˈzeɪʃ ᵊn ˌ·ət‿, -ɪˈ-- ‖ ˌkæθ əţ ər ə- ˌkæθt ər əˈ--

atheteriz|e 'kæθ ɪt ə raɪz '·ət- ‖ kæθ əţ- 'kæθt ə raɪz **~ed** d **~es** ɪz əz **~ing** ɪŋ
athexis kæ 'θeks ɪs kə-, §-əs
athleen 'kæθ liːn ,·'·
athode 'kæθ əʊd ‖ -oʊd **~s** z
,cathode 'ray
athode-ray tube ,kæθ əʊd 'reɪ tjuːb →-tʃuːb ‖ -oʊd 'reɪ tuːb -tjuːb
athodic kæ 'θɒd ɪk kə-, -'θəʊd- ‖ -'θɑːd-
atholic, C~ 'kæθ lɪk 'kæθ əl ɪk, §'kɑːθ- **~s** s
atholicism, c~ kə 'θɒl ə ,sɪz əm -ɪ- ‖ -'θɑːl-
atholicity, C~ ,kæθ ə 'lɪs ət i -ɪt i ‖ -əţ i
at|house 'kæt |haʊs **~houses** haʊz ɪz -əz
:athrine 'kæθ rɪn -rən
:athy 'kæθ i
:atiline 'kæt ə laɪn -ɪ-, -əl aɪn ‖ 'kæţ əl aɪn
ation 'kæt ,aɪ͜ ən ‖ 'kæţ- **~s** z
atkin 'kæt kɪn §-kən **~s** z
:atling, c~ 'kæt lɪŋ
atmint 'kæt mɪnt **~s** s
atnap 'kæt næp **~s** s
atnip 'kæt nɪp **~s** s
:ato 'keɪt əʊ ‖ 'keɪţ oʊ **~'s** z
:aton 'keɪt ən
at-o'-nine tails ,kæt ə 'naɪn teɪəlz ‖ ,kæţ-
:atrina kə 'triːn ə
:atrine 'kætr iːn
:atriona kə 'triː͜ ən ə kæ-; -'triːn ə; ,kætr i 'əʊn ə ‖ -'oʊn-
:AT scan 'kæt skæn ‖ -ər **~er/s** ə/z ‖ ər/z **~s** z
:at's-ear 'kæts ɪə ‖ -ɪr **~s** z
:at's-eye, Catseye *tdmk* 'kæts aɪ **~s** z
:atskill 'kæts kɪl **~s** z
:at's-paw 'kæts pɔː ‖ -pɑː **~s** z
:atsuit 'kæt suːt -sjuːt **~s** s
:atsup 'kæts əp 'ketʃ-, 'kætʃ- *—see also* **ketchup** **~s** s
:attail 'kæt teɪəl **~s** z
:atterick 'kæt͜ ər ɪk ‖ 'kæţ ər ɪk
:atter|y 'kæt ər |i ‖ 'kæţ- **~ies** iz
:attish 'kæt ɪʃ ‖ 'kæţ ɪʃ **~ly** li **~ness** nəs nɪs
:attle 'kæt əl ‖ 'kæţ əl
'cattle cake; **'cattle grid**; **'cattle truck**
:attle|man 'kæt əl mən -mæn ‖ 'kæţ- **~men** mən men
:attleya 'kæt li͜ ə **~s** z
:atto 'kæt əʊ ‖ 'kæţ oʊ
:atton 'kæt ən
catt|y 'kæt |i ‖ 'kæţ |i **~ier** i͜ ə ‖ i͜ ər **~iest** i ,ɪst i͜ əst **~ily** ɪ li əl i ‖ əl i **~iness** i nəs -nɪs
catty-corner 'kæt i ,kɔːn ə ‖ 'kæţ i ,kɔːrn ər
Catullus kə 'tʌl əs
catwalk 'kæt wɔːk ‖ -wɑːk **~s** s
Caucasian kɔː 'keɪz i͜ ən -'keɪʒ-, -'keɪʒ ən ‖ kɔː 'keɪʒ ən kɑː-, -'kæʒ- **~s** z
Caucasoid 'kɔːk ə sɔɪd -zɔɪd ‖ 'kɑːk-
Caucasus 'kɔːk əs əs ‖ 'kɑːk-
caucus 'kɔːk əs ‖ 'kɑːk- **~es** ɪz əz
caudal 'kɔːd əl ‖ 'kɑːd- **~ly** i
caudate 'kɔːd eɪt ‖ 'kɑːd-
caudillo kɔː 'diːl jəʊ kaʊ-, -'dɪl əʊ ‖ kaʊ 'diː joʊ -'dɪl· *—Sp* [kau 'ði ʎo, -jo] **~s** z
Caudine 'kɔːd aɪn ‖ 'kɑːd-
caudle, C~ 'kɔːd əl ‖ 'kɑːd- **~s** z
caught kɔːt ‖ kɑːt
caul kɔːl ‖ kɑːl *(= call)* **~s** z
cauldron 'kɔːldr ən 'kɒldr- ‖ 'kɑːldr- **~s** z
Caulfield 'kɔːl fiːəld 'kɔː- ‖ 'kɑːl-, 'kɔː-
cauliflower 'kɒl i ,flaʊ͜ ə ‖ 'kɑːl i ,flaʊ͜ ər 'kɔːl- **~s** z
,cauli,flower 'cheese; **,cauli,flower 'ear**
caulk kɔːk ‖ kɑːk **caulked** kɔːkt ‖ kɑːkt **caulking** 'kɔːk ɪŋ ‖ 'kɑːk- **caulks** kɔːks ‖ kɑːks
Caunce *(i)* kɔːnts ‖ kɑːnts; *(ii)* kɒnts ‖ kɑːnts
causal 'kɔːz əl ‖ 'kɑːz- **~ly** i
causalit|y kɔː 'zæl ət |i -ɪt- ‖ -əţ |i kɑː- **~ies** iz
causation kɔː 'zeɪʃ ən ‖ kɑː- **~s** z
causative 'kɔːz ət ɪv ‖ -əţ- 'kɑːz- **~ly** li **~s** z
cause kɔːz ‖ kɑːz **caused** kɔːzd ‖ kɑːzd **causes** 'kɔːz ɪz -əz ‖ 'kɑːz- **causing** 'kɔːz ɪŋ ‖ 'kɑːz- *—See also phrases with this word*
cause celebre, cause célèbre ,kəʊz sə 'leb ,kɔːz-, -se-, -sɪ-, ,· ·'·rə ‖ ,kɔːz sə 'leb rə ,kɑːz-, ,koʊz- *—Fr* [koz se lɛbʁ]
causerie 'kəʊz ər i ‖ ,koʊz ə 'riː *—Fr* [koz ʁi] **~s** z
causeway 'kɔːz weɪ ‖ 'kɑːz- **~s** z
caustic 'kɔːst ɪk 'kɒst- ‖ 'kɑːst- **~ally** əl͜ i **~s** s
causticity kɔː 'stɪs ət i kɒ-, -ɪt- ‖ -əţ i kɑː-
Caute kəʊt ‖ koʊt
cauteri... *—see* **cautery**
cauteris... *—see* **cauteriz...**
cauterization ,kɔːt ər aɪ 'zeɪʃ ən -ɪ'- ‖ ,kɔːţ ər ə- ,kɑːţ- **~s** z
cauteriz|e 'kɔːt ə raɪz ‖ 'kɔːţ- 'kɑːţ- **~ed** d **~es** ɪz əz **~ing** ɪŋ
cauter|y 'kɔːt ər |i ‖ 'kɔːţ- 'kɑːţ- **~ies** iz
Cauthen 'kɔːθ ən ‖ 'kɑːθ-
caution 'kɔːʃ ən ‖ 'kɑːʃ- **~ed** d **~ing** ɪŋ **~s** z
cautionary 'kɔːʃ ən ər͜ i -ən͜ ər i ‖ 'kɔːʃ ə ner i 'kɑːʃ-
cautious 'kɔːʃ əs ‖ 'kɑːʃ- **~ly** li **~ness** nəs nɪs
cava 'kɑːv ə *—Sp* ['ka βa]
Cavafy kə 'væf i ‖ -'vɑːf i *—Greek* Kaváfis [ka 'va fis]
cavalcade ,kæv əl 'keɪd ◂ '· · · **~s** z
cavalier ,kæv ə 'lɪə ◂ ‖ -'lɪər **~ly** li **~s** z
cavalla kə 'væl ə **~s** z
Cavalleria Rusticana ,kæv əl ə 'riː͜ ə ,rʊst ɪ 'kɑːn ə kə ,væl-, -,rʌst- *—It* [ka val le 'riː a rus ti 'kaː na]
cavall|y kə 'væl |i **~ies** iz
caval|ry 'kæv əl |ri **~ries** riz
cavalry|man 'kæv əl ri |mən -mæn **~men** mən men
Cavan 'kæv ən
Cavanagh *(i)* 'kæv ən ə, *(ii)* kə 'væn ə
cavatina ,kæv ə 'tiːn ə ‖ ,kɑːv-
cave *n 'watch'* 'keɪv i
cave *n, v 'hollow'* keɪv **caved** keɪvd **caves** keɪvz **caving** 'keɪv ɪŋ
'cave ,painting
cave *interj* ,keɪ 'viː 'keɪv i
Cave *name* keɪv

C

caveat 'kæv i æt 'keɪv-, -ət ‖ 'kɑːv i ɑːt 'kæv-, -æt **~s** s
ˌcaveat 'emptor 'empt ɔː -ə ‖ -ɔːr -ᵊr
cave-in 'keɪv ɪn **~s** z
Cavell *(i)* 'kæv ᵊl*; (ii)* kə 'vel —*Nurse* Edith C~ *was (i).*
cave|man 'keɪv |mæn **~men** men
Cavendish, c~ 'kæv ᵊnd ɪʃ
caver 'keɪv ə ‖ -ᵊr **~s** z
cavern 'kæv ᵊn ‖ -ᵊrn **~ed** d **~ing** ɪŋ **~s** z
cavernous 'kæv ən əs ‖ -ᵊrn- **~ly** li
Caversham 'kæv əʃ əm ‖ -ᵊrʃ-
cavi... —*see* **cavy**

CAVIAR

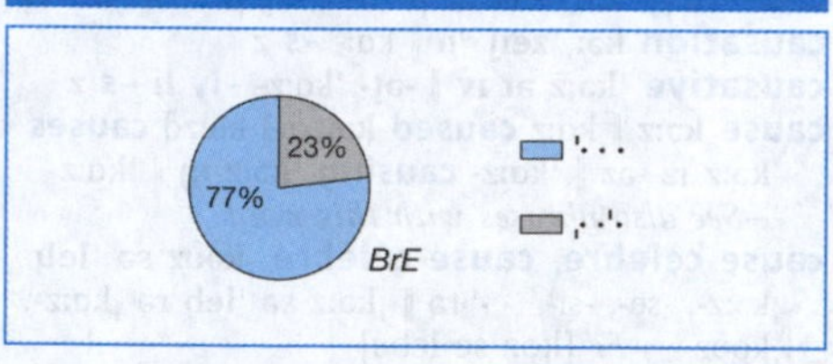

caviar, caviare 'kæv i ɑː ˌ·ˈ·· ‖ -ɑːr 'kɑːv- **~s** z — *Preference poll, BrE:* '· · · *77%,* ˌ· ·'· *23%.*
cavil 'kæv ᵊl -ɪl **~ed, ~led** d **~ing, ~ling** ɪŋ **~s** z
cavitation ˌkæv ɪ 'teɪʃ ᵊn -ə- **~s** z
cavit|y 'kæv ət |i -ɪt- ‖ -əṭ |i **~ies** iz
ca|vort kə |'vɔːt ‖ -|'vɔːrt **~vorted** 'vɔːt ɪd -əd ‖ 'vɔːrṭ əd **~vorting** 'vɔːt ɪŋ ‖ 'vɔːrṭ ɪŋ **~vorts** 'vɔːts ‖ 'vɔːrts
Cavour kə 'vʊə -'vɔː ‖ -'vʊᵊr —*It* [ka 'vuːr]
cavy 'keɪv i **cavies** 'keɪv iz
caw kɔː ‖ kɑː **cawed** kɔːd ‖ kɑːd **cawing** 'kɔːʳ ɪŋ ‖ 'kɔː ɪŋ 'kɑː- **caws** kɔːz ‖ kɑːz *(= cause)*
Cawdor 'kɔːd ə -ɔː ‖ -ᵊr 'kɑːd-, -ɔːr
Cawdrey 'kɔːdr i ‖ 'kɑːdr-
Cawley 'kɔːl i ‖ 'kɑːl-
Cawnpore ˌkɔːn 'pɔː ‖ 'kɔːn pɔːr 'kɑːn-
Cawood 'keɪ wʊd
Caxton 'kækst ən
cay kiː keɪ **cays** kiːz keɪz
cayenne, C~ ⁽ˌ⁾keɪ 'en ⁽ˌ⁾kaɪ- —*Fr* [ka jɛn]
Cayley 'keɪl i
cayman, C~ 'keɪm ən **~s** z
'Cayman ˌIslands ‖ ˌ· '· ·
Caymanian keɪ 'mæn i‿ən **~s** z
Cayuga ki 'uːg ə keɪ-, kaɪ- **~s** z
Cazenove 'kæz ə nəʊv -ɪ- ‖ -noʊv —*but the road in north London is usually* 'keɪz nəʊv
CB ˌsiː 'biː **~er/s** ə/z ‖ ᵊr/z
CBE ˌsiː biː 'iː
CBeebies ˌsiː 'biːb iz
CBS ˌsiː biː 'es ◂
CD ˌsiː 'diː **~s** z
ˌC'D ˌplayer
C. diff. ˌsiː 'dɪf
CD-R ˌsiː diː 'ɑː ‖ -'ɑːr **~s** z
CD-ROM ˌsiː diː 'rɒm ‖ -'rɑːm **~s** z
CD-RW ˌsiː diː ɑː 'dʌb ᵊl ju ‖ -ɑːr'~ -jə; -'dʌb jə **~s** z
céad míle fáilte ˌkeɪd ˌmiːl ə 'fɔːltʃ ə ‖ -'fɑːltʃ- —*Irish* [ˌkʲeːd̪ ˌmʲiːlʲə 'fɑːlʲ tʲə]
ceanothus ˌsiː‿ə 'nəʊθ əs ‖ -'noʊθ- **~es** ɪz əz
cease siːs **ceased** siːst **ceases** 'siːs ɪz -əz **ceasing** 'siːs ɪŋ
cease-fire 'siːs ˌfaɪ‿ə ˌ·'· · ‖ -ˌfaɪ‿ᵊr **~s** z
ceaseless 'siːs ləs -lɪs **~ly** li
Ceausescu tʃaʊ 'ʃesk uː -'tʃesk-, -juː —*Romanian* Ceaușescu [tʃau 'ʃes ku]
cecal 'siːk ᵊl
Cecil *(i)* 'ses ᵊl -ɪl, *(ii)* 'siːs-, *(iii)* 'sɪs- —*In BrE usually (i), though the English landed family is (iii). In AmE usually (ii).*
Cecile 'ses iːᵊl -ᵊl, -ɪl; se 'siːᵊl ‖ se 'siːᵊl
Cecilia sə 'siːl i‿ə sɪ-, -'sɪl- ‖ -'siːl jə -'sɪl-
Cecily *(i)* 'sɪs əl i -ɪl-, *(ii)* 'ses-
cecum 'siːk əm **ceca** 'siːk ə
cedar 'siːd ə ‖ -ᵊr *(= seeder)* **~s** z
ˌCedar 'Rapids
cedarwood 'siːd ə wʊd ‖ -ᵊr- **~s** z
cede siːd *(= seed)* **ceded** 'sid ɪd -əd **cedes** siːdz **ceding** 'siːd ɪŋ
cedi 'siːd i *(= seedy)* **~s** z
cedilla sə 'dɪl ə sɪ- **~s** z
Cedric *(i)* 'sedr ɪk, *(ii)* 'siːdr ɪk —*Usually (i) in BrE, (ii) in AmE*
Ceefax 'siː fæks
Cefn 'kev ᵊn
ceili, ceilidh 'keɪl i **~s** z
ceiling 'siːl ɪŋ *(usually = sealing)* **~s** z
Ceinwen 'kaɪn wen —*Welsh* ['kəin wen]
celadon 'sel əd ən -ə dɒn ‖ -ə dɑːn
'celadon ware
celandine 'sel ən daɪn -diːn **~s** z
Celanese *tdmk* ˌsel ə 'niːz
-cele siːᵊl — **hydrocele** 'haɪdr ə siːᵊl
celeb sə 'leb sɪ- **~s** z
Celebes sə 'liːb iz se-, sɪ-, -'leɪb-; 'sel ɪ biːz, -ə-
celebrant 'sel əb rənt -ɪb- **~s** s
cele|brate 'sel ə |breɪt -ɪ- **~brated** breɪt ɪd -əd ‖ breɪṭ əd **~brates** breɪts **~brating** breɪt ɪŋ ‖ breɪṭ ɪŋ
celebration ˌsel ə 'breɪʃ ᵊn -ɪ- **~s** z
celebrator 'sel ə breɪt ə '·ɪ- ‖ -breɪṭ ᵊr **~s** z
celebratory ˌsel ə 'breɪt ər i ◂ ˌ·ɪ-, '· · · · ·, '· ·brət‿ər i ‖ 'sel əb rə tɔːr i sə 'leb-, -toʊr i
celebrit|y sə 'leb rət |i sɪ-, -rɪt- ‖ -rəṭ |i **~ies** iz
celeriac sə 'ler i æk sɪ-
celerity sə 'ler ət i sɪ-, -ɪt- ‖ -əṭ i
celery 'sel ər i
celesta sə 'lest ə sɪ- **~s** z
Celeste, c~ sə 'lest sɪ- **~'s, ~s** s
celestial sə 'lest i‿əl sɪ- ‖ -'les tʃəl →-'leʃ- **~ly** i
celestite 'sel ə staɪt -ɪ-; sə 'lest aɪt, sɪ-
Celia 'siːl i‿ə
celiac 'siːl i æk
celibacy 'sel əb əs i '·ɪb-
celibate 'sel əb ət -ɪb-, -ɪt **~s** s
Celine, Céline se 'liːn sə-, sɪ-, seɪ-
cell sel *(= sell)* **celled** seld **cells** selz
cell|ar 'sel |ə ‖ -|ᵊr *(= seller)* **~ared** əd ‖ ᵊrd **~aring** ər ɪŋ **~ars** əz ‖ ᵊrz
cellarage 'sel ər ɪdʒ

ellarer 'sel ər ə ‖ -ᵊr ər **~s** z
ellaret, cellarette ˌsel ə 'ret **~s** s
ellar|man 'sel ə mən -mæn ‖ -ᵊr- **~men** mən men
ellini tʃe 'liːn i tʃɪ-, tʃə- —*It* [tʃel 'liː ni]
ellist 'tʃel ɪst §-əst **~s** s
ellmate 'sel meɪt **~s** s
ellnet *tdmk* 'sel net
ello 'tʃel əʊ ‖ -oʊ **~s** z
ellophane, C~ *tdmk* 'sel ə feɪn
ellphone 'sel fəʊn ‖ -foʊn **~s** z
ellular 'sel jʊl ə -jəl- ‖ -jəl ᵊr
ellularity ˌsel ju 'lær ət i ˌ-jə-, -ɪt i ‖ -jə 'lær əţ i -'ler-
ellule 'sel juːl **~s** z
ellulite 'sel ju laɪt -jə-, ˌ· ·'liːt ‖ -jə-
elluloid, C~ *tdmk* 'sel ju lɔɪd -jə- ‖ -jə- -ə-
ellulose 'sel ju ləʊs -jə-, -ləʊz ‖ -jə loʊs
Celsius 'sels i‿əs ‖ 'selʃ əs
elt *'stone implement'* selt **celts** selts
Celt *(i)* kelt, *(ii)* selt **Celts** *(i)* kelts, *(ii)* selts —*In England and Wales usually (i), in Scotland (ii)*
Celtic *(i)* 'kelt ɪk, *(ii)* 'selt ɪk —*The sea is (i), the football, baseball and basketball teams are (ii). The languages are usually (i).*
Cemaes Bay ˌkem aɪs 'beɪ
embalo 'tʃem bə ləʊ ‖ -loʊ **~s** z
ement *n, v* sə 'ment sɪ- **cemented** sə 'ment ɪd sɪ-, -əd ‖ -'menţ əd **cementing** sə 'ment ɪŋ sɪ- ‖ -'menţ ɪŋ **cements** sə 'ments sɪ-
ce'ment ˌmixer
ementation ˌsiːm en 'teɪʃ ᵊn -ən-
ementite sə 'ment aɪt sɪ-
ementum sə 'ment əm sɪ- ‖ -'menţ-
emeter|y 'sem ətr |i -ɪtr-; '·əţ‿ər |i, '·ɪţ‿ ‖ 'sem ə ter |i **~ies** iz
Cemmaes 'kem aɪs
Cenci 'tʃentʃ i —*It* ['tʃɛn tʃi]
CEng ˌsiː 'endʒ
Cenis sə 'niː se- —*Fr* [sə‿ni]
enobite 'siːn əʊ baɪt 'sen- ‖ -ə- **~s** s
enotaph, C~ 'sen ə tɑːf -tæf ‖ -tæf **~s** s
Cenozoic ˌsiːn əʊ 'zəʊ ɪk ◂ ‖ -ə 'zoʊ- ˌsen-
cense senᵗs *(= sense)* **censed** senᵗst **censes** 'senᵗs ɪz -əz **censing** 'senᵗs ɪŋ
censer 'senᵗs ə ‖ -ᵊr *(= censor, sensor)* **~s** z
cens|or 'senᵗs |ə ‖ -|ᵊr **~ored** əd ‖ ᵊrd **~oring** ər ɪŋ **~ors** əz ‖ ᵊrz
censorial sen 'sɔːr i‿əl ‖ -'soʊr-
censorious sen 'sɔːr i‿əs ‖ -'soʊr- **~ly** li **~ness** nəs nɪs
censorship 'senᵗs ə ʃɪp ‖ -ᵊr-
censurab|le 'senᵗʃ ər‿əb |ᵊl **~ly** li
censure 'senᵗʃ ə 'senᵗs jʊə ‖ 'senᵗʃ ᵊr **censured** 'senᵗʃ əd 'senᵗs jʊəd ‖ 'senᵗʃ ᵊrd **censures** 'senᵗʃ əz 'senᵗs jʊəz ‖ 'senᵗʃ ᵊrz **censuring** 'senᵗʃ ər ɪŋ 'senᵗs jʊər ɪŋ
census 'senᵗs əs **~es** ɪz əz
cent sent *(= sent)* **cents** sents
cental 'sent ᵊl **~s** z
centaur 'sent ɔː ‖ -ɔːr **~s** z
Centaur|us sen 'tɔːr |əs **~i** aɪ iː
centaury 'sent ɔːr i
centavo sen 'tɑːv əʊ ‖ -oʊ —*Sp* [sen 'ta βo] **~s** z
centenarian ˌsent ɪ 'neər i‿ən ˌ-ə- ‖ ˌsent ᵊn 'er- **~s** z
centenar|y ₍ₗ₎sen 'tiːn ər |i sᵊn-, -'ten- ‖ -'ten- 'sent ᵊn er |i **~ies** iz
centennial sen 'ten i‿əl sᵊn- **~ly** i **~s** z
center 'sent ə ‖ 'senţ ᵊr **~ed** d **centering** 'sent ər ɪŋ →'sentr ɪŋ ‖ 'senţ ər ɪŋ **~s** z
centerboard 'sent ə bɔːd ‖ 'senţ ᵊr bɔːrd -boʊrd **~s** z
centerfold 'sent ə fəʊld →-fɒʊld ‖ 'senţ ᵊr foʊld **~s** z
centerpiec|e 'sent ə piːs ‖ 'senţ ᵊr- **~es** ɪz əz
centesimal sen 'tes əm ᵊl -ɪm- **~ly** i
centi- ¦sent i -ə ‖ ¦senţ ə ¦sɑːnţ ə
centigrade 'sent ɪ greɪd -ə- ‖ 'senţ ə- 'sɑːnţ-
centigram, centigramme 'sent ɪ græm -ə- ‖ 'senţ ə- 'sɑːnţ- **~s** z
centiliter, centilitre 'sent ɪ ˌliːt ə -ə- ‖ 'senţ ə ˌliːţ ᵊr 'sɑːnţ- **~s** z
centime 'sɒnt iːm 'sɑːnt- ‖ 'sɑːnt- 'sent- —*Fr* [sɑ̃ tim] **~s** z
centimeter, centimetre 'sent ɪ ˌmiːt ə -ə- ‖ 'senţ ə ˌmiːţ ᵊr 'sɑːnţ- **~s** z
centimo 'sent ɪ məʊ -ə- ‖ -moʊ **~s** z —*Sp* céntimo ['θen ti mo, 'sen-]
centipede 'sent ɪ piːd -ə- ‖ 'senţ ə- **~s** z
centner 'sent nə ‖ -nᵊr —*Ger* Zentner ['tsɛnt nɐ] **~s** z
cento 'sent əʊ ‖ -oʊ **~s** z
central, C~ 'sentr əl
ˌCentral 'Africa; ˌCentral ˌAfrican Re'public; ˌcentral 'heating; ˌcentral 'nervous ˌsystem; ˌcentral 'processing ˌunit; ˌcentral ˌreser'vation; 'Central Time
centralis... —*see* **centraliz...**
centralism 'sentr ə ˌlɪz əm
centralist 'sentr əl ɪst -əst
centralistic ˌsentr ə 'lɪst ɪk ◂
centralit|y sen 'træl ət |i -ɪt- ‖ -əţ |i **~ies** iz
centralization ˌsentr əl aɪ 'zeɪʃ ᵊn -ɪ'-- ‖ -əl ə-
centraliz|e 'sentr ə laɪz **~ed** d **~er/s** ə/z ‖ ᵊr/z **~es** ɪz əz **~ing** ɪŋ
centrally 'sentr əl i
centre 'sent ə ‖ 'senţ ᵊr **~d** d **centring** 'sent‿ər ɪŋ ‖ 'senţ ər ɪŋ **~s** z
'centre bit; ˌcentre 'forward
centreboard 'sent ə bɔːd ‖ 'senţ ᵊr bɔːrd -boʊrd **~s** z
centrefold 'sent ə fəʊld →-fɒʊld ‖ 'senţ ᵊr foʊld **~s** z
centrepiec|e 'sent ə piːs ‖ 'senţ ᵊr- **~es** ɪz əz
-centric 'sentr ɪk — **heliocentric** ˌhiːl i‿əʊ 'sentr ɪk ◂ ‖ -oʊ 'sentr-
Centrica *tdmk* 'sentr ɪk ə
centrifugal ˌsentr ɪ 'fjuːg ᵊl ◂ -ə-; sen 'trɪf jʊg ᵊl, -jəg- ‖ sen trɪf jəg ᵊl -əg- **~ly** i
centrifugation ˌsentr ɪ fju 'geɪʃ ᵊn ˌ-ə- ‖ -fjə'--

centrifug|e ˈsentr ɪ fjuːdʒ -ə-, -fjuːʒ **~ed** d **~es** ɪz əz **~ing** ɪŋ
centripetal sen ˈtrɪp ɪt ᵊl -ət-; ˌsentr ɪ ˈpiːt ᵊl, -ə- ‖ -əṱ ᵊl **~ly** i
centrist ˈsentr ɪst §-əst **~s** s
centro- *comb. form with stress-neutral suffix* ˈsentr əʊ ‖ -ə — **centrosome** ˈsentr əʊ səʊm ‖ -ə soʊm
centroid ˈsentr ɔɪd **~s** z
centromere ˈsentr əʊ mɪə ‖ -ə mɪr **~s** z
centum ˈkent əm
centupl|e ˈsent jʊp ᵊl -jəp-; →ˈsentʃ ʊp-, -əp-; sen ˈtjuːp- ‖ sen ˈtuːp ᵊl -ˈtjuːp-, -ˈtʌp- **~ed** d **~es** z **~ing** ˌɪŋ
centurion sen ˈtjʊər i ˌən -ˈtʃʊər-, -ˈtjɔːr-, -ˈtʃɔːr- ‖ -ˈtʊr- -ˈtjʊr- **~s** z
century ˈsentʃ ər ˌi
CEO ˌsiː iː ˈəʊ ‖ -ˈoʊ **~s** z
ceorl tʃeəl ‖ ˈtʃeɪ ɔːrl
cep, cèpe sep **ceps, cèpes** seps
cephalic sə ˈfæl ɪk sɪ-, ke-, kɪ- —*In words containing* (-)cephal-, *the medical profession in Britain generally prefers* **k**. *The alternative pronunciation with* **s** *is nevertheless widespread, and preferred in AmE.*
Cephalonia ˌkef ə ˈləʊn i ˌə ˌsef- ‖ -ˈloʊn- —*ModGk* Kefallinía [cɛ fa li ˈni a]
cephalopod ˈsef əl ə pɒd ‖ -pɑːd **~s** z
cephalosporin ˌsef əl əʊ ˈspɔːr ɪn ˌkef-, §-ən ‖ -ə ˈspɔːr ən -ˈspoʊr-
cephalothorax ˌsef əl əʊ ˈθɔːr æks ‖ -əl ə- -ˈθoʊr-
-cephalous ˈsef əl əs ˈkef- — **autocephalous** ˌɔːt əʊ ˈsef əl əs ◂ ‖ ˌɔːṱ ə- ˌɑːṱ-
-cephaly ˈkef əl i ˈsef- — **microcephaly** ˌmaɪk rəʊ ˈkef əl i -ˈsef- ‖ ˌ·oʊ-
Cephas ˈsiːf æs
Cepheid, c~ ˈsiːf i ɪd ˈsef-, §-əd
Cepheus ˈsiːf juːs ˈsiːf i ˌəs
cepstral ˈkeps trəl
cepstrum ˈkeps trəm **~s** z
ceramic sə ˈræm ɪk sɪ-, kə-, kɪ-, ke- **~s** s
cerastes sə ˈræst iːz sɪ-, se-
Cerberus ˈsɜːb ər ˌəs ‖ ˈsɜ˞ːb-
cercaria sɜː ˈkeər i ˌə sə- ‖ sᵊr ˈker-
cere sɪə ‖ sɪᵊr *(= sere)* **cered** sɪəd ‖ sɪᵊrd
cereal ˈsɪər i ˌəl ‖ ˈsɪr- *(= serial)* **~s** z
cerebell|um ˌser ə ˈbel |əm -ɪ- **~a** ə **~ar** ə ‖ ᵊr
Cerebos *tdmk* ˈser ə bɒs -ɪ- ‖ -bɑːs -boʊs
cerebra sə ˈriːb rə sɪ-; ˈser əb rə, -ɪb-
cerebral ˈser əb rəl -ɪ-; sə ˈriːb rəl, sɪ- **~ly** i
cere|brate ˈser ə |breɪt -ɪ- **~brated** breɪt ɪd -əd ‖ breɪṱ əd **~brates** breɪts **~brating** breɪt ɪŋ ‖ breɪṱ ɪŋ
cerebration ˌser ə ˈbreɪʃ ᵊn -ɪ- **~s** z
cerebrospinal ˌser əb rəʊ ˈspaɪn ᵊl ◂ ˌ·ɪb-; sə ˈriːb- ‖ -əb roʊ-
cerebrovascular ˌser əb rəʊ ˈvæsk jʊl ə ◂ ˌ·ɪb-, -jəl ə; sə ˌriːb- ‖ -roʊ ˈvæsk jəl ᵊr ◂
cerebrum sə ˈriːb rəm sɪ-; ˈser əb-, -ɪb-
Ceredig kə ˈred ɪg —*Welsh* [ke ˈre dig]
Ceredigion ˌker ə ˈdɪg i ɒn ‖ -ɑːn —*Welsh* [ke re ˈdig jon]

cerement ˈsɪə mənt ˈser ə mənt ‖ ˈsɪr- **~s** s
ceremonial ˌser ə ˈməʊn i ˌəl ◂ ˌ·ɪ- ‖ -ˈmoʊn- **~ism** ˌɪz əm **~ist/s** ɪst/s əst/s **~ly** i
ceremonious ˌser ə ˈməʊn i ˌəs ◂ ˌ·ɪ- ‖ -ˈmoʊr **~ly** li **~ness** nəs nɪs
ceremon|y ˈser əm ən |i ˌ·ɪm- ‖ -ə moʊn |i **~ies** iz
Ceres ˈsɪər iːz ‖ ˈsɪr-
Cerf sɜːf ‖ sɜ˞ːf
Ceri ˈker i
cerise sə ˈriːz sɪ-, -ˈriːs
cerium ˈsɪər i ˌəm ‖ ˈsɪr-
CERN sɜːn ‖ sɜ˞ːn
Cerne Abbas ˌsɜːn ˈæb əs ‖ ˌsɜ˞ːn-
Cerrig-y-Drudion ˌker ɪg ə ˈdrɪd jɒn ‖ -jɑːn -jɔːn
cert sɜːt ‖ sɜ˞ːt **certs** sɜːts ‖ sɜ˞ːts
certain ˈsɜːt ᵊn -ɪn ‖ ˈsɜ˞ːt-
certainly ˈsɜːt ᵊn li -ɪn- ‖ ˈsɜ˞ːt-
certain|ty ˈsɜːt ᵊn |ti -ɪn- ‖ ˈsɜ˞ːt- **~ties** tiz
CertEd ˌsɜːt ˈed ‖ ˌsɜ˞ːt-
certes ˈsɜːt ɪz -əz, -iːz; sɜːts ‖ ˈsɜ˞ːṱ iːz sɜ˞ːts
certifiab|le ˈsɜːt ɪ faɪ ˌəb |ᵊl ˈ·ə-, ˌ· · ˈ· · · ‖ ˈsɜ˞ːṱ- **~ly** li
certifi|cate *v* sə ˈtɪf ɪ |keɪt -ə- ‖ sᵊr- **~cated** keɪt ɪd -əd ‖ keɪṱ əd **~cates** keɪts **~cating** keɪt ɪŋ ‖ keɪṱ ɪŋ
certificate *n* sə ˈtɪf ɪk ət -ək-, -ɪt ‖ sᵊr- **~s** s
certification ˌsɜːt ɪf ɪ ˈkeɪʃ ᵊn ˌ·əf-, -ə'- ‖ ˌsɜ˞ːṱ- —*Occasionally also* sə ˌtɪf- ‖ sᵊr-, *but only in the sense 'certificating', not in the sense 'certifying'*
certi|fy ˈsɜːt ɪ |faɪ -ə- ‖ ˈsɜ˞ːṱ- **~fied** faɪd **~fies** faɪz **~fying** faɪ ɪŋ
certiorari ˌsɜːʃ i ˌə ˈreər aɪ ˌsɜːt-, -i ɔː-, -ˈrɑːr i ‖ ˌsɜ˞ːʃ i ˌə ˈrer i ˌ·ə'·
certitude ˈsɜːt ɪ tjuːd -ə-, →-tʃuːd ‖ ˈsɜ˞ːṱ ə tuːd -tjuːd **~s** z
cerulean sə ˈruːl i ˌən sɪ-
Cerullo sə ˈrʊl əʊ se-, -ˈruːl- ‖ -oʊ
cerumen sə ˈruːm en sɪ-, -ən
Cervantes sɜː ˈvænt iːz -ɪz ‖ sᵊr- —*Sp* [θer ˈβan tes]
cervelat ˌsɜːv ə ˈlɑːt -ˈlɑː, -ˈlæt, ˈ· · · ‖ ˈsɜ˞ːv ə lɑːt -lɑː, -læt
cervical sə ˈvaɪk ᵊl sɜː-; ˈsɜːv ɪk ᵊl ‖ ˈsɜ˞ːv ɪk ᵊl
cervices sə ˈvaɪs iːz sɜː-; ˈsɜːv ɪ siːz, -ə- ‖ sᵊr- ˈsɜ˞ːv ə siːz
cervine ˈsɜːv aɪn ‖ ˈsɜ˞ːv-
cervix ˈsɜːv ɪks ‖ ˈsɜ˞ːv- **~es** ɪz əz
Cesar, César ˈseɪz ɑː ‖ seɪ ˈzɑːr —*Fr* [se zaːʁ]
cesarean, cesarian sɪ ˈzeər i ˌən sə-, siː- ‖ -ˈzer- -ˈzær-
Cesarewitch sɪ ˈzær ə wɪtʃ sə-, -ɪ- ‖ -ˈzer-
cesium ˈsiːz i ˌəm ‖ ˈsiːs-
cess ses
cessation se ˈseɪʃ ᵊn sɪ-, sə-
cession ˈseʃ ᵊn *(= session)* **~s** z
Cessna *tdmk* ˈses nə **~s, ~'s** z
cesspit ˈses pɪt **~s** s
cesspool ˈses puːl **~s** z
cesta ˈsest ə **~s** z
c'est la vie ˌseɪ lɑː ˈviː -lə- —*Fr* [sɛ la vi]

cestode 'sest əʊd ‖ -oʊd **~s** z
cestus 'sest əs **~es** ɪz əz
cesur|a sɪ 'zjʊər |ə sə-, siː-, -'zjɔːr-, -'ʒʊər- ‖ -'zʊr- **~ae** iː aɪ **~as** əz
cetacean sɪ 'teɪʃ ən sə-, -'teɪʃ i‿ən, -'teɪs i‿ən **~s** z
cetane 'siːt eɪn
'cetane ˌnumber
ceteris paribus ˌket ə riːs 'pær ɪb əs ˌkeɪt-, ˌset-, -ər ɪs-, -'pɑːr-, -əb-, -ʊs ‖ ˌkeɪţ ər əs- -'per-
Ceti 'siːt aɪ
cetological ˌsiːt ə 'lɒdʒ ɪk əl ◂ ‖ ˌsiːţ ə 'lɑːdʒ-
cetolog|ist siː 'tɒl ədʒ |ɪst sɪ-, §-əst ‖ -'tɑːl- **~ists** ɪsts §əsts **~y** i
cetrimide 'setr ɪ maɪd -ə-
Cetshwayo ketʃ 'waɪ əʊ ‖ -oʊ —*Zulu* [|ɛ 'tʃwaː jɔ]
Cetus 'siːt əs ‖ 'siːţ-
cetyl 'siːt ɪl -əl ‖ 'siːţ əl
Ceuta 'sjuːt ə 'suːt- ‖ 'seɪ uːţ ə —*Sp* ['θeu ta, 'seu-]
Cevennes, Cévennes sɪ 'ven seɪ-, sə —*Fr* [se vɛn]
ceviche sɪ 'viːtʃ eɪ sə-, seɪ-, -i; seɪ 'viːʃ —*AmSp* [se 'βi tʃe]
Ceylon sɪ 'lɒn sə- ‖ -'lɑːn
Ceylonese ˌsel ə 'niːz ◂ ˌsiːl- ‖ -'niːs
Cezanne, Cézanne sɪ 'zæn seɪ-, sə- ‖ seɪ 'zɑːn —*Fr* [se zan]
cf —*see* **compare**
Chablis, c~ 'ʃæb liː 'ʃɑːb-, -li ‖ ʃæ 'bliː ʃɑː-, ʃə- —*Fr* [ʃa bli]
Chabrier 'ʃæb ri eɪ 'ʃɑːb-; ʃɑː 'briː- ‖ ˌʃɑːb ri 'eɪ —*Fr* [ʃa bʁi je]
Chabrol ʃæ 'brɒl ʃə- ‖ ʃɑː 'broʊl —*Fr* [ʃa bʁɔl]
cha-cha 'tʃɑː tʃɑː **~ed** d **cha-chaing** 'tʃɑː tʃɑːr ɪŋ ‖ -tʃɑː ɪŋ **~s** z
cha-cha-cha ˌtʃɑː tʃɑː 'tʃɑː
chacma 'tʃæk mə ‖ 'tʃɑːk- **~s** z
chaconne ʃə 'kɒn ʃæ- ‖ ʃɑː 'kɑːn -kɔːn —*Fr* [ʃa kɔn] **~s** z
chacun à son goût ˌʃæk ɜːn ˌɑː sɒŋ 'guː -ˌæ- ‖ ʃɑː ˌkuːn ɑː sɑːn- -sɔːn- —*Fr* [ʃa kœ̃ a sɔ̃ gu]
Chad, chad tʃæd
Chadband 'tʃæd bænd →'tʃæb-
Chadburn 'tʃæd bɜːn 'tʃæb- ‖ -bɜːn
Chadderton 'tʃæd ət ən ‖ -ərt ən
Chadian 'tʃæd i‿ən **~s** z
Chadic 'tʃæd ɪk
chador 'tʃɑːd ɔː 'tʃʌd-, -ə ‖ -ɔːr
Chadwick 'tʃæd wɪk
chaebol 'tʃeɪ bɒl ‖ -bɔːl -bɑːl, -boʊl —*Kor* [tʃɛ bol]
Chaeronea ˌkaɪər ə 'niː‿ə ˌkɪər-, ˌker-
chaeto- *comb. form*
with stress-neutral suffix |kiːt əʊ ‖ kiːţ ə — **chaetopod** 'kiːt əʊ pɒd ‖ 'kiːţ ə pɑːd
with stress-imposing suffix kiː 'tɒ+ ‖ -'tɑː+ — **chaetophorous** kiː 'tɒf ər əs ‖ -'tɑːf-
chafe tʃeɪf **chafed** tʃeɪft **chafes** tʃeɪfs **chafing** 'tʃeɪf ɪŋ
chafer 'tʃeɪf ə ‖ -ər **~s** z
chaff tʃɑːf tʃæf ‖ tʃæf **chaffed** tʃɑːft tʃæft ‖ tʃæft **chaffing** 'tʃɑːf ɪŋ 'tʃæf- ‖ 'tʃæf- **chaffs** tʃɑːfs tʃæfs ‖ tʃæfs
chaffer 'tʃæf ə ‖ -ər **~ed** d **chaffering** 'tʃæf ər ɪŋ **~s** z
Chaffey 'tʃæf i
chaffinch 'tʃæf ɪntʃ **~es** ɪz əz
chafing 'tʃeɪf ɪŋ
'chafing dish
Chagall ʃæ 'gæl ʃə-, -'gɑːl —*Fr* [ʃa gal] **~s, ~'s** z
Chagas 'ʃɑːg əs —*Port* ['ʃa ɣeʃ] —*The possessive form* **~'** *has the same pronunciation, or sometimes an extra* ɪz əz
'Chagas' diˌsease
Chagford 'tʃæg fəd ‖ -fərd
Chagos 'ʃɑːg ɒs 'ʃæg-, 'tʃɑːg-, 'tʃæg-, -əʊs ‖ 'tʃɑːg oʊs -əs
chagrin 'ʃæg rɪn -rən ‖ ʃə 'grɪn *(*)* **~ed** d
Chagrin 'ʃæg ræ̃ ‖ ʃɑː 'græn —*Fr* [ʃa gʁæ̃]
Chaim haɪm xaɪm —*Hebrew* ['xa jim, xa 'jiːm]
chain, Chain tʃeɪn **chained** tʃeɪnd **chaining** 'tʃeɪn ɪŋ **chains** tʃeɪnz
'chain gang; **'chain ˌletter**; **ˌchain link 'fencing**; **ˌchain re'action**; **'chain stitch**; **'chain store**
chain-link 'tʃeɪn lɪŋk
ˌchain-link 'fence
chainsaw 'tʃeɪn sɔː ‖ -sɑː **~s** z
chain-smok|e tʃeɪn sməʊk ‖ -smoʊk **~ed** t **~er/s** ə/z ‖ ər/z **~es** s **~ing** ɪŋ
chair tʃeə ‖ tʃeər **chaired** tʃeəd ‖ tʃeərd **chairing** 'tʃeər ɪŋ ‖ 'tʃer ɪŋ **chairs** tʃeəz ‖ tʃeərz
'chair lift
chairbound 'tʃeə baʊnd ‖ 'tʃer-
chair|man 'tʃeə |mən ‖ 'tʃer- **~men** mən men **~manship/s** mən ʃɪp/s **~person/s** ˌpɜːs ən/z ‖ ˌpɜːs ən/z **~woman** ˌwʊm ən **~women** ˌwɪm ɪn §-ən
chaise ʃeɪz ‖ tʃeɪs **chaises** 'ʃeɪz ɪz -əz; ʃeɪz ‖ 'tʃeɪs əz
ˌchaise 'longue lɒŋ ‖ lɔːŋ lɑːŋ —*Fr* [ʃɛz lɔ̃ːg] —*The plural,* **~(s) longues**, *is pronounced identically with the singular, or sometimes with added* z. *Particularly in AmE,* longue *is sometimes changed by popular etymology to* lounge.
chakra 'tʃʌk rə 'tʃæk-, 'tʃɑːk-
chalaz|a kə 'leɪz |ə **~ae** iː **~as** əz
Chalcedon 'kæls ɪd ən -əd-; -ɪ dɒn, -ə- ‖ -ə dɑːn
chalcedon|y kæl 'sed ən |i ‖ 'kæls ə doʊn |i **~ies** iz
Chalcidice kæl 'sɪd əs i -ɪs-
Chalcis 'kæls ɪs §-əs
chalcopyrite ˌkælk əʊ 'paɪər aɪt ‖ -ə-
Chalde|a kæl 'diː‿|ə kɔːl- ‖ kɔːl-, kɑːl- **~an/s** ən/z
Chaldee kæl 'diː kɔːl-, '· · ‖ kɔːl-, kɑːl- **~s** z
Chaldon 'tʃɔːld ən 'tʃɒld- ‖ 'tʃɑːld-
chaldron 'tʃɔːldr ən ‖ 'tʃɑːldr- **~s** z

C

chalet 'ʃæl eɪ -i ‖ ʃæ 'leɪ *(*)* **~s** z
Chalfont 'tʃæl fɒnt 'tʃælf ᵊnt ‖ -fɑːnt —*locally also* 'tʃɑːf ᵊnt
chalic|e 'tʃæl ɪs -əs **~es** ɪz əz
chalk, Chalk tʃɔːk ‖ tʃɑːk **chalked** tʃɔːkt ‖ tʃɑːkt **chalking** 'tʃɔːk ɪŋ ‖ 'tʃɑːk- **chalks** tʃɔːks ‖ tʃɑːks
chalkboard 'tʃɔːk bɔːd ‖ -bɔːrd 'tʃɑːk-, -bourd **~s** z
Chalker 'tʃɔːk ə ‖ -ᵊr 'tʃɑːk-
chalkface 'tʃɔːk feɪs ‖ 'tʃɑːk-
chalkstripe 'tʃɔːk straɪp ‖ 'tʃɑːk- **~s** s
chalk|y 'tʃɔːk |i ‖ 'tʃɑːk- **~ier** i‿ə ‖ i‿ᵊr **~iest** i‿ɪst i‿əst **~iness** i nəs i nɪs
challah 'hɑːl ə xɑː 'lɑː **~s** z **challoth** xɑː 'lɒt ‖ -'lout
challeng|e 'tʃæl ɪndʒ -əndʒ **~ed** d **~es** ɪz əz **~ing/ly** ɪŋ /li
challenger, C~ 'tʃæl ɪndʒ ə -əndʒ- ‖ -ᵊr **~s** z
Challenor 'tʃæl ən ə -ɪn- ‖ -ᵊr
Challes, Challis 'tʃæl ɪs -əs
Challock 'tʃɒl ək ‖ 'tʃɑːl-
Challoner 'tʃæl ən ə ‖ -ᵊr
Chalmers *(i)* 'tʃɑːm əz 'tʃɑːlm- ‖ -ᵊrz, *(ii)* 'tʃælm-
chalybeate kə 'lɪb i‿ət ɪt, -eɪt ‖ -'liːb-
Cham *ethnonym* tʃæm **Chams** tʃæmz
chamber 'tʃeɪm bə ‖ -bᵊr **~ed** d **~s** z **'chamber ˌmusic**; **'chamber ˌorchestra**; **'chamber pot**
chamberlain 'tʃeɪm bə lɪn -lən ‖ -bᵊr- **~s** z
Chamberlain, Chamberlaine, Chamberlayne *(i)* 'tʃeɪm bə lɪn -lən ‖ -bᵊr-, *(ii)* -leɪn
chambermaid 'tʃeɪm bə meɪd ‖ -bᵊr- **~s** z
Chambers 'tʃeɪm bəz ‖ -bᵊrz
Chambourcy *tdmk* ʃæm 'bʊəs i ‖ ˌʃɑːm bʊr 'siː —*Fr* [ʃɑ̃ buʁ si]
chambray 'ʃæm breɪ -bri
chambré 'ʃɒm breɪ ‖ ʃɑːm 'breɪ —*Fr* [ʃɑ̃ bʁe]
chameleon kə 'miːl i‿ən **~s** z
chameleonic kə ˌmiːl i 'ɒn ɪk ◂ ‖ -'ɑːn-
chameleon-like kə 'miːl i‿ən laɪk
chamfer 'tʃæmᵖf ə 'ʃæmᵖf- ‖ -ᵊr 'tʃæmp- **~ed** d **chamfering** 'tʃæmᵖf ər‿ɪŋ 'ʃæmᵖf- ‖ 'tʃæmp- **~s** z
chamm|y 'ʃæm |i **~ies** iz
chamois *(i)* 'ʃæm wɑː ‖ ʃæm 'wɑː, *(ii)* 'ʃæm i —*(ii) is used mainly in reference to chamois leather, and is then alternatively spelt* chammy, shammy. *The plural may have* z, *or may — particularly in reference to the goats — be pronounced identically with the singular.*
chamomile 'kæm ə maɪᵊl -miːᵊl
Chamonix 'ʃæm ə niː -ɒ- ‖ ˌʃæm ə 'niː —*Fr* [ʃa mɔ ni]
champ tʃæmp **champed** tʃæmpt **champing** 'tʃæmp ɪŋ **champs** tʃæmps
champagne, C~ ˌʃæm 'peɪn ◂ —*Fr* [ʃɑ̃ paɲ] **ˌchampagne 'cocktail**
Champaign ʃæm 'peɪn
champak 'tʃʌmp ək 'tʃæmp æk
Champernowne 'tʃæmp ə naʊn ‖ -ᵊr-
champers 'ʃæmp əz ‖ -ᵊrz
champerty 'tʃæmp ət i -ɜːt- ‖ -ᵊrt̬ i
champignon 'ʃæmp iːn jɔ̃ ˌ·'·; ʃæm 'pɪn jən ‖ ʃæm 'pɪn jən tʃæm- —*Fr* [ʃɑ̃ pi ɲɔ̃] **~s** z —*or as singular*
champion, C~ 'tʃæmp jən -i‿ən **~ed** d **~ing** ɪŋ **~s** z
championship 'tʃæmp jən ʃɪp -i‿ən- **~s** s
Champlain ₍ˌ₎ʃæm 'pleɪn —*Fr* [ʃɑ̃ plɛ̃]
Champneys 'tʃæmp niz
Champs Elysees, Champs Elysées ˌʃɒnz ə 'liːz eɪ ˌʃɒmz-, ˌʃɔ̃z-, -ɪ-, -eɪ- ‖ ˌʃɑːnz ˌeɪl i 'zeɪ —*Fr* [ʃɑ̃ ze li ze]
Chan tʃæn —*Cantonese* [⁴tsʰɐn]

CHANCE

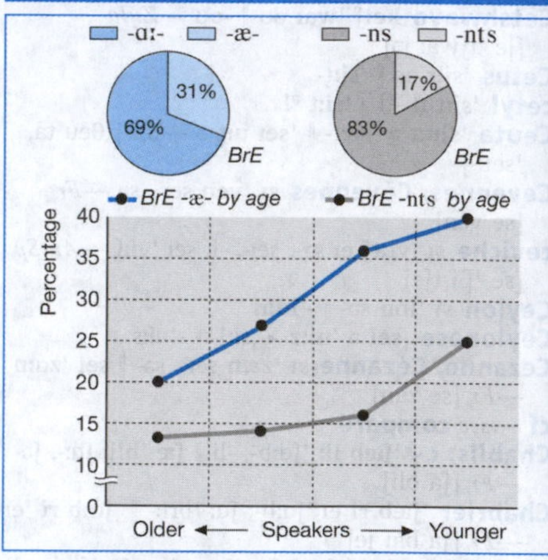

chance tʃɑːnᵗs §tʃænᵗs ‖ tʃænᵗs — *Preference polls, BrE (not restricted to RP):* -ɑː- *69%,* -æ- *31%;* -ns *83%,* -nts *17%.* **chanced** tʃɑːnᵗst §tʃænᵗst ‖ tʃænᵗst **chances** 'tʃɑːnᵗs ɪz §'tʃænᵗs-, -əz ‖ 'tʃænᵗs əz **chancing** 'tʃɑːnᵗs ɪŋ §'tʃænᵗs- ‖ 'tʃænᵗs ɪŋ
chancel 'tʃɑːnᵗs ᵊl §'tʃænᵗs- ‖ 'tʃænᵗs ᵊl **~s** z
chanceller|y 'tʃɑːnᵗs ᵊl‿ər |i §'tʃænᵗs-, '·ᵊl ər‿i ‖ 'tʃænᵗs- **~ies** iz
chancellor, C~ 'tʃɑːnᵗs əl‿ə §'tʃænᵗs- ‖ 'tʃænᵗs ᵊl‿ər **~s** z
chancer 'tʃɑːnᵗs ə §'tʃænᵗs ə ‖ 'tʃænᵗs ᵊr **~s** z
chancer|y 'tʃɑːnᵗs ər‿i §'tʃænᵗs- ‖ 'tʃænᵗs- **~ies** iz
chanciness 'tʃɑːnᵗs i nəs §'tʃænᵗs-, -nɪs ‖ 'tʃænᵗs-
chancre 'ʃæŋk ə ‖ -ᵊr **~s** z
chancroid 'ʃæŋk rɔɪd **~s** z
Chanctonbury 'tʃæŋkt ən bər‿i →'·əm-, -ˌber i ‖ -ˌber i
chanc|y 'tʃɑːnᵗs |i §'tʃænᵗs i ‖ 'tʃænᵗs |i **~ier** i‿ə ‖ i‿ᵊr **~iest** i‿ɪst i‿əst
chandelier ˌʃænd ə 'lɪə ˌʃɒnd-, -ᵊl 'ɪə ‖ -ᵊl 'ɪᵊr **~s** z
chandelle ʃæn 'del ʃɑːn- **~s** z
Chandigarh ˌtʃʌnd i 'gɜː ˌtʃænd-, -'gɑː, '· ·gə ‖ -'gɜː -'gɑːr

chandler, C~ 'tʃɑːnd lə §'tʃænd- ‖ 'tʃænd lᵊr **~s** z
chandler|y 'tʃɑːnd lər |i §'tʃænd-, §-ᵊl r|i ‖ 'tʃænd- **~ies** iz
Chandos *(i)* 'ʃænd ɒs ‖ -oʊs, *(ii)* 'tʃænd-
Chanel ʃə 'nel ʃæ- —*Fr* [ʃa nɛl]
Chang tʃæŋ ‖ dʒɑːŋ —*Chi* Zhāng [¹tʂɑŋ]
Changchun ˌtʃæŋ 'tʃʊn ‖ ˌtʃɑːŋ- —*Chi* Chángchūn [²tʂʰɑŋ ¹tʂʰwən]
change tʃeɪndʒ **changed** tʃeɪndʒd **changes** 'tʃeɪndʒ ɪz -əz **changing** 'tʃeɪndʒ ɪŋ
'change ˌringing
changeability ˌtʃeɪndʒ ə 'bɪl ət i -ɪt i ‖ -əţ i
changeab|le 'tʃeɪndʒ əb |ᵊl **~leness** ᵊl nəs -nɪs **~ly** li
changeless 'tʃeɪndʒ ləs -lɪs **~ly** li **~ness** nəs nɪs
changeling 'tʃeɪndʒ lɪŋ **~s** z
changeover *n* 'tʃeɪndʒ ˌəʊv ə ‖ -ˌoʊv ᵊr **~s** z
changer 'tʃeɪndʒ ə ‖ -ᵊr **~s** z
changeround 'tʃeɪndʒ raʊnd **~s** z
Changi *place in Singapore* 'tʃæŋ i
changing 'tʃeɪndʒ ɪŋ
'changing room
channel, C~ 'tʃæn ᵊl **~ed, ~led** d **~ing, ~ling** ɪŋ **~s** z
'channel ˌhopping; **'Channel ˌIslands**, ˌ· ·'· ·; **'channel ˌsurfing**
Channing 'tʃæn ɪŋ
Channon *(i)* 'tʃæn ən, *(ii)* 'ʃæn ən
chanson 'ʃɒ̃ sɒ̃ 'ʃɒn-, -sɒn ‖ ʃɑːn 'sɔːn -'soʊn, -'sɑːn; 'ʃænᵗs ən —*Fr* [ʃɑ̃ sɔ̃] **~s** z —*or as singular*
chant, Chant tʃɑːnt §tʃænt ‖ tʃænt **chanted** 'tʃɑːnt ɪd §'tʃænt- ‖ 'tʃænţ əd **chanting** 'tʃɑːnt ɪŋ §'tʃænt- ‖ 'tʃænţ ɪŋ
Chantal ʃɑːn 'tæl ˌʃɒn-, ˌʃæn-, -'tɑːl ‖ ʃɑːn 'tɑːl —*Fr* [ʃɑ̃ tal]
Chantelle ˌʃɑːn 'tel ˌʃɒn-, ˌʃæn- —*Fr* [ʃɑ̃ tɛl]
chanter, C~ 'tʃɑːnt ə §'tʃænt- ‖ 'tʃænţ ᵊr **~s** z
chanterelle ˌʃɒnt ə 'rel ˌʃænt-, ˌtʃænt- ‖ ˌʃænţ- ˌʃɑːnţ- **~s** z
chanteus|e ˌʃɒn 'tɜːz ʃɑːn- ‖ ʃɑːn 'tuːz ʃæn- *(*)* —*Fr* [ʃɑ̃ tøːz] **~es** ɪz əz —*or as singular*
chantey 'ʃænt i ‖ 'ʃænţ i **~s** z
chanti... —*see* **chanty**
Chanticleer, c~ 'ʃɑːnt ə klɪə 'ʃɒnt-, 'tʃɑːnt-, 'tʃænt-, -ɪ-, ˌ· · '· ‖ 'tʃænţ ə klɪr **~s, ~'s** z
Chantilly ʃæn 'tɪl i ʃɒn- ‖ ˌʃɑːnt i 'jiː —*Fr* [ʃɑ̃ ti ji]
chantr|y, C~ 'tʃɑːntr |i §'tʃæntr- ‖ 'tʃæntr |i **~ies** iz
'chantry ˌchapel
chant|y 'ʃænt |i 'tʃænt-, 'tʃɑːnt- ‖ 'ʃænţ |i **~ies** iz
Chanukah 'hɑːn ək ə 'hɒn-, 'kɑːn-, -ʊk-, -ɑː —*Hebrew* [xa nu 'ka]
Chao tʃaʊ
ˌChao ˌYuen 'Ren ˌjuː en 'ren —*Chi* Zhào Yuánrèn [⁴tʂɑu ²ɥɛn ⁴ʐən]
chaology keɪ 'ɒl ədʒ i ‖ -'ɑːl-
chaos 'keɪ ɒs ‖ -ɑːs
chaotic keɪ 'ɒt ɪk ‖ -'ɑːţ- **~ally** ᵊl‿i

chap tʃæp **chapped** tʃæpt **chapping** 'tʃæp ɪŋ **chaps** tʃæps
chaparral ˌʃæp ə 'ræl ˌtʃæp-, -'rɑːl
chapati, chapatti tʃə 'pɑːt i -'pæt- ‖ -'pɑːţ i —*Hindi* [tʃə paː ṭi] **~s** z
chapbook 'tʃæp bʊk §-buːk **~s** s
chapel, C~ 'tʃæp ᵊl **~s** z
Chapel-en-le-Frith ˌtʃæp ᵊl ˌen lə 'frɪθ -ᵊl ən lə-
chapelgo|er 'tʃæp ᵊl ˌgəʊ |ə ‖ -ˌgoʊ |ᵊr **~ers** əz ‖ ᵊrz **~ing** ɪŋ
Chapeltown 'tʃæp ᵊl taʊn
chaperon, chaperon|e 'ʃæp ə rəʊn ‖ -roʊn **~ed** d **~es, ~s** z **~ing** ɪŋ
chapfallen 'tʃæp ˌfɔːl ən ‖ -ˌfɑːl-
chaplain 'tʃæp lɪn -lən **~s** z
chaplain|cy 'tʃæp lən |si -lɪn- **~cies** siz
chaplet 'tʃæp lət -lɪt **~s** s
Chaplin 'tʃæp lɪn -lən
Chaplinesque ˌtʃæp lɪ 'nesk ◂ -lə-
Chapman 'tʃæp mən
chapp... —*see* **chap**
chappal 'tʃʌp ᵊl **~s** z
Chappaquiddick ˌtʃæp ə 'kwɪd ɪk
Chappell 'tʃæp ᵊl
chapp|ie, chapp|y, Chappie *tdmk* 'tʃæp |i **~ies** iz
chaps tʃæps
chapstick 'tʃæp stɪk **~s** s
chaptalis... —*see* **chaptaliz...**
chaptalization ˌtʃæpt əl aɪ 'zeɪʃ ᵊn ˌʃæpt-, -ɪ'-- ‖ -əl ə-
chaptaliz|e 'tʃæpt ə laɪz 'ʃæpt- **~ed** d **~es** ɪz əz **~ing** ɪŋ
chapter 'tʃæpt ə ‖ -ᵊr **~s** z
ˌchapter and 'verse; **'chapter house**
char tʃɑː ‖ tʃɑːr **charred** tʃɑːd ‖ tʃɑːrd **charring** 'tʃɑːr ɪŋ **chars** tʃɑːz ‖ tʃɑːrz
charabanc 'ʃær ə bæŋ -bɒŋ ‖ 'ʃer- **~s** z
character 'kær əkt ə -ɪkt- ‖ -ᵊr 'ker- **~s** z
'character sketch
characteris... —*see* **characteriz...**
characteristic ˌkær əkt ə 'rɪst ɪk ◂ ˌ-ɪkt- ‖ ˌker- **~ally** ᵊl‿i **~s** s
characterization ˌkær əkt ər‿aɪ 'zeɪʃ ᵊn ˌ-ɪkt-, ɪ'-- ‖ -ɪkt ər‿ə- ˌker-
characteriz|e 'kær əkt ə raɪz '·ɪkt- ‖ 'ker- **~ed** d **~es** ɪz əz **~ing** ɪŋ
characterless 'kær əkt ə ləs '·ɪkt-, -lɪs ‖ -ᵊr ləs 'ker- **~ly** li
charade ʃə 'rɑːd -'reɪd ‖ -'reɪd **~s** z *The* -'reɪd *form, previously only AmE, is now occasionally also heard in BrE*
charbroil 'tʃɑː brɔɪᵊl ‖ 'tʃɑːr- **~ed** d **~ing** ɪŋ **~s** z
charcoal 'tʃɑː kəʊl →-kɒʊl ‖ 'tʃɑːr koʊl **~ed** d **~ing** ɪŋ **~s** z
charcoal-burner 'tʃɑː kəʊl ˌbɜːn ə →-kɒʊl- ‖ 'tʃɑːr koʊl ˌbɜːn ᵊr **~s** z
Charcot 'ʃɑːk əʊ ‖ ʃɑːr 'koʊ —*Fr* [ʃaʁ ko]
charcuterie ʃɑː 'kuːt ər i -'kjuːt- ‖ ʃɑːr ˌkuːţ ə 'riː -'···· —*Fr* [ʃaʁ ky tʁi]
chard, Chard tʃɑːd ‖ tʃɑːrd

Chardonnay, c~ 'ʃɑːd ə neɪ →-ən eɪ ‖ ˌʃɑːrd ən 'eɪ **~s** z —*Fr* Chardonnet [ʃaʁ dɔ nɛ]
charge tʃɑːdʒ ‖ tʃɑːrdʒ **charged** tʃɑːdʒd ‖ tʃɑːrdʒd **charges** 'tʃɑːdʒ ɪz -əz ‖ 'tʃɑːrdʒ əz **charging** 'tʃɑːdʒ ɪŋ ‖ 'tʃɑːrdʒ ɪŋ **'charge acˌcount**; **'charge card**; **'charge hand**; **'charge nurse**; **'charge sheet**
chargeable 'tʃɑːdʒ əb əl ‖ 'tʃɑːrdʒ-
chargeback 'tʃɑːdʒ bæk ‖ 'tʃɑːrdʒ- **~s** s
chargé d'affaires ˌʃɑːʒ eɪ dæ 'feə -də'· ‖ ʃɑːr ˌʒeɪ də 'feər -dæ'· —*Fr* [ʃaʁ ʒe da fɛːʁ] —*The plural,* **chargés d'affaires**, *is pronounced identically with the singular, as in French; or, alternatively, as* ˌ·eɪz-‖ ·ˌʒeɪz-
charger 'tʃɑːdʒ ə ‖ 'tʃɑːrdʒ ər **~s** z
chargrill 'tʃɑː grɪl ‖ 'tʃɑːr- **~ed** d **~ing** ɪŋ **~s** z
Chari 'tʃɑːr i
chari... —*see* **chary**
Charing 'tʃær ɪŋ 'tʃeər- ‖ 'tʃer- ˌ**Charing 'Cross**
chari|ot 'tʃær i‿|ət ‖ 'tʃer- **~oted** ət ɪd -əd ‖ əṭ əd **~oting** ət ɪŋ ‖ əṭ ɪŋ **~ots** əts
charioteer ˌtʃær i‿ə 'tɪə ‖ -'tɪər ˌtʃer- **~s** z
charisma kə 'rɪz mə **charismata** kə 'rɪz mət ə ˌkær ɪz 'mɑːt ə, -əz- ‖ kə 'rɪz məṭ ə
charismatic ˌkær ɪz 'mæt ɪk ◂ -əz- ‖ -'mæṭ- ˌker- **~ally** əl‿i
charitab|le 'tʃær ɪt əb |əl '·ət- ‖ 'tʃær əṭ- 'tʃer- **~leness** əl nəs -nɪs **~ly** li
charit|y, C~ 'tʃær ət |i -ɪt- ‖ -əṭ |i 'tʃer- **~ies** iz
charivari ˌʃɑːr ɪ 'vɑːr i ˌʃær-, -ə- ‖ ʃə ˌrɪv ə 'riː ˌʃɪv ə 'riː *(*)*
charivaria ˌʃɑːr ɪ 'vɑːr i‿ə ˌʃær-, ˌ·ə-
charka 'tʃɜːk ɑː 'tʃɑːk-, -ə ‖ 'tʃɝːk- **~s** z
charlad|y 'tʃɑː ˌleɪd |i ‖ 'tʃɑːr- **~ies** iz
charlatan 'ʃɑːl ət ən -ə tæn ‖ 'ʃɑːrl ət ən **~ism** ˌɪz əm **~ry** ri **~s** z
Charlbury 'tʃɑːl bər‿i ‖ 'tʃɑːrl ˌber i
Charlecote 'tʃɑːl kəʊt ‖ 'tʃɑːrl koʊt
Charleen *(i)* 'tʃɑːl iːn ₍ₗ₎tʃɑː 'liːn ‖ 'tʃɑːrl-, *(ii)* 'ʃɑːl iːn ₍ₗ₎ʃɑː 'liːn ‖ 'ʃɑːrl iːn ₍ₗ₎ʃɑːr 'liːn
Charlemagne 'ʃɑːl ə meɪn -maɪn, ˌ··'· ‖ 'ʃɑːrl- —*Fr* [ʃaʁ lə manj]
Charlene *(i)* 'tʃɑːl iːn ₍ₗ₎tʃɑː 'liːn ‖ 'tʃɑːrl-, *(ii)* 'ʃɑːl iːn ₍ₗ₎ʃɑː 'liːn ‖ 'ʃɑːrl iːn ₍ₗ₎ʃɑːr 'liːn
Charles tʃɑːlz ‖ tʃɑːrlz —*but as a French name,* ʃɑːl ‖ ʃɑːrl —, *Fr* [ʃaʁl] **Charles', Charles's** 'tʃɑːlz ɪz əz; tʃɑːlz ‖ 'tʃɑːrlz əz tʃɑːrlz
Charleston, c~ 'tʃɑːlst ən 'tʃɑːlz tən ‖ 'tʃɑːrlst ən **~s** z
Charlestown 'tʃɑːlz taʊn ‖ 'tʃɑːrlz-
Charley, Charlie, c~ 'tʃɑːl i ‖ 'tʃɑːrl i **'charley horse**
Charlie, c~ 'tʃɑːl i ‖ 'tʃɑːrl i **~s, ~'s** z
charlock 'tʃɑː lɒk ‖ 'tʃɑːr lɑːk
charlotte, C~ 'ʃɑːl ət ‖ 'ʃɑːrl- **~s, ~'s** s ˌ**Charlotte A'malie** ə 'mɑːl i‿ə ‖ ə 'mɑːl jə; ˌ**charlotte 'russe** ruːs
Charlottenburg ʃɑː 'lɒt ən bɜːg ‖ ʃɑːr 'lɑːt ən bɝːg —*Ger* [ʃaʁ 'lɔt ən bʊʁk]
Charlottesville 'ʃɑːl əts vɪl ‖ 'ʃɑːrl- vəl
Charlottetown 'ʃɑːl ət taʊn ‖ 'ʃɑːrl-
Charlton 'tʃɑːlt ən ‖ 'tʃɑːrlt-
charm tʃɑːm ‖ tʃɑːrm **charmed** tʃɑːmd ‖ tʃɑːrmd **charming** 'tʃɑːm ɪŋ ‖ 'tʃɑːrm ɪŋ **charms** tʃɑːmz ‖ tʃɑːrmz
Charmaine ₍ₗ₎ʃɑː 'meɪn ‖ ʃɑːr-
charmer 'tʃɑːm ə ‖ 'tʃɑːrm ər **~s** z
Charmian *(i)* 'tʃɑːm i‿ən ‖ 'tʃɑːrm-, *(ii)* 'ʃɑːm- ‖ 'ʃɑːrm-, *(iii)* 'kɑːm- ‖ 'kɑːrm-
charming 'tʃɑːm ɪŋ ‖ 'tʃɑːrm ɪŋ **~ly** li
charnel 'tʃɑːn əl ‖ 'tʃɑːrn əl **'charnel house**
Charnock 'tʃɑːn ɒk -ək ‖ 'tʃɑːrn ɑːk
Charnwood 'tʃɑːn wʊd ‖ 'tʃɑːrn-
Charolais, Charollais 'ʃær ə leɪ ‖ ˌʃær ə 'leɪ ˌʃer-, ˌʃɑːr- —*As a pl n, also with final* z
Charon 'keər ən -ɒn ‖ 'ker- 'kær-
charpoy 'tʃɑːp ɔɪ ‖ 'tʃɑːrp- **~s** z
Charrington 'tʃær ɪŋ tən ‖ 'tʃer-
chart, Chart tʃɑːt ‖ tʃɑːrt **charted** 'tʃɑːt ɪd -əd ‖ 'tʃɑːrṭ əd **charting** 'tʃɑːt ɪŋ ‖ 'tʃɑːrṭ ɪŋ
charter 'tʃɑːt ə ‖ 'tʃɑːrṭ ər **~ed** d **chartering** 'tʃɑːt‿ər ɪŋ ‖ 'tʃɑːrṭ ər ɪŋ **~s** z ˌ**chartered ac'countant**; **'charter flight**; ˌ**charter 'member**
charterer 'tʃɑːt‿ər ə ‖ 'tʃɑːrṭ ər ər **~s** z
Charterhouse 'tʃɑːt ə haʊs ‖ 'tʃɑːrṭ ər-
Charteris *(i)* 'tʃɑːt ər ɪs -əs ‖ 'tʃɑːrṭ-, *(ii)* 'tʃɑːt əz ‖ 'tʃɑːrṭ ərz
Chartham 'tʃɑːt əm ‖ 'tʃɑːrṭ-
Chartism 'tʃɑːt ˌɪz əm ‖ 'tʃɑːrṭ-
Chartist 'tʃɑːt ɪst §-əst ‖ 'tʃɑːrṭ- **~s** s
Chartres *place in France* 'ʃɑːtr ə ʃɑːtr, ʃɑːt ‖ 'ʃɑːrtr ə —*Fr* [ʃaʁtχ]
chartreuse, C~ *tdmk* ʃɑː 'trɜːz ‖ ʃɑːr 'truːz -'truːs *(*)* —*Fr* [ʃaʁ tʁøːz]
Chartwell 'tʃɑːt wel -wəl ‖ 'tʃɑːrt-
char|woman 'tʃɑː |ˌwʊm ən ‖ 'tʃɑːr- **~women** ˌwɪm ɪn §-ən
char|y 'tʃeər |i ‖ 'tʃer |i 'tʃær- **~ier** i‿ə ‖ i‿ər **~iest** i‿ɪst i‿əst **~ily** əl i ɪl i **~iness** i nəs i nɪs
Charybdis kə 'rɪbd ɪs §-əs
Chas. tʃæz tʃæs —*or see* Charles
chase, Chase tʃeɪs **chased** tʃeɪst *(= chaste)* **chases** 'tʃeɪs ɪz -əz **chasing** 'tʃeɪs ɪŋ
chaser 'tʃeɪs ə ‖ -ər **~s** z
chasm 'kæz əm *(!)* **~s** z
chassé 'ʃæs eɪ ‖ ʃæ 'seɪ **~d** d **~ing** ɪŋ **~s** z
chasseur ₍ₗ₎ʃæ 'sɜː ‖ -'sɝː —*Fr* [ʃa sœːʁ]
chassis *sing.* 'ʃæs i ‖ 'tʃæs-, ⚠-əs **chassis** *pl* 'ʃæs iz -i ‖ tʃæs-
chaste tʃeɪst *(= chased)* **chaster** 'tʃeɪst ə ‖ -ər **chastest** 'tʃeɪst ɪst -əst
chastely 'tʃeɪst li
chasten 'tʃeɪs ən **~ed** d **~ing** ‿ɪŋ **~s** z
chasteness 'tʃeɪst nəs -nɪs
chastis|e ₍ₗ₎tʃæ 'staɪz ‖ 'tʃæst aɪz **~ed** d **~es** ɪz əz **~ing** ɪŋ
chastisement ₍ₗ₎tʃæ 'staɪz mənt 'tʃæst ɪz mənt, -əz- ‖ 'tʃæst aɪz- **~s** s
chastiser ₍ₗ₎tʃæ 'staɪz ə ‖ -ər **~s** z
chastity, C~ 'tʃæst ət i -ɪt- ‖ -əṭ i **'chastity belt**
chasuble 'tʃæz jʊb əl -jəb- ‖ -jəb- -əb- **~s** z

hat tʃæt **chats** tʃæts **chatted** 'tʃæt ɪd -əd ‖ 'tʃæţ əd **chatting** 'tʃæt ɪŋ ‖ 'tʃæţ ɪŋ
'chat show
hataway 'tʃæt ə weɪ ‖ 'tʃæţ-
hateau, château 'ʃæt əʊ ‖ ʃæ 'toʊ —*Fr* [ʃa to] **~s** z
hateaubriand, c~ ˌʃæt əʊ bri 'ɒn ◂ -'õ, -'ɒnd; -'bri:; ʃæ 'təʊb ri· ‖ ʃæ ˌtoʊ bri 'ɑ:n ◂ —*Fr* [ʃa to bri jɑ̃]
hâteauneuf-du-Pape ˌʃæt əʊ nɜ:f dju 'pæp -du'·, -'pɑ:p ‖ ʃæ ˌtoʊ nʌf du 'pɑ:p —*Fr* [ʃa to nœv dy pap]
hateaux, châteaux 'ʃæt əʊz -əʊ ‖ ʃæ 'toʊz -'toʊ —*Fr* [ʃa to]
hatelain, châtelain 'ʃæt ə leɪn -ᵊl eɪn ‖ 'ʃæţ ᵊl eɪn —*Fr* [ʃat lɛ̃] **~s** z
hatelaine, châtelaine 'ʃæt ə leɪn -ᵊl eɪn ‖ 'ʃæţ ᵊl eɪn —*Fr* [ʃat lɛn] **~s** z
Chater 'tʃeɪt ə ‖ 'tʃeɪţ ᵊr
Chatham 'tʃæt əm ‖ 'tʃæţ-
hatline 'tʃæt laɪn **~s** z
hatroom 'tʃæt ru:m -rʊm **~s** z
Chatsworth 'tʃæts wəθ -wɜ:θ ‖ -wᵊrθ
chatt... —*see* **chat**
Chattahoochee ˌtʃæt ə 'hu:tʃ i ◂ ‖ ˌtʃæţ-
ˌChattaˌhoochee 'River
Chattanooga ˌtʃæt ᵊn 'u:g ə ˌtʃæt ə 'nu:g ə
ˌChattaˌnooga 'choo-choo
chattel 'tʃæt ᵊl ‖ 'tʃæţ- **~s** z
chatter 'tʃæt ə ‖ 'tʃæţ ᵊr **~ed** d **chattering** 'tʃæt‿ər ɪŋ ‖ 'tʃæţ ər ɪŋ **~s** z
chatterbox 'tʃæt ə bɒks ‖ 'tʃæţ ᵊr bɑ:ks **~es** ɪz əz
chatterer 'tʃæt ər ə ‖ 'tʃæţ ər ᵊr **~s** z
Chatteris 'tʃæt ər ɪs §-əs ‖ 'tʃæţ-
Chatterjee, Chatterji 'tʃæt ə dʒi: ‖ 'tʃæţ ᵊr-
Chatterley 'tʃæt ə li -ᵊl i ‖ 'tʃæţ ᵊr- **~'s** z
Chatterton 'tʃæt ət ən ‖ 'tʃæţ ᵊrt ᵊn
chattie...—*see* **chatty**
Chatto 'tʃæt əʊ ‖ 'tʃæţ oʊ
chatt|y 'tʃæt |i ‖ 'tʃæţ |i **~ier** i‿ə ‖ i‿ᵊr **~iest** i‿ɪst i‿əst **~ily** ɪ li əl i **~iness** i nəs i nɪs
chat-up 'tʃæt ʌp ‖ 'tʃæţ-
'chat-up line
Chatwin 'tʃæt wɪn
Chaucer 'tʃɔ:s ə ‖ -ᵊr 'tʃɑ:s-
Chaucerian tʃɔ: 'sɪər i‿ən ‖ -'sɪr- tʃɑ:- **~s** z
chaudfroid 'ʃəʊ fwɑ: -frwɑ: ‖ 'ʃoʊ- —*Fr* [ʃo fʁwa]
Chaudhuri, Chaudhury 'tʃaʊd‿ər i
chauffeur 'ʃəʊf ə ʃəʊ 'fɜ:, ʃə- ‖ ʃoʊ 'fɜ:r **~ed** d **chauffeuring** 'ʃəʊf ər‿ɪŋ ‖ ʃoʊ 'fɜ: ɪŋ **~s** z
chaulmoog|ra tʃɔ:l 'mu:g rə tʃəʊl- ‖ tʃɑ:l- **~ric** rɪk
Chauncey, Chauncy 'tʃɔ:nᵗs i ‖ 'tʃɑ:nᵗs-
chausses ʃəʊs ‖ ʃoʊs
chautauqua, C~ ʃə 'tɔ:k wə ‖ -'tɑ:k- **~s** z
chauvinism 'ʃəʊv ə ˌnɪz əm -ɪ- ‖ 'ʃoʊv-
chauvinist 'ʃəʊv ən‿ɪst -ɪn-, əst ‖ 'ʃoʊv- **~s** s
chauvinistic ˌʃəʊv ə 'nɪst ɪk ◂ -ɪ- ‖ ˌʃoʊv- **~ally** ᵊl‿i
chav tʃæv **chavs** tʃævz
Chavasse ʃə 'væs
Chavez 'tʃæv es ‖ 'tʃɑ:v ez 'ʃɑ:v-, -es —*Sp* Chávez ['tʃa βeθ, -βes]
Chavon, Chavonne ʃə 'vɒn ‖ -'vɑ:n
chaw tʃɔ: ‖ tʃɑ: **chaws** tʃɔ:z ‖ tʃɑ:z
Chawton 'tʃɔ:t ᵊn ‖ 'tʃɑ:t-
Chay tʃeɪ
Chayefsky tʃaɪ 'ef ski
chayote tʃaɪ 'əʊt i ‖ -'oʊţ- **~s** z
Chaz tʃæz
Che tʃeɪ
Cheadle 'tʃi:d ᵊl
Cheam tʃi:m
cheap tʃi:p **cheaper** 'tʃi:p ə ‖ -ᵊr **cheapest** 'tʃi:p ɪst -əst
cheapen 'tʃi:p ən **~ed** d **~ing** ˌɪŋ **~s** z
cheapie 'tʃi:p i **~s** z
cheap-jack 'tʃi:p dʒæk **~s** s
cheap|ly 'tʃi:p |li **~ness** nəs nɪs
cheapo 'tʃi:p əʊ ‖ -oʊ
Cheapside 'tʃi:p saɪd ˌ·'·
cheapskate 'tʃi:p skeɪt **~s** s
cheat tʃi:t **cheated** 'tʃi:t ɪd -əd ‖ 'tʃi:ţ əd **cheating/ly** 'tʃi:t ɪŋ /li ‖ 'tʃi:ţ ɪŋ /li **cheats** tʃi:ts
cheater 'tʃi:t ə ‖ 'tʃi:ţ ᵊr **~s** z
Cheatham 'tʃi:t əm ‖ 'tʃi:ţ-
Chechen 'tʃetʃ en -ən; tʃɪ 'tʃen, tʃe-
Chechenia tʃɪ 'tʃen jə tʃe-
Chechnya tʃetʃ 'njɑ: 'tʃetʃ ni‿ə
check tʃek **checked** tʃekt **checking** 'tʃek ɪŋ **checks** tʃeks
'checking acˌcount
checkbook 'tʃek bʊk §-bu:k **~s** s
checkbox 'tʃek bɒks ‖ -bɑ:ks **~es** ɪz əz
checker, C~ 'tʃek ə ‖ -ᵊr **~ed** d **checkering** 'tʃek ər‿ɪŋ **~s** z
checkerboard 'tʃek ə bɔ:d ‖ -ᵊr bɔ:rd -boʊrd **~s** z
check-in 'tʃek ɪn **~s** z
Checkland 'tʃek lənd
Checkley 'tʃek li
checklist 'tʃek lɪst **~s** s
check|mate 'tʃek |meɪt ˌ·'· **~mated** meɪt ɪd -əd ‖ meɪţ əd **~mates** meɪts **~mating** meɪt ɪŋ ‖ meɪţ ɪŋ
checkout 'tʃek aʊt **~s** s
checkpoint 'tʃek pɔɪnt **~s** s
checkrail 'tʃek reɪᵊl **~s** z
checkrein 'tʃek reɪn **~s** z
checkroom 'tʃek ru:m -rʊm **~s** z
checksum 'tʃek sʌm **~s** z
checkup 'tʃek ʌp **~s** s
Cheddar, c~ 'tʃed ə ‖ -ᵊr
ˌCheddar 'cheese
Chedzoy 'tʃedz ɔɪ
cheek, Cheek tʃi:k **cheeked** tʃi:kt **cheeking** 'tʃi:k ɪŋ **cheeks** tʃi:ks
cheekbone 'tʃi:k bəʊn ‖ -boʊn **~s** z
-cheeked 'tʃi:kt — **rosy-cheeked** ˌrəʊz i 'tʃi:kt ◂ ‖ ˌroʊz-
cheek|y 'tʃi:k |i **~ier** i‿ə ‖ i‿ᵊr **~iest** i‿ɪst i‿əst **~ily** ɪ li əl i **~iness** i nəs i nɪs

cheep tʃiːp *(= cheap)* **cheeped** tʃiːpt **cheeping** ˈtʃiːp ɪŋ **cheeps** tʃiːps
cheer tʃɪə ‖ tʃɪᵊr **cheered** tʃɪəd ‖ tʃɪᵊrd **cheering** ˈtʃɪər ɪŋ ‖ ˈtʃɪr ɪŋ **cheers** tʃɪəz ‖ tʃɪᵊrz
cheerful ˈtʃɪəf ᵊl -ʊl ‖ ˈtʃɪrf- **~ly** ˌi **~ness** nəs nɪs
cheeri... —*see* **cheery**
cheerio, C~ ˌtʃɪər i ˈəʊ ◂ ‖ ˌtʃɪr i ˈoʊ ˈ· · · **~s** z
cheerlead|er ˈtʃɪə ˌliːd ə ‖ ˈtʃɪr ˌliːd ᵊr **~ers** əz ‖ ᵊrz **~ing** ɪŋ
cheerless ˈtʃɪə ləs -lɪs ‖ ˈtʃɪr- **~ly** li **~ness** nəs nɪs
cheers tʃɪəz ‖ tʃɪᵊrz
cheer|y ˈtʃɪər |i ‖ ˈtʃɪr |i **~ier** iˌə ‖ iˌᵊr **~iest** iˌɪst iˌəst **~ily** əl i ɪl i **~iness** i nəs i nɪs
cheese tʃiːz **cheesed** tʃiːzd **cheeses** ˈtʃiːz ɪz -əz
ˌcheesed ˈoff; **ˌcheese ˈstraw**
cheeseboard ˈtʃiːz bɔːd ‖ -bɔːrd -boʊrd **~s** z
cheeseburger ˈtʃiːz ˌbɜːg ə ‖ -ˌbɜːg ᵊr **~s** z
cheesecake ˈtʃiːz keɪk **~s** s
cheesecloth ˈtʃiːz klɒθ -klɔːθ ‖ -klɔːθ -klɑːθ
Cheeseman ˈtʃiːz mən
cheesemonger ˈtʃiːz ˌmʌŋ gə ‖ -gᵊr **~s** z
cheeseparing ˈtʃiːz ˌpeər ɪŋ ‖ -ˌper- -ˌpær-
Cheesewright ˈtʃiːz raɪt
Cheesman ˈtʃiːz mən
cheesy ˈtʃiːz i
cheetah ˈtʃiːt ə ‖ ˈtʃiːţ ə **~s** z
Cheetham ˈtʃiːt əm ‖ ˈtʃiːţ-
Cheetos *tdmk* ˈtʃiːt əʊz ‖ ˈtʃiːţ oʊz
Cheever ˈtʃiːv ə ‖ -ᵊr
Cheez Whiz *tdmk* ˌtʃiːz ˈwɪz
chef ʃef **chefs** ʃefs —*but in French phrases both sing. and pl are* ʃeɪ —*See also phrases with this word*
chef d'oeuvre, chefs d'oeuvre ˌʃeɪ ˈdɜːv rə -ˈdɜːv ‖ ˌʃeɪ ˈdʌv —*Fr* [ʃɛ dœːvʁ]
Chegwin ˈtʃeg wɪn
Cheke tʃiːk
Chekhov ˈtʃek ɒf -ɒv ‖ -ɔːf -ɑːf —*Russ* [ˈtʃɛ xəf]
Chekhovian tʃe ˈkəʊv iˌən -ˈkɒv- ‖ -ˈkoʊv-
Chek Lap Kok ˌtʃek læp ˈkɒk ‖ -lɑːp ˈkoʊk —*Cantonese* [^{3}tsʰɛːk ^{6}laːp ^{3}kɔːk]
chel|a *'claw'* ˈkiːl| ə **~ae** iː
chela *'disciple'* ˈtʃeɪl ə —*Hindi* [tʃeː laː] **~s** z
chelate *v* kiː ˈleɪt kɪ-, kə-, tʃiː-; ˈkiːl eɪt, ˈtʃiːl- ‖ ˈkiːl eɪt **chelated** kiː ˈleɪt ɪd kɪ-, kə-, tʃiː-, -əd; ˈkiːl eɪt-, ˈtʃiːl- ‖ ˈkiːl eɪţ əd
chelate *n, adj* ˈkiːl eɪt ˈtʃiːl- **~s** s
chelation kiː ˈleɪʃ ᵊn kɪ-, kə-, tʃiː-
Chelmer ˈtʃelm ə ‖ -ᵊr
Chelmsford ˈtʃelmz fəd ˈtʃelmᵖs- ‖ -fᵊrd —*locally also* ˈtʃemz-, ˈtʃɒmz-
Chelsea ˈtʃels i
ˌChelsea ˈbun
Cheltenham ˈtʃelt ᵊnˌəm
ˌCheltenham ˈSpa
chemical ˈkem ɪk ᵊl **~ly** ˌi **~s** z
ˌchemical ˌengiˈneering
chemin de fer ʃə ˌmæn də ˈfeə ‖ -ˈfeᵊr —*Fr* [ʃə mɛ̃t fɛːʁ, ʃmɛ̃t fɛːʁ]
chemis|e ʃə ˈmiːz **~es** ɪz əz
chemist ˈkem ɪst §-əst **~s, ~'s** s
chemis|try ˈkem ɪs |tri -əs- **~tries** triz
Chemnitz ˈkem nɪts —*Ger* [ˈkɛm nɪts]
chemo- *comb. form with stress-neutral suffix* |kiːm əʊ |kem əʊ ‖ -oʊ — **chemosynthesis** ˌkiːm əʊ ˈsɪnᵗθ əs ɪs ˌkem-, -ɪs ɪs, §-əs ‖ ˌ·oʊ- *with stress-imposing suffix* kiː ˈmɒ+ ke ˈmɒ+ ‖ -ˈmɑː+ — **chemolysis** kiː ˈmɒl əs ɪs ke-, -ɪs ɪs, §-əs ‖ -ˈmɑːl-
chemotherapy ˌkiːm əʊ ˈθer əp i ˌkem- ‖ ˌ·oʊ
Chenevix *(i)* ˈtʃen ə vɪks, *(ii)* ˈʃen-
Cheney *(i)* ˈtʃeɪn i, *(ii)* ˈtʃiːn i —*The American politician Dick C~ is (i)*
Chengdu ˌtʃeŋ ˈduː ˌtʃʌŋ- —*Chi* Chéngdū [^{2}tʂʰəŋ ^{1}tu]
Chenies *(i)* ˈtʃeɪn iz, *(ii)* ˈtʃiːn iz —*The place in Bucks may be either (i) or (ii).*
chenille ʃə ˈniːᵊl
Chennai ˈtʃen aɪ tʃe ˈnaɪ
cheongsam ˌtʃɒŋ ˈsæm tʃi ˌɒŋ- ‖ ˈtʃɔːŋ sɑːm ˈtʃɑːŋ- **~s** z
Cheops ˈkiː ɒps ‖ -ɑːps
Chepstow ˈtʃep stəʊ ‖ -stoʊ
cheque tʃek *(= check)* **cheques** tʃeks
ˈcheque card
chequebook ˈtʃek bʊk §-buːk **~s** s
chequer ˈtʃek ə ‖ -ᵊr *(= checker)* **~ed** d **chequering** ˈtʃek ər ɪŋ **~s** z
Chequers ˈtʃek əz ‖ -ᵊrz
Cher ʃeə ‖ ʃeᵊr
Cherbourg ˈʃeə bʊəg ˈʃɜː-, -bɔːg, -bɜːg ‖ ˈʃer bʊrg —*Fr* [ʃɛʁ buːʁ]
cherchez la femme ˌʃeəʃ eɪ læ ˈfæm -lɑː·ˈ· ‖ ʃer ˌʃeɪ- —*Fr* [ʃɛʁ ʃe la fam]
Cheremis, Cheremiss ˈtʃer ə mɪs -miːs, ˌ· ·ˈ·
Cherenkov tʃə ˈreŋk ɒf tʃɪ-, -ɒv ‖ -ɑːf —*Russ* [tʃɪ ˈrʲɛn kəf]
Cherie, Chérie ʃə ˈriː ʃe-
Cherilyn *(i)* ˈtʃer əl ɪn -ɪl-, -ən, *(ii)* ˈʃer-
cherimoya ˌtʃer ɪ ˈmɔɪ ə -ə-
cherish ˈtʃer ɪʃ **~ed** t **~es** ɪz əz **~ing** ɪŋ
Cheriton ˈtʃer ɪt ən -ət- ‖ -ᵊn
Chernobyl tʃɜː ˈnəʊb ᵊl tʃə-, -ˈnɒb-, -ɪl; ˈtʃɜːn əb- ‖ tʃᵊr ˈnoʊb- —*Russ* [tʃɪr ˈno bɨlʲ]
Chernomyrdin ˌtʃɜːn ə ˈmɪəd ɪn -ˈmɜːd-, -ᵊn ‖ ˌtʃɪrn ə ˈmɪrd-, ˌtʃɜːn- —*Russ* [tʃɪr nʌ ˈmɨr dʲɪn]
chernozem ˈtʃɜːn əʊ zem ˌ··ˈzjɒm ‖ ˌtʃɜːn ə ˈzem -ˈʒɑːm, -ˈʒɔːm —*Russ* [tʃɪr nʌ ˈzʲɔm]
Cherokee ˈtʃer ə kiː ˌ·ˈ· **~s** z
cheroot ʃə ˈruːt **~s** s
cherr|y, C~ ˈtʃer |i **~ies** iz
cherry-pick ˈtʃer i pɪk **~ed** t **~ing** ɪŋ **~s** s
Chersonese, c~ ˈkɜːs ə niːs -niːz, ˌ· ·ˈ· ‖ ˈkɜːs-
chert tʃɜːt ‖ tʃɜːt **cherts** tʃɜːts ‖ tʃɜːts
Chertsey ˈtʃɜːts i ‖ ˈtʃɜːts i
cherub ˈtʃer əb **~s** z
cherubic tʃə ˈruːb ɪk tʃe- **~ally** ᵊl ˌi

cherubim ˈtʃer ə bɪm ˈker-, -ɪɪ-

Cherubini ˌker u ˈbiːn i -ə-, -iː —*It* [ke ru ˈbiː ni]

chervil ˈtʃɜːv ᵊl -ɪl ‖ ˈtʃɜ˞ːv-

Cherwell ˈtʃɑː wəl -wel ‖ ˈtʃɑːr-

Cheryl *(i)* ˈtʃer əl -ɪl, *(ii)* ˈʃer-

Chesapeake ˈtʃes ə piːk

ˌ**Chesapeake ˈBay**

Chesebrough ˈtʃiːz brə ‖ -broʊ

Chesham ˈtʃeʃ əm —*formerly* ˈtʃes-

Cheshire ˈtʃeʃ ə -ɪə ‖ -ᵊr

ˌ**Cheshire ˈcat, ˌCheshire ˈcheese**

Cheshunt ˈtʃes ᵊnt ˈtʃez- —*There is also a spelling pronunciation* ˈtʃeʃ-

Chesil ˈtʃez ᵊl

ˌ**Chesil ˈBeach**

Chesney *(i)* ˈtʃez ni, *(ii)* ˈtʃes ni

chess tʃes

chessboard ˈtʃes bɔːd ‖ -bɔːrd -boʊrd **~s** z

chess|man ˈtʃes |mæn -mən **~men** men mən

chest tʃest **chested** ˈtʃest ɪd -əd **chests** tʃests

ˌ**chest of ˈdrawers**

chested ˈtʃest ɪd -əd

Chester ˈtʃest ə ‖ -ᵊr

Chesterfield, c~ ˈtʃest ə fiːᵊld ‖ -ᵊr- **~s** z

Chester-le-Street ˈtʃest ə li striːt -ᵊl i-; ˈtʃes li striːt ‖ ˈ·ᵊr·

Chesterton ˈtʃest ət ən ‖ -ᵊrt ᵊn

chestnut, C~ ˈtʃes nʌt ˈtʃest- **~s** s

ˈ**chestnut tree**

chest|y ˈtʃest |i **~ier** i‿ə ‖ i‿ᵊr **~iest** i‿ɪst i‿əst **~iness** i nəs i nɪs

Chet tʃet

Chetham *(i)* ˈtʃiːt əm ‖ ˈtʃiːt̬-, *(ii)* ˈtʃet- ‖ ˈtʃet̬-

Chetnik ˈtʃet nɪk **~s** s

Chetwode ˈtʃet wʊd

Chetwyn ˈtʃet wɪn

Chetwynd ˈtʃet wɪnd

Cheung tʃʌŋ —*Cantonese* [^{1}tsœːŋ]

cheval glass ʃə ˈvæl glɑːs §-glæs ‖ -glæs

chevalier *n* ˌʃev ə ˈlɪə ‖ -ˈlɪᵊr **~s** z

Chevalier *name* ʃə ˈvæl i‿eɪ ʃɪ-

Chevening ˈtʃiːv nɪŋ

Chevette *tdmk* ʃə ˈvet ʃe- **~s** s

Chevington ˈtʃev ɪŋ tən

Cheviot ˈtʃiːv i‿ət ˈtʃev- ‖ ˈʃev- —*locally* ˈtʃiːv- **~s** s

Chevon, Chevonne ʃə ˈvɒn ʃɪ- ‖ -ˈvɑːn

chèvre ˈʃev rə ˈʃeəv- —*Fr* [ʃɛːvʁ]

Chevrolet *tdmk* ˈʃev rə leɪ ˌ· ·ˈ· ‖ ˌʃev rə ˈleɪ **~s** z

chevron ˈʃev rən -rɒn **~s** z

chevv|y, chev|y *v* ˈtʃev |i **~ied** id **~ies** iz **~ying** i‿ɪŋ

Chevvy, Chevy *n 'Chevrolet'* ˈʃev i

chew tʃuː **chewed** tʃuːd **chewing** ˈtʃuː‿ɪŋ **chews** tʃuːz

ˈ**chewing gum**

Chewton ˈtʃuːt ᵊn

chew|y ˈtʃuː|‿i **~iness** i nəs -nɪs

Chex *tdmk* tʃeks

Cheyenne ˌʃaɪ ˈæn ◂ -ˈen **~s** z

Cheyne *(i)* ˈtʃeɪn i, *(ii)* tʃeɪn, *(iii)* tʃiːn

Cheyne-Stokes ˌtʃeɪn ˈstəʊks ‖ -ˈstoʊks

chez ʃeɪ —*Fr* [ʃe]

(ˌ)**chez ˈnous** nuː —*Fr* [nu]

chi *Greek letter* kaɪ **chis** kaɪz

Chiang Kaishek ˌtʃæŋ kaɪ ˈʃek tʃiˌæŋ- ‖ tʃiˌɑːŋ- —*Chi* Jiǎng Jièshí [^{3}tɕjaŋ ^{4}tɕjɛ ^{2}ʂɨ]

Chiang Mai tʃi ˌæŋ ˈmaɪ ‖ -ˌɑːŋ-

Chianti, c~ ki ˈænt i ‖ -ˈɑːnt̬ i —*It* [ˈkjan ti]

~shire ʃə ʃɪə, ˌʃaɪ‿ə ‖ ʃᵊr ʃɪr, ˌʃaɪ ᵊr

Chiapas tʃi ˈæp əs ‖ -ˈɑːp- —*Sp* [ˈtʃja pas]

chiaroscuro ki ˌɑːr ə ˈskʊər əʊ -ˈskjʊər- ‖ -ˈskʊr oʊ -ˈskjʊr- —*It* [kja ros ˈkuː ro] **~s** z

chias|ma kaɪ ˈæz |mə **~mas** məz **~mata** mət ə ‖ mət̬ ə

chiasmus kaɪ ˈæz məs

Chibcha ˈtʃɪb tʃə

Chibchan ˈtʃɪb tʃən

chibouk tʃɪ ˈbuːk tʃə- **~s** s

chic ʃiːk ʃɪk

Chicago ʃɪ ˈkɑːg əʊ ʃə- ‖ -oʊ —*locally also* -ˈkɔːg-

Chicana, c~ tʃɪ ˈkɑːn ə ʃɪ-, tʃə-, ʃə- ‖ -ˈkæn- —*Sp* [tʃi ˈka na] **~s** z

chican|e ʃɪ ˈkeɪn ʃə- **~ed** d **~es** z **~ing** ɪŋ

chicaner|y ʃɪ ˈkeɪn ər |i ʃə- **~ies** iz

Chicano, c~ tʃɪ ˈkɑːn əʊ ʃɪ-, tʃə-, ʃə- ‖ -oʊ -ˈkæn- —*Sp* [tʃi ˈka no] **~s** z

Chichele ˈtʃɪtʃ əl i -ɪl-

Chichén Itzá tʃɪ ˌtʃen ɪt ˈsɑː -iːt- —*AmSp* [tʃi ˌtʃe nit ˈsa]

Chichester ˈtʃɪtʃ ɪst ə -əst- ‖ -ᵊr —*but the place in upstate NY is* ˈtʃaɪ ˌtʃest ᵊr

Chichewa tʃɪ ˈtʃeɪ wə

chi-chi ˈʃiː ʃiː ˈtʃiː tʃiː

chick, Chick tʃɪk **chicks** tʃɪks

chickabidd|y ˈtʃɪk ə bɪd |i **~ies** iz

chickadee ˈtʃɪk ə diː ˌ· ·ˈ· **~s** z

chickaree ˈtʃɪk ə riː **~s** z

Chickasaw ˈtʃɪk ə sɔː ‖ -sɑː **~s** z

chicken ˈtʃɪk ɪn -ən **~ed** d **~ing** ɪŋ **~s** z

ˈ**chicken pox, ˈchicken ˌwire**

chickenfeed ˈtʃɪk ɪn fiːd -ən-

chicken-fried ˈtʃɪk ɪn fraɪd -ən-

chickenhearted ˌtʃɪk ɪn ˈhɑːt ɪd ◂ -ən-, -əd ‖ -ˈhɑːrt̬ əd ◂

chickenlivered ˌtʃɪk ɪn ˈlɪv əd ◂ -ən- ‖ -ᵊrd ◂ ˈ· ·ˌ· ·

chickenshit ˈtʃɪk ɪn ʃɪt -ən-

chickpea ˈtʃɪk piː **~s** z

chickweed ˈtʃɪk wiːd

chicle ˈtʃɪk ᵊl

chicory ˈtʃɪk ər i

chid... —*see* **chide**

Chiddingly *place in Sussex* ˌtʃɪd ɪŋ ˈlaɪ

chide tʃaɪd **chid** tʃɪd **chidden** ˈtʃɪd ᵊn **chided** ˈtʃaɪd ɪd -əd **chides** tʃaɪdz

chief tʃiːf **chiefly** ˈtʃiːf li **chiefs** tʃiːfs

ˌ**chief ˈconstable**; ˌ**Chief Eˈxecutive**; ˌ**chief inˈspector**◂; ˌ**Chief ˈJustice**◂; ˌ**chief of ˈstaff**; ˌ**chief ˌsuperinˈtendent**◂

chieftain ˈtʃiːft ən -ɪn **~s** z

chieftain|cy ˈtʃiːft ən |si -ɪn- **~cies** siz

chiffchaff ˈtʃɪf tʃæf **~s** s

chiffon 'ʃɪf ɒn ʃɪ 'fɒn ‖ ʃɪ 'fɑːn **~s** z

chiffonier, chiffonnier ˌʃɪf ə 'nɪə ‖ -'nɪᵊr **~s** z

chigger 'tʃɪg ə 'dʒɪg- ‖ -ᵊr **~s** z

chignon 'ʃiːn jɒn -jɒ̃ ‖ -jɑːn —*Fr* [ʃi njɔ̃] **~s** z

chigoe 'tʃɪg əʊ ‖ -oʊ 'tʃiːg- **~s** z

Chigwell 'tʃɪg wəl -wel

chihuahua, C~ tʃɪ 'wɑː wə tʃə-, ʃɪ-, ʃə-, -wɑː; -'waʊ ə —*Sp* [tʃi 'wa wa] **~s** z

chikungunya ˌtʃɪk ʊŋ 'gʊn jə

chilblain 'tʃɪl bleɪn **~ed** d **~s** z

child, Child tʃaɪᵊld **children** 'tʃɪldr ən 'tʃʊldr- ‖ 'tʃɪld ᵊrn **children's** 'tʃɪldr ənz 'tʃʊldr- ‖ 'tʃɪld ᵊrnz **child's** tʃaɪᵊldz
'**child aˌbuse**; '**child care**; '**child's play**; ˌ**child 'prodigy**

childbearing 'tʃaɪᵊld ˌbeər ɪŋ ‖ -ˌber- -ˌbær-

childbed 'tʃaɪᵊl*d* bed

childbirth 'tʃaɪᵊl*d* bɜːθ ‖ -bɜːθ

Childe, c~ 'tʃaɪᵊld

childermas, C~ 'tʃɪld ə mæs ‖ -ᵊr-

Childers 'tʃɪld əz ‖ -ᵊrz

childhood 'tʃaɪᵊld hʊd

childish 'tʃaɪᵊld ɪʃ **~ly** li **~ness** nəs nɪs

childless 'tʃaɪl*d* ləs -lɪs **~ness** nəs nɪs

childlike 'tʃaɪᵊl*d* laɪk

childmind|er 'tʃaɪl*d* ˌmaɪnd| ə ‖ -ᵊr **~ers** əz ‖ -ᵊrz **~ing** ɪŋ

childproof 'tʃaɪᵊl*d* pruːf §-prʊf

children 'tʃɪldr ən 'tʃʊldr- ‖ 'tʃɪld ᵊrn **~'s** z
'**children's home**

Childs tʃaɪᵊldz

Childwall 'tʃɪl wɔːl 'tʃɪld- ‖ -wɑːl

Chile, chile 'tʃɪl i ‖ -eɪ —*Sp* ['tʃi le]
ˌ**chile con 'carne** kɒn 'kɑːn i →kɒŋ-, kən-, -eɪ ‖ kɑːn 'kɑːrn i kən-

Chilean 'tʃɪl iˌən ‖ tʃɪ 'liː ən, -'leɪ- **~s** z

chili 'tʃɪl i *(= chilly)* **~es** z
'**chili dog**

chiliad 'kɪl i æd 'kaɪl-, -əd **~s** z

chiliasm 'kɪl i ˌæz əm

chiliast 'kɪl i æst **~s** s

chiliastic ˌkɪl i 'æst ɪk ◂

Chilkoot 'tʃɪl kuːt

chill tʃɪl **chilled** tʃɪld **chilling** 'tʃɪl ɪŋ **chills** tʃɪlz

chiller 'tʃɪl ə ‖ -ᵊr **~s** z

chilli 'tʃɪl i *(= chilly)* **~es** z
ˌ**chilli con 'carne** kɒn 'kɑːn i →kɒŋ-, kən-, -eɪ ‖ kɑːn 'kɑːrn i kən-; '**chilli ˌpowder**

chilling 'tʃɪl ɪŋ **~ly** li

chillness 'tʃɪl nəs -nɪs

Chillon ʃɪ 'lɒn ʃə-; 'ʃɪl ən, -ɒn ‖ ʃə 'lɑːn —*Fr* [ʃi jɔ̃]

chillum 'tʃɪl əm

chill|y 'tʃɪl |i **~ier** iˌə ‖ iˌᵊr **~iest** iˌɪst iˌəst **~ily** ɪ li əl i **~iness** i nəs i nɪs

Chilpruf *tdmk* 'tʃɪl pruːf §-prʊf

Chiltern 'tʃɪlt ən ‖ -ᵊrn **~s** z
ˌ**Chiltern 'Hills**; ˌ**Chiltern 'Hundreds**

Chilton 'tʃɪlt ən ‖ -ᵊn

Chilver 'tʃɪlv ə ‖ -ᵊr **~s** z

chimaera kaɪ 'mɪər ə kɪ-, kə-, ʃɪ-, ʃə-, -'meər-; 'kɪm ər ə, 'ʃɪm- ‖ -'mɪr ə **~s** z

Chimborazo ˌtʃɪm bə 'rɑːz əʊ ˌʃɪm- ‖ -oʊ —*AmSp* [tʃim bo 'ra so]

chime tʃaɪm **chimed** tʃaɪmd **chimes** tʃaɪmz **chiming** 'tʃaɪm ɪŋ

chimer 'tʃaɪm ə ‖ -ᵊr **~s** z

chimera kaɪ 'mɪər ə kɪ-, kə-, ʃɪ-, ʃə-, -'meər-; 'kɪm ər ə, 'ʃɪm- ‖ -'mɪr ə **~s** z

chimeric kaɪ 'mer ɪk kɪ-, kə-, ʃɪ- **~al** ᵊl **~ally** ᵊl i

chimichanga ˌtʃɪm i 'tʃæŋ gə ‖ -'tʃɑːŋ- —*Sp* [tʃi mi 'tʃaŋ ga] **~s** z

chimichurri ˌtʃɪm i 'tʃʊr i -'tʃʌr i

chimney 'tʃɪm ni **~s** z

chimneybreast 'tʃɪm ni brest **~s** s

chimneypiec|e 'tʃɪm ni piːs **~es** ɪz əz

chimneypot 'tʃɪm ni pɒt ‖ -pɑːt **~s** s

chimneystack 'tʃɪm ni stæk **~s** s

chimneysweep 'tʃɪm ni swiːp **~s** s

chimneysweeper 'tʃɪm ni ˌswiːp ə ‖ -ᵊr **~s** z

chimp tʃɪmp **chimps** tʃɪm*p*s

chimpanzee ˌtʃɪmp æn 'ziː ◂ -ən- ‖ ˌʃɪmp-; tʃɪm 'pænz i **~s** z

chin tʃɪn **chinned** tʃɪnd **chinning** 'tʃɪn ɪŋ **chins** tʃɪnz

China, china 'tʃaɪn ə

China|man, c~ 'tʃaɪn ə |mən **~men** mən men

Chinatown 'tʃaɪn ə taʊn

chinaware 'tʃaɪn ə weə ‖ -wer

chinch tʃɪntʃ **chinches** 'tʃɪntʃ ɪz -əz
'**chinch bug**

chincherinchee ˌtʃɪn*t*ʃ ə 'rɪn*t*ʃ i -rɪn 'tʃiː, -rən 'tʃiː **~s** z

chinchilla tʃɪn 'tʃɪl ə **~s** z

chin-chin ˌtʃɪn 'tʃɪn

Chincoteague 'ʃɪŋk ə tiːg 'tʃɪŋk-

Chindit 'tʃɪnd ɪt §-ət **~s** s

chine tʃaɪn **chines** tʃaɪnz

Chinese ˌtʃaɪ 'niːz ◂ ‖ -'niːs ◂
ˌ**Chinese 'chequers**; ˌ**Chinese 'gooseberry**; ˌ**Chinese 'restaurant**

Chingford 'tʃɪŋ fəd ‖ -fᵊrd

chink tʃɪŋk **chinked** tʃɪŋkt **chinking** 'tʃɪŋk ɪŋ **chinks** tʃɪŋ*k*s

chinless 'tʃɪn ləs -lɪs
ˌ**chinless 'wonder**

Chinnor 'tʃɪn ə ‖ -ᵊr

chino 'tʃiːn əʊ 'ʃiːn- ‖ -oʊ **~s** z

chinoiserie ʃɪn 'wɑːz ər i ₍ₗ₎ʃiːn-, -ˌwɑːz ə 'riː —*Fr* [ʃi nwaz ʁi]

chinook, C~ ₍ₗ₎tʃɪ 'nuːk ʃɪ-, §tʃə-, -'nʊk ‖ ʃə 'nʊk ʃɪ- **~s** s

chinquapin 'tʃɪŋk ə pɪn -ɪ- **~s** z

chinstrap 'tʃɪn stræp **~s** s

chintz tʃɪn*t*s **chintzes** 'tʃɪn*t*s ɪz -əz

chintz|y 'tʃɪn*t*s |i **~ier** iˌə ‖ iˌᵊr **~iest** iˌɪst iˌəst

chin-up, chinup 'tʃɪn ʌp **~s** s

chinwag 'tʃɪn wæg **~s** z

chinwagging 'tʃɪn ˌwæg ɪŋ

chionodoxa kaɪ ˌɒn ə 'dɒks ə -ˌəʊn-, ˌkaɪˌən- ‖ kaɪ ˌoʊn ə 'dɑːks ə **~s** z

Chios 'kaɪ ɒs 'kiː- ‖ -ɑːs

chip tʃɪp **chipped** tʃɪpt **chipping** 'tʃɪp ɪŋ **chips** tʃɪps
'chip ˌbasket; 'chip shot
chipboard 'tʃɪp bɔːd ‖ -bɔːrd -bourd
chipmunk 'tʃɪp mʌŋk **~s** s
chipolata ˌtʃɪp ə 'lɑːt ə ‖ -'lɑːṭ ə **~s** z
chipotle tʃɪ 'pɒt leɪ tʃə-, -li ‖ tʃə 'pout- -'pɑːt- —*Sp* [tʃi 'pot le] **~s** z
chipp... —*see* **chip**
Chippendale 'tʃɪp ən deɪᵊl →-m- **~s** z
Chippenham 'tʃɪp ən‿əm
chipper 'tʃɪp ə ‖ -ᵊr
Chippewa 'tʃɪp ɪ wɑː -ə-, -wə
chippi... —*see* **chip; chippy**
chipping, C~ 'tʃɪp ɪŋ **~s** z
ˌChipping 'Sodbury 'sɒd bər‿i →'sɒb- ‖ 'sɑːd ˌber i -bər‿i
chipp|y 'tʃɪp |i **~ies** iz
Chirac 'ʃɪr æk ‖ ʃɪ 'rɑːk —*Fr* [ʃi ʁak]
chiral 'kaɪᵊr əl
chirality kaɪᵊ 'ræl ət i -ɪt- ‖ -əṭ i
Chirk tʃɜːk ‖ tʃɜ˞ːk
chiromancy 'kaɪᵊr əʊ ˌmænᵗs i ‖ -ə-
Chiron 'kaɪᵊr ən -ɒn ‖ -ɑːn
chiropodist kɪ 'rɒp əd ɪst kə-, ʃɪ-, ʃə-, §-əst ‖ kə 'rɑːp- —*formerly also* kaɪᵊ- **~s** s
chiropody kɪ 'rɒp əd i kə-, ʃɪ-, ʃə- ‖ kə 'rɑːp- —*formerly also* kaɪᵊ-
chiropractic ˌkaɪᵊr əʊ 'prækt ɪk ◂ '·ˌ·· ‖ 'kaɪᵊr ə ˌprækt ɪk
chiropractor 'kaɪᵊr əʊ ˌprækt ə ‖ -ə ˌprækt ᵊr **~s** z
chirp tʃɜːp ‖ tʃɜ˞ːp **chirped** tʃɜːpt ‖ tʃɜ˞ːpt **chirping** 'tʃɜːp ɪŋ ‖ 'tʃɜ˞ːp ɪŋ **chirps** tʃɜːps ‖ tʃɜ˞ːps
chirper 'tʃɜːp ə ‖ 'tʃɜ˞ːp ᵊr **~s** z
chirp|y 'tʃɜːp |i ‖ 'tʃɜ˞ːp |i **~ier** i‿ə ‖ i‿ᵊr **~iest** i‿ɪst i‿əst **~ily** ɪ li əl i **~iness** i nəs i nɪs
chirr tʃɜː ‖ tʃɜ˞ː **chirred** tʃɜːd ‖ tʃɜ˞ːd **chirring** 'tʃɜːr ɪŋ ‖ 'tʃɜ˞ː ɪŋ **chirrs** tʃɜːz ‖ tʃɜ˞ːz
chirrup 'tʃɪr əp ‖ 'tʃɜ˞ː- **~ed** t **~ing** ɪŋ **~s** s
chisel 'tʃɪz ᵊl **~ed, ~led** d **~ing, ~ling** ˌɪŋ **~s** z
chiseler, chiseller 'tʃɪz ᵊl‿ə ‖ ər **~s** z
Chisholm 'tʃɪz əm
Chisinau ˌkɪʃ ɪ 'naʊ —*Moldovan* Chişinău [ki ʃi 'nəu]
Chislehurst 'tʃɪz ᵊl hɜːst ‖ -hɜ˞ːst
chi-square 'kaɪ skweə ‖ -skwer **~d** d
'chi-square test
Chiswick 'tʃɪz ɪk §-ək
chit tʃɪt **chits** tʃɪts
chitchat 'tʃɪt tʃæt
chitin 'kaɪt ɪn -ᵊn ‖ -ᵊn
chitinous 'kaɪt ɪn əs -ən- ‖ -ᵊn-
chitlings 'tʃɪt lɪŋz
chitlins 'tʃɪt lɪnz -lənz
chiton 'kaɪt ᵊn -ɒn ‖ -ɑːn **~s** z
Chittagong 'tʃɪt ə gɒŋ ‖ 'tʃɪṭ ə gɔːŋ -gɑːŋ
Chittenden 'tʃɪt ᵊnd ən
chitterling 'tʃɪt ə lɪŋ →-ᵊl ɪŋ ‖ 'tʃɪṭ ᵊr lɪŋ 'tʃɪt lən **~s** z
Chitty, c~ 'tʃɪt i ‖ 'tʃɪṭ i
chiv tʃɪv ʃɪv **chivs** tʃɪvz ʃɪvz
chivalric 'ʃɪv ᵊl rɪk ʃə 'væl-
chivalrous 'ʃɪv ᵊl rəs **~ly** li **~ness** nəs nɪs
chival|ry 'ʃɪv ᵊl |ri **~ries** riz
Chivas *(i)* 'ʃɪv æs, *(ii)* 'ʃiːvəs
chive tʃaɪv **chives** tʃaɪvz
Chivers 'tʃɪv əz ‖ -ᵊrz
chivv|y, chiv|y 'tʃɪv |i **~ied** id **~ies** iz **~ying** i‿ɪŋ
chiz, chizz tʃɪz
chlamydi|a klə 'mɪd i|‿ə **~ae** iː **~al** ‿əl
Chloe, Chloë 'kləʊ i ‖ 'kloʊ i
chloracne ˌklɔːr 'æk ni ‖ ˌkloʊr-
chloral 'klɔːr əl ‖ 'kloʊr-
chlorambucil klɔːr 'æm bju sɪl ‖ -bjə- kloʊr-
chloramine 'klɔːr ə miːn ˌklɔːr 'æm iːn ‖ 'kloʊr-
chloramphenicol ˌklɔːr æm 'fen ɪ kɒl ˌəm-, §-ə kɒl ‖ -koʊl ˌkloʊr-, -kɑːl, -kɔːl
chlorate 'klɔːr eɪt ‖ 'kloʊr- **~s** s
chlordane 'klɔːd eɪn ‖ 'klɔːrd- 'kloʊrd-
chloric 'klɔːr ɪk 'klɒr- ‖ 'kloʊr-
chloride 'klɔːr aɪd ‖ 'kloʊr- **~s** z
chlori|nate 'klɔːr ɪ |neɪt 'klɒr-, -ə- ‖ 'kloʊr- **~nated** neɪt ɪd -əd ‖ neɪṭ əd **~nates** neɪts **~nating** neɪt ɪŋ ‖ neɪṭ ɪŋ
chlorination ˌklɔːr ɪ 'neɪʃ ᵊn ˌklɒr-, -ə- ‖ ˌkloʊr-
chlorine 'klɔːr iːn -ɪn, §-ən ‖ 'kloʊr-
chlorite 'klɔːr aɪt ‖ 'kloʊr-
chloro- *comb. form*
with stress-neutral suffix ¦klɔːr əʊ ¦klɒr- ‖ ¦klɔːr ə ¦kloʊr- — **chlorobenzene** ˌklɔːr əʊ 'benz iːn ˌklɒr- ‖ ˌklɔːr ə- ˌkloʊr-
chlorodyne 'klɔːr ə daɪn 'klɒr- ‖ 'kloʊr-
chlorofluorocarbon ˌklɔːr əʊˌfluəʳ əʊ 'kɑːbən -ˌflɔːr əʊ-; -ˌfluː ə rəʊ- ‖ ˌklɔːr ə ˌflʊr oʊ 'kɑːrb ən ˌkloʊr- **~s** z
chloroform 'klɒr ə fɔːm 'klɔːr- ‖ 'klɔːr ə fɔːrm 'kloʊr- **~ed** d **~ing** ɪŋ **~s** z
chlorophyl, chlorophyll 'klɒr ə fɪl 'klɔːr- ‖ 'klɔːr- 'kloʊr-
chloroplast 'klɔːr əʊ plɑːst -plæst ‖ 'klɔːr ə plæst 'kloʊr- **~s** s
chloroquine, C~ 'klɔːr ə kwɪn 'klɒr-, -kwiːn ‖ 'klɔːr ə kwiːn 'kloʊr-
chlorosis klɔː 'rəʊs ɪs §-əs ‖ klə 'roʊs-
chlorpromazine ˌklɔː 'prəʊm ə ziːn -'prɒm- ‖ ˌklɔːr 'prɑːm ə ziːn ˌkloʊr-
Choat, Choate tʃəʊt ‖ tʃoʊt
Chobham 'tʃɒb əm ‖ 'tʃɑːb-
choc tʃɒk ‖ tʃɑːk *(= chock)* **chocs** tʃɒks ‖ tʃɑːks
chocaholic ˌtʃɒk ə 'hɒl ɪk ◂ ‖ ˌtʃɑːk ə 'hɑːl ɪk ◂ ˌtʃɔːk-, -'hɔːl- **~s** s
choc-bar 'tʃɒk bɑː ‖ 'tʃɑːk bɑːr **~s** z
chocc|y 'tʃɒk |i ‖ 'tʃɑːk |i **~ies** iz
chocho 'tʃəʊ tʃəʊ ‖ 'tʃoʊ tʃoʊ **~s** z
choc-ice 'tʃɒk aɪs ‖ 'tʃɑːk- **~es** ɪz əz
chock tʃɒk ‖ tʃɑːk **chocked** tʃɒkt ‖ tʃɑːkt **chocking** 'tʃɒk ɪŋ ‖ 'tʃɑːk ɪŋ **chocks** tʃɒks ‖ tʃɑːks
chock-a-block ˌtʃɒk ə 'blɒk ◂ ‖ 'tʃɑːk ə blɑːk
chock-full ˌtʃɒk 'fʊl ◂ ‖ ˌtʃɑːk- ˌtʃʌk-

chocoholic ˌtʃɒk ə ˈhɒl ɪk ◂ ‖ ˌtʃɑːk ə ˈhɑːl ɪk ◂ ˌtʃɔːk-, -ˈhɔːl- **~s** s

chocolate ˈtʃɒk lət -lɪt; ˈtʃɒk əl ət, -ɪt ‖ ˈtʃɔːk- ˈtʃɑːk- **~s** s

ˌchocolate ˈbiscuit; ˈchocolate cake, ˌ· · ˈ·; ˌchocolate ˈpudding

chocolate-box ˈtʃɒk lət bɒks -lɪt- ‖ ˈtʃɔːk lət bɑːks ˈtʃɑːk-

chocolatey ˈtʃɒk lət i ‖ ˈtʃɑːk lət̬ i

Choctaw, c~ ˈtʃɒkt ɔː ‖ ˈtʃɑːkt ɔː -ɑː **~s** z

CHOGM ˈtʃɒg əm ‖ ˈtʃɑːg-

choice tʃɔɪs **choicer** ˈtʃɔɪs ə ‖ -ᵊr **choices** ˈtʃɔɪs ɪz -əz **choicest** ˈtʃɔɪs ɪst əst **choicely** ˈtʃɔɪs li **choiceness** ˈtʃɔɪs nəs -nɪs

choir ˈkwaɪ‿ə ‖ ˈkwaɪ‿ᵊr *(! = quire)* **choirs** ˈkwaɪ‿əz ‖ ˈkwaɪ‿ᵊrz

ˈchoir school

choirboy ˈkwaɪ‿ə bɔɪ ‖ ˈkwaɪ‿ᵊr- **~s** z

choirmaster ˈkwaɪ‿ə ˌmɑːst ə §-ˌmæst- ‖ ˈkwaɪ‿ᵊr ˌmæst ᵊr **~s** z

choke tʃəʊk ‖ tʃoʊk **choked** tʃəʊkt ‖ tʃoʊkt **choking** ˈtʃəʊk ɪŋ ‖ ˈtʃoʊk ɪŋ **chokes** tʃəʊks ‖ tʃoʊks

chokeberr|y ˈtʃəʊk ˌber| i ‖ ˈtʃoʊk- **~ies** iz

chokecherr|y ˈtʃəʊk ˌtʃer| i ‖ ˈtʃoʊk- **~ies** iz

choker ˈtʃəʊk ə ‖ ˈtʃoʊk ᵊr **~s** z

chokey, choky ˈtʃəʊk i ‖ ˈtʃoʊk i

cholecystectom|y ˌkɒl ɪ sɪst ˈekt əm |i ˌ·ə- ‖ ˌkoʊl ə- **~ies** iz

choler ˈkɒl ə ‖ ˈkɑːl ᵊr ˈkoʊl- *(usually = collar)*

cholera ˈkɒl ər ə ‖ ˈkɑːl-

choleraic ˌkɒl ə ˈreɪ ɪk ◂ ‖ ˌkɑːl-

choleric ˈkɒl ər ɪk kɒ ˈler- ‖ ˈkɑːl- kə ˈler- **~ally** ᵊl‿i

cholesterol kə ˈlest ə rɒl kɒ-, -ᵊr‿əl ‖ -roʊl -rɑːl, -rɔːl

choline ˈkəʊl iːn ‖ ˈkoʊl-

cholinergic ˌkəʊl ɪ ˈnɜːdʒ ɪk ◂ ˌkɒl-, -ə- ‖ ˌkoʊl ə ˈnɜːdʒ ɪk ◂

cholinesterase ˌkəʊl ɪ ˈnest ə reɪz ˌkɒl-, ˌ·ə-, -reɪs ‖ ˌkoʊl-

cholla ˈtʃɔɪ ə **~s** z

Cholmeley ˈtʃʌm li

Cholmondeley ˈtʃʌm li

Chomolungma ˌtʃəʊm əʊ ˈlʊŋ mə ‖ ˌtʃoʊm oʊ-

chomp tʃɒmp ‖ tʃɑːmp **chomped** tʃɒmpt ‖ tʃɑːmpt **chomping** ˈtʃɒmp ɪŋ ‖ ˈtʃɑːmp ɪŋ **chomps** tʃɒmps ‖ tʃɑːmps

Chomsky ˈtʃɒmᵖsk i ‖ ˈtʃɑːmᵖsk i

Chomskyan ˈtʃɒmᵖsk i‿ən ‖ ˈtʃɑːmᵖsk- **~s** z

chondroma kɒn ˈdrəʊm ə ‖ kɑːn ˈdroʊm ə **~s** z

Chongqing ˌtʃʊŋ ˈtʃɪŋ —*Chi* Chóngqìng [²tʂʰʊŋ ⁴tɕʰiŋ]

Choo tʃuː

choo-choo ˈtʃuː tʃuː **~s** z

chook tʃʊk **chooks** tʃʊks

choose tʃuːz *(= chews)* **chooses** tʃuːz ɪz -əz **choosing** ˈtʃuːz ɪŋ **chose** tʃəʊz ‖ tʃoʊz **chosen** ˈtʃəʊz ᵊn ‖ ˈtʃoʊz ᵊn

chooser ˈtʃuːz ə ‖ -ᵊr **~s** z

choos|y, choos|ey ˈtʃuːz |i **~ier** i‿ə ‖ i‿ᵊr **~iest** i‿ɪst i‿əst **~iness** i nəs i nɪs

chop tʃɒp ‖ tʃɑːp **chopped** tʃɒpt ‖ tʃɑːpt **chopping** ˈtʃɒp ɪŋ ‖ ˈtʃɑːp ɪŋ **chops** tʃɒps ‖ tʃɑːps

ˌchop ˈsuey ˈsuː‿i

chop-chop ˌtʃɒp ˈtʃɒp ‖ ˈtʃɑːp tʃɑːp ˌ·ˈ·

chopfallen ˈtʃɒp ˌfɔːl ən ‖ ˈtʃɑːp- -ˌfɑːl-

chop|house ˈtʃɒp |haʊs ‖ ˈtʃɑːp- **~houses** haʊz ɪz -əz

Chopin ˈʃɒp æ̃ ˈʃəʊp- ‖ ˈʃoʊp æn —*Fr* [ʃɔ pɛ̃]

chopp... —*see* **chop**

chopper ˈtʃɒp ə ‖ ˈtʃɑːp ᵊr **~s** z

chopp|y ˈtʃɒp |i ‖ ˈtʃɑːp |i **~ier** i‿ə ‖ i‿ᵊr **~iest** i‿ɪst i‿əst **~ily** ɪ li əl i **~iness** i nəs -nɪs

chopstick ˈtʃɒp stɪk ‖ ˈtʃɑːp- **~s** s

choral ˈkɔːr əl ‖ ˈkoʊr- **~ly** i

chorale kɒ ˈrɑːl kɔː-, kə- ‖ kə ˈræl -ˈrɑːl **~s** z

-chord kɔːd ‖ kɔːrd — **octachord** ˈɒkt ə kɔːd ‖ ˈɑːkt ə kɔːrd

chord kɔːd ‖ kɔːrd *(= cord)* **chords** kɔːdz ‖ kɔːrdz

chordal ˈkɔːd ᵊl ‖ ˈkɔːrd-

chordate ˈkɔːd eɪt -ɪt, -ət ‖ ˈkɔːrd- **~s** s

chore tʃɔː ‖ tʃɔːr tʃoʊr **chores** tʃɔːz ‖ tʃɔːrz tʃoʊrz

chorea kɔː ˈrɪə kɒ-, kə- ‖ kə ˈriː‿ə

choreograph ˈkɒr i‿ə grɑːf ˈkɔːr-, -græf ‖ ˈkɔːr i‿ə græf ˈkoʊr- **~ed** t **~ing** ɪŋ **~s** s

choreographer ˌkɒr i ˈɒg rəf ə ˌkɔːr- ‖ ˌkɔːr i ˈɑːg rəf ᵊr ˌkoʊr- **~s** z

choreographic ˌkɒr i‿ə ˈgræf ɪk ◂ ˌkɔːr- ‖ ˌkɔːr- ˌkoʊr- **~ally** ᵊl‿i

choreography ˌkɒr i ˈɒg rəf i ˌkɔːr- ‖ ˌkɔːr i ˈɑːg- ˌkoʊr-

choriamb ˈkɒr i æmb ˈkɔːr-, -æm ‖ ˈkɔːr- ˈkoʊr- **~s** z

choriambic ˌkɒr i ˈæm bɪk ◂ ˌkɔːr- ‖ ˌkɔːr- ˌkoʊr-

choriambus ˌkɒr i ˈæm bəs ˌkɔːr- ‖ ˌkɔːr- ˌkoʊr-

choric ˈkɒr ɪk ‖ ˈkɔːr ɪk ˈkɑːr-, ˈkoʊr-

chorine ˈkɔːr iːn ‖ ˈkoʊr- **~s** z

chorion ˈkɔːr i‿ən -ɒn ‖ -i ɑːn ˈkoʊr-

chorionic ˌkɔːr i ˈɒn ɪk ◂ ‖ -ˈɑːn- ˌkoʊr-

chorister ˈkɒr ɪst ə -əst- ‖ ˈkɔːr əst ᵊr ˈkɑːr-, ˈkoʊr- **~s** z

chorizo tʃə ˈriːz əʊ tʃɒ-, -ˈrɪts- ‖ -oʊ -ˈriːs- —*Sp* [tʃo ˈri θo, -so] **~s** z

Chorley ˈtʃɔːl i ‖ ˈtʃɔːrl i

Chorleywood ˌtʃɔːl i ˈwʊd ‖ ˌtʃɔːrl-

Chorlton ˈtʃɔːlt ən ‖ ˈtʃɔːrlt ᵊn

Chorlton-cum-Hardy ˌtʃɔːlt ən kʌm ˈhɑːd i →ˌ·əŋ- ‖ ˌtʃɔːrlt ᵊn kʌm ˈhɑːrd i

choroid ˈkɔːr ɔɪd ˈkoʊr-

chortl|e ˈtʃɔːt ᵊl ‖ ˈtʃɔːrt̬ ᵊl **~ed** d **~es** z **~ing** ‿ɪŋ

chorus ˈkɔːr əs ‖ ˈkoʊr- **~ed** t **~es** ɪz əz **~ing** ɪŋ

ˈchorus girl

chose tʃəʊz ‖ tʃoʊz

chosen ˈtʃəʊz ᵊn ‖ ˈtʃoʊz ᵊn

chota ˈtʃəʊt ə ‖ ˈtʃoʊt̬ ə

Chou En-lai ˌtʃəʊ en ˈlaɪ -ən- ‖ ˌtʃoʊ- —*Chi* Zhou Ēnlái [[1]tʂou [1]ən [2]lai]
chough tʃʌf **choughs** tʃʌfs
choux ʃuː (*= shoe*)
chow tʃaʊ **chows** tʃaʊz
ˈchow chow; **ˌchow ˈmein** meɪn
Chow tʃaʊ —*Cantonese* [[1]tsɐw]
chow-chow ˈtʃaʊ tʃaʊ **~s** z
chowder ˈtʃaʊd ə ‖ -ᵊr **~s** z
chowderhead ˈtʃaʊd ə hed ‖ -ᵊr- **~s** z
chrestomath|y kre ˈstɒm əθ |i ‖ -ˈstɑːm- **~ies** iz
Chrimbo ˈkrɪm bəʊ ‖ -boʊ
Chris krɪs **Chris's** ˈkrɪs ɪz -əz
chrism ˈkrɪz əm
chrisom ˈkrɪz əm **~s** z
Chrissie, Chrissy ˈkrɪs i
Christ kraɪst **Christ's** kraɪsts
Christabel ˈkrɪst ə bel
Christadelphian ˌkrɪst ə ˈdelf i‿ən ◂ **~s** z
Christchurch ˈkraɪst tʃɜːtʃ ‖ -tʃɝːtʃ
christen ˈkrɪs ᵊn **~ed** d **~ing** ‿ɪŋ **~s** z
Christendom ˈkrɪs ᵊn dəm
christening ˈkrɪs ᵊn‿ɪŋ **~s** z
ˈchristening robe
Christi ˈkrɪst i
Christian ˈkrɪs tʃən →ˈkrɪʃ-; ˈkrɪst i‿ən **~s** z
ˈChristian name; **ˌChristian ˈScience**
Christiana ˌkrɪst i ˈɑːn ə ˌkrɪs tʃi- ‖ -ˈæn ə
christiania, C~ ˌkrɪst i ˈɑːn i‿ə **~s** z
Christianis... —*see* **Christianiz...**
Christianit|y ˌkrɪst i ˈæn ət |i ˌkrɪs tʃi-, →ˌkrɪʃ tʃi-, -ɪt i ‖ ˌkrɪs tʃi ˈæn əţ |i **~ies** iz
Christianization ˌkrɪs tʃən aɪ ˈzeɪʃ ᵊn →ˌkrɪʃ-, -ɪˈ--; ˌkrɪst i‿ən aɪ ˈzeɪʃ- ‖ -ə ˈzeɪʃ-
Christianiz|e ˈkrɪs tʃə naɪz →ˈkrɪʃ-; ˈkrɪst i‿ə naɪz **~ed** d **~er/s** ə/z ‖ ᵊr/z **~es** ɪz əz **~ing** ɪŋ
Christianly ˈkrɪs tʃən li →ˈkrɪʃ-; ˈkrɪst i‿ən li
Christie, c~ ˈkrɪst i **~s, ~'s** z
Christina krɪ ˈstiːn ə
Christine ˈkrɪst iːn
Christlike ˈkraɪst laɪk **~ness** nəs nɪs
Christmas ˈkrɪs məs §ˈkrɪz- —*in very careful speech sometimes* ˈkrɪst- **~es** ɪz əz
ˈChristmas box; **ˈChristmas cake**; **ˈChristmas card**; **ˌChristmas ˈcracker**; **ˌChristmas ˈDay**; **ˌChristmas ˈEve**; **ˈChristmas ˌIsland** ‖ ˌ· · ˈ· ·; **ˈChristmas ˌpresent**; **ˌChristmas ˈpudding**; **ˌChristmas ˈstocking**; **ˈChristmas tree**
Christmassy ˈkrɪs məs i
Christmastide ˈkrɪs məs taɪd ˈkrɪst-
Christmastime ˈkrɪs məs taɪm ˈkrɪst-
Christobel ˈkrɪst ə bel
Christophe krɪ ˈstɒf ‖ kriː ˈstɑːf -ˈstɔːf —*Fr* [kʁi stɔf]
christophene ˈkrɪst ə fiːn **~s** z
Christopher ˈkrɪst əf ə ‖ -ᵊr
Christopherson krɪ ˈstɒf əs ən ‖ -ˈstɑːf ᵊrs-
Christy, c~ ˈkrɪst i
chroma ˈkrəʊm ə ‖ ˈkroʊm ə
chromate ˈkrəʊm eɪt ‖ ˈkroʊm- **~s** s
chromatic krə ˈmæt ɪk krəʊ- ‖ kroʊ ˈmæţ ɪk **~ally** ᵊl‿i **~ness** nəs nɪs
chromaticity ˌkrəʊm ə ˈtɪs ət i -ɪt i ‖ ˌkroʊm ə ˈtɪs əţ i
chromatid ˈkrəʊm ət ɪd §-əd ‖ -əţ əd -ə tɪd **~s** z
chromatin ˈkrəʊm ət ɪn §-ən ‖ ˈkroʊm- **~s** z
chromatogram ˈkrəʊm ət ə græm krəʊ ˈmæt- ‖ kroʊ ˈmæţ ə græm krə- **~s** z
chromatographic ˌkrəʊm ət ə ˈgræf ɪk ◂ ‖ kroʊ ˌmæţ ə- krə-
chromatography ˌkrəʊm ə ˈtɒg rəf i ‖ ˌkroʊm ə ˈtɑːg-
chrome krəʊm ‖ kroʊm **chromed** krəʊmd ‖ kroʊmd **chromes** krəʊmz ‖ kroʊmz **chroming** ˈkrəʊm ɪŋ ‖ ˈkroʊm ɪŋ
ˌchrome ˈyellow
chrominance ˈkrəʊm ɪn ənᵗs §-ən- ‖ ˈkroʊm-
chromite ˈkrəʊm aɪt ‖ ˈkroʊm-
chromium ˈkrəʊm i‿əm ‖ ˈkroʊm-
chromo ˈkrəʊm əʊ ‖ ˈkroʊm oʊ **~s** z
chromolithograph ˌkrəʊm əʊ ˈlɪθ ə grɑːf -græf ‖ ˌkroʊm ə ˈlɪθ ə græf **~s** s
chromolithographic ˌkrəʊm əʊ ˌlɪθ ə ˈgræf ɪk ‖ ˌkroʊm ə-
chromolithography ˌkrəʊm əʊ lɪ ˈθɒg rəf i ‖ ˌkroʊm ə lɪ ˈθɑːg-
chromophob|ia ˌkrəʊm əʊ ˈfəʊb |i‿ə ‖ ˌkroʊm ə ˈfoʊb |i‿ə **~ic** ɪk
chromosomal ˌkrəʊm ə ˈsəʊm ᵊl ◂ ‖ ˌkroʊm ə ˈzoʊm ᵊl ◂ -ˈsoʊm- **~ly** i

CHROMOSOME

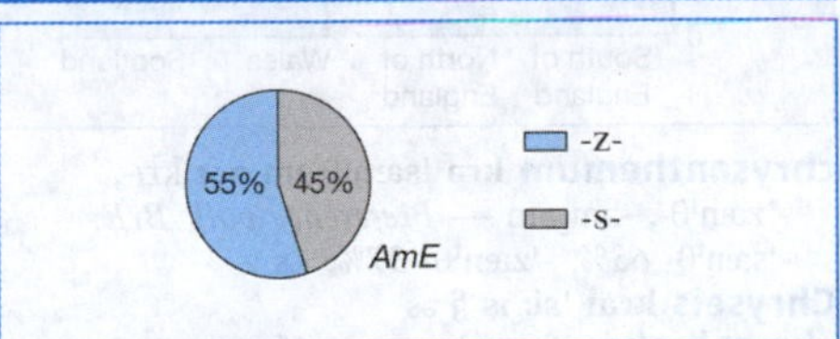

chromosome ˈkrəʊm ə səʊm ‖ ˈkroʊm ə zoʊm -soʊm — *Preference poll, AmE:* -zoʊm *55%,* -soʊm *45%.* **~s** z
chromosphere ˈkrəʊm ə sfɪə ‖ ˈkroʊm ə sfɪr
chronax|ie, chronax|y ˈkrəʊn æks |i krɒn ˈæks i ‖ ˈkroʊn- ˈkrɑːn- **~ies** iz
chroneme ˈkrəʊn iːm ‖ ˈkroʊn- **~s** z
chronemic krəʊ ˈniːm ɪk ‖ kroʊ-
chronic ˈkrɒn ɪk ‖ ˈkrɑːn ɪk **~ally** ᵊl‿i
chronicl|e, C~ ˈkrɒn ɪk ᵊl ‖ ˈkrɑːn- **~ed** d **~es** z **~ing** ‿ɪŋ
chronicler ˈkrɒn ɪk lə ‖ ˈkrɑːn ɪk lᵊr **~s** z
chrono- *comb. form*
with stress-neutral suffix ¦krɒn ə ¦krəʊn əʊ ‖ ¦krɑːn ə ¦kroʊn ə — **chronoscopic** ˌkrɒn ə ˈskɒp ɪk ◂ ˌkrəʊn- ‖ ˌkrɑːn ə ˈskɑːp ɪk ◂ ˌkroʊn-
with stress-imposing suffix krə ˈnɒ+ ‖ krə ˈnɑː+ — **chronoscopy** krə ˈnɒsk əp i ‖ -ˈnɑːsk-
chronograph ˈkrɒn ə grɑːf ˈkrəʊn-, -græf ‖ ˈkrɑːn ə græf ˈkroʊn- **~s** s

chronological ˌkrɒn ə ˈlɒdʒ ɪk ᵊl ◂ ˌkrəʊn-, -ᵊl ˈɒdʒ- ‖ ˌkrɑːn ᵊl ˈɑːdʒ ɪk ᵊl ◂ ˌkroʊn- **~ly** i

chronolog|y krə ˈnɒl ədʒ |i krɒ-, krəʊ- ‖ -ˈnɑːl- **~ies** iz

chronometer krə ˈnɒm ɪt ə krɒ-, krəʊ-, -ət- ‖ -ˈnɑːm əṭ ᵊr **~s** z

chronometric ˌkrɒn ə ˈmetr ɪk ◂ ˌkrəʊn- ‖ ˌkrɑːn- ˌkroʊn- **~al** ᵊl **~ally** ᵊl‿i

chronometry krə ˈnɒm ətr i krɒ-, krəʊ-, -ɪtr- ‖ -ˈnɑːm-

chrysalid ˈkrɪs əl ɪd §-əd **~s** z

chrysalides krɪ ˈsæl ɪ diːz krə-, -ə-

chrysalis ˈkrɪs əl ɪs §-əs **~es** ɪz əz

chrysanth krə ˈsænᵗθ krɪ-, -ˈzænᵗθ **~s** s

CHRYSANTHEMUM

chrysanthemum krə ˈsænᵗθ ɪm əm krɪ-, -ˈzænᵗθ-, -əm‿əm — *Preference poll, BrE:* -ˈsænᵗθ- *63%,* -ˈzænᵗθ- *37%.* **~s** z

Chryseis kraɪ ˈsiː‿ɪs §‿əs

chryselephantine ˌkrɪs ˌel ɪ ˈfænt aɪn -ə-

Chrysler *tdmk* ˈkraɪz lə ‖ ˈkraɪs lᵊr **~s** z

chrysolite ˈkrɪs ə laɪt

chrysoprase ˈkrɪs ə preɪz

Chrysostom ˈkrɪs əst əm

chrysotile ˈkrɪs ə taɪᵊl -tɪl, §-tᵊl

chthonian ˈθəʊn i‿ən ˈkθəʊn- ‖ ˈθoʊn-

chthonic ˈθɒn ɪk ˈkθɒn- ‖ ˈθɑːn-

chub tʃʌb **chubs** tʃʌbz

Chubb tʃʌb

chubb|y ˈtʃʌb |i **~ier** i‿ə ‖ i‿ᵊr **~iest** i‿ɪst i‿əst **~iness** i nəs i nɪs

chuck, Chuck tʃʌk **chucked** tʃʌkt **chucking** ˈtʃʌk ɪŋ **chucks** tʃʌks

chucker-out ˌtʃʌk ər ˈaʊt ‖ -ᵊr- **chuckers-out** ˌtʃʌk əz ˈaʊt ‖ -ᵊrz-

chuckl|e ˈtʃʌk ᵊl **~ed** d **~es** z **~ing** ‿ɪŋ

chucklehead ˈtʃʌk ᵊl hed **~s** z

chuckwalla ˈtʃʌk wɒl ə ‖ -wɑːl ə **~s** z

chuff tʃʌf **chuffed** tʃʌft **chuffing** ˈtʃʌf ɪŋ **chuffs** tʃʌfs

chug tʃʌg **chugged** tʃʌgd **chugging** ˈtʃʌg ɪŋ **chugs** tʃʌgz

chugalug ˈtʃʌg ə lʌg **~ged** d **~ging** ɪŋ **~s** z

Chukchee, Chukchi ˈtʃʊk tʃiː ˈtʃʌk- **~s** z

chukka, chukker ˈtʃʌk ə ‖ -ᵊr **~s** z

Chula Vista ˌtʃuːl ə ˈvɪst ə

chum tʃʌm **chummed** tʃʌmd **chumming** ˈtʃʌm ɪŋ **chums** tʃʌmz

Chumash ˈtʃuːm æʃ

Chumbawamba ˌtʃʌm bə ˈwɑːm bə -ˈwʌm-

chumm|y ˈtʃʌm |i **~ier** i‿ə ‖ i‿ᵊr **~iest** i‿ɪst i‿əst **~ily** ɪ li əl i **~iness** i nəs i nɪs

chump tʃʌmp **chumps** tʃʌm*p*s

chunder ˈtʃʌnd ə ‖ -ᵊr **~ed** d **chundering** ˈtʃʌnd‿ər ɪŋ **~s** z

Chungking ˌtʃʊŋ ˈkɪŋ ˌtʃʌŋ- —*Chi* Chóngqìng [^{2}ʈʂʰʊŋ ^{4}tɕʰiŋ]

chunk tʃʌŋk **chunked** tʃʌŋ*k*t **chunking** ˈtʃʌŋk ɪŋ **chunks** tʃʌŋ*k*s

chunk|y ˈtʃʌŋk |i **~ier** i‿ə ‖ i‿ᵊr **~iest** i‿ɪst i‿əst **~iness** i nəs i nɪs

chunnel, C~ ˈtʃʌn ᵊl

chunter ˈtʃʌnt ə ‖ ˈtʃʌnṭ ᵊr **~ed** d **chuntering** ˈtʃʌnt‿ər ɪŋ ‖ ˈtʃʌnṭ ər ɪŋ **~s** z

church, Church tʃɜːtʃ ‖ tʃɝːtʃ **churched** tʃɜːtʃt ‖ tʃɝːtʃt **churches** ˈtʃɜːtʃ ɪz -əz ‖ ˈtʃɝːtʃ əz **churching** ˈtʃɜːtʃ ɪŋ ‖ ˈtʃɝːtʃ ɪŋ **church's, C~** ˈtʃɜːtʃ ɪz -əz ‖ ˈtʃɝːtʃ əz

ˌChurch ˈArmy; **ˌChurch Comˈmissioners**; **ˌChurch ˈmilitant**; **ˌChurch Slaˈvonic**

Churchdown ˈtʃɜːtʃ daʊn ‖ ˈtʃɝːtʃ-

churchgo|er ˈtʃɜːtʃ ˌgəʊ |ə ‖ ˈtʃɝːtʃ ˌgoʊ |ᵊr **~ers** əz ‖ ᵊrz **~ing** ɪŋ

Churchill ˈtʃɜːtʃ ɪl ‖ ˈtʃɝːtʃ-

Churchillian tʃɜː ˈtʃɪl i‿ən ‖ tʃɝː-

church|man, C~ ˈtʃɜːtʃ |mən ‖ ˈtʃɝːtʃ- **~men** mən men

churchwarden ˌtʃɜːtʃ ˈwɔːd ᵊn ◂ ‖ ˈtʃɝːtʃ ˌwɔːrd ᵊn **~s** z

church|woman ˈtʃɜːtʃ ˌwʊm ən ‖ ˈtʃɝːtʃ- **~women** ˌwɪm ɪn -ən

church|y ˈtʃɜːtʃ| i ‖ ˈtʃɝːtʃ| i **~iness** i nəs -nɪs

churchyard ˈtʃɜːtʃ jɑːd ‖ ˈtʃɝːtʃ jɑːrd **~s** z

churl tʃɜːl ‖ tʃɝːl **churls** tʃɜːlz ‖ tʃɝːlz

churlish ˈtʃɜːl ɪʃ ‖ ˈtʃɝːl- **~ly** li **~ness** nəs nɪs

churn tʃɜːn ‖ tʃɝːn **churned** tʃɜːnd ‖ tʃɝːnd **churning** ˈtʃɜːn ɪŋ ‖ ˈtʃɝːn ɪŋ **churns** tʃɜːnz ‖ tʃɝːnz

chute ʃuːt (= *shoot*) **chutes** ʃuːts

Chuter ˈtʃuːt ə ‖ ˈtʃuːṭ ᵊr

chutney ˈtʃʌt ni

chutzpah ˈhʊts pə ˈxʊts-, -pɑː

Chuvash ˈtʃuːv æʃ tʃu ˈvɑːʃ **~es** ɪz əz

Chuzzlewit ˈtʃʌz ᵊl wɪt

chyle kaɪᵊl

chyme kaɪm

chymotrypsin ˌkaɪm əʊ ˈtrɪps ɪn §-ᵊn ‖ -oʊ-

chypre ˈʃiːp rə —*Fr* [ʃipχ]

CIA ˌsiː aɪ ˈeɪ

ciabatta tʃə ˈbæt ə ˌtʃiː ə-, -ˈbɑːt- ‖ -ˈbæṭ ə —*It* [tʃa ˈbat ta]

Ciampino tʃæm ˈpiːn əʊ ‖ tʃɑːm ˈpiːn oʊ —*It* [tʃam ˈpiː no]

ciao tʃaʊ

Ciaran ˈkɪər ən ‖ ˈkɪr-

Ciba *tdmk* 'siːb ə —*Ger* ['tsiː ba]
Ciba-Geigy *tdmk* ˌsiːb ə 'gaɪg i
Cibber 'sɪb ə ‖ -ᵊr
cibori|um sɪ 'bɔːr i‿|əm sə- ‖ -'boʊr- **~a** ə
cicada sɪ 'kɑːd ə sə- ‖ -'keɪd ə saɪ-, -'kɑːd- **~s** z
cicala sɪ 'kɑːl ə sə- **~s** z
cicatric|e 'sɪk ətr ɪs §-əs **~es** ɪz əz
cicatris... —*see* **cicatriz...**
cicatrix 'sɪk ə trɪks sə 'keɪtr ɪks, sɪ- **cicatrices** ˌsɪk ə 'traɪs iːz
cicatrization ˌsɪk ətr aɪ 'zeɪʃ ᵊn -ətr ɪ- ‖ -ətr ə-
cicatriz|e 'sɪk ə traɪz **~ed** d **~es** ɪz əz **~ing** ɪŋ
cicely, C~ 'sɪs əl‿i -ɪl-
Cicero, c~ 'sɪs ə rəʊ ‖ -roʊ
ciceron|e ˌtʃɪtʃ ə 'rəʊn |i ˌsɪs- ‖ -'roʊn |i **~i** iː
Ciceronian ˌsɪs ə 'rəʊn i‿ən ◂ ‖ -'roʊn- **~s** z
cichlid 'sɪk lɪd §-ləd **~s** z
cicisbe|o ˌtʃɪtʃ ɪz 'beɪ |əʊ ‖ -|oʊ —*It* [tʃi tʃiz 'bɛː o] **~i** iː
Cid sɪd
CID ˌsiː aɪ 'diː
-cidal 'saɪd ᵊl — **genocidal** ˌdʒen ə 'saɪd ᵊl ◂
-cide saɪd — **insecticide** ɪn 'sekt ɪ saɪd -ə-
cider 'saɪd ə ‖ -ᵊr **~s** z
Cif *tdmk* sɪf
cig sɪg **cigs** sɪgz
cigar sɪ 'gɑː sə- ‖ -'gɑːr **~s** z

CIGARETTE

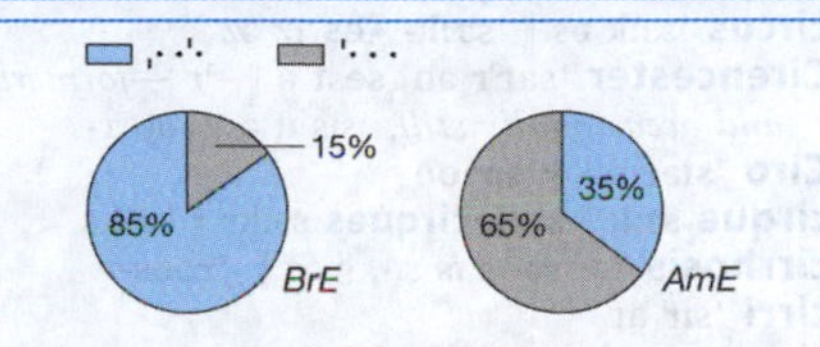

cigaret, cigarette ˌsɪg ə 'ret '··· ‖ '···, ˌ··'· **~s** s —*Preference polls, BrE:* ˌ··'· 85%, '··· 15%; *AmE:* '··· 65%, ˌ··'· 35%.
ˌ**ciga'rette** ˌ**holder**, '··· ˌ··; ˌ**ciga'rette** ˌ**lighter**, '··· ˌ··
cigarillo ˌsɪg ə 'rɪl əʊ ‖ -oʊ -'riː joʊ **~s** z
cigg|ie, cigg|y 'sɪg |i **~ies** iz
ciguatera ˌsɪg wə 'teər ə ˌsiːg-, -'tɪər- ‖ -'ter- —*AmSp* [si ɣwa 'te ɾa]
cilantro sɪ 'læntr əʊ sə- ‖ -'lɑːntr oʊ -'læntr- —*AmSp* [si 'lan tɾo]
Cilcennin kɪl 'ken ɪn §-ən
Cilento sɪ 'lent əʊ sə- ‖ -oʊ
cilia 'sɪl i‿ə 'siːl-
ciliary 'sɪl i‿ər i ‖ -i er i
ciliat|e 'sɪl i eɪt -i‿ət, -i‿ɪt **~ed** ɪd əd **~es** s
Cilic|ia saɪ 'lɪs |i‿ə sɪ-, sə-, -'lɪʃ- ‖ sə 'lɪʃ |ə **~ian/s** i‿ən/z ‖ ᵊn/z
cili|um 'sɪl i‿|əm **~a** ə
cill sɪl *(= sill)* **cills** sɪlz
Cilla 'sɪl ə
Cillit Bang *tdmk* ˌsɪl ɪt 'bæŋ §-ət-
Cimabue ˌtʃɪm ə 'buː eɪ ˌtʃiːm-, -i —*It* [tʃi ma 'buː e]
cimetidine saɪ 'met ɪ diːn sɪ-, sə-, -ə- ‖ -'meţ ə-
Cimmerian sɪ 'mɪər i‿ən sə-, -'mer- ‖ -'mɪr- **~s** z
C-in-C ˌsiː ɪn 'siː §-ən- **~s** z
cinch sɪntʃ **cinched** sɪntʃt **cinches** 'sɪntʃ ɪz -əz **cinching** 'sɪntʃ ɪŋ
cinchona sɪŋ 'kəʊn ə ‖ -'koʊn- **~s** z
Cincinnati ˌsɪnᵗs ə 'næt i ◂ -ɪ- ‖ -'næţ i
Cincinnatus ˌsɪnᵗs ə 'nɑːt əs ◂ -ɪ-, -'neɪt- ‖ -'næţ-
cincture 'sɪŋk tʃə ‖ -tʃᵊr **~s** z
cinder 'sɪnd ə ‖ -ᵊr **~s** z
Cinderella ˌsɪnd ə 'rel ə ◂ §sɪn 'drel ə
Cindy 'sɪnd i
cine 'sɪn i
cine- |sɪn i — **cinephotography** ˌsɪn i fəʊ 'tɒg rəf i ‖ -fə 'tɑːg-
cineaste, cinéaste 'sɪn i æst -eɪ-, ˌ··'· **~s** s
cinecamera 'sɪn i ˌkæm ər‿ə ˌ··'··· **~s** z
cinefilm 'sɪn i fɪlm **~s** z
cinema 'sɪn əm ə -ɪm-; -ə mɑː, -ə- **~s** z
cinemago|er 'sɪn əm ə ˌgəʊ| ə '·ɪm- ‖ -ˌgoʊ| ᵊr **~ers** əz ‖ ᵊrz **~ing** ɪŋ
cinemascope, CinemaScope *tdmk* 'sɪn əm ə skəʊp '·ɪm- ‖ -skoʊp
cinematic ˌsɪn ə 'mæt ɪk ◂ -ə- ‖ -'mæţ- **~ally** ᵊl‿i
cinematograph ˌsɪn ə 'mæt ə grɑːf ˌ·ɪ-, -græf ‖ -'mæţ ə græf **~s** s
cinematography ˌsɪn əm ə 'tɒg rəf i ˌ·ɪm- ‖ -'tɑːg-
cinema verite, cinéma vérité ˌsɪn əm ə 'ver ɪ teɪ ˌ·ɪm-, -ɪ mɑː-, -ə mɑː-, -ə teɪ ‖ -ˌver ə 'teɪ —*Fr* [si ne ma ve ʁi te]
cine-projector 'sɪn i prə ˌdʒekt ə ‖ -ᵊr **~s** z
cineradiographic ˌsɪn i ˌreɪd i‿ə 'græf ɪk **~ally** ᵊl‿i
cineradiography ˌsɪn i ˌreɪd i 'ɒg rəf i ‖ -'ɑːg-
Cinerama *tdmk* ˌsɪn ə 'rɑːm ə -ɪ-
cineraria ˌsɪn ə 'reər i‿ə ‖ -'rer- **~s** z
Cinna 'sɪn ə
cinnabar 'sɪn ə bɑː ‖ -bɑːr
cinnamon 'sɪn əm ən
cinque, C~ sɪŋk *(= sink)*
ˌ**Cinque 'Ports**, '· ·
cinquecento ˌtʃɪŋk wɪ 'tʃent əʊ §-wə- ‖ -oʊ —*It* [tʃiŋ kwe 'tʃen to]
cinquefoil 'sɪŋk fɔɪᵊl 'sæŋk- **~s** z
Cinzano *tdmk* tʃɪn 'zɑːn əʊ sɪn-; tʃɪnt 'sɑːn-, sɪnt- ‖ -oʊ **~s** z
cipher 'saɪf ə ‖ -ᵊr **~ed** d **ciphering** 'saɪf ər‿ɪŋ **~s** z
Cipriani ˌsɪp ri 'ɑːn i
circa 'sɜːk ə ‖ 'sɜ˞ːk ə
circadian sɜː 'keɪd i‿ən ‖ sᵊr-
Circassian sə 'kæs i‿ən sɜː- ‖ sᵊr 'kæʃ ᵊn -i‿ən **~s** z
Circe 'sɜːs i ‖ 'sɜ˞ːs i
circl|e 'sɜːk ᵊl ‖ 'sɜ˞ːk ᵊl **~ed** d **~es** z **~ing** ‿ɪŋ
circlet 'sɜːk lət -lɪt ‖ 'sɜ˞ːk- **~s** s
circlip 'sɜːk lɪp ‖ 'sɜ˞ːk- **~s** s
circs sɜːks ‖ sɜ˞ːks

circu|it ˈsɜːk |ɪt §-ət ‖ ˈsɜ˞ːk |ət **~ited** ɪt ɪd §ət-, -əd ‖ əţ əd **~iting** ɪt ɪŋ §ət- ‖ əţ ɪŋ **~its** ɪts §əts ‖ əts
ˈcircuit ˌbreaker; **ˈcircuit ˌdiagram**; **ˈcircuit judge**

circuitous sɜː ˈkjuː‿ɪt əs sə-, ət- ‖ sᵊr ˈkjuː əţ əs **~ly** li **~ness** nəs nɪs

circuitry ˈsɜːk ətr i -ɪtr- ‖ ˈsɜ˞ːk-

circuity sɜː ˈkjuː‿ət i sə-, ɪt i ‖ sᵊr ˈkjuː əţ i

circular ˈsɜːk jʊl ə -jəl- ‖ ˈsɜ˞ːk jəl ᵊr **~s** z
ˌcircular ˈsaw

circularis... —*see* **circulariz...**

circularit|y ˌsɜːk ju ˈlær ət |i ˌ-jə-, -ɪt i ‖ ˌsɜ˞ːk jə ˈlær əţ |i -ˈler- **~ies** iz

circularization ˌsɜːk jʊl ər aɪ ˈzeɪʃ ᵊn ˌ-jəl-, -ɪˈ-- ‖ ˌsɜ˞ːk jəl ər ə-

circulariz|e ˈsɜːk jʊl ə raɪz ˈ-jəl- ‖ ˈsɜ˞ːk jəl- **~ed** d **~es** ɪz əz **~ing** ɪŋ

circu|late ˈsɜːk ju |leɪt -jə- ‖ ˈsɜ˞ːk jə- **~lated** leɪt ɪd -əd ‖ leɪţ əd **~lates** leɪts **~lating** leɪt ɪŋ ‖ leɪţ ɪŋ

circulation ˌsɜːk ju ˈleɪʃ ᵊn -jə- ‖ ˌsɜ˞ːk jə- **~s** z

circulator ˈsɜːk ju leɪt ə ˈ-jə- ‖ ˈsɜ˞ːk jə leɪţ ᵊr **~s** z

circulatory ˌsɜːk ju ˈleɪt‿ər i ˌ-jə-; ˈsɜːk jʊl ət‿ər i, ˈ-jəl- ‖ ˈsɜ˞ːk jəl ə tɔːr i -toʊr i

circum- *comb. form* ¦sɜːk əm ‖ ¦sɜ˞ːk əm — **circumlunar** ˌsɜːk əm ˈluːn ə ◂ -ˈljuːn- ‖ ˌsɜ˞ːk əm ˈluːn ᵊr ◂

circumcentre, circumcenter ˈsɜːk əm ˌsent ə ‖ ˈsɜ˞ːk əm ˌsen ţ ᵊr **~s** z

circumcis|e ˈsɜːk əm saɪz ‖ ˈsɜ˞ːk- **~ed** d **~er/s** ə/z ‖ ᵊr/z **~es** ɪz əz **~ing** ɪŋ

circumcision ˌsɜːk əm ˈsɪʒ ᵊn ‖ ˌsɜ˞ːk- **~s** z

circumferenc|e sə ˈkʌmᵖf ᵊr‿ənᵗs ‖ sᵊr- sə- **~es** ɪz əz

circumferential sə ˌkʌmᵖf ə ˈrenᵗʃ ᵊl ◂ ‖ sᵊr- sə-

circumflex ˈsɜːk əm fleks ‖ ˈsɜ˞ːk- **~ed** t **~es** ɪz əz **~ing** ɪŋ

circumlocution ˌsɜːk əm lə ˈkjuːʃ ᵊn ‖ ˌsɜ˞ːk əm loʊ- **~s** z

circumlocutory ˌsɜːk əm ˈlɒk jʊt‿ər i -ˈjət‿, -lə ˈkjuːt ər i ‖ ˌsɜ˞ːk əm ˈlɑːk jə tɔːr i -toʊr i

circumnavi|gate ˌsɜːk əm ˈnæv ɪ |geɪt -ˈ-ə- ‖ ˌsɜ˞ːk- **~gated** geɪt ɪd -əd ‖ geɪţ əd **~gates** geɪts **~gating** geɪt ɪŋ ‖ geɪţ ɪŋ

circumnavigation ˌsɜːk əm ˌnæv ɪ ˈgeɪʃ ᵊn -ˌ-ə- ‖ ˌsɜ˞ːk- **~s** z

circumscrib|e ˈsɜːk əm skraɪb ˌ·ˈ· ‖ ˈsɜ˞ːk- **~ed** d **~es** z **~ing** ɪŋ

circumscription ˌsɜːk əm ˈskrɪp ʃᵊn ‖ ˌsɜ˞ːk- **~s** z

circumspect ˈsɜːk əm spekt ‖ ˈsɜ˞ːk- **~ly** li **~ness** nəs nɪs

circumspection ˌsɜːk əm ˈspek ʃᵊn ‖ ˌsɜ˞ːk-

circumstanc|e ˈsɜːk əm stænᵗs -stɑːnᵗs, -stənᵗs ‖ ˈsɜ˞ːk əm stænᵗs **~ed** t **~es** ɪz əz
— *Preference poll, BrE:* -stænᵗs *65%,* -stɑːnᵗs *24%,* -stənᵗs *11%.*

circumstantial ˌsɜːk əm ˈstænᵗʃ ᵊl ◂ -ˈstɑːnᵗʃ- ‖ ˌsɜ˞ːk- **~ly** i

CIRCUMSTANCE

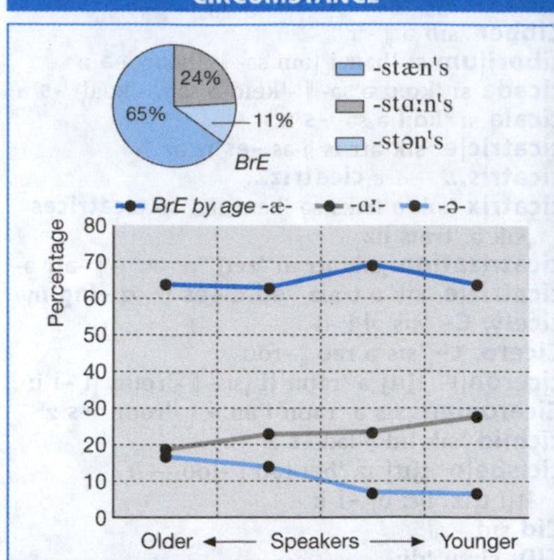

circumvallation ˌsɜːk əm və ˈleɪʃ ᵊn -væˈ-- ‖ ˌsɜ˞ːk- **~s** z

circum|vent ˌsɜːk əm |ˈvent ˈ· · ‖ ˌsɜ˞ːk- **~vented** ˈvent ɪd -əd ‖ ˈvenţ əd **~venting** ˈvent ɪŋ ‖ ˈvenţ ɪŋ **~vents** ˈvents

circumvention ˌsɜːk əm ˈvenᵗʃ ᵊn ‖ ˌsɜ˞ːk- **~s** z

circumventive ˌsɜːk əm ˈvent ɪv ◂ ‖ ˌsɜ˞ːk əm ˈvenţ ɪv ◂

circus ˈsɜːk əs ‖ ˈsɜ˞ːk- **~es** ɪz əz

Cirencester ˈsaɪᵊr ən ˌsest ə ‖ -ᵊr —*formerly, and occasionally still,* ˈsɪs ɪt ə ‖ -əţ ᵊr

Ciro ˈsɪər əʊ ‖ ˈsɪr oʊ

cirque sɜːk ‖ sɜ˞ːk **cirques** sɜːks ‖ sɜ˞ːks

cirrhosis sə ˈrəʊs ɪs sɪ-, §-əs ‖ -ˈroʊs-

cirri ˈsɪr aɪ

cirrocumulus ˌsɪr əʊ ˈkjuːm jʊl əs -jəl əs ‖ ˌsɪr oʊ ˈkjuːm jəl əs

cirrostratus ˌsɪr əʊ ˈstrɑːt əs -ˈstreɪt- ‖ ˌsɪr oʊ ˈstreɪţ əs -ˈstræţ-

cirr|us ˈsɪr |əs **~i** aɪ

cis- *comb. form* ¦sɪs — **cis-butadiene** ˌsɪs ˌbjuːt ə ˈdaɪ iːn ‖ -ˌbjuːţ-

Cisalpine ₍ˌ₎sɪs ˈælp aɪn

cisco ˈsɪsk əʊ ‖ -oʊ **~es, ~s** z

Ciskei ˌsɪs ˈkaɪ ˈ··

cisplatin ₍ˌ₎sɪs ˈplæt ɪn -ᵊn

Cissie ˈsɪs i

cissoid ˈsɪs ɔɪd **~s** z

cissus ˈsɪs əs

ciss|y, Cissy ˈsɪs |i **~ies** iz

Cistercian sɪ ˈstɜːʃ ᵊn sə- ‖ -ˈstɜ˞ːʃ- **~s** z

cistern ˈsɪst ən ‖ -ᵊrn **~s** z

cis-trans ˌsɪs ˈtrænz ◂ -ˈtrɑːnz

cistron ˈsɪs trən -trɒn ‖ -trɑːn **~s** z

cistus ˈsɪst əs

citadel ˈsɪt əd ᵊl -ə del ‖ ˈsɪţ- **~s** z

citation saɪ ˈteɪʃ ᵊn sɪ- **~s** z
ciˈtation form

cite saɪt *(= sight, site)* **cited** ˈsaɪt ɪd -əd ‖ ˈsaɪţ əd **cites** saɪts **citing** ˈsaɪt ɪŋ ‖ ˈsaɪţ ɪŋ

cithara ˈsɪθ ər ə **~s** z

cither ˈsɪθ ə ‖ -ᵊr **~s** z

C

Citation form, dictionary entry and connected speech

1 The *Longman Pronunciation Dictionary* (LPD), like other dictionaries, makes use of various **abbreviatory conventions**. This enables LPD to show a number of possible pronunciations with a single transcription of a word. However, it means that if you want to convert a passage in ordinary spelling into phonetic transcription you must 'unpack' these conventions.

2 For example, some phonetic symbols in LPD are printed in *italic* or raised and in smaller type, to denote OPTIONAL SOUNDS. If you are writing a transcription, you should choose either to include the sound or to omit it. The simplest rule is to convert italic symbols into roman (= plain), and to omit raised symbols.

Dictionary entry **glimpse** glɪm*p*s
You can write glɪmps
Dictionary entry **fail** feɪ^{ə}l
You can write feɪl

3 LPD uses spaces to show SYLLABIFICATION. You will probably want to omit these spaces in your transcription.

Dictionary entry **running** ˈrʌn ɪŋ
You can write ˈrʌnɪŋ

4 The LPD mark ‿, too, shows a syllable boundary, though it is a boundary that may be removed by COMPRESSION. You can ignore this mark.

Dictionary entry **hideous** ˈhɪd i‿əs
You can write ˈhɪdiəs
Dictionary entry **listening** ˈlɪs ^{ə}n‿ɪŋ
You can write ˈlɪsnɪŋ

5 Carrying out the procedure described above will give you a possible **citation** form (= dictionary pronunciation) for a word. This is the way the word might typically be pronounced if spoken in isolation. However, when a word occurs in a phrase or sentence, its pronunciation may sometimes be different from this.

Some of the special phonetic characteristics of **connected speech** are discussed in the articles on ASSIMILATION, COMPOUNDS AND PHRASES, DOUBLE CONSONANTS, ELISION, R-LIAISON, STRESS SHIFT, T-VOICING, and WEAK FORMS.

Citibank *tdmk* 'sɪt i bæŋk ‖ 'sɪţ-
Citicorp *tdmk* 'sɪt i kɔːp ‖ 'sɪţ i kɔːrp
citified 'sɪt i faɪd ‖ 'sɪţ-
Citigroup 'sɪt i gruːp ‖ 'sɪţ-
citizen 'sɪt ɪz ən -əz- ‖ 'sɪţ əz ən -əs- **~s** z
— *Preference poll, AmE: -əz- 64%, -əs- 36%. See chart on p. 150.*
ˌCitizens Ad'vice ˌBureau
citizenry 'sɪt ɪz ən ri '·əz- ‖ 'sɪţ-
citizenship 'sɪt ɪz ən ʃɪp '·əz- ‖ 'sɪţ- **~s** s
citral 'sɪtr əl -æl
citrate 'sɪtr eɪt 'saɪtr-, -ət, -ɪt **~s** s
citric 'sɪtr ɪk
ˌcitric 'acid
citrine 'sɪtr ɪn -iːn, §-ən
Citrine sɪ 'triːn sə-
Citroen, Citroën *tdmk* 'sɪtr əʊ ən 'sɪtr ən ‖ ˌsɪtr oʊ 'en —*Fr* [si tʁɔ ɛn] **~s** z

C

CITIZEN

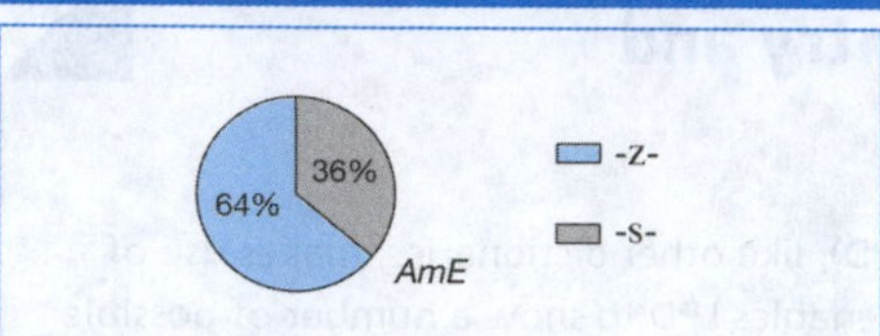

citron 'sɪtr ən **~s** z
citronella ˌsɪtr ə 'nel ə
citrous 'sɪtr əs *(= citrus)*
citrus 'sɪtr əs **~es** ɪz əz
cittern 'sɪt ɜːn -ᵊn ‖ 'sɪţ ᵊrn **~s** z
cit|y 'sɪt |i ‖ 'sɪţ |i **~ies** iz
'city ˌeditor; ˌcity 'fathers; ˌcity 'hall
city-dweller 'sɪt i ˌdwel ə ‖ 'sɪţ i ˌdwel ᵊr **~s** z
cityscape 'sɪt i skeɪp ‖ 'sɪţ- **~s** s
city-state ˌsɪt i 'steɪt ‖ ˌsɪţ- '· · · **~s** s
citywide ˌsɪt i 'waɪd ◂ ‖ ˌsɪţ-
Ciudad θju 'dɑːd ˌθiː u 'dɑːd ‖ sju 'dɑːd ˌsiː u 'dɑːd —*Sp* [θju 'ðað, sju-]
civet 'sɪv ɪt §-ət **~s** s
civic 'sɪv ɪk **~s** s
civies 'sɪv iz
civil 'sɪv ᵊl -ɪl
ˌcivil de'fence; ˌcivil ˌengi'neering; ˌcivil 'liberties; 'civil list; ˌcivil 'partner(ship); ˌcivil 'rights; ˌcivil 'servant; ˌcivil 'war
civilian sə 'vɪl i ən sɪ- **~s** z
civilis... —*see* **civiliz...**
civilit|y sə 'vɪl ət |i sɪ-, -ɪt- ‖ -əţ |i **~ies** iz
civilization ˌsɪv ᵊl aɪ 'zeɪʃ ᵊn ˌ·ɪl-, -ɪ'-- ‖ -ᵊl ə- **~s** z
civiliz|e 'sɪv ə laɪz -ɪ-; -ᵊl aɪz **~ed** d **~er/s** ə/z ‖ ᵊr/z **~es** ɪz əz **~ing** ɪŋ
civilly 'sɪv ᵊl i -ɪl-
civv|y 'sɪv |i **~ies** iz
'civvy street
CJD ˌsiː dʒeɪ 'diː
clachan, C~ 'klæx ən 'klæk-, 'klɑːx-
clack klæk **clacked** klækt **clacking** 'klæk ɪŋ **clacks** klæks
Clackmannan klæk 'mæn ən **~shire** ʃə ʃɪə, ˌʃaɪ ə ‖ ʃᵊr ʃɪr, ˌʃaɪ ᵊr
Clacton 'klækt ən
clad klæd **cladding/s** 'klæd ɪŋ/z **clads** klædz
clade kleɪd **clades** kleɪdz
cladist 'kleɪd ɪst -əst **~s** s
cladistics klə 'dɪst ɪks klæ-
Clady 'klæd i
clafouti, clafoutis klæ 'fuːt i ‖ ˌklɑːf uː 'tiː —*Fr* [kla fu ti]
clag klæg **clagged** klægd **clagging** 'klæg ɪŋ **clags** klægz
claggy 'klæg i
Claiborne 'kleɪ bɔːn ‖ -bɔːrn
claim kleɪm **claimed** kleɪmd **claiming** 'kleɪm ɪŋ **claims** kleɪmz
claimable 'kleɪm əb ᵊl
claimant 'kleɪm ənt **~s** s
claimer 'kleɪm ə ‖ -ᵊr **~s** z
Clair kleə ‖ kleᵊr klæᵊr
clairaudi|ence ₍ₗ₎kleər 'ɔːd i ənᵗs ‖ ₍ₗ₎kler- ₍ₗ₎klær-, 'ɑːd- **~ent/s** ənt/s
Claire kleə ‖ kleᵊr klæᵊr
Clairol *tdmk* 'kleər ɒl ‖ 'kler ɔːl 'klær-, ɑːl
clairvoyance ₍ₗ₎kleə 'vɔɪ ənᵗs ‖ ₍ₗ₎kler- ₍ₗ₎klær-
clairvoyant ₍ₗ₎kleə 'vɔɪ ənt ‖ ₍ₗ₎kler- ₍ₗ₎klær- **~ly** li **~s** s
clam klæm **clammed** klæmd **clamming** 'klæm ɪŋ **clams** klæmz
ˌclam 'chowder
clamant 'kleɪm ənt 'klæm-
clambake 'klæm beɪk **~s** s
clamber 'klæm bə ‖ -bᵊr **~ed** d **clambering** 'klæm bər ɪŋ **~s** z
clamm|y 'klæm |i **~ier** i ə ‖ i ᵊr **~iest** i ɪst i əst **~ily** ɪ li əl i **~iness** i nəs i nɪs
clamor 'klæm ə ‖ -ᵊr **~ed** d **clamoring** 'klæm ər ɪŋ **~s** z
clamorous 'klæm ər əs **~ly** li **~ness** nəs nɪs
clamour 'klæm ə ‖ -ᵊr **~ed** d **clamouring** 'klæm ər ɪŋ **~s** z
clamp, Clamp klæmp **clamped** klæmpt **clamping** 'klæmp ɪŋ **clamps** klæmps
clampdown 'klæmp daʊn **~s** z
clamshell 'klæm ʃel **~s** z
clan klæn **clans** klænz
Clancarty klæn 'kɑːt i →klæŋ- ‖ -'kɑːrţ i
Clancey, Clancy 'klænᵗs i

CLANDESTINE

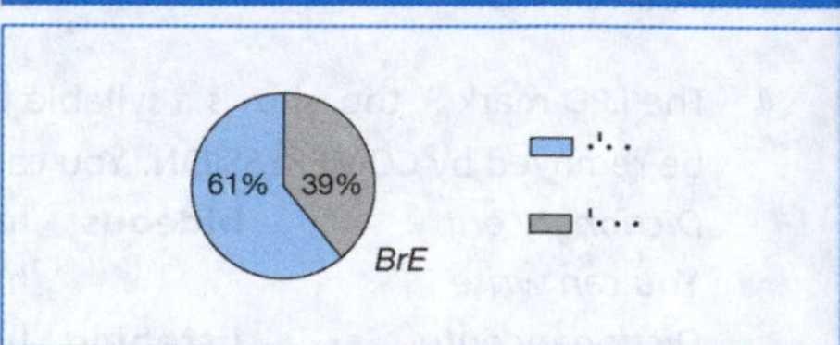

clandestine klæn 'dest ɪn -aɪn, §-ən; 'klænd e staɪn, -ɪ-, -ə-, -stɪn —*Preference poll BrE:* ·'· · 61%, '· · · 39%. **~ly** li **~ness** nəs nɪs
clang klæŋ **clanged** klæŋd **clanging** 'klæŋ ɪŋ **clangs** klæŋz
clanger 'klæŋ ə ‖ -ᵊr **~s** z
clangor 'klæŋ gə -ə ‖ -ᵊr -gᵊr
clangorous 'klæŋ gər əs -ər- **~ly** li
clangour 'klæŋ gə -ə ‖ -ᵊr -gᵊr
clank klæŋk **clanked** klæŋkt **clanking** 'klæŋk ɪŋ **clanks** klæŋks
Clanmaurice, Clanmorris ₍ₗ₎klæn 'mɒr ɪs →₍ₗ₎klæm-, §-əs ‖ -'mɔːr- -'mɑːr-
clannish 'klæn ɪʃ **~ly** li **~ness** nəs nɪs
Clanricarde *(i)* ₍ₗ₎klæn 'rɪk əd ‖ -ᵊrd, *(ii)* ˌklæn rɪ 'kɑːd ◂ ‖ -'kɑːrd ◂
clanship 'klæn ʃɪp
clans|man 'klænz |mən **~men** mən men **~woman** ˌwʊm ən **~women** ˌwɪm ɪn §-ən
clap klæp **clapped** klæpt **clapping** 'klæp ɪŋ **claps** klæps
clapboard 'klæp bɔːd 'klæb əd ‖ 'klæb ᵊrd 'klæp bɔːrd, -boʊrd

lapham 'klæp əm
ˌClapham 'Junction

app... —see clap

apped-out ˌklæpt 'aʊt ◂

apper 'klæp ə ‖ -ᵊr ~s z

apperboard 'klæp ə bɔːd ‖ -ᵊr bɔːrd -bourd ~s z

lapton 'klæpt ən

laptrap 'klæp træp

laque klæk *(= clack)* claques klæks

lara 'kleər ə ‖ 'kler ə 'klær- *—As a foreign name, also* 'klɑːr ə

larabella, C~ ˌklær ə 'bel ə ‖ ˌkler-

lare kleə ‖ kleᵊr klæᵊr

laremont 'kleə mɒnt -mənt ‖ 'kler mɑːnt 'klær-

larence 'klær ənᵗs ‖ 'kler-

larenceux 'klær ən suː -sjuː ‖ 'kler-

larendon, c~ 'klær ənd ən ‖ 'kler-

laret 'klær ət -ɪt ‖ 'kler- ~s s

larges 'klɑːdʒ ɪz -əz ‖ 'klɑːrdʒ əz

larice 'klær ɪs §-əs ‖ 'kler-

laridg|e 'klær ɪdʒ ‖ 'kler- ~e's ɪz əz

larification ˌklær əf ɪ 'keɪʃ ᵊn ˌ·ɪf-, §-ə'·- ‖ ˌkler- ~s z

larificatory ˌklær əf ɪ 'keɪt ər i ◂ ˌ·ɪf-, §-ə'·-; 'klær əf ɪ kət‿ər i, ˌ·ɪf-, §'· ·ə- ‖ 'klær əf ɪk ə tɔːr i 'kler-, klə 'rɪf-, -tour i *(*)*

lari|fy 'klær ə |faɪ -ɪ- ‖ 'kler- ~fied faɪd ~fier/s faɪ‿ə/z ‖ faɪ‿ᵊr/z ~fies faɪz ~fying faɪ ɪŋ

Clarinda klə 'rɪnd ə klæ-

larinet ˌklær ə 'net -ɪ- ‖ ˌkler- ~s s

larinetist, clarinettist ˌklær ə 'net ɪst -ɪ-, §-əst ‖ -'net̬- ˌkler- ~s s

larion 'klær i‿ən ‖ 'kler- ~s z

Clarissa klə 'rɪs ə

larity 'klær ət i -ɪt- ‖ -ət̬ i 'kler-

Clark, Clarke klɑːk ‖ klɑːrk

larkia 'klɑːk i‿ə ‖ 'klɑːrk- ~s z

Clarkson 'klɑːks ᵊn ‖ 'klɑːrks ᵊn

Claro 'kleər əʊ ‖ 'kler oʊ

Clarrie 'klær i ‖ 'kler-

lart klɑːt ‖ klɑːrt clarts klɑːts ‖ klɑːrts

larty 'klɑːt i ‖ 'klɑːrt̬ i

lar|y, Clary 'kleər |i ‖ 'kler |i 'klær- ~ies iz

clase kleɪz kleɪs — orthoclase 'ɔːθ əʊ kleɪz -kleɪs ‖ 'ɔːrθ ə-

clash klæʃ clashed klæʃt clashes 'klæʃ ɪz -əz clashing 'klæʃ ɪŋ

clasp klɑːsp §klæsp ‖ klæsp clasped klɑːspt §klæspt ‖ klæspt clasping 'klɑːsp ɪŋ §'klæsp- ‖ 'klæsp ɪŋ clasps klɑːsps §klæsps ‖ klæsps 'clasp knife

class klɑːs §klæs ‖ klæs classed klɑːst §klæst ‖ klæst classes 'klɑːs ɪz §'klæs-, -əz ‖ 'klæs- classing 'klɑːs ɪŋ §'klæs- ‖ 'klæs ɪŋ ˌclass 'action; 'class ˌsystem; ˌclass 'struggle, '· ˌ··; ˌclass 'war, '· ·

class-conscious ˌklɑːs 'kɒnᵗʃ əs ◂ §ˌklæs- ‖ 'klæs ˌkɑːnᵗʃ əs ~ness nəs nɪs

classi... *—see* classy

classic 'klæs ɪk ~s s

classical 'klæs ɪk ᵊl ~ly ‿i ~ism ˌɪz əm
ˌClassical 'Latin

classicism 'klæs ɪ ˌsɪz əm -ə-

classicist 'klæs ɪs ɪst -əs-, §-əst ~s s

classifiable 'klæs ɪ faɪ‿əb ᵊl '·ə-, ˌ·'·· ··

classification ˌklæs ɪf ɪ 'keɪʃ ᵊn ˌ·əf-, -ə'·- ~s z

classificatory ˌklæs ɪf ɪ 'keɪt ər i ◂ ˌ·əf-, §-ə'·-; '· ·ɪk ət‿ər i ‖ 'klæs əf ɪk ə tɔːr i klə 'sɪf-, klæ 'sɪf-, -tour i *(*)*

classifier 'klæs ɪ faɪ‿ə §'·ə- ‖ -faɪ‿ᵊr ~s z

classi|fy 'klæs ɪ |faɪ -ə- ~fied/s faɪd/z ~fies faɪz ~fying faɪ ɪŋ

classism 'klɑːs ˌɪz əm §'klæs- ‖ 'klæs-

classless 'klɑːs ləs §'klæs-, -lɪs ‖ 'klæs- ~ness nəs nɪs

classmate 'klɑːs meɪt §'klæs- ‖ 'klæs- ~s s

classroom 'klɑːs ruːm §'klæs-, →'klɑːʃ-, →§'klæʃ-, -rʊm ‖ 'klæs- →'klæʃ- ~s z

classwork 'klɑːs wɜːk §'klæs- ‖ 'klæs wɜːk

class|y 'klɑːs |i §'klæs- ‖ 'klæs |i ~ier i‿ə ‖ i‿ᵊr ~iest i‿ɪst i‿əst

clast klæst clasts klæsts

clastic 'klæst ɪk

clathrate 'klæθ reɪt ~s s

clatter 'klæt ə ‖ 'klæt̬ ᵊr ~ed d clattering 'klæt‿ər ɪŋ ‖ 'klæt̬ ər ɪŋ ~s z

Claud klɔːd ‖ klɑːd

Claude *(i)* kləʊd ‖ kloʊd, *(ii)* klɔːd ‖ klɑːd *—Fr* [kloːd]

Claudette ₍ˌ₎klɔː 'det ‖ ₍ˌ₎klɑː-

Claudia 'klɔːd i‿ə ‖ 'klɑːd-

Claudian 'klɔːd i‿ən ‖ 'klɑːd-

claudication ˌklɔːd ɪ 'keɪʃ ᵊn -ə- ‖ ˌklɑːd-

Claudius 'klɔːd i‿əs ‖ 'klɑːd-

Claughton 'klɔːt ᵊn ‖ 'klɑːt- *—but places with this spelling in Lancashire are* 'klæft ən *(near Lancaster) and* 'klaɪt ᵊn *(near Preston)*

clausal 'klɔːz ᵊl ‖ 'klɑːz-

clause klɔːz ‖ klɑːz *(= claws)* clauses 'klɔːz ɪz -əz ‖ 'klɑːz-

Clausewitz 'klaʊz ə vɪts 'klaʊs- *—Ger* ['klau zə vɪts]

claustrophobia ˌklɔːs trə 'fəʊb i‿ə ˌklɒs- ‖ -'foʊb- ˌklɑːs-

claustrophobic ˌklɔːs trə 'fəʊb ɪk ◂ ˌklɒs- ‖ -'foʊb- ˌklɑːs- ~ally ᵊl‿i ~s s

clave kleɪv klɑːv claves kleɪvz klɑːvz

Claverhouse 'kleɪv ə haʊs ‖ -ᵊr-

Clavering *(i)* 'kleɪv ər ɪŋ, *(ii)* 'klæv-

Claverton 'klæv ət ən ‖ -ᵊrt ᵊn

clavichord 'klæv ɪ kɔːd -ə- ‖ -kɔːrd ~s z

clavicle 'klæv ɪk ᵊl ~s z

clavier klə 'vɪə 'klæv i‿ə ‖ -'vɪᵊr ~s z

claviform 'klæv ɪ fɔːm §-ə- ‖ -fɔːrm

Clavius 'kleɪv i‿əs

claw klɔː ‖ klɑː clawed klɔːd ‖ klɑːd clawing 'klɔːʳ ɪŋ ‖ 'klɔː ɪŋ 'klɑː- claws klɔːz ‖ klɑːz
'claw ˌhammer

clawback 'klɔː bæk ‖ 'klɑː- ~s s

Claxton 'klækst ən

clay, Clay kleɪ clays kleɪz
ˌclay 'pigeon, ˌclay 'pigeon ˌshooting

Claydon 'kleɪd ᵊn
clayey 'kleɪ i
claymore 'kleɪ mɔː ‖ -mɔːr -moʊr **~s** z
claypan 'kleɪ pæn **~s** z
Clayton 'kleɪt ᵊn
claytonia kleɪ 'təʊn i‿ə ‖ -'toʊn- **~s** z
clean kliːn **cleaned** kliːnd **cleaning** 'kliːn ɪŋ **cleans** kliːnz
clean-cut ˌkliːn 'kʌt ◂ →ˌkliːŋ-
cleaner 'kliːn ə ‖ -ᵊr **~s, ~'s** z
cleanli... —*see* **cleanly**
clean-limbed ˌkliːn 'lɪmd ◂ ˌ**clean-limbed 'heroes**
cleanliness 'klen li nəs -nɪs
clean-living ˌkliːn 'lɪv ɪŋ ◂
cleanly *adv* 'kliːn li
clean|ly *adj* 'klen |li §'kliːn- **~lier** li‿ə ‖ li‿ᵊr **~liest** li‿ɪst li‿əst
cleanness 'kliːn nəs -nɪs
cleanse klenz **cleansed** klenzd **cleansing** 'klenz ɪŋ **cleanses** 'klenz ɪz -əz
cleanser 'klenz ə ‖ -ᵊr **~s** z
clean-shaven ˌkliːn 'ʃeɪv ᵊn ◂
Cleanthes kli 'ænᵗθ iːz
cleanup 'kliːn ʌp **~s** s
clear klɪə ‖ klɪᵊr **cleared** klɪəd ‖ klɪᵊrd **clearer** 'klɪər ə ‖ 'klɪr ᵊr **clearest** 'klɪər ɪst -əst ‖ 'klɪr əst **clearing** 'klɪər ɪŋ ‖ 'klɪr ɪŋ
clearanc|e 'klɪər ənᵗs ‖ 'klɪr- **~es** ɪz əz **'clearance sale**
Clearasil *tdmk* 'klɪər ə sɪl ‖ 'klɪr-
clearcole 'klɪə kəʊl →-kɒʊl ‖ 'klɪr koʊl
clear-cut ˌklɪə 'kʌt ◂ ‖ ˌklɪr- ˌ**clear-cut de'cision**
clearer 'klɪər ə ‖ 'klɪr ᵊr **~s** z
clear-headed ˌklɪə 'hed ɪd ◂ -əd ‖ ˌklɪr- **~ly** li **~ness** nəs nɪs ˌ**clear-ˌheaded 'attitude**
clearing 'klɪər ɪŋ ‖ 'klɪr ɪŋ **~s** z **'clearing bank**
clearing|house 'klɪər ɪŋ |haʊs ‖ 'klɪr- **~houses** haʊz ɪz -əz
clear|ly 'klɪə |li ‖ 'klɪr |li **~ness** nəs nɪs
clearout 'klɪər aʊt ‖ 'klɪr- **~s** s
clear-sighted ˌklɪə 'saɪt ɪd ◂ -əd ‖ ˌklɪr 'saɪţ əd ◂ **~ly** li **~ness** nəs nɪs
clear-up 'klɪər ʌp ‖ 'klɪr- **~s** s
clearway 'klɪə weɪ ‖ 'klɪr- **~s** z
cleat kliːt **cleated** 'kliːt ɪd -əd ‖ 'kliːţ əd **cleats** kliːts
Cleator 'kliːt ə ‖ 'kliːţ ᵊr
cleavag|e 'kliːv ɪdʒ **~es** ɪz əz
cleave, C~ kliːv **cleaved** kliːvd **cleaves** kliːvz **cleaving** 'kliːv ɪŋ **cleft** kleft **clove** kləʊv ‖ kloʊv **cloven** 'kləʊv ᵊn ‖ 'kloʊv ᵊn
cleaver, C~ 'kliːv ə ‖ -ᵊr **~s** z
Cleckheaton ₍ˌ₎klek 'hiːt ᵊn
Cleddau 'kleð aɪ —*Welsh* ['kle ðai, -ðe]
Cledwyn 'kled wɪn
Clee kliː
cleek kliːk **cleeks** kliːks
Cleese kliːz
Cleethorpes 'kliː θɔːps ‖ -θɔːrps
clef klef **clefs** klefs
cleft kleft **clefts** klefts ˌ**cleft 'palate**; ˌ**cleft 'stick**
cleg kleg **clegs** klegz
Clegg kleg
Cleisthenes 'klaɪsθ ə niːz -ɪ-
cleistogamy klaɪ 'stɒg əm i ‖ -'stɑːg-
Cleland *(i)* 'klel ənd, *(ii)* 'kliːl ənd
Clem, clem klem
clematis 'klem ət ɪs §-əs; klə 'meɪt-, klɪ- ‖ 'klem əţ əs klɪ 'mæţ-, -'meɪţ-, -'mɑːţ- **~es** ɪz əz
Clemence 'klem ənᵗs
Clemenceau 'klem ən səʊ ‖ ˌklem ən 'soʊ —*Fr* [kle mɑ̃ so]
clemenc|y, C~ 'klem ənᵗs |i **~ies** iz
Clemens 'klem ənz
clement, C~ 'klem ənt **~ly** li
Clementina ˌklem ən 'tiːn ə
clementine, C~ 'klem ən taɪn -tiːn **~s** z
clenbuterol klen 'bjuːt ə rɒl ‖ -'bjuːţ ə rɔːl -rɑːl
clench klentʃ **clenched** klentʃt **clenches** 'klentʃ ɪz -əz **clenching** 'klentʃ ɪŋ
Cleo 'kliː‿əʊ ‖ -oʊ
Cleobury *places in Shropshire* 'klɪb ər i 'kleb-, 'klɪəb-
Cleobury *family name (i)* 'kləʊ bər‿i ‖ 'kloʊ ˌber i, *(ii)* 'kliː-
Cleon 'kliː‿ən -ɒn ‖ -ɑːn
Cleopatra, c~ ˌkliː‿ə 'pætr ə -'pɑːtr- **~'s** z
clepsydr|a 'kleps ɪdr |ə -ədr-; klep 'sɪdr |ə **~ae** iː **~as** əz
clerestor|y 'klɪə ˌstɔːr |i 'klɪəst ər‿|i ‖ 'klɪr-ˌstoʊr- **~ies** iz
clerg|y 'klɜːdʒ |i ‖ 'klɝːdʒ |i **~ies** iz
clergy|man 'klɜːdʒ i |mən ‖ 'klɝːdʒ- **~men** mən **~woman** ˌwʊm ən **~women** ˌwɪm ɪn §-ən
cleric 'kler ɪk **~s** s
clerical 'kler ɪk ᵊl **~ly** ‿i
clericalism 'kler ɪk ə ˌlɪz əm -ᵊl ˌɪz-
clerihew, C~ 'kler i hjuː -ə- **~s** z
clerisy 'kler əs i -ɪs-
clerk, Clerk klɑːk ‖ klɝːk *(*)* **clerked** klɑːkt ‖ klɝːkt **clerking** 'klɑːk ɪŋ ‖ 'klɝːk ɪŋ **clerks** klɑːks ‖ klɝːks
Clerkenwell 'klɑːk ən wel -wəl ‖ 'klɝːk- 'klɑːrk-
Clermont 'kleə mɒnt 'klɜː-, -mənt ‖ 'kler mɑːnt 'klɝː-
Clery 'klɪər i ‖ 'klɪr i
Clevedon 'kliːv dən
Cleveland 'kliːv lənd
Cleveleys 'kliːv liz
clever 'klev ə ‖ -ᵊr **cleverer** 'klev ər ə ‖ -ᵊr ər **cleverest** 'klev ər ɪst -əst **~ly** li **~ness** nəs nɪs **'clever dick**, ˌ · · '·
clever-clever ˌklev ə 'klev ə ◂ ‖ -ᵊr 'klev ᵊr
Cleverdon 'klev əd ən ‖ -ᵊrd-

C

Clicks

A **click** is a speech sound made with an air stream set in motion within the mouth rather than by the lungs.

In English, isolated clicks are sometimes used as meaningful noises, but they are not part of the phoneme system and do not form part of the pronunciation of words.

An alveolar click ǀ can be used as a sign of disapproval (see the entry **tut-tut**). If accompanied by a breathy-voiced ŋ, it is a kind of sneer. A lateral click ǁ can be used to encourage horses.

Cleves kliːvz —*Fr* Clèves [klɛːv], *Ger* Kleve ['kleː və]
Clevis 'klev ɪs §-əs **~es** ɪz əz
clew kluː *(= clue)* **clewed** kluːd **clewing** 'kluː‿ɪŋ **clews** kluːz
Clewer 'kluː‿ə ‖ ‿ᵊr
Clewes, Clews kluːz
Cley *(i)* kleɪ, *(ii)* klaɪ
Clibborn 'klɪb ən ‖ -ᵊrn
Cliburn 'klaɪ bɜːn ‖ -bɜːn
cliche, cliché 'kliːʃ eɪ ‖ kliː 'ʃeɪ *(*)* **~d, ~'d** d **~s** z
click klɪk **clicked** klɪkt **clicking** 'klɪk ɪŋ **clicks** klɪks
'click ˌbeetle; **'click ˌlanguage**
clickable 'klɪk əb ᵊl
clicker 'klɪk ə ‖ -ᵊr **~s** z
clickety-|clack ˌklɪk ət i |'klæk ‖ ˌklɪk əţ- **~click** 'klɪk
click-fit 'klɪk fɪt
clickstream 'klɪk striːm **~s** z
click-through 'klɪk θruː **~s** z
client 'klaɪ‿ənt **~s** s
clientele ˌkliː ɒn 'tel -õ-, -ɑːn-, ˌkliː‿ən- ‖ ˌklaɪ‿ən- **~s** z
Clifden 'klɪft ən
cliff klɪf **cliffs** klɪfs
'cliff ˌdweller
Cliff, Cliffe klɪf
cliffhang|er 'klɪf ˌhæŋ ə ‖ -ᵊr **~ers** əz ‖ ᵊrz **~ing** ɪŋ
Clifford 'klɪf əd ‖ -ᵊrd
Clift klɪft
Clifton 'klɪft ən
Cliftonville 'klɪft ən vɪl
climacteric klaɪ 'mækt ər ɪk ˌklaɪ mæk 'ter ɪk **~s** s
climactic klaɪ 'mækt ɪk **~ally** ᵊl‿i
climate 'klaɪm ət -ɪt **~s** s
'climate change
climatic klaɪ 'mæt ɪk ‖ -'mæţ- **~ally** ᵊl‿i
climatologic ˌklaɪm ət ə 'lɒdʒ ɪk ◂ ‖ -əţ ə 'lɑːdʒ- **~al** ᵊl **~ally** ᵊl‿i
climatolog|ist ˌklaɪm ə 'tɒl ədʒ| ɪst §-əst ‖ -'tɑːl- **~ists** ɪsts §əsts **~y** i

climax 'klaɪm æks **climaxed** 'klaɪm ækst **climaxes** 'klaɪm æks ɪz -əz **climaxing** 'klaɪm æks ɪŋ
climb klaɪm *(= clime)* **climbed** klaɪmd **climbing** 'klaɪm ɪŋ **climbs** klaɪmz
climbable 'klaɪm əb ᵊl
climb-down 'klaɪm daʊn **~s** z
climber 'klaɪm ə ‖ -ᵊr **~s** z
climbing 'klaɪm ɪŋ
'climbing frame; **'climbing ˌirons**
clime klaɪm **climes** klaɪmz
clinch, Clinch klɪntʃ **clinched** klɪntʃt **clinches** 'klɪntʃ ɪz -əz **clinching** 'klɪntʃ ɪŋ
clincher 'klɪntʃ ə ‖ -ᵊr **~s** z
cline, Cline klaɪn **clines** klaɪnz
cling klɪŋ **clinging** 'klɪŋ ɪŋ **clings** klɪŋz **clung** klʌŋ
clingfilm 'klɪŋ fɪlm
clingstone 'klɪŋ stəʊn ‖ -stoʊn
cling|y 'klɪŋ |i **~ier** i‿ə ‖ i‿ᵊr **~iest** i‿ɪst i‿əst **~iness** i nəs -nɪs
clinic 'klɪn ɪk **~s** s
clinical 'klɪn ɪk ᵊl **~ly** ‿i
clinician klɪ 'nɪʃ ᵊn klə- **~s** z
clink klɪŋk **clinked** klɪŋkt **clinking** 'klɪŋk ɪŋ **clinks** klɪŋks
clinker 'klɪŋk ə ‖ -ᵊr **~ed** d **clinkering** 'klɪŋk‿ər ɪŋ **~s** z
clinker-built ˌklɪŋk ə 'bɪlt ◂ ‖ -ᵊr-
clinkety-clank ˌklɪŋk ət i 'klæŋk ‖ -əţ i-
clinometer klaɪ 'nɒm ɪt ə klɪ-, -ət- ‖ -'nɑːm əţ ᵊr **~s** z
clint, Clint klɪnt **clints** klɪnts
Clinton 'klɪnt ən ‖ -ᵊn
Clio *(i)* 'klaɪ əʊ ‖ -oʊ, *(ii)* 'kliː- —*The muse is usually (i), the model of car (ii).*
cliometric ˌklaɪ əʊ 'metr ɪk ◂ ‖ -ə- **~s** s
clip klɪp **clipped** klɪpt **clipping** 'klɪp ɪŋ **clips** klɪps
'clip joint
clipboard 'klɪp bɔːd ‖ -bɔːrd -boʊrd **~s** z
clip-clop 'klɪp klɒp ˌ·'· ‖ klɑːp **~ped** t **~ping** ɪŋ **~s** s
clip-on 'klɪp ɒn ‖ -ɑːn -ɔːn
clipper 'klɪp ə ‖ -ᵊr **~s** z
clippie 'klɪp i **~s** z

clipping ˈklɪp ɪŋ **~s** z
Clipsham ˈklɪp ʃəm
Clipstone ˈklɪp stəʊn ‖ -stoʊn
clique kliːk §klɪk **cliques** kliːks §klɪks
cliquey ˈkliːk i §ˈklɪk i
cliquish ˈkliːk ɪʃ §ˈklɪk ɪʃ **~ly** li **~ness** nəs nɪs
cliquy ˈkliːk i §ˈklɪk i
Clissold ˈklɪs əʊld →-ɒʊld, -ᵊld ‖ -oʊld
Clitheroe ˈklɪð ə rəʊ ‖ -roʊ
clitic ˈklɪt ɪk ‖ ˈklɪţ ɪk **~s** s
cliticis... —*see* **cliticiz...**
cliticization ˌklɪt ɪs aɪ ˈzeɪʃ ᵊn ˌ-əs-, -ɪˈ-- ‖ ˌklɪţ əs ə-
cliticiz|e ˈklɪt ɪ saɪz -ə- ‖ ˈklɪţ- **~ed** d **~es** ɪz əz **~ing** ɪŋ
clitoral ˈklɪt ər əl ˈklaɪt- ‖ ˈklɪţ-
clitoridectom|y ˌklɪt ər ɪ ˈdekt əm |i -əˈ-- ‖ ˌklɪţ- **~ies** iz
clitoris ˈklɪt ər ɪs ˈklaɪt-, §-əs ‖ ˈklɪţ-
Clive klaɪv
Cliveden ˈklɪvd ən
clivia ˈklaɪv i̯ə **~s** z
cloac|a kləʊ ˈeɪk |ə ‖ kloʊ- **~ae** iː
cloak kləʊk ‖ kloʊk **cloaked** kləʊkt ‖ kloʊkt **cloaking** ˈkləʊk ɪŋ ‖ ˈkloʊk ɪŋ **cloaks** kləʊks ‖ kloʊks
cloak-and-dagger ˌkləʊk ən ˈdæg ə →-ŋ- ‖ ˌkloʊk ən ˈdæg ᵊr
cloakroom ˈkləʊk ruːm -rʊm ‖ ˈkloʊk-
clobber ˈklɒb ə ‖ ˈklɑːb ᵊr **~ed** d **clobbering** ˈklɒb ər ɪŋ ‖ ˈklɑːb- **~s** z
cloche klɒʃ kləʊʃ ‖ kloʊʃ **cloches** ˈklɒʃ ɪz ˈkləʊʃ-, -əz ˈkloʊʃ əz
clock klɒk ‖ klɑːk **clocked** klɒkt ‖ klɑːkt **clocking** ˈklɒk ɪŋ ‖ ˈklɑːk ɪŋ **clocks** klɒks ‖ klɑːks
ˌclock ˈradio; **ˈclock ˌtower**
clock-watch|er ˈklɒk ˌwɒtʃ |ə ‖ ˈklɑːk ˌwɑːtʃ |ᵊr **~ers** əz ‖ ᵊrz **~ing** ɪŋ
clockwise ˈklɒk waɪz ‖ ˈklɑːk-
clockwork ˈklɒk wɜːk ‖ ˈklɑːk wɜːk
clod klɒd ‖ klɑːd **clods** klɒdz ‖ klɑːdz
Clodagh ˈkləʊd ə ‖ ˈkloʊd ə
cloddish ˈklɒd ɪʃ ‖ ˈklɑːd ɪʃ **~ness** nəs nɪs
clodhopper ˈklɒd ˌhɒp ə ‖ ˈklɑːd ˌhɑːp ᵊr **~s** z
clog klɒg ‖ klɑːg klɔːg **clogged** klɒgd ‖ klɑːgd klɔːgd **clogging** ˈklɒg ɪŋ ‖ ˈklɑːg ɪŋ ˈklɔːg- **clogs** klɒgz ‖ klɑːgz klɔːgz
ˈclog dance
cloggy ˈklɒg i ‖ ˈklɑːg i ˈklɔːg-
Clogher ˈklɒx ə ˈklɒ hə; klɔː ‖ klɔːr
cloisonné klwɑː ˈzɒn eɪ klwʌ- ‖ ˌklɔɪz ə ˈneɪ
cloister ˈklɔɪst ə ‖ -ᵊr **~ed** d **cloistering** ˈklɔɪst ər‿ɪŋ **~s** z
cloistral ˈklɔɪs trəl
clomp klɒmp ‖ klɑːmp **clomped** klɒmpt ‖ klɑːmpt **clomping** ˈklɒmp ɪŋ ‖ ˈklɑːmp ɪŋ **clomps** klɒmps ‖ klɑːmps
clonal ˈkləʊn ᵊl ‖ ˈkloʊn ᵊl **~ly** i
clone kləʊn ‖ kloʊn **cloned** kləʊnd ‖ kloʊnd **clones** kləʊnz ‖ kloʊnz **cloning** ˈkləʊn ɪŋ ‖ ˈkloʊn ɪŋ
Clones *place in Ireland* ˈkləʊn ɪs -əs ‖ ˈkloʊn-
clonic ˈklɒn ɪk ‖ ˈklɑːn ɪk
clonk klɒŋk ‖ klɑːŋk klɔːŋk **clonked** klɒŋkt ‖ klɑːŋkt klɔːŋkt **clonking** ˈklɒŋk ɪŋ ‖ ˈklɑːŋk ɪŋ ˈklɔːŋk- **clonks** klɒŋks ‖ klɑːŋks klɔːŋks
Clonmel, Clonmell ˌklɒn ˈmel →ˌklɒm-, ˈ.. ‖ ˌklɑːn-
clonus ˈkləʊn əs ‖ ˈkloʊn əs **~es** ɪz əz
Clooney ˈkluːn i
clop klɒp ‖ klɑːp **clopped** klɒpt ‖ klɑːpt **clopping** ˈklɒp ɪŋ ‖ ˈklɑːp ɪŋ **clops** klɒps ‖ klɑːps
Clophill ˈklɒp hɪl ‖ ˈklɑːp-
clopp... —*see* **clop**
Clorox *tdmk* ˈklɔːr ɒks ‖ -ɑːks ˈkloʊr-
close *adj, adv* kləʊs ‖ kloʊs **closer** ˈkləʊs ə ‖ ˈkloʊs ᵊr **closest** ˈkləʊs ɪst -əst ‖ ˈkloʊs əst
ˌclose ˈcall; **ˌclose ˈquarters**; **ˌclose ˈshave**; **ˌclose ˈthing**
close *n 'end'* kləʊz ‖ kloʊz **closes** ˈkləʊz ɪz -əz ‖ ˈkloʊz əz
close *v* kləʊz ‖ kloʊz **closed** kləʊzd ‖ kloʊzd **closes** ˈkləʊz ɪz -əz ‖ ˈkloʊz əz **closing** ˈkləʊz ɪŋ ‖ ˈkloʊz ɪŋ
ˌclosed ˈbook; **ˌclosed ˌcircuit ˈteleˌvision**; **ˌclosed ˈshop**
close *n 'courtyard'* kləʊs ‖ kloʊs **closes** ˈkləʊs ɪz -əz ‖ ˈkloʊs əz
Close *family name* kləʊs ‖ kloʊs
close-cropped ˌkləʊs ˈkrɒpt ◂ ‖ ˌkloʊs ˈkrɑːpt ◂
close-cut ˌkləʊs ˈkʌt ◂ ‖ ˌkloʊs-
closed-door ˌkləʊzd ˈdɔː ◂ ‖ ˌkloʊzd ˈdɔːr ◂ -ˈdoʊr
closedown ˈkləʊz daʊn ‖ ˈkloʊz-
closefisted ˌkləʊs ˈfɪst ɪd ◂ -əd ‖ ˌkloʊs-
close-fitting ˌkləʊs ˈfɪt ɪŋ ◂ ‖ ˌkloʊs ˈfɪţ ɪŋ ◂
close-grained ˌkləʊs ˈgreɪnd ◂ ‖ ˌkloʊs-
close-hauled ˌkləʊs ˈhɔːld ◂ ‖ ˌkloʊs- -ˈhɑːld
close-knit ˌkləʊs ˈnɪt ◂ ‖ ˌkloʊs-
close-lipped ˌkləʊs ˈlɪpt ◂ ‖ ˌkloʊs-
closely ˈkləʊs li ‖ ˈkloʊs-
closely-knit ˌkləʊs li ˈnɪt ◂ ‖ ˌkloʊs-
ˌclosely-knit ˈgroup
close-mouthed ˌkləʊs ˈmaʊðd ◂ -ˈmaʊθt ◂ ‖ ˌkloʊs-
closeness ˈkləʊs nəs -nɪs ‖ ˈkloʊs-
closeout ˈkləʊz aʊt ‖ ˈkloʊz-
closer *n* ˈkləʊz ə ‖ ˈkloʊz ᵊr **~s** z
closer *comparative adj* ˈkləʊs ə ‖ ˈkloʊs ᵊr
close-run ˌkləʊs ˈrʌn ◂ ‖ ˌkloʊs-
close season ˈkləʊs ˌsiːz ᵊn ˌ.ˈ.. ‖ ˈkloʊzd-
close-set ˌkləʊs ˈset ◂ ‖ ˌkloʊs-
ˌclose-set ˈeyes
clos|et ˈklɒz |ɪt §-ət ‖ ˈklɑːz |ət **~eted** ɪt ɪd §ət-, -əd ‖ əţ əd **~eting** ɪt ɪŋ §ət- ‖ əţ ɪŋ **~ets** ɪts §-əts ‖ əts
close-up ˈkləʊs ʌp ‖ ˈkloʊs- **~s** s
closing ˈkləʊz ɪŋ ‖ ˈkloʊz ɪŋ
ˈclosing date; **ˈclosing price**; **ˈclosing time**
clostridi|um klɒ ˈstrɪd i̯|əm ‖ klɑː- **~a** ə

C

Clipping

1 A **clipped** vowel is one that is pronounced more quickly than an unclipped vowel. For example, **rice** raɪs has a quick aɪ (and a slow s) when compared with **rise** raɪz (slow aɪ, quicker z).

In English, a vowel (or vowel plus nasal, or vowel plus LIQUID) is clipped when it is followed by one of the consonants p, t, ţ, k, tʃ, f, θ, s, ʃ within the same syllable (when 'syllable' is determined as in this dictionary). These are the FORTIS consonants, and we call this phenomenon **pre-fortis clipping**. It is particularly noticeable with long vowels and diphthongs when they are stressed.

The vowels have pre-fortis clipping in the words

feet fiːt (compare **feed** fiːd)

loose luːs (compare **lose** luːz)

rate reɪt (compare **raid** reɪd).

So do the vowels in the stressed syllables in the words

seeking ˈsiːk ɪŋ (compare **intriguing** ɪn ˈtriːg ɪŋ)

paper ˈpeɪp ə ‖ ˈpeɪp ᵊr (compare **labo(u)r** ˈleɪb ə ‖ -ᵊr)

total ˈtəʊt ᵊl ‖ ˈtoʊţ ᵊl (compare **modal** ˈməʊd ᵊl ‖ ˈmoʊd ᵊl).

The eɪ in **plating** ˈpleɪt ɪŋ has pre-fortis clipping, but the eɪ in **play-time** does not, since here the t is in a different syllable.

2 Clipping does not involve any change of vowel quality ('timbre'). Clipped iː in **teach** tiːtʃ does not sound like ɪ in **rich** rɪtʃ.

3 Both the e and the n of **tent** tent are affected by pre-fortis clipping: compare **tend** tend with no clipping. Both the ɪ and the l of **milk** mɪlk are clipped. In **fierce**, clipping affects the ɪə of BrE fɪəs and the ɪᵊr of AmE fɪᵊrs: compare **fears** fɪəz ‖ fɪᵊrz, where there is no clipping.

4 Another, less noticeable, kind of clipping in English depends on the presence within a word of one or more unstressed syllables after the stressed syllable. The iː in **leader** ˈliːd ə ‖ ˈliːd ᵊr is somewhat clipped in comparison with the iː in **lead** liːd, because in **leader** an unstressed syllable follows. The iː in **leadership** ˈliːd ə ʃɪp ‖ ˈliːd ᵊr ʃɪp is rather more clipped, because two unstressed syllables follow. This kind of clipping is called **rhythmic clipping**.

5 In **teacher** ˈtiːtʃ ə ‖ ˈtiːtʃ ᵊr the iː is affected both by pre-fortis clipping (because of the tʃ) and by rhythmic clipping (because of the **-er**). As a result, it is phonetically quite short. (We still call it a long vowel, because it is still an allophone of the phoneme iː.)

6 The contrary process to clipping may be called **stretching**. This tends to affect the vowel of the last syllable a speaker makes before taking a breath or stopping talking.

closure 'kləʊʒ ə ‖ 'kloʊʒ ᵊr **~d** d **closuring** 'kləʊʒ ər ɪŋ ‖ 'kloʊʒ- **~s** z

clot klɒt ‖ klɑːt **clots** klɒts ‖ klɑːts **clotted** 'klɒt ɪd -əd ‖ 'klɑːţ əd **clotting** 'klɒt ɪŋ ‖ 'klɑːţ ɪŋ
ˌclotted 'cream

cloth klɒθ klɔːθ ‖ klɔːθ klɑːθ **cloths** klɒθs klɒðz, klɔːðz, klɔːθs ‖ klɔːðz klɔːθs, klɑːðz, klɑːθs

clothbound 'klɒθ baʊnd 'klɔːθ- ‖ 'klɔːθ- 'klɑːθ-

clothe *v* kləʊð ‖ kloʊð **clothed** kləʊðd ‖ kloʊðd **clothes** kləʊðz ‖ kloʊðz **clothing** 'kləʊð ɪŋ ‖ 'kloʊð ɪŋ

cloth-eared ˌklɒθ 'ɪəd ◂ ˌklɔːθ- ‖ ˌklɔːθ 'ɪᵊrd ◂ ˌklɑːθ-

clothes *n* kləʊðz kləʊz ‖ kloʊz kloʊðz
'clothes ˌhanger; **'clothes moth**; **'clothes peg**

clothesbasket 'kləʊðz ˌbɑːsk ɪt 'kləʊz-, §-ˌbæsk-, §-ət ‖ 'kloʊz ˌbæsk ət 'kloʊðz- **~s** s

clotheshors|e 'kləʊðz hɔːs 'kləʊz- ‖ 'kloʊz hɔːrs 'kloʊðz- **~es** ɪz əz

clothesline 'kləʊðz laɪn 'kləʊz- ‖ 'kloʊz- 'kloʊðz- **~s** z

clothespin 'kləʊðz pɪn 'kləʊz- ‖ 'kloʊz- 'kloʊðz- **~s** z

clothier, C~ 'kləʊð i‿ə ‖ 'kloʊð i‿ᵊr **~s** z

clothing 'kləʊð ɪŋ ‖ 'kloʊð ɪŋ

Clotho 'kləʊθ əʊ ‖ 'kloʊθ oʊ

clott... —*see* **clot**

cloture 'kləʊtʃ ə ‖ 'kloʊtʃ ᵊr **~s** z

cloud klaʊd **clouded** 'klaʊd ɪd -əd **clouding** 'klaʊd ɪŋ **clouds** klaʊdz
'cloud ˌchamber; **ˌcloud 'nine**

cloudbank 'klaʊd bæŋk →'klaʊb- **~s** s

cloudberr|y 'klaʊd bər‿|i →'klaʊb-, -ˌber |i ‖ -ˌber |i **~ies** iz

cloudburst 'klaʊd bɜːst →'klaʊb- ‖ -bɜ˞ːst **~s** s

cloud-capped ˌklaʊd 'kæpt ◂ →ˌklaʊg-, '· ·
ˌcloud-capped 'mountains

cloud-cuckoo-land ˌklaʊd 'kʊk uː lænd →ˌklaʊg- ‖ -'kuːk-

Cloudesley 'klaʊdz li

cloudi... —*see* **cloudy**

cloudless 'klaʊd ləs -lɪs **~ly** li

cloudscape 'klaʊd skeɪp **~s** s

cloud|y 'klaʊd |i **~ier** i‿ə ‖ i‿ᵊr **~iest** i‿ɪst i‿əst **~ily** ɪ li əl i **~iness** i nəs i nɪs

clough, Clough klʌf —*but the place in Co. Down is* klɒx

Clouseau 'kluːz əʊ ‖ kluː 'zoʊ —*Fr* [klu zo]

clout, Clout klaʊt **clouted** 'klaʊt ɪd -əd ‖ 'klaʊţ əd **clouting** 'klaʊt ɪŋ ‖ 'klaʊţ ɪŋ **clouts** klaʊts

Clouzot 'kluːz əʊ ‖ kluː 'zoʊ —*Fr* [klu zo]

clove kləʊv ‖ kloʊv **cloves** kləʊvz ‖ kloʊvz
ˌclove 'hitch, '· ·

Clovelly klə 'vel i

cloven 'kləʊv ᵊn ‖ 'kloʊv ᵊn

cloven-footed ˌkləʊv ᵊn 'fʊt ɪd ◂ -əd ‖ ˌkloʊv ᵊn 'fʊţ əd ◂

cloven-hoofed ˌkləʊv ᵊn 'huːft ◂ -'hʊft ‖ ˌkloʊv ᵊn 'hʊft ◂ -'huːft, -'hʊvd, -'huːvd

clover 'kləʊv ə ‖ 'kloʊv ᵊr **~s** z

clover|leaf 'kləʊv ə |liːf ‖ 'kloʊv ᵊr- **~leafs** liːfs **~leaves** liːvz

Clovis 'kləʊv ɪs §-əs ‖ 'kloʊv-

Clowes *(i)* klaʊz, *(ii)* kluːz

clown klaʊn **clowned** klaʊnd **clowning** 'klaʊn ɪŋ **clowns** klaʊnz

clownery 'klaʊn ər i

clownish 'klaʊn ɪʃ **~ly** li **~ness** nəs nɪs

cloy klɔɪ **cloyed** klɔɪd **cloying/ly** 'klɔɪ ɪŋ /li **cloys** klɔɪz

cloze kləʊz ‖ kloʊz

club klʌb **clubbed** klʌbd **clubbing** 'klʌb ɪŋ **clubs** klʌbz
ˌClub 'Med; **ˌclub 'sandwich**; **ˌclub 'soda**

clubb... —*see* **club**

clubbable 'klʌb əb ᵊl

clubber 'klʌb ə ‖ -ᵊr **~s** z

clubby 'klʌb i

club|foot ˌklʌb |'fʊt '· · **~feet** 'fiːt **~footed** 'fʊt ɪd ◂ -əd ‖ 'fʊţ əd

club|house 'klʌb |haʊs **~houses** haʊz ɪz -əz

clubland 'klʌb lænd -lənd

club|man 'klʌb |mən -mæn **~men** mən men

clubmate 'klʌb meɪt **~s** s

clubs klʌbz

cluck klʌk **clucked** klʌkt **clucking** 'klʌk ɪŋ **clucks** klʌks

clue kluː **clued** kluːd **clueing, cluing** 'kluː‿ɪŋ **clues** kluːz

clued-in ˌkluːd 'ɪn ◂

Cluedo *tdmk* 'kluːd əʊ ‖ -oʊ

clued-up ˌkluːd 'ʌp ◂

clueless 'kluː ləs -lɪs **~ly** li **~ness** nəs nɪs

Cluj kluːʒ —*Romanian* [kluʒ]

Clumber, c~ klʌm bə ‖ -bᵊr

clump klʌmp **clumped** klʌmpt **clumping** 'klʌmp ɪŋ **clumps** klʌmps

clumpy 'klʌmp i

clums|y 'klʌmz |i **~ier** i‿ə ‖ i‿ᵊr **~iest** i‿ɪst i‿əst **~ily** ɪ li əl i **~iness** i nəs i nɪs

Clun klʌn

Clunes kluːnz

clung klʌŋ

Clunie 'kluːn i

Clunies 'kluːn iz

clunk klʌŋk **clunked** klʌŋkt **clunking** 'klʌŋk ɪŋ **clunks** klʌŋks

clunk-click ˌklʌŋk 'klɪk

clunker 'klʌŋk ə ‖ -ᵊr **~s** z

Cluny 'kluːn i —*Fr* [kly ni]

clupeid 'kluːp i ɪd §-əd **~s** z

clupeoid 'kluːp i ɔɪd

cluster 'klʌst ə ‖ -ᵊr **~ed** d **clustering** 'klʌst ər‿ɪŋ **~s** z
'cluster bomb; **'cluster pine**

clutch klʌtʃ **clutched** klʌtʃt **clutches** 'klʌtʃ ɪz -əz **clutching** 'klʌtʃ ɪŋ
'clutch bag

clutter 'klʌt ə ‖ 'klʌţ ᵊr **~ed** d **cluttering** 'klʌt‿ər ɪŋ ‖ 'klʌţ ər ɪŋ **~s** z

C

lutterbuck 'klʌt ə bʌk ‖ 'klʌt̬ ᵊr-
lutton 'klʌt ᵊn
lwyd 'kluː‿ɪd —*Welsh* [kluid, kloid]
lwydian klu 'ɪd i‿ən
lydach 'klɪd əx 'klʌd-, -ək
lyde klaɪd
lydebank 'klaɪd bæŋk →'klaɪb-
lydella *tdmk* klaɪ 'del ə
lydesdale 'klaɪdz deɪᵊl
lydeside 'klaɪd saɪd
lyne klaɪn
lyro 'klaɪᵊr əʊ ‖ -oʊ
lyst klɪst
lyster 'klɪst ə ‖ -ᵊr **~s** z
lytemnestra ˌklaɪt əm 'niːs trə ˌklɪt-, -ɪm-, -em-, -'nes- ‖ ˌklaɪt̬-
m —*see* **centimeter/s**
'mon kəm 'ɒn ‖ -'ɑːn -'ɔːn
ND ˌsiː en 'diː
nidarian naɪ 'deər i‿ən knaɪ- ‖ -'der- -'dær-
nidus 'naɪd əs 'knaɪd-
NN ˌsiː en 'en
-note 'siː nəʊt ‖ -noʊt **~s** s
nut kə 'njuːt
/o ˌsiː 'əʊ ◂ ‖ -'oʊ —*or see* **care of, carried over**
o *WWW and e-mail* kəʊ ‖ koʊ
o- ¦kəʊ ‖ ¦koʊ —*New compounds in* co- *vary between early and late stress, with a preference for late* (ˌco-ar'ranger) *except when the second element has only one syllable* ('co-heir). *In established words, note however* 'coˌpilot, 'cosine.
o. kəʊ ‖ koʊ —*or see* Company, County
O ˌsiː 'əʊ ◂ ‖ -'oʊ
oach kəʊtʃ ‖ koʊtʃ **coached** kəʊtʃt ‖ koʊtʃt **coaches** 'kəʊtʃ ɪz -əz ‖ 'koʊtʃ əz **coaching** 'kəʊtʃ ɪŋ ‖ 'koʊtʃ ɪŋ **'coach ˌstation**
oachbuilder 'kəʊtʃ ˌbɪld ə ‖ 'koʊtʃ ˌbɪld ᵊr **~s** z
oachella kəʊ 'tʃel ə ‖ koʊ- kə-
oach|man 'kəʊtʃ |mən ‖ 'koʊtʃ- **~men** mən men
oachwork 'kəʊtʃ wɜːk ‖ 'koʊtʃ wɜ˞ːk
oad, Coade kəʊd ‖ koʊd
oadjutor kəʊ 'ædʒ ʊt ə -ət- ‖ koʊ 'ædʒ ət̬ ᵊr ˌkoʊ ə 'dʒuːt̬ ᵊr **~s** z
oagulant kəʊ 'æg jʊl ənt -jəl- ‖ koʊ 'æg jəl- **~s** s
oagu|late kəʊ 'æg ju |leɪt -jə- ‖ koʊ 'æg jə- **~lated** leɪt ɪd -əd ‖ leɪt̬ əd **~lates** leɪts **~lating** leɪt ɪŋ ‖ leɪt̬ ɪŋ
oagulation kəʊ ˌæg ju 'leɪʃ ᵊn -jə- ‖ koʊ ˌæg jə-
oahuila ˌkəʊ ə 'wiːl ə ‖ ˌkoʊ- —*AmSp* [ko a 'wi la]
oal kəʊl →kɒʊl ‖ koʊl **coaled** kəʊld →kɒʊld ‖ koʊld *(= cold)* **coaling** 'kəʊl ɪŋ →'kɒʊl- ‖ 'koʊl ɪŋ **coals** kəʊlz →kɒʊlz ‖ koʊlz **'coal gas**; **'coal tar**; **'coal tit**
oal-black ˌkəʊl 'blæk ◂ →ˌkɒʊl- ‖ ˌkoʊl-

Coalbrookdale ˌkəʊl brʊk 'deɪᵊl →ˌkɒʊl-, §-bruːk- ‖ ˌkoʊl-
coalbunker 'kəʊl ˌbʌŋk ə →'kɒʊl- ‖ 'koʊl ˌbʌŋk ᵊr **~s** z
coalesc|e ˌkəʊ ə 'les ‖ ˌkoʊ- **~ed** t **~es** ɪz əz **~ing** ɪŋ
coalescenc|e ˌkəʊ ə 'les ᵊnᵗs ‖ ˌkoʊ- **~es** ɪz əz
coalescent ˌkəʊ ə 'les ᵊnt ◂ ‖ ˌkoʊ-
coalfac|e 'kəʊl feɪs →'kɒʊl- ‖ 'koʊl- **~es** ɪz əz
coalfield 'kəʊl fiːᵊld →'kɒʊl- ‖ 'koʊl- **~s** z
coal-fired ˌkəʊl 'faɪ‿əd ◂ →ˌkɒʊl- ‖ ˌkoʊl 'faɪ‿ᵊrd ◂
coalfish 'kəʊl fɪʃ →'kɒʊl- ‖ 'koʊl-
coalhole 'kəʊl həʊl →'kɒʊl- ‖ 'koʊl hoʊl **~s** z
coal|house 'kəʊl |haʊs →'kɒʊl- ‖ 'koʊl- **~houses** haʊz ɪz -əz
Coalisland kəʊl 'aɪl ənd ‖ koʊl-
Coalite *tdmk* 'kəʊl aɪt ‖ 'koʊl-
coalition kəʊ ə 'lɪʃ ᵊn ‖ ˌkoʊ- **~s** z
coal|man 'kəʊl mən →'kɒʊl-, -mæn ‖ 'koʊl- **~men** mən men
coalmine 'kəʊl maɪn →'kɒʊl- ‖ 'koʊl- **~s** z
coalminer 'kəʊl ˌmaɪn ə →'kɒʊl- ‖ 'koʊl ˌmaɪn ᵊr **~s** z
coalpit 'kəʊl pɪt →'kɒʊl- ‖ 'koʊl- **~s** s
Coalport 'kəʊl pɔːt →'kɒʊl- ‖ 'koʊl pɔːrt -poʊrt
Coalsack 'kəʊl sæk →'kɒʊl- ‖ 'koʊl-
coalscuttle 'kəʊl ˌskʌt ᵊl →'kɒʊl- ‖ 'koʊl ˌskʌt̬ ᵊl **~s** z
Coalville 'kəʊl vɪl →'kɒʊl-, -vᵊl ‖ 'koʊl-
coaming 'kəʊm ɪŋ ‖ 'koʊm ɪŋ **~s** z
coarse kɔːs ‖ kɔːrs koʊrs *(= course)* **coarser** 'kɔːs ə ‖ 'kɔːrs ᵊr 'koʊrs- **coarsest** 'kɔːs ɪst -əst ‖ 'kɔːrs əst 'koʊrs-
coarse-grained ˌkɔːs 'greɪnd ◂ ‖ ˌkɔːrs- ˌkoʊrs-
coarsely 'kɔːs li ‖ 'kɔːrs- 'koʊrs-
coarsen 'kɔːs ᵊn ‖ 'kɔːrs ᵊn 'koʊrs- **~ed** d **~ing** ɪŋ **~s** z
coarseness 'kɔːs nəs -nɪs ‖ 'kɔːrs- 'koʊrs-
coarticu|late ˌkəʊ ɑː 'tɪk ju |leɪt -jə- ‖ ˌkoʊ ɑːr 'tɪk jə- **~lated** leɪt ɪd -əd ‖ leɪt̬ əd **~lates** leɪts **~lating** leɪt ɪŋ ‖ leɪt̬ ɪŋ
coarticulation ˌkəʊ ɑː ˌtɪk ju 'leɪʃ ᵊn -jə- ‖ ˌkoʊ ɑːr ˌtɪk jə- **~s** z
coarticulatory ˌkəʊ ɑː 'tɪk jʊl ət‿ər i -'•jəl-; -ˌtɪk ju 'leɪt ər i, -ˌjə-, ˌ• •'• • • • ‖ ˌkoʊ ɑːr 'tɪk jəl ə tɔːr i -toʊr i
coast kəʊst ‖ koʊst **coasted** 'kəʊst ɪd -əd ‖ 'koʊst əd **coasting** 'kəʊst ɪŋ ‖ 'koʊst ɪŋ **coasts** kəʊsts ‖ koʊsts
coastal 'kəʊst ᵊl ‖ 'koʊst-
coaster 'kəʊst ə ‖ 'koʊst ᵊr **~s** z
coastguard 'kəʊst gɑːd ‖ 'koʊst gɑːrd **~s** z
coastguards|man 'kəʊst gɑːdz |mən ‖ 'koʊst gɑːrdz- **~men** mən men
coastline 'kəʊst laɪn ‖ 'koʊst-
coastward 'kəʊst wəd ‖ 'koʊst wᵊrd **~s** z
coastwise 'kəʊst waɪz ‖ 'koʊst-

C

coat kəʊt ‖ koʊt **coated** ˈkəʊt ɪd -əd ‖ ˈkoʊţ əd **coating** ˈkəʊt ɪŋ ‖ ˈkoʊţ ɪŋ **coats** kəʊts ‖ koʊts
ˈcoat ˌhanger
Coatbridge ˈkəʊt brɪdʒ ˌ·ˈ· ‖ ˈkoʊt- —*locally* ˌ·ˈ·
coatee ˈkəʊt iː ˌkəʊ ˈtiː ‖ ˌkoʊ ˈtiː **~s** z
Coates, Coats kəʊts ‖ koʊts
coati kəʊ ˈɑːt i ‖ koʊ ˈɑːţ i **~s** z
coati-mundi kəʊ ˌɑːt i ˈmʌnd i -ˈmʊnd- ‖ koʊ ˌɑːţ-
coating ˈkəʊt ɪŋ ‖ ˈkoʊţ ɪŋ **~s** z
coatroom ˈkəʊt ruːm -rʊm ‖ ˈkoʊt- **~s** z
coatstand ˈkəʊt stænd ‖ ˈkoʊt- **~s** z
coat-tail ˈkəʊt teɪəl ‖ ˈkoʊt- **~s** z
coauthor ˌkəʊ ˈɔːθ ə ˈ·ˌ· · ‖ ˌkoʊ ˈɔːθ ər -ˈɑːθ- **~ed** d **coauthoring** ˌkəʊ ˈɔːθ ər ɪŋ ‖ ˌkoʊ- -ˈɑːθ- **~s** z
coax *v* kəʊks ‖ koʊks *(= cokes)* **coaxed** kəʊkst ‖ koʊkst **coaxes** ˈkəʊks ɪz -əz ‖ ˈkoʊks əz **coaxing/ly** ˈkəʊks ɪŋ /li ‖ ˈkoʊks-
coax *n 'cable'* ˈkəʊ æks ‖ ˈkoʊ- **~es** ɪz əz
coaxial ₍ˌ₎kəʊ ˈæks i͜ əl ‖ ₍ˌ₎koʊ- **~ly** i
cob kɒb ‖ kɑːb **cobs** kɒbz ‖ kɑːbz
Cobain kəʊ ˈbeɪn ‖ koʊ- ˈ· ·
cobalt ˈkəʊb ɔːlt -ɒlt ‖ ˈkoʊb- -ɑːlt
Cobb kɒb ‖ kɑːb
cobber ˈkɒb ə ‖ ˈkɑːb ər **~s** z
Cobbett ˈkɒb ɪt §-ət ‖ ˈkɑːb-
cobbl|e ˈkɒb əl ‖ ˈkɑːb- **~ed** d **~es** z **~ing** ͜ɪŋ
Cobbleigh ˈkɒb li ‖ ˈkɑːb li
cobbler ˈkɒb lə ‖ ˈkɑːb lər **~s** z
cobblestone ˈkɒb əl stəʊn ‖ ˈkɑːb əl stoʊn **~s** z
Cobbold ˈkɒb əʊld →-ɒʊld ‖ ˈkɑːb oʊld
Cobden ˈkɒb dən ‖ ˈkɑːb-
cobelligerent ˌkəʊ bə ˈlɪdʒ ər ənt ◂ -bɪ- ‖ ˌkoʊ- **~s** s
Cobh, Cóbh kəʊv ‖ koʊv —*Irish* [koːv]
Cobham ˈkɒb əm ‖ ˈkɑːb-
coble ˈkəʊb əl ˈkɒb- ‖ ˈkoʊb- **~s** z
Cobleigh, Cobley ˈkɒb li ‖ ˈkɑːb-
Coblenz kəʊ ˈblents ‖ koʊ- —*Ger* Koblenz [ˈkoː blɛnts]
cobnut ˈkɒb nʌt ‖ ˈkɑːb- **~s** s
COBOL, Cobol ˈkəʊb ɒl ‖ ˈkoʊb ɔːl -ɑːl
cobra ˈkəʊb rə ˈkɒb- ‖ ˈkoʊb- **~s** z
coburg, C~ ˈkəʊ bɜːg ‖ ˈkoʊ bɜːg —*Ger* [ˈkoː bʊʁk]
cobweb ˈkɒb web ‖ ˈkɑːb- **~bed** d **~s** z
coca ˈkəʊk ə ‖ ˈkoʊk ə
Coca-Cola *tdmk* ˌkəʊk ə ˈkəʊl ə ‖ ˌkoʊk ə ˈkoʊl ə
cocaine ₍ˌ₎kəʊ ˈkeɪn kə- ‖ ₍ˌ₎koʊ- ˈ· ·
coccal ˈkɒk əl ‖ ˈkɑːk əl
cocci ˈkɒks aɪ ˈkɒk- ‖ ˈkɑːks-
coccidiosis kɒk ˌsɪd i ˈəʊs ɪs ˌkɒks ɪd-, §-əs ‖ kɑːk ˌsɪd i ˈoʊs əs ˌkɑːks ɪd-
coccus ˈkɒk əs ‖ ˈkɑːk-
coccyx ˈkɒks ɪks ‖ ˈkɑːks- **coccyges** kɒk ˈsaɪdʒ iːz ‖ kɑːk-
Coch *in Welsh names* kəʊx kəʊk ‖ koʊk —*Welsh* [koːχ]
co|chair ˌkəʊ |ˈtʃeə ˈ· · ‖ ˌkoʊ |ˈtʃeər —*Some speakers stress the v* ˌ·ˈ· *but the n* ˈ· ·. **~chaired** ˈtʃeəd ‖ ˈtʃeərd **~chairing** ˈtʃeər ɪŋ ‖ ˈtʃer ɪŋ **~chairs** ˈtʃeəz ‖ ˈtʃeərz
Cochin ˈkəʊtʃ ɪn ˈkɒtʃ-, §-ən ‖ ˈkoʊtʃ-
cochineal ˌkɒtʃ ɪ ˈniːəl -ə-, ˈ· · · ‖ ˌkɑːtʃ- ˌkoʊtʃ-
Cochise kəʊ ˈtʃiːs -ˈtʃiːz ‖ koʊ-
cochle|a ˈkɒk li͜ ə ‖ ˈkoʊk- ˈkɑːk- **~ae** iː **~ar** ə ‖ ər
Cochran, Cochrane ˈkɒk rən ˈkɒx- ‖ ˈkɑːk-
cock kɒk ‖ kɑːk **cocked** kɒkt ‖ kɑːkt **cocking** ˈkɒk ɪŋ ‖ ˈkɑːk ɪŋ **cocks** kɒks ‖ kɑːks *(= cox)*
ˌcocked ˈhat
cockad|e kɒ ˈkeɪd ‖ kɑː- **~ed** ɪd əd **~es** z
cock-a-doodle-doo ˌkɒk ə ˌduːd əl ˈduː ‖ ˌkɑːk-
cock-a-hoop ˌkɒk ə ˈhuːp ‖ ˌkɑːk-
Cockaigne kɒ ˈkeɪn kə- ‖ kɑː-
cock-a-leekie ˌkɒk ə ˈliːk i ‖ ˌkɑːk-
cockalorum ˌkɒk ə ˈlɔːr əm ‖ ˌkɑːk- -ˈloʊr- **~s** z
cockamamie, cockamamy ˌkɒk ə ˈmeɪm i ◂ ‖ ˌkɑːk-
cock-and-bull ˌkɒk ən ˈbʊl →-ŋ-, →-əm- ‖ ˌkɑːk-
cockateel, cockatiel ˌkɒk ə ˈtiːəl ‖ ˌkɑːk- **~s** z
cockatoo ˌkɒk ə ˈtuː ˈ· · · ‖ ˈkɑːk ə tuː **~s** z
cockatric|e ˈkɒk ə traɪs -trɪs, -trəs ‖ ˈkɑːk- **~es** ɪz əz
Cockayne kɒ ˈkeɪn kə- ‖ kɑː-
Cockburn ˈkəʊb ən -ɜːn ‖ ˈkoʊ bɜːn *(!)*
cockchafer ˈkɒk ˌtʃeɪf ə ‖ ˈkɑːk ˌtʃeɪf ər **~s** z
Cockcroft *(i)* ˈkɒk krɒft -rɒft ‖ ˈkɑːk krɔːft -rɔːft, -krɑːft, -rɑːft; *(ii)* ˈkəʊ krɒft ‖ ˈkoʊ krɔːft -krɑːft
cockcrow ˈkɒk krəʊ ‖ ˈkɑːk kroʊ
cocker, C~ ˈkɒk ə ‖ ˈkɑːk ər **~s** z
ˌcocker ˈspaniel
cockerel ˈkɒk ər͜ əl ‖ ˈkɑːk- **~s** z
Cockermouth ˈkɒk ə maʊθ -məθ ‖ ˈkɑːk ər-
cockeyed ˌkɒk ˈaɪd ◂ ˈ· · ‖ ˌkɑːk-
Cockfield ˈkəʊ fiːəld ‖ ˈkoʊ- *(!)*
cockfight ˈkɒk faɪt ‖ ˈkɑːk- **~s** s
cockfighting ˈkɒk ˌfaɪt ɪŋ ‖ ˈkɑːk ˌfaɪţ ɪŋ
Cockfosters ˈkɒk fɒst əz ˌ·ˈ· · ‖ ˈkɑːk fɔːst ərz -fɑːst-, ˌ·ˈ· ·
cockhorse ˌkɒk ˈhɔːs ◂ ‖ ˌkɑːk ˈhɔːrs ◂
cockieleekie ˌkɒk ə ˈliːk i -i- ‖ ˌkɑːk-
cockle ˈkɒk əl ‖ ˈkɑːk əl **~s** z
cockleshell ˈkɒk əl ʃel ‖ ˈkɑːk- **~s** z
cockney, C~ ˈkɒk ni ‖ ˈkɑːk- **~ism/s** ˌɪz əm/z **~s** z
cock-of-the-rock ˌkɒk əv ðə ˈrɒk ‖ ˌkɑːk əv ðə ˈrɑːk
cockpit ˈkɒk pɪt ‖ ˈkɑːk- **~s** s
cockroach ˈkɒk rəʊtʃ ‖ ˈkɑːk roʊtʃ **~es** ɪz əz
Cockroft *(i)* ˈkɒk rɒft ‖ ˈkɑːk rɔːft -rɑːft, *(ii)* ˈkəʊ krɒft ‖ ˈkoʊ krɔːft -krɑːft
Cocks kɒks ‖ kɑːks
cockscomb ˈkɒks kəʊm ‖ ˈkɑːks koʊm **~s** z
cocksfoot ˈkɒks fʊt ‖ ˈkɑːks- **~s** s
cock|shy ˈkɒk |ʃaɪ ‖ ˈkɑːk- **~shies** ʃaɪz
cockspur ˈkɒk spɜː ‖ ˈkɑːk spɜː **~s** z

C

Coarticulation

1 Speech sounds tend to be influenced by the speech sounds that surround them. **Coarticulation** is the retention of a phonetic feature that was present in a preceding sound, or the anticipation of a feature that will be needed for a following sound. Most ALLOPHONIC variation — though not all — is coarticulatory.

2 For example, a vowel or LIQUID that is adjacent to a nasal tends to be somewhat nasalized. This **coarticulation of nasality** applies to the vowels in **money** ˈmʌn i, and to the l in **elm** elm.

3 The English lenis ('voiced') obstruents tend to lose their voicing when adjacent to a voiceless consonant or to a pause. For example, this applies to the consonants in **good** gʊd when said in isolation, or in a phrase such as **the first good thing**. This is **coarticulation of voicing** (see VOICED AND VOICELESS).

4 Many consonants vary somewhat, depending on which vowel comes after them. Thus the ʃ in **sheep** ʃiːp is more iː-like, the ʃ in **short** ʃɔːt ‖ ʃɔːrt is more ɔː-like. This is **coarticulation of place of articulation**. Other examples are the d in **dream** driːm (post-alveolar because of the r) and the b in **obvious** ˈɒb vi‿əs ‖ ˈɑːb vi‿əs (sometimes labiodental because of the v).

5 For cases where coarticulation is variable, and may result in what sounds like a different phoneme, see ASSIMILATION.

ocksucker ˈkɒk ˌsʌk ə ‖ ˈkɑːk ˌsʌk ᵊr **~s** z

ocksure ˌkɒk ˈʃɔː ◂ -ˈʃʊə ‖ ˌkɑːk ˈʃʊᵊr ◂ -ˈʃɜː **~ly** li **~ness** nəs nɪs

ocktail ˈkɒk terᵊl ‖ ˈkɑːk- **~s** z **ˈcocktail lounge**; **ˈcocktail ˌparty**; **ˈcocktail stick**

ock-up ˈkɒk ʌp ‖ ˈkɑːk- **~s** s

ock|y ˈkɒk |i ‖ ˈkɑːk |i **~ier** i‿ə ‖ i‿ᵊr **~iest** i‿ɪst i‿əst **~ily** ɪ li əl i **~iness** i nəs nɪs

ocky-leeky ˌkɒk i ˈliːk i -ə- ‖ ˌkɑːk-

oco, Coco ˈkəʊk əʊ ‖ ˈkoʊk oʊ **ˌcoco de ˈmer** meə ‖ meᵊr

ocoa ˈkəʊk əʊ ‖ ˈkoʊk oʊ **~s** z

oconut ˈkəʊk ə nʌt ‖ ˈkoʊk- **~s** s **ˌcoconut ˈmatting**; **ˈcoconut shy**

ocoon kə ˈkuːn **~ed** d **~ing** ɪŋ **~s** z

Cocos ˈkəʊk əs -ɒs ‖ ˈkoʊk əs -oʊs

ocotte kə ˈkɒt kɒ-, kəʊ- ‖ koʊ ˈkɑːt kɑː-, -ˈkɔːt —*Fr* [kɔ kɔt] **~s** s

ocoyam ˈkəʊk əʊ jæm ‖ ˈkoʊk oʊ- **~s** z

Cocteau ˈkɒkt əʊ ‖ kɑːk ˈtoʊ kɔːk- —*Fr* [kɔk to]

od kɒd ‖ kɑːd **codded** ˈkɒd ɪd -əd ‖ ˈkɑːd əd **codding** ˈkɒd ɪŋ ‖ ˈkɑːd ɪŋ **cods** kɒdz ‖ kɑːdz

COD *'cash on delivery'* ˌsiː əʊ ˈdiː ‖ -oʊ-

oda ˈkəʊd ə ‖ ˈkoʊd ə **~s** z

oddl|e ˈkɒd ᵊl ‖ ˈkɑːd- **~ed** d **~es** z **~ing** ‿ɪŋ

code kəʊd ‖ koʊd **coded** ˈkəʊd ɪd -əd ‖ ˈkoʊd əd **codes** kəʊdz ‖ koʊdz **coding/s** ˈkəʊd ɪŋ/z ‖ ˈkoʊd ɪŋ/z

codec ˈkəʊd ek ‖ ˈkoʊd- **~s** s

codeine ˈkəʊd iːn ‖ ˈkoʊd-

co-dependenc|e ˌkəʊ di ˈpend ənᵗs ˌ·də- ‖ ˌkoʊ- **~y** i

co-dependent ˌkəʊ di ˈpend ənt ◂ -də- ‖ ˌkoʊ- **~s** s

coder ˈkəʊd ə ‖ ˈkoʊd ᵊr **~s** z

code-|share ˈkəʊd ʃeə ‖ ˈkoʊd ʃer -ʃær **~sharing** ˌʃeər ɪŋ ‖ ˌʃer ɪŋ

codeword ˈkəʊd wɜːd ‖ ˈkoʊd wɜːd **~s** z

codex ˈkəʊd eks ‖ ˈkoʊd- **~es** ɪz əz **codices** ˈkəʊd ɪ siːz ˈkɒd-, -ə- ‖ ˈkoʊd ə- ˈkɑːd-

codfish ˈkɒd fɪʃ ‖ ˈkɑːd-

codger ˈkɒdʒ ə ‖ ˈkɑːdʒ ᵊr **~s** z

codice... —*see* **codex**

codicil ˈkəʊd ɪ sɪl ˈkɒd-, -ə- ‖ ˈkɑːd ə sɪl -əs ᵊl **~s** z

codification ˌkəʊd ɪf ɪ ˈkeɪʃ ᵊn ˌ·əf-, §-əˈ-- ‖ ˌkɑːd- koʊd- **~s** z

codi|fy ˈkəʊd ɪ |faɪ -ə- ‖ ˈkɑːd- ˈkoʊd- **~fied** faɪd **~fier/s** faɪ‿ə/z ‖ faɪ‿ᵊr/z **~fies** faɪz **~fying** faɪ ɪŋ

coding ˈkəʊd ɪŋ ‖ ˈkoʊd- **~s** z

codlin ˈkɒd lɪn §-lən ‖ ˈkɑːd- **~s** z

codling ˈkɒd lɪŋ ‖ ˈkɑːd- **~s** z

cod-liver oil ˌkɒd lɪv ər ˈɔɪəl ◂ ‖ ˈkɑːd lɪv ər ˌɔɪəl

codomain ˌkəʊ də ˈmeɪn -dəʊ-, ˈ· ·ˌ· ‖ ˌkoʊ doʊ- **~s** z

codon ˈkəʊd ɒn ‖ ˈkoʊd ɑːn **~s** z

codpiec|e ˈkɒd piːs →ˈkɒb- ‖ ˈkɑːd- **~es** ɪz əz

Codrington ˈkɒdr ɪŋ tən ‖ ˈkɑːdr-

codriver ˈkəʊ ˌdraɪv ə ˌ·ˈ·· ‖ ˈkoʊ ˌdraɪv ər **~s** z

codswallop ˈkɒdz ˌwɒl əp ‖ ˈkɑːdz ˌwɑːl-

Cody ˈkəʊd i ‖ ˈkoʊd i

Coe kəʊ ‖ koʊ

coed ˈkəʊ ed ˌ·ˈ· ‖ ˈkoʊ- **~s** z

Coed *in Welsh place names* kɔɪd —*Welsh* [kɔid, koːd, koid]

coeducation ˌkəʊ ˌed ju ˈkeɪʃ ən -ˌedʒ u- ‖ ˌkoʊ ˌedʒ ə-

coeducational ˌkəʊ ˌed ju ˈkeɪʃ ən‿əl ◂ -ˌedʒ u- ‖ ˌkoʊ ˌedʒ ə- **~ly** i

coefficient ˌkəʊ ɪ ˈfɪʃ ənt ◂ -ə- ‖ ˌkoʊ- **~s** s

ˌ**coefˌficient of ˈfriction**

coelacanth ˈsiːl ə kænᵗθ **~s** s

coelenterate si ˈlent ə reɪt sə-, -ər ət, -ər ɪt ‖ -ˈlenţ- **~s** s

Coelho ˈkwel juː ku ˈel-, -jəʊ ‖ -joʊ —*BrPort* [ko ˈe ʎu]

coeliac ˈsiːl i æk

ˈ**coeliac diˌsease**

coelom ˈsiːl əm **~s** z

coelomate ˈsiːl ə meɪt **~s** s

coelomic si ˈlɒm ɪk -ˈləʊm- ‖ -ˈlɑːm- -ˈloʊm-

Coen ˈkəʊ ɪn -ən ‖ ˈkoʊ ən

coenobite ˈsiːn əʊ baɪt ‖ -ə- **~s** s

coenzyme ₍ˌ₎kəʊ ˈenz aɪm ‖ ₍ˌ₎koʊ- **~s** z

coequal ₍ˌ₎kəʊ ˈiːk wəl ‖ ₍ˌ₎koʊ- **~ly** i **~s** z

coerc|e kəʊ ˈɜːs ‖ koʊ ˈɝːs **~ed** t **~er/s** ə/z ‖ ər/z **~es** ɪz əz **~ing** ɪŋ

coercible kəʊ ˈɜːs əb əl -ɪb əl ‖ koʊ ˈɝːs-

coercion kəʊ ˈɜːʃ ən ‖ koʊ ˈɝːʃ ən -ˈɝːʒ-

coercive kəʊ ˈɜːs ɪv ‖ koʊ ˈɝːs- **~ly** li **~ness** nəs nɪs

coercivity ˌkəʊ ɜː ˈsɪv ət i -ɪt i ‖ ˌkoʊ ɝː ˈsɪv əţ i

coeternal ˌkəʊ i ˈtɜːn əl ◂ -iː- ‖ ˌkoʊ i ˈtɝːn əl ◂ **~ly** i

Coetzee ₍ˌ₎kuːt ˈsiː‿ə -ˈsiː —*Afrikaans* [ku ˈtsiə]

Coeur d'Alene ˌkɜː də ˈleɪn -dəl ˈeɪn ‖ ˌkɔːrd əl ˈeɪn

Coeur de Lion ˌkɜː də ˈliː ɒ̃ ˌkɜːd əl ˈiː-, -ɒn, ‿ən ‖ ˌkɝː də ˈlaɪ ən ˌkɜːd əl ˈaɪ ən —*Fr* [kœʁ də ljɔ̃]

coeval kəʊ ˈiːv əl ‖ koʊ- **~ly** i **~s** z

coevolution ˌkəʊ iːv ə ˈluːʃ ən -ev ə-, -ˈljuːʃ- ‖ ˌkoʊ ev-

coexist ˌkəʊ ɪg ˈzɪst -ɪk-, -əg-, -ək-, -eg-, -ek- ‖ ˌkoʊ- **~ed** ɪd əd **~ing** ɪŋ **~s** s

coexist|ence ˌkəʊ ɪg ˈzɪst |ənᵗs -ɪk-, -əg-, -ək-, -eg-, -ek- ‖ ˌkoʊ- **~ent/ly** ənt /li

coextensive ˌkəʊ ɪk ˈstenᵗs ɪv -ek-, -ək- ‖ ˌkoʊ- **~ly** li **~ness** nəs nɪs

cofactor ˈkəʊ ˌfækt ə ‖ ˈkoʊ ˌfækt ər **~s** z

CofE ˌsiː‿əv ˈiː

COFFEE

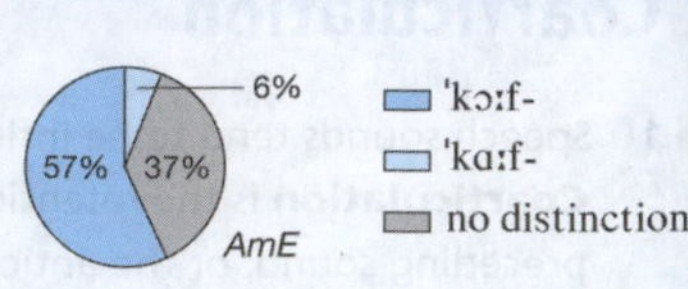

coffee ˈkɒf i ‖ ˈkɔːf i ˈkɑːf- **~s** z — *Preference poll, AmE:* ˈkɔːf- *57%,* ˈkɑːf- *6%; no distinction made between* ɔː *and* ɑː, *37%.*
ˈ**coffee bar**; ˈ**coffee break**; ˈ**coffee cup**; ˈ**coffee klatch** klætʃ ‖ klɑːtʃ, klʌtʃ; ˈ**coffee house**; ˈ**coffee ˌmorning**; ˈ**coffee shop**; ˈ**coffee ˌtable**

coffeemaker ˈkɒf i ˌmeɪk ə ‖ ˈkɔːf i ˌmeɪk ər ˈkɑːf- **~s** z

Coffeemate *tdmk* ˈkɒf i meɪt ‖ ˈkɔːf- ˈkɑːf-

coffeepot ˈkɒf i pɒt ‖ ˈkɔːf i pɑːt ˈkɑːf- **~s** s

coffee-table book ˈkɒf i teɪb əl ˌbʊk §-ˌbuːk ‖ ˈkɔːf- ˈkɑːf-

coffer ˈkɒf ə ‖ ˈkɔːf ər ˈkɑːf- **~s** z

cofferdam ˈkɒf ə dæm ‖ ˈkɔːf ər- ˈkɑːf- **~s** z

Coffey ˈkɒf i ‖ ˈkɔːf i ˈkɑːf-

coffin, C~ ˈkɒf ɪn §-ən ‖ ˈkɔːf ən ˈkɑːf- **~s** z

coffle ˈkɒf əl ‖ ˈkɔːf- ˈkɑːf- **~s** z

cog kɒg ‖ kɑːg **cogs** kɒgz ‖ kɑːgz

Cogan ˈkəʊg ən ‖ ˈkoʊg ən

cogency ˈkəʊdʒ ənᵗs i ‖ ˈkoʊdʒ-

cogent ˈkəʊdʒ ənt ‖ ˈkoʊdʒ- **~ly** li

Coggan ˈkɒg ən ‖ ˈkɑːg-

Coggeshall *(i)* ˈkɒg ɪʃ əl ˈkɒks əl ‖ ˈkɑːg-, *(ii)* ˈkɒgz ɔːl ‖ ˈkɑːgz- -ɑːl —*The place in Essex is (i), the family name (ii)*

Coghill ˈkɒg hɪl -ɪl ‖ ˈkɑːg-

Coghlan *(i)* ˈkəʊl ən ‖ ˈkoʊl-, *(ii)* ˈkɒx lən ˈkɒg- ‖ ˈkɔːk- ˈkɑːk-

cogi|tate ˈkɒdʒ ɪ |teɪt -ə- ‖ ˈkɑːdʒ- **~tated** teɪt ɪd -əd ‖ teɪţ əd **~tates** teɪts **~tating** teɪt ɪŋ ‖ teɪţ ɪŋ

cogitation ˌkɒdʒ ɪ ˈteɪʃ ən -ə- ‖ ˌkɑːdʒ-

cogitative ˈkɒdʒ ɪt ət ɪv ˈ·ət-; -ɪ teɪt-, -ə teɪt- ‖ ˈkɑːdʒ ə teɪţ ɪv **~ly** li **~ness** nəs nɪs

cogito ergo sum ˌkɒg ɪt əʊ ˌɜːg əʊ ˈsʊm §ˌ·ət-, -ˈsʌm ‖ ˌkoʊg ə toʊ ˌɝːg oʊ ˈsʊm -ˌerg-

cognac, C~ ˈkɒn jæk ‖ ˈkoʊn- —*Fr* [kɔ njak] **~s** s

cognate ˈkɒg neɪt ₍ˌ₎·ˈ· ‖ ˈkɑːg- **~ly** li **~s** s

cognis... —*see* **cogniz...**

cognition kɒg ˈnɪʃ ən ‖ kɑːg-

cognitive ˈkɒg nət ɪv -nɪt- ‖ ˈkɑːg nəţ ɪv **~ly** li

cogniz|ance ˈkɒg nɪz |ənᵗs -nəz-; kɒg ˈnaɪz-; ˈkɒn ɪz-, -əz- ‖ ˈkɑːg- **~ant** ənt

cognomen ₍ˌ₎kɒg ˈnəʊm en -ən ‖ ₍ˌ₎kɑːg ˈnoʊm ən ˈkɑːg nəm-

cognoscent|e ˌkɒg nə ˈʃent| i -nəʊ-, -ˈsent-, -iː; ˌkɒn jəʊ- ‖ ˌkɑːn jə ˈʃenţ| i -ə- **~i** i iː

cogwheel ˈkɒg wiːəl -hwiːəl ‖ ˈkɑːg- **~s** z

cohab|it ₍ˌ₎kəʊ ˈhæb |ɪt §-ət ‖ ₍ˌ₎koʊ ˈhæb |ət **~ited** ɪt ɪd §ət-, -əd ‖ əţ əd **~iting** ɪt ɪŋ §ət- ‖ əţ ɪŋ **~its** ɪts §əts ‖ əts

ohabitation (ı)kəʊ ˌhæb ɪ 'teɪʃ ᵊn -ə- ‖ (ı)koʊ-
ohabitee (ı)kəʊ ˌhæb ɪ 'tiː -ə'· ‖ (ı)koʊ- **~s** z
ohen 'kəʊ ɪn §-ən ‖ 'koʊ ən
oher|e kəʊ 'hɪə ‖ koʊ 'hɪᵊr **~ed** d **~es** z
cohering kəʊ 'hɪər ɪŋ ‖ koʊ 'hɪr ɪŋ
oherenc|e kəʊ 'hɪər ənᵗs ‖ koʊ 'hɪr- **~y** i
oherent kəʊ 'hɪər ənt ‖ koʊ 'hɪr- **~ly** li
ohesion kəʊ 'hiːʒ ᵊn ‖ koʊ-
ohesive kəʊ 'hiːs ɪv -'hiːz- ‖ koʊ- **~ly** li **~ness** nəs nɪs
oho 'kəʊ həʊ ‖ 'koʊ hoʊ
oho|bate 'kəʊ həʊ |beɪt ‖ 'koʊ hoʊ- **~bated** beɪt ɪd -əd ‖ beɪt̬ əd **~bates** beɪts **~bating** beɪt ɪŋ ‖ beɪt̬ ɪŋ
ohobation ˌkəʊ həʊ 'beɪʃᵊn ‖ ˌkoʊ hoʊ-
ohoes kə 'həʊz ‖ -'hoʊz
ohort 'kəʊ hɔːt ‖ 'koʊ hɔːrt **~s** s
ohosh 'kəʊ hɒʃ ‖ 'koʊ hɑːʃ **~es** ɪz əz
OHSE 'kəʊz i ‖ 'koʊz i
oif *'headdress'* kɔɪf **coifs** kɔɪfs
oif *'coiffure'* kwɑːf kwæf **coiffed** kwɑːft kwæft **coiffing** 'kwɑːf ɪŋ 'kwæf- **coifs** kwɑːfs kwæfs
oiffeur kwɑː 'fɜː kwɒ-, kwæ-, kwʌ- ‖ -'fɝː —*Fr* [kwa fœːʁ] **~s** z
oiffure kwɑː 'fjʊə kwɒ-, kwæ-, kwʌ- ‖ -'fjʊᵊr —*Fr* [kwa fyːʁ] **~d** d **~s** z
oign kɔɪn *(= coin)*
oil kɔɪᵊl **coiled** kɔɪᵊld **coiling** 'kɔɪl ɪŋ **coils** kɔɪᵊlz
'coil spring
oimbra 'kwɪm brə 'kwiːm- —*Port* ['kwim brɐ]
oin kɔɪn 'kɔɪ ɪn **coined** kɔɪnd 'kɔɪ ɪnd **coining** 'kɔɪn ɪŋ 'kɔɪ ɪn ɪŋ **coins** kɔɪnz 'kɔɪ ɪnz
oinag|e 'kɔɪn ɪdʒ **~es** ɪz əz
oincid|e ˌkəʊ ɪn 'saɪd -ən- ‖ ˌkoʊ- **~ed** ɪd əd **~es** z **~ing** ɪŋ
oincidenc|e kəʊ 'ɪnᵗs ɪd ənᵗs -əd- ‖ koʊ- -ə denᵗs **~es** ɪz əz
oincident kəʊ 'ɪnᵗs ɪd ənt -əd- ‖ koʊ- -ə dent
oincidental kəʊ ˌɪnᵗs ɪ 'dent ᵊl ◂ ·ˌ·· '·-, -ə'-- ‖ koʊ ˌɪnᵗs ə 'dent̬ ᵊl ◂ **~ly** i
oin-op 'kɔɪn ɒp ‖ -ɑːp **~s** s
oinsurance ˌkəʊ ɪn 'ʃʊər ənᵗs ˌ·ən-, -'ʃɔːr- ‖ ˌkoʊ ɪn 'ʃʊr- -'ʃɜː-; ˌkoʊ 'ɪn ʃʊr-
ointreau *tdmk* 'kwɒntr əʊ 'kwɑːntr-, 'kwæntr- ‖ kwɑːn 'troʊ —*Fr* [kwɛ̃ tʁo] **~s** z
oir 'kɔɪ ə ‖ kɔɪᵊr
oit, Coit kɔɪt
oital 'kəʊ ɪt ᵊl §-ət-; 'kɔɪt ᵊl ‖ 'koʊ ət̬ ᵊl
oition kəʊ 'ɪʃ ᵊn ‖ koʊ-
oitus 'kəʊ ɪt əs §-ət-; 'kɔɪt əs ‖ 'koʊ ət̬ əs 'kɔɪt̬ əs
ˌcoitus ˌinter'ruptus ˌɪnt ə 'rʌpt əs ‖ ˌɪnt̬-;
ˌcoitus ˌreser'vatus ˌrez ə 'vɑːt əs ‖ -ɜː-, -'veɪt- -ᵊr 'veɪt̬ əs
ojones kə 'həʊn iz -eɪz ‖ -'hoʊn- -eɪs —*Sp* [ko 'xo nes]
oke kəʊk ‖ koʊk **coked** kəʊkt ‖ koʊkt **cokes** kəʊks ‖ koʊks **coking** 'kəʊk ɪŋ ‖ 'koʊk ɪŋ
Coke *tdmk* kəʊk ‖ koʊk **Cokes** kəʊks ‖ koʊks

Coke *family name (i)* kʊk §kuːk, *(ii)* kəʊk ‖ koʊk
Coker 'kəʊk ə ‖ 'koʊk ᵊr
col, Col kɒl ‖ kɑːl **cols** kɒlz ‖ kɑːlz
col- ¦kɒ, kə ‖ ¦kɑː, kə —*This prefix, found only before* l, *is pronounced stressed* ¦kɒ ‖ ¦kɑː: *(1) if the following syllable is unstressed* (ˌcollo'cation), *(2) in a few two-syllable nouns* ('colleague; *but* col'lapse *with* kə-); *and (3) occasionally, in context, when contrastively stressed* (to select and 'collect). *Otherwise it is usually weak* kə (col'lision).
cola 'kəʊl ə ‖ 'koʊl ə **~s** z
colander 'kʌl ənd ə 'kɒl-, -ɪnd- ‖ -ᵊr 'kɑːl- **~s** z
Colby *(i)* 'kəʊl bi →'kɒʊl- ‖ 'koʊl-, *(ii)* 'kɒl- ‖ 'kɑːl-
colcannon kɒl 'kæn ən ‖ kɑːl-
Colchester 'kəʊltʃ ɪst ə →'kɒʊltʃ-, §'kɒltʃ-, -əst- ‖ 'koʊl ˌtʃest ᵊr
colchicum 'kɒltʃ ɪk əm 'kɒlk- ‖ 'kɑːltʃ- **~s** z
Colchis 'kɒlk ɪs §-əs ‖ 'kɑːlk-
cold kəʊld →kɒʊld ‖ koʊld **colder** 'kəʊld ə →'kɒʊld- ‖ 'koʊld ᵊr **coldest** 'kəʊld ɪst →'kɒʊld, -əst ‖ 'koʊld- **colds** kəʊldz →kɒʊldz ‖ koʊldz
ˌcold 'chisel; **ˌcold 'comfort**; **'cold cream**; **'cold cuts**, ˌ· '·; **ˌcold 'feet**; **ˌcold 'fish**; **'cold frame**; **ˌcold 'front**, '· ·; **'cold snap**; **'cold sore**; **ˌcold 'steel**; **ˌcold 'storage**; **ˌcold 'sweat**; **ˌcold 'turkey**; **ˌcold 'war**◂
cold-blooded ˌkəʊld 'blʌd ɪd ◂ →ˌkɒʊld-, -əd ‖ ˌkoʊld- **~ly** li **~ness** nəs nɪs
cold-drawn ˌkəʊld 'drɔːn ◂ →ˌkɒʊld- ‖ ˌkoʊld- -'drɑːn
Coldfield 'kəʊld fiːᵊld →'kɒʊld- ‖ 'koʊld-
cold-hearted ˌkəʊld 'hɑːt ɪd ◂ →ˌkɒʊld-, -əd ‖ ˌkoʊld 'hɑːrt̬ əd ◂ **~ly** li **~ness** nəs nɪs
coldish 'kəʊld ɪʃ →'kɒʊld- ‖ 'koʊld ɪʃ
Colditz 'kəʊld ɪts →'kɒʊld-, 'kɒld-, §-əts ‖ 'koʊld- 'kɑːld- —*Ger* ['kɔl dɪts]
cold|ly 'kəʊld |li →'kɒʊld- ‖ 'koʊld- **~ness** nəs nɪs
Coldplay 'kəʊld pleɪ →'kɒʊld- ‖ 'koʊld-
cold-shoulder ˌkəʊld 'ʃəʊld ə →ˌkɒʊld 'ʃɒʊld- ‖ ˌkoʊld 'ʃoʊld ᵊr **~ed** d
Coldstream 'kəʊld striːm →'kɒʊld- ‖ 'koʊld-
cole, Cole kəʊl →kɒʊl ‖ koʊl *(= coal)*
Colebrook 'kəʊl brʊk →'kɒʊl- ‖ 'koʊl-
Coleclough *(i)* 'kəʊl klʌf →'kɒʊl- ‖ 'koʊl-, *(ii)* -klaʊ
colectom|y kəʊ 'lekt əm |i ‖ koʊ- **~ies** iz
Coleford 'kəʊl fəd →'kɒʊl- ‖ 'koʊl fᵊrd
Coleherne 'kəʊl hɜːn →'kɒʊl- ‖ 'koʊl hɜːn ·'·
Coleman 'kəʊl mən →'kɒʊl- ‖ 'koʊl-
Colenso kə 'lenz əʊ ‖ -oʊ
coleoptera ˌkɒl i 'ɒpt ər ə ‖ ˌkɑːl i 'ɑːpt-
coleopterous ˌkɒl i 'ɒpt ər əs ◂ ‖ ˌkɑːl i 'ɑːpt-
Coleraine (ı)kəʊl 'reɪn →(ı)kɒʊl- ‖ (ı)koʊl-
Coleridge 'kəʊl ər ˌɪdʒ ‖ 'koʊl- **~'s** ɪz əz
Colerne *(i)* kə 'lɜːn ‖ -'lɜːn; *(ii)* 'kɒl ən ‖ 'kɑːl ᵊrn, *(iii)* 'kʌl ən ‖ -ᵊrn
coleslaw 'kəʊl slɔː →'kɒʊl- ‖ 'koʊl- -slɑː **~s** z
Colet 'kɒl ɪt -ət ‖ 'kɑːl-

C

Colette kɒ ˈlet kə-, ˌkɒ- ‖ koʊ- —*Fr* [kɔ lɛt]
coleus ˈkəʊl i‿əs ‖ ˈkoʊl-
coley ˈkəʊl i ‖ ˈkoʊl i **~s** z
Colgate *tdmk* ˈkəʊl geɪt →ˈkɒʊl-, ˈkɒl-, -gət, -gɪt ‖ ˈkoʊl- ˈkɑːl-
colibri, C~ *tdmk* ˈkɒl ɪb ri -əb- ‖ ˈkɑːl-
colic ˈkɒl ɪk ‖ ˈkɑːl- **~s** s
colicky ˈkɒl ɪk i ‖ ˈkɑːl-
coliform ˈkəʊl i fɔːm ˈkɒl- ‖ ˈkoʊl ə fɔːrm ˈkɑːl-
Colima kə ˈliːm ə —*Sp* [ko ˈli ma]
Colin *(i)* ˈkɒl ɪn -ən ‖ ˈkɑːl-, *(ii)* ˈkəʊ lɪn ‖ ˈkoʊ- —*as a British name, (i).*
Colindale ˈkɒl ɪn deɪᵊl -ən- ‖ ˈkɑːl-
Coliseum ˌkɒl ə ˈsiː‿əm -ɪ- ‖ ˌkɑːl-
colitis kəʊ ˈlaɪt ɪs kɒ-, §-əs ‖ koʊ ˈlaɪţ əs kə-
Coll kɒl ‖ kɑːl
collabo|rate kə ˈlæb ə |reɪt **~rated** reɪt ɪd -əd ‖ reɪţ əd **~rates** reɪts **~rating** reɪt ɪŋ ‖ reɪţ ɪŋ
collaboration kə ˌlæb ə ˈreɪʃ ᵊn **~ist/s** ɪst/s §əst/s **~s** z
collaborative kə ˈlæb ər‿ət ɪv -ə reɪt- ‖ -ə reɪţ ɪv -ər‿əţ- **~ly** li
collaborator kə ˈlæb ə reɪt ə ‖ -reɪţ ᵊr **~s** z
collag|e kɒ ˈlɑːʒ kə-; ˈkɒl ɑːʒ ‖ kə- kɑː-, kɔː-, koʊ- —*Fr* [kɔ laːʒ] **~es** ɪz əz
collagen ˈkɒl ədʒ ən -ɪn ‖ ˈkɑːl-
collaps|e kə ˈlæps **~ed** t **~es** ɪz əz **~ing** ɪŋ
collapsibility kə ˌlæps ə ˈbɪl ət i -ˌɪ-, -ɪt i ‖ -əţ i
collapsible kə ˈlæps əb ᵊl -ɪb-
collar ˈkɒl ə ‖ ˈkɑːl ᵊr **~ed** d **collaring** ˈkɒl ər ɪŋ ‖ ˈkɑːl- **~s** z
ˈ**collar stud**
collarbone ˈkɒl ə bəʊn ‖ ˈkɑːl ᵊr boʊn **~s** z
collard ˈkɒl əd ‖ ˈkɑːl ᵊrd **~s** z
collarette ˌkɒl ə ˈret ‖ ˌkɑːl- **~s** s
collarless ˈkɒl ə ləs -lɪs ‖ ˈkɑːl ᵊr-
col|late kə |ˈleɪt kɒ-, kəʊ- ‖ kɑː-, koʊ-, ˈkɑːl eɪt **~lated** ˈleɪt ɪd -əd ‖ ˈleɪţ əd **~lates** ˈleɪts **~lating** ˈleɪt ɪŋ ‖ ˈleɪţ ɪŋ
collateral kə ˈlæt‿ᵊr əl kɒ- ‖ -ˈlæţ ər əl →-ˈlætr əl **~ly** i
collateraliz|e, collateralis|e kə ˈlæt‿ᵊr ə laɪz ‖ kə ˈlæţ ər ə laɪz **~ed** d **~es** ɪz əz **~ing** ɪŋ
collation kə ˈleɪʃ ᵊn kɒ-, kəʊ- ‖ kɑː-, koʊ- **~s** z
collator kə ˈleɪt ə kɒ-, kəʊ-; ˈkɒl eɪt ə, ˈkəʊl- ‖ kə ˈleɪţ ᵊr kɑː-, koʊ-, ˈkɑːl eɪţ ᵊr **~s** z
colleague ˈkɒl iːg ‖ ˈkɑːl- -ɪg **~s** z
collect *n 'prayer'* ˈkɒl ekt -ɪkt ‖ ˈkɑːl- **~s** s
collect *v, adj, adv* kə ˈlekt **~ed** ɪd əd **~ing** ɪŋ **~s** s
collectable kə ˈlekt əb ᵊl -ɪb- **~s** z
collectanea ˌkɒl ek ˈteɪn i‿ə ‖ ˌkɑːl-
collected kə ˈlekt ɪd -əd **~ly** li **~ness** nəs nɪs
collectible kə ˈlekt əb ᵊl -ɪb- **~s** z
collection kə ˈlek ʃᵊn **~s** z
collective kə ˈlekt ɪv **~ly** li **~ness** nəs nɪs **~s** z
colˌlective ˈ**farm**
collectivis...—*see* **collectiviz...**
collectivism kə ˈlekt ɪ ˌvɪz əm -ə-
collectivist kə ˈlekt ɪv ɪst -əv ɪst, §-əst **~s** s
collectivistic kə ˌlekt ɪ ˈvɪst ɪk ◂ -ə-
collectivit|y ˌkɒl ek ˈtɪv ət |i kə ˌlek-, -ɪt i ‖ kə ˌlek ˈtɪv əţ |i ˌkɑːl ek- **~ies** iz
collectivization kə ˌlekt ɪv aɪ ˈzeɪʃ ᵊn -ˌəv-, -ɪˈ-- ‖ -ɪv ə- **~s** z
collectiviz|e kə ˈlekt ɪ vaɪz -ə- **~ed** d **~es** ɪz əz **~ing** ɪŋ
collector kə ˈlekt ə ‖ -ᵊr **~s** z
colˈ**lector's item**
colleen, C~ kɒ ˈliːn ˈkɒl iːn ‖ kɑː ˈliːn ˈkɑːl iːn **~s** z
colleg|e ˈkɒl ɪdʒ ‖ ˈkɑːl- **~es** ɪz əz
collegial kə ˈliːdʒ i‿əl -ˈliːg-
collegiality kə ˌliːdʒ i ˈæl ət i -ɪt i ‖ -əţ i
collegian kə ˈliːdʒ i‿ən -ˈliːdʒ ən **~s** z
collegiate kə ˈliːdʒ i‿ət kɒ-, ɪt; -ˈliːdʒ ət, -ɪt
collegium kə ˈliːdʒ i‿əm -ˈleg-; -ˈliːdʒ əm **~s** z
collenchyma kə ˈleŋk ɪm ə kɒ-, §-əm-
Colles ˈkɒl ɪs -əs ‖ ˈkɑːl- **Colles'** *same, or with added* ɪz əz
ˌ**Colles' ˈfracture**
collet, Collet, Collett ˈkɒl ɪt -ət ‖ ˈkɑːl- **~s** s
Colley ˈkɒl i ‖ ˈkɑːl i
collid|e kə ˈlaɪd **~ed** ɪd əd **~es** z **~ing** ɪŋ
collie ˈkɒl i ‖ ˈkɑːl i **~s** z
collier, C~ ˈkɒl i‿ə ‖ ˈkɑːl jᵊr **~s** z
collier|y ˈkɒl jər |i ‖ ˈkɑːl- **~ies** iz
colli|gate ˈkɒl ɪ |geɪt -ə- ‖ ˈkɑːl- **~gated** geɪt ɪd -əd ‖ geɪţ əd **~gates** geɪts **~gating** geɪt ɪŋ ‖ geɪţ ɪŋ
colligation ˌkɒl ɪ ˈgeɪʃ ᵊn -ə- ‖ ˌkɑːl- **~s** z
colligative kə ˈlɪg ət ɪv ‖ ˈkɑːl ə geɪţ ɪv
colli|mate ˈkɒl ɪ |meɪt -ə- ‖ ˈkɑːl- **~mated** meɪt ɪd -əd ‖ meɪţ əd **~mates** meɪts **~mating** meɪt ɪŋ ‖ meɪţ ɪŋ
collimation ˌkɒl ɪ ˈmeɪʃ ᵊn -ə- ‖ ˌkɑːl- **~s** z
collimator ˈkɒl ɪ meɪt ə ˈ-ə- ‖ ˈkɑːl ə meɪţ ᵊr **~s** z
Collin ˈkɒl ɪn -ən ‖ ˈkɑːl-
collinear kɒ ˈlɪn i‿ə kə-, kəʊ- ‖ kə ˈlɪn i‿ᵊr kɑː-
Collinge ˈkɒl ɪndʒ -əndʒ ‖ ˈkɑːl-
Collingham ˈkɒl ɪŋ əm ‖ ˈkɑːl-
Collingwood ˈkɒl ɪŋ wʊd ‖ ˈkɑːl-
Collins, c~ ˈkɒl ɪnz -ənz ‖ ˈkɑːl-
Collinson ˈkɒl ɪnᵗs ən -ənᵗs- ‖ ˈkɑːl-
Collis ˈkɒl ɪs -əs ‖ ˈkɑːl-
collision kə ˈlɪʒ ᵊn **~s** z
colˈ**lision course**
collocate *n* ˈkɒl ək ət -ɪt; -ə keɪt ‖ ˈkɑːl- **~s** s
collo|cate *v* ˈkɒl ə |keɪt -əʊ- ‖ ˈkɑːl- **~cated** keɪt ɪd -əd ‖ keɪţ əd **~cates** keɪts **~cating** keɪt ɪŋ ‖ keɪţ ɪŋ
collocation ˌkɒl ə ˈkeɪʃ ᵊn -əʊ- ‖ ˌkɑːl- **~s** z
collocutor kə ˈlɒk jʊt ə -jət-; ˈkɒl ə kjuːt ə ‖ -ˈlɑːk jəţ ᵊr **~s** z
collodi|on kə ˈləʊd i‿|ən ‖ -ˈloʊd- **~um** əm
colloid ˈkɒl ɔɪd ‖ ˈkɑːl- **~s** z
colloidal kə ˈlɔɪd ᵊl kɒ-
collop ˈkɒl əp ‖ ˈkɑːl- **~s** s
colloquia kə ˈləʊk wi‿ə ‖ -ˈloʊk-
colloquial kə ˈləʊk wi‿əl ‖ -ˈloʊk- **~ly** i
colloquialism kə ˈləʊk wi‿ə ˌlɪz əm ‖ -ˈloʊk- **~s** z
colloquium kə ˈləʊk wi‿əm ‖ -ˈloʊk- **~s** z

C

olloq|uy ˈkɒl ək| wi ‖ ˈkɑːl- **~uies** wiz
ollotype ˈkɒl əʊ taɪp ‖ ˈkɑːl ə- **~s** s
olls kɒlz ‖ kɑːlz
ollud|e kə ˈluːd kɒ-, -ˈljuːd **~ed** ɪd əd **~es** z **~ing** ɪŋ
ollusion kə ˈluːʒ ᵊn kɒ-, -ˈljuːʒ- **~s** z
ollusive kə ˈluːs ɪv kɒ-, -ˈljuːs-, -ˈluːz-, -ˈljuːz- **~ly** li **~ness** nəs nɪs
olluvi|um kə ˈluːv i‿|əm kɒ-, -ˈljuːv- **~a** ə **~ums** əmz
olly, Colly ˈkɒl i ‖ ˈkɑːl i
ollyri|um kə ˈlɪr i‿|əm **~a** ə
ollywobbles ˈkɒl i ˌwɒb ᵊlz ‖ ˈkɑːl i ˌwɑːb ᵊlz
olman *(i)* ˈkəʊl mən →ˈkɒʊl- ‖ ˈkoʊl-, *(ii)* ˈkɒl- ‖ ˈkɑːl-
olnaghi kɒl ˈnɑːg i ‖ kɑːl-
olnbrook ˈkəʊln brʊk →ˈkɒʊln-, ˈkəʊn- ‖ ˈkoʊln-
olne kəʊn kəʊln ‖ koʊn
olney ˈkəʊn i ˈkəʊln i ‖ ˈkoʊn i
olobus ˈkɒl əb əs ‖ ˈkɑːl- **~es** ɪz əz
olocynth ˈkɒl ə sɪnᵗθ ‖ ˈkɑːl- **~s** s
ologne, C~ kə ˈləʊn ‖ -ˈloʊn **~s, C~'s** z
olombi|a kə ˈlɒm bi‿|ə -ˈlʌm- ‖ -ˈlʌm- -ˈloʊm- **~an/s** ən/z
olombo kə ˈlʌm bəʊ -ˈlɒm- ‖ -boʊ
Coˈlombo Plan
olon *'colonial farmer'* kɒ ˈlɒn kə- ‖ kə ˈloʊn koʊ- —*Fr* [kɔ lɔ̃] **~s** z
olon *'punctuation mark'; 'part of intestine'* ˈkəʊl ən -ɒn ‖ ˈkoʊl ən **~s** z
Colon, Colón *place in Panama,* **colon, colón** *currency unit* kɒ ˈlɒn kə- ‖ kə ˈloʊn koʊ- —*Sp* [ko ˈlon]
olonel, C~ ˈkɜːn ᵊl ‖ ˈkɝːn ᵊl *(= kernel)* **~s** z
ˌColonel ˈBlimp
olonel|cy ˈkɜːn ᵊl |si ‖ ˈkɝːn- **~cies** siz
oloni... —*see* **colony**
olonial kə ˈləʊn i‿əl ‖ -ˈloʊn- **~ly** i **~s** z
olonialism kə ˈləʊn i‿ə ˌlɪz əm ‖ -ˈloʊn-
olonialist kə ˈləʊn i‿əl ɪst §-əst ‖ -ˈloʊn- **~s** s
olonic kəʊ ˈlɒn ɪk kə- ‖ koʊ ˈlɑːn-
olonis... —*see* **coloniz...**
olonist ˈkɒl ən ɪst §-əst ‖ ˈkɑːl- **~s** s
olonization ˌkɒl ən aɪ ˈzeɪʃ ᵊn -ən ɪ- ‖ ˌkɑːl ən ə- **~s** z
oloniz|e ˈkɒl ə naɪz ‖ ˈkɑːl- **~ed** d **~es** ɪz əz **~ing** ɪŋ
olonizer ˈkɒl ə naɪz ə ‖ ˈkɑːl ə naɪz ᵊr **~s** z
olonnad|e ˌkɒl ə ˈneɪd ˈ· · · ‖ ˌkɑːl- **~ed** ɪd əd **~es** z
olonoscope kə ˈlɒn ə skəʊp ‖ -ˈlɑːn ə skoʊp **~s** s
Colonsay ˈkɒl ənz eɪ -ən seɪ ‖ ˈkɑːl-
Colonus kə ˈləʊn əs -ˈlɒn- ‖ -ˈloʊn-
colon|y ˈkɒl ən |i ‖ ˈkɑːl- **~ies** iz
colophon ˈkɒl ə fɒn -əf ən ‖ ˈkɑːl ə fɑːn -əf ən **~s** z
colophony kɒ ˈlɒf ən i kə- ‖ kə ˈlɑːf-

color ˈkʌl ə ‖ -ᵊr **colored** ˈkʌl əd ‖ -ᵊrd **coloring** ˈkʌl ər ɪŋ **colors** ˈkʌl əz ‖ -ᵊrz
ˈcolor bar, ˈcolor line; ˈcolor scheme; ˌcolor ˈsupplement
Colorado, c~ ˌkɒl ə ˈrɑːd əʊ ◂ ‖ ˌkɑːl ə ˈræd oʊ ◂ -ˈrɑːd-
Coloˌrado ˈbeetle; ˌColoˌrado ˈSprings
colorant ˈkʌl ər ənt **~s** s
coloration ˌkʌl ə ˈreɪʃ ᵊn **~s** z
coloratura ˌkɒl ər ə ˈtʊər ə -ˈtjʊər- ‖ ˌkʌl ər ə ˈtʊr ə -ˈtjʊr- **~s** z
color-blind ˈkʌl ə blaɪnd ‖ -ᵊr- **~ness** nəs nɪs
color-cod|e ˌkʌl ə ˈkəʊd ˈ· · · ‖ ˌkʌl ᵊr ˈkoʊd **~ed** ɪd əd **~ing** ɪŋ **~es** z
color-cod|e ˌkʌl ə ˈkəʊd ˈ· · · ‖ ˈkʌl ᵊr ˌkoʊd ˌ· ˈ· **~ed** ɪd ◂ əd **~ing** ɪŋ **~es** z
color-coordinated ˌkʌl ə kəʊ ˈɔːd ɪ neɪt ɪd ◂ -ˈ·ə-, -ˈ·ᵊn eɪt-, -əd ‖ ˌkʌl ᵊr koʊ ˈɔːrd n eɪţ əd ◂
color-coordination ˌkʌl ə kəʊ ˌɔːd ɪ ˈneɪʃ ᵊn -ə· ·, -ᵊn ˈeɪʃ- ‖ ˌkʌl ᵊr koʊ ˌɔːrd ᵊn ˈeɪʃ ᵊn
colored ˈkʌl əd ‖ -ᵊrd **~s** z
colorfast ˈkʌl ə fɑːst §-fæst ‖ -ᵊr fæst **~ness** nəs nɪs
colorful ˈkʌl ə fᵊl -fʊl ‖ -ᵊr- **~ly** ‿i
colorimeter ˌkʌl ə ˈrɪm ɪt ə -ət ə ‖ -əţ ᵊr **~s** z
colorimetry ˌkʌl ə ˈrɪm ətr i -ɪtr i
coloring ˈkʌl ər ɪŋ
ˈcoloring ˌmatter
colorist ˈkʌl ər ɪst §-əst **~s** s
colorization ˌkʌl ə raɪ ˈzeɪʃ ᵊn
coloriz|e ˈkʌl ə raɪz **~ed** d **~es** ɪz əz **~ing** ɪŋ
colorless ˈkʌl ə ləs -lɪs ‖ -ᵊr- **~ly** li **~ness** nəs nɪs
Coloroll *tdmk* ˈkʌl ə rəʊl →-rɒʊl ‖ -roʊl
colorwash ˈkʌl ə wɒʃ ‖ -ᵊr wɔːʃ -wɑːʃ **~ed** t **~es** ɪz əz **~ing** ɪŋ
colorway ˈkʌl ə weɪ ‖ -ᵊr- **~s** z
Colossae kə ˈlɒs iː -aɪ ‖ -ˈlɑːs-
colossal kə ˈlɒs ᵊl ‖ -ˈlɑːs- **~ly** i
Colosseum, c~ ˌkɒl ə ˈsiː‿əm ‖ ˌkɑːl-
colossi kə ˈlɒs aɪ ‖ -ˈlɑːs-
Colossian kə ˈlɒʃ ᵊn kə ˈlɒs i‿ən, -ˈlɒʃ- ‖ -ˈlɑːʃ- **~s** z
coloss|us kə ˈlɒs |əs ‖ -ˈlɑːs- **~i** aɪ **~uses** əs ɪz -əz
colostom|y kə ˈlɒst əm |i ‖ -ˈlɑːst- **~ies** iz
coˈlostomy bag
colostrum kə ˈlɒs trəm ‖ -ˈlɑːs-
colour ˈkʌl ə ‖ -ᵊr **coloured** ˈkʌl əd ‖ -ᵊrd **colouring** ˈkʌl ər ɪŋ **colours** ˈkʌl əz ‖ -ᵊrz
ˈcolour bar, ˈcolor line; ˈcolour scheme; ˌcolour ˈsupplement
colourant ˈkʌl ər ənt **~s** s
colour-blind ˈkʌl ə blaɪnd ‖ -ᵊr- **~ness** nəs nɪs
colour-coordinated ˌkʌl ə kəʊ ˈɔːd ɪ neɪt ɪd ◂ -ˈ·ə-, -ˈ·ᵊn eɪt-, -əd ‖ ˌkʌl ᵊr koʊ ˈɔːrd ᵊn eɪţ əd ◂
colour-coordination ˌkʌl ə kəʊ ˌɔːd ɪ ˈneɪʃ ᵊn -ə· ·, -ᵊn ˈeɪʃ- ‖ ˌkʌl ᵊr koʊ ˌɔːrd ᵊn ˈeɪʃ ᵊn
coloured ˈkʌl əd ‖ -ᵊrd **~s** z
colourfast ˈkʌl ə fɑːst §-fæst ‖ -ᵊr fæst **~ness** nəs nɪs

colourful 'kʌl ə f^{ə}l -fʊl ‖ -^{ə}r- **~ly** i

colouring 'kʌl ər ɪŋ

'colouring ˌmatter

colourist 'kʌl ər ɪst §-əst **~s** s

colourization, colourisation ˌkʌl ə raɪ 'zeɪʃ ^{ə}n

colouriz|e, colouris|e 'kʌl ə raɪz **~ed** d **~es** ɪz əz **~ing** ɪŋ

colourless 'kʌl ə ləs -lɪs ‖ -^{ə}r- **~ly** li **~ness** nəs nɪs

colourwash 'kʌl ə wɒʃ ‖ -^{ə}r wɔːʃ -wɑːʃ **~ed** t **~es** ɪz əz **~ing** ɪŋ

colourway 'kʌl ə weɪ ‖ -^{ə}r- **~s** z

-colous *stress-imposing* kəl əs — **sanguicolous** sæŋ 'gwɪk əl əs

colpitis kɒl 'paɪt ɪs §-əs ‖ kɑːl 'paɪţ əs

colpo- *comb. form*
with stress-neutral suffix ¦kɒlp əʊ ‖ ¦kɑːlp oʊ — **colpomycosis** ˌkɒlp əʊ maɪ 'kəʊs ɪs §-əs ‖ ˌkɑːlp oʊ maɪ 'koʊs əs
with stress-imposing suffix kɒl 'pɒ+ ‖ kɑːl 'pɑː+ — **colporrhaphy** kɒl 'pɒr əf i ‖ kɑːl 'pɑːr-

colporteur ˌkɒl pɔː 'tɜː ˌkəʊl-; 'kɒl ˌpɔːt ə, 'kəʊl-, ˌ·'· · ‖ ˌkɑːl pɔːr 'tɜː -poʊr-; 'kɑːl ˌpɔːrţ ^{ə}r, -ˌpoʊrţ- —*Fr* [kɔl pɔʁ tœːʁ] **~s** z

colposcope 'kɒlp ə skəʊp ‖ 'kɑːlp ə skoʊp **~s** s

Colquhoun kə 'huːn

Colson 'kəʊls ^{ə}n →'kɒʊls- ‖ 'koʊls-

Colston 'kəʊlst ən →'kɒʊlst- ‖ 'koʊlst-

colt, Colt kəʊlt →kɒʊlt ‖ koʊlt **colts, Colts** kəʊlts →kɒʊlts ‖ koʊlts

coltan 'kɒl tæn ‖ 'kɑːl-

colter 'kəʊlt ə §'kuːt- ‖ 'koʊlt ^{ə}r **~s** z

coltish 'kəʊlt ɪʃ ‖ 'koʊlt- **~ly** li **~ness** nəs nɪs

Coltrane kɒl 'treɪn ‖ koʊl-

coltsfoot 'kəʊlts fʊt →'kɒʊlts- ‖ 'koʊlts- **~s** s

colubrine 'kɒl ju braɪn -brɪn, -brən ‖ 'kɑːl ə- -jə-

Colum, Columb 'kɒl əm ‖ 'kɑːl-

Columba kə 'lʌm bə **~'s** z

columbari|um ˌkɒl əm 'beər i‿əm ‖ ˌkɑːl əm 'ber i‿əm -'bær- **~a** ə

Columbia kə 'lʌm bi‿ə

Columbian kə 'lʌm bi‿ən **~s** z

columbine, C~ 'kɒl əm baɪn ‖ 'kɑːl- **~s** z

columbite kə 'lʌm baɪt 'kɒl əm- ‖ 'kɑːl əm-

columbium kə 'lʌm bi‿əm

Columbo kə 'lʌm bəʊ ‖ -boʊ

Columbus kə 'lʌm bəs

column 'kɒl əm ‖ 'kɑːl əm **~ed** d **~s** z

columnar kə 'lʌm nə ‖ -n^{ə}r

columnist 'kɒl əm nɪst -ɪst, §-nəst, §-əst ‖ 'kɑːl- **~s** s

colure kə 'lʊə -'ljʊə; 'kəʊ· ‖ -'lʊ^{ə}r **~s** z

Colville 'kɒl vɪl ‖ 'koʊl-

Colvin 'kɒlv ɪn §-ən ‖ 'koʊlv ən

Colwich 'kɒl wɪtʃ ‖ 'kɑːl- —*formerly* -ɪtʃ

Colwyn 'kɒl wɪn -wən ‖ 'kɑːl-

ˌColwyn 'Bay

Colyer 'kɒl jə ‖ 'kɑːl j^{ə}r

Colyton 'kɒl ɪt ən -ət- ‖ 'kɑːl ət ^{ə}n

colza 'kɒlz ə ‖ 'kɑːlz ə 'koʊlz-

com *WWW and e-mail* kɒm ‖ kɑːm

com- *This prefix is pronounced stressed* kɒm ‖ kɑːm *(1) if the following syllable is unstressed* (ˌcombi'nation)*; (2) in many disyllabic nouns* ('combine; *but* com'mand)*; and (3) occasionally, in context, when contrastively stressed* (ˌdepartments and 'compartments)*. Otherwise it is usually weak* kəm *in RP and GenAm, though strong in some regional British speech* (com'puter)*. Before a stem beginning* m*, one* m *is lost* ('commerce, com'mit).

coma 'kəʊm ə ‖ 'koʊm ə **~s** z

Comanche kə 'mæntʃ i **~s** z

comatose 'kəʊm ə təʊs -təʊz ‖ 'koʊm ə toʊs **~ly** li

comb kəʊm ‖ koʊm **combed** kəʊmd ‖ koʊmd **combing** 'kəʊm ɪŋ ‖ 'koʊm ɪŋ **combs** kəʊmz ‖ koʊmz

com|bat *v* 'kɒm |bæt 'kʌm-, -bət; kəm '|bæt, $_{(ı)}$kɒm- ‖ kəm |'bæt 'kɑːm bæt **~bated, ~batted** bæt ɪd -əd ‖ 'bæţ əd **~bating, ~batting** bæt ɪŋ ‖ 'bæţ ɪŋ **~bats** bæts ‖ 'bæts

combat *n, adj* 'kɒm bæt 'kʌm-, -bət ‖ 'kɑːm-

'combat faˌtigue

combatant 'kɒm bət ənt 'kʌm-; kəm 'bæt ^{ə}nt $_{(ı)}$kɒm- ‖ kəm 'bæt ^{ə}nt **~s** s

combative 'kɒm bət ɪv 'kʌm-; kəm 'bæt ɪv, $_{(ı)}$kɒm- ‖ kəm 'bæţ ɪv **~ly** li **~ness** nəs nɪs

Combe, combe kuːm —*as a family name, also* kəʊm ‖ koʊm

comber *fish* 'kɒm bə ‖ 'kɑːm b^{ə}r **~s** z

comber *'thing that combs'* 'kəʊm ə ‖ 'koʊm ^{ə}r **~s** z

combination ˌkɒm bɪ 'neɪʃ ^{ə}n -bə- ‖ ˌkɑːm- **~s** z

ˌcombi'nation lock

combinative 'kɒm bɪ nət ɪv ˌ·bə-, -neɪt·ɪv ‖ 'kɑːm bə neɪţ ɪv kəm 'baɪn əţ-

combinatorial ˌkɒm bɪn ə 'tɔːr i‿əl ◂ ˌ·bən- ‖ ˌkɑːm- kəm ˌbaɪn-, -'toʊr-

combine *n* 'kɒm baɪn ‖ 'kɑːm- **~s** z

ˌcombine 'harvester

combin|e *v 'join, unite'* kəm 'baɪn §$_{(ı)}$kɒm- **~ed** d **~er/s** ə/z ‖ ^{ə}r/z **~es** z **~ing** ɪŋ

com'bining form

combin|e *v 'harvest'* 'kɒm baɪn ‖ 'kɑːm- **~ed** d **~es** z **~ing** ɪŋ

combing 'kəʊm ɪŋ ‖ 'koʊm ɪŋ **~s** z

combo 'kɒm bəʊ ‖ 'kɑːm boʊ **~s** z

comb-out 'kəʊm aʊt ‖ 'koʊm- **~s** s

combover 'kəʊm ˌəʊv ə ‖ 'koʊm ˌoʊv ^{ə}r

combust kəm 'bʌst §$_{(ı)}$kɒm- **~ed** ɪd əd **~ing** ɪŋ **~s** s

combustibility kəm ˌbʌst ə 'bɪl ət i §kɒm-, §ˌkɒm bʌst-, -ɪ'--, -ɪt i ‖ -əţ i

combustib|le kəm 'bʌst əb |^{ə}l §$_{(ı)}$kɒm-, -ɪb- **~ly** li

combustion kəm 'bʌs tʃən §$_{(ı)}$kɒm-

com'bustion ˌchamber

C

Combining forms

1 Many literary and scientific words are composed of **combining forms** derived from Greek or Latin. Typically, they consist of a first element and a second element. For example, **microscopic** consists of **micro-** plus **-scopic**. The *Longman Pronunciation Dictionary* has entries for these separate elements, which makes it possible to work out the pronunciation of many rare or new words not listed in this dictionary.

2 One problem is that of deciding the stress pattern of such a word. Most combining form **suffixes** (= second elements) are **stress-neutral** (= they preserve the location of stresses in the first element; the suffix may well be stressed itself). Others are **stress-imposing** (= they cause the main stress to fall on a particular syllable of the first element).

For example, **-graphic** ˈgræf ɪk is stress-neutral, but **-graphy** is stress-imposing (as in **epigraphy** e ˈpɪg rəf i).

3 A first element usually has two different pronunciations, one used with stress-neutral suffixes, the other with stress-imposing suffixes. For the pronunciation of the whole word, the pronunciation for the suffix must be combined with the appropriate pronunciation for the first element.

4 The mark ¦ in the pronunciation of a first element means a stress. This will be a secondary stress (ˌ) if the suffix includes a main stress; if not, it will be a main stress (ˈ). In general, suffixes of two or more syllables are stressed, but those of one syllable are not.

5 For example, take the first element **cata-**.

- With a stress-neutral suffix, it is pronounced ¦kæt ə. Combining this with **-graphic** ˈgræf ɪk we get **catagraphic** ˌkæt ə ˈgræf ɪk. Combining it with **-phyte** faɪt we get **cataphyte** ˈkæt ə faɪt.
- With a stress-imposing suffix, it is pronounced kə ˈtæ⁺. (The sign ⁺ is a reminder that this syllable is incomplete and must attract at least one consonant from the suffix.) Combining **cata-** with **-logy** lədʒ i (stress-imposing) we get **catalogy** kə ˈtæl ədʒ i.

(The words **catagraphic**, **cataphyte**, **catalogy** do not exist. But if they did, we know that this is how they would be pronounced.)

combustive kəm ˈbʌst ɪv §(ˌ)kɒm-
come kʌm —*There is also an occasional weak form* kəm. *See* c'mon **came** keɪm **comes** kʌmz **coming** ˈkʌm ɪŋ
come-all-ye kʌm ˈɔːl ji kə ˈmɔːl-, -jə ‖ -ˈɑːl-
come-at-able ˌkʌm ˈæt əb ᵊl ‖ -ˈæṱ-
comeback ˈkʌm bæk **~s** s
Comecon ˈkɒm i kɒn ‖ ˈkɑːm i kɑːn
comedi... —*see* **comedy**
comedian kə ˈmiːd i‿ən **~s** z
comedic kə ˈmiːd ɪk **~ally** ᵊl‿i
comedienne kə ˌmiːd i ˈen **~s** z
comedo ˈkɒm ɪ dəʊ -ə-; kə ˈmiːd əʊ ‖ ˈkɑːm ə doʊ **~s** z **comedones** ˌkɒm ɪ ˈdəʊn iːz -ə- ‖ ˌkɑːm ə ˈdoʊn iːz
comedown ˈkʌm daʊn **~s** z
comed|y ˈkɒm əd |i -ɪd- ‖ ˈkɑːm- **~ies** iz
come-hither (ˌ)kʌm ˈhɪð ə ‖ -ᵊr -ˈhɪθ-
come|ly ˈkʌm |li **~lier** li‿ə ‖ li‿ᵊr **~liest** li‿ɪst li‿əst **~liness** li nəs li nɪs

Comenius kə ˈmeɪn i‿əs kɒ-, -ˈmiːn-
come-on ˈkʌm ɒn ‖ -ɑːn -ɔːn **~s** z
-comer ˌkʌm ə ‖ -ər — **late-comer** ˈleɪt ˌkʌm ə ‖ -ər **~s** z
comer ˈkʌm ə ‖ -ər **~s** z
Comer *family name* ˈkəʊm ə ‖ ˈkoʊm ər
comestible kə ˈmest əb əl -ɪb- **~s** z
comet ˈkɒm ɪt §-ət ‖ ˈkɑːm- **~s** s
comeuppanc|e ˌkʌm ˈʌp ənts →-mps **~es** ɪz əz
comfit ˈkʌmpf ɪt ˈkɒmpf-, §-ət ‖ ˈkɑːmpf- **~s** s
comf|ort, C~ ˈkʌmpf |ət ‖ -|ərt **~orted** ət ɪd -əd ‖ -ərţ əd **~orting** ət ɪŋ ‖ ərţ ɪŋ **~orts** əts ‖ ərts
ˈcomfort ˌstation
comfortab|le ˈkʌmpft əb |əl ˈkʌmpf ət əb |əl ‖ -ərb-, ˈkʌmpf əţ əb |əl, ˈ·ərţ- **~ly** li **~ness** nəs nɪs
ˌcomfortably ˈoff
comforter ˈkʌmpf ət ə ‖ -ərţ ər -əţ- **~s** z
comfortless ˈkʌmpf ət ləs -lɪs ‖ -ərt-
comfrey ˈkʌmpf ri **~s** z
comf|y ˈkʌmpf |i **~ier** i‿ə ‖ i‿ər **~iest** i‿ɪst i‿əst
comic ˈkɒm ɪk ‖ ˈkɑːm- **~s** s
ˌcomic ˈopera; **ˈcomic strip**
comical ˈkɒm ɪk əl ‖ ˈkɑːm- **~ly** ‿i **~ness** nəs nɪs
Cominform ˈkɒm ɪn ˌfɔːm -ən- ‖ ˈkɑːm ən ˌfɔːrm
coming ˈkʌm ɪŋ **~s** z
coming-out ˌkʌm ɪŋ ˈaʊt
Comintern ˈkɒm ɪn ˌtɜːn -ən- ‖ ˈkɑːm ən ˌtɝːn
Comiskey kə ˈmɪsk i
comit|y ˈkɒm ət |i -ɪt- ‖ ˈkɑːm əţ |i ˈkoʊm- **~ies** iz
comma ˈkɒm ə ‖ ˈkɑːm ə **~s** z
command kə ˈmɑːnd §-ˈmænd ‖ -ˈmænd **~ed** ɪd əd **~ing** ɪŋ **~s** z
comˈmand ˌmodule; **comˌmand perˈformance**
commandant ˈkɒm ən dænt -dɑːnt, ˌ··ˈ· ‖ ˈkɑːm- **~s** s
comman|deer ˌkɒm ən |ˈdɪə -ɑːn-, §-æn- ‖ ˌkɑːm ən |ˈdɪər **~deered** ˈdɪəd ‖ ˈdɪərd **~deering** ˈdɪər ɪŋ ‖ ˈdɪr ɪŋ **~deers** ˈdɪəz ‖ ˈdɪərz
commander kə ˈmɑːnd ə §-ˈmænd- ‖ -ˈmænd ər **~s** z
comˌmander in ˈchief
commanding kə ˈmɑːnd ɪŋ §-ˈmænd- ‖ -ˈmænd- **~ly** li
comˌmanding ˈofficer
commandment kə ˈmɑːn*d* mənt →-ˈmɑːm-, §-ˈmæn*d*- ‖ -ˈmæn*d*- **~s** s
commando kə ˈmɑːnd əʊ §-ˈmænd- ‖ -ˈmænd oʊ **~s** z
comme ci comme ça kɒm ˌsiː kɒm ˈsɑː ‖ kɑːm ˌsiː kɑːm- —*Fr* [kɔm si kɔm sa]
Comme des Garçons *tdmk* ˌkɒm deɪ ˈgɑːs ɒ̃ -gɑː ˈsɒ̃ ‖ ˌkɑːm deɪ gɑːr ˈsoʊn —*Fr* [kɔm de gaʁ sɔ̃]
commedia dell'arte kɒ ˌmeɪd i‿ə del ˈɑːt eɪ kə-, -ˌmed- ‖ kə ˌmeɪd i‿ə del ˈɑːrţ i -ˌmed- —*It* [kom ˈmɛː dja del ˈlar te]
comme il faut ˌkɒm iːəl ˈfəʊ ‖ ˌkʌm iːəl ˈfoʊ ˌkɑːm-, ˌkɔːm- —*Fr* [kɔ mil fo]
commemo|rate kə ˈmem ə |reɪt **~rated** reɪt ɪd -əd ‖ reɪţ əd **~rates** reɪts **~rating** reɪt ɪŋ ‖ reɪţ ɪŋ **~rator/s** reɪt ə/z ‖ reɪţ ər/z
commemoration kə ˌmem ə ˈreɪʃ ən **~s** z
commemorative kə ˈmem ər‿ət ɪv -ə reɪt- ‖ -əţ ɪv -ə reɪţ- **~s** z
commenc|e kə ˈments **~ed** t **~es** ɪz əz **~ing** ɪŋ
commencement kə ˈments mənt **~s** s
commend kə ˈmend **~ed** ɪd əd **~ing** ɪŋ **~s** z
commendab|le kə ˈmend əb |əl **~ly** li
commendation ˌkɒm en ˈdeɪʃ ən -ən- ‖ ˌkɑːm ən- -en- **~s** z
commendatory kə ˈmend ə‿tər i ˌkɒm en ˈdeɪt ər i, ˌ·ən- ‖ -ə tɔːr i -toʊr i
commensal kə ˈments əl **~ism** ˌɪz əm **~ly** i **~s** z
commensurability kə ˌmentʃ ər‿ə ˈbɪl ət i -ˌments-, -jər ə-, -ɪt i ‖ kə ˌments ər‿ə ˈbɪl əţ i
commensurab|le kə ˈmentʃ ər‿əb |əl -ˈments-, -jər əb- ‖ -ˈments- **~ly** li
commensurate kə ˈmentʃ ər‿ət -ˈments-, -jər-, -ɪt ‖ -ˈments- **~ly** li
comment *n* ˈkɒm ent ‖ ˈkɑːm- **~s** s
comm|ent *v* ˈkɒm |ent §kɒ ˈm|ent, kə- ‖ ˈkɑːm- **~ented** ent ɪd -əd ‖ enţ əd **~enting** ent ɪŋ ‖ enţ ɪŋ **~ents** ents
commentar|y ˈkɒm ənt‿ər |i ‖ ˈkɑːm ən ter |i **~ies** iz
commen|tate ˈkɒm ən |teɪt -en- ‖ ˈkɑːm- **~tated** teɪt ɪd -əd ‖ teɪţ əd **~tates** teɪts **~tating** teɪt ɪŋ ‖ teɪţ ɪŋ
commentator ˈkɒm ən teɪt ə ˈ·en- ‖ ˈkɑːm ən teɪţ ər **~s** z
Commer *tdmk* ˈkɒm ə ‖ ˈkɑːm ər **~s** z
commerce ˈkɒm ɜːs ‖ ˈkɑːm ərs kə ˈmɝːs
commercial kə ˈmɜːʃ əl ‖ -ˈmɝːʃ- **~ly** i **~s** z
comˌmercial ˈtraveller
commercialis... —*see* **commercializ...**
commercialism kə ˈmɜːʃ ə ˌlɪz əm -əl ˌɪz- ‖ -ˈmɝːʃ-
commerciality kə ˌmɜːʃ i ˈæl ət i -ɪt i ‖ kə ˌmɝːʃ i ˈæl əţ i
commercialization kə ˌmɜːʃ əl aɪ ˈzeɪʃ ən -əl ɪ- -ˌmɝːʃ əl ə-
commercializ|e kə ˈmɜːʃ ə laɪz -əl aɪz ‖ -ˈmɝːʃ- **~ed** d **~es** ɪz əz **~ing** ɪŋ
commie ˈkɒm i ‖ ˈkɑːm i **~s** z
commination ˌkɒm ɪ ˈneɪʃ ən -ə- ‖ ˌkɑːm-
comminglj|e kɒ ˈmɪŋ gəl kə- ‖ kə- kɑː- **~ed** d **~es** z **~ing** ‿ɪŋ
commi|nute ˈkɒm ɪ |njuːt §-ə- ‖ ˈkɑːm ə |nuːt -njuːt **~nuted** njuːt ɪd -əd ‖ nuːţ əd njuːţ- **~nutes** njuːts ‖ nuːts njuːts **~nuting** njuːt ɪŋ ‖ nuːţ ɪŋ njuːţ-
comminution ˌkɒm ɪ ˈnjuːʃ ən §-ə- ‖ ˌkɑːm ə ˈnuːʃ- -ˈnjuːʃ-
commis ˈkɒm i -ɪs ‖ ˌkɑː ˈmiː ◂ kə-
ˈcommis chef, ˌcommis ˈchef
commise|rate kə ˈmɪz ə |reɪt **~rated** reɪt ɪd -əd ‖ reɪţ əd **~rates** reɪts **~rating** reɪt ɪŋ ‖ reɪţ ɪŋ

ommiseration kə ˌmɪz ə ˈreɪʃ ᵊn **~s** z
ommiserative kə ˈmɪz ər ət ɪv -ə reɪt ɪv ‖ -ə reɪt̬ ɪv **~ly** li
ommissar ˌkɒm ɪ ˈsɑː -ə-, ˈ· · · ‖ ˈkɑːm ə sɑːr **~s** z
ommissariat ˌkɒm ɪ ˈseər i ət ˌ·ə-, -ˈsær-, -ˈsɑːr-, -æt ‖ ˌkɑːm ə ˈser- **~s** s
ommissar|y ˈkɒm ɪs ər |i ˈ·əs- ‖ ˈkɑːm ə ser |i **~ies** iz
ommission kə ˈmɪʃ ᵊn **~ed** d **~ing** ɪŋ **~s** z
comˈmission ˌagent
ommissionaire kə ˌmɪʃ ə ˈneə -ᵊn ˈeə ‖ -ˈneᵊr **~s** z
ommissional kə ˈmɪʃ ᵊn‿əl
ommissionary kə ˈmɪʃ ᵊn‿ər i ‖ -ə ner i
ommissioner kə ˈmɪʃ ᵊn‿ə ‖ ər **~s** z
ommissure ˈkɒm ɪ sjʊə -ə-, -ʃʊə ‖ ˈkɑːm ə ʃʊr **~s** z
ommit kə ˈmɪt **commits** kə ˈmɪts **committed** kə ˈmɪt ɪd -əd ‖ -ˈmɪt̬ əd **committing** kə ˈmɪt ɪŋ ‖ -ˈmɪt̬ ɪŋ
ommitment kə ˈmɪt mənt **~s** s
ommittable kə ˈmɪt əb ᵊl ‖ -ˈmɪt̬-
ommittal kə ˈmɪt ᵊl ‖ -ˈmɪt̬- **~s** z
ommittee kə ˈmɪt i ‖ -ˈmɪt̬ i —*but* ˌkɒm ɪ ˈtiː ‖ ˌkɑːm- *in the obsolete sense 'person to whom someone or something is committed'* **~s** z
comˈmittee ˌstage
ommittee|man kə ˈmɪt i |mən mæn ‖ -ˈmɪt̬- **~men** mən men **~woman** ˌwʊm ən **~women** ˌwɪm ɪn §-ən
ommode kə ˈməʊd ‖ -ˈmoʊd **~s** z
ommodification kə ˌmɒd ɪf ɪ ˈkeɪʃ ᵊn -ˌ·əf-, §-əˈ·- ‖ -ˌmɑːd-
ommodi|fy kə ˈmɒd ɪ| faɪ -ə- ‖ -ˈmɑːd- **~fied** faɪd **~fies** faɪz **~fying** faɪ ɪŋ
ommodious kə ˈməʊd i‿əs ‖ -ˈmoʊd- **~ly** li **~ness** nəs nɪs
ommodit|y kə ˈmɒd ət |i -ɪt- ‖ -ˈmɑːd ət̬ |i **~ies** iz
ommodore ˈkɒm ə dɔː ‖ ˈkɑːm ə dɔːr -doʊr **~s** z
Commodus ˈkɒm əd əs kə ˈməʊd- ‖ ˈkɑːm-
common ˈkɒm ən ‖ ˈkɑːm- **~er** ə ‖ ᵊr **~est** ɪst əst **~ly** li **~ness** nəs nɪs **~s, C~s** z
ˌcommon deˈnominator; ˌCommon ˈMarket; ˌcommon ˈnoun; ˈcommon room; ˌcommon ˈsense
commonage ˈkɒm ən ɪdʒ ‖ ˈkɑːm-
commonalit|y ˌkɒm ə ˈnæl ət |i -ɪt i ‖ ˌkɑːm ə ˈnæl ət̬ |i **~ies** iz
commonal|ty ˈkɒm ən ᵊl |ti ‖ ˈkɑːm- **~ties** tiz
commoner ˈkɒm ən ə ‖ ˈkɑːm ən ᵊr **~s** z
common-law ˌkɒm ən ˈlɔː ◂ ‖ ˌkɑːm- -ˈlɑː
ˌcommon-law ˈmarriage
common-or-garden ˌkɒm ən ɔː ˈgɑːd ᵊn ◂ -əˈ·- ‖ ˌkɑːm ən ᵊr ˈgɑːrd ᵊn ◂
commonplac|e ˈkɒm ən pleɪs →-əm- ‖ ˈkɑːm- **~es** ɪz əz
commonsense ˌkɒm ən ˈsenᵗs ◂ ‖ ˌkɑːm-
ˌcommonsense deˈcision
commonsensical ˌkɒm ən ˈsenᵗs ɪk ᵊl ◂ ‖ ˌkɑːm- **~ly** ˌi
commonsensicality ˌkɒm ən ˌsenᵗs ɪ ˈkæl ət i -ˌ·ə-, -ɪt i ‖ ˌkɑːm ən ˌsenᵗs ɪ ˈkæl ət̬ i
commonweal ˈkɒm ən wiːᵊl ‖ ˈkɑːm-
commonwealth, C~ ˈkɒm ən welθ ‖ ˈkɑːm-
commotion kə ˈməʊʃ ᵊn ‖ -ˈmoʊʃ- **~s** z
commotional kə ˈməʊʃ ᵊn‿əl ‖ -ˈmoʊʃ-
comms kɒmz ‖ kɑːmz

COMMUNAL

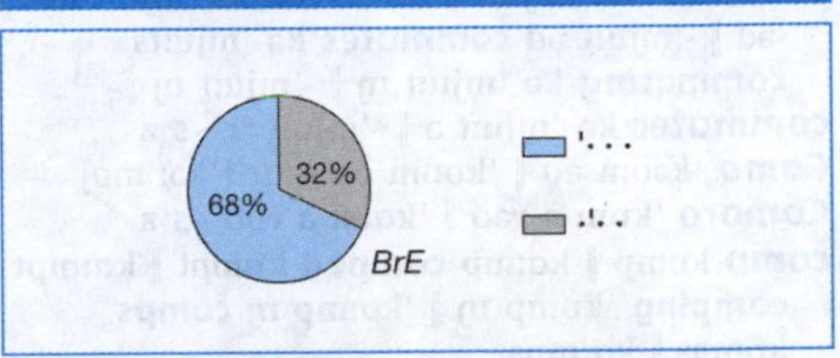

communal ˈkɒm jʊn ᵊl -jən-; kə ˈmjuːn ᵊl ‖ kə ˈmjuːn ᵊl ˈkɑːm jən- — *Preference poll, BrE:* ˈ· · · *68%,* ·ˈ· · *32%.* **~ly** i
communality ˌkɒm ju ˈnæl ət i -ɪt i ‖ ˌkɑːm ju ˈnæl ət̬ i
communard, C~ ˈkɒm ju nɑːd -nɑː ‖ ˈkɑːm ju nɑːrd -nɑːr **~s** z
commun|e *v* kə ˈmjuːn ˈkɒm juːn **~ed** d **~es** z **~ing** ɪŋ
commune, C~ *n* ˈkɒm juːn ‖ ˈkɑːm- kə ˈmjuːn **~s** z
communicability kə ˌmjuːn ɪk ə ˈbɪl ət i -ɪt i ‖ -ət̬ i
communicable kə ˈmjuːn ɪk əb ᵊl **~ness** nəs nɪs
communicant kə ˈmjuːn ɪk ənt **~s** s
communi|cate kə ˈmjuːn ɪ |keɪt -ə- **~cated** keɪt ɪd -əd ‖ keɪt̬ əd **~cates** keɪts **~cating** keɪt ɪŋ ‖ keɪt̬ ɪŋ
communication kə ˌmjuːn ɪ ˈkeɪʃ ᵊn -ə- **~s** z
comˌmuniˈcation cord; comˌmuniˈcations ˌsatellite
communicative kə ˈmjuːn ɪk ət ɪv -ˈ·ək-; -ɪ keɪt-, -ə keɪt- ‖ -ə keɪt̬ ɪv -ɪk ət̬- **~ly** li **~ness** nəs nɪs
comˌmunicative ˈcompetence
communicator kə ˈmjuːn ɪ keɪt ə ‖ -keɪt̬ ᵊr
communion, C~ kə ˈmjuːn i‿ən **~s** z
comˈmunion rail
communique, communiqué kə ˈmjuːn ɪ keɪ -ə- **~s** z
communism, C~ ˈkɒm ju ˌnɪz əm -jə- ‖ ˈkɑːm jə-
communist, C~ ˈkɒm jʊn ɪst -jən-, -juːn-, §-əst ‖ ˈkɑːm jən əst **~s** s
communitarian kə ˌmjuːn ɪ ˈteər i‿ən ◂ -əˈ·- ‖ -ˈter- **~s** z
communit|y kə ˈmjuːn ət |i -ɪt- ‖ -ət̬ |i **~ies** iz
comˈmunity ˌcentre; comˈmunity chest, ·ˌ· · · ˈ·; comˌmunity ˈmedicine; comˌmunity ˈsinging
commutability kə ˌmjuːt ə ˈbɪl ət i -ɪt i ‖ kə ˌmjuːt̬ ə ˈbɪl ət̬ i

C

C

commutable kə ˈmjuːt əb ᵊl ‖ -ˈmjuːt̬-

commu|tate ˈkɒm ju |teɪt ‖ ˈkɑːm jə- **~tated** teɪt ɪd -əd ‖ teɪt̬ əd **~tates** teɪts **~tating** teɪt ɪŋ ‖ teɪt̬ ɪŋ

commutation ˌkɒm ju ˈteɪʃ ᵊn ‖ ˌkɑːm jə- **~s** z

ˌcommu'tation ˌticket

commutative kə ˈmjuːt ət ɪv ˈkɒm ju teɪt ɪv ‖ ˈkɑːm jə teɪt̬ ɪv kə ˈmjuːt̬ ət̬ ɪv **~ly** li

commutator ˈkɒm ju teɪt ə ‖ ˈkɑːm jə teɪt̬ ᵊr **~s** z

commute kə ˈmjuːt **commuted** kə ˈmjuːt ɪd -əd ‖ -ˈmjuːt̬ əd **commutes** kə ˈmjuːts **commuting** kə ˈmjuːt ɪŋ ‖ -ˈmjuːt̬ ɪŋ

commuter kə ˈmjuːt ə ‖ -ˈmjuːt̬ ᵊr **~s** z

Como ˈkəʊm əʊ ‖ ˈkoʊm oʊ —*It* [ˈkɔː mo]

Comoro ˈkɒm ə rəʊ ‖ ˈkɑːm ə roʊ **~s** z

comp kɒmp ‖ kɑːmp **comped** kɒmpt ‖ kɑːmpt **comping** ˈkɒmp ɪŋ ‖ ˈkɑːmp ɪŋ **comps** kɒmps ‖ kɑːmps

compact *v 'press together'* kəm ˈpækt (ˌ)kɒm- ‖ (ˌ)kɑːm- **~ed** ɪd əd **~ing** ɪŋ **~s** s

compact *v 'make an agreement'* ˈkɒm pækt ‖ ˈkɑːm- **~ed** ɪd əd **~ing** ɪŋ **~s** s

compact *adj* kəm ˈpækt (ˌ)kɒm- (ˌ)kɑːm- —*In stress-shifting environments usually* ˌkɒm pækt ‖ ˌkɑːm-, *as if underlyingly* ˌkɒm ˈpækt ◂ ‖ ˌkɑːm- *(even for speakers who otherwise say* kəm ˈpækt*)* **~ly** li **~ness** nəs nɪs

ˌcompact ˈdisc/ˈdisk

compact *n* ˈkɒm pækt ‖ ˈkɑːm-

CompactFlash *tdmk* ˌkɒm pækt ˈflæʃ ‖ ˌkɑːm-

compaction kəm ˈpæk ʃᵊn §(ˌ)kɒm-

compactor kəm ˈpækt ə §(ˌ)kɒm- ‖ -ᵊr **~s** z

compadre kəm ˈpɑːdr eɪ **~s** z

companion kəm ˈpæn jən §(ˌ)kɒm-, -ˈpæn i‿ən **~able** əb ᵊl **~ably** əb li **~ate** ət ɪt **~s** z **~ship** ʃɪp **~way/s** weɪ/z

compan|y ˈkʌmp ən‿|i **~ies** iz

ˌcompany ˈsecretary

Compaq *tdmk* ˈkɒm pæk ‖ ˈkɑːm-

comparability ˌkɒmp ər‿ə ˈbɪl ət i -ɪt i; kəm ˌpær ə-, §kɒm-, -ˌpeər- ‖ ˌkɑːmp ər‿ə ˈbɪl ət̬ i kəm ˌper ə-, -ˌpær-

comparab|le ˈkɒmp ər‿əb |ᵊl kəm ˈpær əb |ᵊl, §(ˌ)kɒm-, -ˈpeər- ‖ ˈkɑːmp- kəm ˈper-, ˈpær- **~ly** li

comparative kəm ˈpær ət ɪv §(ˌ)kɒm- ‖ -ət̬- -ˈper- **~ly** li

comparator kəm ˈpær ət ə §(ˌ)kɒm- ‖ -ət̬ ᵊr -ˈper- **~s** z

com|pare kəm |ˈpeə §(ˌ)kɒm- ‖ -|ˈpeᵊr -ˈpæᵊr **~pared** ˈpeəd ‖ ˈpeᵊrd ˈpæᵊrd **~pares** ˈpeəz ‖ ˈpeᵊrz ˈpæᵊrz **~paring** ˈpeər ɪŋ ‖ ˈper ɪŋ ˈpær-

comparison kəm ˈpær ɪs ən §(ˌ)kɒm-, -əs-, §-ɪz-, §-əz- ‖ -ˈper- **~s** z

comparison-|shop kəm ˈpær ɪs ən |ʃɒp §(ˌ)§kɒm-, -ˈ·əs-, §-·ɪz-, §-·əz- ‖ -|ʃɑːp -ˈper- **~shopping** ˌʃɒp ɪŋ ‖ ˌʃɑːp ɪŋ

compartment *n* kəm ˈpɑːt mənt §(ˌ)kɒm- ‖ -ˈpɑːrt- **~s** s

compartmentalization ˌkɒm pɑːt ˌment ᵊl aɪ ˈzeɪʃ ᵊn -ᵊl ɪ- ‖ kəm ˌpɑːrt ˌment̬ ᵊl ə- ˌkɑːm pɑːrt-

compartmentaliz|e ˌkɒm pɑːt ˈment ᵊl aɪz -ə laɪz ‖ kəm ˌpɑːrt ˈment̬ ᵊl aɪz ˌkɑːm pɑːrt- **~ed** d **~es** ɪz əz **~ing** ɪŋ

compass ˈkʌmp əs §ˈkɒmp- ‖ ˈkɑːmp- **~ed** t **~es** ɪz əz **~ing** ɪŋ

ˈcompass point

compassion kəm ˈpæʃ ᵊn §(ˌ)kɒm-

compassionate kəm ˈpæʃ ᵊn‿ət §(ˌ)kɒm-, ɪt **~ly** li **~ness** nəs nɪs

compatibility kəm ˌpæt ə ˈbɪl ət i §kɒm-, §ˌkɒm pæt-, -ɪˈ·-, -ɪt i ‖ -ˌpæt̬ ə ˈbɪl ət̬ i

compatib|le kəm ˈpæt əb |ᵊl §(ˌ)kɒm-, -ɪb- ‖ -ˈpæt̬- **~ly** li

compatriot kəm ˈpætr i‿ət (ˌ)kɒm- ‖ -ˈpeɪtr- (ˌ)kɑːm-, -ɑːt *(*)* **~s** s

compeer ˈkɒm pɪə ·ˈ· ‖ kəm ˈpɪᵊr (ˌ)kɑːm-, ˈkɑːm pɪr **~s** z

compel kəm ˈpel §(ˌ)kɒm- **~led** d **~ling/ly** ɪŋ /li **~s** z

compellab|le kəm ˈpel əb |ᵊl §(ˌ)kɒm- **~ly** li

compendious kəm ˈpend i‿əs §(ˌ)kɒm- **~ly** li **~ness** nəs nɪs

compendium kəm ˈpend i‿əm §(ˌ)kɒm- **~s** z

compensable kəm ˈpenᵗs əb ᵊl

compen|sate ˈkɒmp ən |seɪt -en- ‖ ˈkɑːmp- **~sated** seɪt ɪd -əd ‖ seɪt̬ əd **~sates** seɪts **~sating** seɪt ɪŋ ‖ seɪt̬ ɪŋ

compensation ˌkɒmp ən ˈseɪʃ ᵊn -en- ‖ ˌkɑːmp- **~s** z

compensatory ˌkɒmp ən ˈseɪt ər i ◂ ˌ·en-, ˈ· · · · ·; kəm ˈpenᵗs ət‿ər i, §(ˌ)kɒm- ‖ kəm ˈpenᵗs ə tɔːr i -toʊr i

compere, compère ˈkɒm peə ‖ ˈkɑːm per **~d** d **~s** z **compering, compèring** ˈkɒm peər ɪŋ ‖ ˈkɑːm per ɪŋ

com|pete kəm |ˈpiːt §(ˌ)kɒm- **~peted** ˈpiːt ɪd -əd ‖ ˈpiːt̬ əd **~petes** ˈpiːts **~peting** ˈpiːt ɪŋ ‖ ˈpiːt̬ ɪŋ

competenc|e ˈkɒmp ɪt ənᵗs -ət- ‖ ˈkɑːmp ət ᵊnᵗs **~y** i

competent ˈkɒmp ɪt ənt -ət- ‖ ˈkɑːmp ət ᵊnt **~ly** li

competition ˌkɒmp ə ˈtɪʃ ᵊn -ɪ- ‖ ˌkɑːmp- **~s** z

competitive kəm ˈpet ət ɪv §(ˌ)kɒm-, -ɪt- ‖ -ˈpet̬ ət̬- **~ly** li **~ness** nəs nɪs

competitor kəm ˈpet ɪt ə §(ˌ)kɒm-, -ət- ‖ -ˈpet̬ ət̬ ᵊr **~s** z

compilation ˌkɒmp ɪ ˈleɪʃ ᵊn -ə-, -aɪ- ‖ ˌkɑːmp- **~s** z

compil|e kəm ˈpaɪᵊl §(ˌ)kɒm- **~ed** d **~es** z **~ing** ɪŋ

compiler kəm ˈpaɪl ə (ˌ)kɒm- ‖ -ᵊr **~s** z

complacenc|e kəm ˈpleɪs ᵊnᵗs §(ˌ)kɒm- **~y** i

complacent kəm ˈpleɪs ᵊnt §(ˌ)kɒm- **~ly** li

complain kəm ˈpleɪn §(ˌ)kɒm- **~ed** d **~er/s** ə/z ‖ ᵊr/z **~ing/ly** ɪŋ /li **~s** z

complainant kəm ˈpleɪn ənt §(ˌ)kɒm- **~s** s

complaint kəm ˈpleɪnt §(ˌ)kɒm- **~s** s

complaisance kəm ˈpleɪz ᵊnᵗs §(ˌ)kɒm- ‖ -ˈpleɪs- -ˈpleɪz-; ˌkɑːm pleɪ ˈzænᵗs, plə-, -ˈzɑːnᵗs, ˌ··ˈ· *(*)*

complaisant kəm ˈpleɪz ᵊnt §(ˌ)kɒm- ‖ -ˈpleɪs- -ˈpleɪz-; ˌkɑːm pleɪ ˈzænt, -plə-, -ˈzɑːnt, ˌ··ˈ· *(*)* **~ly** li

Complan *tdmk* ˈkɒm plæn ‖ ˈkɑːm-

compleat kəm ˈpliːt (ˌ)kɒm-

complected kəm ˈplekt ɪd §(ˌ)kɒm-, -əd

comple|ment *v* ˈkɒmp lɪ |ment -lə-, ˌ··ˈ· ‖ ˈkɑːmp lə- *(= compliment)*—*see note at* -ment **~mented** ment ɪd -əd ‖ menţ əd **~menting** ment ɪŋ ‖ menţ ɪŋ **~ments** ments

complement *n* ˈkɒmp lɪ mənt -lə- ‖ ˈkɑːmp lə- *(= compliment)* **~s** s

complemental ˌkɒmp lɪ ˈment ᵊl ◂ -lə- ‖ ˌkɑːmp lə ˈmenţ ᵊl ◂

complementarity ˌkɒmp lɪ men ˈtær ət i ˌ·lə-, -mən'·-, -ɪt i ‖ ˌkɑːmp lə men ˈtær əţ i -mən'·-, -ˈter-

complementary ˌkɒmp lɪ ˈment ər i ◂ ˌ·lə- ‖ ˌkɑːmp lə ˈmenţ ər i ◂ →-ˈmentr i *(= complimentary)*

ˌcompleˌmentary ˈcolours

complementation ˌkɒmp lɪ men ˈteɪʃ ᵊn ˌ·lə-, -mən'·- ‖ ˌkɑːmp lə-

complementiser, complementizer ˈkɒmp lɪ ment aɪz ə ˈ·lə-, -mən taɪz ə ‖ ˈkɑːmp lə ment aɪz ᵊr -mən taɪz ᵊr **~s** z

com|plete kəm |ˈpliːt §(ˌ)kɒm- **~pleted** ˈpliːt ɪd -əd ‖ ˈpliːţ əd **~pletes** ˈpliːts **~pleting** ˈpliːt ɪŋ ‖ ˈpliːţ ɪŋ

complete|ly kəm ˈpliːt li §(ˌ)kɒm- **~ness** nəs nɪs

completion kəm ˈpliːʃ ᵊn §(ˌ)kɒm- **~s** z

completive kəm ˈpliːt ɪv §(ˌ)kɒm- ‖ -ˈpliːţ-

COMPLEX

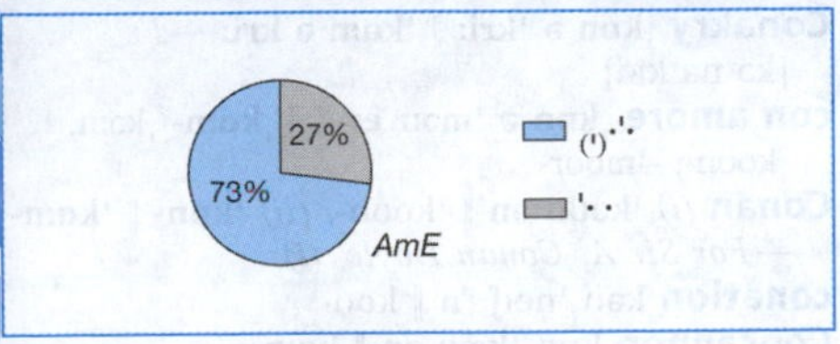

complex *adj* ˈkɒm pleks kəm ˈpleks, ˌkɒm- ‖ ˌkɑːm ˈpleks◂ kəm-, ˈkɑːm pleks — *Preference poll, AmE:* (ˌ)·ˈ· *73%*, ˈ·· *27%*. **~ly** li

ˌcomplex ˈnumber; **ˌcomplex ˈsentence**

complex *n* ˈkɒm pleks ‖ ˈkɑːm- **~es** ɪz əz

complexion kəm ˈplekʃ ᵊn §(ˌ)kɒm- **~ed** d **~s** z

complexit|y kəm ˈpleks ət |i §(ˌ)kɒm-, -ɪt- ‖ -əţ |i **~ies** iz

complianc|e kəm ˈplaɪ‿ənᵗs §(ˌ)kɒm- **~es** ɪz əz **~y** i

compliant kəm ˈplaɪ‿ənt §(ˌ)kɒm- **~ly** li

compli|cate ˈkɒmp lɪ |keɪt -lə- ‖ ˈkɑːmp lə- **~cated** keɪt ɪd -əd ‖ keɪţ əd **~cates** keɪts **~cating** keɪt ɪŋ ‖ keɪţ ɪŋ

complicated ˈkɒmp lɪ keɪt ɪd -əd ‖ ˈkɑːmp lə keɪţ əd **~ly** li **~ness** nəs nɪs

complication ˌkɒmp lɪ ˈkeɪʃ ᵊn -lə- ‖ ˌkɑːmp lə- **~s** z

complicit kəm ˈplɪs ɪt §kɒm-, -ət

complicity kəm ˈplɪs ət i §(ˌ)kɒm-, -ɪt- ‖ -əţ i

complie... —*see* **comply**

compliment *n* ˈkɒmp lɪ mənt -lə- ‖ ˈkɑːmp lə- **~s** s

compli|ment *v* ˈkɒmp lɪ |ment -lə-, ˌ··ˈ· ‖ ˈkɑːmp lə- —*see note at* -ment **~mented** ment ɪd -əd ‖ menţ əd **~menting** ment ɪŋ ‖ menţ ɪŋ **~ments** ments

complimentar|y ˌkɒmp lɪ ˈment‿ər |i ◂ ˌ·lə- ‖ ˌkɑːmp lə ˈmenţ ər |i ◂ →-ˈmentr |i **~ies** iz **~ily** əl i ɪ li **~iness** i nəs i nɪs

complin ˈkɒmp lɪn -lən ‖ ˈkɑːmp-

compline ˈkɒmp lɪn -lən, -laɪn ‖ ˈkɑːmp-

com|ply kəm |ˈplaɪ §(ˌ)kɒm- **~plied** ˈplaɪd **~plies** ˈplaɪz **~plying** ˈplaɪ ɪŋ

compo ˈkɒmp əʊ ‖ ˈkɑːmp oʊ

component kəm ˈpəʊn ənt §(ˌ)kɒm- ‖ -ˈpoʊn- **~s** s

comˌponent ˈparts

componential ˌkɒmp əʊ ˈnenᵗʃ ᵊl ◂ ‖ ˌkɑːmp ə-

com|port *v* kəm |ˈpɔːt §(ˌ)kɒm- ‖ -|ˈpɔːrt -ˈpoʊrt **~ported** ˈpɔːt ɪd -əd ‖ ˈpɔːrţ əd ˈpoʊrţ- **~porting** ˈpɔːt ɪŋ ‖ ˈpɔːrţ ɪŋ ˈpoʊrţ- **~ports** ˈpɔːts ‖ ˈpɔːrts ˈpoʊrts

comportment kəm ˈpɔːt mənt §(ˌ)kɒm- ‖ -ˈpɔːrt- -ˈpoʊrt-

compos|e kəm ˈpəʊz §(ˌ)kɒm- ‖ -ˈpoʊz **~ed** d **~es** ɪz əz **~ing** ɪŋ

composedly kəm ˈpəʊz ɪd li §(ˌ)kɒm-, -əd· ‖ -ˈpoʊz-

composer kəm ˈpəʊz ə §(ˌ)kɒm- ‖ -ˈpoʊz ᵊr **~s** z

Compositae kəm ˈpɒz ɪ taɪ §(ˌ)kɒm-, -ə-, -tiː ‖ -ˈpɑːz-

composite *adj* ˈkɒmp əz ɪt -əs-, §-ət; -ə zaɪt, -saɪt ‖ kəm ˈpɑːz ət kɑːm- **~s** s

composite *v* ˈkɒmp ə zaɪt -saɪt, ˌ··ˈ·; kəm ˈpɒz ɪt ‖ kəm ˈpɑːz ət kɑːm- **composited** ˈkɒmp ə zaɪt ɪd -saɪt ɪd, -əd, ˌ··ˈ·; kəm ˈpɒz ɪt- ‖ kəm ˈpɑːz əţ əd kɑːm- **composites** ˈkɒmp ə zaɪts -saɪts, ˌ··ˈ·; kəm ˈpɒz ɪts ‖ kəm ˈpɑːz əts kɑːm- **compositing** ˈkɒmp ə zaɪt ɪŋ -saɪt ɪŋ, ˌ··ˈ·; kəm ˈpɒz ɪt ɪŋ ‖ kəm ˈpɑːz əţ ɪŋ kɑːm-

composition ˌkɒmp ə ˈzɪʃ ᵊn ‖ ˌkɑːmp- **~s** z

compositional ˌkɒmp ə ˈzɪʃ ᵊn‿əl ◂ ‖ ˌkɑːmp-

compositor kəm ˈpɒz ɪt ə §(ˌ)kɒm-, -ət- ‖ -ˈpɑːz əţ ᵊr **~s** z

compos mentis ˌkɒmp əs ˈment ɪs ˌkɒm pɒs-, §-əs ‖ ˌkɑːmp əs ˈmenţ əs ˌkoʊm poʊs-

compost ˈkɒmp ɒst ‖ ˈkɑːm poʊst *(*)* **~ed** ɪd əd **~ing** ɪŋ **~s** s

composure kəm ˈpəʊʒ ə §(ˌ)kɒm- ‖ -ˈpoʊʒ ᵊr

compote ˈkɒm pəʊt -pɒt ‖ ˈkɑːm poʊt **~s** s

compound *v* kəm ˈpaʊnd (ˌ)kɒm-, ˈ·· **~ed** ɪd əd **~ing** ɪŋ **~s** z

compound *n* ˈkɒm paʊnd ‖ ˈkɑːm- **~s** z

compound *adj* 'kɒm paʊnd ‖ 'kɑːm- kəm 'paʊnd, ˌkɑːm 'paʊnd ◂ ˌ**compound 'fracture**; ˌ**compound 'interest**; ˌ**compound 'tense**
comprehend ˌkɒmp rɪ 'hend -rə- ‖ ˌkɑːm- **~ed** ɪd əd **~ing** ɪŋ **~s** z
comprehensibility ˌkɒmp rɪ ˌhenᵗs ə 'bɪl ət i ˌ·rə-, -ˌ·ɪ-, -ɪt i ‖ ˌkɑːmp rɪ ˌhenᵗs ə 'bɪl əţ i
comprehensib|le ˌkɒmp rɪ 'henᵗs əb |əl ,·rə-, -ɪb əl ‖ ˌkɑːmp- **~ly** li
comprehension ˌkɒmp rɪ 'henᵗʃ ən -rə- ‖ ˌkɑːmp-
comprehensive ˌkɒmp rɪ 'henᵗs ɪv ◂ -rə- ‖ ˌkɑːmp- **~ly** li **~s** z
comprehensivis... —*see* **comprehensiviz...**
comprehensivization ˌkɒmp rɪ ˌhenᵗs ɪv aɪ 'zeɪʃ ən ,·rə-, -ɪ'-- ‖ ˌkɑːmp rɪ ˌhenᵗs ɪv ə-
comprehensiviz|e ˌkɒmp rɪ 'henᵗs ɪ vaɪz ˌ·rə- ‖ ˌkɑːmp- **~ed** d **~es** ɪz əz **~ing** ɪŋ
compress *n* 'kɒm pres ‖ 'kɑːm- **~es** ɪz əz
compress *v* kəm 'pres §₍₁₎kɒm- **~ed** t **~es** ɪz əz **~ing** ɪŋ
com,**pressed 'air**
compressibility kəm ˌpres ə 'bɪl ət i §kɒm-, §ˌkɒm pres-, -ˌ·ɪ-, -ɪt i ‖ -əţ i
compressible kəm 'pres əb əl §₍₁₎kɒm-
compression kəm 'preʃ ən §₍₁₎kɒm- **~s** z
compressor kəm 'pres ə §₍₁₎kɒm- ‖ -ər **~s** z
compris|e kəm 'praɪz §₍₁₎kɒm- **~ed** d **~es** ɪz əz **~ing** ɪŋ
compromis|e 'kɒmp rə maɪz ‖ 'kɑːmp- **~ed** d **~es** ɪz əz **~ing** ɪŋ
comptometer, C~ *tdmk* ˌkɒmp 'tɒm ɪt ə -ət- ‖ ˌkɑːmp 'tɑːm əţ ər **~s** z
Compton *(i)* 'kɒmpt ən ‖ 'kɑːmpt ən, *(ii)* 'kʌmpt ən
comptroller kən 'trəʊl ə kəmp-, ₍₁₎kɒmp-, §₍₁₎kɒn- ‖ -'troʊl ər kɑːmp-, '·,·· **~s** z
compulsion kəm 'pʌlʃ ən §₍₁₎kɒm- **~s** z
compulsive kəm 'pʌls ɪv §₍₁₎kɒm- **~ly** li **~ness** nəs nɪs
compulsor|y kəm 'pʌls ər|i **~ily** əl i ɪ li **~iness** i nəs i nɪs
compunction kəm 'pʌŋk ʃən §₍₁₎kɒm-
computability kəm ˌpjuːt ə 'bɪl ət i §kɒm-, §ˌkɒm pjuːt-, ˌkɒm pjʊt-, -ɪt i ‖ -ˌpjuːţ ə 'bɪl əţ i
computable kəm 'pjuːt əb əl 'kɒm pjʊt- ‖ -'pjuːţ-
computation ˌkɒm pju 'teɪʃ ən ‖ ˌkɑːm- **~s** z
computational ˌkɒm pju 'teɪʃ ən‿əl ◂ ‖ ˌkɑːm- **~ly** i
com|pute kəm |'pjuːt §₍₁₎kɒm- **~puted** 'pjuːt ɪd -əd ‖ 'pjuːţ əd **~putes** 'pjuːts **~puting** 'pjuːt ɪŋ ‖ 'pjuːţ ɪŋ
computer kəm 'pjuːt ə §₍₁₎kɒm- ‖ -'pjuːţ ər **~s** z
com'puter ˌlanguage
computer-aided kəm ˌpjuːt ər'eɪd ɪd ◂ §₍₁₎kɒm-, -əd ‖ -ˌpjuːţ ər-
computer-assisted kəm ˌpjuːt ərə 'sɪst ɪd ◂ §₍₁₎kɒm-, -əd ‖ -ˌpjuːţ ər-
computerate kəm 'pjuːt ər ət §₍₁₎kɒm-, -ɪt ‖ -'pjuːţ-
computer-based kəm ˌpjuːt ə 'beɪst ◂ §₍₁₎kɒm- ‖ -ˌpjuːţ ər-
computeris... —*see* **computeriz...**
computerization kəm ˌpjuːt ə raɪ 'zeɪʃ ən §₍₁₎kɒm-, -ər ɪ- ‖ -ˌpjuːţ ər ə-
computeriz|e kəm 'pjuːt ə raɪz §₍₁₎kɒm- ‖ -'pjuːţ- **~ed** d **~es** ɪz əz **~ing** ɪŋ
comrade 'kɒm reɪd 'kʌm-, -rɪd, -rəd ‖ 'kɑːm ræd -rəd *(*)* **~ly** li **~s** z **~ship** ʃɪp
Comrie 'kɒm ri ‖ 'kɑːm-
coms kɒmz ‖ kɑːmz
comsat, C~ *tdmk* 'kɒm sæt ‖ 'kɑːm- **~s** s
Comstock 'kɒm stɒk 'kʌm- ‖ 'kɑːm stɑːk
comstockery 'kɒm stɒk ər i 'kʌm-, ˌ·'·· ‖ 'kɑːm stɑːk-
Comte kɒnt kɔːnt ‖ koʊnt —*Fr* [kɔ̃ːt]
Comus 'kəʊm əs ‖ 'koʊm-
Comyn 'kʌm ɪn §-ən
Comyns 'kʌm ɪnz §-ənz
con, Con kɒn ‖ kɑːn —*but as an Italian prep, in AmE also* kɔːn, koʊn **conned** kɒnd ‖ kɑːnd **conning** 'kɒn ɪŋ ‖ 'kɑːn ɪŋ **cons** kɒnz ‖ kɑːnz —*see also phrases with this word.*
con- *This prefix is pronounced stressed* **kɒn** ‖ **kɑːn** *(1) if the following syllable is unstressed* (ˌconfron'tation), *(2) in many two-syllable noun* ('contract, *but* con'trol); *and (3) in context, when contrastively stressed* (ˌuniˌformity and 'conˌformity). *Otherwise it is usually weak* **kən** *in RP and GenAm, though strong in some regional British speech* (con'sider). *Before a stem beginning* **n**, *one* **n** *is lost* (con'nect, ˌconno'tation).
Cona *tdmk* 'kəʊn ə ‖ 'koʊn ə
conacre 'kɒn ˌeɪk ə kən 'eɪk ə ‖ 'kɑːn ˌeɪk ər **~s** z
Conakry ˌkɒn ə 'kriː ‖ 'kɑːn ə kriː —*Fr* [kɔ na kʁi]
con amore ˌkɒn ə 'mɔːr eɪ -i ‖ ˌkɑːn- ˌkɔːn, ˌkoʊn-, -'moʊr-
Conan *(i)* 'kəʊn ən ‖ 'koʊn-, *(ii)* 'kɒn- ‖ 'kɑːn- —*For Sir A. Conan Doyle, (i)*
conation kəʊ 'neɪʃ ən ‖ koʊ-
Concannon kɒn 'kæn ən ‖ kɑːn-
concate|nate kən 'kæt ə |neɪt →kəŋ-, ₍₁₎kɒn-, →₍₁₎kɒŋ-, -ɪ-, -ə|n eɪt ‖ kɑːn 'kæt ə|n eɪt **~nated** neɪt ɪd -əd ‖ neɪţ əd **~nates** neɪts **~nating** neɪt ɪŋ ‖ neɪţ ɪŋ
concatenation kən ˌkæt ə 'neɪʃ ən →kəŋ-, kɒn-, ˌkɒn kæt-, ˌɪ'--, -ən eɪʃ- ‖ kɑːn ˌkæt ən 'eɪʃ ən ˌ·--- **~s** z
concatenative kən 'kæt ən‿ət ɪv →kəŋ-, ₍₁₎kɒn-, →₍₁₎kɒŋ-, -'·ɪn-, -ə neɪt-, -ɪ neɪt- ‖ ₍₁₎kɑːn 'kæt ən eɪţ ɪv
concave ₍₁₎kɒn 'keɪv ◂ →₍₁₎kɒŋ-, kən-, →kəŋ-, '·· ‖ ₍₁₎kɑːn- **~ly** li **~ness** nəs nɪs
concavit|y ₍₁₎kɒn 'kæv ət |i →₍₁₎kɒŋ-, kən-, →kəŋ-, -ɪt- ‖ ₍₁₎kɑːn 'kæv əţ |i **~ies** iz
concavo-concave kɒn ˌkeɪv əʊ kɒn 'keɪv ◂ kən-, -kən'· ‖ kɑːn ˌkeɪv oʊ kɑːn 'keɪv

Compounds and phrases

1 A two-element **compound** is typically pronounced with **early stress**: that is to say, its first element has more stress than its second.

ˈbedtime ˈbed taɪm

ˈblockˌbuster ˈblɒk ˌbʌst ə ‖ ˈblɑːk ˌbʌst ᵊr

Although many compounds are written as single words, others are written as two words.

ˈChristmas card

ˈvisitors' book

ˈmusic ˌlessons

ˈbeauty ˌcontest

2 On the other hand, a **phrase** is typically pronounced with **late stress**: that is to say, the second of two words has more stress than the first.

ˌnext ˈtime

ˌprinted ˈcards

ˌseveral ˈbooks

ˌweekly ˈlessons

3 These stress patterns, and all others, can be changed if the speaker wants to emphasize a particular contrast (to focus on a particular element).

I ˌdon't want ˌmusic ˈlessons – ˌjust some ˌtime to ˈpractise!

It ˌwasn't a ˌbeauty ˈcontest – ˌmore a ˌbeauty comˈmercial.

The stress patterns shown in this dictionary are those that apply if *no* special emphasis (no contrastive focus) is required.

4 Some expressions, grammatically compounds, are nevertheless pronounced with late stress (= as if they were phrases). Among them are compounds in which the first element names the **material or ingredient** of which a thing is made.

a ˌrubber ˈduck

ˌpaper ˈplates

ˌcheese ˈsandwiches

a ˌpork ˈpie

a ˌgold ˈring

However, expressions involving **cake, juice** and **water** take early stress.

ˈalmond cake

ˈorange juice

ˈbarley ˌwater

5 Names of roads and streets all take late stress except those involving **street** itself, which take early stress.

ˌMelrose ˈRoad

ˌLavender ˈCrescent

ˌOxford ˈSquare

ˌKing's ˈAvenue but **ˈGower Street**

concavo-convex kɒn ˌkeɪv əʊ kɒn ˈveks ◂ kən-, -kən'· ‖ kɑːn ˌkeɪv oʊ kɑːn ˈveks
conceal kən ˈsiːᵊl §$_{(ı)}$kɒn- **~ed** d **~ing** ɪŋ **~ment** mənt **~s** z
conced|e kən ˈsiːd §$_{(ı)}$kɒn- **~ed** ɪd əd **~es** z **~ing** ɪŋ
conceit kən ˈsiːt §$_{(ı)}$kɒn- **~s** s
conceited kən ˈsiːt ɪd §$_{(ı)}$kɒn-, -əd ‖ -ˈsiːţ əd **~ly** li **~ness** nəs nɪs
conceivab|le kən ˈsiːv əb |ᵊl §$_{(ı)}$kɒn- **~ly** li
conceiv|e kən ˈsiːv §$_{(ı)}$kɒn- **~ed** d **~er/s** ə/z ‖ ᵊr/z **~es** z **~ing** ɪŋ
concele|brate ˌkɒn ˈsel ə |breɪt kən-, -ɪ- ‖ ˌkɑːn- **~brated** breɪt ɪd -əd ‖ breɪţ əd **~brates** breɪts **~brating** breɪt ɪŋ ‖ breɪţ ɪŋ
concelebration ˌkɒn ˌsel ə ˈbreɪʃ ᵊn kən ˌsel-, -ɪ'-- ‖ ˌkɑːn- **~s** z
concen|trate ˈkɒnᵗs ᵊn |treɪt -en- ‖ ˈkɑːnᵗs- **~trated** treɪt ɪd -əd ‖ treɪţ əd **~trates** treɪts **~trating** treɪt ɪŋ ‖ treɪţ ɪŋ
concentration ˌkɒnᵗs ᵊn ˈtreɪʃ ᵊn -en- ‖ ˌkɑːnᵗs- **~s** z
ˌconcen'tration camp
concentrator ˈkɒnᵗs ᵊn treɪt ə ˈ·en- ‖ ˈkɑːnᵗs ᵊn treɪţ ᵊr **~s** z
concentric kən ˈsentr ɪk $_{(ı)}$kɒn- ‖ $_{(ı)}$kɑːn- **~ally** ᵊl‿i
concept ˈkɒn sept ‖ ˈkɑːn- **~s** s
conception kən ˈsep ʃᵊn §$_{(ı)}$kɒn- **~s** z
conceptual kən ˈsep tʃu‿əl §$_{(ı)}$kɒn-, -ʃu‿əl; -ˈsept ju‿ ‖ kɑːn-, -ˈsep tʃəl
conceptualis... —*see* **conceptualiz...**
conceptualization kən ˌsep tʃu‿əl aɪ ˈzeɪʃ ᵊn §kɒn-, -ˌ·ʃu‿əl-, -ˌsept ju‿, -ɪ'-- ‖ -ə ˈzeɪʃ- kɑːn-, -ˌsep tʃəl ə ˈzeɪʃ- **~s** z
conceptualiz|e kən ˈsep tʃu‿ə laɪz §$_{(ı)}$kɒn-, -ˈsept ju‿; -ˈsep tʃu laɪz, -ˈsep tʃə laɪz ‖ kɑːn-, -ˈsep ʃu‿ **~ed** d **~es** ɪz əz **~ing** ɪŋ
conceptually kən ˈsep tʃu‿əl i §$_{(ı)}$kɒn-, -ʃu‿əl i; -ˈsept ju‿ ‖ kɑːn-, -ˈsep tʃəl i
concern kən ˈsɜːn §$_{(ı)}$kɒn- ‖ -ˈsɜ˞ːn **~ed** d **~ing** ɪŋ **~s** z
concerned|ly kən ˈsɜːn ɪd |li §$_{(ı)}$kɒn-, -əd-; -ˈsɜːnd |li ‖ -ˈsɜ˞ːn əd- **~ness** nəs nɪs
con|cert *v* kən |ˈsɜːt §$_{(ı)}$kɒn- ‖ -|ˈsɜ˞ːt **~certed** ˈsɜːt ɪd -əd ‖ ˈsɜ˞ːţ əd **~certing** ˈsɜːt ɪŋ ‖ ˈsɜ˞ːţ ɪŋ **~certs** ˈsɜːts ‖ ˈsɜ˞ːts
concert *n 'agreement'* ˈkɒnᵗs ət ˈkɒn sɜːt ‖ ˈkɑːnᵗs ᵊrt ˈkɑːn sɜ˞ːt
concert *n 'musical performance'* ˈkɒnᵗs ət ‖ ˈkɑːnᵗs ᵊrt **~s** s
ˌconcert 'grand
concertante ˌkɒntʃ ə ˈtænt eɪ -i ‖ ˌkoʊn tʃᵊr ˈtɑːnt eɪ
concerted kən ˈsɜːt ɪd §$_{(ı)}$kɒn-, -əd ‖ -ˈsɜ˞ːţ əd **~ly** li
Concertgebouw $_{(ı)}$kɒn ˈsɜːt gə baʊ kən-, -gɪ baʊ ‖ kɑːn ˈsɜ˞ːt- —*Dutch* [kɔn ˈsɛrt χə ˌbʌu]
concertgo|er ˈkɒnᵗs ət ˌgəʊ |ə ‖ ˈkɑːnᵗs ᵊrt ˌgoʊ |ᵊr **~ers** əz ‖ ᵊrz **~ing** ɪŋ
concerti kən ˈtʃeət iː §$_{(ı)}$kɒn-, -ˈtʃɜːt- ‖ -ˈtʃerţ iː
conˌcerti 'grossi ˈgrɒs iː ‖ ˈgroʊs iː
concertina ˌkɒnᵗs ə ˈtiːn ə ‖ ˌkɑːnᵗs ᵊr- **~ed** d
concertinaing ˌkɒnᵗs ə ˈtiːn əʳ ɪŋ ‖ ˌkɑːnᵗs ᵊr ˈtiːn ə ɪŋ **~s** z
concertin|o ˌkɒntʃ ə ˈtiːn |əʊ ‖ ˌkɑːntʃ ᵊr ˈtiːn |oʊ **~i** iː **~os** əʊz ‖ oʊz
concertmaster ˈkɒnᵗs ət ˌmɑːst ə §-mæst- ‖ ˈkɑːnᵗs ᵊrt ˌmæst ᵊr **~s** z
concert|o kən ˈtʃeət |əʊ §$_{(ı)}$kɒn-, -ˈtʃɜːt- ‖ -ˈtʃerţ |oʊ **~i** iː **~os** əʊz ‖ oʊz
conˌcerto 'grosso ˈgrɒs əʊ ‖ ˈgroʊs oʊ
concession kən ˈseʃ ᵊn §$_{(ı)}$kɒn- **~s** z
concessionaire kən ˌseʃ ə ˈneə §$_{(ı)}$kɒn- ‖ -ˈneᵊr **~s** z
concessionary kən ˈseʃ ᵊn ər‿i -ᵊn‿ər i ‖ -ə ner i
concessive kən ˈses ɪv §$_{(ı)}$kɒn-
conch kɒŋk kɒntʃ ‖ kɑːŋk kɑːntʃ, kɔːŋk **conches** ˈkɒntʃ ɪz -əz ‖ ˈkɑːntʃ ɪz **conchs** kɒŋks ‖ kɑːŋks kɔːŋks
conch|a ˈkɒŋk |ə ‖ ˈkɑːŋk |ə **~ae** iː
conchie ˈkɒnᵗʃ i ‖ ˈkɑːnᵗʃ i **~s** z
Conchobar ˈkɒn u‿ə ˈkɒŋk əʊ ə ‖ ˈkɑːn u‿ᵊr ˈkɑːŋk oʊ ᵊr
conchoid ˈkɒŋk ɔɪd ‖ ˈkɑːŋk- **~s** z
conchoidal kɒŋ ˈkɔɪd ᵊl ‖ kɑːŋ-
conchological ˌkɒŋk ə ˈlɒdʒ ɪk ᵊl ◂ ‖ ˌkɑːŋk ə ˈlɑːdʒ- **~ly** ‿i
conchologist $_{(ı)}$kɒŋ ˈkɒl ədʒ ɪst $_{(ı)}$kɒn-, §-əst ‖ $_{(ı)}$kɑːŋ ˈkɑːl- **~s** s
conchology $_{(ı)}$kɒŋ ˈkɒl ədʒ i $_{(ı)}$kɒn- ‖ $_{(ı)}$kɑːŋ ˈkɑːl-
concierg|e ˈkɒn si eəʒ ˈkɔ̃-, ˌ·ˈ·· ‖ koʊn ˈsjeᵊrʒ —*Fr* [kɔ̃ sjɛʁʒ] **~es** ɪz əz
conciliar kən ˈsɪl i‿ə §$_{(ı)}$kɒn- ‖ ‿ᵊr
concili|ate kən ˈsɪl i |eɪt §$_{(ı)}$kɒn- **~ated** eɪt ɪd -əd ‖ eɪţ əd **~ates** eɪts **~ating** eɪt ɪŋ ‖ eɪţ ɪŋ
conciliation kən ˌsɪl i ˈeɪʃ ᵊn §$_{(ı)}$kɒn- **~s** z
conciliator kən ˈsɪl i eɪt ə ‖ -eɪţ ᵊr **~s** z
conciliatory kən ˈsɪl i‿ət‿ər i §$_{(ı)}$kɒn-, -i eɪt ər i; kən ˌsɪl i ˈeɪt ər i ‖ -i‿ə tɔːr i -toʊr i
concise kən ˈsaɪs §$_{(ı)}$kɒn- **~ly** li **~ness** nəs nɪs
concision kən ˈsɪʒ ᵊn §$_{(ı)}$kɒn-
conclave ˈkɒŋ kleɪv ˈkɒn- ‖ ˈkɑːn- **~s** z
conclud|e kən ˈkluːd →kəŋ-, §$_{(ı)}$kɒn- **~ed** ɪd əd **~es** z **~ing** ɪŋ
conclusion kən ˈkluːʒ ᵊn →kəŋ-, §$_{(ı)}$kɒn- **~s** z
conclusive kən ˈkluːs ɪv →kəŋ-, §$_{(ı)}$kɒn-, §-ˈkluːz- **~ly** li **~ness** nəs nɪs
conclusory kən ˈkluːs ər i →kəŋ-, §(ˌ)kɒn-, -ˈkluːz-
concoct kən ˈkɒkt →kəŋ-, §$_{(ı)}$kɒn- ‖ -ˈkɑːkt **~ed** ɪd əd **~ing** ɪŋ **~s** s
concoction kən ˈkɒk ʃᵊn →kəŋ-, §$_{(ı)}$kɒn- ‖ -ˈkɑːk- **~s** z
concomitanc|e kən ˈkɒm ɪt ənᵗs →kəŋ-, §$_{(ı)}$kɒn-, -ət- ‖ -ˈkɑːm ət ᵊnᵗs **~y** i
concomitant kən ˈkɒm ɪt ənt →kəŋ-, §$_{(ı)}$kɒn-, -ət- ‖ -ˈkɑːm ət ᵊnt **~ly** li **~s** s
concord ˈkɒŋ kɔːd ˈkɒn- ‖ ˈkɑːn kɔːrd →ˈkɑːŋ- **~s** z
Concord *(i)* ˈkɒŋ kɔːd ˈkɒn- ‖ ˈkɑːn kɔːrd →ˈkɑːŋ-, *(ii)* ˈkɒŋk əd ˈkɒn kɔːd, ˈkɒŋ-

Compression

1 Sometimes a sequence of sounds has two possible pronunciations: either as two separate syllables, or **compressed** into a single syllable. Possible compressions are shown in this dictionary by the symbol ‿ between the syllables affected.

lenient	ˈliːn i‿ənt	Two pronunciations are possible: a slower one ˈliːn i ənt, and a faster one ˈliːn jənt.
maddening	ˈmæd ᵊn‿ɪŋ	Two pronunciations are possible: a slower one with three syllables, ˈmæd n ɪŋ or ˈmæd ən ɪŋ and a faster one with two syllables, ˈmæd nɪŋ.
diagram	ˈdaɪ‿ə græm	Two pronunciations are possible: a slower one ˈdaɪ ə græm, and a faster one ˈdaə græm.

2 Generally the uncompressed version is more usual

- in rarer words
- in slow or deliberate speech
- the first time a word is used in a given discourse.

The compressed version is more usual

- in frequently used words
- in fast or casual speech
- if the word has already been used in the discourse.

3 When a syllable is compressed, one of the following phonetic changes takes place. (They are also exemplified in 1 above.)

- A weak vowel i or u is changed into the corresponding semivowel, j or w, producing in combination with the following vowel a crescendo DIPHTHONG.
  influence ˈɪn flu‿ənᵗs (= ˈɪn.flu.ənᵗs or ˈɪn.flwənᵗs)
- A syllabic consonant is changed into a plain non-syllabic consonant. (See SYLLABIC CONSONANTS for this dictionary's use of superscript schwa (ᵊ) to indicate a potential syllabic consonant.)
  doubling ˈdʌb ᵊl‿ɪŋ (= ˈdʌb.l.ɪŋ or ˈdʌb.lɪŋ)
- A long vowel or diphthong changes: iː becomes ɪ, uː becomes ʊ, and a diphthong loses its second element, so that aɪ and aʊ become a. In this dictionary this possibility is shown by printing the length-mark or the second element in italics (i*ː*, a*ɪ*, a*ʊ*). These changes, known as **smoothing**, are often to be heard in BrE RP, but not in GenAm.
  agreeable ə ˈgriː‿əb ᵊl (= ə.ˈgriː.əb.l or ə.ˈgrɪəb.l)
  ruinous ˈruː‿ɪn əs (= ˈruː.ɪn.əs or ˈrʊɪn.əs)
  scientist ˈsaɪ‿ənt ɪst (= ˈsaɪ.ənt.ɪst or ˈsaənt.ɪst)
  nowadays ˈnaʊ‿ə deɪz (= ˈnaʊ.ə.deɪz or ˈnaə.deɪz)

4 In the case of two potential syllabic consonants, it is always the one **before** the mark ‿ that can lose its syllabicity through compression.

national ˈnæʃ ᵊn‿əl (= ˈnæʃ.n.əl or ˈnæʃ.nəl)
liberal ˈlɪb ᵊr‿əl (= ˈlɪb.r.əl or ˈlɪb.rəl)

Compression ▸

Compression continued

5 Sometimes a pronunciation that was originally the result of compression has become the only possibility. For example, the comparative of **simple** ˈsɪmp ᵊl might be expected to be **simpler** ˈsɪmp ᵊl ə ‖ -ər (three syllables). In fact it is always ˈsɪmp lə ‖ -lᵊr (two syllables). There are also words where speakers differ: most people always pronounce **factory** ˈfæk tri with two syllables, but a few may sometimes say it with three, ˈfækt ər i.

Many historical compressions are shown as such in the spelling: **angry, disastrous, remembrance**. In such words an uncompressed pronunciation (e.g. ri ˈmem bər ənᵗs) is not considered standard.

‖ **ˈkɑːŋk ᵊrd** —*The place in NC is (i), that in MA (ii). Authorities disagree about the places in CA and NH.*

concordanc|e kən ˈkɔːd ᵊnᵗs →kəŋ-, §₍ₗ₎kɒn- ‖ -ˈkɔːrd- kɑːn- **~ed** t **~es** ɪz əz **~ing** ɪŋ

concordant kən ˈkɔːd ᵊnt →kəŋ-, §₍ₗ₎kɒn- ‖ -ˈkɔːrd ᵊnt **~ly** li

concordat kɒn ˈkɔːd æt →kɒŋ-, kən-, →kəŋ- ‖ kən ˈkɔːrd æt **~s** s

Concorde *aircraft* ˈkɒŋ kɔːd ˈkɒn- ‖ ˈkɑːn kɔːrd →ˈkɑːŋ-, ·ˈ· **~s** z

concours ˈkɒŋ kʊə ‖ koʊn ˈkʊᵊr —*Fr* [kɔ̃ kuːʁ]

ˌconcours/conˌcours d'eleˈgance, c~ d'éléˈgance ˌdel eɪ ˈgɒnᵗs ‖ ˌdeɪ leɪ ˈgɑːnᵗs —*Fr* [de le gɑ̃ːs]

concours|e ˈkɒŋ kɔːs ˈkɒn- ‖ ˈkɑːn kɔːrs →ˈkɑːŋ-, -koʊrs **~es** ɪz əz

concrete *n; adj 'made of ~'* ˈkɒŋ kriːt ˈkɒn- ‖ ˈkɑːn- ₍ₗ₎·ˈ·

ˌconcrete ˈjungle; **ˈconcrete ˌmixer**

concrete *adj 'not abstract'* ˈkɒŋ kriːt ˈkɒn- ‖ ₍ₗ₎kɑːn ˈkriːt ˈ· ·, kən ˈkriːt **~ly** li **~ness** nəs nɪs

con|crete *v 'cover with ~'* ˈkɒŋ |kriːt ˈkɒn- ‖ ˈkɑːn- ₍ₗ₎·ˈ· **~creted** kriːt ɪd -əd ‖ kriːt̬ əd **~cretes** kriːts **~creting** kriːt ɪŋ ‖ kriːt̬ ɪŋ

con|crete *v 'solidify'* kən |ˈkriːt →kəŋ-, ₍ₗ₎kɒn- ‖ ˈkɑːn |kriːt ₍ₗ₎·ˈ· **~creted** ˈkriːt ɪd -əd ‖ kriːt̬ əd **~cretes** ˈkriːts ‖ kriːts **~creting** ˈkriːt ɪŋ ‖ kriːt̬ ɪŋ

concretion kən ˈkriːʃ ᵊn →kəŋ-, ₍ₗ₎kɒn- ‖ kɑːn- kən- **~s** z

concretis... —*see* **concretiz...**

concretization ˌkɒŋ kriːt aɪ ˈzeɪʃ ᵊn ‖ kɑːn ˌkriːt̬ ə- ˌ· · --

concretiz|e ˈkɒŋ kriːt aɪz ‖ kɑːn ˈkriːt aɪz ˈ· -- **~ed** d **~es** ɪz əz **~ing** ɪŋ

concubinage kɒn ˈkjuːb ɪn ɪdʒ →kɒŋ-, kən-, →kəŋ-, -ən- ‖ kɑːn-

concubine ˈkɒŋ kju baɪn ˈkɒn-, -kjə- ‖ ˈkɑːŋ- **~s** z

concupiscence kən ˈkjuːp ɪs ənᵗs →kəŋ-, kɒn-, →kɒŋ-, §-əs-; ˌkɒŋ kju ˈpɪs- ‖ kɑːn-

concupiscent kən ˈkjuːp ɪs ənt →kəŋ-, kɒn-, →kɒŋ-, §-əs-; ˌkɒŋ kju ˈpɪs- ‖ kɑːn-

con|cur kən |ˈkɜː →kəŋ-, §₍ₗ₎kɒn- ‖ -|ˈkɜ˞ː kɑːn- **~curred** ˈkɜːd ‖ ˈkɜ˞ːd **~curring** ˈkɜːr ɪŋ ‖ ˈkɜ˞ː ɪŋ **~curs** ˈkɜːz ‖ ˈkɜ˞ːz

concurrence kən ˈkʌr ənᵗs →kəŋ-, §₍ₗ₎kɒn- ‖ -ˈkɜ˞ː- kɑːn-

concurrent kən ˈkʌr ənt →kəŋ-, §₍ₗ₎kɒn- ‖ -ˈkɜ˞ː- kɑːn- **~ly** li

concuss kən ˈkʌs →kəŋ-, §₍ₗ₎kɒn- **~ed** t **~es** ɪz əz **~ing** ɪŋ

concussion kən ˈkʌʃ ᵊn →kəŋ-, §₍ₗ₎kɒn-

concussive kən ˈkʌs ɪv →kəŋ-, §₍ₗ₎kɒn-

Conde, Condé ˈkɒnd eɪ ‖ ˈkɑːnd-

ˌCondé ˈNast nɑːst næst ‖ næst

condemn kən ˈdem §₍ₗ₎kɒn- **~ed** d **~ing** ɪŋ **~s** z

conˈdemned cell, ·ˌ· ˈ·

condemnable kən ˈdem nəb ᵊl

condemnation ˌkɒn dem ˈneɪʃ ᵊn -dəm- ‖ ˌkɑːn- **~s** z

condemnatory kən ˈdem nət ər i §₍ₗ₎kɒn-; ˌkɒn dem ˈneɪt ər i ◂, ˌ·dəm- ‖ kən ˈdem nə tɔːr i -toʊr i

condensate ˈkɒn denᵗs eɪt ˈkɒnd ən seɪt; kən ˈdenᵗs eɪt ‖ ˈkɑːn- **~s** s

condensation ˌkɒn den ˈseɪʃ ᵊn -dən- ‖ ˌkɑːn- **~s** z

condens|e kən ˈdenᵗs §₍ₗ₎kɒn- **~ed** t **~es** ɪz əz **~ing** ɪŋ

conˌdensed ˈmilk

condenser kən ˈdenᵗs ə §₍ₗ₎kɒn- ‖ -ᵊr **~s** z

condescend ˌkɒn dɪ ˈsend -də- ‖ ˌkɑːn- **~ed** ɪd əd **~ing/ly** ɪŋ /li **~s** z

condescension ˌkɒn dɪ ˈsenᵗʃ ᵊn -də- ‖ ˌkɑːn-

condign kən ˈdaɪn ˈkɒn daɪn ‖ ˈkɑːn daɪn **~ly** li

condiment ˈkɒnd ɪ mənt -ə- ‖ ˈkɑːnd- **~s** s

condition kən ˈdɪʃ ᵊn §₍ₗ₎kɒn- **~ed** d **~ing** ‿ɪŋ **~s** z

conˌditioned ˈreflex

conditional kən ˈdɪʃ ᵊn‿əl §₍ₗ₎kɒn- **~ly** i

conditionality kən ˌdɪʃ ə ˈnæl ət i §kɒn-, §ˌkɒn ˌdɪʃ-, -ɪt i ‖ -ət̬ i

conditioner kən ˈdɪʃ ᵊn‿ə §₍ₗ₎kɒn- ‖ -ər **~s** z

condo ˈkɒnd əʊ ‖ ˈkɑːnd oʊ **~s** z
condol|e kən ˈdəʊl §(ɪ)kɒn-, →-ˈdɒʊl ‖ -ˈdoʊl **~ed** d **~es** z **~ing** ɪŋ
Condoleezza ˌkɒnd ə ˈliːz ə ‖ ˌkɑːnd-
condolenc|e kən ˈdəʊl ənˈs §(ɪ)kɒn- ‖ -ˈdoʊl- **~es** ɪz əz
condom ˈkɒnd əm ˈkɒn dɒm ‖ ˈkʌnd əm ˈkɑːnd- **~s** z
condominium ˌkɒnd ə ˈmɪn i ˌəm ‖ ˌkɑːnd- **~s** z
Condon ˈkɒnd ən -ɒn ‖ ˈkɑːnd ən
condonation ˌkɒnd ə ˈneɪʃ ən ˌkɒn dəʊ- ‖ ˌkɑːnd- ˌkɑːn doʊ-
condon|e kən ˈdəʊn §(ɪ)kɒn- ‖ -ˈdoʊn **~ed** d **~es** z **~ing** ɪŋ
condor ˈkɒnd ɔː -ə ‖ ˈkɑːnd ər -ɔːr **~s** z
condottier|e ˌkɒn ˌdɒt i ˈeər |eɪ kən ˌdɒt- ‖ ˌkɑːn də ˈtjer |i ˌkɑːn ˌdɑːt̬ i ˈer |i —*It* [kon dot ˈtjɛː re] **~i** iː
Condover ˈkʌnd əʊv ə ‖ -oʊv ər
conduc|e kən ˈdjuːs §(ɪ)kɒn-, →§-ˈdʒuːs ‖ -ˈduːs -ˈdjuːs **~ed** t **~es** ɪz əz **~ing** ɪŋ
conducive kən ˈdjuːs ɪv §(ɪ)kɒn-, →§-ˈdʒuːs- ‖ -ˈduːs- -ˈdjuːs- **~ness** nəs nɪs
conduct *n* ˈkɒn dʌkt -dəkt ‖ ˈkɑːn- **~s** s
conduct *v* kən ˈdʌkt §(ɪ)kɒn- **~ed** ɪd əd **~ing** ɪŋ **~s** s
conductance kən ˈdʌkt ənˈs §(ɪ)kɒn-
conduction kən ˈdʌk ʃən §(ɪ)kɒn-
conductive kən ˈdʌkt ɪv §(ɪ)kɒn- **~ly** li
conductivity ˌkɒn dʌk ˈtɪv ət i ˌ·dək-, -ɪt i ‖ ˌkɑːn dʌk ˈtɪv ət̬ i kən ˌdʌk ˈtɪv-
conductor kən ˈdʌkt ə §(ɪ)kɒn- ‖ -ər **~s** z **~ship/s** ʃɪp/s
conˈductor rail
conductress kən ˈdʌk trəs §(ɪ)kɒn-, -trɪs, -tres **~es** ɪz əz
conduit ˈkɒn dju ɪt ˈkʌn-, -du ɪt, →§-dʒu ɪt, §ˌət; ˈkɒnd ɪt, ˈkʌnd-, §-ət ‖ ˈkɑːn du ət -dju **~s** s
Condy ˈkɒnd i ‖ ˈkɑːnd i
condyle ˈkɒn daɪəl -dɪl, §-dəl ‖ ˈkɑːn- **~s** z
condylom|a ˌkɒnd ɪ ˈləʊm |ə -ə- ‖ ˌkɑːnd ə ˈloʊm |ə **~ata** ət ə ‖ ət̬ ə **~as** əz
cone kəʊn ‖ koʊn **coned** kəʊnd ‖ koʊnd **coning** ˈkəʊn ɪŋ ‖ ˈkoʊn ɪŋ **cones** kəʊnz ‖ koʊnz
conehead ˈkəʊn hed ‖ ˈkoʊn- **~s** z
Conestoga ˌkɒn ɪ ˈstəʊg ə -ə- ‖ ˌkɑːn ə ˈstoʊg ə
coney, Coney ˈkəʊn i ‖ ˈkoʊn i **~s** z
ˌConey ˈIsland
confab *v* kən ˈfæb ˈkɒn fæb ‖ ˈkɑːn fæb **~bed** d **~bing** ɪŋ **~s** z
confab *n* ˈkɒn fæb kən ˈfæb ‖ ˈkɑːn- **~s** z
confabu|late kən ˈfæb ju |leɪt (ɪ)kɒn- ‖ -jə- **~lated** leɪt ɪd -əd ‖ leɪt̬ əd **~lates** leɪts **~lating** leɪt ɪŋ ‖ leɪt̬ ɪŋ
confabulation kən ˌfæb ju ˈleɪʃ ən (ɪ)kɒn- ‖ -jə- **~s** z
confect *v* kən ˈfekt §(ɪ)kɒn- **~ed** ɪd əd **~ing** ɪŋ **~s** s
confection kən ˈfek ʃən §(ɪ)kɒn- **~s** z
confectioner kən ˈfek ʃən ə §(ɪ)kɒn- ‖ ər **~s** z
confectioner|y kən ˈfek ʃən ər |i §(ɪ)kɒn-, -ʃən ər |i ‖ -ʃə ner |i **~ies** iz
confederac|y, C~ kən ˈfed ər əs |i §(ɪ)kɒn- **~ies** iz
confede|rate *v* kən ˈfed ə |reɪt §(ɪ)kɒn- **~rated** reɪt ɪd -əd ‖ reɪt̬ əd **~rates** reɪts **~rating** reɪt ɪŋ ‖ reɪt̬ ɪŋ
confederate *adj, n* kən ˈfed ər ət §(ɪ)kɒn-, -ɪt **~s** s
confederation, C~ kən ˌfed ə ˈreɪʃ ən §kɒn-, §ˌkɒn ˌ·- **~s** z
con|fer kən |ˈfɜː §(ɪ)kɒn- ‖ -|ˈfɜː **~ferred** ˈfɜːd ‖ ˈfɜːd **~ferring** ˈfɜːr ɪŋ ‖ ˈfɜː ɪŋ **~fers** ˈfɜːz ‖ ˈfɜːz
conferee ˌkɒn fə ˈriː -fɜː- ‖ ˌkɑːn- **~s** z
conferenc|e ˈkɒn fər ənˈs ‖ ˈkɑːn- **~es** ɪz əz
conferral kən ˈfɜːr əl §(ɪ)kɒn- ‖ -ˈfɜː- **~s** z
conferv|a kən ˈfɜːv |ə (ɪ)kɒn- ‖ -fɜːv |ə **~ae** iː **~as** əz
confess kən ˈfes §(ɪ)kɒn- **~ed** t **~es** ɪz əz **~ing** ɪŋ
confession kən ˈfeʃ ən §(ɪ)kɒn- **~s** z
confessional kən ˈfeʃ ən əl §(ɪ)kɒn- **~s** z
confessor kən ˈfes ə (ɪ)kɒn-, -ɔː ‖ -ər ˈkɑːn fes-, -ɔːr **~s** z
confetti kən ˈfet i kɒn- ‖ -ˈfet̬ i
confidant, confidante ˈkɒn fɪ dænt -fə-, ˌ· ·ˈ·, ˌ· ·ˈdɑːnt, ˈ· ·dənt ‖ ˈkɑːn- -dɑːnt **~s** s
confid|e kən ˈfaɪd §(ɪ)kɒn- **~ed** ɪd əd **~er/s** ə/z ‖ ər/z **~es** z **~ing** ɪŋ
confidence ˈkɒn fɪd ənˈs -fəd- ‖ ˈkɑːn- **~es** ɪz əz
ˈconfidence ˌlimit; **ˈconfidence trick**
confidence-building ˈkɒn fɪd ənˈs ˌbɪld ɪŋ ‖ ˈkɑːn-
confident ˈkɒn fɪd ənt -fəd- ‖ ˈkɑːn- **~ly** li
confidential ˌkɒn fɪ ˈdenˈʃ əl ◂ -fə- ‖ ˌkɑːn- **~ly** i
confidentiality ˌkɒn fɪ ˌdenˈʃ i ˈæl ət i ˌ·fə- ‖ ˌkɑːn fə ˌdenˈʃ i ˈæl ət̬ i
confiding kən ˈfaɪd ɪŋ §(ɪ)kɒn- **~ly** li
configuration kən ˌfɪg jə ˈreɪʃ ən ˌkɒn ˌfɪg-, -juə-, -ə- ‖ ˌkɑːn fɪg- **~al/ly** əl /i **~s** z
configure kən ˈfɪg ə §(ɪ)kɒn- ‖ -jər (*) **~ed** d **~es** z **configuring** kən ˈfɪg ər ɪŋ (ɪ)kɒn- ‖ -jər ɪŋ
confin|e *v* kən ˈfaɪn §(ɪ)kɒn- **~ed** d **~es** z **~ing** ɪŋ
confine *n* ˈkɒn faɪn ‖ ˈkɑːn- **~s** z
confinement kən ˈfaɪn mənt §(ɪ)kɒn-, →-ˈfaɪm- **~s** s
confirm kən ˈfɜːm §(ɪ)kɒn- ‖ -ˈfɜːm **~ed** d **~ing** ɪŋ **~s** z
confirmation ˌkɒn fə ˈmeɪʃ ən ‖ ˌkɑːn fər- **~s** z
confirmatory kən ˈfɜːm ət ər i ˌkɒn fə ˈmeɪt ər i ◂, ˈ· · · · ‖ -ˈfɜːm ə tɔːr i -toʊr i
con|firmed kən |ˈfɜːmd §(ɪ)kɒn- ‖ -|ˈfɜːmd **~firmedly** ˈfɜːm ɪd li -əd- ‖ ˈfɜːm əd li

C

C

confi|scate *v* 'kɒn fɪ |skeɪt -fə- ‖ 'kɑːn- **~scated** skeɪt ɪd -əd ‖ skeɪţ əd **~scates** skeɪts **~scating** skeɪt ɪŋ ‖ skeɪţ ɪŋ
confiscation ˌkɒn fɪ 'skeɪʃ ən -fə- ‖ ˌkɑːn- **~s** z
confiscatory kən 'fɪsk ət̬ər i kɒn-; ˌkɒn fɪ 'skeɪt ər i, ˌ·fə-, '· · · · · ‖ -ə tɔːr i -tour i
confit 'kɒn fiː ‖ ˌkɔːn 'fiː ˌkɑːn- —*Fr* [kɔ̃ fi]
Confiteor kɒn 'fɪt i ɔː kən- ‖ kən 'fɪţ i ɔːr -'fiːţ-, -i̯ər
conflagration ˌkɒn flə 'greɪʃ ən ‖ ˌkɑːn- **~s** z
con|flate kən |'fleɪt ₍ı₎kɒn- **~flated** 'fleɪt ɪd -əd ‖ 'fleɪţ əd **~flates** 'fleɪts **~flating** 'fleɪt ɪŋ ‖ 'fleɪţ ɪŋ
conflation kən 'fleɪʃ ən ₍ı₎kɒn- **~s** z
conflict *n* 'kɒn flɪkt ‖ 'kɑːn- **~s** s
conflict *v* kən 'flɪkt §₍ı₎kɒn-; 'kɒn flɪkt ‖ 'kɑːn flɪkt **~ed** ɪd əd **~ing/ly** ɪŋ /li **~s** s
confluenc|e 'kɒn flu̯ənᵗs ‖ 'kɑːn- **~es** ɪz əz
confluent 'kɒn flu̯ənt ‖ 'kɑːn- **~s** s
conform kən 'fɔːm §₍ı₎kɒn- ‖ -'fɔːrm **~ed** d **~ing** ɪŋ **~s** z
conformab|le kən 'fɔːm əb |əl §₍ı₎kɒn- ‖ -'fɔːrm- **~leness** əl nəs -nɪs **~ly** li
conformal kən 'fɔːm əl ₍ı₎kɒn- ‖ -'fɔːrm- ₍ı₎kɑːn- **~ly** i
conformance kən 'fɔːm ənᵗs §₍ı₎kɒn- ‖ -'fɔːrm-
conformation ˌkɒn fɔː 'meɪʃ ən -fə- ‖ ˌkɑːn fɔːr- -fər-
conformer kən 'fɔːm ə §₍ı₎kɒn- ‖ -'fɔːrm ər **~s** z
conformist kən 'fɔːm ɪst §₍ı₎kɒn-, §-əst ‖ -'fɔːrm- **~s** s
conformit|y kən 'fɔːm ət |i §₍ı₎kɒn-, -ɪt- ‖ -'fɔːrm əţ |i **~ies** iz
confound kən 'faʊnd ₍ı₎kɒn- ‖ ₍ı₎kɑːn- **~ed** ɪd əd **~ing** ɪŋ **~s** z
confounded kən 'faʊnd ɪd ₍ı₎kɒn-, -əd ‖ ₍ı₎kɑːn- **~ly** li **~ness** nəs nɪs
confraternity ˌkɒn frə 'tɜːn ət i -ɪt i ‖ ˌkɑːn frə 'tɜːn əţ i
confrere, confrère 'kɒn freə ‖ 'kɑːn frer 'koʊn-, ·'· *Fr* [kɔ̃ fʁɛːʁ] **~s** z
con|front kən |'frʌnt §₍ı₎kɒn- **~fronted** 'frʌnt ɪd -əd ‖ 'frʌnţ əd **~fronting** 'frʌnt ɪŋ ‖ 'frʌnţ ɪŋ **~fronts** 'frʌnts
confrontation ˌkɒn frʌn 'teɪʃ ən -frən- ‖ ˌkɑːn-
confrontational ˌkɒn frʌn 'teɪʃ ən̯əl ◂ ˌ·frən- ‖ ˌkɑːn- **~ly** i
confrontationist ˌkɒn frʌn 'teɪʃ ən̯ɪst ˌ·frən-, §əst ‖ ˌkɑːn- **~s** s
Confucian kən 'fjuːʃ ən ₍ı₎kɒn-, -'fjuːʃ i̯ən **~ism** ˌɪz əm
Confucius kən 'fjuːʃ əs ₍ı₎kɒn-, -'fjuːʃ i̯əs —*Chi* Kǒng Fūzǐ [³kʰʊŋ ¹fu ³tsɯ]
confus|e kən 'fjuːz §₍ı₎kɒn- **~ed** d **~es** ɪz əz **~ing/ly** ɪŋ /li
confused|ly kən 'fjuːz ɪd |li §₍ı₎kɒn-, -əd-; -'fjuːzd |li **~ness** nəs nɪs
confusion kən 'fjuːʒ ən §₍ı₎kɒn- **~s** z
confutation ˌkɒn fju 'teɪʃ ən ‖ ˌkɑːn- **~s** z
con|fute kən |'fjuːt §₍ı₎kɒn- **~futed** 'fjuːt ɪd -əd ‖ 'fjuːţ əd **~futes** 'fjuːts **~futing** 'fjuːt ɪŋ ‖ 'fjuːţ ɪŋ
conga 'kɒŋ gə ‖ 'kɑːŋ gə **~ed** d **congaing** 'kɒŋ gəʳ ɪŋ ‖ 'kɑːŋ gə ɪŋ **~s** z
congé 'kɒn ʒeɪ 'kɔ̃- ‖ koʊn 'ʒeɪ kɑːn-, kɔːn-; 'kɑːn ʒeɪ—*Fr* [kɔ̃ ʒe] **~s** z
congeal kən 'dʒiːəl §₍ı₎kɒn- **~ed** d **~ing** ɪŋ **~s** z
congelation ˌkɒn dʒɪ 'leɪʃ ən -dʒə- ‖ ˌkɑːn-
congener kən 'dʒiːn ə kɒn-; 'kɒndʒ ɪn ə, -ən- ‖ 'kɑːndʒ ən ər kən 'dʒiːn ər **~s** z
congenial kən 'dʒiːn i̯əl §₍ı₎kɒn- **~ly** i
congeniality kən ˌdʒiːn i 'æl ət i §ˌkɒn dʒiːn-, -ɪt i ‖ -əţ i
congenital kən 'dʒen ɪt əl §₍ı₎kɒn-, §-ət- ‖ -əţ- **~ly** i
conger 'kɒŋ gə ‖ 'kɑːŋ gər **~s** z
ˌ**conger 'eel**
congeries kɒn 'dʒɪər iːz kən-, -'dʒer-, -ɪz, -'dʒer i iːz ‖ 'kɑːndʒ ə riːz
congest kən 'dʒest §₍ı₎kɒn- **~ed** ɪd əd **~ing** ɪŋ **~s** s
congestion kən 'dʒes tʃən §₍ı₎kɒn-, →-'dʒeʃ-
Congleton 'kɒŋ gəl tən ‖ 'kɑːŋ-
conglomerate *adj, n* kən 'glɒm ər̯ət →kəŋ-, §₍ı₎kɒn-, ɪt, -ə reɪt ‖ -'glɑːm- **~s** s
conglomeration kən ˌglɒm ə 'reɪʃ ən →kəŋ-, §kɒn-, §ˌkɒn ˌglɒm- ‖ -ˌglɑːm- ˌkɑːn ˌglɑːm- **~s** z
Congo 'kɒŋ gəʊ ‖ 'kɑːŋ goʊ
Congolese ˌkɒŋ gə 'liːz ◂ ‖ ˌkɑːŋ- -'liːs
congrats kən 'græts →kəŋ-, §₍ı₎kɒn-
congratters kən 'græt əz →kəŋ-, §₍ı₎kɒn- ‖ -'græţ ərz

CONGRATULATE

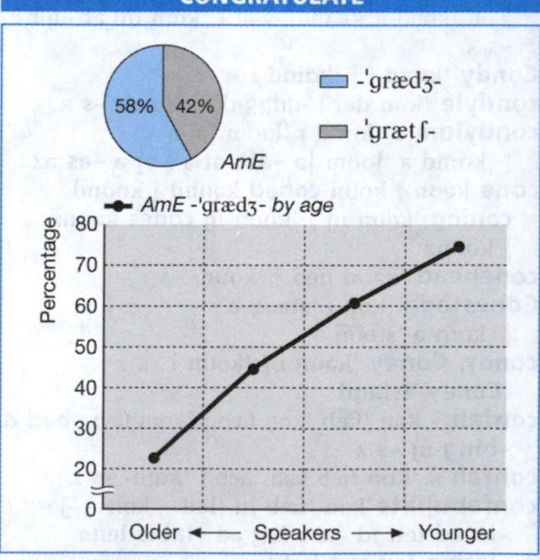

congratu|late kən 'grætʃ u |leɪt →kəŋ-, §₍ı₎kɒn-, -ə-; -'græt ju- ‖ -'grædʒ ə |leɪt 'grætʃ- — *Preference poll, AmE:* -'grædʒ- *58%,* -'grætʃ- *42%.* **~lated** leɪt ɪd -əd ‖ leɪţ əd **~lates** leɪts **~lating** leɪt ɪŋ ‖ leɪţ ɪŋ

congratulation kən ˌgrætʃ u ˈleɪʃ ᵊn →kəŋ-, §kɒn-, §ˌkɒn ˌgrætʃ-, -ə-; -ˌgræt ju- ‖ kən ˌgrætʃ ə- -ˌgrædʒ- **~s** z

congratulatory kən ˌgrætʃ u ˈleɪt ər i ◂ →kəŋ-, §kɒn-, §ˌkɒn ˌgrætʃ-, -əˈ--; -ˌgræt ju-; kən ˈgrætʃ əl ət‿ər i, -ˈ·ʊl- ‖ kən ˈgrætʃ əl‿ə tɔːr i -ˈgrædʒ-, -tour i *(*)*

congregant ˈkɒŋ grɪg ənt -grəg- ‖ ˈkɑːŋ- **~s** s

congre|gate *v* ˈkɒŋ grɪ |geɪt -grə- ‖ ˈkɑːŋ- **~gated** geɪt ɪd -əd ‖ geɪţ əd **~gates** geɪts **~gating** geɪt ɪŋ ‖ geɪţ ɪŋ

congregation ˌkɒŋ grɪ ˈgeɪʃ ᵊn -grə- ‖ ˌkɑːŋ- **~s** z

congregational, C~ ˌkɒŋ grɪ ˈgeɪʃ ᵊn‿əl ◂ ˌ·grə- ‖ ˌkɑːŋ-

Congregationalism ˌkɒŋ grɪ ˈgeɪʃ ᵊn‿ə ˌlɪz əm ˌ·grə-, əl ˌɪz- ‖ ˌkɑːŋ-

Congregationalist ˌkɒŋ grɪ ˈgeɪʃ ᵊn‿əl ɪst ˌ·grə-, §-əst ‖ ˌkɑːŋ- **~s** s

Congresbury ˈkɒnz bər‿i ˈkuːmz- ‖ ˈkɑːnz ber i

congress ˈkɒŋ gres ‖ ˈkɑːŋ grəs -rəs **~es** ɪz əz

congressional kən ˈgreʃ ᵊn‿əl →kəŋ-, $_{(ı)}$kɒn-, →$_{(ı)}$kɒŋ- ‖ $_{(ı)}$kɑːn-

congress|man ˈkɒŋ gres |mən -grɪs-, -grəs- ‖ ˈkɑːŋ grəs- **~men** mən men **~woman** ˌwʊm ən **~women** ˌwɪm ɪn §-ən

Congreve ˈkɒŋ griːv ‖ ˈkɑːn-→ˈkɑːŋ-

congruenc|e ˈkɒŋ gru‿ənᵗs ‖ ˈkɑːŋ- kən ˈgruː‿ **~es** ɪz əz **~y** i

congruent ˈkɒŋ gru‿ənt ‖ ˈkɑːŋ- kən ˈgruː‿ **~ly** li

congruential ˌkɒŋ gru ˈenᵗʃ ᵊl ◂ ‖ ˌkɑːŋ-

congruit|y kən ˈgruː‿ət |i →kəŋ-, $_{(ı)}$kɒn-, →$_{(ı)}$kɒŋ-, ɪt- ‖ əţ |i $_{(ı)}$kɑːn- **~ies** iz

congruous ˈkɒŋ gru‿əs ‖ ˈkɑːŋ- **~ly** li **~ness** nəs nɪs

conic ˈkɒn ɪk ‖ ˈkɑːn ɪk **~s** s

ˌconic ˈsection

conical ˈkɒn ɪk ᵊl ‖ ˈkɑːn-

conidi|um kəʊ ˈnɪd i‿|əm ‖ kə- **~a** ə **~al** əl

conie... —*see* **cony**

conifer ˈkɒn ɪf ə ˈkəʊn-, -əf- ‖ ˈkɑːn əf ᵊr **~s** z

coniferous kəʊ ˈnɪf ər‿əs kɒ- ‖ koʊ- kə-

coning ˈkəʊn ɪŋ ‖ ˈkoʊn ɪŋ

Coningham ˈkʌn ɪŋ əm ‖ -hæm

Coningsby ˈkɒn ɪŋz bi ˈkʌn- ‖ ˈkʌn-

Conisborough, Conisbrough ˈkɒn ɪs bər‿ə ˈ·əs- ‖ ˈkɑːn əs ˌbɜː oʊ

Coniston ˈkɒn ɪst ən §-əst- ‖ ˈkɑːn-

conium ˈkəʊn i‿əm ‖ ˈkoʊn-

conjectural kən ˈdʒek tʃᵊr‿əl §$_{(ı)}$kɒn-, -ʃᵊr‿əl **~ly** i

conjecture kən ˈdʒek tʃə §$_{(ı)}$kɒn-, -ʃə ‖ -tʃᵊr **~d** d **~s** z **conjecturing** kən ˈdʒek tʃər ɪŋ §$_{(ı)}$kɒn-, -ʃər-

conjoin kən ˈdʒɔɪn $_{(ı)}$kɒn- ‖ $_{(ı)}$kɑːn- **~ed** d **~ing** ɪŋ **~s** z

conjoint kən ˈdʒɔɪnt $_{(ı)}$kɒn-, ˈ· · ‖ $_{(ı)}$kɑːn- **~ly** li

conjugal ˈkɒndʒ ʊg ᵊl -əg- ‖ ˈkɑːndʒ əg ᵊl kən ˈdʒuːg- **~ly** i

conjugality ˌkɒndʒ u ˈgæl ət i -ɪt i ‖ ˌkɑːndʒ ə ˈgæl əţ i ˌ·u-

conjugate *adj, n* ˈkɒndʒ ʊg ət -əg-, -ɪt; -u geɪt ‖ ˈkɑːndʒ əg ət -ə geɪt **~ly** li **~s** s

conju|gate *v* ˈkɒndʒ u |geɪt -ə- ‖ ˈkɑːndʒ ə- **~gated** geɪt ɪd -əd ‖ geɪţ əd **~gates** geɪts **~gating** geɪt ɪŋ ‖ geɪţ ɪŋ

conjugation ˌkɒndʒ u ˈgeɪʃ ᵊn -ə- ‖ ˌkɑːndʒ ə- **~al/ly** ‿əl /i **~s** z

conjunct ˈkɒn dʒʌŋkt kən ˈdʒʌŋkt, $_{(ı)}$kɒn- ‖ ˈkɑːn- **~ly** li **~s** s

conjunction kən ˈdʒʌŋk ʃᵊn §$_{(ı)}$kɒn- **~al/ly** ‿əl /i **~s** z

conjunctiv|a ˌkɒn dʒʌŋk ˈtaɪv |ə ‖ ˌkɑːn- kən ˌdʒʌŋk ˈtaɪv |ə **~ae** iː **~al** ᵊl **~as** z

conjunctive kən ˈdʒʌŋkt ɪv $_{(ı)}$kɒn-

conjunctivitis kən ˌdʒʌŋkt ɪ ˈvaɪt ɪs §kɒn-, §ˌkɒn dʒʌŋkt ɪ ˈ--, -əˈ--, §-əs ‖ -ˈvaɪţ əs

conjuncture kən ˈdʒʌŋk tʃə §$_{(ı)}$kɒn- ‖ -tʃᵊr **~s** z

conjuration ˌkɒn dʒu ˈreɪʃ ᵊn ˌkʌndʒ ə- ‖ ˌkɑːndʒ ə-

conjure *'do magic; evoke'* ˈkʌndʒ ə ‖ ˈkɑːndʒ ᵊr **~d** d **~s** z **conjuring** ˈkʌndʒ ər ɪŋ ‖ ˈkɑːndʒ-

conjure *'ask solemnly'* kən ˈdʒʊə $_{(ı)}$kɒn-, -ˈdʒɔː ‖ -ˈdʒʊᵊr **~d** d **~s** z **conjures** kən ˈdʒʊəz $_{(ı)}$kɒn-, -ˈdʒɔːz ‖ -ˈdʒʊᵊrz

conjurer, conjuror ˈkʌndʒ ər‿ə ‖ ˈkɑːndʒ ᵊr ər ˈkʌndʒ- **~s** z

conk kɒŋk ‖ kɑːŋk kɔːŋk **conked** kɒŋkt ‖ kɑːŋkt kɔːŋkt **conking** ˈkɒŋk ɪŋ ‖ ˈkɑːŋk ɪŋ ˈkɔːŋk- **conks** kɒŋks ‖ kɑːŋks kɔːŋks

conked-out ˌkɒŋkt ˈaʊt ◂ ‖ ˌkɑːŋkt- ˌkɔːŋkt-

conker ˈkɒŋk ə ‖ ˈkɑːŋk ᵊr **~s** z

Conleth ˈkɒn ləθ ‖ ˈkɑːn-

con|man ˈkɒn |mæn ‖ ˈkɑːn- **~men** men

con moto $_{(ı)}$kɒn ˈməʊt əʊ ‖ $_{(ı)}$kɑːn ˈmoʊţ oʊ $_{(ı)}$koʊn-

Connacht ˈkɒn ɔːt -ət ‖ ˈkɑːn ɔːt -ɑːt

Connah ˈkɒn ə ‖ ˈkɑːn ə

connate ˈkɒn eɪt kɒ ˈneɪt ‖ ˈkɑːn- kɑː ˈneɪt **~ly** li

Connaught ˈkɒn ɔːt ‖ ˈkɑːn ɔːt -ɑːt

connect kə ˈnekt **~ed** ɪd əd **~ing** ɪŋ **~s** s

conˌnected ˈspeech; **conˈnecting rod**

connected|ly kə ˈnekt ɪd /li -əd- **~ness** nəs nɪs

Connecticut kə ˈnet ɪk ət §-ək- ‖ -ˈneţ- *(!)*

connection kə ˈnek ʃᵊn **~al** ‿əl **~ism** ˌɪz əm **~ist/s** ɪst/s §əst/s ‖ əst/s **~s** z

connective kə ˈnekt ɪv **~ly** li

connectivity ˌkɒn ek ˈtɪv ət i kə ˌnek ˈ--, -ɪt i ‖ ˌkɑːn ek ˈtɪv əţ i

connector kə ˈnekt ə ‖ -ᵊr **~s** z

conned kɒnd ‖ kɑːnd

Connell *(i)* ˈkɒn ᵊl ‖ ˈkɑːn ᵊl; *(ii)* kə ˈnel

Connemara ˌkɒn ɪ ˈmɑːr ə -ə- ‖ ˌkɑːn-

Connery ˈkɒn ər i ‖ ˈkɑːn-

Connex *tdmk* ˈkɒn eks kə ˈneks ‖ ˈkɑːn-

connexion kə ˈnek ʃᵊn **~al** ‿əl **~s** z

Connibere ˈkɒn ɪ bɪə -ə- ‖ ˈkɑːn ə bɪr

Connie ˈkɒn i ‖ ˈkɑːn i

conning ˈkɒn ɪŋ ‖ ˈkɑːn ɪŋ
ˈconning ˌtower
conniption kə ˈnɪp ʃᵊn
connivance kə ˈnaɪv ᵊnᵗs
conniv|e kə ˈnaɪv **~ed** d **~er/s** ə/z ‖ ᵊr/z **~es** z **~ing** ɪŋ
connoisseur ˌkɒn ə ˈsɜː -ɪ- ‖ ˌkɑːn ə ˈsɝː -ˈsʊᵊr **~s** z **~ship** ʃɪp
Connolly ˈkɒn əl i ‖ ˈkɑːn-
Connor ˈkɒn ə ‖ ˈkɑːn ᵊr
Connors ˈkɒn əz ‖ ˈkɑːn ᵊrz
connotation ˌkɒn ə ˈteɪʃ ᵊn -əʊ-, ⚠-ju- ‖ ˌkɑːn- **~s** z
connotative ˈkɒn ə teɪt ɪv ˈ·əʊ-, ⚠ˈ·ju-; kə ˈnəʊt ət ɪv, kɒ- ‖ ˈkɑːn ə teɪţ ɪv kə ˈnoʊţ əţ ɪv **~ly** li
con|note kə |ˈnəʊt kɒ- ‖ -|ˈnoʊt kɑː- **~noted** ˈnəʊt ɪd -əd ‖ ˈnoʊţ əd **~notes** ˈnəʊts ‖ ˈnoʊts **~noting** ˈnəʊt ɪŋ ‖ ˈnoʊţ ɪŋ
connubial kə ˈnjuːb i‿əl kɒ- ‖ -ˈnuːb- -ˈnjuːb- **~ly** i
connubiality kə ˌnjuːb i ˈæl ət i kɒ- ‖ -ˌnuːb i ˈæl əţ i -ˌnjuːb-
conoid ˈkəʊn ɔɪd ‖ ˈkoʊn- **~s** z
Conor ˈkɒn ə ‖ ˈkɑːn ᵊr
conquer ˈkɒŋk ə ‖ ˈkɑːŋk ᵊr *(= conker)* **~ed** d
conquering ˈkɒŋk ər ɪŋ ‖ ˈkɑːŋk- **~s** z
conqueror ˈkɒŋk ər‿ə ‖ ˈkɑːŋk ᵊr‿ər **~s** z
conquest, C~ ˈkɒŋ kwest ‖ ˈkɑːn kwest →ˈkɑːŋ-, -kwəst **~s** s
conquistador kɒn ˈkwɪst ə dɔː →kɒŋ-, ˌ· · ·ˈ·, ·ˌ· ·ˈ· ‖ kɑːn ˈkiːst ə dɔːr kən-, kɔːŋ-, -ˈkwɪst- —*Sp* [koŋ kis ta ˈðor] **conquistadores** kɒn ˌkwɪst ə ˈdɔːr eɪz →kɒŋ-, ˌ· · ·ˈ· · ‖ kɑːn- kən-, kɔːŋ-, -ˌkiːst-, -ˈdoʊr-, -eɪs —*Sp* [koŋ kis ta ˈðo ɾes]
Conrad ˈkɒn ræd ‖ ˈkɑːn-
Conrail, ConRail *tdmk* ˈkɒn reɪᵊl ˌ·ˈ· ‖ ˈkɑːn-
Conran ˈkɒn rən -ræn ‖ ˈkɑːn-
Conroy ˈkɒn rɔɪ ‖ ˈkɑːn-
consanguineous ˌkɒn sæŋ ˈgwɪn i‿əs ◂ ‖ ˌkɑːn- ˌ·sæn- **~ly** li
consanguinity ˌkɒn sæŋ ˈgwɪn ət i -ɪt i ‖ ˌkɑːn sæŋ ˈgwɪn əţ i ˌ·sæn-
conscienc|e ˈkɒnᵗʃ ᵊnᵗs ‖ ˈkɑːnᵗʃ ᵊnᵗs **~es** ɪz əz
ˈconscience clause; **ˈconscience ˌmoney**
conscienceless ˈkɒnᵗʃ ᵊnᵗs ləs -lɪs ‖ ˈkɑːnᵗʃ-
conscience-stricken ˈkɒnᵗʃ ᵊnᵗs ˌstrɪk ən ‖ ˈkɑːnᵗʃ-
conscientious ˌkɒnᵗʃ i ˈenᵗʃ əs ◂ ˌkɒnᵗs- ‖ ˌkɑːnᵗʃ- **~ly** li **~ness** nəs nɪs
ˌconsciˌentious obˈjector
conscionable ˈkɒnᵗʃ ᵊn‿əb əl ‖ ˈkɑːnᵗʃ-
conscious ˈkɒnᵗʃ əs ‖ ˈkɑːnᵗʃ əs **~ly** li
consciousness ˈkɒnᵗʃ əs nəs -nɪs ‖ ˈkɑːnᵗʃ-
ˈconsciousness ˌraising
conscript *n* ˈkɒn skrɪpt ‖ ˈkɑːn- **~s** s
conscript *v* kən ˈskrɪpt §(ɪ)kɒn- **~ed** ɪd əd **~ing** ɪŋ **~s** s
conscription kən ˈskrɪp ʃᵊn §(ɪ)kɒn-
conse|crate ˈkɒnᵗs ɪ |kreɪt -ə- ‖ ˈkɑːnᵗs ə- **~crated** kreɪt ɪd -əd ‖ kreɪţ əd **~crates** kreɪts **~crating** kreɪt ɪŋ ‖ kreɪţ ɪŋ
consecration ˌkɒnᵗs ɪ ˈkreɪʃ ᵊn -ə- ‖ ˌkɑːnᵗs ə-
consecrator ˈkɒnᵗs ɪ kreɪt ə ˈ·ə- ‖ ˈkɑːnᵗs ə kreɪţ ᵊr **~s** z
consecutive kən ˈsek jʊt ɪv §(ɪ)kɒn-, -jət-, §-ət- ‖ -jəţ ɪv -əţ- **~ly** li **~ness** nəs nɪs
consensual kən ˈsenᵗs ju‿əl (ɪ)kɒn-, -ˈsenᵗʃ u‿əl ‖ -ˈsenᵗʃ u‿əl -ˈsenᵗʃ əl **~ly** i
consensus kən ˈsenᵗs əs §(ɪ)kɒn-
con|sent *v, n* kən |ˈsent §(ɪ)kɒn- **~sented** ˈsent ɪd -əd ‖ ˈsenţ əd **~senting** ˈsent ɪŋ ‖ ˈsenţ ɪŋ **~sents** ˈsents
consequenc|e ˈkɒnᵗs ɪk wənᵗs -ək-; §-ɪ kwenᵗs, §-ə- ‖ ˈkɑːnᵗs ə kwenᵗs -ɪk wənᵗs **~es** ɪz əz
consequent ˈkɒnᵗs ɪk wənt -ək-; §-ɪ kwent, §-ə- ‖ ˈkɑːnᵗs ə kwent -ɪk wənt **~ly** li
consequential ˌkɒnᵗs ɪ ˈkwenᵗʃ ᵊl ◂ -ə- ‖ ˌkɑːnᵗs- **~ly** i
conservanc|y kən ˈsɜːv ᵊnᵗs |i §(ɪ)kɒn- ‖ -ˈsɝːv- **~ies** iz
conservation ˌkɒnᵗs ə ˈveɪʃ ᵊn ‖ ˌkɑːnᵗs ᵊr- **~al** ˌəl ◂
conservationism ˌkɒnᵗs ə ˈveɪʃ ə ˌnɪz əm -ᵊn ˌɪz- ‖ ˌkɑːnᵗs ᵊr-
conservationist ˌkɒnᵗs ə ˈveɪʃ ᵊn‿ɪst əst ‖ ˌkɑːnᵗs ᵊr- **~s** s
conservatism kən ˈsɜːv ə ˌtɪz əm §(ɪ)kɒn- ‖ -ˈsɝːv-
conservative, C~ kən ˈsɜːv ət ɪv §(ɪ)kɒn- ‖ -ˈsɝːv əţ ɪv **~ly** li **~s** z
Conˈservative ˌParty
conservatoire kən ˈsɜːv ə twɑː (ɪ)kɒn- ‖ -ˈsɝːv ə twɑːr -ˌ· ·ˈ· **~s** z
conservator kən ˈsɜːv ət ə §(ɪ)kɒn-; ˈkɒnᵗs ə veɪt ə ‖ -ˈsɝːv əţ ᵊr -ə tɔːr; ˈkɑːnᵗs ᵊr veɪţ ᵊr **~s** z
conservator|y kən ˈsɜːv ətr |i -ˈsɜːv ət ər |i ‖ kən ˈsɝːv ə tɔːr |i -toʊr i **~ies** iz
conserv|e *v* kən ˈsɜːv §(ɪ)kɒn- ‖ -ˈsɝːv **~ed** d **~es** z **~ing** ɪŋ
conserve *n* ˈkɒn sɜːv kən ˈsɜːv ‖ ˈkɑːn sɝːv **~s** z
Consett ˈkɒnᵗs ɪt -ət, -et ‖ ˈkɑːnᵗs-
consider kən ˈsɪd ə §(ɪ)kɒn- ‖ -ᵊr **~ed** d
considering kən ˈsɪd‿ər ɪŋ **~s** z
considerab|le kən ˈsɪd‿ər əb |ᵊl §(ɪ)kɒn- **~ly** li
considerate kən ˈsɪd‿ər ət §(ɪ)kɒn-, -ɪt **~ly** li **~ness** nəs nɪs
consideration kən ˌsɪd ə ˈreɪʃ ᵊn §(ɪ)kɒn- **~s** z
Considine ˈkɒnᵗs ɪ daɪn -ə- ‖ ˈkɑːnᵗs-
consigliere ˌkɒn sɪl i ˈeər eɪ -i ‖ ˌkɑːn sɪl i ˈer eɪ —*It* [kon siʎ ˈʎɛː re]
consign kən ˈsaɪn §(ɪ)kɒn- **~ed** d **~ing** ɪŋ **~s** z
consignee ˌkɒnᵗs aɪ ˈniː -ɪ-, -ə- ‖ ˌkɑːnᵗs- **~s** z
consignment kən ˈsaɪn mənt §(ɪ)kɒn-, →-ˈsaɪm- **~s** s
consignor kən ˈsaɪn ə §(ɪ)kɒn-; ˌkɒnᵗs aɪ ˈnɔː, kən ˌsaɪ ˈnɔː ‖ -ᵊr ˌkɑːnᵗs aɪ ˈnɔːr, -ə-; kən ˌsaɪ ˈnɔːr **~s** z
consist kən ˈsɪst §(ɪ)kɒn- **~ed** ɪd əd **~ing** ɪŋ **~s** s
consistence kən ˈsɪst ənᵗs §(ɪ)kɒn-
consistenc|y kən ˈsɪst ənᵗs |i §(ɪ)kɒn- **~ies** iz
consistent kən ˈsɪst ənt **~ly** li

consistorial ˌkɒn sɪ ˈstɔːr i‿əl ‖ ˌkɑːn- -ˈstoʊr-

consistor|y kən ˈsɪst ər‿|i ~ies iz

consolation ˌkɒnᵗs ə ˈleɪʃ ᵊn ‖ ˌkɑːnᵗs- ~s z

ˌconsoˈlation prize

consolatory kən ˈsɒl ət‿ər i §(ı)kɒn-, -ˈsəʊl- ‖ -ˈsoʊl ə tɔːr i -ˈsɑːl-, -toʊr i

consol|e *v* kən ˈsəʊl §(ı)kɒn-, →-ˈsɒʊl ‖ -ˈsoʊl ~ed d ~es z ~ing/ly ɪŋ /li

console *n* ˈkɒn səʊl →-sɒʊl ‖ ˈkɑːn soʊl ~s z

consoli|date kən ˈsɒl ɪ |deɪt §(ı)kɒn-, -ə- ‖ -ˈsɑːl- ~dated deɪt ɪd -əd ‖ deɪţ əd ~dates deɪts ~dating deɪt ɪŋ ‖ deɪţ ɪŋ

consolidation kən ˌsɒl ɪ ˈdeɪʃ ᵊn §kɒn-, §ˌkɒn ˌsɒl-, -ə'·- ‖ -ˌsɑːl-

consolidator kən ˈsɒl ɪ deɪt ə §(ı)kɒn-, -ˈ·ə- ‖ -ˈsɑːl ə deɪţ ᵊr

consols kən ˈsɒlz ˈkɒnᵗs ɒlz, -ᵊlz ‖ -ˈsɑːlz

consomme, consommé kən ˈsɒm eɪ kən-, ˈkɒnᵗs ə meɪ, -ɒ- ‖ ˌkɑːnᵗs ə ˈmeɪ (*) —*Fr* [kɔ̃ sɔ me] ~s z

consonance ˈkɒnᵗs ən‿ənᵗs ‖ ˈkɑːnᵗs-

consonant ˈkɒnᵗs ən‿ənt ‖ ˈkɑːnᵗs- ~s s

consonantal ˌkɒnᵗs ə ˈnænt ᵊl ◂ ‖ ˌkɑːnᵗs ə ˈnænţ ᵊl ◂ ~ly i

con|sort *v* kən |ˈsɔːt (ı)kɒn- ‖ -|ˈsɔːrt (ı)kɑːn-, ˈ· · ~sorted ˈsɔːt ɪd -əd ‖ ˈsɔːrţ əd ~sorting ˈsɔːt ɪŋ ‖ ˈsɔːrţ ɪŋ ~sorts ˈsɔːts ‖ ˈsɔːrts

consort *n* ˈkɒn sɔːt ‖ ˈkɑːn sɔːrt ~s s

consorti|um kən ˈsɔːt i‿|əm §(ı)kɒn-, -ˈsɔːʃ-, -ˈsɔːʃ |əm ‖ -ˈsɔːrt i‿|əm -ˈsɔːrʃ-; -ˈsɔːrʃ |əm ~a ə ~ums əmz

conspecific ˌkɒn spə ˈsɪf ɪk ◂ -spɪ- ‖ ˌkɑːn-

conspectus kən ˈspekt əs §(ı)kɒn- ~es ɪz əz

conspicuous kən ˈspɪk ju‿əs §(ı)kɒn- ~ly li ~ness nəs nɪs

conspirac|y kən ˈspɪr əs |i §(ı)kɒn- ~ies iz

conspirator kən ˈspɪr ət ə §(ı)kɒn- ‖ -əţ ᵊr ~s z

conspiratorial kən ˌspɪr ə ˈtɔːr i‿əl ◂ (ı)kɒn- ‖ -ˈtoʊr- ~ly i

conspire kən ˈspaɪ‿ə §(ı)kɒn- ‖ -ˈspaɪ‿ᵊr ~d d ~s z **conspiring** kən ˈspaɪər ɪŋ §(ı)kɒn- ‖ -ˈspaɪ‿ᵊr ɪŋ

constable, C~ ˈkʌnᵗst əb ᵊl ˈkɒnᵗst- ‖ ˈkɑːnᵗst- ˈkʌnᵗst- ~s z —*The painter* John C~ *was* ˈkʌnᵗst-

constabular|y kən ˈstæb jʊl ər |i §(ı)kɒn-, -ˈ·jəl- ‖ -jə ler |i ~ies iz

Constance ˈkɒnᵗst ənᵗs ‖ ˈkɑːnᵗst-

constancy ˈkɒnᵗst ənᵗs i ‖ ˈkɑːnᵗst-

constant, C~ ˈkɒnᵗst ənt ‖ ˈkɑːnᵗst- ~ly li

Constanta, Constantsa kən ˈstænᵗs ə kɒn- ‖ -ˈstɑːnᵗs ə —*Romanian* Constanţa [kon ˈstan tsa]

Constantine ˈkɒnᵗst ən taɪn -tiːn ‖ ˈkɑːnᵗst-

Constantinople ˌkɒn ˌstænt ɪ ˈnəʊp ᵊl -ə- ‖ ˌkɑːn ˌstænt ᵊn ˈoʊp ᵊl

constatation ˌkɒnᵗst ə ˈteɪʃ ᵊn ‖ ˌkɑːnᵗst- ~s z

constellation ˌkɒnᵗst ə ˈleɪʃ ᵊn -ɪ- ‖ ˌkɑːnᵗst- ~s z

consternation ˌkɒnᵗst ə ˈneɪʃ ᵊn ‖ ˌkɑːnᵗst ᵊr-

consti|pate ˈkɒnᵗst ɪ |peɪt -ə- ‖ ˈkɑːnᵗst- ~pated peɪt ɪd -əd ‖ peɪţ əd ~pates peɪts ~pating peɪt ɪŋ ‖ peɪţ ɪŋ

constipation ˌkɒnᵗst ɪ ˈpeɪʃ ᵊn -ə- ‖ ˌkɑːnᵗst-

constituenc|y kən ˈstɪt ju‿ənᵗs |i §(ı)kɒn-, -ˈstɪtʃ u‿ ‖ -ˈstɪtʃ u‿ ~ies iz

constituent kən ˈstɪt ju‿ənt §(ı)kɒn-, -ˈstɪtʃ u‿ ‖ -ˈstɪtʃ u‿ ~s s

conˌstituent asˈsembly

consti|tute ˈkɒnᵗst ɪ |tjuːt -ə-, →§-tʃuːt ‖ ˈkɑːnᵗst ə |tuːt -tjuːt ~tuted tjuːt ɪd →§tʃuːt-, -əd ‖ tuːţ əd tjuːţ- ~tutes tjuːts →§tʃuːts ‖ tuːts tjuːts ~tuting tjuːt ɪŋ →§tʃuːt- ‖ tuːţ ɪŋ tjuːţ ɪŋ

constitution ˌkɒnᵗst ɪ ˈtjuːʃ ᵊn -ə-, →§-ˈtʃuːʃ- ‖ ˌkɑːnᵗst ə ˈtuːʃ ᵊn -ˈtjuːʃ- ~s z

constitutional ˌkɒnᵗst ɪ ˈtjuːʃ ᵊn‿əl ◂ ˌ·ə-, →§-ˈtʃuːʃ- ‖ ˌkɑːnᵗst ə ˈtuːʃ- -ˈtjuːʃ- ~ly i

constitutionalism ˌkɒnᵗst ɪ ˈtjuːʃ ᵊn‿ə ˌlɪz əm ˌ·ə-, →§-ˈtʃuːʃ-, əl ˌɪz- ‖ ˌkɑːnᵗst ə ˈtuːʃ- -ˈtjuːʃ-

constitutionalist ˌkɒnᵗst ɪ ˈtjuːʃ ᵊn‿əl ɪst ˌ·ə-, →§-ˈtʃuːʃ- ‖ ˌkɑːnᵗst ə ˈtuːʃ- -ˈtjuːʃ-, §-əst ~s s

constitutionality ˌkɒnᵗst ɪ ˌtjuːʃ ə ˈnæl ət i ˌ·ə-, →§-ˌtʃuːʃ-, -ɪt i ‖ ˌkɑːnᵗst ə ˌtuːʃ ə ˈnæl əţ i -ˌtjuːʃ-

constitutive kən ˈstɪt jʊt ɪv §(ı)kɒn-, -ˈstɪtʃ ət-; ˈkɒnᵗst ɪ tjuːt ɪv, ˌ·ə-, -tʃuːt ɪv ‖ ˈkɑːnᵗst ə tuːţ ɪv -tjuːţ ɪv; kən ˈstɪtʃ əţ- ~ly li

constrain kən ˈstreɪn §(ı)kɒn- ~ed d ~ing ɪŋ ~s z

constraint kən ˈstreɪnt §(ı)kɒn- ~s s

constrict kən ˈstrɪkt §(ı)kɒn- ~ed ɪd əd ~ing ɪŋ ~s s

constriction kən ˈstrɪk ʃᵊn §(ı)kɒn- ~s z

constrictive kən ˈstrɪkt ɪv §(ı)kɒn- ~ly li

constrictor kən ˈstrɪkt ə §(ı)kɒn- ‖ -ᵊr ~s z

construct *n* ˈkɒn strʌkt ‖ ˈkɑːn- ~s s

construct *v* kən ˈstrʌkt §(ı)kɒn- ~ed ɪd əd ~ing ɪŋ ~s s

construction kən ˈstrʌk ʃᵊn §(ı)kɒn- ~s z

constructional kən ˈstrʌk ʃᵊn‿əl §(ı)kɒn- ~ly i

constructionist kən ˈstrʌk ʃᵊn‿ɪst §(ı)kɒn-, §‿əst ~s s

constructive kən ˈstrʌkt ɪv §(ı)kɒn- ~ly li ~ness nəs nɪs

constructiv|ism kən ˈstrʌkt ɪv ˌɪz əm §(ı)kɒn- ~ist/s ɪst/s §əst/s

constructor kən ˈstrʌkt ə §(ı)kɒn- ‖ -ᵊr ~s z

construe kən ˈstruː §(ı)kɒn- ~d d ~s z **construing** kən ˈstruː‿ɪŋ §(ı)kɒn-

consubstantial ˌkɒn səb ˈstænᵗʃ ᵊl ◂ §-sʌb-, -ˈstɑːnᵗʃ- ‖ ˌkɑːn-

consubstantiation ˌkɒn səb ˌstænᵗʃ i ˈeɪʃ ᵊn §ˌ·sʌb-, -ˌstænᵗs-, -ˌstɑːnᵗʃ-, -ˌstɑːnᵗs- ‖ ˌkɑːn-

consuetude ˈkɒnᵗs wɪ tjuːd -wə-, →-tʃuːd ‖ ˈkɑːnᵗs wɪ tuːd kən ˈsuː ə-, -tjuːd

consul ˈkɒnᵗs ᵊl ‖ ˈkɑːnᵗs ᵊl ~s z

ˌconsul ˈgeneral

consular ˈkɒnᵗs jʊl ə -jəl- ‖ ˈkɑːnᵗs ᵊl‿ər (*)

consulate ˈkɒnᵗs jʊl ət -jəl-, -ɪt ‖ ˈkɑːnᵗs əl‿ət ~s s

consulship ˈkɒnᵗs ᵊl ʃɪp ‖ ˈkɑːnᵗs- ~s s

consult *v* kən ˈsʌlt §(ı)kɒn- ~ed ɪd əd ~ing ɪŋ ~s s

conˈsulting room

consult *n* kən ˈsʌlt §(ı)kɒn-; ˈkɒn sʌlt ~s s

consultanc|y kən ˈsʌlt ənᵗs |i §(ı)kɒn- **~ies** iz
consultant kən ˈsʌlt ənt §(ı)kɒn- **~s** s
consultation ˌkɒnᵗs ᵊl ˈteɪʃ ᵊn -ʌl- ‖ ˌkɑːnᵗs- **~s** z
consultative kən ˈsʌlt ət ɪv §(ı)kɒn- ‖ -əţ ɪv ˈkɑːnᵗs ᵊl teɪţ ɪv
consultatory kən ˈsʌlt ət‿ər i §(ı)kɒn- ‖ -ə tɔːr i -toʊr i
consumable kən ˈsjuːm əb ᵊl §(ı)kɒn-, -ˈsuːm-, §-ˈʃuːm- ‖ -ˈsuːm- **~s** z
consum|e kən ˈsjuːm §(ı)kɒn-, -ˈsuːm, §-ˈʃuːm ‖ -ˈsuːm **~ed** d **~es** z **~ing** ɪŋ
consumer kən ˈsjuːm ə §(ı)kɒn-, -ˈsuːm-, §-ˈʃuːm- ‖ -ˈsuːm ᵊr **~s** z
conˌsumer ˈdurable; **conˈsumer goods**
consumerism kən ˈsjuːm ə ˌrɪz əm §(ı)kɒn-, -ˈsuːm-, §-ˈʃuːm-, -ᵊr ˌɪz- ‖ -ˈsuːm-
consuming kən ˈsjuːm ɪŋ §(ı)kɒn-, -ˈsuːm-, §-ˈʃuːm- ‖ -ˈsuːm-
consummate *adj* kən ˈsʌm ət §(ı)kɒn-, -ɪt; ˈkɒnᵗs əm-, -jʊm-, -juːm- ‖ ˈkɑːnᵗs əm- **~ly** li
consum|mate *v* ˈkɒnᵗs ə |meɪt -ju- ‖ ˈkɑːnᵗs- **~mated** meɪt ɪd -əd ‖ meɪţ əd **~mates** meɪts **~mating** meɪt ɪŋ ‖ meɪţ ɪŋ
consummation ˌkɒnᵗs ə ˈmeɪʃ ᵊn -ju- ‖ ˌkɑːnᵗs- **~s** z
consumption kən ˈsʌmp ʃᵊn §(ı)kɒn-
consumptive kən ˈsʌmpt ɪv §(ı)kɒn- **~ly** li **~s** z
Contac *tdmk* ˈkɒn tæk ‖ ˈkɑːn-
contact *v* ˈkɒn tækt kən ˈtækt, (ı)kɒn- ‖ ˈkɑːn- **~ed** ɪd əd **~ing** ɪŋ **~s** s
contact *n* ˈkɒn tækt ‖ ˈkɑːn- **~s** s
ˈcontact lens, ˌ· ˈ·
contagion kən ˈteɪdʒ ən §(ı)kɒn-, -ˈteɪdʒ i‿ən **~s** z
contagious kən ˈteɪdʒ əs §(ı)kɒn-, -ˈteɪdʒ i‿əs **~ly** li **~ness** nəs nɪs
contain kən ˈteɪn §(ı)kɒn- **~ed** d **~ing** ɪŋ **~s** z
container kən ˈteɪn ə §(ı)kɒn- ‖ -ᵊr **~s** z
containeris... —*see* **containeriz...**
containerization kən ˌteɪn ər aɪ ˈzeɪʃ ᵊn §kɒn-, ˌkɒn ˌteɪn-, -ər ɪ- ‖ -ər ə-
containeriz|e kən ˈteɪn ə raɪz §(ı)kɒn- **~ed** d **~es** ɪz əz **~ing** ɪŋ
containment kən ˈteɪn mənt §(ı)kɒn-, →-ˈteɪm-
contaminant kən ˈtæm ɪn ənt §(ı)kɒn-, -ən- **~s** s
contami|nate kən ˈtæm ɪ |neɪt §(ı)kɒn-, -ə- **~nated** neɪt ɪd -əd ‖ neɪţ əd **~nates** neɪts **~nating** neɪt ɪŋ ‖ neɪţ ɪŋ
contamination kən ˌtæm ɪ ˈneɪʃ ᵊn §(ı)kɒn-, -ə-
contango kən ˈtæŋ gəʊ kɒn- ‖ -goʊ **~s** z
conte *'story'* kɒnt ‖ koʊnt —*Fr* [kɔ̃ːt] **~s** s
conté *'crayon'* ˈkɒnt eɪ -i ‖ ˈkɑːnt- —*Fr* [kɔ̃ te] **~s** z
Conteh ˈkɒnt eɪ ‖ ˈkɑːnt-
contemn kən ˈtem §(ı)kɒn- **~ed** d **~ing** ɪŋ **~s** z
contem|plate ˈkɒnt əm |pleɪt ˈkɒn tem- ‖ ˈkɑːnţ əm- ˈkɑːn tem- **~plated** pleɪt ɪd -əd ‖ pleɪţ əd **~plates** pleɪts **~plating** pleɪt ɪŋ ‖ pleɪţ ɪŋ
contemplation ˌkɒnt əm ˈpleɪʃ ᵊn ˌkɒn tem- ‖ ˌkɑːnţ əm- ˌkɑːn tem-
contemplative kən ˈtemp lət ɪv §(ı)kɒn-; ˈkɒnt əm pleɪt ɪv, ˈkɒn tem-, -plət ɪv ‖ -ləţ- ˈkɑːnţ əm pleɪţ ɪv, ˈkɑːn tem- —*Some speakers may distinguish between* ·ˈ··· *(with reference to monks and nuns) and* ˈ· · · · *'pensive'.* **~ly** li **~ness** nəs nɪs **~s** z
contemporaneity kən ˌtemp ər‿ə ˈniː‿ət i kɒn-, ˌkɒn ˌtemp-, -ˈneɪ-, ɪt i ‖ -əţ i
contemporaneous kən ˌtemp ə ˈreɪn i‿əs kɒn-, ˌkɒn ˌtemp- **~ly** li **~ness** nəs nɪs
contemporar|y kən ˈtemp ᵊr‿ər |i §(ı)kɒn- ‖ -ə rer |i —*casually also* -ˈtemp r|i **~ies** iz
contempt kən ˈtem*p*t §(ı)kɒn- **~s** s
contemptibility kən ˌtem*p*t ə ˈbɪl ət i §(ı)kɒn-, -ɪt i ‖ -əţ i
contemptib|le kən ˈtem*p*t əb |ᵊl §(ı)kɒn- **~leness** ᵊl nəs -nɪs **~ly** li
contemptuous kən ˈtem*p*t ju‿əs §(ı)kɒn-, -ˈtemp tʃu‿ ‖ -ˈtem*p* tʃu‿əs -ʃu‿əs **~ly** li **~ness** nəs nɪs
contend kən ˈtend §(ı)kɒn- **~ed** ɪd əd **~er/s** ə/z ‖ -ᵊr/z **~ing** ɪŋ **~s** z
con|tent *adj, v, n 'contentment'* kən |ˈtent §(ı)kɒn- **~tented** ˈtent ɪd -əd ‖ ˈtenţ əd **~tenting** ˈtent ɪŋ ‖ ˈtenţ ɪŋ **~tents** ˈten*t*s
content *n 'matter contained'* ˈkɒn tent ‖ ˈkɑːn- **~s** s
contented kən ˈtent ɪd §(ı)kɒn-, -əd ‖ -ˈtenţ əd **~ly** li **~ness** nəs nɪs
contention kən ˈtenᵗʃ ᵊn §(ı)kɒn- **~s** z
contentious kən ˈtenᵗʃ əs §(ı)kɒn- **~ly** li **~ness** nəs nɪs
contentment kən ˈtent mənt §(ı)kɒn-
conterminous kɒn ˈtɜːm ɪn əs kən-, -ən- ‖ -ˈtɜːm- (ı)kɑːn- **~ly** li
contessa kɒn ˈtes ə ‖ kɑːn- —*It* [kon ˈtes sa]
contest *n* ˈkɒn test ‖ ˈkɑːn- **~s** s
contest *v* kən ˈtest §(ı)kɒn-; ˈkɒn test ‖ ˈkɑːn test **~ed** ɪd əd **~ing** ɪŋ **~s** s
contestant kən ˈtest ənt §(ı)kɒn- **~s** s
contestation ˌkɒnt e ˈsteɪʃ ᵊn ‖ ˌkɑːnt-
context ˈkɒn tekst ‖ ˈkɑːn- **~s** s
context-free ˌkɒn teks*t* ˈfriː ◂ ‖ ˌkɑːn-
context-sensitive ˌkɒn teks*t* ˈsenᵗs ət ɪv ◂ -ɪt ɪv ‖ ˌkɑːn teks*t* ˈsenᵗs əţ ɪv ◂
contextual kən ˈtekst ju‿əl §(ı)kɒn-, -ˈteks tʃu‿ ‖ kɑːn ˈteks tʃu‿əl kən-, -ˈteks tʃəl **~ly** i
contextualis... —*see* **contextualiz...**
contextualization kən ˌtekst ju‿əl aɪ ˈzeɪʃ ᵊn §(ı)kɒn-, -ˌteks tʃu‿, -ɪ'- ‖ kɑːn ˌteks tʃu‿əl ə ˈzeɪʃ ᵊn kən-, -ˌteks tʃəl ə ˈzeɪʃ-
contextualiz|e kən ˈtekst ju‿ə laɪz §(ı)kɒn-, -ˈteks tʃu‿ ‖ kɑːn ˈteks tʃu‿ə laɪz kən-, -ˈteks tʃə laɪz **~ed** d **~es** ɪz əz **~ing** ɪŋ
Contiboard *tdmk* ˈkɒnt i bɔːd ‖ ˈkɑːnţ i bɔːrd -boʊrd

contiguit|y ˌkɒnt ɪ ˈgjuː ət |i ˌ·ə-, ɪt i ‖ ˌkɑːnt̬ ə ˈgjuː ət̬ |i **~ies** iz

contiguous kən ˈtɪg ju‿əs §(ı)kɒn- **~ly** li **~ness** nəs nɪs

Contin ˈkɒnt ɪn §-ən ‖ ˈkɑːnt-

continence ˈkɒnt ɪn ənᵗs -ən- ‖ ˈkɑːnt ən-

continent ˈkɒnt ɪn ənt -ən- ‖ ˈkɑːnt ən‿ənt **~ly** li **~s** s

continental ˌkɒnt ɪ ˈnent əl ◂ -ə- ‖ ˌkɑːnt ən ˈent̬ əl ◂ **~ly** i
ˌcontiˌnental ˈbreakfast; **ˌcontiˌnental ˈshelf**

contingenc|y kən ˈtɪndʒ ənᵗs |i §(ı)kɒn- **~ies** iz

contingent kən ˈtɪndʒ ənt §(ı)kɒn- **~ly** li **~s** s

continua kən ˈtɪn ju ə §(ı)kɒn-

continual kən ˈtɪn ju‿əl §(ı)kɒn- **~ly** i

continuance kən ˈtɪn ju‿ənᵗs §(ı)kɒn-

continuant kən ˈtɪn ju‿ənt §(ı)kɒn- **~s** s

continuation kən ˌtɪn ju ˈeɪʃ ən §(ı)kɒn- **~s** z

continuative kən ˈtɪn ju‿ət ɪv -eɪt ɪv ‖ -eɪt̬ ɪv **~ly** li

continu|e kən ˈtɪn juː §(ı)kɒn-, -ju ‖ -ju **~ed** d **~es** z **~ing** ɪŋ

continuit|y ˌkɒnt ɪ ˈnjuː ət |i ˌ·ə-, -ɪt i ‖ ˌkɑːnt ən ˈuː ət̬ |i -ˈjuː- **~ies** iz

continuo kən ˈtɪn ju əʊ (ı)kɒn-, -u- ‖ -oʊ **~s** z

continuous kən ˈtɪn ju‿əs §(ı)kɒn- **~ly** li **~ness** nəs nɪs

continu|um kən ˈtɪn ju‿əm §(ı)kɒn- **~a** ə

contoid ˈkɒnt ɔɪd ‖ ˈkɑːnt- **~s** z

contoidal kɒn ˈtɔɪd əl ‖ kɑːn-

con|tort kən |ˈtɔːt §(ı)kɒn- ‖ -|ˈtɔːrt **~torted** ˈtɔːt ɪd -əd ‖ ˈtɔːrt̬ əd **~torting** ˈtɔːt ɪŋ ‖ ˈtɔːrt̬ ɪŋ **~torts** ˈtɔːts ‖ ˈtɔːrts

contorted kən ˈtɔːt ɪd §(ı)kɒn-, -əd ‖ ˈtɔːrt̬ əd **~ly** li **~ness** nəs nɪs

contortion kən ˈtɔːʃ ən §(ı)kɒn- ‖ -ˈtɔːrʃ ən **~s** z

contortionist kən ˈtɔːʃ ən‿ɪst (ı)kɒn-, §‿əst ‖ -ˈtɔːrʃ- **~s** s

contour ˈkɒn tʊə -ɔː ‖ ˈkɑːn tʊr **~ed** d **contouring** ˈkɒn tʊər ɪŋ ‖ ˈkɑːn tʊr ɪŋ **~s** z
ˈcontour line

contra, C~ ˈkɒntr ə -ɑː ‖ ˈkɑːntr ə **~s** z

contra- *comb. form* ¦kɒntr ə ‖ ¦kɑːntr ə — **contraposition** ˌkɒntr ə pə ˈzɪʃ ən ‖ ˌkɑːntr-

contraband ˈkɒntr ə bænd ‖ ˈkɑːntr- **~ist/s** ɪst/s §əst/s ‖ əst/s

contrabass ˌkɒntr ə ˈbeɪs ˈ· · · ‖ ˈkɑːntr ə beɪs **~ist/s** ɪst/s §əst/s ‖ əst/s

contraception ˌkɒntr ə ˈsep ʃən ‖ ˌkɑːntr-

contraceptive ˌkɒntr ə ˈsept ɪv ◂ ‖ ˌkɑːntr- **~s** z

contract *v* kən ˈtrækt §(ı)kɒn- —*but in the meaning 'agree under contract, make a contract' sometimes* ˈkɒn trækt ‖ ˈkɑːn- **~ed** ɪd əd **~ing** ɪŋ **~s** s

contract *n* ˈkɒn trækt ‖ ˈkɑːn- **~s** s

contractible kən ˈtrækt əb əl §(ı)kɒn-

contractile kən ˈtrækt aɪəl §(ı)kɒn- ‖ -əl -aɪəl

contractility ˌkɒn træk ˈtɪl ət i -ɪt i ‖ ˌkɑːn træk ˈtɪl ət̬ i

contraction kən ˈtræk ʃən §(ı)kɒn- **~s** z

contractor kən ˈtrækt ə §(ı)kɒn-; ˈkɒn trækt ə ‖ ˈkɑːn trækt ər **~s** z

contractual kən ˈtræk tʃu‿əl §(ı)kɒn-, -ˈtrækt ju‿ ‖ kɑːn-, -ˈtræk tʃəl **~ly** i

contracture kən ˈtræk tʃə §(ı)kɒn-, -tjʊə, -ʃə ‖ -tʃər **~s** z

contradict ˌkɒntr ə ˈdɪkt ‖ ˌkɑːntr- **~ed** ɪd əd **~ing** ɪŋ **~s** s

contradiction ˌkɒntr ə ˈdɪk ʃən ‖ ˌkɑːntr- **~s** z

contradictor|y ˌkɒntr ə ˈdɪkt ər‿|i ◂ ‖ ˌkɑːntr- **~ies** iz **~ily** əl i ɪ li **~iness** i nəs i nɪs

contradistinction ˌkɒntr ə dɪ ˈstɪŋk ʃən -ə də- ‖ ˌkɑːntr-

contradistinctive ˌkɒntr ə dɪ ˈstɪŋkt ɪv ◂ -ə də- ‖ ˌkɑːntr- **~ly** li

contrafactual ˌkɒntr ə ˈfæk tʃu‿əl ◂ -ʃu‿əl; -ˈfækt ju‿ ‖ ˌkɑːntr- **~ly** i **~s** z

contraflow ˈkɒntr ə fləʊ ˌ· ·ˈ· ‖ ˈkɑːntr ə floʊ **~s** z

contrail ˈkɒn treɪəl ‖ ˈkɑːn- **~s** z

contraindi|cate ˌkɒntr ə ˈɪnd ɪ |keɪt →ˌ·əʳ- ‖ ˌkɑːntr- **~cated** keɪt ɪd -əd ‖ keɪt̬ əd **~cates** keɪts **~cating** keɪt ɪŋ ‖ keɪt̬ ɪŋ

contraindication ˌkɒntr ə ˌɪnd ɪ ˈkeɪʃ ən →ˌ·əʳ-, ˌ·ˌ·ə- ‖ ˌkɑːntr- **~s** z

contralateral ˌkɒntr ə ˈlæt‿ər əl ◂ ‖ ˌkɑːntr ə ˈlæt̬ ər əl →-ˈlætr əl

contralto kən ˈtrɑːlt əʊ §(ı)kɒn-, -ˈtrælt- ‖ -ˈtrælt oʊ **~s** z

contraption kən ˈtræp ʃən §(ı)kɒn- **~s** z

contrapuntal ˌkɒntr ə ˈpʌnt əl ◂ ‖ ˌkɑːntr ə ˈpʌnt̬ əl ◂ **~ly** i

contrari... —*see* **contrary**

contrariet|y ˌkɒntr ə ˈraɪ‿ət |i -ɪt i ‖ ˌkɑːntr ə ˈraɪ ət̬ |i **~ies** iz

contrarily kən ˈtreər əl i -ɪ li; ˈkɒntr ər- ‖ ˈkɑːn trer əl i ˌ·ˈ·-

contrariwise kən ˈtreər i waɪz §(ı)kɒn-; ˈkɒntr ər- ‖ ˈkɑːn trer- kən ˈtrer-

contrar|y *adj 'perverse, obstinate'* kən ˈtreər |i §(ı)kɒn- ‖ -ˈtrer |i ˈkɑːn trer |i **~iness** i nəs i nɪs

contrar|y *n; adj 'different, opposed'* ˈkɒntr ər |i ‖ ˈkɑːn trer |i **~ies** iz **~iness** i nəs i nɪs

contrast *v* kən ˈtrɑːst §(ı)kɒn-, §-ˈtræst; ˈkɒn trɑːst, §-træst ‖ -ˈtræst ˈkɑːn træst —*The* -ˈtræst *form was apparently used in RP until at least the 1940s.* **~ed** ɪd əd **~ing** ɪŋ **~s** s

contrast *n* ˈkɒn trɑːst §-træst ‖ ˈkɑːn træst **~s** s

contrastive kən ˈtrɑːst ɪv §(ı)kɒn-, §-ˈtræst- ‖ -ˈtræst- **~ly** li **~ness** nəs nɪs

contrasty ˈkɒn trɑːst i §-ˈtræst- ‖ ˈkɑːn træst i

contraven|e ˌkɒntr ə ˈviːn ‖ ˌkɑːntr- **~ed** d **~es** z **~ing** ɪŋ

contravention ˌkɒntr ə ˈvenᵗʃ ən ‖ ˌkɑːntr- **~s** z

contretemps ˈkɒntr ə tɒ̃ -tɒŋ, -tɒm ‖ ˈkɑːntr ə tɑ̃ː —*Fr* [kɔ̃ tʁə tɑ̃] —*The plural (spelled identically) is pronounced with* -z *or, as in French, like the singular.*

C

C

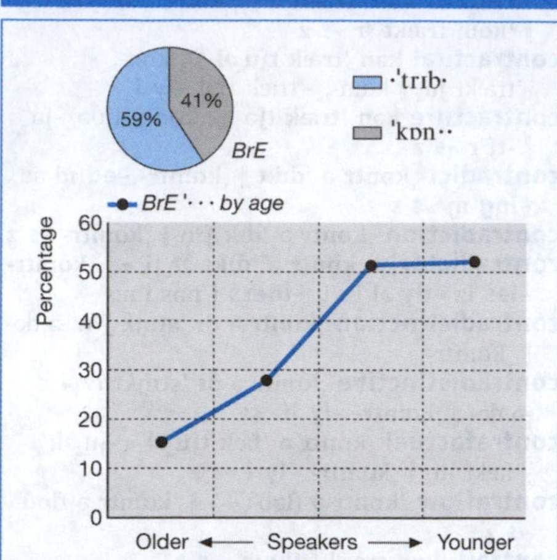

contribute kən ˈtrɪb juːt §₍ₗ₎kɒn-; ˈkɒntr ɪ bjuːt, -ə- ‖ kən ˈtrɪb jət -juːt — *Preference poll, BrE: ·'· · 59%, '· · · 41%; born before 1942, ·'· · 84% '· · · 16%.*

contributed kən ˈtrɪb jʊt ɪd §₍ₗ₎kɒn-; ˈkɒntr ɪ bjuːt ɪd, ˈ·ə- ‖ -ˈtrɪb jəṭ əd -əṭ-, -juːṭ-

contributes kən ˈtrɪb juːts §₍ₗ₎kɒn-; ˈkɒntr ɪ bjuːts, -ə- ‖ -ˈtrɪb jəts -juːts

contributing kən ˈtrɪb jʊt ɪŋ -jət-, §-juːt-; ˈkɒntr ɪ bjuːt ɪŋ, ˈ·ə- ‖ -ˈtrɪb jəṭ ɪŋ -əṭ-, -juːṭ-

contribution ˌkɒntr ɪ ˈbjuːʃ ən -ə- ‖ ˌkɑːntr- **~s** z

contributive kən ˈtrɪb jʊt ɪv §₍ₗ₎kɒn-, -jət-, §-juːt-; ˈkɒntr ɪ bjuːt-, ˈ·ə- ‖ -jəṭ ɪv -əṭ- **~ly** li **~ness** nəs nɪs

contributor kən ˈtrɪb jʊt ə §₍ₗ₎kɒn-, -jət-, §-juːt-; ˈkɒntr ɪ bjuːt ə, ˈ·ə- ‖ -jəṭ ər -əṭ- **~s** z

contributor|y kən ˈtrɪb jʊ‿tər |i §₍ₗ₎kɒn-, -ˈjə-, §-ˈjuː-; ˌkɒntr ɪ ˈbjuːt ər |i, ˌ·ə-‖ -jə tɔːr |i -toʊr i **~ies** iz

contrite ˈkɒn traɪt kən ˈtraɪt ‖ kən ˈtraɪt ˈkɑːn traɪt **~ly** li **~ness** nəs nɪs

contrition kən ˈtrɪʃ ən §₍ₗ₎kɒn-

contrivanc|e kən ˈtraɪv ən̩ts §₍ₗ₎kɒn- **~es** ɪz əz

contriv|e kən ˈtraɪv §₍ₗ₎kɒn- **~ed** d **~es** z **~ing** ɪŋ

control kən ˈtrəʊl §₍ₗ₎kɒn-, →-ˈtrɒʊl ‖ -ˈtroʊl **~led** d **~ling** ɪŋ **~s** z

con'trol freak; **con'trol group**; **con'trol room**; **con'trol ˌtower**

controllable kən ˈtrəʊl əb əl §₍ₗ₎kɒn-, →-ˈtrɒʊl- ‖ -ˈtroʊl-

controller kən ˈtrəʊl ə §₍ₗ₎kɒn-, →-ˈtrɒʊl- ‖ -ˈtroʊl ər **~s** z

controversial ˌkɒntr ə ˈvɜːʃ əl ◂ -ˈvɜːs i‿əl ‖ ˌkɑːntr ə ˈvɝːʃ əl -ˈvɜːs i‿əl **~ist/s** ɪst/s §əst/s ‖ əst/s **~ly** i

controvers|y ˈkɒntr ə vɜːs |i -vəs i; kən ˈtrɒv əs |i, §₍ₗ₎kɒn- ‖ ˈkɑːntr ə vɝːs |i **~ies** iz —*Among RP speakers the* ˈkɒntr- *form perhaps still predominates; but in BrE in general the* -ˈtrɒv- *form is now clearly more*

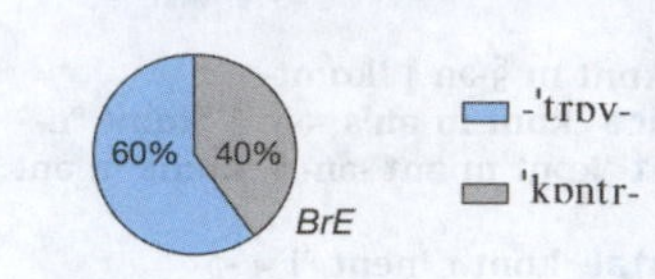

widespread. Preference poll, BrE: -ˈtrɒv- *60%,* ˈkɒntr- *40%. In AmE* ˈkɑːntr- *is the only possibility.*

contro|vert ˌkɒntr ə |ˈvɜːt ◂ ˈ· · · ‖ ˈkɑːntr ə |vɝːt ˌ· ·ˈ· **~verted** ˈvɜːt ɪd -əd ‖ vɝːṭ əd **~verting** ˈvɜːt ɪŋ ‖ vɝːṭ ɪŋ **~verts** ˈvɜːts ‖ vɝːts

contumacious ˌkɒn tju ˈmeɪʃ əs ◂ ‖ ˌkɑːn tə- -tjə-, -tʃə- **~ly** li **~ness** nəs nɪs

contumac|y ˈkɒnt jʊm əs |i ˈ·jəm- ‖ kən ˈtuːm əs |i -ˈtjuːm- **~ies** iz

contumelious ˌkɒn tju ˈmiːl i‿əs ◂ ‖ ˌkɑːn tə- ·tjə-, ·tʃə- **~ly** li

contumely ˈkɒn tjuːm li -tjʊm ɪl i, -əl i; kən ˈtjuːm əl‿i, -ɪl i ‖ kɑːn ˈtuːm əl i kən-, -ˈtjuːm-; ˈkɑːn tə miːl i, ˈ·tjə-, ˈ·tʃə-

contus|e kən ˈtjuːz §₍ₗ₎kɒn-, →§-ˈtʃuːz ‖ -ˈtuːz -ˈtjuːz **~ed** d **~es** ɪz əz **~ing** ɪŋ

contusion kən ˈtjuːʒ ən §₍ₗ₎kɒn-, →§-ˈtʃuːʒ- ‖ -ˈtuːʒ- -ˈtjuːʒ- **~s** z

conundrum kə ˈnʌndr əm **~s** z

conurbation ˌkɒn ɜː ˈbeɪʃ ən -ə- ‖ ˌkɑːn ər- **~s** z

conure ˈkɒn jʊə ‖ ˈkɑːn jʊr **~s** z

Convair *tdmk* ˈkɒn veə ‖ ˈkɑːn ver

convalesc|e ˌkɒn və ˈles ‖ ˌkɑːn- **~ed** t **~es** ɪz əz **~ing** ɪŋ

convalescence ˌkɒn və ˈles ən̩ts ‖ ˌkɑːn-

convalescent ˌkɒn və ˈles ənt ◂ ‖ ˌkɑːn- **~s** s

convect kən ˈvekt §₍ₗ₎kɒn- **~ed** ɪd əd **~ing** ɪŋ **~s** s

convection kən ˈvek ʃən §₍ₗ₎kɒn-

convective kən ˈvekt ɪv §₍ₗ₎kɒn- **~ly** li

convector kən ˈvekt ə §₍ₗ₎kɒn- ‖ -ər **~s** z

conven|e kən ˈviːn §₍ₗ₎kɒn- **~ed** d **~er/s** ə/z ‖ ər/z **~es** z **~ing** ɪŋ

convenienc|e kən ˈviːn i‿ən̩ts §₍ₗ₎kɒn- **~es** ɪz əz

con'venience food

convenient kən ˈviːn i‿ənt §₍ₗ₎kɒn- **~ly** li

convenor kən ˈviːn ə §₍ₗ₎kɒn- ‖ -ər **~s** z

convent ˈkɒn vənt ‖ ˈkɑːn- -vent **~s** s

conventicle kən ˈvent ɪk əl §₍ₗ₎kɒn- ‖ -ˈvenṭ- **~s** z

convention kən ˈvenᵗʃ ən §₍ₗ₎kɒn- **~s** z

conventional kən ˈvenᵗʃ ən‿əl §₍ₗ₎kɒn- **~ism** ɪz əm **~ly** i

conventionalis... —*see* **conventionaliz...**

conventionality kən ˌvenᵗʃ ə ˈnæl ət i §₍ₗ₎kɒn-, -ɪt i ‖ -əṭ i

conventionalized kən ˈvenᵗʃ ən‿ə laɪzd §₍ₗ₎kɒn-

onventio|neer kən ˌventʃ ə ˈnɪə §kɒn- ‖ -ˈnɪᵊr **~ed** d **conventioneering** kən ˌventʃ ə ˈnɪər ɪŋ §(ı)kɒn- ‖ -ˈnɪr ɪŋ **~s** z

onverb ˈkɒn vɜːb ‖ ˈkɑːn vɜ˞ːb **~s** z

onverg|e kən ˈvɜːdʒ §(ı)kɒn- ‖ -ˈvɜ˞ːdʒ —*but in contrast to* diverge, ˈkɒn vɜːdʒ ‖ ˈkɑːn vɜ˞ːdʒ **~ed** d **~es** ɪz əz **~ing** ɪŋ

onvergenc|e kən ˈvɜːdʒ ənᵗs §(ı)kɒn- ‖ -ˈvɜ˞ːdʒ- —*but in contrast to* divergence, ˈkɒn vɜːdʒ- ‖ ˈkɑːn vɜ˞ːdʒ- **~es** ɪz əz **~ies** iz **~y** i

onvergent kən ˈvɜːdʒ ənt §(ı)kɒn- ‖ -ˈvɜ˞ːdʒ- —*but in contrast to* divergent, ˈkɒn vɜːdʒ- ‖ ˈkɑːn vɜ˞ːdʒ- **~ly** li

onversab|le kən ˈvɜːs əb |ᵊl ‖ -ˈvɜ˞ːs- **~leness** ᵊl nəs -nɪs **~ly** li

onversant kən ˈvɜːs ᵊnt §(ı)kɒn- ‖ -ˈvɜ˞ːs- ˈkɑːn vᵊrs- **~ly** li

onversation ˌkɒn və ˈseɪʃ ᵊn ‖ ˌkɑːn vᵊr- **~s** z

ˌ**conver'sation piece**

onversational ˌkɒn və ˈseɪʃ ᵊn‿əl ◂ ‖ ˌkɑːn vᵊr- **~ly** i

onversationalist ˌkɒn və ˈseɪʃ ᵊn‿əl ɪst §-əst ‖ ˌkɑːn vᵊr- **~s** s

onversazion|e ˌkɒn və sæts i ˈəʊn |i ‖ ˌkɑːn vᵊr sɑːts i ˈoʊn |i ˌkoʊn- —*It* [kon ver sat ˈtsjoː ne] **~es** iz **~i** iː

onverse *n* ˈkɒn vɜːs ‖ ˈkɑːn vɜ˞ːs

onvers|e *v* kən ˈvɜːs §(ı)kɒn- ‖ -ˈvɜ˞ːs **~ed** t **~es** ɪz əz **~ing** ɪŋ

onverse *adj* ˈkɒn vɜːs kən ˈvɜːs ‖ kən ˈvɜ˞ːs ˈkɑːn vɜ˞ːs **~ly** li

onversion kən ˈvɜːʃ ᵊn §(ı)kɒn-, §-ˈvɜːʒ- ‖ -ˈvɜ˞ːʒ- -ˈvɜ˞ːʃ- **~s** z

con'version ˌfactor

con|vert *v* kən |ˈvɜːt §(ı)kɒn- ‖ -|ˈvɜ˞ːt **~verted** ˈvɜːt ɪd -əd ‖ ˈvɜ˞ːţ əd **~verts** ˈvɜːts ‖ ˈvɜ˞ːts **~verting** ˈvɜːt ɪŋ ‖ ˈvɜ˞ːţ ɪŋ

convert *n* ˈkɒn vɜːt ‖ ˈkɑːn vɜ˞ːt **~s** s

converter kən ˈvɜːt ə §(ı)kɒn- ‖ -ˈvɜ˞ːţ ᵊr **~s** z

convertibility kən ˌvɜːt ə ˈbɪl ət i §kɒn-, §ˌkɒn ˌvɜːt-, -ɪˈ--, -ɪt i ‖ -ˌvɜ˞ːţ ə ˈbɪl əţ i

convertible kən ˈvɜːt əb ᵊl §(ı)kɒn-, -ɪb- ‖ -ˈvɜ˞ːţ-

convertor kən ˈvɜːt ə §(ı)kɒn- ‖ -ˈvɜ˞ːţ ᵊr **~s** z

convex ˌkɒn ˈveks ◂ kən- ‖ ˌkɑːn- kən-; ˈkɑːn veks **~ly** li

convexit|y kən ˈveks ət |i ˌkɒn-, ɪt- ‖ -əţ |i ˌkɑːn- **~ies** iz

convexo-concave kən ˌveks əʊ kɒn ˈkeɪv ◂ kɒn-, ˌkɒn ˌ--, →-kɒŋˈ-, -kənˈ- ‖ -oʊ kɑːn-

convexo-convex kən ˌveks əʊ kɒn ˈveks ◂ kɒn-, ˌkɒn ˌ--, -kənˈ- ‖ -oʊ kɑːn-

convey kən ˈveɪ §(ı)kɒn- **~ed** d **~ing** ɪŋ **~s** z

conveyanc|e kən ˈveɪ ənᵗs §(ı)kɒn- **~ed** t **~er/s** ə/z ‖ ᵊr/z **~es** ɪz əz **~ing** ɪŋ

conveyer, conveyor kən ˈveɪ ə §(ı)kɒn- ‖ ᵊr **~s** z

con'veyor belt

convict *v* kən ˈvɪkt §(ı)kɒn- **~ed** ɪd əd **~ing** ɪŋ **~s** s

convict *n* ˈkɒn vɪkt ‖ ˈkɑːn- **~s** s

conviction kən ˈvɪk ʃᵊn §(ı)kɒn- **~s** z

convinc|e kən ˈvɪnᵗs §(ı)kɒn- **~ed** t **~es** ɪz əz **~ing/ly** ɪŋ /li

convivial kən ˈvɪv i‿əl §(ı)kɒn- **~ly** i

conviviality kən ˌvɪv i ˈæl ət i §(ı)kɒn-, -ɪt i ‖ -əţ i

convocation, C~ ˌkɒn və ˈkeɪʃ ᵊn ‖ ˌkɑːn- **~s** z

convok|e kən ˈvəʊk §(ı)kɒn- ‖ -ˈvoʊk **~ed** t **~es** s **~ing** ɪŋ

convoluted ˈkɒn və ˌluːt ɪd -ˌljuːt-, -əd, ˌ-ˈ--◂ ‖ ˈkɑːn və ˌluːţ əd **~ly** li

convolution ˌkɒn və ˈluːʃ ᵊn -ˈljuːʃ- ‖ ˌkɑːn- **~s** z

convolv|e kən ˈvɒlv §-ˈvəʊlv ‖ -ˈvɑːlv **~ed** d **~es** z **~ing** ɪŋ

convolv|ulus kən ˈvɒlv |jʊl əs §(ı)kɒn-, -jəl- ‖ -ˈvɑːlv |jəl- -ˈvɔːlv-, -ˈvɑːv-, -ˈvɔːv- **~uli** ju laɪ jə- ‖ jə laɪ **~uluses** jʊl əs ɪz jəl-, -əz ‖ jəl əs əz

convoy *v* ˈkɒn vɔɪ ‖ ˈkɑːn- kən ˈvɔɪ **~ed** d **~ing** ɪŋ **~s** z

convoy *n* ˈkɒn vɔɪ ‖ ˈkɑːn- **~s** z

convulsant kən ˈvʌls ᵊnt §(ı)kɒn- **~s** s

convuls|e kən ˈvʌls §(ı)kɒn- **~ed** t **~es** ɪz əz **~ing** ɪŋ

convulsion kən ˈvʌlʃ ᵊn §(ı)kɒn- **~s** z

convulsive kən ˈvʌls ɪv §(ı)kɒn- **~ly** li **~ness** nəs nɪs

Conway ˈkɒn weɪ ‖ ˈkɑːn-

Conwy ˈkɒn wi ‖ ˈkɑːn- —*Welsh* [ˈkɔn ui]

con|y ˈkəʊn |i ‖ ˈkoʊn |i —*formerly* ˈkʌn i **~ies** iz

Conybeare *(i)* ˈkɒn i bɪə ‖ ˈkɑːn i bɪr, *(ii)* ˈkʌn-

coo kuː **cooed** kuːd **cooing** ˈkuː ɪŋ **coos** kuːz

Coober Pedy ˌkuːb ə ˈpiːd i ‖ -ᵊr-

Cooch kuːtʃ

cooee, cooey ˈkuː iː ˌ-ˈ-; ˈkuː i **~s** z

Coogan ˈkuːg ən

cook, Cook kʊk §kuːk **cooked** kʊkt §kuːkt **cooking** ˈkʊk ɪŋ §ˈkuːk- **cooks** kʊks §kuːks

'cook book

cook-chill ˌkʊk ˈtʃɪl ◂ §ˌkuːk- **~ed** d **~ing** ɪŋ **~s** z

Cooke kʊk §kuːk

Cookeen *tdmk* (ı)kʊ ˈkiːn

cooker ˈkʊk ə §ˈkuːk- ‖ -ᵊr **~s** z

cookery ˈkʊk ər‿i §ˈkuːk-

'cookery book

cook|house ˈkʊk |haʊs §ˈkuːk- **~houses** haʊz ɪz -əz

cookie ˈkʊk i **~s** z

cooking ˈkʊk ɪŋ §ˈkuːk-

'cooking ˌapple

cookout ˈkʊk aʊt §ˈkuːk- **~s** s

Cookson ˈkʊks ᵊn

Cooktown ˈkʊk taʊn

cookware ˈkʊk weə §ˈkuːk- ‖ -wer -wæər **~s** z

cook|y ˈkʊk |i **~ies** iz

cool kuːl **cooled** kuːld **cooler** ˈkuːl ə ‖ -ᵊr **coolest** ˈkuːl ɪst -əst **cooling** ˈkuːl ɪŋ **cools** kuːlz

'cooling ˌtower

C

coolabah 'kuːl ə bɑː **~s** z
coolamon 'kuːl ə mɒn ‖ -mɑːn
Coolangatta ˌkuːl əŋ 'gæt ə -ən- ‖ -'gæţ ə
coolant 'kuːl ənt **~s** s
coolbag 'kuːl bæg **~s** z
coolbox 'kuːl bɒks ‖ -bɑːks **~es** ɪz əz
cooler 'kuːl ə ‖ -ᵊr **~s** z
Cooley 'kuːl i
Coolgardie kuːl 'gɑːd i ‖ -'gɑːrd i
cool-headed ˌkuːl 'hed ɪd ◂ -əd
coolibah, coolibar 'kuːl ə bɑː -ɪ- **~s** z
Coolidge 'kuːl ɪdʒ
coolie 'kuːl i **~s** z
Coolin 'kuːl ɪn §-ən
cooling-off ˌkuːl ɪŋ 'ɒf -'ɔːf ‖ -'ɔːf -'ɑːf
ˌcooling-'off ˌperiod
coolly 'kuːl li -i
coolness 'kuːl nəs -nɪs
Cooloola kə 'luːl ə
coolth kuːlθ
coomb, coombe, C~ kuːm **coombs** kuːmz
Coombes, Coombs, Coomes kuːmz
coon kuːn **coons** kuːnz
Coonawarra ˌkuːn ə 'wɒr ə ‖ -'wɑːr ə -'wɔːr ə
cooncan 'kuːn kæn →'kuːŋ-
Cooney 'kuːn i
coonskin 'kuːn skɪn **~s** z
coontie 'kuːnt i **~s** z
coop kuːp ‖ kʊp **cooped** kuːpt ‖ kʊpt **cooping** 'kuːp ɪŋ ‖ 'kʊp- **coops** kuːps ‖ kʊps
Co-op, co-op 'kəʊ ɒp ‖ 'koʊ ɑːp **~s** s
Coope kuːp
cooper, C~ 'kuːp ə ‖ -ᵊr 'kʊp- **~ed** d
coopering 'kuːp ər ɪŋ ‖ 'kʊp- **~s** z
cooperage 'kuːp ər ɪdʒ ‖ 'kʊp-
coope|rate, co-ope|rate kəʊ 'ɒp ə |reɪt ‖ koʊ 'ɑːp- **~rated** reɪt ɪd -əd ‖ reɪţ əd **~rates** reɪts **~rating** reɪt ɪŋ ‖ reɪţ ɪŋ
cooperation, co-operation kəʊ ˌɒp ə 'reɪʃ ᵊn ˌkəʊ ˌɒp- ‖ koʊ ˌɑːp- ˌkoʊ ˌɑːp-
cooperative, co-operative, C~ kəʊ 'ɒp ər‿ət ɪv ‖ koʊ 'ɑːp ər‿əţ ɪv -ə reɪţ- **~ly** li **~ness** nəs nɪs
coopt, co-opt kəʊ 'ɒpt ‖ koʊ 'ɑːpt **~ed** ɪd əd **~ing** ɪŋ **~s** s
cooptation, co-optation ˌkəʊ ɒp 'teɪʃ ᵊn ‖ ˌkoʊ ɑːp- **~s** z
cooption, co-option kəʊ 'ɒp ʃᵊn ‖ koʊ 'ɑːp- **~s** z
coordin|ate, co-ordin|ate *v* kəʊ 'ɔːd ɪ n|eɪt -ə-, -ᵊn |eɪt ‖ koʊ 'ɔːrd ᵊn |eɪt **~ated** eɪt ɪd -əd ‖ eɪţ əd **~ates** eɪts **~ating** eɪt ɪŋ ‖ eɪţ ɪŋ
coordinate, co-ordinate *adj, n* kəʊ 'ɔːd ɪn ət -ᵊn‿ət, -ɪt ‖ koʊ 'ɔːrd ᵊn‿ət -eɪt **~ly** li **~ness** nəs nɪs **~s** s
coordination, co-ordination kəʊ ˌɔːd ɪ 'neɪʃ ᵊn ˌkəʊ ˌɔːd-, -ə-, -ᵊn 'eɪʃ- ‖ koʊ ˌɔːrd ᵊn 'eɪʃ ᵊn ˌkoʊ ˌɔːrd-
coordinator, co-ordinator kəʊ 'ɔːd ɪ neɪt ə -'-ə-, -ᵊn eɪt- ‖ koʊ 'ɔːrd ᵊn eɪţ ᵊr **~s** z
Coors *tdmk* kɔːz kʊəz ‖ kʊᵊrz
coot kuːt **coots** kuːts
Coot, Coote kuːt
Cootamundra ˌkuːt ə 'mʌndr ə ◂ ‖ ˌkuːţ-
ˌCoota ˌmundra 'wattle
cootie 'kuːt i ‖ 'kuːţ i **~s** z
co-own ˌkəʊ 'əʊn ‖ ˌkoʊ 'oʊn **~ed** d **~er/s** ə/z ‖ -ᵊr/z **~ership** ə ʃɪp ‖ -ᵊr ʃɪp **~ing** ɪŋ **~s** z
cop kɒp ‖ kɑːp **copped** kɒpt ‖ kɑːpt **copping** 'kɒp ɪŋ ‖ 'kɑːp ɪŋ **cops** kɒps ‖ kɑːps
Copacabana ˌkəʊp ə kə 'bæn ə ‖ ˌkoʊp- —*Sp* [ko pa ka 'βa na], *BrazPort* [kɔ pa ka 'bɐ na]
copacetic ˌkəʊp ə 'siːt ɪk ◂ ‖ ˌkoʊp ə 'seţ ɪk ◂ -'siːţ-
copaiba kəʊ 'paɪb ə kɒ- ‖ koʊ-
copal 'kəʊp ᵊl -æl ‖ 'koʊp-
copartner ˌkəʊ 'pɑːt nə ‖ ˌkoʊ 'pɑːrt nᵊr **~s** z **~ship/s** ʃɪp/s
-cope *stress-imposing* kəp i — **apocope** ə 'pɒk əp i ‖ -'pɑːk-
cope, Cope kəʊp ‖ koʊp **coped** kəʊpt ‖ koʊpt **copes** kəʊps ‖ koʊps **coping** 'kəʊp ɪŋ ‖ 'koʊp ɪŋ
copeck 'kəʊp ek ‖ 'koʊp- **~s** s
Copeland 'kəʊp lənd ‖ 'koʊp-
Copenhagen ˌkəʊp ən 'heɪg ən ◂ -'hɑːg-, '· · ˌ· · ‖ 'koʊp ən ˌheɪg ən ˌ· '· ·, -'hɑːg ən —*Danish* København [køb ən 'hauʔn]
coper 'kəʊp ə ‖ 'koʊp ᵊr **~s** z
Copernic|an kəʊ 'pɜːn ɪk |ən ‖ koʊ 'pɝːn- kə- **~us** əs
Copestake 'kəʊp steɪk ‖ 'koʊp-
copestone 'kəʊp stəʊn ‖ 'koʊp stoʊn **~s** z
copi... —*see* **copy**
copier 'kɒp i‿ə ‖ 'kɑːp i‿ᵊr **~s** z
copilot 'kəʊ ˌpaɪl ət ˌ'· · ‖ 'koʊ- **~s** s
coping 'kəʊp ɪŋ ‖ 'koʊp ɪŋ
copingstone 'kəʊp ɪŋ stəʊn ‖ 'koʊp ɪŋ stoʊn **~s** z
copious 'kəʊp i‿əs ‖ 'koʊp- **~ly** li **~ness** nəs nɪs
copita kəʊ 'piːt ə kɒ- ‖ koʊ 'piːţ ə —*Sp* [ko 'pi ta] **~s** z —*Sp* [s]
Copland *(i)* 'kəʊp lənd ‖ 'koʊp-, *(ii)* 'kɒp- ‖ 'kɑːp- —*The composer,* Aaron C~, *is (i)*
Copley 'kɒp li ‖ 'kɑːp-
copolymer (ˌ)kəʊ 'pɒl ɪm ə -əm- ‖ (ˌ)koʊ 'pɑːl əm ᵊr **~s** z
cop-out, copout 'kɒp aʊt ‖ 'kɑːp- **~s** s
copp... —*see* **cop**
copper 'kɒp ə ‖ 'kɑːp ᵊr **~ed** d **~s** z
ˌcopper 'beech; **'Copper Belt**; **ˌcopper 'sulphate**
copperas 'kɒp ər əs ‖ 'kɑːp-
copper-bottomed ˌkɒp ə 'bɒt əmd ◂ ‖ ˌkɑːp ᵊr 'bɑːţ əmd ◂
Copperfield 'kɒp ə fiːᵊld ‖ 'kɑːp ᵊr-
copperhead 'kɒp ə hed ‖ 'kɑːp ᵊr- **~s** z
coppermine, C~ 'kɒp ə maɪn ‖ 'kɑːp ᵊr- **~s** z
copperplate 'kɒp ə pleɪt ˌ· '· ‖ 'kɑːp ᵊr-
coppersmith, C~ 'kɒp ə smɪθ ‖ 'kɑːp ᵊr- **~s** s
coppery 'kɒp ər i ‖ 'kɑːp-
coppic|e 'kɒp ɪs §-əs ‖ 'kɑːp əs **~ed** t **~es** ɪz əz **~ing** ɪŋ

oppola 'kɒp əl ə ‖ 'koʊp- 'kɑːp-
oppull 'kɒp ᵊl ‖ 'kɑːp-
opra 'kɒp rə ‖ 'koʊp- 'kɑːp-
opro- *comb. form*
with stress-neutral suffix ¦kɒp rəʊ ‖ ¦kɑːp rə- — **coprophilia** ˌkɒp rəʊ 'fɪl i̯ə ‖ ˌkɑːp rə-
with stress-imposing suffix kɒ 'prɒ+ ‖ kɑː 'prɑː+ — **coprophagous** kɒ 'prɒf əg əs ‖ kɑː 'prɑːf-
oprocessor, co-processor ˌkəʊ 'prəʊs es ə '·ˌ·· · ‖ ˌkoʊ 'prɑːs es ᵊr -'proʊs- **~s** z
oproduc|e ˌkəʊ prə 'djuːs §-'duːs, →§-'dʒuːs ‖ ˌkoʊ prə 'duːs -'djuːs **~ed** t **~es** ɪz əz **~ing** ɪŋ
oproduction ˌkəʊ prə 'dʌk ʃᵊn ‖ ˌkoʊ-
opse kɒps ‖ kɑːps *(= cops)* **copses** 'kɒps ɪz -əz ‖ 'kɑːps əz
'opt kɒpt ‖ kɑːpt **Copts** kɒpts ‖ kɑːpts
opter, 'copter 'kɒpt ə ‖ 'kɑːpt ᵊr **~s** z
Copthall 'kɒpt ɔːl -hɔːl ‖ 'kɑːpt ɔːl -hɔːl, -ɑːl, -hɑːl
Coptic 'kɒpt ɪk ‖ 'kɑːpt-
op|ula 'kɒp |jʊl ə -jəl- ‖ 'kɑːp |jəl ə **~ulae** ju liː -jə-, -leɪ ‖ jə liː **~ulas** jʊl əz jəl- ‖ jəl əz
opu|late 'kɒp ju |leɪt -jə- ‖ 'kɑːp jə- **~lated** leɪt ɪd -əd ‖ leɪt̬ əd **~lates** leɪts **~lating** leɪt ɪŋ ‖ leɪt̬ ɪŋ
opulation ˌkɒp ju 'leɪʃ ᵊn -jə- ‖ ˌkɑːp jə- **~s** z
opulative 'kɒp jʊl ət ɪv 'jəl-; -ju leɪt-, -jə leɪt- ‖ 'kɑːp jəl ət̬ ɪv -jə leɪt̬- **~ly** li
op|y 'kɒp |i ‖ 'kɑːp |i **~ied** id **~ies** iz **~ying** i ɪŋ
'**copy ˌtaster**; '**copy ˌtypist**
copybook 'kɒp i bʊk §-buːk ‖ 'kɑːp- **~s** s
copyboy 'kɒp i bɔɪ ‖ 'kɑːp- **~s** z
copycat 'kɒp i kæt ‖ 'kɑːp- **~s** s
copydesk 'kɒp i desk ‖ 'kɑːp- **~s** s
Copydex *tdmk* 'kɒp i deks ‖ 'kɑːp-
copy-ed|it 'kɒp i ˌed |ɪt §-ət ‖ 'kɑːp i ˌed |ət **~ited** ɪt ɪd §ət-, -əd ‖ ət̬ əd **~iting** ɪt ɪŋ §ət- ‖ ət̬ ɪŋ **~its** ɪts §əts ‖ əts
copygirl 'kɒp i gɜːl ‖ 'kɑːp i gɜːl **~s** z
copyhold 'kɒp i həʊld →-hɒʊld ‖ 'kɑːp i hoʊld **~s** z
copyholder 'kɒp i ˌhəʊld ə →-ˌhɒʊld- ‖ 'kɑːp i ˌhoʊld ᵊr **~s** z
copyist 'kɒp i ɪst §-əst ‖ 'kɑːp- **~s** s
copyreader 'kɒp i ˌriːd ə ‖ 'kɑːp i ˌriːd ᵊr **~s** z
copy|right 'kɒp i |raɪt ‖ 'kɑːp- **~righted** raɪt ɪd -əd ‖ raɪt̬ əd **~righting** raɪt ɪŋ ‖ raɪt̬ ɪŋ **~rights** raɪts
copywrit|er 'kɒp i ˌraɪt |ə ‖ 'kɑːp i ˌraɪt̬ |ᵊr **~ers** əz ‖ ᵊrz **~ing** ɪŋ
coq au vin ˌkɒk əʊ 'væn -'væ̃ ‖ ˌkoʊk oʊ-, ˌkɑːk- —*Fr* [kɔ ko væ̃]
co|quet kɒ |'ket kəʊ- ‖ koʊ |'ket **~quets** 'kets **~quetted** 'ket ɪd -əd ‖ 'ket̬ əd **~quetting** ket ɪŋ ‖ 'ket̬ ɪŋ
Coquet 'kəʊk ɪt §-ət ‖ 'koʊk-
coquetr|y 'kɒk ɪtr |i 'kəʊk-, -ətr- ‖ 'koʊk- koʊ 'ketr |i **~ies** iz
coquette kɒ 'ket kəʊ- ‖ koʊ- **~s** s
coquettish kɒ 'ket ɪʃ kəʊ- ‖ koʊ 'ket̬ ɪʃ **~ly** li **~ness** nəs nɪs
coquille kɒ 'kiː ‖ koʊ 'kiːᵊl —*Fr* [kɔ kij]
coˌquilles ˌSt 'Jacques ˌsæn 'ʒæk -ˌsæ̃- ‖ ˌsɑːn 'ʒɑːk —*Fr* [sæ̃ ʒak]
coquina kəʊ 'kiːn ə ‖ koʊ-
cor kɔː ‖ kɔːr —*See also phrases with this word*
ˌ**cor 'blimey**
Cora 'kɔːr ə ‖ 'koʊr-
coracle 'kɒr ək ᵊl ‖ 'kɔːr- 'kɑːr- **~s** z
coral, Coral 'kɒr əl ‖ 'kɔːr- 'kɑːr- **~s** z
ˌ**Coral 'Sea**; '**coral snake**
coralline 'kɒr ə laɪn ‖ 'kɔːr- 'kɑːr- **~s** z
coralroot 'kɒr əl ruːt ‖ 'kɔːr- 'kɑːr- **~s** s
Coram 'kɔːr əm
cor anglais ˌkɔːr 'ɒŋ gleɪ -'ɑːŋ- ‖ ˌkɔːr ɑːŋ 'gleɪ ˌkoʊr-, -ɔːŋ- **cors anglais** ˌkɔːz- ‖ ˌkɔːrz- ˌkoʊrz-
corban 'kɔː bæn 'kɔːb ən ‖ 'kɔːr-
corbel 'kɔːb ᵊl ‖ 'kɔːrb- **~ed, ~led** d **~ing, ~ling** ɪŋ **~s** z
Corbet, Corbett 'kɔːb ɪt §-ət ‖ 'kɔːrb-
Corbin 'kɔːb ɪn §-ən ‖ 'kɔːrb-
Corbishley 'kɔːb ɪʃ li ‖ 'kɔːrb-
Corbridge 'kɔː brɪdʒ ‖ 'kɔːr-
Corbusier kɔː 'buːz i eɪ -'bjuːz- ‖ ˌkɔːrb uːz 'jeɪ -uːs- —*Fr* [kɔʁ by zje]
Corby 'kɔːb i ‖ 'kɔːrb i
Corbyn 'kɔːb ɪn §-ən ‖ 'kɔːrb ən
Corcoran 'kɔːk ᵊr ən ‖ 'kɔːrk-
Corcyra kɔː 'saɪᵊr ə ‖ kɔːr- —*ModGk* Kérkira ['cer ci ra]
cord kɔːd ‖ kɔːrd **corded** 'kɔːd ɪd -əd ‖ 'kɔːrd- **cording** 'kɔːd ɪŋ ‖ 'kɔːrd- **cords** kɔːdz ‖ kɔːrdz
cordage 'kɔːd ɪdʒ ‖ 'kɔːrd-
cordate 'kɔːd eɪt ‖ 'kɔːrd- **~ly** li
Cordelia kɔː 'diːl i̯ə ‖ kɔːr-
cordelier, C~ ˌkɔːd ə 'lɪə -ɪ- ‖ ˌkɔːrd ə 'lɪᵊr **~s** z
Cordell ˌkɔː 'del ‖ ˌkɔːr-
cordial 'kɔːd i̯əl ‖ 'kɔːrdʒ əl *(*)* **~ly** i **~s** z
cordiality ˌkɔːd i 'æl ət i -ɪt i ‖ ˌkɔːrdʒ i 'æl ət̬ i kɔːr 'dʒæl ət̬ i *(*)*
cordillera ˌkɔːd ɪl 'jeər ə -ᵊl- ‖ ˌkɔːrd ᵊl 'jer ə kɔːr 'dɪl ər ə —*Sp* [kor ði 'ʎe ra, -'je-]
cordite 'kɔːd aɪt ‖ 'kɔːrd-
cordless 'kɔːd ləs -lɪs ‖ 'kɔːrd-
cordoba, córdoba, C~ 'kɔːd əb ə ‖ 'kɔːrd- —*Sp* Córdoba ['kor ðo βa]
cordon 'kɔːd ᵊn ‖ 'kɔːrd ᵊn **~s** z —*but in French words* -õ, -ɒn, -ɒŋ ‖ kɔːr 'dõː, -'dɑːn, -'dɔːn —*See also phrases with this word*
cordon bleu ˌkɔːd õ 'blɜː◂ -ɒn-, -ɒm-, -ɒŋ- ‖ kɔːr ˌdõː 'blʊ —*Fr* [kɔʁ dɔ̃ blø]
cordon sanitaire ˌkɔːd õ ˌsæn ɪ 'teə ˌ·ɒn-, -ə'· ‖ kɔːr ˌdõː ˌsɑːn i 'teᵊr —*Fr* [kɔʁ dɔ̃ sa ni tɛːʁ]
Cordova 'kɔːd əv ə ‖ 'kɔːrd- —*Sp* Córdoba ['kor ðo βa]
cordovan 'kɔːd əv ᵊn ‖ 'kɔːrd-
corduroy 'kɔːd ə rɔɪ -jʊ-, -jə-; 'kɔːdʒ ə-, -ʊ-; ˌ· ·'·, 'kɔːdr ɔɪ ‖ 'kɔːrd- **~ed** d **~s** z

cordwain ˈkɔːd weɪn ‖ ˈkɔːrd- **~er/s** ə/z ‖ ᵊr/z
core kɔː ‖ kɔːr kour **cored** kɔːd ‖ kɔːrd kourd **cores** kɔːz ‖ kɔːrz kourz **coring** ˈkɔːr ɪŋ ‖ ˈkour-
ˈ**core time**
coreferential ˌkəʊ ˌref ə ˈrenᵗʃ ᵊl ◂ ‖ ˌkou- **~ly** i
Corel *tdmk* kə ˈrel kɒ-; ˈkɒr əl ‖ ˈkɔːr əl, ˈkɑːr-
core|late ˈkɒr ə |leɪt -ɪ-; ˈkəʊ ri-, -rə-, ˌ· ·ˈ· ‖ ˈkou ri- **~lated** leɪt ɪd -əd ‖ leɪţ əd **~lates** leɪts **~lating** leɪt ɪŋ ‖ leɪţ ɪŋ
Coreldraw, CorelDraw! *tdmk* kə ˌrel ˈdrɔː ˌkɒr əl ˈ· ‖ -ˈdrɑː
coreligionist, co-religionist ˌkəʊ rɪ ˈlɪdʒ ən‿ɪst ˌ·rə-, §ˌ·riː-, §‿əst ‖ ˌkou- **~s** s
Corelli kə ˈrel i kɒ- ‖ kou- —*It* [ko ˈrɛl li]
Coren ˈkɒr ən ‖ ˈkɔːr-
coreopsis ˌkɒr i ˈɒps ɪs §-əs ‖ ˌkɔːr i ˈɑːps- ˌkour-
corer ˈkɔːr ə ‖ -ᵊr ˈkour- **~s** z
corespondent, co-respondent ˌkəʊ rɪ ˈspɒnd ənt -rə-, §-riː- ‖ ˌkou rɪ ˈspɑːnd- **~s** s
Corey ˈkɔːr i ‖ ˈkour-
corf kɔːf ‖ kɔːrf **corves** kɔːvz ‖ kɔːrvz
Corfam *tdmk* ˈkɔː fæm ‖ ˈkɔːr-
Corfe kɔːf ‖ kɔːrf
Corfu ˌkɔː ˈfuː -ˈfjuː ‖ ˈkɔːr fuː -fjuː, ˌ·ˈ· —*ModGk* Kérkira [ˈcɛr ci ɾ a]
ˌ**Corfu** ˈ**Channel**
corgi, Corgi ˈkɔːg i ‖ ˈkɔːrg i **~s** z
coriander ˌkɒr i ˈænd ə ˈ· · · · ‖ ˈkɔːr i ænd ᵊr ˈkour-, ˌ·ˌ·ˈ· ·
Corin ˈkɒr ɪn -ən ‖ ˈkɔːr-
Corinne kə ˈrɪn
Corinth *place in Greece* ˈkɒr ɪnᵗθ -ənᵗθ ‖ ˈkɔːr- ˈkɑːr- —*but places in the US are* kə ˈrɪnᵗθ
Corinthian kə ˈrɪnᵗθ i‿ən **~s** z
Coriolanus ˌkɒr i‿əʊ ˈleɪn əs kə ˌraɪ‿ə-, -ˈlɑːn- ‖ ˌkɔːr i‿ə- ˌkɑːr-
Coriolis ˌkɒr i ˈəʊl ɪs §-əs ‖ ˌkɔːr i ˈoul əs ˌkour-, -ə ˈliːs —*Fr* [kɔʁ jɔ lis]
cork, Cork kɔːk ‖ kɔːrk **corked** kɔːkt ‖ kɔːrkt **corking** ˈkɔːk ɪŋ ‖ ˈkɔːrk ɪŋ **corks** kɔːks ‖ kɔːrks
corkage ˈkɔːk ɪdʒ ‖ ˈkɔːrk-
corkboard ˈkɔːk bɔːd ‖ ˈkɔːrk bɔːrd -bourd
corker ˈkɔːk ə ‖ ˈkɔːrk ᵊr **~s** z
corkscrew ˈkɔːk skruː ‖ ˈkɔːrk- **~ed** d **~ing** ɪŋ **~s** z
corkwood ˈkɔːk wʊd ‖ ˈkɔːrk-
cork|y ˈkɔːk |i ‖ ˈkɔːrk |i **~ier** i‿ə ‖ i‿ᵊr **~iest** i‿ɪst i‿əst **~iness** i nəs i nɪs
Corlett ˈkɔːl ɪt -ət ‖ ˈkɔːrl-
Corley ˈkɔːl i ‖ ˈkɔːrl i
corm kɔːm ‖ kɔːrm **corms** kɔːmz ‖ kɔːrmz
Cormac, Cormack ˈkɔːm æk -ək ‖ ˈkɔːrm-
cormel ˈkɔːm ᵊl ‖ ˈkɔːrm ᵊl kɔːr ˈmel **~s** z
cormorant ˈkɔːm ᵊr‿ənt ‖ ˈkɔːrm- -ə rænt **~s** s
corn kɔːn ‖ kɔːrn **corned** kɔːnd ‖ ˈkɔːrnd **corning** ˈkɔːn ɪŋ ‖ ˈkɔːrn ɪŋ **corns** kɔːnz ‖ kɔːrnz
ˈ**corn bread**; ˌ**corned** ˈ**beef**◂; ˌ**corned beef** ˈ**sandwich**; ˈ**corn ex**ˌ**change**; ˈ**Corn Laws**
cornball ˈkɔːn bɔːl →ˈkɔːm- ‖ ˈkɔːrn- -bɑːl **~s** z
corncob ˈkɔːn kɒb →ˈkɔːŋ- ‖ ˈkɔːrn kɑːb **~s** z
corncockle ˈkɔːn ˌkɒk ᵊl →ˈkɔːŋ- ‖ ˈkɔːrn ˌkɑːk ᵊl **~s** z
corncrake ˈkɔːn kreɪk →ˈkɔːŋ- ‖ ˈkɔːrn- **~s** s
corne|a ˈkɔːn i‿|ə kɔː ˈniː‿|ə ‖ ˈkɔːrn i‿|ə **~ae** iː **~al** əl **~as** əz
Corneille kɔː ˈneɪ -ˈneɪᵊl ‖ kɔːr-—*Fr* [kɔʁ nɛj]
cornel ˈkɔːn ᵊl ‖ ˈkɔːrn ᵊl -el **~s** z
Cornelia kɔː ˈniːl i‿ə ‖ kɔːr-
cornelian kɔː ˈniːl i‿ən ‖ kɔːr- **~s** z
Cornelius kɔː ˈniːl i‿əs ‖ kɔːr-
Cornell ˌkɔː ˈnel ‖ ˌkɔːr-
corner, C~ ˈkɔːn ə ‖ ˈkɔːrn ᵊr ˈkɔːn- **~ed** d **cornering** ˈkɔːn ər ɪŋ ‖ ˈkɔːrn ər ɪŋ ˈkɔːn- **~s** z
ˌ**corner** ˈ**shop**, ˈ· · ·
-cornered ˈkɔːn əd ‖ ˈkɔːrn ᵊrd ˈkɔːn- — **three-cornered** ˌθriː ˈkɔːn əd ◂ ‖ -ˈkɔːrn ᵊrd -ˈkɔːn-
cornerstone ˈkɔːn ə stəʊn ‖ ˈkɔːrn ᵊr stoun ˈkɔːn- **~s** z
cornet ˈkɔːn ɪt §-ət ‖ kɔːr ˈnet *(*)* **~s** s
cornetto, C~ *tdmk* ₍ₗ₎kɔː ˈnet əʊ ‖ ₍ₗ₎kɔːr ˈneţ ou **~s** z
corn-fed ˈkɔːn fed ‖ ˈkɔːrn-
cornfield ˈkɔːn fiːᵊld ‖ ˈkɔːrn- **~s** z
cornflakes ˈkɔːn fleɪks ‖ ˈkɔːrn-
cornflour ˈkɔːn ˌflaʊ‿ə ‖ ˈkɔːrn ˌflaʊ‿ᵊr
cornflower ˈkɔːn ˌflaʊ‿ə ‖ ˈkɔːrn ˌflaʊ‿ᵊr **~s** z
Cornford ˈkɔːn fəd ‖ ˈkɔːrn fᵊrd
Cornhill ˌkɔːn ˈhɪl ‖ ˈkɔːrn hɪl
cornic|e ˈkɔːn ɪs §-əs ‖ ˈkɔːrn əs -ɪʃ **~es** ɪz əz
cornich|e, C~ ₍ₗ₎kɔː ˈniːʃ ˈkɔːn iːʃ, -ɪʃ ‖ ₍ₗ₎kɔːr- **~es** ɪz əz
corn|ily ˈkɔːn |ɪ li əl i ‖ ˈkɔːrn- **~iness** i nəs i nɪs
Corning ˈkɔːn ɪŋ ‖ ˈkɔːrn ɪŋ
Cornish ˈkɔːn ɪʃ ‖ ˈkɔːrn-
ˌ**Cornish** ˈ**pasty**
Cornish|man ˈkɔːn ɪʃ |mən ‖ ˈkɔːrn- **~men** mən men **~woman** ˌwʊm ən **~women** ˌwɪm ɪn §-ən
cornmeal ˈkɔːn miːᵊl →ˈkɔːm- ‖ ˈkɔːrn-
corn pone ˈkɔːn pəʊn ‖ ˈkɔːrn poun
cornrow ˈkɔːn rəʊ ‖ ˈkɔːrn rou **~s** z
cornstarch ˈkɔːn stɑːtʃ ‖ ˈkɔːrn stɑːrtʃ
cornucopia ˌkɔːn ju ˈkəʊp i‿ə ‖ ˌkɔːrn ə ˈkoup- ˌ·jə- **~s** z
Cornwall ˈkɔːn wɔːl -wəl ‖ ˈkɔːrn wɑːl -wɔːl
Cornwallis ₍ₗ₎kɔːn ˈwɒl ɪs §-əs ‖ kɔːrn ˈwɑːl-
corn|y ˈkɔːn |i ‖ ˈkɔːrn |i **~ier** i‿ə ‖ i‿ᵊr **~iest** i‿ɪst i‿əst
corolla, C~ kə ˈrɒl ə ‖ -ˈroul ə -ˈrɑːl ə
corollar|y kə ˈrɒl ər |i ‖ ˈkɔːr ə ler |i ˈkɑːr- *(*)* **~ies** iz
Coromandel ˌkɒr əʊ ˈmænd ᵊl ‖ ˌkɔːr ə- ˌkɑːr-
coron|a, C~ kə ˈrəʊn |ə ‖ -ˈroun |ə **~ae** iː **~s** z
coronach ˈkɒr ən ək -əx ‖ ˈkɔːr- ˈkɑːr- **~s** s
Coronado ˌkɒr ə ˈnɑːd əʊ ‖ ˌkɔːr ə ˈnɑːd ou ˌkɑːr-

C

oronal 'kɒr ən ᵊl kə 'rəʊn ᵊl ‖ 'kɔːr- 'kɑːr-; kə 'roʊn- **~s** z
oronar|y 'kɒr ən ər‿|i ‖ 'kɔːr ə ner |i 'kɑːr- **~ies** iz
oronation ˌkɒr ə 'neɪʃ ᵊn ◂ ‖ ˌkɔːr- ˌkɑːr- **~s** z
oroner 'kɒr ən ə ‖ 'kɔːr ᵊn ər 'kɑːr- **~s** z
oronet 'kɒr ən ɪt -ət; -ə net, ˌ··'net ‖ ˌkɔːr ə 'net ˌkɑːr- **~s** s
orot 'kɒr əʊ ‖ kɑː 'roʊ kɔː-, kə- —*Fr* [kɔ ʁo]
orp. kɔːp ‖ kɔːrp —*or see* **Corporal**
orpora 'kɔːp ər‿ə -ə rɑː ‖ 'kɔːrp-
ˌcorpora cal'losa kə 'ləʊs ə ‖ -'loʊs-;
ˌcorpora 'lutea 'luːt i‿ə ‖ 'luːţ-; **ˌcorpora stri'ata** straɪ 'eɪt ə ‖ -'eɪţ-
orporal 'kɔːp ᵊr‿əl ‖ 'kɔːrp- **~s** z
orporate 'kɔːp ər‿ət ɪt ‖ 'kɔːrp- **~ly** li
orporation ˌkɔːp ə 'reɪʃ ᵊn ◂ ‖ ˌkɔːrp- **~s** z
ˌcorpo'ration tax
orporatism 'kɔːp ər‿ə ˌtɪzəm ‿ɪ- ‖ 'kɔːrp-
orporeal kɔː 'pɔːr i‿əl ‖ kɔːr- -'poʊr- **~ly** i
orps *sing.* kɔː ‖ kɔːr koʊr *(= core)* **corps** *pl* kɔːz ‖ kɔːrz koʊrz
ˌcorps de 'ballet ‖ ˌ· ·'·
orpse kɔːps ‖ kɔːrps **corpsed** kɔːpst ‖ kɔːrpst **corpsing** 'kɔːps ɪŋ ‖ 'kɔːrps ɪŋ **corpses** 'kɔːps ɪz -əz ‖ 'kɔːrps əz
orps|man 'kɔːz |mən -mæn ‖ 'kɔːrz- 'koʊrz- **~men** mən
orpulenc|e 'kɔːp jʊl ənᵗs -jəl- ‖ 'kɔːrp jəl- **~y** i
orpulent 'kɔːp jʊl ənt -jəl- ‖ 'kɔːrp jəl- **~ly** li
orpus, Corpus 'kɔːp əs ‖ 'kɔːrp- **~es** ɪz əz
ˌcorpus cal'losum kə 'ləʊs əm ‖ -'loʊs-; **ˌCorpus 'Christi** 'krɪst i; **ˌcorpus de'licti** di 'lɪkt aɪ də-, -iː; **ˌcorpus 'luteum** 'luːt i‿əm ‖ 'luːţ-; **ˌcorpus stri'atum** straɪ 'eɪt əm ‖ -'eɪţ-
orpus-based 'kɔːp əs beɪst ˌ··'·◂ ‖ 'kɔːrp-
orpuscle 'kɔːp ʌs ᵊl kɔː 'pʌs ᵊl ‖ 'kɔːrp- **~s** z
orpuscular kɔː 'pʌsk jʊl ə -jəl- ‖ kɔːr 'pʌsk jəl ᵊr
Corr kɔː ‖ kɔːr **Corrs** kɔːz ‖ kɔːrz
orral kə 'rɑːl kɒ- ‖ -'ræl *(may = chorale)* **~led** d **~ling** ɪŋ **~s** z
orrect kə 'rekt **~ed** ɪd əd **~ing** ɪŋ **~ly** li **~ness** nəs nɪs **~s** s
orrection kə 'rek ʃᵊn **~s** z
orrectional kə 'rek ʃᵊn‿əl
orrectitude kə 'rekt ɪ tjuːd §-ə-, →§-tʃuːd ‖ -tuːd -tjuːd
orrective kə 'rekt ɪv **~ly** li **~s** z
orrector kə 'rekt ə ‖ -ᵊr **~s** z
Correggio kɒ 'redʒ i‿əʊ kə-, -'redʒ əʊ ‖ kə 'redʒ i‿oʊ -'redʒ oʊ —*It* [kor 'red dʒo] **~s, ~'s** z
orre|late *v* 'kɒr ə |leɪt -ɪ- ‖ 'kɔːr- 'kɑːr- **~lated** leɪt ɪd -əd ‖ leɪţ əd **~lates** leɪts **~lating** leɪt ɪŋ ‖ leɪţ ɪŋ
orrelate *n* 'kɒr ə leɪt -ɪ-; -əl ət, -ɪt ‖ 'kɔːr- 'kɑːr- **~s** s
orrelation ˌkɒr ə 'leɪʃ ᵊn -ɪ- ‖ ˌkɔːr- ˌkɑːr- **~s** z
ˌcorre'lation coefˌficient
correlative kə 'rel ət ɪv kɒ- ‖ -əţ ɪv **~ly** li **~ness** nəs nɪs **~s** z
correspond ˌkɒr ə 'spɒnd -ɪ- ‖ ˌkɔːr ə 'spɑːnd ˌkɑːr- **~ed** ɪd əd **~ing/ly** ɪŋ /li **~s** z
correspondenc|e ˌkɒr ə 'spɒnd ənᵗs -ɪ- ‖ ˌkɔːr ə 'spɑːnd- ˌkɑːr- **~es** ɪz əz
ˌcorre'spondence course
correspondent ˌkɒr ə 'spɒnd ənt -ɪ- ‖ ˌkɔːr ə 'spɑːnd- ˌkɑːr- **~ly** li **~s** s
corrida kɒ 'riːd ə kə- ‖ kɔː 'riːð ə —*Sp* [ko 'rri ða] **~s** z
corridor 'kɒr ɪ dɔː -ə-; -ɪd ə, -əd- ‖ 'kɔːr əd ᵊr 'kɑːr-, -ə dɔːr **~s** z
corrie, C~ 'kɒr i ‖ 'kɔːr i 'kɑːr i **~s** z
Corriedale 'kɒr i deɪᵊl ‖ 'kɔːr- 'kɑːr- **~s** z
Corrigan 'kɒr ɪg ən -əg- ‖ 'kɔːr- 'kɑːr-
corrigend|um ˌkɒr ɪ 'dʒend |əm -ə-, -'gend- ‖ ˌkɔːr- ˌkɑːr- **~a** ə
Corris 'kɒr ɪs §-əs ‖ 'kɔːr- 'kɑːr-
corrobo|rate kə 'rɒb ə |reɪt ‖ -'rɑːb- **~rated** reɪt ɪd -əd ‖ reɪţ əd **~rates** reɪts **~rating** reɪt ɪŋ ‖ reɪţ ɪŋ
corroboration kə ˌrɒb ə 'reɪʃ ᵊn ‖ -ˌrɑːb- **~s** z
corroborative kə 'rɒb ər‿ət ɪv -ə reɪt- ‖ -'rɑːb ə reɪţ ɪv -ər‿əţ ɪv **~ly** li
corroborator kə 'rɒb ə reɪt ə ‖ -'rɑːb ə reɪţ ᵊr **~s** z
corroboree kə 'rɒb ər i -ə riː ‖ -'rɑːb- **~s** z
corrod|e kə 'rəʊd ‖ -'roʊd **~ed** ɪd əd **~es** z **~ing** ɪŋ
corrodible kə 'rəʊd əb ᵊl -ɪb- ‖ -'roʊd-
corrosion kə 'rəʊʒ ᵊn ‖ -'roʊʒ-
corrosive kə 'rəʊs ɪv -'rəʊz- ‖ -'roʊs- -'roʊz- **~ly** li **~ness** nəs nɪs
corru|gate 'kɒr ə |geɪt -u-, -ju- ‖ 'kɔːr- 'kɑːr- **~gated** geɪt ɪd -əd ‖ geɪţ əd **~gates** geɪts **~gating** geɪt ɪŋ ‖ geɪţ ɪŋ
corrugation ˌkɒr ə 'geɪʃ ᵊn -u-, -ju- ‖ ˌkɔːr- ˌkɑːr- **~s** z
corrupt kə 'rʌpt **~ed** ɪd əd **~ing** ɪŋ **~s** s
corruptibility kə ˌrʌpt ə 'bɪl ət i -ˌ·ɪ-, -ɪt i ‖ -əţ i
corruptib|le kə 'rʌpt əb |ᵊl -ɪb- **~ly** li
corruption kə 'rʌp ʃᵊn **~s** z
corruptive kə 'rʌpt ɪv **~ly** li
corrupt|ly kə 'rʌpt |li **~ness** nəs nɪs
corruptor kə 'rʌpt ə ‖ -ᵊr **~s** z
Corsa *tdmk* 'kɔːs ə ‖ 'kɔːrs ə
corsag|e (ˌ)kɔː 'sɑːʒ '·· ‖ (ˌ)kɔːr- -'sɑːdʒ, '·· **~es** ɪz əz
corsair 'kɔːs eə (ˌ)kɔː 'seə ‖ 'kɔːrs er (ˌ)kɔːr 'seᵊr **~s** z
corse kɔːs ‖ kɔːrs **corses** 'kɔːs ɪz -əz ‖ 'kɔːrs-
corselet 'kɔːs lət -lɪt ‖ 'kɔːrs- —*but for the undergarment, properly* Corselette *tdmk,* ˌkɔːs ə 'let ‖ ˌkɔːrs- **~s** s
cors|et 'kɔːs |ɪt §-ət ‖ 'kɔːrs |ət **~eted** ɪt ɪd §ət-, -əd ‖ əţ əd **~eting** ɪt ɪŋ §ət- ‖ əţ ɪŋ **~ets** ɪts §əts ‖ əts
corsetry 'kɔːs ɪtr i §-ətr- ‖ 'kɔːrs-
Corsica 'kɔːs ɪk ə ‖ 'kɔːrs-
Corsican 'kɔːs ɪk ən ‖ 'kɔːrs- **~s** z
Corstorphine kə 'stɔːf ɪn §-ᵊn ‖ kᵊr 'stɔːrf-

corteg|e, cortèg|e ₍ᵢ₎kɔː 'teɪʒ -'teʒ, '· · ‖ ₍ᵢ₎kɔːr 'teʒ —*Fr* [kɔʁ tɛːʒ] **~es** ɪz əz
Cortes *'parliament'* 'kɔːt ez -ɪz, -es ‖ 'kɔːrt-
Cortes, Cortés 'kɔːt ez kɔː 'tez ‖ kɔːr 'tez —*Sp* Cortés [kor 'tes]
cortex 'kɔːt eks ‖ 'kɔːrt- **~es** ɪz əz **cortices** 'kɔːt ɪ siːz -ə- ‖ 'kɔːrt̬-
Cortez 'kɔːt ez kɔː 'tez ‖ kɔːr 'tez —*Sp* Cortés [kor 'tes]
Corti 'kɔːt i ‖ 'kɔːrt̬ i —*It* ['kor ti]
cortical 'kɔːt ɪk ᵊl ‖ 'kɔːrt̬-
cortices 'kɔːt ɪ siːz -ə- ‖ 'kɔːrt̬-
corticosteroid ˌkɔːt ɪk əʊ 'stɪər ɔɪd ‖ ˌkɔːrt̬ ɪ koʊ 'stɪr ɔɪd **~s** z
corticosterone ˌkɔːt ɪk əʊ 'stɪər əʊn -ɪ 'kɒst ə rəʊn ‖ ˌkɔːrt̬ ɪ koʊ 'stɪr oʊn -'kɑːst ə roʊn
Cortina kɔː 'tiːn ə ‖ kɔːr- **~s** z
cortisone, C~ 'kɔːt ɪ zəʊn -ə-, -səʊn ‖ 'kɔːrt̬ ə zoʊn -soʊn
Cortland 'kɔːt lənd ‖ 'kɔːrt-
Corton 'kɔːt ᵊn ‖ 'kɔːrt ᵊn
corundum kə 'rʌnd əm
Corunna kə 'rʌn ə kɒ- —*Sp* La Coruña [la ko 'ru ɲa], —*Galician A Coruñha* [a ko 'ru ɲa]
coru|scate 'kɒr ə |skeɪt ‖ 'kɔːr- 'kɑːr- **~scated** skeɪt ɪd -əd ‖ skeɪt̬ əd **~scates** skeɪts **~scating** skeɪt ɪŋ ‖ skeɪt̬ ɪŋ
coruscation ˌkɒr ə 'skeɪʃ ᵊn ‖ ˌkɔːr- ˌkɑːr- **~s** z
corvee, corvée 'kɔːv eɪ ‖ ₍ᵢ₎kɔːr 'veɪ '· —*Fr* [kɔʁ ve] **~s** z
corvette ₍ᵢ₎kɔː 'vet ‖ ₍ᵢ₎kɔːr- **~s** s
corvine 'kɔːv aɪn ‖ 'kɔːrv-
Corvo 'kɔːv əʊ ‖ 'kɔːrv oʊ
Corvus 'kɔːv əs ‖ 'kɔːrv-
Corwen 'kɔː wən ‖ 'kɔːr- —*Welsh* ['kor wen]
Cory 'kɔːr i
corybant, C~ 'kɒr ɪ bænt -ə- ‖ 'kɔːr- **~s** s **corybantes, C~** ˌkɒr ɪ 'bænt iːz -ə- ‖ ˌkɔːr-
Corydon 'kɒr ɪd ən -əd, -ɒn ‖ 'kɔːr-
corymb 'kɒr ɪmb -ɪm, §-əm ‖ 'kɔːr- 'kɑːr- **~s** z
coryphae|us ˌkɒr ɪ 'fiː|əs -ə- ‖ ˌkɔːr- ˌkɑːr- **~i** aɪ iː
Coryton *(i)* 'kɒr ɪt ən -ət- ‖ 'kɔːr ət ᵊn, *(ii)* 'kɔːr- —*in Devon, (i); in Essex, (ii)*
coryza kə 'raɪz ə
cos *'lettuce'* kɒs kɒz ‖ kɑːs koʊs
cos *'cosine'* kɒz kɒs ‖ kɑːs
cos *'because'* kəz kəs, *occasional strong form* kɒz kɒs ‖ kɑːz kɔːz
Cos *island in Greece* kɒs ‖ kɑːs koʊs
Cosa Nostra ˌkəʊz ə 'nɒs trə ‖ ˌkoʊs ə 'noʊs-
Cosby 'kɒz bi ‖ 'kɑːz bi
cosec 'kəʊ sek ‖ 'koʊ-
cosecant ˌkəʊ 'siːk ənt ‖ ˌkoʊ- -ænt **~s** s
cosech 'kəʊ seʃ ‖ 'koʊ- —*or as* cosec h
coset 'kəʊ set ‖ 'koʊ- **~s** s
Cosford 'kɒs fəd ‖ 'kɑːs fᵊrd
Cosgrave 'kɒz greɪv ‖ 'kɑːz-
cosh *'bludgeon'* kɒʃ ‖ kɑːʃ **coshed** kɒʃt ‖ kɑːʃt **coshes** 'kɒʃ ɪz -əz ‖ 'kɑːʃ əz **coshing** 'kɒʃ ɪŋ ‖ 'kɑːʃ ɪŋ
cosh *'hyperbolic cosine'* kɒʃ ‖ kɑːʃ —*or as* cos h
Cosham 'kɒs əm 'kɒʃ- ‖ 'kɑːs əm 'kɑːʃ-
Cosi Fan Tutte, Così Fan Tutte ˌkəʊs i ˌfæn 'tʊt i ˌkəʊz-, kəʊ ˌsiː- ‖ koʊ ˌsiː fɑːn 'tuːt eɪ -'tʊt- —*It* [ko ˌsif fan 'tut te]
co-sign 'kəʊ saɪn ‖ 'koʊ- **~ed** d **~er/s** ə/z ‖ ᵊr/z **~ing** ɪŋ **~s** z
cosignator|y ˌkəʊ 'sɪg nət ər |i ‖ ˌkoʊ 'sɪg nə tɔːr |i -toʊr i **~ies** iz
cosine 'kəʊ saɪn ‖ 'koʊ- **~s** z
CoSIRA kəʊ 'saɪᵊr ə ‖ koʊ-
cosmetic kɒz 'met ɪk ‖ kɑːz 'met̬ ɪk **~ally** ᵊl i **~s** s
cosˌmetic 'surgery
cosmetician ˌkɒz mə 'tɪʃ ᵊn -mɪ- ‖ ˌkɑːz- **~s** z
cosmetolog|ist ˌkɒz mə 'tɒl ədʒ| ɪst -me-, §-əst ‖ ˌkɑːz mə 'tɑːl- **~ists** ɪsts §əsts **~y** i
cosmic 'kɒz mɪk ‖ 'kɑːz- **~ally** ᵊl i
ˌcosmic 'ray
cosmo- *comb. form*
with stress-neutral suffix ¦kɒz məʊ ‖ ¦kɑːz mə -moʊ — **cosmographic** ˌkɒz məʊ 'græf ɪk ◂ ‖ ˌkɑːz mə-
with stress-imposing suffix kɒz 'mɒ+ ‖ kɑːz 'mɑː+ — **cosmographer** kɒz 'mɒg rəf ə ‖ kɑːz 'mɑːg rəf ᵊr
Cosmo 'kɒz məʊ ‖ 'kɑːz moʊ
cosmogon|y kɒz 'mɒg ən |i ‖ kɑːz 'mɑːg- **~ies** iz
cosmography kɒz 'mɒg rəf i ‖ kɑːz 'mɑːg-
cosmological ˌkɒz məʊ 'lɒdʒ ɪk ᵊl ‖ ˌkɑːz mə 'lɑːdʒ- **~ly** i
cosmolog|y kɒz 'mɒl ədʒ |i ‖ kɑːz 'mɑːl- **~ies** iz
cosmonaut 'kɒz mə nɔːt ‖ 'kɑːz- -nɑːt **~s** s
cosmopolitan ˌkɒz mə 'pɒl ɪt ən ◂ ‖ ˌkɑːz mə 'pɑːl ət ᵊn ◂ **~ism** ˌɪz əm **~s** z
cosmos 'kɒz mɒs ‖ 'kɑːz məs -moʊs, -mɑːs
Cossack 'kɒs æk ‖ 'kɑːs- -ək **~s** s
coss|et 'kɒs |ɪt §-ət ‖ 'kɑːs |ət **~eted** ɪt ɪd §ət-, -əd ‖ ət̬ əd **~eting** ɪt ɪŋ §ət- ‖ ət̬ ɪŋ **~ets** ɪts §əts ‖ əts
cossie 'kɒz i ‖ 'kɑːz i **~s** z
cossie 'kɒz i ‖ 'kɑːz i **~s** z
cost kɒst kɔːst ‖ kɔːst kɑːst **costed** 'kɒst ɪd 'kɔːst-, -əd ‖ 'kɔːst əd 'kɑːst- **costing/s** 'kɒst ɪŋ/z 'kɔːst- ‖ 'kɔːst ɪŋ/z 'kɑːst- **costs** kɒsts kɔːsts ‖ kɔːsts kɑːsts
ˌcost of 'living, ˌcost of 'living ˌindex; ˌcost 'price
costa, Costa 'kɒst ə ‖ 'koʊst ə 'kɑːst ə, 'kɔːst ə —*See also phrases with this word* —*Sp* ['kos ta] **~s** z
ˌCosta 'Brava 'brɑːv ə —*Sp* [-'βɾa βa]; ˌCosta del 'Sol del 'sɒl ‖ -'soʊl —*Sp* [-ðel 'sol]
Costain *(i)* 'kɒst eɪn ‖ 'kɑːst-, *(ii)* kɒ 'steɪn ‖ kɑː-
costal 'kɒst ᵊl ‖ 'kɑːst ᵊl
co-star 'kəʊ stɑː ‖ 'koʊ stɑːr **~red** d **co-starring** 'kəʊ stɑːr ɪŋ ‖ 'koʊ- **~s** z
costard 'kʌst əd 'kɒst- ‖ 'kɑːst ᵊrd **~s** z

ostard ˈkɒst əd -ɑːd ‖ ˈkɑːst ᵊrd
osta Ric|a ˌkɒst ə ˈriːk |ə ‖ ˌkoʊst- ˌkɔːst-, ˌkɑːst- —*Sp* [ˌkos ta ˈrri ka] **~an/s** ən/z
ost-benefit ˌkɒst ˈben ɪf ɪt -əf-, §-ət ‖ ˌkɔːst- ˌkɑːst-
ost-effective ˌkɒst ɪ ˈfekt ɪv ◂ ˌkɔːst-, -ə-, ˈ· ·ˌ· · ‖ ˌkɔːst- ˌkɑːst- **~ly** li **~ness** nəs nɪs
ostello *(i)* kɒ ˈstel əʊ kə- ‖ kɑː ˈstel oʊ, *(ii)* ˈkɒst əl əʊ -ɪl- ‖ ˈkɑːst ə loʊ —*In Ireland usually (ii), elsewhere (i)*
ostermonger ˈkɒst ə ˌmʌŋ gə ‖ ˈkɑːst ᵊr ˌmʌŋ gᵊr -ˌmɑːŋ- **~s** z
ostessey *place in Norfolk* ˈkɒs i ‖ ˈkɑːs i *(!)*
ostive ˈkɒst ɪv ‖ ˈkɑːst- ˈkɔːst- **~ly** li **~ness** nəs nɪs
ost|ly ˈkɒst |li ˈkɔːst- ‖ ˈkɔːst |li ˈkɑːst- **~lier** li‿ə ‖ li‿ᵊr **~liest** li‿ɪst li‿əst **~liness** li nəs li nɪs
ostmary ˈkɒst ˌmeər i ‖ ˈkɔːst ˌmer i ˈkɑːst-
ostner ˈkɒst nə ‖ ˈkɑːst nᵊr
ost-plus ˌkɒst ˈplʌs ◂ ˌkɔːst- ‖ ˌkɔːst- ˌkɑːst-
ost-push ˌkɒst ˈpʊʃ ˌkɔːst- ‖ ˌkɔːst- ˌkɑːst-

COSTUME

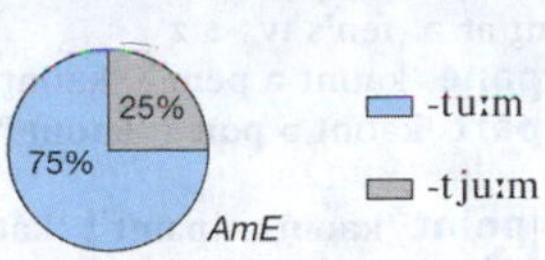

ostume *n, adj* ˈkɒs tjuːm →-tʃuːm, →ˈkɒʃ- ‖ ˈkɑːs tuːm -tjuːm **~d** d **~s** z — *Preference poll, AmE:* -tuːm *75%,* -tjuːm *25%.*
ˈcostume ˌjewellery
ostumier kɒ ˈstjuːm i‿ə →§-ˈstʃuːm-, -i eɪ ‖ kɑː ˈstuːm i eɪ -ˈstjuːm-, -ᵊr **~s** z
os|y ˈkəʊz |i ‖ ˈkoʊz |i **~ier** i‿ə ‖ i‿ᵊr **~ies** iz **~iest** i‿ɪst i‿əst **~ily** ɪ li ə l i **~iness** i nəs i nɪs
ot kɒt ‖ kɑːt **cots** kɒts ‖ kɑːts
ˈcot death
otan ˈkəʊ tæn ‖ ˈkoʊ-
otangent ˌkəʊ ˈtændʒ ənt ˈ·ˌ· · ‖ ˌkoʊ- **~s** s
otanh ˈkəʊ θæn -tænʃ ‖ ˈkoʊ- —*or as* cotan h
ote kəʊt ‖ koʊt *(= coat)* —*formerly also* kɒt ‖ kɑːt **cotes** kəʊts ‖ koʊts
Cote d'Azur, Côte d'Azur ˌkəʊt də ˈzjʊə -dæ- ‖ ˌkoʊt də ˈzʊᵊr —*Fr* [kot da zyːʁ]
Cote d'Ivoire, Côte d'Ivoire ˌkəʊt diː ˈvwɑː ‖ ˌkoʊt diː ˈvwɑːr —*Fr* [kot di vwaːʁ]
oterie ˈkəʊt ər i ˌkəʊt ə ˈriː ‖ ˈkoʊţ ər i ˌkoʊţ ə ˈriː **~s** z
oterminous ₍ˌ₎kəʊ ˈtɜːm ɪn əs -ən- ‖ ₍ˌ₎koʊ ˈtɜːm- **~ly** li
oth kɒθ ‖ kɑːθ *-or as* cot h
Cothi ˈkɒθ i ‖ ˈkɑːθ i ˈkɔːθ-
cothurn|us kəʊ ˈθɜːn |əs kɒ- ‖ koʊ ˈθɜːn |əs **~i** aɪ
cotillion kə ˈtɪl i‿ən kəʊ-, kɒ- ‖ koʊ- **~s** z
cotinga kəʊ ˈtɪŋ gə ‖ koʊ-
Coton ˈkəʊt ᵊn ‖ ˈkoʊt ᵊn

cotoneaster kə ˌtəʊn i ˈæst ə ‖ -ˈtoʊn i ˌæst ᵊr —*There is also a spelling pronunciation, considered incorrect,* ˌkɒt ᵊn ˈiːst ə ‖ ˈkɑːt ᵊn ˌiːst ᵊr **~s** z
Cotopaxi ˌkɒt ə ˈpæks i ˌkəʊt-, -əʊ- ‖ ˌkoʊţ ə- -ˈpɑːks i —*Sp* [ko to ˈpak si]
Cotswold ˈkɒts wəʊld →-wɒʊld, -wəld ‖ ˈkɑːts woʊld **~s** z
cotta ˈkɒt ə ‖ ˈkɑːţ ə **~s** z
cottag|e ˈkɒt ɪdʒ ‖ ˈkɑːţ ɪdʒ **~ed** d **~es** ɪz əz **~ing** ɪŋ
ˌcottage ˈcheese ‖ ˈ· · ·; **ˌcottage ˈhospital**; **ˌcottage ˈindustry**; **ˌcottage ˈloaf**; **ˌcottage ˈpie**
cottager ˈkɒt ɪdʒ ə ‖ ˈkɑːţ ɪdʒ ᵊr **~s** z
cottar ˈkɒt ə ‖ ˈkɑːţ ᵊr **~s** z
Cottenham ˈkɒt ən‿əm ‖ ˈkɑːt ᵊn‿əm
cotter, C~ ˈkɒt ə ‖ kɑːţ ᵊr **~s** z
Cotterell ˈkɒtr əl ‖ ˈkɑːtr-
Cottesloe ˈkɒts ləʊ ˈkɒt əz ləʊ ‖ ˈkɑːts loʊ ˈkɑːţ əz loʊ
Cottesmore ˈkɒts mɔː ‖ ˈkɑːts mɔːr -moʊr
Cottle ˈkɒt ᵊl ‖ ˈkɑːţ ᵊl
cotton, C~ ˈkɒt ᵊn ‖ ˈkɑːt ᵊn **~s** z
ˌcotton ˈcandy; **ˈcotton gin**; **ˈcotton grass**; **ˌcotton ˈwaste**; **ˌcotton ˈwool** ◂
cotton-picking ˈkɒt ᵊn ˌpɪk ɪŋ ‖ ˈkɑːt-
cottonseed ˈkɒt ᵊn siːd ‖ ˈkɑːt-
cottontail ˈkɒt ᵊn teɪᵊl ‖ ˈkɑːt- **~s** z
cottonwood ˈkɒt ᵊn wʊd ‖ ˈkɑːt- **~s** z
cottony ˈkɒt ᵊn i ‖ ˈkɑːt-
cotyledon ˌkɒt ɪ ˈliːd ᵊn -ə-; -ᵊl ˈiːd- ‖ ˌkɑːt ᵊl ˈiːd ᵊn **~ous** əs **~s** z
coucal ˈkuːk ᵊl ˈkʊk-, -æl, -ɑːl **~s** z
couch kaʊtʃ —*but in* **ˈcouch grass** *also* kuːtʃ **couched** kaʊtʃt **couches** ˈkaʊtʃ ɪz -əz **couching** ˈkaʊtʃ ɪŋ
Couch kuːtʃ
couchant ˈkaʊtʃ ənt ˈkuːʃ ᵊnt
couchette ₍ˌ₎kuː ˈʃet **~s** s
Coué ˈkuː eɪ ‖ ku ˈeɪ —*Fr* [kwe, ku e]
cougar ˈkuːg ə -ɑː ‖ -ᵊr **~s** z
cough kɒf kɔːf ‖ kɔːf kɑːf **coughed** kɒft kɔːft ‖ kɔːft kɑːft **coughing** ˈkɒf ɪŋ ˈkɔːf- ‖ ˈkɔːf ɪŋ ˈkɑːf- **coughs** kɒfs kɔːfs ‖ kɔːfs kɑːfs
ˈcough drop; **ˈcough ˌmixture**
Coughlan *(i)* ˈkɒf lən ˈkɒx-, ˈkɒk- ‖ ˈkɔːf- ˈkɑːf-, ˈkoʊk-, *(ii)* ˈkɒg lən ‖ ˈkɔːg- ˈkɑːg-, *(iii)* ˈkəʊl ən ‖ ˈkoʊl ən
Coughton *(i)* ˈkəʊt ᵊn ‖ ˈkoʊt-, *(ii)* ˈkaʊt ᵊn
could *strong form* kʊd, *occasional weak form* kəd
couldn't ˈkʊd ᵊnt —*There is also a form* ˈkʊd ᵊn, *in standard speech used mainly before a consonant. This word has no weak form.*
couldst kʊdst
coulee ˈkuːl i -eɪ **~s** z
coulis *sing.* ˈkuːl i ‖ ku ˈliː **coulis** *pl* ˈkuːl iz -i ‖ ku ˈliːz -ˈliː —*Fr* [ku li]
coulomb, C~ ˈkuːl ɒm ‖ -ɑːm -oʊm —*Fr* [ku lɔ̃] **~s** z
Coulsdon ˈkuːlz dən ˈkəʊlz-

Coulson *(i)* 'kəʊls ᵊn →'kɒʊls- ‖ 'koʊls ᵊn, *(ii)* 'ku:ls ᵊn
Coulston 'ku:lst ən
coulter 'kəʊlt ə →'kɒʊlt-, 'ku:t- ‖ 'koʊlt ᵊr **~s** z
Coulthard *(i)* 'ku:lt ɑ:d ‖ -ɑ:rd, *(ii)* 'kəʊlθ- →'kɒʊlθ- ‖ 'koʊlθ-
Coulton 'kəʊlt ən →'kɒʊlt- ‖ 'koʊlt ᵊn
coumarin 'ku:m ər ɪn §-ən
council 'kaʊnᵗs ᵊl -ɪl *(usually = counsel)* **~s** z
ˌ**Council 'Bluffs**; '**council house**; '**council tax**
councillor, councilor 'kaʊnᵗs ᵊl ə -ɪl- ‖ ər **~s** z
council|man 'kaʊnᵗs ᵊl |mən -ɪl-, -mæn **~men** mən men **~woman** ˌwʊm ən **~women** ˌwɪm ɪn -ən
counsel 'kaʊnᵗs ᵊl **~ed, ~led** d **~ing, ~ling** ˌɪŋ **~s** z
counsellor, counselor 'kaʊnᵗs ᵊl‿ə ‖ ər **~s** z **~ship** ʃɪp
count kaʊnt **counted** 'kaʊnt ɪd -əd ‖ 'kaʊnt̬ əd **counting** 'kaʊnt ɪŋ ‖ 'kaʊnt̬ ɪŋ **counts** kaʊnts
'**count noun**
countab|le 'kaʊnt əb |ᵊl ‖ 'kaʊnt̬- **~ly** li
countdown 'kaʊnt daʊn **~s** z
countenanc|e 'kaʊnt ən ənᵗs -ɪn- ‖ -ᵊn‿ənᵗs **~ed** t **~es** ɪz əz **~ing** ɪŋ
counter 'kaʊnt ə ‖ 'kaʊnt̬ ᵊr **~ed** d **countering** 'kaʊnt‿ər ɪŋ ‖ 'kaʊnt̬ ər ɪŋ **~s** z
counter- *prefix* ¦kaʊnt ə ‖ ¦kaʊnt̬ ᵊr *—In context, this prefix often bears a contrastive nuclear accent (not shown in the entries below).*
counteract ˌkaʊnt ər 'ækt -ə 'rækt ‖ ˌkaʊnt̬ ər- **~ed** ɪd əd **~ing** ɪŋ **~s** s
counteraction ˌkaʊnt ər 'æk ʃᵊn -ə 'ræk-, '.ˌ.. ‖ ˌkaʊnt̬ ər- **~s** z
counterattack *v, n* 'kaʊnt ər ə ˌtæk ˌ..'. ‖ 'kaʊnt̬ ər- **~ed** t **~ing** ɪŋ **~s** s
counterattraction ˌkaʊnt ər ə 'træk ʃᵊn '. . .ˌ. . ‖ ˌkaʊnt̬ ər- **~s** z
counterbalanc|e *v* ˌkaʊnt ə 'bæl ənᵗs ‖ ˌkaʊnt̬ ᵊr- **~ed** t **~es** ɪz əz **~ing** ɪŋ
counterbalanc|e *n* 'kaʊnt ə ˌbæl ənᵗs ‖ 'kaʊnt̬ ᵊr- **~es** ɪz əz
counterbid 'kaʊnt ə bɪd ‖ 'kaʊnt̬ ᵊr- **~ding** ɪŋ **~s** z
counterblast 'kaʊnt ə blɑ:st §-blæst ‖ 'kaʊnt̬ ᵊr blæst **~s** s
countercharg|e *v, n* 'kaʊnt ə tʃɑ:dʒ ‖ 'kaʊnt̬ ᵊr tʃɑ:rdʒ **~ed** d **~es** ɪz əz **~ing** ɪŋ
counterclaim *v, n* 'kaʊnt ə kleɪm ‖ 'kaʊnt̬ ᵊr- **~ed** d **~ing** ɪŋ **~s** z
counterclockwise ˌkaʊnt ə 'klɒk waɪz ‖ ˌkaʊnt̬ ᵊr 'klɑ:k-
counterculture 'kaʊnt ə ˌkʌltʃ ə ‖ 'kaʊn t̬ ᵊr ˌkʌltʃ ᵊr
counterespionage ˌkaʊnt ər 'esp i‿ə nɑ:ʒ -nɑ:dʒ, -nɪdʒ ‖ ˌkaʊnt̬ ər-
counterexample 'kaʊnt ər ɪg ˌzɑ:mp ᵊl -eg,ˌ--, -ɪk,ˌ--, §-ˌzæmp- ‖ 'kaʊn t̬ ᵊr ɪg ˌzæmpᵊl **~s** z
counterfactual ˌkaʊnt ə 'fæk tʃu‿əl -'fæk tju‿əl ‖ ˌkaʊnt̬ ᵊr- -ʃu‿əl, -'fæk tʃə l **~ly** li **~s** z
counter|feit 'kaʊnt ə |fɪt -fi:t ‖ 'kaʊnt̬ ᵊr- **~feited** fɪt ɪd fi:t-, -əd ‖ fɪt̬ əd **~feiting** fɪt ɪŋ fi:t- ‖ fɪt̬ ɪŋ **~feits** fɪts fi:ts
counterfoil 'kaʊnt ə fɔɪᵊl ‖ 'kaʊnt̬ ᵊr- **~s** z
counterinflationary ˌkaʊnt ər ɪn 'fleɪʃ ᵊn ər‿i ◂ -ᵊn‿ər- ‖ ˌkaʊnt̬ ᵊr ɪn 'fleɪʃ ə ner i ◂
counterinsurgency ˌkaʊnt ər ɪn 'sɜ:dʒ ənᵗs i ‖ ˌkaʊnt̬ ər ɪn 'sɝ:dʒ-
counterintelligence ˌkaʊnt ər ɪn 'tel ɪdʒ ənᵗs -dʒ ənᵗs, '. . .ˌ. . . ‖ ˌkaʊnt̬ ər-
counterintuitive ˌkaʊnt ər ɪn 'tju:‿ət ɪv ◂ →§-'tʃu:‿ ‖ ˌkaʊnt̬ ər ɪn 'tu:‿ət̬ ɪv -'tju:‿ **~ly** li
counterirritant ˌkaʊnt ər 'ɪr ɪt ənt §-ət ənt ‖ ˌkaʊnt̬ ər 'ɪr ət ᵊnt **~s** s
countermand ˌkaʊnt ə 'mɑ:nd §-'mænd, '. . . ‖ 'kaʊnt̬ ᵊr mænd ˌ. '. **~ed** ɪd əd **~ing** ɪŋ **~s** z
countermarch 'kaʊnt ə mɑ:tʃ ‖ 'kaʊnt̬ ᵊr mɑ:rtʃ **~ed** t **~es** ɪz əz **~ing** ɪŋ
countermeasure 'kaʊnt ə ˌmeʒ ə ‖ 'kaʊnt̬ ᵊr ˌmeʒ ᵊr -ˌmeɪʒ- **~s** z
counteroffensive ˌkaʊnt ər ə 'fenᵗs ɪv '. . .ˌ. . ‖ 'kaʊnt̬ ər ə ˌfenᵗs ɪv **~s** z
counterpane 'kaʊnt ə peɪn ‖ 'kaʊnt̬ ᵊr- **~s** z
counterpart 'kaʊnt ə pɑ:t ‖ 'kaʊnt̬ ᵊr pɑ:rt **~s** s
counter|point 'kaʊnt ə |pɔɪnt ‖ 'kaʊnt̬ ᵊr- **~pointed** pɔɪnt ɪd -əd ‖ pɔɪnt̬ əd **~pointing** pɔɪnt ɪŋ ‖ pɔɪnt̬ ɪŋ **~points** pɔɪnts
counterpois|e 'kaʊnt ə pɔɪz ‖ 'kaʊnt̬ ᵊr- **~ed** d **~es** ɪz əz **~ing** ɪŋ
counterpresuppositional ˌkaʊnt ə ˌpri: sʌp ə 'zɪʃ ᵊn‿əl ‖ ˌkaʊnt̬ ᵊr- **s** z
counterproductive ˌkaʊnt ə prə 'dʌkt ɪv ◂ ‖ ˌkaʊnt̬ ᵊr- **~ly** li **~ness** nəs nɪs
counterproposal 'kaʊnt ə prə ˌpəʊz ᵊl ‖ 'kaʊnt̬ ᵊr prə ˌpoʊz ᵊl **~s** z
Counter-Reformation ˌkaʊnt ə ˌref ə 'meɪʃ ᵊn ‖ ˌkaʊnt̬ ᵊr ˌref ᵊr-
counterrevolution ˌkaʊnt ə ˌrev ə 'lu:ʃ ᵊn -'lju:ʃ-, '. . .ˌ. . ‖ ˌkaʊnt̬ ᵊr- **~s** z
counterrevolutionar|y ˌkaʊnt ə ˌrev ə 'lu:ʃ ᵊn‿ər |i -'lju:ʃ-, -ᵊn ər‿|i, '. . . .ˌ.- ‖ ˌkaʊnt̬ ᵊr ˌrev ə 'lu:ʃ ə ner |i **~ies** iz
countersank 'kaʊnt ə sæŋk ˌ. '. ‖ 'kaʊnt̬ ᵊr-
countershaft 'kaʊnt ə ʃɑ:ft §-ʃæft ‖ 'kaʊnt̬ ᵊr ʃæft **~s** s
countersign *n* 'kaʊnt ə saɪn ‖ 'kaʊnt̬ ᵊr- **~s** z
countersign *v* 'kaʊnt ə saɪn ˌ. '. ‖ 'kaʊnt̬ ᵊr- **~ed** d **~ing** ɪŋ **~s** z
counter|sink 'kaʊnt ə sɪŋk ˌ. '. ‖ 'kaʊnt̬ ᵊr- **~sank** sæŋk **~sinking** sɪŋk ɪŋ **~sunk** sʌŋk
countertenor ˌkaʊnt ə 'ten ə '. ˌ. ‖ 'kaʊnt̬ ᵊr ˌten ᵊr **~s** z
counterterror|ist ˌkaʊnt ə 'ter ər |ɪst -|əst ‖ ˌkaʊnt̬ ᵊr- **~ism** ˌɪz əm
countervail ˌkaʊnt ə 'veᵊl '. . . ‖ ˌkaʊnt̬ ᵊr- **~ed** d **~ing** ɪŋ **~s** z
counterweight 'kaʊnt ə weɪt ‖ 'kaʊnt̬ ᵊr- **~s** s

ountess 'kaʊnt ɪs -es, -əs, ˌkaʊn 'tes ‖ 'kaʊnt̬ əs **~es** ɪz əz
ounti... —*see* **county**
ounting|house 'kaʊnt ɪŋ |haʊs ‖ 'kaʊnt̬ ɪŋ- **~houses** haʊz ɪz -əz
ountless 'kaʊnt ləs -lɪs
ountrified 'kʌntr i faɪd
ountr|y 'kʌntr |i **~ies** iz
ˌcountry and 'western; **ˌcountry 'bumpkin**; **'country club**; **ˌcountry 'cousin**; **ˌcountry 'dance** ‖ '· · ·; **ˌcountry 'house**; **ˌcountry 'seat**
ountry|man 'kʌntr i |mən **~men** mən
ountryside 'kʌntr i saɪd
ountrywide ˌkʌntr i 'waɪd ◂ '· · ·
ountry|woman 'kʌntr i |ˌwʊm ən **~women** ˌwɪm ɪn §-ən
ount|y 'kaʊnt |i ‖ 'kaʊnt̬ |i **~ies** iz
ˌcounty 'council; **ˌcounty 'court**; **ˌcounty 'town**
oup kuː (!) **coups** kuːz —*See also phrases with this word*
oup de grace, coup de grâce ˌkuː də 'grɑːs —*Fr* [kud gʁas]
oup d'état ˌkuː deɪ 'tɑː —*Fr* [ku de ta]
oup de théâtre ˌkuː də teɪ 'ɑːtr‿ə —*Fr* [kud te ɑːtχ]
oupe *'dish'* kuːp **~s** s
oupe, coupé *'vehicle'* 'kuːp eɪ ‖ kuː 'peɪ kuːp **coupes, coupés** 'kuːp eɪz ‖ kuː 'peɪz kuːps
ouper 'kuːp ə ‖ -ᵊr
ouperin 'kuːp ə ræn -rã —*Fr* [ku pʁɛ̃]
oupland *(i)* 'kuːp lənd, *(ii)* 'kəʊp-
oupl|e 'kʌp ᵊl **~ed** d **~es** z **~ing** ‿ɪŋ
oupler 'kʌp lə ‖ -lᵊr **~s** z
ouplet 'kʌp lət -lɪt **~s** s
oupling *n* 'kʌp lɪŋ **~s** z
oupling *pres part of* **couple** 'kʌp ᵊl‿ɪŋ

COUPON

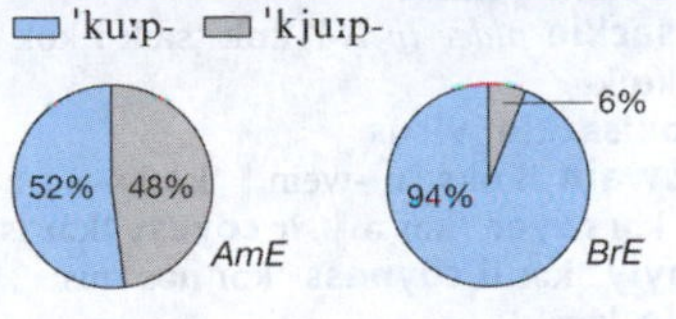

oupon 'kuːp ɒn ⚠ 'kjuːp- ‖ -ɑːn **~s** z — *Preference polls, AmE:* 'kuːp- *52%,* 'kjuːp- *48%; BrE:* 'kuːp- *94%,* 'kjuːp- *6%.*
oups kuːz —*In French phrases usually* kuː, *as singular* —*Fr* [ku] —*See* **coup**
ourage, C~ 'kʌr ɪdʒ ‖ 'kɜː ɪdʒ
ourageous kə 'reɪdʒ əs **~ly** li **~ness** nəs nɪs
Courbet 'kʊə beɪ 'kɔː- ‖ kʊr 'beɪ —*Fr* [kuʁ bɛ]
ourgette ₍ˌ₎kɔː 'ʒet ₍ˌ₎kʊə- ‖ kʊr- **~s** s
ourier 'kʊr i‿ə 'kʊər-, 'kʌr- ‖ 'kɜː i‿ᵊr 'kʊr- **~s** z
Courland 'kʊə lənd -lænd ‖ 'kʊr-
Courrèges ku 'reʒ -'reɪʒ —*Fr* [ku ʁɛːʒ]

course kɔːs ‖ kɔːrs koʊrs (= *coarse*) **coursed** kɔːst ‖ kɔːrst koʊrst **courses** 'kɔːs ɪz -əz ‖ 'kɔːrs əz 'koʊrs- **coursing** 'kɔːs ɪŋ ‖ 'kɔːrs ɪŋ 'koʊrs-
coursebook 'kɔːs bʊk §-buːk ‖ 'kɔːrs- **~s** s
courser 'kɔːs ə ‖ 'kɔːrs ᵊr 'koʊrs- **~s** z
coursework 'kɔːs wɜːk ‖ 'kɔːrs wɜːk 'koʊrs-
court, Court kɔːt ‖ kɔːrt koʊrt **courted** 'kɔːt ɪd -əd ‖ 'kɔːrt̬ əd 'koʊrt̬- **courting** 'kɔːt ɪŋ ‖ 'kɔːrt̬ ɪŋ 'koʊrt̬- **courts** kɔːts ‖ kɔːrts koʊrts
'court card; **ˌcourt 'circular**; **'court shoe**
Courtauld 'kɔːt əʊld →-ɒʊld, -əʊ ‖ 'kɔːrt oʊld 'koʊrt-
court-bouillon ˌkɔːt 'buː jɒn ˌkʊət-, ˌkʊə- ‖ ˌkɔːr 'buːl jɑːn —*Fr* [kuʁ bu jɔ̃]
Courtelle *tdmk* ₍ˌ₎kɔː 'tel ‖ ₍ˌ₎kɔːr- ₍ˌ₎koʊr-
Courtenay 'kɔːt ni ‖ 'kɔːrt- 'koʊrt-
courteous 'kɜːt i‿əs 'kɔːt- ‖ 'kɜːt̬- **~ly** li **~ness** nəs nɪs
courtesan ˌkɔːt ɪ 'zæn -ə-, '· · · ‖ 'kɔːrt̬ əz ən 'koʊrt̬-, -ə zæn **~s** z
courtes|y 'kɜːt əs |i 'kɔːt-, -ɪs- ‖ 'kɜːt̬- **~ies** iz
'courtesy car; **'courtesy light**; **'courtesy ˌtitle**
court|house 'kɔːt |haʊs ‖ 'kɔːrt- 'koʊrt- **~houses** haʊz ɪz -əz
courtier 'kɔːt i‿ə 'kɔːt jə ‖ 'kɔːrt̬ i‿ᵊr 'koʊrt̬-; 'kɔːrtʃ ᵊr, 'koʊrtʃ- **~s** z
court|ly 'kɔːt |li ‖ 'kɔːrt- 'koʊrt- **~liness** li nəs li nɪs
court-martial ˌkɔːt 'mɑːʃ ᵊl ◂ ‖ 'kɔːrt ˌmɑːrʃ ᵊl 'koʊrt-, ˌ·'·· **courts-martial** ˌkɔːts 'mɑːʃ ᵊl ‖ 'kɔːrts ˌmɑːrʃ ᵊl 'koʊrts-, ˌ·'··
Courtneidge 'kɔːt nɪdʒ ‖ 'kɔːrt- 'koʊrt-
Courtney 'kɔːt ni ‖ 'kɔːrt- 'koʊrt-
courtroom 'kɔːt ruːm -rʊm ‖ 'kɔːrt- 'koʊrt- **~s** z
courtship 'kɔːt ʃɪp ‖ 'kɔːrt- 'koʊrt-
courts-martial —*see* **court-martial**
courtyard 'kɔːt jɑːd ‖ 'kɔːrt jɑːrd 'koʊrt- **~s** z
Courvoisier *tdmk* ₍ˌ₎kʊə 'vwæz i eɪ -'vwɑːz- ‖ ˌkɔːrv wɑːs i 'eɪ —*Fr* [kuʁ vwa zje] **~s** z
couscous 'kuːs kuːs
cousin 'kʌz ᵊn **~s** z
Cousins 'kʌz ᵊnz
Cousteau 'kuːst əʊ ‖ ku 'stoʊ —*Fr* [ku sto]
couth kuːθ
Coutts kuːts
couture ku 'tjʊə -'tʊə, →§-'tʃʊə ‖ -'tʊr -'tjʊr —*Fr* [ku tyːʁ]
couturier ku 'tjʊər i eɪ -'tʊər-, →§-'tʃʊər-, -i‿ə ‖ -'tʊr- -i‿ᵊr **~s** z
couvade ₍ˌ₎kuː 'vɑːd
covalenc|y ˌkəʊ 'veɪl ənᵗs |i '·ˌ· · · ‖ ˌkoʊ- **~ies** iz
covalent ˌkəʊ 'veɪl ənt ◂ ‖ ˌkoʊ- **~ly** li
ˌcoˌvalent 'bond
covariance ˌkəʊ 'veər i‿ənᵗs '·ˌ· · · ‖ ˌkoʊ 'ver- -'vær-
cove, Cove kəʊv ‖ koʊv **coves** kəʊvz ‖ koʊvz
coven 'kʌv ᵊn **~s** z
covenant *n* 'kʌv ən‿ənt **~s** s

coven|ant *v* ˈkʌv ən‿ənt ‖ -ə n|ænt **~anted** ənt ɪd -əd ‖ ənţ əd ænţ əd **~anting** ənt ɪŋ ‖ ənţ ɪŋ ænţ ɪŋ **~ants** ənts ‖ ænts
covenanter, covenantor, C~ ˈkʌv ən‿ənt ə ˌkʌv ə ˈnænt ə, ˌkʌv ə næn ˈtɔː ‖ ˈkʌv ə nænţ ər ˌ·ˈ·ˈ·, ˌkʌv ə næn ˈtɔːr **~s** z
Covent ˈkɒv ənt ˈkʌv- ‖ ˈkʌv- ˈkɑːv-
ˌCovent ˈGarden◂
Coventry ˈkɒv əntr i ˈkʌv- ‖ ˈkʌv- ˈkɑːv-
cover ˈkʌv ə ‖ -ər **covered** ˈkʌv əd ‖ -ərd **covering** ˈkʌv ər‿ɪŋ **covers** ˈkʌv əz ‖ -ərz **ˈcover charge**; **ˌcovered ˈwagon**; **ˈcover girl**; **ˈcover ˌletter**; **ˈcover note**; **ˌcover ˈpoint**
Coverack *(i)* ˈkʌv ə ræk -ər ək, *(ii)* ˈkɒv- ‖ ˈkɑːv-
coverage ˈkʌv ər‿ɪdʒ
coverall ˈkʌv ər ɔːl ‖ -ər ɔːl -ɑːl **~s** z
Coverdale ˈkʌv ə deɪəl ‖ -ər-
covering ˈkʌv ər‿ɪŋ **~s** z
ˌcovering ˈletter
cover|let ˈkʌv ə |lət -lɪt ‖ -ər- -lɪd **~lets** ləts lɪts ‖ lɪdz
Coverley ˈkʌv ə li ‖ -ər-
covermount ˈkʌv ə maʊnt ‖ -rə- **~s** s
covert *n* ˈkʌv ət -ə ‖ -ərt ˈkoʊ vɜːt **~s** s

COVERT

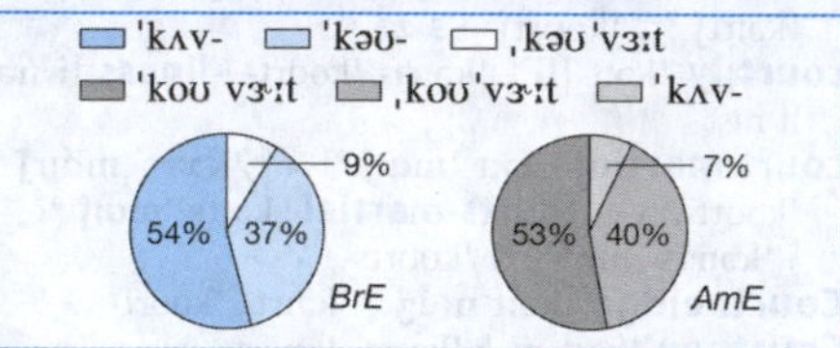

covert *adj* ˈkʌv ət ˈkəʊ vɜːt, ˌkəʊ ˈvɜːt ◂ ‖ ˈkoʊ vɜːt ˌ·ˈ·; ˈkʌv ərt — *Preference polls, BrE:* ˈkʌv- *54%,* ˈkəʊ- *37%,* ˌkəʊ ˈvɜːt *9%; AmE:* ˈkoʊ vɜːt *53%,* ˌkoʊ ˈvɜːt *40%,* ˈkʌv- *7%.* **~ly** li **~ness** nəs nɪs
cover-up ˈkʌv ər ʌp ‖ -ər ʌp **~s** s
cov|et ˈkʌv |ɪt -ət ‖ -|ət **~eted** ɪt ɪd §ət-, -əd ‖ əţ əd **~eting** ɪt ɪŋ §ət- ‖ əţ ɪŋ **~ets** ɪts §əts ‖ əts
covetable ˈkʌv ɪt əb əl ˈ·ət- ‖ ˈ·əţ-
covetous ˈkʌv ɪt əs -ət- ‖ -əţ əs **~ly** li **~ness** nəs nɪs
covey ˈkʌv i **~s** z
coving ˈkəʊv ɪŋ ‖ ˈkoʊv ɪŋ
cow, Cow kaʊ **cows** kaʊz
ˌcow ˈparsley
cowabunga ˌkaʊ ə ˈbʌŋ gə
cowage ˈkaʊ ɪdʒ
Cowan ˈkaʊ‿ən
coward, C~ ˈkaʊ‿əd ‖ ˈkaʊ‿ərd **~s** z
cowardice ˈkaʊ‿əd ɪs §-əs ‖ ˈkaʊ‿ərd-
coward|ly ˈkaʊ‿əd |li ‖ ˈkaʊ‿ərd- **~liness** li nəs li nɪs
cowbell ˈkaʊ bel **~s** z
cowberr|y ˈkaʊ bər‿|i -ˌber |i ‖ -ˌber |i **~ies** iz
cowbird ˈkaʊ bɜːd ‖ -bɜːd **~s** z
cowboy ˈkaʊ bɔɪ **~s** z
Cowbridge ˈkaʊ brɪdʒ
cowcatcher ˈkaʊ ˌkætʃ ə ‖ -ər §-ˌketʃ- **~s** z
Cowdenbeath ˌkaʊd ən ˈbiːθ
Cowdray, Cowdrey ˈkaʊdr i -eɪ
cowed kaʊd
Cowell *(i)* ˈkaʊ‿əl kaʊl ‖ ˈkaʊ‿əl, *(ii)* ˈkəʊ əl ‖ ˈkoʊ əl
Cowen *(i)* ˈkaʊ‿ən -ɪn, *(ii)* ˈkəʊ- ‖ ˈkoʊ-
cower ˈkaʊ‿ə ‖ ˈkaʊ‿ər **cowered** ˈkaʊ‿əd ‖ ˈkaʊ‿ərd **cowering** ˈkaʊ‿ər ɪŋ ‖ ˈkaʊ‿ər ɪŋ **cowers** ˈkaʊ‿əz ‖ ˈkaʊ‿ərz
Cowes kaʊz
Cowgill ˈkaʊ gɪl
cowgirl ˈkaʊ gɜːl ‖ -gɜːl **~s** z
cowhand ˈkaʊ hænd **~s** z
cowheel ˈkaʊ hiːəl
cowherd ˈkaʊ hɜːd ‖ -hɜːd **~s** z
cowhide ˈkaʊ haɪd **~s** z
Cowie ˈkaʊ‿i
cowl kaʊl **cowled** kaʊld **cowling** ˈkaʊl ɪŋ **cowls** kaʊlz
Cowley ˈkaʊl i
cowlick ˈkaʊ lɪk **~s** s
cowling, C~ ˈkaʊl ɪŋ **~s** z
cow|man ˈkaʊ |mən -mæn **~men** mən men
co-worker ˌkəʊ ˈwɜːk ə ˈ·ˌ·· ‖ ˈkoʊ ˌwɜːk ər **~s** z
cowpat ˈkaʊ pæt **~s** s
Cowper *(i)* ˈkuːp ə ‖ -ər, *(ii)* ˈkaʊp-
cowpoke ˈkaʊ pəʊk ‖ -poʊk **~s** s
cowpox ˈkaʊ pɒks ‖ -pɑːks
cowrie, cowry ˈkaʊər i **cowries** ˈkaʊər iz
cowshed ˈkaʊ ʃed **~s** z
cowslip ˈkaʊ slɪp **~s** s
cowtown ˈkaʊ taʊn **~s** z
cox, Cox kɒks ‖ kɑːks *(= cocks)* **coxed** kɒkst ‖ kɑːkst **coxes, Cox's** ˈkɒks ɪz -əz ‖ ˈkɑːks əz **coxing** ˈkɒks ɪŋ ‖ ˈkɑːks ɪŋ **Cox's** ˈkɒks ɪz -əz ‖ ˈkɑːks əz
coxalgia kɒk ˈsældʒ ə -ˈsældʒ i‿ə ‖ kɑːk-
coxcomb ˈkɒks kəʊm ‖ ˈkɑːks koʊm **~s** z
Coxe kɒks ‖ kɑːks
Coxsackie *place in NY* kɒk ˈsæk i kʊk ˈsɑːk i ‖ kɑːk-
Cox'sackie ˌvirus
coxswain ˈkɒks ən -weɪn ‖ ˈkɑːks- **~s** z
coy kɔɪ **coyer** ˈkɔɪ ə ‖ -ər **coyest** ˈkɔɪ ɪst -əst **coyly** ˈkɔɪ li **coyness** ˈkɔɪ nəs -nɪs
Coyle kɔɪəl
coyote kɔɪ ˈəʊt i kaɪ-; ˈkɔɪ əʊt, ˈkaɪ- ‖ kaɪ ˈoʊţ i ˈkaɪ oʊt **coyotes** kɔɪ ˈəʊt iz kaɪ-; ˈkɔɪ əʊts, ˈkaɪ- ‖ kaɪ ˈoʊţ iz ˈkaɪ oʊts
coypu ˈkɔɪp uː -juː; kɔɪ ˈpuː **~s** z
coz kʌz
cozen ˈkʌz ən **~ed** d **~ing** ‿ɪŋ **~s** z
Cozens ˈkʌz ənz
Cozumel ˌkɒz u ˈmel ˌkɒs- ‖ ˌkoʊs- —*AmSp* [ko su ˈmel]
coz|y ˈkəʊz |i ‖ ˈkoʊz |i **~ier** i‿ə ‖ i‿ər **~iest** i‿ɪst i‿əst **~ily** ɪ li əl i **~iness** i nəs i nɪs
CPA ˌsiː piː ˈeɪ **~s** z
CP'er ˌsiː ˈpiː ə ‖ -ər **~s** z
CP/M ˌsiː piː ˈem

PU ˌsiː piː ˈjuː **~s** z
ab, Crab kræb **crabbing** ˈkræb ɪŋ **crabs** kræbz
ˈ**crab** ˌ**apple**; ˈ**crab louse**; ˌ**Crab** ˈ**Nebula**; ˌ**crab** ˈ**paste**
rabb, Crabbe kræb
rabbed ˈkræb ɪd -əd; kræbd **~ly** li **~ness** nəs nɪs
rabb|y ˈkræb |i **~ier** i̯ə ‖ i̯ᵊr **~iest** i̯ɪst i̯əst
rabgrass ˈkræb grɑːs §-græs ‖ -græs
rabtree, C~ ˈkræb triː **~s** z
rabways ˈkræb weɪz
rabwise ˈkræb waɪz
rack kræk **cracked** krækt **cracking** ˈkræk ɪŋ **cracks** kræks
rackbrained ˈkræk breɪnd
rackdown ˈkræk daʊn **~s** z
racker ˈkræk ə ‖ -ᵊr **~s** z
racker-barrel ˈkræk ə ˌbær əl ‖ -ᵊr- -ˌber-
rackerjack ˈkræk ə dʒæk ‖ -ᵊr-
rackhead ˈkræk hed **~s** z
Crackington ˈkræk ɪŋ tən
rackjaw ˈkræk dʒɔː ‖ -dʒɑː
rackl|e ˈkræk ᵊl **~ed** d **~es** z **~ing** ˌɪŋ
rackleware ˈkræk ᵊl weə ‖ -wer -wær
rackling *n 'crisp pork skin'* ˈkræk lɪŋ -lən
crackling *part, verbal n* ˈkræk ᵊl ˌɪŋ
rackly ˈkræk ᵊl ˌi
racknel ˈkræk nᵊl **~s** z
Cracknell ˈkræk nᵊl
rackpot ˈkræk pɒt ‖ -pɑːt **~s** s
cracks|man ˈkræks |mən **~men** mən men
crackup ˈkræk ʌp **~s** s
Cracow ˈkræk aʊ -əʊ, -ɒf ‖ ˈkrɑːk aʊ —*Polish* Kraków [ˈkra kuf]
cracy *stress-imposing* krəs i — **plutocracy** pluː ˈtɒk rəs i ‖ -ˈtɑːk-
Craddock ˈkræd ək
cradl|e ˈkreɪd ᵊl **~ed** d **~es** z **~ing** ˌɪŋ
cradle-rob ˈkreɪd ᵊl rɒb ‖ -rɑːb **~bing** ɪŋ
cradle-snatch|er ˈkreɪd ᵊl ˌsnætʃ |ə ‖ -|ᵊr **~ers** əz ‖ ᵊrz **~ing** ɪŋ
Cradley *(i)* ˈkreɪd li, *(ii)* ˈkræd-
craft krɑːft §kræft ‖ kræft **crafted** ˈkrɑːft ɪd §ˈkræft, -əd ‖ ˈkræft əd **crafting** ˈkrɑːft ɪŋ §ˈkræft- ‖ ˈkræft ɪŋ **crafts** krɑːfts §kræfts ‖ kræfts
ˈ**craft** ˌ**union**
-craft krɑːft §kræft ‖ kræft — **woodcraft** ˈwʊd krɑːft §-kræft ‖ -kræft
crafts|man ˈkrɑːfts |mən §ˈkræfts- ‖ ˈkræfts- **~men** mən men
craftsmanship ˈkrɑːfts mən ʃɪp §ˈkræfts- ‖ ˈkræfts-
crafts|woman ˈkrɑːfts ˌwʊm ən §ˈkræfts- ‖ ˈkræfts- **~women** ˌwɪm ɪn -ən
craft|y ˈkrɑːft |i §ˈkræft- ‖ ˈkræft |i **~ier** i̯ə ‖ i̯ᵊr **~iest** i̯ɪst i̯əst **~ily** ɪ li əl i **~iness** i nəs i nɪs
crag kræg **crags** krægz
Cragg kræg
Craggs krægz
cragg|y ˈkræg |i **~ier** i̯ə ‖ i̯ᵊr **~iest** i̯ɪst i̯əst **~ily** ɪ li əl i **~iness** i nəs i nɪs
craic *Irish spelling of 'crack'* kræk
Craig kreɪg
Craigavon ˌkreɪg ˈæv ᵊn
Craigie ˈkreɪg i
Craignure ₍ˌ₎kreɪg ˈnjʊə ‖ -ˈnʊᵊr -ˈnjʊᵊr
crake kreɪk **crakes** kreɪks
cram, Cram kræm **crammed** kræmd **cramming** ˈkræm ɪŋ **crams** kræmz
crambo ˈkræm bəʊ ‖ -boʊ
cram-full ˌkræm ˈfʊl ◂
crammer ˈkræm ə ‖ -ᵊr **~s** z
Cramond ˈkræm ənd ˈkrɑːm-
cramp kræmp **cramped** kræmpt **cramping** ˈkræmp ɪŋ **cramps** kræmps
crampon ˈkræmp ɒn -ən ‖ -ɑːn **~s** z
cran, Cran kræn **crans** krænz
cranage ˈkreɪn ɪdʒ
cranberr|y ˈkræn bər ˌi →ˈkræm- ‖ -ˌber |i **~ies** iz
Cranborne, Cranbourn, Cranbourne ˈkræn bɔːn →ˈkræm- ‖ -bɔːrn -boʊrn
Cranbrook ˈkræn brʊk →ˈkræm-
crane, Crane kreɪn **craned** kreɪnd **craning** ˈkreɪn ɪŋ **cranes** kreɪnz
ˈ**crane fly**
cranesbill ˈkreɪnz bɪl **~s** z
Cranfield ˈkræn fiːᵊld
Cranford ˈkræn fəd ‖ -fᵊrd
crania ˈkreɪn i̯ə
cranial ˈkreɪn i̯əl
cranio- *comb. form*
with stress-neutral suffix |kreɪn i̯əʊ ‖ oʊ — **craniometric** ˌkreɪn i̯əʊ ˈmetr ɪk ◂ ‖ -oʊˈ--
with stress-imposing suffix ˌkreɪn i ˈɒ+ ‖ -ˈɑː+ — **craniotomy** ˌkreɪn i ˈɒt əm i ‖ -ˈɑːt̬-
crani|um ˈkreɪn i̯|əm **~a** ə
crank, Crank kræŋk **cranked** kræŋkt **cranking** ˈkræŋk ɪŋ **cranks** kræŋks
crankcas|e ˈkræŋk keɪs **~es** ɪz əz
cranki... —*see* **cranky**
Cranko ˈkræŋk əʊ ‖ -oʊ
crankpin ˈkræŋk pɪn **~s** z
crankshaft ˈkræŋk ʃɑːft §-ʃæft ‖ -ʃæft **~s** s
Crankshaw ˈkræŋk ʃɔː ‖ -ʃɑː
crank|y ˈkræŋk |i **~ier** i̯ə ‖ i̯ᵊr **~iest** i̯ɪst i̯əst **~ily** ɪ li əl i **~iness** i nəs i nɪs
Cranleigh, Cranley ˈkræn li
Cranmer ˈkræn mə →ˈkræm- ‖ -mᵊr
crannog ˈkræn əg **~s** z
crann|y ˈkræn |i **~ied** id **~ies** iz
Cranston ˈkrænᵗst ən
Cranwell ˈkræn wəl -wel
crap kræp **crapped** kræpt **crapping** ˈkræp ɪŋ **craps** kræps
crape kreɪp
crapper ˈkræp ə ‖ -ᵊr **~s** z
crappie, crappy ˈkræp i **crappies** ˈkræp iz
crapp|y ˈkræp| i **~ier** i̯ə ‖ i̯ᵊr **~iest** i̯ɪst i̯əst **~ily** ɪ li əl i **~iness** i nəs i nɪs
craps kræps

crapshoot 'kræp ʃuːt **~s** s
crapshooter 'kræp ˌʃuːt ə ‖ -ˌʃuːţ ᵊr **~s** z
crapulence 'kræp jʊl ənᵗs -jəl- ‖ -jəl-
crapulent 'kræp jʊl ənt -jəl- ‖ -jəl- **~ly** li
crapulous 'kræp jʊl əs -jəl- ‖ -jəl- **~ness** nəs nɪs
craquelure 'kræk ə lʊə -ljʊə ‖ -lʊr
crases 'kreɪs iːz
crash kræʃ **crashed** kræʃt **crashes** 'kræʃ ɪz -əz **crashing** 'kræʃ ɪŋ **'crash ˌbarrier**; **'crash ˌhelmet**
Crashaw 'kræʃ ɔː ‖ -ɑː
crash-div|e 'kræʃ daɪv ˌ·'· **~ed** d **~es** z **~ing** ɪŋ **crashdove** 'kræʃ dəʊv ‖ -doʊv
crash-land 'kræʃ lænd ˌ·'· **~ed** ɪd əd **~s** z **~ing/s** ɪŋ/z
crasis 'kreɪs ɪs §-əs **crases** 'kreɪs iːz
crass kræs **crasser** 'kræs ə ‖ -ᵊr **crassest** 'kræs ɪst -əst
crass|ly 'kræs |li **~ness** nəs nɪs
Crassus 'kræs əs
-crat kræt — **plutocrat** 'pluːt əʊ kræt ‖ 'pluːţ ə-
Cratchit 'krætʃ ɪt §-ət
crate kreɪt **crated** 'kreɪt ɪd -əd ‖ 'kreɪţ əd **crates** kreɪts **crating** 'kreɪt ɪŋ ‖ 'kreɪţ ɪŋ
crater 'kreɪt ə ‖ 'kreɪţ ᵊr **~ed** d **cratering** 'kreɪt ər ɪŋ ‖ 'kreɪţ ər ɪŋ **~s** z
Crathes 'kræθ ɪz -əz
Crathorn, Crathorne 'kreɪ θɔːn ‖ -θɔːrn
Crathy 'kræθ i
-cratic 'kræt ɪk ‖ 'kræţ ɪk — **plutocratic** ˌpluːt əʊ 'kræt ɪk ◂ ‖ ˌpluːţ ə 'kræţ ɪk ◂
cra|vat krə|'væt **~vats** 'væts **~vatted** 'væt ɪd -əd ‖ 'væţ əd
crave kreɪv **craved** kreɪvd **craves** kreɪvz **craving** 'kreɪv ɪŋ
craven, Craven 'kreɪv ᵊn **~ly** li **~ness** nəs nɪs
craving 'kreɪv ɪŋ **~s** z
craw krɔː ‖ krɑː **craws** krɔːz ‖ krɑːz
crawdad 'krɔː dæd ‖ 'krɑː- **~s** z
crawfish 'krɔː fɪʃ ‖ 'krɑː-
Crawford 'krɔː fəd ‖ -fᵊrd 'krɑː-
crawl krɔːl ‖ krɑːl **crawled** krɔːld ‖ krɑːld **crawling** 'krɔːl ɪŋ ‖ 'krɑːl- **crawls** krɔːlz ‖ krɑːlz
crawler 'krɔːl ə ‖ -ᵊr 'krɑːl- **~s** z
Crawley 'krɔːl i ‖ 'krɑːl-
crawl|y 'krɔːl |i ‖ 'krɑːl- **~ier** i‿ə ‖ i‿ᵊr **~iest** i‿ɪst i‿əst
Crawshaw 'krɔː ʃɔː ‖ 'krɑː ʃɑː
Crawshay 'krɔː ʃeɪ ‖ 'krɑː-
Cray kreɪ
crayfish 'kreɪ fɪʃ
Crayford 'kreɪ fəd ‖ -fᵊrd
Crayola *tdmk* kreɪ 'əʊl ə ‖ -'oʊl-
crayon 'kreɪ ɒn -ən ‖ -ɑːn -ən; kræn **~ed** d **~ing** ɪŋ **~s** z
craze kreɪz **crazed** kreɪzd **crazes** 'kreɪz ɪz -əz **crazing** 'kreɪz ɪŋ
craz|y 'kreɪz |i **~ier** i‿ə ‖ i‿ᵊr **~iest** i‿ɪst i‿əst **~ily** ɪ li əl i **~iness** i nəs i nɪs **ˌCrazy 'Horse, ˌcrazy 'paving**

CRE ˌsiː ɑːr 'iː ‖ -ɑːr-
Creagh kreɪ
creak kriːk **creaked** kriːkt **creaking** 'kriːk ɪŋ **creaks** kriːks
creak|y 'kriːk |i **~ier** i‿ə ‖ i‿ᵊr **~iest** i‿ɪst i‿əst **~ily** ɪ li əl i **~iness** i nəs i nɪs

CREAM CHEESE

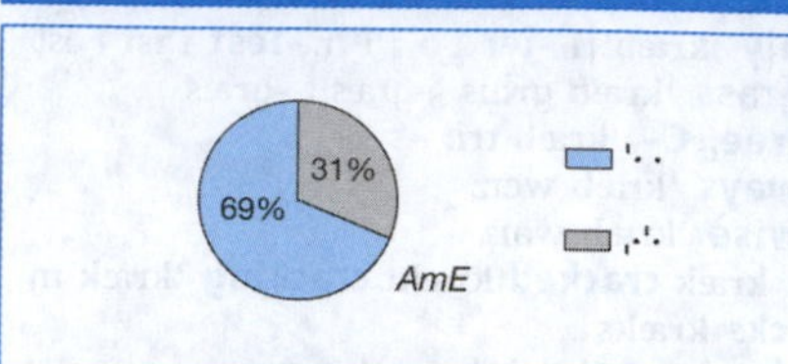

cream kriːm **creamed** kriːmd **creaming** 'kriːm ɪŋ **creams** kriːmz **ˌcream 'cheese, 'cream cheese** — *Preference poll, AmE:* '· · *69%,* ˌ·'· *31%;* **ˌcream 'cracker**; **ˌcream 'puff**; **ˌcream 'sauce**; **ˌcream 'soda**; **ˌcream 'tea**
cream-coloured, cream-colored 'kriːm ˌkʌl əd ‖ -ᵊrd
creamer 'kriːm ə ‖ -ᵊr **~s** z
creamer|y 'kriːm ər |i **~ies** iz
cream|y 'kriːm |i **~ier** i‿ə ‖ i‿ᵊr **~iest** i‿ɪst i‿əst **~ily** ɪ li əl i **~iness** i nəs i nɪs
crease kriːs **creased** kriːst **creases** 'kriːs ɪz -əz **creasing** 'kriːs ɪŋ
crease-resistant 'kriːs ri ˌzɪst ənt -rə-, ˌ· ·'· ◂
Creasey, Creasy 'kriːs i

CREATE

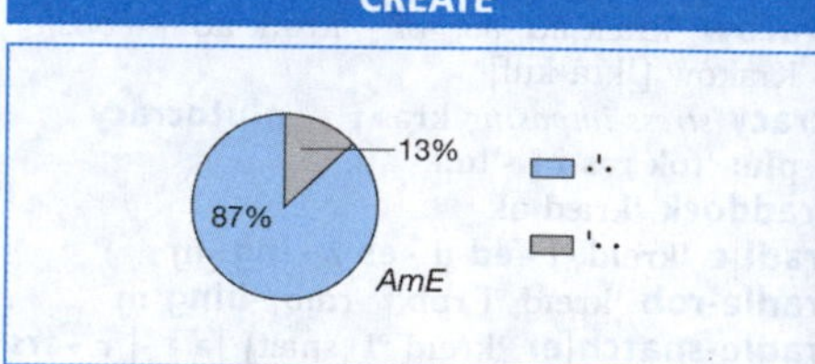

cre|ate kri |'eɪt ˌkriː-, '· · — *Preference poll, AmE:* ·'· *87%,* '· · *13%.* **~ated** 'eɪt ɪd -əd ‖ 'eɪţ əd **~ates** 'eɪts **~ating** 'eɪt ɪŋ ‖ 'eɪţ ɪŋ
creatine 'kriː ə tiːn -tɪn, §-ət ᵊn
creatinine kri 'æt ə niːn -ɪ-; ᵊn iːn; ᵊn ɪn, -ɪn ɪn, §-ᵊn ən ‖ -ᵊn iːn -ən
creation kri 'eɪʃ ᵊn ˌkriː- **~s** z
creationism kri 'eɪʃ ᵊn ˌɪz əm ˌkriː-
creationist kri 'eɪʃ ᵊn‿ɪst ˌkriː-, §‿əst **~s** s
creative kri 'eɪt ɪv ˌkriː- ‖ -'eɪţ ɪv **~ly** li **~ness** nəs nɪs
creativity ˌkriː eɪ 'tɪv ət i ˌkri‿ə-, -ɪt i ‖ -əţ i
creator kri 'eɪt ə ˌkriː-; 'kriː eɪt ə ‖ -'eɪţ ᵊr **~s** z
creature 'kriːtʃ ə ‖ -ᵊr **~s** z **ˌcreature 'comforts** ‖ '· ˌ·
creche, crèche kreʃ kreɪʃ —*Fr* [kʁɛʃ] **creches, crèches** 'kreʃ ɪz 'kreɪʃ-, -əz
Crecy, Crécy 'kres i ‖ kreɪ 'siː —*Fr* [kʁe si]
cred kred
Creda *tdmk* 'kriːd ə
credal 'kriːd ᵊl

edenc|e ˈkriːd ᵊnᵗs **~es** ɪz əz

edential krə ˈdenᵗʃ ᵊl krɪ- **~ed, ~led** d **~s** z

edenza krə ˈdenz ə krɪ **~s** z

ediblity ˌkred ə ˈbɪl ət i ˌ·ɪ-, -ɪt i ‖ -əţ i **ˌcrediˈbility gap**

edib|le ˈkred əb |ᵊl -ɪb- **~ly** li

ed|it ˈkred |ɪt §-ət ‖ -|ət **~ited** ɪt ɪd §ət-, -əd ‖ əţ əd **~iting** ɪt ɪŋ §ət- ‖ əţ ɪŋ **~its** ɪts §əts ‖ əts **ˈcredit acˌcount; ˈcredit card; ˈcredit ˌlimit; ˈcredit note; ˈcredit squeeze**

reditab|le ˈkred ɪt əb |ᵊl §ˈ·ət- ‖ ˈkred əţ- **~ly** li

rediton ˈkred ɪt ən §-ət- ‖ -ət ᵊn

reditor ˈkred ɪt ə §-ət- ‖ -əţ ᵊr **~s** z

reditworth|y ˈkred ɪt ˌwɜːð |i §-ət- ‖ -ˌwɜːð |i **~iness** i nəs i nɪs

redo, Credo ˈkreɪd əʊ ˈkriːd- ‖ -oʊ **~s** z

redulity krə ˈdjuːl ət i krɪ-, kre-, →§-ˈdʒuːl-, -ɪt- ‖ -ˈduːl əţ i -ˈdjuːl-

redulous ˈkred jʊl əs -jəl- ‖ ˈkredʒ əl əs **~ly** li **~ness** nəs nɪs

ree kriː **Crees** kriːz

reed, Creed kriːd **creeds** kriːdz

CREEK

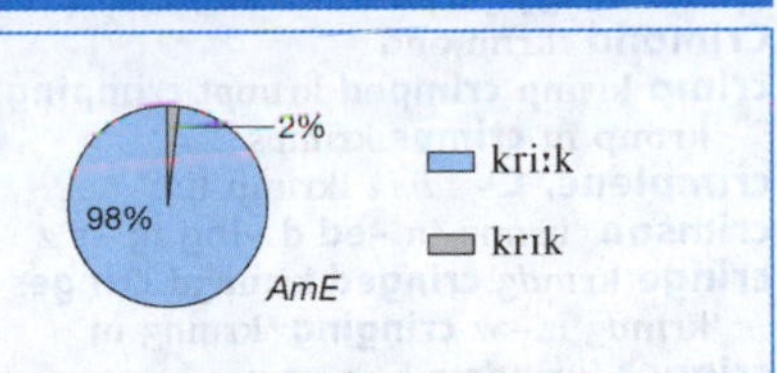

reek kriːk ‖ krɪk — *Preference poll, AmE:* kriːk *98%,* krɪk *2%.* **creeks** kriːks ‖ krɪks

Creek kriːk *(= creak)* **Creeks** kriːks

creel kriːᵊl **creels** kriːᵊlz

Creeley ˈkriːl i

creep kriːp **creeping** ˈkriːp ɪŋ **creeps** kriːps **crept** krept

creeper ˈkriːp ə ‖ -ᵊr **~s** z

creep|y ˈkriːp |i **~ier** i‿ə ‖ i‿ᵊr **~iest** i‿ɪst i‿əst **~ily** ɪ li əl i **~iness** i nəs i nɪs

creepy-crawl|y ˌkriːp i ˈkrɔːl |i ˈ· ·ˌ·· ‖ -ˈkrɑːl- **~ies** iz

Creevey ˈkriːv i

Creighton *(i)* ˈkraɪt ᵊn, *(ii)* ˈkreɪt-

Creigiau ˈkraɪg ə —*Welsh* [ˈkrəig jai, -je]

cremains krə ˈmeɪnz kri-

cremate krə ˈmeɪt kri- ‖ ˈkriːm eɪt **cremated** krə ˈmeɪt ɪd kri-, -əd ‖ ˈkriːm eɪţ əd **cremates** krə ˈmeɪts kri- ‖ ˈkriːm eɪts **cremating** krə ˈmeɪt ɪŋ kri- ‖ ˈkriːm eɪţ ɪŋ

cremation krə ˈmeɪʃ ᵊn kri- ‖ kri- **~s** z

crematori|um ˌkrem ə ˈtɔːr i‿|əm ‖ ˌkriːm-, ˌkrem-, -ˈtoʊr- **~a** ə

cremator|y ˈkrem ət‿ər |i ‖ ˈkriːm ə tɔːr |i ˈkrem-, -toʊr- **~ies** iz

creme, crème krem kreɪm, kriːm —*Fr* [kʁɛm] **cremes, crèmes** kremz kreɪmz, kriːmz —*Fr* [kʁɛm] —*See also phrases with this word*

Creme kriːm

creme brulee, crème brûlée ˌkrem bruː ˈleɪ ˌkreɪm-, ˌ· ˈ· · —*Fr* [kʁɛm bʁy le]

creme caramel, crème caramel ˌkrem ˌkær ə ˈmel ˌkreɪm- ‖ -ˌker-; ˌ·ˈ· · ·

creme de la creme, crème de la crème ˌkrem də lɑː ˈkrem ˌkreɪm-, -ˈkreɪm —*Fr* [kʁɛm də la kʁɛm]

creme de menthe, crème de menthe ˌkrem də ˈmɒnᵗθ ˌkreɪm-, -ˈmɑːnt ‖ -ˈmɑːnt —*Fr* [kʁɛm də mɑ̃ːt]

creme fraiche, crème fraîche ˌkrem ˈfreʃ ˌkreɪm-, -ˈfreɪʃ —*Fr* [kʁɛm fʁɛʃ]

Cremona krɪ ˈməʊn ə krə- ‖ -ˈmoʊn ə —*It* [kre ˈmoː na]

Cremora *tdmk* krɪ ˈmɔːr ə krə-

crenate ˈkriːn eɪt

crenel|ate, crenell|ate ˈkren ə l|eɪt -ᵊl |eɪt ‖ -ᵊl |eɪt **~ated** eɪt ɪd -əd ‖ eɪţ əd **~ates** eɪts ‖ eɪts **~ating** eɪt ɪŋ ‖ eɪţ ɪŋ

crenelation, crenellation ˌkren ə ˈleɪʃ ᵊn -ᵊl ˈeɪʃ- ‖ ˌkren ᵊl ˈeɪʃ ᵊn **~s** z

creole, Creole ˈkriː əʊl ˈkreɪ-, →-ɒʊl ‖ -oʊl **~s** z

creolis... —*see* **creoliz...**

creolization ˌkriː‿əl aɪ ˈzeɪʃ ᵊn ˌkreɪ-, ˈ·əʊl-, -ɪˈ·- ‖ -əl ə-

creoliz|e ˈkriː‿ə laɪz ˈkreɪ-, -əʊ- **~ed** d **~es** ɪz əz **~ing** ɪŋ

Creon ˈkriː‿ən -ɒn ‖ -ɑːn

creosol ˈkriː‿ə sɒl ‖ -soʊl -sɑːl, -sɔːl

creo|sote ˈkriː‿ə |səʊt ‖ -|soʊt **~soted** səʊt ɪd -əd ‖ soʊţ əd **~sotes** səʊts ‖ soʊts **~soting** səʊt ɪŋ ‖ soʊţ ɪŋ **ˈcreosote bush**

crepe, crêpe kreɪp krep —*Fr* [kʁɛp] **crepes, crêpes** kreɪps kreps **ˌcrepe de ˈChine** ʃiːn —*Fr* [də ʃin]; **ˌcrepe ˈpaper** ‖ ˈ· ˌ· ·; **ˌcrepe suˈzette, ˌcrepes suˈzettes** su ˈzet —*Fr* [sy zɛt]

crepi|tate ˈkrep ɪ |teɪt §-ə- **~tated** teɪt ɪd -əd ‖ teɪţ əd **~tates** teɪts **~tating** teɪt ɪŋ ‖ teɪţ ɪŋ

crepitation ˌkrep ɪ ˈteɪʃ ᵊn §-ə- **~s** z

crept krept

crepuscular krɪ ˈpʌsk jʊl ə krə-, kre-, -jəl- ‖ -jəl ᵊr

crescend|o krə ˈʃend |əʊ krɪ- ‖ -|oʊ **~i** iː **~os** əʊz ‖ oʊz

crescent ˈkrez ᵊnt ˈkres- ‖ ˈkres- — *Preference poll, BrE:* ˈkrez- *55%,* ˈkres- *45%. See chart on p. 196.* **~s** s

cresol ˈkriːs ɒl ‖ -ɑːl -ɔːl, -oʊl

cress kres

cresset ˈkres ɪt §-ət **~s** s

Cressida ˈkres ɪd ə -əd-

Cresswell ˈkres wel ˈkrez-, -wəl

crest krest **crested** ˈkrest ɪd -əd **cresting** ˈkrest ɪŋ **crests** krests

Cresta ˈkrest ə

crestfallen ˈkrest ˌfɔːl ən ‖ -ˌfɑːl-

Creswell ˈkres wel ˈkrez-, -wəl

cretaceous, C~ krɪ ˈteɪʃ əs krə-, kre-, -ˈteɪʃ i‿əs

Cretan ˈkriːt ᵊn **~s** z

Crete kriːt

CRESCENT

55% 45% ˈkrez- ˈkres- BrE

BrE ˈkrez- by age

Percentage 100 80 60 40 0

Older ◄— Speakers —► Younger

cretic ˈkriːt ɪk ‖ ˈkriːt̬ ɪk **~s** s
cretin ˈkret ɪn -ᵊn ‖ ˈkriːt ᵊn *(*)* **~ism** ˌɪz əm **~s** z
cretinous ˈkret ɪn əs -ən- ‖ ˈkriːt ᵊn əs *(*)*
cretonne kre ˈtɒn krə-, krɪ-; ˈkret ɒn ‖ ˈkriːt ɑːn krɪ ˈtɑːn
Creutzfeldt-Jakob ˌkrɔɪts felt ˈjæk ɒb ‖ -ˈjɑːk oʊb
ˌ**Creutzfeldt-ˈJakob diˌsease**
crevass|e krə ˈvæs krɪ- **~es** ɪz əz
crevic|e ˈkrev ɪs §-əs **~ed** t **~es** ɪz əz
crew kruː **crewed** kruːd *(= crude)* **crewing** ˈkruː ɪŋ **crews** kruːz
ˈ**crew cut**; ˌ**crew ˈneck**, ˈ.
Crewe kruː
crewel ˈkruː‿əl ɪl
Crewkerne ˈkruː kɜːn ‖ -kɜ˞ːn
crew|man ˈkruː |mən -mæn **~men** mən men
crewmember ˈkruː ˌmem bə ‖ -bᵊr **~s** z
cri kriː **cris** kriː kriːz
ˌ**cri de ˈcoeur** də ˈkɜː ‖ də ˈkɜ˞ː —*Fr* [kʁid kœːʁ]
Crianlarich ˌkriː‿ən ˈlær ɪx -ɪk ‖ -ˈler-
crib krɪb **cribbed** krɪbd **cribbing** ˈkrɪb ɪŋ **cribs** krɪbz
ˈ**crib death**
Cribb krɪb
cribb... —*see* **crib**
cribbage ˈkrɪb ɪdʒ
cribber ˈkrɪb ə ‖ -ᵊr **~s** z
Cribbins ˈkrɪb ɪnz §-ənz
Criccieth ˈkrɪk i‿əθ -eθ —*Welsh* [ˈkrik jeθ]
Crich kraɪtʃ
Crichel ˈkrɪtʃ ᵊl
Crichton ˈkraɪt ᵊn
crick, Crick krɪk **cricked** krɪkt **cricking** ˈkrɪk ɪŋ **cricks, Crick's** krɪks
crick|et ˈkrɪk |ɪt §-ət ‖ -|ət **~eter/s** ɪt ə/z §ət- ‖ ət̬ ᵊr/z **~eting** ɪt ɪŋ ət- ‖ ət̬ ɪŋ
Crickhowell ₍ˌ₎krɪk ˈhaʊ‿əl -ˈhaʊl; krɪ ˈkaʊ‿əl, -ˈkaʊl
cricoid ˈkraɪk ɔɪd **~s** z
cried kraɪd
Crieff kriːf
crier, Crier ˈkraɪ‿ə ‖ ˈkraɪ‿ᵊr **~s** z
cries kraɪz
crikey ˈkraɪk i
crime kraɪm —*but in French expressions* kriːm **crimes** kraɪmz —*See also phrases with this word*
Crimea kraɪ ˈmɪə -ˈmiː ə ‖ -ˈmiː ə
Crimean kraɪ ˈmɪən -ˈmiː ən ‖ -ˈmiː ən **~s** z
crime passionnel ˌkriːm ˌpæs i‿ə ˈnel -ˌpæʃ ə ˈnel —*Fr* [kʁim pa sjɔ nɛl]
criminal ˈkrɪm ɪn ᵊl -ən- **~ly** i **~s** z
criminalis... —*see* **criminaliz...**
criminalit|y ˌkrɪm ɪ ˈnæl ət |i ˌ-ə-, -ɪt i ‖ -ət̬ |i **~ies** iz
criminalization ˌkrɪm ɪn ᵊl aɪ ˈzeɪʃ ᵊn -ᵊn‿əl-, -ɪˈ-- ‖ -ə ˈzeɪʃ-
criminaliz|e ˈkrɪm ɪn ᵊl aɪz -ᵊn‿əl- **~ed** d **~es** ɪz əz **~ing** ɪŋ
crimini ˈkriːm ɪ niː ˈkrɪm-, -ə-
criminological ˌkrɪm ɪn ə ˈlɒdʒ ɪk ᵊl ◂ ˌ-ən- ‖ -ˈlɑːdʒ- **~ly** ‿i
criminologist ˌkrɪm ɪ ˈnɒl ədʒ ɪst ˌ-ə-, §-əst ‖ -ˈnɑːl- **~s** s
criminology ˌkrɪm ɪ ˈnɒl ədʒ i ˌ-ə- ‖ ˈnɑːl-
Crimond ˈkrɪm ənd
crimp krɪmp **crimped** krɪmpt **crimping** ˈkrɪmp ɪŋ **crimps** krɪmps
crimplene, C~ *tdmk* ˈkrɪmp liːn
crimson ˈkrɪmz ᵊn **~ed** d **~ing** ɪŋ **~s** z
cringe krɪndʒ **cringed** krɪndʒd **cringes** ˈkrɪndʒ ɪz -əz **cringing** ˈkrɪndʒ ɪŋ
cringer ˈkrɪndʒ ə ‖ -ᵊr **~s** z
cringle ˈkrɪŋ gᵊl **~s** z
crinkl|e ˈkrɪŋk ᵊl **~ed** d **~es** z **~ing** ‿ɪŋ
crinkle-cut ˈkrɪŋk ᵊl kʌt
crinkly ˈkrɪŋk li
crinoid ˈkraɪn ɔɪd ˈkrɪn- **~s** z
crinoline ˈkrɪn əl ɪn §-ən **~s** z
cripes kraɪps
Crippen ˈkrɪp ɪn -ən
crippl|e ˈkrɪp ᵊl **~ed** d **~es** z **~ing** ‿ɪŋ
Cripplegate ˈkrɪp ᵊl geɪt
Cripps krɪps
Crisco *tdmk* ˈkrɪsk əʊ ‖ -oʊ
crisis ˈkraɪs ɪs §-əs **crises** ˈkraɪs iːz
crisp, Crisp krɪsp **crisped** krɪspt **crisping** ˈkrɪsp ɪŋ **crisps** krɪsps
crispbread ˈkrɪsp bred **~s** z
Crispian ˈkrɪsp i‿ən
Crispin ˈkrɪsp ɪn §-ən
crisply ˈkrɪsp li
crispness ˈkrɪsp nəs -nɪs
crisp|y ˈkrɪsp |i **~ier** i‿ə ‖ i‿ᵊr **~iest** i‿ɪst i‿əst **~ily** ɪ li əl i **~iness** i nəs i nɪs
crisscross ˈkrɪs krɒs -krɔːs ‖ -krɔːs -krɑːs **~ed** t **~es** ɪz əz **~ing** ɪŋ
Cristobal, Cristóbal krɪ ˈstəʊb ᵊl ‖ -ˈstoʊb- —*Sp* [kris ˈto βal]
Critchley ˈkrɪtʃ li
criteri|on kraɪ ˈtɪər i‿|ən ‖ -ˈtɪr- **~a** ə **~al** əl
critic ˈkrɪt ɪk ‖ ˈkrɪt̬ ɪk **~s** s

itical 'krɪt ɪk ᵊl ‖ 'krɪţ- ~ly ˌi
ˌcritical 'mass
iticality ˌkrɪt ɪ 'kæl ət i ˌ-ə-, -ɪt i ‖ ˌkrɪţ ə 'kæl əţ i
iticis|e, criticiz|e 'krɪt ɪ saɪz -ə- ‖ 'krɪţ ə- ~ed d ~es ɪz əz ~ing ɪŋ
iticism 'krɪt ɪ ˌsɪz əm -ə- ‖ 'krɪţ ə- ~s z
itique krɪ 'tiːk krə- ~s s
rittall 'krɪt ɔːl ‖ -ɑːl
ritter 'krɪt ə ‖ 'krɪţ ᵊr ~s z
RO ˌsiː ɑːr 'əʊ ‖ -ɑːr 'oʊ
roak krəʊk ‖ kroʊk croaked krəʊkt ‖ kroʊkt croaking/s 'krəʊk ɪŋ/z ‖ 'kroʊk ɪŋ/z croaks krəʊks ‖ kroʊks
roak|y 'krəʊk |i ‖ 'kroʊk |i ~ily ɪ li əl i ~iness i nəs i nɪs
roat 'krəʊ æt -ət ‖ 'kroʊ- ~s s
roatia krəʊ 'eɪʃ ə ‖ kroʊ-
roatian krəʊ 'eɪʃ ᵊn ‖ kroʊ- ~s z
rochet 'krəʊʃ eɪ -i, §-ə ‖ kroʊ 'ʃeɪ ~ed d ~ing ɪŋ ~s z
rocidolite krəʊ 'sɪd ə laɪt ‖ kroʊ-
rock krɒk ‖ krɑːk crocked krɒkt ‖ krɑːkt crocks krɒks ‖ krɑːks
Crocker 'krɒk ə ‖ 'krɑːk ᵊr
rockery 'krɒk ər i ‖ 'krɑːk-
rocket 'krɒk ɪt §-ət ‖ 'krɑːk- ~s s
Crockett 'krɒk ɪt §-ət ‖ 'krɑːk-
Crockford 'krɒk fəd ‖ 'krɑːk fᵊrd
rocodile 'krɒk ə daɪᵊl ‖ krɑːk- ~s z
'crocodile clip; 'crocodile tears, ˌ· · · '·
rocodilian ˌkrɒk ə 'dɪl i ən ‖ ˌkrɑːk- ~s z
Crocs krɒks ‖ krɑːks *tdmk*
rocus 'krəʊk əs ‖ 'kroʊk əs ~es ɪz əz
Croes- *in Welsh place names* krɔɪs — Croeserw krɔɪs 'er uː
Croesus 'kriːs əs
roft, Croft krɒft krɔːft ‖ krɔːft krɑːft crofting 'krɒft ɪŋ 'krɔːft- ‖ 'krɔːft ɪŋ 'krɑːft- crofts krɒfts krɔːfts ‖ krɔːfts krɑːfts
crofter 'krɒft ə 'krɔːft- ‖ 'krɔːft ᵊr 'krɑːft- ~s z
Crofton 'krɒft ən 'krɔːft- ‖ 'krɔːft- 'krɑːft-
Crohn krəʊn ‖ kroʊn
'Crohn's diˌsease
croiss|ant 'kwæs |ɒ̃ 'krwæs-, 'krwʌs-, 'kwɑːs- ‖ kwɑː 's|ɑ̃ː krə-, krwɑː-, -'s|ɑːnt —*Fr* [kʁwa sɑ̃] ~ants ɒ̃z ‖ ɑ̃ːz ɑːnts
Croix krwɑː kwɑː —*but in the name of the island* St Croix, krɔɪ —*Fr* [kʁwa]
ˌCroix de 'Guerre də 'geə ‖ -'geᵊr —*Fr* [kʁwad gɛːʁ]
Croker 'krəʊk ə ‖ 'kroʊk ᵊr
Cro-Magnon ₍ˌ₎krəʊ 'mæn jɒn -jən; -'mæg nən, -nɒn ‖ ₍ˌ₎kroʊ 'mæg nən -nɑːn —*Fr* [kʁɔ ma njɔ̃]
Cromartie, Cromarty 'krɒm ət i ‖ 'krɑːm ᵊrţ i
Crombie *(i)* 'krɒm bi ‖ 'krɑːm-, *(ii)* 'krʌm-
Crome krəʊm ‖ kroʊm
Cromer 'krəʊm ə ‖ 'kroʊm ᵊr
Cromford 'krɒm fəd ‖ 'krɑːm fᵊrd
cromlech 'krɒm lek ‖ 'krɑːm- ~s s
Crompton *(i)* 'krɒmpt ən ‖ 'krɑːmpt-, *(ii)* 'krʌmpt-
Cromwell 'krɒm wəl -wel ‖ 'krɑːm- —*formerly* 'krʌm-, -ᵊl
Cromwellian ₍ˌ₎krɒm 'wel i ən ‖ ₍ˌ₎krɑːm-
crone krəʊn ‖ kroʊn crones krəʊnz ‖ kroʊnz
Cronin 'krəʊn ɪn §-ən ‖ 'kroʊn-
cronk krɒŋk ‖ krɑːŋk
Cronkite 'krɒŋk aɪt ‖ 'krɑːn kaɪt 'krɑːŋk aɪt
cron|y 'krəʊn |i ‖ 'kroʊn |i ~ies iz ~yism i ˌɪz əm
crook, Crook krʊk §kruːk crooks krʊks §kruːks
crookback, C~ 'krʊk bæk §'kruːk- ~ed t ~s s
Crooke krʊk §kruːk
crooked 'krʊk ɪd §'kruːk-, -əd ~er ə ‖ ᵊr ~est ɪst əst ~ly li ~ness nəs nɪs
Crookes krʊks §kruːks
Croom, Croome kruːm
croon kruːn crooned kruːnd crooning 'kruːn ɪŋ croons kruːnz
crooner 'kruːn ə ‖ -ᵊr ~s z
crop krɒp ‖ krɑːp cropped krɒpt ‖ krɑːpt cropping 'krɒp ɪŋ ‖ 'krɑːp ɪŋ crops krɒps ‖ krɑːps
'crop ˌspraying
crop-dusting 'krɒp ˌdʌst ɪŋ ‖ 'krɑːp-
cropper 'krɒp ə ‖ 'krɑːp ᵊr ~s z
croquet 'krəʊk i -eɪ ‖ kroʊ 'keɪ
croquette krɒ 'ket krəʊ- ‖ kroʊ 'ket ~s s
crore krɔː ‖ krɔːr kroʊr crores krɔːz ‖ krɔːrz kroʊrz
Crosbie, Crosby 'krɒz bi 'krɒs- ‖ 'krɔːz bi 'krɑːz-
crosier, C~ 'krəʊz i ə 'krəʊʒ ə ‖ 'kroʊʒ ᵊr ~s z
Crosland 'krɒs lənd ‖ 'krɔːs- 'krɑːs-
cross, Cross krɒs krɔːs ‖ krɔːs krɑːs crossed krɒst krɔːst ‖ krɔːst krɑːst crosses 'krɒs ɪz 'krɔːs-, -əz ‖ 'krɔːs əz 'krɑːs- crossing 'krɒs ɪŋ 'krɔːs- ‖ 'krɔːs ɪŋ 'krɑːs-
ˌcrossed 'line
cross- ¦krɒs ¦krɔːs ‖ ¦krɔːs ¦krɑːs — cross-cultural ˌkrɒs 'kʌltʃ ᵊr əl ◂ ˌkrɔːs- ‖ ˌkrɔːs- ˌkrɑːs-
crossbar 'krɒs bɑː 'krɔːs- ‖ 'krɔːs bɑːr 'krɑːs- ~s z
crossbeam 'krɒs biːm 'krɔːs- ‖ 'krɔːs- 'krɑːs- ~s z
crossbench 'krɒs bentʃ 'krɔːs-, ˌ·'· ‖ 'krɔːs- 'krɑːs- ~er/s ə/z ‖ ᵊr/z ~es ɪz əz
crossbill 'krɒs bɪl 'krɔːs- ‖ 'krɔːs- 'krɑːs- ~s z
crossbones 'krɒs bəʊnz 'krɔːs- ‖ 'krɔːs boʊnz 'krɑːs-
cross-border ˌkrɒs 'bɔːd ə ◂ ˌkrɔːs- ‖ ˌkrɔːs 'bɔːrd ᵊr ˌkrɑːs-
crossbow 'krɒs bəʊ 'krɔːs- ‖ 'krɔːs boʊ 'krɑːs- ~s z
crossbred 'krɒs bred 'krɔːs- ‖ 'krɔːs- 'krɑːs-
crossbreed 'krɒs briːd 'krɔːs- ‖ 'krɔːs- 'krɑːs- ~s z
cross-channel ˌkrɒs 'tʃæn ᵊl ◂ ˌkrɔːs- ‖ ˌkrɔːs- ˌkrɑːs-

C

crosscheck *v* ˌkrɒs ˈtʃek ˌkrɔːs-, ˈ·· ‖ ˌkrɔːs- ˌkrɑːs- **~ed** t **~ing** ɪŋ **~s** s
crosscheck *n* ˈkrɒs tʃek ˈkrɔːs-, ˌˈ· ‖ ˈkrɔːs- ˈkrɑːs- **~s** s
cross-country ˌkrɒs ˈkʌntr i ◂ ˌkrɔːs- ‖ ˌkrɔːs- ˌkrɑːs- **ˌcross-ˌcountry ˈrunning**
crosscourt ˈkrɒs kɔːt ˈkrɔːs- ‖ ˈkrɔːs kɔːrt ˈkrɑːs-, -kourt
cross-cultural ˌkrɒs ˈkʌltʃ ᵊr‿əl ◂ ˌkrɔːs- ‖ ˌkrɔːs- ˌkrɑːs-
crosscurrent ˈkrɒs ˌkʌr ənt ˈkrɔːs- ‖ ˈkrɔːs ˌkɜː ənt ˈkrɑːs- **~s** s
crosscut *n* ˈkrɒs kʌt ˈkrɔːs- ‖ ˈkrɔːs- ˈkrɑːs- **~s** s
cross|cut *v, adj* ˈkrɒs |kʌt ˈkrɔːs-, ˌ·ˈ· ‖ ˈkrɔːs- ˈkrɑːs- **~cuts** kʌts **~cutting** kʌt ɪŋ ‖ kʌţ ɪŋ
cross-dress|er ˌkrɒs ˈdres |ə ˌkrɔːs- ‖ ˌkrɔːs ˈdres |ᵊr ˌkrɑːs- **~ers** əz ‖ ᵊrz **~ing** ɪŋ
crosse krɒs ‖ krɔːs krɑːs
cross-examination ˌkrɒs ɪg ˌzæm ə ˈneɪʃ ᵊn ˌkrɔːs-, ˌ·ɪk-, ˌ·əg-, ˌ·ək-, ˌ·eg-, ˌ·ek-, -ɪˈ·- ‖ ˌkrɔːs- ˌkrɑːs- **~s** z
cross-examin|e ˌkrɒs ɪg ˈzæm ɪn ˌkrɔːs-, -ɪk-, -əg-, -ək-, -eg-, -ek-, §-ən ‖ ˌkrɔːs- ˌkrɑːs- **~ed** d **~es** z **~ing** ɪŋ
cross-eyed ˌkrɒs ˈaɪd ◂ ˌkrɔːs-, ˈ·· ‖ ˈkrɔːs aɪd ˈkrɑːs-, ˌ·ˈ·
cross-fertilis... —*see* **cross-fertiliz...**
cross-fertilization ˌkrɒs ˌfɜːt ᵊl aɪ ˈzeɪʃ ᵊn ˌkrɔːs-, -ɪl aɪ-, -ɪˈ·-, -əˈ·- ‖ ˌkrɔːs ˌfɜːţ ᵊl ə- ˌkrɑːs-
cross-fertiliz|e ˌkrɒs ˈfɜːt ə laɪz ˌkrɔːs-, -ɪ-, -ᵊl aɪz ‖ ˌkrɔːs ˈfɜːţ ᵊl aɪz ˌkrɑːs- **~ed** d **~es** ɪz əz **~ing** ɪŋ
crossfire ˈkrɒs ˌfaɪ‿ə ˈkrɔːs- ‖ ˈkrɔːs ˌfaɪ ᵊr ˈkrɑːs-
cross-grained ˌkrɒs ˈgreɪnd ◂ ˌkrɔːs- ‖ ˌkrɔːs- ˌkrɑːs-
cross-hatching ˈkrɒs ˌhætʃ ɪŋ ˈkrɔːs- ‖ ˈkrɔːs- ˈkrɑːs-
cross-index ˌkrɒs ˈɪnd eks ˌkrɔːs- ‖ ˌkrɔːs- ˌkrɑːs- **~ed** t **~es** ɪz əz **~ing** ɪŋ
crossing ˈkrɒs ɪŋ ˈkrɔːs- ‖ ˈkrɔːs ɪŋ ˈkrɑːs- **~s** z
crossjack ˈkrɒs dʒæk ˈkrɔːs- ‖ ˈkrɔːs- ˈkrɑːs- —*nautically also* ˈkrɔːdʒ ɪk, ˈkrɒdʒ-, -ək ‖ ˈkrɑːdʒ-, ˈkrɔːdʒ- **~s** s
cross-legged ˌkrɒs ˈlegd ◂ ˌkrɔːs-, ˈ··; -ˈleg ɪd, -əd ‖ ˈkrɔːs legd ˈkrɑːs-, ˌ·ˈ·
Crossley ˈkrɒs li ˈkrɔːs- ‖ ˈkrɔːs- ˈkrɑːs-
Crossmaglen ˌkrɒs mə ˈglen ˌkrɔːs- ‖ ˌkrɔːs- ˌkrɑːs-
Crossman ˈkrɒs mən ˈkrɔːs- ‖ ˈkrɔːs- ˈkrɑːs-
crossmatch ˌkrɒs ˈmætʃ ˌkrɔːs-, ˈ·· ‖ ˌkrɔːs- ˌkrɑːs- **~ed** t **~es** ɪz əz **~ing** ɪŋ
crossover ˈkrɒs ˌəʊv ə ˈkrɔːs- ‖ ˈkrɔːs ˌoʊv ᵊr ˈkrɑːs- **~s** z
crosspatch ˈkrɒs pætʃ ˈkrɔːs- ‖ ˈkrɔːs- ˈkrɑːs- **~es** ɪz əz
crosspiec|e ˈkrɒs piːs ˈkrɔːs- ‖ ˈkrɔːs- ˈkrɑːs- **~es** ɪz əz
cross|ply ˈkrɒs |plaɪ ˈkrɔːs- ‖ ˈkrɔːs- ˈkrɑːs- **~plies** plaɪz

cross-polli|nate ˌkrɒs ˈpɒl ə |neɪt ˌkrɔːs-, -ɪ- ‖ ˌkrɔːs ˈpɑːl- ˌkrɑːs- **~nated** neɪt ɪd -əd ‖ neɪţ əd **~nates** neɪts **~nating** neɪt ɪŋ ‖ neɪţ ɪŋ
cross-pollination ˌkrɒs ˌpɒl ə ˈneɪʃ ᵊn ˌkrɔːs-, -ɪ- ‖ ˌkrɔːs ˌpɑːl- ˌkrɑːs-
cross-purposes ˌkrɒs ˈpɜːp əs ɪz ˌkrɔːs-, -əz ‖ ˌkrɔːs ˈpɜːp- ˌkrɑːs-, ˈ·ˌ···
cross-question ˌkrɒs ˈkwes tʃən ˌkrɔːs-, →-ˈkweʃ- ‖ ˌkrɔːs- ˌkrɑːs- **~ed** d **~ing** ɪŋ **~s** z
cross-re|fer ˌkrɒs rɪ |ˈfɜː ˌkrɔːs-, -rə-, §-riː- ‖ ˌkrɔːs rɪ |ˈfɜː ˌkrɑːs- **~ferred** ˈfɜːd ‖ ˈfɜːd **~ferring** ˈfɜːr ɪŋ ‖ ˈfɜː ɪŋ **~fers** ˈfɜːz ‖ ˈfɜːz
cross-referenc|e ˌkrɒs ˈref ᵊr‿ənᵗs ˌkrɔːs- ‖ ˌkrɔːs- ˌkrɑːs-, ˈ·ˌ··· **~ed** t **~es** ɪz əz **~ing** ɪŋ
crossroad ˈkrɒs rəʊd ˈkrɔːs- ‖ ˈkrɔːs roʊd ˈkrɑːs- **~s** z
cross-section ˈkrɒs ˌsek ʃᵊn ˈkrɔːs-, ˌ·ˈ·· ‖ ˈkrɔːs- ˈkrɑːs- **~ed** d **~s** z
cross-sectional ˌkrɒs ˈsek ʃᵊn‿əl ◂ ˌkrɔːs- ‖ ˌkrɔːs- ˌkrɑːs-
cross-selling ˌkrɒs ˈsel ɪŋ ˌkrɔːs- ‖ ˌkrɔːs- ˌkrɑːs-
cross-stitch ˈkrɒs stɪtʃ ˈkrɔːs- ‖ ˈkrɔːs- ˈkrɑːs-
crosstalk ˈkrɒs tɔːk ˈkrɔːs- ‖ ˈkrɔːs tɔːk ˈkrɑːs tɑːk
crosstown ˌkrɒs ˈtaʊn ◂ ˌkrɔːs- ‖ ˌkrɔːs- ˌkrɑːs-
cross-train ˌkrɒs ˈtreɪn ˌkrɔːs- ‖ ˌkrɔːs- ˌkrɑːs- **~ed** d **~er/s** ə/z ‖ ᵊr/z **~ing** ɪŋ **~s** z
crosstree ˈkrɒs triː ˈkrɔːs- ‖ ˈkrɔːs- ˈkrɑːs- **~s** z
crosswalk ˈkrɒs wɔːk ˈkrɔːs- ‖ ˈkrɔːs wɔːk ˈkrɑːs wɑːk **~s** s
crossways ˈkrɒs weɪz ˈkrɔːs- ‖ ˈkrɔːs- ˈkrɑːs-
crosswind ˈkrɒs wɪnd ˈkrɔːs- ‖ ˈkrɔːs- ˈkrɑːs- **~s** z
crosswise ˈkrɒs waɪz ˈkrɔːs- ‖ ˈkrɔːs- ˈkrɑːs-
crossword ˈkrɒs wɜːd ˈkrɔːs- ‖ ˈkrɔːs wɜːd ˈkrɑːs- **~s** z **ˈcrossword ˌpuzzle**
crosswort ˈkrɒs wɜːt ˈkrɔːs-, -wɔːt ‖ ˈkrɔːs wɜːt ˈkrɑːs-, -wɔːrt
Crosthwaite ˈkrɒs θweɪt ˈkrɔːs- ‖ ˈkrɔːs- ˈkrɑːs-
crostini krɒ ˈstiːn i ‖ krɑː- —*It* [kro ˈstiː ni]
crotch krɒtʃ ‖ krɑːtʃ **crotched** krɒtʃt ‖ krɑːtʃt **crotches** ˈkrɒtʃ ɪz -əz ‖ ˈkrɑːtʃ əz
crotchet ˈkrɒtʃ ɪt -ət ‖ ˈkrɑːtʃ ət **~s** s
crotchet|y ˈkrɒtʃ ət |i -ɪt- ‖ ˈkrɑːtʃ əţ |i **~iness** i nəs i nɪs
croton, Croton ˈkrəʊt ᵊn ‖ ˈkroʊt- **~s** z
crouch, Crouch kraʊtʃ —*but the place in Kent is* kruːtʃ **crouched** kraʊtʃt **crouches** ˈkraʊtʃ ɪz -əz **crouching** ˈkraʊtʃ ɪŋ
Crouchback ˈkraʊtʃ bæk
croup kruːp
croupier ˈkruːp i‿ə -i eɪ ‖ ‿ᵊr **~s** z
croupy ˈkruːp i
crouton ˈkruːt ɒn -õ ‖ -ɑːn kruː ˈtɑːn —*Fr* [kʁu tõ] **~s** z
crow, Crow krəʊ ‖ kroʊ **crew** kruː **crowed** krəʊd ‖ kroʊd **crowing** ˈkrəʊ ɪŋ ‖ ˈkroʊ ɪŋ **crows** krəʊz ‖ kroʊz
crowbar ˈkrəʊ bɑː ‖ ˈkroʊ bɑːr **~s** z

crowborough ˈkrəʊ bər_ə ‖ ˈkroʊ ˌbɜː oʊ
crowd kraʊd **crowded** ˈkraʊd ɪd -əd
crowding ˈkraʊd ɪŋ **crowds** kraʊdz
ˌcrowded ˈout
crowdedness ˈkraʊd ɪd nəs -əd-, -nɪs
crowd-pleas|er ˈkraʊd ˌpliːz ə ‖ -ər **~ers** əz ‖ ərz **~ing** ɪŋ
Crowe krəʊ ‖ kroʊ
crowfoot ˈkrəʊ fʊt ‖ ˈkroʊ- **~s** s
Crowhurst ˈkrəʊ hɜːst ‖ ˈkroʊ hɜːst
Crowley *(i)* ˈkrəʊ li ‖ ˈkroʊ li; *(ii)* ˈkraʊ-
crown kraʊn **crowned** kraʊnd **crowning** ˈkraʊn ɪŋ **crowns** kraʊnz
ˌcrown ˈcolony; **ˌcrown ˈcourt**; **ˌCrown ˈDerby**; **ˌcrowned ˈhead**; **ˌcrown ˈjewels**; **ˌcrown ˈprince◂**, **ˌCrown Prince ˈGeorge**
Crowndale ˈkraʊn deɪəl
Crowne kraʊn
crown-of-thorns ˌkraʊn əv ˈθɔːnz ‖ -ˈθɔːrnz
crow's-|foot ˈkrəʊz| fʊt ‖ ˈkroʊz- **~feet** fiːt
crow's-nest ˈkrəʊz nest ‖ ˈkroʊz- **~s** s
Crowther ˈkraʊð ə ‖ -ər
Crowthorne ˈkrəʊ θɔːn ‖ ˈkroʊ θɔːrn
Croxford ˈkrɒks fəd ‖ ˈkrɑːks fərd
Croyde krɔɪd
Croydon ˈkrɔɪd ən
crozier, C~ ˈkrəʊz i_ə ˈkrəʊʒ ə ‖ ˈkroʊʒ ər **~s** z
cru kruː —*Fr* [kʁy]
cruces ˈkruːs iːz
crucial ˈkruːʃ əl ˈkruːʃ i_əl **~ly** i
cruciality ˌkruːʃ i ˈæl ət i -ɪt i ‖ -əṱ i
crucian ˈkruːʃ ən
cruciate ˈkruːʃ i eɪt ˈkruːs-, ˌət, ˌɪt
crucible ˈkruːs əb əl -ɪb- **~s** z
crucifer ˈkruːs ɪf ə -əf- ‖ -əf ər **~s** z
Cruciferae kruː ˈsɪf ə riː
cruciferous kruː ˈsɪf ər əs
crucifix ˈkruːs ə fɪks -ɪ- **~es** ɪz əz
crucifixion ˌkruːs ə ˈfɪk ʃən -ɪ- **~s** z
cruciform ˈkruːs ɪ fɔːm -ə- ‖ -fɔːrm
cruci|fy ˈkruːs ɪ |faɪ -ə- **~fied** faɪd **~fier/s** faɪ_ə/z ‖ faɪ_ər/z **~fies** faɪz **~fying** faɪ ɪŋ
cruck krʌk **crucks** krʌks
crud krʌd
Cruddas ˈkrʌd əs
cruddy ˈkrʌd i
crude kruːd **cruder** ˈkruːd ə ‖ -ər **crudest** ˈkruːd ɪst -əst
crudely ˈkruːd li
Cruden ˈkruːd ən **~'s** z
crudeness ˈkruːd nəs -nɪs
crudites, crudités ˈkruːd ɪ teɪ -ə- ‖ ˌkruːd ɪ ˈteɪ —*Fr* [kʁy di te]
crudit|y ˈkruːd ət |i -ɪt- ‖ -əṱ |i **~ies** iz
cruel ˈkruː_əl kruːl **crueler, crueller** ˈkruː_əl ə ˈkruːl ə ‖ -ər **cruelest, cruellest** ˈkruː_əl ɪst -əst; ˈkruːl ɪst, -əst
Cruella de Vil kru ˌel ə də ˈvɪl
cruelly ˈkruː_əl i -li; ˈkruːl i, -li
cruel|ty ˈkruː_əl |ti ˈkruːl |ti **~ties** tiz
cruelty-free ˌkruː_əl ti ˈfriː ◂ ˌkruːl ti ˈfriː ◂
cruet ˈkruː_ɪt §_ət **~s** s
Cruft krʌft **Crufts, Cruft's** krʌfts
Cruickshank, Cruikshank ˈkrʊk ʃæŋk §ˈkruːk-
cruise, C~ kruːz *(= crews)* **cruised** kruːzd **cruises** ˈkruːz ɪz -əz **cruising** ˈkruːz ɪŋ
ˌcruise ˈmissile ‖ ˈ·ˌ··
cruiser ˈkruːz ə ‖ -ər **~s** z
cruiserweight ˈkruːz ə weɪt ‖ -ər- **~s** s
cruising ˈkruːz ɪŋ
ˈcruising speed
cruller ˈkrʌl ə ‖ -ər **~s** z
crumb krʌm **crumbed** krʌmd **crumbing** ˈkrʌm ɪŋ **crumbs** krʌmz
crumbl|e ˈkrʌm bəl **~ed** d **~es** z **~ing** _ɪŋ
crum|bly ˈkrʌm |bli **~blier** bli_ə ‖ bli_ər **~bliest** bli_ɪst bli_əst
crumb|y ˈkrʌm |i **~ier** i_ə ‖ i_ər **~iest** i_ɪst i_əst
crumhorn ˈkrʌm hɔːn ‖ -hɔːrn
Crumlin ˈkrʌm lɪn -lən
Crummock ˈkrʌm ək
crumm|y ˈkrʌm |i **~ier** i_ə ‖ i_ər **~iest** i_ɪst i_əst
crump, Crump krʌmp **crumped** krʌm*p*t **crumping** ˈkrʌmp ɪŋ **crumps, Crump's** krʌm*p*s
crumpet ˈkrʌmp ɪt §-ət **~s** s
crumpl|e ˈkrʌmp əl **~ed** d **~es** z **~ing** _ɪŋ
crunch krʌn*t*ʃ **crunched** krʌn*t*ʃt **crunches** ˈkrʌn*t*ʃ ɪz -əz **crunching** ˈkrʌn*t*ʃ ɪŋ
Crunchie *tdmk* ˈkrʌntʃ i **~s** z
crunch|y ˈkrʌn*t*ʃ |i **~iness** i nəs i nɪs
crupper ˈkrʌp ə ‖ -ər
crusad|e kruː ˈseɪd **~ed** ɪd əd **~es** z **~ing** ɪŋ
crusader kruː ˈseɪd ə ‖ -ər **~s** z
cruse, Cruse kruːz ‖ kruːs *(usually = cruise)* **cruses** ˈkruːz ɪz -əz ‖ ˈkruːs-
crush krʌʃ **crushed** krʌʃt **crushes** ˈkrʌʃ ɪz -əz **crushing/ly** ˈkrʌʃ ɪŋ /li
ˈcrush ˌbarrier
crushable ˈkrʌʃ əb əl
Crusoe ˈkruːs əʊ ˈkruːz- ‖ -oʊ
crust krʌst **crusted** ˈkrʌst ɪd -əd **crusting** ˈkrʌst ɪŋ **crusts** krʌsts
crustacean krʌ ˈsteɪʃ ən -ˈsteɪʃ i_ən **~s** z
crustal ˈkrʌst əl
crust|y ˈkrʌst |i **~ier** i_ə ‖ i_ər **~iest** i_ɪst i_əst **~ily** ɪ li əl i **~iness** i nəs i nɪs
crutch, Crutch krʌtʃ **crutched** krʌtʃt **crutches** ˈkrʌtʃ ɪz -əz **crutching** ˈkrʌtʃ ɪŋ
Cruttenden ˈkrʌt ənd ən
Cruttwell, Crutwell ˈkrʌt wəl
crux krʌks krʊks **cruces** ˈkruːs iːz **cruxes** ˈkrʌks ɪz -əz
Cruyff kraɪf —*Dutch* [kʁœyf]
Cruyff krɔɪf kraɪf —*Dutch* [krœyf]
Cruz kruːz —*Sp* [kruθ], *AmSp* [krus], *Port* [kruʃ], *BrazPort* [krus]
cruzeiro kru ˈzeər əʊ ‖ -ˈzer oʊ —*Port* [kru ˈzei ru] **~s** z
crwth kruːθ
cry kraɪ **cried** kraɪd **cries** kraɪz **crying** ˈkraɪ ɪŋ
crybab|y ˈkraɪ ˌbeɪb |i **~ies** iz
Cryer ˈkraɪ_ə ‖ ˈkraɪ_ər
cryo- *comb. form* *with stress-neutral suffix* |kraɪ əʊ -ə ‖ -ə -oʊ

— **cryoscopic** ˌkraɪ əʊ ˈskɒp ɪk ◂ ‖ -ə ˈskɑːp ɪk ◂
with stress-imposing suffix kraɪ ˈɒ+ ‖ -ˈɑː+
— **cryoscopy** kraɪ ˈɒsk əp i ‖ -ˈɑːsk-
cryogenic ˌkraɪ əʊ ˈdʒen ɪk ◂ ‖ -ə- **~s** s
cryonic kraɪ ˈɒn ɪk ‖ -ˈɑːn- **~s** s
cryostat ˈkraɪ‿ə stæt **~s** s
cryotron ˈkraɪ‿ə trɒn ‖ -trɑːn **~s** z
crypt krɪpt **crypts** krɪpts
crypt- *comb. form before vowel* ¦krɪpt —
cryptanalysis ˌkrɪpt ə ˈnæl əs ɪs -ɪs ɪs, §-əs
cryptic ˈkrɪpt ɪk **~ally** ᵊl‿i
crypto ˈkrɪpt əʊ ‖ -oʊ **~s** z
crypto- *comb. form before consonant*
with stress-neutral suffix ¦krɪpt əʊ ‖ -oʊ —
crypto-Fascist ˌkrɪpt əʊ ˈfæʃ ɪst §-əst ‖ -oʊ-
with stress-imposing suffix krɪp ˈtɒ+ ‖ -ˈtɑː+
— **cryptogamous** krɪp ˈtɒg əm əs ‖ -ˈtɑːg-
cryptogam ˈkrɪpt ə gæm **~s** z
cryptogram ˈkrɪpt ə græm **~s** z
cryptographer krɪp ˈtɒg rəf ə ‖ -ˈtɑːg rəf ᵊr **~s** z
cryptographic ˌkrɪpt ə ˈgræf ɪk ◂ **~ally** ᵊl‿i
cryptography krɪp ˈtɒg rəf i ‖ -ˈtɑːg-
cryptorchidism krɪp ˈtɔːk ɪ ˌdɪz əm -ˈ-ə- ‖ -ˈtɔːrk-
crystal, C~ ˈkrɪst ᵊl **~s** z
ˌ**crystal ˈball**; ˌ**crystal ˈclear**◂; ˈ**crystal ˌgazing**; ˌ**Crystal ˈPalace**; ˈ**crystal set**
crystaliz... —*see* **crystalliz...**
crystalline ˈkrɪst ə laɪn -liːn; -ᵊl aɪn, -iːn ‖ -əl ən -ə laɪn, -ə liːn
crystallis... —*see* **crystalliz...**
crystallization ˌkrɪst ᵊl aɪ ˈzeɪʃ ᵊn -ᵊl ɪ-, -ᵊl ə- ‖ -ᵊl ə-
crystalliz|e ˈkrɪst ə laɪz -ᵊl aɪz **~ed** d **~es** ɪz əz **~ing** ɪŋ
crystallographer ˌkrɪst ə ˈlɒg rəf ə -ᵊl ˈɒg- ‖ -ᵊl ˈɑːg rəf ᵊr **~s** z
crystallographic ˌkrɪst ᵊl ə ˈgræf ɪk ◂ **~al** ᵊl **~ally** ᵊl‿i
crystallography ˌkrɪst ə ˈlɒg rəf i -ᵊl ˈɒg- ‖ -ᵊl ˈɑːg-
csardas, csárdás ˈtʃɑːd æʃ -ɑːʃ; ˈzɑːd əs ‖ ˈtʃɑːrd ɑːʃ —*Hung* [ˈtʃaːr daːʃ]
CSE ˌsiː es ˈiː **~s, ˈs** z
C-section ˈsiː ˌsek ʃᵊn
CS gas ˌsiː es ˈgæs
ctenoid ˈtiːn ɔɪd ˈten-
CT scan ˌsiː ˈtiː skæn ˈkæt skæn **~s** z
cub kʌb **cubbing** ˈkʌb ɪŋ **cubs** kʌbz
ˈ**Cub Scout**
Cuba ˈkjuːb ə —*Sp* [ˈku βa]
Cuban ˈkjuːb ən **~s** z
cubbyhole ˈkʌb i həʊl →-hɒʊl ‖ -hoʊl **~s** z
cube kjuːb **cubed** kjuːbd **cubes** kjuːbz **cubing** ˈkjuːb ɪŋ
ˌ**cube ˈroot** ‖ ˈ· ·
cubeb ˈkjuːb eb **~s** z
cubic ˈkjuːb ɪk
cubical ˈkjuːb ɪk ᵊl *(= cubicle)* **~ly** ‿i
cubicle ˈkjuːb ɪk ᵊl **~s** z
cubism ˈkjuːb ˌɪz əm
cubist ˈkjuːb ɪst §-əst **~s** s
cubit ˈkjuːb ɪt §-ət **~s** s
Cubitt ˈkjuːb ɪt §-ət
Cublington ˈkʌb lɪŋ tən
cuboid ˈkjuːb ɔɪd **~s** z
Cuckfield ˈkʊk fiːᵊld
cucking-stool ˈkʌk ɪŋ stuːl **~s** z
Cuckmere ˈkʊk mɪə ‖ -mɪr
Cuckney ˈkʌk ni
cuckold ˈkʌk əʊld →-ɒʊld, ᵊld ‖ -oʊld ᵊld **~ed** ɪd əd **~er/s** ə/z ‖ -ᵊr/z **~ing** ɪŋ **~s** z
cuckoldry ˈkʌk ᵊld ri -əʊld- ‖ -oʊld-
cuckoo ˈkʊk uː ‖ ˈkuːk- ˈkʊk- **~s** z
ˈ**cuckoo clock**
cuckoopint ˈkʊk uː paɪnt -pɪnt ‖ ˈkuːk- ˈkʊk- **~s** s
cuckoo-spit ˈkʊk uː spɪt ‖ ˈkuːk- ˈkʊk-
cucumber ˈkjuːk ʌm bə ‖ -bᵊr **~s** z
cucurbit kju ˈkɜːb ɪt §-ət ‖ -ˈkɜːb- **~s** s
cud kʌd
cudbear ˈkʌd beə →ˈkʌb- ‖ -ber
Cuddesdon ˈkʌdz dən
cuddl|e ˈkʌd ᵊl **~ed** d **~es** z **~ing** ‿ɪŋ
cuddlesome ˈkʌd ᵊl səm
cuddly ˈkʌd ᵊl‿i
Cuddy, cudd|y ˈkʌd |i **~ies** iz
cudgel ˈkʌdʒ əl **~ed, ~led** d **~ing, ~ling** ɪŋ **~s** z
Cudlipp ˈkʌd lɪp
cudweed ˈkʌd wiːd
Cudworth ˈkʌd wəθ -wɜːθ ‖ -wᵊrθ —*locally also* -əθ
cue kjuː **cued** kjuːd **cueing, cuing** ˈkjuː‿ɪŋ **cues** kjuːz
ˈ**cue ball**
cuff, Cuff kʌf **cuffed** kʌft **cuffing** ˈkʌf ɪŋ **cuffs** kʌfs
Cuffley ˈkʌf li
cufflink ˈkʌf lɪŋk **~s** s
cui bono ˌkuː‿i ˈbəʊn əʊ ˌkwiːˈ--, -ˈbɒn- ‖ ˌkwiː ˈboʊn oʊ
Cuillin ˈkuːl ɪn -ən
cuirass kwɪ ˈræs kwə-, kjuᵊ- **~ed** t **~es** ɪz əz
cuirassier ˌkwɪr ə ˈsɪə kjʊər- ‖ -ˈsɪᵊr **~s** z
Cuisenaire, c~ ˌkwiːz ə ˈneə ‖ -ˈneᵊr —*Fr* [kɥiz nɛːʁ]
Cuisinart, c~ ˈkwiːz ɪn ɑːt ˈkwɪz- ‖ -ɑːrt **~s** s
cuisine kwɪ ˈziːn kwə-, ⚠kju- —*Fr* [kɥi zin]
cuiˌ**sine minˈceur** mæn ˈsɜː ‖ -ˈsɜː —*Fr* [mæ̃ sœːʁ]
cuisse kwɪs **cuisses** ˈkwɪs ɪz -əz
Culbertson ˈkʌlb ət sən ‖ -ᵊrt-
Culcheth ˈkʌltʃ əθ -ɪθ
cul-de-sac ˈkʌl də sæk ˈkʊl-, ˌ· ·ˈ· —*Fr* [kyd sak, kyt-] **~s** s
Culham ˈkʌl əm
culinary ˈkʌl ɪn ər‿i ˈkjuːl-, ˈ·ən- ‖ -ə ner i
Culkin ˈkʌlk ɪn §-ən
cull kʌl **culled** kʌld **culling** ˈkʌl ɪŋ **culls** kʌlz
Cullen ˈkʌl ən -ɪn
cullender ˈkʌl ənd ə -ɪnd- ‖ -ᵊr **~s** z
culler, C~ ˈkʌl ə ‖ -ᵊr **~s** z
cullet ˈkʌl ɪt -ət

Cullinan ˈkʌl ɪn ən -ən-
Culloden kə ˈlɒd ən kʌ-, -ˈləʊd- ‖ -ˈlɑːd- -ˈloʊd-
Culˌloden ˈMoor
Cullompton kə ˈlʌmpt ən ˈkʌl əmpt-
culm, Culm kʌlm
culmi|nate ˈkʌlm ɪ |neɪt -ə- **~nated** neɪt ɪd -əd ‖ neɪţ əd **~nates** neɪts **~nating** neɪt ɪŋ ‖ neɪţ ɪŋ
culmination ˌkʌlm ɪ ˈneɪʃ ən -ə- **~s** z
culminative ˈkʌlm ɪn ət ɪv ˈ-ən-; -ɪ neɪt ɪv, -ə · · ‖ ·ə neɪţ ɪv **~ly** li
culotte kju ˈlɒt ku- ‖ ˈkuːl ɑːt ˈkjuːl-; ku ˈlɑːt, kju- —*Fr* [ky lɔt] **~s** s
culpa ˈkʊlp ə -ɑː
culpability ˌkʌlp ə ˈbɪl ət i -ɪt i ‖ -əţ i
culpab|le ˈkʌlp əb |əl **~ly** li
Culpeper, Culpepper ˈkʌl ˌpep ə ‖ -ər
culprit ˈkʌlp rɪt -rət **~s** s
Culross *(i)* ˈkʌl rɒs ,·ˈ·; ˈkuː-, -rəs ‖ -rɔːs -rɑːs; *(ii)* ˈkuː- —*In Scotland, (ii); otherwise usually (i)*
culs-de-sac ˈkʌl də sæk ˈkʊl-, ,· ·ˈ· —*Fr* [kyd sak, kyt-]
Culshaw ˈkʌl ʃɔː ‖ -ʃɑː
cult kʌlt **cults** kʌlts
Culter ˈkuːt ə ‖ ˈkuːţ ər *(!)*
cultic ˈkʌlt ɪk
cultism ˈkʌlt ˌɪz əm
cultist ˈkʌlt ɪst §-əst **~s** s
cultivable ˈkʌlt ɪv əb əl ˈ·əv-
cultivar ˈkʌlt ɪ vɑː -ə- ‖ -vɑːr **~s** z
culti|vate ˈkʌlt ɪ |veɪt -ə- **~vated** veɪt ɪd -əd ‖ veɪţ əd **~vates** veɪts **~vating** veɪt ɪŋ ‖ veɪţ ɪŋ
cultivation ˌkʌlt ɪ ˈveɪʃ ən -ə- **~s** z
cultivator ˈkʌlt ɪ veɪt ə ˈ·ə- ‖ -veɪţ ər **~s** z
cultural ˈkʌltʃ ər‿əl **~ly** i
culture ˈkʌltʃ ə ‖ -ər **~d** d **~s** z **culturing** ˈkʌltʃ ər‿ɪŋ
ˈculture ˌmedium; **ˈculture shock**
Culver ˈkʌlv ə ‖ -ər
culvert ˈkʌlv ət ‖ -ərt **~s** s
Culzean kə ˈleɪn
cum *'come'* kʌm
cum, -cum- *Latin prep* kʌm kʊm —*may be stressed or unstressed —See also phrases with this word*
Cumae ˈkjuːm iː
cumber ˈkʌm bə ‖ -bər **~ed** d **cumbering** ˈkʌm bər‿ɪŋ **~s** z
Cumberland ˈkʌm bə lənd ‖ -bər-
Cumberledge ˈkʌm bə ledʒ -lɪdʒ ‖ -bər-
Cumbernauld ˌkʌm bə ˈnɔːld ˈ· · · ‖ -bər- -ˈnɑːld
cumbersome ˈkʌm bə səm ‖ -bər- **~ly** li **~ness** nəs nɪs
Cumbrae ˈkʌm breɪ
Cumbria ˈkʌm bri‿ə
Cumbrian ˈkʌm bri‿ən **~s** z
cumbrous ˈkʌm brəs
cum grano salis kʌm ˌgreɪn əʊ ˈseɪl ɪs kʊm-, -ˌgrɑːn-, -ˈsɑːl-, -ˈsæl-, §-əs ‖ kʊm ˌgrɑːn oʊ ˈsɑːl əs
cumin ˈkʌm ɪn ˈkuːm-, ˈkjuːm-, §-ən
cum laude (ˌ)kʌm ˈlaʊd eɪ (ˌ)kʊm-, ˈlɔːd-, -i ‖ kʊm ˈlaʊd i -ə
cummerbund ˈkʌm ə bʌnd ‖ ər- **~s** z
cummin, C~ ˈkʌm ɪn §-ən
Cummings, cummings ˈkʌm ɪŋz
Cumnock ˈkʌm nək
Cumnor ˈkʌm nə ‖ -nər
cumquat ˈkʌm kwɒt ‖ -kwɑːt **~s** s
cumshaw ˈkʌm ʃɔː ‖ -ʃɑː **~s** z
cumulative ˈkjuːm jʊl ət ɪv ˈ-jəl-; -ju leɪt-, -jə leɪt- ‖ -jəl əţ ɪv -jə leɪţ ɪv **~ly** li **~ness** nəs nɪs
cumulonimbus ˌkjuːm jʊl əʊ ˈnɪm bəs ˌ·jəl- ‖ -jə loʊ-
cumulostratus ˌkjuːm jʊl əʊ ˈstreɪt əs ˌ·jəl-, -ˈstrɑːt- ‖ -jə loʊ ˈstreɪţ əs -ˈstræţ-
cumulus ˈkjuːm jʊl əs -jəl- ‖ -jəl əs
Cunard (ˌ)kjuː ˈnɑːd ‖ -ˈnɑːrd ˌkuː- **~er/s** ə/z ‖ -ər/z
cunctation (ˌ)kʌŋk ˈteɪʃ ən
cunctator (ˌ)kʌŋk ˈteɪt ə ‖ -ˈteɪţ ər **~s** z
Cundy ˈkʌnd i
cuneal ˈkjuːn i‿əl
cuneate ˈkjuːn i eɪt ət, ɪt
cuneiform ˈkjuːn ɪ fɔːm ˈkjuːn i‿ɪ fɔːm, -i‿ə-; kju ˈneɪ ɪ fɔːm, -ˈniː-, -ə fɔːm ‖ -fɔːrm
Cuningham, Cuninghame ˈkʌn ɪŋ əm ‖ -hæm
Cunliffe ˈkʌn lɪf
cunnilinctus ˌkʌn ɪ ˈlɪŋkt əs -ə-
cunnilingus ˌkʌn ɪ ˈlɪŋ gəs -ə-
cunning ˈkʌn ɪŋ **~ly** li **~ness** nəs nɪs
Cunningham ˈkʌn ɪŋ əm ‖ -hæm
Cunobelin, Cunobeline kju ˈnɒb əl ɪn §-ən ‖ -ˈnoʊb-
Cunobelinus ˌkjuːn əʊ bə ˈlaɪn əs -bɪˈ-, -ˈliːn- ‖ ˌkjuːn oʊ-
cunt kʌnt **cunts** kʌnts
Cunynghame ˈkʌn ɪŋ əm ‖ -hæm
Cuomo ˈkwəʊm əʊ ‖ ˈkwoʊm oʊ
cup kʌp **cupped** kʌpt **cupping** ˈkʌp ɪŋ **cups** kʌps
ˈcup ˌfinal, ˌ· ˈ· ·
Cupar ˈkuːp ə ‖ -ər
cupbearer ˈkʌp ˌbeər ə ‖ -ˌber ər **~s** z
cupboard ˈkʌb əd ‖ -ərd **~s** z
ˈcupboard love
cupcake ˈkʌp keɪk **~s** s
Cupertino ˌkuːp ə ˈtiːn əʊ ‖ -ər ˈtiːn oʊ
cupful ˈkʌp fʊl **~s** z
cupid, Cupid ˈkjuːp ɪd §-əd **~s, ~'s** z
cupidity kju ˈpɪd ət i -ɪt- ‖ -əţ i
Cupit, Cupitt ˈkjuːp ɪt §-ət
cupola ˈkjuːp əl ə **~s** z
cuppa ˈkʌp ə
cupreous ˈkjuːp ri‿əs
cupric ˈkjuːp rɪk
Cuprinol *tdmk* ˈkjuːp rɪ nɒl -rə- ‖ -nɑːl -nɔːl, -noʊl
cupronickel ˌkjuːp rəʊ ˈnɪk əl ˌkuːp- ‖ -roʊ-
cuprous ˈkjuːp rəs
cup-tie ˈkʌp taɪ **~s** z

C

cupule 'kjuːp juːl ~s z
cur kɜː ‖ kɜ˞ː curs kɜːz ‖ kɜ˞ːz
curable 'kjʊər əb ᵊl 'kjɔːr- ‖ 'kjʊr-
curacao, curaçao, C~ 'kjʊər ə səʊ 'kjɔːr-, ˌ· ·'· ‖ 'kjʊr ə soʊ 'kʊr-, -saʊ, ˌ· ·'·
curac|y 'kjʊər əs |i 'kjɔːr- ‖ 'kjʊr- ~ies iz
curare, curari kjuᵊ 'rɑːr i
curassow 'kjʊər ə səʊ 'kjɔːr- ‖ 'kjʊr ə soʊ ~s z
cur|ate *v* kjuᵊ 'r|eɪt ‖ 'kjʊr |eɪt ~ated eɪt ɪd -əd ‖ eɪţ əd ~ates eɪts ~ating eɪt ɪŋ ‖ eɪţ ɪŋ
curate *n* 'kjʊər ət 'kjɔːr-, -ɪt ‖ 'kjʊr- -eɪt ~s s
ˌcurate's 'egg
curative 'kjʊər ət ɪv 'kjɔːr- ‖ 'kjʊr əţ ɪv ~ly li ~ness nəs nɪs
curator kjuᵊ 'reɪt ə ‖ 'kjʊr eɪţ ᵊr -əţ-; kju 'reɪţ ᵊr ~s z
curb kɜːb ‖ kɜ˞ːb curbed kɜːbd ‖ kɜ˞ːbd curbing 'kɜːb ɪŋ ‖ 'kɜ˞ːb ɪŋ curbs kɜːbz ‖ kɜ˞ːbz
curbstone 'kɜːb stəʊn ‖ 'kɜ˞ːb stoʊn ~s z
curd kɜːd ‖ kɜ˞ːd curds kɜːdz ‖ kɜ˞ːdz
ˌcurd 'cheese, '· ·
curdl|e 'kɜːd ᵊl ‖ 'kɜ˞ːd ᵊl ~ed d ~es z ~ing ˌɪŋ
cure kjʊə kjɔː ‖ kjʊᵊr cured kjʊəd kjɔːd ‖ kjʊᵊrd cures kjʊəz kjɔːz ‖ kjʊᵊrz curing 'kjʊər ɪŋ 'kjɔːr- ‖ 'kjʊr ɪŋ
curé 'kjʊər eɪ 'kjɔːr- ‖ kju 'reɪ 'kjʊr eɪ —*Fr* [ky ʁe] ~s z
cure-all 'kjʊər ɔːl 'kjɔːr- ‖ 'kjʊr ɔːl -ɑːl ~s z
curettage kjuᵊ 'ret ɪdʒ ˌkjʊər ɪ 'tɑːʒ, -ə- ‖ ˌkjʊr ə 'tɑːʒ
curette kjuᵊ 'ret ~s s
curfew 'kɜːf juː ‖ 'kɜ˞ːf- ~s z
cur|ia 'kjʊər |i‿ə 'kjɔːr-, 'kʊər- ‖ 'kjʊr- ~iae i iː i aɪ
Curie, curie 'kjʊər i -iː ‖ 'kjʊr i kju 'riː —*Fr* [ky ʁi] ~s z
curing —*see* cure
curio 'kjʊər i əʊ 'kjɔːr- ‖ 'kjʊr i oʊ
curiosa ˌkjʊər i 'əʊs ə ‖ ˌkjʊr i 'oʊs ə -'oʊz-
curiosity ˌkjʊər i 'ɒs ət i ˌkjɔːr-, -ɪt i ‖ ˌkjʊr i 'ɑːs əţ i
curious 'kjʊər i‿əs 'kjɔːr- ‖ 'kjʊr- ~er ə ‖ ᵊr ~ly li ~ness nəs nɪs
curium 'kjʊər i‿əm 'kjɔːr- ‖ 'kjʊr-
curl kɜːl ‖ kɜ˞ːᵊl curled kɜːld ‖ kɜ˞ːᵊld curling 'kɜːl ɪŋ ‖ 'kɜ˞ːl ɪŋ curls kɜːlz ‖ kɜ˞ːᵊlz
curler 'kɜːl ə ‖ 'kɜ˞ːl ᵊr ~s z
curlew 'kɜːl juː -uː ‖ 'kɜ˞ːl- ~s z
curlicue 'kɜːl i kjuː ‖ 'kɜ˞ːl- ~s z
curling 'kɜːl ɪŋ ‖ 'kɜ˞ːl ɪŋ
curl|y 'kɜːl |i ‖ 'kɜ˞ːl |i ~ier i‿ə ‖ i‿ᵊr ~ies iz ~iest i‿ɪst i‿əst ~iness i nəs i nɪs
curlycue 'kɜːl i kjuː ‖ 'kɜ˞ːl- ~s z
curmudgeon kɜː 'mʌdʒ ən kə- ‖ kᵊr- ~ly li ~s z
Curr kɜː ‖ kɜ˞ː
curragh, C~ 'kʌr ə -əx ‖ 'kɜ˞ː ə ~s z
Curran 'kʌr ən ‖ 'kɜ˞ː-
currant 'kʌr ənt ‖ 'kɜ˞ː- *(= current)* ~s s
ˌcurrant 'bun
currawong 'kʌr ə wɒŋ ‖ 'kɜ˞ː ə wɑːŋ ~s z
currenc|y 'kʌr ənᵗs |i ‖ 'kɜ˞ː- ~ies iz
current 'kʌr ənt ‖ 'kɜ˞ː- ~ly li ~ness nəs nɪs ~s s
ˌcurrent af'fairs
curricul|um kə 'rɪk jʊl |əm -jəl- ‖ -jəl- ~a ə ~ar ə ‖ ᵊr
curˌriculum 'vitae 'viːt aɪ -eɪ; 'vaɪt iː ‖ 'vaɪţ 'wiːt aɪ
Currie 'kʌr i ‖ 'kɜ˞ː i
currier 'kʌr i‿ə ‖ 'kɜ˞ː i‿ᵊr ~s z
currish 'kɜːr ɪʃ ‖ 'kɜ˞ː-
curr|y, Curry 'kʌr |i ‖ 'kɜ˞ː |i ~ied id ~ies iz ~ying i‿ɪŋ
'curry ˌpowder
curse kɜːs ‖ kɜ˞ːs cursed kɜːst ‖ kɜ˞ːst curses 'kɜːs ɪz -əz ‖ 'kɜ˞ːs əz cursing 'kɜːs ɪŋ ‖ 'kɜ˞ːs ɪŋ curst kɜːst ‖ kɜ˞ːst
cursed *adj* 'kɜːs ɪd -əd; kɜːst ‖ 'kɜ˞ːs əd kɜ˞ːst ~ly li ~ness nəs nɪs
cursed *past, pp* kɜːst ‖ kɜ˞ːst
cursive 'kɜːs ɪv ‖ 'kɜ˞ːs ɪv ~ly li ~s z
cursor 'kɜːs ə ‖ 'kɜ˞ːs ᵊr ~s z
cursorial kɜː 'sɔːr i‿əl ‖ kᵊr- -'soʊr-
cursor|y 'kɜːs ᵊr‿|i ‖ 'kɜ˞ːs- ~ily əl i ɪ li ~iness i nəs i nɪs
curst kɜːst ‖ kɜ˞ːst
curt, Curt kɜːt ‖ kɜ˞ːt
curtail kɜː 'teɪᵊl kə- ‖ kᵊr- ~ed d ~ing ɪŋ ~ment mənt ~s z
curtain 'kɜːt ᵊn ‖ 'kɜ˞ːt- ~ed d ~ing ˌɪŋ ~s z
'curtain call
curtain-raiser 'kɜːt ᵊn ˌreɪz ə ‖ 'kɜ˞ːt ᵊn ˌreɪz ᵊr ~s z
curtain-up ˌkɜːt ᵊn 'ʌp ‖ ˌkɜ˞ːt-
curtilage 'kɜːt əl ɪdʒ -ɪl- ‖ 'kɜ˞ːţ ᵊl-
Curtin 'kɜːt ɪn §-ᵊn ‖ 'kɜ˞ːt ᵊn
Curtis, Curtiss 'kɜːt ɪs §-əs ‖ 'kɜ˞ːţ-
Curtius 'kɜːt i‿əs ‖ 'kɜ˞ːţ- —*but as a German name sometimes* 'kɜːts- ‖ 'kɜ˞ːts- —*Ger* ['kʊʁ tsi ʊs]
curtly 'kɜːt li ‖ 'kɜ˞ːt-
curtness 'kɜːt nəs -nɪs ‖ 'kɜ˞ːt-
curts|ey, curts|y 'kɜːts |i ‖ 'kɜ˞ːts |i ~eyed, ~ied id ~eying, ~ying i‿ɪŋ ~eys, ~ies iz
curvaceous, curvacious kɜː 'veɪʃ əs ‖ kᵊr- ~ly li ~ness nəs nɪs
curvature 'kɜːv ətʃ ə -ə tjʊə ‖ 'kɜ˞ːv ə tʃʊr -tʃᵊr, -tʊr, -tjʊr
curve kɜːv ‖ kɜ˞ːv curved kɜːvd ‖ kɜ˞ːvd curves kɜːvz ‖ kɜ˞ːvz curving 'kɜːv ɪŋ ‖ 'kɜ˞ːv-
curvet kɜː 'vet ‖ kᵊr- 'kɜ˞ːv ət curveted, curvetted kɜː 'vet ɪd -əd ‖ kᵊr 'veţ əd 'kɜ˞ːv əţ əd curveting, curvetting kɜː 'vet ɪŋ ‖ kᵊr 'veţ ɪŋ 'kɜ˞ːv əţ ɪŋ curvets kɜː 'vets ‖ kᵊr- 'kɜ˞ːv əts
curvilinear ˌkɜːv ɪ 'lɪn i‿ə ◂ ˌ·ə- ‖ ˌkɜ˞ːv ə 'lɪn i‿ᵊr ◂ ~ly li
curvy 'kɜːv i ‖ 'kɜ˞ːv i
Curwen 'kɜː wɪn -wən ‖ 'kɜ˞ː-
Curzon 'kɜːz ᵊn ‖ 'kɜ˞ːz-
Cusack *(i)* 'kjuːs æk, *(ii)* 'kjuːz-
cuscus 'kʌs kʌs 'kʌsk əs ~es ɪz əz
Cush kʌʃ kʊʃ
Cushing 'kʊʃ ɪŋ

C

ushion 'kʊʃ ᵊn ~ed d ~ing ˌɪŋ ~s z
ushite 'kʌʃ aɪt 'kʊʃ- ~s s
ushitic kʌ 'ʃɪt ɪk kʊ- ‖ -'ʃɪţ-
ush|y 'kʊʃ |i ~ier i‿ə ‖ i‿ᵊr ~iest i‿ɪst i‿əst
usp kʌsp cusped kʌspt cusps kʌsps
uspid 'kʌsp ɪd §-əd
uspidor 'kʌsp ɪ dɔː §-ə- ‖ -dɔːr -doʊr ~s z
uss kʌs cussed kʌst cusses 'kʌs ɪz -əz
cussing 'kʌs ɪŋ
ussed *past, pp* kʌst
ussed *adj* 'kʌs ɪd -əd ~ly li ~ness nəs nɪs
Cusson 'kʌs ᵊn
ustard 'kʌst əd ‖ -ᵊrd ~s z
ˌcustard 'apple; ˌcustard 'pie; 'custard ˌpowder
Custer 'kʌst ə ‖ -ᵊr ~'s z
ustodial kʌ 'stəʊd i‿əl kə- ‖ -'stoʊd-
ustodian kʌ 'stəʊd i‿ən kə- ‖ -'stoʊd- ~ship ʃɪp
custod|y 'kʌst əd |i ~ies iz
custom 'kʌst əm ~s z
'custom(s) house
customable 'kʌst əm əb ᵊl
customarily 'kʌst əm ᵊr‿əl i ɪ li, ˌkʌst ə 'mer- ‖ ˌkʌst ə 'mer əl i
customary 'kʌst əm ər‿i ‖ -ə mer i
custom-built ˌkʌst əm 'bɪlt ◂ '. . .
customer 'kʌst əm ə ‖ -ᵊr ~s z
customis|e, customiz|e 'kʌst ə maɪz ~able əb ᵊl ~ed d ~es ɪz əz ~ing ɪŋ
custom-made ˌkʌst əm 'meɪd ◂ '. . .
cut kʌt cuts kʌts cutting 'kʌt ɪŋ ‖ 'kʌţ ɪŋ
ˌcut 'glass ◂, ˌcut glass 'bowls
cut-and-cover ˌkʌt ᵊn 'kʌv ə ◂ ‖ -ᵊr
cut-and-dried ˌkʌt ᵊn 'draɪd ◂
cut-and-dry ˌkʌt ᵊn 'draɪ
cutaneous kju 'teɪn i‿əs ~ly li
cutaway 'kʌt ə ˌweɪ ‖ 'kʌţ- ~s z
cutback 'kʌt bæk ~s s
cutch, Cutch kʌtʃ
cute kjuːt cuter 'kjuːt ə ‖ 'kjuːţ ᵊr cutest 'kjuːt ɪst -əst ‖ 'kjuːţ əst
cute|ly 'kjuːt |li ~ness nəs nɪs
cutesy 'kjuːts i
Cutex *tdmk* 'kjuːt eks
cutey 'kjuːt i ‖ 'kjuːţ i ~s z
Cutforth 'kʌt fɔːθ ‖ -fɔːrθ -foʊrθ
Cuthbert 'kʌθ bət ‖ -bᵊrt
Cuthbertson 'kʌθ bət sən ‖ -bᵊrt-
cuticle 'kjuːt ɪk ᵊl ‖ 'kjuːţ- ~s z
Cuticura *tdmk* ˌkjuːt ɪ 'kjʊər ə -ə-, -'kjɔːr- ‖ ˌkjuːţ ə 'kjʊr ə
cutie 'kjuːt i ‖ 'kjuːţ i ~s z
cutis 'kjuːt ɪs §-əs ‖ 'kjuːţ-
cutlas, cutlass 'kʌt ləs ~es ɪz əz
cutler, C~ 'kʌt lə ‖ -lᵊr ~s z
cutlery 'kʌt lər i -ler i
cutlet 'kʌt lət -lɪt ~s s
cutoff 'kʌt ɒf -ɔːf ‖ 'kʌţ ɔːf -ɑːf ~s s
cutout 'kʌt aʊt ‖ 'kʌţ- ~s s
cut-price ˌkʌt 'praɪs ◂
cutpurse 'kʌt pɜːs ‖ -pɜːs ~es ɪz əz
cut-rate ˌkʌt 'reɪt ◂
cutter, C~ 'kʌt ə ‖ 'kʌţ ᵊr ~s z
cutthroat 'kʌt θrəʊt ‖ -θroʊt ~s s
cutting 'kʌt ɪŋ ‖ 'kʌţ ɪŋ ~ly li ~s z
ˌcutting 'edge
cuttle 'kʌt ᵊl ‖ 'kʌţ ᵊl
cuttlebone 'kʌt ᵊl bəʊn ‖ 'kʌţ ᵊl boʊn
cuttlefish 'kʌt ᵊl fɪʃ ‖ 'kʌţ- ~es ɪz əz
Cutty Sark ˌkʌt i 'sɑːk ‖ ˌkʌţ i sɑːrk
cutup 'kʌt ʌp ‖ 'kʌţ- ~s s
cutwater 'kʌt ˌwɔːt ə ‖ -ˌwɔːţ ᵊr -ˌwɑːţ ᵊr ~s z
cutworm 'kʌt wɜːm ‖ -wɜːm ~s z
Cuvier 'kjuːv i eɪ ‖ ˌ. . '. —*Fr* [ky vje]
Cuxhaven 'kʊks ˌhɑːv ᵊn —*Ger* [kʊks 'haːf ᵊn]
Cuyahoga ˌkaɪ‿ə 'həʊg ə ◂ -'hɒg- ‖ -'hoʊg ə ◂ -'hɔːg-, -'hɑːg-; kə'. ·
ˌCuyaˌhoga 'River
Cuyp kaɪp kɔɪp —*Dutch* [kœyp]
cuz *'because'* kəz
Cuzco 'kʊsk əʊ ‖ 'kuːsk oʊ —*AmSp* ['kus ko]
CV ˌsiː 'viː ~s, ~'s z
CVA ˌsiː viː 'eɪ ~s, ~'s z
cwm, Cwm kʊm kuːm —*Welsh* [kʊm] cwms kʊmz kuːmz
(ˌ)Cwm 'Rhondda
Cwmbran, Cwmbrân kʊm 'brɑːn kuːm-
Cwmyoy kʊm 'jɔɪ
cwt —*see* hundredweight
-cy si — bankruptcy 'bæŋk rʌpts i -rəpts-
Cy saɪ
cyan 'saɪ‿ən -æn
cyanamid saɪ 'æn əm ɪd §-əd; 'saɪ‿ən-
cyanamide saɪ 'æn ə maɪd -əm ɪd, §-əm əd; 'saɪ‿ən- ‖ -əm əd
cyanate 'saɪ‿ə neɪt ~s s
cyanic saɪ 'æn ɪk
cyanide 'saɪ‿ə naɪd ~s z
cyano 'saɪ‿ə nəʊ saɪ 'æn əʊ ‖ 'saɪ ə noʊ
cyanogen saɪ 'æn ədʒ ən -ɪn, -en
cyanosis ˌsaɪ‿ə 'nəʊs ɪs §-əs ‖ -'noʊs-
Cybele 'sɪb əl i -ɪl-
cybercafe, cybercafé 'saɪb ə ˌkæf eɪ -i ‖ -ᵊr kæ ˌfeɪ ˌ. . '. ~s z
cybercrime 'saɪb ə kraɪm ‖ -ᵊr-
cyberfraud 'saɪb ə frɔːd ‖ -ᵊr- -frɑːd
cybernetic ˌsaɪb ə 'net ɪk ◂ ‖ -ᵊr 'neţ- ~ally ᵊl‿i ~s s
cyber|punk 'saɪb ə |pʌŋk ‖ -ᵊr- ~punks pʌŋks
cyberspace 'saɪb ə speɪs ‖ -ᵊr-
cyber-squatt|er 'saɪb ə ˌskwɒt |ə ‖ -ᵊr ˌskwɑːţ |ᵊr ~ers əz ‖ ᵊrz ~ing ɪŋ
cyborg 'saɪb ɔːg ‖ -ɔːrg ~s z
cycad 'saɪk æd -əd ~s z
Cyclades 'sɪk lə diːz
cyclamate 'saɪk lə meɪt 'sɪk- ~s s
cyclamen 'sɪk ləm ən 'saɪk-, -lə men ~s z
cycle 'saɪk ᵊl —*In the senses 'bicycle', 'ride a bicycle' only, there is also an AmE pronunciation* 'sɪk- cycled 'saɪk ᵊld cycles 'saɪk ᵊlz cycling 'saɪk ᵊl‿ɪŋ
'cycle track
cycleway 'saɪk ᵊl weɪ ~s z
cyclic 'saɪk lɪk 'sɪk-

CYCLICAL

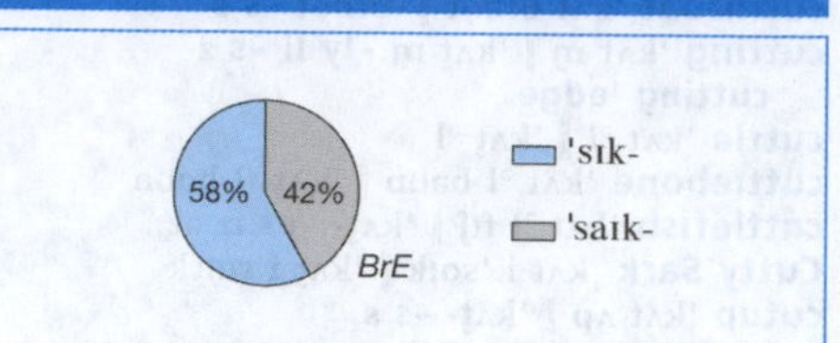

cyclical 'sɪk lɪk ᵊl 'saɪk- — *Preference poll, BrE:* 'sɪk- *58%,* 'saɪk- *42%.* **~ly** ˌi
cycling 'saɪk lɪŋ
cyclist 'saɪk lɪst §-ləst **~s** s
cyclo- *comb. form*
with stress-neutral suffix ¦saɪk ləʊ ¦sɪk ləʊ ‖ -loʊ — **cyclohexane** ˌsaɪk ləʊ 'heks eɪn ˌsɪk- ‖ -loʊ-
with stress-imposing suffix saɪ 'klɒ+ ‖ -'klɑː+ — **cyclometer** saɪ 'klɒm ɪt ə -ət- ‖ -'klɑːm əţ ᵊr
cyclo-cross 'saɪk ləʊ krɒs -krɔːs ‖ -loʊ krɔːs -krɑːs
cycloid 'saɪk lɔɪd **~s** z
cyclometer saɪ 'klɒm ɪt ə -ət- ‖ -'klɑːm əţ ᵊr **~s** z
cyclone 'saɪk ləʊn ‖ -loʊn **~s** z
cyclonic saɪ 'klɒn ɪk ‖ -'klɑːn- **~al** ᵊl
cyclopaedia ˌsaɪk ləʊ 'piːd i‿ə ‖ ˌ·lə- **~s** z
cyclopaedic ˌsaɪk ləʊ 'piːd ɪk ◂ ‖ -lə- **~ally** ᵊl‿i
Cyclopean, c~ ˌsaɪk ləʊ 'piː‿ən ◂ saɪ 'kləʊp i‿ən ‖ -lə-
cyclopedia ˌsaɪk ləʊ 'piːd i‿ə ‖ ˌ·lə- **~s** z
cyclopedic ˌsaɪk ləʊ 'piːd ɪk ◂ ‖ -lə- **~ally** ᵊl‿i
cyclopes, C~ saɪ 'kləʊp iːz ‖ -'kloʊp-
cyclops, C~ 'saɪk lɒps ‖ -lɑːps
cyclorama ˌsaɪk ləʊ 'rɑːm ə ‖ -lə 'ræm ə -'rɑːm- **~s** z
cyclosporin ˌsaɪk ləʊ 'spɔːr ɪn §-ən ‖ -loʊ- -'spoʊr-
cyclostyl|e 'saɪk ləʊ staɪᵊl ‖ -lə- **~ed** d **~es** z **~ing** ɪŋ
cyclothym|ia ˌsaɪk ləʊ 'θaɪm |i‿ə ˌsɪk- ‖ ˌ·lə- **~ic** ɪk ◂
cyclotron 'saɪk ləʊ trɒn ‖ -lə trɑːn **~s** z
cyder 'saɪd ə ‖ -ᵊr **~s** z
Cydrax *tdmk* 'saɪdr æks
Cyfeiliog kə 'vaɪl i ɒg ‖ -ɑːg -ɔːg —*Welsh* [kə 'vəil jog]
cygnet 'sɪg nət -nɪt *(= signet)* **~s** s
Cygnus 'sɪg nəs
cylinder 'sɪl ɪnd ə -ənd- ‖ -ᵊr **~s** z
cylindrical sə 'lɪndr ɪk ᵊl sɪ-, -ək- **~ly** ˌi
cyma 'saɪm ə
cymbal 'sɪm bᵊl *(= symbol)* **~s** z
cymbalist 'sɪm bᵊl ɪst §-əst
cymbalo 'sɪm bə ləʊ ‖ -loʊ **~s** z
Cymbeline 'sɪm bə liːn -bɪ-
cymbidium sɪm 'bɪd i‿əm **~s** z
cyme saɪm **cymes** saɪmz
Cymric 'kɪm rɪk 'kʌm-
Cymru, Cymry 'kʌm ri ⚠'kʊm-, 'kɪm- —*Other pronunciations may be heard from those not familiar with Welsh —Welsh* ['kəm ri, -ri] *(in Welsh these two words are homophones)*
ˌCymru am 'byth æm 'bɪθ —*Welsh* [am 'biθ, -'bɨθ]
Cynan 'kʌn ən —*Welsh* ['kə nan]
Cynara 'sɪn ər ə sɪ 'nɑːr ə
Cyncoed kɪn 'kɔɪd →kɪŋ-
Cynewulf 'kɪn ɪ wʊlf -ə-
cynghanedd kəŋ 'hæn eð kʌŋ-, -'hɑːn- —*Welsh* [kəŋ 'ha neð]
cynic, Cynic 'sɪn ɪk **~s** s
cynical 'sɪn ɪk ᵊl **~ly** ˌi **~ness** nəs nɪs
cynicism 'sɪn ɪ ˌsɪz əm -ə-
Cynon 'kʌn ən —*Welsh* ['kə nɔn]
cynosure 'saɪn ə sjʊə 'sɪn-, -zjʊə, -ʃʊə, -ʒʊə ‖ -ʃʊr **~s** z
Cynthia 'sɪnᵗθ i‿ə
cypher 'saɪf ə ‖ -ᵊr **~s** z
cy pres, cy près ˌsiː 'preɪ ˌsaɪ-
cy pres, cy près ˌsiː 'preɪ ˌsaɪ-
cypress 'saɪp rəs -rɪs **~es** ɪz əz
Cyprian 'sɪp ri‿ən
Cypriot 'sɪp ri‿ət **~s** s
Cypriote 'sɪp ri əʊt ‖ -oʊt **~s** s
cypripedium ˌsɪp rɪ 'piːd i‿əm ˌ·rə- **~s** z
Cyprus 'saɪp rəs
Cyrano de Bergerac ˌsɪr ə nəʊ də 'bɜːʒ ə ræk -'beəʒ- ‖ -noʊ də 'bɜːʒ- -rɑːk —*Fr* [si ʁa nod bɛʁ ʒə ʁak]
Cyrenaic ˌsaɪᵊr ə 'neɪ ɪk ◂ ˌsɪr-, -ɪ- ‖ ˌsɪr-
Cyrenaica ˌsaɪᵊr ə 'neɪ ɪk ə ˌsɪr-, -ɪ-, -'naɪ- ‖ ˌsɪr-
Cyrene saɪᵊ 'riːn i
Cyrenian saɪᵊ 'riːn i‿ən **~s** z
Cyriac 'sɪr i æk
Cyriax 'sɪr i æks
Cyril 'sɪr əl -ɪl
Cyrillic sə 'rɪl ɪk sɪ-, kɪ-
Cyrus 'saɪᵊr əs
-cyst sɪst — **otocyst** 'əʊt əʊ sɪst ‖ 'oʊţ oʊ-
cyst sɪst **cysts** sɪsts
cystectom|y sɪ 'stekt əm |i **~ies** iz
cysteine 'sɪst i iːn -ɪn; 'sɪst eɪn ‖ -ə-
cystic 'sɪst ɪk
cystine 'sɪst iːn -ɪn
cystitis sɪ 'staɪt ɪs §-əs ‖ -'staɪţ-
cysto- *comb. form*
with stress-neutral suffix ¦sɪst ə — **cystoscope** 'sɪst ə skəʊp ‖ -skoʊp
with stress-imposing suffix sɪ 'stɒ+ sə- ‖ -'stɑː+ — **cystoscopy** sɪ 'stɒsk əp i ‖ -'stɑːsk-
-cyte saɪt — **leucocyte** 'luːk ə saɪt 'ljuːk-
Cythera sɪ 'θɪər ə sə- ‖ -'θɪr ə
Cytherea ˌsɪθ ə 'riː‿ə
cyto- *comb. form*
with stress-neutral suffix ¦saɪt əʊ ‖ ¦saɪţ ə -oʊ — **cytolytic** ˌsaɪt əʊ 'lɪt ɪk ◂ ‖ ˌsaɪţ ə 'lɪţ-
with stress-imposing suffix saɪ 'tɒ+ ‖ -'tɑː+ — **cytolysis** saɪ 'tɒl əs ɪs -ɪs-, §-əs ‖ -'tɑːl-
cytogenetic ˌsaɪt əʊ dʒə 'net ɪk ◂ -dʒɪ'- ‖ ˌsaɪţ oʊ dʒə 'neţ- **~s** s **~ally** ᵊl‿i **~s** s

ytological ˌsaɪt ə ˈlɒdʒ ɪk ᵊl ◂ ‖ ˌsaɪţ ə ˈlɑːdʒ- **~ly** ‿i
ytologist saɪ ˈtɒl ədʒ ɪst §-əst ‖ -ˈtɑːl- **~s** s
ytology saɪ ˈtɒl ədʒ i ‖ -ˈtɑːl-
ytomegalovirus ˌsaɪt əʊ ˈmeg ə ləʊ ˌvaɪᵊr əs -ᵊl əʊ- ‖ ˌsaɪţ ə ˈmeg ə loʊ-
ytoplasm ˈsaɪt əʊ ˌplæz əm ‖ ˈsaɪţ ə-
ytoplasmic ˌsaɪt əʊ ˈplæz mɪk ◂ ‖ ˌsaɪţ ə-
ytosine ˈsaɪt əʊ siːn ‖ ˈsaɪţ ə-
ytotoxic ˌsaɪt əʊ ˈtɒks ɪk ◂ ‖ ˌsaɪţ ə ˈtɑːks-
ytotoxin ˌsaɪt əʊ ˈtɒks ɪn §-ᵊn ‖ ˌsaɪţ ə ˈtɑːks ᵊn **~s** z

czar zɑː tsɑː ‖ zɑːr tsɑːr **czars** zɑːz tsɑːz ‖ zɑːrz tsɑːrz
czardas ˈtʃɑːd æʃ -ɑːʃ; ˈzɑːd əs ‖ ˈtʃɑːrd ɑːʃ —*Hung* csárdás [ˈtʃaːr daːʃ]
czardom ˈzɑː dəm ˈtsɑː- ‖ ˈzɑːr- ˈtsɑːr-
czarina zɑː ˈriːn ə tsɑː- **~s** z
czarism ˈzɑːr ˌɪz əm ˈtʃɑːr-
Czech tʃek (= *check*) **Czechs** tʃeks
Czechoslovak ˌtʃek əʊ ˈsləʊv æk ◂ ‖ -oʊ ˈsloʊv- -ə-, -ɑːk **~s** s
Czechoslovaki|a ˌtʃek əʊ sləʊ ˈvæk i‿ə -ˈvɑːk- ‖ -ə sloʊ ˈvɑːk- -ˈvæk- **~an/s** ən/z

Dd

D

d Spelling-to-sound

1 Where the spelling is **d**, the pronunciation is regularly d as in **dead** ded.

2 Where the spelling is double **dd**, the pronunciation is again d as in **middle** ˈmɪd ᵊl.

3 Less frequently, the pronunciation is dʒ as in **gradual** ˈɡrædʒ u‿əl, **procedure** prə ˈsiːdʒ ə ‖ -ᵊr. This pronunciation comes about through yod coalescence (see ASSIMILATION), and applies where the spelling is **du**, most typically where **u** counts as a weak vowel. Some BrE speakers also do this where **u** counts as a strong vowel, and likewise where the spelling is **eu, ew** as in **dew, due** djuː or dʒuː.

4 The verb ending **-ed** has three regular pronunciations (see alphabetic entry at **-ed**). Note that after a voiceless consonant the pronunciation is regularly t as in **clapped** klæpt.

5 **d** is usually silent in **sandwich** and **Wednesday**.

D, d diː **D's, d's, Ds** diːz —*Communications code name:* Delta
-d —*see* **-ed**
-'d d —*This contracted form of* had *and* would *is used only after words (usually pronouns) ending in a vowel sound:* he'd **hiːd**, I'd **aɪd**, she'd **ʃiːd**, they'd **ðeɪd**, we'd **wiːd**, you'd **juːd**, who'd **huːd**, Joe'd **dʒəʊd** ‖ **dʒoʊd**. *After a word ending in a consonant the spelling* 'd *implies merely a weak form,* **əd***:* it'd **ɪt əd** ‖ **ɪṭ əd**. *The occasional contracted form of* did *(esp. AmE) is pronounced in the same way.*
d' d —*This contracted form of* do *is found principally in* d'you **djuː**, →**dʒuː**, **dʒə**
da *in Italian phrases* **dɑː** də —*It* [da] —*See also phrases with this word*
DA ˌdiː ˈeɪ
dab dæb **dabbed** dæbd **dabbing** ˈdæb ɪŋ **dabs** dæbz
ˌ**dab ˈhand**
dabbl|e ˈdæb ᵊl **~ed** d **~er/s** ‿ə/z ‖ ‿ᵊr/z **~es** z **~ing** ‿ɪŋ
dabchick ˈdæb tʃɪk **~s** s
D'Abernon ˈdæb ən ən ˈdɑːb- ‖ -ᵊrn-
dabster ˈdæb stə ‖ -stᵊr **~s** z
da capo dɑː ˈkɑːp əʊ də- ‖ -oʊ —*It* [dak ˈkaː po]
Dacca ˈdæk ə —*see* Dhaka
dace deɪs **daces** ˈdeɪs ɪz -əz
dacha ˈdætʃ ə ‖ ˈdɑːtʃ ə —*Russ* [ˈda tʃə] **~s** z
Dachau ˈdæk aʊ ˈdæx- ‖ ˈdɑːk- —*Ger* [ˈdax au]
dachshund ˈdæks ᵊnd ˈdæʃ-, -hʊnd, -hʊnt ‖ ˈdɑːks hʊnd —*Ger* [ˈdaks hʊnt] **~s** z
Dacia ˈdeɪs i‿ə ˈdeɪʃ ə, ˈdeɪʃ i‿ə
Dacian ˈdeɪs i‿ən ˈdeɪʃ ᵊn, ˈdeɪʃ i‿ən **~s** z
dacoit də ˈkɔɪt **~s** s
Dacre ˈdeɪk ə ‖ -ᵊr
dacron, D~ *tdmk* ˈdæk rɒn ˈdeɪk- ‖ ˈdeɪk rɑːn ˈdæk-
dactyl ˈdækt ɪl -ᵊl **~s** z
dactylic dæk ˈtɪl ɪk **~ally** ᵊl‿i
dactylogram dæk ˈtɪl ə ɡræm **~s** z
dactylographic dæk ˌtɪl ə ˈɡræf ɪk ◂
dactylography ˌdækt ɪ ˈlɒɡ rəf i ˌ-ə- ‖ -ˈlɑːɡ-
-dactylous ˈdækt ɪl əs -əl- — **polydactylous** ˌpɒl i ˈdækt ɪl əs ◂ -əl əs ‖ ˌpɑːl-
dad, Dad dæd **dads, Dad's** dædz
dada, Dada ˈdɑːd ɑː
dadaism, D~ ˈdɑːd ɑːʳ ˌɪz əm ‖ -ɑː-
dadaist, D~ ˈdɑːd ɑːʳ ɪst §-əst ‖ -ɑː- **~s** s
dadaistic, D~ ˌdɑːd ɑːʳ ˈɪst ɪk ◂ ‖ -ɑː-
daddy, Daddy ˈdæd i **daddies, Daddy's** ˈdæd iz
ˌ**daddy ˈlonglegs** ˈlɒŋ leɡz ‖ ˈlɔːŋ- ˈlɑːŋ-
Dade deɪd
dado ˈdeɪd əʊ ‖ -oʊ **~s** z
Daedalus ˈdiːd əl əs ‖ ˈded- *(*)*
daemon ˈdiːm ən ˈdaɪm-, ˈdeɪm- **~s** z

daemonic dɪ ˈmɒn ɪk də-, diː- ‖ -ˈmɑːn- **~ally** ᵊl_i

Daewoo ˈdeɪ uː ‖ ˌdaɪ ˈwuː —*Korean* [dɛ u]

DAF, Daf *tdmk* dæf

daff, Daff dæf **daffs** dæfs

daffodil ˈdæf ə dɪl **~s** z

daff|y, Daffy ˈdæf |i **~ier** i_ə ‖ i_ᵊr **~iest** i_ɪst i_əst

daft dɑːft §dæft ‖ dæft **dafter** ˈdɑːft ə §ˈdæft- ‖ ˈdæft ᵊr **daftest** ˈdɑːft ɪst §ˈdæft-, -əst ‖ ˈdæft-

daft|ly ˈdɑːft |li §ˈdæft- ‖ ˈdæft- **~ness** nəs nɪs

Dafydd ˈdæv ɪð ˈdɑːv- —*Also sometimes* ˈdæf-, -ɪd *by those not familiar with Welsh.* —*Welsh* [ˈda við, -við]

ˌDafydd ap ˈGwilym æp ˈgwɪl ɪm ɑːp-

dag dæg **dags** dægz

da Gama də ˈgɑːm ə ‖ -ˈgæm- —*Port* [dɐ ˈɣɐ mɐ]

Dagenham ˈdæg ən_əm

Dagestan ˌdɑːg ɪ ˈstɑːn -ə-

Dagg dæg

dagga ˈdæx ə ˈdæg-, ˈdʌx-, ˈdɑːg-

dagger ˈdæg ə ‖ -ᵊr **~s** z

Daggett ˈdæg ɪt §-ət

dagg|y ˈdæg |i **~ier** i_ə ‖ i_ᵊr **~iest** i_ɪst i_əst

Daglish ˈdæg lɪʃ

daglock ˈdæg lɒk ‖ -lɑːk **~s** s

Dagmar ˈdæg mɑː ‖ -mɑːr

dago ˈdeɪg əʊ ‖ -oʊ **~es, ~s** z

Dagon ˈdeɪg ɒn -ən ‖ -ɑːn

daguerreotype, daguerrotype də ˈger əʊ taɪp ‖ -ə- **~s** s

Dagwood ˈdæg wʊd

Dahl dɑːl

dahlia, D~ ˈdeɪl i_ə ‖ ˈdæl jə ˈdɑːl- *(*)* **~s** z

Dahmer ˈdɑːm ə ‖ -ᵊr

Dahomey də ˈhəʊm i ‖ -ˈhoʊm i

Dahrendorf ˈdær ən dɔːf ˈdɑːr- ‖ -dɔːrf —*Ger* [ˈdaː ʁən dɔʁf]

Dai daɪ

Daiches *(i)* ˈdeɪʃ ɪz -əz, -ɪs, -əs, *(ii)* ˈdeɪtʃ-, *(iii)* ˈdaɪx- ‖ ˈdaɪk-

Daihatsu *tdmk* daɪ ˈhæts uː ‖ -ˈhɑːts- —*Jp* [da ˌi ha tsɯ]

daikon ˈdaɪk ɒn ‖ -ɑːn —*Jp* [da ˌi koɴ]

Dail, Dáil dɔɪᵊl dɔːl, daɪᵊl —*Irish* [dɑːlʲ]

ˌDail ˈEireann, ˌDáil ˈÉireann ˈeər ən ‖ ˈeɪ rən ˈer- —*Irish* [ˈeː rʲən]

dail|y ˈdeɪl |i **~ies** iz

ˌdaily ˈbread

Daimler ˈdeɪm lə ‖ -lᵊr —*Ger* [ˈdaim lɐ] **~s** z

daimon ˈdaɪm ɒn -ən ‖ -oʊn

daimyo ˈdaɪm jəʊ ‖ -joʊ —*Jp* [da ˌi ˈmjoo]

daint|y, D~ ˈdeɪnt |i ‖ ˈdeɪnt̬ |i **~ier** i_ə ‖ i_ᵊr **~ies** iz **~iest** i_ɪst i_əst **~ily** ɪ li əl i **~iness** i nəs i nɪs

daiquiri, D~ ˈdaɪk ər i ˈdæk-, -ɪr- **~s** z

dair|y ˈdeər |i ‖ ˈder |i ˈdær- **~ies** iz

ˈdairy ˌcattle; **ˈdairy ˌfarmer**

Dairylea *tdmk* ˌdeər i ˈliː◂ ˈ· · · ‖ ˌder-

dairymaid ˈdeər i meɪd ‖ ˈder- ˈdær- **~s** z

dairy|man ˈdeər i |mən -mæn ‖ ˈder- ˈdær- **~men** mən men

dais ˈdeɪ ɪs §-əs; deɪs ‖ ˈdaɪ- **daises** ˈdeɪ ɪs ɪz §-əs-, -əz; ˈdeɪs ɪz, -əz ‖ ˈdaɪ-

daisy, Daisy ˈdeɪz i **daisies, Daisy's** ˈdeɪz iz

ˈdaisy chain; **ˈdaisy wheel**

Daiwa ˈdaɪ wɑː —*Jp* [da ˌi ɰa]

dak dɑːk dɔːk, dæk —*Hindi* [ḍaːk]

Dakar ˈdæk ɑː -ə ‖ də ˈkɑːr —*Fr* [da kaːʁ]

Dakin ˈdeɪk ɪn §-ən

Dakota də ˈkəʊt ə ‖ -ˈkoʊt̬ ə **~s** z

Dakotan də ˈkəʊt ᵊn ‖ -ˈkoʊt- **~s** z

DAKS *tdmk* dæks

dal *in Italian phrases* dæl dɑːl ‖ dɑːl —*It* [dal]

dal *'pulse'* dɑːl

Dalai Lama ˌdæl aɪ ˈlɑːm ə ˌdɑːl- ‖ ˌdɑːl-, -i-

Dalaman ˈdæl ə mæn ˌ· ·ˈ· —*Turkish* [dɑ lɑ ˈmɑn]

dalasi də ˈlɑːs i

Dalbeattie dæl ˈbiːt i dəl- ‖ -ˈbiːt̬ i —*locally* dəl-

Dalberg ˈdæl bɜːg ‖ -bɜːg

Dalby *(i)* ˈdɔːl bi ˈdɒl- ‖ ˈdɑːl-, *(ii)* ˈdæl bi

dale, Dale deɪᵊl **dales, Dales** deɪᵊlz

dalek ˈdɑːl ek **~s** s

dales|man ˈdeɪᵊlz |mən -mæn **~men** mən men **~woman** ˌwʊm ən **~women** ˌwɪm ɪn §-ən

Daley ˈdeɪl i

Dalgarno dæl ˈgɑːn əʊ ‖ -ˈgɑːrn oʊ

Dalgetty, Dalgety ₍ˌ₎dæl ˈget i dəl- ‖ -ˈget̬ i

Dalgleish, Dalglish dæl ˈgliːʃ dəl-

Dalhousie *(i)* dæl ˈhaʊz i, *(ii)* -ˈhuːz i —*(i) is appropriate for the current Earl of D~. The 19th-century governor of Canada is often referred to as (ii).*

Dali ˈdɑːl i —*Sp* Dalí [da ˈli], *Catalan* [də ˈli]

Dalian ˌdɑː li ˈæn —*Chi* Dàlián [⁴da ²ljɛn]

Dalit, dalit ˈdʌl ɪt **~s** s

Dalkeith dæl ˈkiːθ

Dalkey ˈdɔːk i ˈdɔːlk- ‖ ˈdɔːlk i ˈdɑːlk i

Dallaglio də ˈlæl i əʊ ‖ -ˈlɑːl i oʊ

Dallapiccola ˌdæl ə ˈpɪk əl ə —*It* [dal la ˈpik ko la]

Dallas ˈdæl əs

Dallasite ˈdæl ə saɪt **~s** s

Dalles dælz

dalliance ˈdæl i_ənᵗs **~es** ɪz əz

Dalloway ˈdæl ə weɪ

dall|y ˈdæl |i **~ied** id **~ies** iz

Dalmatia dæl ˈmeɪʃ ə -ˈmeɪʃ i_ə

dalmatian, D~ dæl ˈmeɪʃ ᵊn -ˈmeɪʃ i_ən **~s** z

dalmatic dæl ˈmæt ɪk ‖ -ˈmæt̬- **~s** s

Dalmeny dæl ˈmen i dəl-

Dalry dəl ˈraɪ dæl-

Dalrymple dæl ˈrɪmp ᵊl, ˈ· · ·, dəl rɪmp-

dal segno ₍ˌ₎dæl ˈsen jəʊ ₍ˌ₎dɑːl- ‖ ₍ˌ₎dɑːl ˈseɪn joʊ —*It* [dal ˈseɲ ɲo]

Dalston ˈdɔːlst ən ˈdɒlst- ‖ ˈdɑːlst-

Dalton, d~ ˈdɔːlt ən ˈdɒlt- ‖ ˈdɑːlt- **~ism** ˌɪz əm

Daltrey, Daltry ˈdɔːltr i ˈdɒltr- ‖ ˈdɑːltr-

Dalwhinnie dæl ˈwɪn i dəl-, -ˈhwɪn- —*locally* dəl ˈhwɪn i

Daly ˈdeɪl i

D

Dalyell *(i)* di ˈel daɪ-, *(ii)* ˈdæl jəl

Dalzell *(i)* di ˈel, *(ii)* ˈdæl zel

Dalziel *(i)* di ˈel, *(ii)* ˈdæl ziːᵊl

dam dæm **dammed** dæmd **damming** ˈdæm ɪŋ **dams** dæmz

damag|e ˈdæm ɪdʒ **~ed** d **~es** ɪz əz **~ing/ly** ɪŋ /li

Daman ˈdeɪm ən

Damara də ˈmɑːr ə **~s** z

Damaraland də ˈmɑːr ə lænd

Damart *tdmk* ˈdæm ɑːt ˈdeɪm- ‖ -ɑːrt

damascene, D~ ˈdæm ə siːn ˌ··ˈ· **~d** d **~s** z

Damascus də ˈmæsk əs -ˈmɑːsk- —*Arabic* Dimashq [di ˈmaʃq]

damask ˈdæm əsk **~ed** t **~s** s

D'Amato də ˈmɑːt əʊ ‖ -oʊ

dame, Dame deɪm **dames** deɪmz

Damen ˈdeɪm ən

Damian, Damien, Damion ˈdeɪm i‿ən —*As a French name,* Damien *is* [da mjɛ̃]

damm... —*see* **dam**

dammar ˈdæm ə ‖ -ᵊr

dammit ˈdæm ɪt §-ət

damn dæm *(= dam)* **damned** dæmd **damning** ˈdæm ɪŋ -nɪŋ **damns** dæmz

damnab|le ˈdæm nəb |ᵊl **~ly** li

damnation (ˌ)dæm ˈneɪʃ ᵊn

damnedest ˈdæmd ɪst -əst

damn-fool ˈdæm fuːl

Damoclean ˌdæm ə ˈkliː‿ən ◂

Damocles ˈdæm ə kliːz

Damon ˈdeɪm ən

damosel, damozel ˌdæm ə ˈzel **~s** z

damp dæmp **damped** dæm*pt* **damper** ˈdæmp ə ‖ -ᵊr **dampest** ˈdæmp ɪst -əst **damping** ˈdæmp ɪŋ **damps** dæm*ps*

ˈ**damp course**; ˌ**damp** ˈ**squib**

dampen ˈdæmp ən **~ed** d **~ing** ‿ɪŋ **~s** z

damper, D~ ˈdæmp ə ‖ -ᵊr **~s** z

Dampier ˈdæmp i‿ə ˈdæmp ɪə ‖ ‿ᵊr

dampish ˈdæmp ɪʃ

damp|ly ˈdæmp |li **~ness** nəs nɪs

damp-proof ˈdæmp pruːf §-prʊf

damsel ˈdæmz ᵊl ˈdæmᵖs ᵊl **~s** z

damsel|fly ˈdæmz ᵊl |flaɪ **~flies** flaɪz

damson ˈdæmz ᵊn **~s** z

dan dæn —*Jp* [ˈdaɴ]

Dan dæn

Dana *(i)* ˈdɑːn ə, *(ii)* ˈdeɪn ə, *(iii)* ˈdæn ə —*Generally (i) in BrE, (ii) in AmE.*

Danae, Danaë ˈdæn i‿iː -eɪ-

Danaides, Danaïdes də ˈneɪ ɪ diːz dæ-, -ə-

Dan-Air *tdmk* ˌdæn ˈeə ‖ -ˈeᵊr -ˈæᵊr

Da Nang ˌdɑː ˈnæŋ ‖ də ˈnɑːŋ (ˌ)dɑː-, -ˈnæŋ

Danaus, Danaüs ˈdæn i‿əs -eɪ-

Danbury ˈdæn bər‿i →ˈdæm- ‖ -ˌber i

Danby ˈdæn bi →ˈdæm-

dance, Dance dɑːnᵗs §dænᵗs ‖ dænᵗs **danced** dɑːnᵗst §dænᵗst ‖ dænᵗst **dances** ˈdɑːnᵗs ɪz §ˈdænᵗs-, -əz ‖ ˈdænᵗs- **dancing/ly** ˈdɑːnᵗs ɪŋ /li §ˈdænᵗs- ‖ ˈdænᵗs ɪŋ /li

dancer, D~ ˈdɑːnᵗs ə §ˈdænᵗs- ‖ ˈdænᵗs ᵊr **~s** z

Dancy ˈdænᵗs i

dandelion ˈdænd i laɪ‿ən ˈ·ə-, -ᵊl aɪ‿ ‖ -ᵊl aɪ ən **~s** z

Dandenong ˈdænd ə nɒŋ ‖ -nɑːŋ

dander ˈdænd ə ‖ -ᵊr

dandi... —*see* **dandy**

Dandie ˈdænd i

ˌ**Dandie** ˈ**Dinmont** ˈdɪn mənt →ˈdɪm-, -mɒnt

dandi|fy ˈdænd ɪ |faɪ §-ə- **~fied** faɪd **~fier/s** faɪ‿ə/z ‖ faɪ‿ᵊr/z **~fies** faɪz **~fying** faɪ ɪŋ

Dandini dæn ˈdiːn i

dandl|e ˈdænd ᵊl **~ed** d **~es** z **~ing** ‿ɪŋ

Dando ˈdænd əʊ ‖ -oʊ

dandruff ˈdændr əf -ʌf

dand|y, Dandy ˈdænd |i **~ies** iz

Dane deɪn **Danes** deɪnz

Danegeld ˈdeɪn geld →ˈdeɪŋ-

Danelagh, Danelaw ˈdeɪn lɔː ‖ -lɑː

dang dæŋ

danger ˈdeɪndʒ ə ‖ -ᵊr **~s** z

ˈ**danger** ˌ**money**

Dangerfield ˈdeɪndʒ ə fiːᵊld ‖ -ᵊr-

dangerous ˈdeɪndʒ ər‿əs **~ly** li

dangl|e ˈdæŋ gᵊl **~ed** d **~er/s** ‿ə/z ‖ ‿ᵊr/z **~es** z **~ing** ‿ɪŋ

dangly ˈdæŋ gli

Daniel, Daniell ˈdæn jəl

Daniella ˌdæn i ˈel ə dæn ˈjel ə

Danielle ˌdæn i ˈel dæn ˈjel

Daniels ˈdæn jəlz

danio, Danio ˈdeɪn i əʊ ‖ -oʊ

Danish, d~ ˈdeɪn ɪʃ

ˌ**Danish** ˈ**blue**; ˌ**Danish** ˈ**pastry**

dank dæŋk **danker** ˈdæŋk ə ‖ -ᵊr **dankest** ˈdæŋk ɪst -əst **dankly** ˈdæŋk li **dankness** ˈdæŋk nəs -nɪs

Dankworth ˈdæŋk wɜːθ -wəθ ‖ -wᵊrθ

Dannie ˈdæn i

Dannimac *tdmk* ˈdæn i mæk

d'Annunzio dæ ˈnʊnts i əʊ ‖ dɑː ˈnʊnts i oʊ —*It* [dan ˈnun tsjo]

Danny ˈdæn i

Dano-Norwegian ˌdeɪn əʊ nɔː ˈwiːdʒ ən ◂ ‖ -oʊ nɔːr-

danse dɒnᵗs dɑːnᵗs ‖ dɑːnᵗs —*Fr* [dɑ̃ːs]

danseur (ˌ)dɒn ˈsɜː (ˌ)dɑːn- ‖ (ˌ)dɑːn ˈsʊᵊr -ˈsɜː —*Fr* [dɑ̃ sœːʁ] **~s** z

danseuse (ˌ)dɒn ˈsɜːz (ˌ)dɑːn- ‖ (ˌ)dɑːn ˈsuːz -ˈsʊz —*Fr* [dɑ̃ søːz] **~s** *same pronunciation*

Dante ˈdænt i ˈdɑːnt-, -eɪ ‖ ˈdɑːnt eɪ —*It* [ˈdan te]

Dantean ˈdænt i‿ən ˈdɑːnt-; dæn ˈtiː‿ən, dɑːn- **~s** z

Dantesque (ˌ)dæn ˈtesk (ˌ)dɑːn-

Danton ˈdænt ɒn -ən; dɒ̃ ˈtɒ̃ ‖ -ᵊn ˌdɑːn ˈtoʊn —*Fr* [dɑ̃ tɔ̃]

Danube ˈdæn juːb

Danubian dæ ˈnjuːb i‿ən də- ‖ -ˈnuːb- -ˈnjuːb-

Danvers ˈdæn vəz ‖ -vᵊrz

Danville ˈdæn vɪl -vəl

Danzig ˈdænts ɪg -ɪk —*Ger* [ˈdan tsɪç], *Polish* Gdańsk [gdaj̃sk]

Danziger ˈdænts ɪg ə ‖ -ᵊr

dap dæp **daps** dæps

aphne, D~ ˈdæf ni
aphnia ˈdæf ni‿ə
aphnis ˈdæf nɪs §-nəs
apper ˈdæp ə ‖ -ᵊr **~ly** li **~ness** nəs nɪs
appl|e ˈdæp ᵊl **~ed** d **~es** z **~ing** ‿ɪŋ
apple-gray, dapple-grey ˌdæp ᵊl ˈgreɪ◂
apsone ˈdæps əʊn ‖ -oʊn
ar dɑː ‖ dɑːr —*See also phrases with this word*
AR ˌdiː eɪ ˈɑː ‖ -ˈɑːr
ara ˈdɑːr ə
arbishire ˈdɑːb i ʃə -ʃɪə ‖ ˈdɑːrb i ʃᵊr -ʃɪr
'Arblay ˈdɑːb leɪ ‖ ˈdɑːrb-
arby ˈdɑːb i ‖ ˈdɑːrb i
ˌ**Darby and 'Joan club**
'Arc dɑːk ‖ dɑːrk
arcus ˈdɑːk əs ‖ ˈdɑːrk-
arcy, D'Arcy ˈdɑːs i ‖ ˈdɑːrs i
ardanelles ˌdɑːd ə ˈnelz -ᵊn ˈelz ‖ ˌdɑːrd ᵊn ˈelz
ardanus ˈdɑːd ən əs ‖ ˈdɑːrd-
ardic ˈdɑːd ɪk ‖ ˈdɑːrd-
are, Dare deə ‖ deᵊr dæᵊr **dared** deəd ‖ deᵊrd dæᵊrd **dares** deəz ‖ deᵊrz dæᵊrz
daring ˈdeər ɪŋ ‖ ˈder ɪŋ ˈdær-
daredevil ˈdeə ˌdev ᵊl ‖ ˈder- ˈdær- **~ry** ri **~s** z
daren't deənt §ˈdeər ənt ‖ ˈder‿ənt ˈdær‿
Darent ˈdær ənt ‖ ˈder-
Darenth ˈdær ənᵗθ ‖ ˈder-
daresay ˌdeə ˈseɪ◂ ˈdes eɪ ‖ ˌder- ˌdær- —*The* ˈdes eɪ *form is not used at the end of a sentence.*
Daresbury ˈdɑːz bər‿i ‖ ˈdɑːrz- -ˌber i
Dar es Salaam, Dar-es-Salaam ˌdɑːr es sə ˈlɑːm ˌ·ɪs-, ˌ·ez-, ˌ·ɪz-
Darfur ⁽ˌ⁾dɑː ˈfʊə ‖ ⁽ˌ⁾dɑːr ˈfʊᵊr
darg dɑːg ‖ dɑːrg **dargs** dɑːgz ‖ dɑːrgz
daric ˈdær ɪk ‖ ˈder- **~s** s
Darien ˈdeər i‿ən ˈdær- ‖ ˌder i ˈen ˌdær-, ˌdɑːr- —*Sp* Darién [da ˈrjen]
Darin ˈdær ən -ɪn ‖ ˈder-
daring ˈdeər ɪŋ ‖ ˈder- ˈdær- **~ly** li **~ness** nəs nɪs
dariole ˈdær i əʊl →-ɒʊl ‖ -oʊl ˈder-, ˈdɑːr- **~s** z
Darius *(i)* də ˈraɪ‿əs, *(ii)* ˈdeər i‿əs ˈdær- ‖ ˈder-, *(iii)* ˈdɑːr- —*(i) is appropriate for the ancient Persian king*
Darjeeling dɑː ˈdʒiːl ɪŋ ‖ dɑːr-
dark dɑːk ‖ dɑːrk **darker** ˈdɑːk ə ‖ ˈdɑːrk ᵊr **darkest** ˈdɑːk ɪst -əst ‖ ˈdɑːrk-
'Dark ˌAges, ˌ· ˈ· ·; ˌ**dark 'glasses**; ˌ**dark 'horse**
darken ˈdɑːk ən ‖ ˈdɑːrk- **~ed** d **~ing** ‿ɪŋ **~s** z
darkey ˈdɑːk i ‖ ˈdɑːrk i **~s** z
darkie ˈdɑːk i ‖ ˈdɑːrk i **~s** z
darkish ˈdɑːk ɪʃ ‖ ˈdɑːrk-
darkling ˈdɑːk lɪŋ ‖ ˈdɑːrk-
dark|ly ˈdɑːk |li ‖ ˈdɑːrk- **~ness** nəs nɪs
darkroom ˈdɑːk ruːm -rʊm ‖ ˈdɑːrk- **~s** z
dark|y ˈdɑːk |i ‖ ˈdɑːrk |i **~ies** iz
Darlaston ˈdɑːl əst ən ‖ ˈdɑːrl-
Darleen, Darlene ˈdɑːl iːn ‖ ˌdɑːr ˈliːn
Darley ˈdɑːl i ‖ ˈdɑːrl i
darling, D~ ˈdɑːl ɪŋ ‖ ˈdɑːrl- **~s** z
Darlington ˈdɑːl ɪŋ tən ‖ ˈdɑːrl-
Darmstadt ˈdɑːm stæt ‖ ˈdɑːrm- —*Ger* [ˈdaʁm ʃtat]
darmstadtium ˌdɑːm ˈstæt i‿əm -ˈʃtæt- ‖ ˌdɑːrm ˈstæţ i‿əm
darn dɑːn ‖ dɑːrn **darned** dɑːnd ‖ dɑːrnd **darning** ˈdɑːn ɪŋ ‖ ˈdɑːrn- **darns** dɑːnz ‖ dɑːrnz
'darning ˌneedle
darnel ˈdɑːn ᵊl ‖ ˈdɑːrn- **~s** z
darner ˈdɑːn ə ‖ ˈdɑːrn ᵊr **~s** z
Darnley ˈdɑːn li ‖ ˈdɑːrn-
Darrel, Darrell ˈdær əl ‖ ˈder-
Darren, Darron ˈdær ən ‖ ˈder-
Darrow ˈdær əʊ ‖ -oʊ ˈder-
Darryl ˈdær əl -ɪl ‖ ˈder-
dart, Dart dɑːt ‖ dɑːrt **darted** ˈdɑːt ɪd -əd ‖ ˈdɑːrţ əd **darting** ˈdɑːt ɪŋ ‖ ˈdɑːrţ ɪŋ **darts** dɑːts ‖ dɑːrts
D'Artagnan, Dartagnan dɑː ˈtæn jɒn -jən ‖ ˌdɑːrt ᵊn ˈjɑːn —*Fr* [daʁ ta njɑ̃]
dartboard ˈdɑːt bɔːd ‖ ˈdɑːrt bɔːrd -boʊrd **~s** z
darter ˈdɑːt ə ‖ ˈdɑːrţ ᵊr **~s** z
Dartford ˈdɑːt fəd ‖ ˈdɑːrt fᵊrd
Darth Vader ˌdɑːθ ˈveɪd ə ‖ ˌdɑːrθ ˈveɪd ᵊr
Dartmoor ˈdɑːt mɔː -mʊə ‖ ˈdɑːrt mʊr -moʊr
Dartmouth ˈdɑːt məθ ‖ ˈdɑːrt-
dartre ˈdɑːt ə ‖ ˈdɑːrţ ᵊr *(= darter)*
Darwen ˈdɑː wɪn §-wən ‖ ˈdɑːr- —*locally also* ˈdær ən
Darwin ˈdɑː wɪn §-wən ‖ ˈdɑːr-
Darwinian dɑː ˈwɪn i‿ən ‖ dɑːr- **~s** z
Darwinism ˈdɑː wɪn ˌɪz əm -wən- ‖ ˈdɑːr-
Daryll ˈdær əl -ɪl ‖ ˈder-
Daschle ˈdæʃ ᵊl
dash, Dash dæʃ **dashed** dæʃt **dashes** ˈdæʃ ɪz -əz **dashing** ˈdæʃ ɪŋ
dashboard ˈdæʃ bɔːd ‖ -bɔːrd -boʊrd **~s** z
dasheen dæ ˈʃiːn ˈdæʃ iːn
dashiki də ˈʃiːk i dɑː-, dæ- **~s** z
dashing ˈdæʃ ɪŋ **~ly** li **~ness** nəs nɪs
dashpot ˈdæʃ pɒt ‖ -pɑːt **~s** s
Dashwood ˈdæʃ wʊd
dassie ˈdæs i ˈdʌs i **~s** z
dastardly ˈdæst əd li ˈdɑːst- ‖ -ᵊrd-
dasyure ˈdæs i jʊə ˈdæz- ‖ -jʊr **~s** z
DAT dæt ˌdiː eɪ ˈtiː

DATA

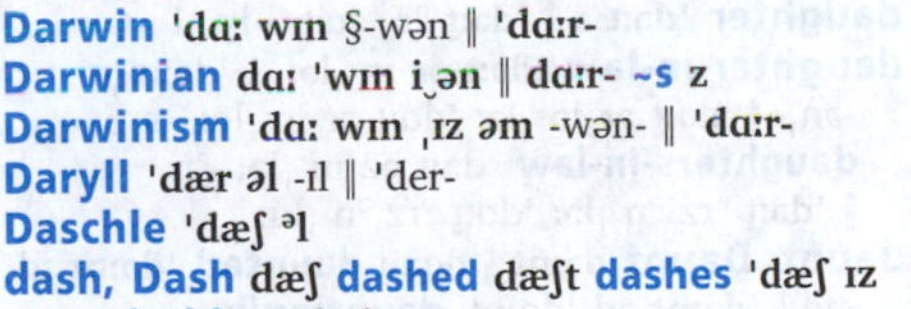

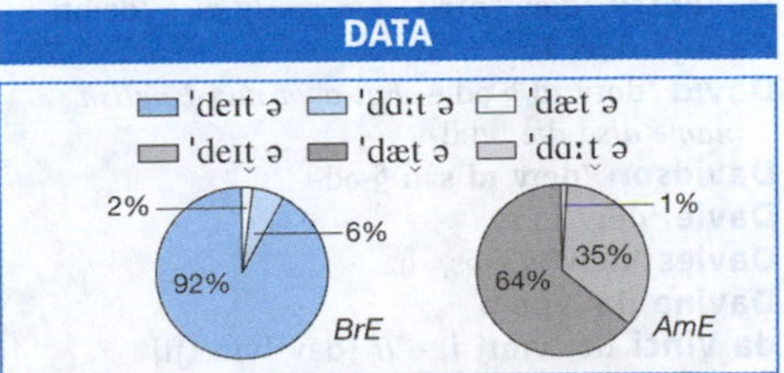

data ˈdeɪt ə ˈdɑːt ə, §ˈdæt ə ‖ ˈdeɪţ ə ˈdæţ ə, ˈdɑːţ ə — *Preference polls, BrE:* ˈdeɪt ə *92%,*

ˈdɑːt ə *6%,* ˈdæt ə *2%; AmE:* ˈdeɪţ ə *64%,* ˈdæţ ə *35%,* ˈdɑːţ ə *1%.*
ˈdata bus; **ˈdata ˌcapture**; **ˌdata ˈprocessing**

databank ˈdeɪt ə bæŋk ˈdɑːt- ‖ ˈdeɪţ- ˈdæţ-, ˈdɑːţ- **~s** s

database ˈdeɪt ə beɪs ˈdɑːt- ‖ ˈdeɪţ- ˈdæţ-, ˈdɑːţ- **~es** ɪz əz

datafile ˈdeɪt ə faɪᵊl ˈdɑːt- ‖ ˈdeɪţ- ˈdæţ-, ˈdɑːţ- **~s** z

Datapost *tdmk* ˈdeɪt ə pəʊst ˈdɑːt- ‖ ˈdeɪţ ə poʊst ˈdæţ-, ˈdɑːţ-

Datchet ˈdætʃ ɪt §-ət

date deɪt **dated** ˈdeɪt ɪd -əd ‖ ˈdeɪţ əd **dates** deɪts **dating** ˈdeɪt ɪŋ ‖ ˈdeɪţ ɪŋ
ˈdate palm; **ˈdating ˌagency**

datebook ˈdeɪt bʊk §-buːk **~s** s

dateline ˈdeɪt laɪn **~d** d **~s** z

date-mark ˈdeɪt mɑːk ‖ -mɑːrk **~ed** t **~ing** ɪŋ **~s** s

date-stamp ˈdeɪt stæmp **~ed** t **~ing** ɪŋ **~s** s

datival də ˈtaɪv ᵊl deɪ- **~ly** i **~s** z

dative ˈdeɪt ɪv ‖ ˈdeɪţ- **~s** z

Datsun *tdmk* ˈdæts ᵊn ‖ ˈdɑːts- —*Jp* [dat ˈto sɑɴ] **~s** z

datum ˈdeɪt əm ˈdɑːt- ‖ ˈdeɪţ- ˈdæţ-, ˈdɑːţ-

datura də ˈtjʊər ə ‖ -ˈtʊr- -ˈtjʊr- **~s** z

daub dɔːb ‖ dɑːb **daubed** dɔːbd ‖ dɑːbd **daubs** dɔːbz ‖ dɑːbz **daubing** ˈdɔːb ɪŋ ‖ ˈdɑːb-

daube dəʊb ‖ doʊb —*Fr* [doːb] **~s** z

Daubeney, Daubney ˈdɔːb ni ‖ ˈdɑːb-

Daudet ˈdəʊd eɪ ‖ doʊ ˈdeɪ —*Fr* [do dɛ]

daughter ˈdɔːt ə ‖ ˈdɔːţ ᵊr ˈdɑːţ- **~ly** li **~s** z

daughter-in-law ˈdɔːt ər ɪn ˌlɔː →ˈdɔːtr-ˌ, -ən,ˌ ‖ ˈdɔːţ ər‿ᵊn ˌlɔː ˈdɑːţ ər‿ᵊn ˌlɑː **~s** z
daughters-in-law ˈdɔːt əz ɪn ˌlɔː -ᵊn,ˌ ‖ ˈdɔːţ ᵊrz ᵊn ˌlɔː ˈdɑːţ ᵊrz ᵊn ˌlɑː

daunt, Daunt dɔːnt ‖ dɑːnt **daunted** ˈdɔːnt ɪd -əd ‖ ˈdɔːnţ əd ˈdɑːnţ- **daunting/ly** ˈdɔːnt ɪŋ /li ‖ ˈdɔːnţ ɪŋ /li ˈdɑːnţ- **daunts** dɔːn*t*s ‖ dɑːn*t*s

dauntless ˈdɔːnt ləs -lɪs ‖ ˈdɑːnt- **~ly** li **~ness** nəs nɪs

dauphin, D~ ˈdɔːf ɪn ˈdəʊf-, §-ᵊn, -æ̃ ‖ doʊ ˈfæn ˈdoʊf ᵊn —*Fr* [do fæ̃] **~s** z

dauphine, D~ ˈdɔːf iːn ˈdəʊf- ‖ doʊ ˈfiːn —*Fr* [do fin] **~s** z

Dave deɪv

davenport, D~ ˈdæv ᵊn pɔːt →-ᵊm- ‖ -pɔːrt -poʊrt **~s** s

Daventry ˈdæv ᵊntr i —*formerly also* ˈdeɪntr i

Davey ˈdeɪv i

David ˈdeɪv ɪd §-əd —*but as a non-English name also* dæ ˈviːd

Davidson ˈdeɪv ɪd sən §-əd-

Davie ˈdeɪv i

Davies ˈdeɪv ɪs §-əs, -iːz

Davina də ˈviːn ə

da Vinci də ˈvɪntʃ i —*It* [dav ˈvin tʃi]

Davis ˈdeɪv ɪs §-əs

Davison ˈdeɪv ɪs ᵊn §-əs-

davit ˈdæv ɪt ˈdeɪv-, §-ət **~s** s

Davos dæ ˈvəʊs ˈdæv ɒs, ˈdɑːv-, -əs ‖ dɑː ˈvoʊs —*Ger* [da ˈvoːs]

Davro ˈdæv rəʊ ‖ -roʊ

Davy ˈdeɪv i
ˌDavy ˌJones's ˈlocker; **ˈDavy lamp**

Davyhulme ˈdeɪv i hjuːm

daw, Daw dɔː ‖ dɑː **daws, Daw's** dɔːz ‖ dɑːz

dawdl|e ˈdɔːd ᵊl ‖ ˈdɑːd- **~ed** d **~er/s** ‿ə/z ‖ ‿ər/z **~es** z **~ing/ly** ‿ɪŋ /li

Dawe dɔː ‖ dɑː

Dawes dɔːz ‖ dɑːz

Dawkins ˈdɔːk ɪnz §-ənz ‖ ˈdɑːk-

Dawlish ˈdɔːl ɪʃ ‖ ˈdɑːl-

dawn, Dawn dɔːn ‖ dɑːn **dawned** dɔːnd ‖ dɑːnd **dawning** ˈdɔːn ɪŋ ‖ ˈdɑːn- **dawns** dɔːnz ‖ dɑːnz
ˌdawn ˈchorus; **ˌdawn ˈredwood**

Dawnay ˈdɔːn i ‖ ˈdɑːn-

Dawson ˈdɔːs ᵊn ‖ ˈdɑːs-

Dax dæks

day, Day deɪ **days** deɪz
ˈday bed; **ˌDay ˈLewis**; **ˈday ˌnursery**; **ˌday of ˈreckoning**; **ˌday reˈlease course**; **ˌday reˈturn**; **ˈday school**

-day deɪ, di —*Although RP and GenAm are both traditionally considered to prefer* **di***, most speakers in practice use both pronunciations for this suffix, often in a strong form—weak form relationship. The* **deɪ** *form is generally preferred in exposed positions, for example at the end of a sentence:* I'll do it on Monday ˈmʌn deɪ*; the* **di** *form is preferred in close-knit expressions such as* Monday morning. ˌmʌnd i ˈmɔːn ɪŋ ‖ -ˈmɔːrn-.

Dayak ˈdaɪ æk **~s** s

Dayan daɪ ˈæn -ˈɑːn ‖ dɑː ˈjɑːn

daybook ˈdeɪ bʊk §-buːk **~s** s

dayboy ˈdeɪ bɔɪ **~s** z

daybreak ˈdeɪ breɪk

day-care ˈdeɪ keə ‖ -ker -kær

daydream ˈdeɪ driːm **~er/s** ə/z ‖ ᵊr/z **~ing** ɪŋ **~s** z

daygirl ˈdeɪ gɜːl ‖ -gɜːl **~s** z

dayglo, Day-Glo *tdmk* ˈdeɪ gləʊ ‖ -gloʊ

Day-Lewis ˌdeɪ ˈluː‿ɪs §‿əs

daylight ˈdeɪ laɪt **~s** s
ˌdaylight ˈrobbery; **ˌdaylight ˈsaving (time)**

daylong ˌdeɪ ˈlɒŋ ◂ ‖ -ˈlɔːŋ ◂ -ˈlɑːŋ ◂

dayroom ˈdeɪ ruːm -rʊm **~s** z

dayspring ˈdeɪ sprɪŋ

daystar ˈdeɪ stɑː ‖ -stɑːr

daytime ˈdeɪ taɪm

day-to-day ˌdeɪ tə ˈdeɪ ◂ ‖ ˌdeɪţ ə-
ˌday-to-ˌday ˈrunning

Dayton ˈdeɪt ᵊn

Daytona deɪ ˈtəʊn ə ‖ -ˈtoʊn ə
Dayˌtona ˈBeach

Daz *tdmk* dæz

daze deɪz **dazed** deɪzd **dazes** ˈdeɪz ɪz -əz **dazing** ˈdeɪz ɪŋ

dazzl|e ˈdæz ᵊl **~ed** d **~er/s** ‿ə/z ‖ ər/z **~es** z **~ing/ly** ‿ɪŋ /li

C ˌdi: 'si:
C10 ˌdi: sI: 'ten **~s, ~'s** z
-day 'di: deɪ
DT ˌdi: di: 'ti:
e *in French phrases* də di *—Fr* [də]
e *in Latin phrases* deɪ di:
e, de *in English family names* də
e- ˌdi:, di, də *—Attached to free forms, meaning 'do the opposite of' or 'remove', this prefix is usually pronounced strong,* ₍ˌ₎di: (ˌde'nasalized). *With these meanings it is freely productive, and most words made this way are not included in the dictionary. Otherwise the prefix is usually weak,* di (de'cide, de'pend), *with variant* də*; but strong* ˌde+ *before an unstressed syllable* ('deference, ˌdere'liction).
eacon, D~ 'di:k ən **~s** z
eaconess ˌdi:k ə 'nes '· · ·; 'di:k ən‿ɪs, əs ‖ 'di:k ən əs **~es** ɪz əz
eacti|vate di 'ækt ɪ |veɪt ˌdi:-, -ə- **~vated** veɪt ɪd -əd ‖ veɪṱ əd **~vates** veɪts **~vating** veɪt ɪŋ ‖ veɪṱ ɪŋ
eactivation di ˌækt ɪ 'veɪʃ ᵊn ˌdi:ˌ-, -ə-
ead ded **deader** 'ded ə ‖ -ᵊr **deadest** 'ded ɪst -əst
ˌ**dead 'centre**; ˌ**dead 'duck**; ˌ**dead 'end**; ˌ**dead 'heat**; ˌ**dead 'letter**; ˌ**dead 'loss**; '**dead march**; '**dead ˌnettle**; ˌ**dead 'reckoning**; ˌ**dead 'ringer**; ˌ**Dead 'Sea**◂; ˌ**Dead Sea 'Scrolls**; ˌ**dead 'weight**
ead-and-alive ˌded ᵊn ə 'laɪv ◂ -ᵊnd ə-
ead beat *adj* ˌded 'bi:t ◂ →ˌdeb-
eadbeat *n* 'ded bi:t →'deb- **~s** s
eadbolt 'ded bəʊlt →'deb-, →-bɒʊlt ‖ -boʊlt **~s** s
eaden 'ded ᵊn **~ed** d **~ing** ‿ɪŋ **~s** z
ead-end ˌded 'end ◂
eadeye 'ded aɪ
eadhead *v* ˌded 'hed '· · ‖ '· · **~ed** ɪd əd **~ing** ɪŋ **~s** z
Deadhead *n* 'ded hed **~s** z
eadli... *—see* **deadly**
eadlight 'ded laɪt **~s** s
eadline 'ded laɪn **~s** z
eadliness 'ded li nəs -nɪs
eadlock 'ded lɒk ‖ -lɑ:k **~ed** t **~s** s
dead|ly 'ded |li **~lier** li‿ə ‖ li‿ᵊr **~liest** li‿ɪst li‿əst
ˌ**deadly 'nightshade**; ˌ**deadly 'sin**
deadman 'ded mæn →'deb-
ˌ**deadman's 'fingers**
deadness 'ded nəs -nɪs
deadpan 'ded pæn →'deb-
deadweight 'ded weɪt
deadwood 'ded wʊd ˌ·'·
deaf def **deafer** 'def ə ‖ -ᵊr **deafest** 'def ɪst -əst
deaf-aid 'def eɪd **~s** z
deaf-and-dumb ˌdef ᵊn 'dʌm ◂
deafen 'def ᵊn **~ed** d **~ing** ‿ɪŋ **~s** z
deafly 'def li
deaf-mute ˌdef 'mju:t ◂ **~s** s

deafness 'def nəs -nɪs
Deakin 'di:k ɪn §-ən
deal, Deal di:ᵊl **dealing/s** 'di:ᵊl ɪŋ/z **deals** di:ᵊlz **dealt** delt *(!)*
dealer 'di:ᵊl ə ‖ -ᵊr **~s** z **~ship/s** ʃɪp/s
dealt delt
dean, Dean di:n **deans, Dean's** di:nz
Deana *(i)* di 'æn ə, *(ii)* 'di:n ə
Deane *(i)* di:n, *(ii)* di 'æn
deaner|y 'di:n ər |i **~ies** iz
deanship 'di:n ʃɪp **~s** s
dear, Dear dɪə ‖ dɪᵊr **dearer** 'dɪər ə ‖ 'dɪr ᵊr **dearest** 'dɪər ɪst -əst ‖ 'dɪr- **dears** dɪəz ‖ dɪᵊrz
Dearborn 'dɪə bɔ:n -bən ‖ 'dɪr bɔ:rn -bᵊrn
Deare dɪə ‖ dɪᵊr
dearie 'dɪər i ‖ 'dɪr i **~s** z
Dearing 'dɪər ɪŋ ‖ 'dɪr ɪŋ
dearly 'dɪə li ‖ 'dɪr li
Dearne dɜ:n ‖ dɜ˞:n
dearness 'dɪə nəs -nɪs ‖ 'dɪr-
dearth dɜ:θ ‖ dɜ˞:θ **dearths** dɜ:θs ‖ dɜ˞:θs
deary 'dɪər i ‖ 'dɪr i
death deθ **deaths** deθs
'**death camp**; '**death cell**; '**death cerˌtificate**; '**death ˌduties**; '**death knell**; '**death mask**; '**death ˌpenalty**; '**death rate**; '**death ˌrattle**; ˌ**death 'row**; '**death squad**; '**death tax**; '**death toll**; '**death trap**; ˌ**Death 'Valley**; '**death ˌwarrant**; '**death wish**
DeAth, De'ath di 'æθ deɪ-, -'ɑ:θ; deɪθ, deθ, di:θ
deathbed 'deθ bed **~s** z
deathblow 'deθ bləʊ ‖ -bloʊ **~s** z
death-dealing 'deθ ˌdi:ᵊl ɪŋ
death-defying 'deθ di ˌfaɪ ɪŋ -də-
deathless 'deθ ləs -lɪs **~ly** li **~ness** nəs nɪs
deathlike 'deθ laɪk
death|ly 'deθ |li **~liness** li nəs -nɪs
death's-head 'deθs hed **~s** z
deathwatch 'deθ wɒtʃ ‖ -wɑ:tʃ **~es** ɪz əz
ˌ**deathwatch 'beetle**
Deauville 'dəʊ vɪl -vi:ᵊl ‖ 'doʊ- *—Fr* [do vil]
Deayton 'di:t ᵊn
deb deb **debs** debz
debacle, débâcle deɪ 'bɑ:k ᵊl dɪ-, də-; -'bɑ:kl; 'deɪb ɑ:k ᵊl; ⚠'deb ək ᵊl *—Fr* [de bɑ:kl] **~s** z *—or as sing.*
debag ˌdi: 'bæg **~ged** d **~ging** ɪŋ **~s** z
de|bar di |'bɑ: də-, ˌdi:- ‖ -|'bɑ:r **~barred** 'bɑ:d ‖ 'bɑ:rd **~barring** 'bɑ:r ɪŋ **~bars** 'bɑ:z ‖ 'bɑ:rz
debark *'strip the bark from (wood)', 'disable vocal cords of (dog)'* ˌdi: 'bɑ:k ‖ -'bɑ:rk **~ed** t **~ing** ɪŋ **~s** s
debark *'disembark'* di 'bɑ:k ˌdi:-, də- ‖ -'bɑ:rk **~ed** t **~ing** ɪŋ **~s** s
debarkation ˌdi: bɑ: 'keɪʃ ᵊn ‖ -bɑ:r- **~s** z
debarment di 'bɑ: mənt də-, ˌdi:- ‖ -'bɑ:r-
debarr... *—see* **debar**
debas|e di 'beɪs də- **~ed** t **~ement/s** mənt/s **~er/s** ə/z ‖ ᵊr/z **~es** ɪz əz **~ing** ɪŋ

D

debatab|le di ˈbeɪt əb |ᵊl də- ‖ -ˈbeɪţ- **~ly** li
de|bate di |ˈbeɪt də- **~bated** ˈbeɪt ɪd -əd ‖ ˈbeɪţ əd **~bater/s** ˈbeɪt ə/z ‖ ˈbeɪţ ᵊr/z **~bates** ˈbeɪts **~bating** ˈbeɪt ɪŋ ‖ ˈbeɪţ ɪŋ
debauch di ˈbɔːtʃ də- ‖ -ˈbɑːtʃ **~ed** t **~es** ɪz əz **~ing** ɪŋ
debauchee ˌdeb ɔː ˈtʃiː -ˈʃiː; dɪ ˌbɔː-, də- ‖ -ɑː- **~s** z
debaucher|y di ˈbɔːtʃ ər‿|i də- ‖ -ˈbɑːtʃ- **~ies** iz
Debbie, Debby ˈdeb i
De Beauvoir də ˈbəʊ vwɑː ‖ -ˌboʊ ˈvwɑːr —*Fr* [də bo vwaːʁ]
De Beer də ˈbɪə ‖ -ˈbɪᵊr
Deben ˈdiːb ən
Debenham ˈdeb ən‿əm
debenture di ˈbentʃ ə də- ‖ -ᵊr **~s** z
debili|tate di ˈbɪl ɪ |teɪt də-, -ə- **~tated** teɪt ɪd -əd ‖ teɪţ əd **~tates** teɪts **~tating** teɪt ɪŋ ‖ teɪţ ɪŋ
debilitation di ˌbɪl ɪ ˈteɪʃ ᵊn də-, -ə-
debilit|y di ˈbɪl ət |i də-, -ɪt- ‖ -əţ |i **~ies** iz
deb|it ˈdeb |ɪt §-ət ‖ -|ət **~ited** ɪt ɪd §ət-, -əd ‖ əţ əd **~iting** ɪt ɪŋ §ət- ‖ əţ ɪŋ **~its** ɪts §əts ‖ əts
debonair, debonaire ˌdeb ə ˈneə◂ ‖ -ˈneᵊr -ˈnæᵊr **~ly** li **~ness** nəs nɪs
debon|e ˌdiː ˈbəʊn ‖ -ˈboʊn **~ed** d **~es** z **~ing** ɪŋ
de Bono də ˈbəʊn əʊ ‖ -ˈboʊn oʊ
Deborah ˈdeb ər‿ə
debouch di ˈbaʊtʃ də-, ˌdiː-, -ˈbuːʃ **~ed** t **~es** ɪz əz **~ing** ɪŋ
Debra ˈdeb rə
Debrett də ˈbret dɪ- **~'s** s
debrid|e di ˈbriːd də-, deɪ- **~ed** ɪd əd **~es** z **~ing** ɪŋ
debridement, débridement dɪ ˈbriːd mənt də-, (ˌ)diː-, deɪ-, ·ˌ·ˈmɒ̃ *Fr* [de bʁid mɑ̃]
debrief ˌdiː ˈbriːf **~ed** t **~ing** ɪŋ **~s** s

DEBRIS

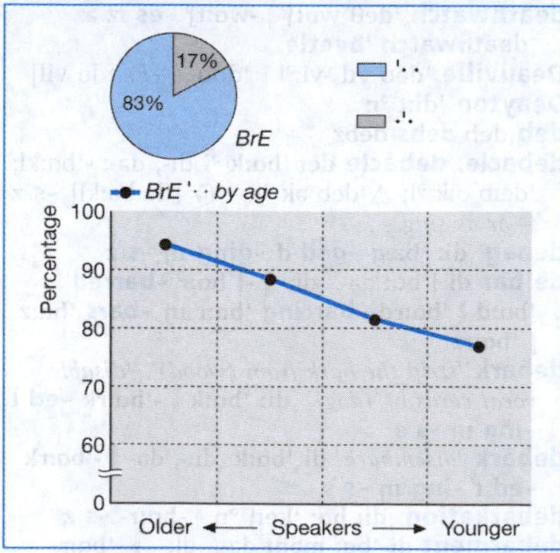

debris, débris ˈdeb riː ˈdeɪb-; də ˈbriː ‖ də ˈbriː ˈdeɪb riː — *Preference poll, BrE:* ˈ·· *83%,* ·ˈ· *17%.*

De Broglie də ˈbrəʊg li ‖ də ˈbrɔɪ —*Fr* [də bʁɔj]
Debs debz
debt det *(!)* **debts** dets
debt-laden ˈdet ˌleɪd ᵊn
debtor ˈdet ə ‖ ˈdeţ ᵊr **~s** z
debt-ridden ˈdet ˌrɪd ᵊn
debug ˌdiː ˈbʌg **~ged** d **~ging** ɪŋ **~s** z
de|bunk ˌdiː |ˈbʌŋk **~bunked** ˈbʌŋkt **~bunker/s** ˈbʌŋk ə/z ‖ ˈbʌŋk ᵊr/z **~bunking** ˈbʌŋk ɪŋ **~bunks** ˈbʌŋks
De Burgh də ˈbɜːg ‖ -ˈbɜ˞ːg
Debussy də ˈbuːs i -ˈbjuːs-, -ˈbʊs-; ˈdeɪb juːs i ‖ ˌdeɪb ju ˈsiː —*Fr* [də by si]

DEBUT

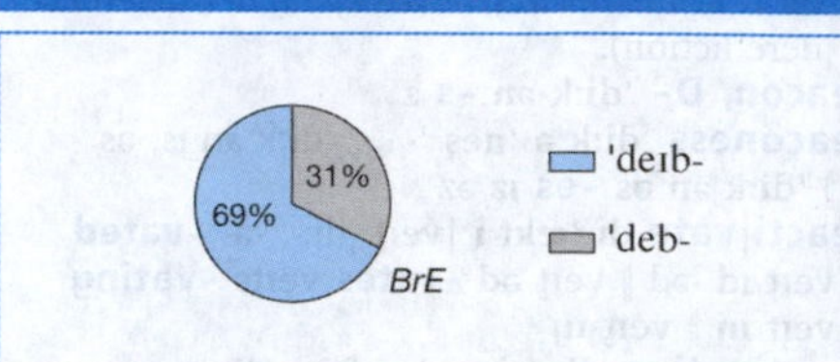

debut, début ˈdeɪb juː -uː; ˈdeb juː ‖ deɪ ˈbjuː — *Preference poll, BrE:* ˈdeɪb- *69%,* ˈdeb- *31%.* —*Fr* [de by] **~s** z
debutant, débutant ˈdeb ju tɒ̃ ˈdeɪb- —*Fr* [de by tɑ̃]
debutante, débutante ˈdeb ju tɑːnt ˈdeɪb-, -tænt, -tɒnt —*Fr* [de by tɑ̃ːt] **~s** s
DEC *tdmk* dek
Dec —*see* **December**
deca- *comb. form*
with stress-neutral suffix ¦dek ə — **decagram** ˈdek ə græm
with stress-imposing suffix dɪ ˈkæ+ də— **Decapolis** dɪ ˈkæp əl ɪs də-, §-əs

DECADE

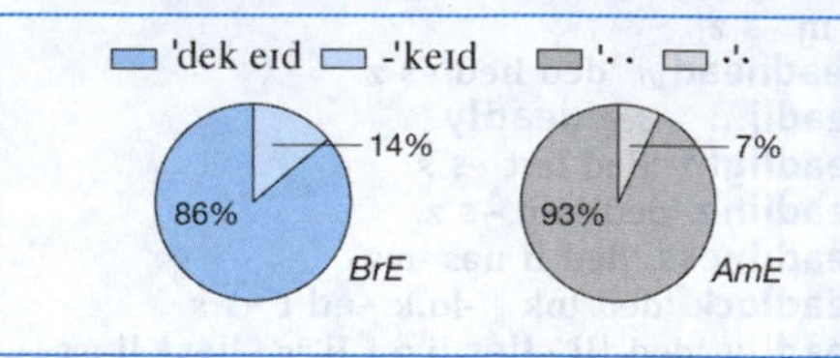

decade ˈdek eɪd di ˈkeɪd, de-; ˈdek əd — *Preference polls, BrE:* ˈdek eɪd *86%,* -ˈkeɪd *14%; AmE:* ˈ·· *93%,* ·ˈ· *7%. The form* ˈdek əd *is associated mainly with the religious sense, 'part of the rosary, set of ten Hail Marys'.* **~s** z
decadence ˈdek əd ənᵗs
decadent ˈdek əd ənt **~ly** li **~s** s
decaf, decaff ˈdiː kæf **~s** s
decaffei|nate ˌdiː ˈkæf ɪ |neɪt dɪ-, -ə- **~nated** neɪt ɪd -əd ‖ neɪţ əd **~nates** neɪts **~nating** neɪt ɪŋ ‖ neɪţ ɪŋ
decagon ˈdek əg ən -ə gɒn ‖ -ə gɑːn **~s** z
decahedr|on ˌdek ə ˈhiːdr |ən -ˈhedr-; ˈ··ˌ·· **~a** ə **~ons** ənz

decal dɪ ˈkæl ˈdiː kæl ‖ ˈdiː kæl dɪ ˈkæl **~s** z
decalcomania dɪ ˌkælk ə ˈmeɪn i‿ə
decalogue ˈdek ə lɒg ‖ -lɔːg -lɑːg
decameron di ˈkæm ᵊr‿ən də-, de-
decamp di ˈkæmp ˌdiː- **~ed** t **~ing** ɪŋ **~s** s
decanal di ˈkeɪn ᵊl də-; ˈdek ən ᵊl **~ly** i
decane ˈdek eɪn
decani di ˈkeɪn aɪ
de|cant di |ˈkænt ˌdiː-, də- **~canted** ˈkænt ɪd -əd ‖ ˈkænţ əd **~canting** ˈkænt ɪŋ ‖ ˈkænţ ɪŋ **~cants** ˈkænts
decanter di ˈkænt ə də-, ˌdiː- ‖ -ˈkænţ ᵊr **~s** z
decapi|tate di ˈkæp ɪ |teɪt də-, ˌdiː-, -ə- **~tated** teɪt ɪd -əd ‖ teɪţ əd **~tates** teɪts **~tating** teɪt ɪŋ ‖ teɪţ ɪŋ
decapitation di ˌkæp ɪ ˈteɪʃ ᵊn ˌdiː ˌkæp-, -ə- **~s** z
decapod ˈdek ə pɒd ‖ -pɑːd **~s** z
decarbonis... —*see* **decarboniz...**
decarbonization ˌdiː ˌkɑːb ən aɪ ˈzeɪʃ ᵊn ·ˌ··-, -ɪˈ·- ‖ diː ˌkɑːrb ən ə- **~s** z
decarboniz|e ₍ˌ₎diː ˈkɑːb ə naɪz ‖ -ˈkɑːrb- **~ed** d **~es** ɪz əz **~ing** ɪŋ
decasyllabic ˌdek ə sɪ ˈlæb ɪk ◂ -səˈ--
decasyllable ˈdek ə ˌsɪl əb ᵊl ˌ·ˈ··· **~s** z
decathlete dɪ ˈkæθ liːt de-, də- **~s** s
decathlon dɪ ˈkæθ lɒn de-, də-, -lən ‖ -lɑːn -lən **~s** z
Decatur dɪ ˈkeɪt ə də- ‖ -ˈkeɪţ ᵊr
decay di ˈkeɪ də- **~ed** d **~ing** ɪŋ **~s** z
Decca *tdmk* ˈdek ə
Deccan ˈdek ən —*Hindi* [d̪ək kʰɪŋ, d̪eː kən]
deceas|e di ˈsiːs də- **~ed** t **~es** ɪz əz **~ing** ɪŋ
decedent di ˈsiːd ᵊnt də- **~s** s
deceit di ˈsiːt də- **~s** s
deceitful di ˈsiːt fᵊl də-, -fʊl **~ly** ‿i **~ness** nəs nɪs
deceiv|e di ˈsiːv də- **~ed** d **~er/s** ə/z ‖ ᵊr/z **~es** z **~ing** ɪŋ
decele|rate ˌdiː ˈsel ə |reɪt **~rated** reɪt ɪd -əd ‖ reɪţ əd **~rates** reɪts **~rating** reɪt ɪŋ ‖ reɪţ ɪŋ
deceleration ˌdiː ˌsel ə ˈreɪʃ ᵊn ·ˌ·- **~s** z
December di ˈsem bə də-, §-ˈzem- ‖ -bᵊr
Decembrist di ˈsem brɪst də-, §-brəst **~s** s
decenc|y ˈdiːs ᵊnᵗs |i **~ies** iz
decennial di ˈsen i‿əl də-, de- **~ly** i
decent ˈdiːs ᵊnt **~ly** li **~ness** nəs nɪs
decentralis... —*see* **decentraliz...**
decentralization ˌdiː ˌsentr əl aɪ ˈzeɪʃ ᵊn ·ˌ·-, -ɪˈ·- ‖ -əl ə- **~s** z
decentraliz|e ₍ˌ₎diː ˈsentr ə laɪz **~ed** d **~es** ɪz əz **~ing** ɪŋ
deception di ˈsep ʃᵊn də- **~s** z
deceptive di ˈsept ɪv də- **~ly** li **~ness** nəs nɪs
deci- ¦des i ‖ ¦des ə — **decimetre** ˈdes i ˌmiːt ə ‖ -ə ˌmiːţ ᵊr
decibel ˈdes ɪ bel -ə-; -ɪb ᵊl, -əb- **~s** z
decid|e di ˈsaɪd də- **~ed** ɪd əd **~er/s** ə/z ‖ ᵊr/z **~es** z **~ing** ɪŋ
decided|ly di ˈsaɪd ɪd |li də-, -əd- **~ness** nəs nɪs
deciduous di ˈsɪd ju‿əs də- ‖ dɪ ˈsɪdʒ u‿əs **~ly** li **~ness** nəs nɪs

decile ˈdes aɪᵊl -ɪl **~s** z
Decima ˈdes ɪm ə -əm-
decimal ˈdes əm ᵊl -ɪm- **~ly** i **~s** z
ˌ**decimal** ˈ**point**; ˈ**decimal** ˌ**system**
decimalis... —*see* **decimaliz...**
decimalization ˌdes əm ᵊl aɪ ˈzeɪʃ ᵊn ˌ·ɪm-, -ɪˈ·- ‖ -ə ˈzeɪʃ-
decimaliz|e ˈdes əm ə laɪz ˈ·ɪm-, -ᵊl aɪz **~ed** d **~es** ɪz əz **~ing** ɪŋ
deci|mate ˈdes ɪ |meɪt -ə- **~mated** meɪt ɪd -əd ‖ meɪţ əd **~mates** meɪts **~mating** meɪt ɪŋ ‖ meɪţ ɪŋ
decimation ˌdes ɪ ˈmeɪʃ ᵊn -ə- **~s** z
Decimus ˈdes ɪm əs -əm-
decipher di ˈsaɪf ə də-, ˌdiː- ‖ -ᵊr **~ed** d **deciphering** di ˈsaɪf ər‿ɪŋ də-, ˌdiː **~s** z
decipherable di ˈsaɪf ər‿əb ᵊl də-, ˌdiː-
decipherer di ˈsaɪf ər‿ə də-, ˌdiː- ‖ -ᵊr‿ər **~s** z
decipherment di ˈsaɪf ə mənt də-, ˌdiː- ‖ -ᵊr- **~s** s
decision di ˈsɪʒ ᵊn də-, -ˈzɪʃ-, -ˈzɪʒ-, -ˈsɪʃ- **~s** z
decision-mak|er di ˈsɪʒ ᵊn ˌmeɪk |ə də-, ˈzɪʃ-, -ˈzɪʒ-, -ˈsɪʃ- ‖ -|ᵊr **~ers** əz ‖ ᵊrz **~ing** ɪŋ
decisive di ˈsaɪs ɪv də-, -ˈsaɪz- **~ly** li **~ness** nəs nɪs
deck dek **decked** dekt **decking** ˈdek ɪŋ **decks** deks
deckchair ˈdek tʃeə ˌ·ˈ· ‖ -tʃer -tʃær **~s** z
-decker ˈdek ə ‖ -ᵊr — **single-decker** ˌsɪŋ gᵊl ˈdek ə ◂ ‖ -ᵊr
Decker ˈdek ə ‖ -ᵊr
deckhand ˈdek hænd **~s** z
deckhouse ˈdek haʊs
deckle ˈdek ᵊl **~s** z
ˌ**deckle** ˈ**edge**
deckle-edged ˌdek ᵊl ˈedʒd ◂
declaim di ˈkleɪm də- **~ed** d **~ing** ɪŋ **~s** z
declamation ˌdek lə ˈmeɪʃ ᵊn **~s** z
declamator|y di ˈklæm ət‿ər |i də- ‖ -ə tɔːr |i -toʊr i **~ily** əl i ɪ li
Declan ˈdek lən
declarable di ˈkleər əb ᵊl də- ‖ -ˈkler- -ˈklær-
declaration ˌdek lə ˈreɪʃ ᵊn **~s** z
declarative di ˈklær ət ɪv də-, -ˈkleər- ‖ -əţ ɪv -ˈkler- **~ly** li
declaratory di ˈklær ət‿ər i də-, -ˈkleər- ‖ -ə tɔːr i -ˈkler-, -toʊr i
declare di ˈkleə də- ‖ dɪ ˈkleᵊr -ˈklæᵊr **~d** d **~s** z **declaring** di ˈkleər ɪŋ də- ‖ dɪ ˈkler ɪŋ -ˈklær-
declaredly di ˈkleər ɪd li də-, -əd- ‖ -ˈkler- -ˈklær-
declasse, déclassé, declassee, déclassée deɪ ˈklæs eɪ -ˈklɑːs-, ˌ·ˈ·ˈ· ‖ ˌdeɪ klæ ˈseɪ -klɑː- —*Fr* [de kla se]
declassifiable ₍ˌ₎diː ˈklæs ɪ faɪ‿əb ᵊl -ˈ·ə-, ˌ·ˌ··ˈ··-
declassification ˌdiː ˌklæs ɪf ɪ ˈkeɪʃ ᵊn ·ˌ·-, -əf ɪˈ·-, §-əˈ· ·
declassi|fy ₍ˌ₎diː ˈklæs ɪ |faɪ -ə- **~fied** faɪd **~fies** faɪz **~fying** faɪ ɪŋ
declension di ˈklenᵗʃ ᵊn də- **~al** ‿əl **~s** z
declinable di ˈklaɪn əb ᵊl də-
declination ˌdek lɪ ˈneɪʃ ᵊn -lə- **~al** ‿əl **~s** z

D

D

decline *n* di ˈklaɪn də- ˈdiː klaɪn **~s** z

declin|e *v* di ˈklaɪn də- **~ed** d **~er/s** ə/z ‖ ᵊr/z **~es** z **~ing** ɪŋ

declivit|y di ˈklɪv ət |i də-, -ɪt- ‖ -əţ |i **~ies** iz

declutch ˌdiː ˈklʌtʃ di-, də- **~ed** t **~es** ɪz əz **~ing** ɪŋ

decoct di ˈkɒkt də- ‖ -ˈkɑːkt **~ed** ɪd əd **~ing** ɪŋ **~s** s

decoction di ˈkɒk ʃᵊn də- ‖ -ˈkɑːk- **~s** z

decod|e ₍ˌ₎diː ˈkəʊd ‖ -ˈkoʊd **~ed** ɪd əd **~er/s** ə/z ‖ ᵊr/z **~es** z **~ing** ɪŋ

decok|e *v* ˌdiː ˈkəʊk dɪ-, də- ‖ -ˈkoʊk **~ed** t **~es** s **~ing** ɪŋ

decoke *n* ˈdiː kəʊk ˌ·ˈ· ‖ -koʊk **~s** s

decolletage, décolletage ˌdeɪ kɒl ˈtɑːʒ deɪ ˈkɒl ɪ tɑːʒ, -ə- ‖ -kɑːl-ˌ· ·əˈ·, ˌdek əl əˈ· —*Fr* [de kɔl taːʒ]

decollete, décolleté deɪ ˈkɒl teɪ -ˈkɒl ɪ teɪ, -ə teɪ ‖ ˌdeɪ kɑːl ˈteɪ ˌ· ·əˈ· —*Fr* [de kɔl te]

decolonis... —*see* **decoloniz...**

decolonization ˌdiː ˌkɒl ən aɪ ˈzeɪʃ ᵊn ˌ·ˌ·-, -ɪˈ·- ‖ diː ˌkɑːl ən ə- **~s** z

decoloniz|e ₍ˌ₎diː ˈkɒl ə naɪz ‖ -ˈkɑːl- **~ed** d **~es** ɪz əz **~ing** ɪŋ

decommission ˌdiː kə ˈmɪʃ ᵊn **~ed** d **~ing** ˌɪŋ **~s** z

decomposable ˌdiː kəm ˈpəʊz əb ᵊl ‖ -ˈpoʊz-

decompos|e ˌdiː kəm ˈpəʊz §-kɒm- ‖ -ˈpoʊz **~ed** d **~er/s** ə/z ‖ ᵊr/z **~es** ɪz əz **~ing** ɪŋ

decomposition ˌdiː ˌkɒmp ə ˈzɪʃ ᵊn ‖ -ˌkɑːmp-

decompress ˌdiː kəm ˈpres §-kɒm- **~ed** t **~es** ɪz əz **~ing** ɪŋ

decompression ˌdiː kəm ˈpreʃ ᵊn §-kɒm- **~s** z
ˌdecomˈpression ˌchamber

decongestant ˌdiː kən ˈdʒest ənt §-kɒn- **~s** s

deconse|crate ˌdiː ˈkɒnᵗs ɪ |kreɪt -ə- ‖ -ˈkɑːnᵗs- **~crated** kreɪt ɪd -əd ‖ kreɪţ əd **~crates** kreɪts **~crating** kreɪt ɪŋ ‖ kreɪţ ɪŋ

deconsecration ˌdiː ˌkɒnᵗs ɪ ˈkreɪʃ ᵊn ˌ·ˌ·- ‖ -ˌkɑːnᵗs- **~s** z

deconstruct ˌdiː kən ˈstrʌkt §-kɒn- **~ed** ɪd əd **~ing** ɪŋ **~s** s

deconstruction ˌdiː kən ˈstrʌk ʃᵊn §-kɒn- **~ism** ˌɪz əm **~ist/s** ɪst/s §əst/s ‖ əst/s **~s** z

decontami|nate ˌdiː kən ˈtæm ɪ |neɪt §ˌkɒn-, -ə neɪt **~nated** neɪt ɪd -əd ‖ neɪţ əd **~nates** neɪts **~nating** neɪt ɪŋ ‖ neɪţ ɪŋ

decontamination ˌdiː kən ˌtæm ɪ ˈneɪʃ ᵊn §ˌ·kɒn-, -əˈ·- **~s** z

decontrol ˌdiː kən ˈtrəʊl §-kɒn-, →-ˈtrɒʊl ‖ -ˈtroʊl **~led** d **~ling** ɪŋ **~s** z

decor, décor ˈdeɪk ɔː ˈdek- ‖ deɪ ˈkɔːr ˈdeɪk ɔːr **~s** z

deco|rate ˈdek ə |reɪt **~rated** reɪt ɪd -əd ‖ reɪţ əd **~rates** reɪts **~rating** reɪt ɪŋ ‖ reɪţ ɪŋ

decoration ˌdek ə ˈreɪʃ ᵊn **~s** z

decorative ˈdek ər‿ət ɪv ‖ əţ ɪv -ə reɪţ- **~ly** li **~ness** nəs nɪs

decorator ˈdek ə reɪt ə ‖ -reɪţ ᵊr **~s** z

decorous ˈdek ər əs —*formerly* dɪ ˈkɔːr əs **~ly** li **~ness** nəs nɪs

decorti|cate ˌdiː ˈkɔːt ɪ |keɪt §-ə- ‖ -ˈkɔːrţ- **~cated** keɪt ɪd -əd ‖ keɪţ əd **~cates** keɪts **~cating** keɪt ɪŋ ‖ keɪţ ɪŋ

decortication ˌdiː ˌkɔːt ɪ ˈkeɪʃ ᵊn §-ə- ‖ diː ˌkɔːrţ ə- **~s** z

decorum dɪ ˈkɔːr əm də- ‖ -ˈkoʊr-

decoupage, découpage ˌdeɪ ku ˈpɑːʒ —*Fr* [de ku paːʒ]

decoupl|e ₍ˌ₎diː ˈkʌp ᵊl **~ed** d **~es** z **~ing** ˌɪŋ

De Courcey, De Courcy *(i)* də ˈkɔːs i ‖ -ˈkɔːrs i -ˈkoʊrs-, *(ii)* -ˈkʊəs i ‖ -ˈkʊrs i, *(iii)* ˌ-ˈkɜːs i ‖ ˈkɜ˞ːs i

decoy *v* di ˈkɔɪ də- **~ed** d **~ing** ɪŋ **~s** z

decoy *n* ˈdiː kɔɪ dɪ ˈkɔɪ, də-, §diː- **~s** z

decreas|e *v* ˌdiː ˈkriːs ◂ di-, də-, ˈ· · **~ed** t **~es** ɪz əz **~ing/ly** ɪŋ /li

decreas|e *n* ˈdiː kriːs di ˈkriːs, də-, ˌdiː- **~es** ɪz əz

decree di ˈkriː də- **~d** d **~ing** ɪŋ **~s** z
deˌcree ˈnisi

decrement *n* ˈdek rɪ mənt -rə- **~s** s

decre|ment *v* ˈdek rɪ |ment -rə- —*See note at* -ment **~mented** ment ɪd -əd ‖ menţ əd **~menting** ment ɪŋ ‖ menţ ɪŋ **~ments** ments

decreolis... —*see* **decreoliz...**

decreolization ˌdiː ˌkriː‿əl aɪ ˈzeɪʃ ᵊn -ˌkreɪ-, -ˌ·əʊl-, -ɪˈ·- ‖ -ə ˈzeɪʃ-

decreoliz|e ˌdiː ˈkriː‿ə laɪz -ˈkreɪ-, -əʊ- **~ed** d **~es** ɪz əz **~ing** ɪŋ

decrepit di ˈkrep ɪt də-, §-ət **~ly** li

decrepi|tate di ˈkrep ɪ |teɪt də-, -ə- **~tated** teɪt ɪd -əd ‖ teɪţ əd **~tates** teɪts **~tating** teɪt ɪŋ ‖ teɪţ ɪŋ

decrepitude di ˈkrep ɪ tjuːd də-, -ə-, →-tʃuːd ‖ -tuːd -tjuːd

decrescendo ˌdiː krə ˈʃend əʊ ˌdeɪ-, -krɪ- ‖ -oʊ **~s** z

De Crespigny *(i)* də ˈkrep ɪn i -ən-, *(ii)* -ˈkresp-

decretal di ˈkriːt ᵊl də- ‖ -ˈkriːţ ᵊl **~s** z

decri... —*see* **decry**

decriminalis... —*see* **decriminaliz...**

decriminalization ˌdiː ˌkrɪm ɪn ᵊl aɪ ˈzeɪʃ ᵊn -ˌ·ᵊn‿əl-, -ˌ·-, -ɪˈ·- ‖ -ə ˈzeɪʃ-

decriminaliz|e ₍ˌ₎diː ˈkrɪm ɪn ə laɪz -ᵊn‿ə-, -əl aɪz **~ed** d **~es** ɪz əz **~ing** ɪŋ

de|cry di |ˈkraɪ də- **~cried** ˈkraɪd **~cries** ˈkraɪz **~crying** ˈkraɪ ɪŋ

decrypt ₍ˌ₎diː ˈkrɪpt **~ed** ɪd əd **~ing** ɪŋ **~s** s

decryption ₍ˌ₎diː ˈkrɪp ʃᵊn **~s** z

decubitus di ˈkjuːb ɪt əs də-, -ət- ‖ -əţ-

decumbent di ˈkʌm bənt də-

decurion de ˈkjʊər i‿ən di- ‖ -ˈkjʊr- **~s** z

decurrent di ˈkʌr ənt də- ‖ -ˈkɜː- **~ly** li

decussate *adj* di ˈkʌs eɪt ˌdiː-, -ət, -ɪt **~ly** li

decuss|ate *v* di ˈkʌs |eɪt ˌdiː-; ˈdek əs- **~ated** eɪt ɪd -əd ‖ eɪţ əd **~ates** eɪts **~ating** eɪt ɪŋ ‖ eɪţ ɪŋ

Dedalus ˈdiːd əl əs ‖ ˈded-

Deddington ˈded ɪŋ tən

Dedham ˈded əm

edi|cate ˈded ɪ |keɪt §-ə- **~cated/ly** keɪt ɪd /li əd /li ‖ keɪţ əd /li **~cates** keɪts **~cating** keɪt ɪŋ ‖ keɪţ ɪŋ
edicatee ˌded ɪk ə ˈtiː ˌ-ək- **~s** z
edication ˌded ɪ ˈkeɪʃ ᵊn §-ə- **~s** z
edicator ˈded ɪ keɪt ə §ˈ-ə- ‖ -keɪţ ᵊr **~s** z
edicatory ˈded ɪk ət‿ər i -ɪ keɪt ər i ‖ -ə tɔːr i -toʊr i
educ|e di ˈdjuːs də-, →§-ˈdʒuːs ‖ -ˈduːs -ˈdjuːs **~ed** t **~es** ɪz əz **~ing** ɪŋ
educible di ˈdjuːs əb ᵊl də-, →§-ˈdʒuːs-, -ɪb- ‖ -ˈduːs- -ˈdjuːs-
educt di ˈdʌkt də- **~ed** ɪd əd **~ing** ɪŋ **~s** s
eductible di ˈdʌkt əb ᵊl də-, -ɪb- **~s** z
eduction di ˈdʌk ʃᵊn də- **~s** z
eductive di ˈdʌkt ɪv də- **~ly** li
ee diː
eed diːd **deeded** ˈdiːd ɪd -əd **deeding** ˈdiːd ɪŋ **deeds** diːdz
ˈdeed poll
eedes diːdz
eejay ˈdiː dʒeɪ ˌ.ˈ. **~s** z
eekes, Deeks diːks
eeko *tdmk* ˈdiːk əʊ ‖ -oʊ
eeley ˈdiːl i
eem diːm **deemed** diːmd **deeming** ˈdiːm ɪŋ **deems** diːmz
Deemer ˈdiːm ə ‖ -ᵊr
Deeming ˈdiːm ɪŋ
de-emphasis|e, de-emphasiz|e ˌdiː ˈemᵖf ə saɪz **~ed** d **~es** ɪz əz **~ing** ɪŋ
eemster ˈdiːm stə ‖ -stᵊr **~s** z
eep diːp **deeper** ˈdiːp ə ‖ -ᵊr **deepest** ˈdiːp ɪst -əst **deeps** diːps
ˈdeep end; **ˌDeep ˈSouth**; **ˌdeep ˈspace**; **ˌdeep ˈwater**
deep-dyed ˌdiːp ˈdaɪd ◂
deepen ˈdiːp ən **~ed** d **~ing** ‿ɪŋ **~s** z
deep-freez|e *n*, **Deepfreeze** *tdmk* ˌdiːp ˈfriːz ‖ ˈdiːp friːz **~es** ɪz əz
deep-freez|e *v* ˌdiːp ˈfriːz **~er/s** ə/z ‖ ᵊr/z **~es** ɪz əz **~ing** ɪŋ
deep-frozen ˌdiːp ˈfrəʊz ᵊn ◂ ‖ -ˈfroʊz-
deep-|fry ˌdiːp |ˈfraɪ ˈ.. **~fried** ˈfraɪd **~fries** ˈfraɪz **~frying** ˈfraɪ ɪŋ
Deeping ˈdiːp ɪŋ
deep-laid ˌdiːp ˈleɪd ◂
deep|ly ˈdiːp |li **~ness** nəs nɪs
deep-pocketed ˌdiːp ˈpɒk ɪt ɪd ◂ -ət-, -əd ‖ -ˈpɑːk əţ əd ◂
deep-rooted ˌdiːp ˈruːt ɪd ◂ -əd ‖ -ˈruːţ- **~ness** nəs nɪs
deep-sea ˌdiːp ˈsiː ◂
deep-seated ˌdiːp siːt ɪd ◂ -əd ‖ -ˈsiːţ-
deep-set ˌdiːp ˈset ◂
deer dɪə ‖ dɪᵊr *(= dear)*
Deer, Deere dɪə ‖ dɪᵊr
deerhound ˈdɪə haʊnd ‖ ˈdɪr- **~s** z
deerskin ˈdɪə skɪn ‖ ˈdɪr- **~s** z
deerstalker ˈdɪə ˌstɔːk ə ‖ ˈdɪr ˌstɔːk ᵊr -ˌstɑːk- **~s** z

de-esca|late ₍ˌ₎diː ˈesk ə |leɪt **~lated** leɪt ɪd -əd ‖ leɪţ əd **~lates** leɪts **~lating** leɪt ɪŋ ‖ leɪţ ɪŋ
de-escalation ˌdiː ˌesk ə ˈleɪʃ ᵊn ·ˌ·- **~s** z
Deeside ˈdiː saɪd
defac|e di ˈfeɪs də- **~ed** t **~es** ɪz əz **~ing** ɪŋ
defacement di ˈfeɪs mənt də- **~s** s
de facto ₍ˌ₎deɪ ˈfækt əʊ di- ‖ -oʊ
defalc|ate ˈdiː fælk |eɪt -fɔːlk- ‖ di ˈfælk- -ˈfɔːlk-; ˈdef ᵊl k|eɪt **~ated** eɪt ɪd -əd ‖ eɪţ əd **~ates** eɪts **~ating** eɪt ɪŋ ‖ eɪţ ɪŋ
defalcation ˌdiːf æl ˈkeɪʃ ᵊn -ɔːl- ‖ ˌdef ᵊl- **~s** z
defamation ˌdef ə ˈmeɪʃ ᵊn ˌdiːf- **~s** z
defamator|y di ˈfæm ə‿tər |i də- ‖ -ə tɔːr |i -toʊr i **~ily** əl i ɪ li
defam|e di ˈfeɪm də- **~ed** d **~es** z **~ing** ɪŋ
default *v* di ˈfɔːlt də-, -ˈfɒlt ‖ -ˈfɑːlt **~ed** ɪd əd **~er/s** ə/z ‖ ᵊr/z **~ing** ɪŋ **~s** s
default *n* di ˈfɔːlt də-, -ˈfɒlt; ˈdiː· ‖ -ˈfɑːlt **~s** s
defeasance di ˈfiːz ᵊnᵗs də-
defeasible di ˈfiːz əb ᵊl də-, -ɪb-
de|feat *v, n* di |ˈfiːt də- **~feated** ˈfiːt ɪd -əd ‖ ˈfiːţ əd **~feating** ˈfiːt ɪŋ ‖ ˈfiːţ ɪŋ **~feats** ˈfiːts
defeatism di ˈfiːt ˌɪz əm də- ‖ -ˈfiːţ-
defeatist di ˈfiːt ɪst də-, §-əst ‖ -ˈfiːţ- **~s** s
defe|cate ˈdef ə |keɪt ˈdiːf-, -ɪ- **~cated** keɪt ɪd -əd ‖ keɪţ əd **~cates** keɪts **~cating** keɪt ɪŋ ‖ keɪţ ɪŋ
defecation ˌdef ə ˈkeɪʃ ᵊn ˌdiːf-, -ɪ- **~s** z

DEFECT

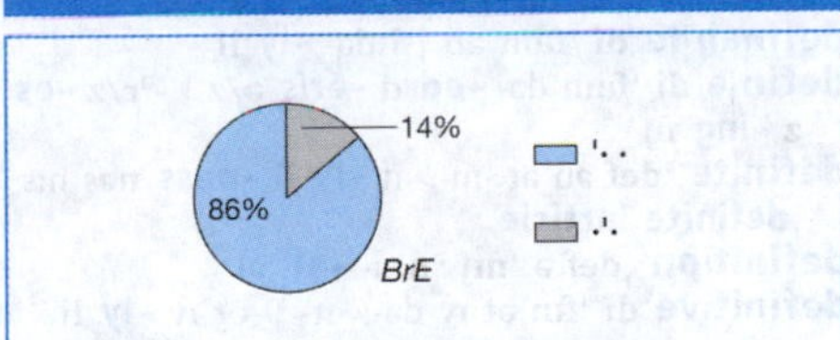

defect *n* ˈdiː fekt di ˈfekt, də- — *Preference poll, BrE:* ˈ·· *86%,* ·ˈ· *14%.* **~s** s
defect *v* di ˈfekt də- **~ed** ɪd əd **~ing** ɪŋ **~s** s
defection di ˈfek ʃᵊn də- **~s** z
defective di ˈfekt ɪv də- **~ly** li **~ness** nəs nɪs
defector di ˈfekt ə də- ‖ -ᵊr **~s** z
defenc|e di ˈfenᵗs də- **~es** ɪz əz
defenceless di ˈfenᵗs ləs də-, -lɪs **~ly** li **~ness** nəs nɪs
defence|man di ˈfenᵗs| mən də- **~men** mən
defend di ˈfend də- **~ed** ɪd əd **~ing** ɪŋ **~s** z
defendant di ˈfend ənt də- ‖ -ænt **~s** s
defender di ˈfend ə də- ‖ -ᵊr **~s** z
defene|strate ₍ˌ₎diː ˈfen ɪ |streɪt -ə- **~strated** streɪt ɪd -əd ‖ streɪţ əd **~strates** streɪts **~strating** streɪt ɪŋ ‖ streɪţ ɪŋ
defenestration ˌdiː ˌfen ɪ ˈstreɪʃ ᵊn -əˈ- **~s** z
defens|e di ˈfenᵗs də- ‖ ˈdiː· **~es** ɪz əz
defenseless di ˈfenᵗs ləs də-, -lɪs **~ly** li **~ness** nəs nɪs
defense|man di ˈfenᵗs| mən də- **~men** mən
defensibility di ˌfenᵗs ə ˈbɪl ət i də-, -ˌ·ɪ-, -ɪt i ‖ -əţ i

defensib|le di 'fen^t^s əb |^ə^l də-, -ɪb- **~ly** li
defensive di 'fen^t^s ɪv də- **~ly** li **~ness** nəs nɪs
de|fer di |'fɜː də- ‖ -|'fɜ˞ː **~ferred** 'fɜːd ‖ 'fɜ˞ːd **~ferring** 'fɜːr ɪŋ ‖ 'fɜ˞ː ɪŋ **~fers** 'fɜːz ‖ 'fɜ˞ːz
deference 'def ^ə^r‿ən^t^s
deferent 'def ^ə^r‿ənt
deferential ˌdef ə 'ren^t^ʃ ^ə^l ◂ **~ly** i
deferment di 'fɜː mənt də- ‖ -'fɜ˞ː- **~s** s
deferral di 'fɜːr əl də- ‖ -'fɜ˞ː- **~s** z
deferrer di 'fɜːr ə də- ‖ -'fɜ˞ː ^ə^r **~s** z
deffo 'def əʊ ‖ -oʊ
defiance di 'faɪ‿ən^t^s də-
defiant di 'faɪ‿ənt də- **~ly** li
defibril|late ₍ˌ₎diː 'fɪb rɪ |leɪt -'faɪb-, -rə- **~lated** leɪt ɪd -əd ‖ leɪt̬ əd **~lates** leɪts **~lating** leɪt ɪŋ ‖ leɪt̬ ɪŋ
defibrillation diː ˌfɪb rɪ 'leɪʃ ^ə^n ˌfaɪb-, ˌ·ˌ·-, -rə'·-
defibrillator ₍ˌ₎diː 'fɪb rɪ leɪt ə -'faɪb-, -'·rə- ‖ -leɪt̬ ^ə^r **~s** z
deficienc|y di 'fɪʃ ^ə^n^t^s |i də- **~ies** iz
  de'ficiency diˌsease
deficient di 'fɪʃ ^ə^nt də- **~ly** li
deficit 'def əs ɪt -ɪs-, -ət; dɪ 'fɪs-, də-, §diː- —*formerly also* 'diːf- **~s** s
de fide di 'faɪd i ˌdiː-; ˌdeɪ 'fiːd eɪ
defie... —*see* **defy**
defilad|e ˌdef ɪ 'leɪd -ə-, '·· · **~ed** ɪd əd **~es** z **~ing** ɪŋ
defile *n* di 'faɪ^ə^l də- 'diː faɪ^ə^l **~s** z
defil|e *v* di 'faɪ^ə^l də- **~ed** d **~es** z **~ing** ɪŋ
defilement di 'faɪ^ə^l mənt də- **~s** s
definab|le di 'faɪn əb |^ə^l də- **~ly** li
defin|e di 'faɪn də- **~ed** d **~er/s** ə/z ‖ -^ə^r/z **~es** z **~ing** ɪŋ
definite 'def ən‿ət -ɪn-, -ɪt **~ly** li **~ness** nəs nɪs
  ˌdefinite 'article
definition ˌdef ə 'nɪʃ ^ə^n -ɪ- **~al** ‿əl
definitive di 'fɪn ət ɪv də-, -ɪt- ‖ -ət̬ ɪv **~ly** li **~ness** nəs nɪs
de|flate ˌdiː |'fleɪt dɪ-, də- **~flated** 'fleɪt ɪd -əd ‖ 'fleɪt̬ əd **~flates** 'fleɪts **~flating** 'fleɪt ɪŋ ‖ 'fleɪt̬ ɪŋ
deflation ˌdiː 'fleɪʃ ^ə^n dɪ-, də- **~s** z
deflationary ˌdiː 'fleɪʃ ^ə^n ər‿i dɪ-, də-, -^ə^n‿ər i ‖ -ə ner i
deflator di 'fleɪt ə də- ‖ -'fleɪt̬ ^ə^r **~s** z
deflect di 'flekt də- **~ed** ɪd əd **~ing** ɪŋ **~s** s
deflection di 'flek ʃ^ə^n də- **~s** z
defloration ˌdiː flɔː 'reɪʃ ^ə^n ˌdef lɔː- ‖ ˌdef lə-, ˌdiːf- **~s** z
deflower ˌdiː 'flaʊ‿ə dɪ-, də- ‖ -'flaʊ‿^ə^r **~ed** d
  deflowering ˌdiː 'flaʊ‿ər ɪŋ dɪ-, də- ‖ -'flaʊ‿^ə^r ɪŋ **~s** z
Defoe di 'fəʊ də- ‖ -'foʊ
defog ˌdiː 'fɒg ◂ ‖ -'fɑːg -'fɔːg **~ged** d **~ger/s** ə/z ‖ ^ə^r/z **~ging** ɪŋ **~s** z
defoliant di 'fəʊl i‿ənt ˌdiː-, də- ‖ -'foʊl- **~s** s
defoli|ate di 'fəʊl i |eɪt ˌdiː-, də- ‖ -'foʊl- **~ated** eɪt ɪd -əd ‖ eɪt̬ əd **~ates** eɪts **~ating** eɪt ɪŋ ‖ eɪt̬ ɪŋ
defoliation di ˌfəʊl i 'eɪʃ ^ə^n də-, ˌdiː ˌfəʊl- ‖ -ˌfoʊl- **~s** z

deforest ˌdiː 'fɒr ɪst dɪ-, də-, -əst ‖ -'fɔːr- -'fɑːr- **~ed** ɪd əd **~ing** ɪŋ **~s** s
deforestation diː ˌfɒr ɪ 'steɪʃ ^ə^n dɪ-, də-, ˌdiː ˌfɒr-, -ə- ‖ -ˌfɔːr- -ˌfɑːr- **~s** z
deform di 'fɔːm də-, ˌdiː- ‖ -'fɔːrm **~ed** d **~ing** ɪŋ **~s** z
deformation ˌdiː fɔː 'meɪʃ ^ə^n ˌdef ə- ‖ ˌdiː fɔːr-, ˌdef ^ə^r- **~s** z
deformit|y di 'fɔːm ət |i də-, -ɪt- ‖ -'fɔːrm ət̬ **~ies** iz
DEFRA 'def rə
defrag *n* 'diː fræg
defrag *v* ˌdiː 'fræg **~ged** d **~ging** ɪŋ **~s** z
defrag|ment ˌdiː fræg 'ment **~mented** 'ment ɪd -əd ‖ 'ment̬- **~menting** 'ment ɪŋ ‖ 'ment̬ ɪŋ **~ments** 'ments
defraud di 'frɔːd də-, ˌdiː- ‖ -'frɑːd **~ed** ɪd əd **~er/s** ə/z ‖ ^ə^r/z **~ing** ɪŋ **~s** z
defraudation ˌdiː frɔː 'deɪʃ ^ə^n ‖ -frɑː- **~s** z
defray di 'freɪ də- **~ed** d **~ing** ɪŋ **~s** z
defrayal di 'freɪ əl də- **~s** z
De Freitas də 'freɪt əs ‖ -'freɪt̬-
defrock ˌdiː 'frɒk ‖ -'frɑːk **~ed** t **~ing** ɪŋ **~s** s
defrost ˌdiː 'frɒst dɪ-, də-, -'frɔːst ‖ -'frɔːst -'frɑːst **~ed** ɪd əd **~ing** ɪŋ **~s** s
deft deft **defter** 'deft ə ‖ -^ə^r **deftest** 'deft ɪst -əst **deftly** 'deft li **deftness** 'deft nəs -nɪs
defunct di 'fʌŋkt də-; 'diː fʌŋkt **~ness** nəs nɪs
defus|e ˌdiː 'fjuːz di-, də- —*Some people disapprove of the pronunciation* di-, *since it can lead to confusion with* diffuse (v). **~ed** d **~es** ɪz əz **~ing** ɪŋ
de|fy di |'faɪ də- **~fied** 'faɪd **~fier/s** 'faɪ‿ə/z ‖ 'faɪ‿^ə^r/z **~fies** 'faɪz **~fying** 'faɪ ɪŋ
degage, dégagé ˌdeɪ gɑː 'ʒeɪ -gæ-; ₍ˌ₎deɪ 'gɑːʒ eɪ
Deganwy dɪ 'gæn wi də- —*Welsh* [de 'ga nui, -nuɨ]
Degas 'deɪg ɑː ‖ də 'gɑː —*Fr* [də ga]
De Gaulle də 'gəʊl di-, →-'gɒʊl, -'gɔːl ‖ -'gɔːl -'goʊl —*Fr* [də gol]
degauss ˌdiː 'gaʊs -'gɔːs **~ed** t **~es** ɪz əz **~ing** ɪŋ
degemi|nate ˌdiː 'dʒem ɪ |neɪt -ə- **~nated** neɪt ɪd -əd ‖ neɪt̬ əd **~nates** neɪts **~nating** neɪt ɪŋ ‖ neɪt̬ ɪŋ
degemination ˌdiː ˌdʒem ɪ 'neɪʃ ^ə^n -ə- **~s** z
degenerac|y di 'dʒen ər‿əs |i də- **~ies** iz
degenerate *adj, n* di 'dʒen ər‿ət də-, -ɪt **~ly** li **~ness** nəs nɪs **~s** s
degene|rate *v* di 'dʒen ə |reɪt də- **~rated** reɪt ɪd -əd ‖ reɪt̬ əd **~rates** reɪts **~rating** reɪt ɪŋ ‖ reɪt̬ ɪŋ
degeneration di ˌdʒen ə 'reɪʃ ^ə^n də- **~s** z
degenerative di 'dʒen ər‿ət ɪv də-, -ə reɪt ɪv ‖ ət̬ ɪv -ə reɪt̬ ɪv **~ly** li
DeGeneres də 'dʒen ər əs di-
deglutition ˌdiː glu 'tɪʃ ^ə^n
degradability di ˌgreɪd ə 'bɪl ət i də-, -ɪt i ‖ -ət̬ i
degradable di 'greɪd əb ^ə^l də-
degradation ˌdeg rə 'deɪʃ ^ə^n **~s** z

egrad|e di ˈɡreɪd də- **~ed** ɪd əd **~es** z **~ing/ly** ɪŋ /li
e|grease ˌdiː |ˈɡriːs -ˈɡriːz **~greased** ˈɡriːst ˈɡriːzd **~greases** ˈɡriːs ɪz ˈɡriːz-, -əz **~greasing** ˈɡriːs ɪŋ ˈ ɡriːz-
egree di ˈɡriː də- **~s** z
e Havilland di ˈhæv ɪl ənd də-, -əl-
ehisc|e di ˈhɪs də- **~ed** t **~es** ɪz əz **~ing** ɪŋ
ehiscence di ˈhɪs ənts də-
ehiscent di ˈhɪs ənt də-
ehorn ˌdiː ˈhɔːn ‖ -ˈhɔːrn **~ed** d **~ing** ɪŋ **~s** z
ehra Dun ˌdeər ə ˈduːn ‖ ˌder-
ehumanis... —*see* **dehumaniz...**
ehumanization ₍ˌ₎diː ˌhjuːm ən aɪ ˈzeɪʃ ən -ən ɪ- ‖ -ən ə- -ˌjuːm-
ehumaniz|e ₍ˌ₎diː ˈhjuːm ə naɪz ‖ -ˈjuːm- **~ed** d **~es** ɪz əz **~ing** ɪŋ
ehumidi|fy ˌdiː hju ˈmɪd ɪ |faɪ §-ˈ-ə- ‖ ˌˌju- **~fied** faɪd **~fier/s** faɪ‿ə/z ‖ faɪ‿ər/z **~fies** faɪz **~fying** faɪ ɪŋ
ehydr|ate ₍ˌ₎diː ˈhaɪdr |eɪt ◂ -haɪ ˈdr|eɪt; ˈ· · · **~ated** eɪt ɪd -əd ‖ eɪţ əd **~ates** eɪts **~ating** eɪt ɪŋ ‖ eɪţ ɪŋ
ehydration ˌdiː haɪ ˈdreɪʃ ən **~s** z
ehydrogenase ˌdiː haɪ ˈdrɒdʒ ə neɪz ˌdiː ˈhaɪdr ədʒ-, -neɪs ‖ -ˈdrɑːdʒ-
eianira ˌdeɪ ə ˈnaɪər ə ˌdiː‿
eic|e, de-ic|e ˌdiː ˈaɪs **~ed** t **~es** ɪz əz **~ing** ɪŋ
eicide ˈdeɪ ɪ saɪd ˈdiː‿, -ə- **~s** z
eictic ˈdaɪkt ɪk ˈdeɪkt- —*Also sometimes, by misanalysis,* di ˈɪkt ɪk, deɪ- **~ally** əl‿i **~s** s
eification ˌdeɪ ɪf ɪ ˈkeɪʃ ən ˌdiː‿, ˌ-əf-, §-əˈ-- **~s** z
ei|fy ˈdeɪ ɪ |faɪ ˈdiː‿, -ə- **~fied** faɪd **~fier/s** faɪ‿ə/z ‖ faɪ‿ər/z **~fies** faɪz **~fying** faɪ ɪŋ
Deighton *(i)* ˈdeɪt ən, *(ii)* ˈdaɪt ən, *(iii)* ˈdiːt ən
deign deɪn *(= Dane)* **deigned** deɪnd **deigning** ˈdeɪn ɪŋ **deigns** deɪnz
Dei gratia ˌdeɪ iː ˈɡrɑːt i‿ə ˌdiː aɪ ˈɡreɪʃ-
Deimos ˈdeɪm ɒs ˈdaɪm- ‖ -ɑːs
deindustriali|sation, ~zation ˌdiː ɪn ˌdʌs tri‿əl aɪ ˈzeɪʃ ən -ɪˈ-- ‖ -əˈ--
deinonychus daɪ ˈnɒn ɪk əs ‖ -ˈnɑːn- **~es** ɪz əz
Deirdre ˈdɪədr i ‖ ˈdɪrdr i —*but in Ireland* -ə —*Ir* [ˈdʲerʲ dʲrʲe]
deism ˈdeɪ ˌɪz əm ˈdiː- ‖ ˈdiː- ˈdeɪ-
deist ˈdeɪ ɪst ˈdiː-, §-əst ‖ ˈdiː- ˈdeɪ- **~s** s

DEITY

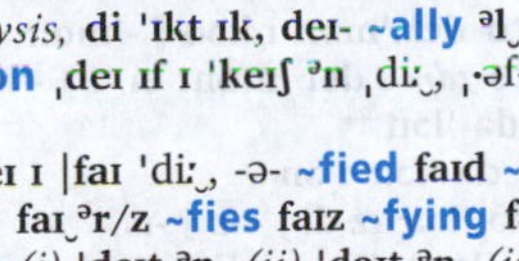

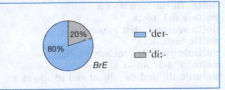

deit|y ˈdeɪ ət |i ˈdiː-, -ɪt- ‖ ˈdiː əţ |i ˈdeɪ- —*Preference poll, BrE:* ˈdeɪ- *80%,* ˈdiː- *20%.* **~ies** iz
deixis ˈdaɪks ɪs ˈdeɪks-, §-əs —*Also sometimes, by misanalysis,* di ˈɪks ɪs, deɪ-, §-əs.

deja vu, déjà vu ˌdeɪʒ ɑː ˈvuː -ˈvjuː *Fr* [de ʒa vy]
dejected di ˈdʒekt ɪd də-, -əd **~ly** li **~ness** nəs nɪs
dejection di ˈdʒek ʃən də- **~s** z
De Jong, De Jongh də ˈjɒŋ ‖ -ˈjɔːŋ -ˈjɑːŋ, -ˈdʒɔːŋ, -ˈdʒɑːŋ
de jure ₍ˌ₎deɪ ˈdʒʊər i di-, -ˈjʊər-, -eɪ ‖ ₍ˌ₎diː ˈdʒʊr i ₍ˌ₎deɪ ˈjʊr eɪ
de Keyser də ˈkaɪz ə ‖ -ər
Dekker ˈdek ə ‖ -ər
dekko ˈdek əʊ ‖ -oʊ **~s** z
de Klerk də ˈkleək ‖ -ˈkleərk —*Afrikaans* [də ˈklɛrk]
De Kooning də ˈkuːn ɪŋ
del, Del del
Delacour ˈdel ə kʊə -kɔː ‖ -kʊr
Delacourt ˈdel ə kɔːt ‖ -kɔːrt -koʊrt
Delacroix ˈdel ə krwɑː ˌ·ˈ· —*Fr* [də la krwa]
Delafield ˈdel ə fiːəld
Delagoa ˌdel ə ˈɡəʊ ə ◂ ‖ -ˈɡoʊ ə
ˌ**Dela**ˌ**goa** ˈ**Bay**
Delahaye ˈdel ə heɪ
de la Mare ˌdel ə ˈmeə də lɑː-; ˈdel ə meə ‖ -ˈmeər -ˈmæər
Delamere ˈdel ə mɪə ˌ· ·ˈ· ‖ -mɪr
Delancey də ˈlænts i
Delaney də ˈleɪn i dɪ-
Delano *(i)* ˈdel ə nəʊ ‖ -noʊ, *(ii)* də ˈleɪn əʊ ‖ -oʊ *-Franklin D~ Roosevelt was (i); the place in CA is (ii).*
De-La-Noy ˈdel ə nɔɪ
Delany də ˈleɪn i dɪ-
de la Renta ˌdel ə ˈrent ə dəl-
Delargy də ˈlɑːɡ i ‖ -ˈlɑːrɡ i
De La Rue, de la Rue ˌdel ə ˈruː dəl ə-; ˈdel ə ruː
delation di ˈleɪʃ ən də- **~s** z
Delaware ˈdel ə weə ‖ -wer -wær
De La Warr ˈdel ə weə ‖ -wer -wær
delay di ˈleɪ də- **~ed** d **~er/s** ə/z ‖ ər/z **~ing** ɪŋ **~s** z
delayed-action di ˌleɪd ˈæk ʃən ◂ də-
Delbert ˈdelb ət ‖ -ərt
Delbridge ˈdel brɪdʒ
del credere ˌdel ˈkreɪd ər i -ˈkred- **~s** z
Delderfield ˈdeld ə fiːəld ‖ -ər-
dele ˈdiːl iː -i **~d** d **~ing** ɪŋ **~s** z
delectab|le di ˈlekt əb |əl də- **~ly** li
delectation ˌdiː lek ˈteɪʃ ən
delegac|y ˈdel ɪɡ əs |i ˈ-əɡ- **~ies** iz
delegate *n* ˈdel ɪɡ ət -əɡ-, -ɪt; -ɪ ɡeɪt, -ə- **~s** s
dele|gate *v* ˈdel ɪ |ɡeɪt -ə- **~gated** ɡeɪt ɪd -əd ‖ ɡeɪţ əd **~gates** ɡeɪts **~gating** ɡeɪt ɪŋ ‖ ɡeɪţ ɪŋ
delegation ˌdel ɪ ˈɡeɪʃ ən -ə- **~s** z
de|lete di |ˈliːt də- **~leted** ˈliːt ɪd -əd ‖ ˈliːţ əd **~letes** ˈliːts **~leting** ˈliːt ɪŋ ‖ ˈliːţ ɪŋ
deleterious ˌdel ɪ ˈtɪər i‿əs ◂ ˌdiːl-, ˌ-ə- ‖ -ˈtɪr- **~ly** li **~ness** nəs nɪs
deletion di ˈliːʃ ən də- **~s** z
delf delf
Delfont ˈdel fɒnt ‖ -fɑːnt

D

delft, Delft delft
delftware 'delft weə ‖ -wer -wær
Delgado del 'gɑːd əʊ ‖ -oʊ
Delhi 'del i
deli 'del i **~s** z
Delia 'diːl i‿ə
Delian 'diːl i‿ən **~s** z
deliberate *adj* di 'lɪb ər‿ət də-, ɪt **~ly** li **~ness** nəs nɪs
delibe|rate *v* di 'lɪb ə |reɪt də- **~rated** reɪt ɪd -əd ‖ reɪţ əd **~rates** reɪts **~rating** reɪt ɪŋ ‖ reɪţ ɪŋ
deliberation di ˌlɪb ə 'reɪʃ ən də- **~s** z
deliberative di 'lɪb ər‿ət ɪv də- ‖ -ə reɪţ ɪv -ər‿əţ- **~ly** li **~ness** nəs nɪs
Delibes də 'liːb dɪ- —*Fr* [də lib]
delicac|y 'del ɪk əs |i '·ək- **~ies** iz
delicate 'del ɪk ət -ək-, -ɪt **~ly** li **~ness** nəs nɪs **~s** s
delicatessen ˌdel ɪk ə 'tes ən ˌ·ək- **~s** z
delicious di 'lɪʃ əs də- **~ly** li **~ness** nəs nɪs
de|light *n, v* di |'laɪt də- **~lighted** 'laɪt ɪd -əd ‖ 'laɪţ əd **~lighting** 'laɪt ɪŋ ‖ 'laɪţ ɪŋ **~lights** 'laɪts
delighted di 'laɪt ɪd də-, -əd ‖ -'laɪţ əd **~ly** li **~ness** nəs nɪs
delightful di 'laɪt fəl də-, -fʊl **~ly** ‿i **~ness** nəs nɪs
Delilah di 'laɪl ə də-
delim|it ₍ₗ₎diː 'lɪm |ɪt dɪ-, də-, §-ət ‖ -|ət **~ited** ɪt ɪd §ət-, -əd ‖ əţ əd **~iting** ɪt ɪŋ §ət- ‖ əţ ɪŋ **~its** ɪts §əts ‖ əts
delimi|tate di 'lɪm ɪ |teɪt də- **~tated** teɪt ɪd -əd ‖ teɪţ əd **~tates** teɪts **~tating** teɪt ɪŋ ‖ teɪţ ɪŋ
delimitation di ˌlɪm ɪ 'teɪʃ ən də- **~s** z
delimitative di 'lɪm ɪt ət ɪv də-, §-'ət-; -ɪ teɪt ɪv, -ə · · ‖ -ə teɪţ ɪv
deline|ate di 'lɪn i |eɪt də- **~ated** eɪt ɪd -əd ‖ eɪţ əd **~ates** eɪts **~ating** eɪt ɪŋ ‖ eɪţ ɪŋ
delineation di ˌlɪn i 'eɪʃ ən də- **~s** z
delineator di 'lɪn i eɪt ə də- ‖ -eɪţ ər **~s** z
delinquenc|y di 'lɪŋk wənts |i də- **~ies** iz
delinquent di 'lɪŋk wənt də- **~ly** li **~s** s
deliquesc|e ˌdel ɪ 'kwes -ə- **~ed** t **~es** ɪz əz **~ing** ɪŋ
deliquescence ˌdel ɪ 'kwes ənts -ə-
deliquescent ˌdel ɪ 'kwes ənt◂ -ə-
delirious di 'lɪr i‿əs də-, 'lɪər- —*Preference poll, BrE:* -'lɪr- *46%,* -'lɪər- *54% (those born since 1973: 80%).* **~ly** li **~ness** nəs nɪs
deliri|um di 'lɪr i‿|əm də-, 'lɪər- **~a** ə **~ums** əmz
deˌ**lirium 'tremens** 'triːm enz 'trem-, -ənz
De Lisle, De L'Isle də 'laɪəl
delist ˌdiː 'lɪst **~ed** ɪd əd **~ing** ɪŋ **~s** s
Delius 'diːl i‿əs
deliver di 'lɪv ə də- ‖ -ər **~ed** d **delivering** dɪ 'lɪv ər‿ɪŋ **~s** z
deliverability di ˌlɪv ər‿ə 'bɪl ət i də-, -ɪt i ‖ -əţ i
deliverable di 'lɪv ər‿əb əl də- **~s** z
deliverance di 'lɪv ər‿ənts də-

DELIRIOUS

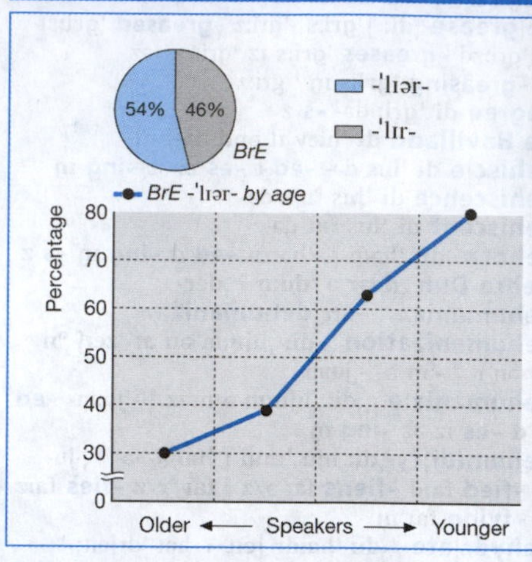

deliverer di 'lɪv ər‿ə də- ‖ -ər‿ər **~s** z
deliver|y di 'lɪv ər‿|i də- **~ies** iz
delivery|man di 'lɪv ər‿i |mæn də-, -mən **~men** men mən
dell, Dell del **dells, Dell's** delz
Della 'del ə
Deller 'del ə ‖ -ər
Dellums 'del əmz
Delmar, Del Mar del 'mɑː '·· ‖ 'del mɑːr ·'·
Delmarva del 'mɑːv ə ‖ -'mɑːrv ə
Delmonico del 'mɒn ɪ kəʊ ‖ -'mɑːn ɪ koʊ
Del Monte *tdmk* del 'mɒnt eɪ -i ‖ -'mɑːnt-
Deloitte də 'lɔɪt
Delorean də 'lɔːr i‿ən
Delores də 'lɔːr ɪz di-, -əz ‖ -ɪs
Delors də 'lɔː ‖ -'lɔːr —*Fr* [də lɔːʁ]
Delos 'diːl ɒs ‖ -ɑːs
de|louse ˌdiː |'laʊs -'laʊz **~loused** 'laʊst 'laʊzd **~louses** 'laʊs ɪz 'laʊz-, -əz **~lousing** 'laʊs ɪŋ 'laʊz-
Delph delf
Delphi 'delf aɪ -i —*Mod Gk* [ðel 'fi]
Delphian 'delf i‿ən
Delphic 'delf ɪk
Delphine del 'fiːn
delphinium del 'fɪn i‿əm **~s** z
Delphinus del 'faɪn əs
Delroy 'del rɔɪ
Delsey *tdmk* 'dels i
delta, Delta 'delt ə **~s** z
deltaic del 'teɪ ɪk
delta-winged ˌdelt ə 'wɪŋd◂
deltic 'delt ɪk
deltiology ˌdelt i 'ɒl ədʒ i ‖ -'ɑːl-
deltoid 'delt ɔɪd **~s** z
delud|e di 'luːd də-, -'ljuːd **~ed** ɪd əd **~es** z **~ing** ɪŋ
delug|e *n, v* 'del juːdʒ -juːʒ **~ed** d **~es** ɪz əz **~ing** ɪŋ
delusion di 'luːʒ ən də-, -'ljuːʒ- **~al** ‿əl **~s** z
delusive di 'luːs ɪv də-, -'ljuːs-, §-'luːz-, §-'ljuːz- **~ly** li **~ness** nəs nɪs

elusory di ˈluːs ər i də-, -ˈljuːs-, -ˈluːz-, -ˈljuːz-
eluxe, de luxe də ˈlʌks di-, -ˈlʊks, -ˈluːks —*Fr* [də lyks]
elve delv **delved** delvd **delver/s** ˈdelv ə/z ‖ -ᵊr/z **delves** delvz **delving** ˈdelv ɪŋ
elwyn ˈdel wɪn
elyn ˈdel ɪn
elyth ˈdel ɪθ
em dem —*or as* Democrat, Democratic
emagnetis... —*see* **demagnetiz...**
emagnetization ˌdiː ˌmæg nət aɪ ˈzeɪʃ ᵊn -ˌ.-ˈ-, -nɪt -ˈ-, -ɪˈ- ‖ -nət̬ ə-
emagnetiz|e ₍ₗ₎diː ˈmæg nə taɪz -nɪ- **~ed** d **~es** ɪz əz **~ing** ɪŋ
emagog ˈdem ə gɒg ‖ -gɑːg **~s** z
emagogic ˌdem ə ˈgɒg ɪk ◂ -ˈgɒdʒ- ‖ -ˈgɑːg- -ˈgɑːdʒ-, -ˈgoʊdʒ- **~ally** ᵊl‿i
emagogue ˈdem ə gɒg ‖ -gɑːg **~s** z
emagoguer|y ˈdem ə gɒg ər |i ˌ· ·ˈ·· ‖ -gɑːg ər |i **~ies** iz
emagogy ˈdem ə gɒg i -gɒdʒ- ‖ -gɑːg i -gɑːdʒ-, -goʊdʒ-
eman ˌdiː ˈmæn **~ned** d **~ning** ɪŋ **~s** z
emand *n, v* di ˈmɑːnd də-, §-ˈmænd ‖ -ˈmænd **~ed** ɪd əd **~ing/ly** ɪŋ /li **~s** z
e Manio də ˈmæn i əʊ ‖ -oʊ
emarc|ate ˈdiː mɑːk |eɪt ‖ di ˈmɑːrk |eɪt ˈdiː mɑːrk eɪt **~ated** eɪt ɪd -əd ‖ eɪt̬ əd **~ates** eɪts **~ating** eɪt ɪŋ ‖ eɪt̬ ɪŋ
emarcation ˌdiː mɑː ˈkeɪʃ ᵊn ‖ -mɑːr-
ˌ**demarˈcation diˌspute**, ˌ· ·ˈ··
emarcative di ˈmɑːk ət ɪv ˌdiː- ‖ -ˈmɑːrk ət̬ ɪv
emarcator ˈdiː mɑːk eɪt ə ‖ di ˈmɑːrk eɪt̬ ᵊr ˈdiː mɑːrk eɪt̬ ᵊr **~s** z
emarch|e, démarch|e ˈdeɪ mɑːʃ ˌ·ˈ· ‖ deɪ ˈmɑːrʃ dɪ- **~es** ɪz əz —*or as sing.* —*Fr* [de maʁʃ]
ematerialis... —*see* **dematerializ...**
ematerialization ˌdiː mə ˌtɪər i‿əl aɪ ˈzeɪʃ ᵊn -ɪˈ- ‖ -ˌtɪr i‿əl ə- **~s** z
ematerializ|e ˌdiː mə ˈtɪər i‿ə laɪz ‖ -ˈtɪr- **~ed** d **~es** ɪz əz **~ing** ɪŋ
eme diːm **demes** diːmz
emean di ˈmiːn də- **~ed** d **~ing** ɪŋ **~s** z
emeanor, demeanour di ˈmiːn ə də- ‖ -ᵊr **~s** z
de|ment *v, n* di |ˈment də- **~mented** ˈment ɪd -əd ‖ ˈment̬ əd **~menting** ˈment ɪŋ ‖ ˈment̬ ɪŋ **~ments** ˈments
demented di ˈment ɪd də-, ₍ₗ₎diː-, -əd ‖ -ˈment̬ əd **~ly** li **~ness** nəs nɪs
dementia di ˈmentʃ ə də-, ₍ₗ₎diː-, -ˈmentʃ i‿ə, -ˈment i‿ə **~s** z
deˌ**mentia ˈpraecox**
demerara, D~ ˌdem ə ˈreər ə ◂ -ˈrɑːr- ‖ -ˈrer ə -ˈrɑːr ə
ˌ**demeˌrara ˈsugar**
demerg|e ˌdiː ˈmɜːdʒ ‖ -mɜːdʒ **~ed** d **~es** ɪz əz **~ing** ɪŋ
demerger ˌdiː ˈmɜːdʒ ə dɪ ˈ·· ‖ -ˈmɜːdʒ ᵊr **~s** z
demerit ₍ₗ₎diː ˈmer ɪt §-ət **~s** s —*but, with contrastive stress,* (ˌmerits and) ˈdeˌmerits

Demerol *tdmk* ˈdem ə rɒl ‖ -roʊl -rɑːl, -rɔːl
demersal di ˈmɜːs ᵊl də- ‖ -ˈmɜːs-
demesne di ˈmeɪn də-, -ˈmiːn **~s** z
Demeter di ˈmiːt ə də- ‖ -ˈmiːt̬ ᵊr
Demetrius di ˈmiːtr i‿əs də-
demi- ¦dem i
demie... —*see* **demy**
demigod ˈdem i gɒd ‖ -gɑːd **~s** z
demigoddess ˈdem i ˌgɒd es -ɪs, -əs ‖ -ˌgɑːd əs **~es** ɪz əz
demijohn ˈdem i dʒɒn ‖ -dʒɑːn **~s** z
demilitaris... —*see* **demilitariz...**
demilitarization ˌdiː ˌmɪl ɪt‿ər aɪ ˈzeɪʃ ᵊn ˌ·ˌ··, -ət‿ər aɪ-, -ɪˈ·- ‖ -ət̬‿ər ə- **~s** z
demilitariz|e ₍ₗ₎diː ˈmɪl ɪt ə raɪz -ˈ·ət- **~ed** d **~es** ɪz əz **~ing** ɪŋ
de Mille də ˈmɪl
demilune ˈdem i luːn -ljuːn **~s** z
demimondaine ˌdem i mɒn ˈdeɪn -ˈmɒnd eɪn ‖ -mɑːn ˈdeɪn -ˈmɑːnd eɪn —*Fr* [də mi mɔ̃ dɛn] **~s** z
demimonde ˌdem i ˈmɒnd ˈ· · · ‖ ˈdem i mɑːnd —*Fr* [də mi mɔ̃ːd]
demin|e ˌdiː ˈmaɪn **~ed** d **~es** z **~ing** ɪŋ
de minimis ₍ₗ₎deɪ ˈmɪn ɪ miːs -ə-
demis|e di ˈmaɪz də-, -ˈmiːz **~ed** d **~es** ɪz əz **~ing** ɪŋ
demisemiquaver ˈdem i sem i ˌkweɪv ə ˌ· ·ˈ·· ‖ -ᵊr **~s** z
demist ˌdiː ˈmɪst **~ed** ɪd əd **~ing** ɪŋ **~s** s
demister ˌdiː ˈmɪst ə ‖ -ᵊr **~s** z
demitasse ˈdem i tæs -tɑːs, ˌ· ·ˈ· —*Fr* [də mi tas]
demiurge ˈdem i ɜːdʒ ˈdiːm- ‖ -ɜːdʒ
demo ˈdem əʊ ‖ -oʊ **~s** z
demo- *comb. form*
with stress-neutral suffix ¦dem ə ¦diːm ə — **demographic** ˌdem ə ˈgræf ɪk ◂ ˌdiːm-
with stress-imposing suffix dɪ ˈmɒ+ də-, diː- ‖ -ˈmɑː+ — **demography** dɪ ˈmɒg rəf i də-, diː- ‖ -ˈmɑːg-
demob ₍ₗ₎diː ˈmɒb ‖ -ˈmɑːb **~bed** d **~bing** ɪŋ **~s** z
demobilis... —*see* **demobiliz...**
demobilization di ˌməʊb əl aɪ ˈzeɪʃ ᵊn ₍ₗ₎diː-, -ɪl aɪ-, -ɪˈ- ‖ -ˌmoʊb əl ə- **~s** z
demobiliz|e di ˈməʊb ə laɪz ₍ₗ₎diː-, -ɪ-, -ᵊl aɪz ‖ -ˈmoʊb- **~ed** d **~es** ɪz əz **~ing** ɪŋ
democrac|y di ˈmɒk rəs |i də- ‖ -ˈmɑːk- **~ies** iz
democrat ˈdem ə kræt **~s** s
democratic ˌdem ə ˈkræt ɪk ◂ ‖ -ˈkræt̬ ɪk ◂ **~ally** ᵊl‿i
democratis... —*see* **democratiz...**
democratization di ˌmɒk rət aɪ ˈzeɪʃ ᵊn də-, -ɪˈ- ‖ -ˌmɑːk rət̬ ə-
democratiz|e di ˈmɒk rə taɪz də- ‖ -ˈmɑːk- **~ed** d **~es** ɪz əz **~ing** ɪŋ
Democritus di ˈmɒk rɪt əs də-, -rət- ‖ -ˈmɑːk rət̬ əs
demode, démodé ₍ₗ₎deɪ ˈməʊd eɪ ‖ ˌdeɪ moʊ ˈdeɪ —*Fr* [de mɔ de]

demodu|late ˌdiː ˈmɒd ju |leɪt di-, -ˈmɒdʒ u- ‖ -ˈmɑːdʒ ə- **~lated** leɪt ɪd -əd ‖ leɪţ əd **~lates** leɪts **~lating** leɪt ɪŋ ‖ leɪţ ɪŋ

demodulation ˌdiː ˌmɒd ju ˈleɪʃ ᵊn -ˌmɒdʒ u-; di ˌmɒd- ‖ -ˌmɑːdʒ ə- dɪ ˌmɑːdʒ ə- **~s** z

demodulator ˌdiː ˈmɒd ju leɪt ə di-, -ˈmɒdʒ u- ‖ -ˈmɑːdʒ ə leɪţ ᵊr **~s** z

demographer di ˈmɒg rəf ə də- ‖ -ˈmɑːg rəf ᵊr **~s** z

demographic ˌdem ə ˈgræf ɪk ◂ ˌdiːm- **~ally** ᵊl‿i

demography di ˈmɒg rəf i də- ‖ -ˈmɑːg-

demoiselle ˌdem wɑː ˈzel -wə- —*Fr* [də mwa zɛl] **~s** z —*or as sing.*

demolish di ˈmɒl ɪʃ də- ‖ -ˈmɑːl- **~ed** t **~es** ɪz əz **~ing** ɪŋ

demolition ˌdem ə ˈlɪʃ ᵊn ˌdiːm- **~s** z

demolitionist ˌdem ə ˈlɪʃ ᵊn‿ɪst ˌdiːm-, §‿əst **~s** s

demon ˈdiːm ən **~s** z

demonetis|e, demonetiz|e (ˌ)diː ˈmʌn ɪ taɪz -ˈmɒn-, -ə- ‖ -ˈmɑːn- -ˈmʌn- **~ed** d **~es** ɪz əz **~ing** ɪŋ

demoniac di ˈməʊn i æk də- ‖ -ˈmoʊn- **~s** s

demoniacal ˌdiːm əʊ ˈnaɪ‿ək ᵊl ◂ ‖ ˌ-ə- **~ly** ‿i

demonic di ˈmɒn ɪk də- ‖ -ˈmɑːn- **~ally** ᵊl‿i

demonis... —*see* **demoniz...**

demonization ˌdiːm ən aɪ ˈzeɪʃ ᵊn -ɪˈ-- ‖ -əˈ-

demoniz|e ˈdiːm ən aɪz **~ed** d **~es** ɪz əz **~ing** ɪŋ

demonology ˌdiːm ə ˈnɒl ədʒ i ‖ -ˈnɑːl-

demonstrability di ˌmɒnᵗs trə ˈbɪl ət i də-, -ɪt i; ˈdem ənᵗs- ‖ di ˌmɑːnᵗs trə ˈbɪl əţ i

DEMONSTRABLE

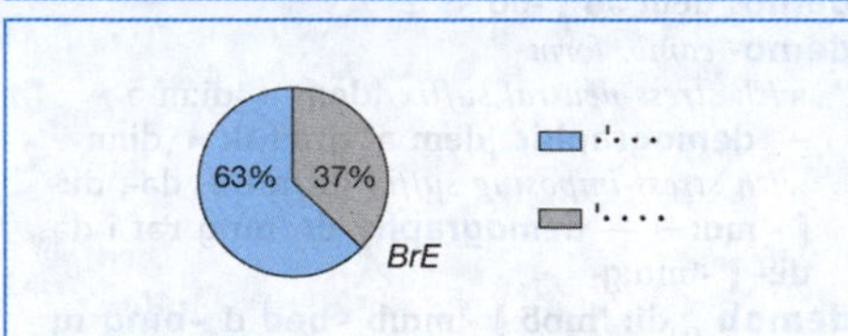

demonstrab|le di ˈmɒnᵗs trəb |ᵊl də-; ˈdem ənᵗs- ‖ dɪ ˈmɑːnᵗs- — *Preference poll, BrE:* ·ˈ·· 63%, ˈ··· 37%. **~ly** li

demon|strate ˈdem ən |streɪt **~strated** streɪt ɪd -əd ‖ streɪţ əd **~strates** streɪts **~strating** streɪt ɪŋ ‖ streɪţ ɪŋ

demonstration ˌdem ən ˈstreɪʃ ᵊn **~s** z

demonstrative di ˈmɒnᵗs trət ɪv də- ‖ -ˈmɑːnᵗs trəţ ɪv **~ly** li **~ness** nəs nɪs

demonstrator ˈdem ən streɪt ə ‖ -streɪţ ᵊr **~s** z

de Montfort də ˈmɒnt fət -fɔːt ‖ di ˈmɑːnt fᵊrt

demoralis... —*see* **demoraliz...**

demoralization di ˌmɒr əl aɪ ˈzeɪʃ ᵊn ˌdiːˌ--, -ɪˈ-- ‖ di ˌmɔːr əl ə- -ˌmɑːr-

demoraliz|e di ˈmɒr ə laɪz (ˌ)diː- ‖ -ˈmɔːr- -ˈmɑːr- **~ed** d **~es** ɪz əz **~ing** ɪŋ

Demos ˈdiːm ɒs ‖ -ɑːs

demosaic ˌdiː məʊ ˈzeɪ ɪk ‖ -moʊ- **~ed, ~ked** t **~ing, ~king** ɪŋ **~s** s

Demosthenes di ˈmɒsθ ə niːz də-, -ɪ- ‖ -ˈmɑːsθ-

de|mote ˌdiː |ˈməʊt dɪ-, də- ‖ -|ˈmoʊt **~moted** ˈməʊt ɪd -əd ‖ ˈmoʊţ əd **~motes** ˈməʊts ‖ ˈmoʊts **~moting** ˈməʊt ɪŋ ‖ ˈmoʊţ ɪŋ

demotic di ˈmɒt ɪk də- ‖ -ˈmɑːţ ɪk

demotion ˌdiː ˈməʊʃ ᵊn dɪ-, də- ‖ -ˈmoʊʃ ᵊn **~s** z

demoti|vate ˌdiː ˈməʊt ɪ |veɪt -ə- ‖ -ˈmoʊţ ə- **~vated** veɪt ɪd -əd ‖ veɪţ əd **~vates** veɪts **~vating** veɪt ɪŋ ‖ veɪţ ɪŋ

demotivation ˌdiː ˌməʊt ɪ ˈveɪʃ ᵊn -ə- ‖ diː ˌmoʊţ ə-

Dempsey ˈdem*p*s i

Dempster, d~ ˈdem*p*st ə ‖ -ᵊr

demulcent di ˈmʌls ənt də- **~s** s

de|mur *v, n* di |ˈmɜː də- ‖ -|ˈmɝː **~murred** ˈmɜːd ‖ ˈmɝːd **~murring** ˈmɜːr ɪŋ ‖ ˈmɝː ɪŋ **~murs** ˈmɜːz ‖ ˈmɝːz

de|mure di |ˈmjʊə də- ‖ -|ˈmjʊᵊr **~murer** ˈmjʊər ə ‖ ˈmjʊr ᵊr **~murest** ˈmjʊər ɪst -əst ‖ ˈmjʊr əst **~murely** ˈmjʊə li ‖ ˈmjʊr li **~mureness** ˈmjʊə nəs nɪs ‖ ˈmjʊr-

demurr... —*see* **demur**

demurrage di ˈmʌr ɪdʒ də- ‖ -ˈmɝː-

demurral di ˈmʌr əl də- ‖ -ˈmɝː- **~s** z

demurrer *'objector'* di ˈmɜːr ə də- ‖ -ˈmɝː ᵊr

demurrer *'objection'* di ˈmʌr ə də- ‖ -ˈmɝː ᵊr

demutualization, demutualisation ˌdiː ˌmjuːtʃ u‿əl aɪ ˈzeɪʃ ᵊn -ɪˈ-· ‖ -əˈ-·

demutualiz|e, demutualis|e ˌdiː ˈmjuːtʃ u‿ə laɪz **~ed** d **~es** ɪz əz **~ing** ɪŋ

de|my di |ˈmaɪ də- **~mies** ˈmaɪz

demystification ˌdiː ˌmɪst ɪf ɪ ˈkeɪʃ ᵊn ˌ-ˌ--, -əf ɪ-, §-əˈ-- ‖ diː ˌmɪst-

demysti|fy (ˌ)diː ˈmɪst ɪ |faɪ -ə- **~fied** faɪd **~fier/s** faɪ‿ə/z ‖ faɪ‿ᵊr/z **~fies** faɪz **~fying** faɪ ɪŋ

demythologis... —*see* **demythologiz...**

demythologization ˌdiː mɪ ˌθɒl ədʒ aɪ ˈzeɪʃ ᵊn ˌmə-, -ɪˈ-- ‖ -ˌθɑːl ədʒ ə-

demythologiz|e ˌdiː mɪ ˈθɒl ə dʒaɪz ˌmə- ‖ -ˈθɑːl- **~ed** d **~es** ɪz əz **~ing** ɪŋ

den, Den den **dens, Den's** denz

Dena ˈdiːn ə

Denaby ˈden əb i

Denali də ˈnɑːl i di-

denari|us di ˈneər i‿əs də-, -ˈnɑːr- ‖ -ˈner- -ˈnær- **~i** aɪ iː

denary ˈdiːn ər i ˈden-

denationalis... —*see* **denationaliz...**

denationalization ˌdiː ˌnæʃ ᵊn‿əl aɪ ˈzeɪʃ ᵊn ·ˌ·-, -ɪˈ-- ‖ diː ˌnæʃ ᵊn‿əl ə- **~s** z

denationaliz|e (ˌ)diː ˈnæʃ ᵊn‿ə laɪz əl aɪz **~ed** d **~es** ɪz əz **~ing** ɪŋ

denaturalization, denaturalisation ˌdiː ˌnætʃ ᵊr‿ə laɪ ˈzeɪʃ ᵊn -ᵊr‿əl aɪ-, -ᵊr‿əl ɪ- ‖ -ᵊr‿əl ə-

denaturaliz|e, denaturalis|e ˌdiː ˈnætʃ ᵊr‿ə laɪz ‿əl aɪz **~ed** d **~es** ɪz əz **~ing** ɪŋ

enature (ˌ)diː ˈneɪtʃ ə ‖ -ᵊr ~d d ~s z
denaturing (ˌ)diː ˈneɪtʃ ər ɪŋ
enaturiz|e (ˌ)diː ˈneɪtʃ ə raɪz ~ed d ~es ɪz əz ~ing ɪŋ
enbigh, Denby ˈden bi →ˈdem-
ench dentʃ
endrite ˈdendr aɪt ~s s
endritic (ˌ)den ˈdrɪt ɪk ‖ -ˈdrɪţ ɪk ~ally ᵊl‿i
endrochronology ˌdendr əʊ krə ˈnɒl ədʒ i ˌ· ·krɒ- ‖ -oʊ krə ˈnɑːl-
endrogram ˈdendr ə græm ~s z
endroid ˈdendr ɔɪd
endrology den ˈdrɒl ədʒ i ‖ -ˈdrɑːl-
ene, Dene *British name* diːn **denes** diːnz
ˈdene hole
ene, Déné *Canadian indigenous people* ˈden i -eɪ
eneb ˈden eb
enebola di ˈneb əl ə də-, de-
engue ˈdeŋ gi -geɪ
eng Xiaoping ˌdʌŋ ʃaʊ ˈpɪŋ ˌdeŋ- —*Chi* Dēng Xiǎopíng [^{1}təŋ ^{3}ɕjɐu ^{2}pʰiŋ]
en Haag den ˈhɑːg dən- —*Dutch* [den ˈhaːx]
enham, Denholm, Denholme ˈden əm —*but Denholme, W.Yks., is usually* -hɒlm ‖ -hoʊlm
eniable di ˈnaɪ‿əb ᵊl
enial di ˈnaɪ‿əl də-, §diː- ~s z
enie... —*see* **deny**
enier *measure of fineness* ˈden i‿ə -eɪ ‖ ˈden jᵊr
enier *coin* ˈden i‿ə -eɪ; də ˈnɪə ‖ də ˈnɪᵊr —*Fr* [də nje] ~s z
enier *'one that denies'* di ˈnaɪ‿ə də- ‖ -ˈnaɪ‿ᵊr ~s z
eni|grate ˈden ɪ |greɪt -ə-; ˈdiː naɪ ˌ|greɪt ~grated greɪt ɪd -əd ‖ greɪţ əd ~grates greɪts ~grating greɪt ɪŋ ‖ greɪţ ɪŋ
enigration ˌden ɪ ˈgreɪʃ ᵊn -ə-; ˌdiː naɪ- ~s z
enigratory ˌden ɪ ˈgreɪt ər i ◂ ˌ·ə-; ˈ· · · · · ‖ ˈden ɪg rə tɔːr i -toʊr i (*)
enim ˈden ɪm -əm ~ed d ~s z
e Niro də ˈnɪər əʊ ‖ -ˈnɪr oʊ
enis ˈden ɪs §-əs ~'s ɪz əz
enise də ˈniːz de-, di-, -ˈniːs
enison ˈden ɪs ən -əs-
enitrification ˌdiː ˌnaɪtr ɪf ɪ ˈkeɪʃ ᵊn -ˌ·əf-, -əˈ· ·
enitri|fy ˌdiː ˈnaɪtr ɪ |faɪ -ə- ~fied faɪd ~fies faɪz ~fying faɪ ɪŋ
enizen ˈden ɪz ən -əz- ~s z
enmark ˈden mɑːk →ˈdem- ‖ -mɑːrk
enne den
ennie ˈden i
enning ˈden ɪŋ
ennis ˈden ɪs §-əs
ennison ˈden ɪs ən §-əs-
enny ˈden i
enominable di ˈnɒm ɪn əb ᵊl də-, -ˈ·ən- ‖ -ˈnɑːm-
enominate *adj* di ˈnɒm ɪn ət də-, -ən-, -ɪt; -ɪ neɪt, -ə- ‖ -ˈnɑːm-

denomi|nate *v* di ˈnɒm ɪ |neɪt də-, -ə- ‖ -ˈnɑːm- ~nated neɪt ɪd -əd ‖ neɪţ əd ~nates neɪts ~nating neɪt ɪŋ ‖ neɪţ ɪŋ
denomination di ˌnɒm ɪ ˈneɪʃ ᵊn də-, -ə- ‖ -ˌnɑːm- ~s z
denominational di ˌnɒm ɪ ˈneɪʃ ᵊn əl ◂ də-, -ˌ·ə- ‖ -ˌnɑːm- ~ism ˌɪz əm ~ly i
denominative di ˈnɒm ɪn ət ɪv ˌdiː-, -ən‿ət- ‖ -ˈnɑːm ən‿əţ ɪv ~s z
denominator di ˈnɒm ɪ neɪt ə də-, -ˈ·ə- ‖ -ˈnɑːm ə neɪţ ᵊr ~s z
denotation ˌdiː nəʊ ˈteɪʃ ᵊn ‖ -noʊ- ~s z
denotative di ˈnəʊt ət ɪv ˌdiː-, də-; ˈdiː nəʊ teɪt ɪv ‖ ˈdiː noʊ teɪţ ɪv di ˈnoʊţ əţ ɪv ~ly li
de|note di |ˈnəʊt də- ‖ -|ˈnoʊt ~noted ˈnəʊt ɪd -əd ‖ ˈnoʊţ əd ~notes ˈnəʊts ‖ ˈnoʊts ~noting ˈnəʊt ɪŋ ‖ ˈnoʊţ ɪŋ
denouement, dénouement deɪ ˈnuː mɒ̃ dɪ-, də- ‖ ˌdeɪ nuː ˈmɑ̃ː —*Fr* [de nu mɑ̃] ~s z —*or as sing.*
denounc|e di ˈnaʊnᵗs də- ~ed t ~er/s ə/z ‖ -ᵊr/z ~es ɪz əz ~ing ɪŋ
de novo (ˌ)deɪ ˈnəʊv əʊ diː-, dɪ-, də ‖ -ˈnoʊv oʊ
Denpasar den ˈpæs ɑː →dem-, -ˈpɑːs- ‖ -ɑːr
dense denᵗs **denser** ˈdenᵗs ə ‖ -ᵊr **densest** ˈdenᵗs ɪst -əst **densely** ˈdenᵗs li **denseness** ˈdenᵗs nəs -nɪs
Denselow ˈdenz ə ləʊ ‖ -loʊ
densit|y ˈdenᵗs ət |i -ɪt- ‖ -əţ i ~ies iz
dent, Dent dent **dented** ˈdent ɪd -əd ‖ ˈdenţ əd **denting** ˈdent ɪŋ ‖ ˈdenţ ɪŋ **dents** dents
dental ˈdent ᵊl ‖ ˈdenţ ᵊl ~ly i ~s z
ˌ**dental ˈfloss**; ˌ**dental ˈsurgeon**, ˈ· · ˌ· ·
dentate ˈdent eɪt ~ly li
denticle ˈdent ɪk ᵊl ‖ ˈdenţ- ~s z
denticulate den ˈtɪk jʊl ət -jəl-, -ɪt; -ju leɪt, -jə- ‖ -jəl ət ~ly li
dentiform ˈdent ɪ fɔːm §-ə- ‖ ˈdenţ ə fɔːrm
dentifric|e ˈdent ɪ frɪs -ə-, §-frəs ‖ ˈdenţə- ~es ɪz əz
dentil ˈdent ɪl -ᵊl ‖ ˈdenţ ᵊl ~s z
dentilabial ˌdent i ˈleɪb i‿əl ◂ ‖ ˌdenţ- ~s z
dentilingual ˌdent i ˈlɪŋ gwəl ◂ -ˈlɪŋ gju‿əl ‖ ˌdenţ- ~s z
dentin ˈdent ɪn §-ən
dentine ˈdent iːn ˌden ˈtiːn
dentist ˈdent ɪst §-əst ‖ ˈdenţ əst ~s s
dentistry ˈdent ɪst ri -əst- ‖ ˈdenţ-
dentition den ˈtɪʃ ᵊn
Denton ˈdent ən ‖ ᵊn
D'Entrecasteaux ˌdɒntr ə kæ ˈstəʊ ◂ ˌ· ·ˈkæst əʊ ‖ ˌdɑːntr ə kæ ˈstoʊ ◂ ˌ· ·ˈkæst oʊ —*Fr* [dɑ̃ tʁə ka sto]
denture ˈdentʃ ə ‖ -ᵊr ~s z
denudation ˌdiː nju ˈdeɪʃ ᵊn §-nu-; ˌden ju- ‖ -nu- -nju- ~s z
denud|e di ˈnjuːd də-, §-ˈnuːd ‖ -ˈnuːd -ˈnjuːd ~ed ɪd əd ~es z ~ing ɪŋ
denumerability di ˌnjuːm ər‿ə ˈbɪl ət i də-, §-ˌnuːm- ‖ -ˌnuːm ər‿ə ˈbɪl əţ i -ˌnjuːm-

denumerab|le di ˈnjuːm ər‿əb |əl də-, §-ˈnuːm- ‖ -ˈnuːm- -ˈnjuːm- **~ly** li

denunciation di ˌnʌnts i ˈeɪʃ ən də- **~s** z

denunciatory di ˈnʌnts i‿ət‿ər i də-, -ˈnʌntʃ- ‖ ‿ə tɔːr i -tour-

Denver ˈden və ‖ -vər

de|ny di |ˈnaɪ də- **~nied** ˈnaɪd **~nies** ˈnaɪz **~nying** ˈnaɪ ɪŋ

Denys ˈden ɪs §-əs

Denzil ˈdenz əl -ɪl

Deo ˈdeɪ əʊ ˈdiː- ‖ -oʊ —*See also phrases with this word*

deoch an doris, deoch an doruis ˌdɒx ən ˈdɒr ɪs ˌdjɒx-, -əs ‖ —

deodand ˈdiː əʊ dænd ‖ -ə- **~s** z

deodar ˈdiː əʊ dɑː ‖ -ə dɑːr **~s** z

deodorant di ˈəʊd‿ər ənt ‖ -ˈoʊd‿ **~s** s

deodoris|e, deodoriz|e di ˈəʊd ə raɪz -ər aɪz ‖ -ˈoʊd- **~ed** d **~er/s** ə/z ‖ -ər/z **~es** ɪz əz **~ing** ɪŋ

deo gratias ˌdeɪ əʊ ˈgrɑːt i‿əs ˌdiː-, -æs, -ɑːs ‖ ˌ·oʊ-

deontic di ˈɒnt ɪk ‖ -ˈɑːnt̬-

deontological di ˌɒnt ə ˈlɒdʒ ɪk əl ◂ ˌdiː- ‖ -ˌɑːnt ə ˈlɑːdʒ- **~ly** ‿i

deontology ˌdiː ɒn ˈtɒl ədʒ i ‖ -ɑːn ˈtɑːl-

deo volente ˌdeɪ əʊ və ˈlent i ˌdiː-, -vɒˈ-, -eɪ ‖ ˌ·oʊ-

deoxy- |diː ɒks i di |ɒks i ‖ di |ɑːks i—
deoxycorticosterone ˌdiː ɒks i ˌkɔːt ɪ kəʊ ˈstɪər əʊn di ˌɒks-, -ˈkɒst ə rəʊn ‖ di ˌɑːks i ˌkɔːrt̬ ɪ ˈkɑːst ə roʊn -ˈkoʊst-

deoxyge|nate ˌdiː ˈɒks ɪdʒ ə |neɪt di-, §-ˈ·ədʒ-; ˌdiː ɒk ˈsɪdʒ- ‖ -ˈɑːks- **~nated** neɪt ɪd -əd ‖ neɪt̬ əd **~nates** neɪts **~nating** neɪt ɪŋ ‖ neɪt̬ ɪŋ

deoxyribonucleic ˌdiː ɒks i ˌraɪb əʊ nju ˈkliː ɪk ◂ di ˌɒks-, -ˈkleɪ- ‖ di ˌɑːks i ˌraɪb oʊ nu- -njuˈ--, -ˈkleɪ-
ˌdeoxy ˌribonu ˌcleic ˈacid

dep —*see* **depart, departure**

Depardieu ˈdep ɑː djɜː ˌ· ·ˈ· ‖ -ɑːr ˈdjʌ —*Fr* [də paʁ djø]

de|part di |ˈpɑːt də- ‖ -|ˈpɑːrt **~parted** ˈpɑːt ɪd -əd ‖ ˈpɑːrt̬ əd **~parts** ˈpɑːts ‖ ˈpɑːrts **~parting** ˈpɑːt ɪŋ ‖ ˈpɑːrt̬ ɪŋ

department di ˈpɑːt mənt də- ‖ -ˈpɑːrt- **~s** s
deˈpartment store

departmental ˌdiː pɑːt ˈment əl ◂ di ˌpɑːt-, də- ‖ ˌdiː pɑːrt ˈment̬ əl di ˌpɑːrt- **~ly** i

departmentaliz|e, departmentalis|e ˌdiː pɑːt ˈment ə laɪz di ˌpɑːt-, də ˌpɑːt-, -əl aɪz ‖ ˌdiː pɑːrt ˈment̬ əl aɪz **~ed** d **~es** ɪz əz **~ing** ɪŋ

departure di ˈpɑːtʃ ə də- ‖ -ˈpɑːrtʃ ər **~s** z
deˈparture lounge; **deˈparture time**

Depeche Mode di ˌpeʃ ˈməʊd də- ‖ -ˈmoʊd

depend di ˈpend də- **~ed** ɪd əd **~ing** ɪŋ **~s** z

dependability di ˌpend ə ˈbɪl ət i də-, -ɪt i ‖ -ət̬ i

dependab|le di ˈpend əb |əl də- **~ly** li

dependanc... —*see* **dependenc...**

dependant di ˈpend ənt də- **~s** s

dependence di ˈpend ənts də- **~es** ɪz əz

dependenc|y di ˈpend ənts |i də- **~ies** iz

dependent di ˈpend ənt də- **~s** s

depict di ˈpɪkt də- **~ed** ɪd əd **~ing** ɪŋ **~s** s

depiction di ˈpɪk ʃən də- **~s** z

depi|late ˈdep ɪ |leɪt -ə- **~lated** leɪt ɪd -əd ‖ leɪt̬ əd **~lates** leɪts **~lating** leɪt ɪŋ ‖ leɪt̬ ɪŋ

depilation ˌdep ɪ ˈleɪʃ ən -ə-

depilator|y di ˈpɪl ət‿ər |i də- ‖ -ə tɔːr |i -tour i **~ies** iz

deplan|e ₍ˌ₎diː ˈpleɪn **~ed** d **~es** z **~ing** ɪŋ

de|plete di |ˈpliːt də- **~pleted** ˈpliːt ɪd -əd ‖ ˈpliːt̬ əd **~pletes** ˈpliːts **~pleting** ˈpliːt ɪŋ ‖ ˈpliːt̬ ɪŋ

depletion di ˈpliːʃ ən də- **~s** z

deplorab|le di ˈplɔːr əb |əl də- ‖ -ˈplour- **~ly** li

deplore di ˈplɔː də- ‖ -ˈplɔːr -ˈplour **~d** d **~s** z
deploring di ˈplɔːr ɪŋ də- ‖ -ˈplour-

deploy di ˈplɔɪ də- **~ed** d **~ing** ɪŋ **~ment** mənt **~s** z

de-policing, depolicing ˌdiː pə ˈliːs ɪŋ

depoliticization, depoliticisation ˌdiː pə ˌlɪt ɪ saɪ ˈzeɪʃ ən -ˌ·ə-, -sɪˈ·- ‖ -ˌlɪt̬ əs ə-

depoliticiz|e, depoliticis|e ˌdiː pə ˈlɪt ɪ saɪz -ə- ‖ -ˈlɪt̬ ə- **~ed** d **~es** ɪz əz **~ing** ɪŋ

deponent di ˈpəʊn ənt də- ‖ -ˈpoʊn- **~s** s

Depo-Provera *tdmk* ˌdep əʊ prəʊ ˈvɪər ə ‖ -oʊ proʊ ˈver ə

depopu|late ₍ˌ₎diː ˈpɒp ju |leɪt -jə- ‖ -ˈpɑːp jə- **~lated** leɪt ɪd -əd ‖ leɪt̬ əd **~lates** leɪts **~lating** leɪt ɪŋ ‖ leɪt̬ ɪŋ

depopulation ˌdiː ˌpɒp ju ˈleɪʃ ən ·ˌ·-, -jəˈ-- ‖ diː ˌpɑːp jə-

de|port di |ˈpɔːt də- ‖ -|ˈpɔːrt -ˈpourt **~ported** ˈpɔːt ɪd -əd ‖ ˈpɔːrt̬ əd ˈpourt̬- **~porting** ˈpɔːt ɪŋ ‖ ˈpɔːrt̬ ɪŋ ˈpourt̬- **~ports** ˈpɔːts ‖ ˈpɔːrts ˈpourts

deportation ˌdiː pɔː ˈteɪʃ ən ‖ -pɔːr- -pər-, -pour- **~s** z

deportee ˌdiː pɔː ˈtiː ‖ -pɔːr- -pour- **~s** z

deportment di ˈpɔːt mənt də- ‖ -ˈpɔːrt- -ˈpourt-

depos|e di ˈpəʊz də- ‖ -ˈpoʊz **~ed** d **~es** ɪz əz **~ing** ɪŋ

depos|it di ˈpɒz |ɪt də-, §-ət ‖ -ˈpɑːz |ət **~ited** ɪt ɪd §ət-, -əd ‖ ət̬ əd **~iting** ɪt ɪŋ §ət- ‖ ət̬ ɪŋ **~its** ɪts §əts ‖ əts
deˈposit acˌcount

depositar|y di ˈpɒz ɪt‿ər |i də-, -ˈət‿ ‖ -ˈpɑːz ə ter |i **~ies** iz

deposition ˌdep ə ˈzɪʃ ən ˌdiː pə- **~s** z

depositor di ˈpɒz ɪt ə də-, -ət- ‖ -ˈpɑːz ət̬ ər **~s** z

depositor|y di ˈpɒz ɪt‿ər |i də-, -ˈət‿ ‖ -ˈpɑːz ə tɔːr |i -tour i **~ies** iz

depot ˈdep əʊ ‖ ˈdiːp oʊ ˈdep— *Preference poll, AmE:* ˈdiːp- 95%, ˈdep- 5%. **~s** z

Depp dep

depravation ˌdep rə ˈveɪʃ ən

deprav|e di ˈpreɪv də- **~ed** d **~es** z **~ing** ɪŋ

depravit|y di ˈpræv ət |i də-, -ɪt- ‖ -ət̬ |i **~ies** iz

DEPOT

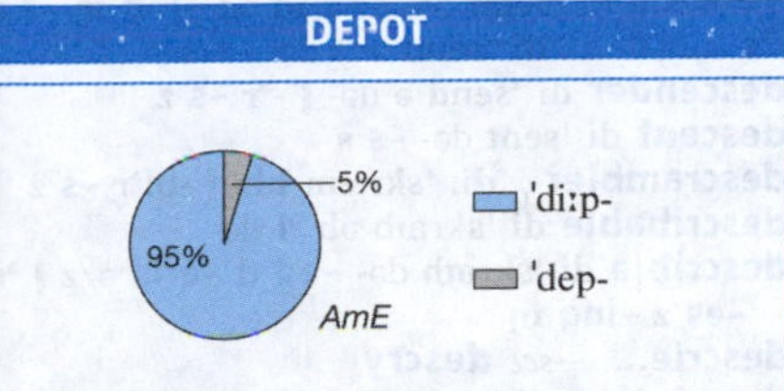

epre|cate ˈdep rə |keɪt -rɪ- **~cated** keɪt ɪd -əd ‖ keɪţ əd **~cates** keɪts **~cating/ly** keɪt ɪŋ /li ‖ keɪţ ɪŋ /li

eprecation ˌdep rə ˈkeɪʃ ən -rɪ-

eprecatory ˈdep rə keɪt ər i ˈ·rɪ-, ˌ· ·ˈ··; -kət ər i ‖ -kə tɔːr i -toʊr i

epreci|ate di ˈpriːʃ i |eɪt də-, -ˈpriːs- **~ated** eɪt ɪd -əd ‖ eɪţ əd **~ates** eɪts **~ating** eɪt ɪŋ ‖ eɪţ ɪŋ

epreciation di ˌpriːʃ i ˈeɪʃ ən də-, -ˌpriːs-

epreciatory di ˈpriːʃ i ət ər i də-, -ˈpriːs-, -ˈpriːʃ ət ər i ‖ ə tɔːr i -toʊr i

epre|date ˈdep rə |deɪt -rɪ- **~dated** deɪt ɪd -əd ‖ deɪţ əd **~dates** deɪts **~dating** deɪt ɪŋ ‖ deɪţ ɪŋ

epredation ˌdep rə ˈdeɪʃ ən -rɪ- **~s** z

epredatory di ˈpred ət ər i də-; ˌdep rə ˈdeɪt ər i, ˌ·rɪ-, ˈ· · ·· ‖ -ə tɔːr i -toʊr i

epress di ˈpres də- **~ed** t **~es** ɪz əz **~ing/ly** ɪŋ /li

epressant di ˈpres ənt də- **~s** s

epression di ˈpreʃ ən də- **~s** z

epressive di ˈpres ɪv də- **~ly** li **~ness** nəs nɪs **~s** z

epressor di ˈpres ə də- ‖ -ər **~s** z

epressuris... —*see* **depressuriz...**

epressurization ˌdiː ˌpreʃ ər aɪ ˈzeɪʃ ən ˌ·-, dɪ,·-, -ɪˈ-- ‖ dɪ ˌpreʃ ər ə- **~s** z

epressuriz|e ₍ˌ₎diː ˈpreʃ ə raɪz dɪ- **~ed** d **~es** ɪz əz **~ing** ɪŋ

DEPRIVATION

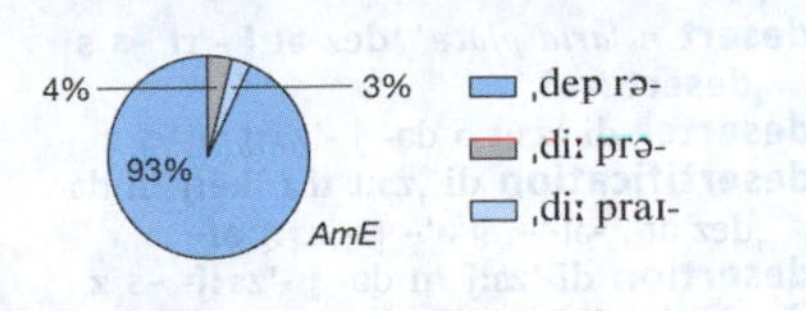

deprivation ˌdep rɪ ˈveɪʃ ən -rə-; ˌdiː prə-, prɪ-, -praɪ-— *Preference poll, AmE:* ˌdep rə- *93%,* ˌdiː prə- *4%,* ˌdiː praɪ- *3%.* **~s** z

depriv|e di ˈpraɪv də- **~ed** d **~es** z **~ing** ɪŋ

de profundis ˌdeɪ prə ˈfʊnd iːs ˌdiː-, -prɒ-, -ˈfʌnd-, -ɪs ‖ -proʊ-

deprogram ˌdiː ˈprəʊ græm §-grəm ‖ -ˈproʊ- **~med** d **~ming** ɪŋ **~s** z

depside ˈdeps aɪd -ɪd, §-əd **~s** z

dept —*see* **department**

Deptford ˈdet fəd ˈdept- ‖ -fərd

depth depθ **depths** depθs ˈ**depth charge**

deputation ˌdep ju ˈteɪʃ ən -jə- ‖ -jə- **~s** z

de|pute di |ˈpjuːt də- **~puted** ˈpjuːt ɪd -əd ‖ ˈpjuːţ əd **~putes** ˈpjuːts **~puting** ˈpjuːt ɪŋ ‖ ˈpjuːţ ɪŋ

deputi... —*see* **deputy**

deputis|e, deputiz|e ˈdep ju taɪz -jə- ‖ -jə- **~ed** d **~es** ɪz əz **~ing** ɪŋ

deput|y ˈdep jʊt |i -jət- ‖ -jəţ |i **~ies** iz

De Quincey də ˈkwɪnˈs i

derail ₍ˌ₎diː ˈreɪəl di- **~ed** d **~ing** ɪŋ **~s** z

derailleur di ˈreɪl jə də-, ˌdiː-, -ə ‖ -ər **~s** z

derailment ₍ˌ₎diː ˈreɪəl mənt dɪ- **~s** s

derang|e di ˈreɪndʒ də- **~ed** d **~es** ɪz əz **~ing** ɪŋ

derangement di ˈreɪndʒ mənt də-

de|rate ˌdiː |ˈreɪt **~rated** ˈreɪt ɪd -əd ‖ ˈreɪţ əd **~rates** ˈreɪts **~rating** ˈreɪt ɪŋ ‖ ˈreɪţ ɪŋ

derb|y ˈdɑːb |i §ˈdɜːb- ‖ ˈdɜːb |i (*) **~ies** iz

Derby *(i)* ˈdɑːb i ‖ ˈdɑːrb i, *(ii)* ˈdɜːb i ‖ ˈdɜːb i —*For the place in England, usually (i); for places in the US, (ii).*

Derbyshire ˈdɑːb i ʃə §ˈdɜːb-, -ʃɪə ‖ ˈdɑːrb i ʃər ˈdɜːb-, -ʃɪr

deregu|late ˌdiː ˈreg ju |leɪt di-, -jə- ‖ -jə- **~lated** leɪt ɪd -əd ‖ leɪţ əd **~lates** leɪts **~lating** leɪt ɪŋ ‖ leɪţ ɪŋ

deregulation ˌdiː ˌreg ju ˈleɪʃ ən -jə- ‖ diː ˌreg jə- ˌ·ˈ--

Dereham ˈdɪər əm ‖ ˈdɪr-

Derek ˈder ɪk

derelict ˈder ə lɪkt -ɪ- **~s** s

dereliction ˌder ə ˈlɪk ʃən -ɪ- **~s** z

derequisition ˌdiː ˌrek wɪ ˈzɪʃ ən -wə- **~ed** d **~ing** ɪŋ **~s** z

derestrict ˌdiː ri ˈstrɪkt -rə- **~ed** ɪd əd **~ing** ɪŋ **~s** s

derestriction ˌdiː ri ˈstrɪk ʃən -rə- **~s** z

De Reszke də ˈresk i

Derg dɜːg ‖ dɜːg

derid|e di ˈraɪd də- **~ed** ɪd əd **~es** z **~ing** ɪŋ

de rigueur ₍ˌ₎də rɪ ˈgɜː ₍ˌ₎deɪ-, ₍ˌ₎diː-, -riː- ‖ -ˈgɜː —*Fr* [də ʁi gœːʁ]

derision di ˈrɪʒ ən də-

derisive di ˈraɪs ɪv də-, -ˈraɪz-, -ˈrɪz- **~ly** li **~ness** nəs nɪs

deris|ory dɪ ˈraɪs |ər i də-, §diː-, -ˈraɪz- **~orily** ər əl i ər ɪ li

derivable di ˈraɪv əb əl də-

derivation ˌder ɪ ˈveɪʃ ən -ə- **~al** əl **~s** z

derivative di ˈrɪv ət ɪv də- ‖ -əţ ɪv **~ly** li **~s** z

deriv|e di ˈraɪv də- **~ed** d **~es** z **~ing** ɪŋ

d'Erlanger ˈdeəl ɒ̃ ʒ eɪ ‖ ˌderl ɑːn ˈʒeɪ

-derm dɜːm ‖ dɜːm — **periderm** ˈper i dɜːm ‖ -dɜːm

derm dɜːm ‖ dɜːm

dermabrasion ˌdɜːm ə ˈbreɪʒ ən ‖ ˌdɜːm-

-dermal ˈdɜːm əl ‖ ˈdɜːm əl — **peridermal** ˌper i ˈdɜːm əl ◂ ‖ -ˈdɜːm-

dermal ˈdɜːm əl ‖ ˈdɜːm-

dermatitis ˌdɜːm ə ˈtaɪt ɪs §-əs ‖ ˌdɜːm ə ˈtaɪţ əs

dermatologist ˌdɜːm ə ˈtɒl ədʒ ɪst §-əst ‖ ˌdɜːm ə ˈtɑːl- **~s** s

D

dermatology ˌdɜːm ə ˈtɒl ədʒ i ‖ ˌdɝːm ə ˈtɑːl-
dermis ˈdɜːm ɪs §-əs ‖ ˈdɝːm-
Dermod ˈdɜːm əd ‖ ˈdɝːm-
Dermot, Dermott ˈdɜːm ət ‖ ˈdɝːm-
dernier cri ˌdɜːn i eɪ ˈkriː ‖ ˌdɝːn- —*Fr* [dɛʁ nje kʁi]
dero|gate ˈder ə |geɪt ˈdiː rəʊ-, |geɪt **~gated** geɪt ɪd -əd ‖ geɪt̬ əd **~gates** geɪts **~gating** geɪt ɪŋ ‖ geɪt̬ ɪŋ
derogation ˌder ə ˈgeɪʃ ᵊn ˌdiː rəʊ- **~s** z
derogator|y di ˈrɒg ət ər |i də- ‖ -ˈrɑːg ə tɔːr |i -toʊr i **~ily** əl i ɪl i **~iness** i nəs i nɪs
Deronda də ˈrɒnd ə di- ‖ -ˈrɑːnd ə
derrick, D~ ˈder ɪk **~s** s
Derrida də ˈriːd ə de-; ˈder ɪd ə, -əd- ‖ ˌder i ˈdɑː ˌ· ·ˈ· —*Fr* [dɛ ʁi da]
Derrie ˈder i
derriere, derrière ˈder i eə ˌ· ·ˈ· ‖ ˌder i ˈeᵊr —*Fr* [dɛʁ jɛːʁ] **~s** z —*or as sing.*
derring-do ˌder ɪŋ ˈduː ˌdeər-, ˌdɜːr-
derringer, D~ ˈder ɪndʒ ə -əndʒ- ‖ -ᵊr **~s** z
derris ˈder ɪs §-əs
Derry, derry ˈder i
Dershowitz ˈdɜːʃ ə wɪts ‖ ˈdɝːʃ-
derv dɜːv ‖ dɝːv
dervish ˈdɜːv ɪʃ ‖ ˈdɝːv- **~es** ɪz əz
Dervla ˈdɜːv lə ‖ ˈdɝːv-
Derwent ˈdɜː wənt -went ‖ ˈdɝː- —*but Baron D~ is* ˈdɑː-
Derwentwater ˈdɜː wənt ˌwɔːt ə -went- ‖ ˈdɝː wənt ˌwɔːt̬ ᵊr -ˌwɑːt̬ ᵊr
Deryck ˈder ɪk
Deryn ˈder ɪn §-ən
Des dez ‖ des —*See also phrases with this word*
DES ˌdiː iː ˈes
Desai de ˈsaɪ ˈdeɪs aɪ
De Sales də ˈsɑːlz
desali|nate ₍ˌ₎diː ˈsæl ɪ |neɪt -ə- **~nated** neɪt ɪd -əd ‖ neɪt̬ əd **~nates** neɪts **~nating** neɪt ɪŋ ‖ neɪt̬ ɪŋ
desalination ˌdiː ˌsæl ɪ ˈneɪʃ ᵊn -ə- ‖ diː ˌsæl ə-
desalinis... —*see* **desaliniz...**
desalinization ˌdiː ˌsæl ɪn aɪ ˈzeɪʃ ᵊn diː ˌsæl-, -ən aɪ-, -ɪˈ·- ‖ -ən ə-
desaliniz|e ₍ˌ₎diː ˈsæl ɪ naɪz -ə- **~ed** d **~es** ɪz əz **~ing** ɪŋ
De Salis *(i)* də ˈsæl ɪs §-əs, *(ii)* -ˈseɪl-, *(iii)* də ˈsɑːlz
desalt ˌdiː ˈsɒlt -ˈsɔːlt ‖ -ˈsɔːlt -ˈsɑːlt **~ed** ɪd əd **~ing** ɪŋ **~s** s
De Saumarez, De Sausmarez də ˈsɒm ər ɪz -ə rez ‖ -ˈsɑːm-
Desborough ˈdez bər‿ə ‖ -ˌbɝː oʊ
descal|e ˌdiː ˈskeɪᵊl **~ed** d **~es** z **~ing** ɪŋ
de|scant *v* di |ˈskænt də-, de- **~scanted** ˈskænt ɪd -əd ‖ ˈskænt̬ əd **~scanting** ˈskænt ɪŋ ‖ ˈskænt̬ ɪŋ **~scants** ˈskænts
descant *n* ˈdesk ænt **~s** s
Descartes ˈdeɪ kɑːt ·ˈ· ‖ deɪ ˈkɑːrt —*Fr* [de kaʁt]
descend di ˈsend də- **~ed** ɪd əd **~ing** ɪŋ **~s** z
descendant di ˈsend ənt də- **~s** s
descender di ˈsend ə də- ‖ -ᵊr **~s** z
descent di ˈsent də- **~s** s
descrambler ₍ˌ₎diː ˈskræm blə ‖ -blᵊr **~s** z
describable di ˈskraɪb əb ᵊl də-
describ|e di ˈskraɪb də- **~ed** d **~er/s** ə/z ‖ ᵊr/z **~es** z **~ing** ɪŋ
descrie... —*see* **descry**
description di ˈskrɪp ʃᵊn də- **~s** z
descriptive di ˈskrɪpt ɪv də- **~ly** li **~ness** nəs nɪs
descriptiv|ism di ˈskrɪpt ɪv |ˌɪz əm də- **~ist/s** ɪst/s §-əst/s
descriptor di ˈskrɪpt ə də- ‖ -ᵊr **~s** z
de|scry di |ˈskraɪ də- **~scried** ˈskraɪd **~scries** ˈskraɪz **~scrying** ˈskraɪ ɪŋ
Desdemona ˌdez dɪ ˈməʊn ə -də- ‖ -ˈmoʊn-
dese|crate ˈdes ɪ |kreɪt -ə- **~crated** kreɪt ɪd -əd ‖ kreɪt̬ əd **~crates** kreɪts **~crating** kreɪt ɪŋ ‖ kreɪt̬ ɪŋ
desecration ˌdes ɪ ˈkreɪʃ ᵊn -ə- **~s** z
deseed ˌdiː ˈsiːd **~ed** ɪd əd **~ing** ɪŋ **~s** z
desegre|gate ₍ˌ₎diː ˈseg rɪ |geɪt -rə- **~gated** geɪt ɪd -əd ‖ geɪt̬ əd **~gates** geɪts **~gating** geɪt ɪŋ ‖ geɪt̬ ɪŋ
desegregation ˌdiː ˌseg rɪ ˈgeɪʃ ᵊn -rə- ‖ diː ˌseg-
deselect ˌdiː sə ˈlekt -si- **~ed** ɪd əd **~ing** ɪŋ **~s** s
deselection ˌdiː sə ˈlek ʃᵊn -si- **~s** z
de Selincourt də ˈsel ɪn kɔːt →-ɪŋ- ‖ -kɔːrt -koʊrt
desensitis... —*see* **desensitiz...**
desensitization ˌdiː ˌsenᵗs ət aɪ ˈzeɪʃ ᵊn -ɪt aɪ-, -ɪˈ·- ‖ diː ˌsenᵗs ət̬ ə- **~s** z
desensitiz|e ₍ˌ₎diː ˈsenᵗs ə taɪz -ɪ- **~ed** d **~es** ɪz əz **~ing** ɪŋ
de|sert *v* di |ˈzɜːt də- ‖ -|ˈzɝːt **~serted** ˈzɜːt ɪd -əd ‖ ˈzɝːt̬ əd **~serting** ˈzɜːt ɪŋ ‖ ˈzɝːt̬ ɪŋ **~serts** ˈzɜːts ‖ ˈzɝːts
desert *n 'what is deserved'* di ˈzɜːt də- ‖ -ˈzɝːt **~s** s
desert *n 'arid place'* ˈdez ət ‖ -ᵊrt **~s** s
ˌdesert ˈrat
deserter di ˈzɜːt ə də- ‖ -ˈzɝːt̬ ᵊr **~s** z
desertification di ˌzɜːt ɪf ɪ ˈkeɪʃ ᵊn də-, ˌdez ət-, -əf·ˈ·-, §-əˈ·- ‖ -ˌzɝːt̬ əf-
desertion di ˈzɜːʃ ᵊn də- ‖ -ˈzɝːʃ- **~s** z
deserv|e di ˈzɜːv də- ‖ -ˈzɝːv **~ed** d **~es** z **~ing** ɪŋ
deserved|ly di ˈzɜːv ɪd |li də-, -əd- ‖ -ˈzɝːv- **~ness** nəs nɪs
desexualization, desexualisation ₍ˌ₎diː ˌsek ʃu‿əl aɪ ˈzeɪʃ ᵊn -ˌseks ju‿, -ɪˈ·- ‖ -əˈ·-
desexualiz|e, desexualis|e ₍ˌ₎diː ˈsek ʃu‿ə laɪz -ˈseks ju‿ **~ed** d **~es** ɪz əz **~ing** ɪŋ
deshabille ˌdez ə ˈbiːᵊl ˌdeɪz-, ˌdes-, -æ-
déshabillé ˌdez ə ˈbiː eɪ ˌdeɪz-, ˌdes-, -æ-; -ˈbiːᵊl —*Fr* [de za bi je]
desiccant ˈdes ɪk ənt -ək- **~s** s

desiccate 'des ɪ |keɪt -ə- **~cated** keɪt ɪd -əd ‖ keɪţ əd **~cates** keɪts **~cating** keɪt ɪŋ ‖ keɪţ ɪŋ
desiccation ˌdes ɪ 'keɪʃ ən -ə- **~s** z
desiccator 'des ɪ keɪt ə '·ə- ‖ -keɪţ ər **~s** z
desiderata di ˌzɪd ə 'rɑːt ə də-, -ˌsɪd-, -'reɪt- ‖ -'rɑːţ ə -'reɪţ-
desiderative di 'zɪd ər ət ɪv də- ‖ -ə reɪţ ɪv ər əţ ɪv **~s** z
desiderat|um di ˌzɪd ə 'rɑːt |əm də-, -ˌsɪd-, -'reɪt- ‖ -'rɑːţ- -'reɪţ- **~a** ə
design di 'zaɪn də- **~ed** d **~ing/ly** ɪŋ /li **~s** z
designate *adj* 'dez ɪg nət -nɪt, -neɪt
desig|nate *v* 'dez ɪg |neɪt **~nated** neɪt ɪd -əd ‖ neɪţ əd **~nates** neɪts **~nating** neɪt ɪŋ ‖ neɪţ ɪŋ
designation ˌdez ɪg 'neɪʃ ən **~s** z
designator 'dez ɪg neɪt ə ‖ -neɪţ ər **~s** z
designedly di 'zaɪn ɪd li də-, -əd-
designer di 'zaɪn ə də- ‖ -ər **~s** z
deˌsigner 'jeans
desinenc|e 'dez ɪn ənts 'des-, -ən- **~es** ɪz əz
desinential ˌdez ɪ 'nentʃ əl ◂ ˌdes-, ə-
desirability di ˌzaɪ ər ə 'bɪl ət i də-, -ɪt i ‖ -ˌzaɪ ər ə 'bɪl əţ i
desirab|le di 'zaɪ ər əb |əl də- ‖ -'zaɪ ər- **~leness** əl nəs -nɪs **~les** əlz **~ly** li
desire di 'zaɪ ə də- ‖ -'zaɪ ər **~d** d **~s** z
desiring dɪ 'zaɪ ər ɪŋ də-, §diː- ‖ -'zaɪ ər ɪŋ
Desiree, Désirée deɪ 'zɪər eɪ de-, dɪ- ‖ ˌdez ə 'reɪ
desirous di 'zaɪ ər əs də- ‖ -'zaɪ ər- **~ly** li **~ness** nəs nɪs
desist di 'zɪst də-, -'sɪst **~ed** ɪd əd **~ing** ɪŋ **~s** s
desk desk **desks** desks
deskill ˌdiː 'skɪl **~ed** d **~ing** ɪŋ **~s** z
desktop 'desk tɒp ˌ·'· ‖ -tɑːp **~s** s
deskwork 'desk wɜːk ‖ -wɜːk
desman 'des mən 'dez- **~s** z
desmid 'dez mɪd §-məd **~s** z
desmoid 'dez mɔɪd 'des- **~s** z
Des Moines də 'mɔɪn di-
Desmond 'dez mənd
desolate *adj* 'des əl ət 'dez-, -ɪt **~ly** li
deso|late *v* 'des ə |leɪt 'dez- **~lated** leɪt ɪd -əd ‖ leɪţ əd **~lates** leɪts **~lating** leɪt ɪŋ ‖ leɪţ ɪŋ
desolation ˌdes ə 'leɪʃ ən ˌdez-
De Soto də 'səʊt əʊ ‖ -'soʊt oʊ —*Sp* [de 'so to]
Desoutter di 'suːt ə də- ‖ -'suːţ ər
De Souza də 'suːz ə
desoxy- ¦dez ˌɒks i ‖ -ˌɑːks- —
desoxymorphine ˌdez ˌɒks i 'mɔːf iːn ‖ dez ˌɑːks i 'mɔːrf-
despair dɪ 'speə də- ‖ -'speər 'spæər **~ed** d
despairing/ly dɪ 'speər ɪŋ /li də- ‖ -'sper- -'spær- **~s** z
Despard 'desp ɑːd ‖ -ɑːrd
despatch *n* di 'spætʃ də-; 'dɪs pætʃ **~es** ɪz əz
despatch *v* di 'spætʃ də- **~ed** t **~es** ɪz əz **~ing** ɪŋ
Despenser dɪ 'spents ə də- ‖ -ər
desperado ˌdesp ə 'rɑːd əʊ ‖ -oʊ -'reɪd- **~es, ~s** z
desperate 'desp ər ət ɪt **~ly** li **~ness** nəs nɪs
desperation ˌdesp ə 'reɪʃ ən
despicability di ˌspɪk ə 'bɪl ət i də-, ˌdesp ɪk-, -ɪt i ‖ -əţ i
despicab|le di 'spɪk əb |əl də- 'desp ɪk- **~leness** əl nəs -nɪs **~ly** li
despis|e di 'spaɪz də- **~ed** d **~es** ɪz əz **~ing** ɪŋ
despite di 'spaɪt də-
Des Plaines *place in IL* des 'pleɪnz
despoil di'spɔɪəl də- **~ed** d **~ing** ɪŋ **~s** z
despoliation di ˌspəʊl i 'eɪʃ ən də- ‖ -ˌspoʊl-
despond di 'spɒnd də- 'desp ɒnd ‖ -'spɑːnd **~ed** ɪd əd **~ing** ɪŋ **~s** z
despondenc|e di 'spɒnd ənts də- ‖ -'spɑːnd- **~ies** iz **~y** i
despondent di 'spɒnd ənt də- ‖ -'spɑːnd- **~ly** li
despot 'desp ɒt -ət ‖ -ɑːt -ət **~s** s
despotic di 'spɒt ɪk də-, de- ‖ -'spɑːţ ɪk **~ally** əl i
despotism 'desp ə ˌtɪz əm
des res ˌdez 'rez
dessert di 'zɜːt də- ‖ -'zɜːt **~s** z
des'sert wine
dessertspoon di 'zɜːt spuːn də- ‖ -'zɜːt- **~s** z
dessert|spoonful di 'zɜːt |spuːn fʊl də- ‖ -'zɜːt- ·ˌ·'· · **~spoonsful** spuːnz fʊl
destabilis... —*see* **destabiliz...**
destabilization ˌdiː ˌsteɪb əl aɪ 'zeɪʃ ən dɪ ˌsteɪb-, -ɪl·'--, -ɪ'-- ‖ diː ˌsteɪb əl ə- **~s** z
destabiliz|e ˌdiː 'steɪb ə laɪz dɪ-, -ɪ-, -əl aɪz **~ed** d **~es** ɪz əz **~ing** ɪŋ
deStalinis... —*see* **deStaliniz...**
deStalinization ˌdiː ˌstɑːl ɪn aɪ 'zeɪʃ ən -ˌstæl-, -ˌ·ən-, -ɪ'-- ‖ diː ˌstɑːl ən ə- -ˌstæl-
deStaliniz|e ˌdiː 'stɑːl ɪ naɪz -'stæl-, -ə- **~ed** d **~es** ɪz əz **~ing** ɪŋ
De Stijl də 'staɪəl —*Dutch* [də 'steil]
destination ˌdest ɪ 'neɪʃ ən -ə- **~s** z
destine 'dest ɪn -ən **~d** d **~s** z
destin|y 'dest ən |i -ɪn- **~ies** iz
destitute 'dest ɪ tjuːt -ə-, →-tʃuːt ‖ -tuːt -tjuːt
destitution ˌdest ɪ 'tjuːʃ ən -ə-, →-'tʃuːʃ- ‖ -'tuːʃ ən -'tjuːʃ-
destroy di 'strɔɪ də- **~ed** d **~ing** ɪŋ **~s** z
destroyer di 'strɔɪ ə də- ‖ -ər **~s** z
destruct di 'strʌkt də- **~ed** ɪd əd **~ing** ɪŋ **~s** s
destructib|le di 'strʌkt əb |əl də-, -ɪb- **~leness** əl nəs -nɪs **~ly** li
destruction di 'strʌk ʃən də- **~s** z
destructive di 'strʌkt ɪv də- **~ly** li **~ness** nəs nɪs
destructor di 'strʌkt ə də- ‖ -ər **~s** z
Destry 'des tri
desuetude 'des wɪ tjuːd →-tʃuːd; di 'sjuː ɪ-, də-, -'suː ə- ‖ -tuːd -tjuːd; di 'suː ə-
desultor|y 'des əlt ər |i 'dez- ‖ -əl tɔːr |i -toʊr i **~ily** əl i ɪ li **~iness** i nəs i nɪs
detach di 'tætʃ də- **~ed** t **~es** ɪz əz **~ing** ɪŋ
detachable di 'tætʃ əb əl də-
detachedly di 'tætʃ ɪd li də-, -əd-; -'tætʃt li

detachment di ˈtætʃ mənt də- **~s** s

DETAIL

25% 75% ˈ. . .ˈ. AmE

detail *n, v* ˈdiː teɪᵊl ; di ˈteɪᵊl, də- **~ed** d **~ing** ɪŋ **~s** z — *Preference poll, AmE:* ˈ. · 75%, .ˈ. 25%.

detain di ˈteɪn də- **~ed** d **~ing** ɪŋ **~s** z

detainee ˌdiː teɪ ˈniː; di ˌteɪ-, də-; ˌdɪt eɪ- **~s** z

detangl|e ˌdiː ˈtæŋ gᵊl **~ed** d **~s** z **~ing** ‿ɪŋ

detect di ˈtekt də- **~ed** ɪd əd **~ing** ɪŋ **~s** s

detectab|le, detectib|le di ˈtekt əb |ᵊl də-, -ɪb- **~ly** li

detection di ˈtek ʃᵊn də-

detective di ˈtekt ɪv də- **~s** z

detector di ˈtekt ə də- ‖ -ᵊr **~s** z

deˈtector van

detent di ˈtent də- **~s** s

detente, détente ˈdeɪ tɒnt -tɑːnt; deɪ ˈtɒnt, -ˈtɑːnt ‖ deɪ ˈtɑːnt —*Fr* [de tɑ̃ːt]

detention di ˈtenᵗʃ ᵊn də- **~s** z

deˈtention ˌcentre

deter di ˈtɜː də- ‖ -ˈtɜː **~red** d **deterring** di ˈtɜːr ɪŋ də- ‖ -ˈtɜː ɪŋ **~s** z

Deterding ˈdet əd ɪŋ ‖ ˈdeţ ᵊrd ɪŋ

detergent di ˈtɜːdʒ ənt də- ‖ -ˈtɜːdʒ- **~s** s

deterior|ate di ˈtɪər i‿ə r|eɪt də-, ⚠-ˈtɪər ə r|eɪt, ⚠-ˈtɪər |eɪt ‖ -ˈtɪr- **~ated** eɪt ɪd -əd ‖ eɪţ əd **~ates** eɪts **~ating** eɪt ɪŋ ‖ eɪţ ɪŋ

deterioration di ˌtɪər i‿ə ˈreɪʃ ᵊn də-, ⚠-ˌtɪər ə ˈreɪʃ ᵊn, ⚠-ˌtɪər i ˈeɪʃ ᵊn ‖ -ˌtɪr- **~s** z

determinable di ˈtɜːm ɪn əb ᵊl də-, -ən‿əb- ‖ -ˈtɜːm-

determinant di ˈtɜːm ɪn ənt də-, -ən- ‖ -ˈtɜːm- **~s** s

determinate di ˈtɜːm ɪn ət də-, -ən-, -ɪt ‖ -ˈtɜːm- **~ly** li **~ness** nəs nɪs

determination di ˌtɜːm ɪ ˈneɪʃ ᵊn də-, -ə- ‖ -ˌtɜːm- **~s** z

determinative di ˈtɜːm ɪn ət ɪv də-, -ən‿ət- ‖ -ˈtɜːm ə neɪţ ɪv -ən‿əţ- **~ness** nəs nɪs **~s** z

determin|e di ˈtɜːm ɪn də-, -ən ‖ -ˈtɜːm- **~ed/ly** d /li **~es** z **~ing** ɪŋ

determiner di ˈtɜːm ɪn ə də-, -ən- ‖ -ˈtɜːm ən ᵊr **~s** z

determinism dɪ ˈtɜːm ɪ ˌnɪz əm də-, §diː-, -ə- ‖ -ˈtɜːm-

deterministic di ˌtɜːm ɪ ˈnɪst ɪk ◂ də-, -ə- ‖ -ˌtɜːm- **~ally** ᵊl‿i

deterrence di ˈter ənᵗs də-, §-ˈtɜːr- ‖ -ˈtɜː- -ˈter-

deterrent di ˈter ənt də-, §-ˈtɜːr- ‖ -ˈtɜː- -ˈter- **~s** s

detest di ˈtest də- **~ed** ɪd əd **~ing** ɪŋ **~s** s

detestab|le di ˈtest əb |ᵊl də- **~leness** ᵊl nəs -nɪs **~ly** li

detestation ˌdiː te ˈsteɪʃ ᵊn

dethron|e di ˈθrəʊn də-, ˌdiː- ‖ -ˈθroʊn **~ed** d **~ement** mənt **~es** z **~ing** ɪŋ

Detmold ˈdet məʊld →-mɒʊld ‖ -moʊld —*G* [ˈdet mɔlt]

deton|ate ˈdet ə n|eɪt -ᵊn |eɪt ‖ ˈdet ᵊn |eɪt ˈdeţ ə n|eɪt **~ated** eɪt ɪd -əd ‖ eɪţ əd **~ates** eɪts **~ating** eɪt ɪŋ ‖ eɪţ ɪŋ

detonation ˌdet ə ˈneɪʃ ᵊn -ᵊn ˈeɪʃ- ‖ ˌdet ᵊn ˈeɪʃ ᵊn ˌdeţ ə ˈneɪʃ- **~s** z

detonator ˈdet ə neɪt ə -ᵊn eɪt- ‖ ˈdet ᵊn eɪţ ᵊr ˈdeţ ə neɪţ ᵊr **~s** z

detour ˈdiː tʊə ˈdeɪ-, -tɔː; ˌdeɪ ˈtʊə, di-, də-, -ˈt… ‖ -tʊr dɪ ˈtʊᵊr **~ed** d **~s** z

detox ˌdiː ˈtɒks di-; ˈdiː tɒks ‖ -ˈtɑːks

detoxi|cate ˌdiː ˈtɒks ɪ |keɪt di-, -ə- ‖ -ˈtɑːks- **~cated** keɪt ɪd -əd ‖ keɪţ əd **~cates** keɪts **~cating** keɪt ɪŋ ‖ keɪţ ɪŋ

detoxication ˌdiː ˌtɒks ɪ ˈkeɪʃ ᵊn di ˌtɒks-, -ə- ‖ diː ˌtɑːks-

detoxification ˌdiː ˌtɒks ɪf ɪ ˈkeɪʃ ᵊn di ˌtɒks- -əf-ˈ.., §-əˈ.. ‖ -ˌtɑːks-

detoxi|fy ˌdiː ˈtɒks ɪ faɪ di-, -ə- ‖ -ˈtɑːks- **~fied** faɪd **~fies** faɪz **~fying** faɪ ɪŋ

detract di ˈtrækt də-, ˌdiː- **~ed** ɪd əd **~ing** ɪŋ **~s** s

detraction di ˈtræk ʃᵊn də-, ˌdiː- **~s** z

detractor di ˈtrækt ə də-, ˌdiː- ‖ -ᵊr **~s** z

detrain ˌdiː ˈtreɪn **~ed** d **~ing** ɪŋ **~s** z

detribalis… —*see* **detribaliz…**

detribalization ˌdiː ˌtraɪb ᵊl aɪ ˈzeɪʃ ᵊn dɪ ˌtraɪb-, -ᵊl ɪ- ‖ -ᵊl ə-

detribaliz|e ˌdiː ˈtraɪb ə laɪz dɪ-, -ᵊl aɪz **~ed** d **~es** ɪz əz **~ing** ɪŋ

detriment ˈdetr ɪ mənt -ə-

detrimental ˌdetr ɪ ˈment ᵊl ◂ -ə- ‖ -ˈmenţ ᵊl ◂ **~ly** i

detritus di ˈtraɪt əs də- ‖ -ˈtraɪţ əs

Detroit di ˈtrɔɪt də-

de trop də ˈtrəʊ ‖ -ˈtroʊ —*Fr* [də tʁo]

Dettol ˈdet ɒl -ᵊl ‖ -ɑːl

Dettori də ˈtɔːr i di-, de-

detumesc|ence ˌdiː tju ˈmes |ᵊnᵗs →-tʃu- ‖ -tu- -tju- **~ent** ᵊnt

Deucalion dju ˈkeɪl i‿ən →dʒu- ‖ du- dju-

deuce djuːs →dʒuːs ‖ duːs djuːs **deuces** ˈdjuːs ɪz →ˈdʒuːs-, -əz ‖ ˈduːs- ˈdjuːs-

deuced djuːst →dʒuːst; ˈdjuːs ɪd, →ˈdʒuːs-, -əd

deucedly ˈdjuːs ɪd li →ˈdʒuːs-, -əd- ‖ ˈduːs- ˈdjuːs-

deus, Deus ˈdeɪ ʊs ˈdiː‿əs

ˌdeus ex ˈmachina ˈmæk ɪn ə ˈmɑːk-, §-ən-; -mə ˈʃiːn ə ‖ -ˈmɑːk ɪ nɑː -ˈmæk-, -ən ə

deuterium dju ˈtɪər i‿əm →dʒu- ‖ du ˈtɪr- dju-

deutero- ¦djuːt ə rəʊ →¦dʒuːt- ‖ ¦duːţ ə roʊ — **Deutero-Isaiah** ˌdjuːt ə rəʊ aɪ ˈzaɪ‿ə →ˌdʒuːt- ‖ ˌduːţ ə roʊ aɪ ˈzeɪ ə

deuteron ˈdjuːt ə rɒn →ˈdʒuːt- ‖ ˈduːţ ə rɑːn ˈdjuːţ- **~s** z

Deuteronomy ˌdjuːt ə ˈrɒn əm i →ˌdʒuːt-; ˈdjuːt ər‿ə nɒm i, →ˈdʒuːt- ‖ ˌduːţ ə ˈrɑːn- ˌdjuːţ-

Deutsch dɔɪtʃ

eutsche Mark ˌdɔɪtʃ ə ˈmɑːk ‖ -ˈmɑːrk —*Ger* [ˌdɔʏ tʃə ˈmaʁk]

eutschland ˈdɔɪtʃ lənd -lænd —*Ger* [ˈdɔʏtʃ lant]

eutschmark, D~ ˈdɔɪtʃ mɑːk ‖ -mɑːrk

eutzia ˈdjuːts i‿ə →ˈdʒuːts-; ˈdɔɪts- ‖ ˈduːts- ˈdjuːts- **~s** z

eva ˈdeɪv ə ˈdiːv- —*Hindi* [d̪eːʋ]

e Valera də və ˈleər ə ˌdev ə-, -ˈlɪər- ‖ -ˈler ə -ˈlɪr-

e Valois də ˈvæl wɑː

evaluation ˌdiː ˌvæl ju ˈeɪʃ ᵊn dɪ ˌvæl- ‖ diː ˌvæl- **~s** z

evalue ˌdiː ˈvæl juː dɪ- **~d** d **~s** z **devaluing** ˌdiː ˈvæl juː‿ɪŋ dɪ-

evanagari ˌdeɪv ə ˈnɑːg ər‿i ˌdev-

evaney di ˈveɪn i də-

eva|state ˈdev ə |steɪt **~stated** steɪt ɪd -əd ‖ steɪţ əd **~states** steɪts **~stating/ly** steɪt ɪŋ /li ‖ steɪţ ɪŋ /li

evastation ˌdev ə ˈsteɪʃ ᵊn

evelop di ˈvel əp də- **~ed** t **~er/s** ə/z ‖ ᵊr/z **~ing** ɪŋ **~s** s

deˈveloping ˌcountry, ·,· · · ˈ· ·

evelopment di ˈvel əp mənt də- **~s** s

deˈvelopment ˌarea

evelopmental di ˌvel əp ˈment ᵊl ◂ də- ‖ -ˈmenţ ᵊl ◂ **~ly** i

everbal ˌdiː ˈvɜːb ᵊl ◂ ‖ -ˈvɜːb- **~s** z

everbative ˌdiː ˈvɜːb ət ɪv di- ‖ -ˈvɜːb əţ ɪv **~s** z

e Vere də ˈvɪə di- ‖ -ˈvɪᵊr

evereux *(i)* ˈdev ə ruːks, *(ii)* -rɜː -ər ə ‖ -ər ə, *(iii)* -reks, *(iv)* -ruː, *(v)* -rəʊ ‖ -roʊ

evianc|e ˈdiːv i‿ənᵗs **~y** i

eviant ˈdiːv i‿ənt **~ly** li **~s** s

eviate *n* ˈdiːv i‿ət -ɪt **~s** s

evi|ate *v* ˈdiːv i |eɪt **~ated** eɪt ɪd -əd ‖ eɪţ əd **~ates** eɪts **~ating** eɪt ɪŋ ‖ eɪţ ɪŋ

eviation ˌdiːv i ˈeɪʃ ᵊn **~ism** ˌɪz əm **~ist/s** ɪst/s §-əst/s **~s** z

eviator ˈdiːv i eɪt ə ‖ -eɪţ ᵊr **~s** z

evic|e di ˈvaɪs də- **~es** ɪz əz

devil ˈdev ᵊl -ɪl **~ed, ~led** d **~ing, ~ling** ɪŋ **~s** z

ˌ**devil's ˈadvocate**; ˈ**devil's food cake**, ˈ· · ˈ· ·; ˌ**devils-on-ˈhorseback**

devilish ˈdev ᵊl ɪʃ **~ly** li **~ness** nəs nɪs

de Villiers də ˈvɪl jəz ‖ -jᵊrz

devil-may-care ˌdev ᵊl meɪ ˈkeə ◂ ‖ -ˈkeᵊr -ˈkæᵊr

devilment ˈdev ᵊl mənt

devil|ry ˈdev ᵊl |ri **~ries** riz

Devine *(i)* di ˈviːn də-, *(ii)* -ˈvaɪn

devious ˈdiːv i‿əs **~ly** li **~ness** nəs nɪs

devis|e di ˈvaɪz də- **~ed** d **~er/s** ə/z ‖ ᵊr/z **~es** ɪz əz **~ing** ɪŋ

devitalis... —*see* **devitaliz...**

devitalization ˌdiː ˌvaɪt ᵊl aɪ ˈzeɪʃ ᵊn -ᵊl ɪ- ‖ diː ˌvaɪţ ᵊl ə-

devitaliz|e ₍ˌ₎diː ˈvaɪt ə laɪz -ᵊl aɪz ‖ -ˈvaɪţ ᵊl aɪz **~ed** d **~es** ɪz əz **~ing** ɪŋ

DeVito də ˈviːt əʊ ‖ də ˈviːţ oʊ

Devizes di ˈvaɪz ɪz də-, -əz

Devlin ˈdev lɪn -lən

devoic|e ₍ˌ₎diː ˈvɔɪs **~ed** t **~es** ɪz əz **~ing** ɪŋ

devoid di ˈvɔɪd də-

devolution ˌdiːv ə ˈluːʃ ᵊn ˌdev-, -ˈljuːʃ- ‖ ˌdev- **~ist/s** ‿ɪst/s **~s** z

devolv|e di ˈvɒlv də-, §-ˈvəʊlv ‖ -ˈvɑːlv **~ed** d **~es** z **~ing** ɪŋ **~ement** mənt

Devon ˈdev ᵊn —*but the river in Notts. is* ˈdiːv-

Devonian de ˈvəʊn i‿ən də-, dɪ- ‖ -ˈvoʊn- **~s** z

Devonish ˈdev ᵊn‿ɪʃ

Devonport ˈdev ᵊn pɔːt →-ᵊm- ‖ -pɔːrt -poʊrt

Devonshire ˈdev ᵊn ʃə -ʃɪə ‖ -ʃᵊr -ʃɪr

de|vote di |ˈvəʊt də- ‖ -|ˈvoʊt **~voted** ˈvəʊt ɪd -əd ‖ ˈvoʊţ əd **~votes** ˈvəʊts ‖ ˈvoʊts **~voting** ˈvəʊt ɪŋ ‖ ˈvoʊţ ɪŋ

devoted|ly di ˈvəʊt ɪd |li də-, -əd- ‖ -ˈvoʊţ əd- **~ness** nəs nɪs

devotee ˌdev əʊ ˈtiː ‖ -ə ˈtiː -ˈteɪ **~s** z

devotion di ˈvəʊʃ ᵊn də- ‖ -ˈvoʊʃ- **~s** z

devotional di ˈvəʊʃ ᵊn‿əl də-ˈvoʊʃ- **~ly** i

devour di ˈvaʊ‿ə də- ‖ ˈvaʊ‿ᵊr **~ed** d

devouring di ˈvaʊ‿ər ɪŋ də- ‖ -ˈvaʊᵊr ɪŋ **~s** z

devout di ˈvaʊt də- **~ly** li **~ness** nəs nɪs

De Vries *(i)* də ˈvriːs, *(ii)* -ˈvriːz

dew djuː →dʒuː ‖ duː djuː **dewed** djuːd →dʒuːd ‖ duːd djuːd **dewing** ˈdjuː ɪŋ →ˈdʒuː- ‖ ˈduː ɪŋ ˈdjuː- **dews** djuːz →dʒuːz ‖ duːz djuːz

ˈ**dew point**

Dewar, dewar ˈdjuː‿ə →ˈdʒuː‿ə ‖ ˈduː ᵊr ˈdjuː ᵊr **~s** z

dewberr|y ˈdjuː bər‿|i →ˈdʒuː- ‖ ˈduː ˌber |i ˈdjuː- **~ies** iz

dewclaw ˈdjuː klɔː →ˈdʒuː- ‖ ˈduː- ˈdjuː-, -klɑː **~s** z

dewdrop ˈdjuː drɒp →ˈdʒuː- ‖ ˈduː drɑːp ˈdjuː- **~s** s

Dewey ˈdjuː‿i →ˈdʒuː‿i ‖ ˈduː i ˈdjuː i

ˌ**Dewey ˈdecimal ˌsystem**

dewfall ˈdjuː fɔːl →ˈdʒuː- ‖ ˈduː- ˈdjuː-, -fɑːl

Dewhurst ˈdjuː hɜːst →ˈdʒuː- ‖ ˈduː hɜːst ˈdjuː-

Dewi ˈde wi —*this Welsh name is occasionally anglicized as* ˈdjuː‿i

dewi... —*see* **dewy**

de Wint də ˈwɪnt

dewlap ˈdjuː læp →ˈdʒuː- ‖ ˈduː- ˈdjuː- **~s** s

dewpond ˈdjuː pɒnd →ˈdʒuː- ‖ ˈduː pɑːnd ˈdjuː- **~s** z

Dewsbury ˈdjuːz bər‿i →ˈdʒuːz- ‖ ˈduːz ˌber i ˈdjuːz-

dew-worm ˈdjuː wɜːm →ˈdʒuː- ‖ ˈduː wɜːm ˈdjuː- **~s** z

dew|y ˈdjuː‿|i →ˈdʒuː‿i ‖ ˈduː |i ˈdjuː i **~ier** i‿ə ‖ i‿ᵊr **~iest** i‿ɪst i‿əst **~ily** ɪ li əl i **~iness** i nəs i nɪs

dewy-eyed ˌdjuː‿i ˈaɪd ◂ →ˌdʒuː- ‖ ˌduː- ˌdjuː-

Dexedrine *tdmk* ˈdeks ɪ driːn -ə-

Dexter, d~ ˈdekst ə ‖ -ᵊr

dexterity dek ˈster ət i -ɪt- ‖ -əţ i

dexterous ˈdeks tər‿əs **~ly** li **~ness** nəs nɪs

dextral ˈdeks trəl **~ly** i

dextrality dek ˈstræl ət i -ɪt- ‖ -əţ i

D

dextrin ˈdeks trɪn
dextro- ¦deks trəʊ ‖ -troʊ
dextrorotatory ˌdeks trəʊ rəʊ ˈteɪt ər i ◂ -ˈrəʊt ət̬ər i ‖ -troʊ ˈroʊt̬ ə tɔːr i ◂ -toʊr i *(*)*
dextrorse ˈdeks trɔːs ₍ˌ₎dek ˈstrɔːs ‖ -trɔːrs **~ly** li
dextrose ˈdeks trəʊz -trəʊs ‖ -troʊs -troʊz
dextrous ˈdeks trəs **~ly** li **~ness** nəs nɪs
dey deɪ *(= day)* **deys** deɪz
De Zoete də ˈzuːt
DFID ˈdɪf ɪd
Dhahran ˌdɑː ˈræn -ˈrɑːn ‖ -ˈrɑːn —*Arabic* [ðˤɑh ˈrɑːn]
Dhaka ˈdæk ə
dhal dɑːl —*Hindi* [dɑːl]
dhansak dʌn ˈsɑːk —*Hindi* [d̪ən̪ saːk]
dharma ˈdɑːm ə ‖ ˈdɑːrm ə —*Hindi* [d̪ʱərm]
Dharug, Dharuk, Dharruk dɑː ˈruːg ˈdʌr ʊk
Dhekelia di ˈkeɪl i‿ə də-
dhobi ˈdəʊb i ‖ ˈdoʊb i —*Hindi* [ˈd̪ʱoː bi] **~s** z **ˈdhobi('s) itch**
dhole dəʊl →dɒʊl ‖ doʊl *(= dole)* **dholes** dəʊlz →dɒʊlz ‖ doʊlz
dhoti ˈdəʊt i ‖ ˈdoʊt̬ i —*Hindi* [ˈd̪ʱoː t̪i] **~s** z
dhow daʊ **dhows** daʊz
dhurrie ˈdʌr i ‖ ˈdɜː i **~s** z
di- ¦daɪ — **dimorphemic** ˌdaɪ mɔː ˈfiːm ɪk ◂ ‖ -mɔːr-
Di daɪ **Di's** daɪz
dia- *comb. form*
with stress-neutral suffix ¦daɪ‿ə — **diatropic** ˌdaɪ‿ə ˈtrɒp ɪk ◂ ‖ -ˈtrɑːp-
with stress-imposing suffix daɪ ˈæ+ — **diatropism** daɪ ˈætr ə ˌpɪz əm
diabesity ˌdaɪ‿ə ˈbiːs ət i -ɪt i ‖ -ət̬ i
diabetes ˌdaɪ‿ə ˈbiːt iːz ◂ -ɪs, §-əs ‖ -ˈbiːt̬ əs -iːz **ˌdiaˌbetes inˈsipidus** ɪn ˈsɪp ɪd əs §-əd əs; **ˌdiaˌbetes melˈlitus** mə ˈlaɪt əs mɪ-, me- ‖ -ˈlaɪt̬- ˈmel ət̬ əs
diabetic ˌdaɪ‿ə ˈbet ɪk ◂ ‖ -ˈbet̬- **~s** s
diablerie di ˈɑːb lər i —*Fr* [dja blə ʁi]
diabolic ˌdaɪ‿ə ˈbɒl ɪk ◂ ‖ -ˈbɑːl- **~al** əl **~ally** əl‿i
diabolism daɪ ˈæb ə ˌlɪz əm
diabolo daɪ ˈæb ə ləʊ di- ‖ -loʊ **~s** z
diachronic ˌdaɪ‿ə ˈkrɒn ɪk ◂ ‖ -ˈkrɑːn- **~ally** əl‿i
diachrony daɪ ˈæk rən i
diacidic ˌdaɪ‿ə ˈsɪd ɪk ◂
diaconal daɪ ˈæk ən əl di-
diaconate daɪ ˈæk ə neɪt di-, -ən ət, -ən ɪt
diacritic ˌdaɪ‿ə ˈkrɪt ɪk ‖ -ˈkrɪt̬- **~al** əl **~ally** əl‿i **~s** s
diadem ˈdaɪ‿ə dem -əd əm **~ed** d **~s** z
Diadochi daɪ ˈæd ə kaɪ
diaer|esis daɪ ˈɪər |əs ɪs -ˈer-, -ɪs ɪs, §-əs ‖ -ˈer- **~eses** ə siːz ɪ-
Diageo *tdmk* di ˈædʒ i əʊ ‖ -oʊ
Diaghilev di ˈæg ə lef -ɪ-

DIAGNOSE

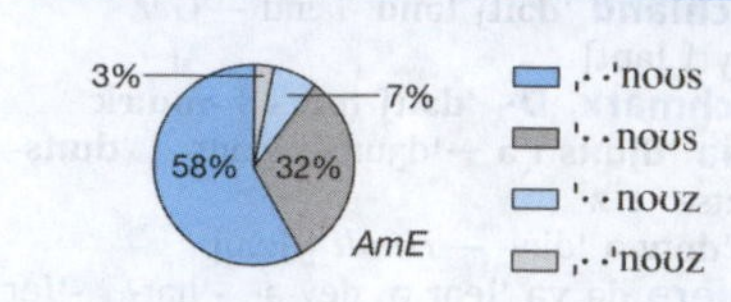

diagnos|e ˈdaɪ‿əg nəʊz -nəʊs, ˌ· ·ˈ· ‖ ˌ· ·ˈnoʊs -ˈnoʊz, ˈ· · · — *Preference poll. AmE:* ˌ· ·ˈnoʊs *58%,* ˈ· ·noʊs *32%,* ˈ· ·noʊz *7%,* ˌ· ·ˈnoʊz *3%.* **~ed** d ‖ t **~es** *v* ɪz əz **~ing** ɪŋ
diagnos|is ˌdaɪ‿əg ˈnəʊs |ɪs -ˈnəʊz-, §-əs ‖ -ˈnoʊs- **~es** *n* iːz
diagnostic ˌdaɪ‿əg ˈnɒst ɪk ◂ ‖ -ˈnɑːst- **~ally** əl‿i **~s** s
diagnostician ˌdaɪ‿əg nɒ ˈstɪʃ ən ‖ -nɑːˈ· · **~s** z
diagonal daɪ ˈæg ən‿əl **~ly** i **~s** z
diagram ˈdaɪ‿ə græm **~ed** d **~ing** ɪŋ **~med** d **~ming** ɪŋ **~s** z
diagrammatic ˌdaɪ‿ə grə ˈmæt ɪk ◂ ‖ -ˈmæt̬- **~al** əl **~ally** əl‿i
dial ˈdaɪ‿əl daɪəl **dialed, dialled** ˈdaɪ‿əld daɪəld **dialing, dialling** ˈdaɪ‿əl ɪŋ ˈdaɪəl ɪŋ **dials** ˈdaɪ‿əlz daɪəlz **ˈdialling code**; **ˈdialling tone**; **ˈdial tone**
dialect ˈdaɪ‿ə lekt **~s** s
dialectal ˌdaɪ‿ə ˈlekt əl ◂ **~ly** i
dialectic ˌdaɪ‿ə ˈlekt ɪk ◂ **~al** əl **~ally** əl‿i **~s** s
dialectician ˌdaɪ‿ə lek ˈtɪʃ ən **~s** z
dialectological ˌdaɪ‿ə lekt ə ˈlɒdʒ ɪk əl ‖ -ˈlɑːdʒ- **~ly** ‿i
dialectologist ˌdaɪ‿ə lek ˈtɒl ədʒ ɪst §-əst ‖ -ˈtɑːl- **~s** s
dialectology ˌdaɪ‿ə lek ˈtɒl ədʒ i ‖ -ˈtɑːl-
dialog, dialogue ˈdaɪ‿ə lɒg ‖ -lɔːg -lɑːg **~s** z
dialup ˈdaɪ‿əl ʌp ˈdaɪəl ʌp
dialys|e ˈdaɪ‿ə laɪz **~ed** d **~es** ɪz əz **~ing** ɪŋ
dialyses *from v* ˈdaɪ‿ə laɪz ɪz -əz
dialyses *n pl* daɪ ˈæl ə siːz -ɪ-
dial|ysis daɪ ˈæl |əs ɪs -ɪs-, §-əs **~yses** ə siːz -ɪ-
diamagnetic ˌdaɪ‿ə mæg ˈnet ɪk ◂ -məgˈ-- ‖ -ˈnet̬-
diamante, diamanté ˌdiː‿ə ˈmɒnt eɪ ˌdaɪ‿, -ˈmænt-, -i ‖ -mɑːn ˈteɪ
diameter daɪ ˈæm ɪt ə -ət- ‖ -ət̬ ər **~s** z
diametral daɪ ˈæm ɪtr əl -ətr-
diametric ˌdaɪ‿ə ˈmetr ɪk ◂ **~al** əl **~ally** əl‿i **ˌdiaˌmetrically opˈposed**
diamond, D~ ˈdaɪ‿əm ənd §ˈdaɪm ənd ‖ ˈdaɪm ənd **~ed** ɪd əd **~s** z **ˌdiamond ˈjubilee**; **ˌdiamond ˈwedding (anniˌversary)**
diamondback ˈdaɪ‿əm ənd bæk §ˈdaɪm· · ‖ ˈdaɪm· · **~s** s
Dian ₍ˌ₎daɪ ˈæn di-
Diana daɪ ˈæn ə
Diane ₍ˌ₎daɪ ˈæn di-
dianetics *tdmk* ˌdaɪ‿ə ˈnet ɪks ‖ -ˈnet̬-
dianoetic ˌdaɪ‿ə nəʊ ˈet ɪk ◂ ‖ -noʊ ˈet̬-
dianthus daɪ ˈænᵗθ əs **~es** ɪz əz

apason ˌdaɪ‿ə ˈpeɪz ᵊn -ˈpeɪs- **~s** z
aper ˈdaɪ‿əp ə §ˈdaɪp ə ‖ ˈdaɪp ᵊr **~ed** d
diapering ˈdaɪ‿əp ər‿ɪŋ §ˈdaɪp ər‿ɪŋ ‖ ˈdaɪp ər‿ɪŋ **~s** z
aphanous daɪ ˈæf ən əs **~ly** li **~ness** nəs nɪs
aphone ˈdaɪ‿ə fəʊn ‖ -foʊn **~s** z
aphoneme ˈdaɪ‿ə ˌfəʊn iːm ˌ···ˈ· ‖ -ˌfoʊn- **~s** z
aphonemic ˌdaɪ‿ə fəʊ ˈniːm ɪk ‖ -fəˈ-- **~ally** ᵊl‿i
aphonic ˌdaɪ‿ə ˈfɒn ɪk ◂ ‖ -ˈfɑːn- **~ally** ᵊl‿i
aphoresis ˌdaɪ‿ə fə ˈriːs ɪs -fɒˈ--, -fɔːˈ--, §-əs
aphoretic ˌdaɪ‿ə fə ˈret ɪk ◂ -fɒˈ--, -fɔːˈ-- ‖ -ˈret̬ ɪk ◂ **~s** s
aphragm ˈdaɪ‿ə fræm **~s** z
aphragmatic ˌdaɪ‿ə fræg ˈmæt ɪk ◂ ‖ -ˈmæt̬- **~ally** ᵊl i
aph|ysis daɪ ˈæf |əs ɪs -ɪs ɪs, §-əs **~yses** ə siːz ɪ-
iarch|y ˈdaɪ ɑːk |i ‖ -ɑːrk |i **~ies** iz
iaries ˈdaɪ‿ər iz
iarist ˈdaɪ‿ər ɪst §-əst; ⚠ˈdaɪ‿ər i ɪst **~s** s
iarrhea, diarrhoea ˌdaɪ‿ə ˈrɪə §-ˈriː‿ə ‖ -ˈriː ə
iar|y ˈdaɪ‿ər |i **~ies** iz
ias ˈdiː‿əs —*Port* [ˈdi ɐʃ]
iaspora, D~ daɪ ˈæsp ər ə ˌdaɪ‿ə ˈspɔːr ə **~s** z
iaspore ˈdaɪ‿ə spɔː ‖ -spɔːr -spoʊr
iastase ˈdaɪ‿ə steɪz -steɪs
iastole daɪ ˈæst əl i
iastolic ˌdaɪ‿ə ˈstɒl ɪk ◂ ‖ -ˈstɑːl-
iathermy ˈdaɪ‿ə ˌθɜːm i ‖ -ˌθɜːm i
iath|esis daɪ ˈæθ |əs ɪs -ɪs ɪs, §-əs **~eses** ə siːz ɪ-
iatom ˈdaɪ‿ə tɒm ət əm ‖ -tɑːm **~s** z
iatomaceous ˌdaɪ‿ət ə ˈmeɪʃ əs ‖ -ət̬ ə-
iatomic ˌdaɪ‿ə ˈtɒm ɪk ◂ ‖ -ˈtɑːm-
iatomite daɪ ˈæt ə maɪt ‖ -ˈæt̬-
iatonic ˌdaɪ‿ə ˈtɒn ɪk ◂ ‖ -ˈtɑːn- **~ally** ᵊl‿i
ˌdiaˌtonic ˈscale
iatribe ˈdaɪ‿ə traɪb **~s** z
Diaz ˈdiː æs -æθ ‖ -ɑːs —*Sp* Díaz [ˈdi aθ], *AmSp* [-as]; *Port* Diaz [ˈdi ɐʃ]
iazepam daɪ ˈeɪz ə pæm -ˈæz-, -ɪ- ‖ -ˈæz-
iazo ₍ₗ₎daɪ ˈeɪz əʊ -ˈæz- ‖ -ˈæz oʊ
iazonium ˌdaɪ‿ə ˈzəʊn i‿əm ‖ -ˈzoʊn-
dib dɪb **dibbed** dɪbd **dibbing** ˈdɪb ɪŋ **dibs** dɪbz
dibber ˈdɪb ə ‖ -ᵊr **~s** z
dibbl|e, D~ ˈdɪb ᵊl **~ed** d **~er/s** ə/z ‖ -ᵊr/z **~es** z **~ing** ‿ɪŋ
Dibden ˈdɪb dən
dibs dɪbz
DiCaprio di ˈkæp ri əʊ ‖ -oʊ
dicast ˈdɪk æst **~s** s
Diccon ˈdɪk ən
dice daɪs **diced** daɪst **dices** ˈdaɪs ɪz -əz **dicing** ˈdaɪs ɪŋ
dicentra ₍ₗ₎daɪ ˈsentr ə **~s** z
dic|ey ˈdaɪs |i **~ier** i‿ə ‖ i‿ᵊr **~iest** i‿ɪst i‿əst
dichlorvos daɪ ˈklɔː vɒs ‖ -ˈklɔːr voʊs -ˈkloʊr-
dichotic ₍ₗ₎daɪ ˈkɒt ɪk dɪ- ‖ -ˈkɑːt̬ ɪk
dichotom|y daɪ ˈkɒt əm |i dɪ- ‖ -ˈkɑːt̬- **~ies** iz
Dick, dick dɪk **Dick's, dicks** dɪks
Dicken ˈdɪk ɪn §-ən
Dickens, d~ ˈdɪk ɪnz §-ənz **D~'** ɪz əz —*or as nominative*
Dickensian dɪ ˈkenz i‿ən də- **~s** z
dicker, D~ ˈdɪk ə ‖ -ᵊr **~ed** d **dickering** ˈdɪk ər‿ɪŋ **~s** z
Dickerson ˈdɪk əs ən ‖ -ᵊrs-
dickey, dickie, D~ ˈdɪk i **~s** z
dickhead ˈdɪk hed **~s** z
Dickie ˈdɪk i
Dickins ˈdɪk ɪnz §-ənz
Dickinson ˈdɪk ɪn sən §-ən-
Dickon ˈdɪk ən
Dickson ˈdɪks ᵊn
dick|y, Dicky ˈdɪk |i **~ies, ~y's** iz
dickybird ˈdɪk i bɜːd ‖ -bɜːd **~s** z
dicotyledon ˌdaɪ ˌkɒt ɪ ˈliːd ᵊn -ə-, -ᵊl ˈiːd- ‖ -ˌkɑːt̬ ᵊl ˈiːd ᵊn ˌ·ˌ··ˈ·· **~s** z
dicoumarol ₍ₗ₎daɪ ˈkuːm ə rɒl ‖ -roʊl -rɑːl, -rɔːl
dicta ˈdɪkt ə
dictaphone, D~ *tdmk* ˈdɪkt ə fəʊn ‖ -foʊn **~s** z
dictate *n* ˈdɪkt eɪt **~s** s
dict|ate *v* ₍ₗ₎dɪk ˈt|eɪt ‖ ˈdɪkt |eɪt dɪk ˈt|eɪt **~ated** eɪt ɪd -əd ‖ eɪt̬ əd **~ates** eɪts **~ating** eɪt ɪŋ ‖ eɪt̬ ɪŋ
dictation dɪk ˈteɪʃ ᵊn **~s** z
dictator dɪk ˈteɪt ə ‖ ˈdɪkt eɪt̬ ᵊr dɪk ˈteɪt̬ ᵊr **~s** z
dictatorial ˌdɪkt ə ˈtɔːr i‿əl ◂ ‖ -ˈtoʊr- **~ly** i **~ness** nəs nɪs
dictatorship dɪk ˈteɪt ə ʃɪp ‖ ˈdɪkt eɪt̬ ᵊr ʃɪp dɪk ˈteɪt̬ ᵊr- **~s** s
diction ˈdɪk ʃᵊn
dictionar|y ˈdɪk ʃən ᵊr‿|i ˈdɪk ʃᵊn‿ər |i, §-ʃə ner |i ‖ ˈdɪk ʃə ner |i **~ies** iz
dict|um ˈdɪkt |əm **~a** ə **~ums** əmz
did dɪd *occasional weak forms* §dəd, d —*see* **ˈd**
didactic daɪ ˈdækt ɪk dɪ-, də- **~ally** ᵊl‿i **~s** s
didacticism daɪ ˈdækt ɪ ˌsɪz əm dɪ-, də-, -ə-
Didcot ˈdɪd kət →ˈdɪg-, -kɒt ‖ -kɑːt
diddl|e ˈdɪd ᵊl **~ed** d **~es** z **~ing** ‿ɪŋ
diddly ˈdɪd ᵊl‿i
diddlysquat ˌdɪd ᵊl‿i ˈskwɒt ˈ· · · · ‖ -ˈskwɑːt
diddums ˈdɪd əmz
diddy, Diddy ˈdɪd i
Diderot ˈdiːd ə rəʊ ‖ ˌdiːd ə ˈroʊ —*Fr* [di dʁo]
didgeridoo ˌdɪdʒ ər‿i ˈduː **~s** z
didicoy, didikoi ˈdɪd ɪ kɔɪ -ə- **~s** z
Didier ˈdɪd i eɪ —*Fr* [di dje]
didn't ˈdɪd ᵊnt ⚠ˈdɪt- —*non-final also* ˈdɪd ᵊn
Dido, dido ˈdaɪd əʊ ‖ -oʊ
didst dɪdst dɪtst
did|y ˈdaɪd |i **~ies** iz
didymous, Didymus ˈdɪd ɪm əs -əm-
die daɪ **died** daɪd **dieing** ˈdaɪ ɪŋ **dies** daɪz **dying** ˈdaɪ ɪŋ
dieback ˈdaɪ bæk
die-cast ˈdaɪ kɑːst §-kæst ‖ -kæst **~ing** ɪŋ **~s** s
dieffenbachia ˌdiːf ᵊn ˈbæk i‿ə →ˌᵊm- ‖ -ˈbɑːk- **~s** z
Diego di ˈeɪg əʊ ‖ -oʊ —*Sp* [ˈdje ɣo]

diehard 'daɪ hɑːd ‖ -hɑːrd **~s** z
dieldrin 'diːəldr ɪn -ən
dielectric ˌdaɪ ɪ 'lek trɪk ◂ -ə- **~ally** əl‿i **~s** s
diene, -diene 'daɪ iːn
Dieppe di 'ep ˌdiː- —*Fr* [djɛp]
dier|esis daɪ 'ɪər |əs ɪs -'er-, -ɪs ɪs, §-əs ‖ -'er- **~eses** ə siːz ɪ-
dies *from* **die** daɪz
dies *Latin, 'day'* 'diː eɪz 'daɪ iːz ‖ -eɪs —*See also phrases with this word*
diesel, D~ 'diːz əl ‖ 'diːs- **~s** z
'**diesel** ˌ**engine**; '**diesel** ˌ**fuel**; '**diesel oil**
diesel-electric ˌdiːz əl ɪ 'lek trɪk ◂ -ə'-- ‖ ˌdiːs- **~s** s
dieselisation, dieselization ˌdiːz əl aɪ 'zeɪʃ ən -əl ɪ- ‖ -əl ə- ˌdiːs-
Dies Irae ˌdiː eɪz 'ɪər aɪ -ez-, -es-, -eɪ ‖ -eɪs 'ɪr eɪ
di|esis 'daɪ‿|əs ɪs ɪs ɪs, §-əs **~eses** ə siːz ɪ-
dies non ˌdaɪ iːz 'nɒn ˌdiː eɪz-, -'nəʊn ‖ -'nɑːn ˌdiː eɪs-, -'noʊn
di|et 'daɪ‿|ət **~eted** ət ɪd -əd ‖ əţ əd **~eting** ət ɪŋ ‖ əţ ɪŋ **~ets** əts
dietar|y 'daɪ‿ət‿ər |i ‖ 'daɪ ə ter |i **~ies** iz
dieter *'one that diets'* 'daɪ‿ət ə ‖ 'daɪ əţ ər **~s** z
Dieter *name* 'diːt ə ‖ 'diːţ ər —*Ger* ['diː tɐ]
dietetic ˌdaɪ‿ə 'tet ɪk ◂ ɪ- ‖ -'teţ- **~ally** əl‿i **~s** s
diethylstil|bestrol, ~boestrol ˌdaɪ ˌeθ əl stɪl 'biːs trɒl -ˌiːθ-, -ˌɪl-, -'bes-, -trəl ‖ daɪ ˌeθ əl stɪl 'bes troʊl -trɑːl, -trɔːl
dietician, dietitian ˌdaɪ‿ə 'tɪʃ ən **~s** z
Dietrich 'diːtr ɪk 'dɪətr-, -ɪx, -ɪʃ —*Ger* ['diː tʁɪç]
Dieu et mon droit ˌdjɜːr eɪ mɒn 'drwɑː ‖ ˌdjʊ eɪ mɔːn 'dwɑː —*Fr* [djø e mɔ̃ dʁwa]
differ 'dɪf ə ‖ -ər **~ed** d **differing** 'dɪf ər‿ɪŋ **~s** z
differenc|e 'dɪf rənts 'dɪf ər‿ənts ‖ 'dɪf ər ənts **~ed** t **~es** ɪz əz **~ing** ɪŋ
different 'dɪf rənt 'dɪf ər‿ənt ‖ 'dɪf ər ənt **~ly** li **~ness** nəs nɪs
different|ia ˌdɪf ə 'rentʃ|i‿ə **~iae** i iː i aɪ, i eɪ
differential ˌdɪf ə 'rentʃ əl ◂ **~ly** i **~s** z
ˌ**diffe**ˌ**rential** '**calculus**; ˌ**diffe**ˌ**rential e'quation**; ˌ**diffe**ˌ**rential** '**gear**
differenti|ate ˌdɪf ə 'rentʃ i |eɪt **~ated** eɪt ɪd -əd ‖ eɪţ əd **~ates** eɪts **~ating** eɪt ɪŋ ‖ eɪţ ɪŋ
differentiation ˌdɪf ə ˌrentʃ i 'eɪʃ ən **~s** z
difficile 'dɪf ɪ sɪl -ə-; ˌdɪf ɪ 'siːəl —*The name of the bacterium Clostridium d~ is Latin, not French* —*Latin* [dif 'fi ki le]
difficult 'dɪf ɪk əlt -ək-; §-ɪ kʌlt, -ə- **~ly** li
difficult|y 'dɪf ɪk əlt |i '-ək-; §-ɪ kʌlt-, §-ə kʌlt- **~ies** iz
diffidence 'dɪf ɪd ənts -əd-
diffident 'dɪf ɪd ənt -əd- **~ly** li
diffract dɪ 'frækt də- **~ed** ɪd əd **~ing** ɪŋ **~s** s
diffraction dɪ 'fræk ʃən də- **~s** z
diffus|e *v* dɪ 'fjuːz də- **~ed** d **~es** ɪz əz **~ing** ɪŋ
diffuse *adj* dɪ 'fjuːs də-, daɪ- **~ly** li **~ness** nəs nɪs
diffuser *n* dɪ 'fjuːz ə də- ‖ -ər **~s** z
diffusion dɪ 'fjuːʒ ən də- **~s** z
diffusive dɪ 'fjuːs ɪv də-, §-'fjuːz- **~ly** li **~ness** nəs nɪs
diffusivity ˌdɪf ju 'sɪv ət i dɪ ˌfjuː-, də ˌfjuː-, -ɪt i ‖ -əţ i
dig dɪg **digging** 'dɪg ɪŋ **digs** dɪgz **dug** dʌg
digamma 'daɪ ˌgæm ə (ˌ)'·· **~s** z
Digbeth 'dɪg bəθ
Digby 'dɪg bi
digerati ˌdɪdʒ ə 'rɑːt i ‖ -'rɑːţ i
digest *v* daɪ 'dʒest dɪ-, də- **~ed** ɪd əd **~ing** ɪŋ **~s** s
digest *n* 'daɪ dʒest **~s** s
digestant daɪ 'dʒest ənt dɪ-, də- **~s** s
digestibility daɪ ˌdʒest ə 'bɪl ət i dɪ-, də-, -ˌɪ -ɪt i ‖ -əţ i
digestib|le daɪ 'dʒest əb |əl dɪ-, də-, -ɪb- **~ly**
digestif dɪ 'ʒest iːf ˌdiːʒ es 'tiːf —*Fr* [di ʒɛs tif] **~s** s
digestion daɪ 'dʒes tʃən dɪ-, də-, →-'dʒeʃ- **~s**
digestive daɪ 'dʒest ɪv dɪ-, də- **~ly** li **~s** z
digger, D~ 'dɪg ə ‖ -ər **~s** z
digging 'dɪg ɪŋ **~s** z
Diggle 'dɪg əl
dight daɪt
digibox, D~ *tdmk* 'dɪdʒ i bɒks ‖ -bɑːks **~es** ɪz əz
digicam 'dɪdʒ ɪ kæm **~s** z
digipack, Digipak *tdmk* 'dɪdʒ i pæk **~s** s
digit 'dɪdʒ ɪt §-ət **~s** s
digital 'dɪdʒ ɪt əl -ət- ‖ -əţ əl **~ly** i **~s** z
digitalin ˌdɪdʒ ɪ 'teɪl ɪn -ə-, §-ən ‖ -'tæl-
digitalis ˌdɪdʒ ɪ 'teɪl ɪs -ə-, §-əs ‖ -'tæl- *(*)*
digitis... —*see* **digitiz...**
digitization ˌdɪdʒ ɪt aɪ 'zeɪʃ ən ˌ·ət-, -ɪ'-- ‖ -əţ ə-
digitiz|e 'dɪdʒ ɪ taɪz -ə- **~ed** d **~er/s** ə/z ‖ ər/z **~es** ɪz əz **~ing** ɪŋ
diglossia (ˌ)daɪ 'glɒs i‿ə ‖ -'glɑːs- -'glɔːs-
diglossic (ˌ)daɪ 'glɒs ɪk ‖ -'glɑːs-
diglot 'daɪ glɒt ‖ -glɑːt **~s** s
digni|fy 'dɪg nɪ |faɪ -nə- **~fied/ly** faɪd /li **~fies** faɪz **~fying** faɪ ɪŋ
dignitar|y 'dɪg nət‿ər |i '-nɪt-‖ -nə ter |i **~ies** iz
dignity 'dɪg nət |i -nɪt- ‖ -nəţ |i **~ies** iz
digoxin dɪ 'dʒɒks ɪn -ən ‖ -'dʒɑːks-
digraph 'daɪ grɑːf -græf ‖ -græf **~s** s
digress daɪ 'gres **~ed** t **~es** ɪz əz **~ing** ɪŋ
digression daɪ 'greʃ ən **~s** z
digressive daɪ 'gres ɪv **~ly** li **~ness** nəs nɪs
dihedral (ˌ)daɪ 'hiːdr əl **~s** z
Dijkstra 'daɪks trə —*Dutch* ['dɛik strɑ]
Dijon 'diːʒ ɒ̃ -ɒn ‖ diː 'ʒɑːn -'ʒɔːn, -'ʒoʊn —*Fr* [di ʒɔ̃]
dik-dik 'dɪk dɪk **~s** s
dike daɪk **diked** daɪkt **dikes** daɪks **diking** 'daɪk ɪŋ
diktat 'dɪkt æt -ɑːt ‖ dɪk 'tɑːt **~s** s
dilapi|date dɪ 'læp ɪ |deɪt də-, -ə- **~dated** deɪt ɪd -əd ‖ deɪţ əd **~dates** deɪts **~dating** deɪt ɪŋ ‖ deɪţ ɪŋ
dilapidation dɪ ˌlæp ɪ 'deɪʃ ən də-, -ə- **~s** z
dilatation ˌdaɪl eɪ 'teɪʃ ən ˌdɪl-, -ə- **~s** z

i|late daɪ ˈ|leɪt dɪ-, də- ‖ ˈdaɪ |leɪt **~lated** leɪt ɪd -əd ‖ leɪţ əd **~lates** leɪts **~lating** leɪt ɪŋ ‖ leɪţ ɪŋ
ilation daɪ ˈleɪʃ ᵊn dɪ-, də- **~s** z
ilator daɪ ˈleɪt ə dɪ-, də- ‖ -ˈleɪţ ᵊr ˈdaɪ leɪţ ᵊr **~s** z
ilator|y ˈdɪl ət‿ər |i ‖ -ə tɔːr |i -toʊr i **~ily** əl i ɪ li **~iness** i nəs i nɪs
ilbert ˈdɪl bət -bɜːt ‖ -bᵊrt
ildo, dildoe ˈdɪld əʊ ‖ -oʊ **~s** z
ildonics dɪl ˈdɒn ɪks ‖ -ˈdɑːn-
ilemma dɪ ˈlem ə daɪ-, də- **~s** z
ilet|tante ˌdɪl ə |ˈtænt i -ɪ- ‖ -|ˈtɑːnt ˈ· · · **~tantes** ˈtænt iz ‖ ˈtɑːnts **~tanti** ˈtænt iː ‖ -ˈtɑːnţ i
ilettantism ˌdɪl ə ˈtænt ˌɪz əm -ɪ- ‖ -ˈtɑːnt- ˈ· · ˌ· ·
Dilhorne ˈdɪl ən -ɔːn ‖ -ᵊrn -hɔːrn
Dili, Díli ˈdiːl i
diligenc|e ˈdɪl ɪdʒ ənᵗs -ədʒ- **~es** ɪz əz
diligent ˈdɪl ɪdʒ ənt -ədʒ- **~ly** li
Dilke dɪlk
dill, Dill dɪl
ˌ**dill ˈpickle**
Diller ˈdɪl ə ‖ -ᵊr
dilli... —*see* **dilly**
Dillinger ˈdɪl ɪndʒ ə ‖ ᵊr
Dillon ˈdɪl ən
Dillwyn ˈdɪl wɪn -ɪn
dill|y, Dilly ˈdɪl |i **~ies** iz
ˈ**dilly bag**
dilly-dall|y ˈdɪl i ˌdæl |i ˌ· ˈ· · **~ied** id **~ies** iz **~ying** i‿ɪŋ
diluent ˈdɪl ju‿ənt **~s** s
di|lute *v, adj* ₍ₗ₎daɪ |ˈluːt dɪ-, də-, -ˈljuːt **~luted** ˈluːt ɪd ˈljuːt-, -əd ‖ ˈluːţ əd **~lutes** ˈluːts ˈljuːts **~luting** ˈlut ɪŋ ˈljuːt- ‖ ˈluːţ ɪŋ
dilution ₍ₗ₎daɪ ˈluːʃ ᵊn dɪ-, də-, -ˈljuːʃ- **~s** z
diluvi|al daɪ ˈluːv i‿|əl dɪ-, də-, -ˈljuːv- **~an** ən **~um** əm
Dilworth ˈdɪl wɜːθ -wəθ ‖ -wᵊrθ
Dilwyn ˈdɪl wɪn
Dilys ˈdɪl ɪs §-əs
dim dɪm **dimmed** dɪmd **dimmer** ˈdɪm ə ‖ -ᵊr **dimmest** ˈdɪm ɪst §-əst **dimming** ˈdɪm ɪŋ **dims** dɪmz —*See also phrases with this word*
DiMaggio dɪ ˈmædʒ i əʊ ‖ -oʊ ·ˈ·oʊ
Dimbleby ˈdɪm bᵊl bi
dime daɪm **dimes** daɪmz
dimension daɪ ˈmenᵗʃ ᵊn dɪ-, də- ‖ də- **~ed** d **~ing** ‿ɪŋ **~s** z
dimensional daɪ ˈmenᵗʃ ᵊn‿əl dɪ-, də- ‖ də- **~ly** i
dimensionality daɪ ˌmenᵗʃ ə ˈnæl ət i dɪ-, də-, -ɪt i ‖ də ˌmenᵗʃ ə ˈnæl əţ i
Diment ˈdaɪm ənt
dimer ˈdaɪm ə ˈdaɪ mɜː ‖ -ᵊr **~s** z
dimercaprol ˌdaɪ mɜː ˈkæp rɒl -mə- ‖ -mᵊr ˈkæp roʊl -rɑːl, -rɔːl
dimerism ˈdɪm ər ˌɪz əm
dimerous ˈdɪm ər əs
dimeter ˈdɪm ɪt ə -ət- ‖ -əţ ᵊr **~s** z
diminish dɪ ˈmɪn ɪʃ də- **~ed** t **~es** ɪz əz **~ing** ɪŋ **~ment** mənt
diˌ**minished reˌsponsiˈbility**; diˌ**minishing reˈturns**
diminuendo dɪ ˌmɪn ju ˈend əʊ də- ‖ -oʊ **~es, ~s** z
diminution ˌdɪm ɪ ˈnjuːʃ ᵊn -ə-, ⚠-ju- ‖ -ˈnuːʃ- -ˈnjuːʃ- **~s** z
diminutive dɪ ˈmɪn jut ɪv də-, -jət- ‖ -jəţ ɪv **~ly** li **~ness** nəs nɪs **~s** z
dimit|y, D~ ˈdɪm ət |i -ɪt- ‖ -əţ |i **~ies** iz
dimly ˈdɪm li
dimmer ˈdɪm ə ‖ -ᵊr **~s** z
ˈ**dimmer switch**
dimmish ˈdɪm ɪʃ
Dimmock ˈdɪm ək
dimness ˈdɪm nəs -nɪs
dimorph|ism ₍ₗ₎daɪ ˈmɔːf |ˌɪz əm ‖ -ˈmɔːrf- **~ous** əs
dimout ˈdɪm aʊt **~s** s
dimpl|e ˈdɪmp ᵊl **~ed** d **~es** z **~ing** ‿ɪŋ
Dimplex *tdmk* ˈdɪmp leks
dimply ˈdɪmp li
dim sum ˌdɪm ˈsʌm -ˈsʊm —*Cantonese* [²dim ¹sem]
dimwit ˈdɪm wɪt **~s** s
dim-witted ˌdɪm ˈwɪt ɪd ◂ -əd ‖ -ˈwɪţ əd ◂ **~ly** li **~ness** nəs nɪs
din, DIN dɪn **dinned** dɪnd **dinning** ˈdɪn ɪŋ **dins** dɪnz
Dina *(i)* ˈdiːn ə, *(ii)* ˈdaɪn-
Dinah ˈdaɪn ə
dinar ˈdiːn ɑː ‖ dɪ ˈnɑːr ˈdiːn ɑːr **~s** z
Dinaric dɪ ˈnær ɪk də-, daɪ- ‖ -ˈner-
Diˌ**naric ˈAlps**
Dinas ˈdiːn æs
din-din ˈdɪn dɪn **~s** z
dine daɪn **dined** daɪnd **dines** daɪnz **dining** ˈdaɪn ɪŋ
Dineen dɪ ˈniːn də-
Dinefwr dɪ ˈnev ʊə ‖ -ʊr
diner ˈdaɪn ə ‖ -ᵊr **~s** z
dinero di ˈneər əʊ ‖ -ˈner oʊ
Dinesen ˈdɪn ɪs ən ˈdiːn-, -əs-, -ɪn
dinette ₍ₗ₎daɪ ˈnet **~s** s
ding dɪŋ **dinged** dɪŋd **dinging** ˈdɪŋ ɪŋ **dings** dɪŋz —*See also phrases with this word*
Dingaan ˈdɪŋ gɑːn
dingaling ˈdɪŋ ə ˈlɪŋ ˈ· · · **~s** z
Ding an sich ˌdɪŋ æn ˈsɪk -ˈsɪx ‖ -ɑːn ˈzɪk —*Ger* [ˌdɪŋ an ˈzɪç]
dingbat ˈdɪŋ bæt **~s** s
dingdong ˈdɪŋ dɒŋ ˌ·ˈ·◂ ‖ -dɔːŋ -dɑːŋ **~s** z
dinge dɪndʒ **dinges** ˈdɪndʒ ɪz -əz
dinger ˈdɪŋ ə ‖ -ᵊr **~s** z
dingh|y ˈdɪŋ |i -g|i **~ies** iz
dingi... —*see* **dingy**
dingle, D~ ˈdɪŋ gᵊl **~s** z
Dingley ˈdɪŋ li
dingo ˈdɪŋ gəʊ ‖ -goʊ **~es** z
dingus ˈdɪŋ əs -gəs **~es** ɪz əz
Dingwall ˈdɪŋ wɔːl -wəl ‖ -wɑːl

D

ding|y ˈdɪndʒ |i **~ier** i‿ə ‖ i‿ᵊr **~iest** i‿ɪst i‿əst **~ily** ɪ li əl i **~iness** i nəs i nɪs

dining ˈdaɪn ɪŋ
 ˈdining car; **ˈdining room**; **ˈdining ˌtable**

dink dɪŋk **dinks** dɪŋks

Dinka ˈdɪŋk ə **~s** z

dinki... —*see* **dinky**

Dinkins ˈdɪŋk ɪnz §-ənz ‖ ˈdɪn kɪnz

dinkum ˈdɪŋk əm

dink|y ˈdɪŋk |i **~ier** i‿ə ‖ i‿ᵊr **~ies** iz **~iest** i‿ɪst i‿əst

dinner ˈdɪn ə ‖ -ᵊr **~s** z
 ˈdinner bell; **ˈdinner ˌjacket**; **ˈdinner ˌparty**; **ˈdinner plate**; **ˈdinner ˌservice**; **ˈdinner set**; **ˈdinner ˌtable**

dinnertime ˈdɪn ə taɪm ‖ -ᵊr- **~s** z

dinoflagellate ˌdaɪn əʊ ˈflædʒ ə leɪt -ˈ-ɪ-; -əl ət, -ɪt ‖ ˌ-oʊ- **~s** s

Dinorwic dɪ ˈnɔː wɪk də- ‖ -ˈnɔːr-

dinosaur ˈdaɪn ə sɔː ‖ -sɔːr **~s** z

dinosaurian ˌdaɪn ə ˈsɔːr i‿ən ◂ **~s** z

dinothere ˈdaɪn əʊ θɪə ‖ -ə θɪr **~s** z

Dinsdale ˈdɪnz deɪᵊl

dint dɪnt

Dinwiddie, Dinwiddy *(i)* dɪn ˈwɪd i, *(ii)* ˈdɪn wɪd i

Dio ˈdaɪ əʊ ‖ -oʊ

diocesan daɪ ˈɒs ɪs ən -əs-, -ɪz-, -əz- ‖ -ˈɑːs- **~s** z

di|ocese ˈdaɪ‿|əs ɪs §-əs; |ə siːz, -siːs **~oceses** ə siːz əs ɪs ɪz, -əz; ə siːz ɪz, ə siːs ɪz, -əz

Diocletian ˌdaɪ‿ə ˈkliːʃ ᵊn -ˈkliːʃ i‿ən

diode ˈdaɪ əʊd ‖ -oʊd **~s** z

Diodorus ˌdaɪ‿ə ˈdɔːr əs ‖ -ˈdoʊr-
 ˌDioˌdorus ˈSiculus ˈsɪk jʊl əs ‖ -jəl əs

dioecious daɪ ˈiːʃ əs **~ly** li

Diogenes daɪ ˈɒdʒ ə niːz -ɪ- ‖ -ˈɑːdʒ-

Diomede ˈdaɪ‿ə miːd

Diomedes ˌdaɪ‿ə ˈmiːd iːz

Dion *modern name* di ˈɒn ˈdiː‿ən -ɒn ‖ di ˈoʊn —*Fr* [djɔ̃]

Dion *classical name* ˈdaɪ‿ən

Dione daɪ ˈəʊn i ‖ -ˈoʊn i

Dionne ˌdiː ˈɒn di- ‖ -ˈɑːn

Dionysia ˌdaɪ‿ə ˈnɪz i‿ə -ˈnɪs- ‖ -ˈnɪʃ-

Dionysiac ˌdaɪ‿ə ˈnɪz i æk ◂ -ˈnɪs- ‖ -ˈnɪʃ-

Dionysian ˌdaɪ‿ə ˈnɪz i‿ən ◂ -ˈnɪs-, -ˈnaɪs- ‖ -ˈnɪʃ ᵊn -ˈnaɪs i‿ən **~s** z

Dionysius ˌdaɪ‿ə ˈnɪz i‿əs -ˈnɪs- ‖ -ˈnɪʃ- *(*)*

Dionysus ˌdaɪ‿ə ˈnaɪs əs -ˈniːs-

Diophantine ˌdaɪ‿əʊ ˈfænt aɪn ◂ ‖ -ə- -ᵊn

Diophantus ˌdaɪ‿əʊ ˈfænt əs ‖ -ə ˈfænt̬ əs

diopside daɪ ˈɒps aɪd ‖ -ˈɑːps-

dioptase daɪ ˈɒpt eɪz -eɪs ‖ -ˈɑːpt-

diopter, dioptre daɪ ˈɒpt ə ‖ -ˈɑːpt ᵊr **~s** z

Dior ˈdiː ɔː ·ˈ· ‖ di ˈɔːr —*Fr* [djɔːʁ]

diorama ˌdaɪ‿ə ˈrɑːm ə ‖ -ˈræm ə -ˈrɑːm ə

dioramic ˌdaɪ‿ə ˈræm ɪk ◂

diorite ˈdaɪ‿ə raɪt

Dioscuri daɪ ˈɒsk jʊr i -aɪ; ˌdaɪ ə ˈskjʊər-, -ɒ- ‖ ˌdaɪ ə ˈskjʊr aɪ

diotic daɪ ˈəʊt ɪk -ˈɒt- ‖ -ˈoʊt̬ ɪk -ˈɑːt- **~ally** ᵊl‿i

dioxide ₍ₗ₎daɪ ˈɒks aɪd ‖ -ˈɑːks- **~s** z

dioxin daɪ ˈɒks ɪn §-ᵊn ‖ -ˈɑːks-

dip, DIP dɪp **dipped** dɪpt **dipping** ˈdɪp ɪŋ **dips** dɪps
 ˈDIP switch

diphenylamine ˌdaɪ ˌfiːn aɪᵊl ˈæm iːn -ˌfen-, -ᵊl-, -ɪn, -ən, -ə ˈmiːn ‖ daɪ ˌfen ᵊl ə ˈmiːn -ˈæm ən

diphone ˈdaɪ fəʊn ‖ -foʊn **~s** z

diphtheria dɪf ˈθɪər i‿ə dɪp- ‖ -ˈθɪr-

DIPHTHONG

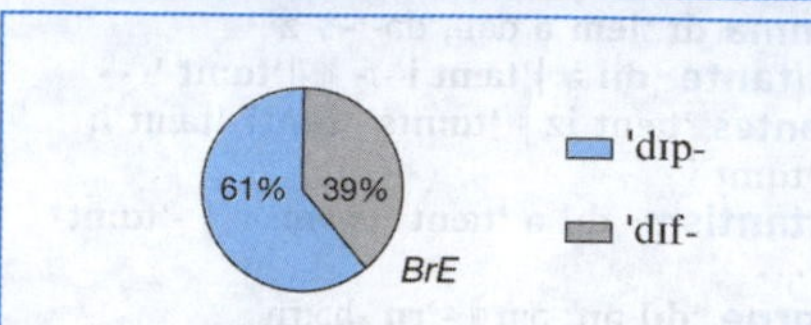

diphthong ˈdɪf θɒŋ ˈdɪp- ‖ -θɔːŋ -θɑːŋ — *Preference poll, BrE:* ˈdɪf- *39%,* ˈdɪp- *61%. Phoneticians, however, prefer* ˈdɪf-. *Native speakers of English do not say* -tɒŋ ‖ -tɔːŋ. **~ed** d **~ing** ɪŋ **~s** z

diphthongal ₍ₗ₎dɪf ˈθɒŋ gᵊl ₍ₗ₎dɪp- ‖ -ˈθɔːŋ- -ˈθɑːŋ- **~ly** i

diphthongis... —*see* **diphthongiz...**

diphthongization ˌdɪf θɒŋ gaɪ ˈzeɪʃ ᵊn ˌdɪp-, -aɪˈ--, -gɪˈ--, -ɪˈ-- ‖ -θɔːŋ ə- -θɑːŋ ə-, -gəˈ- **~s** z

diphthongiz|e ˈdɪf θɒŋ gaɪz ˈdɪp-, -aɪz ‖ -θɔːŋ aɪz -θɑːŋ-, -gaɪz **~ed** d **~es** ɪz əz **~ing** ɪŋ

diplo- *comb. form*
 with stress-neutral suffix ˈdɪp ləʊ ‖ -lə — **diplocardiac** ˌdɪp ləʊ ˈkɑːd i æk ◂ ‖ -lə ˈkɑːrd-

Diplock ˈdɪp lɒk ‖ -lɑːk

diplodocus dɪ ˈplɒd ək əs daɪ-; ˌdɪp ləʊ ˈdəʊk əs ‖ -ˈplɑːd- **~es** ɪz əz

diploid ˈdɪp lɔɪd **~s** z

diploma dɪ ˈpləʊm ə də- ‖ -ˈploʊm ə **~s** z

diplomac|y dɪ ˈpləʊm əs |i də- ‖ -ˈploʊm- **~ies** iz

diplomat ˈdɪp lə mæt **~s** s

diplomate ˈdɪp lə meɪt **~s** s

diplomatic ˌdɪp lə ˈmæt ɪk ◂ ‖ -ˈmæt̬ ɪk ◂ **~ally** ᵊl‿i
 ˌdiploˌmatic ˈbag; **ˌdiploˈmatic corps**; **ˌdiploˌmatic imˈmunity**

diplomatist dɪ ˈpləʊm ət ɪst də-, §-əst ‖ -ət̬- **~s** s

diplophonia ˌdɪp ləʊ ˈfəʊn i‿ə ‖ -lə ˈfoʊn-

diplosis dɪ ˈpləʊs ɪs §də-, §-əs ‖ -ˈploʊs-

dipole ˈdaɪ pəʊl →-pɒʊl ‖ -poʊl **~s** z

dipp.. —*see* **dip**

dipper, D~ ˈdɪp ə ‖ -ᵊr **~s** z

dipp|y ˈdɪp |i **~ier** i‿ə ‖ i‿ᵊr **~iest** i‿ɪst i‿əst

dipshit ˈdɪp ʃɪt **~s** s

dipsomania ˌdɪps əʊ ˈmeɪn i‿ə ‖ ˌ-ə-

dipsomaniac ˌdɪps əʊ ˈmeɪn i æk ‖ ˌ-ə- **~s** s

dipstick ˈdɪp stɪk **~s** s

dipswitch ˈdɪp swɪtʃ **~es** ɪz əz

Dipsy ˈdɪps i

D

Diphthongs

1 A **diphthong** is a complex vowel: a sequence of two vowel qualities within a single syllable. Compare **monophthong**, a vowel whose quality remains constant (as is the case with most vowels).

2 Several English vowel phonemes are diphthongal. The aɪ of **time** taɪm, for example, involves a movement of the tongue from a starting-point a towards an endpoint ɪ.

3 Ordinary diphthongs are **diminuendo** (or **falling**), in that the prominence decreases as we pass from the first element to the second. The a part of aɪ is more prominent than the ɪ part. Compare sequences such as the je in **yes** jes, which is a kind of **crescendo (rising)** diphthong (see also COMPRESSION).

4 In English, the distinction between diphthong and monophthong is not always clear-cut. For example, some speakers pronounce eə as a monophthong, ɛː. In some positions iː and uː may be somewhat diphthongal, ɪi, ʊu.

dipter|al 'dɪpt ər əl **~an** ən **~ous** əs
diptych 'dɪp tɪk **~s** s
Dirac dɪ 'ræk də-; 'dɪr æk
dire 'daɪ‿ə ‖ 'daɪ‿ᵊr **direr** 'daɪ‿ər ə ‖ 'daɪ‿ᵊr ər **direst** 'daɪ‿ər ɪst -əst ‖ 'daɪ‿ᵊr əst

DIRECT

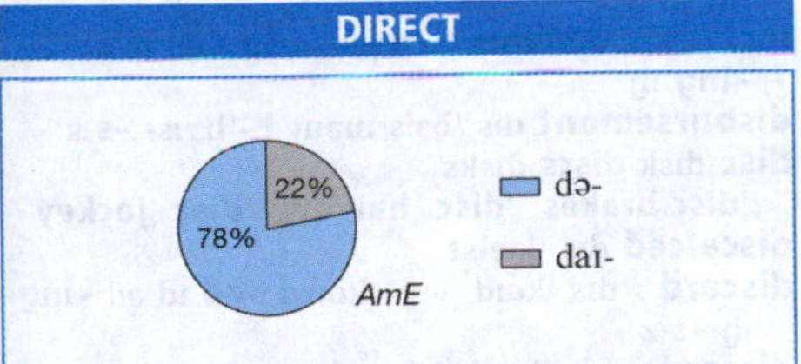

direct *v, adj, adv* ₍ₗ₎daɪᵊ 'rekt də-, dɪ- ‖ də- daɪ- **~ed** ɪd əd **~ing** ɪŋ **~s** s —*In the case of* direct, *the stress-shifted form* ˌdaɪᵊ rekt *is frequent in BrE in phrases such as* ˌdirect 'debit; *but the weak-vowelled variant is also heard,* də 'rekt, dɪ-, *with no stress shift, thus* diˌrect 'debit. — *Preference poll, AmE:* də- *78%,* daɪ- *22%.* **ˌdirect 'debit,** ·ˌ·-·; **ˌdirect 'method,** ·ˌ·-·; **ˌdirect 'object,** ·ˌ·-·; **ˌdirect 'speech,** ·ˌ·-·; **ˌdirect 'tax,** ·ˌ·-
direction daɪᵊ 'rek ʃᵊn də-, dɪ- ‖ də- daɪ- **~s** z — *Preference poll, BrE:* daɪ- *55%,* daɪə- *15%,* dɪ- *15%,* də- *15%*
directional daɪᵊ 'rek ʃᵊn‿əl də-, dɪ- ‖ də- daɪ- **~ly** i
directionality daɪᵊ ˌrek ʃə 'næl ət i də-, dɪ-, -ɪt i; ˌdaɪᵊ·'·- ‖ də ˌrek ʃə 'næl əţ i daɪ-
directionless daɪᵊ'rek ʃᵊn ləs də-, dɪ-, -lɪs ‖ də- daɪ- **~ly** li
directive daɪᵊ 'rekt ɪv də-, dɪ- ‖ də- daɪ- **~s** z
direct|ly daɪᵊ'rekt |li də-, dɪ- ‖ də- daɪ- —*In the senses 'immediately, as soon as' there is also a casual form* 'drek li, *becoming old-fashioned* **~ness** nəs nɪs
Directoire, d~ ˌdɪr ek 'twɑː ˌdɪər-, ˌdiː rek-; də 'rekt wɑː, dɪ-, daɪᵊ- ‖ ˌdiː rek 'twɑːr —*Fr* [di ʁɛk twaːʁ]
director daɪᵊ 'rekt ə də-, dɪ- ‖ də 'rekt ᵊr daɪ- **~s** z
directorate daɪᵊ 'rekt ər‿ət də-, dɪ-, ‿ɪt ‖ də- daɪ- **~s** s
directorial ˌdaɪᵊr ek 'tɔːr i‿əl ◂ də ˌrek-, dɪ- ‖ -'tour-
directorship daɪᵊ 'rekt ə ʃɪp də-, dɪ- ‖ də 'rekt ᵊr- daɪ- **~s** s
director|y daɪᵊ 'rekt ər‿|i də-, dɪ- ‖ də- daɪ- **~ies** iz
directrix daɪᵊ 'rek trɪks də-, dɪ-
direct-to-consumer daɪᵊˌrekt tə kən 'sjuːm ə ◂ də-, dɪ-, §-kɒn'·-, -'suːm-, §-'ʃuːm- ‖ də ˌrekt tə kən 'suːmᵊr ◂ daɪ-
direful 'daɪ‿ə fᵊl -fʊl ‖ 'daɪ‿ᵊr- **~ly** i **~ness** nəs nɪs
dire|ly 'daɪ‿ə |li ‖ 'daɪ‿ᵊr |li **~ness** nəs nɪs
dirge dɜːdʒ ‖ dɝːdʒ **dirges** 'dɜːdʒ ɪz -əz ‖ 'dɝːdʒ-
dirham 'dɪər æm 'dɪr-, -əm ‖ də 'ræm **~s** z

DIRECTION

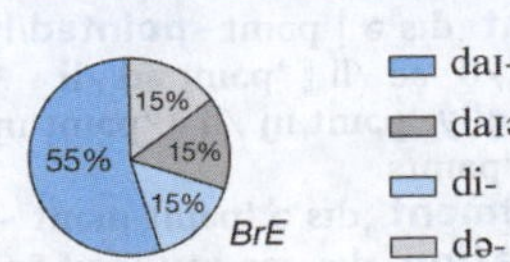

D

dirigible ˈdɪr ɪdʒ əb əl ˈ·ədʒ-, -ɪb əl; də ˈrɪdʒ-, dɪ- **~s** z
dirigisme ˈdɪr ɪ ˌʒɪz əm -ə- —*Fr* [di ʁi ʒism]
dirigiste ˌdɪr ɪ ˈʒiːst ◂ -ə-, ˈdɪr ɪʒ ɪst, -əst —*Fr* [di ʁi ʒist] **~s** s —*or as sing.*
diriment ˈdɪr ɪm ənt -əm-
dirk, Dirk dɜːk ‖ dɜ˞ːk **dirks, Dirk's** dɜːks ‖ dɜ˞ːks
dirndl ˈdɜːnd əl ‖ ˈdɜ˞ːnd- **~s** z
dirt dɜːt ‖ dɜ˞ːt
 ˌdirt ˈcheap; **ˈdirt ˌfarmer**; **ˌdirt ˈroad,** ˈ· ·; **ˈdirt track**
dirtbag ˈdɜːt bæg ‖ ˈdɜ˞ːt- **~s** z
dirt-disher ˈdɜːt ˌdɪʃ ə ‖ ˈdɜ˞ːt ˌdɪʃ ər **~s** z
dirt|y ˈdɜːt |i ‖ ˈdɜ˞ːṭ |i **~ied** id **~ier** i‿ə ‖ i‿ər **~ies** iz **~iest** i‿ɪst i‿əst **~ily** ɪ li əl i **~iness** i nəs i nɪs **~ying** i‿ɪŋ
 ˌdirty old ˈman; **ˌdirty ˈtrick**; **ˌdirty ˈword**; **ˈdirty work**
Dis dɪs
dis dɪs **dissed** dɪst **disses** ˈdɪs ɪz -əz **dissing** ˈdɪs ɪŋ
dis- (ˈ)dɪs —*Stressed when followed by an unstressed syllable, and often even when not:* ˌdisafˈfirm, ₍ˌ₎disˈrelish.
disabilit|y ˌdɪs ə ˈbɪl ət |i -ɪt i ‖ -əṭ |i **~ies** iz
disabl|e dɪs ˈeɪb əl §dɪz- **~ed** d **~ement** mənt **~es** z **~ing** ‿ɪŋ
disabus|e ˌdɪs ə ˈbjuːz **~ed** d **~es** ɪz əz **~ing** ɪŋ
disadvantag|e ˌdɪs əd ˈvɑːnt ɪdʒ §-æd-, §-ˈvænt- ‖ -ˈvænṭ- **~ed** d **~es** ɪz əz **~ing** ɪŋ
disadvantageous ˌdɪs ˌæd vən ˈteɪdʒ əs ·ˌ·-, -vænˈ·-, -vɑːnˈ·- **~ly** li **~ness** nəs nɪs
disaffected ˌdɪs ə ˈfekt ɪd -əd **~ly** li
disaffection ˌdɪs ə ˈfek ʃən
disaffili|ate ˌdɪs ə ˈfɪl i |eɪt **~ated** eɪt ɪd -əd ‖ eɪṭ əd **~ates** eɪts **~ating** eɪt ɪŋ ‖ eɪṭ ɪŋ
disaffiliation ˌdɪs ə ˌfɪl i ˈeɪʃ ən **~s** z
disafforest ˌdɪs ə ˈfɒr ɪst -əst ‖ -ˈfɔːr- -ˈfɑːr- **~ed** ɪd əd **~ing** ɪŋ **~s** s
disafforestation ˌdɪs ə ˌfɒr ɪ ˈsteɪʃ ən -əˈ-- ‖ -ˌfɔːr- -ˌfɑːr- **~s** z
disagree ˌdɪs ə ˈgriː —*Often with contrastive stress:* Do you agree or ˈdɪs əˌgriː ? **~d** d **~ing** ɪŋ **~s** z
disagreeab|le ˌdɪs ə ˈgriː‿əb |əl ◂ **~ly** li
disagreement ˌdɪs ə ˈgriː mənt **~s** s
disallow ˌdɪs ə ˈlaʊ **~ed** d **~ing** ɪŋ **~s** z
disambigu|ate ˌdɪs æm ˈbɪg ju |eɪt **~ated** eɪt ɪd -əd ‖ eɪṭ əd **~ates** eɪts **~ating** eɪt ɪŋ ‖ eɪṭ ɪŋ
disambiguation ˌdɪs æm ˌbɪg ju ˈeɪʃ ən **~s** z
disappear ˌdɪs ə ˈpɪə ‖ -ˈpɪər **~ed** d
 disappearing ˌdɪs ə ˈpɪər ɪŋ ‖ -ˈpɪr ɪŋ **~s** z
disappearanc|e ˌdɪs ə ˈpɪər ənˈs ‖ -ˈpɪr- **~es** ɪz əz
disap|point ˌdɪs ə |ˈpɔɪnt **~pointed/ly** ˈpɔɪnt ɪd /li -əd /li ‖ ˈpɔɪnṭ əd /li **~pointing/ly** ˈpɔɪnt ɪŋ /li ‖ ˈpɔɪnṭ ɪŋ /li **~points** ˈpɔɪnts
disappointment ˌdɪs ə ˈpɔɪnt mənt **~s** s
disapprobation ˌdɪs ˌæp rəʊ ˈbeɪʃ ən ‖ -ə-
disapproval ˌdɪs ə ˈpruːv əl **~s** z
disapprov|e ˌdɪs ə ˈpruːv **~ed** d **~es** z **~ing/ly** ɪŋ /li
disarm dɪs ˈɑːm dɪz- ‖ -ˈɑːrm **~ed** d **~ing/ly** ɪŋ /li **~s** z
disarmament dɪs ˈɑːm ə mənt dɪz- ‖ -ˈɑːrm- **~s** s
disarrang|e ˌdɪs ə ˈreɪndʒ **~ed** d **~ement** mənt **~es** ɪz əz **~ing** ɪŋ
disarray ˌdɪs ə ˈreɪ **~ed** d **~ing** ɪŋ **~s** z
disassembl|e ˌdɪs ə ˈsem bəl **~ed** d **~er/s** ə/z ‖ ər/z **~es** z **~ing** ɪŋ
disassoci|ate ˌdɪs ə ˈsəʊʃ i |eɪt -ˈsəʊs- ‖ -ˈsoʊʃ- -ˈsoʊs- **~ated** eɪt ɪd -əd ‖ eɪṭ əd **~ates** eɪts **~ating** eɪt ɪŋ ‖ eɪṭ ɪŋ
disaster dɪ ˈzɑːst ə də-, §-ˈzæst- ‖ -ˈzæst ər **~s** z
 diˈsaster ˌarea
disastrous dɪ ˈzɑːs trəs də-, §-ˈzæs-, ⚠-ˈzæst ər əs ‖ -ˈzæs- **~ly** li **~ness** nəs nɪs
disavow ˌdɪs ə ˈvaʊ **~ed** d **~ing** ɪŋ **~s** z
disavowal ˌdɪs ə ˈvaʊ‿əl -ˈvaʊl **~s** z
disband dɪs ˈbænd **~ed** ɪd əd **~ing** ɪŋ **~s** z
disbandment dɪs ˈbænd mənt **~s** s
dis|bar dɪs |ˈbɑː ‖ -|ˈbɑːr **~barred** ˈbɑːd ‖ ˈbɑːrd **~barring** ˈbɑːr ɪŋ **~bars** ˈbɑːz ‖ ˈbɑːrz
disbarment dɪs ˈbɑː mənt ‖ -ˈbɑːr- **~s** s
disbelief ˌdɪs bi ˈliːf -bə-
disbeliev|e ˌdɪs bi ˈliːv -bə- **~ed** d **~er/s** ə/z ‖ ər/z **~es** z **~ing/ly** ɪŋ /li
disbud ₍ˌ₎dɪs ˈbʌd **~ded** ɪd əd **~ding** ɪŋ **~s** z
disburden dɪs ˈbɜːd ən ‖ -ˈbɜ˞ːd- **~ed** d **~ing** ‿ɪŋ **~s** z
disburs|e dɪs ˈbɜːs ‖ -ˈbɜ˞ːs **~ed** t **~es** ɪz əz **~ing** ɪŋ
disbursement dɪs ˈbɜːs mənt ‖ -ˈbɜ˞ːs- **~s** s
disc dɪsk **discs** dɪsks
 ˈdisc brakes; **ˈdisc ˌharrow**; **ˈdisc ˌjockey**
discalced dɪs ˈkælst
discard *v* dɪs ˈkɑːd ˌ·- ‖ -ˈkɑːrd **~ed** ɪd əd **~ing** ɪŋ **~s** z
discard *n* ˈdɪs kɑːd ‖-kɑːrd **~s** z
discern dɪ ˈsɜːn də-, -ˈzɜːn‖ ˈsɜ˞ːn -ˈzɜ˞ːn **~ed** d **~ing/ly** ɪŋ /li **~s** z
discernib|le dɪ ˈsɜːn əb |əl də-, -ˈzɜːn-, -ɪb- ‖ -ˈsɜ˞ːn- -ˈzɜ˞ːn- **~ly** li
discernment dɪ ˈsɜːn mənt də-, -ˈzɜːn- ‖ -ˈsɜ˞ːn- -ˈzɜ˞ːn-
discharg|e *n* ˈdɪs tʃɑːdʒ ·ˈ· ‖ -tʃɑːrdʒ **~es** ɪz əz
discharg|e *v* dɪs ˈtʃɑːdʒ ˌ·-, ˈ· · ‖ -ˈtʃɑːrdʒ **~ed** d **~es** ɪz əz **~ing** ɪŋ
disci ˈdɪsk aɪ ˈdɪs-
disciple dɪ ˈsaɪp əl də- **~s** z **~ship** ʃɪp
disciplinarian ˌdɪs ə plɪ ˈneər i‿ən ˌ·ɪ-, -pləˈ-- ‖ -ˈner- **~s** z
disciplinary ˈdɪs ə plɪn ər‿i ˈ·ɪ-, ˈ· ·plən-, ˌ· ·ˈplɪn ər i ‖ -plə ner i
disciplin|e *n, v* ˈdɪs əp lɪn -ɪp-, -lən; §dɪ ˈsɪp-, də- **~ed** d **~es** z **~ing** ɪŋ
disclaim dɪs ˈkleɪm **~ed** d **~ing** ɪŋ **~s** z
disclaimer dɪs ˈkleɪm ə ‖ -ər **~s** z
disclos|e dɪs ˈkləʊz ‖ -ˈkloʊz **~ed** d **~es** ɪz əz **~ing** ɪŋ
disclosure dɪs ˈkləʊʒ ə ‖ -ˈkloʊʒ ər **~s** z

isco 'dɪsk əʊ ‖ -oʊ **~s** z
iscob|olus dɪ 'skɒb |əl əs ‖ -'skɑːb- **~oli** ə laɪ əl aɪ
iscograph|y dɪ 'skɒg rəf |i ‖ -'skɑːg- **~ies** iz
iscolor ₍ₗ₎dɪs 'kʌl ə ‖ -ᵊr **~ed** d **discoloring** dɪs 'kʌl ər ɪŋ **~s** z
iscoloration dɪs ˌkʌl ə 'reɪʃ ᵊn ˌ·ˌ·- **~s** z
iscolour ₍ₗ₎dɪs 'kʌl ə ‖ -ᵊr **~ed** d **discolouring** dɪs 'kʌl ər ɪŋ **~s** z
iscombobu|late ˌdɪsk əm 'bɒb ju |leɪt -jə- ‖ -'bɑːb jə- **~lated** leɪt ɪd -əd ‖ leɪţ əd **~lates** leɪts **~lating** leɪt ɪŋ ‖ leɪţ ɪŋ
iscomf|it dɪs 'kʌmᵖf |ɪt -ət ‖ -|ət **~ited** ɪt ɪd §ət-, -əd ‖ əţ əd **~iting** ɪt ɪŋ §ət- ‖ əţ ɪŋ **~its** ɪts §əts ‖ əts
iscomfiture dɪs 'kʌmᵖf ɪtʃ ə -ətʃ- ‖ -ᵊr **~s** z
iscomfort dɪs 'kʌmᵖf ət ‖ -ᵊrt
iscommod|e ˌdɪs kə 'məʊd ‖ -'moʊd **~ed** ɪd əd **~es** z **~ing** ɪŋ
iscompos|e ˌdɪs kəm 'pəʊz §-kɒm- ‖ -'poʊz **~ed** d **~es** z **~ing/ly** ɪŋ /li
iscomposure ˌdɪs kəm 'pəʊʒ ə §-kɒm- ‖ -'poʊʒ ᵊr
iscon|cert ˌdɪs kən |'sɜːt §-kɒn- ‖ -|'sɜːt **~certed** 'sɜːt ɪd -əd ‖ 'sɜːţ əd **~certing/ly** 'sɜːt ɪŋ /li ‖ 'sɜːţ ɪŋ /li **~certs** 'sɜːts ‖ 'sɜːts
isconfirm ˌdɪs kən 'fɜːm §-kɒn- ‖ -'fɜːm **~ed** d **~ing** ɪŋ **~s** z
disconformit|y ˌdɪs kən 'fɔːm ət |i §ˌ·kɒn-, -ɪt i ‖ -'fɔːrm əţ |i **~ies** iz
disconnect *v* ˌdɪs kə 'nekt **~ed/ly** ɪd /li əd /li **~ing** ɪŋ **~s** s
disconnect *n* ˌdɪs kə 'nekt '· ·ˌ·
disconnection, disconnexion ˌdɪs kə 'nek ʃᵊn **~s** z
disconsolate dɪs 'kɒnᵗs əl ət -ɪt ‖ -'kɑːnᵗs- **~ly** li **~ness** nəs nɪs
discon|tent ˌdɪs kən |'tent §-kɒn- **~tented** 'tent ɪd -əd ‖ 'tenţ əd **~tenting** 'tent ɪŋ ‖ 'tenţ ɪŋ **~tents** tents
discontented ˌdɪs kən 'tent ɪd -əd ‖ -'tenţ əd **~ly** li **~ness** nəs nɪs
discontinuance ˌdɪs kən 'tɪn ju‿ənᵗs §ˌ·kɒn-
discontinuation ˌdɪs kən ˌtɪn ju 'eɪʃ ᵊn §ˌ·kɒn-
discontinu|e ˌdɪs kən 'tɪn juː §-kɒn-, -ju **~ed** d **~es** z **~ing** ɪŋ
discontinuit|y ˌdɪs ˌkɒnt ɪ 'njuː‿ət |i -ə'·, ɪt i ‖ dɪs ˌkɑːnt ᵊn 'uː əţ |i -'juː- **~ies** iz
discontinuous ˌdɪs kən 'tɪn ju‿əs ◂ §ˌ·kɒn- **~ly** li **~ness** nəs nɪs
discord *n* 'dɪs kɔːd ‖ -kɔːrd **~s** z
discordanc|e dɪs 'kɔːd ᵊnᵗs ‖ -'kɔːrd ᵊnᵗs **~es** ɪz əz
discordant dɪs 'kɔːd ᵊnt ‖ -'kɔːrd ᵊnt **~ly** li
discotheque 'dɪsk ə tek ˌ·'· **~s** s
dis|count *v* 'dɪs |kaʊnt ·'· — *Preference poll, AmE:* '· · 82%, ·'· 18%. **~counted** kaʊnt ɪd -əd ‖ kaʊnţ əd **~counting** kaʊnt ɪŋ ‖ kaʊnţ ɪŋ **~counts** kaʊnts

DISCOUNT (verb)

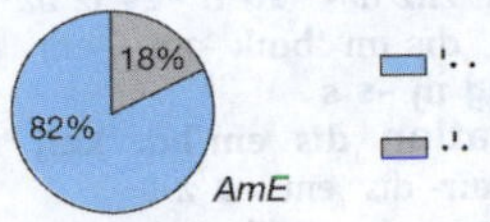

discount *n* 'dɪs kaʊnt **~s** s
'**discount house**; '**discount store**
discountenanc|e dɪs 'kaʊnt ɪn ənᵗs -ən- ‖ -'kaʊnt ᵊn- **~ed** t **~es** ɪz əz **~ing** ɪŋ
discounter 'dɪs kaʊnt ə ‖ -kaʊnţ ᵊr **~s** z
discourag|e dɪs 'kʌr ɪdʒ ‖ -'kɜː- **~ed** d **~es** ɪz əz **~ing/ly** ɪŋ /li
discouragement dɪs 'kʌr ɪdʒ mənt ‖ -'kɜː- **~s** s
discours|e *v* dɪs 'kɔːs ‖ -'kɔːrs -'koʊrs **~ed** t **~es** ɪz əz **~ing** ɪŋ
discours|e *n* 'dɪs kɔːs ·'· ‖ -kɔːrs -koʊrs **~es** ɪz əz
discourteous dɪs 'kɜːt i‿əs ‖ -'kɜːţ- **~ly** li **~ness** nəs nɪs
discourtes|y dɪs 'kɜːt əs |i -'kɜːţ- **~ies** iz
discover dɪ 'skʌv ə də- ‖ -ᵊr **~ed** d **discovering** dɪ 'skʌv ər‿ɪŋ **~s** z
discoverable dɪ 'skʌv ər‿əb ᵊl
discoverer dɪ 'skʌv ər‿ə də- ‖ -ᵊr‿ər **~s** z
discover|y dɪ 'skʌv ər‿|i də- **~ies** iz
discred|it *v, n* ₍ₗ₎dɪs 'kred |ɪt §-ət ‖ -|ət **~ited** ɪt ɪd §ət-, -əd ‖ əţ əd **~iting** ɪt ɪŋ §ət- ‖ əţ ɪŋ **~its** ɪts §əts ‖ əts
discreditab|le ₍ₗ₎dɪs 'kred ɪt əb |ᵊl §-ət əb- ‖ -əţ əb- **~ly** li
discreet dɪ 'skriːt də- **~ly** li **~ness** nəs nɪs
discrepanc|y dɪs 'krep ənᵗs |i **~ies** iz
discrepant dɪs 'krep ənt **~ly** li
discrete dɪ 'skriːt ˌdɪs 'kriːt ◂ *(usually = discreet)* **~ly** li **~ness** nəs nɪs
discretion dɪ 'skreʃ ᵊn
discretionar|y dɪ 'skreʃ ən ᵊr‿|i ᵊn‿ər |i ‖ -ə ner |i **~ily** əl i ɪ li
discriminant dɪ 'skrɪm ɪn ənt də-, -ən‿ənt **~s** s
discrimi|nate dɪ 'skrɪm ɪ |neɪt də-, -ə- **~nated** neɪt ɪd -əd ‖ neɪţ əd **~nates** neɪts **~nating** neɪt ɪŋ ‖ neɪţ ɪŋ
discrimination dɪ ˌskrɪm ɪ 'neɪʃ ᵊn də-, -ə- **~s** z
discriminative dɪ 'skrɪm ɪn ət ɪv də-, -ən‿ət-; -ɪ neɪt ɪv, -ə· · ‖ -ə neɪţ ɪv -ən‿əţ ɪv **~ly** li
discriminator dɪ 'skrɪm ɪ neɪt ə də-, '·ə- ‖ -neɪţ ᵊr **~s** z
discriminator|y dɪ 'skrɪm ɪn ət‿ər |i də-, -'·ən-; -ˌskrɪm ɪ 'neɪt ər |i, -ˌ·ə- ‖ -ə tɔːr |i -toʊr i **~ily** əl i ɪ li
discursive dɪs 'kɜːs ɪv ‖ -'kɜːs- **~ly** li **~ness** nəs nɪs
discus 'dɪsk əs **disci** 'dɪsk aɪ 'dɪs aɪ **~es** ɪz əz
discuss dɪ 'skʌs də- **~ed** t **~es** ɪz əz **~ing** ɪŋ
discussable dɪ 'skʌs əb ᵊl
discussant dɪ 'skʌs ᵊnt də- **~s** s

D

discussion dɪ ˈskʌʃ ən də- **~s** z
disdain *n, v* dɪs ˈdeɪn dɪz- **~ed** d **~ing** ɪŋ **~s** z
disdainful dɪs ˈdeɪn fəl dɪz-, -fʊl **~ly** ˌi
diseas|e dɪ ˈziːz də- **~ed** d **~es** ɪz əz
disembark ˌdɪs ɪm ˈbɑːk -əm-, -em- ‖ -ˈbɑːrk **~ed** t **~ing** ɪŋ **~s** s
disembarkation ˌdɪs ˌem bɑː ˈkeɪʃ ən ˌ·ɪm-, ˌ·əm- ‖ -bɑːr- dɪs ˌem- **~s** z
disembarrass ˌdɪs ɪm ˈbær əs -əm-, -em- ‖ -ˈber- **~ed** t **~es** ɪz əz **~ing** ɪŋ **~ment** mənt
disembod|y ˌdɪs ɪm ˈbɒd |i -əm-, -em- ‖ -ˈbɑːd |i **~ied** id **~ies** iz **~iment** i mənt **~ying** i‿ɪŋ
disembogu|e ˌdɪs ɪm ˈbəʊg -əm-, -em- ‖ -ˈboʊg **~ed** d **~es** z **~ing** ɪŋ
disembowel ˌdɪs ɪm ˈbaʊ‿əl əm-, -em-, ˌ· ·ˈbaʊl ‖ -ˈbaʊ‿əl **~ed, ~led** d **~ing, ~ling** ɪŋ **~ment** mənt **~s** z
disembroil ˌdɪs ɪm ˈbrɔɪəl -əm-, -em- **~ed** d **~ing** ɪŋ **~s** z
disen|chant ˌdɪs ɪn |ˈtʃɑːnt -ən-, -en-, §-|ˈtʃænt ‖ -|ˈtʃænt **~chanted** ˈtʃɑːnt ɪd §ˈtʃænt-, -əd ‖ ˈtʃænṭ əd **~chanting** ˈtʃɑːnt ɪŋ §ˈtʃænt- ‖ ˈtʃænṭ ɪŋ **~chants** ˈtʃɑːnts §ˈtʃænts ‖ ˈtʃænts
disencum|ber ˌdɪs ɪn ˈkʌm |bə →-ɪŋ-, -ən-, -en- ‖ -|bər **~bered** bəd ‖ bərd **~bering** bər‿ɪŋ **~bers** bəz ‖ bərz
disendow ˌdɪs ɪn ˈdaʊ -ən-, -en- **~ed** d **~ing** ɪŋ **~ment** mənt **~s** z
disenfranchis|e ˌdɪs ɪn ˈfræntʃ aɪz -ən-, -en- **~ed** d **~ement** mənt **~es** ɪz əz **~ing** ɪŋ
disengag|e ˌdɪs ɪn ˈgeɪdʒ -ən-, -en- **~ed** d **~ement** mənt **~es** ɪz əz **~ing** ɪŋ
disentangl|e ˌdɪs ɪn ˈtæŋ gəl -ən-, -en- **~ed** d **~ement** mənt **~es** z **~ing** ‿ɪŋ
disequilibrium ˌdɪs ˌiːk wɪ ˈlɪb ri‿əm ˌ·ek-, -wə'-- ‖ dɪs ˌek-
disestablish ˌdɪs ɪ ˈstæb lɪʃ -ə-, -e- **~ed** t **~es** ɪz əz **~ing** ɪŋ **~ment** mənt
disestablishmentarian ˌdɪs ɪ ˌstæb lɪʃ mən ˈteər i‿ən ˌ·ə-, ˌ·e- ‖ -ˈter- **~s** z
disfav|or, disfav|our ₍ˌ₎dɪs ˈfeɪv |ə ‖ -|ər **~ored, ~oured** əd ‖ ərd **~oring, ~ouring** ər‿ɪŋ **~ors, ~ours** əz ‖ ərz
disfig|ure dɪs ˈfɪg |ə ‖ -|jər *(*)* **~ured** əd ‖ jərd **~ures** əz ‖ jərz **~uring** ər‿ɪŋ ‖ jər ɪŋ
disfigurement dɪs ˈfɪg ə mənt ‖ -jər- **~s** z
disforest ₍ˌ₎dɪs ˈfɒr ɪst -əst ‖ -ˈfɔːr- -ˈfɑːr- **~ed** ɪd əd **~ing** ɪŋ **~s** s
disforestation ˌdɪs ˌfɒr ɪ ˈsteɪʃ ən ·ˌ··, -ə- ‖ dɪs ˌfɔːr- -ˌfɑːr-
disfranchis|e dɪs ˈfræntʃ aɪz **~ed** d **~es** ɪz əz **~ing** ɪŋ
disfranchisement dɪs ˈfræntʃ ɪz mənt -əz-, -aɪz- **~s** s
disfrock ˌdɪs ˈfrɒk ‖ -ˈfrɑːk **~ed** t **~ing** ɪŋ **~s** s
disgorg|e dɪs ˈgɔːdʒ ‖ -ˈgɔːrdʒ **~ed** d **~es** ɪz əz **~ing** ɪŋ
disgrac|e *v, n* dɪs ˈgreɪs dɪz-, dəs- **~ed** t **~es** ɪz əz **~ing** ɪŋ
disgraceful dɪs ˈgreɪs fəl dɪz-, dəs-, -fʊl **~ly** ˌi
disgruntled dɪs ˈgrʌnt əld ‖ -ˈgrʌnṭ-
disgruntlement dɪs ˈgrʌnt əl mənt ‖ -ˈgrʌnṭ-
disguis|e *v, n* dɪs ˈgaɪz dɪz-, dəs- **~ed** d **~er/s** ə/z ‖ ər/z **~es** ɪz əz **~ing** ɪŋ
disgust *n, v* dɪs ˈgʌst dɪz-, dəs- **~ed/ly** ɪd /li əd /li **~ing/ly** ɪŋ /li **~s** s
dish dɪʃ **dished** dɪʃt **dishes** ˈdɪʃ ɪz -əz **dishing** ˈdɪʃ ɪŋ
ˈdish ˌtowel
dishabille ˌdɪs ə ˈbiːəl -æ-
disharmonious ˌdɪs hɑː ˈməʊn i‿əs ‖ -hɑːr ˈmoʊn- **~ly** li
disharmon|y ₍ˌ₎dɪs ˈhɑːm ən |i ‖ -ˈhɑːrm- **~ies** iz
dish|cloth ˈdɪʃ |klɒθ -klɔːθ ‖ -|klɔːθ -klɑːθ **~cloths** klɒθs klɒðz, klɔːðz, klɔːθs ‖ klɔːðz klɔːθs, klɑːðz, klɑːθs
dishdasha ˈdɪʃ dæʃ ə ‖ -dɑːʃ- **~s** z
dishearten dɪs ˈhɑːt ən ‖ -ˈhɑːrt- **~ed** d **~ing/ly** ‿ɪŋ /li **~ment** mənt **~s** z
disher ˈdɪʃ ə ‖ -ər **~s** z
dishevel dɪ ˈʃev əl **~ed, ~led** d **~ing, ~ling** ɪŋ **~ment** mənt **~s** z
Dishforth ˈdɪʃ fəθ -fɔːθ ‖ -fərθ -fɔːrθ —*The place in N Yks is locally* -fəθ
dishful ˈdɪʃ fʊl **~s** z
dishi... —*see* **dishy**
dishonest ₍ˌ₎dɪs ˈɒn ɪst dɪz-, -əst ‖ -ˈɑːn- **~ly** li
dishonest|y ₍ˌ₎dɪs ˈɒn əst |i dɪz-, -ɪst- ‖ -ˈɑːn- **~ies** iz
dishon|or, dishon|our *n, v* dɪs ˈɒn |ə dɪz- ‖ -ˈɑːn |ər **~ored, ~oured** əd ‖ ərd **~oring, ~ouring** ər‿ɪŋ **~ors, ~ours** əz ‖ ərz
dishonorab|le, dishonourab|le dɪs ˈɒn ər‿əb |əl dɪz- ‖ -ˈɑːn- **~ly** li
dishpan ˈdɪʃ pæn **~s** z
dishrag ˈdɪʃ ræg **~s** z
dishware ˈdɪʃ weə ‖ -wer -wær
dishwash|er ˈdɪʃ ˌwɒʃ |ə ‖ -ˌwɔːʃ ər -ˌwɑːʃ |ər **~ers** əz ‖ ərz **~ing** ɪŋ
dishwater ˈdɪʃ ˌwɔːt ə ‖ -ˌwɔːṭ ər -ˌwɑːṭ ər
dish|y ˈdɪʃ |i **~ier** i‿ə ‖ i‿ər **~iest** i‿ɪst i‿əst
disillusion ˌdɪs ɪ ˈluːʒ ən -ə-, -ˈljuːʒ- **~ed** d **~ing** ‿ɪŋ **~ment/s** mənt/s **~s** z
disincentive ˌdɪs ɪn ˈsent ɪv ‖ -ˈsenṭ ɪv **~s** z
disinclination ˌdɪs ˌɪn klɪ ˈneɪʃ ən →-ˌɪŋ-, ˌ·ən-, -klə'-- **~s** z
disinclin|e ˌdɪs ɪn ˈklaɪn →-ɪŋ-, -ən- **~ed** d **~es** z **~ing** ɪŋ
disinfect ˌdɪs ɪn ˈfekt -ən- **~ed** ɪd əd **~ing** ɪŋ **~s** s
disinfectant ˌdɪs ɪn ˈfekt ənt -ən- **~s** s
disinfection ˌdɪs ɪn ˈfek ʃən -ən- **~s** z
disinfest ˌdɪs ɪn ˈfest -ən- **~ed** ɪd əd **~ing** ɪŋ **~s** s
disinfestation ˌdɪs ˌɪn fe ˈsteɪʃ ən ˌ·ən- **~s** z
disinflationary ˌdɪs ɪn ˈfleɪʃ ən‿ər i ˌ·ən-, -ˈfleɪʃ ən ri ‖ -ə ner i
disinformation ˌdɪs ˌɪn fə ˈmeɪʃ ən ˌ· ·-, ˌ·ən- ‖ -fər'--
disingenuous ˌdɪs ɪn ˈdʒen ju‿əs ◂ ˌ·ən- **~ly** li **~ness** nəs nɪs

isinher|it ˌdɪs ɪn ˈher |ɪt -ən-, -ət ‖ -|ət **~ited** ɪt ɪd ət-, -əd ‖ əţ əd **~iting** ɪt ɪŋ ət- ‖ əţ ɪŋ **~its** ɪts əts ‖ əts

isinheritance ˌdɪs ɪn ˈher ɪt ənᵗs, ˌən- ‖ -ət ᵊnᵗs

isinte|grate dɪs ˈɪnt ɪ |greɪt -ə- ‖ -ˈɪnţ ə- **~grated** greɪt ɪd -əd ‖ greɪţ əd **~grates** greɪts **~grating** greɪt ɪŋ ‖ greɪţ ɪŋ

isintegration dɪs ˌɪnt ɪ ˈgreɪʃ ᵊn ˌ·ˌ··-, ˌənt-, -əˈ·- ‖ -ˌɪnţ ə- **~s** z

isin|ter ˌdɪs ɪn |ˈtɜː -ən- ‖ -|ˈtɜ˞ **~terred** ˈtɜːd ‖ ˈtɜ˞d **~terring** ˈtɜːr ɪŋ ‖ ˈtɜ˞ ɪŋ **~ters** ˈtɜːz ‖ ˈtɜ˞z

isinterest (ı)dɪs ˈɪntr əst -ɪst, -est; -ˈɪnt ə rest ‖ -ˈɪnţ ər əst, -ə rest

isinterested (ı)dɪs ˈɪntr əst ɪd -ɪst-, -est-, -əd; -ˈɪnt ə rest ɪd, -əd ‖ -ˈɪnţ ər əst əd, -ə rest əd **~ly** li **~ness** nəs nɪs

isintermediation (ı)dɪs ˌɪnt ə miːd i ˈeɪʃ ᵊn ‖ -ˌɪn ţ ᵊr-

isinterment ˌdɪs ɪn ˈtɜː mənt -ən- ‖ -ˈtɜ˞- **~s** s

isinvest ˌdɪs ɪn ˈvest -ən- **~ed** ɪd əd **~ing** ɪŋ **~ment/s** mənt/s **~s** s

isjoin (ı)dɪs ˈdʒɔɪn **~ed** d **~ing** ɪŋ **~s** z

isjoint dɪs ˈdʒɔɪnt **~ly** li

isjointed dɪs ˈdʒɔɪnt ɪd -əd ‖ -ˈdʒɔɪnţ əd **~ly** li **~ness** nəs nɪs

isjunct dɪs ˈdʒʌŋkt ˈ· · **~ly** li **~s** s

isjunction (ı)dɪs ˈdʒʌŋk ʃᵊn **~s** z

isjunctive (ı)dɪs ˈdʒʌŋkt ɪv **~ly** li **~s** z

isjuncture (ı)dɪs ˈdʒʌŋk tʃə -ʃə ‖ -tʃᵊr **~s** z

isk dɪsk **disks** dɪsks
ˈdisk drive

iskette dɪ ˈsket ˌdɪsk ˈet **~s** s

Disley ˈdɪz li

islik|e *v, n* (ı)dɪs ˈlaɪk —*but with contrastive stress,* ˌlikes and ˈdislikes **~ed** t **~es** s **~ing** ɪŋ

dislo|cate ˈdɪs lə |keɪt -ləʊ- ‖ dɪs ˈloʊ|k eɪt **~cated** keɪt ɪd -əd ‖ keɪţ əd **~cates** keɪts **~cating** keɪt ɪŋ ‖ keɪţ ɪŋ

dislocation ˌdɪs lə ˈkeɪʃ ᵊn -ləʊ- ‖ -loʊ- **~s** z

dislodg|e dɪs ˈlɒdʒ ‖ -ˈlɑːdʒ **~ed** d **~es** ɪz əz **~ing** ɪŋ

dislodgement, dislodgment dɪs ˈlɒdʒ mənt ‖ -ˈlɑːdʒ- **~s** s

disloyal (ı)dɪs ˈlɔɪ‿əl **~ly** i

disloyal|ty (ı)dɪs ˈlɔɪ‿əl |ti **~ties** tiz

dismal ˈdɪz məl **~ly** i **~ness** nəs nɪs

dismantl|e dɪs ˈmænt ᵊl **~ed** d **~ement/s** mənt/s **~es** z **~ing** ‿ɪŋ

dismast ˌdɪs ˈmɑːst §-ˈmæst ‖ -ˈmæst **~ed** ɪd əd **~ing** ɪŋ **~s** s

dismay *v, n* dɪs ˈmeɪ dɪz- **~ed** d **~ing** ɪŋ **~s** z

dismember (ı)dɪs ˈmem bə ‖ -bᵊr **~ed** d
dismembering (ı)dɪs ˈmem bər‿ɪŋ **~s** z

dismemberer (ı)dɪs ˈmem bər‿ə ‖ -bᵊr‿ər **~s** z

dismemberment dɪs ˈmem bə mənt ‖ -bᵊr- **~s** s

dismiss dɪs ˈmɪs §(ı)dɪz- **~ed** t **~es** ɪz əz **~ing** ɪŋ

dismissal dɪs ˈmɪs ᵊl §dɪz- **~s** z

dismissive dɪs ˈmɪs ɪv §dɪz- **~ly** li **~ness** nəs nɪs

dis|mount (ı)dɪs |ˈmaʊnt **~mounted** ˈmaʊnt ɪd -əd ‖ ˈmaʊnţ əd **~mounting** ˈmaʊnt ɪŋ ‖ ˈmaʊnţ ɪŋ **~mounts** ˈmaʊnts

Disney ˈdɪz ni
ˌDisney ˈWorld *tdmk,* ˈ·· ·

Disneyland *tdmk* ˈdɪz ni lænd

disobedience ˌdɪs ə ˈbiːd i‿ənᵗs ˌ·əʊ-

disobedient ˌdɪs ə ˈbiːd i‿ənt ◂ ˌ·əʊ- **~ly** li

disobey ˌdɪs ə ˈbeɪ -əʊ- **~ed** d **~ing** ɪŋ **~s** z

disoblig|e ˌdɪs ə ˈblaɪdʒ §-əʊ- **~ed** d **~es** ɪz əz **~ing/ly** ɪŋ /li

disord|er dɪs ˈɔːd |ə dɪz- ‖ -ˈɔːrd |ᵊr **~ered** əd ‖ ᵊrd **~ering** ər‿ɪŋ **~ers** əz ‖ ᵊrz

disorder|ly dɪs ˈɔːd ə |li dɪz-, -ə|l i ‖ -ˈɔːrd ᵊr- **~liness** li nəs -nɪs
disˌorderly ˈconduct; **disˌorderly ˈhouse**

disorganis... —*see* **disorganiz...**

disorganization dɪs ˌɔːg ən aɪ ˈzeɪʃ ᵊn dɪz-, ˌ·ˌ··-, -ɪˈ·- ‖ -ˌɔːrg ən‿ə-

disorganiz|e dɪs ˈɔːg ə naɪz dɪz-, ˌ·ˈ·· ‖ -ˈɔːrg- **~ed** d **~es** ɪz əz **~ing** ɪŋ

disori|ent (ı)dɪs ˈɔːr i |ent ənt ‖ -ˈoʊr- **~ented** ent ɪd ənt-, -əd ‖ enţ əd **~enting** ent ɪŋ ənt- ‖ enţ ɪŋ **~ents** ents ənts

disorien|tate (ı)dɪs ˈɔːr i‿ən |teɪt -ˈɒr-, -i en- ‖ -ˈoʊr- **~tated** teɪt ɪd -əd ‖ teɪţ əd **~tates** teɪts **~tating** teɪt ɪŋ ‖ teɪţ ɪŋ

disorientation dɪs ˌɔːr i‿ən ˈteɪʃ ᵊn -ˌɒr-, ˌ·ˌ··-, -i en- ‖ -ˌoʊr-

disown dɪs ˈəʊn ˌ·ˈ· ‖ -ˈoʊn **~ed** d **~ing** ɪŋ **~s** z

disparag|e dɪ ˈspær ɪdʒ də- ‖ -ˈsper- **~ed** d **~ement/s** mənt/s **~es** ɪz əz **~ing/ly** ɪŋ /li

disparate ˈdɪsp ər‿ət -ɪt; -ə reɪt ‖ dɪs ˈpær-, -ˈper- **~ly** li **~ness** nəs nɪs

disparit|y (ı)dɪs ˈpær ət |i -ɪt- ‖ -əţ |i -ˈper- **~ies** iz

dispassionate dɪs ˈpæʃ ᵊn‿ət ɪt **~ly** li **~ness** nəs nɪs

dispatch *v* dɪ ˈspætʃ də- **~ed** t **~er/s** ə/z ‖ ᵊr/z **~es** ɪz əz **~ing** ɪŋ

dispatch *n* dɪ ˈspætʃ də-; ˈdɪs pætʃ **~es** ɪz əz
diˈspatch box; **diˈspatch ˌrider**

dispel dɪ ˈspel **~led** d **~ling** ɪŋ **~s** z

dispensable dɪ ˈspenᵗs əb ᵊl **~ness** nəs nɪs

dispensar|y dɪ ˈspenᵗs ər‿|i **~ies** iz

dispensation ˌdɪsp ən ˈseɪʃ ᵊn -en- **~s** z

dispens|e dɪ ˈspenᵗs **~ed** t **~er/s** ə/z ‖ ᵊr/z **~es** ɪz əz **~ing** ɪŋ

dispersal dɪ ˈspɜːs ᵊl də- ‖ -ˈspɜ˞s- **~s** z

dispersant dɪ ˈspɜːs ᵊnt də- ‖ -ˈspɜ˞s- **~s** s

dispers|e dɪ ˈspɜːs də- ‖ -ˈspɜ˞s **~ed** t **~es** ɪz əz **~ing** ɪŋ

dispersion, D~ dɪ ˈspɜːʃ ᵊn də-, §-ˈspɜːʒ- ‖ -ˈspɜ˞ʒ- -ˈspɜ˞ʃ- **~s** z

dispersive dɪ ˈspɜːs ɪv də- ‖ -ˈspɜ˞s- -ˈspɜ˞z-

dispir|it dɪ ˈspɪr |ɪt -ət ‖ -|ət **~ited/ly** ɪt ɪd /li ət-, -əd /li ‖ əţ əd /li **~iting** ɪt ɪŋ ət- ‖ əţ ɪŋ **~its** ɪts əts ‖ əts

displac|e (ı)dɪs ˈpleɪs **~ed** t **~es** ɪz əz **~ing** ɪŋ
ˌdisplaced ˈperson, ˌ·ˌ·ˈ··

displacement (ı)dɪs ˈpleɪs mənt **~s** s

D

D

display dɪ ˈspleɪ **~ed** d **~ing** ɪŋ **~s** z
displeas|e (ˌ)dɪs ˈpliːz **~ed** d **~es** ɪz əz **~ing/ly** ɪŋ /li
displeasure (ˌ)dɪs ˈpleʒ ə ‖ -ᵊr
di|sport dɪ |ˈspɔːt ‖ -|ˈspɔːrt -ˈspoʊrt **~sported** ˈspɔːt ɪd -əd ‖ ˈspɔːrt̬ əd ˈspoʊrt̬- **~sporting** ˈspɔːt ɪŋ ‖ ˈspɔːrt̬ ɪŋ ˈspoʊrt̬- **~sports** ˈspɔːts ‖ ˈspɔːrts ˈspoʊrts
disposability dɪ ˌspəʊz ə ˈbɪl ət i də-, -ɪt i ‖ -ˌspoʊz ə ˈbɪl ət̬ i
disposable dɪ ˈspəʊz əb ᵊl də- ‖ -ˈspoʊz-
disposal dɪ ˈspəʊz ᵊl də- ‖ -ˈspoʊz- **~s** z
dispos|e dɪ ˈspəʊz də- ‖ -ˈspoʊz **~ed** d **~es** ɪz əz **~ing** ɪŋ
disposition ˌdɪsp ə ˈzɪʃ ᵊn **~s** z
dispossess ˌdɪs pə ˈzes **~ed** t **~es** ɪz əz **~ing** ɪŋ
dispossession ˌdɪs pə ˈzeʃ ᵊn **~s** z
Disprin *tdmk* ˈdɪsp rɪn -rən **~s** z
disproof (ˌ)dɪs ˈpruːf §-ˈprʊf **~s** s
disproportion ˌdɪs prə ˈpɔːʃ ᵊn ‖ -ˈpɔːrʃ ᵊn -ˈpoʊrʃ- **~al/ly** ‿əl /i **~ed** d **~ing** ‿ɪŋ **~s** z
disproportionate ˌdɪs prə ˈpɔːʃ ᵊn‿ət ◂ ɪt ‖ -ˈpɔːrʃ- -ˈpoʊrʃ- **~ly** li **~ness** nəs nɪs
disprov|e (ˌ)dɪs ˈpruːv **~ed** d **~es** z **~ing** ɪŋ
disputab|le dɪ ˈspjuːt əb |ᵊl də-; ˈdɪs pjʊt- ‖ dɪ ˈspjuːt̬ əb |ᵊl ˈdɪs pjət̬- **~ly** li
disputant dɪ ˈspjuːt ᵊnt də-; ˈdɪs pjʊt ənt ‖ ˈdɪs pjət ᵊnt **~s** s
disputation ˌdɪs pju ˈteɪʃ ᵊn ‖ -pjə- **~s** z
disputatious ˌdɪs pju ˈteɪʃ əs ◂ ‖ -pjə- **~ly** li **~ness** nəs nɪs
di|spute *v* dɪ |ˈspjuːt də- **~sputed** ˈspjuːt ɪd -əd ‖ ˈspjuːt̬ əd **~sputes** ˈspjuːts **~sputing** ˈspjuːt ɪŋ ‖ ˈspjuːt̬ ɪŋ

DISPUTE (noun)

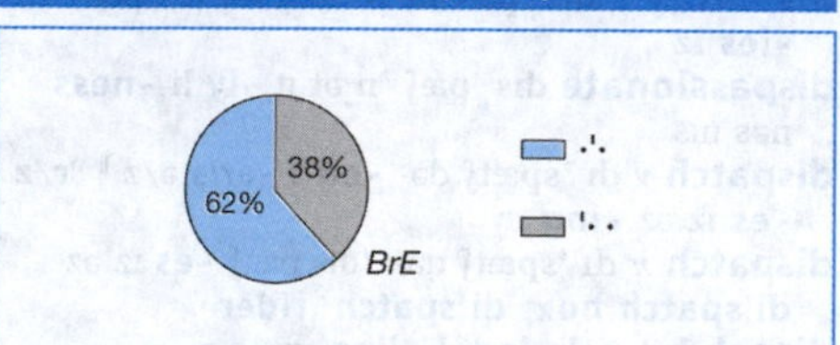

dispute *n* dɪ ˈspjuːt də-; ˈdɪs pjuːt — *Preference poll, BrE:* ·ˈ· *62%,* ˈ·· *38%.* **~s** s
disqualification dɪs ˌkwɒl ɪf ɪ ˈkeɪʃ ᵊn ˌ·ˌ··ˈ··, -əf ɪ-, §-əˈ·- ‖ -ˌkwɑːl- **~s** z
disquali|fy dɪs ˈkwɒl ɪ |faɪ ˌdɪs-, -ə- ‖ -ˈkwɑːl- **~fied** faɪd **~fies** faɪz **~fying** faɪ ɪŋ
disqui|et dɪs ˈkwaɪ‿|ət **~eted** ət ɪd -əd ‖ ət̬ əd **~eting** ət ɪŋ ‖ ət̬ ɪŋ **~ets** əts
disquietude dɪs ˈkwaɪ‿ə tjuːd -ɪ-, →-tʃuːd ‖ -tuːd -tjuːd
disquisition ˌdɪs kwɪ ˈzɪʃ ᵊn -kwə- **~al** ‿əl **~s** z
Disraeli dɪz ˈreɪl i dɪs-
disregard *v, n* ˌdɪs ri ˈgɑːd -rə- ‖ -ˈgɑːrd **~ed** ɪd əd **~ing** ɪŋ **~s** z
disrelish (ˌ)dɪs ˈrel ɪʃ **~ed** t **~es** ɪz əz **~ing** ɪŋ
disremem|ber ˌdɪs ri ˈmem |bə -rə- ‖ -|bᵊr **~bered** bəd ‖ bᵊrd **~bering** bər‿ɪŋ **~bers** bəz ‖ bᵊrz

disrepair ˌdɪs ri ˈpeə -rə- ‖ -ˈpeᵊr -ˈpæᵊr
disreputab|le dɪs ˈrep jʊt əb |ᵊl -jət əb- ‖ -jət̬ əb- **~leness** ᵊl nəs -nɪs **~ly** li
disrepute ˌdɪs ri ˈpjuːt -rə-
disrespect ˌdɪs ri ˈspekt -rə- **~ed** ɪd əd **~ing** ɪ **~s** s
disrespectful ˌdɪs ri ˈspekt fᵊl ◂ -rə-, -fʊl **~ly** li **~ness** nəs nɪs
disrob|e (ˌ)dɪs ˈrəʊb ‖ -ˈroʊb **~ed** d **~es** z **~ing** ɪŋ
disrupt dɪs ˈrʌpt **~ed** ɪd əd **~er/s** ə/z ‖ ᵊr/z **~ing** ɪŋ **~s** s
disruption dɪs ˈrʌp ʃᵊn **~s** z
disruptive dɪs ˈrʌpt ɪv **~ly** li **~ness** nəs nɪs
disruptor dɪs ˈrʌpt ə ‖ -ᵊr **~s** z
Diss dɪs
diss dɪs **dissed** dɪst **disses** ˈdɪs ɪz -əz **dissing** ˈdɪs ɪŋ
dissatisfaction ˌdɪs ˌsæt ɪs ˈfæk ʃᵊn ˌdɪs æt-, dɪ ˌsæt-, -əsˈ·- ‖ ˌdɪs ˌsæt̬ əs- ˌdɪs æt̬-, dɪ ˌsæt̬- **~s** z
dissatis|fy ˌdɪs ˈsæt ɪs |faɪ (ˌ)dɪ-, -əs- ‖ -ˈsæt̬- **~fied/ly** faɪd /li **~fies** faɪz **~fying** faɪ ɪŋ

DISSECT

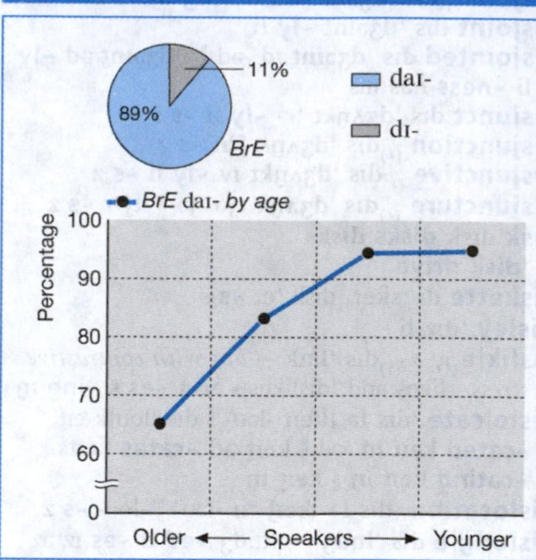

dissect daɪ ˈsekt dɪ-, də- ‖ dɪ-; ˈdaɪ sekt — *Preference poll, BrE:* daɪ- *89% (born since 1981, 95%),* dɪ- *11%.* **~ed** ɪd əd **~ing** ɪŋ **~s** s
dissection dɪ ˈsek ʃᵊn də-, daɪ- **~s** z
dissemblance dɪ ˈsem blənᵗs də-
dissembl|e dɪ ˈsem bᵊl də- **~ed** d **~er/s** ‿ə/z ‖ ər/z **~es** z **~ing** ‿ɪŋ
dissemi|nate dɪ ˈsem ɪ |neɪt də-, -ə- **~nated** neɪt ɪd -əd ‖ neɪt̬ əd **~nates** neɪts **~nating** neɪt ɪŋ ‖ neɪt̬ ɪŋ
dissemination dɪ ˌsem ɪ ˈneɪʃ ᵊn də-, -ə-
disseminator dɪ ˈsem ɪ neɪt ə də-, -ˈ·ə- ‖ -neɪt̬ ᵊr **~s** z
dissension dɪ ˈsenᵗʃ ᵊn də- **~s** z
dis|sent *v, n* dɪ |ˈsent də- *(usually = descent)* **~sented** ˈsent ɪd -əd ‖ ˈsent̬ əd **~senting/ly** ˈsent ɪŋ /li ‖ ˈsent̬ ɪŋ /li **~sents** ˈsents
dissenter, D~ dɪ ˈsent ə də- ‖ -ˈsent̬ ᵊr **~s** z
dissentient dɪ ˈsenᵗʃ i‿ənt də-, -ˈsenᵗʃ ᵊnt **~s** s

dissertation ˌdɪs ə ˈteɪʃ ən -ɜː- ‖ -ər- **~s** z
disservic|e dɪ ˈsɜːv ɪs, (ı)dɪs-, §-əs ‖ -ˈsɜːv- **~es** ɪz əz
dissev|er dɪ ˈsev |ə ‖ -|ər **~ered** əd ‖ ərd **~ering** ər‿ɪŋ **~ers** əz ‖ ərz
dissidence ˈdɪs ɪd ənts -əd-
dissident ˈdɪs ɪd ənt -əd- **~s** s
dissimilar (ı)dɪ ˈsɪm ɪl ə (ı)dɪs-, -əl- ‖ -ər **~ly** li
dissimilarit|y dɪs ɪm ɪ ˈlær ət |i ˌ·əm-, dɪ ˌsɪm-, ˌdɪs ˌsɪm-, -əˈ·-, -ɪt i ‖ -əṭ |i -ˈler- **~ies** iz
dissimi|late (ı)dɪ ˈsɪm ɪ |leɪt -ə- **~lated** leɪt ɪd -əd ‖ leɪṭ əd **~lates** leɪts **~lating** leɪt ɪŋ ‖ leɪṭ ɪŋ
dissimilation ˌdɪs ɪm ɪ ˈleɪʃ ən dɪ ˌsɪm-, ˌdɪs ˌsɪm-, -əˈ·- ‖ dɪ ˌsɪm- **~s** z
dissimilitude ˌdɪs ɪ ˈmɪl ɪ tjuːd ˌ·ə-, ˌ·sɪ-, ˌ·sə-, -ə ·, →-tʃuːd ‖ -tuːd -tjuːd **~s** z
dissimu|late dɪ ˈsɪm ju |leɪt də-, -jə- ‖ -jə- **~lated** leɪt ɪd -əd ‖ leɪṭ əd **~lates** leɪts **~lating** leɪt ɪŋ ‖ leɪṭ ɪŋ
dissimulation dɪ ˌsɪm ju ˈleɪʃ ən də-, -jə- ‖ -jə- **~s** z
dissi|pate ˈdɪs ɪ |peɪt -ə- **~pated** peɪt ɪd -əd ‖ peɪṭ əd **~pates** peɪts **~pating** peɪt ɪŋ ‖ peɪṭ ɪŋ
dissipation ˌdɪs ɪ ˈpeɪʃ ən -ə- **~s** z
dissoci|ate dɪ ˈsəʊs i |eɪt -ˈsəʊʃ- ‖ -ˈsoʊʃ- -ˈsoʊs- **~ated** eɪt ɪd -əd ‖ eɪṭ əd **~ates** eɪts **~ating** eɪt ɪŋ ‖ eɪṭ ɪŋ
dissociation dɪ ˌsəʊʃ i ˈeɪʃ ən -ˌsəʊs- ‖ -ˌsoʊʃ- -ˌsoʊs- **~s** z
dissolubility dɪ ˌsɒl ju ˈbɪl ət i -ˌ·jə-, -ɪt i ‖ dɪ ˌsɑːl jə ˈbɪl əṭ i
dissoluble dɪ ˈsɒl jʊb əl -jəb- ‖ dɪ ˈsɑːl jəb əl **~ness** nəs nɪs
dissolute ˈdɪs ə luːt -ljuːt **~ly** li **~ness** nəs nɪs
dissolution ˌdɪs ə ˈluːʃ ən -ˈljuːʃ- **~s** z
dissolv|e dɪ ˈzɒlv də-, §-ˈzəʊlv ‖ -ˈzɑːlv **~ed** d **~es** z **~ing** ɪŋ
dissonanc|e ˈdɪs ən ənts **~es** ɪz əz
dissonant ˈdɪs ən ənt **~ly** li
dissuad|e dɪ ˈsweɪd **~ed** ɪd əd **~es** z **~ing** ɪŋ
dissuasion dɪ ˈsweɪʒ ən **~s** z
dissuasive dɪ ˈsweɪs ɪv -ˈsweɪz- **~ly** li **~ness** nəs nɪs
dissy... —*see* **disy...**
distaff ˈdɪst ɑːf §-æf ‖ -æf **~s** s
distal ˈdɪst əl **~ly** i
distanc|e ˈdɪst ənts **~ed** t **~es** ɪz əz **~ing** ɪŋ
distant ˈdɪst ənt **~ly** li
distaste (ı)dɪs ˈteɪst **~s** s
distasteful (ı)dɪs ˈteɪst fəl -fʊl **~ly** ‿i **~ness** nəs nɪs
distemp|er dɪ ˈstemp |ə də- ‖ -|ər **~ered** əd ‖ ərd **~ering** ər‿ɪŋ **~ers** əz ‖ ərz
distend dɪ ˈstend də- **~ed** ɪd əd **~ing** ɪŋ **~s** z
distension, distention dɪ ˈstentʃ ən də-
distich ˈdɪst ɪk **~s** s
di|stil, di|still dɪ |ˈstɪl də- **~stilled** ˈstɪld **~stilling** ˈstɪl ɪŋ **~stills, ~stils** ˈstɪlz
distillate ˈdɪst ɪl ət -əl-, -ɪt; -ɪ leɪt, -ə- **~s** s
distillation ˌdɪst ɪ ˈleɪʃ ən -ə-, -əl ˈeɪʃ- **~s** z
ˌdistilˈlation ˌcolumn
distiller dɪ ˈstɪl ə də- ‖ -ər **~s** z
distiller|y dɪ ˈstɪl ər |i də- **~ies** iz
distinct dɪ ˈstɪŋkt də- **~ly** li **~ness** nəs nɪs
distinction dɪ ˈstɪŋk ʃən də- **~s** z
distinctive dɪ ˈstɪŋkt ɪv də- **~ly** li **~ness** nəs nɪs
distingué dɪ ˈstæŋ geɪ də- ‖ ˌdiːst æŋ ˈgeɪ ˌdɪst- —*Fr* [dis tɛ̃ ge]
distinguish dɪ ˈstɪŋ gwɪʃ də-, -wɪʃ **~ed** t **~es** ɪz əz **~ing** ɪŋ
distinguishab|le dɪ ˈstɪŋ gwɪʃ əb |əl də-, -ˈ·wɪʃ- **~ly** li
di|stort dɪ |ˈstɔːt də- ‖ -|ˈstɔːrt **~storted** ˈstɔːt ɪd -əd ‖ ˈstɔːrṭ əd **~storting** ˈstɔːt ɪŋ ‖ ˈstɔːrṭ ɪŋ **~storts** ˈstɔːts ‖ ˈstɔːrts
distortion dɪ ˈstɔːʃ ən də- ‖ -ˈstɔːrʃ ən **~s** z
distract dɪ ˈstrækt də- **~ed/ly** ɪd /li əd /li **~ing/ly** ɪŋ /li **~s** s
distraction dɪ ˈstræk ʃən də- **~s** z
distractor dɪ ˈstrækt ə də- ‖ -ər **~s** z
distrain dɪ ˈstreɪn də- **~ed** d **~ing** ɪŋ **~s** z
distraint dɪ ˈstreɪnt də-
distrait ˈdɪs treɪ dɪ ˈstreɪ, də- ‖ dɪ ˈstreɪ —*Fr* [dis tʁɛ]
distraught dɪ ˈstrɔːt də- ‖ -ˈstrɑːt **~ly** li
distress dɪ ˈstres də- **~ed** t **~es** ɪz əz **~ing/ly** ɪŋ /li
distressful dɪ ˈstres fəl də-, -fʊl **~ly** i **~ness** nəs nɪs

DISTRIBUTE

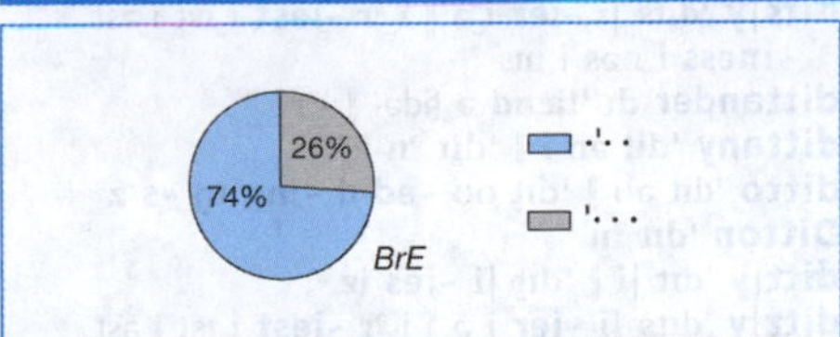

distribute dɪ ˈstrɪb juːt də-; ˈdɪs trɪ bjuːt, -trə- ‖ -jət —*The stressing* ˈ· · ·*, although disliked by many, is widely used in BrE. — Preference poll, BrE:* ·ˈ·· 74%, ˈ· · · 26%. **distributed** dɪ ˈstrɪb jʊt ɪd də-, -jət-, -əd; ˈdɪs trɪ bjuːt ɪd, ˈ·trə-, -əd ‖ -jəṭ əd **distributes** dɪ ˈstrɪb juːts də-; ˈdɪs trɪ bjuːts, -trə- ‖ -jəts **distributing** dɪ ˈstrɪb jʊt ɪŋ də-, -jət-; ˈdɪs trɪ bjuːt ɪŋ, ˈ·trə- ‖ -jəṭ ɪŋ
distribution ˌdɪs trɪ ˈbjuːʃ ən -trə- **~s** z
distributional ˌdɪs trɪ ˈbjuːʃ ən‿əl **~ly** i
distributive dɪ ˈstrɪb jʊt ɪv də-, -jə-; §ˈdɪs trɪ bjuːt ɪv, ˈ·trə- ‖ -jəṭ ɪv **~ly** li **~ness** nəs nɪs
distributor dɪ ˈstrɪb jʊt ə də-, -jət ə; §ˈdɪs trɪ bjuːt ə, ˈ·trə- ‖ -jəṭ ər **~ship/s** ʃɪp/s **~s** z
district ˈdɪs trɪkt **~s** s
ˌdistrict atˈtorney; ˌdistrict ˈnurse; ˌDistrict of Coˈlumbia
distrust (ı)dɪs ˈtrʌst **~ed** ɪd əd **~ing** ɪŋ **~s** s

D

distrustful (ɪ)dɪs 'trʌst fᵊl -fʊl **~ly** i **~ness** nəs nɪs
disturb dɪ 'stɜːb də- ‖ -'stɜ˞ːb **~ed** d **~ing/ly** ɪŋ /li **~s** z
disturbanc|e dɪ 'stɜːb ənᵗs də-, →-mᵖs ‖ -'stɜ˞ːb- **~es** ɪz əz
disunion (ɪ)dɪs 'juːn i‿ən →§(ɪ)dɪʃ-
disu|nite ˌdɪs ju |'naɪt →§ˌdɪʃ- **~nited** 'naɪt ɪd -əd ‖ 'naɪţ əd **~nites** 'naɪts **~niting** 'naɪt ɪŋ ‖ 'naɪţ ɪŋ
disunit|y (ɪ)dɪs 'juːn ət |i →§(ɪ)dɪʃ-, -ɪt- ‖ -əţ |i **~ies** iz
disuse *n* (ɪ)dɪs 'juːs →§(ɪ)dɪʃ-
disused ˌdɪs 'juːzd ◂ dɪs-, →§(ɪ)dɪʃ- **ˌdisused 'railway**
disyllabic ˌdaɪ sɪ 'læb ɪk ◂ -sə-; ˌdɪs ɪ-, -ə- **~ally** ᵊl‿i
disyllable ˌdaɪ 'sɪl əb ᵊl (ɪ)dɪ-, 'ˌ·ˌ·· **~s** z
dit dɪt **dits** dɪts
ditch dɪtʃ **ditched** dɪtʃt **ditches** 'dɪtʃ ɪz -əz **ditching** 'dɪtʃ ɪŋ
ditcher 'dɪtʃ ə ‖ -ᵊr **~s** z
Ditchling 'dɪtʃ lɪŋ
ditchwater 'dɪtʃ ˌwɔːt ə ‖ -ˌwɔːţ ᵊr -ˌwɑːţ ᵊr
dith|er 'dɪð |ə ‖ -|ᵊr **~ered** əd ‖ ᵊrd **~ering** ər‿ɪŋ **~ers** əz ‖ ᵊrz
ditherer 'dɪð ər‿ə ‖ -ᵊr ər **~s** z
dithery 'dɪð ər‿i
dithyramb 'dɪθ ɪ ræm -ə-, -ræmb **~s** z
dithyrambic ˌdɪθ ɪ 'ræm bɪk ◂ -ə-
ditransitive ˌdaɪ 'trænᵗs ət ɪv -'trɑːnᵗs-, -'trænz-, -'trɑːnz-, -ɪt- ‖ -'trænᵗs əţ ɪv -'trænz- **~ly** li **~s** z
dits|y 'dɪts |i **~ier** i‿ə ‖ i‿ᵊr **~iest** i‿ɪst i‿əst **~iness** i nəs i nɪs
dittander dɪ 'tænd ə §də- ‖ -ᵊr
dittany 'dɪt ən i ‖ 'dɪt ᵊn i
ditto 'dɪt əʊ ‖ 'dɪţ oʊ **~ed** d **~ing** ɪŋ **~s** z
Ditton 'dɪt ᵊn
ditt|y 'dɪt |i ‖ 'dɪţ |i **~ies** iz
ditz|y 'dɪts |i **~ier** i‿ə ‖ i‿ᵊr **~iest** i‿ɪst i‿əst **~iness** i nəs i nɪs
diuresis ˌdaɪ juᵊ 'riːs ɪs §-əs ‖ -jə-
diuretic ˌdaɪ juᵊ 'ret ɪk ◂ ‖ -jə 'reţ ɪk **~s** s
diurnal daɪ 'ɜːn ᵊl ‖ -'ɜ˞ːn ᵊl **~ly** i
diva 'diːv ə **~s** z
diva|gate 'daɪv ə |geɪt 'daɪ veɪ-, 'dɪv ə- **~gated** geɪt ɪd -əd ‖ geɪţ əd **~gates** geɪts **~gating** geɪt ɪŋ ‖ geɪţ ɪŋ
divagation ˌdaɪv ə 'geɪʃ ᵊn ˌdaɪ veɪ-, ˌdɪv ə- **~s** z
divalent (ɪ)daɪ 'veɪl ənt 'ˌ·ˌ··
Divali dɪ 'vɑːl i
divan dɪ 'væn də-, (ɪ)daɪ-, 'daɪv æn **~s** z
dive daɪv **dived** daɪvd **dives** daɪvz **diving** 'daɪv ɪŋ **dove** dəʊv ‖ doʊv
dive-bomb 'daɪv bɒm ‖ -bɑːm **~ed** d **~er/s** ə/z ‖ ᵊr/z **~ing** ɪŋ **~s** z
diver, Diver 'daɪv ə ‖ -ᵊr **~s** z
diverg|e daɪ 'vɜːdʒ dɪ-, də- ‖ də 'vɜ˞ːdʒ daɪ- **~ed** d **~es** ɪz əz **~ing** ɪŋ
divergenc|e daɪ 'vɜːdʒ ənᵗs dɪ-, də- ‖ də 'vɜ˞ːdʒ- daɪ- **~es** ɪz əz
divergent (ɪ)daɪ 'vɜːdʒ ənt dɪ-, də- ‖ də 'vɜ˞ːdʒ- daɪ- —*but with contrastive stress, against* convergent, 'daɪˌ·· **~ly** li
divers 'daɪv əz -ɜːz; (ɪ)daɪ 'vɜːs, 'ˌ·· ‖ -ᵊrz
diverse daɪ 'vɜːs ˌdaɪ-, 'ˌ·‖ də 'vɜ˞ːs daɪ-, 'daɪ vɜːs **~ly** li **~ness** nəs nɪs
diversification daɪ ˌvɜːs ɪf ɪ 'keɪʃ ᵊn dɪ-, də-, -ˌ·əf-, §-ə'·- ‖ də ˌvɜ˞ːs- daɪ- **~s** z
diversi|fy daɪ 'vɜːs ɪ |faɪ -ə- ‖ də 'vɜ˞ːs- daɪ- **~fied** faɪd **~fies** faɪz **~fying** faɪ ɪŋ
diversion daɪ 'vɜːʃ ᵊn dɪ-, də-, §-'vɜːʒ- ‖ də 'vɜ˞ːʒ ᵊn daɪ-, -'vɜ˞ːʃ- **~ist/s** ɪst/s §əst/s **~s** z
diversionary daɪ 'vɜːʃ ᵊn ər‿i dɪ-, də-, §-'vɜːʒ-, -ᵊn‿ər- ‖ də 'vɜ˞ːʒ ə ner i daɪ-
diversit|y daɪ 'vɜːs ət |i dɪ-, də-, -ɪt- ‖ də 'vɜ˞ːs əţ |i daɪ- **~ies** iz
di|vert daɪ |'vɜːt dɪ-, də- ‖ də |'vɜ˞ːt daɪ- **~verted** 'vɜːt ɪd -əd ‖ 'vɜ˞ːţ əd **~verting** 'vɜːt ɪŋ ‖ 'vɜ˞ːţ ɪŋ **~verts** 'vɜːts ‖ 'vɜ˞ːts
diverticulitis ˌdaɪv ə ˌtɪk ju 'laɪt ɪs ˌ·ɜː-, §-əs ‖ ˌdaɪv ᵊr ˌtɪk jə 'laɪţ əs
diverticul|um ˌdaɪv ə 'tɪk jʊl |əm ˌ·ɜː-, -jəl əm ‖ ˌdaɪv ᵊr 'tɪk jəl |əm **~a** ə
divertiment|o dɪ ˌvɜːt ɪ 'ment |əʊ -ˌveət-, -ə- ‖ dɪ ˌvɜ˞ːţ ə 'ment |oʊ **~i** iː
divertissement ˌdiː veə 'tiːs mɒ̃ dɪ 'vɜːt ɪs mənt, -əs-, -mɒ̃ ‖ dɪ 'vɜ˞ːţ əs mənt —*Fr* [di vɛʁ tis mɑ̃]
Dives *name* 'daɪv iːz
divest daɪ 'vest dɪ-, də- **~ed** ɪd əd **~ing** ɪŋ **~s** s
divestiture daɪ 'vest ɪtʃ ə dɪ-, də- ‖ -ᵊr -ə tʃʊr **~s** z
divestment daɪ 'vest mənt dɪ-, də- **~s** s
divid|e dɪ 'vaɪd də- **~ed** ɪd əd **~es** z **~ing** ɪŋ
dividend 'dɪv ɪ dend -ə-; -ɪd ənd, -əd- **~s** z
divider dɪ 'vaɪd ə də- ‖ -ᵊr **~s** z
divi-divi ˌdɪv i 'dɪv i ˌdiːv i 'diːv i **~s** z
divination ˌdɪv ɪ 'neɪʃ ᵊn -ə- **~s** z
divin|e *adj, n, v,* **D~** dɪ 'vaɪn də- **~ed** d **~ely** li **~eness** nəs nɪs **~er/s** ə/z ‖ ᵊr/z **~est** ɪst əst **~ing** ɪŋ **diˌvine 'right**; **Diˌvine 'Service**; **di'vining rod**
diving 'daɪv ɪŋ **'diving bell**; **'diving suit**
divingboard 'daɪv ɪŋ bɔːd ‖ -bɔːrd -boʊrd **~s** z
divinit|y, D~ dɪ 'vɪn ət |i də-, -ɪt- ‖ -əţ |i **~ies** iz
Divis 'dɪv ɪs §-əs
divisibility dɪ ˌvɪz ə 'bɪl ət i də-, -ˌ·ɪ-, -ɪt i ‖ -əţ i
divisib|le dɪ 'vɪz əb |ᵊl də-, -ɪb- **~ly** li
division dɪ 'vɪʒ ᵊn də- **~al** ‿əl **~s** z **di'vision ˌlobby**
divisive dɪ 'vaɪs ɪv də-, §-'vaɪz-, §-'vɪz-, §-'vɪs- **~ly** li **~ness** nəs nɪs
divisor dɪ 'vaɪz ə də- ‖ -ᵊr *(= deviser)* **~s** z
divorc|e *n, v* dɪ 'vɔːs də- ‖ -'vɔːrs -'voʊrs **~ed** t **~es** ɪz əz **~ing** ɪŋ

divorcé, divorcee, divorcée dɪ ˌvɔː ˈsiː də-, -ˈseɪ; ˌdɪv ɔː-, ˌdiːv ɔː-, -ˈseɪ; dɪ ˈvɔːs iː, də-, -eɪ ‖ də ˌvɔːr ˈseɪ -ˌvoʊr-, -ˈsiː; -ˈvɔːrs iː, -ˈvoʊrs-, -eɪ **~s** z
divot ˈdɪv ət **~s** s
divulg|e daɪ ˈvʌldʒ dɪ-, də- ‖ də- daɪ- **~ed** d **~es** ɪz əz **~ing** ɪŋ
divulgenc|e daɪ ˈvʌldʒ ənᵗs dɪ-, də- ‖ də- daɪ- **~es** ɪz əz
divv|y ˈdɪv |i **~ied** id **~ies** iz **~ying** i ɪŋ
Diwali dɪ ˈwɑːl i
Dix dɪks
Dixey, Dixie, d~ ˈdɪks i
ˈ**Dixie Cup** *tdmk*
Dixiecrat ˈdɪks i kræt **~s** s
Dixieland, d~ ˈdɪks i lænd
Dixon ˈdɪks ᵊn
DIY, diy ˌdiː aɪ ˈwaɪ **~ing** ɪŋ
ˌ**DIˈY shop**
dizygotic ˌdaɪ zaɪ ˈɡɒt ɪk ◂ ‖ -ˈɡɑːṭ-
dizz|y ˈdɪz |i **~ied** id **~ier** i‿ə ‖ i‿ᵊr **~ies** iz **~iest** i‿ɪst i‿əst **~ily** ɪ li əl i **~iness** i nəs i nɪs **~ying/ly** i‿ɪŋ /li
DJ, D.J. ˌdiː ˈdʒeɪ ‖ ˈ· · **DJs, D.J.s** ˌdiː ˈdʒeɪz ‖ ˈ· ·
Djakarta dʒə ˈkɑːt ə ‖ -ˈkɑːrṭ ə
djellaba, djellabah ˈdʒel əb ə dʒə ˈlɑːb ə **~s** z
Djibouti dʒɪ ˈbuːt i dʒə- ‖ -ˈbuːṭ i **~an/s** ən/z
djinn dʒɪn **djinns** dʒɪnz
DLit, DLitt ˌdiː ˈlɪt **~s, ~'s** s
DNA ˌdiː en ˈeɪ
Dneper, Dnieper ˈniːp ə ˈdniːp- ‖ -ᵊr —*Russ* [dʲnʲepr]
Dnepropetrovsk ˌnep rəʊ pe ˈtrɒfsk -prɪˈ·, -pəˈ· ‖ -roʊ pə ˈtrɔːfsk -ˈtrɑːvsk —*Russ* [dʲnʲɪ prə pʲɪ ˈtrɔfsk]
Dniester ˈniːst ə ˈdniːst- ‖ -ᵊr —*Russ* [dʲnʲestr]
D-notic|e ˈdiː ˌnəʊt ɪs §-əs ‖ -ˌnoʊṭ- **~es** ɪz əz
do *n, other senses* duː **dos, do's** duːz
do *n 'musical note'* dəʊ ‖ doʊ **dos** dəʊz ‖ doʊz
do *v, strong form* duː, *weak forms* dʊ, də, d **did** dɪd **didn't** ˈdɪd ᵊnt **does** dʌz *(see)* **doesn't** ˈdʌz nᵊt **doing** ˈduː‿ɪŋ **done** dʌn **don't** dəʊnt ‖ doʊnt
DOA ˌdiː əʊ ˈeɪ ‖ -oʊ-
doable ˈduː‿əb ᵊl
Doane dəʊn ‖ doʊn
dobbin, D~ ˈdɒb ɪn §-ən ‖ ˈdɑːb- **~s, ~'s** z
Dobbs dɒbz ‖ dɑːbz
Dobell *(i)* dəʊ ˈbel ‖ doʊ-, *(ii)* ˈdəʊb ᵊl ‖ ˈdoʊb-
Doberman, d~ ˈdəʊb ə mən ‖ ˈdoʊb ᵊr mən **~s** z
ˌ**Doberman ˈpinscher** ˈpɪnᵗʃ ə ‖ ᵊr
Dobie ˈdəʊb i ‖ ˈdoʊb i
Dobson ˈdɒb sᵊn ‖ ˈdɑːb-
doc, Doc dɒk ‖ dɑːk **docs, Doc's** dɒks ‖ dɑːks
docent ˈdəʊs ᵊnt dəʊ ˈsent ‖ ˈdoʊs- **~s** s
Docetism dəʊ ˈsiːt ˌɪz əm ˈdəʊs ɪ ˌtɪz əm, -ə- ‖ doʊ ˈsiːṭ-
Docherty ˈdɒx ət i ˈdɒk- ‖ ˈdɑːk ᵊrṭ i
docile ˈdəʊs aɪᵊl ‖ ˈdɑːs ᵊl *(*)* **~ly** li
docility dəʊ ˈsɪl ət i də-, -ɪt- ‖ dɑː ˈsɪl əṭ i doʊ-
dock dɒk ‖ dɑːk **docked** dɒkt ‖ dɑːkt **docking** ˈdɒk ɪŋ ‖ ˈdɑːk ɪŋ **docks** dɒks ‖ dɑːks
docker, D~ ˈdɒk ə ‖ ˈdɑːk ᵊr **~s** z
dock|et ˈdɒk |ɪt §-ət ‖ ˈdɑːk |ət **~eted** ɪt ɪd §ət-, -əd ‖ əṭ əd **~eting** ɪt ɪŋ §ət- ‖ əṭ ɪŋ **~ets** ɪts §əts ‖ əts
dockland, D~ ˈdɒk lənd -lænd ‖ ˈdɑːk- **~s** z
dockside ˈdɒk saɪd ‖ ˈdɑːk-
dockworker ˈdɒk ˌwɜːk ə ‖ ˈdɑːk ˌwɜːk ᵊr **~s** z
dockyard ˈdɒk jɑːd ‖ ˈdɑːk jɑːrd **~s** z
doctor, D~ ˈdɒkt ə ‖ ˈdɑːkt ᵊr **~ed** d **doctoring** ˈdɒkt ər‿ɪŋ ‖ ˈdɑːkt- **~s** z
doctoral ˈdɒkt ər əl →ˈdɒk trəl; dɒk ˈtɔːr əl ‖ ˈdɑːkt-
doctorate ˈdɒkt ər ət -ɪt; →ˈdɒk trət, -trɪt ‖ ˈdɑːkt- **~s** s
Doctorow ˈdɒkt ə rəʊ ‖ ˈdɑːkt ə roʊ
doctrinaire ˌdɒk trɪ ˈneə ◂ -trə- ‖ ˌdɑːk trə ˈneᵊr -ˈnæᵊr **~s** z
doctrinal dɒk ˈtraɪn ᵊl ˈdɒk trɪn ᵊl, -trən- ‖ ˈdɑːk trən ᵊl **~ly** i
doctrinarian ˌdɒk trɪ ˈneər i‿ən ◂ ˌ·trə- ‖ ˌdɑːk trə ˈner- **~s** z
doctrine ˈdɒk trɪn -trən ‖ ˈdɑːk- **~s** z
docudrama ˈdɒk ju ˌdrɑːm ə ‖ ˈdɑːk jə- -ˌdræm ə **~s** z
docu|ment *v* ˈdɒk ju |ment ‖ ˈdɑːk jə- —*See note at* -ment **~mented** ment ɪd -əd ‖ menṭ əd **~menting** ment ɪŋ ‖ menṭ ɪŋ **~ments** mənts
document *n* ˈdɒk ju mənt -jə- ‖ ˈdɑːk jə- **~s** s
documentar|y ˌdɒk ju ˈment‿ər |i ‖ ˌdɑːk jə ˈmenṭ ər |i →-ˈmentr |i **~ies** iz **~ist/s** ɪst/s §əst/s
documentation ˌdɒk ju men ˈteɪʃ ᵊn -mənˈ-- ‖ ˌdɑːk jə-
docusoap ˈdɒk ju səʊp -jə- ‖ ˈdɑːk jə soʊp **~s** s
Docwra ˈdɒk rə ‖ ˈdɑːk-
Dod, Dodd dɒd ‖ dɑːd
dodd|er ˈdɒd |ə ‖ ˈdɑːd |ᵊr **~ered** əd ‖ ᵊrd **~ering/ly** ər ɪŋ /li **~ers** əz ‖ ᵊrz
doddery ˈdɒd ər i ‖ ˈdɑːd-
Doddington ˈdɒd ɪŋ tən ‖ ˈdɑːd-
doddle ˈdɒd ᵊl ‖ ˈdɑːd- **~s** z
dodeca- *comb. form*
with stress-neutral suffix ¦dəʊ ¦dek ə ‖ doʊ ¦dek ə — **dodecasyllable** ˌdəʊ ˌdek ə ˈsɪl əb ᵊl ‖ doʊ ˌdek-
with stress-imposing suffix ˌdəʊd ɪ ˈkæ+ -e-, -ə- ‖ ˌdoʊd- — **dodecagonal** ˌdəʊd ɪ ˈkæɡ ən ᵊl ◂ ˌ·e-, ˌ·ə- ‖ ˌdoʊd-
dodecagon dəʊ ˈdek əɡ ən -ə ɡɒn ‖ doʊ- **~s** z
dodecahedr|on ˌdəʊ ˌdek ə ˈhiːdr |ən -ˈhedr- ‖ doʊ ˌdek- **~a** ə **~ons** ənz
Dodecanese ˌdəʊd ɪk ə ˈniːz ˌ·ek-, §-ˈniːs ‖ doʊ ˈdek ə niːz -niːs, ·ˌ· ·ˈ·
dodecaphonic ˌdəʊd ek ə ˈfɒn ɪk ◂ ˌ·ɪk-, ˌ·ək- ‖ doʊ ˌdek ə ˈfɑːn ɪk ◂

dodge, Dodge dɒdʒ ‖ dɑːdʒ **dodged** dɒdʒd ‖ dɑːdʒd **dodges** ˈdɒdʒ ɪz -əz ‖ ˈdɑːdʒ- **dodging** ˈdɒdʒ ɪŋ ‖ ˈdɑːdʒ ɪŋ

dodgem, D~ *tdmk* ˈdɒdʒ əm ‖ ˈdɑːdʒ- **~s** z **ˈdodgem cars**

dodger ˈdɒdʒ ə ‖ ˈdɑːdʒ ᵊr **~s** z

Dodgson *(i)* ˈdɒdʒ sᵊn ‖ ˈdɑːdʒ-, *(ii)* ˈdɒd sᵊn ‖ ˈdɑːd- —*Lewis Carroll (Charles D~) reportedly was (ii)*

dodg|y ˈdɒdʒ |i ‖ ˈdɑːdʒ |i **~ier** i‿ə ‖ i‿ᵊr **~iest** i‿ɪst i‿əst

Dodi ˈdəʊd i ‖ ˈdoʊd i

dodo ˈdəʊd əʊ ‖ ˈdoʊd oʊ **~es, ~s** z

Dodoma *place in Tanzania* ˈdəʊd əm ə -ə mɑː ‖ ˈdoʊd-

Dodona *place in Greece* dəʊ ˈdəʊn ə ‖ də ˈdoʊn ə

Dodson ˈdɒd sᵊn ‖ ˈdɑːd-

doe, Doe dəʊ ‖ doʊ **does** dəʊz ‖ doʊz

-doer ˌduː‿ə ‖ ˈduː‿ᵊr — **wrong-doer** ˈrɒŋ ˌduː‿ə ‖ ˌrɔːŋ ˈduː ᵊr ˌrɑːŋ-

doer ˈduː‿ə ‖ ˈduː‿ᵊr **~s** z

does *from* **do**, *strong form* dʌz, *weak forms* dəz, dz

does *n, 'female animals'* dəʊz ‖ doʊz

doeskin ˈdəʊ skɪn ‖ ˈdoʊ- **~s** z

doesn't ˈdʌz ᵊnt —*also, when non-final,* ˈdʌz ᵊn

doeth ˈduː‿ɪθ ‿əθ

doff dɒf ‖ dɔːf dɑːf **doffed** dɒft ‖ dɔːft dɑːft **doffing** ˈdɒf ɪŋ ‖ ˈdɔːf ɪŋ ˈdɑːf- **doffs** dɒfs ‖ dɔːfs dɑːfs

dog dɒg ‖ dɔːg dɑːg **dogged** dɒgd ‖ dɔːgd dɑːgd **dogging** ˈdɒg ɪŋ ‖ ˈdɔːg ɪŋ ˈdɑːg- **dogs** dɒgz ‖ dɔːgz dɑːgz **ˈdog ˌbiscuit**; **ˈdog ˌcollar**; **ˈdog days**; **ˌdog in the ˈmanger**; **ˈdog ˌpaddle**; **ˈdog rose**; **ˌdog's ˈbreakfast**; **ˈdog tag**

Dogberry ˈdɒg ˌber i -bər‿i ‖ ˈdɔːg- ˈdɑːg-

dogcart ˈdɒg kɑːt ‖ ˈdɔːg kɑːrt ˈdɑːg- **~s** s

dogcatcher ˈdɒg ˌkætʃ ə §-ˌketʃ- ‖ ˈdɔːg ˌkætʃ ᵊr ˈdɑːg- **~s** z

doge dəʊdʒ dəʊʒ ‖ doʊdʒ **doges** ˈdəʊdʒ ɪz ˈdəʊʒ-, -əz ‖ ˈdoʊdʒ-

dog-eared ˈdɒg ɪəd ˌ·ˈ· ‖ ˈdɔːg ɪrd ˈdɑːg-

dog-eat-dog ˌdɒg iːt ˈdɒg ‖ ˌdɔːg iːt ˈdɔːg ˌdɑːg iːt ˈdɑːg

dog-end ˌdɒg ˈend ˈ· · ‖ ˌdɔːg- ˌdɑːg- **~s** z

dogfight ˈdɒg faɪt ‖ ˈdɔːg- ˈdɑːg- **~s** s

dogfish ˈdɒg fɪʃ ‖ ˈdɔːg- ˈdɑːg- **~es** ɪz əz

dogfood ˈdɒg fuːd ‖ ˈdɔːg- ˈdɑːg- **~s** z

dogged *adj* ˈdɒg ɪd -əd ‖ ˈdɔːg- ˈdɑːg- **~ly** li **~ness** nəs nɪs

dogged *past & pp of* **dog** dɒgd ‖ dɔːgd dɑːgd

dogger, D~ ˈdɒg ə ‖ ˈdɔːg ᵊr ˈdɑːg ᵊr **~s** z

doggerel ˈdɒg ᵊr‿əl ‖ ˈdɔːg- ˈdɑːg-

doggie ˈdɒg i ‖ ˈdɔːg i ˈdɑːg i **~s** z

doggish ˈdɒg ɪʃ ‖ ˈdɔːg- ˈdɑːg- **~ly** li

doggo ˈdɒg əʊ ‖ ˈdɔːg oʊ ˈdɑːg-

doggone ˈdɒg ɒn ‖ ˌdɑːg ˈgɑːn ◂ ˌdɔːg-, -ˈgɔːn **~d** d

dogg|y ˈdɒg |i ‖ ˈdɔːg |i ˈdɑːg- **~ier** i‿ə ‖ i‿ᵊr **~iest** i‿ɪst i‿əst **ˈdoggy bag**; **ˈdoggy ˌpaddle**

doggy-style ˈdɒg i staɪᵊl ‖ ˈdɔːg- ˈdɑːg-

dog|house ˈdɒg |haʊs ‖ ˈdɔːg- ˈdɑːg- **~houses** haʊz ɪz -əz

dogie ˈdəʊg i ‖ ˈdoʊg i **~s** z

dogleg ˈdɒg leg ‖ ˈdɔːg- ˈdɑːg- **~s** z

doglegged ˌdɒg ˈleg ɪd ◂ -əd; -ˈlegd ‖ ˌdɔːg- ˌdɑːg-

dogma ˈdɒg mə ‖ ˈdɔːg- ˈdɑːg- **~s** z

dogmatic dɒg ˈmæt ɪk ‖ dɔːg ˈmæţ ɪk dɑːg- **~ally** ᵊl‿i

dogmatism ˈdɒg mə ˌtɪz əm ‖ ˈdɔːg- ˈdɑːg-

dogmatist ˈdɒg mət ɪst §-əst ‖ ˈdɔːg məţ əst ˈdɑːg- **~s** s

dogmatiz|e, dogmatis|e ˈdɒg mə taɪz ‖ ˈdɔːg- ˈdɑːg- **~ed** d **~es** ɪz əz **~ing** ɪŋ

Dogon ˈdəʊg ɒn ‖ ˈdoʊg ɑːn

do-good|er ˌduː ˈgʊd |ə ‖ ˈduː gʊd |ᵊr **~ers** əz ‖ ᵊrz **~ing** ɪŋ

dogsbod|y ˈdɒgz ˌbɒd |i ‖ ˈdɔːgz ˌbɑːd |i ˈdɑːgz- **~ies** iz

dogsled ˈdɒg sled ‖ ˈdɔːg- ˈdɑːg- **~s** z

dog's-tail ˈdɒgz teɪᵊl ‖ ˈdɔːgz- ˈdɑːgz- **~s** z

dog-tired ˌdɒg ˈtaɪ‿əd ◂ ‖ ˌdɔːg ˈtaɪ‿ᵊrd ◂ ˌdɑːg-

dogtooth ˈdɒg tuːθ §-tʊθ ‖ ˈdɔːg- ˈdɑːg-

dogtrot ˈdɒg trɒt ‖ ˈdɔːg trɑːt ˈdɑːg-

dogwatch ˈdɒg wɒtʃ ‖ ˈdɔːg wɑːtʃ ˈdɑːg-, -wɔːtʃ **~es** ɪz əz

dogwood ˈdɒg wʊd ‖ ˈdɔːg- ˈdɑːg- **~s** z

doh *musical note* dəʊ ‖ doʊ *(= doe)* **dohs** dəʊz ‖ doʊz

doh, d'oh *interjection* dɜː dəʊ ‖ dʌ doʊ

Doha ˈdəʊ hɑː ˈdəʊ ə ‖ ˈdoʊ-

Doherty *(i)* ˈdɒ hət i ˈdɒx ət i ‖ ˈdɑː hᵊrţ i, *(ii)* ˈdəʊ hət i -ət i ‖ ˈdoʊ ᵊrţ i

Dohnányi dɒk ˈnɑːn ji dɒx-, -jiː ‖ ˈdoʊn ɑːn ji —*Hung* [ˈdoh naː ɲi]

Doig *(i)* dɔɪg, *(ii)* ˈdəʊ ɪg ‖ ˈdoʊ-

doil|y ˈdɔɪl |i **~ies** iz

Doi moi ˌdɔɪ ˈmɔɪ

doing ˈduː‿ɪŋ **~s** z

doit dɔɪt **doits** dɔɪts

do-it-yourself ˌduː‿ɪt jə ˈself ◂ →ɪtʃ ə-, -jɔːˈ-, -jʊəˈ-; §ˌ·ət-, §-ətʃ ə- ‖ ˌduː ətʃ ᵊr- **~er/s** ə/z ‖ ᵊr/z

dojo ˈdəʊ dʒəʊ ‖ ˈdoʊ dʒoʊ —*Jp* [ˈdoo dʑoo]

Doktorow ˈdɒkt ər əʊ ‖ ˈdɑːkt ər oʊ

Dolan ˈdəʊl ən ‖ ˈdoʊl-

Dolby ˈdɒl bi ‖ ˈdoʊl- ˈdɔːl-, ˈdɑːl-

dolce ˈdɒltʃ i -eɪ ‖ ˈdoʊltʃ eɪ —*It* [ˈdol tʃe]

ˌdolce ˌfar niˈente ˌfɑː ni ˈent i -eɪ ‖ ˌfɑːr- —*It* [far ˈnjɛn te]; **ˌdolce ˈvita** ˈviːt ə ‖ ˈviːţ ə —*It* [ˈviː ta]

Dolcis *tdmk* ˈdɒls ɪs ˈdɒltʃ-, §-əs ‖ ˈdɑːls-

doldrums ˈdɒldr əmz ˈdəʊldr- ‖ ˈdoʊldr- ˈdɑːldr-, ˈdɔːldr-

dole dəʊl →dɒʊl ‖ doʊl **doled** dəʊld →dɒʊld ‖ doʊld **doles** dəʊlz →dɒʊlz ‖ doʊlz **doling** ˈdəʊl ɪŋ →ˈdɒʊl- ‖ ˈdoʊl ɪŋ

doleful ˈdəʊl fᵊl →ˈdɒl-, -fʊl ‖ ˈdoʊl- **~ly** i **~ness** nəs nɪs
dolerite ˈdɒl ə raɪt ‖ ˈdɑːl-
Dolgellau, Dolgelley dɒl ˈgeθ li -laɪ ‖ dɑːl- —*Welsh* [dol ˈge ɬai, -ɬa, -ɬe]
doli... —*see* **dole**
dolichocephalic ˌdɒl ɪ kəʊ sɪ ˈfæl ɪk ◂ -səˈ--, -keˈ--, -kɪˈ-- ‖ ˌdɑːl ɪ koʊ-
dolichosaur|us ˌdɒl ɪ kəʊ ˈsɔːr |əs ‖ ˌdɑːl ɪ koʊ- **~i** aɪ
Dolin ˈdɒl ɪn §-ən ‖ ˈdoʊl-
dolina dɒ ˈliːn ə dəʊ- ‖ doʊ- **~s** z
doline dɒ ˈliːn dəʊ- ‖ doʊ- **~s** z
Dolittle ˈduː ˌlɪt ᵊl ‖ -ˌlɪṭ-
doll, Doll dɒl ‖ dɑːl dɔːl **dolled** dɒld ‖ dɑːld dɔːld **dolling** ˈdɒl ɪŋ ‖ ˈdɑːl ɪŋ ˈdɔːl- **dolls, doll's** dɒlz ‖ dɑːlz dɔːlz
ˈdoll's house
dollar, D~ ˈdɒl ə ‖ ˈdɑːl ᵊr **~s** z
ˌdollar ˈbill; **ˈdollar sign**
dollarization, dollarisation ˌdɒl ər aɪ ˈzeɪʃᵊn -ɪ- ‖ ˌdɑːl ər ə-
doll|house ˈdɒl |haʊs ‖ ˈdɑːl- ˈdɔːl- **~houses** haʊz ɪz -əz
dollie, D~ ˈdɒl i ‖ ˈdɑːl i ˈdɔːl i **~s** z
Dollond ˈdɒl ənd ‖ ˈdɑːl- ˈdɔːl-
dollop ˈdɒl əp ‖ ˈdɑːl- **~s** s
doll|y, Dolly ˈdɒl |i ‖ ˈdɑːl |i ˈdɔːl- **~ies, ~y's** iz
ˈdolly bird; **ˈdolly ˌmixture**
dolma ˈdɒlm ə -ɑː ‖ ˈdɑːlm- ˈdɔːlm- —*Turkish* [doɫ ˈma] **~s** z **dolmades** dɒl ˈmɑːð ez -ˈmɑːd iːz ‖ dɑːl- dɔːl- —*ModGk* [dol ˈma ðes]
dolman ˈdɒlm ən ‖ ˈdoʊlm- **~s** z
dolmen ˈdɒl men -mən ‖ ˈdoʊlm ən **~s** z
Dolmetsch ˈdɒl metʃ ‖ ˈdɑːl- ˈdɔːl-
Dolmio *tdmk* dɒl ˈmiː əʊ ‖ dɑːl ˈmiː oʊ
dolomite, D~ ˈdɒl ə maɪt ‖ ˈdoʊl- ˈdɑːl- **~s** s
dolor ˈdɒl ə ‖ ˈdoʊl ᵊr ˈdɑːl- **~s** z
Dolores də ˈlɔːr es dɒ-, -ɪs, -əs, -ez, -ɪz, -əz ‖ -əs -ˈloʊr- —*Sp* [do ˈlo ɾes]
doloroso ˌdɒl ə ˈrəʊs əʊ -ˈrəʊz- ‖ ˌdoʊl ə ˈroʊs oʊ —*It* [do lo ˈroː so]
dolorous ˈdɒl ər əs ‖ ˈdoʊl- ˈdɑːl- **~ly** li **~ness** nəs nɪs
dolour ˈdɒl ə ‖ ˈdoʊl ᵊr ˈdɑːl- **~s** z
dolphin, D~ ˈdɒlf ɪn §-ᵊn ‖ ˈdɑːlf- ˈdɔːlf- **~s** z
dolphinarium ˌdɒlf ɪ ˈneər i̯əm ˌ-ə- ‖ ˌdɑːlf ə ˈner- ˌdɔːlf- **~s** z
dolphin-safe ˌdɒlf ɪn ˈseɪf ◂ §-ᵊn- ‖ ˌdɑːlf- ˌdɔːlf-
Dolphus ˈdɒlf əs ‖ ˈdɑːlf-
dolt dəʊlt →dɒʊlt ‖ doʊlt **dolts** dəʊlts →dɒʊlts ‖ doʊlts
doltish ˈdəʊlt ɪʃ →ˈdɒʊlt- ‖ ˈdoʊlt- **~ly** li **~ness** nəs nɪs
dom, Dom dɒm ‖ dɑːm
-dom dəm — **martyrdom** ˈmɑːt ə dəm ‖ ˈmɑːrṭ ᵊr dəm
domain dəʊ ˈmeɪn ‖ doʊ- də- **~s** z
Dombey ˈdɒm bi ‖ ˈdɑːm-
dome dəʊm ‖ doʊm **domed** dəʊmd ‖ doʊmd **domes** dəʊmz ‖ doʊmz
Domecq dəʊ ˈmek ‖ doʊ-
Domesday ˈduːmz deɪ (= *Doomsday*)
ˈDomesday Book
domestic də ˈmest ɪk **~ally** ᵊl i̯ **~s** s
doˌmestic ˈscience; **doˌmestic ˈservice**
domesti|cate də ˈmest ɪ |keɪt **~cated** keɪt ɪd -əd ‖ keɪṭ əd **~cates** keɪts **~cating** keɪt ɪŋ ‖ keɪṭ ɪŋ
domestication də ˌmest ɪ ˈkeɪʃ ᵊn
domesticity ˌdəʊm e ˈstɪs ət i ˌdɒm-, ˌ-ə-, -ɪt i ‖ ˌdoʊm e ˈstɪs əṭ i ˌdɑːm-, ˌ-ə-; də ˌme-
Domestos *tdmk* də ˈmest ɒs dəʊ- ‖ -oʊs
domicil|e ˈdɒm ɪ saɪᵊl ˈdəʊm-, -ə-, əs ɪl, §-əs ᵊl ‖ ˈdɑːm- ˈdoʊm-, -əs ᵊl **~ed** d **~es** z **~ing** ɪŋ
domiciliary ˌdɒm ɪ ˈsɪl i̯ ər i ˌ-ə-, -ˈsɪl ər i ‖ ˌdɑːm ə ˈsɪl i er i ˌdoʊm-
dominance ˈdɒm ɪn ənᵗs -ən- ‖ ˈdɑːm-
dominant ˈdɒm ɪn ənt -ən- ‖ ˈdɑːm- ⚠-ət **~s** s
domi|nate ˈdɒm ɪ |neɪt -ə- ‖ ˈdɑːm- **~nated** neɪt ɪd -əd ‖ neɪṭ əd **~nates** neɪts **~nating** neɪt ɪŋ ‖ neɪṭ ɪŋ
domination ˌdɒm ɪ ˈneɪʃ ᵊn -ə- ‖ ˌdɑːm- **~s** z
dominatr|ix ˌdɒm ɪ ˈneɪtr| ɪks -ə- ‖ ˌdɑːm- **~ices** ɪ siːz ə- **~ixes** ɪks ɪz -əz
domineer ˌdɒm ɪ ˈnɪə -ə- ‖ ˌdɑːm ə ˈnɪᵊr **~ed** d
domineering/ly ˌdɒm ɪ ˈnɪər ɪŋ /li ˌ-ə- ‖ ˌdɑːm ə ˈnɪr ɪŋ /li **~s** z
Domingo də ˈmɪŋ gəʊ dəʊ-, dɒ- ‖ -goʊ —*Sp* [do ˈmiŋ go]
Dominic ˈdɒm ɪ nɪk -ə- ‖ ˈdɑːm-
Dominica *in the Leeward Islands* ˌdɒm ɪ ˈniːk ə -ə- ‖ ˌdɑːm- —*but often called* də ˈmɪn ɪk ə *by those not familiar with the name*
dominical də ˈmɪn ɪk ᵊl dɒ-, dəʊ-
Dominican *'of the D~ Republic'; religious* də ˈmɪn ɪk ən **~s** z
Doˌminican Reˈpublic
Dominican *'of Dominica'* ˌdɒm ɪ ˈniːk ən -ə- ‖ ˌdɑːm- —*see note at* Dominica **~s** z
Dominick ˈdɒm ɪ nɪk -ə- ‖ ˈdɑːm-
dominie ˈdɒm ɪn i -ən- ‖ ˈdɑːm- **~s** z
dominion də ˈmɪn jən -ˈmɪn i̯ən **~s** z
Dominique ˌdɒm ɪ ˈniːk -ə-, ˈ· · · ‖ ˌdɑːm- —*Fr* [dɔ mi nik]
domino, D~ ˈdɒm ɪ nəʊ -ə- ‖ ˈdɑːm ə noʊ **~es, ~s** z
ˈdomino efˌfect; **ˈdomino ˌtheory**
Dominus ˈdɒm ɪn ʊs -ən-, -əs ‖ ˈdoʊm ɪ nuːs ˈdɑːm-, -ə-
ˌdominus voˈbiscum vəʊ ˈbɪsk ʊm -əm ‖ voʊ-
Domitian də ˈmɪʃ ᵊn dəʊ-, dɒ-, -ˈmɪʃ i̯ən
Domremy, Domrémy dɒm ˈreɪm i ‖ ˌdoʊm reɪ ˈmiː —*Fr* [dɔ̃ ʁe mi]
don, Don dɒn ‖ dɑːn —*See also phrases with this word* **donned** dɒnd ‖ dɑːnd **donning** ˈdɒn ɪŋ ‖ ˈdɑːn ɪŋ **dons** dɒnz ‖ dɑːnz
Donaghadee ˌdɒn ə hə ˈdiː ˌ-ək- ‖ ˌdɑːn-
Donahue ˈdɒn ə hjuː ˈdʌn-, -huː ‖ ˈdɑːn-
Donal ˈdəʊn ᵊl ‖ ˈdoʊn ᵊl
Donald ˈdɒn ᵊld ‖ ˈdɑːn ᵊld
Donaldson ˈdɒn ᵊld sən ‖ ˈdɑːn-

Donat 'dəʊn æt ‖ 'doʊn-

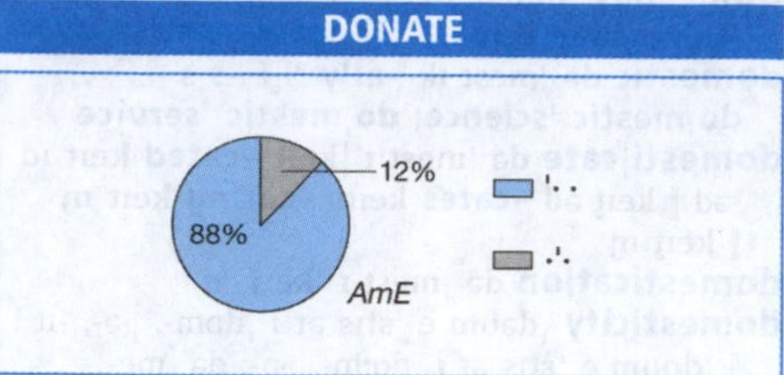

donate dəʊ 'neɪt ‖ 'doʊn eɪt doʊ 'neɪt — *Preference poll, AmE:* '· · 88%, ·'· 12%. **donated** dəʊ 'neɪt ɪd -əd ‖ 'doʊn eɪţ əd doʊ 'neɪţ- **donates** dəʊ 'neɪts ‖ 'doʊn eɪts doʊ 'neɪts **donating** dəʊ 'neɪt ɪŋ ‖ 'doʊn eɪţ ɪŋ doʊ 'neɪţ-

Donatello ˌdɒn ə 'tel əʊ ‖ ˌdɑːn ə 'tel oʊ ˌdoʊn- —*It* [do na 'tɛl lo] **~s, ~'s** z

donation dəʊ 'neɪʃ ᵊn ‖ doʊ- **~s** z

Donatist 'dəʊn ət ɪst 'dɒn-, §-əst ‖ 'doʊn əţ əst 'dɑːn- **~s** z

donative 'dəʊn ət ɪv 'dɒn- ‖ 'doʊn əţ ɪv 'dɑːn- **~s** z

donator dəʊ 'neɪt ə ‖ 'doʊn eɪţ ᵊr doʊ 'neɪţ- **~s** z

Don Carlos ˌdɒn 'kɑːl ɒs →ˌdɒŋ- ‖ ˌdɑːn 'kɑːrl oʊs -əs —*It, Sp* [doŋ 'kar los]

Doncaster 'dɒŋk əst ə 'dɒŋ ˌkɑːst ə, -ˌkæst- ‖ 'dɑːŋ ˌkæst ᵊr 'dɑːn-, -kəst-

done dʌn *(= dun)*

donee ˌ₍ₗ₎dəʊ 'niː ‖ doʊ- **~s** z

Donegal ˌdɒn ɪ 'gɔːl ◂ ˌdʌn-, -ə-, '· · · ‖ ˌdɑːn- -'gɑːl, '· · ·

Donegan 'dɒn ɪg ən -əg- ‖ 'dɑːn-

Donelly 'dɒn əl i ‖ 'dɑːn-

Doner, Döner 'dɒn ə ‖ 'doʊn ᵊr —*Turkish* [dø 'neɾ]

ˌdoner keˈbab

dong dɒŋ ‖ dɑːŋ dɔːŋ **donged** dɒŋd ‖ dɑːŋd dɔːŋd **donging** 'dɒŋ ɪŋ ‖ 'dɑːŋ ɪŋ 'dɔːŋ- **dongs** dɒŋz ‖ dɑːŋz dɔːŋz

donga 'dɒŋ gə ‖ 'dɑːŋ- 'dɔːŋ- **~s** z

Don Giovanni ˌdɒn dʒəʊ 'vɑːn i -'væn i ‖ ˌdɑːn dʒi ə 'vɑːn i —*It* [dɔn dʒo 'van ni]

dongle 'dɒŋ gᵊl ‖ 'dɑːŋ- **~s** z

Donington 'dɒn ɪŋ tən 'dʌn- ‖ 'dɑːn-

Donizetti ˌdɒn ɪ 'zet i -ə-, -ɪd- ‖ˌdɑːn ə 'zeţ i —*It* [do nid 'dzet ti]

donjon 'dɒndʒ ən 'dʌndʒ- ‖ 'dɑːndʒ- **~s** z

Don Juan *(i)* ˌdɒn 'dʒuː‿ən ‖ ˌdɑːn-, *(ii)* -'wɑːn -'hwɑːn —*Sp* [doŋ 'xwan] —*in English literature, including Byron, and usually when used metaphorically, BrE prefers (i); in imitated Spanish, and generally in AmE, (ii) is preferred.*

donkey 'dɒŋk i ‖ 'dɑːŋk i 'dʌŋk-, 'dɔːŋk- **~s** z **'donkey ˌengine**; **'donkey ˌjacket**; **'donkey's years**

donkeywork 'dɒŋk i wɜːk ‖ 'dɑːŋk i wɜːk 'dʌŋk-, 'dɔːŋk-

Donkin 'dɒŋk ɪn ‖ 'dɑːŋk-

Donleavy, Donlevy *(i)* dɒn 'liːv i ‖ dɑːn-, *(ii)* -'lev i

Donmar 'dɒn mɑː →'dɒm- ‖ 'dɑːn mɑːr

donn... —*see* **don**

Donna, donna 'dɒn ə ‖ 'dɑːn ə —*It* ['dɔn na]

Donne *(i)* dʌn, *(ii)* dɒn ‖ dɑːn —*The poet John Donne was probably (i).*

Donnegan 'dɒn ɪg ən -əg- ‖ 'dɑːn-

Donnell 'dɒn ᵊl ‖ dɑːn-

Donnelly 'dɒn əl i ‖ 'dɑːn-

Donner, d~ 'dɒn ə ‖ dɑːn ᵊr

Donnie 'dɒn i ‖ 'dɑːn i

donnish 'dɒn ɪʃ ‖ 'dɑːn- **~ly** li **~ness** nəs nɪs

Donny 'dɒn i ‖ 'dɑːn i

Donnybrook, d~ 'dɒn i brʊk §-bruːk ‖ 'dɑːn- **~s** s

Donoghue, Donohue 'dɒn ə hjuː 'dʌn-, -huː ‖ 'dɑːn-

donor 'dəʊn ə ‖ 'doʊn ᵊr—*but in contrast with* **donee** *also* -ɔː, ˌ₍ₗ₎dəʊ 'nɔː ‖ -ɔːr, ˌ₍ₗ₎doʊ 'nɔːr **~s** z

do-nothing 'duː ˌnʌθ ɪŋ **~s** z

Donovan *(i)* 'dɒn əv ən ‖ 'dɑːn-, *(ii)* 'dʌn-

Don Pasquale ˌdɒn pæ 'skwɑːl eɪ →ˌdɒm-, -pə-, -i ‖ ˌdɑːn- —*It* [dɔm pas 'kwaː le]

Don Quixote ˌdɒn 'kwɪks ət →ˌdɒŋ-, ˌ·kɪ 'həʊt i ‖ ˌdɑːn- ˌ·kiː 'hoʊt eɪ —*Sp* [doŋ ki 'xo te]

don't dəʊnt ‖ doʊnt —*also, non-finally, esp. before a consonant sound,* dəʊn ‖ doʊn. *This word has no weak form except occasionally* də *in* don't mind, don't know *(see* dunno*).* **don'ts** dəʊnts ‖ doʊnts **ˌdon't 'knows**

do|nut 'dəʊ |nʌt ‖ 'doʊ- **~nuts** nʌts **~nutted** nʌt ɪd -əd ‖ nʌţ əd **~nutting** nʌt ɪŋ ‖ nʌţ ɪŋ

doobie 'duːb i **~s** z

doodad 'duː dæd **~s** z

doodah 'duː dɑː **~s** z

doodl|e 'duːd ᵊl **~ed** d **~es** z **~ing** ˌɪŋ

doodlebug 'duːd ᵊl bʌg **~s** z

doo-doo 'duː duː

doofus 'duːf əs **~es** ɪz əz

doohickey 'duː ˌhɪk i **~s** z

doolally ˌ₍ₗ₎duː 'læl i

Doolan 'duːl ən

Dooley 'duːl i

Doolittle 'duː ˌlɪt ᵊl ‖ -ˌlɪţ ᵊl

doom duːm **doomed** duːmd **dooming** 'duːm ɪŋ **dooms** duːmz

doom-laden 'duːm ˌleɪd ᵊn

doomsayer 'duːm ˌseɪ ə ‖ -ᵊr **~s** z

Doomsday, d~ 'duːmz deɪ

doomster 'duːm stə ‖ -stᵊr **~s** z

doomwatch 'duːm wɒtʃ ‖ -wɑːtʃ -wɔːtʃ **~er/s** ə/z ‖ ᵊr/z **~es** ɪz əz

Doon, Doone duːn

Doonesbury 'duːnz bər‿i ‖ -ˌber i

door dɔː ‖ dɔːr doʊr **doors** dɔːz ‖ dɔːrz doʊrz

doorbell 'dɔː bel ‖ 'dɔːr- 'doʊr- **~s** z

doorcas|e 'dɔː keɪs ‖ 'dɔːr- 'doʊr- **~es** ɪz əz

do-or-die ˌduː ɔː 'daɪ ◂ ‖ -ᵊr- -ɔːr-

doorframe 'dɔː freɪm ‖ 'dɔːr- 'doʊr- **~s** z

D

Double consonant letters

1 Double **consonant** letters in English spelling normally correspond to a single sound in pronunciation. So **happy** is pronounced ˈhæp i (not ˈhæp pi), **rabbit** rhymes perfectly with **habit**, **Ellen** rhymes perfectly with **Helen**.

For double **vowel** letters, see **ee** (under **e**), **oo** (under **o**).

2 An exception arises in a few words with **cc** before **i** or **e**, for example **succeed** sək ˈsiːd. See also the article on **s, ss**.

3 The other important exception is where the two letters in question belong to two different parts of a compound word, or one to a stem and one to an affix. Then the two letters usually correspond to two phonemes (see DOUBLE CONSONANT SOUNDS). Examples: **nighttime** ˈnaɪt taɪm, **unnamed** ˌʌn ˈneɪmd, **meanness** ˈmiːn nəs.

Adverbs in **-ly**, however, usually drop one l sound when attached to a stem ending in l: **fully** ˈfʊl i.

doorjamb ˈdɔː dʒæm ‖ ˈdɔːr- ˈdoʊr- **~s** z
doorkeeper ˈdɔː ˌkiːp ə ‖ ˈdɔːr ˌkiːp ᵊr ˈdoʊr- **~s** z
doorknob ˈdɔː nɒb ‖ ˈdɔːr nɑːb ˈdoʊr- **~s** z
doorknocker ˈdɔː ˌnɒk ə ‖ ˈdɔːr ˌnɑːk ᵊr ˈdoʊr- **~s** z
door|man ˈdɔː |mən -mæn ‖ ˈdɔːr- ˈdoʊr- **~men** mən men
doormat ˈdɔː mæt ‖ ˈdɔːr- ˈdoʊr- **~s** s
doornail ˈdɔː neɪᵊl ‖ ˈdɔːr- ˈdoʊr- **~s** z
doorplate ˈdɔː pleɪt ‖ ˈdɔːr- ˈdoʊr- **~s** s
doorpost ˈdɔː pəʊst ‖ ˈdɔːr poʊst ˈdoʊr- **~s** s
doorscraper ˈdɔː ˌskreɪp ə ‖ ˈdɔːr ˌskreɪp ᵊr ˈdoʊr- **~s** z
doorstep ˈdɔː step ‖ ˈdɔːr- ˈdoʊr- **~ped** t **~ping** ɪŋ **~s** s
doorstop ˈdɔː stɒp ‖ ˈdɔːr stɑːp ˈdoʊr- **~per/s** ə/z ‖ ᵊr/z **~s** z
door-to-door ˌdɔː tə ˈdɔː ◂ ‖ ˌdɔːr tə ˈdɔːr ◂ ˌdoʊr tə ˈdoʊr
doorway ˈdɔː weɪ ‖ ˈdɔːr- ˈdoʊr- **~s** z
dooryard ˈdɔː jɑːd ‖ ˈdɔːr jɑːrd ˈdoʊr- **~s** z
dooz|ie, dooz|y ˈduːz i **~ies** iz
dopa ˈdəʊp ə ‖ ˈdoʊp ə -ɑː
dopamine ˈdəʊp ə miːn -mɪn ‖ ˈdoʊp-
dopant ˈdəʊp ənt ‖ ˈdoʊp- **~s** s
dope dəʊp ‖ doʊp **doped** dəʊpt ‖ doʊpt **dopes** dəʊps ‖ doʊps **doping** ˈdəʊp ɪŋ ‖ ˈdoʊp ɪŋ
ˈdope fiend; **ˈdope ˌpeddler**; **ˈdope sheet**
dopehead ˈdəʊp hed ‖ ˈdoʊp- **~s** z
dop|ey ˈdəʊp |i ‖ ˈdoʊp |i **~ier** i‿ə ‖ i‿ᵊr **~iest** i‿ɪst i‿əst
doppelganger, doppelgänger ˈdɒp ᵊl ˌgæŋ ə -ˌgeŋ- ‖ ˈdɑːp ᵊl ˌgæŋ ᵊr —*Ger* [ˈdɔp ᵊl ˌgɛŋ ɐ] **~s** z
Doppler ˈdɒp lə ‖ ˈdɑːp lᵊr
ˈDoppler efˌfect
dopy —*see* **dopey**
Dora ˈdɔːr ə ‖ ˈdoʊr-
Dorabella ˌdɔːr ə ˈbel ə ‖ ˌdoʊr-
dorado də ˈrɑːd əʊ dɒ- ‖ -oʊ **~s** z
Doran ˈdɔːr ən ‖ ˈdoʊr-
Dorcas ˈdɔːk əs ‖ ˈdɔːrk-
Dorchester ˈdɔːtʃ ɪst ə §-est- ‖ ˈdɔːr tʃest ᵊr ˈdɔːrtʃ əst ᵊr
Dordogne ⁽ˌ⁾dɔː ˈdɔɪn ‖ dɔːr ˈdoʊn —*Fr* [dɔʁ dɔnj]
Dore dɔː ‖ dɔːr doʊr
Doré ˈdɔːr eɪ ‖ dɔː ˈreɪ —*Fr* [dɔ ʁe]
Doreen ˈdɔːr iːn dɔː ˈriːn, dɒ-, də- ‖ ˌdɔː ˈriːn
Doria ˈdɔːr i‿ə ‖ ˈdoʊr-
Dorian ˈdɔːr i‿ən ‖ ˈdoʊr-
Doric ˈdɒr ɪk ‖ ˈdɔːr- ˈdɑːr-
dorie... —*see* **dory**
Dorinda də ˈrɪnd ə dɔː-, dɒ-
Doris *in Greece* ˈdɔːr ɪs ˈdɒr-, -əs ‖ ˈdɑːr-, ˈdoʊr-
Doris *personal name* ˈdɒr ɪs -əs ‖ ˈdɔːr- ˈdɑːr-, ˈdoʊr-
Doritos *tdmk* də ˈriːt əʊz ‖ -ˈriːt̬ oʊz
dork dɔːk ‖ dɔːrk **dorks** dɔːks ‖ dɔːrks
Dorking ˈdɔːk ɪŋ ‖ ˈdɔːrk-
dorky ˈdɔːk i ‖ ˈdɔːrk i
Dorling ˈdɔː lɪŋ ‖ ˈdɔːr-
dorm dɔːm ‖ dɔːrm **dorms** dɔːmz ‖ dɔːrmz
Dorman ˈdɔːm ən ‖ ˈdɔːrm-
dormanc|y ˈdɔːm ənᵗs |i ‖ ˈdɔːrm- **~ies** iz
dormant ˈdɔːm ənt ‖ ˈdɔːrm-
dormer, D~ ˈdɔːm ə ‖ ˈdɔːrm ᵊr **~s** z
dormie ˈdɔːm i ‖ ˈdɔːrm i
dormition dɔː ˈmɪʃ ᵊn ‖ dɔːr-

dormitor|y 'dɔːm ətr |i -ɪtr-; 'ət̬ ər |i, 'ɪt̬ ‖ 'dɔːrm ə tɔːr |i **~ies** iz
'**dormitory ˌsuburb**
Dormobile *tdmk* 'dɔːm əʊ biːᵊl ‖ 'dɔːrm ə- **~s** z
dor|mouse 'dɔː |maʊs ‖ 'dɔːr- **~mice** maɪs
dormy 'dɔːm i ‖ 'dɔːrm i
Dornoch 'dɔːn ɒk -ɒx, -ək, -əx ‖ 'dɔːrn ɑːk —*locally* -əx
Dorothea ˌdɒr ə 'θɪə -'θiː ə ‖ ˌdɔːr ə 'θiː ə ˌdɑːr-
Dorothy 'dɒr əθ i ‖ 'dɔːr- 'dɑːr- —*formerly* -ət-
Dorow, Dorrow 'dɒr əʊ ‖ 'dɔːr oʊ 'dɑːr-
dorp dɔːp ‖ dɔːrp **dorps** dɔːps ‖ dɔːrps
Dorr dɔː ‖ dɔːr
Dorrington 'dɒr ɪŋ tən ‖ 'dɔːr- 'dɑːr-
Dorrit 'dɒr ɪt §-ət ‖ 'dɔːr- 'dɑːr-
Dors dɔːz ‖ dɔːrz
dorsal 'dɔːs ᵊl ‖ 'dɔːrs- **~ly** i
Dorset 'dɔːs ɪt -ət ‖ 'dɔːrs-
Dorsey 'dɔːs i ‖ 'dɔːrs i
dorsum 'dɔːs əm ‖ 'dɔːrs-
Dortmund 'dɔːt mənd -mʊnd ‖ 'dɔːrt- —*Ger* ['dɔʁt mʊnt]
dor|y, Dory 'dɔːr |i ‖ 'doʊr- **~ies** iz
do's duːz
DOS dɒs ‖ dɑːs dɔːs
dosag|e 'dəʊs ɪdʒ §'dəʊz- ‖ 'doʊs- **~es** ɪz əz
dose dəʊs §dəʊz ‖ doʊs **dosed** dəʊst §dəʊzd ‖ doʊst **doses** 'dəʊs ɪz §'dəʊz-, -əz ‖ 'doʊs əz **dosing** 'dəʊs ɪŋ §'dəʊz- ‖ 'doʊs ɪŋ
dosh dɒʃ ‖ dɑːʃ
do-si-do ˌdəʊs i 'dəʊ ˌdəʊ saɪ 'dəʊ ‖ ˌdoʊ siː 'doʊ **~s** z
dosimeter dəʊ 'sɪm ɪt ə -ət- ‖ doʊ 'sɪm ət̬ ᵊr **~s** z
dosimetry dəʊ 'sɪm ətr i -ɪtr- ‖ doʊ-
Dos Passos ₍ˌ₎dɒs 'pæs ɒs ‖ doʊs 'pæs oʊs dəs-, -əs
doss dɒs ‖ dɑːs **dossed** dɒst ‖ dɑːst **dosses** 'dɒs ɪz -əz ‖ 'dɑːs əz **dossing** 'dɒs ɪŋ ‖ 'dɑːs ɪŋ
dosser 'dɒs ə ‖ 'dɑːs ᵊr **~s** z
doss|house 'dɒs |haʊs ‖ 'dɑːs- **-houses** haʊz ɪz -əz
dossier 'dɒs i eɪ -i‿ə ‖ 'dɔːs i eɪ 'dɑːs-, -i‿ᵊr —*Fr* [do sje] **~s** z
dost *from* **do** dʌst, *weak form* dəst
Dostoevski, Dostoevsky, Dostoyevski, Dostoyevsky ˌdɒst ɔɪ 'ef ski ‖ ˌdɑːst ə 'jef- ˌdʌst- —*Russ* [də stʌ 'jef skʲɪj]
dot, Dot dɒt ‖ dɑːt **dots** dɒts ‖ dɑːts **dotted** 'dɒt ɪd -əd ‖ 'dɑːt̬ əd **dotting** 'dɒt ɪŋ ‖ 'dɑːt̬ ɪŋ
ˌ**dotted 'line**
dotage 'dəʊt ɪdʒ ‖ 'doʊt̬-
dotard 'dəʊt əd -ɑːd ‖ 'doʊt̬ ᵊrd **~s** z
dot-com ˌdɒt 'kɒm ‖ ˌdɑːt 'kɑːm **~s** z
dote dəʊt ‖ doʊt **doted** 'dəʊt ɪd -əd ‖ 'doʊt̬ əd **dotes** dəʊts ‖ doʊts **doting** 'dəʊt ɪŋ ‖ 'doʊt̬ ɪŋ
doth *from* **do** dʌθ, *weak form* dəθ
Dotheboys 'duː ðə ˌbɔɪz
doting 'dəʊt ɪŋ ‖ 'doʊt̬ ɪŋ **~ly** li
dot-matrix ˌdɒt 'meɪtr ɪks '·ˌ·· ‖ ˌdɑːt-
Dotrice də 'triːs dɒ-
dott... —*see* **dot**
dotterel 'dɒtr əl ‖ 'dɑːtr- **~s** z
Dottie 'dɒt i ‖ 'dɑːt̬ i
dottle 'dɒt ᵊl ‖ 'dɑːt̬ ᵊl
dott|y 'dɒt |i ‖ 'dɑːt̬ |i **~ier** i‿ə ‖ i‿ᵊr **~iest** i‿ɪs i‿əst **~ily** ɪ li əl i **~iness** i nəs i nɪs
Douai 'daʊ i 'duː‿, -eɪ ‖ duː 'eɪ —*but the place in France is* 'duː eɪ ‖ ·'· —*Fr* [dwe, du e]
Douala du 'ɑːl ə —*Fr* [dwa la]
doubl|e 'dʌb ᵊl **~ed** d **~es** z **~ing** ‿ɪŋ **~y** ‿i
ˌ**double 'agent**, ˌ**double 'bar**; ˌ**double 'bass**; ˌ**double 'bed**; ˌ**double 'bind**; ˌ**double 'bluff** —*but* ˌ**bluff and 'double bluff**; ˌ**double 'chin**; ˌ**double 'cream**; ˌ**double 'date**; ˌ**double 'fault**; ˌ**double 'feature**; ˌ**double 'figures**; ˌ**Double 'Gloucester**; '**doubles match**; ˌ**double 'take**, '· · ·; ˌ**double 'time**
double-barreled, double-barrelled ˌdʌb ᵊl 'bær əld ◂ ‖ -'ber-
double-bedded ˌdʌb ᵊl 'bed ɪd ◂ -əd
double-blind ˌdʌb ᵊl 'blaɪnd ◂
double-book ˌdʌb ᵊl 'bʊk §-'buːk **~ed** t **~ing** ɪŋ **~s** s
double-breasted ˌdʌb ᵊl 'brest ɪd ◂ -əd
double-check ˌdʌb ᵊl 'tʃek '· · · **~ed** t **~ing** ɪŋ **~s** s
double-click ˌdʌb ᵊl 'klɪk **~ed** t **~ing** ɪŋ **~s** s
double-clutch 'dʌb ᵊl klʌtʃ **~ed** t **~es** ɪz əz **~ing** ɪŋ
double-cross ˌdʌb ᵊl 'krɒs -'krɔːs ‖ -'krɔːs -'krɑːs **~ed** t **~er/s** ə/z ‖ ᵊr/z **~es** ɪz əz **~ing** ɪŋ
Doubleday 'dʌb ᵊl deɪ
double-deal|er ˌdʌb ᵊl 'diːᵊl |ə ‖ -|ᵊr **~ers** əz ‖ ᵊrz **~ing** ɪŋ
double-decker ˌdʌb ᵊl 'dek ə ◂ ‖ -ᵊr **~s** z
double-declutch ˌdʌb ᵊl diː 'klʌtʃ -dɪ'·, -də'· **~ed** t **~es** ɪz əz **~ing** ɪŋ
double-digit ˌdʌb ᵊl 'dɪdʒ ɪt ◂ §-ət
double-dip ˌdʌb ᵊl 'dɪp **~ped** t **~ping** ɪŋ **~s** s
double-dotted ˌdʌb ᵊl 'dɒt ɪd ◂ -əd ‖ -'dɑːt̬ əd ◂
double-dutch ˌdʌb ᵊl 'dʌtʃ
double-dyed ˌdʌb ᵊl 'daɪd ◂
double-edged ˌdʌb ᵊl 'edʒd ◂
ˌ**double-edged 'compliment**
double entendre ˌduːb ᵊl‿ɒn 'tɒnd‿rə ˌdʌb- ‖ ɑːn 'tɑːnd‿rə —*as if Fr* [du blɑ̃ tɑ̃ːdʁ]
double-entry ˌdʌb ᵊl 'entr i ◂
double-figure ˌdʌb ᵊl 'fɪg ə ◂ ‖ -jᵊr
double-glaz|e ˌdʌb ᵊl 'gleɪz **~ed** d **~es** ɪz əz **~ing** ɪŋ
double-header ˌdʌb ᵊl 'hed ə ‖ -ᵊr
double-jointed ˌdʌb ᵊl 'dʒɔɪnt ɪd ◂ -əd ‖ -'dʒɔɪnt̬ əd ◂
double-park ˌdʌb ᵊl 'pɑːk ‖ -'pɑːrk **~ed** t **~ing** ɪŋ **~s** s
double-quick ˌdʌb ᵊl 'kwɪk ◂
ˌ**double-quick 'time**

Double consonant sounds

1 Double consonant sounds ('geminates') are found in English only across grammatical boundaries: where two words occur next to one another in connected speech, or in the two parts of a compound word, or a stem and an affix. They always straddle a syllable boundary, too. Examples are **a nice sight** ə ˌnaɪs ˈsaɪt, **midday** ˌmɪd ˈdeɪ, **soulless** ˈsəʊl ləs ‖ ˈsoʊl ləs.

2 Although cases like these consist of two identical phonemes in succession, they are not usually pronounced as two distinct complete sounds. The details depend on their manner of ARTICULATION.

- **Fricatives, nasals, liquids**: a geminate is pronounced like a single sound, except that it lasts longer. In **this set** ˌðɪs ˈset the two s's come together to make a long sː between the two vowels, straddling the syllable boundary. In **ten names** ˌten ˈneɪmz we get a long nː.
- **Plosives**: a geminate is pronounced like a single sound, with just one sequence of approach—hold—release (see PLOSIVES); but in a geminate the hold is longer. In **big game** ˌbɪg ˈgeɪm there is a single phonetic gː between the two vowels, straddling the syllable boundary. Exceptionally, because of the possibility of a GLOTTAL STOP, a geminated t may consist phonetically of ʔt: **that time** ˌðæt ˈtaɪm; but a single long alveolar tː is also possible.
- **Affricates** are the only case where two successive complete consonant sounds are pronounced independently, one after the other. In **rich choice** ˌrɪtʃ ˈtʃɔɪs the fricative part of the first tʃ can be separately heard before the beginning of the second tʃ. In **orange juice** there are two separate dʒs.

doubler ˈdʌb əl‿ə ‖ ‿ər **~s** z
double-sided ˌdʌb əl ˈsaɪd ɪd ◂ -əd
double-spac|e ˌdʌb əl ˈspeɪs **~ed** t **~es** ɪz əz **~ing** ɪŋ
doublespeak ˈdʌb əl spiːk
double-stop ˌdʌb əl ˈstɒp ‖ -ˈstɑːp **~ped** t **~ping** ɪŋ **~s** s
doublet ˈdʌb lət -lɪt **~s** s
double-talk ˈdʌb əl tɔːk ‖ -tɑːk **~ed** t **~er/s** ə/z ‖ ər/z **~ing** ɪŋ **~s** s
doublethink ˈdʌb əl θɪŋk
doubleton ˈdʌb əl tən **~s** z
double-tongu|e ˌdʌb əl ˈtʌŋ §-ˈtɒŋ **~ing** ɪŋ
double-wide ˈdʌb əl waɪd **~s** z
doubling ˈdʌb əl‿ɪŋ **~s** z
doubloon dʌ ˈbluːn **~s** z
doubly ˈdʌb li
doubt daʊt **doubted** ˈdaʊt ɪd -əd ‖ ˈdaʊţ əd **doubting** ˈdaʊt ɪŋ ‖ ˈdaʊţ ɪŋ **doubts** daʊts **ˌdoubting ˈThomas**
doubter ˈdaʊt ə ‖ ˈdaʊţ ər **~s** z
doubtful ˈdaʊt fəl -fʊl **~ly** ‿i
doubtless ˈdaʊt ləs -lɪs **~ly** li
douceur duː ˈsɜː ‖ -ˈsɝː —*Fr* [du sœːʁ] **~s** z
douche duːʃ **douched** duːʃt **douches** ˈduːʃ ɪz -əz **douching** ˈduːʃ ɪŋ
Doug dʌg
Dougal, Dougall ˈduːg əl
Dougan ˈduːg ən
dough dəʊ ‖ doʊ (*= doe*) **doughs** dəʊz ‖ doʊz
doughboy ˈdəʊ bɔɪ ‖ ˈdoʊ- **~s** z
Dougherty *(i)* ˈdɒx ət i ˈdɒk- ‖ ˈdɑːk ərţ i, *(ii)* ˈdəʊ- ‖ ˈdoʊ- ˈdɔːrţ i, *(iii)* ˈdaʊ-
dough|nut ˈdəʊ |nʌt ‖ ˈdoʊ- **~nuts** nʌts **~nutted** nʌt ɪd -əd ‖ nʌţ əd **~nutting** nʌt ɪŋ ‖ nʌţ ɪŋ
dought|y, D~ ˈdaʊt |i ‖ ˈdaʊţ |i **~ier** i‿ə ‖ i‿ər **~iest** i‿ɪst i‿əst **~ily** ɪ li əl i **~iness** i nəs i nɪs
dough|y ˈdəʊ |i ‖ ˈdoʊ |i **~ier** i‿ə ‖ i‿ər **~iest** i‿ɪst i‿əst **~iness** i nəs i nɪs
Dougie ˈdʌg i
Douglas, Douglass ˈdʌg ləs
Douglas-Home ˌdʌg ləs ˈhjuːm
Doukhobor ˈduːk ə bɔː ‖ -bɔːr **~s** z
doula ˈduːlə **~s** z
Doulton ˈdəʊlt ən →ˈdɒʊlt- ‖ ˈdoʊlt ən
Doune duːn
Dounreay ˈduːn reɪ ˌ·ˈ·
dour dʊə ˈdaʊ‿ə ‖ dʊər daʊ‿ər

D

dourine ˈduər iːn ‖ du ˈriːn
dour|ly ˈduə |li ˈdau‿ə |li ‖ ˈduᵊr- ˈdau‿ᵊr- **~ness** nəs nɪs
Douro ˈduər əu ‖ ˈdur ou —*Port* [ˈdo ɾu]
douse daus **doused** daust **douses** ˈdaus ɪz -əz **dousing** ˈdaus ɪŋ
Douwe Egberts *tdmk* ˌdau ˈeg bəts -bɜːts ‖ -bᵊrts
dove *n* dʌv **doves** dʌvz
dove *v from* **dive** dəuv ‖ douv
dovecot ˈdʌv kɒt ‖ -kɑːt **~s** s
dovecote ˈdʌv kəut -kɒt ‖ -kout **~s** s
Dovedale ˈdʌv deɪᵊl
dovekey, dovekie ˈdʌv ki **~s** z
Dover ˈdəuv ə ‖ ˈdouv ᵊr **ˌDover ˈsole**
Dovercourt ˈdəuv ə kɔːt ‖ ˈdouv ᵊr kɔːrt -kourt
Doveridge ˈdʌv ər‿ɪdʒ
dovetail *n, v* ˈdʌv teɪᵊl **~ed** d **~ing** ɪŋ **~s** z
Dovey ˈdʌv i —*Welsh* Dyfi [ˈdə vi]
dovish ˈdʌv ɪʃ
Dow dau
dowager ˈdau‿ədʒ ə ɪdʒ- ‖ -ᵊr **~s** z
Dowd daud
Dowdeswell ˈdaudz wəl -wel
Dowding ˈdaud ɪŋ
dowd|y ˈdaud |i **~ier** i‿ə ‖ i‿ᵊr **~ies** iz **~iest** i‿ɪst i‿əst **~ily** ɪ li əl i **~iness** i nəs i nɪs
dowel ˈdau‿əl daul ‖ ˈdau‿əl **doweled, dowelled** ˈdau‿əld dauld ‖ ˈdau‿əld **doweling, dowelling** ˈdau‿əl ɪŋ ˈdaul ɪŋ ‖ ˈdau‿əl ɪŋ **dowels** ˈdauəlz daulz ‖ ˈdau‿əlz
Dowell ˈdau‿əl daul ‖ ˈdau‿əl
dower, Dower ˈdau‿ə ‖ ˈdau‿ᵊr **~s** z
dowitcher ˈdau‿ɪtʃ ə ‖ -ᵊr **~s** z
Dow-Jones ˌdau ˈdʒəunz ◂ ‖ -ˈdʒounz ◂ **ˌDow-Jones ˈaverage**
Dowlais ˈdau laɪs -ləs
Dowland ˈdau lənd
down, Down daun **downed** daund **downing** ˈdaun ɪŋ **downs, Down's** daunz **ˌdown ˈpayment**; **ˈDown's ˌsyndrome**
down- ¦daun
down-and-out ˌdaun ən ˈaut ◂ -ənd- **~s** s
down-and-outer ˌdaun ən ˈaut ə ‖ -ˈauṭ ᵊr **~s** z
down-at-heel ˌdaun ət ˈhiːᵊl ◂
downbeat ˈdaun biːt →ˈdaum- **~s** s
downcast ˈdaun kɑːst →ˈdauŋ-, §-kæst ‖ -kæst
downdraft, downdraught ˈdaun drɑːft §-dræft ‖ -dræft **~s** s
downdrift ˈdaun drɪft
Downe daun
downer ˈdaun ə ‖ -ᵊr **~s** z
Downes daunz
Downey ˈdaun i
downfall ˈdaun fɔːl ‖ -fɑːl **~s** z
downgrad|e *v* ˌdaun ˈgreɪd →ˌdauŋ-; ˈ· · **~ed** ɪd əd **~es** z **~ing** ɪŋ
downgrade *n* ˈdaun greɪd →ˈdauŋ- **~s** z
Downham ˈdaun əm
downhearted ˌdaun ˈhɑːt ɪd ◂ -əd ‖ -ˈhɑːrṭ əd ◂ **~ly** li **~ness** nəs nɪs
downhill ˌdaun ˈhɪl ◂ **~er/s** ə/z ‖ -ᵊr/z
down-home ˌdaun ˈhəum ◂ ‖ -ˈhoum ◂
downi... —*see* **downy**
Downie ˈdaun i
Downing ˈdaun ɪŋ **ˈDowning Street**
downland, D~ ˈdaun lænd -lənd **~s** z
downlighter ˈdaun ˌlaɪt ə ‖ -ˌlaɪṭ ᵊr **~s** z
download ˌdaun ˈləud ˈ· · ‖ ˈdaun loud **~ed** ɪd əd **~ing** ɪŋ **~s** z
downloadable ˌdaun ˈləud əb ᵊl ◂ ˈ· · · · ‖ ˈdaun loud əb ᵊl
downmarket ˌdaun ˈmɑːk ɪt ◂ →ˌdaum-, §-ət ‖ -ˈmɑːrk-
Downpatrick ₍ˌ₎daun ˈpætr ɪk →₍ˌ₎daum-
downpipe ˈdaun paɪp →ˈdaum- **~s** s
downplay ˌdaun ˈpleɪ **~ed** d **~ing** ɪŋ **~s** z
downpour ˈdaun pɔː →ˈdaum- ‖ -pɔːr -pour **~s** z
downrange ˌdaun ˈreɪndʒ ◂
downright ˈdaun raɪt
downriver ˌdaun ˈrɪv ə ◂ ‖ -ᵊr ◂
Downs daunz
downscale ˌdaun ˈskeɪᵊl ◂
downshift ˈdaun ʃɪft ˌ·ˈ· **~ed** ɪd əd **~ing** ɪŋ **~s** s
Downside, d~ ˈdaun saɪd
downsiz|e ˈdaun saɪz ˌ·ˈ· **~ed** d **~es** ɪz əz **~ing** ɪŋ
downspout ˈdaun spaut **~s** s
downstage ˌdaun ˈsteɪdʒ ◂
downstairs ˌdaun ˈsteəz ◂ ‖ -ˈsteᵊrz ◂ -ˈstæᵊrz ◂
downstate *n* ˈdaun steɪt
downstate *adj, adv* ˌdaun ˈsteɪt ◂
downstream ˌdaun ˈstriːm ◂
downstroke ˈdaun strəuk ‖ -strouk **~s** s
downswing ˈdaun swɪŋ **~s** z
downtime ˈdaun taɪm
down-to-earth ˌdaun tu ˈɜːθ ◂ ‖ -ˈɜːθ ◂
downtown ˌdaun ˈtaun ◂
downtrend ˈdaun trend **~s** z
downtrodden ˈdaun ˌtrɒd ᵊn ˌ·ˈ· · ‖ -ˌtrɑːd-
downturn ˈdaun tɜːn ‖ -tɜːn **~s** z
downward ˈdaun wəd ‖ -wᵊrd **~ly** li **~ly** li **~s** z
downwash ˈdaun wɒʃ ‖ -wɔːʃ -wɑːʃ
downwind ˌdaun ˈwɪnd ◂
down|y ˈdaun |i **~ier** i‿ə ‖ i‿ᵊr **~iest** i‿ɪst i‿əst
dowr|y ˈdau‿ᵊr |i **~ies** iz
dowse *'drench', 'extinguish'* daus **dowsed** daust **dowses** ˈdaus ɪz -əz **dowsing** ˈdaus ɪŋ
dowse *'seek underground water or minerals'* dauz **dowsed** dauzd **dowses** ˈdauz ɪz əz **dowsing** ˈdauz ɪŋ
Dowse *name* daus
dowser ˈdauz ə ‖ -ᵊr **~s** z
Dowsing ˈdauz ɪŋ
dowsing rod ˈdauz ɪŋ rɒd ‖ -rɑːd
Dowson ˈdaus ᵊn
doxastic dɒk ˈsæst ɪk ‖ dɑːk-

oxolog|y dɒk 'sɒl ədʒ |i ‖ dɑːk 'sɑːl- ~ies iz
ox|y 'dɒks |i ‖ 'dɑːks |i ~ies iz
oyen 'dɔɪ ən -en —*Fr* [dwa jæ̃] ~s z
oyenne ₍ı₎dɔɪ 'en —*Fr* [dwa jɛn] ~s z
oyle dɔɪᵊl
oyley, D'Oyley, doyly, D'Oyly 'dɔɪl i ~s z
oze dəʊz ‖ doʊz *(= doughs)* dozed dəʊzd ‖ doʊzd dozes 'dəʊz ɪz -əz ‖ 'doʊz əz dozing 'dəʊz ɪŋ ‖ 'doʊz ɪŋ
ozen 'dʌz ᵊn ~s z
ozer 'dəʊz ə ‖ 'doʊz ᵊr ~s z
oz|y 'dəʊz |i ‖ 'doʊz |i ~ier i‿ə ‖ i‿ᵊr ~iest i‿ɪst i‿əst ~ily ɪ li əl i ~iness i nəs i nɪs
Phil ˌdiː 'fɪl
r *'debtor'* 'det ə ‖ 'deţ ᵊr
r *'doctor'* 'dɒkt ə ‖ 'dɑːkt ᵊr
rab dræb drabber 'dræb ə ‖ -ᵊr drabbest 'dræb ɪst -əst drabs dræbz
rabble 'dræb ᵊl
rably 'dræb li
rabness 'dræb nəs -nɪs
racaena drə 'siːn ə ~s z
rachm dræm *(= dram)* drachms dræmz
rach|ma 'dræk |mə ~mae miː meɪ ~mas məz
raco 'dreɪk əʊ ‖ -oʊ
raconian drə 'kəʊn i‿ən dreɪ- ‖ -'koʊn-
raconic drə 'kɒn ɪk dreɪ- ‖ -'kɑːn ɪk ~ally ᵊl‿i
racula 'dræk jʊl ə -jəl- ‖ -jəl ə
raff dræf
raft drɑːft §dræft ‖ dræft drafted 'drɑːft ɪd §'dræft-, -əd ‖ 'dræft əd drafting 'drɑːft ɪŋ §'dræft- ‖ 'dræft ɪŋ drafts drɑːfts §dræfts ‖ dræfts
'draft ˌdodger
raftee ₍ı₎drɑːf 'tiː §₍ı₎dræf- ‖ ₍ı₎dræf- ~s z
rafter 'drɑːft ə §'dræft ə ‖ 'dræft ᵊr ~s z
rafts|man 'drɑːfts |mən §'dræfts- ‖ 'dræfts- ~manship mən ʃɪp ~men mən men
raft|y 'drɑːft |i §'dræft- ‖ 'dræft |i ~ier i‿ə ‖ i‿ᵊr ~iest i‿ɪst i‿əst ~iness i nəs i nɪs
rag dræg dragged drægd dragging 'dræg ɪŋ drags drægz
'drag ˌartist; 'drag race
Drage dreɪdʒ
dragee, dragée dræ 'ʒeɪ ~s z
draggled 'dræg ᵊld
dragg|y 'dræg |i ~ier i‿ə ‖ i‿ᵊr ~iest i‿ɪst i‿əst
dragline 'dræg laɪn ~s z
dragnet 'dræg net ~s s
drago|man 'dræg ə |mən -mæn ~mans mənz mænz ~men mən men
dragon 'dræg ən ~s z
dragonet 'dræg ən ɪt -ət, -ə net ~s s
dragon|fly 'dræg ən |flaɪ →-ŋ- ~flies flaɪz
dragonnad|e ˌdræg ə 'neɪd ~ed ɪd əd ~es z ~ing ɪŋ
dragoon drə 'guːn ~ed d ~ing ɪŋ ~s z
dragster 'dræg stə ‖ -stᵊr ~s z
drail dreɪᵊl drails dreɪᵊlz
drain dreɪn drained dreɪnd draining 'dreɪn ɪŋ drains dreɪnz
'draining board
drainage 'dreɪn ɪdʒ
drainer 'dreɪn ə ‖ -ᵊr ~s z
drainpipe 'dreɪn paɪp →'dreɪm- ~s s
drake, Drake dreɪk drakes, Drake's dreɪks
Drakelow 'dreɪk ləʊ ‖ -loʊ —*locally also* 'ə ·
Drakensberg 'drɑːk ənᵗs bɜːg 'dræk-, -ənz- ‖ -bɜːg
Dralon *tdmk* 'dreɪl ɒn ‖ -ɑːn
dram dræm drams dræmz

DRAMA

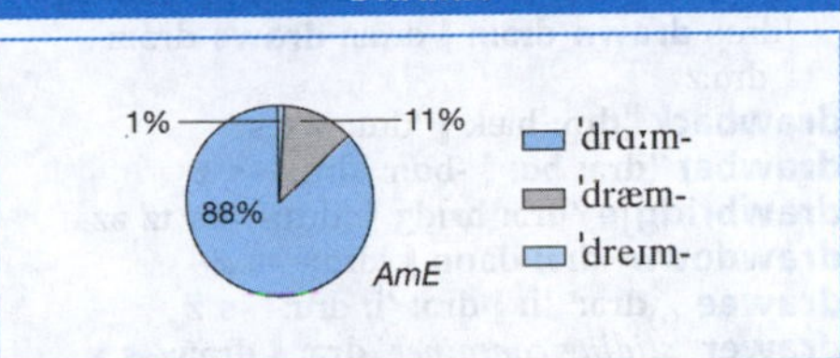

drama 'drɑːm ə ‖ 'dræm ə — *Preference poll, AmE:* 'drɑːm- *88%,* 'dræm- *11%,* 'dreɪm- *1%.* ~s z
drama-doc 'drɑːm ə 'dɒk ‖ -'dɑːk ˌdræm- ~s s
Dramamine *tdmk* 'dræm ə miːn -mɪn ~s z
dramatic drə 'mæt ɪk ‖ -'mæţ- ~ally ᵊl i ~s s
dramatis... *see* dramatiz...
dramatis personae ˌdræm ət ɪs pɜː 'səʊn aɪ ˌdrɑːm-, drə 'mæt-, -iː ‖ -əţ əs pᵊr 'soʊn iː -aɪ
dramatist 'dræm ət ɪst 'drɑːm-, §-əst ‖ -əţ əst ~s s
dramatization ˌdræm ət aɪ 'zeɪʃ ᵊn ˌdrɑːm-, -ət ɪ- ‖ -əţ ə- ~s z
dramatiz|e 'dræm ə taɪz 'drɑːm- ~ed d ~es ɪz əz ~ing ɪŋ
dramaturg|e 'dræm ə tɜːdʒ 'drɑːm- ‖ -tɜːdʒ ~es ɪz əz
dramaturgic ˌdræm ə 'tɜːdʒ ɪk ◂ ˌdrɑːm- ‖ -'tɜːdʒ- ~al ᵊl
dramaturgy 'dræm ə tɜːdʒ i 'drɑːm- ‖ -tɜːdʒ i
Drambuie dræm 'bjuː‿i -'buː‿i ~s z
dramed|y 'drɑːm əd |i ‖ 'dræm- ~ies iz
drank dræŋk
drape dreɪp draped dreɪpt drapes dreɪps draping 'dreɪp ɪŋ
draper, D~ 'dreɪp ə ‖ -ᵊr ~s z
draper|y 'dreɪp ər |i ~ies iz

DRASTIC

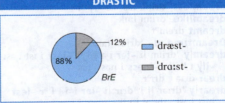

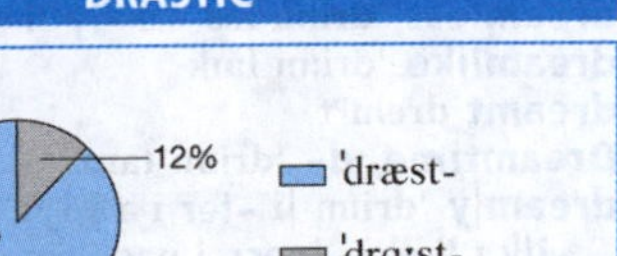

drastic 'dræst ɪk 'drɑːst- — *Preference poll, BrE:* 'dræst- *88% (southerners 92%),* 'drɑːst- *12% (southerners 8%). In AmE always* 'dræst-. ~ally ᵊl‿i
drat dræt dratted 'dræt ɪd -əd ‖ 'dræţ əd
draught drɑːft §dræft ‖ dræft ~s s
'draught exˌcluder

draughtboard ˈdrɑːft bɔːd §ˈdræft- ‖ ˈdræft bɔːrd -boʊrd **~s** z
draughts|man ˈdrɑːfts |mən §ˈdræfts- ‖ˈdræfts- **~manship** mən ʃɪp **~men** mən men
draught|y ˈdrɑːft |i §ˈdræft- ‖ ˈdræft |i **~ier** i‿ə ‖ i‿ər **~iest** i‿ɪst i‿əst **~iness** i nəs i nɪs
Drava ˈdrɑːv ə
Dravidian drə ˈvɪd i‿ən **~s** z
draw drɔː ‖ drɑː **drawing** ˈdrɔːr ɪŋ ‖ ˈdrɔː ɪŋ ˈdrɑː- **drawn** drɔːn ‖ drɑːn **draws** drɔːz ‖ drɑːz
drawback ˈdrɔː bæk ‖ ˈdrɑː- **~s** s
drawbar ˈdrɔː bɑː ‖ -bɑːr ˈdrɑː- **~s** z
drawbridg|e ˈdrɔː brɪdʒ ‖ ˈdrɑː- **~es** ɪz əz
drawdown ˈdrɔː daʊn ‖ ˈdrɑː- **~s** z
drawee ˌdrɔːˈiː ‖ drɔː ˈiː drɑː- **~s** z
drawer *'sliding container'* drɔː ‖ drɔːr **~s** z
drawer *'one that draws'* ˈdrɔːr ə ‖ ˈdrɔː‿ər ˈdrɑː‿ər **~s** z
drawers *'undergarment'* drɔːz ‖ drɔːrz
drawing ˈdrɔːr ɪŋ ‖ ˈdrɔː ɪŋ ˈdrɑː- **~s** z
ˈdrawing board; **ˈdrawing pin**; **ˈdrawing room** *also* ˈdrɔɪŋ
drawl drɔːl ‖ drɑːl **drawled** drɔːld ‖ drɑːld **drawling** ˈdrɔːl ɪŋ ‖ ˈdrɑːl- **drawls** drɔːlz ‖ drɑːlz
drawn drɔːn ‖ drɑːn
drawsheet ˈdrɔː ʃiːt ‖ ˈdrɑː- **~s** s
drawstring ˈdrɔː strɪŋ ‖ ˈdrɑː- **~s** z
Drax dræks
dray, Dray dreɪ **drays** dreɪz
Draycott *(i)* ˈdreɪk ət, *(ii)* ˈdreɪ kɒt ‖ -kɑːt
Drayton ˈdreɪt ən
dread dred **dreaded** ˈdred ɪd -əd **dreading** ˈdred ɪŋ **dreads** dredz
dreadful ˈdred fəl -fʊl **~ly** ‿i **~ness** nəs nɪs
dreadlock ˈdred lɒk ‖ -lɑːk **~ed** t **~s** s
dreadnaught, dreadnought, D~ ˈdred nɔːt ‖ -nɑːt **~s** s
dream driːm **dreamed** drempt driːmd ‖ driːmd **dreaming** ˈdriːm ɪŋ **dreams** driːmz **dreamt** drempt
ˈdream world
dreamboat ˈdriːm bəʊt ‖ -boʊt **~s** s
dreamer ˈdriːm ə ‖ -ər **~s** z
dreamland ˈdriːm lænd
dreamless ˈdriːm ləs -lɪs **~ly** li
dreamlike ˈdriːm laɪk
dreamt drempt
Dreamtime, d~ ˈdriːm taɪm
dream|y ˈdriːm |i **~ier** i‿ə ‖ i‿ər **~iest** i‿ɪst i‿əst **~ily** ɪ li əl i **~iness** i nəs i nɪs
drear drɪə ‖ drɪər
drear|y ˈdrɪər |i ‖ ˈdrɪr |i **~ier** i‿ə ‖ i‿ər **~iest** i‿ɪst i‿əst **~ily** əl i ɪ li **~iness** i nəs i nɪs
dreck drek
dredge dredʒ **dredged** dredʒd **dredges** ˈdredʒ ɪz -əz **dredging** ˈdredʒ ɪŋ
dredger ˈdredʒ ə ‖ -ər **~s** z
dree driː **dreed** driːd **dreeing** ˈdriː ɪŋ **drees** driːz
Dreena ˈdriːn ə
Dreft *tdmk* dreft
dreg dreg **dregs** dregz
dreidel ˈdreɪd əl **~s** z
Dreiser *(i)* ˈdraɪs ə ‖ -ər, *(ii)* ˈdraɪz ə ‖ -ər
drench drentʃ **drenched** drentʃt **drenches** ˈdrentʃ ɪz -əz **drenching** ˈdrentʃ ɪŋ
Drene *tdmk* driːn
Dresden ˈdrezd ən —*Ger* [ˈdʁeːs dən]
dress dres **dressed** drest **dresses** ˈdres ɪz -əz **dressing** ˈdres ɪŋ
ˌdress ˈcircle, ˈ·ˌ··; **ˌdress reˈhearsal**; **ˈdress shield**; **ˌdress ˈsuit** ‖ ˈ· ·
dressage ˈdres ɑːʒ -ɑːdʒ, -ɪdʒ, dre ˈsɑːʒ ‖ drə ˈsɑːʒ dre-
dresser ˈdres ə ‖ -ər **~s** z
dressing ˈdres ɪŋ **~s** z
ˈdressing room; **ˈdressing ˌtable**
dressing-down ˌdres ɪŋ ˈdaʊn
dressing-gown ˈdres ɪŋ gaʊn **~s** z
dressing-up ˌdres ɪŋ ˈʌp
dressmaker ˈdres ˌmeɪk ə ‖ -ər **~s** z
dressmaking ˈdres ˌmeɪk ɪŋ
dress-up ˈdres ʌp
dress|y ˈdres |i **~ier** i‿ə ‖ i‿ər **~iest** i‿ɪst i‿əst **~ily** ɪ li əl i **~iness** i nəs i nɪs
drew, Drew druː
Drexel ˈdreks əl
drey dreɪ **dreys** dreɪz
Dreyfus, Dreyfuss ˈdreɪf əs ˈdraɪf-, -ʊs —*Fr* [dʁɛ fys]
Drian ˈdriː‿ən
dribbl|e ˈdrɪb əl **~ed** d **~er/s** ‿ə/z ‖ ‿ər/z **~es** z **~ing** ‿ɪŋ
Driberg ˈdraɪ bɜːg ‖ -bɜːg
driblet ˈdrɪb lət -lɪt **~s** s
dribs and drabs ˌdrɪbz ən ˈdræbz
dried draɪd
dried-up ˌdraɪd ˈʌp ◂
drier ˈdraɪ‿ə ‖ ˈdraɪ‿ər **~s** z
dries draɪz
driest ˈdraɪ ɪst ˈdraɪ‿əst
Driffield ˈdrɪf iːəld
drift drɪft **drifted** ˈdrɪft ɪd -əd **drifting** ˈdrɪft ɪŋ **drifts** drɪfts
ˈdrift ice
driftage ˈdrɪft ɪdʒ
drifter ˈdrɪft ə ‖ -ər **~s** z
driftnet ˈdrɪft net **~s** s
driftwood ˈdrɪft wʊd
Drighlington ˈdrɪg lɪŋ tən ˈdrɪl ɪŋ-
drill drɪl **drilled** drɪlds **drilling** ˈdrɪl ɪŋ **drills** drɪlz
drillstock ˈdrɪl stɒk ‖ -stɑːk **~s** s
drily ˈdraɪ li
drink drɪŋk **drank** dræŋk **drinking** ˈdrɪŋk ɪŋ **drinks** drɪŋks **drunk** drʌŋk
ˈdrinking ˌfountain; **ˈdrinking ˌwater**
drinkable ˈdrɪŋk əb əl **~s** z
drink-driv|er ˌdrɪŋk ˈdraɪv| ə ‖ -ər **~ers** əz ‖ ərz **~ing** ɪŋ
drinker ˈdrɪŋk ə ‖ -ər **~s** z
drinking-up ˌdrɪŋk ɪŋ ˈʌp
ˌdrinking-ˈup time

rinkwater 'drɪŋk ˌwɔːt ə ‖ -ˌwɔːṱ ᵊr -ˌwɑːṱ-
rip drɪp **dripped** drɪpt **dripping** 'drɪp ɪŋ
drips drɪps
'drip feed; **'drip pan**
rip-|dry *v* 'drɪp |draɪ ˌ·'|·◂ **~dried** draɪd
~dries draɪz **~drying** draɪ ɪŋ
rip-dry *adj* ˌdrɪp 'draɪ ◂
ˌdrip-dry 'shirts
rip-|feed 'drɪp| fiːd ˌ·'|·◂ **~fed** fed **~feeding**
fiːd ɪŋ **~feeds** fiːdz
rip-mat 'drɪp mæt **~s** s
ripping 'drɪp ɪŋ **~s** z
ripp|y 'drɪp |i **~ier** i‿ə ‖ i‿ᵊr **~iest** i‿ɪst i‿əst
riscoll 'drɪsk ᵊl
rive draɪv **driven** 'drɪv ᵊn **drives** draɪvz
driving 'draɪv ɪŋ **drove** drəʊv ‖ droʊv
'drive shaft; **'driving ˌlicence**; **'driving seat**; **'driving test**
riveaway 'draɪv ə ˌweɪ
rive-by 'draɪv baɪ
rive-in 'draɪv ɪn **~s** z
rivel 'drɪv ᵊl **~ed, ~led** d **~ing, ~ling** ɪŋ **~s** z
riveler, driveller 'drɪv ᵊl‿ə ‖ ər **~s** z
riven 'drɪv ᵊn
river, D~ 'draɪv ə ‖ -ᵊr **~s** z
'driver ant; **'driver's ˌlicense**; **'driver's seat**
rive-through, drive-thru 'draɪv θruː **~s** z
rivetime 'draɪv taɪm
riveway 'draɪv weɪ **~s** z
riza-bone *tdmk* 'draɪz ə bəʊn ‖ -boʊn
rizzl|e 'drɪz ᵊl **~ed** d **~es** z **~ing** ‿ɪŋ
rizzly 'drɪz ᵊl‿i
rogheda 'drɔɪ ɪd ə 'drɒh-, -əd-
rogue drəʊg ‖ droʊg **drogues** drəʊgz
‖ droʊgz
roid drɔɪd **droids** drɔɪdz
roit de seigneur ˌdrwɑː də seɪn 'jɜː -sen'-, -siːn'- ‖ -'jɜːː —*Fr* [dʁwad sɛ ɲjœːʁ]
roitwich 'drɔɪt wɪtʃ
roll drəʊl →drɒʊl ‖ droʊl **drolls** drəʊlz
→drɒʊlz ‖ droʊlz
roller|y 'drəʊl ər |i →'drɒʊl- ‖ 'droʊl- **~ies** iz
rollness 'drəʊl nəs →'drɒʊl-, -nɪs ‖ 'droʊl-
rolly 'drəʊl li →'drɒʊl- ‖ 'droʊl-
drome drəʊm ‖ droʊm — **palindrome**
'pæl ɪn drəʊm -ən- ‖ -droʊm
romedar|y 'drɒm əd‿ər |i 'drʌm-, '·ɪd‿;
-ə der i, -ɪ·· ‖ 'drɑːm ə der |i 'drʌm- **~ies** iz
Dromio 'drəʊm i əʊ 'drɒm- ‖ 'droʊm i oʊ
Dromore drə 'mɔː ‖ -'mɔːr -'moʊr
-dromous *stress-imposing* drəm əs
catadromous kə 'tædr əm əs
drone drəʊn ‖ droʊn **droned** drəʊnd
‖ droʊnd **drones** drəʊnz ‖ droʊnz **droning**
'drəʊn ɪŋ ‖ 'droʊn ɪŋ
Dronfield 'drɒn fiːᵊld ‖ 'drɑːn-
drongo 'drɒŋ gəʊ ‖ 'drɑːŋ goʊ **~es, ~s** z
Drood druːd
drool druːl **drooled** druːld **drooling** 'druːl ɪŋ
drools druːlz
droop druːp **drooped** druːpt **drooping/ly**
'druːp ɪŋ /li **droops** druːps
droop|y 'druːp| i **~ier** i‿ə ‖ i‿ᵊr **~iest** i‿ɪst i‿əst
~ily ɪ li əl i **~iness** i nəs -nɪs
drop drɒp ‖ drɑːp **dropped** drɒpt ‖ drɑːpt
dropping 'drɒp ɪŋ ‖ 'drɑːp ɪŋ **drops** drɒps
‖ drɑːps
'drop scone; **'drop shot**
drop-dead ˌdrɒp 'ded ◂ ‖ ˌdrɑːp-
drop-down 'drɒp daʊn ‖ 'drɑːp- **~s** z
drophead 'drɒp hed ‖ 'drɑːp- **~s** z
drop-in 'drɒp ɪn ˌ·'· ‖ 'drɑːp-
dropkick 'drɒp kɪk ‖ 'drɑːp- **~ed** t **~ing** ɪŋ **~s** s
drop-leaf 'drɒp liːf ‖ 'drɑːp-
droplet 'drɒp lət -lɪt ‖ 'drɑːp- **~s** s
drop-off 'drɒp ɒf -ɔːf ‖ 'drɑːp ɔːf -ɑːf **~s** s
dropout 'drɒp aʊt ‖ 'drɑːp- **~s** s
dropper 'drɒp ə ‖ 'drɑːp ᵊr **~s** z
dropping 'drɒp ɪŋ ‖ 'drɑːp- **~s** z
dropsical 'drɒps ɪk ᵊl ‖ 'drɑːps- **~ly** i
dropsy 'drɒps i ‖ 'drɑːps i
dropwort 'drɒp wɜːt §-wɔːt ‖ 'drɑːp wɜːt
-wɔːrt **~s** s
drosh|ky 'drɒʃ |ki ‖ 'drɑːʃ- **~kies** kiz
drosophila drɒ 'sɒf ɪl ə drə-, -əl-
‖ drə 'sɑːf əl ə drə- **~s** z
dross drɒs ‖ drɑːs drɔːs
drought draʊt ‖ ⚠draʊθ **droughts** draʊts
‖ ⚠draʊθs —*The pronunciation with* θ *properly belongs with a now archaic doublet spelled* drouth.
drove drəʊv ‖ droʊv **droves** drəʊvz ‖ droʊvz
drover 'drəʊv ə ‖ 'droʊv ᵊr **~s** z
drown draʊn **drowned** 'draʊnd **drowning**
'draʊn ɪŋ **drowns** draʊnz
drowse draʊz **drowsed** draʊzd **drowses**
'draʊz ɪz -əz **drowsing** 'draʊz ɪŋ
drows|y 'draʊz |i **~ier** i‿ə ‖ i‿ᵊr **~iest** i‿ɪst i‿əst
~ily ɪ li əl i **~iness** i nəs i nɪs
Droylsden 'drɔɪᵊlz dən
drub drʌb **drubbed** drʌbd **drubbing** 'drʌb ɪŋ
drubs drʌbz
Druce druːs
drudge, Drudge drʌdʒ **drudged** drʌdʒd
drudges 'drʌdʒ ɪz -əz **drudging/ly**
'drʌdʒ ɪŋ /li
drudger|y 'drʌdʒ ər‿|i **~ies** iz
drug drʌg **drugged** drʌgd **drugging** 'drʌg ɪŋ
drugs drʌgz
'drug ˌaddict
drugged-out ˌdrʌgd 'aʊt ◂
drugget 'drʌg ɪt §-ət **~s** s
druggie 'drʌg i **~s** z
druggist 'drʌg ɪst §-əst **~s** s
drugg|y 'drʌg| i **~ies** iz
drugstore 'drʌg stɔː ‖ -stɔːr -stoʊr **~s** z
Druid, druid 'druː‿ɪd **~s** z
druidic dru 'ɪd ɪk **~al** ᵊl
drum drʌm **drummed** drʌmd **drumming**
'drʌm ɪŋ **drums** drʌmz
ˌdrum 'major ‖ '· ˌ··; **ˌdrum ˌmajo'rette**
‖ '· · ·ˌ·
Drumalbyn drʌm 'ælb ɪn §-ən
drumbeat 'drʌm biːt **~s** s

Drumcondra drʌm ˈkɒndr ə ‖ -ˈkɑːndr ə
drumfire ˈdrʌm ˌfaɪ͜ə ‖ -ˌfaɪ͜ᵊr
drumhead ˈdrʌm hed **~s** z
drumlin ˈdrʌm lɪn -lən **~s** z
drumm... *—see* **drum**
drummer ˈdrʌm ə ‖ -ᵊr **~s** z
Drummond ˈdrʌm ənd
Drumnadrochit ˌdrʌm nə ˈdrɒx ɪt -ˈdrɒk-, §-ət ‖ -ˈdrɑːk-
Drumochter drə ˈmɒxt ə -ˈmɒkt- ‖ -ˈmɑːkt ᵊr
drum-roll ˈdrʌm rəʊl →-rɒʊl ‖ -roʊl **~s** z
drumstick ˈdrʌm stɪk **~s** s
drunk drʌŋk **drunks** drʌŋ*k*s
drunkard ˈdrʌŋk əd ‖ -ᵊrd **~s** z
drunken ˈdrʌŋk ən **~ly** li **~ness** nəs nɪs
drunkometer drʌŋ ˈkɒm ɪt ə -ət- ‖ -ˈkɑːm əţ ᵊr ˈdrʌŋk ə ˌmiːţ ᵊr **~s** z
drupe druːp *(= droop)* **drupes** druːps
drupel ˈdruːp ᵊl **~s** z
Drury ˈdrʊər i ‖ ˈdrʊr i
Druse, druse druːz **Druses, druses** ˈdruːz ɪz -əz
Drusilla dru ˈsɪl ə
druther ˈdrʌð ə ‖ -ᵊr **~s** z
Druze druːz **Druzes** ˈdruːz ɪz -əz
dry draɪ **dried** draɪd **drier, dryer** ˈdraɪ͜ə ‖ ˈdraɪ͜ᵊr **dries** draɪz **driest, dryest** ˈdraɪ ɪst ˈdraɪ͜əst **drying** ˈdraɪ ɪŋ **ˈdry ˌbattery**, ˌ·ˈ··; **ˌdry ˈcleaner's**; **ˈdry dock**, ˌ·ˈ·; **ˈdry goods**; **ˌdry ˈice**; **ˌdry ˈland**; **ˌdry ˈrot**; **ˌdry ˈrun**
dryad ˈdraɪ æd ˈdraɪ͜əd **dryades** ˈdraɪ͜ə diːz **dryads** ˈdraɪ ædz ˈdraɪ͜ədz
Dryburgh ˈdraɪ bər͜ə ‖ ˈdraɪ bɜːg
dry-clean ˌdraɪ ˈkliːn ◂ **~ed** d **~ing** ɪŋ **~s** z
Dryden ˈdraɪd ᵊn
dryer ˈdraɪ͜ə ‖ ˈdraɪ͜ᵊr **dryest** ˈdraɪ ɪst ˈdraɪ͜əst
dry-eyed ˌdraɪ ˈaɪd ◂
dryish ˈdraɪ ɪʃ
dryly ˈdraɪ li
dryness ˈdraɪ nəs -nɪs
drypoint ˈdraɪ pɔɪnt **~s** s
dry-roasted ˌdraɪ ˈrəʊst ɪd ◂ -əd ◂ ‖ -ˈroʊst-
Drysdale ˈdraɪz deɪᵊl
dry-shod ˌdraɪ ˈʃɒd ◂ ‖ ˈdraɪ ʃɑːd
dry-stone ˈdraɪ stəʊn .ˈ· ‖ -stoʊn
drywall ˈdraɪ wɔːl ‖ -wɑːl
DTI ˌdiː tiː ˈaɪ
DTs, d t's, DT's ˌdiː ˈtiːz
Du *in names (i)* dju →dʒu, *(ii)* du *—See also phrases with this word—This prefix is unstressed.*
dual ˈdjuː͜əl →ˈdʒuː͜, §ˈduː͜; djuːl, →dʒuːl; §duːl ‖ ˈduː əl ˈdjuː- **~s** z **ˌdual ˈcarriageway**
Duala du ˈɑːl ə
dual-band ˌdjuː͜əl ˈbænd ◂ →ˌdʒuː͜, §ˌduː͜; ˌdjuːlˈ·, →ˌdʒuːlˈ·, §ˌduːlˈ· ‖ ˌduː əl- ˌdjuː əl-
dualism ˈdjuː͜əl ˌɪz əm →ˈdʒuː͜, §ˈduː͜ ‖ ˈduː- ˈdjuː- **~s** z
dualist ˈdjuː͜əl ɪst →ˈdʒuː͜, §ˈduː͜ §-əst ‖ ˈduː- ˈdjuː- **~s** s
dualistic ˌdjuː͜ə ˈlɪst ɪk ◂ →ˌdʒuː͜, §ˌdu͜ə͜ ‖ ˌduː- ˌdjuː- **~ally** ᵊl i
dualit|y dju ˈæl ət |i →dʒu-, §du-, -ɪt i ‖ du ˈæl əţ |i dju- **~ies** iz
dual-purpose ˌdjuː͜əl ˈpɜːp əs ◂ →ˌdʒuː͜, §ˌduː͜, ˌdjuːlˈ· ·, →ˌdʒuːlˈ··, §ˌduːlˈ·· ‖ ˌduː əl ˈpɝːp əs ◂ ˌdjuː-
Duane ⁽ˌ⁾duː ˈeɪn dweɪn
dub dʌb **dubbed** dʌbd **dubbing** ˈdʌb ɪŋ **dubs** dʌbz
Dubai ˌduː ˈbaɪ ˌdjuː-, →ˌdʒuː-, du-, dju-, →dʒu-; -ˈbaɪ i *—Arabic* [du ˈbajj]
Dubarry dju ˈbær i du- ‖ du- dju-, -ˈber i
dubbin ˈdʌb ɪn §-ən **~ed** d **~s** z
Dubček ˈdʊb tʃek ‖ ˈduːb- *—Slovak* [ˈdup tʃek]
dubiet|y dju ˈbaɪ͜ət |i →dʒu-, -ɪt- ‖ du ˈbaɪ əţ |i dju- **~ies** iz
dubious ˈdjuːb i͜əs →ˈdʒuːb- ‖ ˈduːb- ˈdjuːb- **~ly** li **~ness** nəs nɪs
Dublin ˈdʌb lɪn §-lən **ˌDublin ˈBay, ˌDublin Bay ˈprawn**
Dubliner ˈdʌb lɪn ə §-lən- ‖ -ᵊr **~s** z
dubnium ˈdʌb ni͜əm ˈduːb-, ˈdʊb-
Dubois, Du Bois *American family name* du ˈbɔɪs də-, -ˈbɔɪz
Dubois *French or Dutch family name* du ˈbwɑː dju- *—Fr* [dy bwa]
Dubonnet *tdmk,* **d~** du ˈbɒn eɪ dju-, →dʒu- ‖ ˌduːb ə ˈneɪ *—Fr* [dy bɔ nɛ] **~s** z
Dubrovnik du ˈbrɒv nɪk dju- ‖ -ˈbrɑːv- *—Croatian* [ˈˈdu broːv niːk]
Dubuque də ˈbjuːk
ducal ˈdjuːk ᵊl →ˈdʒuːk- ‖ ˈduːk ᵊl ˈdjuːk- **~ly** i
Du Cane dju ˈkeɪn du- ‖ du- dju-
Du Cann dju ˈkæn du- ‖ du- dju-
ducat ˈdʌk ət **~s** s
duce ˈduːtʃ eɪ *—It* [ˈdut tʃe]
Duchamp ˈdjuː ʃɒ̃ ˈduː-, -ʃɒm ‖ du ˈʃɑ̃ː -ˈʃɑːm *—Fr* [dy ʃɑ̃]
Duchenne du ˈʃen dju-
Duchesne dju ˈʃeɪn du-
duchess ˈdʌtʃ ɪs -əs, -es, ˌdʌtʃ ˈes **~es** ɪz əz
duchesse dju ˈʃes du- *—Fr* [dy ʃɛs]
duch|y ˈdʌtʃ |i **~ies** iz
Ducie ˈdjuːs i →ˈdʒuːs- ‖ ˈduːs i ˈdjuːs-
duck, Duck dʌk **ducked** dʌkt *(= duct)* **ducking** ˈdʌk ɪŋ **ducks** dʌks **ˈducking stool**; **ˌducks and ˈdrakes**
duckbill ˈdʌk bɪl **~ed** d **~s** z **ˌduckbilled ˈplatypus**
duckboard ˈdʌk bɔːd ‖ -bɔːrd -boʊrd **~s** z
duck-egg ˈdʌk eg **~s** z
Duckett ˈdʌk ɪt §-ət
Duckham ˈdʌk əm **~'s** z
duckie ˈdʌk i **~s** z
duckling ˈdʌk lɪŋ **~s** z
duckweed ˈdʌk wiːd
Duckworth ˈdʌk wəθ -wɜːθ ‖ -wᵊrθ
duck|y ˈdʌk |i **~ier** i͜ə ‖ i͜ᵊr **~ies** iz **~iest** i͜ɪst i͜əst
duct dʌkt **ducted** ˈdʌkt ɪd -əd **ducting** ˈdʌkt ɪŋ **ducts** dʌk*t*s

uctile 'dʌkt aɪᵊl ‖ -ᵊl
uctility dʌk 'tɪl ət i -ɪt- ‖ -əţ i
uctless 'dʌkt ləs -lɪs
ud dʌd **duds** dʌdz
udden, Duddon 'dʌd ᵊn
ude du:d dju:d **dudes** du:dz dju:dz
'dude ranch
udgeon 'dʌdʒ ən
udley 'dʌd li

DUE

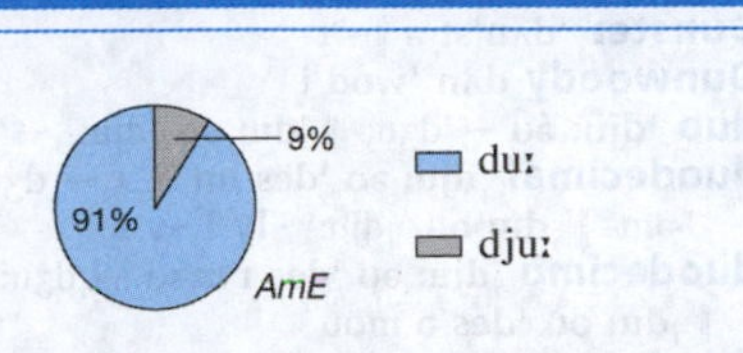

ue dju: →dʒu: ‖ du: dju: — *Preference poll, AmE:* du: *91%,* dju: *9%.* **dues** dju:z →dʒu:z ‖ du:z dju:z
uel 'dju:ˌəl →'dʒu:ˌ; dju:l, →dʒu:l ‖ 'du: əl 'du:- *(= dual)* **~ed, ~led** d **~er/s, ~ler/s** ə/z ‖ ᵊr/z **~ing, ~ling** ɪŋ **~s** z
uelist, duellist 'dju:ˌəl ɪst →'dʒu:ˌ, §-əst; 'dju:l-, →'dʒu:l- ‖ 'du: əl əst 'du:- **~s** s
uenna dju 'en ə du- ‖ du- dju- **~s** z
Duerden 'djʊəd ᵊn ‖ 'dʊrd ᵊn 'djʊrd-
uet dju 'et →dʒu- ‖ du- dju- **~s** s
uettist dju 'et ɪst →dʒu-, §-əst ‖ du 'eţ ɪst dju- **~s** s
uff, Duff dʌf **duffed** dʌft **duffing** 'dʌf ɪŋ **duffs** dʌfs
uffel, D~ *tdmk* 'dʌf ᵊl
uffer 'dʌf ə ‖ -ᵊr **~s** z
Dufferin 'dʌf ərˌɪn -ᵊrˌən
Duffey, Duffie 'dʌf i
Duffield 'dʌf i:ᵊld
uffle 'dʌf ᵊl
'duffle bag; **'duffle coat**
Duffy 'dʌf i
Dufton 'dʌft ən
Dufy 'du:f i ‖ du 'fi: —*Fr* [dy fi]
ug dʌg **dugz** dʌgz
Dugald 'du:g ᵊld
Dugan 'du:g ən
Dugdale 'dʌg deɪᵊl
Duggan 'dʌg ən
Duggleby 'dʌg ᵊl bi
dugong 'du: gɒŋ 'dju:- ‖ -gɑ:ŋ -gɔ:ŋ **~s** z
dugout 'dʌg aʊt **~s** s
Duguid 'dju:g ɪd 'du:g-
duh dɜ: ‖ də dʌ
duiker 'daɪk ə ‖ -ᵊr **~s** z
Duisburg 'dju:z bɜ:g 'dju:s- ‖ 'du:s bɜ:g 'du:z- —*Ger* ['dy:s bʊʁk]
Duisenberg 'daɪz ᵊn bɜ:g 'dɔɪz- ‖ 'du:z ᵊn bɜ:g —*Dutch* ['dœy sᵊn bɛrx]
Dukakis du 'kɑ:k ɪs dju-, də-, §-əs
Dukas 'dju:k ɑ: 'du:k- ‖ du 'kɑ: dju- —*Fr* [dy ka]
duke, Duke dju:k →dʒu:k ‖ du:k dju:k **dukes, Duke's** dju:ks →dʒu:ks ‖ du:ks dju:ks
dukedom 'dju:k dəm →'dʒu:k- ‖ du:k- 'dju:k- **~s** z
Dukeries 'dju:k ər iz →dʒu:k- ‖ 'du:k- 'dju:k-
Dukhobor 'du:k ə bɔ: -əʊ- ‖ -bɔ:r **~s** z
Dukinfield 'dʌk ɪn fi:ᵊld -ən-
Dulais 'dɪl aɪs -əs
dulcet 'dʌls ɪt -ət
dulciana ˌdʌls i 'ɑ:n ə ‖ -'æn ə -'ɑ:n ə
Dulcie 'dʌls i
dulcimer 'dʌls ɪm ə -əm- ‖ -ᵊr **~s** z
Dulcinea ˌdʌls ɪ 'ni:ˌə -ə-, -'neɪ ə
Dulcy 'dʌls i
dulia du 'laɪ ə dju-; 'dju:l iˌə, 'du:l-
dull dʌl **dulled** dʌld **duller** 'dʌl ə ‖ -ᵊr **dullest** 'dʌl ɪst -əst **dulling** 'dʌl ɪŋ **dulls** dʌlz
dullard 'dʌl əd ‖ -ᵊrd **~s** z
Dulles 'dʌl ɪs -əs
dullish 'dʌl ɪʃ
dullness 'dʌl nəs -nɪs
dullsville 'dʌlz vɪl §-vᵊl **~s** z
dull-witted ˌdʌl 'wɪt ɪd ◂ -əd ‖ -'wɪţ əd ◂ **~ness** nəs nɪs
dully 'dʌl li 'dʌl i
dulness 'dʌl nəs -nɪs
dulse dʌls
Duluth də 'lu:θ du-, dju-
Dulux *tdmk* 'dju: lʌks →'dʒu:- ‖ 'du:- 'dju:-
Dulverton 'dʌlv ət ən ‖ -ᵊrt ᵊn
Dulwich 'dʌl ɪdʒ -ɪtʃ
duly 'dju: li →'dʒu:- ‖ 'du: li dju:-
Duma, duma 'du:m ə
Dumaresq, d~ dju 'mer ɪk →dʒu- ‖ du- dju- **~s** s
Dumas 'dju:m ɑ: 'du:m-; du 'mɑ: ‖ du 'mɑ: —*Fr* [dy ma]
Du Maurier du 'mɒr i eɪ dju- ‖ də 'mɔ:r-
dumb dʌm **dumbed** dʌmd **dumber** 'dʌm ə ‖ -ᵊr **dumbest** 'dʌm ɪst -əst **dumbing** 'dʌm ɪŋ **dumbs** dʌmz
'dumb show
Dumbarton ₍ₗ₎dʌm 'bɑ:t ᵊn dəm- ‖ -'bɑ:rt ᵊn ˌ**Dumbarton 'Oaks**; ˌ**Dumbarton 'Bridge** *in CA*
dumbbell 'dʌm bel **~s** z
dumbfound ₍ₗ₎dʌm 'faʊnd '· · **~ed** ɪd əd **~ing** ɪŋ **~s** z
Dumbledore 'dʌm bᵊl dɔ: ‖ -dɔ:r
dumb|ly 'dʌm |li **~ness** nəs nɪs
Dumbo 'dʌm bəʊ ‖ -boʊ
dumbstruck 'dʌm strʌk
dumbwaiter ˌdʌm 'weɪt ə ‖ -'weɪţ ᵊr **~s** z
dumdum, dum-dum 'dʌm dʌm
dumfound ₍ₗ₎dʌm 'faʊnd '· · **~ed** ɪd əd **~ing** ɪŋ **~s** z
Dumfries ₍ₗ₎dʌm 'fri:s dəm-, -'fri:z
Dummer 'dʌm ə ‖ -ᵊr
dumm|y 'dʌm |i **~ies** iz
dump dʌmp **dumped** dʌmpt **dumping** 'dʌmp ɪŋ **dumps** dʌmps
'dump truck
dumper 'dʌmp ə ‖ -ᵊr **~s** z

dumpi... —*see* **dumpy**
dumpling ˈdʌmp lɪŋ **~s** z
dumpster, D~ *tdmk* ˈdʌmpst ə ‖ -ᵊr **~s** z
dump|y ˈdʌmp |i **~ier** i ə ‖ i ᵊr **~iest** i ɪst i əst **~ily** ɪ li əl i **~iness** i nəs i nɪs
dun, Dun dʌn **dunned** dʌnd **dunner** ˈdʌn ə ‖ -ᵊr **dunnest** ˈdʌn ɪst -əst **dunning** ˈdʌn ɪŋ **duns** dʌnz —*See also phrases with this word*
Dunaway ˈdʌn ə weɪ
Dunbar dʌn ˈbɑː →dʌm- ‖ -ˈbɑːr ˈ· ·
Dunblane dʌn ˈbleɪn →dʌm-
Duncan ˈdʌŋk ən
Duncannon dʌn ˈkæn ən →dʌŋ-
dunce dʌnᵗs **dunces, dunce's** ˈdʌnᵗs ɪz -əz
ˈ**dunce's cap**
Dunciad ˈdʌnᵗs i æd
Dundalk *in Ireland* ₍ˌ₎dʌn ˈdɔːk -ˈdɔːlk ‖-ˈdɑːk —*but the place in MD is* ˈ· ·
Dundas dʌn ˈdæs ˈdʌnd əs
Dundee ₍ˌ₎dʌn ˈdiː
₍ˌ₎**Dun'dee cake**; ˌ**Dundee U'nited**, ·ˌ·-
dunderhead ˈdʌnd ə hed ‖ -ᵊr- **~ed** ɪd əd **~s** z
Dundonald dʌn ˈdɒn ᵊld ‖ -ˈdɑːn-
Dundonian dʌn ˈdəʊn i ən ‖ -ˈdoʊn- **~s** z
Dundrear|y, d~ dʌn ˈdrɪər |i ‖ -ˈdrɪr |i **~ies** iz
dune djuːn →dʒuːn ‖ duːn djuːn **dunes** djuːnz →dʒuːnz ‖ duːnz djuːnz
ˈ**dune** ˌ**buggy**
Dunedin dʌn ˈiːd ɪn -ᵊn —*in NZ* -ᵊn
Dunfermline dʌn ˈfɜːm lɪn -lən ‖ -ˈfɜːm-
dung dʌŋ **dunged** dʌŋd **dunging** ˈdʌŋ ɪŋ **dungs** dʌŋz
ˈ**dung** ˌ**beetle**
Dungannon dʌn ˈgæn ən →dʌŋ-
dungaree ˌdʌŋ gə ˈriː ˈ· · · **~s** z
Dungeness ˌdʌndʒ ə ˈnes ◂
ˌ**Dungeness 'B**; ˌ**Dungeness 'crab**
dungeon ˈdʌndʒ ən **~s** z
dunghill ˈdʌŋ hɪl **~s** z
Dunhill ˈdʌn hɪl **~s, ~'s** z
dunk dʌŋk **dunked** dʌŋ*k*t **dunking** ˈdʌŋk ɪŋ **dunks** dʌŋ*k*s
Dunkeld dʌn ˈkeld →dʌŋ-
Dunkery ˈdʌŋk ər i
ˌ**Dunkery 'Beacon**
Dunkirk ₍ˌ₎dʌn ˈkɜːk →₍ˌ₎dʌŋ- ‖ ˈdʌn kɜːk —*Fr* Dunkerque [dœ̃ kɛʁk]
Dunkley ˈdʌŋk li
Dunkling ˈdʌŋk lɪŋ
Dun Laoghaire, Dún Laoghaire, Dún Laoire ₍ˌ₎dʌn ˈlɪər i ₍ˌ₎duːn-, -ˈleər-, -ə ‖ -ˈler- —*Irish* [dun ˈɫeː rʲe]
dunlin ˈdʌn lɪn -lən **~s** z
Dunlop ˈdʌn lɒp ‖ -lɑːp —*but as placename and family name, in BrE usually* ·ˈ·
Dunmail ˌdʌn ˈmeɪᵊl →ˌdʌm-
ˌ**Dunmail 'Raise**
Dunmow ˈdʌn məʊ →ˈdʌm- ‖ -moʊ
Dunn, Dunne dʌn
dunn... —*see* **dun**
dunnage ˈdʌn ɪdʒ
Dunnet, Dunnett ˈdʌn ɪt §-ət
ˌ**Dunnet 'Head**
dunno *'don't know'* də ˈnəʊ ₍ˌ₎dʌ- ‖ -ˈnoʊ
dunnock ˈdʌn ək **~s** s
dunn|y ˈdʌn |i **~ies** iz
Dunoon dʌn ˈuːn də ˈnuːn
Duns dʌnz
ˌ**Duns 'Scotus** ˈskəʊt əs ˈskɒt- ‖ ˈskoʊţ-
Dunsany dʌn ˈseɪn i -ˈsæn-
Dunsinane dʌn ˈsɪn ən —*but in Shakespeare's 'Macbeth'* ˌdʌnᵗs ɪ ˈneɪn, -ə-, ˈ· · ·
Dunstable ˈdʌnᵗst əb ᵊl
Dunstan ˈdʌnᵗst ən
Dunster ˈdʌnᵗst ə ‖ -ᵊr
Dunwoody dʌn ˈwʊd i
duo ˈdjuː əʊ →ˈdʒuː- ‖ ˈduː oʊ ˈdjuː- **~s** z
duodecimal ˌdjuː əʊ ˈdes ɪm ᵊl ◂ →ˌdʒuː-, -ˈəm- ‖ ˌduː oʊ- ˌdjuː- **~ly** i **~s** z
duodecimo ˌdjuː əʊ ˈdes ɪ məʊ →ˌdʒuː-, -ˈ·ə- ‖ ˌduː oʊ ˈdes ə moʊ
duoden|um ˌdjuː əʊ ˈdiːn |əm →ˌdʒuː- ‖ ˌduː ə- ˌdjuː- **~a** ə **~al** ᵊl ◂ **~ums** əmz
ˌ**duo**ˌ**denal 'ulcer**
duologue ˈdjuː ə lɒg →ˈdʒuː ‖ ˈduː ə lɔːg ˈdjuː-, -lɑːg **~s** z
duopol|y dju ˈɒp əl |i →dʒu- ‖ du ˈɑːp- dju- **~ies** iz
dupe djuːp →dʒuːp ‖ duːp djuːp **duped** djuːpt →dʒuːpt ‖ duːpt djuːpt **dupes** djuːps →dʒuːps ‖ duːps djuːps **duping** ˈdjuːp ɪŋ →ˈdʒuːp- ‖ ˈduːp ɪŋ djuːp-
duple ˈdjuːp ᵊl →ˈdʒuːp- ‖ ˈduːp ᵊl ˈdjuːp-
duplex ˈdjuːp leks →ˈdʒuːp- ‖ ˈduːp- ˈdjuːp- **~es** ɪz əz
duplicate *adj, n* ˈdjuːp lɪk ət →ˈdʒuːp-, -lək-, -ɪt ‖ ˈduːp- ˈdjuːp- **~s** s
dupli|cate *v* ˈdjuːp lɪ |keɪt →ˈdʒuːp-, -lə- ‖ ˈduːp- ˈdjuːp- **~cated** keɪt ɪd -əd ‖ keɪţ əd **~cates** keɪts **~cating** keɪt ɪŋ ‖ keɪţ ɪŋ
duplication ˌdjuːp lɪ ˈkeɪʃ ᵊn →ˌdʒuːp-, -lə- ‖ ˌduːp- ˌdjuːp- **~s** z
duplicator ˈdjuːp lɪ keɪt ə →ˈdʒuːp-, ˈ·lə- ‖ ˈduːp lɪ keɪţ ᵊr ˈdjuːp- **~s** z
duplicitous dju ˈplɪs ɪt əs →dʒu-, -ət- ‖ du ˈplɪs əţ əs dju- **~ly** li
duplicity dju ˈplɪs ət i →dʒu-, -ɪt- ‖ du ˈplɪs əţ i dju-
Dupont *(i)* dju ˈpɒnt →dʒu- ‖ du ˈpɑːnt dju-, *(ii)* ˈdjuː pɒnt →ˈdʒuː- ‖ ˈduː pɑːnt ˈdjuː- —*Fr* [dy pɔ̃]
Dupré, Duprée, Duprez du ˈpreɪ dju- —*but as an English name, also* -ˈpriː
Dupuytren du ˈpwiːtr ən dju-; ˈdjuːp i trɒ̃, ˌ· ·ˈ· —*Fr* [dy pɥi tʁɛ̃]
Duquesne du ˈkeɪn dju- —*Fr* [dy kɛn]
durability ˌdjʊər ə ˈbɪl ət i ˌdjɔːr-, →ˌdʒʊər-, -ɪt i ‖ ˌdʊr ə ˈbɪl əţ i ˌdjʊr-
durab|le ˈdjʊər əb |ᵊl ˈdjɔːr-, →ˈdʒʊər- ‖ ˈdʊr- ˈdjʊr- **~leness** ᵊl nəs -nɪs **~les** ᵊlz **~ly** li
Duracell *tdmk* ˈdjʊər ə sel →ˈdʒʊər- ‖ ˈdʊr- ˈdjʊr-
Durack ˈdjʊər æk ‖ ˈdʊr- ˈdjʊr-
Duraglit *tdmk* ˈdjʊər ə glɪt →ˈdʒʊər- ‖ ˈdʊr- ˈdjʊr-

ralumin, D~ *tdmk* djuᵊ ˈræl jʊ mɪn →dʒuᵊ-, -jə-, §-mən ‖ du ˈræl jəm ən dju-

ra mater ˌdjʊər ə ˈmeɪt ə →ˌdʒʊər- ‖ ˌdʊr ə ˈmɑːt̬ ᵊr ˌdjʊr-, ˈ· · ˌ· ·

ran djuᵊ ˈræn duᵊ-, →dʒuᵊ-

rance ˈdjʊər ənˈs ˈdjɔːr-, →ˈdʒʊər- ‖ ˈdʊr- ˈdjʊr-

rango dju ˈræŋ gəʊ →dʒu-, də- ‖ du ˈræŋ goʊ dju-, də-

ration djuᵊ ˈreɪʃ ᵊn djɔː-, →dʒuᵊ- ‖ du- dju- **~s** z

rative ˈdjʊər ət ɪv ˈdjɔːr-, →ˈdʒʊər- ‖ ˈdʊr ət̬ ɪv ˈdjʊr-

rban ˈdɜːb ən ‖ ˈdɝːb-

rbar ˈdɜːb ɑː ˌdɜː ˈbɑː ‖ ˈdɝːb ɑːr **~s** z

rbin ˈdɜːb ɪn §-ən ‖ ˈdɝːb-

rbridge ˈdɜː brɪdʒ ‖ ˈdɝː-

rer, Dürer ˈdjʊər ə ‖ ˈdʊr ᵊr —*Ger* [ˈdyː ʁɐ]

ress djuᵊ ˈres →dʒuᵊ-, ˈdjʊər es ‖ dʊ ˈres

rex, Durex *tdmk* ˈdjʊər eks ˈdjɔːr-, →dʒʊər- ‖ ˈdʊr- ˈdjʊr- **~es** ɪz əz

rham ˈdʌr əm ‖ dɝː-

rian ˈdʊər i ən ˈdjʊr-, -i ɑːn ‖ ˈdʊr- **~s** z

rie ˈdjʊər i ‖ ˈdʊr i ˈdjʊər-

DURING

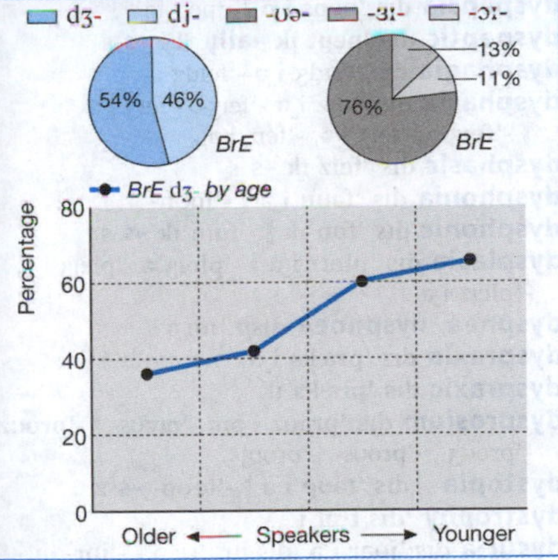

during ˈdʒʊər ɪŋ ˈdjʊər-, ˈdʒɜːr-, ˈdjɜːr-, ˈdʒɔːr-, ˈdjɔːr- ‖ ˈdɝː ɪŋ ˈdʊr-, ˈdjʊr- — *Preference poll, BrE:* ˈdʒ- *54% (born since 1981, 67%)* ˈdj- *46%;* -ʊə- *76%,* -ɜː- *13%,* -ɔː- *10%.*

Durkheim ˈdɜːk haɪm ‖ ˈdɝːk- —*Fr* [dyʁ kɛm]

durmast ˈdɜː mɑːst §-mæst ‖ ˈdɝː mæst **~s** s

Durness ˈdɜːn əs -ɪs ‖ ˈdɝːn-

Durrant *(i)* ˈdʌr ənt ‖ ˈdɝː-, *(ii)* də ˈrænt

Durrell ˈdʌr əl ‖ ˈdɝːr-

Durrenmatt, Dürrenmatt ˈdjʊər ən mæt ˈdʊər- ‖ ˈdʊr ən mɑːt —*Ger* [ˈdʏʁ ən mat]

durr|ie, durr|y ˈdʌr |i ‖ ˈdɝː |i **~ies** iz

durst dɜːst ‖ dɝːst **durstn't** ˈdɜːs ᵊnt ‖ ˈdɝːs-

durum ˈdjʊər əm →ˈdʒʊər- ‖ ˈdʊr- ˈdjʊr-, ˈdɝː-

Dushanbe ˌduː ʃæn ˈbeɪ →-ʃæm- ‖ -ʃɑːn- -ʃæn-, →-ʃɑːm-, →-ʃæm-

dusk dʌsk **dusked** dʌskt **dusking** ˈdʌsk ɪŋ **dusks** dʌsks

dusk|y ˈdʌsk |i **~ier** i‿ə ‖ i‿ᵊr **~iest** i‿ɪst i‿əst **~ily** ɪ li əl i **~iness** i nəs i nɪs

Dusseldorf, Düsseldorf ˈdʊs ᵊl dɔːf ‖ ˈduːs ᵊl dɔːrf ˈdʊs- —*Ger* [ˈdʏs ᵊl dɔʁf]

dust dʌst **dusted** ˈdʌst ɪd -əd **dusting** ˈdʌst ɪŋ **dusts** dʌsts **ˈdust ˌcover**; **ˈdust ˌdevil**; **ˈdusting ˌpowder**; **ˈdust ˌjacket**; **ˈdust storm**

dustbin ˈdʌst bɪn **~s** z

dustbowl ˈdʌst bəʊl →bɒʊl ‖ -boʊl **~s** z

dustcart ˈdʌst kɑːt ‖ -kɑːrt **~s** s

dustcoat ˈdʌst kəʊt ‖ -koʊt **~s** s

duster ˈdʌst ə ‖ -ᵊr **~s** z

dusti... —*see* **dusty**

Dustin ˈdʌst ɪn §-ən

dust|man ˈdʌst |mən **~men** mən men

dustpan ˈdʌst pæn **~s** z

dustsheet ˈdʌst ʃiːt →ˈdʌʃ- **~s** s

dustup ˈdʌst ʌp **~s** s

dust|y, Dusty ˈdʌst |i **~ier** i‿ə ‖ i‿ᵊr **~iest** i‿ɪst i‿əst **~ily** ɪ li əl i **~iness** i nəs i nɪs

Dutch, dutch dʌtʃ **ˌDutch ˈauction**; **ˌDutch ˈcourage**; **ˌDutch ˈelm diˌsease**; **ˌDutch ˈoven**; **ˌDutch ˈtreat**; **ˌDutch ˈuncle**

Dutch|man ˈdʌtʃ |mən **~men** mən men **~woman** ˌwʊm ən **~women** ˌwɪm ɪn §-ən

duteous ˈdjuːt i‿əs →ˈdʒuːt- ‖ ˈduːt̬ i‿əs ˈdjuːt̬- **~ly** li **~ness** nəs nɪs

Duthie ˈdʌθ i

duti... —*see* **duty**

dutiable ˈdjuːt i‿əb ᵊl →ˈdʒuːt- ‖ ˈduːt̬- ˈdjuːt̬-

dutiful ˈdjuːt ɪ fᵊl →dʒuːt-, -ə-, -fʊl ‖ ˈduːt̬- ˈdjuːt̬- **~ly** ‿i **~ness** nəs nɪs

Du Toit dju ˈtwɑː du- ‖ du- dju-

Dutton ˈdʌt ᵊn

dut|y ˈdjuːt |i →ˈdʒuːt i ‖ ˈduːt̬ |i ˈdjuːt̬ i **~ies** iz

duty-free ˌdjuːt i ˈfriː ◂ →ˌdʒuːt-, ˌduːt̬- ˌdjuːt̬- **ˌduty-ˈfree shop, ˌduty-free ˈwhisky**

duum|vir dju ˈʌm |və du-, -ˈʊm- ‖ du ˈʌm |vᵊr **~virate** vər ət vɪr-, -ɪt; -və reɪt, vɪ- **~viri** və riː vɪ-, -raɪ

Duvalier du ˈvæl i eɪ dju- ‖ ˌduː vɑːl ˈjeɪ ·ˈ· · —*Fr* [dy va lje]

duvet ˈduːv eɪ ˈdjuːv- ‖ du ˈveɪ **~s** z

dux dʌks

Duxford ˈdʌks fəd ‖ -fᵊrd

duyker ˈdaɪk ə ‖ -ᵊr **~s** z

DVD ˌdiː viː ˈdiː **~s** z

Dvorak, Dvořák ˈdvɔːʒ æk ˈvɔːʒ-, -ɑːk ‖ ˈdvɔːrʒ ɑːk —*Czech* [ˈdvɔ r̝aːk] —*but as an American family name, and for the keyboard design, also* ˈdvɔːr æk

dwale dweɪᵊl

dwarf dwɔːf ‖ dwɔːrf **dwarfed** dwɔːft ‖ dwɔːrft **dwarfing** ˈdwɔːf ɪŋ ‖ ˈdwɔːrf ɪŋ **dwarfs** dwɔːfs ‖ dwɔːrfs **dwarves** dwɔːvz ‖ dwɔːrvz

dwarfish ˈdwɔːf ɪʃ ‖ ˈdwɔːrf-

dwarfism ˈdwɔːf ˌɪz əm ‖ ˈdwɔːrf-

dwarves dwɔːvz ‖ dwɔːrvz

Dwayne dweɪn

dweeb dwiːb **dweebs** dwiːbz
dwell dwel **dwelled** dweld dwelt **dwelling** ˈdwel ɪŋ **dwells** dwelz **dwelt** dwelt
dweller ˈdwel ə ‖ -ᵊr **~s** z
dwelling ˈdwel ɪŋ **~s** z
ˈdwelling house
dwelt dwelt
Dwight dwaɪt
dwindl|e ˈdwɪnd ᵊl **~ed** d **~es** z **~ing** ‿ɪŋ
Dworkin ˈdwɔːk ɪn §-ən ‖ ˈdwɔːrk-
Dwyer ˈdwaɪ‿ə ‖ ‿ᵊr
Dwynwen ˈduː‿ɪn wen
dyad ˈdaɪ æd **~s** z
dyadic daɪ ˈæd ɪk **~s** s
Dyak ˈdaɪ æk -ək **~s** s
dyarch|y ˈdaɪ ɑːk |i ‖ -ɑːrk |i **~ies** iz
dybbuk ˈdɪb ək diː ˈbuːk **~ed** t **~s** s
Dyce daɪs
Dyck daɪk
dye daɪ *(= die)* **dyed** daɪd **dyes** daɪz **dyeing** ˈdaɪ ɪŋ
dyed-in-the-wool ˌdaɪd ɪn ðə ˈwʊl ◂ ˌ·ᵊn-
dyer, Dyer ˈdaɪ‿ə ‖ ˈdaɪ‿ᵊr **~s** z
dyestuff ˈdaɪ stʌf **~s** s
dyeworks ˈdaɪ wɜːks ‖ -wɜːks
Dyfed ˈdʌv ɪd -ed, -əd —*Welsh* [ˈdə ved] —*Also, by those not familiar with the name,* ˈdɪf-
Dyffryn ˈdʌf rɪn -rən —*Welsh* [ˈdəf rin, -rɨn]
Dyfrig ˈdʌv rɪg —*Welsh* [ˈdəv rig]
dying ˈdaɪ ɪŋ
Dyirbal ˈdʒɪəb ɑːl ‖ ˈdʒɪrb-
dyke daɪk *(= dike)* **dyked** daɪkt **dykes** daɪks **dyking** ˈdaɪk ɪŋ
Dykes daɪks
Dylan ˈdɪl ən ˈdʌl- —*Welsh* [ˈdə lan]
Dymchurch ˈdɪm tʃɜːtʃ ‖ -tʃɜːtʃ
dymo, Dymo *tdmk* ˈdaɪm əʊ ‖ -oʊ **~'d, ~ed** d **~s** z **~ing** ɪŋ
Dymock, Dymoke ˈdɪm ək
Dympna ˈdɪmp nə
dynamic daɪ ˈnæm ɪk dɪ-, də- **~ally** ᵊl‿i **~s** s
dynamism ˈdaɪn ə ˌmɪz əm **~s** z
dyna|mite ˈdaɪn ə |maɪt **~mited** maɪt ɪd -əd ‖ maɪţ əd **~mites** maɪts **~miting** maɪt ɪŋ ‖ maɪţ ɪŋ
dynamo ˈdaɪn ə məʊ ‖ -moʊ **~s** z
dynamometer ˌdaɪn ə ˈmɒm ɪt ə -ət ə ‖ -ˈmɑːm əţ ᵊr **~s** z
dynast ˈdɪn əst ˈdaɪn-, -æst ‖ ˈdaɪn æst -əst **~s** s
dynastic dɪ ˈnæst ɪk də-, daɪ- ‖ daɪ- **~ally** ᵊl‿i
dynast|y ˈdɪn əst |i ‖ ˈdaɪn- *(*)* **~ies** iz
dyne daɪn *(= dine)* **dynes** daɪnz
Dynevor ˈdɪn ɪv ə -əv- ‖ -ᵊr —*but in Wales often* dɪ ˈnev ə. *Welsh* Dinefwr [di ˈne vur]
d'you djuː, dju, djə →dʒuː, →dʒu, →dʒə
dys- (ˌ)dɪs —**dysfunction** (ˌ)dɪs ˈfʌŋ*k* ʃᵊn
Dysart ˈdaɪz ət ˈdaɪs-, -ɑːt ‖ -ɑːrt
dysarthria dɪs ˈɑːθ ri‿ə ‖ -ˈɑːrθ-
dyscalculia ˌdɪs kæl ˈkjuːl i‿ə
dysentery ˈdɪs ᵊntr i ˈdɪs ᵊnt ər i, §-ᵊn ter i ‖ ˈdɪs ᵊn ter i
dysfunction (ˌ)dɪs ˈfʌŋ*k* ʃᵊn **~al** ‿əl **~s** z
dyslalia dɪs ˈleɪl i‿ə -ˈlæl- **~s** z
dyslectic (ˌ)dɪs ˈlekt ɪk **~s** s
dyslexia (ˌ)dɪs ˈleks i‿ə
dyslexic (ˌ)dɪs ˈleks ɪk **~s** s
dysmenorrhea, dysmenorrhoea ˌdɪs ˌmen ə ˈrɪə ‖ -ˈriː ə
Dyson ˈdaɪs ᵊn
dyspepsia dɪs ˈpeps i‿ə ‖ -ˈpep ʃə
dyspeptic dɪs ˈpept ɪk **~ally** ᵊl‿i **~s** s
dysphagia dɪs ˈfeɪdʒ i‿ə -ˈfeɪdʒ ə
dysphasia dɪs ˈfeɪz i‿ə -ˈfeɪʒ-, -ˈfeɪʒ i‿ə ‖ -ˈfeɪʒ ə -ˈfeɪʒ i‿ə, -ˈfeɪz i‿ə
dysphasic dɪs ˈfeɪz ɪk **~s** s
dysphonia dɪs ˈfəʊn i‿ə ‖ -ˈfoʊn-
dysphonic dɪs ˈfɒn ɪk ‖ -ˈfɑːn ɪk **~s** s
dysplasia dɪs ˈpleɪz i‿ə ‖ -ˈpleɪʒ ə -ˈpleɪʒ i‿ə, -ˈpleɪz i‿ə
dyspnea, dyspnoea dɪs*p* ˈniː‿ə
dyspraxia dɪs ˈpræks i‿ə
dyspraxic dɪs ˈpræks ɪk
dysprosium dɪs ˈprəʊz i‿əm -ˈprəʊs- ‖ -ˈproʊz- -ˈproʊʒ-, -ˈproʊs-, -ˈproʊʃ-
dystopia (ˌ)dɪs ˈtəʊp i‿ə ‖ -ˈtoʊp- **~s** z
dystrophy ˈdɪs trəf i
dysuria dɪs ˈjʊər i‿ə ˌdɪs juᵊ ˈriː‿ə ‖ -ˈjʊr- dɪʃ-
dziggetai ˈdʒɪg ə taɪ ˈdzɪg-, ˈzɪg-, -ɪ-, ˌ·ˈ·ˈ· **~s** z

Ee

e Spelling-to-sound

1 Where the spelling is **e**, the pronunciation differs according to whether the vowel is short or long, followed or not by **r**, and strong or weak.

2 The 'strong' pronunciation is regularly
e as in **dress** dres ('short E') or
iː as in **cathedral** kə ˈθiːdr əl ('long E').

3 Where **e** is followed by **r**, the 'strong' pronunciation is
ɜː ‖ ɜ˞ː as in **serve** sɜːv ‖ sɜ˞ːv or
ɪə ‖ ɪ as in **severe** sə ˈvɪə ‖ sə ˈvɪr
or, indeed, there may be the regular 'short' pronunciation
e as in **very** ˈver i.

4 The 'weak' pronunciation is
ɪ as in **wasted** ˈweɪst ɪd or
i as in **review** ri ˈvjuː
(although some speakers use ə instead, thus ˈweɪst əd, rə ˈvjuː) or
ə as in **agent** ˈeɪdʒ ənt (especially where the spelling is **el, ence, ent, er**).

5 Less frequently, the 'strong' pronunciation is
ɪ in the exceptional words **pretty** ˈprɪt i ‖ ˈprɪţ i, **England**, **English** ˈɪŋ-
eə ‖ e in **where** weə ‖ wer, **there** ðeə ‖ ðer (strong forms), and a few others
eɪ, in foreign borrowings such as **suede** sweɪd, and often also in words ending in **-eity**, **-eic** as in **deity** ˈdeɪ- (also ˈdiː-), **nucleic** -ˈkleɪ-
and, in BrE only, ɑː in **clerk** klɑːk, **Derby** ˈdɑːb i, and a few others.

6 **e** is frequently silent. At the end of a word, for example, it is silent if it follows a consonant letter as in **make** meɪk, **life** laɪf, **these** ðiːz, **nice** naɪs, **orange** -ndʒ, **face** feɪs, **huge** hjuːdʒ, **collapse** kə ˈlæps, **twelve** twelv. In this position it may have the function of indicating that the vowel before the consonant is long (**make, life, these**); or that **c** or **g** is 'soft' (**notice, orange**); or both of these (**face, huge**); or neither (**collapse, twelve**).

7 In a few cases at the end of a word after a consonant, the pronunciation is i as in **apostrophe** ə ˈpɒs trəf i ‖ ə ˈpɑːs trəf i.

8 **e** also forms part of the digraphs **ea, ee, ei, eu, ew, ey**.

E

ea Spelling-to-sound

1 Where the spelling is the digraph **ea**, there are several different pronunciations. The most usual are

iː as in **tea** tiː, and

e as in **bread** bred.

Less frequent are

eɪ, notably in **great** ɡreɪt, **steak** steɪk, **break** breɪk

ɪə ‖ iːə, notably in **idea** aɪ ˈdɪə ‖ aɪ ˈdiː ə, **theatre** ˈθɪət ə ‖ ˈθiː ət̬ ər.

2 Where **ea** is followed by **r**, the pronunciation is regularly

ɪə ‖ ɪ as in **near** nɪə ‖ nɪr.

Less frequently it is

ɜː ‖ ɜː as in **early** ˈɜːl i ‖ ˈɜːl i and several others

ɑː notably in **heart** hɑːt ‖ hɑːrt, **hearth**

eə ‖ e notably in **bear** beə ‖ ber, **pear** peə ‖ per, **swear** sweə ‖ swer, **wear** weə ‖ wer, and one meaning of **tear**.

3 **ea** is not a digraph in words such as **creation**, **react**, **area**.

ee Spelling-to-sound

1 Where the spelling is the digraph **ee**, the pronunciation is regularly

iː as in **tree** triː

or, before **r**,

ɪə ‖ ɪ as in **beer** bɪə ‖ bɪr.

2 Exceptionally, the pronunciation is ɪ in AmE **been** bɪn (sometimes also in BrE) and sometimes in **Greenwich** (although here many speakers use e).

3 At the end of a few words the pronunciation is weak i as in **coffee** ˈkɒfi ‖ ˈkɔːfi.

ei, ey Spelling-to-sound

1 Where the spelling is one of the digraphs **ei**, **ey**, the pronunciation is most frequently

eɪ as in **veil** veɪl, **convey** kən ˈveɪ.

2 Less frequently, it is

iː as in **receive** ri ˈsiːv, **key** kiː,

and in a few words

aɪ as in **height** haɪt, **eye** aɪ or

e as in **heifer** ˈhef ə ‖ ˈhef ər, **Reynolds** ˈren əldz.

E

3 Where the spelling is **ei** before **r**, the pronunciation is either
eə ‖ e as in **their** ðeə ‖ ðer or
ɪə ‖ ɪ as in **weird** wɪəd ‖ wɪrd.

4 The exceptional **either**, **neither** may have aɪ or iː, with BrE preferring the former and AmE the latter.

5 **ei** is not a digraph in words such as **atheism**, **deity**.

eu, ew Spelling-to-sound

1 Where the spelling is one of the digraphs **eu**, **ew**, the pronunciation is regularly
juː as in **feudal** ˈfjuːd əl, **few** fjuː or
uː as in **rheumatism** ˈruːm ə tɪz əm, **crew** kruː.
(For the dropping of j, see **u** 3.)

2 Exceptionally, it is also
əʊ ‖ oʊ as in **sew** səʊ ‖ soʊ
ɜː ‖ uː in French words as in **masseuse** mæ ˈsɜːz ‖ mə ˈsuːs or
ɔɪ in German-derived words as in **Freudian** ˈfrɔɪd i ən.
Note also **lieutenant**, BrE lef ˈten ənt.

3 Where the spelling is **eu** before **r**, the pronunciation is regularly
jʊə ‖ jʊ as in **Europe** ˈjʊər əp ‖ ˈjʊr əp,
or when weak
ju as in **neurology** nju ˈrɒl ədʒ i ‖ -ˈrɑːl-.

E, e *name of letter* iː **Es, E's, e's** iːz —*Communications code name:* Echo
ˈE ˌnumber
e *Latin prepn* eɪ iː —*See also phrases with this word*
each iːtʃ
(ˌ)each ˈother; **ˌeach ˈway◂**
Eadie ˈiːd i
Eads iːdz
Eady ˈiːd i
eager ˈiːg ə ‖ -ər **~ly** li **~ness** nəs nɪs
ˌeager ˈbeaver
eagle, Eagle ˈiːg əl **~s** z
eagle-eyed ˌiːg əl ˈaɪd ◂
eaglet ˈiːg lət -lɪt **~s** s
eagre ˈeɪg ə ˈiːg- ‖ -ər **~s** z
Eakins ˈeɪk ɪnz §-ənz
Eakring ˈiːk rɪŋ
Ealing ˈiːl ɪŋ
Eames *(i)* iːmz, *(ii)* eɪmz
Eamon, Eamonn ˈeɪm ən
-ean ˈiː ən, i ən —*In some words this suffix is stressed* (ˌEuroˈpean), *but in others stress-imposing* (Shakeˈspearean). *Both possibilities are heard in* Caribbean.
ear ɪə ‖ ɪər **eared** ɪəd ‖ ɪərd **earing** ˈɪər ɪŋ ‖ ˈɪr ɪŋ **ears** ɪəz ‖ ɪərz
ˈear ˌtrumpet
earache ˈɪər eɪk ‖ ˈɪr-
Eardley ˈɜːd li ‖ ˈɜːd-
eardrop ˈɪə drɒp ‖ ˈɪr drɑːp **~s** s
eardrum ˈɪə drʌm ‖ ˈɪr- **~s** z
eared ɪəd ‖ ɪərd
-eared ˈɪəd ‖ ˈɪərd
earflap ˈɪə flæp ‖ ˈɪr- **~s** s
earful ˈɪə fʊl ‖ ˈɪr-
Earhart ˈeə hɑːt ‖ ˈer hɑːrt
earhole ˈɪə həʊl →-hɒʊl ‖ ˈɪr hoʊl **~s** z
earl, Earl ɜːl ‖ ɜːl **earls, Earl's** ɜːlz ‖ ɜːlz
ˌEarl's ˈCourt; **ˌEarl ˈGrey**

E

earldom 'ɜːl dəm ‖ 'ɝːl- **~s** z

Earle ɜːl ‖ ɝːl

earless 'ɪə ləs -lɪs ‖ 'ɪr-

Earley 'ɜːl i ‖ 'ɝːl i

earli... —*see* **early**

earlobe 'ɪə ləʊb ‖ 'ɪr loʊb **~s** z

earl|y 'ɜːl |i ‖ 'ɝːl |i **~ier** i‿ə ‖ i‿ᵊr **~iest** i‿ɪst i‿əst **~iness** i nəs i nɪs **~ies** iz
'early bird, ˌ· · '·; **ˌearly 'closing day**; **ˌEarly 'English**; **ˌearly 'warning ˌsystem**

earmark 'ɪə mɑːk ‖ 'ɪr mɑːrk **~ed** t **~ing** ɪŋ **~s** s

earmuff 'ɪə mʌf ‖ 'ɪr- **~s** s

earn, Earn ɜːn ‖ ɝːn *(= urn)* **earned** ɜːnd ɜːnt ‖ ɝːnd **earning/s** 'ɜːn ɪŋ/z ‖ 'ɝːn ɪŋ/z **earns** ɜːnz ‖ ɝːnz

earner 'ɜːn ə ‖ 'ɝːn ᵊr **~s** z

earnest 'ɜːn ɪst -əst ‖ 'ɝːn- **~ly** li **~ness** nəs nɪs **~s** s

earnings-related ˌɜːn ɪŋz ri 'leɪt ɪd ◂ -rə'· · ‖ ˌɝːn ɪŋz ri 'leɪţ əd ◂

Earnshaw 'ɜːn ʃɔː ‖ 'ɝːn- -ʃɑː

Earp ɜːp ‖ ɝːp

earphone 'ɪə fəʊn ‖ 'ɪr foʊn **~s** z

earpiec|e 'ɪə piːs ‖ 'ɪr- **~es** ɪz əz

earplug 'ɪə plʌg ‖ 'ɪr- **~s** z

earring 'ɪə rɪŋ 'ɪər ɪŋ ‖ 'ɪr ɪŋ -rɪŋ **~s** z

earshot 'ɪə ʃɒt ‖ 'ɪr ʃɑːt

ear-splitting 'ɪə ˌsplɪt ɪŋ ‖ 'ɪr ˌsplɪţ ɪŋ **~ly** li

earth ɜːθ ‖ ɝːθ **earthed** ɜːθt ‖ ɝːθt **earthing** 'ɜːθ ɪŋ ‖ 'ɝːθ ɪŋ **earths** *v* ɜːθs ‖ ɝːθs **earths** *n pl* ɜːθs ɜːðz ‖ ɝːθs **earth's** ɜːθs ‖ ɝːθs
'earth ˌcloset; **'earth ˌsatellite**; **'earth ˌscience**

Eartha 'ɜːθ ə ‖ 'ɝːθ ə

earthborn 'ɜːθ bɔːn ‖ 'ɝːθ bɔːrn

earthbound 'ɜːθ baʊnd ‖ 'ɝːθ-

earthen 'ɜːθ ᵊn 'ɜːð- ‖ 'ɝːθ-

earthenware 'ɜːθ ᵊn weə 'ɜːð- ‖ 'ɝːθ ᵊn wer -wær

earthi... —*see* **earthy**

earthling 'ɜːθ lɪŋ ‖ 'ɝːθ- **~s** z

earthly 'ɜːθ li ‖ 'ɝːθ-

earth|man 'ɜːθ |mæn ‖ 'ɝːθ- **~men** men

earthnut 'ɜːθ nʌt ‖ 'ɝːθ- **~s** s

earthquake 'ɜːθ kweɪk ‖ 'ɝːθ- **~s** s

earthshaking 'ɜːθ ˌʃeɪk ɪŋ ‖ 'ɝːθ-

earthshattering 'ɜːθ ˌʃæt ər ɪŋ ‖ 'ɝːθ ˌʃæţ ər ɪŋ **~ly** li

earthstar 'ɜːθ stɑː ‖ 'ɝːθ stɑːr **~s** z

earthward 'ɜːθ wəd ‖ 'ɝːθ wᵊrd **~s** z

earthwork 'ɜːθ wɜːk ‖ 'ɝːθ wɝːk **~s** s

earthworm 'ɜːθ wɜːm ‖ 'ɝːθ wɝːm **~s** z

earth|y 'ɜːθ |i ‖ 'ɝːθ |i **~ier** i‿ə ‖ i‿ᵊr **~iest** i‿ɪst i‿əst **~iness** i nəs i nɪs

earwax 'ɪə wæks ‖ 'ɪr-

earwig 'ɪə wɪg ‖ 'ɪr- **~s** z

earworm 'ɪə wɜːm ‖ 'ɪr wɝːm **~s** z

Easdale 'iːz deɪᵊl

ease iːz **eased** iːzd **eases** 'iːz ɪz -əz **easing** 'iːz ɪŋ

easeful 'iːz fᵊl -fʊl **~ly** i **~ness** nəs nɪs

easel 'iːz ᵊl **~s** z

easement 'iːz mənt **~s** s

easi... —*see* **easy**

easily 'iːz ɪ li -əl i

Easington 'iːz ɪŋ tən

Eason 'iːs ᵊn

east, East iːst
ˌEast 'Anglia; **ˌEast 'End**; **ˌEast 'Indies**; **ˌEast 'London**

eastbound 'iːst baʊnd

Eastbourne 'iːst bɔːn ‖ -bɔːrn -boʊrn

Eastcheap 'iːst tʃiːp

East Ender, Eastender ˌiːst 'end ə ‖ -ᵊr **~s** z

Easter 'iːst ə ‖ -ᵊr **~s** z
ˌEaster 'Day; **'Easter egg**; **'Easter ˌIsland** ‖ ˌ· '· ·; **ˌEaster 'Sunday**

Easterbrook 'iːst ə brʊk §-bruːk ‖ -ᵊr-

easterly 'iːst əl i ‖ -ᵊr li **easterlies** 'iːst əl iz ‖ -ᵊr liz

eastern 'iːst ən ‖ -ᵊrn

Easterner, e~ 'iːst ən ə ‖ -ᵊrn ᵊr -ən ᵊr **~s** z

easternmost 'iːst ən məʊst →-əm- ‖ -ᵊrn moʊst

Eastertide 'iːst ə taɪd ‖ -ᵊr- **~s** z

easting 'iːst ɪŋ **~s** z

Eastleigh ˌiːst 'liː ◂ '· ·

Eastman 'iːst mən

east-northeast ˌiːst nɔːθ 'iːst ‖ -nɔːrθ- —*also naut* -nɔːr- ‖ -nɔːr-

Easton 'iːst ən

east-southeast ˌiːst saʊθ 'iːst —*also naut* -saʊ-

eastward 'iːst wəd ‖ -wᵊrd **~ly** li **~s** z

East-West ˌiːst 'west ◂

Eastwood 'iːst wʊd

eas|y 'iːz |i **~ier** i‿ə ‖ i‿ᵊr **~iest** i‿ɪst i‿əst **~ily** ɪ li əl i **~iness** i nəs i nɪs
ˌeasy 'chair, '· · ·; **'easy street**; **ˌeasy 'terms**; **ˌeasy 'virtue**

easygoing ˌiːz i 'gəʊ ɪŋ ◂ ‖ -'goʊ ɪŋ ◂

easyJet *tdmk* 'iːz i dʒet

easy-peasy ˌiːz i 'piːz i ◂

eat iːt **ate** et eɪt ‖ eɪt ⚠et **eaten** 'iːt ᵊn **eating** 'iːt ɪŋ ‖ 'iːţ ɪŋ **eats** iːts
'eating ˌapple; **'eating disˌorder**

eatable 'iːt əb ᵊl ‖ 'iːţ- **~s** z

eaten 'iːt ᵊn

eater 'iːt ə ‖ 'iːţ ᵊr **~s** z

eater|y 'iːt ər |i ‖ 'iːţ- **~ies** iz

eating-|house 'iːt ɪŋ |haʊs ‖ 'iːţ- **~houses** haʊz ɪz -əz

eating-plac|e 'iːt ɪŋ pleɪs ‖ 'iːţ- **~es** ɪz əz

Eaton 'iːt ᵊn
ˌEaton 'Socon 'səʊk ən ‖ 'soʊk-

eau əʊ ‖ oʊ —*Fr* [o]
ˌeau de co'logne də kə 'ləʊn di- ‖ -'loʊn —*Fr* [od kɔ lɔɲ]; **ˌeau de 'nil** də 'niːᵊl —*Fr* [od nil]; **ˌeau de toi'lette** —*Fr* [ot twa lɛt]; **ˌeau de 'vie** də 'viː —*Fr* [od vi]

eaves, Eaves iːvz

eavesdrop 'iːvz drɒp ‖ -drɑːp **~ped** t **~per/s** ə/z ‖ ᵊr/z **~ping** ɪŋ **~s** s

e-banking 'iː ˌbæŋk ɪŋ

eBay 'iː beɪ

ebb eb **ebbed** ebd **ebbing** 'eb ɪŋ **ebbs** ebz
ˌebb 'tide, 'ˑ ˑ
Ebbsfleet 'ebz fliːt
Ebbw 'eb u -ə
ˌEbbw 'Vale
EBCDIC 'eb si dɪk
Ebenezer ˌeb ə 'niːz ə ◂ -ɪ- ‖ -ᵊr 'ˑ ˑ ˑ ˑ
Ebla 'eb lɪs §-ləs
Ebola i 'bəʊl ə ‖ i 'boʊl ə
Ebon 'eb ən
Ebonics i 'bɒn ɪks ‖ -'bɑːn-
Ebonite 'eb ə naɪt
Ebon|y, Ebony 'eb ən |i **~ies** iz
e-book 'iː bʊk **~s** s
Ebor 'iːb ɔː ‖ -ɔːr
Eboracum i 'bɒr ək əm ˌiːb ɔː 'rɑːk- ‖ i 'bɔːr-
i 'bɑːr-
Ebro 'iːb rəʊ 'eb- ‖ -roʊ 'eɪb- —*Sp* ['e βɾo]
ebullience i 'bʌl i‿ən*t*s ə-, -'bʊl-
ebullient i 'bʌl i‿ənt ə-, -'bʊl- **~ly** li
ebullition ˌeb ə 'lɪʃ ᵊn -ʊ-
Ebury 'iːb ər‿i
EC ˌiː 'siː
écarte, écarté eɪ 'kɑːt eɪ ‖ ˌeɪ kɑːr 'teɪ —*Fr* [e kaʁ te]
Ecbatana ek 'bæt ən ə ˌek bə 'tɑːn ə
‖ ek 'bæt ᵊn ə
Ecce Homo ˌek eɪ 'həʊm əʊ ˌeks-, ˌetʃ-, -i-,
-'hɒm- ‖ -'hoʊm oʊ
eccentric ɪk 'sentr ɪk ek-, ək- **~ally** ᵊl‿i **~s** s
eccentricit|y ˌeks en 'trɪs ət |i ˌ-ᵊn-, -ɪt i
‖ -əṭ |i **~ies** iz
Ecclefechan ˌek ᵊl 'fek ən -'fex-
Eccles 'ek ᵊlz
'Eccles cake
ecclesia ɪ 'kliːz i‿ə
Ecclesiastes ɪ ˌkliːz i 'æst iːz ə-
ecclesiastic ɪ ˌkliːz i 'æst ɪk ◂ ə- **~al** ᵊl **~ally**
ᵊl‿i **~s** s
ecclesiasticism ɪ ˌkliːz i 'æst ɪ ˌsɪz əm ə-, -'ˑə-
Ecclesiasticus ɪ ˌkliːz i 'æst ɪk əs ə-
ecclesio- *comb. form*
with stress-neutral suffix ɪ ¦kliːz i‿ə ə-
— **ecclesiological** ɪ ˌkliːz i‿ə 'lɒdʒ ɪk ᵊl ◂ ə-
‖ -'lɑːdʒ-
with stress-imposing suffix ɪ ˌkliːz i 'ɒ+ ə-
‖ ɪ ˌkliːz i 'ɑː+ — **ecclesiology**
ɪ ˌkliːz i 'ɒl ədʒ i ə- ‖ -'ɑːl-
Eccleston 'ek ᵊlst ən
eccrine 'ek rɪn -riːn, -rən, -raɪn
ecdysiast ek 'dɪz i æst **~s** s
ECG ˌiː siː 'dʒiː **~s, ~'s** z
echelon 'eʃ ə lɒn 'eɪʃ- ‖ -lɑːn **~ed** d **~ing** ɪŋ **~s**
z
echeveria, E~ ˌetʃ ɪ 'vɪər i‿ə ˌ-ə-
‖ ˌetʃ əv ə 'riː ə ˌeɪtʃ- **~s** z
echid|na i 'kɪd |nə ə-, e- **~nae** niː **~nas** nəz
echinacea ˌek ɪ 'neɪʃ ə -ə-, ˌˑˑ'eɪs i‿ə
echinoderm i 'kaɪn əʊ dɜːm ə-, -'kɪn-
‖ -ə dɜːm **~s** z
echin|us i 'kaɪn |əs ə-, e-; 'ek ɪn-, -ən- **~i** aɪ
echo, Echo 'ek əʊ ‖ -oʊ **~ed** d **~er/s** ə/z ‖ ᵊr/z
~es z **~ing** ɪŋ

echocardiogram ˌek əʊ 'kɑːd i‿əʊ ɡræm
‖ -oʊ 'kɑːrd i‿ə- **~s** z
echoey 'ek əʊ i ‖ -oʊ i
echoic e 'kəʊ ɪk i-, ə- ‖ -'koʊ- **~ally** ᵊl‿i
echolalia ˌek əʊ 'leɪl i‿ə ‖ ˌˑoʊ-
echolocation ˌek əʊ ləʊ 'keɪʃ ᵊn ‖ -oʊ loʊ-
echt ext ekt —*Ger* [ʔɛçt]
Eckersley 'ek əz li ‖ -ᵊrz-
Eckhart 'ek hɑːt ‖ -hɑːrt —*Ger* ['ʔɛk haʁt]
eclair, éclair i 'kleə eɪ-, 'eɪk leə ‖ eɪ 'kleᵊr i-,
-'klæᵊr —*Fr* [e klɛːʁ] **~s** z
eclampsia ɪ 'klæmps i‿ə e-, ə-
eclat, éclat eɪ 'klɑː 'eɪk lɑː —*Fr* [e kla]
eclectic ɪ 'klekt ɪk e-, ə- **~ally** ᵊl‿i **~s** s
eclecticism ɪ 'klekt ɪ ˌsɪz əm e-, ə-, -ə-
eclips|e ɪ 'klɪps ə-, iː- **~ed** t **~es** ɪz əz **~ing** ɪŋ
eclipsis ɪ 'klɪps ɪs ə-, iː-, §-əs
ecliptic ɪ 'klɪpt ɪk ə-, iː- **~s** s
eclogue 'ek lɒɡ ‖ -lɔːɡ -lɑːɡ **~s** z
Eco 'ek əʊ ‖ -oʊ —*It* ['ɛː ko]
eco- *comb. form* ¦iːk əʊ ¦ek əʊ ‖ ¦iːk oʊ ¦ek-, -ə
— **ecocide** 'iːk əʊ saɪd 'ek- ‖ -ə-
eco-friendly ˌiːk əʊ 'frendli ◂ ˌek- ‖ -oʊ-
E. coli ˌiː 'kəʊl aɪ ‖ -'koʊl-
ecological ˌiːk ə 'lɒdʒ ɪk ᵊl ◂ ˌek- ‖ -'lɑːdʒ- **~ly**
i
ecologist ɪ 'kɒl ədʒ ɪst e-, ə-, iː- ‖ -'kɑːl- **~s** s
ecology i 'kɒl ədʒ i e-, ə- ‖ -'kɑːl-
econometric i ˌkɒn ə 'metr ɪk ◂ ə- ‖ -ˌkɑːn-
~al ᵊl **~s** s
econometrician i ˌkɒn ə me 'trɪʃ ᵊn ə-, iː-,
-mə'-- ‖ -ˌkɑːn ə mə- **~s** z

ECONOMIC

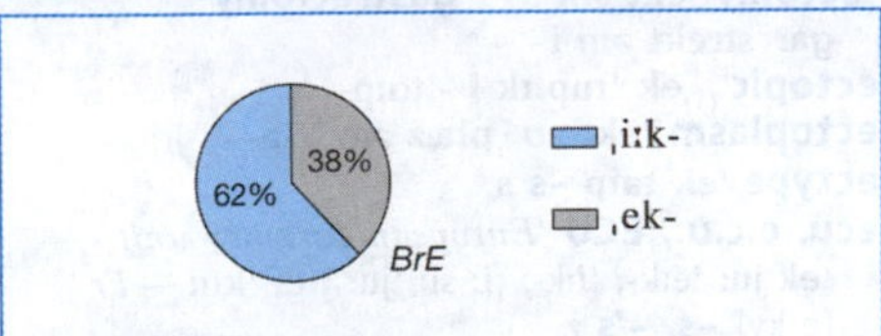

economic ˌiːk ə 'nɒm ɪk ◂ ˌek- ‖ -'nɑːm-
— *Preference poll, BrE:* ˌiːk- *62%,* ˌek- *38%.*
~al ᵊl **~ally** ᵊl‿i **~s** s
economie... —*see* **economy**
economise —*see* **economize**
economist i 'kɒn əm ɪst ə-, §iː-, §-əst ‖ -'kɑːn-
~s s
economiz|e i 'kɒn ə maɪz ə-, §iː- ‖ -'kɑːn- **~ed**
d **~er/s** ə/z ‖ ᵊr/z **~es** ɪz əz **~ing** ɪŋ
econom|y i 'kɒn əm |i ə-, §iː- ‖ -'kɑːn- **~ies** iz
e'conomy class
ecorche, écorché ˌeɪk ɔː 'ʃeɪ ‖ -ɔːr-
Ecorse *place in MI* 'iː kɔːs ɪ 'kɔːs ‖ 'iː kɔːrs
ɪ 'kɔːrs
ecosphere 'iːk əʊ sfɪə 'ek- ‖ -oʊ sfɪr
ecosystem 'iːk əʊ ˌsɪst əm 'ek-, -ɪm ‖ -oʊ- **~s** z
— *Preference poll, BrE:* 'iːk- *88%,* 'ek- *12%.*
See chart on p.262.
ecraseur, écraseur ˌeɪk rɑː 'zɜː ‖ -'zɜ˞ː —*Fr*
[e kʁa zœːʁ] **~s** z
ecru, écru 'eɪk ruː 'ek-

E

ECOSYSTEM

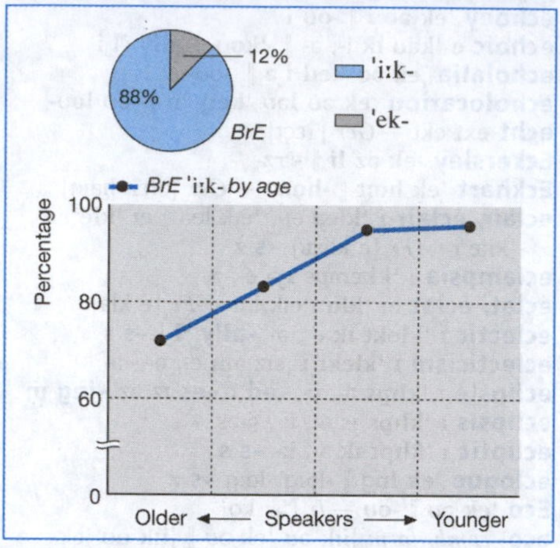

ecstas|y 'ekst əs |i **~ies** iz
ecstatic ɪk 'stæt ɪk ek-, ək- ‖ -'stæţ ɪk **~ally** ᵊl‿i **~s** s
ECT ˌiː siː 'tiː
ecto- *comb. form*
with stress-neutral suffix ¦ekt əʊ ‖ ¦ekt oʊ -ə — **ectogenic** ˌekt əʊ 'dʒen ɪk ◂ ‖ -oʊ- -ə-
with stress-imposing suffix ek 'tɒ+ ‖ ek 'tɑː+ — **ectogenous** ek 'tɒdʒ ən əs -ɪn- ‖ -'tɑːdʒ-
ectoderm 'ekt əʊ dɜːm ‖ -ə dɜ˞ːm **~s** z
ectomorph 'ekt əʊ mɔːf ‖ -ə mɔːrf **~s** s
ectomorphic ˌekt əʊ 'mɔːf ɪk ◂ ‖ -ə 'mɔːrf-
-ectomy 'ekt əm i — **gastrectomy** gæ 'strekt əm i
ectopic (ˌ)ek 'tɒp ɪk ‖ -'tɑːp-
ectoplasm 'ekt əʊ ˌplæz əm ‖ -ə-
ectype 'ek taɪp **~s** s
ecu, e.c.u., ECU *'European currency unit'* 'ek juː 'eɪk-, 'iːk-; ˌiː siː 'juː ‖ eɪ 'kuː —*Fr* [e ky] **~s, ~'s** z
ecu, écu *old coin, 'shield'* 'eɪk juː eɪ 'kjuː ‖ eɪ 'kjuː —*Fr* [e ky] **~s** z
Ecuador 'ek wə dɔː ‖ -dɔːr —*Sp* [e kwa 'ðor]
Ecuadoran ˌek wə 'dɔːr ən ◂ **~s** z
Ecuadorean, Ecuadorian ˌek wə 'dɔːr i‿ən ◂ **~s** z
ecumenical ˌiːk ju 'men ɪk ᵊl ◂ ˌek- ‖ ˌek jə- **~ly** i
ecumenicism ˌiːk ju 'men ɪ ˌsɪz əm -'ə- ‖ ˌek jə-
ecumenism ɪ 'kjuːm ə ˌnɪz əm iː-, 'ek jum-
eczema 'eks ɪm ə -əm‿ə; 'ek zɪm ə ‖ ɪg 'ziːm ə 'egz əm ə, 'eks-
eczematous ek 'sem ət əs ɪk-, -'siːm-; -'zem-, -'ziːm-, ɪg- ‖ ɪg 'zem əţ əs -'ziːm-
Ed ed
-ed, -d t, d, ɪd əd —*This unstressed ending has three regular pronunciations: 1. After* **t** *or* **d** *it is pronounced* **ɪd** *or, less commonly in BrE but regularly in AmE,* **əd**, *as* hated **'heɪt ɪd** ‖ **'heɪţ əd**, needed **'niːd ɪd** ‖ **-əd**. *(In singing, exceptionally, a strong-vowelled variant* **ed** *is usual, as* **'niːd ed**.*)*
2. After the other VOICED consonants or a vowel sound, it is pronounced **d**, *as* called **kɔːld**, seemed **siːmd**, vowed **vaʊd**, tied **taɪd**, feared **fɪəd** ‖ **fɪᵊrd**.
*3. After the other VOICELESS consonants (***p, k, tʃ, f, θ, s, ʃ***), it is pronounced* **t**, *as* gripped **ɡrɪpt**, patched **pætʃt**, knifed **naɪft**.
Certain adjectives have **ɪd, əd** *against these rules, as* wicked **'wɪk ɪd, -əd**. *The same applies also to most words in* -edly, -edness *as* markedly **'mɑːk ɪd li, -əd-** ‖ **'mɑːrk əd li**. *The 'syllabic' pronunciation of the ending formerly applied to all* -ed *formations, and is still heard when people recite older literature, where it may be required for scansion purposes: thus (only in imitated old pronunciation)* seemed **'siːm ɪd**.
Edale 'iː deɪᵊl
Edam 'iːd æm -əm —*Dutch* [eː 'dɑm]
edaphic i 'dæf ɪk ə- **~ally** ᵊl‿i
Edda 'ed ə **~s** z
Eddery 'ed ər i
Eddic 'ed ɪk
Eddie 'ed i
eddie... —*see* **eddy**
Eddington 'ed ɪŋ tən
eddo 'ed əʊ ‖ -oʊ **~es** z
edd|y, Eddy 'ed |i **~ied** id **~ies** iz **~ying** i‿ɪŋ
Eddystone 'ed ɪst ən -əst-; -i stəʊn ‖ -i stoʊn
Ede *family name* iːd
edelweiss 'eɪd ᵊl vaɪs ⚠'aɪd-, -waɪs —*Ger* Edelweiß ['ʔeː dᵊl vais]
edema i 'diːm ə ə- **~s** z
edematous i 'diːm ət əs ə- ‖ -əţ əs
Eden 'iːd ᵊn
Edenbridge 'iːd ᵊn brɪdʒ
Edenfield 'iːd ᵊn fiːᵊld
edentate i 'dent eɪt **~s** s
Edessa i 'des ə
Edexcel ˌed ek 'sel
Edgar 'ed gə →'eg- ‖ -gᵊr
Edgbaston 'edʒ bəst ən -bæst-
edge, Edge edʒ **edged** edʒd **edges** 'edʒ ɪz -əz **edging** 'edʒ ɪŋ
Edgecomb, Edgecombe 'edʒ kəm
-edged 'edʒd — **blunt-edged** ˌblʌnt 'edʒd ◂
Edgehill ˌedʒ 'hɪl —*but as a family name,* '. .
Edgerton 'edʒ ət ən ‖ -ᵊrt ᵊn
edgeways 'edʒ weɪz
edgewise 'edʒ waɪz
Edgeworth 'edʒ wɜːθ -wəθ ‖ -wɜ˞ːθ
edging 'edʒ ɪŋ **~s** z
Edgware 'edʒ weə ‖ -wer
edg|y 'edʒ |i **~ier** i‿ə ‖ i‿ᵊr **~iest** i‿ɪst i‿əst **~ily** ɪ li əl i **~iness** i nəs i nɪs
edh eð **edhs** eðz
Ediacaran ˌiːd i 'æk ər ən ◂ -i‿ə 'kɑːr- ‖ -i‿ə 'kær-
edibility ˌed ə 'bɪl ət i ˌ-ɪ-, -ɪt i ‖ -əţ i
edible 'ed əb ᵊl -ɪb-
edict 'iːd ɪkt **~s** s

die ˈiːd i
dification ˌed ɪf ɪ ˈkeɪʃ ən ˌ·əf-, §-əˈ·-
dific|e ˈed ɪf ɪs -əf-, §-əs **~es** ɪz əz
di|fy ˈed ɪ |faɪ -ə- **~fied** faɪd **~fier/s** faɪ‿ə/z ‖ faɪ‿ər/z **~fies** faɪz **~fying** faɪ ɪŋ
dina *(i)* e ˈdiːn ə ɪ-, *(ii)* i ˈdaɪn ə *—The place in MI is (ii)*
dinburgh ˈed ɪn bər‿ə →ˈ·ɪm-, ˈ·ən-, §-ˌbʌr ə ‖ -ˌbɜː ə -oʊ *—but the place in TX is locally* ˈed ən bɜːg
dington ˈed ɪŋ tən
dison ˈed ɪs ən -əs-
edit ˈed ɪt §-ət **edited** ˈed ɪt ɪd §-ət-, -əd ‖ -əṭ- **editing** ˈed ɪt ɪŋ §-ət- ‖ -əṭ- **edits** ˈed ɪts §-əts
Edith ˈiːd ɪθ -əθ **~'s** s
edition i ˈdɪʃ ən ə- **~s** z
editor ˈed ɪt ə §-ət- ‖ -əṭ ər **~s** z
editorial ˌed ɪ ˈtɔːr i‿əl ◂ ˌ·ə- ‖ -ˈtoʊr- **~ly** i **~s** z
editorialis... *—see* **editorializ...**
editorialization ˌed ɪ ˌtɔːr i‿əl aɪ ˈzeɪʃ ən ˌ·ə-, -ɪˈ·- ‖ -ə ˈzeɪʃ- -ˌtoʊr- **~s** z
editorializ|e ˌed ɪ ˈtɔːr i‿ə laɪz ˌ·ə- ‖ -ˈtoʊr- **~ed** d **~er/s** ə/z ‖ ər/z **~es** ɪz əz **~ing** ɪŋ
editorship ˈed ɪt ə ʃɪp ‖ -əṭ ər- **~s** s
-edly ɪd li əd li — **designedly** di ˈzaɪn ɪd li də-, -əd-
Edmead, Edmeade ˈed miːd →ˈeb-
Edmond ˈed mənd →ˈeb-
Edmonds ˈed mən*d*z →ˈeb-
Edmondson ˈed mən*d* sən →ˈeb-
Edmonton ˈed mən tən →ˈeb-
Edmund ˈed mənd →ˈeb- **~s** z
Edmundson ˈed mən*d* sən →ˈeb-
Edna ˈed nə
Ednyfed ed ˈnʌv ɪd -ed, §-əd *—Welsh* [ed ˈnə ved]
Edo ˈed əʊ ‖ -oʊ *—Jp* [e ˌdo]
Edom ˈiːd əm
Edomite ˈiːd ə maɪt **~s** s
Edrich ˈedr ɪtʃ
Edridge ˈedr ɪdʒ
Edsel ˈed səl
educability ˌed jʊk ə ˈbɪl ət i ˌedʒ ʊk-, ˌedʒ ək-, -ɪt i ‖ ˌedʒ ək ə ˈbɪl əṭ i
educable ˈed jʊk əb əl ˈedʒ ʊk-, ˈedʒ ək- ‖ ˈedʒ ək-
edu|cate ˈed ju |keɪt ˈedʒ u-, ˈedʒ ə- ‖ ˈedʒ ə- **~cated** keɪt ɪd -əd ‖ keɪṭ əd **~cates** keɪts **~cating** keɪt ɪŋ ‖ keɪṭ ɪŋ
education ˌed ju ˈkeɪʃ ən ˌedʒ u-, ˌedʒ ə- ‖ ˌedʒ ə- **~s** z
educational ˌed ju ˈkeɪʃ ən‿əl ◂ ˌedʒ u-, ˌedʒ ə- ‖ ˌedʒ ə- **~ly** i
educationalist ˌed ju ˈkeɪʃ ən‿əl ɪst ˌedʒ u-, ˌedʒ ə-, §-əst ‖ ˌedʒ ə- **~s** s
educative ˈed jʊk ət ɪv ˈedʒ ʊk-, ˈedʒ ək-; ˈed ju keɪt ɪv, ˈedʒ u-, ˈedʒ ə- ‖ ˈedʒ ə keɪṭ ɪv
educator ˈed ju keɪt ə ˈedʒ u-, ˈedʒ ə- ‖ ˈedʒ ə keɪṭ ər **~s** z
educ|e i ˈdjuːs ə-, →-ˈdʒuːs ‖ -ˈduːs -ˈdjuːs **~ed** t **~es** ɪz əz **~ing** ɪŋ
eduction ɪ ˈdʌk ʃən ə-, iː- **~s** z
edutainment ˌed ju ˈteɪn mənt ˌedʒ u-, ˌedʒ ə-, →-ˈteɪm- ‖ ˌedʒ ə-
Edward ˈed wəd ‖ -wərd
Edwardes ˈed wədz ‖ -wərdz
Edwardian ed ˈwɔːd i‿ən -ˈwɑːd- ‖ -ˈwɔːrd- -ˈwɑːrd-
Edwards ˈed wədz ‖ -wərdz
Edwin ˈed wɪn §-wən
Edwina ed ˈwiːn ə
Edwinstowe ˈed wɪn stəʊ §-wən- ‖ -stoʊ
-ee iː, eɪ, i *—Where this is a genuine suffix, it is usually stressed, as* ˌpayˈee, ˌabsenˈtee. *In words spelt -ee where it is not a genuine suffix, it may be stressed* (ˌrefeˈree)*; or unstressed but strong* (ˈpedigree **-griː**)*; or weak* (committee kə ˈmɪt i ‖ -ˈmɪṭ i)*. If alternatively spelt -ée, it is pronounced* eɪ *(see next entry).*
-ee, -ée eɪ *—Often unstressed in BrE, but usually stressed in AmE, as* matinee ˈ· · · ‖ ˌ· ·ˈ·, fiancee ·ˈ· · ‖ ˌ· ·ˈ·
EEC ˌiː iː ˈsiː
EEG ˌiː iː ˈdʒiː **~s** z
eek iːk
eel iːəl **eels** iːəlz
eelgrass ˈiːəl grɑːs §-græs ‖ -græs
eelpout ˈiːəl paʊt **~s** s
eelworm ˈiːəl wɜːm ‖ -wɜːm **~s** z
-een ˈiːn — **velveteen** ˌvelv ə ˈtiːn -ə-
e'en iːn
eeny meeny miny mo ˌiːn i ˌmiːn i ˌmaɪn i ˈməʊ ‖ -ˈmoʊ
-eer ˈɪə ‖ ˈɪər — *This suffix is stressed:* **mountaineer** ˌmaʊnt ɪ ˈnɪə -ə- ‖ -ən ˈɪər
e'er eə ‖ eər æər *(=air)*
eer|ie ˈɪər |i ‖ ˈɪr |i **~ier** i‿ə ‖ i‿ər **~iest** i‿ɪst i‿əst **~ily** əl i ɪ li **~iness** i nəs i nɪs
Eeyore ˈiː ɔː ‖ -ɔːr
eff ef **effed** eft **effing** ˈef ɪŋ **effs** efs
effable ˈef əb əl
effac|e i ˈfeɪs e-, ə- **~ed** t **~es** ɪz əz **~ing** ɪŋ
effaceable i ˈfeɪs əb əl e-, ə-
effacement i ˈfeɪs mənt e-, ə-
effect əˈfekt i- **~ed** ɪd əd **~ing** ɪŋ **~s** s
effective ə ˈfekt ɪv i- **~ly** li **~ness** nəs nɪs
effectual i ˈfek tʃu‿əl ə-, -tju‿əl **~ly** i
effectu|ate i ˈfek tʃu |eɪt ə-, -tju- **~ated** eɪt ɪd -əd ‖ eɪṭ əd **~ates** eɪts **~ating** eɪt ɪŋ ‖ eɪṭ ɪŋ
effectuation i ˌfek tʃu ˈeɪʃ ən ə-, -tju-
effeminacy i ˈfem ɪn əs i ə-, e-, -ˈ·ən-
effeminate i ˈfem ɪn ət ə-, e-, -ˈ·ən-, -ɪt **~ly** li **~s** s
effendi, E~ e ˈfend i i-, ə- **~s** z
efferent ˈef ər ənt ˈiːf-, -er-
effervesc|e ˌef ə ˈves ‖ -ər- **~ed** t **~es** ɪz əz **~ing** ɪŋ
effervescence ˌef ə ˈves ənts ‖ -ər-
effervescent ˌef ə ˈves ənt ◂ ‖ -ər- **~ly** li
effete i ˈfiːt e-, ə- **~ly** li **~ness** nəs nɪs
efficacious ˌef ɪ ˈkeɪʃ əs ◂ -ə- **~ly** li **~ness** nəs nɪs
efficacity ˌef ɪ ˈkæs ət i ˌ·ə-, -ɪt i ‖ -əṭ i
efficacy ˈef ɪk əs i ˈ·ək-

efficienc|y ə 'fɪʃ ᵊnᵗs |i i- **~ies** iz
ef'ficiency bar
efficient ə 'fɪʃ ᵊnt i- **~ly** li
Effie 'ef i
effig|y 'ef ɪdʒ |i -ədʒ- **~ies** iz
Effingham *(i)* 'ef ɪŋ əm §-həm, *(ii)* -hæm *—The place in England is (i), those in the US (ii)*
effleurage 'ef lɜː rɑːʒ -ə-, ˌ·-'· ‖ ˌef lə 'rɑːʒ *—Fr* [ɛ flœ ʁaːʒ]
effloresc|e ˌef lə 'res -lɔː- **~ed** t **~es** ɪz əz **~ing** ɪŋ
efflorescenc|e ˌef lə 'res ᵊnᵗs -lɔː- **~es** ɪz əz
efflorescent ˌef lə 'res ᵊnt ◂ -lɔː-
effluence 'ef lu‿ənᵗs
effluent 'ef lu‿ənt **~s** s
effluvi|um ɪ 'fluːv i‿|əm e-, ə- **~a** ə **~al** əl **~ums** əmz
efflux 'ef lʌks **~es** ɪz əz
effort 'ef ət ‖ -ᵊrt -ɔːrt **~s** s
effortless 'ef ət ləs -lɪs ‖ -ᵊrt- **~ly** li **~ness** nəs nɪs
effronter|y ɪ 'frʌnt ər |i e-, ə- ‖ -'frʌnṭ- **~ies** iz
effulgence i 'fʌldʒ ənᵗs e-, ə-, -'fʊldʒ-
effulgent i 'fʌldʒ ənt e-, ə-, -'fʊldʒ- **~ly** li
effusion i 'fjuːʒ ᵊn e-, ə- **~s** z
effusive i 'fjuːs ɪv e-, ə-, §-'fjuːz- **~ly** li **~ness** nəs nɪs
Efik 'ef ɪk **~s** s
e-fit 'iː fɪt **~s** s
EFL ˌiː ef 'el
eft eft **efts** efts
EFTA 'eft ə
e.g. ˌiː 'dʒiː *or as* for example
egad i 'gæd
egalitarian i ˌgæl ɪ 'teər i‿ən ə-, -ə'-·; ˌiːg æl- ‖ -'ter- **~ism** ˌɪz əm **~s** z
Egan 'iːg ən
Egbert 'eg bɜːt -bət ‖ -bɜ˞ːt
Egeria i 'dʒɪər i‿ə ‖ -'dʒɪr-
Egerton 'edʒ ət ən ‖ -ᵊrt ᵊn
egest i 'dʒest **~ed** ɪd əd **~ing** ɪŋ **~s** s
Egeus ɪ 'dʒiː‿əs iː-; 'iːdʒ uːs, -juːs
egg eg **egged** egd **egging** 'eg ɪŋ **eggs** egz
ˌegg and 'spoon race; **ˌegg 'roll** ‖ '· ·; **'egg ˌtimer**; **'egg white**
eggar, Eggar 'eg ə ‖ -ᵊr **~s** z
eggbeater 'eg ˌbiːt ə ‖ -ˌbiːṭ ᵊr **~s** z
egg-bound 'eg baʊnd
eggcorn 'eg kɔːn ‖ -kɔːrn **~s** z
eggcup 'eg kʌp **~s** s
egghead 'eg hed **~s** z
Egginton 'eg ɪn tən
Eggleton 'eg ᵊl tən
eggnog ˌeg 'nɒg '· · ‖ 'eg nɑːg **~s** z
eggplant 'eg plɑːnt §-plænt ‖ -plænt **~s** s
eggshell 'eg ʃel **~s** z
eggwhisk 'eg wɪsk -hwɪsk **~s** s
Egham 'eg əm
egis 'iːdʒ ɪs §-əs
eglantine 'eg lən taɪn -tiːn **~s** z
Eglon 'eg lɒn ‖ -lɑːn
Eglwys 'eg lu ɪs 'eg lɔɪs *—Welsh* ['e glujs]
Egmont 'eg mɒnt -mənt ‖ -mɑːnt
ego 'iːg əʊ 'eg- ‖ -oʊ **~s** z
'ego trip
egocentric ˌiːg əʊ 'sentr ɪk ◂ ˌeg- ‖ -oʊ- **~ally** ᵊl‿i
egocentricity ˌiːg əʊ sen 'trɪs ət i ˌeg-, -sᵊn'-· -ɪt i ‖ -oʊ sen 'trɪs əṭ i
egocentrism ˌiːg əʊ 'sentr ˌɪz əm ˌeg- ‖ -oʊ-
egoism 'iːg əʊ ˌɪz əm 'eg- ‖ -oʊ-
egoist 'iːg əʊ ɪst 'eg-, §-əst ‖ -oʊ- **~s** s
egoistic ˌiːg əʊ 'ɪst ɪk ◂ ˌeg- ‖ -oʊ- **~ally** ᵊl‿i
egomania ˌiːg əʊ 'meɪn i‿ə ˌeg- ‖ ˌ·oʊ-
egomaniac ˌiːg əʊ 'meɪn i æk ˌeg- ‖ ˌ·oʊ- **~s** s
egomaniacal ˌiːg əʊ mə 'naɪ‿ək ᵊl ◂ ˌeg-, -ɪk ᵊ ‖ ˌ·oʊ-
Egon 'iːg ɒn 'eg-, -ən ‖ 'eɪg ɑːn
egotism 'eg əʊ ˌtɪz əm 'iːg- ‖ 'iːg ə-
egotist 'eg əʊt ɪst 'iːg-, §-əst ‖ 'iːg əṭ əst **~s** s

EGOTISTIC

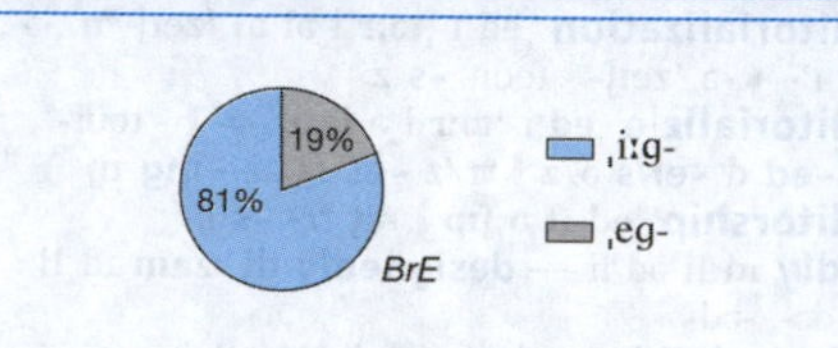

egotistic ˌeg əʊ 'tɪst ɪk ◂ ˌiːg- ‖ ˌiːg ə- *— Preference poll, BrE:* ˌiːg- *81%,* ˌeg- *19%.* **~al** ᵊl **~ally** ᵊl‿i
egregious ɪ 'griːdʒ əs ə-, -'griːdʒ i‿əs **~ly** li **~ness** nəs nɪs
Egremont 'eg rə mənt -rɪ-, -mɒnt ‖ -mɑːnt
egress 'iː gres
egressive i 'gres ɪv *—in contrast to* ingressive, *also* ˌiː-
egret 'iːg rət -rɪt, -ret ‖ 'eg-; iː 'gret, ɪ- **~s** s
Egypt 'iːdʒ ɪpt §-əpt
Egyptian i 'dʒɪp ʃᵊn ə- **~s** z
Egyptological ˌiːdʒ ɪpt ə 'lɒdʒ ɪk ᵊl ◂ §ˌ·əpt-; i ˌdʒɪpt- ‖ -'lɑːdʒ-
Egyptologist ˌiːdʒ ɪp 'tɒl ədʒ ɪst §ˌ·əp-, §-əst ‖ -'tɑːl- **~s** s
Egyptology ˌiːdʒ ɪp 'tɒl ədʒ i §ˌ·əp- ‖ -'tɑːl-
eh eɪ
Ehrlich 'eə lɪk -lɪx ‖ 'er- *—Ger* ['ʔeːɐ lɪç] *—but as an American family name,* 'ɜː- ‖ 'ɜ˞ː-
Eichmann 'aɪk mən 'aɪx- *—Ger* ['ʔaiç man]
Eid iːd
Eid-al-... *—see* Eid-ul-...
eider 'aɪd ə ‖ -ᵊr **~s** z
eiderdown 'aɪd ə daʊn ‖ -ᵊr- **~s** z
eidetic aɪ 'det ɪk ‖ -'deṭ ɪk **~ally** ᵊl‿i
Eid-ul-Adha ˌiːd ʌl 'æd ə -'ʌd ə *—Arabic* [ʕiːd al ʔadˤ 'ħaː]
Eid-ul-Fitr ˌiːd ʌl 'fɪt ə ‖ -fɪṭ ᵊr *—Arabic* [ʕiːd al 'fitˤr]
Eifel, Eiffel 'aɪf ᵊl *—Ger* ['ʔai fᵊl], *Fr* [ɛ fɛl]
ˌEiffel 'Tower
Eifion 'aɪv i ɒn ‖ -ɑːn *—Welsh* ['əiv jon]
eigenfunction 'aɪg ən ˌfʌŋk ʃᵊn →-ŋ- **~s** z
eigenvalue 'aɪg ən ˌvæl juː →-ŋ- **~s** z

iger 'aɪɡ ə ‖ -ᵊr —*Ger* ['ʔai ɡɐ]
igg eɡ
ight eɪt **eights** eɪts
ighteen ˌeɪ 'tiːn ◂ §ˌeɪt-, §ˌeɪt 'iːn
  ˌeighteen 'months
ighteenth ˌeɪ 'tiːnᵗθ ◂ §ˌeɪt-, §ˌeɪt 'iːnᵗθ **~s** s
  ˌeighteenth 'century
ighteen-wheeler ˌeɪ tiːn 'wiːᵊl ə §ˌeɪt-, 'hwiːl- ‖ -ᵊr **~s** z
ightfold 'eɪt fəʊld →-fɒʊld ‖ -foʊld
ighth eɪtθ ‖ eɪθ **eighths** eɪtθs ‖ eɪθs
  'eighth note
eighti... —*see* **eighty**
ightieth 'eɪt i‿əθ §-ti-, ɪθ ‖ 'eɪţ i‿əθ **~s** s
ightsome 'eɪt səm **~s** z
  ˌeightsome 'reel
eight|y 'eɪt |i §'eɪt t|i ‖ 'eɪţ |i **~ies** iz
  ˌeighty-'four◂
Eilat eɪ 'lɑːt
Eilean 'el ən
  ˌEilean 'Donan 'dɒn ən ‖ -'doʊn-
Eileen 'aɪl iːn ‖ ˌaɪ 'liːn ˌeɪ-
Eilidh 'eɪl i
Eiloart 'aɪl əʊ ɑːt ‖ -oʊ ɑːrt
Eindhoven 'aɪnd həʊv ᵊn 'aɪnt- ‖ -hoʊv- —*Dutch* ['ɛint hoː vən]
einkorn 'aɪn kɔːn →'aɪŋ- ‖ -kɔːrn
Einstein 'aɪn staɪn —*Ger* ['ʔain ʃtain]
einsteinium aɪn 'staɪn i‿əm
Eire, Éire 'eər ə ‖ 'er ə 'ær-; 'eɪ rə —*Irish* ['eː rʲə]
eirenicon aɪᵊ 'riːn ɪ kɒn -'ren- ‖ -kɑːn
Eirian 'aɪᵊr i‿ən —*Welsh* ['əir jan]
Eirlys 'aɪ‿ə lɪs -ləs ‖ ᵊr- —*Welsh* ['əir lis, -lis]
Eisenhower 'aɪz ᵊn ˌhaʊ‿ə ‖ -ˌhaʊ‿ᵊr
Eisenstein 'aɪz ᵊn staɪn -ʃtaɪn —*Russ* ['ɛj zʲɪn ʃtʲjn]
eisteddfod aɪ 'steð fəd ɪ-, ə-, -'steð vɒd ‖ -vɑːd —*Welsh* [əi 'sdeð vod] **~s** z

EITHER

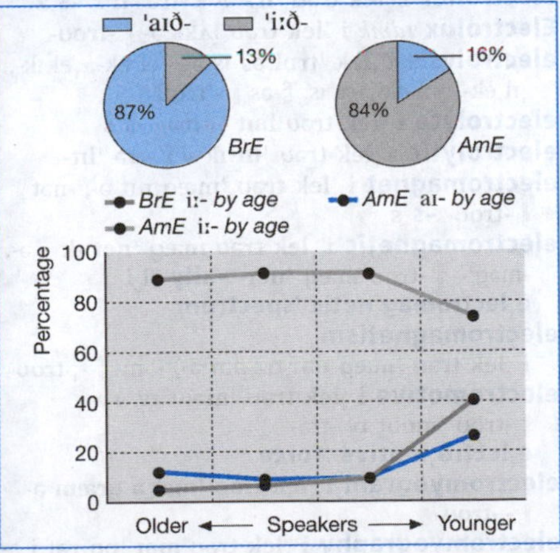

either 'aɪð ə 'iːð- ‖ 'iːð ᵊr 'aɪð- — *Preference polls, BrE:* 'aɪð- *87%,* 'iːð- *13%; AmE:* 'iːð- *84%,* 'aɪð- *16%.*

either-or ˌaɪð ər 'ɔː ˌiːð- ‖ ˌiːð ər 'ɔːr ˌaɪð-
Eithne 'eθ ni —*Irish* ['e hə nə]
ejaculate *n* i 'dʒæk jʊl ət ə-, -jəl-, -ɪt; -ju leɪt, -jə- ‖ -jəl- **~s** s
ejacu|late *v* i 'dʒæk ju |leɪt ə-, -jə- ‖ -jə- **~lated** leɪt ɪd -əd ‖ leɪţ əd **~lates** leɪts **~lating** leɪt ɪŋ ‖ leɪţ ɪŋ
ejaculatio i ˌdʒæk ju 'leɪʃ i əʊ ‖ -jə 'leɪʃ i oʊ
ejaculation i ˌdʒæk ju 'leɪʃ ᵊn ə-, -jə- ‖ -jə- **~s** z
eject i 'dʒekt ə- **~ed** ɪd əd **~ing** ɪŋ **~s** s
ejecta i 'dʒekt ə ə-
ejection i 'dʒek ʃᵊn ə- **~s** z
  e'jection seat
ejective i 'dʒekt ɪv ə- **~ly** li **~s** z
ejectment i 'dʒekt mənt ə- **~s** s
ejector i 'dʒekt ə ə- ‖ -ᵊr **~s** z
  e'jector seat
Ekco *tdmk* 'ek əʊ ‖ -oʊ
eke iːk **eked** iːkt **ekes** iːks **eking** 'iːk ɪŋ
EKG ˌiː keɪ 'dʒiː **~s** z
ekistics i 'kɪst ɪks ə-
Ektachrome *tdmk* 'ekt ə krəʊm ‖ -kroʊm
el el —*See also phrases with this word*
elabo|rate *v* i 'læb ə |reɪt ə- **~rated** reɪt ɪd -əd ‖ reɪţ əd **~rates** reɪts **~rating** reɪt ɪŋ ‖ reɪţ ɪŋ
elaborate *adj* i 'læb ər‿ət ə-, ɪt **~ly** li **~ness** nəs nɪs
elaboration i ˌlæb ə 'reɪʃ ᵊn ə- **~s** z
Elaine ɪ 'leɪn e-, ə-
El Al *tdmk* ˌel 'æl
El Alamein ₍ₗ₎el 'æl ə meɪn ·.·'·
Elam 'iːl əm
Elamite 'iːl ə maɪt **~s** s
elan, élan eɪ 'lɒ̃ i-, -'lɑːn, -'læn; 'eɪl ɒn ‖ eɪ 'lɑːn —*Fr* [e lɑ̃]
  éˌlan vi'tal viː 'tæl -'tɑːl —*Fr* [vi tal]
Elan *valley in Wales* 'iːl ən
Elan *tdmk for car* i' læn eɪ-
eland 'iːl ənd **~s** z
elapid 'el ə pɪd §-æp əd **~s** z
elaps|e i 'læps ə- **~ed** t **~es** ɪz əz **~ing** ɪŋ
elastic i 'læst ɪk ə-, -'lɑːst- **~ally** ᵊl‿i **~s** s
  eˌlastic 'band
elasti|cate i 'læst ɪ |keɪt ə-, -'lɑːst- **~cated** keɪt ɪd -əd ‖ keɪţ əd **~cates** keɪts **~cating** keɪt ɪŋ ‖ keɪţ ɪŋ
elasticity ˌiːl æ 'stɪs ət i ˌel-, ˌ·ɑː-, -ɪt i; i ˌlæ-, ə-, -ˌlɑː- ‖ -əţ i
Elastoplast *tdmk* i 'læst əʊ plɑːst ə-, -'lɑːst-, -plæst ‖ -ə plæst
e|late i |'leɪt ə- **~lated** 'leɪt ɪd -əd ‖ 'leɪţ əd **~lates** 'leɪts **~lating** 'leɪt ɪŋ ‖ 'leɪţ ɪŋ
elated i 'leɪt ɪd ə-, -əd ‖ -'leɪţ əd **~ly** li **~ness** nəs nɪs
elation i 'leɪʃ ᵊn ə-
elative 'iːl ət ɪv i'leɪt- ‖ -əţ- **~s** z
Elba 'elb ə —*It* ['el ba, 'ɛl-]
ElBaradei əl 'bær ə daɪ el-, -deɪ
Elbe elb —*Ger* ['ʔɛl bə]
Elbert 'elb ət ‖ -ᵊrt
elbow 'el bəʊ ‖ -boʊ **~ed** d **~ing** ɪŋ **~s** z
  'elbow grease

elbowroom 'el bəʊ ru:m -rʊm ‖ -boʊ-
Elbrus el 'bru:s -'brʊs, '· · —*Russ* [ɛlʲ 'brus]
El Cajon ˌel kə 'həʊn ‖ -'hoʊn —*Sp* El Cajón [el ka 'xon]
elder, Elder 'eld ə ‖ -ᵊr **~s** z
ˌelder 'brother; **ˌelder 'statesman**
elderberr|y 'eld ə ˌber |i -bər˷|i ‖ -ᵊr ˌber |i **~ies** iz
ˌelderberry 'wine

E

eldercare 'eld ə keə ‖ -ᵊr ker -kær
elderflower 'eld ə ˌflaʊ˷ə ‖ -ᵊr ˌflaʊ˷ᵊr **~s** z
elderl|y 'eld əl |i ‖ -ᵊr l|i **~iness** i nəs i nɪs
eldership 'eld ə ʃɪp ‖ -ᵊr- **~s** s
eldest 'eld ɪst -əst
Eldon 'eld ən
El Dorado ˌel də 'rɑ:d əʊ ‖ -oʊ -'reɪd-
Eldred 'eldr ɪd -ed, -əd
eldrich 'eldr ɪtʃ 'el rɪtʃ
Eldridge 'eldr ɪdʒ
Elea 'i:l i˷ə
Eleanor 'el ən ə -ɪn- ‖ -ᵊr -ə nɔ:r
Eleanora ˌel i˷ə 'nɔ:r ə
Eleatic ˌel i 'æt ɪk ◂ ˌi:l- ‖ -'æţ-
Eleazar ˌel i 'eɪz ə ‖ -ᵊr
elecampane ˌel ɪ kæm 'peɪn ˌ·ə-
elect *adj, n, v* i 'lekt ə- **~ed** ɪd əd **~ing** ɪŋ **~s** s
election i 'lek ʃᵊn ə- **~s** z
electio|neer i ˌlek ʃə |'nɪə ə- ‖ -|'nɪᵊr **~neered** 'nɪəd ‖ 'nɪᵊrd **~neering** 'nɪər ɪŋ ‖ 'nɪr ɪŋ **~neers** 'nɪəz ‖ 'nɪᵊrz
elective i 'lekt ɪv ə- **~ly** li **~s** z
elector i 'lekt ə ə ‖ -ᵊr **~s** z

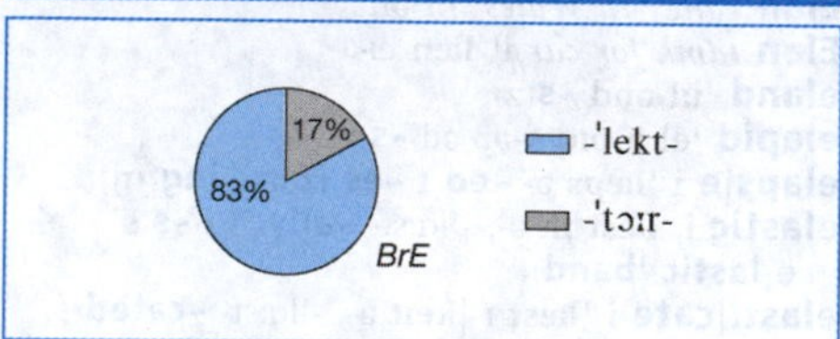

electoral i 'lekt ər əl ə-, →-'lek trəl; -ˌlek 'tɔ:r əl ◂ —*Preference poll, BrE:* -'lekt- *83%,* -'tɔ:r- *17%.* **~ly** i
eˌlectoral 'college
electorate i 'lekt ər˷ət ə-, ɪt **~s** s
Electra i 'lek trə ə-
E'lectra ˌcomplex
electret i 'lek trət ə-, -trɪt, -tret **~s** s
electric i 'lek trɪk ə- **~s** s
eˌlectric 'blanket; **eˌlectric 'chair**; **eˌlectric 'eel**; **eˌlectric 'eye**; **eˌlectric gui'tar**; **eˌlectric 'shock, eˌlectric 'shock ˌtherapy**
electrical i 'lek trɪk ᵊl ə- **~ly** ˷i
eˌlectrical ˌengi'neering
electrician i ˌlek 'trɪʃ ᵊn ə-, ˌel ek-, ˌel ɪk-, ˌɪl ek-, ˌi:l ek-, -'trɪʒ- **~s** z
electricity i ˌlek 'trɪs ət i ə-, ˌel ek-, ˌel ɪk-, ˌɪl ek-, ˌi:l ek-, -'trɪz-, -ɪt i ‖ -əţ i
electrification i ˌlek trɪf ɪ 'keɪʃ ᵊn ə-, -ˌtrəf-, §-ə'·- **~s** z
electri|fy i 'lek trɪ |faɪ ə-, -trə- **~fied** faɪd **~fier/s** faɪ˷ə/z ‖ faɪ˷ᵊr/z **~fies** faɪz **~fying** faɪ ɪŋ
electro- *comb. form*
with stress-neutral suffix i ¦lek trəʊ ə- ‖ i ¦lek troʊ -trə — **electrographic** i ˌlek trəʊ 'græf ɪk ◂ ə- ‖ -troʊ- -trə-
with stress-imposing suffix i ˌlek 'trɒ+ ə-, ˌel ek-, ˌel ɪk-, ˌɪl ek-, ˌi:l ek- ‖ i ˌlek 'trɑ:+ — **electrography** i ˌlek 'trɒg rəf i ə-, ˌel ek-, ˌel ɪk-, ˌɪl ek-, ˌi:l ek- ‖ -'trɑ:g-
electrocardiogram i ˌlek trəʊ 'kɑ:d i˷əʊ græm ə- ‖ -troʊ 'kɑ:rd i˷ə- **~s** z
electrocardiograph i ˌlek trəʊ 'kɑ:d i˷əʊ grɑ:f ə-, -græf ‖ -troʊ 'kɑ:rd i˷ə græf **~s** s
electrocardiography ɪ ˌlek trəʊ ˌkɑ:d i 'ɒg rəf i ə- ‖ -troʊ ˌkɑ:rd i 'ɑ:g-
electroconvulsive iˌlek trəʊ kən 'vʌls ɪv ə- ‖ -ˌtroʊ-
eˌlectroconˌvulsive 'therapy
electro|cute i'lek trə |kju:t ə- **~cuted** kju:t ɪd -əd ‖ kju:ţ əd **~cutes** kju:ts **~cuting** kju:t ɪŋ ‖ kju:ţ ɪŋ
electrocution i ˌlek trə 'kju:ʃ ᵊn ə- **~s** z
electrode i 'lek trəʊd ə- ‖ -troʊd **~s** z
electrodynamic i ˌlek trəʊ daɪ 'næm ɪk ◂ ə-, dɪ'-- ‖ -ˌ·troʊ- **~ally** ᵊl˷i **~s** s
electroencephalogram i ˌlek trəʊ ɪn 'sef əl˷ə græm ə-, -en'--, -'kef-, -əʊ· ‖ -ˌ·troʊ- **~s** z
electroencephalograph i ˌlek trəʊ ɪn 'sef əl˷ə grɑ:f ə-, -en'--, -'kef-, -əʊ·, -græf ‖ -troʊ ɪn 'sef əl˷ə græf **~s** s
electrolier i ˌlek trəʊ 'lɪə ə- ‖ -trə 'lɪᵊr **~s** z
Electrolux *tdmk* i 'lek trəʊ lʌks ə- ‖ -troʊ-
electrolysis i ˌlek 'trɒl əs ɪs ə-, ˌel ek-, ˌel ɪk-, ˌɪl ek-, ˌi:l ek-, -ɪs ɪs, §-əs ‖ -'trɑ:l-
electrolyte i 'lek trəʊ laɪt ‖ -trə- **~s** s
electrolytic i ˌlek trəʊ 'lɪt ɪk ◂ ‖ -trə 'lɪţ-
electromagnet i ˌlek trəʊ 'mæg nɪt ə-, -nət ‖ -troʊ- **~s** s
electromagnetic i ˌlek trəʊ mæg 'net ɪk ◂ ə-, -məg'·- ‖ -troʊ mæg 'neţ- **~ally** ᵊl˷i
eˌlectromagˌnetic 'spectrum
electromagnetism i ˌlek trəʊ 'mæg nə ˌtɪz əm ə-, -'·nɪ- ‖ -ˌ·troʊ-
electromotive i ˌlek trəʊ 'məʊt ɪv ◂ ə- ‖ -troʊ 'moʊţ ɪv -trə-
eˌlectroˌmotive 'force
electromyogram i ˌlek trəʊ 'maɪ˷ə græm ə- ‖ -ˌ·troʊ-
electromyography i ˌlek trəʊ maɪ 'ɒg rəf i ə- ‖ -troʊ maɪ 'ɑ:g-
electron i 'lek trɒn ə- ‖ -trɑ:n **~s** z
eˌlectron 'microscope ‖ ·'· · ˌ· ·

ELECTRONIC

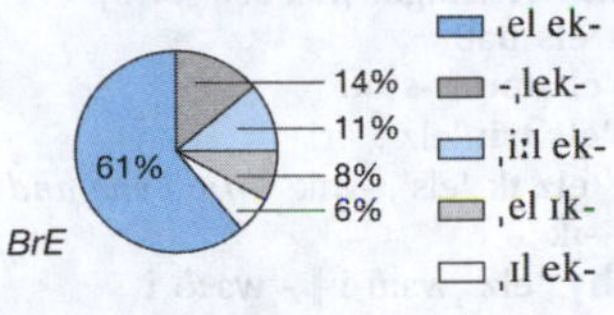

electronic ˌel ek ˈtrɒn ɪk ◂ i ˌlek-, ə-; ˌel ɪk-, ˌɪl ek-, ˌiːl ek- ‖ i ˌlek ˈtrɑːn ɪk ◂ **~a** ə **~ally** ᵊl i **~s** s — *Preference poll, BrE:* ˌel ek- *61%,* ˌlek- *14%,* ˌiːl ek- *11%,* ˌel ɪk- *8%,* ˌɪl ek- *6%*

electropalatogram i ˌlek trəʊ ˈpæl ət ə ɡræm ə-, -ˈə təʊ- ‖ -troʊ ˈpæl əṭ ə-

electropalatography i ˌlek trəʊ ˌpæl ə ˈtɒɡ rəf i ə- ‖ -troʊ ˌpæl ə ˈtɑːɡ-

electro|plate i ˈlek trəʊ |pleɪt ə-, ˌ·ˈ·ˌ· ‖ -trə- **~plated** pleɪt ɪd -əd ‖ pleɪṭ əd **~plates** pleɪts **~plating** pleɪt ɪŋ ‖ pleɪṭ ɪŋ

electroscope i ˈlek trəʊ skəʊp ə- ‖ -trə skoʊp **~s** s

electroshock i ˈlek trəʊ ʃɒk ə- ‖ -troʊ ʃɑːk -trə-

electrostatic i ˌlek trəʊ ˈstæt ɪk ◂ ə- ‖ -trə ˈstæṭ ɪk ◂ **~ally** ᵊl i **~s** s

electrotyp|e i ˈlek trəʊ taɪp ə- ‖ -trə- **~ed** t **~es** s **~ing** ɪŋ

electrum i ˈlek trəm ə-

electuar|y i ˈlekt ju ər |i ə- ‖ i ˈlek tʃu er |i **~ies** iz

eleemosynary ˌel i iː ˈmɒz ɪn ər i ˌel iː ˈmɒz-, ˌ·ɪ-, -ˈmɒs-, -ˈməʊz-, -ˈᵊn- ‖ ˌel ə ˈmɑːs ə ner i ˌ·ɪ-, -ˈmɑːz-, -ˈmoʊs-

elegance ˈel ɪɡ ənᵗs -əɡ-

elegant ˈel ɪɡ ənt -əɡ- **~ly** li

elegiac ˌel ɪ ˈdʒaɪ ək ◂ -ə-, -æk **~s** s
ˌeleˌgiac ˈcouplet

elegis|e, elegiz|e ˈel ə dʒaɪz -ɪ- **~ed** d **~es** ɪz əz **~ing** ɪŋ

elegist ˈel ədʒ ɪst -ɪdʒ-, §-əst **~s** s

eleg|y ˈel ədʒ |i -ɪdʒ- **~ies** iz

element ˈel ɪ mənt -ə- **~s** s

elemental ˌel ɪ ˈment ᵊl ◂ -ə- ‖ -ˈmenṭ ᵊl ◂ **~ly** i

elementar|y ˌel ɪ ˈment ər |i ◂ ˌ·ə- ‖ -ˈmenṭ ər |i ◂ →-ˈmentr |i **~ily** əl ɪ i li **~iness** i nəs i nɪs
ˌeleˌmentary ˈparticle; **ˌeleˈmentary school**

elenchus ɪ ˈleŋk əs ə-

Eleonora ˌel i ə ˈnɔːr ə ɪ ˌleɪ ə-

elephant ˈel ɪf ənt -əf- **~s** s

elephantiasis ˌel ɪf ən ˈtaɪ əs ɪs -əf ən-, -ɪ fæn-, -ə fæn-, §-əs

elephantine ˌel ɪ ˈfænt aɪn ◂ -ə- ‖ -iːn ◂ -aɪn; ˈel əf ən tiːn, -taɪn

Eleusinian ˌel ju ˈsɪn i ən ◂ ˌ·u- **~s** z

Eleusis ɪ ˈljuːs ɪs e-, ə-, -ˈluːs-, §-əs ‖ -ˈluːs-

Eleuthera ɪ ˈluːθ ər ə ə-, e-, -ˈljuːθ-

ele|vate ˈel ɪ |veɪt -ə- **~vated** veɪt ɪd -əd ‖ veɪṭ əd **~vates** veɪts **~vating** veɪt ɪŋ ‖ veɪṭ ɪŋ

elevation ˌel ɪ ˈveɪʃ ᵊn -ə- **~s** z

elevator ˈel ɪ veɪt ə ˈ·ə- ‖ -veɪṭ ᵊr **~s** z
ˈelevator ˌoperator

eleven i ˈlev ᵊn ə- **~s** z

eleven-plus i ˌlev ᵊn ˈplʌs ə-, →-ᵊm-

elevenses i ˈlev ᵊnz ɪz ə-, -əz

eleventh i ˈlev ᵊnᵗθ ə- **~s** s
eˌleventh ˈhour

elf, Elf elf **elf's** elfs **elves** elvz

Elfed ˈelv ed

elfin ˈelf ɪn §-ən

elfish ˈelf ɪʃ **~ly** li **~ness** nəs nɪs

Elfreda, Elfrida el ˈfriːd ə

Elgar ˈelɡ ɑː -ə ‖ -ɑːr -ᵊr

Elgin *(i)* ˈelɡ ɪn §-ən, *(ii)* ˈeldʒ ɪn -ən —*For the marbles, the place in Scotland, and as a British name, (i); for place in IL, and as an American name, (ii).*

El Greco el ˈɡrek əʊ ‖ -oʊ

Eli ˈiːl aɪ

Elia ˈiːl i ə

Elias ɪ ˈlaɪ əs ə-, -æs

elic|it i ˈlɪs |ɪt ə-, §-|ət ‖ -|ət *(usually = illicit)* **~ited** ɪt ɪd §ət-, -əd ‖ əṭ əd **~iting** ɪt ɪŋ §ət- ‖ əṭ ɪŋ **~its** ɪts §əts ‖ əts

elicitation i ˌlɪs ɪ ˈteɪʃ ᵊn ə-, iː-, -ə- **~s** z

elid|e i ˈlaɪd ə-, iː- **~ed** ɪd əd **~es** z **~ing** ɪŋ

eligibility ˌel ɪdʒ ə ˈbɪl ət i ˌ·ədʒ-, -ɪˈ-, -ɪt i ‖ -əṭ i

eligib|le ˈel ɪdʒ əb |ᵊl ˈ·ədʒ-, -ɪb- **~ly** li

Elihu ɪ ˈlaɪ hjuː e-, ə- ‖ ˈel ə hjuː

Elijah ɪ ˈlaɪdʒ ə ə-

Elim ˈiːl ɪm §-əm

elimi|nate i ˈlɪm ɪ |neɪt ə- -ə- **~nated** neɪt ɪd -əd ‖ neɪṭ əd **~nates** neɪts **~nating** neɪt ɪŋ ‖ neɪṭ ɪŋ

elimination i ˌlɪm ɪ ˈneɪʃ ᵊn ə-, -ə- **~s** z

eliminator i ˈlɪm ɪ neɪt ə ə-, ˈ·ə- ‖ -ˈneɪṭ ᵊr **~s** z

Elin ˈel ɪn -ən

Elinor ˈel ən ə -ɪn- ‖ -ən ᵊr -ə nɔːr

Eliot, Eliott ˈel i ət

Elis ˈiːl ɪs §-əs

Elisa i ˈliːs ə ə-, -ˈliːz-, -ˈlɪz-

Elisabeth i ˈlɪz əb əθ ə-

Elise i ˈliːz ə-, e-

Elisha i ˈlaɪʃ ə ə-

elision i ˈlɪʒ ᵊn ə-, §iː- **~s** z

elite, élite i ˈliːt ₍ɪ₎eɪ-, ə- **~s** s

elitism, élitism i ˈliːt ˌɪz əm eɪ-, ə- ‖ -ˈliːṭ-

elitist, élitist i ˈliːt ɪst ə-, §-əst ‖ -ˈliːṭ- **~s** s

elixir i ˈlɪks ə e-, ə-, -ɪə; ˈel ɪk sɪə ‖ -ᵊr **~s** z

Eliza i ˈlaɪz ə ə-

Elizabeth i ˈlɪz əb əθ ə- **~s, ~'s** s

Elizabethan i ˌlɪz ə ˈbiːθ ᵊn ◂ ə- **~s** z

elk elk **elks** elks

Elkan *(i)* ˈelk ən, *(ii)* -ɑːn

elkhound ˈelk haʊnd **~s** z

Elkie ˈelk i

Elkins ˈelk ɪnz

E

E

ell el **ells** elz
Ella 'el ə
Elland 'el ənd
Ellen 'el ən -ɪn
Ellery 'el ər i
Ellesmere 'elz mɪə ‖ -mɪr
  ˌEllesmere 'Port
Ellice 'el ɪs §-əs
Ellie 'el i
Ellington 'el ɪŋ tən
Elliot, Elliott 'el i ˌət
ellips|e i 'lɪps ə-, e- **~es** ɪz əz
ellipses *pl of* **ellipse** i 'lɪps ɪz ə-, e-, -əz
ellipses *pl of* **ellipsis** i 'lɪps iːz ə-, e-
ellips|is i 'lɪps |ɪs ə-, e-, §-əs **~es** iːz
ellipsoid i 'lɪps ɔɪd ə-, e- **~s** z
ellipsoidal ˌel ɪp 'sɔɪd ᵊl ◂ i ˌlɪp-, ə-, e-
ellipt i 'lɪpt ə-, e- **~ed** ɪd əd **~ing** ɪŋ **~s** s
elliptic i 'lɪpt ɪk ə-, e- **~al** ᵊl **~ally** ᵊl ˌi
Ellis 'el ɪs §-əs
Ellison 'el ɪs ən -əs-
Ellsworth 'elz wɜːθ -wəθ ‖ -wɜ˞ːθ
elm elm **elms** elmz
Elmer 'elm ə ‖ -ᵊr
Elmes elmz
Elmet 'elm et -ɪt, §-ət
Elmhurst 'elm hɜːst ‖ -hɜ˞ːst
Elmira el 'marᵊr ə
Elmo 'elm əʊ ‖ -oʊ
El Monte el 'mɒnt i ‖ -'mɑːnt̬ i —*Sp* [el 'mon te]
Elmwood 'elm wʊd
El Niño el 'niːn jəʊ ‖ -joʊ —*Sp* [el 'ni ɲo]
elocution ˌel ə 'kjuːʃ ᵊn
elocutionary ˌel ə 'kjuːʃ ᵊn ər ˌi ◂ -'ᵊn ˌər i ‖ -ə ner i
elocutionist ˌel ə 'kjuːʃ ᵊn ˌɪst §ˌəst **~s** s
Elohim e 'ləʊ hɪm ɪ-, ə-; ˌel əʊ 'hiːm ‖ -'loʊ- ˌel oʊ 'hiːm
Eloise ˌel əʊ 'iːz ‖ -oʊ- '· · ·
elon|gate 'iː lɒŋ |geɪt ‖ i 'lɔːŋ |geɪt -'lɑːŋ *(*)* **~gated** geɪt ɪd -əd ‖ geɪt̬ əd **~gates** geɪts **~gating** geɪt ɪŋ ‖ geɪt̬ ɪŋ
elongation ˌiː lɒŋ 'geɪʃ ᵊn ‖ i ˌlɔːŋ 'geɪʃ ᵊn -ˌlɑːŋ-; ˌiː lɔːŋ-, -lɑːŋ- **~s** z
elop|e i 'ləʊp ə- ‖ -'loʊp **~ed** t **~ement/s** mənt/s **~es** s **~ing** ɪŋ
eloquence 'el ək wənᵗs
eloquent 'el ək wənt **~ly** li **~ness** nəs nɪs
El Paso el 'pæs əʊ ‖ -oʊ —*Sp* [el 'pa so]
Elphick 'elf ɪk
Elphinstone 'elf ɪn stən §-ən-, -stəʊn ‖ -stoʊn
El Portal *place in FL* ˌel pɔː 'tæl ‖ -pɔːr-
Elroy 'el rɔɪ
Elsa 'els ə —*but as a German name, also* 'elz- —*Ger* ['ʔɛl za]
El Salvador ₍ˌ₎el 'sælv ə dɔː ‖ -dɔːr —*Sp* [el sal βa 'ðor]
Elsan *tdmk* 'el sæn
Elsbeth 'els bəθ
else, Else els
elsewhere ˌels 'weə -'hweə, '· · ‖ 'els *h*wer -*h*wær

Elsie 'els i
Elsinore 'els ɪ nɔː -ə-, ˌ· · '· ‖ ˌels ə 'nɔːr -'noʊr —*Danish* Helsingør [hɛl seŋ 'øːʔʁ]
Elspeth 'els pəθ
Elstow 'el stəʊ ‖ -stoʊ
Elstree 'els triː 'elz-, -tri
Elswick 'elz ɪk 'els-, -wɪk —*In Tyne and Wear, locally* -ɪk
Elsworthy 'elz ˌwɜːð i ‖ -ˌwɜ˞ːð i
ELT ˌiː el 'tiː
Eltham *(i)* 'elt əm, *(ii)* 'elθ əm —*The place in London is (i); those in Australia and NZ, (ii)*
Elton 'elt ən
eluci|date i 'luːs ɪ |deɪt ə-, -'ljuːs-, -ə- **~dated** deɪt ɪd -əd ‖ deɪt̬ əd **~dates** deɪts **~dating** deɪt ɪŋ ‖ deɪt̬ ɪŋ
elucidation i ˌluːs ɪ 'deɪʃ ᵊn ə-, -ˌljuːs-, -ə- **~s** z
elucidatory i 'luːs ɪ deɪt ər i ə-, ·ˌ· '· · · ‖ -əd ə tɔːr i -toʊr i
elud|e i 'luːd ə-, -'ljuːd **~ed** ɪd əd **~es** z **~ing** ɪŋ
Eluned e 'lɪn ed -'liːn-
elusion i 'luːʒ ᵊn ə-, -'ljuːʒ-
elusive i 'luːs ɪv ə-, -'ljuːs- **~ly** li **~ness** nəs nɪs
elusory i 'luːs ər ˌi ə-, -'ljuːs-
elute i 'luːt ə-, -'ljuːt **eluted** i 'luːt ɪd ə-, -'ljuːt-, -əd ‖ -'luːt̬- **~s** s **eluting** i 'luːt ɪŋ ə-, -'ljuːt- ‖ -'luːt̬-
Elva 'elv ə
elver 'elv ə ‖ -ᵊr **~s** z
elves elvz
Elvin 'elv ɪn §-ən
Elvira *(i)* el 'vɪər ə ‖ -'vɪr ə, *(ii)* -'varᵊr ə
Elvis 'elv ɪs §-əs
elvish 'elv ɪʃ
Elwes 'el wɪz -wəz
Elwyn 'el wɪn
Ely *American personal name* 'iːl aɪ
Ely *place name* 'iːl i
Elyot 'el i ˌət
Elysee, Elysée eɪ 'liːz eɪ i-, ə- ‖ ˌeɪl iː 'zeɪ —*Fr* [e li ze]
Elysian, e~ i 'lɪz i ˌən ə- ‖ i 'lɪʒ ᵊn -'liːʒ-
Elysium i 'lɪz i ˌəm ə- ‖ i 'lɪʒ- -'liːʒ-, -'lɪz-
elytron 'el ɪ trɒn -ə-; -ɪtr ən, -ətr- ‖ -ə trɑːn
Elzevier, Elzevir 'elz ə vɪə 'els- ‖ -vɪr —*Dutch* ['ɛl zə viːr]
em em
em- ɪm, (ˌ)em —*This prefix is stressed* ˌ**em** *if the following syllable is unstressed* (ˌembro'cation). *Otherwise it is unstressed* (em'balm). *When it is unstressed, a weak-vowel form* **ɪm** *is preferred in RP, although some speakers, particularly regional ones, use a strong-vowel form* **em**.
'em *pronoun* əm —*This variant of* them *has no strong form.*
emaci|ate i 'meɪʃ i |eɪt ə-, -'meɪs- **~ated** eɪt ɪd -əd ‖ eɪt̬ əd **~ates** eɪts **~ating** eɪt ɪŋ ‖ eɪt̬ ɪŋ
emaciation i ˌmeɪʃ i 'eɪʃ ᵊn ə-, -ˌmeɪs-
email, e-mail 'iː meɪᵊl **~ed** d **~ing** ɪŋ **~s** z

Elision

1 **Elision** is the eliding (= omission, deletion) of a sound that would otherwise be present. It is particularly characteristic of rapid or casual speech. It is not random, but follows certain rules, which differ from one language to another.

2 Some types of possible elision can occur within words in isolation. They are shown in this dictionary by the use of *italic* symbols (or occasionally by raised symbols or by transcribing a second pronunciation). In English they include

- the elision of the middle part of ntʃ and ndʒ. For example, **lunch** lʌntʃ is pronounced lʌntʃ or, alternatively, lʌnʃ; **strange** streɪndʒ is streɪndʒ or streɪnʒ.
- the elision of the middle part of mps, mpt, nts, ŋks, ŋkt. For example, **jumped** dʒʌmpt is pronounced dʒʌmpt or, alternatively, dʒʌmt; **lynx** lɪŋks is lɪŋks or lɪŋs.

3 Other types of possible elision apply in compound words and in connected speech. They are shown in this dictionary for compounds, but naturally cannot be shown for connected speech. They include the elision of t and d at the end of a word, before a consonant at the beginning of the next word. Then

- t may be elided in ft, st, and less commonly in pt, kt, tʃt, θt, ʃt
- d may be elided in ld, nd, and less commonly in bd, gd, dʒd, vd, ðd, zd, md, ŋd.

next nekst In isolation, or before a vowel sound, this word is pronounced nekst. But in a phrase such as **next thing, next question** it is often pronounced neks, with elision of the t.

stand stænd In isolation, or before a vowel sound, this word is pronounced stænd. But in a phrase such as **stand clear, stand firm** it is often pronounced stæn, with elision of the d.

4 The contracted negative **n't** ᵊnt is a special case. Its t may be elided in connected speech, no matter what kind of sound follows. Thus when **didn't** ˈdɪd ᵊnt is followed by another word or phrase, it is sometimes pronounced ˈdɪd ᵊn.

5 The consonant h is often elided in unstressed syllables, and especially in weak forms of function words. Thus **him** is hɪm in isolation, or if stressed, but often ɪm when unstressed in a phrase such as **tell him**.

6 The vowel ə is subject to elision as follows.

- often (though not always) when it is followed by a nasal or liquid and then a WEAK vowel. There are two stages: first, the ə combines with the nasal or liquid, making the latter syllabic (see SYLLABIC CONSONANTS); then, the nasal or liquid may become non-syllabic (see COMPRESSION), in which case all trace of the ə has disappeared.

Elision ▸

Elision continued

camera ˈkæm ər‿ə The full form is ˈkæm.ər.ə. If ə is elided, in the first instance it makes the r syllabic: ˈkæm.r.ə. This is usually compressed to give ˈkæm.rə. All three possibilities occur.

- sometimes, in casual speech, in the first syllable of a word in which the second syllable is stressed and begins with a liquid. The first syllable then undergoes compression. Thus **terrific** tə ˈrɪf ɪk sometimes becomes ˈtrɪf ɪk, or **collide** kə ˈlaɪd becomes klaɪd. Since they are not found except in casual speech, these forms are not shown in this dictionary. The same applies to cases of apparent elision of ə in some speakers' occasional pronunciation of words such as **incident** ˈɪnˈs əd ənt, **capacity** kə ˈpæs ət i, where there seems to be a compensatory lengthening of the preceding consonant, giving the effect of ˈɪnˈsː dənt, kə ˈpæsː ti.

7 A pronunciation that originated through elision may become the only possibility for some speakers. Some people have ˈkæm rə as the only pronunciation for **camera**, or pliːs as the only form for **police**. For many people it would feel very artificial to pronounce a t in **postman** ˈpəus mən ‖ ˈpous mən.

ema|nate ˈem ə |neɪt **~nated** neɪt ɪd -əd ‖ neɪţ əd **~nates** neɪts **~nating** neɪt ɪŋ ‖ neɪţ ɪŋ
emanation ˌem ə ˈneɪʃ ən **~s** z
emanative ˈem ə neɪt ɪv -nət ɪv ‖ -neɪţ ɪv
emanatory ˈem ə neɪt ər i ˌ· ·ˈ· · ·; ˈem ən ət‿ər i ‖ -ən ə tɔːr i -tour i
emanci|pate i ˈmænˈs ɪ |peɪt ə-, -ə- **~pated** peɪt ɪd -əd ‖ peɪţ əd **~pates** peɪts **~pating** peɪt ɪŋ ‖ peɪţ ɪŋ
emancipation i ˌmænˈs ɪ ˈpeɪʃ ən ə-, -ə- **~s** z
emancipator i ˈmænˈs ɪ peɪt ə ə-, -ˈ·ə- ‖ -peɪţ ər **~s** z
Emanuel i ˈmæn ju‿əl ə- —*but in singing usually* -el
emascu|late *v* i ˈmæsk ju |leɪt ə- ‖ -jə- **~lated** leɪt ɪd -əd ‖ leɪţ əd **~lates** leɪts **~lating** leɪt ɪŋ ‖ leɪţ ɪŋ
emasculate *adj* i ˈmæsk jʊl ət ə-, -ɪt, -ju leɪt ‖ -jəl-
emasculation i ˌmæsk ju ˈleɪʃ ən ə- ‖ -jə- **~s** z
embalm ɪm ˈbɑːm em-, §-ˈbɑːlm **~ed** d **~er/s** ə/z ‖ ər/z **~ing** ɪŋ **~s** z
embalmment ɪm ˈbɑːm mənt em-, §-ˈbɑːlm- **~s** s
embankment ɪm ˈbæŋk mənt em- **~s** s
embarcadero, E~ em ˌbɑːk ə ˈdeər əu ɪm-, əm- ‖ -ˌbɑːrk ə ˈder ou **~s** z
embargo ɪm ˈbɑːg əu em- ‖ -ˈbɑːrg ou **~ed** d **~es** z **~ing** ɪŋ
embark ɪm ˈbɑːk em- ‖ -ˈbɑːrk **~ed** t **~ing** ɪŋ **~s** s
embarkation ˌem bɑː ˈkeɪʃ ən ‖ -bɑːr- **~s** z
embarras de richesses ɒm ˌbær ɑː də riː ˈʃes ‖ ˌɑːm bɑː ˌrɑː- —*Fr* [ɑ̃ ba ʁa dʁi ʃɛs]
embarrass ɪm ˈbær əs em- ‖ -ˈber- **~ed** t **~es** ɪz əz **~ing/ly** ɪŋ /li **~ment/s** mənt/s
embass|y ˈem bəs |i **~ies** iz
embattl|e ɪm ˈbæt əl em- ‖ -ˈbæţ əl **~ed** d **~es** z **~ing** ‿ɪŋ
embed ɪm ˈbed em- **~ded** ɪd əd **~ding** ɪŋ **~s** z
embellish ɪm ˈbel ɪʃ em- **~ed** t **~es** ɪz əz **~ing** ɪŋ **~ment/s** mənt/s
ember, Ember ˈem bə ‖ -bər **~s** z
ˈEmber day
embezzl|e ɪm ˈbez əl em- **~ed** d **~es** z **~ing** ‿ɪŋ
embezzlement ɪm ˈbez əl mənt em- **~s** s
embezzler ɪm ˈbez əl‿ə em- ‖ ‿ər **~s** z
embitter ɪm ˈbɪt ə em- ‖ -ˈbɪţ ər **~ed** d
embittering ɪm ˈbɪt‿ər ɪŋ em- ‖ -ˈbɪţ ər- **~s** z
embitterment ɪm ˈbɪt ə mənt em- ‖ -ˈbɪţ ər-
emblazon ɪm ˈbleɪz ən em- **~ed** d **~ing** ‿ɪŋ **~ment** mənt **~s** z
emblem ˈem bləm -blɪm **~s** z
emblematic ˌem blə ˈmæt ɪk ◂ -blɪ- ‖ -ˈmæţ- **~ally** əl‿i
emblement ˈem blə mənt -bəl- **~s** s
embodiment ɪm ˈbɒd i mənt em- ‖ -ˈbɑːd- **~s** s
embod|y ɪm ˈbɒd |i em- ‖ -ˈbɑːd |i **~ied** id **~ies** iz **~ying** i‿ɪŋ
embolden ɪm ˈbəuld ən em-, →-ˈbɒuld- ‖ -ˈbould- **~ed** d **~ing** ɪŋ **~s** z
emboli ˈem bə laɪ
embolic em ˈbɒl ɪk ‖ -ˈbɑːl-
embolism ˈem bə ˌlɪz əm **~s** z
em|bolus ˈem |bəl əs **~boli** bə laɪ
embonpoint ˌɒm bɒn ˈpwæ̃ ˌɒ̃-, →-bɒm-, -bɒ̃-, -ˈpwɒ̃ ‖ ˌɑːm boun ˈpwæn —*Fr* [ɑ̃ bɔ̃ pwɛ̃]
embosomed ɪm ˈbuz əmd em-, §-ˈbuːz-

E-mail and the web

In an e-mail address the character @ is read as **at**. The punctuation mark <.> is read as dot, both in e-mail addresses and in URLs (= website addresses). The punctuation mark </> is usually read as **slash** or **forward slash**, and <#> as **hash** (BrE) or **pound sign** (AmE).

So <**j.wells@ucl.ac.uk**> is read as **J dot Wells at U C L dot A C dot U K**.
<**www.pearsonlongman.com/elt-world**> is read as **W W W dot PearsonLongman dot com slash E L T hyphen world**.

E

emboss ɪm ˈbɒs em- ‖ -ˈbɑːs -ˈbɔːs **~ed** t **~es** ɪz əz **~ing** ɪŋ
embouchure ˌɒm bu ˈʃʊə · · · ‖ ˌɑːm bu ˈʃʊᵊr ˈɑːm bə ʃʊr —*Fr* [ɑ̃ bu ʃyːʁ] **~s** z
embourgeoisement ˌɒm bʊəʒ ˈwɑːz mɒ̃ ‖ em ˈbʊrʒ wɑːz mɑːnt ɑːm-, -mənt —*Fr* [ɑ̃ buʁ ʒwaz mɑ̃]
embowered ɪm ˈbaʊ̯ əd em- ‖ -ˈbaʊ̯ ᵊrd
embrac|e ɪm ˈbreɪs em- **~ed** t **~er/s** ə/z ‖ ᵊr/z **~es** ɪz əz **~ing** ɪŋ
embrasure ɪm ˈbreɪʒ ə em- ‖ -ᵊr **~s** z
embrocation ˌem brə ˈkeɪʃ ᵊn **~s** z
embroider ɪm ˈbrɔɪd ə em- ‖ -ᵊr **~ed** d
embroidering ɪm ˈbrɔɪd‿ər ɪŋ **~s** z
embroider|y ɪm ˈbrɔɪd‿ər |i em- **~ies** iz
embroil ɪm ˈbrɔɪᵊl em- **~ed** d **~ing** ɪŋ **~s** z
embryo ˈem bri əʊ ‖ -oʊ **~s** z
embryo- *comb. form*
with stress-neutral suffix ¦em bri əʊ ‖ -ə — **embryotome** ˈem bri əʊ təʊm ‖ -ə toʊm
with stress-imposing suffix ˌem bri ˈɒ+ ‖ -ˈɑː+ — **embryotomy** ˌem bri ˈɒt əm i ‖ -ˈɑːt̬-
embryolog|ist ˌem bri ˈɒl ədʒ| ɪst §-əst ‖ -ˈɑːl- **~ists** ɪsts §əsts **~y** i
embryonic ˌem bri ˈɒn ɪk ◂ ‖ -ˈɑːn- **~ally** ᵊl‿i
Emburey, Embury ˈem bər i -bjʊr-
embus ɪm ˈbʌs em- **~ed, ~sed** t **~es, ~ses** ɪz əz **~ing, ~sing** ɪŋ
emcee ˌem ˈsiː **~d** d **~ing** ɪŋ **~s** z
-eme iːm — **grapheme** ˈgræf iːm —*Although strong-vowelled, this suffix is unstressed.*
Emeline ˈem ə liːn -ɪ-
emend i ˈmend ə- **~ed** ɪd əd **~ing** ɪŋ **~s** z
emendation ˌiːm en ˈdeɪʃ ᵊn ˌem-, -ən- **~s** z
Emeney, Emeny ˈem ən i
emerald ˈem ᵊr‿əld **~s** z
emerg|e i ˈmɜːdʒ ə- ‖ -ˈmɜːdʒ **~ed** d **~es** ɪz əz **~ing** ɪŋ
emergenc|e i ˈmɜːdʒ ənᵗs ə- ‖ -ˈmɜːdʒ- **~es** ɪz əz
emergenc|y i ˈmɜːdʒ ənᵗs |i ə- ‖ -ˈmɜːdʒ- **~ies** iz
emergent i ˈmɜːdʒ ənt ə- ‖ -ˈmɜːdʒ-
emerit|us i ˈmer ɪt| əs ə-, -ət| ‖ -ət̬| əs **~a** ə
Emerson ˈem əs ən ‖ -ᵊrs-
emery, Emery ˈem ər‿i
ˈ**emery ˌpaper**
emetic i ˈmet ɪk ə- ‖ -ˈmet̬ ɪk **~ally** ᵊl‿i **~s** s
emetine ˈem ɪ tiːn -ə-, -tɪn, -taɪn
EMF, emf ˌiː em ˈef
EMG ˌiː em ˈdʒiː
EMI *tdmk* ˌiː em ˈaɪ
emic ˈiːm ɪk **~ally** ᵊl‿i
emigrant ˈem ɪg rənt -əg- **~s** s
emi|grate ˈem ɪ |greɪt -ə- **~grated** greɪt ɪd -əd ‖ greɪt̬ əd **~grates** greɪts **~grating** greɪt ɪŋ ‖ greɪt̬ ɪŋ
emigration ˌem ɪ ˈgreɪʃ ᵊn -ə-
emigre, emigré, émigré ˈem ɪ greɪ -ə- **~s** z
Emil e ˈmiːᵊl eɪ- —*Ger* [ˈʔeː miːl]
Emile, Émile e ˈmiːᵊl eɪ- —*Fr* [e ˈmil]
Emily ˈem əl i -ɪl-
Emin ˈem ɪn
Eminem ˈem ə nem -ɪ-
eminenc|e, E~ ˈem ɪn ənᵗs -ən- **~es** ɪz əz —*but as a French word see next entry*
eminence grise, éminence grise, éminences grises ˌem i nɒ̃s ˈgriːz ‖ ˌeɪm i nɑ̃ːs- —*Fr* [e mi nɑ̃s gʁiːz]
eminent ˈem ɪn ənt -ən- **~ly** li
emir e ˈmɪə ɪ-, ə-, eɪ-; ˈem ɪə ‖ -ˈmɪᵊr **~s** z
emirate ˈem ər ət -ɪər-, -ɪt, -eɪt; e ˈmɪər-, ɪ- ‖ ɪ ˈmɪr- **~s** s
emissar|y ˈem ɪs ər‿|i ‖ -ə ser |i **~ies** iz
emission i ˈmɪʃ ᵊn ə- **~s** z
emissive i ˈmɪs ɪv ə-
emissivity ˌiːm ɪ ˈsɪv ət i ˌem-, ˌ·ə-, -ɪt i ‖ -ət̬ i
e|mit i |ˈmɪt ə- **~mits** ˈmɪts **~mitted** ˈmɪt ɪd -əd ‖ ˈmɪt̬ əd **~mitting** ˈmɪt ɪŋ ‖ ˈmɪt̬ ɪŋ
Emley ˈem li
Emlyn ˈem lɪn §-lən
Emma ˈem ə
Emmanuel i ˈmæn ju‿əl ə-
Emmaus i ˈmeɪ əs e-, ə-
Emmeline ˈem ə liːn -ɪ-
emmenagogue i ˈmen ə gɒg ə-, e-, -ˈmiːn- ‖ -gɑːg **~s** z
Emmental, Emmenthal ˈem ən tɑːl **~er/s** ə/z ‖ -ᵊr/z
emmer ˈem ə ‖ -ᵊr
Emmerdale ˈem ə deɪᵊl ‖ -ᵊr-

Emmerson 'em əs ən ‖ -ᵊrs-
emmet, Emmet, Emmett 'em ɪt §-ət **~s** s
emmetropia ˌem ɪ 'trəʊp i‿ə ˌ·ə- ‖ -'troʊp-
emmetropic ˌem ɪ 'trɒp ɪk ◂ -ə- ‖ -'trɑːp-
Emmie, Emmy 'em i **~s** z
emo 'iːm əʊ ‖ -oʊ
emollient i 'mɒl i‿ənt ə- ‖ -'mɑːl- **~s** s
emolument i 'mɒl ju mənt ə- ‖ -'mɑːl jə-
e-money 'iː ˌmʌn i
Emory 'em ər i
e|mote i |'məʊt ə-, iː- ‖ -|'moʊt **~moted** 'məʊt ɪd -əd ‖ 'moʊţ əd **~motes** 'məʊts ‖ 'moʊts **~moting** 'məʊt ɪŋ ‖ 'moʊţ ɪŋ
emoticon i 'məʊt ɪ kɒn ə-, -'mɒt-, -ɪk ən, -ˌaɪk ɒn ‖ -'moʊţ ɪ kɑːn **~s** z
emotion i 'məʊʃ ᵊn ə- ‖ -'moʊʃ- **~s** z
emotional i 'məʊʃ ᵊn‿əl ə- ‖ -'moʊʃ- **~ism** ˌɪz əm **~ly** i
emotionless i 'məʊʃ ᵊn ləs ə- ‖ -'moʊʃ- **~ly** li
emotive i 'məʊt ɪv ə- ‖ -'moʊţ ɪv **~ly** li **~ness** nəs nɪs
empanada ˌemp ə 'nɑːd ə **~s** z —*Sp* [em pa 'na ða]
empanel ɪm 'pæn ᵊl em- **~ed, ~led** d **~ing, ~ling** ɪŋ **~s** z
empathetic ˌemp ə 'θet ɪk ◂ ‖ -'θeţ- **~ally** ᵊl‿i
empathis|e, empathiz|e 'emp ə θaɪz **~ed** d **~es** ɪz əz **~ing** ɪŋ
empathy 'emp əθ i
Empedocles em 'ped ə kliːz ɪm-
emperor 'emp ər‿ə ‖ -ᵊr‿ər **~s** z **~ship** ʃɪp
emph|asis 'emᵖf |əs ɪs §-əs **~ases** ə siːz
emphasis|e, emphasiz|e 'emᵖf ə saɪz **~ed** d **~es** ɪz əz **~ing** ɪŋ
emphatic ɪm 'fæt ɪk em- ‖ -'fæţ ɪk **~ally** ᵊl‿i **~s** s
emphysema ˌemᵖf ɪ 'siːm ə -ə-, -aɪ-, -'ziːm-; ⚠-'ziːm i‿ə
emphysematous ˌemᵖf ɪ 'sem ət əs ◂ -ə-, -'siːm- ‖ -əţ əs
empire, E~ 'emp aɪ‿ə ‖ 'emp aɪᵊr **~s** z
ˌEmpire 'State ˌBuilding
empire-build|er 'emp aɪ‿ə ˌbɪld| ə ‖ 'emp aɪᵊr ˌbɪld| ᵊr **~ers** əz ‖ ᵊrz **~ing** ɪŋ
empiric ɪm 'pɪr ɪk em- **~s** s
empirical ɪm 'pɪr ɪk ᵊl em- **~ly** ‿i
empiricism ɪm 'pɪr ɪ ˌsɪz əm em-, -'·ə-
emplacement ɪm 'pleɪs mənt em- **~s** s
emplan|e ɪm 'pleɪn em- **~ed** d **~es** z **~ing** ɪŋ
employ ɪm 'plɔɪ em-, əm- **~ed** d **~ing** ɪŋ **~s** z
employable ɪm 'plɔɪ əb ᵊl em-, əm-
employee ɪm 'plɔɪ iː em-, əm-; ˌem plɔɪ 'iː, ˌɪm- ‖ ·.·'· **~s** z
employer ɪm 'plɔɪ ə em-, əm- ‖ -ᵊr **~s** z
employment ɪm 'plɔɪ mənt em-, əm- **~s** s
em'ployment ˌagency
empori|um em 'pɔːr i‿|əm ɪm- ‖ -'poʊr- **~a** ə **~ums** əmz
empower ɪm 'paʊ‿ə em- ‖ -'paʊ‿ᵊr **~ed** d
empowering ɪm 'paʊ‿ər ɪŋ em- ‖ -'paʊ‿ᵊr ɪŋ **~ment** mənt **~s** z
empress 'emp rəs -rɪs **~es** ɪz əz
Empson 'emps ᵊn
empt|y 'empt |i **~ied** id **~ier** i‿ə ‖ i‿ᵊr **~ies** iz **~iest** i‿ɪst i‿əst **~ily** ɪ li əl i **~iness** i nəs i nɪs **~ying** i‿ɪŋ
empty-handed ˌempt i 'hænd ɪd ◂ -əd
empty-headed ˌempt i 'hed ɪd ◂ -əd **~ness** nəs nɪs
empurpled ɪm 'pɜːp ᵊld em- ‖ -'pɜ˞ːp-
empyema ˌemp aɪ 'iːm ə
empyre|al ˌemp ɪ 'riː‿|əl ◂ -aɪᵊ-, -ə- **~an** ən
Emrys 'em rɪs —*Welsh* ['em ris, -rɨs]
Ems emz —*Ger* [ʔɛms]
EMS ˌiː em 'es
Emsworth 'emz wəθ -wɜːθ ‖ -wɜːθ
emu 'iːm juː **~s** z
EMU ˌiː em 'juː 'iːm juː
emu|late 'em ju |leɪt -jə- ‖ -jə- **~lated** leɪt ɪd -əd ‖ leɪţ əd **~lates** leɪts **~lating** leɪt ɪŋ ‖ leɪţ ɪŋ
emulation ˌem ju 'leɪʃ ᵊn -jə- ‖ -jə- **~s** z
emulator 'em ju leɪt ə -'jə- ‖ -jə leɪţ ᵊr **~s** z
emulous 'em jʊl əs -jəl- ‖ -jəl- **~ly** li **~ness** nəs nɪs
emulsification i ˌmʌls ɪf ɪ 'keɪʃ ᵊn ə-, -ˌ·əf-, §-ə'·
emulsi|fy i 'mʌls ɪ |faɪ ə-, -ə- **~fied** faɪd **~fier/s** faɪ‿ə/z ‖ faɪ‿ᵊr/z **~fies** faɪz **~fying** faɪ ɪŋ
emulsion i 'mʌl ʃᵊn ə- **~ed** d **~ing** ‿ɪŋ **~s** z
e'mulsion paint
Emyr 'em ɪə ‖ -ɪr —*Welsh* ['em ir, -ɨr]
en *printer's measure* en **ens** enz
en *in French phrases* ɒ̃ ɒn, ɑːn ‖ ɑ̃ː ɑːn —*Fr* [ɑ̃] —*See also phrases with this word*
en- ɪn ən, (¦)en —*This prefix is stressed* ¦en *if the following syllable is unstressed* (ˌenhar'monic). *Otherwise the prefix is unstressed, and the weak-vowel form* ɪn *is preferred in RP* (en'large), *although some speakers, in Britain particularly regional ones, use* en *or* ən.
-en ᵊn, ən, ən — **wooden** 'wʊd ᵊn **blacken** 'blæk ən **woollen** 'wʊl ən
Ena 'iːn ə
enabl|e ɪn 'eɪb ᵊl en-, ən- **~ed** d **~ement** mənt **~er/s** ‿ə/z ‖ ‿ər/z **~es** z **~ing** ‿ɪŋ
enact ɪn 'ækt en-, ən- **~ed** ɪd əd **~ing** ɪŋ **~ment/s** mənt/s **~s** s
enamel i 'næm ᵊl ə- **~ed, ~led** d **~er/s, ~ler/s** ə/z ‖ ᵊr/z **~ing, ~ling** ɪŋ **~ist/s, ~list/s** ɪst/s §-əst/s **~s** z
enamelware i 'næm ᵊl weə ə- ‖ -wer
enamor, enamour ɪn 'æm ə en-, ən- ‖ -ᵊr **~ed** d
enantio- *comb. form*
with stress-neutral suffix en ¦ænt i‿əʊ ɪn- ‖ ɪn ¦ænţi‿ə — **enantiomorph** en 'ænt i əʊ mɔːf ɪn- ‖ ɪn 'ænţi‿ə mɔːrf
with stress-imposing suffix en ˌænt i 'ɒ+ ɪn- ‖ ɪn ˌænţ i 'ɑː+ — **enantiopathy** en ˌænt i 'ɒp əθ i ɪn- ‖ ɪn ˌænţ i 'ɑːp-
enarthrosis ˌen ɑː 'θrəʊs ɪs §-əs ‖ -ɑːr 'θroʊs-
en bloc ˌɒ̃ 'blɒk ˌɒn-, →ˌɒm-, ˌɑːn-, →ˌɑːm- ‖ ˌɑ̃ː 'blɑːk ˌɑːn- —*Fr* [ɑ̃ blɔk]

n brochette ˌõ brɒ ˈʃet ˌɒn-, →ˌɒm- ‖ ˌɑ̃ː broʊ- —*Fr* [ɑ̃ bʁɔ ʃɛt]
n brosse ˌõ ˈbrɒs ˌɒn-, →ˌɒm- ‖ ˌɑːn ˈbrɔːs -ˈbrɑːs —*Fr* [ɑ̃ bʁɔs]
ncaenia, E~ en ˈsiːn i‿ə
ncamp ɪn ˈkæmp en-, →ɪŋ-, →eŋ- **~ed** t **~ing** ɪŋ **~ment/s** mənt/s **~s** s
ncapsu|late ɪn ˈkæps ju |leɪt en-, ən-, →ɪŋ-, →eŋ-, →əŋ-, §-ə-, §-ˈkæp ʃə-‖ -ə- **~lated** leɪt ɪd -əd ‖ leɪt̬ əd **~lates** leɪts **~lating** leɪt ɪŋ ‖ leɪt̬ ɪŋ
ncapsulation ɪn ˌkæps ju ˈleɪʃ ən en-, ən-, →ɪŋ-, →eŋ-, →əŋ-, §-ə-, §-ˌkæp ʃə- ‖ -ə- **~s** z
Encarta *tdmk* ɪn ˈkɑːt ə en-, →ɪŋ-, →eŋ- ‖ -ˈkɑːrt̬ ə
ncas|e ɪn ˈkeɪs en-, →ɪŋ-, →eŋ- **~ed** t **~ement** mənt **~es** ɪz əz **~ing** ɪŋ
ncash ɪn ˈkæʃ en-, →ɪŋ-, →eŋ- **~able** əb əl **~ed** t **~es** ɪz əz **~ing** ɪŋ **~ment/s** mənt/s
ncaustic ɪn ˈkɔːst ɪk en-, →ɪŋ-, →eŋ-, -ˈkɒst- ‖ -ˈkɔːst- -ˈkɑːst- **~s** s
ence ənts —*The two possible stress-effects of this suffix are illustrated in* ˌcorreˈspondence *and* maˈlevolence. *In a few words it triggers a vowel change and shift of stress in the stem, as* prevail prɪ ˈveɪəl → prevalence ˈprev əl ənts, confide kən ˈfaɪd → confidence ˈkɒn fɪd ənts. *There is fluctuation in* precedence, subsidence.
enceinte ₍ₗ₎ɒn ˈsænt ₍ₗ₎õ- ‖ ₍ₗ₎ɑ̃ː- —*Fr* [ɑ̃ sɛ̃ːt]
Enceladus en ˈsel əd əs
encephalic ˌen kɪ ˈfæl ɪk ◂ →ˌeŋ-, -kə-, -ke-; ˌen sɪ-, -sə-, -se- ‖ -sə-
encepha|litic en ˌkef ə |ˈlɪt ɪk ◂ →eŋ-, en ˌsef-, ɪn-, ˌen kef-, ˌen sef- ‖ ɪn ˌsef ə |ˈlɪt̬ ɪk ◂ **~litis** ˈlaɪt ɪs §-əs ‖ ˈlaɪt̬ əs
encephalo- *comb. form*
with stress-neutral suffix en ¦kef əl əʊ →eŋ-, ɪn-, →ɪŋ-, en ¦sef-, ɪn ¦sef- ‖ ɪn ¦sef əl ə
— **encephalogram** en ˈkef əl əʊ græm →eŋ-, ɪn-, →ɪŋ-, en ˈsef-, ɪn ˈsef- ‖ ɪn ˈsef əl ə græm
with stress-imposing suffix en ˌkef ə ˈlɒ+ →eŋ-, en ˌsef-, ˌ·ˌ·-, ɪn ˌ·- ‖ ɪn ˌsef ə ˈlɑː+
— **encephalopathy** en ˌkef ə ˈlɒp əθ i →eŋ-, en ˌsef-, ˌ·ˌ·-, ɪn ˌ·- ‖ ɪn ˌsef ə ˈlɑːp-
encephalomyelitis en ˌkef ə ləʊ ˌmaɪ‿ə ˈlaɪt ɪs →eŋ-, en ˌsef-, ˌ·ˌ·-, ɪn ˌ·- ‖ ɪn ˌsef ə loʊ ˌmaɪ ə ˈlaɪt̬ əs
enchain ɪn ˈtʃeɪn en-, ən- **~ed** d **~ing** ɪŋ **~ment** mənt **~s** z
en|chant ɪn |ˈtʃɑːnt en-, ən-, §-ˈtʃænt ‖ -|ˈtʃænt **~chanted** ˈtʃɑːnt ɪd §ˈtʃænt-, -əd ‖ ˈtʃænt̬ əd **~chanting** ˈtʃɑːnt ɪŋ §ˈtʃænt- ‖ ˈtʃænt̬ ɪŋ
enchanter ɪn ˈtʃɑːnt ə en-, ən-, §-ˈtʃænt- ‖ -ˈtʃænt̬ ər **~s** z
enchanting ɪn ˈtʃɑːnt ɪŋ en-, ən-, §ˈtʃænt- ‖ -ˈtʃænt̬ ɪŋ **~ly** li
enchantment ɪn ˈtʃɑːnt mənt §-ˈtʃænt- ‖ -ˈtʃænt- **~s** s
enchantress ɪn ˈtʃɑːntr əs en-, ən-, §-ˈtʃæntr-, -ɪs, -es ‖ -ˈtʃæntr- **~es** ɪz əz
enchilada ˌen tʃɪ ˈlɑːd ə -tʃə- **~s** z

Encinitas ˌents ɪ ˈniːt əs -ə- ‖ -ˈniːt̬-
enciph|er ɪn ˈsaɪf |ə en-, ən- ‖ -|ər **~ered** əd ‖ ərd **~ering** ər‿ɪŋ **~ers** əz ‖ ərz
encircl|e ɪn ˈsɜːk əl en-, ən- ‖ -ˈsɜːk- **~ed** d **~ement/s** mənt/s **~es** z **~ing** ‿ɪŋ
enclasp ɪn ˈklɑːsp en-, ən-, →ɪŋ-, →eŋ-, →əŋ-, §-ˈklæsp ‖ -ˈklæsp **~ed** t **~ing** ɪŋ **~s** s
enclave ˈen kleɪv →ˈeŋ-, ˈɒŋ-, ˈ·· ‖ ˈɑːn- **~s** z
enclitic ɪn ˈklɪt ɪk en-, →ɪŋ-, →eŋ- ‖ -ˈklɪt̬ ɪk **~s** s
enclos|e ɪn ˈkləʊz en-, ən-, →ɪŋ-, →eŋ-, →əŋ- ‖ -ˈkloʊz **~ed** d **~es** ɪz əz **~ing** ɪŋ
enclosure ɪn ˈkləʊʒ ə en-, ən-, →ɪŋ-, →eŋ-, →əŋ- ‖ -ˈkloʊʒ ər **~s** z
encod|e ɪn ˈkəʊd ₍ₗ₎en-, →ɪŋ-, →₍ₗ₎eŋ- ‖ -ˈkoʊd **~ed** ɪd əd **~er/s** ə/z ‖ ər/z **~es** z **~ing** ɪŋ
encomiast ɪn ˈkəʊm i æst en-, ən-, →ɪŋ-, →eŋ-, →əŋ-, -əst ‖ -ˈkoʊm- **~s** s
encomienda ɪn ˌkəʊm i ˈend ə en-, ən- ‖ -ˌkoʊm- —*Sp* [eŋ ko ˈmjen da]
encomi|um ɪn ˈkəʊm i‿|əm en-, ən-, →ɪŋ-, →eŋ-, →əŋ- ‖ -ˈkoʊm- **~a** ə **~ums** əmz
encompass ɪn ˈkʌmp əs en-, ən-, →ɪŋ-, →eŋ-, →əŋ- ‖ -ˈkɑːmp- **~ed** t **~es** ɪz əz **~ing** ɪŋ **~ment** mənt
encore ˈɒŋ kɔː ˌ·ˈ· ‖ ˈɑːn kɔːr -koʊr
encounter ɪn ˈkaʊnt ə en-, ən-, →ɪŋ-, →eŋ-, →əŋ- ‖ -ˈkaʊnt̬ ər **~ed** d **encountering** ɪn ˈkaʊnt‿ər ɪŋ en-, ən-, →ɪŋ-, →eŋ-, →əŋ- ‖ -ˈkaʊnt̬ ər ɪŋ →-ˈkaʊntr ɪŋ **~s** z
enˈcounter group
encourag|e ɪn ˈkʌr ɪdʒ en-, ən-, →ɪŋ-, →eŋ-, →əŋ- ‖ -ˈkɜː- **~ed** d **~ement/s** mənt/s **~es** ɪz əz **~ing/ly** ɪŋ /li
encroach ɪn ˈkrəʊtʃ en-, ən-, →ɪŋ-, →eŋ-, →əŋ- ‖ -ˈkroʊtʃ **~ed** t **~es** ɪz əz **~ing** ɪŋ **~ment/s** mənt/s
en croute, en croûte ˌɒn ˈkruːt →ˌɒŋ- ‖ ˌɑːn- —*Fr* [ɑ̃ kʁut]
encrust ɪn ˈkrʌst en-, ən-, →ɪŋ-, →eŋ-, →əŋ- **~ed** ɪd əd **~ing** ɪŋ **~s** s
encrustation ˌɪn krʌs ˈteɪʃ ən ˌen-, →ˌɪŋ-, →eŋ-, ˌ·ˌ·- **~s** z
encrypt ɪn ˈkrɪpt en-, ən-, →ɪŋ-, →eŋ-, →əŋ- **~ed** ɪd əd **~ing** ɪŋ **~s** s
encryption ɪn ˈkrɪp ʃən en-, ən-, →ɪŋ-, →eŋ-, →əŋ- **~s** z
encum|ber ɪn ˈkʌm |bə ən, ən-, →ɪŋ-, →eŋ-, →əŋ- ‖ -|bər **~bered** bəd ‖ bərd **~bering** bər‿ɪŋ **~bers** bəz ‖ bərz
encumbranc|e ɪn ˈkʌm brənts en-, ən-, →ɪŋ-, →eŋ-, →əŋ- **~es** z
-ency ənts i —*Stress always as in the corresponding* -ent *word:* sufˈficiency, ˈurgency, ˈexcellency.
encyclical ɪn ˈsɪk lɪk əl en-, ən- **~s** z
encyclopaed... —*see* **encycloped...**
encyclopedia ɪn ˌsaɪk lə ˈpiːd i‿ə en-, ən- **~s** z
encyclopedic ɪn ˌsaɪk lə ˈpiːd ɪk ◂ en-, ən- **~ally** əl‿i
encyclopedist ɪn ˌsaɪk lə ˈpiːd ɪst en-, ən-, §-əst **~s** s
encyst en ˈsɪst **~ed** ɪd əd **~ing** ɪŋ **~s** s

E

end end **ended** 'end ɪd -əd **ending** 'end ɪŋ **ends** endz
'end ˌmatter; **'end ˌproduct**, ˌ· '· ·; **'end ˌuser**, ˌ· '· ·

endang|er ɪn 'deɪndʒ |ə en-, ən- ‖ -|ᵊr **~ered** əd ‖ ᵊrd **~ering** ər‿ɪŋ **~erment** ə mənt ‖ ᵊr mənt **~ers** əz ‖ ᵊrz

endear ɪn 'dɪə en-, ən- ‖ -'dɪᵊr **~ed** d **endearing/ly** ɪn 'dɪər ɪŋ /li en-, ən- ‖ -'dɪr ɪŋ /li **~ment/s** mənt/s **~s** z

endeavor, endeavour ɪn 'dev ə en-, ən- ‖ -ᵊr **~ed** d **endeavoring, endeavouring** ɪn 'dev ər‿ɪŋ en-, ən- **~s** z

Endell 'end ᵊl

endemic en 'dem ɪk ɪn- **~al** ᵊl **~ally** ᵊl‿i

Enderby 'end ə bi ‖ -ᵊr- **'Enderby Land**

Enders 'end əz ‖ -ᵊrz

endgame 'end geɪm →'eŋ- **~s** z

Endicott 'end ɪ kɒt -ə-; -ɪk ət, -ək- ‖ -kɑːt

ending 'end ɪŋ **~s** z

endive 'end ɪv -aɪv ‖ 'end aɪv 'ɑːnd iːv **~s** z

endless 'end ləs -lɪs **~ly** li **~ness** nəs nɪs

endo- *comb. form*
with stress-neutral suffix ˌend əʊ ‖ ˌend ə — **endocranial** ˌend əʊ 'kreɪn i‿əl ◂ ‖ ˌ·ə- *with stress-imposing suffix* en 'dɒ+ ‖ en 'dɑː+ — **endogenous** en 'dɒdʒ ən əs -ɪn- ‖ -'dɑːdʒ-

endocarditis ˌend əʊ kɑː 'daɪt ɪs §-əs ‖ -oʊ kɑːr 'daɪţ əs

endocarp 'end əʊ kɑːp ‖ -ə kɑːrp **~s** s

endocentric ˌend əʊ 'sentr ɪk ◂ ‖ -oʊ- **~ally** ᵊl‿i

endocrine 'end əʊ kraɪn -krɪn, -kriːn, §-krən ‖ -ə- **~s** z

endocrinology ˌend əʊ krɪ 'nɒl ədʒ i -kraɪ'-- ‖ -oʊ krɪ 'nɑːl-

endogam|ous en 'dɒg əm |əs ‖ -'dɑːg- **~y** i

endogenous en 'dɒdʒ ən əs ɪn-, -ɪn- ‖ -'dɑːdʒ- **~ly** li

endometriosis ˌend əʊ ˌmiːtr i 'əʊs ɪs §-əs ‖ -oʊ ˌmiːtr i 'oʊs əs

endometri|um ˌend əʊ 'miːtr i‿|əm ‖ ˌoʊ- **~a** ə **~al** əl

endomorph 'end əʊ mɔːf ‖ -ə mɔːrf **~s** s

endomorph|ic ˌend əʊ 'mɔːf |ɪk ◂ ‖ -ə 'mɔːrf- **~ism** ˌɪz əm

endoplasm 'end əʊ ˌplæz əm ‖ -ə-

endoplasmic ˌend əʊ 'plæz mɪk ◂ ‖ -oʊ-

Endor 'end ɔː ‖ -ɔːr

endorphin en 'dɔːf ɪn §-ən ‖ -'dɔːrf- **~s** z

endorsable ɪn 'dɔːs əb ᵊl en-, ən- ‖ -'dɔːrs-

endors|e ɪn 'dɔːs en-, ən- ‖ -'dɔːrs **~ed** t **~ement/s** mənt/s **~er/s** ə/z ‖ ᵊr/z **~es** ɪz əz **~ing** ɪŋ

endorsee ˌen dɔː 'siː ‖ -dɔːr- **~s** z

endoscope 'end ə skəʊp ‖ -skoʊp **~s** s

endoscopic ˌend ə 'skɒp ɪk ◂ ‖ -'skɑːp- **~ally** ᵊl‿i

endoscop|y en 'dɒsk əp |i ‖ -'dɑːsk- **~ies** iz

endosmosis ˌend ɒz 'məʊs ɪs -ɒs-, §-əs ‖ -ɑːz 'moʊs- -ɑːs-

endosperm 'end əʊ spɜːm ‖ -oʊ spɜːm

endotherm 'end əʊ θɜːm ‖ -oʊ θɜːm **~s** z

endothermic ˌend əʊ 'θɜːm ɪk ◂ ‖ -ə 'θɜːm- **~ally** ᵊl‿i

endow ɪn 'daʊ en-, ən- **~ed** d **~ing** ɪŋ **~ment/s** mənt/s **~s** z
en'dowment ˌmortgage; **en'dowment ˌpolicy**

endpaper 'end ˌpeɪp ə →'em- ‖ -ᵊr **~s** z

endplay 'end pleɪ →'em- **~ed** d **~ing** ɪŋ **~s** z

Endsleigh 'endz li -liː

end-stopped 'end stɒpt ˌ·'· ‖ -stɑːpt

endu|e ɪn 'djuː en-, ən-, →-'dʒuː ‖ -'duː -'djuː **~ed** d **~es** z **~ing** ɪŋ

endurable ɪn 'djʊər əb ᵊl en-, ən-, →-'dʒʊər-, -'djɔːr- ‖ -'dʊr- -djʊr-, -'dɜːr-

endurance ɪn 'djʊər ənᵗs en-, ən-, -'djɔːr-, →-'dʒʊər- ‖ -'dʊr- -'djʊr-, -'dɜː-

endure ɪn 'djʊə en-, ən-, -'djɔː, →-'dʒʊə ‖ -'dʊᵊr -'djʊᵊr, -'dɜː **~d** d **~s** z **enduring/ly** ɪn 'djʊər ɪŋ /li en-, ən-, -'djɔːr-, →-'dʒʊər- ‖ -'dʊr ɪŋ /li -'djʊr-, -'dɜː-

endways 'end weɪz

endwise 'end waɪz

Endymion en 'dɪm i‿ən ɪn-

-ene iːn — **toluene** 'tɒl ju iːn ‖ 'toʊl- —*Although strong-vowelled, this suffix is unstressed.*

Eneas i 'niː‿əs 'neɪ-, -æs

Eneid 'iːn i‿ɪd ɪ 'niː-, §-əd

enema 'en əm ə -ɪm- **~s** z

enem|y 'en əm |i -ɪm- **~ies** iz **ˌenemy 'alien**

Energen *tdmk* 'en ədʒ ən ‖ -ᵊrdʒ-

energetic ˌen ə 'dʒet ɪk ◂ ‖ -ᵊr 'dʒeţ ɪk ◂ **~ally** ᵊl‿i **~s** s

Energis *tdmk* 'en ədʒ ɪs §-əs ‖ -ᵊrdʒ-

energis|e, energiz|e 'en ə dʒaɪz ‖ -ᵊr- **~ed** d **~es** ɪz əz **~ing** ɪŋ

energ|y 'en ədʒ |i ‖ -ᵊrdʒ |i **~ies** iz

ener|vate 'en ə |veɪt -ɜː- ‖ -ᵊr- **~vated** veɪt ɪd -əd ‖ veɪţ əd **~vates** veɪts **~vating** veɪt ɪŋ ‖ veɪţ ɪŋ

enervation ˌen ə 'veɪʃ ᵊn -ɜː- ‖ -ᵊr-

en famille ˌɒ̃ fæ 'miː ˌɒn-, ˌɑːn- ‖ ˌɑːn fə- —*Fr* [ɑ̃ fa mij]

enfant terrible ˌɒ̃f ɒ̃ tə 'riːb‿lə ˌɒn fɒn-, ˌɑːn fɑːn-, -te'-- ‖ ɑːn ˌfɑːn- —*Fr* [ɑ̃ fɑ̃ tɛ ʁibl] **enfants terribles** *as singular*

enfeebl|e ɪn 'fiːb ᵊl en-, ən- **~ed** d **~ement/s** mənt/s **~es** z **~ing** ‿ɪŋ

enfeoff ɪn 'fiːf en-, ən-, -'fef **~ed** t **~ing** ɪŋ **~s** s

en fete, en fête (ˌ)ɒ̃ 'feɪt (ˌ)ɒn-, -'fet ‖ (ˌ)ɑ̃ː —*Fr* [ɑ̃ fɛt]

Enfield 'en fiːᵊld

enfilad|e *v* ˌen fɪ 'leɪd -fə-, '· · · ‖ 'en fə leɪd -lɑːd **~ed** ɪd əd **~es** z **~ing** ɪŋ

enfilade *n* 'en fɪ leɪd -fə-, ˌ· ·'· ‖ -lɑːd **~s** z

enfold ɪn 'fəʊld en-, ən-, →-'fɒʊld ‖ -'foʊld **~ed** ɪd əd **~ing** ɪŋ **~s** z

enforc|e ɪn 'fɔːs en-, ən- ‖ -'fɔːrs -'foʊrs **~ed** t **~es** ɪz əz **~ing** ɪŋ

nforceab|le ɪn ˈfɔːs əb |əl en-, ən- ‖ -ˈfɔːrs- -ˈfoʊrs- **~ly** li
nforcement ɪn ˈfɔːs mənt en-, ən- ‖ -ˈfɔːrs- -ˈfoʊrs-
nforcer ɪn ˈfɔːs ə en-, ən- ‖ -ˈfɔːrs ər -ˈfoʊrs- **~s** z
nfranchis|e ɪn ˈfræntʃ aɪz en-, ən- **~ed** d **~es** ɪz əz **~ing** ɪŋ
nfranchisement ɪn ˈfræntʃ ɪz mənt en-, ən-, -əz- ‖ -aɪz- -əz- **~s** s
ngadine ˈeŋ gə diːn ˌ· · ˈ·
ngag|e ɪn ˈgeɪdʒ en-, ən-, →ɪŋ-, →eŋ-, →əŋ- **~ed** d **~es** ɪz əz **~ing/ly** ɪŋ /li
ngagé ˌɒŋ gæ ˈʒeɪ -gɑː- ‖ ˌɑːŋ gɑː- —*Fr* [ɑ̃ ga ʒe]
ngagement ɪn ˈgeɪdʒ mənt en-, ən-, →ɪŋ-, →eŋ-, →əŋ- **~s** s
en'gagement book; **en'gagement ring**
en garde ₍ₗ₎ɒ̃ ˈgɑːd ₍ₗ₎ɒn-, →₍ₗ₎ɒŋ- ‖ ₍ₗ₎ɑːn ˈgɑːrd —*Fr* [ɑ̃ gaʁd]
Engelbert ˈeŋ gəl bɜːt ‖ -bɜːt —*Ger* [ˈʔɛŋ əl bɛʁt]
Engels ˈeŋ gəlz —*Ger* [ˈʔɛŋ əls]
engender ɪn ˈdʒend ə en-, ən- ‖ -ər **~ed** d **engendering** ɪn ˈdʒend‿ər ɪŋ **~s** z
engine ˈendʒ ɪn §ɪndʒ-, -ən **~s** z
'engine ˌdriver
engined ˈendʒ ɪnd §ˈɪndʒ-, -ənd — **twin-engined** ˌtwɪn ˈendʒ ɪnd ◂ §-ˈɪndʒ-, -ənd
engi|neer ˌendʒ ɪ |ˈnɪə §ˌɪndʒ-, -ə- ‖ -|ˈnɪər **~neered** ˈnɪəd ‖ ˈnɪərd **~neering** ˈnɪər ɪŋ ‖ ˈnɪr ɪŋ **~neers** ˈnɪəz ‖ ˈnɪrz
England ˈɪŋ glənd -lənd **~'s** z
Englefield ˈeŋ gəl fiːəld
Englewood ˈeŋ gəl wʊd
English ˈɪŋ glɪʃ -lɪʃ **~man** mən **~men** mən men **~ness** nəs nɪs **~woman** ˌwʊm ən **~women** ˌwɪm ɪn §-ən
ˌEnglish 'Channel; **ˌEnglish 'literature**
Eng Lit ˌɪŋ ˈlɪt
Eng. lit. ˌɪŋ ˈlɪt ˌeŋ-
engorg|e ɪn ˈgɔːdʒ en-, ən-, →ɪŋ-, →eŋ-, →əŋ- ‖ -ˈgɔːrdʒ **~ed** d **~ement** mənt **~es** ɪz əz **~ing** ɪŋ
engraft ɪn ˈgrɑːft en-, ən-, →ɪŋ-, →eŋ-, →əŋ-, §-ˈgræft ‖ -ˈgræft **~ed** ɪd əd **~ing** ɪŋ **~s** s
engram ˈen græm →ˈeŋ- **~s** z
engrav|e ɪn ˈgreɪv en-, ən-, →ɪŋ-, →eŋ-, →əŋ- **~ed** d **~er/s** ə/z ‖ ər/z **~es** z **~ing/s** ɪŋ/z
engross ɪn ˈgrəʊs en-, ən-, →ɪŋ-, →eŋ-, →əŋ-, §-ˈgrɒs ‖ -ˈgroʊs **~ed** t **~es** ɪz əz **~ing** ɪŋ
engulf ɪn ˈgʌlf en-, ən-, →ɪŋ-, →eŋ-, →əŋ- **~ed** t **~ing** ɪŋ **~s** s
enhanc|e ɪn ˈhɑːnts en-, ən-, -ˈhænts ‖ -ˈhænts **~ed** t **~ement/s** mənt/s **~er/s** ə/z ‖ ər/z **~es** ɪz əz **~ing** ɪŋ
enharmonic ˌen hɑː ˈmɒn ɪk ◂ ‖ -hɑːr ˈmɑːn- **~ally** əl‿i
Enid ˈiːn ɪd §-əd —*but in Wales sometimes* ˈen-
enigma i ˈnɪg mə e-, ə- **~s** z
enigmatic ˌen ɪg ˈmæt ɪk ◂ ‖ -ˈmæṭ ɪk ◂ **~ally** əl‿i
enjambment ɪn ˈdʒæm mənt en-, ən-, -ˈdʒæmb- —*Fr* enjambement [ɑ̃ ʒɑ̃b mɑ̃] **~s** s
enjoin ɪn ˈdʒɔɪn en-, ən- **~ed** d **~ing** ɪŋ **~s** z
enjoy ɪn ˈdʒɔɪ en-, ən- **~ed** d **~ing** ɪŋ **~s** z
enjoyab|le ɪn ˈdʒɔɪ əb |əl en-, ən- **~ly** li
enjoyment ɪn ˈdʒɔɪ mənt en-, ən- **~s** s
enlarg|e ɪn ˈlɑːdʒ en-, ən- ‖ -ˈlɑːrdʒ **~ed** d **~ement/s** mənt/s **~er/s** ə/z ‖ ər/z **~es** ɪz əz **~ing** ɪŋ
enlighten ɪn ˈlaɪt ən en-, ən- **~ed** d **~ing** ˌɪŋ **~s** z
enlightenment, E~ ɪn ˈlaɪt ən mənt en-, ən-
enlist ɪn ˈlɪst en-, ən- **~ed** ɪd əd **~ing** ɪŋ **~s** s
en'listed man
enlistment ɪn ˈlɪst mənt en-, ən- **~s** s
enliven ɪn ˈlaɪv ən en-, ən- **~ed** d **~ing** ˌɪŋ **~s** z
en masse ₍ₗ₎ɒ̃ ˈmæs ₍ₗ₎ɒn-, →₍ₗ₎ɒm- ‖ ₍ₗ₎ɑːn- -ˈmɑːs —*Fr* [ɑ̃ mas]
enmesh ɪn ˈmeʃ en-, ən-, →ɪm-, →em-, →əm- **~ed** t **~es** ɪz əz **~ing** ɪŋ
enmit|y ˈen mət |i →ˈem-, -mɪt-; ⚠ˈem nət i ‖ ˈen məṭ |i **~ies** iz
Ennals ˈen əlz
enneahedr|on ˌen i‿ə ˈhiːdr |ən -ˈhedr- **~a** ə
Ennerdale ˈen ə deɪəl ‖ -ər-
Ennis ˈen ɪs §-əs
Enniskillen ˌen ɪs ˈkɪl ən ◂ -əs-, -ɪn
Ennius ˈen i‿əs
ennobl|e ɪ ˈnəʊb əl e-, ə-, ɪn-, en-, ən- ‖ -ˈnoʊb- **~ed** d **~ement** mənt **~es** z **~ing** ‿ɪŋ
ennui ˈɒn wiː ·ˈ· ‖ ˌɑːn ˈwiː —*Fr* [ɑ̃ nɥi]
Eno ˈiːn əʊ ‖ -oʊ **~'s** z
Enoch ˈiːn ɒk ‖ -ək -ɑːk
Enola Gay ɪ ˌnəʊl ə ˈgeɪ ‖ -ˌnoʊl-
enology i ˈnɒl ədʒ i ‖ -ˈnɑːl-
Enone i ˈnəʊn i ‖ -ˈnoʊn i
enophile ˈiːn əʊ faɪəl ‖ ˈiːn ə- **~s** z
enormit|y i ˈnɔːm ət |i ə-, -ɪt- ‖ i ˈnɔːrm əṭ |i **~ies** iz
enormous i ˈnɔːm əs ə- ‖ i ˈnɔːrm- **~ly** li **~ness** nəs nɪs
Enos ˈiːn ɒs ‖ -ɑːs
enosis ˈen əʊs ɪs §-əs ‖ ɪ ˈnoʊs-
enough ə ˈnʌf i ˈnʌf —*After* **t, d** *(and sometimes other obstruents) the* **ə** *and* **n** *may combine to give a syllabic consonant, thus* good enough ˌgʊd n ˈʌf.
enounc|e i ˈnaʊnts **~ed** t **~es** ɪz əz **~ing** ɪŋ
enow i ˈnaʊ ə-
en papillote ɒ̃ ˌpæp i ˈɒt ɒn-, →ɒm- ‖ ɑːn ˌpɑːp i ˈoʊt —*Fr* [ɑ̃ pa pi jɔt]
en passant ˌɒn ˈpæs ɒn →ˌɒm-, ˌɒ̃-, -ɒnt, -ɑːnt, -ɒ̃; -pæ ˈsɒnt, -ˈsɑːnt ‖ ˌɑːn pɑː ˈsɑːn -pə- —*Fr* [ɑ̃ pa sɑ̃]
enplan|e ɪn ˈpleɪn en-, →ɪm-, →em- **~ed** d **~es** z **~ing** ɪŋ
enquire ɪn ˈkwaɪ‿ə en-, ən-, →ɪŋ-, →eŋ-, →əŋ- ‖ -ˈkwaɪ‿ər **~d** d **~s** z **enquiring/ly** ɪn ˈkwaɪ‿ər ɪŋ /li en-, ən-, →ɪŋ-, →eŋ-, →əŋ- ‖ -ˈkwaɪ‿ər ɪŋ /li
enquirer ɪn ˈkwaɪ‿ər ə en-, ən-, →ɪŋ-, →eŋ-, →eŋ- ‖ -ˈkwaɪ‿ər ər **~s** z

E

enquir|y ɪn ˈkwaɪ‿ər |i en-, ən-, →ɪŋ-, →eŋ-, →əŋ- ‖ ɪn ˈkwaɪ‿ər |i ˈ· · · ·; ˈɪŋk wər |i **~ies** iz
enrag|e ɪn ˈreɪdʒ en-, ən- **~ed** d **~es** ɪz əz **~ing** ɪŋ
enrapture ɪn ˈræp tʃə en-, ən- ‖ -tʃᵊr **~d** d **~s** z
enrapturing ɪn ˈræp tʃər ɪŋ en-, ən-
enrich ɪn ˈrɪtʃ en-, ən- **~ed** t **~er/s** ə/z ‖ ᵊr/z **~es** ɪz əz **~ing** ɪŋ **~ment/s** mənt/s
Enrico en ˈriːk əʊ ‖ -oʊ —*It* [en ˈriː ko]
Enright ˈen raɪt
enrob|e ɪn ˈrəʊb en-, ən- ‖ -ˈroʊb **~ed** d **~es** z **~ing** ɪŋ
enrol, enroll ɪn ˈrəʊl en-, ən-, →-ˈrɒʊl ‖ -ˈroʊl **~ed** d **~ing** ɪŋ **~ment/s** mənt/s **~s** z
Enron ˈen rɒn ‖ -rɑːn
en route ˌɒn ˈruːt ˌɒ̃- ‖ ˌɑːn- —*Fr* [ɑ̃ ʁut]
ENSA ˈenᵗs ə
ensanguined ɪn ˈsæŋ gwɪnd en-, ən-
Enschede ˈenᵗs kə deɪ —*Dutch* [ˈɛn sxə de]
ensconc|e ɪn ˈskɒnᵗs en-, ən- ‖ -ˈskɑːnᵗs **~ed** t **~es** ɪz əz **~ing** ɪŋ
ensemble ɒn ˈsɒm bᵊl ɒ̃-, -ˈsɒ̃- ‖ ɑːn ˈsɑːm- —*Fr* [ɑ̃ sɑ̃ːbl] **~s** z
enshrin|e ɪn ˈʃraɪn en-, ən- **~ed** d **~ement** mənt **~es** z **~ing** ɪŋ
enshroud ɪn ˈʃraʊd en-, ən- **~ed** ɪd əd **~ing** ɪŋ **~s** z
ensign ˈen saɪn —*but in the sense 'flag', naut, usually* ˈenᵗs ᵊn **~s** z
ensilag|e ˈenᵗs əl ɪdʒ -ɪl-; ɪn ˈsaɪl-, en-, ən- **~ed** d **~es** ɪz əz **~ing** ɪŋ
ensil|e en ˈsaɪᵊl ˈenᵗs aɪᵊl, -ᵊl **~ed** d **~es** z **~ing** ɪŋ
enslav|e ɪn ˈsleɪv en-, ən- **~ed** d **~ement/s** mənt/s **~er/s** ə/z ‖ ᵊr/z **~es** z **~ing** ɪŋ
ensnare ɪn ˈsneə en-, ən- ‖ -ˈsneᵊr -ˈsnæᵊr **~d** d **~ment/s** mənt/s **~s** z **ensnaring** ɪn ˈsneər ɪŋ en-, ən- ‖ -ˈsner ɪŋ -ˈsnær-
Ensor ˈenᵗs ɔː -ə ‖ -ɔːr -ᵊr
enstatite ˈenᵗst ə taɪt
ensu|e ɪn ˈsjuː en-, ən-, -ˈsuː ‖ -ˈsuː **~ed** d **~es** z **~ing** ɪŋ
en suite ˌɒ̃ ˈswiːt ˌɒn-, ˌɑːn- ‖ ˌɑːn- —*Fr* [ɑ̃ sɥit]
ensure ɪn ˈʃɔː en-, ən-, -ˈʃʊə, -ˈsjʊə ‖ -ˈʃʊᵊr -ˈʃɜː **~d** d **~s** z **ensuring** ɪn ˈʃɔːr ɪŋ en-, ən-, -ˈʃʊər-, -ˈsjʊər- ‖ -ˈʃʊr ɪŋ -ˈʃɜː-
ENT ˌiː en ˈtiː
ˌ**EN'T** ˌ**specialist**
-ent ənt —*This suffix has the same stress-effects as* -ence, *thus* adˈjacent, inˈtelligent, ˈeminent; *note* apˈparent. *It triggers a vowel change and change of stress in the stem of some words, as* excel ɪk ˈsel → excellent ˈeks əl ənt, provide prə ˈvaɪd → provident ˈprɒv ɪd ənt ‖ ˈprɑːv-. *Note change of vowel but not of stress in* apˈpear → apˈparent.
entablature en ˈtæb lətʃ ə ɪn-, -lɪtʃ-; -lɪ tʃʊə, lə- ‖ -lə tʃʊr -tʊr; -lətʃ ᵊr **~s** z
entail ɪn ˈteɪᵊl en-, ən- **~ed** d **~ing** ɪŋ **~ment/s** mənt/s **~s** z
entameb|a, entamoeb|a ˌent ə ˈmiːb |ə ‖ ˌenṯ- **~ae** iː **~as** əz

entangl|e ɪn ˈtæŋ gᵊl en-, ən- **~ed** d **~ement/** mənt/s **~es** z **~ing** ‿ɪŋ
entasis ˈent əs ɪs §-əs ‖ ˈenṯ-
Entebbe en ˈteb i ɪn-, ən-
entelech|y en ˈtel ək |i ɪn-, ən- **~ies** iz
entendre —*see* **double entendre**
Entenmann ˈent ən mæn →-əm- ‖ ˈenṯ-
entente ₍ˌ₎ɒn ˈtɒnt ₍ˌ₎ɒ̃- ‖ ₍ˌ₎ɑːn ˈtɑːnt —*Fr* [ɑ̃ tɑ̃ːt]
ˌ**entente** ˌ**cordi'ale**, ·ˌ·· ˌkɔːd i ˈɑːl ‖ ˌkɔːrd- —*Fr* [kɔʁ djal]
enter ˈent ə ‖ ˈenṯ ᵊr **entered** ˈent əd ‖ ˈenṯ ᵊrd **entering** ˈent‿ər ɪŋ ‖ ˈenṯ ər ɪŋ →ˈentr ɪŋ **enters** ˈent əz ‖ ˈenṯ ᵊrz
enteric en ˈter ɪk
enteritis ˌent ə ˈraɪt ɪs §-əs ‖ ˌenṯ ə ˈraɪṯ əs
entero- *comb. form with stress-neutral suffix* ¦ent‿ər əʊ ‖ ¦enṯ ə roʊ — **enterobacterium** ˌent‿ər əʊ bæk ˈtɪər i‿əm ‖ ˌenṯ ə roʊ bæk ˈtɪr- *with stress-imposing suffix* ˌent ə ˈrɒ+ ‖ ˌenṯ ə ˈrɑː+ — **enterostomy** ˌent ə ˈrɒst əm i ‖ ˌenṯ ə ˈrɑːst-
enterpris|e ˈent ə praɪz ‖ˈenṯ ᵊr- **~es** ɪz əz **~ing/ly** ɪŋ /li
entertain ˌent ə ˈteɪn ‖ ˌenṯ ᵊr- **~ed** d **~er/s** ə/z ‖ ᵊr/z **~ing/ly** ɪŋ /li **~s** z
entertainment ˌent ə ˈteɪn mənt →-ˈteɪm- ‖ ˌenṯ ᵊr- **~s** s
enthalpy ˈen θælp i -θᵊlp-; en ˈθælp i, ɪn-, ən-
enthral, enthral|l ɪn ˈθrɔːl en-, ən- ‖ -ˈθrɑːl **~led** d **~ling** ɪŋ **~ment** mənt **~s** z
enthron|e ɪn ˈθrəʊn en-, ən- ‖ -ˈθroʊn **~ed** d **~es** z **~ement** mənt **~ing** ɪŋ
enthus|e ɪn ˈθjuːz en-, ən-, -ˈθuːz ‖ -ˈθuːz **~ed** d **~es** ɪz əz **~ing** ɪŋ
enthusiasm ɪn ˈθjuːz i ˌæz əm en-, ən-, -ˈθuːz-, §-əz- ‖ -ˈθuːz- **~s** z
enthusiast ɪn ˈθjuːz i æst en-, ən-, -ˈθuːz-, §-əst ‖ -ˈθuːz- **~s** s
enthusiastic ɪn ˌθjuːz i ˈæst ɪk ◂ en-, ən-, -ˌθuːz- ‖ -ˌθuːz- **~ally** ᵊl‿i
entia ˈent i‿ə ˈenᵗʃ-
entic|e ɪn ˈtaɪs en-, ən- **~ed** t **~ement/s** mənt/s **~er/s** ə/z ‖ ᵊr/z **~es** ɪz əz **~ing/ly** ɪŋ/ li
entire ɪn ˈtaɪ‿ə en-, ən-, §ˌen-, §ˌɪn- ‖ -ˈtaɪ‿ᵊr **~ly** li **~ness** nəs nɪs
entiret|y ɪn ˈtaɪ‿ər ət |i en-, ən-, -ɪt i, -ˈtaɪ‿ət |i ‖ -ˈtaɪ‿ᵊrṯ |i -ˈtaɪ‿ᵊr əṯ |i **~ies** iz
entiti... —*see* **entity**
entitl|e ɪn ˈtaɪt ᵊl en-, ən- ‖ -ˈtaɪṯ ᵊl **~ed** d **~ement/s** mənt/s **~es** z **~ing** ‿ɪŋ
entit|y ˈent ət |i -ɪt- ‖ ˈenṯ əṯ |i **~ies** iz
entomb ɪn ˈtuːm en-, ən- **~ed** d **~ing** ɪŋ **~ment** mənt **~s** z
entomological ˌent əm ə ˈlɒdʒ ɪk ᵊl ◂ ‖ ˌenṯ əm ə ˈlɑːdʒ- **~ly** ‿i
entomologist ˌent ə ˈmɒl ədʒ ɪst §-əst ‖ ˌenṯ ə ˈmɑːl- **~s** s
entomology ˌent ə ˈmɒl ədʒ i ‖ ˌenṯ ə ˈmɑːl-
entourag|e ˈɒn tuᵊ rɑːʒ ˈɒ̃-, · · ˈ· ‖ ˌɑːn tu ˈrɑːʒ —*Fr* [ɑ̃ tu ʁaːʒ] **~es** ɪz əz

ntracte, entr'acte 'ɒntr ækt 'ɒ̃tr-, ˌ·'· ‖ 'ɑːntr- —*Fr* [ɑ̃ tʁakt] **~s** s
ntrails 'entr erᵊlz ‖ 'entr ᵊlz
ntrain ɪn 'treɪn en-, ən- **~ed** d **~ing** ɪŋ **~ment** mənt **~s** z
ntrammel ɪn 'træm ᵊl en-, ən- **~ed, ~led** d **~ing, ~ling** ɪŋ **~s** z
ntranc|e *n 'way in'* 'entr ənᵗs **~es** ɪz əz
ntranc|e *v 'charm'* ɪn 'trɑːnᵗs en-, ən-, §-'trænᵗs ‖ -'trænᵗs **~ed** t **~ement/s** mənt/s **~es** ɪz əz **~ing/ly** ɪŋ /li
ntrant 'entr ənt **~s** s
ntrap ɪn 'træp en-, ən- **~ment/s** mənt/s **~ped** t **~ping** ɪŋ **~s** s
n|treat ɪn |'triːt en-, ən- **~treated** 'triːt ɪd -əd ‖ 'triːţ əd **~treating/ly** 'triːt ɪŋ /li ‖ 'triːţ ɪŋ /li **~treats** 'triːts
entreatment ɪn 'triːt mənt en-, ən- **~s** s
entreat|y ɪn 'triːt |i en-, ən- ‖ -'triːţ |i **~ies** iz
entrechat 'ɒntr ə ʃɑː 'ɒ̃tr-, 'ɑːntr-, ˌ··'· ‖ ˌɑːntr ə 'ʃɑː —*Fr* [ɑ̃ tʁə ʃa] **~s** z
entrecote, entrecôte 'ɒntr ə kəʊt ˌ··'· ‖ 'ɑːntr ə koʊt ˌ··'· —*Fr* [ɑ̃ tʁə kot] **~s** s
Entre-Deux-Mers ˌɒntr ə ˌdɜː 'meə ‖ ˌɑːntr ə ˌduː 'meᵊr —*Fr* [ɑ̃ tʁə dø mɛːʁ]
entree, entrée 'ɒntr eɪ 'ɒ̃tr- ‖ 'ɑːntr- —*Fr* [ɑ̃ tʁe] **~s** z
entremets *sing.* 'ɒntr ə meɪ 'ɒ̃tr-, 'ɑːntr-, ˌ··'· ‖ 'ɑːntr- —*Fr* [ɑ̃ tʁə mɛ] **~** *pl* z
entrench ɪn 'trentʃ en-, ən- **~ed** t **~es** ɪz əz **~ing** ɪŋ **~ment/s** mənt/s
entre nous ˌɒntr ə 'nuː ˌɒ̃tr-, ɑːntr- ‖ ˌɑːntr- —*Fr* [ɑ̃ tʁə nu]
entrepot, entrepôt 'ɒntr ə pəʊ 'ɒ̃tr- ‖ 'ɑːntr ə poʊ —*Fr* [ɑ̃ tʁə po] **~s** z
entrepreneur ˌɒntr ə prə 'nɜː ˌɒ̃tr-, -pre'-, -'njʊə ‖ ˌɑːntr ə prə 'nɜː -pə'-, -'nʊᵊr —*Fr* [ɑ̃ tʁə pʁə nœːʁ] **~s** z **~ship** ʃɪp
entrepreneurial ˌɒntr ə prə 'nɜːr i‿əl ◂ ˌɒ̃tr-, -pre'--, -'njʊər- ‖ ˌɑːntr ə prə 'nɜː- -'nʊr- **~ly** i
entresol 'ɒntr ə sɒl 'ɒ̃tr- ‖ 'ɑːntr ə sɑːl —*Fr* [ɑ̃ tʁə sɔl] **~s** z
entries 'entr iz
entropic en 'trɒp ɪk ‖ -'trɑːp- **~ally** ᵊl‿i
entropy 'entr əp i
entrust ɪn 'trʌst en-, ən- **~ed** ɪd əd **~ing** ɪŋ **~ment** mənt **~s** s
entr|y 'entr |i **~ies** iz **'entry cerˌtificate**
entryism 'entr i ˌɪz əm
entryist 'entr i ɪst §-əst **~s** s
entryphone 'entr i fəʊn ‖ -foʊn **~s** z
entryway 'entr i weɪ **~s** z
entwin|e ɪn 'twaɪn en-, ən- **~ed** d **~es** z **~ing** ɪŋ
Entwistle 'ent wɪs ᵊl
enucleate *adj* i 'njuːk li ət ə-, -ɪt, -eɪt ‖ i 'nuːk- i 'njuːk-
enucle|ate *v* i 'njuːk li |eɪt ə- ‖ -'nuːk- -'njuːk- **~ated** eɪt ɪd -əd ‖ eɪţ əd **~ates** eɪts **~ating** eɪt ɪŋ ‖ eɪţ ɪŋ
Enugu e 'nuːg uː ɪ-

enumerable i 'njuːm ər‿əb ᵊl ə-, §-'nuːm- ‖ i 'nuːm- i 'njuːm- *(usually = innumerable)*
enume|rate ɪ 'njuːm ə |reɪt ə-, §-'nuːm- ‖ ɪ 'nuːm- ɪ 'njuːm- **~rated** reɪt ɪd -əd ‖ reɪţ əd **~rates** reɪts **~rating** reɪt ɪŋ ‖ reɪţ ɪŋ
enumeration ɪ ˌnjuːm ə 'reɪʃ ᵊn ə-, §-'nuːm- ‖ ɪ ˌnuːm- ɪ ˌnjuːm- **~s** z
enumerator ɪ 'njuːm ə reɪt ə ə-, §-'nuːm- ‖ ɪ 'nuːm ə reɪţ ᵊr ɪ 'njuːm- **~s** z
enunci|ate ɪ 'nʌnᵗs i |eɪt ə-, -'nʌnᵗʃ- **~ated** eɪt ɪd -əd ‖ eɪţ əd **~ates** eɪts **~ating** eɪt ɪŋ ‖ eɪţ ɪŋ
enunciation ɪ ˌnʌnᵗs i 'eɪʃ ᵊn ə-, -ˌnʌnᵗʃ- **~s** z
enunciative ɪ 'nʌnᵗs i‿ət ɪv ə-, -'nʌnᵗʃ-, -eɪt- ‖ -i eɪţ ɪv **~ly** li
enunciator ɪ 'nʌnᵗs i eɪt ə ə-, -'nʌnᵗʃ- ‖ -eɪţ ᵊr **~s** z
enure —*see* **inure**
enuresis ˌen juᵊ 'riːs ɪs §-əs ‖ -jə-
envelop *v* ɪn 'vel əp en-, ən- **~ed** t **~er/s** ə/z ‖ ᵊr/z **~ing** ɪŋ **~s** s

ENVELOPE

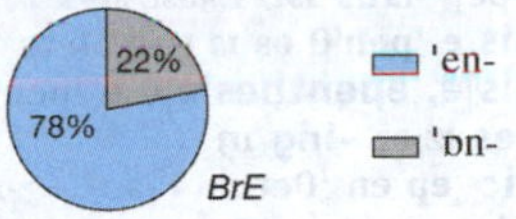

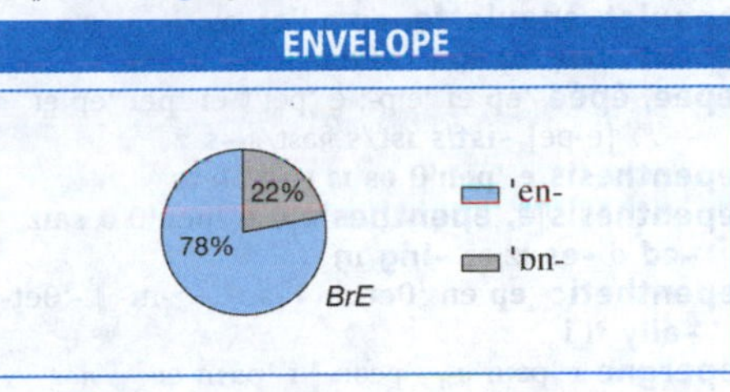

envelope *n* 'en və ləʊp 'ɒn- ‖ -loʊp 'ɑːn- — *Preference poll, BrE:* 'en- *78%,* 'ɒn- *22%.* **~s** s
envelopment ɪn 'vel əp mənt en-, ən-
envenom ɪn 'ven əm en-, ən- **~ed** d **~ing** ɪŋ **~s** z
enviab|le 'en vi‿əb |ᵊl **~ly** li
envie... —*see* **envy**
envious 'en vi‿əs **~ly** li **~ness** nəs nɪs
environ *v* ɪn 'vaɪᵊr ən en-, ən- **~ed** d **~ing** ɪŋ **~s** z
environment ɪn 'vaɪᵊr ən mənt en-, ən-, →-əm-, -ə- **~s** s
environmental ɪn ˌvaɪᵊr ən 'ment ᵊl ◂ en-, ən-, →-əm-, -ə- ‖ -'menţ ᵊl ◂ **~ism** ˌɪz əm **~ist/s** ɪst/s §əst/s **~ly** i
environs *n* ɪn 'vaɪᵊr ənz en-, ən-; 'en vɪr-, -vər-
envisag|e ɪn 'vɪz ɪdʒ en-, ən- **~ed** d **~es** ɪz əz **~ing** ɪŋ
envision ɪn 'vɪʒ ᵊn en-, ən- **~ed** d **~ing** ˌɪŋ **~s** z
envoi, envoy 'en vɔɪ ‖ 'ɑːn- **~s** z
en|vy 'en |vi **~vied** vid **~vies** viz **~vying/ly** vi‿ɪŋ /li
enwrap ɪn 'ræp en-, ən- **~ped** t **~ping** ɪŋ **~s** s
enwreath|e ɪn 'riːð en-, ən- **~ed** d **~es** z **~ing** ɪŋ
Enya 'en jə
enzyme 'en zaɪm **~s** z
Eocene 'iː əʊ siːn ‖ -ə-
eohippus ˌiː əʊ 'hɪp əs ‖ -oʊ-
Eoin *(i)* 'əʊ ɪn -ən ‖ 'oʊ ən, *(ii)* jəʊn ‖ joʊn

E

eolian i ˈəʊl i͜ ən ‖ i ˈoʊl-
Eolic i ˈɒl ɪk -ˈəʊl- ‖ i ˈɑːl ɪk
eolith ˈiː əʊ lɪθ ‖ -ə- **~s** s
eolithic, e~ ˌiː əʊ ˈlɪθ ɪk ◂ ‖ -ə-
eon ˈiː ən -ɒn ‖ -ɑːn **~s** z
Eos ˈiː ɒs ‖ -ɑːs
eosin ˈiː əʊs ɪn §-ən ‖ -əs-
eosinophil ˌiː əʊ ˈsɪn əʊ fɪl ‖ ˌiː ə ˈsɪn ə fɪl **~s** z
Eothen ˈiː əʊ θen i ˈəʊθ en ‖ -ə-
-eous i͜ əs — **piteous** ˈpɪt i͜ əs —*This suffix imposes stress on the preceding syllable:* couˈrageous. *In some words its compressed form* jəs *has coalesced with the final consonant of the stem:* righteous ˈraɪtʃ əs
EP ˌiː ˈpiː **~s, ~'s** z
epact ˈiːp ækt ˈep- **~s** s
Epaminondas e ˌpæm ɪ ˈnɒnd æs ɪ-, -ə- ‖ -ˈnɑːnd əs
eparch ˈep ɑːk ‖ -ɑːrk **~s** s
eparch|y ˈep ɑːk |i ‖ -ɑːrk |i **~ies** iz
epaulet, epaulette ˌep ə ˈlet -ɔː-, ˈ· · · **~s** s
Epcot *tdmk* ˈep kɒt ‖ -kɑːt
epee, épée ˈep eɪ ˈeɪp-; e ˈpeɪ ‖ eɪ ˈpeɪ ˈep eɪ —*Fr* [e pe] **~ist/s** ɪst/s §əst/s **~s** z
epenthesis e ˈpentθ əs ɪs ɪ-, ə-, §-əs
epenthesis|e, epenthesiz|e e ˈpentθ ə saɪz **~ed** d **~es** ɪz əz **~ing** ɪŋ
epenthetic ˌep en ˈθet ɪk ◂ -ən-, →-m- ‖ -ˈθeţ- **~ally** əl͜ i
epergne ɪ ˈpɜːn e-, -ˈpeən ‖ ɪ ˈpɜːn eɪ- —*not actually a French word* **~s** z
epexegesis e ˌpeks ɪ ˈdʒiːs ɪs ɪ-, ə-, -ə-, §-əs
epexegetic e ˌpeks ɪ ˈdʒet ɪk ◂ ɪ-, ə-, -ə- ‖ -ˈdʒeţ- **~ally** əl͜ i
epha, ephah ˈiːf ə ‖ ˈef ə **~s** z
ephebe ˈef iːb ɪ ˈfiːb, e- **~s** z
ephedrine ˈef ɪ driːn -ə-; -ɪdr ɪn, -ədr-, -ən; ɪ ˈfedr ɪn, -ən ‖ ɪ ˈfedr ən e-
ephemera ɪ ˈfem ər͜ ə e-, ə-, -ˈfiːm- **~s** z

EPHEMERAL

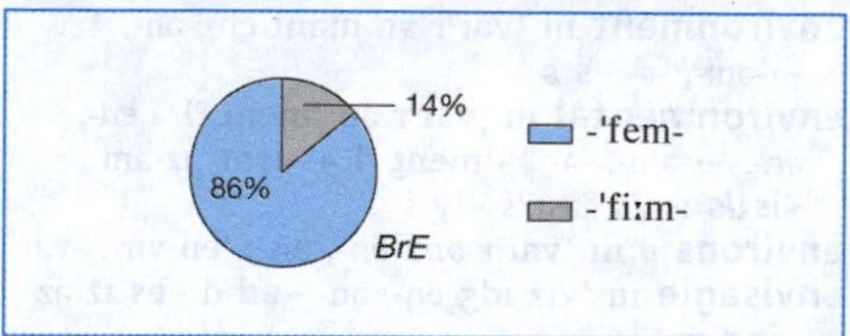

ephemeral ɪ ˈfem ər͜ əl e-, ə-, -ˈfiːm- **~ly** i — *Preference poll, BrE:* -ˈfem- *86%,* -ˈfiːm- *14%*
ephemerality ɪ ˌfem ə ˈræl ət i e-, ə-, -ˌfem- ‖ -əţ i
ephemeris ɪ ˈfem ər ɪs e-, ə-, -ˈfiːm-, §-əs **ephemerides** ˌef ɪ ˈmer ɪ diːz ˌ·ə-, -ˈə-
Ephesian ɪ ˈfiːʒ ən e-, ə-, -ˈfiːʒ i͜ ən **~s** z
Ephesus ˈef ɪs əs -əs-
Ephialtes ˌef i ˈælt iːz
ephod ˈiːf ɒd ˈef- ‖ -ɑːd **~s** z
ephor ˈiːf ɔː ˈef-, -ə ‖ -ɔːr -ər **~s** z
Ephraim ˈiːf reɪ ɪm -ri͜ , -əm; ˈiːf rəm ‖ ˈiːf ri͜ əm

epi- *comb. form*
with stress-neutral suffix ¦ep i ¦ep ə — **epistatic** ˌep ɪ ˈstæt ɪk ◂ -ə- ‖ -ˈstæţ-
with stress-imposing suffix ɪ ˈpɪ + e- — **epistasis** ɪ ˈpɪst əs ɪs e-, §-əs
epic ˈep ɪk **~s** s
epicanth|ic ˌep ɪ ˈkæntθ |ɪk ◂ §-ə- **~us** əs **ˌepiˌcanthic ˈfold**
epicene ˈep ɪ siːn §-ə- **~s** z
epicenter, epicentre ˈep ɪ ˌsent ə §-ə- ‖ -ˌsenţ ər **~s** z
epiclesis ˌep ɪ ˈkliːs ɪs §-ə-, -əs
Epictetus ˌep ɪk ˈtiːt əs ‖ -ˈtiːţ-
epicure ˈep ɪ kjʊə §-ə-, -kjɔː ‖ -kjʊr **~s** z
epicurean, E~ ˌep ɪ kjuə ˈriː͜ ən §ˌ·ə- **~s** z
Epicurus ˌep ɪ ˈkjʊər əs §-ə-, -ˈkjɔːr- ‖ -ˈkjʊr-
epicycle ˈep ɪ ˌsaɪk əl §-ə- **~s** z
epicyclic ˌep ɪ ˈsaɪk lɪk ◂ §-ə-, -ˈsɪk- **ˌepiˌcyclic ˈtrain**
epicycloid ˌep ɪ ˈsaɪk lɔɪd §-ə- **~s** z
Epidaurus ˌep ɪ ˈdɔːr əs §-ə- —*ModGk* Epidhavros [ɛ ˈpi ða vrɔs]
epideictic ˌep ɪ ˈdaɪkt ɪk ◂ -ə-
epidemic ˌep ɪ ˈdem ɪk ◂ §-ə- **~ally** əl͜ i **~s** s
epidemiological ˌep ɪ ˌdiːm i͜ ə ˈlɒdʒ ɪk əl §ˌ·ə-, -ˌdem- ‖ -ˈlɑːdʒ- **~ly** ͜i
epidemiologist ˌep ɪ ˌdiːm i ˈɒl ədʒ ɪst §ˌ·ə-, -ˌdem-, §-əst ‖ -ˈɑːl- **~s** s
epidemiology ˌep ɪ ˌdiːm i ˈɒl ədʒ i §ˌ·ə-, -ˌdem- ‖ -ˈɑːl-
epidermis ˌep ɪ ˈdɜːm ɪs §-ə-, §-əs ‖ -ˈdɝːm-
epidiascope ˌep ɪ ˈdaɪ͜ ə skəʊp §ˌ·ə- ‖ -skoʊp **~s** s
epi|didymis ˌep ɪ |ˈdɪd əm ɪs §ˌ·ə-, -ɪm ɪs, §-əs **~didymides** dɪ ˈdɪm ɪ diːz §də-, -ə-; ˈdɪd əm ɪ diːz, -ə-
epidote ˈep ɪ dəʊt §-ə- ‖ -doʊt
epidural ˌep ɪ ˈdjʊər əl ◂ §-ə-, -ˈdjɔːr-, →-ˈdʒʊər- ‖ -ˈdʊr- -ˈdjʊr- **~ly** i **~s** z
epigastrium ˌep ɪ ˈgæs tri͜ əm §ˌ·ə-
epiglottal ˌep ɪ ˈglɒt əl ◂ -ə- ‖ -ˈglɑːţ əl ◂
epiglottis ˌep ɪ ˈglɒt ɪs -ə-, §-əs, ˈ· · ˌ· · ‖ -ˈglɑːţ- **~es** ɪz əz
epigone ˈep ɪ gəʊn -ə- ‖ -goʊn **~s** z
Epigoni e ˈpɪg ə naɪ ɪ-, -iː
epigram ˈep ɪ græm -ə- **~s** z
epigrammatic ˌep ɪ grə ˈmæt ɪk ◂ ˌ·ə- ‖ -ˈmæţ- **~ally** əl͜ i
epigrammatist ˌep ɪ ˈgræm ət ɪst ˌ·ə-, §-əst ‖ -əţ- **~s** s
epigraph ˈep ɪ grɑːf -ə-, -græf ‖ -græf **~s** s
epigrapher e ˈpɪg rəf ə ɪ- ‖ -ər **~s** z
epigraphic ˌep ɪ ˈgræf ɪk ◂ -ə- **~al** əl **~ally** əl͜ i
epigraphy e ˈpɪg rəf i ɪ-
epilepsy ˈep ɪ leps i ˈ·ə-
epileptic ˌep ɪ ˈlept ɪk ◂ -ə- **~s** s **ˌepiˌleptic ˈfit**
epilog, epilogue ˈep ɪ lɒg -ə- ‖ -lɔːg -lɑːg **~s** z
EpiPen *tdmk* ˈep i pen
epiphan|y, E~ ɪ ˈpɪf ən |i ə- **~ies** iz
epiphenom|enon ˌep ɪ fɪ ˈnɒm |ɪn ən -fəˈ-, -ˈən- ‖ -ˈnɑːm |ə nɑːn -ən ən **~ena** ɪn ə ən- ‖ ən ə **~enal** ɪn əl ən- ‖ ən əl

epiph|ysis e ˈpɪf |əs ɪs ɪ-, §-əs **~yses** ə siːz ɪ-
epiphyte ˈep ɪ faɪt -ə- **~s** s
epiphytic ˌep ɪ ˈfɪt ɪk ◂ -ə- ‖ -ˈfɪţ-
epirus ɪ ˈpaɪᵊr əs e-, ə-
episcopac|y ɪ ˈpɪsk əp əs |i e-, ə- **~ies** iz
episcopal ɪ ˈpɪsk əp ᵊl e-, ə- **~ly** i
episcopalian, E~ ɪ ˌpɪsk ə ˈpeɪl i ̮ən ◂ e-, ə- **~s** z
episcopate ɪ ˈpɪsk əp ət e-, ə-, -ɪt, -eɪt **~s** s
episcope *'projector'* ˈep ɪ skəʊp ‖ -skoʊp **~s** s
episiotom|y ɪ ˌpɪz i ˈɒt əm |i e-, ə-, -ˌpiːz-, ˌep ɪz- ‖ -ˈɑːţ əm |i **~ies** iz
episode ˈep ɪ səʊd -ə- ‖ -soʊd **~s** z
episodic ˌep ɪ ˈsɒd ɪk ◂ -ə- ‖ -ˈsɑːd- **~ally** ᵊl ̮i
epistemic ˌep ɪ ˈstiːm ɪk ◂ -ə-, -ˈstem-
epistemological ɪ ˌpɪst ɪ mə ˈlɒdʒ ɪk ᵊl ◂ e-, ə-, -ˌ·ə-, -ˌ·iː- ‖ -ˈlɑːdʒ- **~ly** ̮i
epistemology ɪ ˌpɪst ɪ ˈmɒl ədʒ i e-, ə-, -ˌ·ə-, -ˌ·iː- ‖ -ˈmɑːl-
epistle, E~ ɪ ˈpɪs ᵊl ə- **~s** z
epistolary ɪ ˈpɪst əl ər i e-, ə-; ˌep ɪ ˈstɒl ər i ◂, §ˌ·ə- ‖ -ə ler i
epistyle ˈep ɪ staɪᵊl -ə- **~s** z
epitaph ˈep ɪ tɑːf -ə-, -tæf ‖ -tæf **~s** s
epitaxial ˌep ɪ ˈtæks i ̮əl ◂ ˌ·ə-
epithalami|um ˌep ɪθ ə ˈleɪm i ̮|əm ˌ·əθ- **~a** ə
epitheli|um ˌep ɪ ˈθiːl i|̮əm ˌ·ə- **~al** əl
epithet ˈep ɪ θet -ə- **~s** s
epitome ɪ ˈpɪt əm i ə- ‖ ɪ ˈpɪţ əm i **~s** z
epitomis|e, epitomiz|e ɪ ˈpɪt ə maɪz ə- ‖ ɪ ˈpɪţ ə- **~ed** d **~es** ɪz əz **~ing** ɪŋ
epizootic ˌep ɪ zəʊ ˈɒt ɪk ◂ ‖ -zoʊ ˈɑːţ ɪk ◂ **~s** s
e pluribus unum eɪ ˌplʊər ɪb əs ˈuːn əm iː-, -ˌplɔːr-, ˌ·ˌ·-, -əb ·ˈ·-, -ʊsˈ·-, -ˈjuːn-, -ʊm ‖ -ˌplʊr-
epoch ˈiːp ɒk ‖ ˈep ək -ɑːk *(*)* **~s** s
epochal ˈep ɒk ᵊl ˈiːp-, -ək-; iː ˈpɒk ᵊl ‖ ˈep ək ᵊl
epoch-making ˈiːp ɒk ˌmeɪk ɪŋ ‖ ˈep ək-
epode ˈep əʊd ‖ -oʊd **~s** z
eponym ˈep ə nɪm **~s** z
eponymous ɪ ˈpɒn ɪm əs ə-, -əm- ‖ ɪ ˈpɑːn- **~ly** li
epos ˈep ɒs ‖ -ɑːs
EPOS ˈiː pɒs ‖ -pɑːs
epox|y ɪ ˈpɒks |i e-, ə- ‖ e ˈpɑːks |i ɪ- **~ies** iz
ˌeˌpoxy ˈresin
epoxide ɪ ˈpɒks aɪd e-, ə- ‖ e ˈpɑːks- ɪ- **~s** z
Epping ˈep ɪŋ
ˌEpping ˈForest
EPROM ˈiː prɒm ‖ -prɑːm **~s** z
epsilon ep ˈsaɪl ən ɪp-, -ɒn; ˈeps ɪ lɒn, -ə-, -lən ‖ ˈeps ə lɑːn -əl ən *(*)* **~s** z
Epsom ˈeps əm
ˌEpsom ˈDowns; ˌEpsom ˈsalts ‖ ˈ· · ·
Epson *tdmk* ˈeps ɒn -ən ‖ -ɑːn
Epstein ˈep staɪn
Epstein-Barr ˌep staɪn ˈbɑː →-staɪm- ‖ -ˈbɑːr
e-publishing ˈiː ˌpʌb lɪʃ ɪŋ
epylli|on e ˈpɪl i ̮|ən ɪ-, ə- **~a** ə
equability ˌek wə ˈbɪl ət i -ɪt i ‖ -əţ i
equab|le ˈek wəb |ᵊl **~leness** ᵊl nəs -nɪs **~ly** li
equal ˈiːk wəl **~ed, ~led** d **~ing, ~ling** ɪŋ **~ly** i **~s** z
ˌEqual ˈRights Aˌmendment; ˈequal(s) sign
equalis... —*see* **equaliz...**
equalitarian ɪ ˌkwɒl ɪ ˈteər i ̮ən ◂ iː-, ə-, -ˌ·ə- ‖ ɪ ˌkwɔːl ə ˈter i ̮ən ◂ -ˌkwɑːl-, -ˈtær- **~s** z
equalit|y iˈkwɒl ət |i ə-, -ɪt- ‖ -ˈkwɑːl əţ- **~ies** iz
equalization ˌiːk wəl aɪ ˈzeɪʃ ᵊn -ɪˈ·- ‖ -əˈ·- **~s** z
equaliz|e ˈiːk wə laɪz **~ed** d **~er/s** ə/z ‖ ᵊr/z **~es** ɪz əz **~ing** ɪŋ
equally ˈiːk wəl i
equanimity ˌek wə ˈnɪm ət i ˌiːk-, -ɪti ‖ -əţ i
equanimous i ˈkwæn ɪm əs e-, -ˈkwɒn-, -əm- **~ly** li
equatable i ˈkweɪt əb ᵊl iː-, ə- ‖ -ˈkweɪţ-
e|quate i |ˈkweɪt ə- **~quated** ˈkweɪt ɪd -əd ‖ ˈkweɪţ əd **~quates** ˈkweɪts **~quating** ˈkweɪt ɪŋ ‖ ˈkweɪţ ɪŋ

EQUATION

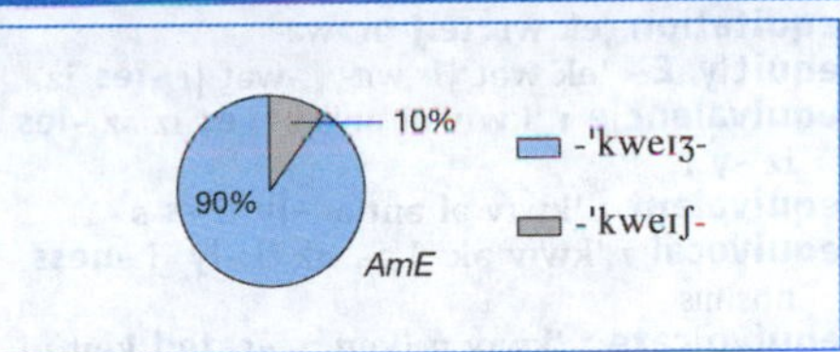

equation i ˈkweɪʒ ᵊn ə-, -ˈkweɪʃ- — *Preference poll, AmE:* -ˈkweɪʒ- *90%*, -ˈkweɪʃ- *10%*. **~s** z
equative i ˈkweɪt ɪv ə- ‖ -ˈkweɪţ- **~s** z
equator, E~ i ˈkweɪt ə ə- ‖ i ˈkweɪţ ᵊr **~s** z
equatorial ˌek wə ˈtɔːr i ̮əl ◂ ˌiːk- ‖ ˌiːk- -ˈtoʊr- **~ly** i
ˌEquaˌtorial ˈGuinea
equerr|y ɪ ˈkwer |i ə-; ˈek wər |i ‖ ˈek wər |i —*at court,* ɪ ˈkwer i **~ies** iz
equestrian ɪ ˈkwes tri ̮ən e-, ə- **~ism** ˌɪz əm **~s** z
equestrienne ɪ ˌkwes tri ˈen e-, ə- **~s** z
equi ˈek wi ˈiːk-
equi- *comb. form*
with stress-neutral suffix ¦iːk wi ¦ek-, -wə- — **equiprobable** ˌiːk wi ˈprɒb əb ᵊl ◂ ˌek-, ˌ·wə- ‖ -ˈprɑːb-
equiangular ˌiːk wi ˈæŋ gjʊl ə ˌek-, -gjəl- ‖ -gjəl ᵊr
equidistant ˌiːk wi ˈdɪst ənt ◂ ˌek-, -wə- **~ly** li
equilateral ˌiːk wi ˈlæt ̮ᵊr əl ◂ ˌ·wə- ‖ -ˈlæţ ər əl →-ˈlætr əl **~ly** i
ˌequiˌlateral ˈtriangle
equilib|rate ˌiːk wi ˈlaɪb |reɪt ˌek-, -wə-, -ˈlɪb-; iː ˈkwɪl ɪ b|reɪt, ɪ-, ə-, -ə- ‖ ɪ ˈkwɪl ə b|reɪt **~rated** reɪt ɪd -əd ‖ reɪţ əd **~rates** reɪts **~rating** reɪt ɪŋ ‖ reɪţ ɪŋ
equilibration ˌiːk wi laɪ ˈbreɪʃ ᵊn ˌek-, ˌ·wə-, -lɪˈ·-; iː ˌkwɪl ɪ-, ɪ-, -əˈ·- ‖ ɪ ˌkwɪl ə-
equilibrium ˌiːk wi ˈlɪb ri ̮əm ˌek-, ˌ·wə-
equine ˈek waɪn ˈiːk- ‖ ˈiːk- ˈek- **~s** z

E

equinoctial ˌiːk wi ˈnɒk ʃəl ◂ ˌek-, -wə- ‖ -ˈnɑːk- **~s** z
ˌ**equiˌnoctial ˈgales**

EQUINOX

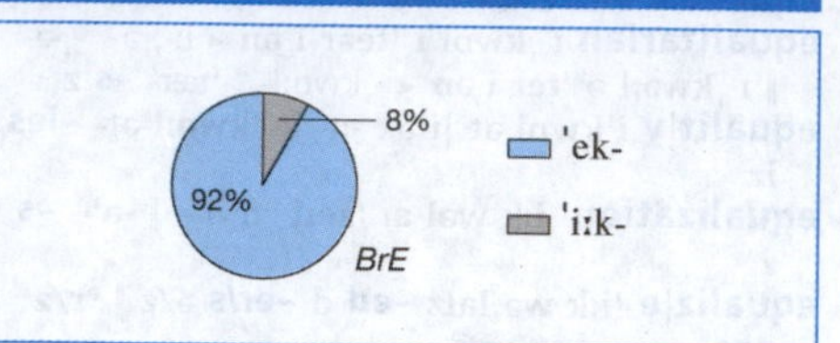

equinox ˈek wi nɒks ˈiːk-, -wə- ‖ -nɑːks **~es** ɪz əz — *Preference poll, BrE:* ˈek- *92%,* ˈiːk- *8%*
equip ɪ ˈkwɪp ə- **~ped** t **~ping** ɪŋ **~s** s
equipag|e ˈek wɪp ɪdʒ -wəp- **~es** ɪz əz
equipment ɪ ˈkwɪp mənt ə-
equipoise ˈek wi pɔɪz ˈiːk-, -wə- **~d** d
equipollent ˌiːk wi ˈpɒl ənt ◂ ˌek-, -wə- ‖ -ˈpɑːl-
equitab|le ˈek wɪt əb |əl ˈ·wət- ‖ -wəţ əb- **~leness** əl nəs -nɪs **~ly** li
equitation ˌek wɪ ˈteɪʃ ən -wə-
equit|y, E~ ˈek wət |i -wɪt- ‖ -wəţ |i **~ies** iz
equivalenc|e ɪ ˈkwɪv əl ənᵗs ə- **~es** ɪz əz **~ies** iz **~y** i
equivalent ɪ ˈkwɪv əl ənt ə- **~ly** li **~s** s
equivocal ɪ ˈkwɪv ək əl ə-, -ɪk əl **~ly** ˌi **~ness** nəs nɪs
equivo|cate ɪ ˈkwɪv ə |keɪt ə- **~cated** keɪt ɪd -əd ‖ keɪţ əd **~cates** keɪts **~cating** keɪt ɪŋ ‖ keɪţ ɪŋ
equivocation ɪ ˌkwɪv ə ˈkeɪʃ ən ə- **~s** z
equus, Equus ˈek wəs
ER ˌiː ˈɑː ‖ -ˈɑːr
er *hesitation noise, BrE* ɜː ə *—The AmE equivalent is written* uh
-er ə ‖ ər **dirtier** ˈdɜːt iˌə ‖ ˈdɜːţ iˌər *—On rare occasions this suffix receives contrastive stress, and is then pronounced* ˈɜː ‖ ˈɜː, *thus* not early, but earliER ˌɜːl i ˈɜː ‖ ˌɜːl i ˈɜː, interviewEE and interviewER ˌɪnt ə vjuː ˈɜː ‖ ˌɪnţ ər vjuː ˈɜː
era ˈɪər ə ‖ ˈɪr ə ˈer ə, ˈiː rə **~s** z
ERA ˌiː ɑːr ˈeɪ ‖ -ɑːr-
eradi|cate ɪ ˈræd ɪ |keɪt ə-, §-ə- **~cated** keɪt ɪd -əd ‖ keɪţ əd **~cates** keɪts **~cating** keɪt ɪŋ ‖ keɪţ ɪŋ
eradication ɪ ˌræd ɪ ˈkeɪʃ ən ə-, §-ə- **~s** z
eradicator ɪ ˈræd ɪ keɪt ə ə-, §-ˈ·ə- ‖ -keɪţ ər **~s** z
erase ɪ ˈreɪz ə- ‖ ɪ ˈreɪs *(*)* **erased** ɪ ˈreɪzd ə- ‖ ɪ ˈreɪst **erases** ɪ ˈreɪz ɪz ə-, -əz ‖ ɪ ˈreɪs əz **erasing** ɪ ˈreɪz ɪŋ ə- ‖ ɪ ˈreɪs ɪŋ
eraser ɪ ˈreɪz ə ə- ‖ ɪ ˈreɪs ər **~s** z
Erasmian ɪ ˈræz miˌən e-, ə- **~s** z
Erasmus ɪ ˈræz məs e-, ə-
Erastian ɪ ˈræst iˌən e-, ə-, ‖ -ˈræs tʃən **~ism** ˌɪz əm **~s** z
erasure ɪ ˈreɪʒ ə ə- ‖ ɪ ˈreɪʃ ər **~s** z
Erato ˈer ə təʊ ‖ -toʊ
Eratosthenes ˌer ə ˈtɒsθ ə niːz ‖ -ˈtɑːsθ-

erbium ˈɜːb iˌəm ‖ ˈɜːb-
Erdington ˈɜːd ɪŋ tən ‖ ˈɜːd-
ere *'before'* eə ‖ eər æər *(= air)*
'ere *'here'* ɪə ‖ ɪər *—a nonstandard form of* her
Erebus ˈer ɪb əs -əb-
Erechtheum ˌer ek ˈθiːˌəm -ɪk-, -ək- ‖ ɪ ˈrek θiˌəm
Erechtheus ɪ ˈrek θjuːs e-, ə-, -ˈ·θiˌəs ‖ -ˈrek θiˌəs
erect *adj, v* ɪ ˈrekt ə- **~ed** ɪd əd **~ing** ɪŋ **~ly** li **~ness** nəs nɪs **~s** s
erectile ɪ ˈrekt aɪəl ə- ‖ -əl -aɪəl
erection ɪ ˈrek ʃən ə- **~s** z
erector ɪ ˈrekt ə ə- ‖ -ər **~s** z
eremite ˈer ə maɪt -ɪ- **~s** s
eremitic ˌer ə ˈmɪt ɪk ◂ -ɪ- ‖ -ˈmɪţ- **~al** əl
e-resume, e-résumé ˈiː ˌrez jʊ meɪ -jə- ‖ -ə- -·ˈmeɪ
erethism ˈer ə ˌθɪz əm -ɪ-
Eretz ˈer ets -ɪts, §-əts *—Hebrew* [ˈɛ rets]
Erewhon ˈer ɪ wɒn -ə-, -hwɒn ‖ *-hwɑːn -hwʌn*
Erfurt ˈeə fɜːt ‖ ˈer- *—Ger* [ˈɛʁ fʊʁt]
erg ɜːg ‖ ɜːg **ergs** ɜːgz ‖ ɜːgz
ergative ˈɜːg ət ɪv ‖ ˈɜːg əţ ɪv **~ly** li **~s** z
ergativity ˌɜːg ə ˈtɪv ət i -ɪt i ‖ ˌɜːg ə ˈtɪv əţ i
ergo ˈɜːg əʊ ˈeəg- ‖ ˈerg oʊ ˈɜːg-
ergonomic ˌɜːg ə ˈnɒm ɪk ◂ ‖ ˌɜːg ə ˈnɑːm ɪk ◂ **~ally** əl ˌi **~s** s
ergonomist ɜː ˈgɒn əm ɪst §-əst ‖ ɜː ˈgɑːn- **~s** s
ergosterol ɜː ˈgɒst ə rɒl ‖ ɜː ˈgɑːst ə roʊl -rɔːl, -rɑːl
ergot ˈɜːg ət -ɒt ‖ ˈɜːg- -ɑːt
ergotism ˈɜːg ə ˌtɪz əm ‖ ˈɜːg-
Eric ˈer ɪk
Erica, erica ˈer ɪk ə **~s, ~'s** z
ericaceous ˌer ɪ ˈkeɪʃ əs ◂ -ə-
Ericsson *tdmk* ˈer ɪks ən *—Swed* [ˈˈeː rik sɔn]
Eridan|us e ˈrɪd ən |əs ɪ-, ə- **~i** aɪ
Erie ˈɪər i ‖ ˈɪr i
ˌ**Erie Caˈnal**
Erik ˈer ɪk
Erika ˈer ɪk ə
Eriksson ˈer ɪks ən
Erin ˈer ɪn ˈɪər-, ˈeər-, §-ən
Eris ˈer ɪs §-əs
Eriskay ˈer ɪ skeɪ -ə-
eristic e ˈrɪst ɪk ɪ-, ə- **~s** s
Erith ˈɪər ɪθ §-əθ ‖ ˈɪr-
Eritre|a ˌer ɪ ˈtreɪ |ə -ə-, -ˈtriːˌ|ə ‖ -ˈtriː |ə **~an/s** ən/z
erk ɜːk ‖ ɜːk *(= irk)* **erks** ɜːks ‖ ɜːks
Erle ɜːl ‖ ɜːl
erlking ˈɜːl kɪŋ ‖ ˈɜːl-
ERM ˌiː ɑːr ˈem ‖ -ɑːr-
ermine ˈɜːm ɪn §-ən ‖ ˈɜːm- **~d** d **~s** z
erne, Erne ɜːn ‖ ɜːn *(= earn)* **ernes** ɜːnz ‖ ɜːnz
Ernest ˈɜːn ɪst -əst ‖ ˈɜːn-
Ernestina ˌɜːn ɪ ˈstiːn ə -ə- ‖ ˌɜːn-
Ernie ˈɜːn i ‖ ˈɜːn i
Ernle ˈɜːn li ‖ ˈɜːn-
Ernst eənᵗst ɜːnᵗst ‖ ɜːnᵗst *—Ger* [ʔɛʁnst]

od|e ɪ 'rəʊd ə- ‖ ɪ 'roʊd **~ed** ɪd əd **~es** z **~ing** ɪŋ

·ogenous ɪ 'rɒdʒ ən əs e-, ə-, -ɪn- ‖ ɪ 'rɑːdʒ-

·oica ɪ 'rəʊ ɪk ə e-, ə- ‖ ɪ 'roʊ-

·os 'ɪər ɒs 'er-, -əʊz ‖ 'er ɑːs 'ɪr-

·osion ɪ 'rəʊʒ ᵊn ə- ‖ ɪ 'roʊʒ ᵊn **~s** z

·osive ɪ 'rəʊs ɪv ə- ‖ ɪ 'roʊs- **~ly** li

·otic ɪ 'rɒt ɪk ə- ‖ ɪ 'rɑːţ ɪk **~ally** ᵊl i

·otica ɪ 'rɒt ɪk ə ə- ‖ ɪ 'rɑːţ ɪk ə

·oticis... *—see* **eroticiz...**

·oticism ɪ 'rɒt ɪ ˌsɪz əm ə-, -ə- ‖ ɪ 'rɑːţ ə-

·oticization ɪ ˌrɒt ɪs aɪ 'zeɪʃ ᵊn ə-, ˌ·əs-, -ɪ'·- ‖ ɪ 'rɑːţ əs ə-

·oticiz|e ɪ 'rɒt ɪ saɪz ə-, -ə- ‖ ɪ 'rɑːţ ə- **~ed** d **~es** ɪz əz **~ing** ɪŋ

·otogenic ɪ ˌrɒt ə 'dʒen ɪk ◂ ə-, -ˌrəʊt- ‖ ɪ ˌroʊţ ə- ɪ ˌrɑːţ ə- **~ally** ᵊl i

rotoman|ia ɪ ˌrɒt əʊ 'meɪn |i ə ə-,ˌrəʊt- ‖ ɪ ˌroʊţ ə- ɪ ˌrɑːţ ə- **~iac/s** i æk/s

rpingham 'ɜːp ɪŋ əm ‖ 'ɜːp ɪŋ hæm

rr ɜː §eə ‖ eᵊr ɜː **erred** ɜːd §eəd ‖ eᵊrd ɜːd **erring** 'ɜːr ɪŋ §'er-, §'eər- ‖ 'er ɪŋ 'ɜː- **errs** ɜːz §eəz ‖ eᵊrz ɜːz

·rrancy 'er ənᵗs i

·rrand 'er ənd **~s** z

·rrant 'er ənt **~ly** li

·rrata e 'rɑːt ə ɪ-, ə-, -'reɪt- ‖ e 'rɑːţ ə -'reɪţ-, -'ræţ-

·rratic ɪ 'ræt ɪk e-, ə- ‖ ɪ 'ræţ ɪk **~ally** ᵊl i **~s** s

·rrat|um e 'rɑːt |əm ɪ-, ə-, -'reɪt- ‖ e 'rɑːţ |əm -'reɪţ-, -'ræţ- **~a** ə

·rrhine 'er aɪn -ɪn

·rring 'ɜːr ɪŋ §'er-, §'eər- ‖ 'er- 'ɜː- **~ly** li

·rrol, Erroll 'er əl

·rroneous ɪ 'rəʊn i əs e-, ə- ‖ ɪ 'roʊn- **~ly** li **~ness** nəs nɪs

error 'er ə ‖ -ᵊr **~s** z

ersatz 'eə zæts 'ɜː-, -sæts, -zɑːts, ·'· ‖ 'er zɑːts 'ɜː-, -sɑːts, -sæts, ·'· *—Ger* [ʔɛɐ 'zats]

Erse ɜːs ‖ ɜːs

Erskine 'ɜːsk ɪn §-ən ‖ 'ɜːsk-

erstwhile 'ɜːst waɪᵊl -hwaɪᵊl ‖ 'ɜːst *h*waɪᵊl

erubescence ˌer u 'bes ᵊnᵗs

erubescent ˌer u 'bes ᵊnt ◂ **~ly** li

eructation ˌiː rʌk 'teɪʃ ᵊn ɪ ˌrʌk-; ˌer ʌk-, -ək- **~s** z

erudite 'er u daɪt -ju- ‖ -jə- -ə- **~ly** li **~ness** nəs nɪs

erudition ˌer u 'dɪʃ ᵊn -ju- ‖ -jə- -ə-

erupt ɪ 'rʌpt ə- **~ed** ɪd əd **~ing** ɪŋ **~s** s

eruption ɪ 'rʌp ʃᵊn ə- **~s** z

eruptive ɪ 'rʌpt ɪv ə- **~ly** li

eruv 'er ʊv ‖ eɪ 'ruːv **eruvin** 'er ʊv ɪn ‖ ˌer u 'viːn

Ervine 'ɜːv ɪn §-ən, -aɪn ‖ 'ɜːv-

-ery ər i *—This stress-neutral suffix is used only after a strong-vowelled syllable* (ma'chinery); *after a weak-vowelled syllable the variant* -ry ri *is used instead* ('dentistry).

Erymanthian ˌer ɪ 'mænᵗθ i ən ◂

erysipelas ˌer ɪ 'sɪp əl əs ˌ·ə-, -ɪl əs

erythema ˌer ɪ 'θiːm ə -ə-

erythrocyte ɪ 'rɪθ rəʊ saɪt ə- ‖ -rə- **~s** s

erythromycin ɪ ˌrɪθ rəʊ 'maɪs ɪn ə-, §-ᵊn ‖ -rə-

erythropoietic ɪ ˌrɪθ rəʊ pɔɪ 'et ɪk ◂ ə- ‖ -rə pɔɪ 'eţ-

-es *ending of pl or 3rd person sing.,* **-es'** *possessive pl ending—There are two pronunciations: 1. After a sibilant sound* (**s, z, ʃ, ʒ, tʃ, dʒ**) *the ending is pronounced* ɪz *or, less commonly in BrE but regularly in AmE,* əz, *as* pushes 'pʊʃ ɪz, -əz, churches' 'tʃɜːtʃ ɪz, -əz. *(In singing a strong-vowelled variant* ez *is occasionally used.) 2. Where the spelling* y *is changed to* i, *this ending is pronounced* z, *as* cry — cries kraɪz *—See also* **-s.**

Esau 'iːs ɔː ‖ -ɑː

Esbjerg 'es bjɜːg ‖ -bjɜːg *—Danish* ['ɛs bjɛɐʔ]

escalad|e ˌesk ə 'leɪd '· · · **~ed** ɪd əd **~es** z **~ing** ɪŋ

esca|late 'esk ə |leɪt **~lated** leɪt ɪd -əd ‖ leɪţ əd **~lates** leɪts **~lating** leɪt ɪŋ ‖ leɪţ ɪŋ

escalation ˌesk ə 'leɪʃ ᵊn **~s** z

escalator 'esk ə leɪt ə ⚠'·jə- ‖ -leɪţ ᵊr **~s** z

escallonia ˌesk ə 'ləʊn i ə ‖ -'loʊn- **~s** z

escallop, escalope 'esk ə lɒp ◂ ˌ··'·; e 'skæl əp, ɪ-, -ɒp ‖ ɪ 'skɑːl əp *(*)* **~s** s

escapade ˌesk ə 'peɪd '· · · ‖ 'esk ə peɪd **~s** z

escap|e ɪ 'skeɪp e-, ə- **~ed** t **~es** s **~ing** ɪŋ **e'scape road**; **e'scape veˌlocity**; **e'scape wheel**

escapee ɪ ˌskeɪ 'piː ˌesk eɪ 'piː **~s** z

escapement ɪ 'skeɪp mənt e-, ə- **~s** s

escapism ɪ 'skeɪp ˌɪz əm e-, ə-

escapist ɪ 'skeɪp ɪst e-, ə-, §-əst **~s** z

escapologist ˌesk ə 'pɒl ədʒ ɪst ˌ·eɪ-, §-əst ‖ -'pɑːl- **~s** z

escapology ˌesk ə 'pɒl ədʒ i ˌ·eɪ- ‖ -'pɑːl-

escargot ɪ 'skɑːg əʊ e- ‖ ˌesk ɑːr 'goʊ *(*) —Fr* [ɛs kaʁ go] **~s** z

escarole 'esk ə rəʊl →-rɒʊl ‖ -roʊl

escarpment ɪ 'skɑːp mənt e-, ə- ‖ ɪ 'skɑːrp- **~s** s

-esce 'es — **opalesce** ˌəʊp ə 'les ‖ ˌoʊp-

-escence 'es ᵊnᵗs — **phosphorescence** ˌfɒs fə 'res ᵊnᵗs ‖ ˌfɑːs-

-escent 'es ᵊnt — **frutescent** fruː 'tes ᵊnt

eschatological ˌesk ət ə 'lɒdʒ ɪk ᵊl ◂ ˌ·æt- ‖ -əţ ə 'lɑːdʒ- **~ly** i

eschatology ˌesk ə 'tɒl ədʒ i ‖ -'tɑːl-

es|cheat ɪs |'tʃiːt es-, əs- **~cheated** 'tʃiːt ɪd -əd ‖ 'tʃiːţ əd **~cheating** 'tʃiːt ɪŋ ‖ 'tʃiːţ ɪŋ **~cheats** 'tʃiːts

Escher 'eʃ ə ‖ -ᵊr *—Dutch* ['ɛʃ ər]

escherichia ˌeʃ ə 'rɪk i ə

eschew ɪs 'tʃuː es-, əs-; i 'ʃuː, ə-; i 'skjuː, ə **~ed** d **~ing** ɪŋ **~s** z

eschscholtzia ɪ 'ʃɒlts i ə e-, ə-, -'skɒlts-; -'skɒlʃ ə, -'skɒltʃ ə ‖ ɪ 'ʃɑːlts- **~s** z

Escoffier ɪ 'skɒf i eɪ e-, ə- ‖ ˌesk ɑːf 'jeɪ *—Fr* [ɛs kɔ fje]

Escondido ˌesk ən 'diːd əʊ ‖ -oʊ -ɑːn-

Escorial e 'skɔːr i æl -ɑːl, -i əl, ˌesk ɒr i 'ɑːl ‖ -i əl -'skoʊr- *—Sp* [es ko 'rjal]

escort *n* 'esk ɔːt ‖ -ɔːrt **~s** s

e|scort *v* ɪ ˈ|skɔːt e-, ə-; ˈe|sk ɔːt ‖ ɪ ˈ|skɔːrt e- **~scorted** skɔːt ɪd -əd ‖ skɔːrṭ əd **~scorting** skɔːt ɪŋ ‖ skɔːrṭ ɪŋ **~scorts** skɔːts ‖ skɔːrts
escritoire ˌesk rə ˈtwɑː -riː-, -rɪ- ‖ -ˈtwɑːr **~s** z
escrow ˈesk rəʊ es ˈkrəʊ ‖ ˈesk roʊ es ˈkroʊ
escudo ɪ ˈʃkuːd əʊ e-, ə-, -ˈskuːd-, -ˈskjuːd- ‖ -oʊ —*Port* [ɪʃ ˈku ðu] **~s** z
esculent ˈesk jʊl ənt ‖ -jəl-
escutcheon ɪ ˈskʌtʃ ən e- **~s** z
Esda ˈes də ˈez-
Esdras ˈez dræs -drəs ‖ -drəs
-ese ˈiːz ‖ -ˈiːs — **journalese** ˌdʒɜːn ə ˈliːz ◂ ‖ ˌdʒɝːn- -ˈliːs **Japanese** ˌdʒæp ə ˈniːz ◂ ‖ -ˈniːs
Esher ˈiːʃ ə ‖ -ᵊr
e-signature ˈiː ˌsɪɡ nətʃ ə -nɪtʃ- ‖ -ᵊr **~s** z
Esk esk
Eskdale ˈesk deɪᵊl
esker ˈesk ə ‖ -ᵊr **~s** z
Eskimo ˈesk ɪ məʊ -ə- ‖ -moʊ **~s** z
ESL ˌiː es ˈel
Esling ˈez lɪŋ
Esme, Esmé ˈez mi
Esmeralda ˌez mə ˈræld ə
Esmond ˈez mənd
ESN ˌiː es ˈen
ESOL ˈiːs ɒl ‖ -ɑːl
esophageal iː ˌsɒf ə ˈdʒiː‿əl ◂ ɪ-, ə-, ˌiːs ɒf- ‖ ɪ ˌsɑːf-
esophagus iː ˈsɒf əɡ əs ɪ-, ə- ‖ ɪ ˈsɑːf- **~es** ɪz əz
esoteric ˌes əʊ ˈter ɪk ◂ ˌiːs- ‖ ˌes ə- **~ally** ᵊl‿i
ESP ˌiː es ˈpiː
espadrille ˌesp ə ˈdrɪl ˈ· · · ‖ ˈesp ə drɪl **~s** z
espalier ɪ ˈspæl i eɪ e-, ə-, ə ‖ -ˈspæl jᵊr -jeɪ **~s** z
esparto e ˈspɑːt əʊ ɪ- ‖ ɪ ˈspɑːrṭ oʊ
especial ɪ ˈspeʃ ᵊl e-, ə-, ⚠ɪk-, ⚠ək- **~ly** i
Esperantist ˌesp ə ˈrænt ɪst ◂ -ˈrɑːnt-, §-əst ‖ -ˈrɑːnṭ- **~s** s
Esperanto ˌesp ə ˈrænt əʊ -ˈrɑːnt- ‖ -ˈrɑːnṭ oʊ —*Esperanto* [es pe ˈran to]
espial ɪ ˈspaɪ‿əl e-, ə-
espie... —*see* **espy**
espionage ˈesp i‿ə nɑːʒ -nɑːdʒ, ˌ· · ·ˈ·, ˈesp i‿ən ɪdʒ
esplanade ˌesp lə ˈneɪd -ˈnɑːd, ˈ· · · ‖ ˈesp lə nɑːd -neɪd **~s** z
Esposito ˌesp ə ˈziːt əʊ -ˈsiːt- ‖ -ˈziːṭ oʊ -ˈsiːṭ- —*Sp* [es po ˈsi to]
espousal ɪ ˈspaʊz ᵊl e-, ə- **~s** z
espouse ɪ ˈspaʊz e-, ə-, §-ˈspaʊs **espoused** ɪ ˈspaʊzd e-, ə-, §-ˈspaʊst **espouses** ɪ ˈspaʊz ɪz e-, ə-, §-ˈspaʊs-, -əz **espousing** ɪ ˈspaʊz ɪŋ e-, ə-, §-ˈspaʊs-
espresso e ˈspres əʊ ‖ -oʊ —*It* [e ˈsprɛs so] **~s** z
esprit, E~ e ˈspriː ɪ-, ə- —*See also phrases with this word*
esprit de corps e ˌspriː də ˈkɔː ɪ-, ə-, ˌesp riː- ‖ -ˈkɔːr -ˈkoʊr —*Fr* [ɛs pʁid kɔːʁ]
esprit d'escalier e ˌspriː de ˈskæl i eɪ ɪ-, ə- ‖ e ˌspriː ˌdesk ɑːl ˈjeɪ —*Fr* [ɛs pʁi dɛs ka lje]

e|spy ɪ ˈ|spaɪ e-, ə- **~spied** ˈspaɪd **~spies** ˈspaɪz **~spying** ˈspaɪ ɪŋ
Espy ˈesp i
Esq. —*see* **Esquire**
-esque ˈesk — **Chaplinesque** ˌtʃæp lɪn ˈesk ◂ -lən-
Esquiline ˈesk wɪ laɪn -wə-
Esquimalt ɪ ˈskwaɪm ɔːlt e-, ə-, -ɒlt ‖ -ɑːlt
esquire ɪ ˈskwaɪ‿ə e-, ə- ‖ ˈesk waɪ‿ᵊr ɪ ˈskwaɪ‿ᵊr, e- **~s** z
ESRC ˌiː es ɑː ˈsiː ‖ -ɑːr ˈ·
-ess ˈes, es, ɪs əs —*There is great inter-speaker variability in the treatment of this suffix. See individual entries.*
essay *v* e ˈseɪ ˈes eɪ **~ed** d **~ing** ɪŋ **~s** z
essay *n 'attempt'* ˈes eɪ e ˈseɪ **~s** z
essay *n 'piece of writing'* ˈes eɪ **~s** z
essayist ˈes eɪ ɪst §-əst **~s** s
esse ˈes i
Essen ˈes ᵊn —*Ger* [ˈʔɛs ᵊn]
essenc|e ˈes ᵊnᵗs **~es** ɪz əz
Essendon ˈes ᵊn dən
Essene ˈes iːn e ˈsiːn ‖ ɪ ˈsiːn e-; ˈes iːn **~s** z
essential ɪ ˈsenᵗʃ ᵊl e-, ə- **~ly** i **~ness** nəs nɪs **~s** z
essentialit|y ɪ ˌsenᵗʃ i ˈæl ət |i e-, ə-, -ɪt |i ‖ -əṭ |i **~ies** iz
Essex ˈes ɪks -əks
essive ˈes ɪv **~s** z
Essling ˈes lɪŋ
Esso *tdmk* ˈes əʊ ‖ -oʊ
Essoldo e ˈsɒld əʊ ɪ-, ə- ‖ -ˈsɑːld oʊ
-est *superlative ending* ɪst əst — **biggest** ˈbɪɡ ɪst -əst **nicest** ˈnaɪs ɪst -əst
-est *archaic and liturgical second person sing. ending* ɪst əst **sendest** ˈsend ɪst -əst **takest** ˈteɪk ɪst -əst
establish ɪ ˈstæb lɪʃ e-, ə- **~ed** t **~er/s** ə/z ‖ ᵊr/z **~es** ɪz əz **~ing** ɪŋ
eˌstablished ˈchurch
establishment, E~ ɪ ˈstæb lɪʃ mənt e-, ə- **~s** s
establishmentarian ɪ ˌstæb lɪʃ mən ˈteər i‿ən ◂ e-, ə- ‖ -ˈter- **~s** z
estaminet e ˈstæm ɪ neɪ ɪ-, -ə- ‖ e ˌstɑːm iː ˈneɪ —*Fr* [ɛs ta mi nɛ] **~s** z
estancia ɪ ˈstænᵗs i‿ə e- ‖ e ˈstɑːnᵗs- —*AmSp* [es ˈtan sja] **~s** z
estate ɪ ˈsteɪt e-, ə- **~s** s
eˈstate ˌagent; **eˈstate car**
Estcourt ˈest kɔːt ‖ -kɔːrt -koʊrt
Este ˈest i —*It* [ˈɛs te]
Estee, Estée ˈest eɪ -i
esteem ɪ ˈstiːm e-, ə- **~ed** d **~ing** ɪŋ **~s** z
Estefan ˈest ə fæn -ɪ-
Estella ɪ ˈstel ə e-, ə-
Estelle ɪ ˈstel e-, ə-
ester ˈest ə ‖ -ᵊr **~s** z
esteras|e ˈest ə reɪz -reɪs **~es** ɪz əz
Esterhazy ˈest ə hɑːz i ‖ ˈ·ᵊr- —*Hung* Eszterházy [ˈɛs tɛr hɑː zi]
Esther ˈest ə ˈesθ- ‖ -ᵊr
esthete ˈiːs θiːt ‖ ˈes- *(*)* **~s** s

sthetic iːs ˈθet ɪk ɪs- ‖ es ˈθeṭ ɪk **~al** ᵊl **~ally** ᵊl‿i **~s** s
stheticism iːs ˈθet ɪ ˌsɪz əm -ə- ‖ es ˈθeṭ ə- ɪs-
sthwaite ˈes θweɪt
stimab|le ˈest ɪm əb |ᵊl ˈ·əm- **~leness** ᵊl nəs -nɪs **~ly** li
sti|mate *v* ˈest ɪ |meɪt -ə-, -mət **~mated** meɪt ɪd -əd ‖ meɪṭ əd **~mates** meɪts **~mating** meɪt ɪŋ ‖ meɪṭ ɪŋ
stimate *n* ˈest ɪm ət -əm-, -ɪt; -ɪ meɪt, -ə- **~s** s
stimation ˌest ɪ ˈmeɪʃ ᵊn -ə- **~s** z
stimator ˈest ɪ meɪt ə ˈ·ə- ‖ -meɪṭ ᵊr **~s** z
stival i ˈstaɪv ᵊl ‖ ˈest əv ᵊl
sti|vate ˈiːst ɪ |veɪt ˈest-, -ə- **~vated** veɪt ɪd -əd ‖ veɪṭ əd **~vates** veɪts **~vating** veɪt ɪŋ ‖ veɪṭ ɪŋ
stivation ˌiːst ɪ ˈveɪʃ ᵊn ˌest-, ə- **~s** z
stoni|a e ˈstəʊn i‿|ə ɪ-, ə- ‖ -ˈstoʊn- **~an/s** ən/z
stop ɪ ˈstɒp e-, ə- ‖ e ˈstɑːp **~ped** t **~ping** ɪŋ **~s** s
stoppel ɪ ˈstɒp ᵊl e-, ə- ‖ e ˈstɑːp-
Storil ˌest ə ˈrɪl ˈ· · · —*Port* [ɪʃ tu ˈril]
stovers ɪ ˈstəʊv əz e-, ə- ‖ e ˈstoʊv ᵊrz ɪ-
strade e ˈstrɑːd ɪ-, ə- **~s** z
stradiol ˌes trə ˈdaɪ ɒl ˌiːs- ‖ -oʊl -ɔːl, -ɑːl
stragon, E~ ˈes trə gɒn ‖ -gɑːn —*Fr* [ɛs tʁa gɔ̃]
strang|e ɪ ˈstreɪndʒ e-, ə- **~ed** d **~es** ɪz əz **~ing** ɪŋ
estrangement ɪ ˈstreɪndʒ mənt e-, ə- **~s** s
estreat ɪ ˈstriːt e- **~s** s
estrogen ˈiːs trədʒ ən ˈes- ‖ ˈes-
estrous, estrus ˈiːs trəs ˈes- ‖ ˈes-
estuarine ˈest ju‿ə raɪn -rɪn ‖ ˈes tʃu‿
estuar|y ˈest jʊr |i ˈ·ju‿ər |i; ˈes tʃʊr |i, ˈeʃ- ‖ ˈes tʃu er |i **~ies** iz
esurienc|e ɪ ˈsjʊər i‿ənᵗs ‖ ɪ ˈsʊr- **~y** i
esurient ɪ ˈsjʊər i‿ənt ‖ ɪ ˈsʊr- **~ly** li
et et —*See also phrases with this word*
ET ˌiː ˈtiː
eta *Greek letter* ˈiːt ə ‖ ˈeɪṭ ə ˈiːṭ ə *(*)*
ETA *'estimated time of arrival'* ˌiː tiː ˈeɪ
ETA *Basque organization* ˈet ə
etagere, étagère ˌeɪt ə ˈʒeə ˌet-, -æ-, -ɑː- ‖ ˌeɪṭ ə ˈʒeᵊr —*Fr* [e ta ʒɛːʁ] **~s** z
et al, et al. ₍ₗ₎et ˈæl ‖ ₍ₗ₎eṭ ˈɑːl -ˈæl, -ˈɔːl
Etam *tdmk* ˈiːt æm
etc., etcetera, et cetera ₍ₗ₎et ˈsetr ə ɪt-, ət-, ⚠₍ₗ₎ek-, -ˈset ər ə ‖ -ˈseṭ ər ə →-ˈsetr ə
etch etʃ **etched** etʃt **etches** ˈetʃ ɪz -əz **etching/s** ˈetʃ ɪŋ/z
etch-a-sketch ˈetʃ ə sketʃ
etcher ˈetʃ ə ‖ -ᵊr **~ers** əz ‖ ᵊrz
Etchingham ˌetʃ ɪŋ ˈhæm
Eteocles ˈet i‿ə kliːz ɪ ˈtiː‿ə- ‖ ɪ ˈtiː ə-
eternal ɪ ˈtɜːn ᵊl iː-, ə- ‖ ɪ ˈtɜ˞ːn ᵊl **~ly** i
eˌternal ˈtriangle
eternalis|e, eternaliz|e ɪ ˈtɜːn ə laɪz iː-, ə-, -ᵊl aɪz ‖ ɪ ˈtɜ˞ːn- **~ed** d **~es** ɪz əz **~ing** ɪŋ
eternit|y ɪ ˈtɜːn ət |i iː-, ə-, -ɪt- ‖ ɪ ˈtɜ˞ːn əṭ |i **~ies** iz
eˈternity ring

Etesian ɪ ˈtiːʒ i‿ən -ˈtiːz-; -ˈtiːʒ ᵊn ‖ ɪ ˈtiːʒ ᵊn
eth *letter name* eð
Eth *woman's name* eθ
-eth *archaic and liturgical third person sing. ending* ɪθ əθ **sendeth** ˈsend ɪθ -əθ, **taketh** ˈteɪk ɪθ -əθ
Ethan ˈiːθ ᵊn
ethane ˈiːθ eɪn ˈeθ- ‖ ˈeθ-
ethanoic ˌeθ ə ˈnəʊ ɪk ◂ ˌiːθ- ‖ -ˈnoʊ-
ethanol ˈeθ ə nɒl ˈiːθ- ‖ -noʊl -nɔːl, -nɑːl
Ethel ˈeθ ᵊl
Ethelbert ˈeθ ᵊl bɜːt ‖ -bɜ˞ːt
Ethelberta ˌeθ ᵊl ˈbɜːt ə ‖ -ˈbɜ˞ːṭ ə
Ethelburga ˌeθ ᵊl ˈbɜːg ə ‖ -ˈbɜ˞ːg ə
Etheldreda ˈeθ ᵊl driːd ə
Ethelred ˈeθ ᵊl red
ether ˈiːθ ə ‖ -ᵊr
ethereal ɪ ˈθɪər i‿əl iː-, ə- ‖ ɪ ˈθɪr- **~ly** i **~ness** nəs nɪs
etherealis|e, etherealiz|e ɪ ˈθɪər i‿ə laɪz iː-, ə- ‖ ɪ ˈθɪr- **~ed** d **~es** ɪz əz **~ing** ɪŋ
Etheredge, Etherege, Etheridge ˈeθ ər ɪdʒ
Ethernet, e~ *tdmk* ˈiːθ ə net ‖ -ᵊr-
ethic ˈeθ ɪk **~s** s
ethical ˈeθ ɪk ᵊl **~ly** ‿i **~ness** nəs nɪs
Ethiop ˈiːθ i ɒp ‖ -ɑːp **~s** s
Ethiope ˈiːθ i əʊp ‖ -oʊp **~s** s
Ethiopi|a ˌiːθ i ˈəʊp i‿|ə ‖ -ˈoʊp- **~an/s** ən/z
Ethiopic ˌiːθ i ˈɒp ɪk ◂ -ˈəʊp- ‖ -ˈɑːp- -ˈoʊp-
ethmoid ˈeθ mɔɪd **~s** z
ethnarch ˈeθ nɑːk ‖ -nɑːrk **~s** s
Ethne ˈeθ ni
ethnic ˈeθ nɪk **~ally** ᵊl‿i **~s** s
ethnicity eθ ˈnɪs ət i -ɪt- ‖ -əṭ i
ethno- *comb. form*
with stress-neutral suffix ˌeθ nəʊ ‖ ˌeθ noʊ — **ethnobotany** ˌeθ nəʊ ˈbɒt ən i ‖ ˌeθ noʊ ˈbɑːt ᵊn i
with stress-imposing suffix eθ ˈnɒ+ ‖ eθ ˈnɑː+ — **ethnogeny** eθ ˈnɒdʒ ən i ‖ -ˈnɑːdʒ-
ethnocentric ˌeθ nəʊ ˈsentr ɪk ◂ ‖ -noʊ-
ethnocentricity ˌeθ nəʊ sen ˈtrɪs ət i -ɪt i ‖ -noʊ sen ˈtrɪs əṭ i
ethnocentrism ˌeθ nəʊ ˈsentr ˌɪz əm ‖ -noʊ-
ethnographer eθ ˈnɒg rəf ə ‖ -ˈnɑːg rəf ᵊr **~s** z
ethnographic ˌeθ nə ˈgræf ɪk ◂ **~al** ᵊl **~ally** ᵊl‿i
ethnography eθ ˈnɒg rəf i ‖ -ˈnɑːg-
ethnological ˌeθ nə ˈlɒdʒ ɪk ᵊl ◂ ‖ -ˈlɑːdʒ- **~ly** ‿i
ethnologist eθ ˈnɒl ədʒ ɪst §-əst ‖ -ˈnɑːl- **~s** s
ethnology eθ ˈnɒl ədʒ i ‖ -ˈnɑːl-
ethnomethodolog|ist ˌeθ nəʊ ˌmeθ ə ˈdɒl ədʒ |ɪst §-əst ‖ -noʊ ˌmeθ ə ˈdɑːl- **~ists** ɪsts §əsts **~y** i
ethnomusicological ˌeθ nəʊ ˌmjuːz ɪk ə ˈlɒdʒ ɪk ᵊl ‖ -noʊ ˌmjuːz ɪk ə ˈlɑːdʒ- **~ly** ‿i
ethnomusicolog|ist ˌeθ nəʊ ˌmjuːz ɪ ˈkɒl ədʒ |ɪst -ˌ·ə-, §-əst ‖ -noʊ ˌmjuːz ɪ ˈkɑːl- **~ists** ɪsts §əsts **~y** i

ethological ˌeθ ə ˈlɒdʒ ɪk əl ◂ ˌiːθ- ‖ -ˈlɑːdʒ- **~ly** ˌi
etholog|ist iː ˈθɒl ədʒ |ɪst ɪ-, §-əst ‖ -ˈθɑːl- **~ists** ɪsts §əsts **~y** i
ethos ˈiːθ ɒs ‖ -ɑːs ˈeθ-, -oʊs
ethyl ˈeθ əl -ɪl; ˈiːθ aɪəl
ˌethyl ˈalcohol
ethylene ˈeθ ə liːn -ɪ-
ˌethylene ˈglycol
etic ˈet ɪk ‖ ˈeţ ɪk **~ally** əl ˌi
e-ticket ˈiː ˌtɪk ɪt §-ət **~s** s
Etienne ˌet i ˈen —*Fr* [e tjɛn]
etio|late ˈiːt i ə |leɪt -i əʊ- ‖ ˈiːţ- **~lated** leɪt ɪd -əd ‖ leɪţ əd **~lates** leɪts **~lating** leɪt ɪŋ ‖ leɪţ ɪŋ
etiolation ˌiːt i ə ˈleɪʃ ən -i əʊ- ‖ ˌiːţ-
etiological ˌiːt i ə ˈlɒdʒ ɪk əl ◂ ‖ ˌiːţ i ə ˈlɑːdʒ- **~ly** ˌi
etiolog|y ˌiːt i ˈɒl ədʒ |i ‖ ˌiːţ i ˈɑːl- **~ies** iz
etiquette ˈet ɪ ket -ɪk ət, ˌet ɪ ˈket ‖ ˈeţ ɪk ət -ɪ ket **~s** s
Etive ˈet ɪv ‖ ˈeţ-
Etna ˈet nə
Eton ˈiːt ən *(= eaten)*
ˌEton ˈcollar
Etonian i ˈtəʊn i ən ‖ -ˈtoʊn- **~s** z
Etruria ɪ ˈtrʊər i ə ə- ‖ ɪ ˈtrʊr-
Etruscan ɪ ˈtrʌsk ən ə- **~s** z
-ette ˈet — **lecturette** ˌlek tʃə ˈret
Ettie ˈet i ‖ ˈeţ i
Ettrick ˈetr ɪk
Etty ˈet i ‖ ˈeţ i
etude, étude ˈeɪ tjuːd →-tʃuːd, ·ˈ· ‖ eɪ ˈtuːd -ˈtjuːd, ˈ· · —*Fr* [e tyd] **~s** z
etui, étui e ˈtwiː ‖ eɪ- —*Fr* [e tɥi] **~s** z
Etwall ˈet wɔːl ‖ -wɑːl
etyma ˈet ɪm ə -əm- ‖ ˈeţ-
etymological ˌet ɪm ə ˈlɒdʒ ɪk əl ◂ ,-əm- ‖ ˌeţ əm ə ˈlɑːdʒ- **~ly** ˌi
etymologis... —*see* **etymologiz...**
etymologist ˌet ɪ ˈmɒl ədʒ ɪst ˌ-ə-, §-əst ‖ ˌeţ ə ˈmɑːl- **~s** s
etymologiz|e ˌet ɪ ˈmɒl ə dʒaɪz ˌ-ə- ‖ ˌeţ ə ˈmɑːl- **~ed** d **~es** ɪz əz **~ing** ɪŋ
etymolog|y ˌet ɪ ˈmɒl ədʒ |i ˌ-ə- ‖ ˌeţ ə ˈmɑːl- **~ies** iz
ety|mon ˈet ɪ |mɒn -ə- ‖ ˈeţ ə |mɑːn **~ma** mə
E-type ˈiː taɪp
EU ˌiː ˈjuː
eu- ¦juː, ju — **eubacteria** ˌjuː bæk ˈtɪər i ə ‖ -ˈtɪr- **eupeptic** ju ˈpept ɪk
Euan ˈjuː ən
Eubank ˈjuː bæŋk
Euboea ju ˈbɪə -ˈbiː ə ‖ -ˈbiː ə
eucalypt ˈjuːk ə lɪpt **~s** s
eucalypt|us ˌjuːk ə ˈlɪpt |əs **~i** aɪ **~uses** əs ɪz -əz
eucharist, E~ ˈjuːk ər ɪst §-əst **~s** s
eucharistic, E~ ˌjuːk ə ˈrɪst ɪk ◂
euch|re ˈjuːk |ə ‖ -|ər **~red** əd ‖ ərd **~res** əz ‖ ərz **~ring** ər ɪŋ
Euclid ˈjuːk lɪd §-ləd
Euclidean, Euclidian, e~ ju ˈklɪd i ən **~s** z
Eucryl *tdmk* ˈjuːk rɪl -rəl
eudiometer ˌjuːd i ˈɒm ɪt ə -ət ə ‖ -ˈɑːm əţ ər
~s z
Eudora ju ˈdɔːr ə ‖ -ˈdoʊr-
Eudoxus ju ˈdɒks əs ‖ -ˈdɑːks-
Euen ˈjuː ən
Eugene ˈjuː dʒiːn -ʒiːn, ·ˈ·; ju ˈʒeɪn
eugenic ju ˈdʒen ɪk **~ally** əl ˌi **~s** s
Eugenie, Eugénie ju ˈʒeɪn i -ˈʒiːn-, -ˈdʒiːn- —*Fr* [ø ʒe ni]
eukaryote ju ˈkær i əʊt -ɒt, -i ət ‖ -oʊt -ˈker- **~s** s
Eulalia ju ˈleɪl i ə
Euler ˈɔɪl ə ˈjuːl- ‖ -ər —*Ger* [ˈʔɔy lɐ]
eulogies ˈjuːl ədʒ iz
eulogis|e ˈjuːl ə dʒaɪz **~ed** d **~es** ɪz əz **~ing** ɪŋ
eulogist ˈjuːl ədʒ ɪst §-əst **~s** s
eulogistic ˌjuːl ə ˈdʒɪst ɪk ◂ **~ally** əl ˌi
eulogi|um ju ˈləʊdʒ i |əm ‖ -ˈloʊdʒ- **~a** ə **~ums** əmz
eulogiz|e ˈjuːl ə dʒaɪz **~ed** d **~es** ɪz əz **~ing** ɪŋ
eulog|y ˈjuːl ədʒ |i **~ies** iz
Eumenides ju ˈmen ɪ diːz -ə-
Eunice ˈjuːn ɪs -əs, ju ˈnaɪs i
Eunson ˈjuːn sən
eunuch ˈjuːn ək **~s** s
euonymus ju ˈɒn ɪm əs -əm- ‖ -ˈɑːn- **~es** ɪz əz
Eupen ˈɜːp ən ˈjuːp-, ˈɔɪp- ‖ ˈɔɪp- —*Fr* [ø pɛn], *Ger* [ˈʔɔy pən]
eupeptic ju ˈpept ɪk
Euphemia ju ˈfiːm i ə
euphemism ˈjuːf ə ˌmɪz əm -ɪ- **~s** z
euphemistic ˌjuːf ə ˈmɪst ɪk ◂ -ɪ- **~ally** əl ˌi
euphonic ju ˈfɒn ɪk ‖ -ˈfɑːn- **~ally** əl ˌi
euphonious ju ˈfəʊn i əs ‖ -ˈfoʊn- **~ly** li **~ness** nəs nɪs
euphonium ju ˈfəʊn i əm ‖ -ˈfoʊn- **~s** z
euphon|y ˈjuːf ən |i **~ies** iz
euphorbia ju ˈfɔːb i ə ‖ -ˈfɔːrb- **~s** z
euphorbiaceous ju ˌfɔːb i ˈeɪʃ əs ◂ ‖ -ˌfɔːrb-
euphoria ju ˈfɔːr i ə -ˈfɒr- ‖ -ˈfoʊr-
euphoric ju ˈfɒr ɪk ‖ -ˈfɔːr- -ˈfɑːr- **~ally** əl ˌi
Euphrates ju ˈfreɪt iːz
Euphrosyne ju ˈfrɒz ɪ niː -ə- ‖ -ˈfrɑːs- -ˈfrɑːz-
Euphues ˈjuːf ju iːz
euphuism ˈjuːf ju ˌɪz əm **~s** z
euphuistic ˌjuːf ju ˈɪst ɪk ◂
euploid ˈjuːp lɔɪd **~s** z
Eurailpass ˈjʊər eɪəl pɑːs ˈjɔːr-, §-pæs; juə ˈreɪəl- ‖ ˈjʊr eɪəl pæs **~es** ɪz əz
Eurasia juə ˈreɪʒ ə -ˈreɪʃ-
Eurasian juə ˈreɪʒ ən -ˈreɪʃ- **~s** z
Euratom juər ˈæt əm ‖ -ˈæţ-
eureka juə ˈriːk ə
eurhythmic juə ˈrɪð mɪk -ˈrɪθ- **~ally** əl ˌi **~s** s
Eurig ˈaɪər ɪg —*Welsh* [ˈəi rig, ˈəi-]
Euripides juə ˈrɪp ɪ diːz -ə-
euripus, E~ juə ˈraɪp əs
euro ˈjʊər əʊ ˈjɔːr- ‖ ˈjʊr oʊ **~s** z
Euro- *comb. form*
with stress-neutral suffix ¦jʊər əʊ ¦jɔːr- ‖ ¦jʊr ə -oʊ — **Eurocrat** ˈjʊər əʊ kræt ˈjɔːr- ‖ ˈjʊr ə-

with stress-imposing suffix juᵊ 'rɒ+ ‖ juᵊ 'rɑː+ — **Eurocracy** juᵊ 'rɒk rəs i ‖ -'rɑːk-
Eurocentric ˌjʊər əʊ 'sentr ɪk ◂ ˌjɔːr- ‖ ˌjʊr oʊ-
Eurocheque 'jʊər əʊ tʃek 'jɔːr- ‖ 'jʊr oʊ- **~s** s
Eurocommunism 'jʊər əʊ ˌkɒm jʊ nɪz əm 'jɔːr-, -ˌjə-; ˌ·'·ˌ·· ‖ 'jʊr oʊ ˌkɑːm jə-
Eurocommunist 'jʊər əʊ ˌkɒm jʊn ɪst 'jɔːr-, -ˌjən-, §-əst; ˌ·'·- ‖ 'jʊr oʊ ˌkɑːm jən əst **~s** s
Eurodisney *tdmk* 'jʊər əʊ ˌdɪz ni 'jɔːr- ‖ 'jʊr oʊ-
Eurodollar 'jʊər əʊ ˌdɒl ə 'jɔːr-, ˌ·'·· ‖ 'jʊr oʊ ˌdɑːl ᵊr **~s** z
Eurofighter 'jʊər əʊ ˌfaɪt ə 'jɔːr-, ˌ·ˌ·'· ‖ 'jʊr oʊ ˌfaɪṱ ᵊr **~s** z
Euroland 'jʊər əʊ lænd 'jɔːr- ‖ 'jʊr oʊ-
Europa juᵊ 'rəʊp ə ‖ -'roʊp ə
Europe 'jʊər əp 'jɔːr- ‖ 'jʊr əp 'jɜː-
European ˌjʊər ə 'piː‿ən ◂ ˌjɔːr- ‖ ˌjʊr- ˌjɜː- **~s** z
ˌ**Euroˌpean Com'munities**; ˌ**Euroˌpean 'Parliament**; ˌ**Euro'pean plan**
europium juᵊ 'rəʊp i‿əm ‖ -'roʊp-
Europoort, Europort 'jʊər əʊ pɔːt 'jɔːr- ‖ 'jʊr oʊ pɔːrt -poʊrt —*Dutch* ['øː roː poːrt]
Eurosceptic ˌjʊər əʊ 'skept ɪk ◂ ˌjɔːr- ‖ ˌjʊr oʊ- **~s** s
Eurostar *tdmk* 'jʊər əʊ stɑː 'jɔːr- ‖ 'jʊr oʊ stɑːr **~s** z
Eurotra juᵊ 'rəʊtr ə ‖ -'roʊtr ə
Eurotrash 'jʊər əʊ træʃ 'jɔːr- ‖ 'jʊr oʊ-
Eurotunnel *tdmk* 'jʊər əʊ ˌtʌn ᵊl 'jɔːr- ‖ 'jʊr oʊ-
Eurovision 'jʊər əʊ ˌvɪʒ ᵊn 'jɔːr- ‖ 'jʊr oʊ-
ˌ**Euroˌvision 'Song ˌContest**
Eurus 'jʊər əs 'jɔːr- ‖ 'jʊr-
Eurydice juᵊ 'rɪd ɪs i -əs-, -iː ˌjʊər ɪ 'diːtʃ i, -eɪ ‖ ˌjʊr- —*Also, where appropriate, pronounced in imitated Italian* Euridice —*It* [eu ri 'diː tʃe]
eurythmic juᵊ 'rɪð mɪk -'rɪθ- **~ally** ᵊl‿i **~s** s
Eusebio, Eusébio ju 'seɪb i əʊ -'seb- ‖ -oʊ —*Port* [eu 'ze bju]
Eusebius ju 'siːb i‿əs
Eustace 'juːst əs -ɪs
eustachian, E~ ju 'steɪʃ ᵊn -'steɪʃ i‿ən; ju 'steɪk i‿ən
Euˌ**stachian 'tube**
Euston 'juːst ən
eutectic ju 'tekt ɪk **~s** s
Eutelsat *tdmk* 'juːt ᵊl sæt 'juː tel- ‖ 'juːṱ-
Euterpe ju 'tɜːp i ‖ -'tɜːp i
euthanas|e 'juːθ ə neɪz **~ed** d **~es** ɪz əz **~ing** ɪŋ
euthanasia ˌjuːθ ə 'neɪz i‿ə -'neɪʒ i‿ə, -'neɪʒ ə ‖ -'neɪʒ ə
euthanis|e, euthaniz|e 'juːθ ə naɪz **~ed** d **~es** ɪz əz **~ing** ɪŋ
eutrophic ju 'trɒf ɪk -'trəʊf- ‖ -'troʊf-
eutrophication ju ˌtrɒf ɪ 'keɪʃ ᵊn juː-, -ə- ‖ -ˌtroʊf-
Euxine 'juːks aɪn ‖ -ᵊn
Euxton 'ekst ən

Eva 'iːv ə —*as a foreign name also* 'eɪv ə *or (esp AmE)* 'ev ə
evacu|ate i'væk ju |eɪt ə- **~ated** eɪt ɪd -əd ‖ eɪṱ əd **~ates** eɪts **~ating** eɪt ɪŋ ‖ eɪṱ ɪŋ
evacuation i ˌvæk ju 'eɪʃ ᵊn ə- **~s** z
evacuee i ˌvæk ju 'iː ə- **~s** z
evad|e i 'veɪd ə- **~ed** ɪd əd **~er/s** ə/z ‖ ᵊr/z **~es** z **~ing** ɪŋ
Evadne ɪ 'væd ni
evalu|ate i 'væl ju |eɪt ə- **~ated** eɪt ɪd -əd ‖ eɪṱ əd **~ates** eɪts **~ating** eɪt ɪŋ ‖ eɪṱ ɪŋ
evaluation i ˌvæl ju 'eɪʃ ᵊn ə- **~s** z
evaluative i 'væl ju‿ət ɪv ə-, -ju eɪt- ‖ -ju eɪṱ ɪv **~ly** li
Evan 'ev ᵊn
Evander ɪ 'vænd ə ə- ‖ -ᵊr
evanescence ˌev ə 'nes ᵊnᵗs ˌiːv-
evanescent ˌev ə 'nes ᵊnt ◂ ˌiːv- **~ly** li
evangel i 'vændʒ əl -el **~s** z
evangelic ˌiːv æn 'dʒel ɪk ◂ ‖ ˌev ᵊn- **~s** s
evangelical ˌiːv æn 'dʒel ɪk ᵊl ◂ ‖ ˌev ᵊn- **~ly** ‿i **~s** s
Evangeline i 'vændʒ ə liːn -ɪ-, -laɪn
evangelis... —*see* **evangeliz...**
evangelism ɪ 'vændʒ ə ˌlɪz əm ə-, -ɪ-
evangelist ɪ 'vændʒ əl ɪst ə-, -ɪl-, §-əst **~s** s
evangelistic ɪ ˌvændʒ ə 'lɪst ɪk ◂ ə-, -ɪ- **~ally** ᵊl‿i
evangelization ɪ ˌvændʒ əl aɪ 'zeɪʃ ᵊn ə-, -ˌ·ɪl-, -ɪ'·- ‖ -əl‿ə-
evangeliz|e ɪ 'vændʒ ə laɪz ə-, -ɪ- **~ed** d **~es** ɪz əz **~ing** ɪŋ
Evans 'ev ᵊnz
Evanston 'ev ᵊnst ən
Evansville 'ev ᵊnz vɪl
evapo|rate i 'væp ə |reɪt ə- **~rated** reɪt ɪd -əd ‖ reɪṱ əd **~rates** reɪts **~rating** reɪt ɪŋ ‖ reɪṱ ɪŋ
eˌ**vaporated 'milk**
evaporation i ˌvæp ə 'reɪʃ ᵊn ə- **~s** z
evaporator i 'væp ə reɪt ə ə- ‖ -reɪṱ ᵊr **~s** z
evasion i 'veɪʒ ᵊn ə- **~s** z
evasive i 'veɪs ɪv ə-, §-'veɪz- **~ly** li **~ness** nəs nɪs
Evatt 'ev ət
eve, Eve iːv
Evelina ˌev ə 'liːn ə -ɪ-
Eveline 'iːv lɪn -lən
Evelyn *(i)* 'iːv lɪn -lən, *(ii)* 'ev- 'ev ə- —*As a man's name, and as an English family name, (i); as a woman's name, either. In AmE usually (ii).*
even 'iːv ᵊn **~ed** d **~ing** ‿ɪŋ **~s** z
even-handed ˌiːv ᵊn 'hænd ɪd ◂ -əd **~ly** li **~ness** nəs nɪs
evening *v 'making even'* 'iːv ᵊn‿ɪŋ
evening *n 'period between afternoon and night'* 'iːv nɪŋ **~s** z
'**evening dress**, ˌ··'·; ˌ**evening 'prayer**; ˌ**evening 'star**
Evenki ɪ 'veŋk i ə-
Evenlode 'iːv ᵊn ləʊd ‖ -loʊd
evenly 'iːv ᵊn li
evenness 'iːv ᵊn nəs -nɪs

E

evensong 'iːv ᵊn sɒŋ ‖ -sɔːŋ -sɑːŋ
even-steven ˌiːv ᵊn 'stiːvᵊn
e|vent ɪ|'vent ə- **~vented** 'vent ɪd -əd ‖ 'vent̬ əd **~venting** 'vent ɪŋ ‖ 'vent̬ ɪŋ **~vents** 'vents
even-tempered ˌiːv ᵊn 'temp əd ◂ ‖ -ᵊrd **~ly** li **~ness** nəs nɪs
eventer ɪ 'vent ə ə- ‖ -ᵊr **~s** z
eventful ɪ 'vent fᵊl ə-, -fʊl **~ly** i **~ness** nəs nɪs
eventide 'iːv ᵊn taɪd
eventual ɪ 'ventʃ u‿əl ə-, -'ventʃ əl —*In formal style also* -'vent ju‿əl
eventualit|y ɪ ˌventʃ u 'æl ət |i ə-, -'vent ju-, -ɪt i ‖ -ət̬ |i **~ies** iz
eventually ɪ 'ventʃ u‿əl i ə-, -'ventʃ əl‿i —*In formal style also* -'vent ju‿əl i
eventu|ate ɪ 'ventʃ u |eɪt ə-, -'vent ju- **~ated** eɪt ɪd -əd ‖ eɪt̬ əd **~ates** eɪts **~ating** eɪt ɪŋ ‖ eɪt̬ ɪŋ
ever 'ev ə ‖ -ᵊr
Everage 'ev ər‿ɪdʒ
Everard 'ev ə rɑːd ‖ -rɑːrd
ever-changing ˌev ə 'tʃeɪndʒ ɪŋ ◂ ‖ -ᵊr- **~ly** li
Everest 'ev ər ɪst -əst, -ə rest
Everett 'ev ər ɪt -ət, -ə ret
Everglades 'ev ə gleɪdz ‖ -ᵊr-
evergreen 'ev ə griːn ‖ -ᵊr- **~s** z
everlasting ˌev ə 'lɑːst ɪŋ ◂ §-'læst- ‖ -ᵊr 'læst- **~ly** li **~ness** nəs nɪs **~s** z
ˌ**everˌlasting 'life**
Everley, Everly 'ev ə li ‖ -ᵊr-
evermore ˌev ə 'mɔː ◂ ‖ -ᵊr 'mɔːr -'moʊr
everpresent ˌev ə 'prez ᵊnt ◂ ‖ -ᵊr-
EverReady *tdmk* ˌev ə 'red i◂ '· ·ˌ· · ‖ '·ᵊrˌ·
Evers 'ev əz ‖ -ᵊrz
Evershed 'ev ə ʃed ‖ -ᵊr-
Eversholt 'ev ə ʃɒlt -ʃəʊlt ‖ -ᵊr ʃoʊlt
eversion i'vɜːʃ ᵊn ə-, -'vɜːʒ- ‖ -'vɜːʒ ᵊn -'vɜːʃ-
e|vert ɪ |'vɜːt iː-, ə- ‖ ɪ |'vɜːt **~verted** 'vɜːt ɪd -əd ‖ 'vɜːt̬ əd **~verting** 'vɜːt ɪŋ ‖ 'vɜːt̬ ɪŋ **~verts** 'vɜːts ‖ 'vɜːts
Evert 'ev ət ‖ -ᵊrt
Everton 'ev ət ən ‖ -ᵊrt ᵊn
every 'ev ri —*In very formal style occasionally also* 'ev ər i *(and in compounds too)*
ˌ**every 'which way**
everybody 'ev ri ˌbɒd i ‖ -ˌbɑːd i
everyday ˌev ri 'deɪ ◂
Everyman 'ev ri mæn
everyone 'ev ri wʌn §-wɒn
everyplace 'ev ri pleɪs
everything 'ev ri θɪŋ ⚠-θɪŋk
everywhere 'ev ri weə -hweə ‖ -*h*wer -*h*wær
Evesham 'iːv ʃəm 'iːv ɪʃ əm, 'iːs əm
Evett 'ev ɪt -ət
Evian *tdmk* 'ev i ɒ̃ ‖ ˌeɪv i 'ɑːn —*Fr* Évian [e vjɑ̃]
evict ɪ 'vɪkt ə- **~ed** ɪd əd **~ing** ɪŋ **~s** s
eviction ɪ 'vɪk ʃᵊn ə- **~s** z
evidenc|e *n, v* 'ev ɪd ənᵗs -əd-; §-ɪ denᵗs, §-ə- **~ed** t **~es** ɪz əz **~ing** ɪŋ
evident 'ev ɪd ənt -əd-; §-ɪ dent, §-ə- **~ly** li
evidential ˌev ɪ 'denᵗʃ ᵊl ◂ -ə- **~ly** i

evil 'iːv ᵊl -ɪl **~s** z
ˌ**evil 'eye; 'Evil One**
evildoer 'iːv ᵊl ˌduː‿ə -ɪl-, ˌ· ·'· · ‖ ᵊr **~s** z
evilly 'iːv əl i -ɪl i
evil-minded ˌiːv ᵊl 'maɪnd ɪd ◂ -ɪl-, -əd **~ly** li **~ness** nəs nɪs
evilness 'iːv ᵊl nəs -ɪl-, -nɪs
evil-tempered ˌiːv ᵊl 'temp əd ◂ -ɪl- ‖ -ᵊrd **~ly** li **~ness** nəs nɪs
evinc|e i 'vɪnᵗs ə- **~ed** t **~es** ɪz əz **~ing** ɪŋ
evisce|rate i 'vɪs ə |reɪt ə- **~rated** reɪt ɪd -əd ‖ reɪt̬ əd **~rates** reɪts **~rating** reɪt ɪŋ ‖ reɪt̬ ɪŋ
evisceration i ˌvɪs ə 'reɪʃ ᵊn ə- **~s** z
Evita e 'viːt ə e-, ə- —*Sp* [e 'βi ta]
evocation ˌiːv əʊ 'keɪʃ ᵊn ˌev- ‖ ˌiːv oʊ- ˌev ə- **~s** z
evocative ɪ 'vɒk ət ɪv ə- ‖ -'vɑːk ət̬ ɪv **~ly** li **~ness** nəs nɪs
evok|e i 'vəʊk ə- ‖ -'voʊk **~ed** t **~es** s **~ing** ɪŋ
evolute 'iːv ə luːt 'ev-, -ljuːt ‖ 'ev-

EVOLUTION

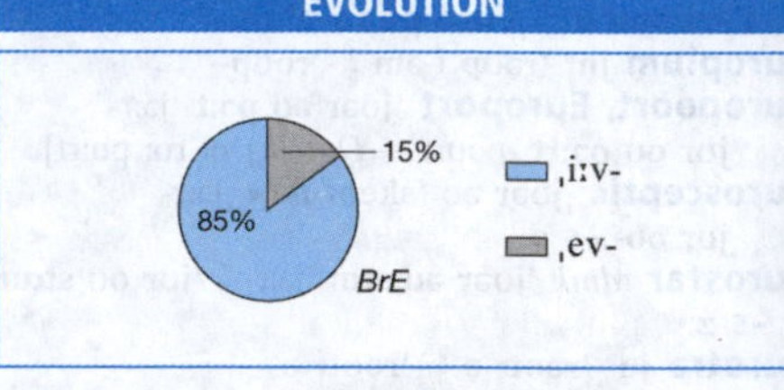

evolution ˌiːv ə 'luːʃ ᵊn ˌev-, -'ljuːʃ- ‖ ˌev- **~s** z — *Preference poll, BrE:* ˌiːv- *85%,* ˌev- *15%*
evolutionar|y ˌiːv ə 'luːʃ ᵊn‿ər |i ◂ ˌev-, -'ljuːʃ-, -ᵊn ᵊr‿|i ‖ ˌev ə 'luːʃ ə ner |i **~ily** əl i ɪ li
evolutive ɪ 'vɒl jʊt ɪv iː-, ə-, -jət- ‖ -'vɑːl jət̬ ɪv
evolv|e i'vɒlv ə-, §-'vəʊlv ‖ -'vɑːlv **~ed** d **~es** z **~ing** ɪŋ
Evonne ˌiː 'vɒn ɪ-, ə- ‖ -'vɑːn
Evo-stik *tdmk* 'iːv əʊ stɪk ‖ -oʊ-
evzone 'ev zəʊn ‖ -zoʊn **~s** z
Ewan 'juː‿ən
Ewart 'juː‿ət ‖ ᵊrt
Ewbank 'juː bæŋk
ewe juː §jəʊ *(= yew, you)* **ewes** juːz
Ewe *loch in Scotland* juː
Ewe *African people and language* 'e weɪ 'eɪ-
Ewell 'juː‿əl juːl
Ewelme 'juː elm
Ewen 'juː‿ən ɪn
ewer 'juː‿ə ‖ ᵊr **~s** z
Ewhurst 'juː hɜːst ‖ -hɜːst
Ewing 'juː‿ɪŋ
Ewins 'juː‿ɪnz
Ewyas 'juː‿əs
ex eks —*See also phrases with this word* **exes, ex's** 'eks ɪz -əz
ex- ¦eks, ɪks, əks, eks —*or with* gz, kz. —*This prefix is always stressed* ¦eks *when it has the specific meaning 'formerly'* (ˌex-'chairman). *When it has no such specific meaning, it is still stressed* ¦eks, ¦egz *(1) if the following syllable is unstressed* (ˌexca'vation), *and (2) in*

some disyllabic nouns and adjectives ('extract). *Otherwise, in RP, the prefix is usually unstressed and weak* **ɪks, ɪgz** (ex'pect). *But both vowel and consonants are subject to variation: some speakers use the weak vowel* **ə** *rather than* **ɪ**, *though others (particularly BrE regional speakers) have strong* **e** *and may even stress it. The forms with* **ks** *are used before a following consonant sound, those with* **gz** *before a vowel sound* (exact **ɪg 'zækt**, exhaust **ɪg 'zɔːst**). *(However, some speakers voice only the second consonant, thus* **ɪk 'zækt, ɪk 'zɔːst**.) *In words with the spellings* exce-, exci- *the consonants are simplified to* **ks** (excite **ɪk 'saɪt**). *Several words are irregular, as shown in the entries below.*

xacer|bate ɪg 'zæs ə |beɪt eg-, əg-, ɪk-, ek-, ək-; ek 'sæs- ‖ -ᵊr- **~bated** beɪt ɪd -əd ‖ beɪţ əd **~bates** beɪts **~bating** beɪt ɪŋ ‖ beɪţ ɪŋ

xacerbation ɪg ˌzæs ə 'beɪʃ ᵊn eg-, əg-, ɪk-, ek-, ək-; ek ˌsæs- ‖ -ᵊr-

xact *adj, v* ɪg 'zækt eg-, əg-, ɪk-, ek-, ək- **~ed** ɪd əd **~ing** ɪŋ **~s** s

xacting ɪg 'zækt ɪŋ eg-, əg-, ɪk-, ek-, ək- **~ly** li **~ness** nəs nɪs

xaction ɪg 'zæk ʃᵊn eg-, əg-, ɪk-, ek-, ək- **~s** z

xactitude ɪg 'zækt ɪ tjuːd eg-, əg-, ɪk-, ek-, ək-, -ə-, →-tʃuːd ‖ -tuːd -tjuːd

xactly ɪg 'zækt li eg-, əg-, ɪk-, ek-, ək- —*In rapid casual speech this word may lose its initial vowel or even the whole initial syllable.*

xactness ɪg 'zækt nəs eg-, əg-, ɪk-, ek-, ək-, -nɪs

x-actor *'former actor'* ˌeks 'ækt ə ‖ -ᵊr **~s** z

xactor *'one that exacts'* ɪg 'zækt ə eg-, əg-, ɪk-, ek-, ək- ‖ -ᵊr **~s** z

xagge|rate ɪg 'zædʒ ə |reɪt eg-, əg-, ɪk-, ek-, ək- **~rated/ly** reɪt ɪd /li -əd /li ‖ reɪţ əd /li **~rates** reɪts **~rating** reɪt ɪŋ ‖ reɪţ ɪŋ

xaggeration ɪg ˌzædʒ ə 'reɪʃ ᵊn eg-, əg-, ɪk-, ek-, ək- **~s** z

xalt ɪg 'zɔːlt eg-, əg-, ɪk-, ek-, ək-, -'zɒlt ‖ -'zɑːlt **~ed** ɪd əd **~ing** ɪŋ **~s** s

xaltation ˌegz ɔːl 'teɪʃ ᵊn ˌeks-, -ɒl- ‖ -ɑːl-

xalted ɪg 'zɔːlt ɪd eg-, əg-, ɪk-, ek-, ək-, -'zɒlt-, -əd ‖ -'zɑːlt- **~ly** li **~ness** nəs nɪs

xam ɪg 'zæm eg- əg-, ɪk-, ek-, ək-; §'egz æm **~s** z

e'xam ˌpaper

xamination ɪg ˌzæm ɪ 'neɪʃ ᵊn eg-, əg-, ɪk-, ek-, ək-, -ə- **~s** z

eˌxami'nation ˌpaper

xamin|e ɪg 'zæm ɪn eg-, əg-, ɪk-, ek-, ək-, §-ən **~ed** d **~es** z **~ing** ɪŋ

xaminee ɪg ˌzæm ɪ 'niː eg-, əg-, ɪk-, ek-, ək-, -ə- **~s** z

xaminer ɪg 'zæm ɪn ə eg-, əg-, ɪk-, ek-, ək-, §-ən- ‖ -ᵊr **~s** z

xample ɪg 'zɑːmp ᵊl eg-, əg-, ɪk-, ek-, ək-, §-'zæmp- ‖ -'zæmp- **~s** z

xanthema ˌeks æn 'θiːm ə ‖ ˌegz æn-

xarch 'eks ɑːk ‖ -ɑːrk **~s** s

exarchate 'eks ɑːk eɪt ‖ -ɑːrk- **~s** s

EXASPERATE

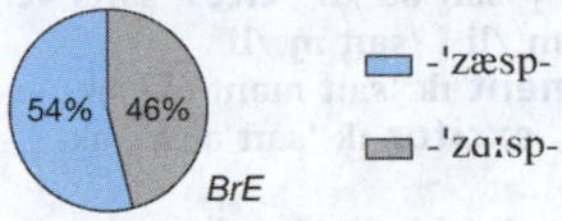

exaspe|rate ɪg 'zæsp ə |reɪt eg-, əg-, ɪk-, ek-, ək-, -'zɑːsp— *Preference poll, BrE:* -'zæsp- *54% (English southerners 33%),* -'zɑːsp- *46% (English southerners 67%). In AmE always* -'zæsp-. **~rated/ly** reɪt ɪd /li -əd /li ‖ reɪţ əd /li **~rates** reɪts **~rating/ly** reɪt ɪŋ /li ‖ reɪţ ɪŋ /li

exasperation ɪg ˌzæsp ə 'reɪʃ ᵊn eg-, əg-, ɪk-, ek-, ək-, -ˌzɑːsp-

Excalibur ek 'skæl ɪb ə -əb- ‖ -ᵊr

ex cathedra ˌeks kə 'θiːdr ə -'θedr-, -'tedr-

exca|vate 'eks kə |veɪt **~vated** veɪt ɪd -əd ‖ veɪţ əd **~vates** veɪts **~vating** veɪt ɪŋ ‖ veɪţ ɪŋ

excavation ˌeks kə 'veɪʃ ᵊn **~s** z

excavator 'eks kə veɪt ə ‖ -veɪţ ᵊr **~s** z

Excedrin *tdmk* ek 'sedr ɪn ɪk-, -ən

exceed ɪk 'siːd ek-, ək- **~ed** ɪd əd **~ing/ly** ɪŋ /li **~s** z

excel ɪk 'sel ek-, ək- **~led** d **~ling** ɪŋ **~s** z

excellence 'eks əl‿ənᵗs

Excellenc|y, e~ 'eks əl‿ənᵗs |i **~ies** iz

excellent 'eks əl‿ənt **~ly** li

excelsior ek 'sels i ɔː ɪk-, -i‿ə ‖ -i‿ᵊr -i ɔːr

except *v, prep, conj* ɪk 'sept ek-, ək- **~ed** ɪd əd **~ing** ɪŋ **~s** s

exception ɪk 'sep ʃᵊn ek-, ək- **~s** z

exceptionab|le ɪk 'sep ʃᵊn‿əb |ᵊl ek-, ək- **~ly** li

exceptional ɪk 'sep ʃᵊn‿əl ek-, ək- **~ly** i

excerpt *n* 'eks ɜːpt ek 'sɜːpt, 'egz ɜːpt ‖ 'eks ɜːpt 'egz ɜːpt **~s** s

excerpt *v* ek 'sɜːpt ɪk-, ək-; ɪg 'zɜːpt ‖ ek 'sɜːpt eg 'zɜːpt, '· · **~ed** ɪd əd **~ing** ɪŋ **~s** s

excess *n* ɪk 'ses ek-, ək-; 'eks es **~es** ɪz əz —*In stress-shifting environments usually* ˌeks es, *as if underlyingly* ˌek 'ses ◂: ˌexcess 'baggage *(see* excess *adj)*

excess *adj* 'eks es ek 'ses, ɪk-, ək-

excessive ɪk 'ses ɪv ek-, ək- **~ly** li

exchang|e *n, v* ɪks 'tʃeɪndʒ eks-, əks- **~ed** d **~es** ɪz əz **~ing** ɪŋ

ex'change rate

exchangeable ɪks 'tʃeɪndʒ əb ᵊl eks-, əks-

exchequer ɪks 'tʃek ə eks-, əks- ‖ -ᵊr **~s** z

excipient ɪk 'sɪp i‿ənt ek-, ək- **~s** s

excise *n 'tax'* 'eks aɪz ɪk 'saɪz, ek-, ək-

excis|e *v 'remove'* ɪk 'saɪz (ˌ)ek-, ək- **~ed** d **~es** ɪz əz **~ing** ɪŋ

excision ɪk 'sɪʒ ᵊn ek-, ək- **~s** z

excitability ɪk ˌsaɪt ə 'bɪl ət i ek-, ək-, -ɪt i ‖ -ˌsaɪţ ə 'bɪl əţ i

E

excitab|le ɪk 'saɪt əb |ᵊl ek-, ək- ‖ -'saɪţ əb- **~leness** ᵊl nəs -nɪs **~ly** li

excitation ˌeks ɪ 'teɪʃ ᵊn -ə-, -aɪ- **~s** z

ex|cite ɪk |'saɪt ek-, ək- **~cited/ly** 'saɪt ɪd /li əd /li ‖ 'saɪţ əd /li **~cites** 'saɪts **~citing/ly** 'saɪt ɪŋ /li ‖ 'saɪţ ɪŋ /li

excitement ɪk 'saɪt mənt ek-, ək- **~s** s

exciter, excitor ɪk 'saɪt ə ek-, ək- ‖ -'saɪţ ᵊr **~s** z

exclaim ɪk 'skleɪm ek-, ək- **~ed** d **~er/s** ə/z ‖ ᵊr/z **~ing** ɪŋ **~s** z

exclamation ˌeks klə 'meɪʃ ᵊn **~s** z
ˌ**excla'mation mark**; ˌ**excla'mation point**

exclamator|y ɪk 'sklæm ət˰ər |i ek-, ək- ‖ -ə tɔːr |i -toʊr i **~ily** əl i ɪ li

exclave 'eks kleɪv **~s** z

exclud|e ɪk 'skluːd ek-, ək- **~ed** ɪd əd **~er/s** ə/z ‖ ᵊr/z **~es** z **~ing** ɪŋ

exclusion ɪk 'skluːʒ ᵊn ek-, ək- **~s** z

exclusionary ɪk 'skluːʒ ᵊn ər˰i -ᵊn˰əri ‖ -ə ner i

exclusive ɪk 'skluːs ɪv ek-, ək-, §-'skluːz- **~ly** li **~ness** nəs nɪs

exclusivity ˌeks klu 'sɪv ət i -ɪt i ‖ -əţ i

excogi|tate eks 'kɒdʒ ɪ |teɪt ɪks-, -ə- ‖ -'kɑːdʒ- **~tated** teɪt ɪd -əd ‖ teɪţ əd **~tates** teɪts **~tating** teɪt ɪŋ ‖ teɪţ ɪŋ

excogitation ˌeks ˌkɒdʒ ɪ 'teɪʃ ᵊn ·ˌ·-, ɪks ˌkɒdʒ- ‖ eks ˌkɑːdʒ- **~s** z

excommunicate *n, adj* ˌeks kə 'mjuːn ɪk ət -ɪt, -ɪ keɪt **~s** s

excommuni|cate *v* ˌeks kə 'mjuːn ɪ |keɪt -'ə- **~cated** keɪt ɪd -əd ‖ keɪţ əd **~cates** keɪts **~cating** keɪt ɪŋ ‖ keɪţ ɪŋ

excommunication ˌeks kə ˌmjuːn ɪ 'keɪʃ ᵊn -ˌə- **~s** z

ex-con ˌeks 'kɒn ‖ -'kɑːn **~s** z

ex-convict ˌeks 'kɒn vɪkt ‖ -'kɑːn- **~s** s

excori|ate ɪk 'skɔːr i |eɪt ek-, ək-, -'skɒr- ‖ -'skoʊr- **~ated** eɪt ɪd -əd ‖ eɪţ əd **~ates** eɪts **~ating** eɪt ɪŋ ‖ eɪţ ɪŋ

excoriation ɪk ˌskɔːr i 'eɪʃ ᵊn ek-, ək-, -ˌskɒr- ‖ -ˌskoʊr- **~s** z

excrement 'eks krɪ mənt -krə-

excremental ˌeks krɪ 'ment ᵊl ◂ -krə- ‖ -'menţ ᵊl ◂

excrescenc|e ɪk 'skres ᵊnᵗs ek-, ək- **~es** ɪz əz

excrescent ɪk 'skres ᵊnt ek-, ək- **~ly** li

excreta ɪk 'skriːt ə ek-, ək- ‖ -'skriːţ ə

ex|crete ɪk |'skriːt ek-, ək- **~creted** 'skriːt ɪd -əd ‖ 'skriːţ əd **~cretes** 'skriːts **~creting** 'skriːt ɪŋ ‖ 'skriːţ ɪŋ

excretion ɪk 'skriːʃ ᵊn ek-, ək-

excretive ɪk 'skriːt ɪv ek-, ək- ‖ -'skriːţ ɪv

excretory ɪk 'skriːt ər i ek-, ək- ‖ 'eks krə tɔːr i -toʊr i

excruciating ɪk 'skruːʃ i eɪt ɪŋ ek-, ək- ‖ -eɪţ ɪŋ **~ly** li

exculp|ate 'eks kʌlp |eɪt ɪks 'kʌlp-, eks- **~ated** eɪt ɪd -əd ‖ eɪţ əd **~ates** eɪts **~ating** eɪt ɪŋ ‖ eɪţ ɪŋ

exculpation ˌeks kʌl 'peɪʃ ᵊn **~s** z

excursion ɪk 'skɜːʃ ᵊn ek-, ək-, -'skɜːʒ- ‖ -'skɜ˞ːʒ ᵊn **~s** z
ex'cursion train

excursive ɪk 'skɜːs ɪv ek-, ək-, §-'skɜːz- ‖ -'skɜ˞ːs- **~ly** li **~ness** nəs nɪs

excursus ek 'skɜːs əs ɪk- ‖ -'skɜ˞ːs- **~es** ɪz əz

excusab|le ɪk 'skjuːz əb |ᵊl ek-, ək- **~ly** li

excusatory ɪk 'skjuːz ət˰ər i ek-, ək-; ˌeks kjuː 'zeɪt ər i ‖ -'skjuːz ə tɔːr i -toʊr i

excus|e *v* ɪk 'skjuːz ek-, ək- **~ed** d **~er/s** ə/z ‖ ᵊr/z **~es** ɪz əz **~ing** ɪŋ

excus|e *n* ɪk 'skjuːs ek-, ək- *(!)* **~es** ɪz əz

excuse-me ɪk 'skjuːz mi ek-, ək-, -miː **~s, ~'s**

ex-directory ˌeks də 'rekt ər˰i ˌ·dɪ-, ˌ·daɪᵊ-

Exe eks

exeat 'eks i æt -eɪ- **~s** s

exec ɪg 'zek eg-, əg-, ɪk-, ek-, ək- **~s** s

execrab|le 'eks ɪk rəb |ᵊl '·ək- **~ly** li

exe|crate 'eks ɪ |kreɪt -ə- **~crated** kreɪt ɪd -əd ‖ kreɪţ əd **~crates** kreɪts **~crating** kreɪt ɪŋ ‖ kreɪţ ɪŋ

execration ˌeks ɪ 'kreɪʃ ᵊn -ə- **~s** z

executable 'eks ɪ kjuːt əb ᵊl ‖ -kjuːţ əb ᵊl

executant ɪg 'zek jʊt ənt eg-, əg-, ɪk-, ek-, ək- -jət-, §-ət- ‖ -jət ᵊnt -ət- **~s** s

exe|cute 'eks ɪ |kjuːt -ə- **~cuted** kjuːt ɪd -əd ‖ 'kjuːţ əd **~cutes** kjuːts **~cuting** kjuːt ɪŋ ‖ kjuːţ ɪŋ

execution ˌeks ɪ 'kjuːʃ ᵊn -ə- **~s** z

executioner ˌeks ɪ 'kjuːʃ ᵊn˰ə ˌ·ə- ‖ ər **~s** z

executive ɪg 'zek jʊt ɪv eg-, əg-, ɪk-, ek-, ək-, -jət-, §-ət- ‖ -jəţ ɪv -əţ- **~s** z
eˌxecutive 'officer

executor ɪg 'zek jʊt ə eg-, əg-, ɪk-, ek-, ək-, -jət-, §-ət- ‖ -jəţ ᵊr -əţ ᵊr —*but in the sense 'performer' also* 'eks ɪ kjuːt ə ‖ -kjuːţ ᵊr **~s** z

executrix ɪg 'zek ju trɪks eg-, əg-, ɪk-, ek-, ək- ‖ -jə- -ə-

exeges|is ˌeks ɪ 'dʒiːs |ɪs -ə-, §-əs **~es** iːz

exegete 'eks ɪ dʒiːt -ə- **~s** s

exegetic ˌeks ɪ 'dʒet ɪk ◂ -ə- ‖ -'dʒeţ- **~al** ᵊl **~s** s

exemplar ɪg 'zemp lɑː eg-, əg-, ɪk-, ek-, ək-, -lə ‖ -lɑːr -lᵊr **~s** z

exemplary ɪg 'zemp lər i eg-, əg-, ɪk-, ek-, ək-

exemplification ɪg ˌzemp lɪf ɪ 'keɪʃ ᵊn eg-, əg-, ɪk-, ek-, ək-, -ˌ·ləf-, §-ə'·- **~s** z

exempli|fy ɪg 'zemp lɪ |faɪ eg-, əg-, ɪk-, ek-, ək-, -lə- **~fied** faɪd **~fier/s** faɪ˰ə/z ‖ faɪ˰ᵊr/z **~fies** faɪz **~fying** faɪ ɪŋ

exempli gratia eg ˌzemp liː 'grɑːt i ɑː ɪg-, əg-; -laɪ 'greɪʃ i˰ə, -eɪ

exempt *adj, v* ɪg 'zem*p*t eg-, əg-, ɪk-, ek-, ək- **~ed** ɪd əd **~ing** ɪŋ **~s** s

exemption ɪg 'zem*p* ʃᵊn eg-, əg-, ɪk-, ek-, ək- **~s** z

exequatur ˌeks ɪ 'kweɪt ə -ə- ‖ -'kweɪţ ᵊr **~s** z

exequies 'eks ɪk wiz -ək-

exercis|e *n, v* 'eks ə saɪz ‖ -ᵊr- **~ed** d **~er/s** ə/z ‖ ᵊr/z **~es** ɪz əz **~ing** ɪŋ
'**exercise bike**; '**exercise book**

exergue ek 'sɜːg 'eks ɜːg ‖ 'eks ɜ˞ːg 'egz- **~s** z

x|ert ɪg |ˈzɜːt eg-, əg-, ɪk-, ek-, ək- ‖ -|ˈzɜːt **~erted** ˈzɜːt ɪd -əd ‖ ˈzɜːt̬ əd **~erting** ˈzɜːt ɪŋ ‖ ˈzɜːt̬ ɪŋ **~erts** ˈzɜːts ‖ ˈzɜːts

xertion ɪg ˈzɜːʃ ən eg-, əg-, ɪk-, ek-, ək- ‖ -ˈzɜːʃ ən **~s** z

xeter ˈeks ɪt ə -ət- ‖ -ət̬ ər

xeunt ˈeks i ʌnt -eɪ-, -ʊnt, -i‿ənt

ˌexeunt ˈomnes ˈɒm neɪz -niːz ‖ ˈɑːm- ˈɔːm-

xfoli|ate (ˌ)eks ˈfəʊl i |eɪt ‖ -ˈfoʊl- **~ated** eɪt ɪd -əd ‖ eɪt̬ əd **~ates** eɪts **~ating** eɪt ɪŋ ‖ eɪt̬ ɪŋ

xfoliation (ˌ)eks ˌfəʊl i ˈeɪʃ ən ‖ -ˌfoʊl-

x gratia (ˌ)eks ˈgreɪʃ ə -ˈgreɪʃ i‿ə

xhalation ˌeks hə ˈleɪʃ ən -ə- **~s** z

xhalatory eks ˈheɪl ət‿ər i ɪks-, əks-, -ˈhæl- ‖ -ə tɔːr i -toʊr i

xhal|e eks ˈheɪəl ɪks-, əks-; eg ˈzeɪəl, ɪg-, əg- **~ed** d **~es** z **~ing** ɪŋ

xhaust *v* ɪg ˈzɔːst eg-, əg-, ɪk-, ek-, ək- ‖ -ˈzɑːst **~ed** ɪd əd **~ing** ɪŋ **~s** s

xhaust *n* ɪg ˈzɔːst eg-, əg-, ɪk-, ek-, ək-, §ˈeg zɔːst ‖ -ˈzɑːst **~s** s

exˈhaust pipe

xhaustion ɪg ˈzɔːs tʃən eg-, əg-, ɪk-, ek-, ək- ‖ -ˈzɑːs-

xhaustive ɪg ˈzɔːst ɪv eg-, əg-, ɪk-, ek-, ək- ‖ -ˈzɑːst- **~ly** li **~ness** nəs nɪs

xhib|it *v* ɪg ˈzɪb |ɪt eg-, əg-, ɪk-, ek-, ək-, §-ət ‖ -|ət **~ited** ɪt ɪd §ət-, -əd ‖ ət̬ əd **~iting** ɪt ɪŋ §ət- ‖ ət̬ ɪŋ **~its** ɪts §əts ‖ əts

xhibit *n* ɪg ˈzɪb ɪt eg-, əg-, ɪk-, ek-, ək-, §-ət; ˈeks ɪb-, -əb- **~s** s

xhibition ˌeks ɪ ˈbɪʃ ən -ə- **~s** z

xhibitioner ˌeks ɪ ˈbɪʃ ən‿ə ˌ-ə- ‖ ər **~s** z

xhibitionism ˌeks ɪ ˈbɪʃ ən ˌɪz əm ˌ-ə-

xhibitionist ˌeks ɪ ˈbɪʃ ən‿ɪst ˌ-ə-, §‿əst **~s** s

xhibitionistic ˌeks ɪ ˌbɪʃ ə ˈnɪst ɪk ˌ-ə- **~ally** əl‿i

xhibitor ɪg ˈzɪb ɪt ə eg-, əg-, §-ət- ‖ -ət̬ ər **~s** z

xhila|rate ɪg ˈzɪl ə |reɪt eg-, əg-, ɪk-, ek-, ək-, ek ˈsɪl- **~rated** reɪt ɪd -əd ‖ reɪt̬ əd **~rates** reɪts **~rating/ly** reɪt ɪŋ /li ‖ reɪt̬ ɪŋ /li

xhilaration ɪg ˌzɪl ə ˈreɪʃ ən eg-, əg-, ɪk-, ek-, ək-, ek ˌsɪl- **~s** z

ex|hort ɪg |ˈzɔːt eg-, əg-, ɪk-, ek-, ək- ‖ -|ˈzɔːrt **~horted** ˈzɔːt ɪd -əd ‖ ˈzɔːrt̬ əd **~horting** ˈzɔːt ɪŋ ‖ ˈzɔːrt̬ ɪŋ **~horts** ˈzɔːts ‖ ˈzɔːrts

exhortation ˌegz ɔː ˈteɪʃ ən ˌeks- ‖ -ɔːr- -ər- **~s** z

exhortative ɪg ˈzɔːt ət ɪv eg-, əg-, ɪk-, ek-, ək- ‖ -ˈzɔːrt̬ ət̬ ɪv

exhortatory ɪg ˈzɔːt ət‿ər i eg-, əg-, ɪk-, ek-, ək- ‖ -ˈzɔːrt̬ ə tɔːr i -toʊr i

exhumation ˌeks hju ˈmeɪʃ ən -ju- ‖ ˌegz ju- **~s** z

exhum|e eks ˈhjuːm ɪg ˈzjuːm, eg-, əg-, ɪk-, ek-, ək-, -ˈzuːm ‖ ɪg ˈzuːm -ˈzjuːm, eks ˈhjuːm **~ed** d **~es** z **~ing** ɪŋ

ex hypothesi ˌeks haɪ ˈpɒθ ə saɪ -əs i ‖ -ˈpɑːθ-

Exide *tdmk* ˈeks aɪd

exigenc|e ˈeks ɪdʒ ənts ˈegz-, -ədʒ- **~es** ɪz əz

exigenc|y ˈeks ɪdʒ ənts |i ˈegz-, -ədʒ-; ɪg ˈzɪdʒ-, eg-, əg-, ɪk-, ek-, ək- **~ies** iz

exigent ˈeks ɪdʒ ənt ˈegz-, -ədʒ- **~ly** li

exiguity ˌeks ɪ ˈgjuː‿ət i ɪt i ‖ ˌegz ɪ ˈgjuː ət̬ i

exiguous ɪg ˈzɪg ju‿əs eg-, əg-, ɪk-, ek-, ək-; ek ˈsɪg-, ɪk-, ək- **~ly** li **~ness** nəs nɪs

exil|e *n, v* ˈeks aɪəl ˈegz- **~ed** d **~es** z **~ing** ɪŋ

exist ɪg ˈzɪst eg-, əg-, ɪk-, ek-, ək- **~ed** ɪd əd **~ing** ɪŋ **~s** s

existence ɪg ˈzɪst ənts eg-, əg-, ɪk-, ek-, ək-

existent ɪg ˈzɪst ənt eg-, əg-, ɪk-, ek-, ək-

existential ˌegz ɪ ˈstentʃ əl ◂ ˌeks-, -ə- **~ism** ˌɪz əm **~ist/s** ɪst/s §əst/s **~ly** i

EXIT

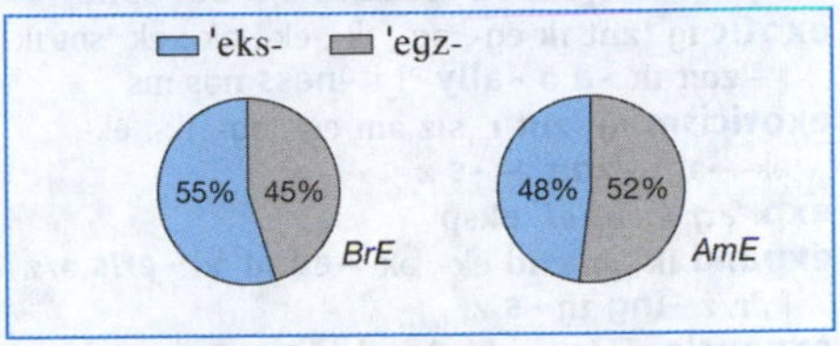

ex|it ˈeks |ɪt ˈegz-, §-ət ‖ -|ət — *Preference polls, BrE:* ˈeks- *55%,* ˈegz- *45%; AmE:* ˈeks- *48%,* ˈegz- *52%.* **~ited** ɪt ɪd §ət-, -əd ‖ ət̬ əd **~iting** ɪt ɪŋ §ət- ‖ ət̬ ɪŋ **~its** ɪts §əts ‖ əts

ˈexit poll

Ex-lax *tdmk* ˈeks læks

ex libris ˌeks ˈliːb rɪs -ˈlaɪb-, -riːs, §-rəs

Exmoor ˈeks mʊə -mɔː ‖ -mʊr

ˌExmoor ˈpony

Exmouth ˈeks məθ -maʊθ

exo- *comb. form*
with stress-neutral suffix ¦eks əʊ ‖ ¦eks oʊ — **exosphere** ˈeks əʊ sfɪə ‖ -oʊ sfɪr
with stress-imposing suffix ek ˈsɒ+ ‖ ek ˈsɑː+ — **exogenous** ek ˈsɒdʒ ən əs -ɪn- ‖ -ˈsɑːdʒ-

exocentric ˌeks əʊ ˈsentr ɪk ◂ ‖ -oʊ- **~ally** əl‿i

Exocet *tdmk* ˈeks əʊ set ‖ -oʊ- **~s** s

exocrine ˈeks əʊ kraɪn -krɪn, §-ək rən ‖ -ək rən

exodus, E~ ˈeks əd əs §ˈegz- **~es** ɪz əz

ex-officio, ex officio ˌeks ə ˈfɪʃ i əʊ ◂ ˌɒ-, -ˈfɪs- ‖ -oʊ

exogamous ek ˈsɒg əm əs ‖ -ˈsɑːg- **~ly** li

exogamy ek ˈsɒg əm i ‖ -ˈsɑːg-

exogenous ek ˈsɒdʒ ən əs ɪk-, -ɪn- ‖ -ˈsɑːdʒ- **~ly** li

exon ˈeks ɒn ‖ -ɑːn **~s** z

exone|rate ɪg ˈzɒn ə |reɪt eg-, əg-, ɪk-, ek-, ək- ‖ -ˈzɑːn- **~rated** reɪt ɪd -əd ‖ reɪt̬ əd **~rates** reɪts **~rating** reɪt ɪŋ ‖ reɪt̬ ɪŋ

exoneration ɪg ˌzɒn ə ˈreɪʃ ən eg-, əg-, ɪk-, ek-, ək- ‖ -ˌzɑːn- **~s** z

exonym ˈeks əʊ nɪm ‖ -ə- **~s** z

exophora ek ˈsɒf ər ə ‖ -ˈsɑːf-

exophoric ˌeks əʊ ˈfɒr ɪk ◂ ‖ -ə ˈfɔːr- -ˈfɑːr-

exophthalm|ic ˌeks ɒf ˈθælm |ɪk ◂ -əf-, -ɒp- ‖ -ɑːf- -əf-, -ɑːp- **~os** əs ɒs ‖ ɑːs

ˌexophˌthalmic ˈgoitre

E

exorbitance ɪg 'zɔːb ɪt ənᵗs eg-, əg-, ɪk-, ek-, ək-, -ət- ‖ -'zɔːrb ət ənᵗs
exorbitant ɪg 'zɔːb ɪt ənt eg-, əg-, ɪk-, ek-, ək-, -ət- ‖ -'zɔːrb ət ənt **~ly** li
exorcis... —*see* **exorciz...**
exorcism 'eks ɔː ˌsɪz əm 'egz-, -ə- ‖ -ɔːr- -ər- **~s** z
exorcist 'eks ɔːs ɪst 'egz-, -əs-, §-əst ‖ -ɔːrs- -ərs- **~s** s
exorciz|e 'eks ɔːs aɪz 'egz-, -ə saɪz ‖ -ɔːrs aɪz -ər saɪz **~ed** d **~es** ɪz əz **~ing** ɪŋ
exordi|um ek 'sɔːd i‿|əm eg 'zɔːd- ‖ eg 'zɔːrd- **~a** ə **~ums** əmz
exoskeleton 'eks əʊ ˌskel ɪt ən -ət- ‖ 'oʊ- **~s** z
exothermic ˌeks əʊ 'θɜːm ɪk ◂ ‖ -oʊ 'θɜːm-
exotic ɪg 'zɒt ɪk eg-, əg-, ɪk-, ek-, ək-; ek 'sɒt ɪk ‖ -'zɑːt̬ ɪk **~a** ə **~ally** əl‿i **~ness** nəs nɪs
exoticism ɪg 'zɒt ɪ ˌsɪz əm eg-, əg-, ɪk-, ek-, ək-, -ə- ‖ -'zɑːt̬ ə- **~s** z
exp *'exponential'* eksp
expand ɪk 'spænd ek-, ək- **~ed** ɪd əd **~er/s** ə/z ‖ ər/z **~ing** ɪŋ **~s** z
expans|e ɪk 'spænᵗs ek-, ək- **~es** ɪz əz
expansibility ɪk ˌspænᵗs ə 'bɪl ət i -ˌ·ɪ-, -ɪt i ‖ -ət̬ i
expansible ɪk 'spænᵗs əb əl ek-, ək-, -ɪb-
expansion ɪk 'spænᵗʃ ən ek-, ək- **~s** z
  ex'pansion bolt
expansionary ɪk 'spænᵗʃ ən‿ər i ek-, ək- ‖ -ə ner i
expansion|ism ɪk 'spænᵗʃ ən| ˌɪz əm ek-, ək- **~ist/s** ɪst/s §əst/s
expansive ɪk 'spænᵗs ɪv ek-, ək- **~ly** li **~ness** nəs nɪs
ex parte ˌeks 'pɑːt i -eɪ ‖ -'pɑːrt̬ i
expat, ex-pat ˌeks 'pæt ◂ **~s** s
expati|ate ek 'speɪʃ i |eɪt ɪk-, əks- **~ated** eɪt ɪd -əd ‖ eɪt̬ əd **~ates** eɪts **~ating** eɪt ɪŋ ‖ eɪt̬ ɪŋ
expatri|ate *v* ₍ˌ₎eks 'pætr i |eɪt ɪks-, 'peɪtr- ‖ -'peɪtr- **~ated** eɪt ɪd -əd ‖ eɪt̬ əd **~ates** eɪts **~ating** eɪt ɪŋ ‖ eɪt̬ ɪŋ
expatriate *n, adj* ₍ˌ₎eks 'pætr i‿ət ɪks-, -'peɪtr-, ɪt, -eɪt ‖ -'peɪtr- **~s** s
expatriation eks ˌpætr i 'eɪʃ ən ɪks-, -ˌpeɪtr-, ˌeks ˌpeɪtr- ‖ -ˌpeɪtr-
expect ɪk 'spekt ₍ˌ₎ek-, ək- **~ed** ɪd əd **~ing** ɪŋ **~s** s
expectanc|e ɪk 'spekt ənᵗs ek-, ək- **~es** ɪz əz **~ies** iz **~y** i
expectant ɪk 'spekt ənt ek-, ək- **~ly** li
expectation ˌeks pek 'teɪʃ ən **~s** z
expectorant ɪk 'spekt ər ənt ek-, ək- **~s** s
expecto|rate ɪk 'spekt ə |reɪt ek-, ək- **~rated** reɪt ɪd -əd ‖ reɪt̬ əd **~rates** reɪts **~rating** reɪt ɪŋ ‖ reɪt̬ ɪŋ
expectoration ɪk ˌspekt ə 'reɪʃ ən ek-, ək- **~s** z
Expedia *tdmk* ɪk 'spiːd i‿ə ek-, ək-
expedienc|e ɪk 'spiːd i‿ənᵗs ek-, ək- **~es** ɪz əz **~ies** iz **~y** i
expedient ɪk 'spiːd i‿ənt ek-, ək- **~ly** li

expe|dite 'eks pə |daɪt -pɪ- **~dited** daɪt ɪd -əd ‖ daɪt̬ əd **~diter/s** daɪt ə/z ‖ daɪt̬ ər/z **~dites** daɪts **~diting** daɪt ɪŋ ‖ daɪt̬ ɪŋ
expedition ˌeks pə 'dɪʃ ən -pɪ- **~s** z
expeditionary ˌeks pə 'dɪʃ ən ər‿i ◂ ˌpɪ-, -ən‿ər i ‖ -ə ner i
expeditious ˌeks pə'dɪʃ əs ◂ -pɪ- **~ly** li **~ness** nəs nɪs
expel ɪk 'spel ek-, ək- **~led** d **~ling** ɪŋ **~s** z
expellee ˌeks pe'liː ɪk ˌspel 'iː, ek-, ək- **~s** z
expend ɪk 'spend ek-, ək- **~ed** ɪd əd **~ing** ɪŋ **~s** z
expendab|le ɪk 'spend əb| əl ek-, ək- **~ly** li
expenditure ɪk 'spend ɪtʃ ə ek-, ək- ‖ -ər -ə tʃʊr **~s** z
expens|e ɪk 'spenᵗs ek-, ək- **~es** ɪz əz
  ex'pense ac,count
expensive ɪk 'spenᵗs ɪv ek-, ək- **~ly** li **~ness** nəs nɪs
experienc|e *n, v* ɪk 'spɪər i‿ənᵗs ek-, ək- ‖ -'spɪr- **~ed** t **~es** ɪz əz **~ing** ɪŋ
experiential ɪk ˌspɪər i 'enᵗʃ əl ◂ ek-, ək- ‖ -ˌspɪr- **~ly** i
experi|ment *v* ɪk 'sper ɪ |ment ek-, ək-, -ə- ‖ -'spɪr- —*See note at* -ment **~mented** ment ɪd -əd ‖ ment̬ əd **~menting** ment ɪŋ ‖ ment̬ ɪŋ **~ments** ments
experiment *n* ɪk 'sper ɪ mənt ek-, ək-, -ə- ‖ -'spɪr- **~s** s
experimental ɪk ˌsper ɪ 'ment əl ◂ ₍ˌ₎ek-, ək-, -ə- ‖ -'ment̬ əl ◂ -ˌspɪr- **~ism** ˌɪz əm **~ist/s** ɪst/s §əst/s **~ly** i
experimentation ɪk ˌsper ɪ men 'teɪʃ ən ek-, ək-, -ˌ·ə-, -mən'·- ‖ -ˌspɪr- **~s** z
expert 'eks pɜːt ˌek 'spɜːt, ɪk-, ək- ‖ 'eks pɜːt ɪk 'spɜːt **~ly** li **~ness** nəs nɪs **~s** s
  ˌ**expert 'system**
expertis|e, expertiz|e *v* 'eks pə taɪz -pɜːt aɪz ‖ -pər- **~ed** d **~es** ɪz əz **~ing** ɪŋ
expertise *n* ˌeks pɜː 'tiːz -pə-, '· · · ‖ -pər 'tiːz -'tiːs
expiable 'eks pi‿əb əl
expi|ate 'eks pi |eɪt **~ated** eɪt ɪd -əd ‖ eɪt̬ əd **~ates** eɪts **~ating** eɪt ɪŋ ‖ eɪt̬ ɪŋ
expiation ˌeks pi 'eɪʃ ən **~s** z
expiatory 'eks pi‿ət‿ər i -eɪt ər i, ˌeks pi 'eɪt ər i ‖ ə tɔːr i -toʊr i
expiration ˌeks pə 'reɪʃ ən -pɪ-, -paɪə- **~s** z
expiratory ɪk 'spaɪər ət‿ər i ₍ˌ₎ek-, ək-, -'spɪr- ‖ -ə tɔːr i -toʊr i
expir|e ɪk 'spaɪ‿ə ₍ˌ₎ek-, ək- ‖ ɪk 'spaɪ‿ər **~ed** d **~es** z **~ing** ɪŋ
expir|y ɪk 'spaɪ‿ər |i ek-, ək- ‖ ɪk 'spaɪ‿ər |i 'eks pər |i **~ies** iz
  ex'piry date
explain ɪk 'spleɪn ek-, ək- **~ed** d **~ing** ɪŋ **~s** z
explainable ɪk 'spleɪn əb əl ek-, ək-
explanation ˌeks plə 'neɪʃ ən **~s** z
explanator|y ɪk 'splæn ət‿ər |i ek-, ək- ‖ -ə tɔːr |i -toʊr i **~ily** əl i ɪ li
expletive ɪk 'spliːt ɪv ek-, ək-; 'eks plət- ‖ 'eks plət̬ ɪv **~s** z
explicable ɪk 'splɪk əb əl ek-, ək-; 'eks plɪk-

xpli|cate 'eks plɪ |keɪt -plə- **~cated** keɪt ɪd -əd ‖ keɪţ əd **~cates** keɪts **~cating** keɪt ɪŋ ‖ keɪţ ɪŋ
xplication ˌeks plɪ 'keɪʃ ən -plə- —*also as a French word, Fr* [ɛks pli ka sjɔ̃] **~s** z
xplicative ek 'splɪk ət ɪv ɪk-, ək-; 'eks plɪk- ‖ -əţ ɪv
xplicatory ek 'splɪk ət‿ər i ɪk-, ək-; ˌeks plɪ 'keɪt ər i ◂ ‖ -ə tɔːr i 'eks plɪk-, -ə tour i
xplicature ek 'splɪk ətʃ ə ɪk-, ək-, -ə tjʊə ‖ -ər **~s** z
xplicit ɪk 'splɪs ɪt ek-, ək-, §-ət —*For contrast with* implicit, *also* ˌeks 'plɪs-, '·ˌ·· **~ly** li **~ness** nəs nɪs
xplod|e ɪk 'spləʊd ek-, ək- ‖ -'sploʊd **~ed** ɪd əd **~er/s** ə/z ‖ ər/z **~es** z **~ing** ɪŋ
xploit *n* 'eks plɔɪt **~s** s
x|ploit *v* ɪk |'splɔɪt ₍ₗ₎ek-, ək- **~ploited** 'plɔɪt ɪd -əd ‖ 'plɔɪţ əd **~ploiting** 'plɔɪt ɪŋ ‖ 'plɔɪţ ɪŋ **~ploits** 'plɔɪts
xploitable ɪk 'splɔɪt əb əl ₍ₗ₎ek-, ək- ‖ -'splɔɪţ-
xploitation ˌeks plɔɪ 'teɪʃ ən **~s** z
xploitative ɪk 'splɔɪt ət ɪv ₍ₗ₎ek-, ək- ‖ -'splɔɪţ əţ ɪv **~ly** li
xploiter ɪk 'splɔɪt ə ₍ₗ₎eks-, əks- ‖ -'splɔɪţ ər **~s** z
xploration ˌeks plə 'reɪʃ ən -plɔː- **~s** z
xplorative ɪk 'splɒr ət ɪv ek-, ək-, -'splɔːr- ‖ -'splɔːr əţ ɪv -'sploʊr- **~ly** li
xploratory ɪk 'splɒr ət‿ər i ek-, ək-, -'splɔːr- ‖ -'splɔːr ə tɔːr i -'sploʊr ə toʊr i
xplore ɪk 'splɔː ek-, ək- ‖ -'splɔːr -'sploʊr **~d** d **~s** z **exploring** ɪk 'splɔːr ɪŋ ek-, ək- ‖ -'sploʊr-
explorer ɪk 'splɔːr ə ek-, ək- ‖ -'splɔːr ər -'sploʊr- **~s** z
explosion ɪk 'spləʊʒ ən ek-, ək- ‖ -'sploʊʒ ən **~s** z
explosive ɪk 'spləʊs ɪv ek-, ək-, -'spləʊz- ‖ -'sploʊs- **~ly** li **~ness** nəs nɪs **~s** z
expo, Expo 'eks pəʊ ‖ -poʊ **~s** z
exponent ɪk 'spəʊn ənt ek-, ək- ‖ ɪk 'spoʊn- 'eks poʊn- **~s** s
exponential ˌeks pə 'nentʃ əl ◂ -pəʊ- ‖ -poʊ- **~ly** i
ˌexpoˌnential 'growth
exponenti|ate ˌeks pə 'nentʃ i |eɪt ˌpəʊ- ‖ ˌpoʊ- **~ated** eɪt ɪd -əd ‖ eɪţ əd **~ates** eɪts **~ating** eɪt ɪŋ ‖ eɪţ ɪŋ
exponentiation ˌeks pə ˌnentʃ i 'eɪʃ ən ˌpəʊ- ‖ ˌpoʊ- **~s** z
ex|port *v* ɪk |'spɔːt ek-, ək-; ˌeks 'pɔːt, '· · ‖ ɪk |'spɔːrt ek-, -'spoʊrt; 'eks pɔːrt, -poʊrt **~ported** 'spɔːt ɪd -əd ‖ 'spɔːrţ əd -'spoʊrţ- **~porting** 'spɔːt ɪŋ ‖ 'spɔːrţ ɪŋ -'spoʊrţ- **~ports** 'spɔːts ‖ 'spɔːrts -'spoʊrts
export *n* 'eks pɔːt ‖ -pɔːrt -poʊrt **~s** s
exportable ɪk 'spɔːt əb əl ek-, ək-; ˌeks 'pɔːt-, '·· ‖ ɪk 'spɔːrţ əb əl ek-, -'spoʊrţ-; 'eks pɔːrţ-, -poʊrţ-
exportation ˌeks pɔː 'teɪʃ ən ‖ -pɔːr- -poʊr-, -pər- **~s** z
exporter ɪk 'spɔːt ə ek-, ək-; 'eks pɔːt ə ‖ -'spɔːrţ ər -'spoʊrţ-; 'eks pɔːrţ- **~s** z
export-import ˌeks pɔːt 'ɪm pɔːt ◂ ‖ ˌeks pɔːrţ 'ɪm pɔːrt ◂ -poʊrt ◂
expos|e *v* ɪk 'spəʊz ek-, ək- ‖ -'spoʊz **~ed** d **~es** ɪz əz **~ing** ɪŋ
exposé *n* ek 'spəʊz eɪ ɪk-, ək- ‖ ˌeks poʊ 'zeɪ —*Fr* [ɛk spo ze] **~s** z
exposition ˌeks pə 'zɪʃ ən **~s** z
expositor ɪk 'spɒz ət ə ek-, ək-, -ɪt- ‖ -'spɑːz əţ ər **~s** z
expository ɪk 'spɒz ət‿ər i ek-, ək-, -'·ɪt‿ ‖ -'spɑːz ə tɔːr i -toʊr i
ex post facto ˌeks ˌpəʊst 'fækt əʊ ·ˌ·· ‖ -ˌpoʊst 'fækt oʊ
expostu|late ɪk 'spɒs tʃu |leɪt ek-, ək-, -tju- ‖ -'spɑːs tʃə- **~lated** leɪt ɪd -əd ‖ leɪţ əd **~lates** leɪts **~lating** leɪt ɪŋ ‖ leɪţ ɪŋ
expostulation ɪk ˌspɒs tʃu 'leɪʃ ən ek-, ək-, -tju- ‖ -ˌspɑːs tʃə- **~s** z
exposure ɪk 'spəʊʒ ə ek-, ək- ‖ -'spoʊʒ ər —*There is also an occasional very careful form* -'spəʊz jə ‖ -'spoʊz jər **~s** z
ex'posure ˌmeter
expound ɪk 'spaʊnd ek-, ək- **~ed** ɪd əd **~ing** ɪŋ **~s** z
express ɪk 'spres ek-, ək- —*In a stress-shifting environment the adj or n is sometimes* ˌeks pres, *as if underlyingly* ˌeks 'pres ◂: ˌExpress 'Dairies. *There is usually no stress-shifting in the v:* to exˌpress 'sympathy **~ed** t **~es** ɪz əz **~ing** ɪŋ **~ly** li
expressible ɪk 'spres əb əl -ɪb-
expression ɪk 'spreʃ ən ek-, ək- **~ism** ˌɪz əm **~ist/s** ɪst/s §əst/s **~s** z
expressionistic ɪk ˌspreʃ ə 'nɪst ɪk ◂ ek-, ək-, →-ən 'ɪst- **~ally** əl i
expressionless ɪk 'spreʃ ən ləs ek-, ək-, -lɪs **~ly** li **~ness** nəs nɪs
expressive ɪk 'spres ɪv ek-, ək- **~ly** li **~ness** nəs nɪs
expressivity ˌeks pre 'sɪv ət i -ɪt i ‖ -əţ i
expressway ɪk 'spres weɪ ek-, ək- **~s** z
expropri|ate ɪk 'sprəʊp ri |eɪt ₍ₗ₎ek-, ək- ‖ -'sproʊp- **~ated** eɪt ɪd -əd ‖ eɪţ əd **~ates** eɪts **~ating** eɪt ɪŋ ‖ eɪţ ɪŋ
expropriation ɪk ˌsprəʊp ri 'eɪʃ ən ek-, ək-, ˌeks ˌprəʊp- ‖ -ˌsproʊp- **~s** z
expulsion ɪk 'spʌlʃ ən ek-, ək- **~s** z
expung|e ɪk 'spʌndʒ ₍ₗ₎ek-, ək- **~ed** d **~es** ɪz əz **~ing** ɪŋ
expur|gate 'eks pə |geɪt -pɜː- ‖ -pər- **~gated** geɪt ɪd -əd ‖ geɪţ əd **~gates** geɪts **~gating** geɪt ɪŋ ‖ geɪţ ɪŋ
expurgation ˌeks pə 'geɪʃ ən -pɜː- ‖ -pər- **~s** z
expurgatory ek 'spɜːg ət‿ər i ‖ -ə tɔːr i -toʊr i

E

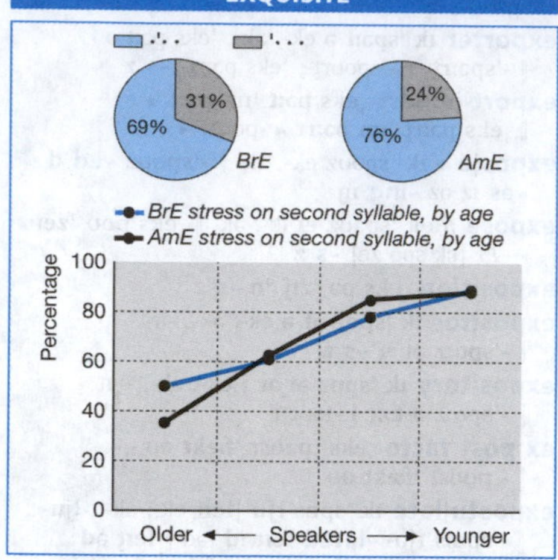

exquisite ɪk ˈskwɪz ɪt ek-, ək-, ˈeks kwɪz-, -ət — *Preference polls, BrE:* ·'·· *69%,* '··· *31%; AmE:* ·'·· *76%,* '··· *24%.* **~ly** li **~ness** nəs nɪs
ex-service ˌeks ˈsɜːv ɪs ◂ ˌek-, §-əs ‖ -ˈsɜ˞ːv əs
ex-service|man ˌeks ˈsɜːv ɪs |mən ˌek-, -əs- ‖ -ˈsɜ˞ːv- **~men** mən men **~woman** ˌwʊm ən **~women** ˌwɪm ɪn §-ən
extant ₍ₗ₎ek ˈstænt ɪk-, ək-; ˈekst ənt
Extel *tdmk* ˈeks tel
extemporaneous ɪk ˌstemp ə ˈreɪn i‿əs ◂ ₍ₗ₎ek-, ək- **~ly** li **~ness** nəs nɪs
extempore ɪk ˈstemp ər i ₍ₗ₎ek-, ək-
extemporis... —*see* **extemporiz...**
extemporization ɪk ˌstemp ər aɪ ˈzeɪʃ ən ek-, ək-, -ər ɪ- ‖ -ər ə- **~s** z
extemporiz|e ɪk ˈstemp ə raɪz ek-, ək- **~ed** d **~es** ɪz əz **~ing** ɪŋ
extend ɪk ˈstend ek-, ək- **~ed** ɪd əd **~ing** ɪŋ **~s** z
exˌtended ˈfamily
extender ɪk ˈstend ə ek-, ək- ‖ -ər **~s** z
extensibility ɪk ˌstenᵗs ə ˈbɪl ət i -ˌɪ-, -ɪt i ‖ -əţ i
extensible ɪk ˈstenᵗs əb əl ek-, ək-, -ɪb-
extension ɪk ˈstenᵗʃ ən ek-, ək- **~s** z
extensional ɪk ˈstenᵗʃ ən‿əl ek-, ək-
extensionality ɪk ˌstenᵗʃ ə ˈnæl ət i ek-, ək-, -ɪt i ‖ -əţ i
extensive ɪk ˈstenᵗs ɪv ek-, ək- **~ly** li **~ness** nəs nɪs
extensor ɪk ˈstenᵗs ə ek-, ək-, -ɔː ‖ -ər **~s** z
extent ɪk ˈstent ek-, ək- **~s** s
extenu|ate ɪk ˈsten ju |eɪt ek-, ək- **~ated** eɪt ɪd -əd ‖ eɪţ əd **~ates** eɪts **~ating** eɪt ɪŋ ‖ eɪţ ɪŋ
extenuation ɪk ˌsten ju ˈeɪʃ ən ek-, ək- **~s** z
exterior ɪk ˈstɪər i‿ə ₍ₗ₎ek-, ək- ‖ -ˈstɪr i‿ər **~ly** li **~s** z
exterioris... —*see* **exterioriz...**
exteriority ɪk ˌstɪər i ˈɒr ət i ek-, ək-, ˌekst ɪər-, -ɪt i ‖ -ˌstɪr i ˈɔːr əţ i -ˈɑːr-
exteriorization ɪk ˌstɪər i‿ər aɪ ˈzeɪʃ ən ek-, ək-, ˌekst ɪər-, -ɪˈ-- ‖ -ˌstɪr i‿ər ə- **~s** z
exterioriz|e ɪk ˈstɪər i‿ə raɪz ₍ₗ₎ek-, ək- ‖ -ˈstɪr- **~ed** d **~es** ɪz əz **~ing** ɪŋ
extermi|nate ɪk ˈstɜːm ɪ |neɪt ek-, ək-, -ə- ‖ -ˈstɜ˞ːm- **~nated** neɪt ɪd -əd ‖ neɪţ əd **~nates** neɪts **~nating** neɪt ɪŋ ‖ neɪţ ɪŋ
extermination ɪk ˌstɜːm ɪ ˈneɪʃ ən ek-, ək-, -ə ‖ -ˌstɜ˞ːm- **~s** z
exterminator ɪk ˈstɜːm ɪ neɪt ə ek-, ək-, -ˈ·ə- ‖ -ˈstɜ˞ːm ə neɪţ ər **~s** z
extern ˈeks tɜːn ‖ -tɜ˞ːn **~s** z **~ship/s** ʃɪp/s
external ɪk ˈstɜːn əl ₍ₗ₎ek-, ək- ‖ -ˈstɜ˞ːn əl **~ly** i **~s** z
externalis... —*see* **externaliz...**
externalit|y ˌekst ɜː ˈnæl ət |i -ɪt i ‖ ˌekst ɜ˞ː ˈnæl əţ |i **~ies** iz
externalization ɪk ˌstɜːn əl aɪ ˈzeɪʃ ən ek-, ək- ekst ɜːn-, -əl ɪ- ‖ -ˌstɜ˞ːn əl ə- **~s** z
externaliz|e ɪk ˈstɜːn ə laɪz ₍ₗ₎ek-, ək-, -əl aɪz ‖ -ˈstɜ˞ːn- **~ed** d **~es** ɪz əz **~ing** ɪŋ
exterritorial ˌeks ˌter ɪ ˈtɔːr i‿əl ◂ ‖ -ˈtoʊr- **~ly** i
extinct ɪk ˈstɪŋkt ₍ₗ₎ek-, ək-
extinction ɪk ˈstɪŋk ʃən ₍ₗ₎ek-, ək- **~s** z
extinguish ɪk ˈstɪŋ gwɪʃ ek-, ək-, §-wɪʃ **~ed** t **~er/s** ə/z ‖ ər/z **~es** ɪz əz **~ing** ɪŋ
extir|pate ˈekst ɜː |peɪt -ə- ‖ -ər- **~pated** peɪt ɪd -əd ‖ peɪţ əd **~pates** peɪts **~pating** peɪt ɪŋ ‖ peɪţ ɪŋ
extirpation ˌekst ɜː ˈpeɪʃ ən -ə- ‖ -ər- **~s** z
extol, extol|l ɪk ˈstəʊl ek-, ək-, →-ˈstɒʊl, -ˈstɒl ‖ -ˈstoʊl **~led** d **~ling** ɪŋ **~s** z
Exton ˈekst ən
ex|tort ɪk |ˈstɔːt ek-, ək- ‖ -|ˈstɔːrt **~storted** ˈstɔːt ɪd -əd ‖ ˈstɔːrţ əd **~storting** ˈstɔːt ɪŋ ‖ ˈstɔːrţ ɪŋ **~storts** ˈstɔːts ‖ ˈstɔːrts
extortion ɪk ˈstɔːʃ ən ek-, ək- ‖ -ˈstɔːrʃ ən **~s** z
extortionate ɪk ˈstɔːʃ ən‿ət ek-, ək-, ɪt ‖ -ˈstɔːrʃ- **~ly** li
extortioner ɪk ˈstɔːʃ ən‿ə ek-, ək- ‖ -ˈstɔːrʃ ən‿ər **~s** z
extortionist ɪk ˈstɔːʃ ən‿ɪst ek-, ək-, §‿əst ‖ -ˈstɔːrʃ- **~s** s
extra ˈeks trə **~s** z
ˌextra ˈcover
extra- *comb. form*
with stress-neutral suffix ˌeks trə — **extracanonical** ˌeks trə kə ˈnɒn ɪk əl ◂ ‖ -ˈnɑːn-
with stress-imposing suffix ɪk ˈstræ+ ek-, ək- — **extrapolate** ɪk ˈstræp ə leɪt ek-, ək-
extracellular ˌeks trə ˈsel jʊl ə ◂ -jəl· ‖ -jəl ər ◂
extract *n* ˈeks trækt **~s** s
extract *v* ɪk ˈstrækt ek-, ək- —*In AmE, in the sense 'select and cite excerpts' also* ˈeks trækt **~ed** ɪd əd **~ing** ɪŋ **~s** s
extraction ɪk ˈstræk ʃən ek-, ək- **~s** z
extractive ɪk ˈstrækt ɪv ek-, ək-
extractor ɪk ˈstrækt ə ek-, ək- ‖ -ər **~s** z
exˈtractor fan

extracurricular ˌeks trə kə ˈrɪk jʊl ə ◂ -jəl ə ‖ -jəl ᵊr
extraditable ˈeks trə daɪt əb ᵊl ˌ· ·ˈ· · · ‖ -daɪţ əb ᵊl
extra|dite ˈeks trə |daɪt **~dited** daɪt ɪd -əd ‖ daɪţ əd **~dites** daɪts **~diting** daɪt ɪŋ ‖ daɪţ ɪŋ
extradition ˌeks trə ˈdɪʃ ᵊn **~s** z
extrados *sing.* ek ˈstreɪd ɒs ‖ ˈeks trə dɑːs **~es** ɪz əz **extrados** *pl* ek ˈstreɪd əʊz ‖ ˈeks trə doʊz
extragalactic ˌek strə gə ˈlækt ɪk ◂
extrajudicial ˌeks trə dʒu ˈdɪʃ ᵊl◂ **~ly** i
extramarital ˌeks trə ˈmær ɪt ᵊl ◂ -ət ᵊl ‖ -əţ ᵊl ◂ -ˈmer- **~ly** i
extrametrical ˌeks trə ˈmetr ɪk ᵊl ◂
extramural ˌeks trə ˈmjʊər əl ◂ -ˈmjɔːr- ‖ -ˈmjʊr əl **~ly** i
extraneous ɪk ˈstreɪn i‿əs ek-, ək- **~ly** li **~ness** nəs nɪs
extranet ˈeks trə net
extraordinaire ɪk ˌstrɔːd ɪ ˈneə ek-, ək-, -ə-, -ᵊn ˈeə ‖ ɪk ˌstrɔːrd ᵊn ˈeᵊr —*Fr* [ɛk stʁa ɔʁ di nɛːʁ]

EXTRAORDINARILY

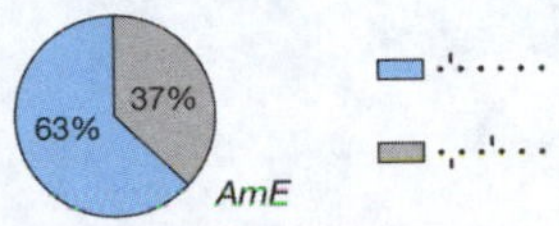

extraordinarily ɪk ˈstrɔːd ᵊn ᵊr‿əl i ek-, ək-, -ˈ·ɪn-, -ᵊn‿ər əl i, §-ˌstrɔːd ᵊn ˈer əl i◂, -ɪ li; ˌeks trə ˈɔːd ᵊn ᵊr‿əl i◂, -ᵊn‿ər əl i, -ɪ li ‖ ɪk ˌstrɔːrd ᵊn ˈer əl i ◂ ·ˈ· · · · · — *Preference poll, AmE:* ·ˈ· · · · · *63%,* ·ˌ· ·ˈ· · · *37% (figures perhaps unreliable because of confusion over possible stress shifting).*
extraordinary ɪk ˈstrɔːd ᵊn ər‿i ek-, ək-, -ˈ·ɪn-, §-er i, -ᵊn‿ər i, ˌeks trə ˈɔːd ᵊn ər‿i◂ , -ᵊn‿ər- ‖ ɪk ˈstrɔːrd ᵊn er i ˌeks trə ˈɔːrd ᵊn er i◂
extrapo|late ɪk ˈstræp ə |leɪt ek-, ək-, ⚠-jə- **~lated** leɪt ɪd -əd ‖ leɪţ əd **~lates** leɪts **~lating** leɪt ɪŋ ‖ leɪţ ɪŋ
extrapolation ɪk ˌstræp ə ˈleɪʃ ᵊn ek-, ək-, ⚠-jə- **~s** z
extrapos|e ˌeks trə ˈpəʊz ‖ -ˈpoʊz **~ed** d **~es** ɪz əz **~ing** ɪŋ
extraposition ˌeks trə pə ˈzɪʃ ᵊn **~s** z
extrasensory ˌeks trə ˈsenᵗs ər‿i ◂ **ˌextraˌsensory perˈception**
extra-special ˌeks trə ˈspeʃ ᵊl ◂ **~ly** ‿i
extraterrestrial ˌeks trə tə ˈres tri‿əl ◂ -tɪˈ·-, -teˈ·-, ⚠-ˈres tʃəl
extraterritorial ˌeks trə ˌter ɪ ˈtɔːr i‿əl -ˌ·ə- ‖ -ˈtoʊr- **~ly** i
extraterritoriality ˌeks trə ˌter ɪ tɔːr i ˈæl ət i -ˌ·ə-, -ɪt i ‖ -əţ i -toʊr iˈ·-
extravaganc|e ɪk ˈstræv əg ənᵗs ek-, ək- **~es** ɪz əz
extravagant ɪk ˈstræv əg ənt ek-, ək- **~ly** li **~ness** nəs nɪs
extravaganza ɪk ˌstræv ə ˈgænz ə ₍ˌ₎ek-, ək- **~s** z
extrava|sate ek ˈstræv ə |seɪt ˌek-, ɪk-, ək- **~sated** seɪt ɪd -əd ‖ seɪţ əd **~sates** seɪts **~sating** seɪt ɪŋ ‖ seɪţ ɪŋ
extravasation ek ˌstræv ə ˈseɪʃ ᵊn ɪk-, ək-, ˌeks træv-, -ˈzeɪʃ- **~s** z
extraversion ˌeks trə ˈvɜːʃ ᵊn -ˈvɜːʒ- ‖ -ˈvɜːʒ ᵊn
extra|vert ˈeks trə |vɜːt ‖ -|vɜːt **~verted** vɜːt ɪd -əd ‖ vɜːţ əd **~verts** ˈvɜːts ‖ ˈvɜːts
extreme ɪk ˈstriːm ek-, ək- —*In a stress-shifting environment occasionally* ˌeks triːm, *as if underlyingly* ˌek ˈstriːm ◂: ˌextreme ˈunction **~ly** li **~ness** nəs nɪs **~s** z
extremis ɪk ˈstriːm ɪs ek-, ək-
extremism ɪk ˈstriːm ˌɪz əm ek-, ək-
extremist ɪk ˈstriːm ɪst ek-, ək-, §-əst **~s** s
extremit|y ɪk ˈstrem ət |i ek-, ək-, -ɪt- ‖ -əţ |i **~ies** iz
extricable ɪk ˈstrɪk əb ᵊl ek-, ək-, ˈeks trɪk-
extri|cate ˈeks trɪ |keɪt -trə- **~cated** keɪt ɪd -əd ‖ keɪţ əd **~cates** keɪts **~cating** keɪt ɪŋ ‖ keɪţ ɪŋ
extrication ˌeks trɪ ˈkeɪʃ ᵊn -trə-
extrinsic ₍ˌ₎eks ˈtrɪnᵗs ɪk ɪks-, -ˈtrɪnz- **~ally** ᵊl‿i
extroversion ˌeks trə ˈvɜːʃ ᵊn -ˈvɜːʒ- ‖ -ˈvɜːʒ ᵊn
extro|vert ˈeks trəʊ |vɜːt ‖ -ə |vɜːt **~verted** vɜːt ɪd -əd ‖ vɜːţ əd **~verts** ˈvɜːts ‖ ˈvɜːts
extrud|e ɪk ˈstruːd ek-, ək- **~ed** ɪd əd **~es** z **~ing** ɪŋ
extrusion ɪk ˈstruːʒ ᵊn ek-, ək- **~s** z
exuberance ɪg ˈzjuːb ᵊr‿ənᵗs eg-, əg-, ɪk-, ek-, ək-, -ˈzuːb- ‖ -ˈzuːb-
exuberant ɪg ˈzjuːb ᵊr‿ənt eg-, əg-, ɪk-, ek-, ək-, -ˈzuːb- ‖ -ˈzuːb- **~ly** li
exudation ˌeks ju ˈdeɪʃ ᵊn ˌegz- ‖ -u-, ˌekʃ u- **~s** z
exud|e ɪg ˈzjuːd eg-, əg-, ɪk-, ek-, ək-, -ˈzuːd ‖ -ˈzuːd **~ed** ɪd əd **~es** z **~ing** ɪŋ
exult ɪg ˈzʌlt eg-, əg-, ɪk-, ek-, ək- **~ed** ɪd əd **~ing** ɪŋ **~s** s
exultant ɪg ˈzʌlt ənt eg-, əg-, ɪk-, ek-, ək- **~ly** li
exultation ˌegz ʌl ˈteɪʃ ᵊn ˌeks-, -ᵊl- **~s** z
Exuma ek ˈsuːm ə
exurb ˈeks ɜːb ˈegz- ‖ -ɜːb **~s** z
exurban ₍ˌ₎eks ˈɜːb ən ₍ˌ₎egz- ‖ ek ˈsɜːb ən eg ˈzɜːb-
exurbanite ₍ˌ₎eks ˈɜːb ə naɪt ₍ˌ₎egz- ‖ ek ˈsɜːb- eg ˈzɜːb- **~s** s
exurbia ₍ˌ₎eks ˈɜːb i‿ə ‖ ek ˈsɜːb- eg ˈzɜːb- **~s** z
exuvi|ae ɪg ˈzjuːv i‿|iː eg-, əg-, ɪk-, ek-, ək-, -ˈzuːv-, -aɪ ‖ -ˈzuːv- **~al** əl
Exxon *tdmk* ˈeks ɒn ‖ -ɑːn
Eyam iːm *(!)*
Eyck aɪk

eye, Eye aɪ *(= I)* **eyed** aɪd **eyeing, eying** 'aɪ ɪŋ **eyes** aɪz
'**eye ˌcontact**; '**eye rhyme**; '**eye ˌshadow**
eyeball 'aɪ bɔːl ‖ -bɑːl **~ed** d **~ing** ɪŋ **~s** z
eyebath 'aɪ bɑːθ §-bæθ ‖ -bæθ **~s** s
eyebright 'aɪ braɪt **~s** s
eyebrow 'aɪ braʊ **~s** z
'**eyebrow ˌpencil**
eye-catching 'aɪ ˌkætʃ ɪŋ ⚠-ˌketʃ- **~ly** li
eyecup 'aɪ kʌp **~s** s
-eyed 'aɪd — **brown-eyed** ˌbraʊn 'aɪd ◂
eyeful 'aɪ fʊl **~s** z
eyeglass 'aɪ glɑːs §-glæs ‖ -glæs **~es** ɪz əz
eyelash 'aɪ læʃ **~es** ɪz əz
eyeless 'aɪ ləs -lɪs
eyelet 'aɪ lət -lɪt **~s** s
eyelevel 'aɪ ˌlev əl ˌ.'. .
eyelid 'aɪ lɪd **~s** z
eyeliner 'aɪ laɪn ə ‖ -ər **~s** z
eye-opener 'aɪ ˌəʊp ən‿ə ‖ -ˌoʊp ən‿ər **~s** z
eyepatch 'aɪ pætʃ **~es** ɪz əz
eyepiec|e 'aɪ piːs **~es** ɪz əz
eye-popping 'aɪ ˌpɒp ɪŋ ‖ -ˌpɑːp-
eyeshade 'aɪ ʃeɪd **~s** z
eyeshot 'aɪ ʃɒt ‖ -ʃɑːt
eyesight 'aɪ saɪt
eyesore 'aɪ sɔː ‖ -sɔːr -soʊr **~s** z
eyestalk 'aɪ stɔːk ‖ -stɑːk **~s** s
eyestrain 'aɪ streɪn
eyeteeth 'aɪ tiːθ
Eyetie 'aɪ taɪ **~s** z
eye|tooth 'aɪ |tuːθ §-tʊθ, ˌ.'. **~teeth** tiːθ
eyewash 'aɪ wɒʃ ‖ -wɑːʃ -wɔːʃ
eyewear 'aɪ weə ‖ -wer -wær
eyewitness 'aɪ ˌwɪt nəs -nɪs, ˌ.'. . **~es** ɪz əz
eying 'aɪ ɪŋ
Eynon 'aɪn ən —*Welsh* ['əi non]
Eynsford 'eɪnz fəd ‖ -fərd
Eynsham 'eɪn ʃəm —*but locally* 'en-
eyot eɪt 'eɪ ət, aɪt **eyots** eɪts 'eɪ əts, aɪts
Eyre, eyre eə ‖ eər æər
eyr|ie, eyr|y 'ɪər |i 'eər-, 'aɪər- ‖ 'er |i 'ɪr-, 'aɪər- **~ies** iz
Eysenck 'aɪz eŋk
Eyton *(i)* 'iːt ən, *(ii)* 'aɪt ən, *(iii)* 'eɪt ən
Ezekiel ɪ 'ziːk i‿əl ə-
e-zine 'iː ziːn **~s** z
Ezra 'ez rə

Ff

f Spelling-to-sound

1 Where the spelling is **f**, the pronunciation is regularly f as in **fifty** ˈfɪft i.

2 Where the spelling is double **ff**, the pronunciation is again f as in **stiff** stɪf.

3 Exceptionally, the word **of** is pronounced with v: **a piece of wood** ə ˌpiːs əv ˈwʊd.

4 **f** is silent in the old pronunciation of **halfpenny** ˈheɪp ni.

5 The sound f is also regularly written **ph** as in **photograph**, and occasionally **gh** as in **rough** rʌf.

F, f ef **Fs, fs, F's, f's** efs —*Communications code name:* Foxtrot
fa fɑː
FA ˌef ˈeɪ ◂
ˌ**FA ˈCup**
fab fæb
Faber ˈfeɪb ə ‖ -ᵊr
Fabergé ˈfæb ə ʒeɪ -dʒeɪ ‖ ˌfæb ᵊr ˈʒeɪ
Fabian ˈfeɪb i‿ən **~s** z
ˈ**Fabian So**ˌ**ciety**
Fabius ˈfeɪb i‿əs
fable ˈfeɪb ᵊl **~d** d **~s** z
fabliau ˈfæb li əʊ ‖ -oʊ **~x** z —*Fr* [fab li jo]
Fablon *tdmk* ˈfæb lɒn -lən ‖ -lɑːn
fabric ˈfæb rɪk **~s** s
fabri|cate ˈfæb rɪ |keɪt -rə- **~cated** keɪt ɪd -əd ‖ keɪṭ əd **~cates** keɪts **~cating** keɪt ɪŋ ‖ keɪṭ ɪŋ
fabrication ˌfæb rɪ ˈkeɪʃ ᵊn -rə- **~s** z
fabricator ˈfæb rɪ keɪt ə ˈ·rə- ‖ -keɪṭ ᵊr **~s** z
fabulist ˈfæb jʊl ɪst -jəl-, §-əst ‖ -jəl- **~s** s
fabulous ˈfæb jʊl əs -jəl- ‖ -jəl- **~ly** li **~ness** nəs nɪs
facade, façade fə ˈsɑːd fæ-; ˈfæs ɑːd **~s** z
face feɪs **faced** feɪst **faces** ˈfeɪs ɪz -əz **facing/s** ˈfeɪs ɪŋ/z
ˈ**face card**; ˈ**face** ˌ**flannel**; ˈ**face pack**; ˈ**face** ˌ**powder**; ˌ**face ˈvalue**, ˈ· ˌ· ·
face-ache ˈfeɪs eɪk **~s** s
Facebook ˈfeɪs bʊk §-buːk
face-|cloth ˈfeɪs |klɒθ -klɔːθ ‖ -|klɔːθ -klɑːθ **~cloths** klɒθs klɔːθs, klɔːðz ‖ klɔːθs klɔːðz, klɑːθs, klɑːðz
-faced ˈfeɪst feɪst — **stony-faced** ˌstəʊn i ˈfeɪst ◂ ˈ· · · ‖ ˌstoʊn-
faceless ˈfeɪs ləs -lɪs
face-lift ˈfeɪs lɪft **~s** s
face-off ˈfeɪs ɒf -ɔːf ‖ -ɔːf -ɑːf **~s** s
faceplate ˈfeɪs pleɪt **~s** s
facer ˈfeɪs ə ‖ -ᵊr **~s** z
face-sav|er ˈfeɪs ˌseɪv |ə ‖ -|ᵊr **~ers** əz ‖ ᵊrz **~ing** ɪŋ
fac|et ˈfæs| ɪt -ət, -et **~eted** ɪt ɪd ət-, et-, -əd ‖ əṭ əd **~ets** ɪts əts, ets
facetiae fə ˈsiːʃ i‿iː
facetious fə ˈsiːʃ əs **~ly** li **~ness** nəs nɪs
face-to-face ˌfeɪs tə ˈfeɪs ◂
facetted ˈfæs ɪt ɪd -ət-, -əd ‖ -əṭ-
Fach vɑːk vɑːx —*Welsh* [vaːχ]
facia ˈfeɪʃ ə ˈfeɪʃ i‿ə **~s** z
facial ˈfeɪʃ ᵊl ˈfeɪʃ i‿əl; ˈfeɪs i‿əl **~ly** i **~s** z
ˈ**facial nerve**
facies ˈfeɪʃ i iːz ˈfeɪʃ iːz
facile ˈfæs aɪᵊl ‖ -ᵊl **~ly** li **~ness** nəs nɪs
facili|tate fə ˈsɪl ə |teɪt -ɪ- **~tated** teɪt ɪd -əd ‖ teɪṭ əd **~tates** teɪts **~tating** teɪt ɪŋ ‖ teɪṭ ɪŋ
facilitation fə ˌsɪl ə ˈteɪʃ ᵊn -ɪ-
facilitative fə ˈsɪl ət ət ɪv -ˈ·ɪt-; -ə teɪt ɪv ‖ -ə teɪṭ ɪv
facilitator fə ˈsɪl ə teɪt ə -ˈ·ɪ- ‖ -teɪṭ ᵊr **~s** z
facilit|y fə ˈsɪl ət |i -ɪt- ‖ -əṭ |i **~ies** iz
facing ˈfeɪs ɪŋ **~s** z
Facit *tdmk* ˈfeɪs ɪt §-ət
facsimile fæk ˈsɪm əl i -ɪl- **~d** d **~ing** ɪŋ **~s** z
fact fækt **facts** fækts
fact-finding ˈfækt ˌfaɪnd ɪŋ
faction ˈfæk ʃᵊn **~s** z
factional ˈfæk ʃᵊn‿əl **~ism** ˌɪz əm
factious ˈfæk ʃəs **~ly** li **~ness** nəs nɪs
factitious fæk ˈtɪʃ əs **~ly** li **~ness** nəs nɪs
factitive ˈfækt ət ɪv -ɪt- ‖ -əṭ ɪv **~ly** li **~s** z
factive ˈfækt ɪv **~s** z
factoid ˈfækt ɔɪd **~s** z

factor 'fækt ə ‖ -ᵊr **~ed** d **factoring** 'fækt ər‿ɪŋ **~s** z
factorage 'fækt ər ɪdʒ
factorial fæk 'tɔːr i‿əl ‖ -'toʊr- **~ly** i **~s** z
factoris... —*see* **factoriz...**
factorization ˌfækt ər aɪ 'zeɪʃ ᵊn -ər ɪ- ‖ -ər ə- **~s** z
factoriz|e 'fækt ə raɪz **~ed** d **~es** ɪz əz **~ing** ɪŋ
factory 'fæk tri 'fækt ər i **factories** 'fæk triz 'fækt ər iz
'**factory farm**; '**factory ship**
factotum fæk 'təʊt əm ‖ -'toʊt̬ əm **~s** z
factual 'fæk tʃu‿əl -ʃu‿əl; 'fækt ju‿əl **~ly** i **~s** z
facula 'fæk jʊl ə -jəl- ‖ -jəl ə
facultative 'fæk ᵊlt ət ɪv -ᵊl teɪt- ‖ 'fæk ᵊl teɪt̬ ɪv **~ly** li
facult|y 'fæk ᵊlt |i **~ies** iz
fad fæd **fads** fædz
Fadden 'fæd ᵊn
faddish 'fæd ɪʃ **~ly** li **~ness** nəs nɪs
faddism 'fæd ˌɪz əm
faddy 'fæd i
fade feɪd **faded** 'feɪd ɪd -əd **fades** feɪdz **fading** 'feɪd ɪŋ
fade-in 'feɪd ɪn **~s** z
fadeless 'feɪd ləs -lɪs **~ly** li
fade-out 'feɪd aʊt **~s** s
fadge fædʒ **fadges** 'fædʒ ɪz -əz
fading 'feɪd ɪŋ **~s** z
fado 'fɑːd əʊ ‖ -oʊ **~s** z —*Port* ['fa ðu]
faecal 'fiːk ᵊl
faeces 'fiːs iːz
faerie 'feɪ ər i 'feər i ‖ 'fer i, 'fær i
Faeroe 'feər əʊ ‖ 'fer oʊ 'fær- *(= pharaoh)* **~s** z
Faeroese ˌfeər əʊ 'iːz ◂ ‖ ˌfer oʊ- ˌfær-, -'iːs ◂
faery 'feɪ ər i 'feər i ‖ 'fer i, 'fær i
faff fæf **faffed** fæft **faffing** 'fæf ɪŋ **faffs** fæfs
fag fæg **fagged** fægd **fagging** 'fæg ɪŋ **fags** fægz
ˌ**fag 'end** ◂, '· ·; ˌ**fagged 'out**
Fagan 'feɪg ən
fagg|ot 'fæg |ət **~oted** ət ɪd -əd ‖ ət̬ əd **~oting** ət ɪŋ ‖ ət̬ ɪŋ **~ots** əts
faggotry 'fæg ətr i
faggotty, faggoty 'fæg ət i ‖ -ət̬ i
fag-hag 'fæg hæg **~s** z
Fagin 'feɪg ɪn §-ən
fag|ot 'fæg |ət **~oted** ət ɪd -əd ‖ ət̬ əd **~oting** ət ɪŋ ‖ ət̬ ɪŋ **~ots** əts
fah fɑː
Fahd fɑːd
Fahrenheit 'fær ən haɪt 'fɑːr- ‖ 'fer-
Fahy 'fɑː hi -i
faience, faïence faɪ 'ɒ̃s feɪ-, -'ɑːnᵗs, -'ɒnᵗs ‖ feɪ 'ɑːnᵗs faɪ- —*Fr* [fa jɑ̃ːs]
fail feɪᵊl **failed** feɪᵊld **failing** 'feɪᵊl ɪŋ **fails** feɪᵊlz
failing *n* 'feɪl ɪŋ **~s** z
fail-safe 'feɪᵊl seɪf ,·'·
Failsworth 'feɪᵊlz wɜːθ -wəθ ‖ -wᵊrθ
fáilte 'fɔːltʃ ə ‖ 'fɑːltʃ ə —*Irish* ['fɑːlʲ tʲə]
failure 'feɪl jə ‖ -jᵊr **~s** z
fain feɪn
faineant, feinéant 'feɪn i‿ənt —*Fr* [fɛ ne ɑ̃]
fainites 'feɪn aɪts
fains feɪnz
faint feɪnt **fainted** 'feɪnt ɪd -əd ‖ 'feɪnt̬ əd **fainter** 'feɪnt ə ‖ 'feɪnt̬ ᵊr **faintest** 'feɪnt ɪst §-əst ‖ 'feɪnt̬ əst **fainting** 'feɪnt ɪŋ ‖ 'feɪnt̬ ɪŋ **faints** feɪnts
faint-hearted ˌfeɪnt 'hɑːt ɪd ◂ -əd ‖ -'hɑːrt̬ əd ◂ **~ly** li **~ness** nəs nɪs
faintly 'feɪnt li
faintness 'feɪnt nəs -nɪs
fair feə ‖ feᵊr fæᵊr **fairer** 'feər ə ‖ 'fer ᵊr 'fær ᵊr **fairest** 'feər ɪst §-əst ‖ 'fer əst 'fær-
ˌ**fair 'copy**; ˌ**fair 'dinkum**; ˌ**fair 'game**; '**Fair Isle**; ˌ**fair 'sex**, '· ·
Fairbairn, Fairbairne 'feə beən ‖ 'fer bern 'fær bærn
Fairbank 'feə bæŋk ‖ 'fer- 'fær-
Fairbanks 'feə bæŋks ‖ 'fer- 'fær-
Fairbourn, Fairbourne 'feə bɔːn ‖ 'fer bɔːrn 'fær-, -bourn
Fairbrother 'feə ˌbrʌðə ‖ 'fer ˌbrʌð ᵊr 'fær-
Fairchild 'feə tʃaɪᵊld ‖ 'fer- 'fær-
Fairclough *(i)* 'feə klʌf ‖ 'fer- 'fær-, *(ii)* -kləʊ ‖ -kloʊ
Fairfax 'feə fæks ‖ 'fer- 'fær-
Fairfield 'feə fiːᵊld ‖ 'fer- 'fær-
Fairford 'feə fəd ‖ 'fer fᵊrd 'fær-
fairground 'feə graʊnd ‖ 'fer- 'fær- **~s** z
fair-haired ˌfeə 'heəd ◂ ‖ ˌfer 'heᵊrd ◂
Fairhaven 'feə ˌheɪv ᵊn ‖ 'fer- 'fær-
fairi... —*see* **fairy**
fairing 'feər ɪŋ ‖ 'fer ɪŋ 'fær- **~s** z
fairish 'feər ɪʃ ‖ 'fer ɪʃ 'fær-
Fairley, Fairlie 'feə li ‖ 'fer- 'fær-
Fairlight 'feə laɪt ‖ 'fer- 'fær-
fairly 'feə li ‖ 'fer- 'fær-
Fairman 'feə mən ‖ 'fer- 'fær-
fair-minded ˌfeə 'maɪnd ɪd ◂ -əd ‖ ˌfer- ˌfær- **~ness** nəs nɪs
Fairmont 'feə mɒnt -mənt ‖ 'fer mɑːnt 'fær-
fairness 'feə nəs -nɪs ‖ 'fer- 'fær-
Fairport 'feə pɔːt ‖ 'fer pɔːrt 'fær-, -poʊrt
fair-to-middling ˌfeə tə 'mɪd ᵊl‿ɪŋ ◂ ‖ ˌfer- ˌfær-
fairway 'feə weɪ ‖ 'fer- 'fær- **~s** z
fair-weather, Fairweather 'feə ˌweð ə ‖ 'fer ˌweð ᵊr 'fær-
fair|y 'feər |i ‖ 'fer |i 'fær- **~ies** iz
'**fairy ˌcycle**, ˌ**fairy 'godˌmother**; '**fairy light**; ˌ**fairy 'ring** ‖ '· · ·; '**fairy ˌstory**
fairyland 'feər i lænd ‖ 'fer- 'fær-
fairy-tale 'feər i teɪᵊl ‖ 'fer- 'fær- **~s** z
Faisal 'faɪs ᵊl
Faisalabad 'faɪs əl ə bæd 'faɪz-, -bɑːd
fait accompli ˌfeɪt ə 'kɒmp liː ˌfet-, -'kʌmp- ‖ ˌfeɪt̬ ə kɑːm 'pliː —*Fr* [fɛ ta kɔ̃ pli] **faits accomplis** ˌfeɪz ə 'kɒmp liː ˌfeɪts-, ˌfeɪt-, ˌfez-, -'kʌmp-, -liːz ‖ ˌfeɪz ə kɑːm 'pliː —*Fr* [fɛ za kɔ̃ pli]
faites vos jeux ˌfeɪt vəʊ 'ʒɜː ˌfet- ‖ -voʊ 'ʒuː —*Fr* [fɛt vo ʒø]

aith, Faith feɪθ **faiths, Faith's** feɪθs
 'faith ˌhealing
aithful 'feɪθ fᵊl -fʊl **~ly** ˌi **~ness** nəs nɪs
aithful, Faithfull 'feɪθ fᵊl -fʊl
aithless 'feɪθ ləs -lɪs **~ly** li **~ness** nəs nɪs
ajita fæ 'hiːt ə fə- ‖ -'hiːt̬ ə fɑː- **~s** z —*Sp* [fa 'xi ta|s]
ake feɪk **faked** feɪkt **fakes** feɪks **faking** 'feɪk ɪŋ
akenham 'feɪk ən‿əm
aker 'feɪk ə ‖ -ᵊr **~s** z
akie 'feɪk i
akir 'feɪk ɪə 'fɑːk-, 'fæk-; fə 'kɪə, fæ- ‖ fə 'kɪᵊr fɑː-; 'feɪk ᵊr **~s** z
Fal fæl
falafel fə 'lɑːf ᵊl
Falange fə 'lændʒ fæ-; 'fæl ændʒ ‖ 'feɪl ændʒ —*Sp* [fa 'laŋ xe]
Falangist fə 'lændʒ ɪst §-əst **~s** s
Falasha fə 'læʃ ə ‖ -'lɑːʃ ə **~s** z
falcate 'fælk eɪt
falchion 'fɔːltʃ ən 'fɔːlʃ- ‖ 'fɑːltʃ- **~s** z
falciform 'fæls ɪ fɔːm -ə- ‖ -fɔːrm

FALCON

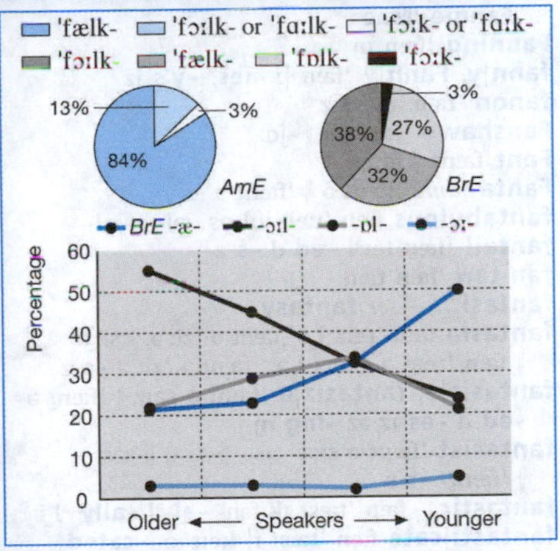

falcon, F~ 'fɔːlk ən 'fælk-, 'fɒlk-, 'fɔːk- ‖ 'fælk- 'fɔːlk-, 'fɑːlk-, 'fɔːk-, 'fɑːk- — *Preference polls, AmE:* 'fælk- *84%,* 'fɔːlk- *or* 'fɑːlk- *13%,* 'fɔːk- *or* 'fɑːk- *3%; BrE:* 'fɔːlk- *38%,* 'fælk- *32%,* 'fɒlk- *27%,* 'fɔːk- *3%.* **~s** z
Falconbridge 'fɔːlk ən brɪdʒ 'fælk-, 'fɒlk-, 'fɔːk-, →-əm- ‖ 'fælk- 'fɔːlk-, 'fɑːlk-
Falconcrest ˌfælk ən 'krest ◂ ˌfɔːlk-, ˌfɔːk-, ˌfɒlk-, →əŋ- ‖ ˌfɔːlk-, ˌfɑːlk-
falconer, F~ 'fɔːlk ən‿ə 'fælk-, 'fɒlk-, 'fɔːk- ‖ 'fælk ᵊn‿ər 'fɔːlk-, 'fɑːlk- **~s** z
falconry 'fɔːlk ən ri 'fælk-, 'fɒlk-, 'fɔːk- ‖ 'fælk- 'fɔːlk-, 'fɑːlk-
Falder 'fɔːld ə 'fɒld- ‖ 'fɔːld ᵊr 'fɑːld-
falderal 'fæld ə ræl -ɪ- ‖ 'fɑːld ə rɑːl **~s** z
Faldo 'fæld əʊ ‖ 'fɑːld oʊ
faldstool 'fɔːl*d* stuːl ‖ 'fɑːl*d*- **~s** z
Falernian fə 'lɜːn i‿ən ‖ -'lɜːn-
Faliscan fə 'lɪsk ən **~s** z

Falk fɔːlk fɔːk ‖ fɑːlk
Falkender 'fɔːlk ənd ə ‖ -ᵊr 'fɑːlk-
Falkirk 'fɔːl kɜːk 'fɒl-, §'fæl, -kək ‖ -kɜːk 'fɑːl-
Falkland 'fɔːlk lənd 'fɔːk-, 'fɒlk- ‖ 'fɔːk- 'fɑːk- **~s** z
 'Falkland ˌIslands ‖ ˌ· '·
Falkner 'fɔːlk nə 'fɔːk-, 'fɒlk-, 'fælk- ‖ 'fɔːk nᵊr 'fɑːk-
Falkus 'fɔːlk əs ‖ 'fɑːlk-
fall, Fall fɔːl ‖ fɑːl **fallen** 'fɔːl ən ‖ 'fɑːl- **falling** 'fɔːl ɪŋ ‖ 'fɑːl- **falls, Falls** fɔːlz ‖ fɑːlz **fell** fel
 'fall guy; **ˌfalling 'star**; **'fall line**
Falla 'fæl ə 'fɑːl-, -jə ‖ 'fɑː jə —*Sp* ['fa ʎa, -ja]
fallacious fə 'leɪʃ əs **~ly** li **~ness** nəs nɪs
fallac|y 'fæl əs |i **~ies** iz
fal-lal ₍ˌ₎fæl 'læl ₍ˌ₎fæ- **~s** z
fallback 'fɔːl bæk ‖ 'fɑːl- **~s** s
fallen 'fɔːl ən ‖ 'fɑːl-
Faller 'fæl ə ‖ -ᵊr
fallibility ˌfæl ə 'bɪl ət i ˌ·ɪ-, -ɪt i ‖ -ət̬ i
fallib|le 'fæl əb |ᵊl -ɪb- **~ly** li
falling-off ˌfɔːl ɪŋ 'ɒf -'ɔːf ‖ -ɔːf ˌfɑːl ɪŋ 'ɑːf
falling-out ˌfɔːl ɪŋ 'aʊt ‖ ˌfɑːl-
fall-off 'fɔːl ɒf -ɔːf ‖ -ɔːf 'fɑːl-, ɑːf **~s** s
Fallon 'fæl ən
fallopian, F~ fə 'ləʊp i‿ən ‖ -'loʊp-
 falˌlopian 'tube
fallout 'fɔːl aʊt ‖ 'fɑːl-
fallow, F~ 'fæl əʊ ‖ -oʊ **~ed** d **~ing** ɪŋ **~s** z
 'fallow deer
Fallowes 'fæl əʊz ‖ -oʊz
Fallowfield 'fæl əʊ fiːᵊld ‖ -oʊ-
Falls fɔːlz ‖ fɑːlz
Falluja fə 'luːdʒ ə —*Arabic* [fa 'luː dʒah]
Falmer 'fælm ə ‖ -ᵊr
Falmouth 'fæl məθ

FALSE

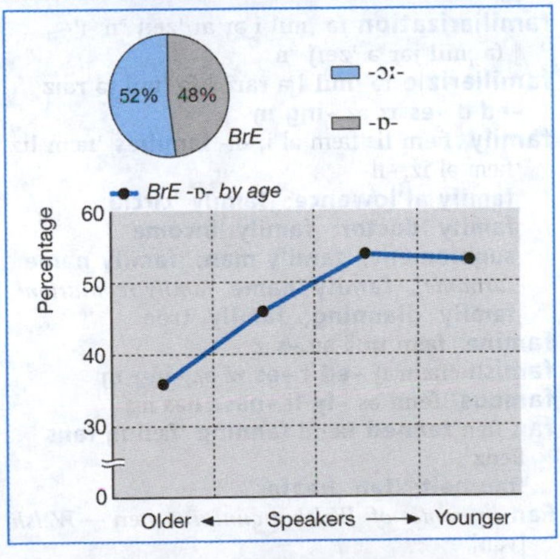

false fɔːls fɒls ‖ fɑːls **falser** 'fɔːls ə 'fɒls ə ‖ 'fɔːls ᵊr 'fɑːls ᵊr **falsest** 'fɔːls ɪst 'fɒls-, §-əst ‖ 'fɔːls əst 'fɑːls- — *Preference poll, BrE:* -ɔː- *52%,* -ɒ- *48%.*

F

ˌ**false aˈlarm**; ˌ**false arˈrest**; ˌ**false ˈbottom**; ˌ**false preˈtenses**; ˌ**false ˈstart**; ˌ**false ˈteeth**
false-hearted ˌfɔːls ˈhɑːt ɪd◂ ˌfɒls-, -əd ‖ ˌfɔːls ˈhɑːrt̬ əd ◂ ˌfɑːls-, ˌ·ˈ·,·
falsehood ˈfɔːls hʊd ˈfɒls- ‖ ˈfɑːls- **~s** z
falsely ˈfɔːls li ˈfɒls- ‖ ˈfɑːls-
falseness ˈfɔːls nəs ˈfɒls-, -nɪs ‖ ˈfɑːls-
falsetto fɔːl ˈset əʊ fɒl- ‖ fɔːl ˈset̬ oʊ fɑːl- **~s** z
falsies ˈfɔːls iz ˈfɒls- ‖ ˈfɑːls-
falsifiability ˌfɔːls ɪ faɪ‿ə ˈbɪl ət i ˌfɒls-, -ɪt i ‖ ˌfɔːls ə faɪ ə ˈbɪl ət̬ i ˌfɑːls-
falsifiab|le ˈfɔːls ɪ faɪ‿əb |ᵊl ˈfɒls-, ˈ·ə-, ˌ··ˈ··· ‖ ˈfɑːls- **~ly** li
falsification ˌfɔːls ɪf ɪ ˈkeɪʃ ᵊn ˌfɒls-, ˌ·əf-, §-əˈ·- ‖ ˌfɑːls- **~s** z
falsi|fy ˈfɔːls ɪ |faɪ ˈfɒls-, -ə- ‖ ˈfɑːls- **~fied** faɪd **~fier/s** faɪ‿ə/z ‖ faɪ‿ᵊr/z **~fies** faɪz **~fying** faɪ ɪŋ
falsit|y ˈfɔːls ət |i ˈfɒls-, -ɪt- ‖ ˈfɔːls ət̬ |i ˈfɑːls- **~ies** iz
Falstaff ˈfɔːlst ɑːf ˈfɒlst-, §-æf ‖ -æf ˈfɑːlst-
Falstaffian (ˌ)fɔːl ˈstɑːf i‿ən (ˌ)fɒl-, §-ˈstæf- ‖ -ˈstæf- (ˌ)fɑːl-
faltboat ˈfælt bəʊt ˈfɑːlt-, ˈfɔːlt-, ˈfɒlt- ‖ ˈfɔːlt boʊt ˈfɑːlt- **~s** s
falter ˈfɔːlt ə ˈfɒlt ə ‖ ˈfɔːlt ᵊr ˈfɑːlt ᵊr **~ed** d **faltering/ly** ˈfɔːlt‿ər ɪŋ /li ˈfɒlt‿ ‖ ˈfɑːlt‿ **~s** z
Falun Gong ˌfɑːl ʊn ˈgɒŋ ˌfæl-, -ˈgʊŋ ‖ -ˈgɔːŋ -ˈgɑːŋ —*Chi* Fǎlún Gōng [^{3}fa ^{2}lwən ^{1}gʊŋ]
Falwell ˈfɔːl wel ‖ ˈfɑːl-
Famagusta ˌfæm ə ˈgʊst ə◂ ˌfɑːm- ‖ ˌfɑːm ə ˈguːst ə
fame feɪm **famed** feɪmd
familial fə ˈmɪl i‿əl ‖ fə ˈmɪl jəl
familiar fə ˈmɪl i‿ə ‖ fə ˈmɪl jᵊr **~ly** li
familiaris... —*see* **familiariz...**
familiarit|y fə ˌmɪl i ˈær ət |i -ɪt i ‖ fə ˌmɪl ˈjær ət̬ |i -ˈjer-; -ˌmɪl i ˈær-, -ˈer- **~ies** iz
familiarization fə ˌmɪl i‿ər aɪ ˈzeɪʃ ᵊn -ɪˈ·- ‖ fə ˌmɪl jər ə ˈzeɪʃ ᵊn
familiariz|e fə ˈmɪl i‿ə raɪz ‖ fə ˈmɪl jə raɪz **~ed** d **~es** ɪz əz **~ing** ɪŋ
family ˈfæm li ˈfæm əl i, -ɪl- **families** ˈfæm liz ˈfæm əl iz, -ɪl-
ˌ**family alˈlowance**; ˌ**family ˈcircle**; ˌ**family ˈdoctor**; ˌ**family ˈincome ˌsupplement**; ˈ**family man**; ˈ**family name** *'surname'*, ˌ**family ˈname** *'family reputation'*; ˌ**family ˈplanning**; ˌ**family ˈtree**
famine ˈfæm ɪn §-ən **~s** z
famish ˈfæm ɪʃ **~ed** t **~es** ɪz əz **~ing** ɪŋ
famous ˈfeɪm əs **~ly** li **~ness** nəs nɪs
fan fæn **fanned** fænd **fanning** ˈfæn ɪŋ **fans** fænz
ˈ**fan belt**; ˈ**fan ˌheater**
Fan *in names of Welsh mountains* væn —*Welsh* [van]
Fanagalo ˌfæn ə gə ˈləʊ ˈ···· ‖ ˌfɑːn ə gə ˈloʊ
fan-assisted ˌfæn ə ˈsɪst ɪd◂ -əd
fanatic fə ˈnæt ɪk ‖ -ˈnæt̬ ɪk **~s** s
fanatical fə ˈnæt ɪk ᵊl ‖ -ˈnæt̬ ɪk- **~ly** ‿i
fanaticism fə ˈnæt ɪ ˌsɪz əm -ə- ‖ -ˈnæt̬ ə-
fanciable ˈfænᵗs i‿əb ᵊl
fancier ˈfænᵗs i‿ə ‖ ᵊr **~s** z
fanciful ˈfænᵗs ɪ fᵊl -ə-, -fʊl **~ly** ‿i **~ness** nəs nɪs
fanc|y, Fanc|y ˈfænᵗs |i **~ied** id **~ier** i‿ə ‖ i‿ᵊr **~ies** iz **~iest** i‿ɪst i‿əst **~ily** ɪ li əl i **~iness** i nəs i nɪs **~ying** i‿ɪŋ
ˌ**fancy ˈdress**; ˈ**fancy goods**; ˈ**fancy man**; ˈ**fancy ˌwoman**
fancy-dress ˌfænᵗs i ˈdres◂
fancy-free ˌfænᵗs i ˈfriː◂
fancywork ˈfænᵗs i wɜːk ‖ -wɜːk
fandango fæn ˈdæŋ gəʊ ‖ -goʊ **~s** z
fane, Fane feɪn **fanes** feɪnz
Faneuil ˈfæn jəl -ᵊl; ˈfæn ju‿əl
ˌ**Faneuil ˈHall**
fanfare ˈfæn feə ‖ -fer -fær **~s** z
fanfaronade ˌfæn fær ə ˈneɪd -fər‿ə-, -ˈnɑːd **~s** z
fanfold ˈfæn fəʊld →-fɒʊld ‖ -foʊld
fang fæŋ **fanged** fæŋd **fangs** fæŋz
Fang *African people and language* fæŋ fɑːŋ
fanlight ˈfæn laɪt **~s** s
Fannie ˈfæn i
ˌ**Fannie ˈMae**
Fanning ˈfæn ɪŋ
fann|y, Fann|y ˈfæn |i **~ies, ~y's** iz
fanon ˈfæn ən **~s** z
Fanshawe ˈfæn ʃɔː ‖ -ʃɑː
Fant fænt ‖ fɑːnt
Fanta *tdmk* ˈfænt ə ‖ ˈfænt̬ ə
fantabulous fæn ˈtæb jʊl əs -jəl- ‖ -jəl-
fantail ˈfæn teɪᵊl **~ed** d **~s** z
fan-tan ˈfæn tæn
fantasi... —*see* **fantasy**
fantasia fæn ˈteɪz i‿ə ˌfænt ə ˈziː‿ə, -ˈsiː‿ə ‖ fæn ˈteɪʒ ə -ˌteɪʒ i‿ə; ˌfænt̬ ə ˈziː ə **~s** z
fantasis|e, fantasiz|e ˈfænt ə saɪz ‖ ˈfænt̬ ə- **~ed** d **~es** ɪz əz **~ing** ɪŋ
fantasist ˈfænt ə sɪst -zɪst, §-səst, §-zəst ‖ ˈfænt̬- **~s** s
fantastic (ˌ)fæn ˈtæst ɪk fən- **~al** ᵊl **~ally** ᵊl‿i
fantasti|cate fæn ˈtæst ɪ| keɪt -ə- **~cated** keɪt ɪd -əd ‖ keɪt̬ əd **~cates** keɪts **~cating** keɪt ɪŋ ‖ keɪt̬ ɪŋ
fantas|y ˈfænt əs |i -əz- ‖ ˈfænt̬- **~ied** id **~ies** iz **~ying** i ɪŋ
Fante, Fanti ˈfænt i ‖ ˈfɑːnt i
Fanthorpe ˈfæn θɔːp ‖ -θɔːrp
fantoccini ˌfænt ə ˈtʃiːn i ‖ ˌfænt̬- ˌfɑːnt̬- —*It* [fan tot ˈtʃiː ni]
Fantom ˈfænt əm ‖ ˈfænt̬-
Fanum ˈfeɪn əm
fanzine ˈfæn ziːn **~s** z
FAO ˌef eɪ ˈəʊ ‖ -ˈoʊ
FAQ ˌef eɪ ˈkjuː **FAQs, FAQ's** ˌef eɪ ˈkjuːz fæks
far fɑː ‖ fɑːr **farther** ˈfɑːð ə ‖ ˈfɑːrð ᵊr **farthest** ˈfɑːð ɪst §-əst ‖ ˈfɑːrð- **further** ˈfɜːð ə ‖ ˈfɜːð ᵊr **furthest** ˈfɜːð ɪst §-əst ‖ ˈfɜːð-
ˌ**Far ˈEast**; ˌ**Far ˈEastern**◂
Fara *island in Orkney* ˈfær ə ‖ ˈfer ə
farad ˈfær əd -æd ‖ ˈfer- **~s** z

araday ˈfær ə deɪ -di ‖ ˈfer-
aradic fə ˈræd ɪk
arandole ˈfær ən dəʊl →-dɒʊl ‖ -doʊl ˈfer- —*Fr* [fa ʁɑ̃ dɔl] **~s** z
arang fæ ˈræŋ fə- **~s** z
araway ˌfɑːr ə ˈweɪ ◂
ˌ**faraway ˈlooks**
arce fɑːs ‖ fɑːrs **farces** ˈfɑːs ɪz -əs ‖ ˈfɑːrs-
arceur ˌfɑː ˈsɜː ‖ ˌfɑːr ˈsɜː —*Fr* [faʁ sœːʁ] **~s** z
arci, farcie ˌfɑː ˈsiː ‖ ˌfɑːr- —*Fr* [faʁ si]
arcical ˈfɑːs ɪk ᵊl -ək- ‖ ˈfɑːrs- **~ly** ‿i **~ness** nəs nɪs
arcy ˈfɑːs i ‖ ˈfɑːrs i
are feə ‖ feᵊr fæᵊr (= *fair*) **fared** feəd ‖ feᵊrd fæᵊrd **fares** feəz ‖ feᵊrz fæᵊrz **faring** ˈfeər ɪŋ ‖ ˈfer ɪŋ ˈfær-
areham ˈfeər əm ‖ ˈfer- ˈfær-
arewell ˌfeə ˈwel ◂ ‖ ˌfer- ˌfær-
arewell *family name* ˈfeə wel -wəl ‖ ˈfer- ˈfær-
arfalle fɑː ˈfæl eɪ ‖ fɑːr- -ˈfɑːl- —*It* [far ˈfal le]
arfetched ˌfɑː ˈfetʃt ◂ ‖ ˌfɑːr-
ar-flung ˌfɑː ˈflʌŋ ◂ ‖ ˌfɑːr-
argo ˈfɑːg əʊ ‖ ˈfɑːrg oʊ
ar-gone ˌfɑː ˈgɒn ◂ §-ˈgɑːn, §-ˈgɔːn ‖ ˌfɑːr ˈgɔːn ◂ -ˈgɑːn ◂
arina fə ˈriːn ə -ˈraɪn ə
arinaceous ˌfær ɪ ˈneɪʃ əs ◂ -ə- ‖ ˌfer-
aringdon ˈfær ɪŋ dən ‖ ˈfer-
arjeon ˈfɑːdʒ ən ‖ ˈfɑːrdʒ-
arl fɑːl ‖ fɑːrl **farls** fɑːlz ‖ fɑːrlz
arleigh, Farley ˈfɑːl i ‖ ˈfɑːrl i
arm fɑːm ‖ fɑːrm **farmed** fɑːmd ‖ fɑːrmd **farming** ˈfɑːm ɪŋ ‖ ˈfɑːrm ɪŋ **farms** fɑːmz ‖ fɑːrmz
armer, F~ ˈfɑːm ə ‖ ˈfɑːrm ᵊr **~s** z
armhand ˈfɑːm hænd ‖ ˈfɑːrm- **~s** z
arm|house ˈfɑːm |haʊs ‖ ˈfɑːrm- **~houses** haʊz ɪz -əz
Farmington ˈfɑːm ɪŋ tən ‖ ˈfɑːrm-
farmland ˈfɑːm lænd -lənd ‖ ˈfɑːrm-
farmstead ˈfɑːm sted ‖ ˈfɑːrm- **~s** z
farmyard ˈfɑːm jɑːd ‖ ˈfɑːrm jɑːrd **~s** z
Farnaby ˈfɑːn əb i ‖ ˈfɑːrn-
Farnborough ˈfɑːn bər‿ə →ˈfɑːm-, §-ˌbʌr- ‖ ˈfɑːrn ˌbɜː oʊ
Farncombe ˈfɑːn kəm →ˈfɑːŋ- ‖ ˈfɑːrn-
Farne fɑːn ‖ fɑːrn
ˈ**Farne ˌIslands**
Farnham ˈfɑːn əm ‖ ˈfɑːrn-
Farnley ˈfɑːn li ‖ ˈfɑːrn-
Farnworth ˈfɑːn wɜːθ ‖ ˈfɑːrn wɜːθ
faro ˈfeər əʊ ‖ ˈfer oʊ ˈfær- (= *pharaoh*)
Faro *place in Portugal* ˈfɑːr əʊ ˈfeər- ‖ -oʊ —*Port* [ˈfa ɾu]
Faroe ˈfeər əʊ ‖ ˈfer oʊ ˈfær- (= *pharaoh*) **~s** z
Faroese ˌfeər əʊ ˈiːz ◂ ‖ ˌfer oʊ- ˌfær-, -ˈiːs◂
far-off ˌfɑːr ˈɒf ◂ -ˈɔːf ‖ ˌfɑːr ˈɔːf ◂ -ˈɑːf
ˌ**far-off ˈlands**
farouche fə ˈruːʃ fæ- —*Fr* [fa ʁuʃ]
Farouk fə ˈruːk
far-out ˌfɑːr ˈaʊt ◂ ‖ ˌfɑːr-
Farquhar ˈfɑːk ə -wə ‖ ˈfɑːrk wᵊr ᵊr, -wɑːr
Farquharson ˈfɑːk əs ən -wəs- ‖ ˈfɑːrk wᵊrs ən -ᵊrs-
Farr fɑː ‖ fɑːr
farraginous fə ˈrædʒ ɪn əs -ˈreɪdʒ-, -ən-
farrago fə ˈrɑːg əʊ -ˈreɪg- ‖ -oʊ **~s** z
Farrah ˈfær ə ‖ ˈfer-
Farrakhan ˈfær ə kæn
Farrant ˈfær ənt ‖ ˈfer-
Farrar ˈfær ə ‖ -ᵊr ˈfer-
far-reaching ˌfɑː ˈriːtʃ ɪŋ ◂ ‖ ˌfɑːr-
ˌ**far-ˌreaching ˈconsequences**
Farrell ˈfær əl ‖ ˈfer-
farrier ˈfær i‿ə ‖ ᵊr ˈfer- **~s** z
Farringdon ˈfær ɪŋ dən ‖ ˈfer-
farrow, F~ ˈfær əʊ ‖ -oʊ ˈfer- **~ed** d **~ing** ɪŋ **~s** z
far-seeing ˌfɑː ˈsiː ɪŋ ◂ ‖ ˌfɑːr-
Farsi ˈfɑːs i ˌfɑː ˈsiː ‖ ˈfɑːrs i
farsighted ˌfɑː ˈsaɪt ɪd ◂ -əd ‖ ˌfɑːr ˈsaɪţ əd ◂ **~ly** li **~ness** nəs nɪs
fart fɑːt ‖ fɑːrt **farted** ˈfɑːt ɪd -əd ‖ ˈfɑːrţ əd **farting** ˈfɑːt ɪŋ ‖ ˈfɑːrţ ɪŋ **farts** fɑːts ‖ fɑːrts
farth|er ˈfɑːð| ə ‖ ˈfɑːrð| ᵊr **~est** ɪst -əst
farthermost ˈfɑːð ə məʊst ‖ ˈfɑːrð ᵊr moʊst
farthing, F~ ˈfɑːð ɪŋ ‖ ˈfɑːrð- **~s** z
farthingale ˈfɑːð ɪŋ geᵊl ‖ ˈfɑːrð- **~s** z
fartlek ˈfɑːt lek ‖ ˈfɑːrt- **~ked** t **~king** ɪŋ **~s** s —*Swedish* [ˈfaʈ lek]
fasces ˈfæs iːz
fascia ˈfeɪʃ ə ˈfeɪʃ i‿ə, ˈfæʃ- ‖ ˈfæʃ i‿ə ˈfeɪʃ ə —*In BrE* ˈfæʃ- *as a medical term, otherwise generally* ˈfeɪʃ-; *as a term in classical architecture, also* ˈfeɪs i‿ə. *In AmE, generally* ˈfæʃ i‿ə, *but* ˈfeɪʃ ə *in the sense of 'board above shopfront'* **~s** z
fasci|ate ˈfæʃ i |eɪt **~ated** eɪt ɪd -əd ‖ eɪţ əd
fascicle ˈfæs ɪk ᵊl -ək- **~s** z
fascicule ˈfæs ɪ kjuːl -ə- **~s** z
fasciitis ˌfæʃ i ˈaɪt ɪs §-əs ‖ -ˈaɪţ əs
fasci|nate ˈfæs ɪ |neɪt -ə- **~nated** neɪt ɪd -əd ‖ neɪţ əd **~nates** neɪts **~nating** neɪt ɪŋ ‖ neɪţ ɪŋ
fascinating ˈfæs ɪ neɪt ɪŋ -ə- ‖ -neɪţ ɪŋ **~ly** li
fascination ˌfæs ɪ ˈneɪʃ ᵊn -ə- **~s** z
fascism ˈfæʃ ˌɪz əm
fascist ˈfæʃ ɪst §-əst **~s** s
fascistic fæ ˈʃɪst ɪk fə-
fash fæʃ **fashed** fæʃt **fashes** ˈfæʃ ɪz -əz **fashing** ˈfæʃ ɪŋ
Fashanu ˈfæʃ ə nuː
fashion ˈfæʃ ᵊn **~ed** d **~ing** ‿ɪŋ **~s** z
ˈ**fashion plate**
-fashion ˌfæʃ ᵊn — **Chinese-fashion** ˌtʃaɪ ˈniːz ˌfæʃ ᵊn
fashionab|le ˈfæʃ ᵊn‿əb |ᵊl **~leness** ᵊl nəs -nɪs **~ly** li
fashionista ˌfæʃ ə ˈniːst ə -ˈnɪst ə; →-ᵊn ˈiːst-, →ᵊn ˈɪst- **-s** z
Fashoda fə ˈʃəʊd ə fæ- ‖ -ˈʃoʊd ə
Faslane fæz ˈleɪn fəs-
Fassbinder ˈfæs bɪnd ə ‖ ˈfɑːs bɪnd ᵊr ˈfæs- —*Ger* Faßbinder [ˈfas bɪn dɐ]

fast fɑːst §fæst ‖ fæst **fasted** 'fɑːst ɪd §'fæst-, -əd ‖ 'fæst əd **faster** 'fɑːst ə §'fæst ə ‖ 'fæst ᵊr **fastest** 'fɑːst ɪst §'fæst-, §-əst ‖ 'fæst- **fasting** 'fɑːst ɪŋ §'fæst- ‖ 'fæst ɪŋ **fasts** fɑːsts §fæsts ‖ fæsts
'fast day; **ˌfast 'food,** '· ·; **ˌfast 'lane**
fastback 'fɑːst bæk §'fæst- ‖ 'fæst- **~s** s
fastball 'fɑːst bɔːl ‖ 'fæst- -bɑːl **~er/s** ə/z ‖ -ᵊr/z
fasten 'fɑːs ᵊn §'fæs- ‖ 'fæs ᵊn **~ed** d **~ing** ˌɪŋ **~s** z
fastener 'fɑːs nə §'fæs-, '·ᵊn ə ‖ 'fæs ᵊn ˌᵊr **~s** z
fastening *n* 'fɑːs nɪŋ §'fæs-, '·ᵊn ɪŋ ‖ 'fæs ᵊn ˌɪŋ **~s** z
fast-forward ˌfɑːst 'fɔː wəd §ˌfæst- ‖ ˌfæst 'fɔːr wᵊrd
fastidious fæ 'stɪd i ˌəs fə- **~ly** li **~ness** nəs nɪs
fastigiate fæ 'stɪdʒ i ˌət -eɪt
fastness 'fɑːst nəs §'fæst-, -nɪs ‖ 'fæst- **~es** ɪz əz
Fastnet 'fɑːst net §'fæst-, -nɪt ‖ 'fæst-
fast-talk ˌfɑːst 'tɔːk §ˌfæst- ‖ ˌfæst- -'tɑːk **~ed** t **~er/s** ə/z ‖ ᵊr/z **~ing** ɪŋ **~s** s
fat fæt **fatted** 'fæt ɪd -əd ‖ 'fæţ əd **fatter** 'fæt ə ‖ 'fæţ ᵊr **fattest** 'fæt ɪst §-əst ‖ 'fæţ əst **fatting** 'fæt ɪŋ ‖ 'fæţ ɪŋ
ˌfat 'cat; **ˌfat 'hen**
Fatah 'fæt ə 'fʌt ə ‖ 'fɑːt ə —*Arabic* ['fa taħ]
fatal 'feɪt ᵊl ‖ 'feɪţ ᵊl **~ism** ˌɪz əm **~ist/s** ɪst/s §-əst/s
fatalistic ˌfeɪt ᵊl 'ɪst ɪk ◂ ‖ ˌfeɪţ- **~ally** ᵊl ˌi
fatalit|y fə 'tæl ət |i feɪ-, -ɪt- ‖ feɪ 'tæl əţ |i fə- **~ies** iz
fatally 'feɪt ᵊl i ‖ 'feɪţ ᵊl i
fata morgana ˌfɑːt ə mɔː 'gɑːn ə ‖ ˌfɑːţ ə mɔːr-
fate, Fate feɪt **fated** 'feɪt ɪd -əd ‖ 'feɪţ əd **fates, Fates** feɪts
fateful 'feɪt fᵊl -fʊl **~ly** i
fat-free ˌfæt 'friː ◂
fathead 'fæt hed **~s** z
fatheaded ˌfæt 'hed ɪd ◂ -əd, '· · · **~ness** nəs nɪs
fath|er 'fɑːð |ə ‖ -|ᵊr **~ered** əd ‖ ᵊrd **~ering** ər ˌɪŋ **~ers** əz ‖ ᵊrz
ˌFather 'Christmas; **'father ˌfigure**; **'Father's Day**; **ˌFather 'Time**
fatherhood 'fɑːð ə hʊd ‖ -ᵊr-
father-in-law 'fɑːð ər ˌɪn ˌlɔː →'·əˌ, ᵊr ˌən- ‖ 'fɑːð ᵊr ˌən ˌlɔː -ər ˌᵊn-, -ˌlɑː **fathers-in-law** 'fɑːð əz ɪn ˌlɔː §-ən ˌ· ‖ -ᵊrz ən ˌlɔː ˌlɑː
fatherland 'fɑːð ə lænd ‖ -ᵊr- **~s** z
fatherly 'fɑːð ə li -ᵊl i ‖ -ᵊr-
fathers-in-law —*see* **father-in-law**
fathom 'fæð əm **~ed** d **~ing** ɪŋ **~s** z
fathomless 'fæð əm ləs -lɪs
fatigu|e fə 'tiːg **~ed** d **~es** z **~ing** ɪŋ
Fatima 'fæt ɪm ə -əm- ‖ 'fæţ-
fatling 'fæt lɪŋ **~s** z
fat|ly 'fæt |li **~ness** nəs nɪs
fatshedera ˌfæts 'hed ər ə **~s** z
fatsia 'fæts i ˌə **~s** z
fatso, Fatso 'fæts əʊ ‖ -oʊ **~es, ~s** z

fat-soluble ˌfæt 'sɒl jʊb ᵊl ◂ -jəb-, '·ˌ·- ‖ 'fæt ˌsɑːl jəb ᵊl
fatstock 'fæt stɒk ‖ -stɑːk
fatt... —*see* **fat**
fatten 'fæt ᵊn **~ed** d **~er/s** ˌə/z ‖ ər/z **~ing** ˌɪŋ **~s** z
fattish 'fæt ɪʃ ‖ 'fæţ ɪʃ **~ness** nəs nɪs
fatt|y 'fæt |i ‖ 'fæţ |i **~ier** iˌə ‖ iˌᵊr **~ies** iz **~iest** iˌɪst iˌəst **~iness** i nəs i nɪs
ˌfatty 'acid
fatuit|y fə 'tjuːˌət |i fæ-, →-'tʃuːˌ, ɪt- ‖ -'tuː əţ |i -'tjuː-, -'tʃuː- **~ies** iz
fatuous 'fæt juˌəs 'fætʃ uˌəs ‖ 'fætʃ uˌəs **~ly** li **~ness** nəs nɪs
fatwa 'fæt wɑː **~s** z —*Arabic* ['fat waː]
faucal 'fɔːk ᵊl ‖ 'fɑːk-
fauces 'fɔːs iːz ‖ 'fɑːs-
faucet 'fɔːs ɪt -ət ‖ 'fɑːs- **~s** s
Faucett, Faucitt 'fɔːs ɪt -ət ‖ 'fɑːs-
faugh fɔː ‖ fɑː —*or non-speech sequences such as* [pɸ, pɸə]
Faulds *(i)* fəʊldz →fɒʊldz ‖ foʊldz, *(ii)* fɔːldz ‖ fɑːldz
Faulkner 'fɔːk nə 'fɔːlk- ‖ -nᵊr 'fɑːk-
Faull fɔːl ‖ fɑːl
fault fɔːlt fɒlt ‖ fɔːlt fɑːlt **faulted** 'fɔːlt ɪd 'fɒlt-, -əd ‖ 'fɔːlt əd 'fɑːlt- **faulting** 'fɔːlt ɪŋ 'fɒlt- ‖ 'fɔːlt ɪŋ 'fɑːlt- **faults** fɔːlts fɒlts ‖ fɔːlts fɑːlts
'fault line; **'fault plane**
faultfind|er 'fɔːlt ˌfaɪnd |ə 'fɒlt- ‖ 'fɔːlt ˌfaɪnd -|ᵊr 'fɑːlt- **~ing** ɪŋ
faultless 'fɔːlt ləs 'fɒlt-, -lɪs ‖ 'fɔːlt- 'fɑːlt- **~ly** li **~ness** nəs nɪs
fault-tolerant 'fɔːlt ˌtɒl ər ənt 'fɒlt-, -ᵊr ˌənt ‖ -ˌtɑːl-
fault|y 'fɔːlt |i 'fɒlt- ‖ 'fɔːlt |i 'fɑːlt- **~ier** iˌə ‖ iˌᵊr **~iest** iˌɪst iˌəst **~ily** ɪ li əl i **~iness** i nəs i nɪs
faun fɔːn ‖ fɑːn *(= fawn)* **fauns** fɔːnz ‖ fɑːnz
fauna 'fɔːn ə 'faʊn- ‖ 'fɑːn ə **~s** z
Fauntleroy 'fɒnt lə rɔɪ 'fɔːnt- ‖ 'fɔːnt- 'fɑːnt-
'Fauntleroy suit
Faure fɔː ‖ fɔːr —*Fr* [fɔːʁ]
Fauré 'fɔːr eɪ 'fɒr- ‖ foʊ 'reɪ fɔː- —*Fr* [fo ʁe]
Faust faʊst —*but the place in NY is* fɔːst
Faustian 'faʊst iˌən
Faustus 'faʊst əs 'fɔːst- ‖ 'fɔːst-, 'fɑːst-
faute de mieux ˌfəʊt də 'mjɜː ‖ ˌfoʊt də 'mjuː —*Fr* [fot də mjø]
Fauve fəʊv ‖ foʊv —*Fr* [foːv]
Fauvism 'fəʊv ˌɪz əm ‖ 'foʊv-
Fauvist 'fəʊv ɪst §-əst ‖ 'foʊv- **~s** s
faux fəʊ ‖ foʊ *see also phrases with this word*
Faux *name (i)* fɔːks ‖ fɑːks, *(ii)* fəʊ ‖ foʊ
faux ami ˌfəʊz æ 'miː ‖ ˌfoʊz- —*Fr* [fo za mi] **~s** z *or as sing.*
faux-naif, faux-naïf ˌfəʊ naɪ 'iːf ◂ ‖ ˌfoʊ nɑː- —*Fr* [fo na if]
faux pas *sing.* ˌfəʊ 'pɑː '· · ‖ ˌfoʊ- —*Fr* [fo pa]
faux pas *pl* ˌfəʊ 'pɑːz -'pɑː, '· · ‖ ˌfoʊ- —*Fr* [fo pa]
fava 'fɑːv ə
'fava bean

ave feɪv
avela fə 'vel ə fæ- **~s** z —*BrPort* [fa 've lɐ, -s]
avell 'feɪv ᵊl
aversham 'fæv əʃ əm ‖ -ᵊrʃ-
avonian, F~ fə 'vəʊn i‿ən feɪ- ‖ -'voʊn-
avor 'feɪv ə ‖ -ᵊr **~ed** d **favoring/ly** 'feɪv ər‿ɪŋ /li **~s** z
avorab|le 'feɪv ər‿əb |ᵊl **~leness** ᵊl nəs -nɪs **~ly** li
avorite 'feɪv rət -rɪt; 'feɪv ər ət, -ɪt ‖ ⚠ 'feɪv ᵊrt **~s** s
ˌ**favorite 'son**
avoritism 'feɪv rə ˌtɪz əm -rɪt-; 'ər əˌ--, -ər ɪ- ‖ ⚠-ᵊr-
avour 'feɪv ə ‖ -ᵊr **~ed** d **favouring/ly** 'feɪv ər‿ɪŋ /li **~s** z
avourab|le 'feɪv ər‿əb |ᵊl **~leness** ᵊl nəs -nɪs **~ly** li
avourite 'feɪv rət -rɪt; 'feɪv ər ət, -ɪt ‖ ⚠ 'feɪv ᵊrt **~s** s
ˌ**favorite 'son**
avouritism 'feɪv rə ˌtɪz əm -rɪt-; 'ər əˌ--, -ər ɪ- ‖ ⚠-ᵊr-
awcett 'fɔːs ɪt -ət ‖ 'fɑːs-
awcus 'fɔːk əs ‖ 'fɑːk-
awkes fɔːks ‖ fɑːks
awley 'fɔːl i ‖ 'fɑːl i
awlty 'fɔːlt i 'fɒlt i ‖ 'fɔːlt i 'fɑːlt i
awn fɔːn ‖ fɑːn **fawned** fɔːnd ‖ fɑːnd **fawner/s** 'fɔːn ə/z ‖ -ᵊr/z 'fɑːn- **fawning/ly** 'fɔːn ɪŋ /li ‖ 'fɑːn- **fawns** fɔːnz ‖ fɑːnz
awr 'vaʊ‿ə ‖ 'vaʊ‿ᵊr —*Welsh* [vaur]
ax, Fax fæks **faxed** fækst **faxes** 'fæks ɪz -əz **faxing** 'fæks ɪŋ
ay, Fay, Faye feɪ
ayed 'faɪ ed
ayette ₍ˌ₎feɪ 'et
ayetteville 'feɪ et vɪl -ɪt-, -ət- ‖ -ət vᵊl -vɪl
aygate 'feɪ geɪt
azackerley, Fazakerley fə 'zæk ə li ‖ -ᵊr-
faze feɪz *(= phase, Fay's)* **fazed** feɪzd **fazes** 'feɪz ɪz -əz **fazing** 'feɪz ɪŋ
Fazeley 'feɪz li
FBI ˌef biː 'aɪ -bi-
feal|ty 'fiː‿əl |ti **~ties** tiz
fear fɪə ‖ fɪᵊr **feared** fɪəd ‖ fɪᵊrd **fearer/s** 'fɪər ə/z ‖ 'fɪr ᵊr/z **fearing** 'fɪər ɪŋ ‖ 'fɪr ɪŋ **fears** fɪəz ‖ fɪᵊrz
fearful 'fɪəf ᵊl 'fɪə fʊl ‖ 'fɪrf ᵊl **~ly** ‿i **~ness** nəs nɪs
Feargal, Fearghal 'fɜːg ᵊl ‖ 'fɜ˞ːg-
Feargus 'fɜːg əs ‖ 'fɜ˞ːg-
fearless 'fɪə ləs -lɪs ‖ 'fɪr- **~ly** li **~ness** nəs nɪs
Fearn, Fearne *(i)* fɜːn ‖ fɜ˞ːn, *(ii)* feən ‖ fern
fearsome 'fɪəs əm ‖ 'fɪrs- **~ly** li **~ness** nəs nɪs
feasibility ˌfiːz ə 'bɪl ət i ˌ·ɪ-, -ɪt i ‖ -əţ i
ˌ**feasi'bility** ˌ**study**
feasib|le 'fiːz əb |ᵊl -ɪb- **~leness** ᵊl nəs -nɪs **~ly** li
feast fiːst **feasted** 'fiːst ɪd -əd **feaster/s** 'fiːst ə/z ‖ -ᵊr/z **feasting** 'fiːst ɪŋ **feasts** fiːsts
'**feast day**

feat fiːt *(= feet)* **feats** fiːts
feath|er 'feð |ə ‖ -|ᵊr **~ered** əd ‖ ᵊrd **~ering** ər‿ɪŋ **~ers** əz ‖ ᵊrz
ˌ**feather 'bed**; ˌ**feather 'boa**; ˌ**feather 'duster**; '**feather star**
featherbed *v* 'feð ə bed ˌ·'·· ‖ -ᵊr- **~ded** ɪd əd **~ding** ɪŋ **~s** z
featherbrained 'feð ə breɪnd ˌ·· '·◂ ‖ -ᵊr-
featheredg|e 'feð ər edʒ ˌ··'· ‖ -ər- **~ed** d **~es** ɪz əz
featheriness 'feð ər‿i nəs -nɪs
featherstitch 'feð ə stɪtʃ ‖ -ᵊr- **~ed** t **~es** ɪz əz **~ing** ɪŋ
Featherstone *(i)* 'feð əst ən -ə stəʊn ‖ -ᵊr stoʊn, *(ii)* 'fɜːst ən ‖ 'fɜ˞ːst-
Featherstonehaugh *(i)* 'feð əst ən hɔː ‖ 'feð ᵊrst- -hɑː, *(ii)* 'fæn ʃɔː ‖ -ʃɑː, *(iii)* 'fest ən hɔː ‖ -hɑː, *(iv)* 'fiːs ᵊn heɪ, *(v)* 'fɪəst ən hɔː ‖ 'fɪrst- -hɑː
featherweight 'feð ə weɪt ‖ -ᵊr- **~s** s
feathery 'feð ər‿i
feature 'fiːtʃ ə ‖ -ᵊr **~ed** d **~es** z **featuring** 'fiːtʃ ər‿ɪŋ
'**feature film**
featureless 'fiːtʃ ə ləs -lɪs ‖ -ᵊr-
Feaver 'fiːv ə ‖ -ᵊr
Febreze *tdmk* fə 'briːz
febrifug|e 'feb rɪ fjuːdʒ -rə- **~es** ɪz əz
febrile 'fiːb raɪᵊl 'feb- ‖ 'feb-

FEBRUARY

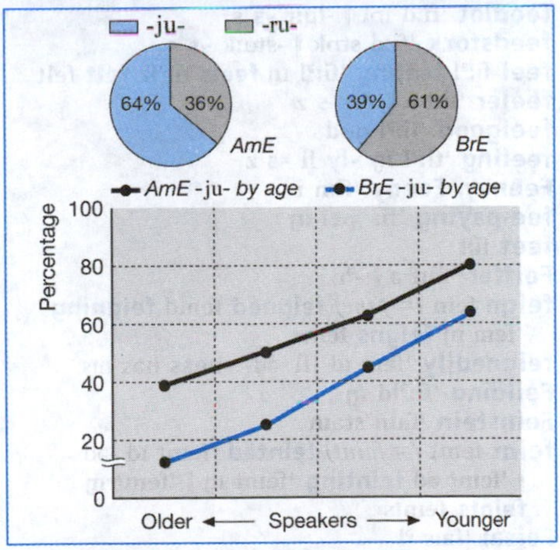

February 'feb ru‿ər i 'feb ju‿, -er i; 'feb rʊr i, -rər-, -jʊr-, -jər- ‖ 'feb ju er i 'feb ru- —*The forms with* j*, although sometimes criticized, are often heard from educated speakers (esp. AmE) and preferred by them. Casually also* 'feb ri. — *Preference polls, AmE:* -ju- *64%,* -ru- *36%; BrE:* -ru- *61%,* -ju- *39%, with vowel in* -ary *weak 57%, strong* -eri *43%.*
fecal 'fiːk ᵊl
feces fiːs iːz
fecit 'feɪk ɪt 'fiːs-, §-ət
feck fek **fecking** 'fek ɪŋ
feckless 'fek ləs -lɪs **~ly** li **~ness** nəs nɪs

F

fecund 'fek ənd 'fi:k-, -ʌnd; fɪ 'kʌnd, fə-
fecun|date 'fek ən |deɪt 'fi:k-, -ʌn- **~dated** deɪt ɪd -əd ‖ deɪţ əd **~dates** deɪts **~dating** deɪt ɪŋ ‖ deɪţ ɪŋ
fecundity fɪ 'kʌnd ət i fə-, fe-, fi:-, -ɪt- ‖ -əţ i
fed, Fed fed **feds, Feds** fedz
ˌfed 'up◂
fedayeen, F~ fə 'dɑ: ji:n fe-, fɪ-; ˌfed aɪ 'i:n ‖ ˌfed ɑ: 'ji:n
federal 'fed‿ər əl **~ism** ˌɪz əm **~ist/s** ɪst/s §əst/s **~ly** li
ˌFederal Re'serve
fede|rate *v* 'fed ə |reɪt **~rated** reɪt ɪd -əd ‖ reɪţ əd **~rates** reɪts **~rating** reɪt ɪŋ ‖ reɪţ ɪŋ
federation ˌfed ə 'reɪʃ ən **~s** z
federative 'fed‿ər ət ɪv -ə reɪt ɪv ‖ 'fed ə reɪţ ɪv ər əţ ɪv **~ly** li
Federer 'fed ər ə ‖ -ər —*Ger* ['fe: də ʁɐ]
Fedex, FedEx *tdmk* 'fed eks **~ed** t **~es** ɪz əz **~ing** ɪŋ
fedora, F~ fɪ 'dɔ:r ə fə- ‖ -'dour- **~s** z
fee fi: **fees** fi:z
feeble 'fi:b əl **~ness** nəs nɪs
feebleminded ˌfi:b əl 'maɪnd ɪd ◂ -əd ‖ '. . . . **~ly** li **~ness** nəs nɪs
feebly 'fi:b li
feed fi:d **fed** fed **feeding** 'fi:d ɪŋ **feeds** fi:dz
'feeding ˌbottle
feedback 'fi:d bæk →'fi:b-
feedbag 'fi:d bæg →'fi:b- **~s** z
feeder 'fi:d ə ‖ -ər **~s** z
feedlot 'fi:d lɒt ‖ -lɑ:t **~s** s
feedstock 'fi:d stɒk ‖ -stɑ:k **~s** s
feel fi:əl **feeling** 'fi:əl ɪŋ **feels** fi:əlz **felt** felt
feeler 'fi:l ə ‖ -ər **~s** z
feelgood 'fi:əl gʊd
feeling 'fi:əl ɪŋ **~ly** li **~s** z
Feeney, Feeny 'fi:n i
fee-paying 'fi: ˌpeɪ ɪŋ
feet fi:t
Feiffer 'faɪf ə ‖ -ər
feign feɪn *(= fane)* **feigned** feɪnd **feigning** 'feɪn ɪŋ **feigns** feɪnz
feigned|ly 'feɪn ɪd |li -əd- **~ness** nəs nɪs
Feilding 'fi:əld ɪŋ
Feinstein 'faɪn staɪn
feint feɪnt *(= faint)* **feinted** 'feɪnt ɪd -əd ‖ 'feɪnţ əd **feinting** 'feɪnt ɪŋ ‖ 'feɪnţ ɪŋ **feints** feɪnts
Feisal 'faɪs əl
feist|y 'faɪst |i —*but the Jamaican word of similar meaning, sometimes so spelt, is* 'feɪst |i **~ier** i‿ə ‖ i‿ər **~iest** i‿ɪst i‿əst **~ily** ɪ li əl i **~iness** i nəs i nɪs
felafel fə 'læf əl fɪ-, fe-, -'lɑ:f- ‖ -'lɑ:f-
feldspar 'feld spɑ: ‖ -spɑ:r **~s** z
feldspathic feld 'spæθ ɪk '. . .
Felice fə 'li:s fɪ-
Felicia fə 'lɪs i‿ə fɪ-, -'lɪʃ- ‖ -'lɪʃ ə -'li:ʃ ə
felici|tate fə 'lɪs ɪ |teɪt fɪ-, fe-, -ə- **~tated** teɪt ɪd -əd ‖ teɪţ əd **~tates** teɪts **~tating** teɪt ɪŋ ‖ teɪţ ɪŋ
felicitation fə ˌlɪs ɪ 'teɪʃ ən fɪ-, fe-, -ə- **~s** z
felicitous fə 'lɪs ɪt əs fɪ-, fe-, -ət- ‖ -əţ əs **~ly** li **~ness** nəs nɪs
felicit|y, F~ fə 'lɪs ət |i fɪ-, fe-, -ɪt- ‖ -əţ |i **~ies** iz
Felindre ve 'lɪndr ə və- —*Welsh* [ve 'lin dre]
feline 'fi:l aɪn **~ly** li **~ness** nəs nɪs **~s** z
Felix 'fi:l ɪks
Felixstowe 'fi:l ɪk stəʊ ‖ -stou
fell, Fell fel **felled** feld **felling** 'fel ɪŋ **fells** felz
fella 'fel ə **~s** z
fellah 'fel ə -ɑ:; fə 'lɑ: **fellaheen, fellahin** ˌfel ə 'hi:n '. . .; fə ˌlɑ: 'hi:n
fel|late fe '|leɪt fə-, fɪ- ‖ 'fe|l eɪt **~lated** leɪt ɪd -əd ‖ leɪţ əd **~later/s** leɪt ə/z ‖ leɪţ ər/z **~lates** leɪts **~lating** leɪt ɪŋ ‖ leɪţ ɪŋ
fellatio fe 'leɪʃ i əʊ fə-, fɪ-, -'lɑ:t- ‖ -oʊ
fellation fe 'leɪʃ ən fə-, fɪ- **~s** z
feller 'fel ə ‖ -ər **~s** z
Felling 'fel ɪŋ
Fellini fe 'li:n i fə-, fɪ- —*It* [fel 'li: ni]
felloe 'fel əʊ ‖ -oʊ *(= fellow)* **~s** z
fellow 'fel əʊ ‖ -oʊ **~s** z
ˌfellow 'creature; **ˌfellow 'feeling**; **ˌfellow 'men**; **ˌfellow 'traveller**
Fellowes, Fellows 'fel əʊz ‖ -oʊz
fellowship 'fel əʊ ʃɪp ‖ -oʊ- **~s** s
felo de se ˌfi:l əʊ di 'si: ˌfel-, -'seɪ; -deɪ 'seɪ ‖ ˌfel oʊ-
felon 'fel ən **~s** z
felonious fə 'ləʊn i‿əs fe-, fɪ- ‖ -'loʊn- **~ly** li **~ness** nəs nɪs
felon|y 'fel ən |i **~ies** iz
Felpham 'felp əm -həm; 'felf-
felspar 'fel spɑ: ‖ -spɑ:r **~s** z
Felstead, Felsted 'fel stɪd -sted
felt felt **felted** 'felt ɪd -əd **felting** 'felt ɪŋ **felts** felts
Feltham 'felt əm —*as a family name, also* 'felθ-
Felton 'felt ən
felt-tip 'felt tɪp ˌ.'. **~s** s
Feltz felts
felucca fe 'lʌk ə fə-, fɪ- ‖ -'lu:k ə -'lʊk ə, -'lʌk ə **~s** z
felwort 'fel wɜ:t -wɔ:t ‖ -wɜ:t -wɔ:rt
fem. fem
FEMA 'fi:m ə
female 'fi:m eɪəl **~ness** nəs nɪs
ˌfemale im'personator
Femidom *tdmk* 'fem ɪ dɒm -ə- ‖ -dɑ:m
Feminax *tdmk* 'fem ɪ næks -ə-
feminine 'fem ən ɪn -ɪn-, §-ən **~ly** li **~ness** nəs nɪs
femininit|y ˌfem ə 'nɪn ət |i ˌ-ɪ-, -ɪt i ‖ -əţ |i **~ies** iz
feminis... —*see* **feminiz...**
feminism 'fem ə ˌnɪz əm -ɪ-
feminist 'fem ən ɪst -ɪn-, §-əst **~s** s
feminization ˌfem ən aɪ 'zeɪʃ ən ˌ-ɪn-, -ɪ'-- ‖ -ən ə-
feminiz|e 'fem ə naɪz -ɪ- **~ed** d **~es** ɪz əz **~ing** ɪŋ

emme fem *but as a French word,* fæm —*Fr* [fam] **femmes** femz

emme fatale ˌfæm fə ˈtɑːl ‖ ˌfem fə ˈtæl ˌfæm-, -ˈtɑːl —*Fr* [fam fa tal] **femmes fatales** —*same pronunciation*

emora ˈfem ər ə ˈfiːm-

emoral ˈfem ^{ə}r‿əl ˈfiːm-

emto- ¦fem^{p}t əʊ ‖ ¦fem^{p}t oʊ — **femtogram** ˈfem^{p}t əʊ græm ‖ -oʊ-

emur ˈfiːm ə ‖ -^{ə}r **~s** z

en fen **fens** fenz

enby ˈfen bi →ˈfem-

ence fen^{t}s **fenced** fen^{t}st **fences** ˈfen^{t}s ɪz -əz **fencing** ˈfen^{t}s ɪŋ

fenced-in ˌfen^{t}st ˈɪn ◂

fence-mending ˈfen^{t}s ˌmend ɪŋ

fencer ˈfen^{t}s ə ‖ -^{ə}r **~s** z

fence-sitter ˈfen^{t}s ˌsɪt ə ‖ -ˌsɪţ ^{ə}r **~s** z

Fenchurch ˈfen tʃɜːtʃ ‖ -tʃɜ˞ːtʃ

fend fend **fended** ˈfend ɪd -əd **fending** ˈfend ɪŋ **fends** fendz

fender, F~ ˈfend ə ‖ -^{ə}r **~s** z

fender-bender ˈfend ə ˌbend ə ‖ -^{ə}r ˌbend ^{ə}r **~s** z

Fenella fə ˈnel ə fɪ-

fenes|trate fə ˈnes |treɪt fɪ-, fe-; ˈfen ɪ s|treɪt, -ə- **~trated** treɪt ɪd -əd ‖ treɪţ əd **~trates** treɪts **~trating** treɪt ɪŋ ‖ treɪţ ɪŋ

fenestration ˌfen ɪ ˈstreɪʃ ^{ə}n -ə- **~s** z

feng shui ˌfʌŋ ˈʃweɪ ˌfʊŋ-, ˌfeŋ-, ˌ·ˈʃuː i —*Chi* fēng shuǐ [¹fəŋ ³ʂwei]

Fenian ˈfiːn i‿ən **~s** z

Fenimore ˈfen ɪ mɔː -ə- ‖ -mɔːr -moʊr

fenland, F~ ˈfen lənd -lænd

Fenn fen

fennec ˈfen ek -ɪk **~s** s

fennel ˈfen ^{ə}l

Fennel, Fennell ˈfen ^{ə}l

Fenner ˈfen ə ‖ -^{ə}r **~'s** z

Fennimore ˈfen ɪ mɔː -ə- ‖ -mɔːr -moʊr

fenny ˈfen i

Fenoulhet ˈfen ə leɪ -^{ə}l eɪ

Fenstanton fen ˈstænt ən

fentanyl ˈfent ə nɪl

Fentiman ˈfent ɪ mən -ə-

Fenton ˈfent ən ‖ -^{ə}n

fenugreek ˈfen ju griːk -u- ‖ -jə-

Fenway ˈfen weɪ

Fenwick *(i)* ˈfen ɪk *(ii)* -wɪk —*The place in Northumberland is (i). The US family name is (ii), the UK one may be either.*

Feodor ˈfiː‿ə dɔː ‖ -dɔːr —*Russ* [fʲɪ ˈɔ dər]

feoff fiːf fef **feoffed** fiːft feft **feoffing** ˈfiːf ɪŋ ˈfef- **feoffs** fiːfs fefs

feoffee fe ˈfiː ₍ı₎fiː- **~s** z

feral ˈfer əl ˈfɪər- ‖ ˈfɪr-

ferbam ˈfɜː bæm ˈfɜːb əm ‖ ˈfɜ˞ː bæm

fer-de-lanc|e ˌfeə də ˈlɑːn^{t}s ˌfɜː-, §-ˈlæn^{t}s ‖ ˌferd ^{ə}l ˈæn^{t}s -ˈɑːn^{t}s **~es** ɪz əz

Ferdinand ˈfɜːd ɪ nænd -ə-, -^{ə}n ænd; -ɪn ənd, -ən‿ənd ‖ ˈfɜ˞ːd ^{ə}n ænd

Ferens ˈfer ənz

Fergal ˈfɜːg ^{ə}l ‖ ˈfɜ˞ːg ^{ə}l

Fergle ˈfɜːg i ‖ ˈfɜ˞ːg i

Fergus ˈfɜːg əs ‖ ˈfɜ˞ːg-

Ferguson, Fergusson ˈfɜːg əs ən ‖ ˈfɜ˞ːg-

ferial ˈfɪər i‿əl ˈfer- ‖ ˈfɪr- ˈfer-

Ferlinghetti ˌfɜːl ɪŋ ˈget i ‖ ˌfɜ˞ːl ɪŋ ˈgeţ i

Fermanagh fə ˈmæn ə fɜː- ‖ f^{ə}r-

Fermat fə ˈmæt fɜː-; ˈfɜːm æt, -ɑː ‖ fer ˈmɑː —*Fr* [fɛʁ ma]

ferment *n* ˈfɜː ment ‖ ˈfɜ˞ː- **~s** s

fer|ment *v* fə |ˈment fɜː- ‖ f^{ə}r- **~mented** ˈment ɪd -əd ‖ ˈmenţ əd **~menting** ˈment ɪŋ ‖ ˈmenţ ɪŋ **~ments** ˈments

fermentation ˌfɜːm en ˈteɪʃ ^{ə}n -ən-, fə ˌmen- ‖ ˌfɜ˞ːm- **~s** z

Fermi ˈfɜːm i ˈfeəm- ‖ ˈfɜ˞ːm i ˈferm i —*It* [ˈfer mi]

fermion ˈfɜːm i ɒn ‖ ˈfɜ˞ːm i ɑːn ˈferm- **~s** z

fermium ˈfɜːm i‿əm ‖ ˈfɜ˞ːm- ˈferm-

Fermor ˈfɜːm ɔː ‖ ˈfɜ˞ːm ɔːr

Fermoy fə ˈmɔɪ fɜː-; ˈfɜːm ɔɪ ‖ f^{ə}r-

fern, Fern fɜːn ‖ fɜ˞ːn **ferns** fɜːnz ‖ fɜ˞ːnz

Fernandez fə ˈnænd ez fɜː-, -ɪz ‖ f^{ə}r- fer- —*Sp* Fernández [fer ˈnan deθ]

Fernando fə ˈnænd əʊ ‖ f^{ə}r ˈnænd oʊ fer-, -ˈnɑːnd- —*Sp* [fer ˈnan do], *Port* [fər ˈnen du]

Ferˌnando ˈPo

Ferndale ˈfɜːn deɪ^{ə}l ‖ ˈfɜ˞ːn-

Ferndown ˈfɜːn daʊn ‖ ˈfɜ˞ːn-

ferner|y ˈfɜːn ər |i ‖ ˈfɜ˞ːn- **~ies** iz

Ferneyhough, Fernihough *(i)* ˈfɜːn i hʌf ‖ ˈfɜ˞ːn-, *(ii)* -həʊ ‖ -hoʊ

Fernley ˈfɜːn li ‖ ˈfɜ˞ːn-

ferny ˈfɜːn i ‖ ˈfɜ˞ːn i

Fernyhalgh *(i)* ˈfɜːn i hʌf ‖ ˈfɜ˞ːn-, *(ii)* -hælʃ

Fernyhough *(i)* ˈfɜːn i hʌf ‖ ˈfɜ˞ːn-, *(ii)* -həʊ ‖ -hoʊ

ferocious fə ˈrəʊʃ əs fɪ- ‖ -ˈroʊʃ- **~ly** li **~ness** nəs nɪs

ferocit|y fə ˈrɒs ət |i fɪ-, -ɪt- ‖ -ˈrɑːs əţ |i **~ies** iz

Ferodo *tdmk* fə ˈrəʊd əʊ fɪ- ‖ -ˈroʊd oʊ

-ferous *stress-imposing* fər əs — **ferriferous** fe ˈrɪf ər əs

Ferranti fə ˈrænt i fɪ-, fe- ‖ -ˈrænţ i -ˈrɑːnţ i

Ferrar *(i)* ˈfer ə ‖ -^{ə}r, *(ii)* fə ˈrɑː ‖ -ˈrɑːr

Ferrara fə ˈrɑːr ə —*It* [fer ˈraː ra]

Ferrari fə ˈrɑːr i —*It* [fer ˈraː ri]

Ferraro fə ˈrɑːr əʊ ‖ -oʊ

ferrel, F~ ˈfer əl **~s, F~'s** z

Ferrer *(i)* ˈfer ə ‖ -^{ə}r, *(ii)* fə ˈreə ‖ -ˈre^{ə}r

Ferrero Rocher *tdmk* fə ˌreər əʊ ˈrɒʃ eɪ -rɒ ˈʃeɪ ‖ fə ˌrer oʊ roʊ ˈʃeɪ

ferr|et ˈfer |ɪt -ət ‖ -|ət **~eted** ɪt ɪd ət-, -əd ‖ əţ əd **~eting** ɪt ɪŋ ət- ‖ əţ ɪŋ **~ets** ɪts əts ‖ əts

ferri- *comb. form*
with stress-neutral suffix ¦fer i -aɪ — **ferricyanide** ˌfer i ˈsaɪ‿ə naɪd ·aɪ-
with stress-imposing suffix fe ˈrɪ+ — **ferriferous** fe ˈrɪf ər əs

ferric ˈfer ɪk

ferrie... —*see* **ferry**

Ferrier ˈfer i‿ə ‖ ^{ə}r

F

Ferris, f~ 'fer ɪs §-əs
'Ferris wheel
ferrite 'fer aɪt
ferro- *comb. form* ˌfer əʊ ‖ -oʊ
— **ferrochromium** ˌfer əʊ 'krəʊm i‿əm ‖ -oʊ 'kroʊm-
ferroconcrete ˌfer əʊ 'kɒŋ kriːt -'kɒn- ‖ -oʊ 'kɑːn- ·-'·
Ferrograph *tdmk* 'fer əʊ grɑːf -græf ‖ -oʊ græf
ferrous 'fer əs
ferruginous fe 'ruːdʒ ɪn əs fə-, fɪ-, -ən-
ferrule 'fer uːl -əl, -juːl ‖ -əl **~s** z
ferr|y, Ferry 'fer |i **~ied** id **~ies** iz **~ying** i‿ɪŋ
ferryboat 'fer i bəʊt ‖ -boʊt **~s** s
ferry|man 'fer i |mən -mæn **~men** mən men
fertile 'fɜːt aɪᵊl ‖ 'fɝːṱ ᵊl *(*)* **~ly** li **~ness** nəs nɪs
fertilis... —*see* **fertiliz...**
fertility fɜː 'tɪl ət i fə-, -ət- ‖ fᵊr 'tɪl əṱ i
fer'tility drug; **fer'tility ˌsymbol**
fertilization ˌfɜːt əl aɪ 'zeɪʃ ᵊn ˌ·ɪl-, -ɪ'-- ‖ ˌfɝːṱ ᵊl ə- **~s** z
fertiliz|e 'fɜːt ə laɪz -ɪ-, -ᵊl aɪz ‖ 'fɝːṱ ᵊl aɪz **~ed** d **~es** ɪz əz **~ing** ɪŋ
fertilizer 'fɜːt ə laɪz ə '·ɪ-, -ᵊl aɪz- ‖ 'fɝːṱ ᵊl aɪz ᵊr **~s** z
ferule 'fer uːl -əl, -juːl ‖ -əl **~s** z
fervenc|y 'fɜːv ᵊnᵗs |i ‖ 'fɝːv- **~ies** iz
fervent 'fɜːv ᵊnt ‖ 'fɝːv- **~ly** li **~ness** nəs nɪs
fervid 'fɜːv ɪd §-əd ‖ 'fɝːv- **~ly** li **~ness** nəs nɪs
fervor, fervour 'fɜːv ə ‖ 'fɝːv ᵊr **~s** z
fescue 'fesk juː **~s** z
fess, Fess, fesse fes **fesses** 'fes ɪz -əz
fest fest **fests** fests
festal 'fest ᵊl **~ly** i
Feste 'fest i
fest|er 'fest |ə ‖ -|ᵊr **~ered** əd ‖ ᵊrd **~ering** ər‿ɪŋ **~ers** əz ‖ ᵊrz
festination ˌfest ɪ 'neɪʃ ᵊn -ə-
Festiniog fe 'stɪn i ɒg ‖ -ɑːg —*Welsh* Ffestiniog [fe 'sdin jog]
festival 'fest ɪv ᵊl -əv- **~s** z
festive 'fest ɪv **~ly** li **~ness** nəs nɪs
festivit|y fe 'stɪv ət |i -ɪt- ‖ -əṱ |i **~ies** iz
festoon ₍ₗ₎fe 'stuːn **~ed** d **~ing** ɪŋ **~s** z
festschrift 'fest ʃrɪft →'feʃ- **~s** s —*Ger* F~ ['fɛst ʃʁɪft]
Festus 'fest əs
feta 'fet ə —*ModGk* ['fɛ ta]
fetal 'fiːt ᵊl ‖ 'fiːṱ ᵊl
fetch fetʃ **fetched** fetʃt **fetches** 'fetʃ ɪz -əz **fetcher/s** 'fetʃ ə/z ‖ -ᵊr/z **fetching/ly** 'fetʃ ɪŋ /li
fete, fête feɪt ‖ fet *(usually = fate)* —*Fr* [fɛt] **feted, fêted** 'feɪt ɪd -əd ‖ 'feɪṱ əd **fetes, fêtes** feɪts **feting, fêting** 'feɪt ɪŋ ‖ 'feɪṱ ɪŋ
ˌfête cham'pêtre, ˌfêtes cham'pêtres ʃɒm 'peɪtr ə -'peɪtr ‖ ʃɑːm- —*Fr* [ʃɑ̃ pɛtχ]
feticide 'fiːt ɪ saɪd §-ə- ‖ 'fiːṱ- **~s** z
fetid 'fet ɪd 'fiːt-, §-əd ‖ 'feṱ əd **~ly** li **~ness** nəs nɪs
fetish 'fet ɪʃ 'fiːt- ‖ 'feṱ ɪʃ **~es** ɪz əz **~ism** ˌɪz əm **~ist/s** ɪst/s §əst/s
fetishistic ˌfet ɪ 'ʃɪst ɪk ◂ ˌfiːt- ‖ ˌfeṱ ɪ- **~ally** ᵊl‿i
fetlock 'fet lɒk ‖ -lɑːk **~s** s
fetor 'fiːt ə -ɔː ‖ 'fiːṱ ᵊr 'fiːt ɔːr **~s** z
fetta 'fet ə —*ModGk* feta ['fɛ ta]
fetter 'fet ə ‖ 'feṱ ᵊr **~ed** d **fettering** 'fet‿ər ɪŋ ‖ 'feṱ ər ɪŋ **~s** z
Fettes 'fet ɪs -ɪz, -əs, -əz ‖ 'feṱ əs
fettl|e 'fet ᵊl ‖ 'feṱ ᵊl **~ed** d **~er/s** ‿ə/z ‖ ‿ər/z **~es** z **~ing** ‿ɪŋ
fettuccin|e, ~i ˌfet u 'tʃiːn i ‖ˌfeṱ ə- —*It* ~e [fet tut 'tʃiː ne]
fetus 'fiːt əs ‖ 'fiːṱ əs **~es** ɪz əz
feu fjuː *(= few)* **feued** 'fjuːd **feuing** 'fjuː ɪŋ **feus** fjuːz
feud fjuːd **feuded** 'fjuːd ɪd -əd **feuding** 'fjuːd ɪŋ **feuds** fjuːdz
feudal 'fjuːd ᵊl **~ly** i
'feudal ˌsystem
feudalism 'fjuːd ᵊl ˌɪz əm
feudalistic ˌfjuːd ᵊl 'ɪst ɪk ◂ -ə 'lɪst- **~ally** ᵊl‿i
feudatory 'fjuːd ə‿tər i ‖ -ə tɔːr i -toʊr i
fever 'fiːv ə ‖ -ᵊr **~ed** d **~s** z
'fever pitch, ˌ· · '·
feverfew 'fiːv ə fjuː ‖ -ᵊr-
feverish 'fiːv ər‿ɪʃ **~ly** li **~ness** nəs nɪs
Feversham 'fev ə ʃəm ‖ -ᵊr-
few fjuː **fewer** 'fjuː‿ə ‖ ᵊr **fewest** 'fjuː‿ɪst §‿əst
Fewkes fjuːks
fewness 'fjuː nəs -nɪs
Fewston 'fjuːst ən
fey, Fey feɪ
Feydeau 'feɪd əʊ ‖ feɪ 'doʊ —*Fr* [fɛ do]
Feyenoord 'faɪ‿ə nɔːd ‖ -nɔːrd —*Dutch* ['fɛi ə noːrt]
Feynman 'faɪn mən
fez, Fez fez **fezes, fezzes** 'fez ɪz -əz
ff..., Ff... *in family names* —*see* **F...**
Ffestiniog fe 'stɪn i ɒg ‖ -ɑːg —*Welsh* [fe 'sdin jog]
Ffion 'fiː ɒn ‖ -ɑːn —*Welsh* ['fi ɔn]
Ffolkes fəʊks ‖ foʊks
Ffoulkes *(i)* fəʊks ‖ foʊks, *(ii)* fuːks
Ffrangcon 'fræŋk ən
Ffynnongroew, Ffynnongroyw ˌfʌn ən 'grɔɪ uː ˌfɪn-, →-əŋ- —*Welsh* [ˌfə non 'groi u, -'groi-]
-fiable faɪ‿əb ᵊl '· · · —*Although this suffix is usually unstressed in RP and GenAm, in some other varieties it is stressed, and this variant is increasingly heard in RP too:* i'dentifiable *or* iˌdenti'fiable
fiance, fiancé, fiancee, fiancée fi 'ɒnᵗs eɪ -'ɑːnᵗs-, -'ɒ̃s- ‖ ˌfiː ɑːn 'seɪ fi 'ɑːnᵗs eɪ —*Fr* [fjɑ̃ se] — *Preference poll, AmE:* ˌ· ·'· *53%,* ·'· · *47%.* **~s** z
Fianna Fail, Fianna Fáil ˌfiː‿ən ə 'fɔɪᵊl -'fɔːl; ˌfiːn ə'· —*Irish* [ˌfiə nə 'fɑːlʲ]
fiasco fi 'æsk əʊ ‖ -oʊ **~es, ~s** z
fiat 'fiː æt 'faɪ-, -ət ‖ -ɑːt
Fiat *tdmk* 'fiː‿ət -æt ‖ -ɑːt **~s** s
fib fɪb **fibbed** fɪbd **fibbing** 'fɪb ɪŋ **fibs** fɪbz
fibber 'fɪb ə ‖ -ᵊr **~s** z

FIANCE

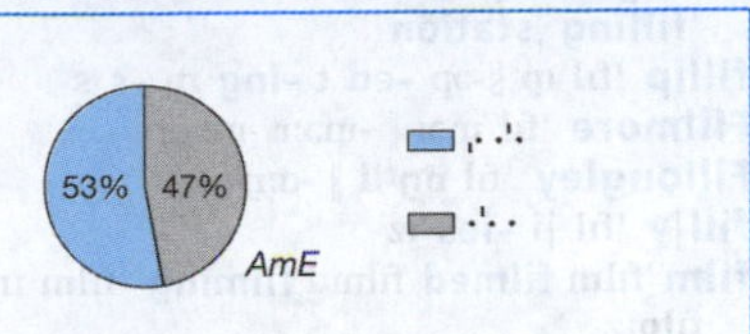

iber 'faɪb ə ‖ -ᵊr **~s** z
ˌfiber 'optics
iberboard 'faɪb ə bɔːd ‖ -ᵊr bɔːrd -bourd
iberfill 'faɪb ə fɪl ‖ -ᵊr-
'iberglas *tdmk,* **fiberglass** 'faɪb ə glɑːs §-glæs ‖ -ᵊr glæs
'ibonacci ˌfɪb ə 'nɑːtʃ i ˌfiːb- —*It* [fi bo 'nat tʃi]
ˌFibo'nacci ˌnumbers
ibre 'faɪb ə ‖ -ᵊr **~s** z
ˌfibre 'optics
ibreboard 'faɪb ə bɔːd ‖ -ᵊr bɔːrd -bourd
ibreglass 'faɪb ə glɑːs §-glæs ‖ -ᵊr glæs
fibril 'faɪb rɪl -rəl **~s** z
fibril|late 'fɪb rɪ |leɪt 'faɪb-, -rə- **~lated** leɪt ɪd -əd ‖ leɪt̬ əd **~lates** leɪts **~lating** leɪt ɪŋ ‖ leɪt̬ ɪŋ
fibrillation ˌfɪb rɪ 'leɪʃ ᵊn ˌfaɪb-, -rə- **~s** z
fibrin 'faɪb rɪn 'fɪb-, §-rən
fibro 'faɪb rəʊ ‖ -roʊ
fibro- *comb. form* ¦faɪb rəʊ ‖ -roʊ — **fibrocement** ˌfaɪb rəʊ sɪ 'ment -sə'. ‖ ˌ·roʊ-
fibroid 'faɪb rɔɪd **~s** z
fibrom|a faɪ 'brəʊm |ə ‖ -'broʊm |ə **~as** əz **~ata** ət ə ‖ ət̬ ə
fibrosis faɪ 'brəʊs ɪs §-əs ‖ -'broʊs-
fibrositis ˌfaɪb rə 'saɪt ɪs §-əs ‖ -'saɪt̬ əs
fibrous 'faɪb rəs
fib|ula 'fɪb |jʊl ə ‖ -|jəl ə **~ulae** ju liː jə- ‖ jə liː **~ulas** jʊl əz ‖ jəl əz
fiche fiːʃ **fiches** 'fiːʃ ɪz -əz
fichu 'fiːʃ uː 'fɪʃ- **~s** z
fickle 'fɪk ᵊl **~ness** nəs nɪs
fiction 'fɪk ʃᵊn **~s** z
fictional 'fɪk ʃᵊn‿əl **~ly** i
fictionalis... —*see* **fictionaliz...**
fictionalization ˌfɪk ʃᵊn‿əl aɪ 'zeɪʃ ᵊn əl ɪ- ‖ əl ə- **~s** z
fictionaliz|e ˌfɪk ʃᵊn‿ə laɪz **~ed** d **~es** ɪz əz **~ing** ɪŋ
fictitious fɪk 'tɪʃ əs **~ly** li **~ness** nəs nɪs
fictive 'fɪkt ɪv **~ness** nəs nɪs
ficus, Ficus 'faɪk əs 'fiːk-
fid fɪd **fids** fɪdz
fiddl|e 'fɪd ᵊl **~ed** d **~es** z **~ing** ‿ɪŋ
fiddleback 'fɪd ᵊl bæk **~s** s
fiddle-de-dee ˌfɪd ᵊl di 'diː
fiddle-faddle 'fɪd ᵊl ˌfæd ᵊl
fiddler, F~ 'fɪd lə 'fɪd ᵊl‿ə ‖ 'fɪd lᵊr 'fɪd ᵊl‿ᵊr **~s** z
'fiddler crab
fiddlestick 'fɪd ᵊl stɪk **~s** s
fiddlewood 'fɪd ᵊl wʊd
fiddling 'fɪd ᵊl‿ɪŋ
fiddl|y 'fɪd ᵊl‿|i **~ier** i‿ə ‖ i‿ᵊr **~iest** i‿ɪst i‿əst
Fidel fɪ 'del (ˌ)fiː-, §fə- —*Sp* [fi 'ðel]
Fidelio fɪ 'deɪl i‿əʊ fə- ‖ oʊ
Fidelis fɪ 'deɪl ɪs fə-, §-əs
fidelit|y fɪ 'del ət |i fə-, faɪ-, -ɪt- ‖ -ət̬ |i **~ies** iz
Fidelma fɪ 'delm ə fə-
fidg|et 'fɪdʒ |ɪt -ət ‖ -|ət **~eted** ɪt ɪd §ət-, -əd ‖ ət̬ əd **~eting** ɪt ɪŋ §ət- ‖ ət̬ ɪŋ **~ets** ɪts §əts ‖ əts
fidget|y 'fɪdʒ ət |i -ɪt- ‖ -ət̬ |i **~iness** i nəs i nɪs
Fidler *(i)* 'fɪd lə ‖ -lᵊr, *(ii)* 'fiːd-
Fido 'faɪd əʊ ‖ -oʊ
fiducial fɪ 'djuːʃ i‿əl fə-, faɪ-, -'djuːs-, →-'dʒuːʃ-, →-'dʒuːs- ‖ fə 'duːʃ ᵊl -'djuːʃ- **~ly** i
fiduciar|y fɪ 'djuːʃ i‿ər |i fə-, faɪ-, -'djuːs-, →-'dʒuːʃ-, →-'dʒuːs-, -'ər |i ‖ fə 'duːʃ i er |i -'djuːʃ-, -'ər |i **~ies** iz
fie faɪ
Fiedler 'fiːd lə ‖ -lᵊr
fief fiːf **fiefs** fiːfs
fiefdom 'fiːf dəm **~s** z
field, Field fiːᵊld **fielded** 'fiːᵊld ɪd -əd **fielding** 'fiːᵊld ɪŋ **fields** fiːᵊldz
'field day; 'field eˌvent; 'field ˌglasses; 'field hand; 'field ˌhockey; ˌfield 'marshal◂, '.ˌ.ˌ.; **'field ˌmushroom; 'field test; 'field ˌtrial; 'field trip**
fieldcraft 'fiːᵊl*d* krɑːft §-kræft ‖ -kræft
Fielden 'fiːᵊld ən
fielder, F~ 'fiːᵊld ə ‖ -ᵊr **~s** z
fieldfare 'fiːᵊld feə ‖ -fer -fær **~s** z
Fielding 'fiːᵊld ɪŋ
field|mouse 'fiːᵊld |maʊs **~mice** maɪs
Fields fiːᵊldz
fields|man 'fiːᵊldz |mən **~men** mən men
field-test 'fiːᵊld test **~ed** ɪd əd **~ing** ɪŋ **~s** s
fieldwork 'fiːᵊld wɜːk ‖ -wɜːk **~er/s** ə/z ‖ ᵊr/z
fiend fiːnd **fiends** fiːndz
fiendish 'fiːnd ɪʃ **~ly** li **~ness** nəs nɪs
Fiennes faɪnz
fierce fɪəs ‖ fɪᵊrs **fiercely** 'fɪəs li ‖ 'fɪrs- **fierceness** 'fɪəsnɪs -nəs ‖ 'fɪrs- **fiercer** 'fɪəs ə ‖ 'fɪrs ᵊr **fiercest** 'fɪəs ɪst -əst ‖ 'fɪrs-
fier|y 'faɪᵊr |i **~ier** i‿ə ‖ i‿ᵊr **~iest** i‿ɪst i‿əst **~ily** əl i ɪ li **~iness** i nəs i nɪs
fiesta, F~ fi 'est ə **~s** z
FIFA 'fiːf ə
fife, Fife faɪf **fifed** faɪft **fifes** faɪfs **fifing** 'faɪf ɪŋ
fife-rail 'faɪf reɪᵊl
Fifi 'fiː fiː
Fifield 'faɪ fiːᵊld
fifteen ˌfɪf 'tiːn ◂ **~s** z
ˌfifteen 'days
fifteenth ˌfɪf 'tiːnθ ◂ **~s** s
fifth fɪfθ fɪftθ, fɪθ **fifths** fɪfθs fɪftθs, fɪfs, fɪθs
ˌFifth A'mendment; ˌfifth 'column
fifth-generation ˌfɪfθ ˌdʒen ə 'reɪʃ ᵊn ◂ ˌfɪftθ-, ˌfɪθ-
fiftieth 'fɪft i‿əθ ɪθ **~s** s
fift|y 'fɪft |i **~ies** iz

F

fifty-fifty ˌfɪft i ˈfɪft i ◂
  ˌfifty-ˌfifty ˈchance
fig fɪɡ **figged** fɪɡd **figging** ˈfɪɡ ɪŋ **figs** fɪɡz
  ˈfig leaf; **ˈfig tree**
Figaro ˈfɪɡ ə rəʊ ‖ -roʊ
Figg fɪɡ
Figgis ˈfɪɡ ɪs §-əs
fight faɪt **fighting** ˈfaɪt ɪŋ ‖ ˈfaɪṭ ɪŋ **fights** faɪts **fought** fɔːt ‖ fɑːt
  ˌfighting ˈchance
fightback ˈfaɪt bæk **~s** s
fighter ˈfaɪt ə ‖ ˈfaɪṭ ᵊr **~s** z
figment ˈfɪɡ mənt **~s** s
Figueroa ˌfɪɡ ə ˈrəʊ ə ‖ -ˈroʊ ə
figurative ˈfɪɡ ər‿ət ɪv ˈ·jʊr- ‖ -jər əṭ ɪv **~ly** li **~ness** nəs nɪs
fig|ure ˈfɪɡ |ə §-|jə ‖ ˈfɪɡ |jᵊr -jʊr *(*) —The pronunciation without* **j**, *standard and usual in BrE, is in AmE generally condemned.* **~ured** əd §jəd ‖ jᵊrd jʊrd **~ures** əz §jəz ‖ jᵊrz jʊrz **~uring** ər ɪŋ §jər- ‖ jər ɪŋ jʊr ɪŋ
  ˌfigured ˈbass; **ˌfigure of ˈeight**; **ˌfigure of ˈspeech**; **ˈfigure ˌskating**
figurehead ˈfɪɡ ə hed ‖ -jᵊr- **~s** z
figurine ˈfɪɡ ə riːn -juᵊ-, ˌ· · ˈ· ‖ ˌfɪɡ jə ˈriːn -ju- **~s** z
figwort ˈfɪɡ wɜːt §-wɔːt ‖ -wɜːt -wɔːrt **~s** s
Fiji ˈfiː dʒiː ˌ·ˈ·
Fijian fi ˈdʒiː‿ən ˌfiː- ‖ ˈfiː dʒi‿ən fɪ ˈdʒiː ən **~s** z
Fila *tdmk* ˈfiːl ɑː -ə
filament ˈfɪl ə mənt **~s** s
filamentous ˌfɪl ə ˈment əs ◂ ‖ -ˈmenṭ-
filari|a fɪ ˈleər i‿|ə fə- ‖ -ˈler- -ˈlær- **~ae** iː
filariasis ˌfɪl ə ˈraɪ‿əs ɪs §-əs; fɪ ˌleər i ˈeɪs-, fə-
filbert ˈfɪlb ət ‖ -ᵊrt **~s** s
filch fɪltʃ **filched** fɪltʃt **filches** ˈfɪltʃ ɪz -əz **filching** ˈfɪltʃ ɪŋ
file faɪᵊl **filed** faɪᵊld **files** faɪᵊlz **filing** ˈfaɪᵊl ɪŋ
  ˈfile ˌserver
filename ˈfaɪᵊl neɪm **~s** z
filet ˈfɪl eɪ -ɪt, §-ət ‖ fɪ ˈleɪ **~s** z
  ˌfilet ˈmignon ˈmiːn jɒn -ˈmɪn- ‖; **fiˌlet miˈgnon** mɪn ˈjɔːn -ˈjɑːn, -ˈjoʊn —*Fr* [fi le mi ɲɔ̃]
Filey ˈfaɪl i
filial ˈfɪl i‿əl **~ly** i **~ness** nəs nɪs
filibeg ˈfɪl ɪ beɡ -ə- **~s** z
filibuster ˈfɪl ɪ bʌst ə ˈ·ə- ‖ -ᵊr **~ed** d **filibustering** ˈfɪl ɪ bʌst ər‿ɪŋ ˈ·ə- **~s** z
filigree ˈfɪl ɪ ɡriː -ə- **~d** d **~ing** ɪŋ **~s** z
filing ˈfaɪᵊl ɪŋ **~s** z
  ˈfiling ˌcabinet; **ˈfiling clerk**
Filioque ˌfiːl i ˈəʊ kwi ˌfɪl-, ˌfaɪl- ‖ -ˈoʊ-
  the ˌFiliˈoque clause
Filipin|o ˌfɪl ɪ ˈpiːn| əʊ ◂ -ə- ‖ -oʊ ◂ **~a** ə ɑː **~as** əz ɑːz **~os** əʊz ‖ oʊz
fill fɪl **filled** fɪld **filling** ˈfɪl ɪŋ **fills** fɪlz
filler ˈfɪl ə ‖ -ᵊr **~s** z
  ˈfiller cap
fill|et ˈfɪl| ɪt §-ət **~eted** ɪt ɪd §ət-, -əd ‖ -əṭ əd **~eting** ɪt ɪŋ §ət- ‖ əṭ ɪŋ **~ets** ɪts §əts
Filleul ˈfɪl i‿əl
fill-in ˈfɪl ɪn **~s** z
filling ˈfɪl ɪŋ **~s** z
  ˈfilling ˌstation
fillip ˈfɪl ɪp §-əp **~ed** t **~ing** ɪŋ **~s** s
Fillmore ˈfɪl mɔː ‖ -mɔːr -moʊr
Fillongley ˈfɪl ɒŋ li ‖ -ɑːŋ-
fill|y ˈfɪl |i **~ies** iz
film fɪlm **filmed** fɪlmd **filming** ˈfɪlm ɪŋ **films** fɪlmz
  ˈfilm ˌpremière ‖ **ˈfilm preˌmière**; **ˈfilm ˌsetting**; **ˈfilm star**; **ˈfilm stock**
filmgoer ˈfɪlm ˌɡəʊ ə ‖ -ˌɡoʊ ᵊr **~s** z
filmic ˈfɪlm ɪk
film-maker ˈfɪlm ˌmeɪk ə ‖ -ᵊr **~s** z
filmstrip ˈfɪlm strɪp **~s** s
film|y ˈfɪlm |i **~ier** i‿ə ‖ i‿ᵊr **~iest** i‿ɪst i‿əst **~ily** ɪ li ə li **~iness** i nəs i nɪs
filo ˈfiːl əʊ ˈfaɪl- ‖ -oʊ —*ModGk* [ˈfi lo]
Filofax *tdmk* ˈfaɪl əʊ fæks ‖ -ə- **~es** ɪz əz
fils *monetary unit, coin* fɪls
fils *'son'* fiːs —*Fr* [fis]
filter ˈfɪlt ə ‖ -ᵊr **~ed** d **filtering** ˈfɪlt‿ər ɪŋ **~s** z
  ˈfilter bed; **ˈfilter ˌpaper**; **ˈfilter tip**, ˌ· · ˈ·
filterable ˈfɪlt‿ər əb ᵊl
filter-tipped ˌfɪlt ə ˈtɪpt ◂ ‖ -ᵊr-
filth fɪlθ
filth|y ˈfɪlθ |i **~ier** i‿ə ‖ i‿ᵊr **~iest** i‿ɪst i‿əst **~ily** ɪ li əl i **~iness** i nəs i nɪs
filtrable ˈfɪltr əb ᵊl
filtrate *n* ˈfɪltr eɪt **~s** s
filtration fɪl ˈtreɪʃ ᵊn **~s** z
fin fɪn —*but as a French word* fæ̃, fæn; *see also phrases with this word* **finned** fɪnd **fins** fɪnz
Fina *tdmk* ˈfiːn ə ˈfaɪn-
finable ˈfaɪn əb ᵊl
finagl|e fɪ ˈneɪɡ ᵊl fə- **~ed** d **~es** z **~ing** ‿ɪŋ
final ˈfaɪn ᵊl **~ly** i **~s** z
finale fɪ ˈnɑːl i fə- ‖ -ˈnæl i -ˈnɑːl i **~s** z
finalis... —*see* **finaliz...**
finalist ˈfaɪn ᵊl ɪst §-əst **~s** s
finality faɪ ˈnæl ət i -ɪt- ‖ -əṭ i
finaliz|e ˈfaɪn ə laɪz -ᵊl aɪz **~ed** d **~es** ɪz əz **~ing** ɪŋ
finally ˈfaɪn əl i

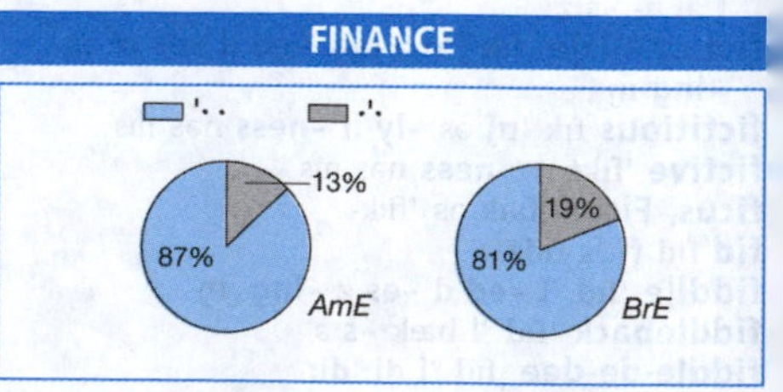

financ|e *n* ˈfaɪn æn^t^s faɪ ˈnæn^t^s, fɪ-, fə- —*Preference polls, AmE:* ˈ· · *87%,* ·ˈ· *13%; BrE:* ˈ· · *81%,* ·ˈ· *19%.* **~es** ɪz əz
financ|e *v* faɪ ˈnæn^t^s fɪ-, fə- ‖ fə- faɪ-; ˈfaɪn æn^t^s **~ed** t **~es** ɪz əz **~ing** ɪŋ

FINANCIAL

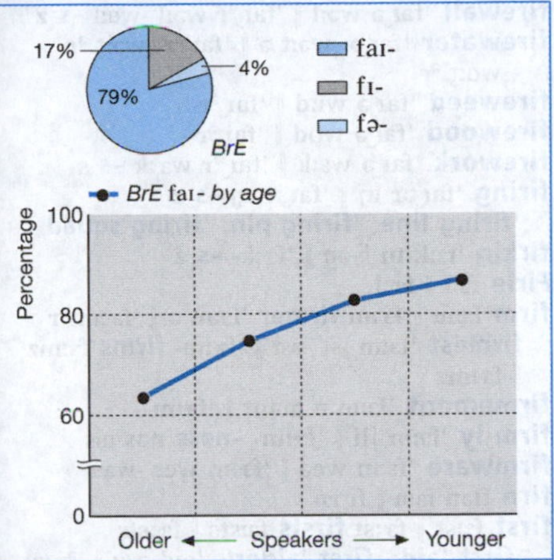

financial faɪ ˈnænᵗʃ əl fɪ-, fə- ‖ fə- faɪ- — *Preference poll, BrE:* faɪ- *79%,* fɪ- *17%,* fə- *4%.* **~ly** i **fiˌnancial ˈyear**
financier faɪ ˈnænᵗs i‿ə fɪ-, fə- ‖ ˌfɪn ən ˈsɪᵊr ˌfaɪn- *(*)* **~s** z
Finbar ˈfɪn bɑː →ˈfɪm- ‖ -bɑːr
Finborough ˈfɪn bər‿ə →ˈfɪm-, §-ˌbʌr ə ‖ -ˌbɜː oʊ
finch, Finch fɪntʃ **finches** ˈfɪntʃ ɪz -əz
Finchale ˈfɪŋk əl
Finchampstead ˈfɪntʃ əm sted -əmp-, -stɪd
Finchingfield ˈfɪntʃ ɪŋ fiːᵊld
Finchley ˈfɪntʃ li
find faɪnd **finding** ˈfaɪnd ɪŋ **finds** faɪndz **found** faʊnd
finder ˈfaɪnd ə ‖ -ᵊr **~s** z
Findern ˈfɪnd ən ‖ -ᵊrn
fin de siècle ˌfæ̃ də ˈsjek lə ˌfæn-, -si ˈeɪk əl —*Fr* [fæ̃d sjɛkl]
Findhorn ˈfɪnd hɔːn ‖ -hɔːrn
finding ˈfaɪnd ɪŋ **~s** z
Findlater ˈfɪn lət ə ˈfɪnd- ‖ -lət̬ ᵊr
Findlay ˈfɪn li ˈfɪnd-
Findon ˈfɪnd ən
Findus *tdmk* ˈfɪnd əs
fine *ordinary senses* faɪn **fined** faɪnd **finer** ˈfaɪn ə ‖ -ᵊr **fines** faɪnz **finest** ˈfaɪn ɪst -əst **fining** ˈfaɪn ɪŋ **ˌfine ˈart; ˌfine ˈprint**
fine *Irish word* ˈfɪn ə —*Irish* [ˈfʲi nʲə] **ˌFine ˈGael**
fine *French word, 'liqueur'* fiːn —*Fr* [fin]
fineable ˈfaɪn əb əl
fine-drawn ˌfaɪn ˈdrɔːn ◂ ‖ -ˈdrɑːn ◂ **ˌfine-drawn ˈfeatures**
finely ˈfaɪn li
finer|y ˈfaɪn ər |i **~ies** iz
fines herbes ˌfiːnz ˈeəb ˌfiːn-, -ˈɜːb ‖ -ˈeᵊrb —*Fr* [fin zɛʁb]
finespun ˌfaɪn ˈspʌn ◂ ˈ· ·
finess|e fɪ ˈnes fə- **~ed** t **~es** ɪz əz **~ing** ɪŋ
fine-tooth ˌfaɪn ˈtuːθ ◂ §-ˈtʊθ, ˈ· · **~ed** t **ˌfine-ˈtooth comb, ˌfine-tooth ˈcomb**
fine-tun|e ˌfaɪn ˈtjuːn →-ˈtʃuːn ‖ -ˈtuːn -ˈtjuːn **~ed** d **~es** z **~ing** ɪŋ
Fingal ˈfɪŋ gəl
finger ˈfɪŋ gə ‖ -gᵊr **fingered** ˈfɪŋ gəd ‖ -gᵊrd **fingering** ˈfɪŋ gər‿ɪŋ **fingers** ˈfɪŋ gəz ‖ gᵊrz **ˈfinger bowl**
fingerboard ˈfɪŋ gə bɔːd ‖ -gᵊr bɔːrd -boʊrd **~s** z
-fingered ˈfɪŋ gəd ‖ -gᵊrd
fingering ˈfɪŋ gər‿ɪŋ **~s** z
fingermark ˈfɪŋ gə mɑːk ‖ -gᵊr mɑːrk **~s** s
fingernail ˈfɪŋ gə neɪᵊl ‖ -gᵊr- **~s** z
finger-|paint ˈfɪŋ gə |peɪnt ‖ -gᵊr- **~painting** ˌpeɪnt ɪŋ ‖ ˌpeɪnt̬ ɪŋ **~paints** peɪnts
fingerplate ˈfɪŋ gə pleɪt ‖ -gᵊr- **~s** s
finger-pointing ˈfɪŋ gə ˌpɔɪnt ɪŋ ‖ -gᵊr ˌpɔɪnt̬ ɪŋ
fingerpost ˈfɪŋ gə pəʊst ‖ -gᵊr poʊst **~s** s
finger|print ˈfɪŋ gə |prɪnt ‖ -gᵊr- **~printed** prɪnt ɪd -əd ‖ prɪnt̬ əd **~printing** prɪnt ɪŋ ‖ prɪnt̬ ɪŋ **~prints** prɪnts
fingerspelling ˈfɪŋ gə ˌspel ɪŋ ‖ -gᵊr-
fingerstall ˈfɪŋ gə stɔːl ‖ -gᵊr- -stɑːl **~s** z
fingertip ˈfɪŋ gə tɪp ‖ -gᵊr- **~s** s
Fingest ˈfɪndʒ ɪst §-əst
finial ˈfaɪn i‿əl ˈfɪn- **~s** z
finical ˈfɪn ɪk əl **~ly** i **~ness** nəs nɪs
finicking ˈfɪn ɪk ɪŋ
finickity fɪ ˈnɪk ət i fə-, -ɪt- ‖ -ət̬ i
finicky ˈfɪn ɪk i
fining ˈfaɪn ɪŋ **~s** z
finis ˈfɪn ɪs ˈfiːn-, ˈfaɪn-, §-əs
finish ˈfɪn ɪʃ **finished** ˈfɪn ɪʃt **finishes** ˈfɪn ɪʃ ɪz -əz **finishing** ˈfɪn ɪʃ ɪŋ **ˈfinishing school; ˌfinishing ˈtouch**
finisher ˈfɪn ɪʃ ə ‖ -ᵊr **~s** z
Finisterre ˌfɪn ɪ ˈsteə ◂ -ə- ‖ -ˈsteᵊr
finite ˈfaɪn aɪt **~ly** li **~ness** nəs nɪs
finito fɪ ˈniːt əʊ fə- ‖ -oʊ —*It* [fi ˈniː to]
fink, Fink, Finke fɪŋk **finked** fɪŋkt **finking** ˈfɪŋk ɪŋ **finks** fɪŋks
Finkelstein ˈfɪŋk əl staɪn
Finland ˈfɪn lənd
Finlandia fɪn ˈlænd i‿ə
Finlandi|sation, ~zation ˌfɪn lənd aɪ ˈzeɪʃ ən -ɪˈ·- ‖ -ə ˈzeɪʃ-
Finlay ˈfɪn li -leɪ
Finlayson ˈfɪn lɪs ən
Finn fɪn **Finns** fɪnz
Finnair *tdmk* ˈfɪn eə ˌ·ˈ· ‖ -er -ær
finnan ˈfɪn ən **ˌfinnan ˈhaddie** ˈhæd i
Finnegan ˈfɪn ɪg ən -əg- **~s, ~'s** z **ˌFinnegans ˈWake**
Finney ˈfɪn i
Finnic ˈfɪn ɪk
Finnish ˈfɪn ɪʃ
Finno-Ugrian ˌfɪn əʊ ˈjuːg ri‿ən ◂ -ˈuːg- ‖ ˌoʊ-
Finno-Ugric ˌfɪn əʊ ˈjuːg rɪk ◂ -ˈuːg- ‖ -oʊ-
Finnuala fɪˈnʊələ ‖ ˌfiːəˈnuːələ
fino ˈfiːn əʊ ‖ -oʊ **~s** z —*Sp* [ˈfi no]

finocchio, finochio fɪ ˈnɒk i əʊ fə- ‖ -ˈnoʊk i oʊ
Finola fɪ ˈnəʊl ə fə- ‖ -ˈnoʊl ə
Finsberg ˈfɪnz bɜːg ‖ -bɝːg
Finsbury ˈfɪnz bər‿i §-ˌber i ‖ -ˌber i
ˌ**Finsbury ˈPark**
Finucane fɪ ˈnuːk ən fə-
Finzi ˈfɪnz i
Fiona fiə ˈnəʊ ə ‖ fiː ə ˈnuː əl ə
Fionnuala fiə ˈnuəl ə ‖ ˈfiːə ˈnu əl ə
fiord fi ˈɔːd ˈfiː ɔːd, fjɔːd ‖ fi ˈɔːrd fjɔːrd **~s** z
fipple ˈfɪp əl **~s** z
fir fɜː ‖ fɝː *(= fur)* **firs** fɜːz ‖ fɝːz
Firbank ˈfɜː bæŋk ‖ ˈfɝː-
fire ˈfaɪ‿ə ‖ ˈfaɪ‿ər **~d** d **firing** ˈfaɪ‿ər ɪŋ ‖ ˈfaɪ‿ər ɪŋ **~s** z
ˈ**fire aˌlarm**; ˈ**fire briˌgade**; ˈ**fire deˌpartment**; ˈ**fire drill**; ˈ**fire ˌengine**; ˈ**fire eˌscape**; ˈ**fire exˌtinguisher**; ˈ**fire ˌfighter**; ˈ**fire ˌfighting**; ˈ**fire hose**; ˈ**fire ˌhydrant**; ˈ**fire inˌsurance**; ˈ**fire ˌirons**; ˈ**fire screen**; ˈ**fire ship**; ˈ**fire ˌstation**; ˈ**fire ˌwarden**
firearm ˈfaɪ‿ər ɑːm ‖ ˈfaɪ‿ər ɑːrm **~s** z
fireball ˈfaɪ‿ə bɔːl ‖ ˈfaɪ‿ər- -bɑːl **~s** z
fireboat ˈfaɪ‿ə bəʊt ‖ ˈfaɪ‿ər boʊt **~s** s
firebomb ˈfaɪ‿ə bɒm ‖ ˈfaɪ‿ər bɑːm **~ed** d **~ing** ɪŋ **~s** z
firebox ˈfaɪ‿ə bɒks ‖ ˈfaɪ‿ər bɑːks **~es** ɪz əz
firebrand ˈfaɪ‿ə brænd ‖ ˈfaɪ‿ər- **~s** z
firebrat ˈfaɪ‿ə bræt ‖ ˈfaɪ‿ər- **~s** s
firebreak ˈfaɪ‿ə breɪk ‖ ˈfaɪ‿ər- **~s** s
firebrick ˈfaɪ‿ə brɪk ‖ ˈfaɪ‿ər- **~s** s
firebug ˈfaɪ‿ə bʌg ‖ ˈfaɪ‿ər- **~s** z
fireclay ˈfaɪ‿ə kleɪ ‖ ˈfaɪ‿ər-
firecracker ˈfaɪ‿ə ˌkræk ə ‖ ˈfaɪ‿ər ˌkræk ər **~s** z
firecrest ˈfaɪ‿ə krest ‖ ˈfaɪ‿ər- **~s** s
firedamp ˈfaɪ‿ə dæmp ‖ ˈfaɪ‿ər-
firedog ˈfaɪ‿ə dɒg ‖ ˈfaɪ‿ər dɔːg -dɑːg **~s** z
fire-eat|er ˈfaɪ‿ər ˌiːt| ə ‖ ˈfaɪ‿ər ˌiːt̬| ər **~ing** ɪŋ **~s** z
firefight ˈfaɪ‿ə faɪt ‖ ˈfaɪ‿ər- **~s** s
fire|fly ˈfaɪ‿ə |flaɪ ‖ ˈfaɪ‿ər- **~flies** flaɪz
firefox, F~ *tdmk* ˈfaɪ‿ə fɒks ‖ ˈfaɪ‿ər fɑːks
fireguard ˈfaɪ‿ə gɑːd ‖ ˈfaɪ‿ər gɑːrd **~s** z
fire|house ˈfaɪ‿ə |haʊs ‖ ˈfaɪ‿ər- **~houses** haʊz ɪz -əz
firelight ˈfaɪ‿ə laɪt ‖ ˈfaɪ‿ər-
firelighter ˈfaɪ‿ə ˌlaɪt ə ‖ ˈfaɪ‿ər ˌlaɪt̬ ər **~s** z
fire|man ˈfaɪ‿ə |mən ‖ ˈfaɪ‿ər- **~man's** mənz **~men** mən men
fireplac|e ˈfaɪ‿ə pleɪs ‖ ˈfaɪ‿ər- **~es** ɪz əz
fireplug ˈfaɪ‿ə plʌg ‖ ˈfaɪ‿ər- **~s** z
firepower ˈfaɪ‿ə ˌpaʊ‿ə ‖ ˈfaɪ‿ər ˌpaʊ‿ər
fireproof ˈfaɪ‿ə pruːf §-prʊf ‖ ˈfaɪ‿ər-
fire-rais|er ˈfaɪ‿ə ˌreɪz |ə ‖ ˈfaɪ‿ər ˌreɪz |ər **~ers** əz ‖ ərz **~ing** ɪŋ
fireside ˈfaɪ‿ə saɪd ‖ ˈfaɪ‿ər- **~s** z
firestone, F~ ˈfaɪ‿ə stəʊn ‖ ˈfaɪ‿ər stoʊn **~s** z
firestorm ˈfaɪ‿ə stɔːm ‖ ˈfaɪ‿ər stɔːrm **~s** z
firethorn ˈfaɪ‿ə θɔːn ‖ ˈfaɪ‿ər θɔːrn **~s** z
firetrap ˈfaɪ‿ə træp ‖ ˈfaɪ‿ər- **~s** s
firewalk|er ˈfaɪ‿ə ˌwɔːk |ə ‖ ˈfaɪ‿ər ˌwɔːk |ər -ˌwɑːk- **~ers** əz ‖ ərz **~ing** ɪŋ
firewall ˈfaɪ‿ə wɔːl ‖ ˈfaɪ‿ər wɔːl -wɑːl **~s** z
firewater ˈfaɪ‿ə ˌwɔːt ə ‖ ˈfaɪ‿ər ˌwɔːt̬ ər -ˌwɑːt̬ ər
fireweed ˈfaɪ‿ə wiːd ‖ ˈfaɪ‿ər-
firewood ˈfaɪ‿ə wʊd ‖ ˈfaɪ‿ər-
firework ˈfaɪ‿ə wɜːk ‖ ˈfaɪ‿ər wɝːk **~s** s
firing ˈfaɪ‿ər ɪŋ ‖ ˈfaɪ‿ər ɪŋ **~s** z
ˈ**firing line**; ˈ**firing pin**; ˈ**firing squad**
firkin ˈfɜːk ɪn §-ən ‖ ˈfɝːk- **~s** z
Firle fɜːl ‖ fɝːl
firm fɜːm ‖ fɝːm **firmer** ˈfɜːm ə ‖ ˈfɝːm ər **firmest** ˈfɜːm ɪst -əst ‖ ˈfɝːm- **firms** fɜːmz ‖ fɝːmz
firmament ˈfɜːm ə mənt ‖ ˈfɝːm-
firm|ly ˈfɜːm |li ‖ ˈfɝːm- **~ness** nəs nɪs
firmware ˈfɜːm weə ‖ ˈfɝːm wer -wær
firn fɪən fɜːn ‖ fɪərn
first fɜːst ‖ fɝːst **firsts** fɜːsts ‖ fɝːsts
ˌ**first ˈaid**; ˌ**first ˈaider/s** ˈeɪd ə/z ‖ -ər/z; ˌ**first ˈbase**; ˌ**first ˈclass**◂; ˌ**first ˈcousin**; ˌ**first-day ˈcover**; ˌ**first ˈfloor**; ˌ**first ˈlady**; ˌ**first lieuˈtenant**◂; ˌ**first ˈmate**; ˈ**first name**; ˌ**first ˈnight**; ˌ**first ofˈfender**; ˌ**first ˌpast the ˈpost**; ˌ**first ˈperson**◂; ˌ**first reˈfusal**; ˌ**first ˈstrike**
firstborn ˈfɜːst bɔːn ‖ ˈfɝːst bɔːrn **~s** z
first-class ˌfɜːst ˈklɑːs ◂ §-ˈklæs ‖ ˌfɝːst ˈklæs ◂
ˌ**first-class hoˈtel**
first-degree ˌfɜːst dɪ ˈgriː ◂ -də- ‖ ˌfɝːst-
ˌ**first-deˌgree ˈmurder**
first-ever ˌfɜːst ˈev ə ◂ ‖ ˌfɝːst ˈev ər ◂
firstfruits ˈfɜːst fruːts ‖ ˈfɝːst-
firsthand ˌfɜːst ˈhænd ◂ ‖ ˌfɝːst-
firstly ˈfɜːst li ‖ ˈfɝːst-
first-nighter ˌfɜːst ˈnaɪt ə ‖ ˌfɝːst ˈnaɪt̬ ər **~s** z
first-person ˌfɜːst ˈpɜːsən ◂ ‖ ˌfɝːst ˈpɝːs n◂
first-rate ˌfɜːst ˈreɪt ◂ ‖ ˌfɝːst-
first-string ˌfɜːst ˈstrɪŋ ◂ ‖ ˌfɝːst-
first-time ˌfɜːst ˈtaɪm ◂ ‖ ˌfɝːst-
ˌ**first-time ˈbuyer**
firth, Firth fɜːθ ‖ fɝːθ **firths** fɜːθs ‖ fɝːθs
firtree ˈfɜː triː ‖ ˈfɝː- **~s** z
fiscal ˈfɪsk əl **~ly** i
ˌ**fiscal ˈyear**
Fischer ˈfɪʃ ə ‖ -ər
fish, Fish fɪʃ **fished** fɪʃt **fishing** ˈfɪʃ ɪŋ **fishes** ˈfɪʃ ɪz -əz
ˈ**fish farm**; ˌ**fish ˈfinger**; ˈ**fishing rod**; ˈ**fish knife**; ˌ**fish ˈnˈ ˈchips**; ˈ**fish slice**; ˈ**fish stick**
Fishbourne ˈfɪʃ bɔːn ‖ -bɔːrn -boʊrn
fishbowl ˈfɪʃ bəʊl →-bɒʊl ‖ -boʊl **~s** z
fishcake ˈfɪʃ keɪk **~s** s
fisher, F~ ˈfɪʃ ə ‖ -ər **~s** z
fisher|man ˈfɪʃ ə |mən ‖ -ər- **~man's** mənz **~men** mən men
fisher|y ˈfɪʃ ər |i **~ies** iz
fish-eye ˈfɪʃ aɪ
ˌ**fish-eye ˈlens**
Fishguard ˈfɪʃ gɑːd ‖ -gɑːrd
fishhook ˈfɪʃ hʊk §-huːk **~s** s

F

ishi... *—see* **fish, fishy**
ishley 'fɪʃ li
ishlock 'fɪʃ lɒk ‖ -lɑːk
ishmonger 'fɪʃ ˌmʌŋ gə ‖ -gᵊr -ˌmɑːŋ- **~s** z
ishnet 'fɪʃ net **~s** s
ishplate 'fɪʃ pleɪt **~s** s
ishpond 'fɪʃ pɒnd ‖ -pɑːnd **~s, F~s** z
ishtail 'fɪʃ teɪᵊl **~ed** d **~ing** ɪŋ **~s** z
ishwick 'fɪʃ wɪk
ish|wife 'fɪʃ |waɪf **~wives** waɪvz
ish|y 'fɪʃ |i **~ier** i‿ə ‖ i‿ᵊr **~iest** i‿ɪst i‿əst **~ily** ɪ li əl i **~iness** i nəs i nɪs
isk, Fiske fɪsk
ison 'faɪs ᵊn
issile 'fɪs aɪᵊl ‖ -ᵊl *(*)*
ission 'fɪʃ ᵊn **~s** z
fissionable 'fɪʃ ᵊn‿əb ᵊl
fissiparous fɪ 'sɪp ər əs fə-
fissure 'fɪʃ ə -ʊə ‖ -ᵊr **~d** d **fissuring** 'fɪʃ ər ɪŋ -ʊər- **~s** z
fist fɪst **fisted** 'fɪst ɪd -əd **fisting** 'fɪst ɪŋ **fists** fɪsts
-fisted 'fɪst ɪd ◂ -əd
fistful 'fɪst fʊl **~s** z
fisticuffs 'fɪst i kʌfs
fistul|a 'fɪst jʊl |ə ‖ 'fɪs tʃəl |ə →'fɪʃ- **~ae** iː **~ar** ə ‖ ᵊr **~as** əz **~ous** əs
fit fɪt **fits** fɪts **fitted** 'fɪt ɪd -əd **fitter** 'fɪt ə ‖ 'fɪţ ᵊr **fittest** 'fɪt ɪst -əst ‖ 'fɪţ əst **fitting** 'fɪt ɪŋ ‖ 'fɪţ ɪŋ
fitch, Fitch fɪtʃ **fitches** 'fɪtʃ ɪz -əz
fitchew, F~ 'fɪtʃ uː **~s** z
fitful 'fɪt fᵊl -fʊl **~ly** i **~ness** nəs nɪs
fitment 'fɪt mənt **~s** s
fitness 'fɪt nəs -nɪs
fitter, F~ 'fɪt ə ‖ 'fɪţ ᵊr **~s** z
fitting 'fɪt ɪŋ ‖ 'fɪţ ɪŋ **~ly** li **~ness** nəs nɪs
Fitz fɪts
Fitzgerald, FitzGerald ₍ˌ₎fɪts 'dʒer əld
Fitzgibbon ₍ˌ₎fɪts 'gɪb ən
Fitzhardinge ₍ˌ₎fɪts 'hɑːd ɪŋ ‖ -'hɑːrd-
Fitzherbert ₍ˌ₎fɪts 'hɜːb ət ‖ -'hɜːb ᵊrt
Fitzjames ₍ˌ₎fɪts 'dʒeɪmz
Fitzjohn ₍ˌ₎fɪts 'dʒɒn ‖ -'dʒɑːn
Fitzpatrick ₍ˌ₎fɪts 'pætr ɪk
Fitzrovia ₍ˌ₎fɪts 'rəʊv i‿ə ‖ -'roʊv-
Fitzroy ₍ˌ₎fɪts 'rɔɪ
Fitzsimmons ₍ˌ₎fɪts 'sɪm ənz
Fitzwalter ₍ˌ₎fɪts 'wɔːlt ə ‖ -'wɔːlt ᵊr -'wɑːlt ᵊr
Fitzwilliam ₍ˌ₎fɪts 'wɪl jəm
five faɪv *—but for clarity in communications code,* fife faɪf **fives** faɪvz
ˌfive-ˌfinger 'exercise; **ˌfive o''clock◂**, **ˌfive oˌclock 'shadow**; **ˌFive-'Year Plan**
five-and-dime ˌfaɪv ᵊnd 'daɪm ◂
five-and-ten ˌfaɪv ən*d* 'ten ◂
five-a-side ˌfaɪv ə 'saɪd ◂
five-barred ˌfaɪv 'bɑːd ◂ ‖ -'bɑːrd ◂
five-eighth ˌfaɪv 'eɪtθ ◂ §-'eɪθ **~s** s
fivefold 'faɪv fəʊld →-fɒʊld ‖ -foʊld
fivepenc|e 'faɪf pənᵗs 'faɪv- **~es** ɪz əz
fivepenn|y 'faɪf pən |i 'faɪv- **~ies** iz
fiver 'faɪv ə ‖ -ᵊr **~s** z
five-spot 'faɪv spɒt ‖ -spɑːt **~s** s
five-star ˌfaɪv 'stɑː ◂ ‖ -'stɑːr ◂
ˌfive-star ho'tel
fix fɪks **fixed** fɪkst **fixes** 'fɪks ɪz -əz **fixing/s** 'fɪks ɪŋ/z
fixable 'fɪks əb ᵊl
fix|ate fɪk 's|eɪt 'fɪks |eɪt ‖ 'fɪks |eɪt **~ated** eɪt ɪd -əd ‖ eɪţ əd **~ates** eɪts **~ating** eɪt ɪŋ ‖ eɪţ ɪŋ
fixation fɪk 'seɪʃ ᵊn **~s** z
fixative 'fɪks ət ɪv ‖ -əţ ɪv **~s** z
fixedly 'fɪks ɪd li -əd-
fixed-rate ˌfɪks*t* 'reɪt ◂
fixer 'fɪks ə ‖ -ᵊr **~s** z
fixit|y 'fɪks ət |i -ɪt- ‖ -əţ |i **~ies** iz
fixture 'fɪks tʃə ‖ -tʃᵊr **~s** z
fizgig 'fɪz gɪg **~s** z
fizz fɪz **fizzed** fɪzd **fizzes** 'fɪz ɪz -əz **fizzing** 'fɪz ɪŋ
fizzl|e 'fɪz ᵊl **~ed** d **~es** z **~ing** ‿ɪŋ
fizz|y 'fɪz |i **~ier** i‿ə ‖ i‿ᵊr **~iest** i‿ɪst i‿əst
fjord fi 'ɔːd 'fiː ɔːd, fjɔːd ‖ fi 'ɔːrd fjɔːrd **~s** z
flab flæb
flabbergast 'flæb ə gɑːst §-gæst ‖ -ᵊr gæst **~ed** ɪd əd **~ing** ɪŋ **~s** s
flabb|y 'flæb |i **~ier** i‿ə ‖ i‿ᵊr **~iest** i‿ɪst i‿əst **~ily** ɪ li əl i **~iness** i nəs i nɪs
flaccid 'flæks ɪd 'flæs-, §-əd **~ly** li **~ness** nəs nɪs
flaccidity flæk 'sɪd ət i flæ-, flə-, -ɪt- ‖ -əţ i
Flack, flack flæk
flag flæg **flagged** flægd **flagging** 'flæg ɪŋ **flags** flægz
'flag day
flagellant 'flædʒ əl ənt -ɪl-; flə 'dʒel- **~s** s
flagellate *n, adj* 'flædʒ əl ət -ɪl-, -ɪt; -ə leɪt **~s** s
flagel|late *v* 'flædʒ ə |leɪt -ɪ- **~lated** leɪt ɪd -əd ‖ leɪţ əd **~lates** leɪts **~lating** leɪt ɪŋ ‖ leɪţ ɪŋ
flagellation ˌflædʒ ə 'leɪʃ ᵊn -ɪ- **~s** z
flagell|um flə 'dʒel| əm flæ- **~a** ə **~ar** ə ‖ ᵊr **~ums** əmz
flageolet ˌflædʒ ə 'let -'leɪ **~s** s
Flagg flæg
flagon 'flæg ən **~s** z
flagpole 'flæg pəʊl →-pɒʊl ‖ -poʊl **~s** z
flagrancy 'fleɪg rənᵗs i
flagrant 'fleɪg rənt **~ly** li
flagrante flə 'grænt i flæ-
flaˌgrante de'licto dɪ 'lɪkt əʊ də-, deɪ- ‖ -oʊ
flagship 'flæg ʃɪp **~s** s
flagstaff, F~ 'flæg stɑːf §-stæf ‖ -stæf **~s** s
flagstone 'flæg stəʊn ‖ -stoʊn **~s** z
flag-waving 'flæg ˌweɪv ɪŋ
Flaherty 'flɑː hət i 'flæ-, -ət-; 'fleət i ‖ 'flæ ᵊrţ i 'flɑːrţ i
flail fleɪᵊl **flailed** fleɪᵊld **flailing** 'fleɪᵊl ɪŋ **flails** fleɪᵊlz
flair fleə ‖ fleᵊr flæᵊr **flairs** fleəz ‖ fleᵊrz flæᵊrz
flak flæk
flake fleɪk **flaked** fleɪkt **flakes** fleɪks **flaking** 'fleɪk ɪŋ

flak|y ˈfleɪk |i **~ier** i‿ə ‖ i‿ᵊr **~iest** i‿ɪst i‿əst **~ily** ɪ li əl i **~iness** i nəs i nɪs

flam flæm **flams** flæmz

flambe, flambé ˈflɒm beɪ ˈflɑːm-, ˈflæm-, -bi ‖ flɑːm ˈbeɪ —*Fr* [flɑ̃ be] **~ed** d

flambeau ˈflæm bəʊ ‖ -boʊ **~x** z

flambee, flambée ˈflɒm beɪ ˈflɑːm-, ˈflæm-, -bi ‖ flɑːm ˈbeɪ —*Fr* [flɑ̃ be] **~d** d

Flamborough ˈflæm bər‿ə ‖ -ˌbɜː oʊ **ˌFlamborough ˈHead**

flamboyance flæm ˈbɔɪ ənᵗs

flamboyant flæm ˈbɔɪ ənt **~ly** li **~s** s

flame fleɪm **flamed** fleɪmd **flames** fleɪmz **flaming/ly** ˈfleɪm ɪŋ /li

flamenco flə ˈmeŋ kəʊ ‖ -koʊ **~s** z

flameproof ˈfleɪm pruːf §-prʊf **~ed** t **~ing** ɪŋ **~s** s

flame-thrower ˈfleɪm ˌθrəʊ ə ‖ -ˌθroʊ ᵊr **~s** z

flaming ˈfleɪm ɪŋ

flamingo flə ˈmɪŋ gəʊ flæ- ‖ -goʊ **~es, ~s** z

Flaminian flə ˈmɪn i‿ən flæ-

flammability ˌflæm ə ˈbɪl ət i -ɪt i ‖ -əţ i

flammable ˈflæm əb ᵊl

Flamsteed ˈflæm stiːd

flan flæn ‖ flɑːn **flans** flænz ‖ flɑːnz

Flanagan ˈflæn əg ən

Flanders ˈflɑːnd əz §ˈflænd- ‖ ˈflænd ᵊrz

flange flændʒ **flanged** flændʒd **flanges** ˈflændʒ ɪz -əz **flanging** ˈflændʒ ɪŋ

flank flæŋk **flanked** flæŋkt **flanking** ˈflæŋk ɪŋ **flanks** flæŋks

flanker ˈflæŋk ə ‖ -ᵊr **~s** z

flannel ˈflæn ᵊl **~ed, ~led** d **~ing, ~ling** ɪŋ **~s** z

flannelboard ˈflæn ᵊl bɔːd ‖ -bɔːrd -boʊrd **~s** z

flannelette ˌflæn ᵊl ˈet -ə ˈlet

flannelgraph ˈflæn ᵊl grɑːf -græf ‖ -græf **~s** s

flannelly ˈflæn ᵊl i

flap flæp **flapped** flæpt **flapping** ˈflæp ɪŋ **flaps** flæps

flapdoodle ˈflæp ˌduːd ᵊl

flapjack ˈflæp dʒæk **~s** s

flapper ˈflæp ə ‖ -ᵊr **~s** z

flare fleə ‖ fleᵊr flæᵊr **flared** fleəd ‖ fleᵊrd flæᵊrd **flares** fleəz ‖ fleᵊrz flæᵊrz **flaring** ˈfleər ɪŋ ‖ ˈfler ɪŋ ˈflær- **ˈflare path**

flare-up ˈfleər ʌp ‖ ˈfler- ˈflær- **~s** s

flash, Flash flæʃ **flashed** flæʃt **flashes** ˈflæʃ ɪz -əz **flashing** ˈflæʃ ɪŋ **ˌflash ˈflood; ˈflash point**

flashback ˈflæʃ bæk **~s** s

flashbulb ˈflæʃ bʌlb **~s** z

flashcard ˈflæʃ kɑːd ‖ -kɑːrd **~s** z

flashcube ˈflæʃ kjuːb **~s** z

flasher ˈflæʃ ə ‖ -ᵊr **~s** z

flashgun ˈflæʃ gʌn **~s** z

flashi... —*see* **flashy**

flashlight ˈflæʃ laɪt **~s** s

Flashman ˈflæʃ mən

flashmob ˈflæʃ mɒb ‖ -mɑːb **~s** z

flashover ˈflæʃ ˌəʊv ə ‖ -ˌoʊv ᵊr **~s** z

flash|y ˈflæʃ |i **~ier** i‿ə ‖ i‿ᵊr **~iest** i‿ɪst i‿əst **~ily** ɪ li əl i **~iness** i nəs i nɪs

flask, Flask flɑːsk §flæsk ‖ flæsk **flasks** flɑːsks §flæsks ‖ flæsks

flat flæt **flats** flæts **flatted** ˈflæt ɪd -əd ‖ ˈflæţ əd **flatter** ˈflæt ə ‖ ˈflæţ ᵊr **flattest** ˈflæt ɪst -əst ‖ ˈflæţ əst **flatting** ˈflæt ɪŋ ‖ ˈflæţ ɪŋ **ˌflat ˈfeet; ˈflat ˌracing; ˌflat ˈspin**

flatbed ˈflæt bed **~s** z

flatboat ˈflæt bəʊt ‖ -boʊt **~s** s

flat-bottomed ˌflæt ˈbɒt əmd ◂ ‖ -ˈbɑːţ əmd ◂

flatbread ˈflæt bred

Flatbush ˈflæt bʊʃ

flatcar ˈflæt kɑː ‖ -kɑːr **~s** z

flat-chested ˌflæt ˈtʃest ɪd ◂ -əd

flatfeet —*see* **flatfoot**

flatfish ˈflæt fɪʃ **~es** ɪz əz

flat|foot ˈflæt |fʊt **~feet** fiːt **~foots** fʊts

flat-footed ˌflæt ˈfʊt ɪd ◂ -əd ‖ -ˈfʊţ əd ◂ **~ly** li **~ness** nəs nɪs

flathead, F~ ˈflæt hed **~s** z

flatiron ˈflæt ˌaɪ‿ən ‖ ˈflæţ ˌaɪ‿ᵊrn **~s** z

Flatland ˈflæt lænd

flatlet ˈflæt lət -lɪt **~s** s

Flatley ˈflæt li

flatlin|e ˈflæt laɪn **~ing** ɪŋ

flatly ˈflæt li

flatmate ˈflæt meɪt **~s** s

flatness ˈflæt nəs -nɪs

flat-pack ˈflæt pæk **~s** s

flatshare ˈflæt ʃeə ‖ -ʃer -ʃær **~s** z

flatten ˈflæt ᵊn **~ed** d **~ing** ‿ɪŋ **~s** z

flatter ˈflæt ə ‖ ˈflæţ ᵊr **~ed** d **flattering/ly** ˈflæt‿ər ɪŋ /li ‖ ˈflæţ- **~s** z

flatterer ˈflæt ər ə ‖ ˈflæţ ər ər **~s** z

flatter|y ˈflæt ər |i ‖ ˈflæţ- **~ies** iz

flattie ˈflæt i ‖ ˈflæţ i **~s** z

flattish ˈflæt ɪʃ ‖ ˈflæţ ɪʃ

flattop ˈflæt tɒp ‖ -tɑːp **~s** s

flatulenc|e ˈflæt jʊl ənᵗs ˈflætʃ ʊl- ‖ ˈflætʃ əl- **~y** i

flatulent ˈflæt jʊl ənt ˈflætʃ ʊl- ‖ ˈflætʃ əl- **~ly** li

flatus ˈfleɪt əs ‖ ˈfleɪţ- **~es** ɪz əz

flatware ˈflæt weə ‖ -wer -wær

flatworm ˈflæt wɜːm ‖ -wɜːm **~s** z

Flaubert ˈfləʊb eə ‖ floʊ ˈbeᵊr —*Fr* [flo bɛːʁ]

flaunt flɔːnt ‖ flɑːnt **flaunted** ˈflɔːnt ɪd -əd ‖ ˈflɔːnţ əd ˈflɑːnţ- **flaunting/ly** ˈflɔːnt ɪŋ /li ‖ ˈflɔːnţ ɪŋ /li ˈflɑːnţ - **flaunts** flɔːnts ‖ flɑːnts

flaunter ˈflɔːnt ə ‖ ˈflɔːnţ ᵊr ˈflɑːnţ- **~s** z

flautist ˈflɔːt ɪst §-əst ‖ ˈflɔːţ- ˈflɑːţ-, ˈflaʊţ- **~s** s

flava ˈfleɪv ə

Flavell *(i)* ˈfleɪv ᵊl, *(ii)* flə ˈvel

Flavia ˈfleɪv i‿ə

Flavian ˈfleɪv i‿ən

flavin ˈfleɪv ɪn ˈflæv-, §-ᵊn **~s** z

flavine ˈfleɪv iːn ˈflæv-, -ɪn

Flavius ˈfleɪv i‿əs

flavone ˈfleɪv əʊn ‖ -oʊn

flavonoid ˈfleɪv ə nɔɪd ˈflæv- **~s** z

flavonol ˈfleɪv ə nɒl ˈflæv- ‖ -nɔːl -nɑːl, -noʊl

avor 'fleɪv ə ‖ -ᵊr **~ed** d **flavoring/s** 'fleɪv ər‿ɪŋ/z **~s** z

avor|ful 'fleɪv ə fʊl -fᵊl ‖ -ᵊr- **~less** ləs lɪs **~some** səm

avour 'fleɪv ə ‖ -ᵊr **~ed** d **flavouring/s** 'fleɪv ər‿ɪŋ/z **~s** z

avour|ful 'fleɪv ə fʊl -fᵊl ‖ -ᵊr- **~less** ləs lɪs **~some** səm

aw flɔː ‖ flɑː **flawed** flɔːd ‖ flɑːd **flawing** 'flɔːʳ ɪŋ ‖ 'flɔː ɪŋ 'flɑː- **flaws** flɔːz ‖ flɑːz

awless 'flɔː ləs -lɪs ‖ 'flɑː- **~ly** li **~ness** nəs nɪs

ax flæks

axen 'flæks ᵊn

laxman 'flæks mən

ay fleɪ **flayed** fleɪd **flaying** 'fleɪ ɪŋ **flays** fleɪz

lea fliː *(= flee)* **fleas** fliːz

'flea ˌmarket

leabag 'fliː bæg **~s** z

leabane 'fliː beɪn **~s** z

leabite 'fliː baɪt **~s** s

lea-bitten 'fliː ˌbɪt ᵊn

leadh flɑː *—Irish* [flʲa(ɣ)]

leapit 'fliː pɪt **~s** s

leawort 'fliː wɜːt §-wɔːt ‖ -wɜːt -wɔːrt **~s** s

leche, flèche fleɪʃ fleʃ **fleches, flèches** 'fleɪʃ ɪz 'fleʃ-, -əz

leck flek **flecked** flekt **flecking** 'flek ɪŋ **flecks** fleks *(= flex)*

lecker 'flek ə ‖ -ᵊr

lection 'flek ʃᵊn **~s** z

lectional 'flek ʃᵊn‿əl

lectionless 'flek ʃᵊn ləs -lɪs

led fled

ledge fledʒ **fledged** fledʒd **fledges** 'fledʒ ɪz -əz **fledging** 'fledʒ ɪŋ

ledgeling, fledgling 'fledʒ lɪŋ **~s** z

lee fliː *(= flea)* **fled** fled **fleeing** 'fliː ɪŋ **flees** fliːz

leece fliːs **fleeced** fliːst **fleeces** 'fliːs ɪz -əz **fleecing** 'fliːs ɪŋ

leec|y 'fliːs |i **~ier** i‿ə ‖ i‿ᵊr **~iest** i‿ɪst i‿əst **~ily** ɪ li əl i **~iness** i nəs i nɪs

leet, Fleet fliːt **fleeted** 'fliːt ɪd -əd ‖ 'fliːt̬ əd **fleeter** 'fliːt ə ‖ 'fliːt̬ ᵊr **fleetest** 'fliːt ɪst -əst ‖ 'fliːt̬- **fleeting** 'fliːt ɪŋ ‖ 'fliːt̬ ɪŋ

'fleet ˌadmiral; **'Fleet Street**

fleeting 'fliːt ɪŋ ‖ 'fliːt̬ ɪŋ **~ly** li **~ness** nəs nɪs

Fleetwood 'fliːt wʊd

Fleming 'flem ɪŋ **~s, ~'s** z

Flemington 'flem ɪŋ tən

Flemish 'flem ɪʃ

flense flenᵗs flenz **flensed** flenᵗst flenzd **flenses** 'flenᵗs ɪz 'flenz-, -əz **flensing** 'flenᵗs ɪŋ 'flenz-

flenser 'flenᵗs ə 'flenz- ‖ -ᵊr **~s** z

flesh fleʃ **fleshed** fleʃt **fleshes** 'fleʃ ɪz -əz **fleshing** 'fleʃ ɪŋ

'flesh wound

flesh-colored, flesh-coloured 'fleʃ ˌkʌl əd ‖ -ᵊrd

fleshi... *—see* **fleshy**

flesh|ly 'fleʃ |li **~lier** li‿ə ‖ li‿ᵊr **~liest** li‿ɪst li‿əst **~liness** li nəs li nɪs

fleshpot 'fleʃ pɒt ‖ -pɑːt **~s** s

flesh|y 'fleʃ |i **~ier** i‿ə ‖ i‿ᵊr **~iest** i‿ɪst i‿əst **~iness** i nəs i nɪs

fletcher, F~ 'fletʃ ə ‖ -ᵊr **~s, ~'s** z

Fletton, f~ 'flet ᵊn

Fleur flɜː ‖ flɜˑː *—Fr* [flœːʁ]

fleur-de-lis, fleur-de-lys *sing.* ˌflɜː də 'liː -'liːs ‖ ˌflɜˑː- *—Fr* [flœʁ də lis]

flew, Flew fluː **flews** fluːz

flex fleks **flexed** flekst **flexes** 'fleks ɪz -əz **flexing** 'fleks ɪŋ

flexibility ˌfleks ə 'bɪl ət i ˌ·ɪ-, -ɪt i ‖ -ət̬ i

flexib|le 'fleks əb |ᵊl -ɪb- **~leness** ᵊl nəs -nɪs **~ly** li

flexion 'flek ʃᵊn

flexional 'flek ʃᵊn‿əl

flexionless 'flek ʃᵊn ləs -lɪs

flexitime 'fleks i taɪm

Flexner 'fleks nə ‖ -nᵊr

flexor 'fleks ə -ɔː ‖ -ᵊr -ɔːr **~s** z

flextime 'fleks taɪm

flexuous 'fleks ju‿əs ‖ 'flek ʃu‿əs **~ly** li

flexure 'flek ʃə 'fleks jʊə ‖ -ʃᵊr **~s** z

flibbertigibbet ˌflɪb ət i 'dʒɪb ɪt -ət ‖ -ᵊrt̬ i- '· · ˌ· · **~s** s

flick flɪk **flicked** flɪkt **flicking** 'flɪk ɪŋ **flicks** flɪks

'flick knife

flicker 'flɪk ə ‖ -ᵊr **~ed** d **flickering** 'flɪk ər‿ɪŋ **~s** z

Flickr *tdmk* 'flɪk ə ‖ -ᵊr

flier 'flaɪ‿ə ‖ 'flaɪ‿ᵊr **~s** z

flies flaɪz

flight flaɪt **flighted** 'flaɪt ɪd -əd ‖ 'flaɪt̬ əd **flighting** 'flaɪt ɪŋ ‖ 'flaɪt̬ ɪŋ **flights** flaɪts

'flight deck; **ˌflight lieu'tenant◂**; **'flight ˌnumber**; **'flight path**; **'flight reˌcorder**; **'flight ˌsergeant**

flighti... *—see* **flighty**

flightless 'flaɪt ləs -lɪs

flight|y 'flaɪt |i ‖ 'flaɪt̬ |i **~ier** i‿ə ‖ i‿ᵊr **~iest** i‿ɪst i‿əst **~ily** ɪ li əl i **~iness** i nəs i nɪs

flimflam 'flɪm flæm **~med** d **~ming** ɪŋ **~s** z

flims|y 'flɪmz |i **~ier** i‿ə ‖ i‿ᵊr **~iest** i‿ɪst i‿əst **~ily** ɪ li əl i **~iness** i nəs i nɪs

flinch flɪntʃ **flinched** flɪntʃt **flinches** 'flɪntʃ ɪz -əz **flinching** 'flɪntʃ ɪŋ

Flinders, f~ 'flɪnd əz ‖ -ᵊrz

fling flɪŋ **flinging** 'flɪŋ ɪŋ **flings** flɪŋz **flung** flʌŋ

Flinn flɪn

flint, Flint flɪnt **flints** flɪnts

flintlock 'flɪnt lɒk ‖ -lɑːk **~s** s

Flintshire 'flɪnt ʃə -ʃɪə ‖ -ʃᵊr -ʃɪr

flintstone, F~ 'flɪnt stəʊn ‖ -stoʊn **~s** z

flint|y 'flɪnt |i ‖ 'flɪnt̬ |i **~ier** i‿ə ‖ i‿ᵊr **~iest** i‿ɪst i‿əst **~ily** ɪ li əl i **~iness** i nəs i nɪs

flip flɪp **flipped** flɪpt **flipping** 'flɪp ɪŋ **flips** flɪps

'flip side

flip-flop 'flɪp flɒp ‖ -flɑːp **~s** s

F

flippancy 'flɪp ənᵗs i
flippant 'flɪp ənt **~ly** li
flipper 'flɪp ə ‖ -ᵊr **~s** z
flirt flɜːt ‖ flɜ˞ːt **flirted** 'flɜːt ɪd -əd ‖ 'flɜ˞ːţ əd **flirting** 'flɜːt ɪŋ ‖ 'flɜ˞ːţ ɪŋ **flirts** flɜːts ‖ flɜ˞ːts
flirtation flɜː 'teɪʃ ᵊn ‖ flɜ˞ː-
flirtatious flɜː 'teɪʃ əs ‖ flɜ˞ː- **~ly** li **~ness** nəs nɪs
flirty 'flɜːt i ‖ 'flɜ˞ːţ i
flit flɪt **flits** flɪts **flitted** 'flɪt ɪd -əd ‖ 'flɪţ əd **flitting** 'flɪt ɪŋ ‖ 'flɪţ ɪŋ
flitch flɪtʃ **flitches** 'flɪtʃ ɪz -əz
flitter 'flɪt ə ‖ 'flɪţ ᵊr **~ed** d **flittering** 'flɪt‿ər ɪŋ ‖ 'flɪţ ər ɪŋ **~s** z
Flitton 'flɪt ᵊn
Flitwick 'flɪt ɪk ‖ 'flɪţ-
flivver 'flɪv ə ‖ -ᵊr **~s** z
Flixton 'flɪkst ən
Flo fləʊ ‖ floʊ
float fləʊt ‖ floʊt **floated** 'fləʊt ɪd -əd ‖ 'floʊţ əd **floating** 'fləʊt ɪŋ ‖ 'floʊţ ɪŋ **floats** fləʊts ‖ floʊts
ˌ**floating 'voter**
floatation fləʊ 'teɪʃ ᵊn ‖ floʊ- **~s** z
floating-point ˌfləʊt ɪŋ 'pɔɪnt ◂ ‖ ˌfloʊţ-
flocculent 'flɒk jʊl ənt ‖ 'flɑːk jəl- **~ly** li
flock flɒk ‖ flɑːk **flocked** flɒkt ‖ flɑːkt **flocking** 'flɒk ɪŋ ‖ 'flɑːk ɪŋ **flocks** flɒks ‖ flɑːks
Flockhart 'flɒk hɑːt ‖ 'flɑːk hɑːrt
Flodden 'flɒd ᵊn ‖ 'flɑːd-
floe fləʊ ‖ floʊ *(= flow)* **floes** fləʊz ‖ floʊz
Floella fləʊ 'el ə ‖ floʊ-
flog flɒg ‖ flɑːg **flogged** flɒgd ‖ flɑːgd **flogging/s** 'flɒg ɪŋ/z ‖ 'flɑːg ɪŋ/z **flogs** flɒgz ‖ flɑːgz
flogger 'flɒg ə ‖ 'flɑːg ᵊr **~s** z
Flo-Jo 'fləʊ dʒəʊ ‖ 'floʊ dʒoʊ
flong flɒŋ ‖ flɔːŋ flɑːŋ **flongs** flɒŋz ‖ flɔːŋz flɑːŋz
flood, Flood flʌd **flooded** 'flʌd ɪd -əd **flooding** 'flʌd ɪŋ **floods** flʌdz
'**flood tide**
floodgate 'flʌd geɪt →'flʌg- **~s** s
flood|light 'flʌd |laɪt **~lighted** laɪt ɪd -əd ‖ laɪţ əd **~lighting** laɪt ɪŋ ‖ laɪţ ɪŋ **~lights** laɪts **~lit** lɪt
floodwater 'flʌd ˌwɔːt ə ‖ -ˌwɔːţ ᵊr -ˌwɑːţ ᵊr
Flook flʊk fluːk
floor flɔː ‖ flɔːr floʊr **floored** flɔːd ‖ flɔːrd floʊrd **flooring** 'flɔːr ɪŋ ‖ 'floʊr- **floors** flɔːz ‖ flɔːrz floʊrz
'**floor cloth**; '**floor ˌmanager**; '**floor show**
floorboard 'flɔː bɔːd ‖ 'flɔːr bɔːrd 'floʊr boʊrd **~s** z
flooring 'flɔːr ɪŋ ‖ 'floʊr-
floor-length 'flɔː leŋᵏθ §-lenᵗθ ‖ 'flɔːr- 'floʊr-
floorspace 'flɔː speɪs ‖ 'flɔːr- 'floʊr-
floortime 'flɔː taɪm ‖ 'flɔːr- 'floʊr-
floorwalker 'flɔː ˌwɔːk ə ‖ 'flɔːr ˌwɔːk ᵊr 'floʊr-, -ˌwɑːk ᵊr **~s** z
floos|ie, floos|y, floozlie, floozly 'fluːz |i **~ies** iz

flop flɒp ‖ flɑːp **flopped** flɒpt ‖ flɑːpt **flopping** 'flɒp ɪŋ ‖ 'flɑːp ɪŋ **flops** flɒps ‖ flɑːps
flop|house 'flɒp |haʊs ‖ 'flɑːp- **~houses** haʊz ɪz -əz
flopp|y 'flɒp |i ‖ 'flɑːp |i **~ier** i‿ə ‖ i‿ᵊr **~ies** iz **~iest** i‿ɪst i‿əst **~ily** ɪ li əl i **~iness** i nəs i nɪs
ˌ**floppy 'disk**
Flopsy, f~ 'flɒps i ‖ 'flɑːps i
flora, Flora 'flɔːr ə ‖ 'floʊr- **~s** z
floral 'flɔːr əl ‖ 'floʊr- **~ly** i
floreat 'flɒr i æt 'flɔːr- ‖ 'flɔːr-
Florence 'flɒr ənᵗs ‖ 'flɔːr- 'flɑːr- **~'s** ɪz əz
Florentine, f~ 'flɒr ən taɪn -tiːn; flə 'rent aɪn ‖ 'flɔːr ən tiːn 'flɑːr- **~s** z
Flores flɔːr ɪz -iːz, -ɪs, §-əs ‖ 'floʊr-
ˌ**Flores 'Sea**
florescence flɔː 'res ᵊnᵗs flɒ-, flə- ‖ floʊ-
floret 'flɒr ət 'flɔːr-, -ɪt ‖ 'flɔːr- 'floʊr- **~s** s
Florey 'flɔːr i 'flɒr- ‖ 'floʊr-
floribunda ˌflɒr ɪ 'bʌnd ə ˌflɔːr-, §-ə- ‖ ˌflɔːr ə- ˌfloʊr- **~s** z
floricultural ˌflɔːr ɪ 'kʌltʃ ᵊr‿əl ˌflɒr-, ˌ-ə- ‖ ˌfloʊr-
floriculture 'flɔːr ɪ ˌkʌltʃ ə 'flɒr-, -ə- ‖ -ᵊr 'floʊr-
floriculturist ˌflɔːr ɪ 'kʌltʃ ər‿ɪst ˌflɒr-, ˌ-ə-, §-əst ‖ ˌfloʊr- **~s** s
florid 'flɒr ɪd §-əd ‖ 'flɔːr- 'flɑːr- **~ly** li **~ness** nəs nɪs
Florida 'flɒr ɪd ə -əd- ‖ 'flɔːr- 'flɑːr-
ˌ**Florida 'Keys**
Floridan 'flɒr ɪd ən -əd- ‖ 'flɔːr- 'flɑːr- **~s** z
Floridian flɒ 'rɪd i‿ən flə- ‖ flə- **~s** z
floridity flɒ 'rɪd ət i flɔː-, flə-, -ɪt- ‖ flə 'rɪd əţ i flɔː-
florin 'flɒr ɪn -ən ‖ 'flɔːr- 'flɑːr- **~s** z
Florio 'flɔːr i əʊ ‖ -oʊ 'floʊr-
florist 'flɒr ɪst 'flɔːr-, §-əst ‖ 'flɔːr- 'flɑːr-, 'floʊr- **~s** s
floristry 'flɒr ɪs tri 'flɔːr-, -əs- ‖ 'flɔːr- 'flɑːr-, 'floʊr-
Florrie 'flɒr i ‖ 'flɔːr i 'flɑːr i
floruit 'flɒr u ɪt 'flɔːr- ‖ 'flɔːr- 'flɑːr-, 'floʊr-, -ju-
floss, Floss flɒs ‖ flɔːs flɑːs **flossed** flɒst ‖ flɔːst flɑːst **flosses** 'flɒs ɪz -əz ‖ 'flɔːs əz 'flɑːs- **flossing** 'flɒs ɪŋ ‖ 'flɔːs ɪŋ 'flɑːs-
Flossie 'flɒs i ‖ 'flɔːs i 'flɑːs i
floss|y 'flɒs |i ‖ 'flɔːs |i 'flɑːs- **~ier** i‿ə ‖ i‿ᵊr **~iest** i‿ɪst i‿əst **~ily** ɪ li əl i **~iness** i nəs i nɪs
flotation fləʊ 'teɪʃ ᵊn ‖ floʊ- **~s** z
flote fləʊt ‖ floʊt
flotilla fləʊ 'tɪl ə ‖ floʊ- **~s** z
flotsam 'flɒts əm ‖ 'flɑːts-
Flotta 'flɒt ə ‖ 'flɑːţ ə
flounce flaʊnᵗs **flounced** flaʊnᵗst **flounces** 'flaʊnᵗs ɪz -əz **flouncing** 'flaʊnᵗs ɪŋ
flounder 'flaʊnd ə ‖ -ᵊr **~ed** d **floundering** 'flaʊnd‿ər ɪŋ **~s** z
flour 'flaʊ‿ə ‖ 'flaʊ‿ᵊr *(= flower)* **floured** 'flaʊ‿əd ‖ 'flaʊ‿ᵊrd **flouring** 'flaʊ‿ər ɪŋ ‖ 'flaʊ‿ᵊr ɪŋ **flours** 'flaʊ‿əz ‖ 'flaʊ‿ᵊrz

ourish 'flʌr ɪʃ ‖ 'flɜː- ~ed t ~es ɪz əz ~ing ɪŋ
ourmill 'flaʊ˽ə mɪl ‖ 'flaʊ˽ᵊr- ~s z
oury 'flaʊ˽ər i ‖ 'flaʊ˽ᵊr i *(= flowery)*
out flaʊt flouted 'flaʊt ɪd -əd ‖ 'flaʊţ əd flouting 'flaʊt ɪŋ ‖ 'flaʊţ ɪŋ flouts flaʊts
ow fləʊ ‖ floʊ flowed fləʊd ‖ floʊd flowing/ly 'fləʊ ɪŋ /li ‖ 'floʊ ɪŋ /li flows fləʊz ‖ floʊz
'flow ˌdiagram
ow|chart 'fləʊ |tʃɑːt ‖ 'floʊ |tʃɑːrt ~charted tʃɑːt ɪd -əd ‖ tʃɑːrţ əd ~charting tʃɑːt ɪŋ ‖ tʃɑːrţ ɪŋ ~charts tʃɑːts ‖ tʃɑːrts
ower 'flaʊ˽ə ‖ 'flaʊ˽ᵊr *(= flour)* flowered 'flaʊ˽əd ‖ 'flaʊ˽ᵊrd flowering/s 'flaʊ˽ər ɪŋ/z ‖ 'flaʊ˽ᵊr ɪŋ/z flowers 'flaʊ˽əz ‖ 'flaʊ˽ᵊrz
'flower girl; ˌflowering 'currant; 'flower ˌpower
owerbed 'flaʊ˽ə bed ‖ 'flaʊ˽ᵊr- ~s z
owerless 'flaʊ˽ə ləs -lɪs ‖ 'flaʊ˽ᵊr-
owerpot 'flaʊ˽ə pɒt ‖ 'flaʊ˽ᵊr pɑːt ~s s
ower|y 'flaʊ˽ər |i ‖ 'flaʊ˽ᵊr |i ~ier i˽ə ‖ i˽ᵊr ~iest i˽ɪst i˽əst ~ily əl i ɪ li ~iness i nəs i nɪs
own fləʊn §'fləʊ ən ‖ floʊn
loyd flɔɪd
lu fluː *(= flew, flue)*
lub flʌb flubbed flʌbd flubbing 'flʌb ɪŋ flubs flʌbz
luck flʌk
luctu|ate 'flʌk tʃu |eɪt -tju- ~ated eɪt ɪd -əd ‖ eɪţ əd ~ates eɪts ~ating eɪt ɪŋ ‖ eɪţ ɪŋ
luctuation ˌflʌk tʃu 'eɪʃ ᵊn -tju- ~s z
lue fluː *(= flew)* flues fluːz
luellen, F~ flu 'el ɪn -ən
luency 'fluː˽ənᵗs i
luent 'fluː˽ənt ~ly li
luff flʌf fluffed flʌft fluffing 'flʌf ɪŋ fluffs flʌfs
luff|y 'flʌf |i ~ier i˽ə ‖ i˽ᵊr ~iest i˽ɪst i˽əst ~ily ɪ li əl i ~iness i nəs i nɪs
flugelhorn, flügelhorn 'fluːg ᵊl hɔːn ‖ -hɔːrn ~s z
fluid 'fluː˽ɪd ~ly li ~ness nəs nɪs ~s z
ˌfluid 'ounce
fluidis|e, fluidiz|e 'fluː˽ɪ daɪz ~ed d ~es ɪz əz ~ing ɪŋ
fluidity flu 'ɪd ət i -ɪt- ‖ -əţ i
fluke fluːk fluked fluːkt flukes fluːks fluking 'fluːk ɪŋ
fluk|ey, fluk|y 'fluːk |i ~ier i˽ə ‖ i˽ᵊr ~iest i˽ɪst i˽əst
flume fluːm flumed fluːmd flumes fluːmz fluming 'fluːm ɪŋ
flummer|y 'flʌm ər˽|i ~ies iz
flummox 'flʌm əks ~ed t ~es ɪz əz ~ing ɪŋ
flung flʌŋ
flunk flʌŋk flunked flʌŋkt flunking 'flʌŋk ɪŋ flunks flʌŋks
flunk|ey, flunk|y 'flʌŋk |i ~eys, ~ies iz
Fluon *tdmk* 'fluː ɒn ‖ -ɑːn
fluor 'fluː ɔː ə ‖ -ɔːr -ᵊr
fluoresc|e flɔː 'res fluᵊ-, flə-; ˌfluː˽ə 'res ‖ floʊ-; ˌfluː ə 'res ~ed t ~es ɪz əz ~ing ɪŋ
fluoresc|ence flɔː 'res |ᵊnᵗs fluᵊ-, flə-; ˌfluː˽ə 'res- ‖ floʊ-; ˌfluː ə 'res- ~ent ᵊnt
fluoric flu 'ɒr ɪk ‖ -'ɔːr ɪk -'ɑːr ɪk
fluori|date 'flɔːr ɪ |deɪt -ə-; 'fluː˽ər ɪ deɪt, -ə deɪt ‖ 'flʊr- 'flɔːr-, 'floʊr- ~dated deɪt ɪd -əd ‖ deɪţ əd ~dates deɪts ~dating deɪt ɪŋ ‖ deɪţ ɪŋ
fluoridation ˌflɔːr ɪ 'deɪʃ ᵊn ˌfluː˽ər ɪ 'deɪʃ-, -ə'-- ‖ ˌflʊr- ˌflɔːr-, ˌfloʊr- ~s z
fluoride 'flʊər aɪd 'flɔːr-; 'fluː ə raɪd ‖ 'flʊr- 'flɔːr-, 'floʊr- ~s z
fluori|nate 'flɔːr ɪ |neɪt 'fluː˽ər ɪ neɪt, -ə neɪt ‖ 'flʊr- 'flɔːr-, 'floʊr- ~nated neɪt ɪd -əd ‖ neɪţ əd ~nates neɪts ~nating neɪt ɪŋ ‖ neɪţ ɪŋ
fluorination ˌflɔːr ɪ 'neɪʃ ᵊn ˌfluː˽ər ɪ 'neɪʃ-, -ə 'neɪʃ- ‖ ˌflʊr- ˌflɔːr-, ˌfloʊr- ~s z
fluorine 'flʊər iːn 'flɔːr-, 'fluː ə riːn ‖ 'flʊr- 'flɔːr-, 'floʊr-
fluorite 'flʊər aɪt 'flɔːr-, 'fluː ə raɪt ‖ 'flʊr- 'flɔːr-, 'floʊr-
fluoro- *comb. form*
with stress-neutral suffix ¦flʊər əʊ ¦flɔːr-; ¦fluː ə rəʊ ‖ ¦flʊr oʊ ¦flɔːr-, ¦floʊr- — fluorocarbon ˌflʊər əʊ 'kɑːb ən ˌflɔːr-; ˌfluː ə rəʊ- ‖ ˌflʊr oʊ 'kɑːrb ən ˌflɔːr-, ˌfloʊr-
with stress-imposing suffix flɔː ¦rɒ+ fluᵊ-, flə-; ˌfluː˽ə 'rɒ+ ‖ flu ¦rɑː+ flɔː-, floʊ- — fluoroscopy flɔː 'rɒsk əp i fluᵊ-, flə-; ˌfluː˽ə'-- ‖ flu 'rɑːsk əp i flɔː-, floʊ-
fluorosis flɔː 'rəʊs ɪs fluᵊ-, flə-; ˌfluː˽ə'--, §-əs ‖ flu 'roʊs əs flɔː-, floʊ-
fluorspar 'flʊə spɑː 'flɔː-; 'fluː ə spɑː ‖ 'flʊr spɑːr 'fluː ᵊr spɑːr, -ɔːr-
fluothane 'fluː˽ə θeɪn
flurr|y, F~ 'flʌr |i ‖ 'flɜː |i ~ied id ~ies iz ~ying i˽ɪŋ
flush flʌʃ flushed flʌʃt flusher 'flʌʃ ə ‖ -ᵊr flushes 'flʌʃ ɪz -əz flushest 'flʌʃ ɪst -əst flushing/s 'flʌʃ ɪŋ/z
Flushing 'flʌʃ ɪŋ
fluster 'flʌst ə ‖ -ᵊr ~ed d flustering 'flʌst ər˽ɪŋ ~s z
flute fluːt fluted 'fluːt ɪd -əd ‖ 'fluːţ əd flutes fluːts fluting/s 'fluːt ɪŋ/z ‖ 'fluːţ ɪŋ/z
flutist 'fluːt ɪst §-əst ‖ 'fluːţ əst ~s s
flutter 'flʌt ə ‖ 'flʌţ ᵊr ~ed d fluttering 'flʌt˽ər ɪŋ ‖ 'flʌţ ər ɪŋ ~s z
fluvial 'fluːv i˽əl
flux flʌks fluxed flʌkst fluxes 'flʌks ɪz -əz fluxing 'flʌks ɪŋ
fluxion 'flʌk ʃᵊn ~s z
fly flaɪ flew fluː flies flaɪz flown fləʊn ‖ floʊn flying 'flaɪ ɪŋ
ˌfly 'half; 'flying boat; ˌflying 'buttress; ˌflying 'colours; ˌflying 'doctor; ˌflying 'fish; ˌflying 'fox; 'flying maˌchine; 'flying ˌofficer; ˌflying 'picket; ˌflying 'saucer; 'flying squad; ˌflying 'start
flyaway 'flaɪ ə ˌweɪ
flyback 'flaɪ bæk
flyblown 'flaɪ bləʊn ‖ -bloʊn
flyboy 'flaɪ bɔɪ ~s z

flyby 'flaɪ baɪ **~s** z
fly-by-night 'flaɪ baɪ ˌnaɪt §-bɪ-, §-bə-
fly-by-wire ˌflaɪ baɪ 'waɪ‿ə ◂ ‖ -'waɪ‿ər ◂
flycatcher 'flaɪ ˌkætʃ ə ⚠ˌketʃ- ‖ -ər **~s** z
fly-drive 'flaɪ draɪv ˌ·'· **~s** z
flyer 'flaɪ‿ə ‖ 'flaɪ‿ər **~s** z
fly-fish 'flaɪ fɪʃ **~er/s** ə/z ‖ ər/z **~ing** ɪŋ
fly|leaf 'flaɪ |liːf **~leaves** liːvz
Flymo *tdmk* 'flaɪ məʊ ‖ -moʊ **~s** z
Flynn flɪn
Flynt flɪnt
fly-on-the-wall ˌflaɪ ɒn ðə 'wɔːl ◂ ‖ -ɑːn-, -ɔːn-, -'wɑːl ◂
flyover 'flaɪ ˌəʊv ə ‖ -ˌoʊv ər **~s** z
flypaper 'flaɪ ˌpeɪp ə ‖ -ər **~s** z
flypast 'flaɪ pɑːst §-pæst ‖ -pæst **~s** s
flypost 'flaɪ pəʊst ‖ -poʊst **~ed** ɪd əd **~er/s** ə/z ‖ -ər/z **~ing** ɪŋ **~s** s
flyscreen 'flaɪ skriːn **~s** z
flysheet 'flaɪ ʃiːt **~s** s
flyspeck 'flaɪ spek **~ed** t **~s** s
flyswatter 'flaɪ ˌswɒt ə ‖ -ˌswɑːṭ ər **~s** z
Flyte flaɪt
flytrap 'flaɪ træp **~s** s
flyweight 'flaɪ weɪt **~s** s
flywheel 'flaɪ wiːəl -hwiːəl **~s** z
flywhisk 'flaɪ wɪsk -hwɪsk **~s** s
FM ˌef 'em ◂
ˌFM 'radio
f-number 'ef ˌnʌm bə ‖ -bər **~s** z
Fo fəʊ ‖ foʊ —*It* [fo]
FO ˌef 'əʊ ‖ -'oʊ
foal fəʊl →fɒʊl ‖ foʊl **foaled** fəʊld →fɒʊld ‖ foʊld **foaling** 'fəʊl ɪŋ →'fɒʊl- ‖ 'foʊl ɪŋ **foals** fəʊlz →fɒʊlz ‖ foʊlz
foam fəʊm ‖ foʊm **foamed** fəʊmd ‖ foʊmd **foaming/ly** 'fəʊm ɪŋ /li ‖ 'foʊm ɪŋ /li **foams** fəʊmz ‖ foʊmz
ˌfoam 'rubber◂
foam|y 'fəʊm |i ‖ 'foʊm |i **~ier** i‿ə ‖ i‿ər **~iest** i‿ɪst i‿əst **~ily** ɪ li əl i **~iness** i nəs i nɪs
fob fɒb ‖ fɑːb **fobbed** fɒbd ‖ fɑːbd **fobbing** 'fɒb ɪŋ ‖ 'fɑːb ɪŋ **fobs** fɒbz ‖ fɑːbz
'fob watch
f.o.b. ˌef əʊ 'biː ‖ -oʊ-
focaccia, foccaccia fəʊ 'kætʃ i‿ə ‖ foʊ 'kɑːtʃ- —*It* focaccia [fo 'kat tʃa]
focal 'fəʊk əl ‖ 'foʊk əl **~ly** i
ˌfocal 'length ‖ '·· ·; **'focal point**
Foch fɒʃ ‖ fɔːʃ fɑːʃ —*Fr* [fɔʃ]
Fochabers 'fɒk əb əz 'fɒx- ‖ 'fɑːk əb ərz
foci 'fəʊs aɪ 'fəʊk-, -iː ‖ 'foʊs- 'foʊk-
fo'c'sle 'fəʊks əl ‖ 'foʊks əl **~s** z
focus 'fəʊk əs ‖ 'foʊk əs **~ed, ~sed** t **~es, ~ses** ɪz əz **~ing, ~sing** ɪŋ
fodder 'fɒd ə ‖ 'fɑːd ər
Foden 'fəʊd ən ‖ 'foʊd-
foe fəʊ ‖ foʊ **foes** fəʊz ‖ foʊz
foehn, föhn fɜːn ‖ feɪn —*Ger* [føːn]
foe|man 'fəʊ |mən ‖ 'foʊ- **~men** mən men
foetal 'fiːt əl ‖ 'fiːṭ əl
foetid 'fet ɪd 'fiːt-, §-əd ‖ 'feṭ əd
foetus 'fiːt əs ‖ 'fiːṭ əs **~es** ɪz əz

fog fɒg ‖ fɑːg fɔːg **fogged** fɒgd ‖ fɑːgd fɔːgd **fogging** 'fɒg ɪŋ ‖ 'fɑːg ɪŋ 'fɔːg- **fogs** fɒgz ‖ fɑːgz fɔːgz
'fog lamp, 'fog light
Fogarty 'fəʊg ət i ‖ 'foʊg ərṭ i
fogbank 'fɒg bæŋk ‖ 'fɑːg- 'fɔːg- **~s** s
fogbound 'fɒg baʊnd ‖ 'fɑːg- 'fɔːg-
Fogerty 'fəʊg ət i ‖ 'foʊg ərṭ i
fogey 'fəʊg i ‖ 'foʊg i **~s** z
Fogg fɒg ‖ fɑːg fɔːg
fogg|y 'fɒg |i ‖ 'fɑːg |i 'fɔːg- **~ier** i‿ə ‖ i‿ər **~iest** i‿ɪst i‿əst **~ily** ɪ li əl i **~iness** i nəs i nɪs
ˌFoggy 'Bottom
foghorn 'fɒg hɔːn ‖ 'fɑːg hɔːrn 'fɔːg- **~s** z
fog|y 'fəʊg |i ‖ 'foʊg |i **~ies** iz
fohn, föhn fɜːn ‖ feɪn —*Ger* [føːn]
foible 'fɔɪb əl **~s** z
foie gras ˌfwɑː 'grɑː —*Fr* [fwa gʁa]
foil fɔɪəl **foiled** fɔɪəld **foiling** 'fɔɪəl ɪŋ **foils** fɔɪəlz
foist fɔɪst **foisted** 'fɔɪst ɪd -əd **foisting** 'fɔɪst ɪŋ **foists** fɔɪsts
Fokker 'fɒk ə ‖ 'fɑːk ər **~s** z
fold fəʊld →fɒʊld ‖ foʊld **folded** 'fəʊld ɪd →'fɒʊld-, -əd ‖ 'foʊld əd **folding** 'fəʊld ɪŋ →'fɒʊld- ‖ 'foʊld ɪŋ **folds** fəʊldz →fɒʊldz ‖ foʊldz
foldaway 'fəʊld ə ˌweɪ →'fɒʊld- ‖ 'foʊld-
folder 'fəʊld ə →'fɒʊld- ‖ 'foʊld ər **~s** z
folderol 'fɒld ə rɒl -ɪ- ‖ 'fɑːld ə rɑːl **~s** z
foldout 'fəʊld aʊt →'fɒʊld- ‖ 'foʊld- **~s** s
Foley 'fəʊl i ‖ 'foʊl i
Folger 'fəʊldʒ ə →'fɒʊldʒ- ‖ 'foʊldʒ ər
folia 'fəʊl i‿ə ‖ 'foʊl-
foliage 'fəʊl i‿ɪdʒ ‖ 'foʊl- **~d** d
'foliage plant
foliar 'fəʊl i‿ə ‖ 'foʊl i‿ər
foliate *adj* 'fəʊl i‿ət ɪt, eɪt ‖ 'foʊl-
foli|ate *v* 'fəʊl i |eɪt ‖ 'foʊl- **~ated** eɪt ɪd -əd ‖ eɪṭ əd **~ates** eɪts **~ating** eɪt ɪŋ ‖ eɪṭ ɪŋ
foliation ˌfəʊl i 'eɪʃ ən ‖ ˌfoʊl- **~s** z
folic 'fəʊl ɪk 'fɒl- ‖ 'foʊl- 'fɑːl-
ˌfolic 'acid
folie à deux ˌfɒl i æ 'dɜː -i ɑː- ‖ foʊ ˌliː ə 'dʌ fɑː- —*Fr* [fɔ li a dø]
folie de grandeur ˌfɒl i də 'grɒnd ɜː ‖ foʊ ˌliː də grɑːn 'dɜː fɑː- —*Fr* [fɔ li də gʁɑ̃ dœːʁ]
Folies Bergere, Folies Bergère ˌfɒl i bɜː 'ʒeə -bə'·, -beə'· ‖ foʊ ˌliː ber 'ʒeər —*Fr* [fɔ li bɛʁ ʒɛːʁ]
folio 'fəʊl i‿əʊ ‖ 'foʊl i‿oʊ **~s** z
foli|um 'fəʊl i‿|əm ‖ 'foʊl- **~a** ə
Foljambe 'fʊldʒ əm
folk fəʊk §fəʊlk ‖ foʊk **folks** fəʊks §fəʊlks ‖ foʊks
'folk dance; **'folk ˌdancer**; **ˌfolk ˌety'mology**; **'folk ˌmedicine**; **'folk ˌsinger**; **'folk song**
Folkestone 'fəʊkst ən ‖ 'foʊkst-
folkie 'fəʊk i ‖ 'foʊk i **~s** z
folklore 'fəʊk lɔː §'fəʊlk- ‖ 'foʊk lɔːr -loʊr
folkloric ˌfəʊk 'lɔːr ɪk ◂ §ˌfəʊlk- ‖ ˌfoʊk- -'loʊr-

olklorist 'fəʊk lɔːr ɪst §'fəʊlk-, §-əst ‖ 'foʊk- -loʊr- **~s** s
olkloristic ˌfəʊk lɔː 'rɪst ɪk ◂ ‖ ˌfoʊk- -loʊ-
olks|y 'fəʊks |i §'fəʊlks- ‖ 'foʊks |i **~ier** i̯ə ‖ i̯ər **~iest** i̯ɪst i̯əst **~iness** i nəs i nɪs
olktale 'fəʊk teɪəl §'fəʊlk- ‖ 'foʊk- **~s** z
olkway 'fəʊk weɪ §'fəʊlk- ‖ 'foʊk- **~s** z
ollett 'fɒl ɪt -ət ‖ 'fɑːl-
ollick 'fɒl ɪk ‖ 'fɑːl-
ollicle 'fɒl ɪk əl ‖ 'fɑːl- **~s** z
ollicular fɒ 'lɪk jʊl ə fə-, -jəl- ‖ fə 'lɪk jəl ər fɑː-
ollie... —*see* **folly**
ollow 'fɒl əʊ ‖ 'fɑːl oʊ **~ed** d **following** 'fɒl əʊ ɪŋ -u̯ɪŋ ‖ 'fɑːl oʊ ɪŋ **~s** z
ollower 'fɒl əʊ ə §-u̯ə ‖ 'fɑːl oʊ ər **~s** z
ollow-my-leader ˌfɒl əʊ mə 'liːd ə -mɪ'--, -maɪ'-- ‖ ˌfɑːl oʊ maɪ 'liːd ər
ollow-on ˌfɒl əʊ 'ɒn ‖ ˌfɑːl oʊ 'ɑːn -'ɔːn **~s** z
ollow-the-leader ˌfɒl əʊ ðə 'liːd ə ‖ ˌfɑːl oʊ ðə 'liːd ər
ollow-through ˌfɒl əʊ 'θruː ‖ ˌfɑːl oʊ- **~s** z
ollow-up 'fɒl əʊ ʌp ‖ 'fɑːl oʊ- **~s** s
oll|y 'fɒl |i ‖ 'fɑːl |i **~ies** iz
olsom *(i)* 'fəʊl səm →'fɒʊl- ‖ 'foʊl səm, *(ii)* 'fɒl- ‖ 'fɑːl- —*The places in CA and NM are (i); the family name may be either.*
omalhaut 'fɒm ə ləʊt 'fəʊm-, -əl hɔːt ‖ 'foʊm əl hɔːt -hɑːt; -ə loʊ
o|ment fəʊ |'ment ‖ foʊ- '· · **~mented** 'ment ɪd -əd ‖ 'menţ əd **~menting** 'ment ɪŋ ‖ 'menţ ɪŋ **~ments** 'ments
omentation ˌfəʊm en 'teɪʃ ən -ən- ‖ ˌfoʊm- **~s** z
ond fɒnd ‖ fɑːnd **fonder** 'fɒnd ə ‖ 'fɑːnd ər **fondest** 'fɒnd ɪst -əst ‖ 'fɑːnd-
onda 'fɒnd ə ‖ 'fɑːnd ə
ondant 'fɒnd ənt ‖ 'fɑːnd- **~s** s
ondl|e 'fɒnd əl ‖ 'fɑːnd- **~ed** d **~es** z **~ing** ‿ɪŋ
ond|ly 'fɒnd |li ‖ 'fɑːnd- **~ness** nəs nɪs
ondu, fondue 'fɒnd juː -uː ‖ fɑːn 'duː -'djuː, '· · —*Fr* [fɔ̃ dy] **~s** z
ongafale ˌfɒŋ ə 'fɑːl eɪ -gə- ‖ ˌfɑːŋ- ˌfɔːŋ-
ont fɒnt ‖ fɑːnt **fonts** fɒnts ‖ fɑːnts
ontaine 'fɒnt eɪn ‖ fɑːn 'teɪn
ontainebleau 'fɒnt ɪn bləʊ →-ɪm-, -ən- ‖ 'fɑːnt ən bloʊ ⚠'faʊnt ən bluː —*Fr* [fɔ̃ tɛn blo]
ontana *tdmk* fɒn 'tɑːn ə ‖ fɑːn 'tæn ə
ontanel, fontanelle ˌfɒnt ə 'nel ‖ ˌfɑːnt ən 'el '· · · **~s** z
onteyn *(i)* ₍ˌ₎fɒn 'teɪn ‖ ₍ˌ₎fɑːn-, *(ii)* 'fɒnt eɪn ‖ 'fɑːn teɪn —*In AmE usually (i).*
Fonz fɒnz ‖ fɑːnz
Foochow ˌfuː 'tʃaʊ —*Chi* Fúzhōu [^{2}fu ^{1}tʂou]
food fuːd §fʊd **foods** fuːdz §fʊdz
'food chain; 'food ˌpoisoning; 'food ˌprocessor; 'food stamp
foodie 'fuːd i **~s** z
foodstuff 'fuːd stʌf §'fʊd- **~s** s
Fookes fuːks

fool fuːl **fooled** fuːld **fooling** 'fuːl ɪŋ **fools** fuːlz
ˌfool's 'errand; ˌfool's 'paradise
fooler|y 'fuːl ər |i **~ies** iz
foolhard|y 'fuːl ˌhɑːd |i ‖ -ˌhɑːrd |i **~ier** i̯ə ‖ i̯ər **~iest** i̯ɪst i̯əst **~ily** ɪ li əl i **~iness** i nəs i nɪs
foolish 'fuːl ɪʃ **~ly** li **~ness** nəs nɪs
foolproof 'fuːl pruːf §-prʊf
foolscap 'fuːl skæp 'fuːlz kæp **~s** s
Foord fɔːd ‖ fɔːrd foʊrd
Foosball 'fuːz bɔːl 'fuːs- ‖ -bɑːl
fooser 'fuːz ə ‖ -ər **~s** z
foot, Foot fʊt **feet** fiːt **footed** 'fʊt ɪd -əd ‖ 'fʊţ əd **footing** 'fʊt ɪŋ ‖ 'fʊţ ɪŋ **foots** fʊts
'foot brake; 'foot fault; 'foot ˌsoldier
footag|e 'fʊt ɪdʒ ‖ 'fʊţ ɪdʒ **~es** ɪz əz
foot-and-mouth ˌfʊt ən 'maʊθ
ˌfoot-and-'mouth diˌsease
football 'fʊt bɔːl §-bəl ‖ -bɑːl **~er/s** ə/z ‖ ər/z **~s** z
'football ˌplayer; 'football pools
foot|bath 'fʊt |bɑːθ §-bæθ ‖ -|bæθ *(not* 'fʊd-*)* **~baths** bɑːðz §bæθs, §bɑːθs, §bæðz ‖ bæðz bæθs
footboard 'fʊt bɔːd ‖ -bɔːrd -boʊrd *(not* 'fʊd-*)* **~s** z
footbridg|e 'fʊt brɪdʒ **~es** ɪz əz
Footdee *place in Grampian* fʊt 'diː —*locally also* 'fɪt i
foot-dragging 'fʊt ˌdræg ɪŋ
Foote fʊt
-footed 'fʊt ɪd -əd ‖ 'fʊţ əd — **splay-footed** ˌspleɪ 'fʊt ɪd ◂ -əd ‖ -'fʊţ əd ◂
-footer 'fʊt ə ‖ 'fʊţ ər — **six-footer** ˌsɪks 'fʊt ə ‖ -'fʊţ ər
footer *n 'football', 'line at end of page'* 'fʊt ə ‖ 'fʊţ ər **~s** z
footfall 'fʊt fɔːl ‖ -fɑːl **~s** z
foot-fault *v* 'fʊt fɔːlt -fɒlt ‖ -fɔːlt -fɑːlt **~ed** ɪd əd **~ing** ɪŋ **~s** s
foothill 'fʊt hɪl **~s** z
foothold 'fʊt həʊld →-hɒʊld ‖ -hoʊld **~s** z
footie 'fʊt i ‖ 'fʊţ i
footing 'fʊt ɪŋ ‖ 'fʊţ ɪŋ **~s** z
footl|e 'fuːt əl ‖ 'fuːţ əl **~ed** d **~es** z **~ing** ‿ɪŋ
footlight 'fʊt laɪt **~s** s
footling 'fuːt lɪŋ
footloose 'fʊt luːs
foot|man 'fʊt |mən **~men** mən
footmark 'fʊt mɑːk ‖ -mɑːrk **~s** s
footnote 'fʊt nəʊt ‖ -noʊt **~s** s
footpad 'fʊt pæd **~s** z
foot|path 'fʊt |pɑːθ §-pæθ ‖ -|pæθ **~paths** pɑːðz §pæθs, §pɑːθs, §pæðz ‖ pæðz pæθs
footplate 'fʊt pleɪt **~man** mən mæn **~men** mən men **~s** s
foot-pound ˌfʊt 'paʊnd '· · **~s** z
foot-pound-second ˌfʊt ˌpaʊnd 'sek ənd →-ŋd **~s** z
footprint 'fʊt prɪnt **~s** s
footrac|e 'fʊt reɪs **~es** ɪz əz
footrest 'fʊt rest **~s** s

F

footsie ˈfʊts i
footslog ˈfʊt slɒɡ ‖ -slɑːɡ **~ged** d **~ger/s** ə/z ‖ ᵊr/z **~ging** ɪŋ **~s** z
footsore ˈfʊt sɔː ‖ -sɔːr -soʊr **~ness** nəs nɪs
footstep ˈfʊt step **~s** s
footstool ˈfʊt stuːl **~s** z
footsure ˈfʊt ʃɔː -ʃʊə ‖ -ʃʊr -ʃɜː **~ness** nəs nɪs
footway ˈfʊt weɪ **~s** z
footwear ˈfʊt weə ‖ -wer -wær
footwork ˈfʊt wɜːk ‖ -wɜ˞ːk
footy ˈfʊt i ‖ ˈfʊṭ i
foo yong, foo yoong, foo young ˌfuː ˈjʌŋ -ˈjɒŋ, -ˈjʊŋ ‖ -ˈjʌŋ -ˈjɔːŋ, -ˈjɑːŋ, -ˈjʊŋ
foozl|e ˈfuːz ᵊl **~ed** d **~er/s** ə/z ‖ ᵊr/z **~es** z **~ing** ˌɪŋ
fop fɒp ‖ fɑːp **fops** fɒps ‖ fɑːps
fopper|y ˈfɒp ər |i ‖ ˈfɑːp- **~ies** iz
foppish ˈfɒp ɪʃ ‖ ˈfɑːp- **~ly** li **~ness** nəs nɪs
for *strong form* fɔː ‖ fɔːr, *weak form* fə ‖ fᵊr — *In both RP and GenAm ELISION gives rise to an occasional prevocalic weak form* fr, *used before weak vowels:* stay for a week ˌsteɪ frə ˈwiːk. *There is also a very casual or rapid weak form* f. *In RP some speakers also have an occasional prevocalic strong form* fɒr, *used (if at all) only in the phrases* for her fɒr ə, for him fɒr ɪm, for it fɒr ɪt, for us fɒr əs.
forag|e ˈfɒr ɪdʒ ‖ ˈfɔːr- ˈfɑːr- **~ed** d **~er/s** ə/z ‖ ᵊr/z **~es** ɪz əz **~ing** ɪŋ
ˈ**forage cap**
foramen fə ˈreɪm en fɒ-, -ən ‖ -ən fɔː- **~s** z
foramina fə ˈræm ɪn ə fɒ-, -ˈreɪm-, §-ən-
foraminifer ˌfɒr ə ˈmɪn ɪf ə -əf ə ‖ ˌfɔːr ə ˈmɪn əf ᵊr ˌfɑːr- **~s** z
foraminif|era fə ˌræm ɪ ˈnɪf |ər‿ə ˌfɒr əm-, ˌfɔːr əm-, -əˈ-- **~eral** ᵊr‿əl **~erous** ər‿əs
forasmuch fər‿əz ˈmʌtʃ ˌfɔːr əz ˈmʌtʃ, ˌfɒr- ‖ ˌfɔːr əz ˈmʌtʃ ˈ· · ·
foray *v, n* ˈfɒr eɪ ‖ ˈfɔːr eɪ ˈfɑːr- **~ed** d **~ing** ɪŋ **~s** z
forbad fə ˈbæd fɔː- ‖ fᵊr- fɔːr-
forbade fə ˈbæd fɔː-, -ˈbeɪd ‖ fᵊr- fɔːr-
for|bear *v 'hold oneself back'* fɔː |ˈbeə fə- ‖ fɔːr |ˈbeᵊr fᵊr-, -ˈbæᵊr **~bearing** ˈbeər ɪŋ ‖ ˈber ɪŋ ˈbær ɪŋ **~bears** ˈbeəz ‖ ˈbeᵊrz ˈbæᵊrz **~bore** ˈbɔː ‖ ˈbɔːr -ˈboʊr **~borne** ˈbɔːn ‖ ˈbɔːrn -ˈboʊrn
forbear *n 'ancestor'* ˈfɔː beə ‖ ˈfɔːr ber ˈfoʊr-, -bær **~s** z
forbearance fɔː ˈbeər ənᵗs fə- ‖ fɔːr ˈber- fᵊr-, -ˈbær-
Forbes fɔːbz ˈfɔːb ɪs, -əs ‖ fɔːrbz —*in Scotland usually as two syllables.*
for|bid fə |ˈbɪd fɔː- ‖ fᵊr- fɔːr- **~bad** ˈbæd **~bade** ˈbæd ˈbeɪd **~bidden** ˈbɪd ᵊn **~bidding** ˈbɪd ɪŋ
forˌbidden ˈfruit
forbidding fə ˈbɪd ɪŋ fɔː- ‖ fᵊr- fɔːr- **~ly** li **~ness** nəs nɪs
forbore fɔː ˈbɔː ‖ fɔːr ˈbɔːr -ˈboʊr
forborne fɔː ˈbɔːn ‖ fɔːr ˈbɔːrn -ˈboʊrn
Forbush ˈfɔː bʊʃ ‖ ˈfɔːr-
force fɔːs ‖ fɔːrs foʊrs **forced** fɔːst ‖ fɔːrst foʊrst **forces** ˈfɔːs ɪz -əz ‖ ˈfɔːrs əz ˈfoʊrs- **forcing** ˈfɔːs ɪŋ ‖ ˈfɔːrs ɪŋ ˈfoʊrs-
ˌ**forced ˈmarch**; ˌ**force maˈjeure** mæ ˈʒɜː mə- ‖ mɑː ˈʒɜː mæ-, mə- —*Fr* [fɔʁs ma ʒœːʁ]
force-|feed ˌfɔːs |ˈfiːd ˈ· · ‖ ˌfɔːrs- ˌfoʊrs- **~fed** ˈfed **~feeding** ˈfiːd ɪŋ **~feeds** ˈfiːdz
forceful ˈfɔːs fᵊl -fʊl ‖ ˈfɔːrs- ˈfoʊrs- **~ly** ‿i **~ness** nəs nɪs
forcemeat ˈfɔːs miːt ‖ ˈfɔːrs- ˈfoʊrs-
forceps ˈfɔːs eps -ɪps, -əps ‖ ˈfɔːrs əps -eps
forcib|le ˈfɔːs əb |ᵊl -ɪb- ‖ ˈfɔːrs- ˈfoʊrs- **~leness** ᵊl nəs -nɪs **~ly** li
ford, Ford fɔːd ‖ fɔːrd foʊrd **forded** ˈfɔːd ɪd -əd ‖ ˈfɔːrd əd ˈfoʊrd- **fording** ˈfɔːd ɪŋ ‖ ˈfɔːrd ɪŋ ˈfoʊrd- **fords, Ford's** fɔːdz ‖ fɔːrdz foʊrdz
fordable ˈfɔːd əb ᵊl ‖ ˈfɔːrd- ˈfoʊrd-
Forde fɔːd ‖ fɔːrd foʊrd
Fordham ˈfɔːd əm ‖ ˈfɔːrd- ˈfoʊrd-
Fordingbridge ˈfɔːd ɪŋ brɪdʒ ‖ ˈfɔːrd- ˈfoʊrd-
Fordyce ˈfɔːd aɪs fɔː ˈdaɪs ‖ ˈfɔːrd- —*in Scotland* ˈ·
fore fɔː ‖ fɔːr foʊr *(= four)*
ˌ**fore and ˈaft**
fore- ¦fɔː ‖ ¦fɔːr- ¦foʊr-
forearm *n 'limb from elbow to wrist'* ˈfɔːr ɑːm ‖ ˈfɔːr ɑːrm ˈfoʊr- **~s** z
forearm *v 'prepare'* ₍ᵢ₎fɔːr ˈɑːm ‖ ₍ᵢ₎fɔːr ˈɑːrm ₍ᵢ₎foʊr- **~ed** d **~ing** ɪŋ **~s** z
forebear *n 'ancestor'* ˈfɔː beə ‖ ˈfɔːr ber ˈfoʊr-, -bær **~s** z
forebod|e fɔː ˈbəʊd fə- ‖ fɔːr ˈboʊd foʊr- **~ed** ɪd əd **~es** z **~ing** ɪŋ
foreboding fɔː ˈbəʊd ɪŋ fə- ‖ fɔːr ˈboʊd ɪŋ foʊr- **~ly** li **~s** z
forebrain ˈfɔː breɪn ‖ ˈfɔːr- ˈfoʊr- **~s** z
forecast *n* ˈfɔː kɑːst §-kæst ‖ ˈfɔːr kæst ˈfoʊr- **~s** s
forecast *v* ˈfɔː kɑːst §-kæst, ₍ᵢ₎·ˈ· ‖ ˈfɔːr kæst ˈfoʊr- **~ed** ɪd əd **~er/s** ə/z ‖ ᵊr/z **~ing** ɪŋ **~s** s
forecastle ˈfəʊks ᵊl ‖ ˈfoʊks- **~s** z
foreclos|e ₍ᵢ₎fɔː ˈkləʊz ‖ ₍ᵢ₎fɔːr ˈkloʊz ₍ᵢ₎foʊr- **~ed** d **~es** ɪz əz **~ing** ɪŋ
foreclosure ₍ᵢ₎fɔː ˈkləʊʒ ə ‖ ₍ᵢ₎fɔːr ˈkloʊʒ ᵊr ₍ᵢ₎foʊr- **~s** z
forecourt ˈfɔː kɔːt ‖ ˈfɔːr kɔːrt ˈfoʊr koʊrt **~s** s
foredeck ˈfɔː dek ‖ ˈfɔːr- ˈfoʊr- **~s** s
foredoomed ₍ᵢ₎fɔː ˈduːmd ‖ ₍ᵢ₎fɔːr- ₍ᵢ₎foʊr-
forefather ˈfɔː ˌfɑːð ə ‖ ˈfɔːr ˌfɑːð ᵊr ˈfoʊr- **~s** z
forefeet ˈfɔː fiːt ‖ ˈfɔːr- ˈfoʊr-
forefinger ˈfɔː ˌfɪŋ ɡə ‖ ˈfɔːr ˌfɪŋ ɡᵊr ˈfoʊr- **~s** z
fore|foot ˈfɔː |fʊt ‖ ˈfɔːr- ˈfoʊr- **~feet** fiːt
forefront ˈfɔː frʌnt ‖ ˈfɔːr- ˈfoʊr-
foregather fɔː ˈɡæð ə ‖ fɔːr ˈɡæð ᵊr **~ed** d
foregathering fɔː ˈɡæð ər‿ɪŋ ‖ fɔːr- **~s** z
fore|go ₍ᵢ₎fɔː |ˈɡəʊ ‖ ₍ᵢ₎fɔːr |ˈɡoʊ foʊr- **~goes** ˈɡəʊz ‖ ˈɡoʊz **~going** ˈɡəʊ ɪŋ ‖ ˈɡoʊ ɪŋ **~gone** ˈɡɒn §ˈɡɔːn, §ˈɡɑːn ‖ ˈɡɔːn ˈɡɑːn **~went** ˈwent

foregoing *adj 'preceding'* 'fɔː ˌɡəʊ ɪŋ (ɪ)'- ‖ (ɪ)fɔːr 'ɡoʊ ɪŋ (ɪ)foʊr-
foregoing *part 'giving up'* (ɪ)fɔː 'ɡəʊ ɪŋ ‖ (ɪ)fɔːr 'ɡoʊ ɪŋ
foregone *pp 'given up'* (ɪ)fɔː 'ɡɒn §-'ɡɔːn, §-'ɡɑːn ‖ (ɪ)fɔːr 'ɡɔːn -'ɡɑːn
foregone *adj, 'certain'* 'fɔː ɡɒn §-ɡɔːn, §-ɡɑːn ‖ 'fɔːr ɡɔːn 'foʊr-, -ɡɑːn
ˌforegone con'clusion
foreground 'fɔː ɡraʊnd ‖ 'fɔːr- 'foʊr- **~ed** ɪd əd **~ing** ɪŋ **~s** z
forehand 'fɔː hænd ‖ 'fɔːr- 'foʊr- **~ed** ɪd əd **~s** z

FOREHEAD

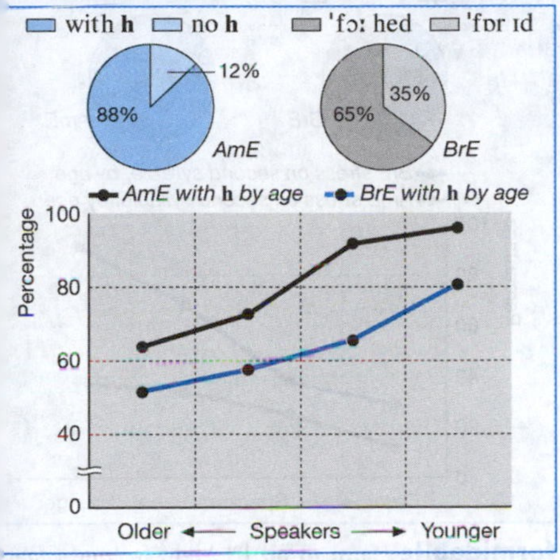

forehead 'fɔː hed 'fɒr ɪd -əd, -ed ‖ 'fɔːr hed 'foʊr-, -ed; 'fɔːr əd, 'fɑːr- —*Preference polls, AmE: with* h *88%, no* h *12%; BrE:* 'fɒr ɪd *35%,* 'fɔː hed *65%. Several BrE respondents said they would have voted for* 'fɒr ed, *an option not offered.* **~s** z
foreign 'fɒr ən -ɪn ‖ 'fɔːr ən 'fɑːr- **~ness** nəs nɪs
ˌforeign af'fairs; **ˌForeign 'Legion**; **ˌforeign 'minister**; **'Foreign ˌOffice**; **ˌForeign 'Secretary**
foreigner 'fɒr ən ə -ɪn- ‖ 'fɔːr ən ᵊr 'fɑːr- **~s** z
foreknowledge (ɪ)fɔː 'nɒl ɪdʒ ‖ (ɪ)fɔːr 'nɑːl- (ɪ)foʊr-
foreland, F~ 'fɔː lənd ‖ 'fɔːr- 'foʊr- **~s** z
foreleg 'fɔː leɡ ‖ 'fɔːr- 'foʊr- **~s** z
forelimb 'fɔː lɪm ‖ 'fɔːr- 'foʊr- **~s** z
forelock 'fɔː lɒk ‖ 'fɔːr lɑːk 'foʊr- **~s** s
fore|man, F~ 'fɔː |mən ‖ 'fɔːr- 'foʊr- **~men** mən men
foremast 'fɔː mɑːst §-mæst, -məst ‖ 'fɔːr mæst 'foʊr-, -məst —*naut* -məst **~s** s
foremost 'fɔː məʊst ‖ 'fɔːr moʊst 'foʊr-
forename 'fɔː neɪm ‖ 'fɔːr- 'foʊr- **~s** z
forenoon 'fɔː nuːn §-nʊn ‖ 'fɔːr- 'foʊr- **~s** z
forensic fə 'renᵗs ɪk fɒ-, -'renz- **~ally** ᵊl‿i **~s** s
foˌrensic 'science
foreordain ˌfɔːr ɔː 'deɪn ‖ ˌfɔːr ɔːr- ˌfoʊr- **~ed** d **~ing** ɪŋ **~ment** mənt **~s** z
forepart 'fɔː pɑːt ‖ 'fɔːr pɑːrt 'foʊr- **~s** s
forepaw 'fɔː pɔː ‖ 'fɔːr- 'foʊr-, -pɑː **~s** z
foreplay 'fɔː pleɪ ‖ 'fɔːr- 'foʊr-
forerunner 'fɔː ˌrʌn ə ‖ 'fɔːr ˌrʌn ᵊr 'foʊr- **~s** z
foresail 'fɔː seɪᵊl -sᵊl ‖ 'fɔːr- 'foʊr- —*naut* -sᵊl **~s** z
fore|see (ɪ)fɔː |'siː fə- ‖ (ɪ)fɔːr- (ɪ)foʊr- **~saw** 'sɔː ‖ 'sɑː **~seeing** 'siː ɪŋ **~seen** 'siːn
foreseeable fɔː 'siː‿əb ᵊl fə- ‖ fɔːr- foʊr-
foreshadow (ɪ)fɔː 'ʃæd əʊ ‖ (ɪ)fɔːr 'ʃæd oʊ (ɪ)foʊr- **~ed** d **~ing** ɪŋ **~s** z
foreshore 'fɔː ʃɔː ‖ 'fɔːr ʃɔːr 'foʊr ʃoʊr **~s** z
foreshorten (ɪ)fɔː 'ʃɔːt ᵊn ‖ (ɪ)fɔːr 'ʃɔːrt ᵊn (ɪ)foʊr- **~ed** d **~ing** ‿ɪŋ **~s** z
foreshow (ɪ)fɔː 'ʃəʊ ‖ (ɪ)fɔːr 'ʃoʊ **~ed** d **~ing** ɪŋ **~n** n **~s** z
foresight 'fɔː saɪt ‖ 'fɔːr- 'foʊr-
foreskin 'fɔː skɪn ‖ 'fɔːr- 'foʊr- **~s** z
forest, F~ 'fɒr ɪst -əst ‖ 'fɔːr əst 'fɑːr- **~s** s
forestall (ɪ)fɔː 'stɔːl ‖ (ɪ)fɔːr- (ɪ)foʊr-, -'stɑːl **~ed** d **~ing** ɪŋ **~s** z
forestation ˌfɒr ə 'steɪʃ ᵊn -ɪ- ‖ ˌfɔːr- ˌfɑːr-
forested 'fɒr ɪst ɪd -əst-, -əd ‖ 'fɔːr- 'fɑːr-
forester, F~ 'fɒr ɪst ə -əst- ‖ 'fɔːr əst ᵊr 'fɑːr- **~s** z
forestry 'fɒr ɪst ri -əst- ‖ 'fɔːr- 'fɑːr-
foretast|e *v* (ɪ)fɔː 'teɪst ‖ (ɪ)fɔːr- (ɪ)foʊr- **~ed** ɪd əd **~es** s **~ing** ɪŋ
foretaste *n* 'fɔː teɪst ‖ 'fɔːr- 'foʊr- **~s** s
fore|tell (ɪ)fɔː |'tel ‖ (ɪ)fɔːr- (ɪ)foʊr- **~telling** 'tel ɪŋ **~tells** 'telz **~told** 'təʊld →'tɒʊld ‖ 'toʊld
forethought 'fɔː θɔːt ‖ 'fɔːr- 'foʊr-, -θɑːt
foretold (ɪ)fɔː 'təʊld →-'tɒʊld ‖ (ɪ)fɔːr 'toʊld (ɪ)foʊr-
forever fər 'ev ə ‖ fər 'ev ᵊr
forewarn (ɪ)fɔː 'wɔːn ‖ (ɪ)fɔːr 'wɔːrn (ɪ)foʊr- **~ed** d **~ing** ɪŋ **~s** z
forewent (ɪ)fɔː 'went ‖ (ɪ)fɔːr- (ɪ)foʊr-
fore|woman 'fɔː |ˌwʊm ən ‖ 'fɔːr- 'foʊr- **~women** ˌwɪm ɪn -ən
foreword 'fɔː wɜːd ‖ 'fɔːr wɜːd 'foʊr- **~s** z
forex 'fɒr eks ‖ 'fɔːr- 'fɑːr-
Forfar 'fɔːf ə ‖ 'fɔːrf ᵊr —*also spelling pronunciation* 'fɔː fɑː ‖ 'fɔːr fɑːr
forf|eit *n, v, adj* 'fɔːf |ɪt -ət ‖ 'fɔːrf |ət **~eited** ɪt ɪd §ət-, -əd ‖ əṭ əd **~eiting** ɪt ɪŋ §ət- ‖ əṭ ɪŋ **~eits** ɪts §əts ‖ əts
forfeitable 'fɔːf ɪt əb ᵊl §'-ət- ‖ 'fɔːrf əṭ əb ᵊl
forfeiter 'fɔːf ɪt ə §-ət ə ‖ 'fɔːrf əṭ ᵊr **~s** z
forfeiture 'fɔːf ɪtʃ ə §-ətʃ- ‖ 'fɔːrf ətʃ ᵊr -ə tʃʊr, -tjʊr **~s** z
forfend fɔː 'fend ‖ fɔːr- **~ed** ɪd əd **~ing** ɪŋ **~s** z
forgather fɔː 'ɡæð ə ‖ fɔːr 'ɡæð ᵊr **~ed** d
forgathering fɔː 'ɡæð ər‿ɪŋ ‖ fɔːr- **~s** z
forgave fə 'ɡeɪv ‖ fᵊr-
forge fɔːdʒ ‖ fɔːrdʒ foʊrdʒ **forged** fɔːdʒd ‖ fɔːrdʒd foʊrdʒd **forges** 'fɔːdʒ ɪz -əz ‖ 'fɔːrdʒ əz 'foʊrdʒ- **forging** 'fɔːdʒ ɪŋ ‖ 'fɔːrdʒ ɪŋ 'foʊrdʒ-
forger 'fɔːdʒ ə ‖ 'fɔːrdʒ ᵊr 'foʊrdʒ- **~s** z
forger|y 'fɔːdʒ ər‿|i ‖ 'fɔːrdʒ- 'foʊrdʒ- **~ies** iz

for|get fə |ˈget ‖ fᵊr- —*but in formal style sometimes* fɔː- ‖ fɔːr- **~gets** ˈgets **~getting** ˈget ɪŋ ‖ ˈgeṱ ɪŋ **~got** ˈgɒt ‖ ˈgɑːt **~gotten** ˈgɒt ᵊn ‖ ˈgɑːt ᵊn

forgetful fə ˈget fᵊl -fʊl ‖ fᵊr- **~ly** i **~ness** nəs nɪs

forget-me-not fə ˈget mi nɒt ‖ fᵊr ˈget mi nɑːt **~s** s

forgettable fə ˈget əb ᵊl ‖ fᵊr ˈgeṱ əb ᵊl

forging ˈfɔːdʒ ɪŋ ‖ ˈfɔːrdʒ ɪŋ ˈfoʊrdʒ- **~s** z

forgivab|le fə ˈgɪv əb |ᵊl fɔː- ‖ fᵊr- fɔːr- **~ly** li

for|give fə |ˈgɪv ‖ fᵊr- —*but in formal style sometimes* fɔː- ‖ fɔːr- **~gave** ˈgeɪv **~given** ˈgɪv ᵊn **~gives** ˈgɪvz **~giving** ˈgɪv ɪŋ

forgiveness fə ˈgɪv nəs fɔː-,-nɪs ‖ fᵊr- fɔːr-

forgiving fə ˈgɪv ɪŋ fɔː- ‖ fᵊr- fɔːr- **~ly** li **~ness** nəs nɪs

for|go ₍ₗ₎fɔː |ˈgəʊ ‖ ₍ₗ₎fɔːr |ˈgoʊ **~goes** ˈgəʊz ‖ ˈgoʊz **~going** ˈgəʊ ɪŋ ‖ ˈgoʊ ɪŋ **~gone** ˈgɒn §ˈgɔːn, §ˈgɑːn ‖ ˈgɔːn ˈgɑːn **~went** ˈwent

forgot fə ˈgɒt ‖ fᵊr ˈgɑːt **~ten** ᵊn

forint ˈfɒr ɪnt §-ənt ‖ ˈfɔːr- —*Hungarian* [ˈfo rint] **~s** s

fork fɔːk ‖ fɔːrk **forked** fɔːkt ‖ fɔːrkt **forking** ˈfɔːk ɪŋ ‖ ˈfɔːrk ɪŋ **forks** fɔːks ‖ fɔːrks
ˌforked ˈlightning

forkful ˈfɔːk fʊl ‖ ˈfɔːrk- **~s** z

forklift ˈfɔːk lɪft ˌ·ˈ· ‖ ˈfɔːrk-
ˌfork-lift ˈtruck ‖ ˈ· ·

forlorn fə ˈlɔːn ₍ₗ₎fɔː- ‖ fᵊr ˈlɔːrn ˌfɔːr- **~ly** li **~ness** nəs nɪs
forˌlorn ˈhope

form fɔːm ‖ fɔːrm **formed** fɔːmd ‖ fɔːrmd **forming** ˈfɔːm ɪŋ ‖ ˈfɔːrm ɪŋ **forms** fɔːmz ‖ fɔːrmz

formal ˈfɔːm ᵊl ‖ ˈfɔːrm ᵊl

formaldehyde fɔː ˈmæld ɪ haɪd -ə- ‖ fɔːr- fᵊr-

formalin, F~ *tdmk* ˈfɔːm ᵊl ɪn §-ən ‖ ˈfɔːrm- -ə liːn

formalis... —*see* **formaliz...**

formalism ˈfɔːm ə ˌlɪz əm -ᵊl ˌɪz- ‖ ˈfɔːrm- **~s** z

formalist ˈfɔːm ᵊl ɪst §-əst ‖ ˈfɔːrm- **~s** s

formalit|y fɔː ˈmæl ət |i -ɪt- ‖ fɔːr ˈmæl əṱ |i **~ies** iz

formalization ˌfɔːm ᵊl aɪ ˈzeɪʃ ᵊn -ɪˈ-- ‖ ˌfɔːrm ᵊl ə- **~s** z

formaliz|e ˈfɔːm ə laɪz -ᵊl aɪz ‖ ˈfɔːrm- **~ed** d **~es** ɪz əz **~ing** ɪŋ

formally ˈfɔːm ᵊl i ‖ ˈfɔːrm-

Forman ˈfɔː mən ‖ ˈfɔːr- ˈfoʊr-

formant ˈfɔːm ənt ‖ ˈfɔːrm- **~s** s
ˈformant ˌstructure

form|at *n, v* ˈfɔːm |æt ‖ ˈfɔːrm- **~ats** æts **~atted** æt ɪd -əd ‖ æṱ əd **~atting** æt ɪŋ ‖ æṱ ɪŋ

for|mate *v 'take one's place in a formation'* fɔː ˈ|meɪt ‖ ˈfɔːr|m eɪt **~mated** meɪt ɪd -əd ‖ meɪṱ əd **~mates** meɪts **~mating** meɪt ɪŋ ‖ meɪṱ ɪŋ

formate *n 'salt or ester of formic acid'* ˈfɔːm eɪt ‖ ˈfɔːrm- **~s** s

formation fɔː ˈmeɪʃ ᵊn ‖ fɔːr- **~al** ˌəl **~s** z

formative ˈfɔːm ət ɪv ‖ ˈfɔːrm əṱ ɪv **~ly** li **~ness** nəs nɪs **~s** z

formatter ˈfɔːm æt ə ‖ ˈfɔːrm æṱ ᵊr **~s** z

formbook ˈfɔːm bʊk ‖ ˈfɔːrm- **~s** s

Formby ˈfɔːm bi ‖ ˈfɔːrm-

forme fɔːm ‖ fɔːrm *(= form)* **formes** fɔːmz ‖ fɔːrmz

former ˈfɔːm ə ‖ ˈfɔːrm ᵊr **~s** z

formerly ˈfɔːm ə li -ᵊl i ‖ ˈfɔːrm ᵊr-

formic ˈfɔːm ɪk ‖ ˈfɔːrm-
ˌformic ˈacid

Formica *tdmk,* **f~** fɔː ˈmaɪk ə ‖ fɔːr-

FORMIDABLE

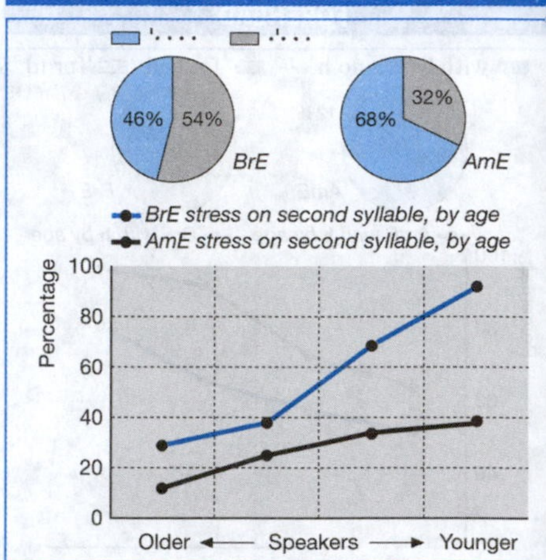

formidab|le ˈfɔːm ɪd əb |ᵊl ˈ-əd-; fə ˈmɪd-, fɔː- ‖ ˈfɔːrm- fᵊr ˈmɪd-, fɔːr- —*Also in an imitated French form,* ˌfɔːm ɪ ˈdɑːb ᵊl ‖ ˌfɔːrm- —*Fr* [fɔʁ mi dabl] — *Preference polls, BrE:* ˈ· · · · *46%,* ·ˈ· · · *54%; AmE:* ˈ· · · · *68%,* ·ˈ· · · *32%.* **~ly** li

formless ˈfɔːm ləs -lɪs ‖ ˈfɔːrm- **~ly** li **~ness** nəs nɪs

Formos|a fɔː ˈməʊs |ə -ˈməʊz- ‖ fɔːr ˈmoʊs |ə **~an/s** ᵊn/z

form|ula ˈfɔːm |jʊl ə -jəl ə ‖ ˈfɔːrm |jəl ə **~ulae** ju liː jə-, -laɪ ‖ jə liː **~ulas** jʊl əz jəl əz ‖ jəl əz

formulaic ˌfɔːm ju ˈleɪ ɪk ◂ -jə- ‖ ˌfɔːrm jə- **~ally** ᵊl ˌi

formular|y ˈfɔːm jʊl ər |i ˈ·jəl- ‖ ˈfɔːrm jə ler |i **~ies** iz

formu|late ˈfɔːm ju |leɪt -jə- ‖ ˈfɔːrm jə- **~lated** leɪt ɪd -əd ‖ leɪṱ əd **~lates** leɪts **~lating** leɪt ɪŋ ‖ leɪṱ ɪŋ

formulation ˌfɔːm ju ˈleɪʃ ᵊn -jə- ‖ ˌfɔːrm jə- **~s** z

Fornax ˈfɔːn æks ‖ ˈfɔːrn-

Forney ˈfɔːn i ‖ ˈfɔːrn i

forni|cate ˈfɔːn ɪ |keɪt -ə- ‖ ˈfɔːrn- **~cated** keɪt ɪd -əd ‖ keɪṱ əd **~cates** keɪts **~cating** keɪt ɪŋ ‖ keɪṱ ɪŋ

fornication ˌfɔːn ɪ ˈkeɪʃ ᵊn -ə- ‖ ˌfɔːrn- **~s** z

fornicator ˈfɔːn ɪ keɪt ə ˈ·ə- ‖ ˈfɔːrn ə keɪṱ ᵊr **~s** z

rnix 'fɔːn ɪks ‖ 'fɔːrn- **fornices** 'fɔːn ɪ siːz -ə- ‖ 'fɔːrn-
rrader, forrarder 'fɒr əd ə ‖ 'fɔːr əd ᵊr 'fɑːr-
rres 'fɒr ɪs -əs ‖ 'fɔːr- 'fɑːr-
rrest 'fɒr ɪst -əst ‖ 'fɔːr- 'fɑːr-
rrester 'fɒr ɪst ə -əst- ‖ 'fɔːr əst ᵊr 'fɑːr-
r|sake fə |'seɪk fɔː- ‖ fᵊr- fɔːr- **~saken** 'seɪk ən **~sakes** 'seɪks **~saking** 'seɪk ɪŋ **~sook** 'sʊk
rsooth fə 'suːθ fɔː- ‖ fᵊr- fɔːr-
rster 'fɔːst ə 'fɒst- ‖ 'fɔːrst ᵊr
r|swear (ı)fɔː |'sweə ‖ (ı)fɔːr |'sweᵊr 'swæᵊr **~swearing** 'sweər ɪŋ ‖ 'swer ɪŋ 'swær ɪŋ **~swears** 'sweəz ‖ 'sweᵊrz 'swæᵊrz **~swore** 'swɔː ‖ 'swɔːr 'swoʊr **~sworn** 'swɔːn ‖ 'swɔːrn 'swoʊrn
rsyte 'fɔː saɪt ‖ 'fɔːr-
rsyth *(i)* fɔː 'saɪθ ‖ fɔːr-, *(ii)* 'fɔː saɪθ ‖ 'fɔːr- *—The Scottish family name is (i).*
rsythia fɔː 'saɪθ i‿ə fə-, -'sɪθ- ‖ fɔːr 'sɪθ i‿ə fᵊr-, -'saɪθ- **~s** z
ort, Fort fɔːt ‖ fɔːrt foʊrt **forts** fɔːts ‖ fɔːrts foʊrts
(ı)**Fort 'Knox**; (ı)**Fort 'Lauderdale**; (ı)**Fort 'William**
orte *loud,* **Forte** *family name* 'fɔːt eɪ -i ‖ 'fɔːrt eɪ **~s** z
orte *'positive characteristic'* 'fɔːt eɪ -i; fɔːt ‖ fɔːrt foʊrt; 'fɔːrţ i, 'fɔːrt eɪ **fortes** 'fɔːt eɪz -iz; fɔːts ‖ fɔːrts foʊrts; 'fɔːrţ iz, 'fɔːrt eɪz
ortean 'fɔːt i‿ən ‖ 'fɔːrţ-
ortepiano, forte-piano ˌfɔːt i pi 'æn əʊ ˌ·eɪ-, -'ɑːn-; ˌ· ·'pjæn-, ˌ· ·'pjɑːn- ‖ ˌfɔːrţ i pi 'ɑːn oʊ ˌfɔːrt eɪ- **~s** z
ortes *—see* **forte, fortis**
ortescue 'fɔːt ɪ skjuː -ə- ‖ 'fɔːrţ-
orth, Forth fɔːθ ‖ fɔːrθ foʊrθ
orthcoming (ı)fɔːθ 'kʌm ɪŋ ‖ (ı)fɔːrθ- (ı)foʊrθ- **~ness** nəs nɪs
orthright 'fɔːθ raɪt ˌ·'· ‖ 'fɔːrθ- 'foʊrθ- **~ly** li **~ness** nəs nɪs
orthwith ˌfɔːθ 'wɪθ -'wɪð ‖ ˌfɔːrθ- ˌfoʊrθ-
orties, F~ 'fɔːt iz §-tiz ‖ 'fɔːrţ iz
ortieth 'fɔːt i‿əθ ɪθ ‖ 'fɔːrţ i‿əθ **~s** s
ortifiable 'fɔːt ɪ faɪ‿əb ᵊl '·ə-, ˌ· ·'· · · ‖ 'fɔːrţ ə-
ortification ˌfɔːt ɪf ɪ 'keɪʃ ᵊn ˌ·əf-, §-ə'·- ‖ ˌfɔːrţ əf- **~s** z
'orti|fy 'fɔːt ɪ |faɪ -ə- ‖ 'fɔːrţ ə- **~fied** faɪd **~fier/s** faɪ‿ə/z ‖ faɪ‿ᵊr/z **~fies** faɪz **~fying** faɪ ɪŋ
Fortinbras 'fɔːt ɪn bræs →-ɪm-, §-ᵊn- ‖ 'fɔːrt ᵊn-
fortis 'fɔːt ɪs §-əs ‖ 'fɔːrţ əs **fortes** 'fɔːt iːz -eɪz ‖ 'fɔːrt-
fortissimo fɔː 'tɪs ɪ məʊ -ə- ‖ fɔːr 'tɪs ə moʊ **~s** z
fortitude 'fɔːt ɪ tjuːd -ə-, →-tʃuːd ‖ 'fɔːrţ ə tuːd -tjuːd
fortnight 'fɔːt naɪt ‖ 'fɔːrt- 'foʊrt- **~s** s
fortnight|ly 'fɔːt naɪt |li ‖ 'fɔːrt- 'foʊrt- **~lies** liz
Fortnum 'fɔːt nəm ‖ 'fɔːrt- **~'s** z

Fortran, FORTRAN 'fɔː træn ‖ 'fɔːr-
fortress 'fɔːtr əs -ɪs ‖ 'fɔːrtr əs **~es** ɪz əz
fortuitous fɔː 'tjuː‿ɪt əs →-'tʃuː‿, ət-, ⚠ˌfɔːtʃ u 'ɪʃ əs ◂ ‖ fɔːr 'tuː əţ əs fᵊr-, -'tjuː- **~ly** li **~ness** nəs nɪs
fortunate 'fɔːtʃ ən‿ət ɪt ‖ 'fɔːrtʃ- **~ly** li
fortune 'fɔːtʃ ən -uːn; 'fɔːt juːn ‖ 'fɔːrtʃ ən **~s** z
'fortune ˌhunter
fortune-tell|er 'fɔːtʃ ən ˌtel |ə -uːn-; 'fɔːt juːn- ‖ 'fɔːrtʃ ən ˌtel |ᵊr **~ers** əz ‖ ᵊrz **~ing** ɪŋ
fort|y, Forty 'fɔːt |i §'fɔːt t|i ‖ 'fɔːrţ |i **~ies** iz
ˌforty 'winks
forty-five ˌfɔːt i 'faɪv ◂ §-ti- ‖ ˌfɔːrţ i- **~s** z
forty-niner ˌfɔːt i 'naɪn ə §-ti- ‖ ˌfɔːrţ i 'naɪn ᵊr **~s** z
forum 'fɔːr əm ‖ 'foʊr- **~s** z
forward 'fɔː wəd ‖ 'fɔːr wᵊrd *—but the adjective and adverb, in BrE nautical use, are* 'fɒr əd **~ed** ɪd əd **~er/s** ə/z ‖ ᵊr/z **~ing** ɪŋ **~s** z
forward-looking ˌfɔː wəd 'lʊk ɪŋ ◂ '·,·· ‖ ˌfɔːr wᵊrd-
ˌforward-ˌlooking 'policies
forward|ly 'fɔː wəd |li ‖ 'fɔːr wᵊrd |li **~ness** nəs nɪs
forwards 'fɔː wədz ‖ 'fɔːr wᵊrdz
forwent (ı)fɔː 'went ‖ (ı)fɔːr-
Fosbury 'fɒz bər‿i ‖ 'fɑːz ˌber i
ˌFosbury 'flop
Fosdick 'fɒz dɪk ‖ 'fɑːz-
Fosdyke 'fɒz daɪk ‖ 'fɑːz-
foss, Foss fɒs ‖ fɑːs **fosses** 'fɒs ɪz -əz ‖ 'fɑːs əz
foss|a 'fɒs |ə ‖ 'fɑːs |ə **~ae** iː **~as** əz
fosse, Fosse fɒs ‖ fɑːs **fosses** 'fɒs ɪz -əz ‖ 'fɑːs əz
ˌFosse 'Way
fossick 'fɒs ɪk ‖ 'fɑːs- **~ed** t **~er/s** ə/z ‖ ᵊr/z **~ing** ɪŋ **~s** s
fossil 'fɒs ᵊl -ɪl ‖ 'fɑːs ᵊl **~s** z
fossilis... *—see* **fossiliz...**
fossilization ˌfɒs ᵊl aɪ 'zeɪʃ ᵊn ˌ·ɪl-, -ɪ'·- ‖ ˌfɑːs ᵊl ə- **~s** z
fossiliz|e 'fɒs ᵊl aɪz -ɪ laɪz ‖ 'fɑːs- **~ed** d **~es** ɪz əz **~ing** ɪŋ
foster, F~ 'fɒst ə ‖ 'fɑːst ᵊr **~ed** d **fostering** 'fɒst ər‿ɪŋ ‖ 'fɑːst ər ɪŋ **~s** z
foster- 'fɒst ə ‖ 'fɑːst ᵊr — **foster-brother** 'fɒst ə ˌbrʌð ə ‖ 'fɑːst ᵊr ˌbrʌð ᵊr
fosterage 'fɒst ər ɪdʒ ‖ 'fɑːst-
fosterling 'fɒst ə lɪŋ ‖ 'fɑːst ᵊr- **~s** z
Fothergill 'fɒð ə gɪl ‖ 'fɑːð ᵊr-
Fotheringay, Fotheringhay 'fɒð ər‿ɪŋ geɪ ‖ 'fɑːð- *—but the Northants village is nowadays called* -heɪ
Fotheringham 'fɒð ər‿ɪŋ əm ‖ 'fɑːð ər‿ɪŋ hæm
Foucault 'fuːk əʊ (ı)fuː 'kəʊ ‖ fuː 'koʊ *—Fr* [fu ko]
fouetté 'fuː‿ə teɪ ‖ ˌfuː ə 'teɪ *—Fr* [fwɛ te] **~s** z
fought fɔːt ‖ fɑːt

foul faʊl (= *fowl*) **fouled** faʊld **fouler** 'faʊl ə ‖ -ᵊr **foulest** 'faʊl ɪst -əst **fouling** 'faʊl ɪŋ **foully** 'faʊl li -i **fouls** faʊlz
ˌfoul 'play
Foula 'fuːl ə
foulard 'fuːl ɑː -ɑːd; fu 'lɑː, -'lɑːd ‖ fu 'lɑːrd **~s** z
Foulds fəʊldz →fɒʊldz ‖ foʊldz
Foulkes *(i)* fəʊks ‖ foʊks, *(ii)* faʊks
foul-mouthed ˌfaʊl 'maʊðd ◂ ‖ -'maʊθt ◂
foulness 'faʊl nəs -nɪs **~es** ɪz əz
Foulness ˌfaʊl 'nes
foul-up 'faʊl ʌp **~s** s
found faʊnd **founded** 'faʊnd ɪd -əd **founding** 'faʊnd ɪŋ **founds** faʊndz
ˌfounding 'father
foundation faʊn 'deɪʃ ᵊn **~s** z
foun'dation course; **foun'dation ˌgarment**; **foun'dation stone**
foundationer faʊn 'deɪʃ ᵊn‿ə ‖ ‿ər **~s** z
founder 'faʊnd ə ‖ -ᵊr **~ed** d **foundering** 'faʊnd‿ər ɪŋ **~s** z
foundling 'faʊnd lɪŋ **~s** z
foundr|y 'faʊndr |i **~ies** iz
fount *'set of printing type'* fɒnt faʊnt ‖ fɑːnt faʊnt **founts** fɒnts faʊnts ‖ fɑːnts faʊnts
fount *'spring, origin'* faʊnt **founts** faʊnts
fountain 'faʊnt ɪn -ən ‖ 'faʊnt ᵊn **~s** z
'fountain pen; **ˌFountains 'Abbey**
Fountain, Fountaine 'faʊnt ɪn -ən ‖ 'faʊnt ᵊn
fountainhead 'faʊnt ɪn hed -ən-, ˌ·'· ‖ 'faʊnt ᵊn- **~s** z
four fɔː ‖ fɔːr foʊr (= *fore*) **fours** fɔːz ‖ fɔːrz foʊrz
'four flush; **ˌfour 'hundred◂**
four by four, 4x4 ˌfɔː baɪ 'fɔː -bi- ‖ 'fɔːr baɪ fɔːr 'foʊr baɪ foʊr **~s** z
Fourcin 'fɔːs ɪn §-ᵊn ‖ 'fɔːrs-
foureyes 'fɔːr aɪz ‖ 'fɔːr- 'foʊr-
fourfold 'fɔː fəʊld →-fɒʊld ‖ 'fɔːr foʊld 'foʊr-
four-footed ˌfɔː 'fʊt ɪd ◂ -əd ‖ ˌfɔːr 'fʊţ əd ◂ ˌfoʊr-
Fourier 'fʊr i‿ə 'fʊər-, -eɪ ‖ 'fʊr i eɪ -i‿ᵊr —*Fr* [fu ʁje]
four-in-hand ˌfɔːr ɪn 'hænd §-ən- ‖ ˌfɔːr ən- ˌfoʊr-
four-|leaf 'fɔː |liːf ‖ 'fɔːr- 'foʊr-
four-leaved ˌfɔː 'liːvd ◂ ‖ ˌfɔːr- ˌfoʊr-
ˌfour-leaved 'clover
four-legged ˌfɔː 'leg ɪd ◂ -əd; -'legd ◂ ‖ ˌfɔːr- ˌfoʊr-
four-letter ˌfɔː 'let ə ◂ ‖ ˌfɔːr 'leţ ᵊr ◂ ˌfoʊr-
ˌfour-ˌletter 'word
four-o'clock ˌfɔːr ə 'klɒk ◂ ‖ ˌfɔːr ə 'klɑːk ◂ ˌfoʊr-
four-part ˌfɔː 'pɑːt ◂ ‖ ˌfɔːr 'pɑːrt ◂ ˌfoʊr-
fourpence 'fɔːp ənᵗs →-mᵖs; 'fɔː penᵗs, ˌ·'· ‖ 'fɔːrp- 'foʊrp-
fourpenny 'fɔːp ən‿i ‖ 'fɔːr ˌpen i 'foʊr-
four-poster ˌfɔː 'pəʊst ə ◂ ‖ ˌfɔːr 'poʊst ᵊr ◂ ˌfoʊr- **~s** z
ˌfour-ˌposter 'bed
four-pounder ˌfɔː 'paʊnd ə ‖ ˌfɔːr 'paʊnd ᵊr ˌfoʊr- **~s** z
fourscore ˌfɔː 'skɔː ◂ '· · ‖ ˌfɔːr 'skɔːr ◂ ˌfoʊr 'skoʊr
ˌfourscore and 'ten
foursome 'fɔː səm ‖ 'fɔːr- 'foʊr- **~s** z
foursquare ˌfɔː 'skweə ◂ '· · ‖ ˌfɔːr 'skweᵊr ˌfoʊr-, -'skwæᵊr
four-star 'fɔː stɑː ‖ 'fɔːr stɑːr 'foʊr-
four-stroke 'fɔː strəʊk ‖ 'fɔːr stroʊk 'foʊr-
fourteen ˌfɔː 'tiːn ◂ §ˌfɔːt- ‖ ˌfɔːr- ˌfɔːrt-, ˌfoʊr ˌfoʊrt- **~s** z
fourteenth ˌfɔː 'tiːnᵗθ ◂ §ˌfɔːt- ‖ ˌfɔːr- ˌfɔːrt-, ˌfoʊr-, ˌfoʊrt- **~s** s
fourth fɔːθ ‖ fɔːrθ foʊrθ (= *forth*) **fourthly** 'fɔːθ li ‖ 'fɔːrθ li 'foʊrθ- **fourths** fɔːθs ‖ fɔːrθs foʊrθs
ˌfourth di'mension; **ˌfourth e'state**; **ˌFourth of Ju'ly**
four-wheel ˌfɔː 'wiːᵊl ◂ -'hwiːᵊl ‖ ˌfɔːr '*h*wiːᵊl ˌfoʊr-
ˌfour-wheel 'drive
four-wheeler ˌfɔː 'wiːl ə ◂ -'hwiːl- ‖ ˌfɔːr '*h*wiːl ᵊr ˌfoʊr- **~s** z
fove|a 'fəʊv i |ə 'fɒv- ‖ 'foʊv- **~ae** iː
Foveaux fə 'vəʊ ‖ -'voʊ
Fowey fɔɪ
Fowke *(i)* fəʊk ‖ foʊk, *(ii)* faʊk
Fowkes *(i)* fəʊks ‖ foʊks, *(ii)* faʊks
fowl faʊl **fowls** faʊlz
'fowl pest
fowler, F~ 'faʊl ə ‖ -ᵊr **~s** z
Fowles faʊlz
Fowlmere 'faʊl mɪə ‖ -mɪr
fox, Fox fɒks ‖ fɑːks **foxed** fɒkst ‖ fɑːkst **foxes** 'fɒks ɪz -əz ‖ 'fɑːks əz **foxing** 'fɒks ɪŋ ‖ 'fɑːks ɪŋ
ˌfox 'terrier
Foxcroft 'fɒks krɒft ‖ 'fɑːks krɔːft -krɑːft
Foxe fɒks ‖ fɑːks
foxfire 'fɒks ˌfaɪ‿ə ‖ 'fɑːks ˌfaɪ‿ᵊr
foxglove 'fɒks glʌv ‖ 'fɑːks- **~s** z
foxhole 'fɒks həʊl →-hɒʊl ‖ 'fɑːks hoʊl **~s** z
foxhound 'fɒks haʊnd ‖ 'fɑːks- **~s** z
foxhunt 'fɒks hʌnt ‖ 'fɑːks- **~s** s
foxhunt|er, F~ 'fɒks ˌhʌnt |ə ‖ 'fɑːks ˌhʌnţ |ᵊr **~ers** əz ‖ ᵊrz **~ing** ɪŋ
foxi... —*see* **foxy**
foxtail 'fɒks teɪᵊl ‖ 'fɑːks- **~s** z
Foxton 'fɒkst ən ‖ 'fɑːkst-
foxtrot 'fɒks trɒt ‖ 'fɑːks trɑːt **~s** s
fox|y 'fɒks |i ‖ 'fɑːks |i **~ier** i‿ə ‖ i‿ᵊr **~iest** i‿ɪst i‿əst **~ily** ɪ li əl i **~iness** i nəs i nɪs
Foy fɔɪ
foyer 'fɔɪ eɪ -ə; 'fwaɪ eɪ ‖ 'fɔɪ ᵊr -eɪ; 'fwɑː jeɪ —*Fr* [fwa je] **~s** z
Foyle fɔɪᵊl **Foyles, Foyle's** fɔɪᵊlz
Fra frɑː —*It* [fra]
frabjous 'fræb dʒəs
fracas *sing.* 'fræk ɑː ‖ 'freɪk əs 'fræk- *(*)*
fracas *pl* 'fræk ɑːz ‖ 'feɪk əs 'fræk- **~es** ɪz əz
fractal 'frækt ᵊl **~s** z
fraction 'fræk ʃᵊn **~s** z

actional 'fræk ʃᵊn‿əl **~ly** i
actio|nate 'fræk ʃə |neɪt **~nated** neɪt ɪd -əd ‖ neɪţ əd **~nates** neɪts **~nating** neɪt ɪŋ ‖ neɪţ ɪŋ
actionation ˌfræk ʃə 'neɪʃ ᵊn **~s** z
actionator 'fræk ʃə neɪt ə ‖ -neɪţ ᵊr **~s** z
actious 'fræk ʃəs **~ly** li **~ness** nəs nɪs
acture 'fræk tʃə -ʃə ‖ -tʃᵊr -ʃᵊr **~d** d **fracturing** 'fræk tʃər‿ɪŋ -ʃər‿ **~s** z
ag fræg **fragged** frægd **fragging** 'fræg ɪŋ **frags** frægz
agile 'frædʒ aɪᵊl ‖ -ᵊl *(*)* **~ly** li **~ness** nəs nɪs
agility frə 'dʒɪl ət i fræ-, -ɪt- ‖ -əţ i
agment *n* 'fræg mənt **~s** s
ag|ment *v* ₍ˌ₎fræg |'ment **~mented** 'ment ɪd -əd ‖ 'menţ əd **~menting** 'ment ɪŋ ‖ 'menţ ɪŋ **~ments** 'ments
agmental fræg 'ment ᵊl ‖ -'menţ ᵊl
agmentary 'fræg mənt‿ər i fræg 'ment- ‖ 'fræg mən ter i
agmentation ˌfræg mən 'teɪʃ ᵊn -men- **~s** z
ragonard 'fræg ə nɑː -ɒ- ‖ ˌfrɑːg oʊ 'nɑːr ˌfræg-, -ə- —*Fr* [fʁa gɔ naːʁ]
ragranc|e 'freɪg rənᵗs **~es** ɪz əz
ragrant 'freɪg rənt **~ly** li **~ness** nəs nɪs
raidy cat 'freɪd i kæt **~s** s
rail freɪᵊl **frailer** 'freɪᵊl ə ‖ -ᵊr **frailest** 'freɪᵊl ɪst -əst **frailly** 'freɪᵊl li **frailness** 'freɪl nəs -nɪs
rail|ty 'freɪᵊl |ti **~ties** tiz
rain freɪn
rame, Frame freɪm **framed** freɪmd **framer/s** 'freɪm ə/z ‖ -ᵊr/z **frames** freɪmz **framing** 'freɪm ɪŋ
ˌframe of 'mind; **ˌframe of 'reference**
rame-up 'freɪm ʌp **~s** s
ramework 'freɪm wɜːk ‖ -wɜːk **~s** s
ramingham *(i)* 'freɪm ɪŋ əm ‖ -hæm, *(ii)* 'fræm-
ramlingham 'fræm lɪŋ əm ‖ -hæm
ramlington 'fræm lɪŋ tən
rampton 'fræmpt ən
ran fræn
ranc fræŋk *(= frank)* —*Fr* [fʁɑ̃] **francs** fræŋks
rance frɑːnᵗs §frænᵗs ‖ frænᵗs **France's** 'frɑːnᵗs ɪz §'frænᵗs-, -əz ‖ 'frænᵗs əz
rances *personal name* 'frɑːnᵗs ɪs §'frænᵗs-, -əs ‖ 'frænᵗs-
Francesca fræn 'tʃesk ə -'sesk- ‖ frɑːn- fræn-
franchis|e 'fræntʃ aɪz 'frɑːntʃ- **~ed** d **~es** ɪz əz **~ing** ɪŋ
franchisee ˌfræntʃ aɪ 'ziː ˌfrɑːntʃ- **~s** z
franchisement 'fræntʃ ɪz mənt 'frɑːntʃ-, §-əz- ‖ -aɪz- -əz- **~s** s
franchisor ˌfræntʃ aɪ 'zɔː ˌfrɑːntʃ-, -ɪ- ‖ -'zɔːr -ə- **~s** z
Francis 'frɑːnᵗs ɪs §'frænᵗs-, -əs ‖ 'frænᵗs-
Franciscan fræn 'sɪsk ən **~s** z
francium 'frænᵗs i‿əm 'frɑːnᵗs-
Franck *composer* frɒŋk frɑːŋk ‖ frɑːŋk —*Fr* [fʁɑ̃ːk]
Franco 'fræŋk əʊ ‖ -oʊ 'frɑːŋk- —*Sp* ['fraŋ ko]

Franco- ¦fræŋk əʊ ‖ -oʊ — **Franco-British** ˌfræŋk əʊ 'brɪt ɪʃ ◂ ‖ -oʊ 'brɪţ ɪʃ ◂
Francois, François 'frɒnᵗs wɑː 'frɑːnᵗs-, 'frænᵗs-, ˌ·'· ‖ frɑːn 'swɑː —*Fr* [fʁɑ̃ swa]
Francoise, Françoise 'frɒnᵗs wɑːz 'frɑːnᵗs-, 'frænᵗs-, ˌ·'· ‖ frɑːn 'swɑːz —*Fr* [fʁɑ̃ swaːz]
francolin 'fræŋk əʊl ɪn §-ən ‖ -əl‿ən **~s** z
Franconi|a fræŋ 'kəʊn i‿|ə ‖ -'koʊn- **~an/s** ən/z
Francophile 'fræŋk əʊ faɪᵊl ‖ -ə- **~s** z
francophobe, F~ 'fræŋk əʊ fəʊb ‖ -ə foʊb **~s** z
francophone, F~ 'fræŋk əʊ fəʊn ‖ -ə foʊn **~s** z
frangible 'frændʒ əb ᵊl -ɪb-
frangipani ˌfrændʒ ɪ 'pɑːn i §-ə-, -'pæn- ‖ -'pæn i **~s** z
Franglais, f~ 'frɒŋ gleɪ 'frɑːŋ- ‖ frɑːn 'gleɪ —*Fr* [fʁɑ̃ glɛ]
frank, Frank fræŋk **franked** fræŋkt **franker** 'fræŋk ə ‖ -ᵊr **frankest** 'fræŋk ɪst -əst **franking** 'fræŋk ɪŋ **franks** fræŋks
Frankau *(i)* 'fræŋk əʊ ‖ -oʊ, *(ii)* -aʊ
frankenfood 'fræŋk ən fuːd **~s** z
Frankenstein 'fræŋk ən staɪn -ɪn- —*Ger* ['fʁaŋk ᵊn ʃtain]
Frankfort *places in US* 'fræŋk fət ‖ -fᵊrt
Frankfurt 'fræŋk fɜːt -fət ‖ -fᵊrt —*Ger* ['fʁaŋk fʊʁt]
frankfurter, F~ 'fræŋk fɜːt ə -fət- ‖ -fᵊrţ ᵊr **~s** z
Frankie 'fræŋk i
frankincense 'fræŋk ɪn ˌsenᵗs -ən-
Frankish 'fræŋk ɪʃ
Frankland 'fræŋk lənd
franklin, F~ 'fræŋk lɪn -lən **~s, ~'s** z
frankly 'fræŋk li
Franklyn 'fræŋk lɪn -lən
frankness 'fræŋk nəs -nɪs
Frannie 'fræn i
Frant frænt
frantic 'frænt ɪk ‖ 'frænţ ɪk **~ally** ᵊl‿i **~ness** nəs nɪs
Franz frænts frɑːnts ‖ frɑːnᵗs —*Ger* [fʁants] —*but as an American name also* frænz
frap fræp **frapped** fræpt **frapping** 'fræp ɪŋ **fraps** fræps
frappe, frappé 'fræp eɪ ‖ fræ 'peɪ —*Fr* [fʁa pe] **~s** z
Frascati fræ 'skɑːt i —*It* [fra 'skaː ti]
Fraser 'freɪz ə ‖ -ᵊr
Fraserburgh 'freɪz ə bər‿ə -ə ˌbʌr ə ‖ -ᵊr ˌbɜː oʊ
Frasier 'freɪz i‿ə 'freɪʒ ə ‖ 'freɪʒ ᵊr
frass fræs
frat fræt **frats** fræts
fratch|y 'frætʃ |i **~iness** i nəs i nɪs
Frater, f~ 'freɪt ə ‖ 'freɪţ ᵊr
fraternal frə 'tɜːn ᵊl ‖ -'tɜːn- **~ism** ˌɪz əm **~ly** i
fraternis... —*see* **fraterniz...**
fraternit|y frə 'tɜːn ət |i -ɪt- ‖ -'tɜːn əţ |i **~ies** iz

F

fraternization ˌfræt ən aɪ ˈzeɪʃ ən -ɪˈ-- ‖ ˌfræţ ərn ə-
fraterniz|e ˈfræt ə naɪz -ən aɪz ‖ -ər- **~ed** d **~er/s** ə/z ‖ ər/z **~es** ɪz əz **~ing** ɪŋ
fratricidal ˌfrætr ɪ ˈsaɪd əl ◂ ˌfreɪtr-, -ə- **~ly** i
fratricide ˈfrætr ɪ saɪd ˈfreɪtr-, -ə- **~s** z
Fratton ˈfræt ən
Frau fraʊ —*Ger* [fʁau]
(ˌ)**Frau ˈBecker**
fraud frɔːd ‖ frɑːd **frauds** frɔːdz ‖ frɑːdz
fraudster ˈfrɔːd stə ‖ -stər ˈfrɑːd- **~s** z
fraudulence ˈfrɔːd jʊl ənts -jəl-, ˈfrɔːdʒ əl- ‖ ˈfrɔːdʒ əl- ˈfrɑːdʒ-
fraudulent ˈfrɔːd jʊl ənt -jəl-, ˈfrɔːdʒ əl- ‖ ˈfrɔːdʒ əl- ˈfrɑːdʒ- **~ly** li
fraught frɔːt ‖ frɑːt
fraulein, fräulein ˈfrɔɪ laɪn ˈfraʊ- —*Ger* Fräulein [ˈfʁɔy lain] **~s** z
Fraunhofer ˈfraʊn həʊf ə ‖ -hoʊf ər —*Ger* [ˈfʁaun hoːf ɐ]
ˈFraunhofer lines
fray freɪ **frayed** freɪd **fraying** ˈfreɪ ɪŋ **frays** freɪz
Fray Bentos ˌfreɪ ˈbent ɒs ‖ -oʊs —*Sp* [frai ˈβen tos]
Frayn, Frayne freɪn
Frazer ˈfreɪz ə ‖ -ər
Frazier ˈfreɪz i‿ə ‖ ˈfreɪʒ ər -i‿ər (*)
frazil ˈfreɪz ɪl ˈfræz-, -əl
frazzl|e ˈfræz əl **~ed** d **~es** z **~ing** ‿ɪŋ
freak friːk **freaked** friːkt **freaking** ˈfriːk ɪŋ **freaks** friːks
freakish ˈfriːk ɪʃ **~ly** li **~ness** nəs nɪs
freak-out ˈfriːk aʊt **~s** s
freak|y ˈfriːk| i **~ier** i‿ə ‖ i‿ər **~iest** i‿ɪst əst **~ily** ɪ li əl i **~iness** i nəs -nɪs
Frean friːn
freckle ˈfrek əl **~d** d **~s** z
Fred fred
Freda ˈfriːd ə
Freddie, Freddy ˈfred i
Frederic ˈfredr ɪk ˈfred ər ɪk
Frederica ˌfred ə ˈriːk ə fre ˈdriːk ə
Frederick ˈfredr ɪk ˈfred ər ɪk
Fredericksburg ˈfred‿ər ɪks bɜːg ‖ -bɜːg
Fredericton ˈfredr ɪk tən ˈfred ər ɪk tən
Fredonia frɪ ˈdəʊn i‿ə frə- ‖ -ˈdoʊn-
free friː **freed** friːd **freeing** ˈfriː ɪŋ **freely** ˈfriː li **freer** ˈfriː‿ə ‖ ər **frees** friːz **freest** ˈfriː‿ɪst əst
ˌfree ˈagent; **ˌfree asˌsociˈation**; **ˌFree ˈChurch**; **ˌfree colˌlective ˈbargaining**; **ˌfree ˈenterprise**; **ˌfree ˈgift**; **ˌfree ˈhand**; **ˌfree ˈhouse**; **ˌfree ˈkick**; **ˌFree ˈKirk**; **ˌfree ˈlove**; **ˌfree ˈpardon**; **ˌfree ˈpass**; **ˌfree ˈport**; **ˌfree ˈspeech**; **ˌfree ˈtrade, ˌFree Trade ˈHall**; **ˌfree ˈverse**; **ˌfree ˈwill**
-free friː —*New formations with this suffix tend to be late-stressed* (ˌlead-ˈfree), *long-established ones early-stressed* (ˈcarefree)
freebas|e ˈfriː beɪs **~ed** t **~es** ɪz əz **~ing** ɪŋ
freebee, freebie ˈfriːb i **~s** z
freeboard ˈfriː bɔːd ‖ -bɔːrd -boʊrd
freebooter ˈfriː ˌbuːt ə ‖ -ˌbuːţ ər **~s** z
freeborn ˌfriː ˈbɔːn ◂ ˈ· · ‖ -ˈbɔːrn ◂
freed friːd
freed|man ˈfriːd |mən -mæn **~men** mən men
freedom ˈfriː dəm **~s** z
ˈfreedom ˌfighter
freed|woman ˈfriːd |ˌwʊm ən **~women** ˌwɪm ɪn -ən
free-fall ˌfriː ˈfɔːl ◂ ˈ· · ‖ -ˈfɑːl **~ing** ɪŋ
free-floating ˌfriː ˈfləʊt ɪŋ ◂ ‖ -ˈfloʊţ ɪŋ
Freefone *tdmk* ˈfriː fəʊn ‖ -foʊn
free-for-all ˈfriː fər ˌɔːl ˌ· · ˈ· ‖ -fər-ˌɑːl **~s** z
freeform ˈfriː fɔːm ‖ -fɔːrm
freehand ˈfriː hænd
freehanded ˌfriː ˈhænd ɪd ◂ -əd **~ly** li **~ness** nəs nɪs
freehold ˈfriː həʊld →-hɒʊld ‖ -hoʊld **~s** z
freeholder ˈfriː həʊld ə →-hɒʊld- ‖ -hoʊld ər **~s** z
freelanc|e ˈfriː lɑːnts §-lænts ‖ -lænts **~ed** t **~es** ɪz əz **~ing** ɪŋ
free-liver ˌfriː ˈlɪv ə ‖ -ər **~s** z
free-living ˌfriː ˈlɪv ɪŋ ◂
freeload ˌfriː ˈləʊd ˈ· · ‖ -ˈloʊd **~ed** ɪd əd **~er/s** ə/z ‖ ər/z **~ing** ɪŋ **~s** z
Freelove ˈfriː lʌv
freely ˈfriː li
free|man, F~ ˈfriː |mən -mæn **~men** mən men
freemartin ˈfriː ˌmɑːt ɪn §-ən ‖ -ˌmɑːrt ən **~s** z
freemason, F~ ˈfriː ˌmeɪs ən ˌ·ˈ· · **~s** z
freemasonry, F~ ˈfriː ˌmeɪs ən ri ˌ·ˈ· · ·
freemen ˈfriː mən -men
freenet ˈfriː net **~s** s
freephone ˈfriː fəʊn ‖ -foʊn
Freeport ˈfriː pɔːt ‖ -pɔːrt -poʊrt
freepost, F~ *tdmk* ˈfriː pəʊst ‖ -poʊst
freer ˈfriː‿ə ‖ ər **~s** z
Freer frɪə ‖ frɪər
free-range ˌfriː ˈreɪndʒ ◂
free-running *adj* ˌfriː ˈrʌn ɪŋ ◂
freerunning *n* ˈfriː ˌrʌn ɪŋ
freesheet ˈfriː ʃiːt **~s** s
freesia ˈfriːz i‿ə ˈfriːʒ ə, ˈfriːʒ i‿ə ‖ ˈfriːʒ ə **~s** z
Freeson ˈfriːs ən
free-spoken ˌfriː ˈspəʊk ən ◂ ‖ -ˈspoʊk- **~ness** nəs nɪs
freest ˈfriː‿ɪst əst
free-standing ˌfriː ˈstænd ɪŋ ◂
freestone, F~ ˈfriː stəʊn ‖ -stoʊn
freestyle ˈfriː staɪəl
freethinker ˌfriː ˈθɪŋk ə ‖ -ər **~s** z
freethinking ˌfriː ˈθɪŋk ɪŋ
free-to-air ˌfriː tu ˈeə ◂ -tə- ‖ -ˈeər ◂ -æər ◂
Freetown ˈfriː taʊn
Freeview *tdmk* ˈfriː vjuː
freeware ˈfriː weə ‖ -wer -wær
freeway ˈfriː weɪ **~s** z
freewheel ˌfriː ˈwiːəl -ˈhwiːəl, ˈ· · **~ed** d **~ing** ɪŋ **~s** z
freewill ˌfriː ˈwɪl ◂
ˌ**freewill ˈofferings**

eeze fri:z *(= frees)* **freezes** 'fri:z ɪz -əz **freezing** 'fri:z ɪŋ **froze** frəʊz ‖ froʊz **frozen** 'frəʊz ᵊn ‖ 'froʊz ᵊn
ˌfreezing 'cold; **'freezing comˌpartment**; **'freezing point**
eeze-|dry ˌfri:z |'draɪ ◂ **~dried** 'draɪd ◂ **~dries** 'draɪz ◂ **~drying** 'draɪ ɪŋ ◂
eeze-frame ˌfri:z 'freɪm '· ·
eezer 'fri:z ə ‖ -ᵊr **~s** z
eeze-up 'fri:z ʌp **~s** s
'eiburg 'fraɪ bɜ:g -bʊəg ‖ -bɜ:g —*Ger* ['fʁai bʊʁk]
eight freɪt **freighted** 'freɪt ɪd -əd ‖ 'freɪţ əd **freighting** 'freɪt ɪŋ ‖ 'freɪţ ɪŋ **freights** freɪts
'eightage 'freɪt ɪdʒ ‖ 'freɪţ-
'eighter 'freɪt ə ‖ 'freɪţ ᵊr **~s** z
'eightliner 'freɪt ˌlaɪn ə ‖ -ᵊr **~s** z
reixenet *tdmk* 'freʃ ə net ˌ· ·'· —*Catalan* [frə ʃə 'nɛt]
remantle 'fri: mænt ᵊl ·'· · ‖ -mænţ ᵊl
remitus 'frem ɪt əs §-ət- ‖ -əţ əs
remont 'fri: mɒnt frɪ 'mɒnt ‖ -mɑ:nt
rench, f~ frentʃ
ˌFrench 'bean; **ˌFrench 'bread**; **ˌFrench Ca'nadian**; **'French doors**, ˌ· '·; **ˌFrench 'dressing**; **ˌFrench 'fries**; **ˌFrench 'horn**; **ˌFrench 'kiss**; **ˌFrench 'leave**; **ˌFrench 'loaf**; **ˌFrench 'polish**; **ˌFrench 'toast**; **ˌFrench 'windows**
renchi|fy, F~ 'frentʃ ɪ |faɪ -ə- **~fied** faɪd **~fies** faɪz **~fying** faɪ ɪŋ
rench|man 'frentʃ |mən **~men** mən **~woman** ˌwʊm ən **~women** ˌwɪm ɪn §-ən
renetic frə 'net ɪk frɪ-, fre- ‖ -'neţ ɪk **~ally** ᵊl‿i
renum 'fri:n əm
renz|y 'frenz |i **~ied/ly** id /li **~ies** iz
reon, Freon *tdmk* 'fri: ɒn ‖ -ɑ:n
requenc|y 'fri:k wənᵗs |i **~ies** iz
'frequency ˌcurve
requent *v* frɪ 'kwent frə-, fri:-; §'fri:k wənt **frequented** frɪ 'kwent ɪd frə-, fri:-, -əd; §'fri:k wənt- ‖ -'kwenţ əd **frequenting** frɪ 'kwent ɪŋ frə-, fri:-; §'fri:k wənt- ‖ -'kwenţ ɪŋ **frequents** frɪ 'kwenᵗs frə-, fri:-; §'fri:k wənᵗs
frequent *adj* 'fri:k wənt **~ly** li **~ness** nəs nɪs
frequentative frɪ 'kwent ət ɪv frə-, fri:- ‖ -'kwenţ əţ ɪv **~s** z
Frere *(i)* frɪə ‖ frɪᵊr, *(ii)* freə ‖ freᵊr
fresco 'fresk əʊ ‖ -oʊ **~ed** d **~es, ~s** z **~ing** ɪŋ
fresh freʃ **freshed** freʃt **fresher** 'freʃ ə ‖ -ᵊr **freshes** 'freʃ ɪz -əz **freshest** 'freʃ ɪst -əst **freshing** 'freʃ ɪŋ
freshen 'freʃ ᵊn **~ed** d **~ing** ‿ɪŋ **~s** z
fresher 'freʃ ə ‖ -ᵊr **~s** z
freshet 'freʃ ɪt -ət **~s** s
fresh-faced ˌfreʃ 'feɪst ◂
freshly 'freʃ li
fresh|man 'freʃ |mən **~men** mən
freshness 'freʃ nəs -nɪs
freshwater, F~ 'freʃ ˌwɔ:t ə ˌ·'· · ‖ -ˌwɔ:ţ ᵊr -ˌwɑ:ţ ᵊr

Fresnel, f~ 'freɪn el 'fren-, -ᵊl, freɪ 'nel ‖ freɪ 'nel —*Fr* [fʁɛ nɛl]
Fresno 'frez nəʊ ‖ -noʊ
fret fret **frets** frets **fretted** 'fret ɪd -əd ‖ 'freţ əd **fretting** 'fret ɪŋ ‖ 'freţ ɪŋ
fretboard 'fret bɔ:d ‖ -bɔ:rd -boʊrd **~s** z
fretful 'fret fᵊl -fʊl **~ly** i **~ness** nəs nɪs
fretsaw 'fret sɔ: ‖ -sɑ: **~s** z
fretwork 'fret wɜ:k ‖ -wɜ:k
Freud frɔɪd —*Ger* [fʁɔʏt]
Freudian 'frɔɪd i‿ən **~s** z
ˌFreudian 'slip
Freya 'freɪ ə
Freycinet 'freɪs ə neɪ —*Fr* [fʁɛ si nɛ]
friability ˌfraɪ‿ə 'bɪl ət i -ɪt i ‖ -əţ i
friable 'fraɪ‿əb ᵊl **~ness** nəs nɪs
friar 'fraɪ‿ə ‖ 'fraɪ‿ᵊr **~s** z
ˌFriar 'Tuck
friar|y 'fraɪ‿ər |i **~ies** iz
fricandeau 'frɪk ən dəʊ ‖ -doʊ ˌ· ·'· **~x** z —*or as sing.*
fricassee *n, v* 'frɪk ə seɪ -si:, ˌ· ·'· ‖ ˌfrɪk ə 'si: **~d** d **~ing** ɪŋ **~s** z
frication frɪ 'keɪʃ ᵊn frə-
fricative 'frɪk ət ɪv ‖ -əţ ɪv **~s** z
fricking 'frɪk ɪŋ
friction 'frɪk ʃᵊn **~s** z
frictional 'frɪk ʃᵊn‿əl **~ly** i **~s** z
Friday 'fraɪ deɪ 'fraɪd i —*see note at* -day **~s** z
fridge frɪdʒ **fridges** 'frɪdʒ ɪz -əz
fridge-freezer ˌfrɪdʒ 'fri:z ə ‖ -ᵊr **~s** z
fried fraɪd
Friedan 'fri:d ᵊn fri: 'dæn
Friedman 'fri:d mən
Friedrich 'fri:dr ɪk —*Ger* ['fʁi:d ʁɪç]
Friel fri:ᵊl
friend, F~ frend **friends** frendz
friendless 'frend ləs -lɪs **~ness** nəs nɪs
friend|ly, F~ 'frend |li **~lies** liz **~liness** li nəs -nɪs
'friendly soˌciety
friendship 'frend ʃɪp **~s** s
frier 'fraɪ‿ə ‖ 'fraɪ‿ᵊr **~s** z
Friern 'fraɪ‿ən 'fri:‿ən ‖ 'fraɪ‿ᵊrn
ˌFriern 'Barnet
fries fraɪz
Fries *American family name* fri:z
Friesian 'fri:z i‿ən 'fri:z-; 'fri:ʒ ᵊn, 'fri:ʒ i‿ən ‖ 'fri:ʒ ᵊn **~s** z
Friesland 'fri:z lənd -lænd —*Dutch* ['fris lɑnt]
frieze fri:z *(= frees)* **friezes** 'fri:z ɪz -əz
frig *v 'masturbate; copulate'* frɪg **frigged** frɪgd **frigging** 'frɪg ɪŋ **frigs** frɪgz
frig *n 'refrigerator'* frɪdʒ
frigate 'frɪg ət -ɪt **~s** s
Frigg frɪg
Frigga 'frɪg ə
fright fraɪt **frights** fraɪts
frighten 'fraɪt ᵊn **~ed** d **~er/s** ‿ə/z ‖ ᵊr/z **~ing/ly** ‿ɪŋ /li **~s** z
fright|ful 'fraɪt |fᵊl -fʊl **~fully** fli fəl i, fʊl i **~fulness** fᵊl nəs fʊl-, -nɪs
frigid 'frɪdʒ ɪd §-əd **~ly** li **~ness** nəs nɪs

F

Frigidaire *tdmk* ˌfrɪdʒ ɪ ˈdeə -ə- ‖ -ˈdeᵊr ˈdæᵊr **~s** z

frigidity frɪ ˈdʒɪd ət i -ɪt- ‖ -əţ i

frijole frɪ ˈhəʊl i -eɪ ‖ -ˈhoʊl i —*Sp* [fri ˈxo le] **~s** z

frill frɪl **frilled** frɪld **frilling** ˈfrɪl ɪŋ **frills** frɪlz

frill|y ˈfrɪl |i **~ier** i‿ə ‖ i‿ᵊr **~iest** i‿ɪst i‿əst **~iness** i nəs i nɪs

Frimley ˈfrɪm li

fringe frɪndʒ **fringed** frɪndʒd **fringes** ˈfrɪndʒ ɪz -əz **fringing** ˈfrɪndʒ ɪŋ
ˈ**fringe** ˌ**benefit**

Frinton ˈfrɪnt ən ‖ -ᵊn

fripper|y ˈfrɪp ər |i **~ies** iz

frisbee, F~ *tdmk* ˈfrɪz bi **~s** z

Frisby ˈfrɪz bi

Frisch frɪʃ —*Ger* [fʁɪʃ]

Frisco ˈfrɪsk əʊ ‖ -oʊ

frise, frisé, frisee, frisée ˈfriːz eɪ ‖ fri ˈzeɪ —*Fr* [fʁi ze]

Frisian ˈfrɪz i‿ən ˈfrɪʒ ᵊn, ˈfrɪʒ i‿ən; ˈfriːz i‿ən; ˈfriːʒ ᵊn, ˈfriːʒ i‿ən ‖ ˈfrɪʒ ᵊn ˈfriːʒ- **~s** z

frisk frɪsk **frisked** frɪskt **frisker/s** ˈfrɪsk ə/z ‖ -ᵊr/z **frisking** ˈfrɪsk ɪŋ **frisks** frɪsks

frisk|y ˈfrɪsk |i **~ier** i‿ə ‖ i‿ᵊr **~iest** i‿ɪst i‿əst **~ily** ɪ li əl i **~iness** i nəs i nɪs

frisson ˈfriːs ɒn ˈfrɪs-, -ɒ̃; friː ˈsɒ̃, frɪ- ‖ friː ˈsoʊn —*Fr* [fʁi sɔ̃] **~s** z

Frist frɪst

frit frɪt **frits** frɪts **fritted** ˈfrɪt ɪd -əd ‖ ˈfrɪţ əd **fritting** ˈfrɪt ɪŋ ‖ ˈfrɪţ ɪŋ

Frith frɪθ

fritillar|y frɪ ˈtɪl ər |i frə- ‖ ˈfrɪţ ᵊl er |i *(*)* **~ies** iz

Frito|-Lay *tdmk* ˈfriːt əʊ| leɪ ‖ ˈfriːţ oʊ- **~s** z

frittata frɪ ˈtɑːt ə —*It* [frit ˈtaː ta]

fritter ˈfrɪt ə ‖ ˈfrɪţ ᵊr **~ed** d **frittering** ˈfrɪt‿ər ɪŋ ‖ ˈfrɪţ ər ɪŋ **~s** z

fritto misto ˌfrɪt əʊ ˈmɪst əʊ ˌfriːt- ‖ ˌfriːt oʊ ˈmiːst oʊ —*It* [ˌfrit to ˈmis to]

Fritz, fritz frɪts

Friuli fri ˈuːl i —*It* [fri ˈuː li]

Friulian fri ˈuːl i‿ən **~s** z

frivolit|y frɪ ˈvɒl ət |i frə-, -ɪt- ‖ -ˈvɑːl əţ |i **~ies** iz

frivolous ˈfrɪv əl‿əs **~ly** li **~ness** nəs nɪs

frizz frɪz **frizzed** frɪzd **frizzes** ˈfrɪz ɪz -əz **frizzing** ˈfrɪz ɪŋ

frizzl|e ˈfrɪz ᵊl **~ed** d **~es** z **~ing** ‿ɪŋ

frizz|ly ˈfrɪz |li **~lier** li‿ə ‖ li‿ᵊr **~liest** li‿ɪst li‿əst

frizz|y ˈfrɪz |i **~ier** i‿ə ‖ i‿ᵊr **~iest** i‿ɪst i‿əst **~ily** ɪ li əl i **~iness** i nəs i nɪs

fro frəʊ ‖ froʊ

Frobisher ˈfrəʊb ɪʃ ə ‖ ˈfroʊb ɪʃ ᵊr
ˌ**Frobisher** ˈ**Bay**

frock frɒk ‖ frɑːk **frocks** frɒks ‖ frɑːks
ˌ**frock** ˈ**coat** ‖ ˈ.

Frodo ˈfrəʊd əʊ ‖ ˈfroʊd oʊ

Frodsham ˈfrɒd ʃəm ‖ ˈfrɑːd-

Froebel, Fröbel ˈfrəʊb ᵊl ˈfrɜːb- ‖ ˈfreɪb- ˈfroʊb- —*Ger* [ˈfʁøː bᵊl]

frog frɒg ‖ frɑːg frɔːg **frogs** frɒgz ‖ frɑːgz frɔːgz

frogbit ˈfrɒg bɪt ‖ ˈfrɑːg- ˈfrɔːg- **~s** s

Froggatt ˈfrɒg ət -ɪt ‖ ˈfrɑːg-

Frogg|ie, frogg|y, F~ ˈfrɒg |i ‖ ˈfrɑːg |i ˈfrɔːg- **~ies** iz

frogging ˈfrɒg ɪŋ ‖ ˈfrɑːg- ˈfrɔːg-

froghopper ˈfrɒg ˌhɒp ə ‖ ˈfrɑːg ˌhɑːp ᵊr ˈfrɔːg- **~s** z

frog|man ˈfrɒg |mən ‖ ˈfrɑːg- ˈfrɔːg- **~men** mən men

frogmarch ˈfrɒg mɑːtʃ ‖ ˈfrɑːg mɑːrtʃ ˈfrɔːg- **~ed** t **~es** ɪz əz **~ing** ɪŋ

Frogmore ˈfrɒg mɔː ‖ ˈfrɑːg mɔːr ˈfrɔːg-, -moᵊr

frogspawn ˈfrɒg spɔːn ‖ ˈfrɑːg- ˈfrɔːg-, -spɑːn

frolic ˈfrɒl ɪk ‖ ˈfrɑːl- **~ked** t **~ker/s** ə/z ‖ ᵊr/z **~king** ɪŋ **~s** s

frolicsome ˈfrɒl ɪk səm ‖ ˈfrɑːl-

from *strong form* frɒm ‖ frʌm frɑːm, *weak form* frəm

fromage frais ˌfrɒm ɑːʒ ˈfreɪ ‖ frə ˌmɑːʒ- —*Fr* [fʁɔ maʒ fʁɛ]

Frome *(i)* fruːm, *(ii)* frəʊm ‖ froʊm —*The places and rivers in England and Jamaica are all (i), although the spelling pronunciation (ii) can be heard from people not familiar with the name. Lake F~ in Australia is (ii).*

Fromm frɒm ‖ frɑːm froʊm

Fron vrɒn ‖ vrɑːn —*Welsh* [vrɔn]

Froncysyllte ˌvrɒn kə ˈsʌlt eɪ →ˌvrɒŋ- ‖ ˌvrɑːn- —*Welsh* [vrɔn kə ˈsəɬ te]

frond frɒnd ‖ frɑːnd **fronded** ˈfrɒnd ɪd -əd ‖ ˈfrɑːnd əd **fronds** frɒndz ‖ frɑːndz

front frʌnt **fronted** ˈfrʌnt ɪd -əd ‖ ˈfrʌnţ əd **fronter** ˈfrʌnt ə ‖ ˈfrʌnţ ᵊr **frontest** ˈfrʌnt ɪst -əst ‖ ˈfrʌnţ əst **fronting** ˈfrʌnt ɪŋ ‖ ˈfrʌnţ ɪŋ **fronts** frʌnts
ˌ**front** ˈ**door**; ˌ**front** ˈ**line**; ˈ**front man**; ˌ**front** ˈ**page**; ˌ**front** ˈ**room**

frontag|e ˈfrʌnt ɪdʒ ‖ ˈfrʌnţ ɪdʒ **~es** ɪz əz

frontal ˈfrʌnt ᵊl ‖ ˈfrʌnţ ᵊl **~ly** i

frontbench ˌfrʌnt ˈbentʃ ◂ ˈ. . **~er/s** ə/z ‖ ᵊr/z

Frontenac ˈfrɒnt ə næk ‖ ˈfrɑːnt ᵊn æk —*Fr* [fʁɔ̃t nak]

frontier ˈfrʌnt ɪə ˈfrɒnt-; frʌn ˈtɪə ‖ frʌn ˈtɪᵊr frɑːn- **~s** z

frontiers|man ˈfrʌnt ɪəz |mən ˈfrɒnt-; frʌn ˈtɪəz- ‖ frʌn ˈtɪrz- **~men** mən **~woman** ˌwʊm ən **~women** ˌwɪm ɪn §-ən

frontispiec|e ˈfrʌnt ɪ spiːs -ə- ‖ ˈfrʌnţ ə- **~es** ɪz əz

front-line ˌfrʌnt ˈlaɪn ◂ ˈ. .
ˌ**front-line** ˈ**troops**

front-loader ˌfrʌnt ˈləʊd ə ‖ -ˈloʊd ᵊr **~s** z

front-loading ˌfrʌnt ˈləʊd ɪŋ ◂ ‖ -ˈloʊd ɪŋ ◂

front-of-house ˌfrʌnt əv ˈhaʊs ◂ ‖ ˌfrʌnţ əv-

front-page ˌfrʌnt ˈpeɪdʒ ◂ ˈ. .

front-rank ˌfrʌnt ˈræŋk ◂

front-runn|er ˌfrʌnt ˈrʌn| ə ˈ.ˌ. . ‖ -ᵊr **~ers** əz ‖ ᵊrz **~ing** ɪŋ

front-wheel ˌfrʌnt ˈwiːᵊl ◂ -ˈhwiːᵊl
ˌ**front-wheel** ˈ**drive**

frosh frɒʃ ‖ frɑːʃ **froshes** ˈfrɒʃ ɪz -əz ‖ ˈfrɑːʃ-

ost, Frost frɒst frɔːst ‖ frɔːst frɑːst **frosted** 'frɒst ɪd 'frɔːst-, -əd ‖ 'frɔːst əd 'frɑːst- **frosting** 'frɒst ɪŋ 'frɔːst- ‖ 'frɔːst ɪŋ 'frɑːst- **frosts** frɒsts frɔːsts ‖ frɔːsts frɑːsts
ostbite 'frɒst baɪt 'frɔːst- ‖ 'frɔːst- 'frɑːst- **~s** s
ostbitten 'frɒst ˌbɪt ᵊn 'frɔːst- ‖ 'frɔːst- 'frɑːst-
ostbound 'frɒst baʊnd 'frɔːst- ‖ 'frɔːst- 'frɑːst-
ost-free ˌfrɒst'friː ◂ ‖ ˌfrɔːst- ˌfrɑːst-
ostie 'frɒst i 'frɔːst- ‖ 'frɔːst i 'frɑːst- **~s, F~s** *tdmk* z
ost|y 'frɒst |i 'frɔːst- ‖ 'frɔːst |i 'frɑːst- **~ier** i͜ə ‖ i͜ᵊr **~iest** i͜ɪst i͜əst **~ily** ɪ li əl i **~iness** i nəs i nɪs
roth *v* frɒθ frɔːθ ‖ frɔːθ frɑːθ, frɔːð **frothed** frɒθt frɔːθt ‖ frɔːθt frɑːθt, frɔːðd **frothing** 'frɒθ ɪŋ 'frɔːθ- ‖ 'frɔːθ ɪŋ 'frɑːθ-, 'frɔːð- **froths** frɒθs frɔːθs ‖ frɔːθs frɑːθs, frɔːðz
roth *n* frɒθ frɔːθ ‖ frɔːθ frɑːθ **froths** frɒθs frɔːθs ‖ frɔːθs frɑːθs
roth|y 'frɒθ |i 'frɔːθ- ‖ 'frɔːθ |i 'frɑːθ-, 'frɔːð- **~ier** i͜ə ‖ i͜ᵊr **~iest** i͜ɪst i͜əst **~ily** ɪ li əl i **~iness** i nəs i nɪs
rottage 'frɒt ɑːʒ -ɪdʒ; frɒ 'tɑːʒ ‖ frɔː 'tɑːʒ frɑː- —*Fr* [fʁɔ taːʒ]
roud fraʊd
roude fruːd
roufrou 'fruː fruː
roward 'frəʊ əd ‖ 'froʊ ᵊrd **~ly** li **~ness** nəs nɪs
rown fraʊn **frowned** fraʊnd **frowner/s** 'fraʊn ə/z ‖ -ᵊr/z **frowning/ly** 'fraʊn ɪŋ /li **frowns** fraʊnz
rowst fraʊst **frowsted** 'fraʊst ɪd -əd **frowsting** 'fraʊst ɪŋ **frowsts** fraʊsts
rowst|y 'fraʊst |i **~ier** i͜ə ‖ i͜ᵊr **~iest** i͜ɪst i͜əst **~ily** ɪ li əl i **~iness** i nəs i nɪs
rows|y, frowz|y 'fraʊz |i **~ier** i͜ə ‖ i͜ᵊr **~iest** i͜ɪst i͜əst **~iness** i nəs -nɪs
froyo 'frəʊ jəʊ ‖ 'froʊ joʊ **~s** z
froze frəʊz ‖ froʊz
frozen 'frəʊz ᵊn ‖ 'froʊz ᵊn **~ly** li **~ness** nəs nɪs
fructification ˌfrʌkt ɪf ɪ 'keɪʃ ᵊn ˌfrʊkt-, ˌ-əf-, §-ə'--
fructi|fy 'frʌkt ɪ |faɪ 'frʊkt-, -ə- **~fied** faɪd **~fies** faɪz **~fying** faɪ ɪŋ
fructose 'frʌkt əʊz 'frʊkt-, -əʊs ‖ -oʊs
frugal 'fruːg ᵊl **~ly** i **~ness** nəs nɪs
frugality fruː 'gæl ət i -ɪt- ‖ -əţ i
fruit fruːt **fruited** 'fruːt ɪd -əd ‖ 'fruːţ əd **fruiting** 'fruːt ɪŋ ‖ 'fruːţ ɪŋ **fruits** fruːts
'fruit bat; **ˌfruit 'cocktail**; **'fruit fly**; **'fruit knife**; **'fruit maˌchine**; **ˌfruit 'salad**
fruitarian fruː 'teər i͜ən ‖ -'ter- -'tær- **~ism** ˌɪz əm **~s** z
fruitcake 'fruːt keɪk **~s** s
fruiterer 'fruːt ər ə ‖ 'fruːţ ər ər **~s** z
fruitful 'fruːt fᵊl -fʊl **~ly** i **~ness** nəs nɪs
fruiti... —*see* **fruity**
fruition fru 'ɪʃ ᵊn
fruitless 'fruːt ləs -lɪs **~ly** li **~ness** nəs nɪs
fruit|y 'fruːt |i ‖ 'fruːţ |i **~ier** i͜ə ‖ i͜ᵊr **~iest** i͜ɪst i͜əst **~iness** i nəs i nɪs
frumenty 'fruːm ənt i
frump frʌmp **frumps** frʌmps
frumpish 'frʌmp ɪʃ **~ly** li **~ness** nəs nɪs
frump|y 'frʌmp |i **~ier** i͜ə ‖ i͜ᵊr **~iest** i͜ɪst i͜əst **~ily** ɪ li əl i **~iness** i nəs i nɪs
frus|trate frʌ 's|treɪt 'frʌs |treɪt ‖ 'frʌs |treɪt **~trated** treɪt ɪd -əd ‖ treɪţ əd **~trater/s** treɪt ə/z ‖ treɪţ ᵊr/z **~trates** treɪts **~trating/ly** treɪt ɪŋ /li ‖ treɪţ ɪŋ /li
frustration frʌ 'streɪʃ ᵊn **~s** z
frust|um 'frʌst |əm **~a** ə **~ums** əmz
frutesc|ence fru 'tes |ᵊn'̮s **~ent** ᵊnt
fry fraɪ **fried** fraɪd **fries** fraɪz **frying** 'fraɪ ɪŋ **'frying pan**
Fry, Frye fraɪ
fryer, frier 'fraɪ͜ə ‖ 'fraɪ͜ᵊr **~s** z
Fryston 'fraɪst ən
fry-up 'fraɪ ʌp **~s** s
f-stop 'ef stɒp ‖ -stɑːp **~s** s
ftp ˌef tiː 'piː **~'d** d **~'ing** ɪŋ **~'s** z
FTSE, FT-SE 'fʊts i
fubs|y 'fʌbz| i **~ier** i͜ə ‖ i͜ᵊr **~iest** i͜ɪst ͜əst
Fuchs *(i)* fʊks, *(ii)* fuːks, *(iii)* fjuːks —*The explorer was (i). (iii) is AmE only.*
fuchsia 'fjuːʃ ə **~s** z
fuchsin 'fuːks ɪn §-ən
fuchsine 'fuːks iːn -ɪn ‖ 'fʊks ᵊn 'fjuːks- *(*)*
fuck fʌk **fucked** fʌkt **fucker/s** 'fʌk ə/z ‖ -ᵊr/z **fucking** 'fʌk ɪŋ **fucks** fʌks **ˌfuck 'all**,'. ·
fucker 'fʌk ə ‖ -ᵊr **~s** z
fuckhead 'fʌk hed **~s** z
fuck-up 'fʌk ʌp **~s** s
fuckwit 'fʌk wɪt **~s** s
fucous 'fjuːk əs
fucus 'fjuːk əs
fuddl|e 'fʌd ᵊl **~ed** d **~es** z **~ing** ͜ɪŋ
fuddy-dudd|y 'fʌd i ˌdʌd |i **~ies** iz
fudge, Fudge fʌdʒ **fudged** fʌdʒd **fudges** 'fʌdʒ ɪz -əz **fudging** 'fʌdʒ ɪŋ
fudgy 'fʌdʒ i
Fuegian 'fweɪdʒ ᵊn 'fweɪg i͜ən **~s** z
fuehrer 'fjʊər ə 'fjɔːr- ‖ 'fjʊr ᵊr —*Ger* Führer ['fyː ʁɐ] **~s** z
fuel 'fjuː͜əl §fjuːl **~ed, ~led** d **~ing, ~ling** ɪŋ **~s** z
'fuel cell; **'fuel oil**
fuel-efficient 'fjuː͜əl i ˌfɪʃ ᵊnt §'fjuːl i-
Fuerteventura ˌfweət i ven 'tjʊər ə ˌ·eɪ, →·'tʃʊər-, →·tʃɔːr- ‖ ˌfwert eɪ ven 'tʊr ə —*Sp* [fwer te βen 'tu ɾa]
fug fʌg **fugs** fʌgz
fugacious fju 'geɪʃ əs **~ly** li **~ness** nəs nɪs
fugacity fju 'gæs ət i -ɪt- ‖ -əţ i
fugal 'fjuːg ᵊl **~ly** i
fuggles, F~ 'fʌg ᵊlz
fugg|y 'fʌg| i **~ier** i͜ə ‖ i͜ᵊr **~iest** i͜ɪst ͜əst **~iness** i nəs -nɪs
fugitive 'fjuːdʒ ət ɪv -ɪt- ‖ -əţ ɪv **~ly** li **~ness** nəs nɪs **~s** z

F

fugu 'fuːg uː —*Jp* ['ɸɯ ŋɯ, -gɯ]
fugue fjuːg **fugues** fjuːgz
fuhrer, führer 'fjʊər ə 'fjɔːr- ‖ 'fjʊr ᵊr —*Ger* Führer ['fyː ʁɐ] **~s** z
Fujairah fu 'dʒaɪᵊr ə
Fuji 'fuːdʒ i —*Jp* ['ɸɯ dʑi]
Fujian ˌfuːdʒ i 'ɑːn 'fuːdʒ i ̮ən —*Chi* Fújiàn [²fu ⁴dʑjɛn]
Fujica *tdmk* 'fuːdʒ ɪk ə
Fujitsu *tdmk* fuː 'dʒɪts uː —*Jp* [ɸɯ 'dʑi tsɯɯ]
Fukuoka ˌfuːk u 'əʊk ə ˌfʊk- ‖ -'oʊk- —*Jp* [ɸɯ̥ 'kɯ o ka]
-ful *(i) suffix to form adjectives,* fᵊl fʊl **painful** 'peɪn fᵊl, -fʊl; *(ii) suffix to form nouns specifying a quantity,* fʊl **spoonful** 'spuːn fʊl
Fula 'fuːl ə **~s** z
Fulani fuː 'lɑːn i 'fuːl ɑːn i
Fulbourn 'fʊl bɔːn ‖ -bɔːrn -boʊrn
Fulbright 'fʊl braɪt
Fulbrighter 'fʊl braɪt ə ‖ -braɪt̬ ᵊr **~s** z
Fulcher 'fʊltʃ ə ‖ -ᵊr
fulc|rum 'fʌlk |rəm 'fʊlk- **~ra** rə
ful|fil, ~fill fʊl| 'fɪl **~filled** fɪld **~filler/s** 'fɪl ə/z ‖ 'fɪl ᵊr/z **~filling** 'fɪl ɪŋ **~fils, ~fills** 'fɪlz
fulfillment, fulfilment fʊl 'fɪl mənt
Fulford 'fʊl fəd ‖ -fᵊrd
Fulham 'fʊl əm
fuliginous fju 'lɪdʒ ɪn əs §-ən- **~ly** li
full fʊl **fuller** 'fʊl ə ‖ -ᵊr **fullest** 'fʊl ɪst -əst
ˌ**full 'dress**; ˌ**full 'house**; ˌ**full 'marks**; ˌ**full 'moon**; ˌ**full 'stop**; ˌ**full 'toss**
fullback ˌfʊl 'bæk '· · ‖ 'fʊl bæk **~s** s
full-blooded ˌfʊl 'blʌd ɪd ◂ -əd **~ness** nəs nɪs
full-blown ˌfʊl 'bləʊn ◂ ‖ -'bloʊn ◂
full-bodied ˌfʊl 'bɒd id ◂ ‖ -'bɑːd-
full-color, full-colour ˌfʊl 'kʌl ə ◂ ‖ -ᵊr◂
full-court ˌfʊl 'kɔːt ◂ ‖ -'kɔːrt ◂ -koʊrt ◂
ˌ**full-court 'press**
full-cream ˌfʊl 'kriːm ◂
ˌ**full-cream 'milk**
full-dress ˌfʊl 'dres ◂
fuller, F~ 'fʊl ə ‖ -ᵊr **~s, ~'s** z
ˌ**fuller's 'earth**
Fullerton 'fʊl ət ən ‖ -ᵊrt ᵊn
full-face ˌfʊl 'feɪs ◂
full-fashioned ˌfʊl 'fæʃ ᵊnd ◂
full-fat ˌfʊl 'fæt ◂
full-figured ˌfʊl 'fɪg əd ◂ ‖ -jᵊrd ◂
full-fledged ˌfʊl 'fledʒd ◂
full-frontal ˌfʊl 'frʌnt ᵊl ◂ ‖ -'frʌnt̬ ᵊl ◂
full-grown ˌfʊl 'grəʊn ◂ ‖ -'groʊn ◂
full-hearted ˌfʊl 'hɑːt ɪd ◂ -əd ‖ -'hɑːrt̬ əd ◂
full-length ˌfʊl 'leŋᵏθ ◂ -'lentθ
ˌ**full-length 'portrait**
fullness 'fʊl nəs -nɪs
full-on ˌfʊl 'ɒn ◂ ‖ -'ɑːn ◂ -'ɔːn ◂
full-page ˌfʊl 'peɪdʒ ◂
full-scale ˌfʊl 'skeɪᵊl ◂
ˌ**full-scale 'war**
full-size ˌfʊl 'saɪz◂
full-term ˌfʊl 'tɜːm ◂ ‖ -'tɜ˞ːm ◂
full-throated ˌfʊl 'θrəʊt ɪd ◂ -əd ‖ -'θroʊt̬ əd ◂
ˌ**full-ˌthroated 'roar**
full-time ˌfʊl 'taɪm ◂
ˌ**full-time 'work**
fully 'fʊl i
-fully fᵊl ̮i fʊl i **painfully** 'peɪn fᵊl ̮i -fʊl i
fully-fashioned ˌfʊl i 'fæʃ ᵊnd ◂
fully-fledged ˌfʊl i 'fledʒd ◂
fully-grown ˌfʊl i 'grəʊn ◂ ‖ -'groʊn ◂
fulmar 'fʊlm ə -ɑː ‖ -ᵊr -ɑːr **~s** z
Fulmer 'fʊlm ə ‖ -ᵊr
fulminant 'fʊlm ɪn ənt 'fʌlm-, -ən-
fulmi|nate 'fʊlm ɪ |neɪt 'fʌlm-, -ə- **~nated** neɪt ɪd -əd ‖ neɪt̬ əd **~nates** neɪts **~nating** neɪt ɪŋ ‖ neɪt̬ ɪŋ
fulmination ˌfʊlm ɪ 'neɪʃ ᵊn ˌfʌlm-, -ə- **~s** z
fulness 'fʊl nəs -nɪs
fulsome 'fʊls əm **~ly** li **~ness** nəs nɪs
Fulton 'fʊlt ən
fulvous fʌlv əs 'fʊlv-
Fulwell 'fʊl wel
Fulwood fʊl wʊd
Fu Manchu ˌfuː mæn 'tʃuː
fumaric fju 'mær ɪk ‖ -'mer-
fumarole 'fjuːm ə rəʊl →-rɒʊl ‖ -roʊl **~s** z
fumbl|e 'fʌm bᵊl **~ed** d **~es** z **~ing** ̮ɪŋ
fumbler 'fʌm blə ‖ -blᵊr **~s** z
fume fjuːm **fumed** fjuːmd **fumes** fjuːmz **fuming** 'fjuːm ɪŋ
fumigant 'fjuːm ɪg ənt -əg- **~s** s
fumi|gate 'fjuːm ɪ |geɪt -ə- **~gated** geɪt ɪd -əd ‖ geɪt̬ əd **~gates** geɪts **~gating** geɪt ɪŋ ‖ geɪt̬ ɪŋ
fumigation ˌfjuːm ɪ 'geɪʃ ᵊn -ə- **~s** z
fumigator 'fjuːm ɪ geɪt ə '·ə- ‖ -geɪt̬ ᵊr **~s** z
fumitor|y 'fjuːm ɪt ər |i '·ət ̮ ‖ -ə tɔːr |i -toʊr i **~ies** iz
fun fʌn
ˈ**fun fur**; ˈ**fun run**
Funafuti ˌfuːn ə 'fuːt i
funambulist fju 'næm bjʊl ɪst -bjəl-, §-əst **~s** s
Funchal ˌfʊn 'tʃɑːl -'ʃɑːl —*Port* [fũ 'ʃal]
function 'fʌŋk ʃᵊn **~ed** d **~ing** ̮ɪŋ **~s** z
functional 'fʌŋk ʃᵊn ̮əl **~ism** ˌɪz əm **~ist/s** ɪst/s §əst/s **~ly** i
functionality ˌfʌŋk ʃə 'næl ət i -ɪt i ‖ -ət̬ i
functionar|y 'fʌŋk ʃᵊn ̮ər |i -ʃᵊn ər ̮|i ‖ -ʃə ner |i **~ies** iz
functor 'fʌŋkt ə ‖ -ᵊr **~s** z
fund fʌnd **funded** 'fʌnd ɪd -əd **funding** 'fʌnd ɪŋ **funds** fʌndz
fundament 'fʌnd ə mənt **~s** s
fundamental ˌfʌnd ə 'ment ᵊl ◂ ‖ -'ment̬ ᵊl ◂ **~ism** ˌɪz əm **~ist/s** ɪst/s §əst/s **~ly** i **~s** z
fund-rais|er 'fʌnd ˌreɪz| ə ‖ -ᵊr **~ers** əz ‖ ᵊrz **~ing** ɪŋ
fund|us 'fʌnd| əs **~i** aɪ
Fundy 'fʌnd i
funeral 'fjuːn ᵊr ̮əl **~s** z
ˈ**funeral diˌrector**; ˈ**funeral home**; ˈ**funeral ˌparlor**

unerary 'fjuːn ᵊr ər i ⚠'fjuːn ər i ‖ -ə rer i
unereal fju 'nɪər i əl ‖ -'nɪr- **~ly** i
unfair 'fʌn feə ‖ -fer -fær **~s** z
ungal 'fʌŋ gᵊl
ungi 'fʌŋ giː -gaɪ; 'fʌndʒ aɪ, -iː
ungible 'fʌndʒ əb ᵊl -ɪb- **~s** z
ungicidal ˌfʌŋ gɪ 'saɪd ᵊl ◂ §-gə-; ˌfʌndʒ ɪ-, §-ə-
ungicide 'fʌŋ gɪ saɪd §-gə-; 'fʌndʒ ɪ-, §-ə- **~s** z
ungoid 'fʌŋ gɔɪd
ungous 'fʌŋ gəs *(= fungus)*
ungus 'fʌŋ gəs **fungi** 'fʌŋ giː -gaɪ; 'fʌndʒ aɪ, -iː **funguses** 'fʌŋ gəs ɪz -əz
unicular fju 'nɪk jʊl ə fə-, -jəl- ‖ -jəl ᵊr **~s** z
  fuˌnicular 'railway
'unk fʌŋk **funked** fʌŋkt **funking** 'fʌŋk ɪŋ **funks** fʌŋks
'unk|y 'fʌŋk |i **~ier** i ə ‖ i ᵊr **~iest** i ɪst i əst **~ily** ɪ li əl i **~iness** i nəs i nɪs
fun-loving 'fʌn ˌlʌv ɪŋ
funnel 'fʌn ᵊl **~ed, ~led** d **~ing, ~ling** ɪŋ **~s** z
funn|y 'fʌn |i **~ier** i ə ‖ i ᵊr **~ies** iz **~iest** i ɪst i əst **~ily** ɪ li əl i **~iness** i nəs i nɪs
  'funny bone; **'funny ˌbusiness**; **'funny farm**; **ˌfunny ha'ha** hɑː 'hɑː '· ·; **ˌfunny 'man** *'strange man'*,; **'funny man** *'comedian'*
funny-looking 'fʌn i ˌlʊk ɪŋ
Funt fʌnt
fur fɜː ‖ fɝː **furred** fɜːd ‖ fɝːd **furring** 'fɜːr ɪŋ ‖ 'fɝː ɪŋ **furs** fɜːz ‖ fɝːz
  'fur seal
furan 'fjʊər æn 'fjɔːr-; fjuᵊ 'ræn ‖ 'fjʊr æn fjʊ 'ræn
furbelow 'fɜːb ə ləʊ -ɪ- ‖ 'fɝːb ə loʊ **~ed** d **~ing** ɪŋ **~s** z
furbish 'fɜːb ɪʃ ‖ 'fɝːb- **~ed** t **~er/s** ə/z ‖ ᵊr/z **~es** ɪz əz **~ing** ɪŋ
Furby *tdmk* 'fɜːb i ‖ 'fɝːb i **~s** z
Furies, f~ 'fjʊər iz 'fjɔːr- ‖ 'fjʊr iz
furious 'fjʊər i əs 'fjɔːr- ‖ 'fjʊr- **~ly** li **~ness** nəs nɪs
furl fɜːl ‖ fɝːl **furled** fɜːld ‖ fɝːld **furling** 'fɜːl ɪŋ ‖ 'fɝːl ɪŋ **furls** fɜːlz ‖ fɝːlz
furlong 'fɜːl ɒŋ ‖ 'fɝːl ɔːŋ -ɑːŋ **~s** z
Furlong, Furlonge 'fɜːl ɒŋ ‖ 'fɝːl ɔːŋ -ɑːŋ
furlough 'fɜːl əʊ ‖ 'fɝːl oʊ **~ed** d **~ing** ɪŋ **~s** z
furnac|e, F~ 'fɜːn ɪs -əs ‖ 'fɝːn- **~es** ɪz əz
Furneaux 'fɜːn əʊ ‖ fɝː 'noʊ
Furnell fɜː 'nel ‖ fɝː-
Furness 'fɜːn ɪs -əs; fɜː 'nes ‖ 'fɝːn əs
furnish 'fɜːn ɪʃ ‖ 'fɝːn- **~ed** t **~er/s** ə/z ‖ ᵊr/z **~es** ɪz əz **~ing/s** ɪŋ/z
furniture 'fɜːn ɪtʃ ə §-ətʃ- ‖ 'fɝːn ɪtʃ ᵊr
Furnival, Furnivall 'fɜːn ɪv ᵊl -əv- ‖ 'fɝːn-
furor 'fjʊər ɔː 'fjɔːr- ‖ 'fjʊr ᵊr -ɔːr, -oʊr **~s** z
furore fjuᵊ 'rɔːr i 'fjʊər ɔː, 'fjɔːr- ‖ 'fjʊr ᵊr -ɔːr, -oʊr **~s** z —*This word sounds different from* furor *in BrE, but not in AmE.*
furph|y, F~ 'fɜːf |i ‖ 'fɝːf |i **~ies** iz
furred fɜːd ‖ fɝːd
furrier 'fʌr i ə ‖ 'fɝː i ᵊr **~s** z
furrier|y 'fʌr i ər| i ‖ 'fɝː i er| i **~ies** iz
furring 'fɜːr ɪŋ ‖ 'fɝː ɪŋ
furrow 'fʌr əʊ ‖ 'fɝː oʊ **~ed** d **~ing** ɪŋ **~s** z
furr|y 'fɜːr |i §'fʌr- ‖ 'fɝː |i **~ier** i ə ‖ i ᵊr **~iest** i ɪst i əst **~iness** i nəs i nɪs
Furtado fɜː 'tɑːd əʊ ‖ fᵊr 'tɑːd oʊ
further 'fɜːð ə ‖ 'fɝːð ᵊr **~ed** d **furthering** 'fɜːð ər ɪŋ ‖ 'fɝːð ər ɪŋ **~s** z
  ˌfurther ˌedu'cation
furtherance 'fɜːð ᵊr ən'ʃs ‖ 'fɝːð-
furtherer 'fɜːð ər ə ‖ 'fɝːð ᵊr ər **~s** z
furthermore ˌfɜːð ə 'mɔː '· · · ‖ 'fɝːð ᵊr mɔːr -moʊr
furthermost 'fɜːð ə məʊst ‖ 'fɝːð ᵊr moʊst
furthest 'fɜːð ɪst -əst ‖ 'fɝːð-
furtive 'fɜːt ɪv ‖ 'fɝːt̬ ɪv **~ly** li **~ness** nəs nɪs
Furtwängler 'fʊət veŋ glə ‖ 'fʊrt weŋ glᵊr —*Ger* ['fʊʁt vɛŋ lɐ]
furuncle 'fjʊər ʌŋk ᵊl 'fjɔːr- ‖ 'fjʊr- **~s** z
fur|y, Fur|y 'fjʊər |i 'fjɔːr- ‖ 'fjʊr |i **~ies** iz
furze fɜːz ‖ fɝːz *(= furs)*
fusarium fju 'zeər i əm ‖ -'zer- -'zær-
  fu'sarium wilt
fuse *n, v* fjuːz **fused** fjuːzd **fuses** 'fjuːz ɪz -əz **fusing** 'fjuːz ɪŋ
  'fuse box; **'fuse wire**
fusee fju 'ziː **~s** z
fusel 'fjuːz ᵊl
  'fusel oil
fuselag|e 'fjuːz ə lɑːʒ 'fjuːs-, -ɪ-, -lɪdʒ ‖ 'fjuːs- 'fjuːz- **~es** ɪz əz
Fuseli 'fjuːz ᵊl i fjuː 'zel i
fusibility ˌfjuːz ə 'bɪl ət i ˌ·ɪ-, -ɪt i ‖ -ət̬ i
fusible 'fjuːz əb ᵊl -ɪb- **~ness** nəs nɪs
fusiform 'fjuːz ɪ fɔːm -ə- ‖ -fɔːrm
fusilier ˌfjuːz ə 'lɪə -ɪ- ‖ -'lɪᵊr **~s** z
fusillad|e ˌfjuːz ə 'leɪd -ɪ-, -'lɑːd, '· · · ‖ 'fjuːs ə leɪd 'fjuːz-, -lɑːd **~ed** ɪd əd **~es** z **~ing** ɪŋ
fusilli fu 'zɪl i fju-, -'sɪl-, -'siːl- —*It* [fu 'zil li, -'sil-]
fusion 'fjuːʒ ᵊn **~al** əl **~ism** ˌɪz əm **~ist/s** ɪst/s §əst/s **~s** z
  'fusion bomb
fuss fʌs **fussed** fʌst **fusses** 'fʌs ɪz -əz **fussing** 'fʌs ɪŋ
fussbudget 'fʌs ˌbʌdʒ ɪt -ət **~s** s
fussi... —*see* **fussy**
fusspot 'fʌs pɒt ‖ -pɑːt **~s** s
fuss|y 'fʌs |i **~ier** i ə ‖ i ᵊr **~iest** i ɪst i əst **~ily** ɪ li əl i **~iness** i nəs i nɪs
fustanella ˌfʌst ə 'nel ə **~s** z
fustian 'fʌst i ən ‖ 'fʌs tʃən
fustic 'fʌst ɪk
fust|y 'fʌst |i **~ier** i ə ‖ i ᵊr **~iest** i ɪst i əst **~ily** ɪ li əl i **~iness** i nəs i nɪs
futharc, futhark 'fuːθ ɑːk ‖ -ɑːrk
futile 'fjuːt aɪᵊl ‖ 'fjuːt̬ ᵊl 'fjuːt aɪᵊl **~ly** li ‖ i li **~ness** nəs nɪs
futilit|y fju 'tɪl ət |i -ɪt- ‖ -ət̬ |i **~ies** iz
futon 'fuːt ɒn 'fjuːt-, 'fʊt-, -ᵊn; ˌfuː 'tɒn ‖ -ɑːn —*Jp* [ɸɯ̥ ˌtoɴ] **~s** z
futtock 'fʌt ək ‖ 'fʌt̬ ək **~s** s
Futura fju 'tjʊər ə →-'tʃʊər ə ‖ -'tʊr ə -'tjʊr ə

future 'fjuːtʃ ə ‖ -ᵊr **~s** z
  ˌfuture 'perfect
future-proof 'fjuːtʃ ə pruːf §-prʊf ‖ -ᵊr- **~ed** t
  ~ing ɪŋ **~s** s
futur|ism 'fjuːtʃ ər |ˌɪz əm **~ist/s** ɪst/s §əst/s
futuristic ˌfjuːtʃ ə 'rɪst ɪk ◂ **~ally** ᵊl_i
futurit|y fju 'tjʊər ət |i -'tjɔːr-, →-'tʃʊər-,
  →§-'tʃɔːr-, -ɪt- ‖ -'tʊr əţ |i **~ies** iz
futurologist ˌfjuːtʃ ə 'rɒl ədʒ ɪst §-əst ‖ -'rɑːl-
  ~s s
futurology ˌfjuːtʃ ə 'rɒl ədʒ i ‖ -'rɑːl-
futz fʌts **futzed** fʌtst **futzes** 'fʌts ɪz -əz
  futzing 'fʌts ɪŋ
fuze fjuːz **fuzed** fjuːzd **fuzes** 'fjuːz ɪz -əz
  fuzing 'fjuːz ɪŋ

Fuzhou ˌfuː 'dʒəʊ ‖ -'dʒoʊ —*Chi* Fúzhōu
  [^{2}fu ^{1}tʂou]
fuzz fʌz **fuzzed** fʌzd **fuzzes** 'fʌz ɪz -əz **fuzzing**
  'fʌz ɪŋ
fuzz|y 'fʌz |i **~ier** i_ə ‖ i_ᵊr **~iest** i_ɪst i_əst **~ily**
  ɪ li əl i **~iness** i nəs i nɪs
fuzzy-wuzz|y 'fʌz i ˌwʌz |i **~ies** iz
f-word 'ef wɜːd ‖ -wɜːd
-fy faɪ —*This suffix imposes antepenultimate stress* (so'lidify, per'sonify).
Fybogel *tdmk* 'faɪb əʊ dʒel ‖ -ə-
Fyfe, Fyffe faɪf
Fylde faɪᵊld
Fylingdales 'faɪl ɪŋ deɪᵊlz
Fyne faɪn

G

g Spelling-to-sound

1 Where the spelling is **g**, the pronunciation is regularly
g as in **gas** gæs ('hard G').
Less frequently, it is
dʒ as in **gentle** ˈdʒent əl ('soft G').
Occasionally, it is ʒ as usually in **garage** ˈgær ɑːʒ ‖ gə ˈrɑːʒ.
g also forms part of the digraphs **gh**, **gu**, and **ng** (see under **n**).

2 Hard G is the usual pronunciation. Soft G and ʒ are found in certain words where **g** is followed by **e**, **i**, **y** — mostly words of French or Latin origin. Thus on the one hand we have
g in **get** get, **give** gɪv
but on the other
dʒ in **general** ˈdʒen rəl, **ginger** ˈdʒɪndʒ ə.

3 Where the spelling is the digraph **dg** before **e**, **i**, **y**, the pronunciation is always dʒ as in **edge** edʒ, **elegy** ˈel ədʒ i.

4 Where the spelling is double **gg**, the pronunciation is again regularly g as in **egg** eg.
Occasionally it is dʒ as in **exaggerate** ɪg ˈzædʒ ə reɪt. Note **suggest** BrE usually sə ˈdʒest but AmE səg ˈdʒest.

5 **g** is silent before **m n** but only at the beginning or end of a word or stem as in **gnat** næt, **sign** saɪn, **phlegm** flem, **foreigner** ˈfɒr ən ə ‖ ˈfɔːr ən ər.

6 The sound g is also occasionally written **gh** as in **ghost** or **gu** as in **guess** ges.

gh Spelling-to-sound

Where the spelling is the occasional digraph **gh** there are several possible pronunciations:
g as in **ghost** gəʊst ‖ goʊst
f as in **rough** rʌf or
silent, after **i** and sometimes other vowel letters as in **high** haɪ, **eight** eɪt, **daughter** ˈdɔːt ə ‖ ˈdɔːt̬ ər.

gu Spelling-to-sound

1 Where the spelling is the digraph **gu**, the pronunciation may be
g as in **guess** ges, **vague** veɪg or
gw as in **language** ˈlæŋ gwɪdʒ.

2 Generally speaking, g is found at the beginning of a word, and at the end of a word before silent **e**; gw is found in the middle of a word.

3 Most instances of **gu** are not a digraph: **gun** gʌn, **regular** ˈreg jəl ə ‖ ˈreg jəl ᵊr, **argue** ˈɑːg juː ‖ ˈɑːrg juː.

G, g dʒiː **Gs, G's, g's** dʒiːz —*Communications code name:* Golf
Ga gɑː
gab gæb **gabbed** gæbd **gabbing** ˈgæb ɪŋ **gabs** gæbz
Gabalfa gə ˈbælv ə -ˈbælf ə —*Welsh* [ga ˈbal va]
gabardine —*see* **gaberdine**
Gabbana gə ˈbɑːn ə -ˈbæn-
Gabbitas ˈgæb ɪ tæs §-ə-
gabbl|e ˈgæb ᵊl **~ed** d **~es** z **~ing** ‿ɪŋ
gabbro ˈgæb rəʊ ‖ -roʊ **~s** z
gabby, Gabby ˈgæb i
gaberdine ˌgæb ə ˈdiːn ◂ ˈ· · · ‖ ˈgæb ᵊr diːn **~s** z
gabfest ˈgæb fest **~s** s
Gabi *name(i)* ˈgæb i, *(ii)* ˈgɑːb i
Gabi *Australian language* ˈgʌb i
gabion ˈgeɪb i‿ən **~s** z
gable, Gable ˈgeɪb ᵊl **~d** d **~s** z
Gabon ˈgæb ɒn gæ ˈbɒn, gə-, -ˈbɒ̃ ‖ gə ˈboʊn —*Fr* [ga bɔ̃]
Gabonese ˌgæb ə ˈniːz ◂ -ɒ-
Gabor *(i)* gə ˈbɔː ‖ -ˈbɔːr, *(ii)* ˈgɑːb ɔː ‖ -ɔːr —*Hungarian* Gábor [ˈgaː bor]
Gaborone ˌgæb ə ˈrəʊn i ˌxæb-, -ˈruːn- ‖ ˌgɑːb ə ˈroʊn i
Gabriel ˈgeɪb ri‿əl
Gabriella ˌgæb ri ˈel ə ˌgeɪb-
Gabrielle ˌgæb ri ˈel ˌgeɪb-, ˈ· · ·
Gaby *(i)* ˈgæb i, *(ii)* ˈgɑːb i
gad, Gad gæd **gadded** ˈgæd ɪd -əd **gadding** ˈgæd ɪŋ **gads** gædz
gadabout ˈgæd ə ˌbaʊt **~s** s
Gadarene ˌgæd ə ˈriːn ◂ ˈ· · · ‖ ˈgæd ə riːn
ˌGadarene ˈswine
Gaddafi gə ˈdɑːf i -ˈdæf- —*Arabic* [ɣað ˈðaː fi]
Gaddesden ˈgædz dən
gad|fly ˈgæd |flaɪ **~flies** flaɪz
gadget ˈgædʒ ɪt -ət **~s** s
gadgetry ˈgædʒ ɪtr i -ətr i
gadolinium ˌgæd ə ˈlɪn i‿əm -ᵊl ˈɪn-
gadroon gə ˈdruːn **~s** z
Gadsby ˈgædz bi
Gadsden, Gadsdon ˈgædz dən
gadwall ˈgæd wɔːl ‖ -wɑːl **~s** z
gadzooks ₍ˌ₎gæd ˈzuːks
Gaea ˈdʒiː‿ə
Gael geɪᵊl **Gaels** geɪᵊlz
Gaelic ˈgeɪl ɪk ˈgæl-, ˈgɑːl-
ˌGaelic ˈfootball
Gaeltacht ˈgeɪᵊl tæxt -təxt —*Irish* [ˈgeːl təxt]
Gaenor ˈgeɪn ə ˈgaɪn-, -ɔː ‖ -ɔːr —*Welsh* [ˈgəi nor]
gaff gæf **gaffed** gæft **gaffing** ˈgæf ɪŋ **gaffs** gæfs
gaffe gæf **gaffes** gæfs
gaffer ˈgæf ə ‖ -ᵊr **~s** z
gag gæg **gagged** gægd **gagging** ˈgæg ɪŋ **gags** gægz
gaga ˈgɑː gɑː
Gagarin gə ˈgɑːr ɪn §-ən —*Russ* [gʌ ˈga rʲin]
Gagauz ˌgæg ɑː ˈuːz
Gagauzi ˌgæg ɑː ˈuːz i ◂
gage, Gage geɪdʒ **gages** ˈgeɪdʒ ɪz -əz
gaggl|e ˈgæg ᵊl **~ed** d **~es** z **~ing** ‿ɪŋ
Gaia ˈgaɪ ə ˈgeɪ ə
Gaidhealtachd ˈgeɪᵊl tək -tæxt —*ScG* [ˈgeːɫ təxk]
gaiet|y ˈgeɪ ət |i -ɪt- ‖ -əţ |i **~ies** iz
gaijin ˌgaɪ ˈdʒɪn -ˈdʒiːn; ˈ· · —*Jp* [ga ˈi dʑiɴ]
Gail, Gaile geɪᵊl
gaillardia geɪ ˈlɑːd i‿ə gə- ‖ -ˈlɑːrd- **~s** z
gaily ˈgeɪ li
gain geɪn **gained** geɪnd **gainer/s** ˈgeɪn ə/z ‖ -ᵊr/z **gaining** ˈgeɪn ɪŋ **gains** geɪnz
gainer ˈgeɪn ə ‖ -ᵊr **~s** z
Gaines geɪnz
Gainesville ˈgeɪnz vɪl -vəl
gainful ˈgeɪn fᵊl -fʊl **~ly** ‿i **~ness** nəs nɪs
gain|say ˌgeɪn |ˈseɪ **~said** ˈsed ˈseɪd **~sayer/s** ˈseɪ ə/z ‖ -ᵊr/z **~saying** ˈseɪ ɪŋ **~says** ˈseɪz ˈsez
Gainsborough ˈgeɪnz bər‿ə ‖ -ˌbɜː oʊ **~s** z
ˈgainst genᵗst geɪnᵗst

airdner *(i)* ˈgeəd nə ‖ ˈgerd nᵊr, *(ii)* ˈgɑːd- ‖ ˈgɑːrd-
airloch ˈgeə lɒx -lɒk ‖ ˈger lɑːk
aisford ˈgeɪs fəd ‖ -fᵊrd
ait geɪt (= *gate*)
aiter ˈgeɪt ə ‖ ˈgeɪt̬ ᵊr **~s** z
aitskell, Gaitskill ˈgeɪt skəl -skɪl
aius ˈgaɪ‿əs
al gæl **gals** gælz
ala ˈgɑːl ə ˈgeɪl ə ‖ ˈgeɪl ə ˈgæl ə **~s** z
alactagogue gə ˈlækt ə gɒg ‖ -gɑːg **~s** z
alactic gə ˈlækt ɪk
alactica gə ˈlækt ɪk ə
alacto- *comb. form*
with stress-neutral suffix gə ¦lækt əʊ ‖ -ə — **galactopoietic** gə ˌlækt əʊ pɔɪ ˈet ɪk ◂ ‖ -ə pɔɪ ˈet̬ ɪk ◂
with stress-imposing suffix ˌgæl æk ˈtɒ+ -æk- ‖ -ˈtɑː+ — **galactometer** ˌgæl æk ˈtɒm ɪt ə ˌ-æk-, -ət ə ‖ -ˈtɑːm ət̬ ᵊr
alactose gə ˈlækt əʊs -əʊz ‖ -oʊs
galah gə ˈlɑː **~s** z
Galahad ˈgæl ə hæd
galantine ˈgæl ən tiːn ˌ· · ˈ· **~s** z
Galapagos, Galápagos gə ˈlæp əg əs -ə gɒs ‖ gə ˈlɑːp ə goʊs -əg əs —*Sp* [ga ˈla pa ɣos]
Galashiels ˌgæl ə ˈʃiːᵊlz
Galatea ˌgæl ə ˈtiː‿ə
Galatia gə ˈleɪʃ ə -ˈleɪʃ i‿ə
Galatian gə ˈleɪʃ ᵊn -ˈleɪʃ i‿ən **~s** z
galax|y ˈgæl əks |i **~ies** iz
Galba ˈgælb ə
galbanum ˈgælb ən əm
Galbraith gæl ˈbreɪθ ‖ ˈgælb reɪθ
gale, Gale geɪᵊl **gales** geɪᵊlz
gale-force ˈgeɪᵊl fɔːs ‖ -fɔːrs -foʊrs
Galen ˈgeɪl ən -ɪn
galena, G~ gə ˈliːn ə
Galenic, g~ geɪ ˈlen ɪk gə-
galere, galère gæ ˈleə ‖ -ˈleᵊr —*Fr* [ga lɛːʁ]
Galicia gə ˈlɪs i‿ə -ˈlɪʃ ə, -ˈlɪʃ i‿ə ‖ -ˈlɪʃ ə -ˈliːʃ-
Galician gə ˈlɪs i‿ən -ˈlɪʃ ᵊn, -ˈlɪʃ i‿ən ‖ -ˈlɪʃ ᵊn -ˈliːʃ- **~s** z
Galilean ˌgæl ɪ ˈliː‿ən ◂ -ə- **~s** z
Galilee ˈgæl ɪ liː -ə-
Galileo ˌgæl ɪ ˈleɪ əʊ -ə-, -ˈliː- ‖ -oʊ —*It* [ga li ˈlɛː o]
galingale ˈgæl ɪŋ geɪᵊl **~s** z
galipot ˈgæl i pɒt ‖ -pɑːt
gall, Gall gɔːl ‖ gɑːl **galled** gɔːld ‖ gɑːld **galling** ˈgɔːl ɪŋ ‖ ˈgɑːl- **galls** gɔːlz ‖ gɑːlz
ˈgall ˌbladder; **ˈgall wasp**
Galla ˈgæl ə **~s** z
Gallacher, Gallaher ˈgæl ə hə -əx ə ‖ -ə hᵊr
Gallagher ˈgæl ə hə -əx ə, -əg ə ‖ -əg ᵊr
gallant *n, adj 'attentive to women'* gə ˈlænt ˈgæl ənt ‖ gə ˈlɑːnt **~ly** li **~s** s
gallant *adj 'brave'* ˈgæl ənt **~ly** li
gallant|ry ˈgæl ənt |ri **~ries** riz
Gallaudet ˌgæl ə ˈdet
galleon ˈgæl i‿ən **~s** z
galleria ˌgæl ə ˈriː‿ə **~s** z
galler|y ˈgæl ər |i **~ies** iz
galley, G~ ˈgæl i **~s** z
ˈgalley proof; **ˈgalley slave**
Galliano ˌgæl i ˈɑːn əʊ ‖ -oʊ
galliard ˈgæl i ɑːd -i‿əd ‖ ˈgæl jᵊrd **~s** z
Gallic, g~ ˈgæl ɪk
gallicism ˈgæl ɪ ˌsɪz əm -ə- **~s** z
gallimauf|ry ˌgæl ɪ ˈmɔːf |ri -ə- ‖ -ˈmɑːf- **~ries** riz
gallinaceous ˌgæl ɪ ˈneɪʃ əs -ə-
galling ˈgɔːl ɪŋ ‖ ˈgɑːl- **~ly** li
gallinule ˈgæl ɪ njuːl -ə- ‖ -nuːl -njuːl **~s** z
Gallipoli gə ˈlɪp əl i
gallipot ˈgæl i pɒt ‖ -pɑːt
gallium ˈgæl i‿əm
galli|vant ˈgæl ɪ |vænt -ə-, vɑːnt, ˌ· · ˈ· ‖ -ə |vænt **~vanted** vænt ɪd vɑːnt-, əd ‖ vænt̬ əd **~vanting** vænt ɪŋ vɑːnt- ‖ vænt̬ ɪŋ **~vants** vænts
Gallo ˈgæl əʊ ‖ -oʊ
Gallo- ¦gæl əʊ ‖ -oʊ — **Gallo-Romance** ˌgæl əʊ rəʊ ˈmænᵗs ◂ ‖ -oʊ roʊ-
gallon ˈgæl ən **~s** z
galloon gə ˈluːn
gallop ˈgæl əp **~ed** t **~er/s** ə/z ‖ ᵊr/z **~ing** ɪŋ **~s** s
Galloway, g~ ˈgæl ə weɪ
gallowglass ˈgæl əʊ glɑːs §-glæs ‖ -oʊ glæs **~es** ɪz əz
gallows ˈgæl əʊz ‖ -oʊz
ˈgallows ˌhumour
gallstone ˈgɔːl stəʊn ‖ -stoʊn ˈgɑːl- **~s** z
Gallup ˈgæl əp
ˌGallup ˈpoll, ˈ· · ‖ ˈ· · ·
gallus ˈgæl əs **~es** ɪz əz
galoot gə ˈluːt **~s** s
galop ˈgæl əp gæ ˈlɒp **~s** s
galore gə ˈlɔː ‖ -ˈlɔːr -ˈloʊr
galosh gə ˈlɒʃ ‖ -ˈlɑːʃ **~es** ɪz əz
Galsworthy *(i)* ˈgɔːlz ˌwɜːð i ‖ -ˌwɜːð i ˈgɑːlz-, *(ii)* ˈgælz-
Galt gɔːlt gɒlt ‖ gɑːlt
Galtieri ˌgælt i ˈeər i ‖ ˌgɑːlt i ˈer i —*Sp* [gal ˈtje ri]
Galton ˈgɔːlt ən ˈgɒlt- ‖ ˈgɑːlt-
galtonia gɔːl ˈtəʊn i‿ə gɒl- ‖ -toʊn- gɑːl- **~s** z
galumph gə ˈlʌmᵖf **~ed** t **~ing** ɪŋ **~s** s
galvanic gæl ˈvæn ɪk **~ally** ᵊl‿i
galvanis... —*see* **galvaniz...**
galvanism ˈgælv ə ˌnɪz əm
galvanization ˌgælv ə naɪ ˈzeɪʃ ᵊn -ən ɪ- ‖ -ən ə-
galvaniz|e ˈgælv ə naɪz **~ed** d **~er/s** ə/z ‖ ᵊr/z **~es** ɪz əz **~ing** ɪŋ
galvano- *comb. form*
with stress-neutral suffix ¦gælv ən ə gæl ¦væn ə — **galvanoscope** ˈgælv ən ə skəʊp gæl ˈvæn- ‖ -skoʊp
with stress-imposing suffix ˌgælv ə ˈnɒ+ ‖ -ˈnɑː+ — **galvanoscopy** ˌgælv ə ˈnɒsk əp i ‖ -ˈnɑːsk-
galvanometer ˌgælv ə ˈnɒm ɪt ə -ət ə ‖ -ˈnɑːm ət̬ ᵊr **~s** z
Galveston, Galvestone ˈgælv əst ən -ɪst-

G

Galway ˈgɔːl weɪ ‖ ˈgɑːl-
gam gæm **gammed** gæmd **gamming** ˈgæm ɪŋ **gams** gæmz
Gama, gama ˈgɑːm ə
Gamage ˈgæm ɪdʒ **~'s** ɪz əz
Gamaliel gə ˈmeɪl i‿əl -ˈmɑːl-
Gambaccini ˌgæm bə ˈtʃiːn i
Gambi|a ˈgæm bi‿|ə **~an/s** ən/z
Gambier, g~ ˈgæm bi‿ə ‖ ‿ər
gambit ˈgæm bɪt §-bət **~s** s
gambl|e, G~ ˈgæm bəl **gambled** ˈgæm bəld **gambler/s** ˈgæm blə/z ‖ -blər/z **gambles** ˈgæm bəlz **gambling** ˈgæm blɪŋ
gamboge gæm ˈbəʊdʒ -ˈbəʊʒ, -ˈbuːʒ ‖ -ˈboʊdʒ
gambol ˈgæm bəl *(= gamble)* **~ed, ~led** d **~ing, ~ling** ɪŋ **~s** z
gambrel ˈgæm brəl **~s** z
game geɪm **gamer** ˈgeɪm ə ‖ -ər **games** geɪmz **gamest** ˈgeɪm ɪst -əst **ˈgame plan**; **ˈgames ˌmistress**
gamecock ˈgeɪm kɒk ‖ -kɑːk **~s** s
gamekeeper ˈgeɪm ˌkiːp ə ‖ -ər **~s** z
gamelan ˈgæm ə læn -ɪ-
gamely ˈgeɪm li
gameplay ˈgeɪm pleɪ
gamesmanship ˈgeɪmz mən ʃɪp
gamete ˈgæm iːt gə ˈmiːt **~s** s
gameto- *comb. form*
with stress-neutral suffix gə ¦miːt əʊ ¦gæm ɪt ə, -ət- ‖ gə ¦miːţ ə ¦gæm əţ ə — **gametocyte** gə ˈmiːt əʊ saɪt ˈgæm ɪt ə-, -ət- ‖ -ˈmiːţ ə- ˈgæm əţ ə-
with stress-imposing suffix ˌgæm ɪ ˈtɒ+ §-ə- ‖ -ˈtɑː+ — **gametogeny** ˌgæm ɪ ˈtɒdʒ ən i ˌ·ə- ‖ -ˈtɑːdʒ-
gamey ˈgeɪm i
gamin ˈgæm ɪn §-ən —*Fr* [ga mæ̃] **~s** z —*or as sing.*
gamine ˈgæm iːn gæ ˈmiːn —*Fr* [ga min] **~s** z
gaming ˈgeɪm ɪŋ **ˈgaming ˌtable**
Gamlen, Gamlin ˈgæm lɪn -lən
gamma ˈgæm ə **~s** z **ˌgamma ˈglobulin**; **ˌgamma ˌradiˈation**; **ˈgamma ray**
Gammell ˈgæm əl
gammer ˈgæm ə ‖ -ər **~s** z
gammon, G~ ˈgæm ən **~ed** d **~ing** ɪŋ **~s** z
gammy ˈgæm i
-gamous *stress-imposing* gəm əs — **bigamous** ˈbɪg əm əs
gamp, Gamp gæmp **gamps** gæmps
gamut ˈgæm ət -ʌt, -ʊt
gam|y ˈgeɪm |i **~ier** i‿ə ‖ i‿ər **~iest** i‿ɪst i‿əst **~iness** i nəs i nɪs
-gamy *stress-imposing* gəm i — **monogamy** mə ˈnɒg əm i ‖ -ˈnɑːg-
gan gæn
Ganda ˈgænd ə ˈgɑːnd ə
Gandalf ˈgænd ælf ‖ -ɑːlf
gander, G~ ˈgænd ə ‖ -ər **~s** z
Gandhi ˈgænd i ˈgɑːnd i —*Hindi* [gɑ̃ː d̪i]
ganef ˈgɑːn əf **~s** s
Ganesh gə ˈneɪʃ -ˈneʃ —*Hindi* [gə neːʃ]
gang gæŋ **ganged** gæŋd **ganging** ˈgæŋ ɪŋ **gangs** gæŋz
gang-bang ˈgæŋ bæŋ **~ed** d **~ing** ɪŋ **~s** z
gangbuster ˈgæŋ ˌbʌst ə ‖ -ər **~s** z
ganger ˈgæŋ ə ‖ -ər **~s** z
Ganges ˈgændʒ iːz
gangland ˈgæŋ lænd -lənd
ganglia ˈgæŋ gli‿ə
gangling ˈgæŋ glɪŋ
gangli|on ˈgæŋ gli‿|ən **~a** ə **~ons** ənz
gan|gly ˈgæŋ |gli **~glier** gli‿ə ‖ gli‿ər **~gliest** gli‿ɪst əst
gangmaster ˈgæŋ ˌmɑːst ə §-ˌmæst- ‖ -mæst ər **~s** z
gangplank ˈgæŋ plæŋk **~s** s
gangren|e ˈgæŋ griːn ‖ ·ˈ· **~ed** d **~es** z **~ing** ɪŋ
gangrenous ˈgæŋ grɪn əs -grən-
gangsta ˈgæŋkst ə **~s** z
gangster ˈgæŋkst ə ‖ -ər **~s** z
gangue gæŋ *(= gang)*
gangway ˈgæŋ weɪ **~s** z
ganister ˈgæn ɪst ə -əst- ‖ -ər
ganja ˈgændʒ ə ˈgɑːndʒ-
gannet ˈgæn ɪt -ət **~s** s
Gannex *tdmk* ˈgæn eks
gansey ˈgænz i **~s** z
Gansu ˌgæn ˈsuː ‖ ˌgɑːn- —*Chi* Gānsù [1kan 4su]
Gant gænt
gantlet ˈgænt lət ˈgɔːnt-, -lɪt ‖ ˈgɔːnt- ˈgɑːnt-, ˈgænt- **~s** s
gantr|y ˈgæntr |i **~ies** iz
Ganymede ˈgæn ɪ miːd -ə-
gaol dʒeɪəl *(= jail)* **gaoled** dʒeɪəld **gaoling** ˈdʒeɪəl ɪŋ **gaols** ˈdʒeɪəlz
gaolbird ˈdʒeɪəl bɜːd ‖ -bɜːd **~s** z
gaoler ˈdʒeɪl ə ‖ -ər **~s** z
gap gæp **gaps** gæps
gape geɪp **gaped** geɪpt **gaper/s** ˈgeɪp ə/z ‖ -ər/z **gapes** geɪps **gaping/ly** ˈgeɪp ɪŋ /li
gap-toothed ˌgæp ˈtuːθt ◂ -ˈtuːðd, §-ˈtʊθt
gar gɑː ‖ gɑːr
garag|e *n, v* ˈgær ɑːʒ -ɑːdʒ, -ɪdʒ; gə ˈrɑːʒ, -ˈrɑːdʒ ‖ gə ˈrɑːʒ -ˈrɑːdʒ *(*)* — *Preference polls, AmE:* -ˈrɑːʒ *52%,* -ˈrɑːdʒ *48%; BrE:* ˈgær ɑːdʒ *56% (*dʒ *31%,* ʒ *25%),* -ɪdʒ *38%,* gə ˈrɑːdʒ *6%.* **~ed** d **~es** ɪz əz **~ing** ɪŋ **ˈgarage sale** ‖ **gaˈrage sale**
garam masala ˌgɑːr əm mə ˈsɑːl ə ˌgʌr-, -mɑːˈ·- —*Hindi-Urdu* [gə rəm mə ʂaː lah]
Garamond ˈgær ə mɒnd ‖ -mɑːnd
Garand ˈgær ənd ‖ ˈger-; gə ˈrænd
Garard ˈgær ɑːd ‖ -ɑːrd ˈger-
garb gɑːb ‖ gɑːrb **garbed** gɑːbd ‖ gɑːrbd
garbage ˈgɑːb ɪdʒ ‖ ˈgɑːrb- **ˈgarbage can**; **ˈgarbage colˌlector**; **ˈgarbage truck**
garbanzo gɑː ˈbænz əʊ ‖ gɑːr ˈbɑːnz oʊ **~s** z
garbl|e ˈgɑːb əl ‖ ˈgɑːrb əl **~ed** d **~es** z **~ing** ‿ɪŋ
Garbo, garbo ˈgɑːb əʊ ‖ ˈgɑːrb oʊ **~s** z

GARAGE

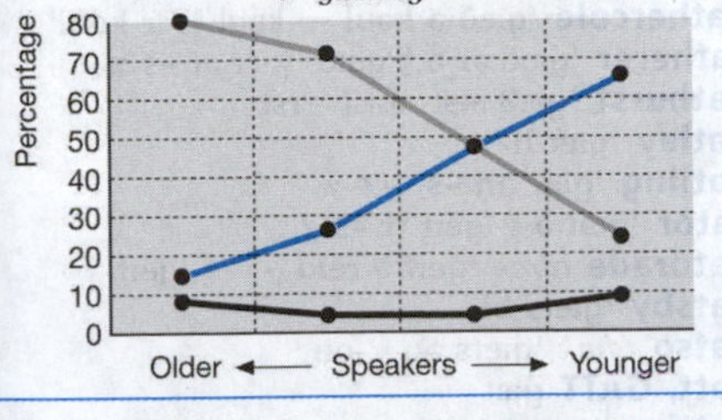

Garcia *English family name (i)* ˈgɑːs i‿ə ‖ ˈgɑːrs-, *(ii)* ˈgɑːʃ- ‖ ˈgɑːrʃ-
Garcia *Spanish name* gɑː ˈsiː‿ə ‖ gɑːr- —*Sp* García [gar ˈθi a], *AmSp* [-ˈsi-]
garcon, garçon ˈgɑːs ɒn -ɒ̃ ‖ gɑːr ˈsoʊn -ˈsɔː; —*Fr* [gaʁ sɔ̃]
garda, Garda *Irish policeman* ˈgɑːd ə ‖ ˈgɑːrd ə —*Irish* [ˈgar də] **gardai, gardaí, G~** ₍ˌ₎gɑː ˈdiː ‖ ₍ˌ₎gɑːr- —*Irish* [ˈgar diː]
ˌGarda ˌSío'chána ˌʃiː‿ə ˈkɔːn ə -ˈxɔːn- ‖ -ˈkɑːn-
Garda *lake in Italy* ˈgɑːd ə ‖ ˈgɑːrd ə —*It* [ˈgar da]
garden, G~ ˈgɑːd ᵊn ‖ ˈgɑːrd ᵊn **~ed** d **~ing** ‿ɪŋ **~s** z
ˈgarden ˌcentre; ˌgarden ˈcity; ˈgarden ˌparty; ˌgarden ˈsuburb
gardener ˈgɑːd nə ‖ ˈgɑːrd nᵊr **~s** z
gardenia gɑː ˈdiːn i‿ə ‖ gɑːr ˈdiːn jə **~s** z
gardening *n* ˈgɑːd nɪŋ ‖ ˈgɑːrd-
garden-variety ˈgɑːd ᵊn və ˌraɪ‿ət i ‖ ˈgɑːrd ᵊn və ˌraɪ əṱ i
Gardiner ˈgɑːd nə ‖ ˈgɑːrd nᵊr
Gardyne gɑː ˈdaɪn ‖ gɑːr-
Gare du Nord ˌgɑː djuː ˈnɔː ‖ ˌgɑːr duː ˈnɔːr —*Fr* [gaʁ dy nɔːʁ]
Garel ˈgær əl ‖ ˈger-
Gareloch ˈgeə lɒx -lɒk ‖ ˈger lɑːk ˈgær-
Gareth ˈgær əθ -ɪθ, -eθ ‖ ˈger- —*Welsh* [ˈga reθ]
Garfield ˈgɑː fiːᵊld ‖ ˈgɑːr-
garfish ˈgɑː fɪʃ ‖ ˈgɑːr-
Garforth ˈgɑː fəθ -fɔːθ ‖ ˈgɑːr fᵊrθ -fɔːrθ, -foʊrθ
Garfunkel gɑː ˈfʌŋk ᵊl ˈgɑːf ʌŋk ᵊl ‖ gɑːr-
garganey ˈgɑːg ən i ‖ ˈgɑːrg- **~s** z
Gargantua gɑː ˈgænt ju‿ə ‖ gɑːr ˈgæntʃ u‿ə
gargantuan gɑː ˈgænt ju‿ən ‖ gɑːr ˈgæntʃ u‿ən
gargl|e ˈgɑːg ᵊl ‖ ˈgɑːrg ᵊl **~ed** d **~es** z **~ing** ‿ɪŋ
gargoyle ˈgɑː gɔɪᵊl ‖ ˈgɑːrg- **~s** z

Garibaldi, g~ ˌgær ɪ ˈbɔːld i -ə-, -ˈbɒld- ‖ ˌger-, -ˈbɑːld i —*It* [ga ri ˈbal di] **~s** z
garish ˈgeər ɪʃ ˈgɑːr- ‖ ˈger- ˈgær- **~ly** li **~ness** nəs nɪs
garland, G~ ˈgɑːl ənd ‖ ˈgɑːrl- **~s** z
garlic, G~, Garlick, Garlicke ˈgɑːl ɪk ‖ ˈgɑːrl-
garlicky ˈgɑːl ɪk i ‖ ˈgɑːrl-
Garman ˈgɑːm ən ‖ ˈgɑːrm-
garment ˈgɑːm ənt ‖ ˈgɑːrm- **~ed** ɪd əd **~s** s
Garmin *tdmk* ˈgɑː mɪn ‖ ˈgɑːr-
Garmisch ˈgɑːm ɪʃ ‖ ˈgɑːrm- —*Ger* [ˈgaʁ mɪʃ]
Garmondsway, Garmonsway ˈgɑːm ənz weɪ ‖ ˈgɑːrm-
garn|er, G~ ˈgɑːn |ə ‖ ˈgɑːrn |ᵊr **~ered** əd ‖ ᵊrd **~ering** ər‿ɪŋ **~ers** əz ‖ ᵊrz
garnet, G~, Garnett ˈgɑːn ɪt -ət ‖ ˈgɑːrn- **~s** s
garnish ˈgɑːn ɪʃ ‖ ˈgɑːrn- **~ed** t **~er/s** ə/z ‖ ᵊr/z **~es** ɪz əz **~ing** ɪŋ
garnishee ˌgɑːn ɪ ˈʃiː §-ə- ‖ ˌgɑːrn- **~s** z
garott... —*see* **garrot...**
Garrard ˈgær ɑːd -əd ‖ -ɑːrd ˈger-, -ᵊrd
Garratt ˈgær ət ‖ ˈger-
Garraway ˈgær ə weɪ ‖ ˈger-
garret, G~, Garrett ˈgær ət -ɪt ‖ ˈger- **~s** s
Garrick ˈgær ɪk ‖ ˈger-
garrison, G~ ˈgær ɪs ən -əs- ‖ ˈger- **~ed** d **~ing** ɪŋ **~s** z
gar|rote, gar|rotte gə |ˈrɒt ‖ -|ˈrɑːt -ˈroʊt **~roted, ~rotted** ˈrɒt ɪd -əd ‖ ˈrɑːṱ əd ˈroʊṱ- **~rotes, ~rottes** ˈrɒts ‖ ˈrɑːts ˈroʊts **~roting, ~rotting** ˈrɒt ɪŋ ‖ ˈrɑːṱ ɪŋ ˈroʊṱ-
garrulity gə ˈruːl ət i gæ-, -ˈrjuːl-, -ɪt- ‖ -əṱ i
garrulous ˈgær əl əs -jʊl- ‖ ˈger- **~ly** li **~ness** nəs nɪs
Garry ˈgær i ‖ ˈger-
garrya ˈgær i‿ə ‖ ˈger- **~s** z
Garryowen, g~ ˌgær i ˈəʊ ɪn -ən ‖ ˌgær i ˈoʊ ən ˌger-
Garscadden gɑː ˈskæd ᵊn ‖ gɑːr-
Garside ˈgɑː saɪd ‖ ˈgɑːr-
Garston ˈgɑːst ən ‖ ˈgɑːrst-
Gartcosh ₍ˌ₎gɑːt ˈkɒʃ ‖ ₍ˌ₎gɑːrt ˈkɑːʃ
garter, G~ ˈgɑːt ə ‖ ˈgɑːrṱ ᵊr **~ed** d **gartering** ˈgɑːt‿ər ɪŋ ‖ ˈgɑːrṱ ər ɪŋ **~s** z
ˈgarter snake
garth, Garth gɑːθ ‖ gɑːrθ **garths, Garth's** gɑːθs ‖ gɑːrθs
Garton ˈgɑːt ᵊn ‖ ˈgɑːrt ᵊn
Garuda *tdmk* gə ˈruːd ə gæ-
Garvagh ˈgɑːv ə ‖ ˈgɑːrv ə
Garvaghy gɑː ˈvæ hi ‖ gɑːr-
Gary *family name* ˈgeər i ‖ ˈger i ˈgær i
Gary *personal name; place in IN* ˈgær i ‖ ˈger-
gas gæs **gases, gasses** ˈgæs ɪz -əz **gassed** gæst **gassing** ˈgæs ɪŋ
ˈgas ˌchamber; ˌgas ˈfire; ˈgas ˌfitter; ˈgas mask; ˈgas ˌpedal; ˈgas ring; ˈgas ˌstation; ˌgas ˈturbine ‖ ˈ· ˌ··
gasbag ˈgæs bæg **~s** z
Gascoigne, Gascoin, Gascoine, Gascoyne ˈgæsk ɔɪn
Gascon ˈgæsk ən **~s** z

G

Gascony ˈgæsk ən i
gaseous ˈgæs i‿əs ˈgeɪs-, ˈgeɪz- ‖ ˈgæʃ əs **~ness** nəs nɪs
gas-fired ˈgæs ˌfaɪ‿əd ‖ -ˌfaɪ‿ᵊrd
gas-guzzl|er ˈgæs ˌgʌz ᵊl|‿ə ‖ ‿ᵊr **~ing** ‿ɪŋ
gash, Gash gæʃ **gashed** gæʃt **gashes** ˈgæʃ ɪz -əz **gashing** ˈgæʃ ɪŋ
gasholder ˈgæs ˌhəʊld ə ‖ -ˌhoʊld ᵊr **~s** z
gasifiable ˈgæs ɪ faɪ‿əb ᵊl §ˈ·ə-; ˌ·.ˈ·.·
gasification ˌgæs ɪf ɪ ˈkeɪʃ ᵊn ˌ·əf-, §-əˈ·-
gasi|fy ˈgæs ɪ |faɪ -ə- **~fied** faɪd **~fier/s** faɪ‿ə/z ‖ faɪ‿ᵊr/z **~fies** faɪz **~fying** faɪ ɪŋ
Gaskell ˈgæsk ᵊl
gasket ˈgæsk ɪt -ət **~s** s
gaskin ˈgæsk ɪn §-ən **~s** z
gaslamp ˈgæs læmp **~s** s
gaslight ˈgæs laɪt **~s** s
gas|man ˈgæs |mæn **~men** men
gasohol ˈgæs ə hɒl ‖ -hɔːl -hɑːl
gasolene, gasoline ˈgæs ə liːn ˌ·.ˈ·
gasometer gæ ˈsɒm ɪt ə gə-, -ət ə ‖ -ˈsɑːm əṱ ᵊr **~s** z
gasp gɑːsp §gæsp ‖ gæsp **gasped** gɑːspt §gæspt ‖ gæspt **gasping** ˈgɑːsp ɪŋ §ˈgæsp- ‖ ˈgæsp ɪŋ **gasps** gɑːsps §gæsps ‖ gæsps
Gaspar ˈgæsp ə -ɑː ‖ -ᵊr -ɑːr
Gaspé ˈgæsp eɪ ‖ gæ ˈspeɪ —*Fr* [gas pe]
gass|y ˈgæs |i **~ier** i‿ə ‖ i‿ᵊr **~iest** i‿ɪst i‿əst **~iness** i nəs i nɪs
gasteropod ˈgæs tər‿ə pɒd ‖ -pɑːd **~s** z
gastrectom|y gæ ˈstrekt əm |i **~ies** iz
gastric ˈgæs trɪk
gastritis gæ ˈstraɪt ɪs §-əs ‖ -ˈstraɪṱ əs
gastro- *comb. form*
with stress-neutral suffix ˌgæs trəʊ ‖ -troʊ — **gastroenteric** ˌgæs trəʊ en ˈter ɪk ◂ ‖ -troʊ-
with stress-imposing suffix gæ ˈstrɒ+ ‖ -ˈstrɑː+ — **gastroscopy** gæ ˈstrɒsk əp i ‖ -ˈstrɑːsk-
gastroenteritis ˌgæs trəʊ ˌent ə ˈraɪt ɪs §-əs ‖ -troʊ ˌenṱ ə ˈraɪṱ əs
gastrointestinal ˌgæs trəʊ ɪn ˈtest ɪn ᵊl ◂ -ᵊn əl; -ˌɪnt es ˈtaɪn- ‖ -troʊ ɪn ˈtest ᵊn‿əl ◂ **~ly** i
gastronome ˈgæs trə nəʊm ‖ -noʊm **~s** z
gastronomic ˌgæs trə ˈnɒm ɪk ◂ ‖ -ˈnɑːm- **~ally** ᵊl‿i
gastronomy gæ ˈstrɒn əm i ‖ -ˈstrɑːn-
gastropod ˈgæs trə pɒd ‖ -pɑːd **~s** z
gastropub ˈgæs trəʊ pʌb ‖ -troʊ- **~s** z
gasworks ˈgæs wɜːks ‖ -wɜːks
gat gæt **gats** gæts
Gatcomb, Gatcombe ˈgæt kəm
gate, Gate geɪt **gated** ˈgeɪt ɪd -əd ‖ ˈgeɪṱ əd **gates** geɪts **gating** ˈgeɪt ɪŋ ‖ ˈgeɪṱ ɪŋ
ˈgate ˌmoney
Gateacre ˈgæt ək ə ‖ -ᵊr
gateau, gâteau ˈgæt əʊ ‖ gæ ˈtoʊ —*Fr* [ga to] **~s, ~x** z *-or as sing.*
gatecrash ˈgeɪt kræʃ **~ed** t **~er/s** ə/z ‖ ᵊr/z **~es** ɪz əz **~ing** ɪŋ
gatefold ˈgeɪt fəʊld →-fɒʊld ‖ -foʊld **~s** z
gate|house, G~ ˈgeɪt |haʊs **~houses** haʊz ɪz -əz
gatekeeper ˈgeɪt ˌkiːp ə ‖ -ᵊr **~s** z
gateleg ˈgeɪt leg **~s** z
gatepost ˈgeɪt pəʊst ‖ -poʊst **~s** s
Gates geɪts
Gateshead ˈgeɪts hed ˌ·ˈ·
gateway ˈgeɪt weɪ **~s** z
Gath gæθ
gather ˈgæð ə §ˈgɑːð- ‖ -ᵊr **~ed** d **gathering** ˈgæð ər‿ɪŋ §ˈgɑːð- **~s** z
Gathercole ˈgæð ə kəʊl →-kɒʊl ‖ -ᵊr koʊl
gatherer ˈgæð ər‿ə §ˈgɑːð- ‖ ᵊr‿ər **~s** z
Gathurst ˈgæθ ɜːst -əst ‖ -ᵊrst
Gatley ˈgæt li
Gatling ˈgæt lɪŋ **~s, ~'s** z
gator ˈgeɪt ə ‖ ˈgeɪṱ ᵊr **~s** z
Gatorade *tdmk* ˈgeɪt ə reɪd ˌ·.ˈ· ‖ ˈgeɪṱ-
Gatsby ˈgæts bi
Gatso *tdmk* ˈgæts əʊ ‖ -oʊ
Gatt, GATT gæt
Gatting ˈgæt ɪŋ ‖ ˈgæṱ ɪŋ
Gatwick ˈgæt wɪk
gauche gəʊʃ ‖ goʊʃ
gauche|ly ˈgəʊʃ |li ‖ ˈgoʊʃ- **~ness** nəs nɪs
Gaucher ˈgəʊ ˈʃeɪ ‖ goʊ ˈʃeɪ **-'s** z —*Fr* [go ʃe]
ˈGoucher's diˌsease
gaucherie ˈgəʊʃ ər i ˌgəʊʃ ə ˈriː ‖ ˌgoʊʃ ə ˈriː —*Fr* [goʃ ʁi] **~s** z
gaucho ˈgaʊtʃ əʊ ‖ -oʊ **~s** z
gaudeamus ˌgaʊd i ˈɑːm ʊs ˌgɔːd-, -ˈeɪm-, -əs
ˌgaudeˌamus ˈigitur
Gaudi, Gaudí gaʊ ˈdiː ˈgaʊd i —*Catalan* [gəu ˈði], *Sp* [gau ˈði]
gaud|y ˈgɔːd |i ‖ ˈgɑːd- **~ier** i‿ə ‖ i‿ᵊr **~iest** i‿ɪst i‿əst **~ily** ɪ li əl i **~iness** i nəs i nɪs
gauge geɪdʒ **gauged** geɪdʒd **gauges** ˈgeɪdʒ ɪz -əz **gauging** ˈgeɪdʒ ɪŋ
Gauguin ˈgəʊg æ̃ -æn ‖ goʊ ˈgæn —*Fr* [go gæ̃] **~s, ~'s** z
Gaul gɔːl ‖ gɑːl **Gauls** gɔːlz ‖ gɑːlz
gauleiter, G~ ˈgaʊ ˌlaɪt ə ‖ -laɪṱ ᵊr —*Ger* [ˈgaʊ lai tɐ] **~s** z
Gaulish ˈgɔːl ɪʃ ‖ ˈgɑːl-
Gaullism ˈgəʊl ˌɪz əm →ˈgɒʊl- ‖ ˈgɔːl- ˈgɑːl-, ˈgoʊl-
Gaullist ˈgəʊl ɪst →ˈgɒʊl-, §-əst ‖ ˈgɔːl- ˈgɑːl-, ˈgoʊl- **~s** s
Gauloise, Gauloises *tdmk* ˈgəʊl wɑːz ˌ·ˈ· ‖ goʊl ˈwɑːz —*Fr* [go lwaːz]
gault, Gault gɔːlt gɒlt ‖ gɑːlt
Gaultier ˈgəʊt i eɪ ˈgɔːlt-, ˌ·.·ˈ· ‖ ˈgoʊt- ˈgoʊlt- —*Fr* [go tje]
Gaumont ˈgəʊ mɒnt -mənt ‖ ˈgoʊ mɑːnt
gaunt, Gaunt gɔːnt ‖ gɑːnt **gaunter** ˈgɔːnt ə ‖ ˈgɔːnṱ ᵊr ˈgɑːnṱ ᵊr **gauntest** ˈgɔːnt ɪst -əst ‖ ˈgɔːnṱ əst ˈgɑːnṱ-
gauntlet ˈgɔːnt lət -lɪt ‖ ˈgɑːnt- **~s** s
gaunt|ly ˈgɔːnt |li ‖ ˈgɑːnt- **~ness** nəs nɪs
Gausden ˈgɔːz dən ‖ ˈgɑːz-
gauss, Gauss gaʊs
Gaussian ˈgaʊs i‿ən

Gautama 'gaʊt əm ə 'gəʊt- ‖ 'goʊt-
Gauteng 'gaʊt eŋ 'xaʊt-
gauze gɔːz ‖ gɑːz **gauzes** 'gɔːz ɪz -əz ‖ 'gɑːz-
gauz|y 'gɔːz |i ‖ 'gɑːz- **~ier** i‿ə ‖ i‿ᵊr **~iest** i‿ɪst i‿əst **~ily** ɪ li əl i **~iness** i nəs i nɪs
Gavan 'gæv ᵊn
gave geɪv
gavel 'gæv ᵊl **~s** z
gavelkind 'gæv ᵊl kaɪnd -kɪnd
Gaveston 'gæv ɪst ən -əst-
gavial 'geɪv i‿əl 'gæv- **~s** z
Gavin 'gæv ɪn -ᵊn
gavotte gə 'vɒt ‖ -'vɑːt **~s** s
Gawain 'gɑː weɪn 'gæ-, -wɪn; gə 'weɪn
gawd gɔːd gɑːd
Gawith *(i)* 'gaʊ‿ɪθ, *(ii)* 'geɪ wɪθ
gawk gɔːk ‖ gɑːk **gawked** gɔːkt ‖ gɑːkt **gawking** 'gɔːk ɪŋ ‖ 'gɑːk- **gawks** gɔːks ‖ gɑːks
gawk|y 'gɔːk |i ‖ 'gɑːk- **~ier** i‿ə ‖ i‿ᵊr **~iest** i‿ɪst i‿əst **~ily** ɪ li əl i **~iness** i nəs i nɪs
Gawler 'gɔːl ə ‖ -ᵊr 'gɑːl-
gawp gɔːp ‖ gɑːp **gawped** gɔːpt ‖ gɑːpt **gawping** 'gɔːp ɪŋ ‖ 'gɑːp- **gawps** gɔːps ‖ gɑːps
gay, Gay geɪ **gaily** 'geɪ li **gayer** 'geɪ ə ‖ -ᵊr **gayest** 'geɪ ɪst -əst **gays** geɪz
gaydar, G~ 'geɪd ɑː ‖ -ɑːr
Gaydon 'geɪd ᵊn
Gaye geɪ
Gayle geᵊl
Gaylord 'geɪ lɔːd ‖ -lɔːrd
Gay-Lussac ˌgeɪ 'luːs æk ‖ -lə 'sæk —*Fr* [gɛ ly sak]
gayness 'geɪ nəs -nɪs
Gaynor 'geɪn ə ‖ -ᵊr
Gayton 'geɪt ᵊn
Gaza 'gɑːz ə ‖ 'gæz- ˌ**Gaza 'Strip**
gazania gə 'zeɪn i‿ə **~s** z
Gazdar 'gæz dɑː ‖ -dɑːr
gaze geɪz **gazed** geɪzd **gazes** 'geɪz ɪz -əz **gazing** 'geɪz ɪŋ
gazebo gə 'ziːb əʊ ‖ -'zeɪb oʊ -'ziːb- **~s** z
gazelle gə 'zel **~s** z
gazer 'geɪz ə ‖ -ᵊr **~s** z
ga|zette gə |'zet **~zetted** 'zet ɪd -əd ‖ 'zeṭ əd **~zettes** 'zets **~zetting** 'zet ɪŋ ‖ 'zeṭ ɪŋ
gazetteer ˌgæz ə 'tɪə -ɪ- ‖ -'tɪᵊr **~s** z
gazillion gə 'zɪl i‿ən ‖ -'zɪl jən **~s** z
gazpacho gæz 'pætʃ əʊ gæs-, gəs-, -'pɑːtʃ- ‖ gə 'spɑːtʃ oʊ —*Sp* [gaθ 'pa tʃo]
gazump gə 'zʌmp **~ed** t **~ing** ɪŋ **~s** s
gazund|er gə 'zʌnd| ə ‖ -ᵊr **~ered** əd ‖ ᵊrd **~ering** ər ɪŋ **~ers** əz ‖ ᵊrz
Gazza 'gæz ə
GB ˌdʒiː 'biː
GCE ˌdʒiː siː 'iː ◂ **~s** z
GCSE ˌdʒiː siː es 'iː **~s** z
Gdansk dænᵗsk gə'dænᵗsk ‖ -'dɑːnᵗsk —*Polish* Gdańsk [gdaj̃sk]
g'day gə 'deɪ
GDP ˌdʒiː diː 'piː
gean giːn **geans** giːnz
gear gɪə ‖ gɪᵊr **geared** gɪəd ‖ gɪᵊrd **gearing** 'gɪər ɪŋ ‖ 'gɪr ɪŋ **gears** gɪəz ‖ gɪᵊrz **'gear ˌlever**; **'gear shift**; **'gear stick**
gearbox 'gɪə bɒks ‖ 'gɪᵊr bɑːks **~es** ɪz əz
Geary 'gɪər i ‖ 'gɪr i
Gebhard 'geb hɑːd ‖ -hɑːrd
gecko 'gek əʊ ‖ -oʊ **~es, ~s** z
Geddes 'ged ɪs §-əs ‖ -iːz
geddit 'ged ɪt §-ət ‖ 'geṭ ət *This non-standard spelling of* get it *reflects a casual pronunciation with* ṭ (= d).
gee, Gee dʒiː **geed** dʒiːd **geeing** 'dʒiː ɪŋ **gees** dʒiːz
geegaw 'dʒiː gɔː 'giː- ‖ -gɑː **~s** z
gee-gee 'dʒiː dʒiː **~s** z
geek giːk **geeks** giːks
geek|y 'giːk| i **~ier** i‿ə ‖ i‿ᵊr **~iest** i‿ɪst ‿əst
Geelong dʒɪ 'lɒŋ dʒə- ‖ -'lɔːŋ -'lɑːŋ
Geen *(i)* giːn, *(ii)* dʒiːn
geese giːs
Geeson *(i)* 'giːs ᵊn, *(ii)* 'dʒiːs ᵊn
Geevor 'giːv ə ‖ -ᵊr
Ge'ez 'giː ez
geezer 'giːz ə ‖ -ᵊr **~s** z
Geffrye 'dʒef ri
gefilte gə 'fɪlt ə
Gehenna gɪ 'hen ə gə-
Gehrig 'geər ɪg ‖ 'ger-
Gehry 'geər i ‖ 'ger i
Geiger 'gaɪg ə ‖ -ᵊr **'Geiger ˌcounter**
Geikie 'giːk i
geisha 'geɪʃ ə —*Jp* [ge ˌe ɕa] **~s** z
Geissler 'gaɪs lə ‖ -lᵊr —*Ger* ['gais lɐ]
gel *'girl'* gel **gels** gelz
gel *'jell, jelly'* dʒel **gelled** dʒeld **gelling** 'dʒel ɪŋ **gels** dʒelz
gelada dʒɪ 'lɑːd ə dʒə-, dʒe- **~s** z
gelatin 'dʒel ət ɪn §-ən
gelatine 'dʒel ə tiːn ˌ. .'.
gelatinous dʒə 'læt ɪn əs dʒɪ-, dʒe-, -ən- ‖ -'læt ᵊn‿əs **~ly** li **~ness** nəs nɪs
geld geld **gelded** 'geld ɪd -əd **gelding** 'geld ɪŋ **gelds** geldz **gelt** gelt
Geldart 'geld ɑːt ‖ -ɑːrt
gelding 'geld ɪŋ **~s** z
Geldof 'geld ɒf ‖ -ɔːf -ɑːf
gelid 'dʒel ɪd §-əd
gelignite 'dʒel ɪg naɪt -əg-
Gell *(i)* dʒel, *(ii)* gel
Geller 'gel ə ‖ -ᵊr
Gelligaer ˌgeθ li 'geə ˌgeɬ i-, -'gaɪ‿ə ‖ -'geᵊr -'gaɪᵊr —*Welsh* [ˌge ɬi 'gair, -'gaɨr]
Gell-Mann ˌgel 'mæn
gelt gelt
gem dʒem **gems** dʒemz
Gemara gə 'mɑːr ə ge-
gemeinschaft gə 'maɪn ʃɑːft -ʃæft —*Ger* [gə 'main ʃaft]
geminate *n, adj* 'dʒem ɪn ət -ən-, -ɪt; -ɪ neɪt, -ə- **~s** s

gemi|nate *v* ˈdʒem ɪ |neɪt -ə- **~nated** neɪt ɪd -əd ‖ neɪţ əd **~nates** neɪts **~nating** neɪt ɪŋ ‖ neɪţ ɪŋ
gemination ˌdʒem ɪ ˈneɪʃ ᵊn -ə- **~s** z
Gemini ˈdʒem ɪ naɪ -ə-, -niː **~s** z
Geminian ˌdʒem ɪ ˈnaɪ‿ən -ə-, ˈniː‿ **~s** z
Gemm|a, gemm|a ˈdʒem |ə **~ae** iː **~as, ~a's** əz
Gemmell, Gemmill ˈgem ᵊl
gemmology, gemology dʒe ˈmɒl ədʒ i ‖ -ˈmɑːl-
gemot, gemote gɪ ˈməʊt gə- ‖ -ˈmoʊt **~s** s
gemsbok ˈgemz bɒk ˈhems-, -bʌk ‖ -bɑːk **~s** s
gemstone ˈdʒem stəʊn ‖ -stoʊn **~s** z
-gen dʒən, dʒen — **glycogen** ˈglaɪk ədʒ ən -əʊ dʒen
gen dʒen **genned** dʒend **genning** ˈdʒen ɪŋ **gens** dʒenz
gendarme ˈʒɒnd ɑːm ˈʒɒ̃d- ‖ ˈʒɑːnd ɑːrm —*Fr* [ʒɑ̃ daʁm] **~s** z
gender ˈdʒend ə ‖ -ᵊr **~s** z
gender-bender ˈdʒend ə ˌbend ə ‖ -ᵊr ˌbend ᵊr **~s** z
gender-neutral ˌdʒend ə ˈnjuːtr əl ◂ §-ˈnuːtr- ‖ -ᵊr ˈnuːtr- -ˈnjuːtr-
gender-specific ˌdʒend ə spə ˈsɪf ɪk ◂ -spɪˈ· ‖ ˌ·ᵊr-
gene, Gene dʒiːn **genes, Gene's** dʒiːnz ˈ**gene pool**
genealogical ˌdʒiːn i‿ə ˈlɒdʒ ɪk ᵊl ◂ ‖ -ˈlɑːdʒ- **~ly** ‿i
genealogist ˌdʒiːn i ˈæl ədʒ ɪst ⚠-ˈɒl-, §-əst ‖ -ˈɑːl- **~s** s
genealog|y ˌdʒiːn i ˈæl ədʒ |i ⚠-ˈɒl- ‖ -ˈɑːl- **~ies** iz
genera ˈdʒen ər ə
general ˈdʒen ᵊr‿əl **~s** z
ˌ**general deˈlivery**; ˌ**general eˈlection**; ˌ**general ˈknowledge**; ˌ**general pracˈtitioner**; ˌ**general ˈstaff**; ˌ**general ˈstrike**
generalis... —*see* **generaliz...**
generalissimo ˌdʒen ᵊr‿ə ˈlɪs ɪ məʊ -ˈə- ‖ -moʊ **~s** z
generalist ˈdʒen ᵊr‿əl ɪst §-əst **~s** s
generalit|y ˌdʒen ə ˈræl ət |i -ɪt i ‖ -əţ |i **~ies** iz
generalization ˌdʒen ᵊr‿əl aɪ ˈzeɪʃ ᵊn əl ɪ- ‖ əl ə- **~s** z
generaliz|e ˈdʒen ᵊr‿ə laɪz **~ed** d **~es** ɪz əz **~ing** ɪŋ
generally ˈdʒen ᵊr‿əl i
general-purpose ˌdʒen ᵊr‿əl ˈpɜːp əs◂ ‖ -ˈpɜːp-
generalship ˈdʒen ᵊr‿əl ʃɪp **~s** s
gene|rate ˈdʒen ə |reɪt **~rated** reɪt ɪd -əd ‖ reɪţ əd **~rates** reɪts **~rating** reɪt ɪŋ ‖ reɪţ ɪŋ
generation ˌdʒen ə ˈreɪʃ ᵊn **~s** z
ˌ**geneˈration gap**
generational ˌdʒen ə ˈreɪʃ ᵊn‿əl **~ly** i
generativ|e ˈdʒen ᵊr‿ət ɪv ‖ -ᵊr‿əţ ɪv -ə reɪţ ɪv **~ely** li **~eness** nəs nɪs **~ist/s** ɪst/s §əst/s
generator ˈdʒen ə reɪt ə ‖ -reɪţ ᵊr **~s** z
generic dʒə ˈner ɪk dʒɪ- **~ally** ᵊl‿i **~s** s
generosity ˌdʒen ə ˈrɒs ət i -ɪt i ‖ -ˈrɑːs əţ i
generous ˈdʒen ᵊr‿əs **~ly** li **~ness** nəs nɪs
Genese dʒə ˈniːs dʒɪ-
Genesee ˌdʒen ə ˈsiː -ɪ-
genesis, G~ ˈdʒen əs ɪs -ɪs-, -ɪz, §-əs
-genesis ˈdʒen əs ɪs -ɪs-, §-əs — **morphogenesis** ˌmɔːf əʊ ˈdʒen əs ɪs -ɪs ɪs, §-əs ‖ ˌmɔːrf oʊ-
genet *animal* ˈdʒen ɪt §-ət **~s** s
Genet *French writer* ʒə ˈneɪ —*Fr* [ʒə nɛ]
genetic dʒə ˈnet ɪk dʒɪ- ‖ -ˈneţ ɪk **~ally** ᵊl‿i **~s** s
geˌ**netic ˈcode**; geˌ**netic** ˌ**engiˈneering**
geneticist dʒə ˈnet ɪs ɪst dʒɪ-, -əs-, §-əst ‖ -ˈneţ- **~s** s
Geneva dʒə ˈniːv ə dʒɪ-
Geˌ**neva conˈvention**
Genevan dʒə ˈniːv ᵊn dʒɪ- **~s** z
Genevieve ˈdʒen ə viːv -ɪ-, ˌ· ·ˈ· —*Fr* Geneviève [ʒən vjɛːv]
Genghis ˈdʒeŋ gɪs ˈgeŋ-, -gɪz, §-gəs, §-gəz
genial *'cheerful'* ˈdʒiːn i‿əl ‖ ˈdʒiːn jəl **~ly** i **~ness** nəs nɪs
genial *'of the chin'* dʒə ˈniː‿əl dʒɪ-, -ˈnaɪ‿əl
geniality ˌdʒiːn i ˈæl ət i -ɪt i ‖ -əţ i
-genic ˈdʒen ɪk ˈdʒiːn ɪk — **mutagenic** ˌmjuːt ə ˈdʒen ɪk ◂ ‖ ˌmjuːţ-
genie, Genie ˈdʒiːn i **genies, Genie's** ˈdʒiːn iz
genii ˈdʒiːn i aɪ
genip ˈgɪn ep **~s** s
genital ˈdʒen ɪt ᵊl -ət- ‖ -əţ ᵊl **~ly** ‿i **~s** z
genitalia ˌdʒen ɪ ˈteɪl i‿ə ˌ-ə-
genitival ˌdʒen ə ˈtaɪv ᵊl ◂ -ɪ- **~ly** i **~s** z
genitive ˈdʒen ət ɪv -ɪt- ‖ -əţ- **~s** z
genitourinary ˌdʒen ɪ təʊ ˈjʊər ɪn ər‿i ˌ-ə-, -ˈjɔːr-, -ˈən- ‖ ˌdʒen ə toʊ ˈjʊr ə ner i
geni|us ˈdʒiːn i‿|əs **~i** i aɪ **~uses** əs ɪz -əz
ˌ**genius ˈloci**
genned-up ˌdʒend ˈʌp ◂
Gennesaret, Gennesareth gə ˈnez ər ɪt gɪ-, ge-, -ət; -ə ret ‖ -ˈnes-
Genoa ˈdʒen əʊ ə dʒə ˈnəʊ ə, dʒɪ-, dʒe- ‖ -oʊ ə —*It* Genova [ˈdʒɛː no va]
genocidal ˌdʒen ə ˈsaɪd ᵊl ◂ -əʊ-
genocide ˈdʒen ə saɪd -əʊ-
Genoese ˌdʒen əʊ ˈiːz ◂ ‖ -oʊ- -ˈiːs ◂
genome ˈdʒiːn əʊm ‖ -oʊm **~s** z
genomic dʒi ˈnəʊm ɪk ‖ -ˈnoʊm-
genotype ˈdʒen ə taɪp ˈdʒiːn- **~s** s
-genous *stress-imposing* dʒən əs — **androgenous** æn ˈdrɒdʒ ən əs ‖ -ˈdrɑːdʒ-
genre ˈʒɒn rə ˈʒɑːn-, ˈʒɒ̃-, ˈdʒɒn- ‖ ˈʒɑːn- —*Fr* [ʒɑ̃ːʁ]
gent, Gent dʒent **gents** dʒents
genteel dʒen ˈtiːᵊl dʒən- **~ly** li **~ness** nəs nɪs
gentian ˈdʒentʃ ᵊn ˈdʒentʃ i‿ən **~s** z
gentile, G~ ˈdʒent aɪᵊl **~s** z
gentility dʒen ˈtɪl ət i -ɪt- ‖ -əţ i
gentle, G~ ˈdʒent ᵊl ‖ ˈdʒenţ ᵊl **gentler** ˈdʒent lə ‖ -lᵊr **gentlest** ˈdʒent lɪst -ləst
gentlefolk ˈdʒent ᵊl fəʊk ‖ ˈdʒenţ ᵊl foʊk **~s** s

gentle|man, G~ ˈdʒent ᵊl |mən ‖ ˈdʒenţ- **~men** mən men —*in rapid casual AmE also* ˈdʒen əm ən
ˌgentleman ˈfarmer; **ˌgentleman's aˈgreement**; **ˌgentleman's ˈgentleman**
gentle|man-at-arms ˌdʒent ᵊl |mən ət ˈɑːmz ‖ ˌdʒenţ ᵊl |mən əţ ˈɑːrmz **~men-at-arms** mən- men-
gentlemanly ˈdʒent ᵊl mən li ‖ ˈdʒenţ-
gentleness ˈdʒent ᵊl nəs -nɪs ‖ ˈdʒenţ-
gentle|woman ˈdʒent ᵊl |ˌwʊm ən ‖ ˈdʒenţ- **~women** ˌwɪm ɪn -ən
gently ˈdʒent li
Gentoo, g~ ˈdʒent uː dʒen ˈtuː **~s** z
gentrification ˌdʒentr ɪf ɪ ˈkeɪʃ ᵊn ˌ-əf-, §-əˈ-- **~s** z
gentri|fy ˈdʒentr ɪ |faɪ -ə- **~fied** faɪd **~fier/s** faɪ‿ə/z ‖ faɪ‿ᵊr/z **~fies** faɪz **~fying** faɪ ɪŋ
gentry, G~ ˈdʒentr i
genuflect ˈdʒen ju flekt -jə- ‖ -jə- **~ed** ɪd əd **~ing** ɪŋ **~s** s
genuflection, genuflexion ˌdʒen ju ˈflek ʃᵊn -jə- ‖ -jə- **~s** z
genuine ˈdʒen ju‿ɪn §‿ən, ⚠-aɪn **~ly** li **~ness** nəs nɪs
genus ˈdʒiːn əs ˈdʒen- **genera** ˈdʒen ər ə
-geny *stress-imposing* dʒən i — **phylogeny** faɪ ˈlɒdʒ ən i ‖ -ˈlɑːdʒ-
geo- *comb. form*
with stress-neutral suffix ¦dʒiː əʊ ‖ ¦dʒiː oʊ — **geothermal** ˌdʒiː əʊ ˈθɜːm ᵊl◂ ‖ -oʊ ˈθɜːm-
with stress-imposing suffix dʒi ˈɒ+ ‖ dʒi ˈɑː+ — **geophagy** dʒi ˈɒf ədʒ i ‖ -ˈɑːf-
geocentric ˌdʒiː əʊ ˈsentr ɪk◂ ‖ -oʊ- **~ally** ᵊl‿i
GeoCities *tdmk* ˌdʒiː əʊ ˈsɪt iz ‖ -oʊ ˈsɪţ-
geode ˈdʒiː əʊd ‖ -oʊd **~s** z
geodesic ˌdʒiː əʊ ˈdiːs ɪk◂ -ˈdes-; dʒɪə ˈdiːs ɪk ‖ -ə ˈdes- -ˈdiːs-
ˌgeoˌdesic ˈdome
geodesist dʒi ˈɒd əs ɪst -ɪs-, -əz-, -ɪz-, §-əst ‖ -ˈɑːd- **~ists** ɪsts §əsts **~y** i
geodetic ˌdʒiː əʊ ˈdet ɪk◂ dʒɪə ˈdet- ‖ ˌdʒiː ə ˈdeţ ɪk◂ **~ally** ᵊl‿i
Geoff dʒef **Geoff's** dʒefs
Geoffrey ˈdʒef ri
Geoghegan *(i)* ˈgeɪg ən, *(ii)* gɪ ˈheɪg ən
geographer dʒi ˈɒg rəf ə ‖ -ˈɑːg rəf ᵊr **~s** z
geographic ˌdʒiː‿ə ˈgræf ɪk dʒɪə ˈgræf- **~al** ᵊl **~ally** ᵊl‿i
geograph|y dʒi ˈɒg rəf |i ˈdʒɒg- ‖ -ˈɑːg- **~ies** iz
geologic ˌdʒiː‿ə ˈlɒdʒ ɪk◂ dʒɪə ˈlɒdʒ- ‖ -ˈlɑːdʒ- **~al** ᵊl **~ally** ᵊl‿i
geologist dʒi ˈɒl ədʒ ɪst §-əst ‖ -ˈɑːl- **~s** s
geolog|y dʒi ˈɒl ədʒ |i ‖ -ˈɑːl- **~ies** iz
geomanc|y ˈdʒiː‿ə mænᵗs| i **~er/s** ə/z ‖ ᵊr/z
geomatic ˌdʒiː‿ə ˈmæt ɪk◂ -əʊ- ‖ -ˈmæţ ɪk **~s** s
geometer dʒi ˈɒm ɪt ə -ət- ‖ -ˈɑːm əţ ᵊr **~s** z
geometric ˌdʒiː‿ə ˈmetr ɪk◂ -əʊ-; dʒɪə ˈmetr- **~al** ᵊl **~ally** ᵊl‿i
ˌgeoˌmetric proˈgression
geometrician ˌdʒiː‿ə me ˈtrɪʃ ᵊn -məˈ--; dʒi ˌɒm ə- ‖ dʒi ˌɑːm ə- **~s** z
geometr|y dʒi ˈɒm ətr |i ˈdʒɒm-, -ɪtr- ‖ -ˈɑːm- **~ies** iz
geophysical ˌdʒiː əʊ ˈfɪz ɪk ᵊl◂ ‖ ˌ-ə- **~ly** ‿i
geophysicist ˌdʒiː əʊ ˈfɪz ɪs ɪst -əs ɪst, §-əst ‖ ˌdʒiː ə- **~s** s
geophysics ˌdʒiː əʊ ˈfɪz ɪks ‖ -ə-
geopolitical ˌdʒiː əʊ pə ˈlɪt ɪk ᵊl◂ ‖ -ə pə ˈlɪţ- **~ly** ‿i
geopolitics ˌdʒiː əʊ ˈpɒl ə tɪks -ˈ-ɪ- ‖ -ə ˈpɑːl-
Geordie ˈdʒɔːd i ‖ ˈdʒɔːrd i **~s** z
George dʒɔːdʒ ‖ dʒɔːrdʒ **George's** ˈdʒɔːdʒ ɪz -əz ‖ ˈdʒɔːrdʒ əz
ˌGeorge ˈCross
Georges ʒɔːʒ dʒɔːdʒ ‖ ʒɔːrʒ dʒɔːrdʒ —*Fr* [ʒɔʁʒ]
Georgetown ˈdʒɔːdʒ taʊn ‖ ˈdʒɔːrdʒ- —*in Guyana locally* -tʌŋ
georgette, G~ ₍ˌ₎dʒɔː ˈdʒet ‖ ₍ˌ₎dʒɔːr- **~s** s
Georgia ˈdʒɔːdʒ ə ˈdʒɔːdʒ i‿ə ‖ ˈdʒɔːrdʒ ə
Georgian ˈdʒɔːdʒ ən ˈdʒɔːdʒ i‿ən ‖ ˈdʒɔːrdʒ ən **~s** z
georgic ˈdʒɔːdʒ ɪk ‖ ˈdʒɔːrdʒ- **~s** s
Georgie ˈdʒɔːdʒ i ‖ ˈdʒɔːrdʒ i
Georgina dʒɔː ˈdʒiːn ə ‖ dʒɔːr-
geostationary ˌdʒiː əʊ ˈsteɪʃ ᵊn ər‿i◂ ᵊn‿ər- ‖ -oʊ ˈsteɪʃ ə ner i
geosynchronous ˌdʒiː əʊ ˈsɪŋk rən əs◂ ‖ ˌdʒiː oʊ-
Gephardt ˈgep hɑːt ‖ -hɑːrt
Geraint ˈger aɪnt ·ˈ· —*Welsh* [ˈge raint]
Gerald ˈdʒer əld
Geraldine ˈdʒer əl diːn —*but* -daɪn *in Coleridge*
Geraldo dʒə ˈræld əʊ ‖ hə ˈrɑːld oʊ —*Sp* [xe ˈral do]
Geraldton ˈdʒer əld tən
geranium dʒə ˈreɪn i‿əm dʒɪ- **~s** z
Gerard ˈdʒer ɑːd -əd; dʒe ˈrɑːd, dʒə- ‖ dʒə ˈrɑːrd
Gerber *(i)* ˈdʒɜːb ə ‖ ˈdʒɜːb ᵊr, *(ii)* ˈgɜːb ə ‖ ˈgɜːb ᵊr —*The tdmk for baby food is usually (ii).*
gerbera ˈdʒɜːb ər ə ˈgɜːb- ‖ ˈdʒɜːb- ˈgɜːb- **~s** z
gerbil ˈdʒɜːb ᵊl -ɪl ‖ ˈdʒɜːb- **~s** z
Gerda ˈgɜːd ə ‖ ˈgɜːd ə
Gere gɪə ‖ gɪᵊr
Gerhardi, Gerhardie dʒə ˈhɑːd i ‖ dʒᵊr ˈhɑːrd i
geriatric ˌdʒer i ˈætr ɪk◂ ‖ ˌdʒɪr- **~s** s
geriatrician ˌdʒer i‿ə ˈtrɪʃ ᵊn ‖ ˌdʒɪr- **~s** z
Gericault, Géricault ˈʒer ɪ kəʊ -ə-, ˌ·ˈ· ‖ ˌʒeɪ rɪ ˈkoʊ —*Fr* [ʒe ʁi ko]
Geritol *tdmk* ˈdʒer ɪ tɒl -ə- ‖ -tɑːl
germ dʒɜːm ‖ dʒɜːm **germs** dʒɜːmz ‖ dʒɜːmz
ˈgerm cell; **ˌgerm ˈwarfare**
Germaine dʒə ˈmeɪn ₍ˌ₎dʒɜː- ‖ dʒᵊr-
German, g~ ˈdʒɜːm ən ‖ ˈdʒɜːm- **~s** z
ˌGerman ˈmeasles; **ˌGerman ˈshepherd**
germander dʒɜː ˈmænd ə dʒə- ‖ dʒᵊr ˈmænd ᵊr **~s** z
germane dʒɜː ˈmeɪn ˈ· ‖ dʒᵊr- **~ly** li **~ness** nəs nɪs
Germanic, g~ dʒɜː ˈmæn ɪk dʒə- ‖ dʒᵊr-

Germanicus dʒɜː ˈmæn ɪk əs dʒə- ‖ dʒᵊr-
germanium dʒɜː ˈmeɪn i‿əm dʒə- ‖ dʒᵊr-
German|y ˈdʒɜːm ən |i ‖ ˈdʒɜ˞ːm- **~ies, ~ys, ~y's** iz
germicidal ˌdʒɜːm ɪ ˈsaɪd ᵊl ◂ -ə- ‖ ˌdʒɜ˞ːm-
germicide ˈdʒɜːm ɪ saɪd -ə- ‖ ˈdʒɜ˞ːm- **~s** z
germinal ˈdʒɜːm ɪn ᵊl -ən- ‖ ˈdʒɜ˞ːm-
germi|nate ˈdʒɜːm ɪ |neɪt -ə- ‖ ˈdʒɜ˞ːm- **~nated** neɪt ɪd -əd ‖ neɪţ əd **~nates** neɪts **~nating** neɪt ɪŋ ‖ neɪţ ɪŋ
germination ˌdʒɜːm ɪ ˈneɪʃ ᵊn -ə- ‖ ˌdʒɜ˞ːm- **~s** z
Germiston ˈdʒɜːm ɪst ən §-əst- ‖ ˈdʒɜ˞ːm-
Germolene *tdmk* ˈdʒɜːm ə liːn ‖ ˈdʒɜ˞ːm-
Gerona dʒə ˈrəʊn ə ‖ -ˈroʊn- —*Sp* [xe ˈɾo na], *Catalan* Girona [ʒi ˈɾo nɐ]
Geronimo dʒə ˈrɒn ɪ məʊ dʒɪ-, dʒe-, -ə- ‖ -ˈrɑːn ə moʊ
Gerontius gə ˈrɒnt i‿əs dʒɪ-, dʒə-, -ˈrɒnᵗʃ- ‖ -ˈrɑːnt-
gerontocrac|y ˌdʒer ɒn ˈtɒk rəs |i ˌ-ən- ‖ -ən ˈtɑːk- **~ies** iz
gerontocratic dʒə ˌrɒnt ə ˈkræt ɪk ◂ ˌdʒer ɒnt-, ˌ-ənt- ‖ dʒə ˌrɑːnţ ə ˈkræţ ɪk ◂
gerontological dʒə ˌrɒnt ə ˈlɒdʒ ɪk ᵊl ◂ ˌdʒer ɒnt-, ˌ-ənt- ‖ dʒə ˌrɑːnţ ə ˈlɑːdʒ-
gerontologist ˌdʒer ɒn ˈtɒl ədʒ ɪst ˌ-ən-, §-əst ‖ -ən ˈtɑːl- **~s** s
gerontology ˌdʒer ɒn ˈtɒl ədʒ i ˌ-ən- ‖ -ən ˈtɑːl-
-gerous *stress-imposing* dʒər əs — **dentigerous** den ˈtɪdʒ ər əs
Gerrard ˈdʒer ɑːd -əd; dʒe ˈrɑːd, dʒə- ‖ dʒə ˈrɑːrd
Gerry ˈdʒer i
gerrymander ˈdʒer i mænd ə ˌ· ·ˈ· · ‖ -ᵊr **~ed** d **gerrymandering** ˈdʒer mænd‿ər ɪŋ ˌ·ˈ· · **~s** z
Gershwin ˈgɜːʃ wɪn §-wən ‖ ˈgɜ˞ːʃ-
Gertie ˈgɜːt i ‖ ˈgɜ˞ːţ i
Gertrude ˈgɜːtr uːd ‖ ˈgɜ˞ːtr- -ʊd
Gerty ˈgɜːt i ‖ ˈgɜ˞ːţ i
gerund ˈdʒer ənd -ʌnd **~s** z
gerundival ˌdʒer ən ˈdaɪv ᵊl ◂ -ʌn-
gerundive dʒə ˈrʌnd ɪv dʒɪ-, dʒe- **~s** z
Gervais dʒə ˈveɪs ‖ dʒᵊr-
Gervaise, Gervase ˈdʒɜːv eɪz -ɪz, -əs; dʒɜː ˈveɪz, -ˈveɪs ‖ ˈdʒɜ˞ːv-
Geryon ˈger i‿ən
gesellschaft gə ˈzel ʃɑːft -ʃæft —*Ger* G~ [gə ˈzɛl ʃaft]
gesso ˈdʒes əʊ ‖ -oʊ
Gest gest
gestalt gə ˈʃtælt -ˈʃtɑːlt; ˈdʒest ælt ‖ gə ˈʃtɑːlt —*Ger* G~ [gə ˈʃtalt] **~en** ən **~s** s
gestapo, G~ ge ˈstɑːp əʊ ‖ gə ˈstɑːp oʊ *Ger* G~ [ge ˈstaː po]
gest|ate dʒe ˈst|eɪt ˈdʒest |eɪt ‖ ˈdʒest |eɪt **~ated** eɪt ɪd -əd ‖ eɪţ əd **~ates** eɪts **~ating** eɪt ɪŋ ‖ eɪţ ɪŋ
gestation dʒe ˈsteɪʃ ᵊn **~s** z **geˈstation ˌperiod**
gestatorial ˌdʒest ə ˈtɔːr i‿əl ◂ ‖ -ˈtoʊr-
gestatory dʒe ˈsteɪt ər i ˈdʒest ə‿tər i ‖ ˈdʒest ə tɔːr i -toʊr i
Gestetner *tdmk* ge ˈstet nə gɪ-, gə- ‖ -nᵊr
gesticu|late dʒe ˈstɪk jʊ |leɪt -jə- ‖ -jə- **~lated** leɪt ɪd -əd ‖ leɪţ əd **~lates** leɪts **~lating** leɪt ɪŋ ‖ leɪţ ɪŋ
gesticulation dʒe ˌstɪk jʊ ˈleɪʃ ᵊn -jə- ‖ -jə- **~s** z
gestural ˈdʒes tʃər əl
ges|ture ˈdʒes |tʃə →ˈdʒeʃ- ‖ -|tʃᵊr **~tured** tʃəd ‖ tʃᵊrd **~tures** tʃəz ‖ tʃᵊrz **~turing** tʃər ɪŋ
gesundheit gə ˈzʊnd haɪt —*Ger* G~ [gə ˈzʊnt hait]
get get **gets** gets **getting** ˈget ɪŋ ‖ ˈgeţ ɪŋ **got** gɒt ‖ gɑːt **gotten** ˈgɒt ᵊn ‖ ˈgɑːt ᵊn
get-at-able get ˈæt əb ᵊl ‖ geţ ˈæţ-
getaway ˈget ə ˌweɪ ‖ ˈgeţ- **~s** z
get-go ˈget gəʊ ‖ -goʊ
Gethin ˈgeθ ɪn
Gething ˈgeθ ɪŋ
Gethsemane geθ ˈsem ən i
getout ˈget aʊt ‖ ˈgeţ- **~s** s
get-rich-quick ˌget rɪtʃ ˈkwɪk ◂
get-together ˈget tə ˌgeð ə ‖ -ᵊr **~s** z
Getty ˈget i ‖ ˈgeţ i
Gettysburg ˈget iz bɜːg ‖ ˈgeţ iz bɜ˞ːg **ˌGettysburg Adˈdress**
getup ˈget ʌp ‖ ˈgeţ- **~s** s
get-up-and-go ˌget ʌp ən ˈgəʊ →-əŋˈ·, →-mˈ· ‖ ˌgeţ ʌp ən ˈgoʊ
geum ˈdʒiː‿əm **~s** z
gewgaw ˈgjuː gɔː ˈguː- ‖ -gɑː **~s** z
Gewurztraminer, Gewürztraminer gə ˈvʊəts trə ˌmiːn ə ‖ -ˈvɜ˞ːts trə ˌmiːn ᵊr —*Ger* [gə ˈvʏʁts tʁa ˌmiːn ɐ]
geyser ˈgiːz ə ˈgaɪz ə ‖ ˈgaɪz ᵊr *(*) —In BrE,* ˈgaɪz ə *(if at all) particularly for the meaning 'hot spring'; the water heater is always* ˈgiːz- **~s** z
Ghan *in Australia* gæn
Ghana ˈgɑːn ə
Ghanaian gɑː ˈneɪ ən gə- ‖ -ˈnaɪ- **~s** z
gharry ˈgær i ‖ ˈger-
ghast|ly ˈgɑːst |li §ˈgæst- ‖ ˈgæst- **~lier** li‿ə ‖ li‿ᵊr **~liest** li‿ɪst əst **~liness** li nəs -nɪs
ghat, ghaut gɑːt gɔːt, gʌt ‖ gɔːt **ghats, Ghats, ghauts** gɑːts gɔːts, gʌts ‖ gɔːts
ghee giː
Ghent gent —*Flemish* Gent [ɣɛnt]
gherkin ˈgɜːk ɪn §-ən ‖ ˈgɜ˞ːk- **~s** z
ghetto ˈget əʊ ‖ ˈgeţ oʊ **~s** z **ˈghetto ˌblaster**
ghettois|e, ghettoiz|e ˈget əʊ aɪz ‖ ˈgeţ oʊ- **~ed** d **~es** ɪz əz **~ing** ɪŋ
ghi giː
Ghia ˈgiː‿ə —*It* [ˈgiː a]
Ghibelline ˈgɪb ə liːn -laɪn ‖ -əl ən
ghillie ˈgɪl i **~s** z
Ghosh gəʊʃ ‖ goʊʃ

ghost gəʊst ‖ goʊst **ghosted** 'gəʊst ɪd -əd ‖ 'goʊst əd **ghosting** 'gəʊst ɪŋ ‖ 'goʊst ɪŋ **ghosts** gəʊsts ‖ goʊsts
'ghost town
Ghostbusters 'gəʊst ˌbʌst əz ‖ 'goʊst ˌbʌst ᵊrz
ghost|ly 'gəʊst |li ‖ 'goʊst |li **~lier** li‿ə ‖ li‿ᵊr **~liest** li‿ɪst əst **~liness** li nəs -nɪs
ghost|write 'gəʊst |raɪt ‖ 'goʊst- **~writer/s** ˌraɪt ə/z ‖ ˌraɪṭ ᵊr/z **~writes** raɪts **~writing** ˌraɪt ɪŋ ‖ ˌraɪṭ ɪŋ
ghoul guːl **ghouls** guːlz
ghoulish 'guːl ɪʃ **~ly** li **~ness** nəs nɪs
GHQ ˌdʒiː eɪtʃ 'kjuː §-heɪtʃ-
ghyll gɪl **ghylls** gɪlz
GI ˌdʒiː 'aɪ ◂ **~s, ~'s** z
Gianni dʒi 'ɑːn i 'dʒɑːn i —*It* ['dʒan ni]
giant 'dʒaɪ‿ənt **~s, ~'s** s
ˌGiant's 'Causeway; **'giant ˌkiller**; **ˌgiant 'panda**
giantess 'dʒaɪ‿ənt es -ɪs, -əs; ˌdʒaɪ‿ən 'tes ‖ 'dʒaɪ ənṭ əs **~es** ɪz əz
giantism 'dʒaɪ‿ənt ˌɪz əm
giant-size 'dʒaɪ‿ənt saɪz
giaour, G~ 'dʒaʊ‿ə ‖ 'dʒaʊ‿ᵊr **giaours, G~** 'dʒaʊ‿əz ‖ 'dʒaʊ‿ᵊrz
giardiasis ˌdʒiː ɑː 'daɪ‿əs ɪs §-əs ‖ ˌ·ɑːr-
Gib *'Gibraltar'* dʒɪb
Gibb gɪb
gibber *'speak incoherently'* 'dʒɪb ə ‖ -ᵊr **~ed** d **gibbering** 'dʒɪb ər‿ɪŋ **~s** z
Gibberd 'gɪb əd ‖ ᵊrd
gibberelic ˌdʒɪb ə 'rel ɪk ◂

GIBBERISH

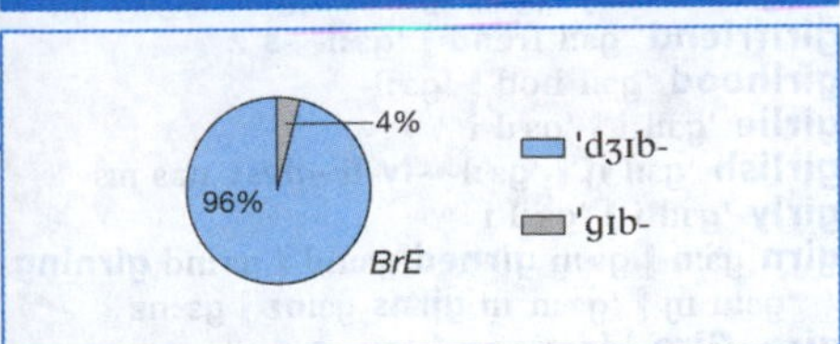

gibberish 'dʒɪb ər‿ɪʃ 'gɪb- — *Preference poll, BrE:* 'dʒɪb- *96%,* 'gɪb- *4%.*
Gibbes gɪbz
gibbet 'dʒɪb ɪt -ət **~s** s
gibbon, G~ 'gɪb ən **~s** z
Gibbons 'gɪb ənz
gibbosit|y gɪ 'bɒs ət |i -ɪt- ‖ -'bɑːs əṭ |i **~ies** iz
gibbous 'gɪb əs **~ly** li **~ness** nəs nɪs
Gibbs gɪbz
gibe dʒaɪb *(= jibe)* **gibed** dʒaɪbd **gibes** dʒaɪbz **gibing/ly** 'dʒaɪb ɪŋ /li
Gibeon 'gɪb i‿ən
Gibeonite 'gɪb i‿ə naɪt **~s** s
giblets 'dʒɪb ləts -lɪts
Gibraltar dʒɪ 'brɔːlt ə dʒə-, -'brɒlt- ‖ -ᵊr -'brɑːlt-
Gibraltarian ˌdʒɪb rɔːl 'teər i‿ən ◂ ˌ·rɒl-; dʒɪ ˌbrɔːl-, dʒə-, -ˌbrɒl- ‖ -'ter- -ˌrɑːl-, -'tær- **~s** z
Gibran ʒɪ 'brɑːn
Gibson 'gɪb sᵊn
gid gɪd
Giddens 'gɪd ᵊnz
Gidding 'gɪd ɪŋ
gidd|y, Giddy 'gɪd |i **~ied** id **~ier** i‿ə ‖ i‿ᵊr **~ies** iz **~iest** i‿ɪst i‿əst **~ily** ɪ li əl i **~iness** i nəs i nɪs **~ying** i‿ɪŋ
Gide ʒiːd —*Fr* [ʒid]
Gidea 'gɪd i‿ə
Gideon 'gɪd i‿ən **~s** z
Gielgud 'giːᵊl gʊd
Gieve giːv
GIF, gif gɪf dʒɪf **GIFs, gifs** gɪfs dʒɪfs
Giffard, Gifford *(i)* 'dʒɪf əd ‖ -ᵊrd, *(ii)* 'gɪf-
gift gɪft **gifted** 'gɪft ɪd -əd **gifting** 'gɪft ɪŋ **gifts** gɪfts
'gift horse; **'gift ˌtoken**
gifted 'gɪft ɪd -əd **~ly** li **~ness** nəs nɪs
giftwrap 'gɪft ræp **~ped** t **~ping** ɪŋ **~s** s
gig gɪg **gigs** gɪgz

GIGA-

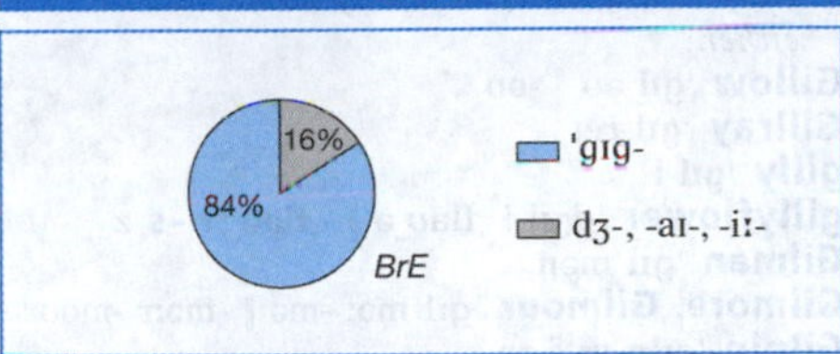

giga- ¦gɪg ə — **gigabyte** 'gɪg ə baɪt — *Preference poll, BrE:* 'gɪg- *84%, others* (dʒ-, -aɪ-, -iː-) *16%.*
gigabit 'gɪg ə bɪt **~s** s
gigabyte 'gɪg ə baɪt **~s** s
gigahertz 'gɪg ə hɜːts ‖ -hɜ˞ːts
gigantic dʒaɪ 'gænt ɪk ‖ -'gænṭ ɪk **~ally** ᵊl‿i
giggl|e 'gɪg ᵊl **~ed** d **~er/s** ‿ə/z ‖ ᵊr/z **~es** z **~ing/ly** ‿ɪŋ /li
Giggleswick 'gɪg ᵊlz wɪk
giggl|y 'gɪg ᵊl‿|i **~ier** i‿ə ‖ i‿ᵊr **~iest** i‿ɪst i‿əst **~iness** i nəs i nɪs
Giggs gɪgz
Gigha 'giː‿ə
Gigi 'ʒiː ʒiː
Gigli 'dʒiːl jiː -iː —*It* ['dʒiʎ ʎi]
gigolo 'dʒɪg ə ləʊ 'ʒɪg- ‖ -loʊ **~s** z
gigot 'dʒɪg ət 'ʒɪg-, -əʊ ‖ ʒiː 'goʊ —*Fr* [ʒi go]
gigue ʒiːg —*Fr* [ʒig] **gigues** ʒiːgz
Gijón hi 'hɒn ‖ -'hoʊn —*Sp* [xi 'xon]
Gikuyu gɪ 'kuː juː
Gil gɪl
Gila 'hiːl ə —*but in BrE a spelling pronunciation* 'giːl ə *is also heard*
Gilbert, g~ 'gɪlb ət ‖ -ᵊrt **~s, ~'s** s
Gilbertian gɪl 'bɜːt i‿ən -'bɜːʃ ᵊn ‖ -'bɜ˞ːṭ- **~s** z
Gilbey 'gɪlb i
Gilchrist 'gɪl krɪst
gild gɪld *(= guild)* **gilded** 'gɪld ɪd -əd **gilding** 'gɪld ɪŋ **gilds** gɪldz **gilt** gɪlt
Gildersleeve 'gɪld ə sliːv ‖ -ᵊr-
Gilead 'gɪl i æd ‖ əd
Giles dʒaɪᵊlz

gilet 'ʒiːl eɪ ‖ ʒə 'leɪ **~s** z —*Fr* [ʒi le]
gilgai 'gɪlg aɪ
Gilgamesh 'gɪlg ə meʃ
Gilhooley gɪl 'huːl i
Gilkes, Gilks dʒɪlks
gill *'organ of breathing', 'wattle', 'ravine', 'stream'* gɪl **gills** gɪlz
gill *'liquid measure'* dʒɪl **gills** dʒɪlz
Gill *name (i)* gɪl, *(ii)* dʒɪl
Gillespie gɪ 'lesp i gə-
Gillette dʒɪ 'let dʒə-
Gilliam 'gɪl i‿əm
Gillian 'dʒɪl i‿ən
Gilliat, Gilliatt 'gɪl i‿ət
Gillick 'gɪl ɪk
gillie, G~ 'gɪl i **~s** z
Gillies 'gɪl iz
gilliflower 'dʒɪl i ˌflaʊ‿ə ‖ -ˌflaʊ‿ᵊr **~s** z
Gilligan 'gɪl ɪg ən
Gillingham *(i)* 'dʒɪl ɪŋ əm, *(ii)* 'gɪl- —*The place in Kent is (i); those in Dorset and Norfolk are (ii). The family name may be either.*
Gillow 'gɪl əʊ ‖ -oʊ
Gillray 'gɪl reɪ
gilly 'gɪl i
gillyflower 'dʒɪl i ˌflaʊ‿ə ‖ -ˌflaʊ‿ᵊr **~s** z
Gilman 'gɪl mən
Gilmore, Gilmour 'gɪl mɔː -mə ‖ -mɔːr -moʊr
Gilpin 'gɪlp ɪn §-ən
Gilroy 'gɪl rɔɪ
gilt gɪlt *(= guilt)* **gilts** gɪlts
gilt-edged ˌgɪlt 'edʒd ◂
Gilwell 'gɪl wəl -wel
gimbals 'dʒɪm bᵊlz 'gɪm-
gimcrack 'dʒɪm kræk
gimlet 'gɪm lət -lɪt **~s** s
gimlet-eyed ˌgɪm lət 'aɪd ◂ -lɪt- ‖ -lət̬-
gimme 'gɪm i
gimmick 'gɪm ɪk **~s** s
gimmickry 'gɪm ɪk ri
gimmicky 'gɪm ɪk i
gimp gɪmp **gimped** gɪm*p*t **gimping** 'gɪmp ɪŋ **gimps** gɪm*p*s
gimpy 'gɪmp i
Gimson *(i)* 'gɪmᵖs ᵊn, *(ii)* 'dʒɪmᵖs- —*The late* Prof. A.C.Gimson, *phonetician, was (i).*
gin dʒɪn **ginned** dʒɪnd **ginning** 'dʒɪn ɪŋ **gins** dʒɪnz
 ˌgin 'rummy; **ˌgin 'sling**; **'gin trap**
Gina 'dʒiːn ə
Gingell 'gɪn*d*ʒ ᵊl
ginger, G~ 'dʒɪn*d*ʒ ə ‖ -ᵊr **~ed** d **gingering** 'dʒɪn*d*ʒ ər‿ɪŋ **~s** z
 ˌginger 'ale; **ˌginger 'beer**; **'ginger group**; **'ginger nut**
gingerbread 'dʒɪn*d*ʒ ə bred ‖ -ᵊr-
ginger|ly 'dʒɪn*d*ʒ ə |li ‖ -ᵊr- **~liness** li nəs -nɪs
gingersnap 'dʒɪn*d*ʒ ə snæp ‖ -ᵊr- **~s** s
gingery 'dʒɪn*d*ʒ ər‿i
gingham 'gɪŋ əm **~s** z
gingival dʒɪn 'dʒaɪv ᵊl 'dʒɪn*d*ʒ ɪv-
gingivitis ˌdʒɪn*d*ʒ ɪ 'vaɪt ɪs -ə- ‖ -'vaɪt̬ əs
Gingold 'gɪŋ gəʊld →-gɒʊld ‖ -goʊld
Gingrich 'gɪŋ grɪtʃ
ginkgo 'gɪŋk əʊ -gəʊ ‖ -oʊ **~es** z
Ginn gɪn
ginner|y 'dʒɪn ər| i **~ies** iz
Ginnie, Ginny 'dʒɪn i
Gino 'dʒiːn əʊ ‖ -oʊ
ginormous dʒaɪ 'nɔːm əs ‖ -'nɔːrm əs **~ly** li
Ginsberg, Ginsburg 'gɪnz bɜːg ‖ -bɜ˞ːg
ginseng 'dʒɪn seŋ
Gioconda ˌdʒiː‿ə 'kɒnd ə ‖ -'kɑːnd- —*It* [dʒo 'kon da]
Giotto 'dʒɒt əʊ 'ʒɒt-; dʒi 'ɒt- ‖ 'dʒɑːt̬ oʊ 'dʒɔːt̬- —*It* ['dʒɔt to]
Giovanni dʒəʊ 'vɑːn i ˌdʒiː‿ə'-, -'væn- ‖ dʒoʊ- dʒə- —*It* [dʒo 'van ni]
gip *'cheat'* dʒɪp **gipped** dʒɪpt **gipping** 'dʒɪp ɪŋ **gips** dʒɪps
gippo 'dʒɪp əʊ ‖ -oʊ **~s** z
Gippsland 'gɪps lænd -lənd
gippy 'dʒɪp i
 ˌgippy 'tummy
gips|y, Gips|y 'dʒɪps |i **~ies, ~y's** iz
giraffe dʒə 'rɑːf dʒɪ-, §-'ræf ‖ -'ræf **~s** s
Giraldus dʒɪ 'ræld əs dʒə-
 Giˌraldus Cam'brensis kæm 'brenᵗs ɪs §-əs
gird gɜːd ‖ gɜ˞ːd **girded** 'gɜːd ɪd -əd ‖ 'gɜ˞ːd əd **girding** 'gɜːd ɪŋ ‖ 'gɜ˞ːd ɪŋ **girds** gɜːdz ‖ gɜ˞ːdz **girt** gɜːt ‖ gɜ˞ːt
girder 'gɜːd ə ‖ 'gɜ˞ːd ᵊr **~s** z
girdl|e 'gɜːd ᵊl ‖ 'gɜ˞ːd ᵊl **~ed** d **~es** z **~ing** ‿ɪŋ
 'girdle cake
girl gɜːl ‖ gɜ˞ːl **girls** gɜːlz ‖ gɜ˞ːlz
 ˌgirl 'Friday; **ˌgirl 'guide**; **ˌgirl 'scout** ‖ '· ·
girlfriend 'gɜːl frend ‖ 'gɜ˞ːl- **~s** z
girlhood 'gɜːl hʊd ‖ 'gɜ˞ːl-
girlie 'gɜːl i ‖ 'gɜ˞ːl i
girlish 'gɜːl ɪʃ ‖ 'gɜ˞ːl- **~ly** li **~ness** nəs nɪs
girly 'gɜːl i ‖ 'gɜ˞ːl i
girn gɜːn ‖ gɜ˞ːn **girned** gɜːnd ‖ gɜ˞ːnd **girning** 'gɜːn ɪŋ ‖ 'gɜ˞ːn ɪŋ **girns** gɜːnz ‖ gɜ˞ːnz
giro, Giro 'dʒaɪᵊr əʊ ‖ -oʊ **~s** z
Girobank *tdmk* 'dʒaɪᵊr əʊ bæŋk ‖ -oʊ-
girt gɜːt ‖ gɜ˞ːt
girth gɜːθ ‖ gɜ˞ːθ **girthed** gɜːθt ‖ gɜ˞ːθt **girthing** 'gɜːθ ɪŋ ‖ 'gɜ˞ːθ ɪŋ **girths** gɜːθs ‖ gɜ˞ːθs
Girton 'gɜːt ᵊn ‖ 'gɜ˞ːt ᵊn
Girtonian gɜː 'təʊn i‿ən ‖ gᵊr- **~s** z
Girvan 'gɜːv ᵊn ‖ 'gɜ˞ːv ᵊn
Gisborne, Gisbourne 'gɪz bən -bɔːn ‖ -bɔːrn -boʊrn
Giscard d'Estaing ˌʒiːsk ɑː de 'stæ̃ -'stæŋ ‖ -ɑːr- —*Fr* [ʒis kaʁ dɛs tæ̃]
Giselle ʒɪ 'zel dʒɪ-, dʒə- —*Fr* [ʒi zɛl]
Gish gɪʃ
gismo 'gɪz məʊ ‖ -moʊ **~s** z
gissa *nonstd 'give us a'* 'gɪs ə
Gissing 'gɪs ɪŋ
gist dʒɪst
git gɪt **gits** gɪts
Gitane *tdmk* ʒɪ 'tɑːn ‖ -'tæn **~s** z —*Fr* [ʒi tan]
gite, gîte ʒiːt —*Fr* [ʒit] **gites, gîtes** ʒiːts

Gittins ˈgɪt ɪnz §-ᵊnz ‖ ˈgɪt ᵊnz
Giuliani ˌdʒuːl i ˈɑːn i
Giulietta ˌdʒuːl i ˈet ə ‖ -ˈeţ ə —*It* [dʒu ˈljet ta]
Giuseppe dʒu ˈsep i —*It* [dʒu ˈzɛp pe]
give gɪv **gave** geɪv **given** ˈgɪv ᵊn **gives** gɪvz
giving ˈgɪv ɪŋ —*The phrase* give me *also has a non-standard casual form* ˈgɪm i, *sometimes written* gimme; *similarly* give us a, *see* gissa
give-and-take ˌgɪv ᵊn ˈteɪk
giveaway ˈgɪv ə ˌweɪ **~s** z
giveback ˈgɪv bæk **~s** s
given ˈgɪv ᵊn
ˈ**given name**
Givenchy *tdmk* ʒiː ˈvɒnᵗʃ i ‖ ˈʒiːv ɑːn ʃiː ˌ· ·ˈ·
giver ˈgɪv ə ‖ -ᵊr **~s** z
Giza ˈgiːz ə
gizmo ˈgɪz məʊ ‖ -moʊ **~s** z
gizzard ˈgɪz əd ‖ -ᵊrd **~s** z
glabell|a glə ˈbel ə **~ae** iː
glabrous ˈgleɪb rəs
glace, glacé ˈglæs eɪ ˈglɑːs-, -i ‖ glæ ˈseɪ **~ed** d **~ing** ɪŋ **~s** z
glacial ˈgleɪʃ ᵊl ˈgleɪʃ i‿əl, ˈgleɪs i‿əl **~ly** i
glaci|ate ˈgleɪs i |eɪt ˈgleɪʃ- ‖ ˈgleɪʃ i |eɪt **~ated** eɪt ɪd -əd ‖ eɪţ əd **~ates** eɪts **~ating** eɪt ɪŋ ‖ eɪţ ɪŋ
glaciation ˌgleɪs i ˈeɪʃ ᵊn ˌgleɪʃ- ‖ ˌgleɪʃ- **~s** z
glacier ˈglæs i‿ə ˈgleɪs- ‖ ˈgleɪʃ ᵊr *(*)* **~s** z
glaciology ˌgleɪs i ˈɒl ədʒ i ‖ ˌgleɪʃ i ˈɑːl-
glacis ˈglæs i -ɪs ,§-əs ‖ glæ ˈsiː **~** *pl* z
glad glæd **gladder** ˈglæd ə ‖ -ᵊr **gladdest** ˈglæd ɪst -əst **glads** glædz
ˌ**glad ˈeye,** ˈ· ·; ˌ**glad ˈhand,** ˈ· ·; ˈ**glad rags**
gladden ˈglæd ᵊn **~ed** d **~ing** ‿ɪŋ **~s** z
glade gleɪd **glades** gleɪdz
glad-hand ˌglæd ˈhænd ˈ· · **~ed** ɪd əd **~er/s** ə/z ‖ ᵊr/z **~ing** ɪŋ **~s** z
gladiator ˈglæd i eɪt ə ‖ -eɪţ ᵊr **~s** z
gladiatorial ˌglæd i‿ə ˈtɔːr i‿əl ◂ ‖ -ˈtoʊr-
gladiol|us ˌglæd i ˈəʊl |əs ‖ -ˈoʊl- **~i** aɪ **~uses** əs ɪz -əz
glad|ly ˈglæd |li **~ness** nəs nɪs
gladsome ˈglæd səm **~ly** li **~ness** nəs nɪs
Gladstone ˈglæd stən ‖ -stoʊn -stən
ˌ**Gladstone ˈbag** ‖ ˈ· · ·
Gladwin ˈglæd wɪn §-wən
Gladys ˈglæd ɪs §-əs
Glagolitic, g~ ˌglæg əʊ ˈlɪt ɪk ◂ ‖ -ə ˈlɪţ ɪk ◂
glair gleə ‖ gleᵊr glæᵊr
glair|y ˈgleər |i ‖ ˈgler |i ˈglær- **~iness** i nəs i nɪs
Glaisher ˈgleɪʃ ə ‖ -ᵊr
Glaister ˈgleɪst ə ‖ -ᵊr
glam, Glam glæm
Glamis ˈglɑːmz *(!)*
glamor ˈglæm ə ‖ -ᵊr
Glamorgan glə ˈmɔːg ən ‖ -ˈmɔːrg-
glamoris... —*see* **glamoriz...**
glamorization ˌglæm ər aɪ ˈzeɪʃ ᵊn -ər ɪ- ‖ -ər ə-
glamoriz|e ˈglæm ə raɪz **~ed** d **~es** ɪz əz **~ing** ɪŋ
glamorous ˈglæm ər‿əs **~ly** li **~ness** nəs nɪs
glamour ˈglæm ə ‖ -ᵊr
glance glɑːnᵗs §glænᵗs ‖ glænᵗs **glanced** glɑːnᵗst §glænᵗst ‖ glænᵗst **glances** ˈglɑːnᵗs ɪz §ˈglænᵗs-, -əz ‖ ˈglænᵗs əz **glancing/ly** ˈglɑːnᵗs ɪŋ/ li §ˈglænᵗs- ‖ ˈglænᵗs-
gland glænd **glands** glændz
glanders ˈglænd əz ˈglɑːnd- ‖ -ᵊrz
glandular ˈglænd jʊl ə ˈglændʒ əl ə ‖ ˈglændʒ əl ᵊr
ˌ**glandular ˈfever**
glans glænz **glandes** ˈglænd iːz
Glanvill, Glanville ˈglæn vɪl -vᵊl
Glanyrafon, Glan-yr-Afon ˌglæn ər ˈæv ᵊn —*Welsh* [glan ər ˈa von]
Glaramara ˌglær ə ˈmɑːr ə ‖ ˌgler-
glare gleə ‖ gleᵊr glæᵊr **glared** gleəd ‖ gleᵊrd glæᵊrd **glares** gleəz ‖ gleᵊrz glæᵊrz
glaring/ly ˈgleər ɪŋ /li ‖ ˈgleᵊr ɪŋ /li ˈglæᵊr-
Glaser ˈgleɪz ə ‖ -ᵊr

GLASGOW

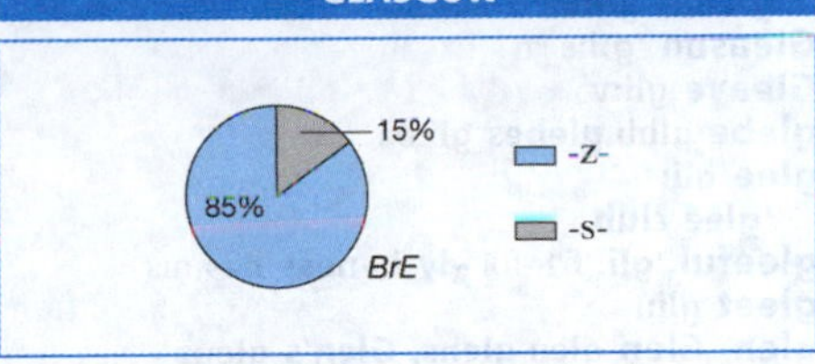

Glasgow ˈglɑːz gəʊ ˈglæz-, ˈglɑːs-, ˈglæs-; ˈglɑːsk əʊ, ˈglæsk- ‖ ˈglæs goʊ ˈglæz- — *Preference poll, BrE:* z *forms 85%,* s *forms 15%.*
Glaslyn ˈglæs lɪn
glasnost ˈglæs nɒst ˈglæz- ‖ ˈglɑːs noʊst —*Russ* [ˈgɫas nəsʲt]
glass, Glass glɑːs §glæs ‖ glæs **glassed** glɑːst §glæst ‖ glæst **glasses** ˈglɑːs ɪz §ˈglæs-, -əz ‖ ˈglæs əz
ˌ**glass ˈeye,** ˌ**glass ˈfibre** ◂
glassblower ˈglɑːs ˌbləʊ ə §ˈglæs- ‖ ˈglæs ˌbloʊ ᵊr **~s** z
glasscutter ˈglɑːs ˌkʌt ə §ˈglæs- ‖ ˈglæs ˌkʌţ ᵊr **~s** z
glassed-in ˌglɑːst ˈɪn ◂ §ˌglæst- ‖ ˌglæst-
glassful ˈglɑːs fʊl §ˈglæs- ‖ ˈglæs- **~s** z
glass|house ˈglɑːs |haʊs §ˈglæs- ‖ ˈglæs- **~houses** haʊz ɪz -əz
glassine ˈglɑːs iːn §ˈglæs- ‖ glæ ˈsiːn
glasspaper ˈglɑːs ˌpeɪp ə §ˈglæs- ‖ ˈglæs ˌpeɪp ᵊr
glassware ˈglɑːs weə §ˈglæs- ‖ ˈglæs wer -wær
glassworks ˈglɑːs wɜːks §ˈglæs- ‖ ˈglæs wɝːks
glasswort ˈglɑːs wɜːt §ˈglæs-, §-wɔːt ‖ ˈglæs wɝːt -wɔːrt **~s** s
glass|y ˈglɑːs |i §ˈglæs- ‖ ˈglæs |i **~ier** i‿ə ‖ i‿ᵊr **~iest** i‿ɪst i‿əst **~ily** ɪ li əl i **~iness** i nəs i nɪs
glassy-eyed ˌglɑːs i ˈaɪd ◂ §ˌglæs- ‖ ˌglæs-
Glastonbury ˈglæst ən bər‿i ˈglɑːst-, →ˈ-əm-, §-ˌber i ‖ -ˌber i
Glaswegian glɑːz ˈwiːdʒ ən glæz-, glɑːs-, glæs-, ˌ-- ‖ glæs- **~s** z

G

Glauber ˈglaʊb ə ˈgləʊb ə, ˈglɔːb ə ‖ -ᵊr **~'s** z

glaucoma glɔː ˈkəʊm ə glaʊ- ‖ glaʊ ˈkoʊm ə glɔː-, glɑː-

glaucomatous glɔː ˈkəʊm ət əs glaʊ-, -ˈkɒm- ‖ glaʊ ˈkoʊm əṱ əs glɔː-, glɑː-, -ˈkɑːm-

glaucous ˈglɔːk əs ‖ ˈglɑːk-

Glaxo *tdmk* ˈglæks əʊ ‖ -oʊ

GlaxoSmithKline *tdmk* ˌglæks əʊ ˌsmɪθ ˈklaɪn ‖ -oʊ-

glaze gleɪz **glazed** gleɪzd **glazes** ˈgleɪz ɪz -əz **glazing** ˈgleɪz ɪŋ

Glazebrook ˈgleɪz brʊk

glazier, G~ ˈgleɪz i‿ə ˈgleɪʒ ə, ˈgleɪʒ i‿ə ‖ ˈgleɪʒ ᵊr **~s** z

Glazunof, Glazunov ˈglæz u nɒf ‖ -ə noʊf -ə nɑːf, -ə nɔːf —*Russian* [glə zu ˈnɔf]

GLC ˌdʒiː el ˈsiː

gleam gliːm **gleamed** gliːmd **gleaming** ˈgliːm ɪŋ **gleams** gliːmz

glean gliːn **gleaned** gliːnd **gleaner/s** ˈgliːn ə/z ‖ -ᵊr/z **gleaning/s** ˈgliːn ɪŋ/z **gleans** gliːnz

Gleason ˈgliːs ᵊn

Gleave gliːv

glebe gliːb **glebes** gliːbz

glee gliː

ˈ**glee club**

gleeful ˈgliː fᵊl -fʊl **~ly** i **~ness** nəs nɪs

gleet gliːt

glen, Glen glen **glens, Glen's** glenz

Glencoe ₍ˌ₎glen ˈkəʊ →₍ˌ₎gleŋ- ‖ -ˈkoʊ

Glenda ˈglend ə

Glendale ˈglen deᵊl

Glendaruel ˌglen də ˈruː‿əl

Glendenning glen ˈden ɪŋ

Glendinning glen ˈdɪn ɪŋ

Glendower glen ˈdaʊ‿ə ‖ -ˈdaʊ‿ᵊr

Gleneagles glen ˈiːg ᵊlz

Glenelg glen ˈelg

Glenfiddich glen ˈfɪd ɪk -ɪx

glengarr|y, G~ glen ˈgær |i →gleŋ- ‖ -ˈger-, ˈ· · · **~ies** iz

Glengormley glen ˈgɔːm li →gleŋ- ‖ -ˈgɔːrm-

Glenice ˈglen ɪs §-əs

Glenlivet glen ˈlɪv ɪt -ət

Glenmorangie ˌglen mə ˈrændʒ i →ˌglem-; ˌ·ˈmɒr əndʒ i

Glenn glen

Glenrothes glen ˈrɒθ ɪs §-əs ‖ -ˈrɑːθ əs

Glenville ˈglen vɪl

Glenys ˈglen ɪs §-əs

gley gleɪ **gleys** gleɪz

glia ˈgliː‿ə ˈglaɪ

glial ˈgliː‿əl ˈglaɪ

glib glɪb **glibber** ˈglɪb ə ‖ -ᵊr **glibbest** ˈglɪb ɪst -əst **glibly** ˈglɪb li **glibness** ˈglɪb nəs -nɪs

glide glaɪd **glided** ˈglaɪd ɪd -əd **glides** glaɪdz **gliding** ˈglaɪd ɪŋ

ˈ**glide path**

glider ˈglaɪd ə ‖ -ᵊr **~s** z

glimmer ˈglɪm ə ‖ -ᵊr **~ed** d **glimmering** ˈglɪm ər‿ɪŋ **~s** z

glimmering ˈglɪm ər‿ɪŋ **~ly** li **~s** z

glimpse glɪmps **glimpsed** glɪmpst **glimpses** ˈglɪmps ɪz -əz **glimpsing** ˈglɪmps ɪŋ

Glinka ˈglɪŋk ə —*Russian* [ˈglʲin kə]

glint glɪnt **glinted** ˈglɪnt ɪd -əd ‖ ˈglɪnṱ əd **glinting** ˈglɪnt ɪŋ ‖ ˈglɪnṱ ɪŋ **glints** glɪnts

glioma glaɪ ˈəʊm ə ‖ -ˈoʊm ə **~s** z

glissad|e *n, v* glɪ ˈsɑːd -ˈseɪd **~ed** ɪd əd **~es** z **~ing** ɪŋ

glissand|o glɪ ˈsænd |əʊ ‖ -ˈsɑːnd |oʊ **~i** iː **~os** əʊz ‖ oʊz

glisten ˈglɪs ᵊn **~ed** d **~ing** ‿ɪŋ **~s** z

glister ˈglɪst ə ‖ -ᵊr **~ed** d **glistering** ˈglɪst ər‿ɪŋ **~s** z

glitch glɪtʃ **glitches** ˈglɪtʃ ɪz -əz

glitter ˈglɪt ə ‖ ˈglɪṱ ᵊr **~ed** d **glittering/ly** ˈglɪt‿ər ɪŋ/ li ‖ ˈglɪṱ ər ɪŋ **~s** z

glitterati ˌglɪt ə ˈrɑːt iː -i ‖ ˌglɪṱ ə ˈrɑːṱ i

glitz glɪts **glitzed** glɪtst **glitzes** ˈglɪts ɪz -əz **glitzing** ˈglɪts ɪŋ

glitz|y ˈglɪts |i **~ier** i‿ə ‖ i‿ᵊr **~iest** i‿ɪst i‿əst **~iness** i nəs i nɪs

Gloag gləʊg ‖ gloʊg

gloaming ˈgləʊm ɪŋ ‖ ˈgloʊm ɪŋ

gloat gləʊt ‖ gloʊt **gloated** ˈgləʊt ɪd -əd ‖ ˈgloʊṱ əd **gloating/ly** ˈgləʊt ɪŋ /li ‖ ˈgloʊṱ ɪŋ /li **gloats** gləʊts ‖ gloʊts

glob glɒb ‖ glɑːb **globs** glɒbz ‖ glɑːbz

global ˈgləʊb ᵊl ‖ ˈgloʊb ᵊl **~ism** ˌɪz əm **~ist/s** ɪst/s §əst/s **~ly** i

ˌ**global ˈwarming**

globalisation, globalization ˌgləʊb ᵊl aɪ ˈzeɪʃ ᵊn -ɪˈ-- ‖ ˌgloʊb ᵊl ə-

globalis|e, globaliz|e ˈgləʊb ə laɪz -ᵊl aɪz ‖ ˈgloʊb- **~ed** d **~es** ɪz əz **~ing** ɪŋ

globe gləʊb ‖ gloʊb **globes** gləʊbz ‖ gloʊbz

ˌ**globe ˈartichoke**

globefish ˈgləʊb fɪʃ ‖ ˈgloʊb- **~es** ɪz əz

globeflower ˈgləʊb ˌflaʊ‿ə ‖ ˈgloʊb ˌflaʊ‿ᵊr **~s** z

globetrott|er ˈgləʊb ˌtrɒt |ə ‖ ˈgloʊb ˌtrɑːṱ |ᵊr **~ers** əz ‖ ᵊrz **~ing** ɪŋ

globose ˈgləʊb əʊs gləʊ ˈbəʊs ‖ ˈgloʊb oʊs **~ly** li **~ness** nəs nɪs

globosity gləʊ ˈbɒs ət i -ɪt- ‖ gloʊ ˈbɑːs əṱ i

globular ˈglɒb jʊl ə -jəl- ‖ ˈglɑːb jəl ᵊr **~ly** li **~ness** nəs nɪs

globule ˈglɒb juːl ‖ ˈglɑːb- **~s** z

globulin ˈglɒb jʊl ɪn -jəl-, §-ən ‖ ˈglɑːb jəl ən **~s** z

glocal ˈgləʊk ᵊl ‖ ˈgloʊk ᵊl

glocalization ˌgləʊk əl aɪ ˈzeɪʃ ᵊn -əl ɪ- ‖ ˌgloʊk əl ə-

glockenspiel ˈglɒk ən spiːᵊl →-ŋ-, ʃpiːᵊl ‖ ˈglɑːk- —*Ger* [ˈglɔk ᵊn ʃpiːl] **~s** z

glom glɒm ‖ glɑːm **glommed** glɒmd ‖ glɑːmd **glomming** ˈglɒm ɪŋ ‖ ˈglɑːm ɪŋ **gloms** glɒmz ‖ glɑːmz

gloom gluːm

gloom|y ˈgluːm |i **~ier** i‿ə ‖ i‿ᵊr **~iest** i‿ɪst i‿əst **~ily** ɪ li əl i **~iness** i nəs i nɪs

gloop gluːp

glop glɒp ‖ glɑːp

gloppy ˈglɒp i ‖ ˈglɑːp i

loria, g~ 'glɔːr i‿ə ‖ 'gloʊr- **~s** z
ˌgloria in ex'celsis ek 'sels ɪs ɪk-; eks 'tʃels-, ek 'ʃels-, -iːs; **ˌGloria 'Patri** 'pɑːtr iː 'pætr-, -i
loriana ˌglɔːr i 'ɑːn ə ‖ ˌgloʊr-, -ˌæn-
lorie... —*see* **glory**
lorification ˌglɔːr ɪf ɪ 'keɪʃ ᵊn ˌ·əf-, §-ə'·- ‖ ˌgloʊr- **~s** z
lori|fy 'glɔːr ɪ |faɪ -ə- ‖ 'gloʊr- **~fied** faɪd **~fier/s** faɪ‿ə/z ‖ faɪ‿ᵊr/z **~fies** faɪz **~fying** faɪ ɪŋ
lorious 'glɔːr i‿əs ‖ 'gloʊr- **~ly** li **~ness** nəs nɪs
lor|y 'glɔːr |i ‖ 'gloʊr- **~ied** id **~ies** iz **~ying** i‿ɪŋ
'glory hole
loss glɒs ‖ glɑːs glɔːs **glossed** glɒst ‖ glɑːst glɔːst **glosses** 'glɒs ɪz -əz ‖ 'glɑːs əz 'glɔːs- **glossing** 'glɒs ɪŋ ‖ 'glɑːs ɪŋ 'glɔːs-
lossal 'glɒs ᵊl ‖ 'glɑːs ᵊl 'glɔːs-
lossar|y 'glɒs ər‿|i ‖ 'glɑːs- 'glɔːs- **~ies** iz
lossectomy glɒ 'sekt əm i ‖ glɑː- glɔː-
lossematic ˌglɒs ɪ 'mæt ɪk ◂ -ə- ‖ ˌglɑːs ə 'mæţ ɪk ◂ ˌglɔːs- **~s** s
lossi... —*see* **glossy**
lossolalia ˌglɒs əʊ 'leɪl i‿ə ‖ ˌglɑːs ə- ˌglɔːs-
Glossop 'glɒs əp ‖ 'glɑːs-
glossopharyngeal ˌglɒs əʊ ˌfær ɪn 'dʒiː‿əl -fə 'rɪndʒ i‿əl ‖ ˌglɑːs oʊ ˌfær ən 'dʒiː əl ˌglɔːs-, -ˌfer-
gloss|y 'glɒs |i ‖ 'glɑːs |i 'glɔːs- **~ier** i‿ə ‖ i‿ᵊr **~iest** i‿ɪst i‿əst **~ily** ɪ li əl i **~iness** i nəs i nɪs
Gloster 'glɒst ə 'glɔːst- ‖ 'glɑːst ᵊr 'glɔːst-
glottal 'glɒt ᵊl ‖ 'glɑːţ ᵊl **~ly** i **~s** z
ˌglottal 'stop
glottalic glɒ 'tæl ɪk ‖ glɑː-
glottalis... —*see* **glottaliz...**
glottalization ˌglɒt ᵊl aɪ 'zeɪʃ ᵊn -ɪ'·- ‖ ˌglɑːţ ᵊl ə- **~s** z
glottaliz|e 'glɒt ᵊl aɪz -ə laɪz ‖ 'glɑːţ ᵊl aɪz **~ed** d **~es** ɪz əz **~ing** ɪŋ
glottis 'glɒt ɪs §-əs ‖ 'glɑːţ əs **~es** ɪz əz
glottochronology ˌglɒt əʊ krə 'nɒl ədʒ i ‖ ˌglɑːţ oʊ krə 'nɑːl-
Gloucester 'glɒst ə 'glɔːst- ‖ 'glɑːst ᵊr 'glɔːst- **~s** z **~shire** ʃə ʃɪə ‖ ʃᵊr ʃɪr
glove glʌv **gloved** glʌvd **gloves** glʌvz **gloving** 'glʌv ɪŋ
'glove comˌpartment; **'glove ˌpuppet**
glover, G~ 'glʌv ə ‖ -ᵊr **~s** z
glow gləʊ ‖ gloʊ **glowed** gləʊd ‖ gloʊd **glowing/ly** 'gləʊ ɪŋ /li ‖ 'gloʊ ɪŋ /li **glows** gləʊz ‖ gloʊz
glower 'glaʊ‿ə ‖ 'glaʊ‿ᵊr **~ed** d **glowering/ly** 'glaʊ‿ər ɪŋ /li ‖ 'glaʊ‿ᵊr ɪŋ /li **~s** z
glowstick 'gləʊ stɪk ‖ 'gloʊ- **~s** s
glow-worm 'gləʊ wɜːm ‖ 'gloʊ wɜːm **~s** z
gloxinia glɒk 'sɪn i‿ə ‖ glɑːk- **~s** z
Gloy *tdmk* glɔɪ
gloze gləʊz ‖ gloʊz **glozed** gləʊzd gloʊzd **glozes** 'gləʊz ɪz -əz ‖ 'gloʊz əz **glozing** 'gləʊz ɪŋ ‖ 'gloʊz ɪŋ
Glubb glʌb
Gluck glʊk —*Ger* [glʊk]
gluco- *comb. form*
with stress-neutral suffix ¦gluːk əʊ ‖ -oʊ — **glucocorticoid** ˌgluːk əʊ 'kɔːt ɪ kɔɪd -'·ə- ‖ -oʊ 'kɔːrţ-
glucose 'gluːk əʊz -əʊs ‖ -oʊs -oʊz
glucoside 'gluːk əʊ saɪd ‖ -ə- **~s** z
glue gluː **glued** gluːd **glues** gluːz **gluing** 'gluː‿ɪŋ
gluer 'gluː‿ə ‖ ᵊr **~s** z
glue-sniff|er 'gluː ˌsnɪf |ə ‖ -|ᵊr **~ers** əz ‖ ᵊrz **~ing** ɪŋ
gluey 'gluː‿i
gluhwein, glühwein 'gluː vaɪn -*Ger* **G~** 'glyː vain
gluing 'gluː‿ɪŋ
glum glʌm **glummer** 'glʌm ə ‖ ᵊr **glummest** 'glʌm ɪst -əst
glume gluːm (= *gloom*) **~s** z
glum|ly 'glʌm |li **~ness** nəs nɪs
gluon 'gluː ɒn ‖ -ɑːn **~s** z
glut glʌt **gluts** glʌts **glutted** 'glʌt ɪd -əd ‖ 'glʌţ əd **glutting** 'glʌt ɪŋ ‖ 'glʌţ ɪŋ
glutamate 'gluːt ə meɪt ‖ 'gluːţ- **~s** s
glutamic gluː 'tæm ɪk
glutamine 'gluːt ə miːn -mɪn ‖ 'gluːţ-
gluteal 'gluːt i‿əl ‖ 'gluːţ-
gluten 'gluːt ᵊn -ɪn
gluteus 'gluːt i‿əs ‖ 'gluːţ-
ˌgluteus 'maximus
glutinous 'gluːt ɪn əs -ᵊn- ‖ 'gluːt ᵊn əs **~ly** li **~ness** nəs nɪs
glutton 'glʌt ᵊn **~s** z
gluttonous 'glʌt ᵊn əs **~ly** li
gluttony 'glʌt ᵊn i
glyceride 'glɪs ə raɪd **~s** z
glycerin, glycerine 'glɪs ər‿ɪn §-ᵊr‿ən; -ə riːn, ˌglɪs ə 'riːn
glycerol 'glɪs ə rɒl ‖ -roʊl -rɑːl, -rɔːl
glycine 'glaɪs iːn
glyco- *comb. form*
with stress-neutral suffix ¦glaɪk əʊ ‖ -oʊ — **glycopeptide** ˌglaɪk əʊ 'pept aɪd ‖ -oʊ-
with stress-imposing suffix glaɪ 'kɒ+ ‖ glaɪ 'kɑː+ — **glycogeny** glaɪ 'kɒdʒ ən i ‖ -'kɑːdʒ-
glycogen 'glaɪk ədʒ ən -əʊ dʒen ‖ -oʊ dʒen
glycol 'glaɪk ɒl ‖ -oʊl -ɑːl, -ɔːl
glycoside 'glaɪk əʊ saɪd ‖ -ə- **~s** z
Glyder 'glɪd ə ‖ -ᵊr —*Welsh* ['glə der] **~s** z
Glyn glɪn
Glynde glaɪnd
Glyndebourne 'glaɪnd bɔːn →'glaɪm- ‖ -bɔːrn -boʊrn
Glynis 'glɪn ɪs §-əs
Glynn, Glynne glɪn
Glynwed *tdmk* 'glɪn wed
glyph glɪf **glyphs** glɪfs
glyptodont 'glɪpt əʊ dɒnt ‖ -ə dɑːnt **~s** s
GM ˌdʒiː 'em ◂
G-man 'dʒiː mæn **G-men** 'dʒiː men
GMT ˌdʒiː em 'tiː
gnarled nɑːld ‖ nɑːrld
gnarly 'nɑːl i ‖ 'nɑːrl i

G

gnash næʃ **gnashed** næʃt **gnasher/s** ˈnæʃ ə/z ‖ -ər/z **gnashes** ˈnæʃ ɪz -əz **gnashing** ˈnæʃ ɪŋ

gnat næt **gnats** næts

gnaw nɔː ‖ nɑː **gnawed** nɔːd ‖ nɑːd **gnawing** ˈnɔːr ɪŋ ‖ ˈnɔː ɪŋ ˈnɑː- **gnawn** nɔːn ‖ nɑːn **gnaws** nɔːz ‖ nɑːz

gneiss naɪs gə ˈnaɪs —*Ger* Gneis [gnais]

gnocchi ˈnɒk i ˈnjɒk i, gə ˈnɒk i ‖ ˈnɑːk i ˈnjɑːk i, ˈnoʊk i —*It* [ˈɲɔk ki]

gnome nəʊm ‖ noʊm **gnomes** nəʊmz ‖ noʊmz

gnomic ˈnəʊm ɪk ‖ ˈnoʊm- **~ally** əl‿i

gnomish ˈnəʊm ɪʃ ‖ ˈnoʊm-

gnomon ˈnəʊm ɒn -ən ‖ ˈnoʊm ɑːn **~s** z

Gnosall ˈnəʊs əl ‖ ˈnoʊs-

gnostic, G~ ˈnɒst ɪk ‖ ˈnɑːst- **~s** s

gnosticism, G~ ˈnɒst ɪ ˌsɪz əm -ə- ‖ ˈnɑːst-

-gnosy *stress-imposing* gnəs i — **pharmacognosy** ˌfɑːm ə ˈkɒg nəs i ‖ ˌfɑːrm ə ˈkɑːg-

GNP ˌdʒiː en ˈpiː

gnu nuː njuː; gə ˈnuː, -ˈnjuː —*The forms with* gə- *are jocular, as generally is the entire word. In serious discourse this animal is called a* wildebeest. **gnus** nuːz njuːz; gə ˈnuːz, -ˈnjuːz

go gəʊ ‖ goʊ —*There are nonstandard weak forms* §gə, §gu **goes** gəʊz ‖ goʊz *There are nonstandard weak forms* §gəz, §gʊz **going** ˈgəʊ ɪŋ ‖ ˈgoʊ ɪŋ —*The phrase* **going to**, *when used as a modal (showing the future), has a casual weak form* (ˈ)gən ə, *also* (ˈ)gəʊ in ə, (ˈ)gən ə, (ˈ)gəʊ ɪnt ə ‖ (ˈ)goʊ‿ən ə, ‿ənt̬ ə. *In RP these are used, if at all, only before words beginning with a consonant sound, being replaced before a vowel sound by* (ˈ)gən u *or other forms with final* u *rather than* ə. *See* gonna. **gone** gɒn §gɔːn, §gɑːn ‖ gɔːn gɑːn **went** went

Goa, goa ˈgəʊ ə ‖ ˈgoʊ ə **~s** z

goad gəʊd ‖ goʊd **goaded** ˈgəʊd ɪd -əd ‖ ˈgoʊd əd **goading** ˈgəʊd ɪŋ ‖ ˈgoʊd ɪŋ **goads** gəʊdz ‖ goʊdz

go-ahead *adj* ˈgəʊ ə ˌhed ˌ· ·ˈ· ◂ ‖ ˈgoʊ-

go-ahead *n* ˈgəʊ ə ˌhed ‖ ˈgoʊ-

goal gəʊl →gɒʊl ‖ goʊl **goals** gəʊlz →gɒʊlz ‖ goʊlz **ˈgoal line**

goalie ˈgəʊl i →ˈgɒʊl- ‖ ˈgoʊl i **~s** z

goalkeep|er ˈgəʊl ˌkiːp| ə →ˈgɒʊl- ‖ ˈgoʊl ˌkiːp| ər **~ers** əz ‖ ərz **~ing** ɪŋ

goalless ˈgəʊl ləs →ˈgɒʊl-, -lɪs ‖ ˈgoʊl-

goalmouth ˈgəʊl maʊθ →ˈgɒʊl- ‖ ˈgoʊl-

goal-oriented ˈgəʊl ˌɔːr i ent ɪd →ˈgɒʊl-, -ˌɒr- ‖ ˈgoʊl ˌɔːr i ent̬ əd -ˌoʊr-

goalpost ˈgəʊl pəʊst →ˈgɒʊl- ‖ ˈgoʊl poʊst **~s** s

goaltend|er ˈgəʊl tend| ə →ˈgɒʊl- ‖ ˈgoʊl tend ər **~ers** əz ‖ ərz **~ing** ɪŋ

Goan ˈgəʊ ən ‖ ˈgoʊ ən **~s** z

Goanese ˌgəʊ ə ˈniːz ◂ ‖ ˌgoʊ- -ˈniːs ◂

goanna gəʊ ˈæn ə ‖ goʊ- **~s** z

go-as-you-please ˌgəʊ əz ju ˈpliːz →ˌəʒ- ‖ ˌgoʊ-

goat gəʊt ‖ goʊt **goats** gəʊts ‖ goʊts

goatee ˌgəʊ ˈtiː ◂ ‖ ˌgoʊ- **~s** z

goatherd ˈgəʊt hɜːd ‖ ˈgoʊt hɜːd **~s** z

Goathland ˈgəʊθ lənd ‖ ˈgoʊθ-

goatsbeard ˈgəʊts bɪəd ‖ ˈgoʊts bɪrd **~s** z

goatskin ˈgəʊt skɪn ‖ ˈgoʊt- **~s** z

goatsucker ˈgəʊt ˌsʌk ə ‖ ˈgoʊt ˌsʌk ər **~s** z

gob gɒb ‖ gɑːb **gobbed** gɒbd ‖ gɑːbd **gobbing** ˈgɒb ɪŋ ‖ ˈgɑːb ɪŋ **gobs** gɒbz ‖ gɑːbz

gobbet ˈgɒb ɪt §-ət ‖ ˈgɑːb- **~s** s

gobbl|e ˈgɒb əl ‖ ˈgɑːb əl **~ed** d **~es** z **~ing** ɪŋ

gobbledegook, gobbledygook ˈgɒb əl di guːk -gʊk ‖ ˈgɑːb-

gobbler ˈgɒb lə ‖ ˈgɑːb lər **~s** z

Gobelin ˈgəʊb əl ɪn ˈgɒb-, §-ən ‖ ˈgoʊb- —*Fr* [gɔb lɛ̃] **~s** z

go-between ˈgəʊ bɪ ˌtwiːn -bə-, §-biː- ‖ ˈgoʊ- **~s** z

Gobi ˈgəʊb i ‖ ˈgoʊb i —*Chi* Gēbì [^{1}kɤ ^{4}pi]

gobie... —*see* **goby**

goblet ˈgɒb lət -lɪt ‖ ˈgɑːb- **~s** s

goblin ˈgɒb lɪn -lən ‖ ˈgɑːb- **~s** z

gobo ˈgəʊb əʊ ‖ ˈgoʊb oʊ **~s** z

Gobowen gɒ ˈbəʊ ɪn -ən ‖ gɑː ˈboʊ-

gobsmack ˈgɒb smæk ‖ ˈgɑːb- **~ed** t **~ing** ɪŋ **~s** s

gobstopper ˈgɒb ˌstɒp ə ‖ ˈgɑːb ˌstɑːp ər **~s** z

go-by *'snub'* ˈgəʊ baɪ ‖ ˈgoʊ-

gob|y *'fish'* ˈgəʊb |i ‖ ˈgoʊb |i **~ies** iz

go-cart ˈgəʊ kɑːt ‖ ˈgoʊ kɑːrt **~s** s

god, God gɒd ‖ gɑːd **gods, God's** gɒdz ‖ gɑːdz

Godalming ˈgɒd əl mɪŋ ‖ ˈgɑːd-

Godard ˈgɒd ɑː -ɑːd ‖ goʊ ˈdɑːr —*Fr* [gɔ daːʁ]

god-awful ˌgɒd ˈɔːf əl ◂ ‖ ˌgɑːd- -ˈɑːf-

Godber ˈgɒd bə →ˈgɒb- ‖ ˈgɑːd bər

god|child ˈgɒd |tʃaɪəld ‖ ˈgɑːd- **~children** ˌtʃɪldr ən ˌtʃʊldr-

goddam, goddamn ˈgɒd æm ‖ ˌgɑːd ˈdæm ◂ **~ed** d

goddammit gɒ ˈdæm ɪt §-ət ‖ ˌgɑːd-

Goddard ˈgɒd ɑːd -əd ‖ ˈgɑːd ərd -ɑːrd

goddaughter ˈgɒd ˌdɔːt ə ‖ ˈgɑːd ˌdɔːt̬ ər -ˌdɑːt̬- **~s** z

goddess ˈgɒd es -ɪs, -əs ‖ ˈgɑːd əs **~es** ɪz əz

Godel, Gödel ˈgɜːd əl ˈgəʊd- ‖ ˈgoʊd- —*Ger* [ˈgøː dəl]

godet ˈgəʊd eɪ -et; gəʊ ˈdet ‖ goʊ ˈdeɪ -ˈdet

godetia gəʊ ˈdiːʃ ə -ˈdiːʃ i‿ə ‖ gə- **~s** z

godfather ˈgɒd ˌfɑːð ə ‖ ˈgɑːd ˌfɑːð ər **~s** z

god-fearing ˈgɒd ˌfɪər ɪŋ ‖ ˈgɑːd ˌfɪr ɪŋ

godforsaken ˈgɒd fə ˌseɪk ən ˌ··ˈ·· ‖ ˈgɑːd fər-

Godfrey ˈgɒd fri ‖ ˈgɑːd-

God-given ˈgɒd ˌgɪv ən →ˈgɑːg- ‖ ˈgɑːd-

godhead, G~ ˈgɒd hed ‖ ˈgɑːd-

Godiva gə ˈdaɪv ə

godless ˈgɒd ləs -lɪs ‖ ˈgɑːd- **~ness** nəs nɪs

Godley ˈgɒd li ‖ ˈgɑːd-

godlike ˈgɒd laɪk ‖ ˈgɑːd-

god|ly ˈgɒd |li ‖ ˈgɑːd- **~liness** li nəs -nɪs

Godmanchester ˈgɒd mən ˌtʃest ə ˌ·ˈ·· ‖ ˈgɑːd mən ˌtʃest ər

Glottal stop

A **glottal stop**, symbolized ʔ, is a PLOSIVE made at the glottis (= made by the vocal folds). In English it is sometimes used as a kind of t-sound, and sometimes has other functions.

1 In certain positions ʔ may be used as an allophone of the phoneme t, as when **pointless** ˈpɔɪnt ləs is pronounced ˈpɔɪnʔ ləs. This is known as **glottalling** or **glottal replacement** of t. It is condemned by some people; nevertheless, it is increasingly heard, especially in BrE. Sometimes the glottal articulation accompanies a simultaneous alveolar articulation.

2 ʔ is found as an allophone of t only

- at the **end** of a syllable, and
- if the preceding sound is a vowel or SONORANT.

Provided these conditions are satisfied, it is widely used in both BrE and AmE where the following sound is an obstruent

football ˈfʊt bɔːl → ˈfʊʔ bɔːl
outside ˌaʊt ˈsaɪd → ˌaʊʔ ˈsaɪd
that faint buzz ˌðæt ˌfeɪnt ˈbʌz → ˌðæʔ ˌfeɪnʔ ˈbʌz

or a nasal

atmospheric ˌæt məs ˈfer ɪk → ˌæʔ məs ˈfer ɪk
button ˈbʌt ən → ˈbʌʔ n
that name ˌðæt ˈneɪm → ˌðæʔ ˈneɪm

or a semivowel or non-syllabic l

Gatwick ˈɡæt wɪk → ˈɡæʔ wɪk
quite well ˌkwaɪt ˈwel → ˌkwaɪʔ ˈwel
brightly ˈbraɪt li → ˈbraɪʔ li

Some speakers of BrE also use it at the end of a word under other circumstances as well:

not only this ˌnɒʔ əʊn li ˈðɪs **but also that** bəʔ ˌɔːl səʊ ˈðæʔ.

Compare AmE ˌnɑːt̬ oʊn li ˈðɪs, bət̬ ˌɔːl soʊ ˈðæt; in this position t̬ is also heard in casual BrE.

3 ʔ is also optionally used as a way of adding emphasis to a syllable that begins with a vowel sound (see HARD ATTACK). It can be used to separate adjacent vowel sounds in successive syllables (= to avoid **hiatus**). In BrE this can be a way of avoiding r (see R-LIAISON), as in one pronunciation of **underexpose** ˌʌnd ə ɪk ˈspəʊz (-ə ʔɪk-).

4 ʔ also forms an essential part of certain interjections, e.g. AmE **uh-uh** ˌʔʌʔ ˈʌʔ.

5 A glottal stop is sometimes used, especially in BrE, to strengthen tʃ or tr at the end of a syllable, and also p, t, k if followed by a consonant or at the end of a word. This is known as **glottal reinforcement**: **teaching** ˈtiːtʃ ɪŋ → ˈtiːʔtʃ ɪŋ, **April** ˈeɪp rəl → ˈeɪʔp rəl, **right!** raɪt → raɪʔt.

Glottal stop ▸

Glottal stop continued

Learners of English should be careful not to apply glottal reinforcement (as opposed to glottal replacement) in words such as **pretty** ˈprɪt i and **jumping** ˈdʒʌmp ɪŋ.

G

godmother ˈgɒd ˌmʌð ə →ˈgɒb- ‖ ˈgɑːd ˌmʌð ər ~s z
Godolphin gə ˈdɒlf ɪn §-ən ‖ gə ˈdɑːlf-
Godot ˈgɒd əʊ ‖ gɑː ˈdoʊ gə- —*Fr* [gɔ do]
godown ˈgəʊ daʊn ‖ ˈgoʊ- ~s z
godparent ˈgɒd ˌpeər ənt →ˈgɒb- ‖ ˈgɑːd ˌper- -ˌpær- ~s s
godsend ˈgɒd send ‖ ˈgɑːd- ~s z
godson ˈgɒd sʌn ‖ ˈgɑːd- ~s z
godspeed, G~ ˌgɒd ˈspiːd ‖ ˌgɑːd-
Godthaab, Godthab ˈgɒt hɑːb -hɔːb ‖ ˈgɑːt hɑːb ˈgoʊt- —*Danish* [ˈgɔd hoːʔb]
Godunov ˈgɒd ə nɒf ˈgʊd-, -u- ‖ ˈgʊd ə nɔːf -nɑːf —*Russ* [gə du ˈnɔf]
Godwin ˈgɒd wɪn §-wən ‖ ˈgɑːd-
godwit ˈgɒd wɪt ‖ ˈgɑːd- ~s s
Godzilla gɒd ˈzɪl ə ‖ gɑːd-
Goebbels ˈgɜːb əlz -əls ‖ ˈgʊb- ˈgɝːb- —*Ger* [ˈgœb əls]
goer ˈgəʊ ə ‖ ˈgoʊ ər ~s z
-goer ˌgəʊ ə ‖ ˌgoʊ ər — **party-goer** ˈpɑːt i ˌgəʊ ə ‖ ˈpɑːrṱ i ˌgoʊ ər
Goering ˈgɜːr ɪŋ ‖ ˈger- ˈgɜː- —*Ger* [ˈgøː ʁɪŋ]
goes gəʊz ‖ goʊz —*There are nonstandard weak forms* §gəz, §gʊz
goest ˈgəʊ ɪst -əst ‖ ˈgoʊ-
goeth ˈgəʊ ɪθ -əθ ‖ ˈgoʊ-
Goethals ˈgəʊθ əlz ‖ ˈgoʊθ-
Goethe ˈgɜːt ə ‖ ˈgeɪṱ ə ˈgɝːṱ-, -i —*Ger* [ˈgøː tə]
gofer ˈgəʊf ə ‖ ˈgoʊf ər ~s z
Goff, Goffe gɒf ‖ gɑːf
goffer ˈgəʊf ə ‖ ˈgɑːf ər *(*)* ~ed d **goffering** ˈgəʊf ər‿ɪŋ ‖ ˈgɑːf ər‿ɪŋ ~s z
Gog gɒg ‖ gɑːg
Gogarty ˈgəʊg ət i ‖ ˈgoʊg ərṱ i
go-gett|er ˈgəʊ ˌget| ə ˌ·ˈ·· ‖ ˈgoʊ ˌgeṱ| ər ~ers əz ‖ ərz ~ing ɪŋ
goggl|e ˈgɒg əl ‖ ˈgɑːg əl ~ed d ~es z ~ing ‿ɪŋ
'**goggle box**
goggle-eyed ˌgɒg əl ˈaɪd ◂ ˈ··· ‖ ˌgɑːg-
Gogmagog ˌgɒg mə ˈgɒg ◂ ‖ ˌgɑːg mə ˈgɑːg ◂
ˌ**Gogmagog 'Hills**
go-go ˈgəʊ gəʊ ‖ ˈgoʊ goʊ
'**go-go ˌdancer**
Gogol ˈgəʊg ɒl ‖ ˈgoʊg ɑːl -əl —*Russ* [ˈgɔ gəlʲ]
Goidel ˈgɔɪd əl
Goidelic, Goidhelic gɔɪ ˈdel ɪk
going ˈgəʊ ɪŋ ‖ ˈgoʊ ɪŋ ~s z —*see note at* go
-going ˌgəʊ ɪŋ ‖ ˌgoʊ ɪŋ — **party-going** ˈpɑːt i ˌgəʊ ɪŋ ‖ ˈpɑːr ṱi ˌgoʊ ɪŋ
going-over ˌgəʊ ɪŋ ˈəʊv ə ˈ·ˌ·ˌ·· ‖ ˌgoʊ ɪŋ ˈoʊv ər
goings-on ˌgəʊ ɪŋz ˈɒn ‖ ˌgoʊ ɪŋz ˈɑːn -ˈɔːn
goiter, goitre ˈgɔɪt ə ‖ ˈgɔɪṱ ər ~s z
goitrous ˈgɔɪtr əs
goji ˈgəʊdʒ i ‖ ˈgoʊdʒ i —*Chi* gǒuqǐ [³kou ³tɕʰi]
go-kart ˈgəʊ kɑːt ‖ ˈgoʊ kɑːrt ~s s
Golan ˈgəʊl æn -ɑːn; gəʊ ˈlɑːn ‖ ˈgoʊl ɑːn
ˌ**Golan 'heights**
Golborne ˈgəʊl bɔːn →ˈgɒʊl- ‖ ˈgoʊl bɔːrn -boʊrn
Golconda gɒl ˈkɒnd ə ‖ gɑːl ˈkɑːnd ə
gold gəʊld →gɒʊld ‖ goʊld **golds** gəʊldz →gɒʊldz ‖ goʊldz
'**Gold Coast**; '**gold ˌdigger**; '**gold dust**; ˌ**gold 'leaf**; ˌ**gold 'medal**; ˌ**gold 'plate**; '**gold reˌserve**; '**gold rush**; '**gold ˌstandard**
Golda ˈgəʊld ə →ˈgɒʊld- ‖ ˈgoʊld ə
goldbeater ˈgəʊl*d* ˌbiːt ə →ˈgɒʊl*d*- ‖ ˈgoʊl*d* ˌbiːṱ ər ~s z
Goldberg ˈgəʊl*d* bɜːg →ˈgɒʊl*d*- ‖ ˈgoʊl*d* bɝːg
Goldblum ˈgəʊl*d* bluːm →ˈgɒʊl*d*- ‖ ˈgoʊl*d*-
goldbrick ˈgəʊl*d* brɪk →ˈgɒʊl*d*- ‖ ˈgoʊl*d*- ~ed t ~ing ɪŋ ~s s
goldcrest ˈgəʊl*d* krest →ˈgɒʊl*d*- ‖ ˈgoʊl*d*- ~s s
golden ˈgəʊld ən →ˈgɒʊld- ‖ ˈgoʊld- ~ly li ~ness nəs nɪs
'**golden age**, ˌ·· ˈ·; ˌ**golden 'eagle**; ˌ**Golden 'Fleece**; ˌ**Golden 'Gate**◂, ˌ**Golden Gate 'Bridge**; ˌ**golden 'handshake**; ˌ**golden 'jubilee**; ˌ**golden 'mean**; ˌ**golden 'oldie**; ˌ**golden 'rule**; ˌ**golden 'syrup**; ˌ**golden 'wedding**
goldeneye ˈgəʊld ən aɪ →ˈgɒʊld- ‖ ˈgoʊld- ~s z
goldenrod ˈgəʊld ən rɒd →ˈgɒʊld-, ˌ·· ˈ· ‖ ˈgoʊld ən rɑːd
goldfield ˈgəʊl*d* fiːəld →ˈgɒʊl*d*- ‖ ˈgoʊl*d*- ~s z
goldfinch ˈgəʊl*d* fɪntʃ →ˈgɒʊl*d*- ‖ ˈgoʊl*d*- ~es ɪz əz
goldfish ˈgəʊl*d* fɪʃ →ˈgɒʊl*d*- ‖ ˈgoʊl*d*- ~es ɪz əz
'**goldfish bowl**
Goldie ˈgəʊld i →ˈgɒʊld- ‖ ˈgoʊld i
Goldilocks, g~ ˈgəʊld i lɒks →ˈgɒʊld- ‖ ˈgoʊld i lɑːks
Golding ˈgəʊld ɪŋ →ˈgɒʊld- ‖ ˈgoʊld-
goldmin|e ˈgəʊl*d* maɪn →ˈgɒʊl*d*- ‖ ˈgoʊl*d*- ~er/s ə/z ‖ ər/z ~es z ~ing ɪŋ
gold-plated ˌgəʊld ˈpleɪt ɪd ◂ →ˌgɒʊld-, -əd ‖ ˌgoʊld ˈpleɪṱ əd ◂
gold-rimmed ˌgəʊl*d*ˈrɪmd ◂ →ˌgɒʊl*d*- ‖ ˌgoʊld-
Goldschmidt ˈgəʊl*d* ʃmɪt →ˈgɒʊl*d*- ‖ ˈgoʊl*d*-

Goldsmith, G~ 'gəʊld smɪθ →'gɒʊld- ‖ 'goʊld- **~s** s
Goldwater 'gəʊld ˌwɔːt ə →'gɒʊld- ‖ 'goʊld ˌwɔːţ ᵊr -ˌwɑːţ ᵊr
Goldwyn 'gəʊld wɪn →'gɒʊld- ‖ 'goʊld-
Golem 'gəʊl əm ‖ 'goʊl- **~s** z
golf gɒlf gɒf, gɔːf, §gəʊlf ‖ gɑːlf gɔːlf
'golf ball; **'golf club**; **'golf course**; **'golf links**
golfer 'gɒlf ə 'gɒf-, 'gɔːf-, §'gəʊlf- ‖ 'gɑːlf ᵊr 'gɔːlf- **~s** z
golfing 'gɒlf ɪŋ 'gɒf-, 'gɔːf-, §'gəʊlf- ‖ 'gɑːlf ɪŋ 'gɔːlf-
Golgi 'gɒldʒ i ‖ 'gɔːldʒ i 'gɑːldʒ i —*It* ['gɔl dʒi]
Golgotha 'gɒlg əθ ə ‖ 'gɑːlg-
Goliath, g~ gə 'laɪ_əθ gəʊ- **~s, ~'s** s
Golightly gəʊ 'laɪt li ‖ goʊ-
Gollancz 'gɒl æŋks -ənts; gə 'lænts, -'læŋks ‖ gə 'lænts
golliwog, golliwogg 'gɒl i wɒg ‖ 'gɑːl i wɑːg **~s** z
Gollum 'gɒl əm ‖ 'gɑːl-
golly 'gɒl i ‖ 'gɑːl i
gollywog 'gɒl i wɒg ‖ 'gɑːl i wɑːg **~s** z
Gomer 'gəʊm ə ‖ 'goʊm ᵊr
Gomes 'gəʊm ez ‖ 'goʊm- —*Port* ['go mɪʃ], *BrPort* ['go mis]
Gomez 'gəʊm ez ‖ 'goʊm- —*Sp* Gómez ['go meθ, -mes]
Gomm, Gomme gɒm ‖ gɑːm
Gomorrah gə 'mɒr ə ‖ -'mɔːr ə -'mɑːr-
Gompers 'gɒmp əz ‖ 'gɑːmp ᵊrz
Gomperts, Gompertz 'gɒmp əts ‖ 'gɑːmp ᵊrts
Gomshall 'gɒm ʃᵊl 'gʌm- ‖ 'gɑːm-
-gon gən gɒn ‖ gɑːn — **hexagon** 'heks əg ən -ə gɒn ‖ -ə gɑːn
gonad 'gəʊn æd 'gɒn- ‖ 'goʊn- **~s** z
gonadotrophin ˌgəʊn əd əʊ 'trəʊf ɪn ˌgɒn-, -'trɒf-, -ᵊn ‖ ˌgoʊn əd ə 'troʊf- **~s** z
-gonal *stress-imposing* gᵊn əl — **isogonal** aɪ 'sɒg ᵊn əl ‖ -'sɑːg-
Goncourt ˌgɒŋ 'kʊə '· · ‖ ˌgoʊn 'kʊᵊr —*Fr* [gɔ̃ kuːʁ]
Gond gɒnd ‖ gɑːnd **Gonds** gɒndz ‖ gɑːndz
Gondi 'gɒnd i ‖ 'gɑːnd i
gondola 'gɒnd əl ə ‖ 'gɑːnd- **~s** z
gondolier ˌgɒnd ə 'lɪə -ᵊl 'ɪə ‖ ˌgɑːnd ə 'lɪᵊr **~s** z
Gondwana gɒn 'dwɑːn ə ‖ gɑːn- **~land** lænd
gone gɒn §gɔːn, §gɑːn ‖ gɔːn gɑːn — *Preference poll, AmE:* gɔːn *76 %,* gɑːn *24% (of those who distinguish these two vowels).*
goner 'gɒn ə ‖ 'gɔːn ᵊr 'gɑːn- **~s** z
Goneril 'gɒn ər ɪl -əl ‖ 'gɑːn-
gonfalon 'gɒn fəl ən ‖ 'gɑːn- **~s** z
gong gɒŋ ‖ gɔːŋ gɑːŋ **gongs** gɒŋz ‖ gɔːŋz gɑːŋz
goniometer ˌgəʊn i 'ɒm ɪt ə -ət ə ‖ ˌgoʊn i 'ɑːm əţ ᵊr **~s** z
goniometric ˌgəʊn i_ə 'metr ɪk ◂ ‖ ˌgoʊn- **~al** ᵊl **~ally** ᵊl_i

GONE

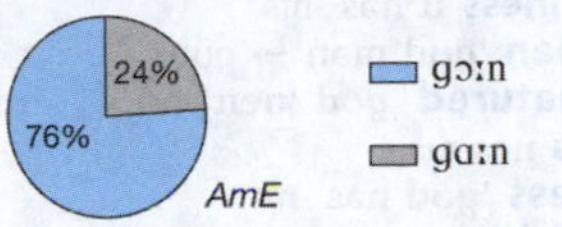

24% ▭ gɔːn
76% ▭ gɑːn
AmE

gonk gɒŋk ‖ gɑːŋk **gonks** gɒŋks ‖ gɑːŋks
gonna *contracted weak form before a consonant* (')gən ə —*There is no real RP strong form for this informal contraction of* going to, *although spelling pronunciations* 'gɒn ə, 'gʌn ə *are sometimes used in reading. There is an AmE strong form* 'gɔːn ə, 'gɑːn ə. —*Before a vowel sound, the contracted weak form* (')gən u *is sometimes used (see discussion at* to*).*
gonococ|cus ˌgɒn əʊ 'kɒk |əs ‖ ˌgɑːn ə 'kɑːk |əs **~ci** saɪ siː, aɪ
gonorrhea, gonorrhoea ˌgɒn ə 'rɪə ‖ ˌgɑːn ə 'riː ə
Gonville 'gɒn vɪl -vᵊl ‖ 'gɑːn-
-gony *stress-imposing* gən i — **cosmogony** kɒz 'mɒg ən i ‖ kɑːz 'mɑːg-
Gonzales, Gonzalez gɒn 'zɑːl ɪz gən-, -ez, -əz ‖ gən 'zɑːl əs gɑːn-, gɔːn-, -'sɑːl-, -es —*Sp* González [gon 'θa leθ, -'sa les]
gonzo 'gɒnz əʊ ‖ 'gɑːnz oʊ **~s** z
goo guː
goober 'guːb ə ‖ -ᵊr **~s** z
Gooch guːtʃ
good, Good gʊd **better** 'bet ə ‖ 'beţ ᵊr **best** best **goods** gʊdz —*In the phrase* a good deal *('quite a lot') a* d *is often lost in RP (providing* deal *is unstressed), thus* a good deal better ə ˌgʊd iːᵊl 'bet ə.
good ˌafter'noon, ˌ·ˌ·'·; **ˌgood 'book**; ₍ᵢ₎**good 'day**; ₍ᵢ₎**good 'evening**; **ˌGood 'Friday**; **ˌgood 'looker**; **ˌgood 'looks**; ₍ᵢ₎**good 'morning**; **ˌgood 'offices**; **ˌgood Sa'maritan**
Goodall 'gʊd ɔːl ‖ -ɑːl
Goodbody 'gʊd ˌbɒd i →'gʊb- ‖ -ˌbɑːd i
good-by, good-bye, goodbye ˌgʊd 'baɪ ◂ →ˌgʊb- **~s** z
Goodchild 'gʊd tʃaɪᵊld
Goode gʊd
Goodenough 'gʊd ɪ ˌnʌf -ə-, -ᵊn ˌʌf
Goodfellow 'gʊd ˌfel əʊ ‖ -oʊ
good-for-nothing ˌgʊd fə 'nʌθ ɪŋ ◂ '· ·ˌ· · ‖ -fᵊr-
Goodge guːdʒ gʊdʒ
Goodhart 'gʊd hɑːt ‖ -hɑːrt
good-hearted ˌgʊd 'hɑːt ɪd ◂ -əd ‖ -'hɑːrţ-
good-humored, good-humoured ˌgʊd 'hjuːm əd ◂ ‖ -ᵊrd ◂ 'juːm- **~ly** li **~ness** nəs nɪs
goodie 'gʊd i **~s** z
goodish 'gʊd ɪʃ
Goodison 'gʊd ɪs ən -əs-
goodli... —*see* **goodly**

G

Goodliffe ˈgʊd lɪf
good-looking ˌgʊd ˈlʊk ɪŋ ◂
good|ly ˈgʊd |li **~lier** li‿ə ‖ li‿ᵊr **~liest** li‿ɪst əst **~liness** li nəs -nɪs
Goodman ˈgʊd mən →ˈgʊb-
good-natured ˌgʊd ˈneɪtʃ əd ◂ ‖ -ᵊrd **~ly** li **~ness** nəs nɪs
goodness ˈgʊd nəs -nɪs
goodnight ₍ˌ₎gʊd ˈnaɪt ◂ gə- **~s** s
good-o, good-oh ˌgʊd ˈəʊ ‖ -ˈoʊ
Goodrich ˈgʊd rɪtʃ
goods gʊdz
good-tempered ˌgʊd ˈtemp əd ◂ ‖ -ᵊrd ◂ **~ly** li **~ness** nəs nɪs
good|wife ˈgʊd |waɪf **~wives** waɪvz
goodwill ˌgʊd ˈwɪl ◂
ˌgoodwill ˈvisit
Goodwin ˈgʊd wɪn §-wən
Goodwood ˈgʊd wʊd
Goodwright ˈgʊd raɪt
good|y ˈgʊd |i **~ies** iz
Goodyear ˈgʊd jə -jɪə, -jɜː ‖ -jᵊr -jɪr; ˈgʊdʒ ɪr
goody-good|y ˈgʊd i ˌgʊd |i ˌ·ˈ·· **~ies** iz
goody-two-shoes ˌgʊd i ˈtuː ʃuːz
goo|ey ˈguː‿|i **~ier** i ə ‖ i ᵊr **~iest** i ɪst i əst **~iness** i nəs i nɪs
goof guːf **goofed** guːft **goofing** ˈguːf ɪŋ **goofs** guːfs
goofball ˈguːf bɔːl ‖ -bɑːl **~s** z
goof-off ˈguːf ɒf ‖ -ɔːf -ɑːf
goof|y ˈguːf |i **~ier** i‿ə ‖ i‿ᵊr **~iest** i‿ɪst i‿əst **~ily** ɪ li əl i **~iness** i nəs i nɪs
Googie ˈguːg i
Googl|e *tdmk* ˈguːg ᵊl **~ed** d **~es** z **~ing** ‿ɪŋ
googlewhack ˈguːg ᵊl wæk -hwæk **~ed** t **~ing** ɪŋ **~s** s
goog|ly ˈguːg |li **~lies** liz
googol ˈguːg ɒl -ᵊl ‖ -ɔːl -ɑːl, -ᵊl **~s** z
googolplex ˈguːg ɒl pleks -ᵊl- ‖ -ɔːl- -ɑːl-, -ᵊl-
goo-goo ˈguː guː
gooi... —*see* **gooey**
gook *'sludge'* gʊk guːk
gook *'SE Asian'* guːk **gooks** guːks
Goole guːl
gool|ie, ~y ˈguːl i **~ies** z
goon guːn **goons** guːnz
gooner|y ˈguːn ər |i **~ies** iz
Goonhilly gʊn ˈhɪl i ˌguːn-, ˈ·ˌ··
goop guːp
goosander guː ˈsænd ə ‖ -ᵊr **~s** z
goose guːs **geese** giːs **goosed** guːst **gooses, goose's** ˈguːs ɪz -əz **goosing** ˈguːs ɪŋ
ˈgoose egg; **ˈgoose ˌpimples**
gooseberr|y ˈgʊz bər‿|i §ˈgʊs-, §ˈguːs-, §ˈguːz- ‖ ˈguːs ˌber |i ˈguːz-, -bər‿|i **~ies** iz
goosebumps ˈguːs bʌmps
goosedown ˈguːs daʊn
gooseflesh ˈguːs fleʃ
goosefoot ˈguːs fʊt **~s** s
goosegog ˈgʊz gɒg ‖ -gɑːg **~s** z
gooseneck ˈguːs nek **~s** s
goosestep ˈguːs step **~ped** t **~ping** ɪŋ **~s** s
Goosnargh ˈguːs nə ‖ -nᵊr

Goossens ˈguːs ᵊnz
GOP ˌdʒiː əʊ ˈpiː ‖ -oʊ-
gopher ˈgəʊf ə ‖ ˈgoʊf ᵊr **~s** z
Gorazde gə ˈræʒ deɪ gɔː-, -də —*Serbian* Goražde [ˈgɔ raʒ dɛ]
Gorbachev, Gorbachov ˈgɔːb ə tʃɒf -tʃɒv, ˌ··ˈ· ‖ ˈgɔːrb ə tʃɔːf -tʃɑːf —*Russ* [gər bʌ ˈtʃɔf]
Gorbals ˈgɔːb ᵊlz ‖ ˈgɔːrb-
gorblimey ₍ˌ₎gɔː ˈblaɪm i ‖ gɔːr-
Gordian ˈgɔːd i‿ən ‖ ˈgɔːrd-
ˌGordian ˈknot
Gordimer ˈgɔːd ɪm ə §-əm ə ‖ ˈgɔːrd əm ᵊr
Gordon ˈgɔːd ᵊn ‖ ˈgɔːrd ᵊn
Gordonstoun ˈgɔːd ᵊnz tən -ᵊnᵗst ən ‖ ˈgɔːrd-
gore, Gore gɔː ‖ gɔːr goʊr **gored** gɔːd ‖ gɔːrd goʊrd **gores** gɔːz ‖ gɔːrz goʊrz **goring** ˈgɔːr ɪŋ ‖ ˈgoʊr-
Gorecki, Górecki gɔː ˈret ski gə- —*Polish* [gu ˈrets ki]
Gore-Tex *tdmk* ˈgɔː teks ‖ ˈgɔːr-
gorge gɔːdʒ ‖ gɔːrdʒ **gorged** gɔːdʒd ‖ gɔːrdʒd **gorges** ˈgɔːdʒ ɪz -əz ‖ ˈgɔːrdʒ əz **gorging** ˈgɔːdʒ ɪŋ ‖ ˈgɔːrdʒ ɪŋ
gorgeous ˈgɔːdʒ əs ‖ ˈgɔːrdʒ- **~ly** li **~ness** nəs nɪs
gorget ˈgɔːdʒ ɪt -ət ‖ ˈgɔːrdʒ- **~s** s
Gorgias ˈgɔːdʒ i‿əs -æs ‖ ˈgɔːrdʒ-
gorgon, G~ ˈgɔːg ən ‖ ˈgɔːrg- **~s, ~'s** z
Gorgonzola ˌgɔːg ən ˈzəʊl ə ◂ →-ŋ- ‖ ˌgɔːrg ən ˈzoʊl ə —*It* [gor gon ˈdzɔː la]
Gorham ˈgɔːr əm
gori... —*see* **gory**
gorilla gə ˈrɪl ə **~s** z
Goring ˈgɔːr ɪŋ
Gorki, Gorky ˈgɔːk i ‖ ˈgɔːrk i —*Russ* [ˈgorʲ kʲɪj]
Gorleston ˈgɔːlst ən ‖ ˈgɔːrlst-
Gorman ˈgɔːm ən ‖ ˈgɔːrm-
gormandis|e, gormandiz|e ˈgɔːm ən daɪz ‖ ˈgɔːrm- **~ed** d **~er/s** ə/z ‖ ᵊr/z **~es** ɪz əz **~ing** ɪŋ
Gormanston ˈgɔːm ənᵗst ən ‖ ˈgɔːrm-
Gormenghast ˈgɔːm ən gɑːst →-əŋ-, §-gæst ‖ ˈgɔːrm ən gæst
gormless ˈgɔːm ləs -lɪs ‖ ˈgɔːrm- **~ly** li **~ness** nəs nɪs
Gormley ˈgɔːm li ‖ ˈgɔːrm-
Goronwy gə ˈrɒn wi gɒ- ‖ -ˈrɑːn- —*Welsh* [go ˈro nuɨ, -nwi]
Gorran ˈgɒr ən ‖ ˈgɔːr-
Gor-Ray *tdmk* ˈgɔː reɪ ‖ ˈgɔːr-
Gorringe ˈgɒr ɪndʒ -əndʒ ‖ ˈgɔːr- ˈgɑːr-
gorse gɔːs ‖ gɔːrs
Gorsedd ˈgɔːs eð ‖ ˈgɔːrs- —*Welsh* [ˈgor seð]
Gorseinon gɔː ˈsaɪn ən ‖ gɔːr- —*Welsh* [gor ˈsəi non]
Gorst gɔːst ‖ gɔːrst
Gorton ˈgɔːt ᵊn ‖ ˈgɔːrt ᵊn
gor|y ˈgɔːr |i ‖ ˈgoʊr- **~ier** i‿ə ‖ i‿ᵊr **~iest** i‿ɪst i‿əst **~ily** əl i ɪ li **~iness** i nəs i nɪs
Gosforth ˈgɒs fəθ -fɔːθ ‖ ˈgɑːs fɔːrθ -foʊrθ
gosh gɒʃ ‖ gɑːʃ
goshawk ˈgɒs hɔːk ‖ ˈgɑːs- -hɑːk **~s** s

oshen ˈgəʊʃ ᵊn ‖ ˈgoʊʃ ᵊn
osling, G~ ˈgɒz lɪŋ ‖ ˈgɑːz- **~s** z
o-slow ˌgəʊ ˈsləʊ ◂ ˈ· · ‖ ˈgoʊ sloʊ **~s** z
ospel, G~ ˈgɒsp ᵊl ‖ ˈgɑːsp ᵊl **~s** z
ˈgospel ˌmusic; ˌgospel ˈtruth
ospeler, gospeller ˈgɒsp əl ə ‖ ˈgɑːsp ᵊl ər **~s** z
osport, g~ ˈgɒs pɔːt ‖ ˈgɑːs pɔːrt -poʊrt **~s** s
oss gɒs ‖ gɔːs gɑːs
ossage ˈgɒs ɪdʒ ‖ ˈgɑːs-
ossamer ˈgɒs əm ə ‖ ˈgɑːs əm ᵊr ˈgɑːz- **~ed** d
osse gɒs ‖ gɔːs gɑːs
ossip ˈgɒs ɪp §-əp ‖ ˈgɑːs əp **~ed** t **~er/s** ə/z ‖ ᵊr/z **~ing** ɪŋ **~s** s
ossipmonger ˈgɒs ɪp ˌmʌŋ gə §-əp- ‖ ˈgɑːs əp ˌmʌŋ gᵊr -ˌmɑːŋ- **~s** z
ossipy ˈgɒs ɪp i §-əp- ‖ ˈgɑːs-
ossypol ˈgɒs i pɒl ‖ ˈgɑːs ə poʊl -pɑːl, -pɔːl
ot gɒt ‖ gɑːt
otcha ˈgɒtʃ ə ‖ ˈgɑːtʃ ə **~s** z
oth gɒθ ‖ gɑːθ **Goths** gɒθs ‖ gɑːθs
otha ˈgəʊθ ə ˈgəʊt- ‖ ˈgoʊt̬ ə —*Ger* [ˈgoː ta]
otham *nickname for NYC* ˈgɒθ əm ˈgəʊθ- ‖ ˈgɑːθ-
otham *place in Notts* ˈgəʊt əm ˈgɒt- ‖ ˈgoʊt̬- ˈgɑːt̬-
othard ˈgɒθ ɑːd ‖ ˈgɑːθ ɑːrd
othenburg ˈgɒθ ᵊn bɜːg ˈgɒt- ‖ ˈgɑːθ ᵊn bɜ˞ːg ˈgɑːt- —*Swedish* Göteborg [ˌjœt ə ˈbɔrj]
othic ˈgɒθ ɪk ‖ ˈgɑːθ ɪk **~ally** ᵊl͜ i
othicism ˈgɒθ ɪ ˌsɪz əm -ə- ‖ ˈgɑːθ-
otta ˈgɒt ə ‖ ˈgɑːt̬ ə —*Although this spelling is nonstandard, particularly in BrE, the pronunciation given is quite usual not only in GenAm but also in informal RP for* got to *('must') before a word beginning with a consonant sound. Before a vowel, the corresponding pronunciation is usually* ˈgɒt u ‖ ˈgɑːt̬ ə *—see discussion at* to
otten ˈgɒt ᵊn ‖ ˈgɑːt ᵊn
otterdammerung ˌgɒt ə ˈdæm ə rʊŋ ˌgɜːt-, -ˈdem-, -rʌŋ ‖ ˌgɑːt̬ ᵊr- —*Ger* Götterdämmerung [ˈgœ tɐ ˌdɛ mə ʁʊŋ]
ottfried ˈgɒt friːd ‖ ˈgɑːt- —*Ger* [ˈgɔt fʁiːt]
otti ˈgɒt i ‖ ˈgɑːt̬ i
ottingen, Göttingen ˈgɜːt ɪŋ ən ˈgɒt- ‖ ˈget̬- ˈgoʊt̬-, ˈgɜːt̬- —*Ger* [ˈgœt ɪŋ ən]
ouach|e gu ˈɑːʃ gwɑːʃ —*Fr* [gwaʃ] **~es** ɪz əz
ouda ˈgaʊd ə ‖ ˈguːd ə —*Dutch* [ˈxɔu daː]
oudge guːdʒ gʊdʒ
oudhurst ˈgaʊd hɜːst ‖ -hɜ˞ːst
ouge gaʊdʒ **gouged** gaʊdʒd **gouges** ˈgaʊdʒ ɪz -əz **gouging** ˈgaʊdʒ ɪŋ
ough gɒf ‖ gɑːf
oujon ˈguːdʒ ən ˈguːʒ-, -ɒn, -õ ‖ gu ˈʒoʊn —*Fr* [gu ʒɔ̃] **~s** z
oulash ˈguːl æʃ ‖ -ɑːʃ -æʃ **~es** ɪz əz
ould guːld gəʊld
ounod ˈguːn əʊ ‖ -oʊ —*Fr* [gu no]
ourami, gouramy gʊ ˈrɑːm i ˈgʊər əm i **~s** z
ourd, gourde gʊəd gɔːd ‖ gɔːrd goʊrd, gʊᵊrd **gourds, gourdes** gʊədz gɔːdz ‖ gɔːrdz goʊrdz, gʊᵊrdz

Gourlay, Gourley ˈgʊəl i ‖ ˈgʊrl i
gourmand ˈgʊəm ənd ˈgɔːm- ‖ ˈgʊrm ɑːnd -ənd; gʊr ˈmɑːnd —*Fr* [guʁ mɑ̃] **~s** z
gourmet ˈgʊəm eɪ ˈgɔːm- ‖ ˈgʊrm eɪ gʊr ˈmeɪ —*Fr* [guʁ mɛ] **~s** z
Gourock ˈgʊər ək ‖ ˈgʊr-
gout gaʊt **gouts** gaʊts
goutweed ˈgaʊt wiːd
gout|y ˈgaʊt |i ‖ ˈgaʊt̬ |i **~ier** i͜ə ‖ i͜ ᵊr **~iest** i͜ ɪst i͜ əst **~ily** ɪ li əl i **~iness** i nəs i nɪs
Govan ˈgʌv ᵊn
gov|ern ˈgʌv |ᵊn ‖ -|ᵊrn **~erned** ᵊnd ‖ ᵊrnd **~erning** ᵊn͜ ɪŋ ‖ ᵊrn ɪŋ **~erns** ᵊnz ‖ ᵊrnz
governance ˈgʌv ᵊn͜ ənᵗs ‖ -ᵊrn ənᵗs
governess ˈgʌv ᵊn͜ əs -ɪs, -es ‖ -ᵊrn əs **~es** ɪz əz
government ˈgʌv ᵊn mənt →-ᵊm-, -ə- ‖ -ᵊrn- —*There are also casual forms* ˈgʌb m mənt, ˈgʌm mənt **~s** s
governmental ˌgʌv ᵊn ˈment ᵊl ◂ →ᵊm-, -ə- ‖ ˌgʌv ᵊrn ˈment̬ ᵊl ◂ **~ly** i
governor ˈgʌv ᵊn͜ ə ‖ ˈgʌv ᵊn͜ ər -ᵊrn ᵊr **~s** z
governor-general ˌgʌv ᵊn͜ ə ˈdʒen rəl -ˈdʒen ər əl ‖ -ᵊn͜ ər- **governors-general** ˌgʌv ᵊn͜ əz- ‖ -ᵊn͜ ərz-
governorship ˈgʌv ᵊn͜ ə ʃɪp ‖ -ᵊn͜ ər- -ᵊrn ᵊr- **~s** s
Govett ˈgʌv ɪt -ət
Gow gaʊ
Gowan, gowan ˈgaʊ͜ ən **~s** z
Gower *(i)* ˈgaʊ͜ ə ‖ ˈgaʊ͜ ᵊr, *(ii)* gɔː ‖ gɔːr *-The peninsula in Wales, and the London street, are (i). The family name is sometimes (ii).*
Gowing ˈgaʊ͜ ɪŋ **~s** z
gown gaʊn **gowned** gaʊnd **gowning** ˈgaʊn ɪŋ **gowns** gaʊnz
Gowrie ˈgaʊᵊr i
goy gɔɪ **goyim** ˈgɔɪ ɪm -jɪm, §-əm **goys** gɔɪz
Goya ˈgɔɪ ə —*Sp* [ˈgo ja] **~s, ~'s** z
Goyt gɔɪt
Gozo ˈgəʊz əʊ ‖ ˈgoʊz oʊ
GP ˌdʒiː ˈpiː **~s, ~'s** z
G-Plan *tdmk* ˈdʒiː plæn
GPO ˌdʒiː piː ˈəʊ ◂ ‖ -ˈoʊ ◂
Graafian ˈgrɑːf i͜ ən ˈgræf-
grab græb **grabbed** græbd **grabbing** ˈgræb ɪŋ **grabs** græbz
ˈgrab bag
grabber ˈgræb ə ‖ -ᵊr **~s** z
grabby ˈgræb i
graben ˈgrɑːb ən **~s** z
Gracch|us ˈgræk |əs **~i** iː aɪ
grace, Grace greɪs **graced** greɪst **graces, Graces, Grace's** ˈgreɪs ɪz -əz **gracing** ˈgreɪs ɪŋ
ˈgrace note
grace-and-favour ˌgreɪs ᵊn ˈfeɪv ə ◂ -ᵊnd- ‖ -ᵊr
Gracechurch ˈgreɪs tʃɜːtʃ ‖ -tʃɜ˞ːtʃ
graceful ˈgreɪs fᵊl -fʊl **~ly** ͜i **~ness** nəs nɪs
Graceland ˈgreɪs lænd -lənd
graceless ˈgreɪs ləs -lɪs **~ly** li **~ness** nəs nɪs
Gracey, Gracie ˈgreɪs i
gracious ˈgreɪʃ əs **~ly** li **~ness** nəs nɪs
grackle ˈgræk ᵊl **~s** z

G

grad græd **grads** grædz
gradability ˌgreɪd ə ˈbɪl ət i -ɪt i ‖ -əţ i
gradable ˈgreɪd əb ᵊl
gradate grə ˈd|eɪt ‖ ˈgreɪd |eɪt **~ated** eɪt ɪd -əd ‖ eɪţ əd **~ates** eɪts **~ating** eɪt ɪŋ ‖ eɪţ ɪŋ
gradation grə ˈdeɪʃ ᵊn greɪ-, græ- **~al** əl **~s** z
grade, Grade greɪd **graded** ˈgreɪd ɪd -əd **grades** greɪdz **grading** ˈgreɪd ɪŋ **ˈgrade ˌcrossing**; **ˈgrade school**
Gradgrind ˈgræd graɪnd →ˈgræg-
gradience ˈgreɪd i‿ənᵗs
gradient ˈgreɪd i‿ənt **~s** s

GRADUAL

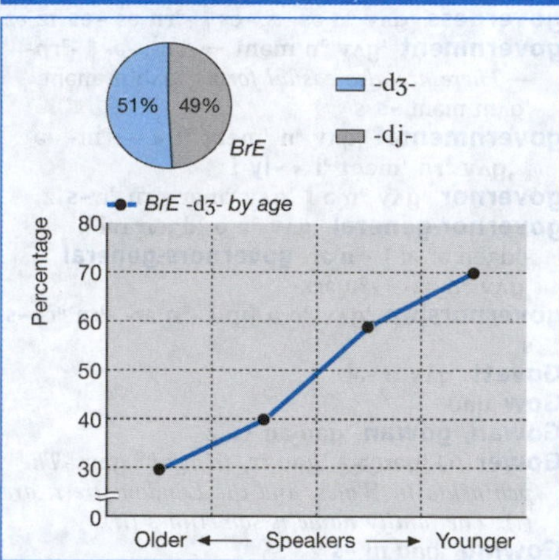

gradual ˈgrædʒ u‿əl ˈgræd ju‿əl; ˈgrædʒ ᵊl **~ly** i **~ness** nəs nɪs — *Preference poll, BrE* (gradually): dʒ *51%,* dj *49%; born since 1973,* dʒ *70%,* dj *30%.*
graduate *adj, n* ˈgrædʒ u‿ət ˈgræd ju‿, ɪt, -eɪt **~s** s
gradu|ate *v* ˈgrædʒ u |eɪt ˈgræd ju- **~ated** eɪt ɪd -əd ‖ eɪţ əd **~ates** eɪts **~ating** eɪt ɪŋ ‖ eɪţ ɪŋ
graduation ˌgrædʒ u ˈeɪʃ ᵊn ˌgræd ju- **~s** z
gradus ˈgræd əs ˈgreɪd- **~es** ɪz əz
Grady ˈgreɪd i
Graeco- ¦griːk əʊ ‖ -oʊ — **Graeco-Roman** ˌgriːk əʊ ˈrəʊm ən ◂ ‖ -oʊ ˈroʊm-
Graeme ˈgreɪ əm greɪm
Graf grɑːf græf —*Ger* [gʁaːf]
graffit|i grə ˈfiːt |i græ- ‖ -ˈfiːţ |i **~o** əʊ ‖ oʊ
Grafham, Graffham ˈgræf əm —*but* Grafham *in Cambridgeshire is* ˈgrɑːf-
graft grɑːft §græft ‖ græft **grafted** ˈgrɑːft ɪd §ˈgræft-, -əd ‖ ˈgræft əd **grafting** ˈgrɑːft ɪŋ §ˈgræft- ‖ ˈgræft ɪŋ **grafts** grɑːfts §græfts ‖ græfts
grafter ˈgrɑːft ə §ˈgræft- ‖ ˈgræft ᵊr **~s** z
Grafton ˈgrɑːft ən §ˈgræft- ‖ ˈgræft-
Graham, g~, Grahame ˈgreɪ əm
Grahamstown ˈgreɪ əmz taʊn
Graig graɪg —*Welsh* [graig]
Grail, grail greɪᵊl **grails** greɪᵊlz

grain greɪn **grained** greɪnd **graining** ˈgreɪn ɪŋ **grains** greɪnz **ˈgrain ˌelevator**
Grainger ˈgreɪndʒ ə ‖ -ᵊr
Grainne, Gráinne ˈgrɔːn jə ‖ ˈgrɑːn-
grain|y ˈgreɪn |i **~ier** i‿ə ‖ i‿ᵊr **~iest** i‿ɪst i‿əst **~iness** i nəs i nɪs
-gram græm — **gorillagram** gə ˈrɪl ə græm
gram, Gram græm **grams** græmz
gramercy, G~ grə ˈmɜːs i ‖ -ˈmɜːs i —*but in NYC* G~ Park *is* ˈgræm əs i ‖ -ᵊrs i
graminaceous ˌgræm ɪ ˈneɪʃ əs ◂ -ə-
grammalogue ˈgræm ə lɒg ‖ -lɔːg -lɑːg **~s** z
grammar ˈgræm ə ‖ -ᵊr **~s** z **ˈgrammar school**
grammarian grə ˈmeər i‿ən ‖ -ˈmer- -ˈmær- **~s** z
grammatical grə ˈmæt ɪk ᵊl ‖ -ˈmæţ- **~ly** i
grammaticality grə ˌmæt ɪ ˈkæl ət i §-ˌə-, -ɪt i ‖ -ˌmæţ ə ˈkæl əţ i
gramme græm **grammes** græmz
Gramm|y ˈgræm |i **~ies, ~ys** iz
Gram-negative ˌgræm ˈneg ət ɪv ◂ ‖ -əţ-
gramophone ˈgræm ə fəʊn ‖ -foʊn **~s** z **ˈgramophone ˌrecord**
Grampian ˈgræmp i‿ən **~s** z
Gram-positive ˌgræm ˈpɒz ət ɪv ◂ -ət- ‖ -ˈpɑːz əţ-
Gramps græmps
grampus ˈgræmp əs **~es** ɪz əz
gran, Gran græn —*See also phrases with this word* **grans, Gran's** grænz
Granada grə ˈnɑːd ə —*Sp* [gra ˈna ða]
granadilla ˌgræn ə ˈdɪl ə ‖ -ˈdiː ə **~s** z
Granados grə ˈnɑːd ɒs ‖ -oʊs —*Sp* [gra ˈna ðos]
granar|y ˈgræn ər |i ‖ ˈgreɪn- **~ies** iz
Granby ˈgræn bi →ˈgræm-
Gran Canaria ˌgræn kə ˈneər i‿ə →ˌgræŋ-, -ˈnɑːr- ‖ ˌgrɑːn kə ˈnɑːr i‿ə -ˈnær-, -ˈner- —*Sp* [graŋ ka ˈna ɾja]
grand, Grand grænd —*but in French expressions* grɒn, grɒ̃ ‖ grɑːn —*Fr* [gʁɑ̃] —*See also phrases with this word* **grander** ˈgrænd ə ‖ -ᵊr **grandest** ˈgrænd ɪst -əst **grands** grændz
ˌGrand ˈCanyon; **ˌgrand ˈjury**; **ˌgrand ˈopera**; **ˌgrand piˈano**; **ˌGrand ˈRapids**; **ˌgrand ˈslam**
grandad, G~ ˈgræn dæd **~s, ~'s** z
grandadd|y ˈgræn ˌdæd |i **~ies, ~y's** iz
grandchild ˈgræn tʃaɪᵊld ˈgrænd- **~'s** z
grandchildren ˈgræn ˌtʃɪldr ən ˈgrænd-, -ˌtʃʊldr- **~'s** z
Grand Coulee ˌgrænd ˈkuːl i
granddad ˈgræn dæd **~s** z
granddadd|y ˈgræn ˌdæd| i **~ies** iz
granddaughter ˈgræn ˌdɔːt ə ˈgrænd- ‖ -ˌdɔːţ ᵊr -ˌdɑːţ- **~s** z
grandduke ˌgrænd ˈdjuːk ◂ →-ˈdʒuːk ‖ -ˈduːk -ˈdjuːk **~s** s
grande dame ˌgrɑːn ˈdæm ‖ -ˈdɑːm —*Fr* [gʁɑ̃d dam]

randee græn ˈdiː **~s** z
randeur ˈgrænd*ʒ* ə ˈgræn djʊə, ˈgrɒ̃-, -djə ‖ -ᵊr -ʊr
randfather, G~ ˈgræn*d* ˌfɑːð ə ‖ -ᵊr **~s, ~'s** z **ˌgrand ˌfather 'clock**
rand Guignol ˌgrɒn ˈgiːn jɒl ˌgrɒ̃- ‖ ˌgrɑːn giːn ˈjoʊl -ˈjɔːl, -ˈjɑːl —*Fr* [-gi ɲɔl]
randiloquence græn ˈdɪl ək wən*t*s
randiloquent græn ˈdɪl ək wənt **~ly** li
randiose ˈgrænd i əʊs -əʊz ‖ -oʊs ˌ· ˈ· **~ly** li **~ness** nəs nɪs
randiosity ˌgrænd i ˈɒs ət i -ɪt i ‖ -ˈɑːs əṭ i
randison ˈgrænd ɪs ən -əs-
randly ˈgrænd li
randma, G~ ˈgræn mɑː ˈgrænd-, →ˈgræm- ‖ -mɔː **~s, ~'s** z
rand mal ˌgrɒn ˈmæl ˌgrɒ̃- ‖ ˌgræn ˈmɑːl ˌgrɑːn-, -ˈmæl, ˈ· · —*Fr* [-mal]
randmama, grandmamma ˈgræn*d* mə ˌmɑː →ˈgræm- **~s, ~'s** z
rand Marnier *tdmk* ˌgrɒn ˈmɑːn i eɪ ˌgrɒ̃- ‖ ˌgrɑːn mɑːrn ˈjeɪ —*Fr* [-maʁ nje]
randmaster ˈgræn*d* ˌmɑːst ə →ˈgræm-, §-ˌmæst-, ˌ·ˈ· · ‖ -ˌmæst ᵊr **~s** z
randmother, G~ ˈgræn ˌmʌð ə ˈgrænd-, →ˈgræm- ‖ -ᵊr **~s, ~'s** z
randness ˈgræn*d* nəs -nɪs
randpa, G~ ˈgræn pɑː →ˈgræm- ‖ -pɔː **~s, ~'s** z
randparent ˈgræn*d* ˌpeər ənt →ˈgræm- ‖ -ˌper- -ˌpær- **~s** s
rand prix ˌgrɒn ˈpriː ˌgrɒ̃-, ˌgrɑːn-, ˌgrɔːn-, →ˌgrɒm-,→grɑːm-, →ˌgrɔːm- ‖ ˌgrɑːn- —*Fr* [gʁɑ̃ pʁi] **grands prix** —*as sing. or with added* z
randsire ˈgræn*d* ˌsaɪ‿ə ‖ -ˌsaɪ‿ᵊr **~s** z
randson ˈgræn sʌn ˈgrænd- **~s** z
rands prix ˌgrɒn ˈpriː ˌgrɒ̃-, ˌgrɑːn-, ˌgrɔːn-, →ˌgrɒm-, →grɑːm-, →ˌgrɔːm-, -ˈpriːz ‖ ˌgrɑːn- —*Fr* [gʁɑ̃ pʁi]
randstand ˈgræn*d* stænd **~ing** ɪŋ **~s** z
grange, G~ greɪnd*ʒ* **granges** ˈgreɪnd*ʒ* ɪz -əz
Grangemouth ˈgreɪnd*ʒ* maʊθ -məθ
Grange-over-Sands ˌgreɪnd*ʒ* əʊv ə ˈsæn*dz* ‖ -oʊv ᵊr-
Granger ˈgreɪnd*ʒ* ə ‖ -ᵊr
granite ˈgræn ɪt -ət **~s** s
granitic grə ˈnɪt ɪk græ- ‖ -ˈnɪṭ ɪk
grannie, granny, G~ ˈgræn i **~s, ~'s** z **'granny flat**; **'granny knot**; **ˌGranny 'Smith**
granola grə ˈnəʊl ə greɪ- ‖ -ˈnoʊl ə
granolithic ˌgræn ə ˈlɪθ ɪk ◂
grant, Grant grɑːnt §grænt ‖ grænt **granted** ˈgrɑːnt ɪd §ˈgrænt-, -əd ‖ ˈgrænṭ əd **granting** ˈgrɑːnt ɪŋ §ˈgrænt- ‖ ˈgrænṭ ɪŋ **grants** grɑːn*ts* §græn*ts* ‖ græn*ts*
Granta ˈgrɑːnt ə ˈgrænt- ‖ ˈgrænṭ ə
grant-aided ˌgrɑːnt ˈeɪd ɪd ◂ §ˌgrænt-, -əd ‖ ˌgrænṭ-
Grantchester ˈgrɑːn tʃɪst ə ˈgræn-, -tʃəst-, §-ˌtʃest- ‖ ˈgræn ˌtʃest ᵊr
grantee ₍ˌ₎grɑːn ˈtiː §₍ˌ₎græn- ‖ ₍ˌ₎græn- **~s** z

Granth grʌnt —*Hindi* [grənt̪ʰ]
Grantham ˈgræn*t*θ əm
grant-in-aid ˌgrɑːnt ɪn ˈeɪd §ˌgrænt- ‖ ˌgrænt ᵊn-
Grantley, Grantly ˈgrɑːnt li §ˈgrænt- ‖ ˈgrænt-
grant-maintaned ˌgrɑːnt meɪn ˈteɪnd ◂ §ˌgrænt-, -men-, -mən- ‖ ˌgrænt-
grantor ₍ˌ₎grɑːn ˈtɔː §₍ˌ₎græn-; ˈgrɑːnt ə, §ˈgrænt- ‖ ₍ˌ₎græn ˈtɔːr ˈgrænṭ ᵊr **~s** z
Grantown-on-Spey ˌgræn taʊn ɒn ˈspeɪ ˌgrænt ən- ‖ -ɑːn ˈspeɪ -ɔːnˈ-
gran turismo ˌgræn tʊə ˈrɪz məʊ -tuᵊ- ‖ ˌgrɑːn tʊ ˈrɪz moʊ -ˈriːz- —*It* [gran tu ˈriz mo]
granular ˈgræn jʊl ə -jəl- ‖ -jəl ᵊr
granularity ˌgræn ju ˈlær ət i ˌjə-, -ɪt i ‖ -jə ˈlær əṭ i -ˈler-
granu|late ˈgræn ju |leɪt -jə- ‖ -jə- **~lated** leɪt ɪd -əd ‖ leɪṭ əd **~lates** leɪts **~lating** leɪt ɪŋ ‖ leɪṭ ɪŋ
granulation ˌgræn ju ˈleɪʃ ᵊn -jə- ‖ -jə- **~s** z
granule ˈgræn juːl **~s** z
Granville ˈgræn vɪl -vᵊl
grape greɪp **grapes** greɪps
grapefruit ˈgreɪp fruːt **~s** s
Grapelli grə ˈpel i
grapeshot ˈgreɪp ʃɒt ‖ -ʃɑːt
grapevine ˈgreɪp vaɪn **~s** z

GRAPH

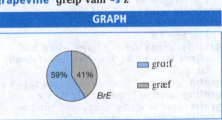

59% 41%
BrE
grɑːf
græf

graph grɑːf græf ‖ græf — *Preference poll, BrE:* grɑːf *59% (English southerners 77%),* græf *41% (English southerners 23%).* **graphed** grɑːft græft ‖ græft **graphing** ˈgrɑːf ɪŋ ˈgræf- ‖ ˈgræf ɪŋ **graphs** grɑːfs græfs ‖ græfs **'graph ˌpaper**
-graph grɑːf græf ‖ græf — **photograph** ˈfəʊt ə grɑːf -græf ‖ ˈfoʊṭ ə græf
grapheme ˈgræf iːm **~s** z
graphemic græ ˈfiːm ɪk grə- **~ally** ᵊl‿i
-grapher *stress-imposing* grəf ə ‖ -ᵊr — **photographer** fəʊ ˈtɒg rəf ə ‖ fə ˈtɑːg rəf ᵊr
-graphic ˈgræf ɪk — **photographic** ˌfəʊt ə ˈgræf ɪk ◂ ‖ ˌfoʊṭ-
graphic ˈgræf ɪk **~al** ᵊl **~ally** ᵊl‿i **~s** s **ˌgraphic de'sign**; **ˌgraphic de'signer**
graphite ˈgræf aɪt
graphological ˌgræf ə ˈlɒdʒ ɪk ᵊl ◂ ‖ -ˈlɑːdʒ- **~ly** ‿i
graphologist græ ˈfɒl ədʒ ɪst grə-, §-əst ‖ -ˈfɑːl- **~s** s
graphology græ ˈfɒl ədʒ i grə- ‖ -ˈfɑːl-
-graphy *stress-imposing* grəf i — **photography** fəʊ ˈtɒg rəf i ‖ fə ˈtɑːg-

grapnel 'græp nᵊl **~s** z
grappa 'græp ə ‖ 'grɑːp ə —*It* ['grap pa]
Grappelli grə 'pel i —*Fr* [gra pɛ li]
grappl|e 'græp ᵊl **~ed** d **~es** z **~ing** ˌɪŋ
'grappling hook; **'grappling ˌiron**
graptolite 'græpt əʊ laɪt ‖ -ə- **~s** s
Grasmere 'grɑːs mɪə §'græs- ‖ 'græs mɪr
grasp grɑːsp §græsp ‖ græsp **grasped** grɑːspt §græspt ‖ græspt **grasping/ly** 'grɑːsp ɪŋ /li §'græsp- ‖ 'græsp ɪŋ /li
grass, Grass grɑːs §græs ‖ græs *Ger* [gras]
grassed grɑːst §græst ‖ græst **grasses** 'grɑːs ɪz §'græs-, -əz ‖ 'græs əz **grassing** 'grɑːs ɪŋ §'græs- ‖ 'græs ɪŋ
ˌgrass 'roots; **ˌgrass 'widow**; **ˌgrass 'widower**
grasshopper 'grɑːs ˌhɒp ə §'græs- ‖ 'græs ˌhɑːp ᵊr **~s** z
Grassington 'grɑːs ɪŋ tən §'græs- ‖ 'græs-
grassland 'grɑːs lænd §'græs-, -lənd ‖ 'græs- **~s** z
grass|y 'grɑːs |i §'græs- ‖ 'græs |i **~ier** i‿ə ‖ i‿ᵊr **~iest** i‿ɪst i‿əst **~iness** i nəs i nɪs
grate greɪt **grated** 'greɪt ɪd -əd ‖ 'greɪţ əd **grates** greɪts **grating** 'greɪt ɪŋ ‖ 'greɪţ ɪŋ
grateful 'greɪt fᵊl -fʊl **~ly** ‿i **~ness** nəs nɪs
grater 'greɪt ə ‖ 'greɪţ ᵊr **~s** z
Gratiano ˌgræʃ i 'ɑːn əʊ ˌgrɑːʃ- ‖ ˌgrɑːʃ 'jɑːn oʊ
graticule 'græt ɪ kjuːl -ə- ‖ 'græţ ə- **~s** z
gratification ˌgræt ɪf ɪ 'keɪʃ ᵊn ˌ·əf-, §-ə'·- ‖ ˌgræţ- **~s** z
grati|fy 'græt ɪ |faɪ -ə- ‖ 'græţ- **~fied** faɪd **~fier/s** faɪ‿ə/z ‖ faɪ‿ᵊr/z **~fies** faɪz **~fying/ly** faɪ ɪŋ /li
gratin 'græt æn ‖ 'grɑːt ᵊn —*Fr* [gʁa tæ̃] **~s** z
grating 'greɪt ɪŋ ‖ 'greɪţ ɪŋ **~ly** li **~s** z
gratis 'græt ɪs 'greɪt-, 'grɑːt-, -əs ‖ 'græţ əs
gratitude 'græt ɪ tjuːd -ə-, →-tʃuːd ‖ 'græţ ə tuːd -tjuːd
Grattan, Gratton 'græt ᵊn
gratuitous grə 'tjuː‿ɪt əs →-'tʃuː‿; ⚠ˌgrætʃ u 'ɪʃ əs ‖ -'tuː əţ əs -'tjuː- **~ly** li **~ness** nəs nɪs
gratuit|y grə 'tjuː‿ət |i →-'tʃuː‿ ɪt- ‖ -'tuː əţ |i -'tjuː- **~ies** iz
graupel 'graʊp ᵊl
gravadlax 'græv əd læks ‖ 'grɑːv əd lɑːks
gravamen grə 'veɪm en -'vɑːm-, -ən; 'græv əm- ‖ -ən
grave *n 'burial place'*; *adj 'serious'*; *v* greɪv **graved** greɪvd **graver** 'greɪv ə ‖ -ᵊr **graves** greɪvz **gravest** 'greɪv ɪst -əst **graving** 'greɪv ɪŋ
'graving dock
grave *accent mark* grɑːv ‖ greɪv grɑːv **graves** grɑːvz ‖ greɪvz grɑːvz
grave *mus* 'grɑːv eɪ —*It* ['grɑː ve]
gravedigger 'greɪv ˌdɪg ə ‖ -ᵊr **~s** z
gravel 'græv ᵊl **~ed, ~led** d **~ing, ~ling** ɪŋ **~s** z
Graveley 'greɪv li
gravelly, G~ 'græv ᵊl i
gravely 'greɪv li
graven 'greɪv ᵊn
graveness 'greɪv nəs -nɪs
Graveney 'greɪv ni
graver 'greɪv ə ‖ -ᵊr **~s** z
graves *pl 'burial places'* greɪvz
graves *pl 'accent marks'* grɑːvz ‖ greɪvz grɑːvz
Graves *wine* grɑːv —*Fr* [gʁaːv]
Graves *family name* greɪvz
Gravesend ˌgreɪvz 'end ◂
graveside 'greɪv saɪd
gravesite 'greɪv saɪt **~s** s
gravestone 'greɪv stəʊn ‖ -stoʊn **~s** z
graveyard 'greɪv jɑːd ‖ -jɑːrd **~s** z
gravid 'græv ɪd §-əd **~ly** li **~ness** nəs nɪs
gravie... —*see* **gravy**
gravitas 'græv ɪ tæs -ə-, -tɑːs
gravi|tate 'græv ɪ |teɪt -ə- **~tated** teɪt ɪd -əd ‖ teɪţ əd **~tates** teɪts **~tating** teɪt ɪŋ ‖ teɪţ ɪŋ
gravitation ˌgræv ɪ 'teɪʃ ᵊn -ə- **~al** ˌəl **~ally** əl i
gravitative 'græv ɪ teɪt ɪv '·ə- ‖ -teɪţ ɪv
gravit|y 'græv ət |i -ɪt- ‖ -əţ |i **~ies** iz
gravlaks 'græv læks ‖ 'grɑːv lɑːks 'græv- —*Swedish* ['grav laks]
gravure grə 'vjʊə -'vjɔː ‖ -'vjʊᵊr
grav|y 'greɪv |i **~ies** iz
'gravy boat, 'gravy train
gray, Gray greɪ **grayed** greɪd **grayer** 'greɪ ə ‖ -ᵊr **grayest** 'greɪ ɪst -əst **graying** 'greɪ ɪŋ **grays, Grays, Gray's** greɪz
ˌgray 'area; **'gray ˌmatter**; **ˌGray's 'Inn**
graybeard 'greɪ bɪəd ‖ -bɪrd **~s** z
grayhound 'greɪ haʊnd **~s** z
grayish 'greɪ ɪʃ
graylag 'greɪ læg **~s** z
grayling 'greɪl ɪŋ **~s** z
gray|ly 'greɪ |li **~ness** nəs nɪs
grayscale 'greɪ skeɪᵊl
Grayson 'greɪs ᵊn
graywacke 'greɪ ˌwæk ə
Graz grɑːts —*Ger* [gʁaːts]
graze greɪz **grazed** greɪzd **grazes** 'greɪz ɪz -əz **grazing** 'greɪz ɪŋ
grazer 'greɪz ə ‖ -ᵊr **~s** z
grazier 'greɪz i‿ə 'greɪʒ ə, 'greɪʒ i‿ə ‖ 'greɪʒ ᵊr *(*)* **~s** z
Grealey 'griːl i
grease *n* griːs
'grease gun
grease *v* griːs griːz **greased** griːst griːzd **greases** 'griːs ɪz 'griːz-, -əz **greasing** 'griːs ɪŋ 'griːz-
ˌgreased 'lightning
greasepaint 'griːs peɪnt
greaseproof 'griːs pruːf §-prʊf
greaser *v* 'griːs ə 'griːz- ‖ -ᵊr **~s** z

GREASY

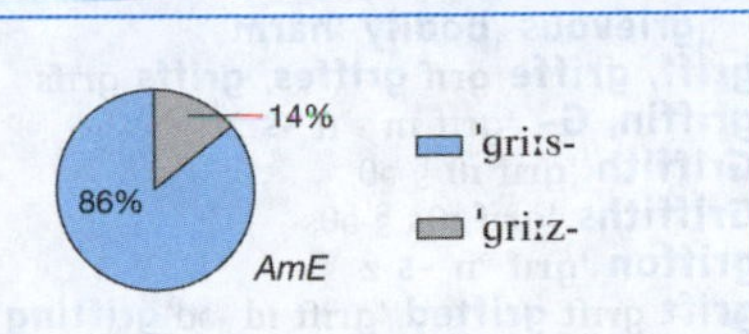

reas|y 'griːs |i 'griːz- — *Preference poll, AmE:* 'griːs- *86%,* 'griːz- *14%.* **~ier** i‿ə ‖ i‿ᵊr **~iest** i‿ɪst i‿əst **~ily** ɪ li əl i **~iness** i nəs i nɪs
ˌgreasy 'spoon

reat greɪt (*= grate*) **greater** 'greɪt ə ‖ 'greɪţ ᵊr **greatest** 'greɪt ɪst -əst ‖ 'greɪţ əst **greats** greɪts
ˌGreat 'Barrier Reef; **ˌGreat 'Bear**; **ˌGreat 'Britain**; **ˌgreat 'circle**; **ˌGreat 'Dane**; **ˌGreater 'London◂**, **ˌGreater ˌLondon 'Council**; **ˌGreat 'Lakes**; **ˌGreat 'Plains**

reat- ¦greɪt —*Compounds in* great- *are usually late-stressed:* ˌgreat-'grandˌdaughter. *However* great-aunt *and* great-uncle, *which are regularly subject to stress-shifting in names* (ˌgreat-'aunt◂, ˌGreat-Aunt 'Mary), *are by some people always given early stress.*

reat-aunt ˌgreɪt 'ɑːnt ◂ §-'ænt, '· · ‖ ˌgreɪţ 'ænt ◂ -'ɑːnt **~s** s

reatcoat 'greɪt kəʊt ‖ -koʊt **~s** s

reat|ly 'greɪt |li **~ness** nəs nɪs

ireatorex 'greɪt ə reks ‖ 'greɪţ-

reat-uncle ˌgreɪt 'ʌŋk ᵊl ◂ '·ˌ· · ‖ ˌgreɪţ- **~s** z

reave, G~ griːv (*= grieve*) **greaves** griːvz

ireaves *(i)* greɪvz, *(ii)* griːvz

rebe griːb **grebes** griːbz

irecian 'griːʃ ᵊn **~s** z

ireco 'grek əʊ ‖ -oʊ

ireco- ¦griːk əʊ ¦grek- ‖ -oʊ — **Greco-Roman** ˌgriːk əʊ 'rəʊm ən ◂ ˌgrek- ‖ -oʊ 'roʊm-

ireece griːs

reed griːd

reed|y 'griːd |i **~ier** i‿ə ‖ i‿ᵊr **~iest** i‿ɪst i‿əst **~ily** ɪ li əl i **~iness** i nəs i nɪs

reedy-guts 'griːd i gʌts

ireek, greek griːk **greeked** 'griːk ɪŋ **greeking** 'griːk ɪŋ **Greeks, greeks** griːks
ˌGreek 'Orthodox

ireeley, Greely 'griːl i

reen, Green griːn **greened** griːnd **greener** 'griːn ə ‖ -ᵊr **greenest** 'griːn ɪst -əst **greening** 'griːn ɪŋ **greens, G~** griːnz
ˌgreen 'bean; **'green belt**; **ˌgreen 'fingers**; **ˌgreen 'light**; **ˌGreen 'Paper**; **ˌgreen 'pepper**; **ˌgreen 'tea**; **ˌgreen 'thumb**

Greenaway 'griːn ə weɪ

greenback 'griːn bæk →'griːm- **~s** s

Greenbaum *(i)* 'griːn baʊm →'griːm-, *(ii)* -bɔːm ‖ -bɑːm, *(iii)* -bəʊm ‖ -boʊm —*The late Prof. Sidney G~, grammarian, claimed not to care which variant people used for his name; he was generally known as (i)*

Greenberg 'griːn bɜːg →'griːm- ‖ -bɜːg

Greene griːn

greener|y 'griːn ər |i **~ies** iz

green-eyed ˌgriːn 'aɪd ◂ ‖ '· ·
ˌgreen-eyed 'monster

Greenfield, G~ 'griːn fiːᵊld

greenfinch 'griːn fɪntʃ **~es** ɪz əz

green|fly 'griːn |flaɪ **~flies** flaɪz

Greenford 'griːn fəd ‖ -fᵊrd

greengag|e 'griːn geɪdʒ →'griːŋ- **~es** ɪz əz

greengrocer 'griːn ˌgrəʊs ə →'griːŋ- ‖ -ˌgroʊs ᵊr **~s** z

greengrocer|y 'griːn ˌgrəʊs ər‿|i →'griːŋ- ‖ -ˌgroʊs- **~ies** iz

Greengross 'griːn grɒs →'griːŋ- ‖ -grɑːs

Greenhalgh 'griːn hælʃ -hɔːlʃ, -hɒlʃ, -hældʒ, -hɔːl

Greenham 'griːn əm

Greenhill 'griːn hɪl

greenhorn 'griːn hɔːn ‖ -hɔːrn **~s** z

Greenhough 'griːn ɒf -hɒf, -həʊ, -haʊ, -hʌf ‖ -hoʊ

green|house 'griːn |haʊs **~houses** haʊz ɪz -əz
'greenhouse efˌfect

greenish 'griːn ɪʃ

Greenland 'griːn lənd -lænd **~er/s** ə/z ‖ ᵊr/z

Greenlandic (ˌ)griːn 'lænd ɪk

green|ly 'griːn |li **~ness** nəs nɪs

Greenock 'griːn ək

Greenough 'griːn əʊ ‖ -oʊ

Greenpeace 'griːn piːs →'griːm-, ˌ·'·

greenroom 'griːn ruːm -rʊm **~s** z

greensand 'griːn sænd **~s** z

greenshank 'griːn ʃæŋk **~s** s

Greenslade 'griːn sleɪd

Greensleeves 'griːn sliːvz

greenstick 'griːn stɪk

greenstone 'griːn stəʊn ‖ -stoʊn

Greenstreet 'griːn striːt

greenstuff 'griːn stʌf

greensward 'griːn swɔːd ‖ -swɔːrd **~s** z

Greenville 'griːn vɪl -vᵊl

greenwash 'griːn wɒʃ ‖ -wɑːʃ -wɔːʃ **~ed** t **~es** ɪz əz **~ing** ɪŋ

Greenwell 'griːn wəl -wel

Greenwich 'gren ɪtʃ 'grɪn-, -ɪdʒ —*This applies both to the London borough, location of the meridian, and to* G~ Village *in NYC; also to the town in CT, though this is sometimes* 'griːn wɪtʃ
ˌGreenwich 'Mean Time, ˌ· · ˌ· '·; **ˌGreenwich 'Village**

greenwood, G~ 'griːn wʊd **~s** z

Greer grɪə ‖ grɪᵊr

greet, Greet griːt **greeted** 'griːt ɪd -əd ‖ 'griːţ əd **greeting** 'griːt ɪŋ ‖ 'griːţ ɪŋ **greets** griːts

greeter 'griːt ə ‖ 'griːţ ᵊr **~s** z

Greg greg

gregarious grɪ 'geər i‿əs grə- ‖ -'ger- -'gær- **~ly** li **~ness** nəs nɪs

Gregg greg

Gregor 'greg ə ‖ -ᵊr

G

Gregorian grɪ 'gɔːr i‿ən grə-, gre- ‖ -'goʊr- **~s** z
Gregory 'greg ər i
Gregson 'greg sən
Gregynog grɪ 'gʌn ɒg grə-, gre- ‖ -ɑːg —*Welsh* [gre 'gə nog]
Greig *(i)* greg, *(ii)* griːg
gremlin 'grem lɪn §-lən **~s** z
grenache grə 'næʃ gre- ‖ -'nɑːʃ
Grenada grɪ 'neɪd ə grə-, gre-
grenade grɪ 'neɪd grə- **~s** z
Grenadian grɪ 'neɪd i‿ən grə-, gre- **~s** z
grenadier ˌgren ə 'dɪə ◂ ‖ -'dɪᵊr ◂ **~s** z
grenadilla ˌgren ə 'dɪl ə **~s** z
grenadine, G~ 'gren ə diːn ˌ·ˈ· **~s** z
Grendel 'grend ᵊl
Grendon 'grend ən
Grenfell 'gren fᵊl -fel
Grenoble grɪ 'nəʊb ᵊl grə- ‖ -'noʊb- —*Fr* [gʁə nɔbl]
Grenville 'gren vɪl -vᵊl
Gresham 'greʃ əm 'gres-
Gresley 'grez li
Greta *(i)* 'griːt ə ‖ 'griːţ ə, *(ii)* 'gret ə ‖ 'greţ ə
Gretchen 'gretʃ ən —*Ger* ['gʁeːt çən]
Gretel 'gret ᵊl ‖ 'greţ ᵊl —*Ger* ['gʁeː tᵊl]
Gretna 'gret nə
ˌ**Gretna 'Green**
Gretzky 'gret ski
Greville 'grev ɪl -ᵊl
grew, Grew gruː
grey, Grey greɪ **greyed** greɪd **greyer** 'greɪ ə ‖ -ᵊr **greyest** 'greɪ ɪst -əst **greying** 'greɪ ɪŋ **greys** greɪz
ˌ**grey 'area**; '**grey ˌmatter**
greybeard 'greɪ bɪəd ‖ -bɪrd **~s** z
greyhound 'greɪ haʊnd **~s** z
greyish 'greɪ ɪʃ
greylag 'greɪ læg **~s** z
grey|ly 'greɪ |li **~ness** nəs nɪs
greyscale 'greɪ skeɪᵊl
Greystoke 'greɪ stəʊk ‖ -stoʊk
greywacke 'greɪ ˌwæk ə
Gribble, g~ 'grɪb ᵊl
Grice graɪs
Gricean 'graɪs i‿ən
gricer 'graɪs ə ‖ -ᵊr **~s** z
grid grɪd **grids** grɪdz
griddl|e 'grɪd ᵊl **~ed** d **~es** z **~ing** ‿ɪŋ
griddlecake 'grɪd ᵊl keɪk **~s** s
gridiron 'grɪd ˌaɪ‿ən ‖ -ˌaɪᵊrn **~ed** d **~ing** ɪŋ **~s** z
Gridley 'grɪd li
gridlock 'grɪd lɒk ‖ -lɑːk **~ed** t **~s** s
grief griːf
grief-stricken 'griːf ˌstrɪk ən
Grieg griːg —*Norw* [gɾiːg]
Grierson 'grɪəs ᵊn ‖ 'grɪᵊrs ᵊn
grievanc|e 'griːv ᵊnᵗs §-i‿ənᵗs **~es** ɪz əz
grieve, G~ griːv **grieved** griːvd **grieves** griːvz **grieving/ly** 'griːv ɪŋ /li
grievous 'griːv əs ⚠'griːv i‿əs **~ly** li **~ness** nəs nɪs
ˌ**grievous ˌbodily 'harm**
griff, griffe grɪf **griffes, griffs** grɪfs
griffin, G~ 'grɪf ɪn -ᵊn **~s** z
Griffith 'grɪf ɪθ §-əθ
Griffiths 'grɪf ɪθs §-əθs
griffon 'grɪf ᵊn **~s** z
grift grɪft **grifted** 'grɪft ɪd -əd **grifting** 'grɪft ɪŋ **grifts** grɪfts
grifter 'grɪft ə ‖ -ᵊr **~s** z
grig, Grig, Grigg grɪg **grigs, Grigg's** grɪgz
Grignard 'griːn jɑː ‖ griːn 'jɑːrd —*Fr* [gʁi njaːʁ]
Grigson 'grɪg sᵊn
grike graɪk **grikes** graɪks
grill grɪl **grilled** grɪld **grilling** 'grɪl ɪŋ **grills** grɪlz
grille grɪl *(= grill)* **grilles** grɪlz
grillroom 'grɪl ruːm -rʊm **~s** z
grilse grɪls
grim grɪm **grimmer** 'grɪm ə ‖ -ᵊr **grimmest** 'grɪm ɪst -əst
ˌ**grim 'reaper**
grimac|e *v, n* grɪ 'meɪs grə-; 'grɪm əs **~ed** t **~es** ɪz əz **~ing** ɪŋ
Grimaldi grɪ 'mɔːld i grə-, -'mɒld- ‖ -'mɑːld-
grimalkin grɪ 'mælk ɪn grə-, -'mɔːlk-, §-ən ‖ -'mɔːlk- **~s** z
grime graɪm **grimed** graɪmd **grimes** graɪmz **griming** 'graɪm ɪŋ
Grimes graɪmz
Grimethorpe 'graɪm θɔːp ‖ -θɔːrp
grimi... —*see* **grimy**
grimly 'grɪm li
Grimm grɪm **Grimm's** grɪmz
grimness 'grɪm nəs -nɪs
Grimond 'grɪm ənd
Grimsargh 'grɪmz ə ‖ -ᵊr
Grimsby 'grɪmz bi
Grimshaw 'grɪm ʃɔː ‖ -ʃɑː
Grimston 'grɪmᵖst ən
grim|y 'graɪm |i **~ier** i‿ə ‖ i‿ᵊr **~iest** i‿ɪst i‿əst **~ily** ɪ li əl i **~iness** i nəs nɪs
grin grɪn **grinned** grɪnd **grinning** 'grɪn ɪŋ **grins** grɪnz
grind graɪnd **grinding** 'graɪnd ɪŋ **grinds** graɪndz **ground** graʊnd
'**grinding wheel**
Grindelwald 'grɪnd ᵊl vɑːld -væld, -wɔːld —*Ger* ['grɪn dᵊl valt]
grinder 'graɪnd ə ‖ -ᵊr **~s** z
Grindon 'grɪnd ən
grindstone 'graɪnd stəʊn ‖ -stoʊn **~s** z
gringo 'grɪŋ gəʊ ‖ -goʊ **~s** z
Grinstead, Grinsted 'grɪn stɪd -sted
Grinton 'grɪnt ən ‖ -ᵊn
griot 'griː əʊ ‖ -oʊ —*Fr* [gʁi o] **~s** z
grip grɪp **gripped** grɪpt **gripping/ly** 'grɪp ɪŋ /li **grips** grɪps
gripe graɪp **griped** graɪpt **gripes** graɪps **griping/ly** 'graɪp ɪŋ /li
griper 'graɪp ə ‖ -ᵊr **~s** z

ipp... —*see* **grip**
ippe grɪp griːp
riqua 'griːk wə 'grɪk- **~land** lænd
isaille grɪ 'zeɪᵊl grə-, griː-, -'zaɪ, -'zaɪᵊl ‖ -'zaɪ -'zeɪᵊl —*Fr* [gʁi zaj]
riselda grɪ 'zeld ə grə-
riseofulvin ˌgrɪz i əʊ 'fʊlv ɪn ˌgrɪs-, -'fʌlv-, §-ᵊn ‖ -i̯ə-
risette grɪ 'zet **~s** s
risewood 'graɪz wʊd
ris|ly 'grɪz |li (= *grizzly*) **~lier** li̯ə ‖ li̯ᵊr **~liest** li̯ɪst li̯əst
rison 'graɪs ᵊn 'grɪz- **~s** z
rissini grɪ 'siːn i grə- —*It* [gris 'siː ni]
rist, Grist grɪst
ristle 'grɪs ᵊl
rist|ly 'grɪs |ᵊl̯ i **~liness** ᵊl̯ i nəs -nɪs
riswold 'grɪz wᵊld -wəʊld, →-wɒʊld ‖ -woʊld
rit grɪt **grits** grɪts **gritted** 'grɪt ɪd -əd ‖ 'grɪţ əd **gritting** 'grɪt ɪŋ ‖ 'grɪţ ɪŋ
ritter 'grɪt ə ‖ 'grɪţ ᵊr **~s** z
ritt|y 'grɪt |i ‖ 'grɪţ |i **~ier** i̯ə ‖ i̯ᵊr **~iest** i̯ɪst i̯əst **~ily** ɪ li əl i **~iness** i nəs nɪs
rizedale 'graɪz deɪᵊl
rizzl|e 'grɪz ᵊl **~ed** d **~es** z **~ing** ɪŋ
rizz|ly 'grɪz |li **~lier** li̯ə ‖ li̯ᵊr **~lies** liz **~liest** li̯ɪst li̯əst
ˌgrizzly 'bear ‖ '. . .
roan grəʊn ‖ groʊn **groaned** grəʊnd ‖ groʊnd **groaning** 'grəʊn ɪŋ ‖ 'groʊn ɪŋ **groans** grəʊnz ‖ groʊnz
groaner 'grəʊn ə ‖ 'groʊn ᵊr **~s** z
groaning 'grəʊn ɪŋ ‖ 'groʊn ɪŋ **~ly** li **~s** z
groat grəʊt ‖ groʊt **groats** grəʊts ‖ groʊts
Gro-Bag *tdmk* 'grəʊ bæg ‖ 'groʊ- **~s** z
grocer 'grəʊs ə ‖ 'groʊs ᵊr **~s** z
grocer|y 'grəʊs ər |i →'grəʊʃ r|i ‖ 'groʊs- →'groʊʃ r|i **~ies** iz
grockle 'grɒk ᵊl ‖ 'grɑːk- **~s** z
Grocott 'grəʊ kɒt ‖ 'groʊ kɑːt
Groening *cartoonist* 'greɪn ɪŋ
grog grɒg ‖ grɑːg
Grogan 'grəʊg ən ‖ 'groʊg-
grogg|y 'grɒg |i ‖ 'grɑːg |i **~ier** i̯ə ‖ i̯ᵊr **~iest** i̯ɪst i̯əst **~ily** ɪ li əl i **~iness** i nəs i nɪs
grogram 'grɒg rəm ‖ 'grɑːg-
groin grɔɪn **groining** 'grɔɪn ɪŋ **groins** grɔɪnz
Grolier 'grəʊl i̯ə ‖ 'groʊl i̯ᵊr —*Fr* [gʁɔ lje]
grommet 'grɒm ɪt 'grʌm-, -ət ‖ 'grɑːm- **~s** s
gromwell 'grɒm wᵊl -wel ‖ 'grɑːm- **~s** z
Gromyko grə 'miːk əʊ ‖ -oʊ —*Russ* [grʌ 'mɨ kə]
Groningen 'grəʊn ɪŋ ən 'grɒn- ‖ 'groʊn- —*Dutch* ['xroː nɪŋ ən]
groom, Groom gruːm grʊm **groomed** gruːmd **grooms** gruːmz grʊmz **grooming** 'gruːm ɪŋ
Groombridge 'gruːm brɪdʒ
grooms|man 'gruːmz |mən 'grʊmz- **~men** mən men
Groote Eylandt 'gruːt ˌaɪl ənd ‖ 'gruːţ-
groove gruːv **grooved** gruːvd **groover/s** 'gruːv ə/z ‖ -ᵊr/z **grooves** gruːvz **grooving** 'gruːv ɪŋ

groov|y 'gruːv |i **~ier** i̯ə ‖ i̯ᵊr **~iest** i̯ɪst i̯əst
grope grəʊp ‖ groʊp **groped** grəʊpt ‖ groʊpt **gropes** grəʊps ‖ groʊps **groping/ly** 'grəʊp ɪŋ /li ‖ 'groʊp-
groper 'grəʊp ə ‖ 'groʊp ᵊr **~s** z
Gropius 'grəʊp i̯əs ‖ 'groʊp-
grosbeak 'grəʊs biːk 'grɒs- ‖ 'groʊs- **~s** s
groschen 'grɒʃ ᵊn 'grəʊʃ- ‖ 'groʊʃ- —*Ger* ['gʁɔʃ ᵊn]
grosgrain 'grəʊ greɪn ‖ 'groʊ-
Grosmont *(i)* 'grəʊ mənt -mɒnt ‖ 'groʊ mɑːnt, *(ii)* 'grəʊs- ‖ 'groʊs-, *(iii)* 'grɒs- ‖ 'grɑːs- —*The place in North Yks is (i) or (ii), that in Gwent (iii)*
gros point ˌgrəʊ 'pɔɪnt ‖ 'groʊ pɔɪnt
gross grəʊs ‖ groʊs **grossed** grəʊst ‖ groʊst **grosser** 'grəʊs ə ‖ 'groʊs ᵊr (= *grocer*) **grosses** 'grəʊs ɪz -əz ‖ 'groʊs əz **grossest** 'grəʊs ɪst -əst ‖ 'groʊs əst **grossing** 'grəʊs ɪŋ ‖ 'groʊs ɪŋ
Gross *(i)* grəʊs ‖ groʊs, *(ii)* grɒs ‖ grɑːs
Grosseteste 'grəʊs teɪt -test ‖ 'groʊs-
grossly 'grəʊs li ‖ 'groʊs li
Grossman 'grəʊs mən ‖ 'groʊs-
Grossmith 'grəʊs mɪθ ‖ 'groʊs-
grossness 'grəʊs nəs -nɪs ‖ 'groʊs-
gross-out 'grəʊs aʊt ‖ 'groʊs-
Grosvenor 'grəʊv nə 'grəʊv ən ə; §'grɒv- ‖ 'groʊv nᵊr
grosz grɒʃ ‖ grɑːʃ —*Polish* [grɔʃ] **groszy** 'grɒʃ i ‖ 'grɑːʃ i —*Polish* ['grɔ ʃi]
Grosz grəʊs ‖ groʊs
grot grɒt ‖ grɑːt **grots** grɒts ‖ grɑːts
Grote grəʊt ‖ groʊt
grotesque grəʊ 'tesk ‖ groʊ- **~ly** li **~ness** nəs nɪs **~s** s
grotesquer|ie, grotesquer|y grəʊ 'tesk ər |i ‖ groʊ- **~ies** iz
Grotius 'grəʊt i̯əs ‖ 'groʊʃ-
grotto 'grɒt əʊ ‖ 'grɑːţ oʊ **~es, ~s** z
grott|y 'grɒt |i ‖ 'grɑːţ |i **~ier** i̯ə ‖ i̯ᵊr **~iest** i̯ɪst i̯əst **~iness** i nəs i nɪs
grouch graʊtʃ **grouched** graʊtʃt **grouches** 'graʊtʃ ɪz -əz **grouching** 'graʊtʃ ɪŋ
Groucho 'graʊtʃ əʊ ‖ -oʊ
grouch|y 'graʊtʃ |i **~ier** i̯ə ‖ i̯ᵊr **~iest** i̯ɪst i̯əst **~ily** ɪ li əl i **~iness** i nəs i nɪs
ground graʊnd **grounded** 'graʊnd ɪd -əd **grounding/s** 'graʊnd ɪŋ/z **grounds** graʊndz **'ground bait**; **'ground conˌtrol**; **'ground crew**; **ˌground 'floor◂**; **ˌground 'glass◂**; **'ground plan**; **'ground rent**; **'ground rule**; **'ground speed**; **'ground staff**; **'ground stroke**
groundbreaking 'graʊnd ˌbreɪk ɪŋ
grounder 'graʊnd ə ‖ -ᵊr **~s** z
groundhog 'graʊnd hɒg ‖ -hɑːg -hɔːg **~s** z
groundless 'graʊnd ləs -lɪs **~ly** li **~ness** nəs nɪs
groundling 'graʊnd lɪŋ **~s** z
groundnut 'graʊnd nʌt **~s** s
groundsel 'graʊnd sᵊl **~s** z
groundsheet 'graʊnd ʃiːt **~s** s

G

grounds|keeper 'graʊndz| ˌkiːp ə ‖ -ᵊr **~keepers** ˌkiːp əz ‖ -ᵊrz **~man** mən mæn **~men** mən men
groundswell 'graʊnd swel **~s** z
groundwater 'graʊnd ˌwɔːt ə ‖ -ˌwɔːţ ᵊr -ˌwɑːţᵊr
groundwork 'graʊnd wɜːk ‖ -wɜːk
group gruːp **grouped** gruːpt **grouping** 'gruːp ɪŋ **groups** gruːps
ˌ**group 'captain**◂; ˌ**group 'practice**; ˌ**group 'therapy**
grouper 'gruːp ə ‖ -ᵊr **~s** z
groupie 'gruːp i **~s** z
grouse graʊs **groused** graʊst **grouses** 'graʊs ɪz -əz **grousing** 'graʊs ɪŋ
grout graʊt **grouted** 'graʊt ɪd -əd ‖ 'graʊţ əd **grouting** 'graʊt ɪŋ ‖ 'graʊţ ɪŋ **grouts** graʊts
grove, Grove grəʊv ‖ groʊv **groves** grəʊvz ‖ groʊvz
grovel 'grɒv ᵊl 'grʌv- ‖ 'grʌv- 'grɑːv- **~ed, ~led** d **~ing, ~ling** ˌɪŋ **~s** z
Grover 'grəʊv ə ‖ 'groʊv ᵊr
Groves grəʊvz ‖ groʊvz
grow grəʊ ‖ groʊ **grew** gruː **growing** 'grəʊ ɪŋ ‖ 'groʊ ɪŋ **grown** grəʊn §'grəʊ ən ‖ groʊn **grows** grəʊz ‖ groʊz
'growing pains; **'growing ˌseason**
growbag 'grəʊ bæg ‖ 'groʊ- **~s** z
grower 'grəʊ ə ‖ 'groʊ ᵊr **~s** z
growl graʊl **growled** graʊld **growling** 'graʊl ɪŋ **growls** graʊlz
growler 'graʊl ə ‖ -ᵊr **~s** z
Growmore *tdmk* 'grəʊ mɔː ‖ 'groʊ mɔːr -moʊr
grown grəʊn §'grəʊ ən ‖ groʊn
grown-up *adj* ˌgrəʊn 'ʌp ◂ ‖ ˌgroʊn- ˌ**grown-up 'sons**
grown-up *n* 'grəʊn ʌp ˌ·'· ‖ 'groʊn- **~s** s
growth grəʊθ ‖ groʊθ **growths** grəʊθs ‖ groʊθs
'growth ˌhormone
groyne grɔɪn *(= groin)* **groynes** grɔɪnz
Grozny 'grɒz ni ‖ 'groʊz- —*Also, misguidedly,* 'grɒʒ- ‖ 'groʊʒ- —*Russ* ['grɔz nʲij]
grub grʌb **grubbed** grʌbd **grubbing** 'grʌb ɪŋ **grubs** grʌbz
grubber 'grʌb ə ‖ -ᵊr **~s** z
grubb|y 'grʌb |i **~ier** i‿ə ‖ i‿ᵊr **~iest** i‿ɪst i‿əst **~ily** ɪ li əl i **~iness** i nəs i nɪs
grubstak|e 'grʌb steɪk **~ed** t **~es** s **~ing** ɪŋ
grudge grʌdʒ **grudged** grʌdʒd **grudges** 'grʌdʒ ɪz -əz **grudging/ly** 'grʌdʒ ɪŋ /li
gruel 'gruː‿əl §gruːl **~ing, ~ling** ɪŋ
gruesome 'gruːs əm **~ly** li **~ness** nəs nɪs
gruff grʌf **gruffer** 'grʌf ə ‖ -ᵊr **gruffest** 'grʌf ɪst -əst **gruffly** 'grʌf li **gruffness** 'grʌf nəs -nɪs
Gruffydd 'grɪf ɪð —*Welsh* ['gri fið, 'grɨ fið]
Gruinard 'grɪn jəd ‖ -jᵊrd —*There is also a spelling pronunciation* 'gruː‿ɪ nɑːd ‖ -nɑːrd
grumbl|e 'grʌm bᵊl **~ed** d **~es** z **grumbling/ly** 'grʌm blɪŋ /li
grumbler 'grʌm blə ‖ -blᵊr **~s** z
grummet 'grʌm ɪt -ət **~s** s
grump grʌmp **grumps** grʌmps
grump|y 'grʌmp |i **~ier** i‿ə ‖ i‿ᵊr **~iest** i‿ɪst i‿əst **~ily** ɪ li əl i **~iness** i nəs i nɪs
Grundig *tdmk* 'grʌnd ɪg 'grʊnd-
Grundy 'grʌnd i
Grundyism 'grʌnd i ˌɪz əm
grunge grʌndʒ
grung|y 'grʌndʒ| i **~ier** i ə ‖ i ᵊr **~iest** i ɪst i əst
grunt grʌnt **grunted** 'grʌnt ɪd -əd ‖ 'grʌnţ əd **grunting** 'grʌnt ɪŋ ‖ 'grʌnţ ɪŋ **grunts** grʌnts
Grunwell 'grʌn wel
Gruyere, Gruyère 'gruː jeə -jə; gru 'jeə ‖ gru 'jeᵊr grɪ- —*Fr* [gʁy jɛːʁ]
gryphon 'grɪf ᵊn **~s** z
g-spot 'dʒiː spɒt ‖ -spɑːt **~s** s
Gstaad gə 'ʃtɑːd -'stɑːd —*Ger* [kʃtaːt]
G-string 'dʒiː strɪŋ **~s** z
GTI ˌdʒiː tiː 'aɪ **~s, ~'s** z
guacamole ˌgwɑːk ə 'məʊl i ‖ -'moʊl i —*Sp* [gwa ka 'mo le]
Guadalajara ˌgwɑːd ᵊl ə 'hɑːr ə —*Sp* [gwa ða la 'xa ɾa]
Guadalcanal ˌgwɑːd ᵊl kə 'næl —*Sp* [gwa ðal ka 'nal]
Guadalquivir ˌgwɑːd ᵊl kwɪ 'vɪə -'kwɪv ə ‖ -'kwɪv ᵊr -kiː 'vɪᵊr —*Sp* [gwa ðal ki 'βiɾ]
Guadeloupe ˌgwɑːd ə 'luːp -ᵊl 'uːp, '· · · —*Fr* [gwad lup]
guaiacol 'gwaɪ‿ə kɒl ‖ -koʊl -kɔːl, -kɑːl
guaiacum 'gwaɪ‿ək əm **~s** z
Guam gwɑːm
guanabana gwə 'nɑːb ən ə ˌgwɑːn ə 'bɑːn ə —*Sp* guanábana [gwa 'na βa na]
guanaco gwə 'nɑːk əʊ gwɑː- ‖ -oʊ **~s** z
Guangdong ˌgwæŋ 'dɒŋ ‖ ˌgwɑːŋ- —*Chi* Guǎngdōng [³kwaŋ ¹tʊŋ]
Guangxi ˌgwæŋ 'ʃiː —*Chi* Guǎngxī [³kwaŋ ¹ɕi]
Guangzhou ˌgwæŋ 'dʒəʊ ‖ ˌgwɑːŋ 'dʒoʊ —*Chi* Guǎngzhōu [³kwaŋ ¹ʈʂou]
guanidine 'gwɑːn ɪ diːn -ə-, -dɪn; §-ɪd ən, -əd-
guanine 'gwɑːn iːn 'guː‿ə niːn
guano 'gwɑːn əʊ ‖ -oʊ
guanosine 'gwɑːn əʊ siːn -ziːn, -sɪn, §-sᵊn ‖ -ə-
Guantanamo gwæn 'tæn ə məʊ gwɑːn-, -'tɑːn- ‖ gwɑːn 'tɑːn ə moʊ —*Sp* Guantánamo [gwan 'ta na mo]
guar 'guː ɑː gwɑː ‖ gwɑːr —*In India,* gwɑː(r)
Guarani, Guaraní, g~ ˌgwɑːr ə 'niː 'gwɑːr ən i —*Sp* [gwa ɾa 'ni] **~s** z
guarantee ˌgær ən 'tiː ◂ ‖ ˌger-, ˌgɑːr- **~d** d **~ing** ɪŋ **~s** z
guarantor ˌgær ən 'tɔː ‖ -'tɔːr ˌger-, ˌgɑːr- **~s** z
guar|anty 'gær |ən tiː -|ənt i ‖ 'ger-, 'gɑːr- **~anties** ən tiːz ənt iz
guard, Guard gɑːd ‖ gɑːrd **guarded** 'gɑːd ɪd -əd ‖ 'gɑːrd əd **guarding** 'gɑːd ɪŋ ‖ 'gɑːrd ɪŋ **guards** gɑːdz ‖ gɑːrdz
'guard's van
guarded 'gɑːd ɪd -əd ‖ 'gɑːrd əd **~ly** li **~ness** nəs nɪs

uard|house 'gɑːd |haʊs ‖ 'gɑːrd- **~houses** haʊz ɪz əz
uardian, G~ 'gɑːd i‿ən ‖ 'gɑːrd- **~s** z **~ship** ʃɪp
ˌguardian 'angel
uardrail 'gɑːd reɪᵊl ‖ 'gɑːrd- **~s** z
uardroom 'gɑːd ruːm -rʊm ‖ 'gɑːrd- **~s** z
uards|man 'gɑːdz |mən -mæn ‖ 'gɑːrdz- **~men** mən men
uatemal|a ˌgwɑːt ə 'mɑːl |ə ˌgwæt-, ˌgwʌt-, -ɪ- ‖ ˌgwɑːţ ə- **~an/s** ən/z
uava 'gwɑːv ə 'gwɔːv- **~s** z
uayaquil ˌgwaɪ‿ə 'kiːᵊl -'kɪl —*Sp* [gwa ja 'kil]
ubba 'gʌb ə
ubbins, g~ 'gʌb ɪnz §-ənz
ubernatorial ˌguːb ən‿ə 'tɔːr i‿əl ◂ ˌgjuːb- ‖ ˌguːb ᵊrn ə- -'toʊr-
ucci *tdmk* 'guːtʃ i
uck gʌk gʊk
udgeon 'gʌdʒ ən **~s** z
'gudgeon pin
udgin 'gʌdʒ ɪn -ən
udrun 'gʊdr uːn
ue gjuː
uelder-ros|e 'geld ə rəʊz ˌ·ˈ· ‖ -roʊz **~es** ɪz əz
Guelf, Guelph gwelf **Guelfs, Guelphs** gwelfs
uenon 'gwen ən -ɒn; gə 'nɒn, -'nɒ̃; 'giːn ən ‖ gə 'noʊn -'nɑːn **~s** z
guerdon 'gɜːd ᵊn ‖ 'gɜːd ᵊn **~s** z
guerilla gə 'rɪl ə ge- —*Normally* = gorilla. *The* ge- *pronunciation aims explicitly to avoid this homophony.* —*Sp* guerrilla [ge 'rri ʎa, -ja]
Guerin 'geər ɪn §-ən ‖ 'ger-
Guernica 'gɜːn ɪk ə 'gwɜːn-, gɜː 'niːk ə ‖ 'gwern- —*Sp* [ger 'ni ka]
Guernsey, g~ 'gɜːnz i ‖ 'gɜːnz i **~s** z
guerrilla gə 'rɪl ə ge-—*see* **guerilla**
guess ges **guessed** gest *(= guest)* **guesses** 'ges ɪz -əz **guessing** 'ges ɪŋ
guesser 'ges ə ‖ -ᵊr **~s** z
guessti|mate *v* 'gest ɪ |meɪt -ə- **~mated** meɪt ɪd -əd ‖ meɪţ əd **~mates** meɪts **~mating** meɪt ɪŋ ‖ meɪţ ɪŋ
guesstimate *n* 'gest ɪm ət -əm-, -ɪt, -eɪt **~s** s
guesswork 'ges wɜːk ‖ -wɜːk
guest, Guest gest **guested** 'gest ɪd -əd **guesting** 'gest ɪŋ **guests** gests
'guest ˌworker
guest|house 'gest |haʊs **~houses** haʊz ɪz -əz
guestroom 'gest ruːm -rʊm **~s** z
Guevara gə 'vɑːr ə gɪ-, ge- —*Sp* [ge 'βa ra]
guff gʌf
guffaw gʌ 'fɔː gə- ‖ -'fɑː; 'gʌf ɔː, -ɑː **~ed** d **guffawing** gʌ 'fɔːʳ ɪŋ gə- ‖ -'fɔː ɪŋ -'fɑː ɪŋ; 'gʌf ɔː ɪŋ, -ɑː- **~s** z
Guggenheim 'gʊg ən haɪm 'guːg-
GUI 'guː i
Guiana gi 'ɑːn ə gaɪ-, -'æn- ‖ -'æn ə -'ɑːn ə **~s** z -*This is appropriate for the name of the general region. Compare* **Guyana**, *formerly British Guiana.*

Guianese ˌgaɪ‿ə 'niːz ◂ ˌgiː‿ ‖ -'niːs
guid gɪd —*or, in Scots dialect pronunciation (perhaps simulated),* [gyd, gyd]
guidance 'gaɪd ᵊnᵗs
guide, Guide gaɪd **guided** 'gaɪd ɪd -əd **guides** gaɪdz **guiding** 'gaɪd ɪŋ
ˌguided 'missile
guidebook 'gaɪd bʊk →'gaɪb-, §-buːk **~s** s
guideline 'gaɪd laɪn **~s** z
guider, G~ 'gaɪd ə ‖ -ᵊr **~s** z
Guido 'gwiːd əʊ 'giːd- ‖ -oʊ —*It* ['gwiː do]
guidon 'gaɪd ᵊn **~s** z
guild gɪld *(= gild)* **guilds** gɪldz
Guildenstern 'gɪld ən stɜːn ‖ -stɜːn
guilder 'gɪld ə ‖ -ᵊr **~s** z
Guildford 'gɪl fəd ‖ -fᵊrd
guildhall, G~ 'gɪld hɔːl ◂ ˌ·ˈ· ‖ -hɔːl -hɑːl **~s** z
guile gaɪᵊl
guileful 'gaɪᵊl fᵊl -fʊl **~ly** i **~ness** nəs nɪs
guileless 'gaɪᵊl ləs -lɪs **~ly** li **~ness** nəs nɪs
Guilford 'gɪl fəd ‖ -fᵊrd
Guilin ˌgweɪ 'lɪn —*Chi* Guìlín [⁴kweɪ ²lɪn]
Guillain-Barré ˌgiː læn 'bær eɪ →-læm-, -jæn-, -lən-, -jən- ‖ gi ˌæ̃ bə 'reɪ -ˌæm- —*Fr* [gi lɛ̃ ba ʁe]
Guillaume 'giː əʊm ‖ giː 'joʊm —*Fr* [gi joːm]
guillemot 'gɪl ɪ mɒt -ə- ‖ -mɑːt **~s** s
guillotin|e 'gɪl ə tiːn 'giː-, -jə-, ˌ· ·ˈ· **~ed** d **~es** z **~ing** ɪŋ
guilt gɪlt
guiltless 'gɪlt ləs -lɪs **~ly** li **~ness** nəs nɪs
guilt-ridden 'gɪlt ˌrɪd ᵊn
guilt|y 'gɪlt |i **~ier** i‿ə ‖ i‿ᵊr **~iest** i‿ɪst i‿əst **~ily** ɪ li əl i **~iness** i nəs i nɪs
guinea, G~ 'gɪn i **~s** z
'guinea fowl; **'guinea pig**; **'guinea worm**
Guinea-Bissau ˌgɪn i bɪ 'saʊ
Guinean 'gɪn i‿ən **~s** z
Guinevere 'gwɪn ɪ vɪə 'gɪn-, -ə- ‖ -vɪr
Guinness 'gɪn ɪs -əs; gɪ 'nes **~es** ɪz əz
guipure gɪ 'pjʊə §gə- ‖ -'pjʊᵊr -'pʊᵊr
Guisborough 'gɪz bər‿ə ‖ -ˌbɜː oʊ
guise, Guise gaɪz *(= guys)* —*but the French name is* giːz **guises** 'gaɪz ɪz -əz
Guiseley 'gaɪz li
guitar gɪ 'tɑː gə- ‖ -'tɑːr **~s** z
guitarist gɪ 'tɑːr ɪst §-əst **~s** s
Guizhou ˌgweɪ 'dʒəʊ ‖ -'dʒoʊ —*Chi* Guìzhōu [⁴kweɪ ¹ţsou]
Gujarat, Gujerat ˌgʊdʒ ə 'rɑːt ˌguːdʒ- —*Hindi* [gʊdʒ raːţ]
Gujarati, Gujerati ˌgʊdʒ ə 'rɑːt i ◂ ˌguːdʒ- —*Hindi* [gʊdʒ raː ţi]
Gulag 'guːl æg -ɑːg ‖ -ɑːg
gular 'gjuːl ə 'guːl- ‖ -ᵊr
Gulbenkian gʊl 'beŋk i‿ən
gulch gʌltʃ **gulches** 'gʌltʃ ɪz -əz
gulden 'gʊld ən **~s** z
gules gjuːlz
gulf, Gulf gʌlf **gulfs** gʌlfs
'Gulf Stream
gull gʌl **gulled** gʌld **gulling** 'gʌl ɪŋ **gulls** gʌlz

Gullah 'gʌl ə **~s** z
Gullane *(i)* 'gɪl ən, *(ii)* 'gʌlən
gullet 'gʌl ɪt -ət **~s** s
Gullett 'gʌl ɪt -ət
gulley 'gʌl i **~s** z
gullibility ˌgʌl ə 'bɪl ət i ˌ·ɪ-, -ɪt i ‖ -əţ i
gullib|le 'gʌl əb |əl -ɪb- **~ly** li
Gulliford 'gʌl i fəd ‖ -fərd
Gullit 'hʊl ɪt 'huːl-, §-ət —*Dutch* ['xʏl ɪt]
Gulliver 'gʌl ɪv ə -əv- ‖ -ər
gull|y, Gully 'gʌl |i **~ies** iz
gulp gʌlp **gulped** gʌlpt **gulping** 'gʌlp ɪŋ **gulps** gʌlps
gum gʌm **gummed** gʌmd **gumming** 'gʌm ɪŋ **gums** gʌmz
ˌgum 'arabic; **'gum tree**
gumball 'gʌm bɔːl ‖ -bɑːl **~s** z
Gumbel 'gʌm bəl
gumbo, Gumbo 'gʌm bəʊ ‖ -boʊ **~s** z
gumboil 'gʌm bɔɪəl **~s** z
gumboot 'gʌm buːt **~s** s
Gumbs gʌmz
gumdrop 'gʌm drɒp ‖ -drɑːp **~s** s
gumma 'gʌm ə **~s** z
Gummer 'gʌm ə ‖ -ər
Gummidge 'gʌm ɪdʒ
gumm|y 'gʌm |i **~ier** i‿ə ‖ i‿ər **~ies** iz **~iest** i‿ɪst i‿əst
gumption 'gʌmp ʃən
gumshield 'gʌm ʃiːəld **~s** z
gumshoe 'gʌm ʃuː **~ing** ɪŋ **~s** z
gun gʌn **gunned** gʌnd **gunning** 'gʌn ɪŋ **guns** gʌnz
'gun ˌcarriage; **'gun ˌcotton**
gunboat 'gʌn bəʊt →'gʌm- ‖ -boʊt **~s** s
gundog 'gʌn dɒg ‖ -dɔːg -dɑːg **~s** z
gundy, Gundy 'gʌnd i
gunfight 'gʌn faɪt **~s** s
gunfighter 'gʌn ˌfaɪt ə ‖ -ˌfaɪţ ər **~s** z
gunfire 'gʌn ˌfaɪ‿ə ‖ -ˌfaɪ‿ər
Gunga Din ˌgʌŋ gə 'dɪn
gunge gʌndʒ
gung-ho ˌgʌŋ 'həʊ ◂ ‖ -'hoʊ
gungy 'gʌndʒ i
gunk gʌŋk
gun|man 'gʌn |mən →'gʌm-, -mæn **~men** mən men
gunmetal 'gʌn ˌmet əl →'gʌm- ‖ -ˌmeţ əl
Gunn gʌn
gunnel 'gʌn əl **~s** z
Gunnell 'gʌn əl
gunner 'gʌn ə ‖ -ər **~s** z
gunnera 'gʌn ər ə **~s** z
Gunnersbury 'gʌn əz bər‿i ‖ -ərz ˌber i
gunnery 'gʌn ər i
Gunnison 'gʌn ɪs ən
gunny 'gʌn i
gunnysack 'gʌn i sæk
gunpoint 'gʌn pɔɪnt →'gʌm-
gunpowder 'gʌn ˌpaʊd ə →'gʌm- ‖ ər
gunrunn|er 'gʌn ˌrʌn |ə ‖ -|ər **~ers** əz ‖ ərz **~ing** ɪŋ
gunship 'gʌn ʃɪp **~s** s
gunshot 'gʌn ʃɒt ‖ -ʃɑːt
gunshy 'gʌn ʃaɪ
gunslinger 'gʌn ˌslɪŋ ə ‖ -ər **~s** z
gunsmith 'gʌn smɪθ **~s** s
Gunter 'gʌnt ə ‖ -ər —*but as a German name,* 'gʊnt ə ‖ -ər —*Ger* Gunter ['gʊn tɐ], Günter ['gʏn tɐ]
Gunther 'gʌnᵗθ ə ‖ -ər —*but as a German name,* 'gʊnt ə ‖ -ər —*Ger* Gunther ['gʊn tɐ], Günther ['gʏn tɐ]
gun-toting 'gʌn ˌtəʊt ɪŋ ‖ -ˌtoʊţ-
gunwale 'gʌn əl **~s** z
gunyah 'gʌn jə **~s** z
guoyu ˌgwɔɪ 'uː -'juː —*Chi* guóyǔ [²kwɔ ³jy]
gupp|y, Guppy 'gʌp |i **~ies** iz
Gupta 'gʊpt ə 'gʌpt- —*Hindi* [gʊp t̪aː]
Gur gʊə ‖ gʊər
gurdwara gɜː 'dwɑːr ə gʊə-,'· · ·; ˌgʊr ə 'dwɑːr ə ‖ 'gɜːd- **~s** z
gurgl|e 'gɜːg əl ‖ 'gɜːg əl **~ed** d **~es** z **~ing** ˌɪŋ
Gurkha 'gɜːk ə 'gʊək- ‖ 'gɜːk ə **~s** z
Gurkhali ₍ₗ₎gɜː 'kɑːl i ₍ₗ₎gʊə- ‖ ₍ₗ₎gɜː-
Gurmukhi 'gʊə mʊk i ‖ 'gʊr-
gurnard 'gɜːn əd ‖ 'gɜːn ərd **~s** z
gurnet 'gɜːn ɪt §-ət ‖ 'gɜːn- **~s** s
Gurney, g~ 'gɜːn i ‖ 'gɜːn i **~'s, ~s** z
guru 'gʊr uː 'gʊər-; 'guː ruː ‖ 'guː ruː —*Hindi* [gʊ ruː] **~s** z
Gus gʌs
gush gʌʃ **gushed** gʌʃt **gushes** 'gʌʃ ɪz -əz **gushing/ly** 'gʌʃ ɪŋ /li
gusher 'gʌʃə ‖ -ər **~s** z
gush|y 'gʌʃ |i **~ier** i‿ə ‖ i‿ər **~iest** i‿ɪst i‿əst **~ily** ɪ li əl i **~iness** i nəs i nɪs
guss|et 'gʌs |ɪt §-ət ‖ -ət **~eted** ɪt ɪd §ət-, -əd ‖ əţ əd **~eting** ɪt ɪŋ §ət- ‖ əţ ɪŋ **~ets** ɪts §əts ‖ əts
Gussie, Gussy, gussy 'gʌs i **gussied** 'gʌs id
gust gʌst **gusted** 'gʌst ɪd -əd **gusting** 'gʌst ɪŋ **gusts** 'gʌsts
gustation gʌ 'steɪʃ ən
gustatory 'gʌst ət ər i gʌs 'teɪt ər i ‖ -ə tɔːr i -toʊr i
Gustav, Gustave 'gʊst ɑːv 'gʌst- ‖ 'gʌst-
Gustavus gʊ 'stɑːv əs gʌ-, gə-
gusto 'gʌst əʊ ‖ -oʊ
gust|y 'gʌst |i **~ier** i‿ə ‖ i‿ər **~iest** i‿ɪst i‿əst **~ily** ɪ li əl i **~iness** i nəs i nɪs
gut gʌt **guts** gʌts **gutted** 'gʌt ɪd -əd ‖ 'gʌţ əd **gutting** 'gʌt ɪŋ ‖ 'gʌţ ɪŋ
Gutenberg 'guːt ən bɜːg ‖ -bɜːg —*Ger* ['guː tən bɛʁk]
Guthrie 'gʌθ ri
gutless 'gʌt ləs -lɪs **~ly** li **~ness** nɪs nəs
Guto 'gɪt əʊ ‖ 'gɪţ oʊ —*Welsh* ['git o]
guts|y 'gʌts |i **~ier** i‿ə ‖ i‿ər **~iest** i‿ɪst i‿əst **~ily** ɪ li əl i **~iness** i nəs i nɪs
gutta 'gʌt ə 'gʊt- ‖ 'gʌţ ə 'gʊţ- **guttae** 'gʌt iː 'gʊt-
gutta-percha ˌgʌt ə 'pɜːtʃ ə ‖ ˌgʌţ ə 'pɜːtʃ ə
gutter 'gʌt ə ‖ 'gʌţ ər **~ed** d **guttering** 'gʌt‿ər ɪŋ ‖ 'gʌţ ər ɪŋ **~s** z
'gutter press, ˌ· · '·

gutteridge ˈgʌt ər ɪdʒ ‖ ˈgʌţ ər-
guttersnipe ˈgʌt ə snaɪp ‖ ˈgʌţ ᵊr- **~s** s
guttural ˈgʌt ər əl ‖ ˈgʌţ ər əl →ˈgʌtr əl **~ism** ˌɪz əm **~ly** i **~ness** nəs nɪs **~s** z
gutturality ˌgʌt ə ˈræl ət i -ɪt i ‖ ˌgʌţ ə ˈræl əţ i
guv, Guv gʌv
guvnor, guv'nor, G~ ˈgʌv nə ‖ -nᵊr **~s** z
guy, Guy gaɪ —*See also phrases with this word* **guyed** gaɪd **guying** ˈgaɪ ɪŋ **guys** gaɪz ˈ**guy line**; ˈ**guy rope**
Guyana gaɪ ˈæn ə -ˈɑːn-
Guyanese ˌgaɪ‿ə ˈniːz ◂
Guy Fawkes ˌgaɪ ˈfɔːks ◂ ˈ· · ‖ -ˈfɑːks ˌ**Guy ˈFawkes night,** ˈ· · ·
Guyler ˈgaɪl ə ‖ -ᵊr
guzzl|e ˈgʌz ᵊl **~ed** d **~es** z **~ing** ˌɪŋ
Gwalia ˈgwɑːl i‿ə
Gwalior ˈgwɑːl i ɔː ‖ -ɔːr —*Hindi* [gʊɑːl jər]
Gwatkin ˈgwɒt kɪn ‖ ˈgwɑːt-
Gwaun-cae-Gurwen ˌgwaɪn kə ˈgɜː wən →ˌgwaɪŋ- ‖ -ˈgɜː- —*Welsh* [gwain kai ˈgir wen]
Gwbert ˈgʊb ət ‖ ˈ-ᵊrt
gweilo ˌgweɪ ˈləʊ ‖ -ˈloʊ —*Cantonese* [^{2}kwɐj ^{2}low]
Gwen gwen
Gwenda ˈgwend ə
Gwendolin, Gwendoline, Gwendolyn ˈgwend ə lɪn -ᵊl ɪn, §-ən ‖ -ᵊl ɪn -ən
Gwendraeth ˈgwen draɪθ
Gwenllian ˈgwen ɬi‿ən -li‿ən ‖ -li‿ən —*Welsh* [ˈgwen ɬjan]
Gwent gwent
Gwilym ˈgwɪl ɪm
Gwydir, Gwydyr *(i)* ˈgwɪd ə -ɪə ‖ -ɪr, *(ii)* ˈgwaɪd-
Gwyn gwɪn
Gwynant ˈgwɪn ænt
Gwynedd ˈgwɪn əð -ɪð, -eð —*Welsh* [ˈgwi neð]
Gwyneth ˈgwɪn əθ -ɪθ, -eθ
Gwynfor ˈgwɪn və -vɔː ‖ -vᵊr -vɔːr —*Welsh* [ˈgwin vor]
gwyniad ˈgwɪn i æd **~s** z
Gwynn, Gwynne gwɪn
Gwynneth ˈgwɪn əθ -ɪθ, -eθ
Gwyther *(i)* ˈgwaɪð ə ‖ -ᵊr, *(ii)* ˈgwɪð ə ‖ -ᵊr
gybe dʒaɪb **gybed** dʒaɪbd **gybes** dʒaɪbz **gybing** ˈdʒaɪb ɪŋ
Gyle gaɪᵊl
Gyles dʒaɪᵊlz
gym dʒɪm **gyms** dʒɪmz ˈ**gym shoe**
gymkhana dʒɪm ˈkɑːn ə **~s** z
gymnasi|um *'hall for gymnastics'* dʒɪm ˈneɪz i‿|əm **~a** ə **~ums** əmz
gymnasium *'secondary school'* gɪm ˈnɑːz i‿əm -ʊm —*Ger* G~ [gym ˈnaː zjʊm] **~s** z
gymnast ˈdʒɪm næst ‖ -nəst **~s** s
gymnastic dʒɪm ˈnæst ɪk **~ally** ᵊl‿i **~s** s
gymnosophist dʒɪm ˈnɒs əf ɪst §-əst ‖ -ˈnɑːs- **~s** s
gymnosperm ˈdʒɪm nəʊ spɜːm ‖ -nə spɜ˞ːm **~s** z
gymslip ˈdʒɪm slɪp **~s** s
gynaec... —*see* **gynec...**
gyneciu|um, gynoeci|um gaɪ ˈniːs i‿|əm dʒaɪ- **~a** ə
gynecological ˌgaɪn ɪk ə ˈlɒdʒ ɪk ᵊl ◂ ˌ·ək- ‖ -ˈlɑːdʒ- ˌdʒaɪn- **~ly** ‿i
gynecologist ˌgaɪn ɪ ˈkɒl ədʒ ɪst ˌ·ə-, §-əst ‖ -ˈkɑːl- ˌdʒaɪn- **~s** s
gynecology ˌgaɪn ɪ ˈkɒl ədʒ i ˌ·ə- ‖ -ˈkɑːl- ˌdʒaɪn-
Gyngell ˈgɪndʒ ᵊl
-gynous *stress-imposing* dʒɪn əs dʒən əs — **androgynous** æn ˈdrɒdʒ ɪn əs -ən- ‖ -ˈdrɑːdʒ-
gyp dʒɪp **gypped** dʒɪpt **gypping** ˈdʒɪp ɪŋ **gyps** dʒɪps
gypsophila dʒɪp ˈsɒf ɪl ə -əl-, ⚠ˌdʒɪps ə ˈfɪl i‿ə ‖ -ˈsɑːf-
gypsum ˈdʒɪps əm
gyps|y, Gyps|y ˈdʒɪps |i **~ies** iz
gyr|ate *v* dʒaɪᵊ ˈr|eɪt dʒɪ-, dʒə-; ˈdʒaɪᵊr |eɪt ‖ ˈdʒaɪᵊr |eɪt **~ated** eɪt ɪd -əd ‖ eɪţ əd **~ates** eɪts **~ating** eɪt ɪŋ ‖ eɪţ ɪŋ
gyration dʒaɪᵊ ˈreɪʃ ᵊn dʒɪ-, dʒə- **~s** z
gyratory dʒaɪᵊ ˈreɪt ər i dʒə-; ˈdʒaɪᵊr ət‿ər i ‖ ˈdʒaɪᵊr ə tɔːr i -toʊr i
gyre ˈdʒaɪ‿ə ‖ ˈdʒaɪ‿ᵊr **gyred** ˈdʒaɪ‿əd ‖ ˈdʒaɪ ᵊrd **gyres** ˈdʒaɪ‿əz ‖ ˈdʒaɪ‿ᵊrz **gyring** ˈdʒaɪ‿ər ɪŋ ‖ ˈdʒaɪ‿ᵊr ɪŋ
gyrfalcon ˈdʒɜː ˌfɔːlk ən ˈdʒɪə-, -ˌfɔːk-, -ˌfælk- ‖ ˈdʒɜ˞ː ˌfælk ən -ˌfɔːlk-, -ˌfɑːlk- **~s** z
gyri ˈdʒaɪᵊr aɪ
gyro *'meat sandwich'* ˈʒɪər əʊ ˈgɪər- ‖ ˈdʒaɪᵊr oʊ **~s** z —*ModGk* [ˈji ɾo]
gyro *'gyroscope, gyrocompass'* ˈdʒaɪᵊr əʊ ‖ -oʊ **~s** z
gyro- *comb. form* *with stress-neutral suffix* ¦dʒaɪᵊr əʊ ‖ -ə — **gyrostatic** ˌdʒaɪᵊr əʊ ˈstæt ɪk ◂ ‖ -ə ˈstæţ ɪk ◂
gyrocompass ˈdʒaɪᵊr əʊ ˌkʌmp əs ‖ -oʊ- -ˌkɑːmp- **~es** ɪz əz
gyromagnetic ˌdʒaɪᵊr əʊ mæg ˈnet ɪk ◂ -məgˈ-- ‖ -oʊ mæg ˈneţ-
gyroscope ˈdʒaɪᵊr ə skəʊp ‖ -skoʊp **~s** s
gyroscopic ˌdʒaɪᵊr ə ˈskɒp ɪk ◂ ‖ -ˈskɑːp- **~ally** ᵊl‿i
gyr|us ˈdʒaɪᵊr |əs **~i** aɪ
Gytha ˈgɪθ ə
gyve dʒaɪv **gyved** dʒaɪvd **gyves** dʒaɪvz **gyving** ˈdʒaɪv ɪŋ

G

h Spelling-to-sound

1 Where the spelling is **h**, the pronunciation is regularly h as in **house** haʊs. The letter **h** may also form part of one of the digraphs **ch, gh, ph, rh, sh, th, wh** (see under **c, g, p, r, s, t, w** respectively).

2 **h** is silent in a number of cases:

- at the beginning of the exceptional words **heir** eə ‖ er, **honest** 'ɒn ɪst ‖ 'ɑːn əst, **hono(u)r** 'ɒn ə ‖ 'ɑːn ᵊr, **hour** aʊ ə ‖ 'aʊ ᵊr and their derivatives; also, in AmE only, in **herb** ɜːb
- at the end of a word after a vowel letter, as in **oh** əʊ ‖ oʊ, **hurrah** hə 'rɑː
- in most cases where it is at the beginning of a weak-vowelled syllable, as in the WEAK FORMs of **he, her, him, his, has, have**; in words such as **annihilate, vehicle**; and sometimes also in words such as **hotel, historic**.

3 The sound h is also occasionally written **wh** as in **who** huː.

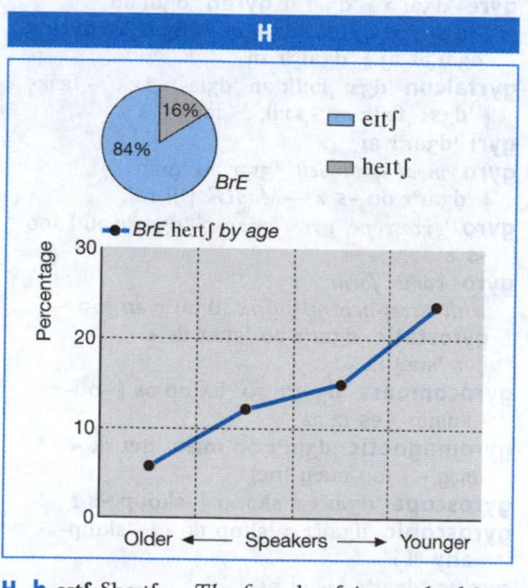

H, h eɪtʃ §heɪtʃ *—The form* heɪtʃ *is standard in Irish English, but traditionally not in BrE or AmE. It is, however, spreading in BrE. Preference poll, BrE:* eɪtʃ *84%,* heɪtʃ *16% (born since 1982, 24%).* **H's, h's** 'eɪtʃ ɪz §'heɪtʃ-, -əz *—Communications code name:* Hotel

H_2O ˌeɪtʃ tuː 'əʊ §ˌheɪtʃ- ‖ -'oʊ

ha *interjection* hɑː

ha *measure —see* **hectare**

Haagen-Dazs, Häagen-Dazs *tdmk* ˌhɑːg ən 'dɑːz -'dɑːs, '· · · ‖ 'hɑːg ən dæs

Haakon 'hɔːk ɒn 'hɑːk-, -ən ‖ -ɑːn 'hɑːk-, -ən *—Norwegian* [ˈˈhoː kɔn]

Haarlem 'hɑːl əm -em ‖ 'hɑːrl- *—Dutch* ['haːr lɛm]

Habakkuk 'hæb ək ək -ə kʌk; hə 'bæk-

habeas corpus ˌheɪb i ˌəs 'kɔːp əs -i æs- ‖ -'kɔːrp-

haberdasher 'hæb ə dæʃ ə ‖ -ᵊr dæʃ ᵊr **~s** z

haberdasher|y 'hæb ə dæʃ ər ˌ|i ‖ 'hæb ᵊr- **~ies** iz

Habgood 'hæb gʊd

Habibie hæ 'biːb i hə- ‖ hɑː-

habiliment hə 'bɪl ɪ mənt hæ-, -ə- **~s** s

habili|tate hə 'bɪl ɪ |teɪt hæ-, -ə- **~tated** teɪt ɪd -əd ‖ teɪṭ əd **~tates** teɪts **~tating** teɪt ɪŋ ‖ teɪṭ ɪŋ

habilitation hə ˌbɪl ɪ 'teɪʃ ᵊn hæ-, -ə-

habit 'hæb ɪt §-ət **~s** s

habitability ˌhæb ɪt ə 'bɪl ət i -ɪt i ‖ -əṭ ə 'bɪl əṭ i

habitab|le 'hæb ɪt əb |ᵊl -ət əb- ‖ -əṭ əb- **~ly** li

habitant *French settler or descendant* ˌæb i 'tɒ̃ ˌhæb- ‖ -'tɑːn **~s** z

habitat, H~ *tdmk* 'hæb ɪ tæt -ə- **~s** s

habitation ˌhæb ɪ 'teɪʃ ᵊn -ə- **~s** z

habit-forming 'hæb ɪt ˌfɔːm ɪŋ §-ət- ‖ -ˌfɔːrm-

habitual hə 'bɪtʃ u ˌəl hæ-, -'bɪt ju ˌ **~ly** i **~ness** nəs nɪs

habitu|ate hə ˈbɪtʃ u |eɪt hæ-, -ˈbɪt ju- **~ated** eɪt ɪd -əd ‖ eɪţ əd **~ates** eɪts **~ating** eɪt ɪŋ ‖ eɪţ ɪŋ
habituation hə ˌbɪtʃ u ˈeɪʃ ᵊn hæ-, -ˌbɪt ju-
habitue, habitué hə ˈbɪtʃ u eɪ ə-, hæ-, -ˈbɪt ju- ‖ ˌ·ˌ·ˈ· —*Fr* [a bi tɥe] **~s** z
Habsburg ˈhæps bɜːg ‖ -bɜːg —*Ger* [ˈhaːps bʊʁk] **~s** z
hacek, háček ˈhɑːtʃ ek **~s** s
hachure hæ ˈʃʊə -ˈʃjʊə ‖ -ˈʃʊᵊr **~s** z
hacienda ˌhæs i ˈend ə ‖ ˌhɑːs- ˌɑːs- —*AmSp* [a ˈsjen da] **~s** z
hack, Hack hæk **hacked** hækt **hacking** ˈhæk ɪŋ **hacks** hæks
ˌ**hacking** ˈ**cough**; ˈ**hacking** ˌ**jacket**
hackamore ˈhæk ə mɔː ‖ -mɔːr -moʊr **~s** z
hackberr|y ˈhæk bər‿i -ˌber |i ‖ -ˌber |i **~ies** iz
hacker, H~ ˈhæk ə ‖ -ᵊr **~s** z
Hackett ˈhæk ɪt §-ət
hackette ˌhæk ˈet **~s** s
hackle ˈhæk ᵊl **~s** z
Hackman ˈhæk mən
hackney, H~ ˈhæk ni **~ed** d **~ing** ɪŋ **~s** z
ˌ**hackney** ˈ**carriage,** ˌ·· ˈ··
hacksaw ˈhæk sɔː ‖ -sɑː **~s** z
hackwork ˈhæk wɜːk ‖ -wɜːk
had *strong form* hæd, *weak forms* həd, əd, d —*The contracted weak form* d *is used mainly after a vowel (and is often written* ˈd*); at the beginning of a sentence the usual weak form is* həd, *or in rapid speech* d.
Haddington ˈhæd ɪŋ tən
haddock ˈhæd ək **~s** s
Haddon ˈhæd ᵊn
hade heɪd **haded** ˈheɪd ɪd -əd **hades** heɪdz **hading** ˈheɪd ɪŋ
Hadeeth —*see* **Hadith**
Haden ˈheɪd ᵊn
Hades *'god of underworld'; 'hell'* ˈheɪd iːz
Hadfield ˈhæd fiːᵊld
Hadith hə ˈdiːθ hæ- ‖ hɑː- —*Arabic* [ˈħa ˈdiːθ]
hadj hædʒ hɑːdʒ
hadji ˈhædʒ i ˈhɑːdʒ-, -iː **~s** z
Hadlee, Hadley ˈhæd li
hadn't ˈhæd ᵊnt
Hadrian ˈheɪdr i‿ən **~'s** z
ˌ**Hadrian's** ˈ**Wall**
hadron ˈhædr ɒn ‖ -ɑːn **~s** z
hadrosaur ˈhædr əʊ sɔː ‖ -ə sɔːr **~s** z
hadst *strong form* hædst, *weak forms* hədst, ədst
hae heɪ
haecceity hek ˈsiː‿ət i hiːk-, haɪk-, -ɪt- ‖ -əţ i
haem hiːm
haematite ˈhiːm ə taɪt
haematologist ˌhiːm ə ˈtɒl ədʒ ɪst §-əst ‖ -ˈtɑːl- **~s** s
haematology ˌhiːm ə ˈtɒl ədʒ i ‖ -ˈtɑːl-
haematom|a ˌhiːm ə ˈtəʊm| ə ‖ -ˈtoʊm| ə **~as** əz **~ata** ət ə ‖ əţ ə
haemo- *comb. form*
with stress-neutral suffix ¦hiːm əʊ ‖ -oʊ — **haemodialysis** ˌhiːm əʊ daɪ ˈæl əs ɪs -ɪs ɪs, §-əs ‖ ˌ-oʊ-
with stress-imposing suffix hiː ˈmɒ+ hɪ- ‖ -ˈmɑː+ — **haemolysis** hiː ˈmɒl əs ɪs hɪ-, -ɪs-, §-əs ‖ -ˈmɑːl-
haemoglobin ˌhiːm ə ˈgləʊb ɪn §-ən, ˈ· · · · ‖ ˈhiːm ə gloʊb ən
haemophilia ˌhiːm ə ˈfɪl i‿ə -ˈfiːl-
haemophiliac ˌhiːm ə ˈfɪl i æk ◂ -ˈfiːl- **~s** s
haemorrhag|e ˈhem ər‿ɪdʒ **~ed** d **~es** ɪz əz **~ing** ɪŋ
haemorrhoid ˈhem ə rɔɪd **~s** z
haemorrhoidal ˌhem ə ˈrɔɪd ᵊl ◂
Haffner, Hafner ˈhæf nə ‖ -nᵊr
hafiz ˈhɑːf ɪz
hafnium ˈhæf ni‿əm
Hafod ˈhæv ɒd ‖ -ɑːd —*Welsh* [ˈha vod]
haft hɑːft §hæft ‖ hæft **hafted** ˈhɑːft ɪd §ˈhæft-, -əd ‖ ˈhæft əd **hafting** ˈhɑːft ɪŋ §ˈhæft- ‖ ˈhæft ɪŋ **hafts** hɑːfts §hæfts ‖ hæfts
hag hæg **hags** hægz
HAG, Hag *tdmk* hɑːg
Hagan ˈheɪg ən
Hagar ˈheɪg ɑː -ə ‖ -ɑːr -ᵊr
Hagerstown ˈheɪg əz taʊn ‖ ᵊrz-
hagfish ˈhæg fɪʃ
Haggai ˈhæg aɪ ˈhæg i aɪ, -eɪ-
haggard, H~ ˈhæg əd ‖ -ᵊrd **~ly** li **~ness** nəs nɪs
Haggerston ˈhæg əst ən ‖ -ᵊrst-
haggis ˈhæg ɪs §-əs **~es** ɪz əz
haggl|e ˈhæg ᵊl **~ed** d **~es** z **~ing** ‿ɪŋ
hagio- *comb. form*
with stress-neutral suffix ¦hæg i‿ə ¦heɪdʒ i‿ə — **hagioscope** ˈhæg i‿ə skəʊp ˈheɪdʒ- ‖ -skoʊp *with stress-imposing suffix* ˌhæg i ˈɒ+ ˌheɪdʒ- ‖ -ˈɑː+ — **hagiolatry** ˌhæg i ˈɒl ətr i ˌheɪdʒ- ‖ -ˈɑːl-
hagiograph|y ˌhæg i ˈɒg rəf |i ˌheɪdʒ- ‖ -ˈɑːg- **~ies** iz
Hagman ˈhæg mən
Hagrid ˈhæg rɪd
hag-ridden ˈhæg ˌrɪd ᵊn
Hague heɪg —*Dutch* Haag [haːx]
hah hɑː
ha-ha *interj* ₍ˌ₎hɑː ˈhɑː hʌ-
ha-ha *n* ˈhɑː hɑː **~s** z
Hahn hɑːn
hahnium ˈhɑːn i‿əm
Haida ˈhaɪd ə
Haifa ˈhaɪf ə
Haig heɪg
Haigh *placename* heɪ
Haigh *family name* heɪg
Haight *(i)* haɪt, *(ii)* heɪt
Haight-Ashbury ˌheɪt ˈæʃ bər‿i ‖ ˈ-ˌber i
Hai Karate *tdmk* ˌhaɪ kə ˈrɑːt i ‖ -ˈrɑːţ i
haiku ˈhaɪk uː —*Jp* [ha‿i kɯ] **~s** z

H

hail heɪᵊl **hailed** heɪᵊld **hailing** 'heɪᵊl ɪŋ **hails** heɪᵊlz
 ˌ**Hail 'Mary**
hailer 'heɪᵊl ə ‖ ᵊr **~s** z
Hailes 'heɪᵊlz
Haile Selassie ˌhaɪl i sə 'læs i -sɪ'--
Hailey 'heɪl i
Haileybury 'heɪl i bər‿i ‖ -ˌber i
hail-fellow-well-met ˌheɪᵊl ˌfel əʊ ˌwel 'met ‖ -oʊ- -ə-
Hailsham 'heɪᵊl ʃəm
hailstone 'heɪᵊl stəʊn ‖ -stoʊn **~s** z
hailstorm 'heɪᵊl stɔːm ‖ -stɔːrm **~s** z
Hailwood 'heɪᵊl wʊd
Hain heɪn
Hainan ˌhaɪ 'næn ‖ -'nɑːn —*Chi* Hǎinán [³hai ²nan]
Hainault 'heɪn ɔːt -ɔːlt, -ɒlt ‖ -ɔːlt -ɑːlt
Haines heɪnz
Haiphong ˌhaɪ 'fɒŋ ‖ -'fɔːŋ -'fɑːŋ —*Vietnamese* [⁴hai ³fɔŋ]
hair heə ‖ heᵊr hæᵊr **hairs** heəz ‖ heᵊrz hæᵊrz
 'hair's breadth; ˌ**hair 'shirt**; **'hair slide**; ˌ**hair 'trigger◂**
hairball 'heə bɔːl ‖ 'her- 'hær-, -bɑːl **~s** z
hairband 'heə bænd ‖ 'her- 'hær- **~s** z
hairbreadth 'heə bredθ -bretθ ‖ 'her- 'hær-
hairbrush 'heə brʌʃ ‖ 'her- 'hær- **~es** ɪz əz
haircare 'heə keə ‖ 'her ker 'hær kær
haircut 'heə kʌt ‖ 'her- 'hær- **~s** s
hairdo 'heə duː ‖ 'her- 'hær- **~s** z
hairdresser 'heə ˌdres ə ‖ 'her ˌdres ᵊr 'hær- **~s, ~'s** z
hairdressing 'heə ˌdres ɪŋ ‖ 'her- 'hær-
hairdryer 'heə ˌdraɪ‿ə ‖ 'her ˌdraɪ‿ᵊr **~s** z
-haired 'heəd ‖ heᵊrd hæᵊrd — **fair-haired** ˌfeə 'heəd ◂ ‖ 'fer heᵊrd 'fær hæᵊrd
hairgrip 'heə grɪp ‖ 'her- 'hær- **~s** s
hairi... —*see* **hairy**
hairless 'heə ləs -lɪs ‖ 'her- 'hær- **~ness** nəs nɪs
hairline 'heə laɪn ‖ 'her- 'hær- **~s** z
hairnet 'heə net ‖ 'her- 'hær- **~s** s
hairpiec|e 'heə piːs ‖ 'her- 'hær- **~es** ɪz əz
hairpin 'heə pɪn ‖ 'her- 'hær- **~s** z
 ˌ**hairpin 'bend**
hair-raising 'heə ˌreɪz ɪŋ ‖ 'her- 'hær-
hair-restorer 'heə ri ˌstɔːr ə -rə- ‖ 'her rɪ ˌstɔːr ᵊr 'hær-, -ˌstoʊr- **~s** z
hair-splitting 'heə ˌsplɪt ɪŋ ‖ 'her ˌsplɪṭ ɪŋ 'hær-
hairspray 'heə spreɪ ‖ 'her- 'hær-
hairspring 'heə sprɪŋ ‖ 'her- 'hær- **~s** z
hairstreak 'heə striːk ‖ 'her- 'hær- **~s** s
hairstyle 'heə staɪᵊl ‖ 'her- 'hær- **~s** z
hairstylist 'heə ˌstaɪᵊl ɪst §-əst ‖ 'her- 'hær- **~s** s
hair|y 'heər |i ‖ 'her |i 'hær- **~ier** i‿ə ‖ i‿ᵊr **~iest** i‿ɪst i‿əst **~iness** i nəs i nɪs
Haiti 'heɪt i 'haɪt-; haɪ 'iːt i, hɑː- ‖ 'heɪṭ i
Haitian 'heɪʃ ᵊn 'haɪʃ-, '·i‿ən; 'heɪt i‿ən; haɪ 'iːʃ ᵊn, hɑː-, -'iːʃ i‿ən **~s** z
Haitink 'haɪt ɪŋk —*Dutch* ['haːi tɪŋk]
haj, hajj hædʒ hɑːdʒ
haji, hajji 'hædʒ i 'hɑːdʒ-, -iː **~s** z
haka 'hɑːk ə **~s** z
hake heɪk **hakes** heɪks
hakim *'judge, ruler'* 'hɑːk ɪm hɑː 'kiːm **~s** z
hakim *'physician'* hə 'kiːm hæ-, hɑː- **~s** z
Hakka 'hæk ə
Hakluyt 'hæk luːt 'hæk ᵊl wɪt
Hal hæl
halal hə 'lɑːl 'hæl æl, hæ 'læl —*Arabic* [ħa 'laːl]
halation hə 'leɪʃ ᵊn **~s** z
halberd 'hæl bəd 'hɔːl-, -bɜːd ‖ -bᵊrd **~s** z
halberdier ˌhæl bə 'dɪə ˌhɔːl- ‖ -bᵊr 'dɪᵊr **~s** z
halcyon 'hæls i‿ən **~s** z
 ˌ**halcyon 'days**
Halcyone hæl 'saɪ‿ən i
Haldane 'hɔːld eɪn 'hɒld- ‖ 'hɑːld-
hale, Hale heɪᵊl *(= hail)* **haler** 'heɪᵊl ə ‖ -ᵊr
 halest 'heɪᵊl ɪst -əst
Haleakala ˌhɑːl i ɑːk ə 'lɑː
haleness 'heɪᵊl nəs -nɪs
Hales heɪᵊlz
Halesowen ₍ˌ₎heɪᵊlz 'əʊ ɪn -ən ‖ -'oʊ-
Halesworth 'heɪᵊlz wɜːθ ‖ -wᵊrθ
Halewood ˌheɪᵊl 'wʊd ◂
Halex *tdmk* 'heɪl eks
Haley 'heɪl i
half hɑːf §hæf ‖ hæf —*See also phrases with this word* **halves** hɑːvz §hævz ‖ hævz
 ˌ**half a 'crown**; ˌ**half 'board**; ˌ**half 'cock**; ˌ**half 'crown**; ˌ**half 'moon**; **'half note**; ˌ**half 'term**; ˌ**half 'volley**
half- ¦hɑːf §¦hæf ‖ ¦hæf
half-a-dozen ˌhɑːf ə 'dʌz ᵊn ◂ §ˌhæf- ‖ ˌhæf-
half-and-half ˌhɑːf ᵊn 'hɑːf ◂ §ˌhæf ᵊn 'hæf ◂ ‖ ˌhæf ᵊn 'hæf ◂
half-arsed ˌhɑːf 'ɑːst ◂ §ˌhæf- ‖ ˌhæf 'ɑːrst ◂ —*See the next entry*
half-assed ˌhɑːf 'ɑːst ◂ §ˌhæf-, -'æst ‖ ˌhæf 'æst ◂
halfback 'hɑːf bæk §'hæf- ‖ 'hæf- **~s** s
half-baked ˌhɑːf 'beɪkt ◂ §ˌhæf- ‖ ˌhæf-
half-breed 'hɑːf briːd §'hæf- ‖ 'hæf- **~s** z
half-brother 'hɑːf ˌbrʌð ə §'hæf- ‖ 'hæf ˌbrʌð ᵊr **~s** z
half-caste 'hɑːf kɑːst §'hæf-, §-kæst ‖ 'hæf kæst **~s** s
half-close ˌhɑːf 'kləʊs ◂ §ˌhæf- ‖ ˌhæf 'kloʊs
half-cocked ˌhɑːf 'kɒkt ◂ §ˌhæf- ‖ ˌhæf 'kɑːkt ◂
half-crazed ˌhɑːf 'kreɪzd ◂ §ˌhæf- ‖ ˌhæf-
half-cup ˌhɑːf 'kʌp §ˌhæf- ‖ ˌhæf- **~s** s
half-cut ˌhɑːf 'kʌt ◂ §ˌhæf- ‖ ˌhæf-
half-day *adj* ˌhɑːf 'deɪ ◂ §ˌhæf- ‖ ˌhæf-
 ˌ**half-day 'closure**
half-day *n* 'hɑːf deɪ §'hæf- ‖ 'hæf- **~s** z
half-gallon ˌhɑːf 'gæl ən ◂ §ˌhæf- ‖ ˌhæf- **~s** z
half-hardy ˌhɑːf 'hɑːd i ◂ §ˌhæf- ‖ ˌhæf 'hɑːrd i ◂
half-hearted ˌhɑːf 'hɑːt ɪd ◂ §ˌhæf-, -əd ‖ ˌhæf 'hɑːrṭ əd ◂ **~ly** li **~ness** nəs nɪs

alf-holiday ˌhɑːf ˈhɒl ə deɪ §ˌhæf-, -ɪ-, ˌdi ‖ ˌhæf ˈhɑːl- **~s** z
alf-hour ˌhɑːf ˈaʊ‿ə ◂ §ˌhæf- ‖ ˌhæf ˈaʊ‿ᵊr ◂ **~ly** li **~s** z
alf-inch ˌhɑːf ˈɪntʃ §ˌhæf- ‖ ˌhæf- **~ed** t **~es** ɪz əz **~ing** ɪŋ
alf-length ˌhɑːf ˈleŋkθ ◂ §ˌhæf-, §-ˈlentθ ‖ ˌhæf-
alf-|life ˈhɑːf |laɪf §ˈhæf- ‖ ˈhæf- **~lives** laɪvz
alf-light ˈhɑːf laɪt §ˈhæf- ‖ ˈhæf-
alf-marathon ˌhɑːf ˈmær əθ ən §ˌhæf-, -ə θɒn ‖ ˌhæf ˈmær ə θɑːn -ˈmer- **~s** z
alf-mast ˌhɑːf ˈmɑːst §ˌhæf-, §-ˈmæst ‖ ˌhæf ˈmæst
alf-measures ˈhɑːf ˌmeʒ əz §ˈhæf-, ˌ·ˈ·· ‖ ˈhæf ˌmeʒ ᵊrz -ˌmeɪʒ-
alf-mile ˌhɑːf ˈmaɪᵊl ◂ §ˌhæf- ‖ ˌhæf-
alf-nelson ˌhɑːf ˈnels ᵊn §ˌhæf- ‖ ˌhæf- ˈ·ˌ·· **~s** z
alf-open ˌhɑːf ˈəʊp ən ◂ §ˌhæf- ‖ ˌhæf ˈoʊp ən
alford ˈhæl fəd ˈhɔːl-, ˈhɒl- ‖ -fᵊrd **~'s** z
alf past *in expressions of time* ˌhɑːf ˈpɑːst ◂ ˌhɑː-, ˌhʌ-, §ˌhæf-, §-ˈpæst ‖ ˌhæf ˈpæst ◂
ˌhalf past ˈten
alfpence ˈheɪp ənˈs →mᵖs
alfpenn|y *n* ˈheɪp n|i ˈheɪp ən |i —*For the British coin in use 1971-85, also* ˌhɑːf ˈpen |i ◂, §ˌhæf- ‖ ˌhæf- **~ies** iz
alfpenny *surname* ˈhɑːf pən i §ˈhæf- ‖ ˈhæf-
alfpennyworth ˈheɪp ni wɜːθ -wəθ; ˈheɪp əθ; ˌhɑːf ˈpen əθ, §ˌhæf- ‖ ˈheɪp ən i wɜːθ —*See* **hap'orth**
alf-pound ˌhɑːf ˈpaʊnd ◂ §ˌhæf- ‖ ˌhæf-
alf-price ˌhɑːf ˈpraɪs ◂ §ˌhæf- ‖ ˌhæf-
alf-sister ˈhɑːf ˌsɪst ə §ˈhæf- ‖ ˈhæf ˌsɪst ᵊr **~s** z
alf-size ˌhɑːf ˈsaɪz ◂ §ˌhæf- ‖ ˌhæf-
alf-timbered ˌhɑːf ˈtɪm bəd ◂ §ˌhæf- ‖ ˌhæf ˈtɪm bᵊrd ◂
alf time ˌhɑːf ˈtaɪm ◂ §ˌhæf- ‖ ˈhæf taɪm
ˌhalf-time ˈscore
alftone ˌhɑːf ˈtəʊn §ˌhæf-, ˈ·· ‖ ˈhæf toʊn **~s** z
alf-track *adj* ˌhɑːf ˈtræk ◂ §ˌhæf- ‖ ˌhæf-
half-track *n* ˈhɑːf træk §ˈhæf- ‖ ˈhæf- **~ed** t **~s** s
alf-|truth ˈhɑːf |truːθ §ˈhæf-, ˌ·ˈ· ‖ ˈhæf- **~truths** truːðz truːθs
halfway ˌhɑːf ˈweɪ ◂ §ˌhæf- ‖ ˌhæf-
ˌhalfway ˈhouse
half-wit ˈhɑːf wɪt §ˈhæf- ‖ ˈhæf- **~s** s
half-witted ˌhɑːf ˈwɪt ɪd ◂ §ˌhæf-, -əd ‖ ˌhæf ˈwɪţ əd ◂ **~ly** li **~ness** nəs nɪs
half-yearly ˌhɑːf ˈjɪə li ◂ §ˌhæf- ‖ ˌhæf ˈjɪr li
halibut ˈhæl ɪb ət -əb- **~s** s
Halicarnassus ˌhæl ɪ kɑː ˈnæs əs ˌ·ə- ‖ -kɑːr ˈ-
halide ˈheɪl aɪd ˈhæl- **~s** z
Halifax ˈhæl ɪ fæks -ə-
halitosis ˌhæl ɪ ˈtəʊs ɪs -ə-, §-əs ‖ -ˈtoʊs-
hall, Hall hɔːl ‖ hɑːl *(= haul)* **halls** hɔːlz ‖ hɑːlz
ˌhall of ˈresidence; **ˌhall ˈporter**

hallal hə ˈlɑːl ˈhæl æl, hæˈlæl —*Arabic* [ħa ˈlaːl]
Hallam ˈhæl əm
Halle, Hallé ˈhæl eɪ -i ‖ ˈhɑːl ə
halleluja, hallelujah ˌhæl ɪ ˈluː jə -ə- **~s** z
Halley *(i)* ˈhæl i; *(ii)* ˈhɔːl i ‖ ˈhɑːl i —*The astronomer andthe comet named after him are usually (i) in educated speech, although some claim that only (ii) is correct. In AmE there is also a popular pronunciation* ˈheɪl i
halliard ˈhæl jəd ‖ -jᵊrd **~s** z
Halliday ˈhæl ɪ deɪ -ə-
Halliwell ˈhæl ɪ wel
hallmark ˈhɔːl mɑːk ‖ -mɑːrk ˈhɑːl- **~ed** t **~ing** ɪŋ **~s** s
hallo hə ˈləʊ ₍ₗ₎hæ-, ₍ₗ₎he-, ₍ₗ₎hʌ- ‖ -ˈloʊ **~es** z
halloo hə ˈluː **~ed** d **~ing** ɪŋ **~s** z
Halloran ˈhæl ər ən
hallow ˈhæl əʊ ‖ -oʊ **~ed** d —*but in the Lord's Prayer also sometimes* ed, ɪd, əd **~ing** ɪŋ **~s** z
Hallowe'en ˌhæl əʊ ˈiːn ◂ ‖ -oʊ- ˌhɑːl-
Hallowes, Hallows ˈhæl əʊz ‖ -oʊz
hallstand ˈhɔːl stænd ‖ ˈhɑːl- **~s** z
halluci|nate hə ˈluːs ɪ |neɪt -ˈljuːs-, -ə- **~nated** neɪt ɪd -əd ‖ neɪţ əd **~nates** neɪts **~nating** neɪt ɪŋ ‖ neɪţ ɪŋ
hallucination hə ˌluːs ɪ ˈneɪʃ ᵊn -ˌljuːs-, -ə- **~s** z
hallucinatory hə ˈluːs ɪn ət‿ər i -ˈljuːs-, -ˈᵊn‿; ·ˌ·ɪ ˈneɪt ər i ◂, ·ˌ·ə-, ·ˈ·· · · · ‖ -ᵊn‿ə tɔːr i -toʊr i
hallucinogen ˌhæl uː ˈsɪn ədʒ ən -ə dʒen; hə ˈluːs ɪn-, -ˈᵊn- **~s** z
hallucinogenic hə ˌluːs ɪn ə ˈdʒen ɪk ◂ -ˌljuːs-, -ˌᵊn‿
hallux ˈhæl əks **~es** ɪz əz
hallway ˈhɔːl weɪ ‖ ˈhɑːl- **~s** z
halma ˈhælm ə
Halmahera ˌhælm ə ˈhɪər ə -ˈhɜːr- ‖ -ˈhɝː ə ˌhɑːlm ə-
halo ˈheɪl əʊ ‖ -oʊ **~ed** d **~es, ~s** z **~ing** ɪŋ
halo- *comb. form*
with stress-neutral suffix |hæl əʊ ‖ -ə —
halophyte ˈhæl əʊ faɪt ‖ -ə-
with stress-imposing suffix hæ ˈlɒ+ ‖ -ˈlɑː+ — **halogenous** hæ ˈlɒdʒ ən əs ‖ -ˈlɑːdʒ-
halogen ˈhæl ə dʒen ˈheɪl-, -ədʒ ən **~s** z
halon ˈheɪl ɒn ‖ -ɑːn **~s** z
haloperidol ˌhæl əʊ ˈper ɪ dɒl ˌheɪl-, -ə- ‖ ˌhæl oʊ ˈper ə dɔːl -dɑːl, -doʊl
halophyte ˈhæl ə faɪt ˈheɪl- **~s** s
halothane ˈhæl əʊ θeɪn ˈheɪl- ‖ -ə-
Halpern ˈhælp ən ‖ -ᵊrn
Hals hæls hælz ‖ hɑːls hɑːlz —*Dutch* [hɑls]
Halsbury ˈhɔːlz bər‿i ˈhɒlz- ‖ ˈhɔːlz ˌber i ˈhɑːlz-
Halse hæls hɔːls, hɒls ‖ hɑːls, hɔːls
Halstead, Halsted *(i)* ˈhæl sted -stɪd, *(ii)* ˈhɔːl- ˈhɒl- ‖ ˈhɑːl-
halt hɔːlt hɒlt ‖ hɑːlt **halted** ˈhɔːlt ɪd ˈhɒlt-, -əd ‖ ˈhɑːlt- **halting/ly** ˈhɔːlt ɪŋ /li ˈhɒlt- ‖ ˈhɑːlt- **halts** hɔːlts hɒlts ‖ hɑːlts — *Preference poll, BrE:* hɒlt *52%,* hɔːlt *48%. See chart on p. 364.*
Haltemprice ˈhɔːlt əm praɪs ˈhɒlt- ‖ ˈhɑːlt-

H

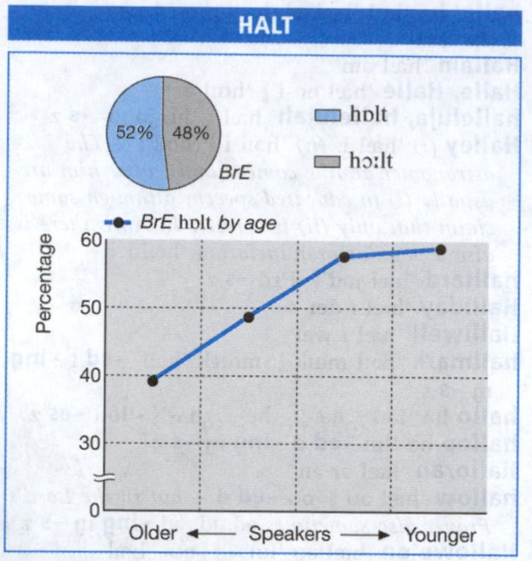

halter ˈhɔːlt ə ˈhɒlt- ‖ -ᵊr ˈhɑːlt- **~s** z
haltere ˈhælt ɪə ˈhɔːlt-, ˈhɒlt- ‖ -ɪr ˈhɔːlt-, ˈhɑːlt- **~s** z
halterneck ˈhɔːlt ə nek ˈhɒlt- ‖ -ᵊr- ˈhɑːlt- **~s** s
Halton ˈhɔːlt ən ˈhɒlt- ‖ ˈhɑːlt-
halva, halvah ˈhælv ə -ɑː ‖ hɑːl ˈvɑː .
halve hɑːv ‖ hæv **halved** hɑːvd ‖ hævd **halves** hɑːvz ‖ hævz **halving** ˈhɑːv ɪŋ ‖ ˈhæv ɪŋ
halves *from* **half, halve** hɑːvz ‖ hævz
halyard ˈhæl jəd ‖ -jᵊrd **~s** z
ham, Ham hæm **hammed** hæmd **hamming** ˈhæm ɪŋ **hams** hæmz
hamadryad ˌhæm ə ˈdraɪ‿əd -æd **~s** z
hamadryas ˌhæm ə ˈdraɪ‿əs -æs **~es** ɪz əz
Haman ˈheɪm ən -æn
Hamas ˈhæm æs hə ˈmæs, hæ-, -ˈmɑːs —*Arabic* [ħa ˈmaːs]
Hamble ˈhæm bᵊl
Hambledon ˈhæm bᵊl dən
Hambletonian ˌhæm bᵊl ˈtəʊn i‿ən ‖ -ˈtoʊn- **~s** z
Hambro ˈhæm brəʊ -brə ‖ -broʊ ˈhɑːm-
Hamburg ˈhæm bɜːg ‖ -bɜːg —*Ger* [ˈham bʊʁk, -bʊʁç]
hamburger, H~ ˈhæm ˌbɜːg ə ‖ -ˌbɜːg ᵊr **~s** z
Hamelin ˈhæm lɪn ˈhæm əl ɪn, -ɪl- —*Ger* Hameln [ˈhaː mᵊln]
Hamersley ˈhæm əz li ‖ -ᵊrz-
ham-fisted ˌhæm ˈfɪst ɪd ◂ -əd **~ly** li **~ness** nəs nɪs
ham-handed ˌhæm ˈhænd ɪd ◂ -əd **~ly** li **~ness** nəs nɪs
Hamilcar hæ ˈmɪl kɑː hə-; ˈhæm ᵊl-, -ɪl- ‖ -kɑːr
Hamill ˈhæm ᵊl -ɪl
Hamilton ˈhæm ᵊl tən -ɪl-
Hamiltonian ˌhæm ᵊl ˈtəʊn i‿ən ◂ ˌ-ɪl- ‖ ˈtoʊn- **~s** z
Hamish ˈheɪm ɪʃ
Hamite ˈhæm aɪt **~s** s
Hamitic hæ ˈmɪt ɪk hə- ‖ -ˈmɪt̬ ɪk
Hamito-Semitic ˌhæm ɪ təʊ sə ˈmɪt ɪk ◂ ˌ-ə-, -sɪˈ-- ‖ ˌhæm ə toʊ sə ˈmɪt̬ ɪk ◂

hamlet, H~ ˈhæm lət -lɪt **~s** s
Hamley ˈhæm li
Hamlin, Hamlyn ˈhæm lɪn §-lən
Hammarskjold ˈhæm ə ʃəʊld →-ʃɒʊld ‖ -ᵊr ʃoʊld ˈhɑːm- —*Swedish* Hamarskjöld [ˈˈha mar ɧœld]
hammer, H~ ˈhæm ə ‖ -ᵊr **~ed** d **hammering** ˈhæm ər‿ɪŋ **~s** z
ˈhammer drill
hammerbeam ˈhæm ə biːm ‖ -ᵊr- **~s** z
Hammerfest ˈhæm ə fest ‖ -ᵊr- ˈhɑːm- —*Norw* [ˈˈham ər fɛst]
hammerhead ˈhæm ə hed ‖ -ᵊr- **~s** z
Hammersley ˈhæm əz li ‖ -ᵊrz-
Hammersmith ˈhæm ə smɪθ ‖ -ᵊr-
Hammerstein *(i)* ˈhæm ə staɪn ‖ -ᵊr-, *(ii)* -stiːn
Hammett ˈhæm ɪt §-ət
hammock ˈhæm ək **~s** s
Hammond ˈhæm ənd
Hammurabi ˌhæm u ˈrɑːb i
hammy ˈhæm i
Hampden ˈhæm dən ˈhæmp-
hamper ˈhæmp ə ‖ -ᵊr **~ed** d **hampering** ˈhæmp ər‿ɪŋ **~s** z
Hampshire ˈhæmp ʃə -ʃɪə ‖ -ʃᵊr -ʃɪr
Hampstead ˈhæmp stɪd -sted, §-stəd
ˌHampstead ˈHeath
Hampton ˈhæmp tən
ˌHampton ˈCourt
hamster ˈhæmᵖst ə ‖ ᵊr **~s** z
hamstring ˈhæm strɪŋ **~ing** ɪŋ **~s** z
hamstrung ˈhæm strʌŋ
Hamtramck hæm ˈtræm ɪk *(!)*
hamza, hamzah ˈhæmz ə **~s** z
Han hæn ‖ hɑːn —*Chi* hàn [⁴xan]
Hanbury ˈhæn bər‿i →ˈhæm-
Hancock ˈhæn kɒk →ˈhæŋ- ‖ -kɑːk
hand hænd **handed** ˈhænd ɪd -əd **handing** ˈhænd ɪŋ **hands** hændz
ˈhand ˌbaggage; **ˈhand greˌnade**; **ˈhand ˌluggage**; **ˌhands ˈoff**; **ˌhands ˈup**; **ˈhand ˌtowel**
handbag ˈhænd bæg →ˈhæm- **~s** z
handball ˈhænd bɔːl →ˈhæm- ‖ -bɑːl **~s** z
handbarrow ˈhænd ˌbær əʊ →ˈhæm- ‖ -oʊ -ˌber- **~s** z
handbasin ˈhænd ˌbeɪs ᵊn →ˈhæm- **~s** z
handbasket ˈhænd ˌbɑːsk ɪt →ˈhæm-, §-ˌbæsk-, -ət ‖ -ˌbæsk- **~s** s
handbell ˈhænd bel →ˈhæm- **~s** z
handbill ˈhænd bɪl →ˈhæm- **~s** z
handbook ˈhænd bʊk →ˈhæm-, §-buːk **~s** s
handbrake ˈhænd breɪk →ˈhæm- **~s** s
handcar ˈhænd kɑː ‖ -kɑːr **~s** z
handcart ˈhænd kɑːt →ˈhæŋ- ‖ -kɑːrt **~s** s
handclap ˈhænd klæp →ˈhæŋ- **~s** s
hand-crafted ˌhænd ˈkrɑːft ɪd ◂ §-ˈkræft-, -əd ‖ -ˈkræft-
handcuff ˈhænd kʌf →ˈhæŋ- **~ed** t **~ing** ɪŋ **~s** s
-handed ˈhænd ɪd ◂ -əd
handedness ˈhænd ɪd nəs -əd-, -nɪs
Handel ˈhænd ᵊl —*Ger* Händel [ˈhɛn dᵊl]

andelian hæn ˈdiːl i‿ən **~s** z
and-eye ˌhænd ˈaɪ
ˌhand-ˌeye coordiˈnation
andful ˈhænd fʊl **~s** z
andgun ˈhænd gʌn →ˈhæŋ- **~s** z
and-held ˈhænd held **~s** z
andhold ˈhænd həʊld →-hɒʊld ‖ -hoʊld **~s** z
andicap ˈhænd i kæp **~ped** t **~per/s** ə/z ‖ ᵊr/z **~ping** ɪŋ **~s** s
andicraft ˈhænd i krɑːft §-kræft ‖ -kræft **~s** s
andie... *—see* **handy**
andily ˈhænd ɪ li -əl i
andiwork ˈhænd i wɜːk ‖ -wɜ˞ːk

HANDKERCHIEF

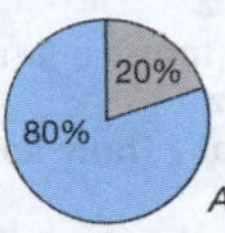

andker|chief ˈhæŋk ə |tʃɪf -tʃəf, -tʃiːf ‖ -ᵊr- — *Preference poll, AmE:* -tʃɪf *80%,* -tʃiːf *20%.* **~chiefs** tʃɪfs tʃəfs, tʃiːfs, tʃiːvz **~chieves** tʃiːvz
andle ˈhænd ᵊl **~d** d **~s** z **handling** ˈhænd lɪŋ ˈhænd ᵊl‿ɪŋ
andlebar ˈhænd ᵊl bɑː ‖ -bɑːr **~s** z
andler ˈhænd lə ˈhænd ᵊl‿ə ‖ -lᵊr -ᵊl‿ər **~s** z
and-lettered ˌhænd ˈlet əd ◂ ‖ -ˈleţ ᵊrd ◂
Handley ˈhænd li
handloom ˈhænd luːm **~s** z
handmade ˌhænd ˈmeɪd ◂ →ˌhæm-
handmaid ˈhænd meɪd →ˈhæm- **~s** z
handmaiden ˈhænd ˌmeɪd ᵊn →ˈhæm- **~s** z
hand-me-down ˈhænd mi daʊn →ˈhæm- **~s** z
handout ˈhænd aʊt **~s** s
handover ˈhænd ˌəʊv ə ‖ -ˌoʊv ᵊr **~s** z
handpick *v* ˌhænd ˈpɪk ◂ →ˌhæm- **~ed** t **~ing** ɪŋ **~s** s
handplant ˈhænd plɑːnt §-plænt ‖ -plænt **~s** s
handrail ˈhænd reɪᵊl **~s** z
handsaw ˈhænd sɔː ‖ -sɑː **~s** z
handset ˈhænd set **~s** s
hands-free ˌhændz ˈfriː ◂ˈ. .
handshak|e ˈhænd ʃeɪk **~es** s **~ing** ɪŋ
hands-off ˌhændz ˈɒf ◂ -ˈɔːf ◂ ‖ -ˈɔːf ◂ -ˈɑːf ◂
handsome ˈhænᵗs əm **~ly** li **~ness** nəs nɪs
hands-on ˌhændz ˈɒn ◂ ‖ -ˈɑːn ◂ -ˈɔːn ◂
handspring ˈhænd sprɪŋ **~s** z
handstand ˈhænd stænd **~s** z
hand-to-hand ˌhænd tə ˈhænd ◂
hand-to-mouth ˌhænd tə ˈmaʊθ ◂
handwash ˈhænd wɒʃ ‖ -wɑːʃ -wɔːʃ **~ed** t **~es** ɪz əz **~ing** ɪŋ
handwork ˈhænd wɜːk ‖ -wɜ˞ːk
hand-wringing ˈhænd ˌrɪŋ ɪŋ
handwriting ˈhænd ˌraɪt ɪŋ ‖ -ˌraɪţ ɪŋ
handwritten ˌhænd ˈrɪt ᵊn ◂
hand|y, Handy ˈhænd |i **~ier** i‿ə ‖ i‿ᵊr **~iest** i‿ɪst i‿əst
handy-dandy ˌhænd i ˈdænd i ◂
handy|man ˈhænd i |mæn **~men** men
hang hæŋ **hanged** hæŋd **hanging/s** ˈhæŋ ɪŋ/z **hangs** hæŋz **hung** hʌŋ
ˌHang ˈSeng (ˌindex) seŋ *—Cantonese* [^{4}hɐŋ ^{1}sɐŋ]
hangar ˈhæŋ ə -gə ‖ -ᵊr -gᵊr *(usually = hanger)* **~s** z
Hangchow ˌhæŋ ˈtʃaʊ *—Chi* Hángzhōu [^{2}xɑŋ ^{1}ʈʂou]
hangdog ˈhæŋ dɒg ‖ -dɔːg -dɑːg **~s** z
hanger ˈhæŋ ə ‖ -ᵊr **s** z
hang|er-on ˌhæŋ |ər ˈɒn ‖ -|ər ˈɑːn -ˈɔːn **~ers-on** əz ˈɒn ‖ ᵊrz ˈɑːn -ˈɔːn
hang-glider ˈhæŋ ˌglaɪd ə ‖ -ᵊr **~s** z
hang-gliding ˈhæŋ ˌglaɪd ɪŋ
hang|man ˈhæŋ |mən **~men** mən
hangnail ˈhæŋ neɪᵊl **~s** z
hangout ˈhæŋ aʊt **~s** s
hangover ˈhæŋ ˌəʊv ə ‖ -ˌoʊv ᵊr **~s** z
hangul, H~ ˈhæŋ gʊl ‖ ˈhɑːn- *—Korean* hangŭl [han gul]
hang-up ˈhæŋ ʌp **~s** s
Hangzhou ˌhæŋ ˈdʒəʊ ‖ -ˈdʒoʊ *—Chi* Hángzhōu [^{2}xɑŋ ^{1}ʈʂou]
Hanif hə ˈniːf
hank, Hank hæŋk **hanks** hæŋks
hanker ˈhæŋk ə ‖ -ᵊr **~ed** d **hankering** ˈhæŋk ər‿ɪŋ **~s** z
hankie ˈhæŋk i **~s** z
Hanks hæŋks
hank|y ˈhæŋk |i **~ies** iz
hanky-panky ˌhæŋk i ˈpæŋk i
Hanley ˈhæn li
Hann hæn
Hanna, Hannah ˈhæn ə
Hannay ˈhæn eɪ
Hannibal ˈhæn ɪb ᵊl -əb-
Hannington ˈhæn ɪŋ tən
Hanoi hæ ˈnɔɪ hə- ‖ hɑː- *—Vietnamese* Hà Nội [^{3}ha ^{6}noi]
Hanover ˈhæn əʊv ə ‖ -oʊv ᵊr *—Ger* Hannover [ha ˈnoː fɐ]
Hanoverian ˌhæn əʊ ˈvɪər i‿ən ◂ -ˈveər- ‖ -ə ˈvɪr- -ˈver- **~s** z
Hanrahan ˈhæn rə hən -hæn
Hanratty hæn ˈræt i ‖ -ˈræţ i ˈ. . .
Hans hænᵗs hænz *—Ger* [hans]
Hansa ˈhænᵗs ə ˈhænz- *—Ger* [ˈhan za]
Hansard ˈhænᵗs ɑːd -əd ‖ -ᵊrd
Hanseatic, h~ ˌhænᵗs i ˈæt ɪk ◂ ˌhænz- ‖ -ˈæţ ɪk ◂
Hansel, Hänsel ˈhænᵗs ᵊl *—Ger* [ˈhan zᵊl, ˈhɛn-]
Hansen ˈhænᵗs ᵊn
hansom, H~ ˈhænᵗs əm *(= handsome)* **~s** z
Hanson ˈhænᵗs ᵊn
Hants hænts *-or as* Hampshire
Hanukah, Hanukkah ˈhɑːn ək ə ˈhɒn-, ˈhæn-, -ʊk-, -uːk-, -ɑː *—Hebrew* [xa nu ˈka]
hanuman, H~ ˌhʌn u ˈmɑːn ˌhɑːn- **~s** z *—Hindi* [hə n̪u maːn]
Hanway ˈhæn weɪ
Hanwell ˈhæn wᵊl -wel

hap hæp **happed** hæpt **happing** ˈhæp ɪŋ **haps** hæps
hapax ˈhæp æks
  ˌhapax leˈgomenon lɪ ˈɡɒm ɪn ən lə-, le-, -ən ən, -ə nɒn ‖ -ˈɡɑːm ə nɑːn
ha'penny ˈheɪp ni ˈheɪp ən i **ha'pennies** ˈheɪp niz ˈheɪp ən iz
haphazard ₍ˌ₎hæp ˈhæz əd ◂ ‖ -ᵊrd **~ly** li **~ness** nəs nɪs
hapless ˈhæp ləs -lɪs
haplography ₍ˌ₎hæp ˈlɒɡ rəf i ‖ -ˈlɑːɡ-
haploid ˈhæp lɔɪd **~y** i
haplolog|y ₍ˌ₎hæp ˈlɒl ədʒ |i ‖ -ˈlɑːl- **~ies** iz
haply ˈhæp li
hap'orth, ha'p'orth ˈheɪp əθ ‖ -ᵊrθ **~s** s
happen ˈhæp ən **happened** ˈhæp ənd →-md
  happening/s ˈhæp ən‿ɪŋ/z **happens** ˈhæp ənz →-mz
happenstance ˈhæp ən stæn^t s →-m-, -stɑːn^t s
happie... —*see* **happy**
happily ˈhæp ɪ li -əl i
happiness ˈhæp i nəs -nɪs
Happisburgh ˈheɪz bər‿ə *(!)*
happ|y, Happy ˈhæp |i **~ier** i‿ə ‖ i‿ᵊr **~iest** i‿ɪst i‿əst
  ˌhappy eˈvent; **ˈhappy ˌhour**; **ˌhappy ˈhunting ground**; **ˌhappy ˈmedium**
happy-clappy ˌhæp i ˈklæp i ◂
happy-go-lucky ˌhæp i ɡəʊ ˈlʌk i ◂ ‖ -ɡoʊˈ--
Hapsburg ˈhæps bɜːɡ ‖ -bɜːɡ —*Ger* Habsburg [ˈhaːps bʊʁk] **~s** z
haptic ˈhæpt ɪk
hara-kiri ˌhær ə ˈkɪr i -ˈkɪər-, ⚠-i ˈkær i, ⚠-i ˈkɑːr i ‖ ˌhɑːr- —*Jp* [ha ˌɾa ki ˈɾi]
haram hæ ˈrɑːm hə-, hɑː- —*Arabic* [ħa ˈraːm]
harangu|e hə ˈræŋ **~ed** d **~es** z **~ing** ɪŋ
Harare hə ˈrɑːr i hɑː-, -eɪ

HARASS

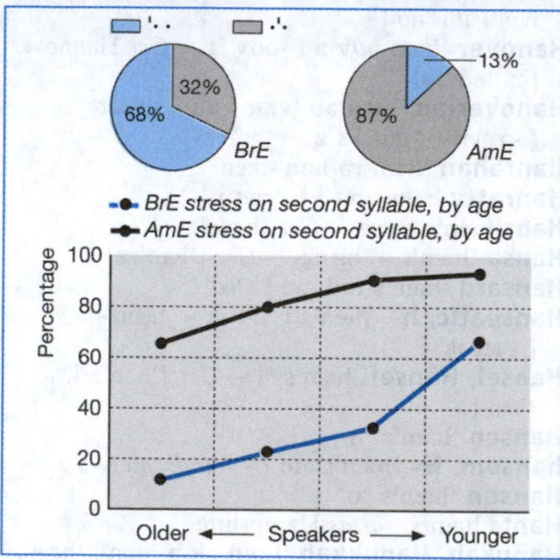

harass ˈhær əs hə ˈræs ‖ hə ˈræs ˈhær əs, ˈher- —*The traditional RP form is* ˈhær əs. *The pronunciation* hə ˈræs, *which originated in the US, was seemingly first heard in Britain in the 1970s. In time it may predominate in BrE, as it already does in AmE. Meanwhile, it evokes negative feelings among those who use the traditional form. Preference polls, BrE:* ˈ· · *68%,* ·ˈ· *32%; AmE:* ·ˈ· *87%,* ˈ· · *13%.* **~ed** t **~er/s** ə/z ‖ ᵊr/z **~es** ɪz əz **~ing** ɪŋ **~ment** mənt
Harben ˈhɑːb ən ‖ ˈhɑːrb-
Harbin ˈhɑː bɪn ˌhɑː ˈbɪn ‖ ˈhɑːrb ən ˌhɑːr ˈbɪn —*Chi* Hā'ěrbīn [¹xa ˌɚ ¹pɪn]
harbinger ˈhɑːb ɪndʒ ə §-əndʒ- ‖ -ᵊr **~s** z
harbor ˈhɑːb ə ‖ ˈhɑːrb ᵊr **~ed** d **harboring** ˈhɑːb ər‿ɪŋ ‖ ˈhɑːrb- **~s** z
harbormaster ˈhɑːb ə ˌmɑːst ə §-ˌmæst- ‖ ˈhɑːrb ᵊr ˌmæst ᵊr **~s** z
Harborough ˈhɑːb ər‿ə ‖ ˈhɑːr ˌbɜː oʊ
harbour ˈhɑːb ə ‖ ˈhɑːrb ᵊr **~ed** d **harbouring** ˈhɑːb ər‿ɪŋ ‖ ˈhɑːrb- **~s** z
harbourmaster ˈhɑːb ə ˌmɑːst ə §-ˌmæst- ‖ ˈhɑːrb ᵊr ˌmæst ᵊr **~s** z
Harcourt ˈhɑː kɔːt ˈhɑːk ət ‖ ˈhɑːr kɔːrt -koʊrt; ˈhɑːrk ᵊrt
hard hɑːd ‖ hɑːrd **harder** ˈhɑːd ə ‖ ˈhɑːrd ᵊr **hardest** ˈhɑːd ɪst -əst ‖ ˈhɑːrd-
  ˌhard ˈby ◂; **ˌhard ˈcash**; **ˌhard ˈcider**; **ˌhard ˈcopy**, ˈ· ·; **ˌhard ˈcore** *'nucleus'*; **ˈhard core** *'broken stones'*; **ˌhard ˈcurrency**; **ˌhard ˈdisk**; **ˌhard ˈdrink**; **ˌhard ˈdrugs**; **ˌhard ˈfeelings**; **ˌhard ˈlabour**; **ˌhard ˈline**; **ˌhard ˈliquor**; **ˌhard ˈluck**; **ˌhard ˈluck ˌstory**, ˌ· ˈ· ˌ· ·; **ˌhard of ˈhearing**; **ˌhard ˈpalate**; **ˌhard ˈrock**; **ˌhard ˈsell**; **ˌhard ˈshoulder**; **ˌhard ˈup** ◂
hard-and-fast ˌhɑːd ᵊn ˈfɑːst ◂ §-ˈfæst ‖ ˌhɑːrd ᵊn ˈfæst ◂
hardback ˈhɑːd bæk →ˈhɑːb- ‖ ˈhɑːrd- **~s** s
hardball ˈhɑːd bɔːl →ˈhɑːb- ‖ ˈhɑːrd- -bɑːl
hard-bitten ˌhɑːd ˈbɪt ᵊn ◂ →ˌhɑːb- ‖ ˌhɑːrd-
hardboard ˈhɑːd bɔːd →ˈhɑːb- ‖ ˈhɑːrd bɔːrd -boʊrd
hard-boiled ˌhɑːd ˈbɔɪᵊld ◂ →ˌhɑːb- ‖ ˌhɑːrd-
  ˌhard-boiled ˈegg
hardbound ˈhɑːd baʊnd →ˈhɑːb- ‖ ˈhɑːrd-
Hardcastle ˈhɑːd ˌkɑːs ᵊl →ˈhɑːɡ-, §-ˌkæs- ‖ ˈhɑːrd ˌkæs ᵊl
hard-core ˌhɑːd ˈkɔː ◂ →ˌhɑːɡ-, ˈ· · ‖ ˌhɑːrd ˈkɔːr ◂ -ˈkoʊr
  ˌhard-core ˈporn
hardcover ˈhɑːd ˌkʌv ə →ˈhɑːɡ- ‖ ˈhɑːrd ˌkʌv ᵊr
hard-done-by ˌhɑːd ˈdʌn baɪ →-ˈdʌm- ‖ ˌhɑːrd-
hard-drinking ˌhɑːd ˈdrɪŋk ɪŋ ◂ ‖ ˌhɑːrd-
hard-earned ˌhɑːd ˈɜːnd ◂ ‖ ˌhɑːrd ˈɝːnd ◂
hard-edged ˌhɑːd ˈedʒd ◂ ‖ ˌhɑːrd-
harden ˈhɑːd ᵊn ‖ ˈhɑːrd ᵊn **~ed** d **~ing** ‿ɪŋ **~s** z
hard-fought ˌhɑːd ˈfɔːt ◂ ‖ ˌhɑːrd- -ˈfɑːt ◂
hard-hat ˈhɑːd hæt ‖ ˈhɑːrd- **~s** s
hardheaded ˌhɑːd ˈhed ɪd ◂ -əd ‖ ˌhɑːrd- **~ly** li **~ness** nəs nɪs
hardhearted ˌhɑːd ˈhɑːt ɪd ◂ -əd ‖ ˌhɑːrd ˈhɑːrţ əd ◂ **~ly** li **~ness** nəs nɪs
hard-hitting ˌhɑːd ˈhɪt ɪŋ ◂ ‖ ˌhɑːrd ˈhɪţ ɪŋ ◂

Hard attack

When a word or syllable begins with a vowel sound, it is possible to start the vowel from a position where the vocal folds are first held closed, then burst open for the vowel: that is, to precede the vowel by a GLOTTAL STOP. This way of starting a vowel is called **hard attack**.

In English, hard attack is not customary. But it is sometimes used for special effect, as a way of emphasizing the importance of a word.

When hard attack is used, and the word in question is preceded by **to**, then the weak form appropriate before a consonant is often used, namely tə. Thus **to eat** is usually tu ˈiːt but sometimes tə ʔiːt.

Hardicanute ˈhɑːd ɪ kə ˌnjuːt ˈ·ə-, ˌ· · ·ˈ· ‖ ˌhɑːrd ə kə ˈnuːt -ˈnjuːt
Hardie ˈhɑːd i ‖ ˈhɑːrd i
hardihood ˈhɑːd i hʊd ‖ ˈhɑːrd-
hardily ˈhɑːd ɪ li -əl i ‖ ˈhɑːrd-
hardiness ˈhɑːd i nəs -nɪs ‖ ˈhɑːrd-
Harding ˈhɑːd ɪŋ ‖ ˈhɑːrd-
Hardinge *(i)* ˈhɑːd ɪŋ ‖ ˈhɑːrd-, *(ii)* -ɪndʒ
hard-line ˌhɑːd ˈlaɪn ◂ ‖ ˌhɑːrd-
hard-liner ˌhɑːd ˈlaɪn ə◂ ˈ· · · ‖ ˌhɑːrd ˈlaɪn ᵊr ◂ **~s** z
hard-luck stor|y ˌhɑːd ˈlʌk ˌstɔːr| i ‖ ˌhɑːrd- -ˌstoʊr| i **~ies** iz
hard|ly ˈhɑːd |li ‖ ˈhɑːrd- **~ness** nəs nɪs
hard-nosed ˌhɑːd ˈnəʊzd ◂ ‖ ˌhɑːrd ˈnoʊzd ◂
hard-on ˈhɑːd ɒn ‖ ˈhɑːrd ɑːn -ɔːn **~s** z
hardpan ˈhɑːd pæn →ˈhɑːb- ‖ ˈhɑːrd-
hard-pressed ˌhɑːd ˈprest ◂ →ˌhɑːb- ‖ ˌhɑːrd-
hard-scrabble ˈhɑːd ˌskræb ᵊl ‖ ˈhɑːrd-
hard-shell ˈhɑːd ʃel ‖ ˈhɑːrd- **~s** z
hardship ˈhɑːd ʃɪp ‖ ˈhɑːrd- **~s** s
hardtack ˈhɑːd tæk ‖ ˈhɑːrd-
hardtop ˈhɑːd tɒp ‖ ˈhɑːrd tɑːp **~s** s
hardware ˈhɑːd weə ‖ ˈhɑːrd wer -wær **~s** z
hardwearing ˌhɑːd ˈweər ɪŋ ◂ ‖ ˌhɑːrd ˈwer ɪŋ ◂ -ˈwær-
ˌhard-ˌwearing ˈfabric
Hardwick, Hardwicke ˈhɑːd wɪk ‖ ˈhɑːrd-
hard-wired ˌhɑːd ˈwaɪ‿əd ◂ ‖ ˌhɑːrd ˈwaɪ‿ᵊrd ◂
hard-won ˌhɑːd ˈwʌn ◂ ‖ ˌhɑːrd-
hardwood ˈhɑːd wʊd ‖ ˈhɑːrd- **~s** z
hard-working ˌhɑːd ˈwɜːk ɪŋ ◂ ‖ ˌhɑːrd ˈwɜːk ɪŋ ◂
hard|y, Hard|y ˈhɑːd |i ‖ ˈhɑːrd |i **~ier** i‿ə ‖ i‿ᵊr **~ies, ~y's** iz **~iest** i‿ɪst i‿əst
hare, Hare heə ‖ heᵊr hæᵊr *(= hair)* **hared** heəd ‖ heᵊrd hæᵊrd **hares** heəz ‖ heᵊrz hæᵊrz **haring** ˈheər ɪŋ ‖ ˈher ɪŋ ˈhær- —*see also phrases with this word*
ˈhare ˌcoursing
harebell ˈheə bel ‖ ˈher- ˈhær- **~s** z
harebrained ˈheə breɪnd ‖ ˈher- ˈhær-
harecloth ˈheə klɒθ -klɔːθ ‖ ˈher klɔːθ ˈhær-, -klɑːθ
Harefield ˈheə fiːᵊld ‖ ˈher-
Hare Krishna ˌhær i ˈkrɪʃ nə ˌhɑːr- ‖ ˌhɑːr- ˌhær-, ˌher-
harelip ˌheə ˈlɪp ˈ· · ‖ ˈher lɪp ˈhær- **~ped** t ◂ **~s** s
harem ˈhɑːr iːm ˈheər-, -əm, ₍ˌ₎hɑː ˈriːm ‖ ˈhær əm ˈher- **~s** z
Harewood ˈheə wʊd ‖ ˈher- ˈhær- —*but* ˈhɑː- ‖ ˈhɑːr- *for the Earl of H~, and for H~ House*
Harford ˈhɑː fəd ‖ ˈhɑːr fᵊrd
Hargraves ˈhɑː greɪvz ‖ ˈhɑːr-
Hargreaves *(i)* ˈhɑː griːvz ‖ ˈhɑːr-, *(ii)* -greɪvz
haricot ˈhær ɪ kəʊ -ə- ‖ -koʊ ˈher- **~s** z
ˌharicot ˈbean, ˈ· · ·
Harijan ˈhʌr ɪdʒ ən ˈhɑːr-, §-ədʒ-; -ɪ dʒɑːn, -ə- ‖ ˈhɑːr ɪ dʒɑːn ˈhær-, ˈher-, -dʒæn **~s** z
Haringey ˈhær ɪŋ geɪ -gi ‖ ˈher-
hark hɑːk ‖ hɑːrk **harked** hɑːkt ‖ hɑːrkt **harking** ˈhɑːk ɪŋ ‖ ˈhɑːrk ɪŋ **harks** hɑːks ‖ hɑːrks
harken ˈhɑːk ən ‖ ˈhɑːrk- **~ed** d **~ing** ‿ɪŋ **~s** z
Harkness ˈhɑːk nəs -nɪs ‖ ˈhɑːrk-
Harlan ˈhɑːl ən ‖ ˈhɑːrl-
Harland ˈhɑːl ənd ‖ ˈhɑːrl-
Harlech ˈhɑːl ək -əx, -ek, -ex ‖ ˈhɑːrl- —*Welsh* [ˈhar lex]
Harlem ˈhɑːl əm ‖ ˈhɑːrl-
Harlemite ˈhɑːl ə maɪt ‖ ˈhɑːrl- **~s** s
harlequin ˈhɑːl ə kwɪn -ɪ-, -kɪn ‖ ˈhɑːrl- **~s** z
harlequinade ˌhɑːl ə kwɪ ˈneɪd ˌ·ɪ-, -kwəˈ-, -kɪˈ- ‖ ˌhɑːrl- **~s** z
Harlesden ˈhɑːlz dən ‖ ˈhɑːrlz-
Harley ˈhɑːl i ‖ ˈhɑːrl i
ˈHarley Street
Harley-Davidson ˌhɑːl i ˈdeɪv ɪd sən -əd· ‖ ˌhɑːrl-
harlot ˈhɑːl ət ‖ ˈhɑːrl- **~s** s
harlot|ry ˈhɑːl ət |ri ‖ ˈhɑːrl- **~ries** riz
Harlow, Harlowe ˈhɑːl əʊ ‖ ˈhɑːrl oʊ
harm hɑːm ‖ hɑːrm **harmed** hɑːmd ‖ hɑːrmd **harming** ˈhɑːm ɪŋ ‖ ˈhɑːrm ɪŋ **harms** hɑːmz ‖ hɑːrmz
Harman ˈhɑːm ən ‖ ˈhɑːrm-

harmattan haː ˈmæt ən ‖ haːr- ˌhaːrm ə ˈtaːn **~s** z
Harmer ˈhaːm ə ‖ ˈhaːrm ər
harmful ˈhaːm fəl -fʊl ‖ ˈhaːrm- **~ly** ˌi **~ness** nəs nɪs
harmless ˈhaːm ləs -lɪs ‖ ˈhaːrm- **~ly** li **~ness** nəs nɪs
Harmon ˈhaːm ən ‖ ˈhaːrm ən
Harmondsworth ˈhaːm əndz wɜːθ ‖ ˈhaːrm əndz wərθ
harmonic haː ˈmɒn ɪk ‖ haːr ˈmaːn ɪk **~ally** əl ˌi **~s** s
harmonica haː ˈmɒn ɪk ə ‖ haːr ˈmaːn- **~s** z
harmonie... —*see* **harmony**
harmonious haː ˈməʊn i ˌəs ‖ haːr ˈmoʊn- **~ly** li **~ness** nəs nɪs
harmonis... —*see* **harmoniz...**
harmonist ˈhaːm ən ɪst §-əst ‖ ˈhaːrm- **~s** s
harmonium haː ˈməʊn i ˌəm ‖ haːr ˈmoʊn- **~s** z
harmonization ˌhaːm ən aɪ ˈzeɪʃ ən -ən ɪ- ‖ ˌhaːrm ən ə- **~s** z
harmoniz|e ˈhaːm ə naɪz ‖ ˈhaːrm- **~ed** d **~es** ɪz əz **~ing** ɪŋ
harmon|y ˈhaːm ən |i ‖ ˈhaːrm- **~ies** iz
Harmsworth ˈhaːmz wɜːθ -wəθ ‖ ˈhaːrmz wərθ
harness ˈhaːn ɪs -əs ‖ ˈhaːrn- **~ed** t **~es** ɪz əz **~ing** ɪŋ
Harold ˈhær əld ‖ ˈher-
harp haːp ‖ haːrp **harped** haːpt ‖ haːrpt **harping** ˈhaːp ɪŋ ‖ ˈhaːrp ɪŋ **harps** haːps ‖ haːrps
Harpenden ˈhaːp ənd ən →-md-
Harper, h~ ˈhaːp ə ‖ ˈhaːrp ər **~s** z
 ˌHarpers ˈFerry
Harpic *tdmk* ˈhaːp ɪk ‖ ˈhaːrp-
harpie... —*see* **harpy**
harpist ˈhaːp ɪst §-əst ‖ ˈhaːrp- **~s** s
harpoon ₍ˌ₎haː ˈpuːn ◂ ‖ ₍ˌ₎haːr- **~ed** d **~ing** ɪŋ **~s** z
harpsichord ˈhaːps ɪ kɔːd -ə- ‖ ˈhaːrps ɪ kɔːrd **~s** z
harp|y ˈhaːp |i ‖ ˈhaːrp |i **~ies** iz
harquebus ˈhaːk wɪb əs -wəb- ‖ ˈhaːrk- **~es** ɪz əz
Harrap ˈhær əp ‖ ˈher-
harridan ˈhær ɪd ən -əd- ‖ ˈher- **~s** z
harrie... —*see* **harry**
harrier ˈhær i ə ‖ ər ˈher- **~s** z
Harries ˈhær ɪs -iz ‖ ˈher-
Harriet ˈhær i ˌət ‖ ˈher-
Harrietsham ˈhær i ˌət ʃəm ‖ ˈher-
Harriman ˈhær ɪ mən -ə- ‖ ˈher-
Harrington ˈhær ɪŋ tən ‖ ˈher-
Harriot, Harriott ˈhær i ˌət ‖ ˈher-
Harris ˈhær ɪs §-əs ‖ ˈher-
 ˌHarris ˈTweed
Harrisburg ˈhær ɪs bɜːg -əs- ‖ -bɜːg ˈher-
Harrison ˈhær ɪs ən -əs- ‖ ˈher-
Harrod ˈhær əd ‖ ˈher- **~s, ~'s** z
Harrogate ˈhær əg ət -əʊg-, -ɪt; -əʊ geɪt ‖ -oʊ geɪt ˈher-
Harrold ˈhær əld ‖ ˈher-
Harrovian hə ˈrəʊv i ˌən hæ- ‖ -ˈroʊv- **~s** z
harrow, H~ ˈhær əʊ ‖ -oʊ ˈher- **~ed** d **~ing/ly** ɪŋ /li **~s** z
harrumph hə ˈrʌmpf **~ed** t **~ing** ɪŋ **~s** s
harr|y ˈhær |i ‖ ˈher- **~ied** id **~ies** iz **~ying** i ɪŋ
Harry ˈhær i ‖ ˈher- **~'s** z
harsh haːʃ ‖ haːrʃ **harsher** ˈhaːʃ ə ‖ ˈhaːrʃ ər **harshest** ˈhaːʃ ɪst -əst ‖ ˈhaːrʃ- **harshly** ˈhaːʃ li ‖ ˈhaːrʃ- **harshness** ˈhaːʃ nəs -nɪs ‖ ˈhaːrʃ-
hart, Hart haːt ‖ haːrt **harts** haːts ‖ haːrts
hartal haː ˈtaːl hɜː-; ˈhaːt aːl ‖ haːr- **~s** z
Harte haːt ‖ haːrt
hartebeest ˈhaːt i biːst -ə-, -bɪəst ‖ ˈhaːrṭ ə- ˈhaːrt biːst **~s** s
Hartfield ˈhaːt fiːəld ‖ ˈhaːrt-
Hartford ˈhaːt fəd ‖ ˈhaːrt fərd
Hartland ˈhaːt lənd ‖ ˈhaːrt-
Hartlepool ˈhaːt li puːl -lə- ‖ ˈhaːrt-
Hartley ˈhaːt li ‖ ˈhaːrt-
Hartnell ˈhaːt nəl ‖ ˈhaːrt-
Hartree, h~ ˈhaː triː ‖ ˈhaːr- **~s** z
hartshorn, H~, Hartshorne ˈhaːts hɔːn ‖ ˈhaːrts hɔːrn
hart's-tongue ˈhaːts tʌŋ §-tɒŋ ‖ ˈhaːrts- **~s** z
harum-scarum ˌheər əm ˈskeər əm ‖ ˌher əm ˈsker əm ˌhær əm ˈskær əm
Harun al-Rashid hæ ˌruːn æl ræ ˈʃiːd haː- ‖ haː ˌruː n aːl raː ˈʃiːd
haruspex hə ˈrʌsp eks hæ-; ˈhær ə speks
Harvard ˈhaːv əd ‖ ˈhaːrv ərd
harvest ˈhaːv ɪst -əst ‖ ˈhaːrv- **~ed** ɪd əd **~er/s** ə/z ‖ ər/z **~ing** ɪŋ **~s** s
 ˌharvest ˈfestival; ˌharvest ˈhome; ˈharvest mite; ˌharvest ˈmoon; ˈharvest mouse
harvest|man ˈhaːv ɪst |mən -əst-, -mæn ‖ ˈhaːrv- **~men** mən men
Harvey, Harvie ˈhaːv i ‖ ˈhaːrv i
Harwell ˈhaː wəl -wel ‖ ˈhaːr-
Harwich ˈhær ɪdʒ -ɪtʃ ‖ ˈher-
Harwood ˈhaː wʊd ‖ ˈhaːr-
Haryana ˌhær i ˈaːn ə ˌhaːr- ‖ ˌhaːr- —*Hindi* [hər ˈjaː ṇə]
Harz haːts ‖ haːrts —*Ger* [haːɐ̯ts]
has *strong form* **hæz**, *weak forms* **həz, əz, z, s** —*Of the weak forms,* **əz** *is not used clause-initially, and* **s, z** *are used in that position only in very fast speech; in other environments* **həz, əz** *are more formal than the contracted forms* **s, z**. *The most usual weak forms are* **əz** *after a word ending in* **s, z, ʃ, ʒ, tʃ, dʒ**; **s** *after one ending in* **p, t, k, f, θ**; *and* **z** *otherwise. The latter two are sometimes shown in writing as the contraction* **'s**. *See note at* have *concerning the choice between strong and weak form.*
has-been ˈhæz biːn -bɪn ‖ -bɪn **~s** z
Hasdrubal ˈhæz druːb əl -druːb-; -dru bæl
Haseldine ˈheɪz əl daɪn

hash hæʃ **hashed** hæʃt **hashes** ˈhæʃ ɪz -əz **hashing** ˈhæʃ ɪŋ
ˌ**hash ˈbrowns**; ˈ**hash mark**
Hashemite ˈhæʃ ɪ maɪt -ə- **~s** s
Hashimoto ˌhæʃ i ˈməʊt əʊ ‖ -ˈmoʊṭ oʊ
hashish ˈhæʃ ɪʃ -iːʃ; hæ ˈʃiːʃ
Hasid ˈhæs ɪd ˈxɑːs-, -əd **Hasidim** ˈhæs ɪd ɪm ˈxɑːs-, -əd-; hæˈsɪd-
Hasidic hæ ˈsɪd ɪk hɑː-
Hasidism ˈhæs ɪd ˌɪz əm hæ ˈsɪd-
Haslam ˈhæz ləm
Haslemere ˈheɪz ᵊl mɪə ‖ -mɪr
haslet ˈheɪz lət ˈhæz-, -lɪt
Haslett *(i)* ˈheɪz lət -lɪt, *(ii)* ˈhæz-
Haslingden ˈhæz lɪŋ dən
Hasmonaean, Hasmonean ˌhæs mə ˈniː̮ ən
hasn't ˈhæz ᵊnt
hasp hɑːsp hæsp ‖ hæsp **hasped** hɑːspt hæspt ‖ hæspt **hasping** ˈhɑːsp ɪŋ ˈhæsp- ‖ ˈhæsp ɪŋ **hasps** hɑːsps hæsps ‖ hæsps
Hassan hə ˈsɑːn hæ-; ˈhæs ᵊn ‖ ˈhɑːs ɑːn
Hasselblad *tdmk* ˈhæs ᵊl blæd ‖ ˈhɑːs ᵊl blɑːd
Hasselhoff ˈhæs ᵊl hɒf ‖ -hɔːf -hɑːf
hassium ˌhæs i̮ əm
hassl|e ˈhæs ᵊl **~ed** d **~es** z **~ing** ̮ɪŋ
hassock ˈhæs ək **~s** s
hast *strong form* hæst, *weak forms* həst, əst, st
hasta la vista ˌæst ə lə ˈvɪst ə -ˈlæ'-, -lɑː'- ‖ ˌɑːst ə lə ˈviːst ə —*Sp* [ˌas ta la ˈβis ta]
hasta mañana ˌæst ə mə ˈnjɑːn ə -mæ'- ‖ ˌɑːst ə mɑː- —*Sp* [ˌas ta ma ˈɲa na]
haste heɪst
hasten ˈheɪs ᵊn **~ed** d **~ing** ̮ɪŋ **~s** z
hasti... —*see* **hasty**
Hastings ˈheɪst ɪŋz
hast|y ˈheɪst |i **~ier** i̮ ə ‖ i̮ ᵊr **~iest** i̮ ɪst i̮ əst **~ily** ɪ li əl i **~iness** i nəs i nɪs
hat hæt **hats** hæts **hatted** ˈhæt ɪd -əd ‖ ˈhæṭ əd **hatting** ˈhæt ɪŋ ‖ ˈhæṭ ɪŋ
ˈ**hat trick**
hatband ˈhæt bænd **~s** z
hatbox ˈhæt bɒks ‖ -bɑːks
hatch, Hatch hætʃ **hatched** hætʃt **hatches** ˈhætʃ ɪz -əz **hatching** ˈhætʃ ɪŋ
hatchback ˈhætʃ bæk **~s** s
hatcheck ˌhæt tʃek
Hatcher ˈhætʃ ə ‖ -ᵊr
hatcher|y ˈhætʃ ər |i **~ies** iz
hatchet ˈhætʃ ɪt §-ət **~s** s
ˈ**hatchet job**; ˈ**hatchet man**
hatchet-faced ˌhætʃ ɪt ˈfeɪst ◂ §-ət-, ˈ· · ·
hatchling ˈhætʃ lɪŋ **~s** z
hatchment ˈhætʃ mənt **~s** s
hatchway ˈhætʃ weɪ **~s** z
hate heɪt **hated** ˈheɪt ɪd -əd ‖ ˈheɪṭ əd **hates** heɪts **hating** ˈheɪt ɪŋ ‖ ˈheɪṭ ɪŋ
hateful ˈheɪt fᵊl -fʊl **~ly** i **~ness** nəs nɪs
hatemonger ˈheɪt ˌmʌŋ gə ‖ -gᵊr -ˌmɑːŋ- **~s** z
hater ˈheɪt ə ‖ ˈheɪṭ ᵊr **~s** z
Hatfield ˈhæt fiːᵊld
hath *strong form* hæθ, *weak forms* həθ, əθ
hatha ˈhæθ ə ˈhʌt- —*Hindi* [hə ṭʰə]
Hathaway ˈhæθ ə weɪ
Hatherleigh ˈhæð ə li -liː ‖ -ᵊr-
Hatherley ˈhæð ə li ‖ -ᵊr-
Hathern ˈhæð ᵊn ‖ -ᵊrn
Hathersage ˈhæð ə seɪdʒ -sɪdʒ, -sedʒ ‖ ˈᵊr-
Hathor ˈhæθ ɔː ‖ -ɔːr
hatpin ˈhæt pɪn **~s** z
hatred ˈheɪtr ɪd -əd **~s** z
Hatshepsut hæt ˈʃep suːt
hatter ˈhæt ə ‖ ˈhæṭ ᵊr **~s** z
Hatteras ˈhæt ər əs ‖ ˈhæṭ-
Hattersley ˈhæt əz li ‖ ˈhæṭ ᵊrz-
Hattie ˈhæt i ‖ ˈhæṭ i
Hatton ˈhæt ᵊn
Hatty ˈhæt i ‖ ˈhæṭ i
hauberk ˈhɔː bɜːk ‖ -bɜːk ˈhɑː- **~s** s
Haugh *(i)* hɔː ‖ hɑː, *(ii)* hɔːf ‖ hɑːf, *(iii)* hɑːx ‖ hɑːk
Haughey ˈhɔː hi ˈhɒ- ‖ ˈhɔːk i ˈhɑːk-
haughti... —*see* **haughty**
Haughton ˈhɔːt ᵊn ‖ ˈhɑːt-
haught|y ˈhɔːt |i ‖ ˈhɔːṭ |i ˈhɑːṭ- **~ier** i̮ ə ‖ i̮ ᵊr **~iest** i̮ ɪst i̮ əst **~ily** ɪ li əl i **~iness** i nəs i nɪs
haul hɔːl ‖ hɑːl **hauled** hɔːld ‖ hɑːld **hauling** ˈhɔːl ɪŋ ‖ ˈhɑːl- **hauls** hɔːlz ‖ hɑːlz
haulage ˈhɔːl ɪdʒ ‖ ˈhɑːl-
ˈ**haulage conˌtractor**
hauler ˈhɔːl ə ‖ -ᵊr ˈhɑːl- **~s** z
haulier ˈhɔːl i̮ ə ‖ ᵊr ˈhɑːl- **~s** z
haulm hɔːm ‖ hɑːm **haulms** hɔːmz ‖ hɑːmz
haunch hɔːntʃ ‖ hɑːntʃ **haunches** ˈhɔːntʃ ɪz -əz ‖ ˈhɑːntʃ-
haunt hɔːnt ‖ hɑːnt **haunted** ˈhɔːnt ɪd -əd ‖ ˈhɔːnṭ əd ˈhɑːnṭ- **haunting/ly** ˈhɔːnt ɪŋ /li ‖ ˈhɔːnṭ ɪŋ /li ˈhɑːnṭ- **haunts** hɔːnts ‖ hɑːnts
Hausa ˈhaʊs ə ˈhaʊz ə
hausfrau, H~ ˈhaʊs fraʊ —*Ger* [ˈhaʊs fʁaʊ] **~en** ən **~s** z
haut|bois *sing.* ˈəʊ |bɔɪ ˈhəʊ-, ˈhɔːt- ‖ ˈhoʊ- ˈoʊ- **~bois** *pl* bɔɪz **~boy** bɔɪ **~boys** bɔɪz
haute əʊt ‖ oʊt —*Fr* [oːt]
ˌ**haute couˈture**; ˌ**haute cuiˈsine**
hauteur əʊ ˈtɜː ˈ· ‖ hoʊ ˈtɜː hɔː-, hɑː- —*Fr* [o tœːʁ]
Havana hə ˈvæn ə -ˈvɑːn ə —*Sp* Habana [a ˈβa na]
Havant ˈhæv ᵊnt
Havasupai ˌhɑːv ə ˈsuːp aɪ ◂
have *strong form* hæv, *weak forms* həv, əv, v —*The weak form* v *is used only after a vowel (when it is often written as the contraction* ʼve*), or in very fast speech at the beginning of a sentence;* əv *is not used at the beginning of a sentence. Weak forms of* have, has, had *are used only when the word functions as the perfective auxiliary, or is the equivalent of* have got *and is used with an object that is not a pronoun, or in the constructions* had better/best/rather. **had** hæd *(see)* **hadn't** ˈhæd ᵊnt **has** hæz *(see)* **hasn't** ˈhæz ᵊnt **haven't** ˈhæv ᵊnt **haves** hævz **having** ˈhæv ɪŋ
Havel ˈhɑːv ᵊl —*Czech* [ˈha vel]
Havelock, h~ ˈhæv lɒk ‖ -lɑːk

H

haven 'heɪv ən **~s** z
have-not 'hæv nɒt ˌ·'· ‖ -nɑːt *—contrastively always* ˌ·'· **~s** s
haven't 'hæv ənt
haver 'heɪv ə ‖ -ər **~ed** d **havering** 'heɪv ər‿ɪŋ **~s** z
Haverfordwest ˌhæv ə fəd 'west ˌhɑː fəd 'west ‖ ˌhæv ər fərd-
Havergal 'hæv əg əl ‖ -ərg-
Haverhill 'heɪv ər‿ɪl ər‿əl, 'heɪv ə hɪl ‖ -ər-
Havering 'heɪv ər‿ɪŋ
Havers 'heɪv əz ‖ -ərz
haversack 'hæv ə sæk ‖ -ər- **~s** s
Haversian, h~ hə 'vɜːʃ ən hæ-,-'vɜːʒ- ‖ -'vɜːʒ ən
haversine 'hæv ə saɪn ‖ -ər- **~s** z
Haverstock 'hæv ə stɒk ‖ -ər stɑːk
haves hævz
Haviland 'hæv ɪ lənd -ə-
Havisham 'hæv ɪʃ əm -əʃ-
havoc 'hæv ək
Havre *place in MT* 'hæv ə ‖ -ər
Havre *place in France* 'ɑːv rə*—Fr* Le Havre [lə aːvʁ]
Havre de Grace *place in MD* ˌhæv ə də 'græs -'greɪs ‖ ˌ·ər-
haw, Haw hɔː ‖ hɑː **hawed** hɔːd ‖ hɑːd **hawing** 'hɔːr ɪŋ ‖ 'hɔː ɪŋ 'hɑː- **haws** hɔːz ‖ hɑːz
Hawaii, Hawai'i hə 'waɪ i hɑː-, -iː ‖ -'wɑː- *—Hawaiian* [ha wai ʔi]
Hawaiian, Hawai'ian hə 'waɪ‿ən -'waɪ i‿ən ‖ -'wɑː jən **~s** z
Hawarden *(i)* 'hɑːd ən ‖ 'hɑːrd ən, *(ii)* 'heɪ ˌwɔːd ən ‖ -ˌwɔːrd- *—The place in Clwyd is (i);* Viscount H~ *and the place in Iowa are (ii)*
Hawes hɔːz ‖ hɑːz
hawfinch 'hɔː fɪntʃ ‖ 'hɑː- **~es** ɪz əz
haw-haw, H~ 'hɔː hɔː ‖ 'hɑː hɑː
Hawick 'hɔː ɪk hɔɪk ‖ 'hɑː-
hawk hɔːk ‖ hɑːk **hawked** hɔːkt ‖ hɑːkt **hawking** 'hɔːk ɪŋ ‖ 'hɑːk- **hawks** hɔːks ‖ hɑːks
'hawk moth
hawkbit 'hɔːk bɪt ‖ 'hɑːk- **~s** s
Hawke hɔːk ‖ hɑːk
hawker 'hɔːk ə ‖ -ər 'hɑːk- **~s** z
Hawker-Siddeley *tdmk* ˌhɔːk ə 'sɪd əl‿i ‖ -ər- ˌhɑːk-
Hawkes hɔːks ‖ hɑːks
hawk-eye 'hɔːk aɪ ‖ 'hɑːk- **~d** d
Hawking 'hɔːk ɪŋ ‖ 'hɑːk-
Hawkinge 'hɔːk ɪndʒ ‖ 'hɑːk-
Hawkins 'hɔːk ɪnz ‖ 'hɑːk-
hawkish 'hɔːk ɪʃ ‖ 'hɑːk- **~ness** nəs nɪs
hawk-nosed ˌhɔːk 'nəʊzd ◂ ‖ -noʊzd ◂ 'hɑːk-
Hawks hɔːks ‖ hɑːks
hawk's-beard 'hɔːks bɪəd ‖ -bɪrd 'hɑːks- **~s** z
hawksbill 'hɔːks bɪl ‖ 'hɑːks- **~s** z
Hawksmoor 'hɔːks mʊə -mɔː ‖ -mʊr 'hɑːks-
hawkweed 'hɔːk wiːd ‖ 'hɑːk- **~s** z
Hawley 'hɔːl i ‖ 'hɑːl i
Hawn hɔːn ‖ hɑːn
Haworth 'haʊ‿əθ 'hɔː- ‖ 'hɔː wərθ 'hɑː-
hawse, Hawse hɔːz ‖ hɑːz **hawses** 'hɔːz ɪz -əz ‖ 'hɑːz-
hawser 'hɔːz ə ‖ -ər 'hɑːz- **~s** z
hawthorn, H~, Hawthorne 'hɔː θɔːn ‖ -θɔːrn 'hɑː- **~s** z
Hawthornden 'hɔː θɔːn dən ‖ -θɔːrn- 'hɑː-
Hawthorne 'hɔː θɔːn ‖ -θɔːrn 'hɑː-
Hawtrey 'hɔːtr i ‖ 'hɑːtr i
Haxey 'hæks i
hay, Hay heɪ **hayed** heɪd **haying** 'heɪ ɪŋ **hays** heɪz
'hay ˌfever, ˌ· '··
Hayakawa ˌhaɪ ə 'kɑː wə ‖ ˌhɑː jə-
haycock, H~ 'heɪ kɒk ‖ -kɑːk **~s** s
Hayden 'heɪd ən
Haydn *Austrian composer* 'haɪd ən *—Ger* ['hai dən] **~'s** z
Haydn *English or Welsh name* 'heɪd ən
Haydock 'heɪ dɒk ‖ -dɑːk
Haydon 'heɪd ən
Hayek 'haɪ ek 'hɑː jek
Hayes heɪz
hayfork 'heɪ fɔːk ‖ -fɔːrk **~s** s
Hayle heɪəl
Hayley 'heɪl i
Hayling 'heɪl ɪŋ
hayloft 'heɪ lɒft -lɔːft ‖ -lɔːft -lɑːft **~s** s
haymak|er 'heɪ ˌmeɪk |ə ‖ -|ər **~ers** əz ‖ ərz **~ing** ɪŋ
Hayman 'heɪ mən
Haymarket 'heɪ ˌmɑːk ɪt §-ət ‖ -ˌmɑːrk-
Haynes heɪnz
hayrick 'heɪ rɪk **~s** s
hayride 'heɪ raɪd **~s** z
Hays heɪz
hayseed 'heɪ siːd **~s** z
haystack 'heɪ stæk **~s** s
Hayter 'heɪt ə ‖ 'heɪţ ər
haywain 'heɪ weɪn **~s** z
Hayward 'heɪ wəd ‖ -wərd
haywire 'heɪ ˌwaɪ‿ə ‖ -ˌwaɪ ər
Haywood 'heɪ wʊd
Hayworth 'heɪ wəθ -wɜːθ ‖ -wərθ
Hazan hə 'zæn
hazard 'hæz əd ‖ -ərd **~ed** ɪd əd **~ing** ɪŋ **~s** z
hazardous 'hæz əd əs ‖ -ərd- **~ly** li **~ness** nəs nɪs
Hazchem 'hæz kem
haze heɪz **hazed** heɪzd **hazes** 'heɪz ɪz -əz **hazing** 'heɪz ɪŋ
hazel, Hazel, Hazell 'heɪz əl **~s** z
hazelnut 'heɪz əl nʌt **~s** s
hazi... *—see* **hazy**
Hazlerigg 'heɪz əl rɪg
Hazlett, Hazlitt 'hæz lɪt 'heɪz-, -lət
hazmat, HazMat 'hæz mæt
haz|y 'heɪz |i **~ier** i‿ə ‖ i‿ər **~iest** i‿ɪst i‿əst **~ily** ɪ li əl i **~iness** i nəs i nɪs
Hazzard 'hæz əd ‖ -ərd
H-block 'eɪtʃ blɒk §'heɪtʃ- ‖ -blɑːk **~s** s
H-bomb 'eɪtʃ bɒm §'heɪtʃ- ‖ -bɑːm **~s** z

HBOS ˈeɪtʃ bɒs §ˈheɪtʃ- ‖ -bɔːs -bɑːs
he *n* hiː
he *pronoun strong form* hiː, *weak forms* hi, i —*The form* i *is not used at the beginning of a sentence or clause.*
he- ˈhiː — **he-goat** ˈhiː gəʊt ‖ -goʊt
Heacham ˈhetʃ əm ˈhiːtʃ-
head, Head hed **headed** ˈhed ɪd -əd **heading** ˈhed ɪŋ **heads** hedz ˌ**head** ˈ**start**; ˌ**head** ˈ**waiter**
headache ˈhed eɪk **~s** s
headachy ˈhed eɪk i
headband ˈhed bænd →ˈheb- **~s** z
headbang|er ˈhed ˌbæŋ| ə →ˈheb- ‖ -ər **~ers** əz ‖ ərz **~ing** ɪŋ
headboard hed bɔːd →ˈheb- ‖ -bɔːrd -boʊrd **~s** z
head|butt ˈhed| bʌt →ˈheb- **~butted** bʌt ɪd -əd ‖ bʌţ- **~butting** bʌt ɪŋ ‖ bʌţ- **~butts** bʌts
headcas|e ˈhed keɪs →ˈheg- **~es** ɪz əz
headcheese ˈhed tʃiːz
headdress ˈhed dres **~es** ɪz əz
-headed ˈhed ɪd -əd — **bullet-headed** ˌbʊl ɪt ˈhed ɪd ◂ -ət-, -əd
header ˈhed ə ‖ -ər **~s** z
headfirst ˌhed ˈfɜːst ◂ ‖ -ˈfɜːst ◂
headgear ˈhed gɪə →ˈheg- ‖ -gɪr
head|hunt ˈhed |hʌnt **~hunted** hʌnt ɪd -əd ‖ hʌnţ əd **~hunting** hʌnt ɪŋ ‖ hʌnţ ɪŋ **~hunts** hʌnts
headhunter ˈhed ˌhʌnt ə ‖ -ˌhʌnţ ər
headi... —*see* **heady**
heading ˈhed ɪŋ **~s** z
Headingley ˈhed ɪŋ li
Headlam ˈhed ləm
headlamp ˈhed læmp **~s** s
headland ˈhed lənd -lænd **~s** z
headless ˈhed ləs -lɪs
Headley ˈhed li
headlight ˈhed laɪt **~s** s
headlin|e ˈhed laɪn **~ed** d **~er/s** ə/z ‖ ər/z **~es** z **~ing** ɪŋ
headline-grabbing ˈhed laɪn ˌgræb ɪŋ
headlock ˈhed lɒk ‖ -lɑːk
headlong ˈhed lɒŋ ˌ·ˈ· ‖ -lɔːŋ -lɑːŋ
head|man ˈhed |mən →ˈheb-, -mæn **~men** mən men
headmaster ˌhed ˈmɑːst ə ◂ →ˌheb-, §-ˈmæst-, ˈ·ˌ·· ‖ -ˈmæst ər ◂ **~s** z
headmistress ˌhed ˈmɪs trəs ◂ →ˌheb-, -trɪs, ˈ·ˌ·· **~es** ɪz əz
head-on ˌhed ˈɒn ◂ ‖ -ˈɑːn ◂ -ˈɔːn ◂
headphone ˈhed fəʊn ‖ -foʊn **~s** z
headpiec|e ˈhed piːs →ˈheb- **~es** ɪz əz
headquarter ˌhed ˈkwɔːt ə ◂ →ˌheg-, ˈ·ˌ·· ‖ ˈhed ˌkwɔːrţ ər -ˌkwɔːţ- **~ed** d **~s** z
headrest ˈhed rest **~s** s
headroom ˈhed ruːm -rʊm
headrush ˈhed rʌʃ
head|scarf ˈhed |skɑːf ‖ -|skɑːrf **~scarves** skɑːvz ‖ skɑːrvz
headset ˈhed set **~s** s
headship ˈhed ʃɪp **~s** s
headshrinker ˈhed ˌʃrɪŋk ə ‖ -ər **~s** z
headstall ˈhed stɔːl ‖ -stɑːl **~s** z
headstand ˈhed stænd **~s** z
headstone, H~ ˈhed stəʊn ‖ -stoʊn **~s** z
headstrong ˈhed strɒŋ ‖ -strɔːŋ -strɑːŋ
heads-up ˈhedz ʌp ˌ·ˈ·
head-to-head ˌhed tə ˈhed ◂
head-up *adj, adv* ˌhed ˈʌp ◂
headwaters ˈhed ˌwɔːt əz ‖ -ˌwɔːţ ərz -ˌwɑːţ-
headway ˈhed weɪ
headwind ˈhed wɪnd **~s** z
headword ˈhed wɜːd ‖ -wɜːd **~s** z
head|y ˈhed |i **~ier** i ə ‖ i ər **~iest** i ɪst i əst **~ily** ɪ li əl i **~iness** i nəs i nɪs
heal, Heal hiːəl **healed** hiːəld **healing** ˈhiːəl ɪŋ **heals, Heal's** hiːəlz
Healaugh ˈhiːl ə
Healdsburg ˈhiːəldz bɜːg ‖ -bɜːg
healer ˈhiːəl ə ‖ -ər **~s** z
Healey ˈhiːl i
health helθ ˈ**health care**; ˈ**health** ˌ**centre**; ˈ**health farm**; ˈ**health food**; ˌ**health** ˈ**maintenance** ˌ**organi**ˌ**zation**; ˈ**health** ˌ**visitor**
healthful ˈhelθ fəl -fʊl **~ly** i **~ness** nəs nɪs
health|y ˈhelθ |i **~ier** i ə ‖ i ər **~iest** i ɪst i əst **~ily** ɪ li əl i **~iness** i nəs i nɪs
Healy ˈhiːl i
Heaney ˈhiːn i
Heanor ˈhiːn ə ˈheɪn ə ‖ -ər
heap hiːp **heaped** hiːpt **heaping** ˈhiːp ɪŋ **heaps** hiːps
hear hɪə ‖ hɪər *(= here)* **heard** hɜːd ‖ hɜːd *(!)* **hearing** ˈhɪər ɪŋ ‖ ˈhɪr ɪŋ **hears** hɪəz ‖ hɪərz
heard, Heard hɜːd ‖ hɜːd *(= herd)*
hearer ˈhɪər ə ‖ ˈhɪr ər **~s** z
hearing ˈhɪər ɪŋ ‖ ˈhɪr ɪŋ **~s** z ˈ**hearing aid**
hearing-impaired ˌhɪər ɪŋ ɪm ˈpeəd ◂ ˈ·····. ‖ ˌhɪr ɪŋ ɪm ˈpeərd ◂ -ˈpæərd ◂
hearken ˈhɑːk ən ‖ ˈhɑːrk ən **~ed** d **~ing** ˌɪŋ **~s** z
Hearn, Hearne hɜːn ‖ hɜːn
hearsay ˈhɪə seɪ ˌ·ˈ· ‖ ˈhɪr-
hearse hɜːs ‖ hɜːs **hearses** ˈhɜːs ɪz -əz ‖ ˈhɜːs əz
Hearst hɜːst ‖ hɜːst
heart hɑːt ‖ hɑːrt *(= hart)* **hearted** ˈhɑːt ɪd -əd ‖ ˈhɑːrţ əd **hearting** ˈhɑːt ɪŋ ‖ ˈhɑːrţ ɪŋ **hearts** hɑːts ‖ hɑːrts ˈ**heart at**ˌ**tack**; ˈ**heart di**ˌ**sease**; ˈ**heart** ˌ**failure**
heartache ˈhɑːt eɪk ‖ ˈhɑːrţ- **~s** s
heartbeat ˈhɑːt biːt ‖ ˈhɑːrt- **~s** s
heartbreak ˈhɑːt breɪk ‖ ˈhɑːrt- **~s** s
heartbreaking ˈhɑːt ˌbreɪk ɪŋ ‖ ˈhɑːrt- **~ly** li
heartbroken ˈhɑːt ˌbrəʊk ən ‖ ˈhɑːrt ˌbroʊk ən **~ly** li **~ness** nəs nɪs
heartburn ˈhɑːt bɜːn ‖ ˈhɑːrt bɜːn
-hearted ˈhɑːt ɪd ◂ -əd ‖ ˈhɑːrţ əd — **tender-hearted** ˌtend ə ˈhɑːt ɪd ◂ -əd ‖ -ər ˈhɑːrţ əd ◂

H

hearten ˈhɑːt ᵊn ‖ ˈhɑːrt ᵊn **~ed** d **~ing/ly** ˌɪŋ /li **~s** z
heartfelt ˈhɑːt felt ‖ ˈhɑːrt-
hearth hɑːθ ‖ hɑːrθ **hearths** hɑːθs hɑːðz ‖ hɑːrθs
hearthrug ˈhɑːθ rʌɡ ‖ ˈhɑːrθ- **~s** z
hearti... —*see* **hearty**
heartland ˈhɑːt lænd ‖ ˈhɑːrt- **~s** z
heartless ˈhɑːt ləs **~ly** li **~ness** nəs nɪs
heart-lung ˌhɑːt ˈlʌŋ ‖ ˌhɑːrt-
ˌ**heart-ˈlung maˌchine**
heartrending ˈhɑːt ˌrend ɪŋ ‖ ˈhɑːrt- **~ly** li
heart-searching ˈhɑːt ˌsɜːtʃ ɪŋ ‖ ˈhɑːrt ˌsɝːtʃ ɪŋ **~s** z
heartsease ˈhɑːts iːz ‖ ˈhɑːrts-
heart-shaped ˈhɑːt ʃeɪpt ‖ ˈhɑːrt-
heartsick ˈhɑːt sɪk ‖ ˈhɑːrt- **~ness** nəs nɪs
heart-stopping ˈhɑːt ˌstɒp ɪŋ ‖ ˈhɑːrt ˌstɑːp ɪŋ
heartstrings ˈhɑːt strɪŋz ‖ ˈhɑːrt-
heartthrob ˈhɑːt θrɒb ‖ ˈhɑːrt θrɑːb **~s** z
heart-to-heart ˌhɑːt tə ˈhɑːt ◂ -tu- ‖ ˌhɑːrt tə ˈhɑːrt ◂
ˌ**heart-to-heart ˈchat**
heartwarming ˈhɑːt ˌwɔːm ɪŋ ‖ ˈhɑːrt ˌwɔːrm ɪŋ **~ly** li
heartwood ˈhɑːt wʊd ‖ ˈhɑːrt-
heartworm ˈhɑːt wɜːm ‖ ˈhɑːrt wɝːm **~s** z
heart|y ˈhɑːt |i ‖ ˈhɑːrţ |i **~ier** i‿ə ‖ i‿ᵊr **~iest** i‿ɪst i‿əst **~ily** ɪ li əl i **~iness** i nəs i nɪs
heat hiːt **heated/ly** ˈhiːt ɪd /li -əd /li ‖ ˈhiːţ əd /li **heating** ˈhiːt ɪŋ ‖ ˈhiːţ ɪŋ **heats** hiːts
ˈ**heat exˌchanger**; ˈ**heat exˌhaustion**; ˈ**heat pump**; ˈ**heat rash**; ˈ**heat shield**; ˈ**heat wave**
heater ˈhiːt ə ‖ ˈhiːţ ᵊr **~s** z
heath, Heath hiːθ **heaths** hiːθs
ˌ**Heath ˈRobinson**
Heathcliff, Heathcliffe ˈhiːθ klɪf
Heathcoat, Heathcote *(i)* ˈheθ kət, *(ii)* ˈhiːθ-
heathen ˈhiːð ᵊn **~dom** dəm **~ish** ɪʃ **~ism** ˌɪz əm
heather, H~ ˈheð ə ‖ -ᵊr —*but the place in Leics is* ˈhiːð- **~s** z
heather-mixture ˈheð ə ˌmɪks tʃə ˌ· ˈ· · ‖ -ᵊr ˌmɪks tʃᵊr
heathery ˈheð ər i
Heathfield ˈhiːθ fiːᵊld
Heathrow ˌhiːθ ˈrəʊ ◂ ˈ· · ‖ ˈhiːθ roʊ
ˌ**Heathrow ˈAirport**
Heaton ˈhiːt ᵊn
heatproof ˈhiːt pruːf §-prʊf
heat-resistant ˈhiːt ri ˌzɪst ənt -rə-
heat-seeking ˈhiːt ˌsiːk ɪŋ
heatstroke ˈhiːt strəʊk ‖ -stroʊk
heave hiːv **heaved** hiːvd **heaves** hiːvz **heaving** ˈhiːv ɪŋ **hove** həʊv ‖ hoʊv
heave-ho ˌhiːv ˈhəʊ ‖ -ˈhoʊ
heaven, H~ ˈhev ᵊn **~s** z
heavenly ˈhev ᵊn li
heaven-sent ˌhev ᵊn ˈsent ◂ ˈ· · ·
heavenward ˈhev ᵊn wəd ‖ -wᵊrd **~s** z

heavi... —*see* **heavy**
Heaviside ˈhev i saɪd
heav|y ˈhev |i **~ier** i‿ə ‖ i‿ᵊr **~iest** i‿ɪst i‿əst **~ily** ɪ li əl i **~iness** i nəs i nɪs
ˌ**heavy ˈhydrogen**; ˌ**heavy ˈindustry**; ˌ**heavy ˈmetal**; ˌ**heavy ˈpetting**; ˌ**heavy ˈwater**
heavy-duty ˌhev i ˈdjuːt i ◂ →-ˈdʒuːt i ◂ ‖ -ˈduːţ i ◂ -ˈdjuːţ i ◂
heavy-handed ˌhev i ˈhænd ɪd ◂ -əd **~ly** li **~ness** nəs nɪs
heavy-hearted ˌhev i ˈhɑːt ɪd ◂ -əd ‖ -ˈhɑːrţ əd ◂
heavy-laden ˌhev i ˈleɪd ᵊn ◂
heavy-set ˌhev i ˈset ◂
heavyweight ˈhev i weɪt **~s** s
Hebburn ˈheb ɜːn -ən ‖ -ᵊrn
Hebden ˈheb dən
hebdomadal heb ˈdɒm əd ᵊl ‖ -ˈdɑːm- **~ly** i
Hebe ˈhiːb i
Hebei ˌhɜː ˈbeɪ ‖ ˌhʌ- —*Chi* Hébĕi [²xɤ ³pei]
hebephrenia ˌhiːb i ˈfriːn i‿ə ˌheb-, ˌ·ə-
Heber ˈhiːb ə ‖ -ᵊr
Hebraic hɪ ˈbreɪ ɪk hə-, hiː-
Hebraist ˈhiːb reɪ ɪst -ri-, §-əst **~s** s
Hebrew ˈhiːb ruː **~s** z
Hebridean ˌheb rə ˈdiː‿ən ◂ -rɪ- **~s** z
Hebrides ˈheb rə diːz -rɪ-
Hebron ˈheb rɒn ˈhiːb-, -rən ‖ -rən
Hecate ˈhek ət i ‖ -əţ i —*in Shakespeare also* ˈhek ət
hecatomb ˈhek ə tuːm -təʊm ‖ -toʊm **~s** z
Hecht hekt
heck, Heck hek
heckelphone ˈhek ᵊl fəʊn ‖ -foʊn **~s** z
heckl|e ˈhek ᵊl **~ed** d **~er/s** ‿ə/z ‖ ‿ᵊr/z **~es** z **~ing** ‿ɪŋ
Heckmondwike ˈhek mənd waɪk
heckuva ˈhek əv ə
hectare ˈhekt eə -ə, -ɑː ‖ -er ær **~s** z
hectic ˈhekt ɪk **~ally** ᵊl‿i
hecto- ¦hekt ə -əʊ — **hectogram** ˈhekt ə ɡræm
hectograph ˈhekt ə ɡrɑːf -əʊ-, -ɡræf ‖ -ɡræf **~s** s
hector, H~ ˈhekt ə ‖ -ᵊr **~ed** d **hectoring** ˈhekt ər ɪŋ **~s** z
Hecuba ˈhek jʊb ə
he'd *strong form* hiːd, *weak forms* hid, id —*The weak form* id *is not used at the beginning of a sentence or clause.*
heddle, H~ ˈhed ᵊl **~s** z
Hedex *tdmk* ˈhed eks
hedge hedʒ **hedged** hedʒd **hedges** ˈhedʒ ɪz -əz **hedging** ˈhedʒ ɪŋ
ˈ**hedge ˌsparrow**
hedgehog ˈhedʒ hɒɡ -ɒɡ ‖ -hɔːɡ -hɑːɡ **~s** z
hedgehop ˈhedʒ hɒp ‖ -hɑːp **~ped** t **~per/s** ə/z ‖ ᵊr/z **~ping** ɪŋ **~s** s
Hedgerley ˈhedʒ ə li ‖ -ᵊr-
hedgerow ˈhedʒ rəʊ ‖ -roʊ **~s** z
Hedges ˈhedʒ ɪz -əz
Hedley ˈhed li

edonic hiː ˈdɒn ɪk hɪ- ‖ -ˈdɑːn ɪk **~s** s
edonism ˈhiːd ᵊn ˌɪz əm ˈhed-
edonist ˈhiːd ᵊn ɪst ˈhed-, §-əst **~s** s
edonistic ˌhiːd ə ˈnɪst ɪk ◂ ˌhed-, -ᵊn ˈɪst-
~ally ᵊl‿i
edy ˈhed i
eebie-jeebies ˌhiːb i ˈdʒiːb iz
eed hiːd **heeded** ˈhiːd ɪd -əd **heeding** ˈhiːd ɪŋ **heeds** hiːdz
eedful ˈhiːd fᵊl -fʊl **~ly** i **~ness** nəs nɪs
eedless ˈhiːd ləs -lɪs **~ly** li **~ness** nəs nɪs
ee-haw ˈhiː hɔː ˌ·ˈ· ‖ -hɑː **~s** z
eel hiːᵊl **heeled** hiːᵊld **heeling** ˈhiːᵊl ɪŋ **heels** hiːᵊlz
eelball ˈhiːᵊl bɔːl ‖ -bɑːl **~s** z
eelbar ˈhiːᵊl bɑː ‖ -bɑːr **~s** z
eelflip ˈhiːl flɪp **~s** s
eenan ˈhiːn ən
eep hiːp
HEFCE ˈhef si -ki, -kə
Heffer ˈhef ə ‖ -ᵊr
Hefner ˈhef nə ‖ -nᵊr
heft heft **hefted** ˈheft ɪd -əd **hefting** ˈheft ɪŋ **hefts** hefts
heft|y ˈheft |i **~ier** i‿ə ‖ i‿ᵊr **~iest** i‿ɪst i‿əst **~ily** ɪ li əl i **~iness** i nəs i nɪs
Hegarty ˈheg ət i ‖ -ᵊrt̬ i
Hegel ˈheɪg ᵊl —*Ger* [ˈheː gᵊl]
Hegelian hɪ ˈgeɪl i‿ən heɪ-, -ˈgiːl- **~s** z
hegemonic ˌheg ə ˈmɒn ɪk ◂ ˌhiːg-, ˌhedʒ-, ˌɪ- ‖ -ˈmɑːn ɪk ◂
hegemon|y hɪ ˈgem ən |i hiː-, -ˈdʒem-; ˈheg ɪm-, ˈhedʒ-, ˈ·əm- ‖ hə ˈdʒem ən |i hɪ-, -ˈgem-; ˈhedʒ ə moʊn |i **~ies** iz
hegira, H~ ˈhedʒ ɪr ə -ər-; hɪ ˈdʒaɪᵊr ə, he- **~s** z
Heidegger ˈhaɪd eg ə -ɪg- ‖ -ᵊr —*Ger* [ˈhai dɛg ɐ]
Heidelberg ˈhaɪd ᵊl bɜːg ‖ -bɜːg —*Ger* [ˈhai dᵊl bɛʁk]
Heidi ˈhaɪd i
heifer ˈhef ə ‖ -ᵊr **~s** z
heigh-ho ˌheɪ ˈhəʊ ˈ· · ‖ -ˈhoʊ —*Usually said with a low-rise nuclear tone.*
height haɪt ⚠haɪtθ **heights** haɪts ⚠haɪtθs
heighten ˈhaɪt ᵊn **~ed** d **~ing** ˌɪŋ **~s** z
Heighway *(i)* ˈhaɪ weɪ, *(ii)* ˈheɪ-
Heilbron, Heilbronn ˈhaɪᵊl brɒn ‖ -brɑːn —*Ger* [hail ˈbʁɔn]
Heilongjiang ˌheɪ lɒŋ ˈdʒæŋ -lʊŋ-, -dʒi ˈæŋ ‖ -lʊŋ dʒi ˈɑːŋ —*Chi* Hēilóngjiāng [¹xei ²lʊŋ ¹tɕjɑŋ]
Heimlich ˈhaɪm lɪk -lɪx —*Ger* [ˈhaɪm lɪç]
ˈHeimlich maˌnoeuvre/maˌneuver
Heine ˈhaɪn ə —*Ger* [ˈhai nə]
Heineken *tdmk* ˈhaɪn ɪk ən -ək-
Heinemann ˈhaɪn ə mən
Heiney ˈhaɪn i
Heinkel ˈhaɪŋk ᵊl
Heinlein ˈhaɪn laɪn
heinous ˈheɪn əs §ˈhiːn-, ⚠ˈ·i‿əs **~ly** li **~ness** nəs nɪs
Heinz *tdmk* haɪnz haɪnʦ

heir eə ‖ eᵊr æᵊr *(= air)* **heirs** eəz ‖ eᵊrz æᵊrz
ˌheir apˈparent; **ˌheir preˈsumptive**
heiress ˈeər es -ɪs, -əs; ˌeər ˈes ‖ ˈer əs ˈær- **~es** ɪz əz
heirless ˈeə ləs -lɪs ‖ ˈer- ˈær- **~ness** nəs nɪs
heirloom ˈeə luːm ‖ ˈer- ˈær- **~s** z
heirship ˈeə ʃɪp ‖ ˈer- ˈær- *(= airship)* **~s** s
Heisenberg ˈhaɪz ᵊn bɜːg ‖ -bɜːg —*Ger* [ˈhai zᵊn bɛʁk]
heist haɪst **heisted** ˈhaɪst ɪd -əd **heisting** ˈhaɪst ɪŋ **heists** haɪsts
hejira, H~ ˈhedʒ ɪr ə -ər-; hɪ ˈdʒaɪᵊr ə, he- **~s** z
Hekla ˈhek lə —*Icelandic* [ˈhɛhk la]
held held
Helen ˈhel ən -ɪn
Helena *(i)* ˈhel ən ə -ɪn-, *(ii)* hə ˈliːn ə hɪ- *—The place in Montana is (i); the personal name was formerly (ii) but is now usually (i). See also* St H~.
Helene he ˈleɪn hə-, hɪ- ‖ -ˈliːn *(*)*
helenium hə ˈliːn i‿əm hɪ-
Helensburgh ˈhel ənz bər‿ə ˈ·ɪnz-, §-ˌbʌr ə ‖ ˈhel ənz bɜːg
Helfgott ˈhelf gɒt ‖ -gɑːt
Helga ˈhelg ə
helianthus ˌhiːl i ˈæn*θ* əs ˌhel- **~es** ɪz əz
helical ˈhel ɪk ᵊl ˈhiːl- **~ly** ‿i
helices ˈhel ɪ siːz ˈhiːl-, -ə-
helicoid ˈhel ɪ kɔɪd -ə- **~s** z
Helicon, h~ ˈhel ɪk ən -ək-; -ɪ kɒn, -ə- ‖ -ə kɑːn -ɪk ən **~s** z
heliconia ˌhel ɪ ˈkəʊn i‿ə ‖ -ˈkoʊn-
helicopter ˈhel ɪ kɒpt ə ˈ·ə-, ˈ·i-; ˌ· ˈ· · ‖ -ə kɑːpt ᵊr ˈhiːl- **~s** z
helideck ˈhel i dek **~s** s
Helier ˈhel i‿ə ‖ ᵊr
Heligoland ˈhel ɪ gəʊ lænd ˈ·ə-, -ɪg ə- ‖ -goʊ-
helio- *comb. form*
with stress-neutral suffix ˈhiːl i əʊ ‖ -oʊ
— **heliocentric** ˌhiːl i əʊ ˈsentr ɪk ◂ ‖ -i oʊ-
with stress-imposing suffix ˌhiːl i ˈɒ+ ‖ -ˈɑː+
— **heliometer** ˌhiːl i ˈɒm ɪt ə -ət ə ‖ -ˈɑːm ət̬ ᵊr
Heliogabalus ˌhiːl i‿ə ˈgæb əl əs -i əʊ- ‖ -i oʊ-
heliograph ˈhiːl i‿ə grɑːf -græf ‖ -græf **~ed** t **~ing** ɪŋ **~s** s
Heliopolis ˌhiːl i ˈɒp əl ɪs §-əs ‖ -ˈɑːp-
Helios ˈhiːl i ɒs ‖ -ɑːs
heliotrope ˈhiːl i‿ə trəʊp ˈhel- ‖ -troʊp **~s** s
heliotropic ˌhiːl i‿ə ˈtrɒp ɪk ◂ ‖ -ˈtrɑːp ɪk ◂ **~ally** ᵊl‿i
heliotropism ˌhiːl i ˈɒtr ə ˌpɪz əm ˈhiːl i‿ə trəʊp ˌɪz-, ˈ· · ·ˌ· · ·, ˌ· · ˈ· · · ‖ -ˈɑːtr-
helipad ˈhel i pæd §-ə- ‖ ˈhiːl- **~s** z
heliport ˈhel i pɔːt §-ə- ‖ -pɔːrt ˈhiːl-, -poʊrt **~s** s
heli-ski|ing ˈhel i ˌskiː| ɪŋ **~er/s** ə/z ‖ ᵊr/z
helium ˈhiːl i‿əm
helix ˈhiːl ɪks **helices** ˈhel ɪ siːz ˈhiːl-, -ə- **~es** ɪz əz
hell, Hell hel **hells, Hell's** helz
ˌHell's ˈAngel

H

he'll *strong form* hiːᵊl, *weak forms* hiᵊl, iᵊl —*The weak form* iᵊl *is not used at the beginning of a sentence or clause.*
hellacious he ˈleɪʃ əs **~ly** li
Helladic he ˈlæd ɪk
Hellas ˈhel æs
hell-bent ˌhel ˈbent ◂
hellcat ˈhel kæt **~s** s
hellebore ˈhel ɪ bɔː -ə- ‖ -bɔːr -bour **~s** z
helleborine ˈhel ɪ bə raɪn ˈ·ə-, -riːn; ˌ· ·ˈbɔːr iːn **~s** z
Hellene ˈhel iːn **~s** z
Hellenic he ˈlen ɪk hɪ-, hə-, -ˈliːn-
Hellenism ˈhel ɪn ˌɪz əm -ən- **~s** z
Hellenistic ˌhel ɪ ˈnɪst ɪk ◂ -ə-
Heller ˈhel ə ‖ -ᵊr
Hellespont ˈhel ɪ spɒnt -ə- ‖ -spɑːnt
hellfire ˌhel ˈfaɪ‿ə ˈ· · ‖ ˈhel ˌfaɪ‿ᵊr
hell-hole ˈhel həʊl →-hɒʊl ‖ -houl **~s** z
Hellicar ˈhel ɪ kɑː -ə- ‖ -kɑːr
hellion ˈhel jən **~s** z
hellish ˈhel ɪʃ **~ly** li **~ness** nəs nɪs
Hellman ˈhel mən
hello hə ˈləʊ he- ‖ -ˈloʊ **~ed** d **~es** z **~ing** ɪŋ
helluva ˈhel əv ə
helm helm **helms** helmz
helm|et ˈhelm |ɪt -ət ‖ -|ət **~eted** ɪt ɪd ət-, -əd ‖ əṭ əd **~ets** ɪts əts ‖ əts
Helmholtz ˈhelm həʊlts →-hɒʊlts ‖ -hoʊlts —*Ger* [ˈhɛlm hɔlts]
helminth ˈhelm ɪnᵗθ **~s** s
helminthiasis ˌhelm ɪn ˈθaɪ‿əs ɪs §ˌ·ən-, §-əs
helminthological ˌhelm ɪnᵗθ ə ˈlɒdʒ ɪk ᵊl ◂ §ˌ·ənᵗθ- ‖ -ˈlɑːdʒ- **~ly** ‿i
helmintholog|ist ˌhelm ɪn ˈθɒl ədʒ |ɪst §ˌ·ən-, §-əst ‖ -ˈθɑːl- **~ists** ɪsts §əsts **~y** i
Helmsdale ˈhelmz deɪᵊl
Helmsley ˈhelmz li ˈhemz-
helms|man ˈhelmz |mən **~men** mən men
Heloise, Héloïse ˈel əʊ iːz ˌ· ·ˈ· ‖ ˈhel oʊ iːz ˈel- —*Fr* [e lɔ iːz]
helot ˈhel ət **~s** s
helotry ˈhel ət ri
help help **helped** helpt **helping/s** ˈhelp ɪŋ/z **helps** helps
ˌ**helping** ˈ**hand**
helpdesk ˈhelp desk **~s** s
helper ˈhelp ə ‖ -ᵊr **~s** z
helpful ˈhelp fᵊl -fʊl **~ly** i **~ness** nəs nɪs
helpless ˈhelp ləs -lɪs **~ly** li
helpline ˈhelp laɪn **~s** z
Helpmann ˈhelp mən
helpmate ˈhelp meɪt **~s** s
helpmeet ˈhelp miːt **~s** s
Helsinki hel ˈsɪŋk i ˈhels ɪŋk i —*Finnish* [ˈhel siŋ ki]
Helston ˈhelst ən
helter-skelter ˌhelt ə ˈskelt ə ‖ -ᵊr ˈskelt ᵊr **~s** z
helve helv **helves** helvz
Helvellyn hel ˈvel ɪn -ən
Helvetia hel ˈviːʃ ə -ˈviːʃ i‿ə
Helvetic hel ˈvet ɪk ‖ -ˈveṭ ɪk
hem hem **hemmed** hemd **hemming** ˈhem ɪŋ **hems** hemz
hemal ˈhiːm ᵊl
he-|man ˈhiː |mæn **~men** men
hematite ˈhiːm ə taɪt ˈhem-
hemato- *comb. form*
with stress-neutral suffix ¦hiːm ə təʊ ¦hem- ‖ -əṭ ə — **hematogenesis** ˌhiːm ət əʊ ˈdʒen əs ɪs ˌhem-, -ɪs ɪs, §-əs ‖ -əṭ ə-
with stress-imposing suffix ˌhiːm ə ˈtɒ+ ˌhem ‖ -ˈtɑː+ — **hematogenous** ˌhiːm ə ˈtɒdʒ ən əs ˌhem- ‖ -ˈtɑːdʒ-
hematologist ˌhiːm ə ˈtɒl ədʒ ɪst §-əst ‖ -ˈtɑːl **~s** s
hematology ˌhiːm ə ˈtɒl ədʒ i ‖ -ˈtɑːl-
hematoma ˌhiːm ə ˈtəʊm ə ‖ -ˈtoʊm ə **~s** z
heme hiːm
Hemel Hempstead ˌhem ᵊl ˈhem*p* stɪd -stəd, -sted
he-men ˈhiː men
hemi- ¦hem i — **hemihydrate** ˌhem i ˈhaɪdr eɪt
hemidemisemiquaver ˌhem i ˌdem i ˈsem i ˌkweɪv ə ‖ -ᵊr **~s** z
Heming ˈhem ɪŋ
Hemingway ˈhem ɪŋ weɪ
hemiplegia ˌhem i ˈpliːdʒ i‿ə -ˈpliːdʒ ə
hemiplegic ˌhem i ˈpliːdʒ ɪk ◂ **~s** s
hemipterous hɪ ˈmɪpt ər əs he-, hə-
hemisphere ˈhem ɪ sfɪə -ə- ‖ -sfɪr **~s** z
hemispheric ˌhem i ˈsfer ɪk ◂ ‖ -ˈsfɪr- **~al** ᵊl **~ally** ᵊl‿i
hemistich ˈhem i stɪk **~s** s
hemline ˈhem laɪn **~s** z
hemlock ˈhem lɒk ‖ -lɑːk **~s** s
Hemmings ˈhem ɪŋz
hemo- *comb. form*
with stress-neutral suffix ¦hiːm əʊ ‖ -oʊ — **hemodialysis** ˌhiːm əʊ daɪ ˈæl əs ɪs -ɪs ɪs, §-əs ‖ ˌ·oʊ-
with stress-imposing suffix hiː ˈmɒ+ hɪ- ‖ -ˈmɑː+ — **hemolysis** hiː ˈmɒl əs ɪs hɪ-, -ɪs-, §-əs ‖ -ˈmɑːl-
hemoglobin ˌhiːm ə ˈgləʊb ɪn §-ən, ˈ· · ·· ‖ ˈhiːm ə gloʊb ən
hemophilia ˌhiːm ə ˈfɪl i‿ə -ˈfiːl-
hemophiliac ˌhiːm ə ˈfɪl i æk ◂ -ˈfiːl- **~s** s
hemorrhag|e ˈhem ər‿ɪdʒ **~ed** d **~es** ɪz əz **~ing** ɪŋ
hemorrhoid ˈhem ə rɔɪd **~s** z
hemorrhoidal ˌhem ə ˈrɔɪd ᵊl ◂
hemp hemp
ˈ**hemp** ˌ**nettle**
Hempel ˈhemp ᵊl
hempen ˈhemp ən
Hempstead ˈhem*p*st ed -ɪd, §-əd
hemstitch ˈhem stɪtʃ **~ed** t **~es** ɪz əz **~ing** ɪŋ
hen hen **hens** henz
ˈ**hen house**; ˈ**hen** ˌ**party**
Henan hɜː ˈnæn ‖ hə ˈnɑːn —*Chi* Hénán [^{2}xɤ ^{2}nan]
henbane ˈhen beɪn →ˈhem-

enbit 'hen bɪt →'hem-
ence henᵗs
enceforth ˌhenᵗs 'fɔːθ '· · ‖ -'fɔːrθ -'fouərθ
enceforward ˌhenᵗs 'fɔː wəd ‖ -'fɔːr wᵊrd
ench|man 'hentʃ |mən **~men** mən
endeca- *comb. form* ¦hen dek ə ·¦ · ·
— **hendecasyllabic** ˌhen dek ə sɪ 'læb ɪk ◂ ·¦ ·-, -sə'·-
endecagon ˌhen 'dek əg ən ‖ -ə gɑːn **~s** z
enderson 'hend əs ən ‖ -ᵊrs-
endiadys hen 'daɪ‿əd ɪs §-əs
endon 'hend ən
endricks, Hendrix 'hendr ɪks
endry 'hendr i
eneage 'hen ɪdʒ
eneghan 'hen ɪg ən
enge hendʒ **henges** 'hendʒ ɪz -əz
engist 'heŋ gɪst -gəst, -dʒɪst
enley 'hen li
enman 'hen mən →'hem-
enna 'hen ə **hennaed** 'hen əd **hennaing** 'hen əʳ ɪŋ ‖ -ə ɪŋ **hennas** 'hen əz
ennessey, Hennessy 'hen əs i -ɪs-
enning 'hen ɪŋ
enpecked 'hen pekt →'hem-
enri ˌɒn 'riː ˌɒ̃-, '· · ‖ ɑːn 'riː —*Fr* [ɑ̃ ʁi] —*but as an American family name,* 'hen ri
enries —*see* **henry**
enrietta ˌhen ri 'et ə ◂ ‖ -'eṭ ə ◂
enriques hen 'riːk ɪz §-əz
en|ry, hen|ry 'hen |ri —*but as a French name,* ˌɒn 'riː ‖ ˌɑːn- —*Fr* [ɑ̃ ʁi] **~ries, ~rys, ~ry's** riz
Henryson 'hen rɪs ən -rəs-
Henslow, Henslowe 'henz ləʊ ‖ -loʊ
Henson 'henᵗs ᵊn
Henton 'hent ən ‖ -ᵊn
Henty 'hent i ‖ 'henṭ i
hep hep
heparin 'hep ər ɪn §-ən
hepatic hɪ 'pæt ɪk he-, hə- ‖ -'pæṭ ɪk **~s** s
hepatica hɪ 'pæt ɪk ə he-, hə- ‖ -'pæṭ- **~s** z
hepatitis ˌhep ə 'taɪt ɪs ◂ -əs ‖ -'taɪṭ əs ◂ , **ˌhepaˌtitis 'B**
Hepburn *(i)* 'hep bɜːn ‖ -bɜ˞ːn; *(ii)* 'heb ɜːn -ən ‖ -ᵊrn
Hephaestus hɪ 'fiːst əs he-, hə- ‖ -'fest- *(*)*
Hephzibah 'hefs ɪ bɑː 'heps-, -ə- ‖ -əb ə
Heppenstall 'hep ən stɔːl →-m- ‖ -stɑːl
Hepplewhite 'hep ᵊl waɪt -hwaɪt
hepta- *comb. form*
with stress-neutral suffix ¦hept ə
— **heptastich** 'hept ə stɪk
with stress-imposing suffix hep 'tæ+
— **heptamerous** hep 'tæm ər əs
heptagon 'hept əg ən -ə gɒn ‖ -ə gɑːn **~s** z
heptagonal hep 'tæg ən ᵊl **~ly** i
heptane 'hept eɪn
heptarch|y 'hept ɑːk |i ‖ -ɑːrk |i **~ies** iz
Heptateuch 'hept ə tjuːk →-tʃuːk ‖ -tuːk -tjuːk
heptathlete hep 'tæθ liːt **~s** s
heptathlon hep 'tæθ lən -lɒn ‖ -lɑːn **~s** z
Hepworth 'hep wɜːθ -wəθ ‖ -wᵊrθ

her *strong form* hɜː ‖ hɜ˞ː, *weak forms* hə, ɜː, ə ‖ hᵊr, ɜ˞ː, ᵊr —*The weak forms* ɜː, ə ‖ ɜ˞ː, ᵊr *are not used at the beginning of a sentence or clause.*
Hera 'hɪər ə ‖ 'hɪr ə
Heraclean ˌher ə 'kliː‿ən ◂
Heracles, Herakles 'her ə kliːz
Heraclitus ˌher ə 'klaɪt əs ˌhɪər- ‖ -'klaɪṭ əs
Heraklion he 'ræk li‿ən hɪ-, hə- —*ModGk* [i 'rak ljon]
herald 'her əld **~ed** ɪd əd **~ing** ɪŋ **~s** z
heraldic hə 'ræld ɪk he-, hɪ- **~ally** ᵊl‿i
herald|ry 'her əld |ri **~ries** riz

HERB

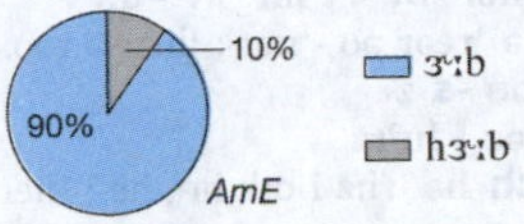

herb hɜːb ‖ ɜ˞ːb hɜ˞ːb — *Preference poll, AmE:* ɜ˞ːb *90%,* hɜ˞ːb *10%.* **herbs** hɜːbz ‖ ɜ˞ːbz hɜ˞ːbz
ˌherb 'bennet; **ˌherb 'Paris**; **ˌherb 'Robert**
Herb *personal name* hɜːb ‖ hɜ˞ːb
herbaceous hə 'beɪʃ əs hɜː- ‖ hɜ˞ː- ɜ˞ː-
herˌbaceous 'border
herbage, H~ 'hɜːb ɪdʒ ‖ 'ɜ˞ːb- 'hɜ˞ːb-
herbal 'hɜːb ᵊl ‖ 'ɜ˞ːb ᵊl 'hɜ˞ːb- **~s** z
herbalist 'hɜːb əl ɪst §-əst ‖ 'ɜ˞ːb- 'hɜ˞ːb- **~s** s
herbari|um hɜː 'beər i‿|əm ‖ hɜ˞ː 'ber- ɜ˞ː-, -'bær- **~a** ə **~ums** əmz
Herbert 'hɜːb ət ‖ 'hɜ˞ːb ᵊrt
herbicide 'hɜːb ɪ saɪd -ə- ‖ 'hɜ˞ːb- 'ɜ˞ːb- **~s** z
Herbie 'hɜːb i ‖ 'hɜ˞ːb i
herbivore 'hɜːb ɪ vɔː -ə- ‖ 'ɜ˞ːb ə vɔːr 'hɜ˞ːb-, -voʊr **~s** z
herbivorous hɜː 'bɪv ər‿əs hə- ‖ ɜ˞ː- hɜ˞ː- **~ly** li
Hercegovina ˌhɜːts ə 'gɒv ɪn ə ˌheəts-, ˌ·ɪ-, -ən ə; gəʊ 'viːn ə ‖ ˌherts ə 'goʊv- —*Serbian* ['hɛr tse gɔ vi na]
Herceptin *tdmk* hɜː 'sept ɪn ‖ hɜ˞ː-
Herculaneum ˌhɜːk ju 'leɪn i‿əm ‖ ˌhɜ˞ːk jə-
Herculean ˌhɜːk ju 'liː‿ən ◂ -jə-; hɜː 'kjuːl i‿ən ‖ ˌhɜ˞ːk jə-
Hercules 'hɜːk ju liːz -jə- ‖ 'hɜ˞ːk jə-
herd, Herd hɜːd ‖ hɜ˞ːd **herded** 'hɜːd ɪd -əd ‖ 'hɜ˞ːd əd **herding** 'hɜːd ɪŋ ‖ 'hɜ˞ːd ɪŋ **herds** hɜːdz ‖ hɜ˞ːdz
herds|man 'hɜːdz |mən ‖ 'hɜ˞ːdz- **~men** mən
Herdwick 'hɜːd wɪk ‖ 'hɜ˞ːd-
here hɪə ‖ hɪᵊr *(= hear)* **here's** hɪəz ‖ hɪᵊrz
hereabout ˌhɪər ə 'baʊt '· · · ‖ 'hɪr ə ˌbaʊt **~s** s
hereafter ˌhɪər 'ɑːft ə §-'æft- ‖ hɪr 'æft ᵊr
hereby ˌhɪə 'baɪ ◂ '· · ‖ ˌhɪr 'baɪ ◂
hereditability hɪ ˌred ɪt ə 'bɪl ət i hə-, he-, -ɪt i ‖ -əṭ ə 'bɪl əṭ i
hereditab|le hɪ 'red ɪt əb |ᵊl hə-, he-, -'ət- ‖ -'red əṭ- **~ly** li
hereditament ˌher ɪ 'dɪt ə mənt ˌ·ə- ‖ -'dɪṭ- **~s** s

hereditarily hə ˈred ət‿ər əl i hɪ-, he-, -ˈ·ɪt‿-ɪ li; ·ˌ·ə ˈter-, -ɪ ˈter- ‖ hə ˌred ə ˈter əl i
hereditar|y hə ˈred ət‿ər |i hɪ-, he-, -ˈ·ɪt‿ ‖ -ə ter |i **~iness** i nəs i nɪs
heredit|y hə ˈred ət |i hɪ-, he-, -ɪt- ‖ -əţ |i **~ies** iz
Hereford *(i)* ˈher ɪ fəd -ə- ‖ -fᵊrd, *(ii)* ˈhɜː fəd ‖ ˈhɜ˞ː fᵊrd —*The city and former county in England are (i); the town in TX is (ii). For the breed of cattle or pigs, and for street names, etc., (i) in BrE, usually (ii) in AmE.* **~shire** ʃə ʃɪə ‖ ʃᵊr
herein ˌhɪər ˈɪn ◂ ‖ hɪr-
hereinafter ˌhɪər ɪn ˈɑːft ə ◂ §-ən-, §-ˈæft- ‖ ˌhɪr ən ˈæft ᵊr ◂
Heren ˈher ən
hereof ˌhɪər ˈɒv ◂ ‖ hɪr ˈʌv -ˈɑːv
Herero hə ˈreər əʊ -ˈrɪər-; ˈhɪər ə rəʊ, ˈheər- ‖ -ˈrer oʊ **~s** z
here's hɪəz ‖ hɪᵊrz
heresiarch hə ˈriːz i ɑːk hɪ-, he-; ˈher əs- ‖ -ɑːrk **~s** s
heres|y ˈher əs |i -ɪs- **~ies** iz
heretic ˈher ə tɪk -ɪ- **~s** s
heretical hə ˈret ɪk ᵊl hɪ-, he- ‖ -ˈreţ- **~ly** ‿i
hereto ˌhɪə ˈtuː ◂ ‖ hɪr-
heretofore ˌhɪə tu ˈfɔː ◂ tə-, -tuː- ‖ ˈhɪrţ ə fɔːr -foʊr, ˌ·ˈ·
hereunder ˌhɪər ˈʌnd ə ◂ ‖ hɪr ˈʌnd ᵊr
hereupon ˌhɪər ə ˈpɒn ◂ ‖ ˈhɪr ə pɑːn -pɔːn, ˌ··ˈ·
Hereward ˈher ɪ wəd -ə- ‖ -wᵊrd
herewith ˌhɪə ˈwɪð ◂ -ˈwɪθ ‖ hɪr-
Herford ˈhɜː fəd ‖ ˈhɜ˞ː fᵊrd
Hergé ˌeə ˈʒeɪ ‖ ˌer- —*Fr* [ɛʁ ʒe]
heriot, H~, Heriott ˈher i‿ət **~s, ~'s** s
Heriot-Watt ˌher i‿ət ˈwɒt ‖ -ˈwɑːt
heritable ˈher ɪt əb ᵊl ˈ·ət- ‖ ˈher əţ-
heritag|e ˈher ɪt ɪdʒ -ət- ‖ -əţ- **~es** ɪz əz
herm hɜːm ‖ hɜ˞ːm **herms** hɜːmz ‖ hɜ˞ːmz
Herman ˈhɜːm ən ‖ ˈhɜ˞ːm-
Hermann ˈhɜːm ən ‖ ˈhɜ˞ːm- —*Ger* [ˈhɛʁ man]
hermaphrodite hɜː ˈmæf rə daɪt hə- ‖ hᵊr- **~s** s
hermaphroditic hɜː ˌmæf rə ˈdɪt ɪk ◂ hə- ‖ hᵊr ˌmæf rə ˈdɪţ ɪk ◂ **~ally** ᵊl‿i
hermeneutic ˌhɜːm ə ˈnjuːt ɪk ◂ -ɪ- ‖ ˌhɜ˞ːm ə ˈnuːţ ɪk ◂ -ˈnjuːţ- **~al** ᵊl **~ally** ᵊl‿i **~s** s
Hermes ˈhɜːm iːz ‖ ˈhɜ˞ːm-
Hermès *tdmk* ˌeə ˈmes ‖ ˌer- —*Fr* [ɛʁ mɛs]
Hermesetas *tdmk* ˌhɜːm ɪ ˈsiːt əs -ə-, -əz, -æs ‖ ˌhɜ˞ːm ə ˈsiːţ əs -əz
hermetic hɜː ˈmet ɪk hə- ‖ hᵊr ˈmeţ ɪk **~ally** ᵊl‿i
Hermia ˈhɜːm i‿ə ‖ ˈhɜ˞ːm-
Hermione hɜː ˈmaɪ‿ən i hə- ‖ hᵊr-
hermit ˈhɜːm ɪt §-ət ‖ ˈhɜ˞ːm- **~s** s
  ˈhermit crab
hermitag|e ˈhɜːm ɪt ɪdʒ -ət- ‖ ˈhɜ˞ːm əţ ɪdʒ —*but the H~ in St Petersburg is usually* ˌeəm ɪ ˈtɑːʒ, -ə- ‖ ˌerm- **~es** ɪz əz
Hermon ˈhɜːm ən ‖ ˈhɜ˞ːm-

hern, Hern, Herne hɜːn ‖ hɜ˞ːn
hernia ˈhɜːn i‿ə ‖ ˈhɜ˞ːn- **~s** z

HERO

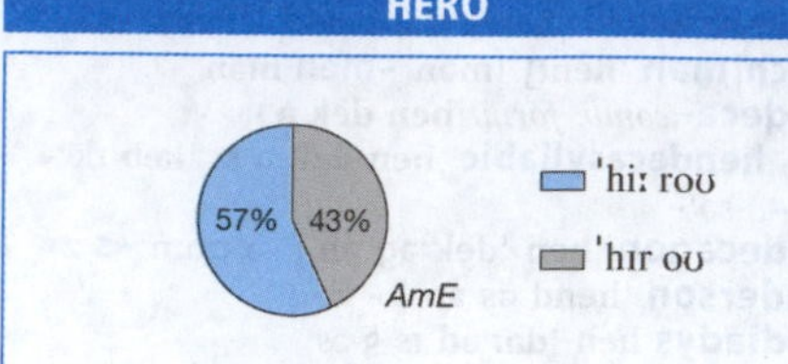

hero, Hero ˈhɪər əʊ ‖ ˈhiː roʊ ˈhɪr oʊ *Preference poll, AmE:* ˈhiː roʊ *57%,* ˈhɪr oʊ *43%.* **~es** z
  ˈhero ˌworship
Herod ˈher əd
Herodias hə ˈrəʊd i æs hɪ-, he-, -əs ‖ -ˈroʊd-
Herodotus hə ˈrɒd ət əs hɪ-, he- ‖ -ˈrɑːd əţ əs
heroic hə ˈrəʊ ɪk hɪ-, he- ‖ -ˈroʊ ɪk **~al** ᵊl **~ally** ᵊl‿i **~s** s
  heˌroic ˈcouplet
heroin ˈher əʊ ɪn §-ən ‖-oʊ ən
heroine ˈher əʊ ɪn ˈhɪər-, -iːn, §-ən ‖ -oʊ ən *(usually = heroin)* **~s** z
heroism ˈher əʊ ˌɪz əm ‖ -oʊ-
heron, Heron ˈher ən **~s** z
heron|ry ˈher ən |ri **~ries** riz
hero-worship *n, v* ˈhɪər əʊ ˌwɜːʃ ɪp §-əp ‖ ˈhiː roʊ ˌwɜ˞ːʃ əp ˈhɪr oʊ- **~ed, ~ped** t **~ing, ~ping** ɪŋ **~s** s
herpes ˈhɜːp iːz ‖ ˈhɜ˞ːp-
herpetological ˌhɜːp ɪt ə ˈlɒdʒ ɪk ᵊl ◂ ˌ·ət- ‖ ˌhɜ˞ːp əţ ə ˈlɑːdʒ- **~ly** ‿i
herpetologist ˌhɜːp ɪ ˈtɒl ədʒ ɪst ˌ·ə-, §-əst ‖ ˌhɜ˞ːp ə ˈtɑːl- **~s** s
herpetology ˌhɜːp ɪ ˈtɒl ədʒ i ˌ·ə- ‖ ˌhɜ˞ːp ə ˈtɑːl-
Herr heə ‖ heᵊr hæᵊr —*Ger* [hɛʁ]
herrenvolk, H~ ˈher ən fəʊk -fɒlk ‖ -foʊk -fɔːlk, -fɑːlk —*Ger* [ˈhɛʁ ən fɔlk]
Herrick ˈher ɪk
Herries ˈher ɪs -ɪz, §-əs, §-əz
herring, H~ ˈher ɪŋ **~s** z
  ˈherring gull
herringbone ˈher ɪŋ bəʊn ‖ -boʊn **~s** z
Herriot ˈher i‿ət
hers hɜːz ‖ hɜ˞ːz
Herschel, Herschell ˈhɜːʃ ᵊl ‖ ˈhɜ˞ːʃ-
herself *strong form* hɜː ˈself ‖ hɜ˞ː-, *weak forms* hə-, ɜː-, ə- ‖ hᵊr-, ᵊr- —*The forms* ɜː-, ə- ‖ ᵊr- *are not used at the beginning of a sentence or clause.*
Hersham ˈhɜːʃ əm ‖ ˈhɜ˞ːʃ-
Hershey ˈhɜːʃ i ‖ ˈhɜ˞ːʃ i
  ˈHershey bar
Herstmonceux ˌhɜːst mən ˈsjuː ◂ -ˈsuː ‖ ˌhɜ˞ːst mən ˈsuː
Herter ˈhɜːt ə ‖ ˈhɜ˞ːţ ᵊr
Hertford *(i)* ˈhɑː fəd ‖ ˈhɑːr fᵊrd, *(ii)* ˈhɑːt- ‖ ˈhɑːrt-, *(iii)* ˈhɜːt- ‖ ˈhɜ˞ːt- —*The traditional pronunciation for the English county town and the Oxford college, (i), has been largely*

superseded by the spelling pronunciation (ii). As an American name, (iii). **~shire** ʃə ʃɪə ‖ ʃᵊr ʃɪr

erts hɑːts ‖ hɑːrts

ertz, Hertz hɜːts ‖ hɜ˞ːts —*Ger* [hɛʁts]

ertzian 'hɜːts i‿ən 'heəts- ‖ 'hɜ˞ːts- 'herts-

ertzog 'hɜːts ɒg ‖ 'hɜ˞ːts ɑːg

ervey *(i)* 'hɑːv i ‖ 'hɑːrv i, *(ii)* 'hɜːv i ‖ 'hɜ˞ːv i

erzegovina ˌhɜːts ə 'gɒv ɪn ə ˌheəts-, ˌ·ɪ-ˌ-ən ə; -gəʊ 'viːn ə ‖ ˌherts ə 'goʊv- —*Serbian* Hercegovina [ˈˈhɛr tsɛ gɔ vi na]

erzl 'hɜːts ᵊl ‖ 'herts- —*Ger* ['hɛʁts ᵊl]

e's *strong form* hiːz, *weak forms* hiz, iːz, iz —*At the beginning of a sentence or clause, only the forms with* h *are used.*

eseltine 'hes ᵊl taɪn 'hez-

eselwood 'hes ᵊl wʊd 'hez-

esiod 'hiːs i‿əd 'hes-, -ɒd

esitance 'hez ɪt ənᵗs -ət- ‖ -ᵊnᵗs

esitanc|y 'hez ɪt ənᵗs |i -ət- ‖ -ᵊnᵗs |i **~ies** iz

esitant 'hez ɪt ənt -ət- ‖ -ᵊnt **~ly** li

esi|tate 'hez ɪ |teɪt -ə- **~tated** teɪt ɪd -əd ‖ teɪţ əd **~tates** teɪts **~tating/ly** teɪt ɪŋ/ li ‖ teɪţ ɪŋ/ li

esitation ˌhez ɪ 'teɪʃ ᵊn -ə- **~s** z

esketh 'hesk əθ -ɪθ

esperia he 'spɪər i‿ə ‖ -'spɪr-

esperian he 'spɪər i‿ən ‖ -'spɪr-

esperides hɪ 'sper ɪ diːz he-, hə-, -ə-

esperus 'hesp ər əs

ess hes

essayon 'hes i‿ən

esse hes 'hes ə —*Ger* ['hɛs ə]

essian, H~ 'hes i‿ən ‖ 'heʃ ᵊn (*) **~s** z

essle *place in Humberside* 'hez ᵊl

ester 'hest ə ‖ -ᵊr

eston 'hest ən

eswall 'hez wəl ‖ -wɔːl -wɑːl

et het **hets** hets

ˌ**het 'up**

etaer|a, hetair|a hɪ 'taɪᵊr |ə he- ‖ -'tɪr |ə **~ae** iː aɪ **~ai** aɪ **~as** əz

heterarch|y 'het ə rɑːk |i ‖ 'heţ ə rɑːrk |i **~ies** iz

hetero 'het‿ər əʊ ‖ 'heţ ə roʊ **~s** z

hetero- *comb. form*
with stress-neutral suffix ¦het‿ər əʊ ‖ ¦heţ ə roʊ — **heterographic** ˌhet‿ər əʊ 'græf ɪk ◂ ‖ ˌheţ ə roʊ-
with stress-imposing suffix ˌhet ə 'rɒ+ ‖ ˌheţ ə 'rɑː+ — **heterography** ˌhet ə 'rɒg rəf i ‖ ˌhet ə 'rɑːg-

heteroclite 'het‿ər əʊ klaɪt ‖ 'heţ ər ə- **~s** s

heterocyclic ˌhet‿ər əʊ 'saɪk lɪk ◂ -'sɪk- ‖ ˌheţ ə roʊ-

heterodox 'het‿ər əʊ dɒks ‖ 'heţ ər ə dɑːks →'hetr ə dɑːks

heterodox|y 'het‿ər əʊ dɒks |i ‖ 'heţ ər ə dɑːks |i →'hetr ə dɑːks |i **~ies** iz

heterodyne 'het‿ər əʊ daɪn ‖ 'heţ ər ə- →'hetr ə daɪn

heterogeneity ˌhet‿ər əʊ dʒə 'niː ət i ˌhet ə ˌrɒdʒ ə-, -dʒɪ'--, -'neɪ-, -ɪt i ‖ ˌheţ ə roʊ dʒə 'niː əţ i →ˌhetr oʊ dʒə'--

heterogeneous ˌhet‿ər əʊ 'dʒiːn i‿əs ◂ ‖ ˌheţ ə roʊ- →ˌhetr oʊ'-, -ə'-- **~ly** li **~ness** nəs nɪs

heteronym 'het‿ər əʊ nɪm ‖ 'heţ ə roʊ- →'hetr oʊ nɪm, -ə nɪm **~s** z

heteronymous ˌhet ə 'rɒn ɪm əs ◂ -əm əs ‖ ˌheţ ə 'rɑːn-

heterorganic ˌhet‿ər ɔː 'gæn ɪk ◂ ‖ ˌheţ ər ɔːr-

heterosexism ˌhet‿ər əʊ 'seks ˌɪz əm ‖ ˌheţ ə roʊ-

heterosexist ˌhet‿ər əʊ 'seks ɪst ◂ §-əst ‖ ˌheţ ə roʊ- **~s** s

heterosexual ˌhet‿ər əʊ 'sek ʃu‿əl ◂ -'seks ju‿əl, -'sekʃ ᵊl ‖ ˌheţ ə roʊ- -ər ə- **~ly** i **~s** z

heterosexuality ˌhet‿ər əʊ ˌsek ʃu 'æl ət i -ˌseks ju- ‖ ˌheţ ə roʊ ˌsekʃu 'æl əţ i -ər ə-

heterozygote ˌhet‿ər əʊ'zaɪg əʊt ‖ ˌheţ ə roʊ 'zaɪg oʊt **~s** s

heterozygous ˌhet‿ər əʊ 'zaɪg əs ‖ ˌheţ ə roʊ-

Hetherington 'heð ər‿ɪŋ tən

Hettie 'het i ‖ 'heţ i

Hetton-le-Hole ˌhet ᵊn lɪ 'həʊl -lə', →-'hoʊl ‖ -'hoʊl

Hetty 'het i ‖ 'heţ i

Heugh *family name* hjuː

Heugh *village in Northumberland* hjuːf

Heulwen 'haɪᵊl wen —*Welsh* ['hail wen, 'hɨil-]

heuristic hjuᵊ 'rɪst ɪk **~ally** ᵊl‿i **~s** s

Hever 'hiːv ə ‖ -ᵊr

hew, Hew hjuː ‖ juː **hewed** hjuːd ‖ juːd **hewing** 'hjuː‿ɪŋ ‖ 'juː‿ **hewn** hjuːn ‖ juːn **hews** hjuːz ‖ juːz

hewer 'hjuː‿ə ‖ ‿ᵊr 'juː‿ **~s** z

Hewett, Hewitt 'hjuː ɪt §‿ət ‖ 'juː-

Hewlett 'hjuːl ɪt §-ət ‖ 'juːl-

hewn hjuːn ‖ juːn

Hewson 'hjuːs ᵊn ‖ 'juːs-

hex heks **hexed** hekst **hexes** 'heks ɪz -əz **hexing** 'heks ɪŋ

hexa- *comb. form*
with stress-neutral suffix ¦heks ə — **hexapod** 'heks ə pɒd ‖ -pɑːd
with stress-imposing suffix hek 'sæ+ — **hexapody** hek 'sæp əd i

hexachlorophene ˌheks ə 'klɔːr ə fiːn 'klɒr- ‖ -'kloʊr-

hexad 'heks æd **~s** z

hexadecimal ˌheks ə 'des ɪm ᵊl ◂ -əm ᵊl **~ly** i **~s** z

hexagon 'heks əg ən ‖ -ə gɑːn **~s** z

hexagonal hek 'sæg ən ᵊl **~ly** i

hexagram 'heks ə græm **~s** z

hexahedron ˌheks ə 'hiːdr ən -'hedr- **~s** z

hexameter hek 'sæm ɪt ə -ət- ‖ -əţ ᵊr **~s** z

hexamine 'heks ə miːn

hexane 'heks eɪn

Hexham 'heks əm

hey heɪ *(= hay)*

heyday 'heɪ deɪ

Heyer ˈheɪ ə ‖ -ər
Heyerdahl ˈheɪ ə dɑːl ˈhaɪ‿ ‖ ˈhaɪ‿ər- —*Norwegian* [ˈhɛi ər dɑːl]
Heyes heɪz
Heyford ˈheɪ fəd ‖ -fərd
Heyhoe ˈheɪ həʊ ‖ -hoʊ
Heys heɪz
Heysel ˈhaɪs əl ˈheɪs- —*Du* [ˈhɛi səl]
Heysham ˈhiːʃ əm —*Often* ˈheɪʃ- *by those not familiar with the name.*
Heythrop ˈhiːθ rəp -rɒp ‖ -rɑːp
Heywood ˈheɪ wʊd
Hezbollah ˌhez bɒ ˈlɑː ˌhɪz- ‖ -bə-
Hezekiah ˌhez ɪ ˈkaɪ‿ə -ə-
hi haɪ *(= high)*
Hialeah ˌhaɪ‿ə ˈliː‿ə
hiatus haɪ ˈeɪt əs hi- ‖ -ˈeɪt̬- **~es** ɪz əz
hiˌatus ˈhernia
Hiawatha ˌhaɪ‿ə ˈwɒθ ə ‖ -ˈwɔːθ ə ˌhiː-, -ˈwɑːθ-
hibachi hɪ ˈbɑːtʃ i —*Jp* [ˈçi ba tɕi] **~s** z
Hibberd ˈhɪb əd ‖ -ərd
Hibbert ˈhɪb ət ‖ -ərt
hibernacul|um ˌhaɪb ə ˈnæk jʊl |əm -jəl əm ‖ -ər ˈnæk jəl- **~a** ə
hiber|nate ˈhaɪb ə |neɪt ‖ -ər- **~nated** neɪt ɪd -əd ‖ neɪt̬ əd **~nates** neɪts **~nating** neɪt ɪŋ ‖ neɪt̬ ɪŋ
hibernation ˌhaɪb ə ˈneɪʃ ən ‖ -ər- **~s** z
Hibernia haɪ ˈbɜːn i‿ə hɪ- ‖ -ˈbɜːn-
Hibernian haɪ ˈbɜːn i‿ən hɪ- ‖ -ˈbɜːn- —*The football team is* hɪ- **~s** z
Hibernicism haɪ ˈbɜːn ɪ ˌsɪz əm -ə- ‖ -ˈbɜːn- **~s** z
hibiscus haɪ ˈbɪsk əs hɪ-, hə- **~es** ɪz əz
Hibs hɪbz
hic hɪk
ˌhic ˈjacet ◂ ˈjæk et ˈdʒeɪs-
hiccough, hiccup ˈhɪk ʌp -əp **~ed** t **~ing** ɪŋ **~s** s
hick, Hick hɪk **hicks** hɪks
Hickey, h~ ˈhɪk i **~s** z
Hickok ˈhɪk ɒk ‖ -ɑːk
hickor|y ˈhɪk ər‿|i **~ies** iz
Hicks hɪks
Hickson ˈhɪks ən
hid hɪd
hidalgo hɪ ˈdælg əʊ ‖ -oʊ —*Sp* [i ˈðal ɣo] **~s** z
Hidatsa hɪ ˈdæts ə ‖ -ˈdɑːts-
Hidcote ˈhɪd kət →ˈhɪg-
hidden ˈhɪd ən
hide haɪd **hidden** ˈhɪd ən **hides** haɪdz **hiding** ˈhaɪd ɪŋ
hide-and-seek ˌhaɪd ən ˈsiːk
hideaway ˈhaɪd ə ˌweɪ **~s** z
hidebound ˈhaɪd baʊnd →ˈhaɪb-
hi-de-hi ˌhaɪ di ˈhaɪ
hideous ˈhɪd i‿əs **~ly** li **~ness** nəs nɪs
hideout ˈhaɪd aʊt **~s** s
hidey-hole ˈhaɪd i həʊl →-hɒʊl ‖ -hoʊl **~s** z
hiding ˈhaɪd ɪŋ **~s** z
hie haɪ *(= high)* **hied** haɪd **hieing, hying** ˈhaɪ ɪŋ **hies** haɪz
hierarch ˈhaɪər ɑːk ‖ -ɑːrk **~s** s
hierarchic ₍ˌ₎haɪə ˈrɑːk ɪk ‖ -ˈrɑːrk- **~al** əl **~ally** əl‿i
hierarch|y ˈhaɪər ɑːk |i ‖ -ɑːrk |i **~ies** iz
hieratic ₍ˌ₎haɪə ˈræt ɪk ‖ -ˈræt̬ ɪk **~al** əl **~ally** əl‿i
hierocratic ˌhaɪər əʊ ˈkræt ɪk ◂ ‖ -ə ˈkræt̬ ɪk **~al** əl **~ally** əl‿i
hieroglyph ˈhaɪər ə glɪf **~s** s
hieroglyphic ˌhaɪər ə ˈglɪf ɪk ◂ **~al** əl **~ally** əl‿i **~s** s
Hieronymus ˌhaɪə ˈrɒn ɪm əs ˌhɪə- ‖ -ˈrɑːn-
hierophant ˈhaɪər əʊ fænt ‖ -ə- haɪ ˈer ə fænt **~s** s
hifalutin, hifalutin' ˌhaɪ fə ˈluːt ɪn ◂ -ən ‖ -ən
hi-fi ˈhaɪ faɪ ˌ·ˈ· **~s** z
Higginbotham *(i)* ˈhɪg ɪn ˌbɒt əm -ən-, →-ɪm- ‖ -ˌbɑːt̬ əm, *(ii)* -ˌbɒθ əm ‖ -ˌbɑːθ əm
Higginbottom ˈhɪg ɪn ˌbɒt əm -ən-, →-ɪm- ‖ -ˌbɑːt̬ əm
Higgins ˈhɪg ɪnz §-ənz
higgl|e ˈhɪg əl **~ed** d **~es** z **~ing** ‿ɪŋ
higgledy-piggledy ˌhɪg əld i ˈpɪg əld i ◂
higgler ˈhɪg əl‿ə ‖ ər **~s** z
Higgs hɪgz
-high ˈhaɪ haɪ — **knee-high** ˌniː ˈhaɪ ◂ ˈ··
high haɪ **higher** ˈhaɪ‿ə ‖ ˈhaɪ‿ər **highest** ˈhaɪ‿ɪst əst **highs** haɪz
ˌhigh ˈchair, ˈ·· ‖ **ˈ··**; **ˌHigh ˈChurch**; **ˌHigh Comˈmission**; **ˌHigh Comˈmissioner, ˌHigh ˈCourt**◂; **ˌhigh exˈplosive**; **ˌhigh fiˈdelity**; **ˌHigh ˈGerman**; **ˌhigh ˈhorse**; **ˌhigh ˈjinks, ˈ· ·**; **ˈhigh jump**; **ˈhigh jumper**; **ˈhigh life**; **ˌhigh ˈmass**; **ˈhigh point**; **ˌhigh ˈpriest**; **ˌhigh ˈpriestess**; **ˌhigh ˈprofile**; **ˌhigh reˈlief**; **ˈhigh road**; **ˈhigh school**; **ˌhigh ˈseas**; **ˌhigh ˈseason**; **ˌHigh ˈSheriff**; **ˈhigh spot**; **ˈhigh street**; **ˌhigh ˈtable**; **ˌhigh ˈtea**; **ˌhigh techˈnology**; **ˌhigh ˈtide**; **ˌhigh ˈtime**; **ˌhigh ˈtreason**; **ˌhigh ˈwater**; **ˌhigh ˈwater mark**; **ˌHigh ˈWycombe**
Higham ˈhaɪ‿əm —*but the place in S.Yorks. is locally also* ˈhɪk-
high-and-mighty ˌhaɪ‿ən ˈmaɪt i ◂ →-əm- ‖ -ˈmaɪt̬ i
highball ˈhaɪ bɔːl ‖ -bɑːl **~s** z
highborn ˈhaɪ bɔːn ˌ·ˈ· ‖ -bɔːrn
highboy ˈhaɪ bɔɪ **~s** z
highbrow ˈhaɪ braʊ **~s** z
Highbury ˈhaɪ bər‿i ‖ -ˌber i
highchair ˌhaɪ ˈtʃeə ‖ ˈhaɪ tʃer **~s** z
high-class ˌhaɪ ˈklɑːs ◂ §-ˈklæs ‖ -ˈklæs ◂
Highclere ˈhaɪ klɪə ‖ -klɪr
Highcliffe ˈhaɪ klɪf
high-definition ˌhaɪ def ə ˈnɪʃ ən ◂ -ɪˈ--
high-density ˌhaɪ ˈdents ət i ◂ -ɪt- ‖ -ət̬ i
high-end ˌhaɪ ˈend ◂
higher ˈhaɪ‿ə ‖ ˈhaɪ‿ər
ˌhigher ˌeduˈcation
higher-end ˌhaɪ‿ərˈend ◂ ‖ ˌhaɪ‿ər-
higher-up ˌhaɪ‿ər ˈʌp ◂ ‖ ˌhaɪ‿ər-
highest ˈhaɪ‿ɪst əst
highfalutin, highfalutin' ˌhaɪ fə ˈluːt ɪn ◂ -ən ‖ -ən

ighfaluting ˌhaɪ fə ˈluːt ɪŋ ◂
igh-five ˌhaɪ ˈfaɪv
igh-flier, high-flyer ˌhaɪ ˈflaɪ‿ə ‖ -ˈflaɪ‿ᵊr **~s** z
igh-flown ˌhaɪ ˈfləʊn ◂ ‖ -ˈfloʊn ◂
ˌhigh-flown ˈlanguage
igh-flying ˌhaɪ ˈflaɪ ɪŋ ◂
ighgate ˈhaɪ geɪt -gɪt, gət
igh-grade ˌhaɪ ˈgreɪd ◂
ighgrove ˈhaɪ grəʊv ‖ -groʊv
igh-handed ˌhaɪ ˈhænd ɪd ◂ -əd **~ly** li **~ness** nəs nɪs
igh-|hat ˈhaɪ |hæt **~hats** hæts **~hatted** hæt ɪd -əd ‖ hæţ əd **~hatting** hæt ɪŋ ‖ hæţ ɪŋ
igh-heeled ˌhaɪ ˈhiːᵊld ◂
igh-keyed ˌhaɪ ˈkiːd ◂
ighland, H~ ˈhaɪl ənd **~s** z
ˌHighland ˈfling
ighlander, H~ ˈhaɪl ənd ə ‖ -ᵊr **~s** z
igh-level ˌhaɪ ˈlev ᵊl ◂
igh|light ˈhaɪ |laɪt **~lighted** laɪt ɪd -əd ‖ laɪţ əd **~lighting** laɪt ɪŋ ‖ laɪţ ɪŋ **~lights** laɪts
ighlighter ˈhaɪ laɪt ə ‖ -laɪţ ᵊr **~s** z
ighly ˈhaɪ li
ighly-strung ˌhaɪ li ˈstrʌŋ ◂
igh-maintenance ˌhaɪ ˈmeɪnt ən‿ənᵗs ◂ ‖ -ᵊn‿
igh-minded ˌhaɪ ˈmaɪnd ɪd ◂ -əd **~ly** li **~ness** nəs nɪs
ighness *'quality of being high'* ˈhaɪ nəs -nɪs
ighness *title* ˈhaɪn əs -ɪs **~es** ɪz əz
igh-octane ˌhaɪ ˈɒkt eɪn ◂ ‖ -ˈɑːkt-
igh-pass ˌhaɪ ˈpɑːs ◂ §-ˈpæs ‖ -ˈpæs ◂
igh-performance ˌhaɪ pə ˈfɔːm ənᵗs ◂ ‖ -pᵊr ˈfɔːrm-
igh-pitched ˌhaɪ ˈpɪtʃt ◂
igh-powered ˌhaɪ ˈpaʊ‿əd ◂ ‖ -ˈpaʊ‿ᵊrd
igh-pressure ˌhaɪ ˈpreʃ ə ◂ ‖ -ᵊr ◂
igh-priced ˌhaɪ ˈpraɪst ◂
igh-principled ˌhaɪ ˈprɪnᵗs ɪp ᵊld ◂ -əp-
igh-profile ˌhaɪ ˈprəʊf aɪᵊl ◂ ‖ -ˈproʊf-
igh-ranking ˌhaɪ ˈræŋk ɪŋ ◂
igh-res ˌhaɪ ˈrez ◂
igh-ris|e ˈhaɪ raɪz ˌ·ˈ·◂ **~es** ɪz əz
igh-risk ˌhaɪ ˈrɪsk ◂
igh-sounding ˌhaɪ ˈsaʊnd ɪŋ ◂
igh-speed ˌhaɪ ˈspiːd ◂
ˌhigh-speed ˈtrain
igh-spirited ˌhaɪ ˈspɪr ɪt ɪd ◂ §-ət-, -əd ‖ -əţ əd ◂ **~ly** li **~ness** nəs nɪs
igh-strung ˌhaɪ ˈstrʌŋ ◂
ightail ˈhaɪ teɪᵊl **~ed** d **~ing** ɪŋ **~s** z
igh-tech ˌhaɪ ˈtek ◂
igh-tension ˌhaɪ ˈtenᵗʃ ᵊn ◂
igh-toned ˌhaɪ ˈtəʊnd ◂ ‖ -ˈtoʊnd ◂
high-top ˈhaɪ tɒp ‖ -tɑːp **~s** s
high-up *n* ˈhaɪ ʌp **~s** s
high-voltage ˌhaɪ ˈvəʊlt ɪdʒ ◂ →-ˈvɒʊlt- ‖ -ˈvoʊlt-
highway ˈhaɪ weɪ **~s** z
ˌHighway ˈCode
highway|man ˈhaɪ weɪ |mən **~men** mən

high-wire ˌhaɪ ˈwaɪ‿ə ◂ ‖ ˈhaɪ waɪᵊr
high-yield ˌhaɪ ˈjiːᵊld ◂ **~er/s** ə/z ◂ ‖ ᵊr/z **~ing** ɪŋ ◂
hijab hɪ ˈdʒɑːb —*Arabic* [hɪ dʒaːb]
hijack ˈhaɪ dʒæk **~ed** t **~er/s** ə/z ‖ ᵊr/z **~ing** ɪŋ **~s** s
hijinks ˈhaɪ dʒɪŋ*ks*
hike haɪk **hiked** haɪkt **hikes** haɪks **hiking** ˈhaɪk ɪŋ
hiker ˈhaɪk ə ‖ -ᵊr **~s** z
hila ˈhaɪl ə
Hilaire hɪ ˈleə ˈhɪl eə ‖ -ˈleᵊr —*Fr* [i lɛːʁ]
hilar ˈhaɪl ə ‖ -ᵊr
hilarious hɪ ˈleər i‿əs hə- ‖ -ˈler- haɪ-, -ˈlær- **~ly** li **~ness** nəs nɪs
hilarity hɪ ˈlær ət i hə-, -ɪt- ‖ -əţ i -ˈler-
Hilary ˈhɪl ər i
Hilbert ˈhɪlb ət ‖ -ᵊrt —*Ger* [ˈhɪl bɐt], *Czech* [ˈɦil bert]
Hilbre ˈhɪlb ri
Hilda ˈhɪld ə
Hildebrand ˈhɪld ə brænd
Hildegarde ˈhɪld ə gɑːd ‖ -gɑːrd
Hildenborough ˈhɪld ən ˌbʌr ə -bər‿ə ‖ -ˌbɜː oʊ
Hilfiger *tdmk* ˈhɪlf ɪg ə ‖ -ᵊr
hill, Hill hɪl **hills** hɪlz
Hillary ˈhɪl ər i
hillbill|y ˈhɪl ˌbɪl |i **~ies** iz
Hillel ˈhɪl el -əl; hɪ ˈleɪᵊl
Hiller ˈhɪl ə ‖ -ᵊr
Hillery ˈhɪl ər i
Hillhead ˌhɪl ˈhed
Hilliard ˈhɪl i‿əd -ɑːd ‖ ᵊrd -ɑːrd
Hillingdon ˈhɪl ɪŋ dən
Hillman ˈhɪl mən
hillock ˈhɪl ək **~s** s
Hills hɪlz
Hillsboro, Hillsborough ˈhɪlz bər‿ə §-ˌbʌr ə ‖ -ˌbɜː oʊ
hillside ˈhɪl saɪd ˌ·ˈ· **~s** z
hilltop ˈhɪl tɒp ‖ -tɑːp **~s** s
hill-walk|er ˈhɪl ˌwɔːk| ə ‖ -ᵊr -ˌwɑːk- **~ers** əz ‖ ᵊrz **~ing** ɪŋ
hilly ˈhɪl i
Hilo *place in Hawaii* ˈhiːl əʊ ‖ -oʊ
hilt hɪlt **hilted** ˈhɪlt ɪd -əd **hilts** hɪlts
Hilton ˈhɪlt ən
hil|um ˈhaɪl |əm **~a** ə **~i** aɪ **~us** əs
Hilversum ˈhɪlv ə səm -sʊm ‖ -ᵊr- —*Dutch* [ˈhɪl vər sʏm]
him *strong form* hɪm, *weak forms* hɪm, ɪm §həm, §əm —*In the rare instances where this word occurs after a pause or at the beginning of a clause, it is always* hɪm.
Himalaya ˌhɪm ə ˈleɪ ə hɪ ˈmɑːl i‿ə —*Hindi* [hɪ maː ləj] **~s** z
Himalayan ˌhɪm ə ˈleɪ ən hɪ ˈmɑːl i‿ən
Himmler ˈhɪm lə ‖ -lᵊr —*Ger* [ˈhɪm lɐ]
himself *strong form* hɪm ˈself §həm-, *weak form* ɪm- §əm- —*The weak form is not used at the beginning of a sentence or clause.*
Himyaritic ˌhɪm jə ˈrɪt ɪk ◂ ‖ -ˈrɪţ-

Hinayana ˌhiːn ə ˈjɑːn ə ˌhɪn-, -ɪ-
Hinchcliffe ˈhɪntʃ klɪf
Hinchinbrook ˈhɪntʃ ɪn brʊk →-ɪm-; -ən-, →-əm-
Hinchingbrooke ˈhɪntʃ ɪŋ brʊk
Hinchley ˈhɪntʃ li
Hinchliffe ˈhɪntʃ lɪf
Hinckley ˈhɪŋk li
hind haɪnd **hinds** haɪndz
Hind *(i)* haɪnd, *(ii)* hɪnd
hindbrain ˈhaɪnd breɪn →ˈhaɪm- **~s** z
Hinde haɪnd
Hindemith ˈhɪnd ə mɪt -mɪθ, §-məθ —*Ger* [ˈhɪn də mɪt]
Hindenburg ˈhɪnd ən bɜːg →-əm- ‖ -bɜːg —*Ger* [ˈhɪn dən bʊʁk]
hinder *adj* ˈhaɪnd ə ‖ -ər **~most** məʊst ‖ moʊst
hinder *v* ˈhɪnd ə ‖ -ər **~ed** d **hindering** ˈhɪnd‿ər ɪŋ **~s** z
hinderer ˈhɪnd‿ər ə ‖ -ər **~s** z
Hindhead ˈhaɪnd hed
Hindi ˈhɪnd i -iː
Hindle ˈhɪnd əl
Hindley *(i)* ˈhɪnd li, *(ii)* ˈhaɪnd li —*The town in Greater Manchester is (i). Otherwise, (ii) is more usual.*
Hindmarsh ˈhaɪnd mɑːʃ →ˈhaɪm- ‖ -mɑːrʃ
hindmost ˈhaɪnd məʊst →ˈhaɪm- ‖ -moʊst
hindquarter ˌhaɪnd ˈkwɔːt ə →ˌhaɪŋ-, ˈkɔːt-, ˈ·ˌ·· ‖ ˈhaɪnd ˌkwɔːrţ ər -ˌkwɔːţ ər **~s** z
hindranc|e ˈhɪndr ənts **~es** ɪz əz
hindsight ˈhaɪnd saɪt
Hindu ˌhɪn ˈduː ◂ ˈ· · ‖ ˈhɪn duː **~s** z
ˌ**Hindu** ˈ**Kush** kʊʃ kuːʃ
Hinduism ˈhɪn du ˌɪz əm ˌ·ˈduː-
Hindustani ˌhɪn du ˈstɑːn i ◂ ‖ -ˈstæn i ◂ -ˈstɑːn i
Hine haɪn
Hines haɪnz
hinge hɪndʒ **hinged** hɪndʒd **hinges** ˈhɪndʒ ɪz -əz **hinging** ˈhɪndʒ ɪŋ
hinn|y ˈhɪn |i **~ied** id **~ies** iz **~ying** i‿ɪŋ
Hinshelwood ˈhɪnt ʃ əl wʊd
hint hɪnt **hinted** ˈhɪnt ɪd -əd ‖ ˈhɪnţ əd **hinting** ˈhɪnt ɪŋ ‖ ˈhɪnţ ɪŋ **hints** hɪnts
hinterland ˈhɪnt ə lænd -lənd ‖ ˈhɪnţ ər-
Hinton ˈhɪnt ən
hip hɪp **hipped** hɪpt **hipper** ˈhɪp ə ‖ -ər **hippest** ˈhɪp ɪst -əst
ˈ**hip flask**; ˈ**hip joint**; ˌ**hip** ˈ**pocket**
hip|bath ˈhɪp |bɑːθ §-bæθ ‖ -|bæθ **~baths** bɑːðz §bɑːθs, §bæθs, §bæðz ‖ bæðz bæθs
hipbone ˈhɪp bəʊn ‖ -boʊn **~s** z
hip-hop ˈhɪp hɒp ‖ -hɑːp
hiphuggers ˈhɪp ˌhʌg əz ‖ -ərz
hipness ˈhɪp nəs -nɪs
Hipparchus hɪ ˈpɑːk əs ‖ -ˈpɑːrk-
hippeastrum ˌhɪp i ˈæs trəm **~s** z
hipped hɪpt
Hippias ˈhɪp i æs -i‿əs
hippie ˈhɪp i **~s** z
hippo, Hippo ˈhɪp əʊ ‖ -oʊ **~s** z
hippocamp|us ˌhɪp ə ˈkæmp |əs **~i** aɪ

Hippocrates hɪ ˈpɒk rə tiːz ‖ -ˈpɑːk-
Hippocratic ˌhɪp əʊ ˈkræt ɪk ◂ ‖ -ə ˈkræţ ɪk ◂
-ˌ**Hippo**ˌ**cratic** ˈ**oath**
Hippocrene ˈhɪp əʊ kriːn ˌ· ˈ·kriːn iː, -i ‖ -ə-
Hippodrome, h~ ˈhɪp ə drəʊm ‖ -droʊm **~s** z
Hippolyta hɪ ˈpɒl ɪt ə -ət- ‖ -ˈpɑːl əţ ə
Hippolyte hɪ ˈpɒl ɪ tiː -ə- ‖ -ˈpɑːl-
Hippolytus hɪ ˈpɒl ɪt əs -ət- ‖ -ˈpɑːl əţ əs
hippopot|amus ˌhɪp ə ˈpɒt |əm əs ‖ -ˈpɑːţ- **~ami** ə maɪ **~amuses** əm əs ɪz -əz
hipp|y ˈhɪp |i **~ies** iz
hipster ˈhɪpst ə ‖ -ər **~s** z
hiragana ˌhɪər ə ˈgɑːn ə ˌhɪr- ‖ ˌhiː rə- —*Jp* [çi ˌɾa ˈŋa na, -ˈga-, -ŋa-]
Hiram ˈhaɪər əm
hircine ˈhɜːs aɪn -ɪn, §-ən ‖ ˈhɜːs-
Hird hɜːd ‖ hɜːd
hire ˈhaɪ‿ə ‖ ˈhaɪ‿ər **hired** ˈhaɪ‿əd ‖ ˈhaɪ‿ərd **hires** ˈhaɪ‿əz ‖ ˈhaɪ‿ərz **hiring/s** ˈhaɪ‿ər ɪŋ/z ‖ ˈhaɪ‿ər ɪŋ/z
ˌ**hire** ˈ**purchase**
hireling ˈhaɪ‿ə lɪŋ ‖ ˈhaɪ‿ər- **~s** z
Hirnant ˈhɜː nænt ‖ ˈhɜː- —*Welsh* [ˈhir nant]
Hirohito ˌhɪr əʊ ˈhiːt əʊ ‖ -oʊ ˈhiːt oʊ —*Jp* [çi ˈɾo çi to]
Hiroshima hɪ ˈrɒʃ ɪm ə hə-, -əm-; ˌhɪr ə ˈʃiːm ə -ɒ- ‖ ˌhɪr oʊ ˈʃiːm ə hə ˈroʊʃ əm ə —*Jp* [çi ˌɾo çi ma]
Hirst hɜːst ‖ hɜːst
hirsute ˈhɜːs juːt -uːt; hɜː ˈsjuːt, -ˈsuːt ‖ ˈhɜːs uː **~ness** nəs nɪs
hirundine hɪ ˈrʌnd aɪn -ɪn, §-ən
Hirwain, Hirwaun ˈhɪə waɪn ‖ ˈhɪr- —*locally also* ˈhɜː wɪn —*Welsh* [ˈhir wain]
his *strong form* hɪz, *weak forms* hɪz, ɪz §həz, §əz —*The forms* ɪz, §əz *are not used at the beginning of a sentence or clause.*
Hiscock *(i)* ˈhɪs kɒk ‖ -kɑːk, *(ii)* -kəʊ ‖ -koʊ
Hislop ˈhɪz ləp -lɒp ‖ -lɑːp
his'n'hers ˌhɪz ən ˈhɜːz ‖ -ˈhɜːz
Hispanic, h~ hɪ ˈspæn ɪk **~s** s
Hispanicism hɪ ˈspæn ɪ ˌsɪz əm -ə- **~s** z
Hispaniola ˌhɪsp æn i ˈəʊl ə hɪ ˌspæn-; ˌhɪsp æn ˈjəʊl ə ‖ ˌhɪsp ən ˈjoʊl ə
Hispano- hɪ ˈspæn əʊ -ˈspɑːn-; ˈhɪsp ən- ‖ -oʊ
Hispano-Suiza *tdmk* hɪ ˌspæn əʊ ˈswiːz ə ‖ -oʊ-
hispid ˈhɪsp ɪd §-əd
hiss hɪs **hissed** hɪst **hisser/s** ˈhɪs ə/z ‖ -ər/z **hisses** ˈhɪs ɪz -əz **hissing** ˈhɪs ɪŋ
hissy fit ˈhɪs i fɪt **~s** s
hist hɪst —*or e.g.* [sːt]
histamine ˈhɪst ə miːn -mɪn
histo- *comb. form*
with stress-neutral suffix ¦hɪst əʊ ‖ -oʊ — **histocompatible** ˌhɪst əʊ kəm ˈpæt əb əl ◂ -ɪb əl ‖ -oʊ kəm ˈpæţ-
with stress-imposing suffix hɪ ˈstɒ+ ‖ -ˈstɑː+ — **histolysis** hɪ ˈstɒl əs ɪs -ɪs-, §-əs ‖ -ˈstɑːl-
histogram ˈhɪst ə græm **~s** z
histological ˌhɪst ə ˈlɒdʒ ɪk əl ‖ -ˈlɑːdʒ- **~ly** ‿i
histology hɪ ˈstɒl ədʒ i ‖ -ˈstɑːl-
Histon ˈhɪst ən

istorian hɪ ˈstɔːr iˌən ‖ -ˈstour- —*sometimes without* h *when after the indefinite article* an **~s** z

HISTORIC

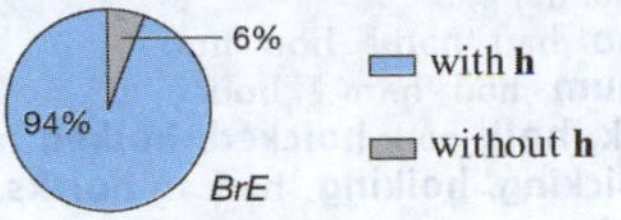

istoric hɪ ˈstɒr ɪk ‖ -ˈstɔːr ɪk -ˈstɑːr- —*sometimes without* h *when after the indefinite article* an — *Preference poll, BrE: with* h *94%, without* h *6%.*

istorical hɪ ˈstɒr ɪk ᵊl ‖ -ˈstɔːr- -ˈstɑːr- —*sometimes without* h *when after the indefinite article* an **~ly** ˌi

istoricism hɪ ˈstɒr ɪ ˌsɪz əm -ə- ‖ -ˈstɔːr- -ˈstɑːr-

istoricity ˌhɪst ə ˈrɪs ət i ˌ-ɒ-, -ɪt i ‖ -əṭ i

istorie... —*see* **history**

istoriographer hɪ ˌstɒr i ˈɒgr əf ə -ˌstɔːr-; ˌhɪst ɔːr-, ˌ-ɒr- ‖ -ˌstɔːr i ˈɑːg rəf ᵊr **~s** z

istoriography hɪ ˌstɒr i ˈɒgr əf i -ˌstɔːr-; ˌhɪst ɔːr-, ˌ-ɒr- ‖ -ˌstɔːr i ˈɑːg-

is|tory ˈhɪs |tri ˈ·|tər i **~tories** triz tər iz

istrionic ˌhɪs tri ˈɒn ɪk ◂ ‖ -ˈɑːn ɪk ◂ **~al** ᵊl **~ally** ᵊl ˌi **~s** s

it hɪt **hits** hɪts **hitting** ˈhɪt ɪŋ ‖ ˈhɪṭ ɪŋ
ˈ**hit list**; ˈ**hit man**; ˈ**hit paˌrade**

itachi *tdmk* hɪ ˈtɑːtʃ i -ˈtætʃ i —*Jp* [ˈçi ta tɕi]

it-and-miss ˌhɪt ᵊn ˈmɪs ◂ -ᵊnd-

it-and-run ˌhɪt ᵊn ˈrʌn ◂ -ᵊnd-

itch, Hitch hɪtʃ **hitched** hɪtʃt **hitches** ˈhɪtʃ ɪz -əz **hitching** ˈhɪtʃ ɪŋ
ˈ**hitching post**

itchcock ˈhɪtʃ kɒk ‖ -kɑːk

itchens ˈhɪtʃ ɪnz -ənz

itchhik|e ˈhɪtʃ haɪk **~ed** t **~er/s** ə/z ‖ ᵊr/z **~es** s **~ing** ɪŋ

itchin ˈhɪtʃ ɪn §-ən

ite haɪt

itech, hi-tech ˌhaɪ ˈtek ◂

ither, H~ ˈhɪð ə ‖ -ᵊr
ˌ**Hither** ˈ**Green**

itherto ˌhɪð ə ˈtuː ◂ ‖ -ᵊr-

Hitler ˈhɪt lə ‖ -lᵊr —*Ger* [ˈhɪt lɐ]

Hitlerian hɪt ˈlɪər iˌən ‖ -ˈlɪr-

Hitlerism ˈhɪt lər ˌɪz əm ‖ ˈhɪt lər-

hi-top ˈhaɪ tɒp ‖ -tɑːp **~s** s

hit-or-miss ˌhɪt ɔː ˈmɪs ◂ ‖ ˌhɪṭ ᵊr-

hitt... —*see* **hit**

hitter ˈhɪt ə ‖ ˈhɪṭ ᵊr **~s** z

Hittite ˈhɪt aɪt **~s** s

HIV ˌeɪtʃ aɪ ˈviː §ˌheɪtʃ-
ˌ**HIˈV inˌfection**; ˌ**HIˌV** ˈ**positive**

hive haɪv **hived** haɪvd **hives** haɪvz **hiving** ˈhaɪv ɪŋ

hiway ˈhaɪ weɪ **~s** z

Hixon ˈhɪks ᵊn

hiya ˈhaɪ jə

Hizbollah ˌhɪz bɒ ˈlɑː ‖ -bə- ˌhez-

Hluhluwe ɬu ˈɬuː weɪ ɬu ˈɬuː- —*Zulu* [ɬu ˈɬuː we]

h'm m, hm —*or e.g.* [mm̩m]

HMO ˌeɪtʃ em ˈəʊ ‖ -ˈoʊ **~s** z

HMS ˌeɪtʃ em ˈes ◂ ⚠ˌheɪtʃ-
ˌ**HMS** ˈ**Hood**

ho həʊ ‖ hoʊ

Hoad həʊd ‖ hoʊd

Hoadley, Hoadly ˈhəʊd li ‖ ˈhoʊd-

hoag|ie, hoag|y ˈhəʊg |i ‖ ˈhoʊg |i **~ies** iz

hoar, Hoar hɔː hɔːr hoʊr

hoard hɔːd ‖ hɔːrd hoʊrd **hoarded** ˈhɔːd ɪd -əd ‖ ˈhɔːrd əd ˈhoʊrd- **hoarding** ˈhɔːd ɪŋ ‖ ˈhɔːrd ɪŋ ˈhoʊrd- **hoards** hɔːdz ‖ hɔːrdz hoʊrdz

hoarder ˈhɔːd ə ‖ ˈhɔːrd ᵊr ˈhoʊrd- **~s** z

hoarding ˈhɔːd ɪŋ ‖ ˈhɔːrd ɪŋ ˈhoʊrd- **~s** z

Hoare hɔː ‖ hɔːr hoʊr

hoar-frost ˌhɔː ˈfrɒst -ˈfrɔːst, ˈ· · ‖ ˈhɔːr frɔːst ˈhoʊr-, -frɑːst

hoarse hɔːs ‖ hɔːrs hoʊrs **hoarsely** ˈhɔːs li ‖ ˈhɔːrs li ˈhoʊrs- **hoarseness** ˈhɔːs nəs -nɪs ‖ ˈhɔːrs- ˈhoʊrs- **hoarser** ˈhɔːs ə ‖ ˈhɔːrs ᵊr ˈhoʊrs- **hoarsest** ˈhɔːs ɪst -əst ‖ ˈhɔːrs əst ˈhoʊrs-

hoar|y ˈhɔːr |i ‖ ˈhoʊr- **~ier** iˌə ‖ iˌᵊr **~iest** iˌɪst iˌəst **~iness** i nəs i nɪs

hoatzin həʊ ˈæts ɪn ˌwɑːt ˈsiːn ‖ hoʊ- **~s** z

hoax həʊks ‖ hoʊks **hoaxed** həʊkst ‖ hoʊkst **hoaxer/s** ˈhəʊks ə/z ‖ ˈhoʊks ᵊr/z **hoaxes** ˈhəʊks ɪz -əz ‖ ˈhoʊks əz **hoaxing** ˈhəʊks ɪŋ ‖ ˈhoʊks ɪŋ

hob hɒb ‖ hɑːb **hobs** hɒbz ‖ hɑːbz

Hobart *(i)* ˈhəʊb ɑːt ‖ ˈhoʊb ɑːrt, *(ii)* -ət ‖ -ᵊrt, *(iii)* ˈhʌb ət ‖ -ᵊrt —*The place in Tasmania is (i), that in IN (ii); the 17th-century judge Sir Henry H~ is believed to have been (iii).*

Hobbes hɒbz ‖ hɑːbz

hobbit ˈhɒb ɪt §-ət ‖ ˈhɑːb- **~s** s

hobbl|e ˈhɒb ᵊl ‖ ˈhɑːb- **~ed** d **~es** z **~ing** ˌɪŋ

hobbledehoy ˌhɒb ᵊl dɪ ˈhɔɪ ˈ· · · · ‖ ˈhɑːb ᵊl dɪ hɔɪ **~s** z

Hobbs hɒbz ‖ hɑːbz

hobb|y ˈhɒb |i ‖ ˈhɑːb |i **~ies** iz

hobbyhors|e ˈhɒb i hɔːs ‖ ˈhɑːb i hɔːrs **~es** ɪz əz

hobbyist ˈhɒb i ɪst §-əst ‖ ˈhɑːb- **~s** s

Hobday, h~ ˈhɒb deɪ ‖ ˈhɑːb-

hobgoblin ₍ˌ₎hɒb ˈgɒb lɪn §-lən, ˈ·ˌ· · ‖ ˈhɑːb ˌgɑːb- **~s** z

Hobley ˈhəʊb li ‖ ˈhoʊb-

hobnail ˈhɒb neɪᵊl ‖ ˈhɑːb- **~ed** d **~s** z

hobnob ˈhɒb nɒb ₍ˌ₎·ˈ· ‖ ˈhɑːb nɑːb **~bed** d **~bing** ɪŋ **~s** z

hobo ˈhəʊb əʊ ‖ ˈhoʊb oʊ **~es, ~s** z

Hoboken ˈhəʊ bəʊk ən ‖ ˈhoʊ boʊk- —*Dutch* [ˈhoː boː kən]

Hobsbawm ˈhɒbz bɔːm ‖ ˈhɑːbz- -bɑːm

Hobson ˈhɒb sᵊn ‖ ˈhɑːb- **~'s** z
ˌ**Hobson's** ˈ**choice**

H

H

Hobson-Jobson ˌhɒb sᵊn ˈdʒɒb sᵊn ‖ ˌhɑːb sᵊn ˈdʒɑːb sᵊn
Ho Chi Minh ˌhəʊ ˌtʃiː ˈmɪn ◂ ‖ ˌhoʊ- —*Vietnamese* [³ho ²tʃi ¹miŋ]
ˌHo Chi ˌMinh ˈCity
Ho Chi Minh ˌhəʊ tʃiː ˈmɪn ◂ ‖ ˌhoʊ-
ˌHo Chi ˌMinh ˈCity
hock hɒk ‖ hɑːk **hocked** hɒkt ‖ hɑːkt **hocking** ˈhɒk ɪŋ ‖ ˈhɑːk ɪŋ **hocks** hɒks ‖ hɑːks
hockey ˈhɒk i ‖ ˈhɑːk i
ˈhockey stick
Hockney ˈhɒk ni ‖ ˈhɑːk- **~s, ~'s** z
hocus-pocus ˌhəʊk əs ˈpəʊk əs ‖ ˌhoʊk əs ˈpoʊk əs
hod hɒd ‖ hɑːd **hods** hɒdz ‖ hɑːdz
Hodder ˈhɒd ə ‖ ˈhɑːd ᵊr
Hoddesdon ˈhɒdz dən ˈhɒd ɪz dən, -əz- ‖ ˈhɑːdz-
Hoddinott ˈhɒd ɪ nɒt -ə- ‖ ˈhɑːd ᵊn ɑːt
Hoddle ˈhɒd ᵊl ‖ ˈhɑːd-
Hodge hɒdʒ ‖ hɑːdʒ
hodge-podge ˈhɒdʒ pɒdʒ ‖ ˈhɑːdʒ pɑːdʒ
Hodges ˈhɒdʒ ɪz -əz ‖ ˈhɑːdʒ-
Hodgkin ˈhɒdʒ kɪn §-kən ‖ ˈhɑːdʒ- **~'s** z
ˈHodgkin's diˌsease
Hodgkinson ˈhɒdʒ kɪn sən §-kən- ‖ ˈhɑːdʒ-
Hodgson ˈhɒdʒ sᵊn ‖ ˈhɑːdʒ-
hodometer hɒ ˈdɒm ɪt ə -ət- ‖ hoʊ ˈdɑːm ət̬ ᵊr
Hodson ˈhɒd sᵊn ‖ ˈhɑːd-
hoe, Hoe həʊ ‖ hoʊ **hoed** həʊd ‖ hoʊd **hoeing** ˈhəʊ ɪŋ ‖ ˈhoʊ ɪŋ **hoes** həʊz ‖ hoʊz
Hoechst hɜːkst ‖ hoʊkst —*Ger* Höchst [høːçst]
hoedown ˈhəʊ daʊn ‖ ˈhoʊ- **~s** z
hoer ˈhəʊ ə ‖ ˈhoʊ ᵊr **~s** z
Hoey ˈhəʊ i ‖ ˈhoʊ i
Hoffa ˈhɒf ə ‖ ˈhɑːf ə
Hoffman, Hoffmann ˈhɒf mən ‖ ˈhɑːf-
Hoffnung ˈhɒf nʊŋ ‖ ˈhɑːf-
Hofmannsthal ˈhɒf mənz tɑːl ‖ ˈhoʊf- —*Ger* [ˈhoːf mans taːl]
Hofmeister ˈhɒf ˌmaɪst ə ‖ ˈhɑːf ˌmaɪst ᵊr —*Ger* [ˈhoːf ˌmai stɐ]
hog hɒg ‖ hɔːg hɑːg **hogged** hɒgd ‖ hɔːgd hɑːgd **hogging** ˈhɒg ɪŋ ‖ ˈhɔːg ɪŋ ˈhɑːg ɪŋ **hogs** hɒgz ‖ hɔːgz hɑːgz
Hogan, hogan ˈhəʊg ən ‖ ˈhoʊg- **~s** z
Hogarth *(i)* ˈhəʊ gɑːθ ‖ ˈhoʊ gɑːrθ, *(ii)* ˈhɒg ət ‖ ˈhɑːg ᵊrt
Hogarthian həʊ ˈgɑːθ i ən ‖ hoʊ ˈgɑːrθ- **~s** z
Hogben ˈhɒg bən ‖ ˈhɔːg- ˈhɑːg-
Hogg, hogg hɒg ‖ hɔːg hɑːg
hogg... —*see* **hog**
Hoggart ˈhɒg ət ‖ ˈhɔːg ᵊrt ˈhɑːg-
hogget ˈhɒg ɪt §-ət ‖ ˈhɔːg- ˈhɑːg- **~s** s
hoggish ˈhɒg ɪʃ ‖ ˈhɔːg- ˈhɑːg- **~ly** li **~ness** nəs nɪs
Hogmanay ˈhɒg mə neɪ ˌ· · ˈ· ‖ ˈhɑːg-
hogshead ˈhɒgz hed ‖ ˈhɔːgz- ˈhɑːgz- **~s** z
hog|tie ˈhɒg |taɪ ‖ ˈhɔːg- ˈhɑːg- **~tied** taɪd **~tieing, ~tying** taɪ ɪŋ **~ties** taɪz
Hogwarts ˈhɒg wɔːts ‖ ˈhɔːg wɔːrts ˈhɑːg-
hogwash ˈhɒg wɒʃ ‖ ˈhɔːg wɑːʃ ˈhɑːg-, -wɔːʃ
hogweed ˈhɒg wiːd ‖ ˈhɔːg- ˈhɑːg- **~s** z

Hohenlinden ˌhəʊ ən ˈlɪnd ən ‖ ˌhoʊ- ˈ· · ˌ· · —*Ger* [hoː ən ˈlɪn dᵊn]
Hohenzollern ˌhəʊ ən ˈzɒl ən ‖ ˈhoʊ ən ˌzɑːl ᵊrn —*Ger* [hoː ən ˈtsɔl ɐn] **~s** z
Hohner *tdmk* ˈhəʊn ə ‖ ˈhoʊn ᵊr —*Ger* [ˈhoː nɐ]
ho-ho ˌhəʊ ˈhəʊ ‖ ˌhoʊ ˈhoʊ
ho-hum ˌhəʊ ˈhʌm ‖ ˌhoʊ-
hoick, hoik hɔɪk **hoicked, hoiked** hɔɪkt **hoicking, hoiking** ˈhɔɪk ɪŋ **hoicks, hoiks** hɔɪks
hoi polloi ˌhɔɪ pə ˈlɔɪ -pɒ-, -ˈpɒl ɔɪ
hoisin ˌhɔɪ ˈsɪn ◂ ˈ· ·
hoist hɔɪst **hoisted** ˈhɔɪst ɪd -əd **hoisting** ˈhɔɪst ɪŋ **hoists** hɔɪsts
hoity-toity ˌhɔɪt i ˈtɔɪt i ‖ ˌhɔɪt̬ i ˈtɔɪt̬ i
hok|ey ˈhəʊk |i ‖ ˈhoʊk |i **~ier** i‿ə ‖ i‿ᵊr **~iest** i‿ɪst i‿əst **~eyness, ~iness** i nəs i nɪs
ˌhokey ˈcokey ˈkəʊk i ‖ ˈkoʊk i
hoki ˈhəʊk i ‖ ˈhoʊk i
Hokkaido hɒ ˈkaɪd əʊ ‖ hoʊ ˈkaɪd oʊ hɑː- —*Jp* [hok ˈkai doo]
Hokonui, h~ ˌhəʊk ə ˈnuː i ‖ ˌhoʊk-
hokum ˈhəʊk əm ‖ ˈhoʊk-
Hokusai ˈhɒk u saɪ ‖ ˈhoʊk- —*Jp* [ˈho kɯ̥ sai]
Holbeach, Holbech, Holbeche ˈhɒl biːtʃ ˈhəʊl- ‖ ˈhoʊl-
Holbeck ˈhɒl bek ˈhəʊl- ‖ ˈhoʊl-
Holbein ˈhɒl baɪn ‖ ˈhoʊl- —*Ger* [ˈhɔl bain] **~s** z
Holborn, Holborne ˈhəʊb ən ˈhəʊlb- ‖ ˈhoʊl bɔːrn —*as a family name, also* ˈhɒlb-; *the place in Scotland is* həʊl ˈbɔːn ‖ hoʊl ˈbɔːrn
Holbrook, Holbrooke ˈhəʊl brʊk →ˈhɒʊl- ‖ ˈhoʊl-
Holby ˈhəʊl bi →ˈhɒʊl- ‖ ˈhoʊl-
Holcomb, Holcombe ˈhəʊl kəm →ˈhɒʊl-; ˈhɒl-, ˈhəʊ- ‖ ˈhoʊl-
hold həʊld →hɒʊld ‖ hoʊld **held** held **holding** ˈhəʊld ɪŋ →ˈhɒʊld- ‖ ˈhoʊld ɪŋ **holds** həʊldz →hɒʊldz ‖ hoʊldz
ˈholding ˌcompany; **ˈholding opeˌration**; **ˈholding ˌpattern**
holdall ˈhəʊld ɔːl →ˈhɒʊld- ‖ ˈhoʊld- ɑːl **~s** z
Holden, h~ ˈhəʊld ən →ˈhɒʊld- ‖ ˈhoʊld-
holder, H~ ˈhəʊld ə →ˈhɒʊld- ‖ ˈhoʊld ᵊr **~s** z
-holder ˌhəʊld ə →ˌhɒʊld- ‖ ˌhoʊld ᵊr — **kettle-holder** ˈket ᵊl ˌhəʊld ə →-ˌhɒʊld- ‖ ˈket̬ ᵊl ˌhoʊld ᵊr
Holderness ˈhəʊld ə nəs →ˈhɒʊld-, -nɪs ‖ ˈhoʊld ᵊr-
holdfast ˈhəʊld fɑːst →ˈhɒʊld-, §-fæst ‖ ˈhoʊld fæst **~s** s
holding ˈhəʊld ɪŋ →ˈhɒʊld- ‖ ˈhoʊld ɪŋ **~s** z
holdover ˈhəʊld ˌəʊv ə →ˈhɒʊld- ‖ ˈhoʊld ˌoʊv ᵊr **~s** z
holdup ˈhəʊld ʌp →ˈhɒʊld- ‖ ˈhoʊld- **~s** s
hole həʊl →hɒʊl ‖ hoʊl **holed** həʊld →hɒʊld ‖ hoʊld *(= hold)* **holes** həʊlz →hɒʊlz ‖ hoʊlz **holing** ˈhəʊl ɪŋ →ˈhɒʊl- ‖ ˈhoʊl ɪŋ
ˌhole in ˈone

ole-and-corner ˌhəʊl ən ˈkɔːn ə →ˌhɒʊl-, -ənd-, →-əŋ- ‖ ˌhoʊl ən ˈkɔːrn ᵊr
ole-in-the-wall ˌhəʊl ɪn ðə ˈwɔːl →ˌhɒʊl- ‖ ˌhoʊl- -ˈwɑːl
oley ˈhəʊl i →ˈhɒʊl- ‖ ˈhoʊl i
olford ˈhəʊl fəd →ˈhɒʊl-, ˈhɒl- ‖ ˈhoʊl fᵊrd
oli... —see **holy**
oliday, H~ ˈhɒl ə deɪ -ɪ-, -di ‖ ˈhɑːl- **~ed** d **~ing** ɪŋ **~s** z
ˈholiday camp; **ˌHoliday ˈInn** *tdmk*
olidaymaker ˈhɒl ə deɪ ˌmeɪk ə ˈ·ɪ-,ˈ· ·di- ‖ ˈhɑːl ə deɪ ˌmeɪk ᵊr **~s** z
olier-than-thou ˌhəʊl i‿ə ðən ˈðaʊ ◂ ‖ ˌhoʊl i‿ᵊr-
oliness, H~ ˈhəʊl i nəs -nɪs ‖ ˈhoʊl-
olinshed ˈhɒl ɪn ʃed ‖ ˈhɑːl- —*This is the usual pronunciation for the 16th-c. chronicler, though he may well actually have been* -ɪnz hed.
olism ˈhəʊl ˌɪz əm →ˈhɒʊl-, ˈhɒl- ‖ ˈhoʊl-
olistic həʊ ˈlɪst ɪk hɒ- ‖ hoʊ- **~ally** ᵊl‿i
olland, h~ ˈhɒl ənd ‖ ˈhɑːl- —*Dutch* [ˈhɔl ɑnt]
ollandaise ˌhɒl ən ˈdeɪz ◂ ‖ ˌhɑːl- ˈ· ·
ˌhollandaise ˈsauce, ‖ ˌ·· ˈ· ˌ ˈ· ·
oll|er ˈhɒl |ə ‖ ˈhɑːl |ᵊr **~ered** əd ‖ ᵊrd **~ering** ər ɪŋ **~ers** əz ‖ ᵊrz
olles ˈhɒl ɪs §-əs ‖ ˈhɑːl-
ollick ˈhɒl ɪk ‖ ˈhɑːl-
olliday ˈhɒl ə deɪ -ɪ-, -di ‖ ˈhɑːl-
ollie ˈhɒl i ‖ ˈhɑːl i
ollinghurst ˈhɒl ɪŋ hɜːst ‖ ˈhɑːl ɪŋ hɜ˞ːst
ollingsworth ˈhɒl ɪŋz wɜːθ -wəθ ‖ ˈhɑːl ɪŋz wɜ˞ːθ
ollins ˈhɒl ɪnz §-ənz ‖ ˈhɑːl-
ollis ˈhɒl ɪs §-əs ‖ ˈhɑːl-
ollow ˈhɒl əʊ ‖ ˈhɑːl oʊ **~ed** d **~ing** ɪŋ **~ly** li **~ness** nəs nɪs **~s** z
olloway ˈhɒl ə weɪ ‖ ˈhɑːl-
ollowed-out ˌhɒl əʊd ˈaʊt ◂ ‖ ˌhɑːl-
olloware ˈhɒl əʊ weə ‖ ˈhɑːl oʊ wer -wær
oll|y, Holly ˈhɒl |i ‖ ˈhɑːl |i **~ies** iz
ollyhock ˈhɒl i hɒk ‖ ˈhɑːl i hɑːk -hɔːk **~s** s
ollywood ˈhɒl i wʊd ‖ ˈhɑːl-
ˌHollywood ˈstars
olm həʊm ‖ hoʊm *(= home)* **holms** həʊmz ‖ hoʊmz
olm həʊm §həʊlm ‖ hoʊm hoʊlm
olman ˈhəʊl mən →ˈhɒʊl- ‖ ˈhoʊl-
olme həʊm §həʊlm ‖ hoʊm hoʊlm
olmes həʊmz §həʊlmz ‖ hoʊmz hoʊlmz
olmesdale ˈhəʊmz deɪᵊl ‖ ˈhoʊmz-
olmfirth ˌhəʊm ˈfɜːθ ‖ ˌhoʊm ˈfɜ˞ːθ
olmium ˈhəʊlm i‿əm →ˈhɒʊlm-, ˈhɒlm- ‖ ˈhoʊlm-
olm-oak ˈhəʊm əʊk ˌ·ˈ· ‖ ˈhoʊm oʊk **~s** s
olmwood ˈhəʊm wʊd ‖ ˈhoʊm-
olness ˈhəʊl nəs →ˈhɒʊl-, -nɪs, -nes ‖ ˈhoʊl-
olo- *comb. form*
with stress-neutral suffix ¦hɒl əʊ ‖ ¦hoʊl ə ¦hɑːl ə — **holoblastic** ˌhɒl əʊ ˈblæst ɪk ◂ ‖ ˌhoʊl ə- ˌhɑːl-
with stress-imposing suffix hɒ ˈlɒ + həʊ- ‖ hoʊ ˈlɑː + hə- — **holopathy** hɒ ˈlɒp əθ i həʊ- ‖ hoʊ ˈlɑːp-
holocaust ˈhɒl ə kɔːst ˈhəʊl- ‖ ˈhoʊl- ˈhɑːl-, -kɑːst **~s** s
Holocene ˈhɒl əʊ siːn ‖ ˈhoʊl ə- ˈhɑːl-
Holofernes ˌhɒl ə ˈfɜːn iːz hə ˈlɒf ə niːz ‖ ˌhɑːl ə ˈfɜ˞ːn iːz ˌhoʊl-
hologram ˈhɒl ə græm ‖ ˈhoʊl- ˈhɑːl- **~s** z
holograph ˈhɒl ə grɑːf -græf ‖ ˈhoʊl ə græf ˈhɑːl- **~s** s
holography hɒ ˈlɒg rəf i həʊ- ‖ hoʊ ˈlɑːg rəf i
holophras|e ˈhɒl əʊ freɪz ‖ ˈhoʊl ə- ˌhɑːl ə- **~es** ɪz əz
holophrastic ˌhɒl əʊ ˈfræst ɪk ◂ ‖ ˌhoʊl ə- ˌhɑːl ə-
holothurian ˌhɒl əʊ ˈθjʊər i‿ən -ˈθjɔːr-, -ˈθʊər- ‖ ˌhoʊl ə ˈθʊr- ˌhɑːl-, -ˈθjʊr- **~s** z
holp həʊlp →hɒʊlp ‖ hoʊlp
holpen ˈhəʊlp ən →ˈhɒʊlp- ‖ ˈhoʊlp-
Holroyd ˈhɒl rɔɪd ˈhəʊl- ‖ ˈhɑːl- ˈhoʊl-
hols *'holidays'* hɒlz ‖ hɑːlz
Holst həʊlst →hɒʊlst ‖ hoʊlst
Holstein, h~ ˈhɒl staɪn ˈhəʊl- ‖ ˈhoʊl stiːn -staɪn —*Ger* [ˈhɔl ʃtain] **~s** z
holster ˈhəʊlst ə →ˈhɒʊlst- ‖ ˈhoʊlst ᵊr **~ed** d **~s** z
Holt həʊlt →hɒʊlt ‖ hoʊlt
Holtby ˈhəʊlt bi →ˈhɒʊlt- ‖ ˈhoʊlt-
holus-bolus ˌhəʊl əs ˈbəʊl əs ‖ ˌhoʊl əs ˈboʊl əs
hol|y ˈhəʊl |i ‖ ˈhoʊl |i **~ier** i‿ə ‖ i‿ᵊr **~iest** i‿ɪst i‿əst **~ily** əl i ɪ li **~iness** i nəs i nɪs
ˌHoly ˈBible; **ˌHoly Comˈmunion**; **ˌHoly ˈFamily**; **ˌHoly ˈGhost**; **ˌHoly ˈGrail**; **the ˈHoly Land**; **holy of ˈholies**; **ˌholy ˈorders**; **ˌHoly ˌRoman ˈEmpire**; **ˌHoly ˈScripture**; **ˌHoly ˈSee**; **ˌHoly ˈSpirit**; **ˈholy ˌwater**, ˌ· · ˈ· ·; **ˈHoly Week**; **ˌHoly ˈWrit**
Holyhead *place in Gwynedd* ˌhɒl i ˈhed ◂ ˈ· · · ‖ ˈhɑːl i hed
Holyoak, Holyoake, Holyoke ˈhəʊl i əʊk ‖ ˈhoʊl i oʊk —*but Holyoke, MA, is usually* ˈhoʊl joʊk
Holyport *place in Berks* ˈhɒl i pɔːt ‖ ˈhɑːl i pɔːrt -poʊrt
Holyrood ˈhɒl i ruːd ‖ ˈhoʊl-
holyston|e ˈhəʊl i stəʊn ‖ ˈhoʊl i stoʊn **~ed** d **~es** z **~ing** ɪŋ
Holywell ˈhɒl i wel -wəl ‖ ˈhɑːl-
homage ˈhɒm ɪdʒ ‖ ˈhɑːm-
hombre ˈɒm breɪ -bri ‖ ˈɑːm bri ˈʌm-, -breɪ —*Sp* [ˈom bre] **~s** z
homburg, H~ ˈhɒm bɜːg ‖ ˈhɑːm bɜ˞ːg —*Ger* [ˈhɔm bʊʁk] **~s** z
home həʊm ‖ hoʊm **homed** həʊmd ‖ hoʊmd **homes** həʊmz ‖ hoʊmz **homing** ˈhəʊm ɪŋ ‖ ˈhoʊm ɪŋ —*The phrase* at home *formerly had an RP variant* ə ˈtəʊm, *now obsolete.*
ˌhome ˈbrew; **ˌHome ˈCounties**; **ˌhome ecoˈnomics**; **ˌhome ˈfront**; **ˌHome ˈGuard**; **ˌhome ˈhelp**; **ˌhome ˈmovie**; **ˈHome ˌOffice**; **ˌhome ˈrule**; **ˌhome ˈrun**; **ˌHome**

H

'Secretary; ˌhome 'straight; ˌhome 'stretch; ˌhome 'truth
Home *family name (i)* həʊm ‖ hoʊm, *(ii)* hjuːm —*The Earls of Home are (ii).*
home-baked ˌhəʊm 'beɪkt ◂ ‖ ˌhoʊm-
Homebase *tdmk* 'həʊm beɪs ‖ 'hoʊm-
homebod|y 'həʊm ˌbɒd |i ‖'hoʊm ˌbaːd |i **~ies** iz
home-bound 'həʊm baʊnd
homeboy 'həʊm bɔɪ ‖ 'hoʊm- **~s** z
home-brewed ˌhəʊm 'bruːd ◂ ‖ ˌhoʊm- ˌ**home-brewed 'beer**
homebuyer 'həʊm ˌbaɪ‿ə ‖-baɪ‿ᵊr **~s** z
homecoming 'həʊm ˌkʌm ɪŋ ‖ 'hoʊm- **~s** z
homegirl 'həʊm gɜːl ‖ -gɜ˞ːl **~s** z
homegrown ˌhəʊm 'grəʊn ◂ ‖ ˌhoʊm 'groʊn ◂ ˌ**homegrown 'cucumbers**
homeland 'həʊm lænd -lənd ‖ 'hoʊm- **~s** z
homeless 'həʊm ləs -lɪs ‖ 'hoʊm- **~ness** nəs nɪs
homelike 'həʊm laɪk ‖ 'hoʊm-
home|ly 'həʊm |li ‖ 'hoʊm- **~lier** li‿ə ‖ li‿ᵊr **~liest** li‿ɪst li‿əst **~liness** li nəs li nɪs
homemade ˌhəʊm 'meɪd ◂ ‖ 'hoʊm meɪd -eɪd
homemaker 'həʊm ˌmeɪk ə ‖ 'hoʊm ˌmeɪk ᵊr **~s** z
homeo- *comb. form*
with stress-neutral suffix ¦həʊm i əʊ ¦hɒm- ‖ ¦hoʊm i‿ə — **homeomorphism** ˌhəʊm i əʊ 'mɔːf ˌɪz əm ˌhɒm- ‖ ˌhoʊm i‿ə 'mɔːrf-
with stress-imposing suffix ˌhəʊm i 'ɒ+ ˌhɒm- ‖ ˌhoʊm i 'ɑː+ — **homeology** ˌhəʊm i 'ɒl ədʒ i ˌhɒm- ‖ˌhoʊm i 'ɑːl-
homeopath 'həʊm i‿ə pæθ 'hɒm- ‖ 'hoʊm- **~s** s
homeopathic ˌhəʊm i‿ə 'pæθ ɪk ◂ ˌhɒm- ‖ ˌhoʊm- **~ally** ᵊl‿i
homeopathist ˌhəʊm i 'ɒp əθ ɪst ˌhɒm-, §-əst ‖ ˌhoʊm i 'ɑːp- **~s** s
homeopathy ˌhəʊm i 'ɒp əθ i ˌhɒm- ‖ˌhoʊm i 'ɑːp- ˌhaːm-
homeostasis ˌhəʊm i əʊ 'steɪs ɪs §-əs; ˌhəʊm i 'ɒst əs ɪs, -əs ‖ ˌhoʊm i oʊ-
homeostatic ˌhəʊm i əʊ 'stæt ɪk ◂ ‖ ˌhoʊm i oʊ 'stæṭ ɪk ◂ **~ally** ᵊl‿i
homeotic ˌhəʊm i 'ɒt ɪk ◂ ˌhɒm- ‖ ˌhoʊm i 'ɑːṭ ɪk ◂
homeowner 'həʊm ˌəʊn ə ‖ 'hoʊm ˌoʊn ᵊr **~s** z
homepag|e 'həʊm peɪdʒ ‖ 'hoʊm- **~es** ɪz əz
Homepride *tdmk* 'həʊm praɪd ‖ 'hoʊm-
Homer, homer 'həʊm ə ‖ 'hoʊm ᵊr **~s, ~'s** z
Homeric həʊ 'mer ɪk ‖ hoʊ- **~ally** ᵊl‿i
Homerton 'hɒm ət ən ‖ 'haːm ᵊrt ᵊn
homeschool 'həʊm skuːl ‖ 'hoʊm- **~ed** d **~ing** ɪŋ **~s** z
homesick 'həʊm sɪk ‖ 'hoʊm- **~ness** nəs nɪs
homespun 'həʊm spʌn ‖ 'hoʊm-
homestay 'həʊm steɪ ‖ 'hoʊm- **~s** z
homestead *n* 'həʊm sted -stɪd, -stəd ‖ 'hoʊm- **~s** z

homestead *v* 'həʊm sted ‖ 'hoʊm- **~ed** ɪd əd **~er/s** ə/z ‖ ᵊr/z **~ing** ɪŋ **~s** z
hometown ˌhəʊm 'taʊn ◂ ‖ ˌhoʊm-
homeward 'həʊm wəd ‖ 'hoʊm wᵊrd **~s** z
homework 'həʊm wɜːk ‖ 'hoʊm wɜ˞ːk **~er/s** ə/z ‖ ᵊr/z **~ing** ɪŋ
hom|ey 'həʊm |i ‖ 'hoʊm |i **~ier** i‿ə ‖ i‿ᵊr **~iest** i‿ɪst i‿əst
homicidal ˌhɒm ɪ 'saɪd ᵊl ◂ -ə- ‖ ˌhaːm- ˌhoʊ- **~ly** i
homicide 'hɒm ɪ saɪd -ə- ‖ 'haːm- 'hoʊm- **~s** z
homiletic ˌhɒm ɪ 'let ɪk ◂ -ə-, ⚠-'lekt- ‖ ˌhaːm ə 'leṭ ɪk ◂ **~ally** ᵊl‿i **~s** s
homil|y 'hɒm əl |i -ɪl- ‖ 'haːm- **~ies** iz
homing 'həʊm ɪŋ ‖ 'hoʊm ɪŋ
'**homing ˌpigeon**
hominid 'hɒm ə nɪd -ɪ-; §-ən əd ‖ 'haːm- **~s** z
hominoid 'hɒm ə nɔɪd -ɪ- ‖ 'haːm- **~s** z
hominy 'hɒm ən i -ɪn- ‖ 'haːm-
homo, Homo 'həʊm əʊ ‖ 'hoʊm oʊ **~s** z
ˌ**Homo 'sapiens** 'sæp i enz 'seɪp-, -i‿ənz
homo- *comb. form*
with stress-neutral suffix ¦həʊm əʊ ¦hɒm- ‖ ¦hoʊm ə — **homotaxis** ˌhəʊm əʊ 'tæks ɪs ˌhɒm-, §-əs ‖ ˌhoʊm ə-
with stress-imposing suffix hə 'mɒ+ hɒ- ‖ hə 'maː+ hoʊ- — **homogonous** hə 'mɒg ən əs hɒ- ‖ hə 'maːg- hoʊ-
homoeo... —*see* **homeo...**
homoerotic ˌhəʊm əʊ ɪ 'rɒt ɪk ◂ ˌhɒm-, -ə'-- ‖ ˌhoʊm oʊ ɪ 'raːṭ ɪk ◂
homoeroticism ˌhəʊm əʊ ɪ 'rɒt ɪ ˌsɪz əm ˌhɒm-, -ə'--, -'-ə- ‖ˌhoʊm oʊ ɪ 'raːṭ ə-
homogeneity ˌhəʊm əʊ dʒə 'niː‿ət i ˌhɒm-, -dʒɪ'--, -'neɪ-, -ɪt i ‖ ˌhoʊm ə dʒə 'niː əṭ i -'neɪ-

HOMOGENEOUS

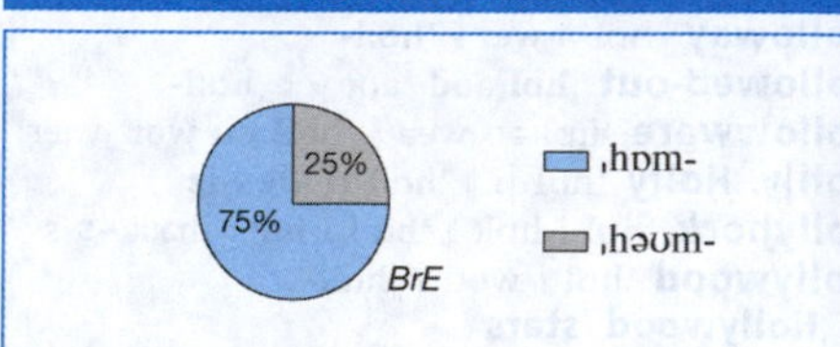

homogeneous ˌhɒm əʊ 'dʒiːn i‿əs ◂ ˌhəʊm- ‖ ˌhoʊm ə- — *Preference poll, BrE:* ˌhɒm- *75%,* ˌhəʊm- *25%.* **~ly** li **~ness** nəs nɪs
homogenis... —*see* **homogeniz...**
homogenization hə ˌmɒdʒ ən aɪ 'zeɪʃ ᵊn hɒ-, -'ɪn-, -ɪ'-- ‖ -ˌmaːdʒ ən ə- hoʊ-
homogeniz|e hə 'mɒdʒ ə naɪz hɒ-, -ɪ- ‖ -'maːdʒ- hoʊ- **~ed** d **~es** ɪz əz **~ing** ɪŋ
homogenous hə 'mɒdʒ ən əs hɒ-, -ɪn- ‖ hoʊ 'maːdʒ-
homograph 'hɒm ə graːf 'həʊm-, -græf ‖ 'haːm ə græf 'hoʊm- **~s** s
homographic ˌhɒm ə 'græf ɪk ◂ ‖ ˌhaːm- ˌhoʊm-
homolog 'hɒm ə lɒg ‖ 'hoʊm ə lɔːg 'haːm-, -laːg **~s** z

omologous hə ˈmɒl əɡ əs hɒ- ‖ hoʊ ˈmɑːl- hə-

omologue ˈhɒm ə lɒɡ ‖ ˈhoʊm ə lɔːɡ ˈhɑːm-, -lɑːɡ **~s** z

omolog|y hə ˈmɒl ədʒ |i hɒ- ‖ hoʊ ˈmɑːl- hə- **~ies** iz

omonym ˈhɒm ə nɪm ˈhəʊm- ‖ ˈhɑːm- ˈhoʊm- **~s** z

omonymous hə ˈmɒn ɪm əs hɒ-, -əm- ‖ hoʊ ˈmɑːn- hə- **~ly** li

omonymy hə ˈmɒn ɪm i hɒ-, -əm- ‖ hoʊ ˈmɑːn- hə-

omophile ˈhəʊm əʊ faɪəl ˈhɒm- ‖ ˈhoʊm ə- **~s** z

omophobe ˈhəʊm əʊ fəʊb ˈhɒm- ‖ ˈhoʊm ə foʊb **~s** z

omophobia ˌhəʊm əʊ ˈfəʊb i‿ə ˌhɒm- ‖ ˌhoʊm ə ˈfoʊb-

omophobic ˌhəʊm əʊ ˈfəʊb ɪk ◂ ˌhɒm- ‖ ˌhoʊm ə ˈfoʊb-

omophone ˈhɒm ə fəʊn ˈhəʊm- ‖ ˈhɑːm ə foʊn ˈhoʊm- **~s** z

omophonic ˌhɒm ə ˈfɒn ɪk ◂ ˌhəʊm- ‖ ˌhɑːm ə ˈfɑːn ɪk ◂ ˌhoʊm-, ˌfoʊn-

omophonous hə ˈmɒf ən əs hɒ- ‖ hoʊ ˈmɑːf- hə-

omophony hə ˈmɒf ən i hɒ- ‖ hoʊ ˈmɑːf- hə-

omorganic ˌhɒm ɔː ˈɡæn ɪk ◂ ˌhəʊm- ‖ ˌhoʊm ɔːr- ˌhɑːm-

HOMOSEXUAL

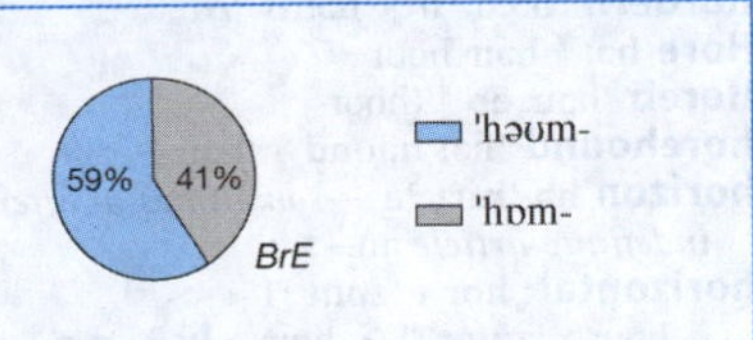

homosexual ˌhəʊm əʊ ˈsek ʃu‿əl ◂ ˌhɒm-, -ˈseks ju‿əl, -ˈsek ʃəl ‖ ˌhoʊm ə ˈsekʃ u‿əl ◂ -ˈ·əl — *Preference poll, BrE:* ˌhəʊm- *59%,* ˌhɒm- *41%.* **~s** z

homosexuality ˌhəʊm əʊ ˌsekʃ u ˈæl ət i ˌhɒm-, -ˌseks ju-, -ɪt i ‖ ˌhoʊm ə ˌsekʃ u ˈæl əṭ i

homozygous ˌhɒm ə ˈzaɪɡ əs ◂ ˌhəʊm- ‖ ˌhoʊm- ˌhɑːm-

homunc|ulus hɒ ˈmʌŋk |jʊl əs hə- ‖ hoʊ ˈmʌŋk |jəl əs **~uli** jʊ laɪ ‖ jə laɪ

hom|y ˈhəʊm |i ‖ ˈhoʊm |i **~ier** i‿ə ‖ i‿ər **~iest** i‿ɪst i‿əst

Hon. *'Honourable'; 'Honorary'* ɒn ‖ ɑːn **Hons** ɒnz ‖ ɑːnz

Hon *'Honey'* hʌn

honcho ˈhɒntʃ əʊ ‖ ˈhɑːntʃ oʊ **~s** z

Honda *tdmk* ˈhɒnd ə ‖ ˈhɑːnd ə —*Jp* [hoˌn da] **~s** z

Honddu ˈhɒn ði ‖ ˈhɑːn-

Hondur|an hɒn ˈdjʊər |ən -ˈdʊər-, →-ˈdʒʊər- ‖ hɑːn ˈdʊr- -ˈdjʊr- **~ans** ənz **~as** əs æs

hone, Hone həʊn ‖ hoʊn **honed** həʊnd ‖ hoʊnd **hones** həʊnz ‖ hoʊnz **honing** ˈhəʊn ɪŋ ‖ ˈhoʊn ɪŋ

Honecker ˈhɒn ek ə -ɪk- ‖ ˈhɑːn ɪk ər —*Ger* [ˈhɔn ɛk ɐ]

Honegger ˈhɒn ɪɡ ə -eɡ- ‖ ˈhɑːn ɪɡ ər —*Fr* [ɔ nɛ ɡɛːʁ]

honest ˈɒn ɪst -əst ‖ ˈɑːn əst **~ly** li

honest-to-goodness ˌɒn ɪst tə ˈɡʊd nəs ◂ ˌ·əst-, -tu ˈ-·, -nɪs ‖ ˌɑːn əst-

honesty ˈɒn əst i -ɪst- ‖ ˈɑːn-

honey, Honey ˈhʌn i **~ed** d **~s** z

honeybee ˈhʌn i biː **~s** z

honeybun ˈhʌn i bʌn **~s** z

honeybunch ˈhʌn i bʌntʃ **~es** ɪz əz

honeycomb ˈhʌn i kəʊm ‖ -koʊm **~ed** d **~ing** ɪŋ **~s** z

Honeycomb, Honeycombe ˈhʌn i kəʊm ‖ -koʊm

honeydew ˈhʌn i djuː →-dʒuː ‖ -duː -djuː
ˌ**honeydew** ˈ**melon**

honeyed ˈhʌn id

honeymoon ˈhʌn i muːn **~ed** d **~er/s** ə/z ‖ ər/z **~ing** ɪŋ **~s** z
ˈ**honeymoon** ˌ**couple**

honeypot ˈhʌn i pɒt ‖ -pɑːt **~s** s

honeysuckle ˈhʌn i ˌsʌk əl **~s** z

Hong Kong ˌhɒŋ ˈkɒŋ ◂ ‖ ˈhɑːŋ kɑːŋ ˈhɔːŋ-, -kɔːŋ, ˌ·ˈ· —*Chi* Xiānggǎng [¹ɕjɑŋ ³kɑŋ], *Cantonese* [¹hœːŋ ²kɔːŋ]

Honiara ˌhəʊn i ˈɑːr ə ˌhɒn- ‖ ˌhoʊn-

honied ˈhʌn id

honi soit qui mal y pense ˌɒn i ˌswɑː kiː ˌmæl i ˈpɒ̃s ‖ ˌɑːn i ˌswɑː kiː ˌmɑːl iː ˈpɑːns ˌɔːn-, ˌoʊn- —*Fr* [ɔ ni swa ki ma li pɑ̃ːs]

Honiton ˈhʌn ɪt ən ˈhɒn-, -ət-

honk hɒŋk ‖ hɑːŋk hɔːŋk **honked** hɒŋkt ‖ hɑːŋkt hɔːŋkt **honking** ˈhɒŋk ɪŋ ‖ ˈhɑːŋk ɪŋ ˈhɔːŋk- **honks** hɒŋks ‖ hɑːŋks hɔːŋks

honk|ie, honk|y ˈhɒŋk |i ‖ ˈhɑːŋk |i ˈhɔːŋk- **~ies** iz

honky-tonk ˈhɒŋk i tɒŋk ˌ· ·ˈ· ‖ ˈhɑːŋk i tɑːŋk ˈhɔːŋk i tɔːŋk **~s** s

Honolulu ˌhɒn ə ˈluːl uː -əl ˈuːl- ‖ ˌhɑːn-

honor, Honor ˈɒn ə ‖ ˈɑːn ər **~ed** d **honoring** ˈɒn ər‿ɪŋ ‖ ˈɑːn ər‿ɪŋ **~s** z
ˈ**honor roll**

honorab|le, H~ ˈɒn ər‿əb |əl ‖ ˈɑːn- ˈ·ərb |əl **~leness** əl nəs -nɪs **~ly** li
ˌ**honorable** ˈ**mention**

honorari|um ˌɒn ə ˈreər i‿|əm -ˈrɑːr- ‖ ˌɑːn ə ˈrer- **~a** ə **~ums** əmz

honorary ˈɒn ər‿ər i ⚠ˈɒn ər‿i ‖ ˈɑːn ə rer i

honoree ˌɒn ə ˈriː ‖ ˌɑːn- **~s** z

honorific ˌɒn ə ˈrɪf ɪk ◂ ‖ ˌɑːn- **~ally** əl‿i **~s** s

honoris causa hɒ ˌnɔːr ɪs ˈkaʊz ɑː ɒ-, -ˈkaʊs-, -ə ‖ oʊ ˌnɔːr əs ˈkaʊs ɑː ɑː-, -ˌnoʊr-, -ə

honour, H~ ˈɒn ə ‖ ˈɑːn ər **~ed** d **honouring** ˈɒn ər‿ɪŋ ‖ ˈɑːn ər‿ɪŋ **~s** z
ˈ**honours list**

honourab|le, H~ ˈɒn ər˽əb |əl || ˈɑːn- ˈərb |əl **~leness** əl nəs -nɪs **~ly** li
ˌ**honourable** ˈ**mention**

Honshu ˈhɒn ʃuː || ˈhɑːn- —*Jp* [ˈhon ɕɯɯ]

Hoo huː

hooch huːtʃ

hoochie ˈhuːtʃ i **~s** z

hood hʊd **hooded** ˈhʊd ɪd -əd **hooding** ˈhʊd ɪŋ **hoods** hʊdz

-hood hʊd — **fatherhood** ˈfɑːð ə hʊd || -ər-

hoodie ˈhʊd i **~s** z

hoodlum ˈhuːd ləm || ˈhʊd- ˈhuːd- **~s** z

hoodoo ˈhuː duː **~ed** d **~ing** ɪŋ **~s** z

hood|wink ˈhʊd |wɪŋk **~winked** wɪŋkt **~winking** wɪŋk ɪŋ **~winks** wɪŋks

hooey ˈhuː˽i

hoof huːf hʊf **hoofed** huːft hʊft **hoofing** ˈhuːf ɪŋ ˈhʊf- **hoofs** huːfs hʊfs **hooves** huːvz hʊvz

hoofer ˈhuːf ə ˈhʊf- || -ər **~s** z

Hoogly, Hooghly ˈhuːg li

hoo-ha ˈhuː hɑː **~s** z

hook, Hook hʊk §huːk **hooked** hʊkt §huːkt **hooking** ˈhʊk ɪŋ §ˈhuːk- **hooks** hʊks §huːks

hooka, hookah ˈhʊk ə **~s** z

Hooke hʊk §huːk

hooker, H~ ˈhʊk ə §ˈhuːk- || -ər **~s** z

hookey ˈhʊk i

hook-nosed ˌhʊk ˈnəʊzd ◂ §ˌhuːk-, ˈ· · || ˈhʊk noʊzd

hookup ˈhʊk ʌp §ˈhuːk- **~s** s

hookworm ˈhʊk wɜːm §ˈhuːk- || -wɜːm **~s** z

hooky ˈhʊk i

Hooley ˈhuːl i

hooligan ˈhuːl ɪg ən -əg- **~s** z

hooliganism ˈhuːl ɪg ən ˌɪz əm ˈ-əg-

Hoon huːn

hoop huːp §hʊp **hooped** huːpt §hʊpt **hooping** ˈhuːp ɪŋ §ˈhʊp- **hoops** huːps §hʊps

Hooper ˈhuːp ə §ˈhʊp- || -ər

hoop-la ˈhuːp lɑː ˈhʊp-

hoopoe ˈhuːp uː -əʊ **~s** z

hooray hu ˈreɪ hə-, ˌhuː- **~ed** d **~ing** ɪŋ **~s** z
hooˌray ˈ**Henry**, ˌ· ˈ· ˌ·

hoosegow ˈhuːs gaʊ **~s** z

Hoosier, h~ ˈhuːʒ ə || -ər **~s** z

Hooson ˈhuːs ən

hoot huːt **hooted** ˈhuːt ɪd -əd || ˈhuːṭ əd **hooting** ˈhuːt ɪŋ || ˈhuːṭ ɪŋ **hoots** huːts

hootch, H~ *tdmk* huːtʃ

hootenann|y ˈhuːt ən æn |i **~ies** iz

hooter ˈhuːt ə || ˈhuːṭ ər **~s** z

Hooton ˈhuːt ən

hoover, H~ ˈhuːv ə || -ər **~ed** d **hoovering** ˈhuːv ər˽ɪŋ **~s** z

hooves huːvz §hʊvz

hop hɒp || hɑːp **hopped** hɒpt || hɑːpt **hopping** ˈhɒp ɪŋ || ˈhɑːp ɪŋ **hops** hɒps || hɑːps

Hopcraft ˈhɒp krɑːft §-kræft || ˈhɑːp kræft

Hopcroft ˈhɒp krɒft -krɔːft || ˈhɑːp krɔːft -krɑːft

hope, Hope həʊp || hoʊp **hoped** həʊpt || hoʊpt **hopes** həʊps || hoʊps **hoping** ˈhəʊp ɪŋ || ˈhoʊp ɪŋ
ˈ**hope chest**

hoped-for ˈhəʊptfɔː || -fɔːr

hopeful ˈhəʊp fəl -fʊl || ˈhoʊp- **~ly** ˽i **~ness** nəs nɪs **~s** z

hopeless ˈhəʊp ləs -lɪs || ˈhoʊp- **~ly** li **~ness** nəs nɪs

Hopi ˈhəʊ piː ˈhəʊp i || ˈhoʊ piː **~s** z

Hopkin ˈhɒp kɪn || ˈhɑːp-

Hopkins ˈhɒp kɪnz || ˈhɑːp-

Hopkinson ˈhɒp kɪn sən || ˈhɑːp-

hoplite ˈhɒp laɪt || ˈhɑːp- **~s** s

hopp... —*see* **hop**

hopped-up ˌhɒpt ˈʌp ◂ || ˌhɑːpt-

hopper, H~ ˈhɒp ə || ˈhɑːp ər **~s** z

hop-picker ˈhɒp ˌpɪk ə || ˈhɑːp ˌpɪk ər **~s** z

Hoppus ˈhɒp əs || ˈhɑːp-

hopsack ˈhɒp sæk || ˈhɑːp- **~ing** ɪŋ

hopscotch ˈhɒp skɒtʃ || ˈhɑːp skɑːtʃ

Hopton ˈhɒpt ən || ˈhɑːpt-

Hopwood ˈhɒp wʊd || ˈhɑːp-

hora ˈhɔːr ə || ˈhoʊr- **~s** z

Horabin ˈhɒr ə bɪn || ˈhɔːr-

Horace ˈhɒr əs -ɪs || ˈhɔːr- ˈhɑːr-

Horatian hə ˈreɪʃ ən hɒ-, -ˈreɪʃ i˽ən

Horatio hə ˈreɪʃ i˽əʊ hɒ- || oʊ -ˈreɪʃ oʊ

Horatius hə ˈreɪʃ i˽əs hɒ-, -ˈreɪʃ əs

Horbury ˈhɔː bər˽i || ˈhɔːr ˌber i

horde hɔːd || hɔːrd hoʊrd *(= hoard)* **hordes** hɔːdz || hɔːrdz hoʊrdz

Hordern ˈhɔːd ən || ˈhɔːrd ərn

Hore hɔː || hɔːr hoʊr

Horeb ˈhɔːr eb || ˈhoʊr-

horehound ˈhɔː haʊnd || ˈhɔːr-

horizon hə ˈraɪz ən —*sometimes* ə- *after the indefinite article* an **~s** z

horizontal ˌhɒr ɪ ˈzɒnt əl ◂ -ə- || ˌhɔːr ə ˈzɑːnṭ əl ◂ ˌhɑːr- **~ly** i **~s** z

Horley ˈhɔːl i || ˈhɔːrl i

Horlick ˈhɔːl ɪk || ˈhɔːrl-

Horlicks *tdmk* ˈhɔːl ɪks || ˈhɔːrl-

hormonal ⁽ˌ⁾hɔː ˈməʊn əl || hɔːr ˈmoʊn əl

hormone ˈhɔːm əʊn || ˈhɔːrm oʊn **~s** z

Hormuz ˌhɔː ˈmuːz ˈhɔːm əz || ˌhɔːr- ˈhɔːrm əz

horn, Horn hɔːn || hɔːrn **horned** hɔːnd || hɔːrnd **horning** ˈhɔːn ɪŋ || ˈhɔːrn ɪŋ **horns** hɔːnz || hɔːrnz

hornbeam ˈhɔːn biːm →ˈhɔːm- || ˈhɔːrn- **~s** z

hornbill ˈhɔːn bɪl →ˈhɔːm- || ˈhɔːrn- **~s** z

hornblende ˈhɔːn blend →ˈhɔːm- || ˈhɔːrn- **~s** z

Hornblower ˈhɔːn ˌbləʊ ə →ˈhɔːm- || ˈhɔːrn ˌbloʊ ər

Hornby ˈhɔːn bi →ˈhɔːm- || ˈhɔːrn-

Horncastle ˈhɔːn ˌkɑːs əl →ˈhɔːŋ-, §-ˌkæs- || ˈhɔːrn ˌkæs əl

Hornchurch ˈhɔːn tʃɜːtʃ || ˈhɔːrn tʃɜːtʃ

Horne hɔːn || hɔːrn

horned *adj* hɔːnd ˈhɔːn ɪd, -əd || hɔːrnd ˈhɔːrn əd

Horner ˈhɔːn ə || ˈhɔːrn ər

ornet ˈhɔːn ɪt -ət ‖ ˈhɔːrn- **~s** s
ˈhornet's nest
orney ˈhɔːn i ‖ ˈhɔːrn i
orni... —*see* **horny**
orniman ˈhɔːn ɪ mən -ə- ‖ ˈhɔːrn-
ornpipe ˈhɔːn paɪp →ˈhɔːm- ‖ ˈhɔːrn- **~s** s
orn-rimmed ˌhɔːn ˈrɪmd ◂ ‖ ˌhɔːrn-
ornsby ˈhɔːnz bi ‖ ˈhɔːrnz-
ornsea ˈhɔːn siː ‖ ˈhɔːrn-
ornsey ˈhɔːnz i ‖ ˈhɔːrnz i
ornswoggl|e ˈhɔːn ˌswɒg ᵊl ‖ ˈhɔːrn ˌswɑːg ᵊl **~ed** d **~es** z **~ing** ‿ɪŋ
orn|y ˈhɔːn |i ‖ ˈhɔːrn |i **~ier** i‿ə ‖ i‿ᵊr **~iest** i‿ɪst i‿əst **~ily** ɪ li əl i **~iness** i nəs i nɪs
orologist hə ˈrɒl ədʒ ɪst hɒ-, hɔː-, §-əst ‖ hə ˈrɑːl- **~s** s
orologium, H~ ˌhɒr ə ˈləʊdʒ i‿əm ˌhɔːr- ‖ ˌhɔːr ə ˈloʊdʒ-
orology hə ˈrɒl ədʒ i hɒ-, hɔː- ‖ hə ˈrɑːl-
oroscope ˈhɒr ə skəʊp ‖ ˈhɔːr ə skoʊp ˈhɑːr- **~s** s
orowitz ˈhɒr ə wɪts -vɪts ‖ ˈhɔːr- ˈhɑːr-
orrendous hɒ ˈrend əs hə- ‖ hɔː- hɑː- **~ly** li **~ness** nəs nɪs
orrib|le ˈhɒr əb |ᵊl -ɪb- ‖ ˈhɔːr- ˈhɑːr- **~leness** ᵊl nəs -nɪs **~ly** li
orrid ˈhɒr ɪd §-əd ‖ ˈhɔːr əd ˈhɑːr- **~ly** li **~ness** nəs nɪs
orrific hɒ ˈrɪf ɪk hə- ‖ hɔː- hɑː- **~ally** ᵊl‿i
orri|fy ˈhɒr ɪ |faɪ -ə- ‖ ˈhɔːr- ˈhɑːr- **~fied/ly** faɪd /li **~fies** faɪz **~fying/ly** faɪ ɪŋ /li
orripilation hɒ ˌrɪp ɪ ˈleɪʃ ᵊn -ə-; ˌhɒr ɪp-, ˌ·əp- ‖ hɔː- hɑː-
orrocks ˈhɒr əks ‖ ˈhɔːr- ˈhɑːr-
orror ˈhɒr ə ‖ ˈhɔːr ᵊr ˈhɑːr- **~s** z
ˈhorror film; **ˈhorror ˌmovie**; **ˈhorror ˌstory**
orror-stricken ˈhɒr ə ˌstrɪk ən ‖ ˈhɔːr ᵊr- ˈhɑːr-
orror-struck ˈhɒr ə strʌk ‖ ˈhɔːr ᵊr- ˈhɑːr-
orsa ˈhɔːs ə ‖ ˈhɔːrs ə
orsbrugh ˈhɔːs brə ˈhɔːz- ‖ ˈhɔːrz-
hors de combat ˌɔː də ˈkɒm bɑː -ˈkɒ̃-, -bæt ‖ ˌɔːr də koʊm ˈbɑː —*Fr* [ɔʁ də kɔ̃ ba]
hors-d'oeuvre, ~s ˌɔː ˈdɜːv ‖ ˌɔːr ˈdɜːv —*Fr* [ɔʁ dœːvʁ]
horse hɔːs ‖ hɔːrs **horsed** hɔːst ‖ hɔːrst **horses** ˈhɔːs ɪz -əz ‖ ˈhɔːrs əz **horsing** ˈhɔːs ɪŋ ‖ ˈhɔːrs ɪŋ
ˈhorse brass; **ˌhorse ˈchestnut** ‖ ˈ· ˌ· ·; **ˈhorse ˌopera**; **ˈhorse sense**
horse-and-buggy ˌhɔːs ᵊn ˈbʌg i -ᵊnd-, →-ᵊm- ‖ ˌhɔːrs-
horse-and-cart ˌhɔːs ᵊn ˈkɑːt -ᵊnd-, →-ᵊŋ- ‖ ˌhɔːrs ᵊn ˈkɑːrt
horseback ˈhɔːs bæk ‖ ˈhɔːrs-
horsebox ˈhɔːs bɒks ‖ ˈhɔːrs bɑːks **~es** ɪz əz
horsedrawn ˈhɔːs drɔːn ‖ ˈhɔːrs- -drɑːn
Horseferry ˈhɔːs ˌfer i -fər‿i ‖ ˈhɔːrs-
horseflesh ˈhɔːs fleʃ ‖ ˈhɔːrs-
horse|fly ˈhɔːs |flaɪ ‖ ˈhɔːrs- **~flies** flaɪz
Horseguard ˈhɔːs gɑːd ‖ ˈhɔːrs gɑːrd **~s** z
horsehair ˈhɔːs heə ‖ ˈhɔːrs her -hær
horsehide ˈhɔːs haɪd ‖ ˈhɔːrs-
horselaugh ˈhɔːs lɑːf §-læf ‖ ˈhɔːrs læf **~s** s
horse|man ˈhɔːs |mən ‖ ˈhɔːrs- **~manship** mən ʃɪp **~men** mən men
horsemastership ˈhɔːs ˌmɑːst ə ʃɪp §-ˌmæst- ‖ ˈhɔːrs ˌmæst ᵊr-
horseplay ˈhɔːs pleɪ ‖ ˈhɔːrs-
horsepower ˈhɔːs ˌpaʊ‿ə ‖ ˈhɔːrs ˌpaʊ‿ᵊr
horseracing ˈhɔːs ˌreɪs ɪŋ ‖ ˈhɔːrs-
horseradish ˈhɔːs ˌræd ɪʃ ‖ ˈhɔːrs- **~es** ɪz əz
horse-rid|ing ˈhɔːs ˌraɪd| ɪŋ ‖ ˈhɔːrs- **~er/s** ə/z ‖ ᵊr/z
horseshit ˈhɔːs ʃɪt →ˈhɔːʃ- ‖ ˈhɔːrs- →ˈhɔːrʃ-, ˈhɔːr-
horseshoe ˈhɔːs ʃuː →ˈhɔːʃ- ‖ ˈhɔːrs- →ˈhɔːrʃ-, ˈhɔːr- **~s** z
horsetail ˈhɔːs teɪᵊl ‖ ˈhɔːrs- **~s** z
horse-trading ˈhɔːs ˌtreɪd ɪŋ ‖ ˈhɔːrs-
horsewhip ˈhɔːs wɪp -hwɪp ‖ ˈhɔːrs- **~ped** t **~ping** ɪŋ **~s** s
horse|woman ˈhɔːs |ˌwʊm ən ‖ ˈhɔːrs- **~women** ˌwɪm ɪn §-ən
hors|ey, H~ ˈhɔːs |i ‖ ˈhɔːrs |i **~ier** i‿ə ‖ i‿ᵊr **~iest** i‿ɪst i‿əst
Horsfall ˈhɒs fɔːl ‖ ˈhɔːrs fɑːl -fɔːl
Horsforth ˈhɔːs fəθ ‖ ˈhɔːrs fᵊrθ
Horsham ˈhɔːʃ əm ‖ ˈhɔːrʃ-
horsi... —*see* **horsey, horsy**
Horsley ˈhɔːz li ‖ ˈhɔːrz-
Horsmonden ˌhɔːz mən ˈden ‖ ˌhɔːrz-
Horsted Keynes ˌhɔːst ɪd ˈkeɪnz -əd- ‖ ˌhɔːrst-
hors|y ˈhɔːs |i ‖ ˈhɔːrs |i **~ier** i‿ə ‖ i‿ᵊr **~iest** i‿ɪst i‿əst
hortative ˈhɔːt ət ɪv hɔː ˈteɪt- ‖ ˈhɔːrţ əţ ɪv **~ly** li
hortatory ˈhɔːt ət‿ər i hɔː ˈteɪt ər i ‖ ˈhɔːrţ ə tɔːr i -toʊr i
Hortensia, h~ hɔː ˈtenᵗs i‿ə -ˈtenᵗʃ- ‖ hɔːr ˈtenᵗʃə **~s** z
horticultural ˌhɔːt ɪ ˈkʌltʃ ᵊr‿əl ◂ ˌ·ə- ‖ ˌhɔːrţ ə- **~ist/s** ɪst/s §əst/s **~ly** i
horticulture ˈhɔːt ɪ ˌkʌltʃ ə -ə-; §ˌ· ·ˈ·· ‖ ˈhɔːrţ ə ˌkʌltʃ ᵊr
horticulturist ˌhɔːt ɪ ˈkʌltʃ ər ɪst ˌ·ə-, §-əst ‖ ˌhɔːrţ ə- **~s** s
Horton ˈhɔːt ᵊn ‖ ˈhɔːrt ᵊn
Horus ˈhɔːr əs ‖ ˈhoʊr-
Horwich ˈhɒr ɪtʃ -ɪdʒ ‖ ˈhɔːr-
Horwood ˈhɔː wʊd ‖ ˈhɔːr-
hosanna həʊ ˈzæn ə ‖ hoʊ- **~s** z
hose, Hose həʊz ‖ hoʊz **hosed** həʊzd ‖ hoʊzd **hoses** ˈhəʊz ɪz -əz ‖ ˈhoʊz əz **hosing** ˈhəʊz ɪŋ ‖ ˈhoʊz ɪŋ
Hosea həʊ ˈzɪə ‖ hoʊ ˈziː ə
Hoseason *(i)* həʊ ˈsiːz ᵊn ˈ·ˌ· · ‖ hoʊ-, *(ii)* ˌhəʊs i ˈeɪs ᵊn -ˈæs- ‖ ˌhoʊs-
hosel ˈhəʊz ᵊl ‖ ˈhoʊz ᵊl **~s** z
hosepipe ˈhəʊz paɪp ‖ ˈhoʊz- **~s** s
hoser ˈhəʊz ə ‖ -ᵊr **~s** z
Hosey ˈhəʊz i ‖ ˈhoʊz i
hosier, H~ ˈhəʊz i‿ə ˈhəʊʒ jə, -ə ‖ ˈhoʊʒ ᵊr **~s** z
hosiery ˈhəʊz i‿ər i ˈhəʊʒ jər i, -ər i ‖ ˈhoʊʒ ər i

Hoskins, Hoskyns ˈhɒsk ɪnz §-ənz ‖ ˈhɑːsk-
hospic|e ˈhɒsp ɪs §-əs ‖ ˈhɑːsp- **~es** ɪz əz

HOSPITABLE

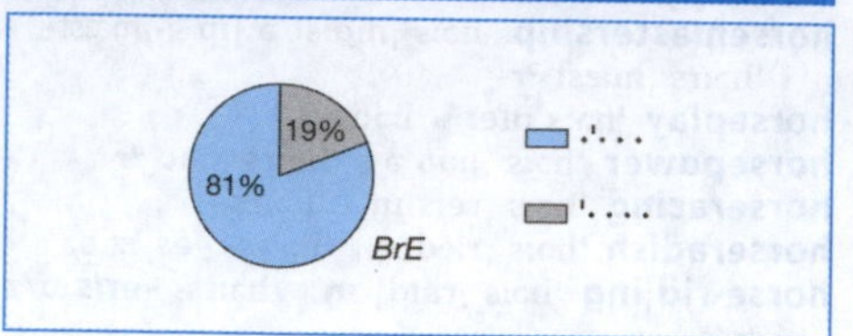

hospitab|le hɒ ˈspɪt əb |əl hə-; ˈhɒsp ɪt-, ˈ-ət- ‖ ˈhɑːsp əṭ- hɑː ˈspɪṭ- — *Preference poll, BrE:* ·ˈ··· 81%, ˈ···· 19%. **~ly** li
hospital ˈhɒsp ɪt əl ‖ ˈhɑːsp ɪṭ əl **~s** z
hospitalis... —*see* **hospitaliz...**
hospitalit|y ˌhɒsp ɪ ˈtæl ət |i ˌ-ə-, -ɪt i ‖ ˌhɑːsp ə ˈtæl əṭ |i **~ies** iz
hospitalization ˌhɒsp ɪt əl aɪ ˈzeɪʃ ən ˌ-ət-, ˌɪˈ- ‖ ˌhɑːsp ɪṭ əl ə-
hospitaliz|e ˈhɒsp ɪt əl aɪz ˈ-ət-, -ə laɪz ‖ ˈhɑːsp ɪṭ- **~ed** d **~es** ɪz əz **~ing** ɪŋ
host, Host həʊst ‖ hoʊst **hosted** ˈhəʊst ɪd -əd ‖ ˈhoʊst əd **hosting** ˈhəʊst ɪŋ ‖ ˈhoʊst ɪŋ **hosts** həʊsts ‖ hoʊsts
hosta ˈhɒst ə ˈhəʊst- ‖ ˈhoʊst ə ˈhɑːst- **~s** z
hostag|e ˈhɒst ɪdʒ ‖ ˈhɑːst- **~es** ɪz əz
hostel ˈhɒst əl ‖ ˈhɑːst- **~ing, ~ling** ɪŋ **~s** z
hosteler, hosteller ˈhɒst əl ə ‖ ˈhɑːst əl ər **~s** z
hostel|ry ˈhɒst əl |ri ‖ ˈhɑːst- **~ries** riz
hostess ˈhəʊst ɪs -əs, -es; ˌhəʊs ˈtes ‖ ˈhoʊst əs **~es** ɪz əz
hostile ˈhɒst aɪəl ‖ ˈhɑːst əl -aɪəl **~ly** li
hostilit|y hɒ ˈstɪl ət |i §hə-, -ɪt- ‖ hɑː ˈstɪl əṭ |i **~ies** iz
hostler ˈɒs lə ˈhɒs- ‖ ˈɑːs lər ˈhɑːs- **~s** z
hot hɒt ‖ hɑːt **hots** hɒts ‖ hɑːts **hotted** ˈhɒt ɪd -əd ‖ ˈhɑːṭ əd **hotting** ˈhɒt ɪŋ ‖ ˈhɑːṭ ɪŋ **ˌhot ˈair**; **ˌhot ˈair balˌloon**; **ˌhot cross ˈbun**; **ˌhot ˈdog** *'frankfurter roll'* ‖ ˈ·.; **ˌhot ˈflash, ˌhot ˈflush**; **ˌhot poˈtato**; **ˈhot rod**; **ˈhot seat**; **ˈhot spot**; **ˌhot ˈstuff**; **ˌhot ˈwater**
hotbed ˈhɒt bed ‖ ˈhɑːt- **~s** z
hot-blooded ˌhɒt ˈblʌd ɪd ◂ -əd ‖ ˌhɑːt- **~ness** nəs nɪs
Hotbot *tdmk* ˈhɒt bɒt ‖ ˈhɑːt bɑːt
hot cake, hotcake ˌhɒt ˈkeɪk ‖ ˈhɑːt keɪk **~s** s
Hotchkiss ˈhɒtʃ kɪs ‖ ˈhɑːtʃ-
hotchpot ˈhɒtʃ pɒt ‖ ˈhɑːtʃ pɑːt **~s** s
hotchpotch ˈhɒtʃ pɒtʃ ‖ ˈhɑːtʃ pɑːtʃ **~es** ɪz əz
hot-dog *v* ˈhɒt dɒg ‖ ˈhɑːt dɔːg -dɑːg **~ged** d **~ging** ɪŋ **~s** z
hotel ˌhəʊ ˈtel ◂ həʊ-, əʊ- ‖ ˌhoʊ- **~s** z
hotelier həʊ ˈtel i eɪ əʊ-, -i‿ə ‖ ˌoʊt əl ˈjeɪ hoʊ ˈtel jər, ˌhoʊṭ əl ˈɪər **~s** z
hot|foot ˌhɒt ˈ|fʊt ◂ ˈ·· ‖ ˈhɑːt |fʊt **~footed** fʊt ɪd -əd ‖ fʊṭ əd **~footing** fʊt ɪŋ ‖ fʊṭ ɪŋ **~foots** fʊts
hot-gospel|er, hot-gospell|er ˌhɒt ˈgɒsp əl |ə ‖ ˌhɑːt ˈgɑːsp əl |ər **~ers** əz ‖ ərz **~ing** ɪŋ
Hotham *(i)* ˈhʌð əm, *(ii)* ˈhɒθ əm ‖ ˈhɑːθ-, *(iii)* ˈhɒt əm ‖ ˈhɑːṭ əm
hothead ˈhɒt hed ‖ ˈhɑːt- **~s** z
hotheaded ˌhɒt ˈhed ɪd ◂ -əd ‖ ˌhɑːt- **~ly** li **~ness** nəs nɪs
hot|house ˈhɒt |haʊs ‖ ˈhɑːt- **~houses** haʊz ɪz -əz
hotline ˈhɒt laɪn ‖ ˈhɑːt- **~s** z
hotlink ˈhɒt lɪŋk ‖ ˈhɑːt- **~s** s
hotly ˈhɒt li ‖ ˈhɑːt-
Hotmail *tdmk* ˈhɒt meɪəl ‖ ˈhɑːt-
hotplate ˈhɒt pleɪt ‖ ˈhɑːt- **~s** s
Hotpoint *tdmk* ˈhɒt pɔɪnt ‖ ˈhɑːt-
hotpot ˈhɒt pɒt ‖ ˈhɑːt pɑːt **~s** s
hotrod ˈhɒt rɒd ‖ ˈhɑːt rɑːd **~ded** ɪd əd **~der/ə/z** ‖ -ər/z **~ding** ɪŋ **~s** z
hotshot ˈhɒt ʃɒt ‖ ˈhɑːt ʃɑːt **~s** s
hotspur, H~ ˈhɒt spɜː -spə ‖ ˈhɑːt spɜː **~s** z
hott.. —*see* **hot**
hot-tempered ˌhɒt ˈtemp əd ◂ ‖ ˌhɑːt ˈtemp ərd ◂
Hottentot ˈhɒt ən tɒt ‖ ˈhɑːt ən tɑːt **~s** s
hottie ˈhɒt i ‖ ˈhɑːṭ i **~s** z
hot-water bottle ˌhɒt ˈwɔːt ə ˌbɒt əl ‖ ˌhɑːt ˈwɔːṭ ər ˌbɑːṭ əl -ˈwɑːṭ- **~s** z
hot-wire *v* ˌhɒt ˈwaɪ‿ə ‖ ˌhɑːt ˈwaɪ‿ər **~d** d **~s** z **hot-wiring** ˌhɒt ˈwaɪ‿ər ɪŋ ‖ ˌhɑːt ˈwaɪ‿ər ɪŋ
Houdini hu ˈdiːn i
hough hɒk ‖ hɑːk **houghed** hɒkt ‖ hɑːkt **houghing** ˈhɒk ɪŋ ‖ ˈhɑːk ɪŋ **houghs** hɒks ‖ hɑːks
Hough *(i)* hʌf, *(ii)* hɒf ‖ hɔːf hɑːf, *(iii)* haʊ
Houghall ˈhɒf əl ‖ ˈhɑːf əl
Hougham ˈhʌf əm
Houghton *(i)* ˈhɔːt ən ‖ ˈhɑːt-, *(ii)* ˈhaʊt ən, *(iii)* ˈhəʊt ən ‖ ˈhoʊt-
Houghton-le-Spring ˌhəʊt ən li ˈsprɪŋ -ləˈ. ‖ ˌhoʊt-
Houlihan ˈhuːl ɪ hən -ə-
houmous ˈhʊm ʊs ˈhuːm-, -əs
hound haʊnd **hounded** ˈhaʊnd ɪd -əd **hounding** ˈhaʊnd ɪŋ **hounds** haʊndz
Houndsditch ˈhaʊndz dɪtʃ
hound's-tooth ˈhaʊndz tuːθ §-tʊθ, ˌ·ˈ·
Hounslow ˈhaʊnz ləʊ ‖ -loʊ
hour ˈaʊ‿ə ‖ ˈaʊə‿r *(= our)* **hours** ˈaʊ‿əz ‖ ˈaʊ‿ərz **ˈhour hand**
hourglass ˈaʊ‿ə glɑːs §-glæs ‖ ˈaʊ‿ər glæs **~es** ɪz əz
houri ˈhʊər i ‖ ˈhʊr i **~s** z
hourly ˈaʊ‿ə li ‖ ˈaʊ‿ər li
Housatonic ˌhuːs ə ˈtɒn ɪk ◂ ˌhuːz- ‖ -ˈtɑːn-
house *n, adj* haʊs **houses** ˈhaʊz ɪz -əz *(!)* **ˈhouse ˌagent**; **ˈhouse arˌrest**, ˌ· ·ˈ·; **ˈhouse ˌhusband**; **ˈhouse lights**; **ˈhouse ˌmartin**; **ˌHouse of ˈCommons**; **ˌHouse of ˈLords**;

ˌHouse of ˌRepreˈsentatives; **ˈhouse ˌparty**; **ˌHouses of ˈParliament**; **ˈhouse ˌsparrow**

ouse *v* haʊz **housed** haʊzd **houses** ˈhaʊz ɪz -əz **housing** ˈhaʊz ɪŋ

ouse *family name* haʊs

ouseboat ˈhaʊs bəʊt ‖ -boʊt **~s** s

ousebound ˈhaʊs baʊnd

ouseboy ˈhaʊs bɔɪ **~s** z

ousebreak ˈhaʊs breɪk **~er/s** ə/z ‖ ᵊr/z **~ing** ɪŋ **housebroken** ˈhaʊs ˌbrəʊk ən ‖ -ˌbroʊk ən

ousebuy|er ˈhaʊs ˌbaɪ|ə ‖ -ˌbaɪ|ᵊr **~ers** əz ‖ ᵊrz **~ing** ɪŋ

ousecoat ˈhaʊs kəʊt ‖ -koʊt **~s** s

ousecraft ˈhaʊs krɑːft §-kræft ‖ -kræft

ousedog ˈhaʊs dɒg ‖ -dɔːg -dɑːg **~s** z

ousefather ˈhaʊs ˌfɑːð ə ‖ -ᵊr **~s** z

ouse|fly ˈhaʊs |flaɪ **~flies** flaɪz

ouseful ˈhaʊs fʊl **~s** z

ousego ˈhaʊs gəʊ ‖ -goʊ

ousehold ˈhaʊs həʊld →-hɒʊld, -əʊld ‖ -hoʊld **~s** z

ˌhousehold ˈname

ouseholder, H~ ˈhaʊs həʊld ə →-hɒʊld-, -əʊld- ‖ -hoʊld ᵊr **~s** z

ousekeeper ˈhaʊs ˌkiːp ə ‖ -ᵊr **~s** z

ousekeeping ˈhaʊs ˌkiːp ɪŋ

ouseleek ˈhaʊs liːk **~s** s

ousemaid ˈhaʊs meɪd **~s** z

ˌhousemaid's ˈknee

ouse|man ˈhaʊs |mən -mæn **~men** mən men

ousemaster ˈhaʊs ˌmɑːst ə §-ˌmæst- ‖ -ˌmæst ᵊr **~ship/s** ʃɪp/s **~s** z

ousemate ˈhaʊs meɪt **~s** s

ousemistress ˈhaʊs ˌmɪs trəs -trɪs **~es** ɪz əz

ousemother ˈhaʊs ˌmʌð ə ‖ -ᵊr **~s** z

ouseparent ˈhaʊs ˌpeər ənt ‖ -ˌper- -ˌpær- **~s** s

housephone ˈhaʊs fəʊn ‖ -foʊn **~s** z

houseplant ˈhaʊs plɑːnt §-plænt ‖ -plænt **~s** s

house-proud ˈhaʊs praʊd

houseroom ˈhaʊs ruːm -rʊm

houses *from* **house** *n, v* ˈhaʊz ɪz -əz *(!)*

house-|sit ˈhaʊs| sɪt **~sitter/s** ˌsɪt ə/z ‖ ˌsɪţ ᵊr/z **~sitting** ˌsɪt ɪŋ ‖ ˌsɪţ ɪŋ

house-to-house ˌhaʊs tə ˈhaʊs ◂ -tu-

housetop ˈhaʊs tɒp ‖ -tɑːp **~s** s

house-train ˈhaʊs treɪn **~ed** d **~ing** ɪŋ **~s** z

houseware ˈhaʊs weə ‖ -wer **~s** z

housewarming ˈhaʊs ˌwɔːm ɪŋ ‖ -ˌwɔːrm ɪŋ **~s** z

house|wife ˈhaʊs |waɪf —*formerly also* ˈhʌz ɪf **~wifely** waɪf li **~wives** waɪvz

housewifery ˈhaʊs wɪf ər‿i ‖ ˈhaʊs waɪf ər i *(*)* —*formerly also* ˈhʌz ɪf ri, -əf-

housework ˈhaʊs wɜːk ‖ -wɜːk

housey-housey, housie-housie ˌhaʊz i ˈhaʊz i

housing ˈhaʊz ɪŋ **~s** z

ˈhousing associˌation; **ˈhousing eˌstate**; **ˈhousing ˌproject**

Housman ˈhaʊs mən

Houston *(i)* ˈhuːst ən, *(ii)* ˈhjuːst ən §ˈjuːst-, *(iii)* ˈhaʊst ən —*The Scottish name is (i), the Texan (ii), the NYC street and GA county (iii).*

Houtman Abrolhos ˌhaʊt mən ə ˈbrɒl əs ‖ -ˈbrɑːl- -ˈbroʊl-

Houyhnhnm ˈhuː‿ɪn əm hu ˈɪn- ‖ ˈhwɪn əm hu ˈɪn əm

hove, Hove həʊv ‖ hoʊv

hovel ˈhɒv ᵊl ˈhʌv- ‖ ˈhʌv ᵊl ˈhɑːv- **~s** z

hov|er ˈhɒv |ə ˈhʌv- ‖ ˈhʌv |ᵊr ˈhɑːv- **~ered** əd ‖ ᵊrd **~ering** ər‿ɪŋ **~ers** əz ‖ ᵊrz

ˈhover fly

hovercraft ˈhɒv ə krɑːft ˈhʌv-, §-kræft ‖ ˈhʌv ᵊr kræft ˈhɑːv- **~s** s

hover|fly ˈhɒv ə |flaɪ ˈhʌv- ‖ ˈhʌv ᵊr- ˈhɑːv- **~flies** flaɪz

Hoveringham ˈhɒv ər‿ɪŋ əm ‖ ˈhʌv- ˈhɑːv-

hoverport ˈhɒv ə pɔːt ˈhʌv- ‖ ˈhʌv ᵊr pɔːrt ˈhɑːv-, -poʊrt **~s** s

hovertrain ˈhɒv ə treɪn ˈhʌv- ‖ ˈhʌv ᵊr- ˈhɑːv- **~s** z

Hovis *tdmk* ˈhəʊv ɪs §-əs ‖ ˈhoʊv-

how haʊ

ˌHow ˈare you? *(greeting)*; **(ˈFine.) ˌHow are ˈyou?** *(reply)*; **ˌHow do you ˈdo?**

Howard ˈhaʊ‿əd ‖ ˈhaʊ‿ᵊrd **~s, ~'s** z

howdah ˈhaʊd ə **~s** z

Howden ˈhaʊd ᵊn

how-do-you-do *n* ˌhaʊ dju ˈduː -djə-, -dʒu-, -dʒə-, -di-, -də ju-; ˈ· · · **~s** z

howdy ˈhaʊd i

how-d'ye-do *n* ˌhaʊ djə ˈduː -dʒə-, -di-; ˈ· · · **~s** z

Howe, howe haʊ

howe'er haʊ ˈeə ‖ -ˈeᵊr

Howell ˈhaʊ‿əl haʊl ‖ ˈhaʊ‿əl

Howells ˈhaʊ‿əlz haʊlz ‖ ˈhaʊ‿əlz

Howerd ˈhaʊ‿əd ‖ ˈhaʊ‿ᵊrd

however haʊ ˈev ə ˌ·- ‖ -ᵊr

Howie ˈhaʊ i

Howitt ˈhaʊ ɪt §-ət

howitzer ˈhaʊ‿ɪts ə §ˌəts- ‖ -ᵊr **~s** z

howl haʊl **howled** haʊld **howling** ˈhaʊl ɪŋ **howls** haʊlz

Howland ˈhaʊ lənd

howler ˈhaʊl ə ‖ ᵊr **~s** z

howsoever ˌhaʊ səʊ ˈev ə ◂ ‖ -soʊ ˈev ᵊr ◂

Howth *place in Co. Dublin* həʊθ ‖ hoʊθ

how-to ˈhaʊ tuː

howzat ₍ˌ₎haʊ ˈzæt

Hoxha ˈhɒdʒ ə ‖ ˈhoʊdʒ ɑː ˈhɑːdʒ-,-ə —*Albanian* [ˈho dʒa]

Hoxton ˈhɒkst ən ‖ ˈhɑːkst-

hoy, Hoy hɔɪ **hoys** hɔɪz

hoya ˈhɔɪ ə **~s** z

hoyden ˈhɔɪd ᵊn **~s** z

hoydenish ˈhɔɪd ən ɪʃ

Hoylake ˈhɔɪ leɪk

Hoyle hɔɪᵊl

HP ˌeɪtʃ ˈpiː ◂ §ˌheɪtʃ-

HQ ˌeɪtʃ ˈkjuː §ˌheɪtʃ-

HRH ˌeɪtʃ ɑːr ˈeɪtʃ §ˌheɪtʃ ɑː ˈheɪtʃ ‖ -ɑːr-

H

HRT ˌeɪtʃ ɑː ˈtiː §ˌheɪtʃ- ‖ -ɑːr-
hryvna, hryvnia ˈrɪv ni‿ə ˈriːv-, -nə —*Ukrainian* [ˈɦrʲiʊ nʲə]
HTML ˌeɪtʃ tiː em ˈel §ˌheɪtʃ-
Hu *Chinese name* huː —*Chi* Hú [²xu]
hub hʌb **hubs** hʌbz
Hubbard ˈhʌb əd ‖ -ərd
hubbi... —*see* **hubby**
Hubble ˈhʌb əl
hubble-bubble ˈhʌb əl ˌbʌb əl **~s** z
hubbub ˈhʌb ʌb **~s** z
hubb|y ˈhʌb |i **~ies** iz
hubcap ˈhʌb kæp **~s** s
Hubei ˌhuː ˈbeɪ —*Chi* Húběi [²xu ³bei]
Hubert ˈhjuːb ət ‖ -ərt
hubris ˈhjuːb rɪs ˈhuːb-, §-rəs
hubristic hju ˈbrɪst ɪk hu- **~ally** əl‿i
Huck hʌk
huckaback ˈhʌk ə bæk
huckleberr|y, H~ ˈhʌk əl bər‿|i -ˌber |i ‖ -ˌber |i **~ies** iz
Hucknall ˈhʌk nəl
huckster ˈhʌkst ə ‖ -ər **huckstering** ˈhʌkst ər ɪŋ **~s** z
hucksterism ˈhʌkst ər ˌɪz əm
Huckvale ˈhʌk verəl
Hudd hʌd
Huddersfield ˈhʌd əz fiːəld ‖ -ərz-
huddl|e ˈhʌd əl **~ed** d **~es** z **~ing** ‿ɪŋ
Huddleston ˈhʌd əl stən
Hudibras ˈhjuːd ɪ bræs -ə-
hudibrastic, H~ ˌhjuːd ɪ ˈbræst ɪk ◂ -ə-
Hudnott ˈhʌd nɒt ‖ -nɑːt
Hudson ˈhʌd sən
ˌHudson ˈBay; **ˌHudson ˈRiver**
hue hjuː (= *hew, Hugh*) **hued** hjuːd **hues** hjuːz
ˌhue and ˈcry
huevos rancheros ˌweɪv ɒs ræn ˈtʃeər ɒs ‖ -oʊs ræn ˈtʃer oʊs —*Sp* [ˌwe βos ran ˈtʃe ros, -βoɾ-]
Huey ˈhjuː‿i
huff, Huff hʌf **huffed** hʌft **huffing** ˈhʌf ɪŋ **huffs** hʌfs
huffish ˈhʌf ɪʃ **~ly** li **~ness** nəs nɪs
huff|y ˈhʌf |i **~ier** i‿ə ‖ i‿ər **~iest** i‿ɪst i‿əst **~ily** ɪ li əl i **~iness** i nəs i nɪs
hug hʌg **hugged** hʌgd **hugging** ˈhʌg ɪŋ **hugs** hʌgz
huge hjuːdʒ §juːdʒ **huger** ˈhjuːdʒ ə §ˈjuːdʒ- ‖ -ər **hugest** ˈhjuːdʒ ɪst §ˈjuːdʒ-, -əst
huge|ly ˈhjuːdʒ |li §ˈjuːdʒ- **~ness** nəs nɪs
huggable ˈhʌg əb əl
hugger ˈhʌg ə ‖ -ər **~s** z
hugger-mugger ˈhʌg ə ˌmʌg ə ‖ -ər ˌmʌg ər
Huggies *tdmk* ˈhʌg iz
Huggins ˈhʌg ɪnz §-ənz
Hugh hjuː
Hughenden ˈhjuː‿ən dən
Hughes hjuːz
Hughey, Hughie ˈhjuː‿i
Hugo ˈhjuːg əʊ ‖ -oʊ
Hugon ˈhjuːg ən -ɒn ‖ -ɑːn
Hugue|not, h~ ˈhjuːg ə |nəʊ ˈhuːg-, -nɒt ‖ -|nɑːt (*) **~nots** nəʊz nɒts ‖ nɑːts
huh hʌ hʌh
huh-uh ˌhʌʔ ˈʌ —*The first syllable is higher-pitched than the second.*
Huhne hjuːn
Huish ˈhjuː‿ɪʃ
hula ˈhuːl ə **~s** z
hula-hoop, Hula-Hoop *tdmk* ˈhuːl ə huːp **~s**
hula-hula ˌhuːl ə ˈhuːl ə **~s** z
Hulbert ˈhʌl bət ‖ -bərt
hulk hʌlk **hulked** hʌlkt **hulking** ˈhʌlk ɪŋ **hulks** hʌlks
hull, Hull hʌl **hulled** hʌld **hulling** ˈhʌl ɪŋ **hulls** hʌlz
hullabaloo ˌhʌl ə bə ˈluː ˈ· · · · **~s** z
hullo hə ˈləʊ ₍ˌ₎hʌ- ‖ -ˈloʊ **~s** z
Hulme *(i)* hjuːm, *(ii)* hʌlm —*In Britain (i), in the US (ii).*
Hulot ˈuːl əʊ ‖ uː ˈloʊ —*Fr* [y lo]
Hulse hʌls
Hulsean hʌl ˈsiː‿ən
hum hʌm **hummed** hʌmd **humming** ˈhʌm ɪŋ **hums** hʌmz
human ˈhjuːm ən §ˈjuːm- **~ly** li **~ness** nəs nɪs **~s** z
ˌhuman ˈbeing; **ˌhuman ˈrace**; **ˌhuman ˈrights**
humana, Humana *tdmk* hju ˈmɑːn ə
humane hju ˈmeɪn ˌhjuː- **~ly** li **~ness** nəs nɪs
humanis... —*see* **humaniz...**
humanism ˈhjuːm ə ˌnɪz əm §ˈjuːm-
humanist ˈhjuːm ən ɪst §ˈjuːm-, §-əst **~s** s
humanistic ˌhjuːm ə ˈnɪst ɪk ◂ §ˌjuːm- **~ally** əl‿i
humanitarian hju ˌmæn ɪ ˈteər i‿ən §ju-, ˌhjuːm æn-, -ə'·- ‖ -ˈter- **~ism** ˌɪz əm
humanit|y hju ˈmæn ət |i §ju-, -ɪt i ‖ -əṭ |i **~ies** iz
humanization ˌhjuːm ən aɪ ˈzeɪʃ ən §ˌjuːm-, -ən ɪ- ‖ -ən ə-
humaniz|e ˈhjuːm ə naɪz §ˈjuːm- **~ed** d **~es** ɪz əz **~ing** ɪŋ
humankind ˌhjuːm ən ˈkaɪnd §ˌjuːm-, →-əŋ-
humanly ˈhjuːm ən li §ˈjuːm-
humanoid ˈhjuːm ə nɔɪd §ˈjuːm- **~s** z
Humber ˈhʌm bə ‖ -bər
Humberside ˈhʌm bə saɪd ‖ -bər-
Humbert ˈhʌm bət ‖ -bərt
humble ˈhʌm bəl **humbled** ˈhʌm bəld **humbler** ˈhʌm blə ‖ -blər **humbles** ˈhʌm bəlz **humblest** ˈhʌm blɪst -bləst **humbling** ˈhʌm bəl‿ɪŋ
ˌhumble ˈpie
humbleness ˈhʌm bəl nəs -nɪs
humbly ˈhʌm bli
Humboldt ˈhʌm bəʊlt ˈhʊm-, →-bɒʊlt ‖ -boʊlt —*Ger* [ˈhʊm bɔlt]
humbug ˈhʌm bʌg **~ged** d **~ging** ɪŋ **~s** z
humbuggery ˈhʌm bʌg ər i
humdinger ˌhʌm ˈdɪŋ ə ‖ -ər **~s** z
humdrum ˈhʌm drʌm
Hume hjuːm

umectant hju ˈmekt ənt **~s** s
umeral ˈhjuːm ər əl **~s** z
um|erus ˈhjuːm |ər əs *(= humorous)* **~eri** ə raɪ
umic ˈhjuːm ɪk
umid ˈhjuːm ɪd §ˈjuːm-, §-əd
umidex ˈhjuːm ɪ deks §ˈjuːm-, -ə-
umidification hju ˌmɪd ɪf ɪ ˈkeɪʃ ən §ju-, ·ˌ·əf-, §-əˈ· ·
umidifier hju ˈmɪd ɪ |faɪ ə ‖ ər **~s** z
umidi|fy hju ˈmɪd ɪ |faɪ §ju-, -ə- **~fied** faɪd **~fies** faɪz **~fying** faɪ ɪŋ
umidity hju ˈmɪd ət i §ju-, -ɪt- ‖ -əţ i
umid|ly ˈhjuːm ɪd |li §ˈjuːm-, §-əd- **~ness** nəs nɪs
umidor ˈhjuːm ɪ dɔː §juːm-, -ə- ‖ -dɔːr **~s** z
umili|ate hju ˈmɪl i |eɪt §ju- **~ated** eɪt ɪd -əd ‖ eɪţ əd **~ates** eɪts **~ating/ly** eɪt ɪŋ /li ‖ eɪţ ɪŋ /li
humiliation hju ˌmɪl i ˈeɪʃ ən ˌhjuːm ɪl-; §ju- **~s** z
humility hju ˈmɪl ət i §ju-, -ɪt- ‖ -əţ i
humm... —*see* **hum**
hummingbird ˈhʌm ɪŋ bɜːd ‖ -bɜːd **~s** z
hummock ˈhʌm ək **~s** s
hummus ˈhʊm ʊs ˈhʌm-, -əs
humongous hju ˈmʌŋ gəs
humor ˈhjuːm ə §ˈjuːm- ‖ -ər **~ed** d **humoring** hjuːm ər ɪŋ §ˈjuːm- **~s** z
humoral ˈhjuːm ər əl
humoresque ˌhjuːm ə ˈresk **~s** s
humorist ˈhjuːm ər ɪst §ˈjuːm-, §-əst **~s** s
humoristic ˌhjuːm ə ˈrɪst ɪk ◂ §ˌjuːm- **~al** əl
humorless ˈhjuːm ə ləs §ˈjuːm-, -lɪs ‖ -ər- **~ly** li **~ness** nəs nɪs
humorous ˈhjuːm ər əs §ˈjuːm- **~ly** li **~ness** nəs nɪs
humour ˈhjuːm ə §ˈjuːm- ‖ -ər **~ed** d **humouring** hjuːm ər ɪŋ §ˈjuːm- **~s** z
humourless ˈhjuːm ə ləs §ˈjuːm-,-lɪs ‖ -ər- **~ly** li **~ness** nəs nɪs
hump hʌmp **humped** hʌmpt **humping** ˈhʌmp ɪŋ **humps** hʌmps
humpback ˈhʌmp bæk **~ed** t
ˌhumpbacked ˈbridge
Humperdinck *German composer* ˈhʊmp ə dɪŋk ˈhʌmp- ‖ -ər- —*Ger* [ˈhʊm pɐ dɪŋk]
Humperdinck *British pop singer* ˈhʌmp ə dɪŋk ‖ -ər-
humph hʌmpf *or e.g.* m̥m, m̥mm̥, həmm̥ *with falling pitch*
Humphrey ˈhʌmpf ri
Humphreys, Humphries, Humphrys ˈhʌmpf riz
humpt|y ˈhʌmpt |i **~ies** iz
ˌHumpty ˈDumpty ˈdʌmpt i
hump|y ˈhʌmp| i **~ier** i ə ‖ i ər **~ies** iz **~iest** i ɪst əst
humungous hju ˈmʌŋ gəs
humus ˈhjuːm əs §ˈjuːm-
Humvee, h~ *tdmk* ˌhʌm ˈviː ˈ· · **~s** z
Hun hʌn **Huns** hʌnz
Hunan ˌhuː ˈnæn ‖ -ˈnɑːn -ˈnæn —*Chi* Húnán [²xu ²nan]
hunch hʌntʃ **hunched** hʌntʃt **hunches** ˈhʌntʃ ɪz -əz **hunching** ˈhʌntʃ ɪŋ
hunchback ˈhʌntʃ bæk **~ed** t **~s** s
hundred ˈhʌndr əd -ɪd ‖ ˈhʌnd ərd **~s** z
ˌhundreds and ˈthousands
hundredfold ˈhʌndr əd fəʊld -ɪd-, →-fɒʊld ‖ -foʊld ˈhʌnd ərd-
hundredth ˈhʌndr ədθ -ɪdθ, -ətθ, -ɪtθ ‖ ˈhʌnd ərdθ **~s** s
hundredweight ˈhʌndr əd weɪt -ɪd- ‖ ˈhʌnd ərd- **~s** s
hung hʌŋ
Hungarian hʌŋ ˈgeər i ən ‖ -ˈger- -ˈgær- **~s** z
Hungary ˈhʌŋ gər i
hunger ˈhʌŋ gə ‖ -gər **~ed** d **hungering** ˈhʌŋ gər ɪŋ **~s** z
ˈhunger march; **ˈhunger ˌmarcher**; **ˈhunger strike**; **ˈhunger ˌstriker**
Hungerford ˈhʌŋ gə fəd -fɔːd ‖ -gər fərd
hungover ˌhʌŋ ˈəʊv ə ◂ ‖ -ˈoʊv ər ◂
hun|gry ˈhʌŋ |gri **~grier** gri ə ‖ gri ər **~griest** gri ɪst əst **~grily** grəl i grɪ li
hung-up ˌhʌŋ ˈʌp ◂
hunk hʌŋk **hunks** hʌŋks
hunker, H~ ˈhʌŋk ə ‖ -ər **~ed** d **hunkering** ˈhʌŋk ər ɪŋ **~s** z
hunk|y ˈhʌŋk| i **~ier** i ə ‖ i ər **~iest** i ɪst əst
hunky-dory ˌhʌŋk i ˈdɔːr i ‖ -ˈdoʊr-
Hunniford ˈhʌn i fəd §-fɔːd ‖ -fərd
Hunnish, h~ ˈhʌn ɪʃ **~ness** nəs nɪs
Hunslet ˈhʌnz lət -lɪt
Hunstanton hʌn ˈstænt ən —*locally also* ˈhʌntst ən
hunt hʌnt **hunted** ˈhʌntɪd -əd ‖ ˈhʌnţ əd **hunting** ˈhʌnt ɪŋ ‖ ˈhʌnţ ɪŋ **hunts** hʌnts
ˈhunting ground
Hunt, Hunte hʌnt
hunter, H~ ˈhʌnt ə ‖ ˈhʌnţ ər **~s** z
hunter-gatherer ˌhʌnt ə ˈgæð ər ə ‖ ˌhʌnţ ər ˈgæð ər ər **~s** z
hunter-killer ˌhʌnt ə ˈkɪl ə ‖ ˌhʌnţ ər ˈkɪl ər **~s** z
Huntingdon ˈhʌnt ɪŋ dən ‖ ˈhʌnţ- **~shire** ʃə ʃɪə ‖ ʃər ʃɪr
Huntingford ˈhʌnt ɪŋ fəd ‖ ˈhʌnţ ɪŋ fərd
Huntington ˈhʌnt ɪŋ tən ‖ ˈhʌnţ- **~'s** z
ˌHuntington ˈBeach; **ˌHuntington's choˈrea**
Huntley, Huntly ˈhʌnt li
huntress ˈhʌntr əs -ɪs, -es **~es** ɪz əz
hunts|man ˈhʌnts |mən **~men** mən men
Huntsville ˈhʌnts vɪl
Huon ˈhjuː ɒn ‖ -ɑːn
Hurd hɜːd ‖ hɜːd
hurdl|e ˈhɜːd əl ‖ ˈhɜːd əl **~ed** d **~es** z **~ing** ɪŋ
hurdler ˈhɜːd lə ‖ ˈhɜːd lər **~s** z
hurdy-gurd|y ˈhɜːd i ˌgɜːd |i ˌ· ˈ· · ‖ ˈhɜːd i ˌgɜːd |i **~ies** iz
Hurford ˈhɜː fəd ‖ ˈhɜː fərd
hurl hɜːl ‖ hɜːl **hurled** hɜːld ‖ hɜːld **hurling** ˈhɜːl ɪŋ ‖ ˈhɜːl ɪŋ **hurls** hɜːlz ‖ hɜːlz

hurler ˈhɜːl ə ‖ ˈhɝːl ər **~s** z
hurley, H~ ˈhɜːl i ‖ ˈhɝːl i **~s** z
Hurlingham ˈhɜːl ɪŋ əm ‖ ˈhɝːl-
hurly-burl|y ˈhɜːl i ˌbɜːl |i ˌ·ˈ·· ‖ ˌhɝːl i ˈbɝːl |i ˈ·ˌ·· **~ies** iz
Hurn hɜːn ‖ hɝːn
Huron ˈhjʊər ən §ˈjʊər-, §ˈhjuːr-, -ɒn ‖ ˈhjʊr ən ˈjʊr-, -ɑːn
hurrah hə ˈrɑː hʊ- ‖ -ˈrɔː **~s** z
hurray hə ˈreɪ hʊ- **~s** z
Hurrell *(i)* ˈhʌr əl ‖ ˈhɝː˛, *(ii)* ˈhʊər əl ‖ ˈhʊr-

HURRICANE

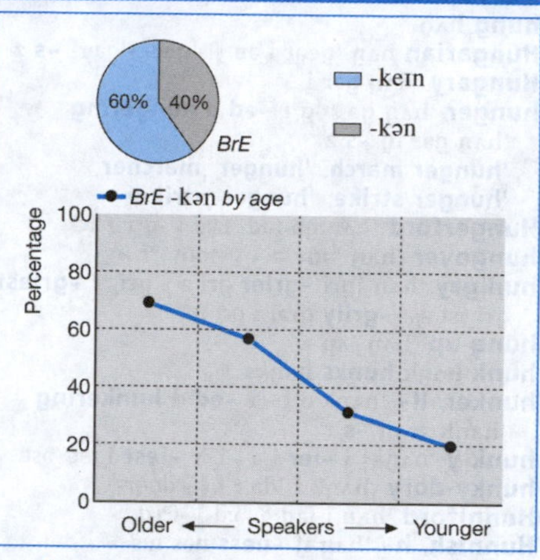

hurricane ˈhʌr ɪk ən -ək-; -ɪ keɪn, -ə- ‖ ˈhɝː ə keɪn — *Preference poll, BrE:* -kən *40% (born before 1942, 70%),* -keɪn *60%.* **~s** z **ˈhurricane lamp**
hurr|y ˈhʌr |i ‖ ˈhɝː |i **~ied/ly** id /li **~ies** iz **~ying** i ɪŋ
Hurst hɜːst ‖ hɝːst
Hurstmonceux ˌhɜːst mən ˈsjuː -ˈsuː, -ˈzuː ‖ ˌhɝːst mən ˈsuː
Hurstpierpoint ˌhɜːst pɪə ˈpɔɪnt ‖ ˌhɝːst pɪr-
hurt, Hurt hɜːt ‖ hɝːt **hurting** ˈhɜːt ɪŋ ‖ ˈhɝːţ ɪŋ **hurts** hɜːts ‖ hɝːts
hurtful ˈhɜːt fəl -fʊl ‖ ˈhɝːt- **~ly** ˌi **~ness** nəs nɪs
hurtl|e ˈhɜːt əl ‖ ˈhɝːţ əl **~ed** d **~es** z **~ing** ˌɪŋ
husband ˈhʌz bənd **~ed** ɪd əd **~ing** ɪŋ **~s** z
husband|man ˈhʌz bənd |mən →-bəm- **~men** mən men
husbandry ˈhʌz bənd ri
hush hʌʃ **hushed** hʌʃt **hushes** ˈhʌʃ ɪz -əz **hushing** ˈhʌʃ ɪŋ
ˈhush ˌmoney; ˈHush ˌPuppies *tdmk*
hushaby, hushabye, hush-a-bye ˈhʌʃ ə baɪ
hush-hush ˌhʌʃ ˈhʌʃ ◂ ˈ· · ‖ ˈhʌʃ hʌʃ
hush-up *n* ˈhʌʃ ʌp
husk hʌsk **husked** hʌskt **husking** ˈhʌsk ɪŋ **husks** hʌsks
huski... —*see* **husky**
Huskisson ˈhʌsk ɪs ən -əs-
husk|y ˈhʌsk |i **~ier** i˛ə ‖ i˛ər **~ies** iz **~iest** i˛ɪst i˛əst **~ily** ɪ li əl i **~iness** i nəs i nɪs
huss hʌs
Huss hʌs hʊs —*German, Czech* [hʊs]
Hussain hu ˈseɪn
hussar hu ˈzɑː hə- ‖ -ˈzɑːr **~s** z
Hussein hu ˈseɪn
Hussey ˈhʌs i
Hussite ˈhʌs aɪt ˈhʊs- **~s** s
huss|y, Hussy ˈhʌs |i ˈhʌz- **~ies** iz
hustings ˈhʌst ɪŋz
hustl|e ˈhʌs əl **~ed** d **~es** z **~ing** ˌɪŋ
hustler ˈhʌs lə ˈhʌs əl˛ə ‖ -lər **~s** z
Huston ˈhjuːst ən
hut hʌt **hutted** ˈhʌt ɪd -əd ‖ ˈhʌţ əd **hutting** ˈhʌt ɪŋ ‖ ˈhʌţ ɪŋ **huts** hʌts
hutch, Hutch hʌtʃ **hutches** ˈhʌtʃ ɪz -əz
Hutchence ˈhʌtʃ əntˢ
Hutcheson ˈhʌtʃ ɪs ən -əs-
Hutchings ˈhʌtʃ ɪŋz
Hutchins ˈhʌtʃ ɪnz
Hutchinson ˈhʌtʃ ɪn sən -ən-
Hutchison ˈhʌtʃ ɪs ən -əs-
hutment ˈhʌt mənt **~s** s
Hutterite ˈhʌt ə raɪt ˈhʊt-, ˈhuːt- ‖ ˈhʌţ- ˈhʊţ-, ˈhuːţ- **~s** s
Hutton ˈhʌt ən
Hutu ˈhuːt uː **~s** z
Huw hjuː —*Welsh* [hiu, hɨu]
Huxley ˈhʌks li
Huxtable ˈhʌkst əb əl
Huygens ˈhaɪg ənz —*Dutch* [ˈhœy xəns]
Huyton ˈhaɪt ən *(= heighten)*
huzza, huzzah hu ˈzɑː hʌ-, hə- **~s** z
Hwang-Ho ˌhwæŋ ˈhəʊ ‖ -ˈhoʊ —*Chi* Huáng Hé [²xwaŋ ²xɤ]
hwyl ˈhuː ɪl əl —*Welsh* [huil, hɨil]
Hy haɪ
hyacinth, H~ ˈhaɪ˛ə sɪntθ **~s** s
hyacinthine ˌhaɪ˛ə ˈsɪntθ aɪn -iːn
Hyacinthus ˌhaɪ˛ə ˈsɪntθ əs
Hyades ˈhaɪ˛ə diːz
hyaena haɪ ˈiːn ə **~s** z
hyalin ˈhaɪ˛ə lɪn
hyaline ˈhaɪ˛ə lɪn -liːn, -laɪn
hyalo- *comb. form*
with stress-neutral suffix ˌhaɪ˛əl əʊ haɪ ¦æl ə ‖ -oʊ haɪ ¦æl ə — **hyaloplasm** ˈhaɪ˛əl əʊ ˌplæz əm haɪ ˈæl ə- ‖ -oʊˌ-
with stress-imposing suffix ˌhaɪ˛ə ˈlɒ+ ‖ -ˈlɑː+ — **hyalophagy** ˌhaɪ˛ə ˈlɒf ədʒ i ‖ -ˈlɑːf-
hyaloid ˈhaɪ˛ə lɔɪd
Hyannis haɪ ˈæn ɪs §-əs
Hyatt ˈhaɪ˛ət
hybrid ˈhaɪb rɪd §-rəd **~s** z **ˌhybrid ˈvigour**
hybridis... —*see* **hybridiz...**
hybridism ˈhaɪb rɪ ˌdɪz əm ‖ -rə-
hybridity haɪ ˈbrɪd ət i -ɪt i ‖ -əţ i
hybridization ˌhaɪb rɪd aɪ ˈzeɪʃ ən ˌ·rəd-, -ɪˈ-- ‖ -rəd ə- **~s** z
hybridiz|e ˈhaɪb rɪ daɪz -rə- **~ed** d **~es** ɪz əz **~ing** ɪŋ
hydatid ˈhaɪd ət ɪd haɪ ˈdæt-, §-əd ‖ -əţ əd **~s** z

Hyde haɪd
ˌ**Hyde ˈPark◂**, ˌ**Hyde ˌPark ˈCorner**

Hyder *tdmk* ˈhaɪd ə ‖ -ᵊr —*Welsh* [ˈhə der]

Hyderabad ˈhaɪd ər‿ə bæd -bɑːd, ˌ· · ˈ·

Hydr|a, Hydra ˈhaɪdr |ə **~ae** iː **~as** əz

hydrangea haɪ ˈdreɪndʒ ə -ˈdreɪndʒ i‿ə ‖ -ˈdrændʒ ə **~s** z

hydrant ˈhaɪdr ənt **~s** s

hydrate *n* ˈhaɪdr eɪt **~s** s

hydr|ate *v* haɪ ˈdr|eɪt ˈhaɪdr |eɪt ‖ ˈhaɪdr |eɪt **~ated** eɪt ɪd -əd ‖ eɪţ əd **~ates** eɪts **~ating** eɪt ɪŋ ‖ eɪţ ɪŋ

hydration haɪ ˈdreɪʃ ᵊn

hydraulic haɪ ˈdrɔːl ɪk -ˈdrɒl- ‖ -ˈdrɑːl- **~ally** ᵊl‿i **~s** s

hydrazine ˈhaɪdr ə ziːn -zɪn, -zaɪn

hydric ˈhaɪdr ɪk

hydride ˈhaɪdr aɪd **~s** z

hydro ˈhaɪdr əʊ ‖ -oʊ **~s** z

hydro- *comb. form*
with stress-neutral suffix ¦haɪdr əʊ ‖ -ə — **hydrotaxis** ˌhaɪdr əʊ ˈtæks ɪs §-əs ‖ -ə-
with stress-imposing suffix haɪ ˈdrɒ+ ‖ -ˈdrɑː+ — **hydrophanous** haɪ ˈdrɒf ən əs ‖ -ˈdrɑːf-

hydrocarbon ˌhaɪdr əʊ ˈkɑːb ən ‖ -ə ˈkɑːrb- **~s** z

hydrocele ˈhaɪdr əʊ siːᵊl ‖ -ə- **~s** z

hydrocephalus ˌhaɪdr əʊ ˈkef əl əs -ˈsef- ‖ -oʊ ˈsef-

hydrochloric ˌhaɪdr əʊ ˈklɒr ɪk◂ -ˈklɔːr- ‖ -ə ˈklɔːr- -ˈkloʊr-
ˌ**hydroˌchloric ˈacid**

hydrochloride ˌhaɪdr əʊ ˈklɔːr aɪd ‖ -ə- -ˈkloʊr- **~s** z

hydrocortisone ˌhaɪdr əʊ ˈkɔːt ɪ zəʊn -ˈə- ‖ -ə ˈkɔːrţ ə zoʊn -soʊn

hydrodynamic ˌhaɪdr əʊ daɪ ˈnæm ɪk◂ -dɪˈ- ‖ ˌhaɪdr oʊ- **~ally** ᵊl‿i **~s** s

hydroelectric ˌhaɪdr əʊ ɪ ˈlek trɪk◂ -əˈ- ‖ ˌhaɪdr oʊ- **~ally** ᵊl‿i

hydroelectricity ˌhaɪdr əʊ i ˌlek ˈtrɪs ət i -əʊ ə-, -əʊ ˌel ek-, -əʊ ˌɪl ek-, -əʊ ˌiː lek-, -ˈtrɪz-, -ɪt i ‖ -oʊ i ˌlek ˈtrɪs əţ i

hydrofoil ˈhaɪdr əʊ fɔɪᵊl ‖ -ə- **~s** z

hydrogen ˈhaɪdr ədʒ ən -ɪdʒ-, -ɪn
ˈ**hydrogen bomb**; ˌ**hydrogen perˈoxide**; ˌ**hydrogen ˈsulphide**

hydroge|nate ˈhaɪdr ədʒ ə |neɪt -ədʒ ɪ-; haɪ ˈdrɒdʒ- ‖ haɪ ˈdrɑːdʒ- ˈhaɪdr ədʒ- **~nated** neɪt ɪd -əd ‖ neɪţ əd **~nates** neɪts **~nating** neɪt ɪŋ ‖ neɪţ ɪŋ

hydrographer haɪ ˈdrɒg rəf ə ‖ -ˈdrɑːg rəf ᵊr **~s** z

hydrographic ˌhaɪdr əʊ ˈgræf ɪk◂ ‖ -ə- **~ally** ᵊl‿i

hydrography haɪ ˈdrɒg rəf i ‖ -ˈdrɑːg-

hydroid ˈhaɪdr ɔɪd **~s** z

hydrologic ˌhaɪdr ə ˈlɒdʒ ɪk ‖ -ˈlɑːdʒ- **~al** ᵊl **~ally** ᵊl‿i

hydrologist haɪ ˈdrɒl ədʒ ɪst §-əst ‖ -ˈdrɑːl- **~s** s

hydrology haɪ ˈdrɒl ədʒ i ‖ -ˈdrɑːl-

hydrolys|e ˈhaɪdr ə laɪz **~ed** d **~es** ɪz əz **~ing** ɪŋ

hydrolysis haɪ ˈdrɒl əs ɪs -ɪs-, §-əs ‖ -ˈdrɑːl-

hydrolytic ˌhaɪdr ə ˈlɪt ɪk◂ ‖ -ˈlɪţ ɪk◂ **~ally** ᵊl‿i

hydrolyz|e ˈhaɪdr ə laɪz **~ed** d **~es** ɪz əz **~ing** ɪŋ

hydrometer haɪ ˈdrɒm ɪt ə -ət- ‖ -ˈdrɑːm əţ ᵊr **~s** z

hydropathy haɪ ˈdrɒp əθ i ‖ -ˈdrɑːp-

hydrophilic ˌhaɪdr əʊ ˈfɪl ɪk◂ ‖ -ə-

hydrophob|ia ˌhaɪdr əʊ ˈfəʊb| i‿ə ‖ -ə ˈfoʊb|- **~ic** ɪk◂

hydrophone ˈhaɪdr ə fəʊn ‖ -foʊn **~s** z

hydrophyte ˈhaɪdr ə faɪt **~s** s

hydroplane ˈhaɪdr əʊ pleɪn ‖ -ə- **~s** z

hydroponic ˌhaɪdr əʊ ˈpɒn ɪk◂ ‖ -ə ˈpɑːn- **~s** s

hydrostatic ˌhaɪdr əʊ ˈstæt ɪk◂ ‖ -ə ˈstæţ ɪk◂ **~ally** ᵊl‿i **~s** s

hydrotherapy ˌhaɪdr əʊ ˈθer əp i ‖ ˌhaɪdr ə-

hydrotropic ˌhaɪdr əʊ ˈtrɒp ɪk◂ ‖ -ə ˈtrɑːp ɪk◂ -ˈtroʊp-

hydrotropism haɪ ˈdrɒtr ə ˌpɪz əm ‖ -ˈdrɑːtr-

hydrous ˈhaɪdr əs

hydroxide haɪ ˈdrɒks aɪd ‖ -ˈdrɑːks- **~s** z

hydroxy haɪ ˈdrɒks i ‖ -ˈdrɑːks i

hydroxyl haɪ ˈdrɒks ɪl -ᵊl ‖ -ˈdrɑːks-

hydrozoan ˌhaɪdr əʊ ˈzəʊ ən ‖ -ə ˈzoʊ- **~s** z

Hydrus ˈhaɪdr əs

hyena haɪ ˈiːn ə **~s** z

hyetograph ˈhaɪ‿ət əʊ grɑːf ˈ-ɪt-, -græf; haɪ ˈet- ‖ -əţ ə græf haɪ ˈeţ- **~s** s

Hygeia haɪ ˈdʒiː‿ə

Hygena *tdmk* haɪ ˈdʒiːn ə

hygiene ˈhaɪdʒ iːn

hygienic haɪ ˈdʒiːn ɪk ‖ ˌhaɪdʒ i ˈen ɪk◂ haɪ ˈdʒen ɪk *(*)* **~ally** ᵊl‿i

hygienist ˈhaɪdʒ iːn ɪst haɪ ˈdʒiːn-, §-əst ‖ haɪ ˈdʒiːn əst -ˈdʒen-; ˈhaɪdʒ iːn əst **~s** s

hygrometer haɪ ˈgrɒm ɪt ə -ət- ‖ -ˈgrɑːm əţ ᵊr **~s** z

hygroscopic ˌhaɪg rə ˈskɒp ɪk◂ ‖ -ˈskɑːp-

Hylas ˈhaɪl əs -æs

Hylda ˈhɪld ə

Hylton ˈhɪlt ən

Hyman ˈhaɪm ən

hymen, Hymen ˈhaɪm en ‖ -ən **~s** z

hymeneal ˌhaɪm e ˈniː‿əl◂ -ɪ-, -ə- ‖ -ə-

hymenopterous ˌhaɪm ə ˈnɒpt ər əs◂ ˌ·ɪ-, ˌ·e- ‖ -ˈnɑːpt-

Hymettus haɪ ˈmet əs ‖ -ˈmeţ əs

Hymie ˈhaɪm i

hymn hɪm *(= him)* **hymned** hɪmd **hymning** ˈhɪm ɪŋ **hymns** hɪmz
ˈ**hymn book**

hymnal ˈhɪm nəl **~s** z

hymnodist ˈhɪm nəd ɪst §-əst **~s** s

hymnod|y ˈhɪm nəd |i **~ies** iz

hymnology hɪm ˈnɒl ədʒ i ‖ -ˈnɑːl-

Hynd haɪnd

hyoid ˈhaɪ ɔɪd

hyoscine ˈhaɪ əʊ siːn ‖ -ə-

H

hyoscyamine ˌhaɪ əʊ ˈsaɪ‿ə miːn -mɪn, §-mən ‖ ˌhaɪ ə-
hypallage haɪ ˈpæl ədʒ i -əg-, -iː **~s** z
Hypatia haɪ ˈpeɪʃ ə -ˈpeɪʃ i‿ə
hype haɪp **hyped** haɪpt **hypes** haɪps **hyping** ˈhaɪp ɪŋ
ˌhyped ˈup
hyper- *comb. form*
with stress-neutral suffix ¦haɪp ə ‖ ¦haɪp ᵊr *—but before a vowel sound,* -ər ‖ -ər;
— **hyperpyrexia** ˌhaɪp ə paɪᵊ ˈreks i‿ə ‖ ˌhaɪp ᵊr-; — **hyperacidity** ˌhaɪp ər ə ˈsɪd ət i -æˈ--, -ɪt i ‖ -ər ə ˈsɪd əţ i
with stress-imposing suffix haɪ ˈpɜː+ ‖ haɪ ˈpɜː+ — **hypergamy** haɪ ˈpɜːg əm i ‖ -ˈpɜːg-
hyperactive ˌhaɪp ər ˈækt ɪv ◂ ‖ -ər- **~ly** li
hyperactivity ˌhaɪp ər æk ˈtɪv ət i -ɪt i ‖ -ər æk ˈtɪv əţ i
hyperbaric ˌhaɪp ə ˈbær ɪk ◂ ‖ -ᵊr- -ˈber-
hyperbaton haɪ ˈpɜːb ə tɒn ‖ -ˈpɜːb ə tɑːn
hyperb|ola haɪ ˈpɜːb|əl ə ‖ -ˈpɜːb|- **~olae** ə liː **~olas** əl əz
hyperbole haɪ ˈpɜːb əl i ⚠ ˈhaɪp ə bəʊl ‖ -ˈpɜːb- **~s** z
hyperbolic ˌhaɪp ə ˈbɒl ɪk ◂ ‖ -ᵊr ˈbɑːl ɪk ◂ **~ally** ᵊl‿i
ˌhyperˌbolic ˈfunction
hyperboloid haɪ ˈpɜːb ə lɔɪd ‖ -ˈpɜːb- **~s** z
hyperborean, H~ ˌhaɪp ə ˈbɔːr i‿ən -bɔː ˈriː‿ən, -bɒˈ-- ‖ ˌhaɪp ᵊr- -ˈboʊr- **~s** z
hypercoristic ˌhaɪp ə kɔː ˈrɪst ɪk ◂ -kɒˈ--, -kəˈ-- ‖ -ᵊr kə- **~ally** ᵊl‿i **~s** s
hypercorrect ˌhaɪp ə kə ˈrekt ◂ ‖ ˌhaɪp ᵊr- **~ly** li **~ness** nəs nɪs
hypercorrection ˌhaɪp ə kə ˈrek ʃᵊn ‖ ˌhaɪp ᵊr- **~s** z
hypercritical ˌhaɪp ə ˈkrɪt ɪk ᵊl ◂ ‖ ˌhaɪp ᵊr ˈkrɪţ- **~ly** ‿i
hypercube ˈhaɪp ə kjuːb ‖ -ᵊr- **~s** z
hyperglycaemia, hyperglycemia ˌhaɪp ə glaɪ ˈsiːm i‿ə ‖ ˌhaɪp ᵊr-
hypericum haɪ ˈper ɪk əm **~s** z
Hyperides haɪ ˈper ə diːz -ə-; ˌhaɪp ə ˈraɪd iːz
hyperinflation ˌhaɪp ər ɪn ˈfleɪʃ ᵊn
Hyperion haɪ ˈpɪər i‿ən -ˈper- ‖ -ˈpɪr-
hyperlink ˈhaɪp ə lɪŋk ‖ -ᵊr- **~s** s
hypermarket ˈhaɪp ə ˌmɑːk ɪt §-ət ‖ -ᵊr ˌmɑːrk- **~s** s
hyperpituitarism ˌhaɪp ə pɪ ˈtjuː‿ɪt ə ˌrɪz əm -pəˈ--, →-ˈtʃuː‿, §-ˈ·‿ət- ‖ -ᵊr pə ˈtuː əţ- -ˈtjuː-
hypersensitive ˌhaɪp ə ˈsenᵗs ət ɪv ◂ -ɪt ɪv ‖ -ᵊr ˈsenᵗs əţ ɪv ◂ **~ness** nəs nɪs
hypersensitivity ˌhaɪp ə ˌsenᵗs ə ˈtɪv ət i -ˌ·ɪ-, -ɪt i ‖ -ᵊr ˌsenᵗs ə ˈtɪv əţ i
hypersonic ˌhaɪp ə ˈsɒn ɪk ◂ ‖ -ᵊr ˈsɑːn ɪk ◂ **~s** s
hyperspace ˈhaɪp ə speɪs ˌ·ˈ· ‖ -ᵊr-
hypertension ˌhaɪp ə ˈtenᵗʃ ᵊn ‖ -ᵊr-
hypertensive ˌhaɪp ə ˈtenᵗs ɪv ‖ -ᵊr-
hypertext ˈhaɪp ə tekst ‖ -ᵊr-
hyperthyroid ˌhaɪp ə ˈθaɪᵊr ɔɪd ◂ ‖ -ᵊr- **~ism** ˌɪz əm
hypertroph|y haɪ ˈpɜːtr əf |i ‖ -ˈpɜːtr- **~ied** id **~ies** iz **~ying** i ɪŋ
hyperventi|late ˌhaɪp ə ˈvent ɪ |leɪt -ə leɪt, -ᵊ|l eɪt ‖ -ᵊr ˈvenţ ᵊ|l eɪt **~lated** leɪt ɪd -əd ‖ leɪţ əd **~lates** leɪts **~lating** leɪt ɪŋ ‖ leɪţ ɪŋ
hyperventilation ˌhaɪp ə ˌvent ɪ ˈleɪʃ ᵊn -əˈ--, -ᵊl ˈeɪʃ- ‖ -ᵊr ˌvenţ ᵊl ˈeɪʃ ᵊn
hyph|a ˈhaɪf |ə **~ae** iː
hyphen ˈhaɪf ᵊn **~s** z
hyphe|nate ˈhaɪf ə |neɪt **~nated** neɪt ɪd -əd ‖ neɪţ əd **~nates** neɪts **~nating** neɪt ɪŋ ‖ neɪţ ɪŋ
hyphenation ˌhaɪf ə ˈneɪʃ ᵊn **~s** z
hypnagogic, hypnogogic ˌhɪp nə ˈgɒdʒ ɪk ◂ -ˈgəʊdʒ- ‖ -ˈgɑːdʒ ɪk ◂ -ˈgoʊdʒ- **~s** s
hypno- *comb. form*
with stress-neutral suffix ¦hɪp nəʊ ‖ -noʊ — **hypnotherapy** ˌhɪp nəʊ ˈθer əp i ‖ ˌhɪp noʊ-
with stress-imposing suffix hɪp ˈnɒ+ ‖ -ˈnɑː+ — **hypnology** hɪp ˈnɒl ədʒ i ‖ -ˈnɑːl-
Hypnos ˈhɪp nɒs ‖ -nɑːs -noʊs, -nəs
hypnos|is hɪp ˈnəʊs |ɪs §-əs ‖ -ˈnoʊs- **~es** iːz
hypnothera|pist ˌhɪp nəʊ ˈθer ə pɪst ‖ ˌnoʊ- **~ists** ɪsts §əsts **~y** i
hypnotic hɪp ˈnɒt ɪk ‖ -ˈnɑːţ ɪk **~ally** ᵊl‿i **~s** s
hypnotis... *—see* **hypnotiz...**
hypnotism ˈhɪp nə ˌtɪz əm
hypnotist ˈhɪp nət ɪst §-əst ‖ -nəţ- **~s** s
hypnotiz|e ˈhɪp nə taɪz **~ed** d **~es** ɪz əz **~ing** ɪŋ
hypo ˈhaɪp əʊ ‖ -oʊ
hypo- *comb. form*
with stress-neutral suffix ¦haɪp əʊ ‖ -ə *—but before a vowel* ¦haɪp əʊ ‖ -oʊ — **hypochlorous** ˌhaɪp əʊ ˈklɔːr əs ◂ ‖ -ə- -ˈkloʊr- — **hypoallergenic** ˌhaɪp əʊ ˌæl ə ˈdʒen ɪk -ɜːˈ-- ‖ -oʊ ˌæl ᵊr-
—The fact that RP ¦haɪp ə *is ambiguous as between* hypo- *and* hyper- *means that for clarity it is arguably better to avoid reducing the second syllable and therefore always to say* ¦haɪp əʊ
with stress-imposing suffix haɪ ˈpɒ+ ‖ -ˈpɑː+ — **hypogynous** haɪ ˈpɒdʒ ɪn əs -ən- ‖ -ˈpɑːdʒ-
hypocaust ˈhaɪp əʊ kɔːst ‖ -ə- -kɑːst **~s** s
hypocenter, hypocentre ˈhaɪp əʊ ˌsent ə ‖ -ə ˌsenţ ᵊr **~s** z
hypochondria ˌhaɪp əʊ ˈkɒndr i‿ə ‖ -ə ˈkɑːndr-
hypochondriac ˌhaɪp əʊ ˈkɒndr i æk ‖ -ə ˈkɑːndr- **~s** s
hypochondriacal ˌhaɪp əʊ kɒn ˈdraɪ‿ək ᵊl ◂ -kənˈ-- ‖ -oʊ kɑːn-
hypocorism haɪ ˈpɒk ə ˌrɪz əm ˌhaɪp ə ˈkɔːr ɪz əm ‖ -ˈpɑːk-
hypocris|y hɪ ˈpɒk rəs |i §haɪ-, -rɪs- ‖ -ˈpɑːk- **~ies** iz
hypocrite ˈhɪp ə krɪt **~s** s
hypocritical ˌhɪp ə ˈkrɪt ɪk ᵊl ◂ ‖ -ˈkrɪţ- **~ly** ‿i

ypodermic ˌhaɪp əʊ ˈdɜːm ɪk ◂ ‖ -ə ˈdɝːm ɪk ◂ **~ally** ᵊl‿i **~s** s
ˌ**hypo**ˌ**dermic** ˈ**needle**
ypodermis ˌhaɪp əʊ ˈdɜːm ɪs §-əs ‖ -ə ˈdɝːm əs
ypogeal ˌhaɪp əʊ ˈdʒiː‿əl ◂ ‖ -oʊ-
ypoglossal ˌhaɪp əʊ ˈglɒs ᵊl ◂ ‖ -ə ˈglɑːs ᵊl ◂
ypoglycaem|ia, hypoglycem|ia ˌhaɪp əʊ glaɪ ˈsiːm| i‿ə ‖ ˌhaɪp oʊ- **~ic** ɪk ◂
ypoid ˈhaɪp ɔɪd **~s** z
yponym ˈhaɪp əʊ nɪm ‖ -ə- **~s** z
yponymy haɪ ˈpɒn əm i -ɪm i ‖ -ˈpɑːn-
ypostasis haɪ ˈpɒst əs ɪs §-əs ‖ -ˈpɑːst-
ypostatic ˌhaɪp ə ˈstæt ɪk ◂ ‖ -ˈstæţ ɪk ◂
ˌ**hypo**ˌ**static** ˈ**union**
ypostatis... —*see* **hypostatiz...**
ypostatization haɪ ˌpɒst ət aɪ ˈzeɪʃ ᵊn -ət ɪ- ‖ -ˌpɑːst əţ ə-
ypostatiz|e haɪ ˈpɒst ə taɪz ‖ -ˈpɑːst- **~ed** d **~es** ɪz əz **~ing** ɪŋ
ypostyle ˈhaɪp əʊ staɪᵊl ‖ -oʊ-
yposulfite, hyposulphite ˌhaɪp əʊ ˈsʌlf aɪt ‖ -oʊ-
ypotactic ˌhaɪp əʊ ˈtækt ɪk ◂ ‖ -ə- -oʊ- **~ally** ᵊl‿i
ypotaxis ˌhaɪp əʊ ˈtæks ɪs §-əs ‖ -ə- -oʊ-
hypo|tension ˌhaɪp əʊ ˈtenʧ ᵊn ‖ ˌhaɪp oʊ- **~tensive** ˈtenᵗs ɪv
hypotenuse haɪ ˈpɒt ə njuːz -ɪ-, -ᵊn juːz ‖ -ˈpɑːt ᵊn uːs -juːs *(*)*
hypothalamic ˌhaɪp əʊ θə ˈlæm ɪk ◂ ‖ ˌhaɪp oʊ-
hypothalamus ˌhaɪp əʊ ˈθæl əm əs ‖ ˌhaɪp oʊ-
hypothe|cate haɪ ˈpɒθ ə |keɪt -ɪ- ‖ -ˈpɑːθ- hɪ- **~cated** keɪt ɪd -əd ‖ keɪţ əd **~cates** keɪts **~cating** keɪt ɪŋ ‖ keɪţ ɪŋ
hypothecation haɪ ˌpɒθ ə ˈkeɪʃ ᵊn -ɪ- ‖ -ˌpɑːθ- hɪ- **~s** z
hypothermia ˌhaɪp əʊ ˈθɜːm i‿ə ‖ -oʊ ˈθɝːm-
hypoth|esis haɪ ˈpɒθ |əs ɪs -ɪs-, §-əs **~eses** ə siːz ɪ-
hypothesis|e, hypothesiz|e haɪ ˈpɒθ ə saɪz ‖ -ˈpɑːθ- **~ed** d **~es** ɪz əz **~ing** ɪŋ
hypothetical ˌhaɪp ə ˈθet ɪk ᵊl ◂ ‖ -ˈθeţ- **~ly** ‿i
hypothyroid ˌhaɪp əʊ ˈθaɪᵊr ɔɪd ◂ ‖ -oʊ- **~ism** ˌɪz əm
hypoxia haɪ ˈpɒks i‿ə ‖ -ˈpɑːks-
hypsometer hɪp ˈsɒm ɪt ə -ət- ‖ -ˈsɑːm əţ ᵊr **~s** z
hypsometry hɪp ˈsɒm ətr i -ɪtr- ‖ -ˈsɑːm-
hyrax ˈhaɪᵊr æks **~es** ɪz əz
Hyrcania hɜː ˈkeɪn i‿ə ‖ hɝː-
Hyslop ˈhɪz ləp
hyssop ˈhɪs əp
hysterectom|y ˌhɪst ə ˈrekt əm |i **~ies** iz
hysteresis ˌhɪst ə ˈriːs ɪs §-əs
hysteria hɪ ˈstɪər i‿ə ‖ -ˈstɪr- -ˈster- **~s** z
hysteric hɪ ˈster ɪk **~s** s
hysterical hɪ ˈster ɪk ᵊl **~ly** ‿i
hysteron proteron ˌhɪst ə rɒn ˈprɒt ə rɒn →-rɒm'-- ‖ ˌhɪst ə rɑːn ˈprɑːţ ə rɑːn
Hythe haɪð
Hyundai *tdmk* ˈhaɪ ən daɪ -ʌn-, -ʊn-, -deɪ; ‖ ˈhʌnd eɪ —*Korean* [hjəːn dɛ]
Hywel ˈhaʊ‿əl —*Welsh* [ˈhə wel]
Hz hɜːts ‖ hɝːts

H

I i

i Spelling-to-sound

1 Where the spelling is **i**, the pronunciation differs according to whether the vowel is short or long, followed or not by **r**, and strong or weak.

2 The 'strong' pronunciation is regularly
ɪ as in **bit** bɪt ('short I'), or
aɪ as in **time** taɪm ('long I').

3 Where **i** is followed by **r**, the 'strong' pronunciation is
ɜː ‖ ɝː as in **firm** fɜːm ‖ fɝːm
aɪ(ə) as in **fire** faɪ‿ə ‖ ˈfaɪ‿ər, **virus** ˈvaɪər əs
or, indeed, the regular 'short' pronunciation ɪ as in **miracle** ˈmɪr ək əl.

4 Less frequently, the 'strong' pronunciation is
iː as in **machine** mə ˈʃiːn.

5 The 'weak' pronunciation is
ɪ as in **rabbit** ˈræb ɪt (although some speakers, especially of AmE, use ə instead, thus ˈræb ət) or
ə as in **admiral** ˈæd mər əl.
Where the following sound is a vowel, the 'weak' pronunciation is
i as in **medium** ˈmiːd i‿əm (see COMPRESSION) or the **i** is silent, serving only to indicate the pronunciation of the consonant as in **special** ˈspeʃ əl (see **c, s, t**).

6 In the rare cases where **i** is found at the end of a word, the pronunciation is either
strong aɪ as in **hi** haɪ or
weak i as in **spaghetti** spə ˈget i ‖ spə ˈgeţ i.

7 **i** also forms part of the digraphs **ai, ei, ie, oi, ui**.

ie Spelling-to-sound

1 Where the spelling is the digraph **ie**, the pronunciation is regularly
iː as in **piece** piːs (especially in the middle of a word) or
aɪ as in **tie** taɪ (especially at the end of a word) or
ɪə ‖ ɪ as in **fierce** fɪəs ‖ fɪrs (before **r**).

2 The 'weak' pronunciation in **-ied, -ies** is usually i as in **buried** 'ber id. Thus the spelling change from **y** to **ie** in inflected forms of words written with **y** at the end does not imply any change in pronunciation.

3 Note the exceptional **friend** frend and **sieve** sɪv; also the usual pronunciation of **handkerchief**, -tʃɪf.

4 **ie** is not a digraph in **science, pliers, society, acquiesce, Viennese, happiest**.

I, i *name of letter* aɪ *(= eye)* **I's, i's** aɪz —*Communications code name:* India

I *pronoun* aɪ *This word has no true weak form in RP, though in rapid casual speech it may become monophthongal* a. *In GenAm it is sometimes weakened to* ə.

I-5 ˌaɪ 'faɪv —*and similarly for the names of other US interstate highways*

Iacoca ˌaɪ‿ə 'kɒk ə ‖ ˌaɪ ə 'kɑːk ə

Iago i 'ɑːg əʊ ‖ -oʊ —*but as a Welsh personal name,* 'jɑːg əʊ ‖ -oʊ —, —*Welsh* ['ja go]

Iain 'iː‿ən

-ial *stress-imposing* i‿əl —*This suffix sometimes causes a change in the stressed vowel:* ˌmana'gerial -'dʒɪər i‿əl ‖ -'dʒɪr-

iamb 'aɪ æm -æmb **~s** z

iambic aɪ 'æm bɪk **~s** s

iam|bus aɪ 'æm |bəs **~bi** baɪ **~buses** bəs ɪz -əz

Ian 'iː‿ən —*In AmE sometimes* 'aɪ ən

-ian *stress-imposing* i‿ən —*This suffix sometimes causes a change in the stressed vowel:* ₍ˌ₎Peck'sniffian ₍ˌ₎Chau'cerian -'sɪər i‿ən ‖ -'sɪr i‿ən

Ianthe aɪ 'ænᵗθ i

Ianucci jæ 'nuːtʃ i jə-

Iapetus aɪ 'æp ɪt əs -ət- ‖ -əṭ əs

IATA i 'ɑːt ə aɪ-

IATEFL ˌaɪ‿ə 'tef ᵊl

iatrogenic aɪ ˌætr əʊ 'dʒen ɪk ◂ ˌ· ·- ‖ -ə-

Ibadan ɪ 'bæd ᵊn ‖ iː 'bɑːd ᵊn -ɑːn —*Yoruba* [i ba dɔ̃]

Ibbotson 'ɪb əts ən

Ibcol *tdmk* 'ɪb kɒl ‖ -koʊl -kɔːl, -kɑːl

I-beam 'aɪ biːm **~s** z

Iberi|a aɪ 'bɪər i‿|ə ‖ -'bɪr- **~an/s** ən/z

ibex 'aɪb eks **~es** ɪz əz

Ibibio ɪ 'bɪb i əʊ -'biːb- ‖ -oʊ **~s** z

ibid 'ɪb ɪd §-əd

ibidem 'ɪb ɪ dem -ə-; ɪ 'baɪd em

-ibility ə 'bɪl ət i ɪ-, -ɪt- ‖ -əṭ i — **visibility** ˌvɪz ə 'bɪl ət i -ɪ'--, -ɪt i ‖ -əṭ i

ibis 'aɪb ɪs §-əs **~es** ɪz əz

Ibiza ɪ 'biːθ ə aɪ-, iː-, -'biːz-, -'biːts- —*Sp* [i 'βi θa], *Catalan* [i 'βi sa, əi-]

-ible əb ᵊl ɪb ᵊl — **visible** 'vɪz əb ᵊl -ɪb-

IBM *tdmk* ˌaɪ biː 'em
ˌ**IBM com'patible**

ibn, Ibn *in Arabic names* 'ɪb ən

Ibo 'iːb əʊ ‖ -oʊ —*Ibo* [i gbo] **~s** z

Ibrahim 'ɪb rə hiːm -hɪm, ˌ· ·'· —*Arabic* [i bra 'hiːm]

Ibrox 'aɪb rɒks ‖ -rɑːks

Ibsen 'ɪb sən —*Norwegian* ['ip sən]

Ibstock 'ɪb stɒk ‖ -stɑːk

ibuprofen ˌaɪb juː 'prəʊf en -ᵊn; aɪ 'bjuːp rəʊ fen ‖ -'proʊf ᵊn

-ic *stress-imposing* ɪk — **periodic** ˌpɪər i 'ɒd ɪk ◂ ‖ ˌpɪr i 'ɑːd ɪk ◂

IC ˌaɪ 'siː **ICs** ˌaɪ 'siːz

-ical *stress-imposing* ɪk ᵊl — **periodical** ˌpɪər i 'ɒd ɪk ᵊl ◂ ‖ ˌpɪr i 'ɑːd ɪk ᵊl ◂

-ically *stress-imposing* ɪk li ɪk əl i — **periodically** ˌpɪər i 'ɒd ɪk li -'ɒd ɪk əl i ‖ ˌpɪr i 'ɑːd- —*shown in entries simply as* ɪk ᵊl i

Icaria ɪ 'keər i‿ə aɪ- ‖ -'ker-

Icarus 'ɪk ər əs 'aɪk-

ICBM ˌaɪ siː biː 'em **~s** z

ICE CREAM

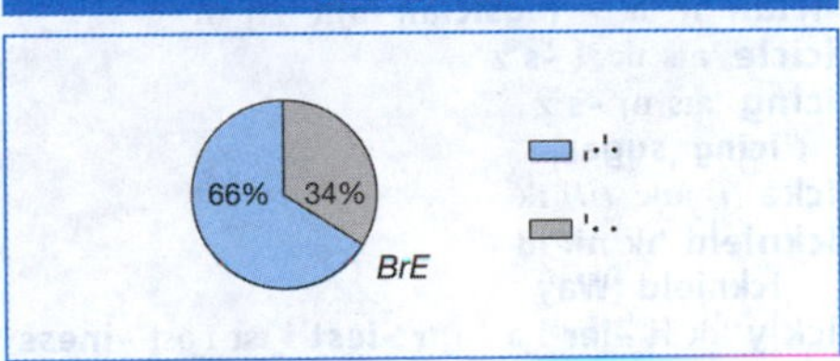

ice aɪs **iced** aɪst **ices** 'aɪs ɪz -əz **icing** 'aɪs ɪŋ
'**ice age**; '**ice axe**; '**ice ˌbucket**; ˌ**ice 'cream** ◂, '· · ‖ '· · — *Preference poll, BrE:* ˌ· '· 66%, '· · 34%; ˌ**ice-cream 'soda**; '**ice field**; '**ice floe**; '**ice ˌhockey**; ˌ**ice 'lolly**, '· ˌ· ·; '**ice pack**; '**ice pick**; '**ice rink**; '**ice sheet**; '**ice ˌwater**

iceball 'aɪs bɔːl ‖ -bɑːl

iceberg 'aɪs bɜːg ‖ -bɜːg **~s** z
ˈ**iceberg 'lettuce**, '· · ˌ· ·

ice-blue ˌaɪs 'bluː ◂

icebound 'aɪs baʊnd

icebox 'aɪs bɒks ‖ -bɑːks **~es** ɪz əz

icebreaker 'aɪs ˌbreɪk ə ‖ -ᵊr **~s** z

icecap 'aɪs kæp **~s** s

ice-cold ˌaɪs 'kəʊld ◂ →-'kɒʊld ‖ -'koʊld ◂

icefall 'aɪs fɔːl ‖ -fɑːl **~s** z

ice|house 'aɪs |haʊs **~houses** haʊz ɪz -əz

Iceland ˈaɪs lənd §-lænd
Icelander ˈaɪs lənd ə -lænd- ‖ -ᵊr **~s** z
Icelandic aɪs ˈlænd ɪk
icemaker ˈaɪs ˌmeɪk ə ‖ -ᵊr **~s** z
ice|man ˈaɪs |mæn -mən **~men** men mən
Iceni aɪ ˈsiːn aɪ -i
ice-|skate ˈaɪs |skeɪt ˈaɪ|s keɪt **~skated** skeɪt ɪd -əd ‖ skeɪţ əd **~skater/s** skeɪt ə/z ‖ skeɪţ ᵊr/z **~skates** skeɪts **~skating** skeɪt ɪŋ ‖ skeɪţ ɪŋ
Ice-T ˌaɪs ˈtiː
ice-tray ˈaɪs treɪ **~s** z
Ichabod ˈɪk ə bɒd ˈɪx- ‖ -bɑːd
ich dien ˌɪx ˈdiːn ˌɪk- ‖ ˌɪk- —*Ger* [ʔɪç ˈdiːn]; *Welsh* eich dyn [əχ ˈdiːn, əiχ-, -ˈdiːn]
I Ching ˌiː ˈtʃɪŋ ˌaɪ-, -ˈdʒɪŋ —*Chi* yì jīng [⁴i ¹tɕiŋ]
ich-laut ˈɪx laʊt ˈɪk- ‖ ˈɪk- —*Ger* Ich-Laut [ˈʔɪç laut] **~s** s
ichneumon ɪk ˈnjuːm ən ‖ -ˈnuːm- -ˈnjuːm- **~s** z
  ichˈneumon fly
ichor ˈaɪk ɔː ‖ -ɔːr
ichthyo- *comb. form*
with stress-neutral suffix ¦ɪkθ i ͜ə -əʊ ‖ -oʊ — **ichthyophobia** ˌɪkθ i ͜ə ˈfəʊb i ͜ə -i əʊ- ‖ -ˈfoʊb- -i oʊ-
with stress-imposing suffix ˌɪkθ i ˈɒ+ ‖ -ˈɑː+ — **ichthyophagous** ˌɪkθ i ˈɒf əg əs ◂ ‖ -ˈɑːf-
ichthyological ˌɪkθ i ͜ə ˈlɒdʒ ɪk ᵊl ◂ -i əʊ- ‖ -ˈlɑːdʒ- -i oʊ- **~ly** ͜i
ichthyolog|ist ˌɪkθ i ˈɒl ədʒ |ɪst -§əst ‖ -ˈɑːl- **~ists** ɪsts §əsts **~y** i
ichthyosaurus ˌɪkθ i ͜ə ˈsɔːr əs **~es** ɪz əz
ichthyosis ˌɪkθ i ˈəʊs ɪs §-əs ‖ -ˈoʊs-
ICI *tdmk* ˌaɪ siː ˈaɪ
ici... —*see* **icy**
-ician ˈɪʃ ᵊn — **musician** mju ˈzɪʃ ᵊn
icicle ˈaɪs ɪk ᵊl **~s** z
icing ˈaɪs ɪŋ **~s** z
  ˈicing ˌsugar
Icke *(i)* aɪk, *(ii)* ɪk
Icknield ˈɪk niːᵊld
  ˌIcknield ˈWay
ick|y ˈɪk |i **~ier** i ͜ə ‖ i ͜ᵊr **~iest** i ͜ɪst i ͜əst **~iness** i nəs -nɪs
icon ˈaɪk ɒn -ən ‖ -ɑːn **~s** z
iconic aɪ ˈkɒn ɪk ‖ -ˈkɑːn-
Iconium aɪ ˈkəʊn i ͜əm ‖ -ˈkoʊn-
icono- *comb. form*
with stress-neutral suffix aɪ ¦kɒn ə ¦aɪk ɒn ə ‖ aɪ ¦kɑːn ə ¦aɪk ɑːn ə — **iconographic** aɪ ˌkɒn ə ˈgræf ɪk ◂ ˌaɪk ɒn- ‖ aɪ ˌkɑːn- ˌaɪk ɑːn-
with stress-imposing suffix ˌaɪk ə ˈnɒ+ -ɒ- ‖ -ˈnɑː+ — **iconology** ˌaɪk ə ˈnɒl ədʒ i ˌ·ɒ- ‖ -ˈnɑːl-
iconoclasm aɪ ˈkɒn ə ˌklæz əm ‖ -ˈkɑːn-
iconoclast aɪ ˈkɒn ə klæst -klɑːst ‖ -ˈkɑːn- **~s** s
iconoclastic aɪ ˌkɒn ə ˈklæst ɪk ◂ ˌaɪk ɒn- ‖ aɪ ˌkɑːn- ˌaɪk ɑːn- **~ally** ᵊl ͜i
iconograph|y ˌaɪk ə ˈnɒg rəf |i ‖ -ˈnɑːg- **~ies** iz
iconost|asis ˌaɪk ə ˈnɒst |əs ɪs ˌ·ɒ-, §-əs ‖ -ˈnɑːst- **~ases** ə siːz
icosahedr|on ˌaɪk əs ə ˈhiːdr |ən ˌ·ɒs-, aɪ ˌkɒs -ˈhedr- ‖ aɪ ˌkoʊs- -ˌkɑːs-; ˌaɪk oʊs-, ˌɑːs- **~a** ə **~ons** ənz
ictal ˈɪkt ᵊl
icteric ɪk ˈter ɪk
icterus ˈɪkt ər əs
ictus ˈɪkt əs **~es** ɪz əz
icy ˈaɪs i **icier** ˈaɪs i ͜ə ‖ ᵊr **iciest** ˈaɪs i ͜ɪst əst
  icily ˈaɪs ɪ li -əl i **iciness** ˈaɪs i nəs -nɪs
-id ɪd §əd — **acarid** ˈæk ər ɪd §-əd **arachnid** ə ˈræk nɪd §-nəd
id *in psychology* ɪd **ids** ɪdz
ID, id *'(proof of) identity'* ˌaɪ ˈdiː
  ˌI'D card
I'd aɪd
Ida ˈaɪd ə
Idaho ˈaɪd ə həʊ ‖ -hoʊ
Idahoan ˈaɪd ə həʊ ən ◂ ˌ· ·ˈ· · ‖ -hoʊ ən **~s** z
Idd *Moslem festival* iːd
Iddesleigh ˈɪdz li
-ide aɪd — **lanthanide** ˈlænᵗθ ə naɪd

IDEA

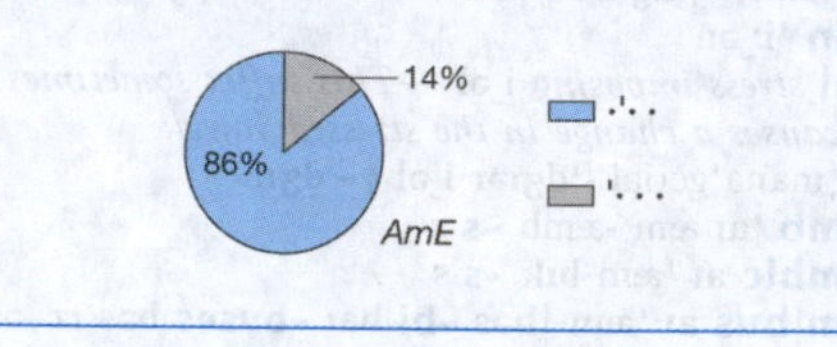

idea aɪ ˈdɪə ˌaɪ-, §-ˈdiː ͜ə ‖ ₍ₗ₎aɪ ˈdiː ə ˈ· · — *Preference poll, AmE:* ·ˈ· 86%, ˈ· · 14%. **~s** z
ideal ₍ₗ₎aɪ ˈdɪəl -ˈdiː ͜əl ‖ ₍ₗ₎aɪ ˈdiː ͜əl **~ly** i li **~s** z
idealis... —*see* **idealiz...**
idealism aɪ ˈdɪəl ˌɪz əm ˌaɪ-, -ˈdiː ͜ə ˌlɪz-; ˈaɪd i ͜ə ˌlɪz ᵊm ‖ aɪ ˈdiː ə ˌlɪz əm **~s** z
idealist aɪ ˈdɪəl ɪst ˌaɪ-, -ˈdiː ͜əl-, ˈaɪd i ͜əl-, §-əst ‖ aɪ ˈdiː əl əst **~s** s
idealistic aɪ ˌdɪə ˈlɪst ɪk ◂ ˌaɪd i ͜ə ˈlɪst ɪk◂, aɪ ˌdiː ͜ə- ‖ aɪ ˌdiː ə ˈlɪst ɪk ◂ ˌaɪd i ͜ə- **~ally** ᵊl ͜i
idealization aɪ ˌdɪəl aɪ ˈzeɪʃ ᵊn ˌaɪ ˌdɪəl-, aɪ ˌdiː ͜əl aɪ'--, §ˌaɪd i ͜əl-, -ɪ'-- ‖ aɪ ˌdiː əl ə ˈzeɪʃ ᵊn **~s** z
idealiz|e aɪ ˈdɪəl aɪz ˌaɪ-; -ˈdiː ͜ə laɪz, §ˈaɪd i ͜ə- ‖ aɪ ˈdiː ə laɪz **~ed** d **~es** ɪz əz **~ing** ɪŋ
ideally ₍ₗ₎aɪ ˈdɪəl i -ˈdiː ͜əl i, -li ‖ ₍ₗ₎aɪ ˈdiː ͜əl i -li
ideate ˈaɪd i |eɪt **~ated** eɪt ɪd -əd ‖ eɪţ əd **~ates** eɪts **~ating** eɪt ɪŋ ‖ eɪţ ɪŋ
ideation ˌaɪd i ˈeɪʃ ᵊn **~al** ͜əl **~ally** ͜əl i
idee, idée ˈiːd eɪ iː ˈdeɪ —*Fr* [i de] **idees, idées** *as sing., or* z
  ˌidee ˈfixe, ˌidée ˈfixe fɪks fiːks —*Fr* [fiks];
  ˌidée reˈçue rə ˈsuː —*Fr* [ʁə sy]
idem ˈɪd em ˈaɪd-, ˈiːd-
ident ˈaɪd ent **~s** s
identical aɪ ˈdent ɪk ᵊl ɪ-, ə- ‖ -ˈdenţ- **~ly** ͜i
  iˌdentical ˈtwin
identifiab|le aɪ ˈdent ɪ faɪ ͜əb |ᵊl -ˈ·ə-, § ·ˌ·ˈ· · · ‖ -ˈdenţ ə- **~ly** li

dentification aɪ ˌdent ɪf ɪ ˈkeɪʃ ən ɪ-, ə-, -ˌ-ˌəf-, §-əˈ-- ‖ -ˌdenṭ- **~s** z
identi|fy aɪ ˈdent ɪ |faɪ ɪ-, ə-, -ə- ‖ -ˈdenṭ ə |faɪ **~fied** faɪd **~fier/s** faɪ‿ə/z ‖ faɪ‿ər/z **~fies** faɪz **~fying** faɪ ɪŋ
identikit, I~ *tdmk* aɪ ˈdent i kɪt ɪ-, ə- ‖ -ˈdenṭ-
identit|y aɪ ˈdent ət |i ɪ-, ə-, -ɪt- ‖ -ˈdenṭ əṭ |i **~ies** iz
iˈdentity card; **iˈdentity ˌcrisis**
ideogram ˈɪd i‿ə græm ˈaɪd-, -i əʊ- **~s** z
ideograph ˈɪd i‿ə grɑːf ˈaɪd-, -i əʊ-, -græf ‖ -græf **~s** s
ideographic ˌɪd i‿ə ˈgræf ɪk ◂ ˌaɪd-, -i əʊ- **~ally** əl‿i
ideography ˌɪd i ˈɒgr əf i ˌaɪd- ‖ -ˈɑːg-
ideological ˌaɪd i‿ə ˈlɒdʒ ɪk əl ◂ ˌɪd- ‖ -ˈlɑːdʒ- **~ly** ‿i
ideologist ˌaɪd i ˈɒl ədʒ ɪst ˌɪd-, §-əst ‖ -ˈɑːl- **~s** s
ideologue ˈaɪd i‿ə lɒg ‖ -lɔːg -lɑːg **~s** z

IDEOLOGY

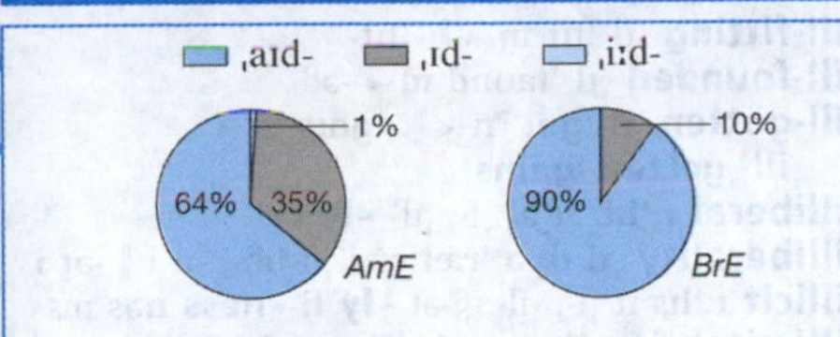

ideolog|y ˌaɪd i ˈɒl ədʒ |i ˌɪd- ‖ -ˈɑːl- — *Preference polls, AmE:* ˌaɪd- *64%,* ˌɪd- *35%,* ˌiːd- *1%; BrE:* ˌaɪd- *90%,* ˌɪd- *10%.* **~ies** iz
ideophone ˈɪd i‿ə fəʊn ˈaɪd-, -i əʊ- ‖ -foʊn **~s** z
ides, Ides aɪdz
idio- *comb. form*
with stress-neutral suffix ˌɪd i əʊ ‖ -ə — **idioglossia** ˌɪd i əʊ ˈglɒs i‿ə ‖ -ə ˈglɑːs- -ˈglɔːs-
with stress-imposing suffix ˌɪd i ˈɒ+ ‖ -ˈɑː+ — **idiopathy** ˌɪd i ˈɒp əθ i ‖ -ˈɑːp-
idioc|y ˈɪd i‿əs |i **~ies** iz
idiolect ˈɪd i‿ə lekt -i əʊ- **~s** s
idiolectal ˌɪd i‿ə ˈlekt əl ◂ -i əʊ- **~ly** i
idiom ˈɪd i‿əm **~s** z
idiomatic ˌɪd i‿ə ˈmæt ɪk ◂ -i əʊ- ‖ -ˈmæṭ- **~ally** əl‿i
idiosyncras|y ˌɪd i‿əʊ ˈsɪŋk rəs |i ‖ -i‿ə- **~ies** iz
idiosyncratic ˌɪd i‿əʊ sɪŋ ˈkræt ɪk -sɪn'- ‖ ə sɪn ˈkræṭ ɪk **~ally** əl‿i
idiot ˈɪd i‿ət **~s** s
idiot savant ˌiːd i əʊ sæ ˈvɒ̃ ˌɪd i‿ət ˈsæv ənt ‖ ˌiːd joʊ sɑː ˈvɑːn -sæˈ- —*Fr* [i djo sa vɑ̃]
idiotic ˌɪd i ˈɒt ɪk ◂ ‖ -ˈɑːṭ ɪk ◂ **~ally** əl‿i
idiot-proof ˈɪd i‿ət pruːf §-prʊf
Idist ˈiːd ɪst §-əst **~s** s
Iditarod *place in AK* aɪ ˈdɪt ə rɒd ‖ aɪ ˈdɪṭ ə rɑːd
idle, Idle ˈaɪd əl **idleness** ˈaɪd əl nəs -nɪs **idler/s** ˈaɪd lə/z ‖ -lər/z **idlest** ˈaɪd lɪst -ləst
idly ˈaɪd li
Ido ˈiːd əʊ ‖ -oʊ
idol ˈaɪd əl *(= idle)* **~s** z
idolater, idolator aɪ ˈdɒl ət ə ‖ -ˈdɑːl əṭ ər **~s** z
idolatrous aɪ ˈdɒl ətr əs ‖ -ˈdɑːl- **~ly** li **~ness** nəs nɪs
idolatr|y aɪ ˈdɒl ətr |i ‖ -ˈdɑːl- **~ies** iz
idolis... —*see* **idoliz...**
idolization ˌaɪd əl aɪ ˈzeɪʃ ən -əl ɪ-, -ə laɪ- ‖ -əl ə-
idoliz|e ˈaɪd əl aɪz -ə laɪz **~ed** d **~er/s** ə/z ‖ ər/z **~es** ɪz əz **~ing** ɪŋ
Idomeneo ɪ ˌdɒm ə ˈneɪ əʊ ‖ ˌiːd oʊm ə ˈneɪ oʊ
Idomeneus aɪ ˈdɒm ɪ njuːs ɪ-, -ə- ‖ -ˈdɑːm ə nuːs -njuːs
Idris ˈɪdr ɪs ˈaɪdr-, §-əs
Idwal ˈɪd wəl
idyl, idyll ˈɪd əl ˈaɪd-, -ɪl ‖ ˈaɪd əl **~s** z
idyllic ɪ ˈdɪl ɪk aɪ- ‖ aɪ- **~ally** əl‿i
-ie i — **sweetie** ˈswiːt i ‖ ˈswiːṭ i
i.e. ˌaɪ ˈiː
iechyd da ˌjæk i ˈdɑː —*Welsh* [ˌje χid ˈdaː, -χid-]
-ier *comparative of* **-y** i‿ə ‖ i‿ər — **dirtier** ˈdɜːt i‿ə ‖ ˈdɜːṭ i‿ər
-ier *suffix forming nouns* ˈɪə ‖ ˈɪər — **brigadier** ˌbrɪg ə ˈdɪə ‖ -ˈdɪər
-ies *pl of* **-y** iz — **doggies** ˈdɒg iz ‖ ˈdɔːg iz ˈdɑːg-
-iest *superlative of* **-y** i‿ɪst əst — **dirtiest** ˈdɜːt i‿ɪst əst ‖ ˈdɜːṭ i‿əst
Iestyn ˈjest ɪn —*Welsh* [ˈje sdin, -sdɪn]
Ieuan ˈjaɪ‿ən -æn —*Welsh* [ˈjə jan]
if ɪf §ɪv —*In RP this word has no separate weak form; but in some other varieties, including GenAm, it may have a weak form* əf **ifs** ɪfs
Ife *place in Nigeria* ˈiː feɪ —*Yoruba* [i fe]
Ife *family name* aɪf
-iferous ˈɪf ər əs — **carboniferous** ˌkɑːb ə ˈnɪf ər əs ‖ ˌkɑːrb-
iff ɪf —*Since* iff *is pronounced identically with plain* if, *its use ('if and only if') is in practice restricted to writing.*
iff|y ˈɪf |i **~iness** i nəs i nɪs
Ifield ˈaɪ fiːəld
Ifor ˈaɪv ə ˈaɪf-; ˈiː vɔː ‖ -ər —*Welsh* [ˈi vor]
-iform ɪ fɔːm ə- ‖ ə fɔːrm — **cruciform** ˈkruːs ɪ fɔːm -ə- ‖ -ə fɔːrm
iftar, I~ ˈɪft ɑː ‖ -ɑːr —*Arabic* [ʔif ˈtˤaːr]
-ify *stress-imposing* ɪ faɪ ə- — **solidify** sə ˈlɪd ɪ faɪ sɒ-, -ə-
Igbo ˈiːb əʊ ‖ -oʊ —*Ibo* [i gbo] **~s** z
Iggy ˈɪg i
Ightham ˈaɪt əm ‖ ˈaɪṭ-
igitur ˈɪg ɪ tʊə ˈɪdʒ-, §-ə-; -ɪt ə, §-ət ə ‖ -tʊr
Iglesias i ˈgleɪz i‿əs —*Sp* [i ˈɣle sjas]
igloo ˈɪg luː **~s** z
Ignatian ɪg ˈneɪʃ i‿ən -ˈneɪʃ ən **~s** z
Ignatieff ɪg ˈnæt i ef ‖ -ˈnæṭ-
Ignatius ɪg ˈneɪʃ əs -ˈneɪʃ i‿əs
igneous ˈɪg ni‿əs
ignimbrite ˈɪg nɪm braɪt §-nəm-

ignis fatuus ˌɪɡ nɪs ˈfæt ju‿əs §ˌ·nəs-, -ˈfætʃ u‿ ‖ -ˈfætʃ u‿əs **ignes fatui** ˌɪɡ neɪz ˈfæt ju iː ˌ·niːz-, -ˈfætʃ u-, -aɪ ‖ -niːz ˈfætʃ u aɪ
ig|nite ɪɡ |ˈnaɪt **~nited** ˈnaɪt ɪd -əd ‖ ˈnaɪţ əd **~nites** ˈnaɪts **~niting** ˈnaɪt ɪŋ ‖ ˈnaɪţ ɪŋ
ignition ɪɡ ˈnɪʃ ən **~s** z
ignitron ɪɡ ˈnaɪtr ɒn ˈɪɡ nɪ trɒn, -nə- ‖ -ɑːn **~s** z
ignob|le ɪɡ ˈnəʊb |əl ˌɪɡ- ‖ -ˈnoʊb- **~ly** li
ignominious ˌɪɡ nə ˈmɪn i‿əs ◂ ˌ·nəʊ- **~ly** li **~ness** nəs nɪs
ignomin|y ˈɪɡ nəm ɪn |i -ən i **~ies** iz
ignoramus ˌɪɡ nə ˈreɪm əs **~es** ɪz əz
ignorance ˈɪɡ nər ənts
ignorant ˈɪɡ nər ənt **~ly** li
ignore ɪɡ ˈnɔː ‖ -ˈnɔːr -ˈnoʊr **~d** d **~s** z **ignoring** ɪɡ ˈnɔːr ɪŋ ‖ -ˈnoʊr-
ignotum per ignotius ɪɡ ˌnəʊt əm ˌpɜːr ɪɡ ˈnəʊt i‿əs -ˌ· ·pər ·ˈ··, -ʊs ‖ ɪɡ ˌnoʊţ əm ˌpɝː ɪɡ ˈnoʊţ-
Igoe ˈaɪɡ əʊ ‖ -oʊ
Igor ˈiːɡ ɔː ‖ -ɔːr —*Russ* [ˈi ɡərʲ]
Igorot ˌiːɡ ə ˈrəʊt ˌɪɡ- ‖ -ˈroʊt **~s** s
Iguaçu, Iguaçú ˌɪɡ wə ˈsuː —*Port* [i ɡwa ˈsu]
iguana ɪ ˈɡwɑːn ə ˌɪɡ ju ˈɑːn ə **~s** z
iguanodon ɪ ˈɡwɑːn ə dɒn ˌɪɡ ju ˈɑːn-, -əd ən ‖ -dɑːn **~s** z
Iguazu, Iguazú ˌɪɡ wə ˈsuː —*Sp* [i ɣwa ˈsu]
IKBS ˌaɪ keɪ biː ˈes
Ike aɪk
IKEA *tdmk* aɪ ˈkiː‿ə ɪ ˈkeɪ ə
ikebana ˌiːk eɪ ˈbɑːn ə ˌɪk-, -i- —*Jp* [i ˈke ba na]
ikon ˈaɪk ɒn -ən ‖ -ɑːn **~s** z
il- (ˌ)ɪ, ˌɪl — **illiberal** ɪ ˈlɪb ər‿əl ˌɪ-, ˌɪl-
Ilchester ˈɪl tʃɪst ə ‖ -ˌtʃest ər
-ile aɪəl ‖ əl *(*) —This BrE-AmE difference is a general tendency; there are several exceptions.* — **agile** ˈædʒ aɪəl ‖ ˈædʒ əl
ILEA ˈɪl i‿ə ˌaɪ el i ˈeɪ ◂
ileac ˈɪl i æk *(= iliac)*
Ile de France ˌiːəl də ˈfrɒ̃s ‖ -ˈfrɑːnts —*Fr* Île-de-France [il də fʁɑ̃ːs]
ileostom|y ˌɪl i ˈɒst əm |i ‖ -ˈɑːst- **~ies** iz
Iles aɪəlz
ileum ˈɪl i‿əm *(= ilium)*
ileus ˈɪl i‿əs
ilex ˈaɪl eks **~es** ɪz əz
Ilford ˈɪl fəd ‖ -fərd
Ilfracombe ˈɪlf rə kuːm
ilia ˈɪl i‿ə
iliac ˈɪl i æk
Iliad ˈɪl i‿əd -i æd
Iliffe ˈaɪl ɪf
ili|um ˈɪl i‿|əm **~a** ə
Ilium *'Troy'* ˈaɪl i‿əm ˈɪl- ‖ ˈɪl-
ilk ɪlk
Ilkeston ˈɪlk ɪst ən -əst-
Ilkley ˈɪlk li
ill ɪl **ills** ɪlz **worse** wɜːs ‖ wɝːs **worst** wɜːst ‖ wɝːst
ˌ**ill at ˈease**; ˌ**ill ˈfeeling**; ˌ**ill ˈwill**
I'll aɪəl
ill-ad|vised ˌɪl əd |ˈvaɪzd ◂ §-æd- **~visedly** ˈvaɪz ɪd li -əd-
ill-assorted ˌɪl ə ˈsɔːt ɪd ◂ -əd ‖ -ˈsɔːrţ əd ◂
illative ɪ ˈleɪt ɪv ˈɪl ət- ‖ ˈɪl əţ ɪv ɪ ˈleɪţ-
Illawarra ˌɪl ə ˈwɒr ə ‖ -ˈwɔːr ə
ill-bred ˌɪl ˈbred ◂
ill-conceived ˌɪl kən ˈsiːvd ◂ §-kɒn-
ill-considered ˌɪl kən ˈsɪd əd ◂ §-kɒn- ‖ -ərd ◂
ill-defined ˌɪl di ˈfaɪnd ◂
ill-disposed ˌɪl dɪ ˈspəʊzd ◂ ‖ -ˈspoʊzd ◂
illegal ɪ ˈliːɡ əl ˌɪ-, ˌɪl- **~ly** i
illegalit|y ˌɪl iː ˈɡæl ət |i ˌ·ɪ-, ˌ·liː-, -ɪt i **~ies** iz
illegibility ɪ ˌledʒ ə ˈbɪl ət i ˌɪ-, ˌɪl-, -ɪˈ··, -ɪt i ‖ -əţ i
illegib|le ɪ ˈledʒ əb |əl ˌɪ-, ˌɪl-, -ɪb- **~ly** li
illegitimac|y ˌɪl ə ˈdʒɪt əm əs |i ˌ·ɪ-, -ˈ·ɪm- ‖ -ˈdʒɪţ əm- **~ies** iz
illegitimate ˌɪl ə ˈdʒɪt əm ət ◂ˌ·ɪ-, -ɪm ət, -ɪt ‖ -ˈdʒɪţ əm- **~ly** li
ill-equipped ˌɪl ɪ ˈkwɪpt ◂ -ə-
ill-fated ˌɪl ˈfeɪt ɪd ◂ -əd ‖ -ˈfeɪţ əd
ill-favored, ill-favoured ˌɪl ˈfeɪv əd ◂ ‖ -ərd ◂
ill-fitting ˌɪl ˈfɪt ɪŋ ◂ ‖ -ˈfɪţ-
ill-founded ˌɪl ˈfaʊnd ɪd ◂ -əd
ill-gotten ˌɪl ˈɡɒt ən ◂ ‖ -ˈɡɑːt ən ◂
ˌ**ill-ˌgotten ˈgains**
illiberal ɪ ˈlɪb ər‿əl ˌɪ-, ˌɪl- **~ly** i
illiberality ˌɪl ɪb ə ˈræl ət i ˌɪl lɪb-, -ɪt i ‖ -əţ i
illicit ɪ ˈlɪs ɪt ˌɪ-, ˌɪl-, §-ət **~ly** li **~ness** nəs nɪs
illimitab|le ɪ ˈlɪm ɪt əb |əl ˌɪ-, ˌɪl-, §-ət əb- ‖ -əţ əb- **~ly** li
ill-informed ˌɪl ɪn ˈfɔːmd ◂ ‖ -ˈfɔːrmd ◂
Illingworth ˈɪl ɪŋ wəθ -wɜːθ ‖ -wɝːθ
illinium ɪ ˈlɪn ɪ‿əm
Illinois ˌɪl ə ˈnɔɪ -ɪ-, -ˈnɔɪz
Illinoisan ˌɪl ə ˈnɔɪ ən ◂ -ɪ-, -ˈnɔɪz ən **~s** z
illiquid ɪ ˈlɪk wɪd ˌɪl-, §-wəd
illiterac|y ɪ ˈlɪt‿ər əs |i ˌɪ-, ˌɪl- ‖ -ˈlɪţ ər əs |i →-ˈlɪtr əs i **~ies** iz
illiterate ɪ ˈlɪt‿ər ət ˌɪ-, ˌɪl-, -ɪt ‖ -ˈlɪţ ər ət →-ˈlɪtr ət **~ly** li **~ness** nəs nɪs **~s** s
ill-judged ˌɪl ˈdʒʌdʒd ◂
ill-mannered ˌɪl ˈmæn əd ◂ ‖ -ərd ◂ **~ly** li
ill-natured ˌɪl ˈneɪtʃ əd ◂ ‖ -ərd◂ **~ly** li **~ness** nəs nɪs
illness ˈɪl nəs -nɪs **~es** ɪz əz
illocution ˌɪl ə ˈkjuːʃ ən **~s** z
illocutionary ˌɪl ə ˈkjuːʃ ən ər‿i ◂ -ən‿ər i ‖ -ə ner i
illogical ɪ ˈlɒdʒ ɪk əl ˌɪ-, ˌɪl- ‖ -ˈlɑːdʒ- **~ly** ‿i **~ness** nəs nɪs
illogicality ɪ ˌlɒdʒ ɪ ˈkæl ət i ˌɪ‚ ·ˈ··, ˌɪl-; -əˈ··, -ɪt i ‖ ɪ ˌlɑːdʒ ə ˈkæl əţ i
ill-omened ˌɪl ˈəʊm end ◂ -ənd ‖ -ˈoʊm-
ill-prepared ˌɪl pri ˈpeəd ◂ -prə- ‖ -ˈpeərd ◂
ill-served ˌɪl ˈsɜːvd ◂ ‖ -ˈsɝːvd ◂
ill-starred ˌɪl ˈstɑːd ◂ ‖ -ˈstɑːrd ◂
ill-suited ˌɪl ˈsuːt ɪd ◂ -ˈsjuːt-, -əd ‖ -ˈsuːţ-
ill-tempered ˌɪl ˈtemp əd ◂ ‖ -ərd ◂ **~ly** li
ill-timed ˌɪl ˈtaɪmd ◂
ill-|treat (ˌ)ɪl |ˈtriːt **~treated** ˈtriːt ɪd -əd ‖ ˈtriːţ əd **~treating** ˈtriːt ɪŋ ‖ ˈtriːţ ɪŋ **~treatment** ˈtriːt mənt **~treats** ˈtriːts

Iltud 'ɪlt ɪd —*Welsh* ['ɪɬ tid, -tɪd]

Illumin|ance ɪ 'lu:m ɪn |ənᵗs -'lju:m-, -ən- **~ant** ənt

Illumi|nate ɪ 'lu:m ɪ |neɪt -'lju:m-, -ə- **~nated** neɪt ɪd -əd ‖ neɪţ əd **~nates** neɪts **~nating** neɪt ɪŋ ‖ neɪţ ɪŋ

Illuminati, i~ ɪ ˌlu:m ɪ 'nɑ:t i: -ə-

Illumination ɪ ˌlu:m ɪ 'neɪʃ ᵊn -ˌlju:m-, -ə- **~s** z

Illumin|e ɪ 'lu:m ɪn -'lju:m-, ən **~ed** d **~es** z **~ing** ɪŋ

Ill-us|e *v* ˌɪl 'ju:z **~ed** d **~es** ɪz əz **~ing** ɪŋ

Ill-use *n* ˌɪl 'ju:s

Illusion ɪ 'lu:ʒ ᵊn -'lju:ʒ- **~s** z

Illusionist ɪ 'lu:ʒ ən ɪst -'lju:ʒ-, ᵊn‿-, §-əst **~s** s

Illusive ɪ 'lu:s ɪv -'lju:s-, §-'lu:z- **~ly** li **~ness** nəs nɪs

Illusory ɪ 'lu:s ər‿i -'lju:s-, -'lu:z-, -'lju:z-

ILLUSTRATE

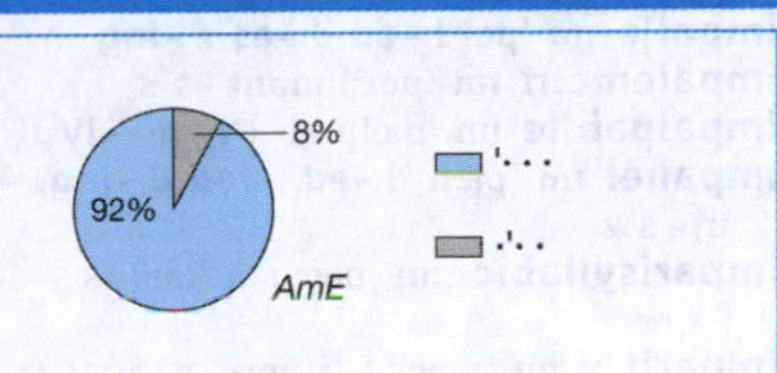

illu|strate 'ɪl ə |streɪt -ju- ‖ ɪ 'lʌs treɪt — *Preference poll, AmE:* '. . . 92%, .'. . 8%. **~strated** streɪt ɪd -əd ‖ streɪţ əd **~strates** streɪts **~strating** streɪt ɪŋ ‖ streɪţ ɪŋ

illustration ˌɪl ə 'streɪʃ ᵊn **~s** z

illustrative 'ɪl ə strət ɪv -streɪt-; ɪ 'lʌs trət ɪv ‖ ɪ 'lʌstr əţ ɪv 'ɪl ə streɪţ ɪv **~ly** li

illustrator 'ɪl ə streɪt ə ‖ -streɪţ ᵊr **~s** z

illustrious ɪ 'lʌs tri‿əs **~ly** li **~ness** nəs nɪs

Illyria ɪ 'lɪr i‿ə -'lɪər-

Illyrian ɪ 'lɪr i‿ən -'lɪər- **~s** z

Illyricum ɪ 'lɪr ɪk əm -'lɪər-

ilmenite 'ɪl mə naɪt -mɪ-

Ilminster 'ɪl mɪnst ə ‖ -ᵊr

Ilocano, Ilokano ˌi:l əʊ 'kɑ:n əʊ ‖ -oʊ 'kɑ:n oʊ **~s** z

Ilona ɪ 'ləʊn ə ‖ -'loʊn ə

Ilson 'ɪls ən

Ilyushin ɪl 'ju:ʃ ɪn -ᵊn —*Russ* [ɪlʲ 'ju ʃɪn]

I'm aɪm —*In casual speech the phrase* I'm going to *before a verb is also* aɪŋ ən ə, aɪm ən ə

im- ɪm —*but before* m *usually* ɪ; *generally stressed only for emphasis or if the following syllable is unstressed:* im'possible, ˌimme'morial

iMac *tdmk* 'aɪ mæk **~s** s

image 'ɪm ɪdʒ **imaged** 'ɪm ɪdʒd **images** 'ɪm ɪdʒ ɪz -əz **imaging** 'ɪm ɪdʒ ɪŋ

image-maker 'ɪm ɪdʒ ˌmeɪk ə ‖ -ᵊr **~s** z

imager 'ɪm ɪdʒ ə -ədʒ- ‖ -ᵊr **~s** z

imager|y 'ɪm ɪdʒ ər‿|i **~ies** iz

imaginab|le ɪ 'mædʒ ɪn əb |ᵊl -ən‿əb- **~ly** li

imaginar|y ɪ 'mædʒ ɪn ᵊr‿|i -ᵊn‿ər |i ‖ -ə ner |i **~ies** iz **~ily** əl ɪ i li **~iness** i nəs i nɪs

imagination ɪ ˌmædʒ ɪ 'neɪʃ ᵊn -ə- **~s** z

imaginative ɪ 'mædʒ ɪn ət ɪv -ən‿ət- ‖ -ən‿əţ ɪv -ə neɪţ ɪv **~ly** li **~ness** nəs nɪs

imagin|e ɪ 'mædʒ ɪn -ən **~ed** d **~es** z **~ing|s** ɪŋ|z

imagines *from* **imagine** ɪ 'mædʒ ɪnz -ənz

imagines *n pl of* **imago** ɪ 'meɪdʒ ɪ ni:z -'mædʒ-, -'mɑ:g-, -ə-

imaging 'ɪm ɪdʒ ɪŋ

imago ɪ 'meɪg əʊ -'mɑ:g- ‖ -oʊ **~es** z

imam ɪ 'mɑ:m 'i: mɑ:m **~s** z

Imax, IMAX *tdmk* 'aɪ mæks

imbalanc|e (ˌ)ɪm 'bæl ənᵗs **~es** ɪz əz

imbecile 'ɪm bə si:ᵊl -bɪ-, -saɪᵊl ‖ -bəs ᵊl -ɪl (*) **~s** z

imbecilic ˌɪm bə 'sɪl ɪk ◂ -bɪ-

imbecilit|y ˌɪm bə 'sɪl ət |i ˌ-bɪ-, -ɪt i ‖ -əţ |i **~ies** iz

imbed ɪm 'bed **~ded** ɪd əd **~ding** ɪŋ **~s** z

Imbert 'ɪm bət ‖ -bᵊrt

imbib|e ɪm 'baɪb **~ed** d **~es** z **~ing** ɪŋ

Imbrium 'ɪm bri‿əm

imbroglio ɪm 'brəʊl i‿əʊ ‖ -'broʊl joʊ **~s** z

Imbros 'ɪm brɒs ‖ -brɑ:s

imbru|e ɪm 'bru: **~ed** d **~es** z **~ing** ɪŋ

imbu|e ɪm 'bju: **~ed** d **~es** z **~ing** ɪŋ

Imelda ɪ 'meld ə

IMF ˌaɪ em 'ef

Imhof 'ɪm həʊf ‖ -hoʊf

imide 'ɪm aɪd **~s** z

imine 'ɪm i:n ɪ 'mi:n **~s** z

imi|tate 'ɪm ɪ |teɪt -ə- **~tated** teɪt ɪd -əd ‖ teɪţ əd **~tates** teɪts **~tating** teɪt ɪŋ ‖ teɪţ ɪŋ

imitation ˌɪm ɪ 'teɪʃ ᵊn -ə- **~s** z

imitative 'ɪm ɪt ət ɪv '-ət-; -ɪ teɪt-, -ə teɪt- ‖ -ə teɪţ ɪv **~ly** li **~ness** nəs nɪs

imitator 'ɪm ɪ teɪt ə '-ə- ‖ -teɪţ ᵊr **~s** z

immaculate ɪ 'mæk jʊl ət ə-, -jəl-, -ɪt ‖ -jəl- **~ly** li **~ness** nəs nɪs

Imˌmaculate Con'ception

immanenc|e 'ɪm ən ənᵗs **~y** i

immanent 'ɪm ən ənt **~ly** li

Immanuel ɪ 'mæn ju‿əl ə-

immaterial ˌɪm ə 'tɪər i‿əl ◂ ‖ -'tɪr- **~ly** i **~ness** nəs nɪs

immature ˌɪm ə 'tjʊə ◂ -'tʃʊə, -'tjɔ:, -'tʃɔ: ‖ -'tʊᵊr -'tʃʊᵊr, -'tjʊᵊr **~ly** li **~ness** nəs nɪs

immaturity ˌɪm ə 'tjʊər ət i -'tʃʊər-, -'tjɔ:r-, -'tʃɔ:r-, -ɪt i ‖ -'tʊr əţ i -'tʃʊr-, -'tjʊr-

immeasurab|le ɪ 'meʒ ər‿əb |ᵊl ˌɪ-, ˌɪm- **~ly** li

immediac|y ɪ 'mi:d i‿əs |i ə-, -'mi:dʒ əs |i **~ies** iz

immediate ɪ 'mi:d i‿ət ə-, -'mi:dʒ ət, -ɪt **~ly** li **~ness** nəs nɪs

Immelmann 'ɪm ᵊl mæn -mən ‖ -mən -mɑ:n —*Ger* ['ʔɪm ᵊl man]

immemorial ˌɪm ə 'mɔ:r i‿əl ◂, ˌɪ- ‖ -'moʊr- **~ly** i

immense ɪ 'menᵗs ə- **~ly** li **~ness** nəs nɪs

immensit|y ɪ 'menᵗs ət |i ə-, -ɪt- ‖ -əţ |i **~ies** iz

immers|e ɪ 'mɜ:s ə- ‖ ɪ 'mɝ:s **~ed** t **~es** ɪz əz **~ing** ɪŋ

immersion ɪ ˈmɜːʃ ᵊn ə-, -ˈmɜːʒ- ‖ ɪ ˈmɝːʒ ᵊn -ˈmɝːʃ- **~s** z
 imˈmersion ˌheater

immigrant ˈɪm ɪɡ rənt -əɡ- **~s** s

immi|grate ˈɪm ɪ |ɡreɪt -ə- **~grated** ɡreɪt ɪd -əd ‖ ɡreɪţ əd **~grates** ɡreɪts **~grating** ɡreɪt ɪŋ ‖ ɡreɪţ ɪŋ

immigration ˌɪm ɪ ˈɡreɪʃ ᵊn -ə- **~s** z

imminenc|e ˈɪm ɪn ənᵗs -ən- **~y** i

imminent ˈɪm ɪn ənt -ən- **~ly** li

Immingham ˈɪm ɪŋ əm §-həm

immiscib|le ɪ ˈmɪs əb |ᵊl -ɪb- **~ly** li

immobile ɪ ˈməʊb aɪᵊl ‖ ɪ ˈmoʊb ᵊl -iːᵊl *(*)*

immobilis... *—see* **immobiliz...**

immobility ˌɪm əʊ ˈbɪl ət i -ɪt i ‖ -oʊ ˈbɪl əţ i

immobilization ɪ ˌməʊb əl aɪ ˈzeɪʃ ᵊn -ˌɪl-, -ɪˈ- ‖ ɪ ˌmoʊb əl ə- **~s** z

immobiliz|e ɪ ˈməʊb ə laɪz -ɪ-, -ᵊl aɪz ‖ ɪ ˈmoʊb- **~ed** d **~er/s** ə/z ‖ ᵊr/z **~es** ɪz əz **~ing** ɪŋ

immoderate ɪ ˈmɒd ər ət ˌɪ-, ˌɪm-, -ɪt ‖ ɪ ˈmɑːd- **~ly** li **~ness** nəs nɪs

immodest ɪ ˈmɒd ɪst ˌɪ-, ˌɪm-, -əst ‖ ɪ ˈmɑːd- **~ly** li

immodesty ɪ ˈmɒd əst i ˌɪ-, ˌɪm-, -ɪst- ‖ ɪ ˈmɑːd-

immo|late ˈɪm əʊ |leɪt ‖ -ə- **~lated** leɪt ɪd -əd ‖ leɪţ əd **~lates** leɪts **~lating** leɪt ɪŋ ‖ leɪţ ɪŋ

immolation ˌɪm əʊ ˈleɪʃ ᵊn ‖ -ə- **~s** z

immoral ɪ ˈmɒr əl ə-, ˌɪ-, ˌɪm- ‖ ɪ ˈmɔːr əl ɪ ˈmɑːr- **~ly** i

immoralit|y ˌɪm ə ˈræl ət |i ˌɒ-, ˌɔː-, -ɪt i ‖ -əţ |i **~ies** iz

immortal ɪ ˈmɔːt ᵊl ə-, ˌɪ-, ˌɪm- ‖ ɪ ˈmɔːrţ ᵊl **~ly** i **~s** z

immortalis... *—see* **immortaliz...**

immortality ˌɪm ɔː ˈtæl ət i -ɪt i ‖ -ɔːr ˈtæl əţ i

immortaliz|e ɪ ˈmɔːt ᵊl aɪz -ə laɪz ‖ ɪ ˈmɔːrţ ᵊl aɪz **~ed** d **~es** ɪz əz **~ing** ɪŋ

immortelle ˌɪm ɔː ˈtel ‖ -ɔːr- **~s** z

immovab|le ɪ ˈmuːv əb |ᵊl ə-, ˌɪ-, ˌɪm- **~ly** li

immune ɪ ˈmjuːn ə-, ˌɪ-
 imˈmune reˌsponse; **imˈmune ˌsystem**

immunis... *—see* **immuniz...**

immunit|y ɪ ˈmjuːn ət |i ə-, -ɪt- ‖ -əţ |i **~ies** iz

immunization ˌɪm ju naɪ ˈzeɪʃ ᵊn ˌjə-, -ɪˈ- ‖ ˌɪm jən ə- ɪ ˌmjuːn ə- **~s** z

immuniz|e ˈɪm ju naɪz -jə- ‖ -jə- **~ed** d **~es** ɪz əz **~ing** ɪŋ

immuno- *comb. form*
with stress-neutral suffix ¦ɪm ju nəʊ ɪ ¦mjuːn əʊ ‖ ¦ɪm jə noʊ ɪ ¦mjuːn oʊ —
 immunodeficiency ˌɪm ju nəʊ dɪ ˈfɪʃ ᵊnᵗs i ɪ ˌmjuːn əʊ-, -dəˈ- ‖ ˌɪm jə noʊ-

immunological ˌɪm jʊn ə ˈlɒdʒ ɪk ᵊl ◂ ɪ ˌmjuːn- ‖ ˌɪm jən ə ˈlɑːdʒ- **~ly** ˌi

immunologist ˌɪm ju ˈnɒl ədʒ ɪst §-əst ‖ ˌɪm jə ˈnɑːl- **~s** s

immunology ˌɪm ju ˈnɒl ədʒ i ‖ ˌɪm jə ˈnɑːl-

immunosuppression ˌɪm ju nəʊ sə ˈpreʃ ᵊn ɪ ˌmjuːn- ‖ ˌɪm jə noʊ-

immunosuppressive ˌɪm ju nəʊ sə ˈpres ɪv ɪ ˌmjuːn- ‖ ˌɪm jə noʊ- **~s** z

immure ɪ ˈmjʊə -ˈmjɔː ‖ ɪ ˈmjʊᵊr **~d** d **~s** z
 immuring ɪ ˈmjʊər ɪŋ -ˈmjɔːr- ‖ ɪ ˈmjʊr ɪŋ

immutability ɪ ˌmjuːt ə ˈbɪl ət i ˌɪ,ˌ··-, ˌɪm,ˌ··-, -ɪt i ‖ -ˌmjuːţ ə ˈbɪl əţ i

immutab|le ɪ ˈmjuːt əb |ᵊl ˌɪ-, ˌɪm- ‖ -ˈmjuːţ- **~ly** li

I-mode ˈaɪ məʊd ‖ -moʊd

Imogen ˈɪm ədʒ ən -ɪn, -ə dʒen ‖ -ə dʒen -ədʒ ən

Imogene ˈɪm ə dʒiːn

imp ɪmp **imps** ɪmps

impact *n* ˈɪm pækt **~s** s

impact *v* ɪm ˈpækt ˈ· · **~ed** ɪd əd **~ing** ɪŋ **~s** s

impair ɪm ˈpeə ‖ -ˈpeᵊr -ˈpæᵊr **~ed** d
 impairing ɪm ˈpeər ɪŋ ‖ -ˈper ɪŋ -ˈpær ɪŋ **~s** z

impairment ɪm ˈpeə mənt ‖ -ˈper- -ˈpær- **~s** s

impala ɪm ˈpɑːl ə ‖ -ˈpæl ə —*Zulu* [i ˈmpʼaː la] **~s** z

impal|e ɪm ˈpeɪᵊl **~ed** d **~es** z **~ing** ɪŋ

impalement ɪm ˈpeɪᵊl mənt **~s** s

impalpab|le ɪm ˈpælp əb |ᵊl ˌɪm- **~ly** li

impanel ɪm ˈpæn ᵊl **~ed, ~led** d **~ing, ~ling** ɪŋ **~s** z

imparisyllabic ˌɪm ˌpær ɪ sɪ ˈlæb ɪk -ˌə-, -səˈ- ‖ -ˌper-

imparit|y ɪm ˈpær ət |i ˌɪm-, -ɪt- ‖ -əţ |i -ˈper- **~ies** iz

im|part ɪm |ˈpɑːt ‖ -|ˈpɑːrt **~parted** ˈpɑːt ɪd -əd ‖ ˈpɑːrţ əd **~parting** ˈpɑːt ɪŋ ‖ ˈpɑːrţ ɪŋ **~parts** ˈpɑːts ‖ ˈpɑːrts

impartial ɪm ˈpɑːʃ ᵊl ˌɪm- ‖ -ˈpɑːrʃ ᵊl **~ly** i

impartiality ˌɪm ˌpɑːʃ i ˈæl ət i ·ˌ· ·ˈ··, -ɪt i ‖ ɪm ˌpɑːrʃ i ˈæl əţ i ˌˌˈ··

impassab|le ɪm ˈpɑːs əb |ᵊl ˌɪm-, §-ˈpæs- ‖ -ˈpæs- **~leness** ᵊl nəs -nɪs **~ly** li

impasse æm ˈpɑːs ɪm-, ɒm-, -ˈpæs, ˈ· · ‖ ˈɪm pæs ·ˈ. —*Fr* [ɛ̃ pas] **~es** ɪz əz

impassibility ɪm ˌpæs ə ˈbɪl ət i -ˌɪ-, -ɪt i ‖ -əţ i

impassib|le ɪm ˈpæs əb |ᵊl ˌɪm-, -ɪb· **~ly** li

impassion ɪm ˈpæʃ ᵊn **~ed** d **~ing** ɪŋ **~s** z

impassive ɪm ˈpæs ɪv **~ly** li **~ness** nəs nɪs

impassivity ˌɪm pæ ˈsɪv ət i -ɪt i ‖ -əţ i

impasto ɪm ˈpæst əʊ -ˈpɑːst- ‖ -oʊ

impatience ɪm ˈpeɪʃ ᵊnᵗs

impatiens ɪm ˈpeɪʃ i enz -ˈpæt- ‖ -ˈpeɪʃ ᵊnz -ᵊnᵗs

impatient ɪm ˈpeɪʃ ᵊnt **~ly** li

impeach ɪm ˈpiːtʃ **~ed** t **~es** ɪz əz **~ing** ɪŋ **~ment/s** mənt/s

impeccab|le ɪm ˈpek əb |ᵊl **~ly** li

impecuniosity ˌɪm pɪ ˌkjuːn i ˈɒs ət i -ɪt i ‖ -ˈɑːs əţ i

impecunious ˌɪm pɪ ˈkjuːn iˌəs ◂ ˌpə- **~ly** li **~ness** nəs nɪs

impedanc|e ɪm ˈpiːd ᵊnᵗs **~es** ɪz əz

imped|e ɪm ˈpiːd **~ed** ɪd əd **~es** z **~ing** ɪŋ

impediment ɪm ˈped ɪ mənt -ə- **~s** s

impedimenta ɪm ˌped ɪ ˈment ə -ə- ‖ -ˈmenţ ə

impel ɪm ˈpel **~led** d **~ling** ɪŋ **~s** z

impeller ɪm ˈpel ə ‖ -ᵊr **~s** z

impend ɪm ˈpend **~ed** ɪd əd **~ing** ɪŋ **~s** z

mpenetrability ɪm ˌpen ɪtr ə ˈbɪl ət i ˌ·ˌ·· ˈ··-, -ətr -ˈ·-, -ɪt i ‖ -əţ i
mpenetrab|le ɪm ˈpen ɪtr əb |ᵊl ˌɪm-, -ˈ·ətr- **~ly** li
mpenitence ɪm ˈpen ɪt ənᵗs ˌɪm-, -ət- ‖ -ᵊnᵗs
mpenitent ɪm ˈpen ɪt ənt ˌɪm-, -ət- ‖ -ᵊnt **~ly** li **~s** s
mperatival ɪm ˌper ə ˈtaɪv ᵊl ◂ **~ly** i
mperative ɪm ˈper ət ɪv ‖ -əţ ɪv **~ly** li **~ness** nəs nɪs **~s** z
mperator ˌɪmp ə ˈrɑːt ɔː -ˈreɪt- ‖ -ɔːr -ˈrɑːţ ᵊr
mperceptibility ˌɪm pə ˌsept ə ˈbɪl ət i -ˌɪ-, -ɪt i ‖ ˌɪm pᵊr ˌsept ə ˈbɪl əţ i
imperceptib|le ˌɪm pə ˈsept əb |ᵊl -ɪb ᵊl ‖ ˌɪm pᵊr- **~ly** li
imperfect ɪm ˈpɜːf ɪkt ˌɪm-, -əkt, -ekt ‖ -ˈpɜ˞ːf- **~ly** li **~ness** nəs nɪs **~s** s
imperfection ˌɪm pə ˈfek ʃᵊn ‖ ˌɪm pᵊr- **~s** z
imperfective ˌɪm pə ˈfekt ɪv ‖ ˌɪm pᵊr- **~ly** li **~s** z
imperforate ɪm ˈpɜːf ər‿ət ˌɪm-, ɪt, -ə reɪt ‖ -ˈpɜ˞ːf- **~s** s
imperial ɪm ˈpɪər i‿əl ‖ -ˈpɪr- **~s** z
imperialism ɪm ˈpɪər i‿ə ˌlɪz əm ‖ -ˈpɪr- **~s** z
imperialist ɪm ˈpɪər i‿əl ɪst §-əst ‖ -ˈpɪr- **~s** s
imperialistic ɪm ˌpɪər i‿əl ˈɪst ɪk ◂ ‖ -ˌpɪr- **~ally** ᵊl‿i
imperially ɪm ˈpɪər i‿əl i ‖ -ˈpɪr-
imperil ɪm ˈper əl -ɪl **~ed, ~led** d **~ing, ~ling** ɪŋ **~s** z
imperious ɪm ˈpɪər i‿əs ‖ -ˈpɪr- **~ly** li **~ness** nəs nɪs
imperishab|le ɪm ˈper ɪʃ əb |ᵊl **~ly** li
imperium ɪm ˈpɪər i‿əm ‖ -ˈpɪr-
impermanenc|e ɪm ˈpɜːm ən ənᵗs ˌɪm- ‖ -ˈpɜ˞ːm- **~y** i
impermanent ɪm ˈpɜːm ən ənt ˌɪm- ‖ -ˈpɜ˞ːm- **~ly** li
impermeability ɪm ˌpɜːm i‿ə ˈbɪl ət i ˌ·ˌ·- ‖ -ˌpɜ˞ːm i‿ə ˈbɪl əţ i
impermeab|le ɪm ˈpɜːm i‿əb |ᵊl ˌɪm- ‖ -ˈpɜ˞ːm- **~leness** ᵊl nəs -nɪs **~ly** li
impermissibility ˌɪm pə ˌmɪs ə ˈbɪl ət i -ɪˈ·-, -ɪt i ‖ -pᵊr ˌmɪs ə ˈbɪl əţ i
impermissib|le ˌɪm pə ˈmɪs əb |ᵊl ◂ -ɪb ᵊl ‖ ˌɪm pᵊr- **~ly** li
impersonal ɪm ˈpɜːs ᵊn‿əl ˌɪm- ‖ -ˈpɜ˞ːs- **~ly** i **~s** z
imperso|nate ɪm ˈpɜːs ə |neɪt ‖ -ˈpɜ˞ːs- **~nated** neɪt ɪd -əd ‖ neɪţ əd **~nates** neɪts **~nating** neɪt ɪŋ ‖ neɪţ ɪŋ
impersonation ɪm ˌpɜːs ə ˈneɪʃ ᵊn ‖ -ˌpɜ˞ːs- **~s** z
impersonator ɪm ˈpɜːs ə neɪt ə ‖ -ˈpɜ˞ːs ə neɪţ ᵊr **~s** z
impertinenc|e ɪm ˈpɜːt ɪn ənᵗs -ᵊn‿ ‖ -ˈpɜ˞ːt ᵊn‿ənᵗs **~es** ɪz əz **~y** i
impertinent ɪm ˈpɜːt ɪn ənt -ᵊn‿ ‖ -ˈpɜ˞ːt ᵊn‿ənt **~ly** li
imperturbability ˌɪm pə ˌtɜːb ə ˈbɪl ət i -ɪt i ‖ -pᵊr ˌtɜ˞ːb ə ˈbɪl əţ i
imperturbab|le ˌɪm pə ˈtɜːb əb |ᵊl ◂ ‖ ˌɪm pᵊr ˈtɜ˞ːb- **~ly** li

impervious ɪm ˈpɜːv i‿əs ˌɪm- ‖ -ˈpɜ˞ːv- **~ly** li **~ness** nəs nɪs
impetigo ˌɪm pɪ ˈtaɪg əʊ -pə-, -pe- ‖ -oʊ
impetuosit|y ɪm ˌpet ju ˈɒs ət |i -ˌpetʃ u- ‖ -ˌpetʃ u ˈɑːs əţ |i **~ies** iz
impetuous ɪm ˈpetʃ u‿əs -ˈpet ju‿ **~ly** li **~ness** nəs nɪs
impetus ˈɪmp ɪt əs -ət- ‖ -əţ- **~es** ɪz əz
Impex ˈɪmp eks
impi ˈɪmp i —*Zulu* [ˈiː mpˈi] **~s** z
impiet|y ɪm ˈpaɪ‿ət |i ˌɪm-, -ɪt- ‖ -əţ |i **~ies** iz
imping|e ɪm ˈpɪndʒ **~ed** d **~ement** mənt **~es** ɪz əz **~ing** ɪŋ

IMPIOUS

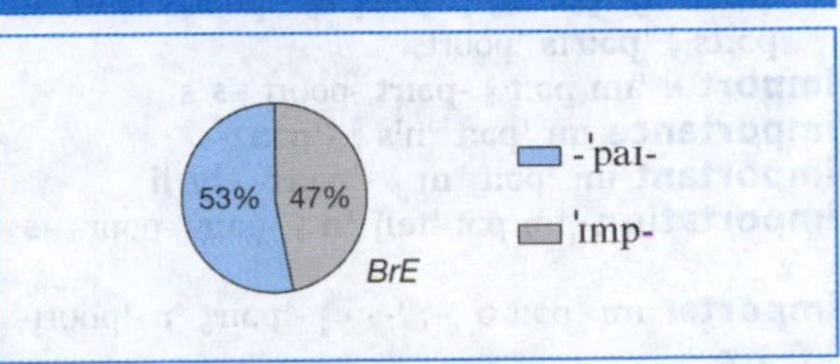

impious ˈɪmp i‿əs (ɪ)ɪm ˈpaɪ‿əs — *Preference poll, BrE:* ˈɪmp- *47% (born before 1942, 63%),* -ˈpaɪ- *53%. The traditional, irregular pronunciation* ˈɪmp i‿əs *has lost ground in favour of* (ɪ)ɪm ˈpaɪ‿əs **~ly** li **~ness** nəs nɪs
impish ˈɪmp ɪʃ **~ly** li **~ness** nəs nɪs
implacability ɪm ˌplæk ə ˈbɪl ət i ˌɪm plæk-, -ɪt i ‖ -əţ i
implacab|le ɪm ˈplæk əb |ᵊl **~leness** ᵊl nəs -nɪs **~ly** li
im|plant *v* ɪm |ˈplɑːnt §-ˈplænt, ˈ· · ‖ -|ˈplænt **~planted** ˈplɑːnt ɪd §ˈplænt-, -əd ‖ ˈplænţ əd **~planting** ˈplɑːnt ɪŋ §ˈplænt- ‖ ˈplænţ ɪŋ **~plants** ˈplɑːnts §ˈplænts ‖ ˈplænts
implant *n* ˈɪm plɑːnt §-plænt ‖ -plænt **~s** s
implantation ˌɪm plɑːn ˈteɪʃ ᵊn -plæn- ‖ -plæn- **~s** z
implausibilit|y ɪm ˌplɔːz ə ˈbɪl ət |i ˌ·ˌ·· ˈ··-, -ɪt i ‖ -əţ i -ˌplɑːz-, ˌ·ˌ·ˈ·-
implausib|le ɪm ˈplɔːz əb |ᵊl ˌɪm-, -ɪb- ‖ -ˈplɑːz- **~ly** li
implement *n* ˈɪmp lɪ mənt -lə- **~s** s
imple|ment *v* ˈɪmp lɪ |ment -lə-, -mənt, §ˌ· · ˈ|ment —*See note at* -ment **~mented** ment ɪd mənt-, -əd ‖ menţ əd **~menting** ment ɪŋ mənt- ‖ menţ ɪŋ **~ments** ments mənts
implementation ˌɪmp lɪ men ˈteɪʃ ᵊn ˌlə-, -mən ˈ·- **~s** z
impli|cate ˈɪmp lɪ |keɪt -lə- **~cated** keɪt ɪd -əd ‖ keɪţ əd **~cates** keɪts **~cating** keɪt ɪŋ ‖ keɪţ ɪŋ
implication ˌɪmp lɪ ˈkeɪʃ ᵊn -lə- **~s** z
implicative ɪm ˈplɪk ət ɪv ˈɪmp lɪ keɪt-, ˈ·lə- ‖ ˈɪmp lə keɪţ ɪv ɪm plɪk əţ- **~ly** li
implicature ɪm ˈplɪk ətʃ ə -ə tjʊə ‖ -ᵊr **~s** z
implicit ɪm ˈplɪs ɪt §-ət **~ly** li **~ness** nəs nɪs
implie... —*see* **imply**
implod|e ɪm ˈpləʊd ‖ -ˈploʊd **~ed** ɪd əd **~es** z **~ing** ɪŋ

implore ɪm ˈplɔː ‖ -ˈplɔːr -ˈploʊr **~d** d **~s** z
imploring/ly ɪm ˈplɔːr ɪŋ /li ‖ -ˈploʊr-
implosion ɪm ˈpləʊʒ ᵊn ‖ -ˈploʊʒ- **~s** z
implosive ɪm ˈpləʊs ɪv ˌɪm-, -ˈpləʊz- ‖ -ˈploʊs- -ˈploʊz- **~ly** li **~s** z
im|ply ɪm |ˈplaɪ **~plied** ˈplaɪd **~plies** ˈplaɪz **~plying** ˈplaɪ ɪŋ
impolite ˌɪm pə ˈlaɪt ◂ **~ly** li **~ness** nəs nɪs
impolitic ɪm ˈpɒl ə tɪk ˌɪm-, -ɪ- ‖ -ˈpɑːl- **~ly** li **~ness** nəs nɪs
imponderab|le ɪm ˈpɒnd‿ər əb |ᵊl ˌɪm- ‖ -ˈpɑːnd‿ **~leness** ᵊl nəs -nɪs **~les** ᵊlz **~ly** li
im|port *v* ɪm |ˈpɔːt ˌ·-, ˈ· · ‖ -|ˈpɔːrt -ˈpoʊrt **~ported** ˈpɔːt ɪd -əd ‖ ˈpɔːrt̬ əd ˈpoʊrt̬- **~porting** ˈpɔːt ɪŋ ‖ ˈpɔːrt̬ ɪŋ -ˈpoʊrt̬- **~ports** ˈpɔːts ‖ ˈpɔːrts ˈpoʊrts
import *n* ˈɪm pɔːt ‖ -pɔːrt -poʊrt **~s** s
importance ɪm ˈpɔːt ᵊnᵗs ‖ -ˈpɔːrt-
important ɪm ˈpɔːt ᵊnt ‖ -ˈpɔːrt- **~ly** li
importation ˌɪm pɔː ˈteɪʃ ᵊn ‖ -pɔːr- -poʊr- **~s** z
importer ɪm ˈpɔːt ə ˌ·-, ˈ· · · ‖ -ˈpɔːrt̬ ᵊr -ˈpoʊrt̬- **~s** z
import-export ˌɪm pɔːt ˈeks pɔːt ‖ -pɔːrt̬ ˈeks pɔːrt -poʊrt̬ ˈeks poʊrt
importunate ɪm ˈpɔːt jʊn ət -ˈpɔːtʃ ən‿ -ɪt ‖ -ˈpɔːrtʃ ən‿ət **~ly** li **~ness** nəs nɪs
importun|e ˌɪmp ə ˈtjuːn ˌɪm pɔː-, →-ˈtʃuːn; ɪm ˈpɔːt juːn, -ˈpɔːtʃ uːn ‖ ˌɪmp ᵊr ˈtuːn -ˈtjuːn; ɪm ˈpɔːrtʃ ən **~ed** d **~es** z **~ing** ɪŋ
importunit|y ˌɪmp ə ˈtjuːn ət |i ˌɪm pɔː-, →-ˈtʃuːn-, -ɪt i ‖ ˌɪmp ᵊr ˈtuːn ət̬ |i ˌɪm pɔːr-, -ˈtjuːn- **~ies** iz
impos|e ɪm ˈpəʊz ‖ -ˈpoʊz **~ed** d **~es** ɪz əz **~ing** ɪŋ
imposing ɪm ˈpəʊz ɪŋ ‖ -ˈpoʊz ɪŋ **~ly** li **~ness** nəs nɪs
imposition ˌɪm pə ˈzɪʃ ᵊn **~s** z
impossibilit|y ɪm ˌpɒs ə ˈbɪl ət |i ˌ·ˌ··ˈ·-, -ɪt i ‖ -ˌpɑːs ə ˈbɪl ət̬ |i **~ies** iz
impossible ɪm ˈpɒs əb ᵊl ˌɪm-, -ɪb- ‖ -ˈpɑːs-
impossibly ɪm ˈpɒs əb li -ɪb- ‖ -ˈpɑːs-
impost ˈɪm pəʊst -pɒst ‖ -poʊst **~s** s
imposter, impostor ɪm ˈpɒst ə ‖ -ˈpɑːst ᵊr **~s** z
imposture ɪm ˈpɒs tʃə ‖ -ˈpɑːs tʃᵊr **~s** z
impotenc|e ˈɪmp ət ənᵗs ‖ -ᵊnᵗs **~y** i
impotent ˈɪmp ət ənt ‖ -ᵊnt **~ly** li
impound ɪm ˈpaʊnd **~ed** ɪd əd **~ing** ɪŋ **~s** z
impoverish ɪm ˈpɒv ər‿ɪʃ ‖ -ˈpɑːv- **~ed** t **~es** ɪz əz **~ing** ɪŋ
impoverishment ɪm ˈpɒv ər‿ɪʃ mənt ‖ -ˈpɑːv- **~s** s
impracticability ɪm ˌprækt ɪk ə ˈbɪl ət i ˌɪmˌ· · ·ˈ·-, -ɪt i ‖ -ət̬ i
impracticab|le ɪm ˈprækt ɪk əb |ᵊl ˌɪm- **~leness** ᵊl nəs -nɪs **~ly** li
impractical ɪm ˈprækt ɪk ᵊl ˌɪm- **~ness** nəs nɪs **~ly** i
impracticality ɪm ˌprækt ɪ ˈkæl ət i ˌɪmˌ· ·ˈ·-, -ɪt i ‖ -ət̬ i
imprecation ˌɪmp rə ˈkeɪʃ ᵊn ˌɪmp ri-, ˌɪm pre- **~s** z
imprecatory ˈɪmp rə keɪt ər i ˈ·ri-, ˌ· ·ˈ·-; ɪm ˈprek ət‿ər i ‖ ˈɪmp rɪk ə tɔːr i ɪm ˈprek-, -toʊr i
imprecise ˌɪm prə ˈsaɪs ◂ -pri- **~ly** li
imprecision ˌɪm prə ˈsɪʒ ᵊn -pri-
impregnability ɪm ˌpreg nə ˈbɪl ət i ˌɪmˌ·ˈ·-, -ɪt i ‖ -ət̬ i
impregnab|le ɪm ˈpreg nəb |ᵊl ˌɪm- **~ly** li
impreg|nate *v* ˈɪm preg |neɪt ·ˈ· ‖ ɪm ˈpreg |neɪt ˈ· · · **~nated** neɪt ɪd -əd ‖ neɪt̬ əd **~nates** neɪts **~nating** neɪt ɪŋ ‖ neɪt̬ ɪŋ
impregnation ˌɪm preg ˈneɪʃ ᵊn ‖ ·ˌ·ˈ· · **~s** z
impresario ˌɪmp rə ˈsɑːr i əʊ ˌ·ri-, ˌɪm pre- ‖ -oʊ -ˈser-, -ˈsær- **~s** z
impress *n* ˈɪm pres **~es** ɪz əz
impress *v* ɪm ˈpres **~ed** t **~es** ɪz əz **~ing** ɪŋ
impression ɪm ˈpreʃ ᵊn **~s** z
impressionability ɪm ˌpreʃ ᵊn‿ə ˈbɪl ət i -ɪt i ‖ -ət̬ i
impressionable ɪm ˈpreʃ ᵊn‿əb ᵊl **~ness** nəs nɪs
impressionism ɪm ˈpreʃ ᵊn ˌɪz əm -ə ˌnɪz-
impressionist ɪm ˈpreʃ ᵊn‿ɪst §‿əst **~s** s
impressionistic ɪm ˌpreʃ ə ˈnɪst ɪk ◂ **~ally** ᵊl‿i
impressive ɪm ˈpres ɪv **~ly** li **~ness** nəs nɪs
imprest ˈɪm prest ·ˈ· **~s** s
imprimatur ˌɪm prɪ ˈmɑːt ə -prə-, -praɪ-, -ˈmeɪt- ‖ -ʊr -ᵊr **~s** z
im|print *v* ɪm |ˈprɪnt ˈ· · **~printed** ˈprɪnt ɪd -əd ‖ ˈprɪnt̬ əd **~printing** ˈprɪnt ɪŋ ‖ ˈprɪnt̬ ɪŋ **~prints** ˈprɪnts
imprint *n* ˈɪm prɪnt **~s** s
imprison ɪm ˈprɪz ᵊn **~ed** d **~ing** ɪŋ **~s** z
imprisonment ɪm ˈprɪz ᵊn mənt →-ˈ·əm-
improbabilit|y ɪm ˌprɒb ə ˈbɪl ət |i ˌ·ˌ· ·ˈ·-, -ɪt i ‖ -ˌprɑːb ə ˈbɪl ət̬ |i **~ies** iz
improbab|le ɪm ˈprɒb əb |ᵊl ˌɪm- ‖ -ˈprɑːb- **~leness** ᵊl nəs -nɪs **~ly** li
impromptu ɪm ˈprɒmpt juː -ˈprɒmp tʃuː ‖ -ˈprɑːmpt uː -juː **~s** z
improper ɪm ˈprɒp ə ˌɪm- ‖ -ˈprɑːp ᵊr **~ly** li **~ness** nəs nɪs
imˌproper ˈfraction, ˌimˌproper ˈfraction
impropriet|y ˌɪm prə ˈpraɪ‿ət |i ⚠ˌ·pə-, -ɪt i ‖ -ət̬ |i **~ies** iz
improv ˈɪm prɒv ‖ -prɑːv
improvability ɪm ˌpruːv ə ˈbɪl ət i -ɪt i ‖ -ət̬ i
improvable ɪm ˈpruːv əb ᵊl
improv|e ɪm ˈpruːv ˌɪm- **~ed** d **~es** z **~ing** ɪŋ
improvement ɪm ˈpruːv mənt **~s** s
improver ɪm ˈpruːv ə ‖ -ᵊr **~s** z
improvidence ɪm ˈprɒv ɪd ənᵗs ˌɪm-, -əd- ‖ -ˈprɑːv- -ə denᵗs
improvident ɪm ˈprɒv ɪd ənt ˌɪm-, -əd- ‖ -ˈprɑːv- -ə dent **~ly** li
improvisation ˌɪm prə vaɪ ˈzeɪʃ ᵊn -prə vɪ-, -prɒv ɪ- ‖ ɪm ˌprɑːv ə-, ˌ· ·ˈ·-, ˌɪm prəv- **~al** ‿əl **~s** z
improvisatory ˌɪm prə ˈvaɪz ət‿ər i ◂ -ˈvɪz-; -vaɪ ˈzeɪt ər i ‖ -ə tɔːr i -toʊr i
improvis|e ˈɪm prə vaɪz ‖ ˌ· ·ˈ· **~ed** d **~es** ɪz əz **~ing** ɪŋ

mprudence ɪm ˈpruːd ᵊnᵗs ˌɪm-
mprudent ɪm ˈpruːd ᵊnt ˌɪm- **~ly** li
mpudenc|e ˈɪmp jʊd ənᵗs ‖ -jəd- **~y** i
mpudent ˈɪmp jʊd ənt ‖ -jəd- **~ly** li
mpugn ɪm ˈpjuːn **~ed** d **~ing** ɪŋ **~s** z
mpuls|e ˈɪm pʌls **~es** ɪz əz
ˈimpulse ˌbuying
mpulsion ɪm ˈpʌl ʃᵊn **~s** z
mpulsive ɪm ˈpʌls ɪv **~ly** li **~ness** nəs nɪs
mpunit|y ɪm ˈpjuːn ət |i -ɪt- ‖ -əţ |i **~ies** iz
mpure ˌɪm ˈpjʊə ◂ ɪm-, -ˈpjɔː ‖ -ˈpjʊᵊr **~ly** li **~ness** nəs nɪs
impurit|y ɪm ˈpjʊər ət |i ˌɪm-, -ɪt- ‖ -ˈpjʊr əţ |i **~ies** iz
imputable ɪm ˈpjuːt əb ᵊl ‖ -ˈpjuːţ-
imputation ˌɪm pju ˈteɪʃ ᵊn ‖ -pjə- -pju- **~s** z
imputation ˌɪm pju ˈteɪʃ ᵊn ‖ -pjə- **~s** z
im|pute ɪm |ˈpjuːt **~puted** ˈpjuːt ɪd -əd ‖ ˈpjuːţ əd **~putes** ˈpjuːts **~puting** ˈpjuːt ɪŋ ‖ ˈpjuːţ ɪŋ
Imran ˈɪm ræn -rɑːn ‖ -rɑːn
Imus ˈaɪm əs
in ɪn *There is no separate weak form in RP. In some other accents, including GenAm, there is a weak form* §ən
in- ɪn *—but before* n *usually* ɪ*; before* k *or* g *assimilates to* ɪŋ*; generally stressed only (i) if meaning 'in' rather than 'not'; or (ii) for emphasis; or (iii) if the following syllable is unstressed:* inˈcredible, ˌinˈside, ˌinatˈtentive
-in ɪn *—but in scientific senses also* §ən — **tannin** ˈtæn ɪn §-ən ‖ -ən — **teach-in** ˈtiːtʃ ɪn
-in' *nonstandard form of* **-ing** ɪn ən *—but after* t *or* d *usually* ᵊn — **likin'** ˈlaɪk ɪn -ən — **eatin'** ˈiːt ᵊn -ɪn
Ina ˈiːn ə ˈaɪn ə
inability ˌɪn ə ˈbɪl ət i -ɪt i ‖ -əţ i
in absentia ˌɪn əb ˈsent i‿ə -ˈsenᵗʃ-, -i ɑː ‖ -ˈsenᵗʃ ə
inaccessibility ˌɪn ək ˌses ə ˈbɪl ət i ˌæk-, ˌɪk-, -ˌ·ɪ-, -ɪt i ‖ -əţ i
inaccessib|le ˌɪn ək ˈses əb |ᵊl ◂ ˌæk-, ˌɪk-, -ɪb ᵊl **~ly** li
inaccurac|y ɪn ˈæk jər əs |i ˌɪn-, -ˈjʊr-, -ɪs i **~ies** iz
inaccurate ɪn ˈæk jər ət ˌɪn-, -jʊr-, -ɪt **~ly** li **~ness** nəs nɪs
inaction ɪn ˈæk ʃᵊn ˌɪn-
inacti|vate ɪn ˈækt ɪ |veɪt -ə- **~vated** veɪt ɪd -əd ‖ veɪţ əd **~vates** veɪts **~vating** veɪt ɪŋ ‖ veɪţ ɪŋ
inactivation ɪn ˌækt ɪ ˈveɪʃ ᵊn ˌ·ˌ· ·ˈ·-, -əˈ·- **~s** z
inactive ɪn ˈækt ɪv ˌɪn- **~ly** li **~ness** nəs nɪs
inactivity ˌɪn æk ˈtɪv ət i -ɪt i ‖ -əţ i
inadequac|y ɪn ˈæd ɪk wəs |i ˌɪn-, -ˈ·ək- **~ies** iz
inadequate ɪn ˈæd ɪk wət ˌɪn-, -ək-, -wɪt **~ly** li
inadmissibility ˌɪn əd ˌmɪs ə ˈbɪl ət i ˌæd-, -ˌ·ɪ-, -ɪt i ‖ -əţ i
inadmissib|le ˌɪn əd ˈmɪs əb |ᵊl ◂ ˌæd-, -ɪb ᵊl **~ly** li
inadvertenc|e ˌɪn əd ˈvɜːt ᵊnᵗs §-æd- ‖ -ˈvɜːt- **~es** ɪz əz **~ies** iz **~y** i
inadvertent ˌɪn əd ˈvɜːt ᵊnt ◂ §-æd- ‖ -ˈvɜːt- **~ly** li
inadvisability ˌɪn əd ˌvaɪz ə ˈbɪl ət i §ˌæd-, -ɪt i ‖ -əţ i
inadvisable ˌɪn əd ˈvaɪz əb ᵊl ◂ §ˌæd-
inalienability ɪn ˌeɪl i‿ən ə ˈbɪl ət i ˌɪnˌ· · ·ˈ·-, -ɪt i ‖ -əţ i
inalienab|le ɪn ˈeɪl i‿ən əb |ᵊl ˌɪn- **~ly** li
inamorata ɪn ˌæm ə ˈrɑːt ə ˌ· · ·ˈ·- ‖ -ˈrɑːţ ə **~s** z
inamorato ɪn ˌæm ə ˈrɑːt əʊ ˌ· · ·ˈ·- ‖ -ˈrɑːţ oʊ **~s** z
inane ɪ ˈneɪn **~ly** li
inanimate ɪn ˈæn ɪm ət -əm- **~ly** li **~ness** nəs nɪs
inanition ˌɪn ə ˈnɪʃ ᵊn
inanit|y ɪ ˈnæn ət |i -ɪt- ‖ -əţ |i **~ies** iz
inapplicability ˌɪn ə ˌplɪk ə ˈbɪl ət i -ɪt i; ˌ·ˌæp lɪk-, ·ˌ·- ‖ ɪn ˌæp lɪk ə ˈbɪl əţ i ˌ·ˌ·
inapplicab|le ˌɪn ə ˈplɪk əb |ᵊl ₍ˌ₎ɪn ˈæp lɪk- ‖ ɪn ˈæp lɪk- ˌɪn- **~ly** li
inappropriate ˌɪn ə ˈprəʊp ri‿ət -ɪt ‖ -ˈproʊpr- **~ly** li **~ness** nəs nɪs
inapt ɪn ˈæpt ˌɪn- **~ly** li **~ness** nəs nɪs
inaptitude ɪn ˈæpt ɪ tjuːd ˌɪn-, -ə-, →-tʃuːd ‖ -ə tuːd -tjuːd
inarticulac|y ˌɪn ɑː ˈtɪk jʊl əs |i -ˈjəl- ‖ -ɑːr ˈtɪk jəl- **~ies** iz
inarticulate ˌɪn ɑː ˈtɪk jʊl ət ◂ -jəl ət, -ɪt ‖ -ɑːr ˈtɪk jəl- **~ly** li **~ness** nəs nɪs
inartistic ˌɪn ɑː ˈtɪst ɪk ◂ ‖ -ɑːr- **~ally** ᵊl‿i
inasmuch ˌɪn əz ˈmʌtʃ
inattention ˌɪn ə ˈtenᵗʃ ᵊn **~s** z
inattentive ˌɪn ə ˈtent ɪv ◂ ‖ -ˈtenţ ɪv ◂ **~ly** li **~ness** nəs nɪs
inaudibility ɪn ˌɔːd ə ˈbɪl ət i ˌɪnˌ· ·ˈ·-, -ɪˈ·-, -ɪt i ‖ -əţ i -ˌɑːd-
inaudib|le ɪn ˈɔːd əb |ᵊl ˌɪn-, -ɪb- ‖ -ˈɑːd- **~ly** li
inaugural ɪ ˈnɔːg jʊr əl -jər-, -ᵊr‿əl ‖ -jər əl ɪ ˈnɑːg-, -ᵊr‿əl **~s** z
inaugu|rate ɪ ˈnɔːg jə |reɪt -juᵊ-, -ə- ‖ ɪ ˈnɑːg- **~rated** reɪt ɪd -əd ‖ reɪţ əd **~rates** reɪts **~rating** reɪt ɪŋ ‖ reɪţ ɪŋ
inauguration ɪ ˌnɔːg jə ˈreɪʃ ᵊn ˌɪn ɔːg-, -juᵊ-, -ə- ‖ ɪ ˌnɑːg- **~s** z
inauspicious ˌɪn ɔː ˈspɪʃ əs ◂ -ɒ- ‖ -ɑː- **~ly** li **~ness** nəs nɪs
in-between ˌɪn bi ˈtwiːn ◂ →ˌɪm-, -bə- **~s** z
inboard ˈɪn bɔːd →ˈɪm- ‖ -bɔːrd -bourd
inborn ˌɪn ˈbɔːn ◂ →ˌɪm- ‖ -ˈbɔːrn
ˌinborn aˈbility
inbound ˈɪn baʊnd →ˈɪm-
in-bounds ˌɪn ˈbaʊndz
inbox ˈɪn bɒks →ˈɪm- ‖ -bɑːks **~es** ɪz əz
inbred ˌɪn ˈbred ◂ →ˌɪm-
ˌinbred ˈcourtesy
inbreeding ˈɪn ˌbriːd ɪŋ →ˈɪm-
in-built ˌɪn ˈbɪlt ◂ →ˌɪm-, ˈ·-
Inc ɪŋk *—see also* **Incorporated**
Inca ˈɪŋk ə **~s** z

incalculab|le ɪn ˈkælk jʊl əb |ᵊl ˌɪn-, →(ˌ)ɪŋ-, -ˈ·jəl ‖ -ˈkælk jəl- **~ly** li
incandesc|e ˌɪn kæn ˈdes →ˌɪŋ-, -kən- ‖ -kən- **~ed** t **~es** ɪz əz **~ing** ɪŋ
incandesc|ence ˌɪn kæn ˈdes |ᵊnᵗs →ˌɪŋ-, -kən- ‖ -kən- **~ent/ly** ᵊnt /li
incantation ˌɪn kæn ˈteɪʃ ᵊn →ˌɪŋ- **~s** z
incantatory ˌɪn kæn ˈteɪt ər i →ˌɪŋ-; ɪn ˈkænt ət‿ər i ‖ ɪn ˈkænt̬ ə tɔːr i -toʊr i
incapability ɪn ˌkeɪp ə ˈbɪl ət i →ɪŋ-, ˌ·ˌ· ·ˈ·-, -ɪt i ‖ -ət̬ i
incapab|le ɪn ˈkeɪp əb |ᵊl →ɪŋ-, ˌ·- **~leness** ᵊl nəs -nɪs **~ly** li
incapaci|tate ˌɪn kə ˈpæs ɪ |teɪt →ˌɪŋ-, -ˈ·ə- **~tated** teɪt ɪd -əd ‖ teɪt̬ əd **~tates** teɪts **~tating** teɪt ɪŋ ‖ teɪt̬ ɪŋ
incapacitation ˌɪn kə ˌpæs ɪ ˈteɪʃ ᵊn →ˌɪŋ-, -əˈ·-
incapacit|y ˌɪn kə ˈpæs ət |i →ˌɪŋ-, -ɪt i ‖ -ət̬ |i **~ies** iz
incapsul... —*see* **encapsul...**
in-car ˌɪn ˈkɑː ◂ →ˌɪŋ- ‖ -ˈkɑːr ◂
incarce|rate ɪn ˈkɑːs ə |reɪt →ɪŋ- ‖ -ˈkɑːrs- **~rated** reɪt ɪd -əd ‖ reɪt̬ əd **~rates** reɪts **~rating** reɪt ɪŋ ‖ reɪt̬ ɪŋ
incarceration ɪn ˌkɑːs ə ˈreɪʃ ᵊn →ɪŋ-, ˌɪn ˌ··ˈ·- ‖ -ˌkɑːrs- **~s** z
incarnadin|e ɪn ˈkɑːn ə daɪn →ɪŋ-, -diːn ‖ -ˈkɑːrn- **~ed** d **~es** z **~ing** ɪŋ
incarnate *adj* ɪn ˈkɑːn ət →ɪŋ-, -ɪt, -eɪt ‖ -ˈkɑːrn-
incarn|ate *v* ˈɪn kɑːn |eɪt →ˈɪŋ-, ·ˈ· · ‖ -kɑːrn- **~ated** eɪt ɪd -əd ‖ eɪt̬ əd **~ates** eɪts **~ating** eɪt ɪŋ ‖ eɪt̬ ɪŋ
incarnation ˌɪn kɑː ˈneɪʃ ᵊn →ˌɪŋ- ‖ -kɑːr- **~s** z
incautious ɪn ˈkɔːʃ əs ˌɪn-, →(ˌ)ɪŋ- ‖ -ˈkɑːʃ- **~ly** li **~ness** nəs nɪs
Ince ɪnᵗs
incendiarism ɪn ˈsend i‿ə ˌrɪz əm §-ˈsendʒ ə ˌrɪz əm
incendiar|y ɪn ˈsend i‿ər |i §ˈsendʒ ər i ‖ -ˈsend i er |i **~ies** iz
incens|e *v 'enrage'* ɪn ˈsenᵗs **~ed** t **~es** ɪz əz **~ing** ɪŋ
incense *n* ˈɪn senᵗs
incentive ɪn ˈsent ɪv ‖ -ˈsent̬ ɪv **~s** z
incentivis|e, incentiviz|e ɪn ˈsent ɪ vaɪz -ə- ‖ -ˈsent̬- **~ed** d **~es** ɪz əz **~ing** ɪŋ
inception ɪn ˈsep ʃᵊn **~s** z
inceptive ɪn ˈsept ɪv **~s** z
incertitude ɪn ˈsɜːt ɪ tjuːd ˌɪn-, -ə-, →-tʃuːd ‖ -ˈsɝːt̬ ə tuːd -tjuːd **~s** z
incessant ɪn ˈses ᵊnt **~ly** li **~ness** nəs nɪs
incest ˈɪn sest
incestuous ɪn ˈsest ju‿əs ‖ -ˈses tʃu- **~ly** li **~ness** nəs nɪs
inch ɪntʃ **inched** ɪntʃt **inches** ˈɪntʃ ɪz -əz **inching** ˈɪntʃ ɪŋ
Inchcape ˈɪntʃ keɪp (ˌ)ˈ·
inchoate *adj* ɪn ˈkəʊ ət →ɪŋ-, -ɪt, -eɪt; ˈɪŋ kəʊ- ‖ -ˈkoʊ- **~ly** li
inchoative ɪn ˈkəʊ ət ɪv →ɪŋ- ‖ -ˈkoʊ ət̬- **~s** z
Inchon ˌɪn ˈtʃɒn ◂ ‖ -ˈtʃɑːn ˈ· · -*Korean* Inchŏn [in tʃŽɔn]
inchworm ˈɪntʃ wɜːm ‖ -wɝːm **~s** z
incidenc|e ˈɪnᵗs ɪd ənᵗs -əd- ‖ -ə denᵗs **~es** ɪz əz
incident ˈɪnᵗs ɪd ənt -əd- ‖ -ə dent **~s** s
incidental ˌɪnᵗs ɪ ˈdent ᵊl ◂ -ə- ‖ -ˈdent̬ ᵊl **~ly** li **~s** z
ˌinciˌdental ˈcomments
incidential ˌɪnᵗs ɪ ˈdenᵗʃ ᵊl ◂ -ə-
incine|rate ɪn ˈsɪn ə |reɪt **~rated** reɪt ɪd -əd ‖ reɪt̬ əd **~rates** reɪts **~rating** reɪt ɪŋ ‖ reɪt̬ ɪŋ
incineration ɪn ˌsɪn ə ˈreɪʃ ᵊn **~s** z
incinerator ɪn ˈsɪn ə reɪt ə ‖ -reɪt̬ ᵊr **~s** z
incipienc|e ɪn ˈsɪp i‿ənᵗs **~y** i
incipient ɪn ˈsɪp i‿ənt **~ly** li
incis|e ɪn ˈsaɪz **~ed** d **~es** ɪz əz **~ing** ɪŋ
incision ɪn ˈsɪʒ ᵊn **~s** z
incisive ɪn ˈsaɪs ɪv §-ˈsaɪz- **~ly** li **~ness** nəs nɪs
incisor ɪn ˈsaɪz ə ‖ -ᵊr **~s** z
in|cite ɪn |ˈsaɪt **~cited** ˈsaɪt ɪd -əd ‖ ˈsaɪt̬ əd **~cites** ˈsaɪts **~citing** ˈsaɪt ɪŋ ‖ ˈsaɪt̬ ɪŋ
incitement ɪn ˈsaɪt mənt **~s** s
incivilit|y ˌɪn sə ˈvɪl ət |i ˌ·sɪ-, -ɪt i ‖ -ət̬ |i **~ies** iz
inclemency ɪn ˈklem ənᵗs i ˌɪn-, →(ˌ)ɪŋ-
inclement ɪn ˈklem ənt ˌɪn-, →(ˌ)ɪŋ-, ⚠ˈɪŋk ᵊl mənt **~ly** li
inclination ˌɪn klɪ ˈneɪʃ ᵊn →ˌɪŋ-, -klə- **~s** z
incline *n* ˈɪn klaɪn →ˈɪŋ- **~s** z
inclin|e *v* ɪn ˈklaɪn →ɪŋ- **~ed** d **~es** z **~ing** ɪŋ
inclinometer ˌɪn klɪ ˈnɒm ɪt ə →ˌɪŋ-, ˌ·klə- ‖ -ˈnɑːm ət̬ ᵊr **~s** z
inclos|e ɪn ˈkləʊz →ɪŋ- ‖ -ˈkloʊz **~ed** d **~es** ɪz əz **~ing** ɪŋ
inclosure ɪn ˈkləʊʒ ə →ɪŋ- ‖ -ˈkloʊʒ ᵊr **~s** z
includ|e ɪn ˈkluːd →ɪŋ- **~ed** ɪd əd **~es** z **~ing** ɪŋ
inclusion ɪn ˈkluːʒ ᵊn →ɪŋ- **~s** z
inclusive ɪn ˈkluːs ɪv →ɪŋ-, §-ˈkluːz- **~ly** li **~ness** nəs nɪs
incognito ˌɪn kɒg ˈniːt əʊ ◂ →ˌɪŋ-; ɪn ˈkɒg nɪ təʊ, →ɪŋ-, -nə- ‖ ˌɪn kɑːg ˈniːt oʊ ɪn ˈkɑːg nə toʊ
incogniz|ance ɪn ˈkɒg nɪz |ənᵗs §-ˈ·nəz- ‖ -ˈkɑːg- **~ant** ənt
incoherenc|e ˌɪn kəʊ ˈhɪər ənᵗs →ˌɪŋ- ‖ -koʊ ˈhɪr- -ˈher- **~y** i
incoherent ˌɪn kəʊ ˈhɪər ənt ◂ →ˌɪŋ- ‖ -koʊ ˈhɪr- -ˈher- **~ly** li **~ness** nəs nɪs
incombustib|le ˌɪn kəm ˈbʌst əb |ᵊl ◂ →ˌɪŋ-, §ˌ·kɒm-, -ɪb ᵊl **~ly** li
income ˈɪn kʌm →ˈɪŋ-, -kəm **~s** z
ˈincome tax
incomer ˈɪn ˌkʌm ə ‖ -ᵊr **~s** z
incoming ˈɪn ˌkʌm ɪŋ →ˈɪŋ-
incommensurab|le ˌɪn kə ˈmenᵗʃ ər‿əb |ᵊl →ˌɪŋ-, -ˈmenᵗs-, -ˈ·jər- **~ly** li
incommensurate ˌɪn kə ˈmenᵗʃ ər‿ət ◂ →ˌɪŋ-, -ˈmenᵗs-, -ˈ·jər-, ɪt **~ly** li **~ness** nəs nɪs
incommod|e ˌɪn kə ˈməʊd →ˌɪŋ- ‖ -ˈmoʊd **~ed** ɪd əd **~es** z **~ing** ɪŋ
incommodious ˌɪn kə ˈməʊd i‿əs ◂ →ɪŋ- ‖ -ˈmoʊd- **~ly** li **~ness** nəs nɪs

ncommunicab|le ˌɪn kə ˈmjuːn ɪk əb |^{ə}l ◂ →ˌɪŋ- **~ly** li

ncommunicado ˌɪn kə ˌmjuːn ɪ ˈkɑːd əʊ →ˌɪŋ-, -ˌ·ə- ‖ -oʊ

ncommunicative ˌɪn kə ˈmjuːn ɪ kət ɪv ◂ -ˈ·ə-, -keɪt ɪv ‖ -ə keɪt̬ ɪv -ɪk ət̬- **~ly** li **~ness** nəs nɪs

ncomparability ɪn ˌkɒmp ər‿ə ˈbɪl ət i →ɪŋ-, ˌ·ˌ·-, -ɪt i; ˌɪn kəm ˌpær ə-, →ˌɪŋ-, §-ˌpeər- ‖ ɪn ˌkɑːmp ər‿ə ˈbɪl ət̬ i ˌ·ˌ·-; ˌɪn kəm ˌpær-, -ˌper-

INCOMPARABLE

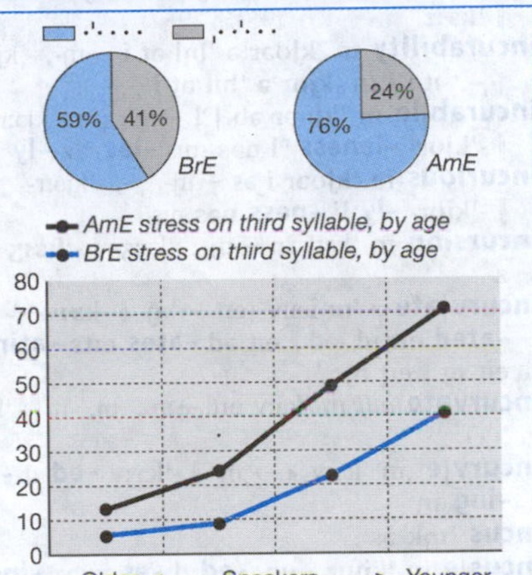

incomparab|le ɪn ˈkɒmp ər‿əb |^{ə}l →ɪŋ-, ˌ·-; ˌɪn kəm ˈpær-, →ˌɪŋ-, §-kɒm-, §-ˈpeər- ‖ ɪn ˈkɑːmp ər‿əb |^{ə}l ˌɪn-; ˌɪn kəm ˈper-, -ˈpær- — *Preference polls, AmE: ·ˈ· · · · 76%, ˌ· ·ˈ· · · 24%; BrE: ·ˈ· · · · 59%, ˌ· ·ˈ· · · 41%.* **~leness** ^{ə}l nəs -nɪs **~ly** li

incompatibilit|y ˌɪn kəm ˌpæt ə ˈbɪl ət |i →ˌɪŋ-, §ˌ·kɒm-, -ˌ·ɪ-, -ɪt i ‖ -ˌpæt̬ ə ˈbɪl ət̬ |i **~ies** iz

incompatib|le ˌɪn kəm ˈpæt əb |^{ə}l ◂ →ˌɪŋ-, §ˌ·kɒm-, -ɪb ^{ə}l ‖ -ˈpæt̬- **~les** ^{ə}lz **~ly** li

incompetenc|e ɪn ˈkɒmp ɪt ən^{t}s →ɪŋ-, ˌ·-, -ət- ‖ -ˈkɑːmp ət ^{ə}n^{t}s **~y** i

incompetent ɪn ˈkɒmp ɪt ənt →ɪŋ-, ˌ·-, -ət- ‖ -ˈkɑːmp ət ^{ə}nt **~ly** li **~s** s

incomplete ˌɪn kəm ˈpliːt ◂ →ˌɪŋ-, §-kɒm- **~ly** li **~ness** nəs nɪs

incomprehensibility ɪn ˌkɒmp rɪ ˌhen^{t}s ə ˈbɪl ət i →ɪŋ-, ˌ·ˌ·-, -rəˌ·- , -ˌ·ɪ-, -ɪt i ‖ ɪn ˌkɑːmp rɪ ˌhen^{t}s ə ˈbɪl ət̬ i ˌ·ˌ·-

incomprehensib|le ɪn ˌkɒmp rɪ ˈhen^{t}s əb |^{ə}l ◂ →ɪŋ-, ˌ·ˌ·-, -rəˈ·-, -ɪb ^{ə}l ‖ ɪn ˌkɑːm- ˌ·ˌ·- **~ly** li

incomprehension ɪn ˌkɒmp rɪ ˈhen^{t}ʃ ^{ə}n →ɪŋ-, ˌ·ˌ·-, -rəˈ·- ‖ ɪn ˌkɑːmp- ˌ·ˌ·-

inconceivability ˌɪn kən ˌsiːv ə ˈbɪl ət i →ˌɪŋ-, §ˌ·kɒn-, -ɪt i ‖ -ət̬ i

inconceivab|le ˌɪn kən ˈsiːv əb |^{ə}l ◂ →ˌɪŋ-, §ˌ·kɒn- **~leness** ^{ə}l nəs -nɪs **~ly** li

inconclusive ˌɪn kən ˈkluːs ɪv ◂ →ˌɪŋ-, →-kəŋ-, §-kɒn-, §-ˈkluːz- **~ly** li **~ness** nəs nɪs

incongruit|y ˌɪn kən ˈgruː‿ət |i →ˌɪŋ-, →ˌ·kəŋ-, ˌ·kɒn-, →ˌ·kɒŋ-, ɪt i ‖ -ət̬ |i **~ies** iz

incongruous ɪn ˈkɒŋ gru‿əs →ɪŋ- ‖ -ˈkɑːŋ- **~ly** li **~ness** nəs nɪs

inconsequence ɪn ˈkɒn^{t}s ɪk wən^{t}s →ɪŋ-, ˌ·-, -ək-; §-ə kwen^{t}s ‖ -ˈkɑːn^{t}s-

inconsequent ɪn ˈkɒn^{t}s ɪk wənt →ɪŋ-, ˌɪn-, -ək-; §-ə kwent ‖ -ˈkɑːn^{t}s- **~ly** li

inconsequential ɪn ˌkɒn^{t}s ɪ ˈkwen^{t}ʃ ^{ə}l ◂ →ɪŋ-, ˌɪnˌ·-, -əˈ·- ‖ -ˌkɑːn^{t}s- **~ly** i **~ness** nəs nɪs

inconsequentiality ɪn ˌkɒn^{t}s ɪ ˌkwen^{t}ʃ i ˈæl ət i →ɪŋ-, ˌ·ˌ·-, -əˌ·-, -ɪt i ‖ -ˌkɑːn^{t}s i ˌkwen^{t}ʃ i ˈæl ət̬ i

inconsiderab|le ˌɪn kən ˈsɪd‿ər əb |^{ə}l ◂ →ˌɪŋ-, §ˌ·kɒn- **~ly** li

inconsiderate ˌɪn kən ˈsɪd‿ər ət ◂ →ˌɪŋ-, §ˌ·kɒn-, -ɪt **~ly** li **~ness** nəs nɪs

inconsideration ˌɪn kən ˌsɪd ə ˈreɪʃ ^{ə}n →ˌɪŋ-, §ˌ·kɒn-

inconsistenc|y ˌɪn kən ˈsɪst ən^{t}s |i →ˌɪŋ-, §ˌ·kɒn- **~ies** iz

inconsistent ˌɪn kən ˈsɪst ənt ◂ →ˌɪŋ-, §-kɒn- **~ly** li

inconsolab|le ˌɪn kən ˈsəʊl əb |^{ə}l ◂ →ˌɪŋ-, §ˌ·kɒn- ‖ -ˈsoʊl- **~leness** ^{ə}l nəs -nɪs **~ly** li

inconspicuous ˌɪn kən ˈspɪk ju‿əs →ˌɪŋ-, §ˌ·kɒn- **~ly** li **~ness** nəs nɪs

inconstanc|y ɪn ˈkɒn^{t}st ən^{t}s |i →ɪŋ-, ˌ·- ‖ -ˈkɑːn^{t}st- **~ies** iz

inconstant ɪn ˈkɒn^{t}st ənt →ɪŋ-, ˌ·- ‖ -ˈkɑːn^{t}st- **~ly** li

incontestability ˌɪn kən ˌtest ə ˈbɪl ət i →ˌɪŋ-, §ˌ·kɒn-, -ɪt i ‖ -ət̬ i

incontestab|le ˌɪn kən ˈtest əb |^{ə}l ◂ →ˌɪŋ-, §ˌ·kɒn- **~ly** li

incontinence ɪn ˈkɒnt ɪn ən^{t}s →ɪŋ-, ˌ·-, -ən‿ ‖ -ˈkɑːnt ^{ə}n‿ən^{t}s

incontinent ɪn ˈkɒnt ɪn ənt →ɪŋ-, ˌ·-, -ən‿ ‖ -ˈkɑːnt ^{ə}n‿ənt **~ly** li

incontrovertib|le ˌɪn ˌkɒntr ə ˈvɜːt əb |^{ə}l →ˌɪŋ-, ·ˌ·- ‖ ˌɪn ˌkɑːntr ə ˈvɝːt̬- **~leness** ^{ə}l nəs -nɪs **~ly** li

inconvenienc|e ˌɪn kən ˈviːn i‿ən^{t}s →ˌɪŋ-, §ˌ·kɒn- **~ed** t **~es** ɪz əz **~ing** ɪŋ

inconvenient ˌɪn kən ˈviːn i‿ənt ◂ →ˌɪŋ-, §ˌ·kɒn- **~ly** li

incorpo|rate *v* ɪn ˈkɔːp ə |reɪt →ɪŋ- ‖ -ˈkɔːrp- **~rated** reɪt ɪd -əd ‖ reɪt̬ əd **~rates** reɪts **~rating** reɪt ɪŋ ‖ reɪt̬ ɪŋ

incorporate *adj* ɪn ˈkɔːp ər‿ət →ɪŋ-, -ɪt, -ə reɪt ‖ -ˈkɔːrp-

incorporation ɪn ˌkɔːp ə ˈreɪʃ ^{ə}n →ɪŋ- ‖ -ˌkɔːrp- **~s** z

incorporeal ˌɪn kɔː ˈpɔːr i‿əl ◂ →ˌɪŋ- ‖ ˌɪn kɔːr- -ˈpoʊr- **~ly** i

incorrect ˌɪn kə ˈrekt ◂ →ˌɪŋ- **~ly** li **~ness** nəs nɪs

incorrigibility ɪn ˌkɒr ɪdʒ ə ˈbɪl ət i →ɪŋ-, ˌ·ˌ·-, -ədʒ ə-, -ɪt i ‖ ɪn ˌkɔːr ədʒ ə ˈbɪl ət̬ i ·ˌkɑːr-, ˌ·ˌ·-

incorrigib|le ɪn ˈkɒr ɪdʒ əb |^{ə}l →ɪŋ-, ˌ·-, -ˈ·ədʒ- ‖ -ˈkɔːr- -ˈkɑːr- **~les** ^{ə}lz **~ly** li

incorrupt ˌɪn kə ˈrʌpt →ˌɪŋ- **~ly** li **~ness** nəs nɪs

incorruptibility ˌɪn kə ˌrʌpt ə ˈbɪl ət i →ˌɪŋ-, -ˌ·ɪ-, -ɪt i ‖ -ət̬ i

incorruptib|le ˌɪn kə ˈrʌpt əb |ᵊl ◂ →ˌɪŋ-, -ɪb ᵊl **~les** ᵊlz **~ly** li

incorruption ˌɪn kə ˈrʌp ʃᵊn →ˌɪŋ-

INCREASE (noun)

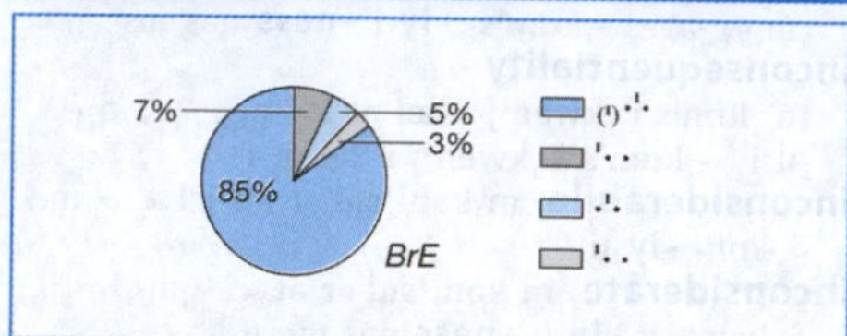

increas|e *n* ˈɪŋ kriːs ˈɪn-, ₍ˌ₎·ˈ· —*The stress distinction between verb ·ˈ· and noun ˈ·· is not always made consistently. Nevertheless, in a BrE preference poll 85% preferred to make this distinction (as against 7% preferring ˈ·· for both verb and noun, 5% ·ˈ· for both, and 3% ˈ·· for the verb, ·ˈ· for the noun).* **~es** ɪz əz

increas|e *v* ɪn ˈkriːs →ɪŋ-, ˌ·-, ˈ·· *(not* -ˈkriːz*)* **~ed** t **~es** ɪz əz **~ing/ly** ɪŋ /li

incredibility ɪn ˌkred ə ˈbɪl ət i →ɪŋ-, ˌ·ˌ·-, -ɪˈ·-, -ɪt i ‖ -ət̬ i

incredib|le ɪn ˈkred əb |ᵊl →ɪŋ-, ˌ·-, -ɪb- **~ly** li

incredulity ˌɪn krə ˈdjuːl ət i →ˌɪŋ-, ˌ·krɪ-, ˌ·kre-, →-ˈdʒuːl-, -ɪt i ‖ -ˈduːl ət̬ i -ˈdjuːl-

incredulous ɪn ˈkred jʊl əs →ɪŋ-, -jəl- ‖ -ˈkredʒ əl əs **~ly** li **~ness** nəs nɪs

incre|ment *v* ˈɪŋ krɪ |ment ˈɪn-, -krə- —*See note at* -ment **~mented** ment ɪd -əd ‖ ment̬ əd **~menting** ment ɪŋ ‖ ment̬ ɪŋ **~ments** men*t*s

increment *n* ˈɪŋ krɪ mənt ˈɪn-, -krə- **~s** s

incremental ˌɪŋ krɪ ˈment ᵊl ◂ ˌɪn-, -krə- ‖ -ˈment̬ ᵊl ◂ **~ly** i

incrimi|nate ɪn ˈkrɪm ɪ |neɪt →ɪŋ-, -ə- **~nated** neɪt ɪd -əd ‖ neɪt̬ əd **~nates** neɪts **~nating** neɪt ɪŋ ‖ neɪt̬ ɪŋ

incrimination ɪn ˌkrɪm ɪ ˈneɪʃ ᵊn →ɪŋ-, -ə-

incriminatory ɪn ˈkrɪm ɪn ət‿ər i →ɪŋ-, -ˈ·ən-; -ˈkrɪm ɪ neɪt ər i, -ˈ·ə-, ˌ·ˌ· ·ˈ··· ‖ -ə tɔːr i -toʊr i

in-crowd ˈɪn kraʊd

incrust ɪn ˈkrʌst →ɪŋ- **~ed** ɪd əd **~ing** ɪŋ **~s** s

incrustation ˌɪn krʌ ˈsteɪʃ ᵊn →ˌɪŋ- **~s** z

incu|bate ˈɪŋ kju |beɪt ˈɪn- ‖ -kjə- **~bated** beɪt ɪd -əd ‖ beɪt̬ əd **~bates** beɪts **~bating** beɪt ɪŋ ‖ beɪt̬ ɪŋ

incubation ˌɪŋ kju ˈbeɪʃ ᵊn ˌɪn- ‖ -kjə- **~s** z

incubator ˈɪŋ kju beɪt ə ˈɪn- ‖ -kjə beɪt̬ ᵊr **~s** z

in|cubus ˈɪŋ |kjʊb əs ˈɪn- **~cubi** kju baɪ **~cubuses** kjʊb əs ɪz -əz

inculc|ate ˈɪn kʌlk |eɪt →ˈɪŋ-, -kᵊl k|eɪt; ɪn ˈkʌlk-, →ɪŋ- ‖ ɪn ˈkʌlk |eɪt ˈ··· **~ated** eɪt ɪd -əd ‖ eɪt̬ əd **~ates** eɪts **~ating** eɪt ɪŋ ‖ eɪt̬ ɪŋ

inculcation ˌɪn kʌl ˈkeɪʃ ᵊn →ˌɪŋ-, -kᵊl- **~s** z

inculp|ate ˈɪn kʌlp |eɪt →ˈɪŋ-; ·ˈ·· ‖ ɪn ˈkʌlp |eɪt ˈ··· **~ated** eɪt ɪd -əd ‖ eɪt̬ əd **~ates** eɪts **~ating** eɪt ɪŋ ‖ eɪt̬ ɪŋ

inculpation ˌɪn kʌl ˈpeɪʃ ᵊn →ˌɪŋ- **~s** z

inculpatory ɪn ˈkʌlp ət‿ər i →ɪŋ-; ˈɪn kʌlp eɪt ər i, →ˈɪŋ-; ˌɪn kʌl ˈpeɪt-, →ˌɪŋ- ‖ -ˈkʌlp ə tɔːr i -toʊr i

incumbenc|y ɪn ˈkʌm bənᵗs |i →ɪŋ- **~ies** iz

incumbent ɪn ˈkʌm bənt →ɪŋ- **~ly** li **~s** s

incunabul|um ˌɪn kju ˈnæb jʊl |əm →ˌɪŋ- **~a** ə **~ar** ə ‖ ᵊr

in|cur ɪn |ˈkɜː →ɪŋ- ‖ -|ˈkɝː **~curred** ˈkɜːd ‖ ˈkɝːd **~curring** ˈkɜːr ɪŋ ‖ ˈkɝː ɪŋ **~curs** ˈkɜːz ‖ ˈkɝːz

incurability ɪn ˌkjʊər ə ˈbɪl ət i →ɪŋ-, -ˌkjɔːr-, ˌ·ˌ·-, -ɪt i ‖ ɪn ˌkjʊr ə ˈbɪl ət̬ i ˌ·ˌ·-

incurab|le ɪn ˈkjʊər əb |ᵊl →ɪŋ-, ˌ·-, -ˈkjɔːr- ‖ -ˈkjʊr- **~leness** ᵊl nəs -nɪs **~les** ᵊlz **~ly** li

incurious ɪn ˈkjʊər i‿əs →ɪŋ-, ˌ·-, -ˈkjɔːr- ‖ -ˈkjʊr- **~ly** li **~ness** nəs nɪs

incursion ɪn ˈkɜːʃ ᵊn →ɪŋ-, -ˈkɜːʒ- ‖ -ˈkɝːʒ ᵊn **~s** z

incurv|ate *v* ˈɪn kɜːv |eɪt →ˈɪŋ- ‖ -kɝːv- ·ˈ·· **~ated** eɪt ɪd -əd ‖ eɪt̬ əd **~ates** eɪts **~ating** eɪt ɪŋ ‖ eɪt̬ ɪŋ

incurvate *adj* ɪn ˈkɜːv eɪt →ɪŋ-, -ət, -ɪt ‖ -ˈkɝːv- ˈ·ˌ··

incurv|e ˌɪn ˈkɜːv ◂ →ˌɪŋ- ‖ -ˈkɝːv **~ed** d **~es** z **~ing** ɪŋ

incus ˈɪŋk əs

incus|e ɪn ˈkjuːz →ɪŋ- **~ed** d **~es** ɪz əz **~ing** ɪŋ

Ind ɪnd aɪnd

ˌ**Ind ˈCoope** *tdmk* kuːp

indaba ɪn ˈdɑːb ə —*Zulu* [i ˈndaː ɓa] **~s** z

indebted ɪn ˈdet ɪd -əd ‖ -ˈdet̬ əd **~ness** nəs nɪs

indecenc|y ɪn ˈdiːs ᵊnᵗs |i ˌɪn- **~ies** iz

indecent ɪn ˈdiːs ᵊnt ˌɪn- **~ly** li

inˌdecent asˈsault, ˌ·ˌ·· ·ˈ·; **inˌdecent exˈposure**

indecipherability ˌɪn di ˌsaɪf ər‿ə ˈbɪl ət i ˌ·də-, -ɪt i ‖ -ət̬ i

indecipherab|le ˌɪn di ˈsaɪf ər‿əb |ᵊl ◂ ˌ·də- **~leness** ᵊl nəs -nɪs **~ly** li

indecision ˌɪn di ˈsɪʒ ᵊn -də-, -ˈzɪʃ-

indecisive ˌɪn di ˈsaɪs ɪv ◂ -də-, -ˈsaɪz- **~ly** li **~ness** nəs nɪs

indeclinab|le ˌɪn di ˈklaɪn əb |ᵊl ◂ ˌ·də- **~leness** ᵊl nəs -nɪs **~ly** li

indecorous ɪn ˈdek ər əs ˌɪn-, §ˌɪn dɪ ˈkɔːr əs ◂, -də- ‖ ˌɪn dɪ ˈkɔːr əs, -ˈkoʊr- **~ly** li **~ness** nəs nɪs

indecorum ˌɪn di ˈkɔːr əm -də- ‖ -ˈkoʊr-

indeed ɪn ˈdiːd ˌɪn-

indefatigab|le ˌɪn di ˈfæt ɪg əb |ᵊl ◂ ˌ·də- ‖ -ˈfæt̬- **~leness** ᵊl nəs -nɪs **~ly** li

indefeasibility ˌɪn di ˌfiːz ə ˈbɪl ət i ˌ·də- ‖ -ət̬ i

indefeasib|le ˌɪn di ˈfiːz əb |ᵊl ◂ ˌ·də-, -ɪb · **~ly** li

indefensib|le ˌɪn di ˈfenᵗs əb |ᵊl ◂ ˌ·də-, -ɪb · **~leness** ᵊl nəs -nɪs **~ly** li

ndefinab|le ˌɪn di ˈfaɪn əb |əl ◂ ˌ·də- **~leness** əl nəs -nɪs **~ly** li

ndefinite ɪn ˈdef ən‿ət ˌɪn-, -ɪn-, -ɪt **~ly** li **~ness** nəs nɪs

inˌdefinite ˈarticle, ˌ·ˌ··· ˈ··

ndelib|le ɪn ˈdel əb |əl ˌɪn-, -ɪb- **~leness** əl nəs -nɪs **~ly** li

ndelicac|y ɪn ˈdel ɪk əs |i ˌɪn-, -ˈək- **~ies** iz

ndelicate ɪn ˈdel ɪk ət ˌɪn-, -ək-, -ɪt **~ly** li **~ness** nəs nɪs

ndemnification ɪn ˌdem nɪf ɪ ˈkeɪʃ ən -ˌ·nəf-, §-əˈ-- **~s** z

ndemni|fy ɪn ˈdem nɪ |faɪ -nə- **~fied** faɪd **~fier/s** faɪ‿ə/z ‖ faɪ‿ər/z **~fies** faɪz **~fying** faɪ ɪŋ

ndemnit|y ɪn ˈdem nət |i -nɪt- ‖ -nəţ |i **~ies** iz

ndene ˈɪnd iːn

ndent *n* ˈɪn dent ·ˈ· **~s** s

n|dent *v* ɪn |ˈdent ˌ·ˈ·◂ **~dented** ˈdent ɪd -əd ‖ ˈdenţ əd **~denting** ˈdent ɪŋ ‖ ˈdenţ ɪŋ **~dents** ˈdents

ndentation ˌɪn den ˈteɪʃ ən **~s** z

ndent|ure *n, v* ɪn ˈdentʃ |ə ‖ -|ər **~ured** əd ‖ ərd **~ures** əz ‖ ərz **~uring** ər ɪŋ

ndependence ˌɪn di ˈpend ənts ◂ -də- **ˌIndeˈpendence Day; ˌIndeˌpendence ˈHall**

ndependent, I~ ˌɪn di ˈpend ənt ◂ -də- **~ly** li **~s** s **ˌindeˌpendent ˈclause**

n-depth ˌɪn ˈdepθ ◂

ndescribability ˌɪn di ˌskraɪb ə ˈbɪl ət i ˌ·də-, -ɪt i ‖ -əţ i

ndescribab|le ˌɪn di ˈskraɪb əb |əl ◂ ˌ·də- **~leness** əl nəs -nɪs **~ly** li

ndesit *tdmk* ˈɪnd ɪ sɪt -ə-, -e-

ndestructibility ˌɪn di ˌstrʌkt ə ˈbɪl ət i ˌ·də-, -ˌ·ɪ-, -ɪt i ‖ -əţ i

indestructib|le ˌɪn di ˈstrʌkt əb |əl ◂ ˌ·də-, -ɪb əl **~leness** əl nəs -nɪs **~ly** li

indeterminab|le ˌɪn di ˈtɜːm ɪn əb |əl ◂ ˌ·də-, -ən‿əb- ‖ -ˈtɝːm- **~ly** li

indeterminac|y ˌɪn di ˈtɜːm ɪn əs |i ˌ·də-, -ən‿əs- ‖ -ˈtɝːm- **~ies** iz

indeterminate ˌɪn di ˈtɜːm ɪn ət ◂ ˌ·də-, -ən‿, -ɪt ‖ -ˈtɝːm- **~ly** li **~ness** nəs nɪs

index *n, v* ˈɪnd eks **~ed** t **~es** ɪz əz **~ing** ɪŋ **indices** ˈɪnd ɪ siːz -ə- **ˈindex ˌfinger; ˈindex ˌnumber**

indexation ˌɪnd ek ˈseɪʃ ən **~s** z

indexer ˈɪnd eks ə ‖ -ər **~s** z

indexical ɪn ˈdeks ɪk əl **~ly** ‿i

index-|linked ˌɪnd eks |ˈlɪŋkt ◂ **~linking** ˈlɪŋk ɪŋ

India, india ˈɪnd i‿ə **ˌindia ˈrubber◂, ˌindia-ˌrubber ˈball**

Indian ˈɪnd i‿ən **~s** z **ˌIndian ˈcorn; ˌIndian ˈink; ˌIndian ˈOcean; ˌIndian ˈsummer**

Indiana ˌɪnd i ˈæn ə -ˈɑːn-

Indianan ˌɪnd i ˈæn ən ◂ -ˈɑːn- **~s** z

Indianapolis ˌɪnd i‿ə ˈnæp əl ɪs §-əs

Indianian ˌɪnd i ˈæn i‿ən ◂ -ˈɑːn- **~s** z

Indic ˈɪnd ɪk

indi|cate ˈɪnd ɪ |keɪt -ə- **~cated** keɪt ɪd -əd ‖ keɪţ əd **~cates** keɪts **~cating** keɪt ɪŋ ‖ keɪţ ɪŋ

indication ˌɪn dɪ ˈkeɪʃ ən -də- **~s** z

indicative ɪn ˈdɪk ət ɪv ‖ -əţ ɪv **~ly** li **~s** z

indicator ˈɪnd ɪ keɪt ə ˈ·ə- ‖ -keɪţ ər **~s** z **ˈindicator board**

indices ˈɪnd ɪ siːz -ə-

in|dict ɪn |ˈdaɪt *(! = indite)* **~dicted** ˈdaɪt ɪd -əd ‖ ˈdaɪţ əd **~dicting** ˈdaɪt ɪŋ ‖ ˈdaɪţ ɪŋ **~dicts** ˈdaɪts

indictable ɪn ˈdaɪt əb əl ‖ -ˈdaɪţ-

indiction ɪn ˈdɪk ʃən **~s** z

indictment ɪn ˈdaɪt mənt **~s** s

indie ˈɪnd i **~s** z

Indies ˈɪnd iz

indifference ɪn ˈdɪf rənts -ˈdɪf ər ənts

indifferent ɪn ˈdɪf rənt -ˈdɪf ər ənt **~ly** li

indigence ˈɪnd ɪdʒ ənts

indigene ˈɪnd ɪ dʒiːn §-ə- **~s** z

indigenous ɪn ˈdɪdʒ ən‿əs -ɪn- **~ly** li **~ness** nəs nɪs

indigent ˈɪnd ɪdʒ ənt **~ly** li **~s** s

indigestibility ˌɪn dɪ ˌdʒest ə ˈbɪl ət i ˌ·də-, ˌ·daɪ-, -ˌ·ɪ-, -ɪt i ‖ -əţ i

indigestib|le ˌɪn dɪ ˈdʒest əb |əl ◂ ˌ·də-, ˌ·daɪ-, -ɪb əl **~ly** li

indigestion ˌɪn dɪ ˈdʒes tʃən -də-, →-ˈdʒeʃ-

indignant ɪn ˈdɪg nənt **~ly** li

indignation ˌɪn dɪg ˈneɪʃ ən

indignit|y ɪn ˈdɪg nət |i -nɪt- ‖ -nəţ |i **~ies** iz

indigo ˈɪnd ɪ gəʊ ‖ -goʊ **~es, ~s** z

Indio ˈɪnd i əʊ ‖ -oʊ

Indira ˈɪnd ɪr ə -ər-; ɪn ˈdɪər ə ‖ -ˈdɪr-

indirect ˌɪn də ˈrekt ◂ -dɪ-, -daɪə- **~ly** li **~ness** nəs nɪs **ˌindiˌrect ˈobject; ˌindiˌrect ˈspeech**

indirection ˌɪn də ˈrek ʃən -dɪ-, -daɪə-

indiscernib|le ˌɪn dɪ ˈsɜːn əb |əl ◂ ˌ·də-, -ˈzɜːn-, -ɪb əl ‖ -ˈsɝːn- -ˈzɝːn- **~ly** li

indiscipline ɪn ˈdɪs əp lɪn ˌɪn-, -ˈɪp-, -lən; §ˌɪn dɪ ˈsɪp-

indiscreet ˌɪn dɪ ˈskriːt ◂ -də- **~ly** li **~ness** nəs nɪs

indiscretion ˌɪn dɪ ˈskreʃ ən -də- **~s** z

indiscriminate ˌɪn dɪ ˈskrɪm ɪn ət ◂ ˌ·də-, -ˈ·ən‿, -ɪt **~ly** li **~ness** nəs nɪs

indispensability ˌɪn dɪ ˌspents ə ˈbɪl ət i ˌ·də-, -ɪt i ‖ -əţ i

indispensab|le ˌɪn dɪ ˈspents əb |əl ◂ ˌ·də- **~les** əlz **~ly** li

indispose ˌɪn dɪ ˈspəʊz -də- ‖ -ˈspoʊz **~ed** d ◂

indisposition ˌɪn ˌdɪsp ə ˈzɪʃ ən ˌ·ˌ·ˈ·· **~s** z

indisputability ˌɪn dɪ ˌspjuːt ə ˈbɪl ət i -ɪt i; ɪn ˌdɪs pjuːt-, ˌ·ˌ··- ‖ -ˌspjuːţ ə ˈbɪl əţ i

indisputab|le ˌɪn dɪ ˈspjuːt əb |əl ◂ ˌ·də-; (ˌ)ɪn ˈdɪs pjuːt- ‖ -ˈspjuːţ- **~ly** li

indissolubility ˌɪn dɪ ˌsɒl ju ˈbɪl ət i ˌ·də-, -ˌjə-, -ɪt i ‖ -ˌsɑːl jə ˈbɪl əţ i

indissolub|le ˌɪn dɪ ˈsɒl jʊb |əl ◂ ˌ·də-, -jəb əl ‖ -ˈsɑːl jəb |əl **~leness** əl nəs -nɪs **~ly** li

I

indistinct ˌɪn dɪ ˈstɪŋkt ◂ -də- **~ly** li **~ness** nəs nɪs
indistinguishab|le ˌɪn dɪ ˈstɪŋ gwɪʃ əb |ᵊl ◂ ˌ·də- **~ly** li
in|dite ɪn |ˈdaɪt **~dited** ˈdaɪt ɪd -əd ‖ ˈdaɪţ əd **~dites** ˈdaɪts **~diting** ˈdaɪt ɪŋ ‖ ˈdaɪţ ɪŋ
indium ˈɪnd i‿əm
individual ˌɪnd ɪ ˈvɪdʒ u‿əl◂ ˌ·ə-, -ˈvɪd ju‿ **~ly** i **~s** z
individualis... —see **individualiz...**
individualism ˌɪnd ɪ ˈvɪdʒ u‿ə ˌlɪz əm ˌ·ə-, -ˈvɪd ju‿; -ˈvɪdʒ u ˌlɪz əm **~s** z
individualist ˌɪnd ɪ ˈvɪdʒ u‿əl ɪst ˌ·ə-, -ˈvɪd ju‿ §-əst; -ˈvɪdʒ ʊl ɪst, -əst **~s** s
individualistic ˌɪnd ɪ ˌvɪdʒ u‿ə ˈlɪst ɪk ˌ·ə-, -ˌvɪd ju‿ -ˌvɪdʒ uˈ·- **~ally** ᵊl‿i
individualit|y ˌɪnd ɪ ˌvɪdʒ u ˈæl ət |i ˌ·ə-, -ˌvɪd ju-, -ɪt i ‖ -əţ |i **~ies** iz
individualization ˌɪnd ɪ ˌvɪdʒ u‿əl aɪ ˈzeɪʃ ᵊn ˌ·ə-, -ˌvɪd ju-, -ɪˈ·- ‖ -əˈ·- **~s** z
individualiz|e ˌɪnd ɪ ˈvɪdʒ u‿ə laɪz ˌ·ə-, -ˈvɪd ju‿; -ˈvɪdʒ u laɪz **~ed** d **~es** ɪz əz **~ing** ɪŋ
individu|ate ˌɪnd ɪ ˈvɪdʒ u |eɪt ˌ·ə-, -ˈvɪd ju- **~ated** eɪt ɪd -əd ‖ eɪţ əd **~ates** eɪts **~ating** eɪt ɪŋ ‖ eɪţ ɪŋ
individuation ˌɪnd ɪ ˌvɪdʒ u ˈeɪʃ ᵊn ˌ·ə-, ˌvɪd ju- **~s** z
indivisibility ˌɪn dɪ ˌvɪz ə ˈbɪl ət i ˌ·də-, ˌ·ɪ-, -ɪt i ‖ -əţ i
indivisib|le ˌɪn dɪ ˈvɪz əb |ᵊl ◂ ˌ·də-, -ɪb ᵊl **~leness** ᵊl nəs -nɪs **~ly** li
Indo- |ɪnd əʊ ‖ -oʊ — **Indo-Pacific** ˌɪnd əʊ pə ˈsɪf ɪk ◂ ‖ ˌ·oʊ-
Indo-Aryan ˌɪnd əʊ ˈeər i‿ən ◂ ‖ -oʊ ˈer- -ˈær-
Indo-China ˌɪnd əʊ ˈtʃaɪn ə ◂ ‖ -oʊ-
Indo-Chinese ˌɪnd əʊ ˌtʃaɪ ˈniːz ‖ -oʊ-
indoctri|nate ɪn ˈdɒk trɪ |neɪt -trə- ‖ -ˈdɑːk- **~nated** neɪt ɪd -əd ‖ neɪţ əd **~nates** neɪts **~nating** neɪt ɪŋ ‖ neɪţ ɪŋ
indoctrination ɪn ˌdɒk trɪ ˈneɪʃ ᵊn ˌ·ˌ·-, -trəˈ·- ‖ -ˌdɑːk- **~s** z
Indo-European ˌɪnd əʊ ˌjʊər ə ˈpiː ən ◂ -ˌjɔːr- ‖ -oʊ ˌjʊr- **~ist/s** ɪst/s -əst/s
ˌIndo-Euroˌpean ˈlanguages
Indo-Germanic ˌɪnd əʊ dʒɜː ˈmæn ɪk ◂ -əʊ dʒə- ‖ -oʊ dʒɜː- -oʊ dʒᵊr-
Indo-Iranian ˌɪnd əʊ ɪ ˈreɪn i‿ən ◂ ‖ ˌ·oʊ-
indole ˈɪnd əʊl →-ɒʊl ‖ -oʊl
indolence ˈɪnd əl ənᵗs
indolent ˈɪnd əl ənt **~ly** li
indomitab|le ɪn ˈdɒm ɪt əb |ᵊl -ˈ·ət- ‖ -ˈdɑːm əţ- **~ly** li
Indonesia ˌɪnd əʊ ˈniːʒ ə -ˈniːz i‿ə, -ˈniːs-; -ˈniːʃ ə
Indonesian ˌɪnd əʊ ˈniːʒ ᵊn ◂ -ˈniːz i‿ən, -ˈniːs-; ˈniːʃ ᵊn **~s** z
indoor ˌɪn ˈdɔː ◂ ‖ -ˈdɔːr ◂ -ˈdoʊr **~s** z
ˌindoor ˈgames
Indore ₍ˌ₎ɪn ˈdɔː ‖ -ˈdɔːr —*Hindi* Indaur [ɪn̪ d̪ɔʊr]
indors|e ɪn ˈdɔːs ən- ‖ -ˈdɔːrs **~ed** t **~es** ɪz əz **~ement/s** mənt/s **~ing** ɪŋ
Indra ˈɪndr ə
indrawn ˌɪn ˈdrɔːn ◂ ‖ -ˈdrɑːn
ˌindrawn ˈbreath
indri ˈɪndr i **~s** z
indubitab|le ɪn ˈdjuːb ɪt əb |ᵊl ˌɪn-, →-ˈdʒuːb- -ˈ·ət- ‖ -ˈduːb əţ- -ˈdjuːb- **~ly** li
induc|e ɪn ˈdjuːs →-ˈdʒuːs ‖ -ˈduːs -ˈdjuːs **~ed** t **~es** ɪz əz **~ing** ɪŋ
inducement ɪn ˈdjuːs mənt →-ˈdʒuːs- ‖ -ˈduːs- -ˈdjuːs- **~s** s
induct ɪn ˈdʌkt **~ed** ɪd əd **~ing** ɪŋ **~s** s
inductanc|e ɪn ˈdʌkt ənᵗs **~es** ɪz əz
inductee ˌɪn dʌk ˈtiː **~s** z
induction ɪn ˈdʌk ʃᵊn **~s** z
inˈduction coil
inductive ɪn ˈdʌkt ɪv **~ly** li **~ness** nəs nɪs
indu|e ɪn ˈdjuː ən-, →-ˈdʒuː ‖ -ˈduː -ˈdjuː **~ed** d **~es** z **~ing** ɪŋ
indulg|e ɪn ˈdʌldʒ **~ed** d **~es** ɪz əz **~ing** ɪŋ
indulgenc|e ɪn ˈdʌldʒ ənᵗs **~es** ɪz əz
indulgent ɪn ˈdʌldʒ ənt **~ly** li
indurate *adj* ˈɪn djʊᵊr ət →-dʒʊᵊr-, -ɪt, -eɪt ‖ -dər- -djər-
indu|rate *v* ˈɪn djuᵊ |reɪt →-dʒuᵊ- ‖ -də- -djə- **~rated** reɪt ɪd -əd ‖ reɪţ əd **~rates** reɪts **~rating** reɪt ɪŋ ‖ reɪţ ɪŋ
induration ˌɪn djuᵊ ˈreɪʃ ᵊn →-dʒuᵊ- ‖ ˌɪn də- -djə-
Indus ˈɪnd əs
industrial ɪn ˈdʌs tri‿əl **~ly** i **~s** z
inˌdustrial ˈaction; inˌdustrial ˌarchaeˈology; inˌdustrial deˈsign; inˌdustrial eˈstate; inˌdustrial ˌrevoˈlution
industrialis... —see **industrializ...**
industrialism ɪn ˈdʌs tri‿əl ˌɪz əm
industrialist ɪn ˈdʌs tri‿əl ɪst §-əst **~s** s
industrialization ɪn ˌdʌs tri‿əl aɪ ˈzeɪʃ ᵊn -ɪˈ·- ‖ -əˈ·- **~s** z
industrializ|e ɪn ˈdʌs tri‿ə laɪz **~ed** d **~es** ɪz əz **~ing** ɪŋ
industrial-strength ɪn ˈdʌs tri‿əl streŋᵏθ §-strenᵗθ
industrious ɪn ˈdʌs tri‿əs **~ly** li **~ness** nəs nɪs
indus|try ˈɪnd əs |tri §-ʌs- **~tries** triz
industry-wide ˌɪnd əs tri ˈwaɪd ◂ §-ʌs-
in|dwell ₍ˌ₎ɪn |ˈdwel **~dwelling** ˈdwel ɪŋ **~dwells** ˈdwelz **~dwelt** ˈdwelt
Indy ˈɪnd i
-ine aɪn, iːn, ɪn §ən —*As a suffix,* iːn *in chemical senses* (ˈbromine, ˈcaffeine), *otherwise usually* aɪn (ˈbovine, ˈcrystalline). *When not felt as a suffix, often* ɪn, §ən (ˈdiscipline, ˈfamine), *sometimes stressed* iːn (rouˈtine).
inebri|ate *v* ɪ ˈniːb ri |eɪt **~ated** eɪt ɪd -əd ‖ eɪţ əd **~ates** eɪts **~ating** eɪt ɪŋ ‖ eɪţ ɪŋ
inebriate *adj, n* ɪ ˈniːb ri‿ət -ɪt, -eɪt **~s** s
inebriation ɪ ˌniːb ri ˈeɪʃ ᵊn
inebriety ˌɪn i ˈbraɪ‿ət i §ˌ·ə-, ‿ɪt i ‖ -əţ i
inedibility ɪn ˌed ə ˈbɪl ət i ˌɪn-ˈ·-, ɪˈ·-, -ɪt i ‖ -əţ i
inedible ɪn ˈed əb ᵊl ˌɪn-, -ɪb ᵊl
ineducable ɪn ˈed jʊk əb ᵊl ˌɪn-, -ˈ·juːk-, -ˈedʒ ʊk-, -ˈ·ək- ‖ -ˈedʒ ək-

neffability ɪn ˌef ə ˈbɪl ət i -ɪt i ‖ -əṭ i
neffab|le ɪn ˈef əb |əl **~leness** əl nəs -nɪs **~ly** li
neffaceab|le ˌɪn i ˈfeɪs əb əl ◂ ˌ·e-, ˌ·ə- **~ly** li
neffective ˌɪn ə ˈfekt ɪv ◂ -i- **~ly** li **~ness** nəs nɪs
neffectual ˌɪn ə ˈfek tʃu‿əl ◂ ˌ·i-, -tju‿əl, -ʃu‿əl **~ly** i **~ness** nəs nɪs
nefficacy ɪn ˈef ɪkəs i
nefficienc|y ˌɪn ə ˈfɪʃ ənts |i ˌ·i- **~ies** iz
nefficient ˌɪn ə ˈfɪʃ ənt ◂ -i- **~ly** li
nelastic ˌɪn i ˈlæst ɪk ◂ -ə-, -ˈlɑːst-
nelasticity ˌɪn i læ ˈstɪs ət i ˌ·ə-, -lɑːˈ--; ˌɪn ˌiːl æˈ--, ˌɪn ˌel æˈ--, -ɑːˈ--, -ɪt i ‖ -əṭ i
nelegance ɪn ˈel ɪg ənts ˌɪn-, -əg-
nelegant ɪn ˈel ɪg ənt ˌɪn-, -əg- **~ly** li
neligibility ɪn ˌel ɪdʒ ə ˈbɪl ət i -ˌ·ədʒ-, ˌ·ˌ·-, -ɪˈ--, -ɪt i ‖ -əṭ i
neligib|le ɪn ˈel ɪdʒ əb |əl ˌɪn-, -ˈ·ədʒ-, -ɪb əl **~ly** li
neluctab|le ˌɪn i ˈlʌkt əb |əl ◂ ˌ·ə- **~ly** li
nept ɪ ˈnept ˌɪn ˈept ◂ **~ly** li **~ness** nəs nɪs
neptitude ɪ ˈnept ɪ tjuːd -ə-, →-tʃuːd ‖ -tuːd -tjuːd
nequalit|y ˌɪn i ˈkwɒl ət |i ˌ·ə-, -ɪt i ‖ -ˈkwɑːl əṭ |i **~ies** iz
nequitab|le ɪn ˈek wɪt əb |əl ˌɪn-, -ˈ·wət- ‖ -ˈek wəṭ- **~leness** əl nəs -nɪs **~ly** li
nequit|y ɪn ˈek wət |i ˌɪn-, -ɪt- ‖ -wəṭ |i **~ies** iz
neradicab|le ˌɪn i ˈræd ɪk əb |əl ◂ ˌ·ə- **~leness** əl nəs -nɪs **~ly** li
nert ɪ ˈnɜːt ‖ ɪ ˈnɝːt **~ly** li **~ness** nəs nɪs
nertance ɪ ˈnɜːt ənts ‖ -ˈnɝːt-
nertia ɪ ˈnɜːʃ ə -ˈnɜːʃ i‿ə ‖ ɪ ˈnɝːʃ ə
 iˈnertia reel; **iˌnertia ˈselling**, ·ˈ· ˌ· ·
nertial ɪ ˈnɜːʃ əl -ˈnɜːʃ i‿əl ‖ ɪ ˈnɝːʃ əl
nescapab|le ˌɪn ɪ ˈskeɪp əb |əl ◂ ˌ·ə- **~ly** li
nessential ˌɪn ɪ ˈsentʃ əl ◂ -ə- **~s** z
nessive ɪn ˈes ɪv ˌɪn- **~s** z
nestimab|le ɪn ˈest ɪm əb |əl ˌɪn-, -ˈ·əm- **~ly** li
nevitability ɪn ˌev ɪt ə ˈbɪl ət i ˌ·ˌ·-, -ət ə-, -ɪt i ‖ -əṭ ə ˈbɪl əṭ i
nevitab|le ɪn ˈev ɪt əb |əl ˌ·-, -ˈ·ət- ‖ -ˈev əṭ- **~leness** əl nəs -nɪs **~ly** li
inexact ˌɪn ɪg ˈzækt ◂ -eg-, -əg-, -ɪk-, -ek-, -ək- **~ly** li **~ness** nəs nɪs
inexactitude ˌɪn ɪg ˈzækt ɪ tjuːd ˌ·eg-, ˌ·əg-, ˌ·ɪk-, ˌ·ek-, ˌ·ək-, -ə ·, →-tʃuːd ‖ -ə tuːd -tjuːd **~s** z
inexcusab|le ˌɪn ɪk ˈskjuːz əb |əl ◂ ˌ·ek-, ˌ·ək- **~leness** əl nəs -nɪs **~ly** li
inexhaustib|le ˌɪn ɪg ˈzɔːst əb |əl ◂ ˌ·eg-, ˌ·əg-, ˌ·ɪk-, ˌ·ek-, ˌ·ək-, -ɪb əl ‖ -ˈzɑːst- **~leness** əl nəs -nɪs **~ly** li
inexorability ɪn ˌeks ər‿ə ˈbɪl ət i §-ˌegz-, -ɪt i ‖ -əṭ i
inexorab|le ɪn ˈeks ər‿əb |əl §-ˈegz- **~leness** əl nəs -nɪs **~ly** li
inexpedienc|e ˌɪn ɪk ˈspiːd i‿ənts ˌ·ek-, ˌ·ək- **~y** i
inexpedient ˌɪn ɪk ˈspiːd i‿ənt ◂ ˌ·ek-, ˌ·ək- **~ly** li
inexpensive ˌɪn ɪk ˈspents ɪv ◂ -ek-, -ək- **~ly** li **~ness** nəs nɪs
inexperience ˌɪn ɪk ˈspɪər i‿ənts ˌ·ek-, ˌ·ək- ‖ -ˈspɪr- **~d** t
inexpert ɪn ˈeks pɜːt ˌɪn-; ˌɪn ek ˈspɜːt ◂, -ɪk-, -ək- ‖ ɪn ˈeks pɝːt ˌɪn-; ˌɪn ɪk ˈspɝːt ◂ **~ly** li **~ness** nəs nɪs
inexpiab|le ɪn ˈeks pi‿əb |əl ˌɪn- **~leness** əl nəs -nɪs **~ly** li
inexplicability ˌɪn ɪk ˌsplɪk ə ˈbɪl ət i ˌ·ek-, ˌ·ək-, -ɪt i; ɪn ˌeks plɪk-, ˌ·ˌ·-- ‖ -əṭ i
inexplicab|le ˌɪn ɪk ˈsplɪk əb |əl ◂ ˌ·ek-, ˌ·ək-; ˌ(ˌ)ɪn ˈeks plɪk- **~leness** əl nəs -nɪs **~ly** li
inexplicit ˌɪn ɪk ˈsplɪs ɪt -ek-, -ək-, §-ət **~ly** li **~ness** nəs nɪs
inexpressib|le ˌɪn ɪk ˈspres əb |əl ◂ ˌ·ek-, ˌ·ək-, -ɪb əl **~leness** əl nəs -nɪs **~ly** li
inexpressive ˌɪn ɪk ˈspres ɪv ◂ -ek-, -ək- **~ly** li **~ness** nəs nɪs
inextinguishab|le ˌɪn ɪk ˈstɪŋ gwɪʃ əb |əl ◂ ˌ·ek-, ˌ·ək-, -ˈ·wɪʃ- **~leness** əl nəs -nɪs **~ly** li
in extremis ˌɪn ɪk ˈstriːm ɪs -ek-, -ək-, §-əs
inextricability ˌɪn ɪk ˌstrɪk ə ˈbɪl ət i ˌ·ek-, ˌ·ək-, -ɪt i; ɪn ˌeks trɪk-, ˌ·ˌ·-- ‖ -əṭ i
inextricab|le ˌɪn ɪk ˈstrɪk əb |əl ◂ ˌ·ek-, ˌ·ək-; ˌ(ˌ)ɪn ˈeks trɪk- **~leness** əl nəs -nɪs **~ly** li
Inez ˈiːn ez ˈaɪn- ‖ ˈaɪn ez aɪ ˈnez, ˈiːn ez; iː ˈnez, ɪ- —*Sp* [ˈi neθ]
infallibility ɪn ˌfæl ə ˈbɪl ət i ˌ·ˌ·-, -ɪˈ--, -ɪt i ‖ -əṭ i
infallib|le ɪn ˈfæl əb |əl ˌɪn-, -ɪb- **~leness** əl nəs -nɪs **~ly** li
infamous ˈɪn fəm əs *(!)* **~ly** li **~ness** nəs nɪs
infam|y ˈɪn fəm |i **~ies** iz
infanc|y ˈɪntf ənts |i **~ies** iz
infant ˈɪntf ənt **~s** s
 ˌinfant ˈprodigy; **ˈinfant school**
infanta ɪn ˈfænt ə —*Sp* [in ˈfan ta] **~s** z
infante ɪn ˈfænt i —*Sp* [in ˈfan te] **~s** z
infanticidal ɪn ˌfænt ɪ ˈsaɪd əl ◂ -ə- ‖ -ˌfænṭ ə-
infanticide ɪn ˈfænt ɪ saɪd -ə- ‖ -ˈfænṭ ə- **~s** z
infantile ˈɪntf ən taɪəl ‖ -təl
 ˌinfantile paˈralysis
infantilism ɪn ˈfænt ɪ ˌlɪz əm -ˈ·ə- ‖ -ˈfænṭ ə-
infantr|y ˈɪntf əntr |i **~ies** iz
infantry|man ˈɪntf əntr i |mən -mæn **~men** mən men
infarct ˈɪn fɑːkt ·ˈ· ‖ -fɑːrkt **~s** s
infarction ɪn ˈfɑːk ʃən ‖ -ˈfɑːrk- **~s** z
infatu|ate ɪn ˈfæt ju |eɪt -ˈfætʃ u- ‖ ɪn ˈfætʃ u- **~ated** eɪt ɪd -əd ‖ eɪṭ əd **~ates** eɪts **~ating** eɪt ɪŋ ‖ eɪṭ ɪŋ
infatuation ɪn ˌfæt ju ˈeɪʃ ən -ˌfætʃ u- ‖ ɪn ˌfætʃ u- **~s** z
infect ɪn ˈfekt **~ed** ɪd əd **~ing** ɪŋ **~s** s
infection ɪn ˈfek ʃən **~s** z
infectious ɪn ˈfek ʃəs **~ly** li **~ness** nəs nɪs
infective ɪn ˈfekt ɪv **~ness** nəs nɪs
infectivity ˌɪn fek ˈtɪv ət i -ɪt i ‖ -əṭ i
infelicitous ˌɪn fə ˈlɪs ɪt əs ◂ ˌ·fɪ-, ˌ·fe-, -ət əs ‖ -əṭ əs **~ly** li
infelicit|y ˌɪn fə ˈlɪs ət |i ˌ·fɪ-, ˌ·fe-, -ɪt i ‖ -əṭ |i **~ies** iz

infer ɪn ˈfɜː ‖ -ˈfɝː **~red** d **inferring** ɪn ˈfɜːr ɪŋ ‖ ɪn ˈfɝː ɪŋ **~s** z
inferab|le ɪn ˈfɜːr əb |əl ˈɪnf ər‿əb |əl ‖ -ˈfɝː- **~ly** li
inferenc|e ˈɪnᵗf ər‿ənᵗs **~es** ɪz əz
inferential ˌɪnᵗf ə ˈrenᵗʃ əl ◂ **~ly** i
inferior ɪn ˈfɪər i‿ə ˌɪn- ‖ -ˈfɪr i‿ər **~s** z
inferiorit|y ɪn ˌfɪər i ˈɒr ət |i ˌ·ˌ-·, -ɪt i ‖ ɪn ˌfɪr i ˈɔːr əṭ |i -ˈɑːr- **~ies** iz
inˌferiˈority ˌcomplex
infernal ɪn ˈfɜːn əl ‖ -ˈfɝːn- **~ly** i
inferno, I~ ɪn ˈfɜːn əʊ ‖ -ˈfɝːn oʊ **~s** z
inferrab|le ɪn ˈfɜːr əb |əl ˈɪnf ər‿əb |əl ‖ -ˈfɝː- **~ly** li
infertile ɪn ˈfɜːt aɪəl ˌɪn- ‖ -ˈfɝːṭ əl *(*)*
infertility ˌɪn fə ˈtɪl ət i ˌ·fɜː-, -ɪt i ‖ -fər ˈtɪl əṭ i
infest ɪn ˈfest **~ed** ɪd əd **~ing** ɪŋ **~s** s
infestation ˌɪn fe ˈsteɪʃ ən **~s** z
infibu|late ɪn ˈfɪb ju |leɪt -jə- ‖ -jə- **~lated** leɪt ɪd -əd ‖ leɪṭ əd **~lates** leɪts **~lating** leɪt ɪŋ ‖ leɪṭ ɪŋ
infibulation ɪn ˌfɪb ju ˈleɪʃ ən -jə- ‖ -jə- **~s** z
infidel ˈɪn fɪd əl -fəd-; -fɪ del, -fə- **~s** z
infidelit|y ˌɪn fɪ ˈdel ət |i ˌ·fə-, -ɪt i ‖ -əṭ |i **~ies** iz
infield ˈɪn fiːəld **~s** z
infielder ˈɪn ˌfiːəld ə ‖ -ər **~s** z
infight|er ˈɪn ˌfaɪt |ə ‖ -ˌfaɪṭ |ər **~ers** əz ‖ ərz **~ing** ɪŋ
infill ˈɪn fɪl **~ed** d **~ing** ɪŋ **~s** z
infil|trate ˈɪn fɪl |treɪt -fəl- ‖ ɪn ˈfɪl|tr eɪt ˈɪn fəl |treɪt *(*)* **~trated** treɪt ɪd -əd ‖ treɪṭ əd **~trates** treɪts **~trating** treɪt ɪŋ ‖ treɪṭ ɪŋ
infiltration ˌɪn fɪl ˈtreɪʃ ən -fəl- **~s** z
infiltrator ˈɪn fɪl treɪt ə ˈ·fəl- ‖ ɪn ˈfɪltr eɪṭ ər ˈɪn fəl treɪṭ- **~s** z
infinite ˈɪn fɪn ət -ɪt; ˈɪnf ən‿ət, ɪt —*but in church music usually* ˈɪn fɪ naɪt, -fə-, -faɪ- **~ly** li **~ness** nəs nɪs
infinitesimal ˌɪn fɪn ɪ ˈtes ɪm əl ◂ -əˈ·-, -əm əl; ˌɪnf ən‿ˈtez- **~ly** i
infiniti... —*see* **infinity**
infinitival ɪn ˌfɪn ɪ ˈtaɪv əl ◂ ˌ· ·-, -əˈ·-
infinitive ɪn ˈfɪn ət ɪv -ɪt- ‖ -əṭ ɪv **~s** z
infinitude ɪn ˈfɪn ɪ tjuːd -ə-, →-tʃuːd ‖ -tuːd -tjuːd **~s** z
infinit|y ɪn ˈfɪn ət |i -ɪt- ‖ -əṭ |i **~ies** iz
infirm ɪn ˈfɜːm ˌɪn- ‖ -ˈfɝːm **~ly** li **~ness** nəs nɪs
infirmar|y ɪn ˈfɜːm ər‿|i ‖ -ˈfɝːm- **~ies** iz
infirmit|y ɪn ˈfɜːm ət |i -ɪt- ‖ -ˈfɝːm əṭ |i **~ies** iz
infix *n* ˈɪn fɪks **~es** ɪz əz
infix *v* ˈɪn fɪks ₍ˌ₎·ˈ· **~ed** t **~es** ɪz əz **~ing** ɪŋ
in flagrante ˌɪn flə ˈgrænt i -eɪ ‖ -ˈgrɑːnt-
in flaˌgrante deˈlicto dɪ ˈlɪkt əʊ də-, diː-, deɪ- ‖ -oʊ
inflam|e ɪn ˈfleɪm **~ed** d **~es** z **~ing** ɪŋ
inflammab|le ɪn ˈflæm əb |əl **~leness** əl nəs -nɪs **~ly** li
inflammation ˌɪn flə ˈmeɪʃ ən **~s** z
inflammatory ɪn ˈflæm ət‿ər i ‖ -ə tɔːr i -toʊr i

inflatable ɪn ˈfleɪt əb əl ‖ -ˈfleɪṭ- **~s** z
in|flate ɪn |ˈfleɪt **~flated** ˈfleɪt ɪd -əd ‖ ˈfleɪṭ əd **~flates** ˈfleɪts **~flating** ˈfleɪt ɪŋ ‖ ˈfleɪṭ ɪŋ
inflation ɪn ˈfleɪʃ ən **~ism** ˌɪz əm **~s** z
inflationary ɪn ˈfleɪʃ ən ər‿i -ən‿ər- ‖ -ə ner i
inˌflationary ˈspiral
inflation-proof ɪn ˈfleɪʃ ən pruːf §-prʊf
inflator ɪn ˈfleɪt ə ‖ ɪn ˈfleɪṭ ər **~s** z
inflect ɪn ˈflekt **~ed** ɪd əd **~ing** ɪŋ **~s** s
inflection ɪn ˈflek ʃən **~al** ‿əl **~s** z
inflexibility ɪn ˌfleks ə ˈbɪl ət i ˌ·ˌ-·, -ɪˈ--, -ɪt i ‖ -əṭ i
inflexib|le ɪn ˈfleks əb |əl ˌɪn-, -ɪb- **~leness** əl nəs -nɪs **~ly** li
inflexion ɪn ˈflek ʃən **~al** ‿əl **~s** z
inflict ɪn ˈflɪkt **~ed** ɪd əd **~ing** ɪŋ **~s** s
infliction ɪn ˈflɪk ʃən
in-flight ˌɪn ˈflaɪt ◂
ˌin-flight ˈmovies
infloresc enc|e ˌɪn flə ˈres ənᵗs -flɔː-, -flɒ- ‖ -flɔː-, -floʊ- **~es** ɪz əz
inflow ˈɪn fləʊ ‖ -floʊ **~s** z
influenc|e ˈɪnᵗf lu‿ənᵗs **~es** ɪz əz
influence-peddling ˈɪnf lu‿ənᵗs ˌped əl‿ɪŋ
influential ˌɪnᵗf lu ˈenᵗʃ əl ◂ **~ly** i
influenza ˌɪnᵗf lu ˈenz ə
influx ˈɪn flʌks **~es** ɪz əz
info ˈɪn fəʊ ‖ -foʊ
infobahn ˈɪn fəʊ bɑːn ‖ -oʊ-
infocom ˈɪn fəʊ kɒm ‖ -oʊ kɑːm **~s** z
infomediary ˌɪn fəʊ ˈmiːd i‿ər i ‖ ˌɪn foʊ ˈmiːd i er i
infomercial ˌɪn fəʊ ˈmɜːʃ əl ‖ ˈɪn foʊ mɝːʃ əl ˈ·fə- **~s** z
inform ɪn ˈfɔːm ‖ -ˈfɔːrm **~ed** d **~ing** ɪŋ **~s** z
informal ɪn ˈfɔːm əl ˌɪn- ‖ -ˈfɔːrm- **~ly** i
informalit|y ˌɪn fɔː ˈmæl ət |i -ɪt i ‖ -fɔːr ˈmæl əṭ |i ˌ·fər- **~ies** iz
informant ɪn ˈfɔːm ənt ‖ -ˈfɔːrm- **~s** s
informatics ˌɪnᵗf ə ˈmæt ɪks -ɔː- ‖ -ər ˈmæṭ-
information ˌɪnᵗf ə ˈmeɪʃ ən ‖ -ər- **~al** əl ◂
ˌinforˈmation reˌtrieval; **ˌinforˈmation techˌnology**, ˌ·ˌ·ˌ· ·ˈ· ·
informative ɪn ˈfɔːm ət ɪv ‖ -ˈfɔːrm əṭ ɪv **~ly** li **~ness** nəs nɪs
informer ɪn ˈfɔːm ə ‖ -ˈfɔːrm ər **~s** z
Infoseek *tdmk* ˈɪn fəʊ siːk ‖ -foʊ-
infotainment ˌɪn fəʊ ˈteɪn mənt →-ˈteɪm- ‖ -foʊ- ˈ· · ·
infowar ˈɪn fəʊ wɔː ‖ -foʊ wɔːr
infra ˈɪnᵗf rə
ˌinfra ˈdig
infra- ¦ɪnᵗf rə — **infrasonic** ˌɪnᵗf rə ˈsɒn ɪk ◂ ‖ -ˈsɑːn-
infraction ɪn ˈfræk ʃən **~s** z
infralapsarian ˌɪnᵗf rə læp ˈseər i‿ən ◂ ‖ -ˈser- -ˈsær- **~ism** ˌɪz əm **~s** z
infrared ˌɪnᵗf rə ˈred ◂
infrastructure ˈɪnᵗf rə ˌstrʌk tʃə ‖ -tʃər **~s** z
infrequency ɪn ˈfriːk wənᵗs i ˌɪn-
infrequent ɪn ˈfriːk wənt ˌɪn- **~ly** li

infring|e ɪn ˈfrɪndʒ **~ed** d **~er/s** ə/z ‖ ər/z **~es** ɪz əz **~ing** ɪŋ
infringement ɪn ˈfrɪndʒ mənt **~s** s
infundibul|um ˌɪn fʌn ˈdɪb jʊl |əm -jəl əm ‖ -jəl |əm **~a** ə **~ar** ə ‖ ər
infuri|ate ɪn ˈfjʊər i |eɪt -ˈfjɔːr- ‖ -ˈfjʊr- **~ated** eɪt ɪd -əd ‖ eɪţ əd **~ates** eɪts **~ating/ly** eɪt ɪŋ /li ‖ eɪţ-
infus|e ɪn ˈfjuːz **~ed** d **~er/s** ə/z ‖ ər/z **~es** ɪz əz **~ing** ɪŋ
infusion ɪn ˈfjuːʒ ən **~s** z
infusori|a ˌɪn fju ˈzɔːr i‿|ə ◂ -ˈsɔːr- ‖ -ˈzoʊr-, -ˈsoʊr- **~al** əl **~an/s** ən/z
-ing ɪŋ —*For* ⚠ɪn, ⚠ən, *see at* -in'. —*Note the typical late/early stress difference between phrases, such as* a ˌsinging caˈnary, *where the* -ing *word is a participial adjective, and compounds, such as* a ˈsinging ˌlesson, *where the* -ing *word is a verbal noun (gerund).*
Inga *(i)* ˈɪŋ ə, *(ii)* ˈɪŋ gə
Ingamells ˈɪŋ gə melz
Ingatestone ˈɪŋ gət stəʊn -geɪt- ‖ -stoʊn
ingathering ˈɪn ˌgæð ər‿ɪŋ →ˈɪŋ-
Inge *family name (i)* ɪŋ, *(ii)* ɪndʒ —*In Britain usually (i), in the US usually (ii).*
Inge *personal name, (i)* ˈɪŋ ə, *(ii)* ˈɪŋ gə
ingenious ɪn ˈdʒiːn i‿əs ˌɪn- **~ly** li **~ness** nəs nɪs
ingenue, ingénue ˈæ̃ʒ ə njuː ˈɒ̃ʒ-, -e-, -eɪ-, -nuː, ˌ·ˈ· ‖ ˈændʒ ə nuː ˈɑːndʒ-, -njuː —*Fr* [æ̃ ʒe ny] **~s** z
ingenuit|y ˌɪndʒ ə ˈnjuː‿ət |i ˌ·ɪ-, §-ˈnuː‿ ɪt i ‖ -ˈnuː əţ |i -ˈnjuː- **~ies** iz
ingenuous ɪn ˈdʒen ju‿əs **~ly** li **~ness** nəs nɪs
Ingersoll *tdmk* ˈɪŋ gə sɒl ‖ -gər sɔːl -sɑːl, -səl
ingest ɪn ˈdʒest ˌɪn- **~ed** ɪd əd **~ing** ɪŋ **~s** s
ingestion ɪn ˈdʒes tʃən ˌɪn-, →-ˈdʒeʃ- **~s** z
Ingham ˈɪŋ əm
ingle, Ingle ɪŋ gəl **~s** z
Ingleborough ˈɪŋ gəl bər‿ə §-ˌbʌr ə ‖ -ˌbɜː oʊ
inglenook ˈɪŋ gəl nʊk §-nuːk **~s** s
Ingleton ˈɪŋ gəl tən
Inglewood ˈɪŋ gəl wʊd
Inglis ˈɪŋ glɪs -gəlz —*in Scotland,* -gəlz
inglorious ɪn ˈglɔːr i‿əs →ɪŋ-, ˌ·- ‖ -ˈgloʊr- **~ly** li **~ness** nəs nɪs
Ingmar ˈɪŋ mɑː ‖ -mɑːr
ingoing ˈɪn ˌgəʊ ɪŋ →ˈɪŋ- ‖ -ˌgoʊ- **~s** z
Ingold ˈɪŋ gəʊld →-gɒʊld ‖ -goʊld
Ingoldsby ˈɪŋ gəldz bi
ingot ˈɪŋ gət -gɒt **~s** s
ingraft ɪn ˈgrɑːft ən-, →ɪŋ-, →əŋ-, §-ˈgræft ‖ -ˈgræft **~ed** ɪd əd **~ing** ɪŋ **~s** s
ingrain ɪn ˈgreɪn →ɪŋ-, ˌ·- **~ed** d **~ing** ɪŋ **~s** z
Ingram ˈɪŋ grəm
Ingrams ˈɪŋ grəmz
ingrate ˈɪn greɪt →ˈɪŋ-, ·ˈ· **~s** s
ingrati|ate ɪn ˈgreɪʃ i |eɪt →ɪŋ- **~ated** eɪt ɪd -əd ‖ eɪţ əd **~ates** eɪts **~ating/ly** eɪt ɪŋ /li ‖ eɪţ ɪŋ /li
ingratitude ɪn ˈgræt ɪ tjuːd →ɪŋ-, ˌ·-, -ˈ·ə-, →§-tʃuːd ‖ -ˈgræţ ə tuːd -tjuːd
Ingrebourne ˈɪŋ grɪ bɔːn -grə- ‖ -bɔːrn -boʊrn
ingredient ɪn ˈgriːd i‿ənt →ɪŋ- **~s** s
Ingres ˈæŋgr ˈæŋ grə —*Fr* [æ̃ːgʁ]
ingress ˈɪn gres →ˈɪŋ- **~es** ɪz əz
ingressive ɪn ˈgres ɪv →ɪŋ-, ˌ·- **~ly** li **~s** z
Ingrid ˈɪŋ grɪd -grəd
in-group *n* ˈɪn gruːp →ˈɪŋ- **~s** s
ingrowing ˌɪn ˈgrəʊ ɪŋ ◂ →ˌɪŋ-, ˈ·ˌ·· ‖ ˈɪn ˌgroʊ ɪŋ
ingrown ˌɪn ˈgrəʊn ◂ →ˌɪŋ- ‖ -ˈgroʊn
inguinal ˈɪŋ gwɪn əl §-gwən-
Ingush ˈɪŋ gʊʃ
Ingushetia ˌɪŋ gʊ ˈʃet i‿ə -ˈʃiːʃ ə
Ingvar ˈɪŋ vɑː ‖ -vɑːr
inhab|it ɪn ˈhæb |ɪt §-ət ‖ -|ət **~ited** ɪt ɪd §ət-, -əd ‖ əţ əd **~iting** ɪt ɪŋ §ət- ‖ əţ ɪŋ **~its** ɪts §əts ‖ əts
inhabitable ɪn ˈhæb ɪt əb əl §-ət əb- ‖ -əţ əb-
inhabitant ɪn ˈhæb ɪt ənt §-ət- ‖ -əţ ənt **~s** s
inhalant ɪn ˈheɪl ənt **~s** s
inhalation ˌɪn hə ˈleɪʃ ən -ə- **~s** z
inhalator ˈɪn hə leɪt ə ‖ -leɪţ ər ˈɪn əl eɪţ- **~s** z
inhal|e ɪn ˈheɪəl ˌɪn- **~ed** d **~er/s** ə/z ‖ ər/z **~es** z **~ing** ɪŋ
inharmonious ˌɪn hɑː ˈməʊn i‿əs ◂ ‖ -hɑːr ˈmoʊn- **~ly** li **~ness** nəs nɪs
inhere ɪn ˈhɪə ‖ -ˈhɪər **~d** d **~s** z **inhering** ɪn ˈhɪər ɪŋ ‖ -ˈhɪr ɪŋ

INHERENT

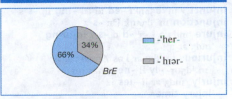

BrE	
-ˈher-	66%
-ˈhɪər-	34%

inherent ɪn ˈher ənt -ˈhɪər- ‖ -ˈhɪr- — *Preference poll, BrE:* -ˈher- *66%,* -ˈhɪər- *34%.* **~ly** li
inher|it ɪn ˈher |ɪt -ət ‖ -|ət **~ited** ɪt ɪd ət-, -əd ‖ əţ əd **~iting** ɪt ɪŋ ət- ‖ əţ ɪŋ **~its** ɪts əts ‖ əts
inheritability ɪn ˌher ɪt ə ˈbɪl ət i -ət ə-, -ɪt i ‖ -əţ ə ˈbɪl əţ i
inheritable ɪn ˈher ɪt əb əl -ət· · ‖ -əţ əb əl
inheritanc|e ɪn ˈher ɪt ənts -ət- ‖ -ət ənts **~es** ɪz əz
inheritor ɪn ˈher ɪt ə -ət- ‖ -əţ ər **~s** z
inhib|it ɪn ˈhɪb |ɪt §-ət ‖ -|ət **~ited/ly** ɪt ɪd /li §ət-, -əd /li ‖ əţ əd /li **~iting** ɪt ɪŋ §ət- ‖ əţ ɪŋ **~its** ɪts §əts ‖ əts
inhibition ˌɪn hɪ ˈbɪʃ ən -ɪ-, -ə- **~s** z
inhibitor ɪn ˈhɪb ɪt ə §-ət- ‖ -əţ ər **~s** z
inhibitory ɪn ˈhɪb ɪt‿ər i -ˈ·ət‿ ‖ -ə tɔːr i -toʊr i
inhospitab|le ˌɪn hɒ ˈspɪt əb |əl ◂ ⁽ˌ⁾ɪn ˈhɒsp ɪt-, -ˈ·ət- ‖ ˌɪn hɑː ˈspɪţ- ⁽ˌ⁾ɪn ˈhɑːsp əţ- **~leness** əl nəs -nɪs **~ly** li
in-house ˌɪn ˈhaʊs ◂
inhuman ɪn ˈhjuːm ən ˌɪn-, §-ˈjuːm- **~ly** li **~ness** nəs nɪs
inhumane ˌɪn hju ˈmeɪn ◂ §-ju- **~ly** li
inhumanit|y ˌɪn hju ˈmæn ət |i §ˌ·ju-, -ɪt i ‖ -əţ |i **~ies** iz

Inigo 'ɪn ɪ gəʊ -ə- ‖ -goʊ
inimical ɪ 'nɪm ɪk ᵊl
inimitab|le ɪ 'nɪm ɪt əb |ᵊl -ət əb- ‖ -əţ əb- **~ly** li
iniquitous ɪ 'nɪk wɪt əs -wət- ‖ -wəţ əs **~ly** li **~ness** nəs nɪs
iniquit|y ɪ 'nɪk wət |i -wɪt- ‖ -wəţ |i **~ies** iz
initial ɪ 'nɪʃ ᵊl **~ed, ~led** d **~ing, ~ling** ɪŋ **~ly** i **~s** z
initialis... —*see* **initializ...**
initialization ɪ ˌnɪʃ əl aɪ 'zeɪʃ ᵊn -əl ɪ- ‖ -əl ə- **~s** z
initializ|e ɪ 'nɪʃ ə laɪz -ᵊl aɪz **~ed** d **~es** ɪz əz **~ing** ɪŋ
initiate *n* ɪ 'nɪʃ i ət ɪt, -eɪt **~s** s
initi|ate *v* ɪ 'nɪʃ i |eɪt **~ated** eɪt ɪd -əd ‖ eɪţ əd **~ates** eɪts **~ating** eɪt ɪŋ ‖ eɪţ ɪŋ
initiation ɪ ˌnɪʃ i 'eɪʃ ᵊn **~s** z
initiative ɪ 'nɪʃ ət ɪv -'nɪʃ i ət ɪv ‖ -əţ ɪv **~s** z
initiator ɪ 'nɪʃ i eɪt ə ‖ -eɪţ ᵊr **~s** z
initiatory ɪ 'nɪʃ i ə tər i ɪ ˌnɪʃ i 'eɪt ər i ◂ ‖ ə tɔːr i ə toʊr i
inject ɪn 'dʒekt **~ed** ɪd əd **~ing** ɪŋ **~s** s
injection ɪn 'dʒek ʃᵊn **~s** z
injector ɪn 'dʒekt ə ‖ -ᵊr **~s** z
in-joke 'ɪn dʒəʊk ‖ -dʒoʊk **~s** s
injudicious ˌɪn dʒu 'dɪʃ əs ◂ **~ly** li **~ness** nəs nɪs
Injun 'ɪndʒ ən **~s** z
injunct *v* ɪn 'dʒʌŋkt **~ed** ɪd əd **~ing** ɪŋ **~s** s
injunction ɪn 'dʒʌŋk ʃᵊn **~s** z
injure 'ɪndʒ ə ‖ -ᵊr **~d** d **~s** z **injuring** 'ɪndʒ ər ɪŋ
injurious ɪn 'dʒʊər i əs ⚠ 'ɪndʒ ər əs ‖ ɪn 'dʒʊr- **~ly** li **~ness** nəs nɪs
injur|y 'ɪndʒ ər |i **~ies** iz
'injury time
injustic|e ɪn 'dʒʌst ɪs ˌɪn-, -əs **~es** ɪz əz
ink ɪŋk **inked** ɪŋkt **inking** 'ɪŋk ɪŋ **inks** ɪŋks
Inkatha ɪn 'kaːt ə →ɪŋ- —*Zulu* [iŋ k'aː tha]
inkblot 'ɪŋk blɒt ‖ -blaːt **~s** s
inkbottle 'ɪŋk ˌbɒt ᵊl ‖ -ˌbaːţ ᵊl **~s** z
ink-cap 'ɪŋk kæp **~s** s
Inkerman 'ɪŋk ə mən ‖ -ᵊr- -maːn —*Russ* [ɪn kʲɪr 'man]
inkhorn 'ɪŋk hɔːn ‖ -hɔːrn **~s** z
inkjet 'ɪŋk dʒet
inkling 'ɪŋk lɪŋ **~s** z
inkpad 'ɪŋk pæd **~s** z
Inkpen 'ɪŋk pen
inkpot 'ɪŋk pɒt ‖ -paːt **~s** s
inkstand 'ɪŋk stænd **~s** z
inkwell 'ɪŋk wel **~s** z
ink|y 'ɪŋk |i **~ier** i ə ‖ i ᵊr **~iest** i ɪst i əst **~iness** i nəs i nɪs
INLA ˌaɪ en el 'eɪ
inlaid ˌɪn 'leɪd ◂
inland *adj* 'ɪn lənd -lænd
ˌInland 'Revenue
inland *adv* ₍ˌ₎ɪn 'lænd '· ·
in-laws 'ɪn lɔːz ‖ -laːz
in|lay *v* ˌɪn |'leɪ '· · **~laid** 'leɪd ◂ **~laying** 'leɪ ɪŋ **~lays** 'leɪz
inlay *n* 'ɪn leɪ **~s** z
inlet 'ɪn lət -lɪt, -let **~s** s
in-line ˌɪn 'laɪn ◂
ˌin-line 'skates
in loco parentis ɪn ˌləʊk əʊ pə 'rent ɪs §-əs ‖ ɪn ˌloʊk oʊ pə 'renţ əs
inly 'ɪn li
Inman 'ɪn mən →'ɪm-
Inmarsat 'ɪn maː sæt →'ɪm- ‖ -maːr-
inmate 'ɪn meɪt →'ɪm- **~s** s
in medias res ɪn ˌmiːd i æs 'reɪz →ɪm-, -ˌmeɪd-, -ˌmed-, -aːs'-, əs'-, 'reɪs
in memoriam ˌɪn mɪ 'mɔːr i əm →ˌɪm-, ˌ·mə-, -æm ‖ -'moʊr-
in-migrant 'ɪn ˌmaɪg rənt →'ɪm- **~s** s
inmost 'ɪn məʊst →'ɪm-, -məst ‖ -moʊst
inn ɪn *(= in)* **inns** ɪnz
ˌInns of 'Court
innards 'ɪn ədz ‖ ᵊrdz
innate ˌɪ 'neɪt ◂ ɪ-, ˌɪn- **~ly** li **~ness** nəs nɪs
ˌinnate 'knowledge, ·ˌ· '··
inner 'ɪn ə ‖ -ᵊr **~s** z
ˌinner 'city; **ˌInner 'Hebrides**; **ˌinner 'man**
'inner tube, ˌ· '·
inner-city ˌɪn ə 'sɪt i ◂ ‖ ˌɪn ᵊr 'sɪţ i ◂
innermost 'ɪn ə məʊst ‖ -ᵊr moʊst
innerv|ate 'ɪn ɜːv |eɪt -ə v|eɪt ‖ ɪ 'nɜːv |eɪt 'ɪn ᵊr v|eɪt **~ated** eɪt ɪd -əd ‖ eɪţ əd **~ates** eɪts **~ating** eɪt ɪŋ ‖ eɪţ ɪŋ
innervation ˌɪn ɜː 'veɪʃ ᵊn -ə- ‖ ˌɪn ᵊr- **~s** z
Innes 'ɪn ɪs -ɪz, -əs, -əz
inning 'ɪn ɪŋ **~s** z **~ses** zɪz zəz
Innisfail ˌɪn ɪs 'feɪᵊl -əs-
Innisfree ˌɪn ɪs 'friː -əs-
innit *nonstd form of* **isn't it** 'ɪn ɪt -ət
innkeeper 'ɪn ˌkiːp ə →'ɪŋ- ‖ -ᵊr **~s** z
innocence 'ɪn əs ənᵗs -əʊs-
innocent, I~ 'ɪn əs ənt -əʊs- **~ly** li **~s** s
innocuous ɪ 'nɒk ju əs ə- ‖ ɪ 'naːk- **~ly** li **~ness** nəs nɪs
innominate ɪ 'nɒm ɪn ət ə-, -ən-, -ɪt; -ɪ neɪt, -ə- ‖ ɪ 'naːm-
inno|vate 'ɪn əʊ |veɪt ‖ -ə- **~vated** veɪt ɪd -əd ‖ veɪţ əd **~vates** veɪts **~vating** veɪt ɪŋ ‖ veɪţ ɪŋ
innovation ˌɪn əʊ 'veɪʃ ᵊn ‖ -ə- **~al** əl ◂ **~s** z

INNOVATIVE

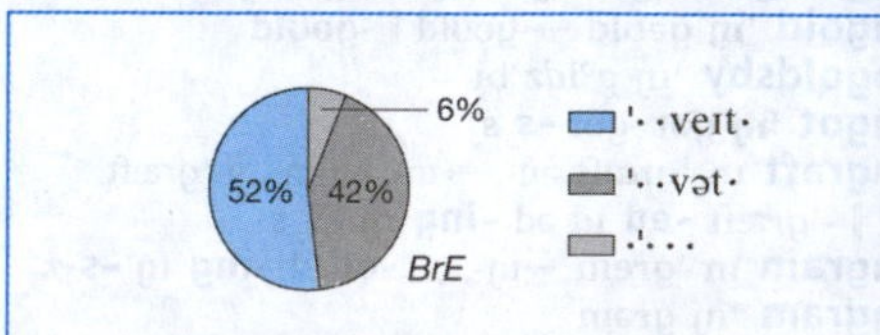

innovative 'ɪn əʊ veɪt ɪv -vət ɪv; ɪ 'nəʊv ət ɪv ‖ 'ɪn ə veɪţ ɪv *Preference poll, BrE:* '· ·veɪt · *52%,* '· ·vət · *42%,* ·'· · · *6%.* **~ly** li **~ness** nəs nɪs
innovator 'ɪn ə veɪt ə ‖ -veɪţ ᵊr **~s** z
innovatory 'ɪn ə veɪt ər i -vət ər i ‖ 'ɪn əv ə tɔːr i -toʊr i

noxa *tdmk* ɪ ˈnɒks ə ‖ ɪ ˈnɑːks ə

nsbruck ˈɪnz brʊk —*Ger* [ˈʔɪnts bʁʊk]

nuendo ˌɪn ju ˈend əʊ ‖ -oʊ **~es** z

nuit ˈɪn u ɪt -ju-, §-ət

numerab|le ɪ ˈnjuːm ər‿əb |əl ə-, §ɪ ˈnuːm- ‖ ɪ ˈnuːm- ɪ ˈnjuːm- **~leness** əl nəs -nɪs **~ly** li

numeracy ɪ ˈnjuːm ər‿əs i §ɪ ˈnuːm- ‖ ɪ ˈnuːm- ɪ ˈnjuːm-

numerate ɪ ˈnjuːm ər‿ət §ɪ ˈnuːm-, ‿ɪt ‖ ɪ ˈnuːm- ɪ ˈnjuːm- **~s** s

nocu|late ɪ ˈnɒk ju |leɪt ə-, -jə- ‖ ɪ ˈnɑːk jə- **~lated** leɪt ɪd -əd ‖ leɪt̬ əd **~lates** leɪts **~lating** leɪt ɪŋ ‖ leɪt̬ ɪŋ

noculation ɪ ˌnɒk ju ˈleɪʃ ən ə-, -jə- ‖ ɪ ˌnɑːk jə- **~s** z

noculator ɪ ˈnɒk ju leɪt ə ə-, -jə- ‖ ɪ ˈnɑːk jə leɪt̬ ər **~s** z

noffensive ˌɪn ə ˈfents ɪv ◂ **~ly** li **~ness** nəs nɪs

noperab|le ɪn ˈɒp ər‿əb |əl ˌɪn- ‖ ɪn ˈɑːp- **~ly** li

noperative ɪn ˈɒp ər‿ət ɪv ˌɪn-, -ə reɪt ɪv ‖ ɪn ˈɑːp ər‿ət̬ ɪv -ə reɪt̬ ɪv **~ness** nəs nɪs

nopportune ɪn ˈɒp ə tjuːn ˌɪn-, →-tʃuːn; ˌ·ˈ·ˈ· ‖ ɪn ˌɑːp ər ˈtuːn ◂ -ˈtjuːn **~ly** li **~ness** nəs nɪs

nordinate ɪn ˈɔːd ɪn ət ən-, -ən‿, -ɪt ‖ -ˈɔːrd ən‿ət **~ly** li **~ness** nəs nɪs

norganic ˌɪn ɔː ˈgæn ɪk ◂ ‖ -ɔːr- **~ally** əl‿i

ˌinorˌganic ˈchemistry

nouye ɪ ˈnuː eɪ

n-patient ˈɪn ˌpeɪʃ ənt →ˈɪm- **~s** s

n|put *v, n* ˈɪn |pʊt →ˈɪm- **~puts** pʊts **~putted** pʊt ɪd -əd ‖ pʊt̬ əd **~putting** pʊt ɪŋ ‖ pʊt̬ ɪŋ

nput/output, input-output ˌɪn pʊt ˈaʊt pʊt →ˌɪm- ‖ -pʊt̬-

nquest ˈɪŋ kwest ˈɪn- **~s** s

nquietude ɪn ˈkwaɪ‿ə tjuːd →ɪŋ-, ɪ tjuːd, →§-tʃuːd ‖ -tuːd -tjuːd

nquire ɪn ˈkwaɪ‿ə →ɪŋ-, ən- ‖ -ˈkwaɪ‿ər **~d** d **~s** z **inquiring/ly** ɪn ˈkwaɪ‿ər ɪŋ /li →ɪŋ-, ən- ‖ -ˈkwaɪ‿ər ɪŋ /li

nquirer ɪn ˈkwaɪər ə →ɪŋ-, ən- ‖ -ər **~s** z

INQUIRY

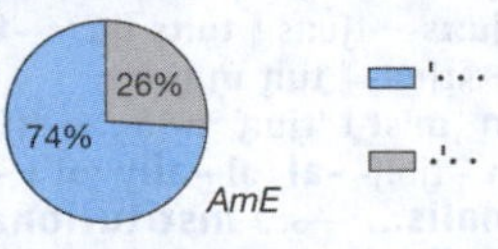

26% ·ˈ· ·
74% ˈ· · ·
AmE

nquir|y ɪn ˈkwaɪər |i →ɪŋ-, ən- ‖ ˈɪn kwər |i , →ˈɪŋ-, -kwaɪər-; ɪn ˈkwaɪər i, →ɪŋ- *Preference poll, AmE:* ˈ· · · *74%,* ·ˈ· · *26%.* **~ies** iz

inquisition, I~ ˌɪŋ kwɪ ˈzɪʃ ən ˌɪn-, -kwə- **~s** z

inquisitive ɪn ˈkwɪz ət ɪv →ɪŋ-, -ɪt- ‖ -ət̬ ɪv **~ly** li **~ness** nəs nɪs

inquisitor ɪn ˈkwɪz ɪt ə →ɪŋ-, -ət- ‖ -ət̬ ər **~s** z

inquisitorial ɪn ˌkwɪz ə ˈtɔːr i‿əl ◂ →ɪŋ-, ˌ·ˌ·-, -ɪˈ·- ‖ -ˈtoʊr- **~ly** i

inquorate ˌɪn ˈkwɔːr eɪt ◂ →ˌɪŋ-, -ət, -ɪt ‖ -ˈkwoʊr-

in re ˌ(ˌ)ɪn ˈriː -ˈreɪ

in-residence ˌ(ˌ)ɪn ˈrez ɪd ənts -əd-

inroad ˈɪn rəʊd ‖ -roʊd **~s** z

inrush ˈɪn rʌʃ **~es** ɪz əz

insalubrious ˌɪn sə ˈluːb ri‿əs ◂ -ˈljuːb- **~ly** li **~ness** nəs nɪs

ins and outs ˌɪnz ən ˈaʊts -ənd-

insane ɪn ˈseɪn ˌɪn- **~ly** li

insanitar|y ɪn ˈsæn ə‿tər |i ˌɪn-, -ˈɪ‿ ‖ -ə ter |i **~iness** i nəs i nɪs

insanit|y ɪn ˈsæn ət |i ˌɪn-, -ɪt i ‖ -ət̬ |i **~ies** iz

insatiab|le ɪn ˈseɪʃ əb |əl -ˈseɪʃ i‿əb |əl **~leness** əl nəs -nɪs **~ly** li

insatiate ɪn ˈseɪʃ i‿ət ɪt, -eɪt **~ly** li **~ness** nəs nɪs

inscape ˈɪn skeɪp **~d** t **~s** s

inscrib|e ɪn ˈskraɪb **~ed** d **~es** z **~ing** ɪŋ

inscription ɪn ˈskrɪp ʃən **~s** z

inscrutability ɪn ˌskruːt ə ˈbɪl ət i ˌ·ˌ·-, -ɪt i ‖ ɪn ˌskruːt̬ ə ˈbɪl ət̬ i

inscrutab|le ɪn ˈskruːt əb |əl ˌɪn- ‖ -ˈskruːt̬- **~leness** əl nəs -nɪs **~ly** li

inseam ˈɪn siːm **~s** z

insect ˈɪn sekt **~s** s

insecticidal ɪn ˌsekt ɪ ˈsaɪd əl ◂ -ə-

insecticide ɪn ˈsekt ɪ saɪd -ə- **~s** z

insectivore ɪn ˈsekt ɪ vɔː -ə- ‖ -vɔːr -voʊr **~s** z

insectivorous ˌɪn sek ˈtɪv ər‿əs ◂

insecure ˌɪn si ˈkjʊə ◂ -sə-, -ˈkjɔː ‖ -ˈkjʊər **~ly** li **~ness** nəs nɪs

insecurit|y ˌɪn si ˈkjʊər ət |i ˌ·sə-, -ˈkjɔːr-, -ɪt i ‖ -ˈkjʊr ət̬ |i **~ies** iz

insemi|nate ɪn ˈsem ɪ |neɪt -ə- **~nated** neɪt ɪd -əd ‖ neɪt̬ əd **~nates** neɪts **~nating** neɪt ɪŋ ‖ neɪt̬ ɪŋ

insemination ɪn ˌsem ɪ ˈneɪʃ ən ˌɪn-, -ə- **~s** z

inseminator ɪn ˈsem ɪ neɪt ə -ˈ·ə- ‖ -ə neɪt̬ ər **~s** z

insensate ɪn ˈsents eɪt ˌɪn-, -ət, -ɪt **~ly** li

insensibility ɪn ˌsents ə ˈbɪl ət i ˌ·ˌ·ˈ·-, -ɪˈ·-, -ɪt i ‖ -ət̬ i

insensib|le ɪn ˈsents əb |əl ˌɪn-, -ɪb- **~ly** li

insensitive ɪn ˈsents ət ɪv ˌɪn-, -ɪt- ‖ -ət̬ ɪv **~ly** li **~ness** nəs nɪs

insensitivity ɪn ˌsents ə ˈtɪv ət i ˌ·ˌ··ˈ·-, -ɪˈ·-, -ɪt i ‖ -ət̬ i

insenti|ence ɪn ˈsentʃ |ənts -ˈsentʃ i‿|ənts **~ent** ənt

inseparability ɪn ˌsep ər‿ə ˈbɪl ət i ˌ·ˌ·-, -ɪt i ‖ -ət̬ i

inseparab|le ɪn ˈsep ər‿əb |əl ˌɪn- **~leness** əl nəs -nɪs **~ly** li

in|sert *v* ɪn |ˈsɜːt -ˈzɜːt ‖ -|ˈsɜːt **~serted** ˈsɜːt ɪd ˈzɜːt-, -əd ‖ ˈsɜːt̬ əd **~serting** ˈsɜːt ɪŋ ˈzɜːt- ‖ ˈsɜːt̬ ɪŋ **~serts** ˈsɜːts ˈzɜːts ‖ ˈsɜːts

insert *n* ˈɪn sɜːt -zɜːt ‖ -sɜːt **~s** s

insertion ɪn ˈsɜːʃ ən -ˈzɜːʃ- ‖ -ˈsɜːʃ- **~s** z

in-service ˌɪn ˈsɜːv ɪs ◂ -əs ‖ -ˈsɜːv-

ˌin-ˌservice ˈtraining

in|set *v* ɪn |ˈset ˈ·· **~sets** ˈsets **~setting** ˈset ɪŋ ‖ ˈset̬ ɪŋ

I

inset *n* ˈɪn set **~s** s

inshallah, insha'allah ɪn ˈʃæl ə -ˈʃɑːl- ‖ ˌɪn ʃɑː ˈlɑː —*Arabic* [ɪn ˌʃaː ʔaɫ ˈɫaːh, ɪn ʃaː ˈɫaːh]

inshore ˌɪn ˈʃɔː ◂ ‖ -ˈʃɔːr ◂ -ˈʃoʊr
ˌinshore ˈfishing

inside ˌɪn ˈsaɪd ◂ —*but* ˈ· · *when contrasted with* outside **~s** z
ˌinside ˈjob, ˈ· · ·; **ˌinside ˈleft**; **ˌinside ˈout**; **ˌinside ˈtrack**

insider ˌɪn ˈsaɪd ə ◂ ‖ -ᵊr **~s** z
inˌsider ˈtrading, ˌ·ˌ· · ˈ· ·

insidious ɪn ˈsɪd i‿əs **~ly** li **~ness** nəs nɪs

insight ˈɪn saɪt **~s** s

insightful ˈɪn saɪt fʊl ·ˈ· · **~ly** i

insignia ɪn ˈsɪɡ ni‿ə **~s** z

insignificanc|e ˌɪn sɪɡ ˈnɪf ɪk ənᵗs **~y** i

insignificant ˌɪn sɪɡ ˈnɪf ɪk ənt ◂ **~ly** li

insincere ˌɪn sɪn ˈsɪə ◂ -sᵊn- ‖ -ˈsɪᵊr **~ly** li

insincerity ˌɪn sɪn ˈser ət i ˌ·sᵊn-, -ɪt i ‖ -əţ i

insinu|ate ɪn ˈsɪn ju |eɪt **~ated** eɪt ɪd -əd ‖ eɪţ əd **~ates** eɪts **~ating** eɪt ɪŋ ‖ eɪţ ɪŋ

insinuation ɪn ˌsɪn ju ˈeɪʃ ᵊn ˌ·ˌ·ˈ·· **~s** z

insipid ɪn ˈsɪp ɪd §-əd **~ly** li **~ness** nəs nɪs

insipidity ˌɪn sɪ ˈpɪd ət i §ˌ·sə-, -ɪt i ‖ -əţ i

insist ɪn ˈsɪst **~ed** ɪd əd **~ing** ɪŋ **~s** s

insistenc|e ɪn ˈsɪst ənᵗs **~y** i

insistent ɪn ˈsɪst ənt **~ly** li

in situ ₍ˌ₎ɪn ˈsɪt juː -ˈsɪtʃ uː, -ˈsaɪt juː, -ˈsaɪtʃ uː ‖ -ˈsaɪt uː -ˈsiːt-, -ˈsɪt-, -juː

insobriety ˌɪn səʊ ˈbraɪ‿ət i ɪt i ‖ ˌɪn sə ˈbraɪ əţ i

insofar ˌɪn səʊ ˈfɑː ◂ ‖ -sə ˈfɑːr

insolation ˌɪn səʊ ˈleɪʃ ᵊn ‖ -soʊ-

insole ˈɪn səʊl →-sɒʊl ‖ -soʊl **~s** z

insolence ˈɪnᵗs əl ənᵗs

insolent ˈɪnᵗs əl ənt **~ly** li

insolubility ɪn ˌsɒl ju ˈbɪl ət i ˌ·ˌ·ˈ··, -ɪt i ‖ ɪn ˌsɑːl jə ˈbɪl əţ i ˌ·ˌ·

insolub|le ɪn ˈsɒl jʊb |ᵊl ˌɪn- ‖ -ˈsɑːl jəb |ᵊl **~leness** ᵊl nəs -nɪs **~ly** li

insolvab|le ɪn ˈsɒlv əb |ᵊl ˌɪn-, §-ˈsəʊlv- ‖ -ˈsɑːlv- **~ly** li

insolvenc|y ɪn ˈsɒlv ənᵗs |i ˌɪn- ‖ -ˈsɑːlv- **~ies** iz

insolvent ɪn ˈsɒlv ənt ˌɪn- ‖ -ˈsɑːlv- **~s** s

insomnia ɪn ˈsɒm ni‿ə ‖ -ˈsɑːm-

insomniac ɪn ˈsɒm ni æk ‖ -ˈsɑːm- **~s** s

insomuch ˌɪn səʊ ˈmʌtʃ ◂ ‖ -sə-

insouciance ɪn ˈsuːs i‿ənᵗs -õs —*Fr* [æ̃ su sjɑ̃ːs]

insouciant ɪn ˈsuːs i‿ənt -õ —*Fr* [æ̃ su sjɑ̃] **~ly** li

inspan ˈɪn spæn ·ˈ· **~ned** d **~ning** ɪŋ **~s** z

inspect ɪn ˈspekt **~ed** ɪd əd **~ing** ɪŋ **~s** s

inspection ɪn ˈspek ʃᵊn **~s** z

inspector ɪn ˈspekt ə ‖ -ᵊr **~s** z

inspectorate ɪn ˈspekt ər‿ət ɪt **~s** s

inspectorship ɪn ˈspekt ə ʃɪp ‖ -ᵊr- **~s** s

inspiration ˌɪn spə ˈreɪʃ ᵊn -spɪ-, -spaɪᵊ- **~s** z

inspirational ˌɪn spə ˈreɪʃ ᵊn‿əl ◂ ˌ·spɪ-, ˌ·spaɪᵊ- **~ly** i

inspiratory ɪn ˈspaɪᵊr ət‿ər i -ˈspɪr- ‖ -ə tɔːr i -toʊri

inspire ɪn ˈspaɪ‿ə ‖ -ˈspaɪ‿ᵊr **~d** d **~s** z
inspiring/ly ɪn ˈspaɪ‿ər ɪŋ /li ‖ -ˈspaɪ‿ᵊr ɪŋ /

inspirer ɪn ˈspaɪ‿ər ə ‖ -ˈspaɪ‿ᵊr ər **~s** z

inspir|it ɪn ˈspɪr |ɪt -ət ‖ -|ət **~ited** ɪt ɪd ət-, - ‖ əţ əd **~iting** ɪt ɪŋ ət- ‖ əţ ɪŋ **~its** ɪts əts ‖ ə

inspiss|ate ɪn ˈspɪs |eɪt ˈ· · · **~ated** eɪt ɪd -əd ‖ eɪţ əd **~ates** eɪts **~ating** eɪt ɪŋ ‖ eɪţ ɪŋ

inst ɪnᵗst *or as* instant, institute

instabilit|y ˌɪn stə ˈbɪl ət |i -ɪt i ‖ -əţ |i **~ies** i

instal, instal|l ɪn ˈstɔːl ‖ -ˈstɑːl **~led** d **~ling** ɪŋ **instals, installs** ɪn ˈstɔːlz ‖ -ˈstɑːlz

installation ˌɪnᵗst ə ˈleɪʃ ᵊn **~s** z

installer ɪn ˈstɔːl ə ‖ -ᵊr -ˈstɑːl- **~s** z

instalment, installment ɪn ˈstɔːl mənt ‖ -ˈstɑːl- **~s** s
inˈstallment plan

Instamatic *tdmk* ˌɪnᵗst ə ˈmæt ɪk ◂ ‖ -ˈmæţ ɪk **~s** s

instanc|e ˈɪnᵗst ənᵗs **~ed** t **~es** ɪz əz **~ing** ɪŋ

instant ˈɪnᵗst ənt **~ly** li

instantaneous ˌɪnᵗst ən ˈteɪn i‿əs ◂ **~ly** li **~ness** nəs nɪs

instanter ɪn ˈstænt ə ‖ -ˈstænţ ᵊr

instanti|ate ɪn ˈstænᵗʃ i |eɪt **~ated** eɪt ɪd -əd ‖ eɪţ əd **~ates** eɪts **~ating** eɪt ɪŋ ‖ eɪţ ɪŋ

instantiation ɪn ˌstænᵗʃ i ˈeɪʃ ᵊn **~s** z

instead ɪn ˈsted

instep ˈɪn step **~s** s

insti|gate ˈɪnᵗst ɪ |ɡeɪt -ə- **~gated** ɡeɪt ɪd -əd ‖ ɡeɪţ əd **~gates** ɡeɪts **~gating** ɡeɪt ɪŋ ‖ ɡeɪţ ɪŋ

instigation ˌɪnᵗst ɪ ˈɡeɪʃ ᵊn -ə- **~s** z

instigator ˈɪnst ɪ ɡeɪt ə ˈ·ə- ‖ -ɡeɪţ ᵊr **~s** z

instil, instil|l ɪn ˈstɪl **~led** d **~ling** ɪŋ **instils, instills** ɪn ˈstɪlz

instillation ˌɪnᵗst ɪ ˈleɪʃ ᵊn -ə-

instiller ɪn ˈstɪl ə ‖ -ᵊr **~s** z

instilment, instillment ɪn ˈstɪl mənt

instinct ˈɪn stɪŋ*k*t **~s** s

instinctive ɪn ˈstɪŋ*k*t ɪv **~ly** li **~ness** nəs nɪs

instinctual ɪn ˈstɪŋ*k*t ju‿əl -ˈstɪŋ*k* tʃu‿əl ‖ -ˈstɪŋ*k* tʃu‿əl **~ly** li

insti|tute ˈɪnᵗst ɪ |tjuːt -ə-, →-tʃuːt ‖ -|tuːt -tjuː **~tuted** tjuːt ɪd →tʃuːt-, -əd ‖ tuːţ əd tjuːţ- **~tutes** tjuːts →tʃuːts ‖ tuːts tjuːts **~tuting** tjuːt ɪŋ →§tʃuːt- ‖ tuːţ ɪŋ tjuːţ-

institution ˌɪnᵗst ɪ ˈtjuːʃ ᵊn -ə-, →-ˈtʃuːʃ- ‖ -ˈtuːʃ ᵊn -ˈtjuːʃ- **~al** ‿əl **~ally** ‿əl i **~s** z

institutionalis... —*see* **institutionaliz...**

institutionalization ˌɪnᵗst ɪ ˌtjuːʃ ᵊn‿əl aɪ ˈzeɪʃ ᵊn ˌ·ə-, →-ˌtʃuːʃ-, -ɪˈ·· ‖ -ˌtuːʃ ᵊn‿əl ə-

institutionaliz|e ˌɪnᵗst ɪ ˈtjuːʃ ᵊn‿ə laɪz ˌ·ə-, →-ˈtʃuːʃ-, əl aɪz ‖ -ˈtuːʃ- -ˈtjuːʃ- **~ed** d **~es** ɪz əz **~ing** ɪŋ

in-store ˌɪn ˈstɔː ◂ ‖ -ˈstɔːr ◂ -ˈstoʊr
ˌin-store ˈbanking

Instow ˈɪn stəʊ ‖ -stoʊ

instruct ɪn ˈstrʌkt **~ed** ɪd əd **~ing** ɪŋ **~s** s

instruction ɪn ˈstrʌk ʃᵊn **~s** z

instructional ɪn ˈstrʌk ʃᵊn‿əl **~ly** i

instructive ɪn ˈstrʌkt ɪv **~ly** li **~ness** nəs nɪs
instructor ɪn ˈstrʌkt ə ‖ -ᵊr **~s** z **~ship/s** ʃɪp/s
instructress ɪn ˈstrʌk trəs -trɪs, -tres **~es** ɪz əz
instru|ment *v* ˈɪnᵗs trə |ment -tru-, ˌ· ·ˈ· — *see note at* -ment **~mented** ment ɪd -əd ‖ menṭ əd **~menting** ment ɪŋ ‖ menṭ ɪŋ **~ments** ments
instrument *n* ˈɪnᵗs trə mənt -tru- **~s** s
ˈinstrument ˌpanel
instrumental ˌɪnᵗs trə ˈment ᵊl ◂ -tru- ‖ -ˈmenṭ ᵊl **~ly** i **~s** z
instrumentalist ˌɪnᵗs trə ˈment ᵊl ɪst ˌ·tru-, §-əst ‖ -ˈmenṭ- **~s** s
instrumentalit|y ˌɪnᵗs trə men ˈtæl ət |i ˌ·tru-, -mənˈ--, -ɪt i ‖ -əṭ |i **~ies** iz
instrumentation ˌɪnᵗs trə men ˈteɪʃ ᵊn ˌ·tru-, -mənˈ--
insubordinate ˌɪn sə ˈbɔːd ɪn ət ◂ -ᵊn‿, -ɪt ‖ -ˈbɔːrd ᵊn‿ət **~ly** li **~s** s
insubordination ˌɪn sə ˌbɔːd ə ˈneɪʃ ᵊn -ˌ·ɪ- ‖ -ˌbɔːrd ᵊn ˈeɪʃ ᵊn
insubstantial ˌɪn səb ˈstænᵗʃ ᵊl ◂ §-sʌb-, -ˈstɑːnᵗʃ- **~ly** i
insufferab|le ɪn ˈsʌf ər‿əb |ᵊl **~leness** ᵊl nəs -nɪs **~ly** li
insufficienc|y ˌɪn sə ˈfɪʃ ᵊnᵗs |i **~ies** iz
insufficient ˌɪn sə ˈfɪʃ ᵊnt ◂ **~ly** li
insuf|flate ˈɪn sə |fleɪt ɪn ˈsʌ|f leɪt, ˈ· ·· **~flated** fleɪt ɪd -əd ‖ fleɪṭ əd **~flates** fleɪts **~flating** fleɪt ɪŋ ‖ fleɪṭ ɪŋ
insufflation ˌɪn sə ˈfleɪʃ ᵊn -sʌ- **~s** z
insular ˈɪnᵗs jʊl ə -jəl-; §ˈɪnᵗʃ ʊl ə, §-əl- ‖ ˈɪnᵗs əl ᵊr -jəl-; ˈɪnᵗʃ- **~ly** li
insularism ˈɪnᵗs jʊl ə ˌrɪz əm ˈ·jəl-; §ˈɪnᵗʃ ʊl-, §ˈ·əl- ‖ ˈɪnᵗs əl- ˈ·jəl-; ˈɪnᵗʃ-
insularity ˌɪnᵗs ju ˈlær ət i ˌ·jə-, -ɪt i; §ˌɪnᵗʃ u- ‖ ˌɪnᵗs ə ˈlær əṭ i ˌ·jə-, -ˈler-; ˌɪnᵗʃ-
insu|late ˈɪnᵗs ju |leɪt -jə-; §ˈɪnᵗʃ u- ‖ -ə- *(*)* **~lated** leɪt ɪd -əd ‖ leɪṭ əd **~lates** leɪts **~lating** leɪt ɪŋ ‖ leɪṭ ɪŋ
ˈinsulating tape
insulation ˌɪnᵗs ju ˈleɪʃ ᵊn -jə-; §ˌɪnᵗʃ u- ‖ -ə-
insulator ˈɪnᵗs ju leɪt ə ˈ·jə-; §ˈɪnᵗʃ u- ‖ -ə leɪṭ ᵊr **~s** z
insulin ˈɪnᵗs jʊl ɪn -jəl-, §-ən; §ˈɪnᵗʃ ʊl-, -əl- ‖ -əl‿ən
insult *v* ɪn ˈsʌlt **~ed** ɪd əd **~ing** ɪŋ **~s** s
insult *n* ˈɪn sʌlt **~s** s
insuperability ɪn ˌsuːp ər‿ə ˈbɪl ət i -ˌsjuːp-, ˌ·ˌ·-, -ɪt i ‖ -əṭ i
insuperab|le ɪn ˈsuːp ər‿əb |ᵊl ˌɪn-, -ˈsjuːp- **~leness** ᵊl nəs -nɪs **~ly** li
insupportab|le ˌɪn sə ˈpɔːt əb |ᵊl ◂ ‖ -ˈpɔːrṭ- -ˈpoʊrṭ- **~leness** ᵊl nəs -nɪs **~ly** li
insurable ɪn ˈʃʊər əb ᵊl -ˈʃɔːr- ‖ -ˈʃʊr- -ˈʃɜː-
insuranc|e ɪn ˈʃʊər ənᵗs -ˈʃɔːr-, ˈʃɜːr- ‖ -ˈʃʊr- -ˈʃɜː-; ˈɪn ʃʊr- — *Preference poll, AmE:* ·ˈ·· *88%,* ˈ··· *12%.* **~es** ɪz əz
inˈsurance ˌpolicy
insure ɪn ˈʃʊə -ˈʃɔː ‖ -ˈʃʊᵊr -ˈʃɜː **~d** d **~s** z
insuring ɪn ˈʃʊər ɪŋ -ˈʃɔːr- ‖ -ˈʃʊr ɪŋ -ˈʃɜː-
insurer ɪn ˈʃʊər ə -ˈʃɔːr ə ‖ -ˈʃʊr ᵊr -ˈʃɜː- **~s** z
insurgenc|e ɪn ˈsɜːdʒ ənᵗs ‖ -ˈsɜːdʒ- **~y** i

INSURANCE

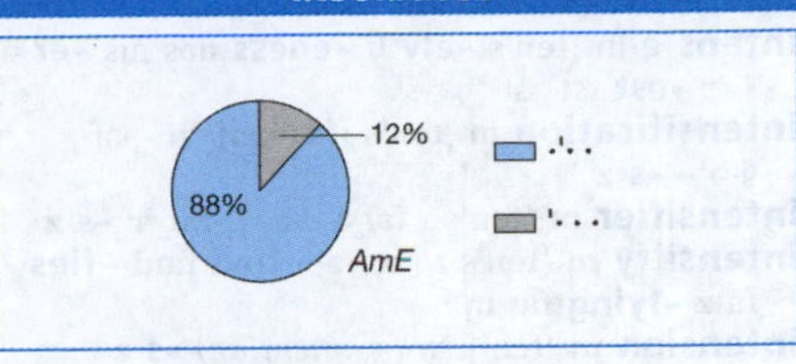

insurgent ɪn ˈsɜːdʒ ənt ‖ -ˈsɜːdʒ- **~s** s
insurmountab|le ˌɪn sə ˈmaʊnt əb |ᵊl ◂ ‖ ˌɪn sᵊr ˈmaʊnṭ- **~ly** li
insurrection ˌɪn sə ˈrek ʃᵊn **~s** z
insurrectionar|y ˌɪn sə ˈrek ʃᵊn‿ər |i -ʃᵊn ər‿|i ‖ -ʃə ner |i **~ies** iz
inswing ˈɪn swɪŋ **~s** z
inswinger ˈɪn ˌswɪŋ ə ‖ -ᵊr **~s** z
intact ɪn ˈtækt ˌɪn- **~ness** nəs nɪs
intaglio ɪn ˈtɑːl i‿əʊ -ˈtæl- ‖ ɪn ˈtæl joʊ -ˈtɑːl- —*It* [in ˈtaʎ ʎo] **~s** z
intake, I~ ˈɪn teɪk **~s** s
intangibility ɪn ˌtændʒ ə ˈbɪl ət i ˌ·ˌ·-, -ɪˈ--, -ɪt i ‖ -əṭ i
intangib|le ɪn ˈtændʒ əb |ᵊl ˌɪn-, -ɪb- **~leness** ᵊl nəs -nɪs **~ly** li
Intasun *tdmk* ˈɪnt ə sʌn
integer ˈɪnt ɪdʒ ə -ədʒ- ‖ -ᵊr **~s** z
integral ˈɪnt ɪg rəl -əg-; ɪn ˈteg-; ⚠ˈɪntr ɪg ᵊl, -əg- ‖ ˈɪnṭ ɪg rəl ɪn ˈteg- **~ly** i **~s** z
ˌintegral ˈcalculus
inte|grate ˈɪnt ɪ |greɪt -ə- ‖ ˈɪnṭ ə- **~grated** greɪt ɪd -əd ‖ greɪṭ əd **~grates** greɪts **~grating** greɪt ɪŋ ‖ greɪṭ ɪŋ
ˌintegrated ˈcircuit
integration ˌɪnt ɪ ˈgreɪʃ ᵊn -ə- ‖ ˌɪnṭ ə- **~s** z
integrative ˈɪnt ɪ greɪt ɪv ˈ·ə-, -grət- ‖ ˈɪnṭ ə greɪṭ ɪv
integrator ˈɪnt ɪ greɪt ə ˈ·ə- ‖ ˈɪnṭ ə greɪṭ ᵊr **~s** z
integrity ɪn ˈteg rət i -rɪt- ‖ -rəṭ i
integument ɪn ˈteg ju mənt ‖ -jə- **~s** s
Intel *tdmk* ˈɪn tel
intellect ˈɪnt ə lekt -ɪ-, -ᵊl ekt ‖ ˈɪnṭ ᵊl ekt **~s** s
intellectual ˌɪnt ə ˈlek tʃu‿əl ◂ ˌ·ɪ-, -ᵊl ˈek-, -tju·, -ʃu · ‖ ˌɪnṭ ᵊl ˈek- **~ly** i **~s** z
intellectualis|e, intellectualiz|e ˌɪnt ə ˈlek tʃu‿ə laɪz ˌ·ɪ-, -ᵊl ˈek-, -tju‿ə-, -ʃu‿ə- ‖ ˌɪnṭ ᵊl ˈek- **~ed** d **~es** ɪz əz **~ing** ɪŋ
intelligenc|e ɪn ˈtel ɪdʒ ənᵗs -ədʒ- **~es** ɪz əz
inˈtelligence ˌofficer; **inˈtelligence ˌquotient**; **inˈtelligence test**
intelligent ɪn ˈtel ɪdʒ ənt -ədʒ- **~ly** li
intelligentsia ɪn ˌtel ɪ ˈdʒent si‿ə ˌ·ˌ·-, -ˈgent- **~s** z
intelligibility ɪn ˌtel ɪdʒ ə ˈbɪl ət i -ˌədʒ-, -ɪˈ--, -ɪt i ‖ -əṭ i
intelligib|le ɪn ˈtel ɪdʒ əb |ᵊl -ˌədʒ-, -ɪb ᵊl **~ly** li
Intelsat ˈɪn tel sæt
intemperance ɪn ˈtemp ᵊr‿ənᵗs ˌɪn-
intemperate ɪn ˈtemp ər‿ət ˌɪn-, ɪt **~ly** li **~ness** nəs nɪs

intend ɪn ˈtend **~ed** ɪd əd **~ing** ɪŋ **~s** z
intendant ɪn ˈtend ənt **~s** s
intens|e ɪn ˈtenᵗs **~ely** li **~eness** nəs nɪs **~er** ə ‖ ᵊr **~est** ɪst əst
intensification ɪn ˌtenᵗs ɪf ɪ ˈkeɪʃ ᵊn -ˌ·əf-, §-əˈ·- **~s** z
intensifier ɪn ˈtenᵗs ɪ faɪ ə -ˈ·ə- ‖ -faɪ ᵊr **~s** z
intensi|fy ɪn ˈtenᵗs ɪ |faɪ -ə- **~fied** faɪd **~fies** faɪz **~fying** faɪ ɪŋ
intension ɪn ˈtenᵗʃ ᵊn *(= intention)* **~s** z
intensional ɪn ˈtenᵗʃ ᵊn əl *(= intentional)*
intensit|y ɪn ˈtenᵗs ət |i -ɪt- ‖ -əţ |i **~ies** iz
intensive ɪn ˈtenᵗs ɪv **~ly** li **~ness** nəs nɪs **~s** z
inˌtensive ˈcare
intent *n, adj* ɪn ˈtent **~ly** li **~ness** nəs nɪs **~s** s
intention ɪn ˈtenᵗʃ ᵊn **~s** z
intentional ɪn ˈtenᵗʃ ᵊn əl **~ly** i
inter *prep, Lat* ˈɪnt ə ‖ ˈɪnţ ᵊr
inter *v 'bury'* ɪn ˈtɜː ‖ -ˈtɜ˞ː **~red** d **interring** ɪn ˈtɜːr ɪŋ ‖ -ˈtɜ˞ː ɪŋ **~s** z
inter- ¦ɪnt ə ‖ ¦ɪnţ ᵊr, *but before a vowel sound* ¦ɪnt ər ‖ ¦ɪnţ ər — **intermesh** *v* ˌɪnt ə ˈmeʃ ‖ ˌɪnţ ᵊr-— **interurban** ˌɪnt ər ˈɜːb ən ◂ ‖ ˌɪnţ ər ˈɜ˞ːb-
interact *v* ˌɪnt ər ˈækt ‖ ˌɪnţ ər- **~ed** ɪd əd **~ing** ɪŋ **~s** s
interaction ˌɪnt ər ˈæk ʃᵊn ‖ ˌɪnţ ər- **~s** z
interactive ˌɪnt ər ˈækt ɪv ◂ ‖ ˌɪnţ ər- **~ly** li
interactivity ˌɪnt ər æk ˈtɪv ət i ‖ ˌɪnţ ᵊr æk ˈtɪv əţ i
interagency ˌɪnt ər ˈeɪdʒənᵗs i ◂ ‖ ˌɪnţ ᵊr-
inter alia ˌɪnt ər ˈeɪl i ə -ˈɑːl-, -ˈæl- ‖ ˌɪnţ ər-
inter|breed *v* ˌɪnt ə |ˈbriːd ‖ ˌɪnţ ᵊr- **~bred** ˈbred **~breeding** ˈbriːd ɪŋ **~breeds** ˈbriːdz
intercalary ɪn ˈtɜːk ᵊl ər i ˌɪnt ə ˈkæl ər i◂, -ˈkeɪl- ‖ ɪn ˈtɜ˞ːk ə ler i ˌɪnţ ᵊr ˈkæl ər i ◂
interca|late ɪn ˈtɜːk ə |leɪt -ᵊ|l eɪt; ˌɪnt ə kə ˈ|leɪt ‖ ɪn ˈtɜ˞ːk ə |leɪt ˌɪnţ ᵊr kə ˈ|leɪt **~lated** leɪt ɪd -əd ‖ leɪţ əd **~lates** leɪts **~lating** leɪt ɪŋ ‖ leɪţ ɪŋ
intercalation ɪn ˌtɜːk ə ˈleɪʃ ᵊn ˌɪnt ə kə- ‖ ɪn ˌtɜ˞ːk ə- ˌɪnţ ᵊr kə- **~s** z
interced|e ˌɪnt ə ˈsiːd ‖ ˌɪnţ ᵊr- **~ed** ɪd əd **~er/s** ə/z ‖ ᵊr/z **~es** z **~ing** ɪŋ
intercept *v* ˌɪnt ə ˈsept ˈ· · · ‖ ˌɪnţ ᵊr- **~ed** ɪd əd **~ing** ɪŋ **~s** s
intercept *n* ˈɪnt ə sept ‖ ˈɪnţ ᵊr- **~s** s
interception ˌɪnt ə ˈsep ʃᵊn ‖ ˌɪnţ ᵊr- **~s** z
interceptor ˌɪnt ə ˈsept ə ‖ ˌɪnţ ᵊr ˈsept ᵊr **~s** z
intercession ˌɪnt ə ˈseʃ ᵊn ‖ ˌɪnţ ᵊr- **~al** əl ◂ **~s** z
intercessor ˌɪnt ə ˈses ə ˈ· · · · ‖ ˌɪnţ ᵊr ˈses ᵊr **~s** z
intercessory ˌɪnt ə ˈses ər i ◂ ‖ ˌɪnţ ᵊr-
interchang|e *v* ˌɪnt ə ˈtʃeɪndʒ ◂ ‖ ˌɪnţ ᵊr- **~ed** d **~es** ɪz əz **~ing** ɪŋ
interchang|e *n* ˈɪnt ə tʃeɪndʒ ‖ ˈɪnţ ᵊr- **~es** ɪz əz
interchangeability ˌɪnt ə ˌtʃeɪndʒ ə ˈbɪl ət i -ɪt i ‖ ˌɪnţ ᵊr ˌtʃeɪndʒ ə ˈbɪl əţ i
interchangeab|le ˌɪnt ə ˈtʃeɪndʒ əb |ᵊl ◂ ‖ ˌɪnţ ᵊr- **~leness** ᵊl nəs -nɪs **~ly** li

inter-city, intercity ˌɪnt ə ˈsɪt i ◂ ‖ ˌɪnţ ᵊr ˈsɪţ i ◂
intercollegiate ˌɪnt ə kə ˈliːdʒ ət ◂ -ɪt, -ˈliːdʒ i ət, ɪt ‖ ˌɪnţ ᵊr-
intercom ˈɪnt ə kɒm ‖ ˈɪnţ ᵊr kɑːm **~s** z
intercommuni|cate ˌɪnt ə kə ˈmjuːn ɪ |keɪt -ˈ·ə- ‖ ˌɪnţ ᵊr- **~cated** keɪt ɪd -əd ‖ keɪţ əd **~cates** keɪts **~cating** keɪt ɪŋ ‖ keɪţ ɪŋ
intercommunication ˌɪnt ə kə ˌmjuːn ɪ ˈkeɪʃ ᵊn -ˌ·ə- ‖ ˌɪnţ ᵊr- **~s** z
intercommunion ˌɪnt ə kə ˈmjuːn i ən ‖ ˌɪnţ ᵊr-
interconnect ˌɪnt ə kə ˈnekt ◂ ‖ ˌɪnţ ᵊr- **~ed** ɪd əd **~ing** ɪŋ **~s** s
interconnection ˌɪnt ə kəˈnek ʃᵊn ‖ ˌɪnţ ᵊr-
intercontinental ˌɪnt ə ˌkɒnt ɪ ˈnent ᵊl ◂ -ˌ·ə- ‖ ˌɪnţ ᵊr ˌkɑːnt ᵊn ˈenţ ᵊl ◂
ˌintercontiˌnental balˌlistic ˈmissile
intercostal ˌɪnt ə ˈkɒst ᵊl ◂ ‖ ˌɪnţ ᵊr ˈkɑːst ᵊl ◂
intercourse ˈɪnt ə kɔːs ‖ ˈɪnţ ᵊr kɔːrs -kours
intercultural ˌɪnt ə ˈkʌltʃ ᵊr əl ◂ ‖ ˌɪnţ ᵊr-
intercurrent ˌɪnt ə ˈkʌr ənt ◂ ‖ ˌɪnţ ᵊr ˈkɜ˞ː- **~ly** li
inter|cut *v* ˌɪnt ə |ˈkʌt ‖ ˌɪnţ ᵊr- **~cuts** ˈkʌts **~cutting** ˈkʌt ɪŋ ‖ ˈkʌţ ɪŋ
interdenominational ˌɪnt ə dɪ ˌnɒm ɪ ˈneɪʃ ᵊn əl ◂ -də,-·, -ˌ·ə- ‖ ˌɪnţ ᵊr dɪ ˌnɑːm ə- **~ism** ˌɪz əm
interdental ˌɪnt ə ˈdent ᵊl ◂ ‖ ˌɪnţ ᵊr ˈdenţ ᵊl ◂ **~ly** i **~s** z
interdepartmental ˌɪnt ə ˌdiː pɑːt ˈment ᵊl ◂ ˌ· ·dɪˌ·ˈ· ·, ˌ· ·dəˌ·ˈ· · ‖ ˌɪnţ ᵊr ˌdiː pɑːrt ˈmenţ ᵊl ˌ· ·dɪˌ·ˈ· · **~ly** i
ˌinterdepartˌmental ˈrivalry
interdependence ˌɪnt ə dɪ ˈpend ənᵗs -dəˈ·-, §-diːˈ·- ‖ ˌɪnţ ᵊr-
interdependent ˌɪnt ə dɪ ˈpend ənt ◂ -dəˈ·-, §-diːˈ·- ‖ ˌɪnţ ᵊr- **~ly** li
interdict *v* ˌɪnt ə ˈdɪkt -ˈdaɪt ‖ ˌɪnţ ᵊr- **~ed** ɪd əd **~ing** ɪŋ **~s** s
interdict *n* ˈɪnt ə dɪkt -daɪt ‖ ˈɪnţ ᵊr- **~s** s
interdiction ˌɪnt ə ˈdɪk ʃᵊn ‖ ˌɪnţ ᵊr- **~s** z
interdisciplinarity ˌɪnt ə ˌdɪs ə plɪ ˈnær ət i -ˌ·ɪ-, -ɪt i ‖ ˌɪnţ ᵊr ˌdɪs ə plə ˈnær əţ i -ˈner-
interdisciplinary ˌɪnt ə ˈdɪs ə plɪn ər i ◂ -ˈ·ɪ-, -plən · ·, ˌ· ·ˌ· ·ˈ· · · ‖ ˌɪnţ ᵊr ˈdɪs ə plə ner i ◂
interest ˈɪntr əst -ɪst, -est; ˈɪnt ə rest ‖ ˈɪnţ ə rest **~ed** ɪd əd **~ing** ɪŋ **~s** s
ˈinterest group
interested ˈɪntr əst ɪd -ɪst-, ˈɪnt ə rest ɪd, -əd ‖ ˈɪnţ ə rest əd **~ly** li **~ness** nəs nɪs
interest-free ˌɪntr əst ˈfriː ◂ -ɪst-, -est; ˌɪnt ə rest- ‖ ˌɪnţ ə rest-
interesting ˈɪntr əst ɪŋ -ɪst-, -est-; ˈɪnt ə rest ɪŋ ‖ ˈɪnţ ə rest ɪŋ **~ly** li
interfac|e *v* ˈɪnt ə feɪs ˌ· ·ˈ· ‖ ˈɪnţ ᵊr- **~ed** t **~es** ɪz əz **~ing** ɪŋ
interfac|e *n* ˈɪnt ə feɪs ‖ ˈɪnţ ᵊr- **~es** ɪz əz
interfaith ˌɪnt ə ˈfeɪθ ◂ ‖ ˌɪnţ ər-
inter|fere ˌɪnt ə |ˈfɪə ‖ ˌɪnţ ᵊr |ˈfɪᵊr -ə- **~fered** ˈfɪəd ‖ ˈfɪᵊrd **~feres** ˈfɪəz ‖ ˈfɪᵊrz **~fering** ˈfɪər ɪŋ ◂ ‖ ˈfɪr ɪŋ ◂
interference ˌɪnt ə ˈfɪər ənᵗs ‖ ˌɪnţ ᵊr ˈfɪr- -ə-

nterferometer ˌɪnt ə fə ˈrɒm ɪt ə -ət ə ‖ ˌɪnṯ ᵊr fə ˈruːm əṯ ᵊr ˌ·ə-, -fɪˈ·- **~s** z

nterferometric ˌɪnt ə ˌfer əʊ ˈmetr ɪk ◂ -ˌfɪər- ‖ ˌɪnṯ ᵊr ˌfɪr ə- **~ally** ᵊl‿i

nterferon ˌɪnt ə ˈfɪər ɒn ‖ ˌɪnṯ ᵊr ˈfɪr ɑːn -ə-

nterflora *tdmk* ˌɪnt ə ˈflɔːr ə ‖ ˌɪnṯ ᵊr- -ˈflour-

ntergalactic ˌɪnt ə gə ˈlækt ɪk ◂ ‖ ˌɪnṯ ᵊr-

ntergenerational ˌɪnt ə ˌdʒen ə ˈreɪʃ ᵊn‿əl ◂ ‖ ˌɪnṯ ᵊr-

nterglacial ˌɪnt ə ˈgleɪs i‿əl ◂ -ˈgleɪʃ-, -ˈgleɪʃ ᵊl ‖ ˌɪnṯ ᵊr ˈgleɪʃ ᵊl ◂

ntergovernmental ˌɪnt ə ˌgʌv ᵊn ˈment ᵊl ◂ -ˌgʌv ᵊm-, -ˌgʌb ᵊm-, -ˌgʌv ə-, -ˌgʌm ˈment- ‖ ˌɪnṯ ᵊr ˌgʌv ᵊrn ˈmenṯ ᵊ l ◂

nterim ˈɪnt ər ɪm §-əm ‖ ˈɪnṯ-

nterior ɪn ˈtɪər i‿ə ‖ -ˈtɪr i‿ᵊr **~ly** li **~s** z

inˌterior ˈdecorator

nterioris|e, interioriz|e ɪn ˈtɪər i‿ə raɪz ‖ -ˈtɪr- **~ed** d **~es** ɪz əz **~ing** ɪŋ

nterject ˌɪnt ə ˈdʒekt ‖ ˌɪnṯ ᵊr- **~ed** ɪd əd **~ing** ɪŋ **~s** s

nterjection ˌɪnt ə ˈdʒek ʃᵊn ‖ ˌɪnṯ ᵊr- **~s** z

nterlac|e ˌɪnt ə ˈleɪs ‖ ˌɪnṯ ᵊr- **~ed** t **~es** ɪz əz **~ing** ɪŋ

nterlaken ˈɪnt ə ˌlɑːk ən ˌ·ˈ·· ‖ ˈɪnṯ ᵊr- —*Ger* [ˈʔɪn tɐ lak ᵊn]

nterlanguag|e ˈɪnt ə ˌlæŋ gwɪdʒ -wɪdʒ ‖ ˈɪnṯ ᵊr- **~es** ɪz əz

nterlard ˌɪnt ə ˈlɑːd ‖ ˌɪnṯ ᵊr ˈlɑːrd **~ed** ɪd əd **~ing** ɪŋ **~s** z

nter|leaf *n* ˈɪnt ə |liːf ‖ ˈɪnṯ ᵊr- **~leaves** liːvz

nterleav|e *v* ˌɪnt ə ˈliːv ‖ ˌɪnṯ ᵊr- **~ed** d **~es** z **~ing** ɪŋ

nterleaves *n pl* ˈɪnt ə liːvz ‖ ˈɪnṯ ᵊr-

nterleaves *from v* ˌɪnt ə ˈliːvz ‖ ˌɪnṯ ᵊr-

nterleukin ˌɪnt ə ˈluːk ɪn -ˈljuːk-, §-ən ‖ ˌɪnṯ ᵊr-

interlin|e *v* ˌɪnt ə ˈlaɪn ‖ ˌɪnṯ ᵊr- **~ed** d **~es** z **~ing** ɪŋ

interlinear ˌɪnt ə ˈlɪn i‿ə ◂ ‖ ˌɪnṯ ᵊr ˈlɪn i‿ᵊr

Interlingua, i~ ˌɪnt ə ˈlɪŋ gwə ˈ·ˌ·· ‖ ˌɪnṯ ᵊr-

interlingue ˌɪnt ə ˈlɪŋ gweɪ ‖ ˌɪnṯ ᵊr-

interlink *v* ˌɪnt ə ˈlɪŋk ‖ ˌɪnṯ ᵊr- **~ed** t **~ing** ɪŋ **~s** s

interlock *v* ˌɪnt ə ˈlɒk ‖ ˌɪnṯ ᵊr ˈlɑːk **~ed** t **~ing** ɪŋ **~s** s

interlock *n* ˈɪnt ə lɒk ‖ ˈɪnṯ ᵊr lɑːk **~s** s

interlocutor ˌɪnt ə ˈlɒk jʊt ə -jət ə ‖ ˌɪnṯ ᵊr ˈlɑːk jəṯ ᵊr **~s** z

interlocutor|y ˌɪnt ə ˈlɒk jʊt‿ər |i -ˈ·jət- ‖ ˌɪnṯ ᵊr ˈlɑːk jə tɔːr |i -tour i **~ies** iz

interloper ˈɪnt ə ləʊp ə ˌ·ˈ·· ‖ ˈɪnṯ ᵊr loʊp ᵊr ˌ·ˈ·· **~s** z

interlude ˈɪnt ə luːd -ljuːd; -ᵊl uːd, -juːd ‖ ˈɪnṯ ᵊr- **~s** z

intermarriage ˌɪnt ə ˈmær ɪdʒ ‖ ˌɪnṯ ᵊr- -ˈmer-

intermarr|y ˌɪnt ə ˈmær |i ‖ ˌɪnṯ ᵊr- -ˈmer- **~ied** id **~ies** iz **~ying** i‿ɪŋ

intermediar|y ˌɪnt ə ˈmiːd i‿ər |i ◂ ‖ ˌɪnṯ ᵊr ˈmiːd i er |i **~ies** iz

intermediate ˌɪnt ə ˈmiːd i‿ət ◂ -ɪt ‖ ˌɪnṯ ᵊr- **~ly** li **~ness** nəs nɪs **~s** s

interment ɪn ˈtɜː mənt ‖ -ˈtɝː- **~s** s

intermezz|o ˌɪnt ə ˈmets |əʊ -ˈmedz- ‖ ˌɪnṯ ᵊr ˈmets |oʊ **~i** i iː **~os** əʊz ‖ oʊz

interminab|le ɪn ˈtɜːm ɪn əb |ᵊl ˌɪn-, ən‿əb- ‖ -ˈtɝːm- **~ly** li

intermingl|e ˌɪnt ə ˈmɪŋ gᵊl ‖ ˌɪnṯ ᵊr- **~ed** d **~es** z **~ing** ‿ɪŋ

intermission ˌɪnt ə ˈmɪʃ ᵊn ‖ ˌɪnṯ ᵊr- **~s** z

inter|mit ˌɪnt ə |ˈmɪt ‖ ˌɪnṯ ᵊr- **~mits** ˈmɪts **~mitted** ˈmɪt ɪd -əd ‖ ˈmɪṯ əd **~mitting** ˈmɪt ɪŋ ‖ ˈmɪṯ ɪŋ

intermittent ˌɪnt ə ˈmɪt ᵊnt ◂ ‖ ˌɪnṯ ᵊr- **~ly** li

intermix ˌɪnt ə ˈmɪks ‖ ˌɪnṯ ᵊr- **~ed** t **~es** ɪz əz **~ing** ɪŋ

intern *v 'confine'* ɪn ˈtɜːn ‖ -ˈtɝːn ˈ· · **~ed** d **~ing** ɪŋ **~s** z

intern *n* ˈɪn tɜːn ‖ -tɝːn **~s** z

intern *v 'act as an intern(e)'* ˈɪn tɜːn ‖ -tɝːn **~ed** d **~ing** ɪŋ **~s** z

internal ɪn ˈtɜːn ᵊl ˌɪn- ‖ -ˈtɝːn- **~ly** i **~s** z

inˌternal comˈbustion; Inˌternal ˈRevenue ˌService

internalis... —*see* **internaliz...**

internalization ɪn ˌtɜːn əl aɪ ˈzeɪʃ ᵊn ˌ·ˌ··-, -ɪˈ·- ‖ ɪn ˌtɝːn ᵊl‿ə- **~s** z

internaliz|e ɪn ˈtɜːn ə laɪz -ᵊl aɪz ‖ -ˈtɝːn ᵊl aɪz **~ed** d **~es** ɪz əz **~ing** ɪŋ

international, I~ ˌɪnt ə ˈnæʃ ᵊn‿əl ◂ ‖ ˌɪnṯ ᵊr- **~ly** i **~s** z

ˌinterˌnational ˈdate line; ˌinterˌnational ˈlaw

Internationale ˌɪnt ə ˌnæʃ ə ˈnɑːl -ˌnæʃ i‿ə ˈnɑːl ‖ ˌɪnṯ ᵊr-

internationalis... —*see* **internationaliz...**

international|ism ˌɪnt ə ˈnæʃ ᵊn‿əl |ˌɪz əm ‖ ˌɪnṯ ᵊr- **~ist/s** ɪst/s §əst/s

internationalization ˌɪnt ə ˌnæʃ ᵊn‿əl aɪ ˈzeɪʃ ᵊn -ɪˈ·- ‖ ˌɪnṯ ᵊr ˌnæʃ ᵊn‿əl ə-

internationaliz|e ˌɪnt ə ˈnæʃ ᵊn‿ə laɪz ‖ ˌɪnṯ ᵊr- **~ed** d **~es** ɪz əz **~ing** ɪŋ

interne ˈɪn tɜːn ‖ -tɝːn **~s** z

internecine ˌɪnt ə ˈniːs aɪn ◂ ‖ ˌɪnṯ ᵊr ˈniːs ᵊn ◂ -ˈnes-, -iːn, -aɪn

internee ˌɪn tɜː ˈniː ‖ -tɝː- **~s** z

Internet, i~ ˈɪnt ə net ‖ ˈɪnṯ ᵊr-

internist ˈɪn tɜːn ɪst §-əst; ·ˈ· · ‖ -tɝːn- **~s** s

internment ɪn ˈtɜːn mənt →-ˈtɜːm- ‖ -ˈtɝːn- **~s** s

internship ˈɪn tɜːn ʃɪp ·ˈ·· ‖ -tɝːn- **~s** s

interoffice ˌɪnt ər ˈɒf ɪs ◂ ‖ ˌɪnṯ ᵊr-

interpel|late ɪn ˈtɜːp ə |leɪt -e-; ˌɪnt ə ˈpe|l eɪt ‖ ˌɪnṯ ᵊr ˈpe|l eɪt ɪn ˈtɝːp ə |leɪt **~lated** leɪt ɪd -əd ‖ leɪṯ əd **~lates** leɪts **~lating** leɪt ɪŋ ‖ leɪṯ ɪŋ

interpellation ɪn ˌtɜːp ə ˈleɪʃ ᵊn -e-; ˌɪnt ə pə-, -peˈ·- ‖ ˌɪnṯ ᵊr pə- ɪn ˌtɝːp ə- **~s** z

interpene|trate ˌɪnt ə ˈpen ɪ |treɪt -ˈ·ə- ‖ ˌɪnṯ ᵊr- **~trated** treɪt ɪd -əd ‖ treɪṯ əd **~trates** treɪts **~trating** treɪt ɪŋ ‖ treɪṯ ɪŋ

interpenetration ˌɪnt ə ˌpen ɪ ˈtreɪʃ ᵊn ˌ·ə- ‖ ˌɪnṯ ᵊr- **~s** z

interpersonal ˌɪnt ə ˈpɜːs ᵊn‿əl ◂ ‖ ˌɪnṯ ᵊr ˈpɝːs-

I

interplanetary ˌɪnt ə ˈplæn ɪt̬ər i ◂ -ˈət̬ ‖ ˌɪnt̬ ər ˈplæn ə ter i
interplay ˈɪnt ə pleɪ ‖ ˈɪnt̬ ər-
Interpol ˈɪnt ə pɒl ‖ ˈɪnt̬ ər poʊl *(*)*
interpo|late ɪn ˈtɜːp ə |leɪt ‖ -ˈtɝːp- **~lated** leɪt ɪd -əd ‖ leɪt̬ əd **~lates** leɪts **~lating** leɪt ɪŋ ‖ leɪt̬ ɪŋ
interpolation ɪn ˌtɜːp ə ˈleɪʃ ən ‖ -ˌtɝːp- **~s** z
interpos|e ˌɪnt ə ˈpəʊz ‖ ˌɪnt̬ ər ˈpoʊz **~ed** d **~es** ɪz əz **~ing** ɪŋ
interposition ˌɪnt ə pə ˈzɪʃ ən ɪn ˌtɜːp ə- ‖ ˌɪnt̬ ər-
interp|ret ɪn ˈtɜːp |rɪt -rət ‖ -ˈtɝːp |rət **~reted** rɪt ɪd rət-, -əd ‖ rət̬ əd **~reting** rɪt ɪŋ rət- ‖ rət̬ ɪŋ **~rets** rɪts rəts ‖ rəts
interpretation ɪn ˌtɜːp rɪ ˈteɪʃ ən -rə- ‖ -ˌtɝːp- **~s** z
interpretative ɪn ˈtɜːp rɪt ət ɪv -ˈrət-; -rɪ teɪt-, -rə teɪt- ‖ -ˈtɝːp rə teɪt̬ ɪv -rət̬ ət̬- **~ly** li
interpreter ɪn ˈtɜːp rɪt ə -rət- ‖ -ˈtɝːp rət̬ ər **~s** z
interpretive ɪn ˈtɜːp rɪt ɪv -rət- ‖ -ˈtɝːp rət̬ ɪv **~ly** li
interquartile ˌɪnt ə ˈkwɔːt aɪəl ◂ ‖ ˌɪnt̬ ər ˈkwɔːrt- -ˈkwɔːrt̬ əl ◂ **~s** z
interracial ˌɪnt ə ˈreɪʃ əl ◂ ‖ ˌɪnt̬ ər- **~ly** i
Inter-Rail ˈɪnt ə reɪəl ‖ ˌɪnt̬ ər-
interreg|num ˌɪnt ə ˈreg |nəm ‖ ˌɪnt̬ ər- **~na** nə **~nums** nəmz
interre|late ˌɪnt ə rɪ |ˈleɪt -rə'-, §-riː'- ‖ ˌɪnt̬ ər- **~lated** ˈleɪt ɪd -əd ‖ ˈleɪt̬ əd **~lates** ˈleɪts **~lating** ˈleɪt ɪŋ ‖ ˈleɪt̬ ɪŋ
interrelation ˌɪnt ə ri ˈleɪʃ ən -rə'- ‖ ˌɪnt̬ ər- **~s** z **~ship/s** ʃɪp/s
interro|gate ɪn ˈter ə |geɪt **~gated** geɪt ɪd -əd ‖ geɪt̬ əd **~gates** geɪts **~gating** geɪt ɪŋ ‖ geɪt̬ ɪŋ
interrogation ɪn ˌter ə ˈgeɪʃ ən **~s** z
in,terro'gation mark
interrogative ˌɪnt ə ˈrɒg ət ɪv ◂ ‖ ˌɪnt̬ ə ˈrɑːg ət̬ ɪv ◂ **~ly** li **~s** z
interrogator ɪn ˈter ə geɪt ə ‖ -geɪt̬ ər **~s** z
interrogator|y ˌɪnt ə ˈrɒg ət̬ər |i ◂ ‖ ˌɪnt̬ ə ˈrɑːg ə tɔːr |i -toʊr i **~ies** iz
interrupt *v* ˌɪnt ə ˈrʌpt ‖ ˌɪnt̬ ə- **~ed** ɪd əd **~ing** ɪŋ **~s** s
interrupt *n* ˈɪnt ə rʌpt ˌ·ˈ· ‖ ˈɪnt̬ ə- **~s** s
interruption ˌɪnt ə ˈrʌp ʃən ‖ ˌɪnt̬ ə- **~s** z
interscholastic ˌɪnt ə skə ˈlæst ɪk ◂ -skɒ'- ‖ ˌɪnt̬ ər-
inter se ˌɪnt ə ˈseɪ -ˈsiː ‖ ˌɪnt̬ ər-
intersect ˌɪnt ə ˈsekt ‖ ˌɪnt̬ ər- **~ed** ɪd əd **~ing** ɪŋ **~s** s
intersection ˌɪnt ə ˈsek ʃən ˈ· ˌ·, · ‖ ˈɪnt̬ ər ˌsek ʃən ˌ· ˈ·· **~s** z
intersession ˈɪnt ə ˌseʃ ən ‖ ˌɪnt̬ ər- **~s** z
intersex ˈɪnt ə seks ‖ ˈɪnt̬ ər- **~es** ɪz əz
interspac|e *v* ˌɪnt ə ˈspeɪs ˈ· · · ‖ ˌɪnt̬ ər- **~ed** t **~es** ɪz əz **~ing** ɪŋ
interspac|e *n* ˈɪnt ə speɪs ˌ· ˈ· ‖ ˈɪnt̬ ər- **~es** ɪz əz
interspers|e ˌɪnt ə ˈspɜːs ‖ ˌɪnt̬ ər ˈspɝːs **~ed** t **~es** ɪz əz **~ing** ɪŋ

interspersion ˌɪnt ə ˈspɜːʃ ən §-ˈspɜːʒ- ‖ ˌɪnt̬ ər ˈspɝːʒ ən
interstate *n* ˈɪnt ə steɪt ‖ ˈɪnt̬ ər- **~s** s
interstate *adj* ˌɪnt ə ˈsteɪt ◂ ˈ· · · ‖ ˌɪnt̬ ər-
ˌinterstate ˈhighway
interstellar ˌɪnt ə ˈstel ə ◂ ‖ ˌɪnt̬ ər ˈstel ər
ˌinterˌstellar ˈdust
interstic|e ɪn ˈtɜːst ɪs -əs ‖ -ˈtɝːst- **~es** ɪz əz
interstitial ˌɪnt ə ˈstɪʃ əl ◂ ‖ ˌɪnt̬ ər- **~ly** i **~s** z
intertextuality ˌɪnt ə ˌteks tju ˈæl ət i -tʃu'-, -ɪt i ‖ ˌɪnt̬ ər ˌteks tʃu ˈæl ət̬ i
intertidal ˌɪnt ə ˈtaɪd əl ◂ ‖ ˌɪnt̬ ər-
intertribal ˌɪnt ə ˈtraɪb əl ◂ ‖ ˌɪnt̬ ər-
intertwin|e ˌɪnt ə ˈtwaɪn ‖ ˌɪnt̬ ər- **~ed** d **~es** z **~ing** ɪŋ
interurban ˌɪnt ər ˈɜːb ən ◂ ‖ ˌɪnt̬ ər ˈɝːb-
interval ˈɪnt əv əl ‖ ˈɪnt̬ ərv əl **~s** z
interven|e ˌɪnt ə ˈviːn ‖ ˌɪnt̬ ər- **~ed** d **~es** z **~ing** ɪŋ
intervention ˌɪnt ə ˈventʃ ən ‖ ˌɪnt̬ ər- **~ism** ˌɪz əm **~ist/s** ɪst/s §əst/s ‖ əst/s **~s** z
inter|view *n, v* ˈɪnt ə |vjuː ‖ ˈɪnt̬ ər- **~viewed** vjuːd **~viewing** vjuː‿ɪŋ **~views** vjuːz
interviewee ˌɪnt ə vju ˈiː ‖ ˌɪnt̬ ər- **~s** z
interviewer ˈɪnt ə vjuː‿ə ‖ ˈɪnt̬ ər vjuː ər **~s** z
intervocalic ˌɪnt ə vəʊ ˈkæl ɪk ◂ ‖ ˌɪnt̬ ər voʊ- **~ally** əl‿i
interwar ˌɪnt ə ˈwɔː ◂ ‖ ˌɪnt̬ ər ˈwɔːr ◂
inter|weave ˌɪnt ə |ˈwiːv ‖ ˌɪnt̬ ər- **~weaves** ˈwiːvz **~weaving** ˈwiːv ɪŋ **~wove** ˈwəʊv ‖ ˈwoʊv **~woven** ˈwəʊv ən ◂ ‖ ˈwoʊv ən ◂
intestacy ɪn ˈtest əs i
intestate ɪn ˈtest eɪt -ət, -ɪt **~s** s
intestinal ɪn ˈtest ɪn əl -ən‿əl; ˌɪnt e ˈstaɪn əl ◂
intestine ɪn ˈtest ɪn -iːn, -ən **~s** z
in-thing ˌɪn ˈθɪŋ
intifada ˌɪnt ɪ ˈfɑːd ə —*Arabic* [in ti ˈfaː dˤa]
intimac|y ˈɪnt ɪm əs |i -ˈəm- ‖ ˈɪnt̬ əm- **~ies** iz
inti|mate *v* ˈɪnt ɪ |meɪt -ə- ‖ ˈɪnt̬ ə- **~mated** meɪt ɪd -əd ‖ meɪt̬ əd **~mates** meɪts **~mating** meɪt ɪŋ ‖ meɪt̬ ɪŋ
intimate *adj, n* ˈɪnt ɪm ət -əm-, -ɪt ‖ ˈɪnt̬ əm ət **~ly** li **~ness** nəs nɪs **~s** s
intimation ˌɪnt ɪ ˈmeɪʃ ən -ə- ‖ ˌɪnt̬ ə- **~s** z
intimi|date ɪn ˈtɪm ɪ |deɪt ˌɪn-, -ə- **~dated** deɪt ɪd -əd ‖ deɪt̬ əd **~dates** deɪts **~dating** deɪt ɪŋ ‖ deɪt̬ ɪŋ
intimidation ɪn ˌtɪm ɪ ˈdeɪʃ ən ˌ·ˌ··, -əˈ-
intimidatory ɪn ˌtɪm ɪ ˈdeɪt ər i ◂ -ˌ·ə-; ·ˈ· · · · ‖ ɪn ˈtɪm əd ə tɔːr i -toʊr i
into *strong form* ˈɪn tuː -tu, *weak forms* (ˈ)ɪnt ə *(especially before a consonant),* (ˈ)ɪnt u *(especially before a vowel)*
intolerab|le ɪn ˈtɒl ər‿əb |əl ‖ -ˈtɑːl- **~leness** əl nəs -nɪs **~ly** li
intoleranc|e ɪn ˈtɒl ər əntˢ ˌɪn- ‖ -ˈtɑːl- **~es** ɪz əz
intolerant ɪn ˈtɒl ər ənt ˌɪn- ‖ -ˈtɑːl- **~ly** li
into|nate ˈɪn təʊ |neɪt ‖ -tə- **~nated** neɪt ɪd -əd ‖ neɪt̬ əd **~nates** neɪts **~nating** neɪt ɪŋ ‖ neɪt̬ ɪŋ
intonation ˌɪn tə ˈneɪʃ ən -təʊ- **~s** z
ˌintoˈnation ˌpatterns

ntonational ˌɪn tə ˈneɪʃ ᵊn‿əl ˌ·təʊ-

ntonative ˈɪn təʊ neɪt ɪv ‖ -tə neɪţ ɪv

nton|e ɪn ˈtəʊn ‖ -ˈtoʊn **~ed** d **~es** z **~ing** ɪŋ

n toto ɪn ˈtəʊt əʊ ‖ -ˈtoʊţ oʊ

ntourist *tdmk* ˈɪn ˌtʊər ɪst -ˌtɔːr-, §-əst ‖ -ˌtʊr-

ntoxicant ɪn ˈtɒks ɪk ənt -ək- ‖ -ˈtɑːks- **~s** s

ntoxi|cate ɪn ˈtɒks ɪ |keɪt -ə- ‖ -ˈtɑːks- **~cated** keɪt ɪd -əd ‖ keɪţ əd **~cates** keɪts **~cating** keɪt ɪŋ ‖ keɪţ ɪŋ

ntoxication ɪn ˌtɒks ɪ ˈkeɪʃ ᵊn -ə- ‖ -ˌtɑːks- **~s** z

ntra- ¦ɪntr ə — **intracardiac** ˌɪntr ə ˈkɑːd i æk ◂ ‖ -ˈkɑːrd-

ntractability ɪn ˌtrækt ə ˈbɪl ət i ˌ·ˌ··-, -ɪt i ‖ -əţ i

ntractab|le ɪn ˈtrækt əb |ᵊl ˌɪn- **~leness** ᵊl nəs -nɪs **~ly** li

ntrados ɪn ˈtreɪd ɒs ‖ ˈɪntr ə dɑːs -doʊ

ntramural ˌɪntr ə ˈmjʊər əl ◂ -ˈmjɔːr- ‖ -ˈmjʊr- **~ly** i

ntramuscular ˌɪntr ə ˈmʌsk jʊl ə ◂ -jəl ə ‖ -jəl ᵊr

ntranet ˈɪntr ə net **~s** s

ntransigenc|e ɪn ˈtrænᵗs ɪdʒ ənᵗs -ˈtrænz-, -ˈtrɑːnᵗs-, -ˈtrɑːnz-, -ədʒ- **~y** i

ntransigent ɪn ˈtrænᵗs ɪdʒ ənt -ˈtrænz-, -ˈtrɑːnᵗs-, -ˈtrɑːnz-, -ədʒ- **~ly** li **~s** s

ntransitive ɪn ˈtrænᵗs ət ɪv ˌɪn-, -ˈtrænz-, -ˈtrɑːnᵗs-, -ˈtrɑːnz-, -ɪt- ‖ -əţ ɪv **~ly** li **~ness** nəs nɪs **~s** z

ntransitivity ɪn ˌtrænᵗs ə ˈtɪv ət i -ˌtrænz-, -ˌtrɑːnᵗs-, -ˌtrɑːnz-, ˌ·ˌ··-, -əˈ--, -ət i ‖ -əţ i

ntrapersonal ˌɪntr ə ˈpɜːs ᵊn‿əl ◂ ‖ -ˈpɜ˞ːs-

ntrapreneur ˌɪntr ə prə ˈnɜː -preˈ·, -ˈnjʊə ‖ -ˈnɜ˞ː -ˈnʊᵊr **~s** z

intrastate ˌɪntr ə ˈsteɪt ◂

intrauterine ˌɪntr ə ˈjuːt ə raɪn ◂ ‖ -ˈjuːţ ər ən -ə raɪn
ˌ**intra**ˌ**uterine deˈvice**

intrava|sate ɪn ˈtræv ə |seɪt ˌ·-- **~sated** seɪt ɪd -əd ‖ seɪţ əd **~sates** seɪts **~sating** seɪt ɪŋ ‖ seɪţ ɪŋ

intravasation ɪn ˌtræv ə ˈseɪʃ ᵊn ˌ·ˌ·-- **~s** z

intravenous ˌɪntr ə ˈviːn əs ◂ ⚠-ˈvin i‿əs **~es** ɪz əz **~ly** li

in-tray ˈɪn treɪ **~s** z

intrench ɪn ˈtrentʃ ən- **~ed** t **~es** ɪz əz **~ing** ɪŋ **~ment/s** mənt/s

intrepid ɪn ˈtrep ɪd §-əd **~ly** li **~ness** nəs nɪs

intrepidity ˌɪn trə ˈpɪd ət i ˌtrɪ-, ˌtre-, -ɪt i ‖ -əţ i

intricac|y ˈɪntr ɪk əs |i ˈ·ək- **~ies** iz

intricate ˈɪntr ɪk ət -ək-, -ɪt **~ly** li **~ness** nəs nɪs

intrigu|e *v* ɪn ˈtriːg **~ed** d **~es** z **~ing** ɪŋ

intrigue *n* ˈɪn triːg -ˈ· **~s** z

intrinsic ɪn ˈtrɪnᵗs ɪk ˌɪn-, -ˈtrɪnz- **~ally** ᵊl‿i

intro ˈɪntr əʊ ‖ -oʊ **~s** z

intro- ¦ɪntr əʊ ‖ -ə — **introgression** ˌɪntr əʊ ˈgreʃ ᵊn ‖ -ə-

introduc|e ˌɪntr ə ˈdjuːs →-ˈdʒuːs ‖ -ˈduːs -ˈdjuːs **~ed** t **~es** ɪz əz **~ing** ɪŋ

introduction ˌɪntr ə ˈdʌk ʃᵊn **~s** z

introductor|y ˌɪntr ə ˈdʌkt‿ər |i ◂ **~ily** əl i ɪ li
ˌ**intro**ˌ**ductory ˈoffer**

introit ˈɪn trɔɪt ɪn ˈtrəʊ ɪt, §-ət ‖ ɪn ˈtroʊ ət, ˈ· · · **~s** s

introject ˌɪntr əʊ ˈdʒekt ‖ -ə- **~ed** ɪd əd **~ing** ɪŋ **~s** s

introjection ˌɪntr əʊ ˈdʒek ʃᵊn ‖ -ə-

intromission ˌɪntr əʊ ˈmɪʃ ᵊn ‖ -ə- **~s** z

intro|mit ˌɪntr əʊ |ˈmɪt ‖ -ə- **~mits** ˈmɪts **~mitted** ˈmɪt ɪd -əd ‖ ˈmɪţ əd **~mitting** ˈmɪt ɪŋ ‖ ˈmɪţ ɪŋ

introspect ˌɪntr əʊ ˈspekt ‖ -ə- **~ed** ɪd əd **~ing** ɪŋ **~s** s

introspection ˌɪntr əʊ ˈspek ʃᵊn ‖ -ə- **~s** z

introspective ˌɪntr əʊ ˈspekt ɪv◂ ‖ -ə- **~ly** li **~ness** nəs nɪs

introversion ˌɪntr əʊ ˈvɜːʃ ᵊn -ˈvɜːʒ- ‖ -ə ˈvɜ˞ːʒ ᵊn

introvert *n* ˈɪntr əʊ vɜːt ‖ -ə vɜ˞ːt **~s** s

introvert *v* ˌɪntr əʊ ˈvɜːt ‖ -ə ˈvɜ˞ːt **~verted** ˈvɜːt ɪd -əd ‖ ˈvɜ˞ːţ əd **~verting** ˈvɜːt ɪŋ ‖ ˈvɜ˞ːţ ɪŋ **~verts** ˈvɜːts ‖ ˈvɜ˞ːts

intrud|e ɪn ˈtruːd **~ed** ɪd əd **~es** z **~ing** ɪŋ

intruder ɪn ˈtruːd ə ‖ -ᵊr **~s** z

intrusion ɪn ˈtruːʒ ᵊn **~s** z

intrusive ɪn ˈtruːs ɪv §-ˈtruːz- **~ly** li **~ness** nəs nɪs

intrust ɪn ˈtrʌst ən- **~ed** ɪd əd **~ing** ɪŋ **~s** s

intu|bate ˈɪn tju |beɪt →-tʃu- ‖ -tu- -tju- **~bated** beɪt ɪd -əd ‖ beɪţ əd **~bates** beɪts **~bating** beɪt ɪŋ ‖ beɪţ ɪŋ

intu|it ɪn ˈtjuː‿|ɪt §→-ˈtʃuː‿, §‿ət ‖ -ˈtuː |ət -ˈtjuː- **~ited** ɪt ɪd §ət-, -əd ‖ əţ əd **~iting** ɪt ɪŋ §ət- ‖ əţ ɪŋ **~its** ɪts §əts ‖ əts

intuition ˌɪn tju ˈɪʃ ᵊn →-tʃu- ‖ -tu- -tju- **~s** z

intuitive ɪn ˈtjuː‿ət ɪv →-ˈtʃuː‿, ɪt ɪv ‖ -ˈtuː əţ ɪv -ˈtjuː- **~ly** li **~ness** nəs nɪs

intumesc|e ˌɪn tju ˈmes →-tʃu- ‖ -tu- -tju- **~ed** t **~es** ɪz əz **~ing** ɪŋ

intumesc|ence ˌɪn tju ˈmes |ᵊnᵗs -tʃu- ‖ -tu- -tju- **~ent** ᵊnt

intussuscept ˌɪnt ə sə ˈsept -əs sə- ‖ ˌɪnţ- **~ed** ɪd əd **~ing** ɪŋ **~s** s

intussusception ˌɪnt ə sə ˈsep ʃᵊn -əs sə- ‖ ˌɪnţ-

Inuit ˈɪn u ɪt -ju-, §-ət **~s** s

Inuk ˈɪn ʊk

Inuktitut ɪ ˈnʊk tɪ tʊt -tə-

inun|date ˈɪn ʌn |deɪt -ən- **~dated** deɪt ɪd -əd ‖ deɪţ əd **~dates** deɪts **~dating** deɪt ɪŋ ‖ deɪţ ɪŋ

inundation ˌɪn ʌn ˈdeɪʃ ᵊn -ən- **~s** z

Inupiaq ɪ ˈnuːp i æk

inure ɪ ˈnjʊə ə-, -ˈnjɔː ‖ ɪn ˈjʊᵊr ɪ ˈnʊᵊr **~d** d **~s** z **inuring** ɪ ˈnjʊər ɪŋ ə-, -ˈnjɔːr- ‖ ɪn ˈjʊr ɪŋ ɪ ˈnʊr-

inurn ɪn ˈɜːn ‖ ɪn ˈɜ˞ːn **~ed** d **~ing** ɪŋ **~ment** mənt **~s** z

in utero ɪn ˈjuːt ə rəʊ ‖ ɪn ˈjuːţ ə roʊ

in vacuo ɪn ˈvæk ju əʊ ‖ -oʊ

invad|e ɪn ˈveɪd **~ed** ɪd əd **~er/s** ə/z ‖ ᵊr/z **~es** z **~ing** ɪŋ

invalid *adj 'not valid'* ɪn ˈvæl ɪd ˌɪn-, §-əd **~ly** li

invalid *n, v, adj 'ill, infirm'* ˈɪn və liːd -lɪd ‖ -vəl əd **~ed** ɪd əd **~ing** ɪŋ **~s** z

invali|date ɪn ˈvæl ɪ |deɪt ˌɪn-, -ə- **~dated** deɪt ɪd -əd ‖ deɪţ əd **~dates** deɪts **~dating** deɪt ɪŋ ‖ deɪţ ɪŋ

invalidation ɪn ˌvæl ɪ ˈdeɪʃ ᵊn -ə-, ˌ·ˌ·-

invalidity ˌɪn və ˈlɪd ət i -ɪt i ‖ -əţ i

invaluab|le ɪn ˈvæl ju͜əb |ᵊl -ˈvæl jʊb |ᵊl **~ly** li

Invar *tdmk* ɪn ˈvɑː ˈ· ·; ˈɪn və ‖ -ˈvɑːr ˈ· ·

invariability ɪn ˌveər i͜ə ˈbɪl ət i ˌ·ˌ·--, -ɪt i ‖ ɪn ˌver i͜ə ˈbɪl əţ i-ˌvær-

invariab|le ɪn ˈveər i͜əb |ᵊl ˌɪn- ‖ -ˈver- -ˈvær- **~leness** ᵊl nəs -nɪs **~ly** li

invariance ɪn ˈveər i͜ənᵗs ˌɪn- ‖ -ˈver- -ˈvær-

invariant ɪn ˈveər i͜ənt ˌɪn- ‖ -ˈver- -ˈvær- **~s** s

invasion ɪn ˈveɪʒ ᵊn **~s** z

invasive ɪn ˈveɪs ɪv §-ˈveɪz- **~ly** li

invective ɪn ˈvekt ɪv **~ly** li **~ness** nəs nɪs

inveigh ɪn ˈveɪ **~ed** d **~ing** ɪŋ **~s** z

inveigl|e ɪn ˈveɪg ᵊl -ˈviːg- **~ed** d **~ement** mənt **~es** z **~ing** ͜ɪŋ

in|vent ɪn |ˈvent **~vented** ˈvent ɪd -əd ‖ ˈvenţ əd **~venting** ˈvent ɪŋ ‖ ˈvenţ ɪŋ **~vents** ˈvents

invention ɪn ˈventʃ ᵊn **~s** z

inventive ɪn ˈvent ɪv ‖ -ˈvenţ ɪv **~ly** li **~ness** nəs nɪs

inventor ɪn ˈvent ə ‖ ˈvenţ ᵊr **~s** z

inventor|y *n, v* ˈɪn vənt͜ər |i ɪn ˈvent ər |i ‖ ˈɪn vən tɔːr |i -toʊr i **~ies** iz

Inver ˈɪn və ‖ -vᵊr

Inveraray ˌɪn vər ˈeər i -ə ‖ -ˈer i -ˈær i

Invercargill ˌɪn və ˈkɑːg ɪl -ᵊl; -kɑː ˈgɪl ‖ -vᵊr ˈkɑːrg ᵊl

Invergarry ˌɪn və ˈgær i ‖ -vᵊr- -ˈger-

Invergordon ˌɪn və ˈgɔːd ᵊn ‖ -vᵊr ˈgɔːrd ᵊn

Inverkeithing ˌɪn və ˈkiːð ɪŋ ‖ -vᵊr-

Invermoriston ˌɪn və ˈmɒr ɪst ən -ˈəst- ‖ -vᵊr ˈmɔːr- -ˈmɑːr-

Inverness ˌɪn və ˈnes ◂ ‖ -vᵊr-
ˌ**Inverness ˈTerrace**

invers|e *adj, n* ˌɪn ˈvɜːs ◂ ɪn- ‖ -ˈvɜːs ˈ· · **~ely** li **~es** ɪz əz
ˌ**inverse proˈportion**

inversion ɪn ˈvɜːʃ ᵊn §-ˈvɜːʒ- ‖ -ˈvɜːʒ ᵊn **~s** z

invert *adj, n* ˈɪn vɜːt ‖ -vɜːt **~s** s

in|vert *v* ɪn |ˈvɜːt ˌɪn- ‖ -|ˈvɜːt **~verted** ˈvɜːt ɪd -əd ‖ ˈvɜːţ əd **~verting** ˈvɜːt ɪŋ ‖ ˈvɜːţ ɪŋ **~verts** ˈvɜːts ‖ ˈvɜːts
inˌ**verted ˈcomma**; **in**ˌ**verted ˈsnob**

invertebrate ɪn ˈvɜːt ɪb rət ˌɪn-, -əb-, -rɪt; -ɪ breɪt, -ə- ‖ -ˈvɜːţ- **~s** s

Inverurie ˌɪn vər ˈʊər i ‖ -ˈʊr i

invest ɪn ˈvest **~ed** ɪd əd **~ing** ɪŋ **~s** s

investi|gate ɪn ˈvest ɪ |geɪt -ə- **~gated** geɪt ɪd -əd ‖ geɪţ əd **~gates** geɪts **~gating** geɪt ɪŋ ‖ geɪţ ɪŋ

investigation ɪn ˌvest ɪ ˈgeɪʃ ᵊn -ˌə- **~s** z

investigative ɪn ˈvest ɪg ət ɪv -ˈəg-; -ɪ geɪt ɪv, -ə · · ‖ -ə geɪţ ɪv

investigator ɪn ˈvest ɪ geɪt ə -ˈə- ‖ -geɪţ ᵊr **~s** z

investigatory ɪn ˈvest ɪg ət ər i ɪn ˌvest ɪ ˈgeɪt ər i ◂ -ˌ·ə-; ·ˈ· · · · · ‖ ɪn ˈvest ɪg ə tɔːr i -toʊr i

investiture ɪn ˈvest ɪtʃ ə -ətʃ ə; -ɪ tjʊə, -ə- ‖ -ətʃ ᵊr -ə tʃʊr **~s** z

investment ɪn ˈvest mənt **~s** s

investor ɪn ˈvest ə ‖ -ᵊr **~s** z

inveterate ɪn ˈvet ͜ər ət -ɪt ‖ ɪn ˈveţ ər ət →ɪn ˈvetr ət **~ly** li **~ness** nəs nɪs

invidious ɪn ˈvɪd i͜əs **~ly** li **~ness** nəs nɪs

invigi|late ɪn ˈvɪdʒ ə |leɪt -ɪ- **~lated** leɪt ɪd -ə ‖ leɪţ əd **~lates** leɪts **~lating** leɪt ɪŋ ‖ leɪţ ɪŋ

invigilation ɪn ˌvɪdʒ ə ˈleɪʃ ᵊn -ɪ- **~s** z

invigilator ɪn ˈvɪdʒ ə leɪt ə -ˈɪ- ‖ -leɪţ ᵊr **~s** z

invigo|rate ɪn ˈvɪg ə |reɪt **~rated** reɪt ɪd -əd ‖ reɪţ əd **~rates** reɪts **~rating** reɪt ɪŋ ‖ reɪţ ɪŋ

invigoration ɪn ˌvɪg ə ˈreɪʃ ᵊn

invincibility ɪn ˌvɪnᵗs ə ˈbɪl ət i ˌ·ˌ·--, -ɪˈ·-, -ɪt i ‖ -əţ i

invincib|le ɪn ˈvɪnᵗs əb |ᵊl ˌɪn-, -ɪb- **~leness** ᵊl nəs -nɪs **~ly** li

inviolability ɪn ˌvaɪ͜əl ə ˈbɪl ət i ˌ·ˌ·--, -ɪt i ‖ -əţ i

inviolab|le ɪn ˈvaɪ͜əl əb |ᵊl ˌɪn- **~leness** ᵊl nəs -nɪs **~ly** li

inviolate ɪn ˈvaɪ͜əl ət -ɪt, ə leɪt **~ly** li **~ness** nəs nɪs

invisibility ɪn ˌvɪz ə ˈbɪl ət i ˌ·ˌ·--, -ɪˈ·-, -ɪt i ‖ -əţ i

invisib|le ɪn ˈvɪz əb |ᵊl ˌɪn-, -ɪb- **~leness** ᵊl nəs -nɪs **~ly** li

invitation ˌɪn vɪ ˈteɪʃ ᵊn -və- **~s** z

in|vite *v* ɪn |ˈvaɪt **~vited** ˈvaɪt ɪd -əd ‖ ˈvaɪţ əd **~vites** ˈvaɪts **~viting/ly** ˈvaɪt ɪŋ /li ‖ ˈvaɪţ-

invite *n* ˈɪn vaɪt **~s** s

invitee ˌɪn vaɪ ˈtiː -vɪ- ‖ -və- **~s** z

in vitro ɪn ˈviːtr əʊ -ˈvɪtr- ‖ -oʊ

in vivo ɪn ˈviːv əʊ -ˈvaɪv- ‖ -oʊ

invocation ˌɪn vəʊ ˈkeɪʃ ᵊn ‖ -və- **~s** z

invoic|e *n, v* ˈɪn vɔɪs **~ed** t **~es** ɪz əz **~ing** ɪŋ

invok|e ɪn ˈvəʊk ‖ -ˈvoʊk **~ed** t **~es** s **~ing** ɪŋ

involucre ˈɪn və luːk ə -ljuːk ə, ˌ· ·ˈ· · ‖ -ᵊr **~s** z

involuntar|ily ɪn ˈvɒl ən͜tər |əl i ˌɪn-, ˌən ter əl i, -ɪ li; ˌ·ˌ· ·ˈter əl i, -ˈtær-, -ɪ li ‖ ɪn ˌvɑːl ən ˈter əl i ˌ·ˌ·-, -ˈtær- **~iness** i nəs i nɪs

involuntar|y ɪn ˈvɒl ənt͜ər |i ˌɪn-, §-ən ter i ‖ -ˈvɑːl ən ter |i

involute ˈɪn və luːt -ljuːt, ˌ· ·ˈ· **~s** s

involution ˌɪn və ˈluːʃ ᵊn -ˈljuːʃ- **~s** z

involv|e ɪn ˈvɒlv §-ˈvəʊlv, →§-ˈvɒʊlv ‖ -ˈvɑːlv — *Preference poll, BrE:* -ˈvɒlv *86%,* -ˈvəʊlv/-ˈvɒʊlv *14%.* **~ed** d **~ement/s** mənt/s **~es** z **~ing** ɪŋ

invulnerability ɪn ˌvʌln ər͜ə ˈbɪl ət i -ˌvʌn-, ˌ·ˌ·--, -ɪt i ‖ -əţ i

invulnerab|le ɪn ˈvʌln ər͜əb |ᵊl ˌɪn-, -ˈvʌn- **~leness** ᵊl nəs -nɪs **~ly** li

inward, I~ ˈɪn wəd ‖ -wᵊrd **~ly** li **~ness** nəs nɪs **~s** z

INVOLVE

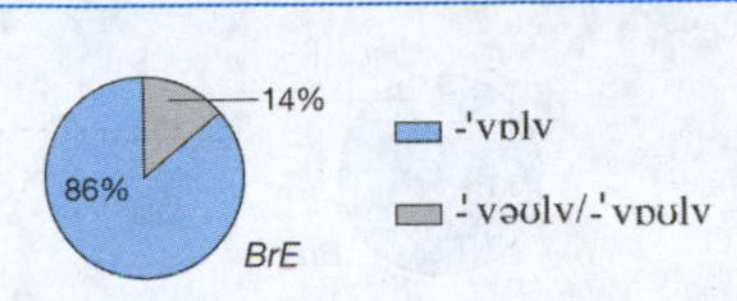

nward-looking ˈɪn wəd ˌlʊk ɪŋ §-ˌluːk-; ˌ· ˈ·· ◂ ‖ -wᵊrd-
nwood ˈɪn wʊd
n-word ˈɪn wɜːd ‖ -wɜ˞ːd **~s** z
inwrought ˌɪn ˈrɔːt ◂ ‖ -ˈrɑːt
INXS ɪn ˈeks es
n-your-face, in-yer-face ˌɪn jə ˈfeɪs ◂ -jɔː ‖ -jᵊr-
/O ˌaɪ ˈəʊ ◂ ‖ -ˈoʊ ◂ *or as* input/output
o ˈaɪ əʊ ‖ -oʊ
oan ˈjəʊ ən ‖ ˈjoʊ- —*Welsh* [ˈjo an]
iodate ˈaɪ‿ə deɪt -əʊ- **~s** s
iodic aɪ ˈɒd ɪk ‖ -ˈɑːd ɪk
iodide ˈaɪ‿ə daɪd -əʊ- **~s** z
iodin ˈaɪ‿əd ɪn -əʊd-, §-ən
iodine ˈaɪ‿ə diːn -əʊ-, -daɪn ‖ -daɪn əd ən
iodis... —*see* **iodiz...**
iodization ˌaɪ‿ə daɪ ˈzeɪʃ ᵊn əd ɪ- ‖ -əd ə-
iodiz|e ˈaɪ‿ə daɪz -əʊ- **~ed** d **~es** ɪz əz **~ing** ɪŋ
iodoform aɪ ˈɒd ə fɔːm ‖ aɪ ˈoʊd ə fɔːrm -ˈɑːd- (*)
iodopsin ˌaɪ əʊ ˈdɒps ɪn §-ən ‖ -ə ˈdɑːps-
iodous aɪ ˈɒd əs ˈaɪ‿əd- ‖ aɪ ˈoʊd- -ˈɑːd-, ˈaɪ əd-
Iolanthe ˌaɪ‿ə ˈlænᵗθ i -əʊ-
Iolo ˈjəʊl əʊ ‖ ˈjoʊl oʊ —*Welsh* [ˈjo lo]
ion ˈaɪ‿ən —*Also occasionally* ˈaɪ ɒn ‖ -ɑːn, *in RP mainly to avoid confusion with* iron **~s** z
-ion *stress-imposing* jən, ən, ən, ᵊn —*often with changes to a stem-final consonant:* inˈjection ɪn ˈdʒek ʃᵊn
Iona aɪ ˈəʊn ə ‖ -ˈoʊn ə
Ione aɪ ˈəʊn i ‖ -ˈoʊn i
Ionesco ˌiː‿ə ˈnesk əʊ -ɒ-; jɒ ˈnesk- ‖ -oʊ —*Fr* [jɔ nɛs ko]
Ionia aɪ ˈəʊn i‿ə ‖ -ˈoʊn-
Ionian aɪ ˈəʊn i‿ən ‖ -ˈoʊn- **~s** z
Ionic aɪ ˈɒn ɪk ‖ -ˈɑːn- **~s** s
ionis... —*see* **ioniz...**
ionization ˌaɪ‿ən aɪ ˈzeɪʃ ᵊn -ɪˈ- ‖ -ə ˈzeɪʃ- **~s** z
ioniz|e ˈaɪ‿ə naɪz **~ed** d **~er/s** ə/z ‖ ᵊr/z **~es** ɪz əz **~ing** ɪŋ
ionosphere aɪ ˈɒn ə sfɪə ‖ -ˈɑːn ə sfɪr
Iorwerth ˈjɔː wɜːθ -weəθ ‖ ˈjɔːr wᵊrθ —*Welsh* [ˈjor werθ]
iota aɪ ˈəʊt ə ‖ -ˈoʊt̬ ə **~s** z
IOU ˌaɪ əʊ ˈjuː ‖ -oʊ- **~s, ~'s** z
Iowa ˈaɪ əʊ ə ˈaɪ‿ə wə ‖ ˈaɪ ə wə
Iowan ˈaɪ əʊ ən ˈaɪ‿ə wən ‖ ˈaɪ ə wən **~s** z
IPA ˌaɪ piː ˈeɪ
ipecac ˈɪp ɪ kæk -ə-
ipecacuanha ˌɪp ɪ kæk ju ˈæn ə ˌ·ə-, -ˈɑːn-
Iphigenia ˌaɪf ɪdʒ ɪ ˈnaɪ‿ə ˌɪf-, ɪ ˌfɪdʒ-, -əˈ‿
iPhone *tdmk* ˈaɪ fəʊn ‖ -foʊn **~s** z
iPod *tdmk* ˈaɪ pɒd ‖ -pɑːd **~s** z
Ipoh ˈiːp əʊ ‖ -oʊ
ipomoea ˌɪp ə ˈmiː‿ə ˌaɪp- **~s** z
ipse dixit ˌɪps i ˈdɪks ɪt -eɪ, §-ət
ipsilateral ˌɪps ɪ ˈlæt‿ᵊr əl ◂ ‖ -ˈlæt̬ ər əl →-ˈlætr əl
ipso facto ˌɪps əʊ ˈfækt əʊ ◂ ‖ -oʊ ˈfækt oʊ ◂
Ipsus ˈɪps əs
Ipswich ˈɪps wɪtʃ
IQ ˌaɪ ˈkjuː **~s, ~'s** z
 ˌIˈQ test
Iqbal ˈɪk bæl ˈɪg-, -bɑːl —*Arabic* [ɪq ˈbaːl]
ir- ɪ —*generally stressed only for emphasis or if the following syllable is unstressed:* ˌirreˈspective
Ira ˈaɪᵊr ə
IRA ˌaɪ ɑːr ˈeɪ ◂ -ɑr-
Irak ɪ ˈrɑːk -ˈræk
Iraki ɪ ˈrɑːk i -ˈræk- **~s** z
Iran ɪ ˈrɑːn -ˈræn
Iranian ɪ ˈreɪn i‿ən aɪᵊ-, -ˈrɑːn- **~s** z
Iraq ɪ ˈrɑːk -ˈræk ‖ aɪ- —*Arabic* [ʕi ˈrɑːq]
Iraqi ɪ ˈrɑːk i -ˈræk- ‖ aɪ- **~s** z
irascibility ɪ ˌræs ə ˈbɪl ət i ˌ·ɪ-, -ɪt i ‖ -ət̬ i
irascib|le ɪ ˈræs əb |ᵊl -ɪb- **~leness** ᵊl nəs -nɪs **~ly** li
irate aɪᵊ ˈreɪt ˌ·ˈ·◂ **~ly** li
ire ˈaɪ‿ə ‖ ˈaɪ‿ᵊr
ireful ˈaɪ‿ə fᵊl -fʊl ‖ ˈaɪ‿ᵊr- **~ly** ‿i **~ness** nəs nɪs
Ireland ˈaɪ‿ə lənd ‖ ˈaɪ‿ᵊr-
Iremonger ˈaɪ‿ə ˌmʌŋ gə ‖ ˈaɪ‿ᵊr ˌmʌŋ gᵊr -ˌmɑːŋ-
Irene ˈaɪᵊ riːn aɪᵊ ˈriːn i ‖ aɪ ˈriːn ˌ·· —*but the name of the Greek goddess is always* -ˈriːn i
irenic aɪᵊ ˈriːn ɪk -ˈren- **~ally** ᵊl‿i
Ireton ˈaɪ‿ə tən ‖ ˈaɪ‿ᵊrt ᵊn
Irian *'New Guinea'* ˈɪr i‿ən ˈɪər-, -ɑːn
 ˌIrian ˈJaya ˈdʒaɪ‿ə ˈdʒɑː jə
iridaceous ˌɪr ɪ ˈdeɪʃ əs ◂ ˌaɪᵊr-, -ə-
iridesc|ence ˌɪr ɪ ˈdes |ᵊnᵗs -ə- **~ent** ᵊnt
iridium ɪ ˈrɪd i‿əm aɪᵊ-
iridolog|ist ˌɪr ɪ ˈdɒl ədʒ |ɪst ˌ·ə-, §-əst ‖ -ˈdɑːl- **~ists** ɪsts §əsts **~y** i
irie ˈaɪᵊr i
iris, Iris ˈaɪᵊr ɪs §-əs **irises, Iris's** ˈaɪᵊr ɪs ɪz §-əs-, -əz
Irish ˈaɪᵊr ɪʃ **~ism** ˌɪz əm
 ˌIrish ˈcoffee; ˌIrish ˈSea; ˌIrish ˈstew
Irish|man ˈaɪᵊr ɪʃ |mən **~men** mən men **~ness** nəs nɪs **~ry** ri **~woman** ˌwʊm ən **~women** ˌwɪm ɪn §-ən
iritis aɪᵊ ˈraɪt ɪs §-əs ‖ -ˈraɪt̬ əs
irk ɜːk ‖ ɜ˞ːk **irked** ɜːkt ‖ ɜ˞ːkt **irking** ˈɜːk ɪŋ ‖ ˈɜ˞ːk ɪŋ **irks** ɜːks ‖ ɜ˞ːks
irksome ˈɜːk səm ‖ ˈɜ˞ːk- **~ly** li **~ness** nəs nɪs
Irkutsk ɜː ˈkʊtsk ɪə- ‖ ɪr- —*Russ* [ɪr ˈkutsk]
Irlam ˈɜːl əm ‖ ˈɜ˞ːl-
Irma ˈɜːm ə ‖ ˈɜ˞ːm ə
Irnbru *tdmk* ˈaɪ‿ən bruː →-əm- ‖ ˈaɪ‿ᵊrn-
iron ˈaɪ‿ən ‖ ˈaɪ‿ᵊrn **ironed** ˈaɪ‿ənd ‖ ˈaɪ‿ᵊrnd **ironing** ˈaɪ‿ən ɪŋ ‖ ˈaɪ‿ᵊrn ɪŋ **irons** ˈaɪ‿ənz ‖ ˈaɪ‿ᵊrnz

'Iron Age; **ˌIron 'Curtain**; **'ironing board**; **'iron mold, 'iron mould**; **ˌiron 'rations**
Ironbridge 'aɪ‿ən brɪdʒ →‿əm- ‖ 'aɪ‿ᵊrn-
ironclad 'aɪ‿ən klæd →‿əŋ- ‖ 'aɪ‿ᵊrn- **~s** z
iron-gray, iron-grey ˌaɪ‿ən 'greɪ ◂ →‿əŋ- ‖ ˌaɪ‿ᵊrn-
ironic aɪᵊ 'rɒn ɪk ‖ -'rɑːn- **~al** ᵊl **~ally** ᵊl‿i
ironie... —*see* **irony**
ironist *'user of irony'* 'aɪᵊr ən ɪst §-əst **~s** s
ironmaster 'aɪ‿ən ˌmɑːst ə →-əm-, §-ˌmæst- ‖ 'aɪ‿ᵊrn ˌmæst ᵊr **~s** z
ironmonger 'aɪ‿ən ˌmʌŋ gə →-əm- ‖ 'aɪ‿ᵊrn ˌmʌŋ gᵊr -ˌmɑːŋ- **~s** z
ironmonger|y 'aɪ‿ən ˌmʌŋ gər |i →'·əm- ‖ 'aɪ‿ᵊrn- ˌmɑːŋ- **~ies** iz
iron-on 'aɪ‿ən ɒn ˌ· '·◂ ‖ 'aɪ‿ᵊrn ɑːn -ɔːn **~s** z
Ironside 'aɪ‿ən saɪd ‖ 'aɪ‿ᵊrn- **~s** z
ironstone 'aɪ‿ən stəʊn ‖ 'aɪ‿ᵊrn stoʊn
ironware 'aɪ‿ən weə ‖ 'aɪ‿ᵊrn wer -wær
ironwood 'aɪ‿ən wʊd ‖ 'aɪ‿ᵊrn-
ironwork 'aɪ‿ən wɜːk ‖ 'aɪ‿ᵊrn wɜːk **~s** s
irony *adj 'like iron'* 'aɪ‿ən i ‖ 'aɪ‿ᵊrn i
iron|y *n* 'aɪᵊr ən |i **~ies** iz
Iroquoian ˌɪr ə 'kwɔɪ ən ◂ **~s** z
Iro|quois *sing.* 'ɪr ə |kwɔɪ -kwɔɪz **~quois** *pl* kwɔɪz kwɔɪ
irradi|ate ɪ 'reɪd i |eɪt **~ated** eɪt ɪd -əd ‖ eɪţ əd **~ates** eɪts **~ating** eɪt ɪŋ ‖ eɪţ ɪŋ
irradiation ɪ ˌreɪd i 'eɪʃ ᵊn **~s** z
irrational ɪ 'ræʃ ᵊn‿əl ˌɪ- ‖ ˌɪr- **~ly** i
irrationalit|y ɪ ˌræʃ ə 'næl ət |i ˌɪˌ·-, -ɪt i ‖ -əţ |i ˌɪrˌ·- **~ies** iz
Irrawaddy ˌɪr ə 'wɒd i ‖ -'wɑːd i
irrealis ˌɪr i 'ɑːl ɪs §-əs
irreconcilability ɪr ˌek ən ˌsaɪl ə 'bɪl ət i ˌɪˌ·-, -ŋˌ·-, -ɪt i ‖ -əţ i
irreconcilab|le ˌɪr ˌek ən 'saɪl əb |ᵊl ◂ ɪˌ·-, ·'· · · ·, →-ŋ'·- **~ly** li
irrecoverab|le ˌɪr i 'kʌv ər‿əb |ᵊl ◂ ˌ·ə- **~leness** ᵊl nəs -nɪs **~ly** li
irredeemability ˌɪr i ˌdiːm ə 'bɪl ət i ˌ·ə-, -ɪt i ‖ -əţ i
irredeemab|le ˌɪr i 'diːm əb |ᵊl ◂ ˌ·ə- **~les** ᵊlz **~ly** li
irredentism, I~ ˌɪr i 'dent ɪz əm ˌ·ə-
irredentist, I~ ˌɪr i 'dent ɪst ◂ -ə-, §-əst ‖ -'denţ əst **~s** s
irreducibility ˌɪr i ˌdjuːs ə 'bɪl ət i ˌ·ə-, →-ˌdʒuːs-, -ɪt i ‖ -ˌduːs ə 'bɪl əţ i -ˌdjuːs-
irreducib|le ˌɪr i 'djuːs əb |ᵊl ◂ ˌ·ə-, →-'dʒuːs- ‖ -'duːs- -'djuːs- **~leness** ᵊl nəs -nɪs **~ly** li
irrefutab|le ˌɪr i 'fjuːt əb |ᵊl ˌ·ə-; ɪ 'ref jʊt-, -'·jət- ‖ ˌɪr i 'fjuːţ əb |ᵊl ɪ 'ref jəţ-, ˌɪ-, ˌɪr- — *Preference poll, BrE:* ˌ·'·· 93%, '·· · · 7%. **~ly** li
irregardless ˌɪr i 'gɑːd ləs ◂ -ə-, -lɪs ‖ -'gɑːrd-
irregular ɪ 'reg jʊl ə ˌɪ-, -jəl-, §-əl- ‖ -jəl ᵊr ˌɪr- **~ly** li **~s** z
irregularit|y ɪ ˌreg jʊ 'lær ət |i ˌɪr eg-, -jə'·-, -ɪt i ‖ ɪ ˌreg jə 'lær əţ |i ˌɪrˌ·-, -'ler- **~ies** iz
irrelevanc|e ɪ 'rel əv ənᵗs ˌɪ-, -'·ɪv- ‖ ˌɪr- **~ies** iz **~y** i
irrelevant ɪ 'rel əv ənt ˌɪ-, -ɪv- ‖ ˌɪr- **~ly** li

IRREFUTABLE

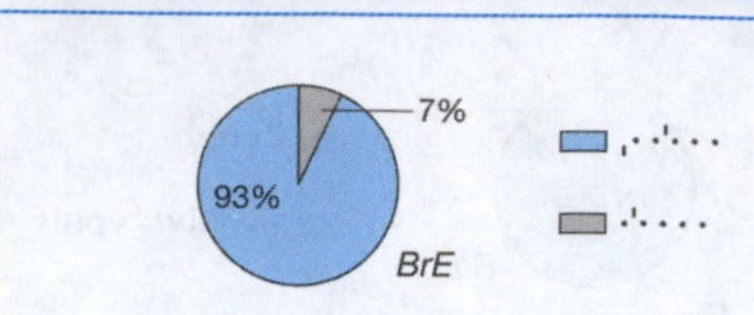

irreligion ˌɪr i 'lɪdʒ ən ◂ -ə-
irreligious ˌɪr i 'lɪdʒ əs ◂ -ə- **~ly** li **~ness** nəs nɪs
irremediab|le ˌɪr i 'miːd i‿əb |ᵊl ◂ ˌ·ə- **~ly** li
irremovab|le ˌɪr i 'muːv əb |ᵊl ◂ ˌ·ə- **~ly** li
irreparab|le ɪ 'rep ər‿əb |ᵊl §ˌɪr i 'peər əb |ᵊl ◂, ˌ·ə- ‖ ˌɪr-; ˌɪr ɪ 'per-, -'pær- **~leness** ᵊl nəs -nɪs **~ly** li
irreplaceable ˌɪr i 'pleɪs əb ᵊl ◂ ˌ·ə-
irrepressib|le ˌɪr i 'pres əb |ᵊl ◂ ˌ·ə-, -ɪb ᵊl **~leness** ᵊl nəs -nɪs **~ly** li
irreproachab|le ˌɪr i 'prəʊtʃ əb |ᵊl ◂ ˌ·ə- ‖ -'proʊtʃ- **~leness** ᵊl nəs -nɪs **~ly** li
irresistibility ˌɪr i ˌzɪst ə 'bɪl ət i ˌ·ə-, -ɪt i ‖ -əţ i
irresistib|le ˌɪr i 'zɪst əb |ᵊl ◂ ˌ·ə-, -ɪb ᵊl **~leness** ᵊl nəs -nɪs **~ly** li
irresolute ɪ 'rez ə luːt ˌɪ-, -ljuːt ‖ -əl ət **~ly** li **~ness** nəs nɪs
irresolution ɪ ˌrez ə 'luːʃ ᵊn ˌɪ rez ə'·-, -'ljuːʃ-
irrespective ˌɪr i 'spekt ɪv ◂ -ə- **~ly** li
irresponsibility ˌɪr i ˌspɒnᵗs ə 'bɪl ət i ˌ·ə-, -ɪ'·-, -ɪt i ‖ -ˌspɑːnᵗs ə 'bɪl əţ i
irresponsib|le ˌɪr i 'spɒnᵗs əb |ᵊl ◂ ˌ·ə-, ɪb ᵊl ‖ -'spɑːnᵗs- **~leness** ᵊl nəs -nɪs **~ly** li
irretrievab|le ˌɪr i 'triːv əb |ᵊl ◂ ˌ·ə- **~leness** ᵊl nəs -nɪs **~ly** li
irreverence ɪ 'rev ᵊr‿ənᵗs ˌɪ- ‖ ˌɪr-
irreverent ɪ 'rev ᵊr‿ənt ˌɪ- ‖ ˌɪr- **~ly** li
irreversibility ˌɪr i ˌvɜːs ə 'bɪl ət i ˌ·ə-, -ɪ'·-, -ɪt i ‖ -ˌvɜːs ə 'bɪl əţ i
irreversib|le ˌɪr i 'vɜːs əb |ᵊl ◂ ˌ·ə-, -ɪb ᵊl ‖ -'vɜːs- **~leness** ᵊl nəs -nɪs **~ly** li
irrevocability ɪ ˌrev ək ə 'bɪl ət i ˌɪr i ˌvəʊk-, -ɪt i ‖ -əţ i ˌɪr ˌrev ək ə'·-
irrevocab|le ɪ 'rev ək əb |ᵊl ˌɪr i 'vəʊk-, ˌ·ə- ‖ ˌɪr-; ˌɪr i 'voʊk- **~leness** ᵊl nəs -nɪs **~ly** li
irrigable 'ɪr ɪg əb ᵊl '·əg-
irri|gate 'ɪr ɪ |geɪt -ə- **~gated** geɪt ɪd -əd ‖ geɪţ əd **~gates** geɪts **~gating** geɪt ɪŋ ‖ geɪţ ɪŋ
irrigation ˌɪr ɪ 'geɪʃ ᵊn -ə- **~al** ‿əl ◂
irritability ˌɪr ɪt ə 'bɪl ət i ˌ·ət-, -ɪt i ‖ ˌɪr əţ ə 'bɪl əţ i
irritab|le 'ɪr ɪt əb |ᵊl -ət əb- ‖ -əţ əb- **~leness** ᵊl nəs -nɪs **~ly** li
irritant 'ɪr ɪt ənt -ət- ‖ -ət ᵊnt **~s** s
irri|tate 'ɪr ɪ |teɪt -ə- **~tated** teɪt ɪd -əd ‖ teɪţ əd **~tates** teɪts **~tating/ly** teɪt ɪŋ /li ‖ teɪţ ɪŋ /li
irritation ˌɪr ɪ 'teɪʃ ᵊn -ə- **~s** z
irrupt ɪ 'rʌpt ˌɪ- ‖ ˌɪr- *(usually = erupt)* **~ed** ɪd əd **~ing** ɪŋ **~s** s

rruption ɪ ˈrʌp ʃən ˌɪ- ‖ ˌɪr- **~s** z
rruptive ɪ ˈrʌpt ɪv ˌɪ- ‖ ˌɪr-
rvine *(i)* ˈɜːv ɪn §-ən ‖ ˈɜːv-, *(ii)* -aɪn —*The place in Strathclyde is (i), that in CA (ii). As a personal name, usually (i).*
rving ˈɜːv ɪŋ ‖ ˈɜːv-
rwell ˈɜː wel ‖ ˈɜː-
rwin ˈɜː wɪn §-wən ‖ ˈɜː-
s *strong form* ɪz, *weak forms* z, s —*After a word ending in* s, z, ʃ, ʒ, tʃ, dʒ *there is no distinct weak form in RP, though in some varieties* §əz *is used. Otherwise, the contracted form* s *may be used after a word ending in* p, t, k, f, θ, *while* z *may be used after one ending in a vowel sound or* b, d, g, v, ð, m, n, ŋ, l *and AmE* r; s *and* z *may be shown in orthography as* 's. *No contraction is possible when this word is stranded: is is always strong and uncontracted in* Tell me what it is.
ISA ˈaɪs ə **ISAs, ISA's** ˈaɪs əz
Isaac ˈaɪz ək
Isaacs ˈaɪz əks
Isabel ˈɪz ə bel
Isabella ˌɪz ə ˈbel ə
Isador, Isadore ˈɪz ə dɔː ‖ -dɔːr -dour
Isadora ˌɪz ə ˈdɔːr ə ‖ -ˈdour-
isagogic ˌaɪs ə ˈgɒdʒ ɪk ◂ ‖ -ˈgɑːdʒ- **~s** s
Isaiah aɪ ˈzaɪ‿ə §-ˈzeɪ ə ‖ aɪ ˈzeɪ ə *(*)*
Isambard ˈɪz əm bɑːd ‖ -bɑːrd
-isation aɪ ˈzeɪʃ ən ɪ- ‖ ə ˈzeɪʃ ən *(*)* — **canonisation** ˌkæn ən aɪ ˈzeɪʃ ən -ən ɪ- ‖ -ən ə-
Isbister *(i)* ˈaɪz bɪst ə ‖ -ər, *(ii)* ˈɪz-
ISBN ˌaɪ es biː ˈen
Iscariot ɪ ˈskær i‿ət ə- ‖ ɪ ˈsker-
ischaem|ia, ischem|ia ɪ ˈskiːm |i‿ə **~ic** ɪk
ischi|um ˈɪsk i‿|əm **~a** ə **~al** əl
ISDN ˌaɪ es diː ˈen
-ise aɪz —*see also* **-ize**
isenthalpic ˌaɪs en ˈθælp ɪk ◂ ˌaɪz-, -ɪn-, -ən-
isentropic ˌaɪs en ˈtrɒp ɪk ◂ ˌaɪz-, -ɪn-, ən- ‖ -ˈtrɑːp ɪk -ˈtroup-
Iseult i ˈzuːlt -ˈsuːlt
-ish ɪʃ — **boyish** ˈbɔɪ ɪʃ —*also informally as a separate word, 'approximately, to a certain extent'* **ish** ɪʃ
Isham ˈaɪʃ əm
Isherwood ˈɪʃ ə wʊd ‖ -ər-
Ishiguro ˌɪʃ i ˈgʊər əʊ ‖ -ˈgʊr oʊ
Ishihara ˌɪʃ i ˈhɑːr ə
Ishmael ˈɪʃ meɪəl -mi‿əl
Ishmaelite ˈɪʃ mi‿ə laɪt ˈɪʃ meɪəl aɪt; ˈɪʃ mə laɪt, -mɪ- **~s** s
Ishtar ˈɪʃt ɑː ‖ -ɑːr
Isidor, Isidore ˈɪz ə dɔː -ɪ- ‖ -dɔːr -dour
isinglass ˈaɪz ɪŋ glɑːs §-glæs ‖ -ən glæs -ɪŋ-
Isis ˈaɪs ɪs §-əs
Isla ˈaɪl ə
Islam ˈɪs lɑːm ˈɪz-, -læm, -ləm; ɪs ˈlɑːm, ɪz-, -ˈlæm —*Arabic* [is ˈlaːm]
Islamabad ɪs ˈlɑːm ə bæd ɪz-, -ˈlæm-, -bɑːd
Islamic ɪs ˈlæm ɪk ɪz-, -ˈlɑːm-
Islam|ism ˈɪs ləm ˌɪz əm ˈɪz-, -lɑːm-, -læm- **~ist/s** ɪst/s §əst/s
Islamophobia ɪs ˌlæm əʊ ˈfəʊb i‿ə ɪz-, -ˌlɑːm-; ˌ- - ‖ -ˈfoub-
island ˈaɪl ənd **~ed** ɪd əd **~ing** ɪŋ **~s** z
islander ˈaɪl ənd ə ‖ ər **~s** z
Islay ˈaɪl ə -eɪ
isle aɪəl **isles** aɪəlz
ˌIsle of ˈMan; ˌIsle of ˈWight
islet ˈaɪl ət -ɪt **~s** s
Isleworth ˈaɪz əl wɜːθ -wəθ ‖ -wərθ
Islington ˈɪz lɪŋ tən
Islip *(i)* ˈaɪs lɪp, *(ii)* ˈɪz- —*The places in England and NY are (i); the family name is usually (ii)*
Islwyn ˈɪs lu ɪn ɪz ˈluː‿, ɪs- —*Welsh* [ˈis lujn, -luin]
ism ˈɪz əm **isms** ˈɪz əmz
-ism ˌɪz əm — **Darwinism** ˈdɑː wɪ ˌnɪz əm -wə- ‖ ˈdɑːr-
Ismaili, Isma'ili ˌɪz mɑː ˈiːl i ◂ ɪz ˈmaɪl i ‖ ˌɪs meɪ ˈɪl i ˌɪz- —*Arabic* [ɪs maː ˈʕiː liː] **~s** z
Ismailia, Ismailiya ˌɪz maɪ ˈliː‿ə ˌɪs- ‖ ˌɪz meɪ ə ˈliː ə
Ismay ˈɪz meɪ
isn't *contracted form* ˈɪz ənt
ISO ˌaɪ es ˈəʊ ‖ -ˈoʊ
iso- *comb. form*
with stress-neutral suffix ¦aɪs əʊ ‖ -oʊ — **isoseismal** ˌaɪs əʊ ˈsaɪz məl ◂ ‖ -oʊ-
with stress-imposing suffix aɪ ˈsɒ+ ‖ aɪ ˈsɑː+ — **isogonal** aɪ ˈsɒg ən əl ‖ -ˈsɑːg-
isobar ˈaɪs əʊ bɑː ‖ -ə bɑːr **~s** z
isobaric ˌaɪs əʊ ˈbær ɪk ◂ ‖ -ə- -ˈber-
isobath ˈaɪs əʊ bæθ -bɑːθ ‖ ə bæθ **~s** s
Isobel ˈɪz ə bel
isochromatic ˌaɪs əʊ krəʊ ˈmæt ɪk ◂ ‖ ˌaɪs ə kroʊ ˈmæţ ɪk ◂
isochronal aɪ ˈsɒk rən əl ‖ -ˈsɑːk- **~ly** i
isochronicit|y aɪ ˌsɒk rə ˈnɪs ət |i ˌaɪs əʊ krə-, -ɪt i ‖ aɪ ˌsɑːk rə ˈnɪs əţ |i **~ies** iz
isochronis|e, isochroniz|e aɪ ˈsɒk rə naɪz ‖ -ˈsɑːk- **~ed** d **~es** ɪz əz **~ing** ɪŋ
isochronous aɪ ˈsɒk rən əs ‖ -ˈsɑːk- **~ly** li
isochron|y aɪ ˈsɒk rən |i ‖ -ˈsɑːk- **~ies** iz
isoclinal ˌaɪs əʊ ˈklaɪn əl ◂ ‖ -ə-
isocline ˈaɪs əʊ klaɪn ‖ -ə- **~s** z
isoclinic ˌaɪs əʊ ˈklɪn ɪk ◂ ‖ -ə-
Isocrates aɪ ˈsɒk rə tiːz ‖ -ˈsɑːk-
isogloss ˈaɪs əʊ glɒs ‖ -ə glɑːs -glɔːs **~es** ɪz əz
isohyet ˌaɪs əʊ ˈhaɪ‿ət -ɪt ‖ -oʊ- **~s** s
iso|late *v* ˈaɪs ə |leɪt ‖ ˈɪs- **~lated** leɪt ɪd -əd ‖ leɪţ əd **~lates** leɪts **~lating** leɪt ɪŋ ‖ leɪţ ɪŋ
isolate *n, adj* ˈaɪs əl ət -ɪt; -ə leɪt ‖ ˈɪs- **~s** s
isolation ˌaɪs ə ˈleɪʃ ən ‖ ˌɪs- **~ism** ɪz əm **~ist/s** ɪst/s §əst/s
isolative ˈaɪs əl ət ɪv -ə leɪt- ‖ ˈaɪs ə leɪţ ɪv ˈɪs- **~ly** li
Isolda ɪ ˈzɒld ə ‖ ɪ ˈsoʊld ə -ˈzoʊld ə
Isolde ɪ ˈzɒld ə ‖ ɪ ˈsoʊld ·ˈə —*Ger* [ʔi ˈzɔl də]
isomer ˈaɪs əm ə ‖ -ər **~s** z
isomeric ˌaɪs əʊ ˈmer ɪk ◂ ‖ -ə-

isomerism aɪ 'sɒm ə ˌrɪz əm ‖ -'sɑːm- **~s** z
isometric ˌaɪs əʊ 'met rɪk ◂ ‖ -ə- **~s** s
isomorph 'aɪs əʊ mɔːf ‖ -ə mɔːrf **~s** s
isomorphic ˌaɪs əʊ 'mɔːf ɪk ◂ ‖ -ə 'mɔːrf- **~ally** ᵊl‿i
isomorphism ˌaɪs əʊ 'mɔːf ˌɪz əm ‖ ˌ-ə 'mɔːrf- **~s** z
Ison 'aɪs ᵊn
isophone 'aɪs əʊ fəʊn ‖ -ə foʊn **~s** z
isopleth 'aɪs əʊ pleθ ‖ -ə- **~s** s
isoprene 'aɪs əʊ priːn ‖ -ə-
isopropyl ˌaɪs əʊ 'prəʊp ɪl ◂ -ᵊl ‖ -ə 'proʊp ᵊl ◂
isosceles aɪ 'sɒs ə liːz -ɪ- ‖ -'sɑːs-
isospora aɪ 'sɒsp ər ə ‖ -'sɑːsp- **~s** z
isotherm 'aɪs əʊ θɜːm ‖ -ə θɜːm **~s** z
isotonic ˌaɪs əʊ 'tɒn ɪk ◂ ‖ -ə 'tɑːn-
isotope 'aɪs ə təʊp -əʊ- ‖ -ə toʊp **~s** s
isotopic ˌaɪs əʊ 'tɒp ɪk ◂ ‖ -ə 'tɑːp- **~ally** ᵊl‿i
ISP ˌaɪ es 'piː **~s** z
I-Spy, I-spy ˌaɪ 'spaɪ
Israel 'ɪz reɪᵊl 'ɪz ri‿əl ‖ 'ɪz ri‿əl —*in singing usually* 'ɪz reɪ el
Israeli ɪz 'reɪl i **~s** z
Israelite 'ɪz ri‿ə laɪt 'ɪz reɪᵊl aɪt; 'ɪz rə laɪt, -rɪ- **~s** s
Issigonis ˌɪs ɪ 'gəʊn ɪs -ə-, §-əs ‖ -'goʊn-
issuable 'ɪʃ u‿əb ᵊl 'ɪs ju‿, 'ɪʃ ju‿
issuance 'ɪʃ u‿ənᵗs 'ɪs ju‿, 'ɪʃ ju‿

ISSUE

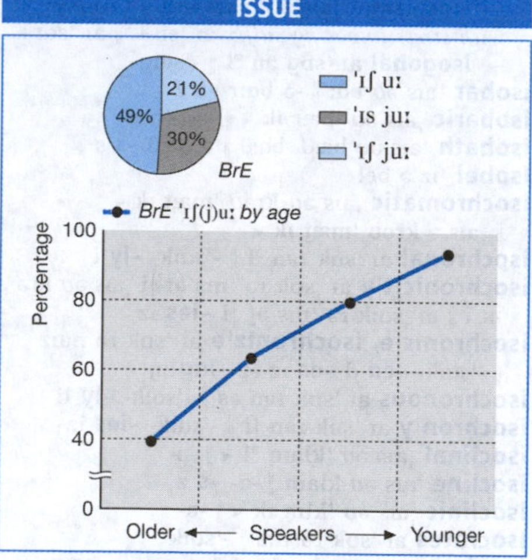

issue 'ɪʃ uː 'ɪs juː, 'ɪʃ juː — *Preference poll, BrE:* 'ɪʃ uː *49%,* 'ɪs juː *30%,* 'ɪʃ juː *21%. In AmE always* 'ɪʃ uː. **issued** 'ɪʃ uːd 'ɪs juːd, 'ɪʃ- **issues** 'ɪʃ uːz 'ɪs juːz, 'ɪʃ- **issuing** 'ɪʃ uː‿ɪŋ 'ɪs juː‿ɪŋ, 'ɪʃ-
issuer 'ɪʃ uː‿ə 'ɪs juː‿ə, 'ɪʃ- ‖ ‿ᵊr **~s** z
Issus 'ɪs əs
Issy 'ɪs i
-ist ɪst §-əst ‖ əst — **machinist** mə 'ʃiːn ɪst §-əst ‖ -əst
-istan ɪ 'stɑːn ə-, -'stæn — **Londonistan** ˌlʌnd ən ɪ 'stɑːn -ən ə-, -'stæn
Istanbul ˌɪst æn 'bʊl ◂ -ɑːn-, →-æm-, -'buːl ‖ '· · · —*Turkish* İstanbul [is 'tɑn bul]
Isthmian 'ɪsθ mi‿ən 'ɪs-, 'ɪst-
isthmus 'ɪs məs 'ɪsθ-, 'ɪst- **~es** ɪz əz
-istic 'ɪst ɪk — **impressionistic** ɪm ˌpreʃ ə 'nɪst ɪk ◂
istle 'ɪst li
Istria 'ɪs tri‿ə
Isuzu *tdmk* i 'suːz uː aɪ- —*Jp* [i ˌsɯ dzɯ]
it *strong form* ɪt —*There is no distinct weak form in RP, but in some other varieties, including most GenAm, there is a weak form* §ət. —*The phrases* it is, it isn't *are often syllabified irregularly, as* ɪ 'tɪz, ɪ 'tɪz ᵊnt.
IT *'information technology'* ˌaɪ 'tiː
ITA, i.t.a. ˌaɪ tiː 'eɪ ◂
Italian ɪ 'tæl jən ə- **~s** z
italianate, I~ ɪ 'tæl jə neɪt ə-
italic, I~ ɪ 'tæl ɪk ə-, aɪ- **~s** s
italicis... —*see* **italiciz...**
italicization ɪ ˌtæl ɪ saɪ 'zeɪʃ ᵊn ə-, aɪ-, ˌ·ə-, -sɪ'·- ‖ -ə sə- **~s** z
italiciz|e ɪ 'tæl ɪ saɪz ə-, aɪ-, -ə- **~ed** d **~es** ɪz əz **~ing** ɪŋ
Italo- ɪ ¦tæl əʊ ə-; ¦ɪt əl əʊ ‖ ɪ ¦tæl oʊ ¦ɪţ ᵊl oʊ — **Italo-German** ɪ ˌtæl əʊ 'dʒɜːm ən ◂ ˌɪt əl əʊ- ‖ -oʊ 'dʒɜːm ən ◂ ˌɪţ ᵊl oʊ-
Italy 'ɪt əl i ‖ 'ɪţ ᵊl i
Itasca *lake in MN* aɪ 'tæsk ə
itch ɪtʃ **itched** ɪtʃt **itches** 'ɪtʃ ɪz -əz **itching** 'ɪtʃ ɪŋ
Itchen 'ɪtʃ ɪn -ən
itch|y 'ɪtʃ |i **~ier** i‿ə ‖ i‿ᵊr **~iest** i‿ɪst i‿əst **~iness** i nəs i nɪs
ˌ**itchy 'feet**; ˌ**itchy 'palm**
it'd *'it would', 'it had'* ɪt əd ‖ ɪţ əd
-ite aɪt — **Luddite** 'lʌd aɪt
item 'aɪt əm -ɪm, -em ‖ 'aɪţ əm **~s** z
itemis|e, itemiz|e 'aɪt ə maɪz -ɪ- ‖ 'aɪţ- **~ed** d **~es** ɪz əz **~ing** ɪŋ
ite|rate 'ɪt ə |reɪt ‖ 'ɪţ- **~rated** reɪt ɪd -əd ‖ reɪţ əd **~rates** reɪts **~rating** reɪt ɪŋ ‖ reɪţ ɪŋ
iteration ˌɪt ə 'reɪʃ ᵊn ‖ ˌɪţ- **~s** z
iterative 'ɪt‿ər ət ɪv 'ɪt ə reɪt- ‖ 'ɪţ ə reɪţ ɪv -ər əţ- **~ly** li **~ness** nəs nɪs
iterativity ˌɪt‿ər ə 'tɪv ət i -ɪt i ‖ ˌɪţ ər ə 'tɪv əţ i
Ithaca 'ɪθ ək ə
Ithon 'aɪθ ɒn ‖ -ɑːn —*Welsh* ['əj θon]
ithyphallic ˌɪθ i 'fæl ɪk ◂ ˌaɪθ- **~s** s
-itides *pl of* **-itis** 'ɪt ɪ diːz -ə- ‖ -'ɪţ ə diːz — **meningitides** ˌmen ɪn 'dʒɪt ɪ diːz §ˌ·ən-, §-'·ə- ‖ -'dʒɪţ ə diːz
itinerancy aɪ 'tɪn ər ənᵗs i ɪ-
itinerant aɪ 'tɪn ər ənt ɪ- **~s** s
itinerar|y aɪ 'tɪn ᵊr‿ər |i ⚠-'tɪn ər‿|i ‖ -ə rer |i **~ies** iz
-ition 'ɪʃ ᵊn — **opposition** ˌɒp ə 'zɪʃ ᵊn ‖ ˌɑːp-
-itious 'ɪʃ əs — **adventitious** ˌæd vən 'tɪʃ əs ◂ -ven-
-itis 'aɪt ɪs §-əs ‖ 'aɪţ əs — **enteritis** ˌent ə 'raɪt ɪs §-əs ‖ ˌenţ ə 'raɪţ əs

tive *stress-imposing* ət ɪv ɪt- ‖ əţ ɪv — **competitive** kəm ˈpet ət ɪv -ɪt- ‖ -ˈpeţ əţ ɪv

t'll *'it will'* ɪt ᵊl ‖ ɪţ ᵊl

tma ˈɪt mɑː

TN ˌaɪ tiː ˈen

tory *stress-imposing* ət‿ər i ɪt‿ər i ‖ ə tɔːr i ə toʊr i *(*)* — **territory** ˈter ət‿ər i ˈ-ɪt‿ ‖ ˈter ə tɔːr i -toʊr i

ts ɪts —*non-RP weak form* əts

t's *'it is'; 'it has'* ɪts —*non-RP weak form* əts

tself ɪt ˈself §ət-

tsy-bitsy ˌɪts i ˈbɪts i ◂

tty-bitty ˌɪt i ˈbɪt i ◂ ‖ ˌɪţ i ˈbɪţ i ◂

Tunes *tdmk* ˈaɪ tjuːnz →-tʃuːnz, §-tuːnz ‖ -tuːnz -tjuːnz

TV ˌaɪ tiː ˈviː ◂

ity *stress-imposing* ət i ɪt i ‖ əţ i — **modernity** mɒ ˈdɜːn ət i mə-, -ɪt i ‖ mɑː ˈdɜːn əţ i

UD ˌaɪ juː ˈdiː **~s, ~'s** z

van ˈaɪv ᵊn —*but as a foreign name also* ˌiː ˈvæn ◂, ɪ-, -ˈvɑːn

vana ɪ ˈvɑːn ə -ˈvæn-

vanhoe ˈaɪv ᵊn həʊ ‖ -hoʊ

-ive ɪv — **prohibitive** prəʊ ˈhɪb ɪt ɪv -ət- ‖ proʊ ˈhɪb əţ ɪv

've *'I have'* aɪv

veagh ˈaɪv ə -eɪ

veco *tdmk* ɪ ˈveɪk əʊ aɪ ˈviːk- ‖ -oʊ

Ivens ˈaɪv ᵊnz

Iver ˈaɪv ə ‖ -ᵊr

Ives aɪvz

ivi... —*see* **ivy**

ivied ˈaɪv id

Ivor ˈaɪv ə ‖ -ᵊr

Ivorian aɪ ˈvɔːr i‿ən ɪ- **~s** z

ivor|y, Ivor|y ˈaɪv ər‿|i **~ies, ~y's** iz **ˌIvory ˈCoast; ˌivory ˈtower**

ivy, Ivy ˈaɪv i **ivied** ˈaɪv id **ivies** ˈaɪv iz **ˈIvy ˌLeague**

Iwan ˈjuː‿ən —*Welsh* [ˈi wan]

Iwo ˈiː wəʊ ‖ -woʊ -wə **ˌIwo ˈJima** ˈdʒiːm ə —*Jp* [i ˌoo dzi ma]

ixia ˈɪks i‿ə **~s** z

Ixion ɪk ˈsaɪ‿ən

Izaak ˈaɪz ək

Izal *tdmk* ˈaɪz ᵊl

izard, Izard ˈɪz əd ‖ -ᵊrd **~s** z

-ization aɪ ˈzeɪʃ ᵊn ɪ- ‖ ə ˈzeɪʃ ᵊn *(*)* — **velarization** ˌviːl ər aɪ ˈzeɪʃ ᵊn -ɪˈ-- ‖ -ə ˈzeɪʃ ᵊn

-ize aɪz —*This suffix is unstressed (though strong) in RP and GenAm, but sometimes stressed in other varieties* —**velarize** ˈviːl ə raɪz §ˌ· ·ˈ·

Izzard, i~ *(i)* ˈɪz əd ‖ -ᵊrd, *(ii)* -ɑːd ‖ -ɑːrd

Izzy ˈɪz i

Jj

j Spelling-to-sound

1 Where the spelling is **j**, the pronunciation is regularly dʒ as in **jump** dʒʌmp.

2 Occasionally, in words of foreign origin, it is ʒ as in **jabot** ˈʒæb əʊ ‖ ʒæ ˈboʊ or j as in **hallelujah** ˌhæl ɪ.ˈluː jə.

3 The sound dʒ is also regularly written **dg** or **g**, as in **hedge** hedʒ, **large** lɑːdʒ ‖ lɑːrdʒ.

J, j dʒeɪ **Js, J's, j's** dʒeɪz —*Communications code name:* Juliet
jab dʒæb **jabbed** dʒæbd **jabbing** ˈdʒæb ɪŋ **jabs** dʒæbz
jabber ˈdʒæb ə ‖ -ᵊr **~ed** d **jabbering** ˈdʒæb ər ɪŋ **~s** z
jabberer ˈdʒæb ər ə ‖ -ᵊr **~s** z
Jabberwock, j~ ˈdʒæb ə wɒk ‖ -ᵊr wɑːk **~y** i
Jabez ˈdʒeɪb ez -ɪz
jabiru ˌdʒæb ə ˈruː -ɪ-, ˈ· · · **~s** z
jaborandi ˌdʒæb ə ˈrænd i ˌʒæb-, -ræn ˈdiː **~s** z
jabot ˈʒæb əʊ ‖ ʒæ ˈboʊ —*Fr* [ʒa bo] **~s** z
jacamar ˈdʒæk ə mɑː ˈʒæk- ‖ -mɑːr **~s** z
jacana dʒə ˈkɑːn ə ˈdʒæk ən ə; ˌdʒæs ə ˈnɑː, ˌʒæs- —*Port* jaçanã [ʒɐ sɐ ˈnɐ̃] **~s** z
jacaranda ˌdʒæk ə ˈrænd ə **~s** z
Jacinta dʒə ˈsɪnt ə —*but as a foreign name also* hæ- —*Sp* [xa ˈθin ta, -ˈsin-]
jacinth, J~ ˈdʒæs ɪnᵗθ ˈdʒeɪs-, §-ᵊnᵗθ ‖ ˈdʒeɪs- ˈdʒæs- **~s** s
Jacintha dʒə ˈsɪnᵗθ ə dʒæ-
jack, Jack dʒæk **jacked** dʒækt **jacking** ˈdʒæk ɪŋ **jacks, Jack's** dʒæks
ˌ**Jack ˈFrost**; ˈ**jack knife**; ˈ**jack plug**; ˌ**Jack ˈRobinson**; ˌ**Jack ˈRussell**; ˌ**jack ˈtar**; ˌ**Jack the ˈLad**
jackal ˈdʒæk ɔːl -ᵊl ‖ -ᵊl -ɔːl, -ɑːl **~s** z
jackanapes ˈdʒæk ə neɪps
jackaroo ˌdʒæk ə ˈruː **~ed** d **~ing** ɪŋ **~s** z
jackass ˈdʒæk æs -ɑːs **~es** ɪz əz
jack|boot ˈdʒæk| buːt **~booted** buːt ɪd -əd ‖ -buːt̬- **~boots** buːts
jackdaw ˈdʒæk dɔː ‖ -dɑː **~s** z
jackeroo ˌdʒæk ə ˈruː **~ed** d **~ing** ɪŋ **~s** z
jacket ˈdʒæk ɪt §-ət **~s** s
jackfruit ˈdʒæk fruːt **~s** s
jackhammer ˈdʒæk ˌhæm ə ‖ -ᵊr **~s** z
Jackie ˈdʒæk i
jack-in-office ˈdʒæk ɪn ˌɒf ɪs §-ən-, §-əs ‖ -ˌɑːf əs -ˌɔːf-
jack-in-the-box ˈdʒæk ɪn ðə ˌbɒks §ˈ·ən- ‖ -ˌbɑːks **~es** ɪz əz
jack-in-the-pulpit ˌdʒæk ɪn ðə ˈpʊlp ɪt §-ˈpʌlp-, §-ət
jack|knife *n, v* ˈdʒæk |naɪf **~knifed** naɪft **~knifes** naɪfs **~knifing** naɪf ɪŋ
Jacklin ˈdʒæk lɪn §-lən
Jackman ˈdʒæk mən
Jacko ˈdʒæk əʊ ‖ -oʊ
jack-of-all-trades ˌdʒæk əv ˈɔːl treɪdz ˌ· ·ˌ·ˈ· ‖ -ˈɑːl-
jack-o'-lantern ˌdʒæk ə ˈlænt ən ˈ· ·ˌ· · ‖ -ᵊrn **~s** z
jackpot ˈdʒæk pɒt ‖ -pɑːt **~s** s
jackrabbit ˈdʒæk ˌræb ɪt §-ət **~s** s
jacksnipe ˈdʒæk snaɪp **~s** s
Jackson ˈdʒæks ən
Jacksonian dʒæk ˈsəʊn i‿ən ‖ -ˈsoʊn- **~s** z
Jacksonville ˈdʒæks ən vɪl
jack-the-lad ˌdʒæk ðə ˈlæd **~s** z
Jacky ˈdʒæk i
Jacob ˈdʒeɪk əb -ʌb **~'s** z
Jacobean ˌdʒæk əʊ ˈbiː ən ◂ ‖ -ə- **~s** z
Jacobethan ˌdʒæk əʊ ˈbiːθ ᵊn ◂ ‖ -ə-
Jacobi *(i)* ˈdʒæk əb i, *(ii)* dʒə ˈkəʊb i ‖ -ˈkoʊb i
jacobian, J~ dʒə ˈkəʊb i‿ən ‖ -ˈkoʊb- **~s** z
Jacobin ˈdʒæk əb ɪn §-ən **~ism** ˌɪz əm **~s** z
Jacobite ˈdʒæk ə baɪt **~s** s
Jacobs ˈdʒeɪk əbz -ʌbz
Jacobson ˈdʒeɪk əb sən
jacobus, J~ dʒə ˈkəʊb əs ‖ -ˈkoʊb- **~es** ɪz əz
Jacoby *(i)* dʒə ˈkəʊb i ‖ -ˈkoʊb-, *(ii)* ˈdʒæk əb i

acquard 'dʒæk ɑːd dʒə 'kɑːd ‖ -ɑːrd —*Fr* [ʒa kaːʁ] **~s** z

acqueline 'dʒæk ə liːn -lɪn; 'dʒæk liːn, 'ʒæk-, -lɪn

acquelyn 'dʒæk əl ɪn §-ən

acques dʒeɪks dʒæks, ʒæk ‖ ʒɑːk —*Fr* [ʒak]

acqui 'dʒæk i

acuzzi, J~ *tdmk* dʒə 'kuːz i dʒæ- **~s** z

ade, Jade dʒeɪd **jaded** 'dʒeɪd ɪd -əd **jades** dʒeɪdz **jading** 'dʒeɪd ɪŋ

adeite 'dʒeɪd aɪt **~s** s

'adoube ʒæ 'duːb ʒə-, ʒɑː-

aeger, J~ *tdmk* 'jeɪg ə 'dʒeɪg- ‖ -ᵊr **~s** z

ael 'dʒeɪ əl -el

affa, jaffa 'dʒæf ə **jaffas** 'dʒæf əz
ˌ**Jaffa 'orange**

affle 'dʒæf ᵊl **~s** z

affna 'dʒæf nə

ag, Jag dʒæg **jagged** *v* dʒægd **jagging** 'dʒæg ɪŋ **jags, Jags** dʒægz

agan 'dʒeɪg ən

agged *adj* 'dʒæg ɪd -əd **~ly** li **~ness** nəs nɪs

agger 'dʒæg ə ‖ -ᵊr

agg|y 'dʒæg |i **~ier** i ə ‖ i ᵊr **~iest** i ɪst i əst

ago 'dʒeɪg əʊ ‖ -oʊ

aguar, J~ 'dʒæg ju ə §-ɑː ‖ 'dʒæg wɑːr 'dʒæg ju ɑːr **~s** z

jaguarondi ˌdʒæg wə 'rɒnd i ˌʒæg- ‖ -'rɑːnd i ˌdʒɑːg-, ˌʒɑːg- **~s** z

jaguarundi ˌdʒæg wə 'rʌnd i ˌʒæg- ‖ ˌdʒɑːg-, ˌʒɑːg- **~s** z

Jah dʒɑː

jai dʒaɪ —*Hindi* [dʒæ]

jai alai ˌhaɪ ə 'laɪ '· · ·; ˌhaɪ 'laɪ, '· · ‖ 'haɪ laɪ ˌhaɪ ə 'laɪ

jail dʒeɪᵊl **jailed** dʒeɪᵊld **jailing** 'dʒeɪᵊl ɪŋ **jails** dʒeɪᵊlz

jailbait 'dʒeɪᵊl beɪt

jailbird 'dʒeɪᵊl bɜːd ‖ -bɜːd **~s** z

jailbreak 'dʒeɪᵊl breɪk **~er/s** ə/z ‖ ᵊr/z **~s** s

jailer, jailor 'dʒeɪl ə ‖ -ᵊr **~s** z

jailhouse 'dʒeɪᵊl haʊs

Jaime 'dʒeɪm i —*but as a Spanish name,* 'haɪm i —*Sp* ['xai me]

Jain dʒaɪn dʒeɪn **~ism** ˌɪz əm **~s** z

Jaipur ˌdʒaɪ 'pʊə -'pɔː ‖ 'dʒaɪ pʊr —*Hindi* [dʒəi pʊr]

Jairus 'dʒaɪᵊr əs dʒeɪ 'aɪᵊr əs

Jakarta dʒə 'kɑːt ə ‖ -'kɑːrṱ ə

Jake, jake dʒeɪk **Jake's, jakes, Jakes** dʒeɪks

Jakobson 'jɑːk əb sən

JAL *tdmk* dʒæl dʒɑːl

Jalalabad dʒə 'lɑːl ə bɑːd -'læl-, -bæd, ·,· ·'· —*Hindi* [dʒə lɑː lɑː bɑːḍ]

jalap 'dʒæl əp 'dʒɒl- ‖ 'dʒɑːl-

jalapeno, jalapeño ˌhæl ə 'peɪn jəʊ ‖ ˌhɑːl ə 'peɪn joʊ ˌhæl- —*Sp* [xa la 'pe ɲo] **~s** z

jalfrezi dʒæl 'freɪz i

jalop|y dʒə 'lɒp |i ‖ -'lɑːp |i **~ies** iz

jalousie 'ʒæl u ziː ,· ·'·; §dʒə 'luːs i ‖ 'dʒæl əs i *(*)* **~s** z

jam dʒæm **jammed** dʒæmd **Jamming** 'dʒæm ɪŋ **jams** dʒæmz
'jam ˌsession

Jamaica dʒə 'meɪk ə

Jamaican dʒə 'meɪk ən **~s** z

Jamal dʒə 'mɑːl

jamb dʒæm dʒæmb *(usually = jam)* **jambs** dʒæmz dʒæmbz

jambalaya ˌdʒæm bə 'laɪ ə ˌdʒʌm- **~s** z

jamboree ˌdʒæm bə 'riː ◂ **~s** z

Jamelia dʒə 'miːl i ə

James dʒeɪmz **James', James's** 'dʒeɪmz ɪz -əz; dʒeɪmz

Jamesian 'dʒeɪm zi ən **~s** z

Jameson 'dʒeɪm sən 'dʒem ɪs ən, 'dʒɪm-, 'dʒæm-, 'dʒeɪm-, -əs-

Jamestown 'dʒeɪmz taʊn

Jamie 'dʒeɪm i

Jamieson 'dʒeɪm ɪs ən 'dʒem-, 'dʒɪm-, 'dʒæm-

Jamiroquai dʒə 'mɪr ə kwaɪ

jamm... —*see* **jam**

jammer 'dʒæm ə ‖ -ᵊr **~s** z

jammies 'dʒæm iz

Jammu 'dʒæm uː 'dʒʌm-

jamm|y 'dʒæm |i **~ier** i ə ‖ i ᵊr **~iest** i ɪst i əst

jam-packed ˌdʒæm 'pækt ◂

Jamshid, Jamshyd ˌdʒæm 'ʃiːd '· ·, -ʃɪd

Jan dʒæn —*but as a male name also* jæn ‖ jɑːn —*and by confusion also* ʒɒ̃, ʒæn —*Polish, Czech, Swedish, Norwegian* [jan], *Dutch* [jɑn]

Jan. dʒæn —*see also* **January**

Janacek, Janáček 'jæn ə tʃek -ɑː- —*Czech* ['ja naː tʃek]

Jancis 'dʒænᵗs ɪs §-əs

Jane dʒeɪn

Janet 'dʒæn ɪt -ət

Janette dʒə 'net dʒæ-

jangl|e 'dʒæŋ gᵊl **~ed** d **~es** z **~ing** ɪŋ

Janice 'dʒæn ɪs -əs

Janie 'dʒeɪn i

Janine dʒə 'niːn

Janis 'dʒæn ɪs -əs

janissar|y 'dʒæn ɪs ər |i -əs- ‖ -ə ser |i **~ies** iz

janitor 'dʒæn ɪt ə -ət- ‖ -əṱ ᵊr **~s** z

janitorial ˌdʒæn ɪ 'tɔːr i əl ◂ ˌ·ə- ‖ -'toʊr-

janizar|y 'dʒæn ɪz ər |i '·əz- ‖ -ə zer |i **~ies** iz

Jansen 'dʒænᵗs ən **~ism** ˌɪz əm **~ist/s** ɪst/s §əst/s

Jansky, j~ 'dʒænᵗs ki

Janson 'dʒænᵗs ən

Jantzen *tdmk* 'dʒænts ᵊn 'jænts-

January 'dʒæn ju ər i 'dʒæn jʊr i, §'dʒæn ju er i ‖ -ju er i

Janus 'dʒeɪn əs

Janvrin 'dʒæn vrɪn -vrən

Jap dʒæp **Japs** dʒæps

Japan, japan dʒə 'pæn **~ned** d **~ning** ɪŋ **~s, ~'s** z

Japanese ˌdʒæp ə 'niːz ◂
ˌ**Japanese 'lantern**; ˌ**Japanese 'maple**; ˌ**Japanese 'people**

jape dʒeɪp **japes** dʒeɪps

Japhet 'dʒeɪf et -ɪt, §-ət

J

Japheth ˈdʒeɪf eθ -ɪθ, §-əθ
Japhetic dʒeɪ ˈfet ɪk dʒə- ‖ -ˈfeṭ ɪk
japonica dʒə ˈpɒn ɪk ə ‖ -ˈpɑːn- **~s** z
Jaques *(i)* dʒeɪks, *(ii)* dʒæks —*but in Shakespeare* ˈdʒeɪk wɪz
jar dʒɑː ‖ dʒɑːr **jarred** dʒɑːd ‖ dʒɑːrd **jarring** ˈdʒɑːr ɪŋ **jars** dʒɑːz ‖ dʒɑːrz
Jardine ˈdʒɑːd iːn ‖ dʒɑːr ˈdiːn
jardiniere, jardinière ˌʒɑːd ɪn i ˈeə ˌʒɑːd ɪn ˈjeə ‖ ˌdʒɑːrd ən ˈɪər ˌʒɑːrd-, -ˈjeər —*Fr* [ʒaʁ di njɛːʁ] **~s** z
Jared ˈdʒær əd ‖ˈdʒer-
jargon ˈdʒɑːg ən ‖ ˈdʒɑːrg- -ɑːn **~s** z
jargonistic ˌdʒɑːg ə ˈnɪst ɪk ◂ ‖ ˌdʒɑːrg-
jarhead ˈdʒɑː hed ‖ ˈdʒɑːr- **~s** z
Jarlsberg *tdmk* ˈjɑːlz bɜːg ‖ ˈjɑːrlz bɜːg
Jarman ˈdʒɑːm ən ‖ ˈdʒɑːrm-
Jarndyce ˈdʒɑːnd aɪs ‖ ˈdʒɑːrnd-
Jarrad ˈdʒær əd ‖ ˈdʒer-
jarrah ˈdʒær ə ‖ ˈdʒer- **~s** z
Jarratt, Jarrett ˈdʒær ət -ɪt ‖ ˈdʒer-
Jarrold ˈdʒær əld ‖ ˈdʒer-
Jarrow ˈdʒær əʊ ‖ -oʊ ˈdʒer-
Jaruzelski ˌjær u ˈzel ski ‖ ˌjɑːr- —*Polish* [ja ru ˈzel ski]
Jarvik ˈdʒɑːv ɪk ‖ ˈdʒɑːrv-
Jarvis ˈdʒɑːv ɪs §-əs ‖ ˈdʒɑːrv-
Jas. dʒæs —*see also* **James**
jasmine, J~ ˈdʒæz mɪn ˈdʒæs-, §-mən **~s, ~'s** z
Jason ˈdʒeɪs ən
jasper, J~ ˈdʒæsp ə ‖ -ər **~s, ~'s** z
jaundice ˈdʒɔːnd ɪs §-əs ‖ ˈdʒɑːnd- **~d** t
jaunt dʒɔːnt ‖ dʒɑːnt **jaunted** ˈdʒɔːnt ɪd -əd ‖ ˈdʒɔːnṭ əd ˈdʒɑːnṭ- **jaunting** ˈdʒɔːnt ɪŋ ‖ ˈdʒɔːnṭ ɪŋ ˈdʒɑːnṭ- **jaunts** dʒɔːnts ‖ dʒɑːnts **ˈjaunting car**
jaunt|y ˈdʒɔːnt |i ‖ ˈdʒɔːnṭ |i ˈdʒɑːnṭ- **~ier** i ə ‖ i ər **~iest** i ɪst i əst **~ily** ɪ li əl i **~iness** i nəs i nɪs
Java ˈdʒɑːv ə ‖ ˈdʒæv ə —*in AmE the computer language is* ˈdʒɑːv ə, *and this is also the most usual pronunciation for the island; but coffee is often* ˈdʒæv ə, *while the places in NY are* ˈdʒeɪv ə
Javan ˈdʒɑːv ən ‖ ˈdʒæv- **~s** z
Javanese ˌdʒɑːv ə ˈniːz ◂ ‖ ˌdʒæv- ˌdʒɑːv-, -ˈniːs ◂
JavaScript ˈdʒɑːv ə skrɪpt ‖ ˈdʒæv-
javelin ˈdʒæv əl ɪn § ən **~s** z
Javits ˈdʒæv ɪts §-əts
jaw dʒɔː ‖ dʒɑː **jawed** dʒɔːd ‖ dʒɑːd **jawing** ˈdʒɔːr ɪŋ ‖ ˈdʒɔː ɪŋ ˈdʒɑː-
jawbone ˈdʒɔː bəʊn ‖ -boʊn ˈdʒɑː- **~s** z
jawbreaker ˈdʒɔː ˌbreɪk ə ‖ -ər ˈdʒɑː- **~s** z
jawline ˈdʒɔː laɪn ‖ ˈdʒɑː-
jay, Jay dʒeɪ **jays, Jay's** dʒeɪz
jaybird ˈdʒeɪ bɜːd ‖ -bɜːd
Jaycee ˌdʒeɪ ˈsiː
Jayne dʒeɪn
jaywalk ˈdʒeɪ wɔːk ‖ -wɑːk **~ed** t **~er/s** ə/z ‖ ər/z **~ing** ɪŋ **~s** s
Jaywick ˈdʒeɪ wɪk
jazz dʒæz **jazzed** dʒæzd **jazzes** ˈdʒæz ɪz -əz **jazzing** ˈdʒæz ɪŋ
jazzed-up ˌdʒæzd ˈʌp ◂
jazz|man ˈdʒæz| mæn **~men** men
jazz|y ˈdʒæz |i **~ier** i ə ‖ i ər **~iest** i ɪst i əst **~ily** ɪ li əl i **~iness** i nəs i nɪs
JCB *tdmk* ˌdʒeɪ siː ˈbiː **~s, ~'s** z
jealous ˈdʒel əs **~ly** li **~ness** nəs nɪs
jealous|y ˈdʒel əs |i **~ies** iz
Jean *male name, French* ʒɒ̃ ‖ ʒɑːn —*Fr* [ʒɑ̃]
Jean *female name* dʒiːn
Jeanette dʒɪ ˈnet dʒə-
Jeanie, Jeannie ˈdʒiːn i
Jeannine dʒɪ ˈniːn dʒə-
jeans, Jeans dʒiːnz
Jeavons ˈdʒev ənz
Jeb, Jebb dʒeb
Jebusite ˈdʒeb ju zaɪt ‖ -jə saɪt **~s** s
Jed dʒed
Jedburgh ˈdʒed bər ə →ˈdʒeb-
Jedda, Jeddah ˈdʒed ə —*Arabic* [ˈdʒed da]
Jedediah ˌdʒed ɪ ˈdaɪ ə ◂ -ə-
Jedi ˈdʒed aɪ
jeep, Jeep *tdmk* dʒiːp **jeeps** dʒiːps
jeepers ˈdʒiːp əz ‖ -ərz
jeepney ˈdʒiːp ni **~s** z
Jeeps dʒiːps
jeer dʒɪə ‖ dʒɪər **jeered** dʒɪəd ‖ dʒɪərd **jeering** ˈdʒɪər ɪŋ ‖ ˈdʒɪr ɪŋ **jeers** dʒɪəz ‖ dʒɪərz
Jeeves dʒiːvz
jeez dʒiːz
Jeff dʒef
Jefferies ˈdʒef riz
Jeffers ˈdʒef əz ‖ -ərz
Jefferson ˈdʒef əs ən ‖ -ərs-
Jeffersonian ˌdʒef ə ˈsəʊn i ən ◂ ‖ -ər ˈsoʊn- **~s** z
Jeffery, Jeffrey ˈdʒef ri
Jeffreys, Jeffries dʒef riz
Jeger ˈdʒeɪg ə ‖ -ər
Jehoshaphat dʒɪ ˈhɒʃ ə fæt dʒə-, -ˈhɒs- ‖ -ˈhɑːs-
Jehovah dʒɪ ˈhəʊv ə dʒə- ‖ -ˈhoʊv ə **~'s** z **Jeˌhovah's ˈWitness**
Jehu ˈdʒiː hjuː ‖ -huː
jejune dʒɪ ˈdʒuːn dʒə- **~ly** li **~ness** nəs nɪs
jejunum dʒɪ ˈdʒuːn əm dʒə- **~s** z
Jekyll *(i)* ˈdʒek əl -ɪl, *(ii)* ˈdʒiːk-
jell dʒel **jelled** dʒeld **jelling** ˈdʒel ɪŋ **jells** dʒelz
jellaba, jellabah ˈdʒel əb ə dʒə ˈlɑːb ə **~s** z
Jellicoe ˈdʒel ɪ kəʊ -ə- ‖ -koʊ
jellie... —*see* **jelly**
jello, Jello, Jell-O *tdmk* ˈdʒel əʊ ‖ -oʊ **~s** z
jell|y ˈdʒel |i **~ied** id **~ies** iz **~ying** i ɪŋ **ˌjellied ˈeels**; **ˈjelly ˌbaby**; **ˈjelly bean**; **ˈjelly roll**
jellyfish ˈdʒel i fɪʃ **~es** ɪz əz
Jemima dʒɪ ˈmaɪm ə dʒə-
jemm|y, Jemmy ˈdʒem |i **~ied** id **~ies** iz **~ying** i ɪŋ
Jena ˈjeɪn ə —*Ger* [ˈjeː na]

Je ne sais quoi ˌʒə nə seɪ ˈkwɑː —*Fr* [ʒən sɛ kwa]
Jenga ˈdʒeŋ ɡə
Jenifer ˈdʒen ɪf ə -əf- ‖ -ᵊr
Jenkin ˈdʒeŋk ɪn §-ən
Jenkins ˈdʒeŋk ɪnz §-ənz
Jenkinson ˈdʒeŋk ɪn sən §-ən-
Jenks dʒeŋks
Jenner ˈdʒen ə ‖ -ᵊr
jennet ˈdʒen ɪt §-ət **~s** s
Jennie ˈdʒen i
jennie... —*see* **jenny**
Jennifer ˈdʒen ɪf ə -əf- ‖ -ᵊr
Jennings ˈdʒen ɪŋz
jenny, Jenny ˈdʒen i **jennies, Jenny's** ˈdʒen iz
Jensen ˈdʒenᵗs ən —*but as a non-English name also* ˈjenᵗs- —*Danish* [ˈjɛn sən], *German* [ˈjɛn zᵊn]
Jenůfa ˈjen uːf ə —*Czech* [ˈje nuː fa]
jeopardis|e, jeopardiz|e ˈdʒep ə daɪz ‖ -ᵊr- **~ed** d **~es** ɪz əz **~ing** ɪŋ
jeopardy ˈdʒep əd i ‖ -ᵊrd i
Jephthah ˈdʒefθ ə
jequirity dʒɪ ˈkwɪr ət i dʒə-, -ɪt- ‖ -əṭ i
jeˈquirity bean
jerboa dʒɜː ˈbəʊ ə dʒə- ‖ dʒᵊr ˈboʊ ə **~s** z
jeremiad ˌdʒer ɪ ˈmaɪ əd -ə-, -æd **~s** z
Jeremiah ˌdʒer ɪ ˈmaɪ ə ◂ -ə- **~s, ~'s** z
Jeremy ˈdʒer əm ɪ -ɪm-
Jerez hə ˈrez he-, -ˈreθ, -ˈres —*Sp* [xe ˈɾeθ]
Jericho ˈdʒer ɪ kəʊ ‖ -koʊ
jerk dʒɜːk ‖ dʒɜ˞ːk **jerked** dʒɜːkt ‖ dʒɜ˞ːkt **jerking** ˈdʒɜːk ɪŋ ‖ ˈdʒɜ˞ːk ɪŋ **jerks** dʒɜːks ‖ dʒɜ˞ːks
jerkin ˈdʒɜːk ɪn §-ən ‖ ˈdʒɜ˞ːk- **~s** z
jerkwater ˈdʒɜːk ˌwɔːt ə ‖ ˈdʒɜ˞ːk ˌwɔːṭ ᵊr ˌwɑːṭ ᵊr
jerk|y ˈdʒɜːk |i ‖ ˈdʒɜ˞ːk |i **~ier** i ə ‖ i ᵊr **~iest** i ɪst i əst **~ily** ɪ li əl i **~iness** i nəs i nɪs
Jermaine dʒə ˈmeɪn ‖ dʒᵊr-
Jermyn ˈdʒɜːm ɪn §-ən ‖ ˈdʒɜ˞ːm-
jeroboam, J~ ˌdʒer ə ˈbəʊ əm ‖ -ˈboʊ- **~s** z
Jerome dʒə ˈrəʊm dʒɪ-, dʒe- ‖ -ˈroʊm
Jerrold ˈdʒer əld
jerr|y, Jerr|y ˈdʒer |i **~ies, ~y's** iz
ˈjerry can
jerry-|build ˈdʒer i |bɪld **~builder/s** bɪld ə/z ‖ -ᵊrz **~building** bɪld ɪŋ **~builds** bɪldz **~built** bɪlt
jersey, J~ ˈdʒɜːz i ‖ ˈdʒɜ˞ːz i **~s** z
ˌJersey ˈCity
Jerusalem dʒə ˈruːs əl əm dʒɪ-, dʒe- ‖ -ˈruːz-
Jeˌrusalem ˈartichoke
Jervaulx ˈdʒɜːv əʊ ‖ ˈdʒɜ˞ːv oʊ —*but as a family name* -ɪs, -əs
Jervis ˈdʒɜːv ɪs ˈdʒɑːv-, §-əs ‖ ˈdʒɜ˞ːv-
Jerwood ˈdʒɜː wʊd ‖ ˈdʒɜ˞ː-
Jespersen ˈjesp əs ən ˈdʒesp- ‖ -ᵊrs- —*Danish* [ˈjes bɐ sən]
Jess, jess dʒes **jessed** dʒest *(= jest)* **jesses** ˈdʒes ɪz -əz **jessing** ˈdʒes ɪŋ
jessamine, J~ ˈdʒes əm ɪn §-ən
Jesse ˈdʒes i —*sometimes also* dʒes
Jessel ˈdʒes ᵊl
Jessica ˈdʒes ɪk ə
Jessie ˈdʒes i
Jessop ˈdʒes əp
jest dʒest **jested** ˈdʒest ɪd -əd **jesting/ly** ˈdʒest ɪŋ /li **jests** dʒests
jester ˈdʒest ə ‖ -ᵊr **~s** z
Jesu ˈdʒiːz juː ‖ -uː —*in singing also* ˈjeɪz uː, ˈjeɪs- **~'s** z
Jesuit ˈdʒez ju ɪt ˈdʒeʒ-, -u , § ət ‖ ˈdʒeʒ u ət ˈdʒez- **~s** s
jesuitic, J~ ˌdʒez ju ˈɪt ɪk ◂ ˌdʒeʒ-, -u- ‖ ˌdʒeʒ u ˈɪṭ ɪk ◂ dʒez- **~al** ᵊl **~ally** ᵊl i
Jesus ˈdʒiːz əs ‖ -əz **Jesus'** ˈdʒiːz əs ‖ -əz
ˌJesus ˈChrist
jet dʒet **jets** dʒets **jetted** ˈdʒet ɪd -əd ‖ ˈdʒeṭ əd **jetting** ˈdʒet ɪŋ ‖ ˈdʒeṭ ɪŋ
ˌjet ˈengine; **ˈjet lag**; **ˌjet proˈpulsion**; **ˈjet set**; **ˈjet stream**
jet-black ˌdʒet ˈblæk ◂
jete, jeté ʒə ˈteɪ —*Fr* [ʒə te, ʃte] **~s** z
jetfoil ˈdʒet fɔɪᵊl **~s** z
Jethro ˈdʒeθ rəʊ ‖ -roʊ
jet-lagged ˈdʒet læɡd
jetliner ˈdʒet ˌlaɪn ə ‖ -ᵊr **~s** z
jet-propelled ˌdʒet prə ˈpeld ◂
jetsam ˈdʒet səm -sæm
jet-setter ˈdʒet set ə ‖ -seṭ ᵊr
jet-ski, jetski, Jet Ski *tdmk* ˈdʒet skiː **~ed** d **~es** z **~ing** ɪŋ **~s** z
jettison ˈdʒet ɪs ən -ɪz-, -əs-, -əz- ‖ ˈdʒeṭ- **~ed** d **~ing** ɪŋ **~s** z
jett|y ˈdʒet |i ‖ ˈdʒeṭ |i **~ies** iz
Jeuda ˈdʒuːd ə
jeu d'esprit, jeux d'esprit ˌʒɜː de ˈspriː ‖ ˌʒuː- —*Fr* [ʒø dɛs pʁi]
jeunesse dor|ee, ~ée ˌʒɜːn es ˈdɔːr eɪ ʒɜː ˌnes dɔː ˈreɪ ‖ ʒuː ˌnes dɔː ˈreɪ —*Fr* [ʒœ nɛs dɔ ʁe, -nɛz-]
Jevons ˈdʒev ᵊnz
Jew dʒuː **Jews** dʒuːz
jewel ˈdʒuː əl dʒuːl **~led, ~ed** d **~s** z
Jewel, Jewell ˈdʒuː əl dʒuːl
jeweller, jeweler ˈdʒuː əl ə ˈdʒuːl ə ‖ -ᵊr **~s** z
jewellery, jewelry ˈdʒuː əl ri ˈdʒuːl ri; §ˈdʒuːl ər i
Jewess ˈdʒuː es -ɪs, -əs, ˌdʒuː ˈes ‖ -əs **~es** ɪz əz
Jewett ˈdʒuː ɪt § ət
Jewish ˈdʒuː ɪʃ **~ness** nəs nɪs
Jewry ˈdʒʊər i §ˈdʒuː ri ‖ ˈdʒuː ri
jew's-harp ˌdʒuːz ˈhɑːp ‖ ˈdʒuːz hɑːrp ˈdʒuːs-
Jewson ˈdʒuːs ᵊn
Jeyes dʒeɪz
Jezebel ˈdʒez ə bel -ɪ-, -bᵊl
Jezreel ˈdʒez ri əl dʒez ˈriːᵊl
Jiang Qing ˌdʒæŋ ˈtʃɪŋ dʒiˌæŋ- ‖ dʒi ˌɑːŋ- —*Chi* Jiāng Qīng [¹tɕjaŋ ¹tɕʰiŋ]
Jiangsu ˌdʒæŋ ˈsuː dʒiˌæŋ- ‖ dʒi ˌɑːŋ- —*Chi* Jiāngsū [¹tɕjaŋ ¹su]
Jiangxi ˌdʒæŋ ˈʃiː dʒiˌæŋ- ‖ dʒi ˌɑːŋ- —*Chi* Jiāngxī [¹tɕjaŋ ¹ɕi]

J

Jiang Zemin ˌdʒæŋ zə ˈmɪn dʒi ˌæŋ-, -zi- ‖ ˌdʒɑːŋ- ˌʒɑːŋ-, dʒi ˌɑːŋ- —*Chi* Jiāng Zémín [¹tɕjaŋ ²tsɤ ²mɪn]
jib dʒɪb **jibbed** dʒɪbd **jibbing** ˈdʒɪb ɪŋ **jibs** dʒɪbz
jibe dʒaɪb **jibed** dʒaɪbd **jibes** dʒaɪbz **jibing** ˈdʒaɪb ɪŋ
jicama ˈhiːk əm ə ˈhɪk-
JICTAR ˈdʒɪkt ɑː ‖ -ɑːr
Jif *tdmk* dʒɪf
jiff dʒɪf **jiffs** dʒɪfs
Jiffi *tdmk* ˈdʒɪf i
jiffy ˈdʒɪf i **jiffies** ˈdʒɪf iz
jig dʒɪg **jigged** dʒɪgd **jigging** ˈdʒɪg ɪŋ **jigs** dʒɪgz
jigger ˈdʒɪg ə ‖ -ᵊr **~ed** d **~s** z
jiggery-pokery ˌdʒɪg ər i ˈpəʊk ər i ‖ -ˈpoʊk-
jiggl|e ˈdʒɪg ᵊl **~ed** d **~es** z **~ing** ɪŋ
jiggly ˈdʒɪg ᵊl i
jiggy ˈdʒɪg i
jigsaw ˈdʒɪg sɔː ‖ -sɑː **~s** z
ˈjigsaw ˌpuzzle
jihad dʒɪ ˈhæd dʒə-, -ˈhɑːd ‖ -ˈhɑːd **~i/z** i/z —*Arabic* [dʒɪ ˈhaːd] **~s** z
jilbab dʒɪl ˈbæb -ˈbɑːb **~s** z —*Arabic* [dʒɪl ˈbaːb]
Jilin ˌdʒiː ˈlɪn ˈdʒɪl ɪn —*Chi* Jílín [²tɕi ²lɪn]
Jill dʒɪl
jilt dʒɪlt **jilted** ˈdʒɪlt ɪd -əd **jilting** ˈdʒɪlt ɪŋ **jilts** dʒɪlts
Jim dʒɪm
ˌjim ˈcrow, ˌJim ˈCrow law
jim-dandy ˌdʒɪm ˈdænd i ◂
jiminy ˈdʒɪm ən i -ɪn-
jimjams ˈdʒɪm dʒæmz
Jimmi, Jimmie, Jimmy, jimm|y ˈdʒɪm |i **~ies** iz
jimson weed ˈdʒɪmᵖs ən wiːd **~s** z
Jin *dynasty* dʒɪn —*Chi* Jìn [³tɕɪn]
Jinan ˌdʒiː ˈnæn ‖ -ˈnɑːn —*Chi* Jìnán [⁴tɕi ²nan]
Jindiworobak ˌdʒɪnd i ˈwɒr ə bæk ‖ -ˈwɔːr- **~s** s
jingl|e ˈdʒɪŋ gᵊl **~ed** d **~es** z **~ing** ɪŋ
jingo ˈdʒɪŋ gəʊ ‖ -goʊ **~es** z **~ism** ˌɪz əm **~ist/s** ɪst/s §əst/s ‖ əst/s
jingoistic ˌdʒɪŋ gəʊ ˈɪst ɪk ◂ ‖ -goʊ- **~ally** ᵊl‿i
jinks dʒɪŋks
jinn dʒɪn
Jinnah ˈdʒɪn ə
jinni ˈdʒɪn i dʒɪ ˈniː
Jinnie, Jinny ˈdʒɪn i
jinricksha, jinrikisha dʒɪn ˈrɪk ʃə ˌ-ˈ-, ʃɔː ‖ -ʃɔː ʃɑː —*Jp* [dʑiˌn ɾi ˈki ɕa, -ˈɾi ki-] **~s** z
jinx dʒɪŋks **jinxed** dʒɪŋkst **jinxes** ˈdʒɪŋks ɪz -əz **jinxing** ˈdʒɪŋks ɪŋ
jipijapa ˌhɪp i ˈhɑːp ə **~s** z
jitney ˈdʒɪt ni **~s** z
jitter ˈdʒɪt ə ‖ ˈdʒɪţ ᵊr **~ed** d **jittering** ˈdʒɪt ər ɪŋ ‖ ˈdʒɪţ ər ɪŋ **~s** z
jitterbug ˈdʒɪt ə bʌg ‖ ˈdʒɪţ ᵊr- **~ged** d **~ging** ɪŋ **~s** z
jittery ˈdʒɪt ər i ‖ ˈdʒɪţ-

jiujitsu ˌdʒuː ˈdʒɪts uː —*Jp* [ˈdʑɯɯ dʑɯ tsɯ]
jive dʒaɪv **jived** dʒaɪvd **jives** dʒaɪvz **jiving** ˈdʒaɪv ɪŋ
jizz dʒɪz
Jnr —*see* **Junior**
Jo, jo dʒəʊ ‖ dʒoʊ
Joab ˈdʒəʊ æb ‖ ˈdʒoʊ-
Joachim ˈjəʊ ə kɪm ‖ ˈjoʊ- —*Ger* [jo ˈʔax ɪm, ˈjoː ax ɪm]
Joad dʒəʊd ‖ dʒoʊd
Joan dʒəʊn ‖ dʒoʊn
Joanna dʒəʊ ˈæn ə ‖ dʒoʊ-
Joanne ₍ˌ₎dʒəʊ ˈæn ‖ ₍ˌ₎dʒoʊ-
job *'employment, task'* dʒɒb ‖ dʒɑːb **jobbed** dʒɒbd ‖ dʒɑːbd **jobbing** ˈdʒɒb ɪŋ ‖ ˈdʒɑːb ɪŋ **jobs** dʒɒbz ‖ dʒɑːbz
ˌjob ˈlot, ˈ· ·; **ˈjob share**
Job *name* dʒəʊb ‖ dʒoʊb **Job's** dʒəʊbz ‖ dʒoʊbz
ˌJob's ˈcomforter; **ˌJob's ˈtears**
jobber ˈdʒɒb ə ‖ ˈdʒɑːb ᵊr **~s** z
jobbery ˈdʒɒb ər i ‖ ˈdʒɑːb-
Jobcentre ˈdʒɒb ˌsent ə ‖ ˈdʒɑːb ˌsenţ ᵊr **~s** z
jobholder ˈdʒɒb ˌhəʊld ə →-ˌhɒʊld- ‖ ˈdʒɑːb ˌhoʊld ᵊr **~s** z
job-hunt|er/s ˈdʒɒb ˌhʌnt| ə/z ‖ ˈdʒɑːb ˌhʌnţ ᵊr/z **~ing** ɪŋ
jobless ˈdʒɒb ləs -lɪs ‖ ˈdʒɑːb- **~ness** nəs nɪs
Jobs *(i)* dʒəʊbz ‖ dʒoʊbz *(ii)* dʒɒbz ‖ dʒɑːbz
job-sharing ˈdʒɒb ˌʃeər ɪŋ ‖ ˈdʒɑːb ˌʃer ɪŋ ˌʃær-
Jobson ˈdʒɒb sᵊn ‖ ˈdʒɑːb-
jobsworth ˈdʒɒbz wɜːθ ‖ ˈdʒɑːbz wɜːθ **~s** s
Jo'burg ˈdʒəʊ bɜːg ‖ ˈdʒoʊ bɜˑːg
Jocasta dʒəʊ ˈkæst ə ‖ dʒoʊ-
Jocelyn ˈdʒɒs lɪn -lən; ˈdʒɒs əl ɪn, -ən ‖ ˈdʒɑːs-
Jock, jock dʒɒk ‖ dʒɑːk **Jock's, jocks** dʒɒks ‖ dʒɑːks
jockey ˈdʒɒk i ‖ ˈdʒɑːk i **~ed** d **~ing** ɪŋ **~s** z
jockstrap ˈdʒɒk stræp ‖ ˈdʒɑːk- **~s** s
jocose dʒəʊ ˈkəʊs ‖ dʒoʊ ˈkoʊs dʒə- **~ly** li
jocosity dʒəʊ ˈkɒs ət i -ɪt- ‖ dʒoʊ ˈkɑːs əţ i dʒə-
jocular ˈdʒɒk jʊl ə -jəl- ‖ ˈdʒɑːk jəl ᵊr **~ly** li
jocularity ˌdʒɒk ju ˈlær ət i ˌ-jə-, -ɪt i ‖ ˌdʒɑːk jə ˈlær əţ i -ˈler-
jocund ˈdʒɒk ənd ˈdʒəʊk-, -ʌnd ‖ ˈdʒɑːk- ˈdʒoʊk- **~ly** li
jocundity dʒə ˈkʌnd ət i dʒɒ-, dʒəʊ-, -ɪt- ‖ dʒoʊ ˈkʌnd əţ i dʒɑː-
jod jɒd ‖ jɑːd jɔːd, jʊd **jods** jɒdz ‖ jɑːdz jɔːdz, jʊdz
jodhpurs ˈdʒɒd pəz ‖ ˈdʒɑːd pᵊrz
Jodi, Jodie ˈdʒəʊd i ‖ ˈdʒoʊd i
Jodrell ˈdʒɒdr əl ‖ ˈdʒɑːdr-
ˌJodrell ˈBank
Jody ˈdʒəʊd i ‖ ˈdʒoʊd i
Joe, joe dʒəʊ ‖ dʒoʊ
ˌJoe ˈBloggs; **ˌJoe ˈpublic**
Joel ˈdʒəʊ əl -el ‖ ˈdʒoʊ-
Joey, joey ˈdʒəʊ i ‖ ˈdʒoʊ i **~s, ~'s** z

og dʒɒg ‖ dʒɑːg **jogged** dʒɒgd ‖ dʒɑːgd **jogging** 'dʒɒg ɪŋ ‖ 'dʒɑːg ɪŋ **jogs** dʒɒgz ‖ dʒɑːgz
ˌ**jog trot**
ogger 'dʒɒg ə ‖ 'dʒɑːg ᵊr **~s** z
oggl|e 'dʒɒg ᵊl ‖ 'dʒɑːg- **~ed** d **~es** z **~ing** ɪŋ
ohannesburg dʒəʊ 'hæn ɪs bɜːg §-'hɒn-, -ɪz- ‖ dʒoʊ 'hæn əs bɝːg
Johannine dʒəʊ 'hæn aɪn ‖ -ən
John, john dʒɒn ‖ dʒɑːn **John's, johns** dʒɒnz ‖ dʒɑːnz
ˌ**John 'Bull**; ˌ**John 'Doe**
Johnian 'dʒəʊn i ən ‖ 'dʒoʊn- **~s** z
Johnnie 'dʒɒn i ‖ 'dʒɑːn i
johnn|y, J~ 'dʒɒn |i ‖ 'dʒɑːn |i **~ies** iz
johnnycake 'dʒɒn i keɪk ‖ 'dʒɑːn- **~s** s
johnny-come-late|ly ˌdʒɒn i kʌm 'leɪt |li ‖ ˌdʒɑːn- **~lies** liz
Johnny-on-the-spot ˌdʒɒn i ɒn ðə 'spɒt ‖ ˌdʒɑːn i ɑːn ðə 'spɑːt -ɔːn-
John o'Groats ˌdʒɒn ə 'grəʊts ‖ ˌdʒɑːn ə 'groʊts
Johns dʒɒnz ‖ dʒɑːnz
Johnson 'dʒɒnᵗs ᵊn ‖ 'dʒɑːnᵗs-
Johnsonian dʒɒn 'səʊn i ən ‖ dʒɑːn 'soʊn-
Johnston *(i)* 'dʒɒnᵗst ən ‖ 'dʒɑːnᵗst-, *(ii)* 'dʒɒnᵗs ᵊn ‖ 'dʒɑːnᵗs-
Johnstone *(i)* 'dʒɒnᵗst ən ‖ 'dʒɑːnᵗst-, *(ii)* 'dʒɒnᵗs ᵊn ‖ 'dʒɑːnᵗs-, *(iii)* 'dʒɒn stəʊn ‖ 'dʒɑːn stoʊn
Johor, Johore dʒəʊ 'hɔː ‖ dʒə 'hɔːr -'hoʊr
joie de vivre ˌʒwɑː də 'viːv rə -'viːv —*Fr* [ʒwad viːvʁ]
join dʒɔɪn **joined** dʒɔɪnd **joining** 'dʒɔɪn ɪŋ **joins** dʒɔɪnz
joined-up ˌdʒɔɪnd 'ʌp ◂
joiner 'dʒɔɪn ə ‖ -ᵊr **~s** z
joinery 'dʒɔɪn ər i
joint dʒɔɪnt **jointed** 'dʒɔɪnt ɪd -əd ‖ 'dʒɔɪnt̬ əd **jointing** 'dʒɔɪnt ɪŋ ‖ 'dʒɔɪnt̬ ɪŋ **jointly** 'dʒɔɪnt li
joint-stock ˌdʒɔɪnt 'stɒk ˈ · · ‖ -'stɑːk
ˌ**joint-'stock ˌcompany**
joist dʒɔɪst **joists** dʒɔɪsts
Jojo, jo-jo 'dʒəʊ dʒəʊ ‖ 'dʒoʊ dʒoʊ
jojoba həʊ 'həʊb ə ‖ hoʊ 'hoʊb ə —*Sp* [xo 'xo βa]
joke dʒəʊk ‖ dʒoʊk **joked** dʒəʊkt ‖ dʒoʊkt **jokes** dʒəʊks ‖ dʒoʊks **joking/ly** 'dʒəʊk ɪŋ /li ‖ 'dʒoʊk ɪŋ /li
joker 'dʒəʊk ə ‖ 'dʒoʊk ᵊr **~s** z
jok|ey, jok|y 'dʒəʊk |i ‖ 'dʒoʊk |i **~ily** ɪ li əl i **~iness** i nəs i nɪs
Jolie ʒəʊ 'liː ‖ ʒoʊ-
Joliet *place in IL* ˌdʒəʊl i 'et ˈ · · · ‖ ˌdʒoʊl-
Jolley, Jollie 'dʒɒl i ‖ 'dʒɑːl i
jolli... —*see* **jolly**
Jolliffe 'dʒɒl ɪf §-əf ‖ 'dʒɑːl-
jollification ˌdʒɒl ɪf ɪ 'keɪʃ ᵊn ˌ-əf-, §-ə'- ‖ ˌdʒɑːl- **~s** z
jollity 'dʒɒl ət i -ɪt- ‖ 'dʒɑːl ət̬ i

joll|y, Jolly 'dʒɒl |i ‖ 'dʒɑːl |i **~ied** id **~ier** i ə ‖ i ᵊr **~ies** iz **~iest** i ɪst i əst **~ily** ɪ li əl i **~iness** i nəs i nɪs **~ying** i ɪŋ
ˌ**Jolly 'Roger**
jollyboat 'dʒɒl i bəʊt ‖ 'dʒɑːl i boʊt **~s** s
Jolson 'dʒəʊl sən →'dʒɒʊl-; 'dʒɒl- ‖ 'dʒoʊl-
jolt dʒəʊlt →dʒɒʊlt ‖ dʒoʊlt **jolted** 'dʒəʊlt ɪd →'dʒɒʊlt-, -əd ‖ 'dʒoʊlt əd **jolting** 'dʒəʊlt ɪŋ →'dʒɒʊlt- ‖ 'dʒoʊlt ɪŋ
jolty 'dʒəʊlt i →'dʒɒʊlt- ‖ 'dʒoʊlt i
Jolyon 'dʒəʊl i ən 'dʒɒl- ‖ 'dʒoʊl jən
Jon dʒɒn ‖ dʒɑːn
Jonah, jonah 'dʒəʊn ə ‖ 'dʒoʊn ə
Jonas 'dʒəʊn əs ‖ 'dʒoʊn-
Jonathan 'dʒɒn əθ ən ‖ 'dʒɑːn-
Jones dʒəʊnz ‖ dʒoʊnz **Joneses** 'dʒəʊnz ɪz -əz ‖ 'dʒoʊnz əz
Jonesian 'dʒəʊnz i‿ən ‖ 'dʒoʊnz- **~s** z
Jonestown 'dʒəʊnz taʊn ‖ 'dʒoʊnz-
Jong jɒŋ ‖ jɑːŋ
jongleur ˌʒɒŋ 'glɜː ˌdʒɒŋ- ‖ 'dʒɑːŋ glᵊr **~s** z *or as sing.* —*Fr* [ʒɔ̃ glœːʁ]
Joni 'dʒəʊn i ‖ 'dʒoʊn i
jonquil 'dʒɒŋk wɪl -wəl ‖ 'dʒɑːŋk- 'dʒɑːn kwəl **~s** z
Jonson, Jonsson 'dʒɒnᵗs ən ‖ 'dʒɑːnᵗs-
Jools dʒuːlz
Joplin 'dʒɒp lɪn §-lən ‖ 'dʒɑːp-
Jopling 'dʒɒp lɪŋ ‖ 'dʒɑːp-
Joppa 'dʒɒp ə ‖ 'dʒɑːp ə
Jopson 'dʒɒps ən ‖ 'dʒɑːps-
Jordan 'dʒɔːd ᵊn ‖ 'dʒɔːrd-
Jordanhill ˌdʒɔːd ᵊn 'hɪl ◂ ‖ ˌdʒɔːrd-
Jordanian dʒɔː 'deɪn i ən ‖ dʒɔːr- **~s** z
Jorge 'hɔː heɪ ‖ 'hɔːr- —*Sp* ['xoɾ xe]
Jorrocks 'dʒɒr əks ‖ 'dʒɔːr- 'dʒɑːr-
jorum 'dʒɔːr əm ‖ 'dʒoʊr- **~s** z
José *(i)* həʊ 'zeɪ -'seɪ ‖ hoʊ- —*Sp* [xo 'se], *(ii)* 'ʒəʊs eɪ ‖ ʒoʊ 'seɪ —*Fr* [ʒo se]
Joseph 'dʒəʊz ɪf §'dʒəʊs-, -əf ‖ 'dʒoʊz əf 'dʒoʊs-
Josephine 'dʒəʊz ɪ fiːn §'dʒəʊs-, -ə- ‖ 'dʒoʊz ə- 'dʒoʊs-
Josephson 'dʒəʊz ɪf sən 'dʒəʊs-, -əf- ‖ 'dʒoʊz- 'dʒoʊs-
Josephus dʒəʊ 'siːf əs ‖ dʒoʊ-
josh, Josh dʒɒʃ ‖ dʒɑːʃ **joshed** dʒɒʃt ‖ dʒɑːʃt **joshes** 'dʒɒʃ ɪz -əz ‖ 'dʒɑːʃ əz **joshing** 'dʒɒʃ ɪŋ ‖ 'dʒɑːʃ ɪŋ
Joshua 'dʒɒʃ ju ə -u ə ‖ 'dʒɑːʃ u ə
'**Joshua tree**
Josiah dʒəʊ 'saɪ ə -'zaɪ ə ‖ dʒoʊ-
Josie 'dʒəʊz i ‖ 'dʒoʊz i
joss, Joss dʒɒs ‖ dʒɑːs
'**joss stick**
jostl|e 'dʒɒs ᵊl ‖ 'dʒɑːs- **~ed** d **~es** z **~ing** ɪŋ
Jost van Dyke ˌjəʊst væn 'daɪk ‖ ˌjoʊst-
jot dʒɒt ‖ dʒɑːt **jots** dʒɒts ‖ dʒɑːts **jotted** 'dʒɒt ɪd -əd ‖ 'dʒɑːt̬ əd **jotting** 'dʒɒt ɪŋ ‖ 'dʒɑːt̬ ɪŋ
jotter 'dʒɒt ə ‖ 'dʒɑːt̬ ᵊr **~s** z
jotting 'dʒɒt ɪŋ ‖ 'dʒɑːt̬ ɪŋ **~s** z
joule, Joule dʒuːl dʒaʊl, dʒəʊl **~s, ~'s** z

J

jounce dʒaʊnᵗs **jounced** dʒaʊnᵗst **jounces** ˈdʒaʊnᵗs ɪz -əz **jouncing** ˈdʒaʊnᵗs ɪŋ

journal ˈdʒɜːn ᵊl ‖ ˈdʒɜːn- **~s** z

journalese ˌdʒɜːn ə ˈliːz -ᵊl ˈiːz ‖ ˌdʒɜːn ᵊl ˈiːz -ˈiːs

journalism ˈdʒɜːn ə ˌlɪz əm -ᵊl ˌɪz- ‖ ˈdʒɜːn-

journalist ˈdʒɜːn əl ɪst §-əst ‖ ˈdʒɜːn- **~s** s

journalistic ˌdʒɜːn ə ˈlɪst ɪk ◂ -ᵊl ˈɪst- ‖ ˌdʒɜːn ᵊl ˈɪst ɪk ◂ **~ally** ᵊl i

journey ˈdʒɜːn i ‖ ˈdʒɜːn i **~ed** d **~ing/s** ɪŋ/z **~s** z

journey|man ˈdʒɜːn i |mən ‖ ˈdʒɜːn- **~men** mən men

journo ˈdʒɜːn əʊ ‖ ˈdʒɜːn oʊ **~s** z

joust dʒaʊst **jousted** ˈdʒaʊst ɪd -əd **jousting** ˈdʒaʊst ɪŋ **jousts** dʒaʊsts

Jove dʒəʊv ‖ dʒoʊv

jovial ˈdʒəʊv i əl ‖ ˈdʒoʊv- **~ly** i

joviality ˌdʒəʊv i ˈæl ət i -ɪt i ‖ ˌdʒoʊv i ˈæl əṭ i

Jovian ˈdʒəʊv i ən ‖ ˈdʒoʊv-

Jowell *(i)* ˈdʒaʊ‿əl *(ii)* ˈdʒəʊ əl ‖ ˈdʒoʊ- —*The British politician Tessa J~ is (i)*

Jowett, Jowitt *(i)* ˈdʒaʊ ɪt -ət, *(ii)* ˈdʒəʊ- ‖ ˈdʒoʊ-

jowl dʒaʊl **jowls** dʒaʊlz

-jowled ˈdʒaʊld

joy, Joy dʒɔɪ **joys** dʒɔɪz

Joyce dʒɔɪs

joyful ˈdʒɔɪf ᵊl ˈdʒɔɪ fʊl **~ly** i **~ness** nəs nɪs

joyless ˈdʒɔɪ ləs -lɪs **~ly** li **~ness** nəs nɪs

Joyner ˈdʒɔɪn ə ‖ -ᵊr

Joynson ˈdʒɔɪnᵗs ən

joyous ˈdʒɔɪ əs **~ly** li **~ness** nəs nɪs

joyrid|e ˈdʒɔɪ raɪd **~er/s** ə/z ‖ ᵊr/z **~ing** ɪŋ **~s** z

joystick ˈdʒɔɪ stɪk **~s** s

JP ˌdʒeɪ ˈpiː **~s, ~'s** z

jpeg, jpg ˈdʒeɪ peg **~s, ~'s** z

Jr —*see* **Junior**

Juan wɑːn hwɑːn, ˈdʒuː ən ‖ *h*wɑːn —*Sp* [xwan]

Juanita wə ˈniːt ə xwə-; ˌdʒuː ə ˈniːt ə ‖ *h*wɑː ˈniːṭ ə —*Sp* [xwa ˈni ta]

jubilant ˈdʒuːb ɪl ənt -əl- **~ly** li

Jubilate ˌdʒuːb ɪ ˈlɑːt i ˌjuːb-, -ə-, -eɪ ‖ -ˈleɪṭ i **~s** z

jubilation ˌdʒuːb ɪ ˈleɪʃ ᵊn -ə- **~s** z

jubilee ˈdʒuːb ɪ liː -ə-, ˌ· · ˈ· **~s** z

Judaea dʒu ˈdɪə -ˈdiː ə ‖ dʒu ˈdiː ə

Judaean dʒu ˈdɪən -ˈdiː ən ‖ dʒu ˈdiː ən **~s** z

Judaeo- dʒu ¦diː əʊ -¦deɪ- ‖ -oʊ — **Judaeo-Spanish** dʒu ˌdiː əʊ ˈspæn ɪʃ ◂ -ˌdeɪ- ‖ -oʊ-

Judah ˈdʒuːd ə

Judaic dʒu ˈdeɪ ɪk **~a** ə **~ally** ᵊl i

judais... —*see* **judaiz...**

Judaism ˈdʒuːd eɪ ˌɪz əm -i-; ˈdʒuːd ˌɪz əm ‖ -ə-

judaiz|e ˈdʒuːd eɪ aɪz **~ed** d **~es** ɪz əz **~er/s** ə/z ‖ -ᵊr/z **~ing** ɪŋ

Judas, judas ˈdʒuːd əs **~es, 's** ɪz əz **'Judas tree**

Judd dʒʌd

judder ˈdʒʌd ə ‖ -ᵊr **~ed** d **juddering** ˈdʒʌd ər ɪŋ **~s** z

Jude dʒuːd **Jude's** dʒuːdz

Judea dʒu ˈdɪə -ˈdiː ə ‖ dʒu ˈdiː ə

Judean dʒu ˈdɪən -ˈdiː ən ‖ dʒu ˈdiː ən **~s** z

Judeo- dʒu ¦diː əʊ -¦deɪ- ‖ -oʊ — **Judeo-Spanish** dʒu ˌdiː əʊ ˈspæn ɪʃ ◂ -ˌdeɪ- ‖ -oʊ-

judge dʒʌdʒ **judged** dʒʌdʒd **judges** ˈdʒʌdʒ ɪz -əz **judging** ˈdʒʌdʒ ɪŋ

judgement ˈdʒʌdʒ mənt **~s** s

judgemental dʒʌdʒ ˈment ᵊl ‖ -ˈmenṭ ᵊl **~ly** i

judgeship ˈdʒʌdʒ ʃɪp **~s** s

judgment ˈdʒʌdʒ mənt **~s** s **'judgment day**

judgmental dʒʌdʒ ˈment ᵊl ‖ -ˈmenṭ ᵊl **~ly** i

Judi ˈdʒuːd i

judicative ˈdʒuːd ɪk ət ɪv ˈ·ək- ‖ -ɪ keɪṭ ɪv

judicature ˈdʒuːd ɪk ə tʃə -tjʊə; dʒu ˈdɪk- ‖ -ɪ keɪtʃ ᵊr -ɪk ə tʃʊr **~s** z

judicial dʒu ˈdɪʃ ᵊl **~ly** i

judiciar|y dʒu ˈdɪʃ ər |i -ˈdɪʃ i ər |i ‖ -ˈdɪʃ i er |i **~ies** iz

judicious dʒu ˈdɪʃ əs **~ly** li **~ness** nəs nɪs

Judith ˈdʒuːd ɪθ -əθ

judo ˈdʒuːd əʊ ‖ -oʊ —*Jp* [ˈdʑɯɯ doo]

Jud|y, jud|y ˈdʒuːd |i **~y's, ~ies** iz

jug dʒʌg **jugged** dʒʌgd **jugging** ˈdʒʌg ɪŋ **jugs** dʒʌgz

jug-eared ˌdʒʌg ˈɪəd ◂ ‖ ˈdʒʌg ɪrd

jugful ˈdʒʌg fʊl **~s** z

juggernaut, J~ ˈdʒʌg ə nɔːt ‖ -ᵊr- -nɑːt **~s** s

juggins ˈdʒʌg ɪnz §-ənz

juggl|e ˈdʒʌg ᵊl **~ed** d **~es** z **~ing** ɪŋ

juggler ˈdʒʌg lə ˈdʒʌg ᵊl ə ‖ ˈdʒʌg lᵊr -ᵊl ər **~s** z

jugglery ˈdʒʌg lər i

Jugoslav ˈjuːg əʊ slɑːv ˌ· ·ˈ· ‖ -oʊ slɑːv -slæv **~s** z

Jugoslavi|a ˌjuːg əʊ ˈslɑːv i |ə ‖ ˌ·oʊ- **~an/s** ən/z

jugular ˈdʒʌg jʊl ə -jəl- ‖ -jəl ᵊr **~s** z **ˌjugular 'vein**

Jugurtha dʒu ˈgɜːθ ə ju- ‖ -ˈgɜːθ ə

juice dʒuːs **juiced** dʒuːst **juices** ˈdʒuːs ɪz -əz **juicing** ˈdʒuːs ɪŋ

juicer ˈdʒuːs ə ‖ -ᵊr **~s** z

juic|y ˈdʒuːs |i **~ier** i ə ‖ i ᵊr **~iest** i ɪst i əst **~ily** ɪ li əl i **~iness** i nəs i nɪs

Juilliard ˈdʒuːl i ɑːd ‖ -ɑːd

jujitsu dʒu ˈdʒɪts uː ˌdʒuː- —*Jp* [ˈdʑɯɯ dʑi tsɯ]

juju ˈdʒuːdʒ uː **~ism** ˌɪz əm **~s** z

jujube ˈdʒuːdʒ uːb ‖ ˈ·ʊb i **~s** z

juke dʒuːk **juked** dʒuːkt **jukes** dʒuːks **juking** ˈdʒuːk ɪŋ

jukebox ˈdʒuːk bɒks ‖ -bɑːks **~es** ɪz əz

Jukes dʒuːks

julep ˈdʒuːl ɪp -ep, -əp **~s** s

Jules dʒuːlz —*Fr* [ʒyl]

Julia ˈdʒuːl i ə ‖ ˈdʒuːl jə

Julian ˈdʒuːl i ən ‖ ˈdʒuːl jən

Juliana ˌdʒuːl i ˈɑːn ə ‖ -ˈæn ə
Julie ˈdʒuːl i
Julien ˈdʒuːl i ən ‖ ˈdʒuːl jən
Julienne ˌdʒuːl i ˈen ◂ ˌʒuːl- —*Fr* [ʒy ljɛn]
Juliet *(i)* ˈdʒuːl i ət ‖ ˈdʒuːl jət, *(ii)* ˌdʒuːl i ˈet ˈ. . . —*In Shakespeare, traditionally (i)*
Juliette ˌdʒuːl i ˈet
Julius ˈdʒuːl i əs ‖ ˈdʒuːl jəs
July dʒu ˈlaɪ dʒə-, ˌdʒuː- **~s** z
jumbl|e ˈdʒʌm bᵊl **~ed** d **~es** z **~ing** ɪŋ
 ˈjumble sale
jum|bly ˈdʒʌm |bli **~blies** bliz
jumbo, Jumbo ˈdʒʌm bəʊ ‖ -boʊ **~s** z
 ˈjumbo jet, ˌ. . ˈ.
jumbo-sized ˈdʒʌm bəʊ saɪzd ‖ -boʊ-
JumboTron *tdmk* ˈdʒʌm bəʊ trɒn ‖ -boʊ trɑːn
jumbuck ˈdʒʌm bʌk **~s** s

JUMPED

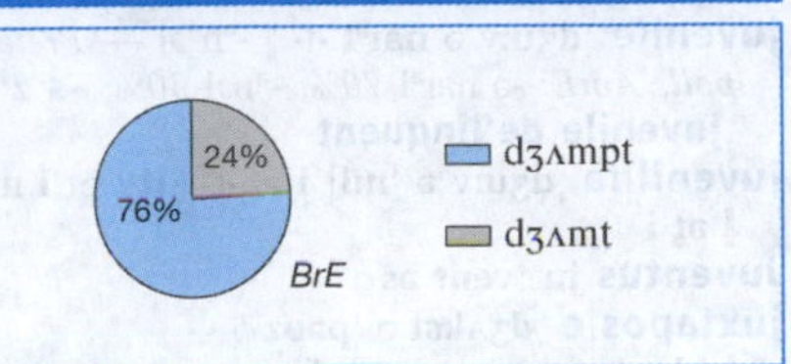

jump dʒʌmp **jumped** dʒʌmpt — *Preference poll, BrE* dʒʌmpt *76%,* dʒʌmt *24%.* **jumping** ˈdʒʌmp ɪŋ **jumps** dʒʌmps
 ˈjump jet; **ˈjump leads**; **ˈjump seat**
jumped-up ˌdʒʌmpt ˈʌp ◂
jumper ˈdʒʌmp ə ‖ -ᵊr **~s** z
jumping-off ˌdʒʌmp ɪŋ ˈɒf -ˈɔːf ‖ -ˈɔːf -ˈɑːf
 ˌjumping-ˈoff place
jump-off ˈdʒʌmp ɒf -ɔːf ‖ -ɔːf -ɑːf **~s** s
jump-|start ˈdʒʌmp| stɑːt ˌ·ˈ· ‖ -stɑːrt **~started** stɑːt ɪd -əd ‖ stɑːrţ əd **~starting** stɑːt ɪŋ ‖ stɑːrţ ɪŋ **~starts** stɑːts ‖ stɑːrts
jumpsuit ˈdʒʌmp suːt -sjuːt **~s** s
jump-up ˈdʒʌmp ʌp **~s** s
jump|y ˈdʒʌmp |i **~ier** i ə ‖ i ᵊr **~iest** i ɪst i əst **~ily** ɪ li əl i **~iness** i nəs i nɪs
junction ˈdʒʌŋk ʃən **~s** z
 ˈjunction box
juncture ˈdʒʌŋk tʃə -ʃə ‖ -tʃᵊr **~s** z
June dʒuːn **Junes, June's** dʒuːnz
Juneau ˈdʒuːn əʊ dʒu ˈnəʊ ‖ -oʊ
Jung jʊŋ —*Ger* [jʊŋ]
Jungfrau ˈjʊŋ fraʊ —*Ger* [ˈjʊŋ fʁaʊ]
Jungian ˈjʊŋ i ən **~s** z
jungle ˈdʒʌŋ gᵊl **~s** z
 ˈjungle gym
Juninho dʒu ˈniːn jəʊ ‖ -joʊ —*Port* [ʒu ˈni ɲu]
junior, J~ ˈdʒuːn i ə ‖ ˈdʒuːn jᵊr **~s** z
 ˌJunior ˈCollege; **ˈjunior school**
juniper ˈdʒuːn ɪp ə -əp- ‖ -ᵊr **~s** z
Junipero hu ˈniːp ə rəʊ ‖ -roʊ —*Sp* Junípero [xu ˈni pe ɾo]
Junius ˈdʒuːn i əs ‖ ˈdʒuːn jəs

junk dʒʌŋk **junked** dʒʌŋkt **junking** ˈdʒʌŋk ɪŋ **junks** dʒʌŋks
 ˈjunk bond; **ˈjunk food**; **ˈjunk mail**; **ˈjunk shop**
Junker ˈjʊŋk ə ‖ -ᵊr —*Ger* [ˈjʊŋ kɐ] **~s** z
junk|et ˈdʒʌŋk |ɪt §-ət ‖ -|ət **~eted** ɪt ɪd §ət-, -əd ‖ əţ əd **~eting** ɪt ɪŋ §ət- ‖ əţ ɪŋ **~ets** ɪts §əts ‖ əts
junkie ˈdʒʌŋk i **~s** z
Junkin ˈdʒʌŋk ɪn §-ən
junk|y ˈdʒʌŋk |i **~ies** iz
junkyard ˈdʒʌŋk jɑːd ‖ -jɑːrd **~s** z
Juno ˈdʒuːn əʊ ‖ -oʊ
Junoesque ˌdʒuːn əʊ ˈesk ◂ ‖ -oʊ-
Junor ˈdʒuːn ə ‖ -ᵊr
junta ˈdʒʌnt ə ˈhʊnt-, ˈdʒʊnt- ‖ ˈhʊnt ə —*Sp* [ˈxun ta] **~s** z
Jupiter ˈdʒuːp ɪt ə -ət- ‖ -əţ ᵊr
Jura, jura ˈdʒʊər ə ‖ ˈdʒʊr ə —*Fr* [ʒy ʁa]
Jurassic dʒuᵊ ˈræs ɪk
Jurgen, Jürgen ˈjɜːg ən ˈjʊəg- ‖ ˈjɜːg ən —*Ger* [ˈjʏʁ gᵊn]
juridical dʒuᵊ ˈrɪd ɪk ᵊl **~ly** i
jurie... —*see* **jury**
jurisdiction ˌdʒʊər ɪs ˈdɪk ʃᵊn ˈdʒɜːr-, ˈdʒɔːr-, -əs-, -ɪz-, -əz- ‖ ˌdʒʊr- **~s** z
jurisprudence ˌdʒʊər ɪs ˈpruːd ᵊnᵗs ˈdʒɜːr-, ˈdʒɔːr-, -əs-, ˈ.ˌ.ˈ.. ‖ ˌdʒʊr-
jurist ˈdʒʊər ɪst ˈdʒɜːr-, ˈdʒɔːr-, §-əst ‖ ˈdʒʊr- **~s** s
juror ˈdʒʊər ə ˈdʒɜːr-, ˈdʒɔːr- ‖ ˈdʒʊr ᵊr **~s** z

JURY

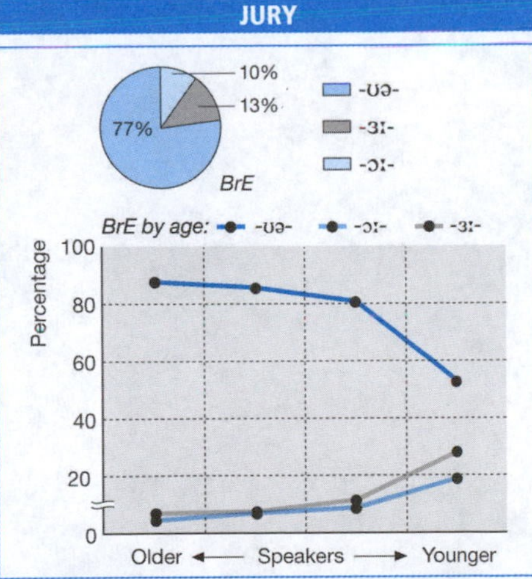

jur|y, Jury ˈdʒʊər |i ˈdʒɜːr-, ˈdʒɔːr- ‖ ˈdʒʊr |i — *Preference poll, BrE* -ʊə- *77%,* -ɜː- *13%,* -ɔː- *10%.* **~ies** iz
jury|man ˈdʒʊər i |mən ˈdʒɜːr-, ˈdʒɔːr- ‖ ˈdʒʊr- **~men** mən men
jurymast ˈdʒʊər i mɑːst ˈdʒɜːr-, ˈdʒɔːr-, -məst, §-mæst ‖ ˈdʒʊr i mæst —*naut* -məst
jury|men ˈdʒʊər i |mən ˈdʒɜːr-, ˈdʒɔːr-, -men ‖ ˈdʒʊr- **~woman** ˌwʊm ən **~women** ˌwɪm ɪn -ən
jus *'law'* dʒʌs juːs

J

jussive 'dʒʌs ɪv **~s** z
just *adv strong form* dʒʌst dʒəst, dʒest, *weak form* dʒəst §dʒɪst
just *adj* dʒʌst
justic|e, J~ 'dʒʌst ɪs §-əs **~es** ɪz əz
ˌ**Justice of the 'Peace**
justiciable dʒʌ 'stɪʃ iˌəb ᵊl -'stɪʃ əb ᵊl
justiciar|y dʒʌ 'stɪʃ i ər |i -'stɪʃ ər |i ‖ -i er |i **~ies** iz
justifiability ˌdʒʌst ɪ faɪ ə 'bɪl ət i -ɪt i ‖ -əṱ i

JUSTIFIABLE

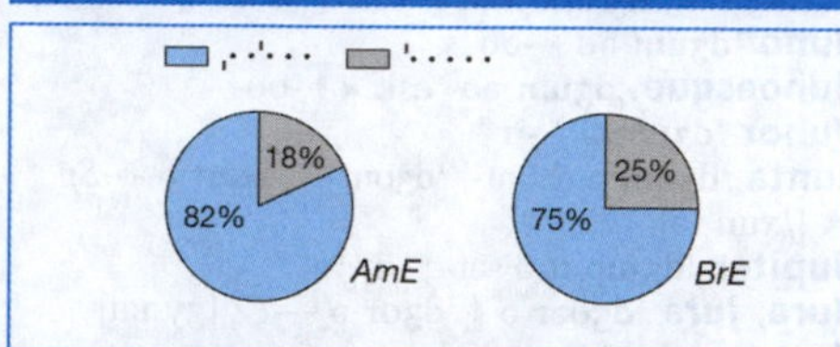

justifiab|le ˌdʒʌst ɪ 'faɪ əb |ᵊl ˌ·ə-, '· · · · · — *Preference polls: AmE,* ˌ· ·'· · · *82%,* '· · · · · *18%; BrE,* ˌ· ·'· · · *75%,* '· · · · · *25%.* **~ly** li
justification ˌdʒʌst ɪf ɪ 'keɪʃ ᵊn ˌ·əf-, §-ə'·- **~s** z
justificatory 'dʒʌst ɪf ɪ keɪt ər i '·əf-, §'·.ə-, ˌ· ·'· · ·, '· ·ɪk ət ər i ‖ dʒʌ 'stɪf ɪk ə tɔːr i -toʊr i; 'dʒʌst əf ə keɪṱ ər i
justi|fy 'dʒʌst ɪ |faɪ -ə- **~fied** faɪd **~fier/s** faɪ ə/z ‖ faɪ ᵊr/z **~fies** faɪz **~fying** faɪ ɪŋ
Justin 'dʒʌst ɪn §-ən
Justine 'dʒʌst iːn dʒʌ 'stiːn ‖ dʒʌ 'stiːn —*Fr* [ʒy stin]
Justinian dʒʌ 'stɪn i ən
just-in-time ˌdʒʌst ɪn 'taɪm ◂ §-ən-
just|ly 'dʒʌst |li **~ness** nəs nɪs
jut dʒʌt **juts** dʒʌts **jutted** 'dʒʌt ɪd -əd ‖ 'dʒʌṱ əd **jutting** 'dʒʌt ɪŋ ‖ 'dʒʌṱ ɪŋ
jute, Jute dʒuːt **jutes, Jutes** dʒuːts
Jutland 'dʒʌt lənd —*Danish* Jylland ['jyl anʔ]
Juvenal 'dʒuːv ᵊn əl -ɪn-

JUVENILE

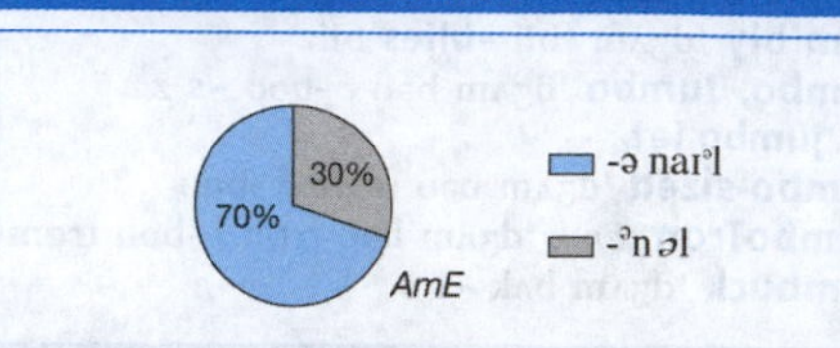

juvenile 'dʒuːv ə naɪᵊl -ɪ- ‖ -ᵊn əl — *Preference poll, AmE:* -ə naɪᵊl *70%,* -ᵊnəl *30%.* **~s** z
ˌ**juvenile de'linquent**
juvenil|ia ˌdʒuːv ə 'nɪl| i ə ˌ·ɪ- **~ity** ət i ɪt i ‖ əṱ i
Juventus ju 'vent əs
juxtapos|e ˌdʒʌkst ə 'pəʊz '· · · ‖ 'dʒʌkst ə poʊz **~ed** d **~es** ɪz əz **~ing** ɪŋ
juxtaposition ˌdʒʌkst ə pə 'zɪʃ ᵊn **~s** z
JVC *tdmk* ˌdʒeɪ viː 'siː
Jyväskylä 'juːv ə skjuːl ə —*Finnish* ['jy væs ky læ]

k Spelling-to-sound

1 Where the spelling is **k**, the pronunciation is regularly k as in **kind** kaɪnd. In the digraph **ck**, the pronunciation is again k as in **back** bæk.

2 **k** is silent at the beginning of a word when followed by **n** as in **knee** niː.

3 The sound k is also regularly written **c** as in **cat**, and **ck** as in **back**. It is sometimes also written **cc** as in **account**, **qu** as in **queue**, and in various other ways.

K, k keɪ **k's, Ks, K's** keɪz —*Communications code name:* Kilo
Kaaba ˈkɑːb ə ˈkɑː əb ə
kabaddi kə ˈbæd i —*Hindi* [kə bəɖ ɖi]
Kabaka kə ˈbɑːk ə
kabala kæ ˈbɑːl ə kə-
Kabardian kə ˈbɑːd i ən ‖ -ˈbɑːrd-
kabbala, Kabbalah kæ ˈbɑːl ə kə-
kabob kə ˈbɒb ‖ -ˈbɑːb **~s** z
kaboom kə ˈbuːm
kabuki kə ˈbuːk i kæ- —*Jp* [ka ˌbɯ ki]
Kabul ˈkɑːb ʊl ˈkɔːb-, -əl; kə ˈbʊl
Kabyle kə ˈbaɪəl
Kaddish, k~ ˈkæd ɪʃ ‖ ˈkɑːd-
Kadett *tdmk* kə ˈdet
Kadima kə ˈdiːm ə
kaffeeklatsch ˈkæf i klætʃ ‖ ˈkɔːf- ˈkɑːf-
Kaffir ˈkæf ə ‖ -ər **~s** z
Kaffraria kæ ˈfreər i ə kə- ‖ -ˈfrer-
Kafir ˈkæf ə ‖ -ər **~s** z
Kafka ˈkæf kə ‖ ˈkɑːf- —*Czech, Ger* [ˈkaf ka]
Kafkaesque ˌkæf kər ˈesk ◂ ‖ ˌkɑːf kə-
kaftan ˈkæft æn -ɑːn ‖ -ən kæf ˈtæn **~s** z
Kagan ˈkeɪg ən
kagoul, kagoule kə ˈguːl **~s** z
Kahan kə ˈhɑːn
Kahlo ˈkɑːl əʊ ‖ -oʊ
Kahlua, Kahlúa *tdmk* kə ˈluː ə kɑː-
Kahn kɑːn
kahuna kə ˈhuːn ə **~s** z
Kai kaɪ
ˌKai ˈTak tæk ‖ tɑːk —*Cantonese* [^{2}kʰɐj ^{1}tɐk]
kail keɪəl
kailyard ˈkeɪəl jɑːd ‖ -jɑːrd
kainite ˈkaɪn aɪt ˈkeɪn-
Kaiser ˈkaɪz ə ‖ -ər —*Ger* [ˈkai zɐ] **~s** z
Kaiserslautern ˌkaɪz əz ˈlaʊt ɜːn -ən, ˌ··ˈ·· ‖ -ərz ˈlaʊt ərn —*Ger* [kai zɐs ˈlau tɐn]
kaka ˈkɑːk ɑː -ə **~s** z
Kakadu ˌkæk ə ˈduː ◂ ˈ···
kakapo ˈkɑːk ə pəʊ ‖ -poʊ **~s** z
kakemono ˌkæk ɪ ˈməʊn əʊ ‖ ˌkɑːk ə ˈmoʊn oʊ —*Jp* [ka ˈke mo no]
kala-azar ˌkæl ər ə ˈzɑː ˌkɑːl- ‖ ˌkɑːl ə ə ˈzɑːr ˌkæl-
Kalahari ˌkæl ə ˈhɑːr i ◂ ‖ ˌkɑːl-
Kalamazoo, k~ ˌkæl əm ə ˈzuː ◂
kalanchoe ˌkæl ən ˈkəʊ i →-əŋ- ‖ -ˈkoʊ i kə ˈlæŋk u i **~s** z
Kalashnikov *tdmk* kə ˈlæʃ nɪ kɒf -nə- ‖ -ˈlɑːʃ nɪ kɑːf **~s** s
kale keɪəl
kaleidoscope kə ˈlaɪd ə skəʊp ‖ -skoʊp **~s** s
kaleidoscopic kə ˌlaɪd ə ˈskɒp ɪk ◂ ‖ -ˈskɑːp- **~ally** əl i
kalends ˈkæl endz -ɪndz, -əndz
Kalevala ˌkɑːl ɪ ˈvɑːl ə ˌkæl-, -ə-, -ɑː, ˈ···· —*Finnish* [ˈkɑ le vɑ lɑ]
Kalgoorlie kæl ˈgʊəl i ‖ -ˈgʊrl i
kali *plant* ˈkeɪl aɪ ˈkæl i
Kali *Hindu goddess of destruction* ˈkɑːl i —*Skt* [ˈkɑː liː]
Kalimantan ˌkæl ɪ ˈmænt ən -æn ‖ ˌkɑːl i ˈmɑːnt ɑːn
Kalispel, Kalispell ˈkæl ə spel -ɪ-, ˌ··ˈ·
kalmia ˈkælm i̯ ə **~s** z
Kalmuck ˈkæl mʌk -mək **~s** s
Kalmyk ˈkæl mɪk **~s** s
Kama ˈkɑːm ə
Kamasutra ˌkɑːm ə ˈsuːtr ə
Kamchatka kæm ˈtʃæt kə ‖ kɑːm-, ˈtʃɑːt- —*Russ* [kʌm ˈtʃat kə]
kameez kə ˈmiːz
Kamen ˈkeɪm ən
kamikaze ˌkæm ɪ ˈkɑːz i ◂ -ə- ‖ ˌkɑːm- —*Jp* [ka ˈmi ka dze] **~s** z
Kampala kæm ˈpɑːl ə ‖ kɑːm-
kampong, K~ ˈkæm pɒŋ ˌ·ˈ· ‖ ˈkɑːm pɔːŋ -pɑːŋ
Kampuche|a ˌkæmp u ˈtʃiː‿ə **~an/s** ən/z
kana ˈkɑːn ə —*Jp* [ka ˌna]

Kanak kə ˈnɑːk -ˈnæk **~s** s
kanaka, K~ kə ˈnæk ə -ˈnɑːk ə; ˈkæn ək ə **~s** z
Kanarese ˌkæn ə ˈriːz ◂ ‖ -ˈriːs ◂
kanban ˈkæn bæn →ˈkæm- —*Jp* [ka ̩m baɴ]
Kanchenjunga ˌkæntʃ ən ˈdʒʊŋ ɡə -ˈdʒʌŋ- ‖ ˌkɑːntʃ-
Kandahar ˌkænd ə ˈhɑː ‖ -ˈhɑːr ˈ· · ·
Kandinsky kæn ˈdɪnᵗsk i —*Russ* [kʌn ˈdʲin skʲij]
Kandy ˈkænd i ‖ ˈkɑːnd i
Kane keɪn
Kanga, kanga ˈkæŋ ɡə
kangaroo ˌkæŋ ɡə ˈruː ◂ **~s** z
ˌkangaroo ˈcourt, ˌ· ·ˈ· ·
kanji ˈkændʒ i ˈkɑːndʒ i ‖ ˈkɑːndʒ i —*Jp* [ka ̩n dʑi] **~s** z
Kannada ˈkɑːn əd ə ˈkæn-
Kano ˈkɑːn əʊ ‖ -oʊ
Kansan ˈkænz ən **~s** z
Kansas ˈkænz əs ˈkænᵗs-
ˌKansas ˈCity ◂, ˌKansas ˌCity ˈsteak
Kant kænt ‖ kɑːnt —*Ger* [kant]
Kantian ˈkænt i ən ‖ ˈkɑːnt- ˈkænt- **~s** z
Kaohsiung ˌkaʊ ˈʃʊŋ -ʃi ˈʊŋ —*Chi* Gāoxióng [¹kɑu ²ɕjʊŋ]
kaolin ˈkeɪ əl ɪn §-ən
kaon ˈkeɪ ɒn ‖ -ɑːn **~s** z
kapellmeister kə ˈpel ˌmaɪst ə kæ- ‖ -ər **~s** z
Kaplan ˈkæp lən
kapok ˈkeɪp ɒk ‖ -ɑːk
Kapoor kə ˈpʊə ‖ kə ˈpʊər
Kaposi kə ˈpəʊz i kæ-, kɑː-, -ˈpəʊs-; ˈkɑːp əʃ i, ˈkæp- ‖ kə ˈpoʊs i ˈkæp əs i —*Hungarian* [ˈkɒ po ʃi]
kappa ˈkæp ə **~s** z
kaput kə ˈpʊt kæ- ‖ kɑː-, -ˈpuːt
kara ˈkʌr ə —*Punjabi* [kə raː]
karabiner ˌkær ə ˈbiːn ə ‖ -ər ˌker- **~s** z
Karachi kə ˈrɑːtʃ i
Karadzic ˈkær ə dʒɪtʃ ‖ ˈkɑːr- —*Serbian* Karadžić [ˈka ɾa dʒitɕ]
Karajan ˈkær ə jɑːn ‖ ˈkɑːr- -jən —*Ger* [ˈkaː ʁa jan, ˈka-]
Karakoram, Karakorum ˌkær ə ˈkɔːr əm ‖ ˌkɑːr- -ˈkoʊr-
karakul ˈkær ək əl -ə kʊl ‖ ˈker- **~s** z
karaoke ˌkær i ˈəʊk i -eɪ-, -ə- ‖ -ˈoʊk- ˌker- —*Jp* [ka ̩ɾa o ke]
karat ˈkær ət ‖ ˈker- (*= carrot*) **~s** s
karate kə ˈrɑːt i ‖ -ˈrɑːṭ i —*Jp* [ka ̩ɾa te]
Kardomah *tdmk* kɑː ˈdəʊm ə ‖ kɑːr ˈdoʊm ə
karela kə ˈrel ə **~s** z
Kareli|a kə ˈriːl i |ə **~an/s** ən/z
Karen *female name (i)* ˈkær ən ‖ ˈker-, *(ii)* ˈkɑːr ən
Karen *Myanmar people* kə ˈren ˌkæ- **~s** z
Karenina kə ˈren ɪn ə §-ən- —*Russ* [kʌ ˈrʲe nʲɪ nə]
Kariba kə ˈriːb ə kæ-
Karin *(i)* ˈkær ɪn -ən ‖ ˈker-, *(ii)* ˈkɑːr-
Karl kɑːl ‖ kɑːrl
Karla ˈkɑːl ə ‖ ˈkɑːrl ə
Karloff ˈkɑːl ɒf ‖ ˈkɑːrl ɔːf -ɑːf
Karlsruhe ˈkɑːlz ruː ə ‖ ˈkɑːrlz- —*Ger* [ˈkaʁls ʁuː ə]
karm|a ˈkɑːm| ə ˈkɜːm|- ‖ ˈkɑːrm| ə —*Hindi* [kərm] **~ic** ɪk
Karnataka kə ˈnɑːt ək ə ‖ kɑːr ˈnɑːṭ-
Karno ˈkɑːn əʊ ‖ ˈkɑːrn oʊ
Karol ˈkær əl ‖ ˈker-
Karoo kə ˈruː
Karpeles ˈkɑːp ə liːz -ɪ- ‖ ˈkɑːrp-
Karpov ˈkɑːp ɒf -ɒv ‖ ˈkɑːrp ɑːf —*Russ* [ˈkaɾ pəf]
karst kɑːst ‖ kɑːrst
kart kɑːt ‖ kɑːrt **karting** ˈkɑːt ɪŋ ‖ ˈkɑːrṭ ɪŋ **karts** kɑːts ‖ kɑːrts
karyo- *comb. form* *with stress-neutral suffix* ¦kær i əʊ ‖ -ə ¦ker- — **karyotype** ˈkær i əʊ taɪp ‖ -i ə- ˈker- *with stress-imposing suffix* ˌkær i ˈɒ+ ‖ -ˈɑː+ ˌker- — **karyogamy** ˌkær i ˈɒɡ əm i ‖ -ˈɑːɡ- ˌker-
kasbah ˈkæz bɑː -bə ‖ ˈkɑːz-
kasha ˈkæʃ ə ˈkɑːʃ- ‖ ˈkɑːʃ ə
Kashmir ˌkæʃ ˈmɪə ◂ ‖ -ˈmɪər ˌkæʒ-; ˈ· ·
Kashmiri kæʃ ˈmɪər i ‖ -ˈmɪr i ˌkæʒ- **~s** z
Kasparov kæ ˈspɑːr ɒf -ɒv; ˈkæsp ə rɒf ‖ -ɑːf -ɔːf —*Russ* [kʌ ˈspa rəf]
kat kæt kɑːt ‖ kɑːt
kata... —*see* **cata...**
katabatic ˌkæt ə ˈbæt ɪk ◂ ‖ ˌkæṭ ə ˈbæṭ ɪk ◂ **~s** s
katakana ˌkæt ə ˈkɑːn ə ‖ ˌkɑːṭ- —*Jp* [ka ̩ta ˈka na, -ˈta ka-]
Katanga kə ˈtæŋ ɡə ‖ -ˈtɑːŋ-
Katarina ˌkæt ə ˈriːn ə ‖ ˌkæṭ-
Kate keɪt
Katerina ˌkæt ə ˈriːn ə ‖ ˌkæṭ-
Kath kæθ
Katharevousa, Katharevusa, k~ ˌkæθ ə ˈrev ʊs ə -əs ə ‖ ˌkɑːθ- —*ModGk* [ka θa ˈɾe vu sa]
Katharine, Katherine ˈkæθ ər ɪn §-ər ən —*but the river and town in N.Terr, Australia, are* -ə raɪn
Kathie ˈkæθ i
Kathleen ˈkæθ liːn ‖ ˌ·ˈ· —*formerly* ˌ·ˈ· *in BrE too*
Kathmandu ˌkæt mæn ˈduː ◂ ˌkɑːt-, -mən-, -mɑːn-
Kathryn ˈkæθ rɪn -rən
Kathy ˈkæθ i
Katie ˈkeɪt i ‖ ˈkeɪṭ i
Katin ˈkeɪt ɪn §-ən ‖ -ən
Katmai ˈkæt maɪ
Katmandu ˌkæt mæn ˈduː ◂ ˌkɑːt-, -mən-, -mɑːn-
Katowice ˌkæt əʊ ˈviːts ə -ˈvɪts-, -eɪ ‖ -oʊ- -ə- —*Polish* [ka to ˈvi tse]
Katrina kə ˈtriːn ə
Katrine *name of loch* ˈkætr ɪn §-ən
Katy ˈkeɪt i ‖ ˈkeɪṭ i
katydid ˈkeɪt i dɪd ‖ ˈkeɪṭ- **~s** z
Katyn ˈkæt ɪn ‖ kɑː ˈtiːn kə- —*Russ* [kʌ ˈtinʲ]
Katyusha kə ˈtjuːʃ ə kæ-

atz kæts
auai, Kaua'i kaʊ ˈɑː i —*Hawaiian* [kau a ʔi]
aufman ˈkɔːf mən ˈkaʊf- ‖ ˈkɑːf-
aunas ˈkaʊn əs —*Lith* [ˈˈkau nas]
aunda kɑː ˈʊnd ə -ˈuːnd-
aur kɔː ˈkaʊ‿ə ‖ kɔːr ˈkaʊ‿ᵊr
auri ˈkaʊᵊr i **~s** z
ava ˈkɑːv ə
avanagh *(i)* ˈkæv ən ə, *(ii)* kə ˈvæn ə, *(iii)* ˈkæv ə nɑː
awasaki, k~ ˌkaʊ ə ˈsɑːk i ˌkɑː wə- —*Jp* [ka ˌɰa sa ki]
ay keɪ
ayak ˈkaɪ æk **~er/s** ə/z ‖ ᵊr/z **~s** s
aye keɪ
ayo ˌkeɪ ˈəʊ ‖ -ˈoʊ **~ed** d **~ing** ɪŋ **~s** z
ayser Bondor *tdmk* ˌkeɪz ə ˈbɒnd ə ‖ -ᵊr ˈbɑːnd ᵊr
azakh kə ˈzæk -ˈzɑːk, ˈkæz æk ‖ kə ˈzɑːk **~s** s
azakhstan ˌkæz æk ˈstɑːn ˌkɑːz-, -ɑːk-, kə ˌzɑːk-, -ˈstæn
azan kə ˈzæn -ˈzɑːn —*Russ* [kʌ ˈzanʲ]
azi ˈkɑːz i **~s** z
azoo kə ˈzuː **~s** z
byte ˈkɪl əʊ baɪt ‖ -ə- **~s** s
KC ˌkeɪ ˈsiː **~s** z
kea ˈkiː ə ˈkeɪ- **~s** z
Keady ˈkiːd i
Kean, Keane *(i)* kiːn, *(ii)* keɪn
Keanu ki ˈɑːn uː
Kearney, Kearny *(i)* ˈkɑːn i ‖ ˈkɑːrn i, *(ii)* ˈkɜːn i ‖ ˈkɝːn i —*The places in NB and NJ are (i); the places in Co. Down and CA are (ii); as family names, both pronunciations are found.*
Keating ˈkiːt ɪŋ ‖ ˈkiːt̬ ɪŋ **~'s** z
Keaton ˈkiːt ᵊn
Keats kiːts
Keatsian ˈkiːts i ən **~s** z
Keays kiːz
kebab kɪ ˈbæb kə- ‖ -ˈbɑːb **~s** z
Keble ˈkiːb ᵊl
kebob kɪ ˈbɒb kə- ‖ -ˈbɑːb **~s** z
ked ked **keds** kedz
kedge kedʒ **kedged** kedʒd **kedges** ˈkedʒ ɪz -əz **kedging** ˈkedʒ ɪŋ
kedgeree ˌkedʒ ə ˈriː ˈ· · · ‖ ˈkedʒ ə riː **~s** z
Kedleston ˈked ᵊlst ən —*locally also* -ləst-
Kedron ˈkedr ɒn ˈkiːdr-, -ən ‖ ˈkiːdr ən
Keds *tdmk* kedz
Keeble ˈkiːb ᵊl
Keeffe kiːf
Keegan ˈkiːg ən
keel kiːᵊl **keeled** kiːᵊld **keeling** ˈkiːᵊl ɪŋ **keels** kiːᵊlz
Keele kiːᵊl
Keeler ˈkiːl ə ‖ -ᵊr
Keeley ˈkiːl i
keelhaul ˈkiːᵊl hɔːl ‖ -hɑːl **~ed** d **~ing** ɪŋ **~s** z
Keeling ˈkiːl ɪŋ
keelson ˈkels ᵊn ˈkiːᵊls- **~s** z
keema ˈkiːm ə
keen, Keen kiːn **keened** kiːnd **keener** ˈkiːn ə ‖ -ᵊr **keenest** ˈkiːn ɪst -əst **keening** ˈkiːn ɪŋ **keens** kiːnz
Keenan ˈkiːn ən
Keene kiːn
keenly ˈkiːn li **keenness** ˈkiːn nəs -nɪs
keep kiːp **keeping** ˈkiːp ɪŋ **keeps** kiːps **kept** kept
keep-away ˈkiːp ə ˌweɪ
keeper ˈkiːp ə ‖ -ᵊr **~s** z
keepie-uppie ˌkiːp i ˈʌp i
keepnet ˈkiːp net **~s** s
keepsake ˈkiːp seɪk **~s** s
keeshond ˈkeɪs hɒnd ‖ -hɑːnd **~s** z
Keewatin ki ˈweɪt ɪn §-ᵊn
kef kef keɪf
keffiya ke ˈfiː ə
Keflavik ˈkef lə vɪk —*Icelandic* Keflavík [ˈcɛp la viːk]
keg keg **kegs** kegz
Kegan ˈkiːg ən
kegger ˈkeg ə ‖ -ᵊr **~s** z
kegler ˈkeg lə ‖ -lᵊr **~s** z
Keig kiːg
Keighley *(i)* ˈkiːθ li, *(ii)* ˈkiː li —*The place in WYks is (i); the family or personal name may be either (i) or (ii).*
Keigwin ˈkeg wɪn
Keiller, Keillor ˈkiːl ə ‖ -ᵊr
Keir kɪə ‖ kɪᵊr
Keira ˈkɪər ə ‖ ˈkɪr ə
keister ˈkiːst ə ˈkaɪst ə ‖ -ᵊr **~s** z
Keitel ˈkaɪt ᵊl
Keith kiːθ
Kekule, Kekulé ˈkek ju leɪ -jə- ‖ ˈkeɪk ə- —*Ger* [ˈkeː ku le]
Kekwick ˈkek wɪk
Keller, k~ ˈkel ə ‖ -ᵊr **~s** z
Kellett ˈkel ɪt §-ət
Kelley, Kellie ˈkel i
Kellogg ˈkel ɒg ‖ -ɔːg -ɑːg **~'s** *tdmk* z
Kells kelz
Kelly ˈkel i
keloid ˈkiːl ɔɪd **~s** z
kelp kelp
kelper ˈkelp ə ‖ -ᵊr **~s** z
kelp|ie, kelp|y ˈkelp |i **~ies** iz
Kelsey ˈkels i
Kelso ˈkels əʊ ‖ -oʊ
Kelton ˈkelt ən
Kelvin, k~ ˈkelv ɪn §-ᵊn
Kelvinator *tdmk* ˈkelv ɪ neɪt ə ˈ-ə- ‖ -ə neɪt̬ ᵊr
Kelvinside ˌkelv ɪn ˈsaɪd -ᵊn-
Kemble ˈkem bᵊl
Kemp, kemp kemp
ˈKemp Town
Kempis ˈkemp ɪs §-əs
Kempson ˈkemps ən
kempt kem*p*t
Kemsley ˈkemz li
ken, Ken ken
Kenco *tdmk* ˈken kəʊ →ˈkeŋ- ‖ -koʊ
Kendal, Kendall ˈkend ᵊl

kendo 'kend əʊ ‖ -oʊ —*Jp* ['ken doo]
Kendrick 'kendr ɪk
Keneally kɪ 'ni:l i kə-, ke-
Kenelm 'ken elm
Kenilworth 'ken ᵊl wɜ:θ -ɪl-, -wəθ ‖ -wɜ˞:θ
Kenmare ken 'meə ‖ -'meᵊr
Kennebunkport ˌken ə 'bʌŋk pɔ:t ‖ -pɔ:rt -pourt
Kennedy 'ken əd i -ɪd- **~s, ~'s** z
kennel 'ken ᵊl **~ed, ~led** d **~ing, ~ling** ɪŋ **~s** z
Kennelly 'ken əl i
Kennet 'ken ɪt -ət
Kenneth 'ken ɪθ -əθ
kenning, K~ 'ken ɪŋ **~s** z
Kennington 'ken ɪŋ tən
Kenny 'ken i
keno 'ki:n əʊ ‖ -oʊ
Kenosha kɪ 'nəʊʃ ə kə- ‖ kə 'noʊʃ ə
kenosis ke 'nəʊs ɪs kɪ-, §-əs ‖ -'noʊs-
Kenrick 'ken rɪk
Kensal 'kens ᵊl 'kenz-
Kenshole *(i)* 'ken ʃəʊl →-ʃɒʊl ‖ -ʃoʊl, *(ii)* 'kenz həʊl →-hɒʊl ‖ -hoʊl
Kensington 'kenz ɪŋ tən
Kensit 'kenz ɪt 'kenᵗs-, §-ət
Kensitas *tdmk* 'kenz ɪ tæs
Kent kent
kentia 'kent i͜ ə **~s** z
Kentigern 'kent ɪg ən -ɪ gɜ:n ‖ 'kenţ ɪ gɜ˞:rn
Kentish 'kent ɪʃ
Kenton 'kent ən ‖ -ᵊn
Kentucky ken 'tʌk i ˌ-- ‖ kən- *(*)*
Kenwood 'ken wʊd
Kenworthy 'ken ˌwɜ:ð i ‖ -ˌwɜ˞:ð i
Kenya 'ken jə 'ki:n- —*Mostly* 'ki:n- *before independence,* 'ken- *since.*
Kenyan 'ken jən 'ki:n- **~s** z
Kenyatta ken 'jæt ə ‖ -'jɑ:ţ ə
Kenyon 'ken jən
Keogh, Keough 'ki: əʊ kjəʊ ‖ 'ki: oʊ
Keown 'ki: əʊn kjəʊn, ki 'əʊn ‖ ki 'oʊn kjoʊn, 'ki: oʊn
kepi 'keɪp i —*Fr* képi [ke pi] **~s** z
Kepler 'kep lə ‖ -lᵊr —*Ger* ['kɛp lɐ]
Keppel 'kep ᵊl
kept kept
Ker *(i)* kɜ: ‖ kɜ˞:, *(ii)* kɑ: ‖ kɑ:r, *(iii)* keə ‖ keᵊr —*In the US, (i); in Scotland,* kɛ:r *(= iii).*
Kerala 'ker əl ə kə 'rɑ:l ə
keratin 'ker ət ɪn §-ən ‖ -ᵊn
keratitis ˌker ə 'taɪt ɪs §-əs ‖ -'taɪţ əs
kerato- *comb. form*
with stress-neutral suffix ¦ker ət əʊ ‖ -əţ oʊ — **keratoplasty** 'ker ət əʊ ˌplæst i ‖ -əţ oʊ-
with stress-imposing suffix ˌker ə 'tɒ+ ‖ -'tɑ:+ — **keratogenous** ˌker ə 'tɒdʒ ən əs ◂ ‖ -'tɑ:dʒ-
keratosis ˌker ə 'təʊs ɪs §-əs ‖ -'toʊs əs
kerb kɜ:b ‖ kɜ˞:b **kerbed** kɜ:bd ‖ kɜ˞:bd **kerbing** 'kɜ:b ɪŋ ‖ 'kɜ˞:b ɪŋ **kerbs** kɜ:bz ‖ kɜ˞:bz
'kerb ˌcrawler, 'kerb ˌcrawling
kerbstone 'kɜ:b stəʊn ‖ 'kɜ˞:b stoʊn **~s** z

kerchief 'kɜ: tʃɪf -tʃəf, -tʃi:f ‖ 'kɜ˞:- **~s** s
kerching kə 'tʃɪŋ ‖ kᵊr-
Kerenski, Kerensky kə 'renᵗsk i —*Russ* ['kʲe rʲin skʲij]
kerf kɜ:f ‖ kɜ˞:f **kerfs** kɜ:fs ‖ kɜ˞:fs
kerfuffle kə 'fʌf ᵊl ‖ kᵊr-
Kerguelen 'kɜ:g əl ɪn -ɪl-, -ən ‖ 'kɜ˞:g-
Kermadec 'kɜ:m ə dek ‖ 'kɜ˞:m-
kermes 'kɜ:m i:z -ɪz ‖ 'kɜ˞:m-
kermess 'kɜ:m es ‖ 'kɜ˞:m əs kᵊr 'mes
kermis 'kɜ:m ɪs §-əs ‖ 'kɜ˞:m-
Kermit 'kɜ:m ɪt §-ət ‖ 'kɜ˞:m-
Kermode *(i)* 'kɜ:m əʊd ‖ 'kɜ˞:m oʊd, *(ii)* kɜ: 'məʊd ‖ kɜ˞: 'moʊd
kern, Kern kɜ:n ‖ kɜ˞:n **kerned** kɜ:nd ‖ kɜ˞:nd **kerning** 'kɜ:n ɪŋ ‖ 'kɜ˞:n ɪŋ **kerns** kɜ:nz ‖ kɜ˞:nz
kernel 'kɜ:n ᵊl ‖ 'kɜ˞:n ᵊl **~s** z
kerosene, kerosine 'ker ə si:n ˌ-·'·
Kerouac 'ker u æk
Kerr *(i)* kɜ: ‖ kɜ˞:, *(ii)* kɑ: ‖ kɑ:r, *(iii)* keə ‖ keᵊr —*In the US, (i).*
kerria 'ker i ə **~s** z
Kerrigan 'ker ɪg ən §-əg-
Kerrin 'ker ɪn §-ən
Kerry 'ker i
kersey, K~ 'kɜ:z i ‖ 'kɜ˞:z i **~s** z
Kershaw 'kɜ: ʃɔ: ‖ 'kɜ˞:- -ʃɑ:
kerygma kə 'rɪg mə
Kes kes
kesh *'Sikh beard and hair'* keɪʃ
Kesh keʃ
Kesteven ke 'sti:v ᵊn kɪ-; 'kest ɪv ən, -əv-
Keston 'kest ən
kestrel 'kes trəl **~s** z
Keswick *place in Cumbria* 'kez ɪk
Keswick *family name(i)* 'kez ɪk, *(ii)* -wɪk
ketamine 'ket ə mi:n ‖ 'keţ-
ketch, Ketch ketʃ **ketches** 'ketʃ ɪz -əz
Ketchikan 'ketʃ ɪ kæn -ə-
ketchup 'ketʃ əp -ʌp **~s** s
ketone 'ki:t əʊn ‖ -oʊn **~s** z
ketonuria ˌki:t əʊ 'njʊər i ə ‖ -oʊ 'nʊr- -'njʊr-
ketosis ki: 'təʊs ɪs kɪ-, §-əs ‖ -'toʊs əs
Kettering 'ket ər ɪŋ ‖ 'keţ ər ɪŋ
kettle, K~ 'ket ᵊl ‖ 'keţ ᵊl **~s** z
kettledrum 'ket ᵊl drʌm ‖ 'keţ- **~s** z
Kettley 'ket li
Ketton 'ket ᵊn
Kev kev
Kevin 'kev ɪn §-ᵊn
kevlar, K~ *tdmk* 'kev lɑ: ‖ -lɑ:r
Kevorkian kə 'vɔ:k i͜ ən ‖ -'vɔ:rk-
Kew kju:
ˌKew 'Gardens
kewpie, K~ *tdmk* 'kju:p i
kex keks
key, Key ki: **keyed** ki:d **keying** 'ki: ɪŋ **keys** ki:z
ˌkeyed 'up ◂; **'key ˌmoney**; **'key ring**; **'key ˌsignature**; **ˌKey 'West**

eyboard 'ki: bɔ:d ‖ -bɔ:rd -bourd **~ed** ɪd əd **~er/s** ə/z ‖ ᵊr/z **~ing** ɪŋ **~ist/s** ɪst/s §əst/s **~s** z
eyes ki:z
eyholder 'ki: ˌhəʊld ə →-ˌhɒʊld ə ‖ -ˌhoʊld ᵊr **~s** z
eyhole 'ki: həʊl →-hɒʊl ‖ -hoʊl **~s** z
eylog|ger 'ki: ˌlɒg ə ‖ -ˌlɔ:g ᵊr -ˌlɑ:g- **~gers** əz ‖ ᵊrz **~ging** ɪŋ
eynes *(i)* keɪnz, *(ii)* ki:nz *—as a family name, and for the economist, usually (i); in the placename* Horsted K~, *(i), but in* Milton K~, *(ii).*
eynesian 'keɪnz i ən **~ism** ˌɪz əm **~s** z
eynote 'ki: nəʊt ‖ -noʊt **~s** s
eynsham 'keɪn ʃəm
eyonna ki 'ɒn ə ‖ -'ɑ:n ə
eypad 'ki: pæd **~s** z
eypal 'ki: pæl **~s** z
eypunch 'ki: pʌntʃ **~ed** t **~es** ɪz əz **~ing** ɪŋ
eyser *(i)* 'ki:z ə ‖ -ᵊr, *(ii)* 'kaɪz-
eystone 'ki: stəʊn ‖ -stoʊn **~s** z
eystroke 'ki: strəʊk ‖ -stroʊk **~s** s
eyword 'ki: wɜ:d ‖ -wɜ:d **~s** z
g *sing.* 'kɪl ə græm **~** *pl* z
Khachaturian ˌkætʃ ə 'tʊər i ən ˌkɑ:tʃ-, -'tjʊər- ‖ ˌkɑ:tʃ ə 'tʊr- *—Russ* [xə tʃɪ tu 'rʲan]
khaki 'kɑ:k i ‖ 'kæk i **~s** z
Khalid 'kɑ:l ɪd *—Arabic* ['xa: lɪd]
khalif 'keɪl ɪf 'kæl-, §-əf; kæ 'li:f **~s** s
khalifate 'kæl ɪ feɪt 'keɪl-, -ə- **~s** s
Khalsa 'kʌls ə *—Hindi-Urdu* [kʰəl sa:]
Khamenei, Khamene'i ˌkɑ:m ə 'neɪ -neɪ 'i: *—Farsi* [xɑ: me neʔ 'i:]
khan, Khan kɑ:n **khans** kɑ:nz
khanate 'kɑ:n eɪt **~s** s
Khartoum, Khartum ˌkɑ: 'tu:m kɑ:- ‖ ₍ˌ₎kɑ:r- *—Arabic* [xɑr 'tˤu:m]
Khayyam kaɪ 'æm -'ɑ:m ‖ -'jɑ:m
khazi 'kɑ:z i **~s** z
khedive, K~ kɪ 'di:v kə-, ke- **~s** z
Khmer kmeə kə 'meə ‖ kə 'meᵊr **Khmers** kmeəz kə 'meəz ‖ kə 'meᵊrz
Khoisan ˌkɔɪ 'sɑ:n -'sæn
Khomeini kɒ 'meɪn i kəʊ-, həʊ- ‖ koʊ- kə-
Khrushchev 'krʊs tʃɒf 'krʊʃ-, ·'· ‖ 'kru:s tʃef -tʃɔ:f, -tʃɑ:f, ·'· *—Russ* [xrʊ 'ɕtɕɔf]
Khyber 'kaɪb ə ‖ -ᵊr
ˌKhyber 'Pass
kHz 'kɪl əʊ hɜ:ts ‖ -ə hɜ:ts
kiang ki 'æŋ 'ki: æŋ ‖ -'ɑ:ŋ 'ki: æŋ, -ɑŋ **~s** z
Kia-Ora *tdmk* ˌki: ə 'ɔ:r ə
kibbl|e 'kɪb ᵊl **~ed** d **~es** z **~ing** ɪŋ
kibbutz kɪ 'bʊts **kibbutzim** ˌkɪb ʊt 'si:m
kibitz 'kɪb ɪts **~ed** t **~er/s** ə/z ‖ ᵊr/z **~es** ɪz əz **~ing** ɪŋ
kibla, kiblah 'kɪb lə *—Arabic* ['qɪb lah]
kibosh 'kaɪ bɒʃ ‖ -bɑ:ʃ
kick kɪk **kicked** kɪkt **kicking/s** 'kɪk ɪŋ/z **kicks** kɪks
kickabout 'kɪk ə ˌbaʊt **~s** s
Kickapoo 'kɪk ə pu: **~s** z
kick-ass 'kɪk æs
kickback 'kɪk bæk **~s** s
kickball 'kɪk bɔ:l ‖ -bɑ:l
kickbox|er 'kɪk ˌbɒks| ə ‖ -ˌbɑ:ks| ᵊr **~ers** əz ‖ ᵊrz **~ing** ɪŋ
kickdown 'kɪk daʊn
kicker 'kɪk ə ‖ -ᵊr **~s** z
kickflare 'kɪk fleə ‖ -fler **~s** z
kickflip 'kɪk flɪp **~s** s
kick-off 'kɪk ɒf -ɔ:f ‖ -ɔ:f -ɑ:f **~s** s
kickshaw 'kɪk ʃɔ: ‖ -ʃɑ: **~s** z
kickstand 'kɪk stænd **~s** z
kick-|start 'kɪk |stɑ:t ˌ·'· ‖ -|stɑ:rt **~started** stɑ:t ɪd -əd ‖ stɑ:rṱ əd **~starting** stɑ:t ɪŋ ‖ stɑ:rṱ ɪŋ **~starts** stɑ:ts ‖ stɑ:rts
kicky 'kɪk i
kid kɪd **kidded** 'kɪd ɪd -əd **kidding** 'kɪd ɪŋ **kids** kɪdz
ˌkid 'gloves
Kidd kɪd
kidder 'kɪd ə ‖ ᵊr **~s** z
Kidderminster 'kɪd ə ˌmɪnst ə ‖ -ᵊr ˌmɪnᵗst ᵊr
kiddie 'kɪd i **~s** z
kiddie-cam 'kɪd i kæm
kiddo 'kɪd əʊ
kidd|y 'kɪd |i **~ies** iz
kid-glove ˌkɪd 'glʌv ◂ →ˌkɪg-
Kidlington 'kɪd lɪŋ tən
Kidman 'kɪd mən
kidnap 'kɪd næp **~ed, ~ped** t **~er/s, ~per/s** ə/z ‖ ᵊr/z **~ing, ~ping** ɪŋ **~s** s
kidney 'kɪd ni **~s** z
'kidney bean; **'kidney maˌchine**; **'kidney stone**
kidney-shaped 'kɪd ni ʃeɪpt
Kidsgrove 'kɪdz grəʊv ‖ -groʊv
kidskin 'kɪd skɪn
kidult 'kɪd ʌlt **~s** s
Kidwelly kɪd 'wel i
Kiel ki:ᵊl *—Ger* [ki:l]
kielbasa ki:ᵊl 'bɑ:s ə kɪl-, -'bæs- *—Polish* kiełbasa [kʲew 'ba sa]
Kielder 'ki:ᵊld ə ‖ -ᵊr
Kieran, Kieron 'kɪər ən ‖ 'kɪr-
Kierkegaard 'kɪək ə gɑ:d ‖ 'kɪrk ə gɑ:rd -ɪ- *—Danish* ['kiʁ gə gɔ:ʔʁ]
kieselguhr 'ki:z ᵊl gʊə ‖ -gʊr
Kiev, ki|ev 'ki: |ev -|ef, ·'· **~s** evz efs *—Russ* ['kʲi jɪf], *Ukrainian* Kyiv ['ki jɪf]
Kigali kɪ 'gɑ:l i kə-
kike kaɪk **kikes** kaɪks
Kikuyu kɪ 'ku: ju: **~s** z
Kilauea ˌkɪl ə 'weɪ ə ˌki:l aʊ 'eɪ ə
Kilbracken kɪl 'bræk ən
Kilbride kɪl 'braɪd
Kilburn 'kɪlb ən 'kɪl bɜ:n ‖ -ᵊrn
Kildare kɪl 'deə ‖ -'deᵊr -'dæᵊr
kilderkin 'kɪld ək ɪn §-ən ‖ -ᵊrk- **~s** z
Kilfedder kɪl 'fed ə ‖ -ᵊr
Kilian 'kɪl i ən
kilim, K~ kɪ 'li:m
Kilimanjaro ˌkɪl ɪm ən 'dʒɑ:r əʊ ˌ·ə-, -ɪ mæn-, -ə mæn- ‖ -oʊ
Kilkenny kɪl 'ken i

K

kill kɪl **killed** kɪld **killing** 'kɪl ɪŋ **kills** kɪlz
Killamarsh 'kɪl ə mɑːʃ ‖ -mɑːrʃ
Killanin kɪ 'læn ɪn kə-, §-ən
Killarney kɪ 'lɑːn i kə- ‖ -'lɑːrn i
killdeer 'kɪl dɪə ‖ -dɪᵊr **~s** z
killer 'kɪl ə ‖ -ᵊr **~s** z
ˌkiller 'whale, '· ·
Killiecrankie ˌkɪl i 'kræŋk i
Killin kɪ 'lɪn kə-
Killiney kɪ 'laɪn i kə-
killing 'kɪl ɪŋ **~ly** li **~s** z
killjoy 'kɪl dʒɔɪ **~s** z
Kilmainham kɪl 'meɪn əm
Kilmarnock kɪl 'mɑːn ək -ɒk ‖ -'mɑːrn ək
Kilmuir kɪl 'mjʊə ‖ -'mjʊᵊr
kiln kɪln kɪl **kilns** kɪlnz kɪlz
Kilner, k~ 'kɪl nə ‖ -nᵊr
Kilnsey 'kɪlnz i
kilo 'kiːl əʊ ‖ -oʊ 'kɪl- **~s** z
kilo- 'kɪl əʊ- ‖ 'kɪl ə 'kiːl ə — **kilocalorie** 'kɪl əʊ ˌkæl ər i ‖ 'ə- 'kiːl-
kilobyte 'kɪl əʊ baɪt ‖ -ə- **~s** s
kilocycle 'kɪl əʊ ˌsaɪk ᵊl ‖ -ə- **~s** z
kilogram, kilogramme 'kɪl ə græm 'kiːl- **~s** z
kilohertz 'kɪl əʊ hɜːts ‖ -ə hɝːts
kilojoule 'kɪl ə dʒuːl **~s** z
kiloliter, kilolitre 'kɪl əʊ ˌliːt ə ‖ -ə ˌliːţ ᵊr **~s** z

KILOMETER, KILOMETRE

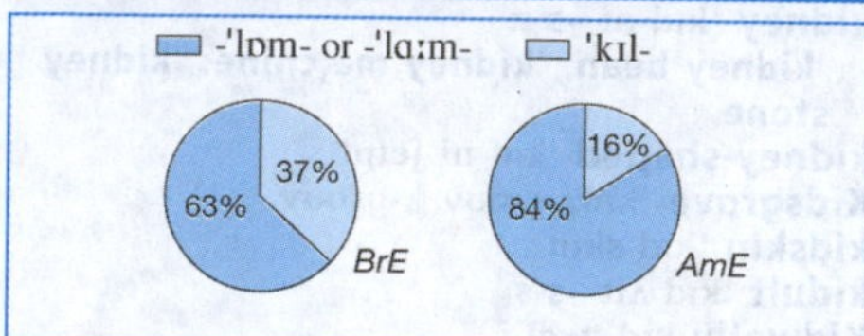

kilometer, kilometre kɪ 'lɒm ɪt ə kə-, ət-; 'kɪl ə ˌmiːt ə ‖ kə 'lɑːm əţ ᵊr kɪ-; 'kɪl ə ˌmiːţ ᵊr —*On the analogy of* 'centiˌmetre, 'milliˌmetre, *it is clear that the stressing* 'kiloˌmetre *is logical and might be expected to predominate. Nevertheless, it does not. Preference polls, BrE:* -'lɒm- *63%,* 'kɪl- *37%; AmE:* -'lɑːm- *84%,* 'kɪl- *16%* -'lɒm- *57%.* **~s** z
kiloton 'kɪl əʊ tʌn ‖ -ə- **~s** z
kilovolt 'kɪl əʊ vəʊlt →-vɒʊlt ‖ -ə voʊlt **~s** s
kilowatt 'kɪl ə wɒt ‖ -ə wɑːt **~s** s
kilowatt-hour ˌkɪl ə wɒt 'aʊ ə ‖ ˌkɪl ə wɑːţ 'aʊ ᵊr **~s** z
Kilpatrick kɪl 'pætr ɪk
Kilroy ₍ˌ₎kɪl 'rɔɪ '· ·
Kilsby 'kɪlz bi
kilt kɪlt **kilted** 'kɪlt ɪd -əd **kilts** kɪlts
kilter 'kɪlt ə ‖ -ᵊr
Kim kɪm
Kimball 'kɪm bᵊl
Kimber 'kɪm bə ‖ -bᵊr
Kimberley 'kɪm bə li ‖ -bᵊr-
kimberlite 'kɪm bə laɪt ‖ -bᵊr-
Kimberly 'kɪm bə li ‖ -bᵊr-
Kimbolton kɪm 'bəʊlt ən →-'bɒʊlt- ‖ -'boʊlt ᵊn
kimchee, kimchi, kimch'i 'kɪm tʃiː —*Korean* [g̊im tʃʰi]
Kimmeridge 'kɪm ə rɪdʒ
kimono kɪ 'məʊn əʊ kə-; §'kɪm ə nəʊ ‖ -'moʊn ə -oʊ —*Jp* [ki ˌmo no]
kin kɪn
-kin kɪn §kən — **lambkin** 'læm kɪn §-kən
kina 'kiːn ə
Kinabalu ˌkɪn ə 'baːl uː -bə 'luː
kinaesthesia ˌkɪn iːs 'θiːz i ə ˌkaɪn-, ˌɪs-, ˌəs- ‖ ˌkɪn əs 'θiːʒ ə
kinaesthetic ˌkɪn iːs 'θet ɪk ◂ ˌkaɪn-, ɪs-, -əs- ‖ -əs 'θeţ- **~ally** ᵊl i
Kincaid kɪn 'keɪd →kɪŋ-
Kincardine kɪn 'kɑːd ɪn →kɪŋ-, -ᵊn ‖ -'kɑːrd ᵊn
Kincora kɪn 'kɔːr ə →kɪŋ-
kind kaɪnd **kinds** kaɪndz
kinda 'kaɪnd ə
Kinder 'kɪnd ə ‖ -ᵊr
kindergarten 'kɪnd ə ˌgɑːt ᵊn ‖ -ᵊr ˌgɑːrt ᵊn **~s** z
kindergartner 'kɪnd ə ˌgɑːt nə ‖ -ᵊr ˌgɑːrt nᵊr -ˌgɑːrd- **~s** z
Kindersley 'kɪnd əz li ‖ -ᵊrz-
kind-hearted ˌkaɪnd 'hɑːt ɪd ◂ -əd ‖ -'hɑːrţ əd ◂ **~ly** li **~ness** nəs nɪs
kindl|e 'kɪnd ᵊl **~ed** d **~es** z **~ing** ɪŋ
kindling *n* 'kɪnd lɪŋ
kind|ly 'kaɪnd |li **~lier** li ə ‖ li ᵊr **~liest** li ɪst əst **~liness** li nəs -nɪs
kindness 'kaɪnd nəs -nɪs **~es** ɪz əz
kindred 'kɪndr əd -ɪd **~ness** nəs nɪs
kine kaɪn
kinematic ˌkɪn ɪ 'mæt ɪk ◂ ˌkaɪn-, -ə- ‖ -'mæţ- **~s** s
kinesics kaɪ 'niːs ɪks kɪ-, -'niːz-
kinesiology kɪˌniːz i 'ɒl ədʒ | i ‖ -'ɑːl **~ist** | s ɪst | s ‖ əst | s
kinesthesia ˌkɪn iːs 'θiːz i ə ˌkaɪn-, ˌɪs-, ˌəs- ‖ ˌkɪn əs 'θiːʒ ə
kinesthetic ˌkɪn iːs 'θet ɪk ◂ˌkaɪn-, -ɪs-, -əs- ‖ -əs 'θeţ- **~ally** ᵊl i
kinetic kaɪ 'net ɪk kɪ-, kə- ‖ kə 'neţ ɪk kɪ-, kaɪ- **~ally** ᵊl i **~s** s
kiˌnetic 'energy
kinfolk 'kɪn fəʊk ‖ -foʊk **~s** s
king, King kɪŋ **kings, King's** kɪŋz
₍ˌ₎**King 'George**; **King ˌJames 'version**, ₍ˌ₎· '· ˌ· ·; ₍ˌ₎**King 'Lear**; **ˌKing's 'Bench**, **ˌKing's 'Bench Diˌvision**; **ˌKing's 'Counsel**; **ˌKings 'Cross**◂; **ˌKing's 'English**; **ˌking's 'evidence**; **king's 'evil**; **ˌKing's 'Lynn**
kingcup 'kɪŋ kʌp **~s** s
kingdom 'kɪŋ dəm **~s** z
Kingdon 'kɪŋ dən
kingfisher 'kɪŋ ˌfɪʃ ə ‖ -ᵊr **~s** z
Kingham 'kɪŋ əm
kinglet 'kɪŋ lət -lɪt **~s** s
king|ly 'kɪŋ |li **~lier** li ə ‖ li ᵊr **~liest** li ɪst əst **~liness** li nəs -nɪs
kingmaker 'kɪŋ ˌmeɪk ə ‖ -ᵊr **~s** z

K

ingpin 'kɪŋ pɪn ˌ·ˈ· **~s** z
Kingsbridge 'kɪŋz brɪdʒ
Kingsbury 'kɪŋz bər i ‖ -ˌber i
Kingsford 'kɪŋz fəd ‖ -fᵊrd
kingship 'kɪŋ ʃɪp **~s** s
king-size 'kɪŋ saɪz **~d** d
Kingsley 'kɪŋz li
Kingston 'kɪŋᵏst ən 'kɪŋz tən
ˌKingston upon 'Thames
Kingstown 'kɪŋz taʊn
Kingsway 'kɪŋz weɪ
Kingswear 'kɪŋz wɪə ‖ -wɪr
Kingswinford kɪŋ 'swɪn fəd ‖ -fᵊrd
Kingswood 'kɪŋz wʊd
Kington 'kɪŋ tən
Kingussie kɪŋ 'juːs i *(!)*
kink kɪŋk **kinked** kɪŋkt **kinking** 'kɪŋk ɪŋ **kinks** kɪŋks
kinkajou 'kɪŋk ə dʒuː **~s** z
kink|y 'kɪŋk |i **~ier** i ə ‖ i ᵊr **~iest** i ɪst i əst **~ily** ɪ li əl i **~iness** i nəs i nɪs
Kinloch ₍ˌ₎kɪn 'lɒk -'lɒx ‖ -'lɑːk
Kinloss ₍ˌ₎kɪn 'lɒs ‖ -'lɔːs -'lɑːs
Kinnear kɪ 'nɪə -'neə ‖ -'nɪᵊr
Kinnock 'kɪn ək
Kinross ₍ˌ₎kɪn 'rɒs ‖ -'rɔːs -'rɑːs
Kinsale ₍ˌ₎kɪn 'seɪᵊl
Kinsella *(i)* ₍ˌ₎kɪn 'sel ə, *(ii)* 'kɪnᵗs əl ə
Kinsey 'kɪnz i
kinsfolk 'kɪnz fəʊk ‖ -foʊk
Kinshasa kɪn 'ʃɑːs ə -'ʃæs-, -'ʃɑːz-
kinship 'kɪn ʃɪp
kins|man 'kɪnz |mən **~men** mən men **~woman** ˌwʊm ən **~women** ˌwɪm ɪn §-ən
Kintyre ₍ˌ₎kɪn 'taɪ ə ‖ kɪn 'taɪ ᵊr
kiosk 'kiː ɒsk §'kaɪ- ‖ 'kiː ɑːsk ki 'ɑːsk **~s** s
Kiowa 'kiː ə wɑː -wə, -weɪ **~s** z
kip kɪp **kipped** kɪpt **kipping** 'kɪp ɪŋ **kips** kɪps
Kipling 'kɪp lɪŋ
Kiplingesque ˌkɪp lɪŋ 'esk ◂
Kipp kɪp
kippa, kippah kɪ 'pɑː **kippot** kɪ 'pəʊt ‖ -'poʊt
Kippax 'kɪp əks -æks
kipper 'kɪp ə ‖ -ᵊr **~ed** d **kippering** 'kɪp ər ɪŋ **~s** z
Kipps kɪps
kir kɪə ‖ kɪᵊr —*Fr* [kiːʁ]
Kirbigrip *tdmk* 'kɜːb i grɪp ‖ 'kɜ˞ːb- **~s** s
Kirby 'kɜːb i ‖ 'kɜ˞ːb i
Kirchhoff 'kɜːk ɒf -hɒf ‖ 'kɪrk hɔːf 'kɜ˞ːk-, -hɑːf —*Ger* ['kɪʁç hɔf]
Kirghiz, Kirgiz 'kɜː gɪz 'kɪə- ‖ kɪr 'giːz
Kirghizia kɜː 'gɪz i̯ə kɪə- ‖ kɪr 'giːʒ ə -i̯ə
Kiribati ˌkɪr ɪ 'bɑːt i ˌkɪər-, -ə-, -'bæt i; ˌ·· 'bæs, '· · · —*The pronunciation recommended by all reference books is* -bæs, -'bæs; *but the influence of orthography is such that this form has not established itself in the face of spelling pronunciations.*
Kiri Te Kanawa ˌkɪr i ti 'kɑːn ə wə ˌkɪər-, -'kæn-
kirk, Kirk kɜːk ‖ kɜ˞ːk **kirks, Kirk's** kɜːks ‖ kɜ˞ːks
Kirkbride ₍ˌ₎kɜːk 'braɪd ‖ ₍ˌ₎kɜ˞ːk-
Kirkby *(i)* 'kɜːk bi ‖ 'kɜ˞ːk-, *(ii)* 'kɜːb i ‖ 'kɜ˞ːb i —*The place in Merseyside is (ii) (!), as are other places in the north of England; places in the Midlands are (i); the family name may be either.*
Kirkcaldy kə 'kɒd i kɜː-, -'kɔːd- ‖ kᵊr 'kɑːd i -'kɔːd-, -'kɑːld-, -'kɔːld- *(!)*
Kirkcudbright kə 'kuːb ri kɜː- ‖ kᵊr- *(!)*
Kirkdale 'kɜːk deɪᵊl ‖ 'kɜ˞ːk-
Kirkgate *streets in Leeds, Bradford* 'kɜːg ət 'kɜː geɪt ‖ 'kɜ˞ːk geɪt
Kirkham 'kɜːk əm ‖ 'kɜ˞ːk-
Kirkland 'kɜːk lənd ‖ 'kɜ˞ːk-
Kirklees ₍ˌ₎kɜːk 'liːz ‖ ₍ˌ₎kɜ˞ːk-
Kirkpatrick ₍ˌ₎kɜːk 'pætr ɪk ‖ ₍ˌ₎kɜ˞ːk-
Kirkstall *place in W Yks* 'kɜːk stɔːl -stəl ‖ 'kɜ˞ːk- -stɑːl
Kirkstone 'kɜːk stən -stəʊn ‖ 'kɜ˞ːk stoʊn
Kirkuk kɪə 'kʊk kɜː- ‖ kɪr- kᵊr- —*Arabic* [kɪr 'kuːk]
Kirkup 'kɜːk əp -ʌp ‖ 'kɜ˞ːk-
Kirkwall 'kɜːk wɔːl ‖ 'kɜ˞ːk- -wɑːl
Kirov 'kɪər ɒv -ɒf ‖ 'kɪr ɔːf -ɑːf —*Russ* ['kʲi rəf]
kirpan kɪə 'pɑːn kɜː- ‖ kɪr- —*Punjabi* [kɪr pɑːn] **~s** z
Kirriemuir ˌkɪr i 'mjʊə ‖ -'mjʊᵊr
kirsch kɪəʃ kɜːʃ ‖ kɪrʃ—*Ger* [kɪʁʃ]
Kirsten 'kɜːst ɪn -ən ‖ 'kɜ˞ːst- —*but as a foreign name also* 'kɪəst- ‖ 'kɪrst-
Kirstie, Kirsty 'kɜːst i ‖ 'kɜ˞ːst i
kirtle 'kɜːt ᵊl ‖ 'kɜ˞ːt̬ ᵊl **~s** z
Kirton 'kɜːt ᵊn ‖ 'kɜ˞ːt-
Kisangani ˌkɪs æŋ 'gɑːn i ‖ ˌkiːs ɑːn-
kish, Kish kɪʃ
Kishinev 'kɪʃ ɪ nev -ə-, -nef *Moldovan* Chișinău [ki ʃi 'nəu]
kishke 'kɪʃ kə **~s** z
kismet 'kɪz met 'kɪs-, -mɪt, -mət
kiss kɪs **kissed** kɪst **kisses** 'kɪs ɪz -əz **kissing** 'kɪs ɪŋ
'kissing bug; **'kissing gate**; **ˌkiss of 'death**; **ˌkiss of 'life**
kissable 'kɪs əb ᵊl
kissagram 'kɪs ə græm **~s** z
kisser 'kɪs ə ‖ -ᵊr **~s** z
Kissimmee kɪ 'sɪm i
Kissinger 'kɪs ɪndʒ ə -əndʒ-; '·ɪŋ ə ‖ -ᵊr
kiss-me-quick ˌkɪs mi 'kwɪk ◂
kissoff 'kɪs ɒf -ɔːf ‖ -ɔːf -ɑːf
kissogram 'kɪs ə græm **~s** z
kit, Kit kɪt **kits** kɪts **kitted** 'kɪt ɪd -əd ‖ 'kɪt̬ əd **kitting** 'kɪt ɪŋ ‖ 'kɪt̬ ɪŋ
Kitaj kɪ 'taɪ
kitbag 'kɪt bæg **~s** z
Kit-Cat, kit-cat 'kɪt kæt **~s** s
kitchen, K~ 'kɪtʃ ən -ɪn **~s** z
ˌkitchen 'garden
Kitchener 'kɪtʃ ən ə -ɪn- ‖ -ᵊn ər
kitchenette ˌkɪtʃ ə 'net -ɪ- **~s** s
kitchen-sink ˌkɪtʃ ən 'sɪŋk ◂ -ɪn-
kitchenware 'kɪtʃ ən weə -ɪn- ‖ -wer

K

kite, Kite kaɪt **kited** ˈkaɪt ɪd -əd ‖ ˈkaɪţ- **kites** kaɪts **kiting** ˈkaɪt ɪŋ ‖ ˈkaɪţ-
kite-flying ˈkaɪt ˌflaɪ ɪŋ
Kit-E-Kat *tdmk* ˈkɪt i kæt ‖ ˈkɪţ-
Kitemark ˈkaɪt mɑːk ‖ -mɑːrk
kith kɪθ
 ˌkith and ˈkin
kiting ˈkaɪt ɪŋ ‖ ˈkaɪţ ɪŋ
Kit-Kat *tdmk* ˈkɪt kæt **~s** s
kitsch kɪtʃ
Kitson ˈkɪts ən
Kitt kɪt
kitten ˈkɪt ᵊn **~ed** d **~ing** ɪŋ **~s** z
kittenish ˈkɪt ᵊn ɪʃ **~ly** li **~ness** nəs nɪs
Kittitian kɪ ˈtɪʃ ᵊn **~s** z
kittiwake ˈkɪt i weɪk ‖ ˈkɪţ- **~s** s
Kitto ˈkɪt əʊ ‖ ˈkɪţ oʊ
Kitts kɪts
kitt|y, Kitt|y ˈkɪt |i ‖ ˈkɪţ |i **~ies, ~y's** iz
 ˈKitty Hawk
kitty-corner ˈkɪt i ˌkɔːn ə ‖ ˈkɪţ i ˌkɔːr nᵊr -ˌkɔːn-
Kitzbuehel, Kitzbuhel, Kitzbühel ˈkɪts bjuˌəl -buˌəl; ˈ-bjuːl, -buːl —*Ger* [ˈkɪts byː əl]
kiva ˈkiːv ə **~s** z
Kiveton *place in SYks* ˈkɪv ɪt ən -ət-
Kiwanian ki ˈwɑːn i ən §kə- **~s** z
Kiwanis kɪ ˈwɑːn ɪs §kə-, §-əs
kiwi, Kiwi ˈkiː wiː **~s** z
 ˈkiwi fruit
Kizzy ˈkɪz i
Klamath ˈklæm əθ **~s** s
 ˌKlamath ˈFalls; **ˈKlamath weed**
klan, Klan klæn
Klans|man ˈklænz |mən **~men** mən men
klatsch klætʃ
Klatt klæt
Klaus klaʊs —*Ger* [klaus]
klavier klæ ˈvɪə klə- ‖ -ˈvɪᵊr **~s** z
klaxon, K~ *tdmk* ˈklæks ən **~s** z
Klebs-Loffler, Klebs-Löffler ˌklebz ˈlʌf lə -ˈlɜːf- ‖ -ˈlef lᵊr —*Ger* [ˌkleːps ˈlœf lɐ]
Klee kleɪ —*Ger* [kleː]
Kleenex *tdmk* ˈkliːn eks **~es** ɪz əz
Klein klaɪn
Kleinwort ˈklaɪn wɔːt ‖ -wɔːrt
Klemperer ˈklemp ər ə ‖ -ᵊr ər —*Ger* [ˈklɛmp əʁ ɐ]
klepht kleft *(= cleft)* **klephts** klefts
kleptomania ˌklept əʊ ˈmeɪn i ə ‖ ˌ-ə-
kleptomaniac ˌklept əʊ ˈmeɪn i æk ◂ ‖ ˌ-ə- **~s** s
klezmer ˈklez mə ‖ -mᵊr
klieg kliːg
 ˈklieg light
Klim *tdmk* klɪm
Klimt klɪmᵖt
Kline klaɪn
Klinefelter ˈklaɪn felt ə ‖ -ᵊr **~'s** z
Klingon ˈklɪŋ ɒn ‖ -ɑːn -ɔːn
klipspringer ˈklɪp ˌsprɪŋ ə ‖ -ᵊr **~s** z
Klondike ˈklɒnd aɪk ‖ ˈklɑːnd-

kloof kluːf **kloofs** kluːfs
Klosters ˈkləʊst əz ˈklɒst- ‖ ˈkloʊst ᵊrz —*Ger* [ˈkloː stɐs]
kludge kluːdʒ klʌdʒ **kludged** kluːdʒd klʌdʒd **kludging** ˈkluːdʒ ɪŋ ˈklʌdʒ- **kludges** ˈkluːdʒ ɪz ˈklʌdʒ-, -əz
kludgey, kludgy ˈkluːdʒ i ˈklʌdʒ i
klutz klʌts **klutzes** ˈklʌts ɪz -əz
klutz|y ˈklʌts |i **~ier** i ə ‖ i ᵊr **~iest** i ɪst i əst **~iness** i nəs i nɪs
klystron, K~ *tdmk* ˈklaɪs trɒn ˈklɪs- ‖ -trɑːn **~s** z
km —*see* **kilometre**
K-Mart *tdmk* ˈkeɪ mɑːt ‖ -mɑːrt
knack næk **knacks** næks
knacker ˈnæk ə ‖ -ᵊr **~ed** d **knackering** ˈnæk ər ɪŋ **~s** z
 ˈknacker's yard
knackwurst ˈnæk vʊəst ‖ ˈnɑːk wɜːst -wʊrst —*Ger* [ˈknak vʊʁst]
knap næp *(= nap)* **knapped** næpt **knapping** ˈnæp ɪŋ **knaps** næps
Knapp næp
knapsack ˈnæp sæk **~s** s
knapweed ˈnæp wiːd **~s** z
Knaresborough ˈneəz bər ə ‖ ˈnerz ˌbɜː oʊ
Knatchbull ˈnætʃ bʊl
knave neɪv *(= nave)* **knaves** neɪvz
knaver|y ˈneɪv ər |i **~ies** iz
knavish ˈneɪv ɪʃ **~ly** li **~ness** nəs nɪs
knawel nɔːl ˈnɔː əl ‖ nɑːl
knead niːd *(= need)* **kneaded** ˈniːd ɪd -əd **kneading** ˈniːd ɪŋ **kneads** niːdz
Knebworth ˈneb wəθ -wɜːθ ‖ -wᵊrθ
knee niː **kneed** niːd *(= need)* **kneeing** ˈniː ɪŋ **knees** niːz
 ˈknee ˌbreeches
Kneebone ˈniː bəʊn ‖ -boʊn
kneecap ˈniː kæp **~ped** t **~ping** ɪŋ **~s** s
knee-deep ˌniː ˈdiːp ◂
knee-high ˌniː ˈhaɪ ◂
kneehole ˈniː həʊl →-hɒʊl ‖ -hoʊl **~s** z
knee-jerk ˈniː dʒɜːk ‖ -dʒɜːk
kneel niːᵊl **kneeled** niːᵊld **kneeling** ˈniːᵊl ɪŋ **kneels** niːᵊlz **knelt** nelt
knee-length ˈniː leŋᵏθ -lenᵗθ
kneeler ˈniːᵊl ə ‖ -ᵊr **~s** z
knees-up ˈniːz ʌp
knell nel **knells** nelz
Kneller ˈnel ə ‖ -ᵊr
knelt nelt
Knesset ˈknes et -ɪt, -ət; kə ˈnes·
knew njuː ‖ nuː njuː *(= new)*
K'nex *tdmk* kə ˈneks
knicker ˈnɪk ə ‖ -ᵊr **~s** z
knickerbocker, K~ ˈnɪk ə bɒk ə ‖ -ᵊr bɑːk ᵊr **~s** z
 ˌknickerbocker ˈglory
knick-knack ˈnɪk næk **~s** s
Knieval kə ˈniːv ᵊl
knife naɪf **knifed** naɪft **knifes** naɪfs **knifing** ˈnaɪf ɪŋ **knives** naɪvz
knife-edge ˈnaɪf edʒ

K

nife-point 'naɪf pɔɪnt
night, K~ naɪt *(= night)* **knighted** 'naɪt ɪd -əd ‖ 'naɪţ əd **knighting** 'naɪt ɪŋ ‖ 'naɪţ ɪŋ **knights, Knight's** naɪts
night-errant ˌnaɪt 'er ənt ‖ ˌnaɪţ- **knights-errant** ˌnaɪts 'er ənt
nighthood 'naɪt hʊd **~s** z
night|ly 'naɪt |li *(= nightly)* **~liness** li nəs -nɪs
Knighton 'naɪt ən
Knightsbridge 'naɪts brɪdʒ
niphofia nɪ 'fəʊf i ə naɪ- ‖ -'foʊf- **~s** z
nish kə 'nɪʃ knɪʃ **knishes** kə 'nɪʃ ɪz -əz; 'knɪʃ·
nit nɪt *(= nit)* **knits** nɪts **knitted** 'nɪt ɪd -əd ‖ 'nɪţ əd **knitter** 'nɪt ə ‖ 'nɪţ ər **~s** z **knitting** 'nɪt ɪŋ ‖ 'nɪţ ɪŋ
'knitting ˌneedle
knitwear 'nɪt weə ‖ -wer
knives naɪvz
knob nɒb ‖ nɑːb **knobbed** nɒbd ‖ nɑːbd **knobs** nɒbz ‖ nɑːbz
knobbly 'nɒb əl i ‖ 'nɑːb-
knobby 'nɒb i ‖ 'nɑːb i
knobkerrie 'nɒb ˌker i -kər- ‖ 'nɑːb- **~s** z
knock, Knock nɒk ‖ nɑːk **knocked** nɒkt ‖ nɑːkt **knocking** 'nɒk ɪŋ ‖ 'nɑːk ɪŋ **knocks** nɒks ‖ nɑːks
knockabout 'nɒk ə ˌbaʊt ‖ 'nɑːk- **~s** s
knockback 'nɒk bæk ‖ 'nɑːk- **~s** s
knockdown 'nɒk daʊn ‖ 'nɑːk- **~s** z
knock-down-drag-out ˌnɒk daʊn 'dræg aʊt ◂ ‖ ˌnɑːk-
knocker 'nɒk ə ‖ 'nɑːk ər **~s** z
knock|er-up ˌnɒk |ər 'ʌp ‖ ˌnɑːk ər- **~ers-up** əz 'ʌp ‖ ərz 'ʌp
knock-for-knock ˌnɒk fə 'nɒk ◂ ‖ ˌnɑːk fər 'nɑːk ◂
knock-forward ˌnɒk 'fɔː wəd ‖ ˌnɑːk 'fɔːr wərd **~s** z
Knockholt 'nɒk həʊlt →-hɒʊlt ‖ 'nɑːk hoʊlt
knock-knee ˌnɒk 'niː ‖ ˌnɑːk- **~d** d ◂
knock-knock ˌnɒk 'nɒk ‖ ˌnɑːk 'nɑːk
ˌknock-'knock joke
knockoff 'nɒk ɒf -ɔːf ‖ 'nɑːk ɔːf -ɑːf **~s** s
knock-on ˌnɒk 'ɒn '· · ‖ ˌnɑːk 'ɑːn -'ɔːn
ˌknock-'on efˌfect, ˌknock-on ef'fect, 'knock-on efˌfect
knockout 'nɒk aʊt ‖ 'nɑːk- **~s** s
knock-up 'nɒk ʌp ‖ 'nɑːk- **~s** s
knockwurst 'nɒk wɜːst ‖ 'nɑːk wɜːst -vʊrst
Knole nəʊl →nɒʊl ‖ noʊl
knoll, Knoll nəʊl →nɒʊl ‖ noʊl **knolls** nəʊlz →nɒʊlz ‖ noʊlz
Knollys nəʊlz →nɒʊlz ‖ noʊlz
Knopf knɒpf ‖ knɑːpf
Knorr nɔː ‖ nɔːr
Knossos 'knɒs ɒs 'nɒs-, -əs ‖ 'nɑːs əs
knot nɒt ‖ nɑːt *(= not)* **knots** nɒts ‖ nɑːts **knotted** 'nɒt ɪd -əd ‖ 'nɑːţ əd **knotting** 'nɒt ɪŋ ‖ 'nɑːţ ɪŋ
knotgrass 'nɒt grɑːs §-græs ‖ 'nɑːt græs
knothole 'nɒt həʊl →-hɒʊl ‖ 'nɑːt hoʊl **~s** z
Knott nɒt ‖ nɑːt
knott... *—see* **knot**
Knottingley 'nɒt ɪŋ li ‖ 'nɑːţ-
knott|y 'nɒt |i ‖ 'nɑːţ |i **~ier** i ə ‖ i ər **~iest** i ɪst i əst **~iness** i nəs i nɪs
knout naʊt **knouts** naʊts
know nəʊ ‖ noʊ *(= no)* **knew** njuː ‖ nuː njuː **knowing** 'nəʊ ɪŋ ‖ 'noʊ ɪŋ **known** nəʊn §'nəʊ ən ‖ noʊn **knows** nəʊz ‖ noʊz
knowable 'nəʊ əb əl ‖ 'noʊ-
know-all 'nəʊ ɔːl ‖ 'noʊ- -ɑːl **~s** z
know-how 'nəʊ haʊ ‖ 'noʊ-
knowing 'nəʊ ɪŋ ‖ 'noʊ ɪŋ **~ly** li **~ness** nəs nɪs
know-it-all 'nəʊ ɪt ɔːl §-ət- ‖ 'noʊ əţ- -ɑːl **~s** z
Knowle nəʊl →nɒʊl ‖ noʊl
knowledge 'nɒl ɪdʒ ‖ 'nɑːl- *(!)*
knowledgeab|le 'nɒl ɪdʒ əb |əl ‖ 'nɑːl- **~ly** li
Knowles nəʊlz →nɒʊlz ‖ noʊlz
known nəʊn §'nəʊ ən ‖ noʊn
know-nothing 'nəʊ ˌnʌθ ɪŋ ‖ 'noʊ- **~s** z
Knowsley 'nəʊz li ‖ 'noʊz-
Knox nɒks ‖ nɑːks
Knoxville 'nɒks vɪl ‖ 'nɑːks-
Knoydart 'nɔɪd ɑːt -ət ‖ -ɑːrt
knuckl|e 'nʌk əl **~ed** d **~es** z **~ing** ɪŋ
knuckleball 'nʌk əl bɔːl ‖ -bɑːl **~s** z
knucklebone 'nʌk əl bəʊn ‖ -boʊn **~s** z
knuckle-dragger 'nʌk əl ˌdræg ə ‖ -ər **~s** z
knuckle-duster 'nʌk əl ˌdʌst ə ‖ -ər **~s** z
knucklehead 'nʌk əl hed **~s** z
knurl nɜːl ‖ nɜːl **knurled** nɜːld ‖ nɜːld **knurls** nɜːlz ‖ nɜːlz
Knuston 'nʌst ən
Knutsford 'nʌts fəd ‖ -fərd
KO, k.o. ˌkeɪ 'əʊ ‖ -'oʊ **~'d** d **~'ing** ɪŋ **~'s** z
koa 'kəʊ ə ‖ 'koʊ ə **~s** z
koala kəʊ 'ɑːl ə ‖ koʊ- **~s** z
koan 'kəʊ æn -ən, -ɑːn ‖ 'koʊ ɑːn *—Jp* [koˌo ɑɴ] **~s** z
Kobe *American personal name* kəʊb ‖ koʊb
Kobe *place in Japan* 'kəʊb eɪ -i ‖ 'koʊb eɪ *—Jp* ['ko̞o be]
Koblenz kəʊ 'blents ‖ 'koʊ blents *—Ger* ['koː blɛnts]
Koch *(i)* kəʊk ‖ koʊk, *(ii)* kɒtʃ ‖ kɑːtʃ, *(iii)* kɒx ‖ kɔːk kɑːk *—Ger* [kɔx]
Kochel, Köchel 'kɜːk əl 'kɜːx- ‖ 'kɜːʃ əl 'kɜːk- *—Ger* ['kœç əl]
'Köchel ˌnumber
Kodachrome *tdmk* 'kəʊd ə krəʊm ‖ 'koʊd ə kroʊm
Kodak, kodak *tdmk* 'kəʊd æk ‖ 'koʊd- **~s, ~'s** s
Kodaly, Kodály 'kəʊd aɪ ‖ koʊ 'daɪ *—Hung* ['ko daːj]
Kodiak 'kəʊd i æk ‖ 'koʊd-
Koestler 'kɜːst lə ‖ 'kest lər
Kofi 'kəʊf i ‖ 'koʊf i
Koh-i-noor ˌkəʊ i 'nʊə ◂ -'nɔː, '· · · ‖ 'koʊ ə nʊr
kohl, Kohl kəʊl →kɒʊl ‖ koʊl *—Ger* [koːl]
kohlrabi ˌkəʊl 'rɑːb i →ˌkɒʊl- ‖ ˌkoʊl-
koi kɔɪ *—Jp* ['ko i]
koine, koiné 'kɔɪn eɪ -iː, -i **~s** z

K

Kojak ˈkəʊdʒ æk ‖ ˈkoʊdʒ-
Kokomo ˈkəʊk ə məʊ ‖ ˈkoʊk ə moʊ
Kokoschka kəʊ ˈkɒʃ kə ‖ kə ˈkɑːʃ- -ˈkɔːʃ- —*Ger* [ko ˈkɔʃ ka, ˈkɔ kɔʃ ka]
kola, Kola ˈkəʊl ə ‖ ˈkoʊl ə
Kolkata kɒl ˈkʌt ə -ˈkæt- ‖ kɔːl- kɑːl-, koʊl- —*Bengali* [ˈkol ka ṯa]
kolkhoz ˌkɒl ˈkɒz -ˈkɔːz, -ˈhɔːz ‖ kɑːl ˈkɑːz -ˈkɔːz —*Russ* [kʌɫ ˈxɔs] **~es** ɪz əz
Kolynos *tdmk* ˈkɒl ɪ nɒs -ə- ‖ ˈkɑːl ə nɑːs
Komi ˈkəʊm i ‖ ˈkoʊm i **~s** z
Komodo kə ˈməʊd əʊ ‖ -ˈmoʊd oʊ
Koˌmodo ˈdragon
Komsomol ˈkɒm sə mɒl ˌ· ·ˈ· ‖ ˈkɑːm sə mɑːl -mɔːl, ˌ· ·ˈ· —*Russ* [kəm sʌ ˈmoɫ]
Kondratieff, Kondratiev kɒn ˈdræt i ef ‖ kɑːn ˈdrɑːt- —*Russ* [kʌn ˈdra tʲɪf]
Kongo ˈkɒŋ gəʊ ‖ ˈkɑːŋ goʊ
Konica *tdmk* ˈkɒn ɪk ə ˈkəʊn- ‖ ˈkɑːn- ˈkoʊn- —*Jp* [ˈko ɲi ka]
Konigsberg, Königsberg ˈkɜːn ɪgz bɜːg ˈkəʊn-, -beəg ‖ ˈkeɪn ɪgz bɝːg ˈkʊn- —*Ger* [ˈkøː nɪçs bɛʁk]
Konkani ˈkɒŋk ən i ‖ ˈkɑːŋk-
Konrad ˈkɒn ræd ‖ ˈkɑːn-
Kon-Tiki ˌkɒn ˈtiːk i -ˈtɪk- ‖ ˌkɑːn-
Koo kuː
kook kuːk **kooks** kuːks
kookaburra ˈkʊk ə bʌr ə ‖ -bɜː ə **~s** z
Kookai, Kookaï *tdmk* ˈkuː kaɪ
kook|y ˈkuːk |i **~ier** i ə ‖ i ᵊr **~iest** i ɪst i əst **~iness** i nəs i nɪs
Kool *tdmk* kuːl
Kool-Aid *tdmk* ˈkuːl eɪd
Koontz kuːnts
Kootenay ˈkuːt ə neɪ -ᵊn eɪ ‖ -ᵊn eɪ
kop, Kop kɒp ‖ kɑːp *(= cop)* **kops** kɒps ‖ kɑːps
kopeck, kopek ˈkəʊp ek ˈkɒp- ‖ ˈkoʊp- **~s** s
kopje ˈkɒp i ‖ ˈkɑːp i **~s** z
koppa ˈkɒp ə ‖ ˈkɑːp ə **~s** z
Koppel ˈkɒp ᵊl ‖ ˈkɑːp ᵊl
koppie ˈkɒp i ‖ ˈkɑːp i **~s** z
Koran kɔː ˈrɑːn kɒ-, kə- ‖ kə- —*Arabic* [qurˈʔaːn]
Koranic kɔː ˈræn ɪk kɒ-, kə- ‖ kə-
Kordofan ˌkɔːd əʊ ˈfæn -ˈfɑːn ‖ ˌkɔːrd oʊ ˈfɑːn
Kordofanian ˌkɔːd əʊ ˈfeɪn i ən ◂ -ˈfɑːn- ‖ ˌkɔːrd oʊ ˈfæn-
Korea kə ˈrɪə kɒ-, §-ˈriː ə ‖ kə ˈriː ə
Korean kə ˈrɪən kɒ-, §-ˈriː ən ‖ kə ˈriː ən **~s** z
korfball ˈkɔːf bɔːl ‖ ˈkɔːrf- -bɑːl
korma ˈkɔːm ə ‖ ˈkɔːrm ə **~s** z
Korsakoff, Korsakov, Korsakow ˈkɔːs ə kɒf ‖ ˈkɔːrs ə kɑːf -kɔːf —*Russ* [ˈkor sə kəf]
Kos *Greek island* kɒs ‖ kɑːs kɔːs, koʊs
kos *Indian measure of distance* kəʊs ‖ koʊs
Kosciusko *name of mountain* ˌkɒs i ˈʌsk əʊ -ˈʊsk- ‖ ˌkɑːs i ˈʌsk oʊ ˌkɑːsk- —*Polish* Kościuszko [kɔɕ ˈtɕuʃ kɔ]
kosher ˈkəʊʃ ə ‖ ˈkoʊʃ ᵊr
Kosovar ˈkɒs ə vɑː ‖ ˈkoʊs ə vɑːr ˈkɑːs-, ˈkɔːs- **~s** z
Kosovo ˈkɒs ə vəʊ ‖ ˈkoʊs ə voʊ ˈkɑːs-, ˈkɔːs- —*Serbian* [ˈkɔ sɔ vɔ], *Albanian* Kosova [ˈkɔ sɔ va]
Kosset *tdmk* ˈkɒs ɪt §-ət ‖ ˈkɑːs-
Kossoff ˈkɒs ɒf ‖ ˈkɑːs ɔːf -ɑːf
Kotex *tdmk* ˈkəʊt eks ‖ ˈkoʊt-
kotow ˌkəʊ ˈtaʊ ‖ koʊ ˈtoʊ ˈ· · **~ed** d **~ing** ɪŋ **~s** z
koumis, koumiss ˈkuːm ɪs -əs
kour|os ˈkʊər ɒs ‖ ˈkʊr- **~oi** ɔɪ
Kowloon ˌkaʊ ˈluːn ◂ —*Cantonese* [²kɐw ⁴loŋ]
kowtow ˌkaʊ ˈtaʊ ‖ ˈ· · **~ed** d **~ing** ɪŋ **~s** z
Koštunica kɒʃ ˈtuːn ɪts ə ‖ kɔːʃ-, kɑːʃ-, koʊʃ- —*Serbian* [ko ˈʃtu ni tsa]
kraal krɑːl krɔːl —*in South African English*, krɔːl **kraals** krɑːlz krɔːlz
Kraft *tdmk* krɑːft §kræft ‖ kræft
krait kraɪt **kraits** kraɪts
Krakatoa ˌkræk ə ˈtəʊ ə ˌkrɑːk- ‖ -ˈtoʊ ə
kraken ˈkrɑːk ən ˈkreɪk-, ˈkræk- **~s** z
Krakow ˈkræk aʊ -əʊ, -ɒf ‖ ˈkrɑːk aʊ —*Polish* Kraków [ˈkra kuf]
Kramer ˈkreɪm ə ‖ -ᵊr
kraut, Kraut kraʊt **krauts** kraʊts
Kray kreɪ
Krebs krebz
Kremlin, k~ ˈkrem lɪn §-lən
Kreutzer ˈkrɔɪts ə ‖ -ᵊr —*Ger* [ˈkʁɔʏ tsɐ]
krill krɪl
krimmer ˈkrɪm ə ‖ -ᵊr
Kringle ˈkrɪŋ gᵊl
Krio ˈkriː əʊ ‖ -oʊ **~s** z
kris *'knife'* kriːs krɪs
Kris *personal name* krɪs
Krishna ˈkrɪʃ nə
Krishnamurti ˌkrɪʃ nə ˈmɜːt i -ˈmʊət i ‖ -ˈmɝːṱ i
Krispie ˈkrɪsp i **~s** z
Krista ˈkrɪst ə
Kristen ˈkrɪst ən
Kristi, Kristie ˈkrɪst i
Kristle ˈkrɪst ᵊl
Kristy ˈkrɪst i
Krona *tdmk*, **krona** ˈkrəʊn ə ‖ ˈkroʊn ə —*Swedish* [ˈkru na] **kronor** ˈkrəʊn ɔː ‖ ˈkroʊn ɔːr —*Swedish* [ˈkru nur]
krone ˈkrəʊn ə ‖ ˈkroʊn ə —*Danish* [ˈkʁo nə] **kroner** ˈkrəʊn ə ‖ ˈkroʊn ᵊr —*Danish* [ˈkʁo nɒ]
Kru kruː **Krus** kruːz
Kruger ˈkruːg ə ‖ -ᵊr —*Afrikaans* [ˈkry xər]
Krugerrand, k~ ˈkruːg ə rænd **~s** z
Krupp krʊp krʌp —*Ger* [kʁʊp] **Krupp's** krʊps krʌps
Kruschen *tdmk* ˈkrʊʃ ᵊn ˈkrʌʃ-
Krushchev ˈkrʊs tʃɒf ˈkrʊʃ-, ·ˈ· ‖ ˈkruːs tʃef -tʃɔːf, -tʃɑːf, ·ˈ· —*Russ* [xru ˈɕːɔf]
krypton ˈkrɪpt ɒn -ən ‖ -ɑːn
kryptonite ˈkrɪpt ə naɪt
Kshatriya ˈkʃætr i ə
Kuala Lumpur ˌkwɑːl ə ˈlʊmp ʊə ˌkwɒl-, -ˈlʌmp-, -ə ‖ -lʊm ˈpʊᵊr
Kublai ˈkuːb lə ˈkʊb-, -laɪ

ubla Khan ˌku:b lə 'kɑ:n ˌkʊb-
ubrick 'kju:b rɪk
uccha 'kʌtʃ ə —*Punjabi* [kət tʃə]
udos 'kju:d ɒs ‖ -oʊz 'ku:d-, -oʊs, -ɑ:s
udu 'ku:d u: 'kʊd- **~s** z
udzu 'kʊd zu: —*Jp* ['kɯ dzɯ]
ufic 'ku:f ɪk 'kju:f-
uhn ku:n
uhnian 'ku:n i‿ən
uiper 'kaɪp ə ‖ -ᵊr
u Klux Klan ˌku: klʌks 'klæn ˌkju:-, ⚠ˌklu:-
ukri 'kʊk ri **~s** z
ulak 'ku:l æk ‖ ku 'lɑ:k -'læk; 'ku:l ɑ:k, -æk —*Russ* [ku 'łak] **~s** s
ultur kʊl 'tʊə ‖ -'tʊᵊr —*Ger* [kʊl 'tu:ɐ]
umis, kumiss 'ku:m ɪs §-əs
ummel, kümmel 'kʊm ᵊl ‖ 'kɪm- *(*)* —*Ger* ['kʏm ᵊl]
umquat 'kʌm kwɒt ‖ -kwɑ:t **~s** s
Kung, !xũ kʊŋ —*In the language so named, the exclamation mark denotes a post-alveolar ('palatal') click. This accompanies a voiceless velar affricate* [kx]. *The vowel is a nasalized* [ũ]. *The syllable is said on a low rising tone.*
ung fu ˌkʌŋ 'fu: ˌkʊŋ- —*Chi* gōngfū [¹kʊŋ ¹fu]
unming ˌkʊn 'mɪŋ —*Chi* Kūnmíng [¹kʰuən ²miŋ]
uomintang ˌkwəʊ mɪn 'tæŋ ˌgwəʊ- ‖ ˌkwoʊ mɪn 'tɑ:ŋ ˌgwoʊ-, -'tæŋ —*Chi* Guómíndǎng [²kwɔ ²mɪn ³taŋ]
uoni *tdmk* ku 'əʊn i ‖ -'oʊn i
urath 'kjʊər æθ ‖ 'kjʊr-
urd kɜ:d kʊəd ‖ kɜ˞:d kʊᵊrd **Kurds** kɜ:dz kʊədz ‖ kɜ˞:dz kʊᵊrdz
urdish 'kɜ:d ɪʃ ‖ 'kɜ˞:d-
urdistan ˌkɜ:d ɪ 'stɑ:n -ə-, -'stæn ‖ 'kɜ˞:d ə stæn
ureishi ku 'reʃ i -'reɪʃ-
uril, Kurile kʊ 'ri:ᵊl kju- ‖ 'kʊr ɪl 'kjʊr-
urosawa ˌkʊər əʊ 'sɑ: wə ‖ ˌkʊr oʊ- —*Jp* [ku ˌɾo sa wa]
ursaal 'kɜ:z ᵊl 'kɜ:s-; 'kɜ: sɑ:l, 'kʊə-, -sᵊl, -zɑ:l ‖ 'kʊr sɑ:l
ursk kʊəsk ‖ kʊᵊrsk —*Russ* [kursk]
urt kɜ:t kʊət ‖ kɜ˞:t —*Ger* [kʊʁt]
urtosis kɜ: 'təʊs ɪs kə-, §-əs ‖ kɜ˞: 'toʊs əs
uru 'kʊr u:
urus ku 'rʊʃ -'ru:ʃ *Turkish* kuruş [ku 'ruʃ]
urus kʊ 'rʊʃ -'ru:ʃ

Kurzweil 'kɜ:z waɪᵊl 'kɜ:ts-, -vaɪᵊl ‖ 'kɜ˞:z-
Kutch kʌtʃ
Kuwait ku 'weɪt kju-, kə- —*Arabic* [ku 'we:t]
Kuwaiti ku 'weɪt i kju-, kə- ‖ -'weɪţ i **~s** z
Kvaerner, Kværner kə 'vɜ:n ə -'vɑ:n- ‖ -'vɜ˞:n ᵊr
kvas, kvass kvɑ:s kvæs ‖ kwɑ:s
kvetch kvetʃ **kvetched** kvetʃt **kvetches** 'kvetʃ ɪz -əz **kvetching** 'kvetʃ ɪŋ
Kwa kwɑ:
Kwajalein 'kwɑ:dʒ ə leɪn -əl ən
Kwakiutl ˌkwɑ:k i 'u:t ᵊl ◂ ‖ -'u:ţ-
Kwandebele, KwaNdebele ˌkwɒnd ɪ 'bel i ˌkwɑ:nd-, -'beɪl-, -eɪ ‖ ˌkwɑ:nd-
Kwanza, Kwanzaa 'kwɑ:nz ə 'kwænz-, -ɑ:
kwashiorkor ˌkwɒʃ i 'ɔ:k ɔ: ˌkwæʃ-, -ə ‖ ˌkwɑ:ʃ i 'ɔ:rk ᵊr -ɔ:r
kwatcha 'kwɑ:tʃ ə
KwaZulu kwɑ: 'zu:l u:
kwela 'kweɪl ə
Kwells *tdmk* kwelz
KWIC kwɪk
Kwik-Fit *tdmk* 'kwɪk fɪt
Kwiksave *tdmk* 'kwɪk seɪv
Kyd kɪd
Kyle, kyle kaɪᵊl
Kyleakin ₍ₗ₎kaɪᵊl 'æk ɪn
Kylie 'kaɪl i
kymogram 'kaɪm əʊ græm ‖ -ə- **~s** z
kymograph 'kaɪm əʊ grɑ:f -græf ‖ -ə græf **~s** s
kymographic ˌkaɪm əʊ 'græf ɪk ◂ ‖ -ə- **~ally** ᵊl i
Kynance 'kaɪn æntˢ
Kynaston 'kɪn əst ən
Kyocera *tdmk* ˌkaɪ ə 'sɪər ə ‖ -'sɪr ə —*Jp* [kjo ˌo se ɾa]
Kyoto ki 'əʊt əʊ ‖ -'oʊt oʊ —*Jp* ['kjoo to]
kyphosis kaɪ 'fəʊs ɪs §-əs ‖ -'foʊs-
kyphotic kaɪ 'fɒt ɪk ‖ -'fɑ:ţ-
Kyrgyz 'kɜ:g ɪz 'kɪəg- ‖ 'kɜ˞:g- 'kɪrg-
Kyrgyzstan ˌkɜ:g ɪ 'stɑ:n ˌkɪəg-, -'stæn ‖ ˌkɜ˞:g- ˌkɪrg-, '. . .
kyrie 'kɪr i eɪ 'kɪər-, -i:
kyrie e'leison ɪ 'leɪs ɒn e-, -ᵊn; -'leɪ ə sɒn ‖ -ɑ:n
Kyushu ki 'u:ʃ u: 'kju:ʃ u: —*Jp* ['kjɯɯ ɕɯɯ]
Kyzyl Kum kə ˌzɪl 'ku:m -'kʊm —*Russ* [kɨ ˌziɫ 'kum]

K

Ll

l Spelling-to-sound

1 Where the spelling is **l**, the pronunciation is regularly l as in **little** 'lɪt ᵊl.

2 Where the spelling is double **ll**, the pronunciation is again regularly l as in **silly** 'sɪl i.

3 **l** is silent in a fair number of words, expecially when it stands between

- **a** and **f** as in **half** hɑːf ‖ hæf
- **a** and **k** as in **talk** tɔːk ‖ tɔːk or
- **a** and **m** as in **salmon** 'sæm ən.

Note also **could** kʊd, **should** ʃʊd, **would** wʊd.

L

L, l el *(= ell)* **Ls, l's, L's** elz *—Communications code name:* Lima 'liːm ə
ˌL'1; **ˌL'2**
la lɑː *—but in French, Italian, and Spanish expressions also* lə, læ *— Fr, It, Sp* [la]; *in family names usually* lə *—See also phrases with this word*
LA ˌel 'eɪ ◂ *—see also* **Los Angeles**
ˌLA 'Law
laager 'lɑːg ə ‖ -ᵊr *(= lager)* **~ed** d **~s** z
Laa-Laa 'lɑː lɑː
lab læb **labs** læbz
Laban *(i)* 'leɪb ən -æn, *(ii)* 'lɑːb-, *(iii)* lə 'bæn *—The biblical figure is (i), the dance notation system and its inventor (ii).*
label 'leɪb ᵊl **~ed, ~led** d **~ing, ~ling** ɪŋ **~s** z
labia 'leɪb i‿ə
ˌlabia ma'jora mə 'dʒɔːr ə ‖ -'dʒoʊr-; **ˌlabia mi'nora** mɪ 'nɔːr ə mə- ‖ -'noʊr-
labial 'leɪb i‿əl **~ly** i **~s** z
labialis... *—see* **labializ...**
labiality ˌleɪb i 'æl ət i -ɪt i ‖ -əţ i
labialization ˌleɪb i‿əl aɪ 'zeɪʃ ᵊn -ɪ'-- ‖ -ə 'zeɪʃ- **~s** z
labializ|e 'leɪb i‿ə laɪz **~ed** d **~es** ɪz əz **~ing** ɪŋ
labial-velar ˌleɪb i‿əl 'viːl ə ◂ ‖ -ᵊr ◂ **~s** z
labiate 'leɪb i eɪt -ət, -ɪt **~s** s
labile 'leɪb aɪᵊl ‖ -ᵊl
lability leɪ 'bɪl ət i lə-, -ɪt i ‖ -əţ i
labiodental ˌleɪb i əʊ 'dent ᵊl ◂ ‖ -oʊ 'denţ ᵊl ◂ **~ly** i **~s** z
labiopalatal ˌleɪb i əʊ 'pæl ət ᵊl ◂ ‖ -oʊ 'pæl əţ ᵊl ◂ **~ly** i **~s** z
labiovelar ˌleɪb i əʊ 'viːl ə ◂ ‖ -oʊ 'viːl ᵊr ◂ **~s** z
labiovelaris... *—see* **labiovelariz...**
labiovelarization ˌleɪb i əʊ ˌviːl ər aɪ 'zeɪʃ ᵊn -ɪ'-- ‖ -i oʊ ˌviːl ər ə- **~s** z
labiovelariz|e ˌleɪb i əʊ 'viːl ə raɪz ‖ -i oʊ- **~ed** d **~es** ɪz əz **~ing** ɪŋ
labi|um 'leɪb i‿|əm **~a** ə
La Boheme, La Bohème ˌlɑː bəʊ 'em ˌlæ-, -'eɪm ‖ -boʊ- *—Fr* [la bo ɛm]
labor 'leɪb ə ‖ -ᵊr **~ed** d **laboring** 'leɪb ər‿ɪŋ **~s** z
'labor camp; **'Labor Day**; **'labor exˌchange**; **'labor ˌmarket**; **ˌlabor of 'love**; **'Labor ˌParty**; **'labor ˌunion**
laborator|y lə 'bɒr ət‿ər |i ‖ 'læb ᵊr‿ə tɔːr |i -toʊr i *(*) —In BrE formerly also* 'læb ər‿ət‿ər i **~ies** iz
laborer 'leɪb ər‿ə ‖ -ᵊr ər **~s** z
labor-intensive ˌleɪb ər ɪn 'tenᵗs ɪv ◂ ‖ ˌər-
laborious lə 'bɔːr i‿əs ‖ -'boʊr- **~ly** li **~ness** nəs nɪs
Laborite 'leɪb ə raɪt **~s** s
labor-saving 'leɪb ə ˌseɪv ɪŋ ‖ -ᵊr-
Labouchere ˌlæb uː 'ʃeə '· · · ‖ -'ʃeᵊr
labour 'leɪb ə ‖ -ᵊr **~ed** d **labouring** 'leɪb ər‿ɪŋ **~s** z
'labour camp; **'Labour Day**; **'labour exˌchange**; **'labour ˌmarket**; **ˌlabour of 'love**; **'Labour ˌParty**; **'labour ˌunion**
labourer 'leɪb ər‿ə ‖ -ᵊr‿ər **~s** z
labour-intensive ˌleɪb ər ɪn 'tenᵗs ɪv ◂ ‖ ˌər-
Labourite 'leɪb ə raɪt **~s** s
labour-saving 'leɪb ə ˌseɪv ɪŋ ‖ -ᵊr-
Labov lə 'bɒv -'bəʊv ‖ -'boʊv
Labovian lə 'bəʊv i‿ən ‖ -'boʊv-
Labrador 'læb rə dɔː ‖ -dɔːr **~s** z
ˌLabrador re'triever
Labuan lə 'buː‿ən ‖ ˌlɑːb u 'ɑːn

burnum lə 'bɜːn əm ‖ -'bɝːn- **~s** z
byrinth 'læb ə rɪnᵗθ -ɪ- **~s** s
byrinthine ˌlæb ə 'rɪnᵗθ aɪn ◂ -ɪ- ‖ -ən -iːn, -aɪn
byrinthitis ˌlæb ər‿ɪn 'θaɪt ɪs -ᵊr‿ən-, §-əs ‖ -'θaɪţ əs
c *'100 000'* lɑːk læk **lacs** lɑːks læks
c *'resin'* læk *(= lack)* **lacs** læks
acan læ 'kɒ̃ -'kɑːn ‖ lə 'kɑːn —*Fr* [la kɑ̃]
accadive 'læk əd ɪv 'lɑːk-, ə diːv, -daɪv
ce leɪs **laced** leɪst **laces** 'leɪs ɪz -əz **lacing** 'leɪs ɪŋ
acedaemon ˌlæs ə 'diːm ən -ɪ-
acedaemonian ˌlæs ə dɪ 'məʊn i‿ən ◂ ˌ·ɪ-, -də'-- ‖ -'moʊn- **~s** z
ace|rate *v* 'læs ə |reɪt **~rated** reɪt ɪd -əd ‖ reɪţ əd **~rates** reɪts **~rating** reɪt ɪŋ ‖ reɪţ ɪŋ
aceration ˌlæs ə 'reɪʃ ᵊn **~s** z
acert|a lə 'sɜːt |ə ‖ -'sɝːţ |ə **~ae** iː
ace-up 'leɪs ʌp **~s** s
acewing 'leɪs wɪŋ **~s** z
acey 'leɪs i
aches 'lætʃ ɪz 'leɪtʃ-, -əz
achesis 'læk ɪs ɪs ⚠'lætʃ-, -əs-, §-əs
achlan 'lɒk lən 'læk- ‖ 'lɑːk-
achryma Christi ˌlæk rɪm ə 'krɪst i ˌ·rəm-
achrymal 'læk rɪm əl -rəm- **~s** z
achrymator 'læk rɪ meɪt ə '·rə- ‖ -meɪţ ᵊr **~s** z
achrymator|y ˌlæk rɪ 'meɪt ər |i ◂ ˌ·rə-, '·-·-, '·-mət‿ər |i ‖ 'læk rəm ə tɔːr |i -toʊr i **~ies** iz
achrymose 'læk rɪ məʊs -rə-, -məʊz ‖ -moʊs **~ly** li
a Cienega ˌlɑː si 'en əg ə
ack læk **lacked** lækt **lacking** 'læk ɪŋ **lacks** læks
ackadaisical ˌlæk ə 'deɪz ɪk ᵊl ◂ **~ly** ‿i **~ness** nəs nɪs
ackawanna ˌlæk ə 'wɒn ə ‖ -'wɑːn ə
ackey 'læk i **~s** z
ackluster, lacklustre 'læk ˌlʌst ə ˌ·'· · ‖ -ᵊr
acock 'leɪk ɒk ‖ -ɑːk
aconia lə 'kəʊn i‿ə ‖ -'koʊn-
aconic lə 'kɒn ɪk ‖ -'kɑːn- **~ally** ᵊl‿i
acquer 'læk ə ‖ -ᵊr **~ed** d **lacquering** 'læk ər ɪŋ **~s** z
acrim... —*see* **lachrym...**
acrosse lə 'krɒs ‖ -'krɔːs -'krɑːs
acrymal 'læk rɪm əl -rəm- **~s** z
act|ate *v* ₍ₗ₎læk 't|eɪt 'lækt |eɪt ‖ 'lækt |eɪt **~ated** eɪt ɪd -əd ‖ eɪţ əd **~ates** eɪts **~ating** eɪt ɪŋ ‖ eɪţ ɪŋ
actate *n* 'lækt eɪt **~s** s
actation ₍ₗ₎læk 'teɪʃ ᵊn **~s** z
acteal 'lækt i‿əl **~s** z
actic 'lækt ɪk
ˌ**lactic 'acid**
actobacill|us ˌlækt əʊ bə 'sɪl |əs ‖ ˌ·oʊ- **~i** aɪ
actose 'lækt əʊs -əʊz ‖ -oʊs -oʊz
acun|a lə 'kjuːn |ə læ-, -'kuːn- **~ae** iː aɪ
ac|y, Lacy 'leɪs |i **~ier** i‿ə ‖ i‿ᵊr **~iest** i‿ɪst i‿əst **~iness** i nəs i nɪs
ad læd **lads** lædz
Lada *tdmk* 'lɑːd ə **~s** z

Ladakh lə 'dɑːk 'dɔːk
Ladbroke 'læd brʊk →'læb-, -brəʊk ‖ -broʊk **~'s** s
Ladd læd
ladder 'læd ə ‖ -ᵊr **~ed** d **laddering** 'læd ər ɪŋ **~s** z
ladd|ie, ladd|y 'læd |i **~ies** iz
ladd|ish 'læd| ɪʃ **~ism** ˌɪz əm
lade leɪd *(= laid)* **laded** 'leɪd ɪd -əd **laden** 'leɪd ᵊn **lades** leɪdz **lading** 'leɪd ɪŋ
Ladefoged 'læd ɪ fəʊg ɪd '·ə-, -əd ‖ -foʊg-
laden 'leɪd ᵊn
Laden 'lɑːd ᵊn —*Arabic* ['laː dɪn]
ladette læ'det **~s** s
Ladhar Bheinn ˌlɑː 'ven ‖ ˌlɑːr-—*ScG* [ˌɫaar 'vjeɲ]
la-di-da ˌlɑː di 'dɑː ◂
ladies 'leɪd iz
ladies-in-waiting ˌleɪd iz ɪn 'weɪt ɪŋ §-ᵊn'-- ‖ -ᵊn 'weɪţ ɪŋ
ladieswear 'leɪd iz weə ‖ -wer -wær
Ladin læ 'diːn lə-
lading 'leɪd ɪŋ
Ladino, l~ lə 'diːn əʊ læ- ‖ -oʊ
ladl|e 'leɪd ᵊl **~ed** d **~es** z **~ing** ‿ɪŋ
lad|y, Lad|y 'leɪd |i **~ies, ~ies', ~y's** iz **'ladies' man**; **'ladies' room**; **'Lady ˌChapel**; **'Lady Day**; **'lady's ˌfingers**, ˌ· · '·
ladybird 'leɪd i bɜːd ‖ -bɝːd **~s** z
ladybug 'leɪd i bʌg **~s** z
ladyfinger 'leɪd i ˌfɪŋ gə ‖ -gᵊr **~s** z
lady|-in-waiting ˌleɪd i|‿ɪn 'weɪt ɪŋ §-ən'-- ‖ -ən 'weɪţ ɪŋ **ladies~** ˌleɪd iz-
lady-killer 'leɪd i ˌkɪl ə ‖ -ᵊr **~s** z
ladylike 'leɪd i laɪk
ladyship 'leɪd i ʃɪp **~s** s
Ladysmith 'leɪd i smɪθ
lady's-slipper ˌleɪd iz 'slɪp ə ‖ -ᵊr **~s** z
Lae leɪ 'leɪ i, 'lɑː eɪ
Laertes leɪ 'ɜːt iːz ‖ -'ɝːt iːz
Laetitia li 'tɪʃ ə lə-, -'tɪʃ i‿ə
laetrile, L~ *tdmk* 'leɪ ə traɪᵊl -trɪl; -ətr əl ‖ -ətr əl -ə trɪl
laevo- ¦liːv əʊ ‖ -ə — **laevorotation** ˌliːv əʊ rəʊ 'teɪʃ ᵊn ‖ -ə roʊ-
laevulose 'liːv ju ləʊz 'lev-, -jə-, -ləʊs ‖ -jə loʊs -loʊz
Lafayette ˌlɑː faɪ 'et -feɪ- ‖ ˌlæf i-ˌlɑːf-, -eɪ- —*Fr* [la fa jɛt]
Lafcadio læf 'kɑːd i əʊ ‖ lɑːf 'kɑːd i oʊ
Laffan lə 'fæn
Laffer 'læf ə ‖ -ᵊr
'Laffer curve
Lafford 'læf əd ‖ -ᵊrd
LaFontaine ˌlæf ɒn 'ten ˌlɑː fɒn-, -'teɪn ‖ ˌlɑː fɔːn 'ten -foʊn- —*Fr* [la fɔ̃ tɛn]
lag læg **lagged** lægd **lagging** 'læg ɪŋ **lags** lægz
Lagan, lagan 'læg ən
lager 'lɑːg ə ‖ -ᵊr 'lɔːg- **~s** z
Lagerfeld 'lɑːg ə felt ‖ -ᵊr-
laggard 'læg əd ‖ -ᵊrd **~ly** li **~s** z
lagnappe, lagniappe 'læn jæp ·'· **~s** s

lagomorph 'læg ə mɔːf ‖ -mɔːrf **~s** s
Lagonda *tdmk* lə 'gɒnd ə ‖ -'gɑːnd ə **~s** z
lagoon lə 'guːn **~s** z
Lagos *in Nigeria* 'leɪg ɒs ‖ -ɑːs —*Those not familiar with Nigeria also sometimes say* 'lɑːg ɒs ‖ -oʊs
Lagrange lə 'grɒ̃ʒ læ-, lɑː-, -'grɑːnʒ, -'greɪndʒ ‖ -'grɑːndʒ —*Fr* [la gʁɑ̃ːʒ]
La Guardia lə 'gwɑːd i ə ‖ -'gwɑːrd-
Laguna *tdmk* lə 'guːn ə
La,guna 'Beach
lahar 'lɑː hɑː ‖ -hɑːr **~s** z
lah-di-dah ˌlɑː di 'dɑː ◂
Lahnda 'lɑːnd ə
Lahore lə 'hɔː ‖ -'hɔːr -'hoʊr —*Urdu* [laː hoːr]
laic 'leɪ ɪk **~al** ᵊl **~ally** ᵊl i **~s** s
laicis... —*see* **laiciz...**
laicization ˌleɪ ɪs aɪ 'zeɪʃ ᵊn ˌ·əs-, -ɪ'·- ‖ -əs ə- **~s** z
laiciz|e 'leɪ ɪ saɪz -ə- **~ed** d **~es** ɪz əz **~ing** ɪŋ
laid leɪd
laid-back ˌleɪd 'bæk ◂ →ˌleɪb-
Laidlaw 'leɪd lɔː ‖ -lɑː
lain leɪn *(= lane)*
Laindon 'leɪnd ən
Laing *(i)* læŋ, *(ii)* leɪŋ
Laingian 'læŋ i ən **~s** z
lair leə ‖ leᵊr læᵊr **lairs** leəz ‖ leᵊrz læᵊrz
laird, Laird leəd ‖ leᵊrd læᵊrd **lairds** leədz ‖ leᵊrdz læᵊrdz
Lairg leəg ‖ leᵊrg læᵊrg
lairy 'leər i ‖ 'ler i
laisser-faire, laissez-faire ˌleɪs eɪ 'feə ˌles- ‖ -'feᵊr -'fæᵊr —*Fr* [lɛ se fɛːʁ]
lait|y 'leɪ ət |i -ɪt- ‖ -əţ |i **~ies** iz
Laius 'leɪ i əs 'laɪ əs, 'leɪ- ‖ 'leɪ əs 'leɪ i əs
La Jolla lə 'hɔɪ ə
lake, Lake leɪk **lakes** leɪks
Lake 'Charles; **'Lake ˌDistrict**; **'Lake ˌPoets**; **ˌLake Suc'cess**
lakebed 'leɪk bed **~s** z
lakeland, L~ 'leɪk lənd -lænd **~s** z
Lakenheath 'leɪk ən hiːθ
Laker 'leɪk ə ‖ -ᵊr
Lakesha lə 'keʃ ə
lakeside, L~ 'leɪk saɪd
lakh lɑːk læk —*Hindi* [laːkh] **lakhs** lɑːks læks
Lakme, Lakmé 'læk meɪ -mi
Lakshadweep læk 'ʃæd wiːp
Lakshmi 'lʌk ʃmi 'læk-, 'lɑːk- —*Sanskrit* [lək ʂmiː]
Lalage 'læl əg i -ədʒ-
la-la land 'lɑː lɑː lænd
Laleham 'leɪl əm
-lalia 'leɪl i ə — **coprolalia** ˌkɒp rəʊ 'leɪl i ə ‖ ˌkɑːp rə-
Lalique *tdmk* læ 'liːk lə- ‖ lɑː- —*Fr* [la lik]
Lallans 'læl ənz
lallation læ 'leɪʃ ᵊn **~s** z
lalling 'læl ɪŋ
Lalo 'lɑːl əʊ ‖ -oʊ —*Fr* [la lo]
lam læm **lammed** læmd **lamming** 'læm ɪŋ **lams** læmz
lama 'lɑːm ə **~s** z
Lamaism 'lɑːm əʳ ˌɪz əm ‖ -ə-
Lamarck lə 'mɑːk læ-, lɑː- ‖ -'mɑːrk —*Fr* [la maʁk]
Lamarckian lə 'mɑːk i ən læ-, lɑː- ‖ -'mɑːrk- **~s** z
Lamarr lə 'mɑː ‖ -'mɑːr
lamaser|y 'lɑːm əs ər |i ‖ -ə ser |i **~ies** iz
Lamaze lə 'meɪz
Lamaze lə 'meɪz —*Fr* [la maz]
lamb, Lamb læm *(= lam)* **lambed** læmd **lambing** 'læm ɪŋ **lambs, Lamb's** læmz
ˌlamb 'chop ‖ 'lamb chop
lambad|a læm 'bɑːd| ə ‖ lɑːm- **~aed** əd **~aing** əʳ ɪŋ ‖ ə ɪŋ **~as** əz
Lambarene ˌlæm bə 'riːn i ‖ ˌlɑːm- —*Fr* Lambaréné [lɑ̃ ba ʁe ne]
lambast læm 'bæst -'bɑːst **~ed** ɪd əd **~ing** ɪŋ **~s** s
lambast|e læm 'beɪst **~ed** ɪd əd **~ing** ɪŋ **~es** s
lambda 'læmd ə **~s** z
lambdacism 'læmd ə ˌsɪz əm **~s** z
Lambeg, l~ læm 'beg **~s** z
lambent 'læm bənt **~ly** li
Lambert, l~ 'læm bət ‖ -bᵊrt **~s, ~'s** s
Lambeth 'læm bəθ
ˌLambeth 'Conference; **ˌLambeth 'Palace**; **ˌLambeth 'Walk**
lambkin 'læm kɪn §-kən **~s** z
lamblike 'læm laɪk
Lamborghini *tdmk* ˌlæm bɔː 'giːn i -bə- ‖ ˌlɑːm bɔːr- -bᵊr- —*It* [lam bor 'giː ni] **~s** z
Lamborn, Lambourne 'læm bɔːn ‖ -bɔːrn -boʊrn
Lambretta *tdmk* læm 'bret ə ‖ -'breţ ə **~s** z
Lambrusco, l~ læm 'brʊsk əʊ ‖ -'bruːsk oʊ —*It* [lam 'brus ko]
lambskin 'læm skɪn **~s** z
lambswool 'læmz wʊl
Lambton 'læmᵖt ən
LAMDA 'læmd ə
lame leɪm **lamed** leɪmd **lamer** 'leɪm ə ‖ -ᵊr **lames** leɪmz **lamest** 'leɪm ɪst -əst **laming** 'leɪm ɪŋ
ˌlame 'duck
lamé 'lɑːm eɪ 'læm- ‖ lɑː 'meɪ læ-
lamebrain 'leɪm breɪn **~ed** d **~s** z
lamell|a lə 'mel |ə **~ae** iː **~as** əz
lamellibranch lə 'mel ɪ bræŋk §-'·ə-
lame|ly 'leɪm |li **~ness** nəs nɪs
lament *v, n* lə 'ment **lamented** lə 'ment ɪd -əd ‖ lə 'menţ əd **lamenting** lə 'ment ɪŋ ‖ lə 'menţ ɪŋ **laments** lə 'ments
lamentab|le lə 'ment əb |ᵊl 'læm ənt-, '·ɪnt- ‖ lə 'menţ- 'læm ənţ- — *Preference poll, BrE:* -'ment- *72%,* 'læm- *28% (born before 1942, 44%).* **~ly** li
lamentation ˌlæm ən 'teɪʃ ᵊn -ɪn-, -en- **~s, L~s** z
lame-o 'leɪm əʊ ‖ -oʊ **~s** z
La Mesa *place in CA* lə 'meɪs ə
lamin|a 'læm ɪn |ə -ən- **~ae** iː **~as** əz
laminal 'læm ɪn ᵊl -ən- **~s** z

LAMENTABLE

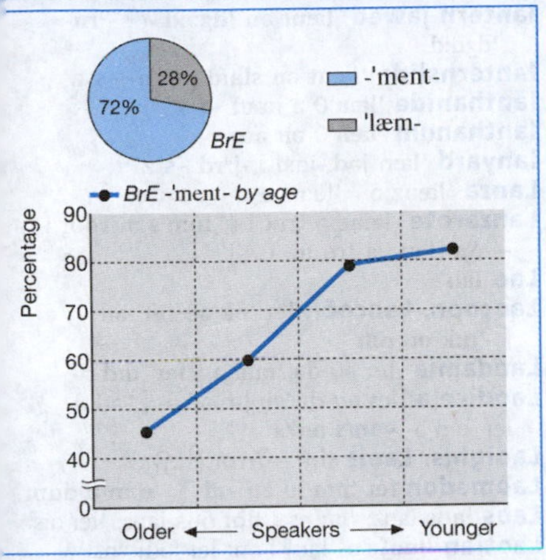

aminar 'læm ɪn ə -ən- ‖ -ᵊr
ˌlaminar 'flow
aminaria ˌlæm ɪ 'neər i ə ˌ·ə- ‖ -'ner- -'nær-
ami|nate *v* 'læm ɪ |neɪt -ə- **~nated** neɪt ɪd -əd ‖ neɪţ əd **~nates** neɪts **~nating** neɪt ɪŋ ‖ neɪţ ɪŋ
aminate *n, adj* 'læm ɪ neɪt -ə-; -ən ət, -ɪt **~s** s
amination ˌlæm ɪ 'neɪʃ ᵊn -ə- **~s** z
aminator 'læm ɪ neɪt ə '·ə- ‖ -neɪţ ᵊr **~s** z
aming *(i)* 'leɪm ɪŋ, *(ii)* 'læm-
amington, l~ 'læm ɪŋ tən **~s** z
ammas 'læm əs
ammergeier, lammergeyer 'læm ə gaɪ ə ‖ -ᵊr gaɪ ᵊr **~s** z
ammermoor 'læm ə mʊə -mɔː, ˌ· ·'· ‖ -mʊr -mɔːr, -moʊr
ammermuir 'læm ə mjʊə -mjɔː ‖ -ᵊr mjʊr
ˌLammermuir 'Hills
amond 'læm ənd
amont *(i)* 'læm ənt, *(ii)* lə 'mɒnt ‖ -'mɑːnt —*In AmE, (ii).*
amorna lə 'mɔːn ə ‖ -'mɔːrn ə
amp læmp **lamps** læmps
amp-black 'læmp blæk
Lampedusa ˌlæmp ɪ 'djuːz ə -ə-, →-'dʒuːz-, -'duːz- ‖ -ə 'duːz ə -'duːs- —*It* [lam pe 'duː za]
ampern 'læmp ən ‖ -ᵊrn **~s** z
Lampeter 'læmp ɪt ə -ət- ‖ -əţ ᵊr
amplight 'læmp laɪt
amplighter 'læmp ˌlaɪt ə ‖ -ˌlaɪţ ᵊr **~s** z
Lamplugh 'læmp luː -lə
ampoon ⁽ˌ⁾læm 'puːn **~ed** d **~ing** ɪŋ **~s** z
amp-post 'læmp pəʊst ‖ -poʊst **~s** s
amprey 'læmp ri **~s** z
ampshade 'læmp ʃeɪd **~s** z
LAN læn *or as* local area network
Lana 'lɑːn ə ‖ 'læn ə
Lanagan 'læn əg ən
Lanai, lanai lə 'naɪ lɑː-, -'nɑː i **~s** z
Lanark 'læn ək ‖ -ᵊrk **~shire** ʃə ʃɪə, ˌʃaɪ ə ‖ ʃᵊr ʃɪr

Lancashire 'læŋk ə ʃə -ʃɪə ‖ -ʃᵊr -ʃɪə
Lancaster 'læŋk əst ə 'læŋ kɑːst ə, -kæst- ‖ -ᵊr 'læŋ kæst ᵊr
Lancastrian læŋ 'kæs tri ən **~s** z
lance, Lance lɑːnᵗs §lænᵗs ‖ lænᵗs **lanced** lɑːnᵗst §lænᵗst ‖ lænᵗst **lances, Lance's** 'lɑːnᵗs ɪz §'lænᵗs-, -əz ‖ 'lænᵗs əz **lancing** 'lɑːnᵗs ɪŋ §'lænᵗs- ‖ 'lænᵗs ɪŋ
ˌlance 'corporal ◂
lancelet 'lɑːnᵗs lət §'lænᵗs-, -lɪt ‖ 'lænᵗs- **~s** s
Lancelot 'lɑːnᵗs ə lɒt §'lænᵗs-, -əl ət ‖ 'lænᵗs ə lɑːt -əl ət
lanceolate 'lɑːnᵗs i ə leɪt §'lænᵗs-, -lət, -lɪt ‖ 'lænᵗs-
lancer 'lɑːnᵗs ə §'lænᵗs- ‖ 'lænᵗs ᵊr **~s** z
lancet 'lɑːnᵗs ɪt §'lænᵗs-, -ət ‖ 'lænᵗs ət **~s** s
Lanchester 'lɑːntʃ ɪst ə 'læntʃ-, -əst-, §'læn ˌtʃest ə ‖ 'læn ˌtʃest ᵊr
Lancia *tdmk* 'lɑːnᵗs i ə §'lænᵗs- —*It* ['lan tʃa] **~s** z
lanci|nate 'lænᵗs ɪ |neɪt 'lɑːnᵗs-, -ə- **~nated** neɪt ɪd -əd ‖ neɪţ əd **~nates** neɪts **~nating** neɪt ɪŋ ‖ neɪţ ɪŋ
Lancing 'lɑːnᵗs ɪŋ §'lænᵗs- ‖ 'lænᵗs ɪŋ
Lancome, Lancôme *tdmk* 'lɒŋ kəʊm ‖ lɑːŋ 'koʊm lɔːŋ-
Lancs. læŋks
land, Land lænd **landed** 'lænd ɪd -əd **landing** 'lænd ɪŋ **lands** lændz
'land ˌagent; 'land crab; ˌlanded 'gentry; ˌLand's 'End
landau, L~ 'lænd ɔː -aʊ ‖ -aʊ -ɔː, -ɑː **~s** z
landaulet, landaulette ˌlænd ɔː 'let ‖ -ɑː- **~s** s
landbank 'lænd bæŋk →'læmb-
land-based 'lænd beɪst →'læmb-
lander, L~ 'lænd ə ‖ -ᵊr **~s** z
Landers 'lænd əz ‖ -ᵊrz
landfall 'lænd fɔːl ‖ -fɑːl **~s** z
landfill 'lænd fɪl **~s** z
land-form 'lænd fɔːm ‖ -fɔːrm **~s** z
land-hold|er/s 'lænd ˌhəʊld ə/z →ˌhɒʊld- ‖ -ˌhoʊld ᵊr/z **~ing** ɪŋ
landing 'lænd ɪŋ **~s** z
'landing craft; 'landing field; 'landing gear; 'landing net; 'landing stage; 'landing strip
Landis 'lænd ɪs §-əs
landlad|y 'lænd leɪd |i **~ies** iz
landless 'lænd ləs -lɪs
landline 'lænd laɪn **~s** z
landlocked 'lænd lɒkt ‖ -lɑːkt
landlord 'lænd lɔːd ‖ -lɔːrd **~ism** ˌɪz əm **~s** z
landlubber 'lænd ˌlʌb ə ‖ -ᵊr **~ly** li **~s** z
landmark 'lænd mɑːk →'læm- ‖ -mɑːrk **~s** s
landmass 'lænd mæs →'læm- **~es** ɪz əz
landmine 'lænd maɪn →'læm- **~s** z
Landor 'lænd ɔː -ə ‖ -ɔːr -ᵊr
landowner 'lænd ˌəʊn ə ‖ -ˌoʊn ᵊr **~s** z
landrail 'lænd reɪᵊl **~s** z
land rover, Land-Rover *tdmk* 'lænd ˌrəʊv ə ‖ -ˌroʊv ᵊr **~s** z
Landsat 'lænd sæt

L

landscap|e ˈlænd skeɪp **~ed** t **~er/s** ə/z ‖ ᵊr/z **~es** s **~ing** ɪŋ
ˌlandscape ˈgardening; **ˈlandscape mode**
Landseer ˈlænd sɪə ‖ -sɪr
landslide ˈlænd slaɪd **~s** z
landslip ˈlænd slɪp **~s** s
landward ˈlænd wəd ‖ -wᵊrd **~s** z
Landy ˈlænd i
lane, Lane leɪn **lanes** leɪnz
Lanfranc ˈlæn fræŋk
Lang læŋ
Langan ˈlæŋ ən
Langbaurgh ˈlæŋ bɑːf -bɑː ‖ -bɑːrf -bɑːr
Langdale ˈlæŋ deɪᵊl
Lange *(i)* læŋ *(ii)* ˈlɒŋ i ‖ ˈlɑːŋ i *-The NZ politician is (ii)*
Langer ˈlæŋ ə ‖ -ᵊr
Langerhans ˈlæŋ ə hænz -hænᵗs ‖ ˈlɑːŋ ᵊr hɑːnz -hɑːnᵗs *—Ger* [ˈlaŋ ɐ hanᵗs]
Langford ˈlæŋ fəd ‖ -fᵊrd
Langham ˈlæŋ əm
Langholm *place in Dumfries & Galloway* ˈlæŋ əm *—often called* -həʊm ‖ -hoʊm *by those not familiar with the name*
Langland ˈlæŋ lənd
langlauf ˈlæŋ laʊf ‖ ˈlɑːŋ- **~er/s** ə/z ‖ -ᵊr/z
Langley ˈlæŋ li
Langmuir ˈlæŋ mjʊə ‖ -mjʊr
Langobardic ˌlæŋ gəʊ ˈbɑːd ɪk ◂ ‖ -ə ˈbɑːrd-
langouste ˌlɒŋ ˈguːst ˈ· · ‖ ˌlɑːŋ- *—Fr* [lɑ̃ gust] **~s** s
langoustine ˌlɒŋ gu ˈstiːn ‖ ˌlɑːŋ- *—Fr* [lɑ̃ gu stin] **~s** z
langsyne, lang syne ₍ˌ₎læŋ ˈsaɪn
Langton ˈlæŋᵏt ən
Langtry ˈlæŋ tri
languag|e ˈlæŋ gwɪdʒ §ˈlæŋ wɪdʒ **~es** ɪz əz
ˈlanguage laˌboratory ‖ **- ˌlaboratory**; **ˈlanguage ˌteaching**
langue lɒŋg lɑːŋg, lɑːŋ, lɒ̃g ‖ lɑːŋg *—Fr* [lɑ̃ːg]
ˌlangue de ˈchat də ˈʃɑː *—Fr* [də ʃa]
Languedoc ˌlɒŋ gə ˈdɒk ˌlɑːŋ-, ˈ··· ‖ ˌlɑːŋ gə ˈdɑːk -ˈdɔːk, -ˈdoʊk *—Fr* [lɑ̃g dɔk]
languid ˈlæŋ gwɪd §-gwəd **~ly** li **~ness** nəs nɪs
languish, L~ ˈlæŋ gwɪʃ **~ed** t **~es** ɪz əz **~ing/ly** ɪŋ/li **~ment** mənt
languor ˈlæŋ gə ‖ -gᵊr
languorous ˈlæŋ gər əs **~ly** li **~ness** nəs nɪs
langur læŋ ˈgʊə lʌŋ-; ˈlæŋ gə ‖ -ˈgʊᵊr **~s** z
Lanigan ˈlæn ɪg ən -əg-
La Niña lə ˈniːn jə lɑː-, læ- ‖ lɑː- *—Sp* [la ˈni ɲa]
lank læŋk
Lankester ˈlæŋk ɪst ə -əst- ‖ -ᵊr
lank|ly ˈlæŋk |li **~ness** nəs nɪs
lank|y ˈlæŋk |i **~ier** i‿ə ‖ i‿ᵊr **~iest** i‿ɪst i‿əst **~ily** ɪ li əl i **~iness** i nəs i nɪs
lanner ˈlæn ə ‖ -ᵊr **~s** z
lanolin ˈlæn əl ɪn §-ən
lanoline ˈlæn ə liːn -lɪn
Lansbury ˈlænz bər‿i ‖ -ˌber i
Lansdown, Lansdowne ˈlænz daʊn
Lansing ˈlɑːnᵗs ɪŋ §ˈlænᵗs- ‖ ˈlænᵗs ɪŋ
lansker, L~ ˈlæn skə ‖ -skᵊr
lantern ˈlænt ən ‖ -ᵊrn **~s** z
lantern-jawed ˌlænt ən ˈdʒɔːd ◂ ‖ -ᵊrn- -ˈdʒɑːd
lanternslide ˈlænt ən slaɪd ‖ -ᵊrn- **~s** z
lanthanide ˈlænᵗθ ə naɪd **~s** z
lanthanum ˈlænᵗθ ən əm
lanyard ˈlæn jəd -jɑːd ‖ -jᵊrd **~s** z
Lanza ˈlænz ə ‖ ˈlɑːnz ə
Lanzarote ˌlænz ə ˈrɒt i ‖ ˌlɑːnᵗs ə ˈroʊt̬ i *—Sp* [lan θa ˈɾo te, -sa-]
Lao laʊ
Laocoon, Laocoön leɪ ˈɒk əʊ ɒn -ən ‖ -ˈɑːk oʊ ɑːn
Laodamia ˌleɪ əʊ də ˈmaɪ‿ə ‖ leɪ ˌɑːd ə-
Laodice|a ˌleɪ əʊ dɪ ˈsiː‿|ə -əd ə- ‖ -əd ə- leɪ ˌɑːd ə- **~an/s** ən/z
Laoighis, Laois liːʃ *—Irish* [ɫiːʃ]
Laomedon leɪ ˈɒm ɪd ən -əd- ‖ -ˈɑːm ə dɑːn
Laos laʊs laʊz; ˈlɑː ɒs ‖ ˈlɑː oʊs laʊs; ˈleɪ ɑːs
Laotian ˈlaʊʃ ᵊn ˈlaʊʃ i‿ən; leɪ ˈəʊʃ ᵊn, -ˈəʊʃ i‿ən ‖ leɪ ˈoʊʃ ᵊn ˈlaʊʃ ᵊn **~s** z
Lao-tse, Lao-tsze, Lao-tzu ˌlaʊ ˈtseɪ -ˈtsiː, -ˈtsuː *—Chi* Lǎo Zǐ [^{3}lɐu ^{3}tsɯ]
lap læp **lapped** læpt **lapping** ˈlæp ɪŋ **laps** læps
laparoscope ˈlæp ər‿ə skəʊp ‖ -skoʊp **~s** s
laparoscop|y ˌlæp ə ˈrɒsk əp |i ‖ -ˈrɑːsk- **~ies** iz
laparotom|y ˌlæp ə ˈrɒt əm |i ‖ -ˈrɑːt̬ əm |i **~ies** iz
La Paz lə ˈpæz ‖ lə ˈpɑːz *—AmSp* [la ˈpas]
lapdanc|er/s ˈlæp ˌdɑːnᵗs ə/z §-ˌdænᵗs- ‖ -ˌdænᵗs ər/z **~ing** ɪŋ
lapdog ˈlæp dɒg ‖ -dɔːg -dɑːg **~s** z
lapel lə ˈpel læ- **~s** z
lap-held ˈlæp held
Laphroaig lə ˈfrɔɪg lɑː-, læ-
lapidar|y ˈlæp ɪd‿ər |i ˈ·əd‿ ‖ -ə der |i **~ies** iz
lapilli lə ˈpɪl aɪ
lapis lazuli ˌlæp ɪs ˈlæz jʊl i §ˌ·əs-, -jəl i, -aɪ ‖ -ə liː -ˈlæʒ-
Lapith ˈlæp ɪθ **~s** s
Laplace lə ˈplɑːs læ-, lɑː-, -ˈplæs *—Fr* [la plas]
Lapland ˈlæp lænd -lənd
Laplander ˈlæp lænd ə -lənd- ‖ -ᵊr **~s** z
Lapotaire ˌlæp ɒ ˈteə -ə- ‖ -oʊ ˈteᵊr -ˈtæᵊr
Lapp læp
lappet ˈlæp ɪt §-ət **~s** s
Lappin ˈlæp ɪn §-ən
Lappish ˈlæp ɪʃ
Lapsang Souchong ˌlæp sæŋ suː ˈʃɒŋ -ˈtʃɒŋ ‖ ˌlɑːp sɑːŋ ˈsuː ʃɑːŋ
lapse læps *(= laps)* **lapsed** læpst **lapses** ˈlæps ɪz -əz **lapsing** ˈlæps ɪŋ
lapsus linguae ˌlæps əs ˈlɪŋ gwaɪ -gwiː
laptop ˈlæp tɒp ‖ -tɑːp **~s** s
Laputa lə ˈpjuːt ə ‖ -ˈpjuːt̬ ə
Laputan lə ˈpjuːt ᵊn **~s** z
lapwing ˈlæp wɪŋ **~s** z
Lar, lar lɑː ‖ lɑːr **lares** ˈlɑːr eɪz ˈleər iːz ‖ ˈlær iːz ˈler-
lars lɑːz ‖ lɑːrz

ara 'lɑːr ə

aramie 'lær əm i ‖ 'ler-

arbert 'lɑːb ət ‖ 'lɑːrb ᵊrt

rboard 'lɑːb əd 'lɑː bɔːd ‖ 'lɑːrb ᵊrd

rcenous 'lɑːs ən əs -ɪn- ‖ 'lɑːrs- **~ly** li

rcen|y 'lɑːs ən |i -ɪn- ‖ 'lɑːrs- **~ies** iz

rch lɑːtʃ ‖ lɑːrtʃ **larches** 'lɑːtʃ ɪz -əz ‖ 'lɑːrtʃ əz

rd lɑːd ‖ lɑːrd **larded** 'lɑːd ɪd -əd ‖ 'lɑːrd əd **larding** 'lɑːd ɪŋ ‖ 'lɑːrd ɪŋ **lards** lɑːdz ‖ lɑːrdz

rd-ass 'lɑːd ɑːs -æs ‖ 'lɑːrd æs **~es** ɪz əz

arder 'lɑːd ə ‖ 'lɑːrd ᵊr **~s** z

ardner 'lɑːd nə ‖ 'lɑːrd nᵊr

ardy 'lɑːd i ‖ 'lɑːrd i

'lardy cake

aredo lə 'reɪd əʊ ‖ -oʊ

ares 'lɑːr eɪz 'leər iːz ‖ 'lær iːz 'ler-

argactil, l~ *tdmk* lɑː 'gækt ɪl -ᵊl ‖ lɑːr-

arge, Large lɑːdʒ ‖ lɑːrdʒ **larger** 'lɑːdʒ ə ‖ 'lɑːrdʒ ᵊr **largest** 'lɑːdʒ ɪst -əst ‖ 'lɑːrdʒ-

arge-hearted ˌlɑːdʒ 'hɑːt ɪd ◂ -əd ‖ ˌlɑːrdʒ 'hɑːrṭ əd ◂ **~ness** nəs nɪs

argely 'lɑːdʒ li ‖ 'lɑːrdʒ li

arge-minded ˌlɑːdʒ 'maɪnd ɪd ◂ -əd ‖ ˌlɑːrdʒ- **~ness** nəs nɪs

argeness 'lɑːdʒ nəs -nɪs ‖ 'lɑːrdʒ-

arge-scale ˌlɑːdʒ 'skeɪᵊl ◂ ‖ ˌlɑːrdʒ-

argess, largesse (ˌ)lɑː 'dʒes -'ʒes; 'lɑːdʒ es ‖ (ˌ)lɑːr-

arghetto lɑː 'get əʊ ‖ lɑːr 'geṭ oʊ **~s** z

argish 'lɑːdʒ ɪʃ ‖ 'lɑːrdʒ-

argo 'lɑːg əʊ ‖ 'lɑːrg oʊ **~s** z

.args lɑːgz ‖ lɑːrgz

ariat 'lær i‿ət ‖ 'ler- **~s** s

.arisa, Larissa lə 'rɪs ə

.arium, l~ 'leər i‿əm ‖ 'ler- 'lær-

ark, Lark lɑːk ‖ lɑːrk **larked** lɑːkt ‖ lɑːrkt **larking** 'lɑːk ɪŋ ‖ 'lɑːrk ɪŋ **larks** lɑːks ‖ lɑːrks

Larkhall 'lɑːk hɔːl ‖ 'lɑːrk- -hɑːl

Larkin 'lɑːk ɪn §-ən ‖ 'lɑːrk-

larkspur 'lɑːk spɜː ‖ 'lɑːrk spɜː **~s** z

larky 'lɑːk i ‖ 'lɑːrk i

Larmor 'lɑːm ə -ɔː ‖ 'lɑːrm ᵊr -ɔːr

larn lɑːn ‖ lɑːrn **larned** lɑːnd ‖ lɑːrnd **larning** 'lɑːn ɪŋ ‖ 'lɑːrn ɪŋ **larns** lɑːnz ‖ lɑːrns *This is a non-standard variant of* learn, *sometimes used humorously.*

Larnaca 'lɑːn ək ə ‖ 'lɑːrn-

Larne lɑːn ‖ lɑːrn

Larousse læ 'ruːs ‖ lɑː- —*Fr* [la ʁus]

larrikin 'lær ɪk ɪn -ək-, §-ən ‖ 'ler- **~s** z

larrup 'lær əp ‖ 'ler- **~ed** t **~ing** ɪŋ **~s** s

Larry 'lær i ‖ 'ler-

Lars lɑːz ‖ lɑːrz lɑːrs —*Swedish* [laʂ]

ˌLars 'Porsena 'pɔːs ɪn ə -ən- ‖ 'pɔːrs-

LARSP lɑːsp ‖ lɑːrsp

larv|a 'lɑːv |ə ‖ 'lɑːrv |ə **~ae** iː eɪ **~al** ᵊl

Larwood 'lɑː wʊd ‖ 'lɑːr-

laryngal lə 'rɪŋ gᵊl læ- **~s** z

laryngeal lə 'rɪndʒ əl læ-, -'rɪndʒ i‿əl; ˌlær ɪn 'dʒiː‿əl ◂, -ən- ‖ ˌlær ən 'dʒiː əl, ˌler- **~s** z

laryngealis... —*see* **laryngealiz...**

laryngealization lə ˌrɪndʒ əl aɪ 'zeɪʃ ᵊn læ-, -əl ɪ- ‖ -əl ə-

laryngealiz|e lə 'rɪndʒ ə laɪz læ- **~ed** d **~es** ɪz əz **~ing** ɪŋ

laryngectomee ˌlær ɪn 'dʒekt ə miː ˌ·ən-, ˌ·ˌ·ˌ·'· ‖ ˌler- **~s** z

laryngectom|y ˌlær ɪn 'dʒekt əm |i ˌ·ən- ‖ ˌler- **~ies** iz

larynges læ 'rɪndʒ iːz lə-

laryngitis ˌlær ɪn 'dʒaɪt ɪs -ən-, §-əs ‖ -'dʒaɪṭ əs ˌler-

laryngo- *comb. form*
with stress-neutral suffix lə ¦rɪŋ gəʊ ‖ -goʊ — **laryngophantom** lə ˌrɪŋ gəʊ 'fænt əm ‖ -goʊ 'fænṭ-
with stress-imposing suffix ˌlær ɪŋ 'gɒ+ ‖ ˌlær ən 'gɑː+ ˌler-, →-ɪŋ- — **laryngopathy** ˌlær ɪŋ 'gɒp əθ i ‖ -ən 'gɑːp əθ i ˌler-, →ˌ·ɪŋ-

laryngograph, L~ *tdmk* lə 'rɪŋ gəʊ grɑːf læ-, -græf ‖ -gə græf **~s** s

laryngographic lə ˌrɪŋ gəʊ 'græf ɪk ◂ læ- ‖ -gə- **~ally** ᵊl‿i

laryngography ˌlær ɪŋ 'gɒg rəf i ‖ ˌlær ən 'gɑːg- ˌler-, →ˌ·ɪŋ-

laryngological lə ˌrɪŋ gə 'lɒdʒ ɪk ᵊl ◂ læ- ‖ -'lɑːdʒ- **~ly** ‿i

laryngolog|ist/s ˌlær ɪŋ 'gɒl ədʒ |ɪst/s §-əst/s ‖ ˌlær ən 'gɑːl- ˌler-, →ˌ·ɪŋ- **~y** i

laryngoscope lə 'rɪŋ gə skəʊp læ- ‖ -skoʊp **~s** s

laryngoscopic lə ˌrɪŋ gə 'skɒp ɪk ◂ læ- ‖ -'skɑːp ɪk ◂ **~ally** ᵊl‿i

laryngoscop|y ˌlær ɪŋ 'gɒsk əp |i ‖ ˌlær ən 'gɑːsk- ˌler-, →ˌ·ɪŋ- **~ies** iz

larynx 'lær ɪŋks ‖ 'ler- **~es** ɪz əz **larynges** læ 'rɪndʒ iːz lə-

Las *Spanish article* læs ‖ lɑːs —*usually unstressed. See also phrases with this word* —*Sp* [las]

lasagn|a lə 'zæn |jə -'sæn-, -'zɑːn-, -'sɑːn- ‖ -'zɑːn- —*It* [la 'zaɲ ɲa] **~e** jə jeɪ —*It* [-ɲe]

lascar, L~ 'læsk ə ‖ -ᵊr **~s** z

Lascaux 'læsk əʊ læ 'skəʊ ‖ lɑː 'skoʊ læ- —*Fr* [las ko]

Lascelles 'læs ᵊlz lə 'selz

lascivious lə 'sɪv i‿əs **~ly** li **~ness** nəs nɪs

Lasdun 'læzd ən

laser 'leɪz ə ‖ -ᵊr **~s** z

'laser ˌprinter

laserjet 'leɪz ə dʒet ‖ -ᵊr- **~s** s

lash læʃ **lashed** læʃt **lashes** 'læʃ ɪz -əz **lashing/s** 'læʃ ɪŋ/z

Lasham 'læʃ əm —*locally also* 'læs-

lash-up 'læʃ ʌp **~s** s

LASIK 'leɪz ɪk

Laski 'læsk i

Las Palmas læs 'pæl məs ˌ·-, -'pɑːl- ‖ lɑːs 'pɑːlm əs —*Sp* [las 'pal mas]

lass, Lass læs **lasses** 'læs ɪz -əz

Lassa 'læs ə 'lɑːs-
ˌ**Lassa 'fever**
Lassen 'læs ᵊn
lassi 'læs i 'lʌs- ‖ lɑː 'siː —*Hindi* [lə si]
lassie, L~ 'læs i **~s** z
lassitude 'læs ɪ tjuːd -ə-, →-tʃuːd ‖ -tuːd -tjuːd
lasso lə 'suː læ-; 'læs əʊ ‖ 'læs oʊ læ 'suː *(*)* **~ed** d **~ing** ɪŋ **~es, ~s** z
last, Last lɑːst §læst ‖ læst **lasted** 'lɑːst ɪd §'læst-, -əd ‖ 'læst əd **lasting** 'lɑːst ɪŋ §'læst- ‖ 'læst ɪŋ **lasts** lɑːsts §læsts ‖ læsts
ˌ**last 'judgment**; ˌ**last 'minute**; **'last name,** ˌ·'·; ˌ**last 'night**; ˌ**last 'post**; ˌ**last 'straw**; ˌ**last 'week**; ˌ**last 'word**
last-ditch ˌlɑːst 'dɪtʃ ◂ §ˌlæst- ‖ ˌlæst-
last-gasp ˌlɑːst'gɑːsp ◂ §ˌlæst-, §-'gæsp ‖ ˌlæst 'gæsp ◂
lasting 'lɑːst ɪŋ §'læst- ‖ 'læst ɪŋ **~ly** li **~ness** nəs nɪs
lastly 'lɑːst li §'læst- ‖ 'læst li
last-minute ˌlɑːst 'mɪn ɪt ◂ §-ət ‖ ˌlæst-
Las Vegas læs 'veɪg əs ˌ·- ‖ lɑːs-
lat læt **lats** læts
Latakia ˌlæt ə 'kiːˌə ‖ ˌlæţ- ˌlɑːţ-
Latasha lə 'tæʃ ə
latch lætʃ **latched** lætʃt **latches** 'lætʃ ɪz -əz **latching** 'lætʃ ɪŋ
latchet 'lætʃ ɪt -ət **~s** s
latchkey 'lætʃ kiː **~s** z
'latchkey child
late leɪt **later** 'leɪt ə ‖ 'leɪţ ᵊr **latest** 'leɪt ɪst -əst ‖ 'leɪţ əst
late-breaking 'leɪt ˌbreɪk ɪŋ
latecomer 'leɪt ˌkʌm ə ‖ -ᵊr **~s** z
lateen lə 'tiːn **~s** z
lately 'leɪt li
latenc|y 'leɪt ᵊnᵗs |i **~ies** iz
lateness 'leɪt nəs -nɪs **~es** ɪz əz
late-night 'leɪt naɪt
latent 'leɪt ᵊnt **~ly** li
ˌ**latent 'heat**
later 'leɪt ə ‖ 'leɪţ ᵊr
lateral 'lætˌᵊr əl ‖ 'læţ ər əl →'lætr əl **~ly** i **~s** z
ˌ**lateral 'fricative**; ˌ**lateral 'thinking**
laterality ˌlæt ə 'ræl ət i -ɪt i ‖ ˌlæţ ə 'ræl əţ i
Lateran 'læt ər ən ‖ 'læţ-
laterite 'læt ə raɪt ‖ 'læţ-
latest 'leɪt ɪst -əst ‖ 'leɪţ-
latex 'leɪt eks **~es** ɪz əz
LaTeX, LaTEX *computing* 'leɪ tek
lath lɑːθ læθ ‖ læθ **laths** lɑːθs lɑːðz; læθs, læðz ‖ læðz læθs
Latham *(i)* 'leɪð əm, *(ii)* 'leɪθ-
lathe leɪð **lathes** leɪðz
lath|er 'lɑːð |ə 'læð- ‖ 'læð |ᵊr — *Preference poll, BrE:* 'lɑːð- *72% (southerners 88%),* 'læð- *28% (southerners 12%).* **~ered** əd ‖ ᵊrd **~ering** ər ˌɪŋ **~ers** əz ‖ ᵊrz
lathery 'lɑːð ər i 'læð- ‖ 'læð-
lathi 'lɑːt i —*Hindi* [laː ʈʰi] **~s** z
Lathom *(i)* 'leɪð əm, *(ii)* 'leɪθ-
Latimer 'læt ɪm ə -əm- ‖ 'læţ əm ᵊr

LATHER

Latin 'læt ɪn §-ᵊn ‖ 'læt ᵊn **~s** z
ˌ**Latin A'merican**◂
Latina læ 'tiːn ə lə- ‖ lɑː-, -ɑː **~s** z s
Latinate 'læt ɪ neɪt §-ə- ‖ ᵊn eɪt
latinis... —*see* **latiniz...**
latin|ism 'læt ɪn |ˌɪz əm §-ᵊn- ‖ 'læt ᵊn- **~ist/s** ɪst/s §əst/s ‖ əst/s
latinization ˌlæt ɪn aɪ 'zeɪʃ ᵊn §ˌ·ᵊn-, -ɪ'·- ‖ ˌlæt ᵊn ə-
latiniz|e 'læt ɪ naɪz §-ᵊn aɪz ‖ -ᵊn aɪz **~ed** d **~es** ɪz əz **~ing** ɪŋ
Latino læ 'tiːn əʊ lə- ‖ -oʊ **~s** z s
latish 'leɪt ɪʃ ‖ 'leɪţ ɪʃ
latitude 'læt ɪ tjuːd -ə-, →-tʃuːd ‖ 'læţ ə tuːd -tjuːd **~s** z
latitudinal ˌlæt ɪ 'tjuːd ɪn ᵊl ◂ ˌ·ə-, →-'tʃuːd-, -ᵊnˌəl ‖ ˌlæţ ə 'tuːd ᵊnˌəl ◂ -'tjuːd-
latitudinarian ˌlæt ɪ ˌtjuːd ɪ 'neər i ən ˌ·ə-, →-ˌtʃuːd-, -ˌ·ə- ‖ ˌlæţ ə ˌtuːd ᵊn 'er i ən -ˌtjuːd **~s** z
Latium 'leɪʃ iˌəm
latke 'lɑːt kə **~s** z
Latona lə 'təʊn ə ‖ -'toʊn ə
Latoya lə 'tɔɪ ə
latria lə 'traɪˌə
latrine lə 'triːn **~s** z
Latrobe, La Trobe lə 'trəʊb ‖ -'troʊb
-latry *stress-imposing* lətr i — **hagiolatry** ˌhæg i 'ɒl ətr i ˌheɪdʒ- ‖ -'ɑːl-
latte 'læt eɪ 'lɑːt- ‖ 'lɑːt eɪ **~s** z —*It* ['lat te]
latter 'læt ə ‖ 'læţ ᵊr
latter-day ˌlæt ə 'deɪ◂ ‖ ˌlæţ ᵊr-
ˌ**latter-day 'hero**
latterly 'læt ə li -ᵊl i ‖ 'læţ ᵊr li
lattic|e 'læt ɪs -əs ‖ 'læţ əs **~ed** t **~es** ɪz əz **~ework** wɜːk ‖ wɜːk **~ing** ɪŋ
Lattimore 'læt ɪ mɔː -ə- ‖ 'læţ ə mɔːr -moʊr
Latvi|a 'læt viˌ|ə ‖ 'lɑːt- **~an/s** ən/z
laud, Laud lɔːd ‖ lɑːd **lauded** 'lɔːd ɪd -əd ‖ 'lɑːd- **lauding** 'lɔːd ɪŋ ‖ 'lɑːd- **lauds, Lauds** lɔːdz ‖ lɑːdz
Lauda 'laʊd ə —*Ger* ['lau da]
laudability ˌlɔːd ə 'bɪl ət i -ɪt i ‖ -əţ i ˌlɑːd-
laudab|le 'lɔːd əb |ᵊl ‖ 'lɑːd- **~ly** li
laudanum 'lɔːd ᵊnˌəm 'lɒd- ‖ 'lɑːd-
laudatory 'lɔːd ət ˌər i ‖ -ə tɔːr i 'lɑːd-, -toʊri
Lauder 'lɔːd ə ‖ -ᵊr 'lɑːd-
Lauderdale 'lɔːd ə deɪᵊl ‖ -ᵊr- 'lɑːd-
laugh lɑːf §læf ‖ læf **laughed** lɑːft §læft ‖ læft **laughing** 'lɑːf ɪŋ §'læf- ‖ 'læf ɪŋ **laughs** lɑːfs §læfs ‖ læfs
'laughing gas; ˌ**laughing 'jackass**
laughab|le 'lɑːf əb |ᵊl §'læf- ‖ 'læf- **~ly** li

Laugharne lɑːn ‖ lɑːrn
laughingly ˈlɑːf ɪŋ li §ˈlæf- ‖ ˈlæf ɪŋ li
laughingstock ˈlɑːf ɪŋ stɒk ˈ§læf- ‖ ˈlæf ɪŋ stɑːk
laughter ˈlɑːft ə §ˈlæft- ‖ ˈlæft ᵊr
Laughton ˈlɔːt ᵊn ‖ ˈlɑːt-
Launceston ˈlɔːnᵗst ən ˈlɑːnᵗst-; ˈlɑːnᵗs ᵊn, ˈlɔːnᵗs- ‖ ˈlɔːnᵗs əst ən ˈlɑːnᵗs- *-but in Tasmania,* ˈlɒnᵗs əst ən ‖ ˈlɑːnᵗs-
launch lɔːntʃ ‖ lɑːntʃ *—In RP formerly also* ˈlɑːntʃ. **launched** lɔːntʃt ‖ lɑːntʃt **launcher/s** ˈlɔːntʃ ə/z ‖ -ᵊr/z ˈlɑːntʃ- **launches** ˈlɔːntʃ ɪz -əz ‖ ˈlɑːntʃ- **launching** ˈlɔːntʃ ɪŋ ‖ ˈlɑːntʃ- **ˈlaunching pad, ˈlaunch pad**; **ˈlaunch ˌvehicle**
laund|er ˈlɔːnd| ə ‖ -ᵊr ˈlɑːnd|- **~ered** əd ‖ ᵊrd **~ering** ər ɪŋ **~ers** əz ‖ ᵊrz
launderette, L~ *tdmk* ˌlɔːnd ə ˈret ˌlɔːn ˈdret ‖ ˌlɑːnd- **~s** s
laundress ˈlɔːndr es -əs, -ɪs ‖ ˈlɑːndr- **~es** ɪz əz
laundrette ˌlɔːn ˈdret ‖ ˌlɑːn- **~s** s
laundromat, L~ *tdmk* ˈlɔːndr ə mæt ‖ ˈlɑːndr- **~s** s
laundr|y ˈlɔːndr |i ‖ ˈlɑːndr- **~ies** iz **ˈlaundry ˌbasket**
Lauper ˈlaʊp ə ‖ -ᵊr
Laura ˈlɔːr ə
lauraceous lɒ ˈreɪʃ əs lɔː- ‖ lɔː- lɑː-
Laurasia lɔː ˈreɪʃ ə -ˈreɪʒ-, -ˈreɪʒ i‿ə ‖ lɔː ˈreɪʒ ə lɑː-, -ˈreɪʃ-
Laurasian lɔː ˈreɪʃ ᵊn -ˈreɪʒ-, -ˈreɪʒ i‿ən ‖ lɔː ˈreɪʒ ᵊn lɑː-, -ˈreɪʃ-
laureate ˈlɔːr i‿ət ˈlɒr-, -ɪt ‖ ˈlɑːr- **~s** s **~ship** ʃɪp
laurel, L~ ˈlɒr əl ‖ ˈlɔːr- ˈlɑːr- **~s** z
Lauren ˈlɔːr ən ˈlɒr- ‖ ˈlɑːr-
Laurence ˈlɒr ənᵗs ‖ ˈlɔːr- ˈlɑːr-
Laurentian lɒ ˈrenᵗʃ ᵊn lɔː- ‖ lɔː- lɑː- **~s** z
Lauretta lə ˈret ə lɔː- ‖ -ˈreţ ə
lauric ˈlɔːr ɪk ˈlɒr- ‖ ˈlɑːr-
Laurie ˈlɒr i ‖ ˈlɔːr i
Laurier ˈlɒr i‿ə -eɪ ‖ ˈlɔːr i‿ᵊr ˌlɔːr i ˈeɪ
Lauriston ˈlɒr ɪst ən -əst- ‖ ˈlɔːr- ˈlɑːr-
laurustinus ˌlɒr ə ˈstaɪn əs ˌlɔːr- ‖ ˌlɔːr-
lauryl ˈlɒr ɪl ˈlɔːr-, -əl ‖ ˈlɔːr əl ˈlɑːr-
Lausanne ləʊ ˈzæn ‖ loʊ- *—Fr* [lo zan, lɔ-]
lav læv **lavs** lævz
lava ˈlɑːv ə
lavabo lə ˈvɑːb əʊ -ˈveɪb- ‖ -oʊ **~es** z
lavage ˈlæv ɪdʒ -ɑːʒ; læ ˈvɑːʒ ‖ lə ˈvɑːʒ ˈlæv ɪdʒ
Laval lə ˈvæl læ- *—Fr* [la val]
lavaliere lə ˌvæl i ˈeə ‖ ˌlæv ə ˈlɪᵊr ˌlɑːv- **~s** z
lavatorial ˌlæv ə ˈtɔːr i‿əl ◂ ‖ -ˈtoʊr-
lavator|y ˈlæv ət‿ər |i ‖ -ə tɔːr |i -toʊr i **~ies** iz
lave leɪv **laved** leɪvd **laves** leɪvz **laving** ˈleɪv ɪŋ
lavender, L~ ˈlæv ənd ə -ɪnd- ‖ -ᵊr **~s** z
Lavengro lə ˈveŋ grəʊ ‖ -groʊ
Lavenham ˈlæv ən‿əm
laver *'basin'* ˈleɪv ə ‖ -ᵊr **~s** z
laver *'seaweed'* ˈlɑːv ə ‖ -ᵊr ˈleɪv-
Laver *family name* ˈleɪv ə ‖ -ᵊr
Lavern, Laverne lə ˈvɜːn ‖ -ˈvɜːn
Lavers ˈleɪv əz ‖ -ᵊrz
Lavinia lə ˈvɪn i‿ə
lavish ˈlæv ɪʃ **~ed** t **~es** ɪz əz **~ing** ɪŋ **~ly** li **~ness** nəs nɪs
Lavoisier lə ˈvwɑːz i eɪ læ-, -ˈvwæz- ‖ ˌlæv wɑː zi ˈeɪ *—Fr* [la vwa zje]
lavv|y ˈlæv |i **~ies** iz
law, Law lɔː ‖ lɑː **laws** lɔːz ‖ lɑːz
law-abiding ˈlɔːʳ ə ˌbaɪd ɪŋ ‖ ˈlɔː- ˈlɑː-
law-breaker ˈlɔː ˌbreɪk ə ‖ -ᵊr ˈlɑː- **~s** z
Lawes lɔːz ‖ lɑːz
Lawford ˈlɔː fəd ‖ -fᵊrd ˈlɑː-
lawful ˈlɔː fᵊl -fʊl ‖ ˈlɑː- **~ly** i **~ness** nəs nɪs
Lawler ˈlɔːl ə ‖ -ᵊr ˈlɑːl-
lawless, L~ ˈlɔː ləs -lɪs ‖ ˈlɑː- **~ly** li **~ness** nəs nɪs
Lawley ˈlɔː li ‖ ˈlɑː-
lawmaker ˈlɔː meɪk ə ‖ -ᵊr ˈlɑː- **~s** z
law|man ˈlɔː| mæn ‖ ˈlɑː- **~men** men
lawn lɔːn ‖ lɑːn **lawns** lɔːnz ‖ lɑːnz **ˈlawn ˌparty**; **ˌlawn ˈtennis** ‖ ˈ· ˌ·
lawnmower ˈlɔːn ˌməʊ ə ‖ -ˌmoʊ ᵊr ˈlɑːn- **~s** z
Lawrance, Lawrence ˈlɒr ənᵗs ‖ ˈlɔːr- ˈlɑːr-
lawrencium lə ˈrenᵗs i‿əm lɔː-, lɒ- ‖ lɔː- lɑː-
Lawrentian lɒ ˈrenᵗʃ ᵊn lɔː-, -ˈrenᵗʃ i‿ən ‖ lɔː- lɑː- **~s** z
Lawrie, Lawry ˈlɒr i ‖ ˈlɔːr i ˈlɑːr i
Lawson ˈlɔːs ᵊn ‖ ˈlɑːs-
lawsuit ˈlɔː suːt -sjuːt ‖ ˈlɑː- **~s** s
Lawton ˈlɔːt ᵊn ‖ ˈlɑːt-

LAWYER

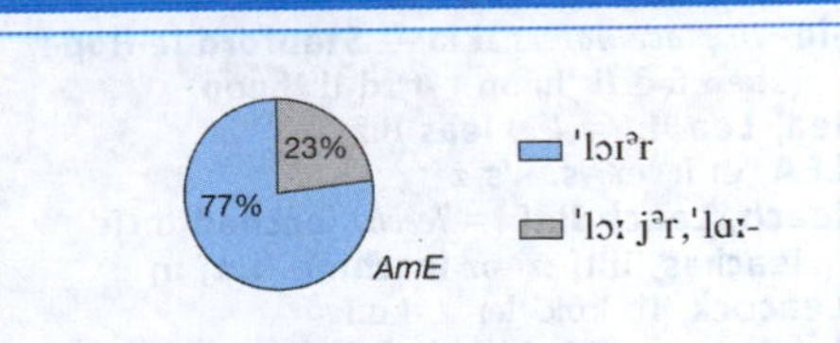

lawyer ˈlɔː jə ˈlɔɪ ə ‖ ˈlɔɪ ᵊr ˈlɔː jᵊr, ˈlɑː- **~s** z *— Preference poll, AmE:* ˈlɔɪ ᵊr *77%,* ˈlɔː jᵊr, ˈlɑː jᵊr *23%.*
lax læks **laxed** lækst **laxer** ˈlæks ə ‖ -ᵊr **laxes** ˈlæks ɪz -əz **laxest** ˈlæks ɪst -əst **laxing** ˈlæks ɪŋ
Laxalt ˈlæks ɔːlt ‖ -ɑːlt
laxative ˈlæks ət ɪv ‖ -əţ ɪv **~s** z
Laxey ˈlæks i
laxity ˈlæks ət i -ɪt- ‖ -əţ i
lax|ly ˈlæks |li **~ness** nəs nɪs
lay leɪ **laid** leɪd **laying** ˈleɪ ɪŋ **lays** leɪz **ˌlay ˈbrother**; **ˌlay ˈfigure** ‖ ˈ· ˌ· ·; **ˌlay ˈreader**; **ˌlay ˈsister**
layabout ˈleɪ ə ˌbaʊt **~s** s
layaway ˈleɪ əˌweɪ
lay-by ˈleɪ baɪ **~s** z
Laycock ˈleɪ kɒk ‖ -kɑːk
layer ˈleɪ ə leə ‖ -ᵊr leᵊr **~ed** d **layering** ˈleɪ ər ɪŋ ˈleər ɪŋ ‖ ˈler ɪŋ **~s** z **ˈlayer cake**
layette leɪ ˈet **~s** s

lay|man 'leɪ |mən **~men** mən
lay-off 'leɪ ɒf -ɔːf ‖ -ɔːf -ɑːf **~s** s
layout 'leɪ aʊt **~s** s
layover 'leɪ ˌəʊv ə ‖ -ˌoʊv ᵊr **~s** z
layperson 'leɪ ˌpɜːs ᵊn ‖ -ˌpɜ˞ːs- **~s** z
layshaft 'leɪ ʃɑːft §-ʃæft ‖ -ʃæft **~s** s
Layton 'leɪt ᵊn
lay-up 'leɪ ʌp **~s** s
lay|woman 'leɪ ˌwʊm ən **~women** ˌwɪm ɪn §-ən
Lazard 'læz ɑːd ‖ lə 'zɑːrd **~s** z
lazaretto ˌlæz ə 'ret əʊ ‖ -'ret̬ oʊ **~s** z
Lazarus 'læz ər‿əs
laze leɪz *(= lays)* **lazed** leɪzd **lazes** 'leɪz ɪz -əz **lazing** 'leɪz ɪŋ
Lazenby 'leɪz ᵊn bi →-ᵊm-
lazi... —*see* **lazy**
Lazio 'læts i əʊ ‖ 'lɑːts i oʊ —*It* ['lat tsjo]
Lazonby 'leɪz ᵊn bi →-ᵊm-
lazulite 'læz ju laɪt 'læʒ-, -jə- ‖ 'læʒ ə- (*)
laz|y 'leɪz |i **~ier** i‿ə ‖ i‿ᵊr **~iest** i‿ɪst i‿əst **~ily** ɪ li əl i **~iness** i nəs i nɪs
lazybones 'leɪz i bəʊnz ‖ -boʊnz
lb *sing.* paʊnd **lb** *pl* paʊndz **lbs** paʊndz
lbw ˌel biː 'dʌb ᵊl ju
LCD ˌel siː 'diː **~s, ~'s** z
LCM ˌel siː 'em **~s, ~'s** z
LDC ˌel diː 'siː **~s, ~'s** z
L-dopa, L-Dopa ˌel 'dəʊp ə ‖ -'doʊp ə
L-driver 'el ˌdraɪv ə ‖ -ᵊr **~s** z
Le, le *in family names* lə —*See also phrases with this word—and note occasional exceptions, e.g.* Le Fanu
-le- *in place names* li lə — **Stanford-le-Hope** ˌstæn fəd li 'həʊp ‖ -fᵊrd li 'hoʊp
lea, Lea liː *(= lee)* **leas** liːz
LEA ˌel iː 'eɪ **~s, ~'s** z
leach, Leach liːtʃ *(= leech)* **leached** liːtʃt **leaches** 'liːtʃ ɪz -əz **leaching** 'liːtʃ ɪŋ
Leacock 'liː kɒk 'leɪ- ‖ -kɑːk
lead *n 'metal'* led **leaded** 'led ɪd -əd **leading** 'led ɪŋ **leads** ledz
lead *v; n 'guiding, first place/act/actor, leash, cord, flex'* liːd **leading** 'liːd ɪŋ **leads** liːdz **led** led
Leadbetter 'led ˌbet ə →'leb-; ˌ·'·· ‖ -ˌbet̬ ᵊr
Leadbitter 'led ˌbɪt ə →'leb- ‖ -ˌbɪt̬ ᵊr
leaded 'led ɪd -əd
leaden 'led ᵊn **~ly** li **~ness** nəs nɪs
Leadenhall 'led ᵊn hɔːl ‖ -hɑːl
leader 'liːd ə ‖ -ᵊr **~s** z
leadership 'liːd ə ʃɪp ‖ -ᵊr- **~s** s
lead-free ˌled 'friː ◂
lead-in 'liːd ɪn ˌ·'· **~s** z
leading *adj 'main', 'guiding'* 'liːd ɪŋ **~ly** li ˌ**leading 'article**; ˌ**leading 'edge**; ˌ**leading 'lady**; ˌ**leading 'light**; ˌ**leading 'question**
leading *n 'metal', 'space between rows of type'* 'led ɪŋ
lead-off 'liːd ɒf -ɔːf ‖ -ɔːf -ɑːf
lead poisoning ˌled 'pɔɪz ᵊn‿ɪŋ
lead time 'liːd taɪm **~s** z
lead-up 'liːd ʌp **~s** s

leaf liːf **leafed** liːft **leafing** 'liːf ɪŋ **leafs** liːfs **leaves** liːvz **'leaf mould**
leafage 'liːf ɪdʒ
leafi... —*see* **leafy**
leafless 'liːf ləs -lɪs **~ness** nəs nɪs
leaf|let 'liːf |lət -lɪt **~leted, ~letted** lət ɪd lɪt-, -əd ‖ lət̬ əd **~leting, ~letting** lət ɪŋ lɪt- ‖ lət̬ ɪŋ **~lets** ləts lɪts ‖ ləts
leaf|y 'liːf |i **~ier** i‿ə ‖ i‿ᵊr **~iest** i‿ɪst i‿əst **~iness** i nəs i nɪs
Leagrave 'liː greɪv
league liːg —*In AmE there is also a non-standard pronunciation* lɪg. **leagued** liːgd **leagues** liːgz **leaguing** 'liːg ɪŋ
Leah liː‿ə
Leahy 'liː hi 'leɪ-, -i
leak liːk *(= leek)* **leaked** liːkt **leaking** 'liːk ɪŋ **leaks** liːks
leakag|e 'liːk ɪdʒ **~es** ɪz əz
Leakey 'liːk i
leak|y 'liːk |i **~ier** i‿ə ‖ i‿ᵊr **~iest** i‿ɪst i‿əst **~iness** i nəs i nɪs
Leamington *(i)* 'lem ɪŋ tən, *(ii)* 'liːm- —*The place in England is (i); that in Canada, (ii).* ˌ**Leamington 'Spa**
lean, Lean liːn **leaned** liːnd lent **leaning** 'liːn ɪŋ **leans** liːnz **leant** lent
Leander li 'ænd ə ‖ -ᵊr
Leane liːn
leaned liːnd lent
LeAnn, Leanne li 'æn
leanness 'liːn nəs -nɪs
leant lent *(= lent)*
lean-to 'liːn tuː ˌ·'· **~s** z
leap liːp **leaped** lept liːpt ‖ liːpt **leaping** 'liːp ɪŋ **leaps** liːps **leapt** lept **'leap year**
leaped lept liːpt ‖ liːpt
leapfrog 'liːp frɒg ‖ -frɔːg -frɑːg **~ged** d **~ging** ɪŋ **~s** z
leapt lept
Lear lɪə ‖ lɪᵊr
Learjet *tdmk* 'lɪə dʒet ‖ 'lɪr- **~s** s
learn lɜːn ‖ lɜ˞ːn **learned** lɜːnd lɜːnt ‖ lɜ˞ːnd **learning** 'lɜːn ɪŋ ‖ 'lɜ˞ːn ɪŋ **learns** lɜːnz ‖ lɜ˞ːnz **learnt** lɜːnt ‖ lɜ˞ːnt
learned *past & pp of* learn; *adj 'acquired by experience'* lɜːnd lɜːnt ‖ lɜ˞ːnd
learned *adj 'scholarly', 'well-informed'* 'lɜːn ɪd -əd ‖ 'lɜ˞ːn əd **~ly** li **~ness** nəs nɪs
learner 'lɜːn ə ‖ 'lɜ˞ːn ᵊr **~s** z ˌ**learner 'driver**
learnt lɜːnt ‖ lɜ˞ːnt
Leary 'lɪər i ‖ 'lɪr i
leasable 'liːs əb ᵊl
lease liːs **leased** liːst **leases** 'liːs ɪz -əz **leasing** 'liːs ɪŋ
leaseback 'liːs bæk **~s** s
leasehold 'liːs həʊld →-hɒʊld ‖ -hoʊld **~er/s** ə/z ‖ ᵊr/z **~s** z
leash liːʃ **leashed** liːʃt **leashes** 'liːʃ ɪz -əz **leashing** 'liːʃ ɪŋ

Leason ˈliːs ᵊn
least liːst
leastways ˈliːst weɪz
leastwise ˈliːst waɪz
leat liːt **leats** liːts
Leatham *(i)* ˈliːθ əm, *(ii)* ˈliːð-
leather, L~ ˈleð ə ‖ -ᵊr **~ed** d **leathering** ˈleð ər‿ɪŋ **~s** z
leatherback ˈleð ə bæk ‖ -ᵊr- **~s** s
leatherette, L~ *tdmk* ˌleð ə ˈret ◂
Leatherhead ˈleð ə hed ‖ -ᵊr-
leatherjacket ˈleð ə ˌdʒæk ɪt §-ət ‖ -ᵊr- **~s** s
leatherneck ˈleð ə nek ‖ -ᵊr- **~s** s
leather|y ˈleð ər‿|i **~iness** i nəs i nɪs
leave liːv **leaves** liːvz **leaving** ˈliːv ɪŋ **left** left **ˈleave ˌtaking**
leaved liːvd
leaven ˈlev ᵊn **~ed** d **~ing** ‿ɪŋ **~s** z
Leavenworth ˈlev ᵊn wɜːθ -wəθ ‖ -wɜːθ
leaves liːvz
leave-taking ˈliːv ˌteɪk ɪŋ
leaving ˈliːv ɪŋ **~s** z
Leavis ˈliːv ɪs -əs
Leavisite ˈliːv ɪ saɪt -ə- **~s** s
Leavitt ˈlev ɪt §-ət
Lebanese ˌleb ə ˈniːz ◂ ‖ -ˈniːs ◂
Lebanon ˈleb ən ən -ə nɒn ‖ -ə nɑːn
lebensraum, L~ ˈleɪb ənz raʊm →-mz-, -ənᵗs- —*Ger* [ˈleː bəns ʁaum, -bms-]
Le Bon lə ˈbɒn ‖ -ˈbɑːn -ˈbɔːn
Lebon ˈliːb ən
Lebowa lə ˈbəʊ ə ‖ -ˈboʊ ə
Lec *tdmk* lek
Le Carré lə ˈkær eɪ ‖ lə kɑː ˈreɪ
leccy *'electricity'* ˈlek i
lech letʃ **leched** letʃt **leches** ˈletʃ ɪz -əz **leching** ˈletʃ ɪŋ
lecher ˈletʃ ə ‖ -ᵊr **~s** z
lecherous ˈletʃ ər‿əs **~ly** li **~ness** nəs nɪs
lecher|y ˈletʃ ər |i **~ies** iz
Lechlade ˈletʃ leɪd
Lechmere ˈletʃ mɪə ˈleʃ- ‖ -mɪr
lecithin ˈles ɪθ ɪn -əθ-, -ən
Leckhampton ˈlek ˌhæmᵖt ən
Lecky ˈlek i
Leconfield ˈlek ən fiːᵊld
Le Corbusier lə kɔː ˈbuːz i eɪ -ˈbjuːz- ‖ lə ˌkɔːrb uːz ˈjeɪ -uːs- —*Fr* [lə kɔʁ by zje]
Le Creuset *tdmk* lə ˈkruːz eɪ ‖ lə kruː ˈzeɪ —*Fr* [lə kʁø zɛ]
lect lekt **lects** lekts
lectal ˈlekt ᵊl
lectern ˈlekt ən -ɜːn ‖ -ᵊrn **~s** z
lectionar|y ˈlek ʃᵊn ər‿|i -ʃᵊn‿ər |i ‖ -ʃə ner |i **~ies** iz
lector ˈlekt ɔː ‖ -ɔːr -ᵊr **~s** z
lecture ˈlek tʃə -ʃə ‖ -tʃᵊr -ʃᵊr **~d** d **~s** z **lecturing** ˈlek tʃər‿ɪŋ -ʃər‿ɪŋ
lecturer ˈlek tʃər‿ə -ʃər‿ə ‖ -tʃᵊr ər -ʃᵊr‿ər **~s** z
lectureship ˈlek tʃə ʃɪp -ʃə- ‖ -tʃᵊr- -ʃᵊr- **~s** s
led led
LED ˌel iː ˈdiː **~s, ~'s** z
Leda ˈliːd ə ˈleɪd ə
Ledbury ˈled bər‿i →ˈleb- ‖ -ˌber i
lederhosen ˈleɪd ə ˌhəʊz ᵊn ‖ -ᵊr ˌhoʊz ᵊn —*Ger* [ˈleː dɐ ˌhoːz ᵊn]
Ledgard ˈledʒ ɑːd ‖ -ɑːrd
ledge ledʒ **ledged** ledʒd **ledges** ˈledʒ ɪz -əz
ledger, L~ ˈledʒ ə ‖ -ᵊr **~s** z
lee, Lee liː **lees, Lee's** liːz **ˌlee ˈshore** ‖ ˈ· ·; **ˌlee ˈtide** ‖ ˈ· ·
leech, Leech liːtʃ **leeched** liːtʃt **leeches** ˈliːtʃ ɪz -əz **leeching** ˈliːtʃ ɪŋ
Leeds liːdz
Lee-Enfield ˌliː ˈen fiːᵊld
leek, Leek liːk **leeks** liːks
Leeming ˈliːm ɪŋ
leer lɪə ‖ lɪᵊr **leered** lɪəd ‖ lɪᵊrd **leering** ˈlɪər ɪŋ ‖ ˈlɪr ɪŋ **leers** lɪəz ‖ lɪᵊrz
leer|y ˈlɪər |i ‖ ˈlɪr |i **~ier** i‿ə ‖ i‿ᵊr **~iest** i‿ɪst i‿əst **~ily** əl i ɪ li **~iness** i nəs i nɪs
lees, Lees liːz
Leeson ˈliːs ᵊn
leet liːt **leets** liːts
leeward, L~ ˈliː wəd ‖ -wᵊrd —*also nautical* ˈluː‿əd, ˈljuː‿ ‖ ‿ᵊrd **~s** z **ˈLeeward ˌIslands** ‖ ˌ· · ˈ· ·
leeway ˈliː weɪ
Lefanu, Le Fanu *(i)* ˈlef ə njuː -nuː ‖ -nuː -njuː, *(ii)* lə ˈfɑːn uː
Lefevre lə ˈfiːv ə ‖ -ᵊr —*but as a French name,* lə ˈfev —*Fr* Lefebvre, Lefèvre [lə fɛːvʁ]
left left **ˌleft ˈluggage ˌoffice**; **ˌleft ˈwing**◂
left-click ˌleftˈklɪk ◂ **~ed** t **~ing** ɪŋ **~s** s
left-hand ˌleft ˈhænd ◂ **ˌleft-hand ˈside**
left-handed ˌleft ˈhænd ɪd ◂ -əd **~ly** li **~ness** nəs nɪs
left-hander ˌleft ˈhænd ə ‖ -ᵊr **~s** z
leftie... —*see* **lefty**
leftist ˈleft ɪst §-əst **~s** s
left-of-centre, left-of-center ˌleft əv ˈsent ə ◂‖ -ˈsenṱ ᵊr
leftover ˈleft ˌəʊv ə ‖ -ˌoʊv ᵊr **~s** z
leftward ˈleft wəd ‖ -wᵊrd **~s** z
left-winger ˌleft ˈwɪŋ ə ‖ -ᵊr **~s** z
left|y ˈleft |i **~ies** iz
leg leg **legged** legd **legging** ˈleg ɪŋ **legs** legz **ˌleg ˈside**
legac|y ˈleg əs |i **~ies** iz
legal ˈliːg ᵊl **~ly** i **ˌlegal ˈaid**; **ˌlegal ˈtender**
legalese ˌliːg ə ˈliːz -ᵊl ˈiːz ‖ -ˈliːs
legalis... —*see* **legaliz...**
legalism ˈliːg ə ˌlɪz əm -ᵊl ˌɪz-
legalistic ˌliːg ə ˈlɪst ɪk ◂ -ᵊl ˈɪst- **~ally** ᵊl‿i
legalit|y lɪ ˈgæl ət |i liː-, -ɪt- ‖ -əṱ |i **~ies** iz
legalization ˌliːg əl aɪ ˈzeɪʃ ᵊn -əl ɪ- ‖ -əl ə- **~s** z
legaliz|e ˈliːg ə laɪz -ᵊl aɪz **~ed** d **~es** ɪz əz **~ing** ɪŋ
legal-size ˈliːg ᵊl saɪz
Legard ˈledʒ əd ‖ -ᵊrd
legate *n* ˈleg ət -ɪt, -eɪt **~s** s
legatee ˌleg ə ˈtiː **~s** z

legation lɪ ˈgeɪʃ ən lə- **~s** z
legato lɪ ˈgɑːt əʊ lə-, le- ‖ -oʊ **~s** z
legator lɪ ˈgeɪt ə lə-, le- ‖ -ˈgeɪţ ər **~s** z
LegCo ˈledʒ kəʊ ‖ -koʊ
legend ˈledʒ ənd -ɪnd **~s** z
legendary ˈledʒ ənd‿ər i ˈ· ɪnd- ‖ -ən der i
leger, Leger ˈledʒ ə ‖ -ər **~s** z
ˈleger line
legerdemain ˌledʒ ə də ˈmeɪn ‖ ˌ·ər-
Legg, Legge leg
Leggatt ˈleg ət
legged *adj* ˈleg ɪd -əd; legd
leggings ˈleg ɪŋz
legg|y ˈleg |i **~ier** i‿ə ‖ i‿ər **~iest** i‿ɪst i‿əst **~iness** i nəs i nɪs
Legh liː
leghorn *'straw; hat; breed of fowl'* le ˈgɔːn ˌleg ˈhɔːn, ˈ· · ‖ ˈleg hɔːrn -ərn
Leghorn *place: old name for Livorno* ˈleg hɔːn ˌ·ˈ· ‖ -hɔːrn
legibility ˌledʒ ə ˈbɪl ət i ˌ·ɪ-, -ɪt i ‖ -əţ i
legib|le ˈledʒ əb |əl -ɪb- **~ly** li
legion ˈliːdʒ ən **~s** z
legionar|y ˈliːdʒ ən ər‿|i ‖ -ə ner |i **~ies** iz
legionell|a ˌliːdʒ ə ˈnel |ə **~ae** iː **~as** əz
legionnaire ˌliːdʒ ə ˈneə ‖ -ˈneər -ˈnæər **~s** z
ˌlegion'naires' diˌsease
legi|slate ˈledʒ ɪ |sleɪt -ə- **~slated** sleɪt ɪd -əd ‖ sleɪţ əd **~slates** sleɪts **~slating** sleɪt ɪŋ ‖ sleɪţ ɪŋ
legislation ˌledʒ ɪ ˈsleɪʃ ən -ə-
legislative ˈledʒ ɪs lət ɪv ˈ·əs-; -ɪ sleɪt-, -ə sleɪt- ‖ -ə sleɪţ ɪv -əs ləţ ɪv **~ly** li **~s** z
legislator ˈledʒ ɪ sleɪt ə ˈ·ə- ‖ -ə sleɪţ ər **~s** z
legislature ˈledʒ ɪs lətʃ ə ˈ·əs-; -lə tʃʊə; -ɪ sleɪtʃ ə, -ə · · ‖ -ə sleɪtʃ ər ˌ· ˈ· · **~s** z
legit lɪ ˈdʒɪt lə-
legitimacy lɪ ˈdʒɪt əm əs i lə-, ˈ·ɪm- ‖ -ˈdʒɪţ-
legiti|mate *v* lɪ ˈdʒɪt ə |meɪt lə-, -ɪ- ‖ -ˈdʒɪţ- **~mated** meɪt ɪd -əd ‖ meɪţ əd **~mates** meɪts **~mating** meɪt ɪŋ ‖ meɪţ ɪŋ
legitimate *adj* lɪ ˈdʒɪt əm ət lə-, -ɪm-, -ɪt ‖ -ˈdʒɪţ- **~ly** li
legitimation lɪ ˌdʒɪt ə ˈmeɪʃ ən lə-, -ɪ- ‖ -ˌdʒɪţ-
legitimatis... —*see* **legitimatiz...**
legitimatization lɪ ˌdʒɪt əm ət aɪ ˈzeɪʃ ən lə-, -ˌɪm-, -ɪˈ·- ‖ -ˌdʒɪţ əm əţ ə-
legitimatiz|e lɪ ˈdʒɪt əm ə taɪz lə-, ˈ·ɪm- ‖ -ˈdʒɪţ- **~ed** d **~es** ɪz əz **~ing** ɪŋ
legitimis... —*see* **legitimiz...**
legitimization lɪ ˌdʒɪt əm aɪ ˈzeɪʃ ən lə-, -ˌɪm-, -ɪˈ·- ‖ -ˌdʒɪţ əm ə-
legitimiz|e lɪ ˈdʒɪt ə maɪz lə-, -ɪ- ‖ -ˈdʒɪţ- **~ed** d **~es** ɪz əz **~ing** ɪŋ
legless ˈleg ləs -lɪs
Lego *tdmk* ˈleg əʊ ‖ -oʊ —*Danish* [ˈleː go]
leg-of-mutton ˌleg əv ˈmʌt ən ◂
leg-over ˈleg ˌəʊv ə ‖ -ˌoʊv ər
leg-pull ˈleg pʊl **~ing** ɪŋ **~s** z
Legree lɪ ˈgriː lə-
legroom ˈleg ruːm -rʊm
legume ˈleg juːm lɪ ˈgjuːm, lə- **~s** z
leguminous lɪ ˈgjuːm ɪn əs lə-, le-, -ən-
leg-up ˈleg ʌp
leg-warmer ˈleg ˌwɔːm ə ‖ -ˌwɔːrm ər
legwork ˈleg wɜːk ‖ -wɜːk
Lehar, Lehár leɪ ˈhɑː lɪ-, lə-, ˈleɪ hɑː ‖ ˈleɪ hɑːr —*Hungarian* [ˈlɛ haːr]
Le Havre lə ˈɑːv rə -ˈhɑːv-, -ə ‖ -ər —*Fr* [lə aːvʁ]
Lehigh ˈliː haɪ
Lehman, Lehmann *(i)* ˈleɪ mən, *(ii)* ˈliː- —*Usually (i).*
Lehrer ˈleər ə ˈlɪər- ‖ ˈlɪr ər
lei leɪ ˈleɪ i **leis** leɪz ˈleɪ iz
Leibnitz, Leibniz ˈlaɪb nɪts ˈliːb- —*Ger* [ˈlaib nɪts]
Leica *tdmk* ˈlaɪk ə —*Ger* [ˈlai ka] **~s** z
Leicester ˈlest ə ‖ -ər *(!)* —*Sometimes called* ˈlaɪ sest ər *by those not familiar with the name.*
Leicestershire, Leics, Leics. ˈlest ə ʃə -ʃɪə ‖ -ər ʃər -ʃɪr
Leiden ˈlaɪd ən ˈleɪd- —*Dutch* [ˈlei dən]
Leif liːf
Leigh *(i)* liː, *(ii)* laɪ —*Usually (i); but some places in the south of England are (ii).*
Leighton ˈleɪt ən
Leila ˈliːl ə ˈleɪl ə
Leinster ˈlentst ə ‖ -ər —*but the Duke of L~ is* ˈlɪntst-
Leintwardine ˈlent wə daɪn -diːn; ˈlænt ə diːn ‖ -wər-
Leipzig ˈlaɪp sɪg -sɪk —*Ger* [ˈlaip tsɪç]
Leishman ˈliːʃ mən ˈlɪʃ-
leishmania ˌ(ˌ)liːʃ ˈmeɪn i‿ə
leishmaniasis ˌliːʃ mə ˈnaɪ‿əs ɪs §-əs
leister *'spear'* ˈliːst ə ‖ -ər
Leister *name* ˈlest ə ‖ -ər
leisure ˈleʒ ə ‖ ˈliːʒ ər ˈleʒ-, ˈleɪʒ- **~d** d **~liness** li nəs -nɪs **~ly** li
leisurewear ˈleʒ ə weə ‖ ˈliːʒ ər wer ˈleʒ-, ˈleɪʒ-, -wær
Leith liːθ
leitmotif, leitmotiv, leitmotive ˈlaɪt məʊ ˌtiːf ˈ·ˌməʊt ɪv ‖ -moʊ- —*Ger* [ˈlait mo ˌtiːf]
Leitrim ˈliːtr ɪm §-əm
Leix liːʃ
lek lek **lekked** lekt **lekking** ˈlek ɪŋ **leks** leks
lekker ˈlek ə ‖ -ər
Leland ˈliːl ənd
Lely ˈliːl i
leman ˈlem ən ˈliːm- **~s** z
Leman *surname; street name in London* ˈlem ən ˈliːm-
Le Mans lə ˈmɒ̃ ‖ -ˈmɑːn —*Fr* [lə mɑ̃]
Lemesurier lə ˈmeʒ ər‿ə ‖ -ər ər lə ˌmeʒ ər‿i ˈeɪ
lemm|a ˈlem |ə **~as** əz **~ata** ət ə ‖ əţ ə
lemmatis... —*see* **lemmatiz...**
lemmatization ˌlem ət aɪ ˈzeɪʃ ən -ət ɪ- ‖ -əţ ə- **~s** z
lemmatiz|e ˈlem ə taɪz **~ed** d **~es** ɪz əz **~ing** ɪŋ

emme 'lem i —*This is a non-standard or casual form of* let me
emming 'lem ɪŋ **~s** z
emming-like 'lem ɪŋ laɪk
emmon 'lem ən
em|niscus lem |'nɪsk əs **~nisci** 'nɪs aɪ 'nɪsk-, -iː
emnos 'lem nɒs ‖ -nɑːs -noʊs
emon, Lemon 'lem ən **~s** z ˌ**lemon 'curd**; '**lemon grass**; ˌ**lemon meˌringue 'pie**; ˌ**lemon 'sole**; ˌ**lemon 'squash**; ˌ**lemon 'yellow◂**
emonade ˌlem ə 'neɪd ◂ **~s** z
e Monde lə 'mɒnd ‖ -'mɔːnd -'mɑːnd —*Fr* [lə mɔ̃ːd]
emony 'lem ən i
empert 'lemp ət ‖ -ᵊrt
empriere 'lemp ri eə ‖ ˌlemp ri 'eᵊr
emsip *tdmk* 'lem sɪp
emuel 'lem ju‿əl
emur 'liːm ə -jʊə ‖ -ᵊr **~s** z
en len
ena *river* 'leɪn ə 'liːn- —*Russ* ['lʲɛ nə]
ena *personal name* 'liːn ə
end lend **lending** 'lend ɪŋ **lends** lendz **lent** lent '**lending ˌlibrary**
ender 'lend ə ‖ -ᵊr **~s** z
end-lease, Lend-Lease ˌlend 'liːs ‖ '..
enes 'liːn iːz 'leɪn-, -eɪz

LENGTH

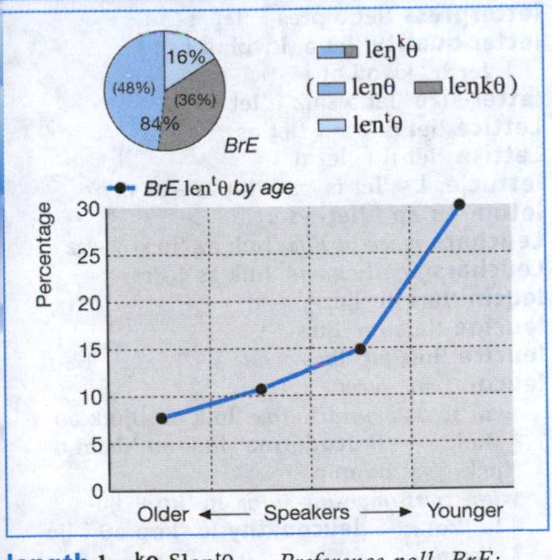
16%
(48%)
(36%)
84%
leŋᵏθ
(leŋθ
leŋkθ)
lenᵗθ
BrE
BrE lenᵗθ by age
Percentage
30
25
20
15
10
5
0
Older
Speakers
Younger

length leŋᵏθ §lenᵗθ — *Preference poll, BrE:* leŋᵏθ *84%* (leŋθ *48%,* leŋkθ *36%*), lenᵗθ *16%.* **lengths** leŋᵏθs §lenᵗθs
lengthen 'leŋᵏθ ən §'lenᵗθ- **~ed** d **~ing** ‿ɪŋ **~s** z
length|ways 'leŋᵏθ |weɪz §'lenᵗθ- **~wise** waɪz
length|y 'leŋᵏθ |i §'lenᵗθ- **~ier** i‿ə ‖ i‿ᵊr **~iest** i‿ɪst i‿əst **~ily** ɪ li əl i **~iness** i nəs i nɪs
lenienc|e 'liːn i‿ənᵗs **~y** i
lenient 'liːn i‿ənt **~ly** li
Lenihan 'len ə hən
Lenin 'len ɪn §-ən —*Russ* ['lʲe nʲɪn]
Leningrad 'len ɪn græd →-ɪŋ-, §-ən- —*Russ* [lʲɪ nʲɪn 'grat]
Lenin|ism 'len ɪn |ˌɪz əm §-ən- **~ist/s** ɪst/s §əst/s ‖ əst/s
lenis 'liːn ɪs 'leɪn-, §-əs **lenes** 'liːn iːz 'leɪn-, -eɪz
le|nite lɪ |'naɪt lə- **~nited** 'naɪt ɪd -əd ‖ 'naɪţ əd **~nites** 'naɪts **~niting** 'naɪt ɪŋ ‖ 'naɪţ ɪŋ
lenition lɪ 'nɪʃ ᵊn lə- **~s** z
lenity 'len ət i 'liːn-, -ɪt- ‖ -əţ i
Lennie 'len i
Lennon 'len ən
Lennox 'len əks
Lenny 'len i
leno 'liːn əʊ ‖ -oʊ **~s** z
Leno *(i)* 'liːn əʊ ‖ -oʊ, *(ii)* 'len- —*Jay Leno, TV personality, is (ii)*
Lenor *tdmk* lɪ 'nɔː lə- ‖ -'nɔːr
Lenore lɪ 'nɔː lə- ‖ -'nɔːr -'noʊr
Lenox 'len əks
lens lenz **lenses** 'lenz ɪz -əz
lent, Lent lent
lenten 'lent ən ‖ -ᵊn
Lentheric, Lenthéric *tdmk* 'lɒnᵗθ ər ɪk 'lɒ̃θ- ‖ 'lɑːnᵗθ-
lenticel 'lent ɪ sel §-ə- ‖ 'lenţ ə- **~s** z
lenticular len 'tɪk jʊl ə -jəl- ‖ -jəl ᵊr
lentigo len 'taɪg əʊ ‖ -oʊ
lentil 'lent ɪl -ᵊl ‖ 'lenţ ᵊl **~s** z
lentivirus 'lent i ˌvaɪ‿ər əs ‖ 'lenţ ə ˌvaɪrᵊ əs **~es** ɪz əz
lento 'lent əʊ ‖ -oʊ **~s** z
Leo 'liː‿əʊ ‖ 'liː oʊ
Leofric 'lef rɪk 'leɪ əf rɪk ‖ li 'ɑːf rɪk
Leominster *(i)* 'lemᵖst ə ‖ -ᵊr, *(ii)* 'lem ɪnᵗst ə ‖ -ənᵗst ᵊr —*The place in England is (i), that in MA (ii).*
Leon *personal name* 'liː‿ən 'leɪ-, -ɒn ‖ -ɑːn
León *place in Spain* leɪ 'ɒn ‖ -'oʊn —*Sp* [le 'on]
Leona li 'əʊn ə ‖ -'oʊn ə
Leonard 'len əd ‖ -ᵊrd
Leonardo ˌliː‿əʊ 'nɑːd əʊ ˌleɪ- ‖ ˌliː ə 'nɑːrd oʊ
Leonid 'liː‿əʊn ɪd 'leɪ-, §-əd ‖ -ən-
Leonidas li 'ɒn ɪ dæs -ə- ‖ -'ɑːn əd əs
Leonie *(i)* 'liː‿ən i, *(ii)* li 'əʊn i ‖ -'oʊn i
leonine, L~ 'liː‿əʊ naɪn ‖ -ə-
Leonora ˌliː‿ə 'nɔːr ə ‖ -'noʊr-
Leontes li 'ɒnt iːz leɪ- ‖ -'ɑːnt-
leopard 'lep əd ‖ -ᵊrd **~s** z
leopardess 'lep əd es -ɪs, -əs ‖ -ᵊrd əs **~es** ɪz əz
leopard-skin 'lep əd skɪn ‖ -ᵊrd-
Leopold 'liː‿ə pəʊld →-pɒʊld ‖ -poʊld —*but as a foreign name also* 'leɪ-
leotard 'liː‿ə tɑːd 'leɪ-, -əʊ- ‖ -tɑːrd **~s** z
Lepanto lɪ 'pænt əʊ lə- ‖ -oʊ —*It* ['leː pan to]
Le Pen lə 'pen —*Fr* [lə pɛn]
leper 'lep ə ‖ -ᵊr **~s** z
lepidopter|a, L~ ˌlep ɪ 'dɒpt ər |ə ˌ-ə- ‖ -'dɑːpt- **~ist/s** ɪst/s §əst/s ‖ əst/s **~ous** əs
Lepidus 'lep ɪd əs -əd-
Lepontine lə 'pɒnt aɪn lɪ- ‖ -'pɑːnt-

Leppard ˈlep ɑːd ‖ -ɑːrd
leprechaun ˈlep rə kɔːn -rɪ-, -hɔːn ‖ -kɑːn **~s** z
leprosari|um ˌlep rə ˈseər i‿|əm ‖ -ˈser- **~a** ə **~ums** əmz
leprosy ˈlep rəs i
leprous ˈlep rəs **~ly** li **~ness** nəs nɪs
Lepsius ˈleps i‿əs
leptokurtic ˌlept əʊ ˈkɜːt ɪk ◂ ‖ -ə ˈkɝːt̬ ɪk ◂
lepton ˈlept ɒn ‖ -ɑːn **~s** z
leptospirosis ˌlept əʊ spaɪᵊ ˈrəʊs ɪs §-əs ‖ -ə spaɪ ˈroʊs əs
Lepus ˈliːp əs ˈlep-
Lermontov ˈleə mɒnt ɒf ‖ ˈler mɑːnt ɔːf —*Russ* [ˈlʲer mən təf]
Lerner ˈlɜːn ə ‖ ˈlɝːn ᵊr
Leroy *(i)* ˈliː rɔɪ, *(ii)* lə ˈrɔɪ —*As a family name, (ii).*
Lerwick ˈlɜː wɪk ‖ ˈlɝː-
Les *personal name (i) short for* **Leslie** lez, *(ii) short for* **Lester** les
les *French plural 'the'* leɪ —*but before a vowel sound* leɪz —*See also phrases with this word.* —*Fr* [le, lez]
Le Saux lə ˈsəʊ ‖ -ˈsoʊ
Lesbia ˈlez bi‿ə
lesbian, L~ ˈlez bi‿ən **~ism** ˌɪz əm **~s** z
lesbo ˈlez bəʊ ‖ -boʊ **~s** z
Lesbos ˈlez bɒs ‖ -bɑːs -boʊs
lèse-majesté ˌleɪz ˈmædʒ ə steɪ ˌliːz-, -ˈmæʒ-, -ɪ-, -e- ‖ ˌliːz ˈmædʒ əst i —*Fr* [lɛz ma ʒɛs te]
lese-majesty ˌliːz ˈmædʒ əst i ˌleɪz-, -ɪst-
lesion ˈliːʒ ᵊn **~s** z
Lesley, Leslie ˈlez li ‖ ˈles-
Lesmahagow ˌles mə ˈheɪg əʊ ‖ -oʊ
Lesney *tdmk* ˈlez ni
Lesotho lə ˈsuːt uː lɪ-, leɪ-, -ˈsəʊt əʊ ‖ -ˈsoʊt oʊ —*Sotho* [lɪ ˈsʊː tʰʊ]
less les

-LESS

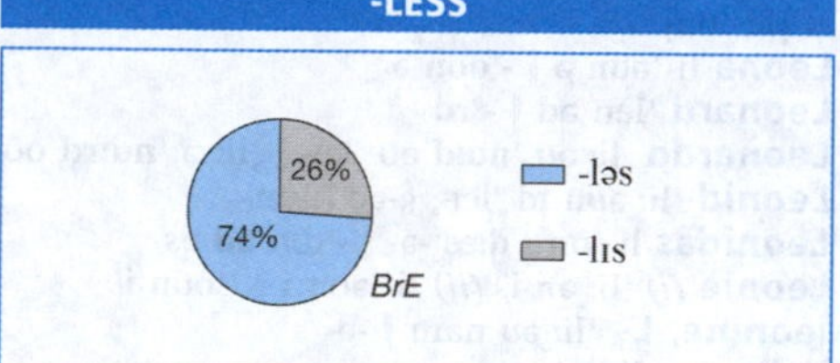

-less ləs lɪs —*In singing, a strong-vowelled form* les *is usual.* — *Preference poll, BrE (for the word* careless, *disregarding votes for* -les *and from respondents who do not distinguish* ɪ *from* ə *in this position):* -ləs *74%,* -lɪs *26%* — **faithless** ˈfeɪθ ləs -lɪs, *in singing* -les
lessee ₍ˌ₎le ˈsiː **~s** z
lessen ˈles ᵊn *(= lesson)* **~ed** d **~ing** ˌɪŋ **~s** z
Lesseps ˈles əps -eps —*Fr* [lɛ sɛps]
lesser, L~ ˈles ə ‖ -ᵊr
Lessing ˈles ɪŋ
lesson ˈles ᵊn **~s** z
lessor ₍ˌ₎le ˈsɔː ˈles ɔː ‖ ₍ˌ₎le ˈsɔːr ˈles ɔːr **~s** z
lest lest
Lester ˈlest ə ‖ -ᵊr

Lestrange, L'Estrange lɪ ˈstreɪndʒ lə-
let let —*The phrase* let me *has a non-standard casual form* ˈlem i, *sometimes written* lemme **lets, let's** lets **letting** ˈlet ɪŋ ‖ ˈlet̬ ɪŋ
-let lət lɪt — **leaflet** ˈliːf lət -lɪt
letch letʃ **letched** letʃt **letches** ˈletʃ ɪz -əz **letching** ˈletʃ ɪŋ
Letchworth ˈletʃ wəθ -wɜːθ ‖ -wɝːθ
letdown ˈlet daʊn **~s** z
lethal ˈliːθ ᵊl
lethality liː ˈθæl ət i -ɪt- ‖ -ət̬ i
lethally ˈliːθ əl i
lethargic lə ˈθɑːdʒ ɪk lɪ-, le- ‖ -ˈθɑːrdʒ- **~ally** ᵊl‿i
lethargy ˈleθ ədʒ i ‖ -ᵊrdʒ i
Lethbridge ˈleθ brɪdʒ
Lethe ˈliːθ i -iː
Le Tissier lə ˈtɪs i eɪ
Letitia lə ˈtɪʃ ə lɪ-, -ˈtɪʃ i‿ə ‖ -ˈtiːʃ ə
Letraset *tdmk* ˈletr ə set
let's *contracted form* lets
Lett let **Letts, Lett's** lets
letter ˈlet ə ‖ ˈlet̬ ᵊr **~ed** d **lettering** ˈlet ər ɪŋ ‖ ˈlet̬ ər ɪŋ **~s** z
ˈletter bomb; **ˌletter of ˈcredit**; **ˈletter ˌopener**
letterbox ˈlet ə bɒks ‖ ˈlet̬ ᵊr bɑːks **~es** ɪz əz **~ing** ɪŋ
letterhead ˈlet ə hed ‖ ˈlet̬ ᵊr- **~s** z
Letterman ˈlet ə mən ‖ ˈlet̬ ᵊr-
letter-perfect ˌlet ə ˈpɜːf ɪkt ◂ -ekt, §-əkt ‖ ˌlet̬ ᵊr ˈpɝːf ɪkt ◂
letterpress ˈlet ə pres ‖ ˈlet̬ ᵊr-
letter-quality ˈlet ə ˌkwɒl ət i -ɪt i ‖ ˈlet̬ ᵊr ˌkwɑːl ət̬ i
letter-size ˈlet ə saɪz ‖ ˈlet̬ ᵊr-
Lettice ˈlet ɪs §-əs ‖ ˈlet̬ əs
Lettish ˈlet ɪʃ ‖ ˈlet̬ ɪʃ
lettuc|e, L~ ˈlet ɪs -əs ‖ ˈlet̬ əs **~es** ɪz əz
letup ˈlet ʌp ‖ ˈlet̬- **~s** s
Leuchars *place in Fife* ˈluːk əz ˈluːx- ‖ -ᵊrz
Leuchars *family name* ˈluːk əs ‖ -ᵊrs
leucin ˈluːs ɪn ˈljuːs-, §-ən
leucine ˈluːs iːn ˈljuːs-
leucite ˈluːs aɪt ˈljuːs-
leuco- *comb. form*
with stress-neutral suffix ¦luːk əʊ ¦ljuːk əʊ ‖ ¦luːk ə — **leucoderma** ˌluːk əʊ ˈdɜːm ə ˌljuːk- ‖ -ə ˈdɝːm ə
with stress-imposing suffix lu ˈkɒ+ lju- ‖ lu ˈkɑː+ — **leucopathy** lu ˈkɒp əθ i lju- ‖ -ˈkɑːp-
leucocyte ˈluːk əʊ saɪt ˈljuːk- ‖ -ə- **~s** s
leucopenia ˌluːk əʊ ˈpiːn i‿ə ˌljuːk- ‖ ˌ-ə-
leucotomis|e, leucotomiz|e lu ˈkɒt ə maɪz lju- ‖ lu ˈkɑːt̬- **~ed** d **~es** ɪz əz **~ing** ɪŋ
leucotom|y lu ˈkɒt əm |i lju- ‖ lu ˈkɑːt̬- **~ies** iz
leukaemia, leukemia lu ˈkiːm i‿ə lju- **~s** z
leuko... —*see* **leuco...**
le|vant, L~ lə |ˈvænt lɪ- **~vanted** ˈvænt ɪd -əd ‖ ˈvænt̬ əd **~vanting** ˈvænt ɪŋ ‖ ˈvænt̬ ɪŋ **~vants** ˈvænts

evantine ˈlev ən taɪn -tiːn ‖ lə ˈvænt ən, -aɪn **~s** z
evator lə ˈveɪt ə lɪ-, -ɔː ‖ -ˈveɪţ ər **~s** z
evee, levée ˈlev i -eɪ **~s** z
evel ˈlev əl **~ed, ~led** d **~ing, ~ling** ɪŋ **~s** z
 ˌlevel ˈcrossing
eveler, L~ ˈlev əl ə ‖ -ər **~s** z
evel-headed ˌlev əl ˈhed ɪd ◂ ‖ ˈ· ·ˌ· · **~ly** li **~ness** nəs nɪs
eveller, L~ ˈlev əl ə ‖ -ər **~s** z
evel-pegging ˌlev əl ˈpeg ɪŋ
.even *(i)* ˈlev ən, *(ii)* ˈliːv ən —*Most rivers of this name, and the Loch, are (ii), but the river in Cumbria is (i). The family name may be either.*
.evens ˈlev ənz
ev|er ˈliːv |ə ‖ ˈlev |ər ˈliːv- **~ered** əd ‖ ərd **~ering** ər‿ɪŋ **~ers** əz ‖ ərz
.ever ˈliːv ə ‖ -ər
everag|e ˈliːv ər‿ɪdʒ ˈlev- ‖ ˈlev- **~ed** d **~es** ɪz əz **~ing** ɪŋ
everet ˈlev ər‿ət -ɪt **~s** s
Leverhulme ˈliːv ə hjuːm ‖ -ər-
Levett ˈlev ɪt -ət
Levi *personal or family name, (i)* ˈlev i, *(ii)* ˈliːv i
Levi *biblical name* ˈliːv aɪ
levi... —*see* **levy**
leviathan, L~ lə ˈvaɪ‿əθ ən lɪ- **~s** z
Levin, levin ˈlev ɪn §-ən **~s** z
Levine lə ˈviːn
levirate ˈliːv ər ət ˈlev-, -ɪr-, -ɪt; -ə reɪt
Levi's *tdmk*, **Levis** *'jeans'* ˈliːv aɪz
Levi Strauss *clothing manufacturer* ˌliːv aɪ ˈstrɔːs -ˈstraʊs
Levi-Strauss, Lévi-Strauss *French anthropologist* ˌlev i ˈstraʊs ˌleɪv- —*Fr* [le vi stroːs]
levi|tate ˈlev ɪ |teɪt -ə- **~tated** teɪt ɪd -əd ‖ teɪţ əd **~tates** teɪts **~tating** teɪt ɪŋ ‖ teɪţ ɪŋ
levitation ˌlev ɪ ˈteɪʃ ən -ə- **~s** z
Levite ˈliːv aɪt **~s** s
Levitic|us lə ˈvɪt ɪk |əs lɪ- ‖ -ˈvɪţ- **~al** əl
Levitra *tdmk* lə ˈviːtr ə le-
Levittown ˈlev ɪt taʊn -ət-
levit|y ˈlev ət |i -ɪt- ‖ -əţ |i **~ies** iz
levodopa ˌliːv əʊ ˈdəʊp ə ˌlev- ‖ -ə ˈdoʊp ə ˌ· ·ˌ· ·
lev|y *v, n* ˈlev |i **~ied** id **~ies** iz **~ying** i‿ɪŋ
Levy *name, (i)* ˈliːv i, *(ii)* ˈlev i
Lew luː ljuː
lewd luːd ljuːd **lewder** ˈluːd ə ˈljuːd- ‖ -ər **lewdest** ˈluːd ɪst ˈljuːd-, -əst
lewd|ly ˈluːd |li ˈljuːd- **~ness** nəs nɪs
Lewes ˈluː‿ɪs §‿əs
Lewin ˈluː‿ɪn §‿ən
Lewinsky lə ˈwɪn ski
Lewis, lewis ˈluː‿ɪs §‿əs
Lewisham ˈluː‿ɪʃ əm
lewisite ˈluː‿ɪ saɪt §‿ə-
Lex, lex leks
lexeme ˈleks iːm **~s** z
lexemic lek ˈsiːm ɪk
lexical ˈleks ɪk əl **~ly** ‿i
lexico- *comb. form*
 with stress-neutral suffix ˌleks ɪ kəʊ ‖ -koʊ
 — **lexicostatistics** ˌleks ɪ kəʊ stə ˈtɪst ɪks ‖ ˌ· ·koʊ-
 with stress-imposing suffix ˌleks ɪ ˈkɒ+ -ə- ‖ -ˈkɑː+ — **lexicology** ˌleks ɪ ˈkɒl ədʒ i ˌ·ə- ‖ -ˈkɑːl-
lexicographer ˌleks ɪ ˈkɒg rəf ə ˌ·ə- ‖ -ˈkɑːg rəf ər **~s** z
lexicographic ˌleks ɪk ə ˈgræf ɪk ◂ ˌ·ək- **~ally** əl‿i
lexicography ˌleks ɪ ˈkɒg rəf i ˌ·ə- ‖ -ˈkɑːg-
lexicological ˌleks ɪk ə ˈlɒdʒ ɪk əl ◂ ˌ·ək- ‖ -ˈlɑːdʒ- **~ly** ‿i
lexicologist ˌleks ɪ ˈkɒl ədʒ ɪst ˌ·ə-, §-əst ‖ -ˈkɑːl- **~s** s
lexicology ˌleks ɪ ˈkɒl ədʒ i ˌ·ə- ‖ -ˈkɑːl-
lexicon ˈleks ɪk ən -ək-; -ɪ kɒn, -ə- ‖ -ə kɑːn **~s** z
Lexington ˈleks ɪŋ tən
lexis ˈleks ɪs §-əs
Lexmark *tdmk* ˈleks mɑːk ‖ -mɑːrk
Lexus *tdmk* ˈleks əs
ley leɪ liː
Ley *(i)* liː, *(ii)* leɪ
Leyburn ˈleɪ bɜːn ‖ -bɝːn
Leyden ˈlaɪd ən
Leyland ˈleɪ lənd
leylandii leɪ ˈlænd i aɪ ·ˈ· aɪ
Leys liːz
Leysdown ˈleɪz daʊn
Leystonstone ˈleɪt ən stəʊn ‖ -stoʊn
Leyton ˈleɪt ən
lezzie ˈlez i **~s** z
Lhasa ˈlɑːs ə ˈlæs- —*Chi* Lāsà [1la 4sa]
 ˌLhasa ˈapso ˈæps əʊ ‖ ˈɑːps oʊ
li liː
LI ˌel ˈaɪ —*see also* **Long Island**
liabilit|y ˌlaɪ‿ə ˈbɪl ət |i -ɪt i ‖ -əţ |i **~ies** iz
liable ˈlaɪ‿əb əl
liais|e li ˈeɪz laɪ- **~ed** d **~es** ɪz əz **~ing** ɪŋ
liaison li ˈeɪz ən laɪ-, -ɒn, -õ ‖ ˈliː ə zɑːn ˌ·ˈ·; ⚠ˈleɪ-; li ˈeɪz ɑːn —*Fr* [ljɛ zɔ̃] **~s** z
Liam ˈliː‿əm
liana li ˈɑːn ə -ˈæn- **~s** z
liane li ˈɑːn -ˈæn **~s** z
Lianne li ˈæn
Liao *dynasty* li ˈaʊ —*Chi* Liáo [2ljau]
Liaoning li ˌaʊ ˈnɪŋ —*Chi* Liáoníng [2ljau 2niŋ]
liar ˈlaɪ‿ə ‖ ˈlaɪ‿ər **~s** z
Lias, lias ˈlaɪ‿əs
liassic, L~ laɪ ˈæs ɪk
LIAT *airline* ˈliː æt ˈliː‿ət
lib, Lib lɪb
 ˌLib ˈDem/s dem/z
Libanus ˈlɪb ən əs
libation laɪ ˈbeɪʃ ən lɪ- **~s** z
libber ˈlɪb ə ‖ -ər **~s** z
Libbie, Libby ˈlɪb i
Lib-Dem, Libdem ˌlɪb ˈdem ◂ **~s** z
libel ˈlaɪb əl **~ed, ~led** d **~ing, ~ling** ɪŋ **~s** z

L

libellous, libelous ˈlaɪb ᵊl əs **~ly** li
Liberace ˌlɪb ə ˈrɑːtʃ i
liberal, L~ ˈlɪb ᵊr‿əl **~ly** i **~s** z
ˌ**liberal ˈarts**; ˌ**Liberal ˈDemocrat**; ˈ**Liberal ˌParty**; ˌ**liberal ˈstudies**
liberalis... —*see* **liberaliz...**
liberalism ˈlɪb ᵊr‿əl ˌɪz əm
liberalit|y ˌlɪb ə ˈræl ət |i -ɪt i ‖ -əţ |i **~ies** iz
liberalization ˌlɪb ᵊr‿əl aɪ ˈzeɪʃ ᵊn -ɪˈ-- ‖ -əˈ-- **~s** z
liberaliz|e ˈlɪb ᵊr‿ə laɪz **~ed** d **~es** ɪz əz **~ing** ɪŋ
liberally ˈlɪb ᵊr‿əl i
libe|rate ˈlɪb ə |reɪt **~rated** reɪt ɪd -əd ‖ reɪţ əd **~rates** reɪts **~rating** reɪt ɪŋ ‖ reɪţ ɪŋ
liberation ˌlɪb ə ˈreɪʃ ᵊn ◂ **~ist/s** ‿ɪst/s §‿əst/s ‖ ‿əst/s
ˌ**libeˌration theˈology**, ˌ· ·ˈ· · ·ˌ· · ·
liberator ˈlɪb ə reɪt ə ‖ -reɪţ ᵊr **~s** z
Liberi|a laɪ ˈbɪər i‿|ə ‖ -ˈbɪr- **~an/s** ən/z
libertarian ˌlɪb ə ˈteər i‿ən ◂ ‖ -ᵊr ˈter- **~s** z
liberti... —*see* **liberty**
libertine ˈlɪb ə tiːn -taɪn ‖ -ᵊr- **~s** z
Liberton ˈlɪb ət ən ‖ -ᵊrt ᵊn
libert|y, L~ ˈlɪb ət |i ‖ ᵊrţ |i **~ies** iz
Libeskind ˈliːb ə skɪnd
libidinal lɪ ˈbɪd ɪn ᵊl lə-, -ᵊn‿əl ‖ -ᵊn‿əl
libidinous lɪ ˈbɪd ɪn əs lə-, -ən‿əs ‖ -ən‿əs
libido lɪ ˈbiːd əʊ lə- ‖ -oʊ ˈlɪb ə doʊ **~s** z
LIBOR ˈlaɪb ɔː ‖ -ɔːr
Libra ˈliːb rə ˈlɪb-, ˈlaɪb-
Libran ˈliːb rən ˈlɪb-, ˈlaɪb- **~s** z
librarian laɪ ˈbreər i‿ən lɪ-, lə- ‖ -ˈbrer- **~s** z **~ship** ʃɪp
librar|y ˈlaɪb rər |i ˈlaɪb ər‿i ‖ ˈlaɪb rer |i -rər i, ⚠-er i, -ər‿i **~ies** iz —*The awkwardness of two* **r** *s in the same unstressed syllable makes people tend to drop the first of them. While perhaps condemned by the speech-conscious, such reduced pronunciations are nevertheless often heard from educated speakers. Where in AmE the second syllable has a strong vowel, the reduction is more noticeable, hence less frequently heard and more strongly disapproved of.*
librate laɪ ˈb|reɪt ˈlaɪb |reɪt ‖ ˈlaɪb |reɪt **~rated** reɪt ɪd -əd ‖ reɪţ əd **~rates** reɪts **~rating** reɪt ɪŋ ‖ reɪţ ɪŋ
libration laɪ ˈbreɪʃ ᵊn **~s** z
librettist lɪ ˈbret ɪst lə-, §-əst ‖ -ˈbreţ əst **~s** s
librett|o lɪ ˈbret |əʊ lə- ‖ -ˈbreţ |oʊ **~i** iː **~os** əʊz ‖ oʊz
Libreville ˈliːb rə vɪl -viːl
Librium *tdmk* ˈlɪb ri‿əm
Liby|a ˈlɪb i‿|ə **~an/s** ən/z
lice laɪs
licenc|e, licens|e ˈlaɪs ᵊnᵗs **~ed** t **~es** ɪz əz **~ing** ɪŋ
ˌ**licensed ˈpremises**; ˌ**licensed ˌpractical ˈnurse**; ˌ**licensed ˈvictualler**; ˈ**license plate**; ˈ**licensing laws**
licensee ˌlaɪs ᵊn ˈsiː **~s** z
licenser, licensor ˈlaɪs ᵊnᵗs ə ‖ -ᵊr **~s** z
licentiate laɪ ˈsenᵗʃ i‿ət lɪ-, -ˈsenᵗs-, ɪt **~s** s
licentious laɪ ˈsenᵗʃ əs **~ly** li **~ness** nəs nɪs
lichee ˌlaɪ ˈtʃiː ˈlɪtʃ iː, ˈliːtʃ-, -i ‖ ˈliːtʃ i ˈlaɪtʃ i **~s** z
lichen ˈlaɪk ən ˈlɪtʃ ᵊn, -ɪn **~s** z
Lichfield ˈlɪtʃ fiːᵊld
Lichtenstein *family name* ˈlɪkt ən staɪn -stiːn —*Ger* [ˈli çᵊn ʃtain]
licit ˈlɪs ɪt §-ət **~ly** li **~ness** nəs nɪs
lick lɪk **licked** lɪkt **licking** ˈlɪk ɪŋ **licks** lɪks
lickerish ˈlɪk ər ɪʃ
lickety-split ˌlɪk ət i ˈsplɪt -ɪt i- ‖ -əţ i-
lickspittle ˈlɪk ˌspɪt ᵊl ‖ -ˌspɪţ ᵊl **~s** z
licorice ˈlɪk ər‿ɪs ‿ɪʃ, §‿əs
lictor ˈlɪkt ə -ɔː ‖ -ᵊr **~s** z
lid lɪd **lidded** ˈlɪd ɪd -əd **lids** lɪdz
Liddell *(i)* ˈlɪd ᵊl, *(ii)* lɪ ˈdel
Liddle ˈlɪd ᵊl
Liddon ˈlɪd ᵊn
Lidl *tdmk* ˈlɪd ᵊl
lido ˈliːd əʊ ‖ -oʊ **~s** z
lie laɪ **lain** leɪn **lay** leɪ **lied** laɪd **lies** laɪz **lying** ˈlaɪ ɪŋ
ˈ**lie deˌtector**
Liebfraumilch, l~ ˈliːb fraʊ mɪlk -mɪlx, -mɪlʃ —*Ger* Liebfrauenmilch [liːp ˈfʁaʊ ən mɪlç]
Liebig ˈliːb ɪg —*Ger* [ˈliː bɪç]
Liechtenstein ˈlɪkt ən staɪn ˈlɪxt- —*Ger* [ˈlɪçt ᵊn ʃtain] **~er/s** ə/z ‖ ᵊr/z
lied *‘musical setting’* liːd —*Ger* [liːt] **lieder** ˈliːd ə ‖ -ᵊr —*Ger* [ˈliː dɐ]
lied *past and pp of* **lie** laɪd
lie-down ˌlaɪ ˈdaʊn ˈ· · **~s** z
lief liːf *(= leaf)*
liege liːdʒ liːʒ **lieges** ˈliːdʒ ɪz ˈliːʒ-, -əz
ˌ**liege ˈlord**; ˈ**liege man**
Liege, Liège li ˈeɪʒ -ˈeʒ —*Fr* [ljɛːʒ]
lie-in ˌlaɪ ˈɪn ˈ· · **~s** z
lien ˈliː‿ən liːn **liens** ˈliː‿ənz liːnz
lieu luː ljuː
lieutenanc|y lef ˈten ənᵗs |i ləf- ‖ luː- *(*)* **~ies** iz
lieutenant lef ˈten ənt ləf- ‖ luː- *(*)* **~s** s
life laɪf **life's** laɪfs **lives** laɪvz
ˈ**life belt**; ˈ**life ˌcycle**; ˌ**life exˈpectancy**, ˈ· ·ˌ· · ·; ˌ**life imˈprisonment**; ˈ**life inˌsurance**; ˈ**life ˌjacket**; ˌ**life ˈpeer**, ˌ**life ˈpeeress**; ˈ**life preˌserver**; ˈ**life raft**; ˌ**life ˈsavings**; ˈ**life ˌstory**; ˌ**life ˈwork**, ˌ**life's ˈwork**
life-affirming ˈlaɪf ə ˌfɜːm ɪŋ ‖ -ˌfɜːm-
life-and-death ˌlaɪf ᵊn ˈdeθ ◂
lifeblood ˈlaɪf blʌd
lifeboat ˈlaɪf bəʊt ‖ -boʊt **~s** s
lifebuoy ˈlaɪf bɔɪ **~s** z
life-giving ˈlaɪf ˌgɪv ɪŋ
lifeguard ˈlaɪf gɑːd ‖ -gɑːrd **~s** z
lifeless ˈlaɪf ləs -lɪs **~ly** li **~ness** nəs nɪs
lifelike ˈlaɪf laɪk
lifeline ˈlaɪf laɪn **~s** z
lifelong ˈlaɪf lɒŋ ˌ·ˈ·◂ ‖ -lɔːŋ -lɑːŋ
lifer ˈlaɪf ə ‖ -ᵊr **~s** z

life-sav|er 'laɪf ˌseɪv| ə ‖ -ər **~ers** əz ‖ ərz **~ing** ɪŋ
life-size 'laɪf saɪz ˌ'◂ **~d** d
lifespan 'laɪf spæn **~s** z
lifestyle 'laɪf staɪəl **~s** z
life-support 'laɪf sə ˌpɔːt ˌ· ·'· ‖ -ˌpɔːrt -ˌpoʊrt
life-threatening 'laɪf ˌθret ən‿ɪŋ
lifetime 'laɪf taɪm **~s** z
lifework ˌlaɪf 'wɜːk '·· ‖ -'wɜːk
LIFFE laɪf
Liffey 'lɪf i
Lifford 'lɪf əd ‖ -ərd
lift lɪft **lifted** 'lɪftɪd -əd **lifting** 'lɪft ɪŋ **lifts** lɪfts
liftboy 'lɪft bɔɪ **~s** z
lift|man 'lɪft |mæn **~men** men
liftoff 'lɪft ɒf -ɔːf ‖ -ɔːf -ɑːf **~s** s
ligament 'lɪg ə mənt **~s** s
ligamental ˌlɪg ə 'ment əl ◂ ‖ -'ment̬ əl ◂
ligand 'lɪg ənd 'laɪg- **~s** z
lig|ate 'laɪg |eɪt **~ated** eɪt ɪd -əd ‖ eɪt̬ əd **~ates** eɪts **~ating** eɪt ɪŋ ‖ eɪt̬ ɪŋ
ligature 'lɪg ətʃ ə -ə tjʊə, -ə tʃʊə ‖ -ə tʃʊr -ətʃ ər, -ə tʊr **~s** z
liger 'laɪg ə ‖ -ər **~s** z
ligger 'lɪg ə ‖ -ər **~s** z
light laɪt **lighted** 'laɪt ɪd -əd ‖ 'laɪt̬ əd **lighter** 'laɪt ə ‖ 'laɪt̬ ər **lightest** 'laɪt ɪst -əst ‖ 'laɪt̬ əst **lighting** 'laɪt ɪŋ ‖ 'laɪt̬ ɪŋ **lights** laɪts **lit** lɪt
ˌ**light 'aircraft**; ˌ**light 'ale**; '**light bulb**; ˌ**light 'heavyweight**; ˌ**lighting-'up time**; '**light ˌmeter**; '**light pen**; '**light year**
lighten 'laɪt ən **~ed** d **~ing** ‿ɪŋ **~s** z
lighter 'laɪt ə ‖ 'laɪt̬ ər **~s** z
lighterage 'laɪt ər ɪdʒ ‖ 'laɪt̬-
lighter|man 'laɪt ə mən ‖ 'laɪt̬ ər- **~men** mən men
lightface 'laɪt feɪs
light-fingered ˌlaɪt 'fɪŋ gəd ◂ ‖ -gərd ◂ **~ness** nəs nɪs
Lightfoot 'laɪt fʊt
light-headed ˌlaɪt 'hed ɪd ◂ -əd **~ly** li **~ness** nəs nɪs
light-hearted ˌlaɪt 'hɑːt ɪd ◂ -əd ‖ -'hɑːrt̬ əd ◂ **~ly** li **~ness** nəs nɪs
light|house 'laɪt |haʊs **~houses** haʊz ɪz -əz
lightly 'laɪt li
light-minded ˌlaɪt 'maɪnd ɪd ◂ -əd **~ly** li **~ness** nəs nɪs
lightness 'laɪt nəs -nɪs **~es** ɪz əz
lightning 'laɪt nɪŋ
'**lightning bug**; '**lightning conˌductor**; ˌ**lightning 'strike** *'sudden stoppage'*; '**lightning strike** *'atmospheric discharge'*
lightship 'laɪt ʃɪp **~s** s
lights-out ˌlaɪts 'aʊt '· ·
lightstick 'laɪt stɪk **~s** s
lightweight 'laɪt weɪt **~s** s
ligneous 'lɪg ni‿əs
lignification ˌlɪg nɪf ɪ 'keɪʃ ən ˌ·nəf-, §-ə'·-
ligni|fy 'lɪg nɪ |faɪ -nə- **~fied** faɪd **~fies** faɪz **~fying** faɪ ɪŋ
lignin 'lɪg nɪn §-nən
lignite 'lɪg naɪt
lignocaine 'lɪg nəʊ keɪn ‖ -ə-
lignum vitae ˌlɪg nəm 'vaɪt i -'viːt aɪ ‖ -'vaɪt̬ i -ə
Liguri|a lɪ 'gjʊər i‿|ə ‖ -'gjʊr- **~an/s** ən/z
likable 'laɪk əb əl **~ness** nəs nɪs
like laɪk **liked** laɪkt **likes** laɪks **liking** 'laɪk ɪŋ
-like laɪk — **springlike** 'sprɪŋ laɪk
likeable 'laɪk əb əl **~ness** nəs nɪs
likelihood 'laɪk li hʊd **~s** z
likely 'laɪk li
like-minded ˌlaɪk 'maɪnd ɪd ◂ -əd **~ly** li **~ness** nəs nɪs
liken 'laɪk ən **~ed** d **~ing** ‿ɪŋ **~s** z
likeness 'laɪk nəs -nɪs **~es** ɪz əz
likewise 'laɪk waɪz
liking 'laɪk ɪŋ **~s** z
Likud lɪ 'kʊd -'kuːd ‖ -'kuːd
lilac, Lilac 'laɪl ək ‖ -ɑːk, -æk **~s** s
Lilburne 'lɪl bɜːn ‖ -bɜːn
Lilian 'lɪl i‿ən
Lilias 'lɪl i‿əs
Liliburlero ˌlɪl i bə 'leər əʊ ‖ -bər 'ler oʊ
lilie... —*see* **lily**
Lilith 'lɪl ɪθ -əθ
Lille liːəl —*Fr* [lil]
Lillee 'lɪl i
Lillehammer 'lɪl ɪ hæm ə ‖ -ə hɑːm ər -hæm· —*Norw* [''li lə ha mər]
Lil-lets *tdmk* lɪ 'lets
Lilley 'lɪl i
Lillian 'lɪl i‿ən
Lillibullero ˌlɪl i bə 'leər əʊ ‖ -'ler oʊ
Lillie 'lɪl i
Lilliput 'lɪl ɪ pʌt -ə-, -pʊt; -ɪp ət, -əp-
lilliputian, L~ ˌlɪl ɪ 'pjuːʃ ən ◂ -ə-, -'pjuːʃ i‿ən **~s** z
Lilly 'lɪl i
Lillywhite 'lɪl i waɪt -hwaɪt
lilo, li-lo, Lilo, Li-lo *tdmk* 'laɪ ləʊ ‖ -loʊ **~s** z
Lilongwe lɪ 'lɒŋ weɪ ‖ -'lɔːŋ- -'lɑːŋ-
lilt, Lilt *tdmk* lɪlt **lilted** 'lɪlt ɪd -əd **lilting** 'lɪlt ɪŋ **lilts** lɪlts
lilting 'lɪlt ɪŋ **~ly** li **~ness** nəs nɪs
lil|y, Lil|y 'lɪl |i **~ies, ~y's** iz
ˌ**lily of the 'valley**
lily-livered ˌlɪl i 'lɪv əd ◂ ‖ -ərd ◂
lily-white ˌlɪl i 'waɪt ◂ -'hwaɪt
Lima, lima *(i)* 'liːm ə, *(ii)* 'laɪm ə *The place in Peru* —*Sp* ['li ma] *—and the communications code name for the letter* L *are (i); the place in Ohio is (ii); the bean is (ii) in AmE, either in BrE.*
'**lima bean**
limacon, limaçon 'lɪm ə sɒn ‖ -sɑːn ˌliːm ə 'soʊn —*Fr* [li ma sɔ̃] **~s** z
Limassol 'lɪm ə sɒl ‖ -sɔːl -sɑːl, -soʊl, ˌ· ·'·
Limavady ˌlɪm ə 'væd i
limb lɪm **limbs** lɪmz
Limbaugh 'lɪm bɔː ‖ -bɑː
limber 'lɪm bə ‖ -bər **~ed** d **limbering** 'lɪm bər‿ɪŋ **~s** z

L

limbic ˈlɪm bɪk
limbless ˈlɪm ləs -lɪs
limbo, Limbo ˈlɪm bəʊ ‖ -boʊ **~s** z
Limburger ˈlɪm bɜːg ə ‖ -bɜːg ᵊr
lim|bus ˈlɪm |bəs **~bi** baɪ
lime laɪm **limed** laɪmd **limes** laɪmz **liming** ˈlaɪm ɪŋ
ˌlime ˈgreen◂; ˈlime tree
limeade ˌlaɪm ˈeɪd **~s** z
Limehouse ˈlaɪm haʊs
limejuic|e ˈlaɪm dʒuːs **~es** ɪz əz
limekiln ˈlaɪm kɪln -kɪl **~s** z
limelight ˈlaɪm laɪt **~s** s
limen ˈlaɪm en -ən **~s** z **limina** ˈlɪm ɪn ə §-ən ə
limerick, L~ ˈlɪm ər‿ɪk **~s** s
limescale ˈlaɪm skeɪᵊl
limestone ˈlaɪm stəʊn ‖ -stoʊn
limey, Limey ˈlaɪm i **~s** z
limin|a ˈlɪm ɪn |ə §-ən- **~al** ᵊl
lim|it ˈlɪm |ɪt §-ət -|ət **~ited** ɪt ɪd §ət-, -əd ‖ əţ əd **~iting** ɪt ɪŋ §ət- ‖ əţ ɪŋ **~its** ɪts §əts ‖ əts
ˌlimited ˌliaˈbility
limitation ˌlɪm ɪ ˈteɪʃ ᵊn -ə- **~s** z
limitless ˈlɪm ɪt ləs §-ət-, -lɪs **~ly** li **~ness** nəs nɪs
limn lɪm *(= limb)* **limned** lɪmd **limning** ˈlɪm ɪŋ -nɪŋ **limns** lɪmz
limo ˈlɪm əʊ ‖ -oʊ **~s** z
Limoges lɪ ˈməʊʒ ‖ -ˈmoʊʒ —*Fr* [li mɔːʒ]
Limousin ˌlɪm u ˈzæn -ˈzæ̃ —*Fr* [li mu zɛ̃]
limousine ˌlɪm ə ˈziːn ˈ· · · ‖ ˈlɪm ə ziːn ˌ· ·ˈ· **~s** z
limp lɪmp **limped** lɪmpt **limping** ˈlɪmp ɪŋ **limps** lɪmps
limpet ˈlɪmp ɪt §-ət **~s** s
limpid ˈlɪmp ɪd §-əd **~ly** li **~ness** nəs nɪs
limpidity lɪm ˈpɪd ət i -ɪt- ‖ -əţ i
limp|ly ˈlɪmp |li **~ness** nəs nɪs
Limpopo lɪm ˈpəʊp əʊ ‖ -ˈpoʊp oʊ
limp-wristed ˌlɪmp ˈrɪst ɪd◂ -əd◂
lim|y ˈlaɪm |i **~ier** i‿ə ‖ i‿ᵊr **~iest** i‿ɪst i‿əst
Linacre ˈlɪn ək ə ‖ -ᵊr
linage ˈlaɪn ɪdʒ
Lin Biao ˌlɪn bi ˈaʊ —*Chi* Lín Biāo [²lɪn ¹pjɑu]
Linch lɪntʃ
linchpin ˈlɪntʃ pɪn **~s** z
Lincoln ˈlɪŋk ən **~'s** z **~shire** ʃə ʃɪə ‖ ʃᵊr ʃɪr
ˌLincoln's ˈInn
Lincs, Lincs. lɪŋks
linctus ˈlɪŋkt əs **~es** ɪz əz
Lind lɪnd
Linda ˈlɪnd ə
lindane ˈlɪnd eɪn
Lindbergh ˈlɪnd bɜːg ‖ -bɜːg
linden, L~ ˈlɪnd ən **~s** z
Lindisfarne ˈlɪnd ɪs fɑːn -əs- ‖ -fɑːrn
Lindley ˈlɪnd li
Lindo ˈlɪnd əʊ ‖ -oʊ
Lindon ˈlɪnd ən
Lindsay, Lindsey ˈlɪndz i
Lindwall ˈlɪnd wɔːl ‖ -wɑːl
Lindy ˈlɪnd i
line, Line laɪn **lined** laɪnd **lines** laɪnz **lining** ˈlaɪn ɪŋ
ˈline ˌdrawing; ˈline ˌprinter
lineag|e *'descent'* ˈlɪn i‿ɪdʒ **~es** ɪz əz
lineag|e *'number of lines'* ˈlaɪn ɪdʒ
lineal ˈlɪn i‿əl **~ly** i
lineament ˈlɪn i‿ə mənt **~s** s
linear ˈlɪn i‿ə ‖ ᵊr **~ly** li
ˌLinear ˈB; ˌlinear ˈprogramming
linearit|y ˌlɪn i ˈær ət |i -ɪt i ‖ -əţ |i -ˈer- **~ies** iz
lineation ˌlɪn i ˈeɪʃ ᵊn **~s** z
linebacker ˈlaɪn ˌbæk ə ‖ -ᵊr **~s** z
Lineker ˈlɪn ɪk ə -ək- ‖ -ᵊr
line|man ˈlaɪn |mən **~men** mən
linen ˈlɪn ɪn §-ən **~s** z
ˈlinen ˌbasket
lineout ˈlaɪn aʊt **~s** s
liner ˈlaɪn ə ‖ -ᵊr **~s** z
linertrain ˈlaɪn ə treɪn ‖ -ᵊr- **~s** z
lineshoot|er ˈlaɪn ˌʃuːt |ə ‖ -ˌʃuːţ |ᵊr **~ers** əz ‖ ᵊrz **~ing** ɪŋ
lines|man ˈlaɪnz |mən **~men** mən men
lineup ˈlaɪn ʌp **~s** s
Linford ˈlɪn fəd ‖ -fᵊrd
-ling lɪŋ — **underling** ˈʌnd ə lɪŋ ‖ -ᵊr-
ling, Ling lɪŋ **lings** lɪŋz
Lingala lɪŋ ˈgɑːl ə
lingam ˈlɪŋ gəm **~s** z
linger ˈlɪŋ gə ‖ -gᵊr **~ed** d **lingering/ly** ˈlɪŋ gər‿ɪŋ /li **~s** z
lingerie ˈlænʒ ər i ˈlɒndʒ-; -ə reɪ ‖ ˌlɑːndʒ ə ˈreɪ -ˈriː, ˈ· · · —*Fr* [læ̃ʒ ʁi]
Lingfield ˈlɪŋ fiːᵊld
lingo ˈlɪŋ gəʊ ‖ -goʊ **~es** z
lingua ˈlɪŋ gwə
ˌlingua ˈfranca ˈfræŋk ə
lingual ˈlɪŋ gwəl §-gju‿əl **~s** z
Linguaphone *tdmk* ˈlɪŋ gwə fəʊn ‖ -foʊn
Linguarama *tdmk* ˌlɪŋ gwə ˈrɑːm ə ‖ -ˈræm- -ˈrɑːm-
linguine, linguini lɪŋ ˈgwiːn i —*It* [liŋ ˈgwiː ne]
linguist ˈlɪŋ gwɪst §-gwəst **~s** s
linguistic lɪŋ ˈgwɪst ɪk **~ally** ᵊl‿i **~s** s
liniment ˈlɪn ə mənt -ɪ- **~s** s
lining ˈlaɪn ɪŋ **~s** z
link, Link lɪŋk **linked** lɪŋkt **linking** ˈlɪŋk ɪŋ **links** lɪŋks
linkag|e ˈlɪŋk ɪdʒ **~es** ɪz əz
Linklater *(i)* ˈlɪŋk ˌleɪt ə ‖ -leɪţ ᵊr, *(ii)* -lət ə ‖ -ləţ ᵊr —*The author* Eric L~ *and his son* Magnus L~ *are (ii).*
link|man ˈlɪŋk |mæn —*but in the obsolete sense 'torchbearer' was usually* -mən **~men** men
linkup ˈlɪŋk ʌp **~s** s
Linley ˈlɪn li
Linlithgow lɪn ˈlɪθ gəʊ ‖ -goʊ
Linnae|us, Linne|us lɪ ˈniː‿|əs -ˈneɪ |əs **~an/s** ən/z
linnet ˈlɪn ɪt §-ət **~s** s
Linnhe ˈlɪn i

Liquids

The English **liquids** are l and r. Both are usually voiced APPROXIMANTS. The difference between them is that

- l is ALVEOLAR and **lateral** (= the air escapes over one or both sides of the tongue, passing round the tongue tip)
- r is POST-ALVEOLAR and **median** (= the air escapes over the tongue tip, while the sides of the tongue are pressed firmly against the roof of the mouth).

In both cases there is some ALLOPHONIC variation:

- Both may be voiceless because of the ASPIRATION of a preceding plosive, e.g. **play** pleɪ, **pray** preɪ.
- In RP l is **clear** (= has e-resonance) before a vowel sound or j, but **dark** (= has ʊ-resonance; allophonic symbol ɫ) elsewhere. Hence **like** laɪk, **value** ˈvæl juː (clear), **milk** mɪlk (= mɪɫk), **fall** fɔːl (= fɔːɫ). In AmE, l may be fairly dark everywhere.
- In a consonant cluster after t or d, r is made FRICATIVE instead of approximant. The result is that tr and dr form AFFRICATES, e.g. **train** treɪn, **drain** dreɪn.

lino ˈlaɪn əʊ ‖ -oʊ **~s** z
linocut ˈlaɪn əʊ kʌt ‖ -oʊ- **~s** s
linoleic ˌlɪn əʊ ˈliː ɪk ◂ -ˈleɪ- ‖ -ə-
linoleum lɪ ˈnəʊl i əm lə- ‖ -ˈnoʊl- **~s** z
Linotype *tdmk* ˈlaɪn əʊ taɪp ‖ -ə-
linseed ˈlɪn siːd
ˈlinseed oil, ˌ· · ˈ·
linsey-woolsey ˌlɪnz i ˈwʊlz i **~s** z
lint lɪnt
lintel ˈlɪnt əl **~s** z
Linton ˈlɪnt ən ‖ -ən
Lintott ˈlɪn tɒt ‖ -tɑːt
Linus ˈlaɪn əs
Linux ˈlɪn əks ˈlaɪn-
Linwood ˈlɪn wʊd
Linz lɪnts —*Ger* [lɪnts]
lion ˈlaɪ ən **~s** z
Lionel ˈlaɪ ən əl
lioness ˈlaɪ ən es -ɪs, -əs; ˌlaɪ ə ˈnes ‖ -əs **~es** ɪz əz
Lionheart ˈlaɪ ən hɑːt ‖ -hɑːrt
lion-hearted ˌlaɪ ən ˈhɑːt ɪd ◂ -əd, ˈ· ·ˌ· · ‖ -ˈhɑːrţ əd ◂
lionis... —*see* **lioniz...**
lionization ˌlaɪ ən aɪ ˈzeɪʃ ən ən ɪ- ‖ -ən ə-
lioniz|e ˈlaɪ ə naɪz **~ed** d **~er/s** ə/z ‖ ər/z **~es** ɪz əz **~ing** ɪŋ
lip lɪp **lipped** lɪpt **lipping** ˈlɪp ɪŋ **lips** lɪps
ˈlip gloss; **ˈlip ˌservice**
Lipari ˈlɪp ər i —*It* [ˈliː pa ri]
lipase ˈlaɪp eɪs ˈlɪp-, -eɪz
lipid ˈlɪp ɪd §-əd **~s** z
Lipitor *tdmk* ˈlɪp ɪ tɔː -ə- ‖ -tɔːr
Lipman, Lipmann ˈlɪp mən
lipo- *comb. form*
with stress-neutral suffix ¦lɪp əʊ ¦laɪp- ‖ -ə — **lipochrome** ˈlɪp əʊ krəʊm ˈlaɪp- ‖ -ə kroʊm
with stress-imposing suffix lɪ ˈpɒ+ laɪ- ‖ -ˈpɑː+ — **lipolysis** lɪ ˈpɒl əs ɪs -ɪs-, §-əs ‖ -ˈpɑːl-
lipoid ˈlɪp ɔɪd ˈlaɪp- **~s** z
lipom|a lɪ ˈpəʊm |ə lə-, laɪ- ‖ -ˈpoʊm |ə **~as** əz **~ata** ət ə ‖ əţ ə
liposome ˈlɪp əʊ səʊm ˈlaɪp- ‖ -ə soʊm **~s** z
liposuction ˈlɪp əʊ ˌsʌk ʃən ˈlaɪp- ‖ -oʊ- -ə-
Lippizaner ˌlɪp ɪt ˈsɑːn ə ◂ -ət- ‖ -ər ◂ **~s** z
Lippmann ˈlɪp mən
lipp|y ˈlɪp |i **~ier** i ə ‖ i ər **~iest** i ɪst i əst
lip-|read *present* ˈlɪp |riːd **~read** *past, pp* red **~reader/s** riːd ə/z ‖ -ər/z **~reading** riːd ɪŋ **~reads** riːdz
lip-smacking ˈlɪp ˌsmæk ɪŋ
lipstick ˈlɪp stɪk **~s** s
lip-sync, lip-synch ˈlɪp sɪŋk
Lipton ˈlɪpt ən
liquefaction ˌlɪk wɪ ˈfæk ʃən -wə-
lique|fy ˈlɪk wɪ |faɪ -wə- **~fied** faɪd **~fier/s** faɪ ə/z ‖ faɪ ər/z **~fies** faɪz **~fying** faɪ ɪŋ
liquescenc|e lɪ ˈkwes ənts **~y** i
liquescent lɪ ˈkwes ənt
liqueur lɪ ˈkjʊə lə-, -ˈkjɔː, -ˈkjɜː ‖ -ˈkɜː -ˈkjʊr —*Fr* [li kœːʁ] **~s** z
liquid ˈlɪk wɪd §-wəd **~ly** li **~s** z
ˌ**liquid ˈcrystal**; ˌ**liquid ˈoxygen**
liquidambar ˌlɪk wɪd ˈæm bə §-wəd-, ˈ· · · · ‖ -bər **~s** z

liqui|date 'lɪk wɪ |deɪt -wə- **~dated** deɪt ɪd -əd ‖ deɪţ əd **~dates** deɪts **~dating** deɪt ɪŋ ‖ deɪţ ɪŋ
liquidation ˌlɪk wɪ 'deɪʃ ən -wə- **~s** z
liquidator 'lɪk wɪ deɪt ə '·wə- ‖ -deɪţ ər **~s** z
liquidis|e, liquidiz|e 'lɪk wɪ daɪz -wə- **~ed** d **~er/s** ə/z ‖ ər/z **~es** ɪz əz **~ing** ɪŋ
liquidity lɪ 'kwɪd ət i lə-, -ɪt- ‖ -əţ i
liquitab 'lɪk wɪ tæb §-wə- **~s** z
liquor 'lɪk ə ‖ -ər —*also (med, pharm)* 'laɪk-, -wɔː ‖ -wɔːr **~ed** d **liquoring** 'lɪk ər ɪŋ **~s** z

LIQUORICE

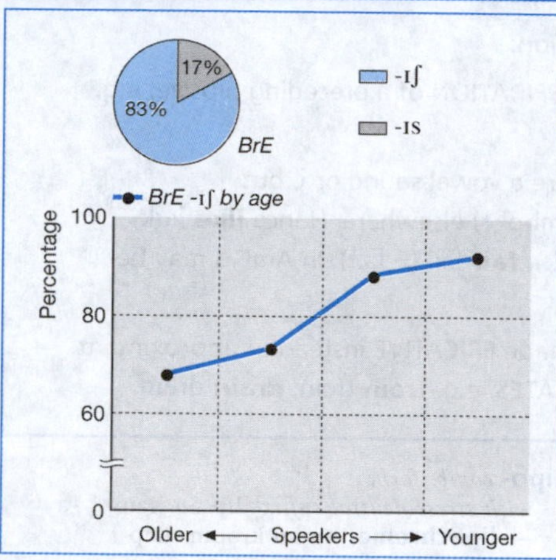

liquorice 'lɪk ər ɪʃ ɪs, §əs *Preference poll, BrE: -ɪʃ 83% (born since 1981, 92%), -ɪs 17%.*
ˌ**liquorice 'allsorts**
lira 'lɪər ə ‖ 'lɪr ə —*It* ['liː ra] **lire** 'lɪər ə -eɪ, -i ‖ 'lɪr eɪ —*It* ['liː re]
liriodendron ˌlɪr i əʊ 'dendr ən ‖ -i ə- **~s** z
liripipe 'lɪr i paɪp -ə- **~s** s
Lisa *(i)* 'liːs ə, *(ii)* 'liːz ə, *(iii)* 'laɪz ə
Lisbet 'lɪz bət -bet, -bɪt
Lisbeth 'lɪz bəθ -beθ, -bɪθ
Lisbon 'lɪz bən —*Port* Lisboa [liʒ 'βoʌ]
Lisburn 'lɪz bɜːn ‖ -bərn
Liskeard lɪ 'skɑːd ‖ -'skɑːrd
lisle, Lisle laɪəl —*but as a French name,* liːəl —*Fr* [lil]
lisp, LISP lɪsp **lisped** lɪspt **lisping** 'lɪsp ɪŋ **lisps** lɪsps
lisper 'lɪsp ə ‖ -ər **~s** z
Lissajous 'liːs ə ʒuː 'lɪs-; ˌ· ·'· —*Fr* [li sa ʒu]
lissom, lissome 'lɪs əm **~ly** li **~ness** nəs nɪs
Lisson 'lɪs ən
list lɪst **listed** 'lɪst ɪd -əd **listing** 'lɪst ɪŋ **lists** lɪsts
'**list price**
listel 'lɪst əl **~s** z
listen 'lɪs ən **~ed** d **~ing** ɪŋ **~s** z
listenable 'lɪs ən əb əl
listener 'lɪs ən ə ‖ ər **~s** z
Lister, l~ 'lɪst ə ‖ -ər **~s, ~'s** z
listeria lɪ 'stɪər i ə ‖ -'stɪr- **~s** z
Listerine *tdmk* 'lɪst ə riːn ‖ ˌ· ·'·
listeriosis lɪ ˌstɪər i 'əʊs ɪs -əs; ˌlɪst ɪər·'· · ‖ lɪ ˌstɪr i 'oʊs əs
listing 'lɪst ɪŋ **~s** z
'**listing ˌpaper**
listless 'lɪst ləs -lɪs **~ly** li **~ness** nəs nɪs
Liston 'lɪst ən
Listowel lɪ 'stəʊ əl ‖ -'stoʊ-
listserv 'lɪst sɜːv ‖ -sɜːv **~s** z
Liszt lɪst —*Hung* [list]
lit lɪt
Lita 'liːt ə ‖ 'liːţ ə
Li Tai Po ˌliː ˌtaɪ 'pəʊ ‖ -'poʊ —*Chi* Lǐ Dài Bái [³li ⁴tai ²pai]
litan|y 'lɪt ən |i ‖ -ən |i **~ies** iz
Litchfield 'lɪtʃ fiːəld
litchi ˌlaɪ 'tʃiː 'lɪtʃ iː, 'liːtʃ-, -i ‖ 'liːtʃ i 'laɪtʃ i **~s** z
lit crit ˌlɪt 'krɪt
lite laɪt
-lite laɪt — **chrysolite** 'krɪs ə laɪt
liter 'liːt ə ‖ 'liːţ ər **~s** z
literacy 'lɪt ər əs i ‖ 'lɪţ ər- →'lɪtr əs i
literal 'lɪt ər əl ‖ 'lɪţ ər əl →'lɪtr əl **~ism** ˌɪz əm **~ist/s** ɪst/s §əst/s ‖ əst/s **~ly** i **~ness** nəs nɪs **~s** z
literar|y 'lɪt ər ər |i ⚠ 'lɪtr |i ‖ 'lɪţ ə rer |i **~ily** əl i ɪ li **~iness** i nəs -nIs
literate 'lɪt ər ət -ɪt ‖ 'lɪţ ər ət →'lɪtr ət **~s** s
literati ˌlɪt ə 'rɑːt iː ‖ ˌlɪţ ə 'rɑːţ i
literatim ˌlɪt ə 'rɑːt ɪm -'reɪt-, §-əm ‖ ˌlɪţ ə 'reɪţ əm -'rɑːţ-
literature 'lɪtr ətʃ ə -ɪtʃ-; -ə tjʊə, -ɪ-; 'lɪt ər· · ‖ 'lɪţ ər ətʃ ər -ə tʃʊr, →'lɪtr· · **~s** z
-lith lɪθ — **megalith** 'meg ə lɪθ
litharge 'lɪθ ɑːdʒ ‖ -ɑːrdʒ lɪ 'θɑːrdʒ
lithe laɪð ‖ laɪθ
lithe|ly 'laɪð |li ‖ 'laɪθ- **~ness** nəs nɪs
lithesome 'laɪð səm ‖ 'laɪθ-
Lithgow 'lɪθ gəʊ ‖ -goʊ
lithia 'lɪθ i ə
lithic 'lɪθ ɪk
-lithic 'lɪθ ɪk — **megalithic** ˌmeg ə 'lɪθ ɪk ◂
lithium 'lɪθ i əm
litho 'laɪθ əʊ ‖ -oʊ
litho- *comb. form*
with stress-neutral suffix |lɪθ əʊ ‖ -ə — **lithosphere** 'lɪθ əʊ sfɪə ‖ -ə sfɪr
with stress-imposing suffix lɪ 'θɒ+ ‖ -'θɑː+ — **lithotomy** lɪ 'θɒt əm i ‖ -'θɑːţ-
lithograph 'lɪθ əʊ grɑːf 'laɪθ-, -græf ‖ -ə græf **~s** s
lithographer lɪ 'θɒg rəf ə laɪ- ‖ -'θɑːg rəf ər **~s** z
lithographic ˌlɪθ əʊ 'græf ɪk ◂ ˌlaɪθ- ‖ -ə- **~ally** əl i
lithography lɪ 'θɒg rəf i laɪ- ‖ -'θɑːg-
Lithuania ˌlɪθ ju 'eɪn i ə ˌ-u- ‖ ˌlɪθ u-
Lithuanian ˌlɪθ ju 'eɪn i ən ◂ ˌ-u- ‖ ˌlɪθ u- **~s** z
litigant 'lɪt ɪg ənt -əg- ‖ 'lɪţ ɪg- **~s** s
liti|gate 'lɪt ɪ |geɪt -ə- ‖ 'lɪţ ə- **~gated** geɪt ɪd -əd ‖ geɪţ əd **~gates** geɪts **~gating** geɪt ɪŋ ‖ geɪţ ɪŋ
litigation ˌlɪt ɪ 'geɪʃ ən -ə- ‖ ˌlɪţ- **~s** z

litigious lɪ 'tɪdʒ əs lə- **~ly** li **~ness** nəs nɪs
litmus 'lɪt məs
'litmus ˌpaper; **'litmus test**
litotes 'laɪt əʊ tiːz laɪ 'təʊt iːz ‖ 'laɪţ ə tiːz 'lɪţ-; laɪ 'toʊt iːz
litre 'liːt ə ‖ 'liːţ ər **~s** z
litter 'lɪt ə ‖ 'lɪţ ər **~ed** d **littering** 'lɪt ər ɪŋ ‖ 'lɪţ ər ɪŋ **~s** z
litterateur, littérateur ˌlɪt ər ə 'tɜː ‖ ˌlɪţ ər ə 'tɜː -'tʊər; →ˌlɪtr ə'· —*Fr* [li te ʁa tœːʁ] **~s** z
litterbag 'lɪt ə bæg ‖ 'lɪţ ər- **~s** z
litterbin 'lɪt ə bɪn ‖ 'lɪţ ər- **~s** z
litterbug 'lɪt ə bʌg ‖ 'lɪţ ər- **~s** z
litterlout 'lɪt ə laʊt ‖ 'lɪţ ər- **~s** s
little, L~ 'lɪt əl ‖ 'lɪţ əl **least** liːst **less** les
littler 'lɪt əl‿ə ‖ ər
ˌlittle 'finger; **'little ˌpeople**; **'Little Rock** *place in AR*; **ˌlittle 'woman**
Littlehampton ˌlɪt əl 'hæmp tən ◂ '·ˌ·· ‖ ˌlɪţ-
Littlejohn 'lɪt əl dʒɒn ‖ 'lɪţ əl dʒɑːn
Littler 'lɪt lə ‖ -lər
Littlestone 'lɪt əl stən -stəʊn ‖ 'lɪţ əl stoʊn
Littleton 'lɪt əl tən ‖ 'lɪţ-
Litton 'lɪt ən
littoral 'lɪt ər əl ‖ 'lɪţ- ˌlɪţ ə 'ræl, -'rɑːl **~s** z
liturgic lɪ 'tɜːdʒ ɪk lə- ‖ -'tɜːdʒ- **~al** əl **~ally** əl‿i **~s** s
liturgist 'lɪt ədʒ ɪst §-əst ‖ 'lɪţ ərdʒ- **~s** s
liturg|y 'lɪt ədʒ |i ‖ 'lɪţ ərdʒ |i **~ies** iz
livability ˌlɪv ə 'bɪl ət i -ɪt i ‖ -əţ i
livable 'lɪv əb əl
live *adj, adv* laɪv
ˌlive per'formance; **ˌlive 'wire**
live *v* lɪv **lived** lɪvd **lives** lɪvz **living** 'lɪv ɪŋ
liveability ˌlɪv ə 'bɪl ət i -ɪt i ‖ -əţ i
liveable 'lɪv əb əl
lived-in 'lɪvd ɪn
live-in ˌlɪv 'ɪn ◂
ˌlive-in 'lover
livelihood 'laɪv li hʊd **~s** z
livelong 'lɪv lɒŋ 'laɪv- ‖ -lɔːŋ -lɑːŋ
live|ly, L~ 'laɪv |li **~lier** li‿ə ‖ li‿ər **~liest** li‿ɪst li‿əst **~liness** li nəs -nɪs
liven 'laɪv ən **~ed** d **~ing** ‿ɪŋ **~s** z
Livens 'lɪv ənz
liver 'lɪv ə ‖ -ər **~s** z
'liver salts; **'liver ˌsausage**; **'liver spot**
Liver *Building, bird, symbol of Liverpool* 'laɪv ə ‖ -ər
liverie... —*see* **livery**
liverish 'lɪv ər ɪʃ **~ness** nəs nɪs
Livermore 'lɪv ə mɔː ‖ -ər mɔːr -moʊr
Liverpool 'lɪv ə puːl ‖ -ər-
Liverpudlian ˌlɪv ə 'pʌd li‿ən ◂ ‖ ˌ·ər- **~s** z
Liversedge 'lɪv ə sedʒ ‖ -ər-
liverwort 'lɪv ə wɜːt §-wɔːt ‖ -ər wɜːt -wɔːrt **~s** s
liverwurst 'lɪv ə wɜːst ‖ -ər wɜːst -wʊrst, -wʊʃt
liver|y 'lɪv ər‿|i **~ied** id **~ies** iz
'livery ˌcompany; **'livery ˌstable**
livery|man 'lɪv ər‿i |mən **~men** mən men
lives *pl of* **life** laɪvz
lives *3 sing. of* **live** lɪvz
Livesey *(i)* 'lɪv si, *(ii)* -zi
livestock 'laɪv stɒk ‖ -stɑːk
Livia 'lɪv i‿ə
livid 'lɪv ɪd §-əd **~ly** li **~ness** nəs nɪs
living 'lɪv ɪŋ **~s** z
ˌliving 'fossil; **ˌliving 'memory**; **'living room**; **'living ˌstandard**; **ˌliving 'wage**
Livings 'lɪv ɪŋz
Livingston 'lɪv ɪŋ stən
Livingstone 'lɪv ɪŋ stən -stəʊn ‖ -stoʊn
Livoni|a lɪ 'vəʊn i‿|ə ‖ -'voʊn- **~an/s** ən/z
Livy 'lɪv i
lixivi|ate lɪk 'sɪv i |eɪt **~ated** eɪt ɪd -əd ‖ eɪţ əd **~ates** eɪts **~ating** eɪt ɪŋ ‖ eɪţ ɪŋ
Liz lɪz
Liza *(i)* 'laɪz ə *(ii)* 'liːz ə
lizard, L~ 'lɪz əd ‖ -ərd **~s** z
Lizzie 'lɪz i
Ljubljana ˌlʊb li 'ɑːn ə ‖ ˌluːb- —*Slovene* [lʲu 'blʲaː na]
'll əl, əl —*Following a word other than a pronoun, this contracted form is pronounced as a separate syllable, thus* Jim'll do it **'dʒɪm əl ˌduː ɪt**, Lucy'll do it **'luːs i‿əl ˌduː ɪt**. *See, however, the entries* I'll, he'll, she'll, there'll, they'll, we'll, you'll.
llama 'lɑːm ə **~s** z
Llan *prefix in Welsh names* **læn θlæn, ɬæn** —*In Welsh this is* **ɬan**, *usually anglicized as* **læn** *or, when unstressed,* **lən**. *The Welsh sound (a voiceless alveolar lateral fricative) is however sometimes imitated by the non-Welsh as the cluster* **θl**, *or even as* **xl**. *No AmE forms are given for the Welsh names that follow.*
Llanberis læn 'ber ɪs θlæn- —*Welsh* [ɬan 'be ris]
Llandaff 'lænd əf 'ɬæn dæf, 'θlæn-, ˌ·'· —*Welsh* Llandaf [ɬan 'daːv]
Llandeilo læn 'daɪl əʊ 'θlæn- ‖ -oʊ —*Welsh* [ɬan 'dəi lo]
Llandovery læn 'dʌv ər‿i θlæn- —*Welsh* Llanymddyfri [ˌɬan əm 'ðəv ri]
Llandrindod læn 'drɪn dɒd θlæn- ‖ -dɑːd —*Welsh* [ɬan 'drin dod]
Llandudno læn 'dɪd nəʊ θlæn-, -'dʌd- ‖ -noʊ —*Welsh* [ɬan 'dïd no, -'did-]
Llanelli lə 'neθ li ɬə-, læ-, θlæ-, θlə- —*Welsh* [ɬan 'eɬ i]
Llanfairfechan ˌlæn feə 'fek ən ˌθlæn-, fə-, ˌ·vaɪ‿ə'·· ‖ -fer- —*Welsh* [ˌɬan vair 've χan]
Llanfairpwll ˌlæn feə 'puːl -ˌvaɪ‿ə-, -'pʊɬ ‖ -fer- *Also* **Llanfairpwllgwyngyll** ˌlæn vaɪ‿ə puːɬ 'gwɪn gɪɬ →-'gwɪŋ- ‖ ˌ·vaɪər- —*usually called* **Llanfair P.G.** ˌlæn feə ˌpiː 'dʒiː ˌθlæn-, ˌ·ˌvaɪ‿əˌ·'· ‖ -fer- —*The full form, famous for its length, is* Llanfairpwllgwyngyllgogerychwyrndrobwll-llandysiliogogogoch —*Welsh* [ˌɬan vair pʊɬ ˌgwin giɬ go ˌger ə ˌχwərn ˌdro buɬ ˌɬan də ˌsil jo ˌgo go 'goːχ -pʊɬ-, -ˌgwɪn gɪɬ-, -bʊɬ-]

L

Llangollen læn ˈgɒθ lən θlæn-, →læŋ- ‖ -ˈgɔːθ- —*Welsh* [ɬan ˈgo ɬen]

Llangranog læn ˈgræn ɒg θlæn-, →læŋ-, -əg ‖ -ɔːg —*Welsh* [ɬan ˈgra nog]

Llangurig læn ˈgɪr ɪg θlæn-, →læŋ- —*Welsh* [ɬan ˈgɨ rɪg, -ˈgi-]

Llanrwst læn ˈruːst θlæn- —*Welsh* [ɬan ˈruːst]

Llantrisant læn ˈtrɪs ᵊnt

Llanuwchllyn læn ˈjuːk lɪn θlæn-, lən-, θlən-, -ˈjuːx- —*Welsh* [ɬan ˈiuχ ɬɨn, -ˈiuχ ɬɪn]

Llanwrtyd læn ˈʊət ɪd θlæn- ‖ -ˈʊrt- —*Welsh* [ɬan ˈʊr tɪd, -tɨd]

Llareggub lə ˈreg əb læ-, θlə-, θlæ-, -ʌb —*not a real Welsh name*

Llewelyn lə ˈwel ɪn θlə-; lu ˈel-, θlu- —*Welsh* [ˈɬwe lɨn; ɬe ˈwe lɨn, -lin]

Lleyn liːn θliːn, leɪn, θleɪn —*Welsh* Llŷn [ɬiːn, ɬiːn]

Lloret lə ˈret —*Sp* [ʎo ˈret, jo-], *Catalan* [ʎu ˈret]

Lloyd lɔɪd

Llywelyn lə ˈwel ɪn θlə-, §-ən; lu ˈel-, θlu- —*Welsh* [ɬə ˈwe lɨn, -lin]

lo ləʊ ‖ loʊ

ˌlo and beˈhold

loach, Loach ləʊtʃ ‖ loʊtʃ **loaches** ˈləʊtʃ ɪz -əz ‖ ˈloʊtʃ əz

load ləʊd ‖ loʊd **loaded** ˈləʊd ɪd -əd ‖ ˈloʊd əd **loading** ˈləʊd ɪŋ ‖ ˈloʊd ɪŋ **loads** ləʊdz ‖ loʊdz

ˈload ˌfactor

load-bearing ˈləʊd ˌbeər ɪŋ ‖ ˈloʊd ˌber ɪŋ

loadmaster ˈləʊd ˌmɑːst ə §-ˌmæst- ‖ -ˌmæst ᵊr **~s** z

loadsamoney ˈləʊdz ə ˌmʌn i ‖ ˈloʊdz-

loadstar ˈləʊd stɑː ‖ ˈloʊd stɑːr **~s** z

loadstone ˈləʊd stəʊn ‖ ˈloʊd stoʊn **~s** z

loaf ləʊf ‖ loʊf **loafed** ləʊft ‖ loʊft **loafing** ˈləʊf ɪŋ ‖ ˈloʊf ɪŋ **loafs** ləʊfs ‖ loʊfs **loaves** ləʊvz ‖ loʊvz

loafer ˈləʊf ə ‖ ˈloʊf ᵊr **~s** z

loafsugar ˈləʊf ˌʃʊg ə ‖ ˈloʊf ʃʊg ᵊr

loam ləʊm ‖ loʊm

loamy ˈləʊm i ‖ ˈloʊm i

loan ləʊn ‖ loʊn **loaned** ləʊnd ‖ loʊnd **loaning** ˈləʊn ɪŋ ‖ ˈloʊn ɪŋ **loans** ləʊnz ‖ loʊnz

loaner ˈləʊn ə ‖ ˈloʊn ᵊr **~s** z

loanword ˈləʊn wɜːd ‖ ˈloʊn wɜːd **~s** z

loath ləʊθ ⚠ləʊð ‖ loʊθ loʊð

loathe ləʊð ‖ loʊð **loathed** ləʊðd ‖ loʊðd **loather/s** ˈləʊð ə/z ‖ ˈloʊð ᵊr/z **loathes** ləʊðz ‖ loʊðz **loathing/ly** ˈləʊð ɪŋ /li ‖ ˈloʊð ɪŋ /li

loathsome ˈləʊð səm ˈləʊθ- ‖ ˈloʊð- ˈloʊθ- **~ly** li **~ness** nəs nɪs

loaves ləʊvz ‖ loʊvz

lob lɒb ‖ lɑːb **lobbed** lɒbd ‖ lɑːbd **lobbing** ˈlɒb ɪŋ ‖ ˈlɑːb ɪŋ **lobs** lɒbz ‖ lɑːbz

lobate ˈləʊb eɪt ‖ ˈloʊb-

lobb|y ˈlɒb |i ‖ ˈlɑːb |i **~ied** id **~ies** iz **~ying** i‿ɪŋ

lobbyist ˈlɒb i ɪst -əst ‖ ˈlɑːb- **~s** s

lobe ləʊb ‖ loʊb **lobed** ləʊbd ‖ loʊbd **lobes** ləʊbz ‖ loʊbz

lobelia ləʊ ˈbiːl i‿ə ‖ loʊ- **~s** z

lobeline ˈləʊb ə liːn ‖ ˈloʊb-

loblol|y ˈlɒb ˌlɒl |i ‖ ˈlɑːb ˌlɑːl |i **~ies** iz

lobotomis|e, lobotomiz|e ləʊ ˈbɒt ə maɪz ‖ loʊ ˈbɑːţ- lə- **~ed** d **~es** ɪz əz **~ing** ɪŋ

lobotom|y ləʊ ˈbɒt əm |i ‖ loʊ ˈbɑːţ- lə- **~ies** iz

lobscouse ˈlɒb skaʊs ‖ ˈlɑːb-

lobster ˈlɒb stə ‖ ˈlɑːb stᵊr **~s** z

lobster|man ˈlɒb stə| mən -mæn ‖ ˈlɑːb stᵊr|- **~men** mən men

lobsterpot ˈlɒb stə pɒt ‖ ˈlɑːb stᵊr pɑːt **~s** s

lobular ˈlɒb jʊl ə ‖ ˈlɑːb jəl ᵊr

lobule ˈlɒb juːl ‖ ˈlɑːb- **~s** z

local, Local ˈləʊk ᵊl ‖ ˈloʊk ᵊl **~ly** i **~s** z

ˌlocal ˌarea ˈnetwork; **ˌlocal auˈthority**; **ˌlocal ˈcolour**; **ˌlocal ˈderby**; **ˌlocal ˈoption**; **ˈlocal time, ˌ·ˈ·**

lo-cal *'low-calorie'* ˌləʊ ˈkæl ◂ ‖ ˌloʊ-

locale ləʊ ˈkɑːl ‖ loʊ ˈkæl **~s** z

localis... —*see* **localiz...**

localism ˈləʊk ᵊl ˌɪz əm ‖ ˈloʊk- **~s** z

localit|y ləʊ ˈkæl ət |i -ɪt- ‖ loʊ ˈkæl əţ |i **~ies** iz

localization ˌləʊk əl aɪ ˈzeɪʃ ᵊn -əl ɪ- ‖ ˌloʊk əl ə- **~s** z

localiz|e ˈləʊk ə laɪz -ᵊl aɪz ‖ ˈloʊk- **~ed** d **~es** ɪz əz **~ing** ɪŋ

locally ˈləʊk ᵊl i ‖ ˈloʊk-

lo-carb ˌləʊ ˈkɑːb ◂ ‖ ˌloʊ ˈkɑːrb ◂

Locarno ləʊ ˈkɑːn əʊ lɒ- ‖ loʊ ˈkɑːrn oʊ —*It* [lo ˈkar no]

loc|ate ləʊ ˈk|eɪt ‖ ˈloʊk |eɪt loʊ ˈk|eɪt **~ated** eɪt ɪd -əd ‖ eɪţ əd **~ates** eɪts **~ating** eɪt ɪŋ ‖ eɪţ ɪŋ

location ləʊ ˈkeɪʃ ᵊn ‖ loʊ- **~s** z

locative ˈlɒk ət ɪv ‖ ˈlɑːk əţ ɪv **~s** z

loch lɒx lɒk ‖ lɑːk lɑːx **lochs** lɒxs lɒks ‖ lɑːks lɑːxs

Lochearnhead lɒx ˌɜːn ˈhed lɒk- ‖ lɑːk ˌɜːn- lɑːx-

Lochgilphead lɒx ˈgɪlp hed lɒk- ‖ lɑːk- lɑːx-

Lochinvar ˌlɒx ɪn ˈvɑː ˌlɒk- ‖ ˌlɑːk ən ˈvɑːr

Lochinver lɒ ˈxɪn və -ˈkɪn- ‖ lɑː ˈkɪn vᵊr

loci ˈləʊs aɪ ˈləʊk-, ˈlɒk-, -iː ‖ ˈloʊs aɪ ˈloʊk-, -iː

lock, Lock lɒk ‖ lɑːk **locked** lɒkt ‖ lɑːkt **locking** ˈlɒk ɪŋ ‖ ˈlɑːk ɪŋ **locks** lɒks ‖ lɑːks

ˈlock ˌkeeper

lockable ˈlɒk əb ᵊl ‖ ˈlɑːk-

Locke lɒk ‖ lɑːk

locker ˈlɒk ə ‖ ˈlɑːk ᵊr **~s** z

ˈlocker room

Lockerbie ˈlɒk əb i ‖ ˈlɑːk ᵊrb i

locker-room ˈlɒk ə ruːm -rʊm ‖ ˈlɑːk ᵊr-

locket ˈlɒk ɪt §-ət ‖ ˈlɑːk- **~s** s

Lockhart *(i)* ˈlɒk ət ‖ ˈlɑːk ᵊrt, *(ii)* -hɑːt ‖ -hɑːrt

Lockheed ˈlɒk hiːd ‖ ˈlɑːk-

lockjaw ˈlɒk dʒɔː ‖ ˈlɑːk- -dʒɑː

locknut ˈlɒk nʌt ‖ ˈlɑːk- **~s** s

lockout ˈlɒk aʊt ‖ ˈlɑːk- **~s** s

Locksley ˈlɒks li ‖ ˈlɑːks-
locksmith ˈlɒk smɪθ ‖ ˈlɑːk- **~s** s
lockstep ˈlɒk step ‖ ˈlɑːk-
lockstitch ˈlɒk stɪtʃ ‖ ˈlɑːk- **~ed** t **~es** ɪz əz **~ing** ɪŋ
lockup ˈlɒk ʌp ‖ ˈlɑːk- **~s** s
Lockwood ˈlɒk wʊd ‖ ˈlɑːk-
Lockyer ˈlɒk jə ‖ ˈlɑːk jᵊr
loco ˈləʊk əʊ ‖ ˈloʊk oʊ **~s** z
locomotion ˌləʊk ə ˈməʊʃ ᵊn ‖ ˌloʊk ə ˈmoʊʃ ᵊn
locomotive ˌləʊk ə ˈməʊt ɪv ◂ ˈ· · · · ‖ ˌloʊk ə ˈmoʊţ ɪv ◂ **~s** z
locomotor ˌləʊk əʊ ˈməʊt ə ◂ ‖ ˌloʊk ə ˈmoʊţ ᵊr ◂ **ˌloco ˌmotor aˈtaxia**
locoweed ˈləʊk əʊ wiːd ‖ ˈloʊk oʊ-
Locris ˈləʊk rɪs ˈlɒk-, -rəs ‖ ˈloʊk-
locum ˈləʊk əm ˈlɒk- ‖ ˈloʊk- **~s** z **ˌlocum ˈtenens** ˈten enz ˈtiːn- ‖ -ənz
locus ˈləʊk əs ˈlɒk- ‖ ˈloʊk- **ˌlocus ˈclassicus** ˈklæs ɪk əs; **ˌlocus ˈstandi** ˈstænd aɪ
locust ˈləʊk əst ‖ ˈloʊk- **~s** s
locution ləʊ ˈkjuːʃ ᵊn lɒ- ‖ loʊ- **~s** z
locutionary ləʊ ˈkjuːʃ ᵊn ər‿i -ᵊn‿ər i ‖ loʊ ˈkjuːʃ ə ner i
Lod lɒd ‖ loʊd
lode, Lode ləʊd ‖ loʊd *(= load)* **lodes** ləʊdz ‖ loʊdz
loden ˈləʊd ᵊn ‖ ˈloʊd ᵊn
lodestar ˈləʊd stɑː ‖ ˈloʊd stɑːr **~s** z
lodestone ˈləʊd stəʊn ‖ ˈloʊd stoʊn **~s** z
lodge, Lodge lɒdʒ ‖ lɑːdʒ **lodged** lɒdʒd ‖ lɑːdʒd **lodges** ˈlɒdʒ ɪz -əz ‖ ˈlɑːdʒ- **lodging** ˈlɒdʒ ɪŋ ‖ ˈlɑːdʒ ɪŋ
lodger ˈlɒdʒ ə ‖ ˈlɑːdʒ ᵊr **~s** z
lodging ˈlɒdʒ ɪŋ ‖ ˈlɑːdʒ ɪŋ **~s** z **ˈlodging house**
lodgment ˈlɒdʒ mənt ‖ ˈlɑːdʒ- **~s** s
Lodi *places in US* ˈləʊd aɪ ‖ ˈloʊd-
Lodore ləʊ ˈdɔː ‖ loʊ ˈdɔːr
Lodz wʊdʒ wuːtʃ ‖ loʊdz lɑːdz, wuːdʒ —*Polish* Łódź [wutɕ]
Loeb ləʊb lɜːb ‖ loʊb —*Ger* [løːp]
loess, löss ˈləʊ es -ɪs, -əs; lɜːs ‖ les lʌs, ˈloʊ əs, lɜːs —*Ger* [lœs, løːs]
Loewe ˈləʊ i ‖ loʊ
Lofoten ləʊ ˈfəʊt ᵊn ˈ·ˌ· · ‖ ˈloʊ foʊt ᵊn —*Norw* [ˈluː fut ən]
loft lɒft ‖ lɔːft lɑːft **lofts** lɒfts ‖ lɔːfts lɑːfts
Lofthouse ˈlɒft haʊs -əs ‖ ˈlɔːft- ˈlɑːft-
Lofting ˈlɒft ɪŋ ‖ ˈlɔːft ɪŋ ˈlɑːft-
Loftus ˈlɒft əs ‖ ˈlɔːft- ˈlɑːft-
loft|y ˈlɒft |i ‖ ˈlɔːft |i ˈlɑːft- **~ier** i‿ə ‖ i‿ᵊr **~iest** i‿ɪst i‿əst **~ily** ɪ li əl i **~iness** i nəs i nɪs
log lɒg ‖ lɔːg lɑːg **logged** lɒgd ‖ lɔːgd lɑːgd **logging** ˈlɒg ɪŋ ‖ ˈlɔːg ɪŋ ˈlɑːg- **ˌlog ˈcabin**
-log lɒg ‖ lɔːg lɑːg — **catalog** ˈkæt ə lɒg ‖ ˈkæţ ᵊl ɔːg -ɑːg
Logan ˈləʊg ən ‖ ˈloʊg-
loganberr|y ˈləʊg ən bər‿|i →ˈ·ŋ-, →ˈ·əm-, -ˌber |i ‖ ˈloʊg ən ˌber |i **~ies** iz
logarithm ˈlɒg ə rɪð əm -rɪθ əm ‖ ˈlɔːg- ˈlɑːg- **~s** z
logarithmic ˌlɒg ə ˈrɪð mɪk ◂ -ˈrɪθ- ‖ ˌlɔːg- ˌlɑːg- **~al** ᵊl **~ally** ᵊl‿i
logbook ˈlɒg bʊk §-buːk ‖ ˈlɔːg- ˈlɑːg- **~s** s
loge ləʊʒ ‖ loʊʒ **loges** ˈləʊʒ ɪz -əz ‖ ˈloʊʒ-
logg... —*see* **log**
logger ˈlɒg ə ‖ ˈlɔːg ᵊr ˈlɑːg- **~s** z
loggerhead ˈlɒg ə hed ‖ ˈlɔːg ᵊr- ˈlɑːg- **~s** z
loggia ˈlɒdʒ i‿ə ˈləʊdʒ- ‖ ˈloʊdʒ ə ˈloʊdʒ i‿ə **~s** z
logi... —*see* **logy**
logic ˈlɒdʒ ɪk ‖ ˈlɑːdʒ- **~s** s
Logica *tdmk* ˈlɒdʒ ɪk ə ‖ ˈlɑːdʒ-
logical ˈlɒdʒ ɪk ᵊl ‖ ˈlɑːdʒ- **~ly** ‿i **~ness** nəs nɪs
-logical ˈlɒdʒ ɪk ᵊl ‖ ˈlɑːdʒ- — **cytological** ˌsaɪt əʊ ˈlɒdʒ ɪk ᵊl ◂ ‖ ˌsaɪţ ə ˈlɑːdʒ-
logicality ˌlɒdʒ ɪ ˈkæl ət i §ˌ·ə-, -ɪt i ‖ ˌlɑːdʒ ə ˈkæl əţ i
logician ləʊ ˈdʒɪʃ ᵊn lɒ- ‖ loʊ- **~s** z
Logie ˈləʊg i ‖ ˈloʊg i
-logist *stress-imposing* lədʒ ɪst §-əst — **physiologist** ˌfɪz i ˈɒl ədʒ ɪst §-əst ‖ -ˈɑːl-
logistic ləʊ ˈdʒɪst ɪk lɒ- ‖ loʊ- **~al** ᵊl **~ally** ᵊl‿i **~s** s
logjam ˈlɒg dʒæm ‖ ˈlɔːg- ˈlɑːg- **~s** z
loglog ˌlɒg ˈlɒg ‖ ˌlɔːg ˈlɔːg ˌlɑːg ˈlɑːg
logo, Logo, LOGO ˈləʊg əʊ ˈlɒg- ‖ ˈloʊg oʊ **~s** z
logo- *comb. form*
with stress-neutral suffix ˌlɒg əʊ ‖ ˌlɔːg ə ˈlɑːg ə — **logographic** ˌlɒg əʊ ˈgræf ɪk ◂ ‖ ˌlɔːg ə- ˌlɑːg-
with stress-imposing suffix lɒ ˈgɒ+ ‖ loʊ ˈgɑː+ — **logography** lɒ ˈgɒg rəf i ‖ loʊ ˈgɑːg-
logogram ˈlɒg ə græm ‖ ˈlɔːg- ˈlɑːg- **~s** z
logon ˌlɒg ˈɒn ‖ ˌlɔːg ˈɑːn ˌlɑːg-, ˈɔːn **~s** z
logopaed|ic, logoped|ic ˌlɒg ə ˈpiːd|ɪk ◂ ‖ ˌlɔːg- ˌlɑːg- **~ics** ɪks **~ist/s** ɪst/s əst/s
logorrhea, logorrhoea ˌlɒg ə ˈriː‿ə ‖ ˌlɔːg- ˌlɑːg-
Logos, logos ˈlɒg ɒs ˈləʊg- ‖ ˈloʊg ɑːs -ɔːs, -oʊs
logotype ˈlɒg əʊ taɪp ‖ ˈlɔːg- ˈlɑːg- **~s** s
logroll|er ˈlɒg ˌrəʊl |ə →-ˌrɒʊl- ‖ ˈlɔːg ˌroʊl |ᵊr ˈlɑːg- **~ers** əz ‖ ᵊrz **~ing** ɪŋ
Logue ləʊg ‖ loʊg
-logue lɒg ‖ lɔːg lɑːg — **monologue** ˈmɒn ə lɒg ‖ ˈmɑːn ə lɔːg -lɑːg
logwood ˈlɒg wʊd ‖ ˈlɔːg- ˈlɑːg-
log|y ˈləʊg |i ‖ ˈloʊg |i **~ier** i‿ə ‖ i‿ᵊr **~iest** i‿ɪst i‿əst **~ily** ɪ li əl i **~iness** i nəs i nɪs
-logy *stress-imposing* lədʒ i — **analogy** ə ˈnæl ədʒ i
Lohengrin ˈləʊ ən grɪn -ɪn-, →-əŋ- ‖ ˈloʊ- —*Ger* [ˈloː ən gʁiːn]
loin lɔɪn **loins** lɔɪnz
loin|cloth ˈlɔɪn |klɒθ →ˈlɔɪŋ-, -klɔːθ ‖ -|klɔːθ -klɑːθ **~cloths** klɒθs klɒðz, klɔːðz, klɔːθs ‖ klɔːðz klɔːθs, klɑːðz, klɑːθs

Loire lwɑː ‖ lwɑːr —*Fr* [lwaːʁ]
Lois ˈləʊ ɪs §-əs ‖ ˈloʊ-
loiter ˈlɔɪt ə ‖ ˈlɔɪţ ər **~ed** d **loitering** ˈlɔɪt‿ər ɪŋ ‖ ˈlɔɪţ ər ɪŋ **~s** z
loiterer ˈlɔɪt‿ər ə ‖ ˈlɔɪţ ər ər **~s** z
Loki ˈləʊk i ‖ ˈloʊk i
Lola ˈləʊl ə ‖ ˈloʊl ə
Lolita lɒ ˈliːt ə ləʊ- ‖ loʊ ˈliːţ ə **~s** z
loll lɒl ‖ lɑːl **lolled** lɒld ‖ lɑːld **lolling** ˈlɒl ɪŋ ‖ ˈlɑːl ɪŋ **lolls** lɒlz ‖ lɑːlz
Lollard ˈlɒl əd -ɑːd ‖ ˈlɑːl ərd **~s** z
lollie... —*see* **lolly**
lollipop ˈlɒl i pɒp ‖ ˈlɑːl i pɑːp **~s** s
ˈlollipop man, ˈlollipop ˌwoman
lollop ˈlɒl əp ‖ ˈlɑːl- **~ed** t **~ing** ɪŋ **~s** s
lollo rosso ˌlɒl əʊ ˈrɒs əʊ ‖ ˌlɑːl oʊ ˈrɑːs oʊ ˌloʊl-, -ˈroʊs- —*It* [ˌlol lo ˈros so]
loll|y ˈlɒl |i ‖ ˈlɑːl |i **~ies** iz
lollygag ˈlɒl i gæg ‖ ˈlɑːl- **~ged** d **~ging** ɪŋ **~s** z
lollypop ˈlɒl i pɒp ‖ ˈlɑːl i pɑːp **~s** s
Loma Prieta ˌləʊm ə pri ˈet ə ‖ ˌloʊm ə pri ˈeɪţ ə -ˈeţ ə
Lomas ˈləʊm əs -æs ‖ ˈloʊm æs
Lomax ˈləʊm æks -əks ‖ ˈloʊm-
Lombard ˈlɒm bəd ˈlʌm-, -bɑːd ‖ ˈlɑːm bərd -bɑːrd **~s** z
ˈLombard Street
Lombardi lɒm ˈbɑːd i ‖ lɑːm ˈbɑːrd i
Lombardo lɒm ˈbɑːd əʊ ‖ lɑːm ˈbɑːrd oʊ —*It* [lom ˈbar do]
Lombardy ˈlɒm bəd i ˈlʌm- ‖ ˈlɑːm bərd i -bɑːrd i
ˌLombardy ˈpoplar
Lombok ˈlɒm bɒk ‖ ˈlɑːm bɑːk ˈ.
Lombrosian lɒm ˈbrəʊz i‿ən ‖ lɑːm ˈbroʊz- -ˈbroʊʒ ən **~s** z
Lombroso lɒm ˈbrəʊz əʊ ‖ lɑːm ˈbroʊz oʊ —*It* [lom ˈbroː so]
Lome, Lomé ˈləʊ meɪ ‖ loʊ ˈmeɪ —*Fr* [lɔ me]
Lomond ˈləʊm ənd ‖ ˈloʊm-
Lomu ˈləʊm uː ‖ ˈloʊm-
London ˈlʌnd ən *(!)*
ˌLondon ˈAirport; **ˌLondon ˈBridge**; **ˌLondon ˈpride**
Londonderry ˈlʌnd ən ˌder i -ənd‿ər i; ˌlʌnd ən ˈder i◂ —*Lord L~ iss* ˈlʌnd ənd‿ər i
Londoner ˈlʌnd ən ə ‖ -ər **~s** z
lone ləʊn ‖ loʊn
ˌLone ˈRanger; **ˌlone ˈwolf**
lone|ly ˈləʊn |li ‖ ˈloʊn- **~lier** li‿ə ‖ li‿ər **~liest** li‿ɪst li‿əst **~liness** li nəs li nɪs
ˌlonely ˈhearts, ˈ. .
loner ˈləʊn ə ‖ ˈloʊn ər **~s** z
lonesome ˈləʊn səm ‖ ˈloʊn- **~ly** li **~ness** nəs nɪs
long, Long lɒŋ ‖ lɔːŋ lɑːŋ **longed** lɒŋd ‖ lɔːŋd lɑːŋd **longer** ˈlɒŋ gə ‖ ˈlɔːŋ gər ˈlɑːŋ- **longest** ˈlɒŋ gɪst -gəst ‖ ˈlɔːŋ gəst ˈlɑːŋ- **longing** ˈlɒŋ ɪŋ ‖ ˈlɔːŋ ɪŋ ˈlɑːŋ- **longs** lɒŋz ‖ lɔːŋz lɑːŋz
ˈLong Beach; **ˌlong diˈvision**; **ˌlong ˈhaul**; ₍ˌ₎**Long ˈIsland, Long ˌIsland ˈSound,** .ˈ. . ˈ.; **ˈlong johns**; **ˈlong jump, ˈlong ˌjumper**; **ˈlong shot**; **ˌlong ˈsuit**; **ˌlong ˈton**; **ˌlong ˈvac, ˌlong vaˈcation**; **ˌlong ˈwave,** ˈ. .
Longannet lɒŋ ˈæn ɪt -ət ‖ lɔːŋ- lɑːŋ-
long-awaited ˌlɒŋ ə ˈweɪt ɪd ◂ -əd ‖ ˌlɔːŋ ə ˈweɪţ əd ◂ ˌlɑːŋ-
longboat ˈlɒŋ bəʊt ‖ ˈlɔːŋ boʊt ˈlɑːŋ- **~s** s
longbow ˈlɒŋ bəʊ ‖ ˈlɔːŋ boʊ ˈlɑːŋ- **~s** z
Longbridge ˈlɒŋ brɪdʒ ‖ ˈlɔːŋ- ˈlɑːŋ-
long-distance ˌlɒŋ ˈdɪst ənᵗs ◂ ‖ ˌlɔːŋ- ˌlɑːŋ-
long-drawn-out ˌlɒŋ drɔːn ˈaʊt ◂ ‖ ˌlɔːŋ- ˌlɑːŋ drɑːn-
longed-for ˈlɒŋd fɔː ‖ ˈlɔːŋd fɔːr ˈlɑːŋd-
longer *comparative adj* ˈlɒŋ gə ‖ ˈlɔːŋ gər ˈlɑːŋ- —*But the agent noun* longer *'one that longs', if ever used, is pronounced without* g, *as* -ə ‖ -ər
longeron ˈlɒndʒ ər ən ‖ ˈlɑːndʒ ə rɑːn **~s** z
longest ˈlɒŋ gɪst -gəst ‖ ˈlɔːŋ- ˈlɑːŋ-
longevity lɒn ˈdʒev ət i lɒŋ-, -ɪt- ‖ lɑːn ˈdʒev əţ i lɔːn-
long-expected ˌlɒŋ ɪk ˈspekt ɪd ◂ -ek-, -ək-, -əd ‖ ˌlɔːŋ- ˌlɑːŋ-
Longfellow ˈlɒŋ ˌfel əʊ ‖ ˈlɔːŋ ˌfel oʊ ˈlɑːŋ-
Longford ˈlɒŋ fəd ‖ ˈlɔːŋ fərd ˈlɑːŋ-
longhair ˈlɒŋ heə ‖ ˈlɔːŋ her ˈlɑːŋ- **~s** z
long-haired ˌlɒŋ ˈheəd ◂ ‖ ˌlɔːŋ ˈheərd ◂ ˌlɑːŋ-
longhand ˈlɒŋ hænd ‖ ˈlɔːŋ- ˈlɑːŋ-
long-haul ˌlɒŋ ˈhɔːl ◂ ˈ. . ‖ ˌlɔːŋ- ˌlɑːŋ ˈhɑːl◂
long-headed ˌlɒŋ ˈhed ɪd ◂ -əd ‖ ˌlɔːŋ- ˌlɑːŋ-
longhop ˈlɒŋ hɒp ‖ ˈlɔːŋ hɑːp ˈlɑːŋ- **~s** s
longhorn ˈlɒŋ hɔːn ‖ ˈlɔːŋ hɔːrn ˈlɑːŋ- **~s** z
long|house ˈlɒŋ| haʊs ‖ ˈlɔːŋ- ˈlɑːŋ- **~houses** haʊz ɪz -əz
Longhurst ˈlɒŋ hɜːst ‖ ˈlɔːŋ hɜːst ˈlɑːŋ-
Longines *tdmk* ˈlɒndʒ iːn ‖ lɑːn ˈdʒiːn
longing ˈlɒŋ ɪŋ ‖ ˈlɔːŋ ɪŋ ˈlɑːŋ- **~ly** li **~s** z
Longinus lɒn ˈdʒaɪn əs lɒŋ ˈgiːn- ‖ lɑːn-
longish ˈlɒŋ ɪʃ ˈlɒŋg- ‖ ˈlɔːŋ- ˈlɑːŋ-

LONGITUDE

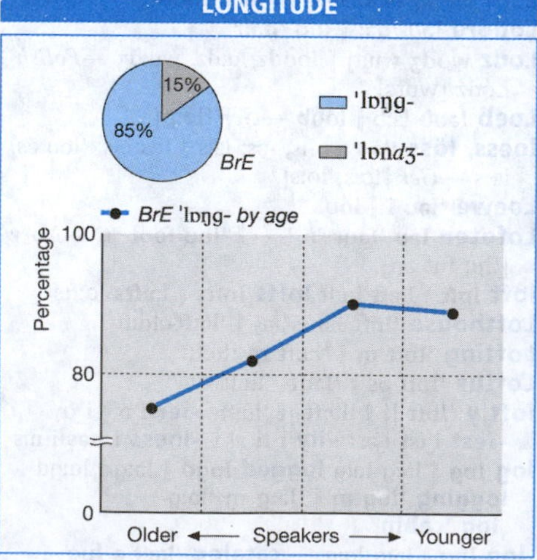

longitude ˈlɒŋ gɪ tjuːd -gə-, -dɪ-, -tɪ-, →-tʃuːd; ˈlɒndʒ ɪ-, -ə- ‖ ˈlɑːndʒ ə tuːd -tjuːd

— Preference poll, BrE: ˈlɒŋg- 85%, ˈlɒndʒ- 15%. Several respondents spontaneously mentioned ˈlɒŋ dɪ-, which was not given as an option in the questionnaire. **~s** z

ongitudinal ˌlɒŋ gɪ ˈtjuːd ɪn ᵊl ◂ ˌ·gə-, ˌlɒndʒ ɪ-, ˌ·ə-, →-ˈtʃuːd-, -ᵊn‿əl ‖ ˌlɑːndʒ ə ˈtuːd ᵊn‿əl ◂ -ˈtjuːd- **~ly** i

ongland ˈlɒŋ lənd ‖ ˈlɔːŋ- ˈlɑːŋ-

ong-lasting ˌlɒŋ ˈlɑːst ɪŋ ◂ §-ˈlæst- ‖ ˌlɔːŋ ˈlæst ɪŋ ◂ ˌlɑːŋ-

ongleat ˈlɒŋ liːt ‖ ˈlɔːŋ- ˈlɑːŋ-

ong-life ˌlɒŋ ˈlaɪf ◂ ‖ ˌlɔːŋ- ˌlɑːŋ-

ong-lived ˌlɒŋ ˈlɪvd ◂ ‖ ˌlɔːŋ ˈlaɪvd ◂ ˌlɑːŋ-, -ˈlɪvd ◂ *(*)*

ong-lost ˌlɒŋ ˈlɒst ◂ -ˈlɔːst ◂ ‖ ˌlɔːŋ ˈlɔːst ◂ ˌlɑːŋ-, -ˈlɑːst ◂

ongman ˈlɒŋ mən ‖ ˈlɔːŋ- ˈlɑːŋ-

ongobardi ˌlɒŋ gəʊ ˈbɑːd i -iː ‖ ˌlɔːŋ gə ˈbɑːrd i ˌlɑːŋ-, -aɪ

ong-playing ˌlɒŋ ˈpleɪ ɪŋ ◂ ‖ ˌlɔːŋ- ˌlɑːŋ-
 ˌlong-ˌplaying ˈrecord

ong-range ˌlɒŋ ˈreɪndʒ ◂ ‖ ˌlɔːŋ- ˌlɑːŋ-
 ˌlong-range ˈmissiles

ongridge ˈlɒŋ grɪdʒ -rɪdʒ ‖ ˈlɔːŋ- ˈlɑːŋ-

ong-running ˌlɒŋ ˈrʌn ɪŋ ◂ ‖ ˌlɔːŋ- ˌlɑːŋ-

ong-serving ˌlɒŋ ˈsɜːv ɪŋ ◂ ‖ ˌlɔːŋ ˈsɜːv- ˈlɑːŋ-

ongship ˈlɒŋ ʃɪp ‖ ˈlɔːŋ- ˈlɑːŋ- **~s** s

ongshore|man ˈlɒŋ ʃɔː |mən ‖ ˈlɔːŋ ʃɔːr- ˈlɑːŋ-, -ʃour- **~men** mən men

longsighted ˌlɒŋ ˈsaɪt ɪd ◂ -əd ‖ ˌlɔːŋ ˈsaɪţ əd ◂ ˌlɑːŋ- **~ness** nəs nɪs

longstanding ˌlɒŋ ˈstænd ɪŋ ◂ ‖ ˌlɔːŋ- ˌlɑːŋ-

long-stay ˌlɒŋ ˈsteɪ ◂ ‖ ˌlɔːŋ- ˌlɑːŋ-

longstop ˈlɒŋ stɒp ‖ ˈlɔːŋ stɑːp ˈlɑːŋ- **~s** s

longsuffering ˌlɒŋ ˈsʌf ər‿ɪŋ ◂ ‖ ˌlɔːŋ- ˌlɑːŋ- **~ly** li

long-term ˌlɒŋ ˈtɜːm ◂ ‖ ˌlɔːŋ ˈtɜːm ◂ ˌlɑːŋ-

long-time, longtime ˈlɒŋ taɪm ‖ ˈlɔːŋ- ˈlɑːŋ-

Longton ˈlɒŋ tən ‖ ˈlɔːŋ- ˈlɑːŋ-

Longtown ˈlɒŋ taʊn ‖ ˈlɔːŋ- ˈlɑːŋ-

longueur ₍ˌ₎lɒŋ ˈgɜː ‖ loʊn ˈgɜː *—Fr* [lɔ̃ gœːʁ] **~s** z

Longus ˈlɒŋ gəs ‖ ˈlɔːŋ- ˈlɑːŋ-

longways ˈlɒŋ weɪz ‖ ˈlɔːŋ- ˈlɑːŋ-

longwearing ˌlɒŋ ˈweər ɪŋ ◂ ‖ ˌlɔːŋ ˈwer ɪŋ ◂ ˌlɑːŋ-

longwinded ˌlɒŋ ˈwɪnd ɪd ◂ -əd ‖ ˌlɔːŋ- ˌlɑːŋ- **~ly** li **~ness** nəs nɪs

longwise ˈlɒŋ waɪz ‖ ˈlɔːŋ- ˈlɑːŋ-

Longyearbyen ˈlɒŋ jɪə ˌbjuː ən ˈ·jɜː, -ˌbuː ‖ ˈlɔːŋ jɪr- ˈlɑːŋ- *—Norw* [ˈlɔŋ jiːr byː ən]

lonicera lɒ ˈnɪs ər‿ə lə- ‖ loʊ-

Lonnie ˈlɒn i ‖ ˈlɑːn i

Lonrho *tdmk* ˈlɒn rəʊ ˈlʌn- ‖ ˈlɑːn roʊ

Lonsdale ˈlɒnz deɪᵊl ‖ ˈlɑːnz-

loo luː **loos** luːz

Looe luː

loofa, loofah ˈluːf ə **~s** z

loogie ˈluːg i

look lʊk §luːk **looked** lʊkt §luːkt **looking** ˈlʊk ɪŋ §ˈluːk- **looks** lʊks §luːks
 ˈlooking glass

look-alike ˈlʊk ə ˌlaɪk §ˈluːk- **~s** s

looker ˈlʊk ə §ˈluːk- ‖ -ᵊr **~s** z

looker-on ˌlʊk ər ˈɒn §ˌluːk- ‖ -ᵊr ˈɑːn -ˈɔːn
 lookers-on ˌlʊk əz ˈɒn §ˌluːk- ‖ -ᵊrz ˈɑːn -ˈɔːn

look-in ˈlʊk ɪn §ˈluːk-

lookit ˈlʊk ɪt §-ət

lookout ˈlʊk aʊt §ˈluːk- **~s** s

look-over ˈlʊk ˌəʊv ə §ˈluːk- ‖ -ˌoʊv ᵊr

look-see ˌlʊk ˈsiː §ˌluːk-, ˈ· ·

lookup ˈlʊk ʌp §ˈluːk- **~s** s

loom luːm **loomed** luːmd **looming** ˈluːm ɪŋ **looms** luːmz

loon luːn **loons** luːnz

loon|ey, loon|ie, loonly ˈluːn |i **~ier** i‿ə ‖ i‿ᵊr **~ies, ~eys** iz **~iest** i‿ɪst i‿əst
 ˈloony bin

looong, loooong *emphatic version of* long lɒŋ ‖ lɔːŋ lɑːŋ *with the vowel considerably extended*

loop luːp **looped** luːpt **looper/s** ˈluːp ə/z ‖ -ᵊr/z **looping** ˈluːp ɪŋ **loops** luːps

loophole ˈluːp həʊl →-hɒʊl ‖ -hoʊl **~s** z

loop-the-loop ˌluːp ðə ˈluːp

loopy ˈluːp i

loose luːs **loosed** luːst **looser** ˈluːs ə ‖ -ᵊr **looses** ˈluːs ɪz -əz **loosest** ˈluːs ɪst -əst **loosing** ˈluːs ɪŋ
 ˌloose ˈchange; **ˌloose ˈend**

loosebox ˈluːs bɒks ‖ -bɑːks **~es** ɪz əz

loose-fitting ˌluːs ˈfɪt ɪŋ ◂ ‖ -ˈfɪţ ɪŋ ◂

loose-jointed ˌluːs ˈdʒɔɪnt ɪd ◂ -əd ‖ -ˈdʒɔɪnţ əd ◂

loose-knit ˌluːs ˈnɪt ◂

loose-leaf ˌluːs ˈliːf ◂

loose-limbed ˌluːs ˈlɪmd ◂

loosely ˈluːs li

loosen ˈluːs ᵊn **~ed** d **~ing** ‿ɪŋ **~s** z

looseness ˈluːs nəs -nɪs

loosestrife ˈluːs straɪf -traɪf **~s** s

loosey-goosey ˌluːs i ˈguːs i ◂

loot luːt **looted** ˈluːt ɪd -əd ‖ ˈluːţ əd **looting** ˈluːt ɪŋ ‖ ˈluːţ ɪŋ **loots** luːts

looter ˈluːt ə ‖ ˈluːţ ᵊr **~s** z

lop lɒp ‖ lɑːp **lopped** lɒpt ‖ lɑːpt **lopping** ˈlɒp ɪŋ ‖ ˈlɑːp ɪŋ **lops** lɒps ‖ lɑːps

lope ləʊp ‖ loʊp **loped** ləʊpt ‖ loʊpt **lopes** ləʊps ‖ loʊps **loping** ˈləʊp ɪŋ ‖ ˈloʊp ɪŋ

lop-eared ˌlɒp ˈɪəd ◂ ‖ ˌlɑːp ˈɪᵊrd ◂

loperamide ləʊ ˈper ə maɪd ‖ loʊ-

Lopez, López ˈləʊp ez ‖ ˈloʊp- *—Sp* [ˈlo peθ, -pes]

Lop Nur ˌlɒp ˈnʊə ‖ ˌlɔːp ˈnʊᵊr ˌlɑːp-, ˌloʊp- *—Chi* Luóbùbó [²lwɔ ⁴pu ²pɔ]

lop-sided ˌlɒp ˈsaɪd ɪd ◂ -əd ‖ ˌlɑːp- **~ly** li **~ness** nəs nɪs

loquacious ləʊ ˈkweɪʃ əs lɒ- ‖ loʊ- **~ly** li **~ness** nəs nɪs

loquacity ləʊ ˈkwæs ət i lɒ-, -ɪt- ‖ loʊ ˈkwæs əţ i

loquat ˈləʊ kwɒt -kwət ‖ ˈloʊ kwɑːt **~s** s

lor lɔː ‖ lɔːr

Lora ˈlɔːr ə

Loraine lə ˈreɪn lɒ-

Loram ˈlɔːr əm

loran ˈlɔːr ən **~s** z
Lorca ˈlɔːk ə ‖ ˈlɔːrk ə —*Sp* [ˈlor ka]
Lorcan ˈlɔːk ən ‖ ˈlɔːrk-
lord, Lord lɔːd ‖ lɔːrd —*but as a vocative in a court of law,* my lord *is also* mɪ ˈlʌd, mə-
lorded ˈlɔːd ɪd -əd ‖ ˈlɔːrd əd **lording** ˈlɔːd ɪŋ ‖ ˈlɔːrd ɪŋ **lords, Lords, Lord's** lɔːdz ‖ lɔːrdz
ˌLord ˈChancellor; **ˌLord Chief ˈJustice**; **₍ₗ₎Lord ˈMayor**; **ˌLord's ˈPrayer**
lordling ˈlɔːd lɪŋ ‖ ˈlɔːrd- **~s** z
lord|ly ˈlɔːd |li ‖ ˈlɔːrd- **~lier** li‿ə ‖ li‿ər **~liest** li‿ɪst li‿əst **~liness** li nəs li nɪs
lordosis lɔː ˈdəʊs ɪs §-əs ‖ lɔːr ˈdoʊs əs
lordship, L~ ˈlɔːd ʃɪp ‖ ˈlɔːrd- **~s** s
lordy ˈlɔːd i ‖ ˈlɔːrd i
lore lɔː ‖ lɔːr loʊr
L'Oréal *tdmk* ˌlɒr i ˈæl ˈ· · · ‖ ˌlɔːr i ˈæl -ˈɑːl
Lorelei, Loreley ˈlɒr ə laɪ ˈlɔːr- ‖ ˈlɔːr- —*Ger* [loː ʁə ˈlaɪ]
Loren ˈlɔːr en -ən; lɔː ˈren, lə- ‖ ˈlɔːr ən —*It* [ˈlɔː ren]
Lorentz ˈlɒr ənts ˈlɔːr- ‖ ˈlɔːr- ˈloʊr- —*Dutch* [ˈloː rɛnts]
Lorenz ˈlɒr ənz ‖ ˈlɔːr- ˈloʊr- —*but as a German name,* ˈlɔːr ənts, ˈlɒr- —*Ger* [ˈloː ʁɛnts]
Lorenzo lə ˈrenz əʊ lɒ- ‖ -oʊ lɔː-
Loretta lə ˈret ə lɒ-, lɔː- ‖ lə ˈreţ ə lɔː-
Loretto lə ˈret əʊ lɔː- ‖ lə ˈreţ oʊ lɔː
lorgnette ₍ₗ₎lɔːn ˈjet ‖ lɔːrn- —*Fr* [lɔʁ njɛt] **~s** s
Lorie ˈlɒr i ‖ ˈlɔːr i
lorie... —*see* **lory**
lorikeet ˈlɒr ɪ kiːt -ə-, ˌ· ·ˈ· ‖ ˈlɔːr- ˈlɑːr- **~s** s
lorimer, L~ ˈlɒr ɪm ə -əm- ‖ ˈlɔːr əm ər **~s** z
loris, Loris ˈlɔːr ɪs §-əs ‖ ˈloʊr- **~es** ɪz əz
lorn lɔːn ‖ lɔːrn
Lorna ˈlɔːn ə ‖ ˈlɔːrn ə
Lorne lɔːn ‖ lɔːrn
Lorraine lə ˈreɪn lɒ-, lɔː-—*Fr* [lɔ ʁɛn]
lorr|y ˈlɒr |i §ˈlʌr- ‖ ˈlɔːr |i ˈlɑːr- **~ies** iz
ˈlorry park
lor|y ˈlɔːr |i ‖ ˈloʊr- **~ies** iz
Los Alamos lɒs ˈæl ə mɒs ‖ lɔːs ˈæl ə moʊs lɑːs-
Los Angeles lɒs ˈændʒ ə liːz -ɪ-, -lɪs, -ləs ‖ lɔːs ˈændʒ əl əs lɑːs-, -ˈæŋ gəl-, -ə liːz
lose luːz **loses** ˈluːz ɪz -əz **losing** ˈluːz ɪŋ **lost** lɒst lɔːst ‖ lɔːst lɑːst
Loseley ˈləʊz li ‖ ˈloʊz-
loser ˈluːz ə ‖ -ər **~s** z
Losey ˈləʊz i ‖ ˈloʊz i
Los Gatos lɒs ˈgæt əʊs ‖ loʊs ˈgɑːţ oʊs lɔːs-, lɑːs-
loss lɒs lɔːs ‖ lɔːs lɑːs **losses** ˈlɒs ɪz ˈlɔːs-, -əz ‖ ˈlɔːs əz ˈlɑːs-
ˈloss adˌjuster; **ˈloss ˌleader**
Lossiemouth ˌlɒs i ˈmaʊθ ‖ ˌlɔːs- ˌlɑːs-
loss-making ˈlɒs ˌmeɪk ɪŋ ˈlɔːs- ‖ ˈlɔːs- ˈlɑːs-
lossy ˈlɒs i ‖ ˈlɔːs i ˈlɑːs-
lost lɒst lɔːst ‖ lɔːst lɑːst
ˌlost ˈcause; **ˌlost ˈproperty**
lost-and-found ˌlɒst ən ˈfaʊnd ˌlɔːst- ‖ ˌlɔːst- ˈlɑːst-
Lostwithiel lɒst ˈwɪθ i‿əl ‖ lɔːst- lɑːst-
lot, Lot lɒt ‖ lɑːt **lots** lɒts ‖ lɑːts
loth ləʊθ ‖ loʊθ
Lothario ləʊ ˈθɑːr i əʊ lɒ-, -ˈθeər- ‖ loʊ ˈθer i oʊ -ˈθær-
Lothbury ˈləʊθ bər‿i ˈlɒθ- ‖ ˈloʊθ ˌber i
Lothian ˈləʊð i‿ən ‖ ˈloʊð- **~s** z
lotic ˈləʊt ɪk ‖ ˈloʊţ ɪk
lotion ˈləʊʃ ən ‖ ˈloʊʃ- **~s** z
lotsa *'lots of'* ˈlɒts ə ‖ ˈlɑːts ə
lotta *'lot of'* ˈlɒt ə ‖ ˈlɑːţ ə
lotter|y ˈlɒt‿ər |i ‖ ˈlɑːţ ər |i →ˈlɑːtr |i **~ies** iz
Lottie, Lotty ˈlɒt i ‖ ˈlɑːţ i
lotto, Lotto ˈlɒt əʊ ‖ ˈlɑːţ oʊ
lotus ˈləʊt əs ‖ ˈloʊţ əs **~es** ɪz əz
lotus-eater ˈləʊt əs ˌiːt ə ‖ ˈloʊţ əs ˌiːţ ər **~s** z
Lou luː
louche luːʃ
loud laʊd **louder** ˈlaʊd ə ‖ -ər **loudest** ˈlaʊd ɪst -əst
Loudan, Loudon, Loudoun ˈlaʊd ən
louden ˈlaʊd ən **~ed** d **~ing** ˌɪŋ **~s** z
loudhailer ˌlaʊd ˈheɪl ə ‖ -ər **~s** z
loudly ˈlaʊd li
loud|mouth ˈlaʊd |maʊθ **~mouths** maʊðz maʊθs
loudmouthed ˌlaʊd ˈmaʊðd ◂ -ˈmaʊθt, ˈ· ·
loudness ˈlaʊd nəs -nɪs **~es** ɪz əz
loudspeaker ˌlaʊd ˈspiːk ə ˈ· ˌ· · ‖ -ər **~s** z
Loudwater ˈlaʊd ˌwɔːt ə ‖ -ˌwɔːţ ər -ˌwɑːţ-
Louella lu ˈel ə
lough, Lough lɒx lɒk ‖ lɑːk lɑːx —*but as a family name also* lʌf, ləʊ ‖ loʊ **loughs** lɒxs lɒks ‖ lɑːks lɑːxs
Loughboro', Loughborough ˈlʌf bər‿ə §-ˌbʌr- ‖ -ˌbɜː oʊ
Loughlin ˈlɒx lɪn ˈlɒk-, -lən ‖ ˈlɑːf- lɑːk-
Loughor ˈlʌx ə ‖ ˈlʌk ər
Loughton ˈlaʊt ən
Louie ˈluː‿i
Louis *(i)* ˈluː‿i, *(ii)* ‿ɪs §‿əs —*Fr* [lwi, lu i]
ˌLouis Quaˈtorze kə ˈtɔːz kæ- ‖ -ˈtɔːrz —*Fr* [ka tɔrz]; **ˌLouis ˈQuinze** kænz —*Fr* [kɛ̃ːz]; **ˌLouis ˈSeize** sez seɪz —*Fr* [sɛːz]; **ˌLouis ˈTreize** trez treɪz —*Fr* [tʁɛːz]
Louisa lu ˈiːz ə
Louisburg ˈluː‿ɪs bɜːg §‿əs- ‖ -bɜːg
louis d'or ˌluː‿i ˈdɔː ‖ -ˈdɔːr **~s** z
Louise lu ˈiːz
Louisiana lu ˌiːz i ˈæn ə ˌluː‿ɪz-, -ˈɑːn-
Louisville ˈluː‿i vɪl §‿ə-
lounge laʊndʒ **lounged** laʊndʒd **lounges** ˈlaʊndʒ ɪz -əz **lounging** ˈlaʊndʒ ɪŋ
ˈlounge bar, ˌ· ˈ·; **ˈlounge suit**
lounger ˈlaʊndʒ ə ‖ -ər **~s** z
Lounsbury ˈlaʊnz bər‿i ‖ -ˌber i
loupe luːp *(= loop)* **loupes** luːps
lour ˈlaʊ‿ə ‖ ˈlaʊ‿ər **~ed** d **louring** ˈlaʊ‿ər ɪŋ ‖ ˈlaʊ‿ər ɪŋ **~s** z
Lourdes lʊəd lʊədz, lɔːdz ‖ lʊərd —*Fr* [luʁd]

louse *v* laʊz laʊs **loused** laʊzd laʊst **louses** 'laʊz ɪz 'laʊs-, -əz **lousing** 'laʊz ɪŋ 'laʊs-
louse *n* laʊs **lice** laɪs
lous|y 'laʊz |i **~ier** i‿ə ‖ i‿ᵊr **~iest** i‿ɪst i‿əst **~ily** ɪ li əl i **~iness** i nəs i nɪs
lout laʊt **louts** laʊts
Louth *(i)* laʊθ, *(ii)* laʊð —*The place in England is (i), the place in Ireland (ii)*
loutish 'laʊt ɪʃ ‖ 'laʊţ ɪʃ **~ly** li **~ness** nəs nɪs
Louvain lu 'væn -'vɛ̃; 'luːv æn, -ǣ —*Fr* [lu vɛ̃]
louv|er, louv|re 'luːv |ə ‖ -|ᵊr **~ered, ~red** əd ‖ ᵊrd **~ers, ~res** əz ‖ ᵊrz
Louvre *museum* 'luːv‿rə luːv ‖ 'luːv ᵊr —*Fr* [luːvʁ]
lovab|le 'lʌv əb |ᵊl **~leness** ᵊl nəs -nɪs **~ly** li
lovage 'lʌv ɪdʒ
lovat, Lovat 'lʌv ət
love, Love lʌv **loved** lʌvd **loves** lʌvz **loving** 'lʌv ɪŋ
'**love af**ˌ**fair**; '**love match**; '**love nest**; '**love** ˌ**story**
loveab|le 'lʌv əb |ᵊl **~leness** ᵊl nəs -nɪs **~ly** li
lovebird 'lʌv bɜːd ‖ -bɜːd **~s** z
lovebite 'lʌv baɪt **~s** s
love|child 'lʌv |tʃaɪᵊld **~children** ˌtʃɪldr ən
loveday 'lʌv deɪ
loved-up ˌlʌvd 'ʌp ◂
lovefest 'lʌv fest **~s** s
love-hate ˌlʌv 'heɪt
ˌ**love-'hate re**ˌ**lationship**
love-in-a-mist ˌlʌv ɪn ə 'mɪst §ˌ·ən-
Lovejoy 'lʌv dʒɔɪ
Lovelace 'lʌv leɪs
loveless 'lʌv ləs -lɪs **~ly** li **~ness** nəs nɪs
loveli... —*see* **lovely**
love-lies-bleeding ˌlʌv laɪz 'bliːd ɪŋ
Lovell 'lʌv ᵊl
lovelock, L~ 'lʌv lɒk ‖ -lɑːk **~s** s
lovelorn 'lʌv lɔːn ‖ -lɔːrn
love|ly 'lʌv |li **~lier** li‿ə ‖ li‿ᵊr **~lies** liz **~liest** li‿ɪst li‿əst **~liness** li nəs -nɪs
lovemaking 'lʌv ˌmeɪk ɪŋ
lover 'lʌv ə ‖ -ᵊr **~ly** li **~s** z
Loveridge 'lʌv rɪdʒ
lovesick 'lʌv sɪk **~ness** nəs nɪs
lovey 'lʌv i **~s** z
lovey-dovey ˌlʌv i 'dʌv i ◂ '·ˌ··
Lovibond 'lʌv i bɒnd ‖ -bɑːnd
loving 'lʌv ɪŋ **~ly** li
'**loving cup**; ˌ**loving 'kindness**
low, Low ləʊ ‖ loʊ *(= lo)* **lowed** ləʊd ‖ loʊd **lower** 'ləʊ ə ‖ 'loʊ ᵊr **lowest** 'ləʊ ɪst -əst ‖ 'loʊ əst **lowing** 'ləʊ ɪŋ ‖ 'loʊ ɪŋ **lows** ləʊz ‖ loʊz
ˌ**Low 'Church**; ˌ**Low 'German**; '**low life**; ˌ**low 'profile**; '**low** ˌ**season**; ˌ**low 'tide**; ˌ**low 'water,** ˌ**low 'water mark**
lowborn ˌləʊ 'bɔːn ◂ ‖ 'loʊ bɔːrn
lowboy 'ləʊ bɔɪ ‖ 'loʊ-
lowbred ˌləʊ 'bred ◂ ‖ ˌloʊ- '· ·
lowbrow 'ləʊ braʊ ‖ 'loʊ- **~s** z
low-budget ˌləʊ 'bʌdʒ ɪt ◂ §-ət ‖ ˌloʊ-
low-cal ˌləʊ 'kæl ◂ ‖ ˌloʊ-
low-class ˌləʊ 'klɑːs ◂ §-'klæs ◂ ‖ ˌloʊ 'klæs ◂
low-cost ˌləʊ 'kɒst ◂ -'kɔːst ‖ ˌloʊ 'kɔːst ◂ -'kɑːst ◂
low-cut ˌləʊ 'kʌt ◂ ‖ ˌloʊ-
low-down *adj* ˌləʊ 'daʊn ◂ ‖ ˌloʊ-
lowdown *n* 'ləʊ daʊn ‖ 'loʊ-
Lowe ləʊ ‖ loʊ
Lowell 'ləʊ əl ‖ 'loʊ əl
Lowenbrau, Löwenbräu *tdmk* 'ləʊ ən braʊ ‖ 'loʊ- —*Ger* ['løː vᵊn bʁɔʏ]
low-end ˌləʊ 'end ◂ ‖ ˌloʊ-
lower *v 'threaten'* 'laʊ‿ə ‖ 'laʊ‿ᵊr **~ed** d **lowering** 'laʊ‿ər ɪŋ ‖ 'laʊ‿ᵊr ɪŋ **~s** z
lower *adj, comp of* low 'ləʊ ə ‖ 'loʊ ᵊr
ˌ**lower 'case**◂; ˌ**lower 'class**◂; ˌ**Lower East 'Side**; ˌ**Lower 'House**
lower *v 'bring down'* 'ləʊ ə ‖ 'loʊ ᵊr **~ed** d **lowering** 'ləʊ ər ɪŋ ‖ 'loʊ ᵊr ɪŋ **~s** z
lower-end ˌləʊ ər 'end ◂ ‖ ˌloʊ ᵊr-
lowermost 'ləʊ ə məʊst ‖ 'loʊ ᵊr moʊst
Lowestoft 'ləʊst ɒft 'ləʊ ɪst ɒft, -əst-, -əft, -əf ‖ 'loʊst ɔːft -ɑːft, -əf
low-fat ˌləʊ 'fæt ◂ ‖ ˌloʊ-
low-flying ˌləʊ 'flaɪ ɪŋ ◂ ‖ ˌloʊ-
low-grade ˌləʊ 'greɪd ◂ ‖ ˌloʊ-
low-income ˌləʊ 'ɪn kʌm ◂ →-'ɪŋ-, -kəm ‖ ˌloʊ-
low-key ˌləʊ 'kiː ◂ ‖ ˌloʊ-
lowland, L~ 'ləʊ lənd ‖ 'loʊ- **~s** z
lowlander 'ləʊ lənd ə ‖ 'loʊ lənd ᵊr **~s** z
low-level ˌləʊ 'lev ᵊl ◂ ‖ ˌloʊ-
low-life 'ləʊ laɪf ‖ 'loʊ- **~s** s
lowlight 'ləʊ laɪt ‖ 'loʊ- **~s** s
low-loader ˌləʊ 'ləʊd ə ‖ ˌloʊ 'loʊd ᵊr **~s** z
low|ly 'ləʊ |li ‖ 'loʊ |li **~lier** li‿ə ‖ li‿ᵊr **~liest** li‿ɪst li‿əst **~liness** li nəs li nɪs
low-lying ˌləʊ 'laɪ ɪŋ ◂ ‖ ˌloʊ-
Lowman 'ləʊ mən ‖ 'loʊ-
low-minded ˌləʊ 'maɪnd ɪd ◂ -əd ‖ ˌloʊ- **~ly** li **~ness** nəs nɪs
Lowndes laʊndz
low-necked ˌləʊ 'nekt ◂ ‖ ˌloʊ-
lowness 'ləʊ nəs -nɪs ‖ 'loʊ-
low-paid ˌləʊ 'peɪd ◂ ‖ ˌloʊ-
low-pass ˌləʊ 'pɑːs ◂ §-'pæs ‖ ˌloʊ 'pæs ◂
low-paying ˌləʊ 'peɪ ɪŋ ◂ ‖ ˌloʊ-
low-pitched ˌləʊ 'pɪtʃt ◂ ‖ ˌloʊ-
low-powered ˌləʊ 'paʊ‿əd ◂ ‖ ˌloʊ 'paʊ‿ᵊrd ◂
low-price ˌləʊ 'praɪs ◂ ‖ ˌloʊ-
low-profile ˌləʊ 'prəʊf aɪᵊl ◂ ‖ ˌloʊ 'proʊf-
low-ranking ˌləʊ 'ræŋk ɪŋ ◂ ‖ ˌloʊ-
low-rent ˌləʊ 'rent ◂ ‖ ˌloʊ-
lowrider 'ləʊ ˌraɪd ə ‖ 'loʊ ˌraɪd ᵊr **~s** z
Lowrie, Lowry 'laʊᵊr i
low-rise 'ˌləʊ 'raɪz ◂ ‖ ˌloʊ-
low-risk ˌləʊ 'rɪsk ◂ ‖ ˌloʊ-
low-slung ˌləʊ 'slʌŋ◂ ‖ ˌloʊ-
low-spirited ˌləʊ 'spɪr ɪt ɪd ◂ -ət-, -əd ‖ ˌloʊ 'spɪr əţ əd ◂
low-tech ˌləʊ 'tek ◂ ‖ ˌloʊ-
Lowther 'laʊð ə ‖ -ᵊr —*but as a family name sometimes* 'ləʊð- ‖ 'loʊð-

Lowton ˈləʊt ᵊn ‖ ˈloʊt ᵊn
lox lɒks ‖ lɑːks
Loxene *tdmk* ˈlɒks iːn ‖ ˈlɑːks-
Loxley ˈlɒks li ‖ ˈlɑːks-
loxodromic ˌlɒks ə ˈdrɒm ɪk ◂ ‖ ˌlɑːks ə ˈdrɑːm ɪk ◂ **~ally** ᵊl̮ i
Loy lɔɪ
loyal ˈlɔɪ̯əl
loyalism ˈlɔɪ ə ˌlɪz əm
loyalist, L~ ˈlɔɪ əl ɪst §-əst
loyally ˈlɔɪ əl i
loyal|ty ˈlɔɪ̯əl |ti **~ties** tiz
Loyd lɔɪd
Loyola ˈlɔɪ əl ə lɔɪ ˈəʊl- ‖ lɔɪ ˈoʊl ə —*Sp* [lo ˈjo la]
Lozells ləʊ ˈzelz ‖ loʊ-
lozeng|e ˈlɒz ɪndʒ -əndʒ ‖ ˈlɑːz- **~es** ɪz əz
LP ˌel ˈpiː **~s, ~'s** z
LPC ˌel piː ˈsiː
LPG ˌel piː ˈdʒiː
L-plate ˈel pleɪt **~s** s
LSD ˌel es ˈdiː
LSE ˌel es ˈiː
Ltd —*see* **Limited**
Luanda lu ˈænd ə ‖ -ˈɑːnd- —*Port* [ˈlwen dɐ]
luau ˈluː aʊ *Hawaiian* lūʻau [ˈluː ʔau]
Luba ˈluːb ə
Lubavitcher ˈluːb ə vɪtʃ ə ‖ -ᵊr **~s** z
lubber ˈlʌb ə ‖ -ᵊr **~s** z
Lubbock ˈlʌb ək
lube luːb **lubed** luːbd **lubes** luːbz **lubing** ˈluːb ɪŋ
Lubeck, Lübeck ˈluː bek ˈljuː- —*Ger* [ˈlyː bɛk, -beːk]
lubricant ˈluːb rɪk ənt ˈljuːb-, -rək- **~s** s
lubri|cate ˈluːb rɪ |keɪt ˈljuːb-, -rə- **~cated** keɪt ɪd -əd ‖ keɪţ əd **~cates** keɪts **~cating** keɪt ɪŋ ‖ keɪţ ɪŋ
lubrication ˌluːb rɪ ˈkeɪʃ ᵊn ˌljuːb-, -rə- **~s** z
lubricator ˈluːb rɪ keɪt ə ˈljuːb-, ˈ·rə- ‖ -keɪţ ᵊr **~s** z
lubricious luː ˈbrɪʃ əs ljuː- **~ly** li **~ness** nəs nɪs
lubricity luː ˈbrɪs ət i ljuː-, -ɪt- ‖ -əţ i
Lucan ˈluːk ən
Lucas ˈluːk əs
Luce luːs
Lucent *tdmk* ˈluːs ᵊnt
lucerne, L~ lu ˈsɜːn ‖ -ˈsɜːn —*Fr* [ly sɛʁn]
Lucia ˈluːs i̯ə ˈluːʃ-, ˈluːʃ ə —*but as an Italian name* lu ˈtʃiː̯ə —*It* [lu ˈtʃiː a] —*see also* **St Lucia**
Lucian ˈluːs i̯ən ˈluːʃ- ‖ ˈluːʃ ᵊn
lucid ˈluːs ɪd ˈljuːs-, §-əd **~ly** li **~ness** nəs nɪs
lucidity luː ˈsɪd ət i ljuː-, -ɪt- ‖ -əţ i
Lucie ˈluːs i
Lucifer, l~ ˈluːs ɪf ə -əf- ‖ -ᵊr **~s** z
luciferin luː ˈsɪf ər ɪn §-ən
Lucille lu ˈsiːᵊl
Lucinda luː ˈsɪnd ə
Lucite *tdmk* ˈluːs aɪt
Lucius ˈluːs i̯əs ˈluːʃ- ‖ ˈluːʃ əs
luck, Luck lʌk **lucked** lʌkt **lucking** ˈlʌk ɪŋ **lucks** lʌks
luckless ˈlʌk ləs -lɪs **~ly** li **~ness** nəs nɪs
Lucknow ˈlʌk naʊ ˌ·ˈ· —*Hindi* [ləkʰ nəw]
luck|y, Lucky ˈlʌk |i **~ier** i̯ə ‖ i̯ᵊr **~iest** i̯ɪst i̯əst **~ily** ɪ li əl i **~iness** i nəs i nɪs
ˌ**lucky** ˈ**dip**
Lucozade *tdmk* ˈluːk əʊ zeɪd ‖ -ə-
lucrative ˈluːk rət ɪv ˈljuːk- ‖ -rəţ ɪv
lucre ˈluːk ə ˈljuːk- ‖ -ᵊr
Lucrece lu ˈkriːs ljuː-
Lucretia lu ˈkriːʃ ə lju-, -ˈkriːʃ i̯ə
Lucretius lu ˈkriːʃ əs lju-, -ˈkriːʃ i̯əs
lucu|brate ˈluːk ju |breɪt ˈljuːk- ‖ -jə- **~brated** breɪt ɪd -əd ‖ breɪţ əd **~brates** breɪts **~brating** breɪt ɪŋ ‖ breɪţ ɪŋ
lucubration ˌluːk ju ˈbreɪʃ ᵊn ‖ -jə- **~s** z
Lucull|us lu ˈkʌl |əs lju- **~an** ən
Lucy ˈluːs i
Lud, lud lʌd
Luddite, l~ ˈlʌd aɪt **~s** s
lude luːd **ludes** luːdz
Ludgate ˈlʌd gət -gɪt, -geɪt
ludic ˈluːd ɪk ˈljuːd-
ludicrous ˈluːd ɪk rəs ˈljuːd-, -ək- **~ly** li **~ness** nəs nɪs
Ludlow ˈlʌd ləʊ ‖ -loʊ
Ludlum ˈlʌd ləm
Ludmila, Ludmilla lʊd ˈmɪl ə
ludo, Ludo ˈluːd əʊ ‖ -oʊ
Ludovic ˈluːd ə vɪk
Ludwig ˈlʊd vɪg ˈluːd- ‖ ˈlʌd wɪg ˈlʊd-, -vɪg —*Ger* [ˈluːt vɪç]
luff lʌf **luffed** lʌft **luffing** ˈlʌf ɪŋ **luffs** lʌfs
Lufthansa *tdmk* ˈlʊft ˌhænz ə -ˌhænᵗs- ‖ -ˌhɑːnz ə —*Ger* [ˈlʊft ˌhan za]
Luftwaffe ˈlʊft ˌwæf ə -ˌvæf-, -ˌwɑːf-, -ˌvɑːf- ‖ -ˌvɑːf ə —*Ger* [ˈlʊft ˌvaf ə]
lug lʌg **lugged** lʌgd **lugging** ˈlʌg ɪŋ **lugs** lʌgz
Luganda lu ˈgænd ə -ˈgɑːnd- ‖ -ˈgɑːnd ə
Lugano luː ˈgɑːn əʊ lə- ‖ -oʊ —*It* [lu ˈgaː no]
Lugard ˈluː gɑːd ˌ·ˈ· ‖ -gɑːrd
luge luːʒ luːdʒ **luged** luːʒd luːdʒd **luges** ˈluːʒ ɪz ˈluːdʒ-, -əz **luging** ˈluːʒ ɪŋ ˈluːdʒ-
Luger *tdmk* ˈluːg ə ‖ -ᵊr —*Ger* [ˈluː gɐ] **~s** z
lugg... —*see* **lug**
luggage ˈlʌg ɪdʒ
ˈ**luggage** ˌ**label**; ˈ**luggage rack**; ˈ**luggage van**
lugger ˈlʌg ə ‖ ᵊr **~s** z
Lughnasa, Lughnasadh ˈluːn əs ə
lughole ˈlʌg həʊl →-hɒʊl ‖ -hoʊl —*humorously also BrE* -əʊl **~s** z
Lugosi lu ˈgəʊs i ‖ -ˈgoʊs-
lugsail ˈlʌg seɪᵊl —*naut* -sᵊl **~s** z
lugubrious lə ˈguːb ri̯əs lu-, -ˈgjuːb- **~ly** li **~ness** nəs nɪs
lugworm ˈlʌg wɜːm ‖ -wɜːm **~s** z
Luigi lu ˈiːdʒ i
Lukacs, Lukács ˈluːk ætʃ ‖ -ɑːtʃ —*Hungarian* [ˈlu kaːtʃ]
Luke luːk
lukewarm ˌluːk ˈwɔːm ◂ ˈ· · ‖ -ˈwɔːrm **~ly** li **~ness** nəs nɪs
lull lʌl **lulled** lʌld **lulling** ˈlʌl ɪŋ **lulls** lʌlz

ulla|by ˈlʌl ə |baɪ **~bied** baɪd **~bies** baɪz **~bying** baɪ ɪŋ
ulu, lulu ˈluːl uː **~s, ~'s** z
ulworth ˈlʌl wəθ -wɜːθ ‖ -wɜːθ
um lʌm **lumz** lʌmz
umbago lʌm ˈbeɪg əʊ ‖ -oʊ
umbar ˈlʌm bə -bɑː ‖ -bᵊr -bɑːr
umber ˈlʌm bə ‖ -bᵊr **~ed** d **lumbering** ˈlʌm bər‿ɪŋ **~s** z
umberjack ˈlʌm bə dʒæk ‖ -bᵊr- **~s** s
umber|man ˈlʌm bə |mən -mæn ‖ -bᵊr- **~men** mən men
umbermill ˈlʌm bə mɪl ‖ -bᵊr- **~s** z
umber-room ˈlʌm bə ruːm -rʊm ‖ -bᵊr- **~s** z
umberyard ˈlʌm bə jɑːd ‖ -bᵊr jɑːrd **~s** z
umen ˈluːm ɪn -ən, -en ‖ -ən **~s** z
umiere, lumière, L~ ˈluːm i eə ˌ· ˈ· ‖ ˌluːm i ˈeᵊr —*Fr* [ly mjɛːʁ]
luminanc|e ˈluːm ɪn ənᵗs ˈljuːm-, -ən- **~es** ɪz əz
luminar|y ˈlum ɪn ər‿i ˈljuːm-, ˈ·ən- ‖ -ə ner |i **~ies** iz
luminesc|e ˌluːm ɪ ˈnes ˌljuːm-, -ə- **~ed** t **~es** ɪz əz **~ing** ɪŋ
luminescence ˌluːm ɪ ˈnes ᵊnᵗs ˌljuːm-, -ə-
luminescent ˌluːm ɪ ˈnes ᵊnt ◂ ˌljuːm-, -ə-
luminosit|y ˌluːm ɪ ˈnɒs ət |i ˌljuːm-, ˌ·ə-, -ɪt i ‖ -ˈnɑːs ət̬ |i **~ies** iz
luminous ˈluːm ɪn əs ˈljuːm-, -ən- **~ly** li **~ness** nəs nɪs
Lumley ˈlʌm li
lumme ˈlʌm i
lummox ˈlʌm əks **~es** ɪz əz
lummy ˈlʌm i
lump lʌmp **lumped** lʌmpt **lumping** ˈlʌmp ɪŋ **lumps** lʌmps
ˌ**lump** ˈ**sum**
lumpectom|y ˌlʌmp ˈekt əm |i **~ies** iz
lumpen ˈlʌmp ən ˈlʊmp-
lumpenproletariat ˌlʌmp ən ˌprəʊl ə ˈteər i‿ət ˌlʊmp-, →ˌ·əm-, -ˌ·ɪ-, -æt ‖ -ˌproʊl ə ˈter-
lumpfish ˈlʌmp fɪʃ **~es** ɪz əz
lumpish ˈlʌmp ɪʃ **~ly** li **~ness** nəs nɪs
Lumpkin ˈlʌmp kɪn §-kən
lump|y ˈlʌmp |i **~ier** i‿ə ‖ i‿ᵊr **~iest** i‿ɪst i‿əst
Lumsden ˈlʌmz dən
Lumumba lu ˈmʊm bə -ˈmuːm-
Luna, luna ˈluːn ə ˈljuːn-
ˈ**luna moth**
lunac|y ˈluːn əs |i **~ies** iz
lunar ˈluːn ə ‖ -ᵊr
lunate ˈluːn eɪt -ət, -ɪt
lunatic ˈluːn ə tɪk **~s** s
ˈ**lunatic a**ˌ**sylum**; ˌ**lunatic** ˈ**fringe**
lunation luː ˈneɪʃ ᵊn **~s** z
lunch lʌntʃ **lunched** lʌntʃt **lunches** ˈlʌntʃ ɪz -əz **lunching** ˈlʌntʃ ɪŋ
lunchbox ˈlʌntʃ bɒks ‖ -bɑːks **~es** ɪz əz
luncheon ˈlʌntʃ ən **~s** z
ˈ**luncheon meat**; ˈ**luncheon** ˌ**voucher**
luncheonette ˌlʌntʃ ə ˈnet **~s** s
lunchroom ˈlʌntʃ ruːm -rʊm **~s** z
lunchtime ˈlʌntʃ taɪm **~s** z

Lund *family name* lʌnd
Lund *place in Sweden* lʊnd —*Swedish* [lʊnd], *Danish* [lonʔ]
Lundy ˈlʌnd i
lune, Lune luːn ljuːn **lunes** luːnz ljuːnz
Luneburg ˈluːn ə bɜːg ‖ -bɜːg —*Ger* Lüneburg [ˈlyː nə bʊʁk]
lunette ₍ˌ₎luː ˈnet ₍ˌ₎ljuː- **~s** s
lung lʌŋ **lunged** lʌŋd **lungs** lʌŋz
lunge lʌndʒ **lunged** lʌndʒd **lunges** ˈlʌndʒ ɪz -əz **lunging** ˈlʌndʒ ɪŋ
lunged *'having lungs'* lʌŋd
lunged *past & pp of* **lunge** lʌndʒd
lungfish ˈlʌŋ fɪʃ **~es** ɪz əz
lungful ˈlʌŋ fʊl **~s** z
lungi ˈlʊŋ gi **~s** z
lungpower ˈlʌŋ ˌpaʊ‿ə ‖ -ˌpaʊ‿ᵊr
lunkhead ˈlʌŋk hed **~s** z
Lunn lʌn
Lunt lʌnt
Luo ˈluː əʊ ‖ -oʊ
lupanar lu ˈpeɪn ə -ˈpɑːn-, -ɑː ‖ -ᵊr **~s** z
Lupercal ˈluːp ə kæl ˈljuːp-, -ɜː- ‖ -ᵊr-
Lupercalia ˌluːp ə ˈkeɪl i‿ə ˌljuːp-, ˌ·ɜː- ‖ ˌ·ᵊr-
lupin, lupine *n, flower* ˈluːp ɪn §-ən **~s** z
lupine *adj* ˈluːp aɪn ˈljuːp-
lupus, Lupus ˈluːp əs ˈljuːp-
lur lʊə lɜː ‖ lʊᵊr **lurs** lʊəz lɜːz ‖ lʊᵊrz
lurch lɜːtʃ ‖ lɜːtʃ **lurched** lɜːtʃt ‖ lɜːtʃt **lurches** ˈlɜːtʃ ɪz -əz ‖ ˈlɜːtʃ əz **lurching** ˈlɜːtʃ ɪŋ ‖ ˈlɜːtʃ ɪŋ
lurcher ˈlɜːtʃ ə ‖ ˈlɜːtʃ ᵊr **~s** z

LURE

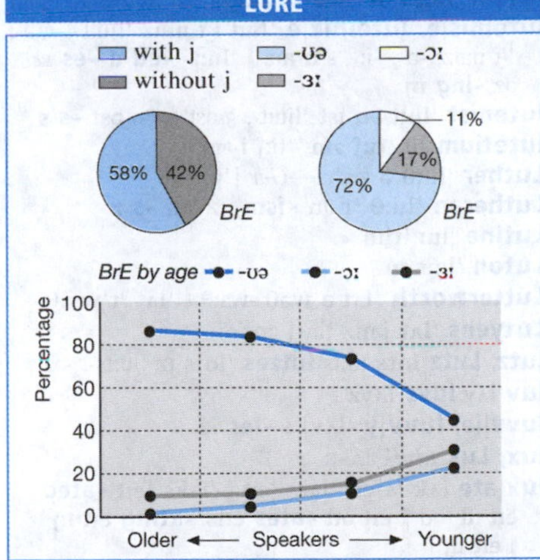

lure ljʊə lʊə, ljɜː, ljɔː ‖ lʊᵊr — *Preference poll, BrE: with* j *58%, without* j *42%;* -ʊə *72%,* -ɜː *17%,* -ɔː *11%.* **lured** ljʊəd lʊəd, ljɜːd, ljɔːd ‖ lʊᵊrd **lures** ljʊəz lʊəz, ljɜːz, ljɔːz ‖ lʊᵊrz **luring** ˈljʊər ɪŋ ˈlʊər-, ˈljɜːr-, ˈljɔːr- ‖ ˈlʊr ɪŋ
Lurex *tdmk* ˈljʊər eks ˈlʊər-, ˈljɜːr-, ˈljɔːr- ‖ ˈlʊr-
Lurgan ˈlɜːg ən ‖ ˈlɜːg-
lurgy ˈlɜːg i ‖ ˈlɜːg i
lurid ˈljʊər ɪd ˈlʊər-, ˈljɜːr-, ˈljɔːr-, §-əd ‖ ˈlʊr əd **~ly** li **~ness** nəs nɪs

lurk lɜːk ‖ lɜˑːk **lurked** lɜːkt ‖ lɜˑːkt **lurking** ˈlɜːk ɪŋ ‖ ˈlɜˑːk ɪŋ **lurks** lɜːks ‖ lɜˑːks
lurker ˈlɜːk ə ‖ ˈlɜˑːk ᵊr **~s** z
Lurpak *tdmk* ˈlɜː pæk ‖ ˈlɜˑː-
Lusaka lu ˈsɑːk ə lʊ-, -ˈzɑːk-
Lusatia lu ˈseɪʃ ə -ˈseɪʃ i‿ə
Lusatian lu ˈseɪʃ ᵊn -ˈseɪʃ i‿ən **~s** z
luscious ˈlʌʃ əs **~ly** li **~ness** nəs nɪs
lush, Lush lʌʃ **lusher** ˈlʌʃ ə ‖ -ᵊr **lushes** ˈlʌʃ ɪz -əz **lushest** ˈlʌʃ ɪst -əst
Lushington ˈlʌʃ ɪŋ tən
lush|ly ˈlʌʃ |li **~ness** nəs nɪs
Lusiad ˈluːs i æd ˈljuːs- **~s** z
Lusitani|a ˌluːs ɪ ˈteɪn i‿|ə ˌ-ə- **~an/s** ən/z
lust lʌst **lusted** ˈlʌst ɪd -əd **lusting** ˈlʌst ɪŋ **lusts** lʌsts
luster ˈlʌst ə ‖ -ᵊr **~s** z
lustful ˈlʌst fᵊl -fʊl **~ly** i **~ness** nəs nɪs
lusti... —*see* **lusty**
lustral ˈlʌs trəl
lus|trate lʌ ˈs|treɪt ˈlʌs |treɪt ‖ ˈlʌs |treɪt **~trated** treɪt ɪd -əd ‖ treɪţ əd **~trates** treɪts **~trating** treɪt ɪŋ ‖ treɪţ ɪŋ
lustration lʌ ˈstreɪʃ ᵊn **~s** z
lustre ˈlʌst ə ‖ -ᵊr **~s** z
lustrous ˈlʌs trəs **~ly** li **~ness** nəs nɪs
lus|trum ˈlʌs |trəm **~tra** trə **~trums** trəmz
lust|y ˈlʌst |i **~ier** i‿ə ‖ i‿ᵊr **~iest** i‿ɪst i‿əst **~ily** ɪ li əl i **~iness** i nəs i nɪs
lutanist ˈluːt ən ɪst ˈljuːt-, §-əst ‖ -ᵊn‿əst **~s** s
lute luːt ljuːt **lutes** luːts ljuːts
luteal ˈluːt i‿əl ˈljuːt- ‖ ˈluːţ-
luteinis|e, luteiniz|e ˈluːt i‿ɪ naɪz ˈljuːt-, -i‿ə-; ˈ·ɪ naɪz, -ə-, -iː-, -ᵊn aɪz ‖ ˈluːţ- **~ed** d **~es** ɪz əz **~ing** ɪŋ
lutenist ˈluːt ən ɪst ˈljuːt-, §-əst ‖ -ᵊn‿əst **~s** s
lutetium lu ˈtiːʃ əm -ˈtiːʃ i‿əm
Luther ˈluːθ ə ‖ -ᵊr —*Ger* [ˈlʊt ɐ]
Lutheran ˈluːθ ᵊr‿ən **~ism** ˌɪz əm **~s** z
Lutine ˌluː ˈtiːn ◂
Luton ˈluːt ᵊn
Lutterworth ˈlʌt ə wəθ -wɜːθ ‖ ˈlʌţ ᵊr wɜˑːθ
Lutyens ˈlʌt jənz ˈlʌtʃ ənz
lutz, Lutz lʊts luːts **lutzes** ˈlʊts ɪz ˈluːts-, -əz
luv lʌv **luvs** lʌvz
luvv|ie, luvv|y ˈlʌv| i **~ies** iz
lux, Lux *tdmk* lʌks
lux|ate lʌk ˈs|eɪt ˈlʌks |eɪt ‖ ˈlʌks |eɪt **~ated** eɪt ɪd -əd ‖ eɪţ əd **~ates** eɪts **~ating** eɪt ɪŋ ‖ eɪţ ɪŋ
luxation lʌk ˈseɪʃ ᵊn **~s** z
luxe lʌks lʊks, luːks ‖ lʊks lʌks, luːks —*Fr* [lyks]
Luxemburg, Luxembourg ˈlʌks əm bɜːg ‖ -bɜˑːg —*Ger* [ˈlʊks ᵊm bʊʁk], *Fr* Luxembourg [lyk sɑ̃ buːʁ] **~er/s** ə/z ‖ ᵊr/z
Luxor ˈlʌks ɔː ‖ -ɔːr
luxuri|ance lʌg ˈzjʊər i‿|ənᵗs ləg-, lʌk-, -ˈʒʊər-; lʌk ˈsjʊər-, -ˈʃʊər- ‖ lʌg ˈʒʊr- lʌk ˈʃʊr- **~ant/ly** ənt /li
luxuri|ate lʌg ˈzjʊər i |eɪt ləg-, lʌk-, -ˈʒʊər-; lʌk ˈsjʊər-, -ˈʃʊər- ‖ lʌg ˈʒʊr- lʌk ˈʃʊr- **~ated** eɪt ɪd -əd ‖ eɪţ əd **~ates** eɪts **~ating** eɪt ɪŋ ‖ eɪţ ɪŋ

LUXURIOUS

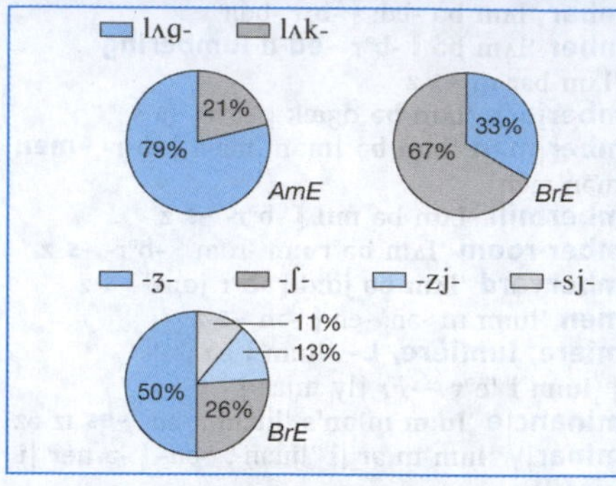

luxurious lʌk ˈʒʊər i‿əs lək-, lʌg-, ləg-, -ˈʃʊər-, -ˈzjʊər-, -ˈsjʊər- ‖ lʌg ˈʒʊr- lʌk ˈʃʊr- — *Preference polls, AmE:* lʌg- *79%,* lʌk- *21%; BrE:* lʌk- *67%,* lʌg- *33%;* -ʒ- *50%,* -ʃ- *26%,* -zj- *13%,* -sj- *11%.* **~ly** li **~ness** nəs nɪs

LUXURY

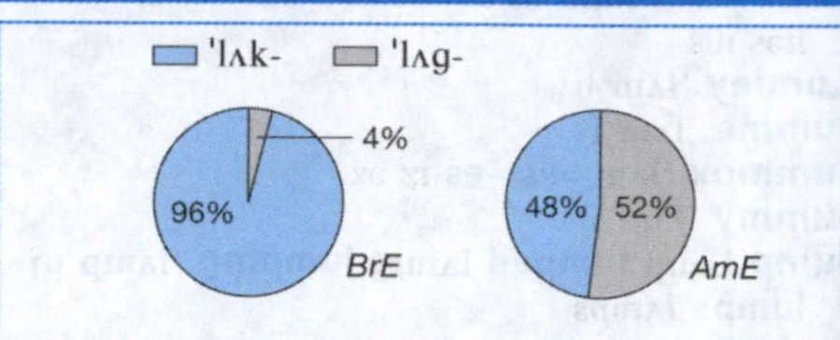

luxur|y ˈlʌk ʃər‿|i §ˈlʌg ʒər‿|i ‖ ˈlʌg ʒər‿|i ˈlʌk ʃər‿|i — *Preference polls, BrE:* ˈlʌk- *96%,* ˈlʌg- *4%; AmE:* ˈlʌk- *48%,* ˈlʌg- *52%.* **~ies** iz
Luzon ˌluː ˈzɒn ‖ -ˈzɑːn
Lvov lə ˈvɒf ‖ -ˈvɑːf -ˈvɔːf —*Ukrainian* Lviv [lʲvʲiw], *Polish* Lwów [lvuf], *Russian* [lʲvof]
-ly li —*After a stem ending in* l, *one* l *is usually lost, together with any* ə, *thus* fully ˈfʊl i, gently ˈdʒent li.
Lyall ˈlaɪ‿əl
Lybrand ˈlaɪ brænd
lycanthrope ˈlaɪk ən θrəʊp laɪ ˈkænᵗθ rəʊp ‖ -θroʊp **~s** s
lycanthropy laɪ ˈkænᵗθ rəp i
lycee, lycée ˈliːs eɪ ‖ liː ˈseɪ —*Fr* [li se] **~s** z
Lyceum laɪ ˈsiː‿əm
lychee ˌlaɪ ˈtʃiː ˈ· ·; ˈlɪtʃ i ‖ ˈliːtʃ i **~s** z
lychgate ˈlɪtʃ geɪt **~s** s
lychnis ˈlɪk nɪs §-nəs
Lyci|a ˈlɪs i‿|ə ‖ ˈlɪʃ- **~an/s** ən/z
Lycidas ˈlɪs ɪ dæs -ə-
lycopene ˈlaɪk əʊ piːn ‖ -oʊ-
lycopodium ˌlaɪk ə ˈpəʊd i‿əm ‖ -ˈpoʊd-
Lycos *tdmk* ˈlaɪk ɒs ‖ -ɑːs
Lycra *tdmk* ˈlaɪk rə
Lycurgus laɪ ˈkɜːg əs ‖ -ˈkɜˑːg-
Lydd lɪd

yddite ˈlɪd aɪt
ydgate ˈlɪd geɪt →ˈlɪg-, -gɪt —*but in Sheffield,* ˈlɪdʒ ɪt
ydi|a ˈlɪd i‿|ə **~an/s** ən/z
ye laɪ *(= lie)*
yell ˈlaɪ‿əl
ygon ˈlɪg ən
ying ˈlaɪ‿ɪŋ
ying-in ˌlaɪ‿ɪŋ ˈɪn **lyings-in** ˌlaɪ‿ɪŋz ˈɪn
yle laɪᵊl
yly ˈlɪl i
yme laɪm
yme-grass ˈlaɪm grɑːs §-græs ‖ -græs
ymeswold *tdmk* ˈlaɪmz wəʊld →-wɒʊld ‖ -woʊld
ymington ˈlɪm ɪŋ tən
ymm lɪm
ympany ˈlɪmp ən i
ymph lɪmᵖf **lymphs** lɪmᵖfs
  ˈlymph node
lymphadenopath|y ˌlɪmᵖf ˌæd ɪ ˈnɒp əθ |i -ˌ·ə-, -ᵊn ˈɒp- ‖ -ᵊn ˈɑːp- **~ies** iz
lymphatic lɪm ˈfæt ɪk ‖ -ˈfæţ- **~s** s
lympho- *comb. form*
  with stress-neutral suffix |lɪmᵖf əʊ ‖ -ə
  — **lymphocyte** ˈlɪmᵖf əʊ saɪt ‖ -ə-
  with stress-imposing suffix lɪm ˈfɒ+ ‖ -ˈfɑː+
  — **lymphopathy** lɪm ˈfɒp əθ i ‖ -ˈfɑːp-
lymphoma lɪm ˈfəʊm ə ‖ -ˈfoʊm ə **~s** z
Lympne lɪm
Lynam ˈlaɪn əm
lynch, Lynch lɪntʃ **lynched** lɪntʃt **lynches** ˈlɪntʃ ɪz -əz **lynching** ˈlɪntʃ ɪŋ
  ˈlynch law; **ˈlynch mob**
Lynchburg ˈlɪntʃ bɜːg ‖ -bɝːg
lynchpin ˈlɪntʃ pɪn **~s** z
Lyndhurst ˈlɪnd hɜːst ‖ -hɝːst
Lyndon ˈlɪnd ən
Lyneham ˈlaɪn əm
Lynette lɪ ˈnet
Lynmouth ˈlɪn məθ →ˈlɪm-
Lynn, Lynne lɪn
Lynton ˈlɪnt ən ‖ -ᵊn
lynx, Lynx lɪŋks **lynxes** ˈlɪŋks ɪz -əz
lynx-eyed ˌlɪŋks ˈaɪd ◂ ˈ· ·

lyo- *comb. form*
  with stress-neutral suffix |laɪ əʊ ‖ -ə
  — **lyophilic** ˌlaɪ əʊ ˈfɪl ɪk ◂ ‖ -ə-
  with stress-imposing suffix laɪ ˈɒ+ ‖ -ˈɑː+
  — **lyophilize** laɪ ˈɒf ɪ laɪz -ə- ‖ -ˈɑːf ə-
Lyon *surname* ˈlaɪ‿ən
Lyonesse ˌlaɪ‿ə ˈnes
lyonnaise ˌliː‿ə ˈneɪz ◂ ˌlaɪ‿ —*Fr* [ljɔ nɛːz]
Lyonnesse ˌlaɪ‿ə ˈnes
Lyons *place in France* ˈliː ɒ̃ -ɒn; ˈlaɪ‿ənz ‖ liː ˈɑːn -ˈɔːn —*Fr* Lyon [ljɔ̃]
Lyons *family name* ˈlaɪ‿ənz
Lyra ˈlaɪᵊr ə
lyre ˈlaɪ‿ə ‖ ˈlaɪ‿ᵊr *(= liar)* **lyres** ˈlaɪ‿əz ‖ ˈlaɪ‿ᵊrz
lyrebird ˈlaɪ‿ə bɜːd ‖ ˈlaɪ‿ᵊr bɝːd **~s** z
lyric ˈlɪr ɪk **~al** ᵊl **~ally** ᵊl‿i **~s** s
lyricism ˈlɪr ɪ ˌsɪz əm -ə-
lyricist ˈlɪr ɪs ɪst -əs-, §-əst **~s** s
lyrist *'lyric poet'* ˈlɪr ɪst §-əst **~s** s
lyrist *'lyre player'* ˈlaɪ‿ər ɪst ˈlɪr ɪst; §-əst **~s** s
Lysander laɪ ˈsænd ə ‖ -ᵊr
-lyse laɪz — **paralyse** ˈpær ə laɪz ‖ ˈper-
Lysenko lɪ ˈseŋk əʊ lə- ‖ -oʊ —*Russian* [lʲɨ ˈsʲen kə]
lysergic laɪ ˈsɜːdʒ ɪk lɪ-, lə- ‖ -ˈsɝːdʒ-
  lyˌsergic ˈacid
Lysias ˈlɪs i æs ‖ -əs
lysis ˈlaɪs ɪs §-əs
-lysis *stress-imposing* ləs ɪs lɪs-, §-əs
  — **paralysis** pə ˈræl əs ɪs -ɪs-, §-əs
Lysistrata laɪ ˈsɪs trət ə ˌlɪs ɪ ˈstrɑːt ə, ˌlɪz- ‖ ˌlɪs ə ˈstrɑːţ ə laɪ ˈsɪs trəţ ə
lysol, Lysol *tdmk* ˈlaɪs ɒl ‖ -ɔːl -ɑːl, -oʊl
lysosome ˈlaɪs əʊ səʊm ‖ -ə soʊm -zoʊm **~s** z
lysozyme ˈlaɪz əʊ zaɪm ‖ -ə zaɪm
Lystra ˈlɪs trə
lystrosaur ˈlɪs trəʊ sɔː ‖ -trə sɔːr
-lyte laɪt — **electrolyte** ɪ ˈlek trəʊ laɪt ə- ‖ -trə-
Lytham ˈlɪð əm
-lytic ˈlɪt ɪk ‖ ˈlɪţ ɪk — **electrolytic** ɪ ˌlek trəʊ ˈlɪt ɪk ◂ ‖ -trə ˈlɪţ ɪk ◂
Lyttelton ˈlɪt ᵊl tən ‖ ˈlɪţ-
Lytton ˈlɪt ᵊn

m Spelling-to-sound

1 Where the spelling is **m**, the pronunciation is regularly m as in **medium** ˈmiːd i‿əm.

2 Where the spelling is double **mm**, the pronunciation is again regularly m as in **hammer** ˈhæm ə ‖ ˈhæm ər.

M, m em **M's, m's, Ms** emz —*Communications code name:* Mike

'm m —*see* **I'm**

M'…, M'… *in this dictionary listed alphabetically as if written* **Mac…**

M1 ˌem ˈwʌn §-ˈwɒn **M25** ˌem ˌtwent i ˈfaɪv ⚠-ˌtwen i- ‖ -ˌtwenţ i- **M40** ˌem ˈfɔːt i ‖ -ˈfɔːrţ i —*and similarly for other British motorway numbers*

ma, Ma mɑː **mas, Ma's** mɑːz

MA —*see* **Massachusetts**

MA *'master of arts'* ˌem ˈeɪ

Maalox *tdmk* ˈmeɪ lɒks ‖ -lɑːks

ma'am *strong form* **mæm** mɑːm, *weak form* **məm** —*After* yes *there is also a weak form* **əm.**

Maas mɑːs —*Dutch* [maːs]

Maastricht ˈmɑːs trɪkt -trɪxt —*Dutch* [maː ˈstrɪxt]

Mab, Mabb mæb

Mabel ˈmeɪb əl

Mabinogion ˌmæb ɪ ˈnɒg i ɒn ˌ-ə-, -i‿ən ‖ -ˈnoʊg i ɑːn —*Welsh* [ma bi ˈnog jon]

Mablethorpe ˈmeɪb əl θɔːp ‖ -θɔːrp

Mableton ˈmeɪb əl tən

Mabley *(i)* ˈmeɪb li, *(ii)* ˈmæb li

Mabon *(i)* ˈmeɪb ən, *(ii)* ˈmæb ən

Mac, mac mæk

Mac-, Mc- *prefix in names:(i) usually, unstressed* **mək**, *or sometimes* **mæk** *(perhaps depending on degree of formality):* Mc'Donald, Mac'Donald, Mac'donald*; but (ii)* ¦mæk *before an unstressed syllable:* 'McEnroe, 'MacEnroe*; (iii)* mə *before* **k, g**: Mc'Gill, Mac'Gill, Mac'gill, Mac'Gill. *This prefix is spelt sometimes* Mac, *sometimes* Mc, *sometimes* M' *or* M', *and the stem which follows may be spelt with a capital letter or with a small one. Particularly in Ireland, the prefix is sometimes written as a separate word. To save repetition, many entries below are shown only in the* Mc- *form, with a capital letter for the stem, all written as one word.* Mc- *is in any case listed here alphabetically as if it were* Mac-.

macabre mə ˈkɑːb‿rə -ə ‖ -ər **~ly** li

macadam, McAdam mə ˈkæd əm

macadamia ˌmæk ə ˈdeɪm i‿ə **~s** z
  ˌmacaˈdamia nut

macadamis|e, macadamiz|e mə ˈkæd ə maɪz **~ed** d **~es** ɪz əz **~ing** ɪŋ

Macafee, McAfee *(i)* ˌmæk ə ˈfiː ˈ• • •, *(ii)* mə ˈkæf i -ˈkɑːf-

McAleese ˌmæk ə ˈliːs

McAlery ˌmæk ə ˈlɪər i ‖ -ˈlɪr i

McAlinden, McAlindon ˌmæk ə ˈlɪnd ən

McAlister, McAllister mə ˈkæl ɪst ə -əst- ‖ -ər

McAloon ˌmæk ə ˈluːn

McAlpine mə ˈkælp aɪn -ɪn, §-ən

McAnally ˌmæk ə ˈnæl i

McAnespie ˌmæk ə ˈnesp i

McAnulty ˌmæk ə ˈnʌlt i

Macao mə ˈkaʊ —*Port* Macáu [mɐ ˈkau], *Chi* Ào Mén [⁴au ²mən]

macaque mə ˈkɑːk -ˈkæk; ˈmæk æk **~s** s

McArdle mə ˈkɑːd əl ‖ -ˈkɑːrd-

macarena ˌmæk ə ˈreɪn ə ‖ ˌmɑːk- —*Sp* macareña [ma ka ˈre ɲa]

macaroni ˌmæk ə ˈrəʊn i ◂ ‖ -ˈroʊn i ◂ **~es, ~s** z
  ˌmacaˌroni ˈcheese

macaronic ˌmæk ə ˈrɒn ɪk ◂ ‖ -ˈrɑːn ɪk ◂ **~s** s

macaroon ˌmæk ə ˈruːn **~s** z

McArthur mə ˈkɑːθ ə ‖ -ˈkɑːrθ ər

Macassar, m~ mə ˈkæs ə ‖ -ər
  Maˈcassar oil

McAteer ˌmæk ə ˈtɪə ˈ• • • ‖ -ˈtɪər

Macau, Macáu mə ˈkaʊ —*Port* [mɐ ˈkau], *Chi* Ào Mén [⁴au ²mən]

Macaulay, McAulay, McAuley mə ˈkɔːl i ‖ -ˈkɑːl-

McAuliffe mə ˈkɔːl ɪf §-əf ‖ -ˈkɑːl-

Macavity mə ˈkæv ət i -ɪt- ‖ -əţ i

McAvoy ˈmæk ə vɔɪ

macaw mə ˈkɔː ‖ -ˈkɑː **~s** z

cBain mək ˈbeɪn §mæk-

cBeal mək ˈbiːəl

acbeth, McBeth mək ˈbeθ mæk-

cBrain, McBrayne mək ˈbreɪn §mæk-

cBrearty mək ˈbrɪət i §mæk- ‖ -ˈbrɪrt̬ i

cBride mək ˈbraɪd §mæk-

acca ˈmæk ə

accabae|an, Maccabe|an ˌmæk ə ˈbiː|ən ◂ -ˈbeɪ- **~us** əs

cCabe mə ˈkeɪb

accabees ˈmæk ə biːz

accabeus ˌmæk ə ˈbiː‿əs ◂ -ˈbeɪ-

cCaffray, McCaffrey mə ˈkæf ri

cCain mə ˈkeɪn

cCall mə ˈkɔːl ‖ -ˈkɑːl

cCallum mə ˈkæl əm

cCambridge mə ˈkeɪm brɪdʒ

cCanlis mə ˈkæn lɪs -ləs

cCann mə ˈkæn

cCarran mə ˈkær ən ‖ -ˈker-

McCarthy mə ˈkɑːθ i ‖ -ˈkɑːrθ i **~ism** ˌɪz əm

McCarthyite mə ˈkɑːθ i aɪt ‖ -ˈkɑːrθ- **~s** s

McCartney mə ˈkɑːt ni ‖ -ˈkɑːrt-

McCaskill mə ˈkæsk əl -ɪl

McCavish mə ˈkæv ɪʃ

macchiato ˌmæk i ˈɑːt əʊ ‖ ˌmɑːk i ˈɑːt̬ oʊ —*It* [mak ˈkjaː to]

McCleary, McCleery mə ˈklɪər i ‖ -ˈklɪr i

McClellan mə ˈklel ən

McClelland mə ˈklel ənd

Macclesfield ˈmæk əlz fiːəld

McClintock mə ˈklɪnt ɒk -ək ‖ -ɑːk

McCloskey mə ˈklɒsk i ‖ -ˈklɑːsk i

McClure mə ˈklʊə ‖ -ˈklʊər

McCluskie mə ˈklʌsk i

Maccoby ˈmæk əb i

McColl mə ˈkɒl ‖ -ˈkɑːl

McConachie, McConachy, McConaghy, McConochie mə ˈkɒn ək i -əx i, -ə hi ‖ -ˈkɑːn-

McCool mə ˈkuːl

McCormack mə ˈkɔːm ək -æk ‖ -ˈkɔːrm-

McCormick mə ˈkɔːm ɪk §-ək ‖ -ˈkɔːrm-

McCorquodale mə ˈkɔːk ə deɪəl ‖ -ˈkɔːrk-

McCowan mə ˈkaʊ‿ən

McCoy mə ˈkɔɪ

McCrae, McCrea mə ˈkreɪ

McCreadie, McCready *(i)* mə ˈkriːd i, *(ii)* mə ˈkred i

McCrindell, McCrindle mə ˈkrɪnd əl

McCrum mə ˈkrʌm

McCullers mə ˈkʌl əz ‖ -ərz

McCulloch, McCullough mə ˈkʌl ək -əx

McCurtain, McCurtin mə ˈkɜːt ɪn -ən ‖ -ˈkɜːt ən

McCusker mə ˈkʌsk ə ‖ -ər

McDade mək ˈdeɪd

McDermot, McDermott mək ˈdɜːm ət ‖ -ˈdɝːm-

McDiarmid mək ˈdɜːm ɪd §mæk-, -ˈdeəm-, §-əd ‖ -ˈdɝːm-

McDonagh mək ˈdɒn ə ‖ -ˈdɑːn ə

McDonald, Macdonald mək ˈdɒn əld mæk- ‖ -ˈdɑːn- **~'s** *tdmk* z

McDonnell *(i)* ˌmæk də ˈnel, *(ii)* mək ˈdɒn əl §mæk- ‖ -ˈdɑːn-

McDougal, McDougall mək ˈduːg əl mæk-

McDowall, McDowell *(i)* mək ˈdaʊ‿əl ‖ -ˈdaʊ‿əl, *(ii)* -ˈdəʊ- ‖ ˈdoʊ-

McDuff, Macduff mək ˈdʌf mæk-

mace, Mace meɪs **Maced** meɪst **maces, Maces** ˈmeɪs ɪz -əz **Macing** ˈmeɪs ɪŋ

mace-bearer ˈmeɪs ˌbeər ə ‖ ˌber ər ˌbær- **~s** z

macedoine, macédoine ˌmæs ɪ ˈdwɑːn -ə-, ˈ· · · **~s** z

Macedon ˈmæs ɪd ən -əd- ‖ -ə dɑːn

Macedoni|a ˌmæs ɪ ˈdəʊn i‿|ə ˌ-ə- ‖ -ˈdoʊn- **~an/s** ən/z

McElderry, McEldery ˈmæk əl ˌder i ˌ·ˈ··

McElhone ˈmæk əl həʊn ‖ -hoʊn

McElligott mə ˈkel ɪg ət -əg-

McElroy ˈmæk əl rɔɪ —*but in AmE also* mə ˈkel-

McElwain *(i)* ˈmæk əl weɪn, *(ii)* mə ˈkel weɪn mæk-

McEnroe ˈmæk ɪn rəʊ -ən- ‖ -roʊ

mace|rate ˈmæs ə |reɪt **~rated** reɪt ɪd -əd ‖ reɪt̬ əd **~rates** reɪts **~rating** reɪt ɪŋ ‖ reɪt̬ ɪŋ

maceration ˌmæs ə ˈreɪʃ ən **~s** z

macerator ˈmæs ə reɪt ə ‖ -reɪt̬ ər **~s** z

McEvoy ˈmæk ɪ vɔɪ -ə-

McEwan, McEwen mə ˈkjuː‿ən

McFadden mək ˈfæd ən

McFadyean, McFadyen, McFadzean mək ˈfæd jən §mæk-

McFarland mək ˈfɑːl ənd ‖ -ˈfɑːrl-

McFarlane mək ˈfɑːl ɪn §mæk-, -ən ‖ -ˈfɑːrl-

McFee, McFie mək ˈfiː mæk-

McGahey mə ˈgɑː hi -ˈgæ-, -ˈgæx i

McGee mə ˈgiː

McGill mə ˈgɪl

McGillicuddy *(i)* ˈmæg lɪ ˌkʌd i, *(ii)* mə ˈgɪl i ˌkʌd i

McGilligan mə ˈgɪl ɪg ən -əg-

McGillivray mə ˈgɪl ɪv ri -əv-, -reɪ

McGillycuddy *(i)* ˈmæg lɪ ˌkʌd i, *(ii)* mə ˈgɪl i ˌkʌd i ˌ**Macgilly,cuddy's ˈReeks**

McGinn mə ˈgɪn

McGinty mə ˈgɪnt i ‖ -ˈgɪnt̬ i

McGlashan mə ˈglæʃ ən

McGoldrick mə ˈgəʊld rɪk →-ˈgɒʊld- ‖ -ˈgoʊld-

McGonagall mə ˈgɒn əg əl ‖ -ˈgɑːn-

McGoohan mə ˈguː‿ən -hən

McGough mə ˈgɒf ‖ -ˈgɑːf -ˈgɔːf

McGovern mə ˈgʌv ən ‖ -ərn

McGowan mə ˈgaʊ‿ən

McGrady mə ˈgræd i *(!)*

McGrath mə ˈgrɑːθ -ˈgræθ, -ˈgrɑː ‖ -ˈgræθ —*In Ireland also* -ˈgræh

McGraw mə ˈgrɔː ‖ -ˈgrɑː

McGregor mə ˈgreg ə ‖ -ər

McGuffey mə ˈgʌf i

M

McGuffin mə 'gʌf ɪn §-ᵊn
McGuigan mə 'gwiːg ən -'gwɪg-
McGuinness mə 'gɪn ɪs §-əs
McGuire mə 'gwaɪ‿ə ‖ -'gwaɪ‿ᵊr
McGurk mə 'gɜːk ‖ -'gɜːk
McGwire mə 'gwaɪ‿ə ‖ -'gwaɪ‿ᵊr
Mach, mach mɑːk mæk, mɒk —*Ger* [max]
McHale mək 'heɪᵊl
Macheath mək 'hiːθ mæk-
Machen *(i)* 'meɪtʃ ɪn -ən, *(ii)* 'mæk-, *(iii)* 'mæx-—*The place in Gwent is (iii)*
McHenry mək 'hen ri
machete mə 'ʃet i -'tʃet-, -'tʃeɪt-; mə 'ʃet ‖ mə 'ʃeţ i -'tʃeţ-; mə 'ʃet **machetes** mə 'ʃet iz -'tʃet-, -'tʃeɪt-; mə 'ʃets ‖ mə 'ʃeţ iz -'tʃeţ-; mə 'ʃets
Machiavelli ˌmæk i‿ə 'vel i —*It* [ma kja 'vɛl li]
Machiavellian ˌmæk i‿ə 'vel i‿ən◂ **~ism** ˌɪz əm **~s** z
machico|late mə 'tʃɪk əʊ |leɪt mæ- ‖ -ə- **~lated** leɪt ɪd -əd ‖ leɪţ əd **~lates** leɪts **~lating** leɪt ɪŋ ‖ leɪţ ɪŋ
machicolation mə ˌtʃɪk əʊ 'leɪʃ ᵊn mæ- ‖ -ə- **~s** z
Machin 'meɪtʃ ɪn §-ən
machi|nate 'mæk ɪ |neɪt 'mæʃ-, -ə- **~nated** neɪt ɪd -əd ‖ neɪţ əd **~nates** neɪts **~nating** neɪt ɪŋ ‖ neɪţ ɪŋ
machination ˌmæk ɪ 'neɪʃ ᵊn ˌmæʃ-, -ə- **~s** z
machine mə 'ʃiːn **machined** mə 'ʃiːnd **machines** mə 'ʃiːnz **machining** mə 'ʃiːn ɪŋ **ma'chine code**; **ma'chine ˌgunner**; **ma'chine tool**
machinegun mə 'ʃiːn gʌn →-'ʃiːŋ- **~ned** d **~ning** ɪŋ **~s** z
machine-head mə 'ʃiːn hed **~s** z
machine-made mə 'ʃiːn meɪd →-'ʃiːm-
machine-readable mə ˌʃiːn 'riːd əb ᵊl◂
machiner|y mə 'ʃiːn ər‿|i **~ies** iz
machine-wash mə ˌʃiːn 'wɒʃ ‖ -'wɔːʃ -'wɑːʃ **~ed** t **~es** ɪz əz **~ing** ɪŋ
machine-washable mə ˌʃiːn 'wɒʃ əb ᵊl ‖ -'wɔːʃ- -'wɑːʃ-
machinist mə 'ʃiːn ɪst §-əst **~s** s
machismo mə 'tʃɪz məʊ mæ-, ⚠-'kɪz- ‖ mɑː 'tʃiːz moʊ mə-, 'tʃɪz-—*Sp* [ma 'tʃis mo]
macho 'mætʃ əʊ 'mɑːtʃ- ‖ 'mɑːtʃ oʊ ⚠'mɑːk- **~s** z
Machrihanish ˌmæk rɪ 'hæn ɪʃ ˌmæx-, -rə-
Machu Picchu ˌmætʃ uː 'pɪk tʃuː ˌmɑːtʃ-, -'piːk- ‖ ˌmɑːtʃ uː 'piːk tʃu —*Sp* ['ma tʃu 'pik tʃu]
Machynlleth mə 'kʌn ɬəθ ‖ -ləθ —*Welsh* [ma 'χən ɬeθ]
McIlroy 'mæk ɪl rɔɪ -ᵊl-, ˌ·'·
McIlvaney ˌmæk ᵊl 'veɪn i -ɪl-
McIlvenny ˌmæk ᵊl 'ven i -ɪl-
McIlwain 'mæk ᵊl weɪn -ɪl-
McIlwraith 'mæk ᵊl reɪθ -ɪl-
McIndoe 'mæk ɪn dəʊ ən- ‖ -doʊ
McInnes, McInnis mə 'kɪn ɪs §-əs
McIntosh, macintosh 'mæk ɪn tɒʃ §-ən- ‖ -tɑːʃ **~es** ɪz əz
McIntyre 'mæk ɪn taɪ‿ə §'·ən- ‖ -taɪ‿ᵊr
McIver, McIvor *(i)* mə 'kaɪv ə ‖ -ᵊr, *(ii)* mə 'kiːv ə ‖ -ᵊr
MacJob ₍ˌ₎mək 'dʒɒb ‖ -'dʒɑːb —*also* '·, *whe in contrast to* (real) job **~s** z
mack, Mack mæk **macks** mæks
Mackay, McKay *(i)* mə 'kaɪ, *(ii)* mə 'keɪ —*In BrE usually (i).*
McKechnie mə 'kex ni -'kek- ‖ -'kek-
McKee mə 'kiː
McKellar mə 'kel ə ‖ -ᵊr
McKellen mə 'kel ən
McKendrick mə 'kendr ɪk
McKenna mə 'ken ə
Mackenzie, McKenzie mə 'kenz i
McKeown mə 'kjəʊn ‖ -'kjoʊn
mackerel 'mæk rəl 'mæk ər əl **~s** z
McKern mə 'kɜːn ‖ -'kɜːn
McKerras mə 'ker əs
Mackeson 'mæk ɪs ən -əs-
Mackie 'mæk i
McKie *(i)* mə 'kaɪ, *(ii)* mə 'kiː
Mackin 'mæk ɪn §-ən
Mackinac, Mackinaw, m~ 'mæk ɪ nɔː -ə- ‖ -nɑː **~s** z
McKinlay, McKinley mə 'kɪn li
McKinnon mə 'kɪn ən
mackintosh, M~ 'mæk ɪn tɒʃ §-ən- ‖ -tɑːʃ **~es, ~'s** ɪz əz
McKittrick mə 'kɪtr ɪk
McLachlan mə 'klɒx lən -'klɒk- ‖ -'klɑːk-
MacLaine mə 'kleɪn
Maclaren, McLaren mə 'klær ən ‖ -'kler-
McLaughlin mə 'klɒx lɪn -'klɒk-, -'glɒx-, §-lən ‖ -'klɑːk-
McLaurin mə 'klɔːr ɪn -'klɒr-, §-ən
McLean, Maclean *(i)* mə 'kleɪn, *(ii)* mə 'kliːn
Macleans *tdmk* mə 'kliːnz
McLehose 'mæk ᵊl həʊz -lɪ-, -lə- ‖ -hoʊz
McLeish, MacLeish mə 'kliːʃ mæk 'liːʃ
McLennan mə 'klen ən
Macleod, McLeod mə 'klaʊd *(!)*
McLiammoir mə 'klɪəm ɔː ‖ -'kliː ə mɔːr
McLintock mə 'klɪnt ɒk -ək ‖ -ɑːk
McLoughlin mə 'klɒx lɪn -'klɒk-, -'glɒk-, §-lən ‖ -'klɑːk-
McLuhan mə 'kluː‿ən
McLysaght mə 'klaɪs ət -ə, -əkt
McMahon mək 'mɑːn §mæk-, -'mɑː ən, -'mæ hən ‖ -'mæn
McManaman mək 'mæn əm ən
McManus mək 'mæn əs §mæk-, -'mɑːn-, -'meɪn-
McMartin mək 'mɑːt ɪn mæk-, §-ᵊn ‖ -'mɑːrt ᵊn
McMaster mək 'mɑːst ə mæk-, §-'mæst- ‖ -'mæst ᵊr
McMenemey, McMenemy mək 'men əm i
McMichael mək 'maɪk ᵊl
Macmillan, McMillan mək 'mɪl ən mæk-
McMullan, McMullen mək 'mʌl ən

McMurdo mək 'mɜːd əʊ ‖ -'mɝːd oʊ
McMurray mək 'mʌr i ‖ -'mɝː i
McMurtry mək 'mɜːtr i ‖ -'mɝːtr i
McNab mək 'næb §mæk-
McNaghten, McNaghton mək 'nɔːt ən mæk- ‖ -'nɑːt-
McNair mək 'neə ‖ -'neər
McNally mək 'næl i
Macnamara, McNamara ˌmæk nə 'mɑːr ə ‖ 'mæk nə ˌmær ə -ˌmer ə
McNamee ˌmæk nə 'miː
McNaughten, McNaughton mək 'nɔːt ən mæk- ‖ -'nɑːt-
McNeice mək 'niːs
McNeil mək 'niːəl
McNeilage mək 'niːl ɪdʒ
McNeill mək 'niːəl
McNestry mək 'nes tri
MacNugget *tdmk* mək 'nʌg ɪt mæk-, §-ət **~s** s
Macon *place in France; wine* 'mɑːk ɒ̃ 'mæk-, -ɒn ‖ mɑː 'koʊn —*Fr* Mâcon [mɑ kɔ̃]
Macon *place in Georgia* 'meɪk ən
Maconachie mə 'kɒn ək i -əx i, -ə hi ‖ -'kɑːn-
Maconchy mə 'kɒŋk i ‖ -'kɑːŋk i
Maconochie mə 'kɒn ək i -əx- ‖ -'kɑːn-
McPhail mək 'feɪəl
McPhee mək 'fiː
McPherson mək 'fɜːs ən mæk-, -'fɪəs- ‖ -'fɝːs ən
McQuade mə 'kweɪd
Macquarie, McQuarrie mə 'kwɒr i ‖ -'kwɔːr i -'kwɑːr i
McQueen mə 'kwiːn
McRae mə 'kreɪ
macrame, macramé mə 'krɑːm i -eɪ ‖ 'mæk rə meɪ *(*)*
Macready, McReady mə 'kriːd i
macro 'mæk rəʊ ‖ -roʊ **~s** z
macro- *comb. form*
with stress-neutral suffix ˌmæk rəʊ ‖ -roʊ — **macroclimatic** ˌmæk rəʊ klaɪ 'mæt ɪk ◂ ‖ ˌmæk roʊ klaɪ 'mæṱ ɪk ◂
with stress-imposing suffix mæ 'krɒ+ ‖ mæ 'krɑː+ — **macropterous** mæ 'krɒpt ər əs ‖ -'krɑːpt-
macrobiotic ˌmæk rəʊ baɪ 'ɒt ɪk ◂ -bi'- ‖ -rə baɪ 'ɑːṱ ɪk ◂ **~ally** əl ˌi **~s** s
macrocarpa ˌmæk rəʊ 'kɑːp ə ‖ -roʊ 'kɑːrp ə
macrocosm 'mækr əʊ ˌkɒz əm ‖ -ə ˌkɑːz əm
macroeconomic ˌmæk rəʊ ˌiːk ə 'nɒm ɪk ◂ -ˌek- ‖ -roʊ ˌek ə 'nɑːm- -ˌiːk- **~s** s
macron 'mæk rɒn 'meɪk-, -rən ‖ -rɑːn **~s** z
macrophag|e 'mæk rəʊ feɪdʒ ‖ -rə- **~es** ɪz əz
macroscopic ˌmækr əʊ'skɒp ɪk ◂ ‖ -oʊ 'skɑːp-
Macrossan mə 'krɒs ən ‖ -'krɔːs- -'krɑːs-
McShea mək 'ʃeɪ §mæk-
McSorley mək 'sɔːl i ‖ -'sɔːrl i
McSwiney mək 'swiːn i mæk-, -'swɪn-
McTaggart mək 'tæg ət mæk- ‖ -ərt
McTavish mək 'tæv ɪʃ mæk-
McTeague mək 'tiːg mæk-
McTeer mək 'tɪə mæk-, mə- ‖ 'tɪər

mac|ula 'mæk |jʊl ə jəl- ‖ -|jəl ə **~ulae** ju liː jə- ‖ jə liː
ˌ**macula 'lutea** 'luːt i ə ‖ 'luːṱ-
McVay, McVeagh, McVeigh, McVey mək 'veɪ
McVicar mək 'vɪk ə ‖ -ər
McVitie, McVittie mək 'vɪt i mæk- ‖ -'vɪṱ i
McWhirter mək 'wɜːt ə mæk-, -'hwɜːt- ‖ -'hwɝːṱ ər
McWilliams mək 'wɪl jəmz mæk-
Macy 'meɪs i **Macy's** *tdmk* 'meɪs iz
mad, Mad mæd **madder** 'mæd ə ‖ -ər **maddest** 'mæd ɪst -əst
Madagascan ˌmæd ə 'gæsk ən ◂ **~s** z
Madagascar ˌmæd ə 'gæsk ə ‖ -ər
madam, Madam 'mæd əm **~s, ~'s** z
Madame, m~ 'mæd əm ‖ mə 'dɑːm, -'dæm —*Fr* [ma dam] **~s, ~'s** z
Madang mə 'dæŋ ‖ mɑː 'dɑːŋ
madcap 'mæd kæp →'mæg- **~s** s
madden, M~ 'mæd ən **~ed** d **~ing/ly** ˌɪŋ /li **~s** z
madder 'mæd ə ‖ -ər
Maddie 'mæd i
madding 'mæd ɪŋ
Maddison 'mæd ɪs ən -əs-
Maddock 'mæd ək
Maddocks, Maddox 'mæd əks
made meɪd
Madeira mə 'dɪər ə ‖ -'dɪr ə —*Port* [mɐ 'ðei ɾɐ, ma 'dei ɾa]
Ma'deira cake
Madejski mə 'deɪsk i
Madeleine, m~ 'mæd əl ɪn §-ən; -ə leɪn, -əl eɪn **~s** z
Madeley 'meɪd li
Madeline 'mæd əl ɪn §ən —*formerly also* -ə laɪn
mademoiselle, M~ ˌmæd əm wə 'zel ◂ -ə'-; ˌmæm wə 'zel —*Fr* [mad mwa zɛl, man-] **~s** z
made-to-measure ˌmeɪd tə 'meʒ ə ◂ ‖ -ər ◂
made-to-order ˌmeɪd tu 'ɔːd ə ◂ -tə- ‖ -'ɔːrd ər ◂
made-up ˌmeɪd 'ʌp
ˌ**made-up 'story**
Madge mædʒ
mad|house 'mæd |haʊs **~houses** haʊz ɪz -əz
Madingley 'mæd ɪŋ li
Madison 'mæd ɪs ən -əs-
ˌ**Madison 'Avenue**
Madley 'mæd li
madly 'mæd li
mad|man 'mæd |mən →'mæb- **~men** mən men
madness 'mæd nəs -nɪs **~es** ɪz əz
madonna, M~ mə 'dɒn ə ‖ -'dɑːn ə —*It* [ma 'dɔn na] **~s, ~'s** z
madras *'cotton'* 'mædr əs mə 'drɑːs -'dræs
Madras mə 'drɑːs -'dræs —*but the place in OR is* 'mædr əs
madrasa, madrasah, madrassa mə 'dræs ə **~s** z

madrepore ˈmædr ɪ pɔː -ə-, ˌ· ·ˈ· ‖ -pɔːr -pour **~s** z
Madrid mə ˈdrɪd —*Sp* [ma ˈðrið]
madrigal ˈmædr ɪɡ əl -əɡ- **~s** z
madrilene, madrilène ˌmædr ɪ ˈlen -ə-, -ˈleɪn, ˈ· · · —*Fr* [ma dʁi lɛn] **~s** z
madrona, madrone mə ˈdrəʊn ə ‖ -ˈdroʊn ə **~s** z
mad|woman ˈmæd |ˌwʊm ən **~women** ˌwɪm ɪn -ən
Mae meɪ
ˌMae ˈWest
Maecenas maɪ ˈsiːn æs miː-, -əs ‖ -əs
Maelor ˈmaɪl ɔː ‖ -ɔːr —*Welsh* [ˈməi lor, ˈməi-]
maelstrom, M~ ˈmeɪəl strɒm -strəm, -strəʊm ‖ -strəm -strɑːm **~s** z
maenad ˈmiːn æd **~s** z
Maendy ˈmeɪnd i ˈmaɪnd- —*Welsh* [ˈməin di]
Maentwrog maɪn ˈtʊər ɒɡ ‖ -ˈtʊr ɑːɡ —*Welsh* [məin ˈtu roɡ, məi-n-]
Maerdy ˈmɑːd i ‖ ˈmɑːrd i —*but some places of this name have an alternative pronunciation* ˈmeɪ əd i ‖ -ərd i *or* ˈmaɪ‿əd i ‖ ˈmaɪərd i
Maersk, Mærsk meəsk ‖ meərsk
Maesteg ˌmaɪs ˈteɪɡ —*Welsh* [mais ˈteːɡ, maːs-]
maestoso maɪ ˈstəʊs əʊ -ˈstəʊz- ‖ -ˈstoʊs oʊ -ˈstoʊz- —*It* [ma es ˈtoː so]
maestro ˈmaɪs trəʊ ‖ -troʊ —*It* [ma ˈɛs tro, -ˈes-] **~s** z
Maeterlinck ˈmeɪt ə lɪŋk ‖ ˈmeɪt̬ ər- —*Fr* [mɛ tɛʁ lɛ̃ːk]
Maev, Maeve meɪv
Mafeking ˈmæf ɪk ɪŋ -ək-
maffia, mafia, Mafia ˈmæf i‿ə ˈmɑːf- ‖ ˈmɑːf- ˈmæf-
mafios|o ˌmæf i ˈəʊs |əʊ ˌmɑːf-, -ˈəʊz- ‖ ˌmɑːf i ˈoʊs |oʊ ˌmæf-, -ˈoʊz- **~i** iː
mag mæɡ **mags** mæɡz
Magarshack ˈmæɡ ə ʃæk ‖ -ər-
magazine ˌmæɡ ə ˈziːn ˈ· · · ‖ ˈmæɡ ə ziːn ˌ· ·ˈ· **~s** z
Magda ˈmæɡd ə
Magdala ˈmæɡd əl ə mæɡ ˈdɑːl ə
Magdalen ˈmæɡd əl ɪn -ən —*but the Oxford college is* ˈmɔːd lɪn, -lən ‖ ˈmɔːd-, ˈmɑːd-
Magdalene ˌmæɡd ə ˈliːn i ˈmæɡd ə liːn, -lɪn —*but the Cambridge college is* ˈmɔːd lɪn, -lən ‖ ˈmɔːd-, ˈmɑːd-
Magdalenian ˌmæɡd ə ˈliːn i‿ən ◂
mage meɪdʒ **mages** ˈmeɪdʒ ɪz -əz
Magee mə ˈɡiː
Magellan mə ˈɡel ən -ˈdʒel- ‖ -ˈdʒel ən
Magellanic ˌmæɡ ɪ ˈlæn ɪk ◂ ˌmædʒ-, -ə- ‖ ˌmædʒ-
ˌMagelˌlanic ˈcloud
magenta, M~ mə ˈdʒent ə ‖ -ˈdʒent̬ ə
Maggie, m~ ˈmæɡ i
maggot ˈmæɡ ət **~s** s
maggoty ˈmæɡ ət i ‖ -ət̬ i
Maggs mæɡz
Maghera ˌmæk ə ˈrɑː ˌmæ hə-
Magherafelt ˌmæk ər‿ə ˈfelt ˌmæ hər‿
Maghreb ˈmɑːɡ reb ˈmæɡ-, ˈmʌɡ-, -rɪb, -rəb; mɑː ˈɡreb, mə-
Maghull mə ˈɡʌl
magi, Magi ˈmeɪdʒ aɪ ˈmeɪɡ-
magic ˈmædʒ ɪk **~ked** t **~king** ɪŋ **~s** s
ˌmagic ˈcarpet; **ˌmagic ˈeye**; **ˌmagic ˈlantern**; **ˌMagic ˈMarker** *tdmk*; **ˌmagic ˈsquare**; **ˌmagic ˈwand**
magical ˈmædʒ ɪk əl **~ly** i
magician mə ˈdʒɪʃ ən **~s** z
Magilligan mə ˈɡɪl ɪɡ ən
Maginnis mə ˈɡɪn ɪs §-əs
Maginot ˈmæʒ ɪ nəʊ ˈmædʒ-, -ə- ‖ -noʊ —*Fr* [ma ʒi ˈno]
ˈMaginot Line
magisteri|al ˌmædʒ ɪ ˈstɪər i‿|əl ◂ ˌ·ə- ‖ -ˈstɪr- **~ally** əl i **~um** əm
magistrac|y ˈmædʒ ɪs trəs |i ˈ·əs- **~ies** iz
magistral ˈmædʒ ɪs trəl -əs-; mə ˈdʒɪs-, mæ-
magistrate ˈmædʒ ɪ streɪt -ə-; -əs trət, -trɪt **~s** s
maglev, M~ ˈmæɡ lev
mag|ma ˈmæɡ |mə **~mas** məz **~mata** mət ə ‖ mət̬ ə
Magna, magna ˈmæɡ nə
ˌMagna ˈCarta, ˌMagna ˈCharta ˈkɑːt ə ‖ -ˈkɑːrt̬ ə
magna cum laude ˌmæɡ nə kʊm ˈlaʊd eɪ ˌnɑː-
magnanimity ˌmæɡ nə ˈnɪm ət i -ɪt i ‖ -ət̬ i
magnanimous mæɡ ˈnæn ɪm əs məɡ-, -əm- **~ly** li **~ness** nəs nɪs
magnate ˈmæɡ neɪt -nət, -nɪt **~s** s
magnesia, M~ mæɡ ˈniːʃ ə məɡ-, -ˈniːs i‿ə, -ˈniːʒ ə, -ˈniːz i‿ə
magnesite ˈmæɡ nɪ saɪt -nə-
magnesium mæɡ ˈniːz i‿əm məɡ-, -ˈniːʒ əm, -ˈniːs i‿əm, -ˈniːʃ əm
magˌnesium hyˈdroxide
magnet ˈmæɡ nɪt -nət **~s** s
magnetic mæɡ ˈnet ɪk məɡ- ‖ -ˈnet̬ ɪk **~ally** əl i
magˌnetic ˈfield; **magˌnetic ˈnorth**; **magˌnetic ˈpole**; **magˌnetic ˈtape**
magnetis... —*see* **magnetiz...**
magnetism ˈmæɡ nə ˌtɪz əm -nɪ-
magnetite ˈmæɡ nə taɪt -nɪ-
magnetization ˌmæɡ nət aɪ ˈzeɪʃ ən ˌ·nɪt-, -ɪˈ-‖ -nət̬ ə- **~s** z
magnetiz|e ˈmæɡ nə taɪz -nɪ- **~ed** d **~es** ɪz əz **~ing** ɪŋ
magneto mæɡ ˈniːt əʊ məɡ- ‖ -ˈniːt̬ oʊ **~s** z
magneto- *comb. form*
with stress-neutral suffix mæɡ |niːt əʊ ‖ -|niːt̬ ə — **magnetosphere** mæɡ ˈniːt əʊ sfɪə ‖ -ˈniːt̬ ə sfɪr
with stress-imposing suffix ˌmæɡ nə ˈtɒ+ -nɪ- ‖ -ˈtɑː+ — **magnetometer** ˌmæɡ nə ˈtɒm ɪt ə ˌnɪ-, -ət ə ‖ -ˈtɑːm ət̬ ər
magnetron ˈmæɡ nə trɒn -nɪ- ‖ -trɑːn **~s** z
Magnificat mæɡ ˈnɪf ɪ kæt məɡ-, -ə- **~s** s

magnification ˌmæg nɪf ɪ ˈkeɪʃ ᵊn ˌ·nəf-, §-əˈ·- **~s** z
magnificence mæg ˈnɪf ɪs ən*t*s məg-, -əs-
magnificent mæg ˈnɪf ɪs ənt məg-, -əs- **~ly** li
magnifico mæg ˈnɪf ɪ kəʊ §-ə- ‖ -koʊ **~s** z
magnifier ˈmæg nɪ faɪ‿ə ˈ·nə- ‖ -faɪ‿ᵊr **~s** z
magni|fy ˈmæg nɪ |faɪ -nə- **~fied** faɪd **~fies** faɪz **~fying** faɪ ɪŋ
ˈmagnifying glass
magniloquence mæg ˈnɪl ək wən*t*s
magniloquent mæg ˈnɪl ək wənt **~ly** li
magnitude ˈmæg nɪ tjuːd -nə-, →-tʃuːd ‖ -tuːd -tjuːd **~s** z
magnolia, M~ mæg ˈnəʊl i‿ə məg- ‖ -ˈnoʊl- **~s** z
Magnox, m~ ˈmæg nɒks ‖ -nɑːks
magnum ˈmæg nəm **~s** z
ˌmagnum ˈopus
Magnus ˈmæg nəs
ˈMagnus hitch
Magnusson ˈmæg nəs ən
Magog ˈmeɪ gɒg ‖ -gɑːg
Magoo mə ˈguː
magpie ˈmæg paɪ **~s** z
Magrath mə ˈgrɑː -ˈgrɑːθ, -ˈgræθ
Magraw mə ˈgrɔː ‖ -ˈgrɑː
Magri ˈmæg ri
Magritte mæ ˈgriːt mə- ‖ mɑː- —*Fr* [ma gʁit]
Magruder mə ˈgruːd ə ‖ -ᵊr
magstripe ˈmæg straɪp **~s** s
maguey mə ˈgeɪ ˈmæg weɪ
Maguire mə ˈgwaɪ‿ə ‖ -ˈgwaɪ‿ᵊr
magus, Magus ˈmeɪg əs **magi, Magi** ˈmeɪdʒ aɪ ˈmeɪg-
Magwitch ˈmæg wɪtʃ
Magyar ˈmæg jɑː ‖ -jɑːr **~s** z —*Hung* [ˈmɒ ɟɒr]
Mahabharata mə ˌhɑː ˈbɑːr ət ə ˌmɑː hə-, ˌmæ hə-,-ˈbær- —*Hindi* [mə hɑː bʱɑː rət̪]
Mahaffy mə ˈhæf i
Mahalia mə ˈheɪl i‿ə
maharaja, maharajah ˌmɑː hə ˈrɑːdʒ ə -ə- —*Hindi* [mə hɑː rɑː dʒɑː, mɑː-] **~s** z
maharanee, maharani ˌmɑː hə ˈrɑːn i -ə- —*Hindi* [mə hɑː rɑː ni, mɑː-] **~s** z
Maharashtra ˌmɑː hə ˈræʃ trə -ə-, -ˈrɑːʃ- —*Hindi* [mə hɑː rəʃtr]
Maharishi ˌmɑː hə ˈrɪʃ i -ə- —*Hindi* [mə hər ʃi]
Mahathir ˌmæ hə ˈtɪə ˌmɑː- ‖ ˌmɑː hə ˈtɪᵊr
mahatma, M~ mə ˈhɑːt mə -ˈhæt- —*Hindi* [mə hɑːt̪ mɑː] **~s** z
Mahayana ˌmɑː hə ˈjɑːn ə mə ˌhɑː ˈ· · —*Hindi* [mə hɑː jən]
Mahdi ˈmɑːd i -iː
Mahé ˈmɑː eɪ -heɪ —*Fr* [ma e]
Maher *(i)* mɑː ‖ mɑːr, *(ii)* meɪ ə ‖ ᵊr
Mahfouz mɑː ˈfuːz —*Arabic* [mah ˈfuːzˤ]
mah-jong, mah-jongg ˌmɑː ˈdʒɒŋ ‖ -ˈʒɑːŋ -ˈdʒɑːŋ, -ˈʒɔːŋ, -ˈdʒɔːŋ; ˈ· ·
Mahler ˈmɑːl ə ‖ -ᵊr —*Ger* [ˈmaː lɐ]
mahlstick ˈmɔːl stɪk ‖ ˈmɑːl- ˈmɔːl- **~s** s
Mahmud mɑː ˈmuːd
mahoe ˈmɑː həʊ i ‖ mə ˈhoʊ ˈmɑː hoʊ
mahogan|y mə ˈhɒg ən |i ‖ -ˈhɑːg- **~ies** iz
Mahomet mə ˈhɒm ɪt -et, §-ət ‖ -ˈhɑːm-
Mahommed mə ˈhɒm ɪd -ed, §-ət ‖ -ˈhɑːm-
Mahommedan mə ˈhɒm ɪd ən -əd- ‖ -ˈhɑːm- **~s** z
Mahon *family name* mɑːn ˈmæ hən ‖ mæn
Mahoney, Mahony *(i)* ˈmɑː ən i, *(ii)* mə ˈhəʊn i ‖ -ˈhoʊn i
mahonia mə ˈhəʊn i‿ə ‖ -ˈhoʊn- **~s** z
Mahood mə ˈhʊd
mahout mə ˈhaʊt mɑː-, -ˈhuːt **~s** s
Mai *(i)* meɪ, *(ii)* maɪ
Maia ˈmaɪ‿ə ˈmeɪ ə
maid meɪd *(= made)* **maids** meɪdz
ˌMaid ˈMarian
Maida ˈmeɪd ə
maidan maɪ ˈdɑːn mæ- **~s** z
maiden, M~ ˈmeɪd ᵊn **~s** z
ˈmaiden name; **ˌmaid of ˈhonour**; **ˌmaiden ˈover**
maidenhair ˈmeɪd ᵊn heə ‖ -her -hær
maidenhead, M~ ˈmeɪd ᵊn hed **~s** z
maidenhood ˈmeɪd ᵊn hʊd
maiden|ly ˈmeɪd ᵊn |li **~liness** li nəs -nɪs
Maidment ˈmeɪd mənt →ˈmeɪb-
maidservant ˈmeɪd ˌsɜːv ᵊnt ‖ -ˌsɜːv- **~s** s
Maidstone ˈmeɪd stən -stəʊn ‖ -stoʊn
maieutic meɪ ˈjuːt ɪk maɪ- ‖ -ˈjuːt̬-
maigre ˈmeɪg ə ‖ -ᵊr
Maigret ˈmeɪg reɪ ‖ ˌmeɪ ˈgreɪ —*Fr* [mɛ gʁɛ]
mail meɪᵊl *(= male)* **mailed** meɪᵊld **mailing** ˈmeɪᵊl ɪŋ **mails** meɪᵊlz
ˈmailing list; **ˌmail ˈorder◂**; **ˈmail train**
mailbag ˈmeɪᵊl bæg **~s** z
mailbomb ˈmeɪᵊl bɒm ‖ -bɑːm **~s** z
mailbox ˈmeɪᵊl bɒks ‖ -bɑːks **~es** ɪz əz
Mailer ˈmeɪl ə ‖ -ᵊr
Mailgram *tdmk* ˈmeɪᵊl græm **~s** z
mail|man ˈmeɪᵊl |mæn **~men** men
mailshot ˈmeɪᵊl ʃɒt ‖ -ʃɑːt **~s** s
maim meɪm **maimed** meɪmd **maiming** ˈmeɪm ɪŋ **maims** meɪmz
Maimonides maɪ ˈmɒn ɪ diːz -ə- ‖ -ˈmɑːn-
main meɪn **mains** meɪnz
ˌmain ˈchance; **ˌmain ˈclause**; **ˌmain ˈdrag**; **ˌmain ˈline◂**; **ˈMain Street**; **ˌmain ˈverb**
Main *river in Germany* maɪn meɪn —*Ger* [main]
Maine meɪn
mainframe ˈmeɪn freɪm **~s** z
Maingay ˈmeɪn geɪ →ˈmeɪŋ-
mainland ˈmeɪn lənd -lænd
mainlin|e ˈmeɪn laɪn ˌ·ˈ· **~ed** d **~er/s** ə/z ‖ ᵊr/z **~es** z **~ing** ɪŋ
mainly ˈmeɪn li
mainmast ˈmeɪn mɑːst →ˈmeɪm-, §-mæst, -məst ‖ -mæst —*naut* -məst **~s** s
mainsail ˈmeɪn seɪᵊl -sᵊl —*naut* -sᵊl **~s** z
mainspring ˈmeɪn sprɪŋ **~s** z
mainstay ˈmeɪn steɪ **~s** z
mainstream ˈmeɪn striːm

M

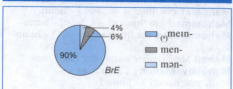

MAINTAIN

4%
6%
90%
(ı)meın-
men-
mən-
BrE

maintain (ı)meın ˈteın men-, mən- — *Preference poll, BrE:* (ı)meın- *90%,* men- *6%,* mən- *4%.* **~ed** d **~ing** ɪŋ **~s** z

maintenance ˈmeɪnt ən‿ənᵗs -ɪn-; ⚠(ı)meın ˈteın- ‖ -ən‿- **ˈmaintenance ˌorder**

Mainwaring *(i)* ˈmæn ər ɪŋ, *(ii)* ˈmeın ˌweər ɪŋ -wər-; ˌ·ˈ· · ‖ -ˌwer-

Mainz maınts —*Ger* [maints]

Mair ˈmaɪ‿ə ‖ ˈmaɪ‿ᵊr —*Welsh* [mair] —*but as a family name,* meə ‖ meᵊr

Maire ˈmær i ‖ ˈmer- —*but as a family name,* meə ‖ meᵊr

Mairead mə ˈreɪd

Maisie ˈmeɪz i

maisonette, maisonnette ˌmeɪz ə ˈnet ˌmeɪs-, ˌᵊn ˈet **~s** s

Maitland ˈmeɪt lənd

maitre d', maître d' ˌmeɪtr ə ˈdiː ˌmetr- ‖ ˌmeɪţ ᵊr- **~s** z

maitre d'hotel, maître d'hôtel ˌmeɪtr ə dəʊ ˈtel ◂ ˌmetr- ‖ -doʊ ˈtel ˌmeɪţ ᵊr- —*Fr* [mɛ tʁə do tɛl] **maitres d'hotel, maîtres d'hôtel** ˌmeɪtr əz- ˌmetr əz- ‖ ˌmeɪţ ᵊrz-

maize meɪz *(= maze)*

majestic, M~ mə ˈdʒest ɪk **~al** ᵊl **~ally** ᵊl‿i

majest|y, M~ ˈmædʒ əst |i ɪst- **~ies** iz

majolica mə ˈdʒɒl ɪk ə -ˈjɒl- ‖ -ˈdʒɑːl-

major, Major ˈmeɪdʒ ə ‖ -ᵊr **~ed** d **majoring** ˈmeɪdʒ ər‿ɪŋ **~s** z **ˌmajor ˈgeneral◂**; **ˌmajor ˈkey**; **ˌmajor ˈleague◂**; **ˌmajor ˈsuit**

Majorc|a mə ˈjɔːk |ə maɪ ˈɔːk-, mə ˈdʒɔːk- ‖ -ˈjɔːrk |ə -ˈdʒɔːrk ə —*Sp* Mallorca [ma ˈʎor ka, -ˈjor-] **~an/s** ən/z

majordomo ˌmeɪdʒ ə ˈdəʊm əʊ ‖ -ᵊr ˈdoʊm oʊ **~s** z

majorette ˌmeɪdʒ ə ˈret **~s** s

majoritarian mə ˌdʒɒr ɪ ˈteər i‿ən ◂ -ˌ·ə- ‖ -ˌdʒɔːr ə ˈter- -ˌdʒɑːr- **~s** z

majorit|y mə ˈdʒɒr ət |i -ɪt- ‖ -ˈdʒɔːr əţ |i -ˈdʒɑːr- **~ies** iz **maˈjority ˌleader**

majorly ˈmeɪdʒ ə li ‖ -ᵊr-

Majuro mə ˈdʒʊər əʊ ‖ mə ˈdʒʊr oʊ

majuscule ˈmædʒ ə skjuːl ‖ mə ˈdʒʌsk juːl **~s** z

Makarios mə ˈkɑːr i ɒs -ˈkær- ‖ -oʊs -ɑːs, əs

Makaton *tdmk* ˈmæk ə tɒn ˈmɑːk- ‖ -tɑːn -toʊn

make meɪk **made** meɪd **makes** meɪks **making** ˈmeɪk ɪŋ

make-believe ˈmeɪk bɪ ˌliːv -bə-, §bi:-, ˌ· ·ˈ·

make-or-break ˌmeɪk ɔː ˈbreɪk ◂ ‖ -ᵊr-

makeover ˈmeɪk ˌəʊv ə ‖ -ˌoʊv ᵊr **~s** z

Makepeace ˈmeɪk piːs

maker, Maker ˈmeɪk ə ‖ -ᵊr **~s** z

Makerere mə ˈker ər i

makeshift ˈmeɪk ʃɪft

make-up ˈmeɪk ʌp **~s** s

makeweight ˈmeɪk weɪt **~s** s

make-work ˈmeɪk wɜːk ‖ -wɜːk

making ˈmeɪk ɪŋ **~s** z

-making ˌmeɪk ɪŋ — **sick-making** ˈsɪk ˌmeɪk ɪŋ

Makins ˈmeɪk ɪnz §-ənz

mako ˈmɑːk əʊ ˈmeɪk- ‖ -oʊ **~s** z

mal- mæl — **maladaptive** ˌmæl ə ˈdæpt ɪv ◂

Malabar ˈmæl ə bɑː ˌ· ·ˈ◂ ‖ -bɑːr

malacca, M~ mə ˈlæk ə ‖ -ˈlɑːk ə **~s** z

Malachi ˈmæl ə kaɪ

malachite ˈmæl ə kaɪt

Malachy ˈmæl ək i

maladi... —*see* **malady**

maladjust|ed ˌmæl ə ˈdʒʌst |ɪd ◂ -əd **~ment** mənt

maladministration ˌmæl əd ˌmɪn ɪ ˈstreɪʃ ᵊn ˌ·æd-, -əˈ-

maladroit ˌmæl ə ˈdrɔɪt ◂ **~ly** li **~ness** nəs nɪs

malad|y ˈmæl əd |i **~ies** iz

Malaga ˈmæl əg ə —*Sp* Málaga [ˈma la ɣa]

Malagasy ˌmæl ə ˈgæs i ◂ -ˈgɑːz i

Malahide ˈmæl ə haɪd

malaise mə ˈleɪz mæ-

Malamud ˈmæl ə mʊd

malamute ˈmæl ə mjuːt -muːt **~s** s

Malaprop, m~ ˈmæl ə prɒp ‖ -prɑːp

malapropism ˈmæl ə prɒp ˌɪz əm ‖ ˈ· ·prɑːp- **~s** z

malapropos ˌmæl ˌæp rə ˈpəʊ ˌ·ˈ· ·ˈ· ‖ -ˈpoʊ

malar ˈmeɪl ə ‖ -ᵊr

malaria mə ˈleər i‿ə ‖ -ˈler-

malari|al mə ˈleər i‿|əl ‖ -ˈler- **~ous** əs

malarkey, malarky mə ˈlɑːk i ‖ -ˈlɑːrk i

Malathion *tdmk* ˌmæl ə ˈθaɪ‿ən

Malawi, Malaw i mə ˈlɑː wi **~an/s** ən/z

Malay mə ˈleɪ ‖ ˈmeɪ leɪ mə ˈleɪ **~s** z

Malaya mə ˈleɪ ə

Malayalam ˌmæl eɪ ˈɑːl əm ◂ -i-, -ə ˈjɑːl-

Malayan mə ˈleɪ ən **~s** z

Malayo-Polynesian mə ˌleɪ əʊ ˌpɒl i ˈniːz i‿ən -ˈniːʒ-, -ˈniːʒ ᵊn ‖ -oʊ ˌpɑːl ə ˈniːʒ ᵊn -ˈniːʃ ᵊn

Malaysia mə ˈleɪz i‿ə -ˈleɪʒ-, -ˈleɪʒ ə ‖ mə ˈleɪʒ ə -ˈleɪʃ ə

Malaysian mə ˈleɪz i‿ən -ˈleɪʒ-, -ˈleɪʒ ᵊn ‖ mə ˈleɪʒ ᵊn -ˈleɪʃ ᵊn **~s** z

Malcolm ˈmælk əm —*rarely also* ˈmɔːlk-

malcontent ˈmæl kən ˌtent §-kɒn- ‖ ˌmæl kən ˈtent **~s** s

malcontented ˌmæl kən ˈtent ɪd ◂ §-kɒn-, -əd ‖ -ˈtenţ əd ◂

mal de mer ˌmæl də ˈmeə ‖ -ˈmeᵊr —*Fr* [mal də mɛːʁ]

Malden ˈmɔːld ən ˈmɒld- ‖ ˈmɑːld-

Maldive ˈmɔːld iːv ˈmɒld-, ˈmɑːld-, -ɪv, -aɪv ‖ ˈmɑːld-, ˈmæld- **~s** z

Maldivian mɔːl ˈdɪv i‿ən mɒl-, mɑːl- ‖ mɑːl-, mæl- **~s** z
Maldon ˈmɔːld ən ˈmɒld- ‖ ˈmɑːld-
Maldwyn *(i)* ˈmæld wɪn, *(ii)* ˈmɔːld- ˈmɒld- ‖ ˈmɑːld-
male, Male meɪᵊl **males** meɪᵊlz
ˌ**male ˈchauvinist◂**, ˌ**male ˌchauvinist ˈpig**
Male, Malé *capital of Maldives* ˈmɑːl eɪ
malediction ˌmæl ɪ ˈdɪk ʃən -ə- **~s** z
male-dominated ˌmeɪᵊl ˈdɒm ɪ neɪt ɪd ◂ -ˈ·ə- ‖ -ˈdɑːm ə neɪt̬-
malefactor ˈmæl ɪ fækt ə ˈ-ə- ‖ -ᵊr **~s** z
malefic mə ˈlef ɪk
malefic|ence mə ˈlef ɪs |ənᵗs mæ-, §-əs- **~ent** ənt
maleic mə ˈleɪ ɪk -ˈliː-
maleness ˈmeɪᵊl nəs -nɪs
Malet ˈmæl ɪt -ət
male-voice ˈmeɪᵊl vɔɪs
malevolence mə ˈlev əl ənᵗs mæ-
malevolent mə ˈlev əl ənt mæ- **~ly** li
malfeasance ₍ˌ₎mæl ˈfiːz ᵊnᵗs
Malfi ˈmælf i
malformation ˌmæl fɔː ˈmeɪʃ ᵊn -fə- ‖ -fɔːr- -fᵊr- **~s** z
malformed ˌmæl ˈfɔːmd ◂ ‖ -ˈfɔːrmd ◂
malfunction ˌmæl ˈfʌŋk ʃᵊn **~ed** d **~ing** ˌɪŋ **~s** z
Malham ˈmæl əm
Malhotra məl ˈhəʊtr ə ‖ -ˈhoʊtr-
Mali ˈmɑːl i
Malian ˈmɑːl i‿ən **~s** z
Malibu ˈmæl ɪ buː -ə-
malic ˈmæl ɪk ˈmeɪl-
malice ˈmæl ɪs §-əs
malicious mə ˈlɪʃ əs **~ly** li **~ness** nəs nɪs
malign mə ˈlaɪn **~ed** d **~ing** ɪŋ **~ly** li **~s** z
malignanc|y mə ˈlɪg nənᵗs |i **~ies** iz
malignant mə ˈlɪg nənt **~ly** li
maligner mə ˈlaɪn ə ‖ -ᵊr **~s** z
malignit|y mə ˈlɪg nət |i -nɪt- ‖ -nət̬ |i **~ies** iz
Malik ˈmæl ɪk
Malin ˈmæl ɪn §-ən
malinger mə ˈlɪŋ gə ‖ -gᵊr **~ed** d **malingering** mə ˈlɪŋ gər‿ɪŋ **~s** z
malingerer mə ˈlɪŋ gər ə ‖ -gᵊr ər
Malinowski ˌmæl ɪ ˈnɒf ski -ə- ‖ -ˈnɑːf- -ˈnɔːf-
malkin, M~ ˈmɔːk ɪn ˈmɔːlk-, ˈmɒlk-, §-ən ‖ ˈmɑːk-, ˈmælk- **~s** z
mall, Mall mɔːl mæl, mɒl ‖ mɑːl — *Preference poll, BrE, in the sense 'shopping centre':* mɔːl *50% (born since 1973: 76%),* mæl *50%. Several respondents voted for* mɒl, *not an option offered. Always* mæl *in the London place names* The Mall, Chiswick Mall, Pall Mall. **malls** mɔːlz mælz ‖ mɑːlz
Mallaig ˈmæl eɪg
Mallalieu ˈmæl ə ljuː -ljɜː, -luː ‖ -luː
Mallam ˈmæl əm
mallard ˈmæl ɑːd -əd ‖ -ᵊrd **~s** z
Mallarmé ˈmæl ɑː meɪ ‖ ˌmæl ɑːr ˈmeɪ —*Fr* [ma laʁ me]
malleability ˌmæl i‿ə ˈbɪl ət i -ɪt i ‖ -ət̬ i

MALL

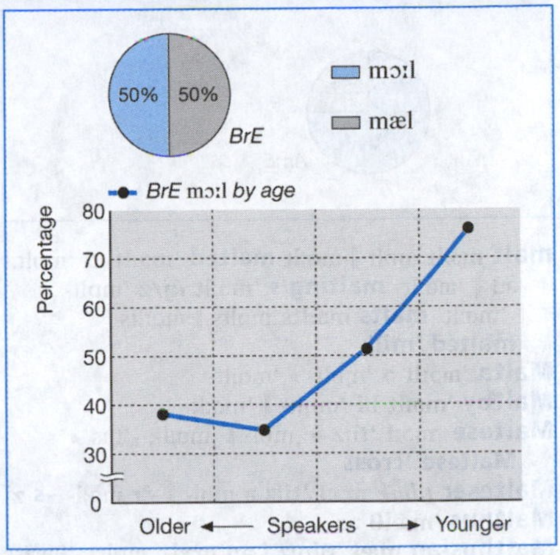

malleab|le ˈmæl i‿əb |ᵊl **~leness** ᵊl nəs -nɪs **~ly** li
mallee ˈmæl i **~s** z
mallei ˈmæl i aɪ
malle|olus mə ˈliː‿|əl əs **~oli** ə laɪ
Malleson ˈmæl ɪs ən -əs-
mallet ˈmæl ɪt -ət **~s** s
Mallet, Mallett ˈmæl ɪt -ət
malle|us ˈmæl i|‿əs **~i** aɪ
Malling *places in Kent* ˈmɔːl ɪŋ ‖ ˈmɑːl- —*Occasionally also, inappropriately,* ˈmæl-
Mallinson ˈmæl ɪn sən -ən-
Mallorca mə ˈjɔːk ə məl- ‖ -ˈjɔːrk ə
Mallory ˈmæl ər i
mallow, M~ ˈmæl əʊ ‖ -oʊ **~s** z
mall-rat ˈmɔːl ræt ‖ ˈmɑːl- **~s** s
Malmesbury ˈmɑːmz bər‿i §ˈmɒlmz- ‖ -ˌber i
Malmo, Malmö, Malmoe ˈmælm əʊ ‖ -oʊ —*Swed* Malmö [ˈˈmalm øː]
malmsey ˈmɑːmz i §ˈmɒlmz-
malnourished ˌmæl ˈnʌr ɪʃt ◂ ‖ -ˈnɜː-
malnutrition ˌmæl nju ˈtrɪʃ ᵊn ‖ -nu- -nju-
malodorous mæl ˈəʊd ər əs ‖ -ˈoʊd- **~ly** li **~ness** nəs nɪs
Malone mə ˈləʊn ‖ -ˈloʊn
Malory ˈmæl ər i
Malpas *(i)* ˈmɔːlp əs ˈmɔːp- ‖ ˈmɑːlp-, *(ii)* ˈməʊp əs ‖ ˈmoʊp-, *(iii)* ˈmælp əs —*The place in Cheshire is (i) or (iii), that in Cornwall (ii), that in Gwent (iii); the family name is usually (iii).*
Malpighi mæl ˈpiːg i —*It* [mal ˈpiː gi]
Malpighian mæl ˈpɪg i‿ən -ˈpiːg-
Malplaquet ˈmæl plə keɪ ˌ·ˈ· —*Fr* [mal pla kɛ]
malpractice ˌmæl ˈprækt ɪs §-əs, ˈ·ˌ·· — *Preference poll, AmE:* ˌ·ˈ·· *75%,* ˈ·ˌ·· *25%.* *See chart on p.486.*
ˌ**malˈpractice inˌsurance**
Malraux ˌmæl ˈrəʊ ‖ -ˈroʊ ˌmɑːl- —*Fr* [mal ʁo]

MALPRACTICE

malt mɔːlt mɒlt ‖ mɑːlt **malted** ˈmɔːlt ɪd ˈmɒlt, -əd ‖ ˈmɑːlt- **malting/s** ˈmɔːlt ɪŋ/z ˈmɒlt- ‖ ˈmɑːlt- **malts** mɔːlts mɒlts ‖ mɑːlts
ˌmalted ˈmilk

Malta ˈmɔːlt ə ˈmɒlt- ‖ ˈmɑːlt-

Maltby ˈmɔːlt bi ˈmɒlt- ‖ ˈmɑːlt-

Maltese ˌmɔːl ˈtiːz ◂ ˌmɒl- ‖ ˌmɑːl-, -ˈtiːs ◂
ˌMaltese ˈcross

Malteser *tdmk* mɔːl ˈtiːz ə mɒl- ‖ -ᵊr mɑːl- **~s** z

Malthus ˈmælθ əs

Malthusian mæl ˈθjuːz i‿ən mɔːl-, mɒl-, -ˈθuːz- ‖ -ˈθuːʒ ᵊn mɔːl-, mɑːl- **~s** z

Malton ˈmɔːlt ən ˈmɒlt- ‖ ˈmɑːlt-

Maltravers mæl ˈtræv əz ‖ -ᵊrz

mal|treat ˌmæl |ˈtriːt **~treated** ˈtriːt ɪd -əd ‖ ˈtriːṱ əd **~treating** ˈtriːt ɪŋ ‖ ˈtriːṱ ɪŋ **~treatment** ˈtriːt mənt **~treats** ˈtriːts

maltster ˈmɔːlt stə ˈmɒlt- ‖ -stᵊr ˈmɑːlt- **~s** z

Malvern *(i)* ˈmɔːlv ən ˈmɔːv-, ˈmɒlv- ‖ -ᵊrn ˈmɑːlv-, *(ii)* ˈmælv ən ‖ -ᵊrn *—In England (i), in the US (ii).*

malversation ˌmæl vɜː ˈseɪʃ ᵊn -və- ‖ -vᵊr-

Malvinas mæl ˈviːn əz mɔːl-, mɒl- *—AmSp* [mal ˈβi nas, -nah]

Malvolio mæl ˈvəʊl i‿əʊ ‖ -ˈvoʊl i‿oʊ

malware ˈmæl weə ‖ -wer

Malyon ˈmæl jən

mam, Mam mæm **mams, Mam's** mæmz

mama, Mama mə ˈmɑː ˈmæm ə ‖ ˈmɑːm ə *(*)* **~s, ~'s** z
ˈMama's boy

Mamaroneck mə ˈmær ə nek ‖ -ˈmer-

mamba ˈmæm bə ‖ ˈmɑːm- ˈmæm-, -bɑː **~s** z

mambo ˈmæm bəʊ ‖ ˈmɑːm boʊ **~ed** d **~es, ~s** z **~ing** ɪŋ

Mameluke ˈmæm ɪ luːk -ə-, -ljuːk

Mamet ˈmæm ɪt -ət

Mamie ˈmeɪm i

mamm|a *'breast'* ˈmæm |ə **~ae** iː

mamma, Mamma *'mother'* mə ˈmɑː ‖ ˈmɑːm ə **~s, ~'s** z

mammal ˈmæm ᵊl **~s** z

mammalian mə ˈmeɪl i‿ən mæ- **~s** z

mammar|y ˈmæm ər |i **~ies** iz
ˈmammary gland

mammee mæ ˈmiː -ˈmeɪ ‖ mɑː-

mammogram ˈmæm ə græm **~s** z

mammography mæ ˈmɒg rəf i ‖ -ˈmɑːg-

mammon, M~ ˈmæm ən

mammoth ˈmæm əθ **~s** s

mamm|y, Mammy ˈmæm |i **~ies** iz

man, Man mæn **manned** mænd **manning** ˈmæn ɪŋ **man's** mænz **men** men **men's** menz
ˌman ˈFriday; ˌman in the ˈmoon; ˌman in the ˈstreet; ˌman ˈjack; ˌman of ˈletters; ˌman of ˈstraw

-man mən, mæn *—This suffix may be weak or strong. (i) In most well-established formations written as one word, it is weak,* mən*:* policeman pə ˈliːs mən. *(ii) Where written hyphenated or as two words, and in new formations, it is usually strong,* mæn*:* spaceman ˈspeɪs mæn. *Note* batman *'army servant'* ˈbæt mən, *but* Batman *(cartoon character)* ˈbæt mæn

mana ˈmɑːn ə

man-about-town ˌmæn ə baʊt ˈtaʊn
men-about-town ˌmen-

manacl|e ˈmæn ək ᵊl **~ed** d **~es** z **~ing** ˌɪŋ

manag|e ˈmæn ɪdʒ -ədʒ **~ed** d **~es** ɪz əz **~ing** ɪŋ

manageability ˌmæn ɪdʒ ə ˈbɪl ət i ˌ-ədʒ-, -ɪt i ‖ -əṱ i

manageab|le ˈmæn ɪdʒ əb |ᵊl ˈ-ədʒ- **~ly** li

management ˈmæn ɪdʒ mənt -ədʒ- **~s** s

manager ˈmæn ɪdʒ ə -ədʒ- ‖ -ᵊr **~s** z

manageress ˌmæn ɪdʒ ə ˈres ˌ-ədʒ-, ˈ-·· ‖ ˈmæn ɪdʒ ər əs *(*)* **~es** ɪz əz

managerial ˌmæn ə ˈdʒɪər i‿əl ◂ ‖ -ˈdʒɪr- **~ly** i

managership ˈmæn ɪdʒ ə ʃɪp ˈ-ədʒ- ‖ -ᵊr- **~s** s

Managua mə ˈnæg wə -ˈnɑːg- ‖ -ˈnɑːg- *—Sp* [ma ˈna ɣwa]

manana, mañana mæn ˈjɑːn ə mən- ‖ mən- mɑːn- *—Sp* [ma ˈɲa na]

Manasseh mə ˈnæs i -ə ‖ -ə

man-at-arms ˌmæn ət ˈɑːmz ‖ -əṱ ˈɑːrmz
men-at-arms ˌmen-

manatee ˌmæn ə ˈtiː ‖ ˈmæn ə tiː **~s** z

man-bag ˈmæn bæg **~s** z

-mancer ˌmænᵗs ə ‖ -ᵊr — **necromancer** ˈnek rə ˌmænᵗs ə ‖ -ᵊr

Manchester ˈmæntʃ ɪst ə -əst-; ˈmæn ˌtʃest- ‖ -ᵊr

manchineel ˌmæntʃ ɪ ˈniːᵊl -ə- **~s** z

Manchu ˌmæn ˈtʃuː ◂ *—Chi* Mǎn Zhōu [^{3}man ^{1}ʈʂou]

Manchukuo ˌmæn tʃuː ˈkwəʊ ‖ -ˈkwoʊ *—Chi* Mǎn Zhōu Guó [^{3}man ^{1}ʈʂou ^{2}kwɔ]

Manchuri|a mæn ˈtʃʊər i‿|ə ‖ -ˈtʃʊr- **~an/s** ən/z

manciple ˈmænᵗs ɪp ᵊl -əp- **~s** z

mancozeb ˈmæŋk əʊ zeb ‖ -ə-

Mancunian mæn ˈkjuːn i‿ən →mæŋ- **~s** z

-mancy ˌmænᵗs i — **necromancy** ˈnek rə ˌmænᵗs i

Manda ˈmænd ə

mandala ˈmænd əl ə ˈmʌnd-; mæn ˈdɑːl ə **~s** z

Mandalay ˌmænd ə ˈleɪ ◂ -ᵊl ˈeɪ; ˈ· · ·

mandamus mæn ˈdeɪm əs **~es** ɪz əz

mandarin, M~ ˈmænd ər ɪn §-ən, ˌmænd ə ˈrɪn **~s** z
ˌmandarin ˈduck; ˌmandarin ˈorange

mandarinate ˈmænd‿ər ɪ neɪt ər ə- **~s** s

mandatar|y ˈmænd ət‿ər |i ˈ·ɪt‿, mæn ˈdeɪt ər |i ‖ -ə ter |i **~ies** iz
mand|ate *v* ˌmæn ˈd|eɪt ˈmænd |eɪt ‖ ˈmænd |eɪt **~ated** eɪt ɪd -əd ‖ eɪţ əd **~ates** eɪts **~ating** eɪt ɪŋ ‖ eɪţ ɪŋ
mandate *n* ˈmænd eɪt -ɪt, -ət **~s** s
mandator|y ˈmænd ət‿ər |i ˈ·ɪt‿, mæn ˈdeɪt ər |i ‖ -ə tɔːr |i -toʊr i **~ies** iz
man-day ˈmæn deɪ ˌ·ˈ· **~s** z
Mande ˈmænd eɪ ˈmɑːnd- ‖ ˈmɑːnd eɪ mɑːn ˈdeɪ **~s** z
Mandela mæn ˈdel ə -ˈdeɪl- —*Xhosa* [ma ˈndɛː la]
Mandelbaum ˈmænd ᵊl baʊm
Mandelbrot ˈmænd ᵊl brəʊt ‖ ˈmɑːnd ᵊl broʊt ˈmænd-
Mandelson ˈmænd ᵊl sən
Mandelstam ˈmænd ᵊl stæm -stəm
Mandeville ˈmænd ə vɪl -ɪ-
mandible ˈmænd ɪb ᵊl -əb- **~s** z
Mandingo mæn ˈdɪŋ gəʊ ‖ -goʊ **~s** z
mandolin, mandoline ˌmænd ə ˈlɪn -ᵊl ˈɪn; ˈmænd ᵊl ɪn, §-ən **~s** z
mandorla mæn ˈdɔːl ə ‖ -ˈdɔːrl ə **~s** z
mandragora mæn ˈdræg ər ə
mandrake ˈmændr eɪk **~s** s
mandrax, M~ *tdmk* ˈmændr æks **~es** ɪz əz
mandrel, mandril ˈmændr əl -ɪl **~s** z
mandrill ˈmændr ɪl -əl **~s** z
Mandy ˈmænd i
mane meɪn *(= main)* **maned** meɪnd **manes** meɪnz
Manea ˈmeɪn i
man-eat|er ˈmæn ˌiːt |ə ‖ -ˌiːţ |ᵊr **~ers** əz ‖ ᵊrz **~ing** ɪŋ
maneb ˈmæn eb
maneg|e, manèg|e mæ ˈneɪʒ -ˈneʒ —*Fr* [ma nɛːʒ] **~es** ɪz əz
manes, Manes *'shades of the dead'* ˈmɑːn eɪz -eɪs; ˈmeɪn iːz
Manet ˈmæn eɪ ‖ mæ ˈneɪ mə- —*Fr* [ma nɛ] **~s, ~'s** z
maneuvrability, maneuverability mə ˌnuːv ər‿ə ˈbɪl ət i -ɪt i ‖ -əţ i
maneuvrable, maneuverable mə ˈnuːv ər‿əb ᵊl
maneuv|re, maneuv|er mə ˈnuːv |ə ‖ -|ᵊr **~ered, ~red** əd ‖ ᵊrd **~ering, ~ring** ər‿ɪŋ **~ers, ~res** əz ‖ ᵊrz
Manfred ˈmæn frɪd -frəd, -fred
manful ˈmæn fᵊl -fʊl **~ly** i **~ness** nəs nɪs
manga ˈmæŋ gə ‖ ˈmɑːŋ- —*Jp* [ma ˌŋ ŋa]
mangabey ˈmæŋ gə beɪ -biː **~s** z
manganate ˈmæŋ gə neɪt **~s** s
manganese ˈmæŋ gə niːz ˌ· ·ˈ·◂ ‖ niːs
manganic mæn ˈgæn ɪk →mæŋ-
manganous ˈmæŋ gən əs mæn ˈgæn əs, →mæŋ-
mange meɪndʒ
mangel-wurzel ˈmæŋ gᵊl ˌwɜːz ᵊl ‖ -ˌwɝːz- **~s** z
manger ˈmeɪndʒ ə ‖ -ᵊr **~s** z
mangetout ˌmɒndʒ ˈtuː ˌmɑːndʒ-, ˌmɒ̃ʒ-; ˈ· · ‖ ˌmɑːndʒ- —*Fr* [mɑ̃ʃ tu]
mangl|e ˈmæŋ gᵊl **~ed** d **~es** z **~ing** ‿ɪŋ
mango ˈmæŋ gəʊ ‖ -goʊ **~es, ~s** z
mangold, M~ ˈmæŋ gəʊld →-gɒʊld ‖ -goʊld **~s** z
mangosteen ˈmæŋ gəʊ stiːn **~s** z
Mangotsfield ˈmæŋ gəts fiːᵊld
mangrove ˈmæŋ grəʊv ˈmæn- ‖ -groʊv **~s** z
 ˈmangrove swamp
mang|y ˈmeɪndʒ |i **~ier** i‿ə ‖ i‿ᵊr **~iest** i‿ɪst i‿əst **~ily** ɪ li əl i **~iness** i nəs i nɪs
manhandl|e ˈmæn ˌhænd ᵊl ˌ·ˈ· **~ed** d **~es** z **~ing** ‿ɪŋ
Manhattan, m~ mæn ˈhæt ᵊn mən- **~s, ~'s** z
manhole ˈmæn həʊl →-hɒʊl ‖ -hoʊl **~s** z
 ˈmanhole ˌcover
manhood ˈmæn hʊd
manhour ˈmæn ˌaʊ‿ə ‖ -ˌaʊ‿ᵊr **~s** z
manhunt ˈmæn hʌnt **~s** s
mania ˈmeɪn i‿ə **~s** z
-mania ˈmeɪn i‿ə — **pyromania** ˌpaɪᵊr ə ˈmeɪn i‿ə
maniac ˈmeɪn i æk **~s** s
-maniac ˈmeɪn i æk — **pyromaniac** ˌpaɪᵊr ə ˈmeɪn i æk
maniacal mə ˈnaɪ‿ək ᵊl **~ly** ‿i
manic ˈmæn ɪk **~s** s
manic-depressive ˌmæn ɪk di ˈpres ɪv ◂ -də'-- **~s** z
Manichaean, Manichean ˌmæn ɪ ˈkiː‿ən ◂ -ə- **~s** z
Manichaeism, Manicheism ˌmæn ɪ ˈkiː‿ˌɪz əm -ə-
manicure ˈmæn ɪ kjʊə -ə-, -kjɔː ‖ -kjʊr -kjɝː **~d** d **~s** z **manicuring** ˈmæn ɪ kjʊər ɪŋ ˈ·ə-, -kjɔːr ɪŋ ‖ -kjʊr ɪŋ -kjɝː ɪŋ
manicurist ˈmæn ɪ kjʊər ɪst ˈ·ə-, -kjɔːr ɪst, §-əst ‖ -kjʊr əst **~s** s
manifest *adj, n, v* ˈmæn ɪ fest -ə- **~ed** ɪd əd **~ing** ɪŋ **~s** s
manifestation ˌmæn ɪ fe ˈsteɪʃ ᵊn ˌ·ə-, fə'-- **~s** z
manifestly ˈmæn ɪ fest li ˈ·ə-
manifesto ˌmæn ɪ ˈfest əʊ -ə- ‖ -oʊ **~es, ~s** z
manifold, M~ ˈmæn ɪ fəʊld -ə-, →-fɒʊld ‖ -foʊld **~ed** ɪd əd **~ing** ɪŋ **~ly** li **~ness** nəs nɪs **~s** z
manikin ˈmæn ɪk ɪn -ək-, §-ən **~s** z
manila, M~, manilla mə ˈnɪl ə **~s** z
 Maˌnila ˈhemp
Manilow ˈmæn ɪ ləʊ -əl əʊ ‖ -loʊ
manioc ˈmæn i ɒk ‖ -ɑːk
maniple ˈmæn ɪp ᵊl -əp- **~s** z
manipulability mə ˌnɪp jʊl ə ˈbɪl ət i -ˌjəl-, -ɪt i ‖ -jəl ə ˈbɪl əţ i
manipulab|le mə ˈnɪp jʊl əb |ᵊl -jəl əb- ‖ -jəl əb- **~ly** li
manipu|late mə ˈnɪp ju |leɪt -jə- ‖ -jə- **~lated** leɪt ɪd -əd ‖ leɪţ əd **~lates** leɪts **~lating** leɪt ɪŋ ‖ leɪţ ɪŋ
manipulation mə ˌnɪp ju ˈleɪʃ ᵊn -jə- ‖ -jə- **~s** z

M

manipulative mə ˈnɪp jʊl ət ɪv -jəl ət-; -ju leɪt-, -jə leɪt- ‖ -jə leɪt̬ ɪv -jə lət̬- **~ly** li **~ness** nəs nɪs
manipulator mə ˈnɪp ju leɪt ə -jə- ‖ -jə leɪt̬ ᵊr **~s** z
Manitoba ˌmæn ɪ ˈtəʊb ə -ə- ‖ -ˈtoʊb ə
manitou ˈmæn ɪ tuː §-ə-
Manitoulin ˌmæn ɪ ˈtuːl ɪn -ə-, §-ən
mankind mæn ˈkaɪnd →mæŋ-, ˌ·ˈ· —*but in the rare sense 'men as distinct from women',* ˈ··
mank|y ˈmæŋk |i **~ier** i‿ə ‖ i‿ᵊr **~iest** i‿ɪst i‿əst
Manley, Manly ˈmæn li
man|ly ˈmæn |li **~lier** li‿ə ‖ li‿ᵊr **~liest** li‿ɪst əst **~liness** li nəs -nɪs
man-made ˌmæn ˈmeɪd ◂ →ˌmæm- ˌ**man-made ˈfibres**
Mann mæn
manna ˈmæn ə
mannequin ˈmæn ɪk ɪn -ək-, §-ən **~s** z
manner ˈmæn ə ‖ -ᵊr **~ed** d **~s** z
mannerism ˈmæn ər ˌɪz əm **~s** z
manner|ly ˈmæn ə |li ‖ -ᵊr- **~liness** li nəs -nɪs
Manners ˈmæn əz ‖ -ᵊrz
Mannheim ˈmæn haɪm —*Ger* [ˈman haim]
mannikin ˈmæn ɪk ɪn -ək-, §-ən **~s** z
Manning ˈmæn ɪŋ
Manningham ˈmæn ɪŋ əm
mannish ˈmæn ɪʃ **~ly** li **~ness** nəs nɪs
mannitol ˈmæn ɪ tɒl §-ə- ‖ -toʊl -tɑːl, -tɔːl
Manny ˈmæn i
mano a mano ˌmæn əʊ ɑː ˈmæn əʊ ‖ ˌmɑːn oʊ ɑː ˈmɑːn oʊ —*Sp* [ˌma no a ˈma no]
manoeuvrability mə ˌnuːv ər‿ə ˈbɪl ət i -ɪt i ‖ -ət̬ i
manoeuvrable mə ˈnuːv ər‿əb ᵊl
manoeuv|re, maneuv|er mə ˈnuːv |ə ‖ -|ᵊr **~ered, ~red** əd ‖ ᵊrd **~ering, ~ring** ər‿ɪŋ **~ers, ~res** əz ‖ ᵊrz
man-of-war ˌmæn əv ˈwɔː -ə- ‖ -ˈwɔːr **men-of-war** ˌmen-
manometer məˈnɒm ɪt ə mæ-, §-ət- ‖ -ˈnɑːm ət̬ ᵊr **~s** z
manometric ˌmæn əʊ ˈmetr ɪk ◂ ‖ -ə- **~al** ᵊl **~ally** ᵊl‿i
Manon Lescaut mæ ˌnɒ̃ le ˈskəʊ ‖ mɑː ˌnoʊn le ˈskoʊ —*Fr* [ma nɔ̃ lɛs ko]
manor ˈmæn ə ‖ -ᵊr *(= manner)* **~s** z ˈ**manor house**
Manorbier ˌmæn ə ˈbɪə ‖ -ᵊr ˈbɪᵊr
manorial mə ˈnɔːr i‿əl mæ- ‖ -ˈnoʊr-
man-o'-war ˌmæn ə ˈwɔː ‖ -ˈwɔːr **men-o'-war** ˌmen-
manpower ˈmæn ˌpaʊ‿ə →ˈmæm- ‖ -ˌpaʊ‿ᵊr
manque, manqué ˈmɒŋk eɪ ˈmɑːŋk- ‖ mɑːŋ ˈkeɪ —*Fr* [mɑ̃ ke]
Manresa mæn ˈreɪs ə -ˈreɪz- ‖ mɑːn- mæn- —*Sp* [man ˈre sa]
mansard ˈmænᵗs ɑːd -əd ‖ -ɑːrd -ᵊrd **~s** z
manse mænᵗs **manses** ˈmænᵗs ɪz -əz
Mansel, Mansell ˈmænᵗs ᵊl
manservant ˈmæn ˌsɜːv ᵊnt ‖ -ˌsɜːv- **~s** s
Mansfield ˈmænᵗs fiːᵊld
-manship mən ʃɪp — **gamesmanship** ˈgeɪmz mən ʃɪp
mansion ˈmænᵗʃ ᵊn **~s** z ˌ**Mansion ˈHouse,** ˈ· · ·
man-size ˈmæn saɪz **~d** d
manslaughter ˈmæn ˌslɔːt ə ‖ -ˌslɔːt̬ ᵊr -ˌslɑːt̬-
Manson ˈmænᵗs ᵊn
Manston ˈmænᵗst ən
manta, Manta ˈmænt ə ‖ ˈmænt̬ ə **~s** z
mantel ˈmænt ᵊl ‖ ˈmænt̬ ᵊl *(= mantle)* **~s** z
mantelpiec|e ˈmænt ᵊl piːs ‖ ˈmænt̬- **~es** ɪz əz
mantel|shelf ˈmænt ᵊl |ʃelf ‖ ˈmænt̬ ᵊl- **~shelves** ʃelvz
mantic ˈmænt ɪk ‖ ˈmænt̬ ɪk
mantilla mæn ˈtɪl ə ‖ -ˈtiː ə —*Sp* [man ˈti ʎa, -ja] **~s** z
Mantinea ˌmænt ɪ ˈniː‿ə -ə-, -ˈneɪ-
mantis ˈmænt ɪs §-əs ‖ ˈmænt̬ əs **~es** ɪz əz
mantissa mæn ˈtɪs ə **~s** z
mantl|e ˈmænt ᵊl ‖ ˈmænt̬ ᵊl **~ed** d **~es** z **~ing** ɪŋ
man-to-man ˌmæn tə ˈmæn ◂
Mantovani ˌmænt ə ˈvɑːn i
mantra ˈmæntr ə ˈmʌntr- **~s** z
mantrap ˈmæn træp **~s** s
Mantu|a, m~ ˈmænt ju‿|ə -u‿; ˈmæntʃ u‿|ə ‖ ˈmæntʃ u‿|ə **~an/s** ən/z
manual ˈmæn ju‿əl **~ly** i **~s** z
Manuel *forename* ˌmæn ˈwel ˈ··; ˈmæn ju‿əl ‖ mæn ˈwel —*Sp* [ma ˈnwel]
Manuel *family name* ˈmæn ju‿əl -el
manufac|ture ˌmæn ju ˈfæk |tʃə -jə-, -ə-, -ʃə ‖ -jə ˈfæk |tʃᵊr -ʃᵊr **~tured** tʃəd ‖ tʃᵊrd **~tures** tʃəz ‖ tʃᵊrz **~turing** tʃər ɪŋ
manufacturer ˌmæn ju ˈfæk tʃər‿ə ·ˈjə-, ·ˈə-, -ʃər‿ə ‖ -jə ˈfæk tʃᵊr‿ər -ʃᵊr‿ər **~s** z
manumission ˌmæn ju ˈmɪʃ ᵊn -jə- ‖ -jə- **~s** z
manu|mit ˌmæn ju |ˈmɪt -jə- ‖ -jə- **~mits** ˈmɪts **~mitted** ˈmɪt ɪd -əd ‖ ˈmɪt̬ əd **~mitting** ˈmɪt ɪŋ ‖ ˈmɪt̬ ɪŋ
manure mə ˈnjʊə -ˈnjɔː ‖ -ˈnʊᵊr ˈnjʊᵊr **~d** d **manuring** mə ˈnjʊər ɪŋ -ˈnjɔːr- ‖ -ˈnʊr ɪŋ -ˈnjʊər- **~s** z
manuscript ˈmæn ju skrɪpt -jə- ‖ -jə- **~s** s
Manwaring ˈmæn ər ɪŋ ‖ -wɔːr-
Manx mæŋ*k*s ˌ**Manx ˈcat**
Manx|man ˈmæŋ*k*s |mən -mæn **~men** mən men
many ˈmen i —*There are occasional weak forms* mən i, mni *(esp. in* how many*); in AmE also* ˈmɪn i. —*In Ireland often* ˈmæn i **more** mɔː ‖ mɔːr moʊr **most** məʊst ‖ moʊst
man-year ˈmæn jɪə ˌ·ˈ· ‖ -jɪᵊr **~s** z
many-faceted ˌmen i ˈfæs ɪt ɪd -ət-, -et ◂, -əd ‖ -ət̬-
many-sided ˌmen i ˈsaɪd ɪd ◂ -əd **~ness** nəs nɪs
manzanilla, M~ ˌmænz ə ˈnɪl ə ‖ -ˈniː ə —*Sp* [man θa ˈni ʎa, -ja] **~s** z

Mao maʊ
Mao Tsetung ˌmaʊt sɪ ˈtʊŋ -tseɪ; **Mao Zedong** ˌmaʊd zə ˈdʊŋ —*Chi* Máo Zédōng [²mɐu ²tsɤ ¹tʊŋ]
Maoism ˈmaʊ ˌɪz əm
Maoist ˈmaʊ ɪst §-əst **~s** s
Maori ˈmaʊᵊr i —*Maori* [ˈma o ɾi] **~s** z
map mæp **mapped** mæpt **mapping/s** ˈmæp ɪŋ/z **maps** mæps
maple ˈmeɪp ᵊl **~s** z
ˈmaple leaf; **ˌmaple ˈsyrup**
Maplin ˈmæp lɪn -lən
Mapp mæp
Mappin ˈmæp ɪn §-ən
Mapplethorpe ˈmeɪp ᵊl θɔːp ˈmæp- ‖ -θɔːrp
map-read|er ˈmæp ˌriːd |ə ‖ -|ᵊr **~ers** əz ‖ ᵊrz **~ing** ɪŋ
Maputo mə ˈpuːt əʊ ‖ -oʊ
maquette mæ ˈket **~s** s
maquillage ˌmæk i ˈɑːʒ -ˈjɑːʒ —*Fr* [ma ki jaːʒ]
maquis mæ ˈkiː mɑː-; ˈmæk iː, ˈmɑːk- —*Fr* [ma ki]
mar, Mar mɑː ‖ mɑːr **marred** mɑːd ‖ mɑːrd **marring** ˈmɑːr ɪŋ **mars** mɑːz ‖ mɑːrz
Mar. —*see* **March**
marabou, marabout ˈmær ə buː ‖ ˈmer- **~s** z
maraca mə ˈræk ə ‖ -ˈrɑːk ə -ˈræk- **~s** z
Maradona ˌmær ə ˈdɒn ə ‖ -ˈdɑːn- ˌmer- —*Sp* [ma ɾa ˈðo na]
maraschino, M~ ˌmær ə ˈskiːn əʊ ◂ -ˈʃiːn- ‖ -oʊ ◂ ˌmer-, -ˈʃiːn- **~s** z
maras|mus mə ˈræz |məs **~mic** mɪk
Marat ˈmær ɑː ‖ mə ˈrɑː —*Fr* [ma ʁa]
Marathi mə ˈrɑːt i ‖ -ˈrɑːt̬ i —*Hindi* [mə raː ʈʰi] **~s** z
marathon, M~ ˈmær əθ ən -ə θɒn ‖ -ə θɑːn ˈmer- **~er/s** ə/z ‖ -ᵊr/z **~s** z
maraud mə ˈrɔːd ‖ -ˈrɑːd **~ed** ɪd əd **~er/s** ə/z ‖ ᵊr/z **~ing** ɪŋ **~s** z
Marazion ˌmær ə ˈzaɪ‿ən ‖ ˌmer-
Marbella *place in Spain* mɑː ˈbeɪ ə -jə ‖ mɑːr- —*There is also a spelling pronunciation* ⚠-ˈbel ə —*Sp* [mar ˈβe ʎa, -ja]
marbl|e ˈmɑːb ᵊl ‖ ˈmɑːrb- **~ed** d **~es** z **~ing** ‿ɪŋ
Marblehead ˈmɑːb ᵊl hed ˌ·ˈ·ˌ· ‖ ˈmɑːrb-
Marburg ˈmɑː bɜːg ‖ ˈmɑːr bɜːg —*Ger* [ˈmaːɐ bʊʁk]
marc, Marc mɑːk ‖ mɑːrk *(= mark)*
Marcan ˈmɑːk ən ‖ ˈmɑːrk-
marcasite ˈmɑːk ə saɪt ‖ ˈmɑːrk-
Marceau ˌmɑː ˈsəʊ ‖ ˌmɑːr ˈsoʊ —*Fr* [maʁ so]
Marcel, m~ ₍ₗ₎mɑː ˈsel ‖ ₍ₗ₎mɑːr- **~led** d **~ling** ɪŋ **~s** z
Marcella ₍ₗ₎mɑː ˈsel ə ‖ ₍ₗ₎mɑːr-
Marcelle ₍ₗ₎mɑː ˈsel ‖ ₍ₗ₎mɑːr-
Marcellus mɑː ˈsel əs ‖ mɑːr-
march, March mɑːtʃ ‖ mɑːrtʃ **marched** mɑːtʃt ‖ mɑːrtʃt **marches, March's** ˈmɑːtʃ ɪz -əz ‖ ˈmɑːrtʃ əz **marching** ˈmɑːtʃ ɪŋ ‖ ˈmɑːrtʃ ɪŋ
ˈmarching ˌorders
Marchant ˈmɑːtʃ ənt ‖ ˈmɑːrtʃ-
marcher ˈmɑːtʃ ə ‖ ˈmɑːrtʃ ᵊr **~s** z
marchioness ˌmɑːʃ ə ˈnes ˈmɑːʃ ən‿ɪs, əs ‖ ˈmɑːrʃ ən‿əs **~es** ɪz əz
Marchmont ˈmɑːtʃ mənt ‖ ˈmɑːrtʃ-
march-past ˈmɑːtʃ pɑːst §-pæst ‖ ˈmɑːrtʃ pæst **~s** s
Marcia ˈmɑːs i‿ə ˈmɑːʃ ə ‖ ˈmɑːrʃ ə
Marciano ˌmɑːs i ˈɑːn əʊ ‖ ˌmɑːrs i ˈæn oʊ
Marco ˈmɑːk əʊ ‖ ˈmɑːrk oʊ
Marconi mɑː ˈkəʊn i ‖ mɑːr ˈkoʊn i —*It* [mar ˈkoː ni]
Marcos ˈmɑːk ɒs ‖ ˈmɑːrk oʊs
Marcus ˈmɑːk əs ‖ ˈmɑːrk-
Marcuse mɑː ˈkuːz ə ‖ mɑːr-
Marden ˈmɑːd ᵊn ‖ ˈmɑːrd- —*The place in Kent is sometimes* ₍ₗ₎mɑː ˈden ‖ ₍ₗ₎mɑːr-
Mardi Gras ˌmɑːd i ˈgrɑː ‖ ˈmɑːrd i grɑː -grɔː; ˌ· ·ˈ·
mardy ˈmɑːd i ‖ ˈmɑːrd i
mare *'lunar plain', 'sea'* ˈmɑːr eɪ ˈmær-, -i
maria ˈmɑːr i‿ə ˈmær-
mare *'she-horse'* meə ‖ meᵊr mæᵊr **mares, mare's** meəz ‖ meᵊrz mæᵊrz
ˈmare's nest
Maree mə ˈriː
Marengo mə ˈreŋ gəʊ ‖ -goʊ —*It* [ma ˈreŋ go]
mare's-tail ˈmeəz teɪᵊl ‖ ˈmerz- ˈmærz- **~s** z
marg mɑːdʒ ‖ mɑːrdʒ
Margach ˈmɑːg ə ‖ ˈmɑːrg ə
Margam ˈmɑːg əm ‖ ˈmɑːrg-
Margaret ˈmɑːg rət -rɪt; ˈmɑːg ər ət, -ɪt ‖ ˈmɑːrg-
Margaretting ˌmɑːg ə ˈret ɪŋ ‖ ˌmɑːrg ə ˈret̬ ɪŋ
margarine ˌmɑːdʒ ə ˈriːn ˌmɑːg-, ˈ· · · ‖ ˈmɑːrdʒ ᵊr‿ən -ə riːn *(*)*
Margarita, m~ ˌmɑːg ə ˈriːt ə ‖ ˌmɑːrg ə ˈriːt̬ ə **~s, ~'s** z
margarite ˈmɑːg ə raɪt ‖ ˈmɑːrg-
Margary ˈmɑːg ər i ‖ ˈmɑːrg-
Margate ˈmɑː geɪt -gɪt, -gət ‖ ˈmɑːr-
margay ˈmɑːg eɪ ‖ ˈmɑːrg- mɑːr ˈgeɪ **~s** z
marge mɑːdʒ ‖ mɑːrdʒ
Margerison *(i)* ˈmɑːdʒ ər ɪs ən əs ən ‖ ˈmɑːrdʒ-, *(ii)* mɑː ˈdʒer- ‖ mɑːr-
margin ˈmɑːdʒ ɪn §-ən ‖ ˈmɑːrdʒ- **~s** z
marginal ˈmɑːdʒ ɪn ᵊl -ᵊn ə̩l ‖ ˈmɑːrdʒ- **~ly** i
marginalia ˌmɑːdʒ ɪ ˈneɪl i‿ə ˌ·ə- ‖ ˌmɑːrdʒ-
marginalis... —*see* **marginaliz...**
marginality ˌmɑːdʒ ɪ ˈnæl ət i ˌ·ə-, -ɪt i ‖ ˌmɑːrdʒ ə ˈnæl ət̬ i
marginalization ˌmɑːdʒ ɪn ᵊl aɪ ˈzeɪʃ ᵊn ˌ·ᵊn‿əl-, -ɪˈ-- ‖ ˌmɑːrdʒ ᵊn‿əl ə-
marginaliz|e ˈmɑːdʒ ɪn ə laɪz -ᵊn‿ə-, -əl aɪz **~ed** d **~es** ɪz əz **~ing** ɪŋ
Margo ˈmɑːg əʊ ‖ ˈmɑːrg oʊ
Margolis mɑː ˈgəʊl ɪs §-əs ‖ mɑːr ˈgoʊl-
Margot ˈmɑːg əʊ -ət ‖ ˈmɑːrg oʊ
margrave ˈmɑː greɪv ‖ ˈmɑːr- **~s** z
marguerite, M~ ˌmɑːg ə ˈriːt ‖ ˌmɑːrg- **~s, ~'s** s

M

Marham *(i)* ˈmær əm ‖ ˈmer-, *(ii)* ˈmɑːr əm —*Both (i) and (ii) are heard for the place in Norfolk.*
Mari ˈmɑːr i **~s** z
Maria *personal name(i)* mə ˈriː‿ə, *(ii)* mə ˈraɪ‿ə —*Always (ii) in the phrase* Black Maria
maria, Maria *Latin pl of* **mare** ˈmɑːr i‿ə ˈmær-
mariachi ˌmær i ˈɑːtʃ i ‖ ˌmɑːr- ˌmær- —*Sp* [ma ˈɾja tʃi]
Marian *adj, n* ˈmeər i‿ən ‖ ˈmer-
Marian *forename* ˈmær i‿ən §-æn ‖ ˈmer-
Mariana ˌmær i ˈɑːn ə ◂ ˌmeər-, -ˈæn- ‖ -ˈæn ə ◂ ˌmer-; ˌmɑːr i ˈɑːn ə **~s** z
ˌMariana ˈTrench
Marianne ˌmær i ˈæn ‖ ˌmer- —*Fr* [maʁ jan]
Marie *(i)* mə ˈriː, *(ii)* ˈmɑːr i, *(iii)* ˈmær i —*In AmE (i).*
ˌMarie ˌAntoiˈnette ‖ Maˌrie-
Marienbad ˈmær i‿ən bæd mə ˈriː‿ən-, →‿əm- ‖ ˈmer- *Ger* [ma ˈʁiː ən baːt]
Marietta ˌmær i ˈet ə ‖ -ˈeţ ə ˌmer-
marigold, M~ ˈmær i gəʊld §-ə-, →-gɒʊld ‖ -ə goʊld ˈmer- **~s** z
marihuana, marijuana ˌmær ɪ ˈwɑːn ə -ə-, -ˈhwɑːn-; ˌmær i ju ˈɑːn ə ‖ ˌmer-
Marilyn ˈmær əl ɪn -ɪl-, -ən ‖ ˈmer-
marimba mə ˈrɪm bə **~s** z
Marin *(i)* ˈmɑːr ɪn §-ən, *(ii)* ˈmær- ‖ ˈmer-, *(iii)* mə ˈrɪn —*The county in CA is (iii).*
marina, M~ mə ˈriːn ə **~s** z
marinad|e ˌmær ɪ ˈneɪd -ə-, ˈ· · · ‖ ˌmer- **~ed** ɪd əd **~es** z **~ing** ɪŋ
marinara ˌmær ɪ ˈnɑːr ə -ə- ‖ -ˈner ə ˌmer-, ˌmɑːr-, -ˈnɑːr-, -ˈnær- —*It* [ma ɾi ˈnaː ɾa]
mari|nate ˈmær ɪ |neɪt -ə- ‖ ˈmer- **~nated** neɪt ɪd -əd ‖ neɪţ əd **~nates** neɪts **~nating** neɪt ɪŋ ‖ neɪţ ɪŋ
marine mə ˈriːn **~s** z
Maˈrine Corps
mariner, M~ ˈmær ɪn ə -ən- ‖ -ən ər ˈmer- **~s** z
mariniere ˌmær ɪn ˈjeə ‖ ˌmɑːr ən ˈjeər ˌmær-, ˌmer- —*Fr* marinière [ma ʁi njɛːʁ]
Marino mə ˈriːn əʊ ‖ -oʊ
Mario ˈmær i əʊ ˈmɑːr- ‖ ˈmɑːr i oʊ ˈmær-, ˈmer-
mariolatry, M~ ˌmeər i ˈɒl ətr i ˌmær- ‖ ˌmer i ˈɑːl- ˌmær-
Mariology ˌmeər i ˈɒl ədʒ i ˌmær- ‖ ˌmer i ˈɑːl- ˌmær-
Marion ˈmær i‿ən ˈmeər- ‖ ˈmer-
marionette ˌmær i‿ə ˈnet ‖ ˌmer- **~s** s
mariposa ˌmær ɪ ˈpəʊz ə ‖ -ˈpoʊz ə ˌmer-, -ˈpoʊs-
ˌmariˈposa ˌlily
Marischal ˈmɑːʃ əl ‖ ˈmɑːrʃ-
Marist ˈmeər ɪst §-əst ‖ ˈmer- ˈmær- **~s** s
marital ˈmær ɪt əl -ət- ‖ -əţ əl ˈmer- —*In BrE formerly also* mə ˈraɪt- **~ly** i
maritime, M~ ˈmær ɪ taɪm -ə- ‖ ˈmer- **~s** z
Marius ˈmær i‿əs ˈmɑːr-, ˈmeər- ‖ ˈmer-, ˈmɑːr-
marjoram, M~ ˈmɑːdʒ ər‿əm ‖ ˈmɑːrdʒ-
Marjoribanks ˈmɑːtʃ bæŋks ‖ ˈmɑːrtʃ-
Marjorie, Marjory ˈmɑːdʒ ər‿i ‖ ˈmɑːrdʒ-
mark, Mark mɑːk ‖ mɑːrk **marked** mɑːkt ‖ mɑːrkt **marking** ˈmɑːk ɪŋ ‖ ˈmɑːrk ɪŋ **marks** mɑːks ‖ mɑːrks
(ˌ)Mark ˈAntony
markdown ˈmɑːk daʊn ‖ ˈmɑːrk- **~s** z
marked|ly ˈmɑːk ɪd |li -əd- ‖ ˈmɑːrk- **~ness** nəs nɪs
marker, M~ ˈmɑːk ə ‖ ˈmɑːrk ər **~s** z
mark|et ˈmɑːk |ɪt §-ət ‖ ˈmɑːrk |ət **~eted** ɪt ɪd §ət-, -əd ‖ əţ əd **~eting** ɪt ɪŋ §ət- ‖ əţ ɪŋ **~ets** ɪts §əts ‖ əts
ˌmarket ˈforces; **ˌmarket ˈgarden** ‖ ˈ· · ˌ· ·, **~er/s, ~ing**; **ˌmarket ˈprice** ‖ ˈ· · ·; **ˌmarket reˈsearch, -ˈresearch** ‖ ˈ· · ˌ· ·, ˌ· ˌ· ·; **ˈmarket town**; **ˌmarket ˈvalue**, ˈ· · ˌ· ·
marketability ˌmɑːk ɪt ə ˈbɪl ət i §ˌət-, -ɪt i ‖ ˌmɑːrk əţ ə ˈbɪl əţ i
marketable ˈmɑːk ɪt əb əl §ˈət- ‖ ˈmɑːrk əţ-
market-driven ˈmɑːk ɪt ˌdrɪv ən -ət- ‖ ˈmɑːrk-
marketeer ˌmɑːk ɪ ˈtɪə -ə- ‖ ˌmɑːrk ə ˈtɪər **~s** z
market-maker ˈmɑːk ɪt ˌmeɪk ə -ət- ‖ ˈmɑːrk ət ˌmeɪk ər **~s** z
market-oriented ˈmɑːk ɪt ˌɔːr i ent ɪd ˈ-ət-, ˌɒr-, -əd ‖ ˈmɑːrk əţ ˌɔːr i enţ əd -ˌoʊr-
marketplac|e ˈmɑːk ɪt pleɪs §-ət- ‖ ˈmɑːrk- **~es** ɪz əz
Market Rasen ˌmɑːk ɪt ˈreɪz ən §-ət- ‖ ˌmɑːrk-
Markey ˈmɑːk i ‖ ˈmɑːrk i
Markham ˈmɑːk əm ‖ ˈmɑːrk-
marking ˈmɑːk ɪŋ ‖ ˈmɑːrk ɪŋ **~s** z
ˈmarking ink
markka ˈmɑːk ə ‖ ˈmɑːrk ə —*Finnish* [ˈmark ka]
Markov ˈmɑːk ɒv -ɒf ‖ ˈmɑːrk ɑːf -ɔːf —*Russ* [ˈmar kəf]
ˌMarkov ˈprocess ‖ ˈ· · ˌ· ·
Markova mɑː ˈkəʊv ə ‖ mɑːr ˈkoʊv ə —*Russ* [ˈmar kə və]
Marks mɑːks ‖ mɑːrks
ˌMarks and ˈSpencer *tdmk*
marks|man ˈmɑːks |mən ‖ ˈmɑːrks- **~manship** mən ʃɪp **~men** mən men **~woman** ˌwʊm ən **~women** ˌwɪm ɪn §-ən
markup ˈmɑːk ʌp ‖ ˈmɑːrk- **~s** s
marl mɑːl ‖ mɑːrl
Marlboro *tdmk* ˈmɑːl bər‿ə ˈmɔːl- ‖ ˈmɑːrl ˌbɜː oʊ
Marlboro, Marlborough *place name, family name* ˈmɔːl bər‿ə ˈmɑːl- ‖ ˈmɑːrl ˌbɜː oʊ ˈmɔːrl-, -ə
Marlene *(i)* ˈmɑːl iːn ˌmɑː ˈliːn ‖ mɑːr ˈliːn, *(ii)* mɑː ˈleɪn ə ‖ mɑːr- —*As an English name, (i); as a German name, (ii).* —*Ger* [maʁ ˈleː nə]
Marler ˈmɑːl ə ‖ ˈmɑːrl ər
Marley ˈmɑːl i ‖ ˈmɑːrl i
marlin, marline ˈmɑːl ɪn §-ən ‖ ˈmɑːrl- **~s** z
marlinespike, marlinspike ˈmɑːl ɪn spaɪk -ən- ‖ ˈmɑːrl- **~s** s
Marlon ˈmɑːl ən -ɒn ‖ ˈmɑːrl-
Marlow, Marlowe ˈmɑːl əʊ ‖ ˈmɑːrl oʊ
Marmaduke ˈmɑːm ə djuːk →-dʒuːk ‖ ˈmɑːrm ə duːk -djuːk

marmalade ˈmɑːm ə leɪd ‖ ˈmɑːrm- **~s** z
ˌmarmalade ˈcat
Marmara ˈmɑːm ər ə ‖ ˈmɑːrm-
Marmion ˈmɑːm i̯ ən ‖ ˈmɑːrm-
marmite, M~ *tdmk* ˈmɑːm aɪt ‖ ˈmɑːrm-
Marmora ˈmɑːm ər ə ‖ ˈmɑːrm-
marmoreal mɑː ˈmɔːr i̯ əl ‖ mɑːr- -ˈmoʊr-
marmoset ˈmɑːm ə zet -set, ˌ· ·ˈ· ‖ ˈmɑːrm- **~s** s
marmot ˈmɑːm ət ‖ ˈmɑːrm- **~s** s
Marn, Marne mɑːn ‖ mɑːrn
Marner ˈmɑːn ə ‖ ˈmɑːrn ᵊr
Marnie ˈmɑːn i ‖ ˈmɑːrn i
marocain ˈmær ə keɪn ˌ· ·ˈ· ‖ ˈmer-
Maronite ˈmær ə naɪt ‖ ˈmer- **~s** s
maroon mə ˈruːn **~ed** d **~ing** ɪŋ **~s** z
Marplan *tdmk* ˈmɑː plæn ‖ ˈmɑːr-
Marple ˈmɑːp ᵊl ‖ ˈmɑːrp ᵊl
Marprelate ˈmɑː ˌprel ət -ɪt ‖ ˈmɑːr-
Marquand ˈmɑːk wənd ‖ ˌmɑːr ˈkwɑːnd
marque mɑːk ‖ mɑːrk *(= mark)* **marques** mɑːks ‖ mɑːrks
marquee ₍ˌ₎mɑː ˈkiː ‖ ₍ˌ₎mɑːr- **~s** z
Marquesan mɑː ˈkeɪz ᵊn -ˈkeɪs- ‖ mɑːr- **~s** z
Marquesas mɑː ˈkeɪz əz -ˈkeɪs əs, -æs ‖ mɑːr-
marquess ˈmɑːk wɪs -wəs ‖ ˈmɑːrk- **~es** ɪz əz
marquetry ˈmɑːk ɪtr i -ətr- ‖ ˈmɑːrk-
marquis, M~ ˈmɑːk wɪs -wəs; ₍ˌ₎mɑː ˈkiː ‖ ˈmɑːrk wəs ₍ˌ₎mɑːr ˈkiː **~es** ɪz əz
marquis|e ₍ˌ₎mɑː ˈkiːz ‖ ₍ˌ₎mɑːr- **~es** ɪz əz
Marr mɑː ‖ mɑːr
Marrakech, Marrakesh ˌmær ə ˈkeʃ mə ˈræk eʃ ‖ ˌmer-
marram ˈmær əm ‖ ˈmer-
ˈmarram grass
marriag|e ˈmær ɪdʒ ‖ ˈmer- **~es** ɪz əz
ˈmarriage ˌbroker; **ˌmarriage ˈguidance**; **ˈmarriage lines**
marriageability ˌmær ɪdʒ ə ˈbɪl ət i ˌ·ədʒ-, -ɪt i ‖ -əţ i ˌmer-
marriageable ˈmær ɪdʒ əb ᵊl ˈ·ədʒ- ‖ ˈmer- **~ness** nəs nɪs
married ˈmær id ‖ ˈmer- **~s** z
Marriner ˈmær ɪn ə -ən- ‖ -ᵊr
Marriott ˈmær i̯ ət ‖ ˈmer-, -ɑːt
marron ˈmær ən -õ ‖ ˈmer-; mə ˈroʊn, mæ- —*Fr* [ma ʁɔ̃] **~s** z —*or as sing.*
marrow ˈmær əʊ ‖ -oʊ ˈmer- **~s** z
marrowbone ˈmær əʊ bəʊn ‖ -ə boʊn ˈmer-, -oʊ- **~s** z
marrowfat ˈmær əʊ fæt ‖ -oʊ- ˈmer-, -ə-
ˌmarrowfat ˈpea
marr|y ˈmær |i ‖ ˈmer- — *Preference poll, AmE:* ˈmer- *53%,* ˈmær- *47%.* **~ied** id **~ies** iz **~ying** i̯ ɪŋ
Marryat ˈmær i̯ ət ‖ ˈmer-
Mars mɑːz ‖ mɑːrz
Marsala, m~ mɑː ˈsɑːl ə ‖ mɑːr- —*It* [mar ˈsaː la]
Marsden ˈmɑːz dən ‖ ˈmɑːrz-
Marseillaise ˌmɑːs eɪ ˈeɪz -ˈjeɪz, -ˈez; -ᵊl-; -ə ˈleɪz, -ˈlez ‖ ˌmɑːrs- —*Fr* [maʁ sɛ jɛːz]

MARRY

53% ˈmer-
47% ˈmær-
AmE

Marseilles ₍ˌ₎mɑː ˈseɪ -ˈseɪlz ‖ ₍ˌ₎mɑːr- —*Fr* Marseille [maʁ sɛj]
marsh, Marsh mɑːʃ ‖ mɑːrʃ **marshes** ˈmɑːʃ ɪz -əz ‖ ˈmɑːrʃ əz
ˈmarsh gas; **ˌmarsh ˈmarigold**
Marsha ˈmɑːʃ ə ‖ ˈmɑːrʃ ə
marshal ˈmɑːʃ ᵊl ‖ ˈmɑːrʃ ᵊl **~ed, ~led** d **~ing, ~ling** ˌɪŋ **~s** z
ˈmarshalling yard; **ˌmarshal of the ˌRoyal ˈAir Force**
Marshall ˈmɑːʃ ᵊl ‖ ˈmɑːrʃ ᵊl
ˈMarshall Plan
Marshalsea ˈmɑːʃ ᵊl si -siː ‖ ˈmɑːrʃ-
Marsham ˈmɑːʃ əm ‖ ˈmɑːrʃ-
marshiness ˈmɑːʃ i nəs -nɪs ‖ ˈmɑːrʃ-
marshland ˈmɑːʃ lænd -lənd ‖ ˈmɑːrʃ- **~s** z
marshmallow ₍ˌ₎mɑːʃ ˈmæl əʊ ‖ ˈmɑːrʃ ˌmel oʊ ˌmæl-, -ə *(*)* **~s** z
marshy ˈmɑːʃ i ‖ ˈmɑːrʃ i
Marsilius mɑː ˈsɪl i̯ əs ‖ mɑːr-
Marson ˈmɑːs ᵊn ‖ ˈmɑːrs ᵊn
Marston ˈmɑːst ən ‖ ˈmɑːrst ən
ˌMarston ˈMoor
marsupial mɑː ˈsuːp i̯ əl -ˈsjuːp- ‖ mɑːr- **~s** z
marsupi|um mɑː ˈsuːp i̯ |əm -ˈsjuːp- ‖ mɑːr- **~a** ə
mart mɑːt ‖ mɑːrt **marts** mɑːts ‖ mɑːrts
martagon ˈmɑːt əg ən ‖ ˈmɑːrţ- **~s** z
Martel, Martell mɑː ˈtel ‖ mɑːr-
martello, M~ mɑː ˈtel əʊ ‖ mɑːr ˈtel oʊ **~s** z
Marˌtello ˈtower
marten ˈmɑːt ɪn -ᵊn ‖ ˈmɑːrt ᵊn **~s** z
Martens *(i)* ˈmɑːt ɪnz -ᵊnz ‖ ˈmɑːrt ᵊnz, *(ii)* mɑː ˈtenz ‖ mɑːr-
Martha ˈmɑːθ ə ‖ ˈmɑːrθ ə
Marti ˈmɑːt i ‖ ˈmɑːrţ i
martial, M~ ˈmɑːʃ ᵊl ‖ ˈmɑːrʃ ᵊl *(= marshal)* **~ly** i
ˌmartial ˈarts; **ˌmartial ˈlaw**
Martian, m~ ˈmɑːʃ ᵊn ˈmɑːʃ i̯ ən ‖ ˈmɑːrʃ- **~s** z
Martin, m~ ˈmɑːt ɪn §-ᵊn ‖ ˈmɑːrt ᵊn **~s, ~'s** z
Martina mɑː ˈtiːn ə ‖ mɑːr-
Martineau ˈmɑːt ɪ nəʊ -ə-, -ᵊn əʊ ‖ ˈmɑːrt ᵊn oʊ
martinet ˌmɑːt ɪ ˈnet -ə-, -ᵊn ˈet ‖ ˌmɑːrt ᵊn ˈet **~s** s
Martinez mɑː ˈtiːn ez ‖ mɑːr ˈtiːn es -əs —*Sp* Martínez [mar ˈti neθ, -nes]
martingale ˈmɑːt ɪn geɪᵊl →-ɪŋ-, §-ᵊn- ‖ ˈmɑːrt ᵊn- **~s** z
martini, M~ *tdmk* mɑː ˈtiːn i ‖ mɑːr- **~s** z
Martinique ˌmɑːt ɪ ˈniːk -ə-, -ᵊn ˈiːk ‖ ˌmɑːrt ᵊn ˈiːk

M

Martinmas ˈmɑːt ɪn məs →-ɪm-, §-ᵊn-, -mæs ‖ ˈmɑːrt ᵊn-
Martinu ˈmɑːt ɪ nuː §-ə- ‖ ˈmɑːrt ᵊn uː —*Czech* Martinů [ˈmar ci nuː]
Martland ˈmɑːt lənd ‖ ˈmɑːrt-
martlet ˈmɑːt lət -lɪt ‖ ˈmɑːrt- **~s** s
Marty ˈmɑːt i ‖ ˈmɑːrt̬ i
Martyn ˈmɑːt ɪn §-ᵊn ‖ ˈmɑːrt ᵊn
martyr ˈmɑːt ə ‖ ˈmɑːrt̬ ᵊr **~ed** d **martyring** ˈmɑːt ər ɪŋ ‖ ˈmɑːrt̬ ər ɪŋ **~s** z
martyrdom ˈmɑːt ə dəm ‖ ˈmɑːrt̬ ᵊr- **~s** z
martyrolog|y ˌmɑːt ə ˈrɒl ədʒ |i ‖ ˌmɑːrt̬ ə ˈrɑːl- **~ies** iz
marvel ˈmɑːv ᵊl ‖ ˈmɑːrv ᵊl **~ed, ~led** d **~ing, ~ling** ɪŋ **~s** z
Marvell ˈmɑːv ᵊl ‖ ˈmɑːrv ᵊl
marvellous, marvelous ˈmɑːv ləs ˈmɑːv əl əs ‖ ˈmɑːrv- **~ly** li **~ness** nəs nɪs
Marvin ˈmɑːv ɪn §-ᵊn ‖ ˈmɑːrv ᵊn
Marwick ˈmɑː wɪk ‖ ˈmɑːr-
Marx mɑːks ‖ mɑːrks **Marx's** ˈmɑːks ɪz -əz ‖ ˈmɑːrks əz
ˈMarx ˌBrothers
Marxian ˈmɑːks i‿ən ‖ ˈmɑːrks-
Marxism ˈmɑːks ˌɪz əm ‖ ˈmɑːrks-
Marxism-Leninism ˌmɑːks ˌɪz əm ˈlen ɪn ˌɪz əm §-ˈ·ən- ‖ ˌmɑːrks-
Marxist ˈmɑːks ɪst §-əst ‖ ˈmɑːrks- **~s** s
Marxist-Leninist ˌmɑːks ɪst ˈlen ɪn ɪst §-əst ˈlen ɪn əst, §-ən· ‖ ˌmɑːrks- **~s** s
Mary ˈmeər i ‖ ˈmer i ˈmær i
ˌMary ˌQueen of ˈScots
Maryland ˈmeər ɪ lənd ˈmer-, -ə-, -lænd ‖ ˈmer əl ənd ˈmær-
Marylebone ˈmær əl ə bən ˈ·ɪ-, -lɪ·, -bəʊn; ˈmær ɪb ən, ˈmɑːl-, -əb- ‖ ˈmer əl ə boʊn ˈmær-
Maryport ˈmeər i pɔːt ‖ ˈmer i pɔːrt -poʊrt
marzipan ˈmɑːz ɪ pæn -ə-, ˌ··ˈ· ‖ ˈmɑːrz- ˈmɑːrts-, -pɑːn
Masada mə ˈsɑːd ə
Masai ˈmɑː saɪ ˌ·ˈ·, mə ˈsaɪ
masala mə ˈsɑːl ə
Mascagni mæ ˈskæn ji -ˈskɑːn- ‖ mɑː ˈskɑːn ji mæ- —*It* [ma ˈskaɲ ɲi]
Mascall ˈmæsk ᵊl
mascara mæ ˈskɑːr ə mə- ‖ -ˈskær ə -ˈsker- *(*)* **~'d, ~ed** d **~s** z
Mascarene, m~ ˌmæsk ə ˈriːn ◂ **~s** z
mascarpone ˌmæsk ɑː ˈpəʊn i -ə-, -eɪ; -ˈpəʊn ‖ ˌmɑːsk ɑːr ˈpoʊn eɪ —*It* [ma skar ˈpoː ne]
mascot ˈmæsk ət -ɒt ‖ -ɑːt -ət **~s** s
masculine ˈmæsk jʊl ɪn ˈmɑːsk-, -jəl-, §-ən, §-ju laɪn, -jə- ‖ -jəl ən **~ly** li **~ness** nəs nɪs **~s** z
masculinis... —*see* **masculiniz...**
masculinity ˌmæsk ju ˈlɪn ət i ˌmɑːsk-, ˌjə-, -ɪt i ‖ -jə ˈlɪn ət̬ i
masculinization ˌmæsk jʊl ɪn aɪ ˈzeɪʃ ᵊn ˌmɑːsk-, ˌjəl-, ˌ· ·ən-, -ɪˈ- ‖ ˌmæsk jəl ən ə-
masculiniz|e ˈmæsk jʊl ɪ naɪz ˈmɑːsk-, ˈjəl-, §-ə · ‖ ˈmæsk jəl ə- **~ed** d **~es** ɪz əz **~ing** ɪŋ
Masefield ˈmeɪs fiːᵊld ˈmeɪz-
maser ˈmeɪz ə ‖ -ᵊr **~s** z
Maserati *tdmk* ˌmæz ə ˈrɑːt i ‖ ˌmɑːs ə ˈrɑːt̬ i ˌmæz ə- **~s** z
Maseru mə ˈsɪər uː -ˈseər- ‖ ˈmæz ə ruː ˈmɑːs-
mash mæʃ **mashed** mæʃt **mashes** ˈmæʃ ɪz -əz **mashing** ˈmæʃ ɪŋ
Masham *(i)* ˈmæs əm, *(ii)* ˈmæʃ əm —*The place in NYks. is (i), the breed of sheep and the family name either (i) or (ii).*
masher ˈmæʃ ə ‖ -ᵊr **~s** z
mashie ˈmæʃ i **~s** z
Mashonaland mə ˈʃɒn ə lænd -ˈʃəʊn- ‖ -ˈʃɑːn- -ˈʃoʊn-
masjid ˈmæs dʒɪd ˈmʌs-
mask mɑːsk §mæsk ‖ mæsk **masked** mɑːskt §mæskt ‖ mæskt **masking** ˈmɑːsk ɪŋ §ˈmæsk- ‖ ˈmæsk ɪŋ **masks** mɑːsks §mæsks ‖ mæsks
ˈmasking tape
Maskall, Maskell ˈmæsk ᵊl
masochism ˈmæs ə ˌkɪz əm ˈmæz-
masochist ˈmæs ək ɪst ˈmæz-, §-əst **~s** s
masochistic ˌmæs ə ˈkɪst ɪk ◂ ˌmæz- **~ally** ᵊl‿i
mason, Mason ˈmeɪs ᵊn **~s** z
ˈMason jar
Mason-Dixon meɪs ᵊn ˈdɪks ᵊn
ˌMason-ˈDixon line
masonic, M~ mə ˈsɒn ɪk -ˈzɒn- ‖ -ˈsɑːn-
Masonite *tdmk* ˈmeɪs ə naɪt
mason|ry ˈmeɪs ᵊn |ri **~ries** riz
Masora, Masorah mə ˈsɔːr ə ‖ -ˈsoʊr-
Masorete ˈmæs ə riːt **~s** s
Masoretic ˌmæs ə ˈret ɪk ◂ ‖ -ˈret̬-
masque mɑːsk mæsk ‖ mæsk *(= mask)* **masques** mɑːsks mæsks ‖ mæsks

MASQUERADE

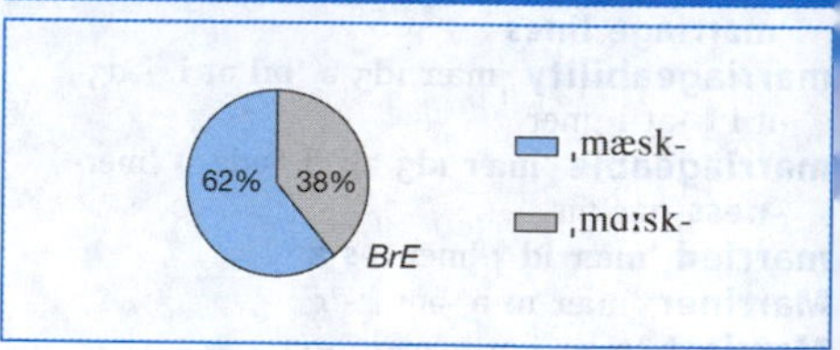

masquerad|e *n, v* ˌmæsk ə ˈreɪd ˌmɑːsk- — *Preference poll, BrE:* ˌmæsk- *62% (English southerners 48%),* ˌmɑːsk- *38% (English southerners 52%). In AmE always* ˌmæsk-. **~ed** ɪd əd **~er/s** ə/z ‖ ᵊr/z **~es** z **~ing** ɪŋ
mass *common n, v, adj* mæs **massed** mæst **masses** ˈmæs ɪz -əz **massing** ˈmæs ɪŋ
ˌmass ˈmedia; **ˌmass proˈduction**
Mass *'eucharist', 'music for the Mass'* mæs mɑːs **Masses** ˈmæs ɪz ˈmɑːs-, -əz
Mass. *'Massachusetts'* mæs —*or as* Massachusetts
Massachusetts ˌmæs ə ˈtʃuːs ɪts -ˈtʃuːz-, -əts — *Preference poll, AmE:* -ˈtʃuːs- *87%,* -ˈtʃuːz- *13%.*
massacre ˈmæs ək ə -ɪk- ‖ -ᵊr **~d** d **~s** z **massacring** ˈmæs ək ər‿ɪŋ

MASSACHUSETTS

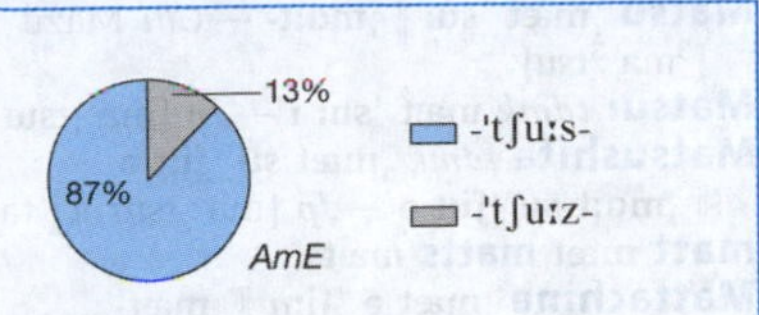

massag|e 'mæs ɑːʒ -ɑːdʒ ‖ mə 'sɑːʒ -'sɑːdʒ *(*)* **~ed** d **~es** ɪz əz **~ing** ɪŋ
'massage ˌparlour ‖ **mas'sage ˌparlor**
Massapequa ˌmæs ə 'piːk wə ◂ **ˌMassaˌpequa 'Park**
massasauga ˌmæs ə 'sɔːg ə ‖ -'sɑːg- **~s** z
Masscomp *tdmk* 'mæs kɒmp ‖ -kɑːmp **~s** s
massé 'mæs i ‖ mæ 'seɪ **~s** z
Massenet 'mæs ə neɪ ‖ ˌmæs ə 'neɪ —*Fr* [mas nɛ]
Massereene 'mæs ə riːn
masseter mæ 'siːt ə mə-; 'mæs ɪt ə, -ət- ‖ -'siːt̬ ᵊr **~s** z
masseur mæ 'sɜː mə- ‖ -'sʊᵊr **~s** z
masseus|e mæ 'sɜːz mə- ‖ -'suːz -'suːs, -'sʊz **~es** ɪz əz
Massey, Massie 'mæs i
massif 'mæs iːf mæ 'siːf ‖ mæ 'siːf —*Fr* [ma sif] **~s** s
massiness 'mæs i nəs -nɪs
Massinger 'mæs ɪndʒ ə -əndʒ- ‖ -ᵊr
massive 'mæs ɪv **~ly** li **~ness** nəs nɪs
massless 'mæs ləs -lɪs **~ness** nəs nɪs
mass-market 'mæs ˌmɑːk ɪt -ət ‖ -ˌmɑːrk-
Masson 'mæs ᵊn
mass-produc|e ˌmæs prə 'djuːs ◂ →-'dʒuːs ‖ -'duːs -'djuːs **~ed** t **~es** ɪz əz **~ing** ɪŋ
massy 'mæs i
mast mɑːst §mæst ‖ mæst **masts** mɑːsts §mæsts ‖ mæsts
mastectom|y mæ 'stekt əm |i mə- **~ies** iz
master, M~ 'mɑːst ə §'mæst- ‖ 'mæst ᵊr **~ed** d **mastering** 'mɑːst ər ɪŋ →'mɑːs trɪŋ; §'mæst ər ɪŋ, →§'mæs trɪŋ ‖ 'mæst ər ɪŋ →'mæs trɪŋ **~s, ~'s** z
'master card; **'master key**, ˌ· · '·; **ˌMaster of 'Arts**; **ˌmaster of 'ceremonies**; **ˌMaster of 'Science**; **'master race**; **'master's deˌgree**; **ˌmaster 'sergeant**◂
master-at-arms ˌmɑːst ər ət 'ɑːmz §ˌmæst- ‖ ˌmæst ər ət̬ 'ɑːrmz **masters-at-arms** -əz ət- ‖ -ᵊrz ət̬-
MasterCard *tdmk* 'mɑːst ə kɑːd §'mæst- ‖ 'mæst ᵊr kɑːrd **~s** z
masterclass 'mɑːst ə klɑːs §'mæst ə klæs ‖ 'mæst ᵊr klæs
masterful 'mɑːst ə fᵊl §'mæst-, -fʊl ‖ mæst ᵊr- **~ly** ˌi **~ness** nəs nɪs
master|ly 'mɑːst ə |li §'mæst-, -ᵊ|l i ‖ 'mæst ᵊr- **~liness** li nəs li nɪs
Masterman 'mɑːst ə mən §'mæst- ‖ 'mæst ᵊr-
mastermind *n, v* 'mɑːst ə maɪnd §'mæst-, ˌ· ·'· ‖ 'mæst ᵊr- **~ed** ɪd əd **~ing** ɪŋ **~s** z
masterpiec|e 'mɑːst ə piːs §'mæst- ‖ 'mæst ᵊr- **~es** ɪz əz
Masters 'mɑːst əz §'mæst- ‖ 'mæst ᵊrz
masterstroke 'mɑːst ə strəʊk §'mæst- ‖ 'mæst ᵊr stroʊk **~s** s
masterwork 'mɑːst ə wɜːk §'mæst- ‖ 'mæst ᵊr wɜːk **~s** s
mastery 'mɑːst ər |i →'mɑːs tr|i; §'mæst ər |i, →§'mæs tr|i ‖ 'mæst ər |i →'mæs tr|i **~ies** iz
masthead 'mɑːst hed §'mæst- ‖ 'mæst- **~s** z
mastic 'mæst ɪk
masti|cate 'mæst ɪ |keɪt §-ə- **~cated** keɪt ɪd -əd ‖ keɪt̬ əd **~cates** keɪts **~cating** keɪt ɪŋ ‖ keɪt̬ ɪŋ
mastication ˌmæst ɪ 'keɪʃ ᵊn §-ə- **~s** z
masticator|y 'mæst ɪ kət ər |i -keɪt ər |i, ˌ· ·'keɪt ər |i ‖ -kə tɔːr |i -toʊr i **~ies** iz
mastiff 'mæst ɪf 'mɑːst-, §-əf **~s** s
mastitis mæ 'staɪt ɪs mə-, §-əs ‖ -'staɪt̬ əs
mastodon 'mæst ə dɒn -əd ən ‖ -dɑːn **~s** z
mastoid 'mæst ɔɪd **~s** z
mastoiditis ˌmæst ɔɪ 'daɪt ɪs §-əs ‖ -'daɪt̬ əs
Mastroianni ˌmæs trəʊ 'jɑːn i ˌmɑːs-, -'jæn- ‖ -trə- -troʊ- —*It* [mas tro 'jan ni]
mastur|bate 'mæst ə |beɪt 'mɑːst- ‖ -ᵊr- **~bated** beɪt ɪd -əd ‖ beɪt̬ əd **~bates** beɪts **~bating** beɪt ɪŋ ‖ beɪt̬ ɪŋ
masturbation ˌmæst ə 'beɪʃ ᵊn ˌmɑːst- ‖ -ᵊr- **~s** z
masturbatory ˌmæst ə 'beɪt ər i ◂ ˌmɑːst-, '· · · · · ‖ 'mæst ᵊrb ə tɔːr i -toʊr i
mat mæt **mats** mæts **matted** 'mæt ɪd -əd ‖ 'mæt̬ əd **matting** 'mæt ɪŋ ‖ 'mæt̬ ɪŋ
Matabele ˌmæt ə 'biːl i ◂ -'bel- ‖ ˌmæt̬- **~land** lænd **~s** z
matador 'mæt ə dɔː ‖ 'mæt̬ ə dɔːr **~s** z
Mata Hari ˌmɑːt ə 'hɑːr i ‖ ˌmɑːt̬-
Matapan 'mæt ə pæn ˌ· ·'· ‖ 'mæt̬-
match mætʃ **matched** mætʃt **matches** 'mætʃ ɪz -əz **matching** 'mætʃ ɪŋ
ˌmatch 'point ‖ '· ·
matchboard 'mætʃ bɔːd ‖ -bɔːrd -boʊrd
matchbook 'mætʃ bʊk §-buːk **~s** s
matchbox 'mætʃ bɒks ‖ -bɑːks **~es** ɪz əz
match-fit ˌmætʃ 'fɪt ◂ **~ness** nəs nɪs
matchless 'mætʃ ləs -lɪs **~ly** li **~ness** nəs nɪs
matchlock 'mætʃ lɒk ‖ -lɑːk **~s** s
matchmaker 'mætʃ ˌmeɪk |ə ‖ -|ᵊr **~ers** əz ‖ ᵊrz **~ing** ɪŋ
matchplay 'mætʃ pleɪ
matchstick 'mætʃ stɪk **~s** s
matchwood 'mætʃ wʊd
mate meɪt **mated** 'meɪt ɪd -əd ‖ 'meɪt̬ əd **mates** meɪts **mating** 'meɪt ɪŋ ‖ 'meɪt̬ ɪŋ
maté 'mæt eɪ 'mɑːt- ‖ 'mɑːt eɪ mɑː 'teɪ
matelot 'mæt ləʊ 'mæt əl əʊ ‖ -loʊ **~s** z
mater, Mater 'meɪt ə 'mɑːt- ‖ 'meɪt̬ ᵊr 'mɑːt̬- **~s, ~'s** z
ˌMater ˌDolo'rosa ˌdɒl ə 'rəʊs ə -'rəʊz- ‖ ˌdoʊl ə 'roʊs ə -ɑː
materia mə 'tɪər iˌə ‖ -'tɪr-
maˌteria 'medica 'med ɪk ə
material mə 'tɪər iˌəl ‖ -'tɪr- **~s** z

M

materialis... —*see* **materializ...**
materialism mə ˈtɪər i‿ə ˌlɪz əm ‖ -ˈtɪr-
materialist mə ˈtɪər i‿əl ɪst §-əst ‖ -ˈtɪr- **~s** s
materialistic mə ˌtɪər i‿ə ˈlɪst ɪk ◂ ‖ -ˌtɪr- **~ally** əl‿i
materialization mə ˌtɪər i‿əl aɪ ˈzeɪʃ ən -ɪˈ-- ‖ mə ˌtɪr i‿əl ə- **~s** z
materializ|e mə ˈtɪər i‿ə laɪz ‖ -ˈtɪr- **~ed** d **~es** ɪz əz **~ing** ɪŋ
material|ly mə ˈtɪər i‿əl |i ‖ -ˈtɪr- **~ness** nəs nɪs
materiel, matériel mə ˌtɪər i ˈel -ˈtɪər i‿əl ‖ -ˌtɪr- —*Fr* [ma te ʁjɛl]
maternal mə ˈtɜːn əl ‖ -ˈtɜːn əl **~ly** i
maternity mə ˈtɜːn ət i -ɪt- ‖ -ˈtɜːn əṱ i
mateship ˈmeɪt ʃɪp
matey ˈmeɪt i ‖ ˈmeɪṱ i **~ness** nəs nɪs
math mæθ
mathematical ˌmæθ ə ˈmæt ɪk əl ◂ ˌ-ɪ-; mæθ ˈmæt- ‖ -ˈmæṱ- **~ly** ‿i
mathematician ˌmæθ əm‿ə ˈtɪʃ ən ˌ-ɪm- **~s** z
mathematics ˌmæθ ə ˈmæt ɪks -ɪ-; mæθ ˈmæt- ‖ -ˈmæṱ ɪks
Mather *(i)* ˈmeɪð ə ‖ -ər, *(ii)* ˈmæð-, *(iii)* ˈmeɪθ-
Matheson ˈmæθ ɪs ən -əs-
Mathew ˈmæθ juː
Mathias mə ˈθaɪ‿əs
Mathis ˈmæθ ɪs §-əs
maths mæθs
Matilda mə ˈtɪld ə
matinee, matinée ˈmæt ɪ neɪ §-ə-, §-ən eɪ ‖ ˌmæt ən ˈeɪ *(*)* **~s** z
ˈ**matinee ˌidol** ‖ ˌ**matiˈnee ˌidol**
matins ˈmæt ɪnz §-ənz ‖ -ənz
Matisse mæ ˈtiːs —*Fr* [ma tis]
Matlock ˈmæt lɒk ‖ -lɑːk
Mato Grosso ˌmæt əʊ ˈgrɒs əʊ ˌmɑːt- ‖ ˌmæṱ ə ˈgroʊs oʊ —*Port* [ˌma tu ˈgro su]
matriarch ˈmeɪtr i ɑːk ˈmætr- ‖ -ɑːrk **~s** s
matriarch|al ˌmeɪtr i ˈɑːk |əl ◂ ˌmætr-, ˈ· · · · ‖ -ˈɑːrk |əl ◂ **~ic** ɪk ◂
matriarch|y ˈmeɪtr i ɑːk |i ˈmætr- ‖ -ɑːrk |i **~ies** iz
matric mə ˈtrɪk
matrices ˈmeɪtr ɪ siːz ˈmætr-, -ə-
matricide ˈmeɪtr ɪ saɪd ˈmætr-, -ə- ‖ ˈmætr- ˈmeɪtr- **~s** z
matriculant mə ˈtrɪk jʊl ənt -jəl- ‖ -jəl- **~s** s
matricu|late mə ˈtrɪk ju |leɪt -jə- ‖ -jə- **~lated** leɪt ɪd -əd ‖ leɪṱ əd **~lates** leɪts **~lating** leɪt ɪŋ ‖ leɪṱ ɪŋ
matriculation mə ˌtrɪk ju ˈleɪʃ ən -jə- ‖ -jə- **~s** z
matrilineal ˌmætr ɪ ˈlɪn i‿əl ◂ ˌmeɪtr-, ˌ-ə- **~ly** i
matrilocal ˌmætr ɪ ˈləʊk əl ◂ ˌmeɪtr-, -ə-, ˈ·ˌ·ˌ· · ‖ -ə ˈloʊk əl ◂ **~ly** i
matrimonial ˌmætr ɪ ˈməʊn i‿əl ◂ ˌ-ə- ‖ -ˈmoʊn- **~ly** i
matrimon|y ˈmætr ɪm ən |i ˈ-əm- ‖ -ə moʊn |i *(*)* **~ies** iz
matrix ˈmeɪtr ɪks —*in printing also* ˈmætr- **~es** ɪz əz

matron, M~ ˈmeɪtr ən **~liness** li nəs -nɪs **~ly** li **~s** z
Matsu ˌmæt ˈsuː ‖ ˌmɑːt- —*Chi* Mǎzǔ [3ma 3tsu]
Matsui *tdmk* mæt ˈsuː i —*Jp* [ma ˌtsɯ i]
Matsushita *tdmk* ˌmæt su ˈʃiːt ə ‖ ˌmɑːt su ˈʃiːṱ ə —*Jp* [ma ˌtsɯ̥ ˈçi̥ ta]
matt mæt **matts** mæts
Mattachine ˌmæt ə ˈʃiːn ‖ ˌmæṱ-
matte mæt **mattes** mæts
matted ˈmæt ɪd -əd ‖ ˈmæṱ əd **~ly** li **~ness** nəs nɪs
Mattel mə ˈtel mæ-
matter ˈmæt ə ‖ ˈmæṱ ər **~ed** d **~s** z
Matterhorn ˈmæt ə hɔːn ‖ ˈmæṱ ər hɔːrn
matter-of-course ˌmæt‿ər əv ˈkɔːs ◂ ‖ ˌmæṱ ər əv ˈkɔːrs ◂ -ˈkoʊrs ◂
matter-of-fact ˌmæt‿ər əv ˈfækt ◂ -əˈ- ‖ ˌmæṱ ər- **~ly** li **~ness** nəs nɪs
Matthäus mə ˈteɪ əs —*Ger* [ma ˈtɛː ʊs]
Matthean mæ ˈθiː‿ən mə-
Matthes ˈmæθ ɪz -əz, -əs
Matthew ˈmæθ juː
Matthews ˈmæθ juːz
Matthey ˈmæθ i ˈmæt- ‖ ˈmæṱ-
Matthias mə ˈθaɪ‿əs
Matthiessen ˈmæθ ɪs ən §-əs-
Mattie ˈmæt i ‖ ˈmæṱ i
matting ˈmæt ɪŋ ‖ ˈmæṱ ɪŋ
mattins ˈmæt ɪnz §-ənz ‖ -ənz
mattock ˈmæt ək ‖ ˈmæṱ- **~s** s
mattress ˈmætr əs -ɪs **~es** ɪz əz
matu|rate ˈmætʃ u |reɪt -ə-; ˈmæt juə-, -jə- ‖ -ə- **~rated** reɪt ɪd -əd ‖ reɪṱ əd **~rates** reɪts **~rating** reɪt ɪŋ ‖ reɪṱ ɪŋ
maturation ˌmætʃ u ˈreɪʃ ən -ə-; ˌmæt juə-, -jə- ‖ -ə- **~s** z
mature *adj, v* mə ˈtʃʊə -ˈtjʊə, -ˈtjɔː, -ˈtʃɔː ‖ -ˈtʊər -ˈtʃʊər, -ˈtjʊər **~d** d **~ly** li **~ness** nəs nɪs **maturer** mə ˈtʃʊər ə -ˈtjʊər-, -ˈtjɔːr-, -ˈtʃɔːr- ‖ -ˈtʊr ər -ˈtʃʊr-, -ˈtjʊr- **~s** z **maturest** mə ˈtʃʊər ɪst -ˈtjʊər-, -ˈtjɔːr-, -ˈtʃɔːr-, -əst ‖ -ˈtʊr əst -ˈtʃʊr-, -ˈtjʊr- **maturing** mə ˈtʃʊər ɪŋ -ˈtjʊər-, -ˈtjɔːr-, -ˈtʃɔːr- ‖ -ˈtʊr ɪŋ -ˈtʃʊr-, -ˈtjʊr-
maˌture ˈstudent
maturit|y mə ˈtʃʊər ət |i -ˈtjʊər-, -ˈtjɔːr-, -ˈtʃɔːr-, -ɪt- ‖ -ˈtʊr əṱ |i -ˈtʃʊr-, -ˈtjʊr- **~ies** iz
matutinal ˌmæt ju ˈtaɪn əl ◂ ˌmætʃ u-, §-ə-; mə ˈtjuːt ɪn-, ˌənəl ‖ ˌmætʃ u- mə ˈtuːt ən‿əl, -ˈtjuːt- **~ly** i
matza, matzah ˈmɒts ə ˈmɑːts-, ˈmæts- ‖ ˈmɑːts ə **~s** z
matzo, matzoh ˈmɒts ə ˈmɑːts-, ˈmæts-, -əʊ ‖ ˈmɑːts ə -oʊ **~s** z
mauby ˈmɔːb i ‖ ˈmɑːb-
Maud, maud, Maude mɔːd ‖ mɑːd **mauds, Maud's** mɔːdz ‖ mɑːdz
maudlin ˈmɔːd lɪn §-lən ‖ ˈmɑːd- **~ly** li
Maudling ˈmɔːd lɪŋ ‖ ˈmɑːd-
Maudsley ˈmɔːdz li ‖ ˈmɑːdz-
Maufe mɔːf ‖ mɑːf
Mauger ˈmeɪdʒ ə ‖ -ər

Maugham mɔːm ‖ mɑːm *(!) —occasionally also* ˈmɒf əm ‖ ˈmɔːf-, ˈmɑːf-
Maughan mɔːn ‖ mɑːn
Maui ˈmaʊ i
maul mɔːl ‖ mɑːl **mauled** mɔːld ‖ mɑːld **mauling** ˈmɔːl ɪŋ ‖ ˈmɑːl-
Mauleverer mə ˈlev ər ə mɔː- ‖ -ᵊr ər
maulstick ˈmɔːl stɪk ‖ ˈmɑːl- **~s** s
Mau Mau ˈmaʊ maʊ ˌ·ˈ· **~s** z
Maumee mɔː ˈmiː ˈ· · ‖ mɑː-
Mauna Kea ˌmaʊn ə ˈkeɪ ə
Mauna Loa ˌmaʊn ə ˈləʊ ə ‖ -ˈloʊ ə
maunder, M~ ˈmɔːnd ə ‖ -ᵊr ˈmɑːnd- **~ed** d **maundering** ˈmɔːnd ər ɪŋ ‖ ˈmɑːnd‿ **~s** z
Maundy, m~ ˈmɔːnd i ‖ ˈmɑːnd- **ˈMaundy ˌmoney**; **ˌMaundy ˈThursday**
Maupassant ˈməʊp ə sõ -æ- ‖ ˈmoʊp ə sɑːnt ˌ·ˈ· —*Fr* [mo pa sɑ̃]
Maupin ˈmɔːp ɪn -ən ‖ ˈmɑːp-
Maureen ˈmɔːr iːn mɔː ˈriːn ‖ mɔː ˈriːn mɑː-
Mauretani|a ˌmɒr ɪ ˈteɪn i‿|ə ˌmɔːr-, ˌ·ə- ‖ ˌmɔːr ə- **~an/s** ən/z
Mauriac ˈmɔːr i æk ˈməʊ ri- ‖ ˌmɔːr i ˈɑːk —*Fr* [mɔ ʁjak]
Maurice *(i)* ˈmɒr ɪs §-əs ‖ ˈmɔːr əs ˈmɑːr-, *(ii)* mɒ ˈriːs mə- ‖ mɔː- mɑː-
Mauritani|a ˌmɒr ɪ ˈteɪn i‿|ə ˌmɔːr-, ˌ·ə- ‖ ˌmɔːr ə- **~an/s** ən/z
Maurit|ian mə ˈrɪʃ |ᵊn mɒ-, mɔː- ‖ mɔː- mɑː-, -ˈrɪʃ |i‿ən **~ians** ᵊnz i‿ənz **~ius** əs ‖ i‿əs
Mauser ˈmaʊz ə ‖ -ᵊr —*Ger* [ˈmau zɐ] **~s** z
mausoleum ˌmɔːs ə ˈliː‿əm ˌmɔːz-, ˌmaʊz-, -ˈleɪ- ‖ ˌmɑːs-, ˌmɔːz-, ˌmɑːz- **~s** z
mauve məʊv ‖ moʊv mɔːv, mɑːv *(!)*
maven ˈmeɪv ᵊn **~s** z
maverick ˈmæv ər‿ɪk **~s** s
Mavis, mavis ˈmeɪv ɪs §-əs **~es, ~'s** ɪz əz
Mavor ˈmeɪv ə ‖ -ᵊr
maw, Maw mɔː ‖ mɑː **maws** mɔːz ‖ mɑːz
Mawddach ˈmaʊð əx -ək ‖ -ək —*Welsh* [ˈmau ðaχ]
Mawdesley, Mawdsley ˈmɔːdz li ‖ ˈmɑːdz-
Mawer mɔː ˈmɔː‿ə ‖ ˈmɔː‿ᵊr ˈmɑː‿
Mawgan ˈmɔːg ən ‖ ˈmɑːg-
Mawhinny mə ˈwɪn i -ˈhwɪn- ‖ -ˈ*h*wɪn-
mawkish ˈmɔːk ɪʃ ‖ ˈmɑːk- **~ly** li **~ness** nəs nɪs
Mawson ˈmɔːs ᵊn ‖ ˈmɑːs-
Max, max mæks **Max's** ˈmæks ɪz -əz **ˌMax ˈFactor** *tdmk*
Maxell *tdmk* ˈmæks el mæk ˈsel
maxi ˈmæks i **~s, ~'s** z
maxill|a mæk ˈsɪl |ə **~ae** iː
maxillary mæk ˈsɪl ər i ‖ ˈmæks ə ler i *(*)*
maxim, Maxim ˈmæks ɪm §-əm **~s** z
maxima ˈmæks ɪm ə -əm-
maximal ˈmæks ɪm ᵊl -ᵊm‿əl **~ly** i
maximalist ˈmæks ɪm əl ɪst ˈ·ᵊm-, §-əst **~s** s
Maximilian ˌmæks ɪ ˈmɪl i‿ən ˌ·ə- ‖ ˌmæks ə ˈmɪl jən
maximin ˈmæks i mɪn ˌ· ·ˈ· ‖ -ə-
maximis... —*see* **maximiz...**
maximization ˌmæks ɪm aɪ ˈzeɪʃ ᵊn ˌ·əm-, -ɪˈ·- ‖ -əm ə- **~s** z
maximiz|e ˈmæks ɪ maɪz -ə- **~ed** d **~es** ɪz əz **~ing** ɪŋ
maxim|um ˈmæks ɪm |əm -əm- **~a** ə **~ums** əmz
Maximus, m~ ˈmæks ɪm əs -əm-
Maxine ˌmæks ˈiːn ˈ· ·
Maxton ˈmækst ən
Maxwell, m~ ˈmæks wel -wəl **~s** z
may, May meɪ **ˈMay Day**
Maya *Central American people* ˈmaɪ‿ə ˈmɑː jə **~s** z
Maya *Hindu deity*, **maya** *'illusion'* maɪ‿ə ˈmɑː jə
Maya *personal name (i)* ˈmeɪ ə, *(ii)* ˈmaɪ‿ə
Mayall ˈmeɪ ɔːl əl ‖ -ɑːl
Mayan ˈmaɪ‿ən **~s** z
maybe ˈmeɪb i ˈmeɪ biː, ₍ˌ₎·ˈ· —*There is also a casual form* **ˈmeb i**. *The stress pattern* ₍ˌ₎·ˈ· *is usual only when the word is at the end of a clause or sentence, with a concessive meaning:* They will try, ₍ˌ₎mayˈbe; but they will not succeed.
maybeetle ˈmeɪ ˌbiːt ᵊl ‖ -ˌbiːṭ- **~s** z
Maybelline *tdmk* ˈmeɪb ə liːn -e-, ˌ· · ˈ·
maybug ˈmeɪ bʌg **~s** z
mayday, M~ ˈmeɪ deɪ
Mayer *(i)* ˈmeɪ ə meə ‖ ᵊr, *(ii)* ˈmaɪ‿ə ‖ ᵊr *—(i) is an English form, (ii) a German form —Ger* [ˈmai ɐ]
mayest ˈmeɪ ɪst -əst; meɪst
Mayfair ˈmeɪ feə ‖ -fer -fær
Mayfield ˈmeɪ fiːᵊld
Mayflower, m~ ˈmeɪ ˌflaʊ‿ə ‖ -ˌflaʊ‿ᵊr **~s** z
may|fly ˈmeɪ |flaɪ **~flies** flaɪz
mayhem ˈmeɪ hem
Mayhew ˈmeɪ hjuː
Maynard ˈmeɪn əd -ɑːd ‖ -ᵊrd -ɑːrd
Mayne meɪn
Maynooth mə ˈnuːθ meɪ-
mayn't meɪnt ˈmeɪ ənt
Mayo, mayo ˈmeɪ əʊ ‖ -oʊ *—in Irish English the placename is also* ·ˈ·

MAYONNAISE

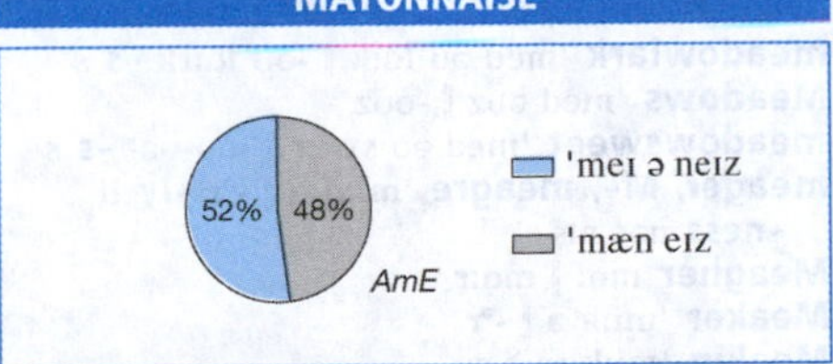

mayonnaise ˌmeɪ ə ˈneɪz ◂ ‖ ˈmeɪ ə neɪz ˌ· ·ˈ·; ˈmæn eɪz — *Preference poll, AmE:* ˈmeɪ ə- *52%,* ˈmæ- *48%.*
mayor, Mayor meə ‖ ˈmeɪ‿ᵊr meᵊr **mayors, Mayor's** meəz ‖ ˈmeɪ‿ᵊrz meᵊrz
mayoral ˈmeər əl meɪ ˈɔːr əl ‖ ˈmeɪ‿ər əl
mayoralty ˈmeər əl ti ‖ ˈmeɪ‿ər əl ti ˈmer əl ti
mayoress ˌmeər ˈes ˈ· ·; ˈmeər ɪs, -əs ‖ ˈmeɪ‿ər əs ˈmer əs
mayorship ˈmeə ʃɪp ‖ ˈmeɪ‿ᵊr ʃɪp ˈmeᵊr· **~s** s

M

Mayotte maɪ ˈɒt -ˈjɒt ‖ -ˈjɑːt —*Fr* [ma jɔt]
maypole ˈmeɪ pəʊl →-pɒʊl ‖ -poʊl **~s** z
Mays meɪz
mayst meɪst
may've ˈmeɪ əv
mayweed ˈmeɪ wiːd **~s** z
mazard ˈmæz əd ‖ -ᵊrd **~s** z
Mazarin ˈmæz ə rɪn -ræn —*Fr* [ma za ʁɛ̃]
mazarine ˈmæz ə riːn ˌ· · ˈ·◂
Mazawattee *tdmk* ˌmæz ə ˈwɒt i ‖ -ˈwɑːt̬ i
Mazda *tdmk* ˈmæz də
Mazdaism ˈmæz dəʳ ˌɪz əm ‖ -ə-
maze meɪz **mazes** ˈmeɪz ɪz -əz
mazel tov ˈmæz ᵊl tɒf -tɒv ‖ ˈmɑːz ᵊl tɑːf -tɑːv
Mazeppa mə ˈzep ə
Mazola *tdmk* mə ˈzəʊl ə ‖ mə ˈzoʊl ə
mazuma mə ˈzuːm ə
mazurka mə ˈzɜːk ə ‖ -ˈzɜ˞ːk ə -ˈzʊrk- —*Polish* [ma ˈzur ka] **~s** z
maz|y ˈmeɪz |i **~ier** i‿ə ‖ i‿ᵊr **~iest** i‿ɪst i‿əst **~ily** ɪ li əl i **~iness** i nəs i nɪs
MBA ˌem biː ˈeɪ
Mbabane ˌem bə ˈbɑːn i əm ˌbæ-, -bæˈ· ·, -bɑː· · —*siSwati* [mba ˈbaː ne]
MBE ˌem biː ˈiː
Mbeki əm ˈbek i —*Xhosa* [ˈmbeː ki]
mbyte, Mbyte ˈmeg ə baɪt **~s** s
MC ˌem ˈsiː **~'d** d **~'ing** ɪŋ **~'s** z
Mc... —*see* **Mac...** —*Names beginning Mc- are listed in this dictionary as if written Mac-*
MCC ˌem siː ˈsiː
m-commerce ˈem ˌkɒm ɜːs ‖ -ˌkɑːm ᵊrs
MCP ˌem siː ˈpiː **~s, ~'s** z
MD ˌem ˈdiː
me miː, *weak form* mi
ˈ**me gene**ˌ**ration**
ME *medical condition* ˌem ˈiː
Meacham ˈmiːtʃ əm
Meacher ˈmiːtʃ ə ‖ -ᵊr
mea culpa ˌmeɪ ə ˈkʊlp ə -ɑː ˈkʊlp ɑː
mead miːd
Mead, Meade miːd
meadow ˈmed əʊ ‖ -oʊ **~s** z
Meadowcroft ˈmed əʊ krɒft ‖ -oʊ krɔːft -krɑːft
meadowlark ˈmed əʊ lɑːk ‖ -oʊ lɑːrk **~s** s
Meadows ˈmed əʊz ‖ -oʊz
meadowsweet ˈmed əʊ swiːt ‖ -oʊ- -ə- **~s** s
meager, M~, meagre ˈmiːg ə ‖ -ᵊr **~ly** li **~ness** nəs nɪs
Meagher mɑː ‖ mɑːr
Meaker ˈmiːk ə ‖ -ᵊr
Meakin ˈmiːk ɪn §-ən
meal miːᵊl **meals** miːᵊlz
ˈ**meal** ˌ**ticket**
mealie ˈmiːl i **~s** z
meals-on-wheels ˌmiːᵊlz ɒn ˈwiːᵊlz -ˈhwiːlz ‖ -ɑːn ˈ*h*wiːᵊlz -ɔːn-
mealtime ˈmiːᵊl taɪm **~s** z
mealworm ˈmiːᵊl wɜːm ‖ -wɜ˞ːm **~s** z
meal|y ˈmiːl |i **~ier** i‿ə ‖ i‿ᵊr **~iest** i‿ɪst i‿əst **~iness** i nəs i nɪs
mealybug ˈmiːl i bʌg **~s** z
mealy-mouthed ˌmiːl i ˈmaʊðd◂ ‖ -ˈmaʊθt◂
mean miːn **meaner** ˈmiːn ə ‖ -ᵊr **meanest** ˈmiːn ɪst -əst **meaning** ˈmiːn ɪŋ **means** miːnz **meant** ment *(!)*
ˈ**means test**; ˌ**mean** ˈ**time**
meander, M~ mi ˈænd ə ‖ -ᵊr **~ed** d **meandering/ly** mi ˈænd‿ər ɪŋ /li **~s** z
meanie ˈmiːn i **~s** z
meaning ˈmiːn ɪŋ **~s** z
meaningful ˈmiːn ɪŋ fᵊl -fʊl **~ly** i **~ness** nəs nɪs
meaningless ˈmiːn ɪŋ ləs -lɪs **~ly** li **~ness** nəs nɪs
mean|ly ˈmiːn |li **~ness** nəs nɪs
mean-spirited ˌmiːn ˈspɪr ɪt ɪd◂ -ət-, -əd ‖ -ət̬-
meant ment *(!)*
meantime ˈmiːn taɪm ˌ·ˈ·
meanwhile ˈmiːn waɪᵊl -hwaɪᵊl, ˌ·ˈ· ‖ -*h*waɪᵊl
mean|y ˈmiːn| i **~ies** iz
Meara *(i)* ˈmɪər ə ‖ ˈmɪr ə, *(ii)* ˈmɑːr ə
Mearns *place in Grampian* meənz ‖ meᵊrnz
Mears mɪəz ‖ mɪᵊrz
Measham ˈmiːʃ əm
measles ˈmiːz ᵊlz
meas|ly ˈmiːz |li ˈmiːz ᵊ|l i **~liness** li nəs -nɪs
measurable ˈmeʒ ər‿əb ᵊl ‖ ˈmeɪʒ-

MEASURE

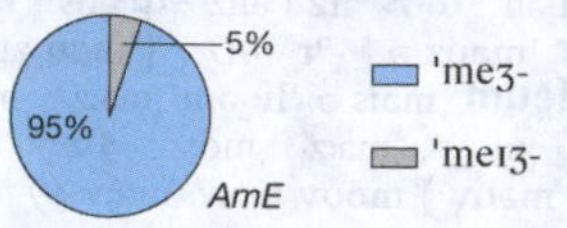

meas|ure ˈmeʒ |ə ‖ -|ᵊr ˈmeɪʒ- — *Preference poll, AmE:* ˈmeʒ- *95%,* ˈmeɪʒ- *5%.* **~ured** əd ‖ ᵊrd **~uring** ər‿ɪŋ **~ures** əz ‖ ᵊrz
ˈ**measuring jug**
measureless ˈmeʒ ə ləs -lɪs ‖ -ᵊr- ˈmeɪʒ- **~ly** li
measurement ˈmeʒ ə mənt ‖ -ᵊr- ˈmeɪʒ- **~s** s
measurer ˈmeʒ ər ə ‖ -ər ˈmeɪʒ- **~s** z
meat miːt *(= meet)* **meats** miːts
ˌ**meat** ˈ**loaf** ‖ ˈ· ·
meat-and-potatoes ˌmiːt ᵊn pə ˈteɪt əʊz◂ -əm pə- ‖ -ˈteɪt̬ oʊz◂
meat-ax, meat-ax|e ˈmiːt æks ‖ ˈmiːt̬- **~ed** t **~es** ɪz əz **~ing** ɪŋ
meatball ˈmiːt bɔːl ‖ -bɑːl **~s** z
Meath *county in Ireland* miːð —*but by outsiders often called* miːθ
meati... —*see* **meaty**
meatless ˈmiːt ləs -lɪs
meat-packing ˈmiːt ˌpæk ɪŋ
meatus mi ˈeɪt əs ‖ -ˈeɪt̬- **~es** ɪz əz
meat|y ˈmiːt |i ‖ ˈmiːt̬ |i **~ier** i‿ə ‖ i‿ᵊr **~iest** i‿ɪst i‿əst **~ily** ɪ li əl i **~iness** i nəs i nɪs
Mebyon Kernow ˌmeb i‿ən ˈkɜːn əʊ ‖ -ˈkɜ˞ːn oʊ
Mecca, mecca ˈmek ə —*Arabic* [ˈmak ka]
meccano, M~ *tdmk* mɪ ˈkɑːn əʊ mə-, me- ‖ -oʊ
Mecham ˈmiːk əm

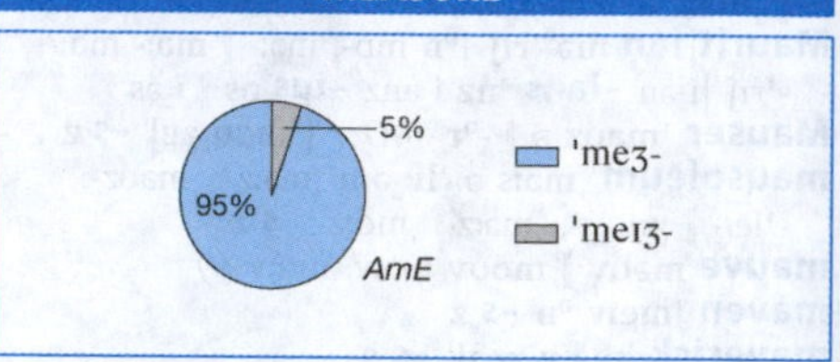

mechanic mɪ ˈkæn ɪk mə- **~s** s

mechanical mɪ ˈkæn ɪk ᵊl mə- **~ly** ˌi **~ness** nəs nɪs **~s** z
meˌchanical ˌengiˈneering

mechanis... —*see* **mechaniz...**

mechanism ˈmek ə ˌnɪz əm **~s** z

mechanist ˈmek ən ɪst §-əst **~s** s

mechanistic ˌmek ə ˈnɪst ɪk◂ **~ally** ᵊlˌi

mechanization ˌmek ən aɪ ˈzeɪʃ ᵊn -ən ɪ- ‖ -ən ə-

mechaniz|e ˈmek ə naɪz **~ed** d **~es** ɪz əz **~ing** ɪŋ

Mechlin ˈmek lɪn §-lən —*Dutch* Mechelen [ˈmɛ xə lən], *French* Malines [ma lin]

Mecklenburg ˈmek lən bɜːg -lɪn-, →-ləm- ‖ -bɜːg —*Ger* [ˈmeː klən bʊʁk, ˈmɛ-]

meconium mi ˈkəʊn i‿əm mə- ‖ -ˈkoʊn-

Med, med med **meds** medz

MEd ˌem ˈed

medal ˈmed ᵊl **~s** z

medalist ˈmed ᵊl ɪst §-əst **~s** s

medallion mə ˈdæl i‿ən mɪ- ‖ -ˈdæl jən **~s** z

medallist ˈmed ᵊl ɪst §-əst **~s** s

Medan ˈmeɪd æn -ɑːn ‖ meɪ ˈdɑːn

Medau ˈmed aʊ

Medawar ˈmed ə wə ‖ -wᵊr

meddl|e ˈmed ᵊl *(= medal)* **~ed** d **~er/s** ˌə/z ‖ ər/z **~es** z **~ing** ɪŋ

meddlesome ˈmed ᵊl səm **~ly** li **~ness** nəs nɪs

Mede miːd **Medes** miːdz

Medea mə ˈdɪə mɪ-, -ˈdiː‿ə ‖ mə ˈdiː ə

Medellin, Medellín ˌmed əl ˈjiːn ◂-el- —*Sp* [me ðe ˈʎin, -ˈjiːn]

Medevac ˈmed ɪ ˌvæk -ə-

medfly ˈmed flaɪ

media *other senses; Latin adj* ˈmiːd i‿ə ˈmed-

media *pl of* **medium**, *'means of communication'* ˈmiːd i‿ə

Media *'country of the Medes'* ˈmiːd i‿ə

mediaeval ˌmed i ˈiːv ᵊl ◂ me ˈdiːv ᵊl ‖ ˌmiːd-ˌmed-, ˌmɪd-; mɪ ˈdiːv ᵊl *(*)* **~ism** ˌɪz əm **~ist/s** ɪst/s §əst/s ‖ əst/s **~ly** i

medial ˈmiːd i‿əl **~ly** i

median ˈmiːd i‿ən **~ly** li **~s** z

mediant ˈmiːd i‿ənt **~s** s

mediastin|um ˌmiːd i‿ə ˈstaɪn |əm **~a** ə **~al** ᵊl ◂

medi|ate *v* ˈmiːd i |eɪt **~ated** eɪt ɪd -əd ‖ eɪţ əd **~ates** eɪts **~ating** eɪt ɪŋ ‖ eɪţ ɪŋ

mediation ˌmiːd i ˈeɪʃ ᵊn **~s** z

mediator ˈmiːd i eɪt ə ‖ -eɪţ ᵊr **~s** z

medic ˈmed ɪk **~s** s

Medicaid, m~ ˈmed ɪ keɪd

medical ˈmed ɪk ᵊl **~ly** ˌi **~s** z
ˈmedical card; **ˈmedical cerˌtificate**

medicament mə ˈdɪk ə mənt mɪ-, me-; ˈmed ɪk- **~s** s

Medicare, m~ ˈmed ɪ keə ‖ -ker -kær

medi|cate ˈmed ɪ |keɪt §-ə- **~cated** keɪt ɪd -əd ‖ keɪţ əd **~cates** keɪts **~cating** keɪt ɪŋ ‖ keɪţ ɪŋ

medication ˌmed ɪ ˈkeɪʃ ᵊn §-ə- **~s** z

Medici ˈmed ɪtʃ i §-ətʃ-; me ˈdiːtʃ i, mə-, mɪ- —*It* [ˈmeː di tʃi]

medicinal mə ˈdɪs ᵊn‿əl mɪ-, me-, -ɪn- —*formerly also* ˌmed ɪ ˈsaɪn ᵊl, ˈmed sᵊn‿əl **~ly** i

medicine ˈmed sᵊn -sɪn, ˈmed ɪs ən, -əs-, -ɪn **~s** z
ˈmedicine chest; **ˈmedicine man**

medick ˈmed ɪk **~s** s

medico ˈmed ɪ kəʊ ‖ -koʊ **~s** z

medieval ˌmed i ˈiːv ᵊl ◂ me ˈdiːv ᵊl ‖ ˌmiːd-ˌmed-, ˌmɪd-; mɪ ˈdiːv ᵊl *(*)* **~ism** ˌɪz əm **~ist/s** ɪst/s §əst/s ‖ əst/s **~ly** i

Medina, m~ *(i)* me ˈdiːn ə mə-, mɪ-, *(ii)* -ˈdaɪn ə —*The place in Saudi Arabia is (i)* —*Arabic* [me ˈdiː na]*; that in OH, (ii).*

mediocre ˌmiːd i ˈəʊk ə ◂ ˌmed-, ˈ·· ‖ -ˈoʊk ᵊr

mediocrit|y ˌmiːd i ˈɒk rət |i ˌmed-, -ɪt i ‖ -ˈɑːkr əţ |i **~ies** iz

medi|tate ˈmed ɪ |teɪt -ə- **~tated** teɪt ɪd -əd ‖ teɪţ əd **~tates** teɪts **~tating** teɪt ɪŋ ‖ teɪţ ɪŋ

meditation ˌmed ɪ ˈteɪʃ ᵊn -ə- **~s** z

meditative ˈmed ɪt ət ɪv -ət ət-; -ɪ teɪt-, -ə teɪt- ‖ -ə teɪţ ɪv **~ly** li **~ness** nəs nɪs

Mediterranean ˌmed ɪ tə ˈreɪn i‿ən ◂ ˌ-ə- **~s** z
ˌMediterˌranean ˈSea

medi|um ˈmiːd i‿|əm **~a** ə **~ums** əmz
ˌmedium ˈwave◂

medium-sized ˌmiːd i‿əm ˈsaɪzd ◂ ˈ··

medium-term ˌmiːd i‿əm ˈtɜːm ◂ ‖ ˈtɜːm ◂

medlar ˈmed lə ‖ -lᵊr **~s** z

medley ˈmed li **~s** z

Medlicott ˈmed lɪ kɒt ‖ -kɑːt

Medlock ˈmed lɒk ‖ -lɑːk

Medoc, Médoc ˈmed ɒk meɪ ˈdɒk ‖ meɪ ˈdɑːk —*Fr* [me dɔk]

Medresco me ˈdresk əʊ mə-, mɪ- ‖ -oʊ

medulla me ˈdʌl ə mə-, mɪ-
meˌdulla ˌoblonˈgata ˌɒb lɒŋ ˈgɑːt ə ‖ ˌɑːb lɔːŋ ˈgɑːţ ə -lɑːŋ-

medullary me ˈdʌl ər i mə-, mɪ- ‖ ˈmed ᵊl er i ˈmedʒ-; mə ˈdʌl ər i *(*)*

Medusa, m~ mə ˈdjuːz ə me-, mɪ-, -ˈdjuːs-, →-ˈdʒuːz- ‖ -ˈduːs ə -ˈdjuːs-, -ˈduːz-, -ˈdjuːz- **~s, ~'s** z

Medway ˈmed weɪ

Medwin ˈmed wɪn

Mee miː

meed miːd **meeds** miːdz

Meehan ˈmiː‿ən

meek, Meek miːk

meek|ly ˈmiːk |li **~ness** nəs nɪs

meerkat ˈmɪə kæt ‖ ˈmɪr- **~s** s

meerschaum ˈmɪəʃ əm ˈmɪə ʃaʊm ‖ ˈmɪrʃ əm ˈmɪr ʃɔːm, -ʃɑːm

Meerut ˈmɪər ət —*Hindi* [meː rəʈʱ]

meet miːt **meeting** ˈmiːt ɪŋ ‖ ˈmiːţ ɪŋ **meets** miːts **met** met

meet-and-greet ˌmiːt ᵊn ˈgriːt ◂

meeting ˈmiːt ɪŋ ‖ ˈmiːţ ɪŋ **~s** z
ˈmeeting point

M

meeting|house ˈmiːt ɪŋ |haʊs ‖ ˈmiːt̬- **~houses** haʊz ɪz -əz
mefloquine ˈmef lə kwiːn -kwɪn ‖ -kwaɪn
meg, Meg meg **megs** megz
mega ˈmeg ə
mega- *comb. form* ¦meg ə — **megastar** ˈmeg ə stɑː ‖ -stɑːr
megabit ˈmeg ə bɪt **~s** s
megabuck ˈmeg ə bʌk **~s** s
megabyte ˈmeg ə baɪt **~s** s
megacycle ˈmeg ə ˌsaɪk ᵊl **~s** z
megadeath ˈmeg ə deθ **~s** s
megahertz ˈmeg ə hɜːts ‖ -hɝːts
megalith ˈmeg ə lɪθ **~s** s
megalithic ˌmeg ə ˈlɪθ ɪk ◂
megalo- *comb. form*
with stress-neutral suffix ¦meg ə ləʊ -ᵊl əʊ ‖ -loʊ — **megaloblastic** ˌmeg ə ləʊ ˈblæst ɪk ◂ -ᵊl əʊ- ‖ -ə loʊ-
with stress-imposing suffix ˌmeg ə ˈlɒ+ ‖-ˈlɑː+ — **megalopolis, M~** ˌmeg ə ˈlɒp əl ɪs §-əs ‖ -ˈlɑːp-
megalomania ˌmeg əl əʊ ˈmeɪn i ə ‖ -əl ə-
megalomaniac ˌmeg əl əʊ ˈmeɪn i æk ‖ -əl ə- **~s** s
megalosaur ˈmeg əl əʊ sɔː ‖ -ə sɔːr **~s** z
Megan *(i)* ˈmeg ən, *(ii)* ˈmiːg-, *(iii)* ˈmeɪg- —*In BrE always (i).*
Megane, Mégane mə ˈgæn me- ‖ -ˈgɑːn —*Fr* [me gan]

megaphone ˈmeg ə fəʊn ‖ -foʊn **~s** z
megapixel ˈmeg ə ˌpɪks ᵊl **~s** z
megaplex ˈmeg ə pleks **~es** ɪz əz
Megara, m~ ˈmeg ər ə
megaron ˈmeg ə rɒn ‖ -rɑːn
megastar ˈmeg ə stɑː ‖ -stɑːr **~s** z
megastore ˈmeg ə stɔː ‖ -stɔːr **~s** z
megatheri|um ˌmeg ə ˈθɪər i |əm ‖ -ˈθɪr- **~a** ə
megaton ˈmeg ə tʌn **~s** z
megawatt ˈmeg ə wɒt ‖ -wɑːt **~s** s
Megger *tdmk* ˈmeg ə ‖ -ᵊr
Meggeson ˈmeg ɪs ən -əs-
Meggezones *tdmk* ˈmeg ɪ zəʊnz -ə- ‖ -zoʊnz
Meggison ˈmeg ɪs ən -əs-
Megillah, m~ mə ˈgɪl ə **~s** z
megilp mə ˈgɪlp
megohm ˈmeg əʊm ‖ -oʊm **~s** z
megrim ˈmiːg rɪm -rəm **~s** z
Mehmet ˈmem et —*Turkish* [mɛh ˈmɛt]
Mehta ˈmeɪt ə
Meier ˈmaɪ ə ‖ ˈmaɪ ᵊr
Meikle ˈmiːk ᵊl
Meiklejohn *(i)* ˈmiːk ᵊl dʒɒn ‖ -dʒɑːn, *(ii)* ˈmɪk-
Mein Kampf ˌmaɪn ˈkæmpf —*Ger* [main ˈkampf]
meios|is maɪ ˈəʊs |ɪs meɪ-, §-əs ‖ -ˈoʊs- **~es** iːz
Meir mɪə ‖ mɪᵊr —*but as an Israeli name,* meɪ ˈɪə ‖ -ˈɪᵊr
Meirion ˈmaɪᵊr i ɒn ‖ -ɑːn —*Welsh* [ˈməir jon]
Meirionnydd ˌmer i ˈɒn ɪð -ɪθ, -əθ ‖ -ˈɑːn- —*Welsh* [məir ˈjɔn ɨ ð, -ɪð]
meishi ˈmeɪʃ i —*Jp* [me ˌe ɕi] **~s** z
Meissen ˈmaɪs ᵊn —*Ger* [ˈmai sᵊn]
ˈ**Meissen ware**
Meistersinger ˈmaɪst ə ˌsɪŋ ə ‖ -ᵊr ˌsɪŋ ᵊr —*Ger* [ˈmai stɐ ˌzɪŋ ɐ] **~s** z
meitnerium ˌmaɪt ˈnɪər i əm -ˈneər- ‖ -ˈnɪr- -ˈner-
Mekka ˈmek ə
Mekong ˌmiː ˈkɒŋ ◂ ˌmeɪ- ‖ ˌmeɪ ˈkɔːŋ ◂ -ˈkɑːŋ
ˌ**Mekong** ˈ**Delta**
Mel, mel mel **mels, Mel's** melz
melamine ˈmel ə miːn -mɪn, -maɪn
melancholia ˌmel ən ˈkəʊl i ə →ˌ·əŋ- ‖ -ˈkoʊl-
melancholic ˌmel ən ˈkɒl ɪk ◂ →·əŋ- ‖ -ˈkɑːl- **~ally** ᵊl i
melancholy ˈmel ən kəl i →ˈ·əŋ-, -kɒl i ‖ -kɑːl i
Melanchthon mə ˈlæŋk θən mɪ-, me-, θɒn ‖ -θɑːn —*Ger* [me ˈlanç tɔn]
Mela|nesia ˌmel ə| ˈniːz i ə -ˈniːʒ ə, -ˈniːs i ə, ˈniːʃ ə ‖ -ˈniːʒ ə -ˈniːʃ ə **~nesian/s** ˈniːz i ən/z ◂ ˈniːʒ ᵊn/z, ˈniːs i ən/z, ˈniːʃ ᵊn/z ‖ ˈniːʒ ᵊn/z ◂ ˈniːʃ ᵊn/z
melang|e, mélang|e meɪ ˈlɑːnʒ me-, -ˈlɒ̃ʒ —*Fr* [me lɑ̃ːʒ] **~es** ɪz əz
Melanie ˈmel ən i
melanin ˈmel ən ɪn §-ən
melanism ˈmel ə ˌnɪz əm
melano- *comb. form* ¦mel ə nəʊ ‖ -ə noʊ -ən ə — **melanocyte** ˈmel ə nəʊ saɪt ‖ -ə noʊ- -ə nə-
melanoma ˌmel ə ˈnəʊm ə ‖ -ˈnoʊm ə **~s** z
melanuria ˌmel ə ˈnjʊər i ə ‖ -ˈnʊr- -ˈnjʊr-
melatonin ˌmel ə ˈtəʊn ɪn -ən ‖ -ˈtoʊn-
Melba ˈmelb ə
Melbourne *(i)* ˈmel bɔːn ‖ -bɔːrn -boʊrn, *(ii)* ˈmelb ən ‖ -ᵊrn —*The places in Cambridgeshire and Derbyshire are (i). The place in Australia is (ii) locally, but is often called (i) by non-Australians.*
Melchers ˈmeltʃ əz ‖ -ᵊrz
Melchett ˈmeltʃ ɪt -ət
Melchior ˈmelk i ɔː ‖ -ɔːr
Melchizedek mel ˈkɪz ə dek
meld meld **melded** ˈmeld ɪd -əd **melding** ˈmeld ɪŋ **melds** meldz
Meldrew ˈmeldr uː
Meldrum ˈmeldr əm
Meleager ˌmel i ˈeɪg ə ‖ -ˈeɪdʒ ᵊr
melee, mêlée ˈmel eɪ me ˈleɪ ‖ ˈmeɪl eɪ meɪ ˈleɪ *(*)* **~s** z
Melhuish *(i)* ˈmel ɪʃ, *(ii)* ˈmel hju ɪʃ -ju-, -u-, *(iii)* mel ˈhjuː ɪʃ
Melia ˈmiːl i ə
melic ˈmel ɪk
Melilla me ˈliː ə -jə —*Sp* [me ˈli ja, -ʎa]
melilot ˈmel ɪ lɒt -ə- ‖ -lɑːt **~s** s
Melina mə ˈliːn ə me-, mɪ-
melinite ˈmel ɪ naɪt -ə-
melio|rate ˈmiːl i ə |reɪt **~rated** reɪt ɪd -əd ‖ reɪt̬ əd **~rates** reɪts **~rating** reɪt ɪŋ ‖ reɪt̬ ɪŋ
melioration ˌmiːl i ə ˈreɪʃ ᵊn **~s** z
meliorative ˈmiːl i ər ət ɪv ə reɪt- ‖ ə reɪt̬ ɪv
meliorism ˈmiːl i ə ˌrɪz əm

meliorist ˈmiːl iˌər ɪst §-əst **~s** s
melisma mə ˈlɪz mə mɪ-, me- **~s** z
melismatic ˌmel ɪz ˈmæt ɪk ◂ §,·əz- ‖ -ˈmæṭ ɪk ◂
Melissa mə ˈlɪs ə mɪ-, me-
Melksham ˈmelk ʃəm
melliflu|ence mə ˈlɪf luˌ|ənᵗs mɪ-, me- **~ent** ənt
mellifluous mə ˈlɪf luˌəs mɪ-, me- **~ly** li **~ness** nəs nɪs
Mellish ˈmel ɪʃ
Mellony ˈmel ən i
Mellor ˈmel ə ‖ -ᵊr
Mellors ˈmel əz ‖ -ᵊrz
mellow ˈmel əʊ ‖ -oʊ **~ed** d **~er** ə ‖ ᵊr **~est** ɪst əst **~ing** ɪŋ **~ly** li **~ness** nəs nɪs **~s** z
Melly ˈmel i
melodeon mə ˈləʊd iˌən mɪ-, me- ‖ -ˈloʊd- **~s** z
melodic mə ˈlɒd ɪk mɪ-, me- ‖ -ˈlɑːd- **~ally** ᵊlˌi
melodica mə ˈlɒd ɪk ə mɪ-, me- ‖ -ˈlɑːd- **~s** z
melodie... —*see* **melody**
melodion mə ˈləʊd iˌən mɪ-, me- ‖ -ˈloʊd- **~s** z
melodious mə ˈləʊd iˌəs mɪ-, me- ‖ -ˈloʊd- **~ly** li **~ness** nəs nɪs
melodis... —*see* **melodize**
melodist ˈmel əd ɪst §-əst **~s** s
melodiz|e ˈmel ə daɪz **~ed** d **~es** ɪz əz **~ing** ɪŋ
melodrama ˈmel ə ˌdrɑːm ə -əʊ- ‖ -ˌdræm- **~s** z
melodramatic ˌmel ə drə ˈmæt ɪk ◂ ˌ·əʊ- ‖ -ˈmæṭ ɪk ◂ **~ally** ᵊlˌi **~s** s
melod|y, M~ ˈmel əd |i —*Occasionally, and particularly in singing, also* -əʊd- ‖ -oʊd- **~ies** iz
Meloids *tdmk* ˈmel ɔɪdz
melon ˈmel ən **~s** z
Melos ˈmiːl ɒs ˈmel- ‖ -ɑːs
Melpomene mel ˈpɒm ən i -ɪn i, -iː ‖ -ˈpɑːm-
Melrose ˈmel rəʊz ‖ -roʊz
melt melt **melted** ˈmelt ɪd -əd **melting/ly** ˈmelt ɪŋ /li **melts** melts
ˈmelting point; **ˈmelting pot**
meltag|e ˈmelt ɪdʒ **~es** ɪz əz
meltdown ˈmelt daʊn **~s** z
Melton, m~ ˈmelt ən
ˌMelton ˈMowbray
Meltonian *tdmk* mel ˈtəʊn iˌən ‖ -ˈtoʊn-
meltwater ˈmelt ˌwɔːt ə ‖ -ˌwɔːṭ ᵊr -ˌwɑːṭ- **~s** z
Melville ˈmel vɪl
Melvin, Melvyn ˈmelv ɪn §-ən
member ˈmem bə ‖ -bᵊr **~s** z
ˌMember of ˈParliament
membership ˈmem bə ʃɪp ‖ -bᵊr- **~s** s
membrane ˈmem breɪn **~s** z
membranous ˈmem brən əs mem ˈbreɪn-
meme miːm **memes** miːmz
memento mə ˈment əʊ mɪ-, me-, ⚠məʊ- ‖ -ˈmenṭ oʊ **~es, ~s** z
meˌmento ˈmori ˈmɒr iː ˈmɔːr-, -i, -aɪ ‖ ˈmɔːr-
Memnon ˈmem nɒn -nən ‖ -nɑːn
memo ˈmem əʊ ˈmiːm- ‖ -oʊ **~s** z
ˈmemo pad
memoir ˈmem wɑː ‖ -wɑːr -wɔːr **~s** z
memorabilia ˌmem ərˌə ˈbɪl iˌə -ˈbiːl-
memorab|le ˈmem ərˌəb |ᵊl **~leness** ᵊl nəs -nɪs **~ly** li
memorand|um ˌmem ə ˈrænd |əm **~a** ə **~s** z
memorial mə ˈmɔːr iˌəl mɪ-, me- ‖ -ˈmoʊr- **~ly** i **~s** z
memorialis|e, memorializ|e mə ˈmɔːr iˌə laɪz mɪ-, me- ‖ -ˈmoʊr- **~ed** d **~es** ɪz əz **~ing** ɪŋ
memorie... —*see* **memory**
memoris... —*see* **memoriz...**
memorization ˌmem ər aɪ ˈzeɪʃ ᵊn -ə'- ‖ -ə'-
memoriz|e ˈmem ə raɪz **~ed** d **~es** ɪz əz **~ing** ɪŋ
memor|y ˈmem ərˌ|i **~ies** iz
ˈmemory span
memory-hogging ˈmem ərˌi ˌhɒg ɪŋ ‖ -ˌhɑːg ɪŋ
Memphis ˈmemᵖf ɪs §-əs
memsahib ˈmem sɑːb ˈmem ˌsɑː ɪb, -hɪb **~s** z
men men **men's** menz
ˈmen's room
-men mən, men —*See note at* -man. *The pronunciation* men *is used for the plural rather more widely than* mæn *is for the singular.*
menac|e ˈmen əs -ɪs **~ed** t **~er/s** ə/z ‖ ᵊr/z **~es** ɪz əz **~ing/ly** ɪŋ /li
menag|e, ménag|e ₍ˌ₎me ˈnɑːʒ ₍ˌ₎meɪ-, mə-, mɪ-, -ˈnæʒ; ˈmeɪn ɑːʒ ‖ meɪ ˈnɑːʒ mə- —*Fr* [me naːʒ] **~es** ɪz əz
méˌnage à ˈtrois, ˌ· · ·ˈ· ɑː ˈtrwɑː —*Fr* [a tʁwa]
menagerie mə ˈnædʒ ərˌi mɪ-, me- -ˈnæʒ- -ˈnɑːʒ- **~s** z
Menai ˈmen aɪ —*Welsh* [ˈme nai, -ne]
ˌMenai ˈBridge; **ˌMenai ˈStrait**
Menander mə ˈnænd ə mɪ-, me- ‖ -ᵊr
menarche me ˈnɑːk i mɪ-, mə-; ˈmen ɑːk ‖ -ˈnɑːrk i
men-at-arms ˌmen ət ˈɑːmz ‖ -əṭ ˈɑːrmz
Mencap ˈmen kæp →ˈmeŋ-
Mencius ˈmen ʃiˌəs ˈmenᵗʃ əs —*Chi* Mèngzi [⁴mʌŋ tsɯ]
Mencken ˈmeŋk ən
mend mend **mended** ˈmend ɪd -əd **mending** ˈmend ɪŋ **mends** mendz
mendacious men ˈdeɪʃ əs **~ly** li **~ness** nəs nɪs
mendacity men ˈdæs ət i -ɪt- ‖ -əṭ i
Mende ˈmend eɪ
Mendel ˈmend ᵊl
Mendeleev ˌmend ə ˈleɪ ev ˌ·ɪ-, -ef, -əf; -ᵊl ˈeɪ- —*Russ* [mʲɪnʲ dʲɪ ˈlʲe jɪf]
mendelevium ˌmend ə ˈliːv iˌəm ˌ·ɪ-; -ᵊl ˈiːv-
Mendeleyev ˌmend ə ˈleɪ ev ˌ·ɪ-, -ef, -əf; -ᵊl ˈeɪ- —*Russ* [mʲɪnʲ dʲɪ ˈlʲe jɪf]
Mendelian men ˈdiːl iˌən
Mendelism ˈmend ᵊl ˌɪz əm -ə ˌlɪz-
Mendelssohn ˈmend ᵊl sən —*Ger* [ˈmɛn dᵊl zoːn, -dᵊls zoːn]

M

mender ˈmend ə ‖ -ᵊr **~s** z
Mendez, Méndez ˈmend ez ‖ men ˈdez —*Sp* [ˈmen deθ, -des]
mendicant ˈmend ɪk ənt §-ək- **~s** s
Mendip ˈmend ɪp **~s** s
 ˌMendip ˈHills
Mendocino ˌmend ə ˈsiːn əʊ ‖ -oʊ
Mendoza men ˈdəʊz ə ‖ -ˈdoʊz ə —*AmSp* [men ˈdo sa]
Menelaus ˌmen ɪ ˈleɪ əs -ə-, -ᵊl ˈeɪ-
Menem ˈmen em
mene mene tekel upharsin ˌmiːn i ˈmiːn i ˌtek ᵊl ju ˈfɑːs ɪn §-ᵊn ‖ -ˈfɑːrs- -ˌtiːk-, -ˈfers-
Menevia mɪ ˈniːv i‿ə mə-
menfolk ˈmen fəʊk ‖ -foʊk
Mengele ˈmeŋ əl ə —*German* [mɛŋ l ə]
Mengistu meŋ ˈgɪst uː men-
menhaden men ˈheɪd ᵊn mən- **~s** z
menhir ˈmen hɪə ‖ -hɪr **~s** z
menial ˈmiːn i‿əl **~ly** i **~s** z
Meniere, Ménière ˈmen i eə ˈmeɪn-, ˌ·ˈ· ‖ mən ˈjeᵊr ˌmeɪn-; ˈmen jᵊr —*Fr* [me njɛːʁ]
 ˈMénière's diˌsease ‖ **Mén'ière's-**
meningeal me ˈnɪndʒ i‿əl mə-, mɪ-; ˌmen ɪn ˈdʒiː‿əl ◂, -ən-
meninges me ˈnɪndʒ iːz mə-, mɪ-
meningitis ˌmen ɪn ˈdʒaɪt ɪs -ən-, §-əs ‖ -ˈdʒaɪt̬ əs
meningococc|al mə ˌnɪndʒ əʊ ˈkɒk |ᵊl ◂ -ˌnɪŋ gəʊ- ‖ -ə ˈkɑːk |ᵊl ◂ **~us** əs
meninx ˈmen ɪŋks **meninges** me ˈnɪndʒ iːz mə-, mɪ-
me|niscus mə |ˈnɪsk əs mɪ-, me- **~nisci** ˈnɪs aɪ ˈnɪsk-, -iː
Menlo ˈmen ləʊ ‖ -loʊ
Mennonite ˈmen ə naɪt **~s** s
men-of-war ˌmen əv ˈwɔː -ə- ‖ -ˈwɔːr
Menominee, Menomini, Menomonee, Menomonie mə ˈnɒm ən i mɪ-, me- ‖ -ˈnɑːm- **~s** z
menopausal ˌmen əʊ ˈpɔːz ᵊl ◂ ˌmiːn- ‖ -ə- -ˈpɑːz-
menopause ˈmen əʊ pɔːz ˈmiːn- ‖ -ə- -pɑːz
menorah mə ˈnɔːr ə mɪ- ‖ -ˈnoʊr- **~s** z
menorrhagia ˌmen ə ˈreɪdʒ i‿ə ˌmiːn-; -ˈreɪdʒ ə
menorrhoea ˌmen ə ˈriː‿ə ˌmiːn-
Menotti mə ˈnɒt i mɪ-, ne- ‖ -ˈnɑːt i —*It* [me ˈnɔt ti]
mens menz
 ˌmens ˈrea ˈriː‿ə ˈreɪ ə; **ˌmens ˈsana** ˈsɑːn ə ˈsæn- **(in ˌcorpore ˈsano)** ɪn ˌkɔːp ər i ˈsɑːn əʊ →ɪŋ-, -ˌ·ə reɪ-, -ˈsæn- ‖ ɪn ˌkɔːrp ər i ˈsɑːn oʊ
Mensa ˈmenᵗs ə
mensch menᵗʃ **menschen** ˈmenᵗʃ ən **mensches** ˈmenᵗʃ ɪz -əz
menses ˈmenᵗs iːz
Menshevik ˈmenᵗʃ ə vɪk -ɪ-, -viːk **~s** s
Menshevism ˈmenᵗʃ ə ˌvɪz əm -ɪ-
Menston ˈmenᵗst ən

menstrual ˈmenᵗs tru‿əl
 ˌmenstrual ˈperiod
menstru|ate ˈmenᵗs tru |eɪt ‖ ˈmen str|eɪt **~ated** eɪt ɪd -əd ‖ eɪt̬ əd **~ates** eɪts **~ating** eɪt ɪŋ ‖ eɪt̬ ɪŋ
menstruation ˌmenᵗs tru ˈeɪʃ ᵊn ‖ men ˈstreɪʃ- **~s** z
mensurability ˌmenᵗʃ ər‿ə ˈbɪl ət i ˌmenᵗs-, ˌjər-, -ɪt i ‖ -ət̬ i
mensurable ˈmenᵗʃ ər‿əb ᵊl ˈmenᵗs-, ˈ·jər-
mensural ˈmenᵗʃ ər əl ˈmenᵗs-, -jər-
mensuration ˌmenᵗʃ ə ˈreɪʃ ᵊn ˌmenᵗs-, -jə-
menswear ˈmenz weə ‖ -wer -wær
-ment *noun ending* mənt, *verb ending* ment — **ornament** *n* ˈɔːn ə mənt ‖ ˈɔːrn-, *v* ˈɔːn ə ment ‖ ˈɔːrn- —*This ending is usually weak in nouns, strong in verbs (although this standard distinction is not always observed by native speakers). In most cases* -ment *is unstressed and has no effect on stress. In two-syllable verbs, however, it is stressed: compare the noun* ˈsegment *and the verb to* segˈment. *There are various exceptions, including* ˈcomment *v., n.,* laˈment *v., n.,* torment, ferment *(in these latter two the ending is always strong, unstressed in the noun but stressed in the verb).*
Mentadent *tdmk* ˈment ə dent ‖ ˈment̬-
mental ˈment ᵊl ‖ ˈment̬ ᵊl **~ly** i
 ˌmental ˈage◂, a ˌmental age of ˈten; **ˌmental deˈfective**; **ˌmental ˈhealth**; **ˈmental ˌhospital**; **ˌmental ˈnote**
-mental ˈment ᵊl ‖ ˈment̬ ᵊl — **ornamental** ˌɔːn ə ˈment ᵊl ◂ ‖ ˌɔːrn ə ˈment̬ ᵊl ◂
mentalism ˈment ᵊl ˌɪz əm -ə ˌlɪz- ‖ ˈment̬-
mentalist ˈment ᵊl ɪst §-əst; -ə lɪst, §-ləst ‖ ˈment̬- **~s** s
mentalistic ˌment ə ˈlɪst ɪk ◂ ˌment ᵊl ˈɪst- ‖ ˌment̬ ᵊl ˈɪst ɪk ◂ **~ally** ᵊl‿i
mentalit|y men ˈtæl ət |i -ɪt- ‖ -ət̬ |i **~ies** iz
mentee ˌmen ˈtiː **~s** z
menthol ˈmenᵗθ ɒl ‖ -ɔːl -ɑːl
mentholated ˈmenᵗθ ə leɪt ɪd -əd ‖ -leɪt̬ əd
mention ˈmenᵗʃ ᵊn **~ed** d **~ing** ɪŋ **~s** z
mentor, M~ ˈment ɔː -ə ‖ ˈment ɔːr ˈment̬ ᵊr **~ed** d **mentoring** ˈment ər ɪŋ -ɔːr- ‖ ˈment̬ ᵊr ɪŋ ˈment ɔːr- **~s** z
menu ˈmen juː ‖ ˈmeɪn- **~s** z
menu-driven ˈmen juː ˌdrɪv ᵊn ˌ·ˈ·· ‖ ˈmeɪn-
Menuhin ˈmen ju‿ɪn §‿ən
Menzies ˈmenz iz —*but in Scotland usually* ˈmɪŋ ɪs, -ɪz
Meols *(i)* miːᵊlz, *(ii)* melz —*Places near Southport, Merseyside (formerly Lancs), are (i); that near Hoylake, Merseyside (formerly Cheshire), is (ii).*
Meon *place in Hampshire* ˈmiː‿ən
Meopham *place in Kent* ˈmep əm
meow mi ˈaʊ **~ed** d **~ing** ɪŋ **~s** z
MEP ˌem iː ˈpiː **~s** z
mepacrine ˈmep ə krɪn -kriːn
Mephisto mə ˈfɪst əʊ mɪ-, me- ‖ -oʊ

Mephistophelean, m~ ˌmef ɪst ə ˈfiːl i̯ən ◂ ˌəst-; mə ˌfɪst-, mɪ-, me-; ˌmef ɪ ˌstɒf ə ˈliː̯ən ‖ -əˌstɑːf ə ˈliː ən

Mephistopheles ˌmef ɪ ˈstɒf ə liːz ˌ-ə-, -ˈɪ- ‖ -ˈstɑːf-

mephitic mɪ ˈfɪt ɪk mə-, me- ‖ -ˈfɪţ-

meprobamate ˌmep rəʊ ˈbæm eɪt me ˈprəʊb ə meɪt, mɪ-, mə- ‖ ˌmep roʊ-

-mer mə ‖ mᵊr — **monomer** ˈmɒn əʊm ə ‖ ˈmɑːn əm ᵊr

Merc mɜːk ‖ mɜ˞ːk

mercantile ˈmɜːk ən taɪᵊl →-ŋ- ‖ ˈmɜ˞ːk ən tiːᵊl -taɪᵊl, -tᵊl

mercantilism ˈmɜːk ənt ɪ ˌlɪz əm →ˈŋt-, -ə˛-, -əl ˌɪz-, -ən taɪ ˌlɪz- ‖ ˈmɜ˞ːk ən tiː ˌlɪz əm -taɪ ˌ-

mercantilist ˈmɜːk ənt ɪl ɪst →ˈ-ŋt-, -əl ɪst, -aɪl ɪst, §-əst; mɜː ˈkænt əl- ‖ ˈmɜ˞ːk ən tiːl əst -taɪl əst **~s** s

mercaptan mɜː ˈkæpt æn ‖ mᵊr-

Mercator mɜː ˈkeɪt ə mə-, -ɔː ‖ mᵊr ˈkeɪţ ᵊr **~'s** z

Merˌcator proˈjection, Merˌcator's proˈjection

Merced *place in CA* mɜː ˈsed ‖ mᵊr-

Mercedes mə ˈseɪd ɪz mɜː-, -iːz ‖ mᵊr- —*The pl of the tdmk is pronounced the same as the sing., or with* -iːz.

mercenar|y ˈmɜːs ᵊn ər ˌi ˈ-ɪn- ‖ ˈmɜ˞ːs ᵊn er |i **~ies** iz

mercer, M~ ˈmɜːs ə ‖ ˈmɜ˞ːs ᵊr **~s** z

merceris|e, merceriz|e ˈmɜːs ə raɪz ‖ ˈmɜ˞ːs- **~ed** d **~es** ɪz əz **~ing** ɪŋ

merchandis|e, merchandiz|e *v* ˈmɜːtʃ ən daɪz ‖ ˈmɜ˞ːtʃ- **~ed** d **~er/s** ə/z ‖ ᵊr/z **~es** ɪz əz **~ing** ɪŋ

merchandise *n* ˈmɜːtʃ ən daɪz -daɪs ‖ ˈmɜ˞ːtʃ-

merchant, M~ ˈmɜːtʃ ənt ‖ ˈmɜ˞ːtʃ- **~s** s **ˌmerchant ˈbank, ~er, ~ing**; **ˌmerchant maˈrine**; **ˌmerchant ˈnavy**; **ˌmerchant ˈseaman**

merchantable ˈmɜːtʃ ənt əb ᵊl ‖ ˈmɜ˞ːtʃ ənţ-

merchant|man ˈmɜːtʃ ənt |mən ‖ ˈmɜ˞ːtʃ- **~men** mən men

Mercia ˈmɜːs i̯ə ˈmɜːʃ-, ˈmɜːʃ ə ‖ ˈmɜ˞ːʃ i̯ə ˈmɜ˞ːʃ ə

Mercian ˈmɜːs i̯ən ˈmɜːʃ-, ˈmɜːʃ ᵊn ‖ ˈmɜ˞ːʃ i̯ən ˈmɜ˞ːʃ ᵊn **~s** z

mercie... —*see* **mercy**

merciful ˈmɜːs ɪ fᵊl -ə-, -fʊl ‖ ˈmɜ˞ːs- **~ly** ˌi **~ness** nəs nɪs

merciless ˈmɜːs ɪ ləs -ə- ‖ ˈmɜ˞ːs- **~ly** li **~ness** nəs nɪs

Merck mɜːk ‖ mɜ˞ːk

mercurial mɜː ˈkjʊər i̯əl ‖ mᵊr ˈkjʊr- **~ly** i **~s** z

mercuric mɜː ˈkjʊər ɪk ‖ mᵊr ˈkjʊr-

Mercurochrome *tdmk* mɜː ˈkjʊər ə krəʊm ‖ mᵊr ˈkjʊr ə kroʊm

mercurous ˈmɜːk juᵊr əs -jər- ‖ ˈmɜ˞ːk jər-

mercur|y, M~ ˈmɜːk juᵊr |i -jər- ‖ ˈmɜ˞ːk jər |i **~ies, ~y's** iz

Mercutio mə ˈkjuːʃ i əʊ mɜː- ‖ mᵊr ˈkjuːʃ i oʊ

merc|y, Merc|y ˈmɜːs |i ‖ ˈmɜ˞ːs |i **~ies, ~y's** iz **ˈmercy ˌkilling**

merde meəd ‖ meᵊrd *Fr* [mɛʁd]

mere mɪə ‖ mɪᵊr **meres** mɪəz ‖ mɪᵊrz **merest** ˈmɪər ɪst -əst ‖ ˈmɪr əst

Meredith ˈmer əd ɪθ -ɪd-, §-əθ —*In Wales* me ˈred ɪθ

Meredydd mə ˈred ɪð -ɪθ —*Welsh* [me ˈre dið]

merely ˈmɪə li ‖ ˈmɪr-

merest ˈmɪər ɪst -əst ‖ mɪr-

meretricious ˌmer ə ˈtrɪʃ əs ◂ -ɪ- **~ly** li **~ness** nəs nɪs

Merfyn ˈmɜːv ɪn ‖ ˈmɜ˞ːv- —*Welsh* [ˈmer vin, -vɨn]

merganser mɜː ˈgænᵗs ə -ˈgænz- ‖ mᵊr ˈgænᵗs ᵊr **~s** z

merge mɜːdʒ ‖ mɜ˞ːdʒ **merged** mɜːdʒd ‖ mɜ˞ːdʒd **merges** ˈmɜːdʒ ɪz -əz ‖ ˈmɜ˞ːdʒ əz **merging** ˈmɜːdʒ ɪŋ ‖ ˈmɜ˞ːdʒ ɪŋ

merger ˈmɜːdʒ ə ‖ ˈmɜ˞ːdʒ ᵊr **~s** z

Merida ˈmer ɪd ə -əd- *Sp* Mérida [ˈme ri ða]

Meriden ˈmer ɪd ən -əd-

meridian mə ˈrɪd i̯ən mɪ- **~s** z

meridional mə ˈrɪd i̯ən ᵊl mɪ- **~s** z

meringue mə ˈræŋ **~s** z

merino mə ˈriːn əʊ ‖ -oʊ **~s** z

Merioneth ˌmer i ˈɒn əθ -ɪθ, -eθ ‖ -ˈɑːn- —*Welsh* Meirionnydd [məir ˈjɔn ɨð, -ɪð]

meristem ˈmer i stem -ə- **~s** z

mer|it ˈmer |ɪt -ət ‖ -|əţ **~ited** ɪt ɪd ət-, -əd ‖ əţ əd **~iting** ɪt ɪŋ ət- ‖ əţ ɪŋ **~its** ɪts əts ‖ əts

meritocrac|y ˌmer ɪ ˈtɒk rəs |i ˌ-ə- ‖ -ˈtɑːk- **~ies** iz

meritocrat ˈmer ɪt əʊ kræt §ˈ-ət- ‖ -əţ ə- **~s** s

meritocratic ˌmer ɪt əʊ ˈkræt ɪk ◂ §ˌ-ət- ‖ -əţ ə ˈkræţ- **~ally** ᵊl ˌi

meritorious ˌmer ɪ ˈtɔːr i̯əs ◂ ˌ-ə- ‖ -ˈtoʊr- **~ly** li **~ness** nəs nɪs

Merkel ˈmeək ᵊl ˈmɜːk ‖ ˈmerk- ˈmɜ˞ːk- —*Ger* [ˈmɛʁ kl]

merkin ˈmɜːk ɪn §-ən ‖ ˈmɜ˞ːk- **~s** z

Merle, merle mɜːl ‖ mɜ˞ːl **merles, Merle's** mɜːlz ‖ mɜ˞ːlz

merlin, M~ ˈmɜːl ɪn §-ən ‖ ˈmɜ˞ːl- **~s, ~'s** z

merlot, M~ ˈmɜːl əʊ ˈmeəl- ‖ mᵊr ˈloʊ mer- —*Fr* [mɛʁ lo]

mermaid ˈmɜː meɪd ‖ ˈmɜ˞ː- **~s** z

mer|man ˈmɜː |mæn ‖ ˈmɜ˞ː- **~men** men

Merman ˈmɜːm ən ‖ ˈmɜ˞ːm-

-merous *stress-imposing* mər əs — **polymerous** pə ˈlɪm ər əs

Merovingian ˌmer əʊ ˈvɪndʒ i̯ən ◂ ‖ ˌ-ə- **~s** z

merri... —*see* **merry**

Merrick ˈmer ɪk

Merrilies ˈmer əl iz -ɪl-

Merrill ˈmer əl -ɪl

Merrimac, Merrimack ˈmer ɪ mæk -ə-

Merriman ˈmer i mən

merriment ˈmer i mənt

Merrion ˈmer i̯ən

merr|y, Merry ˈmer |i **~ier** i̯ə ‖ i̯ᵊr **~iest** i̯ɪst i̯əst **~ily** ɪ li əl i **~iness** i nəs i nɪs

M

Merrydown *tdmk* 'mer i daʊn
merry-go-round 'mer i gəʊ ˌraʊnd ‖ -i goʊ-ɪ gə- **~s** z
merrymak|er 'mer i ˌmeɪk |ə ‖ -|ᵊr **~ers** əz ‖ ᵊrz **~ing** ɪŋ
merrythought 'mer i θɔːt ‖ -θɑːt **~s** s
Merryweather 'mer i ˌweð ə ‖ -ᵊr
Mersey 'mɜːz i ‖ 'mɜ˞ːz i
Merseyside 'mɜːz i saɪd ‖ 'mɜ˞ːz-
Merstham 'mɜːst əm ‖ 'mɜ˞ːst-
Merthiolate *tdmk* 'mɜːθ i‿ə leɪt ‖ 'mɜ˞ːθ-
Merthyr 'mɜːθ ə ‖ 'mɜ˞ːθ ᵊr —*Welsh* ['mer θɪr, -θɨr]
ˌ**Merthyr 'Tydfil** 'tɪd vɪl —*Welsh* ˌMerthyr 'Tudful ['tɪd vɪl]
Merton 'mɜːt ᵊn ‖ 'mɜ˞ːt ᵊn
Mervin, Mervyn 'mɜːv ɪn §-ᵊn ‖ 'mɜ˞ːv-
Meryl 'mer əl -ɪl
mesa, Mesa 'meɪs ə **~s** z
mesallianc|e, mésallianc|e me 'zæl i‿ənᵗs meɪ-, -ɒ̃s ‖ meɪ- ˌmeɪz ə 'laɪ ənᵗs —*Fr* [me za ljɑ̃ːs] **~es** ɪz əz
mescal 'mesk æl me 'skæl
mescalin, mescaline 'mesk əl ɪn §-ən, -ə liːn
Mesdames, m~ 'meɪ dæm -dæmz ‖ meɪ 'dɑːm —*Fr* [me dam]
mesdemoiselles ˌmeɪd əm‿wə 'zel —*Fr* [med mwa zɛl]
meseemed mi 'siːmd **meseems** mi 'siːmz
mesembryanthemum mə ˌzem bri 'ænᵗθ ɪm əm mɪ-, -əm‿əm **~s** z
mesencephalon ˌmes en 'kef ə lɒn ˌmez-, →ˌ·eŋ-; -'sef- ‖ -'sef ə lɑːn
mesenchyme 'mes eŋ kaɪm 'mez-
mesh meʃ **meshed** meʃt **meshes** 'meʃ ɪz -əz **meshing** 'meʃ ɪŋ
Meshach 'miːʃ æk
meshuga, meshugga mə 'ʃʊg ə
mesial 'miːz i‿əl 'miːs-
mesmeric mez 'mer ɪk
mesmeris... —*see* **mesmeriz...**
mesmerism 'mez mə ˌrɪz əm
mesmerist 'mez mər ɪst §-əst **~s** s
mesmeriz|e 'mez mə raɪz **~ed** d **~er/s** ə/z ‖ ᵊr/z **~es** ɪz əz **~ing** ɪŋ
mesne miːn *(= mean)*
meso- *comb. form*
with stress-neutral suffix ¦mes əʊ ¦mez-, ¦miːs-, ¦miːz- ‖ -ə — **mesophyte** 'mes əʊ faɪt 'mez-, 'miːs-, 'miːz- ‖ -ə-
mesolect 'mes əʊ lekt 'mez-, 'miːs-, 'miːz- ‖ -ə- **~s** s
mesolectal ˌmes əʊ 'lekt ᵊl ◂ ˌmez-, ˌmiːs-, ˌmiːz- ‖ -ə- **~ly** i
Mesolithic, m~ ˌmes əʊ 'lɪθ ɪk ◂ ˌmez-, ˌmiːs-, ˌmiːz- ‖ -ə-
mesomorph 'mes əʊ mɔːf 'mez-, 'miːs-, 'miːz- ‖ -oʊ mɔːrf -ə- **~s** s
mesomorphic ˌmes əʊ 'mɔːf ɪk ◂ ˌmez-, ˌmiːs-, ˌmiːz- ‖ -ə 'mɔːrf- -oʊ'--
meson 'miːz ɒn 'miːs-, 'mez-, 'mes-, 'meɪz- ‖ -ɑːn
Mesopotamia ˌmes ə pə 'teɪm i‿ə ˌmesp ə'--
mesothelioma ˌmes əʊ ˌθiːl i 'əʊm ə ˌmez-, ˌmiːs-, ˌmiːz- ‖ -ə ˌθiːl i 'oʊm ə **~s** z
mesothelium ˌmes əʊ 'θiːl i‿əm ˌmez-, ˌmiːs-, ˌmiːz- ‖ -ə-
mesozoic ˌmes əʊ 'zəʊ ɪk ◂ ˌmez-, ˌmiːs-, ˌmiːz- ‖ -ə 'zoʊ-
mesquite, M~ me 'skiːt mə-, mɪ-; 'mesk iːt
mess mes **messed** mest **messes** 'mes ɪz -əz **messing** 'mes ɪŋ
'mess ˌjacket; **'mess kit**
messag|e 'mes ɪdʒ **~es** ɪz əz **~ing** ɪŋ
Messalina ˌmes ə 'liːn ə -'laɪn-
messenger, M~ 'mes ᵊnd͜ʒ ə -ɪndʒ- ‖ -ᵊr **~s** z
Messer 'mes ə ‖ -ᵊr
Messerschmidt *tdmk* 'mes ə ʃmɪt ⚠'meʃ ə smɪt ‖ -ᵊr- —*Ger* ['mɛs ɐ ʃmɪt]
messi... —*see* **messy**
Messiaen 'mes jɒ̃ -jɑːn ‖ mes 'jɑːn —*Fr* [mɛ sjɑ̃, -sjæ̃]
messiah, M~ mə 'saɪ‿ə mɪ-, me- **~s** z
messianic, M~ ˌmes i 'æn ɪk ◂ **~ally** ᵊl‿i
Messieurs, m~ meɪ 'sjɜːz me-; 'mes əz ‖ meɪs 'jɜ˞ːz məs-, -'juː —*Fr* [me sjø]
Messina me 'siːn ə mə-, mɪ- —*It* [mes 'siː na]
messmate 'mes meɪt **~s** s
Messrs 'mes əz ‖ -ᵊrz
messuag|e 'mes wɪdʒ 'mes ju‿ɪdʒ **~es** ɪz əz
mess|y 'mes |i **~ier** i‿ə ‖ i‿ᵊr **~iest** i‿ɪst i‿əst **~ily** ɪ li əl i **~iness** i nəs i nɪs
mestizo me 'stiːz əʊ mɪ-, mə- ‖ -oʊ -'stiːs- **~s** z
met, Met met
'Met ˌOffice
meta *in Roman circus* 'miːt ə 'meɪt- ‖ 'miːţ ə
meta *fuel* 'miːt ə ‖ 'miːţ ə
meta- *comb. form*
with stress-neutral suffix ¦met ə ‖ ¦meţ ə — **metastatic** ˌmet ə 'stæt ɪk ◂ ‖ ˌmeţ ə 'stæţ ɪk ◂
with stress-imposing suffix mə 'tæ+ mɪ-, me- — **metastasis** mə 'tæst əs ɪs mɪ-, me-, §-əs
Meta *river in Colombia* 'meɪt ə ‖ 'meɪţ ə —*Sp* ['me ta]
Meta *forename* 'miːt ə ‖ 'miːţ ə
metabolic ˌmet ə 'bɒl ɪk ◂ ‖ ˌmeţ ə 'bɑːl ɪk ◂ **~ally** ᵊl‿i
metabolis... —*see* **metaboliz...**
metabolism mə 'tæb ə ˌlɪz əm mɪ-, me- **~s** z
metabolite mə 'tæb ə laɪt mɪ-, me- **~s** s
metaboliz|e mə 'tæb ə laɪz mɪ-, me- **~ed** d **~es** ɪz əz **~ing** ɪŋ
metacarpal ˌmet ə 'kɑːp ᵊl ◂ ‖ ˌmeţ ə 'kɑːrp ᵊl ◂ **~s** z
metacarpus ˌmet ə 'kɑːp əs ‖ ˌmeţ ə 'kɑːrp əs
metacenter, metacentre 'met ə ˌsent ə ‖ 'meţ ə ˌsenţ ᵊr **~s** z
metadata 'met ə ˌdeɪt ə -ˌdɑːt-, §-ˌdæt- ‖ 'meţ ə ˌdeɪţ ə -ˌdæţ-, -ˌdɑːţ-
metal 'met ᵊl ‖ 'meţ ᵊl **~ed, ~led** d **~ing, ~ling** ɪŋ **~s** z
metalanguag|e 'met ə ˌlæŋ gwɪdʒ §-wɪdʒ ‖ 'meţ- **~es** ɪz əz
metaldehyde me 'tæld ɪ haɪd mə-, mɪ-, ə-

metalinguistic ˌmet ə lɪŋ ˈgwɪst ɪk ◂ ‖ ˌmeţ- **~ally** ᵊl_i **~s** s
metallic me ˈtæl ɪk mə-, mɪ- **~ally** ᵊl_i
Metallica me ˈtæl ɪk ə mə-, mɪ-
metalliferous ˌmet ə ˈlɪf ər əs ◂ -ᵊl ˈɪf- ‖ ˌmeţ ᵊl ˈɪf-
metalloid ˈmet ə lɔɪd -ᵊl ɔɪd ‖ ˈmeţ ᵊl ɔɪd **~s** z
metallurgical ˌmet ə ˈlɜːdʒ ɪk ᵊl ◂ -ᵊl ˈɜːdʒ- ‖ ˌmeţ ᵊl ˈɝːdʒ- **~ally** ᵊl_i
metallurgist me ˈtæl ədʒ ɪst mə-, mɪ-, §-əst; ˈmet ᵊl ɜːdʒ- ‖ ˈmeţ ᵊl ɝːdʒ əst **~s** s
metallurgy me ˈtæl ədʒ i mə-, mɪ-; ˈmet ᵊl ɜːdʒ- ‖ ˈmeţ ᵊl ɝːdʒ i
metalwork ˈmet ᵊl wɜːk ‖ ˈmeţ ᵊl wɝːk
metalwork|er ˈmet ᵊl ˌwɜːk |ə ‖ ˈmeţ ᵊl ˌwɝːk |ᵊr **~ers** əz ‖ ᵊrz **~ing** ɪŋ
metamere ˈmet ə mɪə ‖ ˈmeţ ə mɪr **~s** z
metamerism me ˈtæm ə ˌrɪz əm mɪ-, mə-
metamorphic ˌmet ə ˈmɔːf ɪk ◂ ‖ ˌmeţ ə ˈmɔːrf ɪk ◂
metamorphism ˌmet ə ˈmɔːf ˌɪz əm ‖ ˌmeţ ə ˈmɔːrf- **~s** z
metamorphos|e ˌmet ə ˈmɔːf əʊz ‖ ˌmeţ ə ˈmɔːrf oʊz -oʊs **~ed** d **~es** ɪz əz **~ing** ɪŋ
metamorphoses *from v* ˌmet ə ˈmɔːf əʊz ɪz -əz ‖ ˌmeţ ə ˈmɔːrf oʊz əz -ˈoʊs-
metamorphoses *n pl* ˌmet ə ˈmɔːf ə siːz -mɔː ˈfəʊs iːz ‖ ˌmeţ ə ˈmɔːrf-
metamorphos|is ˌmet ə ˈmɔːf əs |ɪs -mɔː ˈfəʊs-, §-əs ‖ ˌmeţ ə ˈmɔːrf- **~es** iːz
metaphor ˈmet əf ə -ə fɔː ‖ ˈmeţ ə fɔːr -əf ᵊr **~s** z
metaphorical ˌmet ə ˈfɒr ɪk ᵊl ◂ ‖ ˌmeţ ə ˈfɔːr- -ˈfɑːr- **~ly** _i
metaphras|e ˈmet ə freɪz ‖ ˈmeţ- **~ed** d **~es** ɪz əz **~ing** ɪŋ
metaphysical, M~ ˌmet ə ˈfɪz ɪk ᵊl ◂ ‖ ˌmeţ- **~ly** _i **~s** z
metaphysics ˌmet ə ˈfɪz ɪks ‖ ˌmeţ-
metastable ˌmet ə ˈsteɪb ᵊl ◂ ‖ ˌmeţ-
metast|asis me ˈtæst |əs ɪs mɪ-, mə-, §-əs **~ases** ə siːz
metastasis|e, metastasiz|e me ˈtæst ə saɪz mɪ-, mə- **~ed** d **~es** ɪz əz **~ing** ɪŋ
metastatic ˌmet ə ˈstæt ɪk ◂ ‖ ˌmeţ ə ˈstæţ ɪk ◂
metatarsal ˌmet ə ˈtɑːs ᵊl ◂ ‖ ˌmeţ ə ˈtɑːrs ᵊl ◂ **~s** z
metatars|us ˌmet ə ˈtɑːs |əs ‖ ˌmeţ ə ˈtɑːrs |əs **~i** aɪ
metath|esis me ˈtæθ |əs ɪs mɪ-, mə-, §-əs **~eses** ə siːz
metathesis|e, metathesiz|e me ˈtæθ ə saɪz mɪ-, mə- **~ed** d **~es** ɪz əz **~ing** ɪŋ
Metaxa *tdmk* me ˈtæks ə mɪ-, mə-
metazoa ˌmet ə ˈzəʊ ə ‖ ˌmeţ ə ˈzoʊ ə
Metcalf, Metcalfe ˈmet kɑːf §-kæf, -kəf ‖ -kæf
mete miːt *(= meet)* **meted** ˈmiːt ɪd -əd ‖ ˈmiːţ əd **metes** miːts **meting** ˈmiːt ɪŋ ‖ ˈmiːţ ɪŋ
metempsychosis ˌmet emp saɪ ˈkəʊs ɪs ˌ-əm-, §-əs ‖ ˌmeţ əm saɪ ˈkoʊs əs mə ˌtemps ə-
meteor ˈmiːt i_ə -ɔː ‖ ˈmiːţ i_ᵊr -ɔːr **~s** z ˈmeteor ˌshower
meteoric ˌmiːt i ˈɒr ɪk ◂ ‖ ˌmiːţ i ˈɔːr ɪk ◂ -ˈɑːr- **~ally** ᵊl_i
meteorite ˈmiːt i_ə raɪt ‖ ˈmiːţ- **~s** s
meteoroid ˈmiːt i_ə rɔɪd ‖ ˈmiːţ- **~s** z
meteorological ˌmiːt i_ər ə ˈlɒdʒ ɪk ᵊl ◂ ⚠ˌmiːt_ər ə'-- ‖ ˌmiːţ i_ər ə ˈlɑːdʒ- **~ly** _i
meteorologist ˌmiːt i_ə ˈrɒl ədʒ ɪst ⚠ˌmiːt əˈ--, §-əst ‖ ˌmiːţ i_ə ˈrɑːl- **~s** s
meteorology ˌmiːt i_ə ˈrɒl ədʒ i ⚠ˌmiːt əˈ-- ‖ ˌmiːţ i_ə ˈrɑːl-
meter ˈmiːt ə ‖ ˈmiːţ ᵊr **~ed** d **metering** ˈmiːt ər ɪŋ ‖ ˈmiːţ ər ɪŋ **~s** z
-meter *(i)* ˌmiːt ə ‖ ˌmiːţ ᵊr, *(ii)* mɪt ə -mət ə ‖ məţ ᵊr *—Pronunciation (i) is used (a) in units of length (also spelt* -metre*):* ˈcentiˌmeter/ˈcentiˌmetre, *and sometimes (b) in the meaning 'measuring device':* ˈvoltˌmeter. *The stress-imposing pronunciation (ii) is used (c) with reference to versification:* penˈtameter, *and sometimes (d) for 'measuring device':* baˈrometer. *(Hence the different pronunciations of the two senses of* micrometer.*) In the words* altimeter *and* kilometer/kilometre *the two types have been confused, giving rise to competing pronunciations with different stressings.*
meth- *comb. form before vowel* **meθ** *—or, in BrE only,* miːθ *—see following*
methacrylate meθ ˈæk rɪ leɪt -ˈrə-
methadone ˈmeθ ə dəʊn ‖ -doʊn
methamphetamine ˌmeθ æm ˈfet ə miːn -mɪn, §-mən ‖ -ˈfeţ-
methane ˈmiːθ eɪn ‖ ˈmeθ- *(*)*
methanoic ˌmeθ ə ˈnəʊ ɪk ◂ ‖ -ˈnoʊ-
methanol ˈmeθ ə nɒl ˈmiːθ- ‖ -nɔːl -nɑːl, -noʊl
metheglin me ˈθeg lɪn mɪ-, mə-, §-lən
methinks mi ˈθɪŋks
method ˈmeθ əd **~s** z
methodical mə ˈθɒd ɪk ᵊl mɪ-, me- ‖ -ˈθɑːd- **~ly** _i **~ness** nəs nɪs
methodics mə ˈθɒd ɪks mɪ-, me- ‖ -ˈθɑːd-
Methodism ˈmeθ ə ˌdɪz əm
Methodist ˈmeθ əd ɪst §-əst **~s** s
Methodius me ˈθəʊd i_əs mɪ-, mə- ‖ -ˈθoʊd-
methodological ˌmeθ əd ə ˈlɒdʒ ɪk ᵊl ◂ ‖ -ˈlɑːdʒ- **~ly** _i
methodologist ˌmeθ ə ˈdɒl ədʒ ɪst §-əst ‖ -ˈdɑːl- **~s** s
methodolog|y ˌmeθ ə ˈdɒl ədʒ |i ‖ -ˈdɑːl- **~ies** iz
methought mi ˈθɔːt ‖ -ˈθɑːt
meths meθs
Methuen *(i)* ˈmeθ ju_ən -u_, ɪn, *(ii)* mə ˈθjuː_ən mɪ-, me-, -ˈθuː_, ɪn *—The English family name is (i); the place in MA is (ii).*
Methuselah, m~ mə ˈθjuːz əl ə mɪ-, -ˈθuːz- ‖ -ˈθuːz- **~s, ~'s** z
Methven ˈmeθ vən
methyl ˈmeθ ᵊl -ɪl *—in BrE technical usage also* ˈmiːθ aɪᵊl
ˌmethyl ˈalcohol

M

methylamine me 'θaɪl ə miːn miː-, mɪ-, mə-; ˌmeθ ɪl 'æm iːn, -ᵊl- ‖ ˌmeθ ᵊl ə 'miːn -'æm ən; mə 'θɪl ə miːn

methy|late *n, v* 'meθ ə |leɪt -ɪ- **~lated** leɪt ɪd -əd ‖ leɪţ əd **~lates** leɪts **~lating** leɪt ɪŋ ‖ leɪţ ɪŋ

ˌmethylated 'spirits

methylene 'meθ ə liːn ɪ-

metic 'met ɪk ‖ 'meţ- **~s** s

meticulous mə 'tɪk jʊl əs mɪ-, me-, -jəl- ‖ -jəl- **~ly** li **~ness** nəs nɪs

metier, métier 'met i eɪ 'meɪt- ‖ 'meɪt jeɪ -'. —*Fr* [me tje] **~s** z

metis, métis *sing.* meɪ 'tiː -'tiːs, *pl* -'tiː -'tiːs, -'tiːz

Metonic me 'tɒn ɪk mɪ-, mə- ‖ -'tɑːn-

Meˌtonic 'cycle

metonym 'met ə nɪm ‖ 'meţ- **~s** z

metonym|y me 'tɒn əm |i mə-, mɪ-, -ɪm- ‖ -'tɑːn- **~ies** iz

me-too ˌmiː 'tuː **~ism** ˌɪz əm

met|ope 'met |əʊp -|əp i ‖ 'meţ |əp i **~opes** əʊps əp iz ‖ əp iz

metre 'miːt ə ‖ 'miːţ ᵊr **~s** z

-metre ˌmiːt ə ‖ ˌmiːţ ᵊr —*see note at* **-meter**

metric 'metr ɪk **~s** s

ˌmetric 'ton

-metric 'metr ɪk — **parametric** ˌpær ə 'metr ɪk ◂ ‖ ˌper-

-metrical 'metr ɪk ᵊl — **parametrical** ˌpær ə 'metr ɪk ᵊl ◂ ‖ ˌper-

metrical 'metr ɪk ᵊl **~ly** ˌi

metricality ˌmetr ɪ 'kæl ət i ˌ-ə-, -ɪt i ‖ -əţ i

metri|cate 'metr ɪ |keɪt -ə- **~cated** keɪt ɪd -əd ‖ keɪţ əd **~cates** keɪts **~cating** keɪt ɪŋ ‖ keɪţ ɪŋ

metrication ˌmetr ɪ 'keɪʃ ᵊn -ə-

metricis|e, metriciz|e 'metr ɪ saɪz -ə- **~ed** d **~es** ɪz əz **~ing** ɪŋ

metro, Metro 'metr əʊ ‖ -oʊ me 'troʊ **~s** z

metro- *comb. form*
with stress-neutral suffix(i) ¦metr əʊ ‖ -ə, *(ii)* ¦miːtr əʊ ‖ -ə —*(i) particularly in the senses 'measurement', 'mother'; (ii) particularly in the sense 'uterus'* — **metronymic** ˌmetr əʊ 'nɪm ɪk ◂ ‖ -ə-
with stress-imposing suffix mɪ 'trɒ+ mə-, me- ‖ -'trɑː+ — **metrology** mɪ 'trɒl ədʒ |i mə-, me- ‖ -'trɑːl- **~ies** iz

Metro-Goldwyn-Mayer ˌmetr əʊ ˌgəʊld wɪn 'meɪ ə →-ˌgɒʊld-, →-wɪm'· · ‖ -oʊ ˌgoʊld wɪn 'meɪ ᵊr

Metroland 'metr əʊ lænd ‖ -oʊ-

metronidazole ˌmetr əʊ 'naɪd ə zəʊl -ɒn 'aɪd-, →-zɒʊl ‖ -ə 'naɪd ə zoʊl

metronome 'metr ə nəʊm ‖ -noʊm **~s** z

metronomic ˌmetr ə 'nɒm ɪk ◂ ‖ -'nɑːm-

Metropole 'metr ə pəʊl →-pɒʊl ‖ -poʊl **~s** z

metropolis, M~ mə 'trɒp əl ɪs mɪ-, me-, §-əs ‖ -'trɑːp- **~es** ɪz əz

metropolitan, M~ ˌmetr ə 'pɒl ɪt ən ◂ -'-ət- ‖ -'pɑːl ət ᵊn ◂ **~s** z

metrorrhagia ˌmiːtr əʊ 'reɪdʒ i‿ə ˌmetr-, ˌ-ɔː-, -'reɪdʒ ə ‖ ˌ-ə-

metrosexual ˌmetr əʊ 'sek ʃu‿əl ◂ ‖ ˌ-oʊ- **~s** z

-metry *stress-imposing* mətr i mɪtr i — **chronometry** krə 'nɒm ətr i -ɪtr- ‖ -'nɑːm-

Metternich 'met ə nɪk -nɪx ‖ 'meţ ᵊr- —*Ger* ['mɛt ɐ nɪç]

mettle 'met ᵊl ‖ 'meţ ᵊl *(= metal)*

mettlesome 'met ᵊl səm ‖ 'meţ-

Mettoy *tdmk* 'met ɔɪ

Metuchen mɪ 'tʌtʃ ən mə-

Metz mets —*Fr* [mɛs]

meuniere, meunière ˌmɜːn i 'eə '· · ‖ mʌn 'jeᵊr —*Fr* [mø njɛːʁ]

Meurig 'maɪᵊr ɪg —*Welsh* ['məi rig, 'məi-]

Meuse mɜːz ‖ mjuːz mʊz —*Fr* [møːz]

Meux *(i)* mjuːks, *(ii)* mjuːz, *(iii)* mjuː

Mevagissey ˌmev ə 'gɪs i -'gɪz-

mew mjuː **mewed** mjuːd **mewing** 'mjuː ɪŋ **mews** mjuːz *(= muse)*

Mewes *(i)* 'mev ɪs §-əs, *(ii)* 'mjuː‿ɪs §‿əs

mewl mjuːl *(= mule)* **mewled** mjuːld **mewling** 'mjuːl ɪŋ **mewls** mjuːlz

mews mjuːz

Mexboro', Mexborough 'meks bər‿ə ‖ -ˌbɜː oʊ

Mexicali ˌmeks ɪ 'kæl i -'kɑːl- —*Sp* [me xi 'ka li]

Mexican 'meks ɪk ən **~s** z

Mexico 'meks ɪk əʊ ‖ -oʊ —*Sp* México, Méjico ['me xi ko]

ˌMexico 'City

Mey meɪ

Meyer *(i)* 'maɪ‿ə ‖ 'maɪ‿ᵊr, *(ii)* 'meɪ ə ‖ -ᵊr, *(iii)* meə ‖ meᵊr, *(iv)* mɪə ‖ mɪᵊr

Meynell *(i)* 'men ᵊl, *(ii)* meɪ 'nel

Meyrick 'mer ɪk

meze 'mez eɪ ‖ me 'zeɪ 'meɪz eɪ —*Turkish* [me 'ze]

mezereon mə 'zɪər i‿ən mɪ-, me- ‖ -'zɪr- **~s** z

mezuzah mə 'zʊz ə -'zuːz- **~s** z

mezzanine 'mets ə niːn 'mez- ‖ 'mez- **~s** z

mezzo 'mets əʊ 'medz- ‖ -oʊ **~s** z

mezzo-soprano ˌmets əʊ sə 'prɑːn əʊ ˌmedz- ‖ -oʊ sə 'præn oʊ -'prɑːn- **~s** z

mezzo|tint 'mets əʊ |tɪnt 'medz- ‖ -oʊ- **~tinted** tɪnt ɪd -əd ‖ tɪnţ əd **~tinting** tɪnt ɪŋ ‖ tɪnţ ɪŋ **~tints** tɪnts

mg —*see* **milligram(s)**

MGM *tdmk* ˌem dʒiː 'em

Mhairi 'vɑːr i

mho məʊ ‖ moʊ **mhos** məʊz ‖ moʊz

MHz —*see* **megahertz**

mi miː

MI5 ˌem aɪ 'faɪv

MI6 ˌem aɪ 'sɪks

Mia 'miː‿ə

Miami maɪ 'æm i

miaow mi 'aʊ ˌmiː- **~ed** d **~ing** ɪŋ **~s** z

miasma mi 'æz mə maɪ- **~s** z

mica 'maɪk ə

micaceous maɪ 'keɪʃ əs

Micah 'maɪk ə

icawber, m~ mə ˈkɔːb ə mɪ- ‖ -ᵊr -ˈkɑːb-
icawberish mə ˈkɔːb ər ɪʃ mɪ- ‖ -ˈkɑːb-
ice maɪs
ichael ˈmaɪk ᵊl
ichaela *(i)* mɪ ˈkeɪl ə mə-, *(ii)* maɪ-
ichaelis *(i)* mɪ ˈkeɪl ɪs mə-, §-əs, *(ii)* -ˈkaɪl-
ichaelmas ˈmɪk ᵊl məs
ˌ**Michaelmas ˈdaisy**
ichel mɪ ˈʃel miː- —*Fr* [mi ʃɛl]
ichelangelo ˌmaɪk ᵊl ˈændʒ ə ləʊ ˌmɪk-, -ˈ·ɪ- ‖ -loʊ —*It* [mi ke ˈlan dʒe lo]
icheldever ˈmɪtʃ əl dev ə ‖ -ᵊr
ichele, Michèle mɪ ˈʃel miː- —*Fr* [mi ʃɛl]
ichelin *tdmk* ˈmɪtʃ əl‿ɪn ˈmɪʃ- —*Fr* [miʃ lɛ̃] —*In BrE the* M~ Guide *is usually pronounced as if French.*
ichelle mɪ ˈʃel miː-
ichelmore ˈmɪtʃ əl mɔː ‖ -mɔːr -moʊr
ichelob *tdmk* ˈmɪk ə ləʊb -ᵊl əʊb ‖ -ᵊl oʊb
ichelson *(i)* ˈmaɪk ᵊl sən, *(ii)* ˈmɪtʃ- —*The physicist A A M~ was (i).*
ichener *(i)* ˈmɪʃ nə ‖ -nᵊr, *(ii)* ˈmɪtʃ ən‿ə ‖ -ᵊn‿ər —*The novelist* James M~ *is (ii).*
ichie ˈmɪk i ˈmɪx-, ˈmiːx-
ichigan ˈmɪʃ ɪg ən ⚠ˈmɪtʃ-
ichigander ˌmɪʃ ɪ ˈgænd ə ‖ -ᵊr **~s** z
ick, mick mɪk **micks, Mick's** mɪks
ickey, mickey, Mickie ˈmɪk i
ˌ**mickey ˈfinn**; ˌ**Mickey ˈMouse**
ickle ˈmɪk ᵊl
ickleham ˈmɪk ᵊl əm
ickleover ˈmɪk ᵊl ˌəʊv ə ‖ -ˌoʊv ᵊr
icklethwaite ˈmɪk ᵊl θweɪt
icklewhite ˈmɪk ᵊl waɪt -hwaɪt ‖ -*h*waɪt
icky, micky ˈmɪk i
icmac ˈmɪk mæk **~s** s
icra, Micra *tdmk* ˈmaɪk rə
icro ˈmaɪk rəʊ ‖ -roʊ **~s** z
icro- *comb. form*
with stress-neutral suffix ¦maɪk rəʊ ‖ -roʊ — **microfossil** ˌmaɪk rəʊ ˈfɒs ᵊl ‖ -ˈfɑːs-
with stress-imposing suffix maɪ ˈkrɒ+ ‖ -ˈkrɑː+ — **micrography** maɪ ˈkrɒg rəf i ‖ -ˈkrɑːg-
microbe ˈmaɪk rəʊb ‖ -roʊb **~s** z
microbial maɪ ˈkrəʊb i‿əl ‖ -ˈkroʊb-
microbiological ˌmaɪk rəʊ ˌbaɪ‿ə ˈlɒdʒ ɪk ᵊl ‖ -roʊ ˌbaɪ ə ˈlɑːdʒ- **~ly** ‿i
microbiologist ˌmaɪk rəʊ baɪ ˈɒl ədʒ ɪst §-əst ‖ -roʊ baɪ ˈɑːl- **~s** s
microbiology ˌmaɪk rəʊ baɪ ˈɒl ədʒ i ‖ -roʊ baɪ ˈɑːl-
microbrew ˈmaɪk rəʊ bruː ‖ -roʊ- **~s** z
microbrewer|y ˈmaɪk rəʊ ˌbruː‿ər |i ‖ -roʊ- **~ies** iz
microchip ˈmaɪk rəʊ tʃɪp ‖ -roʊ- **~s** s
microclimate ˈmaɪk rəʊ ˌklaɪm ət -ɪt ‖ -roʊ- **~s** s
microcline ˈmaɪk rəʊ klaɪn ‖ -roʊ- **~s** z
microcomputer ˈmaɪk rəʊ kəm ˌpjuːt ə §-kɒm,·- ‖ -roʊ kəm ˌpjuːt̬ ᵊr **~s** z
microcosm ˈmaɪk rəʊ ˌkɒz əm ‖ -rə ˌkɑːz- **~s** z
microcosmic ˌmaɪk rəʊ ˈkɒz mɪk ◂ ‖ -rə ˈkɑːz-

microdot ˈmaɪk rəʊ dɒt ‖ -rə dɑːt -roʊ- **~s** s
microeconomic ˌmaɪk rəʊ ˌiːk ə ˈnɒm ɪk ◂ ˌ·ˌek- ‖ -roʊ ˌek ə ˈnɑːm- -ˌiːk- **~s** s
microelectronic ˌmaɪk rəʊ ɪ ˌlek ˈtrɒn ɪk ˌ·ə-, -ˌel ek'·-, -ˌɪl ek'·-, -ˌiːl ek'·- ‖ -roʊ ɪ ˌlek ˈtrɑːn- **~s** s
microfarad ˈmaɪk rəʊ ˌfær əd -æd ‖ -roʊ- -ˌfer- **~s** z
microfich|e ˈmaɪk rəʊ fiːʃ -fɪʃ ‖ -rə- **~es** ɪz əz
microfilm ˈmaɪk rəʊ fɪlm ‖ -rə- **~ed** d **~ing** ɪŋ **~s** z
microgram ˈmaɪk rəʊ græm ‖ -rə- **~s** z
microgroove ˈmaɪk rəʊ gruːv ‖ -rə- -roʊ- **~s** z
microlight ˈmaɪk rəʊ laɪt ‖ -rə- -roʊ- **~s** s
micromanag|e ˈmaɪk rəʊ ˌmæn ɪdʒ -ədʒ ‖ -roʊ- **~ed** d **~ement** mənt **~es** ɪz əz **~ing** ɪŋ
micromesh ˈmaɪk rəʊ meʃ ‖ -roʊ-
micrometer, micrometre *'micron'* ˈmaɪk rəʊ ˌmiːt ə maɪ ˈkrɒm ɪt ə, -ət ə ‖ -roʊ ˌmiːt̬ ᵊr **~s** z
micrometer *'instrument'* maɪ ˈkrɒm ɪt ə -ət- ‖ -ˈkrɑːm ət̬ ᵊr **~s** z
microminiaturis... —*see* **microminiaturiz...**
microminiaturization ˌmaɪk rəʊ ˌmɪn ətʃ ər aɪ ˈzeɪʃ ᵊn -ˌɪtʃ-, -ˌ·i‿ətʃ · ·'·-, -ɪ'·- ‖ -roʊ ˌmɪn i‿ətʃ ər ə- -ˌ·ətʃ · ·'·-
microminiaturiz|e ˌmaɪk rəʊ ˈmɪn ətʃ ə raɪz -ˈɪtʃ-, -ˈ·i‿ətʃ · · ‖ -roʊ ˈmɪn i‿ətʃ- -ˈ·ətʃ · · **~ed** d **~es** ɪz əz **~ing** ɪŋ
micron ˈmaɪk rɒn -rən ‖ -rɑːn **~s** z
Micronesia ˌmaɪk rəʊ ˈniːz i‿ə -ˈniːʒ ə, -ˈniːs i‿ə, -ˈniːʃ ə ‖ -rə ˈniːʒ ə -ˈniːʃ-
Micronesian ˌmaɪk rəʊ ˈniːz i‿ən ◂ -ˈniːʒ ᵊn, -ˈniːs i‿ən, -ˈniːʃ ᵊn ‖ -rə ˈniːʒ ᵊn -ˈniːʃ- **~s** z
microorganism ˌmaɪk rəʊ ˈɔːg ə ˌnɪz əm ˈ·ˌ·ˌ· · · ‖ -roʊ ˈɔːrg- **~s** z
Micropal ˈmaɪk rəʊ pæl ‖ -roʊ-
microphone ˈmaɪk rə fəʊn ‖ -foʊn **~s** z
microprocessor ˈmaɪk rəʊ ˌprəʊs es ə -ɪs ə, §-əs ə; ˌ·ˈ·ˌ· · · ‖ -rə ˌprɑːs es ᵊr -əs ᵊr **~s** z
microscope ˈmaɪk rə skəʊp ‖ -skoʊp **~s** s
microscopic ˌmaɪk rə ˈskɒp ɪk ◂ ‖ -ˈskɑːp ɪk ◂ **~ally** ᵊl‿i
microscopy maɪ ˈkrɒsk əp i ‖ -ˈkrɑːsk-
microsecond ˈmaɪk rəʊ ˌsek ənd ˌ·ˈ·ˌ· ‖ -rə- -roʊ-, ⚠-ənt **~s** z
Microsoft *tdmk* ˈmaɪk rəʊ sɒft ‖ -rə sɔːft -sɑːft
microsurgery ˈmaɪk rəʊ ˌsɜːdʒ ər‿i ‖ -roʊ ˌsɜ˞ːdʒ-
microtome ˈmaɪk rəʊ təʊm ‖ -rə toʊm **~s** z
microwav|e ˈmaɪk rə weɪv -rəʊ- ‖ -rə- -roʊ- **~able** əb ᵊl **~ed** d **~es** z **~ing** ɪŋ
mictu|rate ˈmɪk tjuᵊ |reɪt -tʃə- ‖ -tʃə- -tə- **~rated** reɪt ɪd -əd ‖ reɪt̬ əd **~rates** reɪts **~rating** reɪt ɪŋ ‖ reɪt̬ ɪŋ
micturation ˌmɪk tju ˈreɪʃ ᵊn -tʃə- ‖ -tʃə- -tə- **~s** z
micturition ˌmɪk tju ˈrɪʃ ᵊn -tʃə- ‖ -tʃə- -tə- **~s** z
mid mɪd
ˌ**Mid Glaˈmorgan**
mid- ¦mɪd — **mid-Atlantic** ˌmɪd ət ˈlænt ɪk ◂ ‖ -ˈlænt̬-

M

midair ˌmɪd ˈeə ◂ ‖ -ˈeᵊr ◂ -ˈæᵊr
Midas ˈmaɪd əs -æs
mid-Atlantic ˌmɪd ət ˈlænt ɪk ◂ ‖ -ˈlænt̬-
midbrain ˈmɪd breɪn
midcourse ˌmɪd ˈkɔːs ◂ →ˌmɪg- ‖ -ˈkɔːrs ◂ -ˈkoʊrs
midday ˌmɪd ˈdeɪ ◂ ˈ..
midden ˈmɪd ᵊn **~s** z
middie... —*see* **middy**
middle ˈmɪd ᵊl **~s** z
ˌ**middle ˈage**; ˌ**Middle ˈAges**; ˌ**middle ˈC**; ˌ**middle ˈclass**; ˌ**middle ˈcourse**, ˈ. . .; ˌ**middle ˈdistance**; ˌ**middle ˈear**; ˌ**Middle ˈEast**; ˌ**Middle ˈEastern**◂; ˌ**Middle ˈEnglish**; ˌ**middle ˈfinger**; ˌ**middle ˈmanagement**; ˌ**middle ˈname**; ˌ**middle of ˈnowhere**; ˈ**middle school**; ˌ**Middle ˈWest**
middle-aged ˌmɪd ᵊl ˈeɪdʒd ◂
ˌ**middle-aged ˈspread**
middlebrow ˈmɪd ᵊl braʊ **~s** z
Middlebury *place in VT* ˈmɪd ᵊl ˌber i
middle-class ˌmɪd ᵊl ˈklɑːs ◂ §-ˈklæs ‖ -ˈklæs ◂
middle-distance ˌmɪd ᵊl ˈdɪst ənᵗs ◂
Middleham ˈmɪd ᵊl əm
middle|man ˈmɪd ᵊl |mæn **~men** men
Middlemarch ˈmɪd ᵊl mɑːtʃ ‖ -mɑːrtʃ
Middlemast ˈmɪd ᵊl mɑːst §-mæst ‖ -mæst
middlemen ˈmɪd ᵊl men
middle-of-the-road ˌmɪd ᵊl‿əv ðə ˈrəʊd ◂ -ᵊl‿ə ðə- ‖ -ˈroʊd ◂
middle-ranking ˌmɪd ᵊl ˈræŋk ɪŋ ◂
Middlesboro, Middlesborough *place in KY* ˈmɪd ᵊlz bər‿ə ‖ -ˌbɜː oʊ
Middlesbrough *place in England* ˈmɪd ᵊlz brə
Middlesex ˈmɪd ᵊl seks
middle-sized ˌmɪd ᵊl ˈsaɪzd◂
Middleton ˈmɪd ᵊl tən
Middletown ˈmɪd ᵊl taʊn
middleweight ˈmɪd ᵊl weɪt **~s** s
Middlewich ˈmɪd ᵊl wɪtʃ
middling ˈmɪd ᵊl‿ɪŋ **~ly** li
Middx —*see* **Middlesex**
midd|y ˈmɪd |i **~ies** iz
Mideast ˌmɪd ˈiːst
midfield ˈmɪd fiːᵊld ˌ.ˈ. **~er/s** ə/z ‖ -ᵊr/z
midge mɪdʒ **midges** ˈmɪdʒ ɪz -əz
midget ˈmɪdʒ ɪt §-ət **~s** s
Midgley ˈmɪdʒ li
midgut ˈmɪd gʌt →ˈmɪg- **~s** s
Midhurst ˈmɪd hɜːst ‖ -hɜːst
midi *'mid-length (garment)'* ˈmɪd i **~s** z
Midi *'south of France'* mɪ ˈdiː miː-—*Fr* [mi di]
MIDI, Midi *computer interface* ˈmɪd i **~s** z
Midian ˈmɪd i‿ən
Midianite ˈmɪd i‿ə naɪt **~s** s
midinette ˌmɪd i ˈnet —*Fr* [mi di nɛt] **~s** s
midiron ˈmɪd ˌaɪ‿ən ‖ -ˌaɪ‿ᵊrn **~s** z
midland, M~ ˈmɪd lənd **~er/s** ə/z ‖ ᵊr/z **~s** z
Midler ˈmɪd lə ‖ -lᵊr
mid-life ˌmɪd ˈlaɪf ◂
ˌ**mid-life ˈcrisis**
Midlothian mɪd ˈləʊð i‿ən ‖ -ˈloʊð-
midmost ˈmɪd məʊst →ˈmɪb- ‖ -moʊst

midnight ˈmɪd naɪt
ˌ**midnight ˈsun**
mid-off ˌmɪd ˈɒf -ˈɔːf ‖ -ˈɔːf -ˈɑːf **~s** s
mid-on ˌmɪd ˈɒn ‖ -ˈɑːn -ˈɔːn **~s** z
midpoint ˈmɪd pɔɪnt →ˈmɪb- **~s** s
mid-range ˌmɪd ˈreɪndʒ ◂
midriff ˈmɪd rɪf **~s** s
midsection ˈmɪd ˌsek ʃᵊn **~s** z
midship ˈmɪd ʃɪp **~s** s
midship|man ˈmɪd ʃɪp |mən **~men** mən
midsize ˈmɪd saɪz
midst mɪdst mɪtst
midstream ˌmɪd ˈstriːm ◂
midsummer ˌmɪd ˈsʌm ə ◂ ˈ.ˌ. . ‖ -ᵊr **~s, ~'s** z
ˌ**Midˌsummer ˈDay**; ˌ**midˌsummer ˈmadness**
midterm ˌmɪd ˈtɜːm ◂ ‖ -ˈtɜːm ◂—*but in the sense '~ examination' usually* ˈ. .
— **midterms** ˈmɪd tɜːmz ‖ -tɜːmz
midtown ˈmɪd taʊn
midway *n,* **M~** ˈmɪd weɪ
midway *adj, adv* ˌmɪd ˈweɪ◂
midweek ˌmɪd ˈwiːk ◂
Midwest ˌmɪd ˈwest
Midwestern ˌmɪd ˈwest ən ◂ ‖ -ᵊrn ◂
Midwesterner ˌmɪd ˈwest ən ə ‖ -ᵊrn ᵊr **~s** z
midwicket ˌmɪd ˈwɪk ɪt §-ət
mid|wife ˈmɪd |waɪf **~wives** waɪvz
midwifery ˌmɪd ˈwɪf ər‿i ˈ. . . ‖ ˈmɪd waɪf-
midwinter ˌmɪd ˈwɪnt ə ◂ ‖ -ˈwɪnt̬ ᵊr◂
midwives ˈmɪd waɪvz
midyear ˈmɪd jɪə ‖ -jɪr
Miele *tdmk* ˈmiːl ə
mien miːn *(= mean)* **miens** miːnz
Miers ˈmaɪ‿əz ‖ ˈmaɪ‿ᵊrz
Mies van der Rohe ˌmiːz væn də ˈrəʊ ə ˌmiːs ‖ -dᵊr ˈroʊ ə ˌ-vɑːn-; ˌ. . ˌ. .
miff mɪf **miffed** mɪft **miffing** ˈmɪf ɪŋ **miffs** mɪfs
MiG mɪg **MiGs, MiG's** mɪgz
might maɪt
might-have-beens ˈmaɪt əv biːnz -ə-, -bɪnz ‖ ˈmaɪt̬ əv bɪnz
mighti... —*see* **mighty**
mightily ˈmaɪt ɪ li -ᵊl i ‖ ˈmaɪt̬ ᵊl i
mightn't ˈmaɪt ᵊnt
might|y ˈmaɪt |i ‖ ˈmaɪt̬ |i **~ier** i‿ə ‖ i‿ᵊr **~iest** i‿ɪst i‿əst **~iness** i nəs i nɪs
mignon ˈmɪn jɒn ˌ.ˈ. ‖ miːn ˈjoʊn -ˈjɑːn, -ˈjɔːn —*Fr* [mi ɲjɔ̃]
mignonette, M~ ˌmiːn jə ˈnet **~s** s
migraine ˈmiːg reɪn ˈmaɪg-, ˈmɪg- ‖ ˈmaɪg-
— *Preference poll, BrE:* ˈmiːg- *61%,* ˈmaɪg- *39%.* **~s** z
migrant ˈmaɪg rənt **~s** s
mig|rate ₍₁₎maɪ ˈg|reɪt ˈmaɪg |reɪt ‖ ˈmaɪg |reɪt **~rated** reɪt ɪd -əd ‖ reɪt̬ əd **~rates** reɪts **~rating** reɪt ɪŋ ‖ reɪt̬ ɪŋ
migration ₍₁₎maɪ ˈgreɪʃ ᵊn **~al** ‿əl **~s** z
migratory ˈmaɪg rət‿ər i ₍₁₎maɪ ˈgreɪt ər i ‖ ˈmaɪg rə tɔːr i -toʊr i
Miguel miː ˈgel mɪ-—*Sp, Port* [mi ˈɣel]

MIGRAINE

39% 'miːg-
61% 'maɪg-
BrE

BrE by 'maɪg- by age

Speakers	Percentage
Older	15
	31
	42
Younger	72

Percentage: 0 10 20 30 40 50 60 70 80
Older ⟵ Speakers ⟶ Younger

mikado, M~ mɪ ˈkɑːd əʊ mə- ‖ -oʊ —*Jp* [mi ˌka do] **~s** z
Mikardo mɪ ˈkɑːd əʊ mə- ‖ -ˈkɑːrd oʊ
mike, Mike maɪk **mikes, Mike's** maɪks
Mikey ˈmaɪk i
Mikhail mɪ ˈkaɪəl -ˈxaɪəl —*Russ* [mʲɪ xʌ ˈiɫ]
mil mɪl *(= mill)* **mils** mɪlz
milad|y mɪ ˈleɪd |i mə- **~ies** iz
milag|e ˈmaɪl ɪdʒ ˈmaɪəl- **~es** ɪz əz
Milan mɪ ˈlæn mə-, -ˈlɑːn —*formerly* ˈmɪl ən; *but the place in IN is* ˈmaɪl æn —*It* Milano [mi ˈlaː no]
Milanese ˌmɪl ə ˈniːz ◂ -ˈneɪz ‖ -ˈniːs —*but as a cookery term also* ˌ· ·ˈneɪz eɪ
milch mɪltʃ
ˈmilch cow
mild maɪəld **milder** ˈmaɪəld ə ‖ -ər **mildest** ˈmaɪəld ɪst -əst
milden ˈmaɪəld ən **~ed** d **~ing** ɪŋ **~s** z
Mildenhall ˈmɪld ən hɔːl ‖ -hɑːl
mildew ˈmɪl djuː →-dʒuː ‖ -duː -djuː **~ed** d **~ing** ɪŋ **~s** z
mildewy ˈmɪl djuː i →-dʒuː‿ ‖ -duː i -djuː-
mildly ˈmaɪəld li
mild-mannered ˌmaɪld ˈmæn əd ◂ ‖ -ərd ◂
Mildmay ˈmaɪəld meɪ
mildness ˈmaɪəld nəs -nɪs
Mildred ˈmɪldr əd -ɪd
mile maɪəl **miles** maɪəlz
mileag|e ˈmaɪl ɪdʒ ˈmaɪəl- **~es** ɪz əz
mileometer maɪ ˈlɒm ɪt ə ˌmaɪəl ˈɒm-, -ət- ‖ -ˈlɑːm ət̬ ər **~s** z
milepost ˈmaɪəl pəʊst ‖ -poʊst **~s** s
miler ˈmaɪl ə ˈmaɪəl- ‖ -ər **~s** z
miles *pl of* **mile** maɪəlz
miles *Latin, 'soldier'* ˈmiːl eɪz -eɪs ‖ -eɪs
ˌmiles ˌgloriˈosus ˌglɔːr i ˈəʊs əs -ʊs ‖ -ˈoʊs- ˌgloʊr-
Miles *name* maɪəlz
Milesian maɪ ˈliːz i‿ən mɪ-, -ˈliːʒ-, -ˈliːʒ ən ‖ -ˈliːʒ ən -ˈliːʃ- **~s** z
milestone ˈmaɪəl stəʊn ‖ -stoʊn **~s** z

Miletus maɪ ˈliːt əs mɪ-, mə- ‖ -ˈliːt̬-
milfoil ˈmɪl fɔɪəl **~s** z
Milford ˈmɪl fəd ‖ -fərd
ˌMilford ˈHaven
Milhaud ˈmiː əʊ -jəʊ ‖ miː ˈoʊ -ˈjoʊ —*Fr* [mi jo, -lo]
miliaria ˌmɪl i ˈeər i‿ə ‖ -ˈer- -ˈær-
miliary ˈmɪl i‿ər i ‖ -i er i
Miliband ˈmɪl ɪ bænd -ə-
milieu ˈmiːl jɜː ˌ(ɪ)·ˈ· ‖ miːl ˈjuː mɪl- —*Fr* [mi ljø] **~s** z **~x** z *or as sing.*
militancy ˈmɪl ɪt ənts i ˈ·ət-
militant ˈmɪl ɪt ənt -ət- **~ly** li **~s** s
militaria ˌmɪl ɪ ˈteər i‿ə ˌ·ə- ‖ -ˈter- -ˈtær-
militarily ˈmɪl ɪt‿ər əl i li; ˌmɪl ɪ ˈter-, ˌ·ə- ‖ ˌmɪl ə ˈter-
militaris... —*see* **militariz...**
militarism ˈmɪl ɪt ə ˌrɪz əm ˈ·ət- ‖ ˈmɪl ət̬-
militarist ˈmɪl ɪt ər ɪst ˈ·ət-, §-əst ‖ ˈmɪl ət̬- **~s** s
militaristic ˌmɪl ɪt ə ˈrɪst ɪk ◂ ˌ·ət- ‖ ˌmɪl ət̬- **~ally** əl‿i
militarization ˌmɪl ɪt ər aɪ ˈzeɪʃ ən ˌ·ət- ‖ -ət̬ ər ə·- **~s** z
militariz|e ˈmɪl ɪt ə raɪz ˈ·ət- ‖ -ət̬ ə- **~ed** d **~es** ɪz əz **~ing** ɪŋ
military ˈmɪl ɪ‿tər i ˈ·ə‿ ‖ -ə ter i
ˌmilitary poˈlice
mili|tate ˈmɪl ɪ |teɪt -ə- **~tated** teɪt ɪd -əd ‖ teɪt̬ əd **~tates** teɪts **~tating** teɪt ɪŋ ‖ teɪt̬ ɪŋ
militia mə ˈlɪʃ ə mɪ- **~man** mən **~men** mən men **~s** z
milk mɪlk **milked** mɪlkt **milking** ˈmɪlk ɪŋ **milks** mɪlks
ˌmilk ˈchocolate; **ˈmilk float**; **ˈmilking maˌchine**; **ˈmilking stool**; **ˌmilk ˈpudding**; **ˈmilk run**; **ˌmilk ˈshake**, ‖ ˈ· ·; **ˈmilk tooth**
milki... —*see* **milky**
milkmaid ˈmɪlk meɪd **~s** z
milk|man ˈmɪlk |mən **~men** mən men
milksop ˈmɪlk sɒp ‖ -sɑːp **~s** s
milkweed ˈmɪlk wiːd **~s** z
milkwort ˈmɪlk wɜːt §-wɔːt ‖ -wɜːt -wɔːrt **~s** s
milk|y ˈmɪlk |i **~ier** i‿ə ‖ i‿ər **~iest** i‿ɪst i‿əst **~iness** i nəs i nɪs
ˌMilky ˈWay
mill, Mill mɪl **milled** mɪld **milling** ˈmɪl ɪŋ **mills** mɪlz
Millais ˈmɪl eɪ mɪ ˈleɪ ‖ mɪ ˈleɪ
Millan ˈmɪl ən
Millar ˈmɪl ə ‖ -ər
Millard ˈmɪl ɑːd ‖ -ərd
Millbank ˈmɪl bæŋk
millboard ˈmɪl bɔːd ‖ -bɔːrd -boʊrd
milldam ˈmɪl dæm **~s** z
millefeuille ˌmiːəl ˈfɔɪ ˌmɪl-, -ˈfɜː jə —*Fr* [mil fœj]
millefiori ˌmɪl i fi ˈɔːr i ˌmɪl i ˈfjɔːr i
Millen ˈmɪl ən
millenarian ˌmɪl ə ˈneər i‿ən ◂ ˌ·ɪ- ‖ -ˈner- -ˈnær- **~ism** ˌɪz əm **~s** z
millenni|um mɪ ˈlen i‿|əm mə- **~a** ə **~al** əl **~ums** əmz

M

millepede 'mɪl ɪ piːd -ə- **~s** z
millepore 'mɪl ɪ pɔː -ə- ‖ -pɔːr -poʊr **~s** z
miller, M~ 'mɪl ə ‖ -ᵊr **~s** z
millet 'mɪl ɪt §-ət **~s** s
Millet *French name* 'miː eɪ -jeɪ ‖ miː 'jeɪ —*Fr* [mi jɛ, -lɛ]
Millett 'mɪl ɪt §-ət
milli- ¦mɪl ɪ §-ə — **millisecond** 'mɪl ɪ ˌsek ənd §-ə-, →-ŋd ‖ ⚠-ənt
milliard 'mɪl i ɑːd 'mɪl jɑːd ‖ -ɑːrd **~s** z
millibar 'mɪl i bɑː ‖ -bɑːr **~s** z
Millicent 'mɪl ɪs ənt -əs-
Millie 'mɪl i
Milligan 'mɪl ɪg ən
milligram, milligramme 'mɪl i græm -ə- **~s** z
Millikan 'mɪl ɪk ən
milliliter, millilitre 'mɪl i ˌliːt ə -ə- ‖ -ə ˌliːţ ᵊr **~s** z
millimeter, millimetre 'mɪl i ˌmiːt ə -ə- ‖ -ə ˌmiːţ ᵊr **~s** z
milliner 'mɪl ɪn ə -ən- ‖ -ᵊr **~s** z
millinery 'mɪl ɪn ər‿i 'ən- ‖ -ə ner i
Millington 'mɪl ɪŋ tən
million 'mɪl jən 'mɪl i‿ən **~s** z
millionaire ˌmɪl jə 'neə ◂ -i‿ə- ‖ -'neᵊr -'næᵊr; '. . . **~s** z
millionairess ˌmɪl jə 'neər ɪs -əs, -es; -neə 'res ‖ -'ner əs -'nær- **~es** ɪz əz
millionth 'mɪl jənᵗθ 'mɪl i‿ənᵗθ **~s** s
millipede 'mɪl ɪ piːd -ə- **~s** z
millisec|ond 'mɪl ɪ ˌsek |ənd -ə-, →-ŋd ‖ ⚠-ənt **~onds** əndz →ŋdz ‖ ⚠ənts
Millom 'mɪl əm
millpond 'mɪl pɒnd ‖ -pɑːnd **~s** z
millrace 'mɪl reɪs
Mills mɪlz
millstone 'mɪl stəʊn ‖ -stoʊn **~s** z
Millwall 'mɪl wɔːl -wəl, ˌmɪl 'wɔːl ‖ -wɑːl
millwheel 'mɪl wiːᵊl -hwiːᵊl ‖ -*h*wiːᵊl **~s** z
millwright 'mɪl raɪt **~s** s
Milman 'mɪl mən
Milne mɪln mɪl
Milner 'mɪln ə ‖ -ᵊr
Milnes mɪlnz mɪlz
Milngavie mɪl 'gaɪ mʌl- *(!)*
Milo, milo 'maɪl əʊ 'miːl- ‖ -oʊ
milometer maɪ 'lɒm ɪt ə -ət- ‖ -'lɑːm əţ ᵊr **~s** z
milord mi 'lɔːd mə- ‖ -'lɔːrd **~s** z
Milos 'miːl ɒs ‖ -ɑːs -oʊs
Milosevic mɪ 'lɒʃ ə vɪtʃ -'lɒs- ‖ -'loʊs- -'lɑːs- —*Serbian* Milošević [mi 'lo ʃe vitɕ]
Milport 'mɪl pɔːt ‖ -pɔːrt -poʊrt
milquetoast, M~ 'mɪlk təʊst ‖ -toʊst **~s** s
milt, Milt mɪlt **milted** 'mɪlt ɪd -əd **milting** 'mɪlt ɪŋ **milts** mɪlts
Miltiades mɪl 'taɪ‿ə diːz
Milton 'mɪlt ən
ˌMilton 'Keynes kiːnz
Miltonic mɪl 'tɒn ɪk ‖ -'tɑːn-
Milupa *tdmk* mi 'luːp ə
Milwaukee mɪl 'wɔːk i -iː ‖ -'wɑːk-
Mimas 'maɪm əs -æs
mime maɪm **mimed** maɪmd **mimes** maɪmz **miming** 'maɪm ɪŋ
mimeo 'mɪm i əʊ ‖ -oʊ **~ed** d **~ing** ɪŋ **~s** z
mimeograph, M~ 'mɪm i‿ə grɑːf -græf ‖ -græf **~ed** t **~ing** ɪŋ **~s** s
mimesis mɪ 'miːs ɪs mə-, maɪ-, §-əs
mimetic mɪ 'met ɪk mə-, maɪ- ‖ -'meţ- **~ally** ᵊl‿i
Mimi 'miːm i 'miː miː
mimic 'mɪm ɪk **~ked** t **~king** ɪŋ **~s** s
mimic|ry 'mɪm ɪk |ri -ək- **~ries** riz
mimosa mɪ 'məʊz ə §mə-, -'məʊs- ‖ -'moʊs ə -'moʊz- **~s** z
mims|y 'mɪmz| i **~ier** i‿ə ‖ i‿ᵊr **~iest** i‿ɪst ‿əst **~ily** ɪ li əl i **~iness** i nəs -nɪs
mimulus 'mɪm jʊl əs -jəl- ‖ -jəl-
min. —*see (i)* **minimum,** —*(ii)* **minute/s**
Min *river* mɪn —*Chi* Mín [²mɪn]
min|a 'maɪn |ə **~ae** iː **~as** əz
minaret ˌmɪn ə 'ret '. . . **~s** s
minator|y 'mɪn ət‿ər |i 'maɪn- ‖ -ə tɔːr |i -toʊr i **~ily** əl i -ɪ li
mince mɪnᵗs **minced** mɪnᵗst **minces** 'mɪnᵗs ɪz -əz **mincing/ly** 'mɪnᵗs ɪŋ /li
ˌmince 'pie; **'mincing maˌchine**
mincemeat 'mɪnᵗs miːt
mincer 'mɪnᵗs ə ‖ -ᵊr **~s** z
Minch mɪntʃ **Minches** 'mɪntʃ ɪz -əz
mind maɪnd **minded** 'maɪnd ɪd -əd **minding** 'maɪnd ɪŋ **minds** maɪndz
'mind ˌreader, 'mind ˌreading; **ˌmind's 'eye**
Mindanao ˌmɪnd ə 'naʊ ‖ -'nɑː oʊ
mind-bending 'maɪn*d* ˌbend ɪŋ →'maɪm- **~ly** li
mind-blowing 'maɪn*d* ˌbləʊ ɪŋ →'maɪm- ‖ -ˌbloʊ-
mind-boggling 'maɪn*d* ˌbɒg ᵊl‿ɪŋ →'maɪm- ‖ -ˌbɑːg- **~ly** li
minder 'maɪnd ə ‖ -ᵊr **~s** z
mind-expanding 'maɪnd ɪk ˌspænd ɪŋ -ek-, -ək-
mindful 'maɪn*d* fᵊl -fʊl **~ly** ‿i **~ness** nəs nɪs
mindless 'maɪn*d* ləs -lɪs **~ly** li **~ness** nəs nɪs
mindset 'maɪn*d* set **~s** s
Mindy 'mɪnd i
mine maɪn **mined** maɪnd *(= mind)* **mines** maɪnz **mining** 'maɪn ɪŋ
'mine deˌtector
minefield 'maɪn fiːᵊld **~s** z
Minehead 'maɪn hed ˌ.'.
minelayer 'maɪn ˌleɪ ə ‖ -ᵊr **~s** z
minelaying 'maɪn ˌleɪ ɪŋ
Minelli mɪ 'nel i mə-
miner 'maɪn ə ‖ -ᵊr **~s** z
mineral 'mɪn ᵊr‿əl **~s** z
'mineral oil; **'mineral ˌwater**
mineralogical ˌmɪn ᵊr‿ə 'lɒdʒ ɪk ᵊl ◂ ‖ -'lɑːdʒ- **~ly** ‿i
mineralogist ˌmɪn ə 'ræl ədʒ ɪst ⚠-'rɒl-, §-əst ‖ -'rɑːl- **~s** s
mineralogy ˌmɪn ə 'ræl ədʒ i ⚠-'rɒl- ‖ -'rɑːl-
Minerva mɪ 'nɜːv ə mə- ‖ -'nɜːv-

ineshaft ˈmaɪn ʃɑːft §-ʃæft ‖ -ʃæft **~s** s
inestrone ˌmɪn ə ˈstrəʊn i -ɪ- ‖ -ˈstroʊn i
⚠-ˈstroʊn
inesweeper ˈmaɪn ˌswiːp ə ‖ -ᵊr **~s** z
inesweeping ˈmaɪn ˌswiːp ɪŋ
ineworker ˈmaɪn ˌwɜːk ə ‖ -ˌwɜːk ᵊr **~s** z
ning mɪŋ **minging** ˈmɪŋ ɪŋ
Ming *dynasty* mɪŋ —*Chi* Míng [²miŋ]
ninge mɪndʒ
minger ˈmɪŋ ə ‖ -ᵊr **~s** z
Minghella mɪŋ ˈgel ə
mingl|e ˈmɪŋ gᵊl **~ed** d **~er/s** ə/z ‖ ər/z **~es** z
~ing ˌɪŋ
mingogram ˈmɪŋ gəʊ græm ‖ -gə- **~s** z
mingograph, M~ ˈmɪŋ gəʊ grɑːf -græf
‖ -gə græf **~s** s
Mingrelian mɪn ˈgriːl i ən →mɪŋ-
Mingulay ˈmɪŋ gʊ leɪ
Mingus ˈmɪŋ gəs
ming|y ˈmɪndʒ |i **~ier** i ə ‖ i ᵊr **~iest** i ɪst i əst
mini, Mini ˈmɪn i **~s, ~'s** z
mini- ¦mɪn i —**minilecture** ˈmɪn i ˌlek tʃə -ʃə
‖ -tʃᵊr -ʃᵊr
miniature ˈmɪn ətʃ ə -ɪtʃ-, -i ətʃ ə
‖ ˈmɪn i ətʃ ᵊr ə tʃʊr; ˈmɪn ɪ tʃʊr **~s** z
miniaturis... —*see* **miniaturiz...**
miniaturist ˈmɪn ətʃ ər ɪst ˈ·ɪtʃ-, ˈ·i ətʃ · ·, §-əst
‖ ˈmɪn i ətʃ ər əst ə tʃʊr əst; ˈmɪn ɪ tʃʊr əst **~s**
s
miniaturization ˌmɪn ətʃ ər aɪ ˈzeɪʃ ᵊn
ˌmɪn ɪtʃ-, -i ətʃ ər aɪ-, -ɪ'·-
‖ ˌmɪn i ətʃ ər ə ˈzeɪʃ ᵊn ˌmɪn ətʃ ər ə'·- **~s** z
miniaturiz|e ˈmɪn ətʃ ə raɪz ˈ·ɪtʃ-, -i ətʃ ə-
‖ ˈmɪn i ətʃ ə raɪz -ətʃ ə raɪz **~ed** d **~es** ɪz əz
~ing ɪŋ
minibar ˈmɪn i bɑː ‖ -bɑːr **~s** z
minibus ˈmɪn i bʌs **~ed, ~sed** t **~es, ~ses** ɪz
əz **~ing, ~sing** ɪŋ
minicab ˈmɪn i kæb **~s** z
minicam ˈmɪn i kæm **~s** z
minicomputer ˈmɪn i kəm ˌpjuːt ə §-kɒm ˌ·-,
ˌ· · ˈ· · ‖ -ˌpjuːţ ᵊr **~s** z
minim ˈmɪn ɪm §-əm **~s** z
minima ˈmɪn ɪm ə -əm-
minimal ˈmɪn ɪm ᵊl -əm- **~ly** i
ˌminimal ˈpair
minimalism ˈmɪn ɪm ᵊl ˌɪz əm
minimalist ˈmɪn ɪm ᵊl ɪst ˈ·əm-, §-əst **~s** s
mini-mart ˈmɪn i mɑːt ‖ -mɑːrt **~s** s
minimax ˈmɪn ɪ mæks -ə-
mini-me ˌmɪn i ˈmiː
minimis... —*see* **minimiz...**
minimization ˌmɪn ɪ maɪ ˈzeɪʃ ᵊn ˌ·ə- ‖ -əm ə-
minimiz|e ˈmɪn ɪ maɪz -ə- **~ed** d **~es** ɪz əz
~ing ɪŋ
minim|um ˈmɪn ɪm |əm -əm- **~a** ə **~ums** əmz
ˌminimum ˈwage
minimum-security
ˌmɪn ɪm əm sɪ ˈkjʊər ət i ◂ ˌ·əm-, -sə'·, -ət i
‖ -ˈkjʊr əţ i
minimus ˈmɪn ɪm əs -əm-
mining ˈmaɪn ɪŋ
minion ˈmɪn jən ˈmɪn i ən **~s** z

mini-roundabout ˌmɪn i ˈraʊnd ə ˌbaʊt **~s** s
miniscule, minuscule ˈmɪn ə skjuːl -ɪ- **~s** z
miniseries ˈmɪn i ˌsɪər iːz -ɪz ‖ -ˌsɪr-
minisite ˈmɪn i saɪt **~s** s
mini|skirt ˈmɪn i |skɜːt ‖ -|skɜːt **~skirted**
skɜːt ɪd -əd ‖ skɜːţ əd **~skirts** skɜːts ‖ skɜːts
minister ˈmɪn ɪst ə -əst- ‖ -ᵊr **~ed** d
ministering ˈmɪn ɪst ər ɪŋ ˈ·əst-;
→ˈmɪn ɪ strɪŋ, -ə- **~s** z
ˌministering ˈangel
ministerial ˌmɪn ɪ ˈstɪər i əl ◂ ˌ·ə- ‖ -ˈstɪr- **~ly** i
ministrant ˈmɪn ɪs trənt -əs- **~s** s
ministration ˌmɪn ɪ ˈstreɪʃ ᵊn -ə- **~s** z
minis|try ˈmɪn ɪs |tri -əs- **~tries** triz
minium ˈmɪn i əm
minivan ˈmɪn i væn **~s** z
miniver, M~ ˈmɪn ɪv ə -əv- ‖ -ᵊr
mink mɪŋk **minks** mɪŋks
minke ˈmɪŋk i -ə ‖ -ə **~s** z
Minkowski mɪŋ ˈkɒf ski ‖ -ˈkɑːf- -ˈkɔːf-
Minna ˈmɪn ə
Minneapolis ˌmɪn i ˈæp əl ɪs §-əs
Minnehaha ˌmɪn i ˈhɑː hɑː
Minnelli mɪ ˈnel i mə-
minneola ˌmɪn i ˈəʊl ə ‖ -ˈoʊl ə **~s** z
minnesinger ˈmɪn ɪ ˌsɪŋ ə -ə- ‖ -ᵊr **~s** z
Minnesota ˌmɪn ɪ ˈsəʊt ə -ə- ‖ -ˈsoʊţ ə
Minnesotan ˌmɪn ɪ ˈsəʊt ᵊn ◂ -ə- ‖ -ˈsoʊt ᵊn ◂
~s z
Minnie ˈmɪn i
minnow ˈmɪn əʊ ‖ -oʊ **~s** z
Minoan mɪ ˈnəʊ ən mə-, maɪ- ‖ -ˈnoʊ ən **~s** z
Minogue mɪ ˈnəʊg mə- ‖ -ˈnoʊg
Minolta *tdmk* mɪ ˈnɒlt ə mə-, -ˈnəʊlt-
‖ -ˈnɑːlt ə -ˈnoʊlt- —*Jp* [mi ˌno ɾɯ ta]
minor, Minor ˈmaɪn ə ‖ -ᵊr *(= miner)* **~ed** d
minoring ˈmaɪn ər ɪŋ **~s** z
ˌminor ˈplanet; **ˌminor ˈsuit**
Minorca mɪ ˈnɔːk ə mə- ‖ -ˈnɔːrk ə —*Sp*
Menorca [me ˈnor ka]
Minories ˈmɪn ər iz
minorit|y maɪ ˈnɒr ət |i mɪ-, mə-, -ɪt-
‖ mə ˈnɔːr əţ |i maɪ-, ˈnɑːr- **~ies** iz
minor-league ˈmaɪn ə liːg ‖ -ᵊr-
Minos ˈmaɪn ɒs ‖ -əs -ɑːs
Minotaur ˈmaɪn ə tɔː ‖ ˈmɪn ə tɔːr ˈmaɪn- **~s** z
Minsk mɪnᵗsk
minster, M~ ˈmɪnᵗst ə ‖ -ᵊr **~s** z
minstrel ˈmɪnᵗs trəl **~s** z
minstrel|sy ˈmɪnᵗs trəl |si **~sies** siz
mint mɪnt **minted** ˈmɪnt ɪd -əd ‖ ˈmɪnţ əd
minting ˈmɪnt ɪŋ ‖ ˈmɪnţ ɪŋ **mints** mɪnts
ˌmint ˈjulep; **ˌmint ˈsauce** ‖ ˈ· ·
mintag|e ˈmɪnt ɪdʒ ‖ ˈmɪnţ- **~es** ɪz əz
Minter ˈmɪnt ə ‖ ˈmɪnţ ᵊr
Minto ˈmɪnt əʊ ‖ -oʊ
Minton ˈmɪnt ən ‖ -ᵊn
minty, Minty ˈmɪnt i ‖ ˈmɪnţ i
minuend ˈmɪn ju end **~s** z
minuet ˌmɪn ju ˈet **~s** s
minus ˈmaɪn əs **~es** ɪz əz
ˌminus ˈone; **ˈminus sign**
minuscule ˈmɪn ə skjuːl -ɪ- ‖ mɪ ˈnʌsk juːl **~s** z

M

minute *adj 'tiny'* maɪ 'njuːt ˌ'· ‖ -'nuːt -'njuːt **~ly** li
min|ute *n, v* 'mɪn |ɪt §-ət ‖ -|ət **~uted** ɪt ɪd §ət-, -əd ‖ əṭ əd **~utes** ɪts §əts ‖ əts **~uting** ɪt ɪŋ §ət- ‖ əṭ ɪŋ
'minute hand; **'minute steak**
minute|man, M~ 'mɪn ɪt |mæn §-ət- **~men** men
minuteness maɪ 'njuːt nəs ˌ·-, -nɪs ‖ -'nuːt- -'njuːt-
minuti|a maɪ 'njuːʃ i‿|ə mɪ-, mə-, -'nuːʃ-, -'njuːt-, -'nuːt- ‖ -'nuːʃ- -'njuːʃ- **~ae** iː aɪ
minx mɪŋks **minxes** 'mɪŋks ɪz -əz
Miocene 'maɪ‿ə siːn
MIPS, mips mɪps
Miquelon 'miːk ə lɒn ‖ -lɑːn -lɔːn —*Fr* [mi klɔ̃]
Mir mɪə ‖ mɪᵊr —*Russ* [mʲir]
Mira 'maɪᵊr ə 'mɪr-
Mirabeau 'mɪr ə bəʊ ‖ -boʊ —*Fr* [mi ʁa bo]
Mirabel 'mɪr ə bel
miracle 'mɪr ək ᵊl -ɪk- **~s** z
'miracle drug; **'miracle play**
miraculous mə 'ræk jʊl əs mɪ-, -jəl- ‖ -jəl- **~ly** li **~ness** nəs nɪs
mirag|e, M~ 'mɪr ɑːʒ mə 'rɑːʒ, mɪ- ‖ mə 'rɑːʒ **~es** ɪz əz
Miranda mə 'rænd ə mɪ-
MIRAS 'maɪᵊr əs -æs
mire 'maɪ‿ə ‖ 'maɪ‿ᵊr **mired** 'maɪ‿əd ‖ 'maɪ‿ᵊrd **mires** 'maɪ‿əz ‖ 'maɪ‿ᵊrz **miring** 'maɪ‿ər ɪŋ ‖ 'maɪ‿ᵊr ɪŋ
mirepoix ˌmɪə 'pwɑː ‖ mɪr- —*Fr* [miʁ pwa]
Mirfield 'mɜː fiːᵊld ‖ 'mɜ˞ː-
Mirfin 'mɜːf ɪn §-ᵊn ‖ 'mɜ˞ːf-
Miriam 'mɪr i‿əm
mirk mɜːk ‖ mɜ˞ːk
mirk|y 'mɜːk |i ‖ 'mɜ˞ːk |i **~ier** i‿ə ‖ i‿ᵊr **~iest** i‿ɪst i‿əst **~ily** ɪ li əl i **~iness** i nəs i nɪs
Miró mɪ 'rəʊ ‖ -'roʊ —*Sp, Catalan* [mi 'ro]
Mirren 'mɪr ən
Mirro *tdmk* 'mɪr əʊ ‖ -oʊ
mirror 'mɪr ə ‖ -ᵊr **~ed** d **mirroring** 'mɪr ər ɪŋ **~s** z
ˌmirror 'image, '· · ˌ· ·; **'mirror ˌwriting**
mirth mɜːθ ‖ mɜ˞ːθ
mirthful 'mɜːθ fᵊl -fʊl ‖ 'mɜ˞ːθ-
mirthless 'mɜːθ ləs -lɪs ‖ 'mɜ˞ːθ- **~ly** li
MIRV mɜːv ‖ mɜ˞ːv **~ed** d **~ing** ɪŋ **~s** z
mir|y 'maɪᵊr |i **~ier** i‿ə ‖ i‿ᵊr **~iest** i‿ɪst i‿əst **~iness** i nəs i nɪs
mis- ˌmɪs
misadventure ˌmɪs əd 'ventʃ ə §-æd- ‖ -ᵊr **~s** z
misadvis|e ˌmɪs əd 'vaɪz §-æd- **~ed** d **~es** ɪz əz **~ing** ɪŋ
misalign ˌmɪs ə 'laɪn **~ed** d **~ing** ɪŋ **~ment/s** mənt/s **~s** z
misallianc|e ˌmɪs ə 'laɪ‿ənᵗs **~es** ɪz əz
misandry mɪs 'ændr i 'mɪs ᵊndr i
misanthrope 'mɪs ᵊn θrəʊp 'mɪz-, -æn- ‖ -θroʊp **~s** s
misanthropic ˌmɪs ᵊn 'θrɒp ɪk ◂ ˌmɪz-, æn- ‖ -'θrɑːp- **~ally** ᵊl‿i
misanthropist mɪs 'ænᵗθ rəp ɪst mɪz-, §-əst **~s** s
misanthropy mɪs 'ænᵗθ rəp i mɪz-
misapplication ˌmɪs ˌæp lɪ 'keɪʃ ᵊn -lə'- **~s** z
misap|ply ˌmɪs ə |'plaɪ **~plied** 'plaɪd **~plies** 'plaɪz **~plying** 'plaɪ ɪŋ
misapprehend ˌmɪs ˌæp rɪ 'hend -rə- **~ed** ɪd əd **~ing** ɪŋ **~s** z
misapprehension ˌmɪs ˌæp rɪ 'henᵗʃ ᵊn -rə- **~s** z
misappropri|ate ˌmɪs ə 'prəʊp ri |eɪt ‖ -'proʊp- **~ated** eɪt ɪd -əd ‖ eɪṭ əd **~ates** eɪts **~ating** eɪt ɪŋ ‖ eɪṭ ɪŋ
misappropriation ˌmɪs ə ˌprəʊp ri 'eɪʃ ᵊn ‖ -ˌproʊp- **~s** z
misbegotten ˌmɪs bi 'gɒt ᵊn ◂ -bə- ‖ -'gɑːt ᵊn
misbehav|e ˌmɪs bi 'heɪv -bə- **~ed** d **~es** z **~ing** ɪŋ
misbehavior, misbehaviour ˌmɪs bi 'heɪv jə -bə- ‖ -jᵊr **~s** z
misc. —*see* **miscellaneous**
miscalcu|late ˌmɪs 'kælk ju |leɪt -jə- ‖ -jə- **~lated** leɪt ɪd -əd ‖ leɪṭ əd **~lates** leɪts **~lating** leɪt ɪŋ ‖ leɪṭ ɪŋ
miscalculation ˌmɪs ˌkælk ju 'leɪʃ ᵊn -jə- ‖ -jə- **~s** z
miscall ˌmɪs 'kɔːl ‖ -'kɑːl **~ed** d **~ing** ɪŋ **~s** z
Miscampbell mɪ 'skæm bᵊl
miscarriag|e ₍ˌ₎mɪs 'kær ɪdʒ ◂ 'ˌ· · ‖ 'ˌ· · · ˌker- **~es** ɪz əz
misˌcarriage of 'justice ‖ ˌ·ˌ·-
miscarr|y ₍ˌ₎mɪs 'kær |i 'ˌ· · ‖ -'ker- **~ied** id **~ies** iz **~ying** i ɪŋ
miscast ˌmɪs 'kɑːst §-'kæst ‖ -'kæst **~ing** ɪŋ **~s** s
miscegenation ˌmɪs ɪdʒ ə 'neɪʃ ᵊn ˌ·ədʒ-, -ɪ'-; mɪ ˌsedʒ-, mə-
miscellanea ˌmɪs ə 'leɪn i‿ə
miscellaneous ˌmɪs ə 'leɪn i‿əs ◂ **~ly** li **~ness** nəs nɪs
miscellanist mɪ 'sel ən ɪst mə-, §-əst; 'mɪs ə leɪn- ‖ 'mɪs ə leɪn- **~s** s
miscellan|y mɪ 'sel ən |i mə-, 'mɪs ə leɪn |i ‖ 'mɪs ə leɪn |i *(*)* **~ies** iz
mischance ˌmɪs 'tʃɑːnᵗs →§ˌmɪʃ-, §-'tʃænᵗs, '· · ‖ -'tʃænᵗs
mischief 'mɪs tʃɪf →§'mɪʃ-, §-tʃəf, §-tʃiːf **~s** s
mischief-mak|er 'mɪs tʃɪf ˌmeɪk| ə →§'mɪʃ-, §-tʃəf-, §-tʃiːf- ‖ -ᵊr **~ers** əz ‖ ᵊrz **~ing** ɪŋ
mischievous 'mɪs tʃɪv əs →§'mɪʃ-, -tʃəv-; mɪs 'tʃiːv-, -i‿əs — *Preference polls, (stress) AmE:* 'mɪs- *67%,* -'tʃiːv əs *22%* -'tʃiːv i‿əs *11%; BrE:* 'mɪs- *65% (born since 1981: 49%),* -'tʃiːv əs *20% (born since 1981: 22%);* 'tʃiːv i‿əs *15% (born since 1981: 29%);* -i‿əs *40%.* **~ly** li **~ness** nəs nɪs
miscible 'mɪs əb ᵊl -ɪb-
misconceiv|e ˌmɪs kən 'siːv §-kɒn- **~ed** d **~es** z **~ing** ɪŋ
misconception ˌmɪs kən 'sep ʃᵊn §-kɒn- **~s** z
misconduct *n* ˌmɪs 'kɒn dʌkt ‖ -'kɑːn-
misconduct *v* ˌmɪs kən 'dʌkt §-kɒn- **~ed** ɪd əd **~ing** ɪŋ **~s** s

MISCHIEVOUS

misconstruction ˌmɪs kən 'strʌk ʃᵊn §-kɒn- **~s** z
misconstru|e ˌmɪs kən 'struː §-kɒn- **~ed** d **~es** z **~ing** ɪŋ
miscount *n* 'mɪs kaʊnt ˌ·'· **~s** s
mis|count *v* ˌmɪs |'kaʊnt **~counted** 'kaʊnt ɪd -əd ‖ 'kaʊnṱ əd **~counting** 'kaʊnt ɪŋ ‖ 'kaʊnṱ ɪŋ **~counts** 'kaʊnts
miscreant 'mɪs kri̯ənt **~s** s
miscu|e *v, n* mɪs 'kjuː **~ed** d **~es** z **~ing** ɪŋ
mis|date *v* ˌmɪs |'deɪt **~dated** 'deɪt ɪd -əd ‖ 'deɪṱ əd **~dates** 'deɪts **~dating** 'deɪt ɪŋ ‖ 'deɪṱ ɪŋ
misdeal *n* ˌmɪs 'diːᵊl '· · **~s** z
misdeal *v* ˌmɪs 'diːᵊl **~ing** ɪŋ **~s** z **misdealt** ˌmɪs 'delt
misdeed ˌmɪs 'diːd '· · **~s** z
misdemeanor, misdemeanour ˌmɪs di 'miːn ə -də- ‖ -ᵊr **~s** z
misdiagnos|e ˌmɪs 'daɪ‿əg nəʊz -nəʊz, -ˌ·ˌ·'· ‖ -ˌdaɪ əg 'noʊs -'·. **~ed** d **~es** ɪz əz **~ing** ɪŋ
misdirect ˌmɪs də 'rekt -dɪ-, -daɪᵊ- **~ed** ɪd əd **~ing** ɪŋ **~s** s
misdirection ˌmɪs də 'rek ʃᵊn -dɪ-, -daɪᵊ- **~s** z
misdoing ˌmɪs 'duː‿ɪŋ '·ˌ·· **~s** z
mise-en-scene, mise-en-scène ˌmiːz ɒn 'seɪn -'sen ‖ -ɑːn- —*Fr* [mi zɑ̃ sɛn]
miser 'maɪz ə ‖ -ᵊr **~s** z
miserab|le 'mɪz ər‿əb |ᵊl →'mɪʒ rəb |ᵊl ‖ 'mɪz ᵊrb |ᵊl **~leness** ᵊl nəs -nɪs **~ly** li
misere, misère mɪ 'zeə §mə- ‖ -'zeᵊr
miserere, M~ ˌmɪz ə 'reər i -'rɪər-, -eɪ ‖ -'rer- -'rɪr-
misericord mɪ 'zer ɪ kɔːd mə-, -ə- ‖ -kɔːrd **~s** z
miserie... —*see* **misery**
miser|ly 'maɪz ə |li -ᵊ|l i ‖ -ᵊr- **~liness** li nəs li nɪs
miser|y 'mɪz ər‿|i →'mɪʒ r|i **~ies** iz
misfeasanc|e ₍ˌ₎mɪs 'fiːz ᵊnᵗs **~es** ɪz əz
misfield *n.* 'mɪs fiːᵊld **~s** z
misfield *v.* ˌmɪs 'fiːᵊld **~ed** d **~ing** ɪŋ **~s** z
misfire *v* ˌmɪs 'faɪ‿ə ‖ -'faɪ‿ᵊr **~d** d **~s** z
misfiring ˌmɪs 'faɪ‿ər ɪŋ ‖ -'faɪ‿ᵊr ɪŋ
misfire *n* ˌmɪs 'faɪ‿ə '·ˌ· ‖ -'faɪ‿ᵊr '·ˌ· **~s** z
misfit 'mɪs fɪt ˌ·'· **~s** s
misfortune mɪs 'fɔːtʃ ən -uːn ‖ -'fɔːrtʃ- **~s** z
misgiving ₍ˌ₎mɪs 'gɪv ɪŋ **~s** z
misgovern ˌmɪs 'gʌv ᵊn ‖ -ᵊrn **~ed** d **~ing** ɪŋ **~s** z
misguided ₍ˌ₎mɪs 'gaɪd ɪd -əd **~ly** li
mishandl|e ˌmɪs 'hænd ᵊl **~ed** d **~es** z **~ing** ɪŋ
mishap 'mɪs hæp ₍ˌ₎·'· **~s** s
Mishcon 'mɪʃ kɒn ‖ -kɑːn
ˌ**Mishcon de 'Reya** də 'reɪ ə
mis|hear ˌmɪs |'hɪə ‖ -|'hɪᵊr **~heard** 'hɜːd ◂ ‖ 'hɜːd ◂ **~hearing** 'hɪər ɪŋ ‖ 'hɪr ɪŋ **~hears** 'hɪəz ‖ 'hɪᵊrz
Mishima 'mɪʃ ɪm ə 'miːʃ- —*Jp* [mi ˌɕi ma]
mis|hit *v* ˌmɪs |'hɪt **~hits** 'hɪts **~hitting** 'hɪt ɪŋ ‖ 'hɪṱ ɪŋ
mishit *n* 'mɪs hɪt ˌ·'· **~s** s
mishmash 'mɪʃ mæʃ ‖ -mɑːʃ -mæʃ *(*)*
Mishna, Mishnah mɪʃ nə
misinform ˌmɪs ɪn 'fɔːm §-ᵊn- ‖ -'fɔːrm **~ed** d **~ing** ɪŋ **~s** z
misinformation ˌmɪs ɪn fə 'meɪʃ ᵊn §ˌ·ᵊn- ‖ -ɪn fᵊr-
misinterp|ret ˌmɪs ɪn 'tɜːp |rɪt §-ᵊn-, -rət ‖ -'tɜːp |rət -ət **~reted** rɪt ɪd §rət-, -əd ‖ rəṱ əd əṱ- **~reting** rɪt ɪŋ §rət- ‖ rəṱ ɪŋ əṱ- **~rets** rɪts §rəts ‖ rəts əts
misinterpretation ˌmɪs ɪn ˌtɜːp rɪ 'teɪʃ ᵊn §ˌ·ᵊn-, -rə'- ‖ -ˌtɜːp rə- -ˌtɜːp ə- **~s** z
misjudg|e ˌmɪs 'dʒʌdʒ **~ed** d **~es** ɪz əz **~ing** ɪŋ
misjudgement, misjudgment ₍ˌ₎mɪs 'dʒʌdʒ mənt **~s** s
miskick *v*, ˌmɪs 'kɪk **~ed** t **~ing** ɪŋ **~s** s
miskick *n.* 'mɪs kɪk **~s** s
Miskin 'mɪsk ɪn §-ən
Miskito mɪ 'skiːt əʊ ‖ -oʊ
mis|lay ₍ˌ₎mɪs |'leɪ **~laid** 'leɪd **~laying** 'leɪ ɪŋ **~lays** 'leɪz
mis|lead ₍ˌ₎mɪs |'liːd **~leading/ly** 'liːd ɪŋ /li **~leads** 'liːdz **~led** 'led
mismanag|e ˌmɪs 'mæn ɪdʒ **~ed** d **~es** ɪz əz **~ing** ɪŋ
mismanagement ˌmɪs 'mæn ɪdʒ mənt
mismatch *v* ˌmɪs 'mætʃ **~ed** t **~es** ɪz əz **~ing** ɪŋ
mismatch *n* 'mɪs mætʃ ˌ·'· **~es** ɪz əz
mismeasure ˌmɪs 'meʒ ə ‖ -ᵊr -'meɪʒ- **~ment** mənt
misnam|e ˌmɪs 'neɪm **~ed** d **~es** z **~ing** ɪŋ
misnomer ˌmɪs 'nəʊm ə ‖ -'noʊm ᵊr **~s** z
miso 'miːs əʊ ‖ -oʊ —*Jp* ['mi so]
misogynist mɪ 'sɒdʒ ən ɪst maɪ-, mə-, -ɪn-, §-əst ‖ -'sɑːdʒ- **~s** s
misogynistic mɪ ˌsɒdʒ ə 'nɪst ɪk ◂ maɪ-, mə-, -ɪn-, §-əst ‖ ˌsɑːdʒ-
misogyny mɪ 'sɒdʒ ən i maɪ-, mə-, -ɪn- ‖ -'sɑːdʒ-
misplac|e ˌmɪs 'pleɪs **~ed** t ◂ **~es** ɪz əz **~ing** ɪŋ

M

misplacement ˌmɪs ˈpleɪs mənt
misprint *n* ˈmɪs prɪnt **~s** s
mis|print *v* ˌmɪs |ˈprɪnt **~printed** ˈprɪnt ɪd -əd ‖ ˈprɪnt̬ əd **~printing** ˈprɪnt ɪŋ ‖ ˈprɪnt̬ ɪŋ **~prints** ˈprɪnts
misprision ˌmɪs ˈprɪʒ ᵊn
mispronounc|e ˌmɪs prə ˈnaʊⁿts **~ed** t **~es** ɪz əz **~ing** ɪŋ
mispronunciation ˌmɪs prə ˌnʌⁿts i ˈeɪʃ ᵊn ⚠-ˌnaʊⁿts- **~s** z
misquotation ˌmɪs kwəʊ ˈteɪʃ ᵊn ‖ -kwoʊ- **~s** z
mis|quote ˌmɪs |ˈkwəʊt ‖ -|ˈkwoʊt **~quoted** ˈkwəʊt ɪd -əd ‖ ˈkwoʊt̬ əd **~quotes** ˈkwəʊts ‖ ˈkwoʊts **~quoting** ˈkwəʊt ɪŋ ‖ ˈkwoʊt̬ ɪŋ
mis|read *v pres* ˌmɪs |ˈriːd **~read** *v past & pp* ˈred **~reading** ˈriːd ɪŋ **~reads** ˈriːdz
misre|port ˌmɪs ri |ˈpɔːt -rə- ‖ -|ˈpɔːrt -|ˈpoʊrt **~ported** ˈpɔːt ɪd -əd ‖ ˈpɔːrt̬ əd ˈpoʊrt̬- **~porting** ˈpɔːt ɪŋ ‖ ˈpɔːrt̬ ɪŋ ˈpoʊrt̬- **~ports** ˈpɔːts ‖ ˈpɔːrts ˈpoʊrts
misrepre|sent ˌmɪs ˌrep ri |ˈzent -rə- ‖ ˌ·ˌ·- **~sented** ˈzent ɪd -əd ‖ ˈzent̬ əd **~senting** ˈzent ɪŋ ‖ ˈzent̬ ɪŋ **~sents** ˈzents
misrepresentation ˌmɪs ˌrep ri zen ˈteɪʃ ᵊn -ˌrə-, -zᵊn'-‖ ˌ·ˌ·- **~s** z
misrul|e *v, n* ˌmɪs ˈruːl **~ed** d **~es** z **~ing** ɪŋ
miss, Miss mɪs —*For the noun, when used with a name, there is also an occasional weak form* §məs **missed** mɪst **misses** ˈmɪs ɪz -əz **missing** ˈmɪs ɪŋ
⁽ˌ⁾**Miss ˈAbbott**; ˌ**missing ˈlink**
missa ˈmɪs ə
ˌ**missa ˈbrevis** ˈbrev ɪs ˈbreɪv-, §-əs
missal ˈmɪs ᵊl **~s** z
missel ˈmɪs ᵊl ˈmɪz-
mis-|sell ˌmɪs |ˈsel **~selling** ˈsel ɪŋ **~sells** ˈselz **~sold** ˈsəʊld →ˈsɒʊld ‖ -ˈsoʊld
Missenden ˈmɪs ᵊnd ən
misshape *n* ˈmɪs ʃeɪp →ˈmɪʃ- **~s** s
misshap|e *v* ˌmɪs ˈʃeɪp →ˌmɪʃ- **~ed** t **~en** ən **~es** s **~ing** ɪŋ
missile ˈmɪs aɪᵊl -ᵊl ‖ -ᵊl **~s** z
mission ˈmɪʃ ᵊn **~s** z
missionar|y ˈmɪʃ ᵊn ər‿|i -ᵊn‿ər- ‖ -ə ner |i **~ies** iz
ˈ**missionary poˌsition**
missioner ˈmɪʃ ᵊn‿ə ‖ ər **~s** z
missis ˈmɪs ɪz §-əz
Mississauga ˌmɪs ɪ ˈsɔːg ə -ə- ‖ -ˈsɑːg-
Mississippi ˌmɪs ɪ ˈsɪp i -ə-
ˌ**MissisˌsippiˈDelta**
Mississippian ˌmɪs ɪ ˈsɪp i‿ən ◂ ˌ·ə- **~s** z
missive ˈmɪs ɪv **~s** z
Missolonghi ˌmɪs ə ˈlɒŋ gi ‖ -ˈlɔːŋ- -ˈlɑːŋ-
Missoula mɪ ˈzuːl ə mə-
Missouri mɪ ˈzʊər i mə-, -ˈsʊər- ‖ -ˈzʊr i -ˈzɜː-, -ə
Missourian mɪ ˈzʊər i‿ən mə-, -ˈsʊər- ‖ -ˈzʊr- -ˈzɜː- **~s** z
misspell ˌmɪs ˈspel **~ed** d **~ing** ɪŋ **~s** z **misspelt** ˌmɪs ˈspelt ◂
misspend ˌmɪs ˈspend **~ing** ɪŋ **~s** z **misspent** ˌmɪs ˈspent ◂
ˌ**misspent ˈyouth**
mis|state ˌmɪs |ˈsteɪt **~stated** ˈsteɪt ɪd -əd ‖ ˈsteɪt̬ əd **~states** ˈsteɪts **~stating** ˈsteɪt ɪŋ ‖ ˈsteɪt̬ ɪŋ
misstatement ˌmɪs ˈsteɪt mənt **~s** s
misstep *n.* ˈmɪs step **~s** s
missus ˈmɪs ɪz §-əz ‖ ˈmɪs əz ˈmɪz-, -əs
miss|y, Missy ˈmɪs |i **~ies** iz
mist mɪst **misted** ˈmɪst ɪd -əd **misting** ˈmɪst ɪŋ **mists** mɪsts
mistak|e *v, n* mɪ ˈsteɪk mə- **~en** ən **~es** s **~ing** ɪŋ **mistook** mɪ ˈstʊk mə-, §-ˈstuːk
mistaken mɪ ˈsteɪk ən mə- **~ly** li **~ness** nəs nɪs
mister, M~ ˈmɪst ə ‖ -ᵊr **~s** z
⁽ˌ⁾**Mister ˈJones**
misti... —*see* **misty**
mistim|e ˌmɪs ˈtaɪm **~ed** d **~es** z **~ing** ɪŋ
mistle ˈmɪs ᵊl ˈmɪz-
ˈ**mistle thrush**
mistletoe ˈmɪs ᵊl təʊ ˈmɪz- ‖ -toʊ
mistook mɪ ˈstʊk mə-, §-ˈstuːk
mistral ˈmɪs trəl -trɑːl; mɪ ˈstrɑːl, mə- —*Fr* [mis tʁal]
mistrans|late ˌmɪs trænz ˈ|leɪt -trɑːnz-, -trænᵗs-, -trɑːnᵗs-, -trənz-, -trənᵗs- ‖ -ˈ|·ˌ· **~lated** leɪt ɪd -əd ‖ leɪt̬ əd **~lates** leɪts **~lating** leɪt ɪŋ ‖ leɪt̬ ɪŋ
mistranslation ˌmɪs trænz ˈleɪʃ ᵊn -trɑːnz-, -trænᵗs-, -trɑːnᵗs-, -trənz-, -trənᵗs- **~s** z
mis|treat ˌmɪs |ˈtriːt **~treated** ˈtriːt ɪd -əd ‖ ˈtriːt̬ əd **~treating** ˈtriːt ɪŋ ‖ ˈtriːt̬ ɪŋ **~treats** ˈtriːts
mistreatment ˌmɪs ˈtriːt mənt **~s** s
mistress, M~ ˈmɪs trəs -trɪs **~es** ɪz əz
mistrial ˌmɪs ˈtraɪ‿əl ˈ·ˌ·· **~s** z
mistrust *v, n* ˌmɪs ˈtrʌst **~ed** ɪd əd **~ing/ly** ɪŋ /li **~s** s
mistrustful ˌmɪs ˈtrʌst fᵊl -fʊl **~ly** ‿i **~ness** nəs nɪs
mist|y ˈmɪst |i **~ier** i‿ə ‖ i‿ᵊr **~iest** i‿ɪst i‿əst **~ily** ɪ li əl i **~iness** i nəs i nɪs
misty-eyed ˌmɪst i ˈaɪd ◂
misunder|stand ˌmɪs ˌʌnd ə |ˈstænd ‖ -ᵊr- ·ˌ·- **~standing/s** ˈstænd ɪŋ/z **~stands** ˈstændz **~stood** ˈstʊd
misus|e *n* ˌmɪs ˈjuːs →§ˌmɪʃ- **~es** ɪz əz
misus|e *v* ˌmɪs ˈjuːz →§ˌmɪʃ- **~ed** d **~es** ɪz əz **~ing** ɪŋ
MIT ˌem aɪ ˈtiː ◂
Mita ˈmiːt ə ‖ ˈmiːt̬ ə
Mitch, mitch mɪtʃ
Mitcham ˈmɪtʃ əm
Mitchel, Mitchell ˈmɪtʃ əl
Mitchison ˈmɪtʃ ɪs ən -əs-
Mitchum ˈmɪtʃ əm
mite maɪt *(= might)* **mites** maɪts
miter ˈmaɪt ə ‖ ˈmaɪt̬ ᵊr **~ed** d **mitering** ˈmaɪt ər ɪŋ ‖ ˈmaɪt̬ ər ɪŋ **~s** z
Mitford ˈmɪt fəd ‖ -fᵊrd
Mithraic mɪ ˈθreɪ ɪk
Mithraism ˈmɪθ reɪ ˌɪz əm -rə-; mɪθ ˈreɪˌ··

Mithraist 'mɪθ reɪ ɪst -rə-, §-əst; mɪθ 'reɪ- **~s** s
Mithras 'mɪθ ræs -rəs
Mithridates ˌmɪθ rə 'deɪt iːz -rɪ-
mitiǀgate 'mɪt ɪ ǀgeɪt §-ə- ‖ 'mɪţ ə- **~gated** geɪt ɪd -əd ‖ geɪţ əd **~gates** geɪts **~gating** geɪt ɪŋ ‖ geɪţ ɪŋ
mitigation ˌmɪt ɪ 'geɪʃ ən §-ə- ‖ ˌmɪţ ə-
mitochondriǀon ˌmaɪt əʊ 'kɒndr i̯ǀən ‖ ˌmaɪţ ə 'kɑːndr- **~a** ə **~al** əl
mitosis ₍ˌ₎maɪ 'təʊs ɪs §-əs ‖ -'toʊs əs
mitrailleuse ˌmɪtr aɪ 'ɜːz ‖ -ə 'jɜːz —*Fr* [mi tʁa jøːz]
mitral 'maɪtr əl
mitrǀe 'maɪt ə ‖ 'maɪţ ər **~ed** d **~es** z **mitring** 'maɪt ˌər ɪŋ ‖ 'maɪţ ər ɪŋ
'mitre joint
Mitsubishi *tdmk* ˌmɪts u 'bɪʃ i ‖ ˌmiːts uː 'biːʃ iː —*Jp* [mi ˌtsɯ 'bi ɕi]
mitt mɪt **mitts** mɪts
mitten 'mɪt ən **~s** z
Mitterand 'miːt ə rõ 'mɪt- ‖ -rɑːn —*Fr* [mi tɛ ʁɑ̃]
Mitton 'mɪt ən
Mitty 'mɪt i ‖ 'mɪţ i **~ish** ɪʃ
Mitylene ˌmɪt ə 'liːn i -ɪ-, →-əl 'iːn- ‖ ˌmɪţ-
Mitzi 'mɪts i
mitzvah 'mɪts və
Miwok 'miː wɒk ‖ -wɑːk **~s** s
mix mɪks **mixed** mɪkst **mixes** 'mɪks ɪz -əz **mixing** 'mɪks ɪŋ
ˌmixed 'bag; **ˌmixed 'blessing**; **ˌmixed 'doubles**; **ˌmixed e'conomy**; **ˌmixed 'farming**; **ˌmixed 'grill**; **ˌmixed 'marriage**; **ˌmixed 'metaphor**
mix-and-match ˌmɪks ən 'mætʃ ◂ -ənd-
mixed-ability ˌmɪkst ə 'bɪl ət i -ɪt i ‖ -əţ i
mixed up, mixed-up ˌmɪkst 'ʌp ◂
ˌmixed-up 'kid
mixer 'mɪks ə ‖ -ər **~s** z
mixologist mɪk 'sɒl ədʒ ɪst §-əst ‖ -'sɑːl- **~s** s
mixtape 'mɪks teɪp **~s** s
Mixtec 'miːs tek **~s** s
mixture 'mɪks tʃə ‖ -tʃər **~s** z
mix-up 'mɪks ʌp **~s** s
Miyake mɪ 'jæk i ‖ mɪ 'jɑːk i —*Jp* [mi ˌja ke]
mizen, mizzen 'mɪz ən **~s** z
mizuna mɪ 'zuːn ə
mizzenmast 'mɪz ən mɑːst →-əm-, §-mæst ‖ -mæst **~s** s
mizzlǀe 'mɪz əl **~ed** d **~es** z **~ing** ˌɪŋ
ml *sing.* 'mɪl i ˌliːt ə -ə- ‖ -ə ˌliːţ ər *pl* z
m'lady mɪ 'leɪd i mə-
M'lord mɪ 'lɔːd mə- ‖ -'lɔːrd
M'lud mɪ 'lʌd mə-
mm *sing.* 'mɪl i ˌmiːt ə -ə- ‖ -ə ˌmiːţ ər *pl* z
mnemonic nɪ 'mɒn ɪk nə-, niː-, mnɪ- ‖ -'mɑːn- **~ally** əl i̯ **~s** s
Mnemosyne ni 'mɒz ɪn i nə-, mni-, -'mɒs-, -ən- ‖ -'mɑːs ən i -'mɑːz-
mo, Mo məʊ ‖ moʊ
MO ˌem 'əʊ ‖ -'oʊ —*also see* Missouri
-mo məʊ ‖ moʊ — **twelvemo** 'twelv məʊ ‖ -moʊ

moa 'məʊ ə ‖ 'moʊ ə **~s** z
Moab 'məʊ æb ‖ 'moʊ-
Moabite 'məʊ ə baɪt ‖ 'moʊ- **~s** s
moan məʊn ‖ moʊn **moaned** məʊnd ‖ moʊnd **moaning** 'məʊn ɪŋ ‖ 'moʊn ɪŋ **moans** məʊnz ‖ moʊnz
moaner 'məʊn ə ‖ 'moʊn ər **~s** z
moat, Moat məʊt ‖ moʊt **moated** 'məʊt ɪd -əd ‖ 'moʊţ əd **moating** 'məʊt ɪŋ ‖ 'moʊţ ɪŋ **moats** məʊts ‖ moʊts
mob mɒb ‖ mɑːb **mobbed** mɒbd ‖ mɑːbd **mobbing** 'mɒbɪŋ ‖ 'mɑːb ɪŋ **mobs** mɒbz ‖ mɑːbz
Mobberley 'mɒb ə li ‖ 'mɑːb ər-
mobcap 'mɒb kæp ‖ 'mɑːb- **~s** s
mobe məʊb ‖ moʊb **mobes** məʊbz ‖ moʊbz
Moberly 'məʊb ə li ‖ 'moʊb ər-
Mobil *tdmk* 'məʊb əl -ɪl ‖ 'moʊb-
mobile 'məʊb aɪəl ‖ 'moʊb əl -iːəl, -aɪəl **~s** z
ˌmobile 'home ‖ '. . .; **ˌmobile 'library**; **ˌmobile 'phone**
Mobile *place in AL* məʊ 'biːəl 'məʊb iːəl ‖ moʊ 'biːəl 'moʊb iːəl
mobilis... *see* **mobiliz...**
mobility məʊ 'bɪl ət i -ɪt i ‖ moʊ 'bɪl əţ i
mobilization ˌməʊb əl aɪ 'zeɪʃ ən ˌ·ɪl-, -ɪ'·- ‖ ˌmoʊb əl ə- **~s** z
mobilizǀe 'məʊb ə laɪz -ɪ-, -əl aɪz ‖ 'moʊb- **~ed** d **~es** ɪz əz **~ing** ɪŋ
Mobius, Möbius, m~ 'mɜːb i̯əs 'məʊb- ‖ 'moʊb- 'meɪb- —*Ger* ['møː bi ʊs]
ˌMobius 'strip ‖ '. . . .
mobster 'mɒb stə ‖ 'mɑːb stər **~s** z
Mobutu məʊ 'buːt uː ‖ moʊ-
Moby 'məʊb i ‖ 'moʊb i
ˌMoby 'Dick
Mocatta məʊ 'kæt ə ‖ moʊ 'kæţ ə
moccasin 'mɒk əs ɪn §-ən ‖ 'mɑːk- **~s** z
mocha, Mocha 'mɒk ə 'məʊk- ‖ 'moʊk ə
mochaccino ˌmɒk ə 'tʃiːn əʊ ‖ ˌmoʊk ə 'tʃiːn oʊ **~s** z
mock mɒk ‖ mɑːk mɔːk **mocked** mɒkt ‖ mɑːkt mɔːkt **mocking/ly** 'mɒk ɪŋ /li ‖ 'mɑːk ɪŋ /li 'mɔːk- **mocks** mɒks ‖ mɑːks mɔːks
ˌmock ˌturtle 'soup
mocker 'mɒk ə ‖ 'mɑːk ər 'mɔːk- **~s** z
mockerǀy 'mɒk ər ǀi ‖ 'mɑk- 'mɔːk- **~ies** iz
mock-heroic ˌmɒk hə 'rəʊ ɪk ◂ -hɪ-, -he- ‖ ˌmɑːk hɪ 'roʊ ɪk ◂ ˌmɔːk- **~ally** əl i̯ **~s** s
mockingbird 'mɒk ɪŋ bɜːd ‖ 'mɑːk ɪŋ bɜːd 'mɔːk- **~s** z
mockney 'mɒk ni ‖ 'mɑːk-
mock-up 'mɒk ʌp ‖ 'mɑːk- 'mɔːk- **~s** s
mod, Mod *'Gaelic meeting'* mɒd məʊd ‖ moʊd —*ScG* Mòd [moːd]
mod, Mod *'modern; (adherent of, pertaining to) fashion style'* mɒd ‖ mɑːd **mods** mɒdz ‖ mɑːdz
ˌmod 'con
MoD *'Ministry of Defence'* ˌem əʊ 'diː ◂ ‖ -oʊ-
modacrylic ˌmɒd ə 'krɪl ɪk ◂ ‖ ˌmɑːd-
ˌmodaˌcrylic 'fibre

M

modal ˈməʊd ᵊl ‖ ˈmoʊd ᵊl **~s** z
ˌ**modal auˈxiliary**
modalit|y məʊ ˈdæl ət |i -ɪt- ‖ moʊ ˈdæl əţ |i **~ies** iz
modally ˈməʊd ᵊl i ‖ ˈmoʊd ᵊl i
mode məʊd ‖ moʊd **modes** məʊdz ‖ moʊdz
model ˈmɒd ᵊl ‖ ˈmɑːd ᵊl **~ed, ~led** d **~er/s, ~ler/s** ‿ə/z ‖ ‿ᵊr/z **~ing, ~ling** ‿ɪŋ **~z** z
modem ˈməʊd em -əm ‖ ˈmoʊd- **~s** z
Modena ˈmɒd ɪn ə -ᵊn ə; mɒ ˈdeɪn ə, mə- ‖ ˈmoʊd ᵊn ə ˈmɔːd-, ˈmɑːd-, -ɑː —*It* [ˈmɔː de na]
moderate *adj, n* ˈmɒd ‿ər ət -ɪt ‖ ˈmɑːd ‿ **~ly** li **~ness** nəs nɪs **~s** s
mode|rate *v* ˈmɒd ə |reɪt ‖ ˈmɑːd- **~rated** reɪt ɪd -əd ‖ reɪţ əd **~rates** reɪts **~rating** reɪt ɪŋ ‖ reɪţ ɪŋ
moderation ˌmɒd ə ˈreɪʃ ᵊn ‖ ˌmɑːd- **~s** z
moderato ˌmɒd ə ˈrɑːt əʊ ‖ ˌmɑːd ə ˈrɑːţ oʊ **~s** z
moderator ˈmɒd ə reɪt ə ‖ ˈmɑːd ə reɪţ ᵊr **~s** z
modern ˈmɒd ᵊn ‖ ˈmɑːd ᵊrn **~ly** li **~ness** nəs nɪs **~s** z
ˌ**Modern ˈEnglish◂, ˌModern ˌEnglish ˈLanguage**; ˌ**Modern ˈGreek**; ˌ**modern ˈjazz**; ˌ**modern penˈtathlon**
modern-day ˌmɒd ᵊn ˈdeɪ◂ ‖ ˌmɑːd ᵊrn-
modernis... —*see* **moderniz...**
modernism ˈmɒd ə ˌnɪz əm -ᵊn ˌɪz- ‖ ˈmɑːd ᵊr-
modernist ˈmɒd ən ɪst §-əst ‖ ˈmɑːd ᵊrn- **~s** s
modernistic ˌmɒd ə ˈnɪst ɪk ◂ -ᵊn ˈɪst- ‖ ˌmɑːd ᵊr- **~ally** ᵊl ‿i
modernit|y mɒ ˈdɜːn ət |i mə-, -ɪt- ‖ mɑː ˈdɜːn əţ |i moʊ-, mə- **~ies** iz
modernization ˌmɒd ə naɪ ˈzeɪʃ ᵊn -nɪˈ--; -ᵊn ‿aɪ-, -ᵊn ‿ɪ- ‖ ˌmɑːd ᵊrn ə- **~s** z
moderniz|e ˈmɒd ə naɪz -ᵊn aɪz ‖ ˈmɑːd ᵊr- **~ed** d **~er/s** ə/z ‖ ᵊr/z **~es** ɪz əz **~ing** ɪŋ
modest ˈmɒd ɪst §-əst ‖ ˈmɑːd əst **~ly** li
Modestine ˈmɒd ɪ stiːn -ə-, ˌ· ·ˈ· ‖ ˈmɑːd-
Modesto mə ˈdest əʊ ‖ -oʊ
modest|y, M~ ˈmɒd əst |i -ɪst- ‖ ˈmɑːd- **~ies** iz
modicum ˈmɒd ɪk əm -ək- ‖ ˈmɑːd- ˈmoʊd- **~s** z
modification ˌmɒd ɪf ɪ ˈkeɪʃ ᵊn ˌ-əf-, §-əˈ-- ‖ ˌmɑːd- **~s** z
modi|fy ˈmɒd ɪ |faɪ -ə- ‖ ˈmɑːd- **~fied** faɪd **~fier/s** faɪ ‿ə/z ‖ faɪ ‿ᵊr/z **~fies** faɪz **~fying** faɪ ɪŋ
Modigliani ˌmɒd ɪl ˈjɑːn i ‖ ˌmoʊd iːl- moʊ ˌdiːl i ˈɑːn i —*It* [mo diʎ ˈʎaː ni]
modiolus məʊ ˈdiː‿əl əs -ˈdaɪ‿ ‖ moʊ ˈdaɪ əl əs mə-
modish ˈməʊd ɪʃ ‖ ˈmoʊd- **~ly** li **~ness** nəs nɪs
modiste məʊ ˈdiːst ‖ moʊ- **~s** s
modular ˈmɒd jʊl ə -jəl-; →ˈmɒdʒ ʊl ə, -əl- ‖ ˈmɑːdʒ əl ᵊr
modularis... —*see* **modulariz...**
modularity ˌmɒd ju ˈlær ət i →ˌmɒdʒ u-, -ɪt i ‖ ˌmɑːdʒ ə ˈlær əţ i -ˈler-
modularization ˌmɒd jʊl ər aɪ ˈzeɪʃ ᵊn ˌjəl-, -ɪˈ--; →ˌmɒdʒ ʊl-, ˌ·əl- ‖ ˌmɑːdʒ əl ər ə-
modulariz|e ˈmɒd jʊl ə raɪz ˈ·jəl-; →ˈmɒdʒ ʊl-, ˈ·əl- ‖ ˈmɑːdʒ əl ə raɪz **~ed** d **~es** ɪz əz **~ing** ɪŋ
modu|late ˈmɒd ju |leɪt →ˈmɒdʒ u-, -ə- ‖ ˈmɑːdʒ ə- **~lated** leɪt ɪd -əd ‖ leɪţ əd **~lates** leɪts **~lating** leɪt ɪŋ ‖ leɪţ ɪŋ
modulation ˌmɒd ju ˈleɪʃ ᵊn →ˌmɒdʒ u-, ˌ·ə- ‖ ˌmɑːdʒ ə- **~s** z
module ˈmɒd juːl →ˈmɒdʒ uːl ‖ ˈmɑːdʒ uːᵊl **~s** z
modulo ˈmɒd ju ləʊ -jə- ‖ ˈmɑːdʒ ə loʊ
modulus ˈmɒd jʊl əs -jəl- ‖ ˈmɑːdʒ əl əs
moduli mɒd ju laɪ -liː ‖ ˈmɑːdʒ ə laɪ
modus ˈməʊd əs ˈmɒd- ‖ ˈmoʊd əs
ˌ**modus ˌopeˈrandi** ˌɒp ə ˈrænd i -aɪ ‖ ˌɑːp-;
ˌ**modus viˈvendi** vɪ ˈvend i §və-, -aɪ
Moesia ˈmiːs i‿ə ˈmiːz-; ˈmiːʃ ə, ˈmiːʒ ə ‖ ˈmiːʃ-
Moët et Chandon ˌməʊ ɪt eɪ ˈʃɒ̃d ɒ̃ ,· eɪ- ‖ ˌmoʊ ət eɪ ʃɑːn ˈdɔːn —*Fr* [mo e e ʃɑ̃ dɔ̃]
Moffat, Moffatt ˈmɒf ət ‖ ˈmɑːf-
mog, Mog mɒg ‖ mɑːg **mogs** mɒgz ‖ mɑːgz
Mogadishu ˌmɒg ə ˈdɪʃ uː ‖ ˌmɑːg- ˌmɔːg-, -ˈdiːʃ-
Mogadon *tdmk* ˈmɒg ə dɒn ‖ ˈmɑːg ə dɑːn
Mogador ˌmɒg ə ˈdɔː ˈ· · · ‖ ˌmɑːg ə ˈdɔːr -ˈdoʊr
Mogford ˈmɒg fəd ‖ ˈmɑːg fᵊrd
Mogg mɒg ‖ mɑːg
Moggach ˈmɒg əx -ək ‖ ˈmɑːg ək
mogg|ie, mogg|y ˈmɒg |i ‖ ˈmɑːg |i **~ies** iz
Mogollon ˌməʊg ə ˈjəʊn ‖ ˌmoʊg ə ˈjoʊn
mogul, Mogul ˈməʊg ᵊl -ʊl, -ʌl ‖ ˈmoʊg- moʊ ˈgʌl **~s** z
mohair ˈməʊ heə ‖ ˈmoʊ her -hær
Mohamma... —*see* **Mohamme...**
Mohammed məʊ ˈhæm ɪd -əd, -ed ‖ moʊ- —*Arabic* [mu ˈħam mad]
Mohammedan məʊ ˈhæm ɪd ən -əd- ‖ moʊ- **~ism** ˌɪz əm **~s** z
Mohan ˈməʊ hæn -hən, -ən ‖ ˈmoʊ-
Mohave məʊ ˈhɑːv i ‖ mə- moʊ- **~s** z
Mohawk, m~ ˈməʊ hɔːk ‖ ˈmoʊ- -hɑːk **~s** s
mohel ˈməʊ hel ‖ ˈmoʊ- -əl; mɔɪᵊl **~s** z
Mohican, m~ məʊ ˈhiːk ən ˈməʊ ɪk- ‖ moʊ- mə- **~s** z
Moho ˈməʊ həʊ ‖ ˈmoʊ hoʊ
Mohole ˈməʊ həʊl →-hɒʊl ‖ ˈmoʊ hoʊl
Mohorovicic ˌməʊ hə ˈrəʊv ɪ tʃɪtʃ -ˈ·ə- ‖ ˌmoʊ hə ˈroʊv- —*Serbo-Croat* Mohorovičić [mɔ xɔ ˈrɔ vi tʃit ɕ]
Mohs məʊz ‖ moʊz —*Ger* [moːs]
Mohun *(i)* ˈməʊ ən -hən ‖ ˈmoʊ hən; *(ii)* muːn
moi mwɑː —*Fr* [mwa]
Moi *African name* mɔɪ
moidore ˌmɔɪ ˈdɔː ˈmɔɪd ɔː ‖ ˈmɔɪd ɔːr -oʊr **~s** z
moiet|y ˈmɔɪ ət |i -ɪ- ‖ -əţ |i **~ies** iz
Moir ˈmɔɪ ə ‖ mɔɪᵊr
Moira ˈmɔɪᵊr ə
moire mwɑː ‖ mwɑːr mɔːr, moʊr
moiré ˈmwɑːr eɪ ‖ mwɑː ˈreɪ ˈmɔːr eɪ, ˈmoʊr-
Moiseivich, Moiseiwitsch mɔɪ ˈzeɪ ɪ vɪtʃ -ˈseɪ-

moist mɔɪst **moister** ˈmɔɪst ə ‖ -ᵊr **moistest** ˈmɔɪst ɪst -əst

moisten ˈmɔɪs ᵊn

moist|ly ˈmɔɪst |li **~ness** nəs nɪs

moisture ˈmɔɪs tʃə ‖ -tʃᵊr

moisturis|e, moisturiz|e ˈmɔɪs tʃə raɪz **~er/s** ə/z ‖ ᵊr/z

moither ˈmɔɪð ə ‖ -ᵊr **~ed** d **moithering** ˈmɔɪð ər ɪŋ **~s** z

Mojave məʊ ˈhɑːv i ‖ mə- moʊ-

Moˌjave ˈDesert

mojito məʊ ˈhiːt əʊ ‖ moʊ ˈhiːţ oʊ **~s** z s —*AmSp* [mo ˈhi to]

mojo ˈməʊdʒ əʊ ‖ ˈmoʊdʒ oʊ **~s** z

moke məʊk ‖ moʊk **mokes** məʊks ‖ moʊks

molal ˈməʊl əl →ˈmɒʊl- ‖ ˈmoʊl-

molar ˈməʊl ə ‖ ˈmoʊl ᵊr **~s** z

molasses məʊ ˈlæs ɪz -əz ‖ mə-

mold, Mold məʊld →mɒʊld ‖ moʊld **molded** ˈməʊld ɪd →ˈmɒʊld-, -əd ‖ ˈmoʊld əd

molding/s ˈməʊld ɪŋ/z →ˈmɒʊld- ‖ ˈmoʊld ɪŋ/z **molds** məʊldz →mɒʊldz ‖ moʊldz

Moldavi|a mɒl ˈdeɪv i‿|ə ‖ mɑːl- **~an/s** ən/z

mold|er ˈməʊld |ə →ˈmɒʊld- ‖ ˈmoʊld |ᵊr **~ered** əd ‖ ᵊrd **~ering** ər ɪŋ **~ers** əz ‖ ᵊrz

Moldov|a mɒl ˈdəʊv |ə ‖ mɑːl ˈdoʊv |ə **~an/s** ᵊn/z

mold|y ˈməʊld |i →ˈmɒʊld- ‖ ˈmoʊld |i **~ier** i‿ə ‖ i‿ᵊr **~iest** i‿ɪst i‿əst **~iness** i nəs i nɪs

mole, Mole məʊl →mɒʊl ‖ moʊl **moles** məʊlz →mɒʊlz ‖ moʊlz

Molech ˈməʊl ek ‖ ˈmoʊl-

molecular mə ˈlek jʊl ə məʊ-, mɒ-, -jəl- ‖ -jəl ᵊr

molecule ˈmɒl ɪ kjuːl ˈməʊl-, -ə- ‖ ˈmɑːl- **~s** z

molehill ˈməʊl hɪl →ˈmɒʊl- ‖ ˈmoʊl- **~s** z

Molesey ˈməʊlz i →ˈmɒʊlz- ‖ ˈmoʊlz i

moleskin ˈməʊl skɪn →ˈmɒʊl- ‖ ˈmoʊl- **~s** z

molest mə ˈlest məʊ- **~ed** ɪd əd **~ing** ɪŋ **~s** s

molestation ˌməʊl e ˈsteɪʃ ᵊn ‖ ˌmoʊl- **~s** z

molester mə ˈlest ə məʊ- ‖ -ᵊr **~s** z

Molesworth ˈməʊlz wɜːθ →ˈmɒʊlz-, -wəθ ‖ ˈmoʊlz wᵊrθ

Moliere, Molière ˈmɒl i eə ˈməʊl- ‖ moʊl ˈjeᵊr —*Fr* [mɔ ljɛːʁ]

Molina məʊ ˈliːn ə ‖ moʊ- mə-

Moline məʊ ˈliːn ‖ moʊ-

moll, Moll mɒl ‖ mɑːl **molls** mɒlz ‖ mɑːlz

Mollie, mollie ˈmɒl i ‖ ˈmɑːl i **~s, ~'s** z

mollifiable ˈmɒl ɪ faɪ‿əb ᵊl §ˌ·-ˈ·-·- ‖ ˈmɑːl-

mollification ˌmɒl ɪf ɪ ˈkeɪʃ ᵊn ˌ-əf-, §-əˈ·- ‖ ˌmɑːl-

molli|fy ˈmɒl ɪ |faɪ -ə- ‖ ˈmɑːl- **~fied** faɪd **~fier/s** faɪ‿ə/z ‖ faɪ‿ᵊr/z **~fies** faɪz **~fying/ly** faɪ ɪŋ /li

Molloy mə ˈlɔɪ

mollusc, mollusk ˈmɒl əsk -ʌsk ‖ ˈmɑːl- **~s** s

Mollweide ˈmɒl vaɪd ə ‖ ˈmɔːl- ˈmɑːl- —*Ger* [ˈmɔl vai də]

Moll|y, moll|y ˈmɒl |i ‖ ˈmɑːl |i **~ies, ~y's** iz

mollycoddl|e ˈmɒl i ˌkɒd ᵊl ‖ ˈmɑːl i ˌkɑːd ᵊl **~ed** d **~es** z **~ing** ‿ɪŋ

Moloch, m~ ˈməʊl ɒk ‖ ˈmoʊl ɑːk ˈmɑːl ək **~s** s

Moloney, Molony mə ˈləʊn i ‖ -ˈloʊn i

Molotov ˈmɒl ə tɒf ‖ ˈmɑːl ə tɔːf ˈmoʊl-, ˈmɔːl-, -tɑːf —*Russ* [ˈmɔ łə təf]

ˌMolotov ˈcocktail

molt məʊlt →mɒʊlt ‖ moʊlt **molted** ˈməʊlt ɪd →ˈmɒʊlt-, -əd ‖ ˈmoʊlt əd **molting** ˈməʊlt ɪŋ →ˈmɒʊlt- ‖ ˈmoʊlt ɪŋ **molts** məʊlts →mɒʊlts ‖ moʊlts

molten ˈməʊlt ən →ˈmɒʊlt- ‖ ˈmoʊlt-

molto ˈmɒlt əʊ ‖ ˈmoʊlt oʊ —*It* [ˈmɔl to]

Molton ˈməʊlt ən →ˈmɒʊlt- ‖ ˈmoʊlt-

Molucc|a məʊ ˈlʌk |ə ‖ mə- **~an/s** ən/z **~as** əz

moly ˈməʊl i ‖ ˈmoʊl i

molybdate mə ˈlɪbd eɪt mɒ-, məʊ- **~s** s

molybdenum mə ˈlɪbd ən əm mɒ-, məʊ-

molybdic mə ˈlɪbd ɪk mɒ-, məʊ-

Molyneaux ˈmɒl ɪ nəʊ -ə- ‖ ˈmɑːl ə noʊ

Molyneux *(i)* ˈmɒl ɪ njuː -ə- ‖ ˈmɑːl-, *(ii)* ˈmʌl-, *(iii)* -njuːks

mom, Mom mɒm ‖ mɑːm **moms, Mom's** mɒmz ‖ mɑːmz

mom-and-pop ˌmɒm ən ˈpɒp →-əm- ‖ ˌmɑːm ən ˈpɑːp

Mombasa mɒm ˈbæs ə -ˈbɑːs- ‖ mɑːm ˈbɑːs ə -ˈbæs- —*Swahili* [mo ˈmba sa]

moment ˈməʊm ənt ‖ ˈmoʊm- **~ly** li **~s** s

momenta məʊ ˈment ə ‖ moʊ ˈmenţ ə

momentarily ˈməʊm ənt‿ər əl i -ɪ li; ˌməʊm ən ˈter əl i, -ɪ li ‖ ˌmoʊm ən ˈter əl i

momentar|y ˈməʊm ənt‿ər |i ‖ ˈmoʊm ən ter |i **~iness** i nəs i nɪs

momentous məʊ ˈment əs ‖ moʊ ˈmenţ əs mə- **~ly** li **~ness** nəs nɪs

moment|um məʊ ˈment |əm ‖ moʊ ˈmenţ |əm mə- **~a** ə

momma, Momma ˈmɒm ə ‖ ˈmɑːm ə **~s, ~'s** z

momm|ie, momm|y, M~ ˈmɒm |i ‖ ˈmɑːm |i **~ies, ~y's** iz

Momus ˈməʊm əs ‖ ˈmoʊm-

Mon *name of language or people* məʊn mɒn ‖ moʊn

Mon. —*see* **Monday**

Mona, mona ˈməʊn ə ‖ ˈmoʊn ə **~s, ~'s** z

ˌMona ˈLisa

Monacan ˈmɒn ək ən mə ˈnɑːk- ‖ ˈmɑːn ək- mə ˈnɑːk- **~s** z

Monaco ˈmɒn ə kəʊ mə ˈnɑːk əʊ ‖ ˈmɑːn ə koʊ mə ˈnɑːk oʊ —*Fr* [mɔ na ko], *It* [ˈmɔː na ko]

monad ˈmɒn æd ˈməʊn- ‖ ˈmoʊn- **~s** z

Monadhliadh ˌməʊn ə ˈliː‿ə ‖ ˌmoʊn-

monadic mɒ ˈnæd ɪk məʊ- ‖ moʊ- mə-

monadism ˈmɒn ə ˌdɪz əm ˈməʊn-, -æd ˌɪz- ‖ ˈmoʊn æd ˌɪz-

monadnock, M~ mə ˈnæd nɒk ‖ -nɑːk **~s** s

Monaghan, Monahan ˈmɒn ə hən ‖ ˈmɑːn- -hæn

monandrous mɒ ˈnændr əs mə- ‖ mə-

monarch ˈmɒn ək §-ɑːk ‖ ˈmɑːn ᵊrk -ɑːrk **~s** s

monarchal mə ˈnɑːk əl mɒ- ‖ mə ˈnɑːrk- mɑː- **~ly** i
monarchic mə ˈnɑːk ɪk mɒ- ‖ mə ˈnɑːrk- mɑː- **~ally** əl‿i
monarchism ˈmɒn ə ˌkɪz əm ‖ ˈmɑːn ər- -ɑːr-
monarchist ˈmɒn ək ɪst §-əst ‖ ˈmɑːn ərk- -ɑːrk- **~s** s
monarch|y ˈmɒn ək |i ‖ ˈmɑːn ərk |i -ɑːrk- **~ies** iz
Monash ˈmɒn æʃ ‖ ˈmɑːn-
monasterial ˌmɒn ə ˈstɪər i‿əl ◂ ‖ ˌmɑːn ə ˈstɪr-
monastery ˈmɒn əs tər‿i ‖ ˈmɑːn ə ster i
monastic mə ˈnæst ɪk mɒ- **~ally** əl‿i **~s** s
monasticism mə ˈnæst ɪ ˌsɪz əm mɒ-, -ə-
Monastir ˌmɒn ə ˈstɪə ‖ ˌmɑːn ə ˈstɪər
monatomic ˌmɒn ə ˈtɒm ɪk ◂ ‖ ˌmɑːn ə ˈtɑːm-
monaural ˌmɒn ˈɔːr əl ◂ ‖ ˌmɑːn- **~ly** i
Monbiot ˈmɒn bi əʊ →ˈmɒm- ‖ ˈmɑːn bi oʊ
Monchen-Gladbach, Mönchen-Gladbach ˌmʌntʃ ən ˈglæd bæk →-əŋ- —*Ger* [ˌmœn çən ˈglat bax]
Monck mʌŋk
Monckton ˈmʌŋkt ən
Moncreiff, Moncreiffe, Moncrieff, Moncrieffe mən ˈkriːf →məŋ-, mɒn- ‖ mɑːn-
Mond mɒnd ‖ mɑːnd —*Ger* [moːnt]
Mondale ˈmɒn deɪəl ‖ ˈmɑːn-
Monday ˈmʌnd eɪ -i —*See note at* -day **~s, ~'s** z
ˌMonday ˈmorning, that ˌMonday ˈmorning ˌfeeling; **ˈMonday Club**
Mondeo *tdmk* ₍ˌ₎mɒn ˈdeɪ əʊ ‖ ˌmɑːn ˈdeɪ oʊ **~s** z
mondo, Mondo ˈmɒnd əʊ ‖ ˈmɑːnd oʊ
Mondrian ˌmɒndr i ˈɑːn ‖ ˈmɔːndr i ɑːn ˈmɑːndr- —*Dutch* [ˈmɔn driː aːn]
monecious mɒ ˈniːʃ əs mə- ‖ mɑː-
Monegasque, Monégasque ˌmɒn ɪ ˈgæsk ◂ -ə- ‖ ˌmɑːn- **~s** s —*Fr* [mɔ ne gask]
moneme ˈmɒn iːm ˈməʊn- ‖ ˈmoʊn- **~s** z
monera, M~ mə ˈnɪər ə mɒ-, məʊ- ‖ mə ˈnɪr ə mɑː-, moʊ-
Monet ˈmɒn eɪ ‖ moʊ ˈneɪ —*Fr* [mɔ nɛ]
monetarism ˈmʌn ɪt ə ˌrɪz əm ˈmɒn-, ˈ·ət- ‖ ˈmɑːn ə tə- ˈmʌn-
monetarist ˈmʌn ɪt‿ər ɪst ˈmɒn-, ˈ·ət‿, §-əst ‖ ˈmɑːn- ˈmʌn- **~s** s
monetary ˈmʌn ɪt‿ər i ˈmɒn-, ˈ·ət‿ ‖ ˈmɑːn ə ter i ˈmʌn-
monetis|e, monetiz|e ˈmʌn ɪ taɪz ˈmɒn-, -ə- ‖ ˈmɑːn- ˈmʌn- **~ed** d **~es** ɪz əz **~ing** ɪŋ
money, Money ˈmʌn i **moneyed, monied** ˈmʌn id **moneys, monies** ˈmʌn iz
ˈmoney ˌmarket; **ˈmoney ˌorder**; **ˈmoney ˌspider**; **ˈmoney supˌply**
moneybags ˈmʌn i bægz
moneybox ˈmʌn i bɒks ‖ -bɑːks **~es** ɪz əz
moneychanger ˈmʌn i ˌtʃeɪndʒ ə ‖ -ər **~s** z
moneygrab|ber ˈmʌn i ˌgræb ə ‖ -ər **~bers** əz ‖ ərz **~bing** ɪŋ
moneygrub|ber ˈmʌn i ˌgrʌb |ə ‖ -|ər **~bers** əz ‖ ərz **~bing** ɪŋ
moneylend|er ˈmʌn i ˌlend |ə ‖ -|ər **~ers** əz ‖ ərz **~ing** ɪŋ
moneymak|er ˈmʌn i ˌmeɪk |ə ‖ -|ər **~ers** əz ‖ ərz **~ing** ɪŋ
Moneypenny ˈmʌn i ˌpen i ˈmɒn- ‖ ˈmɑːn-
moneyspinner ˈmʌn i ˌspɪn ə ‖ -ər **~s** z
moneywort ˈmʌn i wɜːt §-wɔːt ‖ -wɜːt -wɔːrt
monger ˈmʌŋ gə ‖ ˈmɑːŋ gər ˈmʌŋ- **~s** z
Mongol, m~ ˈmɒŋ gəl -gɒl ‖ ˈmɑːŋ- ˈmɑːn goʊl, →ˈmɑːŋ- **~s** z
Mongoli|a mɒŋ ˈgəʊl i‿|ə ‖ mɑːŋ ˈgoʊl- mɑːn- **~an/s** ən/z
Mongolic mɒŋ ˈgɒl ɪk ‖ mɑːn ˈgɑːl ɪk →mɑːŋ-
mongolism ˈmɒŋ gə ˌlɪz əm -gɒ- ‖ ˈmɑːn- →ˈmɑːŋ-
Mongoloid, m~ ˈmɒŋ gə lɔɪd ‖ ˈmɑːn- →ˈmɑːŋ- **~s** z
mongoos|e ˈmɒŋ guːs ˈmʌŋ- ‖ ˈmɑːn- →ˈmɑːŋ **~es** ɪz əz
mongrel ˈmʌŋ grəl ‖ ˈmɑːŋ- **~ism** ˌɪz əm **~s** z
mongrelis... —*see* **mongreliz...**
mongrelization ˌmʌŋ grəl aɪ ˈzeɪʃ ən -ɪ'·- ‖ -ə'·- ˌmɑːŋ-
mongreliz|e ˈmʌŋ grə laɪz ‖ ˈmɑːŋ- **~ed** d **~es** ɪz əz **~ing** ɪŋ
Monica ˈmɒn ɪk ə §-ək- ‖ ˈmɑːn-
monicker ˈmɒn ɪk ə ‖ ˈmɑːn ɪk ər **~s** z
monie... —*see* **money**
Monifieth ˌmʌn ɪ ˈfiːθ
moniker ˈmɒn ɪk ə ‖ ˈmɑːn ɪk ər **~s** z
monilia mɒ ˈnɪl| i‿ə mə- ‖ moʊ-
moniliform mɒ ˈnɪl ɪ fɔːm mə-, -ə- ‖ moʊ ˈnɪl ə fɔːrm
Monique mɒ ˈniːk ‖ moʊ- mə- —*Fr* [mɔ nik]
monism ˈmɒn ˌɪz əm ‖ ˈmoʊn- ˈmɑːn-
monist ˈmɒn ɪst §-əst ‖ ˈmoʊn- ˈmɑːn- **~s** s
monistic mɒ ˈnɪst ɪk mə- ‖ moʊ- mɑː- **~ally** əl‿i
monitor ˈmɒn ɪt ə -ət- ‖ ˈmɑːn əṭ ər **~ed** d
monitoring ˈmɒn ɪt‿ər ɪŋ ˈ·ət‿ ‖ˈmɑːn əṭ ər ɪŋ →ˈmɑːn ətr ɪŋ **~s** z
monk, Monk mʌŋk **monks** mʌŋks
monkey ˈmʌŋk i **~ed** d **~ing** ɪŋ **~s** z
ˈmonkey ˌbusiness; **ˈmonkey nut**; **ˈmonkey wrench**
monkey-puzzle ˈmʌŋk i ˌpʌz əl **~s** z
monkfish ˈmʌŋk fɪʃ
Mon-Khmer ˌməʊn ˈkmeə ◂ ˌməʊn kə ˈmeə ‖ ˌmoʊn ˈkmeər ˌmoʊn kə ˈmeər
monkhood ˈmʌŋk hʊd
Monkhouse ˈmʌŋk haʊs
monkish ˈmʌŋk ɪʃ **~ly** li **~ness** nəs nɪs
Monkton ˈmʌŋk tən
Monmouth ˈmɒn məθ ˈmʌn-, →ˈmɒm- ‖ ˈmɑːn-
Monmouthshire ˈmɒn məθ ʃə ˈmʌn-, →ˈmɒm-, -ʃɪə ‖ ˈmɑːn məθ ʃər -ʃɪr
Monnow ˈmɒn əʊ ˈmʌn- ‖ ˈmɑːn oʊ
mono ˈmɒn əʊ ‖ ˈmɑːn oʊ
Mono *lake in CA* ˈməʊn əʊ ‖ ˈmoʊn oʊ
mono- *comb. form with stress-neutral suffix* |mɒn əʊ ‖ |mɑːn ə -oʊ, *but before a vowel always* -əʊ ‖ -oʊ;

— **monochord** 'mɒn əʊ kɔːd ‖ 'mɑːn ə kɔːrd; — **monoacidic** ˌmɒn əʊ ə 'sɪd ɪk ◂ -æ'-- ‖ ˌmɑːn oʊ- *with stress-imposing suffix* mə 'nɒ+ mɒ- ‖ mə 'nɑː+ mɑː-; — **monology** mə 'nɒl ədʒ i mɒ- ‖ mə 'nɑːl- mɑː-

Monoceros mə 'nɒs ər əs ‖ -'nɑːs-

monochromatic ˌmɒn əʊ krə 'mæt ɪk ◂ ‖ -'mæṭ ɪk ◂

monochrome 'mɒn ə krəʊm -əʊ- ‖ 'mɑːn ə kroʊm

monocle 'mɒn ək ᵊl ‖ 'mɑːn ɪk- **~d** d **~s** z

monoclonal ˌmɒn əʊ 'kləʊn ᵊl ◂ ‖ ˌmɑːn ə 'kloʊn ᵊl ◂ -oʊ-

monocoque 'mɒn əʊ kɒk ‖ 'mɑːn ə koʊk -kɑːk **~s** s

monocot 'mɒn əʊ kɒt ‖ 'mɑːn ə kɑːt **~s** s

monocotyledon ˌmɒn əʊ ˌkɒt ə 'liːd ᵊn -ɪ'--, -ᵊl 'iːd- ‖ ˌmɑːn ə ˌkɑːṭ ᵊl 'iːd ᵊn **~s** z

monocular mɒ 'nɒk jʊl ə mə-, -jəl- ‖ mɑː 'nɑːk jəl ᵊr

monoculture 'mɒn əʊ ˌkʌltʃ ə ‖ 'mɑːn ə ˌkʌltʃ ᵊr

monod|y 'mɒn əd |i ‖ 'mɑːn- **~ies** iz

monoecious mɒ 'niːʃ əs mə- ‖ mɑː- **~ly** li

monofil 'mɒn əʊ fɪl ‖ 'mɑːn ə-

monogamist mə 'nɒg əm ɪst mɒ-, §-əst ‖ -'nɑːg- **~s** s

monogamous mə 'nɒg əm əs mɒ- ‖ -'nɑːg- **~ly** li

monogamy mə 'nɒg əm i mɒ- ‖ -'nɑːg-

monogenetic ˌmɒn əʊ dʒə 'net ɪk ◂ -dʒɪ'-- ‖ ˌmɑːn ə dʒə 'neṭ ɪk ◂

monoglot 'mɒn əʊ glɒt ‖ 'mɑːn ə glɑːt **~s** s

monogram 'mɒn ə græm ‖ 'mɑːn- **~med** d **~s** z

monograph 'mɒn ə grɑːf -græf ‖ 'mɑːn ə græf **~s** s

monogyny mə 'nɒdʒ ən i mɒ-, -ɪn- ‖ -'nɑːdʒ-

monokini 'mɒn əʊ ˌkiːn i ‖ 'mɑːn ə- **~s** z

monolingual ˌmɒn əʊ 'lɪŋ gwəl ◂ ,· ·'lɪŋ gju‿əl ‖ ˌmɑːn ə- ˌmoʊn- **~s** z

monolith 'mɒn ə lɪθ -ᵊl ɪθ ‖ 'mɑːn- **~s** s

monolithic ˌmɒn ə 'lɪθ ɪk ◂ -ᵊl 'ɪθ- ‖ ˌmɑːn- **~ally** ᵊl‿i

monolog, monologue 'mɒn ə lɒg -ᵊl ɒg ‖ 'mɑːn ᵊl ɔːg -ɑːg **~s** z

monologuist 'mɒn ə lɒg ɪst -ᵊl ɒg-, §-əst ‖ 'mɑːn ᵊl ɔːg əst -ɑːg- **~s** s

monomania ˌmɒn əʊ 'meɪn i‿ə ‖ ˌmɑːn ə-

monomaniac ˌmɒn əʊ 'meɪn i æk ‖ ˌmɑːn ə- **~s** s

monomark, M~ *tdmk* 'mɒn əʊ mɑːk ‖ 'mɑːn ə mɑːrk **~s** s

monomer 'mɒn əm ə ‖ 'mɑːn əm ᵊr **~s** z

monomeric ˌmɒn ə 'mer ɪk ◂ ‖ ˌmɑːn-

monomial mɒ 'nəʊm i‿əl mə- ‖ mɑː 'noʊm- **~s** z

monomorphemic ˌmɒn əʊ mɔː 'fiːm ɪk ◂ ‖ ˌmɑːn ə mɔːr-

Monongahela mə ˌnɒŋ gə 'hiːl ə ◂ ‖ -ˌnɑːŋ- **Moˌnongaˌhela 'River**

mononucleosis ˌmɒn əʊ ˌnjuːk li 'əʊs ɪs §-ˌnuːk-, §-əs ‖ ˌmɑːn oʊ ˌnuːk li 'oʊs əs -ˌnjuːk-

monophonic ˌmɒn əʊ 'fɒn ɪk ◂ ‖ ˌmɑːn ə 'fɑːn ɪk ◂ -'foʊn- **~ally** ᵊl‿i

monophthong 'mɒn əf θɒŋ -əp-, -ə- ‖ 'mɑːn əf θɔːŋ -ə-, -θɑːŋ **~ing** ɪŋ **~s** z

monophthongal ˌmɒn əf 'θɒŋ gᵊl ◂ -əp-, -ə- ‖ ˌmɑːn əf 'θɔːŋ gᵊl ◂ -ə-, -'θɑːŋ- **~ly** i

monophthongis... —*see* **monophthongiz...**

monophthongization ˌmɒn əf θɒŋ gaɪ 'zeɪʃ ᵊn ,·əp-, ,·ə-, -aɪ'--, -gɪ'--, -ɪ'-- ‖ ˌmɑːn əf θɔːŋ gə- ,· ·θɑːŋ-, -ə'-- **~s** z

monophthongiz|e 'mɒn əf θɒŋ gaɪz '·əp-, -aɪz ‖ 'mɑːn əf θɔːŋ gaɪz '·ə-, ·θɑːŋ ·, -aɪz **~ed** d **~es** ɪz əz **~ing** ɪŋ

Monophysite mə 'nɒf ɪ saɪt -ə- ‖ mə 'nɑːf ə- **~s** s

monoplane 'mɒn ə pleɪn ‖ 'mɑːn- **~s** z

Monopole, m~ 'mɒn ə pəʊl →-pɒʊl ‖ 'mɑːn ə poʊl **~s** z

monopolie... —*see* **monopoly**

monopolis... —*see* **monopoliz...**

monopolist mə 'nɒp əl ɪst §-əst ‖ -'nɑːp- **~s** s

monopolistic mə ˌnɒp ə 'lɪst ɪk ◂ ‖ -ˌnɑːp- **~ally** ᵊl‿i

monopolization mə ˌnɒp ə laɪ 'zeɪʃ ᵊn -ɪ'-- ‖ -ˌnɑːp əl ə- **~s** z

monopoliz|e mə 'nɒp ə laɪz ‖ -'nɑːp- **~ed** d **~es** ɪz əz **~ing** ɪŋ

monopol|y, M~ *tdmk* mə 'nɒp əl |i ‖ -'nɑːp- **~ies** iz

monopson|y mə 'nɒps ən |i ‖ -'nɑːps- **~ies** iz

monorail 'mɒn əʊ reɪᵊl ‖ 'mɑːn ə- **~s** z

monosodium ˌmɒn əʊ 'səʊd i‿əm ◂ ‖ ˌmɑːn ə 'soʊd- **ˌmonoˌsodium 'glutamate**

monospac|e 'mɒn əʊ speɪs ‖ 'mɑːn oʊ- **~ed** t **~es** ɪz əz **~ing** ɪŋ

monosyllabic ˌmɒn əʊ sɪ 'læb ɪk ◂ -sə'-- ‖ ˌmɑːn ə sə- **~ally** ᵊl‿i

monosyllable 'mɒn əʊ ˌsɪl əb ᵊl ,·'·· ‖ 'mɑːn ə- **~s** z

monotheism 'mɒn əʊ θi ˌɪz əm '·ˌθiː ɪz əm; mə 'nɒθ i ˌɪz əm ‖ 'mɑːn ə-

monotheist 'mɒn əʊ θi ɪst -ˌθiː ɪst, §-əst; mə 'nɒθ i· ‖ 'mɑːn ə- **~s** s

monotheistic ˌmɒn əʊ θi 'ɪst ɪk ◂ ,· ·θiː'·-; mə ˌnɒθ i'-- ‖ ˌmɑːn ə-

monotone 'mɒn ə təʊn ‖ 'mɑːn ə toʊn **~s** z

monotonous mə 'nɒt ən əs ‖ -'nɑːt ᵊn‿əs **~ly** li **~ness** nəs nɪs

monotony mə 'nɒt ən i ‖ -'nɑːt ᵊn i

monotreme 'mɒn əʊ triːm ‖ 'mɑːn ə- **~s** z

monotype, M~ *tdmk* 'mɒn əʊ taɪp ‖ 'mɑːn ə- **~s** s

monounsaturated ˌmɒn əʊ ʌn 'sætʃ ə reɪt ɪd ◂ -əd ‖ ˌmɑːn oʊ-

monoxide mə 'nɒks aɪd mɒ- ‖ mə 'nɑːks- mɑː- **~s** z

Monro, Monroe mən 'rəʊ ˌmʌn-, ˌmɒn- ‖ -'roʊ

Monrovia mən 'rəʊv i‿ə mɒn- ‖ -'roʊv-

M

mons, Mons mɒnz ‖ mɑːnz —*Fr* [mɔ̃ːs]
ˌmons ˈveneris ˈven ər ɪs §-əs
Monsanto *tdmk* mɒn ˈsænt əʊ ‖ mɑːn ˈsænṭ oʊ
Monsarrat ˈmɒn sə ræt ˌ·ˈ·ˈ· ‖ ˌmɑːn sə ˈrɑːt -ˈræt
Monsieur, m~ mə ˈsjɜː ˈmʊs jɜː, -jə ‖ məs ˈjuː →məʃ-, -ˈjɜː; mə ˈsɪᵊr —*There is an occasional weak form* mə sjə —*Fr* [mə sjø]
Monsignor, m~ mɒn ˈsiːn jə ‖ mɑːn ˈsiːn jᵊr —*It* [mon siɲ ˈɲoːr]
monsoon ˌmɒn ˈsuːn ◂ mɒn-, mən- ‖ ˌmɑːn- **~s** z
ˌmonsoon ˈlow
monster ˈmɒnᵗst ə ‖ ˈmɑːnᵗst ᵊr **~s** z
monstera mɒn ˈstɪər ə ˈmɒnᵗst ər ə ‖ ˈmɑːnᵗst ər ə **~s** z
monstranc|e ˈmɒnᵗs trənᵗs ‖ ˈmɑːnᵗs- **~es** ɪz əz
monstrosit|y mɒn ˈstrɒs ət |i mən-, -ɪt- ‖ mɑːn ˈstrɑːs əṭ |i **~ies** iz
monstrous ˈmɒnᵗs trəs ‖ ˈmɑːnᵗs- **~ly** li **~ness** nəs nɪs
Mont mɒnt ‖ mɑːnt —*but in names of mountains* mɔ̃, mɒn ‖ mɔːn, mɑːn, moʊn —*Fr* [mɔ̃]
ˌMont ˈBlanc blɔ̃ blɒŋ ‖ blɑːŋ —*Fr* [blɑ̃]
montag|e mɒn ˈtɑːʒ mɔ̃-, ˈ·· ‖ mɑːn- moʊn- —*Fr* [mɔ̃ taːʒ] **~es** ɪz əz
Montagu, Montague ˈmɒnt ə gjuː ‖ ˈmɑːnṭ- **~s, ~'s** z
Montaigne mɒn ˈteɪn ‖ mɑːn- moʊn- —*Fr* [mɔ̃ tɛnj]
montan ˈmɒnt ən -æn ‖ ˈmɑːnt ᵊn
Montan|a mɒn ˈtæn |ə -ˈtɑːn- ‖ mɑːn- **~an/s** ən/z
montane ˈmɒnt eɪn ‖ˌmɑːn ˈteɪn ˈ··
Montauk ˈmɒnt ɔːk ‖ ˈmɑːnt- -ɑːk
montbretia mɒn ˈbriːʃ ə →mɒm- ‖ mɑːn- **~s** z
Monte, monte ˈmɒnt i ‖ ˈmɑːnṭ i —*It* [ˈmon te]
ˌMonte ˈCarlo —*Fr* [mɔ̃ te kaʁ lo]
Montebello ˌmɒnt i ˈbel əʊ -ə- ‖ ˌmɑːnṭ ə ˈbel oʊ
Montefiore ˌmɒnt i fi ˈɔːr i -ə-, -eɪ ‖ ˌmɑːnṭ-
Montego mɒn ˈtiːg əʊ ‖ mɑːn ˈtiːg oʊ
MonˌtegoˈBay
Monteith, m~ mɒn ˈtiːθ ‖ mɑːn- **~s** s
Montel ˌmɒn ˈtel ◂ ‖ ˌmɑːn-
Montenegrin ˌmɒnt i ˈniːg rɪn ◂ -ə-, -ˈneɪg-, -ˈneg-, §-rən ‖ ˌmɑːnṭ ə- **~s** z
Montenegro ˌmɒnt i ˈniːg rəʊ ə-, -ˈneɪg-, -ˈneg- ‖ ˌmɑːnṭ ə ˈniːg roʊ -ˈneg-
Monterey *place in CA,* **Monterrey** *place in Mexico* ˌmɒnt ə ˈreɪ -ɪ- ‖ ˌmɑːnṭ- —*Sp* [mon te ˈrrei]
Montesquieu ˌmɒnt e ˈskjɜː -ˈskjuː, ˈ··· ‖ ˌmɑːnṭ ə ˈskjuː ˌmoʊnṭ- —*Fr* [mɔ̃ tɛs kjø]
Montessori ˌmɒnt ə ˈsɔːr i -e-, -ɪ- ‖ ˌmɑːnṭ- -ˈsoʊr- —*It* [mon tes ˈsɔː ri]
Monteux mɒn ˈtɜː ‖ moʊn ˈtʌ —*Fr* [mɔ̃ tø]
Monteverdi ˌmɒnt i ˈveəd i -ə-, -ˈvɜːd- ‖ ˌmɑːnṭ ə ˈverd i ˌmɔːnṭ-, -ˈvɜːd- —*It* [mon te ˈver di]
Montevideo ˌmɒnt i vɪ ˈdeɪ əʊ ˌ·ə-, §-və ˈ-, ˌ··ˈvɪd i əʊ ‖ ˌmɑːnṭ ə və ˈdeɪ oʊ ˌ··ˈvɪd i oʊ
Montezuma ˌmɒnt i ˈzuːm ə -ə-, -ˈzjuːm- ‖ ˌmɑːnṭ-
Montfort ˈmɒnt fət -fɔːt ‖ ˈmɑːnt fᵊrt —*Fr* [mɔ̃ fɔːʁ]
Montgolfier, m~ mɒnt ˈgɒlf i‿ə →mɒŋk-, -eɪ ‖ mɑːnt ˈgɑːlf i‿ᵊr ·,·i ˈeɪ —*Fr* [mɔ̃ gɔl fje] **~s** z
Montgomerie, Montgomery *(i)* mənt ˈgʌm ər‿i mən-, mɒnt-, mɒn- ‖ mɑːnt-, *(ii)* -ˈgɒm- ‖ -ˈgɑːm-
month mʌnᵗθ **months** mʌnᵗθs →mʌnᵗs
month|ly ˈmʌnᵗθ |li **~lies** liz
Monticello ˌmɒnt i ˈtʃel əʊ -ˈsel- ‖ ˌmɑːnṭ ɪ ˈtʃel oʊ -ˈsel-
Montmartre mɒn ˈmɑːtr →mɒm-, -ˈmɑːtr ə ‖ moʊn ˈmɑːr trə mɔːn- —*Fr* [mɔ̃ maʁtχ]
Montmorency ˌmɒnt mə ˈrenᵗs i ‖ ˌmɑːnt-
Montoya mɒn ˈtɔɪ ə ‖ mɑːn- —*Sp* [mon ˈto ja]
Montpelier, Montpellier mɒnt ˈpel i‿ə mɒm-, -eɪ ‖ ˌmoʊn pel ˈjeɪ ˌmɔːn-, ˌmɑːn- —*but the place in VT is* -ˈpiːl i‿ə ‖ mɑːnt ˈpiːl i‿ᵊr —*Fr* [mɔ̃ pə lje, -pɛ-]
Montreal ˌmɒntr i ˈɔːl ◂ ‖ ˌmɑːntr- ˌmʌntr-, -ˈɑːl —*Fr* Montréal [mɔ̃ ʁe al]
Montreux mɒn ˈtrɜː -ˈtrəʊ ‖ moʊn ˈtrʊ -ˈtruː —*Fr* [mɔ̃ tʁø]
Montrose mɒn ˈtrəʊz mən- ‖ mɑːn ˈtroʊz
Mont-Saint-Michel ˌmɒnt ˌsæn mɪ ˈʃel ˌmɔ̃-, →-ˌsæm-, -miː- ‖ ˌmoʊn- ˌmɔːn-, ˌmɑːn- —*Fr* [mɔ̃ sɛ̃ mi ʃɛl]
Montserrat ˌmɒnts ə ˈræt -se-, ˈ··· ‖ ˌmɑːnts- -ˈrɑːt —*In the West Indies, locally usually* ˈ··· —*Catalan* [munt sə ˈrrat]
Montserratian ˌmɒnts ə ˈreɪʃ ᵊn ◂ -se- ‖ ˌmɑːnts- **~s** z
Monty ˈmɒnt i ‖ ˈmɑːnt i
monument, M~ ˈmɒn ju mənt -jə ‖ ˈmɑːn jə- **~s** s
monumental ˌmɒn ju ˈment ᵊl ◂ -jə- ‖ ˌmɑːn jə ˈmenṭ ᵊl ◂ **~ly** i
Monymusk ˌmɒn i ˈmʌsk ‖ ˌmɑːn-
Monza ˈmɒnz ə ‖ ˈmɑːnz ə —*It* [ˈmon tsa]
Monzie mɒ ˈniː mə- ‖ mɑː-
moo muː **mooed** muːd *(= mood)* **mooing** ˈmuː ɪŋ **moos** muːz
mooch muːtʃ **mooched** muːtʃt **mooches** ˈmuːtʃ ɪz -əz **mooching** ˈmuːtʃ ɪŋ
moocow ˈmuː kaʊ **~s** z
mood muːd **moods** muːdz
mood-altering ˈmuːd ˌɔːlt‿ər ɪŋ -ˌɒlt‿ ‖ -ˌɑːlt‿
Moodey, Moodie ˈmuːd i
mood|y, Moody ˈmuːd |i **~ier** i‿ə ‖ i‿ᵊr **~iest** i‿ɪst i‿əst **~ily** ɪ li əl i **~iness** i nəs i nɪs
Moog *tdmk* məʊg muːg ‖ moʊg —*Robert M~ preferred* məʊg ‖ moʊg
ˌMoog ˈsynthesizer
moola, moolah ˈmuːl ə

mooli ˈmuːl i
moon, Moon muːn **mooned** muːnd **mooning** ˈmuːn ɪŋ **moons** muːnz
ˈmoon shot
moonbeam ˈmuːn biːm →ˈmuːm- **~s** z
moon|calf ˈmuːn |kɑːf →ˈmuːŋ-, §-kæf ‖ -|kæf **~calves** kɑːvz §kævz ‖ kævz
Moonee, Mooney, Moonie ˈmuːn i **~s** z
moon-faced ˈmuːn feɪst
mooni... —*see* **moony**
moonless ˈmuːn ləs -lɪs
moon|light ˈmuːn |laɪt **~lighter/s** laɪt ə/z ‖ laɪṱ ər/z **~lighting** laɪt ɪŋ ‖ laɪṱ ɪŋ
ˌmoonlight ˈflit
moonlit ˈmuːn lɪt
moonrise ˈmuːn raɪz
moon-roof ˈmuːn ruːf -rʊf
moonscape ˈmuːn skeɪp **~s** s
moonshine ˈmuːn ʃaɪn
moonshiner ˈmuːn ʃaɪn ə ‖ -ər **~s** z
moonstone ˈmuːn stəʊn ‖ -stoʊn **~s** z
moonstruck ˈmuːn strʌk
moon|y ˈmuːn |i **~ier** i‿ə ‖ i‿ər **~iest** i‿ɪst i‿əst **~ily** ɪ li əl i
moor, Moor mʊə mɔː ‖ mʊər **moored** mʊəd mɔːd ‖ mʊərd **mooring** ˈmʊər ɪŋ ˈmɔːr- ‖ ˈmʊər ɪŋ
moorcock, M~ ˈmʊə kɒk ˈmɔː- ‖ ˈmʊr kɑːk
Moorcroft ˈmʊə krɒft ˈmɔː- ‖ ˈmʊr krɔːft -krɑːft
Moore mʊə mɔː ‖ mʊər mɔːr, moʊr
Moorgate ˈmʊə geɪt ˈmɔː- ‖ ˈmʊr-
Moorhead ˈmʊə hed ˈmɔː- ‖ ˈmʊr-
moorhen ˈmʊə hen ˈmɔː- ‖ ˈmʊr- **~s** z
Moorhouse ˈmʊə haʊs ˈmɔː- ‖ ˈmʊr-
moorings ˈmʊər ɪŋz ˈmɔːr- ‖ ˈmʊr ɪŋz
Moorish ˈmʊər ɪʃ ˈmɔːr- ‖ ˈmʊr ɪʃ
moorland, M~ ˈmʊə lənd ˈmɔː-, -lænd ‖ ˈmʊr- **~s** z
moose muːs
moot muːt **mooted** ˈmuːt ɪd -əd ‖ ˈmuːṱ əd **mooting** ˈmuːt ɪŋ ‖ ˈmuːṱ ɪŋ **moots** muːts
ˌmoot ˈpoint; ˌmoot ˈquestion
Moots muːts
mop mɒp ‖ mɑːp **mopped** mɒpt ‖ mɑːpt **mopping** ˈmɒp ɪŋ ‖ ˈmɑːp ɪŋ **mops** mɒps ‖ mɑːps
mope məʊp ‖ moʊp **moped** məʊpt ‖ moʊpt **mopes** məʊps ‖ moʊps **moping** ˈməʊp ɪŋ ‖ ˈmoʊp ɪŋ
moped *n* ˈməʊ ped ‖ ˈmoʊ- **~s** z
mopoke ˈməʊp əʊk ‖ ˈmoʊp oʊk **~s** s
mopp... —*see* **mop**
moppet ˈmɒp ɪt §-ət ‖ ˈmɑːp- **~s** s
Mopsy ˈmɒps i ‖ ˈmɑːps i
mop-up ˈmɒp ʌp ‖ ˈmɑːp- **~s** s
moquette mɒ ˈket məʊ- ‖ moʊ-
mor|a ˈmɔːr |ə ‖ ˈmoʊr- **~ae** iː **~as** əz
Morag ˈmɔːr æg ‖ ˈmoʊr-
moraic mɔː ˈreɪ ɪk ‖ moʊ-
moraine mə ˈreɪn mɒ- **~s** z
moral ˈmɒr əl ‖ ˈmɔːr əl ˈmɑːr- **~s** z
ˌMoral Maˈjority; ˌMoral Reˈarmament
morale mə ˈrɑːl mɒ- ‖ mə ˈræl *(*)*
morale-boosting mə ˈrɑːl ˌbuːst ɪŋ mɒ- ‖ mə ˈræl-
moralis... —*see* **moraliz...**
moralism ˈmɒr ə ˌlɪz əm ‖ ˈmɔːr- ˈmɑːr-
moralist ˈmɒr əl ɪst §-əst ‖ ˈmɔːr- ˈmɑːr- **~s** s
moralistic ˌmɒr ə ˈlɪst ɪk ◂ ‖ ˌmɔːr- ˌmɑːr- **~ally** əl‿i
moralit|y mə ˈræl ət |i mɒ-, -ɪt- ‖ mə ˈræl əṱ |i mɔː- **~ies** iz
moˈrality play
moraliz|e ˈmɒr ə laɪz ‖ ˈmɔːr- ˈmɑːr- **~ed** d **~er/s** ə/z ‖ ər/z **~es** ɪz əz **~ing** ɪŋ
morally ˈmɒr əl i ‖ ˈmɔːr- ˈmɑːr-
Moran *(i)* ˈmɔːr ən ˈmɒr-, *(ii)* mə ˈræn mɒ- ‖ mɔː-
Morant mə ˈrænt mɒ- ‖ mɔː-
morass mə ˈræs mɒ- ‖ mɔː- **~es** ɪz əz
moratori|um ˌmɒr ə ˈtɔːr i‿|əm ‖ ˌmɔːr- ˌmɑːr-, -ˈtoʊr- **~a** ə **~ums** əmz
Moravi|a mə ˈreɪv i‿|ə mɒ- **~an/s** ən/z
moray *'kind of eel'* ˈmɒr eɪ ˈmɔːr-; mə ˈreɪ, mɒ- ‖ ˈmɔːr eɪ ˈmoʊr-; mə ˈreɪ **~s** z
Moray ˈmʌr i ⚠ˈmɒr-, -eɪ ‖ ˈmɝː i *(= Murray)*
morbid ˈmɔːb ɪd §-əd ‖ ˈmɔːrb- **~ly** li **~ness** nəs nɪs
morbidezza ˌmɔːb ɪ ˈdets ə §-ə- ‖ ˌmɔːrb- —*It* [mor bi ˈdet tsa]
morbidit|y mɔː ˈbɪd ət |i -ɪt- ‖ mɔːr ˈbɪd əṱ |i **~ies** iz
mordancy ˈmɔːd ənts i ‖ ˈmɔːrd-
mordant ˈmɔːd ənt ‖ ˈmɔːrd- **~ly** li **~s** s
Mordecai ˈmɔːd ɪ kaɪ -ə-; ˌ· · ˈkeɪ aɪ, ˌ· · ˈkaɪ i ‖ ˈmɔːrd-
Morden ˈmɔːd ən ‖ ˈmɔːrd-
mordent ˈmɔːd ənt ‖ ˈmɔːrd- **~s** s
Mordor ˈmɔːd ɔː ‖ ˈmɔːrd ɔːr
Mordred ˈmɔːdr ɪd -əd, -ed ‖ ˈmɔːrdr-
Mordvin ˈmɔːd vɪn ‖ ˈmɔːrd-
more, More mɔː ‖ mɔːr moʊr
Morea mɔː ˈrɪə mɒ-, mə- ‖ mɔː ˈriː ə moʊ-
Morecambe, Morecombe ˈmɔːk əm ‖ ˈmɔːrk-
moreish ˈmɔːr ɪʃ ‖ ˈmoʊr-
morel mə ˈrel mɒ- ‖ mɔː- **~s** z
morello mə ˈrel əʊ mɒ- ‖ -oʊ **~s** z
moreover mɔːr ˈəʊv ə mər- ‖ -ˈoʊv ər moʊr-; ˈ· ˌ· ·
mores ˈmɔːr eɪz -iːz ‖ ˈmoʊr-
Moresby ˈmɔːz bi ‖ ˈmɔːrz- ˈmoʊrz- —*but the place in Cumbria is* ˈmɒr ɪs bi
Moresque ₍ˌ₎mɔː ˈresk mə-
Moreton ˈmɔːt ən ‖ ˈmɔːrt- ˈmoʊrt-
Moretonhampstead ˌmɔːt ən ˈhæmp stɪd -sted ‖ ˌmɔːrt- ˌmoʊrt-
Morfa ˈmɔːv ə ‖ ˈmɔːrv ə —*Welsh* [ˈmɔr va]
Morfudd, Morfydd ˈmɔːv ɪð ‖ ˈmɔːrv- —*Welsh* [ˈmɔr við, -vɨð]
Morgan ˈmɔːg ən ‖ ˈmɔːrg-
morganatic ˌmɔːg ə ˈnæt ɪk ◂ ‖ ˌmɔːrg ə ˈnæṱ ɪk ◂ **~ally** əl‿i
morgen ˈmɔːg ən ‖ ˈmɔːrg- **~s** z
Morgenthau ˈmɔːg ən θɔː ‖ ˈmɔːrg- -θɑː

M

morgue mɔːg ‖ mɔːrg **morgues** mɔːgz ‖ mɔːrgz
MORI 'mɔːr i 'mɒr-
Moriarty ˌmɒr i 'ɑːt i ‖ ˌmɔːr i 'ɑːrţ i
moribund 'mɒr ɪ bʌnd -ə-; -ɪb ənd, -əb- ‖ 'mɔːr- 'mɑːr- **~ly** li
Morison 'mɒr ɪs ən -əs- ‖ 'mɔːr- 'mɑːr-
Morissette ˌmɒr ɪ 'set -ə- ‖ ˌmɔːr- ˌmɑːr-
Morland 'mɔː lənd ‖ 'mɔːr-
Morley 'mɔːl i ‖ 'mɔːrl i
Mormon 'mɔːm ən ‖ 'mɔːrm- **~ism** ˌɪz əm **~s** z
morn mɔːn ‖ mɔːrn **morns** mɔːnz ‖ mɔːrnz
Morna 'mɔːn ə ‖ 'mɔːrn ə
mornay, M~ 'mɔːn eɪ ‖ mɔːr 'neɪ —*Fr* [mɔʁ nɛ]
morning 'mɔːn ɪŋ ‖ 'mɔːrn ɪŋ **~s** z
'morning coat; **'morning dress**, ,.. '.; **ˌmorning 'glory** ‖ '.. ,. ; **ˌMorning 'Prayer**; **'morning ˌsickness**; **ˌmorning 'star**
morning-after ˌmɔːn ɪŋ 'ɑːft ə ◂ §-'æft- ‖ ˌmɔːrn ɪŋ 'æft ᵊr ◂
ˌmorning-'after pill
Mornington 'mɔːn ɪŋ tən ‖ 'mɔːrn-
ˌMornington 'Crescent
Moroccan mə 'rɒk ən ‖ -'rɑːk- **~s** z
Morocco, m~ mə 'rɒk əʊ ‖ -'rɑːk oʊ
moron 'mɔːr ɒn ‖ 'mɔːr ɑːn 'moʊr- **~s** z
Moroni mə 'rəʊn i ‖ -'roʊn i mɔː-
moronic mə 'rɒn ɪk mɒ-, mɔː- ‖ -'rɑːn ɪk **~ally** ᵊl‿i
morose mə 'rəʊs mɒ- ‖ -'roʊs mɔː- **~ly** li **~ness** nəs nɪs
Morpeth 'mɔːp əθ ‖ 'mɔːrp-
morph mɔːf ‖ mɔːrf **morphed** mɔːft ‖ mɔːrft **morphing** 'mɔːf ɪŋ ‖ 'mɔːrf ɪŋ **morphs** mɔːfs ‖ mɔːrfs
morph- *comb. form before vowel*
with unstressed suffix 'mɔːf ‖ 'mɔːrf — **morphon** 'mɔːf ɒn ‖ 'mɔːrf ɑːn
with stressed suffix mɔːf ‖ mɔːrf — **morphosis** mɔː 'fəʊs ɪs §-əs ‖ mɔːr 'foʊs-
-morph mɔːf ‖ mɔːrf — **isomorph** 'aɪs əʊ mɔːf ‖ -ə mɔːrf
morpheme 'mɔːf iːm ‖ 'mɔːrf- **~s** z
morphemic mɔː 'fiːm ɪk ‖ mɔːr- **~ally** ᵊl‿i **~s** s
Morphett 'mɔːf ɪt §-ət ‖ 'mɔːrf ət
Morpheus 'mɔːf juːs 'mɔːf i‿əs ‖ 'mɔːrf-
morphia 'mɔːf i‿ə ‖ 'mɔːrf-
-morphic 'mɔːf ɪk ‖ 'mɔːrf ɪk — **isomorphic** ˌaɪs əʊ 'mɔːf ɪk ◂ ‖ -ə 'mɔːrf-
morphine 'mɔːf iːn ‖ 'mɔːrf-
morpho- *comb. form before cons*
with stress-neutral suffix ¦mɔːf əʊ ‖ ¦mɔːrf oʊ — **morphotectonics** ˌmɔːf əʊ tek 'tɒn ɪks ‖ ˌmɔːrf oʊ tek 'tɑːn-
with stress-imposing suffix mɔː 'fɒ+ ‖ mɔːr 'fɑː+ — **morphometry** mɔː 'fɒm ətr i -ɪtr- ‖ mɔːr 'fɑːm-
morphological ˌmɔːf ə 'lɒdʒ ɪk ᵊl ◂ ‖ ˌmɔːrf ə 'lɑːdʒ- **~ly** ‿i
morpholog|y mɔː 'fɒl ədʒ |i ‖ mɔːr 'fɑːl- **~ies** iz
morphophoneme ˌmɔːf əʊ 'fəʊn iːm ‖ ˌmɔːrf oʊ 'foʊn- **~s** z
morphophonemic ˌmɔːf əʊ fəʊ 'niːm ɪk ◂ ‖ ˌmɔːrf oʊ fə- **~ally** ᵊl‿i **~s** s
morphophonology ˌmɔːf əʊ fəʊ 'nɒl ədʒ i ‖ ˌmɔːrf oʊ fə 'nɑːl-
morphosyntactic ˌmɔːf əʊ sɪn 'tækt ɪk ◂ ‖ ˌmɔːrf oʊ-
-morphous 'mɔːf əs ‖ 'mɔːrf əs — **isomorphous** ˌaɪs əʊ 'mɔːf əs ◂ ‖ -ə 'mɔːrf-
-morphy mɔːf i ‖ mɔːrf i — **isomorphy** 'aɪs əʊ mɔːf i ‖ -ə mɔːrf i
Morphy 'mɔːf i ‖ 'mɔːrf i
Morpurgo mɔː 'pɜːg əʊ ‖ mɔːr 'pɜːg oʊ
Morrell *(i)* mə 'rel mɒ-, *(ii)* 'mʌr əl ‖ 'mɜː-
Morrill 'mɒr ɪl -əl ‖ 'mɔːr- 'mɑːr-
Morris, m~ 'mɒr ɪs §-əs ‖ 'mɔːr- 'mɑːr- **'morris dance**; **'morris ˌdancer**; **'morris men**
Morrison 'mɒr ɪs ən §-əs- ‖ 'mɔːr- 'mɑːr-
Morrissey 'mɒr ɪs i -əs- ‖ 'mɔːr- 'mɑːr-
Morristown 'mɒr ɪs taʊn §-əs- ‖ 'mɔːr- 'mɑːr-
morrow, M~ 'mɒr əʊ ‖ 'mɔːr oʊ 'mɑːr- **~s** z
Morse, morse mɔːs ‖ mɔːrs **morses, Morse's** 'mɔːs ɪz -əz ‖ 'mɔːrs əz
ˌMorse 'code
morsel 'mɔːs ᵊl ‖ 'mɔːrs- **~s** z
Mort, mort mɔːt ‖ mɔːrt **morts, Mort's** mɔːts ‖ mɔːrts
mortadella ˌmɔːt ə 'del ə ‖ ˌmɔːrţ ə- **~s** z
mortal 'mɔːt ᵊl ‖ 'mɔːrţ ᵊl **~s** z
ˌmortal 'sin
mortalit|y mɔː 'tæl ət |i -ɪt- ‖ mɔːr 'tæl əţ |i **~ies** iz
mortally 'mɔːt əl i ‖ 'mɔːrţ ᵊl i
mortar 'mɔːt ə ‖ 'mɔːrţ ᵊr **~ed** d **mortaring** 'mɔːt ər ɪŋ ‖ 'mɔːrţ ər ɪŋ **~s** z
mortarboard 'mɔːt ə bɔːd ‖ 'mɔːrţ ᵊr bɔːrd -boʊrd **~s** z
Morte d'Arthur ˌmɔːt 'dɑːθ ə ‖ ˌmɔːrt 'dɑːrθ ᵊr
Mortehoe 'mɔːt həʊ ‖ 'mɔːrt hoʊ
mortem 'mɔːt əm -em ‖ 'mɔːrţ-
mortgag|e 'mɔːg ɪdʒ ‖ 'mɔːrg- **~ed** d **~es** ɪz əz **~ing** ɪŋ
mortgagee ˌmɔːg ɪ 'dʒiː -ə- ‖ ˌmɔːrg- **~s** z
mortgagor ˌmɔːg ɪ 'dʒɔː -ə-; 'mɔːg ɪdʒ ə, -ədʒ- ‖ ˌmɔːrg ə 'dʒɔːr 'mɔːrg ədʒ ᵊr **~s** z
mortic|e 'mɔːt ɪs §-əs ‖ 'mɔːrţ əs **~ed** t **~es** ɪz əz **~ing** ɪŋ
mortician mɔː 'tɪʃ ᵊn ‖ mɔːr- **~s** z
mortification ˌmɔːt ɪf ɪ 'keɪʃ ᵊn ˌ·əf-, §-ə'·- ‖ ˌmɔːrţ əf- **~s** z
morti|fy 'mɔːt ɪ |faɪ -ə- ‖ 'mɔːrţ ə- **~fied** faɪd **~fies** faɪz **~fying/ly** faɪ ɪŋ /li
Mortimer 'mɔːt ɪm ə -əm- ‖ 'mɔːrţ əm ᵊr
mortis|e 'mɔːt ɪs §-əs ‖ 'mɔːrţ əs **~ed** t **~es** ɪz əz **~ing** ɪŋ
'mortise lock
Mortlake 'mɔːt leɪk ‖ 'mɔːrt-
mortmain 'mɔːt meɪn ‖ 'mɔːrt-
Morton 'mɔːt ᵊn ‖ 'mɔːrt ᵊn

M

mortuar|y 'mɔːtʃ u˽ər |i 'mɔːtʃ ər |i; 'mɔːt ju˽ər i, 'mɔːt jʊr |i ‖ 'mɔːrtʃ u er |i **~ies** iz
mosaic, M~ məʊ 'zeɪ ɪk ‖ moʊ- **~s** s
moschatel ˌmɒsk ə 'tel ‖ ˌmɑːsk- '· · · **~s** z
Moscow 'mɒsk əʊ ‖ 'mɑːsk aʊ -oʊ
Moseley 'məʊz li ‖ 'moʊz-
Moselle məʊ 'zel ‖ moʊ- —*Fr* [mo zɛl], *Ger* Mosel ['moː zᵊl]
Moses 'məʊz ɪz -əz ‖ 'moʊz-
mosey 'məʊz i ‖ 'moʊz i **~ed** d **~ing** ɪŋ **~s** z
mosh mɒʃ ‖ mɑːʃ **moshed** mɒʃt ‖ mɑːʃt **moshes** 'mɒʃ ɪz -əz ‖ 'mɑːʃ əz **moshing** 'mɒʃ ɪŋ ‖ 'mɑːʃ ɪŋ
Moskva 'mɒsk və ‖ mɑːsk 'vɑː —*Russ* [mʌ 'skva]
Moskvich *tdmk* 'mɒsk vɪtʃ ‖ 'mɑːsk- —*Russ* [mʌ 'skvʲitʃ] **~es** ɪz əz
Moslem 'mɒz ləm 'mʊz-, -lɪm, -lem ‖ 'mɑːz- 'mɑːs- **~s** z
Mosley *family name(i)* 'məʊz li ‖ 'moʊz-, *(ii)* 'mɒz- ‖ 'mɑːz-
mosque mɒsk ‖ mɑːsk **mosques** mɒsks ‖ mɑːsks
mosquito mə 'skiːt əʊ mɒ- ‖ -'skiːţ oʊ **~es, ~s** z
mo'squito net
moss, Moss mɒs ‖ mɔːs mɑːs **mosses** 'mɒs ɪz -əz ‖ 'mɔːs əz 'mɑːs-
Mossad 'mɒs æd ‖ mə 'sɑːd mɑː-, moʊ-
Mossbauer, Mössbauer 'mɒs ˌbaʊ˽ə ‖ 'mɔːs ˌbaʊ ᵊr 'mɑːs- —*Ger* ['mœs bau ɐ]
'Mössbauer ef,fect
moss-grown 'mɒs grəʊn ‖ 'mɔːs groʊn 'mɑːs-
Mossi 'mɒs i ‖ 'mɑːs i
Mossman 'mɒs mən ‖ 'mɔːs- 'mɑːs-
Mossop 'mɒs əp ‖ 'mɔːs- 'mɑːs-
moss|y 'mɒs |i ‖ 'mɔːs |i 'mɑːs- **~ier** i˽ə ‖ i˽ᵊr **~iest** i˽ɪst i˽əst **~iness** i nəs i nɪs
most məʊst ‖ moʊst **mostly** 'məʊst li ‖ 'moʊst-
ˌmost of 'all
-most məʊst ‖ moʊst — **innermost** 'ɪn ə məʊst ‖ -ᵊr moʊst
Mostar 'mɒst ɑː ‖ 'mɑːst ɑːr 'moʊst- —*Croatian* [''mɔ staːr]
most-favoured, most-favored ˌməʊst 'feɪv əd ◂ ‖ ˌmoʊst'feɪv ᵊrd ·'· ·
Mostyn 'mɒst ɪn §-ən ‖ 'mɑːst-
Mosul 'məʊ sᵊl 'muːs- ‖ 'moʊs-
mot məʊ ‖ moʊ —*Fr* [mo] **mots** məʊz ‖ moʊz
ˌmot 'juste ʒuːst —*Fr* [ʒyst]
M.o.T., MOT ˌem əʊ 'tiː ‖ -oʊ- **~'d** d **~'ing** ɪŋ **~s, ~'s** z
mote məʊt ‖ moʊt *(= moat)* **motes** məʊts ‖ moʊts
motel ₍ˌ₎məʊ 'tel ‖ ₍ˌ₎moʊ- **~s** z
motet ₍ˌ₎məʊ 'tet ‖ ₍ˌ₎moʊ- **~s** s
moth mɒθ ‖ mɔːθ mɑːθ **moths** mɒθs ‖ mɔːðz mɑːðz, mɔːθs, mɑːθs
Mothaks *tdmk* 'mɒθ æks ‖ 'mɔːθ- 'mɑːθ-
mothball 'mɒθ bɔːl ‖ 'mɔːθ- 'mɑːθ bɑːl **~ed** d **~ing** ɪŋ **~s** z
moth-eaten 'mɒθ ˌiːt ᵊn ‖ 'mɔːθ- 'mɑːθ-
mother, M~ 'mʌð ə ‖ -ᵊr **~ed** d **mothering** 'mʌð ər˽ɪŋ **~s** z
'mother ˌcountry; **ˌMother 'Goose**, **ˌMother 'Goose rhyme**; **ˌmother 'hen**; **'Mothering ˌSunday**; **ˌMother 'Nature**; **'mother's boy**; **'Mother's Day**; **ˌmother's 'ruin**; **ˌmother su'perior**; **ˌmother 'tongue,** '· ·
motherboard 'mʌð ə bɔːd ‖ -ᵊr bɔːrd -boʊrd **~s** z
Mothercare *tdmk* 'mʌð ə keə ‖ -ᵊr ker
mothercraft 'mʌð ə krɑːft §-kræft ‖ -ᵊr kræft
motherese ˌmʌð ə 'riːz
motherfuck|er 'mʌð ə ˌfʌk| ə ‖ -ᵊr ˌfʌk| ᵊr **~ers** əz ‖ ᵊrz **~ing** ɪŋ
motherhood 'mʌð ə hʊd ‖ -ᵊr-
mother-in-law 'mʌð ər˽ɪn ˌlɔː '·ə-, -ᵊr˽ən- ‖ -ᵊr˽ən- -ˌlɑː **~s, ~'s** z **mothers-in-law** 'mʌð əz ɪn ˌlɔː §-ən ˌ· ‖ -ᵊrz ən- ˌlɑː
motherland 'mʌð ə lænd ‖ -ᵊr-
motherless 'mʌð ə ləs -lɪs ‖ -ᵊr- **~ness** nəs nɪs
mother|ly 'mʌð ə |li ‖ -ᵊr- **~liness** li nəs -nɪs
mother-of-pearl ˌmʌð ər˽əv 'pɜːl ◂ ‖ -'pɜ˞ːl
mother-of-thousands ˌmʌð ər˽əv 'θaʊz ᵊndz
mothers- —*see* **mother-**
mother-to-be ˌmʌð ə tə 'biː ‖ ˌ·ᵊr- **mothers-to-be** ˌmʌð əz tə 'biː ‖ ˌ·ᵊrz-
Motherwell 'mʌð ə wəl -wel ‖ -ᵊr-
mothproof 'mɒθ pruːf §-prʊf ‖ 'mɔːθ- 'mɑːθ- **~ed** t **~ing** ɪŋ **~s** s
moth|y 'mɒθ |i ‖ 'mɔːθ |i 'mɑːθ- **~ier** i˽ə ‖ i˽ᵊr **~iest** i˽ɪst i˽əst
motif ₍ˌ₎məʊ 'tiːf mɒ- ‖ moʊ- **~s** s
motile 'məʊt aɪᵊl ‖ 'moʊţ ᵊl 'moʊt aɪᵊl *(*)*
motility məʊ 'tɪl ət i -ɪt- ‖ moʊ 'tɪl əţ i
motion, M~ 'məʊʃ ᵊn ‖ 'moʊʃ ᵊn **~ed** d **~ing** ˽ɪŋ **~s** z
ˌmotion 'picture◂; **'motion ˌsickness**
motionless 'məʊʃ ᵊn ləs -lɪs ‖ 'moʊʃ- **~ly** li **~ness** nəs nɪs
moti|vate 'məʊt ɪ |veɪt -ə- ‖ 'moʊţ ə- **~vated** veɪt ɪd -əd ‖ veɪţ əd **~vates** veɪts **~vating** veɪt ɪŋ ‖ veɪţ ɪŋ
motivation ˌməʊt ɪ 'veɪʃ ᵊn -ə- ‖ ˌmoʊţ ə- **~s** z
motivational ˌməʊt ɪ 'veɪʃ ᵊn˽əl ˌ·ə- ‖ ˌmoʊţ ə- **~ly** i
motivator 'məʊt ɪ veɪt ə -ə- ‖ 'moʊţ ə veɪţ ᵊr **~s** z
motive 'məʊt ɪv ‖ 'moʊţ ɪv **~less** ləs lɪs **~s** z
motley, M~ 'mɒt li ‖ 'mɑːt-
motmot 'mɒt mɒt ‖ 'mɑːt mɑːt **~s** s
motocross 'məʊt əʊ krɒs -krɔːs ‖ 'moʊţ oʊ krɔːs -krɑːs
motor 'məʊt ə ‖ 'moʊţ ᵊr **~ed** d **motoring** 'məʊt˽ər ɪŋ ‖ 'moʊţ ər ɪŋ **~s** z
'motor lodge; **'motor ˌscooter**; **ˌmotor 'vehicle**
motorbike 'məʊt ə baɪk ‖ 'moʊţ ᵊr- **~s** s
motorboat 'məʊt ə bəʊt ‖ 'moʊţ ᵊr boʊt **~s** s
motorcade 'məʊt ə keɪd ‖ 'moʊţ ᵊr- **~s** z
motorcar 'məʊt ə kɑː ‖ 'moʊţ ᵊr kɑːr **~s** z

M

motorcoach 'məʊt ə kəʊtʃ ‖ 'moʊţ ᵊr koʊtʃ **~es** ɪz əz
motorcycle 'məʊt ə ˌsaɪk ᵊl ‖ 'moʊţ ᵊr- **~s** z
motorcyclist 'məʊt ə ˌsaɪk lɪst §-ləst ‖ 'moʊţ ᵊr- **~s** s
motoris... —*see* **motoriz...**
motorist 'məʊt ər ɪst §-əst ‖ 'moʊţ ər- **~s** s
motoriz|e 'məʊt ə raɪz ‖ 'moʊţ ə- **~ed** d **~es** ɪz əz **~ing** ɪŋ
motor|man 'məʊt ə |mən -mæn ‖ 'moʊţ ᵊr- **~men** mən men
motor|mouth 'məʊt ə |maʊθ ‖ 'moʊţ ᵊr- **~mouths** maʊðz
motorway 'məʊt ə weɪ ‖ 'moʊţ ᵊr- **~s** z
Motown 'məʊ taʊn ‖ 'moʊ-
Motson 'mɒts ᵊn ‖ 'mɑːts-
Mott mɒt ‖ mɑːt
motte mɒt ‖ mɑːt **mottes** mɒts ‖ mɑːts
mottl|e 'mɒt ᵊl ‖ 'mɑːţ ᵊl **~ed** d **~es** z **~ing** ˌɪŋ
motto 'mɒt əʊ ‖ 'mɑːţ oʊ **~es, ~s** z
Mottram 'mɒtr əm ‖ 'mɑːtr-
Motu 'məʊt uː ‖ 'moʊt-
motu proprio ˌməʊt uː 'prɒp ri əʊ -'prəʊp- ‖ ˌmoʊt uː 'proʊp ri oʊ
moue muː *(= moo)* —*Fr* [mu] **moues** muːz
moufflon, mouflon 'muːf lɒn ‖ -lɑːn **~s** z
mouille, mouillé 'mwiː eɪ 'muː jeɪ ‖ muː 'jeɪ —*Fr* [mu je]
mould, Mould məʊld →mɒʊld ‖ moʊld **moulded** 'məʊld ɪd →'mɒʊld-, -əd ‖ 'moʊld əd **moulding/s** 'məʊld ɪŋ/z →'mɒʊld- ‖ 'moʊld ɪŋ/z **moulds** məʊldz →mɒʊldz ‖ moʊldz
mould|er 'məʊld |ə →'mɒʊld- ‖ 'moʊld |ᵊr **~ered** əd ‖ ᵊrd **~ering** ər ɪŋ **~ers** əz ‖ ᵊrz
mould|y 'məʊld |i →'mɒʊld- ‖ 'moʊld |i **~ier** i‿ə ‖ i‿ᵊr **~iest** i‿ɪst i‿əst **~iness** i nəs i nɪs
Moulinex *tdmk* 'muːl ɪ neks -ə-
Moulin Rouge ˌmuːl æn 'ruːʒ —*Fr* [mu læ̃ ʁuːʒ]
moult, Moult məʊlt →mɒʊlt ‖ moʊlt **moulted** 'məʊlt ɪd →'mɒʊlt-, -əd ‖ 'moʊlt əd **moulting** 'məʊlt ɪŋ →'mɒʊlt- ‖ 'moʊlt ɪŋ **moults** məʊlts →mɒʊlts ‖ moʊlts
Moulton 'məʊlt ən →'mɒʊlt- ‖ 'moʊlt-
mound maʊnd **mounds** maʊndz
mount, Mount maʊnt **mounted** 'maʊnt ɪd -əd ‖ 'maʊnţ əd **mounting** 'maʊnt ɪŋ ‖ 'maʊnţ ɪŋ **mounts** maʊnts
ˌMount 'Everest; **ˌMount 'Pleasant**; **ˌMount 'Rushmore**; **ˌMount 'Vernon**
mountain 'maʊnt ɪn -ən ‖ -ᵊn —*In singing sometimes* -eɪn **~s** z
'mountain ˌlion; **'mountain range**; **ˌMountain 'Standard Time, 'Mountain Time**
mountaineer ˌmaʊnt ɪ 'nɪə -ə- ‖ -ᵊn 'ɪᵊr **~ed** d **mountaineering** ˌmaʊnt ɪ 'nɪər ɪŋ ˌ-ə- ‖ -ᵊn 'ɪr ɪŋ **~s** z
mountainous 'maʊnt ɪn əs -ən- ‖ -ᵊn-
mountainside 'maʊnt ɪn saɪd -ən- ‖ -ᵊn- **~s** z
mountaintop 'maʊnt ɪn tɒp -ən- ‖ -ᵊn tɑːp **~s** s
Mountbatten maʊnt 'bæt ᵊn ‖ '·ˌ··
mountebank 'maʊnt ɪ bæŋk -ə- ‖ 'maʊnţ- **~s** s
Mountford 'maʊnt fəd ‖ -fᵊrd
Mountie 'maʊnt i ‖ 'maʊnţ i **~s** z
Mountjoy maʊnt 'dʒɔɪ '··
Mountsorrel ˌmaʊnt 'sɒr əl ‖ -'sɔːr- -'sɑːr-
Mount|y 'maʊnt |i ‖ 'maʊnţ |i **~ies** iz
Moureen 'mɔːr iːn mɔː 'riːn
Mourinho mə 'riːn jəʊ mu-, -ju —*Port* [mo 'ri ɲu]
mourn mɔːn mʊən ‖ mɔːrn moʊrn **mourned** mɔːnd mʊənd ‖ mɔːrnd moʊrnd **mourning** 'mɔːn ɪŋ 'mʊən- ‖ 'mɔːrn ɪŋ 'moʊrn- **mourns** mɔːnz mʊənz ‖ mɔːrnz moʊrnz
Mourne mɔːn ‖ mɔːrn moʊrn
mourner 'mɔːn ə 'mʊən- ‖ 'mɔːrn ᵊr 'moʊrn- **~s** z
mournful 'mɔːn fᵊl 'mʊən-, -fʊl ‖ 'mɔːrn- 'moʊrn- **~ly** ˌi **~ness** nəs nɪs
mourning 'mɔːn ɪŋ 'mʊən- ‖ 'mɔːrn ɪŋ 'moʊrn-
Mousa *place in Shetland* 'muːz ə
mouse *v* maʊz maʊs **moused** maʊzd maʊst **mouses** 'maʊz ɪz 'maʊs-, -əz **mousing** 'maʊz ɪŋ 'maʊs-
mouse *n* maʊs **mice** maɪs **mice's** 'maɪs ɪz -əz **mouse's** 'maʊs ɪz -əz
'mouse mat; **'mouse pad**
mousehole 'maʊs həʊl →-hɒʊl ‖ -hoʊl **~s** z
Mousehole *place in Cornwall* 'maʊz ᵊl
mouselike 'maʊs laɪk
mouser 'maʊz ə 'maʊs- ‖ -ᵊr **~s** z
mousetrap 'maʊs træp **~s** s
mous|ey 'maʊs |i **~ier** i‿ə ‖ i‿ᵊr **~iest** i‿ɪst i‿əst **~iness** i nəs i nɪs
moussaka mu 'sɑːk ə —*ModGk* [mu sa 'ka] **~s** z
mousse muːs *(= moose)* **mousses** 'muːs ɪz -əz
Moussec *tdmk* ˌmuː 'sek
Moussorgsky mu 'sɔːg ski mə-, -'zɔːg- ‖ -'sɔːrg- -'zɔːrg- —*Russ* ['mu sərk skʲɪj]
moustach|e mə 'stɑːʃ mu-, §-'stæʃ, §-'stɒʃ ‖ 'mʌst æʃ mə 'stæʃ *(*)* **~ed** t **~es** ɪz əz
moustachio mə 'stɑːʃ i əʊ -'stæʃ- ‖ mə 'stæʃ i oʊ **~ed** d **~s** z
mous|y 'maʊs |i **~ier** i‿ə ‖ i‿ᵊr **~iest** i‿ɪst i‿əst **~iness** i nəs i nɪs
mouth *v* maʊð **mouthed** maʊðd **mouths** maʊðz **mouthing** 'maʊð ɪŋ
mouth *n* maʊθ **mouths** maʊðz §maʊθs
'mouth ˌorgan; **'mouth ˌulcer**
-mouthed 'maʊðd 'maʊθt — **foul-mouthed** ˌfaʊl 'maʊðd ◂ -'maʊθt
mouthful 'maʊθ fʊl **~s** z
mouthorgan 'maʊθ ˌɔːg ən ‖ -ˌɔːrg- **~s** z
mouthpart 'maʊθ pɑːt ‖ -pɑːrt **~s** s
mouthpiec|e 'maʊθ piːs **~es** ɪz əz
mouth-to-mouth ˌmaʊθ tə 'maʊθ ◂ -tu-
ˌmouth-to-ˌmouth reˌsusci'tation
mouthwash 'maʊθ wɒʃ ‖ -wɔːʃ -wɑːʃ **~es** ɪz əz
mouthwatering 'maʊθ ˌwɔːt‿ər ɪŋ ‖ -ˌwɔːţ ər ɪŋ -ˌwɑːţ-

mouth|y ˈmaʊð| i ˈmaʊθ| i **~ier** i‿ə ‖ i‿ᵊr **~iest** i‿ɪst ‿əst
movable ˈmuːv əb ᵊl
ˌmovable ˈfeast
move muːv *(!)* **moved** muːvd **moves** muːvz
moving ˈmuːv ɪŋ
ˌmoving ˈpicture; **ˌmoving ˈstaircase**;
ˈmoving van *'removal van'*
moveable ˈmuːv əb ᵊl
movement ˈmuːv mənt **~s** s
mover ˈmuːv ə ‖ -ᵊr **~s** z
movie ˈmuːv i **~s** z
ˈmovie star
moviego|er ˈmuːv i ˌgəʊ| ə ‖ -ˌgoʊ ᵊr **~ers** əz ‖ ᵊrz **~ing** ɪŋ
moviemak|er ˈmuːv i ˌmeɪk ə ‖ -ᵊr **~ers** əz ‖ ᵊrz **~ing** ɪŋ
Movietone *tdmk* ˈmuːv i təʊn ‖ -toʊn
moving ˈmuːv ɪŋ **~ly** li
mow *'stack', v 'store hay'* maʊ **mowed** maʊd **mowing** ˈmaʊ ɪŋ **mows** maʊz *—but usually* məʊ ‖ moʊ *in the inn name* ˌBarley ˈMow
mow *'grimace'* maʊ **mowed** maʊd **mowing** ˈmaʊ ɪŋ **mows** maʊz
mow *'cut down'* məʊ ‖ moʊ *(= mo)* **mowed** məʊd ‖ moʊd **mowing** ˈməʊ ɪŋ ‖ ˈmoʊ ɪŋ **mown** məʊn ‖ moʊn **mows** məʊz ‖ moʊz
ˈmowing maˌchine
Mowat, Mowatt *(i)* ˈməʊ ət ‖ ˈmoʊ-, *(ii)* ˈmaʊ-
Mowbray ˈməʊb ri -reɪ ‖ ˈmoʊb-
mower, Mower ˈməʊ ə ‖ ˈmoʊ ᵊr **~s** z
Mowgli ˈmaʊg li
Mowlam, Mowlem ˈməʊl əm ‖ ˈmoʊl-
mown məʊn ‖ moʊn *(= moan)*
moxa ˈmɒks ə ‖ ˈmɑːks ə
moxibustion ˌmɒks ɪ ˈbʌs tʃən -ə- ‖ ˌmɑːks-
moxie ˈmɒks i ‖ ˈmɑːks i
Moy mɔɪ
Moya ˈmɔɪ ə
Moygashel mɔɪ ˈgæʃ ᵊl ˈmɔɪg əʃ-
Moynahan ˈmɔɪn ə hən -hæn
Moyne mɔɪn
Moynihan ˈmɔɪn i‿ən -ɪ hæn, -ə-
Moyra ˈmɔɪᵊr ə
Mozambican, Mozambiquan ˌməʊz əm ˈbiːk ən ◂ -æm- ‖ ˌmoʊz- **~s** z
Mozambique ˌməʊz əm ˈbiːk -æm- ‖ ˌmoʊz-
Mozarab məʊ ˈzær əb ‖ moʊ- -ˈzer- **~s** z
Mozarabic məʊ ˈzær əb ɪk ‖ moʊ- -ˈzer-
Mozart ˈməʊts ɑːt ‖ ˈmoʊts ɑːrt *—Ger* [ˈmoː tsaʁt]
Mozartian ˌməʊt ˈsɑːt i‿ən ◂ ‖ moʊt ˈsɑːrt̬ i‿ən **~s** z
mozzarella ˌmɒts ə ˈrel ə ◂ ‖ ˌmɑːt- ˌmoʊt- *—It* [mot tsa ˈrɛl la]
mozzie ˈmɒz i ‖ ˈmɑːz i **~s** z
MP ˌem ˈpiː **MPs, MP's** ˌem ˈpiːz
mp3 ˌem piː ˈθriː **~s** z
MPEG, mpg ˈem peg **~s** z
mph ˌem piː ˈeɪtʃ §-ˈheɪtʃ *—or as* miles per hour, miles an hour
MPhil ˌem ˈfɪl
Mpumalanga ᵊm ˌpuːm ə ˈlæŋ gə *—siSwati* [mpú má ˈlàː ŋgà]
Mr ˈmɪst ə ‖ -ᵊr
Mrs ˈmɪs ɪz §-əz ‖ ˈmɪz-
MRSA ˌem ɑːr es ˈeɪ ‖ ˌem ɑːr-
ms *—see* **manuscript**
Ms mɪz məz, məs *—As a self-designation,* **mɪz** *seems to be preferred. Those who say* **məz, məs** *may use it in stressed as well as unstressed position. Some claim the word is unpronounceable.*
MS *'multiple sclerosis'* ˌem ˈes
MSc ˌem es ˈsiː
MS-DOS *tdmk* ˌem es ˈdɒs ‖ -ˈdɔːs -ˈdɑːs
mss *—see* **manuscripts**
Mt *—see* **Mount**
MTV ˌem tiː ˈviː
mu mjuː *(= mew)*
Mubarak mu ˈbɑːr æk -ˈbær-, -ək *—Arabic* [mu ˈbaː rak]
much, Much mʌtʃ **more** mɔː ‖ mɔːr moʊr **most** məʊst ‖ moʊst **muchness** ˈmʌtʃ nəs -nɪs
much-heralded ˌmʌtʃ ˈher əld ɪd ◂ -əd
mucho ˈmuːtʃ əʊ ‖ -oʊ *—Sp* [ˈmu tʃo]
much-vaunted ˌmʌtʃ ˈvɔːnt ɪd ◂ -əd ‖ -ˈvɔːnt̬- -ˈvɑːnt̬-
mucic ˈmjuːs ɪk
mucilag|e ˈmjuːs ɪl ɪdʒ -əl- **~es** ɪz əz
mucilaginous ˌmjuːs ɪ ˈlædʒ ɪn əs ◂ ˌ-ə-, -ən əs
mucin ˈmjuːs ɪn §-ᵊn **~s** z
muck, Muck mʌk **mucked** mʌkt **mucking** ˈmʌk ɪŋ **mucks** mʌks
mucker ˈmʌk ə ‖ -ᵊr **~s** z
muckety-muck ˌmʌk ət i ˈmʌk ‖ -ət̬- **~s** s
muckheap ˈmʌk hiːp **~s** s
muckle ˈmʌk ᵊl
ˌMuckle ˈFlugga ˈflʌg ə
muckluck ˈmʌk lʌk **~s** s
muckrak|er ˈmʌk reɪk |ə ‖ -|ᵊr **~ers** əz ‖ ᵊrz **~ing** ɪŋ
muck-spread|er ˈmʌk ˌspred| ə ‖ -ᵊr **~ers** əz ‖ ᵊrz **~ing** ɪŋ
muck|y ˈmʌk |i **~ier** i‿ə ‖ i‿ᵊr **~iest** i‿ɪst i‿əst
muco- *comb. form*
with stress-neutral suffix ˌmjuːk əʊ ‖ -oʊ — **mucofibrous** ˌmjuːk əʊ ˈfaɪb rəs ◂ ‖ -oʊ-
with stress-imposing suffix mju ˈkɒ+ ‖ -ˈkɑː+ — **mucoclasis** mju ˈkɒk ləs ɪs §-əs ‖ -ˈkɑːk-
mucous ˈmjuːk əs *(= mucus)*
ˌmucous ˈmembrane
Mu-cron *tdmk* ˈmjuː krɒn ‖ -krɑːn
mucus ˈmjuːk əs
mud mʌd **muds** mʌdz
ˈmud bath; **ˌmud ˈpie**; **ˈmud ˌpuppy**
mudbank ˈmʌd bæŋk →ˈmʌb- **~s** s
mud|bath ˈmʌd| bɑːθ →ˈmʌb-, §-bæθ ‖ -bæθ **~baths** bɑːðz §bɑːθs, §bæθs, §bæðz ‖ bæðz bæθs
Mudd mʌd
muddi... *—see* **muddy**
muddl|e ˈmʌd ᵊl **~ed** d **~es** z **~ing** ‿ɪŋ

M

muddle-headed ˌmʌd ᵊl ˈhed ɪd ◂ -əd **~ly** li **~ness** nəs nɪs
mudd|y ˈmʌd |i **~ied** id **~ier** i‿ə ‖ i‿ᵊr **~ies** iz **~iest** i‿ɪst i‿əst **~ily** ɪ li əl i **~iness** i nəs i nɪs **~ying** i‿ɪŋ
Mudeford ˈmʌd i fəd ‖ -fᵊrd *(!)*
mudfish ˈmʌd fɪʃ **~es** ɪz əz
mudflap ˈmʌd flæp **~s** s
mudflat ˈmʌd flæt **~s** s
Mudge mʌdʒ
mudguard ˈmʌd gɑːd →ˈmʌg- ‖ -gɑːrd **~s** z
Mudie ˈmjuːd i
mudlark ˈmʌd lɑːk ‖ -lɑːrk **~s** s
mudpack ˈmʌd pæk →ˈmʌb- **~s** s
mudskipper ˈmʌd ˌskɪp ə ‖ -ᵊr **~s** z
mudslide ˈmʌd slaɪd **~s** z
mudsling|er ˈmʌd ˌslɪŋ |ə ‖ -|ᵊr **~ers** əz ‖ ᵊrz **~ing** ɪŋ
mud-wrestling ˈmʌd ˌres ᵊl‿ɪŋ ‖ ˌræs-
muesli ˈmjuːz li ˈmuːz- ‖ ˈmjuːs- **~s** z —*Ger* Müsli [ˈmyːs li]
muezzin mu ˈez ɪn mju-, §-ᵊn **~s** z
muff mʌf **muffed** mʌft **muffing** ˈmʌf ɪŋ **muffs** mʌfs
muffin ˈmʌf ɪn §-ᵊn **~s** z
muffl|e ˈmʌf ᵊl **~ed** d **~es** z **~ing** ‿ɪŋ
muffler ˈmʌf lə ‖ -lᵊr **~s** z
Muffy ˈmʌf i
mufti, Mufti ˈmʌft i **~s** z
mug mʌg **mugged** mʌgd **mugging/s** ˈmʌg ɪŋ/z **mugs** mʌgz
ˈmug's game
Mugabe mu ˈgɑːb i -eɪ
mugful ˈmʌg fʊl **~s** z
mugger ˈmʌg ə ‖ -ᵊr **~s** z
Muggeridge ˈmʌg ər‿ɪdʒ
muggins, M~ ˈmʌg ɪnz §-ənz
muggle ˈmʌg ᵊl **~s** z
Muggleton ˈmʌg ᵊl tən
Muggletonian ˌmʌg ᵊl ˈtəʊn i‿ən ‖ -ˈtoʊn- **~s** z
mugg|y ˈmʌg |i **~ier** i‿ə ‖ i‿ᵊr **~iest** i‿ɪst i‿əst **~ily** ɪ li əl i **~iness** i nəs i nɪs
mugho ˈmjuːg əʊ ˈmuːg- ‖ -oʊ **~s** z
mugshot ˈmʌg ʃɒt ‖ -ʃɑːt **~s** s
mugwort ˈmʌg wɜːt -wɔːt ‖ -wɜːt -wɔːrt **~s** s
mugwump ˈmʌg wʌmp **~s** s
Muhammed mu ˈhæm ɪd -əd, -ed —*Arabic* [mu ˈħam mad]
Muhammedan mu ˈhæm ɪd ən -əd- **~ism** ˌɪz əm **~s** z
Muir mjʊə mjɔː ‖ mjʊᵊr
Muirhead ˈmjʊə hed ˈmjɔː- ‖ ˈmjʊr-
mujaheddin, mujahedeen ˌmuːdʒ ə he ˈdiːn ˌmʊdʒ-, ˌmuːʒ-, ˌ·ɑː-, -həˈ· —*Arabic* [mu dʒaː hi ˈdiːn]
Mukden ˈmʊk dən
mukluk ˈmʌk lʌk **~s** s
muktuk ˈmʌk tʌk
mulatto mju ˈlæt əʊ mu-, mə- ‖ -ˈlæţ oʊ -ˈlɑːţ- **~s** z
mulberr|y ˈmʌl bər‿|i ‖ -ˌber |i **~ies** iz
Mulcaghey mʌl ˈkæ hi -ˈkæx i
Mulcahy mʌl ˈkæ hi
mulch mʌltʃ **mulched** mʌltʃt **mulches** ˈmʌltʃ ɪz -əz **mulching** ˈmʌltʃ ɪŋ
mulct mʌlkt **mulcted** ˈmʌlkt ɪd -əd **mulcting** ˈmʌlkt ɪŋ **mulcts** mʌlkts
Mulder ˈmʌld ə ‖ -ᵊr
Muldoon mʌl ˈduːn
mule mjuːl **mules** mjuːlz
Mules mjuːlz
muleteer ˌmjuːl ə ˈtɪə -ɪ- ‖ -ˈtɪᵊr **~s** z
mulga ˈmʌlg ə **~s** z
Mulhearn mʌl ˈhɜːn ‖ -ˈhɜːn
Mulholland mʌl ˈhɒl ənd ‖ -ˈhɑːl-
mulish ˈmjuːl ɪʃ **~ly** li **~ness** nəs nɪs
mull, Mull mʌl **mulled** mʌld **mulling** ˈmʌl ɪŋ **mulls** mʌlz
mulla, mullah ˈmʌl ə ˈmʊl- **~s** z
Mullan ˈmʌl ən
mullein ˈmʌl ɪn -eɪn, -ən **~s** z
Muller ˈmʌl ə ‖ -ᵊr —*but as a German name* ˈmʊl-, ˈmuːl-, ˈmjuːl- —*Ger* Müller [ˈmʏl ɐ]
mullet ˈmʌl ɪt -ət **~s** s
Mulley ˈmʌl i
Mulligan, m~ ˈmʌl ɪg ən -əg- **~s** z
mulligatawny ˌmʌl ɪg ə ˈtɔːn i ◂ ˌ·əg- ‖ -ˈtɑːn-
Mulliken ˈmʌl ɪk ən
mullion ˈmʌl i‿ən ‖ ˈmʌl jən **~ed** d **~s** z
Mulroney mʌl ˈrəʊn i ‖ -ˈroʊn i
multi- *comb. form*
with stress-neutral suffix ¦mʌlt i ‖ -aɪ — **multiethnic** ˌmʌlt i ˈeθ nɪk ◂ ‖ -aɪ-
with stress-imposing suffix mʌl ˈtɪ+ — **multiparous** mʌl ˈtɪp ər əs
multicellular ˌmʌlt i ˈsel jʊl ə ◂ -jəl· ‖ -jəl ᵊr
multicolored, multicoloured ˈmʌlt i ˌkʌl əd ˌ·ˈ·· ‖ -ᵊrd -aɪ-
multicultural ˌmʌlt i ˈkʌltʃ ᵊr‿əl ◂ ‖ ˌ·aɪ- **~ism** ˌɪz əm **~ist/s** ɪst/s §əst/s **~ly** i
multidimensional ˌmʌlt i daɪ ˈmenʃ ᵊn‿əl ◂ -i dɪ-, -i də- ‖ -i də-
multidirectional ˌmʌlt i daɪᵊ ˈrek ʃᵊn‿əl ◂ -i dɪ-, -i də- ‖ -i də-
multidisciplinary ˌmʌlt i ˈdɪs ə plɪn ər‿i ◂ -ˈ·ɪ-, -ˈ·plən-, -ˌ·ˈplɪn ər i◂ ‖ -plə ner i
multifaceted ˌmʌlt i ˈfæs ɪt ɪd ◂ -ət·, -əd◂ ‖ -əţ əd ◂
multi-faith ˌmʌlt i ˈfeɪθ ◂
multifamily ˌmʌlt i ˈfæm əl‿i ◂ -ɪl i ◂
multifarious ˌmʌlt ɪ ˈfeər i‿əs ◂ ˌ·ə- ‖ -ˈfer- -ˈfær- **~ly** li **~ness** nəs nɪs
multiform ˈmʌlt i fɔːm -ə- ‖ -fɔːrm
multiformity ˌmʌlt i ˈfɔːm ət i ˌ·ə-, -ɪt i ‖ -ˈfɔːrm əţ i
multifunction ˌmʌlt i ˈfʌŋkʃᵊn ◂ **~al** əl ◂
multigrav|ida ˌmʌlt i ˈgræv |ɪd ə -əd ə **~idae** ɪ diː ə-
multilateral ˌmʌlt i ˈlæt‿ᵊr əl ◂ ‖ -ˈlæţ ər əl◂ →-ˈlætr əl ◂ **~ly** i
ˌmultiˌlateral ˈtrade
multilevel ˌmʌlt i ˈlev ᵊl ◂
multilingual ˌmʌlt i ˈlɪŋ gwəl ◂ -ˈlɪŋ gju‿əl ‖ ˌ·aɪ- **~ism** ɪz əm **~ly** i
ˌmultiˌlingual ˈsecretary

multimedia ˌmʌlt i ˈmiːd i‿ə ‖ ˌ·aɪ-
multimillion ˌmʌlt i ˈmɪl jən ◂
multimillionaire ˌmʌlt i ˌmɪl jə ˈneə ‖ -ˈneᵊr ˌ·aɪ-, -ˈnæᵊr; ˌ·ˌ·ˈ·· ~s z
multinational ˌmʌlt i ˈnæʃ ᵊn‿əl ◂ ‖ ˌ·aɪ- ~s z
multip|ara mʌl ˈtɪp |ər ə ~arae ə riː ~arous ər əs
multiparty ˌmʌlt i ˈpɑːt i ◂ ‖ -ˈpɑːrţ i ◂
multi-player ˌmʌlt i ˈpleɪ ə ◂ ‖ -ᵊr ◂
multiple ˈmʌlt ɪp ᵊl -əp- ~s z
ˌmultiple scleˈrosis
multiple-choice ˌmʌlt ɪp ᵊl ˈtʃɔɪs ˌ·əp-
ˌmultiple-ˈchoice ˌquestion
multiplex ˈmʌlt ɪ pleks -ə-, -i- ~ed t ~es ɪz əz ~ing ɪŋ
multiplexer, multiplexor ˈmʌlt ɪ pleks ə ˈ·ə- ‖ -ᵊr ~s z
multiplicand ˌmʌlt ɪ plɪ ˈkænd ˌ·ə-, §-pləˈ· ~s z
multiplication ˌmʌlt ɪ plɪ ˈkeɪʃ ᵊn ˌ·ə-, §-pləˈ·- ~s z
ˌmultipliˈcation sign; ˌmultipliˈcation ˌtable
multiplicative ˌmʌlt ɪ ˈplɪk ət ɪv ˌ·ə-; ˈ· ·plɪ keɪt ɪv, -plə · · ‖ -ˈplɪk əţ ɪv ˈ· ·plə keɪţ ɪv ~ly li
multiplicit|y ˌmʌlt ɪ ˈplɪs ət |i ˌ·ə-, -ɪt i ‖ -əţ |i ~ies iz
multi|ply *v* ˈmʌlt ɪ |plaɪ -ə- ~plied plaɪd ~plier/s plaɪ‿ə/z ‖ plaɪ‿ᵊr/z ~plies plaɪz ~plying plaɪ ɪŋ
multiply *adv* ˈmʌlt əp li -ɪp-
multipolar ˌmʌlt i ˈpəʊl ə ◂ ‖ -ˈpoʊl ᵊr ◂
multipurpose ˌmʌlt i ˈpɜːp əs ◂ ‖ -ˈpɜːp əs ◂ -aɪ-
multiraci|al ˌmʌlt i ˈreɪʃ |ᵊl ◂ ‖ aɪ- ~alism ə ˌlɪz əm ~ally əl i
multiskilling ˈmʌlt i ˌskɪl ɪŋ
multistage ˈmʌlt i steɪdʒ
multistorey, multistory ˌmʌlt i ˈstɔːr i ◂ ‖ -aɪ-, -ˈstoʊr-
ˌmultiˌstorey ˈcarpark
multitask ˈmʌlt i tɑːsk §-tæsk, ˌ·ˈ· ‖ -ˈtæsk ~er/s ə/z ‖ ᵊr/z ~ing ɪŋ
multitude ˈmʌlt ɪ tjuːd -ə-, →tʃuːd ‖ -tuːd -tjuːd ~s z
multitudinous ˌmʌlt ɪ ˈtjuːd ɪn əs ◂ ˌ·ə-, →ˈtʃuːd-, -ən‿əs ‖ -ˈtuːd ᵊn‿əs -ˈtjuːd- ~ly li
multivitamin ˈmʌlt i ˌvɪt əm ɪn -ˌvaɪt-, §-ən ‖ -ˌvaɪţ- ~s z
multum in parvo ˌmʊlt ʊm ɪn ˈpɑːv əʊ ˌmʌlt-, ˌ·əm-, →-ɪmˈ·-, §-ənˈ·- ‖ -ˈpɑːrv oʊ -ˈpɑːr woʊ
mum, Mum mʌm **mums, Mum's** mʌmz
Mumbai ˌmʊm ˈbaɪ
mumbl|e ˈmʌm bᵊl ~ed d ~es z ~ing ‿ɪŋ
Mumbles ˈmʌm bᵊlz
mumbling ˈmʌm bᵊl‿ɪŋ ~ly li
mumbo jumbo ˌmʌm bəʊ ˈdʒʌm bəʊ ‖ -boʊ ˈdʒʌm boʊ
Mumford ˈmʌm fəd ‖ -fᵊrd
Mumm mʌm mʊm
mummer ˈmʌm ə ‖ -ᵊr ~s z
Mummerset, m- ˈmʌm ə set ‖ -ᵊr-
mummer|y ˈmʌm ər |i ~ies iz
mummie... —*see* **mummy**
mummification ˌmʌm ɪf ɪ ˈkeɪʃ ᵊn ˌ·əf-, §-əˈ·-
mummi|fy ˈmʌm ɪ |faɪ -ə- ~fied faɪd ~fies faɪz ~fying faɪ ɪŋ
mumming ˈmʌm ɪŋ
mumm|y, M~ ˈmʌm |i ~ies, ~y's iz
mumpish ˈmʌmp ɪʃ ~ly li ~ness nəs nɪs
mumps mʌmps
mumsy, Mumsy ˈmʌmz i
mum-to-be ˌmʌm tə ˈbiː
Muncaster ˈmʌŋk əst ə §ˈmʌŋ ˌkɑːst ə, §-ˌkæst- ‖ ˈmʌn ˌkæst ᵊr
munch mʌntʃ **munched** mʌntʃt **munches** ˈmʌntʃ ɪz -əz **munching** ˈmʌntʃ ɪŋ
Munch mʊŋk —*Norwegian* [mʊŋk]
Munchausen, Munchhausen, Münchhausen ˈmʌntʃ aʊz ᵊn ˈmʊntʃ-, -haʊz-; mʌn ˈtʃɔːz ᵊn —*Ger* [ˈmʏnç haʊ zᵊn]
munchies, M~ *tdmk* ˈmʌntʃ iz
munchkin, M~ ˈmʌntʃ kɪn ~s z
Muncie ˈmʌnᵗs i
Munda ˈmʊnd ə
mundane ₍ˌ₎mʌn ˈdeɪn ˈ· · ~ly li ~ness nəs nɪs
Munday ˈmʌn deɪ
Mundesley ˈmʌnz li
mung mʌŋ **munged** mʌŋd **munging** ˈmʌŋ ɪŋ **mungs** mʌŋz
Mungo, mungo ˈmʌŋ gəʊ ‖ -goʊ
Munich ˈmjuːn ɪk -ɪx —*Ger* München [ˈmʏn çən]
municipal mju ˈnɪs ɪp ᵊl -əp-; §ˌmjuːn ɪ ˈsɪp-, -ə- ~ly i
municipalis... —*see* **municipaliz...**
municipalit|y mju ˌnɪs ɪ ˈpæl ət |i ˌmjuːn ɪs-, -əˈ·-, -ət i ‖ -əţ |i ~ies iz
municipalization mju ˌnɪs ɪp əl aɪ ˈzeɪʃ ᵊn -ˌ·əp-; §ˌmjuːn ɪ ˌsɪp-, -ə- ‖ -əˈ·- ~s z
municipaliz|e mju ˈnɪs ɪp ə laɪz -ˈ·əp-; §ˌmjuːn ɪ ˈsɪp-, -ə- ~ed d ~es ɪz əz ~ing ɪŋ
munificence mju ˈnɪf ɪs ənᵗs -əs-
munificent mju ˈnɪf ɪs ənt -əs- ~ly li
muniment ˈmjuːn ɪ mənt -ə- ~s s
munition mju ˈnɪʃ ᵊn ~s z
Munn mʌn
Munro, Munroe, Munrow mən ˈrəʊ mʌn- ‖ -ˈroʊ
Munsell ˈmʌnᵗs ᵊl
Munster, Münster *place in Germany* ˈmʊnᵗst ə ‖ -ᵊr —*Ger* [ˈmʏn stɐ]
Munster *province of Ireland* ˈmʌnᵗst ə ‖ -ᵊr
munt mʊnt **munts** mʊnts
muntjac, muntjak ˈmʌnt dʒæk ˈmʌntʃ æk ~s s
Muntz mʌnts
muon ˈmjuː ɒn ‖ -ɑːn ~s z
muppet, M~ ˈmʌp ɪt §-ət ~s s
muraena mjuᵊ ˈriːn ə ~s z
mural ˈmjʊər əl ˈmjɔːr- ‖ ˈmjʊr əl ~s z
Murchison *(i)* ˈmɜːtʃ ɪs ən §-əs- ‖ ˈmɜːtʃ-, *(ii)* ˈmɜːk- ‖ ˈmɜːk-

M

Murcia ˈmɜːθ i‿ə ˈmʊəθ- ‖ ˈmɝːs- —*Sp* [ˈmur θja]
murder ˈmɜːd ə ‖ ˈmɝːd ᵊr **~ed** d **murdering** ˈmɜːd‿ər ɪŋ ‖ ˈmɝːd‿ər ɪŋ **~s** z
murderer ˈmɜːd‿ər ə ‖ ˈmɝːd ər ᵊr **~s** z
murderess ˈmɜːd ə res -ər ɪs, -ər əs; ˌmɜːd ə ˈres ‖ ˈmɝːd ər əs **~es** ɪz əz
murderous ˈmɜːd‿ər əs ‖ ˈmɝːd‿ **~ly** li **~ness** nəs nɪs
Murdo ˈmɜːd əʊ ‖ ˈmɝːd oʊ
Murdoch ˈmɜːd ɒk -əx ‖ ˈmɝːd ɑːk
Murdock ˈmɜːd ɒk ‖ ˈmɝːd ɑːk
murex ˈmjʊər eks ˈmjɔːr- ‖ ˈmjʊr- **~es** ɪz əz
Murfin ˈmɜːf ɪn §-ᵊn ‖ ˈmɝːf-
Murfreesboro ˈmɜːf riz ˌbʌr ə ‖ ˈmɝːf riz ˌbɝː oʊ -iz-, ə
Murgatroyd ˈmɜːg ə trɔɪd ‖ ˈmɝːg-
Muriel ˈmjʊər i‿əl ˈmjɔːr- ‖ ˈmjʊr-
Murillo mjuᵊ ˈrɪl əʊ -jəʊ ‖ -oʊ —*Sp* [mu ˈri ʎo, -jo]
murine ˈmjʊər aɪn -ɪn, §-ən ‖ ˈmjʊr-
murk mɜːk ‖ mɝːk
murk|y ˈmɜːk |i ‖ ˈmɝːk |i **~ier** i‿ə ‖ i‿ᵊr **~iest** i‿ɪst i‿əst **~ily** ɪ li əl i **~iness** i nəs i nɪs
Murmansk mɜː ˈmænᵗsk mə- ‖ mʊr ˈmɑːnᵗsk ˈ· · —*Russ* [ˈmur mənsk]
murmur ˈmɜːm ə ‖ ˈmɝːm ᵊr **~ed** d **murmuring/ly** ˈmɜːm ər‿ɪŋ /li ‖ ˈmɝːm ər ɪŋ /li **~s** z
Murph|y, murph|y ˈmɜːf |i ‖ ˈmɝːf |i **~ies, ~y's** iz
ˈ**Murphy's Law**, ˌ· · ˈ·
murrain ˈmʌr ɪn -ən, -eɪn ‖ ˈmɝː ən **~s** z
Murray ˈmʌr i -eɪ ‖ ˈmɝː i
Murrayfield ˈmʌr i fiːᵊld ‖ ˈmɝː-
murre mɜː ‖ mɝː (= *myrrh*) **murres** mɜːz ‖ mɝːz
Murrell (*i*) ˈmʌr əl ‖ˈmɝː‿əl, (*ii*) mʌ ˈrel mə-
Murrow ˈmʌr əʊ ‖ ˈmɝː oʊ
Murrumbidgee ˌmʌr əm ˈbɪdʒ i ‖ ˌmɝː əm-
Mururoa ˌmʊr ə ˈrəʊ ə ‖ˌmuː ruː ˈroʊ ə
musaceous mju ˈzeɪʃ əs
Muscadet, m~ ˈmʌsk ə deɪ ˌ· · ˈ·. —*Fr* [my ska de] **~s** z
muscadine ˈmʌsk ə daɪn -əd ɪn, -əd ən **~s** z
muscae volitantes ˌmʌsk i ˌvɒl ɪ ˈtænt iːz ˌmʊsk-, ˌmʌs-, ˌ·aɪ-, -ə'·-, -eɪz ‖ -ˌvɑːl-
muscat ˈmʌsk ət -æt **~s** s
Muscat ˈmʌsk æt mʌ ˈskæt —*Arabic* [ˈmas qatˤ]
muscatel ˌmʌsk ə ˈtel **~s** z
muscl|e ˈmʌs ᵊl (= *mussel*) **~ed** d **~es** z **~ing** ‿ɪŋ
muscle-bound ˈmʌs ᵊl baʊnd
muscle|man ˈmʌs ᵊl |mæn **~men** men
muscly ˈmʌs ᵊl‿i
muscovado ˌmʌsk ə ˈvɑːd əʊ -ˈveɪd- ‖ -oʊ
Muscovite, m~ ˈmʌsk ə vaɪt **~s** s
Muscovy ˈmʌsk əv i
muscular ˈmʌsk jʊl ə -jəl- ‖ -jəl ᵊr **~ly** li
ˌ**muscular** ˈ**dystrophy**
muscularity ˌmʌsk ju ˈlær ət i -ɪt i ‖ -jə ˈlær əṭ i -ˈler-
musculature ˈmʌsk jʊl ətʃ ə ˈ·jəl-, -ə tjʊə ‖ -jəl ə tʃʊr -ətʃ ᵊr **~s** z
muse, Muse mjuːz **mused** mjuːzd **muses, Muses** ˈmjuːz ɪz -əz **musing/ly** ˈmjuːz ɪŋ /li
musette mju ˈzet —*Fr* [my zɛt] **~s** s
museum mju ˈziː‿əm ˌmjuː- —*Occasionally also* -ˈzeɪ- **~s** z
mu'seum piece
Museveni mu ˈsev ən i ˌmuːs ə ˈveɪn i
Musgrave ˈmʌz greɪv
Musgrove ˈmʌz grəʊv ‖ -groʊv
mush *'soft mass, porridge'* mʌʃ ‖ mʊʃ
mush *'face; fellow'* mʊʃ
mush *'travel by dog team'; interj* mʌʃ **mushed** mʌʃt **musher/s** ˈmʌʃ ə/z ‖ -ᵊr/z **mushes** ˈmʌʃ ɪz -əz **mushing** ˈmʌʃ ɪŋ
Musharraf mu ˈʃær əf —*Urdu* [mu ʃər əf]
mushroom ˈmʌʃ rʊm -ruːm ‖ -ruːm -rʊm, -ruːn, ˈmʌʃ ə- **~ed** d **~ing** ɪŋ **~s** z
mush|y ˈmʌʃ |i ‖ ˈmʊʃ- **~ier** i‿ə ‖ i‿ᵊr **~iest** i‿ɪst i‿əst **~ily** ɪ li əl i **~iness** i nəs i nɪs
music ˈmjuːz ɪk
ˈ**music box**; ˈ**music** ˌ**center**, ˈ**music** ˌ**centre**; ˈ**music hall**; ˈ**music stand**
musical ˈmjuːz ɪk ᵊl **~ly** ‿i **~s** z
ˈ**musical box**; ˌ**musical** ˈ**chairs**; ˌ**musical** ˈ**instrument**
musicale ˌmjuːz ɪ ˈkɑːl -ˈkæl ‖ ˈkæl **~s** z
musically ˈmjuːz ɪk ᵊl‿i
musicassette ˌmjuːz ɪ kə ˈset -kæˈ· **~s** s
musician mju ˈzɪʃ ᵊn **~s** z **~ship** ʃɪp
musicological ˌmjuːz ɪk ə ˈlɒdʒ ɪk ᵊl ◂ ˌ·ək- ‖ -ˈlɑːdʒ- **~ly** ‿i
musicolog|ist ˌmjuːz ɪ ˈkɒl ədʒ |ɪst ˌ·ə-, §-əst ‖ -ˈkɑːl- **~ists** ɪsts §əsts **~y** i
musique concrète mju ˌziːk kɒŋ ˈkret ‖ -koʊŋ- -kɔːŋ-, -kɑːŋ- —*Fr* [my zik kɔ̃ kʁɛt]
musk mʌsk
ˈ**musk deer**
muskeg ˈmʌsk eg -eɪg
muskellung|e ˈmʌsk ə lʌndʒ **~es** ɪz əz
musket ˈmʌsk ɪt -ət **~s** s
musketeer ˌmʌsk ə ˈtɪə -ɪ- ‖ -ˈtɪᵊr **~s** z
musketry ˈmʌsk ɪtr i -ətr-
Muskie ˈmʌsk i
muskmelon ˈmʌsk ˌmel ən **~s** z
Muskogean mʌ ˈskəʊg i‿ən ‖ -ˈskoʊg-
Muskogee mʌ ˈskəʊg i ‖ -ˈskoʊg i **~s** z
muskrat ˈmʌsk ræt **~s** s
musk|y ˈmʌsk |i **~ier** i‿ə ‖ i‿ᵊr **~iest** i‿ɪst i‿əst **~iness** i nəs i nɪs
Muslim ˈmʊz lɪm ˈmʌz-, ˈmʊs-, -ləm ‖ ˈmuːz-, ˈmuːs-, ˈmʌs- — *Preference poll, BrE:* ˈmʊ- *70%*, ˈmʌ- *30%*, -z- *89%*, -s- *11%*, -lɪm *91%*, -ləm *9%*. **~s** z
muslin ˈmʌz lɪn -lən **~s** z
muso ˈmjuːz əʊ ‖ -oʊ **~s** z
musquash ˈmʌsk wɒʃ ‖ -wɑːʃ -wɔːʃ **~es** ɪz əz
muss mʌs **mussed** mʌst (= *must*) **musses** ˈmʌs ɪz -əz **mussing** ˈmʌs ɪŋ
mussel ˈmʌs ᵊl **~s** z
Musselburgh ˈmʌs ᵊl bər‿ə -ˌbʌr ə ‖ -ˌbɝː oʊ

MUSLIM

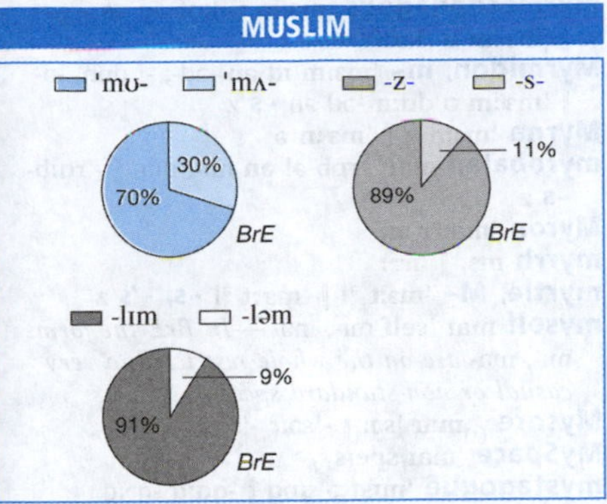

Mussolini ˌmʊs ə 'liːn i ˌmʌs- ‖ ˌmuːs- —*It* [mus so 'liː ni]
Mussorgsky mu 'sɔːg ski mə-, -'zɔːg- ‖ -'sɔːrg- -'zɔːrg- —*Russ* ['mu sərk skʲɪj]
must *strong form* mʌst, *weak forms* məst, məs
mustach|e mə 'stɑːʃ mʊ-, §-'stæʃ, §-'stɒʃ ‖ 'mʌst æʃ mə 'stæʃ **~ed** t **~es** ɪz əz
mustachio mə 'stɑːʃ i əʊ -'stæʃ- ‖ -i oʊ **~ed** d **~s** z
Mustafa 'mʊst əf ə 'mʌst-, -ə fɑː; mu 'stɑːf ə, mə-
mustang 'mʌst æŋ **~s** z
Mustapha 'mʊst əf ə 'mʌst-, -ə fɑː; mu 'stɑːf ə, mə-
mustard 'mʌst əd ‖ -ᵊrd **~s** z
'mustard gas; **'mustard ˌplaster**
muster 'mʌst ə ‖ -ᵊr **~ed** d **mustering** 'mʌst ər ɪŋ →'mʌs trɪŋ **~s** z
musth mʌst
musti... —*see* **musty**
Mustique mu 'stiːk
mustn't 'mʌs ᵊnt →-ᵊn
must-see ˌmʌst 'siː ◂ **~s** z
must|y 'mʌst |i **~ier** i‿ə ‖ i‿ᵊr **~iest** i‿ɪst i‿əst **~ily** ɪ li əl i **~iness** i nəs i nɪs
mutability ˌmjuːt ə 'bɪl ət i -ɪt i ‖ ˌmjuːţ ə 'bɪl əţ i
mutab|le 'mjuːt əb |ᵊl ‖ 'mjuːţ- **~leness** ᵊl nəs -nɪs **~ly** li
mutagen 'mjuːt ədʒ ən -ə dʒen ‖ 'mjuːţ- **~s** z
mutagenic ˌmjuːt ə 'dʒen ɪk ◂ ‖ ˌmjuːţ- **~ally** ᵊl‿i
mutagenicity ˌmjuːt ə dʒe 'nɪs ət i -ɪt i ‖ ˌmjuːţ ədʒ ə 'nɪs əţ i
mutant 'mjuːt ᵊnt **~s** s
mutate mju '|teɪt ‖ 'mjuː|t eɪt **~tated** teɪt ɪd -əd ‖ teɪţ əd **~tates** teɪts **~tating** teɪt ɪŋ ‖ teɪţ ɪŋ
mutation mju 'teɪʃ ᵊn **~s** z
mutatis mutandis mu ˌtɑːt ɪs mu 'tænd ɪs mju-, -ˌteɪt-, -ˌiːs-, -mju'--, -iːs ‖ -'tɑːnd-
Mutch, mutch mʌtʃ **mutches** 'mʌtʃ ɪz -əz
mute mjuːt **muted** 'mjuːt ɪd -əd ‖ 'mjuːţ əd **mutely** 'mjuːt li **muteness** 'mjuːt nəs -nɪs
muter 'mjuːt ə ‖ 'mjuːţ ᵊr **mutes** mjuːts **mutest** 'mjuːt ɪst -əst ‖ 'mjuːţ əst **muting** 'mjuːt ɪŋ ‖ 'mjuːţ ɪŋ
muti|late 'mjuːt ɪ |leɪt -ə-, -ᵊ|l eɪt ‖ 'mjuːţ ᵊ|l eɪt **~lated** leɪt ɪd -əd ‖ leɪţ əd **~lates** leɪts **~lating** leɪt ɪŋ ‖ leɪţ ɪŋ
mutilation ˌmjuːt ɪ 'leɪʃ ᵊn -ə-, -ᵊl 'eɪʃ- ‖ ˌmjuːţ ᵊl 'eɪʃ ᵊn **~s** z
mutineer ˌmjuːt ɪ 'nɪə -ə-, -ᵊn 'ɪə ‖ ˌmjuːt ᵊn 'ɪᵊr **~s** z
mutini... —*see* **mutiny**
mutinous 'mjuːt ɪn əs -ən- ‖ -ᵊn‿əs **~ly** li **~ness** nəs nɪs
mutin|y 'mjuːt ən |i -ɪn- ‖ -ᵊn |i **~ied** id **~ies** iz **~ying** i ɪŋ
mutism 'mjuːt ˌɪz əm ‖ 'mjuːţ-
mutt mʌt **mutts** mʌts
mutter, M~ 'mʌt ə ‖ 'mʌţ ᵊr **~ed** d **muttering/ly** 'mʌt‿ər ɪŋ /li ‖ 'mʌţ ər ɪŋ /li →'mʌtr ɪŋ /li **~s** z
mutterer 'mʌt ər ə ‖ 'mʌţ ər ᵊr **~s** z
mutton 'mʌt ᵊn
muttonchop ˌmʌt ᵊn 'tʃɒp ◂ ‖ 'mʌt ᵊn tʃɑːp **~s** s
ˌmuttonchop 'whiskers
muttonhead 'mʌt ᵊn hed **~s** z
mutual 'mjuːtʃ u‿əl 'mjuːt ju‿; 'mjuːtʃ əl **~ly** i **~s** z
'mutual fund
mutuality ˌmjuːtʃ u 'æl ət i ˌmjuːt ju- -ɪt i ‖ -əţ i
muu-muu 'muː muː **~s** z
Muxworthy 'mʌks ˌwɜːð i ‖ -ˌwɜˑð i
Muybridge 'maɪ brɪdʒ
muzak, Muzak *tdmk* 'mjuːz æk
muzz mʌz **muzzed** mʌzd **muzzes** 'mʌz ɪz -əz **muzzing** 'mʌz ɪŋ
muzzl|e 'mʌz ᵊl **~ed** d **~es** z **~ing** ‿ɪŋ
muzzle-loader 'mʌz ᵊl ˌləʊd ə ‖ -ˌloʊd ᵊr **~s** z
muzz|y 'mʌz |i **~ier** i‿ə ‖ i‿ᵊr **~iest** i ɪst i‿əst **~ily** ɪ li əl i **~iness** i nəs i nɪs
mwa, mwah mwɑː mwʌ
my maɪ —*There are also weak forms* **mi, mə,** *found mainly in British regional (non-RP) speech (where it may be shown in spelling as* me*), but also sometimes, mainly in set phrases, in casual RP. Otherwise, there is no distinct weak form.*
myalgia maɪ 'ældʒ ə -i‿ə
myalgic maɪ 'ældʒ ɪk
myall, Myall 'maɪ ɔːl ‖ -ɑːl **~s** z
Myanmar 'miː‿ən mɑː →‿əm-; mi 'æn mɑː ‖ -mɑːr mi ˌɑːn 'mɑːr
myasthenia ˌmaɪ‿əs 'θiːn i‿ə
myasthenic ˌmaɪ‿əs 'θen ɪk ◂
myceli|um maɪ 'siːl i‿|əm **~a** ə
mycella maɪ 'sel ə
Mycenae maɪ 'siːn i -iː
Mycenaean ˌmaɪs ə 'niː‿ən ◂ -ɪ-, -iː- **~s** z
myco- *comb. form* *with stress-neutral suffix* ¦maɪk əʊ ‖ -ə — **mycotoxin** ˌmaɪk əʊ 'tɒks ɪn §-ᵊn ‖ -ə 'tɑːks ᵊn

with stress-imposing suffix maɪ ˈkɒ+ ‖ -ˈkɑː+ — **mycologist** maɪ ˈkɒl ədʒ ɪst §-əst ‖ -ˈkɑːl-
mycology maɪ ˈkɒl ədʒ i ‖ -ˈkɑːl-
mycosis maɪ ˈkəʊs ɪs §-əs ‖ -ˈkoʊs əs
mydriasis mɪ ˈdraɪ‿əs ɪs mə-, §-əs
mydriatic ˌmɪdr i ˈæt ɪk ‖ -ˈæṭ ɪk **~s** s
myelin ˈmaɪ‿əl ɪn -ɪl-, §-ən
ˌmyelin ˈsheath
myelitis ˌmaɪ‿ə ˈlaɪt ɪs -ɪ-, §-əs ‖ -ˈlaɪṭ əs
myelo- *comb. form*
with stress-neutral suffix ¦maɪ‿əl əʊ maɪ ¦el əʊ ‖ ¦maɪ əl ə — **myelogram** ˈmaɪ‿əl əʊ græm maɪ ˈel- ‖ ˈmaɪ əl ə-
with stress-imposing suffix ˌmaɪ‿ə ˈlɒ+ ‖ -ˈlɑː+ — **myelography** ˌmaɪ‿ə ˈlɒg rəf i ‖ -ˈlɑːg-
myeloid ˈmaɪ‿ə lɔɪd
myelom|a ˌmaɪ‿ə ˈləʊm |ə ‖ -ˈloʊm |ə **~as** əz **~ata** ət ə ‖ əṭ ə
Myer ˈmaɪ‿ə ‖ ˈmaɪ‿ᵊr
Myers ˈmaɪ‿əz ‖ ˈmaɪ‿ᵊrz
Myfanwy mə ˈvæn wi mɪ-, -ˈfæn- —*Welsh* [mə ˈvan wi, -ˈva nui]
Mykonos ˈmiːk ə nɒs ‖ -nɑːs -noʊs, -nɔːs —*ModGk* [ˈmi kɔ nɔs]
mylar, Mylar *tdmk* ˈmaɪl ɑː ‖ -ɑːr
Myleene ˈmaɪl iːn
Myles maɪᵊlz
mylonite ˈmaɪl ə naɪt ˈmɪl-
myna, mynah ˈmaɪn ə **~s** z
ˈmynah bird
Mynd mɪnd
Mynett, Mynott ˈmaɪn ət
myo- *comb. form*
with stress-neutral suffix ¦maɪ əʊ ‖ -ə — **myocardial** ˌmaɪ əʊ ˈkɑːd i‿əl ◂ ‖ -ə ˈkɑːrd-
with stress-imposing suffix maɪ ˈɒ+ ‖ -ˈɑː+ — **myopathy** maɪ ˈɒp əθ i ‖ -ˈɑːp-
myocardiogram ˌmaɪ əʊ ˈkɑːd i‿ə græm ‖ -ə ˈkɑːrd- **~s** z
myoclonic ˌmaɪ əʊ ˈklɒn ɪk ◂ ‖ -ə ˈklɑːn ɪk ◂
ˌmyoˌclonic ˈspasm
myoelastic ˌmaɪ əʊ ɪ ˈlæst ɪk ◂ -əˈ--, -ˈlɑːst- ‖ ˌmaɪ oʊ-
myope ˈmaɪ əʊp ‖ -oʊp **~s** s
myopia maɪ ˈəʊp i‿ə ‖ -ˈoʊp-
myopic maɪ ˈɒp ɪk -ˈəʊp- ‖ -ˈɑːp ɪk -ˈoʊp- **~ally** ᵊl‿i
myosin ˈmaɪ əʊ sɪn -əs ən ‖ -əs ən
myosotis ˌmaɪ‿ə ˈsəʊt ɪs §-əs ‖ -ˈsoʊṭ əs
Myra ˈmaɪᵊr ə
myriad ˈmɪr i‿əd **~s** z
myriapod ˈmɪr i‿ə pɒd ‖ -pɑːd **~s** z
myrmecophagous ˌmɜːm ɪ ˈkɒf əg əs ◂ ˌ-ə- ‖ ˌmɝːm ə ˈkɑːf-
Myrmidon, m~ ˈmɜːm ɪd ən -əd-; -ɪ dɒn, -ə- ‖ ˈmɝːm ə dɑːn -əd ən **~s** z
Myrna ˈmɜːn ə ‖ ˈmɝːn ə
myrobalan maɪᵊ ˈrɒb əl ən mɪ-, mə- ‖ -ˈrɑːb- **~s** z
Myron ˈmaɪᵊr ən
myrrh mɜː ‖ mɝː
myrtle, M~ ˈmɜːt ᵊl ‖ ˈmɝːṭ ᵊl **~s, ~'s** z
myself maɪ ˈself mɪ-, mə- —*In BrE the forms* mɪ-, mə- *are on the whole restricted to very casual or non-standard speech.*
Mysore ₍ₗ₎maɪ ˈsɔː ‖ -ˈsɔːr -ˈsoʊr
MySpace ˈmaɪ speɪs
mystagogue ˈmɪst ə gɒg ‖ -gɑːg -gɔːg
mysterious mɪ ˈstɪər i‿əs mə- ‖ -ˈstɪr- **~ly** li **~ness** nəs nɪs
myster|y ˈmɪs tr|i ˈmɪst ər |i **~ies** iz
ˈmystery play; **ˈmystery tour**
mystic, M~ ˈmɪst ɪk **~s** s
mystical ˈmɪst ɪk ᵊl **~ly** ‿i **~ness** nəs nɪs
mysticism ˈmɪst ɪ ˌsɪz əm -ə-
mystification ˌmɪst ɪf ɪ ˈkeɪʃ ᵊn ˌ-əf-, §-əˈ-- **~s** z
mysti|fy ˈmɪst ɪ |faɪ -ə- **~fied** faɪd **~fier/s** faɪ‿ə/z ‖ faɪ‿ᵊr/z **~fies** faɪz **~fying** faɪ ɪŋ
mystique mɪ ˈstiːk ˌmɪs ˈtiːk **~s** s
myth mɪθ **myths** mɪθs
mythic ˈmɪθ ɪk **~al** ᵊl **~ally** ᵊl i
mytho- *comb. form*
with stress-neutral suffix ¦mɪθ əʊ ‖ -ə — **mythopoeic** ˌmɪθ əʊ ˈpiː ɪk ◂ ‖ -ə-
with stress-imposing suffix mɪ ˈθɒ+ mə-, maɪ- ‖ -ˈθɑː+ — **mythography** mɪ ˈθɒg rəf i mə-, maɪ- ‖ -ˈθɑːg-
Mytholmroyd ˌmaɪð əm ˈrɔɪd
mythological ˌmɪθ ə ˈlɒdʒ ɪk ᵊl ◂ ˌmaɪθ- ‖ -ˈlɑːdʒ- **~ly** ‿i
mythologist mɪ ˈθɒl ədʒ ɪst mə-, maɪ-, §-əst ‖ -ˈθɑːl- **~s** s
mytholog|y mɪ ˈθɒl ədʒ |i mə-, maɪ- ‖ -ˈθɑːl- **~ies** iz
mytho|poeia ˌmɪθ əʊ |ˈpiː‿ə ‖ -ə- **~poeic** ˈpiː ɪk ◂
Mytilene ˌmɪt ɪ ˈliːn i -ə-, -ᵊl ˈiːn-, -iː ‖ ˌmɪṭ ᵊl ˈiːn i
Mytton ˈmɪt ᵊn
myxedema, myxoedema ˌmɪks i ˈdiːm ə §-ə-
myxomatosis ˌmɪks əm ə ˈtəʊs ɪs §-əs ‖ -ˈtoʊs əs
myxomycete ˌmɪks əʊ maɪ ˈsiːt ˌ·ˈ·· ‖ ˌ·oʊ- **~s** s
myxovirus ˈmɪks əʊ ˌvaɪᵊr əs ˌ·ˈ·· ‖ -ə- **~es** ɪz əz

Nn

n Spelling-to-sound

1 Where the spelling is **n**, the pronunciation is regularly n as in **nation** ˈneɪʃ ᵊn or ŋ as in **think** θɪŋk. **n** also forms part of the digraph **ng**.

2 The pronunciation is n everywhere *except*

- before the sound k (written **c, g, k, q, x**), and
- where the spelling is the digraph **ng** (see **ng** 2, 3 below),

in which cases the pronunciation is regularly ŋ.

Examples:

n in **net** net, **fan** fæn, **unit** ˈjuːn ɪt, **enter** ˈent ə ‖ ˈenţ ᵊr

ŋ in **uncle** ˈʌŋk ᵊl, **anger** ˈæŋ gə ‖ ˈæŋ gᵊr, **thanks** θæŋks, **conquer** ˈkɒŋ kə ‖ ˈkɑːŋ kᵊr, **anxious** ˈæŋkʃ əs, **win** wɪŋ.

3 Where the spelling is double **nn**, the pronunciation is again regularly n as in **funny** ˈfʌn i.

4 **n** is silent when it follows **m** at the end of a word, and in the corresponding inflected forms as in **column** ˈkɒl əm ‖ ˈkɑːl əm, **condemned** kən ˈdemd (but **hymnal** ˈhɪm nəl).

ng Spelling-to-sound

1 Where the spelling is the digraph **ng**, the pronunciation is regularly

ŋ as in **singing** ˈsɪŋ ɪŋ

ŋg as in **angle** ˈæŋ gᵊl or

ndʒ as in **strange** streɪndʒ.

2 The pronunciation is ŋ when **ng** is at the end of a word or stem. Examples: **hang** hæŋ, **singer** ˈsɪŋ ə ‖ ˈsɪŋ ᵊr, **strongly** ˈstrɒŋ li ‖ ˈstrɔːŋ li. (Although in this position plain ŋ is standard in RP and GenAm, some speakers use ŋg.)

3 The pronunciation is usually ŋg when **ng** is in the middle of a word (and not at the end of a stem). Examples: **hungry** ˈhʌŋ gri, **finger** ˈfɪŋ gə ‖ ˈfɪŋ gᵊr, **single** ˈsɪŋ gᵊl.

4 The pronunciation is ndʒ

where the spelling is **nge** at the end of a word as in **challenge** ˈtʃæl ɪndʒ,

and sometimes before **e, i, y** in the middle of a word as in **danger** ˈdeɪndʒ ə ‖ ˈdeɪndʒ ᵊr.

5 The three pronunciations corresponding to the spelling **ng** are illustrated in the same context in the sets
singer ˈsɪŋ ə ‖ -ᵊr
finger ˈfɪŋ gə ‖ -gᵊr
ginger ˈdʒɪndʒ ə ‖ -ᵊr
hanger ˈhæŋ ə ‖ -ᵊr
anger ˈæŋ gə ‖ -gᵊr
danger ˈdeɪndʒ ə ‖ -ᵊr.

6 Where **n** belongs to a prefix and **g** to a stem, they do not form a digraph. Consequently, the pronunciation is usually n as in **ingenious** ɪn ˈdʒiːn i‿əs. However, where the **g** is hard, then the n may become ŋ by ASSIMILATION. This is regular where the syllable containing the nasal is stressed as in **congress** ˈkɒŋ gres ‖ ˈkɑːŋ grəs, and otherwise optional as in **conclusion** kən ˈkluːʒ ᵊn → kəŋ-. (The assimilation seems to be usually made in BrE but rarely in AmE.)

N, n en **N's, n's, Ns** enz *Communications code name:* November
N *—see* **North, northerly, Northern**
'n, 'n' *conventional spelling for the weak form of* **and** ən, ən, ᵊn
 ˌfish 'n' 'chips
Naafi, NAAFI ˈnæf i
naan nɑːn næn
Naas *place in Co. Kildare* neɪs
nab næb **nabbed** næbd **nabbing** ˈnæb ɪŋ **nabs** næbz
Nabarro nə ˈbɑːr əʊ ‖ -oʊ
Nabataean, Nabatean ˌnæb ə ˈtiː‿ən ◂ **~s** z
nabb... *—see* **nab**
Nabbs næbz
Nabisco *tdmk* nə ˈbɪsk əʊ næ- ‖ -oʊ
Nablus ˈnɑːb ləs ˈnæb-, -lʊs
nabob ˈneɪb ɒb ‖ -ɑːb **~s** z
Nabokov nə ˈbəʊk ɒf ˈnæb ə kɒf ‖ -ˈbɔːk əf -ˈbɑːk-; ˈnæb ə kɑːf, ˈnɑːb-, -kɔːf
Naboth ˈneɪb ɒθ ‖ -ɑːθ -oʊθ
Nabucco nə ˈbuːk əʊ ‖ -oʊ *—It* [na ˈbuk ko]
nacelle nə ˈsel næ- **~s** z
nacho ˈnɑːtʃ əʊ ‖ -oʊ **~s** z
Nacogdoches *place in TX* ˌnæk ə ˈdəʊtʃ ɪz -əz ‖ -ˈdoʊtʃ əz
nacre ˈneɪk ə ‖ -ᵊr
nacreous ˈneɪk ri‿əs
NACRO ˈnæk rəʊ ‖ -roʊ
nad næd **nads** nædz
nada ˈnɑːd ə *—Sp* [ˈna ða]
Na-Dene, Na-Déné ˌnɑː ˈdeɪn i -ˈden-, -eɪ; -də ˈneɪ; nə ˈdiːn
Nader ˈneɪd ə ‖ -ᵊr
Nadi *place in Fiji* ˈnænd i ˈnɑːnd i *—Fijian* [ˈna ndi]
Nadia *(i)* ˈneɪd i‿ə, *(ii)* ˈnɑːd i‿ə
Nadine neɪ ˈdiːn nə-
nadir ˈneɪd ɪə ˈnæd- ‖ -ɪr -ᵊr **~s** z
Nadir næ ˈdɪə ‖ -ˈdɪᵊr
nae neɪ
naev|us ˈniːv |əs **~i** aɪ
naff næf **naffer** ˈnæf ə ‖ -ᵊr **naffest** ˈnæf ɪst -əst
 ˌnaff ˈoff
NAFTA ˈnæft ə
nag næg **nagged** nægd **nagger/s** ˈnæg ə/z ‖ -ᵊr/z **nagging** ˈnæg ɪŋ **nags** nægz
Naga ˈnɑːg ə ‖ -ɑː **~s** z
Nagaland ˈnɑːg ə lænd
nagana nə ˈgɑːn ə
Nagano ˈnæg ə nəʊ ˈnɑːg- ‖ -noʊ nə ˈgɑːn oʊ *—Jp* [ˈna ŋa no, -ga-]
Nagari ˈnɑːg ər i
Nagasaki ˌnæg ə ˈsɑːk i ˌnɑːg- ‖ -ˈsæk- *—Jp* [na ˈŋa sa ki, -ˈga-]
nagg... *—see* **nag**
Nagorno-Karabakh nə ˌgɔːn əʊ ˌkær ə ˈbæk -ˈbɑːk ‖ nə ˌgɔːrn oʊ ˌkɑːr ə ˈbɑːk *—Russ* [nə ˌgor nə kə rɐ ˈbax]
Nagoya nə ˈgɔɪ ə *—Jp* [ˈna ŋo ja, -go-]
Nagpur ˌnæg ˈpʊə ˌnɑːg-, ˈpɔː ‖ ˌnɑːg ˈpʊᵊr
Nagy nɒdʒ ‖ nɑːdʒ *—Hung* [nɒɟ]
nah *informal, 'no'* næː nʌː ‖ nɑː
Na h-Eileanan an Iar nə ˌhɪl ən ən ən ˈjɪə ‖ -ˈjɪᵊr
Nahuatl ˈnɑː wɑːt ᵊl ·ˈ· · **~an** ‿ən **~s** z
Nahum ˈneɪ həm -hʌm, -əm
naiad ˈnaɪ æd ˈnaɪ‿əd **naiades** ˈnaɪ‿ə diːz **~s** z
naif, naïf naɪ ˈiːf nɑː-
nail, Nail neɪᵊl **nailed** neɪᵊld **nailing** ˈneɪᵊl ɪŋ **nails** neɪᵊlz
 ˈnail file; **ˈnail ˌpolish**; **ˈnail ˌscissors**; **ˈnail ˌvarnish**

nail-bit|er ˈneɪᵊl ˌbaɪt |ə ‖ -ˌbaɪt̬ |ᵊr **~ers** əz ‖ ᵊrz **~ing/ly** ɪŋ /li

nailbrush ˈneɪᵊl brʌʃ **~es** ɪz əz

nailclipper ˈneɪᵊl ˌklɪp ə ‖ -ᵊr **~s** z

nailgun ˈneɪᵊl gʌn **~s** z

Nailsea ˈneɪᵊl siː

Nailsworth ˈneɪᵊlz wəθ -wɜːθ ‖ -wᵊrθ -wɜːθ

Naipaul ˈnaɪ pɔːl

naira ˈnaɪᵊr ə

Nairn neən ‖ neᵊrn næᵊrn

Nairobi naɪᵊ ˈrəʊb i ‖ -ˈroʊb i

Naish *(i)* neɪʃ, *(ii)* næʃ

Naismith ˈneɪ smɪθ

naive, naïve naɪ ˈiːv nɑː- **~ly** li **~ness** nəs nɪs

naiveté, naïveté naɪ ˈiːv ə teɪ nɑː-; -ˈiːv teɪ —*Fr* [na if te]

naivet|y, naïvet|y naɪ ˈiːv ət |i nɑː-, -ɪt-; -ˈiːv t|i ‖ -ət̬ |i **~ies** iz

naked ˈneɪk ɪd -əd *(!)* **~ly** li **~ness** nəs nɪs

naker ˈneɪk ə ˈnæk- ‖ -ᵊr **~s** z

Nakhichevan ˌnɑːk ɪ tʃɪ ˈvɑːn ˌnæk-, ˌ·ə-, -tʃəˈ-, -ˈvæn —*Russ* [nə xʲi tʃɪ ˈvanʲ]

NALGO ˈnælg əʊ ‖ -oʊ

Nam, 'Nam *'Vietnam'* næm nɑːm

Nama ˈnɑːm ə ‖ -ɑː **~s** z

Namaland ˈnɑːm ə lænd

Namaqualand nə ˈmɑːk wə lænd

Namath ˈneɪm əθ

namby-pam|by ˌnæm bi ˈpæm |bi ◂ **~bies** biz

name neɪm **named** neɪmd **names** neɪmz **naming** ˈneɪm ɪŋ **ˈname day**

name-calling ˈneɪm ˌkɔːl ɪŋ ‖ -ˌkɑːl-

name-check ˈneɪm tʃek **~ing** ɪŋ

namedrop ˈneɪm drɒp ‖ -drɑːp **~ped** t **~per/s** ə/z ‖ ᵊr/z **~ping** ɪŋ **~s** s

nameless ˈneɪm ləs -lɪs **~ly** li **~ness** nəs nɪs

namely ˈneɪm li

nameplate ˈneɪm pleɪt **~s** s

namesake ˈneɪm seɪk **~s** s

nametag ˈneɪm tæg **~s** z

name-tape ˈneɪm teɪp **~s** s

Namib ˈnɑːm ɪb

Namibi|a nə ˈmɪb i‿|ə **~an/s** ən/z

Namier ˈneɪm ɪə ˈneɪm i‿ə ‖ -ɪr

Namur næ ˈmjʊə -ˈmʊə ‖ nə ˈmjʊᵊr -ˈmʊᵊr —*Fr* [na myːʁ]

nan *'bread'* nɑːn næn

nan *'grandmother',* **Nan** *personal name* næn **nans, Nan's** nænz

Nanaimo nə ˈnaɪm əʊ næ- ‖ -oʊ

Nanak ˈnɑːn ək

Nancarrow næn ˈkær əʊ →næŋ- ‖ -oʊ -ˈker-

Nance, nance nænᵗs

Nanchang ˌnæn ˈtʃæŋ ◂ ‖ ˌnɑːn ˈtʃɑːŋ ◂ *Chi* Nánchāng [^{1}nan ^{3}tʃɑŋ]

Nanci, Nancie, Nancy *personal name,* **n~** ˈnænᵗs i

Nancy *place in France* ˌnɒ̃ ˈsiː ˌnɑːn-, ˈ· · —*Fr* [nɑ̃ si]

NAND nænd **ˈNAND gate**

Nandi *place in Fiji, properly* Nadi ˈnænd i ˈnɑːnd i

nandina næn ˈdiːn ə **~s** z

nandrolone ˈnændr ə ləʊn ‖ -loʊn

Nanette næ ˈnet nə-

nang næŋ

nan Gàidheal nən ˈgeɪᵊl

Nanga Parbat ˌnʌŋ gə ˈpɜːb ət ˌnæŋ-, -ˈpɑːb-, -æt ‖ -ˈpɝːb- -ˈpɑːrb-

Nanjing ˌnæn ˈdʒɪŋ ‖ nɑːn- —*Chi* Nánjīng [^{2}nan ^{1}tɕiŋ]

nankeen ₍ˌ₎næn ˈkiːn ◂ →næŋ- **ˌnankeen ˈkestrel**

Nanking ˌnæn ˈkɪŋ ◂ →ˌnæŋ- ‖ ˌnɑːn- —*Chi* Nánjīng [^{2}nan ^{1}tɕiŋ]

nanna ˈnæn ə **~s** z

Nannie ˈnæn i

Nanning ˌnæn ˈnɪŋ ◂ ‖ ˌnɑːn- —*Chi* Nánníng [^{2}nan ^{2}niŋ]

nann|y, Nann|y ˈnæn |i **~ies, ~y's** iz **ˈnanny goat**

nannygai ˈnæn i gaɪ **~s** z

nano ˈnɑːn əʊ ‖ -oʊ

nano- ¦næn əʊ ‖ -ə — **nanosecond** ˈnæn əʊ ˌsek ənd →-ŋd ‖ -ə- **nanotechnology** ˌnæn əʊ tek ˈnɒl ədʒ i ‖ -oʊ tek ˈnɑːl-

nanobot ˈnæn əʊ bɒt ‖ -ə bɑːt **~s** s

nanomachine ˈnæn əʊ mə ˌʃiːn ‖ -oʊ mə- **~s** z

Nanook ˈnæn uːk -ʊk

nanopublish|er ˈnæn əʊ ˌpʌb lɪʃ |ə ‖ -oʊ ˌpʌb lɪʃ ᵊr **~ers** əz ‖ ᵊrz **~ing** ɪŋ

nanoscience ˈnæn əʊ ˌsaɪ‿ənᵗs ‖ -oʊ-

nanosecond ˈnæn əʊ ˌsek ənd ‖ -oʊ- **~s** z

Nansen ˈnænᵗs ᵊn ‖ ˈnɑːnᵗs-

Nant *in Welsh place names* nænt —*Welsh* [nant]

Nantes nɑːnt nænts, nɒnt —*Fr* [nɑ̃ːt]

Nantffrancon nænt ˈfræŋk ən —*Welsh* [nant ˈfraŋ kon]

Nantgarw nænt ˈgær uː —*Welsh* [nant ˈga ru]

Nantucket næn ˈtʌk ɪt -ət

Nantwich ˈnænt wɪtʃ

Naoise ˈniːʃ ə -i

Naomi *(i)* ˈneɪ əm i ‖ -aɪ, *(ii)* neɪ ˈəʊm i ‖ -ˈoʊm i -aɪ

nap næp **napped** næpt **napping** ˈnæp ɪŋ **naps** næps

Napa ˈnæp ə **ˌNapa ˈValley◂**

napalm ˈneɪp ɑːm ˈnæp-, §-ɑːlm **~ed** d **~ing** ɪŋ **~s** z

nape neɪp **napes** neɪps

Naphtali ˈnæft ə laɪ

naphtha ˈnæfθ ə ˈnæpθ-

naphthalene ˈnæfθ ə liːn ˈnæpθ-

naphthol ˈnæfθ ɒl ˈnæpθ- ‖ -ɔːl -ɑːl, -oʊl

Napier ˈneɪp i‿ə ‖ ᵊr —*but a few people with this surname call it* nə ˈpɪə ‖ -ˈpɪᵊr

Napierian nə ˈpɪər i‿ən neɪ- ‖ -ˈpɪr-

napkin ˈnæp kɪn §-kən **~s** z **ˈnapkin ring**

Naples ˈneɪp ᵊlz

Napoleon, n~ nə ˈpəʊl i‿ən ‖ -ˈpoʊl- **~s, ~'s** z
Napoleonic nə ˌpəʊl i ˈɒn ɪk ◂ ‖ nə ˌpoʊl i ˈɑːn ɪk ◂
napolitaine, N~ næ ˌpɒl ɪ ˈteɪn nə-, -ə- ‖ -ˌpɑːl- —*Fr* [na pɔ li tɛn]
nappe næp
napp|y ˈnæp |i **~ies** iz
ˈnappy rash; **ˈnappy ˌliner**
Napster *tdmk* ˈnæpst ə ‖ -ᵊr
Nara ˈnɑːr ə —*Jp* [ˈna ɾa]
Narayan nə ˈraɪ‿ən
Narbonne ₍ˌ₎nɑː ˈbɒn ‖ ₍ˌ₎nɑːr ˈbɔːn -ˈbɑːn, -ˈbʌn —*Fr* [naʁ bɔn]
narc nɑːk ‖ nɑːrk **narcs** nɑːks ‖ nɑːrks
narciss|i nɑː ˈsɪs |aɪ -iː ‖ nɑːr- **~ism** ˌɪz əm **~ist** ɪst §əst
narcissistic ˌnɑːs ɪ ˈsɪst ɪk ◂ -ə- ‖ ˌnɑːrs- **~ally** ᵊl‿i
narciss|us, N~ nɑː ˈsɪs |əs ‖ nɑːr- **~i** aɪ
narcolepsy ˈnɑːk əʊ leps i ‖ ˈnɑːrk ə-
narcoleptic ˌnɑːk əʊ ˈlept ɪk ◂ ‖ -ə-
narcos|is nɑː ˈkəʊs |ɪs §-əs ‖ nɑːr ˈkoʊs |əs **~es** iːz
narcotic nɑː ˈkɒt ɪk ‖ nɑːr ˈkɑːţ ɪk **~ally** ᵊl‿i **~s** s
narcotis... —*see* **narcotiz...**
narcotism ˈnɑːk ə ˌtɪz əm ‖ ˈnɑːrk-
narcotiz|e ˈnɑːk ə taɪz ‖ ˈnɑːrk- **~ed** d **~es** ɪz əz **~ing** ɪŋ
nard nɑːd ‖ nɑːrd
nardoo ˌnɑː ˈduː ‖ ˌnɑːr-
nareal ˈneər i‿əl ‖ ˈner- ˈnær-
Narelle nə ˈrel
nares ˈneər iːz ‖ ˈner- ˈnær-
narghile, nargile, nargileh ˈnɑːg ə leɪ -ɪ-, -li ‖ ˈnɑːrg- **~s** z
narial ˈneər i‿əl ‖ ˈner- ˈnær-
Narita ˈnær ɪt ə -ət-; nə ˈriːt ə —*Jp* [ˈna ɾi ta]
nark nɑːk ‖ nɑːrk **narked** nɑːkt ‖ nɑːrkt **narking** ˈnɑːk ɪŋ ‖ ˈnɑːrk ɪŋ **narks** nɑːks ‖ nɑːrks
nark|y ˈnɑːk |i ‖ ˈnɑːrk |i **~ier** i‿ə ‖ i‿ᵊr **~iest** i‿ɪst i‿əst
Narnia ˈnɑːn i‿ə ‖ ˈnɑːrn-
Narraganset, Narrangansett ˌnær ə ˈgænᵗs ɪt ◂ -ət ‖ ˌner- **ˌNarraˌgansett ˈBay**
Narrandera *place in NSW* nə ˈrænd ər ə
narrate nə ˈreɪt næ- ‖ ˈnær eɪt ˈner-; næ ˈreɪt **narrated** nə ˈreɪt ɪd næ-, -əd ‖ ˈnær eɪţ əd ˈner-; næ ˈreɪţ- **narrates** nə ˈreɪts næ- ‖ ˈnær eɪts ˈner-; næ ˈreɪts **narrating** nə ˈreɪt ɪŋ næ- ‖ ˈnær eɪţ ɪŋ ˈner-; næ ˈreɪţ-
narration nə ˈreɪʃ ᵊn næ- ‖ næ- **~s** z
narrative ˈnær ət ɪv ‖ -əţ ɪv ˈner- **~ly** li **~s** z
narrator nə ˈreɪt ə næ-; ˈnær ət ə ‖ ˈnær eɪţ ᵊr ˈner-, -əţ-; næ ˈreɪţ-, nə- **~s** z (*)
narrow ˈnær əʊ ‖ -oʊ ˈner- **~ed** d **~er** ə ‖ ᵊr **~est** ɪst əst **~ing** ɪŋ **~ly** li **~ness** nəs nɪs **~s** z
ˈnarrow boat; **ˌnarrow ˈgauge◂**, ˈ· · ·; **ˌnarrow ˈsqueak**
narrowband ˈnær əʊ bænd ‖ -oʊ-
narrowcast ˈnær əʊ kɑːst §-kæst ‖ -oʊ kæst ˈner- **~er/s** ə/z ‖ ᵊr/z **~ing** ɪŋ
narrow-gauge ˌnær əʊ ˈgeɪdʒ ◂ ‖ -oʊ-
narrow-minded ˌnær əʊ ˈmaɪnd ɪd ◂ -əd ‖ -oʊ- ˌner- **~ly** li **~ness** nəs nɪs
narthex ˈnɑːθ eks ‖ ˈnɑːrθ- **~es** ɪz əz
narwhal ˈnɑː wəl ‖ ˈnɑːr *h*wɑːl **~s** z
n-ary ˈen ər i
nary ˈneər i ‖ ˈner i ˈnær-
NASA ˈnæs ə ˈnɑːs-
nasal ˈneɪz ᵊl **~s** z
nasalis... —*see* **nasaliz...**
nasality neɪ ˈzæl ət i -ɪt- ‖ -əţ i
nasalization ˌneɪz əl aɪ ˈzeɪʃ ᵊn -əl ɪ- ‖ -əl ə- **~s** z
nasaliz|e ˈneɪz ə laɪz -ᵊl aɪz **~ed** d **~es** ɪz əz **~ing** ɪŋ
nasally ˈneɪz ᵊl i
nascent ˈnæs ᵊnt ˈneɪs-
Nasdaq, NASDAQ *tdmk* ˈnæz dæk
naseberr|y ˈneɪz ˌber |i **~ies** iz
Naseby ˈneɪz bi
Naseem ₍ˌ₎næ ˈsiːm
Nash, Nashe næʃ
Nashua ˈnæʃ u‿ə
Nashville ˈnæʃ vɪl -vəl
nasi goreng ˌnɑːs i gə ˈreŋ ˌnæs-, ˌnɑːz-, -ˈgɒr eŋ, -ˈgɔːr eŋ —*Bahasa Ind* [ˌna si ˈgo reŋ]
nasion ˈneɪz i‿ən -ɒn ‖ -ɑːn **~s** z
Nasmyth *(i)* ˈneɪs mɪθ *(ii)* ˈneɪz- *(iii)* ˈnæs-
nasofrontal ˌneɪz əʊ ˈfrʌnt ᵊl ◂ ‖ -oʊ ˈfrʌnţ ᵊl ◂
nasopharyngeal ˌneɪz əʊ ˌfær ɪn ˈdʒiː‿əl -ˌən-; -fə ˈrɪndʒ i‿əl, -fæˈ- ‖ ˌ·oʊ-, fer-
nasopharynx ˈneɪz əʊ ˌfær ɪŋks ˌ·ˈ·· ‖ -oʊ- -ˌfer- **~es** ɪz əz
Nassau *places in Bahamas and the US* ˈnæs ɔː ‖ -ɑː
Nassau *region of Germany* ˈnæs aʊ ‖ ˈnɑːs- —*Ger* [ˈna sau]
Nassau *princely family* ˈnæs ɔː -aʊ ‖ ˈnɑːs aʊ
Nasser ˈnæs ə ˈnɑːs- ‖ -ᵊr —*Arabic* [ˈnaː sˤir]
Nastase nə ˈstɑːz i næ-, -eɪ
nastic ˈnæst ɪk
nasturtium nə ˈstɜːʃ əm ‖ næ ˈstɝːʃ- nə- **~s** z
nast|y ˈnɑːst |i §ˈnæst- ‖ ˈnæst |i **~ier** i‿ə ‖ i‿ᵊr **~ies** iz **~iest** i‿ɪst i‿əst **~ily** ɪ li əl i **~iness** i nəs i nɪs
Nat næt **Nats, Nat's** næts
natal ˈneɪt ᵊl ‖ ˈneɪţ ᵊl
Natal *province of South Africa* nə ˈtæl -ˈtɑːl
Natalie ˈnæt əl i ‖ ˈnæţ ᵊl i
natalit|y neɪ ˈtæl ət |i nə-, -ɪt- ‖ -əţ |i **~ies** iz
Natasha nə ˈtæʃ ə ‖ -ˈtɑːʃ ə
natch nætʃ
Natchez ˈnætʃ ɪz -əz
Natchitoches *place in Louisiana* ˈnæk ə tɒʃ -ət əʃ ‖ -ə tɑːʃ -əţ əʃ (!)
nates ˈneɪt iːz
NATFHE ˈnæt fi -fiː
Nathan ˈneɪθ ᵊn
Nathanael, Nathaniel nə ˈθæn i‿əl

Natick ˈneɪt ɪk
nation ˈneɪʃ ən **~s** z
 ˌ**nation ˈstate**, ˈ· ·
national ˈnæʃ ən‿əl **~s** z
 ˌ**national ˈanthem**; ˌ**national ˈdebt**; ˌ**National ˈFront**; ˌ**national ˈgovernment**; ˌ**National ˈHealth ˌService**; ˌ**National Inˈsurance**; ˌ**national ˈpark**; ˌ**national ˈservice**; ˌ**National ˈTrust**
nationalis... —*see* **nationaliz...**
nationalism ˈnæʃ ən‿əl ˌɪz əm **~s** z
nationalist ˈnæʃ ən‿əl ɪst §-əst **~s** s
nationalistic ˌnæʃ ən‿ə ˈlɪst ɪk ◂ əl ˈɪst- **~ally** əl‿i
nationalit|y ˌnæʃ ə ˈnæl ət |i ˌnæʃˈ· ·, -ɪt i ‖ -əţ |i **~ies** iz
nationalization ˌnæʃ ən‿əl aɪ ˈzeɪʃ ən -ɪˈ·- ‖ -ə ˈzeɪʃ- **~s** z
nationaliz|e ˈnæʃ ən‿ə laɪz əl aɪz **~ed** d **~es** ɪz əz **~ing** ɪŋ
nationally ˈnæʃ ən‿əl i
nationhood ˈneɪʃ ən hʊd
nation-state ˌneɪʃ ən ˈsteɪt ‖ ˈ· ·
nationwide, N~ ˌneɪʃ ən ˈwaɪd ◂ ˈ· · ·
 ˌ**nationwide ˈbroadcast**
native ˈneɪt ɪv ‖ ˈneɪţ ɪv **~s** z
 ˌ**Native ˈAmerican**; ˌ**native ˈspeaker**
native-born ˌneɪt ɪv ˈbɔːn ◂ ˈ· · · ‖ ˌneɪţ ɪv ˈbɔːrn ◂
native|ly ˈneɪt ɪv |li ‖ ˈneɪţ ɪv |li **~ness** nəs nɪs
nativit|y, N~ nə ˈtɪv ət |i -ɪt- ‖ -əţ |i neɪ- **~ies** iz
 naˈtivity play
NATO, Nato ˈneɪt əʊ ‖ ˈneɪţ oʊ ˈneɪ toʊ
natron ˈneɪtr ən -ɒn ‖ -ɑːn
NATSOPA næt ˈsəʊp ə ‖ -ˈsoʊp ə
natter ˈnæt ə ‖ ˈnæţ ər **~ed** d **nattering** ˈnæt‿ər ɪŋ ‖ ˈnæţ ər ɪŋ **~s** z
natterjack ˈnæt ə dʒæk ‖ ˈnæţ ər- **~s** s
natt|y ˈnæt |i ‖ ˈnæţ |i **~ier** i‿ə ‖ i‿ər **~iest** i‿ɪst i‿əst **~ily** ɪ li əl i **~iness** i nəs i nɪs
natural ˈnætʃ ər‿əl **~s** z
 ˌ**natural ˈgas**; ˌ**natural ˈhistory**; ˌ**natural phiˈlosophy**; ˌ**natural ˈscience**; ˌ**natural seˈlection**
natural-born ˌnætʃ ər‿əl ˈbɔːn ◂ ‖ -ˈbɔːrn ◂
naturalis... —*see* **naturaliz...**
naturalism ˈnætʃ ər‿ə ˌlɪz əm
naturalist ˈnætʃ ər‿əl ɪst §-əst **~s** s
naturalistic ˌnætʃ ər‿ə ˈlɪst ɪk ◂ **~ally** əl‿i
naturalization ˌnætʃ ər‿ə laɪ ˈzeɪʃ ən -ər‿əl aɪ-, -ər‿əl ɪ- ‖ -ər‿əl ə- **~s** z
naturaliz|e ˈnætʃ ər‿ə laɪz əl aɪz **~ed** d **~es** ɪz əz **~ing** ɪŋ
natural|ly ˈnætʃ ər‿əl |i **~ness** nəs nɪs
nature ˈneɪtʃ ə ‖ -ər **~d** d **~s** z
 ˈ**nature reˌserve**; ˈ**nature ˌstudy**
naturism ˈneɪtʃ ər ˌɪz əm
naturist ˈneɪtʃ ər ɪst §-əst **~s** s
naturopath ˈneɪtʃ ər əʊ pæθ ˈnætʃ- ‖ -ər ə- **~s** s
naturopathic ˌneɪtʃ ər əʊ ˈpæθ ɪk ◂ ˌnætʃ- ‖ -ər ə- **~ally** əl‿i
naturopathy ˌneɪtʃ ə ˈrɒp əθ i ˌnætʃ- ‖ -ˈrɑːp-
NatWest *tdmk* ˌnæt ˈwest◂
Naucratis ˈnɔːk rət ɪs §-əs ‖ -rəţ-
Naugahyde *tdmk* ˈnɔːg ə haɪd ‖ ˈnɑːg-
naught nɔːt ‖ nɑːt **naughts** nɔːts ‖ nɑːts
Naughtie ˈnɒxt i ‖ ˈnɔːkt i
naught|y ˈnɔːt |i ‖ ˈnɔːţ |i ˈnɑːţ- **~ier** i‿ə ‖ i‿ər **~iest** i‿ɪst i‿əst **~ily** li əl i **~iness** i nəs i nɪs
Naunton ˈnɔːnt ən ‖ ˈnɔːnt ən ˈnɑːnt-
naupli|us ˈnɔːp li‿əs ‖ ˈnɑːp- **~i** aɪ iː
Nauru nə ˈruː naʊ-, nɑː-, ˈ· ·; nɑː ˈuː ruː **~an/s** ən/z
nausea ˈnɔːs i‿ə ˈnɔːz- ‖ ˈnɔːz- ˈnɑːz-, nɔːs-, ˈnɑːs-; ˈnɔːʃ ə, ˈnɑːʃ-, ˈnɔːʒ-, ˈnɑːʒ-
nause|ate ˈnɔːs i |eɪt ˈnɔːz- ‖ ˈnɔːz- ˈnɑːz-, ˈnɔːs-, ˈnɑːs-, ˈnɔːʃ-, ˈnɑːʃ-, ˈnɔːʒ-, ˈnɑːʒ- **~ated** eɪt ɪd -əd ‖ eɪţ əd **~ates** eɪts **~ating/ly** eɪt ɪŋ /li ‖ eɪţ ɪŋ /li
nauseous ˈnɔːs i‿əs ˈnɔːz- ‖ ˈnɔːʃ əs ˈnɑːʃ-; ˈnɔːz i‿əs, ˈnɑːz- **~ly** li **~ness** nəs nɪs
Nausicaa, Nausicaä nɔː ˈsɪk i‿ə -eɪ ə ‖ nɑː-
nautch nɔːtʃ ‖ nɑːtʃ **nautches** ˈnɔːtʃ ɪz -əz ‖ ˈnɑːtʃ-
nautical ˈnɔːt ɪk əl ‖ ˈnɔːţ ɪk əl ˈnɑːţ- **~ly** ‿i
 ˌ**nautical ˈmile**
naut|ilus, N~ *tdmk* ˈnɔːt |ɪl əs -əl- ‖ ˈnɔːţ |əl əs ˈnɑːţ- **~ili** ɪ laɪ əl aɪ, ɪ liː, əl iː ‖ əl aɪ əl iː **~iluses** ɪl əs ɪz əl-, -əz ‖ əl əs əz
Navaho, Navajo ˈnæv ə həʊ ‖ -hoʊ ˈnɑːv- **~s** z
naval ˈneɪv əl
Navan ˈnæv ən
navarin ˈnæv ər‿ɪn §-ər‿ən —*Fr* [na va ʁæ̃] **~s** z
Navarino ˌnæv ə ˈriːn əʊ ‖ -oʊ
Navarone ˈnæv ə rəʊn ˌ· ·ˈ· ‖ -roʊn
Navarre nə ˈvɑː ‖ -ˈvɑːr —*Fr* [na vaːʁ]
nave neɪv **naves** neɪvz
navel ˈneɪv əl *(= naval)* **~s** z
 ˈ**navel ˌorange**; ˈ**navel ˌgazing**
navicular nə ˈvɪk jʊl ə -jəl- ‖ -jəl ər
navie... —*see* **navy**
navigability ˌnæv ɪg ə ˈbɪl ət i -ɪt i ‖ -əţ i
navigab|le ˈnæv ɪg əb |əl **~leness** əl nəs -nɪs **~ly** li
navi|gate ˈnæv ɪ |geɪt -ə- **~gated** geɪt ɪd -əd ‖ geɪţ əd **~gates** geɪts **~gating** geɪt ɪŋ ‖ geɪţ ɪŋ
navigation ˌnæv ɪ ˈgeɪʃ ən -ə-
navigational ˌnæv ɪ ˈgeɪʃ ən‿əl ◂ ˌ·ə- **~ly** i
navigator ˈnæv ɪ geɪt ə ˈ·ə- ‖ -geɪţ ər **~s** z
Navratilova næv ˌræt ɪ ˈləʊv ə nəv-, ˌnæv rə- ‖ ˌnæv rə tɪ ˈloʊv ə ˌ·ræ- —*Czech* Navratilová [ˈna vra ci lo vaː]
navv|y ˈnæv |i **~ies** iz
nav|y ˈneɪv |i **~ies** iz
 ˌ**navy ˈblue**◂
nawab nə ˈwɑːb -ˈwɔːb ‖ -ˈwɔːb **~s** z
Naxalite ˈnæks ə laɪt ˈnʌks- **~s** z
Naxos ˈnæks ɒs ‖ -ɑːs ˈnɑːks-, -oʊs, -əs
nay neɪ **nays** neɪz

Nayland ˈneɪl ənd
Nayler, Naylor ˈneɪl ə ‖ -ᵊr
naysayer ˈneɪ ˌseɪ ə ‖ -ᵊr **~s** z
Nazarene ˌnæz ə ˈriːn ˈ· · · **~s** z
Nazareth ˈnæz ər əθ -ɪθ
Nazarite ˈnæz ə raɪt -ᵊr aɪt **~s** z
Nazca ˈnæz kə ‖ ˈnɑːsk ə —*AmSp* [ˈnas ka]
Naze neɪz
Nazeing ˈneɪz ɪŋ
Nazi, nazi ˈnɑːts i ˈnæts-, ˈnɑːz- **~s** z
Naziism ˈnɑːts i ˌɪz əm ˈnæts-, ˈnɑːz-
Nazism ˈnɑːts ˌɪz əm ˈnæts-, ˈnɑːz-
NB ˌen ˈbiː —*see also* **nota bene, Nebraska, New Brunswick**
NBA ˌen biː ˈeɪ →ˌem-
NBC ˌen biː ˈsiː →ˌem-
NCO ˌen si ˈəʊ ‖ -ˈoʊ **~s, ~'s** z
NCP ˌen siː ˈpiː
Ncube ˈnuːb eɪ —*Ndebele* [ˈŋ|uː ɓe]
Ndebele ᵊn dɪ ˈbel i ˌen-, -də-, -deɪ-, -ˈbeɪl-, -ˈbiːl-, -eɪ **~s** z
N'Djamena, N'Djaména ᵊn dʒæ ˈmeɪn ə ‖ -dʒɑː-
Ndola ᵊn ˈdəʊl ə ‖ -ˈdoʊl-
NE —*see* **northeast, northeastern**
Neagh neɪ
Neagle ˈniːg ᵊl
Neal, Neale, Neall niːᵊl
Neanderthal ni ˈænd ə tɑːl neɪ-, -θɔːl; -ət ᵊl ‖ -ᵊr θɔːl -ˈɑːnd-, -tɔːl, -tɑːl —*Ger* [ne ˈan dɐ taːl] **~s** z
Neˈanderthal man, ·ˌ· · · ˈ·
neap niːp **neaps** niːps
ˈneap tide
Neapolis ni ˈæp əl ɪs §-əs
neapolitan, N~ nɪə ˈpɒl ɪt ən ˌniː‿əˈ· · ·◂, -ət ən ‖ ˌniː ə ˈpɑːl ət ᵊn ◂ **~s** z
near nɪə ‖ nɪᵊr **neared** nɪəd ‖ nɪᵊrd **nearer** ˈnɪər ə ‖ ˈnɪr ᵊr **nearest** ˈnɪər ɪst -əst ‖ ˈnɪr əst **nearing** ˈnɪər ɪŋ ‖ ˈnɪr ɪŋ **nears** nɪəz ‖ nɪᵊrz
ˌNear ˈEast, ˌNear ˈEastern; **ˌnearest and ˈdearest**; **ˌnear ˈmiss**; **ˌnear ˈthing**
nearby *adj, adv* ˌnɪə ˈbaɪ ◂ ‖ ˌnɪr-
a ˌnearby ˈrestaurant
Nearctic ˌniː ˈɑːkt ɪk ◂ ‖ -ˈɑːrkt- -ˈɑːrţ-
near|ly ˈnɪə |li ‖ ˈnɪr |li **~ness** nəs nɪs
nearside ˈnɪə saɪd ˌ·ˈ· ‖ ˈnɪr-
nearsighted ˌnɪə ˈsaɪt ɪd ◂ -əd, ˈ·ˌ· · ‖ ˌnɪr ˈsaɪţ əd ◂ **~ly** li **~ness** nəs nɪs
Neasden ˈniːzd ən
neat niːt **neater** ˈniːt ə ‖ ˈniːţ ᵊr **neatest** ˈniːt ɪst -əst ‖ ˈniːţ əst
neaten ˈniːt ᵊn **~ed** d **~ing** ˌɪŋ **~s** z
neath, 'neath niːθ
Neath niːθ
neat|ly ˈniːt |li **~ness** nəs nɪs
Neave niːv
neb neb **nebs** nebz
nebbich, nebbish ˈneb ɪʃ **~es** ɪz əz
Nebo *mountain in Jordan* ˈniːb əʊ ‖ -oʊ
Nebo *places in Wales* ˈneb əʊ ‖ -oʊ
Nebrask|a nə ˈbræsk |ə nɪ- **~an/s** ən/z
Nebuchadnezzar, n~ ˌneb jʊk əd ˈnez ə ˌ·jək- ‖ ˌneb ək əd ˈnez ᵊr ˌ·jək- **~s** z
neb|ula ˈneb |jʊl ə -jəl- ‖ -|jəl ə **~ulae** ju liː jə ‖ jə liː **~ular** jʊl ə jəl- ‖ jəl ᵊr **~ulas** jʊl əz jəl- ‖ jəl əz
nebuliser, nebulizer ˈneb ju laɪz ə ‖ -jə laɪz ᵊr **~s** z
nebulosit|y ˌneb ju ˈlɒs ət |i ˌ·jə-, -ɪt i ‖ -jə ˈlɑːs əţ |i **~ies** iz
nebulous ˈneb jʊl əs -jəl- ‖ -jəl əs **~ly** li **~ness** nəs nɪs
NEC ˌen iː ˈsiː

NECESSARILY

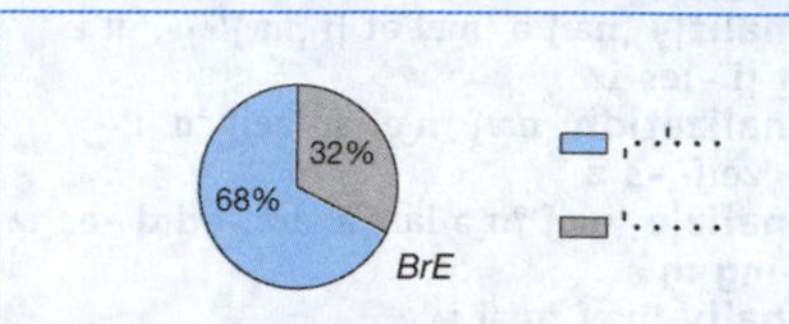

necessarily ˌnes ə ˈser əl i ˌ·ɪ-; ˈnes əs ᵊr‿əl i, ˈ·ɪs-, ‿ɪ li — *Preference poll, BrE:* ˌ··ˈ·· *68%,* ˈ· · · · *32%. Compare* voluntarily.

NECESSARY

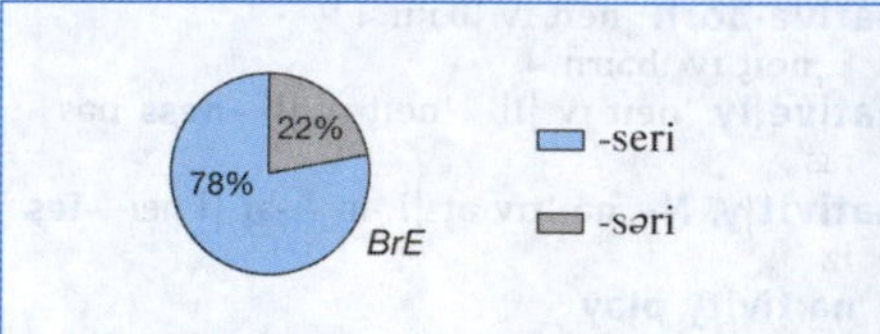

necessar|y ˈnes ə ser |i ˈ·ɪ-; ˈnes əs ᵊr‿|i, ˈ·ɪs- — *Preference poll, BrE:* -seri *78%,* -səri *22%.* **~ies** iz
ˌnecessary ˈevil
necessi|tate nə ˈses ɪ |teɪt nɪ-, ne-, -ə- **~tated** teɪt ɪd -əd ‖ teɪţ əd **~tates** teɪts **~tating** teɪt ɪŋ ‖ teɪţ ɪŋ
necessitous nə ˈses ɪt əs nɪ-, ne-, -ət- ‖ -əţ əs **~ly** li **~ness** nəs nɪs
necessit|y nə ˈses ɪt |i nɪ-, ne-, -ət- ‖ -əţ |i **~ies** iz
Nechells ˈniːtʃ ᵊlz
neck nek **necked** nekt **necking** ˈnek ɪŋ **necks** neks
neck-and-neck ˌnek ən ˈnek ◂
Neckar ˈnek ə -ɑː ‖ -ᵊr —*Ger* [ˈnɛk aʁ]
neckband ˈnek bænd **~s** z
-necked ˈnekt — **long-necked** ˌlɒŋ ˈnekt ◂ ‖ ˌlɔːŋ- ˌlɑːŋ-
Necker ˈnek ə ‖ -ᵊr —*Fr* [nɛ kɛːʁ]
neckerchief ˈnek ə tʃɪf -tʃiːf ‖ -ᵊr- -tʃəf **~s** s
necklac|e ˈnek ləs -lɪs **~ed** t **~es** ɪz əz **~ing** ɪŋ
necklet ˈnek lət -lɪt **~s** s
neckline ˈnek laɪn **~s** z
necktie ˈnek taɪ **~s** z
neckwear ˈnek weə ‖ -wer -wær
necro- *comb. form*
with stress-neutral suffix ˈnek rəʊ ‖ -roʊ —

necrobiosis ˌnek rəʊ baɪ ˈəʊs ɪs §-əs ‖ -roʊ baɪ ˈoʊs-
with stress-imposing suffix ne ˈkrɒ+ nɪ-, nə- ‖ -ˈkrɑː+ — **necrology** ne ˈkrɒl ədʒ |i nɪ-, nə- ‖ -ˈkrɑːl- **~ies** iz
necromancer ˈnek rəʊ mænᵗs ə ‖ -rə mænᵗs ᵊr **~s** z
necromancy ˈnek rəʊ mænᵗs i ‖ -rə mænᵗs i
necrophilia ˌnek rəʊ ˈfɪl i ə -ˈfiːl- ‖ ˌ·rə-
necrophiliac ˌnek rəʊ ˈfɪl i æk -ˈfiːl- ‖ ˌ·rə- **~s** s
necrophilism ne ˈkrɒf ɪ ˌlɪz əm nə-, nɪ-, -ˈ·ə- ‖ -ˈkrɑːf-
necropolis ne ˈkrɒp əl ɪs nə-, nɪ-, §-əs ‖ -ˈkrɑːp- **~es** ɪz əz
necrops|y ˈnek rɒps |i ‖ -rɑːps- **~ies** iz
necrosis ne ˈkrəʊs ɪs nə-, nɪ-, §-əs ‖ -ˈkroʊs-
necrotic ne ˈkrɒt ɪk nə-, nɪ- ‖ -ˈkrɑːţ ɪk
necrotis|e, necrotiz|e ˈnek rə taɪz **~ed** d **~es** ɪz əz **~ing** ɪŋ
nectar ˈnekt ə ‖ -ᵊr **~s** z
nectarine ˈnekt ə riːn -ər ɪn, §-ər ən **~s** z
nectar|y ˈnekt ər |i **~ies** iz
ned, Ned ned **neds** nedz
Neddie, Neddy ˈned i **~s, ~'s** z
nee, née neɪ ⚠niː *(= nay)*
need niːd **needed** ˈniːd ɪd -əd **needing** ˈniːd ɪŋ **needs** niːdz
needful ˈniːd fᵊl -fʊl **~ly** i **~ness** nəs nɪs
Needham ˈniːd əm
needl|e, N~ ˈniːd ᵊl **~ed** d **~es** z **~ing** ˌɪŋ
needlecord ˈniːd ᵊl kɔːd ‖ -kɔːrd **~s** z
needlecraft ˈniːd ᵊl krɑːft §-kræft ‖ -kræft
needlefish ˈniːd ᵊl fɪʃ
needlepoint ˈniːd ᵊl pɔɪnt
needless ˈniːd ləs -lɪs **~ly** li **~ness** nəs nɪs
needle|woman ˈniːd ᵊl |ˌwʊm ən **~women** ˌwɪm ɪn -ən
needlework ˈniːd ᵊl wɜːk ‖ -wɜːk
needn't ˈniːd ᵊnt →-ᵊn
need-to-know ˌniːd tə ˈnəʊ ‖ -ˈnoʊ
need|y ˈniːd |i **~ier** i ə ‖ i ᵊr **~iest** i ɪst i əst **~ily** ɪ li əl i **~iness** i nəs i nɪs
neem niːm
neep niːp **neeps** niːps
ne'er neə ‖ neᵊr næᵊr
ne'er-do-well ˈneə du ˌwel ‖ ˈner- ˈnær- **~s** z
Neeson ˈniːs ᵊn
Neet, NEET niːt
nefarious nɪ ˈfeər i əs nə-, ne- ‖ -ˈfer- -ˈfær- **~ly** li **~ness** nəs nɪs
Nefertiti ˌnef ə ˈtiːt i ‖ -ᵊr ˈtiːţ i
Neff nef
Nefyn ˈnev ɪn
NEG, neg. neg
negate nɪ |ˈgeɪt nə-, ne- **~gated** ˈgeɪt ɪd -əd ‖ ˈgeɪţ əd **~gates** ˈgeɪts **~gating** ˈgeɪt ɪŋ ‖ ˈgeɪţ ɪŋ
negation nɪ ˈgeɪʃ ᵊn nə-, ne- **~s** z
negativ|e ˈneg ət ɪv ‖ -əţ ɪv **~ed** d **~ely** li **~eness** nəs nɪs **~es** z **ing** ɪŋ
negativism ˈneg ət ɪv ˌɪz əm -ət əv- ‖ -əţ ɪv-
negativistic ˌneg ət ɪ ˈvɪst ɪk ◂ -ət ə- ‖ -əţ ɪ- **~ally** ᵊl i
negativity ˌneg ə ˈtɪv ət i -ɪt i ‖ -əţ i
negator nɪ ˈgeɪt ə nə-, ne- ‖ -ˈgeɪţ ᵊr **~s** z
Negeb ˈneg eb
Negev ˈneg ev nɪ ˈgev, nə-
neglect *v, n* nɪ ˈglekt nə-, §₍ᵢ₎ne- **~ed** ɪd əd **~ing** ɪŋ **~s** s
neglectful nɪ ˈglekt fᵊl nə-, §₍ᵢ₎ne-, -fʊl **~ly** i **~ness** nəs nɪs
negligee, negligée ˈneg lɪ ʒeɪ -lə-, -liː- ‖ ˌneg lə ˈʒeɪ ˈ· · · —*Fr* négligée [ne gli ʒe] **~s** z
negligenc|e ˈneg lɪdʒ ənᵗs -lədʒ- **~es** ɪz əz
negligent ˈneg lɪdʒ ənt -lədʒ- **~ly** li
negligib|le ˈneg lɪdʒ əb |ᵊl ˈ·lədʒ-, -ɪb ᵊl **~leness** ᵊl nəs -nɪs **~ly** li
negotiability nɪ ˌgəʊʃ i ə ˈbɪl ət i nə-, -ɪt i; -ˌgəʊʃ ə ˈbɪl- ‖ nɪ ˌgoʊʃ i ə ˈbɪl əţ i -ˌgoʊʃ ə ˈbɪl-
negotiable nɪ ˈgəʊʃ i əb ᵊl nə-, -ˈgəʊʃ əb ᵊl ‖ -ˈgoʊʃ- -ˈ·əb ᵊl
negoti|ate nɪ ˈgəʊʃ i |eɪt nə-, -ˈgəʊs- ‖ -ˈgoʊʃ- **~ated** eɪt ɪd -əd ‖ eɪţ əd **~ates** eɪts **~ating** eɪt ɪŋ ‖ eɪţ ɪŋ
negotiation nɪ ˌgəʊʃ i ˈeɪʃ ᵊn nə-, -ˌgəʊs- ‖ -ˌgoʊʃ- -ˌgoʊs- **~s** z
negotiator nɪ ˈgəʊʃ i eɪt ə nə-, -ˈgəʊs- ‖ -ˈgoʊʃ i eɪţ ᵊr **~s** z
negress, Negress ˈniːg res -rəs, -rɪs **~es** ɪz əz
Negri ˈneg ri
Negrillo nɪ ˈgrɪl əʊ nə-, ne- ‖ -oʊ -ˈgriː-, -joʊ **~s** z
negritude, négritude ˈneg rɪ tjuːd ˈniːg-, -rə-, →-tʃuːd ‖ -tuːd -tjuːd
negro, Negro *person* ˈniːg rəʊ ‖ -roʊ **~es** z
Negro *name of river* ˈneɪg rəʊ ˈneg- ‖ -roʊ
negroid, N~ ˈniːg rɔɪd **~s** z
negroni, N~ nɪ ˈgrəʊn i ne-, nə- ‖ -ˈgroʊn i **~s** z
negus, Negus ˈniːg əs **~es** ɪz əz
Nehemiah ˌniː ə ˈmaɪ ə ˌneɪ-, -hə-, -ɪ-, -hɪ-
Nehru ˈneər uː ‖ ˈneɪ ruː ˈner uː —*Hindi* [n̥eh ruː]
neigh neɪ *(= nay)* **neighed** neɪd **neighing** ˈneɪ ɪŋ **neighs** neɪz
neighbo... —*see* **neighbou...**
neighbour ˈneɪb ə ‖ -ᵊr **~s** z
neighbourhood ˈneɪb ə hʊd ‖ -ᵊr- **~s** z
ˌneighbourhood ˈwatch
neighbouring ˈneɪb ər ɪŋ
neighbour|ly ˈneɪb ə |li ‖ -ᵊr- **~liness** li nəs -nɪs
Neil, Neill niːᵊl
Neilson ˈniːl sən
Neiman ˈniːm ən
Neisse ˈnaɪs ə —*Ger* Neisse, Neiße [ˈnai sə]
neither ˈnaɪð ə ˈniːð- ‖ ˈniːð ᵊr ˈnaɪð- —*See preference poll figures at* either
Nejd neʒd
Nekrasov ne ˈkrɑːs ɒv nɪ- ‖ -oʊv —*Russ* [nʲɪ ˈkra səf]
nekton ˈnekt ɒn -ən ‖ -ɑːn

N

Nell nel
Nellie ˈnel i
Nellis ˈnel ɪs §-əs
nelly, N~ ˈnel i
Nelson, n~ ˈnels ən **~s, ~'s** z
nematic nɪ ˈmæt ɪk nə-, ne- ‖ -ˈmæṭ- **~s** s
nematocyst ˈnem ət əʊ sɪst nɪ ˈmæt-, nə-, ne- ‖ ˈnem əṭ ə- nɪ ˈmæṭ ə- **~s** s
nematode ˈnem ə təʊd ‖ -toʊd **~s** z
nembutal, N~ *tdmk* ˈnem bju tæl -bjə-, -tɒl, -tɑːl ‖ -bjə tɔːl -tɑːl, -tæl **~s** z
nem con, nem. con. ˌnem ˈkɒn ‖ -ˈkɑːn
Nemea nɪ ˈmiː‿ə nə-, ne-; ˈnem i‿ə, ˈniːm-
Nemean nɪ ˈmiː‿ən nə-, ne-; ˈnem i‿ən, ˈniːm- **~s** z
nem|esis, N~ ˈnem |əs ɪs -ɪs-, §-əs **~eses** ə siːz ɪ-
Nemo ˈniːm əʊ ‖ -oʊ
nemophila nɪ ˈmɒf ɪl ə nə-, -əl- ‖ -ˈmɑːf- **~s** z
nene *kind of bird* ˈneɪn eɪ **~s** z
Nene *name of river* niːn nen —*The river in the English midlands is known as the* nen *upstream (e.g. at Northampton) but as the* niːn *downstream (e.g. at Peterborough and Wisbech).*
Nennius ˈnen i‿əs
neo- *comb. form*
with stress-neutral suffix ¦niː əʊ ‖ -ə -oʊ — **neophilia** ˌniː əʊ ˈfɪl i‿ə ‖ ˌ·ə-
with stress-imposing suffix ni ˈɒ+ ‖ -ˈɑː+ — **neophilism** ni ˈɒf ɪ ˌlɪz əm -ˈ·ə- ‖ -ˈɑːf-
Neocene, n~ ˈniː əʊ siːn ‖ -ə-
neoclassic ˌniː əʊ ˈklæs ɪk ◂ ‖ ˌ·oʊ- **~al** əl ◂
neoclassicism ˌniː əʊ ˈklæs ɪ ˌsɪz əm -ˈ·ə- ‖ ˌ·oʊ-
neoclassicist ˌniː əʊ ˈklæs ɪs ɪst -əs ɪst, §-əst ‖ ˌ·oʊ- **~s** s
neocolonialism ˌniː əʊ kə ˈləʊn i‿ə ˌlɪz əm ‖ ˌniː oʊ kə ˈloʊn jə ˌlɪz əm
neocolonialist ˌniː əʊ kə ˈləʊn i‿əl ɪst ◂ §-əst ◂ ‖ ˌniː oʊ kə ˈloʊn jəl əst ◂ **~s** s
neocon ˈniː əʊ kɒn ‖ ˈniː oʊ kɑːn **~s** z
neoconservative ˌniː əʊ kən ˈsɜːv ət ɪv ◂ ‖ ˌniː oʊ kən ˈsɜːv əṭ ɪv ◂ **~s** z
neocortex ˌniː əʊ ˈkɔːt eks ‖ -oʊ ˈkɔːrt-
neodymium ˌniː əʊ ˈdɪm i‿əm ‖ ˌ·oʊ-
neofascist ˌniː əʊ ˈfæʃ ɪst ◂ §-əst ‖ -oʊ- **~s** s
Neogaea ˌni əʊ ˈdʒiː‿ə ‖ -ə-
neoimpressionism ˌniː əʊ ɪm ˈpreʃ ən ˌɪz əm -ə ˌnɪz- ‖ ˌ·oʊ-
neoimpressionist ˌniː əʊ ɪm ˈpreʃ ən‿ɪst §əst ‖ ˌ·oʊ- **~s** s
Neo-Latin ˌniː əʊ ˈlæt ɪn ◂ §-ən ‖ -oʊ ˈlæt ən
neolithic, N~ ˌniː əʊ ˈlɪθ ɪk ◂ ‖ -ə-
neologis|e, neologiz|e ni ˈɒl ə dʒaɪz ‖ -ˈɑːl- **~ed** d **~es** ɪz əz **~ing** ɪŋ
neologism ni ˈɒl ə ˌdʒɪz əm ˈniː‿əl- ‖ -ˈɑːl- **~s** z
Neo-Melanesian ˌniː əʊ ˌmel ə ˈniːz i‿ən ◂ -ˈniːʒ ən, -ˈniːs i‿ən, -ˈniːʃ ən ‖ ˌ·oʊ-
neomycin ˌniː əʊ ˈmaɪs ɪn §-ən ‖ -oʊ- -ə-
neon ˈniː ɒn -ən ‖ -ɑːn
ˈneon light
neonatal ˌniː əʊ ˈneɪt əl ◂ ‖ -oʊ ˈneɪṭ- **~ly** i
neonate ˈniː əʊ neɪt ‖ -ə- **~s** s
neo-Nazi ˌniː əʊ ˈnɑːts i ◂ ‖ -oʊ- **~s** z
neophyte ˈniː əʊ faɪt ‖ -ə- **~s** s
neoplasm ˈniː əʊ ˌplæz əm ‖ -ə- **~s** z
neoprene ˈniː əʊ priːn ‖ -ə-
Neoptolemus ˌniː ɒp ˈtɒl əm əs -ɪm əs ‖ -ɑːp ˈtɑːl-
neotame ˈniː əʊ teɪm ‖ -ə-
neotenous ni ˈɒt ən əs ‖ -ˈɑːt ən əs
neoteny ni ˈɒt ən i ‖ -ˈɑːt ən i
neoteric ˌniː əʊ ˈter ɪk ◂ ‖ -ə- **~s** s
Neozoic ˌniː əʊ ˈzəʊ ɪk ◂ ‖ -oʊ ˈzoʊ-
Nepal nɪ ˈpɔːl nə-, ne-, -ˈpɑːl ‖ nə ˈpɔːl -ˈpɑːl, -ˈpæl
Nepalese ˌnep ə ˈliːz ◂ -ɔː-, -ɑː-; -əl ˈiːz◂
Nepali nɪ ˈpɔːl i nə-, ne-, -ˈpɑːl- ‖ nə ˈpɔːl i -ˈpɑːl-, -ˈpæl- **~s** z
Nepean nɪ ˈpiː‿ən nə-
nepenthe nɪ ˈpentθ i ne-, nə-

NEPHEW

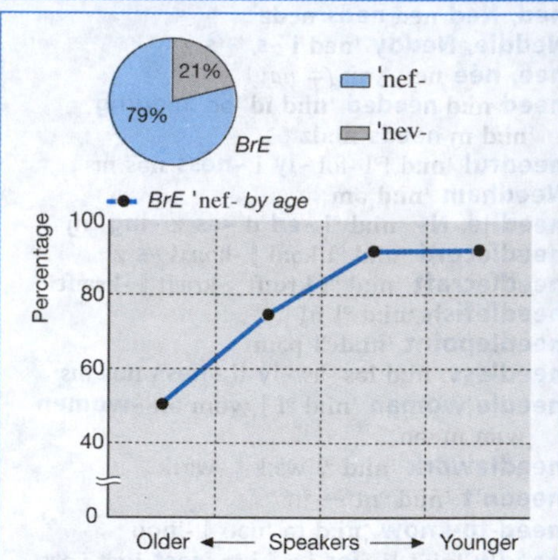

nephew ˈnef juː ˈnev- — *Preference poll, BrE:* ˈnef- *79%,* ˈnev- *21%. It is evident that the traditional form with* v *has been largely displaced by the spelling pronunciation, as has long been the case in AmE.* **~s** z
nephrite ˈnef raɪt
nephritic nɪ ˈfrɪt ɪk nə-, ne- ‖ -ˈfrɪṭ ɪk
nephritis nɪ ˈfraɪt ɪs nə-, ne-, §-əs ‖ -ˈfraɪṭ əs
nephro- *comb. form*
with stress-neutral suffix ¦nef rəʊ ‖ -rə — **nephrolith** ˈnef rəʊ lɪθ ‖ -rə-
with stress-imposing suffix ne ˈfrɒ+ nɪ-, nə- ‖ nɪ ˈfrɑː+ — **nephrotomy** ne ˈfrɒt əm i nɪ-, nə- ‖ nɪ ˈfrɑːṭ əm i
ne plus ultra ˌneɪ plʊs ˈʊltr ɑː ˌniː-, -plʌs-, -ˈʌltr-, -ə
nepotism ˈnep ə ˌtɪz əm
nepotistic ˌnep ə ˈtɪst ɪk ◂ **~al** əl ◂
Neptune, n~ ˈnep tjuːn -tʃuːn ‖ -tuːn -tjuːn **~s, ~'s** z

eptunian, n~ nep ˈtjuːn i‿ən →-ˈtʃuːn- ‖ -ˈtuːn- ˈtjuːn-
eptunium nep ˈtjuːn i‿əm →-ˈtʃuːn- ‖ -ˈtuːn- -ˈtjuːn-
erd nɜːd ‖ nɜ˞ːd **nerds** nɜːdz ‖ nɜ˞ːdz
ereid, n~ ˈnɪər i ɪd ‖ ˈnɪr- **~s** z
ereus ˈnɪər i uːs ‿əs ‖ ˈnɪr-
erf, NERF *tdmk* nɜːf ‖ nɜ˞ːf
ero ˈnɪər əʊ ‖ ˈniː roʊ ˈnɪr oʊ
eruda nə ˈruːd ə ne-, nɪ- —*Sp* [ne ˈru ða]
erurkar nɪ ˈrɜːk ə nə- ‖ -ˈrɜ˞ːk ᵊr
erva ˈnɜːv ə ‖ ˈnɜ˞ːv ə
erve nɜːv ‖ nɜ˞ːv **nerved** nɜːvd ‖ nɜ˞ːvd **nerves** nɜːvz ‖ nɜ˞ːvz **nerving** ˈnɜːv ɪŋ ‖ ˈnɜ˞ːv ɪŋ
ˈnerve cell; ˈnerve ˌcentre; ˈnerve gas; ˈnerve ˌimpulse
erveless ˈnɜːv ləs -lɪs ‖ ˈnɜ˞ːv- **~ly** li **~ness** nəs nɪs
erve-racking, nerve-wracking ˈnɜːv ˌræk ɪŋ ‖ ˈnɜ˞ːv-
ervine ˈnɜːv iːn -aɪn ‖ ˈnɜ˞ːv-
ervous ˈnɜːv əs ‖ ˈnɜ˞ːv əs **~ly** li **~ness** nəs nɪs
ˌnervous ˈbreakdown; ˈnervous ˌsystem
ervure ˈnɜːv jʊə -jə ‖ ˈnɜ˞ːv jʊr -jᵊr **~s** z
erv|y ˈnɜːv |i ‖ ˈnɜ˞ːv |i **~ier** i‿ə ‖ i‿ᵊr **~iest** i‿ɪst i‿əst **~ily** ɪ li əl i **~iness** i nəs i nɪs
Nerys ˈner ɪs §-əs
Nesbit, Nesbitt ˈnez bɪt
Nescafe, Nescafé *tdmk* ˈnes kæ ˌfeɪ -ˌkæf i, -eɪ; ˈnes kæf ‖ ˌ• ˈ•
nescience ˈnes i‿ənᵗs ‖ ˈneʃ ᵊnᵗs ˈneʃ i‿ənᵗs
nescient ˈnes i‿ənt ‖ ˈneʃ ᵊnt ˈneʃ i‿ənt **~s** s
nesh neʃ
Nesquik *tdmk* ˈnes kwɪk
ness, Ness nes **nesses, Ness's** ˈnes ɪz -əz
-ness nəs nɪs —*The noun-forming suffix has no effect upon word stress:* ˈcareless, ˈcarelessness. —*In singing, a strong-vowelled form* **nes** *is customary.*
-ness *in place names* ˈnes — **Sheerness** ˌʃɪə ˈnes ◂ ‖ ˌʃɪr-
Nesselrode, n~ ˈnes ᵊl rəʊd ‖ -roʊd —*Russ* [nʲi sɪɫ ˈrɔ də]
Nessie ˈnes i
Nessler ˈnes lə ‖ -lᵊr —*Ger* [ˈnɛs lɐ]
nessun dorma ˌnes uːn ˈdɔːm ə ‖ -ˈdɔːrm ə —*It* [ˌnes sun ˈdɔr ma]
Nessus ˈnes əs
nest, Nest nest **nested** ˈnest ɪd -əd **nesting** ˈnest ɪŋ **nests** nests
ˈnest egg
Nesta ˈnest ə
nestl|e ˈnes ᵊl **~ed** d **~es** z **~ing** ‿ɪŋ
Nestlé *tdmk* ˈnes leɪ -li, -ᵊl ‖ -li
nestling *part of* **nestle** ˈnes ᵊl‿ɪŋ
nestling *n 'young bird'* ˈnest lɪŋ **~s** z
Neston ˈnest ən
Nestor ˈnest ɔː -ə ‖ -ᵊr -ɔːr
Nestorian ne ˈstɔːr i‿ən ‖ -ˈstoʊr- **~ism** ˌɪz əm **~s** z
Nestorius ne ˈstɔːr i‿əs ‖ -ˈstoʊr-

net net **nets** nets **netted** ˈnet ɪd -əd ‖ ˈneţ əd **netting** ˈnet ɪŋ ‖ ˈneţ ɪŋ
Netanyahu ˌnet ᵊn ˈjɑː huː -æn-
netball ˈnet bɔːl ‖ -bɑːl
nether ˈneð ə ‖ -ᵊr
Netherlander ˈneð əl ənd ə -ə lænd ə ‖ -ᵊr lənd ᵊr -lænd- **~s** z
Netherlands ˈneð əl əndz ‖ -ᵊr ləndz
ˌNetherlands Anˈtilles
nethermost ˈneð ə məʊst ‖ -ᵊr moʊst
Netherton ˈneð ət ən ‖ -ᵊrt ᵊn
netherworld ˈneð ə wɜːld ‖ -ᵊr wɜ˞ːld
netiquette ˈnet ɪ ket -ɪk ət, ˌnet ɪ ˈket ‖ ˈneţ ɪk ət -ɪ ket
netizen ˈnet ɪz ən -əz- ‖ ˈneţ əz ən -əs- **~s** z
Netley ˈnet li
netpreneur ˈnet prə nɜː -pre- ‖ -nɜ˞ː **~s** z
netrepreneur ˈnetr ə prə nɜː -ə pre- ‖ -nɜ˞ː **~s** z
Netscape *tdmk* ˈnet skeɪp
netspeak ˈnet spiːk
netsuke ˈnet ski -skeɪ; ˈnets ʊk i, -eɪ —*Jp* [ne ˌtsɯ̥ ke] **~s** z
netsurfing ˈnet ˌsɜːf ɪŋ ‖ -ˌsɜ˞ːf-
nett net
nett... —*see* **net**
Nettie ˈnet i ‖ ˈneţ i
netting ˈnet ɪŋ ‖ ˈneţ ɪŋ
nettl|e, N~ ˈnet ᵊl ‖ ˈneţ ᵊl **~ed** d **~es** z **~ing** ɪŋ
ˈnettle rash
Nettlefold ˈnet ᵊl fəʊld →-fɒʊld ‖ ˈneţ ᵊl foʊld
Nettleship ˈnet ᵊl ʃɪp ‖ ˈneţ-
nettlesome ˈnet ᵊl səm ‖ ˈneţ-
network ˈnet wɜːk ‖ -wɜ˞ːk **~ed** t **~er/s** ə/z ‖ ᵊr/z **~ing** ɪŋ **~s** s
Neubrandenburg ˌnɔɪ ˈbrænd ən bɜːg ‖ -ˈbrɑːnd ən bɜ˞ːg —*Ger* [nɔy ˈbʁan dᵊn bʊʁk]
Neuchâtel, Neufchâtel ˌnɜː ʃæ ˈtel ◂ -ʃə- ‖ ˌnuː- ˌnʊ- —*Fr* [nø ʃa tɛl]
neum, neume njuːm §nuːm ‖ nuːm njuːm **neums, neumes** njuːmz §nuːmz ‖ nuːmz njuːmz
Neumann ˈnjuː mən §ˈnuː- ‖ ˈnuː- ˈnjuː —*but as a German name,* ˈnɔɪ- —*Ger* [ˈnɔy man]
neural ˈnjʊər ə l ˈnjɔːr- §ˈnʊər- ‖ ˈnʊr əl ˈnjʊr-, nɜ˞ː-
neuralgia njuᵊ ˈrældʒ ə njə-, njɔː-, §nuᵊ- ‖ nu- nə-, nju-
neuralgic njuᵊ ˈrældʒ ɪk njə-, njɔː-, §nuᵊ- ‖ nu- nə-, nju-
neurasthenia ˌnjʊər əs ˈθiːn i‿ə ˌnjɔːr-, §ˌnʊər-, ˌ-æs- ‖ ˌnʊr- ˌnjʊr-
neurasthenic ˌnjʊər əs ˈθen ɪk ◂ ˌnjɔːr-, §ˌnʊər-, -æs- ‖ ˌnʊr- ˌnjʊr- **~ally** ᵊl‿i
neuritis njuᵊ ˈraɪt ɪs njə-, njɔː-, §nuᵊ-, §-əs ‖ nu ˈraɪţ əs nə-, nju-
neuro- *comb. form*
with stress-neutral suffix ¦njʊər əʊ ¦njɔːr-, §¦nʊər- ‖ ¦nʊr oʊ ¦njʊr- — **neurobiology** ˌnjʊər əʊ baɪ ˈɒl ədʒ i ˌnjɔːr-, §ˌnʊər- ‖ ˌnʊr oʊ baɪ ˈɑːl- ˌnjʊr-

N

with stress-imposing suffix njuᵊ ˈrɒ+ njə-, njɔː-, §nuᵊ- ‖ nu ˈrɑː+ nə-, nju-
neuropathy njuᵊ ˈrɒp əθ i njə-, §nuᵊ- ‖ nu ˈrɑːp- nə-, nju-

neuroinformatics ˌnjʊər əʊ ˌɪn fə ˈmæt ɪks ˌnjɔːr-, §ˌnʊər- ‖ ˌnʊr oʊ ˌɪn fᵊr ˈmæţ ɪks ˌnjʊr-

neurological ˌnjʊər ə ˈlɒdʒ ɪk ᵊl ◂ ˌnjɔːr-, §ˌnʊər- ‖ ˌnʊr ə ˈlɑːdʒ- ˌnjʊr- **~ly** ‿i

neurologist njuᵊ ˈrɒl ədʒ ɪst njə-, njɔː-, §nuᵊ-, §-əst ‖ nu ˈrɑːl- nə-, nju- **~s** s

neurology njuᵊ ˈrɒl ədʒ i njə-, njɔː-, §nuᵊ- ‖ nu ˈrɑːl- nə-, nju-

neuroma njuᵊ ˈrəʊm ə ‖ -ˈroʊm ə **~s** z

neuron ˈnjʊər ɒn ˈnjɔːr-, §ˈnʊər- ‖ ˈnʊr ɑːn ˈnjʊr-; ˈnjuː rɑːn **~s** z

neurone ˈnjʊər əʊn ˈnjɔːr-, §ˈnʊər- ‖ ˈnʊr oʊn ˈnjʊr-; ˈnjuː roʊn **~s** z

neuropath|y njuᵊ ˈrɒp əθ |i njə-, njɔː-, §nuᵊ- ‖ nu ˈrɑːp- nə-, nju- **~ies** iz

neurosci|ence ˌnjʊər əʊ ˈsaɪ‿|ənᵗs ˌnjɔːr-, §ˌnʊər-, ˈ·ˌ·· ‖ ˌnʊr oʊ- ˌnjʊr- **~ences** ənᵗs ɪz -əz **~entist/s** ənt ɪst/s §-əst/s ‖ ənţ əst/s

neuros|is njuᵊ ˈrəʊs |ɪs njə-, njɔː-, §nuᵊ-, §-əs ‖ nu ˈroʊs- nə-, nju- **~es** iːz

neurosurgeon ˌnjʊər əʊ ˈsɜːdʒ ən ˌnjɔː-, §ˌnʊər-, ˈ·ˌ·· ‖ ˌnʊr oʊ ˈsɝːdʒ ən ˌnjʊr- **~s** z

neurosurgery ˌnjʊər əʊ ˈsɜːdʒ ər‿i ˌnjɔː-, §ˌnʊər-, ˈ·ˌ·· ‖ ˌnʊr oʊ ˈsɝːdʒ-

neurosurgical ˌnjʊər əʊ ˈsɜːdʒ ɪk ᵊl ◂ ˌnjɔː-, §ˌnʊər-, ˈ·ˌ··· ‖ ˌnʊr oʊ ˈsɝːdʒ- **~ly** ‿i

neurotheology ˌnjʊər əʊ θi ˈɒl ədʒ i ˌnjɔːr-, §ˌnʊər- ‖ ˌnʊr oʊ θi ˈɑːl- ˌnjʊr-

neurotic njuᵊ ˈrɒt ɪk njə-, njɔː-, §nuᵊ- ‖ nu ˈrɑːţ ɪk nə-, nju- **~ally** ᵊl‿i **~s** s

neuroticism njuᵊ ˈrɒt ɪ ˌsɪz əm njə-, njɔː-, §nuᵊ-, -ˈ·ə- ‖ nu ˈrɑːţ ə- nə-, nju-

neurotransmitter ˌnjʊər əʊ trænz ˈmɪt ə ˌnjɔːr, §ˌnʊər-, -trɑːnzˈ··, -trænᵗsˈ··, -trɑːnᵗsˈ··, ˈ····ˌ·· ‖ ˌnʊr oʊ trænᵗs ˈmɪţ ᵊr -trænzˈ··, ˈ····ˌ··

neut|er ˈnjuːt |ə §ˈnuːt- ‖ ˈnuːţ |ᵊr ˈnjuːţ- **~ered** əd ‖ ᵊrd **~ering** ər ɪŋ **~ers** əz ‖ ᵊrz

neutral ˈnjuːtr əl §ˈnuːtr- ‖ ˈnuːtr əl ˈnjuːtr- **~s** z

neutralis... *—see* **neutraliz...**

neutralism ˈnjuːtr ə ˌlɪz əm §ˈnuːtr-, -ᵊl ˌɪz- ‖ ˈnuːtr- ˈnjuːtr-

neutralist ˈnjuːtr əl ɪst §ˈnuːtr-, §-əst ‖ ˈnuːtr- ˈnjuːtr- **~s** s

neutrality nju ˈtræl ət i §nu-, -ɪt- ‖ nu ˈtræl əţ i nju-

neutralization ˌnjuːtr əl aɪ ˈzeɪʃ ᵊn §ˌnuːtr-, -ɪˈ·· ‖ ˌnuːtr əl ə- ˌnjuːtr- **~s** z

neutraliz|e ˈnjuːtr ə laɪz §ˈnuːtr- ‖ ˈnuːtr- ˈnjuːtr- **~ed** d **~es** ɪz əz **~ing** ɪŋ

neutrally ˈnjuːtr əl i §ˈnuːtr- ‖ ˈnuːtr- ˈnjuːtr-

neutrino nju ˈtriːn əʊ §nu- ‖ nu ˈtriːn oʊ nju- **~s** z

neutron ˈnjuːtr ɒn §ˈnuːtr- ‖ ˈnuːtr ɑːn ˈnjuːtr- **~s** z **ˈneutron bomb**; **ˈneutron star**

neutropenia ˌnjuːtr əʊ ˈpiːn i‿ə §ˌnuːtr- ‖ ˌnuːtr oʊ ˈpiːn jə ˌnjuːtr-

neutrophil ˈnjuːtr əʊ fɪl §ˈnuːtr- ‖ ˈnuːtr ə- ˈnjuːtr-

Neva *river in USSR* ˈneɪv ə ˈniːv- *—Russ* [nʲɪ ˈva]

Nevad|a nɪ ˈvɑːd |ə nə-, ne- ‖ nɪ ˈvæd |ə -ˈvɑːd- *—but places in AR, IA, MO are also* -ˈveɪd- **~an/s** ᵊn/z

Nevard nə ˈvɑːd nɪ- ‖ -ˈvɑːrd

Neve niːv

névé ˈnev eɪ ‖ neɪ ˈveɪ *—Fr* [ne ve]

never ˈnev ə ‖ -ᵊr

never-ending ˌnev ᵊr ˈend ɪŋ ◂ -ə-

nevermore ˌnev ə ˈmɔː ‖ -ᵊr ˈmɔːr -ˈmoʊr

never-never ˌnev ə ˈnev ə ‖ -ᵊr ˈnev ᵊr **ˌnever-ˈnever land**

nevertheless ˌnev ə ðə ˈles ‖ ˌnev ᵊr-

Nevil, Nevill, Neville ˈnev ᵊl -ɪl

Nevin ˈnev ɪn -ᵊn

Nevinson ˈnev ɪnᵗs ən -ənᵗs-

Nevis *mountain and loch in Scotland* ˈnev ɪs §-əs

Nevis *island in West Indies* ˈniːv ɪs §-əs

nev|us ˈniːv |əs **~i** aɪ **~uses** əs ɪz -əz

NEW

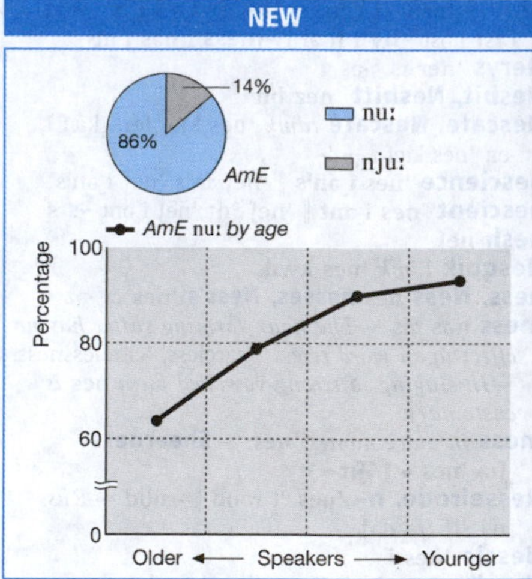

new njuː §nuː ‖ nuː njuː *— Preference poll, AmE:* nuː *86%,* njuː *14%.—See also phrases with this word* **newer** ˈnjuː‿ə ‖ ˈnuː ᵊr ˈnjuː- **newest** ˈnjuː‿ɪst §ˈnuː‿, əst ‖ ˈnuː əst ˈnjuː- **ˌNew ˈAge◂**, **ˌNew Age ˈtraveller**; **ˌnew ˈblood**; **ˌnew ˈbroom**; **(ˌ)New ˈBrunswick**; **ˌNew ˌCaleˈdonia**; **ˌnew ˈdeal**, **ˌNew ˈDeal**; **(ˌ)New ˈDelhi**; **(ˌ)New ˈEngland**; **ˌNew ˈForest◂**, **ˌNew ˌForest ˈpony**; **(ˌ)New ˈGuinea**; **(ˌ)New ˈHampshire**; **New ˈHaven** *place in CN, also* ˈ·ˌ··; **(ˌ)New ˈJersey**; **(ˌ)New ˈMexico**; **ˌnew ˈmoon**; **New ˈOrleans**, **ˌNew Orˈleans**; **ˌNew ˈQuay** *place in Dyfed*; **ˌNew ˈRight**; **ˌNew ˌScotland ˈYard**; **ˌNew South ˈWales**; **ˌNew ˈTestament**; **ˈnew town**, **ˌ·ˈ·**; **ˌNew ˈWave◂**, **ˌNew Wave ˈmusic**; **ˌNew**

Neutralization

1 Two PHONEMES may, in certain phonetic environments, not be distinguishable. We say the **opposition** between them is **neutralized**.

2 In most environments English p and b are in opposition: that is, they carry a potential difference in meaning. This can be seen in pairs such as **pin** pɪn and **bin** bɪn, **cup** kʌp and **cub** kʌb. After s, however, the opposition is neutralized (since p here has no ASPIRATION). Conventionally, we write **spin** phonemically as spɪn; but since there is no possible difference between p and b here we could just as well write sbɪn.

3 One type of neutralization is symbolized explicitly in LPD by the use of the symbols i and u. The opposition between iː and ɪ operates in most environments, as seen in **green** griːn and **grin** grɪn, **leap** liːp and **lip** lɪp. But there are two environments in which it is neutralized:

- when the vowel is in a WEAK syllable at the end of a word (or at the end of part of a compound word or of a stem), as in **happy** ˈhæp i, **valley** ˈvæl i, **babies** ˈbeɪb iz.
- when the vowel is in a weak syllable before another vowel, as in **radiation** ˌreɪd i ˈeɪʃ ᵊn, **glorious** ˈglɔːr i‿əs.

In these positions the vowel is traditionally identified with ɪ. But in fact some speakers use ɪ, some use iː, some use something intermediate or indeterminate, and some fluctuate between the two possibilities. Modern pronunciation dictionaries use the symbol i, which reflects this.

Similarly, in this dictionary the symbol u represents the neutralization of the opposition between uː and ʊ. This neutralization is found not only in i environments, but also in certain others, for example, in one pronunciation of **stimulate** ˈstɪm ju leɪt.

Do not confuse neutralization with the term **neutral vowel**, a name sometimes used for ə.

ˈWorld; **ˌnew ˈyear◂**, **ˌNew Year's ˈDay**, **ˌNew Year's ˈEve**; **₍ˌ₎New ˈYork**, **ˌNew York ˈCity**, ; **₍ˌ₎New ˈYorker**, **ˌNew York ˈState**

Newark **ˈnjuː‿ək** §ˈnuː- ‖ **ˈnuː ᵊrk** ˈnjuː- *—but the place in DE is* -ɑːk ‖ -ɑːrk

newbie **ˈnjuːb i** §ˈnuːb- ‖ **ˈnuːb i** ˈnjuːb- **~s** **z**

Newbiggin **ˈnjuː ˌbɪg ɪn** §ˈnuː-, §-ən ‖ **ˈnuː-** ˈnjuː-

Newbold **ˈnjuː bəʊld** §ˈnuː-, →-bɒʊld ‖ **ˈnuː boʊld** ˈnjuː-

Newbolt **ˈnjuː bəʊlt** §ˈnuː-, →-bɒʊlt ‖ **ˈnuː boʊlt** ˈnjuː-

newborn **ˈnjuː bɔːn** §ˈnuː-; ˌ·ˈ·◂ ‖ **ˈnuː bɔːrn** ˈnjuː-

Newbridge **ˈnjuː brɪdʒ** §ˈnuː- ‖ **ˈnuː-** ˈnjuː-

Newbrough **ˈnjuː brʌf** §ˈnuː- ‖ **ˈnuː-** ˈnjuː-

newbuild **ˈnjuː bɪld** §ˈnuː ‖ **ˈnuː-** njuː-

Newburg, n~ **ˈnjuː bɜːg** §ˈnuː- ‖ **ˈnuː bɝːg** ˈnjuː-

Newburgh **ˈnjuː bər‿ə** §ˈnuː- ‖ **ˈnuː bɝːg** ˈnjuː-

Newbury **ˈnjuː bər‿i** §ˈnuː- ‖ **ˈnuː ˌber i** ˈnjuː-, -bər‿i

Newby **ˈnjuːb i** §ˈnuːb- ‖ **ˈnuːb i** ˈnjuːb-

Newcastle **ˈnjuː ˌkɑːs ᵊl** §ˈnuː-, §-ˌkæs-, §·ˈ· · ‖ **ˈnuː ˌkæs ᵊl** ˈnjuː- *—In Tyne & Wear, locally* njuː ˈkæs ᵊl
ˌNewcastle-(up)on-ˈTyne, *locally* **Newˌcastle-**; **ˌNewcastle-ˌunder-ˈLyme**

Newcomb, Newcombe, Newcome **ˈnjuːk əm** §ˈnuːk- ‖ **ˈnuːk-** ˈnjuːk-

newcomer **ˈnjuː ˌkʌm ə** §ˈnuː- ‖ **ˈnuː ˌkʌm ᵊr** ˈnjuː- **~s** **z**

Newdigate ˈnjuːd ɪ geɪt §ˈnuːd-, -ə-, -gɪt, -gət ‖ ˈnuːd- ˈnjuːd-
Newe njuː §nuː ‖ nuː njuː
newel ˈnjuː‿əl §ˈnuː- ‖ ˈnuː əl ˈnjuː- **~s** z
New Englander nju ˈɪŋ glənd ə -lənd ə ‖ nu ˈɪŋ glənd ər nju- **~s** z
newfangled ˌnjuː ˈfæŋ gəld ◂ §ˌnuː- ‖ ˌnuː- ˌnjuː-; ˈ·ˌ··
Newfie ˈnjuːf i §ˈnuːf- ‖ ˈnuːf i ˈnjuːf- **~s** z
new-found ˌnjuː-ˈfaʊnd ◂ §ˌnuː- ‖ ˌnuː- ˌnjuː-
Newfoundland ˈnjuːf ənd lənd §ˈnuːf-, -lænd, ˌ··ˈ·; nju ˈfaʊnd-, §nu- ‖ ˈnuːf ənd lənd ˈnjuːf-, -lænd; nu ˈfaʊnd-, nju- —*Locally* ˌ··ˈ·. *The breed of dog is usually* ·ˈ··. **~s, ~'s** z
Newfoundlander ˌnjuːf ənd ˈlænd ə §ˌnuːf-; ˈ····, -lənd ə; nju ˈfaʊnd lənd ə, §nu- ‖ ˈnuːf ənd lənd ər ˈnjuːf-, -lænd ər **~s** z
Newgate ˈnjuː geɪt §ˈnuː-, -gɪt, -gət ‖ ˈnuː- ˈnjuː-
Newham ˈnjuː‿əm §ˈnuː‿, -hæm; ˌ·ˈhæm ◂ ‖ ˈnuː- ˈnjuː-
Newhaven *place in Sussex* ˈnjuː ˌheɪv ən §ˈnuː-, ·ˈ·· ‖ ˈnuː- ˈnjuː-
Newington ˈnjuː‿ɪŋ tən §ˈnuː- ‖ ˈnuː- ˈnjuː-
newish ˈnjuː‿ɪʃ §ˈnuː‿ ‖ ˈnuː- ˈnjuː-
new-laid ˌnjuː ˈleɪd ◂ §ˌnuː- ‖ ˌnuː- ˌnjuː-
ˌnew-laid ˈeggs
Newlands ˈnjuː ləndz §ˈnuː- ‖ ˈnuː- ˈnjuː-
new-look ˌnjuː ˈlʊk ◂ §ˌnuː- ‖ ˌnuː- ˌnjuː-
newly ˈnjuː li §ˈnuː- ‖ ˈnuː- ˈnjuː-
Newlyn ˈnjuː lɪn §ˈnuː- ‖ ˈnuː- ˈnjuː-
newlywed ˈnjuː li wed §ˈnuː-, ˌ··ˈ·◂ ‖ ˈnuː- ˈnjuː- **~s** z
Newman ˈnjuː mən §ˈnuː- ‖ ˈnuː- ˈnjuː-
Newmark ˈnjuː mɑːk §ˈnuː- ‖ ˈnuː mɑːrk ˈnjuː-
Newmarket, n~ ˈnjuː ˌmɑːk ɪt §ˈnuː-, §-ət ‖ ˈnuː ˌmɑːrk ət ˈnjuː-
new-mown ˌnjuː ˈməʊn ◂ §ˌnuː- ‖ ˌnuː ˈmoʊn ◂ ˌnjuː-
ˌnew-mown ˈhay
Newnes njuːnz §nuːnz ‖ ˈnuːnz ˈnjuːnz
newness ˈnjuː nəs §ˈnuː-, -nɪs ‖ ˈnuː- ˈnjuː-
Newnham ˈnjuːn əm §ˈnuːn- ‖ ˈnuːn- ˈnjuːn-
New Orleans ˌnjuː ˈɔːl i‿ənz §ˌnuː-, -ˈɔːl ənz, -ɔː ˈliːnz ‖ ˌnuː ˈɔːrl ənz ˌnjuː-; ˌnuː ɔːr ˈliːnz, ˌnjuː-
Newport ˈnjuː pɔːt §ˈnuː- ‖ nuː pɔːrt ˈnjuː-, -poʊrt
—*but in* **ˌNewport ˈNews** *place in VA, sometimes* -pət ‖ -pərt
Newquay *place in Cornwall* ˈnjuː kiː §ˈnuː- ‖ ˈnuː- ˈnjuː-
Newry ˈnjʊər i §ˈnʊər- ‖ ˈnuː ri ˈnjuː-
news njuːz §nuːz ‖ nuːz njuːz
ˈnews ˌagency; **ˈnews ˌconference**
newsagent ˈnjuːz ˌeɪdʒ ənt §ˈnuːz- ‖ ˈnuːz- ˈnjuːz- **~s** s
newsboy ˈnjuːz bɔɪ §ˈnuːz- ‖ ˈnuːz- ˈnjuːz- **~s** z
newscast ˈnjuːz kɑːst §ˈnuːz-, §-kæst ‖ ˈnuːz kæst ˈnjuːz- **~er/s** ə/z ‖ ər/z **~ing** ɪŋ **~s** s
newsflash ˈnjuːz flæʃ §ˈnuːz- ‖ ˈnuːz- ˈnjuːz- **~es** ɪz əz
newsgroup ˈnjuːz gruːp §ˈnuːz- ‖ ˈnuːz- njuːz- **~s** s
newshawk ˈnjuːz hɔːk §ˈnuːz- ‖ ˈnuːz- ˈnjuːz-, -hɑːk **~s** s
newshound ˈnjuːz haʊnd §ˈnuːz- ‖ ˈnuːz- ˈnjuːz- **~s** z
newsletter ˈnjuːz ˌlet ə §ˈnuːz- ‖ ˈnuːz ˌleţ ər ˈnjuːz- **~s** z
newsmaker ˈnjuːz ˌmeɪk ə §ˈnuːz- ‖ ˈnuːz ˌmeɪk ər ˈnjuːz- **~s** z
news|man ˈnjuːz| mæn -mən ‖ ˈnuːz- ˈnjuːz- **~men** men mən
newsmonger ˈnjuːz ˌmʌŋ gə §ˈnuːz- ‖ ˈnuːz ˌmɑːŋ gər ˈnjuːz-, -ˌmʌŋ- **~s** z
Newsnight ˈnjuːz naɪt §ˈnuːz- ‖ ˈnuːz- ˈnjuːz-
Newsom, Newsome *family name* ˈnjuːs əm §ˈnuːs- ‖ ˈnuːs- ˈnjuːs-
Newsome *place in West Yorks.* ˈnjuːz əm §ˈnuːz- ‖ ˈnuːz- ˈnjuːz-

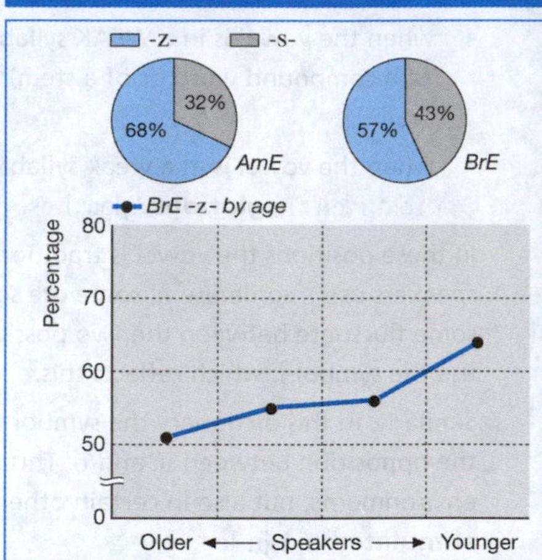

newspaper ˈnjuːz ˌpeɪp ə ˈnjuːs-, §ˈnuːz-, §ˈnuːs- ‖ ˈnuːz ˌpeɪp ər ˈnjuːz-, ˈnuːs-, ˈnjuːs- — *Preference polls, AmE:* z *68%,* s *32%; BrE:* z *57%,* s *43%.* **~man** mæn **~men** men **~s** z **~woman** ˌwʊm ən **~women** ˌwɪm ɪn §-ən
newspeak, N~ ˈnjuː spiːk §ˈnuː- ‖ ˈnuː- ˈnjuː-
news|person ˈnjuːz ˌpɜːs ən §ˈnuːz- ‖ ˈnuːz ˌpɜːs ən ˈnjuːz- **~people** ˌpiːp əl
newsprint ˈnjuːz prɪnt §ˈnuːz- ‖ ˈnuːz- ˈnjuːz-
newsreader ˈnjuːz ˌriːd ə §ˈnuːz- ‖ ˈnuːz ˌriːd ər ˈnjuːz- **~s** z
newsreel ˈnjuːz riːəl §ˈnuːz- ‖ ˈnuːz- ˈnjuːz- **~s** z
newsroom ˈnjuːz ruːm §ˈnuːz-, -rʊm ‖ ˈnuːz- ˈnjuːz- **~s** z
newssheet ˈnjuːz ʃiːt §ˈnuːz-, →ˈnjuːʒ- ‖ ˈnuːz- ˈnjuːz- **~s** s
newsstand ˈnjuːz stænd §ˈnuːz- ‖ ˈnuːz- ˈnjuːz- **~s** z
Newstead ˈnjuːst ɪd -ed ‖ ˈnuːst- ˈnjuːst-

ewsvendor 'nju:z ˌvend ə §'nu:z- ‖ 'nu:z ˌvend ᵊr 'nju:z- **~s** z

ews|woman 'nju:z ˌwʊm ən §'nu:z- ‖ 'nu:z- 'nju:z- **~women** ˌwɪm ɪn §-ən

ewsworthy 'nju:z ˌwɜ:ð i §'nu:z- ‖ 'nu:z ˌwɝ:ð i 'nju:z-

ewswriter 'nju:z ˌraɪt ə §'nu:z- ‖ 'nu:z ˌraɪţ ᵊr 'nju:z- **~s** z

ews|y 'nju:z |i §'nu:z- ‖ 'nu:z |i 'nju:z- **~ier** i‿ə ‖ i‿ᵊr **~ies** iz **~iest** i‿ɪst i‿əst **~iness** i nəs i nɪs

ewt nju:t §nu:t ‖ nu:t nju:t **newts** nju:ts §nu:ts ‖ nu:ts nju:ts

ewton, n~ 'nju:t ᵊn §'nu:t- ‖ 'nu:t ᵊn 'nju:t- **~s, ~'s** z

ewtonian nju 'təʊn i‿ən §nu- ‖ nu 'toʊn- nju-

ewton-le-Willows ˌnju:t ᵊn li 'wɪl əʊz §ˌnu:t- ‖ ˌnu:t ᵊn li 'wɪl oʊz ˌnju:t-

ewtonmore ˌnju:t ᵊn 'mɔ: §ˌnu:t- ‖ ˌnu:t ᵊn 'mɔ:r ˌnju:-, -'moʊr

ewtown 'nju: taʊn §'nu:- ‖ 'nu:- 'nju:- —*but in Irish compound place-names,* ¦nju:t ᵊn, §¦nu:t- ‖ ¦nu:t ᵊn, ¦nju:t- — **Newtownabbey** ˌnju:t ᵊn 'æb i §ˌnu:t- ‖ ˌnu:t- ˌnju:t- , **Newtownards** ˌnju:t ᵊn 'ɑ:dz §ˌnu:t- ‖ ˌnu:t ᵊn 'ɑ:rdz ˌnju:t-

ew York ˌnju: 'jɔ:k◂ §ˌnu:- ‖ ₍ˌ₎nu: 'jɔ:rk ◂ ₍ˌ₎nju:- **~er/s** ə/z ‖ ᵊr/z

ˌNew York 'City

ew Zealand nju 'zi:l ənd ˌnju:-, §nu-, §ˌnu:- ‖ nu- nju-, ˌnu:-, ˌnju:- —*locally sometimes* -'zɪl-

New ˌZealand 'flax

ew Zealander nju 'zi:l ənd ə ˌnju:-, §nu-, §ˌnu:- ‖ nu 'zi:l ənd ᵊr nju-, ˌnu:-, ˌnju:- **~s** z

ext nekst

ext-door ˌnekst 'dɔ: ◂ ‖ -'dɔ:r ◂ -'doʊr ◂

ˌnext-door 'neighbour

exus 'neks əs **~es** ɪz əz

ey neɪ —*Fr* [nɛ]

ez Perce, Nez Percé ˌnez 'pɜ:s ˌnes-, -'peəs, -'peəs eɪ ‖ -'pɝ:s —*Fr* [ne pɛʁ se]

g ɪŋ eŋ —*Cantonese* [⁴ŋ, ⁴m]

gaio, ngaio 'naɪ əʊ ‖ -oʊ —*Maori* ['ŋai o] **~s, ~'s** z

giyambaa, Ngiyampaa *Australian language* 'ŋeəm bɑ: ‖ 'ŋeɪ əm bɑ:

guni ᵊŋ 'gu:n i

NHS ˌen eɪtʃ 'es §-heɪtʃ-

Nhulunbuy *place in Australia* 'nu:l ən bɔɪ →-əm-

Ni *'nickel'* ˌen 'aɪ

Ni, Ní *in Irish names* ni: —*Irish* [ɲi:]

niacin 'naɪ‿əs ɪn §-ᵊn

Niagara naɪ 'æg ər‿ə ni-

Niˌagara 'Falls

Niall *(i)* ni:ᵊl, *(ii)* 'naɪ‿əl

Niamey ni 'ɑ:m eɪ ˌnɪə 'meɪ ‖ ˌni: ə 'meɪ —*Fr* [nja mɛ]

Niamh ni:v 'ni:‿əv

nib nɪb **nibs** nɪbz

nibbl|e 'nɪb ᵊl **~ed** d **~es** z **~ing** ˌɪŋ

Nibelung 'ni:b ə lʊŋ —*Ger* ['ni: bə lʊŋ]

Nibelungenlied 'ni:b ə lʊŋ ən li:d -li:t —*Ger* ['ni: bə lʊŋ ən li:t]

niblick 'nɪb lɪk **~s** s

NiCad, NiCd 'naɪ kæd

Nicaea naɪ 'si:‿ə

NiCam *tdmk* 'naɪ kæm

Nicarag|ua ˌnɪk ə 'ræg| ju‿ə -'rɑ:g|-, -'•wə ‖ -'rɑ:g| wə —*Sp* [ni ka 'ra ɣwa] **~an/s** ən/z ◂

nice naɪs **nicer** 'naɪs ə ‖ -ᵊr **nicest** 'naɪs ɪst -əst

Nice *place in France* ni:s —*Fr* [nis]

nice-looking ˌnaɪs 'lʊk ɪŋ ◂ §-'lu:k-

nicely 'naɪs li

Nicene ˌnaɪ 'si:n ◂

ˌNicene 'Creed

niceness 'naɪs nəs -nɪs

nicet|y 'naɪs ət |i -ɪt- ‖ -əţ |i **~ies** iz

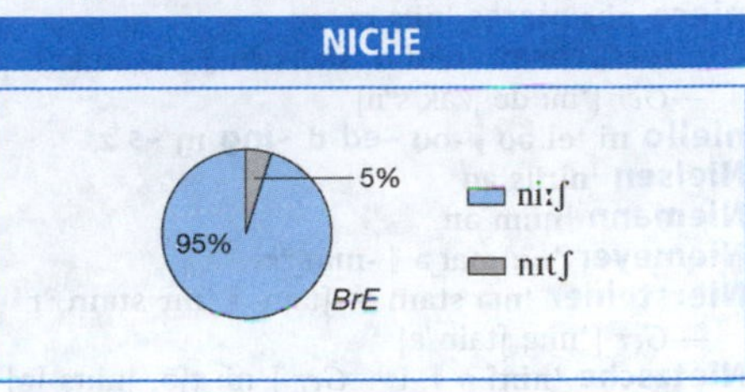

NICHE

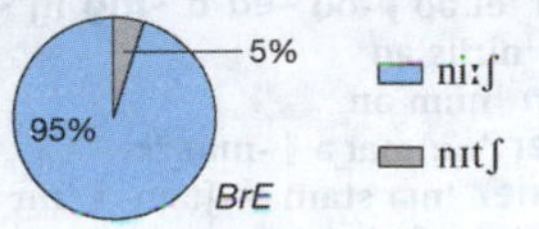

niche ni:ʃ nɪtʃ ‖ nɪtʃ — *Preference poll, BrE:* ni:ʃ *95%,* nɪtʃ *5%. In AmE only* nɪtʃ. **niches** 'ni:ʃ ɪz 'nɪtʃ-, 'nɪʃ-, -əz ‖ 'nɪtʃ əz

Nichiren ˌnɪtʃ ɪ 'ren ˌ• •'•; 'nɪʃ ər ən —*Jp* ['ɲi tɕi ɾeɴ]

Nichol 'nɪk ᵊl

Nichola 'nɪk əl ə

Nicholas 'nɪk əl‿əs

Nicholls, Nichols 'nɪk ᵊlz

Nicholson 'nɪk ᵊl sən

Nicias 'nɪs i‿əs

nick, Nick nɪk **nicked** nɪkt **nicking** 'nɪk ɪŋ **nicks, Nick's** nɪks

nickel 'nɪk ᵊl **~s** z

ˌnickel 'silver

nickel-and-dime ˌnɪk ᵊl ən 'daɪm

nickelodeon ˌnɪk ə 'ləʊd i‿ən ‖ -'loʊd- **~s** z

nickel-|plate ˌnɪk ᵊl |'pleɪt ◂ **~plated** 'pleɪt ɪd -əd ‖ 'pleɪţ əd **~plates** 'pleɪts **~plating** 'pleɪt ɪŋ ‖ 'pleɪţ ɪŋ

nicker 'nɪk ə ‖ -ᵊr **~ed** d **nickering** 'nɪk ər ɪŋ **~s** z

Nicki 'nɪk i

Nickleby 'nɪk ᵊl bi

nicknack 'nɪk næk **~s** s

nicknam|e 'nɪk neɪm **~ed** d **~es** z **~ing** ɪŋ

Nicky 'nɪk i

Nicobar 'nɪk əʊ bɑ: ‖ -ə bɑ:r

Nicodemus ˌnɪk ə 'di:m əs

nicoise, niçoise ₍ˌ₎ni: 'swɑ:z nɪ- —*Fr* [ni swa:z]

Nicol 'nɪk ᵊl

Nicola 'nɪk əl ə

Nicole nɪ 'kəʊl →'kɒʊl ‖ -'koʊl

Nicolette ˌnɪk ə 'let

N

Nicoll ˈnɪk ᵊl
Nicolson ˈnɪk ᵊl sən
Nicomachean naɪ ˌkɒm ə ˈkiː‿ən ◂ ˌ·ˌ··ˈ· · ‖ -ˌkɑːm-
Nicomachus ₍ˌ₎naɪ ˈkɒm ək əs ‖ -ˈkɑːm-
Nicosia ˌnɪk ə ˈsiː‿ə
nicotinamide ˌnɪk ə ˈtɪn ə maɪd -ˈtiːn- ‖ -mɪd
nicotine ˈnɪk ə tiːn ˌ·ˈ·
nic|tate nɪk ˈ|teɪt ‖ ˈnɪk|t eɪt **~tated** teɪt ɪd -əd ‖ teɪţ əd **~tates** teɪts **~tating** teɪt ɪŋ ‖ teɪţ ɪŋ
nicti|tate ˈnɪkt ɪ |teɪt -ə- **~tated** teɪt ɪd -əd ‖ teɪţ əd **~tates** teɪts **~tating** teɪt ɪŋ ‖ teɪţ ɪŋ
Niddrie, Niddry ˈnɪdr i
nidicolous nɪ ˈdɪk əl əs
nidifugous nɪ ˈdɪf jʊg əs -jəg-
nid|us ˈnaɪd |əs **~i** aɪ **~uses** əs ɪz -əz
Niebuhr ˈniː bʊə ‖-bʊr —*Ger* [ˈniː buːɐ]
niece niːs **nieces** ˈniːs ɪz -əz
Niedersachsen ˈniːd ə ˌsæks ᵊn ‖ -ᵊr ˌsɑːks- —*Ger* [ˈniː dɐ ˌzak sᵊn]
niello ni ˈel əʊ ‖ -oʊ **~ed** d **~ing** ɪŋ **~s** z
Nielsen ˈniːᵊls ən
Niemann ˈniːm ən
Niemeyer ˈniː maɪ‿ə ‖ -maɪ‿ᵊr
Niersteiner ˈnɪə staɪn ə -ʃtaɪn- ‖ ˈnɪr staɪn ᵊr —*Ger* [ˈniːɐ ʃtain ɐ]
Nietzsche ˈniːtʃ ə ‖ -i —*Ger* [ˈniː tʃə, ˈniːts ʃə]
niff nɪf **niffed** nɪft **niffing** ˈnɪf ɪŋ **niffs** nɪfs
niffy ˈnɪf i
nift|y ˈnɪft |i **~ier** i‿ə ‖ i‿ᵊr **~ies** iz **~iest** i‿ɪst i‿əst **~ily** ɪ li əl i
Nige naɪdʒ
Nigel ˈnaɪdʒ əl
nigella, N~ naɪ ˈdʒel ə
Niger *country* niː ˈʒeə ˈnaɪdʒ ə ‖ ˈnaɪdʒ ᵊr —*Fr* [ni ʒɛːʁ]
Niger *river* ˈnaɪdʒ ə ‖ -ᵊr
Niger-Congo ˌnaɪdʒ ə ˈkɒŋ gəʊ ◂ ‖ -ᵊr ˈkɑːŋ goʊ
Nigeria naɪ ˈdʒɪər i‿ə ‖ -ˈdʒɪr-
Nigerian naɪ ˈdʒɪər i‿ən ‖ -ˈdʒɪr- **~s** z
Nigerien, Nigérien niː ˈʒeər i‿ən ‖ -ˈʒer- —*Fr* [ni ʒe ʁjɛ̃] **~s** z —*or as singular*
Nigerois ˌniːʒ eə ˈwɑː ◂ ˌnɪʒ- ‖ -er- —*not a French word*
niggard ˈnɪg əd ‖ -ᵊrd **~s** z
niggard|ly ˈnɪg əd |li ‖ -ᵊrd- **~liness** li nəs -nɪs
nigger ˈnɪg ə ‖ -ᵊr **~s** z
niggl|e ˈnɪg ᵊl **~ed** d **~es** z **~ing** ‿ɪŋ
niggler ˈnɪg lə ‖ -lᵊr **~s** z
nigg|ly ˈnɪg |li **~liness** li nəs -nɪs
nigh naɪ
night naɪt **nights** naɪts
 ˈnight ˌblindness, ˌ·ˈ··; **ˈnight owl**; **ˈnight school**; **ˈnight shift**; **ˈnight soil**; **ˈnight watch**, ˌ·ˈ·; **ˌnight ˈwatchman**
nightcap ˈnaɪt kæp **~s** s
nightclothes ˈnaɪt kləʊðz -kləʊz ‖ -kloʊz -kloʊðz
nightclub ˈnaɪt klʌb **~bed** d **~ber/s** ə/z ‖ ᵊr/z **~bing** ɪŋ **~s** z
nightcrawler ˈnaɪt ˌkrɔːl ə ‖ -ᵊr -ˌkrɑːl- **~s** z
nightdress ˈnaɪt dres **~es** ɪz əz
nightfall ˈnaɪt fɔːl ‖ -fɑːl
nightgown ˈnaɪt gaʊn **~s** z
nighthawk ˈnaɪt hɔːk ‖ -hɑːk **~s** s
nightie ˈnaɪt i ‖ ˈnaɪţ i **~s** z
nightingale, N~ ˈnaɪt ɪŋ geɪᵊl ‖ ˈnaɪt ᵊn- ˈnaɪţ ɪŋ- **~s** z
nightjar ˈnaɪt dʒɑː ‖ -dʒɑːr **~s** z
nightlife ˈnaɪt laɪf
nightlight ˈnaɪt laɪt **~s** s
nightline ˈnaɪt laɪn **~s** z
nightlong ˌnaɪt ˈlɒŋ ◂ ˈ· · ‖ -ˈlɔːŋ -ˈlɑːŋ
nightly ˈnaɪt li
nightmare ˈnaɪt meə ‖ -mer -mær **~s** z
nightmarish ˈnaɪt meər ɪʃ ‖ -mer- -mær- **~ly** li **~ness** nəs nɪs
night-night ˌnaɪt ˈnaɪt
nightrider ˈnaɪt raɪd ə ‖ -ᵊr **~s** z
nightshade ˈnaɪt ʃeɪd **~s** z
nightshirt ˈnaɪt ʃɜːt ‖ -ʃɜːt **~s** s
nightsoil ˈnaɪt sɔɪl
nightspot ˈnaɪt spɒt ‖ -spɑːt **~s** s
nightstand ˈnaɪt stænd **~s** z
nightstick ˈnaɪt stɪk **~s** s
nighttime ˈnaɪt taɪm
nightwear ˈnaɪt weə ‖-wer
nig-nog ˈnɪg nɒg ‖ -nɑːg **~s** z
nihil ˈnaɪ hɪl ˈniː-, ˈnɪ-, -həl
nihilism ˈnaɪ ɪ ˌlɪz əm ˈniː-, -hɪ-, -ə-, -hə-; ˈnɪ hɪ-, -hə-
nihilist ˈnaɪ ɪl ɪst ˈniː-, -hɪl-, -əl-, -həl-, §-əst; ˈnɪ hɪl-, -həl- **~s** s
nihilistic ˌnaɪ ɪ ˈlɪst ɪk ◂ ˌniː-, -hɪ-, -ə-, -hə-; ˌnɪ hɪ-, -hə-
nihil obstat ˌnaɪ hɪl ˈɒb stæt ˌniː-, ˌnɪ-, -həl- ‖ -ˈɑːb-
Nijinsky nɪ ˈdʒɪnʲsk i nə-, -ˈʒɪnʲsk- —*Russ* [nʲɪ ˈʒɨn skʲɪj]
Nijmegen ˈnaɪ meɪg ən ˈ·· · —*Dutch* [ˈnɛi meː xən]
-nik nɪk — **refusenik** rɪ ˈfjuːz nɪk rə-, §riː-
Nike ˈnaɪk i naɪk
Nikita nɪ ˈkiːt ə nə- ‖ -ˈkiːţ ə —*Russ* [nʲɪˈkʲi tə]
Nikkei nɪ ˈkeɪ ˈniːk eɪ ‖ ˈniːk eɪ —*Jp* [ɲik ˌkei, -ˌkee]
Nikki ˈnɪk i
Nikon *tdmk* ˈnɪk ɒn ‖ ˈnaɪk ɑːn ˈniːk- —*Jp* [ˈɲi koɴ]
nil nɪl
 ˌnil ˌdespeˈrandum ˌdesp ə ˈrænd əm
Nile naɪᵊl
nilgai ˈnɪlg aɪ **~s** z
Nilo-Saharan ˌnaɪl əʊ sə ˈhɑːr ən ◂ ‖ ˌnaɪl oʊ sə ˈhær ən ◂ -ˈher-, -ˈhɑːr-
Nilotic naɪ ˈlɒt ɪk ‖ -ˈlɑːţ ɪk
Nilsen, Nilsson ˈniːᵊls ᵊn ˈnɪls-
nim nɪm
nimbi ˈnɪm baɪ
nim|ble ˈnɪm |bᵊl **~bler** blə ‖ blᵊr **~blest** blɪst bləst **~bleness** bᵊl nəs -nɪs **~bly** bli

nimbostratus ˌnɪm bəʊ ˈstreɪt əs ‖ -boʊ ˈstreɪţ- -ˈstræţ-
nim|bus ˈnɪm |bəs **~bi** baɪ **~buses** bəs ɪz -əz
nim|by, NIM|BY ˈnɪm| bi **~bies** biz **~byism** bi ˌɪz əm
Nîmes niːm —*Fr* [nim]
nimini-piminy, niminy-piminy ˌnɪm ən i ˈpɪm ən i ◂ -ɪn i ˈpɪm ɪn-
Nimitz ˈnɪm ɪts §-əts
Nimmo ˈnɪm əʊ ‖ -oʊ
Nimrod, n~ ˈnɪm rɒd ‖ -rɑːd **~s, ~'s** z
Nin nɪn niːn
Nina ˈniːn ə
nincompoop ˈnɪŋk əm puːp ˈnɪn kəm- **~s** s
nine naɪn —*but for clarity in communication code,* niner ˈnaɪn ə ‖ -ᵊr **nines** naɪnz
ˌnine days' ˈwonder
ninefold ˈnaɪn fəʊld →-fɒʊld ‖ -foʊld
ninepin ˈnaɪn pɪn →ˈnaɪm- **~s** z
nineteen ˌnaɪn ˈtiːn ◂ —*occasionally, when stress-shifted, also* ˈnaɪn tən **~s** z
ˌnineteen ˈpeople; ˌnineteen ˌninety-ˈnine
nineteenth ˌnaɪn ˈtiːnᵗθ ◂ **~s** s
ˌnineteenth ˈhole
ninetieth ˈnaɪnt i əθ -ɪθ ‖ ˈnaɪnţ i əθ **~s** s
nine-to-five ˌnaɪn tə ˈfaɪv
Ninette nɪ ˈnet niː-
ninet|y ˈnaɪnt |i ‖ ˈnaɪnţ |i **~ies** iz
ninety-nine ˌnaɪnt i ˈnaɪn ◂ ‖ ˌnaɪnţ-
ninety-ninth ˌnaɪnt i ˈnaɪnᵗθ ◂ ‖ ˌnaɪnţ-
Nineveh ˈnɪn ɪv ə -əv-
Ningbo ˌnɪŋ ˈbəʊ ‖ -ˈboʊ —*Chi* Níngbō [²niŋ ¹po]
Ningxia ˌnɪŋ ʃi ˈɑː —*Chi* Níngxià [²niŋ ⁴ɕja]
Ninian ˈnɪn i ə̯n
ninish ˈnaɪn ɪʃ
ninja ˈnɪndʒ ə **~s** z
ninn|y ˈnɪn |i **~ies** iz
Nintendo *tdmk* nɪn ˈtend əʊ ‖ -oʊ
ninth naɪnᵗθ **ninthly** ˈnaɪnᵗθ li **ninths** naɪnᵗθs
niobate ˈnaɪ əʊ beɪt ‖ -ə-
Niobe ˈnaɪ̯əb i -əʊb i ‖ -ə biː
niobic naɪ ˈəʊb ɪk ‖ -ˈoʊb-
niobium naɪ ˈəʊb i̯əm ‖ -ˈoʊb-
nip, Nip nɪp **nipped** nɪpt **nipping/ly** ˈnɪp ɪŋ /li **nips** nɪps
nipper ˈnɪp ə ‖ -ᵊr **~s** z
nippi... —*see* **nippy**
nipple ˈnɪp ᵊl **~s** z
nipplewort ˈnɪp ᵊl wɜːt §-wɔːt ‖ -wɝːt -wɔːrt **~s** s
Nippon ˈnɪp ɒn ‖ -ɑːn nɪ ˈpɑːn —*Jp* [ɲip ˈpoɴ]
Nipponese ˌnɪp ə ˈniːz ◂ ‖ -ˈniːs ◂
nipp|y ˈnɪp |i **~ier** i̯ə ‖ i̯ᵊr **~iest** i̯ɪst i̯əst **~ily** ɪ li əl i **~iness** i nəs i nɪs
niqab nɪ ˈkɑːb —*Arabic* [nɪ ˈqaːb]
NIREX, Nirex *tdmk* ˈnaɪᵊr eks
nirvana, N~ nɪə ˈvɑːn ə nɜː- ‖ nɪr- -ˈvæn- —*Hindi* [ɲɪr ʋaːɳ]
Nis, Niš nɪʃ niːʃ
Nisan ˈnaɪs æn ˈnɪs-, -ɑːn ‖ ˈniːs ɑːn ˈnɪs ᵊn
Nisbet, Nisbett ˈnɪz bət -bɪt
Nisei, nisei ˈniː seɪ —*Jp* [ˈɲi seː]
nisi ˈnaɪs aɪ ˈniːs i
ˌnisi ˈprius ˈpraɪ̯əs ˈpriː̯əs
Nissan *tdmk* ˈnɪs æn ‖ -ɑːn ˈniːs- —*Jp* [ɲis ˌsaɴ]
Nissen ˈnɪs ᵊn
ˈNissen hut
Nistelrooy ˈnɪst ᵊl rɔɪ
nit nɪt **nits** nɪts
Nita ˈniːt ə ‖ ˈniːţ ə
nite naɪt
niter ˈnaɪt ə ‖ ˈnaɪţ ᵊr
niterie ˈnaɪt ər i ‖ ˈnaɪţ- **~s** z
nitpick ˈnɪt pɪk **~ed** t **~er/s** ə/z ‖ ᵊr/z **~ing** ɪŋ **~s** s
nitrate ˈnaɪtr eɪt -ət, -ɪt **~s** s
nitrazepam naɪ ˈtræz ɪ pæm -ˈtreɪz-, -ə-
nitre ˈnaɪt ə ‖ ˈnaɪţ ᵊr
nitric ˈnaɪtr ɪk
ˌnitric ˈacid
nitride ˈnaɪtr aɪd **~s** z
nitrification ˌnaɪtr ɪf ɪ ˈkeɪʃ ᵊn ˌ-əf-, ˌ-əˈ- ·
nitrif|y ˈnaɪtr ɪ faɪ -ə- **~ied** aɪd **~ies** aɪz **~ying** aɪ ɪŋ
nitrile ˈnaɪtr aɪᵊl -ɪl, §-əl **~s** z
nitrite ˈnaɪtr aɪt **~s** s
nitro ˈnaɪtr əʊ ‖ -oʊ
nitro- *comb. form*
with stress-neutral suffix ¦naɪtr əʊ ‖ -oʊ — **nitrobenzene** ˌnaɪtr əʊ ˈbenz iːn ‖ -oʊ-ben ˈziːn
with stress-imposing suffix naɪ ˈtrɒ+ ‖ -ˈtrɑː+ — **nitrometer** naɪ ˈtrɒm ɪt ə -ət- ‖ -ˈtrɑːm əţ ᵊr
nitrocellulose ˌnaɪtr əʊ ˈsel ju ləʊs -ˈ-jə-, -ləʊz ‖ -oʊ ˈsel jə loʊs -loʊz
nitrochalk, Nitro-chalk *tdmk* ˈnaɪtr əʊ tʃɔːk ‖ -oʊ- -tʃɑːk
nitrogen ˈnaɪtr ədʒ ən
nitrogenous naɪ ˈtrɒdʒ ən əs -ɪn- ‖ -ˈtrɑːdʒ-
nitroglycerin, nitroglycerine ˌnaɪtr əʊ ˈglɪs ər ɪn ˌ-ə-, -iːn, §-ən ‖ ˌ-ə-
nitrosamine naɪ ˈtrəʊz ə miːn -ˈtrəʊs-; ˌnaɪtr əʊs ə ˈmiːn, -ˈæm iːn, ˈ· · · · ‖ -ˈtroʊs-
nitrous ˈnaɪtr əs
nitty ˈnɪt i ‖ ˈnɪţ i
nitty-gritty ˌnɪt i ˈgrɪt i ‖ ˌnɪţ i ˈgrɪţ i
nitwit ˈnɪt wɪt **~s** s
Niue ˈnjuː eɪ ni ˈuː eɪ ‖ ni ˈuː eɪ
Niu Gini ₍ˌ₎njuː ˈgɪn i
Nivea *tdmk* ˈnɪv i̯ə -eɪ
Niven ˈnɪv ᵊn
nix nɪks **nixed** nɪkst **nixes** ˈnɪks ɪz -əz **nixing** ˈnɪks ɪŋ
Nixdorf *tdmk* ˈnɪks dɔːf ‖ -dɔːrf
nixie ˈnɪks i **~s** z
Nixon ˈnɪks ən
Nixonian nɪk ˈsəʊn i̯ən ‖ -ˈsoʊn-
Nizam, nizam nɪ ˈzɑːm naɪ-, -ˈzæm **~s** z
Nizhni Novgorod ˌnɪʒ ni ˈnɒv gə rɒd ‖ -ˈnɑːv gə rɑːd —*Russ* [ˌnʲiʒ nʲi ˈnɔv gə rət]
Nkomo ᵊn ˈkəʊm əʊ →ᵊŋ- ‖ -ˈkoʊm oʊ —*Ndebele* [ŋkʼɔː mɔ]
Nkrumah ᵊn ˈkruːm ə →ᵊŋ-

N

no nəʊ ‖ noʊ —*There is also an occasional weak form* nə **noes** nəʊz ‖ noʊz
ˈno ball; **ˌno ˈway**
no., No. —*see* **number; North nos.** —*see* **numbers**
no-account ˌnəʊ ə ˈkaʊnt ◂ ‖ ˌnoʊ-
Noachian nəʊ ˈeɪk i‿ən ‖ noʊ-
Noah ˈnəʊ ə ‖ ˈnoʊ ə
ˌNoah's ˈark
Noakes nəʊks ‖ noʊks
Noam ˈnəʊ əm nəʊm ‖ ˈnoʊ əm noʊm
nob nɒb ‖ nɑːb **nobs** nɒbz ‖ nɑːbz
no-ball ˌnəʊ ˈbɔːl ‖ ˌnoʊ- **~ed** d **~ing** ɪŋ **~s** z
nobbl|e ˈnɒb ᵊl ‖ ˈnɑːb ᵊl **~ed** d **~es** z **~ing** ˌɪŋ
nobbut ˈnɒb ət ‖ ˈnɑːb-
nobby, Nobby ˈnɒb i ‖ ˈnɑːb i
Nobel ₍ˌ₎nəʊ ˈbel ‖ ₍ˌ₎noʊ- —*Swedish* [nɔ ˈbɛl]
NoˌbeI ˈprize, ˌNobel ˈprize
nobelium nəʊ ˈbiːl i‿əm ‖ noʊ- -ˈbel-
nobiliary nəʊ ˈbɪl i‿ər i ‖ noʊ ˈbɪl i er i -ˈbɪl jər i
nobilit|y nəʊ ˈbɪl ət |i -ɪt- ‖ noʊ ˈbɪl əṭ |i **~ies** iz
noble, Noble ˈnəʊb ᵊl ‖ ˈnoʊb ᵊl **nobler** ˈnəʊb lə ‖ ˈnoʊb lᵊr **nobles** ˈnəʊb ᵊlz ‖ ˈnoʊb ᵊlz **noblest** ˈnəʊb lɪst -ləst ‖ ˈnoʊb ləst
noble|man ˈnəʊb ᵊl |mən ‖ ˈnoʊb- **~men** mən
noble-minded ˌnəʊb ᵊl ˈmaɪnd ɪd ◂ -əd ‖ ˌnoʊb-
nobleness ˈnəʊb ᵊl nəs -nɪs ‖ ˈnoʊb-
noblesse oblige nəʊ ˌbles əʊ ˈbliːʒ ˌ·ˈ·ˈ· ‖ noʊ ˌbles oʊ- —*Fr* [nɔb lɛ sɔ bliːʒ]
noble|woman ˈnəʊb ᵊl |ˌwʊm ən ‖ ˈnoʊb- **~women** ˌwɪm ɪn §-ən
nobly ˈnəʊb li ‖ ˈnoʊb li
nobod|y ˈnəʊb əd |i ˈnəʊ ˌbɒd |i ‖ ˈnoʊb əd |i ˈnoʊ ˌbɑːd |i, -bʌd i **~ies, ~y's** iz
no-brainer ˌnəʊ ˈbreɪn ə ‖ ˌnoʊ ˈbreɪn ᵊr ˌ·ˈ·· **~s** z
nock nɒk ‖ nɑːk *(= knock)* **nocked** nɒkt ‖ nɑːkt **nocking** ˈnɒk ɪŋ ‖ ˈnɑːk ɪŋ **nocks** nɒks ‖ nɑːks
no-claim ˌnəʊ ˈkleɪm ‖ ˌnoʊ- **~s** z
ˌno-claim(s) ˈbonus, ˌ·ˈ·ˌ··
no-confidence ˌnəʊ ˈkɒn fɪd ᵊnᵗs -fəd- ‖ ˌnoʊ ˈkɑːn-
no-count ˈnəʊ kaʊnt ‖ ˈnoʊ-
noctilucent ˌnɒkt ɪ ˈluːs ᵊnt §-ə-, -ˈljuːs- ‖ ˌnɑːkt ə-
noctuid ˈnɒkt ju‿ɪd ˈnɒk tʃu‿, §‿əd ‖ˈnɑːk tʃu əd -tu- **~s** z
nocturn ˈnɒkt ɜːn ˌnɒk ˈtɜːn ‖ ˈnɑːkt ɜːn **~s** z
nocturnal nɒk ˈtɜːn ᵊl ‖ nɑːk ˈtɜːn ᵊl **~ly** i
nocturne ˈnɒkt ɜːn ˌnɒk ˈtɜːn ‖ ˈnɑːkt ɜːn **~s** z
nod nɒd ‖ nɑːd **nodded** ˈnɒd ɪd -əd ‖ ˈnɑːd əd **nodding** ˈnɒd ɪŋ ‖ ˈnɑːd ɪŋ **nods** nɒds ‖ nɑːdz
ˌnodding acˈquaintance
nodal ˈnəʊd ᵊl ‖ ˈnoʊd ᵊl
nodality nəʊ ˈdæl ət i -ɪt- ‖ noʊ ˈdæl əṭ i
nodd... —*see* **nod**
noddle ˈnɒd ᵊl ‖ ˈnɑːd ᵊl **~s** z
Nodd|y, nodd|y ˈnɒd |i ‖ ˈnɑːd |i **~ies, ~y's** iz
node nəʊd ‖ noʊd **nodes** nəʊdz ‖ noʊdz
nodular ˈnɒd jʊl ə -jəl- ‖ ˈnɑːdʒ əl ᵊr
nodule ˈnɒd juːl ‖ ˈnɑːdʒ uːl **~s** z
Noel, Noël *personal name* ˈnəʊ‿əl -el ‖ ˈnoʊ-
Noel, Noël *'Christmas'* nəʊ ˈel ‖ noʊ-
Noele ˌnəʊ ˈel◂ ‖ ˌnoʊ-
noes *pl of* **no** nəʊz ‖ noʊz *(= nose)*
noesis nəʊ ˈiːs ɪs §-əs ‖ noʊ-
noetic nəʊ ˈet ɪk ‖ noʊ ˈeṭ ɪk
no-fault ˌnəʊ ˈfɔːlt ◂ -ˈfɒlt ◂ ‖ ˌnoʊ ˈfɔːlt ◂ -ˈfɑːlt ◂
no-fly ˌnəʊ ˈflaɪ ◂ ‖ ˌnoʊ-
ˌno-ˈfly zone, ˌ··ˈ·
no-frills ˌnəʊ ˈfrɪlz ◂ ‖ ˌnoʊ-
nog nɒg ‖ nɑːg **nogs** nɒgz ‖ nɑːgz
noggin ˈnɒg ɪn §-ən ‖ ˈnɑːg- **~s** z
no-go ˌnəʊ ˈgəʊ ◂ ‖ ˌnoʊ ˈgoʊ
ˌno-ˈgo ˌarea, ˌ·ˈ·ˌ···
no-good ˌnəʊ ˈgʊd ◂ ‖ ˌnoʊ-
Noh nəʊ ‖ noʊ —*Jp* [no‿o]
no-hitter ˌnəʊ ˈhɪt ə ‖ ˌnoʊ ˈhɪṭ ᵊr **~s** z
no-holds-barred ˌnəʊ həʊldz ˈbɑːd◂ →-hɒʊldz- ‖ ˌnoʊ hoʊldz ˈbɑːrd ◂
no-hope ˌnəʊ ˈhəʊp ◂ ‖ ˌnoʊ ˈhoʊp ◂
no-hoper ˌnəʊ ˈhəʊp ə ‖ ˌnoʊ ˈhoʊp ᵊr **~s** z
nohow ˈnəʊ haʊ ‖ ˈnoʊ-
noir nwɑː ‖ nwɑːr —*Fr* [nwaːʁ]
noise nɔɪz **noised** nɔɪzd **noises** ˈnɔɪz ɪz -əz **noising** ˈnɔɪz ɪŋ
noiseless ˈnɔɪz ləs -lɪs **~ly** li **~ness** nəs nɪs
noise-maker ˈnɔɪz ˌmeɪk ə ‖ -ᵊr **~s** z
noisette nwɑː ˈzet nwæ- —*Fr* [nwa zɛt] **~s** s —*or as singular*
noisi... —*see* **noisy**
noisome ˈnɔɪs əm **~ly** li **~ness** nəs nɪs
nois|y ˈnɔɪz |i **~ier** i‿ə ‖ i‿ᵊr **~iest** i‿ɪst i‿əst **~ily** ɪ li əl i **~iness** i nəs i nɪs
Nokia *tdmk* ˈnɒk i‿ə ‖ ˈnoʊk i‿ə
Nola ˈnəʊl ə ‖ ˈnoʊl ə
Nolan ˈnəʊl ən ‖ ˈnoʊl ən
nolens volens ˌnəʊl enz ˈvəʊl enz ‖ ˌnoʊl enz ˈvoʊl-
noli-me-tangere, noli me tangere ˌnəʊl i ˌmeɪ ˈtæŋ gər i -ˌmiː-, -ˈtændʒ ər-, -gə reɪ ‖ ˌnoʊl-
nolle prosequi ˌnɒl i ˈprɒs ɪ kwaɪ -ˈ·ə-, -kwiː ‖ ˌnɑːl i ˈprɑːs-
no-load ˌnəʊ ˈləʊd◂ ‖ ˌnoʊ ˈloʊd ◂
nolo contendere ˌnəʊl əʊ kən ˈtend ər i -kɒn'·-, -ə reɪ ‖ ˌnoʊl oʊ-
nomad ˈnəʊm æd ‖ ˈnoʊm- **~s** z
nomadic nəʊ ˈmæd ɪk ‖ noʊ- **~ally** ᵊl‿i
nomadism ˈnəʊm æd ˌɪz əm ‖ ˈnoʊm-
no-man's-land ˈnəʊ mænz lænd ‖ ˈnoʊ-
nom de guerre ˌnɒm də ˈgeə ˌnõ- ‖ ˌnɑːm də ˈgeᵊr -dɪ- —*Fr* [nõd gɛːʁ] **noms de guerre** *same pronunciation*
nom de plume ˌnɒm də ˈpluːm ˌnõ-; ˈ··· ‖ ˌnɑːm- —*Fr* [nõd plym] **noms de plume** *same pronunciation*
Nome nəʊm ‖ noʊm

omenclature nəʊ ˈmeŋk lətʃ ə; ˈnəʊm ən kleɪtʃ ə, ˈnɒm-, →-əŋ, ˈ·cn-, →-eŋ- ‖ ˈnoʊm ən kleɪtʃ ər noʊ ˈmen klə tʃʊr, →-ˈmeŋ-, -klətʃ ər **~s** z

ominal ˈnɒm ɪn əl -ən-, -ən‿əl ‖ ˈnɑːm ən əl -ən‿əl **~s** z

ominally ˈnɒm ɪn əl i -ən‿əl i ‖ ˈnɑːm ən əl i -ən‿əl-

omi|nate ˈnɒm ɪ |neɪt -ə- ‖ ˈnɑːm- **~nated** neɪt ɪd -əd ‖ neɪţ əd **~nates** neɪts **~nating** neɪt ɪŋ ‖ neɪţ ɪŋ

omination ˌnɒm ɪ ˈneɪʃ ən -ə- ‖ ˌnɑːm- **~s** z

ominative ˈnɒm ən‿ət ɪv ˈ·ɪn- ‖ ˈnɑːm ən‿əţ ɪv **~s** z

ominator ˈnɒm ɪ neɪt ə -ə- ‖ -neɪţ ər **~s** z

ominee ˌnɒm ɪ ˈniː ◂ -ə- ‖ˌnɑːm- **~s** z

omo- *comb. form*
with stress-neutral suffix ¦nɒm ə¦nəʊm- ‖¦nɑːm ə ¦noʊm- — **nomogram** ˈnɒm ə græm ˈnəʊm- ‖ ˈnɑːm- ˈnoʊm-
with stress-imposing suffix nɒ ˈmɒ+ nəʊ- ‖ noʊ ˈmɑː+ — **nomology** nɒ ˈmɒl ədʒ i nəʊ- ‖ noʊ ˈmɑːl-

Nomura nəʊ ˈmjʊər ə -ˈmʊər- ‖ noʊ ˈmjʊr ə —*Jp* [no ˌmɯ ɾa]

nomy *stress-imposing* nəm i — **taxonomy** tæk ˈsɒn əm i ‖ -ˈsɑːn-

non nɒn nəʊn ‖ nɑːn noʊn —*See also phrases with this word*

non- ¦nɒn ‖¦nɑːn —*Also occasionally* ¦nʌn — **nonacademic** ˌnɒn ˌæk ə ˈdem ɪk ˌnʌn- ‖ˌnɑːn-

nonage ˈnəʊn ɪdʒ ˈnɒn- ‖ ˈnoʊn- ˈnɑːn-

nonagenarian ˌnəʊn ə dʒə ˈneər i‿ən ◂ˌnɒn-, -dʒɪˈ·- ‖ ˌnoʊn ə dʒə ˈner- ˌnɑːn- **~s** z

nonaggression ˌnɒn ə ˈgreʃ ən ‖ ˌnɑːn-

nonagon ˈnɒn əg ən ˈnəʊn-, -ə gɒn ‖ ˈnɑːn ə gɑːn ˈnoʊn- **~s** z

nonalcoholic ˌnɒn ˌælk ə ˈhɒl ɪk ◂ ‖ ˌnɑːn ˌælk ə ˈhɔːl ɪk ◂ -ˈhɑːl-
ˌnonalcoˌholic ˈbeverage

nonaligned ˌnɒn ə ˈlaɪnd ◂ -əl ˈaɪnd ◂ ‖ ˌnɑːn-

nonalignment ˌnɒn ə ˈlaɪn mənt →-laɪm-; -əl ˈaɪn- ‖ ˌnɑːn-

no-name ˌnəʊ ˈneɪm ◂ ‖ ˌnoʊ-

nonappearanc|e ˌnɒn ə ˈpɪər ənts ‖ ˌnɑːn ə ˈpɪr- **~es** ɪz əz

nonary ˈnəʊn ər i ˈnɒn- ‖ ˈnoʊn- ˈnɑːn-

nonassertive ˌnɒn ə ˈsɜːt ɪv ◂ ‖ ˌnɑːn ə ˈsɜːţ ɪv ◂

non-attendance ˌnɒn ə ˈtend ənts ◂ ‖ ˌnɑːn-

nonbeliever ˌnɒn bi ˈliːv ə →ˌnɒm-, -bə- ‖ ˌnɑːn bi ˈliːv ər **~s** z

non-binding ˌnɒn ˈbaɪnd ɪŋ ◂→ˌnɒm- ‖ ˌnɑːn-

non-biological ˌnɒn ˌbaɪ‿ə ˈlɒdʒ ɪk əl ◂ →ˌnɒm- ‖ ˌnɑːn-

nonce nɒnts ‖ nɑːnts **nonces** ˈnɒnts ɪz -əz ‖ ˈnɑːnts əz
ˈnonce word

nonchalance ˈnɒntʃ əl ənts ‖ ˌnɑːn ʃə ˈlɑːnts ˈ· · · (*)

nonchalant ˈnɒntʃ əl ənt ‖ ˌnɑːn ʃə ˈlɑːnt ◂ ˈ· · · **~ly** li

non-com ˈnɒn kɒm →ˈnɒŋ- ‖ ˈnɑːn kɑːm **~s** z

non-combat ˌnɒn ˈkɒm bæt ◂ →ˌnɒŋ- ‖ ˌnɑːn ˈkɑːm-

noncombatant ˌnɒn ˈkɒm bət ənt →ˌnɒŋ-, -ˈkʌm-; ˌ·kəm ˈbæt ənt, §-kɒm- ‖ ˌnɑːn kəm ˈbæt ənt ˌ·ˈkɑːm bət ənt **~s** s

noncommissioned ˌnɒn kə ˈmɪʃ ənd ◂ →ˌnɒŋ- ‖ ˌnɑːn-
ˌnoncomˌmissioned ˈofficer

noncommittal ˌnɒn kə ˈmɪt əl ◂ →ˌnɒŋ- ‖ ˌnɑːn kə ˈmɪţ əl ◂ **~ly** i

noncompetitive ˌnɒn kəm ˈpet ət ɪv ◂ →ˌnɒŋ-, §-kɒmˈ·, -ɪt · ‖ ˌnɑːn kəm ˈpeţ-

noncompli|ance ˌnɒn kəm ˈplaɪ‿|ənts →ˌnɒŋ-, §-kɒm- ‖ ˌnɑːn- **~ant** ənt

non compos mentis ˌnɒn ˌkɒmp əs ˈment ɪs →ˌnɒŋ-, ˌnəʊn-, -ˌ·ɒs- ‖ nɑːn ˌkɑːmp əs ˈmenţ əs noʊn-, ˌ·ˌ· ˈ· ·

nonconductor ˌnɒn kən ˈdʌkt ə →ˌnɒŋ-, §-kɒn- ‖ ˌnɑːn kən ˈdʌkt ər **~s** z

nonconformism ˌnɒn kən ˈfɔːm ˌɪz əm →ˌnɒŋ-, §ˌ·kɒn- ‖ ˌnɑːn kən ˈfɔːrm-

nonconformist, N~ ˌnɒn kən ˈfɔːm ɪst ◂ →ˌnɒŋ-, §-kɒn-, §-əst ‖ ˌnɑːn kən ˈfɔːrm əst ◂ **~s** s

nonconformity, N~ ˌnɒn kən ˈfɔːm ət i →ˌnɒŋ-, §ˌ·kɒn-, -ɪt i ‖ ˌnɑːn kən ˈfɔːrm əţ i

noncontributory ˌnɒn kən ˈtrɪb jʊt‿ər i◂ →ˌnɒŋ-, §ˌ·kɒn-; ˌ·ˌkɒn trɪ ˈbjuːt ər i, -trəˈ·- ‖ ˌnɑːn kən ˈtrɪb jə tɔːr i ◂ -toʊr i

non-controversial ˌnɒn ˌkɒntr ə ˈvɜːʃ əl◂ ‖ ˌnɑːn ˌkɑːntr ə ˈvɜːʃ əl ◂

noncooperation, non-co-operation ˌnɒn kəʊ ˌɒp ə ˈreɪʃ ən ˌnɒŋ- ‖ˌnɑːn koʊ ˌɑːp-

non-count ˌnɒn ˈkaʊnt ◂ →ˌnɒŋ- ‖ ˌnɑːn-

noncustodial ˌnɒn kʌ ˈstəʊd i‿əl ◂→ˌnɒŋ-, -kə- ‖ ˌnɑːn-

non-dairy ˌnɒn ˈdeər i ◂‖ ˌnɑːn ˈder i ◂ -ˈdær-

non-deductible ˌnɒn di ˈdʌkt əb əl ◂ ˌ·də- ‖ ˌnɑːn-

nondenominational ˌnɒn di ˌnɒm ɪ ˈneɪʃ ən‿ə l ◂ˌ·də-, -əˈ· ‖ ˌnɑːn di ˌnɑːm-

nondescript ˈnɒn dɪ skrɪpt -də-, †-diː- ‖ ˌnɑːn dɪ ˈskrɪpt◂ **~s** s

nondisclosure ˌnɒn dɪs ˈkləʊʒ ə -dəs- ‖ˌnɑːn dɪs ˈkloʊʒ ər

nondrip ˌnɒn ˈdrɪp ◂ ‖ ˌnɑːn-

non-durable ˌnɒn ˈdjʊər əb l ◂ →-dʒʊər-, -ˈdjɔːr- ‖ ˌnɑːn ˈdʊr- -ˈdjʊr- **~s** z

none nʌn §nɒn *(= nun)*

nonentit|y nɒ ˈnent ət |i nə-, -ɪt- ‖ nɑː ˈnenţ əţ |i **~ies** iz

nones nəʊnz ‖ noʊnz

nonessential ˌnɒn ɪ ˈsentʃ əl ◂ -ə- ‖ ˌnɑːn-

nonesuch ˈnʌn sʌtʃ §ˈnɒn-

nonet ₍ˌ₎nəʊ ˈnet nɒ- ‖ noʊ- **~s** s

nonetheless ˌnʌn ðə ˈles ◂ §ˌnɒn-

non-event ˌnɒn ɪ ˈvent -ə-, §-iː-; ˈ· · · ‖ ˌnɑːn- **~s** s

non-executive ˌnɒn ɪg ˈzek jʊt ɪv ◂ ˌ·eg-, ˌ·əg-, ˌ·ɪk-, ˌ·ek-, ˌ·ək-, -jət ·, §-ət · ‖ ˌnɑːn ɪg ˈzek jəṱ ɪv ◂ §-əṱ ɪv **~s** z
nonexistent ˌnɒn ɪg ˈzɪst ənt ◂ -eg-, -əg-, -ɪk-, -ek-, -ək- ‖ ˌnɑːn-
nonfat ˌnɒn ˈfæt ◂ ‖ ˌnɑːn-
non-feasance ˌnɒn ˈfiːz ᵊnᵗs ‖ ˌnɑːn-
non-ferrous ˌnɒn ˈfer əs ◂ ‖ ˌnɑːn-
nonfiction ˌnɒn ˈfɪk ʃᵊn ‖ ˌnɑːn-
non-finite ˌnɒn ˈfaɪn aɪt ◂ ‖ ˌnɑːn-
nonflammable ˌnɒn ˈflæm əb ᵊl ◂ ‖ ˌnɑːn-
non-governmental ˌnɒn ˌgʌv ᵊn ˈment l ◂ →ˌnɒŋ-, →ᵊmˈ·-, -əˈ·- ‖ ˌnɑːn ˌgʌv ᵊrn ˈmenṱ ᵊl ◂
non-immigrant ˌnɒn ˈɪm ɪg rənt ◂ -əg- ‖ ˌnɑːn- **~s** s
noninterference ˌnɒn ˌɪnt ə ˈfɪər ənᵗs ‖ ˌnɑːn ˌɪnṱ ᵊr ˈfɪr ənᵗs
nonintervention ˌnɒn ˌɪnt ə ˈvenᵗʃ ᵊn ‖ ˌnɑːn ˌɪnṱ ᵊr- **~ist/s** ɪst/s §əst/s
noninvolvement ˌnɒn ɪn ˈvɒlv mənt -ən-, §-ˈvəʊlv- ‖ ˌnɑːn ɪn ˈvɑːlv-
non-iron ˌnɒn ˈaɪ͜ən ◂ ‖ ˌnɑːn ˈaɪ͜ᵊrn ◂
non-judgmental, non-judgemental ˌnɒn dʒʌdʒ ˈment ᵊl ◂ ‖ ˌnɑːn dʒʌdʒ ˈmenṱ ᵊl ◂
nonjuror ˌnɒn ˈdʒʊər ə ‖ ˌnɑːn ˈdʒʊr ᵊr **~s** z
nonlinear ˌnɒn ˈlɪn i͜ə ◂ ‖ ˌnɑːn ˈlɪn i͜ᵊr ◂
non-member ˌnɒn ˈmem bə →ˌnɒm- ‖ ˌnɑːn ˈmem bᵊr **~s** z
non-negotiable ˌnɒn nɪ ˈgəʊʃ i͜əb ᵊl ◂ ˌ·nə-, -ˈ·əb ᵊl ‖ ˌnɑːn nɪ ˈgoʊʃ-
no-no ˈnəʊ nəʊ ‖ ˈnoʊ noʊ **~s** z
nonobservance ˌnɒn əb ˈzɜːv ᵊnᵗs §-ɒb- ‖ ˌnɑːn əb ˈzɝːv-
no-nonsense ˌnəʊ ˈnɒnᵗs ənᵗs ◂ ‖ ˌnoʊ ˈnɑːn senᵗs ◂ -ˈnɑːnᵗs ənᵗs
nonoxynol nəʊ ˈnɒks ɪ nɒl -ə- ‖ noʊ ˈnɑːks ə nɑːl -nɔːl, -noʊl
nonpareil ˌnɒn pə ˈrerᵊl →ˌnɒm-; ˈnɒn pᵊr ˌəl, →ˈnɒm- ‖ ˌnɑːn pə ˈrel ◂
non-partisan ˌnɒn ˌpɑːt ɪ ˈzæn ◂ →ˌnɒm- ‖ ˌnɑːn ˈpɑːrṱ ə zæn ◂ -sæn ◂
nonpayment ˌnɒn ˈpeɪ mənt ◂ →ˌnɒm- ‖ ˌnɑːn-
non-playing ˌnɒn ˈpleɪ ɪŋ ◂ →ˌnɒm-‖ˌnɑːn- **ˌnon-ˌplaying ˈcaptain**
nonplus ˌnɒn ˈplʌs →ˌnɒm-, ˈ· · ‖ ˌnɑːn- **~sed** t **~ses** ɪz əz **~sing** ɪŋ
non-prescription ˌnɒn pri ˈskrɪp ʃᵊn ◂ →ˌnɒm-, -prə- ‖ ˌnɑːn-
non-profit ˌnɒn ˈprɒf ɪt →ˌnɒm-, §-ət ‖ ˌnɑːn ˈprɑːf-
non-profit-making ˌnɒn ˈprɒf ɪt ˌmeɪk ɪŋ →ˌnɒm-, §-ˈ·ət- ‖ ˌnɑːn ˈprɑːf-
nonproliferation ˌnɒn prəʊ ˌlɪf ə ˈreɪʃ ᵊn →ˌnɒm- ‖ ˌnɑːn prə-
non-refundable ˌnɒn ri ˈfʌnd əb l ◂ ˌ·rə- ‖ ˌnɑːn-
non-renewable ˌnɒn ri ˈnjuː əb ᵊl ◂ ˌ·rə-, §-ˈnuː- ‖ ˌnɑːn ri ˈnuː- ˌ·rə-, -ˈnjuː-
nonresident ˌnɒn ˈrez ɪd ənt ◂ -əd- ‖ ˌnɑːn- **~s** s
non-residential ˌnɒn rez ɪ ˈdenᵗʃᵊl◂ -rez ə- ‖ ˌnɑːn- -res ə-
nonrestrictive ˌnɒn ri ˈstrɪkt ɪv ◂ -rə- ‖ ˌnɑːn
nonreturnable ˌnɒn ri ˈtɜːn əb ᵊl ◂ ˌ·rə- ‖ ˌnɑːn ri ˈtɝːn-
nonrhotic ˌnɒn ˈrəʊt ɪk ◂ ‖ ˌnɑːn ˈroʊṱ ɪk ◂
nonrhoticity ˌnɒn rəʊ ˈtɪs ət i -ɪt i ‖ ˌnɑːn roʊ ˈtɪs əṱ i
non-scientific ˌnɒn saɪ͜ən ˈtɪf ɪk ‖ ˌnɑːn-
nonsectarian ˌnɒn sek ˈteər i͜ən ◂ ‖ ˌnɑːn sek ˈter- -ˈtær-
nonsense ˈnɒnᵗs ənᵗs ‖ ˈnɑːn senᵗs ˈnɑːnᵗs ənᵗs
nonsensical nɒn ˈsenᵗs ɪk ᵊl ‖ nɑːn- **~ly** ˌi
non sequitur ˌnɒn ˈsek wɪt ə ˌnəʊn-, -wət- ‖ ˌnɑːn ˈsek wəṱ ᵊr -wə tʊr **~s** z
non-shrink ˌnɒn ˈʃrɪŋk ◂ ‖ ˌnɑːn-
nonskid ˌnɒn ˈskɪd ◂ ‖ ˌnɑːn-
non-slip ˌnɒn ˈslɪp ◂ ‖ ˌnɑːn-
nonsmok|er ˌnɒn ˈsməʊk| ə ‖ ˌnɑːn ˈsmoʊk| ᵊr **~ers** əz ‖ ᵊrz **~ing** ɪŋ ◂
non-specific ˌnɒn spə ˈsɪf ɪk ◂ -spɪ- ‖ ˌnɑːn- **ˌnon-speˌcific ˌureˈthritis**
nonstandard ˌnɒn ˈstænd əd ◂ ‖ ˌnɑːn ˈstænd ᵊrd
nonstarter ˌnɒn ˈstɑːt ə ‖ ˌnɑːn ˈstɑːrṱ ᵊr **~s** z
nonstick ˌnɒn ˈstɪk ◂ ‖ ˌnɑːn- **ˌnon-stick ˈfrying-pan**
nonstop ˌnɒn ˈstɒp ◂ ‖ ˌnɑːn ˈstɑːp ◂
Nonsuch ˈnɒn sʌtʃ ˈnʌn- ‖ ˈnɑːn- ˈnʌn-
non-swimmer ˌnɒn ˈswɪm ə ‖ ˌnɑːn ˈswɪm ᵊr **~s** z
nonthreatening ˌnɒn ˈθret ᵊn͜ ɪŋ ◂ ‖ ˌnɑːn-
nontoxic ˌnɒn ˈtɒks ɪk ◂ ‖ ˌnɑːn ˈtɑːks ɪk ◂
non-traditional ˌnɒn trə ˈdɪʃ ᵊn͜ əl ◂ ‖ ˌnɑːn-
non troppo ˌnɒn ˈtrɒp əʊ ˌnəʊn- ‖ ˌnɑːn ˈtrɑːp oʊ ˌnoʊn-, ˈtroʊp- —*It* [non ˈtrɔp po]
non-U ˌnɒn ˈjuː ◂ ‖ ˌnɑːn-
nonunion ˌnɒn ˈjuːn i͜ən ◂ ‖ ˌnɑːn- **~ised, ~ized** aɪzd ◂
nonverbal ˌnɒn ˈvɜːb ᵊl ◂ ‖ ˌnɑːn ˈvɝːb ᵊl ◂
nonviolence ˌnɒn ˈvaɪ͜əl ənᵗs ‖ ˌnɑːn-
nonviolent ˌnɒn ˈvaɪ͜əl ənt ◂ ‖ ˌnɑːn- **~ly** li
nonwhite, non-White ˌnɒn ˈwaɪt ◂ -ˈhwaɪt ‖ ˌnɑːn- **~s** s
noodle ˈnuːd ᵊl **~s** z
noogie ˈnuːg i
nook nʊk §nuːk **nooks** nʊks §nuːks
nookie, nooky ˈnʊk i
noon nuːn **noons** nuːnz
Noonan ˈnuːn ən
noonday ˈnuːn deɪ
no one *pronoun*, **no-one** ˈnəʊ wʌn §-wɒn **no one's, no-one's** ˈnəʊ wʌnz §-wɒnz
noontide ˈnuːn taɪd
noose nuːs **noosed** nuːst **nooses** ˈnuːs ɪz -əz **noosing** ˈnuːs ɪŋ
Nootka ˈnʊt kə ˈnuːt-
nopal ˈnəʊp ᵊl ‖ ˈnoʊp ᵊl **~s** z
nope nəʊp ‖ noʊp —*usually said with the* **p** *unreleased*
noplace ˈnəʊ pleɪs ‖ ˈnoʊ-

nor nɔː ‖ nɔːr —*There is also an occasional weak form* nə ‖ nᵊr

nor-, nor'- nɔː ‖ nɔːr —*but in RP before a vowel,* nɔːr — **nor'-east** ˌnɔːr 'iːst ◂ ‖ ˌnɔːr-

NOR nɔː ‖ nɔːr

Nora 'nɔːr ə

noradrenalin, noradrenaline ˌnɔːr ə 'dren əl ɪn -iːn, §-ən

Norah 'nɔːr ə

Noraid 'nɔːr eɪd

Norbert 'nɔːb ət ‖ 'nɔːrb ᵊrt

Norden 'nɔːd ᵊn ‖ 'nɔːrd ᵊn

Nordic, n~ 'nɔːd ɪk ‖ 'nɔːrd ɪk **~s** s

Nordrhein-Westfalen ˌnɔːd raɪn vest 'fɑːl ən ‖ ˌnɔːrd- —*Ger* [ˌnɔʁt rain vest 'faː lən]

Nordstrom *tdmk* 'nɔːd strɒm -strəm ‖ 'nɔːrd strəm -stroum

Nore nɔː ‖ nɔːr

nor'easter ˌnɔːr 'iːst ə -ᵊr **~s** z

Noreen 'nɔːr iːn nɔː 'riːn ‖ nɔː 'riːn

Norfolk *place in England* 'nɔːf ək ‖ 'nɔːrf- —*but places in the US are also* -ɔːk, -ɑːk. *The island off Australia is locally* 'nɔː fəʊk.
ˌ**Norfolk 'Broads, ˌNorfolk 'jacket**; ˌ**Norfolk 'terrier**

nori 'nɔːr i 'nɒr- —*Jp* [no 'ri]

noria 'nɔːr i‿ə ‖ 'nour- **~s** z

Noricum 'nɒr ɪk əm ‖ 'nɔːr- 'nɑːr-

Noriega ˌnɒr i 'eɪg ə ‖ ˌnɔːr- —*Sp* [no 'rje ɣa]

Norland, n~ 'nɔː lənd ‖ 'nɔːr-

norm, Norm nɔːm ‖ nɔːrm **norms, Norm's** nɔːmz ‖ nɔːrmz

Norma 'nɔːm ə ‖ 'nɔːrm ə

normal, N~ 'nɔːm ᵊl ‖ 'nɔːrm ᵊl **~s** z

normalcy 'nɔːm ᵊl si ‖ 'nɔːrm-

normalis... —*see* **normaliz...**

normality nɔː 'mæl ət i -ɪt- ‖ nɔːr 'mæl əţ i

normalization ˌnɔːm əl aɪ 'zeɪʃ ᵊn -əl ɪ- ‖ ˌnɔːrm əl ə- **~s** z

normaliz|e 'nɔːm ə laɪz ‖ 'nɔːrm- **~ed** d **~es** ɪz əz **~ing** ɪŋ

normally 'nɔːm əl i ‖ 'nɔːrm-

Norman 'nɔːm ən ‖ 'nɔːrm ən
ˌ**Norman 'Conquest**

Normanby 'nɔːm ən bi →-əm- ‖ 'nɔːrm-

Normand 'nɔːm ænd -ənd ‖ 'nɔːrm-

Normandy 'nɔːm ənd i ‖ 'nɔːrm-

Normanton 'nɔːm ən tən ‖ 'nɔːrm-

normative 'nɔːm ət ɪv ‖ 'nɔːrm əţ ɪv **~ly** li **~ness** nəs nɪs

Norn nɔːn ‖ nɔːrn

Norplant *tdmk* 'nɔː plɑːnt §-plænt ‖ 'nɔːr plænt

Norrie 'nɒr i ‖ 'nɔːr i 'nɑːr-

Norris 'nɒr ɪs §-əs ‖ 'nɔːr əs 'nɑːr-

Norrköping 'nɔː tʃɜːp ɪŋ ‖ 'nɔːr tʃoup- —*Swed* ['nɔr çøː piŋ]

Norroy 'nɒr ɔɪ ‖ 'nɔːr- 'nɑːr-

Norse nɔːs ‖ nɔːrs

Norse|man 'nɔːs |mən ‖ 'nɔːrs- **~men** mən -men

north, North nɔːθ ‖ nɔːrθ
ˌ**North ˌCaro'lina**; ˌ**North Da'kota**; ˌ**North Ko'rea**; ˌ**North 'Pole**; ˌ**North 'Sea**; ˌ**North 'Star**; ˌ**North 'Yorkshire**

Northallerton nɔːθ 'æl ət ən nɔː-ð- ‖ nɔːrθ 'æl ᵊrt ᵊn

Northampton nɔː 'θæmpt ən nə-, nɔːθ 'hæmpt- ‖ nɔːr- **~shire** ʃə ʃɪə ‖ ʃᵊr ʃɪr

Northanger nɔː 'θæŋ gə 'nɔːθ ˌæŋ gə, -ˌhæŋ-, -ə ‖ nɔːr 'θæŋ gᵊr 'nɔːrθ ˌæŋ-, ˌhæŋ-

Northants 'nɔːθ ænts nɔː 'θænts ‖ 'nɔːrθ-

northbound 'nɔːθ baʊnd ‖ 'nɔːrθ-

Northbrook 'nɔːθ brʊk ‖ 'nɔːrθ-

Northcliffe 'nɔːθ klɪf ‖ 'nɔːrθ-

Northcote 'nɔːθ kət -kɒt, -kəʊt ‖ 'nɔːrθ kout

north-country ˌnɔːθ 'kʌntr i ◂ ‖ ˌnɔːrθ- **~men** mən men **~man** mən mæn

northeast, N~ ˌnɔːθ 'iːst ◂ ‖ ˌnɔːrθ- —*also naut* ˌnɔːr- **~er/s** ə/z ‖ ᵊr/z **~erlies** əl iz ‖ ᵊr liz **~erly** əl i ‖ ᵊr li **~ern** ən ‖ ᵊrn **~erner/s** ən ə/z ‖ ᵊrn ᵊr/z **~ward/s** wəd/z ‖ wᵊrd/z

Northenden 'nɔːð ᵊnd ən ‖ 'nɔːrð-

norther|ly 'nɔːð ə |li -ə|l i ‖ 'nɔːrð ᵊr |li **~lies** liz

northern, N~ 'nɔːð ᵊn ‖ 'nɔːrð ᵊrn
ˌ**Northern 'Ireland**; ˌ**northern 'lights**; ˌ**Northern 'Territory**

northerner, N~ 'nɔːð ən ə ‖ 'nɔːrð ᵊrn ᵊr -ᵊn- **~s** z

northernmost 'nɔːð ᵊn məʊst →-ᵊm- ‖ -ᵊrn moust

Northfield 'nɔːθ fiːᵊld ‖ 'nɔːrθ- **~s** z

Northfleet 'nɔːθ fliːt ‖ 'nɔːrθ-

Northiam 'nɔːð i‿əm ‖ 'nɔːrð-

northing 'nɔːð ɪŋ 'nɔːθ- ‖ 'nɔːrθ ɪŋ 'nɔːrð- **~s** z

North|man 'nɔːθ mən ‖ 'nɔːrθ- **~men** mən men

north-north-|east ˌnɔːθ nɔːθ| 'iːst ‖ ˌnɔːrθ nɔːrθ- **~west** 'west

Northolt 'nɔːθ əʊlt →-ɒʊlt ‖ 'nɔːrθ oult

Northrop, Northrup 'nɔːθ rəp ‖ 'nɔːrθ-

Northumberland nɔː 'θʌm bə lənd nə- ‖ nɔːr 'θʌm bᵊr-

Northumbri|a nɔː 'θʌm bri‿|ə ‖ nɔːr- **~an/s** ən/z

northward 'nɔːθ wəd ‖ 'nɔːrθ wᵊrd **~s** z

northwest, N~ ˌnɔːθ 'west ◂ ‖ ˌnɔːrθ- —*also naut* ˌnɔː- ‖ ˌnɔːr- **~er/s** ə/z ‖ ᵊr/z **~erlies** əl iz ‖ ᵊr liz **~erly** əl i ‖ ᵊr li **~ern** ən ‖ ᵊrn **~ward/s** wəd/z ‖ wᵊrd/z
ˌ**Northwest 'Territories**

Northwich 'nɔːθ wɪtʃ ‖ 'nɔːrθ-

Northwood 'nɔːθ wʊd ‖ 'nɔːrθ-

Norton 'nɔːt ᵊn ‖ 'nɔːrt ᵊn

Norvic *tdmk* 'nɔː vɪk ‖ 'nɔːr-

Norwalk 'nɔː wɔːk ‖ 'nɔːr- -wɑːk

Norway 'nɔː weɪ ‖ 'nɔːr weɪ
ˌ**Norway 'spruce**

Norwegian nɔː 'wiːdʒ ᵊn ‖ nɔːr- **~s** z

Norwich *place in England* 'nɒr ɪdʒ -ɪtʃ ‖ 'nɔːr- 'nɑːr-

Norwich *place in CT* 'nɔː wɪtʃ ‖ 'nɔːr-

N

Norwood ˈnɔː wʊd ‖ ˈnɔːr-
nos, nos., Nos. ˈnʌm bəz ‖ -bᵊrz
nose nəʊz ‖ noʊz **nosed** nəʊzd ‖ noʊzd **noses** ˈnəʊz ɪz -əz ‖ ˈnoʊz əz **nosing** ˈnəʊz ɪŋ ‖ ˈnoʊz ɪŋ
nosebag ˈnəʊz bæɡ ‖ ˈnoʊz- **~s** z
nosebleed ˈnəʊz bliːd ‖ ˈnoʊz- **~s** z
nosecone ˈnəʊz kəʊn ‖ ˈnoʊz koʊn **~s** z
nose|dive ˈnəʊz |daɪv ‖ ˈnoʊz- **~dived** daɪvd **~dives** daɪvz **~diving** daɪv ɪŋ **~dove** dəʊv ‖ doʊv
no-see-um ˌnəʊ ˈsiː əm ‖ ˌnoʊ- **~s** z
nosegay ˈnəʊz ɡeɪ ‖ ˈnoʊz- **~s** z
nosey —*see* **nosy**
Nosferatu ˌnɒs fə ˈrɑːt uː -fe- ‖ ˌnɑːs-
nosh nɒʃ ‖ nɑːʃ **noshed** nɒʃt ‖ nɑːʃt **noshes** ˈnɒʃ ɪz -əz ‖ ˈnɑːʃ əz **noshing** ˈnɒʃ ɪŋ ‖ ˈnɑːʃ ɪŋ
nosher|y ˈnɒʃ ər |i ‖ ˈnɑːʃ- **~ies** iz
no-show ˈnəʊ ʃəʊ ‖ ˈnoʊ ʃoʊ **~s** z
nosh-up ˈnɒʃ ʌp ‖ ˈnɑːʃ- **~s** s
no-side ˌnəʊ ˈsaɪd ‖ ˌnoʊ-
no-smoking ˌnəʊ ˈsməʊk ɪŋ ‖ ˌnoʊ ˈsmoʊk ɪŋ
ˌno-ˈsmoking sign
noso- *comb. form*
with stress-neutral suffix ¦nɒs əʊ ‖ ¦nous ə ¦nɑːs oʊ — **nosographic** ˌnɒs əʊ ˈɡræf ɪk ◂ ‖ ˌnous ə- ˌnɑːs oʊ-
with stress-imposing suffix nɒ ˈsɒ+ ‖ noʊ ˈsɑː+ — **nosology** nɒ ˈsɒl ədʒ i ‖ noʊ ˈsɑːl-
nostalgia nɒ ˈstældʒ ə -ˈstældʒ i‿ə ‖ nɑː- nə-
nostalgic nɒ ˈstældʒ ɪk ‖ nɑː- nə- **~ally** ᵊl‿i
Nostradamus ˌnɒs trə ˈdɑːm əs -ˈdeɪm- ‖ ˌnɑːs- ˌnous-
Nostratic nɒ ˈstræt ɪk ‖ nɑː ˈstræţ ɪk nɔː-
nostril ˈnɒs trəl -trɪl ‖ ˈnɑːs- **~s** z
nostrum ˈnɒs trəm ‖ ˈnɑːs- **~s** z
nos|y ˈnəʊz |i ‖ ˈnoʊz |i **~ier** i‿ə ‖ i‿ᵊr **~iest** i‿ɪst i‿əst **~ily** ɪ li əl i **~iness** i nəs i nɪs
ˌnosy ˈparker
not nɒt ‖ nɑːt —*There is no weak form other than the contracted* n't *used with certain modals.*
nota bene ˌnəʊt ə ˈben i -ɑː-, -ˈbiːn-, -eɪ ‖ ˌnoʊţ ə- -ˈbeɪn eɪ
notabilit|y ˌnəʊt ə ˈbɪl ət |i -ɪt i ‖ ˌnoʊţ ə ˈbɪl əţ |i **~ies** iz
notab|le ˈnəʊt əb |ᵊl ‖ ˈnoʊţ- **~les** ᵊlz **~ly** li
notarie... —*see* **notary**
notaris... —*see* **notariz...**
notarization ˌnəʊt ər aɪ ˈzeɪʃ ᵊn -ər ɪ- ‖ ˌnoʊţ ər ə-
notariz|e ˈnəʊt ə raɪz ‖ ˈnoʊţ- **~ed** d **~es** ɪz əz **~ing** ɪŋ
notar|y ˈnəʊt ər |i ‖ ˈnoʊţ- **~ies** iz
no|tate nəʊ ˈ|teɪt ‖ ˈnoʊ|t eɪt **~tated** teɪt ɪd -əd ‖ teɪţ əd **~tates** teɪts **~tating** teɪt ɪŋ ‖ teɪţ ɪŋ
notation nəʊ ˈteɪʃ ᵊn ‖ noʊ- **~s** z
notch nɒtʃ ‖ nɑːtʃ **notched** nɒtʃt ‖ nɑːtʃt **notches** ˈnɒtʃ ɪz -əz ‖ ˈnɑːtʃ əz **notching** ˈnɒtʃ ɪŋ ‖ ˈnɑːtʃ ɪŋ
note nəʊt ‖ noʊt **noted** ˈnəʊt ɪd -əd ‖ ˈnoʊţ əd **notes** nəʊts ‖ noʊts **noting** ˈnəʊt ɪŋ ‖ ˈnoʊţ ɪŋ
notebook ˈnəʊt bʊk §-buːk ‖ ˈnoʊt- **~s** s
notecas|e ˈnəʊt keɪs ‖ ˈnoʊt- **~es** ɪz əz
noted ˈnəʊt ɪd -əd ‖ ˈnoʊţ əd **~ly** li **~ness** nəs nɪs
notelet ˈnəʊt lət -lɪt ‖ ˈnoʊt- **~s** s
notepad ˈnəʊt pæd ‖ ˈnoʊt- **~s** z
notepaper ˈnəʊt ˌpeɪp ə ‖ ˈnoʊt ˌpeɪp ᵊr
noteworth|y ˈnəʊt ˌwɜːð |i ‖ ˈnoʊt ˌwɜːð |i **~ily** ɪ li əl i **~iness** i nəs i nɪs
not-for-profit ˌnɒt fə ˈprɒf ɪt §-ət ‖ ˌnɑːt fᵊr ˈprɑːf ət
nother ˈnʌð ə ‖ -ᵊr
nothing ˈnʌθ ɪŋ §ˈnɒθ- **~ness** nəs nɪs
ˌnothing ˈdoing; **(there's) ˌnothing ˈfor it**; **(there's) ˌnothing ˈto it**
notic|e ˈnəʊt ɪs §-əs ‖ ˈnoʊţ əs **~ed** t **~es** ɪz əz **~ing** ɪŋ
ˈnotice board
noticeab|le ˈnəʊt ɪs əb |ᵊl ˈ·əs- ‖ ˈnoʊţ əs- **~ly** li
notifiable ˈnəʊt ɪ faɪ‿əb ᵊl ˈ·ə-, ˌ·ˈ·· ‖ ˈnoʊţ-
notification ˌnəʊt ɪf ɪ ˈkeɪʃ ᵊn ˌ·əf-, §-əˈ·- ‖ ˌnoʊţ- **~s** z
noti|fy ˈnəʊt ɪ |faɪ -ə- ‖ ˈnoʊţ ə- **~fied** faɪd **~fier/s** faɪ‿ə/z ‖ faɪ‿ᵊr/z **~fies** faɪz **~fying** faɪ ɪŋ
notion ˈnəʊʃ ᵊn ‖ ˈnoʊʃ ᵊn **~s** z
notional ˈnəʊʃ ᵊn‿əl ‖ ˈnoʊʃ- **~ly** i
notoriety ˌnəʊt ə ˈraɪ‿ət i ‖ ˌnoʊţ ə ˈraɪ əţ i
notorious nəʊ ˈtɔːr i‿əs ‖ noʊ- nə-, -ˈtour- **~ly** li **~ness** nəs nɪs
Notre Dame *(i)* ˌnəʊtr ə ˈdɑːm ◂ ˌnɒtr- ‖ ˌnoʊţ ᵊr ˈdɑːm ˈnoʊtr ə- *(ii)* -ˈdeɪm —*for the Paris cathedral, and for the religious order in France and Britain, (i); in the United States (ii).* —*Fr* [nɔ tʁə dam]
no-trump ˌnəʊ ˈtrʌmp ◂ ‖ ˌnoʊ- **~s** s
Nott nɒt ‖ nɑːt
Nottingham ˈnɒt ɪŋ əm §-həm ‖ ˈnɑːţ- -hæm **~shire** ʃə ʃɪə ‖ ʃᵊr ʃɪr
Notting Hill ˌnɒt ɪŋ ˈhɪl ◂ ‖ ˌnɑːţ-
Notts nɒts ‖ nɑːts
Notus ˈnəʊt əs ‖ ˈnoʊţ əs
notwithstanding ˌnɒt wɪð ˈstænd ɪŋ ◂ -wɪθ- ‖ ˌnɑːt-
Nouakchott ˌnuː æk ˈʃɒt ‖ -ɑːk ˈʃɑːt —*Fr* [nwak ʃɔt]
nougat ˈnuːɡ ɑː §ˈnʌɡ ət ‖ ˈnuːɡ ət (*)
nought nɔːt ‖ nɑːt **noughts** nɔːts ‖ nɑːts
ˌnoughts and ˈcrosses
Noumea, Nouméa nuː ˈmiː‿ə -ˈmeɪ‿ə —*Fr* [nu me a]
noumenon ˈnuːm ən ən ˈnaʊm-, -ɪn-; -ə nɒn, -ɪ- ‖ -ə nɑːn
noun naʊn **nouns** naʊnz
nourish ˈnʌr ɪʃ ‖ ˈnɜː ɪʃ **~ed** t **~es** ɪz əz **~ing/ly** ɪŋ/li **~ment** mənt
nous naʊs

ouveau, ~x ˈnuːv əʊ ‖ ˌnuː ˈvoʊ —*Fr* [nu vo]
ˌnouveau(x) ˈriche(s) riːʃ —*Fr* [ʁiʃ]
ouvelle cuisine ˌnuːv el kwɪ ˈziːn nu ˌvel·ˈ·, -kwiː·ˈ· —*Fr* [nu vɛl kɥi zin]
ouvelle vague ˌnuːv el ˈvɑːg —*Fr* [nu vɛl vag]
Nov —*see* **November**
ov|a, Nov|a ˈnəʊv |ə ‖ ˈnoʊv |ə **~ae** iː **~as** əz
ˌNova ˈScotia ˈskəʊʃ ə ‖ ˈskoʊʃ ə
Novartis *tdmk* nəʊ ˈvɑːt ɪs §-əs ‖ noʊ ˈvɑːrţ əs
Novaya Zemlya ˌnəʊv ə jə ˈzem li̯ ə ˌnɒv-, ˌɑː- ‖ ˌnoʊv- —*Russ* [ˌnɔ və jə zʲɪm ˈlʲa]
novel ˈnɒv əl §ˈnʌv- ‖ ˈnɑːv əl **~s** z
novelette ˌnɒv ə ˈlet əl ˈet ‖ ˌnɑːv- **~s** s
novelettish ˌnɒv ə ˈlet ɪʃ ◂ əl ˈet- ‖ ˌnɑːv ə ˈleţ ɪʃ ◂ əl ˈeţ-
novelist ˈnɒv əl ɪst §-əst ‖ ˈnɑːv- **~s** s
novelistic ˌnɒv ə ˈlɪst ɪk ◂ -əl ˈɪst- ‖ ˌnɑːv-
novelization, novelisation ˌnɒv əl aɪ ˈzeɪʃ ən -ɪˈ· ·, -ə · · ‖ ˌnɑːv əl ə-
novell|a nəʊ ˈvel |ə ‖ noʊ- **~as** əz **~e** iː eɪ
Novello nə ˈvel əʊ ‖ -oʊ
novelt|y ˈnɒv əlt |i ‖ ˈnɑːv- **~ies** iz
November nəʊ ˈvem bə ‖ noʊ ˈvem bər nə- **~s** z
novena nəʊ ˈviːn ə ‖ noʊ- **~s** z
Novgorod ˈnɒv gə rɒd ‖ ˈnɑːv gə rɑːd —*Russ* [ˈnɔv gə rət]
Novial ˈnəʊv i̯ əl ‖ ˈnoʊv-
novic|e ˈnɒv ɪs §-əs ‖ ˈnɑːv əs **~es** ɪz əz
noviciate, novitiate nəʊ ˈvɪʃ i̯ ət -ɪt, -eɪt ‖ noʊ ˈvɪʃ ət nə-, -ˈvɪʃ i̯ ət, -i eɪt **~s** s
novocain, novocaine, N~ *tdmk* ˈnəʊv əʊ keɪn ˈnɒv- ‖ ˈnoʊv ə-
Novosibirsk ˌnəʊv əʊ sɪ ˈbɪəsk -səˈ· ‖ ˌnoʊv ə sə ˈbɪərsk —*Russ* [nə və sʲɪ ˈbʲirsk]
Novotel *tdmk* ˈnəʊv əʊ ˌtel ‖ ˈnoʊv oʊ- -ə-
now naʊ
nowadays ˈnaʊ ə deɪz
Nowell *'Christmas'* nəʊ ˈel ‖ noʊ-
Nowell *personal name* ˈnəʊ əl -el ‖ ˈnoʊ-
nowhere ˈnəʊ weə -hweə ‖ ˈnoʊ wer -hwer, -wær, -hwær —*Occasionally also* -wə, -hwə ‖ -wər , -hwər
no-win ˌnəʊ ˈwɪn ◂ ‖ ˌnoʊ-
ˌno-ˈwin situˌation, ˌ· ·ˌ· ·ˈ· ·
nowise ˈnəʊ waɪz ‖ ˈnoʊ-
nowt naʊt nəʊt
noxious ˈnɒk ʃəs ‖ ˈnɑːk- **~ly** li **~ness** nəs nɪs
Noyes *family name* nɔɪz
Noyes Fludde ˌnɔɪ əz ˈflʊd
nozzle ˈnɒz əl ‖ ˈnɑːz əl **~s** z
NPR ˌen piː ˈɑː ‖ -ˈɑːr
nr —*see* **near**
NSAID ˈen sed -seɪd **~s** z
NSPCC ˌen es ˌpiː siː ˈsiː
NSU ˌen es ˈjuː
-n't ənt —*This contraction of* **not** *does not receive stress, even for contrast:* either you DID or you DIDN'T ˈdɪd ənt
nth entθ
n-tuple ˈen tjʊp əl ˌeɪ ˈtjuːp əl, →-ˈtʃuːp- ‖ ˈen tʊp əl -tjʊp-; ˌen ˈtuːp əl, -ˈtjuːp- **~s** z
n-type ˈen taɪp
nu *name of Greek letter* njuː §nuː ‖ nuː njuː
Nuala ˈnʊəl ə ‖ ˈnuː əl ə
nuanc|e ˈnjuː ɑːnts ˈnuː-, -ɒnts, -ɒ̃s, ˌ·ˈ· ‖ ˈnuː- ˈnjuː- —*Fr* [nɥɑ̃ːs] **~es** ɪz əz
nub nʌb **nubs** nʌbz
Nuba ˈnjuːb ə §ˈnuːb- ‖ ˈnuːb ə ˈnjuːb-
nubbin ˈnʌb ɪn §-ən **~s** z
nubble ˈnʌb əl **~s** z
nubbly ˈnʌb əl i
nubby ˈnʌb i
Nubi|a ˈnjuːb i̯ |ə §ˈnuːb- ‖ ˈnuːb- ˈnjuːb- **~an/s** ən/z
ˌNubian ˈDesert
nubile ˈnjuːb aɪəl §ˈnuːb- ‖ ˈnuːb əl ˈnjuːb-, -aɪəl

NUCLEAR

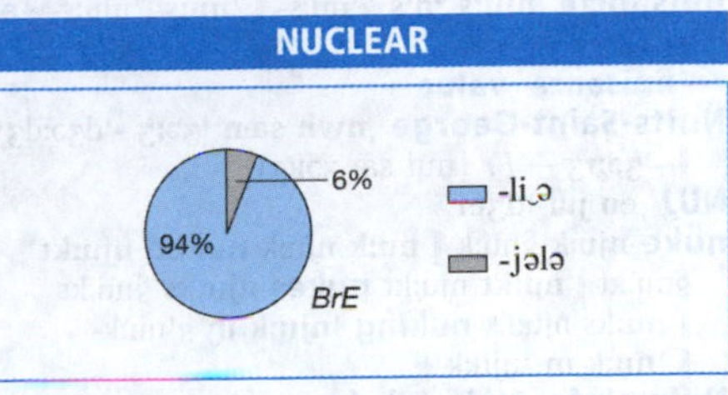

nuclear ˈnjuːk li̯ ə §ˈnuːk-, ⚠-jəl ə ‖ ˈnuːk li̯ ər ˈnjuːk-, ⚠-jəl ər — *Preference poll, BrE:* -li̯ ə *94%,* -jələ *6%.*
ˌnuclear ˈenergy; **ˌnuclear reˈactor**; **ˌnuclear ˈtone**; **ˌnuclear ˈwinter**
nuclear-free ˌnjuːk li ə ˈfriː ◂ §ˌnuːk-, ⚠ˌjəl- ‖ ˌnuːk li̯ ər- ˌnjuːk-, ⚠ˌjəl-
nuclei ˈnjuːk li aɪ §ˈnuːk-, -iː ‖ ˈnuːk- ˈnjuːk-
nucleic nju ˈkliː ɪk §nu-, -ˈkleɪ- ‖ nu- nju-
nuˌcleic ˈacid
nucleo- *comb. form*
with stress-neutral suffix ¦njuːk li əʊ §¦nuːk- ‖ ¦nuːk li ə ¦njuːk- — **nucleoplasm** ˈnjuːk li əʊ ˌplæz əm §ˈnuːk- ‖ ˈnuːk li ə- ˈnjuːk-
with stress-imposing suffix ˌnjuːk li ˈɒ+ ˌnuːk- ‖ ˌnuːk li ˈɑː+ ˌnjuːk- — **nucleofugal** ˌnjuːk li ˈɒf jʊg əl ◂ §ˌnuːk- ‖ ˌnuːk li ˈɑːf jəg əl ◂ ˌnjuːk-
nucleol|us nju ˈkliː əl |əs §nu-; ˌnjuːk li ˈəʊl |əs, §ˌnuːk- ‖ nu- nju- **~i** aɪ
nucleon ˈnjuːk li ɒn §ˈnuːk- ‖ ˈnuːk li ɑːn ˈnjuːk- **~s** z
nucleonic ˌnjuːk li ˈɒn ɪk ◂ §ˌnuːk- ‖ ˌnuːk li ˈɑːn ɪk ◂ ˌnjuːk- **~s** s
nucleoside ˈnjuːk li̯ ə saɪd §ˈnuːk- ‖ ˈnuːk- ˈnjuːk- **~s** z
nucleotide ˈnjuːk li̯ ə taɪd §ˈnuːk- ‖ ˈnuːk- ˈnjuːk- **~s** z
nucle|us ˈnjuːk li̯ |əs §ˈnuːk-, ⚠-jəl- ‖ ˈnuːk- ˈnjuːk-, , ⚠-jəl- **~i** aɪ iː
nuclide ˈnjuːk laɪd §ˈnuːk- ‖ ˈnuːk- ˈnjuːk- **~s** z
nuddy ˈnʌd i
nude njuːd §nuːd ‖ nuːd njuːd **nudes** njuːdz §nuːdz ‖ nuːdz njuːdz

nudge nʌdʒ **nudged** nʌdʒd **nudges** ˈnʌdʒ ɪz -əz **nudging** ˈnʌdʒ ɪŋ

nudibranch ˈnjuːd ɪ bræŋk §ˈnuːd-, §-ə- ‖ ˈnuːd- ˈnjuːd- **~s** s

nudie ˈnjuːd i §ˈnuːd i ‖ ˈnuːd i ˈnjuːd i

nudism ˈnjuːd ˌɪz əm §ˈnuːd- ‖ ˈnuːd- ˈnjuːd-

nudist ˈnjuːd ɪst §ˈnuːd-, §-əst ‖ ˈnuːd əst ˈnjuːd- **~s** s

nudit|y ˈnjuːd ət |i §ˈnuːd-, -ɪt- ‖ ˈnuːd əṭ |i ˈnjuːd- **~ies** iz

nudnik ˈnʊd nɪk **~s** s

'nuff nʌf

Nuffield ˈnʌf iːᵊld

nugatory ˈnjuːg ət ̮ər i §ˈnuːg-; njuː ˈgeɪt ər i ‖ ˈnuːg ə tɔːr i ˈnjuːg-, -toʊr-

Nugent ˈnjuːdʒ ənt §ˈnuːdʒ- ‖ ˈnuːdʒ- ˈnjuːdʒ-

nugget ˈnʌg ɪt §-ət **~s** s

nuisanc|e ˈnjuːs ᵊnᵗs §ˈnuːs- ‖ ˈnuːs- ˈnjuːs- **~es** ɪz əz
ˈnuisance ˌvalue

Nuits-Saint-George ˌnwiː sæn ˈʒɔːʒ -ˈdʒɔːdʒ ‖ -ˈʒɔːrʒ —*Fr* [nɥi sɛ̃ ʒɔʁʒ]

NUJ ˌen juː ˈdʒeɪ

nuke njuːk §nuːk ‖ nuːk njuːk **nuked** njuːkt §nuːkt ‖ nuːkt njuːkt **nukes** njuːks §nuːks ‖ nuːks njuːks **nuking** ˈnjuːk ɪŋ §ˈnuːk- ‖ ˈnuːk ɪŋ ˈnjuːk-

Nukualofa, Nuku'alofa ˌnuː kuː ə ˈləʊf ə ‖ -ˈloʊf ə —*Tongan* [nu ku ʔa ˈlo fa]

null nʌl
ˌnull and ˈvoid

nullah ˈnʌl ə -ɑː **~s** z

nulla-nulla ˈnʌl ə ˌnʌl ə **~s** z

Nullarbor ˈnʌl ə bɔː ‖ -bɔːr
ˌNullarbor ˈPlain

nullification ˌnʌl ɪf ɪ ˈkeɪʃ ᵊn ˌ-əf-, §-əˈ--

nulli|fy ˈnʌl ɪ |faɪ -ə- **~fied** faɪd **~fier/s** faɪ ̮ə/z ‖ faɪ ̮ᵊr/z **~fies** faɪz **~fying** faɪ ɪŋ

nullip|ara nʌ ˈlɪp |ər ə **~arae** ə riː

nullit|y ˈnʌl ət |i -ɪt- ‖ -əṭ |i **~ies** iz

nul points ˌnʊl ˈpwæ̃ ‖ -ˈpwæŋ —*Fr* [nyl pwɛ̃]

NUM ˌen ju ˈem

Numa ˈnjuːm ə ˈnuːm- ‖ ˈnuːm ə ˈnjuːm-

numb nʌm **numbed** nʌmd **number** ˈnʌm ə ‖ -ᵊr **numbest** ˈnʌm ɪst -əst **numbing/ly** ˈnʌm ɪŋ /li **numbs** nʌmz

numbat ˈnʌm bæt **~s** s

number *n, v* ˈnʌm bə ‖ -bᵊr **~ed** d **numbering** ˈnʌm bər ̮ɪŋ **~s** z
ˌnumber ˈone◂; **ˌNumber ˈTen◂**, **ˌNumber Ten ˈDowning Street**

number *adj 'more numb'* ˈnʌm ə ‖ -ᵊr

number-crunch|er ˈnʌm bə ˌkrʌntʃ |ə ‖ -bᵊr ˌkrʌntʃ |ᵊr **~ers** əz ‖ ᵊrz **~ing** ɪŋ

numberless ˈnʌm bə ləs -lɪs ‖ -bᵊr-

numberplate ˈnʌm bə pleɪt ‖ -bᵊr- **~s** s

Numbers ˈnʌm bəz ‖ -bᵊrz

numbly ˈnʌm li

numbskull ˈnʌm skʌl **~s** z

numerable ˈnjuːm ər ̮əb ᵊl §ˈnuːm- ‖ ˈnuːm- ˈnjuːm-

numeracy ˈnjuːm ər ̮əs i §ˈnuːm- ‖ ˈnuːm- njuːm-

numeral ˈnjuːm ᵊr ̮əl §ˈnuːm- ‖ ˈnuːm- ˈnjuːm- **~s** z

numerate *adj* ˈnjuːm ər ̮ət §ˈnuːm-, -ɪt, -ə reɪt ‖ ˈnuːm- ˈnjuːm-

numeration ˌnjuːm ə ˈreɪʃ ᵊn §ˌnuːm- ‖ ˌnuːm- ˌnjuːm-

numerator ˈnjuːm ə reɪt ə §ˈnuːm- ‖ ˈnuːm ə reɪṭ ᵊr ˈnjuːm- **~s** z

numeric nju ˈmer ɪk §nu- ‖ nu- nju- **~al** ᵊl **~ally** ᵊl ̮i **~s** s

numerological ˌnjuːm ər ̮ə ˈlɒdʒ ɪk ᵊl ◂ §ˌnuːm- ‖ ˌnuːm ər ̮ə ˈlɑːdʒ- ˌnjuːm- **~ly** ̮i

numerology ˌnjuːm ə ˈrɒl ədʒ i §ˌnuːm- ‖ ˌnuːm ə ˈrɑːl- ˌnjuːm-

numero uno ˌnuːm ə rəʊ ˈuːn əʊ njuː- ‖ ˌnuːm ə roʊ ˈuːn oʊ ˌnjuːm-

numerous ˈnjuːm ər ̮əs §ˈnuːm- ‖ ˈnuːm- ˈnjuːm- **~ly** li **~ness** nəs nɪs

Numidi|a nju ˈmɪd i ̮|ə §nu- ‖ nu- nju- **~an/s** ən/z

numinous ˈnjuːm ɪn əs §ˈnuːm-, -ən- ‖ ˈnuːm- ˈnjuːm-

numismatic ˌnjuːm ɪz ˈmæt ɪk ◂ §ˌnuːm- ‖ ˌnuːm əz ˈmæṭ ɪk ◂ ˌnjuːm-, ˌ-əs- **~s** s

numismatist njuː ˈmɪz mət ɪst §nuː-, §-əst ‖ nuː ˈmɪz məṭ əst nju-, -ˈmɪs- **~s** s

nummary ˈnʌm ər i

nummular ˈnʌm jʊl ə -jəl- ‖ -jəl ᵊr

nump|tie, nump|ty ˈnʌm*p*| ti **~ties** tiz

numskull ˈnʌm skʌl **~s** z

nun nʌn **nuns** nʌnz

nunatak ˈnʌn ə tæk **~s** s

Nunavut ˈnuːn ə vuːt

Nunawading ˈnʌn ə wɒd ɪŋ ‖ -wɑːd·

Nunc Dimittis ˌnʌŋk dɪ ˈmɪt ɪs ˌnʊŋk-, -daɪ-, -də-, §-əs ‖ -ˈmɪṭ əs

nunchaku nʌn ˈtʃæk uː ‖ -ˈtʃɑːk- —*Jp* [ˈnɯn tɕa kɯ] **~s** z

nunciature ˈnʌnᵗs i ̮ə tjʊə ̮ətʃ ə ‖ ̮ə tjʊr ̮ətʃ ᵊr **~s** z

nuncio ˈnʌnᵗs i əʊ ˈnʌnᵗʃ-, ˈnʊnᵗs-, ˈnʊnᵗʃ- ‖ -oʊ **~s** z

Nuneaton nʌn ˈiːt ᵊn

Nunn nʌn

nunner|y ˈnʌn ər |i **~ies** iz

Nupe *African language and people* ˈnuːp eɪ

NUPE *trade union* ˈnjuːp ˈnuːp-

nuptial ˈnʌp ʃᵊl -tʃəl; ⚠ˈnʌp ʃu ̮əl, ⚠-tʃu ̮əl **~ly** i **~s** z

Nuremberg ˈnjʊər əm bɜːg ˈnjɔːr- ‖ ˈnʊr əm bɜːg ˈnjʊr- —*Ger* Nürnberg [ˈnʏʁn bɛʁk]

Nureyev ˈnjʊər i ef njuᵊ ˈreɪ-, -ev ‖ nu ˈreɪ- —*Russ* [nu ˈrʲe jɪf]

Nuristan ˌnʊər ɪ ˈstɑːn -ˈstæn ‖ ˌnʊr ɪ ˈstæn -ˈstɑːn

Nurofen *tdmk* ˈnjʊər əʊ fen §ˈnʊər- ‖ ˈnʊr ə- ˈnjʊr-

nurse, Nurse nɜːs ‖ nɜːs **nursed** nɜːst ‖ nɜːst **nurses** ˈnɜːs ɪz -əz ‖ ˈnɜːs əz **nursing** ˈnɜːs ɪŋ ‖ ˈnɜːs ɪŋ

nurseling 'nɜːs lɪŋ ‖ 'nɜːs- **~s** z
nursemaid 'nɜːs meɪd ‖ 'nɜːs- **~s** z
nurser|y 'nɜːs ᵊr‿|i →'nɜːʃ ri ‖ 'nɜːs ᵊr‿|i **~ies** iz
'nursery rhyme; **'nursery school**
nurserymaid 'nɜːs ᵊr‿i meɪd →'nɜːʃ ri- ‖ 'nɜːs- **~s** z
nursery|man 'nɜːs ᵊr‿i |mən →'nɜːʃ ri- ‖ 'nɜːs- **~men** mən
nursing 'nɜːs ɪŋ ‖ 'nɜːs ɪŋ
'nursing home; **ˌnursing 'mother**
nursling 'nɜːs lɪŋ ‖ 'nɜːs- **~s** z
nurturance 'nɜːtʃ ᵊr‿ənᵗs ‖ 'nɜːtʃ-
nurture 'nɜːtʃ ə ‖ 'nɜːtʃ ᵊr **~ed** d **~s** z
nurturing 'nɜːtʃ ər ɪŋ ‖ 'nɜːtʃ ər ɪŋ
NUS ˌen ju 'es
Nussbaum 'nʊs baʊm
nut nʌt **nuts** nʌts **nutted** 'nʌt ɪd -əd ‖ 'nʌţ əd
nutting 'nʌt ɪŋ ‖ 'nʌţ ɪŋ
NUT *trades union* ˌen juː 'tiː
nutation njuː 'teɪʃ ᵊn §nuː- ‖ nuː- njuː- **~s** z
nut-brown ˌnʌt 'braʊn ◂
ˌnut-brown 'hair
nutcas|e 'nʌt keɪs **~es** ɪz əz
nutcracker 'nʌt ˌkræk ə ‖ -ᵊr **~s** z
nuthatch 'nʌt hætʃ **~es** ɪz əz
nut|house 'nʌt |haʊs **~houses** haʊz ɪz -əz
Nutkin 'nʌt kɪn
Nutley 'nʌt li
nutmeg 'nʌt meg
nutraceuticals ˌnjuːtr ə 'suːt ɪk ᵊlz §ˌnuːtr-, -'sjuːt- ‖ ˌnuːtr ə 'suːţ- ˌnjuːtr-
Nutrasweet, NutraSweet *tdmk* 'njuːtr ə swiːt §'nuːtr- ‖ 'nuːtr- 'njuːtr-
nutria 'njuːtr i‿ə §'nuːtr- ‖ 'nuːtr- 'njuːtr- **~s** z
nutrient 'njuːtr i‿ənt §'nuːtr- ‖ 'nuːtr- 'njuːtr- **~s** s
nutrigenomics ˌnjuːtr ɪ dʒi 'nəʊm ɪks §ˌnuːtr-, -ɪ dʒə-, -'nɒm- ‖ ˌnuːtr ə dʒi 'noʊm ɪks ˌnjuːtr-
nutriment 'njuːtr ɪ mənt §'nuːtr-, -ə- ‖ 'nuːtr- 'njuːtr- **~s** s
nutrition nju 'trɪʃ ᵊn §nu- ‖ nu- nju- **~al** ‿əl **~ally** ‿əl i
nutritionist nju 'trɪʃ ᵊn ɪst §nu-, §‿əst ‖ nu- nju- **~s** s
nutritious nju 'trɪʃ əs §nu- ‖ nu- nju- **~ly** li **~ness** nəs nɪs
nutritive 'njuːtr ət ɪv §'nuːtr-, -ət- ‖ 'nuːtr əţ ɪv 'njuːtr- **~ly** li **~s** z
nuts nʌts
nutshell 'nʌt ʃel **~s** z
Nutt nʌt
nutt... —*see* **nut**
Nuttall 'nʌt ɔːl ‖ -ɑːl
nutter, N~ 'nʌt ə ‖ 'nʌţ ᵊr **~s** z
Nutting, n~ 'nʌt ɪŋ ‖ 'nʌţ ɪŋ
Nutton 'nʌt ᵊn
nutt|y 'nʌt |i ‖ 'nʌţ |i **~ier** i‿ə ‖ i‿ᵊr **~iest** i‿ɪst i‿əst **~ily** ɪ li əl i **~iness** i nəs i nɪs
Nuuk 'nuːk
nux vomica ˌnʌks 'vɒm ɪk ə ‖ -'vɑːm-
Nuyts nɔɪts
nuzzl|e 'nʌz ᵊl **~ed** d **~es** z **~ing** ‿ɪŋ
NVQ ˌen viː 'kjuː **~s** z
N-word 'en wɜːd ‖ -wɜːd **~s** z
NY —*see* **New York**
Nyack 'naɪ æk
Nyanja ni 'ændʒ ə
nyanza, N~ ni 'ænz ə naɪ-
Nyasaland naɪ 'æs ə lænd ni-
NYC —*see* **New York City**
Nye, nye naɪ **nyes, Nye's** naɪz
Nyerere njə 'reər i nɪ-, nɪə-, -'rer- ‖ -'rer-
nylon 'naɪl ɒn ‖ -ɑːn **~s** z
nymph nɪmᵖf **nymphs** nɪmᵖfs
nymphet 'nɪmᵖf ɪt -ət, -et; nɪm 'fet **~s** s
nympho 'nɪmᵖf əʊ ‖ -oʊ **~s** z
nymphomania ˌnɪmᵖf ə 'meɪn i‿ə
nymphomaniac ˌnɪmᵖf ə 'meɪn i æk **~s** s
Nynorsk 'niː nɔːsk ‖ -nɔːrsk —*Norw* ['nyː nɔʂk]
Nyree 'naɪᵊr iː
nystagmus nɪ 'stæg məs
nystatin 'nɪst ə tɪn §-ət ən
NZ ˌen 'zed ◂ ‖ -'ziː ◂ —*see* **New Zealand**

N

Oo

o Spelling-to-sound

1 Where the spelling is **o**, the pronunciation differs according to whether the vowel is

- short or long
- followed or not by **r**, and
- strong or weak.

2 The 'strong' pronunciation is regularly

ɒ ‖ ɑː as in **lot** lɒt ‖ lɑːt ('short O')

əʊ ‖ oʊ as in **nose** nəʊz ‖ noʊz ('long O').

3 Less frequently, it is

ʌ as in **come** kʌm (especially before **m, n, v, th**)

uː as in **move** muːv

ʊ as in **woman** ˈwʊm ən (note also ɪ in **women**) or

ɒ ‖ ɔː as in **cross** krɒs ‖ krɔːs (but some speakers of AmE use ɑː instead, thus krɑːs).

Note also the exceptional **gone** gɒn ‖ gɔːn.

4 Where the spelling is **or**, the 'strong' pronunciation is

ɔː as in **north** nɔːθ ‖ nɔːrθ

or, indeed, especially in BrE, the regular 'short' pronunciation

ɒ ‖ ɑː as in **moral** ˈmɒr əl (AmE ˈmɔːr əl, ˈmɑːr əl).

5 Less frequently, it is

ɜː ‖ ɜ˞ː as in **work** wɜːk ‖ wɜ˞ːk (especially after **w**) or

ʌ ‖ ɜ˞ː as in **worry** ˈwʌr i ‖ ˈwɜ˞ː i.

6 The 'weak' pronunciation is

ə as in **method** ˈmeθ əd, **Oxford** ˈɒks fəd ‖ ˈɑːks fᵊrd.

In unstressed syllables there are often two possibilities, ə or əʊ ‖ oʊ, the second being associated with careful speech or unfamiliar words, thus **phonetics** fəʊ ˈnet ɪks ‖ foʊ ˈneţ ɪks as a little-used word but fə ˈnet ɪks ‖ -neţ- as an everyday word.

7 **o** also forms part of the digraphs **oa, oe, oi, oo, ou, ow, oy** (see below).

oa Spelling-to-sound

1 Where the spelling is the digraph **oa**, the pronunciation is regularly
əʊ ‖ oʊ as in **road** rəʊd ‖ roʊd or
ɔː as in **board** bɔːd ‖ bɔːrd (before **r**).

2 Note the exceptional words **broad** brɔːd (and derivatives **abroad**, **broaden**), **cupboard** ˈkʌb əd ‖ ˈkʌb ᵊrd.

3 **oa** is not a digraph in **oasis**, **Noah**, **coalescence**, **protozoa**.

oe Spelling-to-sound

1 Where the spelling is the digraph **oe**, the pronunciation is regularly
əʊ ‖ oʊ as in **toe** təʊ ‖ toʊ.

2 Exceptionally, it is
uː in **shoe** ʃuː, **canoe** kə ˈnuː
ʌ in **does** (from **do**) dʌz
iː in **phoenix** ˈfiːn ɪks and other words of Greek origin.

3 **oe** is not a digraph in **poem**, **poetic**, **coerce**, **Noel**.

oi, oy Spelling-to-sound

1 Where the spelling is one of the digraphs **oi** and **oy**, the pronunciation is regularly
ɔɪ as in **noise** nɔɪz, **boy** bɔɪ.

2 In words of French origin, the pronunciation is often
wɑː as in **patois** ˈpæt wɑː.

3 Occasionally **oi** is weak, as in the usual pronunciation of **tortoise** ˈtɔːt əs ‖ ˈtɔːrṭ əs.

4 Note the exceptional words **choir** ˈkwaɪ‿ə ‖ ˈkwaɪ‿ᵊr, **buoy** bɔɪ (AmE also ˈbuː i).

5 **oi** is not a digraph in **coincidence**, **soloist**.

oo Spelling-to-sound

1 Where the spelling is the digraph **oo**, the pronunciation is regularly either
uː as in **food** fuːd or ʊ as in **good** gʊd.
There is no rule, although ʊ is commoner before **k** (**book** bʊk). In some words both pronunciations are in use as in **room** ruːm or rʊm.

O

2 Less frequently, the pronunciation is
ʌ as in **blood** blʌd, **flood** flʌd.

3 Where the spelling is **oor**, the pronunciation is
ɔː as in **door** dɔː ‖ dɔːr or
ʊə ‖ ʊ as in **moor** mʊə ‖ mʊr (but BrE now often mɔː).

4 Note the exceptional word **brooch** brəʊtʃ ‖ broʊtʃ (AmE also bruːtʃ).

5 **oo** is not a digraph in **zoology**, **cooperate**.

ou, ow Spelling-to-sound

1 Where the spelling is one of the digraphs **ou** and **ow**, the pronunciation is regularly
aʊ as in **round** raʊnd, **cow** kaʊ.

2 Less frequently, it is
əʊ ‖ oʊ as in **soul** səʊl ‖ soʊl, **own** əʊn ‖ oʊn
ʌ as in **touch** tʌtʃ or
uː as in **group** gruːp.

3 Note also the exceptional **could** kʊd, **should** ʃʊd, **would** wʊd.

4 Where the spelling is the notorious **ough**, the pronunciation may be any of the following:
ɔː as in **thought** θɔːt
uː as in **through** θruː
aʊ as in **bough** baʊ
əʊ ‖ oʊ as in **though** ðəʊ ‖ ðoʊ
ʌf as in **rough** rʌf
ɒf ‖ ɔːf as in **cough** kɒf ‖ kɔːf
ə ‖ oʊ as in **thorough** ˈθʌr ə ‖ ˈθɜː oʊ.
There are also other possibilities in **lough**, **hiccough** (more usually written **loch**, **hiccup**).

5 Where the spelling is **our**, the pronunciation may be strong
aʊ ə as in **flour** ˈflaʊ‿ə ‖ ˈflaʊ‿ər
ɔː as in **four** fɔː ‖ fɔːr
ɜː ‖ ɜ˞ː as in **journey** ˈdʒɜːn i ‖ ˈdʒɜ˞ːn i
ʌr ‖ ɜ˞ː as in **courage** ˈkʌr ɪdʒ ‖ ˈkɜ˞ː ɪdʒ or
ʊə ‖ ʊ as in **tourist** ˈtʊər ɪst ‖ ˈtʊr əst (BrE also ɔː); also
ʊ in the exceptional **courier**, usually ˈkʊr i‿ə ‖ ˈkʊr i‿ər.
or weak ə ‖ ər as in **colour** (BrE spelling) ˈkʌl ə ‖ -ər.

6 In the adjective ending **-ous** the pronunciation is weak əs, as in **famous** ˈfeɪm əs, **jealousy** ˈdʒel əs i.

O, o əʊ ‖ oʊ **O's, o's, Os** əʊz ‖ oʊz —*Communications code name:* Oscar **ˈO ˌlevel**; **ˌO'V ˌlanguage**
O, O' *in family names* əʊ ‖ oʊ —*This prefix is unstressed; it is occasionally reduced to* ə
o' ə —*weak form only; see* of
Oadby ˈəʊd bi →ˈəʊb- ‖ ˈoʊd-
oaf əʊf ‖ oʊf **oafs** əʊfs ‖ oʊfs
oafish ˈəʊf ɪʃ ‖ ˈoʊf ɪʃ **~ly** li **~ness** nəs nɪs
Oahu, O'ahu əʊ ˈɑː huː ‖ oʊ ˈɑː huː ə ˈwɑː- —*Hawaiian* [o ˈʔa hu]
oak əʊk ‖ oʊk **oaks** əʊks ‖ oʊks **ˌOak ˈRidge**; **ˈoak tree**
oak-apple ˈəʊk ˌæp əl ‖ ˈoʊk-
oaken ˈəʊk ən ‖ ˈoʊk ən
Oakengates ˈəʊk ən geɪts →-ŋ- ‖ ˈoʊk-
Oakes əʊks ‖ oʊks
Oakham ˈəʊk əm ‖ ˈoʊk-
Oakhampton ˌəʊk ˈhæmp tən ◂ ‖ ˈoʊk ˌ· ·
Oakland ˈəʊk lənd ‖ ˈoʊk-
Oakleigh, Oakley ˈəʊk li ‖ ˈoʊk-
Oaks əʊks ‖ oʊks
Oaksey ˈəʊks i ‖ ˈoʊks i
oakum ˈəʊk əm ‖ ˈoʊk-
Oakville ˈəʊk vɪl ‖ ˈoʊk-
Oamaru ˈɒm ə ruː ‖ ˈɑːm-
OAP ˌəʊ eɪ ˈpiː ‖ ˌoʊ- **~s, ~'s** z
oar ɔː ‖ ɔːr oʊr *(= ore)* **oared** ɔːd ‖ ɔːrd oʊrd **oaring** ˈɔːr ɪŋ ˈoʊr- **oars** ɔːz ‖ ɔːrz oʊrz
oarfish ˈɔː fɪʃ ‖ ˈɔːr- ˈoʊr-
oarlock ˈɔː lɒk ‖ ˈɔːr lɑːk ˈoʊr- **~s** s
oars|man ˈɔːz |mən ‖ ˈɔːrz- ˈoʊrz- **~manship** mən ʃɪp **~men** mən **~woman** ˌwʊm ən **~women** ˌwɪm ɪn §-ən
oarweed ˈɔː wiːd ‖ ˈɔːr- ˈoʊr-
OAS ˌəʊ eɪ ˈes ‖ ˌoʊ-
oas|is, O~ əʊ ˈeɪs |ɪs §-əs ‖ oʊ- **~es** iːz
oast əʊst ‖ oʊst **ˈoast house**
oat əʊt ‖ oʊt **oats** əʊts ‖ oʊts
oatcake ˈəʊt keɪk ‖ ˈoʊt- **~s** s
oaten ˈəʊt ən ‖ ˈoʊt ən
Oates əʊts ‖ oʊts
oath əʊθ ‖ oʊθ **oaths** əʊðz əʊθs ‖ oʊðz oʊθs
oatmeal ˈəʊt miːəl ‖ ˈoʊt-
oats əʊts ‖ oʊts
OAU ˌəʊ eɪ ˈjuː ‖ ˌoʊ-
Oaxaca wə ˈhɑːk ə wɑː- —*Sp* [wa ˈxa ka]
Ob *river in USSR* ɒb ‖ oʊb ɑːb, ɔːb —*Russ* [ɔpʲ]
Obadiah ˌəʊb ə ˈdaɪ ə ‖ ˌoʊb-
Obama əʊ ˈbɑːm ə -ˈbæm- ‖ oʊ-
Oban ˈəʊb ən ‖ ˈoʊb-
obbligat|o ˌɒb lɪ ˈgɑːt |əʊ -lə- ‖ ˌɑːb lə ˈgɑːt̬ |oʊ **~i** iː **~os** əʊz ‖ oʊz
obcordate ɒb ˈkɔːd eɪt ‖ ɑːb ˈkɔːrd-
obduracy ˈɒb djʊr əs i ˈ·djər- ‖ ˈɑːb dʊr əs i ˈ·djʊr-, ˈ·dər-, ˈ·djər-
obdurate ˈɒb djʊr ət -djər-, -ɪt ‖ ˈɑːb dʊr ət -djʊr-, -dər-, -djər- **~ly** li **~ness** nəs nɪs
OBE ˌəʊ bi ˈiː ‖ ˌoʊ- **~s, ~'s** z
obeah ˈəʊb i ə ‖ ˈoʊb-
obedience ə ˈbiːd i ənts əʊ- ‖ oʊ- ə-
obedient ə ˈbiːd i ənt əʊ- ‖ oʊ- ə- **~ly** li
obeisanc|e əʊ ˈbeɪs ənts -ˈbiːs- ‖ oʊ- ə- **~es** ɪz əz
obelisk ˈɒb əl ɪsk §-əsk ‖ ˈɑːb ə lɪsk ˈoʊb- **~s** s
ob|elus ˈɒb |əl əs -ɪl- ‖ ˈɑːb- **~eli** ə laɪ ɪ-
Oberammergau ˌəʊb ər ˈæm ə gaʊ ‖ ˌoʊb ər ˈɑːm ər gaʊ —*Ger* [ˌʔoː bɐ ˈʔam ɐ gaʊ]
Oberland ˈəʊb ə lænd ‖ ˈoʊb ər- —*Ger* [ˈʔoː bɐ lant]
Oberlin ˈəʊb ə lɪn ‖ ˈoʊb ər- —*Fr* [ɔ bɛʁ lɛ̃]
Oberon ˈəʊb ər ən -ə rɒn ‖ ˈoʊb ə rɑːn
obese əʊ ˈbiːs ‖ oʊ- **~ness** nəs nɪs
obesity əʊ ˈbiːs ət i -ɪt- ‖ oʊ ˈbiːs ət̬ i
obey ə ˈbeɪ əʊ- ‖ oʊ- ə- **~ed** d **~ing** ɪŋ **~s** z
obfusc|ate ˈɒb fʌsk |eɪt -fə sk|eɪt ‖ ˈɑːb- ·ˈ·. **~ated** eɪt ɪd -əd ‖ eɪt̬ əd **~ates** eɪts **~ating** eɪt ɪŋ ‖ eɪt̬ ɪŋ
obfuscation ˌɒb fʌ ˈskeɪʃ ən -fə- ‖ ˌɑːb- **~s** z
ob-gyn, ob/gyn ˌəʊ biː ˈgaɪn -ˈdʒɪn; -ˌdʒiː waɪ ˈen ‖ ˌoʊb-
obi *'sash'* ˈəʊb i ‖ ˈoʊb i —*Jp* [ˈo bi] **~s** z
obi *'witchcraft'* ˈəʊb i ‖ ˈoʊb i
obit ˈəʊb ɪt ˈɒb-, §-ət ‖ ˈoʊb- —*as a shortening of* obituary, *also* əʊ ˈbɪt ‖ oʊ- **~s** s
obiter ˈɒb ɪt ə ˈəʊb-, -ət- ‖ ˈoʊb ət̬ ər ˈɑːb- **ˌobiter ˈdictum**
obituaris|e, obituariz|e ə ˈbɪtʃ u ə raɪz əʊ-, ɒ-, -ˈbɪt ju ˌ, -ˈbɪtʃ ə raɪz **~ed** d **~es** ɪz əz **~ing** ɪŋ
obituarist ə ˈbɪtʃ u ər ɪst əʊ-, ɒ-, -ˈbɪt ju ˌ, §-əst; -ˈbɪtʃ ər ɪst ‖ -u er əst **~s** s
obituar|y ə ˈbɪtʃ u ər |i əʊ-, ɒ-, -ˈbɪt ju ; -ˈbɪtʃ ər |i ‖ -u er |i **~ies** iz
object *v* əb ˈdʒekt §₍₁₎ɒb- ‖ ₍₁₎ɑːb- **~ed** ɪd əd **~ing** ɪŋ **~s** s
object *n* ˈɒb dʒekt -dʒɪkt ‖ ˈɑːb- **~s** s **ˈobject ˌlesson**
objecti|fy *v* əb ˈdʒekt ɪ |faɪ §₍₁₎ɒb-, -ə- ‖ ₍₁₎ɑːb- **~fied** faɪd **~fies** faɪz **~fying** faɪ ɪŋ
objection əb ˈdʒek ʃən §₍₁₎ɒb- ‖ ₍₁₎ɑːb- **~s** z
objectionab|le əb ˈdʒek ʃən əb |əl §₍₁₎ɒb- ‖ ₍₁₎ɑːb- **~ly** li
objectival ˌɒb dʒɪk ˈtaɪv əl ◂ -dʒek- ‖ ˌɑːb-
objective əb ˈdʒekt ɪv ₍₁₎ɒb- ‖ ₍₁₎ɑːb- —*When contrastively stressed, as opposed to* subjective, *usually* ˈɒb· · ‖ ˈɑːb· · **~ly** li **~ness** nəs nɪs **~s** z

objectivism əb ˈdʒekt ɪv ˌɪz əm ₍ₗ₎ɒb-, -əv- ‖ ₍ₗ₎ɑːb-
objectivity ˌɒb dʒek ˈtɪv ət i ˌ·dʒɪk-, -ɪt i ‖ ˌɑːb dʒek ˈtɪv əţ i
objector əb ˈdʒekt ə §₍ₗ₎ɒb- ‖ -ᵊr ₍ₗ₎ɑːb- **~s** z
object-oriented ˌɒb dʒekt ˈɔːr i ent ɪd ◂ ˌ·dʒɪkt-, -ˈɒr-, -əd ‖ ˌɑːb dʒɪkt ˈɔːr i enţ əd ◂
objet, objets ˈɒb ʒeɪ ‖ ˌɔːb ˈʒeɪ ◂ ˌɑːb- —*Fr* [ɔb ʒɛ]
ˌobjet(s) ˈd'art dɑː ‖ dɑːr —*Fr* [daːʁ]; **ˌobjet(s) ˈtrouvé(s)** ‖ **-trouˈvé(s)** ˈtruːv eɪ ‖ truː ˈveɪ —*Fr* [tʁu ve]
objur|gate ˈɒb dʒə |geɪt -dʒɜː- ‖ ˈɑːb dʒᵊr- **~gated** geɪt ɪd -əd ‖ geɪţ əd **~gates** geɪts **~gating** geɪt ɪŋ ‖ geɪţ ɪŋ
objurgation ˌɒb dʒə ˈgeɪʃ ᵊn -dʒɜː- ‖ ˌɑːb dʒᵊr- **~s** z
objurgatory ɒb ˈdʒɜːg ət‿ər i əb-; ˈɒb dʒə geɪt ər i, ˈdʒɜː-, ˌ·ˈ·· ‖ əb ˈdʒɝːg ə tɔːr i -toʊr i
oblast ˈɒb lɑːst -læst ‖ ˈɑːb- **~s** s —*Russ* [ˈɔ bləsʲtʲ]
oblate *n, adj* ˈɒb leɪt əʊ ˈbleɪt, ɒ- ‖ ˈɑːb leɪt ɑː ˈbleɪt, oʊ- **~ly** li **~ness** nəs nɪs **~s** s
ˌoblate ˈsphere
oblation ə ˈbleɪʃ ᵊn əʊ-, ɒ- ‖ oʊ- **~s** z
obli|gate ˈɒb lɪ |geɪt -lə- ‖ ˈɑːb- **~gated** geɪt ɪd -əd ‖ geɪţ əd **~gates** geɪts **~gating** geɪt ɪŋ ‖ geɪţ ɪŋ
obligation ˌɒb lɪ ˈgeɪʃ ᵊn -lə- ‖ ˌɑːb- **~s** z
obligator|y ə ˈblɪg ət‿ər |i ɒ- ‖ ə ˈblɪg ə tɔːr |i ɑː-, -toʊr i; ˈɑːb lɪg- **~ily** əl i ɪ li
oblig|e ə ˈblaɪdʒ əʊ- **~ed** d **~es** ɪz əz **~ing** ɪŋ
obligee ˌɒb lɪ ˈdʒiː -lə- ‖ ˌɑːb- **~s** z
obliging ə ˈblaɪdʒ ɪŋ əʊ- **~ly** li **~ness** nəs nɪs
obligor ˌɒb lɪ ˈgɔː -lə- ‖ ˌɑːb lə ˈgɔːr ˈ··· **~s** z
oblique ə ˈbliːk əʊ-, ɒ- ‖ oʊ-, -ˈblaɪk —*The AmE pronunciation* -ˈblaɪk *is esp. military.* **~ly** li **~ness** nəs nɪs **~s** s
oˌblique ˈangle
obliquit|y ə ˈblɪk wət |i əʊ-, ɒ-, -ɪt- ‖ -wəţ |i oʊ- **~ies** iz
oblite|rate ə ˈblɪt ə |reɪt ɒ- ‖ ə ˈblɪţ- oʊ- **~rated** reɪt ɪd -əd ‖ reɪţ əd **~rates** reɪts **~rating** reɪt ɪŋ ‖ reɪţ ɪŋ
obliteration ə ˌblɪt ə ˈreɪʃ ᵊn ɒ- ‖ ə ˌblɪţ- oʊ- **~s** z
oblivion ə ˈblɪv i‿ən ɒ-, əʊ- ‖ oʊ-, ɑː-
oblivious ə ˈblɪv i‿əs ɒ-, əʊ- ‖ oʊ-, ɑː- **~ly** li **~ness** nəs nɪs
oblong ˈɒb lɒŋ ‖ ˈɑːb lɔːŋ -lɑːŋ **~s** z
obloq|uy ˈɒb lək |wi ‖ ˈɑːb- **~uies** wiz
obnoxious əb ˈnɒk ʃəs ɒb- ‖ ɑːb ˈnɑːk- əb- **~ly** li **~ness** nəs nɪs
oboe ˈəʊb əʊ ‖ ˈoʊb oʊ **~s** z
ˌoboe d'aˈmore də ˈmɔːr i dɑː-, -eɪ
oboist ˈəʊb əʊ ɪst §-əst ‖ ˈoʊb oʊ- **~s** s
obol ˈɒb ɒl -ᵊl ‖ ˈɑːb ᵊl ˈoʊb- **~s** z
ob|olus ˈɒb |əl əs ‖ ˈɑːb- **~oli** ə laɪ
Obote əʊ ˈbəʊt eɪ -i ‖ oʊ ˈboʊt-
O'Boyle əʊ ˈbɔɪᵊl ‖ oʊ-
O'Brady *(i)* əʊ ˈbreɪd i ‖ oʊ-, *(ii)* əʊ ˈbrɔːd i ‖ oʊ- -ˈbrɑːd- —*In AmE, (i).*
Ó Briain əʊ ˈbriːn ‖ oʊ- —*Irish* [oː ˈbrʲɪənʲ]
O'Brien, O'Bryan əʊ ˈbraɪ‿ən ‖ oʊ-
obscene əb ˈsiːn ₍ₗ₎ɒb- ‖ ₍ₗ₎ɑːb- **~ly** li
obscenit|y əb ˈsen ət |i ɒb-, -ˈsiːn-, -ɪt- ‖ -əţ |i ɑːb- **~ies** iz
obscurantism ˌɒb skjuᵊ ˈrænt ˌɪz əm ˌ·skjə- ‖ əb ˈskjʊr ən ˌtɪz əm ɑːb-; ˌɑːb skju ˈræn- *(*)*
obscurantist ˌɒb skjuᵊ ˈrænt ɪst ◂ -skjə-, §-əst ‖ əb ˈskjʊr ənt əst ɑːb-; ˌɑːb skju ˈrænţ- *(*)* **~s** s
obscure *adj, v* əb ˈskjʊə ɒb-, -ˈskjɔː ‖ -ˈskjʊᵊr ɑːb- **~d** d **~ly** li **~ness** nəs nɪs **obscurer** əb ˈskjʊər ə ɒb-, -ˈskjɔːr- ‖ -ˈskjʊr ᵊr ɑːb- **obscures** əb ˈskjʊəz ɒb-, -ˈskjɔːz ‖ -ˈskjʊᵊrz ɑːb- **obscurest** əb ˈskjʊər ɪst ɒb-, -ˈskjɔːr-, -əst ‖ -ˈskjʊr əst ɑːb- **obscuring** əb ˈskjʊər ɪŋ ɒb-, -ˈskjɔːr- ‖ -ˈskjʊr ɪŋ ɑːb-
obscurit|y əb ˈskjʊər ət |i ɒb-, -ˈskjɔːr-, -ɪt- ‖ -ˈskjʊr əţ |i ɑːb- **~ies** iz
obse|crate ˈɒb sɪ |kreɪt -sə- ‖ ˈɑːb- **~crated** kreɪt ɪd -əd ‖ kreɪţ əd **~crates** kreɪts **~crating** kreɪt ɪŋ ‖ kreɪţ ɪŋ
obsecration ˌɒb sɪ ˈkreɪʃ ᵊn -sə- ‖ ˌɑːb- **~s** z
obsequies ˈɒb sək wiz -sɪk-; ɒb ˈsiːk- ‖ ˈɑːb-
obsequious əb ˈsiːk wi‿əs ɒb-, ⚠-ju‿əs ‖ ɑːb- **~ly** li **~ness** nəs nɪs
observab|le əb ˈzɜːv əb |ᵊl §₍ₗ₎ɒb- ‖ -ˈzɝːv- **~les** ᵊlz **~ly** li
observanc|e əb ˈzɜːv ᵊnᵗs §₍ₗ₎ɒb- ‖ -ˈzɝːv- **~es** ɪz əz
observant əb ˈzɜːv ᵊnt §₍ₗ₎ɒb- ‖ -ˈzɝːv- **~ly** li
observation ˌɒbz ə ˈveɪʃ ᵊn ˌɒb sə- ‖ ˌɑːbz ᵊr- ˌɑːb sᵊr- **~al** ‿əl **~ally** ‿əl i **~s** z
ˌobserˈvation car; **ˌobserˈvation post**
observator|y əb ˈzɜːv ətr |i §₍ₗ₎ɒb-, -ˈzɜːv ət ər |i ‖ -ˈzɝːv ə tɔːr |i -toʊr i **~ies** iz
observ|e əb ˈzɜːv §₍ₗ₎ɒb- ‖ -ˈzɝːv **~ed** d **~es** z **~ing/ly** ɪŋ /li
observer, O~ əb ˈzɜːv ə §₍ₗ₎ɒb- ‖ ˈzɝːv ᵊr **~s** z
obsess əb ˈses ɒb- ‖ ɑːb- **~ed** t **~es** ɪz əz **~ing** ɪŋ
obsession əb ˈseʃ ᵊn ɒb- ‖ ɑːb- **~al** ‿əl **~s** z
obsessive əb ˈses ɪv ɒb- ‖ ɑːb- **~ly** li **~ness** nəs nɪs **~s** z
obsessive-compulsive əb ˌses ɪv kəm ˈpʌls ɪv ◂ ɒb-, §-kɒm ˈ·-
obsidian əb ˈsɪd i‿ən ɒb-
obsolescence ˌɒb sə ˈles ᵊnᵗs ‖ ˌɑːb-
obsolescent ˌɒb sə ˈles ᵊnt ◂ ‖ ˌɑːb- **~ly** li
obsolete ˈɒb sə liːt ˌ·ˈ· ‖ ˌɑːb sə ˈliːt ◂ ˈ··· **~ly** li **~ness** nəs nɪs
obstacle ˈɒb stək ᵊl -stɪk- ‖ ˈɑːb- **~s** z
ˈobstacle course; **ˈobstacle race**
obstetric əb ˈstetr ɪk ɒb- ‖ ɑːb- **~al** ᵊl **~ally** ᵊl‿i **~s** s
obstetrician ˌɒb stə ˈtrɪʃ ᵊn -stɪ-, -ste- ‖ ˌɑːb- **~s** z
obstinacy ˈɒb stɪn əs i ˈ·stən- ‖ ˈɑːb-
obstinate ˈɒb stɪn ət -stən-, -ɪt ‖ ˈɑːb- **~ly** li **~ness** nəs nɪs
obstipation ˌɒb stɪ ˈpeɪʃ ᵊn -stə- ‖ ˌɑːb-
obstreperous əb ˈstrep ər əs ɒb- ‖ ɑːb- **~ly** li **~ness** nəs nɪs

obstruct əb ˈstrʌkt §(ˌ)ɒb- ‖ (ˌ)ɑːb- **~ed** ɪd əd **~ing** ɪŋ **~s** s
obstruction əb ˈstrʌk ʃᵊn §(ˌ)ɒb- ‖ (ˌ)ɑːb- **~ism** ˌɪz əm **~ist/s** ɪst/s §‿əst/s ‖ əst/s **~s** z
obstructive əb ˈstrʌkt ɪv §(ˌ)ɒb- ‖ (ˌ)ɑːb- **~ly** li **~ness** nəs nɪs
obstruent ˈɒb stru‿ənt ‖ ˈɑːb- **~s** s
obtain əb ˈteɪn §(ˌ)ɒb- ‖ (ˌ)ɑːb- **~ed** d **~er/s** ə/z ‖ ᵊr/z **~ing** ɪŋ **~s** z
obtainable əb ˈteɪn əb ᵊl §(ˌ)ɒb- ‖ (ˌ)ɑːb-
obtrud|e əb ˈtruːd ɒb- ‖ ɑːb- **~ed** ɪd əd **~es** z **~ing** ɪŋ
obtrusion əb ˈtruːʒ ᵊn ɒb- ‖ ɑːb- **~s** z
obtrusive əb ˈtruːs ɪv ɒb-, §-ˈtruːz- ‖ ɑːb- **~ly** li **~ness** nəs nɪs
obtu|rate ˈɒb tjuᵊ |reɪt -tʃə- ‖ ˈɑːb tə |reɪt -tjə- **~rated** reɪt ɪd -əd ‖ reɪţ əd **~rates** reɪts **~rating** reɪt ɪŋ ‖ reɪţ ɪŋ
obturation ˌɒb tjuᵊ ˈreɪʃ ᵊn ‖ ˌɑːb tə- -tjə- **~s** z
obturator ˈɒb tjuᵊ reɪt ə ‖ ˈɑːb tə reɪţ ᵊr ˈ-tjə- **~s** z
obtuse əb ˈtjuːs ɒb- ‖ əb ˈtuːs ɑːb-, -ˈtjuːs **~ly** li **~ness** nəs nɪs
obvers|e ˈɒb vɜːs ‖ ˈɑːb vɜ˞ːs ˌ-ˈ-, əb ˈ- **~es** ɪz əz **~ely** li
ob|vert ɒb |ˈvɜːt ‖ ɑːb |ˈvɜ˞ːt **~verted** ˈvɜːt ɪd -əd ‖ ˈvɜ˞ːţ əd **~verting** ˈvɜːt ɪŋ ‖ ˈvɜ˞ːţ ɪŋ **~verts** ˈvɜːts ‖ ˈvɜ˞ːts
obvi|ate ˈɒb vi |eɪt ‖ ˈɑːb- **~ated** eɪt ɪd -əd ‖ eɪţ əd **~ates** eɪts **~ating** eɪt ɪŋ ‖ eɪţ ɪŋ
obviative ˈɒb vi‿ət ɪv ‖ ˈɑːb vi eɪţ ɪv
obvious ˈɒb vi‿əs ‖ ˈɑːb- **~ly** li **~ness** nəs nɪs
obvolute ˈɒb və luːt -ljuːt, ˌ-ˈ- ‖ ˈɑːb-
obvolution ˌɒb və ˈluːʃ ᵊn -ˈljuːʃ- ‖ ˌɑːb-
O'Byrne əʊ ˈbɜːn ‖ oʊ ˈbɜ˞ːn
Ocado *tdmk* əʊ ˈkɑːd əʊ ‖ oʊ ˈkɑːd oʊ
O'Callaghan əʊ ˈkæl ə hən -gən, -hæn ‖ oʊ-
ocarina ˌɒk ə ˈriːn ə ‖ ˌɑːk- **~s** z
O'Casey əʊ ˈkeɪs i ‖ oʊ-
Occam ˈɒk əm ‖ ˈɑːk- **~s** z
ˌOccam's ˈrazor
occasion ə ˈkeɪʒ ᵊn §əʊ- **~ed** d **~ing** ‿ɪŋ **~s** z
occasional ə ˈkeɪʒ ᵊn‿əl §əʊ- **~ly** i
Occident, o~ ˈɒks ɪd ənt -əd- ‖ ˈɑːks- -ə dent
occidental, O~ ˌɒks ɪ ˈdent ᵊl ◂ -ə- ‖ ˌɑːks ə ˈdenţ ᵊl ◂ **~s** z
occipital ɒk ˈsɪp ɪt ᵊl -ət- ‖ ɑːk ˈsɪp əţ ᵊl **~s** z
occiput ˈɒks ɪ pʌt -ə-, -pət ‖ ˈɑːks- **~s** s
Occitan ˈɒks ɪt ən ‖ ˈɑːks- -ə tæn —*Fr* [ɔk si tɑ̃]
occlud|e ə ˈkluːd ɒ- ‖ ɑː- **~ed** ɪd əd **~es** z **~ing** ɪŋ
occlusal ə ˈkluːz ᵊl ɒ-, -ˈkluːs- ‖ ɑː-
occlusion ə ˈkluːʒ ᵊn ɒ- ‖ ɑː- **~s** z
occlusive ə ˈkluːs ɪv ɒ-, §-ˈkluːz- ‖ ɑː- **~s** z
occult *v* ə ˈkʌlt ɒ- ‖ ɑː- **~ed** ɪd əd **~ing** ɪŋ **~s** s
occult *adj, n* ˈɒk ʌlt ɒ ˈkʌlt, ə- ‖ ə ˈkʌlt ɑː-, oʊ-; ˈɑːk ʌlt
occultation ˌɒk ʌl ˈteɪʃ ᵊn -ᵊl- ‖ ˌɑːk- **~s** z
occultism ˈɒk ʌl ˌtɪz əm -ᵊl-; ɒ ˈkʌl-, ə- ‖ ə ˈkʌl- ɑː-; ˈɑːk ᵊl-
occultist ˈɒk ʌlt ɪst -ᵊlt-, §-əst; ɒ ˈkʌlt-, ə- ‖ ə ˈkʌlt əst ɑː-; ˈɑːk ᵊlt- **~s** s
occupanc|y ˈɒk jʊp ənᵗs |i ˈ-jəp- ‖ ˈɑːk jəp- **~ies** iz
occupant ˈɒk jʊp ənt -jəp- ‖ ˈɑːk jəp- **~s** s
occupation ˌɒk ju ˈpeɪʃ ᵊn -jə- ‖ ˌɑːk jə- **~s** z
occupational ˌɒk ju ˈpeɪʃ ᵊn‿əl ◂ ˌ-jə- ‖ ˌɑːk jə- **~ly** i
ˌoccuˌpational ˈtherapy
occu|py ˈɒk ju |paɪ -jə- ‖ ˈɑːk jə |paɪ **~pied** paɪd **~pier/s** paɪ‿ə/z ‖ paɪ‿ᵊr/z **~pies** paɪz **~pying** paɪ ɪŋ
oc|cur ə |ˈkɜː §əʊ- ‖ ə |ˈkɜ˞ː **~curred** ˈkɜːd ‖ ˈkɜ˞ːd **~curring** ˈkɜːr ɪŋ ‖ ˈkɜ˞ː ɪŋ **~curs** ˈkɜːz ‖ ˈkɜ˞ːz
occurrenc|e ə ˈkʌr ənᵗs §əʊ-, §-ˈkɜːr- ‖ ə ˈkɜ˞ː ənᵗs **~es** ɪz əz
ocean ˈəʊʃ ᵊn ‖ ˈoʊʃ ᵊn **~s** z
oceanari|um ˌəʊʃ ə ˈneər i‿|əm ‖ ˌoʊʃ ə ˈner- -ˈnær- **~a** ə **~ums** əmz
oceanfront ˈəʊʃ ᵊn frʌnt ‖ ˈoʊʃ- **~s** s
oceangoing ˈəʊʃ ᵊn ˌgəʊ ɪŋ ‖ ˈoʊʃ ᵊn ˌgoʊ ɪŋ
Oceani|a ˌəʊs i ˈɑːn i‿|ə ˌəʊʃ-, -ˈeɪn- ‖ ˌoʊʃ i ˈæn i‿|ə -ˈɑːn- **~an/s** ən/z ◂
oceanic, O~ ˌəʊʃ i ˈæn ɪk ◂ ˌəʊs- ‖ ˌoʊʃ-
Oceanid, o~ əʊ ˈsiː‿ən ɪd -ˈʃiː‿, §-əd ‖ oʊ- **~s** z
oceanographer ˌəʊʃ ə ˈnɒg rəf ə ˌəʊʃ i‿əˈ- ‖ ˌoʊʃ ə ˈnɑːg rəf ᵊr **~s** z
oceanographic ˌəʊʃ ən‿ə ˈgræf ɪk ◂ -i‿ən ə- ‖ ˌoʊʃ-
oceanography ˌəʊʃ ə ˈnɒg rəf i ˌəʊʃ i‿əˈ- ‖ ˌoʊʃ ə ˈnɑːg rəf i
Oceanside ˈəʊʃ ᵊn saɪd ‖ ˈoʊʃ-
Oceanus əʊ ˈsiː‿ən əs -ˈʃiː‿ ‖ oʊ-
ocell|us əʊ ˈsel |əs ‖ oʊ- **~i** aɪ iː
ocelot ˈɒs ə lɒt ˈəʊs-, -ɪ- ‖ ˈɑːs ə lɑːt ˈoʊs- **~s** s
och ɒx ‖ ɑːk
oche ˈɒk i ‖ ˈɑːk i **~s** z
ocher ˈəʊk ə ‖ ˈoʊk ᵊr **~s** z
ocherous ˈəʊk ər‿əs ‖ ˈoʊk-
Ochil ˈəʊk ᵊl ˈəʊx- ‖ ˈoʊk-
Ochiltree ˈɒk ᵊl triː ˈɒx-, ˈəʊk-, ˈəʊx-, -ɪl-, -tri ‖ ˈɑːk- ˈoʊk-
ochlocracy ɒ ˈklɒk rəs i ‖ ɑː ˈklɑːk-
ochone ɒx ˈəʊn ‖ ɔː ˈxoʊn
Ocho Rios *place in Jamaica* ˌəʊtʃ əʊ ˈriː əʊs ˌɒtʃ- ‖ ˌoʊtʃ oʊ ˈriː oʊs —*locally also* -ˈraɪ-
ochre ˈəʊk ə ‖ ˈoʊk ᵊr **~s** z
ochreous ˈəʊk ri‿əs -ər- ‖ ˈoʊk ər‿əs -ri‿əs
ochry ˈəʊk ər‿i ‖ ˈoʊk-
ocker, Ocker ˈɒk ə ‖ ˈɑːk ᵊr **~dom** dəm **~s** z
Ockham ˈɒk əm ‖ ˈɑːk-
Ockley ˈɒk li ‖ ˈɑːk-
o'clock ə ˈklɒk §əʊ- ‖ ə ˈklɑːk
O'Connell əʊ ˈkɒn ᵊl ‖ oʊ ˈkɑːn ᵊl
O'Conner, O'Connor əʊ ˈkɒn ə ‖ oʊ ˈkɑːn ᵊr
ocotillo ˌɒk ə ˈtiːl jəʊ -ˈtiː-, -ˈtiː əʊ ‖ ˌoʊk ə ˈtiːl joʊ -ˈtiː oʊ **~s** z
OCR ˌəʊ siː ˈɑː ‖ ˌoʊ siː ˈɑːr
Ocracoke ˈəʊk rə kəʊk ‖ ˈoʊk rə koʊk
oct- *comb. form before vowel* |ɒkt ‖ |ɑːkt — **octad** ˈɒkt æd ‖ ˈɑːkt-
octa- *comb. form with stress-neutral suffix* |ɒkt ə ‖ |ɑːkt ə — **octachord** ˈɒkt ə kɔːd ‖ ˈɑːkt ə kɔːrd *with stress-imposing suffix*

ɒk ˈtæ+ ‖ ɑːk ˈtæ+ —**octameter** ɒk ˈtæm ɪt ə -ət- ‖ ɑːk ˈtæm əṭ ᵊr
octad ˈɒkt æd ‖ ˈɑːkt- **~s** z
octagon ˈɒkt əg ən ‖ ˈɑːkt ə gɑːn *(*)* **~s** z
octagonal ɒk ˈtæg ᵊn əl ‖ ɑːk- **~ly** i
octahedral ˌɒkt ə ˈhiːdr əl ◂ -ˈhedr- ‖ ˌɑːkt-
octahedr|on ˌɒkt ə ˈhiːdr |ən -ˈhedr- ‖ ˌɑːkt- **~a** ə **~ons** ənz
octal ˈɒkt ᵊl ‖ ˈɑːkt ᵊl
octane ˈɒkt eɪn ‖ ˈɑːkt-
Octans ˈɒkt ænz ‖ ˈɑːkt-
octant ˈɒkt ənt ‖ ˈɑːkt- **~s** s
Octateuch ˈɒkt ə tjuːk §-tʃuːk ‖ ˈɑːkt ə tuːk -tjuːk
octave ˈɒkt ɪv §-əv, -eɪv ‖ ˈɑːkt- *—Generally* -ɪv, §-əv *as a musical or literary term, but* -eɪv *in the sense 'period of eight days'* **~s** z
Octavia ɒk ˈteɪv i‿ə -ˈtɑːv- ‖ ɑːk-
Octavian ɒk ˈteɪv i‿ən -ˈtɑːv- ‖ ɑːk-
Octavius ɒk ˈteɪv i‿əs -ˈtɑːv- ‖ ɑːk-
octavo ɒk ˈteɪv əʊ -ˈtɑːv- ‖ ɑːk ˈteɪv oʊ -ˈtɑːv- **~s** z
octennial ɒk ˈten i‿əl ‖ ɑːk-
octet ɒk ˈtet ‖ ɑːk- **~s** s
octo- *comb. form with stress-neutral suffix* |ɒkt əʊ ‖ |ɑːkt ə —**octosyllable** ˈɒkt əʊ ˌsɪl əb ᵊl ˌ·ˈ·· ‖ ˈɑːkt ə-
October ɒk ˈtəʊb ə ‖ ɑːk ˈtoʊb ᵊr **~s** z
octodecimo ˌɒkt əʊ ˈdes ɪ məʊ -ə- ‖ ˌɑːkt oʊ ˈdes ə moʊ
octogenarian ˌɒkt əʊ dʒə ˈneər i‿ən ◂ ˌ· ·dʒɪ- ‖ ˌɑːkt ə dʒə ˈner- **~s** z
octopod ˈɒkt ə pɒd ‖ ˈɑːkt ə pɑːd **~s** z
oct|opus ˈɒkt |əp əs -|ə pʊs ‖ ˈɑːkt- **~opi** ə paɪ **~opuses** əp əs ɪz -pʊs-, -əz
octoroon ˌɒkt ə ˈruːn ‖ ˌɑːkt- **~s** z
octosyllabic ˌɒkt əʊ sɪ ˈlæb ɪk ◂ -sə'-- ‖ ˌɑːkt ə-
octosyllable ˈɒkt əʊ ˌsɪl əb ᵊl ˌ·ˈ·· ‖ ˈɑːkt oʊ-
octuple ˈɒkt jʊp ᵊl -jəp-, §-əp-; ɒk ˈtjuːp ᵊl ‖ ˈɑːkt ʊp ᵊl -jʊp-; ɑːk ˈtuːp-, -ˈtjuːp- **~s** z
ocular ˈɒk jʊl ə -jəl- ‖ ˈɑːk jəl ᵊr **~ly** li **~s** z
oculist ˈɒk jʊl ɪst -jəl-, §-əst ‖ ˈɑːk jəl əst **~s** s
oculogyric ˌɒk ju ləʊ ˈdʒɪr ɪk ◂ ˌ·jə- ‖ ˌɑːk jə loʊ-
oculomotor ˌɒk ju ləʊ ˈməʊt ə ◂ ˌ·jə- ‖ ˌɑːk jə loʊ ˈmoʊṭ ᵊr ◂
OD ˌəʊ ˈdiː ‖ ˌoʊ- **~'d, ~ed, ~'ed** d **~ing, ~'ing** ɪŋ **~s, ~'s** z
odalisk, odalisque ˈəʊd ə lɪsk ˈɒd-, →-ᵊl ɪsk ‖ ˈoʊd ᵊl ɪsk **~s** s
O'Daly əʊ ˈdeɪl i ‖ oʊ-
odd ɒd ‖ ɑːd **odder** ˈɒd ə ‖ ˈɑːd ᵊr **oddest** ˈɒd ɪst -əst ‖ ˈɑːd əst **odds** ɒdz ‖ ɑːdz
ˈodd ˈbod; ˌodd man ˈout; ˌodds and ˈends
oddball ˈɒd bɔːl →ˈɒb- ‖ ˈɑːd- -bɑːl **~s** z
Oddbins *tdmk* ˈɒd bɪnz →ˈɒb- ‖ ˈɑːd-
Oddfellow ˈɒd ˌfel əʊ ‖ ˈɑːd ˌfel oʊ **~s** z
Oddie ˈɒd i ‖ ˈɑːd i
oddish ˈɒd ɪʃ ‖ ˈɑːd ɪʃ
oddit|y ˈɒd ət |i -ɪt- ‖ ˈɑːd əṭ |i **~ies** iz
odd-job |man ˌɒd ˈdʒɒb |mən ‖ ˌɑːd ˈdʒɑːb- **~men** men
oddly ˈɒd li ‖ ˈɑːd li
oddment ˈɒd mənt →ˈɒb- ‖ ˈɑːd-
oddness ˈɒd nəs -nɪs ‖ ˈɑːd nəs **~es** ɪz əz
oddsmaker ˈɒdz ˌmeɪk ə ‖ ˈɑːdz ˌmeɪk ᵊr **~s** z
odds-on ˌɒdz ˈɒn ◂ ‖ ˌɑːdz ˈɑːn ◂ -ˈɔːn
-ode əʊd ‖ oʊd — **pentode** ˈpent əʊd ‖ -oʊd
ode əʊd ‖ oʊd **odes** əʊdz ‖ oʊdz
O'Dea *(i)* əʊ ˈdeɪ ‖ oʊ-, *(ii)* əʊ ˈdiː ‖ oʊ-
Odell *(i)* ˈəʊd ᵊl ‖ ˈoʊd ᵊl, *(ii)* əʊ ˈdel ‖ oʊ-
Odense ˈəʊd ᵊnᵗs ə ‖ ˈoʊd- *—Danish* [ˈoːʔ ðn̩ sə]
Odeon ˈəʊd i‿ən ‖ ˈoʊd- **~s** z
Oder ˈəʊd ə ‖ ˈoʊd ᵊr *—Ger* [ˈʔoː dɐ]
Oder-Neisse Line ˌəʊd ə ˈnaɪs ə laɪn ‖ ˌoʊd ᵊr-
Odessa əʊ ˈdes ə ‖ oʊ- *—Russ* [ʌ ˈdʲɛ sə]
Odets əʊ ˈdets ‖ oʊ-
Odette əʊ ˈdet ‖ oʊ- *—Fr* [ɔ dɛt]
Odeum, odeum əʊ ˈdiː‿əm ˈəʊd i‿əm ‖ oʊ ˈdiː əm ˈoʊd i‿əm
Odgers ˈɒdʒ əz ‖ ˈɑːdʒ ᵊrz
Odham ˈɒd əm ‖ ˈɑːd-
Odiham ˈəʊd i‿əm -həm ‖ ˈoʊd-
Odile əʊ ˈdiːᵊl ‖ oʊ-
Odin ˈəʊd ɪn §-ᵊn ‖ ˈoʊd-
odious ˈəʊd i‿əs ‖ ˈoʊd- **~ly** li **~ness** nəs nɪs
odium ˈəʊd i‿əm ‖ ˈoʊd-
Odo ˈəʊd əʊ ‖ ˈoʊd oʊ
Odoacer ˌɒd əʊ ˈeɪs ə ˌəʊd- ‖ ˌoʊd oʊ ˈeɪs ᵊr
O'Doherty əʊ ˈdɒx ət i -ˈdəʊ-, -ˈdɒ hət- ‖ oʊ ˈdɑː hᵊrṭ i -ˈdɔːrṭ i
odometer əʊ ˈdɒm ɪt ə ɒ-, -ət- ‖ oʊ ˈdɑːm əṭ ᵊr **~s** z
O'Donnell əʊ ˈdɒn ᵊl ‖ oʊ ˈdɑːn ᵊl
O'Donovan əʊ ˈdʌn əv ən -ˈdɒn- ‖ oʊ ˈdɑːn-
odontolog|ist ˌɒd ɒn ˈtɒl ədʒ ɪst ˌəʊd-, §-əst ‖ ˌoʊd ɑːn ˈtɑːl- ˌɑːd- **~ists** ɪsts §əsts **-y** i
odor ˈəʊd ə ‖ ˈoʊd ᵊr **~ed** d **~s** z
odoriferous ˌəʊd ə ˈrɪf ər əs ◂ ‖ ˌoʊd- **~ly** li **~ness** nəs nɪs
odorless ˈəʊd ə ləs -lɪs; ᵊl əs, -ɪs ‖ ˈoʊd ᵊr-
Odo-Ro-No *tdmk* ˌəʊd əʊ ˈrəʊn əʊ ‖ ˌoʊd ə ˈroʊn oʊ
odorous ˈəʊd ər əs ‖ ˈoʊd- **~ly** li **~ness** nəs nɪs
odour ˈəʊd ə ‖ ˈoʊd ᵊr **~ed** d **~s** z
odourless ˈəʊd ə ləs -lɪs; -ᵊl əs, -ɪs ‖ ˈoʊd ᵊr-
O'Dowd əʊ ˈdaʊd ‖ oʊ-
O'Dwyer əʊ ˈdwaɪ‿ə ‖ oʊ ˈdwaɪ‿ᵊr
Odysseus ə ˈdɪs juːs ɒ-, əʊ-, -ˈdɪs i‿əs ‖ oʊ ˈdɪs i‿əs -ˈdɪʃ-, ə ˈdɪs juːs
Odyssey, o~ ˈɒd əs i -ɪs- ‖ ˈɑːd- **~s** z
oec... *—see* **ec...**
OECD ˌəʊ iː siː ˈdiː ‖ ˌoʊ-
oecumenic ˌiːk ju ˈmen ɪk ◂ ˌek- ‖ ˌek jə- **~al/ly** ᵊl /ˌi
OED ˌəʊ iː ˈdiː ‖ ˌoʊ-
oedem|a i ˈdiːm |ə **~as** əz **~ata** ət ə ‖ əṭ ə
oedematous i ˈdiːm ət əs ‖ -əṭ əs
Oedipal, o~ ˈiːd ɪp ᵊl -əp- ‖ ˈed əp ᵊl ˈiːd- *(*)*

Oedipus 'iːd ɪp əs -əp- ‖ 'ed əp əs 'iːd-
'Oedipus ˌcomplex
oeil-de-boeuf ˌɜː i də 'bɜːf ˌ-jə- ‖ ˌʌd ə 'bʌf —*Fr* [œj də bœf]
oenology i 'nɒl ədʒ i ‖ -'nɑːl-
Oenone i 'nəʊn i ‖ i 'noʊn i
oenophile 'iːn əʊ faɪᵊl ‖ 'iːn ə- **~s** z
o'er ɔː 'əʊ ə ‖ ɔːr oʊr
oersted 'ɜːst ɪd -ed, -əd ‖ 'ɜːst əd —*Danish* Ørsted ['œʁ sdəð] **~s** z
oesophageal i ˌsɒf ə 'dʒiː‿əl ◂ ə-, ˌiːs ɒf ə'·- ‖ i ˌsɑːf- ˌiːs ə 'fædʒ i‿əl ◂
oesoph|agus i 'sɒf |əg əs ə- ‖ i 'sɑːf- **~agi** ə gaɪ -dʒaɪ **~aguses** əg əs ɪz -əz
oestradiol ˌiːs trə 'daɪ ɒl ˌes-, -əl; iː 'stræd i ɒl ‖ ˌes trə 'daɪ ɔːl -ɑːl, -oʊl
oestrogen 'iːs trədʒ ən 'es-, -trə dʒen ‖ 'es- **~s** z
oestrous, oestrus 'iːs trəs 'es- ‖ 'es- *(*)*
oeuvre 'ɜːv rə 'ɜːv ə ‖ 'ʊv rə 'ʊv ᵊr —*Fr* [œːvʁ]
of *strong form* ɒv ‖ ʌv ɑːv *(*), weak form* əv —*There is also an informal rapid-speech or nonstandard weak form, used before consonants only,* ə. *It is sometimes written* o'.
O'Faolain, O'Faoláin əʊ 'feɪl ən -'fæl-, -ɔɪn ‖ oʊ-
off ɒf ɔːf ‖ ɔːf ɑːf
'off chance; **ˌoff 'colour◂**; **ˌoff 'line◂**
off- ¦ɒf ¦ɔːf ‖ ¦ɔːf ¦ɑːf — **off-air** ˌɒf 'eə ◂ ‖ ˌɔːf 'eᵊr ◂ ˌɑːf-, -'æᵊr
Offa 'ɒf ə ‖ 'ɔːf ə 'ɑːf-
off-air ˌɒf 'eə ◂ ˌɔːf- ‖ ˌɔːf 'eᵊr ◂ ˌɑːf-
offal 'ɒf ᵊl ‖ 'ɔːf ᵊl 'ɑːf-
Offaly 'ɒf əl i ‖ 'ɔːf- 'ɑːf-
off-balance ˌɒf 'bæl ənᵗs ◂ ˌɔːf- ‖ ˌɔːf- ˌɑːf-
offbeat *adj* ˌɒf 'biːt ◂ ˌɔːf-, '· · ‖ ˌɔːf- ˌɑːf-
offbeat *n* 'ɒf biːt 'ɔːf- ‖ 'ɔːf- 'ɑːf- **~s** s
off-brand 'ɒf brænd 'ɔːf- ‖ 'ɔːf- 'ɑːf- **~s** z
off-Broadway ˌɒf 'brɔːd weɪ ◂ ˌɔːf- ‖ ˌɔːf- ˌɑːf-, -'brɑːd-
off-campus ˌɒf 'kæmp əs ◂ ˌɔːf- ‖ ˌɔːf- ˌɑːf-
off-centre, off-center ˌɒf 'sent ə ˌɔːf- ‖ ˌɔːf 'senṱ ᵊr ˌɑːf-
off-chance 'ɒf tʃɑːnᵗs 'ɔːf-, §-tʃænᵗs ‖ 'ɔːf tʃænᵗs 'ɑːf-
off-color, off-colour ˌɒf 'kʌl ə ◂ ˌɔːf- ‖ ˌɔːf 'kʌl ᵊr ◂ ˌɑːf-
offcut 'ɒf kʌt 'ɔːf- ‖ 'ɔːf- 'ɑːf- **~s** s
off-duty ˌɒf 'djuːt i ◂ ˌɔːf-, 'dʒuːt-, §-'duːt- ‖ ˌɔːf 'duːṱ i ◂ ˌɑːf-, -'djuːṱ-
Offenbach 'ɒf ᵊn bɑːk ‖ 'ɔːf- 'ɑːf- —*Fr* [ɔ fɛn bak], *Ger* ['ʔɔf ᵊn bax]
offenc|e ə 'fenᵗs §əʊ- **~eless** ləs lɪs **~es** ɪz əz
offend ə 'fend §əʊ- **~ed** ɪd əd **~er/s** ə/z ᵊr/z **~ing** ɪŋ **~s** z
offens|e ə 'fenᵗs §əʊ- —*but in AmE in the sporting meaning 'attack, attacking side' often* 'ɑːf enᵗs, 'ɔːf- **~eless** ləs lɪs **~es** ɪz əz
offensive ə 'fenᵗs ɪv əʊ- —*but in the sense 'relating to attack' also* 'ɒf enᵗs ɪv ‖ 'ɔːf-, 'ɑːf- **~ly** li **~ness** nəs nɪs **~s** z
offer 'ɒf ə ‖ 'ɔːf ᵊr 'ɑːf- **~ed** d **offering/s** 'ɒf ər‿ɪŋ/z ‖ 'ɔːf ər‿ɪŋ/z 'ɑːf- **~s** z
offertor|y 'ɒf ət‿ər |i ‖ 'ɔːf ᵊr tɔːr |i 'ɑːf-, -toʊr i **~ies** iz
off-glide 'ɒf glaɪd 'ɔːf- ‖ 'ɔːf- 'ɑːf- **~s** z
off-guard ˌɒf 'gɑːd ˌɔːf- ‖ ˌɔːf 'gɑːrd ˌɑːf-
offhand ˌɒf 'hænd ◂ ˌɔːf- ‖ ˌɔːf- ˌɑːf-
offhanded ˌɒf 'hænd ɪd ˌɔːf-, -əd ‖ ˌɔːf- ˌɑːf- **~ly** li **~ness** nəs nɪs
offic|e 'ɒf ɪs §-əs ‖ 'ɑːf əs 'ɔːf- **~es** ɪz əz
'office block; **'office boy**, **'office girl**; **'office hours**, ˌ· ·'·
office-bearer 'ɒf ɪs ˌbeər ə §-əs- ‖ 'ɑːf əs ˌber ᵊr **~s** z
officeholder 'ɒf ɪs ˌhəʊld ə §-əs- ‖ 'ɑːf əs ˌhoʊld ᵊr 'ɔːf- **~s** z
officer 'ɒf ɪs ə §-əs- ‖ 'ɑːf əs ᵊr 'ɔːf- **~ed** d **~s** z
official ə 'fɪʃ ᵊl §əʊ- **~dom** dəm **~s** z
officialese ə ˌfɪʃ ə 'liːz §əʊ-, ·ˌ· · '· ‖ 'liːs
officialis|e, officializ|e ə 'fɪʃ ə laɪz §əʊ- **~ed** d **~es** ɪz əz **~ing** ɪŋ
officially ə 'fɪʃ əl i §əʊ-
officiant ə 'fɪʃ i‿ənt §əʊ- **~s** s
offici|ate ə 'fɪʃ i |eɪt §əʊ- **~ated** eɪt ɪd -əd ‖ eɪṱ əd **~ates** eɪts **~ating** eɪt ɪŋ ‖ eɪṱ ɪŋ
officiation ə ˌfɪʃ i 'eɪʃ ᵊn §əʊ-
officious ə 'fɪʃ əs §əʊ- **~ly** li **~ness** nəs nɪs
offing 'ɒf ɪŋ 'ɔːf- ‖ 'ɔːf ɪŋ 'ɑːf-
offish 'ɒf ɪʃ 'ɔːf- ‖ 'ɔːf ɪʃ 'ɑːf- **~ly** li **~ness** nəs nɪs
off-key ˌɒf 'kiː ◂ ˌɔːf- ‖ ˌɔːf- ˌɑːf-
off-kilter ˌɒf 'kɪlt ə ◂ ˌɔːf- ‖ ɔːf 'kɪlt ᵊr ◂ ˌɑːf-
off-licenc|e 'ɒf ˌlaɪs ᵊnᵗs 'ɔːf-, ˌ·'· · ‖ 'ɔːf- 'ɑːf- **~es** ɪz əz
off-load ˌɒf 'ləʊd ˌɔːf- ‖ ˌɔːf 'loʊd ˌɑːf- **~ed** ɪd əd **~ing** ɪŋ **~s** z
off-message ˌɒf 'mes ɪdʒ ◂ ˌɔːf- ‖ ˌɔːf- ˌɑːf-
off-off-Broadway ˌɒf ɒf 'brɔːd weɪ ◂ ˌɔːf ɔːf- ‖ ˌɔːf ɔːf- ˌɑːf ɑːf-
off-peak ˌɒf 'piːk ◂ ˌɔːf- ‖ ˌɔːf- ˌɑːf-
off-piste ˌɒf 'piːst ◂ ˌɔːf- ‖ ˌɔːf- ˌɑːf-
offprint 'ɒf prɪnt 'ɔːf- ‖ 'ɔːf- 'ɑːf- **~s** s
off-putting 'ɒf ˌpʊt ɪŋ 'ɔːf-, ˌ·'· · ‖ 'ɔːf ˌpʊṱ ɪŋ 'ɑːf-
off-ramp 'ɒf ræmp 'ɔːf- ‖ 'ɔːf- 'ɑːf- **~s** s
off-road ˌɒf 'rəʊd ◂ ˌɔːf- ‖ ˌɔːf 'roʊd ◂ ˌɑːf-
offscouring 'ɒf skaʊᵊr ɪŋ 'ɔːf- ‖ 'ɔːf- 'ɑːf- **~s** z
off-screen ˌɒf 'skriːn ◂ ˌɔːf- ‖ ˌɔːf- ˌɑːf-
off-season *n* 'ɒf ˌsiːz ᵊn 'ɔːf- ‖ 'ɔːf- 'ɑːf-
off-season *adj* ˌɒf 'siːz ᵊn ◂ ˌɔːf- ‖ ˌɔːf- ˌɑːf-
offset *n* 'ɒf set 'ɔːf- ‖ 'ɔːf- 'ɑːf- **~s** s
off|set *v* ˌɒf |'set ˌɔːf-, '· · ‖ ˌɔːf- ˌɑːf- **~sets** 'sets **~setting** 'set ɪŋ ‖ 'seṱ ɪŋ
offshoot 'ɒf ʃuːt 'ɔːf- ‖ 'ɔːf- 'ɑːf- **~s** s
offshore ˌɒf 'ʃɔː ◂ ˌɔːf- ‖ ˌɔːf 'ʃɔːr ◂ ˌɑːf-, -'ʃoʊr
offsid|e ˌɒf 'saɪd ◂ ˌɔːf- ‖ ˌɔːf- ˌɑːf- **~er/s** ə/z ‖ ᵊr/z **~es** z
off-site ˌɒf 'saɪt ◂ ˌɔːf- ‖ ˌɔːf- ˌɑːf-
offspring 'ɒf sprɪŋ 'ɔːf- ‖ 'ɔːf- 'ɑːf-
offstage ˌɒf 'steɪdʒ ◂ ˌɔːf- ‖ ˌɔːf- ˌɑːf-
off-street ˌɒf 'striːt ◂ ˌɔːf- ‖ ˌɔːf- ˌɑːf-
ˌoff-street 'parking
off-the-cuff ˌɒf ðə 'kʌf ◂ ˌɔːf- ‖ ˌɔːf- ˌɑːf-

off-the-peg ˌɒf ðə ˈpeg ◂ ‖ ˌɔːf-ˌɑːf-
off-the-rack ˌɒf ðə ˈræk ◂ ˌɔːf- ‖ ˌɔːf-ˌɑːf-
off-the-record ˌɒf ðə ˈrek ɔːd ◂ ˌɔːf-, §-əd ‖ ˌɔːf ðə ˈrek ərd ◂ ˌɑːf-
off-the-shelf ˌɒf ðə ˈʃelf ◂ ‖ ˌɔːf- ˌɑːf-
off-the-shoulder ˌɒf ðə ˈʃəʊld ə ◂ ˌɔːf-, →-ˈʃɒʊld- ‖ ˌɔːf ðə ˈʃoʊld ər ◂
off-the-wall ˌɒf ðə ˈwɔːl ◂ ˌɔːf- ‖ ˌɔːf- ˌɑːf-, -ˈwɑːl
offtrack ˌɒf ˈtræk ◂ ˌɔːf- ‖ ˌɔːf- ˌɑːf-
off-white ˌɒf ˈwaɪt ◂ ˌɔːf-, -ˈhwaɪt ‖ ˌɔːf *h*waɪt ◂ ˌɑːf-
off-year ˈɒf jɪə ˈɔːf- ‖ ˈɔːf jɪr ˈɑːf-
Ofgas ˈɒf gæs ‖ ˈɔːf- ˈɑːf-
Ofgem ˈɒf dʒem ‖ ˈɔːf- ˈɑːf-
O'Fiaich əʊ ˈfiː ‖ oʊ- —*Irish* [oː ˈfʲiə]
Ofili ə ˈfiːl i
oflag ˈɒf læg -lɑːg ‖ ˈɑːf- ˈɔːf- —*Ger* [ˈʔɔf laːk]
O'Flaherty əʊ ˈflɑː hət i -ˈflæ-, -ət-; -ˈfleət i ‖ oʊ ˈflæ ərṭ i -ˈflerṭ i
O'Flynn əʊ ˈflɪn ‖ oʊ-
Ofsted ˈɒf sted ‖ ˈɑːf- ˈɔːf-
oft ɒft ɔːft ‖ ɔːft ɑːft
Oftel ˈɒf tel ‖ ˈɑːf- ˈɔːf-

OFTEN

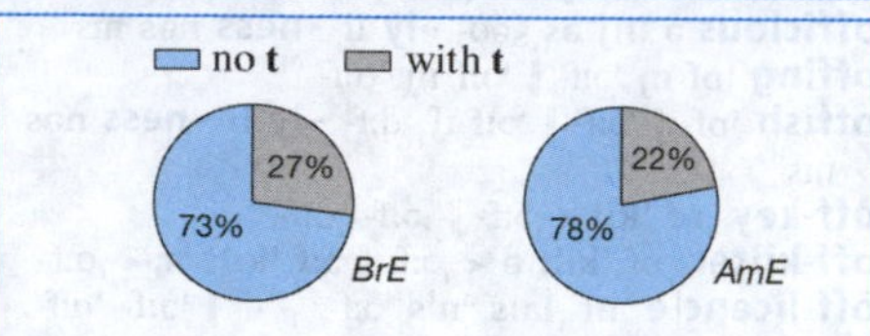

often ˈɒf ən ˈɒft ən, ˈɔːf ən, ˈɔːft ən ‖ ˈɔːf ən ˈɑːf-; ˈɔːft ən, ˈɑːft- —*Many speakers use both the form without* t *and the form with it. Preference polls, Br: no* t *73%, with* t *27%; with* ɒ *99%, with* ɔː *1%; AmE, no* t *78%, with* t *22%.* **~er** ‿ə ‖ ər **~est** ‿ɪst əst **~times** taɪmz
ofttimes ˈɒft taɪmz ˈɔːft- ‖ ˈɔːft- ˈɑːft-
Ofwat ˈɒf wɒt ‖ ˈɑːf wɑːt
Og ɒg ‖ ɔːg ɑːg
Ogaden ˌɒg ə ˈden ‖ ˌɑːg- ˌoʊg-
ogam ˈɒg əm ˈəʊg-; ɔːm ‖ ˈɑːg- ˈɔːg-, ˈoʊg-
Ogbomosho ˌɒg bə ˈməʊʃ əʊ ‖ ˌɑːg bə ˈmoʊʃ oʊ
Ogden, Ogdon ˈɒgd ən ‖ ˈɔːgd- ˈɑːgd-
ogee ˈəʊdʒ iː ‖ ˈoʊdʒ iː oʊ ˈdʒiː **~s** z
Ogen ˈəʊg en ‖ ˈoʊg-
Ogg ɒg ‖ ɔːg ɑːg
ogham ˈɒg əm ˈəʊg-; ɔːm ‖ ˈɑːg- ˈɔːg-, ˈoʊg-
Ogilvie, Ogilvy ˈəʊg əlv i ‖ ˈoʊg-
ogival əʊ ˈdʒaɪv əl ‖ oʊ-
ogive ˈəʊdʒ aɪv ‖ ˈoʊdʒ- **~s** z
og|le ˈəʊg |əl ˈɒg- ‖ ˈoʊg |əl ˈɑːg- — *Preference poll. BrE:* ˈəʊg- *76%,* ˈɒg- *24%.* **~led** əld **~les** əlz **~ling** əl‿ɪŋ
Oglethorpe ˈəʊg əl θɔːp ‖ ˈoʊg əl θɔːrp
Ogmore ˈɒg mɔː ‖ ˈɔːg mɔːr ˈɑːg-, -moʊr
ogonek ɒ ˈgɒn ek ə- ‖ oʊ ˈgɑːn- -ˈgoʊn- **~s** s —*Polish* [o ˈgo nek]
Ogoni əʊ ˈgəʊn i ‖ oʊ ˈgoʊn i **~land** lænd

OGLE

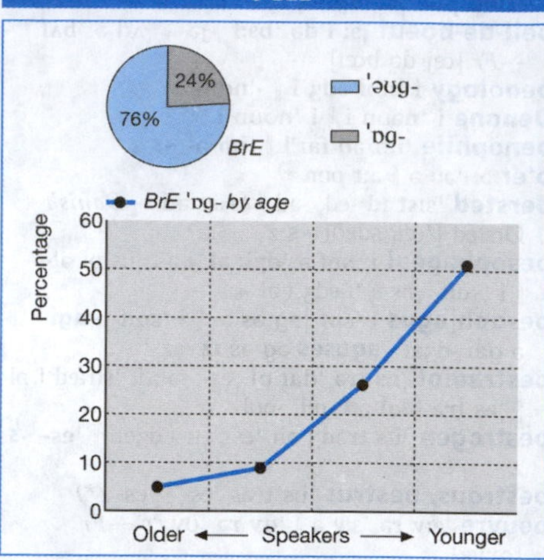

O'Grady əʊ ˈgreɪd i ‖ oʊ-
ogre ˈəʊg ə ‖ ˈoʊg ər **~s** z
ogreish ˈəʊg ər ɪʃ ‖ ˈoʊg-
ogress ˈəʊg rɪs -rəs, -res ‖ ˈoʊg ər‿əs **~es** ɪz əz
Ogwen ˈɒg wen ‖ ˈɔːg- ˈɑːg-
Ogwr ˈɒg ʊə ‖ ˈɔːg ʊr ˈɑːg- —*Welsh* [ˈo gur]
oh əʊ ‖ oʊ *(= O)* **oh's, ohs** əʊz ‖ oʊz
OH —*see* **Ohio**
O'Hagan əʊ ˈheɪg ən ‖ oʊ-
O'Halloran əʊ ˈhæl ər ən ‖ oʊ-
O'Hanlon əʊ ˈhæn lən ‖ oʊ-
O'Hara əʊ ˈhɑːr ə ‖ oʊ ˈhær ə -ˈher-
O'Hare əʊ ˈheə ‖ oʊ ˈheər -ˈhæər
O'Higgins əʊ ˈhɪg ɪnz §-ənz ‖ oʊ-
Ohio əʊ ˈhaɪ əʊ ‖ oʊ ˈhaɪ oʊ **~an/s** ən/z
ohm, Ohm əʊm ‖ oʊm —*Ger* [ʔoːm] **ohms** əʊmz ‖ oʊmz
ohmic ˈəʊm ɪk ‖ ˈoʊm-
ohmmeter ˈəʊm ˌmiːt ə ‖ ˈoʊm ˌmiːṭ ər **~s** z
OHMS ˌəʊ eɪtʃ em ˈes §ˌ· heɪtʃ- ‖ ˌoʊ-
oho əʊ ˈhəʊ ‖ oʊ ˈhoʊ
OHP ˌəʊ eɪtʃ ˈpiː ‖ ˌoʊ- **~s** z
oi ɔɪ
oick ɔɪk **oicks** ɔɪks
-oid ɔɪd — **planetoid** ˈplæn ə tɔɪd -ɪ-
oidi|um əʊ ˈɪd i |əm ‖ oʊ- **~a** ə
oik ɔɪk **oiks** ɔɪks
oil ɔɪəl **oiled** ɔɪəld **oiling** ˈɔɪəl ɪŋ **oils** ɔɪəlz
 ˈoil drum; **ˈoil paint**; **ˈoil ˌpainting**; **ˈoil slick**; **ˈoil ˌtanker**; **ˈoil well**
oil-based ˈɔɪəl beɪst
oil-bearing ˈɔɪəl ˌbeər ɪŋ ‖ -ˌber- -ˌbær-
oilbird ˈɔɪəl bɜːd ‖ -bɜ˞ːd **~s** z
oilcake ˈɔɪəl keɪk
oilcan ˈɔɪəl kæn **~s** z
oilcloth ˈɔɪəl klɒθ -klɔːθ ‖ -klɔːθ -klɑːθ
oiler ˈɔɪəl ə ‖ -ər **~s** z
oilfield ˈɔɪəl fiːəld **~s** z
oil-fired ˈɔɪəl ˌfaɪ‿əd ˌ·ˈ· ◂ ‖ -ˌfaɪ‿ərd
oil-free ˌɔɪəl ˈfriː ◂
oili... —*see* **oily**

oil|man ˈɔɪəl |mæn -mən **~men** men mən
oil-rich ˌɔɪəl ˈrɪtʃ ◂
oilrig ˈɔɪəl rɪɡ **~s** z
oilseed ˈɔɪəl siːd
oilskin ˈɔɪəl skɪn **~s** z
oilstone ˈɔɪəl stəʊn ‖ -stoʊn
oil|y ˈɔɪl |i **~ier** i‿ə ‖ i‿ər **~iest** i‿ɪst i‿əst **~iness** i nəs i nɪs
oink ɔɪŋk **oinks** ɔɪŋks
ointment ˈɔɪnt mənt **~s** s
Oireachtas ˈer əkθ əs ˈeər-, -əkt- —*Irish* [ˈɛ rʲəx təs]
Oise wɑːz —*Fr* [waːz]
Oistrakh ˈɔɪs trɑːk -trɑːx —*Russ* [ˈɔj strəx]
Ojibwa, Ojibway əʊ ˈdʒɪb weɪ -wə ‖ oʊ- **~s** z
OK, O.K. ₍ˌ₎əʊ ˈkeɪ ‖ ₍ˌ₎oʊ- **~'d** d **~'ing** ɪŋ **~'s** z
okapi əʊ ˈkɑːp i ‖ oʊ- **~s** z
Okavango ˌɒk ə ˈvæŋ ɡəʊ ◂ ‖ ˌoʊk ə ˈvæŋ ɡoʊ ◂ -ˈvɑːŋ-
 ˌOkaˌvango "Swamp
okay ₍ˌ₎əʊ ˈkeɪ ‖ ₍ˌ₎oʊ- **~ed** d **~ing** ɪŋ **~s** z
Okayama ˌəʊk ə ˈjɑːm ə ‖ ˌɒk- ‖ ˌoʊk- —*Jp* [o ˈka ja ma]
Okazaki ˌəʊk ə ˈzɑːk i ‖ ˌoʊk- —*Jp* [o ˌka dza ki]
Okeechobee ˌəʊk ɪ ˈtʃəʊb i ‖ ˌoʊk ə ˈtʃoʊb i
O'Keefe, O'Keeffe əʊ ˈkiːf ‖ oʊ-
Okefenokee ˌəʊk ɪf ɪ ˈnəʊk i ◂, -əf-, -əˈ- ‖ ˌoʊk əf ə ˈnoʊk i
 ˌOkefeˌnokee 'Swamp
Okehampton ˌəʊk ˈhæmpt ən ‖ ˈəʊk ˌ· ·
okey-doke ˌəʊk i ˈdəʊk ‖ ˌoʊk i ˈdoʊk
okey-dokey ˌəʊk i ˈdəʊk i ‖ ˌoʊk i ˈdoʊk i
Okhotsk əʊ ˈkɒtsk ɒ-, ˈ· · ‖ oʊ ˈkɑːtsk —*Russ* [ʌ ˈxɔtsk]
Okie ˈəʊk i ‖ ˈoʊk i **~s** z
Okina|wa ˌɒk i ˈnɑː |wə ˌəʊk-, -ə- ‖ ˌoʊk ə-ˈnaʊ ə —*Jp* [o ˌki na wa] **~wan/s** wən/z ◂
Oklahom|a ˌəʊk lə ˈhəʊm |ə ◂ ‖ ˌoʊk lə ˈhoʊm |ə **~an/s** ən/z ◂
 ˌOklaˌhoma 'City
okra ˈəʊk rə ˈɒk- ‖ ˈoʊk rə
Okri ˈɒk ri ‖ ˈɑːk-
-ol ɒl ‖ ɔːl ɑːl, oʊl — **glycerol** ˈɡlɪs ə rɒl ‖ -rɔːl -rɑːl, -roʊl
ol' *elided form of* old əʊl →ɒʊl ‖ oʊl
Olaf ˈəʊl əf -æf, -ɑːf ‖ ˈoʊl- —*Norw* [ˈˈuː laf]
Olav ˈəʊl æv -əv ‖ ˈoʊl-
Olave ˈɒl əv -ɪv, -eɪv ‖ ˈɑːl-
Olbers ˈɒlb əz ‖ ˈoʊlb ərz —*Ger* [ˈʔɔl bɐs]
Olbia ˈɒlb i‿ə ‖ ˈɑːlb- —*It* [ˈɔl bja]
old əʊld →ɒʊld ‖ oʊld **older** ˈəʊld ə →ˈɒʊld- ‖ ˈoʊld ər **oldest** ˈəʊld ɪst →ˈɒʊld-, -əst ‖ ˈoʊld əst
 ˌold 'age◂, ˌold age 'pension, ˌold age 'pensioner; ˌOld 'Bailey; ˌold boy *'former pupil'*, **ˌold 'boy** *'old chap'*, **ˌold-'boy ˌnetwork; ˌOld 'Catholic; ˌOld Church Slaˈvonic; ˌOld 'English ◂; ˌold 'flame; ˈold girl** *' 'former pupil'*; **ˌold 'guard,** ˈ· ·; **ˌold 'hand; ˌold 'hat; ˌold 'lady; ˌold 'lag; ˌold 'maid; ˌold 'man; ˌold 'master; ˌOld 'Nick; ˌold 'people's home; ˈold school** *'conservative attitudes'*, **ˌold 'school ◂** *'former place of learning'*, **ˌold school 'tie; ˌOld 'Testament ◂; ˌold 'wives' tale; ˌold 'woman; ˌOld 'World** ◂
Oldbury ˈəʊld bər‿i →ˈɒʊld- ‖ ˈoʊld ˌber i
Oldcastle ˈəʊld ˌkɑːs əl →ˈɒʊld-, §-ˌkæs- ‖ ˈoʊld ˌkæs əl
olde ˈəʊld i →ˈɒʊld ‖ ˈoʊld i
 ˌolde 'worlde ˈwɜːld i ‖ ˈwɜːld i
olden ˈəʊld ən ˈɒʊld- ‖ ˈoʊld ən
Oldenburg ˈəʊld ən bɜːɡ →ˈɒʊld-, →-əm- ‖ ˈoʊld ən bɜːɡ —*Ger* [ˈʔɔl dən bʊʁk, -bʊʁç]
old-established ˌəʊld ɪ ˈstæb lɪʃt ◂ →ˌɒʊld-, -ə- ‖ ˌoʊld-
old-fashioned ˌəʊld ˈfæʃ ənd ◂ →ˌɒʊld- ‖ ˌoʊld-
Oldfield ˈəʊld fiːəld →ˈɒʊld- ‖ ˈoʊld-
old-fogeyish, old-fogyish ˌəʊld ˈfəʊɡ i ɪʃ →ˌɒʊld- ‖ ˌoʊld ˈfoʊɡ-
old-growth ˌəʊld ˈɡrəʊθ ◂ →ˌɒʊld- ‖ ˌoʊld ˈɡroʊθ ◂
Oldham ˈəʊld əm →ˈɒʊld- ˈoʊld-
oldie ˈəʊld i →ˈɒʊld- ‖ ˈoʊld i **~s** z
oldish ˈəʊld ɪʃ →ˈɒʊld- ‖ ˈoʊld-
old-line ˌəʊld ˈlaɪn ◂ →ˌɒʊld- ‖ ˌoʊld-
old-maidish ˌəʊld ˈmeɪd ɪʃ ◂ →ˌɒʊld- ‖ ˌoʊld-
Oldman ˈəʊld mən →ˈɒʊld- ‖ ˈoʊld-
Oldrey ˈəʊldr i ˈɒʊldr- ‖ ˈoʊldr i
Oldsmobile *tdmk* ˈəʊldz məʊ ˌbiːəl →ˈɒʊldz- ‖ ˈoʊldz mə ˌbiːəl **~s** z
old-stager ˌəʊld ˈsteɪdʒ ə →ˌɒʊld- ‖ ˌoʊld ˈsteɪdʒ ər **~s** z
oldster ˈəʊld stə →ˈɒʊld- ‖ ˈoʊld stər **~s** z
old-style ˌəʊld ˈstaɪəl ◂ →ˌɒʊld- ‖ ˌoʊld-
old-tim|e ˌəʊld ˈtaɪm ◂ →ˌɒʊld-, ˈ· · ‖ ˌoʊld- **~er/s** ə/z ‖ ər/z
 ˌold-time 'dancing
Olduvai ˈɒld ə vaɪ ˈəʊld-, -u-, -ju- ‖ ˈɔːld- ˈɑːld-, ˈoʊld-
 ˌOlduvai 'Gorge
old-womanish ˌəʊld ˈwʊm ən ɪʃ ◂ →ˌɒʊld- ‖ ˌoʊld-
old-world ˌəʊld ˈwɜːld ◂ →ˌɒʊld- ‖ ˌoʊld ˈwɜːld ◂
-ole əʊl →ɒʊl ‖ oʊl — **benzole** ˈbenz əʊl →-ɒʊl ‖ -oʊl —*but note also words such as* hyperbole, systole *with* əl i
olé əʊ ˈleɪ ‖ oʊ-
oleaginous ˌəʊl i ˈædʒ ɪn əs -ən- ‖ ˌoʊl- **~ly** li **~ness** nəs nɪs
oleander ˌəʊl i ˈænd ə ‖ ˈoʊl i ænd ər ˌ·ˈ· · **~s** z
olearia ˌɒl i ˈeər i‿ə ˌəʊl- ‖ ˌoʊl i ˈer- -ˈær- **~s** z
O'Leary əʊ ˈlɪər i ‖ oʊ ˈlɪr i
oleaster ˌəʊl i ˈæst ə ‖ ˈoʊl i æst ər ˌ·ˈ· · **~s** z
oleate ˈəʊl i eɪt ‖ ˈoʊl- **~s** s
olecranon əʊ ˈlek rə nɒn ˌəʊl ɪ ˈkreɪn ən, -ə- ‖ oʊ ˈlek rə nɑːn
olefin ˈəʊl ɪ fɪn -ə-, -fiːn, -fən ‖ ˈoʊl- **~s** z
olefine ˈəʊl ɪ fiːn -ə-, -fɪn ‖ ˈoʊl- **~s** z
Oleg ˈəʊl eɡ ˈɒl- ‖ ˈoʊl- —*Russ* [ʌ ˈlʲek]
oleic əʊ ˈliː ɪk -ˈleɪ- ‖ oʊ-
oleo ˈəʊl i əʊ ‖ ˈoʊl i oʊ

oleo- *comb. form* ¦əʊl i əʊ ‖ ¦oʊl i oʊ — **oleoresin** ˌəʊl i əʊ ˈrez ɪn §-ᵊn ‖ ˌoʊl i oʊ ˈrezᵊn

oleograph ˈəʊl i͜ə grɑːf -græf ‖ ˈoʊl i͜ə græf **~s** s

olfaction ɒl ˈfæk ʃᵊn ‖ ɑːl- oʊl-

olfactory ɒl ˈfækt ər͜ i ‖ ɑːl- oʊl-

Olga ˈɒlg ə ‖ ˈoʊlg ə —*Russ* [ˈɔlʲ gə]

Olifant ˈɒl ɪf ənt -əf- ‖ ˈɑːl-

oligarch ˈɒl ɪ gɑːk -ə- ‖ ˈɑːl ə gɑːrk ˈoʊl- **~s** s

oligarchic ˌɒl ɪ ˈgɑːk ɪk ◂ -ə- ‖ ˌɑːl ə ˈgɑːrk ɪk ◂ ˌoʊl-

oligarch|y ˈɒl ɪ gɑːk |i ˈ·ə-‖ ˈɑːl ə gɑːrk |i ˈoʊl- **~ies** iz

oligo- *comb. form with stress-neutral suffix* ¦ɒl ɪ gəʊ -ə- ‖ ¦ɑːl ɪ goʊ ¦oʊl- — **oligosaccharide** ˌɒl ɪ gəʊ ˈsæk ə raɪd ˌ·ə- ‖ ˌɑːl ɪ goʊ-, ˌoʊl-, -ər əd *with stress-imposing suffix* ˌɒl ɪ ˈgɒ+ -ə- ‖ ˌɑːl ə ˈgɑː+ ˌoʊl- — **oligopsony** ˌɒl ɪ ˈgɒps ən i ˌ·ə- ‖ ˌɑːl ə ˈgɑːps- ˌoʊl-

Oligocene ˈɒl ɪ gəʊ siːn ɒ ˈlɪg əʊ- ‖ ˈɑːl ɪ goʊ- ˈoʊl-; ə ˈlɪg ə-

oligomer ˌɒl ɪ ˈgəʊm ə ɒ ˈlɪg əm ə, ə-; ˈɒl ɪg əm ə, ˈ·əg- ‖ ə ˈlɪg əm ᵊr **~s** z

oligopol|y ˌɒl ɪ ˈgɒp əl |i ˌ·ə- ‖ ˌɑːl ə ˈgɑːp- **~ies** iz

olio ˈəʊl i əʊ ‖ ˈoʊl i oʊ **~s** z

Oliphant ˈɒl ɪf ənt -əf- ‖ ˈɑːl-

olivaceous ˌɒl ɪ ˈveɪʃ əs ◂ -ə- ‖ ˌɑːl-

olivary ˈɒl ɪv ər i ˈ·əv- ‖ ˈɑːl ə ver i

olive, Olive ˈɒl ɪv §-əv ‖ ˈɑːl ɪv -əv **~s, ~'s** z **ˈolive branch**; **ˌolive ˈdrab**; **ˌolive ˈoil**, ˈ·· ‖ ˈ· · ·

olivenite ɒ ˈlɪv ə naɪt əʊ-, ˈɒl ɪv- ‖ oʊ-

Oliver ˈɒl ɪv ə -əv- ‖ ˈɑːl əv ᵊr

Olivet ˈɒl ɪ vet -ə-; -ɪv ət, -ɪt ‖ ˈɑːl-

Olivetti *tdmk* ˌɒl ɪ ˈvet i -ə- ‖ ˌɑːl ə ˈveţ i —*It* [o li ˈvet ti]

Olivia ə ˈlɪv i͜ə ɒ-, əʊ- ‖ oʊ-

Olivier ə ˈlɪv i eɪ ɒ-, -ə ‖ oʊ-

olivine ˈɒl ɪ viːn -ə-, ˌ· ˈ·

olla podrida ˌɒl ə pə ˈdriːd ə ˌ· jə-, -pɒˈ-- ‖ ˌɑːl- ˌɔɪ- —*Sp* [ˌo ʎa po ˈðri ða, ˌo ja-]

Ollerenshaw *(i)* ˈɒl ər ən ʃɔː ‖ ˈɑːl- -ʃɑː, *(ii)* ˌɒl ə ˈren- ‖ ˌɑːl-

Ollerton ˈɒl ət ən ‖ ˈɑːl ᵊrt ᵊn

Ollie ˈɒl i ‖ ˈɑːl i

olm əʊlm →ɒʊlm, ɒlm ‖ oʊlm

Olmec ˈɒl mek ˈəʊl-, →ˈɒʊl- ‖ ˈoʊl-

Olney ˈəʊln i →ˈɒʊln- ‖ ˈoʊln i

olog|y ˈɒl ədʒ |i ‖ ˈɑːl- **~ies** iz —*see also* **-logy**

Olomouc ˈɒl ə maʊts -ɒ- ‖ ˈoʊl oʊ- —*Czech* [ˈo lo mouts]

oloroso ˌɒl ə ˈrəʊs əʊ ˌəʊl-, -ˈrəʊz- ‖ ˌoʊl ə ˈroʊs oʊ **~s** z —*Sp* [o lo ˈro so]

Olsen, Olson ˈəʊls ᵊn →ˈɒʊls- ‖ ˈoʊls-

Olwen ˈɒl wen -wɪn, §-wən ‖ ˈɑːl- —*Welsh* [ˈɔl wen]

Olwyn ˈɒl wɪn §-wən ‖ ˈɑːl-

Olympia ə ˈlɪmp i͜ə əʊ- ‖ oʊ-

Olympiad ə ˈlɪmp i æd əʊ- ‖ oʊ- **~s** z

Olympian ə ˈlɪmp i͜ən əʊ- ‖ oʊ- **~s** z

Olympic ə ˈlɪmp ɪk əʊ- ‖ oʊ- **~s** s **Oˌlympic ˈGames**

Olympus ə ˈlɪmp əs əʊ- ‖ oʊ-

Olynthus əʊ ˈlɪnᵗθ əs ‖ oʊ-ə-

om, Om əʊm ɒm ‖ oʊm ɔːm, ɑːm —*Skt* [oːm]

-oma ˈəʊm ə ‖ ˈoʊm ə — **melanoma** ˌmel ə ˈnəʊm ə ‖ -ˈnoʊm ə

Omagh ˈəʊm ə -ɑː ‖ ˈoʊm-

Omaha ˈəʊm ə hɑː ‖ ˈoʊm- -hɔː

O'Mahoney əʊ ˈmɑː ən i ‖ oʊ- ˌoʊ mə ˈhoʊn i

O'Malley *(i)* əʊ ˈmæl i ‖ oʊ-, *(ii)* -ˈmeɪl i

Oman *name of country* əʊ ˈmɑːn ‖ oʊ- —*Arabic* [ʕu ˈmaːn]

Oman *family name* ˈəʊm ən ‖ ˈoʊm-

Omani əʊ ˈmɑːn i ‖ oʊ- **~s** z

Omar ˈəʊm ɑː ‖ ˈoʊm ɑːr -ᵊr **ˌOmar Khayˈyam, ˌOmar Khayˈyám** kaɪ ˈæm -ˈɑːm ‖ kaɪ ˈjɑːm -ˈjæm

O'Mara əʊ ˈmɑːr ə ‖ oʊ-

omas|um əʊ ˈmeɪs |əm ‖ oʊ- **~a** ə

ombuds|man ˈɒm bʊdz |mən -bʌdz-, -mæn ‖ ˈɑːm- **~men** mən men

Omdurman ˌɒm dɜː ˈmɑːn -də-, -ˈmæn; ˈɒm də mən ‖ ˌɑːm dᵊr ˈmɑːn -dʊr- —*Arabic* [um durˈmaːn]

-ome əʊm ‖ oʊm — **phyllome** ˈfɪl əʊm ‖ -oʊm

O'Meara *(i)* əʊ ˈmɑːr ə ‖ oʊ-, *(ii)* -ˈmeər ə ‖ -ˈmer ə -ˈmær-, *(iii)* -ˈmɪər ə ‖ -ˈmɪr ə

OMEGA

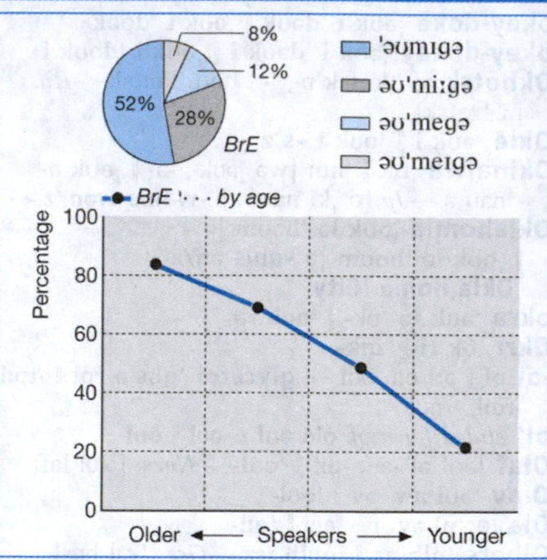

omega, Omega ˈəʊm ɪg ə -əg-; əʊ ˈmiːg ə, -ˈmeg-, -ˈmeɪg- ‖ oʊ ˈmeɪg ə -ˈmeg-, -ˈmiːg- *Preference poll, BrE:* ˈəʊm- *52% (born before 1942, 83%)*, -ˈmiːg- *28%*, -ˈmeg- *12%*, -ˈmeɪg- *8%*. **~s** z

omelet, omelette ˈɒm lət -lɪt, -let ‖ ˈɑːm- ˈɑːm əl ət **~s** s

omen ˈəʊm en -ən ‖ ˈoʊm ən **~s** z

oment|um əʊ ˈment |əm ‖ oʊ ˈmenţ |əm **~a** ə

omer, Omer ˈəʊm ə ‖ ˈoʊm ᵊr **~s** z

omerta, omertà əʊ ˈmɜːt ə -ˈmeət-; ˌəʊm ə ˈtɑː ‖ oʊ ˈmert ə ˌoʊm ᵊr ˈtɑː —*It* [o merˈta]

omicron əʊ ˈmaɪk rɒn -rən; ˈɒm ɪk- ‖ ˈɑːm ə krɑːn ˈoʊm- *(*)* **~s** z

OMINOUS

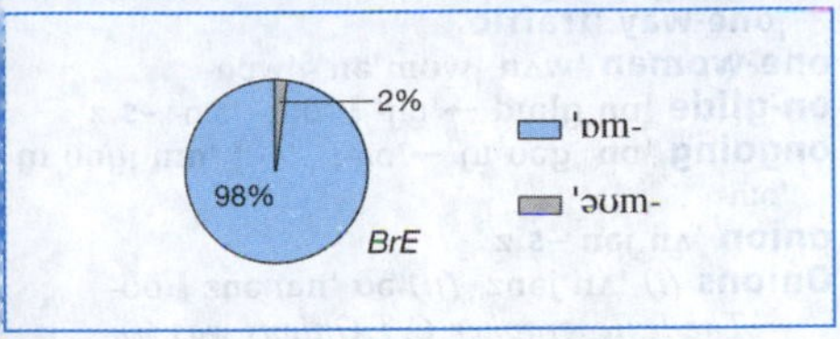

ominous ˈɒm ɪn əs ˈəʊm-, -ən- ‖ ˈɑːm- — *Preference poll, BrE:* ˈɒm- *98%,* ˈəʊm- *2%.* **~ly** li **~ness** nəs nɪs

omissible əʊ ˈmɪs əb ᵊl -ɪb- ‖ oʊ-

omission əʊ ˈmɪʃ ᵊn ‖ oʊ- ə- **~s** z

o|mit əʊ |ˈmɪt ‖ oʊ- ə- **~mits** ˈmɪts **~mitted** ˈmɪt ɪd -əd ‖ ˈmɪţ əd **~mitting** ˈmɪt ɪŋ ‖ ˈmɪţ ɪŋ

ommatidi|um ˌɒm ə ˈtɪd i‿|əm ‖ˌɑːm- **~a** ə **~al** əl

omni- *comb. form with stress-neutral suffix* ¦ɒm nɪ -nə ‖ ¦ɑːm- — **omnicompetent** ˌɒm nɪ ˈkɒmp ɪt ənt ◂ §ˌ·nə-, -ˈ·ət- ‖ ˌɑːm nɪ ˈkɑːmp ət ᵊnt ◂ ˌ·nə- *with stress-imposing suffix* ɒm ˈnɪ+ ‖ ɑːm- — **omnivorous** ɒm ˈnɪv ər‿əs ‖ ɑːm-

omnibus ˈɒm nɪb əs -nəb-; -nɪ bʌs, -nə- ‖ ˈɑːm- **~es** ɪz əz

omnifarious ˌɒm nɪ ˈfeər i‿əs ◂ ˌ·nə- ‖ ˌɑːm nə ˈfer- -ˈfær-

omnipotence ɒm ˈnɪp ət ənᵗs ‖ ɑːm ˈnɪp ət ᵊnᵗs

omnipotent ɒm ˈnɪp ət ənt ‖ ɑːm ˈnɪp ət ᵊnt **~ly** li

omnipresence ˌɒm nɪ ˈprez ᵊnᵗs -nə- ‖ˌɑːm-

omnipresent ˌɒm nɪ ˈprez ᵊnt ◂ -nə-‖ˌɑːm-

omniscience ɒm ˈnɪs i‿ənᵗs -ˈnɪʃ-, -ˈnɪʃ ᵊnᵗs ‖ ɑːm ˈnɪʃ ᵊnᵗs

omniscient ɒm ˈnɪs i‿ənt -ˈnɪʃ-, -ˈnɪʃ ᵊnt ‖ ɑːm ˈnɪʃ ᵊnt **~ly** li

omnium, O~ ˈɒm ni‿əm ‖ ˈɑːm-

omnium-gatherum ˌɒm ni‿əm ˈgæð ər əm ‖ ˌɑːm-

omnivore ˈɒm nɪ vɔː -nə- ‖ ˈɑːm nɪ vɔːr -voʊr **~s** z

omnivorous ɒm ˈnɪv ər‿əs ‖ ɑːm- **~ly** li **~ness** nəs nɪs

Omo *tdmk* ˈəʊm əʊ ‖ ˈoʊm oʊ

Omotic əʊ ˈmɒt ɪk ‖ oʊ ˈmɑːţ ɪk

omph|alos ˈɒmᵖf |ə lɒs ‖ ˈɑːmᵖf |əl əs **~ali** ə laɪ

Omsk ɒmᵖsk ‖ ɔːmᵖsk ɑːmᵖsk —*Russ* [ɔmsk]

on ɒn ‖ ɑːn ɔːn
ˈon side *'leg side'*

on- ¦ɒn ‖ ¦ɑːn ¦ɔːn — **on-going** ˌɒn ˈgəʊ ɪŋ ◂ ‖ ˈɑːn ˌgoʊ ɪŋ ɔːn-

-on ɒn, ən ‖ ɑːn, ən —*When this is a true suffix* (eˈlectron), *it is usually strong. When it is a mere ending* (ˈcommon) *it is usually weak, but there are a number of exceptions* (ˈcoupon) *and words where speakers disagree* (ˈlexicon). *In many cases BrE prefers a weak vowel, AmE a strong vowel* (ˈAmazon).

on-again off-again ˌɒn ə ˌgen ˈɒf ə ˌgen ◂ -ˌgeɪn·-ˌgeɪn, -ˈɔːf-ˌ·‖ ɑːn-,·ˈɔːf-ˌ· -ˈɑːf-ˌ·; ɔːn-ˌ·ˈɔːf-

onager ˈɒn ədʒ ə -əg- ‖ ˈɑːn ɪdʒ ᵊr **~s** z **onagri** ˈɒn ə graɪ ‖ ɑːn-

on-air ˌɒn ˈeə ◂ ‖ ˌɑːn ˈeᵊr ◂ ˌɔːn-, -ˈæᵊr

Onan ˈəʊn æn -ən ‖ ˈoʊn-

onanism ˈəʊn ə ˌnɪz əm æ- ‖ ˈoʊn-

Onassis əʊ ˈnæs ɪs §-əs ‖ oʊ- -ˈnɑːs-

on-board ˈɒn bɔːd ‖ ˈɑːn bɔːrd ˈɔːn-, -boʊrd

ONC ˌəʊ en ˈsiː ‖ ˌoʊ- **~s, ~'s** z

once wʌnᵗs §wɒnᵗs

once-over ˈwʌnᵗs ˌəʊv ə §ˈwɒnᵗs-, ˌ·ˈ·· ‖ -ˌoʊv ᵊr

oncer ˈwʌnᵗs ə §ˈwɒnᵗs- ‖ -ᵊr **~s** z

onchocerciasis ˌɒŋk əʊ sɜː ˈkaɪ‿əs ɪs ˌ·sə-, -ˈsaɪ-, §-əs ‖ ˌɑːŋk oʊ sɜː-

onco- *comb. form with stress-neutral suffix* ¦ɒŋk əʊ ‖ ¦ɑːŋk oʊ -ə — **oncocyte** ˈɒŋk əʊ saɪt ‖ ˈɑːŋk oʊ- -ə- *with stress-imposing suffix* ɒŋ ˈkɒ+ ‖ ɑːn ˈkɑː+ →ɑːŋ- — **oncology** ɒŋ ˈkɒl ədʒ i ‖ ɑːn ˈkɑːl- →ɑːŋ-

oncogene ˈɒŋk əʊ dʒiːn ‖ ˈɑːŋk oʊ- -ə- **~s** z

oncoming ˈɒn ˌkʌm ɪŋ →ˈɒŋ- ‖ ˈɑːn- ˈɔːn-

oncost ˈɒn kɒst →ˈɒŋ-, -kɔːst ‖ ˈɑːn kɔːst ˈɔːn-; -kɑːst **~s** s

OND ˌəʊ en ˈdiː ‖ ˌoʊ- **~s, ~'s** z

Ondaatje ɒn ˈdɑːtʃ ə ‖ ɑːn-

on-deck ɒn ˈdek ‖ ɑːn- ɔːn-

ONE

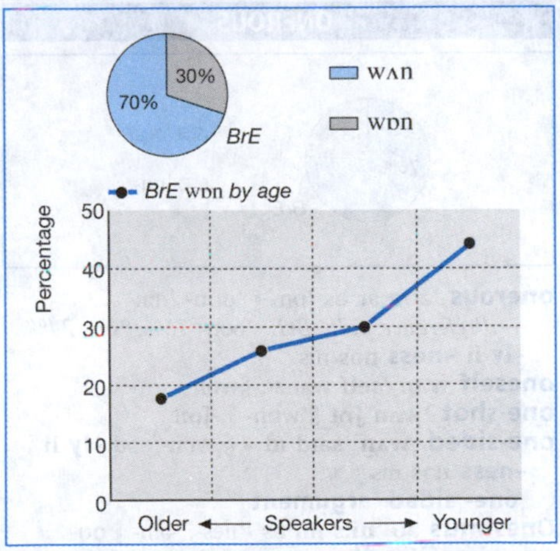

one wʌn §wɒn — *Preference poll, BrE:* wʌn *70%,* wɒn *30%.* —*In standard speech this word has no weak form. See, however,* ˈun.

ones, one's wʌnz §wɒnz

ˌone aˈnother

one- ¦wʌn §¦wɒn — **one-tailed** ˌwʌn ˈteɪᵊld ◂ §ˌwɒn-

one-acter ˌwʌn ˈækt ə §ˌwɒn- ‖ -ᵊr **~s** z

O'Neal əʊ ˈniːᵊl ‖ oʊ-

O

one-armed ˌwʌn ˈɑːmd ◂ §ˌwɒn- ‖ -ˈɑːrmd ◂

ˌ**one-armed ˈbandit**

one-day ˈwʌn deɪ §ˈwɒn-

one-dimensional ˌwʌn daɪ ˈmenᵗʃ ᵊnˌəl ◂ ˌ·dɪ-, ˌ·də-

one-eyed ˌwʌn ˈaɪd ◂ §ˌwɒn-

Onega ɒ ˈneɪɡ ə -ˈneɡ- ‖ oʊ ˈneɡ ə -ˈniːɡ; oʊn ˈjeɪɡ ə —*Russ* [ʌ ˈnʲɛ ɡə]

Onegin ɒ ˈneɪɡ ɪn əʊ-, ɒn ˈjeɪɡ-, -ən ‖ oʊ- ɑː-

one-horse ˌwʌn ˈhɔːs ◂ §ˌwɒn- ‖ -ˈhɔːrs ◂

ˌ**one-horse ˈtown**

Oneida əʊ ˈnaɪd ə ‖ oʊ- **~s** z

O'Neil, O'Neill əʊ ˈniːᵊl ‖ oʊ-

oneiromancy əʊ ˈnaɪᵊr ə mænᵗs i ‖ oʊ-

one-legged ˌwʌn ˈleɡ ɪd ◂ §ˌwɒn-, -əd, ˌ·ˈleɡd

one-liner ˌwʌn ˈlaɪn ə §ˌwɒn- ‖ -ᵊr **~s** z

one-man ˌwʌn ˈmæn ◂ →ˌwʌm-, §ˌwɒn-

ˌ**one-man ˈband**

oneness ˈwʌn nəs §ˈwɒn-, -nɪs

one-night ˌwʌn ˈnaɪt ◂ §ˌwɒn-

ˌ**one-night ˈstand**

one-off ˌwʌn ˈɒf ◂ §ˌwɒn- ‖ -ˈɔːf ◂ -ˈɑːf **~s** s

one-on-one ˌwʌn ɒn ˈwʌn §ˌwɒn·ˈwɒn ‖ -ɑːn- -ɔːn-

Oneonta ˌəʊn i ˈɒnt ə ‖ ˌoʊn i ˈɑːnt̬ ə

one-parent ˌwʌn ˈpeər ənt ◂ →ˌwʌm-, §ˌwɒn- ‖ -ˈper- -ˈpær-

ˌ**one-ˌparent ˈfamily**

one-percent ˈwʌn pə ˌsent →ˈwʌm-, §ˈwɒn- ‖ -pᵊr-

one-piece ˌwʌn ˈpiːs ◂ →ˌwʌm-, §ˌwɒn-

ˌ**one-piece ˈsnowsuit**

one-resource ˌwʌn ri ˈzɔːs ◂ §ˌwɒn-, -rə-, -ˈsɔːs ◂; ˈriː sɔːs ◂ ‖ -ˈriː sɔːrs ◂ -ri ˈsɔːrs ◂

O

ONEROUS

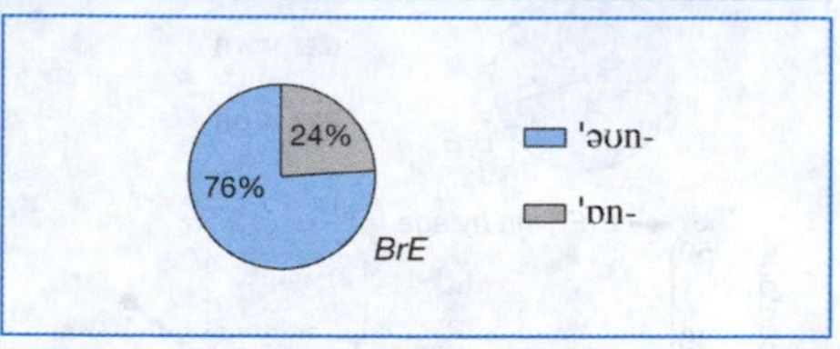

onerous ˈəʊn ər əs ˈɒn- ‖ ˈoʊn- ˈɑːn- — *Preference poll, BrE:* ˈəʊn- *76%,* ˈɒn- *24%.* **~ly** li **~ness** nəs nɪs

oneself wʌn ˈself wʌnz-, §wɒn-

one-shot ˈwʌn ʃɒt §ˈwɒn- ‖ -ʃɑːt

one-sided ˌwʌn ˈsaɪd ɪd ◂ §ˌwɒn-, -əd **~ly** li **~ness** nəs nɪs

ˌ**one-ˌsided ˈargument**

Onesimus əʊ ˈniːs ɪm əs -ˈnes-, -əm- ‖ oʊ-

one-size-fits-all ˌwʌn ˌsaɪz ˌfɪts ˈɔːl §ˌwɒn- ‖ -ˈɑːl

one-star ˌwʌn ˈstɑː ◂ ˌwɒn- ‖ -ˈstɑːr ◂

ˌ**one-star hoˈtel**

one-step ˈwʌn step §ˈwɒn-

one-stop ˈwʌn stɒp §ˈwɒn- ‖ -stɑːp

onetime ˈwʌn taɪm §ˈwɒn-

one-to-one ˌwʌn tə ˈwʌn ◂ §ˌwɒn·ˈwɒn, -tu-

one-track ˌwʌn ˈtræk ◂ §ˈwɒn-

ˌ**one-track ˈmind**

one-two ˌwʌn ˈtuː §ˌwɒn-

one-up ˌwʌn ˈʌp §ˌwɒn- **~ping** ɪŋ

one-upmanship (ˌ)wʌn ˈʌp mən ʃɪp §(ˌ)wɒn-

one-way ˌwʌn ˈweɪ ◂ §ˌwɒn-

ˌ**one-way ˈtraffic**

one-woman ˈwʌn ˌwʊm ən §ˈwɒn-

on-glide ˈɒn ɡlaɪd →ˈɒŋ- ‖ ˈɑːn- ˈɔːn- **~s** z

ongoing ˈɒn ˌɡəʊ ɪŋ →ˈɒŋ-, ˌ·ˈ·· ‖ ˈɑːn ˌɡoʊ ɪŋ ˈɔːn-

onion ˈʌn jən **~s** z

Onions *(i)* ˈʌn jənz, *(ii)* əʊ ˈnaɪˌənz ‖ oʊ- —*The lexicographer C. T. Onions was (i).*

onionskin ˈʌn jən skɪn

onium ˈəʊn iˌəm ‖ ˈoʊn-

onkaparinga, O~ ˌɒŋk ə pə ˈrɪŋ ɡə ‖ ˌɑːŋk-

online, on-line ˌɒn ˈlaɪn ◂ ‖ ˌɑːn- ˌɔːn-

ˌ**online ˈhelp**

onlooker ˈɒn ˌlʊk ə ‖ ˈɑːn ˌlʊk ᵊr ˈɔːn- **~s** z

only ˈəʊn li §-i ‖ ˈoʊn li *(!)*

on-message ˌɒn ˈmes ɪdʒ ‖ ˌɑːn- ˌɔːn-

o.n.o. —*see* **or near offer**

Ono ˈəʊn əʊ ‖ ˈoʊn oʊ —*Jp* [o ˌno]

on-off ˌɒn ˈɒf ◂ -ˈɔːf ◂ ‖ ˌɑːn ˈɔːf ◂ ˌɔːn-, -ˈɑːf ◂

onomastic ˌɒn əʊ ˈmæst ɪk ◂ ‖ ˌɑːn oʊ- -ə- **~s** s

onomatopoeia ˌɒn əʊ mæt ə ˈpiːˌə ‖ ˌɑːn ə mæt̬ ə ˈpiː ə ˌ·mɑːt̬-

onomatopoeic ˌɒn əʊ mæt ə ˈpiː ɪk ◂ ‖ ˌɑːn ə mæt̬- ˌ·mɑːt̬- **~ally** ᵊlˌi

Onondaga ˌɒn ən ˈdɑːɡ ə ◂ -ˈdɔːɡ- ‖ ˌɑːn- -ˈdɔːɡ- **~s** z

on-ramp ˈɒn ræmp ‖ ˈɑːn- ˈɔːn- **~s** s

onrush ˈɒn rʌʃ ‖ ˈɑːn- ˈɔːn- **~es** ɪz əz

onrushing ˈɒn ˌrʌʃ ɪŋ ‖ ˈɑːn- ˈɔːn-

on-screen ˌɒn ˈskriːn ◂ ‖ ˌɑːn- ˌɔːn-

onset ˈɒn set ‖ ˈɑːn- ˈɔːn- **~s** s

onshore ˌɒn ˈʃɔː ◂ ‖ ˌɑːn ˈʃɔːr ◂ ˌɔːn-, -ˈʃoʊr

onside ˌɒn ˈsaɪd ◂ ‖ ˌɑːn- ˌɔːn-

on-site ˌɒn ˈsaɪt ◂ ‖ ˌɑːn- ˌɔːn-

onslaught ˈɒn slɔːt ‖ ˈɑːn- ˈɔːn-; -slɑːt **~s** s

Onslow ˈɒnz ləʊ ‖ ˈɑːnz loʊ

on-stage ˌɒn ˈsteɪdʒ ◂ ‖ ˌɑːn- ˌɔːn-

onstream ˌɒn ˈstriːm ◂ ‖ ˌɑːn- ˌɔːn-

Ontario ɒn ˈteər i əʊ ‖ ɑːn ˈter i oʊ -ˈtær-

on-the-job ˌɒn ðə ˈdʒɒb ◂ ‖ ˌɑːn ðə ˈdʒɑːb ◂ ˌɔːn-

onto *before a consonant* ˈɒn tə ‖ ˈɑːn tə ˈɔːn-, *elsewhere* ˈɒn tu -tuː ‖ ˈɑːn tu ˈɔːn-, -tə

ontogenesis ˌɒnt əʊ ˈdʒen əs ɪs -ɪs·, §-əs ‖ ˌɑːnt̬ oʊ-

ontogenetic ˌɒnt əʊ dʒə ˈnet ɪk ◂ -dʒɪˈ· · ‖ ˌɑːnt̬ oʊ dʒə ˈnet̬ ɪk ◂ **~ally** ᵊlˌi

ontogen|y ɒn ˈtɒdʒ ən |i -ɪn- ‖ ɑːn ˈtɑːdʒ- **~ies** iz

ontological ˌɒnt ə ˈlɒdʒ ɪk ᵊl ◂ ˌɒnt ᵊl ˈɒdʒ- ‖ ˌɑːnt̬ ᵊl ˈɑːdʒ- **~ly** i

ontology ɒn ˈtɒl ədʒ i ‖ ɑːn ˈtɑːl-

onus ˈəʊn əs ‖ ˈoʊn əs **~es** ɪz əz

onward ˈɒn wəd ‖ ˈɑːn wᵊrd ˈɔːn- **~s** z

-onym *stress-imposing* ən ɪm §-əm ‖ ə nɪm — **acronym** ˈæk rən ɪm §-əm ‖ -ə nɪm

onyx ˈɒn ɪks ˈəʊn- ‖ ˈɑːn ɪks

oo-, oö- *comb. form with stress-neutral suffix* |əʊ ə ‖ |oʊ ə — **oocyte, oöcyte** ˈəʊ ə saɪt ‖ ˈoʊ- *with stress-imposing suffix* əʊ ˈɒ+ ‖ oʊ ˈɑː+ — **oogamy, oögamy** əʊ ˈɒg əm i ‖ oʊ ˈɑːg-
oodles ˈuːd əlz
oof uːf
ooh uː **oohed** uːd **oohing** ˈuː ɪŋ **oohs** uːz
ooh-la-la, oo-la-la ˌuː lɑː ˈlɑː
oolite ˈəʊ ə laɪt ‖ ˈoʊ- **~s** s
oolith ˈəʊ ə lɪθ ˈuː‿ ‖ ˈoʊ- **~s** s
oolitic ˌəʊ ə ˈlɪt ɪk ◂ ‖ ˌoʊ ə ˈlɪţ ɪk ◂
oological ˌəʊ ə ˈlɒdʒ ɪk əl ◂ ‖ ˌoʊ ə ˈlɑːdʒ-
oolog|y əʊ ˈɒl ədʒ |i ‖ oʊ ˈɑːl- **~ist/s** ɪst/s §əst/s
oolong, O~ ˈuː lɒŋ ·ˈ· ‖ -lɔːŋ -lɑːŋ
oompah ˈuːm pɑː ˈʊm- **~s** z
oomph ʊmpf uːmpf
Oona, Oonagh ˈuːn ə
oops ʊps wʊps, uːps
oops-a-daisy ˌʊps ə ˈdeɪz i ˌwʊps-, ˌuːps-, ˈ· · ˌ· · ‖ ˈ· · ˌ· ·
Oort ɔːt ‖ ɔːrt oʊrt —*Dutch* [oːrt]
Oosterhuis ˈəʊst ə haʊs ‖ ˈoʊst ər- —*Dutch* [ˈoː stər hœys]
ooze uːz **oozed** uːzd **oozes** ˈuːz ɪz -əz **oozing** ˈuːz ɪŋ
ooz|y ˈuːz |i **~ier** i‿ə ‖ i‿ər **~iest** i‿ɪst i‿əst **~ily** ɪ li əl i **~iness** i nəs i nɪs
op ɒp ‖ ɑːp
ˈop art
Op —*see* **Opus**
opacit|y əʊ ˈpæs ət |i -ɪt- ‖ oʊ ˈpæs əţ |i **~ies** iz
opal ˈəʊp əl ‖ ˈoʊp əl **~s** z
opalescence ˌəʊp ə ˈles ənts ˌɒp-, →ˌ·əl ˈes- ‖ ˌoʊp-
opalescent ˌəʊp ə ˈles ənt ◂ ˌɒp-, →ˌ·əl ˈes- ‖ ˌoʊp-
opaline ˈəʊp ə laɪn -liːn, →-əl aɪn, →-əl iːn ‖ ˈoʊp-
opaque əʊ ˈpeɪk ‖ oʊ- **~ly** li **~ness** nəs nɪs
op. cit. ˌɒp ˈsɪt ‖ ˌɑːp-
ope əʊp ‖ oʊp **oped** əʊpt ‖ oʊpt **opes** əʊps ‖ oʊps **oping** ˈəʊp ɪŋ ‖ ˈoʊp ɪŋ
OPEC ˈəʊp ek ‖ ˈoʊp-
op-ed ˌɒp ˈed ‖ ˌɑːp-
Opel *tdmk* ˈəʊp əl ‖ ˈoʊp əl —*Ger* [ˈʔoː pəl] **~s** z
op|en ˈəʊp |ən ‖ ˈoʊp |ən **~ened** ənd →md **~ener** ən‿ə ‖ ən‿ər **~enest** ən‿ɪst əst **~ening** ən‿ɪŋ **~ens** ənz →mz
ˈopen day; **ˌopen ˈhouse**; **ˌopen ˈletter**; **ˌopen ˈsandwich**; **ˈopen ˌseason**; **ˌopen ˈsecret**; **ˌopen ˈsesame**; **ˌOpen Uniˈversity**; **ˌopen ˈverdict**
open-air ˌəʊp ən ˈeə ◂ ‖ ˌoʊp ən ˈeər -ˈæər
open-and-shut ˌəʊp ən‿ən ˈʃʌt ◂ -ən‿ənd- ‖ ˌoʊp-
opencast ˈəʊp ən kɑːst →-m-, →-əŋ-, §-kæst ‖ ˈoʊp ən kæst
open-door ˌəʊp ən ˈdɔː ◂ →-m- ‖ ˌoʊp ən ˈdɔːr ◂ -ˈdoʊr
open-ended ˌəʊp ən ˈend ɪd ◂ -əd ‖ ˌoʊp- **~ness** nəs nɪs
opener ˈəʊp ən‿ə ‖ ˈoʊp ən‿ər **~s** z
open-eyed ˌəʊp ən ˈaɪd ◂ ‖ ˌoʊp-
open-faced ˌəʊp ən ˈfeɪst ◂ →-m- ‖ ˌoʊp-
open-handed ˌəʊp ən ˈhænd ɪd ◂ -əd ‖ ˌoʊp- ˈ· ˌ· · **~ly** li **~ness** nəs nɪs
open-heart ˌəʊp ən ˈhɑːt ◂ ‖ ˌoʊp ən ˈhɑːrt ◂
ˌopen-ˌheart ˈsurgery
open-hearted ˌəʊp ən ˈhɑːt ɪd ◂ -əd ‖ ˌoʊp ən ˈhɑːrţ əd ◂ ˈ· ˌ· ·
open-hearth ˌəʊp ən ˈhɑːθ ◂ ‖ ˌoʊp ən ˈhɑːrθ ◂
opening ˈəʊp ən‿ɪŋ ‖ ˈoʊp ən‿ɪŋ **~s** z
ˈopening time
opening-up ˌəʊp ən‿ɪŋ ˈʌp ‖ ˌoʊp-
open-jaw ˌəʊp ən ˈdʒɔː ◂ ‖ ˌoʊp- -ˈdʒɑː ◂
openly ˈəʊp ən li →-m- ‖ ˈoʊp-
open-minded ˌəʊp ən ˈmaɪnd ɪd ◂ →-m-, -əd ‖ ˌoʊp- ˈ· ˌ· · **~ly** li **~ness** nəs nɪs
open-mouthed ˌəʊp ən ˈmaʊðd ◂ →-m-, §-ˈmaʊθt ‖ ˌoʊp- ˈ· ˌ· ·
open-necked ˌəʊp ən ˈnekt ◂ ‖ ˌoʊp-
openness ˈəʊp ən nəs →-m-, -nɪs ‖ ˈoʊp-
open-plan ˌəʊp ən ˈplæn ◂ →-m- ‖ ˌoʊp-
Openshaw ˈəʊp ən ʃɔː →-m- ‖ ˈoʊp- -ʃɑː
open-toed ˌəʊp ən ˈtəʊd ◂ ‖ ˌoʊp ən ˈtoʊd ◂
openwork ˈəʊp ən wɜːk →-m- ‖ ˈoʊp ən wɜːk
opera ˈɒp ər‿ə ‖ ˈɑːp ər‿ə ⚠‿i —*also as an Italian word, It* [ˈɔː pe ra] *or as a French word, Fr* opéra [ɔ pe ʁa] —*but as the plural of* opus, *sometimes* ˈəʊp- ‖ ˈoʊp- **~s** z
ˌopéra ˈbouffe buːf —*Fr* [buf]; **ˌopera ˈbuffa** ˈbuːf ə —*It* [ˈbuf fa]; **ˌopéra coˈmique** kɒ ˈmiːk ‖ kɑː-; **ˈopera ˌglasses**; **ˈopera house**; **ˌopera ˈseria** ˈsɪər i‿ə ‖ ˈsɪr- —*It* [ˈsɛː rja]
operability ˌɒp ər‿ə ˈbɪl ət i -ɪt i ‖ ˌɑːp ər‿ə ˈbɪl əţ i
operable ˈɒp ər‿əb əl ‖ ˈɑːp-
operand ˈɒp ə rænd -ər ənd ‖ ˈɑːp- **~s** z
operant ˈɒp ər ənt ‖ ˈɑːp- **~s** s
ope|rate ˈɒp ə |reɪt ‖ ˈɑːp- **~rated** reɪt ɪd -əd ‖ reɪţ əd **~rates** reɪts **~rating** reɪt ɪŋ ‖ reɪţ ɪŋ
ˈoperating ˌsystem; **ˈoperating ˌtable**; **ˈoperating ˌtheatre**
operatic ˌɒp ə ˈræt ɪk ◂ ‖ ˌɑːp ə ˈræţ ɪk ◂ **~ally** əl‿i **~s** s
operation ˌɒp ə ˈreɪʃ ən ‖ ˌɑːp- **~s** z
ˌopeˈrations reˌsearch, -ˌresearch; **opeˈrations room**
operational ˌɒp ə ˈreɪʃ ən‿əl ◂ ‖ ˌɑːp- **~ly** i
ˌopeˌrational reˈsearch, -ˈresearch
operative ˈɒp ər‿ət ɪv -ə reɪt- ‖ ˈɑːp ər‿əţ ɪv -ə reɪţ- —*The pronunciation* -reɪt ɪv ‖ -reɪţ ɪv *is heard more often for the noun than for the adj.* **~s** z
operator ˈɒp ə reɪt ə ‖ ˈɑːp ə reɪţ ər **~s** z
opercul|um əʊ ˈpɜːk jʊl |əm ɒ-, -jəl- ‖ oʊ ˈpɜːk jəl |əm **~a** ə
operetta ˌɒp ə ˈret ə ‖ ˌɑːp ə ˈreţ ə **~s** z
operettist ˌɒp ə ˈret ɪst §-əst ‖ ˌɑːp ə ˈreţ əst **~s** s

O

Ophelia ə ˈfiːl i‿ə əʊ-, ɒ- ‖ oʊ-

ophicleide ˈɒf ɪ klaɪd §-ə- ‖ ˈɑːf- **~s** z

ophidian ɒ ˈfɪd i‿ən əʊ- ‖ oʊ- **~s** z

Ophir ˈəʊf ə ‖ ˈoʊf ᵊr

Ophiuchus ɒ ˈfjuːk əs ˌɒf i ˈuːk əs ‖ ˌɑːf i ˈjuːk əs ˌoʊf-

ophthalmia ɒf ˈθælm i‿ə ɒp- ‖ ɑːf- ɑːp-

ophthalmic ɒf ˈθælm ɪk ɒp- ‖ ɑːf- ɑːp-

ophthalmo- *comb. form* *with stress-neutral suffix* ɒf ¦θælm əʊ ɒp- ‖ ɑːf ¦θælm ə ɑːp- — **ophthalmoscopic** ɒf ˌθælm əʊ ˈskɒp ɪk ◂ ɒp- ‖ ɑːf ˌθælm ə ˈskɑːp ɪk ◂ ɑːp- *with stress-imposing suffix* ˌɒfθ æl ˈmɒ+ ˌɒpθ- ‖ ˌɑːfθ æl ˈmɑː+ ˌɑːpθ- — **ophthalmoscopy** ˌɒfθ æl ˈmɒsk əp i ˌɒpθ- ‖ ˌɑːfθ æl ˈmɑːsk- ˌɑːpθ-

ophthalmolog|ist ˌɒfθ æl ˈmɒl ədʒ |ɪst ˌɒpθ-, §-əst ‖ ˌɑːfθ æl ˈmɑːl- ˌɑːpθ- **~ists** ɪsts §əsts **~y** i

ophthalmoscope ɒf ˈθælm ə skəʊp ɒp- ‖ ɑːf ˈθælm ə skoʊp ɑːp- **~s** s

Ophüls ˈəʊf ᵊlz ‖ oʊ ˈfʊlz —*Ger* [ˈɔ fʏls]

-opia ˈəʊp i‿ə ‖ ˈoʊp i‿ə — **diplopia** dɪ ˈpləʊp i‿ə ‖ -ˈploʊp-

opiate ˈəʊp i‿ət -ɪt, -eɪt ‖ ˈoʊp- **~s** s

Opie ˈəʊp i ‖ ˈoʊp i

opin|e əʊ ˈpaɪn ‖ oʊ- **~ed** d **~es** z **~ing** ɪŋ

opinion ə ˈpɪn jən §əʊ- **~s** z **oˈpinion poll**

opinionated ə ˈpɪn jə neɪt ɪd §əʊ-, -əd ‖ -neɪṭ əd

opinion-maker ə ˈpɪn jən ˌmeɪk ə §əʊ- ‖ -ᵊr **~s** z

opioid ˈəʊp i ɔɪd ‖ ˈoʊp- **~s** z

opisthobranch əʊ ˈpɪs θə bræŋk ‖ ə- oʊ- **~s** s

opium ˈəʊp i‿əm ‖ ˈoʊp- **ˈopium den**; **ˈopium ˌpoppy**

Opodo *tdmk* əʊ ˈpəʊd əʊ ‖ oʊ ˈpoʊd oʊ

Oporto əʊ ˈpɔːt əʊ ‖ oʊ ˈpɔːrṭ oʊ -ˈpoʊrṭ- —*Port* [u ˈpor tu]

opossum ə ˈpɒs əm ‖ ə ˈpɑːs əm ˈpɑːs əm **~s** z

Oppenheim ˈɒp ən haɪm ‖ ˈɑːp-

Oppenheimer ˈɒp ən haɪm ə ‖ ˈɑːp ən haɪm ᵊr

oppidan ˈɒp ɪd ən §-əd- ‖ ˈɑːp- **~s** z

opponent ə ˈpəʊn ənt ‖ ə ˈpoʊn ənt **~s** s

opportune ˈɒp ə tjuːn →-tʃuːn, ˌ· ·ˈ· ‖ ˌɑːp ᵊr ˈtuːn ◂ -ˈtjuːn (*) **~ly** li **~ness** nəs nɪs

opportun|ism ˌɒp ə ˈtjuːn |ˌɪz əm →-ˈtʃuːn-, ˈ· · ·ˌ· · ‖ ˌɑːp ᵊr ˈtuːn- -ˈtjuːn- **~ist/s** ɪst/s ◂ §əst/s

opportunistic ˌɒp ə tjuː ˈnɪst ɪk ◂ →-tʃuːˈ-- ‖ ˌɑːp ᵊr tuː- -tjuːˈ-- **~ally** ᵊl‿i

opportunit|y ˌɒp ə ˈtjuːn ət |i →-ˈtʃuːn-, -ɪt i ‖ ˌɑːp ᵊr ˈtuːn əṭ |i -ˈtjuːn- **~ies** iz

opposable ə ˈpəʊz əb ᵊl ‖ ə ˈpoʊz-

oppos|e ə ˈpəʊz ‖ ə ˈpoʊz **~ed** d **~es** ɪz əz **~ing** ɪŋ

OPPOSITE

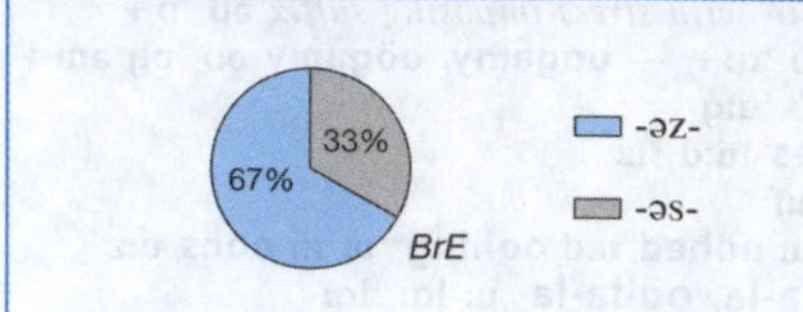

opposite ˈɒp əz ɪt -əs-, §-ət ‖ ˈɑːp- — *Preference poll, BrE: -əz- 67%, -əs- 33%.* **~ly** li **~ness** nəs nɪs **~s** s **ˌopposite ˈnumber**; **ˌopposite ˈsex**

opposition ˌɒp ə ˈzɪʃ ᵊn ‖ ˌɑːp- **~al** ‿əl ◂ **~s** z

oppress ə ˈpres §əʊ- **~ed** t **~es** ɪz əz **~ing** ɪŋ

oppression ə ˈpreʃ ᵊn §əʊ- **~s** z

oppressive ə ˈpres ɪv §əʊ- **~ly** li **~ness** nəs nɪs

oppressor ə ˈpres ə §əʊ- ‖ -ᵊr **~s** z

opprobrious ə ˈprəʊb ri‿əs ‖ ə ˈproʊb- **~ly** li **~ness** nəs nɪs

opprobrium ə ˈprəʊb ri‿əm ‖ ə ˈproʊb-

oppugn ə ˈpjuːn **~ed** d **~er/s** ə/z ‖ ᵊr/z **~ing** ɪŋ **~s** z

Oprah ˈəʊp rə ‖ ˈoʊp rə

Opren *tdmk* ˈəʊp rən -ren ‖ ˈɑːp- ˈoʊp-

opsonic ɒp ˈsɒn ɪk ‖ ɑːp ˈsɑːn ɪk

opsonin ˈɒps ən ɪn §-ən ‖ ˈɑːps-

opt ɒpt ‖ ɑːpt **opted** ˈɒpt ɪd -əd ‖ ˈɑːpt əd **opting** ˈɒpt ɪŋ ‖ ˈɑːpt ɪŋ **opts** ɒpts ‖ ɑːpts

Optacon *tdmk* ˈɒpt ək ən ‖ ˈɑːpt ə kɑːn

optative ˈɒpt ət ɪv ɒp ˈteɪt ɪv ‖ ˈɑːpt əṭ ɪv **~s** z

optic ˈɒpt ɪk ‖ ˈɑːpt ɪk **~s** s

optical ˈɒpt ɪk ᵊl ‖ ˈɑːpt- **~ly** ‿i **ˌoptical ˈcharacter recogˌnition**; **ˌoptical ˈfibre**; **ˌoptical ilˈlusion**

optician ɒp ˈtɪʃ ᵊn ‖ ɑːp- **~s** z

optim|a ˈɒpt ɪm |ə -əm- ‖ ˈɑːpt- **~al/ly** ᵊl /i

optimality ˌɒpt ɪ ˈmæl ət i ˌ-ə-, -ɪt i ‖ ˌɑːpt ə ˈmæl əṭ i

optimis... —*see* **optimiz...**

optimism ˈɒpt ɪ ˌmɪz əm -ə- ‖ ˈɑːpt-

optimist ˈɒpt ɪm ɪst -əm-, §-əst ‖ ˈɑːpt- **~s** s

optimistic ˌɒpt ɪ ˈmɪst ɪk ◂ -ə- ‖ ˌɑːpt- **~ally** ᵊl‿i

optimization ˌɒpt ɪm aɪ ˈzeɪʃ ᵊn ˌ-əm-, -ɪˈ-- ‖ ˌɑːpt ə- **~s** z

optimiz|e ˈɒpt ɪ maɪz -ə- ‖ ˈɑːpt- **~ed** d **~es** ɪz əz **~ing** ɪŋ

optim|um ˈɒpt ɪm |əm -əm- ‖ ˈɑːpt- **~a** ə **~ums** əmz

option ˈɒp ʃᵊn ‖ ˈɑːp ʃᵊn **~s** z

optional ˈɒp ʃᵊn‿əl ‖ ˈɑːp- **~ly** i

optoelectronic ˌɒpt əʊ ɪ ˌlek ˈtrɒn ɪk -əˌ--; ˌ· ·ˌel ek-, -ˌel ɪk-, -ˌɪl ek-, -ˌiːl ek- ‖ ˌɑːpt oʊ ɪ ˌlek ˈtrɑːn ɪk **~s** s

optometr|ist ɒp ˈtɒm ətr |ɪst -ɪtr-, §-əst ‖ ɑːp ˈtɑːm- **~ists** ɪsts §əsts **~y** i

opt-out ˈɒpt aʊt ‖ ˈɑːpt- **~s** s

Optrex *tdmk* ˈɒp treks ‖ ˈɑːp-

opul|ence ˈɒp jʊl |ənᵗs -jəl- ‖ ˈɑːp jəl- **~ent/ly** ənt /li

Optional sounds

1 **Optional sounds** are sounds that are pronounced by some speakers or on some occasions, but are omitted by other speakers or on other occasions. In the *Longman Pronunciation Dictionary* (LPD) they are indicated in two ways: by **italics** and by **raised letters** in smaller type.

2 Sounds shown in **italics** are sounds which the foreign learner is recommended to include (although native speakers sometimes omit them). They denote sounds that may optionally be **elided**.

lunch	lʌn*t*ʃ	Some say lʌntʃ, others say lʌnʃ. LPD recommends lʌntʃ.
bacon	ˈbeɪk *ə*n	Some say ˈbeɪk ən, others say ˈbeɪk n. LPD recommends ˈbeɪk ən.

3 Sounds shown with **raised letters** are sounds which the foreign learner is recommended to ignore (although native speakers sometimes include them). They denote sounds that may optionally be inserted.

fence	fenᵗs	Some say fens, others say fents. LPD recommends fens.
sadden	ˈsæd ᵊn	Some say ˈsæd n, others say ˈsæd ən. LPD recommends ˈsæd n.

4 The number of syllables, as shown by the spacing, is not affected by omitting an optional sound. Thus there are still two syllables in **bacon**, if pronounced ˈbeɪk n, and in **sadden**, if pronounced ˈsæd n. In such cases the n is termed **syllabic** (see SYLLABIC CONSONANTS).

5 An italic length mark, as in **agreeable** ə ˈgriː‿əb ᵊl, means that as COMPRESSION occurs the vowel changes to the corresponding short vowel, producing a diphthong. This process is called **smoothing** — see COMPRESSION 3.

opuntia əʊ ˈpʌnᵗʃ i‿ə ɒ- ‖ oʊ- -ˈpʌnᵗʃ ə **~s** z

opus ˈəʊp əs ˈɒp- ‖ ˈoʊp əs **opera** ˈəʊp ər ə ˈɒp- ‖ ˈoʊp- ˈɑːp- **~es** ɪz əz
  ˌOpus ˈDei ˈdeɪ iː

or ɔː ‖ ɔːr —*In AmE* ɔːr *is a strong form, paired with a weak form* ᵊr. *In BrE, however,* ɔː *normally has no weak form: there is only an occasional weak form* ə, *used chiefly in set phrases.*

-or ə ‖ ᵊr —*also occasionally for emphasis* ɔː ‖ ɔːr — **generator** ˈdʒen ə reɪt ə ‖ -reɪţ ᵊr

ora, Ora ˈɔːr ə ‖ ˈoʊr-

orach, orach|e ˈɒr ɪtʃ -ətʃ ‖ ˈɔːr ɪtʃ ˈɑːr- **~es** ɪz əz

oracle ˈɒr ək ᵊl -ɪk- ‖ ˈɔːr- ˈɑːr- **~s** z

oracular ɒ ˈræk jʊl ə ə-, ɔː-, -jəl- ‖ ɔː ˈræk jəl ᵊr oʊ-, ə- **~ly** li

oracy ˈɔːr əs i ˈɒr- ‖ ˈoʊr-

Oradea ɒ ˈrɑːd i‿ə ɔː- ‖ ɔː- —*Romanian* [o ˈra dea̯]

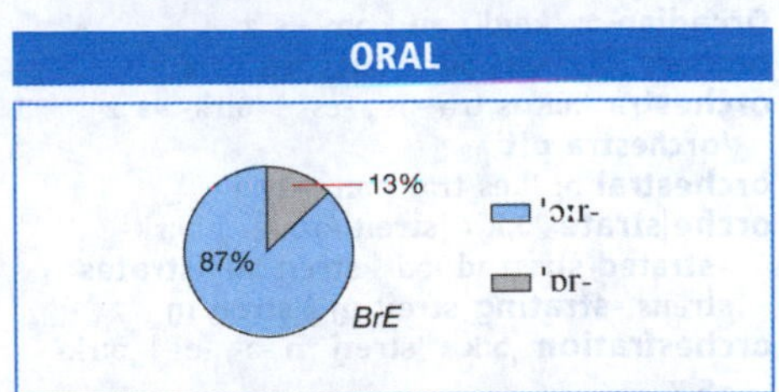

oral ˈɔːr əl §ˈɒr- ‖ ˈoʊr- — *Preference poll, BrE:* ˈɔːr- *87%,* ˈɒr- *13%.* **~ly** i **~s** z

Oran ə ˈræn ɔː-, -ˈrɑːn ‖ ɔː-, oʊ- —*Fr* [ɔ ʁɑ̃]

Orana ə ˈrɑːn ə

orang|e, O~ ˈɒr ɪn*d*ʒ -ən*d*ʒ ‖ ˈɔːr- ˈɑːr- — *Preference poll, AmE:* ˈɔːr- *80%,* ˈɑːr- *20%. See chart on p. 568.* **~es** ɪz əz
  ˈorange ˌblossom; **ˌOrange Free ˈState,** ˌ. . ˈ. .

orangeade ˌɒr ɪn*d*ʒ ˈeɪd -ən*d*ʒ- ‖ ˌɔːr- ˌɑːr- **~s** z

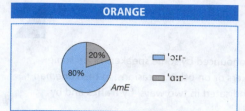

ORANGE

20% ˈɔːr-
80% ˈɑːr-
AmE

Orange|man ˈɒr ɪndʒ |mən -əndʒ-, -mæn ‖ ˈɔːr- ˈɑːr- **~men** mən men
oranger|y ˈɒr ɪndʒ ər‿|i ˈ·əndʒ- ‖ ˈɔːr- ˈɑːr- **~ies** iz
orangoutan, orangoutang, orangutan, orangutang ɔː ˈræŋ ə tæn ɒ-, ə-, -u-, -tæŋ, ˌ·ˌ·ˈ·; ˌ·ˈuː tæn, -ˈjuː-, -tɑːn ‖ ə- **~s** z
o|rate ɔː |ˈreɪt ɒ-, ə- ‖ oʊ- **~rated** ˈreɪt ɪd -əd ‖ ˈreɪţ əd **~rates** ˈreɪts **~rating** ˈreɪt ɪŋ ‖ ˈreɪţ ɪŋ
oration ə ˈreɪʃ ən ɔː-, ɒ- ‖ oʊ- **~s** z
orator ˈɒr ət ə ‖ ˈɔːr əţ ər ˈɑːr- **~s** z
oratorical ˌɒr ə ˈtɒr ɪk əl ◂ ‖ ˌɔːr ə ˈtɔːr- ˌɑːr ə ˈtɑːr- **~ly** ‿i
oratorio ˌɒr ə ˈtɔːr i əʊ ‖ ˌɔːr ə ˈtɔːr i oʊ ˌɑːr-, -ˈtoʊr- **~s** z
oratory, O~ ˈɒr ət‿ər i ‖ ˈɔːr ə tɔːr i ˈɑːr-, -toʊr i
orb ɔːb ‖ ɔːrb **orbs** ɔːbz ‖ ɔːrbz
Orbach ˈɔː bæk ‖ ˈɔːr bɑːk
orbed ɔːbd ‖ ɔːrbd —*in poetry also* ˈɔːb ɪd, -əd ‖ ˈɔːrb-
orbicular ɔː ˈbɪk jʊl ə -jəl- ‖ ɔːr ˈbɪk jəl ər
Orbison ˈɔːb ɪs ən -əs- ‖ ˈɔːrb-
orb|it ˈɔːb |ɪt §-ət ‖ ˈɔːrb |ət **~ited** ɪt ɪd §ət-, -əd ‖ əţ əd **~iting** ɪt ɪŋ §ət- ‖ əţ ɪŋ **~its** ɪts §əts ‖ əts
orbital ˈɔːb ɪt əl §-ət- ‖ ˈɔːrb əţ əl **~ly** i
orbitale ˌɔːb ɪ ˈtɑːl i -ə-, -ˈteɪl- ‖ ˌɔːrb-
orbiter ˈɔːb ɪt ə §-ət- ‖ ˈɔːrb əţ ər **~s** z
orc ɔːk ‖ ɔːrk **orcs** ɔːks ‖ ɔːrks
Orcadian ɔː ˈkeɪd i‿ən ‖ ɔːr- **~s** z
orchard, O~ ˈɔːtʃ əd ‖ ˈɔːrtʃ ərd **~s** z
orchestra ˈɔːk ɪs trə -əs-, -es- ‖ ˈɔːrk- **~s** z
ˈorchestra pit
orchestral ɔː ˈkes trəl ‖ ɔːr- **~ly** i
orche|strate ˈɔːk ɪ |streɪt -ə-, -e- ‖ ˈɔːrk- **~strated** streɪt ɪd -əd ‖ streɪţ əd **~strates** streɪts **~strating** streɪt ɪŋ ‖ streɪţ ɪŋ
orchestration ˌɔːk ɪ ˈstreɪʃ ən -ə-, -e- ‖ ˌɔːrk- **~s** z
orchestrina ˌɔːk ɪ ˈstriːn ə -ə- ‖ ˌɔːrk- **~s** z
orchestrion ɔː ˈkes tri‿ən ‖ ɔːr -ɑːn **~s** z
orchid ˈɔːk ɪd §-əd ‖ ˈɔːrk əd **~s** z
orchidaceous ˌɔːk ɪ ˈdeɪʃ əs §-ə- ‖ ˌɔːrk-
orchidectom|y ˌɔːk ɪ ˈdekt əm |i -ə- ‖ ˌɔːrk- **~ies** iz
orchil ˈɔːk ɪl ˈɔːtʃ-, §-əl ‖ ˈɔːrk- ˈɔːrtʃ-
orchis ˈɔːk ɪs §-əs ‖ ˈɔːrk-
orchitis ɔː ˈkaɪt ɪs §-əs ‖ ɔːr ˈkaɪţ əs
Orcus ˈɔːk əs ‖ ˈɔːrk əs
Orczy ˈɔːts i ˈɔːks i, ˈɔːk zi ‖ ˈɔːrts i
Ord ɔːd ‖ ɔːrd
ordain ₍ˌ₎ɔː ˈdeɪn ‖ ɔːr- **~ed** d **~ing** ɪŋ **~s** z
Orde ɔːd ‖ ɔːrd
ordeal ɔː ˈdiːəl ˈɔːd iːəl ‖ ɔːr- **~s** z
order ˈɔːd ə ‖ ˈɔːrd ər **~ed** d **ordering** ˈɔːd‿ər ɪŋ ‖ ˈɔːrd‿ər ɪŋ **~s** z
ˈorder ˌpaper
order|ly ˈɔːd ə|l i ‖ ˈɔːrd ər |li **~lies** liz **~liness** li nəs -nɪs
ordinaire ˌɔːd ɪ ˈneə -ə-, -ən ˈeə ‖ ˌɔːrd ən ˈeər -ˈæər —*Fr* [ɔʁ di nɛːʁ]
ordinal ˈɔːd ɪn əl -ən‿əl ‖ ˈɔːrd ən‿əl **~s** z
ordinanc|e ˈɔːd ɪn ənᵗs -ən‿ənᵗs ‖ ˈɔːrd ən‿ənᵗs **~es** ɪz əz
ordinand ˈɔːd ɪ nænd -ə-, -ən ænd, ˌ·ˈ·ˈ· ‖ ˈɔːrd ən ænd ˌ·ˈ·ˈ· **~s** z
ordinarily ˈɔːd ən ər‿əl i ˈ·ɪn-, ˈ·ən‿ər əl i, -ɪ li; ˌ·ˈ·er əl i, -ɪ li ‖ ˌɔːrd ən ˈer ə l i

ORDINARY

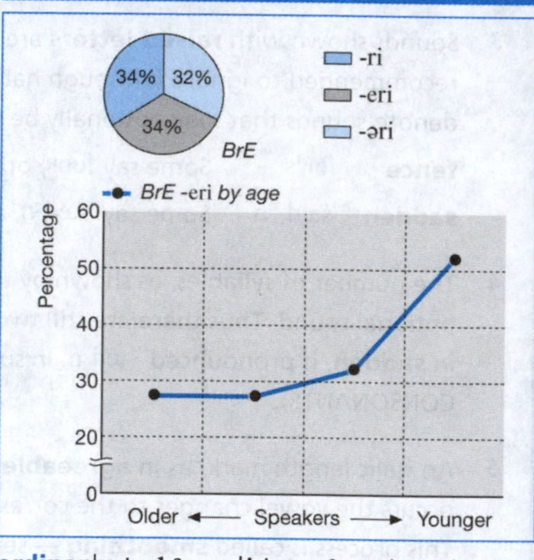

ordinar|y ˈɔːd ən ər‿|i ˈ·ɪn-, -ən‿ər i; -er i ‖ ˈɔːrd ən er |i — *Preference poll, BrE:* -ri *34%,* -əri *32%,* -eri *34%.* **~ies** iz **~iness** i nəs i nɪs
ˈordinary ˌlevel; **ˌordinary ˈseaman**
ordinate ˈɔːd ən‿ət -ɪn-, ɪt, -eɪt ‖ ˈɔːrd- **~s** s
ordination ˌɔːd ɪ ˈneɪʃ ən -ə-, -ən ˈeɪʃ- ‖ ˌɔːrd ən ˈeɪʃ ən **~s** z
ordines ˈɔːd ɪ niːz -ə- ‖ ˈɔːrd-
ordnance ˈɔːd nənᵗs ‖ ˈɔːrd-
ˌOrdnance ˈSurvey
ordo ˈɔːd əʊ ‖ ˈɔːrd oʊ **ordines** ˈɔːd ɪ niːz -ə- ‖ ˈɔːrd-
Ordovician ˌɔːd əʊ ˈvɪʃ i‿ən ◂ -ˈvɪs-, -ˈvɪʃ ən ‖ ˌɔːrd ə ˈvɪʃ ən ◂
ordure ˈɔːd jʊə ‖ ˈɔːrdʒ ər ˈɔːrd jʊr
Ordzhonikidze ˌɔːdʒ ɒn i ˈkɪdz i ˌən- ‖ ˌɔːrdʒ ɑːn- —*Russ* [ar dʒə nʲi ˈki dzʲi]
ore, Ore ɔː ‖ ɔːr oʊr **ores** ɔːz ‖ ɔːrz oʊrz
öre ˈɜːr ə ‖ ˈɜː ə —*Swedish* [ˈøː rə]
oread ˈɔːr i æd **~s** z
Örebro ˈɜːr ə bruː ‖ ˈɜː- —*Swedish* [œː rə ˈbruː]
orectic ɒ ˈrekt ɪk ə- ‖ ɔː-
oregano ˌɒr ɪ ˈɡɑːn əʊ -ə- ‖ ə ˈreɡ ə noʊ ɔː- (*)

Oregon 'ɒr ɪɡ ən -əɡ- ‖ 'ɔːr- 'ɑːr-, -ə ɡɑːn
ˌOregon 'grape; ˌOregon 'Trail
Oregonian ˌɒr ɪ 'ɡəʊn i‿ən ◂ ˌ-ə- ‖ ˌɔːr ə 'ɡoʊn- ˌɑːr- **~s** z
O'Reilly əʊ 'raɪl i ‖ oʊ-
Oreo *tdmk,* **oreo** 'ɔːr i əʊ ‖ -oʊ 'oʊr- **~s** z
Oresteia ˌɒr ɪ 'staɪ‿ə ˌɔːr-, -ə-, -'steɪ ə, -'stiː‿ə ‖ ˌɔːr- ˌoʊr-
Orestes ɒ 'rest iːz ɔː-, ə- ‖ ɔː-
orfe ɔːf ‖ ɔːrf **orfes** ɔːfs ‖ ɔːrfs
Orfeo ɔː 'feɪ əʊ 'ɔːf i əʊ ‖ ɔːr 'feɪ oʊ 'ɔːrf i oʊ —*It* [or 'fɛː o]
Orff ɔːf ‖ ɔːrf —*Ger* [ʔɔʁf]
Orford 'ɔːf əd ‖ 'ɔːrf ᵊrd
org *WWW and e-mail* ɔːɡ ‖ ɔːrɡ
organ 'ɔːɡ ən ‖ 'ɔːrɡ ən **~s** z
'organ ˌgrinder; 'organ pipe
organa 'ɔːɡ ən ə ‖ 'ɔːrɡ-
organd|ie, organd|y 'ɔːɡ ənd |i ‖ 'ɔːrɡ- **~ies** iz
organelle ˌɔːɡ ə 'nel ‖ ˌɔːrɡ- **~s** z
organic ɔː 'ɡæn ɪk ‖ ɔːr- **~ally** ᵊl‿i
organis... —*see* **organiz...**
organism 'ɔːɡ ə ˌnɪz əm -ən ˌɪz- ‖ 'ɔːrɡ- **~s** z
organist 'ɔːɡ ən ɪst §-əst ‖ 'ɔːrɡ- **~s** s
organization ˌɔːɡ ən aɪ 'zeɪʃ ᵊn -ɪ'-- ‖ ˌɔːrɡ ən‿ə- **~s** z
organizational ˌɔːɡ ən aɪ 'zeɪʃ ᵊn‿əl ◂ -ɪ'-- ‖ ˌɔːrɡ ən‿ə- **~ly** i
organiz|e 'ɔːɡ ə naɪz -ən aɪz ‖ 'ɔːrɡ- **~ed** d **~es** ɪz əz **~ing** ɪŋ
ˌorganized 'crime
organizer 'ɔːɡ ə naɪz ə -ən aɪz- ‖ 'ɔːrɡ ə naɪz ᵊr **~s** z
organo- *comb. form*
with stress-neutral suffix ɔː ¦ɡæn əʊ ¦ɔːɡ ən əʊ ‖ ɔːr ¦ɡæn ə ɔːrɡ ən ə — **organochlorine** ɔː ˌɡæn əʊ 'klɔːr iːn ˌɔːɡ ən- ‖ ɔːr ˌɡæn ə- ˌɔːrɡ ən-, -'kloʊr-, -ən
with stress-imposing suffix ˌɔːɡ ə 'nɒ+ ‖ ˌɔːrɡ ə 'nɑː+ — **organography** ˌɔːɡ ə 'nɒɡ rəf i ‖ ˌɔːrɡ ə 'nɑːɡ-
organogram ɔː 'ɡæn ə ɡræm ‖ ɔːr- **~s** z
organon 'ɔːɡ ə nɒn ‖ 'ɔːrɡ ə nɑːn **~s** z **organa** 'ɔːɡ ən ə ‖ 'ɔːrɡ-
organ|um 'ɔːɡ ən |əm ‖ 'ɔːrɡ- **~a** ə
organza ɔː 'ɡænz ə ‖ ɔːr-
orgasm 'ɔːɡ æz əm ‖ 'ɔːrɡ- **~ed** d **~ing** ˌɪŋ **~s** z
orgasmic ɔː 'ɡæz mɪk ‖ ɔːr- **~ally** ᵊl‿i
orgeat 'ɔːʒ ɑː ‖ 'ɔːrʒ- —*Fr* [ɔʁ ʒa]
orgi... —*see* **orgy...**
orgiastic ˌɔːdʒ i 'æst ɪk ◂ ‖ ˌɔːrdʒ- **~ally** ᵊl‿i
orgone 'ɔːɡ əʊn ‖ 'ɔːrɡ oʊn
Orgreave 'ɔː ɡriːv ‖ 'ɔːr-
org|y 'ɔːdʒ |i ‖ 'ɔːrdʒ |i **~ies** iz
Oriana ˌɔːr i 'ɑːn ə ˌɒr-
oriel, Oriel 'ɔːr i‿əl ‖ 'oʊr- **~s** z
ˌoriel 'window, ˌ. . . ˌ. .
ori|ent *v* 'ɔːr i |ent 'ɒr- ‖ 'oʊr- **~ented** ent ɪd -əd ‖ enţ əd **~enting** ent ɪŋ ‖ enţ ɪŋ **~ents** ents
orient, O~ *adj, n* 'ɔːr i‿ənt 'ɒr- ‖ 'oʊr-
ˌOrient Ex'press
oriental, O~ ˌɔːr i 'ent ᵊl ◂ ˌɒr- ‖ -'enţ ᵊl ◂ ˌoʊr- **~ism** ˌɪz əm **~ist/s** ɪst/s §əst/s ‖ əst/s **~s** z
orien|tate 'ɔːr i‿ən |teɪt 'ɒr-, -i en- ‖ 'oʊr- **~tated** teɪt ɪd -əd ‖ teɪţ əd **~tates** teɪts **~tating** teɪt ɪŋ ‖ teɪţ ɪŋ
orientation ˌɔːr i‿ən 'teɪʃ ᵊn ˌɒr-, -i en- ‖ ˌoʊr- **~s** z
orien|teer ˌɔːr i‿ən |'tɪə ˌɒr-, -i en|- ‖ -'tɪr ˌoʊr- **~teering** 'tɪər ɪŋ ‖ 'tɪr ɪŋ **~teered** 'tɪəd ‖ 'tɪrd **~teers** 'tɪəz ‖ 'tɪrd
orific|e 'ɒr əf ɪs -ɪf-, §-əs ‖ 'ɔːr əf əs 'ɑːr- **~es** ɪz əz
oriflamme 'ɒr ɪ flæm -ə- ‖ 'ɔːr ə- 'ɑːr- **~s** z
origami ˌɒr ɪ 'ɡɑːm i ˌɔːr-, -ə- ‖ ˌɔːr ə- —*Jp* [o 'ri ŋa mi, -ɡa-]
origanum ə 'rɪɡ ən əm ɒ-; ˌɒr ɪ 'ɡɑːn-, -ə-
Origen 'ɒr ɪ dʒen -ə- ‖ 'ɔːr- 'ɑːr-
origin 'ɒr ɪdʒ ɪn -ədʒ-, -ən ‖ 'ɔːr- 'ɑːr- **~s** z
original ə 'rɪdʒ ᵊn‿əl ɒ-, -ɪn- **~s** z
oˌriginal 'sin
originalit|y ə ˌrɪdʒ ə 'næl ət |i ɒ-, -ˌɪ-, -ɪt i ‖ -əţ |i **~ies** iz
originally ə 'rɪdʒ ᵊn‿əl i ɒ-, -'ɪn-
origi|nate ə 'rɪdʒ ə |neɪt ɒ-, -ɪ- **~nated** neɪt ɪd -əd ‖ neɪţ əd **~nates** neɪts **~nating** neɪt ɪŋ ‖ neɪţ ɪŋ
origination ə ˌrɪdʒ ə 'neɪʃ ᵊn ɒ-, -ɪ-
originative ə 'rɪdʒ ə neɪt ɪv ɒ-, -ɪ- ·, -ən‿ət ɪv, -ɪn ət ɪv ‖ -neɪţ ɪv **~ly** li
originator ə 'rɪdʒ ə neɪt ə ɒ-, -'·ɪ- ‖ -neɪţ ᵊr **~s** z
O-ring 'əʊ rɪŋ ‖ 'oʊ- **~s** z
Orinoco ˌɒr ɪ 'nəʊk əʊ -ə- ‖ ˌɔːr ə 'noʊk oʊ ˌoʊr- —*Sp* [o ri 'no ko]
Orinthia ə 'rɪnᵗθ i‿ə ɒ-
oriole 'ɔːr i əʊl →-ɒʊl, əl ‖ -oʊl 'oʊr- **~s** z
Orion ə 'raɪ‿ən ɒ-, ɔː- ‖ oʊ- **Orionis** ˌɔːr i 'əʊn ɪs §-əs ‖ -'oʊn-
O'Riordan *(i)* əʊ 'rɪəd ᵊn ‖ oʊ 'rɪrd ᵊn, *(ii)* əʊ 'raɪ‿əd ᵊn ‖ oʊ 'raɪ‿ᵊrd ᵊn
orison 'ɒr ɪz ən -əz- ‖ 'ɔːr əs- 'ɑːr-, -əz- **~s** z
Orissa ɒ 'rɪs ə ɔː-, ə- ‖ oʊ-
Oriya ɒ 'riː‿ə ɔː-, ə- ‖ ɔː-
ork ɔːk ‖ ɔːrk **orks** ɔːks ‖ ɔːrks
Orkney 'ɔːk ni ‖ 'ɔːrk- **~s** z
ˌOrkney 'Islands ‖ '. . ˌ. .
Orlando ɔː 'lænd əʊ ‖ ɔːr 'lænd oʊ
orle ɔːl ‖ ɔːrl **orles** ɔːlz ‖ ɔːrlz
Orleans, Orléans ɔː 'liː‿ənz 'ɔːl i‿ənz, ˌɔːl eɪ 'ɒ̃ ‖ 'ɔːrl i‿ənz ɔːr 'liːnz —*Fr* [ɔʁ le ɑ̃]
Orlon, orlon *tdmk* 'ɔːl ɒn ‖ 'ɔːrl ɑːn
orlop 'ɔː lɒp ‖ 'ɔːr lɑːp **~s** s
Orly 'ɔːl i ‖ 'ɔːrl i ɔːr 'liː —*Fr* [ɔʁ li]
Orm, Orme ɔːm ‖ ɔːrm
Ormandy 'ɔːm ənd i ‖ 'ɔːrm-
Ormeau 'ɔːm əʊ ·'· ‖ 'ɔːrm oʊ
ormer 'ɔːm ə ‖ 'ɔːrm ᵊr **~s** z
Ormerod 'ɔːm ᵊr‿ɒd ‖ 'ɔːrm ᵊr‿ɑːd
Ormesby 'ɔːmz bi ‖ 'ɔːrmz-
ormolu 'ɔːm ə luː -ljuː ‖ 'ɔːrm-

O

Ormond, Ormonde 'ɔːm ənd ‖ 'ɔːrm-

Ormrod 'ɔːm rɒd ‖ 'ɔːrm rɑːd

Ormsby 'ɔːmz bi ‖ 'ɔːrmz-

Ormskirk 'ɔːmz kɜːk 'ɔːmᵖs- ‖ 'ɔːrmz kɜ˞ːk

Ormulum 'ɔːm jʊl əm -jəl- ‖ 'ɔːrm-

orna|ment *v* 'ɔːn ə |ment ‖ 'ɔːrn- —*See note at* -ment **~mented** ment ɪd -əd ‖ menṱ əd **~menting** ment ɪŋ ‖ menṱ ɪŋ **~ments** ments

ornament *n* 'ɔːn ə mənt ‖ 'ɔːrn- **~s** s

ornamental ˌɔːn ə 'ment ᵊl ◂ ‖ˌɔːrn ə 'menṱ ᵊl ◂ **~ly** i

ornamentation ˌɔːn ə men 'teɪʃ ᵊn -əm ən- ‖ˌɔːrn- **~s** z

ornate ₍ˌ₎ɔː 'neɪt ‖ ₍ˌ₎ɔːr- **~ly** li **~ness** nəs nɪs

orner|y 'ɔːn ər‿|i ‖ 'ɔːrn- 'ɑːn- **~ier** i‿ə ‖ i‿ᵊr **~iest** i‿ɪst i‿əst **~iness** i nəs i nɪs

ornitho- *comb. form with stress-neutral suffix* ¦ɔːn ɪθ əʊ -əθ- ‖ ¦ɔːrn əθ ə — **ornithomancy** 'ɔːn ɪθ əʊ ˌmænᵗs i ‖ 'ɔːrn əθ ə- *with stress-imposing suffix* ˌɔːn ɪ 'θɒ+ -ə- ‖ ˌɔːrn ə 'θɑː+ — **ornithoscopy** ˌɔːn ɪ 'θɒsk əp i ˌ·ə- ‖ ˌɔːrn ə 'θɑːsk-

ornithological ˌɔːn ɪθ ə 'lɒdʒ ɪk ᵊl ◂ ˌ·əθ- ‖ ˌɔːrn əθ ə 'lɑːdʒ- **~ly** ‿i

ornitholog|ist ˌɔːn ɪ 'θɒl ədʒ |ɪst ˌ·ə-, §-əst ‖ ˌɔːrn ə 'θɑːl- **~ists** ɪsts §əsts **~y** i

ornithopter 'ɔːn ɪ θɒpt ə 'ˌ·ə- ‖ 'ɔːrn ə θɑːpt ᵊr **~s** z

ornithosis ˌɔːn ɪ 'θəʊs ɪs -ə-, §-əs ‖ ˌɔːrn ə 'θoʊs əs

oro- *comb. form with stress-neutral suffix* ¦ɒr əʊ ¦ɔːr- ‖ ¦ɔːr ə ¦ɑːr-, ¦oʊr- — **orographic** ˌɒr əʊ 'græf ɪk ◂ ˌɔːr- ‖ ˌɔːr ə-, ˌɑːr-, ˌoʊr- *with stress-imposing suffix* ɒ 'rɒ+ ɔː- ‖ ɔː 'rɑː+ ɑː-, oʊ- — **orology** ɒ 'rɒl ədʒ i ɔː- ‖ ɔː 'rɑːl ədʒ i ɑː-, oʊ-

oronasal ˌɔːr əʊ 'neɪz ᵊl ◂ ‖ -oʊ- ˌoʊr-

Oronsay 'ɒr ən seɪ -zeɪ ‖ 'ɔːr-

Orontes ə 'rɒnt iːz ɒ- ‖ ɔː 'rɑːnt iːz ɑː-, oʊ-

oropharynx 'ɔːr əʊ ˌfær ɪŋks ˌ· ·'· ‖ 'ɔːr oʊ ˌfær- 'oʊr-, -ə-, -ˌfer-

orotund 'ɒr əʊ tʌnd 'ɔːr- ‖ 'ɔːr ə- 'ɑːr-, 'oʊr-

orotundity ˌɒr əʊ 'tʌnd ət i ˌɔːr-, -ɪt i ‖ ˌɔːr ə 'tʌnd əṱ i ˌɑːr-, ˌoʊr-

O'Rourke əʊ 'rɔːk -'rʊək ‖ oʊ 'rɔːrk

orphan 'ɔːf ᵊn ‖ 'ɔːrf ᵊn **~ed** d **~ing** ɪŋ **~s** z

orphanag|e 'ɔːf ən ɪdʒ ‖ 'ɔːrf- **~es** ɪz əz

orphanhood 'ɔːf ᵊn hʊd ‖ 'ɔːrf-

Orphean ɔː 'fiː‿ən 'ɔːf i‿ən ɔːr 'fiː ən 'ɔːrf i‿ **~s** z

Orpheus 'ɔːf juːs 'ɔːf i‿əs ‖ 'ɔːrf-

Orphic 'ɔːf ɪk ‖ 'ɔːrf-

Orphism 'ɔːf ˌɪz əm ‖ 'ɔːrf-

orphrey 'ɔːf ri ‖ 'ɔːrf- **~s** z

orpiment 'ɔːp ɪ mənt §-ə- ‖ 'ɔːrp-

orpin 'ɔːp ɪn §-ən ‖ 'ɔːrp- **~s** z

orpine 'ɔːp aɪn -ɪn, §-ən ‖ 'ɔːrp ən **~s** z

Orpington 'ɔːp ɪŋ tən ‖ 'ɔːrp- **~s** z

Orr ɔː ‖ ɔːr

Orrell 'ɒr əl ‖ 'ɔːr- 'ɑːr-

orrer|y 'ɒr ər |i ‖ 'ɔːr- 'ɑːr- **~ies** iz

orris 'ɒr ɪs §-əs ‖ 'ɔːr- 'ɑːr-

Orsini ɔː 'siːn i ‖ ɔːr- —*It* [or 'siː ni]

Orsino ɔː 'siːn əʊ ‖ ɔːr 'siːn oʊ

Orson 'ɔːs ᵊn ‖ 'ɔːrs ᵊn

ortanique ˌɔːt ə 'niːk -ᵊn 'iːk ‖ ˌɔːrt ᵊn 'iːk **~s** s

Ortega ɔː 'teɪg ə ‖ ɔːr- —*Sp* [or 'te ɣa]

orthicon 'ɔːθ ɪ kɒn -ə- ‖ 'ɔːrθ ɪ kɑːn **~s** z

ortho- *comb. form with stress-neutral suffix* ¦ɔːθ əʊ ‖ ¦ɔːrθ ə -oʊ — **orthotone** 'ɔːθ əʊ təʊn ‖ 'ɔːrθ ə toʊn -oʊ- *with stress-imposing suffix* ɔː 'θɒ+ ‖ ɔːr 'θɑː+ — **orthotropous** ɔː 'θɒtr əp əs ‖ ɔːr 'θɑːtr-

orthocenter, orthocentre 'ɔːθ əʊ ˌsent ə ‖ 'ɔːrθ ə ˌsenṱ ᵊr -oʊ- **~s** z

orthochromatic ˌɔːθ əʊ krəʊ 'mæt ɪk ◂ ‖ ˌɔːrθ ə kroʊ 'mæṱ ɪk **~ally** ᵊl‿i

orthoclase 'ɔːθ əʊ kleɪz -kleɪs ‖ 'ɔːrθ ə- -oʊ-

orthodontic ˌɔːθ əʊ 'dɒnt ɪk ◂ ‖ ˌɔːrθ ə 'dɑːnṱ ɪk ◂ **~s** s

orthodontist ˌɔːθ əʊ 'dɒnt ɪst §-əst ‖ ˌɔːrθ ə 'dɑːnṱ əst **~s** s

orthodox, O~ 'ɔːθ ə dɒks ‖ 'ɔːrθ ə dɑːks ˌ**Orthodox 'Church**

orthodox|y 'ɔːθ ə dɒks |i ‖ 'ɔːrθ ə dɑːks |i **~ies** iz

orthoepic ˌɔːθ əʊ 'ep ɪk ‖ ˌɔːrθ oʊ-

orthoep|ist 'ɔːθ əʊ ˌep |ɪst §-əst, ˌ· ·'· ·; ɔː 'θəʊ ɪp-, -'·əp- ‖ 'ɔːrθ oʊ- **~ists** ɪsts §əsts **~y** i

orthogonal ɔː 'θɒg ən ᵊl ‖ ɔːr 'θɑːg- **~ly** i

orthographer ɔː 'θɒg rəf ə ‖ ɔːr 'θɑːg rəf ᵊr **~s** z

orthographic ˌɔːθ ə 'græf ɪk ◂ ‖ ˌɔːrθ- **~ally** ᵊl‿i

orthograph|y ɔː 'θɒg rəf |i ‖ ɔːr 'θɑːg- **~ies** iz

orthopaed|ic, orthoped|ic ˌɔːθ ə 'piːd |ɪk/s ◂ ‖ ˌɔːrθ- **~ics** ɪks **~ist** ɪst §əst ‖ əst **~ists** ɪsts §əsts **~y** i

orthopter|a ɔː 'θɒpt ər |ə ‖ ɔːr 'θɑːpt- **~an** ən **~ous** əs

orthoptic ɔː 'θɒpt ɪk ‖ ɔːr 'θɑːpt ɪk **~s** s

orthos|is ɔː 'θəʊs| ɪs §-əs ‖ ɔːr 'θoʊs| əs **~es** iːz

orthostich|ous ɔː 'θɒst ɪk |əs -ək- ‖ ɔːr 'θɑːst- **~y** i

orthotic ɔː 'θɒt ɪk ‖ ɔːr 'θɑːṱ ɪk **~s** s

ortolan 'ɔːt əl ən -ə læn ‖ 'ɔːrṱ ᵊl ən **~s** z

Orton 'ɔːt ᵊn ‖ 'ɔːrt ᵊn

Ortonesque ˌɔːt ə 'nesk ◂ →-ᵊn 'esk ‖ ˌɔːrt ᵊn 'esk ◂

orts ɔːts ‖ ɔːrts

Orville 'ɔː vɪl 'ɔːv ᵊl ‖ 'ɔːrv ᵊl

Orwell 'ɔː wel -wəl ‖ 'ɔːr-

Orwellian ɔː 'wel i‿ən ‖ ɔːr-

-ory ər i ‖ ər i, ɔːr i oʊr i —*This suffix is usually stress-neutral when attached to a free stem* (di'rectory, 'promissory)*; otherwise it imposes stress on one of the two preceding syllables* (per'functory, 'repertory)*. It has a strong vowel in AmE* (-ɔːr i) *if the preceding vowel is weak* ('dormitory)*; otherwise, and always in BrE, it has a weak vowel.*

oryx 'ɒr ɪks ‖ 'ɔːr- 'ɑːr-, 'oʊr- **~es** ɪz əz

orzo 'ɔːz əʊ 'ɔːdz- ‖ -oʊ

os *'bone'; 'mouth'* ɒs ‖ ɑːs

Osag|e ₍ˌ₎əʊ 'seɪdʒ '· · ‖ ₍ˌ₎oʊ- **~es** ɪz əz
Osaka əʊ 'sɑːk ə '· · ·, 'ɔːs ək ə ‖ oʊ- —*Jp* [oˌo sa ka]
Osama bin Laden əʊ ˌsɑːm ə bɪn 'lɑːd ᵊn -en ‖ oʊ- —*Arabic* [u 'saː ma bin 'laː dan]
Osbert 'ɒz bət -bɜːt ‖ 'ɑːz bᵊrt
Osborn, Osborne, Osbourne 'ɒz bɔːn -bən ‖ 'ɑːz bɔːrn
Oscan 'ɒsk ən ‖ 'ɑːsk-
Oscar, oscar 'ɒsk ə ‖ 'ɑːsk ᵊr
oscil|late 'ɒs ɪ |leɪt -ə-, -ᵊ|l eɪt ‖ 'ɑːs- **~lated** leɪt ɪd -əd ‖ leɪţ əd **~lates** leɪts **~lating** leɪt ɪŋ ‖ leɪţ ɪŋ
oscillation ˌɒs ɪ 'leɪʃ ᵊn -ə-, -ᵊl 'eɪʃ- ‖ ˌɑːs- **~s** z
oscillator 'ɒs ɪ leɪt ə '·ə-, -ᵊl eɪt- ‖ 'ɑːs ə leɪţ ᵊr **~s** z
oscillatory 'ɒs ɪl ət‿ər i '·əl-; ˌɒs ɪ 'leɪt ər i, ˌ·ə-, '· · · · · ‖ 'ɑːs əl ə tɔːr i -toʊr i
oscillo- *comb. form with stress-neutral suffix* ə ¦sɪl əʊ ɒ- ‖ ɑː ¦sɪl ə — **oscillographic** əˌsɪl əʊ 'græf ɪk ◂ ɒ- ‖ ɑː ˌsɪl ə- *with stress-imposing suffix* ˌɒs ɪ 'lɒ+ -ə- ‖ ˌɑːs ə 'lɑː+ **oscillography** ˌɒs ɪ 'lɒg rəf i -ə- ‖ ˌɑːs ə 'lɑːg-
oscillogram ə 'sɪl ə græm ɒ- ‖ ɑː- **~s** z
oscillograph ə 'sɪl ə grɑːf ɒ-, -græf ‖ -græf ɑː- **~s** s
oscilloscope ə 'sɪl ə skəʊp ɒ- ‖ -skoʊp ɑː- **~s** s
Osco-Umbrian ˌɒsk əʊ 'ʌm bri‿ən ◂ ‖ ˌɑːsk oʊ-
osculant 'ɒsk jʊl ənt -jəl- ‖ 'ɑːsk jəl-
oscular 'ɒsk jʊl ə -jəl- ‖ 'ɑːsk jə lᵊr
oscu|late 'ɒsk ju |leɪt ‖ 'ɑːsk jə- **~lated** leɪt ɪd -əd ‖ leɪţ əd **~lates** leɪts **~lating** leɪt ɪŋ ‖ leɪţ ɪŋ
osculation ˌɒsk ju 'leɪʃ ᵊn -jə- ‖ ˌɑːsk jə- **~s** z
osculatory 'ɒsk jʊl ət‿ər i '·jəl-, ˌɒsk ju 'leɪt‿ər i ‖ 'ɑːsk jəl ə tɔːr i -toʊr i
oscul|um 'ɒsk jʊl |əm -jəl- ‖ 'ɑːsk jəl- **~a** ə
-oses 'əʊs iːz ‖ 'oʊs iːz — **fibroses** faɪ 'brəʊs iːz ‖ -'broʊs-
Osgood 'ɒz gʊd ‖ 'ɑːz-
O'Shaughnessy əʊ 'ʃɔːn əs i -ɪs- ‖ oʊ- -'ʃɑːn-
O'Shea *(i)* əʊ 'ʃeɪ ‖ oʊ-, *(ii)* -'ʃiː
Oshkosh 'ɒʃ kɒʃ ‖ 'ɑːʃ kɑːʃ
osier 'əʊz i‿ə 'əʊʒ ə, 'əʊʒ i‿ə ‖ 'oʊʒ ᵊr 'oʊz i‿ᵊr **~s** z
Osijek 'ɒs i ek ‖ 'oʊs- —*Croatian* ['ɔ si jɛk]
Osiris əʊ 'saɪᵊr ɪs ɒ-, §-əs ‖ oʊ-
-osis 'əʊs ɪs §-əs ‖ 'oʊs əs — **ornithosis** ˌɔːn ɪ 'θəʊs ɪs -ə-, §-əs ‖ ˌɔːr nə 'θoʊs əs
-osity 'ɒs ət i -ɪt i ‖ 'ɑːs əţ i **verbosity** vɜː 'bɒs ət i -ɪt i ‖ vɜː 'bɑːs əţ i
Oslo 'ɒz ləʊ 'ɒs- ‖ 'ɑːz loʊ 'ɑːs- —*Norw* [''us lu]
Osman ɒz 'mɑːn ɒs-; 'ɒz mən ‖ 'ɑːz mən 'ɑːs-
Osmanli ɒz 'mæn li ɒs-, -'mɑːn- ‖ ɑːz- ɑːs- **~s** z
Osmiroid *tdmk* 'ɒz mə rɔɪd -mɪ- ‖ 'ɑːz-
osmium 'ɒz mi‿əm ‖ 'ɑːz-
Osmond 'ɒz mənd ‖ 'ɑːz- **~s** z
osmosis ɒz 'məʊs ɪs ɒs-, §-əs ‖ ɑːs 'moʊs əs ɑːz-
Osmotherley, Osmotherly ɒz 'mʌð ə li ‖ ɑːz 'mʌð ᵊr-
osmotic ɒz 'mɒt ɪk ɒs- ‖ ɑːz 'mɑːţ ɪk ɑːs- **~ally** ᵊl‿i
Osmund, o~ 'ɒz mənd ‖ 'ɑːz- ɑːs-
osmunda ɒz 'mʌnd ə ‖ ɑːz- ɑːs-
Osnabruck, Osnabrück 'ɒz nə brʊk ‖ 'ɑːz- —*Ger* [ʔɔs na 'bʁʏk]
Osnaburg, Osnaburgh, o~ 'ɒz nə bɜːg ‖ 'ɑːz nə bɜːg
osprey 'ɒsp ri -reɪ ‖ 'ɑːsp- **~s** z
Ossa 'ɒs ə ‖ 'ɑːs ə
osseous 'ɒs i‿əs ‖ 'ɑːs- **~ly** li
Osset 'ɒs ɪt §-ət ‖ 'ɑːs- **~s** s
Ossetia ɒ 'set i‿ə ɒ 'siːʃ ə ‖ ɑː 'seţ i‿ə ɑː 'siːʃ ə
Ossetian ɒ 'set i‿ən ɒ 'siːʃ ᵊn ‖ ɑː 'seţ i‿ən ɑː 'siːʃ ᵊn **~s** z
Ossetic ɒ 'set ɪk ‖ ɑː 'seţ ɪk
Ossett 'ɒs ɪt §-ət ‖ 'ɑːs-
Ossian 'ɒs i‿ən ‖ 'ɑːʃ ᵊn 'ɑːs i‿ən
Ossianic ˌɒs i 'æn ɪk ◂ ‖ ˌɑːs- ˌɑːʃ-
ossicle 'ɒs ɪk ᵊl ‖ 'ɑːs- **~s** z
ossification ˌɒs ɪf ɪ 'keɪʃ ᵊn ˌ·əf-, §-ə'-- ‖ ˌɑːs-
ossifrag|e 'ɒs ɪf rɪdʒ -ə-; -ɪ freɪdʒ, -ə- ‖ 'ɑːs- **~es** ɪz əz
ossi|fy 'ɒs ɪ |faɪ -ə- ‖ 'ɑːs- **~fied** faɪd **~fies** faɪz **~fying** faɪ ɪŋ
Ossining 'ɒs ᵊn ɪŋ -ɪn- ‖ 'ɑːs-
osso bucco, osso buco ˌɒs əʊ 'bʊk əʊ -'buːk- ‖ ˌoʊs oʊ 'buːk oʊ ˌɑːs- —*It* [ˌɔs so 'bu ko]
ossuar|y 'ɒs ju‿ər |i ‖ 'ɑːs ju er |i **~ies** iz
osteitis ˌɒst i 'aɪt ɪs §-əs ‖ ˌɑːst i 'aɪţ əs
Ostend ₍ˌ₎ɒst 'end ‖ ₍ˌ₎ɑːst- —*Dutch* Oostende [oːst 'ɛn də], *Fr* Ostende [ɔs 'tɑ̃ːd]
ostensib|le ɒ 'stenᵗs əb |ᵊl -ɪb- ‖ ɑː- ə- **~ly** li
ostensive ɒ 'stenᵗs ɪv ‖ ɑː- **~ly** li
ostentation ˌɒst en 'teɪʃ ᵊn -ən- ‖ ˌɑːst-
ostentatious ˌɒst en 'teɪʃ əs ◂ -ən- ‖ ˌɑːst- **~ly** li **~ness** nəs nɪs
osteo- *comb. form with stress-neutral suffix* ¦ɒst i‿əʊ ‖ ¦ɑːst i‿ə — **osteoclast** 'ɒst i‿əʊ klæst ‖ 'ɑːst i‿ə- *with stress-imposing suffix* ˌɒst i 'ɒ+ ‖ ˌɑːst i 'ɑː+ — **osteology** ˌɒst i 'ɒl ədʒ i ‖ ˌɑːst i 'ɑːl-
osteoarthritis ˌɒst i‿əʊ ɑː 'θraɪt ɪs §-əs ‖ ˌɑːst i‿oʊ ɑːr 'θraɪţ əs
osteomalacia ˌɒst i‿əʊ mə 'leɪʃ i‿ə -'leɪʃ ə ‖ ˌɑːst i‿oʊ-
osteomyelitis ˌɒst i‿əʊ ˌmaɪ‿ə 'laɪt ɪs §-əs ‖ ˌɑːst i‿oʊ ˌmaɪ ə 'laɪţ əs
osteopath 'ɒst i‿əʊ pæθ ‖ 'ɑːst i‿ə- **~s** s
osteopathic ˌɒst i‿əʊ 'pæθ ɪk ◂ ‖ ˌɑːst i‿ə- **~ally** ᵊl‿i
osteopathy ˌɒst i 'ɒp əθ i ‖ ˌɑːst i 'ɑːp-
osteoporosis ˌɒst i‿əʊ pɔː 'rəʊs ɪs §-əs ‖ ˌɑːst i‿oʊ pə 'roʊs əs
Osterley 'ɒst ə li →-ᵊl i ‖ 'ɑːst ᵊr-
Ostermilk *tdmk* 'ɒst ə mɪlk ‖ 'ɑːst ᵊr-
Ostia 'ɒst i‿ə ‖ 'ɑːst-
ostiar|y 'ɒst i‿ər |i ‖ 'ɑːst i er |i **~ies** iz
ostinato ˌɒst ɪ 'nɑːt əʊ -ə- ‖ ˌɑːst ə 'nɑːţ oʊ ˌɔːst- **~s** z
osti|um 'ɒst i‿|əm ‖ 'ɑːst- **~a** ə

O

ostler, O~ 'ɒs lə ‖ 'ɑːs lᵊr **~s** z
ostom|y 'ɒst əm| i ‖ 'ɑːst- **~ies** iz —*see also* **-stomy**
ostracis... —*see* **ostraciz...**
ostracism 'ɒs trə ˌsɪz əm ‖ 'ɑːs- **~s** z
ostraciz|e 'ɒs trə saɪz ‖ 'ɑːs- **~ed** d **~es** ɪz əz **~ing** ɪŋ
Ostrava 'ɒs trəv ə ‖ 'ɔːs- 'ɑːs-, 'oʊs- —*Czech* ['ɔ stra va]
ostrich 'ɒs trɪtʃ -trɪdʒ ‖ 'ɑːs- 'ɔːs- **~es** ɪz əz **'ostrich egg**; **'ostrich ˌfeather**
Ostrogoth 'ɒs trəʊ gɒθ ‖ 'ɑːs trə gɑːθ **~s** s
Ostrogothic ˌɒs trəʊ 'gɒθ ɪk ◂ ‖ ˌɑːs trə 'gɑːθ ɪk ◂
Ostwald 'ɒst vælt ‖ 'ɑːst- —*Ger* ['ɔst valt]
Ostyak 'ɒst jæk 'ɒst i æk ‖ 'ɑːst jɑːk -i ɑːk, -æk **~s** s
O'Sullivan əʊ 'sʌl ɪv ən -əv- ‖ oʊ-
Oswald 'ɒz wəld ‖ 'ɑːz-
Oswaldtwistle 'ɒz wəld ˌtwɪs ᵊl -ᵊl- ‖ 'ɑːz-
Oswego ɒ 'swiːg əʊ -'zwiːg- ‖ ɑː 'swiːg oʊ
Oswestry 'ɒz wəs tri -wɪs- ‖ 'ɑːz-
Osyth 'əʊz ɪθ 'əʊs- ‖ 'oʊz-
Otago əʊ 'tɑːg əʊ ɒ- ‖ oʊ 'tɑːg oʊ
Otaheite ˌəʊt ə 'hiːt i -'heɪt- ‖ ˌoʊt̬ ə 'hiːt̬ i
otarine 'əʊt ə raɪn ‖ 'oʊt̬-
otar|y 'əʊt ər| i ‖ 'oʊt̬- **~ies** iz
O tempora! O mores ₍ᵢ₎əʊ 'temp ər ə ₍ᵢ₎əʊ 'mɔːr iːz -eɪz, -eɪs ‖ ₍ᵢ₎oʊ 'temp ər ə ₍ᵢ₎oʊ- -'moʊr-
Otford 'ɒt fəd ‖ 'ɑːt fᵊrd
Othello əʊ 'θel əʊ ɒ- ‖ ə 'θel oʊ oʊ-
other 'ʌð ə ‖ 'ʌð ᵊr **others** 'ʌð əz ‖ -ᵊrz
otherness 'ʌð ə nəs -nɪs ‖ -ᵊr-
otherwise 'ʌð ə waɪz ‖ -ᵊr-
otherworld|ly ˌʌð ə 'wɜːld |li ◂ ‖ -ᵊr 'wɜːld- **~liness** li nəs -nɪs
Othman ɒθ 'mɑːn ‖ ɑːθ-
Otho 'əʊθ əʊ ‖ 'oʊθ oʊ
-otic 'ɒt ɪk ‖ 'ɑːt̬ ɪk —*but* 'əʊt ɪk ‖ 'oʊt̬ ɪk *when not related to a noun in* -osis — **symbiotic** ˌsɪm baɪ 'ɒt ɪk ◂ ‖ -'ɑːt ɪk ◂ — **periotic** ˌper i 'əʊt ɪk ◂ ‖ -'oʊt̬ ɪk ◂
otic 'əʊt ɪk 'ɒt- ‖ 'oʊt̬ ɪk 'ɑːt̬-
otiose 'əʊt i ˌəʊs 'əʊʃ-, -əʊz; 'əʊʃ i ˌəs ‖ 'oʊʃ i oʊs 'oʊt̬- **~ly** li
otiosity ˌəʊt i 'ɒs ət i ˌəʊʃ-, -ɪt i ‖ ˌoʊʃ i 'ɑːs ət̬ i ˌoʊt̬-
Otis 'əʊt ɪs §-əs ‖ 'oʊt̬ əs
otitis əʊ 'taɪt ɪs §-əs ‖ oʊ 'taɪt̬ əs
Otley 'ɒt li ‖ 'ɑːt-
oto- *comb. form with stress-neutral suffix* ¦əʊt əʊ ‖ ¦oʊt̬ ə — **otocyst** 'əʊt əʊ sɪst ‖ 'oʊt̬ ə- *with stress-imposing suffix* əʊ 'tɒ+ ‖ oʊ 'tɑː+ — **otology** əʊ 'tɒl ədʒ i ‖ oʊ 'tɑːl-
otolaryngolog|ist ˌəʊt əʊˌlær ɪŋ 'gɒl ədʒ |ɪst §-əst ‖ ˌoʊt̬ oʊ ˌlær ɪŋ 'gɑːl- -ˌler- **~ists** ɪsts §əsts **~y** i
Otomanguean ˌəʊt ə 'mæŋ gi ˌən -geɪ ən ‖ ˌoʊt̬-
O'Toole əʊ 'tuːl ‖ oʊ-
Otranto ɒ 'trænt əʊ 'ɒtr ən təʊ ‖ oʊ 'trɑːnt oʊ —*It* ['ɔː tran to]
OTT ˌəʊ tiː 'tiː ‖ ˌoʊ-
ottar 'ɒt ə ‖ 'ɑːt̬ ᵊr
ottava əʊ 'tɑːv ə ɒ- ‖ oʊ- **otˌtava 'rima** 'riːm ə
Ottawa 'ɒt ə wə ‖ 'ɑːt̬ ə wə -wɑː, -wɔː
otter 'ɒt ə ‖ 'ɑːt̬ ᵊr **~s** z
Otterburn 'ɒt ə bɜːn ‖ 'ɑːt̬ ᵊr bɜːn
Ottery 'ɒt ər i ‖ 'ɑːt̬-
Ottfur 'ɒt fə ‖ 'ɑːt fᵊr
Otto, otto 'ɒt əʊ ‖ 'ɑːt̬ oʊ
Ottoline 'ɒt ə lɪn -ᵊl ɪn ‖ 'ɑːt̬-
ottoman, O~ 'ɒt ə mən -əʊ- ‖ 'ɑːt̬- **~s** z
Otway 'ɒt weɪ ‖ 'ɑːt-
Ötzi 'əʊts i 'ɜːts i ‖ 'oʊts i —*Ger* ['œts i]
ouabain ˌwɑː 'beɪ ɪn -'bɑː-, '· · ·
Ouachita 'wɒʃ ə tɔː ‖ 'wɑːʃ- -tɑː **~s** z
Ouagadougou ˌwɑːg ə 'duːg uː ˌwæg-
oubliette ˌuːb li 'et **~s** s
ouch aʊtʃ
oud uːd **ouds** uːdz
Oudenaarde, Oudenarde 'uːd ə nɑːd -ᵊn ɑːd ‖ -nɑːrd —*Dutch* ['ɔu də naːr də]
Oudh aʊd
ought ɔːt ‖ ɑːt —*The combination* ought to *is often pronounced with a single* **t**, *as* 'ɔːt ə ‖ 'ɔːt̬ ə *(esp. before a consonant sound; also, esp. BrE,* 'ɔːt u *before a vowel sound).*
oughta = *ought to* 'ɔːt ə ‖ 'ɔːt̬ ə 'ɑːt̬ ə
Oughtershaw 'aʊt ə ʃɔː ‖ 'aʊt̬ ᵊr- -ʃɑː
Oughterside 'aʊt ə saɪd ‖ 'aʊt̬ ᵊr-
oughtn't 'ɔːt ᵊnt →-ᵊn ‖ 'ɑːt-
Oughton *(i)* 'aʊt ᵊn, *(ii)* 'ɔːt ᵊn ‖ 'ɑːt-
Ouida 'wiːd ə
ouija, O~ *tdmk* 'wiːdʒ ə -ɑː, -i **'ouija board**
ould *dialectal form of* old aʊld
Ould *family name (i)* əʊld →ɒʊld ‖ oʊld, *(ii)* uːld
Oulton 'əʊlt ən →'ɒʊlt- ‖ 'oʊlt ᵊn
ounce aʊnᵗs **ounces** 'aʊnᵗs ɪz -əz
Oundle 'aʊnd ᵊl
our 'aʊ‿ə ɑː ‖ 'aʊ‿ᵊr ɑːr —*Some speakers use* ɑː ‖ ɑːr *as the weak form,* 'aʊ‿ə ‖ 'aʊ‿ᵊr *as the strong; others use only one or only the other. In RP the latter form in any case readily undergoes smoothing (see COMPRESSION) to* aː, ɑː.
ˌOur 'Father; **₍ᵢ₎Our 'Lady**; **₍ᵢ₎Our 'Lord**
-our ə ‖ ᵊr — **armour** 'ɑːm ə ‖ 'ɑːrm ᵊr
ours 'aʊ‿əz ɑːz ‖ aʊ‿ᵊrz ɑːrz
our|self ₍ᵢ₎aʊ‿ə |'self ɑː |'self ‖ ₍ᵢ₎aʊ‿ᵊr |'self ɑːr |'self **~selves** 'selvz
-ous əs — **hazardous** 'hæz əd əs ‖ -ᵊrd- **carnivorous** kɑː 'nɪv ər‿əs ‖ kɑːr-
Ouse uːz
ousel 'uːz ᵊl **~s** z
Ouseley, Ousley 'uːz li
Ouspensky u 'spenᵗsk i —*Russ* [u 'sʲpʲenʲ sʲkʲij]
oust aʊst **ousted** 'aʊst ɪd -əd **ousting** 'aʊst ɪŋ **ousts** aʊsts

ouster ˈaʊst ə ‖ -ᵊr **~s** z
out aʊt **outed** ˈaʊt ɪd -əd ‖ ˈaʊt̬ əd **outing** ˈaʊt ɪŋ ‖ ˈaʊt̬ ɪŋ **outs** aʊts
out- ¦aʊt
outag|e ˈaʊt ɪdʒ ‖ ˈaʊt̬- **~es** ɪz əz
out-and-out ˌaʊt ᵊn ˈaʊt ◂ -ᵊnd-
ˌout-and-ˌout ˈfailure
outback, O~ ˈaʊt bæk
outbalanc|e ˌaʊt ˈbæl ənᵗs **~ed** t **~es** ɪz əz **~ing** ɪŋ
outbid ˌaʊt ˈbɪd **~ding** ɪŋ **~s** z
outboard ˈaʊt bɔːd ‖ -bɔːrd -bourd **~s** z
ˌoutboard ˈmotor
outbound ˈaʊt baʊnd
outbox *n.* ˈaʊt bɒks ‖ -bɑːks **~es** ɪz əz
outbrav|e ˌaʊt ˈbreɪv **~ed** d **~es** z **~ing** ɪŋ
outbreak ˈaʊt breɪk **~s** s
outbuilding ˈaʊt ˌbɪld ɪŋ **~s** z
outburst ˈaʊt bɜːst ‖ -bɜːst **~s** s
outcast, outcaste ˈaʊt kɑːst §-kæst ‖ -kæst **~s** s
outclass ˌaʊt ˈklɑːs §-ˈklæs ‖ -ˈklæs **~ed** t **~es** ɪz əz **~ing** ɪŋ
outcome ˈaʊt kʌm **~s** z
outcrop ˈaʊt krɒp ‖ -krɑːp **~ped** t **~ping** ɪŋ **~s** s
out|cry ˈaʊt |kraɪ **~cries** kraɪz
out|date ˌaʊt |ˈdeɪt **~dated** ˈdeɪt ɪd ◂ -əd ‖ ˈdeɪt̬ əd ◂ **~dates** ˈdeɪts **~dating** ˈdeɪt ɪŋ ‖ ˈdeɪt̬ ɪŋ
outdid ˌaʊt ˈdɪd
outdistanc|e ˌaʊt ˈdɪst ənᵗs **~ed** t **~es** ɪz əz **~ing** ɪŋ
out|do ˌaʊt |ˈduː **~did** ˈdɪd **~does** ˈdʌz **~done** ˈdʌn
outdoor ˌaʊt ˈdɔː ◂ ‖ -ˈdɔːr ◂ -ˈdour **~s** z **~sy** zi
ˌoutdoor ˈshoes
out|draw ˌaʊt| ˈdrɔː ‖ -ˈdrɑː **~drawing** ˈdrɔːʳ ɪŋ ‖ ˈdrɔː ɪŋ ˈdrɑː ɪŋ **~drawn** ˈdrɔːn ‖ ˈdrɑːn **~draws** ˈdrɔːz ‖ ˈdrɑːz **~drew** ˈdruː
outer ˈaʊt ə ‖ ˈaʊt̬ ᵊr
ˌOuter ˈHebrides
outermost ˈaʊt ə məʊst ‖ ˈaʊt̬ ᵊr moust
outerwear ˈaʊt ə weə ‖ ˈaʊt̬ ᵊr wer
outfac|e ˌaʊt ˈfeɪs **~ed** t **~es** ɪz əz **~ing** ɪŋ
outfall ˈaʊt fɔːl ‖ -fɑːl **~s** z
outfield ˈaʊt fiːᵊld
outfielder ˈaʊt fiːᵊld ə ‖ -ᵊr **~s** z
out|fight ˌaʊt |ˈfaɪt **~fighting** ˈfaɪt ɪŋ ‖ ˈfaɪt̬ ɪŋ **~fights** ˈfaɪts **~fought** ˈfɔːt ‖ ˈfɑːt
out|fit ˈaʊt |fɪt **~fits** fɪts **~fitted** fɪt ɪd -əd ‖ fɪt̬ əd **~fitting** fɪt ɪŋ ‖ fɪt̬ ɪŋ
outfitter ˈaʊt fɪt ə ‖ -fɪt̬ ᵊr **~s** z
outflank ˌaʊt ˈflæŋk **~ed** t **~ing** ɪŋ **~s** s
outflow *n* ˈaʊt fləʊ ‖ -flou **~s** z
outflow *v* ˌaʊt ˈfləʊ ‖ -ˈflou **~ed** d **~ing** ɪŋ **~s** z
outfought ˌaʊt ˈfɔːt ‖ -ˈfɑːt
outfox ˌaʊt ˈfɒks ‖ -ˈfɑːks **~ed** t **~es** ɪz əz **~ing** ɪŋ
outgeneral ˌaʊt ˈdʒen ᵊr‿əl **~ed, ~led** d **~ing, ~ling** ɪŋ **~s** z
outgo *n* ˈaʊt gəʊ ‖ -gou **~es** z
outgoing *n* ˈaʊt gəʊ ɪŋ ‖ -goʊ- **~s** z
outgoing *adj* ˌaʊt ˈgəʊ ɪŋ ◂ ˈ,· · ‖ -ˈgou-
outgrew ˌaʊt ˈgruː
out-group *n* ˈaʊt gruːp **~s** s
out|grow ˌaʊt |ˈgrəʊ ‖ -|ˈgrou **~grew** ˈgruː **~growing** ˈgrəʊ ɪŋ ‖ ˈgrou ɪŋ **~grown** ˈgrəʊn ‖ ˈgroun **~grows** ˈgrəʊz ‖ ˈgrouz
outgrowth ˈaʊt grəʊθ ‖ -grouθ **~s** s
outguess ˌaʊt ˈges **~ed** t **~es** ɪz əz **~ing** ɪŋ
outgun ˌaʊt ˈgʌn **~ned** d **~ning** ɪŋ **~s** z
out-Herod ˌaʊt ˈher əd **~ed** ɪd əd **~ing** ɪŋ **~s** z
out|house ˈaʊt |haʊs **~houses** haʊz ɪz -əz
Outhwaite *(i)* ˈaʊθ weɪt, *(ii)* ˈəʊθ- ‖ ˈoʊθ-, *(iii)* ˈuːθ-
outing ˈaʊt ɪŋ ‖ ˈaʊt̬ ɪŋ **~s** z
outlaid ˌaʊt ˈleɪd ˈ· ·
outlander, O~ ˈaʊt lænd ə ‖ -ᵊr **~s** z
outlandish ₍ˌ₎aʊt ˈlænd ɪʃ **~ly** li **~ness** nəs nɪs
outlast ˌaʊt ˈlɑːst §-ˈlæst ‖ -ˈlæst **~ed** ɪd əd **~ing** ɪŋ **~s** s
outlaw *n, v* ˈaʊt lɔː ‖ -lɑː **~ed** d **outlawing** ˈaʊt lɔːʳ ɪŋ ‖ -lɔː ɪŋ -lɑː- **~s** z
outlaw|ry ˈaʊt lɔː |ri ‖ -lɑː- **~ries** riz
outlay *n* ˈaʊt leɪ **~s** z
out|lay *v* ˌaʊt |ˈleɪ ˈ· · **~laid** ˈleɪd **~laying** ˈleɪ ɪŋ **~lays** ˈleɪz
outlet ˈaʊt let -lət, -lɪt **~s** s
outlier ˈaʊt ˌlaɪ‿ə ‖ -ˌlaɪ ᵊr **~s** z
outlin|e *v* ˈaʊt laɪn ˌ·ˈ· **~ed** d **~es** z **~ing** ɪŋ
outline *n* ˈaʊt laɪn **~s** z
outliv|e ˌaʊt ˈlɪv **~ed** d **~es** z **~ing** ɪŋ
outlook ˈaʊt lʊk §-luːk **~s** s
outlying ˈaʊt ˌlaɪ ɪŋ ˌ·ˈ·
outman ˌaʊt ˈmæn **~ned** d **~ning** ɪŋ **~s** z
outmaneuve|r, outmanoeuv|re ˌaʊt mə ˈnuːv |ə ‖ -|ᵊr -ˈnjuːv- **~red** əd ‖ ᵊrd **~res** əz ‖ ᵊrz **~ring** ər‿ɪŋ ‖ ᵊr‿ɪŋ
outmarch ˌaʊt ˈmɑːtʃ ‖ -ˈmɑːrtʃ **~ed** t **~es** ɪz əz **~ing** ɪŋ
outmatch ˌaʊt ˈmætʃ **~ed** t **~es** ɪz əz **~ing** ɪŋ
outmoded ˌaʊt ˈməʊd ɪd ◂ -əd ‖ -ˈmoud- **~ly** li **~ness** nəs nɪs
outmost ˈaʊt məʊst ‖ -moust
outnumber ˌaʊt ˈnʌm bə ‖ -bᵊr **~ed** d **outnumbering** ˌaʊt ˈnʌm bər‿ɪŋ **~s** z
out-of-body ˌaʊt əv ˈbɒd i ◂ ‖ ˌaʊt̬ əv ˈbɑːd i ◂
out-of-court ˌaʊt əv ˈkɔːt ◂ ‖ ˌaʊt̬ əv ˈkɔːrt ◂ -ˈkourt ◂
out-of-date ˌaʊt əv ˈdeɪt ◂ ‖ ˌaʊt̬-
out-of-door ˌaʊt əv ˈdɔː ◂ ‖ ˌaʊt̬ əv ˈdɔːr ◂ -ˈdour
out-of-pocket ˌaʊt əv ˈpɒk ɪt ◂ §-ət ‖ ˌaʊt̬ əv ˈpɑːk-
ˌout-of-ˌpocket exˈpenses
out-of-sight ˌaʊt əv ˈsaɪt ◂ ‖ ˌaʊt̬-
out-of-state ˌaʊt əv ˈsteɪt ◂ ‖ ˌaʊt̬-
out-of-the-way ˌaʊt əv ðə ˈweɪ ◂ -ə ðə- ‖ ˌaʊt̬-
ˌout-of-the-ˌway ˈplaces
out-of-town ˌaʊt əv ˈtaʊn ◂ ‖ ˌaʊt̬-
out-of-work ˌaʊt əv ˈwɜːk ◂ ‖ ˌaʊt̬ əv ˈwɜːk ◂
outpac|e ˌaʊt ˈpeɪs **~ed** t **~es** ɪz əz **~ing** ɪŋ

O

outpatient ˈaʊt ˌpeɪʃ ənt **~s** s
outperform ˌaʊt pə ˈfɔːm ‖ -pər ˈfɔːrm **~ed** d **~ing** ɪŋ **~s** z
outplacement ˈaʊt ˌpleɪs mənt **~s** s
outplay ˌaʊt ˈpleɪ **~ed** d **~ing** ɪŋ **~s** z
out|point ˌaʊt |ˈpɔɪnt **~pointed** ˈpɔɪnt ɪd -əd ‖ ˈpɔɪnţ əd **~pointing** ˈpɔɪnt ɪŋ ‖ ˈpɔɪnţ ɪŋ **~points** ˈpɔɪnts
outpoll ˌaʊt ˈpəʊl ◂ →ˈpɒʊl ◂ ‖ -ˈpoʊl ◂ **~ed** d **~ing** ɪŋ **~s** z
outport ˈaʊt pɔːt ‖ -pɔːrt -poʊrt **~s** s
outpost ˈaʊt pəʊst ‖ -poʊst **~s** s
outpour *v* ˌaʊt ˈpɔː ‖ -ˈpɔːr -ˈpoʊr **~ed** d
outpouring ˌaʊt ˈpɔːr ɪŋ ‖ -ˈpoʊr- **~s** z
outpour *n* ˈaʊt pɔː ‖ -pɔːr -poʊr **~s** z
outpouring *n* ˈaʊt ˌpɔːr ɪŋ ˌ·ˈ·· ‖ -ˌpoʊr- **~s** z
out|put *n, v* ˈaʊt |pʊt **~puts** pʊts **~putted** pʊt ɪd -əd ‖ pʊţ əd **~putting** pʊt ɪŋ ‖ pʊţ ɪŋ
outrag|e *v* ˈaʊt reɪdʒ ˌ·ˈ· **~ed** d **~es** ɪz əz **~ing** ɪŋ
outrag|e *n* ˈaʊt reɪdʒ **~es** ɪz əz
outrageous ₍ˌ₎aʊt ˈreɪdʒ əs **~ly** li **~ness** nəs nɪs
Outram *(i)* ˈuːtr əm, *(ii)* ˈaʊtr əm
outran ˌaʊt ˈræn
outrang|e ˌaʊt ˈreɪndʒ **~ed** d **~es** ɪz əz **~ing** ɪŋ
out|rank ˌaʊt |ˈræŋk **~ranked** ˈræŋkt **~ranking** ˈræŋk ɪŋ **~ranks** ˈræŋks
outre, outré ˈuːtr eɪ ‖ uː ˈtreɪ —*Fr* [u tʁe]
outreach *n* ˈaʊt riːtʃ **~es** ɪz əz
outreach *v* ˌaʊt ˈriːtʃ **~ed** t **~es** ɪz əz **~ing** ɪŋ
out|ride ˌaʊt |ˈraɪd **~ridden** ˈrɪd ən **~rides** ˈraɪdz **~rode** ˈrəʊd ‖ ˈroʊd
outrider ˈaʊt ˌraɪd ə ‖ -ər **~s** z
outrigger ˈaʊt ˌrɪɡ ə ‖ -ər **~s** z
outright *adj* ˈaʊt raɪt
outright *adv* ₍ˌ₎aʊt ˈraɪt ˈ··
outrival ˌaʊt ˈraɪv əl **~ed, ~led** d **~ing, ~ling** ɪŋ **~s** z
outrode ˌaʊt ˈrəʊd ‖ -ˈroʊd
out|run ˌaʊt |ˈrʌn **~ran** ˈræn **~running** ˈrʌn ɪŋ **~runs** ˈrʌnz
outrush ˈaʊt rʌʃ **~es** ɪz əz
out|sell ˌaʊt |ˈsel **~selling** ˈsel ɪŋ **~sells** ˈselz **~sold** ˈsəʊld →ˈsɒʊld ‖ ˈsoʊld
outset ˈaʊt set
out|shine ˌaʊt |ˈʃaɪn **~shines** ˈʃaɪnz **~shining** ˈʃaɪn ɪŋ **~shone** ˈʃɒn ‖ ˈʃoʊn *(*)*
out|shoot ˌaʊt| ˈʃuːt ◂ **~shooting** ˈʃuːţ ɪŋ **~shoots** ˈʃuːts **~shot** ˈʃɒt ‖ ˈʃɑːt
outside ˌaʊt ˈsaɪd ◂ —*stressed* ˈ· · *whenever contrasted with* inside **~s** z
ˌoutside ˈbroadcast; **ˌoutside ˈworld**
outsider ˌaʊt ˈsaɪd ə ‖ -ər **~s** z
outsize ˌaʊt ˈsaɪz ◂ ˈ· · **~d** d
outskirts ˈaʊt skɜːts ‖ -skɜːts
out|smart ˌaʊt |ˈsmɑːt ‖ -|ˈsmɑːrt **~smarted** ˈsmɑːt ɪd -əd ‖ ˈsmɑːrţ əd **~smarting** ˈsmɑːt ɪŋ ‖ ˈsmɑːrţ ɪŋ **~smarts** ˈsmɑːts ‖ ˈsmɑːrts
outsourc|e ˈaʊt sɔːs ‖ -sɔːrs -soʊrs **~ed** t **~es** ɪz əz **~ing** ɪŋ

outspan, O~ *n* ˈaʊt spæn **~s** z
outspan *v* ˌaʊt ˈspæn **~ned** d **~ning** ɪŋ **~s** z
outspend ˌaʊt ˈspend **~ing** ɪŋ **~s** z **outspent** ˌaʊt ˈspent
outspoken ₍ˌ₎aʊt ˈspəʊk ən ‖ -ˈspoʊk- **~ly** li **~ness** nəs nɪs
outspread *v, adj* ˌaʊt ˈspred ◂ **~ing** ɪŋ **~s** z
outspread *n* ˈaʊt spred
outstanding ₍ˌ₎aʊt ˈstænd ɪŋ **~ly** li
outstare ₍ˌ₎aʊt ˈsteə ‖ -ˈsteər -ˈstæər **~d** d **~s** z
outstaring ˌaʊt ˈsteər ɪŋ ‖ -ˈster ɪŋ -ˈstær-
outstation ˈaʊt ˌsteɪʃ ən **~ed** d **~s** z
outstay ˌaʊt ˈsteɪ **~ed** d **~ing** ɪŋ **~s** z
outstretched ˌaʊt ˈstretʃt ◂
outstrip ˌaʊt ˈstrɪp **~ped** t **~ping** ɪŋ **~s** s
outswing ˈaʊt swɪŋ **~er/s** ə/z ‖ ər/z **~s** z
outta *'out of'* ˈaʊt ə ‖ ˈaʊţ ə
out-take ˈaʊt teɪk **~s** s
outtalk ˌaʊt ˈtɔːk ‖ -ˈtɑːk **~ed** t **~ing** ɪŋ **~s** s
out-tray ˈaʊt treɪ **~s** z
outturn ˈaʊt tɜːn ‖ -tɜːn **~s** z
out|vote ˌaʊt |ˈvəʊt ‖ -|ˈvoʊt **~voted** ˈvəʊt ɪd -əd ‖ ˈvoʊţ əd **~votes** ˈvəʊts ‖ ˈvoʊts **~voting** ˈvəʊt ɪŋ ‖ ˈvoʊţ ɪŋ
outward ˈaʊt wəd ‖ -wərd **~ly** li **~ness** nəs nɪs **~s** z
ˌOutward ˈBound
out|wear ˌaʊt |ˈweə ‖ -|ˈweər -ˈwæər **~wearing** ˈweər ɪŋ ‖ ˈwer ɪŋ ˈwær- **~wears** ˈweəz ‖ ˈweərz ˈwæərz **~worn** ˈwɔːn ◂ ‖ ˈwɔːrn ◂ ˈwoʊrn
outweigh ˌaʊt ˈweɪ **~ed** d **~ing** ɪŋ **~s** z
out|wit ˌaʊt |ˈwɪt **~wits** ˈwɪts **~witted** ˈwɪt ɪd -əd‖ ˈwɪţ əd **~witting** ˈwɪt ɪŋ ‖ ˈwɪţ ɪŋ
outwith ˌaʊt ˈwɪθ ◂ -ˈwɪð —*Since this is mainly a Scottish word, it tends to be said with the* θ *of Scottish* with
outwore ˌaʊt ˈwɔː ‖ -ˈwɔːr -ˈwoʊr
outwork *n* ˈaʊt wɜːk ‖ -wɜːk **~er/s** ə/z ‖ ər/z
outworn ˌaʊt ˈwɔːn ◂ ‖ -ˈwɔːrn ◂ -ˈwoʊrn
ouzel ˈuːz əl **~s** z
ouzo ˈuːz əʊ ‖ -oʊ —*Gk* [ˈu zɔ]
ova ˈəʊv ə ‖ ˈoʊv ə
oval, Oval ˈəʊv əl ‖ ˈoʊv- **~ly** i **~ness** nəs nɪs **~s** z
ˌOval ˈOffice, ˈ· · ˌ· ·
Ovaltine *tdmk* ˈəʊv əl tiːn ‖ ˈoʊv-
Ovambo əʊ ˈvæm bəʊ ‖ oʊ ˈvɑːm boʊ
ovarian əʊ ˈveər iˌən ‖ oʊ ˈver- -ˈvær-
ovar|y ˈəʊv ər |i ‖ ˈoʊv- **~ies** iz
ovate *Welsh title* ˈɒv ət -ɪt; ˈəʊv eɪt ‖ ˈɑːv- **~s** s
ovate *'egg-shaped'* ˈəʊv eɪt -ət, -ɪt ‖ ˈoʊv- **~ly** li
ovation əʊ ˈveɪʃ ən ‖ oʊ- **~s** z
Ove Arup ˌəʊv ˈær əp ‖ ˌoʊv- -ˈer-
oven ˈʌv ən **~s** z
ovenbird ˈʌv ən bɜːd →-əm- ‖ -bɜːd **~s** z
Ovenden *(i)* ˈɒv ən dən ‖ ˈɑːv-, *(ii)* ˈəʊv- ‖ ˈoʊv-
ovenproof ˈʌv ən pruːf →-əm-, §-prʊf
oven-ready ˌʌv ən ˈred i ◂
ˌoven-ˌready ˈturkey
Ovens ˈʌv ənz
ovenware ˈʌv ən weə ‖ -wer -wær

over, Over ˈəʊv ə ‖ ˈoʊv ᵊr **~s** z
ˌover and ˈdone with
over- ¦əʊv ə ‖ ¦oʊv ᵊr —*but before a vowel sound,* ¦əʊv ər ‖ ¦oʊv ər
overabundance ˌəʊv ər ə ˈbʌnd ənᵗs ˌ·rə'·· ‖ˌoʊv ər‿
overachiever ˌəʊv ər ə ˈtʃiːv ə ˌ·rə'·· ‖ ˌoʊv ər‿ə ˈtʃiːv ᵊr **~s** z
overact ˌəʊv ər ˈækt ‖ ˌoʊv ər- **~ed** ɪd əd **~ing** ɪŋ **~s** s
overactive ˌəʊv ər ˈækt ɪv ‖ ˌoʊv ər-
overactivity ˌəʊv ər æk ˈtɪv ət i -ɪt i ‖ ˌoʊv ər æk ˈtɪv əṭ i
overage *n 'surplus'* ˈəʊv ər ɪdʒ ‖ ˈoʊv-
overage *adj 'too old'* ˌəʊv ər ˈeɪdʒ ◂ ‖ ˌoʊv ər-
overall *n* ˈəʊv ər ɔːl ‖ ˈoʊv ər- -ɑːl **~s** z
overall *adj, adv* ˌəʊv ər ˈɔːl ◂ ‖ ˌoʊv ər-ˈɑːl
overambitious ˌəʊv ər æm ˈbɪʃ əs ◂ ‖ ˌoʊv ər- **~ly** li
overanxiety ˌəʊv ər æŋ ˈzaɪ‿ət i ˌ·æŋg-, ‿ɪt i ‖ ˌoʊv ər æŋ ˈzaɪ əṭ i
overanxious ˌəʊv ər ˈæŋk ʃəs ◂ ‖ ˌoʊv ər- **~ly** li **~ness** nəs nɪs
overarch ˌəʊv ər ˈɑːtʃ ‖ ˌoʊv ər ˈɑːrtʃ **~ed** t **~es** ɪz əz **~ing** ɪŋ
overarm ˈəʊv ər ɑːm ‖ ˈoʊv ər ɑːrm
over|awe ˌəʊv ər ˈɔː ‖ ˌoʊv ər- -ˈɑː **~awed** ˈɔːd ‖ ˈɑːd **~awes** ˈɔːz ‖ ˈɑːz **~awing** ˈɔːʳ ɪŋ ‖ˈɔː ɪŋ ˈɑː-
overbalanc|e ˌəʊv ə ˈbæl ənᵗs ‖ ˌoʊv ᵊr- **~ed** t **~es** ɪz əz **~ing** ɪŋ
over|bear ˌəʊv ə |ˈbeə ‖ ˌoʊv ᵊr |ˈbeᵊr -ˈbæᵊr **~bearing/ly** ˈbeər ɪŋ /li ‖ ˈber ɪŋ /li ˈbær- **~bore** ˈbɔː ‖ ˈbɔːr ˈboʊr **~borne** ˈbɔːn ‖ ˈbɔːrn ˈboʊrn
overbid *n* ˈəʊv ə bɪd ‖ ˈoʊv ᵊr- **~s** z
overbid *v* ˌəʊv ə ˈbɪd ‖ˌoʊv ᵊr- **~ding** ɪŋ **~s** z
overbite ˈəʊv ə baɪt ‖ ˈoʊv ᵊr-
over|blow *v* ˌəʊv ə |ˈbləʊ ‖ ˌoʊv ᵊr |ˈbloʊ '·· **~blew** ˈbluː **~blowing** ˈbləʊ ɪŋ ‖ ˈbloʊ ɪŋ **~blown** ˈbləʊn ‖ ˈbloʊn **~blows** ˈbləʊz ‖ ˈbloʊz
overboard ˈəʊv ə bɔːd ˌ· ·ˈ· ‖ ˈoʊv ᵊr bɔːrd -boʊrd
overbook ˌəʊv ə ˈbʊk §-ˈbuːk ‖ˌoʊv ᵊr- **~ed** t **~ing** ɪŋ **~s** s
overbor... —*see* **overbear**
overbridg|e ˈəʊv ə brɪdʒ ‖ ˈoʊv ᵊr- **~es** ɪz əz
overburden *v* ˌəʊv ə ˈbɜːd ᵊn ‖ˌoʊv ᵊr ˈbɜːd ᵊn **~ed** d **~ing** ‿ɪŋ **~s** z
overburden *n* ˈəʊv ə ˌbɜːd ᵊn ‖ ˈoʊv ᵊr ˌbɜːd ᵊn **~s** z
overcall *v* ˌəʊv ə ˈkɔːl ‖ ˌoʊv ᵊr- -ˈkɑːl **~ed** d **~ing** ɪŋ **~s** z
overcall *n* ˈəʊv ə kɔːl‖ ˈoʊv ᵊr- -kɑːl **~s** z
overcame ˌəʊv ə ˈkeɪm ‖ ˌoʊv ᵊr-
overcapacity ˌəʊv ə kə ˈpæs ət i -ɪt i ‖ ˌoʊv ᵊr kə ˈpæs əṭ i
overcast *adj* ˌəʊv ə ˈkɑːst ◂ §-ˈkæst, '· · ‖ ˌoʊv ᵊr ˈkæst ◂
overcast *n* ˈəʊv ə kɑːst §-kæst ‖ ˈoʊv ᵊr kæst
overcautious ˌəʊv ə ˈkɔːʃ əs ◂ ‖ ˌoʊv ᵊr- -ˈkɑːʃ-
overcharg|e *v* ˌəʊv ə ˈtʃɑːdʒ ‖ ˌoʊv ᵊr ˈtʃɑːrdʒ **~ed** d **~es** ɪz əz **~ing** ɪŋ
overcharg|e *n* ˈəʊv ə tʃɑːdʒ ‖ ˈoʊv ᵊr tʃɑːrdʒ **~es** ɪz əz
overcloud ˌəʊv ə ˈklaʊd ‖ ˌoʊv ᵊr- **~ed** ɪd əd **~ing** ɪŋ **~s** z
overcoat ˈəʊv ə kəʊt ‖ ˈoʊv ᵊr koʊt **~s** s
over|come ˌəʊv ə |ˈkʌm ‖ ˌoʊv ᵊr- **~came** ˈkeɪm **~comes** ˈkʌmz **~coming** ˈkʌm ɪŋ
overcom|mit ˌəʊv ə kə |ˈmɪt ‖ ˌoʊv ᵊr- **~mits** ˈmɪts **~mitted** ˈmɪt ɪd -əd ‖ ˈmɪṭ əd **~mitting** ˈmɪt ɪŋ ‖ ˈmɪṭ ɪŋ
overcompen|sate ˌəʊv ə ˈkɒmp ən |seɪt -en- ‖ ˌoʊv ᵊr ˈkɑːmp- **~sated** seɪt ɪd -əd ‖ seɪṭ əd **~sates** seɪts **~sating** seɪt ɪŋ ‖ seɪṭ ɪŋ
overcompensation ˌəʊv ə ˌkɒmp ən ˈseɪʃ ᵊn -ˌ·en- ‖ˌoʊv ᵊr ˌkɑːmp- **~s** z
overconfid|ence ˌəʊv ə ˈkɒn fɪd |ənᵗs -fəd- ‖ˌoʊv ᵊr ˈkɑːn- **~ent/ly** ənt /li
overcook ˌəʊv ə ˈkʊk ◂ §-ˈkuːk ‖ ˌoʊv ᵊr- **~ed** t **~ing** ɪŋ **~s** s
overcrop ˌəʊv ə ˈkrɒp ‖ ˌoʊv ᵊr ˈkrɑːp **~ped** t **~ping** ɪŋ **~s** s
overcrowd ˌəʊv ə ˈkraʊd ‖ ˌoʊv ᵊr- **~ed** ɪd əd **~ing** ɪŋ **~s** z
overdevelop ˌəʊv ə dɪ ˈvel əp -ə də-, §-ə diː- ‖ ˌoʊv ᵊr- **~ed** t **~ing** ɪŋ **~ment** mənt **~s** s
over|do ˌəʊv ə |ˈduː ‖ˌoʊv ᵊr- **~did** ˈdɪd **~does** ˈdʌz **~done** ˈdʌn ◂ **~doing** ˈduː‿ɪŋ
overdos|e *n* ˈəʊv ə dəʊs §-dəʊz‖ ˈoʊv ᵊr doʊs **~es** ɪz əz
overdos|e *v* ˌəʊv ə ˈdəʊs §-ˈdəʊz ‖ ˌoʊv ᵊr ˈdoʊs **~ed** t **~es** ɪz əz **~ing** ɪŋ
overdraft ˈəʊv ə drɑːft §-dræft ‖ ˈoʊv ᵊr dræft **~s** s
over|draw ˌəʊv ə| ˈdrɔː ‖ ˌoʊv ᵊr|- -ˈdrɑː; '·. . **~drawing** ˈdrɔːʳ ɪŋ ‖ ˈdrɔː ɪŋ ˈdrɑː- **~drawn** ˈdrɔːn ◂ ‖ ˈdrɑːn **~draws** ˈdrɔːz ‖ ˈdrɑːz **~drew** ˈdruː
overdress ˌəʊv ə ˈdres ‖ ˌoʊv ᵊr- **~ed** t ◂ **~es** ɪz əz **~ing** ɪŋ
overdrew ˌəʊv ə ˈdruː ‖ ˌoʊv ᵊr- ˈ· ·
overdrive *n* ˈəʊv ə draɪv ‖ ˈoʊv ᵊr-
overdue ˌəʊv ə ˈdjuː ◂ →§-ˈdʒuː ‖ˌoʊv ᵊr ˈduː ◂ -ˈdjuː
ˌoverdue ˈbills
over-easy ˌəʊv ər ˈiːz i ◂ ‖ ˌoʊv ᵊr-
over|eat ˌəʊv ər| ˈiːt ‖ ˌoʊv ər| ˈiːt **~ate** ˈet ˈeɪt ‖ ˈeɪt **~eaten** ˈiːt ᵊn **~eating** ˈiːt ɪŋ ‖ ˈiːṭ ɪŋ **~eats** ˈiːts
overegg ˌəʊv ər ˈeg ‖ ˌoʊv ᵊr- **~ed** d **~ing** ɪŋ **~s** z
overempha|sis ˌəʊv ərˈemᵖf ə |sɪs ‖ ˌoʊv ᵊr- **~ses** siːz
overemphasis|e, overemphasiz|e ˌəʊv ərˈemᵖf ə saɪz ‖ ˌoʊv ᵊr- **~ed** d **~es** ɪz əz **~ing** ɪŋ
overesti|mate *v* ˌəʊv ər ˈest ɪ |meɪt -ˈ·ə- ‖ ˌoʊv ər- **~mated** meɪt ɪd -əd ‖ meɪṭ əd **~mates** meɪts **~mating** meɪt ɪŋ ‖ meɪṭ ɪŋ
overestimate *n* ˌəʊv ər ˈest ɪm ət -ˈ·əm-, -ɪt; -ɪ meɪt, -ə meɪt ‖ ˌoʊv ər- **~s** s

overex|cite ˌəʊv ər ɪk |ˈsaɪt -ekˈ·, -əkˈ·, ˌ·rɪkˈ·, ˌ·rəkˈ· ‖ ˌoʊv ər- **~cited** ˈsaɪt ɪd -əd ‖ ˈsaɪţ əd **~citement** ˈsaɪt mənt **~cites** ˈsaɪts **~citing** ˈsaɪt ɪŋ ‖ ˈsaɪţ ɪŋ
overe|xert ˌəʊv ər ɪg |ˈzɜːt -egˈ·, -əgˈ·, -ɪkˈ·, -ekˈ·, -əkˈ·, ˌ·rɪgˈ·, ˌ·rəgˈ· ‖ ˌoʊv ər ɪg |ˈzɜːt **~xerted** ˈzɜːt ɪd -əd ‖ ˈzɜːţ əd **~xerting** ˈzɜːt ɪŋ ‖ ˈzɜːţ ɪŋ **~xerts** ˈzɜːts ‖ ˈzɜːts
overexertion ˌəʊv ər ɪg ˈzɜːʃ ən -egˈ·, -əgˈ·, -ɪkˈ·, -ekˈ·, -əkˈ·, ˌ·rɪgˈ·, ˌ·rəgˈ· ‖ ˌoʊv ər ɪg ˈzɜːʃ ən **~s** z
overexpos|e ˌəʊv ər ɪk ˈspəʊz -ekˈ·, -əkˈ·, ˌ·rɪkˈ·, ˌ·rəkˈ· ‖ ˌoʊv ər ɪk ˈspoʊz **~ed** d **~es** ɪz əz **~ing** ɪŋ
overexposure ˌəʊv ər ɪk ˈspəʊʒ ə -ekˈ·-, -əkˈ·-, ˌ·rɪkˈ·, ˌ·rəkˈ· ‖ ˌoʊv ər ɪk ˈspoʊʒ ər **~s** z
overextend ˌəʊv ər ɪk ˈstend -ekˈ·, -əkˈ·, ˌ·rɪkˈ·, ˌ·rəkˈ· ‖ ˌoʊv ər‿ **~ed** ɪd ◂ əd **~ing** ɪŋ **~s** z
over|feed ˌəʊv ə |ˈfiːd ‖ ˌoʊv ər- **~fed** ˈfed **~feeding** ˈfiːd ɪŋ **~feeds** ˈfiːdz
overfill ˌəʊv ə ˈfɪl ◂ ‖ ˌoʊv ər- **~ed** d **~ing** ɪŋ **~s** z
overfish ˌəʊv ə ˈfɪʃ ◂ ‖ ˌoʊv ər- **~ed** t **~es** ɪz əz **~ing** ɪŋ
over|flew ˌəʊv ə |ˈfluː ‖ ˌoʊv ər- **~flies** ˈflaɪz
overflight ˈəʊv ə flaɪt ‖ ˈoʊv ər- **~s** s
overflow *v* ˌəʊv ə ˈfləʊ ‖ ˌoʊv ər ˈfloʊ **~ed** d **~ing** ɪŋ **~s** z
overflow *n* ˈəʊv ə fləʊ ‖ ˈoʊv ər floʊ **~s** z
over|fly ˌəʊv ə |ˈflaɪ ◂ ‖ ˌoʊv ər- **~flew** ˈfluː **~flies** ˈflaɪz **~flown** ˈfləʊn ‖ ˈfloʊn **~flying** ˈflaɪ ɪŋ
overfond ˌəʊv ə ˈfɒnd ◂ ‖ ˌoʊv ər ˈfɑːnd ◂
overgarment ˈəʊv ə ˌgɑːm ənt ‖ ˈoʊv ər ˌgɑːrm ənt **~s** s
overgeneralis... —*see* **overgeneraliz...**
overgeneralization ˌəʊv ə ˌdʒen ər‿əl aɪ ˈzeɪʃ ən ‿əl ɪ- ‖ ˌoʊv ər ˌdʒen ər‿əl ə ˈzeɪʃ ən
overgeneraliz|e ˌəʊv ə ˈdʒen ər‿ə laɪz ‖ ˌoʊv ər- **~ed** d **~es** ɪz əz **~ing** ɪŋ
overgraz|e ˌəʊv ə ˈgreɪz ‖ ˌoʊv ər- **~ed** d **~es** ɪz əz **~ing** ɪŋ
overground ˈəʊv ə graʊnd ‖ ˈoʊv ər-
overgrown ˌəʊv ə ˈgrəʊn ◂ ‖ ˌoʊv ər ˈgroʊn ◂ **ˌovergrown ˈgarden**
overgrowth ˈəʊv ə grəʊθ ‖ ˈoʊv ər groʊθ
overhand ˈəʊv ə hænd ‖ ˈoʊv ər-
over|hang *v* ˌəʊv ə |ˈhæŋ ‖ ˌoʊv ər- **~hanging** ˈhæŋ ɪŋ ◂ **~hangs** ˈhæŋz **~hung** ˈhʌŋ ◂
overhang *n* ˈəʊv ə hæŋ ‖ ˈoʊv ər- **~s** z
overhast|y ˌəʊv ə ˈheɪst |i ‖ ˌoʊv ər- **~ily** ɪ li əl i **~iness** i nəs i nɪs
overhaul *v* ˌəʊv ə ˈhɔːl ‖ ˌoʊv ər- -ˈhɑːl **~ed** d **~ing** ɪŋ **~s** z
overhaul *n* ˈəʊv ə hɔːl ‖ ˈoʊv ər- -hɑːl **~s** z
overhead *adj, adv* ˌəʊv ə ˈhed ◂ ‖ ˌoʊv ər- **ˌoverhead ˈcamshaft**; **ˌoverhead proˈjector**
overhead *n* ˈəʊv ə hed ‖ ˈoʊv ər- **~s** z
over|hear ˌəʊv ə |ˈhɪə ‖ ˌoʊv ər |ˈhɪər **~heard** ˈhɜːd ◂ ‖ ˈhɜːd ◂ *(!)* **~hearing** ˈhɪər ɪŋ ‖ ˈhɪr ɪŋ **~hears** ˈhɪəz ‖ ˈhɪərz
over|heat ˌəʊv ə |ˈhiːt ‖ ˌoʊv ər- **~heated** ˈhiːt ɪd -əd ‖ ˈhiːţ əd **~heating** ˈhiːt ɪŋ ‖ ˈhiːţ ɪŋ **~heats** ˈhiːts
overhung ˌəʊv ə ˈhʌŋ ◂ ‖ ˌoʊv ər-
overindulg|e ˌəʊv ər ɪn ˈdʌldʒ ‖ ˌoʊv ər- **~ed** d **~ence** ənts **~ent/ly** ənt /li **~es** ɪz əz **~ing** ɪŋ
overjoyed ˌəʊv ə ˈdʒɔɪd ◂ ‖ ˌoʊv ər-
overkill ˈəʊv ə kɪl ‖ ˈoʊv ər-
overladen ˌəʊv ə ˈleɪd ən ◂ ‖ ˌoʊv ər-
overlaid ˌəʊv ə ˈleɪd ◂ ‖ ˌoʊv ər-
overland ˈəʊv ə lænd ˌ·ˈ·◂ ‖ ˈoʊv ər- **~er/s** ə/z ‖ ər/z
overlap *n* ˈəʊv ə læp ‖ ˈoʊv ər- **~s** s
overlap *v* ˌəʊv ə ˈlæp ‖ ˌoʊv ər- **~ped** t **~ping** ɪŋ **~s** s
overlay *n* ˈəʊv ə leɪ ‖ ˈoʊv ər- **~s** z
over|lay *v* ˌəʊv ə |ˈleɪ ‖ ˌoʊv ər- **~laid** ˈleɪd **~laying** ˈleɪ ɪŋ **~lays** ˈleɪz
overleaf ˌəʊv ə ˈliːf ˈ· ·· ‖ ˈoʊv ər liːf
over|leap ˌəʊv ə |ˈliːp ‖ ˌoʊv ər- **~leaped** ˈlept ˈliːpt ‖ ˈliːpt **~leaping** ˈliːp ɪŋ **~leaps** ˈliːps **~leapt** ˈlept
over|lie ˌəʊv ə |ˈlaɪ ‖ ˌoʊv ər- **~lain** ˈleɪn **~lay** ˈleɪ **~lies** ˈlaɪz **~lying** ˈlaɪ ɪŋ
overload *v* ˌəʊv ə ˈləʊd ‖ ˌoʊv ər ˈloʊd **~ed** ɪd əd **~ing** ɪŋ **~s** z
overload *n* ˈəʊv ə ləʊd ‖ ˈoʊv ər loʊd **~s** z
overlong ˌəʊv ə ˈlɒŋ ◂ ‖ ˌoʊv ər ˈlɔːŋ -ˈlɑːŋ
overlook *v* ˌəʊv ə ˈlʊk §-ˈluːk ‖ ˌoʊv ər- **~ed** t **~ing** ɪŋ **~s** s
overlook *n* ˈəʊv ə lʊk §-luːk ‖ ˈoʊv ər- **~s** s
overlord ˈəʊv ə lɔːd ‖ ˈoʊv ər lɔːrd **~s** z **~ship** ʃɪp
overly ˈəʊv ə li ‖ ˈoʊv ər-
overlying ˌəʊv ə ˈlaɪ ɪŋ ◂ ‖ ˌoʊv ər-
overman *v* ˌəʊv ə ˈmæn ‖ ˌoʊv ər- **~ned** d **~ning** nɪŋ **~s** z
overmast|er ˌəʊv ə ˈmɑːst |ə §-ˈmæst- ‖ ˌoʊv ər ˈmæst |ər **~ered** əd ‖ ərd **~ering** ər‿ɪŋ **~ers** əz ‖ ərz
overmuch ˌəʊv ə ˈmʌtʃ ◂ ‖ ˌoʊv ər-
overnight *adj, adv* ˌəʊv ə ˈnaɪt ◂ ‖ ˌoʊv ər- **ˌovernight ˈbag**
overoptimistic ˌəʊv ər ˌɒpt ɪ ˈmɪst ɪk ◂ -ˌ·ə- ‖ ˌoʊv ər ˌɑːpt- **~ally** əl‿i
overpaid ˌəʊv ə ˈpeɪd ◂ ‖ ˌoʊv ər-
overpass ˈəʊv ə pɑːs §-pæs ‖ ˈoʊv ər pæs **~es** ɪz əz
over|pay *v* ˌəʊv ə |ˈpeɪ ‖ ˌoʊv ər- **~paid** ˈpeɪd ◂ **~paying** ˈpeɪ ɪŋ **~ment/s** mənt/s **~pays** ˈpeɪz
overplay ˌəʊv ə ˈpleɪ ‖ ˌoʊv ər- **~ed** d **~ing** ɪŋ **~s** z
overplus ˈəʊv ə plʌs ‖ ˈoʊv ər-
overpopu|late ˌəʊv ə ˈpɒp ju |leɪt -ˈ·jə- ‖ ˌoʊv ər ˈpɑːp jə- **~lated** leɪt ɪd -əd ‖ leɪţ əd **~lates** leɪts **~lating** leɪt ɪŋ ‖ leɪţ ɪŋ
overpopulation ˌəʊv ə ˌpɒp ju ˈleɪʃ ən -jəˈ·- ‖ ˌoʊv ər ˌpɑːp jə-
overpower ˌəʊv ə ˈpaʊ‿ə ‖ ˌoʊv ər ˈpaʊ‿ər **~ed** d **overpowering/ly** ˌəʊv ə ˈpaʊ‿ər ɪŋ /li ‖ ˌoʊv ər ˈpaʊ‿ər ɪŋ /li **~s** z

overpressure ˈəʊv ə ˌpreʃ ə ‖ ˈoʊv ᵊr ˌpreʃ ᵊr

overpriced ˌəʊv ə ˈpraɪst ◂ ‖ ˌoʊv ᵊr-

over|print *v* ˌəʊv ə |ˈprɪnt ‖ ˌoʊv ᵊr- **~printed** ˈprɪnt ɪd -əd ‖ ˈprɪnṭ əd **~printing** ˈprɪnt ɪŋ ‖ ˈprɪnṭ ɪŋ **~prints** ˈprɪnts

overprint *n* ˈəʊv ə prɪnt ‖ ˈoʊv ᵊr- **~s** s

overproduc|e ˌəʊv ə prə ˈdjuːs §-ˈduːs §→ˈdʒuːs ‖ ˌoʊv ᵊr prə ˈduːs -ˈdjuːs **~ed** t **~es** ɪz əz **~ing** ɪŋ

overproduction ˌəʊv ə prə ˈdʌk ʃᵊn ‖ ˌoʊv ᵊr-

overproof ˌəʊv ə ˈpruːf ‖ ˌoʊv ᵊr-

overprotect ˌəʊv ə prəʊ ˈtekt ‖ ˌoʊv ᵊr prə- **~ed** ɪd əd **~ing** ɪŋ **~s** s

overprotective ˌəʊv ə prəʊ ˈtekt ɪv ◂ ‖ ˌoʊv ᵊr prə-

overqualified ˌəʊv ə ˈkwɒl ɪ faɪd ◂ -ˈ·ə- ‖ ˌoʊv ᵊr ˈkwɑːl-

overran ˌəʊv ə ˈræn ‖ ˌoʊv ᵊr-

over|rate ˌəʊv ə |ˈreɪt ‖ ˌoʊv ᵊr- **~rated** ˈreɪt ɪd ◂ -əd ‖ ˈreɪṭ əd ◂ **~rates** ˈreɪts **~rating** ˈreɪt ɪŋ ‖ ˈreɪṭ ɪŋ

overreach ˌəʊv ə ˈriːtʃ ‖ ˌoʊv ᵊr- **~ed** t **~es** ɪz əz **~ing** ɪŋ

overreact ˌəʊv ə ri ˈækt ‖ ˌoʊv ᵊr- **~ed** ɪd əd **~ing** ɪŋ **~s** s

overreaction ˌəʊv ə ri ˈæk ʃᵊn ‖ ˌoʊv ᵊr- **~s** z

override *n* ˈəʊv ə raɪd ‖ ˈoʊv ᵊr- **~s** z

over|ride *v* ˌəʊv ə |ˈraɪd ‖ ˌoʊv ᵊr- **~ridden** ˈrɪd ᵊn **~rides** ˈraɪdz **~riding/ly** ˈraɪd ɪŋ /li **~rode** ˈrəʊd ‖ ˈroʊd

overrider ˈəʊv ə raɪd ə ‖ ˈoʊv ᵊr raɪd ᵊr **~s** z

overripe ˌəʊv ə ˈraɪp ‖ ˌoʊv ᵊr- **~ness** nəs nɪs

overrul|e ˌəʊv ə ˈruːl ‖ ˌoʊv ᵊr- **~ed** d **~es** z **~ing** ɪŋ

overrun *n* ˈəʊv ə rʌn ‖ ˈoʊv ᵊr- **~s** z

over|run *v* ˌəʊv ə |ˈrʌn ‖ ˌoʊv ᵊr- **~ran** ˈræn **~running** ˈrʌn ɪŋ **~runs** ˈrʌnz

oversaw ˌəʊv ə ˈsɔː ‖ ˌoʊv ᵊr- -ˈsɑː

oversea ˌəʊv ə ˈsiː ◂ ‖ ˌoʊv ᵊr- **~s** z

ˌoverseas ˈposting

over|see ˌəʊv ə |ˈsiː ‖ ˌoʊv ᵊr- **~saw** ˈsɔː ‖ ˈsɑː **~seeing** ˈsiː ɪŋ **~seen** ˈsiːn **~sees** ˈsiːz

overseer ˈəʊv ə sɪə ˈ··ˌsiː ə ‖ ˈoʊv ᵊr sɪr ˈ··ˌsiː ᵊr **~s** z

over|sell ˌəʊv ə |ˈsel ‖ ˌoʊv ᵊr- **~selling** ˈsel ɪŋ **~sells** ˈselz **~sold** ˈsəʊld →ˈsɒʊld ‖ ˈsoʊld

oversensitive ˌəʊv ə ˈsenᵗs ət ɪv -ɪt ɪv ‖ ˌoʊv ᵊr ˈsenᵗs əṭ ɪv

oversensitivity ˌəʊv ə ˌsenᵗs ə ˈtɪv ət i -ɪˈ·-, -ɪt i ‖ ˌoʊv ᵊr ˌsenᵗs ə ˈtɪv əṭ i

oversew ˈəʊv ə səʊ ˌ·ˈ· ‖ ˈoʊv ᵊr soʊ **~ed** d **~ing** ɪŋ **~n** n **~s** z

oversexed ˌəʊv ə ˈsekst ◂ ‖ ˌoʊv ᵊr-

overshadow ˌəʊv ə ˈʃæd əʊ ‖ ˌoʊv ᵊr ˈʃæd oʊ **~ed** d **~ing** ɪŋ **~s** z

overshoe ˈəʊv ə ʃuː ‖ ˈoʊv ᵊr- **~s** z

overshoot *n* ˈəʊv ə ʃuːt ‖ ˈoʊv ᵊr- **~s** s

over|shoot *v* ˌəʊv ə |ˈʃuːt ‖ ˌoʊv ᵊr- **~shooting** ˈʃuːt ɪŋ ‖ ˈʃuːṭ ɪŋ **~shoots** ˈʃuːts **~shot** ˈʃɒt ◂ ‖ ˈʃɑːt ◂

overside ˈəʊv ə saɪd ‖ ˈoʊv ᵊr-

oversight ˈəʊv ə saɪt ‖ ˈoʊv ᵊr- **~s** s

oversimplification ˌəʊv ə ˌsɪmp lɪf ɪ ˈkeɪʃ ᵊn -ˌ·ləf-, §-əˈ-- ‖ ˌoʊv ᵊr- **~s** z

oversimpli|fy ˌəʊv ə ˈsɪmp lɪ |faɪ -ˈ·lə- ‖ ˌoʊv ᵊr- **~fied** faɪd **~fies** faɪz **~fying** faɪ ɪŋ

oversize *adj* ˌəʊv ə ˈsaɪz ◂ ‖ ˌoʊv ᵊr- **~d** d

ˌoversize ˈboots

over|sleep *v* ˌəʊv ə |ˈsliːp ‖ ˌoʊv ᵊr- **~sleeping** ˈsliːp ɪŋ **~sleeps** ˈsliːps **~slept** ˈslept

oversold ˌəʊv ə ˈsəʊld →-ˈsɒʊld ‖ ˌoʊv ᵊr ˈsoʊld

overspend *n* ˈəʊv ə spend ‖ ˈoʊv ᵊr- **~s** z

over|spend *v* ˌəʊv ə |ˈspend ‖ ˌoʊv ᵊr- **~spending** ˈspend ɪŋ **~spends** ˈspendz **~spent** ˈspent

overspill *n* ˈəʊv ə spɪl ‖ ˈoʊv ᵊr- **~s** z

overstaff ˌəʊv ə ˈstɑːf §-ˈstæf ‖ ˌoʊv ᵊr ˈstæf **~ed** t **~ing** ɪŋ **~s** s

over|state ˌəʊv ə |ˈsteɪt ‖ ˌoʊv ᵊr- **~stated** ˈsteɪt ɪd -əd ‖ ˈsteɪṭ əd **~states** ˈsteɪts **~stating** ˈsteɪt ɪŋ ‖ ˈsteɪṭ ɪŋ

overstatement ˌəʊv ə ˈsteɪt mənt ˈ··ˌ·· ‖ ˈoʊv ᵊr ˌsteɪt- **~s** s

overstay ˌəʊv ə ˈsteɪ ‖ ˌoʊv ᵊr- **~ed** d **~er/s** ə/z ‖ ᵊr/z **~ing** ɪŋ **~s** z

oversteer *v* ˌəʊv ə ˈstɪə ‖ ˌoʊv ᵊr ˈstɪᵊr **~ed** d

oversteering ˌəʊv ə ˈstɪər ɪŋ ‖ ˌoʊv ᵊr ˈstɪr ɪŋ **~s** z

oversteer *n* ˈəʊv ə stɪə ‖ ˈoʊv ᵊr stɪr

overstep *v* ˌəʊv ə ˈstep ‖ ˌoʊv ᵊr- **~ped** t **~ping** ɪŋ **~s** s

overstock *v* ˌəʊv ə ˈstɒk ‖ ˌoʊv ᵊr ˈstɑːk **~ed** t **~ing** ɪŋ **~s** s

overstrain *v* ˌəʊv ə ˈstreɪn ‖ ˌoʊv ᵊr- **~ed** d **~ing** ɪŋ **~s** z

overstrain *n* ˈəʊv ə streɪn ˌ·ˈ· ‖ ˈoʊv ᵊr-

overstretch ˌəʊv ə ˈstretʃ ‖ ˌoʊv ᵊr- **~ed** t **~es** ɪz əz **~ing** ɪŋ

overstrung ˌəʊv ə ˈstrʌŋ ◂ ˈ· · · ‖ ˌoʊv ᵊr-

overstuffed ˌəʊv ə ˈstʌft ◂ ‖ ˌoʊv ᵊr-

oversubscrib|e ˌəʊv ə səb ˈskraɪb §-sʌbˈ· ‖ ˌoʊv ᵊr- **~ed** d **~es** z **~ing** ɪŋ

oversup|ply *v* ˌəʊv ə sə |ˈplaɪ ‖ ˌoʊv ᵊr- **~plied** ˈplaɪd **~plies** ˈplaɪz **~plying** ˈplaɪ ɪŋ

oversupply *n* ˌəʊv ə sə ˈplaɪ ˈ· · ·ˌ· ‖ ˈoʊv ᵊr sə ˌplaɪ

overt əʊ ˈvɜːt ˈəʊv ɜːt ‖ oʊ ˈvɝːt ˈoʊv ɝːt **~ly** li

overtake ˌəʊv ə ˈteɪk ‖ ˌoʊv ᵊr- **~taken** ˈteɪk ən ◂ **~takes** ˈteɪks **~taking** ˈteɪk ɪŋ **~took** ˈtʊk §ˈtuːk

overtax *v* ˌəʊv ə ˈtæks ‖ ˌoʊv ᵊr- **~ed** t **~es** ɪz əz **~ing** ɪŋ

over-the-counter ˌəʊv ə ðə ˈkaʊnt ə ◂ ‖ ˌoʊv ᵊr ðə ˈkaʊnṭ ᵊr ◂

over-the-top ˌəʊv ə ðə ˈtɒp ◂ ‖ ˌoʊv ᵊr ðə ˈtɑːp ◂

overthrow *n* ˈəʊv ə θrəʊ ‖ ˈoʊv ᵊr θroʊ **~s** z

over|throw *v* ˌəʊv ə |ˈθrəʊ ◂ ‖ ˌoʊv ᵊr |ˈθroʊ **~threw** ˈθruː **~throwing** ˈθrəʊ ɪŋ ‖ ˈθroʊ ɪŋ **~thrown** ˈθrəʊn ◂ §ˈθrəʊ ən ‖ ˈθroʊn ◂ **~throws** ˈθrəʊz ‖ ˈθroʊz

overthrust ˈəʊv ə θrʌst ‖ ˈoʊv ᵊr- **~s** s

overtime *n, adv* 'əʊv ə taɪm ‖ 'oʊv ᵊr-
'overtime ban
overtire ˌəʊv ə 'taɪ̯ə ◂ ‖ ˌoʊv ᵊr 'taɪ̯ᵊr ◂ **~d** d
overtiring ˌəʊv ə 'taɪ̯ər ɪŋ ‖ ˌoʊv ᵊr 'taɪ̯ᵊr ɪŋ **~s** z
Overton 'əʊv ət ən ‖ 'oʊv ᵊrt ᵊn
overtone 'əʊv ə təʊn ‖ 'oʊv ᵊr toʊn **~s** z
overtook ˌəʊv ə 'tʊk §-'tuːk ‖ ˌoʊv ᵊr-
overtop ˌəʊv ə 'tɒp ‖ ˌoʊv ᵊr 'tɑːp **~ped** t **~ping** ɪŋ **~s** s
overtrick 'əʊv ə trɪk ‖ 'oʊv ᵊr- **~s** s
overtrump ˌəʊv ə 'trʌmp ‖ ˌoʊv ᵊr- **~ed** t **~ing** ɪŋ **~s** s
overture 'əʊv ə tjʊə -tʃʊə, -tʃə ‖ 'oʊv ᵊr tʃʊr -tʃᵊr, -tjʊr **~s** z
overturn *v* ˌəʊv ə 'tɜːn ‖ ˌoʊv ᵊr 'tɜːn **~ed** d **~ing** ɪŋ **~s** z
overus|e *v* ˌəʊv ə 'juːz ‖ ˌoʊv ᵊr- **~ed** d **~es** ɪz əz **~ing** ɪŋ
overuse *n* ˌəʊv ə 'juːs ‖ ˌoʊv ᵊr-
overvalu|e ˌəʊv ə 'væl juː ‖ ˌoʊv ᵊr- **~ed** d **~es** z **~ing** ɪŋ
overview 'əʊv ə vjuː ‖ 'oʊv ᵊr- **~s** z
overweening ˌəʊv ə 'wiːn ɪŋ ◂ ‖ ˌoʊv ᵊr- **~ly** li
overweight *n* 'əʊv ə weɪt ‖ 'oʊv ᵊr-
over|weight *v, adj* ˌəʊv ə |'weɪt ◂ ‖ ˌoʊv ᵊr- **~weighted** 'weɪt ɪd -əd ‖ 'weɪţ əd **~weighting** 'weɪt ɪŋ ‖ 'weɪţ ɪŋ **~weights** 'weɪts
overwhelm ˌəʊv ə 'welm -'hwelm ‖ ˌoʊv ᵊr '*h*welm **~ed** d **~ing/ly** ɪŋ /li **~s** z
over|wind ˌəʊv ə 'waɪnd ‖ ˌoʊv ᵊr- **~winding** 'waɪnd ɪŋ **~winds** 'waɪndz **~wound** 'waʊnd
overwint|er ˌəʊv ə 'wɪnt |ə ‖ ˌoʊv ᵊr 'wɪnţ |ᵊr **~ered** əd ‖ ᵊrd **~ering** ər ɪŋ ‖ ər ɪŋ **~ers** əz ‖ ᵊrz
overwork *n* ˌəʊv ə 'wɜːk '· · · ‖ ˌoʊv ᵊr 'wɜːk
overwork *v* ˌəʊv ə 'wɜːk ‖ ˌoʊv ᵊr 'wɜːk **~ed** t **~ing** ɪŋ **~s** s
overwound ˌəʊv ə 'waʊnd ◂ ‖ ˌoʊv ᵊr-
over|write ˌəʊv ə |'raɪt ‖ ˌoʊv ᵊr- **~writes** 'raɪts **~writing** 'raɪt ɪŋ ‖ 'raɪţ ɪŋ **~written** 'rɪt ᵊn **~wrote** 'rəʊt ‖ 'roʊt
overwrought ˌəʊv ə 'rɔːt ◂ ‖ ˌoʊv ᵊr- -'rɑːt
overzealous ˌəʊv ə 'zel əs ◂ ‖ ˌoʊv ᵊr- **~ly** li **~ness** nəs nɪs
Ovett 'əʊv et əʊ 'vet ‖ 'oʊv et oʊ 'vet
Ovid *(i)* 'ɒv ɪd §-əd ‖ 'ɑːv-; *(ii)* 'əʊv ɪd §-əd ‖ 'oʊv- —*The Latin poet is known as (i); the American place name and personal name is (ii).*
Ovidian ɒ 'vɪd i̯ən əʊ- ‖ oʊ- ɑː-
oviduct 'əʊv i dʌkt §-ə- ‖ 'oʊv ə- **~s** s
Oviedo ˌɒv i 'eɪd əʊ ˌəʊv- ‖ ˌoʊv i 'eɪd oʊ —*Sp* [o 'βje ðo]
oviform 'əʊv i fɔːm §-ə- ‖ 'oʊv ə fɔːrm
ovine 'əʊv aɪn ‖ 'oʊv-
Oving 'əʊv ɪŋ ‖ 'oʊv-
Ovingdean 'əʊv ɪŋ diːn 'ɒv- ‖ 'oʊv-
oviparous əʊ 'vɪp ər əs ‖ oʊ- **~ly** li
ovipositor ˌəʊv i 'pɒz ɪt ə §ˌ·ə-, §-ət ə ‖ ˌoʊv ə 'pɑːz əţ ᵊr '· ·ˌ· · **~s** z

ovoid 'əʊv ɔɪd ‖ 'oʊv- **~s** z
ovo|lo 'əʊv ə |ləʊ ‖ 'oʊv ə |loʊ **~li** liː
ovoviviparity ˌəʊv əʊ ˌvɪv ɪ 'pær ət i -ə'-, -ət i ‖ ˌoʊv oʊ ˌvɪv ə 'pær əţ i
ovoviviparous ˌəʊv əʊ vɪ 'vɪp ər əs ◂ -və'-, -vaɪ'- ‖ ˌoʊv oʊ vaɪ-
ovular 'ɒv jʊl ə 'əʊv-, -jəl- ‖ 'ɑːv jəl ᵊr 'oʊv-
ovu|late *v* 'ɒv ju |leɪt 'əʊv-, -jə- ‖ 'ɑːv jə- 'oʊv **~lated** leɪt ɪd -əd ‖ leɪţ əd **~lates** leɪts **~lating** leɪt ɪŋ ‖ leɪţ ɪŋ
ovulation ˌɒv ju 'leɪʃ ᵊn ˌəʊv-, -jə- ‖ ˌɑːv jə- ˌoʊv- **~s** z
ovule 'ɒv juːl 'əʊv- ‖ 'ɑːv- 'oʊv- **~s** z
ov|um 'əʊv |əm ‖ 'oʊv |əm **~a** ə
ow aʊ
Owain 'əʊ aɪn ‖ 'oʊ- —*Welsh* ['ə waɪn, 'o-]
Owbridge 'əʊ brɪdʒ ‖ 'oʊ-
owe əʊ ‖ oʊ *(= oh, O)* **owed** əʊd ‖ oʊd **owes** əʊz ‖ oʊz **owing** 'əʊ ɪŋ ‖ 'oʊ ɪŋ
Owen 'əʊ ɪn -ən ‖ 'oʊ ən
Owens 'əʊ ɪnz -ənz ‖ 'oʊ ənz
Ower *(i)* 'aʊ̯ə ‖ 'aʊ̯ᵊr, *(ii)* 'əʊ ə ‖ 'oʊ ᵊr —*Usually (i).* **~s** z
owie 'aʊ i **~s** z
owing 'əʊ ɪŋ ‖ 'oʊ ɪŋ
owl aʊl **owls** aʊlz
owlet 'aʊl ət -ɪt, -et **~s** s
owlish 'aʊl ɪʃ **~ly** li **~ness** nəs nɪs
owl-like 'aʊl laɪk
own əʊn ‖ oʊn **owned** əʊnd ‖ oʊnd **owning** 'əʊn ɪŋ ‖ 'oʊn ɪŋ **owns** əʊnz ‖ oʊnz **ˌon your 'own**; **ˌown 'goal**
own-brand ˌəʊn 'brænd ◂ →ˌəʊm-, '· · ‖ ˌoʊn- **~s** z
owner 'əʊn ə ‖ 'oʊn ᵊr **~s** z
owner-driver ˌəʊn ə 'draɪv ə ‖ ˌoʊn ᵊr 'draɪv ᵊr **~s** z
owner-occu|pied ˌəʊn ər 'ɒk ju |paɪd ◂ -'jə- ‖ ˌoʊn ər 'ɑːk jə- **~pier/s** paɪ̯ə/z ‖ paɪ̯ᵊr/z
owner-operator ˌəʊn ər 'ɒp ə reɪt ə ‖ ˌoʊn ᵊr 'ɑːp ə reɪţᵊr **~s** z
ownership 'əʊn ə ʃɪp ‖ 'oʊn ᵊr-
own-label ˌəʊn 'leɪb ᵊl ◂ ‖ ˌoʊn-
owt aʊt əʊt —*This is a non-standard variant of* aught
ox ɒks ‖ ɑːks **oxen** 'ɒks ᵊn ‖ 'ɑːks ᵊn **ox's** 'ɒks ɪz -əz ‖ 'ɑːks əz
oxalate 'ɒks ə leɪt →-ᵊl eɪt ‖ 'ɑːks-
oxalic ₍ˌ₎ɒk 'sæl ɪk ‖ ₍ˌ₎ɑːk-
oxalis ɒk 'sæl ɪs -'sɑːl-, 'ɒks əl-, §-əs ‖ ɑːk 'sæl əs 'ɑːks əl-
oxblood 'ɒks blʌd ‖ 'ɑːks-
oxbow 'ɒks bəʊ ‖ 'ɑːks boʊ **~s** z
Oxbridge 'ɒks brɪdʒ ‖ 'ɑːks-
oxcart 'ɒks kɑːt ‖ 'ɑːks kɑːrt **~s** s
oxen 'ɒks ᵊn ‖ 'ɑːks ᵊn
Oxenden 'ɒks ᵊnd ən ‖ 'ɑːks-
Oxenford 'ɒks ᵊn fɔːd -fəd ‖ 'ɑːks ᵊn fɔːrd -fᵊrd
Oxenham 'ɒks ᵊn̩ əm ‖ 'ɑːks-
Oxenholme 'ɒks ᵊn həʊm ‖ 'ɑːks ᵊn hoʊm
oxer 'ɒks ə ‖ 'ɑːks ᵊr **~s** z
oxeye 'ɒks aɪ ‖ 'ɑːks- **~s** z
ˌoxeye 'daisy

Oxfam ˈɒks fæm ‖ ˈɑːks-
Oxford, o~ ˈɒks fəd ‖ ˈɑːks fᵊrd **~shire** ʃə ʃɪə ‖ ʃᵊr ʃɪr **~s, ~'s** z
ˌ**Oxford ˈCircus**; ˌ**Oxford ˈEnglish**; ˈ**Oxford ˌmovement**; ˈ**Oxford Street**
Oxhey ˈɒks i -heɪ ‖ ˈɑːks-
oxhide ˈɒks haɪd ‖ ˈɑːks-
oxidant ˈɒks ɪd ənt -əd- ‖ ˈɑːks- *(usually = occident)* **~s** s
oxidas|e ˈɒks ɪ deɪz -ə-, -deɪs ‖ ˈɑːks- **~es** ɪz əz
oxidation ˌɒks ɪ ˈdeɪʃ ᵊn -ə- ‖ ˌɑːks- **~s** z
oxidative ˈɒks ɪ deɪt ɪv ˈ·ə-‖ ˈɑːks ə deɪţ ɪv
oxide ˈɒks aɪd ‖ ˈɑːks- **~s** z
oxidis... —*see* **oxidiz...**
oxidization ˌɒks ɪd aɪ ˈzeɪʃ ᵊn ˌ·əd-, -ɪˈ-- ‖ ˌɑːks əd ə- **~s** z
oxidiz|e ˈɒks ɪ daɪz -ə- ‖ ˈɑːks ə- **~ed** d **~es** ɪz əz **~ing** ɪŋ
oxime ˈɒks iːm -aɪm ‖ ˈɑːks- **~s** z
Oxley ˈɒks li ‖ ˈɑːks-
oxlip ˈɒks lɪp ‖ ˈɑːks- **~s** s
Oxnard *(i)* ˈɒks nəd ‖ ˈɑːks nᵊrd, *(ii)* -nɑːd ‖ -nɑːrd —*The place in CA is (ii).*
Oxo *tdmk* ˈɒks əʊ ‖ ˈɑːks oʊ
Oxon ˈɒks ɒn -ᵊn, ɒk ˈsɒn ‖ ˈɑːks ɑːn
Oxonian ɒk ˈsəʊn i‿ən ‖ ɑːk ˈsoʊn- **~s** z
oxonium ɒk ˈsəʊn i‿əm ‖ ɑːk ˈsoʊn-
oxpecker ˈɒks ˌpek ə ‖ ˈɑːks ˌpek ᵊr **~s** z
Oxshott ˈɒk ʃɒt ˈɒks- ‖ ˈɑːk ʃɑːt
oxtail ˈɒks teɪᵊl ‖ ˈɑːks- **~s** z
Oxted ˈɒkst ɪd -əd, -ed ‖ ˈɑːkst əd
Oxton ˈɒkst ən ‖ ˈɑːkst-
oxtongue ˈɒks tʌŋ §-tɒŋ ‖ ˈɑːks- **~s** z
Oxus ˈɒks əs ‖ ˈɑːks əs
oxy- *comb. form with stress-neutral suffix* ¦ɒks i ‖ ¦ɑːks i — **oxychloride** ˌɒks i ˈklɔːr aɪd ‖ ˌɑːks i ˈklɔːr aɪd -ˈkloʊr- *with stress-imposing suffix* ɒk ˈsɪ+ ‖ ɑːk ˈsɪ+ — **oxypathy** ɒk ˈsɪp əθ i ‖ ɑːk-
oxyacetylene ˌɒks i‿ə ˈset ə liːn ◂ -ˈ·ɪ-, -lɪn; -ᵊl iːn, -ɪn ‖ ˌɑːks i ə ˈseţ ᵊl iːn ◂ -ən
Oxydol *tdmk* ˈɒks ɪ dɒl ‖ ˈɑːks ə dɔːl -dɑːl
oxygen ˈɒks ɪdʒ ən -ədʒ- ‖ ˈɑːks-
ˈ**oxygen mask**; ˈ**oxygen tent**
oxyge|nate ˈɒks ɪdʒ ə |neɪt ˈ·ədʒ-; ɒk ˈsɪdʒ- ‖ ˈɑːks- **~nated** neɪt ɪd -əd ‖ neɪţ əd **~nates** neɪts **~nating** neɪt ɪŋ ‖ neɪţ ɪŋ
oxygenation ˌɒks ɪdʒ ə ˈneɪʃ ᵊn ɒk ˌsɪdʒ ə- ‖ ˌɑːks- **~s** z
oxygenis|e, oxygeniz|e ˈɒks ɪdʒ ə naɪz ˈ·ədʒ- ‖ ˈɑːks- **~ed** d **~es** ɪz əz **~ing** ɪŋ
oxymor|on ˌɒks i ˈmɔːr |ɒn -ən ‖ ˌɑːks i ˈmɔːr |ɑːn -ˈmoʊr- **~a** ə **~ons** ɒnz ənz ‖ ɑːnz
Oxyrhynchus ˌɒks i ˈrɪŋk əs ‖ ˌɑːks-
oxytocic ˌɒks i ˈtəʊs ɪk ◂ ‖ ˌɑːks i ˈtoʊs ɪk ◂ **~s** s
oxytocin ˌɒks i ˈtəʊs ɪn §-ən ‖ ˌɑːks i ˈtoʊs ᵊn
oxytone ˈɒks i təʊn ‖ ˈɑːks i toʊn **~s** z
oyer ˈɔɪ ə ‖ ˈɔɪ ᵊr
oyes, oyez əʊ ˈjez -ˈjes, -ˈjeɪ, ˈ· · ‖ oʊ-
oyster ˈɔɪst ə ‖ -ᵊr **~s** z
ˈ**oyster bed**
oyster-catcher ˈɔɪst ə ˌkætʃ ə §-ˌketʃ- ‖ -ᵊr ˌkætʃ ᵊr **~s** z
Oystermouth ˈɔɪst ə maʊθ ‖ -ᵊr-
oz, oz. *sing.* aʊnᵗs, *pl* ˈaʊnᵗs ɪz -əz
Oz ɒz ‖ ɑːz
Ozalid *tdmk* ˈɒz əl ɪd ˈəʊz- ‖ ˈɑːz-
Ozanne əʊ ˈzæn ‖ oʊ-
Ozark ˈəʊz ɑːk ‖ ˈoʊz ɑːrk **~s** s
ozocerite əʊ ˈzəʊk ə raɪt -ˈzəʊs-; ˌəʊz əʊ ˈsɪər aɪt ‖ oʊ ˈzoʊk- -ˈzoʊs-; ˌoʊz oʊ ˈsɪr aɪt
ozokerite əʊ ˈzəʊk ə raɪt ˌəʊz əʊ ˈkɪər aɪt ‖ oʊ ˈzoʊk- ˌoʊz oʊ ˈkɪr aɪt
ozone ˈəʊz əʊn əʊ ˈzəʊn ‖ ˈoʊz oʊn oʊ ˈzoʊn
ˈ**ozone ˌlayer**, ·ˈ· ˌ··
ozone-friendly ˌəʊz əʊn ˈfrend li ◂ ‖ ˌoʊz oʊn-
ozonic əʊ ˈzɒn ɪk ‖ oʊ ˈzɑːn ɪk
ozoniferous ˌəʊz əʊ ˈnɪf ər əs ‖ ˌoʊz ə-
ozonosphere əʊ ˈzəʊn ə sfɪə -ˈzɒn- ‖ oʊ ˈzoʊn ə sfɪr -ˈzɑːn-
ozs, ozs. ˈaʊnᵗs ɪz -əz
Ozymandias ˌɒz i ˈmænd i‿əs ˌ·ə-, -æs ‖ ˌɑːz-
Ozzie ˈɒz i ‖ ˈɑːz i

Pp

p Spelling-to-sound

1 Where the spelling is **p**, the pronunciation is regularly p as in **pipe** paɪp. **p** also forms part of the digraph **ph**.

2 Where the spelling is double **pp**, the pronunciation is regularly p as in **happy** ˈhæp i.

3 **p** is normally silent at the beginning of a word before **n**, **s**, **t** as in **pneumonia** ˈnjuː- ‖ ˈnuː-, **psychiatrist** saɪ-, **pterodactyl** ˌter-.

ph Spelling-to-sound

1 Where the spelling is the digraph **ph**, the pronunciation is regularly f as in **photograph** ˈfəʊt ə grɑːf ‖ ˈfoʊṭ ə græf.

2 Exceptionally, it is

p as in **shepherd** ˈʃep əd ‖ ˈʃep ᵊrd, **Clapham** ˈklæp əm (in these words the **h** was originally part of a suffix, and hence silent)

v as in **Stephen** ˈstiːv ᵊn and the older pronunciation of **nephew** ˈnev juː (now usually ˈnef-).

P

P, p piː **P's, p's, Ps** piːz —*Communications code name:* Papa

p *'penny, pence'* piː —*See note at* **pence**

pa, Pa pɑː ‖ pɔː **pas, Pa's** pɑːz ‖ pɔːz

PA ˌpiː ˈeɪ —*but see also* Pennsylvania

pa'anga pɑː ˈæŋ ə -gə ‖ -ˈɑːŋ-

Pablo ˈpæb ləʊ ‖ ˈpɑːb loʊ —*Sp* [ˈpa βlo]

pablum ˈpæb ləm

pabulum ˈpæb jʊl əm -jəl- ‖ -jəl-

PABX ˌpiː eɪ biː ˈeks

paca ˈpɑːk ə ˈpæk ə **~s** z

pace *n, v* peɪs **paced** peɪst **paces** ˈpeɪs ɪz -əz **pacing** ˈpeɪs ɪŋ **ˈpace ˌbowler**

pace *prep 'with due deference to'* ˈpeɪs i ˈpɑːtʃ eɪ, ˈpɑːk-

Pace *family name* peɪs

pacemaker ˈpeɪs ˌmeɪk ə ‖ -ᵊr **~s** z

pacer ˈpeɪs ə ‖ -ᵊr **~s** z

pacesetter ˈpeɪs ˌset ə ‖ -ˌseṭ ᵊr **~s** z

pac|ey ˈpeɪs |i **~ier** i‿ə ‖ i‿ᵊr **~iest** i‿ɪst i‿əst **~ily** ɪ li əl i

Pachelbel ˈpæk ᵊl bel ˈpæx-, ˈpɑːk-, ˈpɑːx- ‖ ˈpɑːk- —*Ger* [pa ˈxɛl bᵊl; ˈpax ɛl-, -bɛl]

pachinko pə ˈtʃɪŋk əʊ ‖ -oʊ —*Jp* [pa ˈtɕiŋ ko]

pachisi pə ˈtʃiːz i pæ-, -ˈtʃiːs-

Pachuco pə ˈtʃuːk əʊ ‖ -oʊ **~s** z —*Sp* [pa ˈtʃu ko]

pachyderm ˈpæk i dɜːm ‖ -dɝːm **~s** z

pachydermatous ˌpæk i ˈdɜːm ət əs ◂ ‖ -ˈdɝːm əṭ əs ◂

pacific, P~ pə ˈsɪf ɪk **~ally** ᵊl‿i **Paˌcific ˌNorthˈwest**; **Paˌcific ˈOcean**; **Paˌcific ˈrim**

pacification ˌpæs ɪf ɪ ˈkeɪʃ ᵊn ˌ·əf-, §-əˈ-- **~s** z

pacificatory ˌpæs ɪf ɪ ˈkeɪt ər i ◂ ˌ·əf-, -əˈ--, pə ˈsɪf ɪk ət‿ər i ‖ pə ˈsɪf ɪk ə tɔːr i -toʊr i

pacificist pə ˈsɪf ɪs ɪst pæ-, -əs-, §-əst **~s** s

pacifier ˈpæs ɪ faɪ‿ə ˌ·ə- ‖ faɪ‿ᵊr **~s** z

pacifism ˈpæs ɪ ˌfɪz əm -ə-

pacifist ˈpæs ɪf ɪst -əf-, §-əst **~s** s

paci|fy ˈpæs ɪ |faɪ -ə- **~fied** faɪd **~fies** faɪz **~fying** faɪ ɪŋ

Pacino pə ˈtʃiːn əʊ ‖ -oʊ

pack pæk **packed** pækt (= *pact*) **packing** 'pæk ɪŋ **packs** pæks
'pack ˌanimal; **'pack ice**; **'packing case**

packag|e 'pæk ɪdʒ **~ed** d **~es** ɪz əz **~ing** ɪŋ
'package deal; **ˌpackage 'holiday**; **'package store**; **'package tour**, ˌ· · '·.

Packard 'pæk ɑːd -ᵊrd ‖ -ᵊrd

packed-out ˌpækt 'aʊt ◂

packer, P~ 'pæk ə ‖ -ᵊr **~s** z

pack|et 'pæk |ɪt §-ət ‖ -|ət **~eted** ɪt ɪd §ət-, -əd ‖ ət̬ əd **~eting** ɪt ɪŋ §ət- ‖ ət̬ ɪŋ **~ets** ɪts §əts ‖ əts

packet-switching 'pæk ɪt ˌswɪtʃ ɪŋ §-ət-

packhors|e 'pæk hɔːs ‖ -hɔːrs **~es** ɪz əz

pack|man 'pæk| mən -mæn **~men** mən men

packsaddle 'pæk ˌsæd ᵊl **~s** z

Pac-man *tdmk* 'pæk mæn

pact pækt **pacts** pækts

pac|y 'peɪs |i **~ier** i‿ə ‖ i‿ᵊr **~iest** i‿ɪst i‿əst **~ily** ɪ li əl i

pad pæd **padded** 'pæd ɪd -əd **padding** 'pæd ɪŋ **pads** pædz

Padang 'pɑː dæŋ -dɑːŋ

Padarn 'pæd ᵊn -ɑːn ‖ -ᵊrn -ɑːrn —*Welsh* ['pa darn]

padauk pə 'daʊk

Padbury 'pæd bər‿i →'pæb- ‖ -ˌber i

padd... —*see* **pad**

Paddick 'pæd ɪk

paddie... —*see* **paddy**

Paddington 'pæd ɪŋ tən

paddl|e 'pæd ᵊl **~ed** d **~es** z **~ing** ‿ɪŋ
'paddle boat; **'paddle ˌsteamer**; **'paddling pool**; **'paddle wheel**

paddock, P~ 'pæd ək **~s** s

padd|y, Padd|y 'pæd |i **~ies, ~y's** iz
'paddy field; **'paddy ˌwagon**

paddymelon 'pæd i ˌmel ən **~s** z

paddywhack 'pæd i wæk -hwæk ‖ -*h*wæk **~s** s

pademelon 'pæd i ˌmel ən **~s** z

Paderborn ˌpɑːd ə 'bɔːn '· · · ‖ -ᵊr 'bɔːrn —*Ger* [paː dɐ 'bɔʁn]

Paderewski ˌpæd ə 'ref ski -'rev- ‖ ˌpɑːd- —*Polish* [pa dɛ 'rɛf ski]

Padfield 'pæd fiːᵊld

Padiham 'pæd i‿əm

padlock 'pæd lɒk ‖ -lɑːk **~ed** t **~ing** ɪŋ **~s** s

Padmore 'pæd mɔː →'pæb- ‖ -mɔːr -moʊr

Padraic 'pɑːdr ɪk -ɪɡ

Padraig 'pɑːdr ɪɡ —*Irish* ['pɑ rɪɡ]

padre 'pɑːdr i -eɪ **~s** z

padron|e pə 'drəʊn |i pæ-, -eɪ ‖ -'droʊn |i **~es** iz **~i** iː

padsaw 'pæd sɔː ‖ -sɑː **~s** z

Padstow 'pæd stəʊ ‖ -stoʊ

Padu|a 'pæd ju‿|ə ‖ 'pædʒ u‿|ə —*It* Padova ['paː do va] **~an/s** ən/z

Paducah pə 'duːk ə -'djuːk-

paean 'piː‿ən **~s** z

paederast 'ped ə ræst 'piːd- **~s** s

paederastic ˌped ə 'ræst ɪk ◂ ˌpiːd- **~ally** ᵊl‿i

paederasty 'ped ə ræst i 'piːd-

paediatric ˌpiːd i 'ætr ɪk ◂ **~ally** ᵊl‿i **~s** s

paediatrician ˌpiːd i‿ə 'trɪʃ ᵊn **~s** z

paedophile 'piːd əʊ faɪᵊl ‖ 'ped ə- 'piːd- **~s** z

paedophilia ˌpiːd əʊ 'fɪl i‿ə ‖ ˌped ə- ˌpiːd-

paedophiliac ˌpiːd əʊ 'fɪl i æk ‖ ˌped ə- ˌpiːd- **~s** s

paella paɪ 'el ə ‖ pɑː- -'eɪl jə, -'eɪ-—*Sp* [pa 'e ʎa, -ja] **~s** z

paeon 'piː‿ən ‖ -ɑːn **~s** z

paeon|y 'piː‿ən |i **~ies** iz

pagan 'peɪɡ ən **~dom** dəm **~s** z

Paganini ˌpæɡ ə 'niːn i ‖ ˌpɑːɡ- —*It* [pa ɡa 'niː ni]

paganism 'peɪɡ ən ˌɪz əm

page, Page peɪdʒ **paged** peɪdʒd **pages, Page's** 'peɪdʒ ɪz -əz **paging** 'peɪdʒ ɪŋ
'page boy

pageant 'pædʒ ənt **~s** s

pageantr|y 'pædʒ əntr |i **~ies** iz

page-jack 'peɪdʒ dʒæk **~ing** ɪŋ

pager 'peɪdʒ ə ‖ -ᵊr **~s** z

Paget 'pædʒ ɪt -ət **~'s** s
'Paget's diˌsease

Pagham 'pæɡ əm

paginate 'pædʒ ɪ |neɪt -ə- **~nated** neɪt ɪd -əd ‖ neɪt̬ əd **~nates** neɪts **~nating** neɪt ɪŋ ‖ neɪt̬ ɪŋ

pagination ˌpædʒ ɪ 'neɪʃ ᵊn -ə- **~s** z

Paglia 'pɑːl jə 'pæɡ li‿ə

Pagliacci ˌpæl i 'ɑːtʃ i ‖ ˌpɑːl 'jɑːtʃ i —*It* [paʎ 'ʎat tʃi]

Pagnell 'pæɡ nᵊl

Pagnol pæn 'jɒl ‖ -'joʊl —*Fr* [pa 'ɲjɔl]

pagoda pə 'ɡəʊd ə ‖ -'ɡoʊd ə **~s** z
pa'goda tree

Pago Pago ˌpɑːɡ əʊ 'pɑːɡ əʊ ˌpæŋ ɡəʊ 'pæŋ ɡəʊ, ˌpeɪɡ əʊ 'peɪɡ əʊ ‖ ˌpɑːŋ ɡoʊ 'pɑːŋ ɡoʊ, ˌpɑːɡ oʊ 'pɑːɡ oʊ

pah pɑː

Pahang pə 'hʌŋ -'hæŋ ‖ -'hɑːŋ

Pahari pə 'hɑːr i

Pahlavi 'pɑːl əv i

paid peɪd

paid-up ˌpeɪd 'ʌp ◂
ˌpaid-up 'members

Paige peɪdʒ

paigle 'peɪɡ ᵊl **~s** z

Paignton 'peɪnt ən ‖ -ᵊn

pail peɪᵊl **pails** peɪᵊlz

pailful 'peɪl fʊl **~s** z

paillass|e 'pæl i æs ˌ· · '· ‖ pæl 'jæs **~es** ɪz əz

paillette (ˌ)pæl 'jet ˌpæl i 'et ‖ paɪ 'jet —*Fr* [pa jɛt] **~s** s

pain, Pain peɪn **pained** peɪnd **paining** 'peɪn ɪŋ **pains** peɪnz

pain au chocolat ˌpæn əʊ 'ʃɒk ə lɑː ‖ -oʊ ˌʃɑːk ə 'lɑː —*Fr* [pɛ̃ o ʃɔ kɔ la]

Paine peɪn

painful 'peɪn fᵊl -fʊl **~ly** ‿i **~ness** nəs nɪs

painkill|er 'peɪn ˌkɪl |ə →'peɪŋ- ‖ -ᵊr **~ers** əz ‖ ᵊrz **~ing** ɪŋ

painless 'peɪn ləs -lɪs **~ly** li **~ness** nəs nɪs

painstaking 'peɪnz ˌteɪk ɪŋ **~ly** li

Painswick 'peɪnz wɪk

paint peɪnt **painted** 'peɪnt ɪd -əd ‖ 'peɪnt̬ əd **painting/s** 'peɪnt ɪŋ/z ‖ 'peɪnt̬ ɪŋ/z **paints** peɪnts
paintball 'peɪnt bɔːl ‖ -bɑːl **~er/s** ə/z ‖ ᵊr/z **~ing** ɪŋ
paintbox 'peɪnt bɒks ‖ -bɑːks **~es** ɪz əz
paintbrush 'peɪnt brʌʃ **~es** ɪz əz
painter, P~ 'peɪnt ə ‖ 'peɪnt̬ ᵊr **~s** z
painterly 'peɪnt ə li →ᵊl i ‖ 'peɪnt̬ ᵊr li
paintwork 'peɪnt wɜːk ‖ -wɜːk
pair peə ‖ peᵊr pæᵊr **paired** peəd ‖ peᵊrd pæᵊrd **pairing** 'peər ɪŋ ‖ 'per ɪŋ 'pær- **pairs** peəz ‖ peᵊrz pæᵊrz
pais|a 'paɪs ɑː **~as** ɑːz **~e** eɪ
Paish peɪʃ
Paisley, p~ 'peɪz li **~s, ~'s** z
Paiute ˌpaɪ 'uːt -'juːt, '· · **~s** s

PAJAMAS

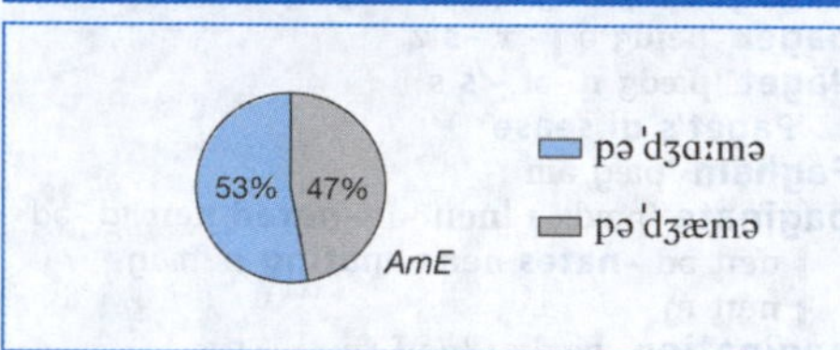

pajama pə 'dʒɑːm ə ⚠bə- ‖ -'dʒæm ə — *Preference poll, AmE:* 'dʒɑːm- *53%,* -'dʒæm- *47%.* **~ed** d **~s** z
pakapoo ˌpæk ə 'puː ◂ **~s** z
ˌ**pakapoo 'ticket**, ˌ· · ˈ· ˌ· ·
pak-choi ˌpæk 'tʃɔɪ ˌpɑːk- ˌbɒk- ‖ ˌpɑːk- ˌbɑːk-
pakeha, P~ 'pɑːk i hɑː -ə-, ˌ· ·ˈ· **~s** z
Pakenham *place in Suffolk* 'peɪk ən‿əm
Pakenham *family name* 'pæk ən‿əm
Paki 'pæk i 'pɑːk i **~s** z
Paki-bashing 'pæk i ˌbæʃ ɪŋ 'pɑːk-
Pakistan ˌpɑːk ɪ 'stɑːn ˌpæk-, -ə- ‖ 'pæk ɪ stæn 'pɑːk ɪ stɑːn, ˌ· ·ˈ· *(*)*
Pakistani ˌpɑːk ɪ 'stɑːn i ◂ -ə-, -'stæn- ‖ ˌpæk ɪ 'stæn i ◂ ˌpɑːk ɪ 'stɑːn i **~s** z
pakora pə 'kɔːr ə ‖ -'koʊr-
pal, Pal, PAL pæl **palled** pæld **palling** 'pæl ɪŋ **pals** pælz
palac|e 'pæl əs -ɪs **~es** ɪz əz
ˌ**palace ˌrevo'lution**
paladin 'pæl əd ɪn §-ən **~s** z
Palaearctic ˌpæl i 'ɑːkt ɪk ◂ ˌpeɪl- ‖ ˌpeɪl i 'ɑːrkt ɪk ◂ -'ɑːrt̬-
palaeo- *comb. form with stress-neutral suffix* ¦pæl i əʊ ¦peɪl- ‖ ¦peɪl i oʊ — **palaeomagnetism** ˌpæl i əʊ 'mæg nə ˌtɪz əm ˌpeɪl-, -'·nɪ- ‖ ˌpeɪl i oʊ- *with stress-imposing suffix* ˌpæl i 'ɒ+ ˌpeɪl- ‖ ˌpeɪl i 'ɑː+ — **palaeographer** ˌpæl i 'ɒg rəf ə ˌpeɪl- ‖ ˌpeɪl i 'ɑːg rəf ᵊr **~s** z
palaeobotany ˌpæl i əʊ 'bɒt ən i ˌpeɪl- ‖ ˌpeɪl i oʊ 'bɑːt ᵊn‿i
Palaeocene, p~ 'pæl i əʊ siːn 'peɪl- ‖ 'peɪl i ə-
palaeographic ˌpæl i əʊ 'græf ɪk ◂ ˌpeɪl- ‖ ˌpeɪl i ə-
palaeography ˌpæl i 'ɒg rəf i ˌpeɪl- ‖ ˌpeɪl i 'ɑːg-
Palaeolithic, p~ ˌpæl i əʊ 'lɪθ ɪk ◂ ˌpeɪl- ‖ ˌpeɪl i ə-
palaeontological ˌpæl i ˌɒnt ə 'lɒdʒ ɪk ᵊl ˌpeɪl- ‖ ˌpeɪl i ˌɑːnt̬ ᵊl 'ɑːdʒ ɪk ᵊl
palaeontolog|ist ˌpæl i ɒn 'tɒl ədʒ |ɪst ˌpeɪl-, §-əst ‖ ˌpeɪl i ɑːn 'tɑːl ədʒ |əst **~ists** ɪsts §əsts **~y** i
Palaeozoic, p~ ˌpæl i əʊ 'zəʊ ɪk ◂ ˌpeɪl- ‖ ˌpeɪl i ə 'zoʊ ɪk ◂
palaes|tra pə 'laɪs |trə -'liːs-, -'les- ‖ -'les- **~trae** triː traɪ **~tras** trəz
palais *sing* 'pæl eɪ -i ‖ pæ 'leɪ **palais** *pl* 'pæl eɪz ‖ pæ 'leɪz
ˌ**palais de 'danse** ‖ ·ˌ·-də 'dɑːnᵗs -'dɒ̃s, §-'dænᵗs‖ də 'dænᵗs
palankeen, palanquin ˌpæl ən 'kiːn →-əŋ- **~s** z
palatability ˌpæl ət ə 'bɪl ət i ˌ·ɪt-, -ɪt i ‖ ˌpæl ət̬ ə 'bɪl ət̬ i
palatab|le 'pæl ət əb |ᵊl -ɪt əb- ‖ -ət̬ əb- **~leness** ᵊl nəs -nɪs **~ly** li
palatal 'pæl ət ᵊl pə 'leɪt ᵊl ‖ -ət̬ ᵊl —*In phonetics* '· · ·*, in anatomy (BrE) sometimes* ·'· · **~ly** i **~s** z
palatalis... —*see* **palataliz...**
palatalization ˌpæl ət əl aɪ 'zeɪʃ ᵊn pə ˌleɪt-, -ɪ'·- ‖ -ət̬ ᵊl ə- **~s** z
palataliz|e 'pæl ət ə laɪz pə 'leɪt-, →-ᵊl aɪz ‖ -ət̬ ᵊl aɪz **~ed** d **~es** ɪz əz **~ing** ɪŋ
palate 'pæl ət -ɪt **~s** s
palatial pə 'leɪʃ ᵊl -'leɪʃ i‿əl **~ly** i
palatinate, P~ pə 'læt ɪn ət -ən-, -ɪt ‖ -ᵊn ət **~s** s
palatine, P~ 'pæl ə taɪn **~s** z
palatoalveolar ˌpæl ət əʊˌælv i 'əʊl ə ◂ -æl 'viː‿əl ə ◂ ‖ -ət̬ oʊ æl 'viː əl ᵊr **~s** z
palatogram 'pæl ət əʊ græm ‖ -ət̬ ə- **~s** z
palatographic ˌpæl ət əʊ 'græf ɪk ◂ ‖ -ət̬ ə- **~ally** ᵊl‿i
palatography ˌpæl ə 'tɒg rəf i ‖ -'tɑːg-
Palau pə 'laʊ pɑː-
palaver pə 'lɑːv ə ‖ -ᵊr -'læv- **~s** z
Palawan pə 'lɑː wən
palazz|o pə 'læts |əʊ ‖ -'lɑːts |oʊ **~i** iː **~os** əʊz ‖ oʊz —*It* [pa 'lat tso]
pale peɪᵊl *(= pail)* **paler** 'peɪᵊl ə ‖ -ᵊr **palest** 'peɪᵊl ɪst -əst
ˌ**pale 'ale**
Pale *in eastern Ireland* peɪᵊl
Pale *place in Bosnia* 'pɑːl eɪ —*Serbian* ['pa le]
Palearctic ˌpæl i 'ɑːkt ɪk ◂ ˌpeɪl- ‖ ˌpeɪl i 'ɑːrkt ɪk ◂ -'ɑːrt̬-
palefac|e 'peɪᵊl feɪs **~es** ɪz əz
pale|ly 'peɪᵊl |li **~ness** nəs nɪs
paleo-, palaeo- *comb. form with stress-neutral suffix* ¦pæl i əʊ ¦peɪl- ‖ ¦peɪl i oʊ — **paleomagnetism** ˌpæl i əʊ 'mæg nə ˌtɪz əm ˌpeɪl-, -'·nɪ- ‖ ˌpeɪl i oʊ- *with stress-imposing suffix* ˌpæl i 'ɒ+ ˌpeɪl- ‖ ˌpeɪl i 'ɑː+ — **paleographer** ˌpæl i 'ɒg rəf ə ˌpeɪl- ‖ ˌpeɪl i 'ɑːg rəf ᵊr **~s** z

P

paleobotany ˌpæl i əʊ ˈbɒt ən i ˌpeɪl- ‖ ˌpeɪl i oʊ ˈbɑːt ən i
Paleocene, p~ ˈpæl i əʊ siːn ˈpeɪl- ‖ ˈpeɪl i ə-
paleographic ˌpæl i əʊ ˈɡræf ɪk ◂ ˌpeɪl- ‖ ˌpeɪl i ə-
paleography ˌpæl i ˈɒɡ rəf i ˌpeɪl- ‖ ˌpeɪl i ˈɑːɡ-
Paleolithic, p~ ˌpæl i əʊ ˈlɪθ ɪk ◂ ˌpeɪl- ‖ ˌpeɪl i ə-
paleontological ˌpæl i ˌɒnt ə ˈlɒdʒ ɪk əl ˌpeɪl- ‖ ˌpeɪl i ˌɑːnt əl ˈɑːdʒ ɪk əl
paleontolog|ist ˌpæl i ɒn ˈtɒl ədʒ |ɪst ˌpeɪl-, §-əst ‖ ˌpeɪl i ɑːn ˈtɑːl ədʒ |əst **~ists** ɪsts §əsts **~y** i
paleotype ˈpæl i əʊ taɪp ˈpeɪl- ‖ ˈpeɪl i oʊ-
Paleozoic, p~ ˌpæl i əʊ ˈzəʊ ɪk ◂ ˌpeɪl- ‖ ˌpeɪl i ə ˈzoʊ ɪk ◂
Palermo pə ˈleəm əʊ -ˈlɜːm- ‖ -ˈlerm oʊ -ˈlɜːm- —*It* [pa ˈlɛr mo]
Palestine ˈpæl ə staɪn -ɪ-
Palestinian ˌpæl ə ˈstɪn i ən ◂ ˌ·ɪ- **~s** z
pales|tra pə ˈles |trə -ˈliːs- **~trae** triː traɪ, treɪ **~tras** trəz
Palestrina ˌpæl ə ˈstriːn ə -ɪ-, -e- —*It* [pa les ˈtriː na]
Palethorp, Palethorpe ˈpeɪəl θɔːp ‖ -θɔːrp
palette ˈpæl ət -ɪt, -et **~s** s
ˈ**palette knife**
Paley ˈpeɪl i
palfrey, P~ ˈpɔːlf ri ˈpɒlf- ‖ ˈpɑːlf- **~s** z
Palfreyman ˈpɔːlf ri mən ˈpɒlf- ‖ ˈpɑːlf-
Palgrave ˈpæl ɡreɪv ˈpɔːl- ‖ ˈpɔːl-, ˈpɑːl-
Pali ˈpɑːl i
Palikir ˈpæl ɪk ə ‖ -ər
palimony ˈpæl ɪm ən i ˈ·ə- ‖ -ə moʊn i (*)
palimpsest ˈpæl ɪm*p* sest -əm*p*- **~s** s
Palin ˈpeɪl ɪn §-ən
palindrome ˈpæl ɪn drəʊm -ən- ‖ -droʊm **~s** z
palindromic ˌpæl ɪn ˈdrɒm ɪk ◂ -ən- ‖ -ˈdroʊm ɪk ◂ -ˈdrɑːm-
paling, P~ ˈpeɪl ɪŋ **~s** z
palingenesis ˌpæl ɪn ˈdʒen əs ɪs ˌ·ən-, -ɪs ɪs, §-əs
palinode ˈpæl ɪ nəʊd -ə- ‖ -noʊd **~s** z
palisad|e ˌpæl ɪ ˈseɪd -ə- **~ed** ɪd əd **~es** z **~ing** ɪŋ
palish ˈpeɪl ɪʃ
Palitoy *tdmk* ˈpæl ɪ tɔɪ -ə-
Palk pɔːk pɔːlk ‖ pɑːk, pɔːlk, pɑːlk
pall pɔːl ‖ pɑːl **palled** pɔːld ‖ pɑːld **palling** ˈpɔːl ɪŋ ‖ ˈpɑːl- **palls** pɔːlz ‖ pɑːlz
Palladian pə ˈleɪd i ən -ˈlɑːd-
palladic pə ˈlæd ɪk -ˈleɪd-
Palladio pə ˈlæd i əʊ -ˈlɑːd- ‖ -ˈlɑːd i oʊ —*It* [pal ˈlaː djo, -di o]
palladium, P~ pə ˈleɪd i əm
palladous pə ˈleɪd əs ˈpæl əd-
Pallas ˈpæl əs -æs
ˌ**Pallas Aˈthene**
pallbearer ˈpɔːl ˌbeər ə ‖ -ˌber ər ˈpɑːl-, ˌbær- **~s** z
pallet ˈpæl ət -ɪt **~s** s
palletis... —*see* **palletiz...**
palletization ˌpæl ət aɪ ˈzeɪʃ ən ˌ·ɪt-, -ɪ·- ‖ -ət̬ ə-
palletiz|e ˈpæl ə taɪz -ɪ- **~ed** d **~es** ɪz əz **~ing** ɪŋ
palliass|e ˈpæl i æs ˌ· ·ˈ· ‖ pæl ˈjæs **~es** ɪz əz
palli|ate ˈpæl i |eɪt **~ated** eɪt ɪd -əd ‖ eɪt̬ əd **~ates** eɪts **~ating** eɪt ɪŋ ‖ eɪt̬ ɪŋ
palliation ˌpæl i ˈeɪʃ ən **~s** z
palliative ˈpæl i ət ɪv ‖ -i eɪt̬ ɪv -i ət̬ ɪv **~s** z
pallid ˈpæl ɪd §-əd **~ly** li **~ness** nəs nɪs
Palliser ˈpæl ɪs ə -əs- ‖ -ər
palli|um ˈpæl i |əm **~a** ə **~ums** əmz
Pall Mall ˌpæl ˈmæl ◂ —*Formerly also* ˌpel ˈmel◂
pallor ˈpæl ə ‖ -ər
pally ˈpæl i

PALM

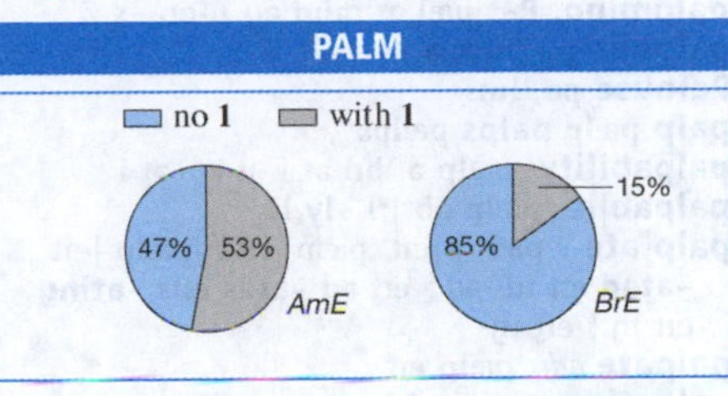

palm pɑːm §pɑːlm, §pælm, §pɒlm ‖ **pɑːlm** pɑːm, pɔːlm, pɔːm — *Preference polls, AmE: no* l *47%, with* l *53%; BrE: no* l *85%, with* l *15%.*
palmed pɑːmd §pɑːlmd, §pælmd, §pɒlmd ‖ **pɑːlmd** pɑːmd, pɔːlmd, pɔːmd **palming** ˈpɑːm ɪŋ §ˈpɑːlm-, §ˈpælm-, §ˈpɒlm- ‖ ˈ**pɑːlm ɪŋ** ˈpɑːm-, pɔːlm-, pɔːm- **palms** pɑːmz §pɑːlmz, §pælmz, §pɒlmz ‖ **pɑːlmz** pɑːmz, pɔːlmz, pɔːmz
ˌ**Palm ˈBeach**; ˈ**palm oil**; ˌ**Palm ˈSprings**; ˌ**Palm ˈSunday**; ˌ**palm ˈwine**
Palma ˈpælm ə ˈpɑːm-, ˈpɑːlm-, §ˈpɒlm- ‖ ˈ**pɑːlm ə** -ɑː —*Sp* [ˈpal ma]
palmar ˈpælm ə §ˈpɑːlm-, §ˈpɒlm-, -ɑː ‖ -ər
palmate ˈpælm eɪt ˈpɑːm-, §ˈpɑːlm-, §ˈpɒlm-, -ət, -ɪt **~ly** li
palmcorder ˈpɑːm ˌkɔːd ə §ˈpɑːlm-, §ˈpælm-, §ˈpɒlm-; ˌ·ˈ· · ‖ ˈ**pɑːlm ˌkɔːrd ər** ˈpɑːm-, pɔːlm-, ˈpɔːm- **~s** z
Palme ˈpɑːlm ə —*Swedish* [ˈˈpal mə]
palmer, P~ ˈpɑːm ə §ˈpɑːlm-, §ˈpælm-, §ˈpɒlm- ‖ ˈ**pɑːlm ər** ˈpɑːm-, ˈpɔːlm-, ˈpɔːm- **~s, ~'s** z
Palmerston ˈpɑːm əst ən §ˈpɑːlm-, §ˈpælm-, §ˈpɒlm- ‖ ˈ**pɑːlm ərst-** ˈpɑːm-, ˈpɔːlm-, ˈpɔːm-
ˌ**Palmerston ˈNorth**
palmetto pæl ˈmet əʊ pɑː-, §pɑːl-, §pɒl- ‖ -ˈmet̬ oʊ **~s** z
palmist ˈpɑːm ɪst §ˈpɑːlm-, §ˈpælm-, §ˈpɒlm-, §-əst ‖ ˈ**pɑːlm ɪst** ˈpɑːm-, ˈpɔːlm-, ˈpɔːm- **~s** s
palmistry ˈpɑːm ɪs tri §ˈpɑːlm-, §ˈpælm-, §ˈpɒlm-, -əs- ‖ ˈ**pɑːlm əs tri** ˈpɑːm-, ˈpɔːlm-, ˈpɔːm-
palmitate ˈpælm ɪ teɪt ˈpɑːm-, §ˈpɑːlm-, §ˈpɒlm-, -ə- **~s** s
palmitic pæl ˈmɪt ɪk pɑː-, §pɑːl-, §pɒl- ‖ -ˈmɪt̬ ɪk

palmitin ˈpælm ɪt ɪn ˈpɑːm-, §ˈpɑːlm-, §ˈpɒlm-, -ət-, §-ən ‖ -ət ᵊn
Palmolive *tdmk* ˌpɑːm ˈɒl ɪv §ˌpɑːlm-, §ˈpælm-, §ˈpɒlm-, §-əv ‖ ˌpɑːlm ˈɑːl ɪv ˌpɑːm-, ˌpɔːlm-, ˌpɔːm-
palm-sized ˈpɑːm saɪzd §ˈpɑːlm-, §ˈpælm-, §ˈpɒlm- ‖ ˈpɑːlm- ˈpɑːm-, ˈpɔːlm-, ˈpɔːm-
palmtop ˈpɑːm tɒp §ˈpɑːlm-, §ˈpælm-, §ˈpɒlm- ‖ ˈpɑːlm tɑːp ˈpɑːm-, ˈpɔːlm-, ˈpɔːm- **~s** s
palm|y ˈpɑːm |i §ˈpɑːlm-, §ˈpælm-, §ˈpɒlm- ‖ ˈpɑːlm |i ˈpɑːm-, ˈpɔːlm-, ˈpɔːm- **~ier** i‿ə ‖ i‿ᵊr **~iest** i‿ɪst i‿əst
Palmyra, p~ ₍ˌ₎pæl ˈmaɪᵊr ə **~s** z
Palo Alto ˌpæl əʊ ˈælt əʊ ‖ ˌpæl oʊ ˈælt oʊ
palolo pə ˈləʊl əʊ ‖ -ˈloʊl oʊ
Palomar ˈpæl əʊ mɑː ‖ -ə mɑːr ˌ·ˈ·
palomino, P~ ˌpæl ə ˈmiːn əʊ ‖ -oʊ **~s** z
palooka pə ˈluːk ə **~s** z
Palouse pə ˈluːs
palp pælp **palps** pælps
palpability ˌpælp ə ˈbɪl ət i -ɪt i ‖ -əţ i
palpab|le ˈpælp əb |ᵊl **~ly** li
palp|ate *v* pæl ˈp|eɪt ˈpælp |eɪt ‖ ˈpælp |eɪt **~ated** eɪt ɪd -əd ‖ eɪţ əd **~ates** eɪts **~ating** eɪt ɪŋ ‖ eɪţ ɪŋ
palpate *adj* ˈpælp eɪt
palpation pæl ˈpeɪʃ ᵊn
palpebral ˈpælp ɪb rəl -əb-; pæl ˈpiːb-, -ˈpeb-
palpi ˈpælp aɪ -iː
palpi|tate ˈpælp ɪ |teɪt -ə- **~tated** teɪt ɪd -əd ‖ teɪţ əd **~tates** teɪts **~tating** teɪt ɪŋ ‖ teɪţ ɪŋ
palpitation ˌpælp ɪ ˈteɪʃ ᵊn -ə- **~s** z
palsgrave, P~ ˈpɔːlz greɪv ‖ ˈpɑːlz-
pals|y ˈpɔːlz |i ˈpɒlz- ‖ ˈpɑːlz- **~ied** id **~ies** iz **~ying** i ɪŋ
palsy-walsy ˌpælz i ˈwælz i ◂
palt|er ˈpɔːlt |ə ˈpɒlt- ‖ -|ᵊr ˈpɑːlt- **~ered** əd ‖ ᵊrd **~ering** ər ɪŋ **~ers** əz ‖ ᵊrz
Paltrow ˈpæltr əʊ ‖ -oʊ
paltr|y ˈpɔːltr |i ˈpɒltr- ‖ ˈpɑːltr- **~ier** i‿ə ‖ i‿ᵊr **~iest** i‿ɪst i‿əst **~ily** ɪ li əl i **~iness** i nəs i nɪs
paludal pə ˈluːd ᵊl -ˈljuːd-; ˈpæl jʊd-, -jəd-
Paludrine, p~ ˈpæl ju drɪn -u-, -jə-, -driːn
palynolog|ist ˌpæl ɪ ˈnɒl ədʒ |ɪst ˌ-ə-, §-əst ‖ -ˈnɑːl- **~ists** ɪsts §əsts **~y** i
Pam pæm
Pama-Nyungan ˌpɑːm ə ˈnjʊŋ ən ◂ -gən
Pamela ˈpæm əl‿ə -ɪl ə
Pamir pə ˈmɪə ‖ -ˈmɪᵊr **~s** z
Pamlico ˈpæm lɪ kəʊ -lə- ‖ -koʊ
ˌ**Pamlico ˈSound**
pampa, Pampa ˈpæmp ə —*Sp* [ˈpam pa]
pampas ˈpæmp əs -əz
ˈ**pampas grass**
pamper ˈpæmp ə ‖ -ᵊr **~ed** d **pampering** ˈpæmp ər ɪŋ **~s** z
Pampers *tdmk* ˈpæmp əz ‖ -ᵊrz
pamphlet ˈpæmᵖf lət -lɪt **~s** s
pamphle|teer ˌpæmᵖf lə |ˈtɪə -lɪ- ‖ -|ˈtɪᵊr **~teered** ˈtɪəd ‖ ˈtɪᵊrd **~teering** ˈtɪər ɪŋ ‖ ˈtɪr ɪŋ **~teers** ˈtɪəz ‖ ˈtɪᵊrz
Pamphyli|a pæm ˈfɪl i‿|ə **~an/s** ən/z
Pamplona pæm ˈpləʊn ə ‖ -ˈploʊn ə —*Sp* [pam ˈplo na]
pan, Pan pæn —*but in the sense 'betel leaf'*, pɑːn **panned** pænd **panning** ˈpæn ɪŋ **pans** pænz
ˌ**Pan ˈAm** *tdmk*
pan- ¦pæn — **Pan-Arabism** ˌpæn ˈær əb ɪz əm
panacea ˌpæn ə ˈsɪə -ˈsiː‿ə ‖ -ˈsiː ə **~s** z
panache pə ˈnæʃ pæ-, -ˈnɑːʃ
panada pə ˈnɑːd ə **~s** z
Panadol *tdmk* ˈpæn ə dɒl ‖ -dɑːl **~s** z
pan-African ˌpæn ˈæf rɪk ən ◂ **~ism** ˌɪz əm
Panama, p~ ˈpæn ə mɑː ˌ·ˈ· ‖ -mɔː — *Sp* Panamá [pa na ˈma] **~s, ~'s** z
ˌ**Panama Caˈnal**; ˌ**Panama ˈhat**
Panamanian ˌpæn ə ˈmeɪn i‿ən ◂ **~s** z
Panasonic *tdmk* ˌpæn ə ˈsɒn ɪk ‖ -ˈsɑːn ɪk
panatela, panatella ˌpæn ə ˈtel ə **~s** z
Panathenaea ˌpæn ˌæθ ɪ ˈniː‿ə ·ˌ··ˈ··, -ə'-
pancak|e ˈpæn keɪk ˈpæŋk eɪk **~ed** t **~es** s **~ing** ɪŋ
ˈ**Pancake Day**; ˌ**pancake ˈlanding**; ˌ**pancake ˈroll**; ˌ**Pancake ˈTuesday**
pancetta pæn ˈtʃet ə ‖ -ˈtʃeţ- —*It* [pan ˈtʃet ta]
panchax ˈpæn tʃæks **~es** ɪz əz
Pancho ˈpæntʃ əʊ ‖ -oʊ —*Sp* [ˈpan tʃo]
panchromatic ˌpæn krəʊ ˈmæt ɪk◂ →ˌpæŋ- ‖ -kroʊ ˈmæţ ɪk ◂ -krə-
Pancras ˈpæŋk rəs
pancreas ˈpæŋk ri‿əs -æs ‖ˈpæn kri- **~es** ɪz əz
pancreatic ˌpæŋk ri ˈæt ɪk ◂ ‖ -ˈæţ ɪk ˌpæn kri-
pancreatin ˈpæŋk ri‿ət ɪn pæn ˈkriː‿ →pæŋ-, §-ən ‖ -ən
pancreatitis ˌpæŋk ri‿ə ˈtaɪt ɪs §-əs ‖ -ˈtaɪţ əs
pancuronium ˌpæn kjuᵊ ˈrəʊn i‿əm →ˌpæŋ-, -kjə- ‖ -ˈroʊn-
panda ˈpænd ə **~s** z
ˈ**panda car**; ˌ**panda ˈcrossing**
pandanus pæn ˈdeɪn əs -ˈdæn- **~es** ɪz əz
Pandarus ˈpænd ər əs
pandect ˈpæn dekt **~s** s
pandemic ₍ˌ₎pæn ˈdem ɪk **~s** s
pandemonium ˌpænd ə ˈməʊn i‿əm ˌ·ɪ- ‖ -ˈmoʊn-
pander ˈpænd ə ‖ -ᵊr **~ed** d **pandering** ˈpænd‿ər ɪŋ **~s** z
pandialectal ˌpæn ˌdaɪ‿ə ˈlekt ᵊl◂
pandit, P~ ˈpænd ɪt ˈpʌnd-, §-ət —*Hindi* [pəɳ ɖɪţ] **~s** s
Pandora, p~ ₍ˌ₎pæn ˈdɔːr ə ‖ -ˈdoʊr- **~s, ~'s** z
Panˌ**dora's ˈbox**
pandowd|y pæn ˈdaʊd |i **~ies** iz
pane, Pane peɪn *(= pain)* **paned** peɪnd **panes** peɪnz
panegyric ˌpæn ə ˈdʒɪr ɪk -ɪ- ‖ -ˈdʒaɪr- **~s** s
panegyris|e, panegyriz|e ˈpæn ədʒ ə raɪz ˈ-ɪdʒ-, -ɪ · **~ed** d **~es** ɪz əz **~ing** ɪŋ
panegyrist ˌpæn ə ˈdʒɪr ɪst -ɪ-, §-əst, ˈ···· ‖ -ˈdʒaɪr- **~s** s
panel ˈpæn ᵊl **~ed, ~led** d **~ing, ~ling** ɪŋ **~s** z
ˈ**panel ˌbeater**; ˈ**panel saw**

panelist, panellist 'pæn ^{ə}l ɪst §-əst **~s** z
Panesar 'pæn ə sɑɪ ‖ -sɑːr
panetton|e ˌpæn ə 'təʊn |i -ɪ- ‖ -'toʊn |i ˌpɑːn- —*It* [pa net 'toː ne] **~es** iz **~i** iː
pan-|fry 'pæn |fraɪ **~fried** fraɪd **~fries** fraɪz **~frying** fraɪ ɪŋ
panful 'pæn fʊl **~s** z
pang pæŋ **pangs** pæŋz
panga 'pæŋ gə ‖ 'pɑːŋ gə **~s** z
Pangaea pæn 'dʒiː‿ə
Pangbourne 'pæŋ bɔːn ‖ -bɔːrn -boʊrn
Pangloss 'pæn glɒs →'pæŋ- ‖ -glɑːs -glɔːs
Panglossian, p~ $_{(ı)}$pæn 'glɒs i‿ən →$_{(ı)}$pæŋ- ‖ -'glɑːs- -'glɔːs-
pangolin pæŋ 'gəʊl ɪn §-ən; 'pæŋg əʊ lɪn, §-lən ‖ 'pæŋ gəl ən 'pæn-, -'goʊl- **~s** z
panhandl|e 'pæn ˌhænd ^{ə}l **~ed** d **~er/s** ‿ə/z ‖ ‿ər/z **~es** z **~ing** ‿ɪŋ
panhellenic ˌpæn hɪ 'len ɪk ◂ -he-, -hə-, -ɪ-, -ə-, -'liːn-
panhellenism ˌpæn 'hel ɪn ˌɪz əm -ən-
panic 'pæn ɪk **~ked** t **~king** ɪŋ **~s** s
'**panic** ˌ**button**; '**panic** ˌ**stations**
panicky 'pæn ɪk i
panicle 'pæn ɪk ^{ə}l **~s** z
panicle 'pæn ɪk ^{ə}l **~s** z
panic-|stricken 'pæn ɪk |ˌstrɪk ən **~struck** strʌk
panini, P~ *'sandwich(es)'; 'prickly pear'; Italian name* pə 'niːn i —*It* [pa 'niː ni] **~s** z
Panini *Sanskrit name* 'pɑːn ɪ niː -ni —*Skt* ['paː ɳi ɳi]
Panjab ˌpʌn 'dʒɑːb '··
Panjabi $_{(ı)}$pʌn 'dʒɑːb i pən-, -iː **~s** z
panjandrum pæn 'dʒændr əm pən- **~s** z
Pankhurst 'pæŋk hɜːst ‖ -hɜ˞ːst
panlectal ˌpæn 'lekt ^{ə}l ◂
Panmunjom ˌpæn mʊn 'dʒɒm ‖ ˌpɑːn mʊn 'dʒɑːm —*Korean* [p^{h}an mun dʒɔm]
pannage 'pæn ɪdʒ
Pannal, Pannell 'pæn ^{ə}l
panne pæn *(= pan)*
pannier 'pæn i‿ə ‖ ^{ə}r **~ed** d **~s** z
pannikin 'pæn ɪ kɪn -ə-, §-kən **~s** z
Pannonia pə 'nəʊn i‿ə pæ- ‖ -'noʊn-
panoch|a pə 'nəʊtʃ |ə ‖ -'noʊtʃ- **~e** i
panop|ly 'pæn əp |li **~lied** lid **~lies** liz
panoptic $_{(ı)}$pæn 'ɒpt ɪk ‖ -'ɑːpt- **~al** ^{ə}l
panopticon $_{(ı)}$pæn 'ɒpt ɪk ən §-ək- ‖ -'ɑːpt ə kɑːn **~s** z
panorama, P~ ˌpæn ə 'rɑːm ə ‖ -'ræm ə -'rɑːm- **~s** z
panoramic ˌpæn ə 'ræm ɪk ◂ -'rɑːm- **~ally** ^{ə}l‿i
panpipes 'pæn paɪps →'pæm-
pan-roasted 'pæn ˌrəʊst ɪd -əd ‖ -ˌroʊst-
Pan-Slavism ˌpæn 'slɑːv ˌɪz əm -'slæv-
pans|y, Pans|y 'pænz |i **~ies, ~y's** iz
pant pænt **panted** 'pænt ɪd -əd ‖ 'pæn̬t əd **panting/ly** 'pænt ɪŋ /li ‖ 'pæn̬t ɪŋ /li **pants** pænts

Pantagruel ˌpænt ə gru 'el '· ·gru‿əl ‖ pæn 'tæg ru el ˌpæn̬t ə 'gruː‿əl —*Fr* [pɑ̃ ta gʁy ɛl]
Pantagruelian ˌpænt ə gru 'el i‿ən ◂ ˌpænt ə 'gruːl i‿ən ‖ ˌpæn̬t ə-
pantalette ˌpænt ə 'let -^{ə}l 'et ‖ ˌpæn̬t ^{ə}l 'et **~s** s
pantaloon, P~ ˌpænt ə 'luːn ◂ -^{ə}l 'uːn, '· · ‖ ˌpæn̬t ^{ə}l 'uːn ◂ **~s** z
pantechnicon pæn 'tek nɪk ən **~s** z
Pantelleria ˌpæn tel ə 'riː‿ə ·,·- —*It* [pan tel le 'riː a]
Pantene *tdmk* ˌpæn 'ten
pantheism 'pæn^{t}θ i ˌɪz əm
pantheist 'pæn^{t}θ i ɪst §-əst **~s** s
pantheistic ˌpæn^{t}θ i 'ɪst ɪk ◂ **~al** ^{ə}l **~ally** ^{ə}l‿i
pantheon 'pæn^{t}θ i‿ən pæn 'θiː‿, -ɒn ‖ -ɑːn **~s** z
panther 'pæn^{t}θ ə ‖ -^{ə}r **~s** z
pantie girdle 'pænt i ˌgɜːd ^{ə}l ‖ 'pæn̬t i ˌgɜ˞ːd ^{ə}l **~s** z
panties 'pænt iz ‖ 'pæn̬t iz
pantihose 'pænt i həʊz ‖ 'pæn̬t i hoʊz
pantile 'pæn taɪ^{ə}l **~s** z
panto 'pænt əʊ ‖ -oʊ **~s** z
pantograph 'pænt əʊ grɑːf -græf ‖ 'pæn̬t ə græf **~s** s
pantomime 'pænt ə maɪm ‖ 'pæn̬t- **~s** z
pantomimic ˌpænt ə 'mɪm ɪk ◂ ‖ ˌpæn̬t-
pantomimist 'pænt ə maɪm ɪst §-əst, ˌ··'·· ‖ 'pæn̬t- **~s** s
Panton 'pænt ən ‖ -^{ə}n
pantothenic ˌpænt ə 'θen ɪk ◂ ‖ ˌpæn̬t-
pantr|y 'pæntr |i **~ies** iz
pants pænts
pantsuit 'pænt suːt -sjuːt
pant|y 'pænt |i ‖ 'pæn̬t |i **~ies** iz
'**panty hose**; '**panty raid**
Pantycelyn ˌpænt ə 'kel ɪn —*Welsh* [ˌpant ə 'ke lin]
pantyliner 'pænt i ˌlaɪn ə ‖ 'pæn̬t i ˌlaɪn ^{ə}r **~s** z
pantywaist 'pænt i weɪst ‖ 'pæn̬t- **~s** s
Pan Yan *tdmk* ˌpæn 'jæn ◂
Panza 'pænz ə —*Sp* ['pan θa]
panzer 'pænz ə ‖ -^{ə}r —*Ger* ['pan tsɐ] **~s** z
pap, Pap pæp **paps** pæps
papa, Papa pə 'pɑː ‖ 'pɑːp ə —*but as code name for the letter* P, *usually* 'pɑːp ə *even in BrE* **~s** z
papabile pɑː 'pɑːb ɪ leɪ —*It* [pa 'paː bi le]
papac|y 'peɪp əs |i **~ies** iz
Papadopoulos ˌpæp ə 'dɒp əl əs ‖ ˌpɑːp ə 'dɑːp- —*Greek* [pa pa 'ðo pu los]
papadum 'pæp əd əm 'pʌp-, 'pɒp-, -ə dʌm **~s** z
Papagen|a ˌpæp ə 'geɪn ə **~o** -əʊ ‖ -oʊ
papain pə 'peɪ ɪn -'paɪ-, §-ən
papal 'peɪp ^{ə}l **~ly** i
Papandreou ˌpæp æn 'dreɪ uː ‖ ˌpɑːp ɑːn- —*Greek* [pa pan 'ðre u]

P

paparazz|o ˌpæp ə ˈræts |əʊ -ˈrɑːts- ‖ ˌpɑːp ə ˈrɑːts |oʊ -ˈrɑːz- **~i** i -iː —*It* [pa pa ˈrat tso]
papaverine pə ˈpæv ə riːn -ˈpeɪv-, -rɪn, -rən
papaw ˈpɔːp ɔː pə ˈpɔː ‖ ˈpɑːp-, -ɑː **~s** z
papaya pə ˈpaɪ‿ə **~s** z
Papeete ˌpɑːp i ˈeɪt i -ə-, -ˈiːt-; pə ˈpiːt i ‖ -ˈeɪt eɪ pə ˈpiːţ i
paper ˈpeɪp ə ‖ -ər **~ed** d **papering** ˈpeɪp ər‿ɪŋ **~s** z
ˌ**paper 'bag** *(bag made of paper),* **'paper bag** *(bag for newspapers);* **'paper chase**; **'paper clip**; **'paper knife**; **'paper ˌmoney**; ˌ**paper 'tiger**; **'paper trail**
paperback ˈpeɪp ə bæk ‖ -ər- **~s** s
paperboard ˈpeɪp ə bɔːd ‖ -ər bɔːrd -boʊrd
paperboy ˈpeɪp ə bɔɪ ‖ -ər- **~s** z
paperclip ˈpeɪp ə klɪp ‖ -ər- **~s** s
paperhanger ˈpeɪp ə ˌhæŋ ə ‖ -ər ˌhæŋ ər **~s** z
paperless ˈpeɪp ə ləs -lɪs ‖ -ər-
paper-pusher ˈpeɪp ə ˌpʊʃ ə ‖ -ər ˌpʊʃ ər **~s** z
paper-thin ˌpeɪp ə ˈθɪn ◂ ‖ -ər-
paperweight ˈpeɪp ə weɪt ‖ -ər- **~s** s
paperwork ˈpeɪp ə wɜːk ‖ -ər wɜːk
papery ˈpeɪp ər i
Paphlagoni|a ˌpæf lə ˈgəʊn i‿ə ‖ -ˈgoʊn- **~an/s** ən/z
Paphos ˈpæf ɒs ˈpeɪf- ‖ -oʊs ˈpɑːf- —*Greek* [ˈpa fos]
Papiament|o ˌpæp i‿ə ˈment |əʊ ˌpɑːp- ‖ ˌpɑːp jə ˈment |oʊ **~u** uː
papier-mache, papier-mâché ˌpæp i eɪ ˈmæʃ eɪ ◂ ˌpeɪp ə ˈmæʃ- ‖ ˌpeɪp ər mə ˈʃeɪ ◂ -mæˈ· *(*)* —*Fr* [pa pje ma ʃe]
papill|a pə ˈpɪl |ə **~ae** iː
papillary pə ˈpɪl ər i ‖ ˈpæp ə ler i
papillate ˈpæp ɪ leɪt -ə-, →-əl eɪt, pə ˈpɪl eɪt
papillom|a ˌpæp ɪ ˈləʊm |ə -ə- ‖ -ˈloʊm |ə **~as** əz **~ata** ət ə ‖ əţ ə
papillon, P~ ˈpæp ɪ lɒn -ə- ‖ -lɑːn ˌpɑːp- —*Fr* [pa pi jɔ̃] **~s** z
papillote ˈpæp ɪ lɒt -ə-, -ləʊt ‖ ˌpæp ɪ ˈjoʊt ˌpɑːp- —*Fr* [pa pi jɔt] **~s** s
papist ˈpeɪp ɪst §-əst **~s** s
papistic peɪ ˈpɪst ɪk pə- **~al** əl
papistry ˈpeɪp ɪs tri -əs-
papoos|e pə ˈpuːs ‖ pæ- pə- **~es** ɪz əz
pappardelle ˌpæp ə ˈdel eɪ -ɑː-, -i ‖ -ər- -ɑːr- —*It* [pap parˈdɛl le]
papp|ous, ~us ˈpæp| əs **~i** aɪ
papp|y ˈpæp |i **~ier** i‿ə ‖ i‿ər **~iest** i‿ɪst i‿əst **~ies** iz
paprika ˈpæp rɪk ə; pə ˈpriːk ə, pæ- ‖ pə ˈpriːk ə pæ- *(*)*
Papu|a ˈpæp u‿|ə ˈpɑːp-, -ju- **~an/s** ən/z
ˌ**Papua New 'Guinea**
papule ˈpæp juːl **~s** z
Papworth ˈpæp wɜːθ -wəθ ‖ -wərθ
papyr|us pə ˈpaɪər |əs **~i** aɪ **~uses** əs ɪz -əz
par, Par pɑː ‖ pɑːr
ˌ**par 'value**

para *'paratrooper', 'paragraph'* ˈpær ə ‖ ˈper ə **~s** z
para *monetary unit* ˈpɑːr ə **~s** z
para- *comb. form with stress-neutral suffix* ¦pær ə ‖ ¦per ə — **parapraxis** ˌpær ə ˈpræks ɪs §-əs ‖ ˌper- *with stress-imposing suffix* pə ˈræ+ — **parabasis** pə ˈræb əs ɪs §-əs
Pará *river in Brazil* pə ˈrɑː —*Port* [pɐ ˈra]
parable ˈpær əb əl ‖ ˈper- **~s** z
parabola pə ˈræb əl ə **~s** z
parabolic ˌpær ə ˈbɒl ɪk ◂ ‖ ˌpær ə ˈbɑːl ɪk ◂ ˌper- **~al** əl **~ally** əl‿i
paraboloid pə ˈræb ə lɔɪd **~s** z
Paraburdoo ˌpær ə bə ˈduː ‖ -bər ˈ· ˌper-
Paracel ˌpær ə ˈsel **~s** z
Paracelsus ˌpær ə ˈsels əs ‖ ˈper-
paracetamol ˌpær ə ˈsiːt ə mɒl -ˈset- ‖ -ˈsiːţ ə mɑːl ˌper-, -ˈseţ-, -mɔːl, -moʊl **~s** z
para|chute ˈpær ə |ʃuːt ‖ ˈper- **~chuted** ʃuːt ɪd -əd ‖ ʃuːţ əd **~chutes** ʃuːts **~chuting** ʃuːt ɪŋ ‖ ʃuːţ ɪŋ
parachutist ˈpær ə ʃuːt ɪst §-əst, ˌ·ˈ·· ‖ -ʃuːţ əst ˈper- **~s** s
Paraclete, p~ ˈpær ə kliːt ‖ ˈper-
parad|e pə ˈreɪd **~ed** ɪd əd **~es** z **~ing** ɪŋ
paˈ**rade ground**
paradichlorobenzene ˌpær ə ˌdaɪ klɔːr əʊ ˈbenz iːn ˌ···ˌ·- ‖ -oʊˈ·· ˌper-, -kloʊr·ˈ·, -ben ˈziːn
paradigm ˈpær ə daɪm ‖ ˈper-, -dɪm **~s** z
paradigmatic ˌpær ə dɪg ˈmæt ɪk ◂ ‖ -ˈmæţ ɪk ◂ ˌper- **~ally** əl‿i
paradisal ˌpær ə ˈdaɪs əl ◂ -ˈdaɪz- ‖ ˌper-
paradise, P~ ˈpær ə daɪs ‖ ˈper-, -daɪz
paradisiac ˌpær ə ˈdɪz i æk ◂; -ˈdɪs-; -dɪ ˈsaɪ‿ək, -dəˈ·· ‖ ˌper-
paradisiacal ˌpær ə dɪ ˈsaɪ‿ək əl ◂ -dəˈ·· ‖ ˌper-
parador ˈpær ə dɔː ‖ ˌpɑːr ɑː ˈdɔːr —*Sp* [pa ra ˈðor] **~s** z
parados ˈpær ə dɒs ‖ -dɑːs ˈper- **~es** ɪz əz
paradox ˈpær ə dɒks ‖ -dɑːks ˈper- **~es** ɪz əz
paradoxical ˌpær ə ˈdɒks ɪk əl ◂ ‖ -ˈdɑːks- ˌper- **~ly** ‿i **~ness** nəs nɪs
paraffin ˈpær ə fɪn -fiːn, ˌ··ˈ·; §ˈpær əf ən ‖ ˈper-
'paraffin wax, ˌ···ˈ·
paraglid|er ˈpær ə ˌglaɪd ə ‖ -ər ˈper- **~ers** əz ‖ ərz **~ing** ɪŋ
paragoge ˌpær ə ˈgəʊdʒ i ‖ -ˈgoʊdʒ i ˌper-
paragogic ˌpær ə ˈgɒdʒ ɪk ◂ ‖ -ˈgɑːdʒ- ˌper-
paragon ˈpær əg ən ‖ -ə gɑːn ˈper-, -əg ən *(*)* **~s** z
paragraph ˈpær ə grɑːf -græf ‖ -græf ˈper- **~ed** t **~ing** ɪŋ **~s** s
paragraphia ˌpær ə ˈgræf i‿ə -ˈgrɑːf- ‖ ˌper-
Paraguay ˈpær ə gwaɪ ˌ·ˈ· ‖ ˈper-, -gweɪ —*Sp* [pa ra ˈɣwai]
Paraguayan ˌpær ə ˈgwaɪ‿ən ◂ ‖ ˌper-, -ˈgweɪ- **~s** z
parakeet ˈpær ə kiːt ˌ·ˈ· ‖ ˈper- **~s** s
paralanguage ˈpær ə ˌlæŋ gwɪdʒ -wɪdʒ ‖ ˈper-
paraldehyde pə ˈræld ɪ haɪd -ˈə-

paralegal ˌpær ə ˈliːɡ əl ◂ ‖ ˌper- **~s** z
paralinguistic ˌpær ə lɪŋ ˈɡwɪst ɪk ◂ ‖ ˌper- **~ally** əl ˌi **~s** s
parallactic ˌpær ə ˈlækt ɪk ◂ ‖ ˌper- **~ally** əl ˌi
parallax ˈpær ə læks ‖ ˈper- **~es** ɪz əz
parallel ˈpær ə lel -əl əl ‖ ˈper- **~ed, ~led** d **~ing, ~ling** ɪŋ **~s** z
ˌ**parallel ˈbars**
parallelepiped ˌpær ə lel ə ˈpaɪp ed ˌ· · ·ˈep ɪ ped, -ə- ‖ ˌper- **~s** z
parallelism ˈpær ə lel ˌɪz əm -ləl ˌ·-; ⚠ˈpær ə ˌlɪz əm ‖ ˈper- **~s** z
parallelogram ˌpær ə ˈlel ə ɡræm ‖ ˌper- **~s** z
paralogism pə ˈræl ə ˌdʒɪz əm **~s** z
Paralympics ˌpær ə ˈlɪmp ɪks ‖ ˌper-
paralysation ˌpær ə laɪ ˈzeɪʃ ən ‖ -lə ˈ-- ˌper-
paralys|e ˈpær ə laɪz ‖ ˈper- **~ed** d **~es** ɪz əz **~ing/ly** ɪŋ/ li
paralyses *from v* ˈpær ə laɪz ɪz -əz ‖ ˈper-
paralyses *n pl* pə ˈræl ə siːz -ɪ-
paral|ysis pə ˈræl |əs ɪs -ɪs-, §-əs **~yses** ə siːz ɪ-
paralytic ˌpær ə ˈlɪt ɪk ◂ ‖ -ˈlɪt̬ ɪk ◂ ˌper- **~ally** əl ˌi **~s** s
paralyzation ˌpær ə laɪ ˈzeɪʃ ən ‖ -lə ˈ-- ˌper-
paralyz|e ˈpær ə laɪz ‖ ˈper- **~ed** d **~es** ɪz əz **~ing** ɪŋ
paramagnetic ˌpær ə mæɡ ˈnet ɪk ◂ -məɡ ˈ-- ‖ -ˈnet̬ ɪk ◂ ˌper-
paramagnetism ˌpær ə ˈmæɡ nə ˌtɪz əm -ˈ·nɪ- ‖ ˌper-
Paramaribo ˌpær ə ˈmær ɪ bəʊ §-ˈ·ə- ‖ -boʊ ˌper- —*Dutch* [paː raː ˈmaː ri boː]
paramatta ˌpær ə ˈmæt ə ‖ -ˈmæt̬ ə ˌper-
parameci|um ˌpær ə ˈmiːs i ˌ|əm ‖ ˌper-, -ˈmiːʃ- **~a** ə **~ums** əmz
paramedic ˌpær ə ˈmed ɪk ‖ ˌper- **~al** əl ◂ **~s** s
parameter pə ˈræm ɪt ə -ət- ‖ -ət̬ ər **~s** z
parameteris... —*see* **parameteriz...**
parameterization pə ˌræm ɪt ər aɪ ˈzeɪʃ ən -ˌət ˌ-ɪˈ-- ‖ -ət̬ ər ə- → -ˌ·ətr əˈ-
parameteriz|e pə ˈræm ɪt ə raɪz -ˈ·ət-; → ·ˈ·ɪ traɪz, -ə- ‖ -ət̬ ə- **~ed** d **~es** ɪz əz **~ing** ɪŋ
parametric ˌpær ə ˈmetr ɪk ◂ ‖ ˌper- **~ally** əl ˌi
parametris... —*see* **parametris...**
parametrization pə ˌræm ətr aɪ ˈzeɪʃ ən -ˌ·ɪtr-, -ɪˈ-- ‖ -əˈ--
parametriz|e pə ˈræm ə traɪz -ɪ- **~ed** d **~es** ɪz əz **~ing** ɪŋ
paramilitar|y ˌpær ə ˈmɪl ɪt ər |i ◂ -ˈ·ət ˌ ‖ -ə ter |i ˌper- **~ies** iz
paramnesia ˌpær æm ˈniːz i ˌə -ˈniːʒ ə ‖ -ˈniːʒ ə ˌper-
paramount ˈpær ə maʊnt ‖ ˈper- **~cy** si **~ly** li
paramour, P~ ˈpær ə mʊə -mɔː ‖ ˈpær ə mɔːr ˈper- **~s** z
Paramus pə ˈræm əs
Paraná ˌpær ə ˈnɑː ‖ ˌper-, ˌpɑːr- —*Port* [pɐ rɐ ˈna], *Sp* [pa ra ˈna]
parang ˈpɑːr æŋ **~s** z
paranoi|a ˌpær ə ˈnɔɪ |ə ‖ ˌper- **~ac** æk ◂ ɪk **~acally** æk əl ˌi ɪk-
paranoid ˈpær ə nɔɪd ‖ ˈper- **~s** z
paranormal ˌpær ə ˈnɔːm əl ◂ ‖ -ˈnɔːrm əl ◂ ˌper- **~ly** i
parapet ˈpær əp ɪt -ət, -ə pet ‖ ˈper- **~s** s
paraph ˈpær æf -əf ‖ ˈper-; pə ˈræf **~s** s
paraphernalia ˌpær ə fə ˈneɪl i ˌə ‖ -ə fər- ˌper-
paraphilia ˌpær ə ˈfɪl i ˌə ‖ ˌper- **~s** z
paraphras|e *n, v* ˈpær ə freɪz ‖ ˈper- **~ed** d **~es** ɪz əz **~ing** ɪŋ
paraphrastic ˌpær ə ˈfræst ɪk ◂ ‖ ˌper- **~ally** əl ˌi
paraplegia ˌpær ə ˈpliːdʒ ə -ˈpliːdʒ i ˌə ‖ ˌper-
paraplegic ˌpær ə ˈpliːdʒ ɪk ◂ ‖ ˌper- **~s** s
paraprax|is ˌpær ə ˈpræks |ɪs ˌper- **~es** iːz
parapsychologic ˌpær ə ˌsaɪk ə ˈlɒdʒ ɪk -ˌpsaɪk- ‖ -ˈlɑːdʒ- ˌper- **~al/ly** əl/ ˌi
parapsycholog|ist ˌpær ə saɪ ˈkɒl ədʒ |ɪst -psaɪˈ--, §-əst ‖ -ˈkɑːl- ˌper- **~ists** ɪsts §əsts **~y** i
paraquat, P~ *tdmk* ˈpær ə kwɒt -kwæt ‖ -kwɑːt ˈper-
paras ˈpær əz ‖ ˈper-
parasailing ˈpær ə ˌseɪəl ɪŋ ‖ ˈper-
parasang ˈpær ə sæŋ ‖ ˈper- **~s** z
parascend|ing ˈpær ə ˌsend| ɪŋ ‖ ˈper- **~er/s** ə/z ‖ ər/z
para|shah, P~ ˈpær ə |ʃɑː ‖ ˈpɑːr- **~shoth** ʃəʊt ‖ ʃoʊt
parasite ˈpær ə saɪt ‖ ˈper- **~s** s
parasitic ˌpær ə ˈsɪt ɪk ◂ ‖ -ˈsɪt̬ ɪk ◂ ˌper- **~al** əl **~ally** əl ˌi
parasitism ˈpær ə saɪt ˌɪz əm -sɪ ˌtɪz- ‖ -ə saɪt̬- ˈper-, -sə ˌtɪz-
parasitology ˌpær ə saɪ ˈtɒl ədʒ i -sɪ ˈtɒl- ‖ -saɪ ˈtɑːl- ˌper-, -sə-
parasol ˈpær ə sɒl ˌ· ·ˈ· ‖ -sɔːl ˈper-, -sɑːl **~s** z
parasympathetic ˌpær ə ˌsɪmp ə ˈθet ɪk ◂ ‖ -ˈθet̬ ɪk ◂ ˌper-
parasynthesis ˌpær ə ˈsɪnᵗθ əs ɪs -ɪs ɪs, §-əs ‖ ˌper-
parasynthetic ˌpær ə sɪn ˈθet ɪk ◂ ‖ -ˈθet̬ ɪk ◂ ˌper- **~ally** əl ˌi
paratactic ˌpær ə ˈtækt ɪk ◂ ‖ ˌper- **~ally** əl ˌi
parataxis ˌpær ə ˈtæks ɪs §-əs, ˈ· · · · ‖ ˌper-
parathion ˌpær ə ˈθaɪ ɒn -ˈθaɪ ˌən ‖ -ɑːn ˌper-
parathyroid ˌpær ə ˈθaɪər ɔɪd ◂ ‖ ˌper- **~s** z
ˌ**paraˈthyroid gland**, · · ˈ · · ˈ·
paratroop ˈpær ə truːp ‖ ˈper- **~er/s** ə/z ‖ ər/z **~s** s
paratyphoid ˌpær ə ˈtaɪf ɔɪd ‖ ˌper-
paravane ˈpær ə veɪn ‖ ˈper- **~s** z
parboil ˈpɑː bɔɪəl ‖ ˈpɑːr- **~ed** d **~ing** ɪŋ **~s** z
parbuckle ˈpɑː bʌk əl ‖ ˈpɑːr- **~s** z
parcel ˈpɑːs əl ‖ ˈpɑːrs əl **~ed, ~led** d **~ing, ~ling** ˌɪŋ **~s** z
ˈ**parcel post**; ˈ**parcel bomb**
Parcelforce ˈpɑːs əl fɔːs ‖ ˈpɑːrs əl fɔːrs -foʊrs
parch pɑːtʃ ‖ pɑːrtʃ **parched** pɑːtʃt ‖ pɑːrtʃt **parches** ˈpɑːtʃ ɪz -əz ‖ ˈpɑːrtʃ əz **parching** ˈpɑːtʃ ɪŋ ‖ ˈpɑːrtʃ ɪŋ
parchedness ˈpɑːtʃt nəs -nɪs ‖ ˈpɑːrtʃt-
parcheesi, parchesi pɑː ˈtʃiːz i -ˈtʃiːs i ‖ pɑːr-
parchment ˈpɑːtʃ mənt ‖ ˈpɑːrtʃ- **~s** s
pard pɑːd ‖ pɑːrd **pards** pɑːdz ‖ pɑːrdz

P

pardalote ˈpɑːd ə ləʊt →-ᵊl əʊt ‖ ˈpɑːrd ᵊl oʊt **~s** s

pardner, P~ ˈpɑːd nə ‖ ˈpɑːrd nᵊr **~s** z

Pardoe ˈpɑːd əʊ ‖ ˈpɑːrd oʊ

pardon ˈpɑːd ᵊn ‖ ˈpɑːrd ᵊn **~ed** d **~ing** ˌɪŋ **~s** z

pardonab|le ˈpɑːd ᵊn‿əb |ᵊl ‖ ˈpɑːrd- **~ly** li

pardoner ˈpɑːd ᵊn‿ə ‖ ˈpɑːrd ᵊn‿ər **~s** z

pare peə ‖ peᵊr pæᵊr *(= pair)* **pared** peəd ‖ peᵊrd pæᵊrd **pares** peəz ‖ peᵊrz pæᵊrz **paring** ˈpeər ɪŋ ‖ ˈper ɪŋ ˈpær-

pared-down ˌpeəd ˈdaʊn ◂ ‖ ˌperd- ˌpærd-

paregoric ˌpær ə ˈgɒr ɪk ◂ -ɪ- ‖ -ˈgɔːr ɪk ◂ ˌper-, ˈgɑːr-

parenchyma pə ˈreŋk ɪm ə §-əm-

par|ent *n, v* ˈpeər |ənt ‖ ˈper |ənt ˈpær- **~ented** ənt ɪd -əd ‖ ənṭ əd **~enting** ənt ɪŋ ‖ ənṭ ɪŋ **~ents** ənts **ˈparent ˌcompany,** ˌ··ˈ··

parentag|e ˈpeər ənt ɪdʒ ‖ ˈper ənṭ ɪdʒ ˈpær- **~es** ɪz əz

parental pə ˈrent ᵊl ‖ -ˈrenṭ ᵊl **~ly** i

parenteral pæ ˈrent ər əl pə- ‖ -ˈrenṭ-

parenth|esis pə ˈrenᵗθ |əs ɪs -ɪs-, §-əs **~eses** ə siːz ɪ-

parenthesis|e, parenthesiz|e pə ˈrenᵗθ ə saɪz **~ed** d **~es** ɪz əz **~ing** ɪŋ

parenthetic ˌpær ən ˈθet ɪk ◂ -en- ‖ -ˈθeṭ ɪk ◂ ˌper- **~al** ᵊl **~ally** ᵊl‿i

parenthood ˈpeər ənt hʊd ‖ ˈper- ˈpær-

parentless ˈpeər ənt ləs -lɪs ‖ ˈper- ˈpær-

parent-teacher ˌpeər ənt ˈtiːtʃ ə ‖ ˌper ənt ˈtiːtʃ ᵊr ˌpær- **ˌparent-ˈteacher associˌation**

pareo ˈpɑːr eɪ əʊ pɑː ˈreɪ- ‖ -oʊ **~s** z

parer ˈpeər ə ‖ ˈper ᵊr ˈpær- **~s** z

parerg|on pə ˈrɜːg |ɒn -ˈeəg-, -|ən ‖ -ˈrɜᵊːg ɑːn -ˈrerg- **~a** ə

paresis pə ˈriːs ɪs §-əs; ˈpær əs-, -ɪs-

paretic pə ˈret ɪk ‖ -ˈreṭ-

pareu ˈpɑːr eɪ uː pɑː ˈreɪ- **~s** z

par excellence ˌ₍ₗ₎pɑːʳ ˈeks ə lɑːnᵗs -lɒ̃s, -əl‿ənᵗs ‖ ˌpɑːr ˌeks ə ˈlɑːnᵗs —*Fr* [pa ʁɛk sɛ lɑ̃ːs]

parfait ˌpɑː ˈfeɪ ˈ·· ‖ ˌpɑːr- **~s** z

Parfitt ˈpɑːf ɪt §-ət ‖ ˈpɑːrf-

parfum pɑː ˈfʌ̃ -ˈfʌm ‖ pɑːr- —*Fr* [paʁ fœ̃]

parg|et ˈpɑːdʒ |ɪt §-ət ‖ ˈpɑːrdʒ |ət **~eted** ɪt ɪd §ət-, -əd ‖ əṭ əd **~eting** ɪt ɪŋ §ət- ‖ əṭ ɪŋ **~ets** ɪts §əts ‖ əts

Pargiter ˈpɑːdʒ ɪt ə §-ət- ‖ ˈpɑːrdʒ əṭ ᵊr

Parham ˈpær əm

parhelia pɑː ˈhiːl i‿ə ‖ pɑːr-

parheliacal ˌpɑː hɪ ˈlaɪ‿ək ᵊl ◂ §-hə- ‖ ˌpɑːr-

parhelic ₍ₗ₎pɑː ˈhiːl ɪk ‖ ₍ₗ₎pɑːr-

parheli|on pɑː ˈhiːl i‿|ən -ɒn ‖ pɑːr- **~a** ə

pariah pə ˈraɪ‿ə ˈpær i‿ə **~s** z

Parian ˈpeər i‿ən ‖ ˈper- ˈpær- **~s** z

parietal pə ˈraɪ‿ət ᵊl -ɪt- ‖ -əṭ ᵊl **~s** z

pari-mutuel ˌpær i ˈmjuːtʃ u‿əl -ˈmjuːt ju‿əl, -ˈmjuːtʃ əl ‖ ˌper- **~s** z

paring ˈpeər ɪŋ ‖ ˈper- ˈpær- **~s** z *(= pairing)*

pari passu ˌpær i ˈpæs uː ˌpɑːr-, -juː ‖ ˌpɑːr i ˈpɑːs uː

paripinnate ˌpær i ˈpɪn eɪt ◂ -ə- ‖ ˌper-

Paris ˈpær ɪs §-əs ‖ ˈper- —*Fr* [pa ʁi]

parish, P~ ˈpær ɪʃ ‖ ˈper- **~es** ɪz əz **ˌparish ˈclerk**; **ˌparish ˈpriest**; **ˌparish ˈregister**

parishioner pə ˈrɪʃ ᵊn‿ə ‖ ‿ər **~s** z

parish-pump ˌpær ɪʃ ˈpʌmp ‖ ˌper-

Parisian pə ˈrɪz i‿ən ‖ pə ˈrɪʒ ᵊn -ˈriːʒ- *(*)* **~s** z

parisyllabic ˌpær ɪ sɪ ˈlæb ɪk ◂ ˌ·ə-, -sə'- ‖ ˌper-

parit|y ˈpær ət |i -ɪt- ‖ -əṭ |i ˈper- **~ies** iz

park, Park pɑːk ‖ pɑːrk **parked** pɑːkt ‖ pɑːrkt **parking** ˈpɑːk ɪŋ ‖ ˈpɑːrk ɪŋ **parks** pɑːks ‖ pɑːrks **ˌPark ˈAvenue**

parka ˈpɑːk ə ‖ ˈpɑːrk ə **~s** z

park-and-ride ˌpɑːk ənd ˈraɪd ‖ ˌpɑːrk-

Parke pɑːk ‖ pɑːrk

Parker ˈpɑːk ə ‖ ˈpɑːrk ᵊr

Parkes pɑːks ‖ pɑːrks

Parkeston, Parkestone ˈpɑːkst ən ‖ ˈpɑːrkst-

Parkgate *(i)* ˈpɑːk geɪt ‖ ˈpɑːrk-, *(ii)* ˌ·ˈ· —*In Co. Antrim, (i); in Cheshire, (ii).*

Parkhouse ˈpɑːk haʊs ‖ ˈpɑːrk-

Parkhurst ˈpɑːk hɜːst ‖ ˈpɑːrk hɜᵊːst

parkin, P~ ˈpɑːk ɪn §-ən ‖ ˈpɑːrk-

parking ˈpɑːk ɪŋ ‖ ˈpɑːrk ɪŋ **ˈparking ˌgarage** ‖ ˈ· ··ˌ·; **ˈparking light**; **ˈparking lot**; **ˈparking ˌmeter**; **ˈparking space**; **ˈparking ˌticket**; **ˈpark ˌkeeper**

Parkinson ˈpɑːk ɪn sən §-ən- ‖ ˈpɑːrk- **~'s** z **ˈParkinson's diˌsease**; **ˈParkinson's law**

parkinsonian ˌpɑːk ɪn ˈsəʊn i‿ən ◂ ‖ ˌpɑːrk ən ˈsoʊn-

parkinsonism ˈpɑːk ɪn sə ˌnɪz əm §ˈ·ən-, -sən ˌɪz- ‖ ˈpɑːrk-

parkland ˈpɑːk lænd ‖ ˈpɑːrk- **~s** z

Parkray *tdmk* ˈpɑːk reɪ ‖ ˈpɑːrk-

Parks pɑːks ‖ pɑːrks

Parkstone ˈpɑːkst ən ‖ ˈpɑːrk stoʊn

parkway ˈpɑːk weɪ ‖ ˈpɑːrk- **~s** z

park|y ˈpɑːk |i ‖ ˈpɑːrk |i **~ier** i‿ə ‖ i‿ᵊr **~iest** i‿ɪst i‿əst

parlance ˈpɑːl ənᵗs ‖ ˈpɑːrl-

parlando pɑː ˈlænd əʊ ‖ pɑːr ˈlɑːnd oʊ —*It* [par ˈlan do]

parlay ˈpɑːl i ‖ ˈpɑːrl eɪ -i **~ed** d **~ing** ɪŋ **~s** z

parley ˈpɑːl i ‖ ˈpɑːrl i **~ed** d **~ing** ɪŋ **~s** z

parleyvoo ˌpɑːl i ˈvuː -eɪ- ‖ ˌpɑːrl-

parliament, P~ ˈpɑːl ə mənt -ɪ-, -jə- ‖ ˈpɑːrl- **~s** s

parliamentarian ˌpɑːl ə men ˈteər i‿ən ˌ·ɪ-, ˌ·jə-, -mən'·- ‖ ˌpɑːrl ə men ˈter- -mən'·- **~ism** ˌɪz əm **~s** z

parliamentary ˌpɑːl ə ˈment‿ər i ◂ ˌ·ɪ-, ˌ·jə- ‖ ˌpɑːrl ə ˈmenṭ-

Parlophone *tdmk* ˈpɑːl ə fəʊn ‖ ˈpɑːrl ə foʊn

parlor, parlour ˈpɑːl ə ‖ ˈpɑːrl ᵊr **~s** z **ˈparlor car**; **ˈparlour game**; **ˈparlour maid**

parlous ˈpɑːl əs ‖ ˈpɑːrl əs **~ly** li **~ness** nəs nɪs

parlyaree ˌpɑːl i ˈɑːr i ‖ ˌpɑːrl-

Parma ˈpɑːm ə ‖ ˈpɑːrm ə —*It* [ˈpar ma]
Parmenides pɑː ˈmen ɪ diːz -ə- ‖ pɑːr-
Parmenter ˈpɑːm ɪnt ə -ənt- ‖ ˈpɑːrm ənt ᵊr
Parmentier pɑː ˈment i‿ə -ˈmɒnt i eɪ; ˈpɑːm ənt jeɪ ‖ ˌpɑːrm ən ˈtjeɪ —*Fr* [paʁ mɑ̃ tje] *(*)*
Parmesan ˌpɑːm ɪ ˈzæn ◂ -ə- ‖ ˈpɑːrm ə zɑːn -ʒɑːn, -zæn; -əz ən *(*)*
ˌ**Parmesan ˈcheese**
parmigiana ˌpɑːm ɪ ˈdʒɑːn ə -ˈʒɑːn- ‖ ˌpɑːrm- —*It* [par mi ˈdʒaː na]
Parminter ˈpɑːm ɪnt ə -ənt- ‖ ˈpɑːrm ənt ᵊr
Parmiter ˈpɑːm ɪt ə -ət- ‖ ˈpɑːrm əţ ᵊr
Parnassian pɑː ˈnæs i‿ən ‖ pɑːr- **~s** z
Parnassus pɑː ˈnæs əs ‖ pɑːr- —*ModGk* Parnassos [par na ˈsɔs]
Parnell *(i)* pɑː ˈnel ‖ pɑːr-, *(ii)* ˈpɑːn ᵊl ‖ ˈpɑːrn ᵊl
Parnes pɑːnz ‖ pɑːrnz
parochial pə ˈrəʊk i‿əl ‖ -ˈroʊk- **~ism** ˌɪz əm **~ly** i
parodist ˈpær əd ɪst §-əst ‖ ˈper- **~s** s
parod|y ˈpær əd |i ‖ ˈper- **~ied** id **~ies** iz **~ying** i ɪŋ
paroecious pə ˈriːʃ əs
parol ˈpær əl pə ˈrəʊl, →-ˈrɒʊl ‖ ˈper-
parol|e pə ˈrəʊl →-ˈrɒʊl ‖ -ˈroʊl **~ed** d **~es** z **~ing** ɪŋ
parolee pə ˌrəʊ ˈliː ‖ -ˌroʊ- pə ˈroʊl iː **~s** z
paronomasia ˌpær ən ə ˈmeɪz i‿ə -ə nəʊ-, -ˈmeɪs- ‖ ˌpær ə noʊ ˈmeɪʒ ə ˌper-, -ˈmeɪʒ i‿ə
paronychia ˌpær ə ˈnɪk i‿ə ‖ ˌper-
paronym ˈpær ə nɪm ‖ ˈper- **~s** z
paronym|ous pə ˈrɒn ɪm |əs pæ-, -əm- ‖ -ˈrɑːn- **~ously** əs li **~y** i
Paroo ˈpɑːr uː
Paros ˈpeər ɒs ˈpær-, ˈpɑːr- ‖ ˈper ɑːs ˈpær-
parotid pə ˈrɒt ɪd §-əd ‖ -ˈrɑːţ əd
parotitis ˌpær ə ˈtaɪt ɪs §-əs ‖ -ˈtaɪţ əs ˌper-
-parous *stress-imposing* pər əs — **oviparous** əʊ ˈvɪp ər əs ‖ oʊ-
parousia, P~ pə ˈruːz i‿ə -ˈruːs-
paroxysm ˈpær ək ˌsɪz əm -ɒk-; pə ˈrɒks ˌɪz- ‖ ˈper-; pə ˈrɑːks ˌɪz- **~s** z
paroxysmal ˌpær ək ˈsɪz məl ◂ -ɒk- ‖ ˌper- **~ly** i
paroxytone pə ˈrɒks ɪ təʊn pæ-, -ə- ‖ -ˈrɑːks ə toʊn **~s** z
Parozone *tdmk* ˈpær ə zəʊn ‖ -zoʊn ˈper-
parquet ˈpɑːk eɪ -i ‖ pɑːr ˈkeɪ *(*)* **~ed** d **~ing** ɪŋ **~s** z
parquetr|y ˈpɑːk ɪtr |i -ətr- ‖ ˈpɑːrk- **~ies** iz
parr, Parr pɑː ‖ pɑːr *(= par)* **parrs, Parr's** pɑːz ‖ pɑːrz
Parracombe ˈpær ə kuːm ‖ ˈper-
Parramatta, p~ ˌpær ə ˈmæt ə ‖ -ˈmæţ ə ˌper-
parrel ˈpær əl ‖ ˈper- **~s** z
Parret, Parrett ˈpær ɪt §-ət ‖ˈper-
parricidal ˌpær ɪ ˈsaɪd ᵊl ◂ -ə- ‖ ˌper-
parricide ˈpær ɪ saɪd -ə- ‖ ˈper- **~s** z
Parrish ˈpær ɪʃ ‖ ˈper-
parr|ot, P~ ˈpær |ət ‖ ˈper- **~oted** ət ɪd -əd ‖ əţ əd **~oting** ət ɪŋ ‖ əţ ɪŋ **~ots** əts
parrot-fashion ˈpær ət ˌfæʃ ᵊn ‖ ˈper-
parrotfish ˈpær ət fɪʃ ‖ ˈper- **~es** ɪz əz
Parrott ˈpær ət ‖ ˈper-
parr|y, Parry ˈpær |i ‖ ˈper- **~ied** id **~ies** iz **~ying** i ɪŋ
parsable ˈpɑːz əb ᵊl ‖ ˈpɑːrs-
parse pɑːz ‖ pɑːrs *(*)* **parsed** pɑːzd ‖ pɑːrst **parses** ˈpɑːz ɪz -əz ‖ ˈpɑːrs əz **parsing** ˈpɑːz ɪŋ ‖ ˈpɑːrs ɪŋ
parsec ˈpɑː sek ‖ ˈpɑːr- **~s** s
Parsee ˈpɑːs iː ˌpɑː ˈsiː ‖ ˈpɑːrs iː ˌpɑːr ˈsiː —*In India,* ˌˈ· **~s** z
parser ˈpɑːz ə ‖ ˈpɑːrs ᵊr **~s** z
Parsi —*see* **Parsee**
Parsifal ˈpɑːs ɪf ᵊl -əf-; -ɪ fɑːl, -ə-, -fæl ‖ ˈpɑːrs- —*Ger* [ˈpaʁ zi fal]
parsimonious ˌpɑːs ɪ ˈməʊn i‿əs ◂ ˌ·ə- ‖ˌpɑːrs ə ˈmoʊn- **~ly** li **~ness** nəs nɪs
parsimony ˈpɑːs ɪm ən i ˈ·əm- ‖ ˈpɑːrs ə moʊn i *(*)*
Parsippany pə ˈsɪp ən i ‖ pᵊr-
parsley ˈpɑːs li ‖ ˈpɑːrs li
Parsley *family name* ˈpɑːz li ‖ ˈpɑːrz-
Parslow ˈpɑːz ləʊ ‖ ˈpɑːrz loʊ ˈpɑːrs-
parsnip ˈpɑːs nɪp §-nəp ‖ ˈpɑːrs- **~s** s
parson ˈpɑːs ᵊn ‖ ˈpɑːrs ᵊn **~s** z
ˌ**parson's ˈnose**
parsonag|e ˈpɑːs ən‿ɪdʒ ‖ ˈpɑːrs- **~es** ɪz əz
parsonic pɑː ˈsɒn ɪk ‖ pɑːr ˈsɑːn ɪk **~al** ᵊl
Parsons ˈpɑːs ᵊnz ‖ ˈpɑːrs-
part pɑːt ‖ pɑːrt **parted** ˈpɑːt ɪd -əd ‖ ˈpɑːrţ əd **parting** ˈpɑːt ɪŋ ‖ ˈpɑːrţ ɪŋ **parts** pɑːts ‖ pɑːrts
ˌ**part exˈchange**; ˌ**part of ˈspeech**; ˈ**part work**
par|take pɑː |ˈteɪk ‖ pɑːr- pᵊr- **~taken** ˈteɪk ən **~taker/s** ˈteɪk ə/z ‖ ˈteɪk ᵊr/z **~takes** ˈteɪks **~taking** ˈteɪk ɪŋ **~took** ˈtʊk §ˈtuːk
parterre pɑː ˈteə ‖ pɑːr ˈteᵊr —*Fr* [paʁ tɛːʁ] **~s** z
Parthenia pɑː ˈθiːn i‿ə ‖ pɑːr-
parthenium pɑː ˈθiːn i‿əm ‖ pɑːr- **~s** z
parthenogenesis ˌpɑːθ ə nəʊ ˈdʒen əs ɪs ˌ·ɪ-, -ɪs ɪs, §-əs ‖ ˌpɑːrθ ə noʊ-
Parthenon ˈpɑːθ ən ən -ɪn-; -ə nɒn, -ɪ- ‖ ˈpɑːrθ ə nɑːn
Parthenope pɑː ˈθen əp i ‖ pɑːr-
Parthi|a ˈpɑːθ i‿|ə ‖ ˈpɑːrθ- **~an/s** ən/z
partial ˈpɑːʃ ᵊl ‖ ˈpɑːrʃ ᵊl **~ness** nəs nɪs **~s** z
partialit|y ˌpɑːʃ i ˈæl ət |i -ɪt i ‖ ˌpɑːrʃ i ˈæl əţ |i **~ies** iz
partially ˈpɑːʃ əl‿i ‖ˈpɑːrʃ-
participant pɑː ˈtɪs ɪp ənt -əp- ‖ pᵊr- pɑːr- **~s** s
partici|pate pɑː ˈtɪs ɪ |peɪt -ə- ‖ pɑːr- pᵊr- **~pated** peɪt ɪd -əd ‖ peɪţ əd **~pates** peɪts **~pating** peɪt ɪŋ ‖ peɪţ ɪŋ
participation pɑː ˌtɪs ɪ ˈpeɪʃ ᵊn ˌpɑːt ɪs-, -əˈ- ‖ pɑːr- pᵊr-
participative pɑː ˈtɪs ɪ peɪt ɪv -ˈə, -pət ɪv ‖ pɑːr ˈtɪs ə pəţ ɪv pᵊr-, -peɪţ ɪv
participator pɑː ˈtɪs ɪ |peɪt ə -ə- ‖ pɑːr ˈtɪs ə peɪţ ᵊr pᵊr- **~s** z

participatory pɑː ˌtɪs ɪ ˈpeɪt ər i ◂ ˌpɑːt ɪs-, -əˈ--; pɑː ˈtɪs ɪ pət̬ər i, -ˈ·ə- ‖ pɑːr ˈtɪs əp ə tɔːr i pᵊr-, -toʊr i

participial ˌpɑːt ɪ ˈsɪp i‿əl ◂ ˌ·ə- ‖ ˌpɑːrt̬ ə- **~ly** i

participle ˈpɑːt ɪs ɪp ᵊl ˈ·əs-, -əp ·; pɑː ˈtɪs-; ˈpɑːts ɪp ᵊl, -əp- ‖ ˈpɑːrt̬ ə sɪp ᵊl **~s** z

Partick ˈpɑːt ɪk ‖ ˈpɑːrt̬ ɪk

particle ˈpɑːt ɪk ᵊl ‖ ˈpɑːrt̬- **~s** z

parti-colored, parti-coloured ˌpɑːt i ˈkʌl əd ◂ ˈ· ·ˌ· · ‖ ˌpɑːrt̬ i ˈkʌl ᵊrd ◂

particular pə ˈtɪk jʊl ə -jəl-; ⚠ -ˈtɪk lə ‖ pᵊr ˈtɪk jəl ᵊr pə- **~s** z

particularis... —*see* **particulariz...**

particularism pə ˈtɪk jʊl ər ˌɪz əm -ˈ·jəl- ‖ pᵊr ˈtɪk jəl- pə-, pɑːr-

particularit|y pə ˌtɪk ju ˈlær ət |i -ˌ·jə-, -ɪt i ‖ pᵊr ˌtɪk jə ˈlær ət̬ |i pə-, ˌpɑːr ˌtɪk·ˈ--, -ˈler- **~ies** iz

particularization pə ˌtɪk jʊl ər aɪ ˈzeɪʃ ᵊn -ˌ·jəl-, -ɪˈ-- ‖ pᵊr ˌtɪk jəl ər ə- pə-, pɑːr-

particulariz|e pə ˈtɪk jʊl ə raɪz -ˈ·jəl- ‖ pᵊr ˈtɪk jəl- pə-, pɑːr- **~ed** d **~es** ɪz əz **~ing** ɪŋ

particularly pə ˈtɪk jʊl ə li -ˈ·jəl- ‖ pᵊr ˈtɪk jəl ᵊr pə- —*in casual speech sometimes also* -ˈtɪk jəl‿i

particulate pɑː ˈtɪk jʊl ət pə-, -ɪt, -ju leɪt ‖ pɑːr ˈtɪk jəl ət pᵊr-, -jə leɪt

parting ˈpɑːt ɪŋ ‖ ˈpɑːrt̬ ɪŋ **~s** z
ˌ**parting** ˈ**shot**

Partington ˈpɑːt ɪŋ tən ‖ ˈpɑːrt̬-

parti pris ˌpɑːt i ˈpriː ‖ ˌpɑːrt̬- —*Fr* [paʁ ti pʁi]

partisan ˌpɑːt ɪ ˈzæn ◂ -ə-, ˈ· · · ‖ ˈpɑːrt̬ əz ən -əs-; -ə zæn *(*)* **~s** z **~ship** ʃɪp

partita pɑː ˈtiːt ə ‖ pɑːr ˈtiːt̬ ə

-partite ˈpɑːt aɪt ‖ ˈpɑːrt- — **tripartite** ₍ı₎traɪ ˈpɑːt aɪt ‖ -ˈpɑːrt-

partition pɑː ˈtɪʃ ᵊn pə- ‖ pɑːr- pᵊr- **~ed** d **~ing** ‿ɪŋ **~s** z

partitive ˈpɑːt ət ɪv -ɪt- ‖ ˈpɑːrt̬ ət̬ ɪv **~ly** li **~s** z

partiz... —*see* **partis...**

partly ˈpɑːt li ‖ ˈpɑːrt-

partner ˈpɑːt nə ‖ ˈpɑːrt nᵊr **~ed** d **partnering** ˈpɑːt nər ɪŋ ‖ ˈpɑːrt nər ɪŋ **~less** ləs lɪs **~s** z **~ship/s** ʃɪp/s

Parton ˈpɑːt ᵊn ‖ ˈpɑːrt ᵊn

partook pɑː ˈtʊk §-ˈtuːk ‖ pɑːr-

partridg|e, P~ ˈpɑːtr ɪdʒ ‖ ˈpɑːrtr ɪdʒ **~es** ɪz əz

part-singing ˈpɑːt ˌsɪŋ ɪŋ ‖ ˈpɑːrt-

part-song ˈpɑːt sɒŋ ‖ ˈpɑːrt sɔːŋ -sɑːŋ **~s** z

part-time ˌpɑːt ˈtaɪm ◂ ‖ ˌpɑːrt-
ˌ**part-time** ˈ**job**

part-timer ˌpɑːt ˈtaɪm ə ‖ ˌpɑːrt ˈtaɪm ᵊr **~s** z

parturient pɑː ˈtjʊər i‿ənt ‖ pɑːr ˈtʊr- -ˈtjʊr-

parturition ˌpɑːt juᵊ ˈrɪʃ ᵊn -jə-, ˌpɑːtʃ ə- ‖ ˌpɑːrt̬ ə- ˌpɑːrtʃ ə-, ˌpɑːrt ju-

partway ˌpɑːt ˈweɪ ◂ ˈ· · ‖ ˌpɑːrt-

part|y ˈpɑːt |i ‖ ˈpɑːrt̬ |i **~ied** id **~ies** iz **~ying** i ɪŋ
ˌ**party** ˈ**line** *'political view'*, ˈ**party line** *'shared phone line'*; ˈ**party piece**; ˌ**party** ˈ**politics**; ˈ**party** ˌ**pooper**; ˌ**party** ˈ**wall**

party-col... —*see* **parti-col...**

partygoer ˈpɑːt i ˌɡəʊ ə ‖ ˈpɑːrt̬ i ˌɡoʊ ᵊr **~s** z

parvenu, parvenue ˈpɑːv ə njuː -nuː ‖ ˈpɑːrv ə nuː -njuː —*Fr* [paʁ və ny] **~s** z

parvo ˈpɑːv əʊ ‖ ˈpɑːrv oʊ **~s** z

parvovirus ˈpɑːv əʊ ˌvaɪᵊr əs ‖ ˈpɑːrv oʊ- **~es** ɪz əz

Parzival ˈpɑːts ɪ fɑːl -ə- ‖ ˈpɑːrts- —*Ger* [ˈpar tsi fal]

pas pɑː —*Fr* [pa] —*see also phrases with this word*

Pasadena ˌpæs ə ˈdiːn ə

Pasargadae pə ˈsɑːɡ ə diː ‖ -ˈsɑːrɡ-

pascal *unit of pressure* ˈpæsk ᵊl ₍ı₎pæ ˈskæl ‖ ₍ı₎pɑː ˈskɑːl **~s** z

Pascal *proper name; computer language* ₍ı₎pæ ˈskæl -ˈskɑːl; ˈpæsk æl, -ɑːl, -ᵊl —*Fr* [pas kal]

Pascale ₍ı₎pæ ˈskɑːl -ˈskæl

paschal ˈpæsk ᵊl ˈpɑːsk-

Pasco, Pascoe ˈpæsk əʊ ‖ -oʊ

pas de basque ˌpɑː də ˈbɑː -ˈbɑːsk ‖ -ˈbæsk —*Fr* [pad bask]

pas de deux ˌpɑː də ˈdɜː ‖ -ˈduː -ˈdɜː —*Fr* [pad dø]

paseo pæ ˈseɪ əʊ ‖ -oʊ pɑː- —*Sp* [pa ˈse o]

pash pæʃ **pashes** ˈpæʃ ɪz -əz

pasha, Pasha ˈpɑːʃ ə ˈpæʃ-, pə ˈʃɑː **~s** z

pashmina pæʃ ˈmiːn ə pʌʃ- **~s** z

Pashto ˈpʌʃt əʊ ˈpæʃt- ‖ -oʊ

pasigraph|y pə ˈsɪɡ rəf |i **~ies** iz

Pasiphae, Pasiphaë pə ˈsɪf i iː -eɪ- ‖ -ə-

Pasmore ˈpɑːs mɔː ˈpæs- ‖ ˈpæs mɔːr -moʊr

paso doble ˌpæs əʊ ˈdəʊb leɪ ‖ ˌpɑːs oʊ ˈdoʊb- —*Sp* [ˌpa so ˈðoβ le]

Pasolini ˌpæs əʊ ˈliːn i ‖ -oʊ- —*It* [pa zo ˈliː ni]

pasqueflower ˈpæsk ˌflaʊ‿ə ˈpɑːsk- ‖ -ˌflaʊ‿ᵊr **~s** z

pasquinad|e ˌpæsk wɪ ˈneɪd -wə- **~ed** ɪd əd **~es** z **~ing** ɪŋ

pass pɑːs §pæs ‖ pæs **passed** pɑːst §pæst ‖ pæst **passes** ˈpɑːs ɪz -əz ‖ ˈpæs əz **passing** ˈpɑːs ɪŋ §ˈpæs- ‖ ˈpæs ɪŋ
ˈ**pass de**ˌ**gree**; ˌ**pass** ˈ**out** *v*; ˈ**pass out** *n*

passab|le ˈpɑːs əb |ᵊl §ˈpæs- ‖ ˈpæs- **~leness** ᵊl nəs -nɪs **~ly** li

passacaglia ˌpæs ə ˈkɑːl i‿ə ‖ ˌpɑːs- -ˈkæl- —*Not actually an Italian word.*

passade pæ ˈseɪd pə-

passag|e ˈpæs ɪdʒ —*but as a move in dressage, also* pæ ˈsɑːʒ **~es** ɪz əz

passageway ˈpæs ɪdʒ weɪ **~s** z

Passaic pə ˈseɪ ɪk

Passamaquoddy ˌpæs əm ə ˈkwɒd i ‖ -ˈkwɑːd i

passant ˈpæs ᵊnt ˈpɑːs-, -ɒ̃t —*Fr* [pa sɑ̃]

Passat *tdmk* pæ ˈsæt -ˈsɑːt

passbook ˈpɑːs bʊk §ˈpæs-, §-buːk ‖ ˈpæs- **~s** s

Passchendaele ˈpæʃ ᵊn deɪᵊl

passe, passé, passée ˈpɑːs eɪ ˈpæs- ‖ pæ ˈseɪ —*Fr* [pa se] *(*)*
passel ˈpæs ᵊl **~s** z
passenger, P~ ˈpæs ɪndʒ ə -əndʒ- ‖ -ᵊr **~s** z
passe-partout ˌpæs pɑː ˈtuː ˌpɑːs-, -pə-, ˈ· · · ‖ -pɑːr ˈtuː -pᵊr- —*Fr* [pas paʁ tu]
pass|erby ˌpɑːs |ə ˈbaɪ §ˌpæs- ‖ ˌpæs |ᵊr ˈbaɪ ˈ· · · **~ersby** əz ˈbaɪ ‖ ᵊrz ˈbaɪ
passerine ˈpæs ə raɪn -riːn
Passfield ˈpɑːs fiːᵊld ˈpæs- ‖ ˈpæs-
passible *'capable of feeling'* ˈpæs ɪb ᵊl -əb-
passim ˈpæs ɪm §-əm
passing ˈpɑːs ɪŋ §ˈpæs- ‖ ˈpæs ɪŋ **'passing note**; **ˌpassing 'off**; **ˌpassing 'out**; **'passing shot**
passion, P~ ˈpæʃ ᵊn **~s** z **'passion play**; **ˌPassion 'Sunday**; **ˌPassion 'week**
passionate ˈpæʃ ᵊn‿ət **~ly** li
passionflower ˈpæʃ ᵊn ˌflaʊ‿ə ‖ -ˌflaʊ‿ᵊr **~s** z
passionfruit ˈpæʃ ᵊn fruːt **~s** s
passionless ˈpæʃ ᵊn ləs -lɪs **~ly** li **~ness** nəs nɪs
Passiontide ˈpæʃ ᵊn taɪd
passive ˈpæs ɪv §-əv **~ly** li **~ness** nəs nɪs **~s** z
passivis... —*see* **passiviz...**
passivity pæ ˈsɪv ət i pə-, -ɪt- ‖ -əṭ i
passivization ˌpæs ɪv aɪ ˈzeɪʃ ᵊn ˌ-əv-, -ɪˈ-- ‖ -ɪv ə-
passiviz|e ˈpæs ɪ vaɪz -ə- **~ed** d **~es** ɪz əz **~ing** ɪŋ
passkey ˈpɑːs kiː §ˈpæs- ‖ ˈpæs- **~s** z
Passmore ˈpɑːs mɔː ˈpæs- ‖ ˈpæs mɔːr -moʊr
passover, P~ ˈpɑːs ˌəʊv ə §ˈpæs- ‖ ˈpæs ˌoʊv ᵊr **~s** z
passport ˈpɑːs pɔːt §ˈpæs- ‖ ˈpæs pɔːrt -poʊrt **~s** s
password ˈpɑːs wɜːd §ˈpæs- ‖ ˈpæs wɜːd **~s** z
Passy pæ ˈsiː ‖ pɑː- —*Fr* [pa si]
past pɑːst §pæst ‖ pæst **ˌpast 'master**; **ˌpast 'participle**, --ˈ· · ·; **ˌpast 'perfect**; **ˌpast 'tense**
pasta ˈpæst ə ‖ ˈpɑːst ə *(*)*
past|e peɪst **~ed** ɪd əd **~es** s **~ing** ɪŋ
pasteboard ˈpeɪst bɔːd ‖ -bɔːrd -boʊrd
pastel ˈpæst ᵊl ₍ˌ₎pæ ˈstel ‖ pæ ˈstel **~s** z
pastelist, pastellist ˈpæst ᵊl ɪst §-əst ‖ pæ ˈstel- **~s** s
pastern ˈpæst ən -ɜːn ‖ -ᵊrn **~s** z
Pasternak ˈpæst ə næk ‖ -ᵊr- —*Russ* [pə sʲtʲɪr ˈnak]
paste-up ˈpeɪst ʌp **~s** s
Pasteur ₍ˌ₎pæ ˈstɜː ˌpɑː- ‖ -ˈstɜː —*Fr* [pa stœːʁ]
pasteuris... —*see* **pasteuriz...**
pasteurization ˌpɑːs tʃər aɪ ˈzeɪʃ ᵊn ˌpæs-; ˌpɑːst ər-, ˌpæst-, ˌ·jʊr-; -ɪˈ-- ‖ ˌpæs tʃər ə-ˌ·tər-
pasteuriz|e ˈpɑːs tʃə raɪz ˈpæs-; ˈpɑːst ə-, ˈpæst-, -juᵊ-, -jə- ‖ ˈpæs tʃə raɪz -tə- **~ed** d **~es** ɪz əz **~ing** ɪŋ
pastich|e pæ ˈstiːʃ ˈpæst iːʃ ‖ pɑː- **~es** ɪz əz
pastil, pastille ˈpæst ᵊl -ɪl; ₍ˌ₎pæ ˈstiːᵊl **~s** z
pastime ˈpɑːs taɪm §ˈpæs- ‖ ˈpæs- **~s** z
pasting ˈpeɪst ɪŋ **~s** z
pastis pæ ˈstiːs -ˈstɪs —*Fr* [pa stis]
past-master ˈpɑːst ˌmɑːst ə §-ˌmæst-, ˌ·ˈ· · ‖ ˈpæst ˌmæst ᵊr
Paston ˈpæst ən
pastor ˈpɑːst ə §ˈpæst- ‖ ˈpæst ᵊr **~s** z
pastoral ˈpɑːst ᵊr‿əl ˈpæst-; §pɑː ˈstɔːr əl, §pæ- ‖ ˈpæst- —*but as a noun, sometimes* ˌ·əˈrɑːl **~s** z
pastorale ˌpæst ə ˈrɑːl ˌpɑːst-, -ˈræl; -ˈ·i **~s** z
pastoral|ism ˈpɑːst ᵊr‿əl |ˌɪz əm ˈpæst- ‖ ˈpæst- **~ist/s** ɪst/s §əst/s ‖ əst/s **~ly** i
pastorate ˈpɑːst ər ət §ˈpæst-, -ɪt ‖ ˈpæst- **~s** s
pastrami pə ˈstrɑːm i pæ-
pas|try ˈpeɪs |tri **~tries** triz
pastrycook ˈpeɪs tri kʊk §-kuːk **~s** s
pasturage ˈpɑːs tʃər ɪdʒ §ˈpæs-, -tjʊr-, -tjər- ‖ ˈpæs-
pasture *n, v* ˈpɑːs tʃə §ˈpæs-, -tjə, -tjʊə ‖ ˈpæs tʃᵊr **~d** d **~s** z **pasturing** ˈpɑːs tʃər ɪŋ §ˈpæs-, -tjər-, -tjʊr- ‖ ˈpæs tʃər ɪŋ
pastureland ˈpɑːs tʃə lænd §ˈpæs- ‖ ˈpæs tʃᵊr- **~s** z
past|y *n 'pie'* ˈpæst |i ˈpɑːst- **~ies** iz
past|y *adj 'paste-like'* ˈpeɪst |i **~ier** i‿ə ‖ i‿ᵊr **~iest** i‿ɪst i‿əst **~iness** i nəs i nɪs
pasty-faced ˈpeɪst i feɪst ˌ· ·ˈ·
pat, Pat pæt **pats, Pat's** pæts **patted** ˈpæt ɪd -əd ‖ ˈpæṭ əd **patting** ˈpæt ɪŋ ‖ ˈpæṭ ɪŋ
pat-a-cake ˈpæt ə keɪk ‖ ˈpæṭ-
patagi|um pə ˈteɪdʒ i‿|əm ˌpæt ə ˈdʒaɪ‿|əm ‖ ˌpæṭ- **~a** ə
Patagoni|a ˌpæt ə ˈgəʊn i‿|ə ‖ ˌpæṭ ə ˈgoʊn- **~an/s** ən/z ◂
pataka *'Maori storehouse'* ˈpɑːt ə kɑː ‖ ˈpɑːṭ- **~s** z
Pataki pə ˈtæk i
pat-ball ˈpæt bɔːl ‖ -bɑːl
patch, Patch pætʃ **patched** pætʃt **patches, Patch's** ˈpætʃ ɪz -əz **patching** ˈpætʃ ɪŋ **ˌpatch 'pocket**
patchouli ˈpætʃ ʊl i -əl-; pə ˈtʃuːl-, -iː
patchwork ˈpætʃ wɜːk ‖ -wɜːk **~s** s
patch|y ˈpætʃ |i **~ier** i‿ə ‖ i‿ᵊr **~iest** i‿ɪst i‿əst **~ily** ɪ li əl i **~iness** i nəs i nɪs
Pate peɪt
pate *'top of the head'* peɪt **pates** peɪts
pate, paté, pâté *'meat spread'* ˈpæt eɪ -i ‖ pɑː ˈteɪ pæ- —*Fr* [pa te] *(*)* **pates, patés, pâtés** ˈpæt eɪz -iz ‖ pɑː ˈteɪz pæ- —*see also phrases with this word*
pâte *'paste for porcelain'* pɑːt —*Fr* [pat]
pâté de foie ˌpæt eɪ də ˈfwɑː ˌ·i- ‖ pɑː ˌteɪ- pæ- —*Fr* [pa ted fwa] **ˌpâté de ˌfoie 'gras** ˈgrɑː —*Fr* [gʁa]
Patel *(i)* pə ˈtel, *(ii)* pə ˈteɪᵊl
Pateley ˈpeɪt li
patell|a pə ˈtel |ə **~ae** iː **~ar** ə ‖ ᵊr **~as** əz
paten ˈpæt ᵊn **~s** z
patency ˈpeɪt ᵊnᵗs i
pat|ent *n, adj, v* ˈpeɪt |ᵊnt ˈpæt- ‖ ˈpæt |ᵊnt ˈpeɪt- *(*)* —*In BrE the pronunciation* ˈpæt- *is mainly restricted to technical use; in AmE the*

pronunciation 'peɪt- *is used only in the sense 'open, obvious'*. **~ented** ᵊnt ɪd -əd ‖ ᵊnţ əd **~enting** ᵊnt ɪŋ ‖ ᵊnţ ɪŋ **~ents** ᵊnts **ˌpatent 'leather◂**; **ˌpatent 'medicine**; **'Patent ˌOffice**

patentable 'peɪt ᵊnt əb ᵊl 'pæt- ‖ 'pæt ᵊnţ-

patentee ˌpeɪt ᵊn 'tiː ˌpæt- ‖ ˌpæt- **~s** z

patently 'peɪt ᵊnt li

pater *'prayer'* 'pæt ə 'pɑːt- ‖ 'pɑːt er 'pɑːţ ᵊr **~s** z

Pater, pater *'father'* 'peɪt ə ‖ 'peɪţ ᵊr **~s, ~'s** z

paterfamilias ˌpeɪt ə fə 'mɪl i æs ˌpæt-, -əs ‖ ˌpɑːţ ᵊr fə 'miːl i‿əs ˌpeɪţ-, ˌpæţ- **~es** ɪz əz

paternal pə 'tɜːn ᵊl ‖ -'tɝːn-

paternalism pə 'tɜːn əl ˌɪz əm -ə ˌlɪz- ‖ -'tɝːn-

paternalistic pə ˌtɜːn ə 'lɪst ɪk◂ -ᵊl 'ɪst- ‖ pə ˌtɝːn ᵊl 'ɪst ɪk◂ **~ally** ᵊl‿i

paternally pə 'tɜːn əl i ‖ -'tɝːn-

paternity pə 'tɜːn ət i -ɪt- ‖ -'tɝːn əţ i —*In contrast with* maternity, *sometimes* 'pəˌ• • • **pa'ternity test**

paternoster, P~ ˌpæt ə 'nɒst ə◂ ‖ ˌpɑːţ ᵊr 'nɑːst ᵊr◂ ˌpæţ-, -'nɔːst-, '• •ˌ• • **~s** z **ˌPaternoster 'Row**

Paterson 'pæt əs ən ‖ 'pæţ ᵊrs ən

path *'way'* pɑːθ §pæθ ‖ pæθ *(*)* **paths** pɑːðz §pæðz, §pɑːθs, §pæθs ‖ pæðz pæθs

path *'pathology'* pæθ **'path lab**

PATH *NY-NJ subway system* pæθ

-path pæθ — **osteopath** 'ɒst i əʊ pæθ ‖ 'ɑːst i ə pæθ

Pathan pə 'tɑːn —*Hindi* [pə tʰaːn] **~s** z

Pathé 'pæθ eɪ

pathetic pə 'θet ɪk ‖ -'θeţ ɪk **~ally** ᵊl‿i

pathfinder 'pɑːθ ˌfaɪnd ə §'pæθ- ‖ 'pæθ ˌfaɪnd ᵊr **~s** z

pathic 'pæθ ɪk **~s** s

-pathic 'pæθ ɪk — **psychopathic** ˌsaɪk əʊ 'pæθ ɪk◂ ‖ -ə-

pathless 'pɑːθ ləs §'pæθ-, -lɪs ‖ 'pæθ- **~ness** nəs nɪs

Pathmark *tdmk* 'pæθ mɑːk ‖ -mɑːrk

patho- *comb. form with stress-neutral suffix* ¦pæθ əʊ ‖ -oʊ — **pathopsychology** ˌpæθ əʊ saɪ 'kɒl ədʒ i ‖ -oʊ saɪ 'kɑːl- *with stress-imposing suffix* pə 'θɒ+ ‖ -'θɑː+ — **patholysis** pə 'θɒl əs ɪs -ɪs ɪs, §-əs ‖ -'θɑːl-

pathogen 'pæθ ədʒ ən -ə dʒen **~s** z

pathogenic ˌpæθ ə 'dʒen ɪk◂ **~ally** ᵊl‿i

pathognomy pə 'θɒg nəm i ‖ -'θɑːg-

pathological ˌpæθ ə 'lɒdʒ ɪk ᵊl◂ ‖ -'lɑːdʒ- **~ly** ‿i

pathologist pə 'θɒl ədʒ ɪst §-əst ‖ -'θɑːl- **~s** s

patholog|y pə 'θɒl ədʒ |i ‖ -'θɑːl- **~ies** iz

pathos 'peɪθ ɒs ‖ -ɑːs -ɔːs, -oʊs

pathway 'pɑːθ weɪ §'pæθ- ‖ 'pæθ- **~s** z

-pathy *stress-imposing* pəθ i — **telepathy** tə 'lep əθ i tɪ-, te-

Patiala ˌpʌt i 'ɑːl ə ‖ ˌpʌţ- —*Panjabi* [pə ţi aː lə]

patience, P~ 'peɪʃ ᵊnᵗs

patient 'peɪʃ ᵊnt **~ly** li **~s** s

patina 'pæt ɪn ə -ən-, pə 'tiːn ə ‖ pə 'tiːn ə *(*)* **~s** z

patio 'pæt i əʊ ‖ 'pæţ i oʊ 'pɑːţ- **~s** z

patisserie, pâtisserie pə 'tiːs ər‿i pæ-, -'tɪs- —*Fr* [pa tis ʁi] **~s** z

Patmore 'pæt mɔː ‖ -mɔːr -moʊr

Patmos 'pæt mɒs ‖ -məs -mɑːs, -moʊs

Patna 'pæt nə 'pʌt- —*Hindi* [pəʈ naː]

pat|ois *sing.* 'pæt |wɑː ‖ 'pɑːt- —*Fr* [pa twa] **~ois** *pl* wɑːz —*Fr* [pa twa]

Paton 'peɪt ᵊn

Patras 'pætr æs -əs; pə 'træs —*Gk* ['pa tras]

patrial 'peɪtr i‿əl 'pætr- **~s** z

patriality ˌpeɪtr i 'æl ət i ˌpætr- ‖ -əţ i

patriarch 'peɪtr i ɑːk 'pætr- ‖ -ɑːrk **~s** s

patriarchal ˌpeɪtr i 'ɑːk ᵊl◂ ˌpætr- ‖ -'ɑːrk ᵊl◂ **~ism** ˌɪz əm **~ly** i

patriarchate 'peɪtr i ɑːk ət 'pætr-, -ɪt, -eɪt ‖ -ɑːrk- **~s** s

patriarch|y 'peɪtr i ɑːk |i 'pætr- ‖ -ɑːrk |i **~ies** iz

Patrice pə 'triːs

Patricia pə 'trɪʃ ə -'trɪʃ i‿ə ‖ -'triːʃ-

patrician pə 'trɪʃ ᵊn **~s** z

patriciate pə 'trɪʃ i‿ət -eɪt

patricide 'pætr ɪ saɪd 'peɪtr-, -ə- **~s** z

Patrick 'pætr ɪk

patriclinous pə 'trɪk lɪn əs -lən-; ˌpætr ɪ 'klaɪn əs◂, -ə-

Patricroft 'pætr ɪ krɒft -ə- ‖ -krɔːft -krɑːft

patrilineal ˌpætr ə 'lɪn i‿əl◂ ˌ•ɪ-

patrilocal ˌpætr ə 'ləʊk ᵊl◂ ˌ•ɪ-, '• ˌ• • ‖ -'loʊk ᵊl◂

patrimonial ˌpætr ə 'məʊn i‿əl◂ ˌ•ɪ- ‖ -'moʊn- **~ly** i

patrimon|y 'pætr ɪm ən |i '•əm- ‖ -ə moʊn |i *(*)* **~ies** iz

patriot 'pætr i‿ət 'peɪtr- ‖ 'peɪtr- **~s** s

PATRIOTIC

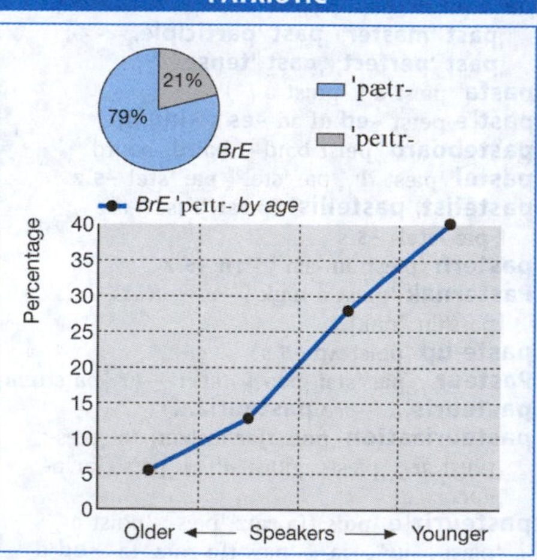

patriotic ˌpætr i 'ɒt ɪk◂ ˌpeɪtr- ‖ ˌpeɪtr i 'ɑːţ ɪk◂ — *Preference poll, BrE:* 'pætr- *79%,* 'peɪtr- *21%.* **~ally** ᵊl‿i

patriotism 'pætr i‿ə ˌtɪz əm 'peɪtr- ‖ 'peɪtr-

patristic pə ˈtrɪst ɪk pæ- **~s** s
Patroclus pə ˈtrɒk ləs ‖ -ˈtroʊk-
patrol pə ˈtrəʊl →-ˈtrɒʊl ‖ -ˈtroʊl **~led** d **~ling** ɪŋ **~s** z
  pa'trol car; pa'trol ˌwagon
patrol|man pə ˈtrəʊl |mən →-ˈtrɒʊl-, -mæn ‖ -ˈtroʊl- **~men** mən men **~woman** ˌwʊm ən **~women** ˌwɪm ɪn -ən
patrology pə ˈtrɒl ədʒ i pæ- ‖ -ˈtrɑːl-
patron ˈpeɪtr ən **~s** z
  ˌpatron 'saint
patronage ˈpætr ən ɪdʒ
patronal pə ˈtrəʊn əl pæ- ‖ ˈpeɪtr ən‿əl (*)
patroness ˌpeɪtr ə ˈnes ˈ· · ·; -ən əs, -ɪs ‖ ˈpeɪtr ən əs **~es** ɪz əz

PATRONISE

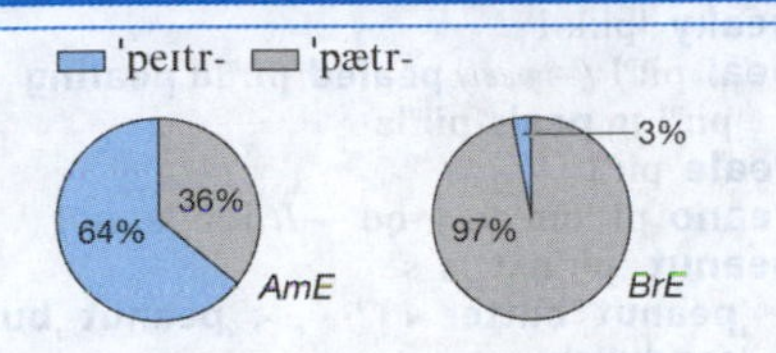

patronis|e, patroniz|e ˈpætr ə naɪz ‖ ˈpeɪtr- ˈpætr- — *Preference polls, AmE:* ˈpeɪtr- *64%,* ˈpætr- *36%; BrE:* ˈpætr- *97%,* ˈpeɪtr- *3%.* **~ed** d **~es** ɪz əz **~ing** ɪŋ
patronymic ˌpætr ə ˈnɪm ɪk ◂ **~ally** əl‿i **~s** s
pats|y, Pats|y ˈpæts |i **~ies, ~y's** iz
Pattaya ˈpæt eɪ ə -ɑː
patten, P~ ˈpæt ən **~s** z
patter ˈpæt ə ‖ ˈpæṭ ər **~ed** d **pattering** ˈpæt ər ɪŋ ‖ ˈpæṭ ər ɪŋ **~s** z
Patterdale ˈpæt ə deɪəl ‖ ˈpæṭ ər-
pattern ˈpæt ən ‖ ˈpæṭ ərn **~ed** d **~ing** ɪŋ ‖ ɪŋ **~s** z
Patterson ˈpæt əs ən ‖ ˈpæṭ ərs ən
Patti, Pattie ˈpæt i ‖ ˈpæṭ i
Pattison ˈpæt ɪs ən -əs- ‖ ˈpæṭ-
Patton ˈpæt ən
patt|y, Patt|y ˈpæt |i ‖ ˈpæṭ |i **~ies, ~y's** iz
patulous ˈpæt jʊl əs -jəl- ‖ ˈpætʃ əl əs **~ly** li **~ness** nəs nɪs
patzer ˈpɑːts ə ˈpæts- ‖ -ər **~s** z
paua ˈpaʊ‿ə **~s** z
paucal ˈpɔːk əl ‖ ˈpɑːk-
paucity ˈpɔːs ət i -ɪt- ‖ əṭ i ˈpɑːs-
Paul pɔːl ‖ pɑːl **Paul's** pɔːlz ‖ pɑːlz
Paula ˈpɔːl ə ‖ ˈpɑːl-
Paulette (ˌ)pɔː ˈlet ‖ (ˌ)pɑː-
Pauli *(i)* ˈpaʊl i, *(ii)* ˈpɔːl i ‖ ˈpɑːl
Pauline *adj 'relating to St Paul'; n 'pupil of St Paul's School'* ˈpɔːl aɪn ‖ ˈpɑːl- **~s** z
Pauline *forename* ˈpɔːl iːn ‖ (ˌ)pɔː ˈliːn (ˌ)pɑː- (*)
Pauling ˈpɔːl ɪŋ ‖ ˈpɑːl-
Paulinus pɔː ˈlaɪn əs ‖ pɑː-
Paull pɔːl ‖ pɑːl
paulownia pɔː ˈləʊn i‿ə ‖ -ˈloʊn- pɑː- **~s** z
Pauncefote ˈpɔːnts fət -fʊt ‖ ˈpɑːnts-
paunch pɔːntʃ ‖ pɑːntʃ **paunches** ˈpɔːntʃ ɪz -əz ‖ ˈpɑːntʃ-
paunch|y ˈpɔːntʃ |i ‖ ˈpɑːntʃ- **~iness** i nəs i nɪs
pauper ˈpɔːp ə ‖ -ər ˈpɑːp- **~s** z
pauperis... —*see* **pauperiz...**
pauperism ˈpɔːp ər ˌɪz əm ‖ ˈpɑːp-
pauperization ˌpɔːp ər aɪ ˈzeɪʃ ən -ɪˈ-- ‖ -ər ə- ˌpɑːp-
pauperiz|e ˈpɔːp ə raɪz ‖ ˈpɑːp- **~ed** d **~es** ɪz əz **~ing** ɪŋ
paupiette ˌpəʊp i ˈet ‖ ˌpoʊp- **~s** s —*or as singular* —*Fr* [po pjɛt]
Pausanias pɔː ˈseɪn i æs -əs ‖ pɑː-
pause pɔːz ‖ pɑːz **paused** pɔːzd ‖ pɑːzd **pauses** ˈpɔːz ɪz -əz ‖ ˈpɑːz- **pausing** ˈpɔːz ɪŋ ‖ ˈpɑːz-
pavan, pavane pə ˈvæn -ˈvɑːn, ˈpæv ən ‖ pə ˈvɑːn -ˈvæn **~s** z
Pavarotti ˌpæv ə ˈrɒt i ‖ -ˈrɑːṭ i —*It* [pa va ˈrɔt ti]
pave peɪv **paved** peɪvd **paves** peɪvz **paving** ˈpeɪv ɪŋ
pavé ˈpæv eɪ ‖ pæ ˈveɪ —*Fr* [pa ve]
pavement ˈpeɪv mənt **~s** s
  ˈpavement ˌartist
Pavey ˈpeɪv i
pavilion pə ˈvɪl i‿ən ‖ pə ˈvɪl jən **~ed** d **~ing** ɪŋ **~s** z
paving ˈpeɪv ɪŋ
  ˈpaving stone
pavior, paviour, P~ ˈpeɪv jə ‖ -jər **~s** z
Pavitt ˈpæv ɪt §-ət
Pavlov ˈpæv lɒv ‖ -lɑːv ˈpɑːv- —*Russ* [ˈpav ɫəf]
Pavlova, p~ pæv ˈləʊv ə ˈpæv ləv ə ‖ -ˈloʊv ə pɑːv- —*Russ* [ˈpav ɫə və] **~s** z
Pavlovian (ˌ)pæv ˈləʊv i‿ən ‖ -ˈloʊv- (ˌ)pɑːv-
Pavlow ˈpæv ləʊ ‖ -loʊ
Pavo ˈpɑːv əʊ ‖ -oʊ
Pavonia pə ˈvəʊn i‿ə ‖ -ˈvoʊn-
pavonine ˈpæv əʊ naɪn ‖ -ə-
paw pɔː ‖ pɑː **pawed** pɔːd ‖ pɑːd **pawing** ˈpɔːr ɪŋ ‖ ˈpɔː ɪŋ ˈpɑː- **paws** pɔːz ‖ pɑːz
pawk|y ˈpɔːk |i ‖ ˈpɑːk- **~ier** i‿ə ‖ i‿ər **~iest** i‿ɪst i‿əst **~ily** ɪ li əl i **~iness** i nəs i nɪs
pawl pɔːl ‖ pɑːl *(= pall, Paul)* **pawls** pɔːlz ‖ pɑːlz
pawn pɔːn ‖ pɑːn **pawned** pɔːnd ‖ pɑːnd **pawning** ˈpɔːn ɪŋ ‖ ˈpɑːn- **pawns** pɔːnz ‖ pɑːnz
pawnbrok|er ˈpɔːn ˌbrəʊk |ə ‖ -ˌbroʊk |ər ˈpɑːn- **~ers** əz ‖ ərz **~ing** ɪŋ
Pawnee pɔː ˈniː ‖ pɑː- **~s** z
pawnshop ˈpɔːn ʃɒp ‖ -ʃɑːp ˈpɑːn- **~s** s
pawpaw, paw-paw ˈpɔː pɔː ‖ ˈpɑː pɑː **~s** z
Pawtucket pɔː ˈtʌk ɪt pə-, §-ət ‖ pə- pɔː-, pɑː-
pax, Pax pæks ‖ pɑːks
  ˌPax ˈChristi ˈkrɪst i; **ˌPax Roˈmana** rəʊ ˈmɑːn ə ‖ roʊ-; **ˌpax voˈbiscum** vəʊ ˈbɪsk əm -ʊm ‖ voʊ-
Paxman ˈpæks mən
Paxo *tdmk* ˈpæks əʊ ‖ -oʊ
Paxos ˈpæks ɒs ‖ -oʊs —*Gk* [pa ˈksos]
Paxton ˈpækst ən

P

pay peɪ **paid** peɪd **paying** ˈpeɪ ɪŋ **pays** peɪz
 ˈpay claim; **ˈpay dirt**; **ˈpay ˌenvelope**; **ˌpaying ˈguest**; **ˈpay ˌpacket**; **ˈpay phone**; **ˈpay ˌstation**; **ˈpay train**

payable ˈpeɪ əb ᵊl

pay-as-you-go ˌpeɪ əz ju ˈgəʊ ◂ -əz jə-, →-əʒ ju-, →-əʒ jə, →-əʒ u-, →-əʒ ə- ‖ -əʒ ə ˈgoʊ ◂

payback ˈpeɪ bæk

paybed ˈpeɪ bed **~s** z

paycheck, paycheque ˈpeɪ tʃek **~s** s

payday ˈpeɪ deɪ **~s** z

PAYE ˌpiː eɪ waɪ ˈiː

payee ˌpeɪ ˈiː **~s** z

payer ˈpeɪ ə ‖ ᵊr **~s** z

paying-in ˌpeɪ ɪŋ ˈɪn
 ˌpaying ˈin slip

payload ˈpeɪ ləʊd ‖ -loʊd **~s** z

paymaster ˈpeɪ ˌmɑːst ə §-ˌmæst- ‖ -ˌmæst ᵊr **~s** z
 ˌpaymaster ˈgeneral

payment ˈpeɪm ənt **~s** s

Payn, Payne peɪn

paynim, P~ ˈpeɪn ɪm

Paynter ˈpeɪnt ə ‖ ˈpeɪnţ ᵊr

payoff ˈpeɪ ɒf -ɔːf ‖ -ɔːf -ɑːf **~s** s

payola peɪ ˈəʊl ə ‖ -ˈoʊl ə

payout ˈpeɪ aʊt **~s** s

Paypal *tdmk* ˈpeɪ pæl

pay-per-|click ˌpeɪ pə |ˈklɪk ◂ ‖ -pᵊr- **~view** ˈvjuː ◂

payphone ˈpeɪ fəʊn ‖ -foʊn **~s** z

payroll ˈpeɪ rəʊl →-rɒʊl ‖ -roʊl **~s** z

payslip ˈpeɪ slɪp **~s** s

Payton ˈpeɪt ᵊn

pay-TV ˌpeɪ tiː ˈviː ˈ· ·ˌ·

Paz pæz ‖ pɑːz —*AmSp* [pas, pah]

pazazz pə ˈzæz

PBS ˌpiː biː ˈes

PC, P.C. ˌpiː ˈsiː ◂ **~s, ~'s** z

PCB ˌpiː siː ˈbiː **~s** z

PE ˌpiː ˈiː

pea piː **peas** piːz
 ˌpea ˈgreen◂; **ˈpea ˌjacket**; **ˌpea ˈsouper**

Peabody ˈpiː ˌbɒd i ˈpeɪ-; ˈpiːb əd i ‖ -ˌbɑːd i

pea-brained ˈpiː breɪnd

peace, Peace piːs
 ˈPeace Corps; **ˈpeace ˌoffering**; **ˈpeace pipe**

peaceab|le ˈpiːs əb |ᵊl **~leness** ᵊl nəs -nɪs **~ly** li

peaceful ˈpiːs fᵊl -fʊl **~ly** ̮i **~ness** nəs nɪs

Peacehaven ˈpiːs ˌheɪv ᵊn

peacekeep|er ˈpiːs ˌkiːp| ə ‖ -ᵊr **~ers** əz ‖ -ᵊrz **~ing** ɪŋ

peace-loving ˈpiːs ˌlʌv ɪŋ

peacemak|er ˈpiːs ˌmeɪk| ə ‖ -ᵊr **~ers** əz ‖ -ᵊrz **~ing** ɪŋ

peacenik ˈpiːs nɪk **~s** s

peacetime ˈpiːs taɪm

peach, Peach piːtʃ **peaches** ˈpiːtʃ ɪz -əz
 ˌPeach ˈMelba

peaches-and-cream ˌpiːtʃ ɪz ᵊn ˈkriːm ◂ →-ᵊŋ-

Peachey ˈpiːtʃ i

peachick ˈpiː tʃɪk **~s** s

Peachum ˈpiːtʃ əm

peach|y ˈpiːtʃ |i **~ier** i ̮ə ‖ i ̮ᵊr **~iest** i ̮ɪst i ̮əst **~iness** i nəs i nɪs

peacock, P~ ˈpiːk ɒk ˈpiː kɒk ‖ ˈpiː kɑːk **~s** s
 ˌpeacock ˈblue◂

peafowl ˈpiː faʊl **~s** z

peahen ˈpiː hen **~s** z

peak piːk *(= peek)* **peaked** piːkt **peaking** ˈpiːk ɪŋ **peaks** piːks

Peak, Peake piːk
 ˈPeak ˌDistrict; **ˌpeak ˈtime◂**

peaked *adj 'having a peak'; past and pp of* **peak** piːkt

peaked *adj 'peaky, pale'* — ‖ ˈpiːk əd

Peaker ˈpiːk ə ‖ -ᵊr

peaky ˈpiːk i

peal piːᵊl *(= peel)* **pealed** piːᵊld **pealing** ˈpiːᵊl ɪŋ **peals** piːᵊlz

Peale piːᵊl

Peano pi ˈɑːn əʊ ‖ -oʊ —*It* [pe ˈaː no]

peanut ˈpiː nʌt **~s** s
 ˌpeanut ˈbutter ◂ ‖ ˈ· · ˌ· ·; **ˌpeanut ˌbutter ˈsandwich**

pear peə ‖ peᵊr pæᵊr *(= pair)* **pears** peəz ‖ peᵊrz pæᵊrz

Pear *family name* pɪə ‖ peᵊr

Pearce pɪəs ‖ pɪᵊrs

pearl, Pearl pɜːl ‖ pɜˑl **pearled** pɜːld ‖ pɜˑld **pearling** ˈpɜːl ɪŋ ‖ ˈpɜˑl ɪŋ **pearls** pɜːlz ‖ pɜˑlz
 ˈpearl ˌdiver; **ˌPearl ˈHarbor**

pearlite ˈpɜːl aɪt ‖ ˈpɜˑl-

pearlwort ˈpɜːl wɜːt -wɔːt ‖ ˈpɜˑl wɜˑt

pearl|y ˈpɜːl |i ‖ ˈpɜˑl |i **~ier** i ̮ə ‖ i ̮ᵊr **~ies** iz **~iest** i ̮ɪst i ̮əst **~iness** i nəs i nɪs
 ˌpearly ˈgates

pearmain, P~ ˈpeə meɪn ˈpɜː- ‖ ˈper- **~s** z

Pearn pɜːn ‖ pɜˑn

Pears *family name (i)* pɪəz ‖ pɪᵊrz, *(ii)* peəz ‖ peᵊrz pæᵊrz —*The singer* Sir Peter Pears *was (i), but the brand of soap is (ii)*

Pearsall pɪəs ᵊl -ɔːl ‖ ˈpɪrs ɔːl -ɑːl

Pearse pɪəs ‖ pɪᵊrs

pear-shaped ˈpeə ʃeɪpt ‖ ˈper- ˈpær-

Pearson ˈpɪəs ᵊn ‖ ˈpɪrs ᵊn

Peart pɪət ‖ pɪᵊrt

Peary ˈpɪər i ‖ ˈpɪr i

peasant ˈpez ᵊnt **~s** s
 ˌPeasants' Reˈvolt

peasantry ˈpez ᵊntr i

pease, Pease piːz
 ˌpease ˈpudding

Peaseblossom ˈpiːz ˌblɒs əm ‖ -ˌblɑːs əm

peasecod ˈpiːz kɒd ‖ -kɑːd **~s** z

peashooter ˈpiː ʃuːt ə ‖ -ʃuːţ ᵊr **~s** z

pea-souper ˌpiː ˈsuːp ə ‖ -ᵊr **~s** z

peat, Peat, Peate piːt
 ˈpeat bog

peat|y ˈpiːt |i ‖ ˈpiːţ |i **~ier** i ̮ə ‖ i ̮ᵊr **~iest** i ̮ɪst ̮əst **~iness** i nəs -nɪs

Peaudouce *tdmk* ˌpəʊ ˈduːs ‖ ˌpoʊ-

peav|ey, peav|y, P~ ˈpiːv |i **~eys, ~ies** iz

pebbl|e ˈpeb ᵊl **~ed** d **~es** z **~ing** ɪŋ

pebble-dash ˈpeb ᵊl dæʃ **~ed** t **~es** ɪz əz **~ing** ɪŋ

pebbly ˈpeb ᵊl‿i

pec pek **pecs** peks

pecan pɪ ˈkæn ˈpiːk æn, -ən ‖ pɪ ˈkɑːn -ˈkæn; ˈpiːk æn **~s** z

peccadillo ˌpek ə ˈdɪl əʊ ‖ -oʊ **~s** z

peccar|y ˈpek ər |i **~ies** iz

peccavi pe ˈkɑːv iː —*Formerly* -ˈkeɪv aɪ

peck, Peck pek **pecked** pekt **pecking** ˈpek ɪŋ **pecks** peks
ˈ**pecking** ˌ**order**

pecker ˈpek ə ‖ -ᵊr **~s** z

Peckham ˈpek əm

Peckinpah ˈpek ɪn pɑː -ən-

peckish ˈpek ɪʃ **~ly** li **~ness** nəs nɪs

Peckitt ˈpek ɪt §-ət

Pecksniff ˈpek snɪf

Pecksniffian (ˌ)pek ˈsnɪf i‿ən

Peconic pɪ ˈkɒn ɪk ‖ -ˈkɑːn-

pecorino ˌpek ə ˈriːn əʊ ‖ -oʊ —*It* [pe ko ˈriː no]

Pecos ˈpeɪk əs -ɒs ‖ -ɑːs -oʊs

Pécs petʃ ‖ peɪtʃ —*Hungarian* [peːtʃ]

pecten ˈpekt ɪn -en, §-ən

pectic ˈpekt ɪk

pectin ˈpekt ɪn §-ən

pecti|nate ˈpekt ɪ |neɪt -ə- **~nated** neɪt ɪd -əd ‖ neɪt̬ əd **~nately** neɪt li

pectoral ˈpekt ᵊr‿əl **~s** z
ˌ**pectoral** ˈ**cross**; ˌ**pectoral** ˈ**fin**

pecu|late ˈpek ju |leɪt -jə- ‖ -jə- **~lated** leɪt ɪd -əd ‖ leɪt̬ əd **~lates** leɪts **~lating** leɪt ɪŋ ‖ leɪt̬ ɪŋ

peculation ˌpek ju ˈleɪʃ ᵊn -jə- ‖ -jə- **~s** z

peculator ˈpek ju leɪt ə ˈ·jə- ‖ -jə leɪt̬ ᵊr **~s** z

peculiar pɪ ˈkjuːl i‿ə pə-, ⚠bə- ‖ -ˈkjuːl jᵊr **~s** z

peculiarit|y pɪ ˌkjuːl i ˈær ət |i pə-, ⚠bə-, -ɪt i ‖ -ət̬ |i -ˈer-; ·ˌ·ˈjær-, -ˈjer- **~ies** iz

peculiarly pɪ ˈkjuːl i‿ə li pə-, ⚠bə- ‖ -ˈkjuːl jᵊr li

pecuniar|y pɪ ˈkjuːn i‿ər |i pə-, -ˈkjuːn ər |i ‖ -i er |i **~ily** əl i ɪ li

-ped ped — **biped** ˈbaɪ ped

pedagogic ˌped ə ˈgɒdʒ ɪk ◂ -ˈgəʊdʒ-, -ˈgɒg- ‖ -ˈgɑːdʒ ɪk -ˈgoʊdʒ- **~al** ᵊl ◂ **~ally** ᵊl‿i

pedagogue ˈped ə gɒg ‖ -gɑːg **~s** z

pedagogy ˈped ə gɒdʒ i -gəʊdʒ-, -gɒg- ‖ -goʊdʒ i -gɑːdʒ-

pedal *n, v* ˈped ᵊl *(= peddle)* **~ed, ~led** d **~ing, ~ling** ‿ɪŋ **~s** z

pedal *adj* ˈpiːd ᵊl ˈped-

pedalo ˈped ə ləʊ → -ᵊl əʊ ‖ -ᵊl oʊ **~s** z

pedant ˈped ᵊnt **~s** s

pedantic pɪ ˈdænt ɪk pə-, pe- ‖ -ˈdænt̬ ɪk **~ally** ᵊl‿i

pedantr|y ˈped ᵊntr |i **~ies** iz

Pedder ˈped ə ‖ -ᵊr

peddl|e ˈped ᵊl **~ed** d **~es** z **~ing** ‿ɪŋ

peddler ˈped lə ‖ -lᵊr **~s** z

-pede piːd — **millipede** ˈmɪl ɪ piːd -ə-

Peden ˈpiːd ᵊn

pederast ˈped ə ræst ˈpiːd- **~s** s

pederastic ˌped ə ˈræst ɪk ◂ ˌpiːd- **~ally** ᵊl‿i

pederasty ˈped ə ræst i ˈpiːd-

pedestal ˈped ɪst ᵊl -əst- **~s** z

pedestrian pə ˈdes tri‿ən pɪ- **~s** z
peˌ**destrian** ˈ**crossing**

pedestrianis... —*see* **pedestrianiz...**

pedestrianization pə ˌdes tri‿ən aɪ ˈzeɪʃ ᵊn pɪ-, -ɪˈ·· ‖ -əˈ··

pedestrianiz|e pə ˈdes tri‿ə naɪz pɪ- **~ed** d **~es** ɪz əz **~ing** ɪŋ

Pedi ˈped i

pediatric ˌpiːd i ˈætr ɪk ◂ **~ally** ᵊl‿i **~s** s

pediatrician ˌpiːd i‿ə ˈtrɪʃ ᵊn **~s** z

pedicab ˈped i kæb **~s** z

pedicel ˈped i sel -ə- **~s** z

pedicle ˈped ɪk ᵊl **~s** z

pedicular pɪ ˈdɪk jʊl ə pe-, pə-, -jəl- ‖ -jəl ᵊr

pedicure ˈped i kjʊə -ə-, -kjɔː ‖ -kjʊr **~s** z

pedicurist ˈped i kjʊər ɪst ˈ·ə-, -ə kjɔːr-, §-əst ‖ -kjʊr əst **~s** s

pediform ˈped i fɔːm ‖ -fɔːrm

pedigree ˈped ɪ griː -ə- **~d** d **~s** z

pediment ˈped ɪ mənt -ə- **~s** s

pedimented ˈped ɪ ment ɪd ˈ·ə-, -mənt-, -əd ‖ -ment̬ əd

pedipalp ˈped i pælp **~s** s

pedlar ˈped lə ‖ -lᵊr **~s** z

pedogenesis ˌped əʊ ˈdʒen əs ɪs ˌpiːd-, -ɪs ɪs, §-əs ‖ ˌ·ə-

pedometer pɪ ˈdɒm ɪt ə pə-, pe-, -ət- ‖ -ˈdɑːm ət̬ ᵊr **~s** z

pedophile ˈpiːd əʊ faɪᵊl ‖ -ə- ˈped- **~s** z

pedophilia ˌpiːd əʊ ˈfɪl i‿ə ‖ ˌ·ə- ˌped-

pedophiliac ˌpiːd əʊ ˈfɪl i æk ‖ ˌ·ə- ˌped- **~s** s

Pedro, p~ ˈpedr əʊ ˈpeɪdr-, ˈpiːdr- ‖ ˈpeɪdr oʊ —*Sp* [ˈpe ðro]

Peds *tdmk* pedz

peduncle pɪ ˈdʌŋk ᵊl pə-, pe- ‖ ˈpiːd ʌŋk ᵊl **~s** z

peduncular pɪ ˈdʌŋk jʊl ə pə-, pe-, -jəl- ‖ -jəl ᵊr

pedunculate pɪ ˈdʌŋk ju leɪt pə-, pe-, -jə-, -lət, -lɪt ‖ -jə-

pee piː **peed** piːd **peeing** ˈpiː ɪŋ **pees** piːz

Peeb|les ˈpiːb |ᵊlz **~lesshire** ᵊlz ʃə →ᵊlʒ-, -ʃɪə, §-ˌʃaɪ‿ə

Pee Dee ˌpiː ˈdiː ◂
ˌ**Pee Dee** ˈ**River**

peek, Peek piːk **peeked** piːkt **peeking** ˈpiːk ɪŋ **peeks** piːks

peekaboo ˌpiːk ə ˈbuː ˈ· · ·

peel, Peel, Peele piːᵊl **peeled** piːᵊld **peeling/s** ˈpiːᵊl ɪŋ/z **peels** piːᵊlz

peeler ˈpiːl ə ‖ -ᵊr **~s** z

peen piːn

peep piːp **peeped** piːpt **peeping** ˈpiːp ɪŋ **peeps** piːps
ˌ**peeping** ˈ**Tom**

peepbo ˈpiːp bəʊ -əʊ, ˌ·ˈ· ‖ -boʊ

pee-pee ˈpiː piː **~s** z

peeper ˈpiːp ə ‖ -ᵊr **~s** z

peephole 'pi:p həʊl →-hɒʊl ‖ -hoʊl **~s** z
peepshow 'pi:p ʃəʊ ‖ -ʃoʊ **~s** z
peep-toe 'pi:p təʊ ‖ -toʊ
peepul 'pi:p ᵊl *(= people)* **~s** z
peer pɪə ‖ pɪᵊr **peered** pɪəd ‖ pɪᵊrd **peering** 'pɪər ɪŋ ‖ 'pɪr ɪŋ **peers** pɪəz ‖ pɪᵊrz
'peer group; **ˌpeer re'view**
peerag|e 'pɪər ɪdʒ ‖ 'pɪr- **~es** ɪz əz
peeress ˌpɪər 'es '· ·, -əs, -ɪs ‖ 'pɪr əs **~es** ɪz əz
peerie 'pɪər i ‖ 'pɪr i
peerless 'pɪə ləs -lɪs ‖ 'pɪr- **~ly** li **~ness** nəs nɪs
peer-to-peer ˌpɪə tə 'pɪə ◂ ‖ ˌpɪr tə 'pɪᵊr ◂
peeve pi:v **peeved** pi:vd **peeving** 'pi:v ɪŋ **peeves** pi:vz
peevish 'pi:v ɪʃ **~ly** li **~ness** nəs nɪs
peewee, P~ 'pi: wi: **~s** z
peewit 'pi: wɪt **~s** s
peg, Peg, Pegg peg **pegged** pegd **pegging** 'peg ɪŋ **pegs** pegz
ˌpeg 'leg ‖ '·.
Pegasus 'peg əs əs
pegboard 'peg bɔ:d ‖ -bɔ:rd -bourd **~s** z
Peggie 'peg i
Peggotty 'peg ət i ‖ -əţ i
Peggy 'peg i
Pegler 'peg lə ‖ -lᵊr
pegmatite 'peg mə taɪt
Pei peɪ
peignoir 'peɪn wɑ: ‖ peɪn 'wɑ:r —*Fr* [pɛn waːʁ, pɛnj-] **~s** z
Peiping ˌpeɪ 'pɪŋ
Peirce pɪəs ‖ pɪᵊrs
pejoration ˌpi:dʒ ə 'reɪʃ ᵊn ˌpedʒ-
pejorative pɪ 'dʒɒr ət ɪv pə-, -'dʒɔ:r-; 'pi:dʒ ər‿ət- ‖ -'dʒɔ:r əţ ɪv -'dʒɑ:r-; 'pedʒ ə reɪţ ɪv **~ly** li **~s** z
peke pi:k *(= peak)* **pekes** pi:ks
Pekin ˌpi: 'kɪn ◂
Pekines|e ˌpi:k ɪ 'ni:z ◂ -ə- ‖ -'ni:s **~es** ɪz əz
Peking ˌpi: 'kɪŋ ◂ —*see also* **Beijing**
Pekingese ˌpi:k ɪ 'ni:z ◂ -ɪŋ 'i:z ◂, -ə- ‖ -'ni:s, -ɪŋ 'i:s, '· · ·
pekoe 'pi:k əʊ ‖ -oʊ
pelag|e 'pel ɪdʒ **~es** ɪz əz
pelagian, P~ pɪ 'leɪdʒ i‿ən pə-, pe-, -'leɪdʒ ən **~ism** ˌɪz əm **~s** z
pelagic pə 'lædʒ ɪk pɪ-, pe-
Pelagius pɪ 'leɪdʒ i‿əs pə-, pe-
pelargonium ˌpel ə 'gəʊn i‿əm ˌ·ɑ:- ‖ -ɑ:r 'goʊn- **~s** z
Pelasgian pe 'læz dʒi‿ən pɪ-, pə-, -gi‿ən; -'læz dʒən **~s** z
Pele, Pelé, Pelee, Pelée *place name, mountain* 'pel eɪ pə 'leɪ ‖ pə 'leɪ 'peɪ leɪ —*Fr* [pə le]
Pele, Pelé *footballer* 'pel eɪ ‖ 'peɪl eɪ —*Port* [pɛ 'lɛ]
pelerine 'pel ə ri:n -rɪn **~s** z
Peleus 'pi:l ju:s 'pi:l i‿əs, 'pel-
pelf pelf
Pelham, p~ 'pel əm **~s, ~'s** z
Pelias 'pi:l i æs -əs

pelican, P~ 'pel ɪk ən **~s** z
ˌpelican 'crossing
Pelion 'pi:l i‿ən -ɒn
peliss|e pə 'li:s pe-, pɪ- **~es** ɪz əz
Pella 'pel ə
pellagra pə 'læg rə pɪ-, pe-, -'leɪg-, -'lɑ:g-
Pelleas, Pelléas 'pel eɪ æs -i- —*Fr* [pɛ le ɑ:s]
Pelles 'pel i:z
pell|et 'pel |ɪt §-ət ‖ -|ət **~eted** ɪt ɪd §ət-, -əd ‖ əţ əd **~eting** ɪt ɪŋ §ət- ‖ əţ ɪŋ **~ets** ɪts §əts ‖ əts
Pelletier 'pel ət i eɪ ‖ ˌpel ə 'tɪᵊr —*Fr* [pɛl 'tje]
pellicle 'pel ɪk ᵊl **~s** z
pellicular pə 'lɪk jʊl ə pe-, pɪ-, -jəl- ‖ -jəl ᵊr
pellitor|y 'pel ɪt‿ər |i '·ət‿ ‖ ə tɔ:r |i -tour i **~ies** iz
pell-mell ˌpel 'mel ◂
pellucid pɪ 'lu:s ɪd pə-, pe-, -'lju:s-, §-əd **~ly** li **~ness** nəs nɪs
Pelman 'pel mən **~ism** ˌɪz əm
pelmet 'pelm ɪt -ət **~s** s
Peloponnese 'pel əp ə ni:s ˌ· · '· ‖ ˌpel əp ə 'ni:z -'ni:s —*ModGk* Peloponnesos [pe lo 'po ni sos]
Peloponnesian ˌpel əp ə 'ni:ʃ ᵊn ◂ -'ni:ʃ i‿ən ‖ -'ni:ʒ- **~s** z
ˌPeloponˌnesian 'War
Peloponnesus ˌpel əp ə 'ni:s əs
Pelops 'pi:l ɒps pel- ‖ -ɑ:ps
pelorus pə 'lɔ:r əs pɪ- ‖ -'lour- **~es** ɪz əz
Pelosi pə 'ləʊs i ‖ -'loʊs i
pelota pə 'lɒt ə pɪ-, pe-, -'ləʊt- ‖ -'loʊţ ə —*Sp* [pe 'lo ta]
peloton 'pel ət ən -ə tɒn ‖ -ə tɑ:n ˌ· ·'· **~s** z
pelt pelt **pelted** 'pelt ɪd -əd **pelting** 'pelt ɪŋ **pelts** pelts
peltast 'pelt æst **~s** s
peltate 'pelt eɪt **~ly** li
Peltier 'pelt i eɪ —*Fr* [pɛl tje]
Pelton 'pelt ən
pelvic 'pelv ɪk
pelv|is 'pelv |ɪs §-əs **~es** i:z **~ises** ɪs ɪz §əs ɪz, -əz
Pemba 'pem bə
Pemberton 'pem bət ən ‖ -bᵊrt ᵊn
Pembrey ₍ˌ₎pem 'breɪ 'pem bri
Pembridge 'pem brɪdʒ
Pembroke 'pem brʊk -brək, -brəʊk ‖ -broʊk -brʊk **~shire** ʃə ʃɪə ‖ ʃᵊr ʃɪr
Pembury 'pem bər‿i
pemican, pemmican 'pem ɪk ən
pemphigus 'pemᵖf ɪg əs §-əg-; pem 'faɪg-
pen pen **penned** pend *(= pend)* **penning** 'pen ɪŋ **pens** penz
'pen friend; **'pen name**; **'pen pal**; **'pen ˌpusher**
penal 'pi:n ᵊl
'penal ˌcolony
penalis... —*see* **penaliz...**
penalization ˌpi:n əl aɪ 'zeɪʃ ᵊn -ɪ'·- ‖ -əl ə- ˌpen- **~s** z

penaliz|e ˈpiːn ə laɪz -ᵊl aɪz ‖ ˈpiːn ᵊl aɪz ˈpen- **~ed** d **~es** ɪz əz **~ing** ɪŋ
penally ˈpiːn əl i
penalt|y ˈpen ᵊlt |i **~ies** iz **ˈpenalty ˌarea**; **ˈpenalty box**; **ˈpenalty goal**; **ˈpenalty kick**
penanc|e ˈpen ənᵗs **~es** ɪz əz
pen-and-ink ˌpen ən ˈɪŋk ◂ -ənd-
Penang pə ˈnæŋ pe-
Penarth pe ˈnɑːθ pə- ‖ -ˈnɑːrθ —*Welsh* [pe ˈnarθ]
penates pe ˈnɑːt eɪz pɪ-, pə-, -iːz, -ˈneɪt iːz ‖ ˈneɪt- -ˈnɑːt-
pence penᵗs —*There is a BrE weak form* pənᵗs, *but it is now fairly rare. Prices are usually quoted with the strong form* penᵗs *or with* **p** piː, *usually stressed:* **15p** ˌfɪf tiːn ˈpenᵗs, ˌfɪf tiːn ˈpiː
penchant ˈpɒ̃ ʃɒ̃ ˈpɒn ʃɒn, ˈpɒŋ ʃɒŋ ‖ ˈpentʃ ənt *(*)* —*Fr* [pɑ̃ ʃɑ̃] **~s** z ‖ s
pencil ˈpenᵗs ᵊl -ɪl **~ed, ~led** d **~ing, ~ling** ɪŋ **~s** z **ˈpencil case**; **ˈpencil ˌsharpener**
pencil-thin ˌpenᵗs ᵊl ˈθɪn ◂ -ɪl-
Pencoed ₍ˌ₎pen ˈkɔɪd →₍ˌ₎peŋ-
pend pend **pending** ˈpend ɪŋ
pendant ˈpend ənt **~s** s
Pendennis pen ˈden ɪs §-əs
pendent ˈpend ənt **~ly** li **~s** s
pendente lite pen ˌdent i ˈlaɪt iː -i
pendentive pen ˈdent ɪv ‖ -ˈdenṭ ɪv **~s** z
Pender ˈpend ə ‖ -ᵊr
Penderecki ˌpend ə ˈret ski —*Polish* [pen de ˈrets ki]
Pendergast ˈpend ə gɑːst §-gæst ‖ -ᵊr gæst
Pendine ₍ˌ₎pen ˈdaɪn
pending ˈpend ɪŋ
Pendle ˈpend ᵊl
Pendlebury ˈpend ᵊl bər‿i ‖ -ˌber i
Pendleton ˈpend ᵊl tən
Pendolino *tdmk* ˌpend ə ˈliːn əʊ ‖ -oʊ
pendragon, P~ pen ˈdræg ən **~s** z
pendulous ˈpend jʊl əs -jəl- ‖ ˈpendʒ əl əs **~ly** li **~ness** nəs nɪs
pendulum ˈpend jʊl əm -jəl- ‖ ˈpendʒ əl əm **~s** z
Penelope pə ˈnel əp i pɪ-
peneplain, peneplane ˈpiːn ɪ pleɪn ˈpen-, -ə-, ˌ· ·ˈ· **~s** z
penetrability ˌpen ətr ə ˈbɪl ət i ˌ·ɪtr-, -ɪt i ‖ -əṭ i
penetrab|le ˈpen ətr əb |ᵊl ˈ·ɪtr- **~ly** li
penetralia ˌpen ə ˈtreɪl i‿ə ˌ·ɪ-
penetrance ˈpen ətr ənᵗs -ɪtr-
pene|trate ˈpen ə |treɪt -ɪ- **~trated** treɪt ɪd -əd ‖ treɪṭ əd **~trates** treɪts **~trating/ly** treɪt ɪŋ /li ‖ treɪṭ ɪŋ /li
penetration ˌpen ə ˈtreɪʃ ᵊn -ɪ- **~s** z
penetrative ˈpen ətr ət ɪv ˈ·ɪtr-, -ə treɪt-, -ɪ treɪt- ‖ -ə treɪṭ ɪv **~ly** li **~ness** nəs nɪs
Penfold ˈpen fəʊld →-fɒʊld ‖ -foʊld
penfriend ˈpen frend **~s** z
Pengam ˈpeŋ gəm
Penge pendʒ
Pengelly pen ˈgel i →peŋ-
penguin, P~ ˈpeŋ gwɪn §-gwən **~s** z
Penhaligon pen ˈhæl ɪg ən
penicillin ˌpen ə ˈsɪl ɪn -ɪ-, §-ən
penicillium ˌpen ə ˈsɪl i‿əm ˌ·ɪ-
Penicuik ˈpen i kʊk
penile ˈpiːn aɪᵊl ‖ -ᵊl
penillion pe ˈnɪθ li‿ən pɪ-, pə-, -ˈnɪl i‿ —*Welsh* [pe ˈniɬ jon]
peninsula pə ˈnɪnᵗs jʊl ə pɪ-, pe-, -ˈnɪnᵗʃ ʊl ə ‖ -əl ə **~s** z
peninsular pə ˈnɪnᵗs jʊl ə pɪ-, pe-, -ˈnɪnᵗʃ ʊl ə ‖ -ᵊl ər
penis ˈpiːn ɪs §-əs **~es** ɪz əz
Penistone ˈpen ɪst ən
penitence ˈpen ɪt ənᵗs -ət- ‖ -ət ᵊnᵗs
penitent ˈpen ɪt ənt -ət- ‖ -ət ᵊnt **~ly** li **~s** s
penitential ˌpen ɪ ˈtenᵗʃ ᵊl ◂ -ə- **~ly** i
penitentiar|y ˌpen ɪ ˈtenᵗʃ ər |i ˌ·ə- **~ies** iz
Penk peŋk
Penkhull ˈpeŋk ᵊl -hʌl
pen|knife ˈpen |naɪf **~knives** naɪvz
Penkridge ˈpeŋk rɪdʒ
Penlee ₍ˌ₎pen ˈliː
Penmaenmawr, Penmaen-mawr ˌpen mən ˈmaʊ‿ə →ˌpem-, →ˌ·məm-, ˌ·maɪn-; ˌ· ·ˈmɔː ‖ -ˈmaʊ‿ᵊr —*Welsh* [ˌpɛn maɨn ˈmaur, -mən-]
pen|man ˈpen mən →ˈpem- **~manship** mən ʃɪp **~men** mən men
Penn pen
Penn. pen *or as* Pennsylvania
penn|a ˈpen |ə **~ae** iː
pennant, P~ ˈpen ənt **~s** s
penne ˈpen eɪ -i —*It* [ˈpen ne]
Penney, Pennie ˈpen i
penni... —*see* **penny**
penniless ˈpen ɪ ləs -ə-, -lɪs; -ᵊl əs, -ɪs **~ly** li **~ness** nəs nɪs
Pennine ˈpen aɪn **~s** z **ˌPennine ˈWay**
Pennington ˈpen ɪŋ tən
pennon ˈpen ən **~ed** d **~s** z
pennorth, penn'orth ˈpen əθ ‖ -ᵊrθ
Pennsylvania ˌpenᵗs ᵊl ˈveɪn i‿ə ◂ ˌ·ɪl- ‖ ˌ· ·ˈ·jə ◂ **ˌPennsylˌvania ˈDutch**
Pennsylvanian ˌpenᵗs ᵊl ˈveɪn i‿ən ◂ ˌ·ɪl- ‖ ˌ· ·ˈ·jən ◂ **~s** z
penn|y, Penn|y ˈpen |i **~ies, ~y's** iz **ˌpenny ˈblack**; **ˌpenny ˈdreadful**; **ˌpenny ˈwhistle**
-penny *adj-forming suffix* pən i, ˌpen i — **tenpenny** ˈten pən i ˈtemp ən‿i, ˈten ˌpen i —*These are pre-1971. Since decimalization the equivalent is* pence, p *thus* **a 10p packet** ə ˌten piː ˈpæk ɪt *: see note at* pence
penny-ante ˌpen i ˈænt i ◂ ‖ -ˈænṭ i ◂
pennycress ˈpen i kres
Pennycuick *(i)* ˈpen i kʊk, *(ii)* -kwɪk, *(iii)* -kjuːk
penny-farthing ˌpen i ˈfɑːð ɪŋ ‖ -ˈfɑːrð- **~s** z

P

Pennyfeather 'pen i ˌfeð ə ‖ -ᵊr
penny-halfpen|ny ˌpen i 'heɪp |ni **~nies** niz
penny-pinch|er 'pen i ˌpɪntʃ| ə ‖ ᵊr **~ers** əz ‖ ᵊrz **~ing** ɪŋ
pennyroyal ˌpen i 'rɔɪ̯əl **~s** z
pennyweight 'pen i weɪt **~s** s
penny-wise ˌpen i 'waɪz ◂
pennywort 'pen i wɜːt -wɔːt ‖ -wɜːt -wɔːrt
pennyworth 'pen əθ 'pen i wɜːθ, -wəθ ‖ 'pen i wɜːθ **~s** s
Penobscot pə 'nɒb skɒt pe-, pɪ-, -skət ‖ -'nɑːb skɑːt -skət
penological ˌpiːn ə 'lɒdʒ ɪk ᵊl ‖ -'lɑːdʒ- **~ly** ˌi
penology ₍ₗ₎piː 'nɒl ədʒ i pɪ- ‖ -'nɑːl-
Pen-rhos *places in Gwynedd, Gwent, Powys* ˌpen 'rəʊs ◂ ‖ -'roʊs —*Welsh* [ˌpɛn 'hroːs]
Penrhos *place in Gwynedd* 'pen rəʊs -rɒs ‖ -roʊs —*Welsh* ['pɛn hroːs]
Penrhyn 'pen rɪn —*Welsh* ['pɛn hrɨn, -hrin]
Penrhyndeudraeth ˌpen rɪn 'daɪdr əθ -aɪθ —*Welsh* [ˌpɛn hrɨn 'dəi draiθ]
Penrith *place in NSW* 'pen rɪθ -rəθ —*locally* -rəθ
Penrith *place in Cumbria* 'pen rɪθ ˌ·'· —*locally also* 'pɪər ɪθ
Penrose 'pen rəʊz ₍ₗ₎·'· ‖ -roʊz
Penry 'pen ri
Penryn ₍ₗ₎pen 'rɪn
Pensacola ˌpenᵗs ə 'kəʊl ə ‖ -'koʊl ə
Pen-sarn *places in Clwyd and Gwynedd* pen 'sɑːn ‖ -'sɑːrn
Pensarn *place in Dyfed* 'pen sɑːn ‖ -sɑːrn
pensée 'pɒ̃s eɪ ˌpɒ̃ 'seɪ ‖ ˌpɑːn 'seɪ —*Fr* [pɑ̃ se] **~s** z *or as sing.*
penseroso ˌpenᵗs ə 'rəʊz əʊ -'rəʊs- ‖ -'roʊs oʊ
Penshurst 'penz hɜːst ‖ -hɜːst
pensile 'penᵗs aɪᵊl ‖ -ᵊl
pension *'payment'* 'penᵗʃ ᵊn **~ed** d **~ing** ˌɪŋ **~s** z
 'pension fund
pension *'boarding-house'* 'pɒ̃s jɒ̃ ‖ pɑːns 'joʊn —*Fr* [pɑ̃ sjɔ̃] **~s** z
pensionable 'penᵗʃ ᵊn̩əb ᵊl
pensioner 'penᵗʃ ᵊn̩ə ‖ ər **~s** z
pensive 'penᵗs ɪv **~ly** li **~ness** nəs nɪs
penstemon pen 'stiːm ən 'penᵗst ɪm-, -əm- **~s** z
penstock 'pen stɒk ‖ -stɑːk **~s** s
pent pent
 ˌpent 'up◂
pent- *comb. form* ¦pent — **pentoxide** ˌpent 'ɒks aɪd ‖ -'ɑːks-
penta, Penta 'pent ə ‖ 'pent̬ ə
penta- *comb. form with stress-neutral suffix* ¦pent ə ‖¦pent̬ ə — **pentaprism** 'pent ə ˌprɪz əm ‖ 'pent̬ ə- *with stress-imposing suffix* pen 'tæ+ — **pentamerous** pen 'tæm ər əs
pentacle 'pent ək ᵊl ‖ 'pent̬- **~s** z
pentad 'pent æd **~s** z
pentagon, P~ 'pent əg ən -ə gɒn ‖ 'pent̬ ə gɑːn **~s** z
pentagonal pen 'tæg ən ᵊl
pentagram 'pent ə græm ‖ 'pent̬- **~s** z
pentahedr|on ˌpent ə 'hiːdr |ən -'hedr- ‖ ˌpent̬- **~a** ə **~al** əl **~ons** ənz
pentamerous pen 'tæm ər əs
pentameter pen 'tæm ɪt ə -ət- ‖ -ət̬ ᵊr **~s** z
pentane 'pent eɪn
pentangle 'pent ˌæŋ gᵊl **~s** z
Pentateuch 'pent ə tjuːk →-tʃuːk ‖ 'pent̬ ə tuːk -tjuːk
pentathlete pen 'tæθ liːt **~s** s
pentathlon pen 'tæθ lən -lɒn ‖ -lɑːn
pentatonic ˌpent ə 'tɒn ɪk ◂ ‖ ˌpent̬ ə 'tɑːn ɪk ◂
Pentax *tdmk* 'pent æks
Pentecost 'pent ɪ kɒst -ə- ‖ 'pent̬ ə kɔːst -kɑːst
pentecostal ˌpent ɪ 'kɒst ᵊl ◂ -ə- ‖ ˌpent̬ ə 'kɔːst ᵊl ◂ -'kɑːst- **~ism** ˌɪz əm **~ist/s** ɪst/s §əst/s
Pentel *tdmk* 'pen tel
Pentelicus pen 'tel ɪk əs
Pentelikon pen 'tel ɪk ən -kɒn ‖ -ɪ kɑːn
Penthesilea ˌpenᵗθ es ɪ 'leɪ ə ˌ·əs-, -ə'·-, -'liː̯ə
Pentheus 'penᵗθ juːs 'penᵗθ i̯ əs
pent|house 'pent |haʊs **~houses** haʊz ɪz -əz
pentiment|o ˌpent ɪ 'ment |əʊ -ə- ‖ ˌpent̬ ə 'ment |oʊ **~i** iː *It* [pɛn ti 'mɛn t|o, -i]
Pentire pen 'taɪ̯ə ‖ -'taɪ̯ᵊr
Pentium *tdmk* 'pent i̯əm ‖ 'pent̬-
Pentland 'pent lənd
 ˌPentland 'Firth
pentobarbitone ˌpent əʊ 'bɑːb ɪ təʊn -'·ə- ‖ ˌpent̬ ə 'bɑːrb ə toʊn
pentode 'pent əʊd ‖ -oʊd **~s** z
Penton 'pent ən ‖ -ᵊn
Pentonville 'pent ən vɪl ˌ··'· ‖ -ᵊn-
pentose 'pent əʊz -əʊs ‖ -oʊs -oʊz
Pentothal *tdmk* 'pent ə θæl -θɒl, -θɔːl ‖ 'pent̬ ə θɔːl -θɑːl
Pentre 'pentr ə 'pen treɪ —*Welsh* ['pɛn trɛ]
Pentreath pen 'triːθ
pentstemon pent 'stiːm ən pen-, -'stem-; 'pentst ɪm-, -əm- **~s** z
pent-up ˌpent 'ʌp ◂ ‖ ˌpent̬-
 ˌpent-up e'motions
penuche pə 'nuːtʃ i
penult pə 'nʌlt pɪ-, pe- ‖ 'piːn ʌlt *(*)*
penultimate pə 'nʌlt ɪm ət pɪ-, pe-, -əm ət, -ɪt **~ly** li **~s** s
penum|bra pə 'nʌm |brə pɪ-, pe- **~brae** briː **~bral** brəl **~bras** brəz
penurious pə 'njʊər i̯əs pɪ-, pe- ‖ -'nʊr- -'njʊr- **~ly** li **~ness** nəs nɪs
penury 'pen jər i -jʊr-
Penutian pɪ 'njuːt i̯ən pe-, pə-, -'nuːt-; -'njuːʃ ᵊn, -'nuːʃ- ‖ -'nuːʃ-
Penwith ₍ₗ₎pen 'wɪθ
Penwortham 'pen wəð əm ‖ -wᵊrð-
Penybont, Pen-y-bont ˌpen ə 'bɒnt -i- ‖ -'bɑːnt —*Welsh* [ˌpɛn ə 'bɔnt]
Penyghent ˌpen i 'gent '··
Pen-y-groes ˌpen ə 'grɔɪs -i-, -'grəʊs —*Welsh* [ˌpɛn ə 'grois]

Penzance pen ˈzænᵗs pən-, -ˈzɑːnᵗs
peon ˈpiː‿ən -ɒn ‖ -ɑːn —*formerly, and in India,* pjuːn **~s** z
peonage ˈpiː‿ən ɪdʒ
peon|y ˈpiː‿ən |i **~ies** iz
peopl|e ˈpiːp ᵊl **~ed** d **~es** z **~ing** ‿ɪŋ
people-watching ˈpiːp ᵊl ˌwɒtʃ ɪŋ ‖ -ˌwɑːtʃ- -ˌwɔːtʃ-
Peoria pi ˈɔːr i‿ə ‖ -ˈoʊr-
Peover ˈpiːv ə ‖ -ᵊr
pep, PEP pep **pepped** pept **pepping** ˈpep ɪŋ **peps** peps
ˈpep pill; **ˈpep talk**
Pepe ˈpep eɪ —*Sp* [ˈpe pe]
peperomia ˌpep ə ˈrəʊm i‿ə ‖ -ˈroʊm- **~s** z
peperoni ˌpep ə ˈrəʊn i ‖ -ˈroʊn i
Pepin ˈpep ɪn §-ən
Pepita pe ˈpiːt ə pə- —*Sp* [pe ˈpi ta]
peplum ˈpep ləm **~s** z
pepp... —*see* **pep**
Peppard ˈpep ɑːd ‖ pe ˈpɑːrd
pepper, P~ ˈpep ə ‖ -ᵊr **~ed** d **peppering** ˈpep ər‿ɪŋ **~s** z
ˈpepper mill; **ˈpepper pot**
pepper-and-salt ˌpep ᵊr‿ən ˈsɒlt ◂ ˌ·ə-, -ənd ˈ·, -ˈsɔːlt ‖ -ˈsɔːlt -ˈsɑːlt
pepperbox ˈpep ə bɒks ‖ -ᵊr bɑːks **~es** ɪz əz
peppercorn ˈpep ə kɔːn ‖ -ᵊr kɔːrn **~s** z
ˌpeppercorn ˈrent
Pepperidge ˈpep ə rɪdʒ
peppermint ˈpep ə mɪnt ‖ -ᵊr- **~s** s
pepperoni ˌpep ə ˈrəʊn i ‖ -ˈroʊn i
pepper|y ˈpep ər |i **~iness** i nəs i nɪs
Peppiatt ˈpep i‿ət
pepp|y ˈpep |i **~iness** i nəs i nɪs
Pepsi *tdmk* ˈpeps i **~s** z
Pepsi-Cola *tdmk* ˌpeps i ˈkəʊl ə ‖ -ˈkoʊl ə
pepsin ˈpeps ɪn §-ən **~s** z
Pepsodent *tdmk* ˈpeps əʊ dent -əd ənt ‖ -əd ənt
peptic ˈpept ɪk
ˌpeptic ˈulcer
peptide ˈpept aɪd **~s** z
Pepto-Bismol *tdmk* ˌpept əʊ ˈbɪz mɒl ‖ -toʊ ˈbɪz mɑːl
peptone ˈpept əʊn ‖ -oʊn **~s** z
Pepys *(i)* piːps, *(ii)* ˈpep ɪs, *(iii)* peps —*the diarist is (i)*
Pequot ˈpiː kwɒt ‖ -kwɑːt **~s** s
per pɜː ‖ pɜ˞ː, *weak form* pə ‖ pᵊr —*see also phrases with this word*
per- pə ‖ pᵊr *(but before a vowel* pər*), or* ¦pɜː ‖ ¦pɜ˞ː *(but in RP before a vowel* ¦pɜːr*)*
peradventure ˌpɜːr əd ˈventʃ ə ˌper-, pər‿, §-æd- ‖ ˈpɜ˞ː əd ˌventʃ ᵊr ˈper-; ˌ·ˈ· ·
Perahia pə ˈraɪ‿ə
Perak ˈpeər ə ˈpɪər ə ‖ ˈper ə —*There are also spelling pronunciations* pə ˈræk, pe-, pɪ- ‖ -ˈrɑːk, ˈpeɪ ræk —*Malay* [pe raʔ]
perambu|late pə ˈræm bju |leɪt -bjə- ‖ -bjə- **~lated** leɪt ɪd -əd ‖ leɪţ əd **~lates** leɪts **~lating** leɪt ɪŋ ‖ leɪţ ɪŋ
perambulation pə ˌræm bju ˈleɪʃ ᵊn -bjə- ‖ -bjə- **~s** z
perambulator pə ˈræm bju leɪt ə -ˈ·bjə- ‖ -bjə leɪţ ᵊr **~s** z
per annum pər ˈæn əm ‖ pər-
perborate pə ˈbɔːr eɪt pɜː-; ˈpɜːb ə reɪt ‖ pᵊr- -ˈboʊr- **~s** s
percale pə ˈkerᵊl -ˈkɑːl ‖ pᵊr-
per capita pə ˈkæp ɪt ə ˌpɜː-, §-ət- ‖ pᵊr ˈkæp əţ ə
perceivab|le pə ˈsiːv əb |ᵊl ‖ pᵊr- **~ly** li
perceiv|e pə ˈsiːv ‖ pᵊr- **~ed** d **~es** z **~ing** ɪŋ
percent, per cent pə ˈsent ‖ pᵊr-
percentag|e pə ˈsent ɪdʒ ‖ pᵊr ˈsenţ ɪdʒ **~es** ɪz əz
percentile pə ˈsent aɪᵊl ‖ pᵊr- -ˈsenţ ᵊl **~s** z
percept ˈpɜː sept ‖ ˈpɜ˞ː- **~s** s
perceptibility pə ˌsept ə ˈbɪl ət i -ˌ·ɪ-, -ɪt i ‖ pᵊr ˌsept ə ˈbɪl əţ i
perceptib|le pə ˈsept əb |ᵊl -ˈ·ɪb- ‖ pᵊr- **~ly** li
perception pə ˈsep ʃᵊn ‖ pᵊr- **~s** z
perceptive pə ˈsept ɪv ‖ pᵊr- **~ly** li **~ness** nəs nɪs
perceptivity ˌpɜː sep ˈtɪv ət i pə ˌsep-, -ɪt i ‖ ˌpɜ˞ː sep ˈtɪv əţ i
perceptual pə ˈsep tʃu‿əl -ʃu‿; -ˈsept ju‿ ‖ pᵊr- **~ly** i
Perceval ˈpɜːs ɪv ᵊl -əv- ‖ ˈpɜ˞ːs-
perch pɜːtʃ ‖ pɜ˞ːtʃ **perched** pɜːtʃt ‖ pɜ˞ːtʃt **perches** ˈpɜːtʃ ɪz -əz ‖ ˈpɜ˞ːtʃ əz **perching** ˈpɜːtʃ ɪŋ ‖ ˈpɜ˞ːtʃ ɪŋ
perchance pə ˈtʃɑːnᵗs ˌpɜː-, §-ˈtʃænᵗs ‖ pᵊr ˈtʃænᵗs
Percheron ˈpɜːʃ ə rɒn ‖ ˈpɜ˞ːtʃ ə rɑːn ˈpɜ˞ːʃ- —*Fr* [pɛʁ ʃə ʁɔ̃] **~s** z
percipience pə ˈsɪp i‿ənᵗs ‖ pᵊr-
percipient pə ˈsɪp i‿ənt ‖ pᵊr- **~ly** li **~s** s
Percival ˈpɜːs ɪv ᵊl -əv- ‖ ˈpɜ˞ːs-
perco|late ˈpɜːk ə |leɪt ⚠-ju-, ⚠-jə- ‖ ˈpɜ˞ːk- **~lated** leɪt ɪd -əd ‖ leɪţ əd **~lates** leɪts **~lating** leɪt ɪŋ ‖ leɪţ ɪŋ
percolation ˌpɜːk ə ˈleɪʃ ᵊn ⚠-ju-, ⚠-jə- ‖ ˌpɜ˞ːk- **~s** z
percolator ˈpɜːk ə leɪt ə ⚠ˈ·ju-, ⚠ˈ·jə- ‖ ˈpɜ˞ːk ə leɪţ ᵊr **~s** z
per contra ˌpɜː ˈkɒntr ə pə- ‖ ˌpɜ˞ː ˈkɑːntr ə
percuss pə ˈkʌs ‖ pᵊr- **~ed** t **~es** ɪz əz **~ing** ɪŋ
percussion pə ˈkʌʃ ᵊn ‖ pᵊr- **~s** z
perˈcussion cap
percussionist pə ˈkʌʃ ᵊn‿ɪst §‿əst ‖ pᵊr- **~s** s
percussive pə ˈkʌs ɪv ‖ pᵊr- **~ly** li **~ness** nəs nɪs
percutaneous ˌpɜː kju ˈteɪn i‿əs ‖ ˌpɜ˞ː- **~ly** li
Percy ˈpɜːs i ‖ ˈpɜ˞ːs i
per diem ˌpɜː ˈdiː em pə-, -ˈdaɪ-, -əm ‖ pᵊr- ˌpɜ˞ː-
Perdita ˈpɜːd ɪt ə §-ət- ‖ ˈpɜ˞ːd əţ ə pᵊr ˈdiːţ ə
perdition pə ˈdɪʃ ᵊn pɜː- ‖ pᵊr-
Perdue, p~ ˈpɜːd juː ‖ pᵊr ˈduː -ˈdjuː
pere, père, Père peə ‖ peᵊr —*Fr* [pɛːʁ]
peregri|nate ˈper əg rɪ |neɪt ˈ·ɪg-, -rə · **~nated** neɪt ɪd -əd ‖ neɪţ əd **~nates** neɪts **~nating** neɪt ɪŋ ‖ neɪţ ɪŋ

P

peregrination ˌper əg rɪ ˈneɪʃ ən ˌ·ɪg-, -rəˈ·- **~s** z

peregrine, P~ ˈper əg rɪn -ɪg-, §-rən; -griːn, -ə- **~s** z
ˌperegrine ˈfalcon

pereira, P~ pə ˈreər ə -ˈrɪər- ‖ -ˈrer ə
peˈreira bark

Perelman *(i)* ˈper əl mən, *(ii)* ˈpɜːl mən ‖ ˈpɝːl- —*Usually (i).*

peremptor|y pə ˈrempt ər‿|i pɪ-; ˈper əmpt- —*Both stressings are in use among English lawyers.* **~ily** əl i ɪ li **~iness** i nəs i nɪs

perennial pə ˈren i‿əl **~ly** i **~s** z

perentie pəˈrent i ‖ -ˈrenţ i **~s** z

Peres pə ˈrez

perestroika ˌper ə ˈstrɔɪk ə -ɪ- — *Russ* [pʲɪ rʲɪ ˈstroj kə]

Pérez de Cuéllar ˌper əz də ˈkweɪl jɑː ˌ·ɪz-, ˌ·ez- -ˈkweɪ- ‖ -jɑːr —*AmSp* [ˌpe res de ˈkwe jar, ˌ·reh-]

perfect *v* pə ˈfekt pɜː- ‖ pər- **~ed** ɪd əd **~ing** ɪŋ **~s** s

perfect *adj, n* ˈpɜːf ɪkt -ekt, §-əkt ‖ ˈpɝːf- **~s** s
ˌperfect ˈtense; **ˌperfect ˈparticiple**

perfectibility pə ˌfekt ə ˈbɪl ət i pɜː-, -ˌ·ɪ-, -ɪt i ‖ pər ˌfekt ə ˈbɪl əţ i

perfectib|le pə ˈfekt əb |əl pɜː-, -ˈ·ɪb- ‖ pər- **~ly** li

perfection pə ˈfek ʃən ‖ pər- **~s** z

perfectionism pə ˈfek ʃən ˌɪz əm ‖ pər-

perfectionist pə ˈfek ʃən‿ɪst §‿əst ‖ pər- **~s** s

perfective pə ˈfekt ɪv ‖ pər- **~ly** li **~ness** nəs nɪs **~s** z

perfect|ly ˈpɜːf ɪkt li -ekt-, §-əkt- ‖ ˈpɝːf- **~ness** nəs nɪs

perfecto pə ˈfekt əʊ ‖ pər ˈfekt oʊ **~s** z

perfervid pɜː ˈfɜːv ɪd pə-, §-əd ‖ pər ˈfɝːv- **~ly** li **~ness** nəs nɪs

perfidious pə ˈfɪd i‿əs pɜː- ‖ pər- **~ly** li **~ness** nəs nɪs

perfid|y ˈpɜːf əd |i -ɪd- ‖ ˈpɝːf- **~ies** iz

perfoliate pə ˈfəʊl i‿ət ət, -eɪt ‖ pər ˈfoʊl-

perforate *adj* ˈpɜːf ər‿ət ɪt, -ə reɪt ‖ ˈpɝːf-

perfo|rate *v* ˈpɜːf ə |reɪt ‖ ˈpɝːf- **~rated** reɪt ɪd -əd ‖ reɪţ əd **~rates** reɪts **~rating** reɪt ɪŋ ‖ reɪţ ɪŋ

perforation ˌpɜːf ə ˈreɪʃ ən ‖ ˌpɝːf- **~s** z

perforator ˈpɜːf ə reɪt ə ‖ ˈpɝːf ə reɪţ ər **~s** z

perforce pə ˈfɔːs pɜː- ‖ pər ˈfɔːrs -ˈfoʊrs

perform pə ˈfɔːm ‖ pər ˈfɔːrm **~ed** d **~ing** ɪŋ **~s** z

performanc|e pə ˈfɔːm ənts ‖ pər ˈfɔːrm- **~es** ɪz əz

performance-enhancing pə ˈfɔːm ənts ɪn ˌhɑːnts ɪŋ -·en-, - ·ən-, -ˌhænts- ‖ pr ˈfɔːrm ənts ɪn ˌhænts ɪŋ

performance-related pə ˌfɔːm əns ri ˈleɪt ɪd ◂ -rəˈ·- ‖ pər ˈfɔːrm əns rə ˌleɪţ əd

performative pə ˈfɔːm ət ɪv ‖ pər ˈfɔːrm əţ ɪv **~s** z

performer pə ˈfɔːm ə ‖ pər ˈfɔːrm ər **~s** z

perfume *n* ˈpɜː fjuːm ‖ ˈpɝː fjuːm pər ˈfjuːm **~s** z

perfum|e *v* ˈpɜː fjuːm pə ˈfjuːm, pɜː- ‖ pər ˈfjuːm ˈpɝː fjuːm **~ed** d **~es** z **~ing** ɪŋ

perfumer pə ˈfjuːm ə pɜː-; ˈpɜː fjuːm ə ‖ pər ˈfjuːm ər ˈpɝː fjuːm ər **~s** z

perfumer|y pə ˈfjuːm ər |i pɜː- ‖ pər- **~ies** iz

perfumier pə ˈfjuːm i‿ə pɜː-, -eɪ ‖ pər ˈfjuːm i‿ər **~s** z

perfunctor|y pə ˈfʌŋkt ər‿|i pɜː- ‖ pər- **~ily** əl i ɪ li **~iness** i nəs i nɪs

perfus|e pə ˈfjuːz pɜː- ‖ pər- **~ed** d **~es** ɪz əz **~ing** ɪŋ

perfusion pə ˈfjuːʒ ən pɜː- ‖ pər- **~s** z

Pergamon ˈpɜːg əm ən ‖ ˈpɝːg- -ə mɑːn

Pergamum ˈpɜːg əm əm ‖ ˈpɝːg-

pergola ˈpɜːg əl ə pə ˈgəʊl ə ‖ ˈpɝːg əl ə pər ˈgoʊl ə **~s** z

Pergolesi ˌpɜːg əʊ ˈleɪz i ‖ ˌpɝːg ə- -ˈleɪs- —*It* [per go ˈleː si]

Perham ˈper əm

perhaps pə ˈhæps ‖ pər- —*informally also* pər ˈæps, præps

peri ˈpɪər i ‖ ˈpɪr i **~s** z

peri- *comb. form with stress-neutral suffix* ¦per i —*but before a consonant sound often* ¦per ɪ, §¦per ə ‖ ¦per ə — **perinatal** ˌper i ˈneɪt əl ◂ ‖ ˌper ə ˈneɪţ əl ◂ *with stress-imposing suffix* pə ˈrɪ+ pɪ-, pe- — **pericope** pə ˈrɪk əp i pɪ-, pe-

perianth ˈper i ænʰθ **~s** s

pericarditis ˌper i kɑː ˈdaɪt ɪs §-əs ‖ ˌper ə kɑːr ˈdaɪţ əs

pericardi|um ˌper i ˈkɑːd i‿|əm ‖ -ə ˈkɑːrd- **~a** ə **~ums** əmz

pericarp ˈper i kɑːp -ə- ‖ -ə kɑːrp **~s** s

Periclean ˌper ɪ ˈkliː‿ən ◂ -ə-

Pericles ˈper ɪ kliːz -ə-

pericynthion ˌper i ˈsɪnʰθ i‿ən ‖ -ə ˈsɪnʰθ i ɑːn

peridot ˈper i dɒt ‖-ə dɑːt -doʊ

perigee ˈper ɪ dʒiː -i-, -ə- **~s** z

Perigord, Périgord ˈper ɪ gɔː -ə- ‖ ˌper ə ˈgɔːr —*Fr* [pe ʁi gɔːʁ]

periheli|on ˌper i ˈhiːl i‿|ən ‖ ˌ·ə- **~a** ə

peril ˈper əl -ɪl **~s** z

perilous ˈper əl əs -ɪl- **~ly** li **~ness** nəs nɪs

perilune ˈper i luːn -ljuːn ‖ -ə-

perimeter pə ˈrɪm ɪt ə pɪ-, pe-, -ət- ‖ -əţ ər **~s** z

perinatal ˌper ɪ ˈneɪt əl -ə- ‖ -ˈneɪţ-

perineal ˌper ɪ ˈniː‿əl -ə-

perine|um ˌper ɪ ˈniː‿|əm -ə- **~a** ə

period ˈpɪər i‿əd ‖ ˈpɪr- **~s** z
ˈperiod piece

periodate pər ˈaɪ‿ə deɪt ‖ pər- **~s** s

periodic *'recurring at intervals'* ˌpɪər i ˈɒd ɪk ◂ ‖ ˌpɪr i ˈɑːd ɪk ◂
ˌperiˌodic ˈtable

periodic *'derived by addition of water to* I_2O_7*'* ˌpɜːr aɪ ˈɒd ɪk ◂ ‖ ˌpɝː aɪ ˈɑːd-

periodical ˌpɪər i ˈɒd ɪk əl ◂ ‖ ˌpɪr i ˈɑːd ɪk əl ◂ **~ly** ‿i **~s** z

periodicity ˌpɪər i‿ə ˈdɪs ət i ‖ ˌpɪr i‿ə ˈdɪs əţ i

periodont|al ˌper i əʊ ˈdɒnt |ᵊl ◂ ‖ ˌper i oʊ ˈdɑːnt̬ |ᵊl ◂ -ə'-- **~ic** -ɪk ◂ **~ics** ɪks **~ist/s** ɪst/s §-əst/s
perioste|um ˌper i ˈɒst i‿|əm ‖ -ˈɑːst- **~a** ə **~al** əl
periotic ˌper i ˈəʊt ɪk ◂ -ˈɒt- ‖ -ˈoʊt̬-
peripatetic, P~ ˌper ɪ pə ˈtet ɪk ◂ ˌ·ə-, ˌ·i- ‖ -ˈtet̬- **~ally** ᵊl‿i **~s** s
peripeteia, peripetia ˌper ɪ pə ˈtiː‿ə ˌ·ə-, ˌ·i-, -ˈtaɪ‿ə **~s** z
peripet|y pə ˈrɪp ət |i pe-, pɪ- ‖ -ət̬ |i **~ies** iz
peripheral pə ˈrɪf ᵊr‿əl pɪ-, pe- **~s** z
peˌripheral ˈnervous ˌsystem
peripherality pə ˌrɪf ə ˈræl ət i pɪ-, pe-, -ɪt i ‖ -ət̬ i
peripherally pə ˈrɪf ᵊr‿əl i pɪ-, pe-
peripher|y pə ˈrɪf ər‿|i pɪ-, pe- **~ies** iz
periph|rasis pə ˈrɪf |rəs ɪs pɪ-, pe-, §-əs **~rases** rə siːz
periphrastic ˌper ɪ ˈfræst ɪk ◂ -ə-, -i- **~ally** ᵊl‿i
perique pə ˈriːk
periscope ˈper ɪ skəʊp -ə- ‖ -skoʊp **~s** s
periscopic ˌper ɪ ˈskɒp ɪk ◂ -ə- ‖ -ˈskɑːp ɪk ◂
perish ˈper ɪʃ **~ed** t **~es** ɪz əz **~ing/ly** ɪŋ /li
perishability ˌper ɪʃ ə ˈbɪl ət i -ɪt i ‖ -ət̬ i
perishable ˈper ɪʃ əb ᵊl **~ness** nəs nɪs **~s** z
perisher ˈper ɪʃ ə ‖ -ᵊr **~s** z
perispom|enon ˌper i ˈspəʊm |ə nɒn ‖ -ˈspoʊm |ə nɑːn **~ena** ən ə
perissodactyl pə ˌrɪs əʊ ˈdækt ɪl pɪ-, pe-, §-ᵊl, ·ˌ· ·ˌ· · ‖ -ə'-- **~s** z
peristalsis ˌper ɪ ˈstæls ɪs -ə-, §-əs ‖ -ˈstɔːls əs -ˈstɑːls-, -ˈstæls-
peristaltic ˌper ɪ ˈstælt ɪk ◂ -ə- ‖ ˈstɔːlt ɪk ◂ -ˈstɑːlt-, -ˈstælt-
peristyle ˈper ɪ staɪᵊl -ə-, -i- **~s** z
peritone|um ˌper ɪ təʊ ˈniː‿|əm ˌ·ə- ‖ ˌper ət ᵊn ˈiː |əm **~a** ə
peritonitis ˌper ɪ təʊ ˈnaɪt ɪs ˌ·ə-, §-əs ‖ ˌper ət ᵊn ˈaɪt̬ əs
Perivale ˈper ɪ veɪᵊl -i-, -ə-
periwig ˈper i wɪg **~ged** d **~s** z
periwinkle ˈper i ˌwɪŋk ᵊl **~s** z
perjure ˈpɜːdʒ ə ‖ ˈpɜ˞ːdʒ ᵊr **~d** d **perjuring** ˈpɜːdʒ ər‿ɪŋ ‖ ˈpɜ˞ːdʒ ər ɪŋ **~s** z
perjurer ˈpɜːdʒ ər‿ə ‖ ˈpɜ˞ːdʒ ᵊr‿ər **~s** z
perjurious pɜː ˈdʒʊər i‿əs pə-, -ˈdʒɔːr- ‖ pɜ˞ː ˈdʒʊr- pᵊr- **~ly** li **~ness** nəs nɪs
perjur|y ˈpɜːdʒ ər‿|i **~ies** iz
perk pɜːk ‖ pɜ˞ːk **perked** pɜːkt ‖ pɜ˞ːkt **perking** ˈpɜːk ɪŋ ‖ ˈpɜ˞ːk ɪŋ **perks** pɜːks ‖ pɜ˞ːks
perki... —*see* **perky**
Perkin ˈpɜːk ɪn §-ən ‖ ˈpɜ˞ːk-
Perkins ˈpɜːk ɪnz §-ənz ‖ ˈpɜ˞ːk-
Perks pɜːks ‖ pɜ˞ːks
perk|y, Perky ˈpɜːk |i ‖ ˈpɜ˞ːk |i **~ier** i‿ə ‖ i‿ᵊr **~iest** i‿ɪst i‿əst **~ily** ɪ li əl i **~iness** i nəs i nɪs
perlative ˈpɜːl ət ɪv ‖ ˈpɜ˞ːl ət̬-
Perlis ˈpɜːl ɪs §-əs ‖ ˈpɜ˞ːl- —*Malay* [ˈper lis]
perlite ˈpɜːl aɪt ‖ ˈpɜ˞ːl-
Perlman ˈpɜːl mən ‖ ˈpɜ˞ːl-
perlocution ˌpɜː ləʊ ˈkjuːʃ ᵊn -lɒ- ‖ ˌpɜ˞ː lə-
perlocutionary ˌpɜː ləʊ ˈkjuːʃ ᵊn ər‿i ◂ ˌ·lɒ- ‖ ˌpɜ˞ː lə ˈkjuːʃ ə ner i ◂
perm pɜːm ‖ pɜ˞ːm **permed** pɜːmd ‖ pɜ˞ːmd **perming** ˈpɜːm ɪŋ ‖ ˈpɜ˞ːm ɪŋ **perms** pɜːmz ‖ pɜ˞ːmz
Perm *place in Russia* pɜːm ‖ pɜ˞ːm —*Russ* [pʲermʲ]
permaculture ˈpɜːm ə ˌkʌltʃ ə ‖ ˈpɜ˞ːm ə ˌkʌltʃ ᵊr
permafrost ˈpɜːm ə frɒst -frɔːst ‖ ˈpɜ˞ːm ə frɔːst -frɑːst
permalloy ˈpɜːm ə lɔɪ pɜːm ˈæl ɔɪ ‖ ˌpɜ˞ːm ˈæl ɔɪ ˈpɜ˞ːm ə lɔɪ
permanenc|e ˈpɜːm ən‿ənᵗs ‖ ˈpɜ˞ːm- **~ies** iz **~y** i
permanent ˈpɜːm ən‿ənt ‖ ˈpɜ˞ːm- **~ly** li **~s** s
ˌpermanent ˈwave; ˌpermanent ˈway
permanganate pə ˈmæŋ gə neɪt pɜː-, -gən ɪt, -ət ‖ pᵊr- **~s** s
permanganic ˌpɜː mæn ˈgæn ɪk ◂ →-mæŋ- ‖ ˌpɜ˞ː-
permeability ˌpɜːm i‿ə ˈbɪl ət i -ɪt i ‖ ˌpɜ˞ːm i‿ə ˈbɪl ət̬ i
permeab|le ˈpɜːm i‿əb |ᵊl ‖ ˈpɜ˞ːm- **~ly** li
permeance ˈpɜːm i‿ənᵗs ‖ ˈpɜ˞ːm-
perme|ate ˈpɜːm i |eɪt ‖ ˈpɜ˞ːm- **~ated** eɪt ɪd -əd ‖ eɪt̬ əd **~ates** eɪts **~ating** eɪt ɪŋ ‖ eɪt̬ ɪŋ
permeation ˌpɜːm i ˈeɪʃ ᵊn ‖ ˌpɜ˞ːm-
Permian ˈpɜːm i‿ən ‖ ˈpɜ˞ːm-
permissib|le pə ˈmɪs əb |ᵊl -ˈ·ɪb- ‖ pᵊr- **~leness** ᵊl nəs -nɪs **~ly** li
permission pə ˈmɪʃ ᵊn ‖ pᵊr- **~s** z
permissive pə ˈmɪs ɪv ‖ pᵊr- **~ly** li **~ness** nəs nɪs
per|mit *v* pə |ˈmɪt ‖ pᵊr- **~mits** ˈmɪts **~mitted** ˈmɪt ɪd -əd ‖ ˈmɪt̬ əd **~mitting** ˈmɪt ɪŋ ‖ ˈmɪt̬ ɪŋ
permit *n* ˈpɜːm ɪt ‖ ˈpɜ˞ː mɪt pᵊr ˈmɪt **~s** s
permittivity ˌpɜːm ɪ ˈtɪv ət i ˌ·ə- ‖ ˌpɜ˞ːm ɪ ˈtɪv ət̬ i
permu|tate ˈpɜːm ju |teɪt -jə- ‖ ˈpɜ˞ːm- pᵊr ˈmjuː|t eɪt **~tated** teɪt ɪd -əd ‖ teɪt̬ əd **~tates** teɪts **~tating** teɪt ɪŋ ‖ teɪt̬ ɪŋ
permutation ˌpɜːm ju ˈteɪʃ ᵊn -jə- ‖ ˌpɜ˞ːm- **~al** ‿əl **~s** z
per|mute pə |ˈmjuːt ‖ pᵊr- **~muted** ˈmjuːt ɪd -əd ‖ ˈmjuːt̬ əd **~mutes** ˈmjuːts **~muting** ˈmjuːt ɪŋ ‖ ˈmjuːt̬ ɪŋ
Permutit *tdmk* pə ˈmjuːt ɪt §-ət; ˈpɜːm jʊt- ‖ pᵊr ˈmjuːt̬-
Pernambuco ˌpɜːn əm ˈbuːk əʊ -æm-, -ˈbjuːk- ‖ ˌpɜ˞ːn əm ˈbuːk oʊ —*Port* [per nem ˈbu ku]
pernicious pə ˈnɪʃ əs pɜː- ‖ pᵊr- **~ly** li **~ness** nəs nɪs
perˌnicious aˈnaemia
pernickety pə ˈnɪk ət i -ɪt- ‖ pᵊr ˈnɪk ət̬ i
Pernod *tdmk* ˈpɜːn əʊ ˈpeən- ‖ per ˈnoʊ —*Fr* [pɛʁ no]
Peron, Perón pə ˈrɒn pe-, pɪ- ‖ -ˈroʊn —*Sp* [pe ˈɾon]
perone|al ˌper əʊ ˈniː‿|əl ◂ ‖ -oʊ- -ə- **~us** əs

P

pero|rate ˈper ə |reɪt -ɒ-, -ɔː- ‖ ˈpɜː- **~rated** reɪt ɪd -əd ‖ reɪţ əd **~rates** reɪts **~rating** reɪt ɪŋ ‖ reɪţ ɪŋ

peroration ˌper ə ˈreɪʃ ᵊn **~s** z

Perowne pə ˈrəʊn pe- ‖ -ˈroʊn

peroxide pə ˈrɒks aɪd ‖ -ˈrɑːks- **~s** z
peˌroxide ˈblonde

perp pɜːp ‖ pɝːp **perps** pɜːps ‖ pɝːps

perpend *n* ˈpɜː pend ‖ ˈpɝː- **~s** z

perpendicular ˌpɜːp ən ˈdɪk jʊl ə ◂ →ˌ·m-, -jəl ə ‖ ˌpɝːp ən ˈdɪk jəl ᵊr **~ly** li **~s** z

perpendicularity ˌpɜːp ən ˌdɪk ju ˈlær ət i →ˌ·m-, -ˌ·jə-, -ɪt i ‖ ˌpɝːp ən ˌdɪk jə ˈlær əţ i -ˈler-

perpe|trate ˈpɜːp ə |treɪt -ɪ- ‖ ˈpɝːp- **~trated** treɪt ɪd -əd ‖ treɪţ əd **~trates** treɪts **~trating** treɪt ɪŋ ‖ treɪţ ɪŋ

perpetration ˌpɜːp ə ˈtreɪʃ ᵊn -ɪ- ‖ ˌpɝːp- **~s** z

perpetrator ˈpɜːp ə treɪt ə ˈ·ɪ- ‖ ˈpɝːp ə treɪţ ᵊr **~s** z

PERPETUAL

6%
-tju‿əl
-tʃu‿əl
-tʃəl
57% 37%
BrE
BrE -tʃ- by age
Percentage
60 50 40 30 20 0
Older ← Speakers → Younger

perpetual pə ˈpet ju‿əl →-ˈpetʃ u‿, -ˈpetʃ əl ‖ pᵊr ˈpetʃ u‿əl — *Preference poll, BrE:* -tju‿əl *57%,* -tʃu‿əl *37%,* -tʃəl *6%.* **~ly** i

perpetu|ate pə ˈpet ju |eɪt -ˈpetʃ u- ‖ pᵊr ˈpetʃ u |eɪt **~ated** eɪt ɪd -əd ‖ eɪţ əd **~ates** eɪts **~ating** eɪt ɪŋ ‖ eɪţ ɪŋ

perpetuation pə ˌpet ju ˈeɪʃ ᵊn -ˌpetʃ u- ‖ pᵊr ˌpetʃ u-

perpetuit|y ˌpɜːp ə ˈtjuː‿ət |i ˌ·ɪ-, →-ˈtʃuː‿, ɪt i ‖ ˌpɝːp ə ˈtuː əţ |i -ˈtjuː- **~ies** iz

perpetuum mobile pə ˌpet ju‿əm ˈməʊb əl i pɜː-, -ˌpetʃ u‿, -ˌpet u‿, -ɪl·, -eɪ ‖ pᵊr ˌpetʃ u əm ˈmoʊb-

Perpignan ˈpɜːp iːn jɒ̃ ‖ ˌpɝːp iːn ˈjɑːn —*Fr* [pɛʁ pi ɲɑ̃]

perplex pə ˈpleks ‖ pᵊr- **~ed** t **~es** ɪz əz **~ing** ɪŋ

perplexed|ly pə ˈpleks ɪd |li -əd-; pə ˈplekst |li ‖ pᵊr- **~ness** nəs nɪs

perplexit|y pə ˈpleks ət |i -ɪt- ‖ pᵊr ˈpleks əţ |i **~ies** iz

per pro ˌpɜː ˈprəʊ ◂ ‖ ˌpɝː ˈproʊ ◂

perquisite ˈpɜːk wɪz ɪt -wəz-, §-ət ‖ ˈpɝːk- **~s** s

Perranporth ˌper ən ˈpɔːθ →-əm- ‖ -ˈpɔːrθ

Perrault ˈper əʊ ‖ pe ˈroʊ —*Fr* [pɛ ʁo]

Perrier *tdmk* ˈper i eɪ ‖ ˌ··ˈ· —*Fr* [pɛ ʁje] **~s** z

Perrin ˈper ɪn §-ən —*but as a French name, also* -æ̃, *Fr* [pɛ ʁɛ̃]

perruquier pə ˈruːk i eɪ —*Fr* [pɛ ʁy kje] **~s** z

perr|y, Perr|y ˈper |i **~ies, ~y's** iz

Persaud pə ˈsɔːd ‖ pᵊr- -ˈsɑːd

Perse, perse pɜːs ‖ pɝːs

per se ˌpɜː ˈseɪ ‖ ˌpɝː-, ˌper-, -ˈsiː

perse|cute ˈpɜːs ɪ |kjuːt -ə- ‖ ˈpɝːs- **~cuted** kjuːt ɪd -əd ‖ kjuːţ əd **~cutes** kjuːts **~cuting** kjuːt ɪŋ ‖ kjuːţ ɪŋ

persecution ˌpɜːs ɪ ˈkjuːʃ ᵊn -ə- ‖ ˌpɝːs- **~s** z

persecutor ˈpɜːs ɪ kjuːt ə ˈ·ə- ‖ ˈpɝːs ɪ kjuːţ ᵊr **~s** z

persecutory ˌpɜːs ɪ ˈkjuːt ər i ˌ·ə-, ˈ···· ‖ ˈpɝːs ɪ kjuːţ ər i -kju tɔːr i, -kju toʊr i

Perseid ˈpɜːs i ɪd §-əd ‖ ˈpɝːs- **~s** z

Persephone pɜː ˈsef ən i pə- ‖ pᵊr-

Persepolis pɜː ˈsep əl ɪs pə-, §-əs ‖ pᵊr-

Perseus ˈpɜːs juːs ˈpɜːs i‿əs ‖ ˈpɝːs i‿əs ˈpɝːs juːs, -uːs

perseverance ˌpɜːs ɪ ˈvɪər ənᵗs -ə- ‖ ˌpɝːs ə ˈvɪr-

perseve|rate pə ˈsev ə |reɪt ‖ pᵊr- **~rated** reɪt ɪd -əd ‖ reɪţ əd **~rates** reɪts **~rating** reɪt ɪŋ ‖ reɪţ ɪŋ

perseveration pə ˌsev ə ˈreɪʃ ᵊn pɜː- ‖ pᵊr- **~s** z

perseverative pə ˈsev ər‿ət ɪv ‖ pᵊr ˈsev ə reɪţ ɪv **~ly** li

persevere ˌpɜːs ɪ ˈvɪə -ə- ‖ ˌpɝːs ə ˈvɪᵊr **~d** d **~s** z **persevering/ly** ˌpɜːs ɪ ˈvɪər ɪŋ /li ˌ·ə- ‖ ˌpɝːs ə ˈvɪr ɪŋ /li

Pershing ˈpɜːʃ ɪŋ ‖ ˈpɝːʃ ɪŋ

Pershore ˈpɜː ʃɔː ‖ ˈpɝː ʃɔːr -ʃoʊr

Persi|a ˈpɜːʃ |ə ˈpɜːʒ- ‖ ˈpɝːʒ |ə **~an/s** ᵊn/z
ˌPersian ˈcat

persienne ˌpɜːs i ˈen ‖ ˌpɝːz- —*Fr* [pɛʁ sjɛn] **~s** z

persiflage ˈpɜːs ɪ flɑːʒ ˈpeəs-, -ə-, ˌ··ˈ· ‖ ˈpɝːs- ˈpers- —*Fr* [pɛʁ si flaːʒ]

Persil *tdmk* ˈpɜːs ɪl -ᵊl ‖ ˈpɝːs-

persimmon pə ˈsɪm ən pɜː- ‖ pᵊr- **~s** z

Persis ˈpɜːs ɪs §-əs ‖ ˈpɝːs-

persist pə ˈsɪst ‖ pᵊr- -ˈzɪst **~ed** ɪd əd **~ing** ɪŋ **~s** s

persistenc|e pə ˈsɪst ənᵗs ‖ pᵊr- -ˈzɪst- **~y** i

persistent pə ˈsɪst ənt ‖ pᵊr- -ˈzɪst- **~ly** li

persnickety pə ˈsnɪk ət i -ɪt- ‖ pᵊr ˈsnɪk əţ i

person ˈpɜːs ᵊn ‖ ˈpɝːs ᵊn **~s** z

person|a pə ˈsəʊn |ə pɜː- ‖ pᵊr ˈsoʊn |ə -ɑː **~ae** iː aɪ **~as** əz
ˌpersona ˈgrata ˈgrɑːt ə ˈgreɪt- ‖ ˈgrɑːţ ə ˈgræţ-, ˈgreɪţ-; **perˌsona ˌnon ˈgrata** nəʊn nɒn ‖ nɑːn noʊn

personable ˈpɜːs ᵊn‿əb ᵊl ‖ ˈpɝːs- **~leness** ᵊl nəs -nɪs

personag|e ˈpɜːs ᵊn ɪdʒ ‖ ˈpɝːs- **~es** ɪz əz

personal ˈpɜːs ᵊn‿əl ‖ ˈpɝːs- **~s** z
ˌpersonal asˈsistant; ˈpersonal ˌcolumn;

ˌpersonal comˈputer; **ˌpersonal eˈstate**; **ˌpersonal ˈpronoun**; **ˌpersonal ˈproperty**; **ˌpersonal ˈstereo**

personalis... —*see* **personaliz...**

personalit|y ˌpɜːs ə ˈnæl ət |i -ɪt i ‖ ˌpɜ˞ːs ə ˈnæl əṱ |i **~ies** iz
ˌpersoˈnality cult; **ˌpersoˈnality test**

personalization ˌpɜːs ᵊn‿əl aɪ ˈzeɪʃ ᵊn -ɪˈ-- ‖ ˌpɜ˞ːs ᵊn‿əl ə-

personaliz|e ˈpɜːs ᵊn‿ə laɪz -əl aɪz ‖ ˈpɜ˞ːs- **~ed** d **~es** ɪz əz **~ing** ɪŋ

personally ˈpɜːs ᵊn‿əl i ‖ ˈpɜ˞ːs-

perso|nate *v* ˈpɜːs ə |neɪt -ᵊ|n eɪt ‖ ˈpɜ˞ːs- **~nated** neɪt ɪd -əd ‖ neɪṱ əd **~nates** neɪts **~nating** neɪt ɪŋ ‖ neɪṱ ɪŋ

personation ˌpɜːs ə ˈneɪʃ ᵊn ‖ ˌpɜ˞ːs- **~s** z

personator ˈpɜːs ə neɪt ə →-ᵊn eɪt- ‖ ˈpɜ˞ːs ᵊn eɪṱ ᵊr **~s** z

personification pə ˌsɒn ɪf ɪ ˈkeɪʃ ᵊn pɜː-, -ˌ-ˌəf-, §-əˈ-- ‖ pᵊr ˌsɑːn- **~s** z

personi|fy pə ˈsɒn ɪ |faɪ pɜː-, -ə- ‖ pᵊr ˈsɑːn- **~fied** faɪd **~fier/s** faɪ‿ə/z ‖ faɪ‿ᵊr/z **~fies** faɪz **~fying** faɪ ɪŋ

personnel ˌpɜːs ə ˈnel -ᵊn ˈel ‖ ˌpɜ˞ːs-
ˌpersonˈnel ˌmanager

person-to-person ˌpɜːs ᵊn tə ˈpɜːs ᵊn ◂ -ᵊn tu- ‖ ˌpɜ˞ːs ᵊn tə ˈpɜ˞ːs ᵊn ◂

perspective pə ˈspekt ɪv ‖ pᵊr- **~ly** li **~s** z

perspex, P~ *tdmk* ˈpɜːsp eks ‖ ˈpɜ˞ːsp-

perspicacious ˌpɜːsp ɪ ˈkeɪʃ əs ◂ -ə- ‖ ˌpɜ˞ːsp- **~ly** li **~ness** nəs nɪs

perspicacity ˌpɜːsp ɪ ˈkæs ət i ˌ-ə-, -ɪt i ‖ ˌpɜ˞ːsp ə ˈkæs əṱ i

perspicuity ˌpɜːsp ɪ ˈkjuː‿ət i ˌ-ə-, ɪt i ‖ ˌpɜ˞ːsp ə ˈkjuː əṱ i

perspicuous pə ˈspɪk ju‿əs ‖ pᵊr- **~ly** li **~ness** nəs nɪs

perspiration ˌpɜːsp ə ˈreɪʃ ᵊn ‖ ˌpɜ˞ːsp-

perspiratory pə ˈspaɪ‿ər ət‿ər i -ˈspɪr-; ˈpɜːsp ər‿ə ·, ·ɪr- ‖ pᵊr ˈspaɪr ə tɔːr i ˈpɜ˞ːsp ər‿ə-, -toʊr i

perspire pə ˈspaɪ‿ə ‖ pᵊr ˈspaɪ‿ᵊr **~d** d **~s** z
perspiring pə ˈspaɪ‿ər ɪŋ ‖ pᵊr ˈspaɪ‿ᵊr ɪŋ

persuad|e pə ˈsweɪd ‖ pᵊr- **~ed** ɪd əd **~er/s** ə/z ‖ ᵊr/z **~es** z **~ing** ɪŋ

persuasion pə ˈsweɪʒ ᵊn ‖ pᵊr- **~s** z

persuasive pə ˈsweɪs ɪv -ˈsweɪz- ‖ pᵊr- **~ly** li **~ness** nəs nɪs

pert pɜːt ‖ pɜ˞ːt **perter** ˈpɜːt ə ‖ ˈpɜ˞ːṱ ᵊr **pertest** ˈpɜːt ɪst -əst ‖ ˈpɜ˞ːṱ əst

pertain pə ˈteɪn pɜː- ‖ pᵊr- **~ed** d **~ing** ɪŋ **~s** z

Perth pɜːθ ‖ pɜ˞ːθ

Perthite ˈpɜːθ aɪt ‖ ˈpɜ˞ːθ- **~s** s

Perthshire ˈpɜːθ ʃə -ʃɪə, -ˌʃaɪ‿ə ‖ ˈpɜ˞ːθ ʃᵊr -ʃɪr, -ˌʃaɪ‿ᵊr

pertinacious ˌpɜːt ɪ ˈneɪʃ əs ◂ -ə- ‖ ˌpɜ˞ːt ᵊn ˈeɪʃ əs **~ly** li **~ness** nəs nɪs

pertinacity ˌpɜːt ɪ ˈnæs ət i ˌ-ə-, -ɪt i ‖ ˌpɜ˞ːt ᵊn ˈæs əṱ i

pertinence ˈpɜːt ɪn ənᵗs -ən- ‖ ˈpɜ˞ːt ᵊn‿ənᵗs

pertinent ˈpɜːt ɪn ənt -ən- ‖ ˈpɜ˞ːt ᵊn‿ənt **~ly** li

pert|ly ˈpɜːt| li ‖ ˈpɜ˞ːt| li **~ness** nəs -nɪs

perturb pə ˈtɜːb pɜː ‖ pᵊr ˈtɜ˞ːb **~ed** d **~ing** ɪŋ **~s** z

perturbation ˌpɜːt ə ˈbeɪʃ ᵊn ˌpɜː tɜː- ‖ ˌpɜ˞ːṱ ᵊr- ˌpɜ˞ː tɜ˞ː- **~s** z

pertussis pə ˈtʌs ɪs §-əs ‖ pᵊr-

Pertwee ˈpɜːt wiː ‖ ˈpɜ˞ːt-

Peru pə ˈruː —*Sp* Perú [pe ˈɾu] **~'s** z

Perugia pə ˈruːdʒ ə pɪ-, pe-, -ˈruːdʒ i‿ə —*It* [pe ˈruː dʒa]

Perugino ˌper u ˈdʒiːn əʊ ‖ -oʊ —*It* [pe ru ˈdʒiː no]

peruke pə ˈruːk pe- **~s** s

perusal pə ˈruːz ᵊl pe- **~s** z

perus|e pə ˈruːz pe- **~ed** d **~es** ɪz əz **~ing** ɪŋ

Perutz pə ˈrʊts -ˈruːts —*Ger* [ˈpɛʁ ʊts]

Peruvian pə ˈruːv i‿ən pe- **~s** z

Peruzzi pə ˈruːts i —*It* [pe ˈrut tsi]

perv, perve pɜːv ‖ pɜ˞ːv **perved** pɜːvd ‖ pɜ˞ːvd **perves** pɜːvz ‖ pɜ˞ːvz **perving** ˈpɜːv ɪŋ ‖ ˈpɜ˞ːv ɪŋ

pervad|e pə ˈveɪd pɜː- ‖ pᵊr- **~ed** ɪd əd **~es** z **~ing** ɪŋ

pervasion pə ˈveɪʒ ᵊn ‖ pᵊr-

pervasive pə ˈveɪs ɪv pɜː-, -ˈveɪz- ‖ pᵊr- **~ly** li **~ness** nəs nɪs

perverse pə ˈvɜːs ‖ pᵊr ˈvɜ˞ːs **~ly** li **~ness** nəs nɪs

perversion pə ˈvɜːʃ ᵊn -ˈvɜːʒ- ‖ pᵊr ˈvɜ˞ːʒ ᵊn -ˈvɜ˞ːʃ- **~s** z

perversit|y pə ˈvɜːs ət |i -ɪt- ‖ pᵊr ˈvɜ˞ːs əṱ |i **~ies** iz

perversive pə ˈvɜːs ɪv ‖ pᵊr ˈvɜ˞ːs ɪv

per|vert *v* pə |ˈvɜːt ‖ pᵊr |ˈvɜ˞ːt **~verted** ˈvɜːt ɪd -əd ‖ ˈvɜ˞ːṱ əd **~verting** ˈvɜːt ɪŋ ‖ ˈvɜ˞ːṱ ɪŋ **~verts** ˈvɜːts ‖ ˈvɜ˞ːts

pervert *n* ˈpɜː vɜːt ‖ ˈpɜ˞ː vɜ˞ːt **~s** s

perverter pə ˈvɜːt ə ‖ pᵊr ˈvɜ˞ːṱ ᵊr **~s** z

pervious ˈpɜːv i‿əs ‖ ˈpɜ˞ːv- **~ness** nəs nɪs

Pery *(i)* ˈpeər i ‖ ˈper i ˈpær-, *(ii)* ˈpɪər i ‖ ˈpɪr i, *(iii)* ˈper i

Pesach ˈpeɪs ɑːk -ɑːx

Pescadores ˌpesk ə ˈdɔːr iːz ‖ -ˈdoʊr-

peseta pə ˈseɪt ə ‖ -ˈseɪṱ ə —*Sp* [pe ˈse ta] **~s** z

pesewa pe ˈsiː wə pɪ-, pə- **~s** z

Peshawar pə ˈʃɑː wə pe-, -ˈʃɔː- ‖ -wᵊr

pesk|y ˈpesk |i **~ier** i‿ə ‖ i‿ᵊr **~iest** i‿ɪst i‿əst **~ily** ɪ li əl i **~iness** i nəs i nɪs

peso ˈpeɪs əʊ ‖ -oʊ —*Sp* [ˈpe so] **~s** z

pessar|y ˈpes ər |i **~ies** iz

pessimism ˈpes ə ˌmɪz əm ˈpez-, -ɪ-

pessimist ˈpes əm ɪst ˈpez-, -ɪm-, §-əst **~s** s

pessimistic ˌpes ə ˈmɪst ɪk ◂ ˌpez-, -ɪ- **~ally** ᵊl‿i

pest pest **pests** pests

Pest *place in Hungary* pest peʃt —*Hung* [pɛʃt]

Pestalozzi ˌpest ə ˈlɒts i ‖ -ˈlɑːts i —*It* [pes ta ˈlɔt tsi]

pester ˈpest ə ‖ -ᵊr **~ed** d **pestering** ˈpest ər‿ɪŋ **~s** z

pesticide ˈpest ɪ saɪd -ə- **~s** z

pestiferous pes ˈtɪf ər‿əs **~ly** li

pestilenc|e ˈpest ɪl |ənᵗs -əl-, ⚠-jʊl- **~es** ɪz əz

pestilent ˈpest ɪl |ənt -əl-, ⚠-jʊl- **~ly** li

pestilential ˌpest ɪ ˈlenᵗʃ əl ◂ -ə-, →-əl ˈenᵗʃ- **~ly** i
pestl|e ˈpes əl ˈpest- **~ed** d **~es** z **~ing** ˌɪŋ
pesto ˈpest əʊ ‖ -oʊ —*It* [ˈpes to]
pet, PET pet **pets** pets **petted** ˈpet ɪd -əd ‖ ˈpeţ əd **petting** ˈpet ɪŋ ‖ ˈpeţ ɪŋ **ˈpet name,** ˌ· ˈ·; **ˈPET ˌscan(ner)**
Peta ˈpiːt ə ‖ ˈpiːţ ə
peta- ˈpet ə ‖ ˈpeţ ə
petaflop ˈpet ə flɒp ‖ ˈpeţ ə flɑːp **~s** s
Pétain ˈpet æ̃ ˈpeɪt- ‖ peɪ ˈtæ̃ —*Fr* [pe tɛ̃]
petal ˈpet əl ‖ ˈpeţ əl **~ed, ~led** d **~s** z
petanque, pétanque ˌpeɪ ˈtɒŋk ‖ -ˈtɑːŋk —*Fr* [pe tɑ̃k]
petard pe ˈtɑːd pɪ-, pə-; ˈpet ɑːd ‖ -ˈtɑːrd **~s** z
petasus ˈpet əs əs ‖ ˈpeţ- **~es** ɪz əz
Pete piːt
petechi|a pe ˈtiːk i|ə pɪ-, pə- **~ae** iː
Peter, peter ˈpiːt ə ‖ ˈpiːţ ər **~ed** d **petering** ˈpiːt ər ɪŋ ‖ ˈpiːţ ər ɪŋ **~s, ~'s** z **ˌPeter ˈPan**
Peterboro', Peterborough ˈpiːt ə bər ə -ˌbʌr ə ‖ ˈpiːţ ər ˌbɜː oʊ
Peterhead ˌpiːtə ˈhed ‖ ˌpiːţ ər-
Peterkin ˈpiːt ə kɪn ‖ ˈpiːţ ər-
Peterlee ˌpiːt ə ˈliː ˈ· · · ‖ ˌpiːţ ər-
Peterloo ˌpiːt ə ˈluː ◂ ‖ ˌpiːţ ər- **ˌPeterloo ˈmassacre**
peter|man ˈpiːt ə |mən -mæn ‖ ˈpiːţ ər- **~men** mən men
Peters ˈpiːt əz ‖ ˈpiːţ ərz
Petersburg ˈpiːt əz bɜːg ‖ ˈpiːţ ərz bɜːg
Petersfield ˈpiːt əz fiːəld ‖ ˈpiːţ ərz-
Petersham, p~ ˈpiːt əʃ əm ‖ ˈpiːţ ərʃ- ər ʃæm
Peterson ˈpiːt əs ən ‖ ˈpiːţ ərs ən
Petherick ˈpeθ ər ɪk
Pethick ˈpeθ ɪk
pethidine ˈpeθ ɪ diːn -ə-
petillant, pétillant ˈpet i ɒ̃ -ɪl ənt, §-əl- ‖ ˌpeɪţ i ˈjɑːn —*Fr* [pe ti jɑ̃]
petiole ˈpet i əʊl ˈpiːt-, →-ɒʊl ‖ ˈpeţ i oʊl **~s** z
petit ˈpet i pə ˈtiː ‖ ˈpeţ i —*Fr* [pə ti] **ˌpetit ˈbourgeois,** ˌ· · ˈ·; **ˌpetit ˌbourgeoiˈsie**; **ˌpetit ˈfour** fʊə fɔː ‖ fɔːr foʊr —*Fr* [fuʁ]; **ˌpetit ˈmal** mæl ‖ mɑːl mæl —*Fr* [mal]; **ˌpetit ˈpoint**; **ˌpetit(s) ˈpois** pwɑː —*Fr* [pwa]; **ˌpetit ˈpain** pæ̃ —*Fr* [pɛ̃]
petite pə ˈtiːt —*Fr* [pə tit]
petition pə ˈtɪʃ ən pɪ- **~ed** d **~ing** ˌɪŋ **~s** z
petitioner pə ˈtɪʃ ən ə pɪ- ‖ ər **~s** z
petitio principii pɪ ˌtɪʃ i əʊ prɪn ˈsɪp i aɪ pe-, pə-, -ˌtɪt-, -ˈkɪp-, -iː ‖ -ˌ· ·oʊ-
Peto ˈpiːt əʊ ‖ ˈpiːţ oʊ
Petofi, Petöfi ˈpet əf i -ɜːf i ‖ ˈpeţ əf i —*Hung* Petőfi [ˈpɛ tøː fi]
Petra ˈpetr ə ˈpiːtr-
Petrarch ˈpetr ɑːk ‖ -ɑːrk
Petrarchan pe ˈtrɑːk ən pɪ-, pə- ‖ -ˈtrɑːrk-
petrel ˈpetr əl *(= petrol)* **~s** z
Petri ˈpiːtr i ˈpetr i —*Ger* [ˈpeː tʁi]
Petrie ˈpiːtr i
petrifaction ˌpetr ɪ ˈfæk ʃən -ə-
petri|fy ˈpetr ɪ |faɪ -ə- **~fied** faɪd **~fies** faɪz **~fying** faɪ ɪŋ
Petrine ˈpiːtr aɪn
petro- *comb. form with stress-neutral suffix* ˈpetr əʊ ‖ -ə — **petrological** ˌpetr əʊ ˈlɒdʒ ɪk əl ◂ ‖ -ə ˈlɑːdʒ- *with stress-imposing suffix* pe ˈtrɒ+ pɪ-, pə- ‖ -ˈtrɑː+ — **petrography** pe ˈtrɒg rəf i pɪ-, pə- ‖ -ˈtrɑːg-
Petroc ˈpetr ɒk ‖ -ɑːk
petrochemical ˌpetr əʊ ˈkem ɪk əl ◂ ‖ ˌ·oʊ- **~s** z
petrodollar ˈpetr əʊ ˌdɒl ə ‖ -oʊ ˌdɑːl ər **~s** z
Petrofina *tdmk* ˌpetr əʊ ˈfiːn ə ‖ -oʊ-
petroglyph ˈpetr əʊ glɪf ‖ -ə- **~s** s
Petrograd ˈpetr ə græd —*Russ* [pʲɪ trʌ ˈgrat]
petrol ˈpetr əl **ˈpetrol ˌstation**; **ˈpetrol tank**
petrolatum ˌpetr ə ˈleɪt əm ‖ -ˈleɪţ əm -ˈlɑːţ-
petrol-bomb ˈpetr əl bɒm ‖ -bɑːm **~ed** d **~ing** ɪŋ **~s** z
petroleum pə ˈtrəʊl i əm pɪ- ‖ -ˈtroʊl- **peˌtroleum ˈjelly**
petrologist pə ˈtrɒl ədʒ ɪst pɪ-, pe-, §-əst ‖ -ˈtrɑːl- **~s** s
petrology pə ˈtrɒl ədʒ i pɪ-, pe- ‖ -ˈtrɑːl-
Petronas pe ˈtrəʊn æs pɪ-, pə-, -əs ‖ -ˈtroʊn-ɑːs
Petronella, p~ ˌpetr ə ˈnel ə
Petronius pɪ ˈtrəʊn i əs pə-, pe- ‖ -ˈtroʊn-
Petropavlovsk ˌpetr əʊ ˈpæv lɒfsk ‖ -ə ˈpæv lɔːfsk -lɑːfsk —*Russ* [pʲɪ trʌ ˈpav ləfsk]
Petruchio pɪ ˈtruːtʃ i əʊ pə-, pe-, -ˈtruːk- ‖ -oʊ
pe-tsai ˌpeɪt ˈsaɪ
petticoat ˈpet i kəʊt ‖ ˈpeţ i koʊt **~s** s **ˌPetticoat ˈLane**
Pettifer ˈpet ɪf ə -əf- ‖ ˈpeţ əf ər
pettifog ˈpet i fɒg ‖ ˈpeţ i fɔːg -fɑːg **~ged** d **~ger/s** ə/z ‖ ər/z **~gery** ər i **~ging** ɪŋ **~s** z
Pettigrew ˈpet i gruː ‖ ˈpeţ-
pettish ˈpet ɪʃ ‖ ˈpeţ ɪʃ **~ly** li **~ness** nəs nɪs
Pettit ˈpet ɪt §-ət ‖ ˈpeţ ət
pettitoes ˈpet i təʊz ‖ ˈpeţ i toʊz
Pettitt ˈpet ɪt §-ət ‖ ˈpeţ ət
pett|y, Petty ˈpet |i ‖ ˈpeţ |i **~ier** i ə ‖ i ər **~iest** i ɪst i əst **~ily** ɪ li əl i **~iness** i nəs i nɪs **ˌpetty ˈbourgeois,** ˌ· · ˈ·; **ˌpetty ˈcash**; **ˌpetty ˈlarceny**; **ˌpetty ˈofficer**◂
Petula pə ˈtjuːl ə pɪ-, pe-, →-ˈtʃuːl- ‖ -ˈtuːl ə -ˈtjuːl-
petulanc|e ˈpet jʊl ənᵗs ˈpetʃ əl- ‖ ˈpetʃ əl- **~y** i
petulant ˈpet jʊl ənt ˈpetʃ əl- ‖ ˈpetʃ əl- **~ly** li
Petulengro ˌpet ju ˈleŋ grəʊ -ə-, ˌpetʃ ə- ‖ ˌpetʃ ə ˈleŋ groʊ
petunia pə ˈtjuːn i ə pɪ-, pe-, →-ˈtʃuːn- ‖ pɪ ˈtuːn jə -ˈtjuːn- **~s** z
petuntse peɪ ˈtʊnts ə pɪ-, -ˈtʌnts-, -i —*Chi* báidūn zi [²pai ¹tuən ·tsɯ]
Petworth ˈpet wɜːθ -wəθ ‖ -wərθ
Peugeot *tdmk* ˈpɜːʒ əʊ ˈpjuːʒ-, ˈpjuːdʒ-, -ɒt ‖ pjuː ˈʒoʊ puː-, pɜː- —*Fr* [pø ʒo]

Pevensey 'pev ᵊnz i
Peveril 'pev ᵊr‿əl ɪl
Pevsner 'pevz nə ‖ -nᵊr
pew pjuː **pews** pjuːz
pewit 'piː wɪt ‖ 'pjuː ət **~s** s
Pewsey 'pjuːz i
pewter 'pjuːt ə ‖ 'pjuːṭ ᵊr
pewterer 'pjuːt ər ə ‖ 'pjuːṭ ər ᵊr **~s** z
peyote peɪ 'əʊt i pi- ‖ -'oʊṭ i —*Sp* [pe 'jo te]
Peyronie's 'per ən iz ‖ ˌper ə 'niːz —*Fr* [pɛ ʁɔ ni]
Peyton 'peɪt ᵊn
Pfeiffer 'faɪf ə 'pfaɪf ə ‖ -ᵊr
pfennig 'fen ɪg 'pfen-, -ɪk —*Ger* ['pfɛn ɪç] **~igs** ɪgz ɪks
Pfizer 'faɪz ə ‖ -ᵊr
PG ˌpiː 'dʒiː **~s, ~'s** z
PGA ˌpiː dʒiː 'eɪ
pH ˌpiː 'eɪtʃ §-'heɪtʃ
Phaeacian fi 'eɪʃ ᵊn **~s** z
Phaedo 'fiːd əʊ 'faɪd- ‖ -oʊ 'fed-
Phaedra 'fiːdr ə 'faɪdr- ‖ 'fedr ə
Phaedrus 'fiːdr əs 'faɪdr- ‖ 'fedr əs
phaen... —*see* **phen...**
Phaethon, Phaëthon 'feɪ əθ ᵊn -ɪθ- ‖ -ə θɑːn
phaeton 'feɪt ᵊn ‖ 'feɪ ət ᵊn **~s** z
phage feɪdʒ **phages** 'feɪdʒ ɪz -əz
phagocyte 'fæg əʊ saɪt ‖ -ə- **~s** s
phagocytosis ˌfæg əʊ saɪ 'təʊs ɪs §-əs ‖ -oʊ saɪ 'toʊs-
-phagous *stress-imposing* fəg əs — **saprophagous** sæ 'prɒf əg əs ‖ -'prɑːf-
-phagy *stress-imposing* fədʒ i — **geophagy** dʒi 'ɒf ədʒ i ‖ -'ɑːf-
Phaidon *tdmk* 'faɪd ᵊn
phalange 'fæl ændʒ fə 'lændʒ ‖ 'feɪl- **~es** ɪz əz
phalanger fə 'lændʒ ə ‖ -ᵊr **~s** z
Phalangist fə 'lændʒ ɪst fæ-, §-əst; 'fæl əndʒ- ‖ feɪ- **~s** s
phalanx 'fæl æŋks ‖ 'feɪl- 'fæl- **phalanges** fə 'lændʒ iːz fæ- ‖ feɪ-
phalaris 'fæl ər ɪs §-əs
phalarope 'fæl ə rəʊp ‖ -roʊp **~s** s
phalli 'fæl aɪ -iː
phallic 'fæl ɪk
phallocrat 'fæl əʊ kræt ‖ -ə- **~s** s
phallocratic ˌfæl əʊ 'kræt ɪk ◂ ‖ -ə 'kræṭ-
phallus 'fæl əs **~i** aɪ -iː **~uses** əs ɪz -əz
phanerogam 'fæn ər əʊ gæm fə 'ner- ‖ -ər ə- **~s** z
phanerogamic ˌfæn ər əʊ 'gæm ɪk ◂ ‖ -ə'--
phanerogamous ˌfæn ə 'rɒg əm əs ◂ ‖ -'rɑːg-
phanerozoic, P~ ˌfæn ər əʊ 'zəʊ ɪk ◂ ‖ -ə 'zoʊ-
phantasm 'fæn ˌtæz əm **~s** z
phantasmagoria ˌfænt æz mə 'gɒr i‿ə fæn ˌtæz-, -'gɔːr- ‖ fæn ˌtæz mə 'gɔːr i‿ə -'goʊr-
phantasmagoric ˌfænt æz mə 'gɒr ɪk ◂ fæn ˌtæz- ‖ fæn ˌtæz mə 'gɔːr ɪk ◂ -'gɑːr- **~al** ᵊl
phantasmal fæn 'tæz məl
phantasmic fæn 'tæz mɪk
phantasy 'fænt əs i ‖ 'fænṭ- **~ies** iz
phantom 'fænt əm ‖ 'fænṭ əm **~s** z
ˌ**phantom 'limb**
-phany *stress-imposing* fən i — **theophany** θi 'ɒf ən i ‖ -'ɑːf-
Pharaoh, p~ 'feər əʊ ‖ 'fer oʊ 'fær-; 'feɪ roʊ **~s** z
'**pharaoh ant**
Pharaonic ˌfeər eɪ 'ɒn ɪk ◂ feə 'rɒn- ‖ ˌfer eɪ 'ɑːn ɪk ◂ ˌfær-
pharisaic, P~ ˌfær ɪ 'seɪ ɪk ◂ -ə- ‖ˌfer- **~al** ᵊl **~ally** ᵊl‿i **~alness** ᵊl nəs -nɪs
Pharisaism 'fær ɪ seɪ ˌɪz əm '-ə- ‖ 'fer-
pharisee, P~ 'fær ɪ siː -ə- ‖ 'fer- **~s** z
pharma 'fɑːm ə ‖ 'fɑːrm ə
pharmaceutic ˌfɑːm ə 'suːt ɪk ◂ -'sjuːt-, -'kjuːt- ‖ ˌfɑːrm ə 'suːṭ ɪk ◂ **~al** ᵊl **~ally** ᵊl‿i **~s** s
pharmacist 'fɑːm əs ɪst §-əst ‖ 'fɑːrm- **~s** s
pharmaco- *comb. form with stress-neutral suffix* ¦fɑːm ə kəʊ ‖ ¦fɑːrm ə koʊ — **pharmacodynamic** ˌfɑːm ə kəʊ daɪ 'næm ɪk ◂ ‖ ˌfɑːrm ə koʊ- *with stress-imposing suffix* ˌfɑːm ə 'kɒ+ ‖ ˌfɑːrm ə 'kɑː+ — **pharmacognosy** ˌfɑːm ə 'kɒg nəs i ‖ ˌfɑːrm ə 'kɑːg-
pharmacological ˌfɑːm ə kə 'lɒdʒ ɪk ᵊl ◂ ‖ ˌfɑːrm ək ə 'lɑːdʒ- **~ly** ‿i
pharmacologist ˌfɑːm ə 'kɒl ədʒ ɪst §-əst ‖ ˌfɑːrm ə 'kɑːl- **~s** s
pharmacology ˌfɑːm ə 'kɒl ədʒ i ‖ ˌfɑːrm ə 'kɑːl-
pharmacopoeia, pharmacopeia ˌfɑːm ə kə 'piː‿ə -əʊ'-- ‖ ˌfɑːrm- **~al** əl **~as** əz
pharmacy 'fɑːm əs i ‖ 'fɑːrm- **~ies** iz
Pharos 'feər ɒs ‖ 'fer ɑːs 'fær-
Pharsalus fɑː 'seɪl əs ‖ fɑːr-
pharyngal fə 'rɪŋ gᵊl fæ- **~s** z
pharyngeal ˌfær ən 'dʒiː‿əl ◂ -ɪn-; fə 'rɪndʒ i‿əl, fæ- ‖ ˌfer- **~s** z
pharynges fæ 'rɪndʒ iːz fə-
pharyngitis ˌfær ən 'dʒaɪt ɪs -ɪn-, §-əs ‖ -'dʒaɪṭ əs ˌfer-
pharyngo- *comb. form with stress-neutral suffix* fə ¦rɪŋ gəʊ ‖ -gə — **pharyngoscope** fə 'rɪŋ gəʊ skəʊp ‖ -gə skoʊp *with stress-imposing suffix* ˌfær ɪŋ 'gɒ+ ‖ -'gɑː+ ˌfer- — **pharyngotomy** ˌfær ɪŋ 'gɒt əm i ‖ -'gɑːṭ- ˌfer-
pharynx 'fær ɪŋks ‖ 'fer- **~es** ɪz əz **pharynges** fæ 'rɪndʒ iːz fə-
phase feɪz **phased** feɪzd **phases** 'feɪz ɪz -əz **phasing** 'feɪz ɪŋ
phase-out 'feɪz aʊt **~s** s
phaser 'feɪz ə ‖ -ᵊr **~s** z
phasmid 'fæz mɪd §-məd **~s** z
phat fæt
phat-ass 'fæt æs ‖ 'fæṭ-
phatic 'fæt ɪk ‖ 'fæṭ ɪk
PhD ˌpiː eɪtʃ 'diː §-heɪtʃ- **~s, ~'s** z
pheasant 'fez ᵊnt **~s** s
Phebe, p~ 'fiːb i **~s, ~'s** z
Phebus 'fiːb əs

Phedo 'fiːd əʊ 'faɪd- ‖ -oʊ
Phedra 'fiːdr ə 'faɪdr-
Phedrus 'fiːdr əs 'faɪdr-
Pheidippides faɪ 'dɪp ɪ diːz -ə-
Phelan *(i)* 'fiːl ən, *(ii)* 'feɪl ən
phellem 'fel em -əm
Phelps felps
phenacetin fə 'næs ət ɪn fɪ-, fe-, -ɪt ɪn, §-ən
phenetic fə 'net ɪk fɪ- ‖ -'neţ- **~s** s
Phenicia fə 'nɪʃ ə fɪ-; -'nɪʃ i‿ə ‖ -'niːʃ-
Phenician fə 'nɪʃ ᵊn fɪ-; -'nɪʃ i‿ən ‖ -'niːʃ- **~s** z
phenobarbital ˌfiːn əʊ 'bɑːb ɪt ᵊl -ə ᵊl ‖ -oʊ 'bɑːrb ə tɔːl -tɑːl
phenobarbitone ˌfiːn əʊ 'bɑːb ɪ təʊn -'·ə- ‖ -oʊ 'bɑːrb ə toʊn
phenol 'fiːn ɒl ‖ -oʊl -ɔːl, -ɑːl **~s** z
phenolic fɪ 'nɒl ɪk §fə- ‖ -'noʊl- -'nɑːl-
phenolphthalein ˌfiːn ɒl 'θeɪl i‿ɪn ˌ·ᵊl-, -'θæl-, -'fθæl-, ən, -'·iːn ‖ ˌfiːn ᵊl 'θæl i ən
phenom fɪ 'nɒm fə- ‖ 'fiːn ɑːm fɪ 'nɑːm **~s** z
phenomena fə 'nɒm ɪn ə fɪ-, -ən- ‖ -'nɑːm-
phenomenal fə 'nɒm ɪn ᵊl fɪ-, -ən- ‖ -'nɑːm- **~ly** i
phenomenological fə ˌnɒm ɪn ə 'lɒdʒ ɪk ᵊl ◂ fɪ-, -ˌ·ən- ‖ -ˌnɑːm ən ə 'lɑːdʒ- **~ly** ˌi
phenomenology fə ˌnɒm ɪ 'nɒl ədʒ i fɪ-, -ˌ·ə- ‖ -ˌnɑːm ə 'nɑːl-
phenom|enon fə 'nɒm| ɪn ən fɪ-, -ən- ‖ -'nɑːm| ə nɑːn -ən ən **~ena** ən ə *(*)*
phenotype 'fiːn əʊ taɪp ‖ -ə- **~s** s
phenotypic ˌfiːn əʊ 'tɪp ɪk ◂ ‖ -ə- **~al** ᵊl **~ally** ᵊl‿i
Phensic *tdmk* 'fenᵗs ɪk 'fenz-
phenyl 'fiːn aɪᵊl 'fen-, -ᵊl, -ɪl ‖ 'fen ᵊl 'fiːn-
phenylalanine ˌfiːn ɪl 'æl ə niːn ˌfen-, ˌ·ᵊl-, ˌ·aɪᵊl- ‖ ˌfen ᵊl-
phenylketonuria ˌfiːn ɪl ˌkiːt əʊ 'njʊər i‿ə ˌfen-, ˌ·-ᵊl-, ˌ·aɪᵊl- ‖ ˌfen ᵊl ˌkiːţ oʊ 'nʊr i‿ə -ˌkiːt ᵊn 'ʊr-, -'jʊr-
pheromonal ˌfer ə 'məʊn ᵊl ◂ ‖ -'moʊn-
pheromone 'fer ə məʊn ‖ -moʊn **~s** z
phew fjuː —*and non-speech sounds such as* [ʍ, ʍu, ʍʊ, ɸ, pɸː]
phi faɪ **phis** faɪz
ˌ**Phi** ˌ**Beta** '**Kappa**
phial 'faɪ‿əl **~s** z
Phibbs fɪbz
Phidias 'fɪd i æs 'faɪd- ‖ -əs
Phidippides faɪ 'dɪp ɪ diːz -ə-
Phil fɪl
phil- *comb. form before vowel before unstressed syllable* ¦fɪl — **philatelic** ˌfɪl ə 'tel ɪk ◂ *before stressed syllable* fɪ 'l+ fə- ‖ fə 'l+ — **philately** fɪ 'læt əl i fə- ‖ fə 'læţ ᵊl i
-phil fɪl — **Francophil** 'fræŋk əʊ fɪl ‖ -oʊ- -ə-
Philadelphia ˌfɪl ə 'delf i‿ə
Philadelphian ˌfɪl ə 'delf i‿ən ◂ **~s** z
philadelphus ˌfɪl ə 'delf əs **~es** ɪz əz
philander fɪ 'lænd ə fə- ‖ -ᵊr **~ed** d
philandering fɪ 'lænd‿ər ɪŋ fə- **~s** z
philanderer fɪ 'lænd‿ər ə fə- ‖ -ᵊr **~s** z
philanthrope 'fɪl ən θrəʊp -æn- ‖ -θroʊp **~s** s
philanthropic ˌfɪl ən 'θrɒp ɪk ◂ -æn- ‖ -'θrɑːp- **~al** ᵊl **~ally** ᵊl‿i
philanthropist fɪ 'lænᵗθ rəp ɪst fə-, §-əst **~s** s
philanthrop|y fɪ 'lænᵗθ rəp |i fə- **~ies** iz
philatelic ˌfɪl ə 'tel ɪk ◂ **~ally** ᵊl‿i
philatelist fɪ 'læt əl ɪst fə-, §-əst ‖ fə 'læţ ᵊl əst **~s** s
philately fɪ 'læt əl i fə- ‖ fə 'læţ ᵊl i
Philbin 'fɪl bɪn
Philby 'fɪl bi
-phile faɪᵊl — **Anglophile** 'æŋ gləʊ faɪᵊl ‖ -ə-
Phileas 'fɪl i‿əs
Philemon fɪ 'liːm ɒn faɪ-, fə-, -mən ‖ -ən
Philharmonia ˌfɪl hɑː 'məʊn i‿ə ˌ·ɑː-, ˌ·ə- ‖ -hɑːr 'moʊn-
philharmonic ˌfɪl ɑː 'mɒn ɪk ◂ -ə-, -hɑː- ‖ -hɑːr 'mɑːn- -ᵊr- **~s** s
philhellene ˌfɪl 'hel iːn '·ˌ·· **~s** z
philhellenic ˌfɪl he 'liːn ɪk ◂ -hə-, -'len-
philhellenism ˌfɪl 'hel ə ˌnɪz əm -ɪ-
-philia 'fɪl i‿ə — **necrophilia** ˌnek rəʊ 'fɪl i‿ə ‖ ˌ·ə-
-philiac 'fɪl i æk — **coprophiliac** ˌkɒp rəʊ 'fɪl i æk ‖ ˌkɑːp rə-
-philic 'fɪl ɪk — **photophilic** ˌfəʊt əʊ 'fɪl ɪk ◂ ‖ ˌfoʊţ ə-
Philip 'fɪl ɪp §-əp
Philippa 'fɪl ɪp ə -əp-
Philippe fɪ 'liːp —*Fr* [fi lip]
Philippi fɪ 'lɪp aɪ fə-; 'fɪl ɪ paɪ, -ə-
Philippian fɪ 'lɪp i‿ən fə- **~s** z
philippic fɪ 'lɪp ɪk fə- **~s** s
Philippine 'fɪl ə piːn -ɪ-; ˌ··'· **~s** z
Philips 'fɪl ɪps §-əps
Philipson 'fɪl ɪps ən §-əps-
Philistia fɪ 'lɪst i‿ə fə-
philistine, P~ 'fɪl ɪ staɪn -ə- ‖ -stiːn fɪ 'lɪst ən, -iːn *(*)* **~s** z
philistinism 'fɪl ɪst ɪ ˌnɪz əm '·əst-, -əˌ·- ‖ 'fɪl ə stiː-
Phillip, Phillipp 'fɪl ɪp §-əp
Phillips 'fɪl ɪps §-əps
Phillis 'fɪl ɪs §-əs
Phillpot, Phillpott 'fɪl pɒt ‖ -pɑːt
phillumenist fɪ 'luːm ən ɪst fə-, -'ljuːm-, -ɪn-, §-əst **~s** s
phillumeny fɪ 'luːm ən i fə-, -'ljuːm-, -ɪn-
Philly 'fɪl i
philo- *comb. form*
with stress-neutral suffix ¦fɪl əʊ ‖ -ə — **philosophical** ˌfɪl əʊ 'sɒf ɪk ᵊl ◂ ‖ -ə 'sɑːf-
with stress-imposing suffix fɪ 'lɒ+ ‖ -'lɑː+ — **philogyny** fɪ 'lɒdʒ ən i fə-, -ɪn- ‖ -'lɑːdʒ-
Philo 'faɪl əʊ ‖ -oʊ
Philoctetes ˌfɪl ək 'tiːt iːz -ɒk-
philodendron, P~ ˌfɪl ə 'dendr ən **~s** z
philological ˌfɪl əʊ 'lɒdʒ ɪk ᵊl ◂ ‖ -ə 'lɑːdʒ- **~ly** ˌi
philologist fɪ 'lɒl ədʒ ɪst fə-, §-əst ‖ -'lɑːl- **~s** s
philology fɪ 'lɒl ədʒ i fə- ‖ -'lɑːl-
Philomel, p~ 'fɪl əʊ mel ‖ -ə- **~s** z
Philomela ˌfɪl əʊ 'miːl ə ‖ -ə-
Philomena ˌfɪl əʊ 'miːn ə ‖ -ə-

P

philoprogenitive ˌfɪl əʊ prəʊ ˈdʒen ət ɪv ◂ -ɪt ɪv ‖ -ə proʊ ˈdʒen əṭ ɪv **~ly** li **~ness** nəs nɪs

philosopher fə ˈlɒs əf ə fɪ- ‖ -ˈlɑːs əf ər **~s** z

phiˌlosopher's ˈstone

philosophic ˌfɪl ə ˈsɒf ɪk ◂ -ˈzɒf- ‖ -ˈsɑːf- -ˈzɑːf- **~al** əl ◂ **~ally** əl‿i

philosophis|e, philosophiz|e fə ˈlɒs ə faɪz fɪ- ‖ -ˈlɑːs- **~ed** d **~er/s** ə/z ‖ ər/z **~es** ɪz əz **~ing** ɪŋ

philosoph|y fə ˈlɒs əf |i fɪ- ‖ -ˈlɑːs- **~ies** iz

Philostratus fɪ ˈlɒs trət əs fə- ‖ -ˈlɑːs trəṭ əs

-philous *stress-imposing* fɪl əs -fəl- ‖ fəl əs — **acidophilous** ˌæs ɪ ˈdɒf ɪl əs ◂ §ˌ-ə-, -əl əs ‖ ˌæs ə ˈdɑːf əl əs ◂

Philp fɪlp

Philpot ˈfɪl pɒt ‖ -pɑːt

Philpotts ˈfɪl pɒts ‖ -pɑːts

philter, philtre ˈfɪlt ə ‖ -ər *(= filter)* **~s** z

phimosis faɪ ˈməʊs ɪs §-əs ‖ -ˈmoʊs əs

Phineas ˈfɪn i‿əs -æs

Phipps fɪps

phish fɪʃ **phishing** ˈfɪʃ ɪŋ

phiz, Phiz fɪz *(= fizz)*

Phizackerley fɪ ˈzæk əl i fə- ‖ -ər li

phizog ˈfɪz ɒg ‖ -ɑːg

phlebitic flɪ ˈbɪt ɪk flə- ‖ -ˈbɪṭ-

phlebitis flɪ ˈbaɪt ɪs flə-, §-əs ‖ -ˈbaɪṭ əs

phlebotom|y flɪ ˈbɒt əm |i flə- ‖ -ˈbɑːṭ- **~ies** iz **~ist/s** ɪst/s §əst/s

Phlegethon ˈfleg ɪθ ən -əθ-; -ɪ θɒn, -ə- ‖ -ə θɑːn

phlegm flem

phlegmatic fleg ˈmæt ɪk ‖ -ˈmæṭ ɪk **~ally** əl‿i

phlegmy ˈflem i

phloem ˈfləʊ ɪm -em, §-əm ‖ ˈfloʊ em

phlogistic flɒ ˈdʒɪst ɪk ‖ floʊ-

phlogiston flɒ ˈdʒɪst ən -ɒn ‖ floʊ- -ɑːn

phlox flɒks ‖ flɑːks *(= flocks)* **phloxes** ˈflɒks ɪz -əz ‖ ˈflɑːks əz

Phnom Penh ˌnɒm ˈpen ˌpnɒm-, pə ˌnɒm ˈpen ‖ ˌnɑːm- —*Khmer* [pʰnɔm ˈpɨɲ]

-phobe fəʊb ‖ foʊb — **Anglophobe** ˈæŋ gləʊ fəʊb ‖ -glə foʊb

phobia ˈfəʊb i‿ə ‖ ˈfoʊb i‿ə **~s** z

-phobia ˈfəʊb i‿ə ‖ ˈfoʊb i‿ə — **Francophobia** ˌfræŋ kəʊ ˈfəʊb i‿ə ‖ -ə ˈfoʊb-

phobic ˈfəʊb ɪk ‖ ˈfoʊb ɪk **~ally** əl‿i **~s** s

-phobic ˈfəʊb ɪk ‖ ˈfoʊb ɪk — **Russophobic** ˌrʌs əʊ ˈfəʊb ɪk ◂ ‖ -ə ˈfoʊb-

Phobos ˈfəʊb ɒs ‖ ˈfoʊb ɑːs

Phocaea fəʊ ˈsiː‿ə ‖ foʊ-

Phocian ˈfəʊʃ i‿ən ˈfəʊs- ‖ ˈfoʊʃ- **~s** z

phocine ˈfəʊs aɪn ‖ ˈfoʊs-

Phocion ˈfəʊs i‿ən ‖ ˈfoʊʃ i‿ən -ɑːn

Phocis ˈfəʊs ɪs §-əs ‖ ˈfoʊs-

phocomelia ˌfəʊk əʊ ˈmiːl i‿ə ‖ ˌfoʊk oʊ-

phocomely fəʊ ˈkɒm əl i -ɪl- ‖ foʊ ˈkɑːm-

Phoebe, p~ ˈfiːb i **~s, ~'s** z

Phoebus ˈfiːb əs

Phoenicia fə ˈnɪʃ ə fɪ-; -ˈnɪʃ i‿ə ‖ -ˈniːʃ-

Phoenician fə ˈnɪʃ ən fɪ-; -ˈnɪʃ i‿ən ‖ -ˈniːʃ- **~s** z

phoenix, P~ ˈfiːn ɪks **~es, ~'s** ɪz əz **~like** laɪk

phon fɒn ‖ fɑːn **phons** fɒnz ‖ fɑːnz

phon- *comb. form*
before vowel before unstressed syllable ¦fəʊn- ¦fɒn- ‖ ¦foʊn — **phoniatric** ˌfəʊn i ˈætr ɪk ◂ ˌfɒn- ‖ ˌfoʊn-
before stressed syllable fəʊ ˈn+ ‖ foʊ ˈn+ — **phonendoscope** fəʊ ˈnend ə skəʊp ‖ foʊ ˈnend ə skoʊp

phonaesthesia ˌfəʊn iːs ˈθiːz i‿ə ˌ·ɪs-, ˌ·əs-, -ˈθiːʒ- ‖ ˌfoʊn əs ˈθiːʒ ə

phon|ate fəʊ ˈn|eɪt ‖ ˈfoʊn |eɪt **~ated** eɪt ɪd -əd ‖ eɪṭ əd **~ates** eɪts **~ating** eɪt ɪŋ ‖ eɪṭ ɪŋ

phonation fəʊ ˈneɪʃ ən ‖ foʊ-

phoˈnation type

phonatory fəʊ ˈneɪt ər i ˈfəʊn ət‿ər i ‖ ˈfoʊn ə tɔːr i -toʊr i

phone fəʊn ‖ foʊn **phoned** fəʊnd ‖ foʊnd **phones** fəʊnz ‖ foʊnz **phoning** ˈfəʊn ɪŋ ‖ ˈfoʊn ɪŋ

ˈphone book; **ˈphone box**; **ˈphone call**

-phone fəʊn ‖ foʊn — **anglophone** ˈæŋ gləʊ fəʊn ‖ -ə foʊn

phonecard, P~ ˈfəʊn kɑːd →ˈfəʊŋ- ‖ ˈfoʊn kɑːrd **~s** z

phone-in ˈfəʊn ɪn ‖ ˈfoʊn- **~s** z

phonematic ˌfəʊn ɪ ˈmæt ɪk ◂ -iː-, -ə- ‖ ˌfoʊn ə ˈmæṭ ɪk ◂

phoneme ˈfəʊn iːm ‖ ˈfoʊn- **~s** z

phonemic fəʊ ˈniːm ɪk ‖ fə- foʊ- **~ally** əl‿i **~s** s

phonemicis... —*see* **phonemiciz...**

phonemicist fəʊ ˈniːm ɪs ɪst -əs-, §-əst ‖ fə- foʊ- **~s** s

phonemicization fəʊ ˌniːm ɪs aɪ ˈzeɪʃ ən -ˌəs-, -ɪˈ-- ‖ fə ˌniːm əs ə- foʊ- **~s** z

phonemiciz|e fəʊ ˈniːm ɪ saɪz -ə- ‖ fə- foʊ- **~ed** d **~es** ɪz əz **~ing** ɪŋ

phonesthesia ˌfəʊn iːs ˈθiːz i‿ə ˌ·ɪs-, ˌ·əs-, -ˈθiːʒ- ‖ ˌfoʊn əs ˈθiːʒ ə

phone-tapping ˈfəʊn ˌtæp ɪŋ ‖ ˈfoʊn- **~s** z

phonetic fə ˈnet ɪk fəʊ- ‖ -ˈneṭ ɪk **~ally** əl‿i **~s** s

phoˌnetic ˈsymbol

Phonetica fəʊ ˈnet ɪk ə ‖ fə ˈneṭ-

phonetician ˌfəʊn ɪ ˈtɪʃ ən ˌfɒn-, -ə- ‖ ˌfoʊn- ˌfɑːn- **~s** z

phoneticis... —*see* **phoneticiz...**

phoneticization fəʊ ˌnet ɪs aɪ ˈzeɪʃ ən -ˌəs- ‖ foʊ ˌneṭ əs ə- fə-

phoneticiz|e fəʊ ˈnet ɪ saɪz -ə- ‖ foʊ ˈneṭ- fə- **~ed** d **~es** ɪz əz **~ing** ɪŋ

phon|ey, phon|y ˈfəʊn |i ‖ ˈfoʊn |i **~eyness, ~iness** i nəs i nɪs **~eys, ~ies** iz **~ier** i‿ə ‖ i‿ər **~iest** i‿ɪst i‿əst **~ily** ɪ li əl i

ˌphoney ˈwar

phoniatric ˌfəʊn i ˈætr ɪk ◂ ˌfɒn- ‖ ˌfoʊn- ˌfɑːn- **~s** s

phonic ˈfɒn ɪk ˈfəʊn- ‖ ˈfɑːn ɪk ˈfoʊn- **~s** s

phono- *comb. form*
with stress-neutral suffix ¦fəʊn əʊ ¦fɒn- ‖ ¦foʊn ə — **phonoscope** ˈfəʊn əʊ skəʊp ˈfɒn- ‖ ˈfoʊn ə skoʊp
with stress-imposing suffix fəʊ ˈnɒ+ ‖ fə ˈnɑː+ foʊ- — **phonometer** fəʊ ˈnɒm ɪt ə -ət- ‖ fə ˈnɑːm əṭ ər foʊ-

P

phonogram ˈfəʊn ə ɡræm ‖ ˈfoʊn- **~s** z
phonograph ˈfəʊn ə ɡrɑːf -ɡræf ‖ ˈfoʊn ə ɡræf **~s** s
phonographic ˌfəʊn ə ˈɡræf ɪk ◂ ‖ ˌfoʊn- **~ally** əl‿i
phonological ˌfəʊn ə ˈlɒdʒ ɪk əl ◂ ˌfɒn-, -əl ˈɒdʒ- ‖ ˌfoʊn əl ˈɑːdʒ- ˌfɑːn- **~ly** ‿i
phonologist fəʊ ˈnɒl ədʒ ɪst §-əst ‖ fə ˈnɑːl- foʊ- **~s** s
phonolog|y fəʊ ˈnɒl ədʒ |i ‖ fə ˈnɑːl- foʊ- **~ies** iz
phonotactic ˌfəʊn əʊ ˈtækt ɪk ◂ ˌfɒn- ‖ ˌfoʊn- ˌfɑːn- **~ally** əl‿i **~s** s
-phonous *stress-imposing* fən əs — **homophonous** hə ˈmɒf ən əs hɒ- ‖ hə ˈmɑːf-
phon|y ˈfəʊn |i ‖ ˈfoʊn |i **~iness** i nəs i nɪs **~ies** iz **~ier** i‿ə ‖ i‿ər **~iest** i‿ɪst i‿əst **~ily** ɪ li əl i
-phony *stress-imposing* fən i — **cacophony** kæ ˈkɒf ən i ‖ -ˈkɑːf-
phooey ˈfuː‿i
-phore fɔː ‖ fɔːr foʊr — **anthophore** ˈæntθ əʊ fɔː ‖ -ə fɔːr -foʊr
-phoresis fə ˈriːs ɪs §-əs — **electrophoresis** ɪ ˌlek trəʊ fə ˈriːs ɪs ə-, §-əs ‖ -ˌ·trə-
phormium ˈfɔːm i‿əm ‖ ˈfɔːrm-
-phorous *stress-imposing* fər əs — **anthophorous** æn ˈθɒf ər əs ‖ -ˈθɑːf-
phosgene ˈfɒz dʒiːn ˈfɒs- ‖ ˈfɑːz-
phosphatas|e ˈfɒs fə teɪz -teɪs ‖ ˈfɑːs- **~es** ɪz əz
phosphate ˈfɒs feɪt ‖ ˈfɑːs- **~s** s
phosphatic ₍ˌ₎fɒs ˈfæt ɪk ‖ ₍ˌ₎fɑːs ˈfæt̬ ɪk -ˈfeɪt̬-
phosphene ˈfɒs fiːn ‖ ˈfɑːs- **~s** z
phosphide ˈfɒs faɪd ‖ ˈfɑːs- **~s** z
phosphite ˈfɒs faɪt ˈfɑːs- **~s** s
phospho- *comb. form*
with stress-neutral suffix ¦fɒs fəʊ ‖ ¦fɑːs foʊ — **phospholipid** ˌfɒs fəʊ ˈlɪp ɪd §-əd ‖ ˌfɑːs foʊ- **~s** z
phosphor ˈfɒs fə ‖ ˈfɑːs fər -fɔːr **~s** z
phosphoresc|e ˌfɒs fə ˈres ‖ ˌfɑːs- **~ed** t **~es** ɪz əz **~ing** ɪŋ
phosphorescence ˌfɒs fə ˈres ənts ‖ ˌfɑːs-
phosphorescent ˌfɒs fə ˈres ənt ◂ ‖ ˌfɑːs- **~ly** li
phosphoric ₍ˌ₎fɒs ˈfɒr ɪk ‖ ₍ˌ₎fɑːs ˈfɔːr ɪk -ˈfɑːr-
phosphorous ˈfɒs fər‿əs ‖ ˈfɑːs-
phosphorus, P~ ˈfɒs fər‿əs ‖ ˈfɑːs-
phosphory|late fɒs ˈfɒr ə |leɪt ˈfɒs fər-, -ɪ- ‖ fɑːs ˈfɔːr- -ˈfɑːr- **~lated** leɪt ɪd -əd ‖ leɪt̬ əd **~lates** leɪts **~lating** leɪt ɪŋ ‖ leɪt̬ ɪŋ
phosphorylation fɒs ˌfɒr ə ˈleɪʃ ən ˌ· · ·ˈ· ·, ˌ·fər-, -ɪˈ·- ‖ fɑːs ˌfɔːr- -ˌfɑːr-, ˌ· · ·ˈ· ·
phossy ˈfɒs i ‖ ˈfɑːs i
photic ˈfəʊt ɪk ‖ ˈfoʊt̬ ɪk
photo ˈfəʊt əʊ ‖ ˈfoʊt̬ oʊ **~s** z
ˈphoto call; **ˌphoto ˈfinish**; **ˈphoto op, ˈphoto opporˌtunity**
photo- *comb. form*
with stress-neutral suffix ¦fəʊt əʊ ‖ ¦foʊt̬ oʊ — **photomicrograph** ˌfəʊt əʊ ˈmaɪk rəʊ ɡrɑːf -ɡræf ‖ ˌfoʊt̬ oʊ ˈmaɪk rə ɡræf
with stress-imposing suffix fəʊ ˈtɒ+ ‖ foʊ ˈtɑː+ — **photometry** fəʊ ˈtɒm ətr i -ɪtr- ‖ foʊ ˈtɑːm-
photocell ˈfəʊt əʊ sel ‖ ˈfoʊt̬ oʊ- **~s** z
photochemical ˌfəʊt əʊ ˈkem ɪk əl ◂ ‖ ˌfoʊt̬ oʊ- **~ly** ‿i
photochromic ˌfəʊt əʊ ˈkrəʊm ɪk ◂ ‖ ˌfoʊt̬ oʊ ˈkroʊm ɪk ◂ **~s** s
photocomposition ˌfəʊt əʊ ˌkɒmp ə ˈzɪʃ ən ‖ ˌfoʊt̬ oʊ ˌkɑːmp-
photocopier ˈfəʊt əʊ ˌkɒp i‿ə ˌ·ˈ· · · ‖ ˈfoʊt̬ oʊ ˌkɑːp i‿ər ·ə- **~s** z
photocop|y *n, v* ˈfəʊt əʊ ˌkɒp |i ˌ·ˈ· · ‖ ˈfoʊt̬ oʊ ˌkɑːp |i -ə- **~ied** id **~ies** iz **~ying** i ɪŋ
photoelectric ˌfəʊt əʊ ɪ ˈlek trɪk ◂ -əˈ·- ‖ ˌfoʊt̬ oʊ- **~ally** əl‿i
ˌphotoeˌlectric ˈcell
Photofit *tdmk* ˈfəʊt əʊ fɪt ‖ ˈfoʊt̬ oʊ-
photoflood ˈfəʊt əʊ flʌd ‖ ˈfoʊt̬ oʊ- **~s** z
photogenic ˌfəʊt əʊ ˈdʒen ɪk ◂ -ˈdʒiːn- ‖ ˌfoʊt̬ ə- **~ally** əl‿i
photogrammetr|ist ˌfəʊt əʊ ˈɡræm ətr |ɪst -ɪtr-, §-əst ‖ ˌfoʊt̬ oʊ- **~ists** ɪsts §əsts **~y** i
photograph *n, v* ˈfəʊt ə ɡrɑːf -ɡræf ‖ ˈfoʊt̬ ə ɡræf **~ed** t **~ing** ɪŋ **~s** s
photographer fə ˈtɒɡ rəf ə ‖ -ˈtɑːɡ rəf ər **~s** z
photographic ˌfəʊt ə ˈɡræf ɪk ◂ ‖ ˌfoʊt̬ ə- **~ally** əl‿i
ˌphotoˌgraphic ˈmemory
photography fə ˈtɒɡ rəf i ‖ -ˈtɑːɡ-
photogravure ˌfəʊt əʊ ɡrə ˈvjʊə ‖ ˌfoʊt̬ ə ɡrə ˈvjʊər **~s** z
photojournalism ˌfəʊt əʊ ˈdʒɜːn əl ˌɪz əm ˈ· ˌ· ˌ· · · ‖ ˌfoʊt̬ oʊ ˈdʒɝːn-
photokinesis ˌfəʊt əʊ kaɪ ˈniːs ɪs -kɪˈ·-, §-əs ‖ ˌfoʊt̬ oʊ-
photolitho ˌfəʊt əʊ ˈlaɪθ əʊ ‖ ˌfoʊt̬ oʊ ˈlɪθ oʊ
photolithography ˌfəʊt əʊ lɪ ˈθɒɡ rəf i -laɪˈ·-, §-ləˈ·- ‖ ˌfoʊt̬ oʊ lɪ ˈθɑːɡ-
photometer fəʊ ˈtɒm ɪt ə §-ət- ‖ foʊ ˈtɑːm ət̬ ər **~s** z
photomontag|e ˌfəʊt əʊ mɒn ˈtɑːʒ ‖ ˌfoʊt̬ oʊ mɑːn- ˌ·ə- **~es** ɪz əz
photon ˈfəʊt ɒn ‖ ˈfoʊt ɑːn **~s** z
photonasty ˈfəʊt əʊ ˌnæst i ‖ ˈfoʊt̬ oʊ-
photophobia ˌfəʊt əʊ ˈfəʊb i‿ə ‖ ˌfoʊt̬ ə ˈfoʊb-
photo-reconnaissance ˌfəʊt əʊ ri ˈkɒn ɪs ənts -rəˈ·-, -ˈ·əs- ‖ ˌfoʊt̬ oʊ ri ˈkɑːn əz ənts -ˈ·əs-
photosensitis... —*see* **photosensitiz...**
photosensitive ˌfəʊt əʊ ˈsents ət ɪv ◂ -ɪt ɪv ‖ ˌfoʊt̬ oʊ ˈsents ət̬ ɪv ◂
photosensitivity ˌfəʊt əʊ ˌsents ə ˈtɪv ət i -ɪˈ·-, -ɪt i ‖ ˌfoʊt̬ oʊ ˌsents ə ˈtɪv ət̬ i
photosensitization ˌfəʊt əʊ ˌsents ət aɪ ˈzeɪʃ ən -ˌ·ɪt-, -ɪˈ·- ‖ ˌfoʊt̬ oʊ ˌsents ət̬ ə-
photosensitiz|e ˌfəʊt əʊ ˈsents ə taɪz -ˈ·ɪ- ‖ ˌfoʊt̬ oʊ- **~ed** d **~es** ɪz əz **~ing** ɪŋ

Phoneme and allophone

1 A **phoneme** is one of the basic distinctive units in the phonetics of a language. The actual speech sounds which represent it are its **allophones**. Phonemes have the power of distinguishing words in the language (e.g. p and b, as in **pit** pɪt and **bit** bɪt); allophones, as such, do not (e.g. clear and dark varieties of l).

2 Each language has its own phonemic system and its own rules for determining the allophones appropriate to the phonemes in various phonetic environments. In English, for example, the phoneme p comprises both aspirated and unaspirated allophones (see ASPIRATION). In some other languages, e.g. Hindi, aspirated and unaspirated plosives represent distinct phonemes. English ʃ varies according to its surroundings (see COARTICULATION). The phoneme iː comprises both clipped and unclipped allophones (see CLIPPING).

3 The allophones of a phoneme are phonetically similar to one another. More importantly, their distribution is either **complementary** (= predictable by rule from the context) or else **random** (= in free variation). When it is important to distinguish phonemic transcription from allophonic or impressionistic transcription, it is usual to enclose the former in slants / /, the latter in square brackets [ ].

4 The phonetic notation in this dictionary is phonemic, with the following minor exceptions:

- The symbols i, u are employed to reflect the NEUTRALIZATION of /iː - ɪ/ and /uː - ʊ/ in certain positions.
- For AmE, the allophone [ţ] of /t/ is symbolized explicitly.
- The optional allophone [oʊ] of /əʊ/ (BrE) is symbolized explicitly.
- For some speakers (not of RP), ʌ and ə are not in contrast.
- Italic and raised symbols show the possibility of omission or insertion of a sound.
- The marks ‿, ◂, §, ⚠ are added.

photoset 'fəʊt əʊ set ‖ 'foʊţ oʊ- **~s** s
photosphere 'fəʊt əʊ sfɪə ‖ 'foʊţ oʊ sfɪr
photostat, P~ *tdmk* 'fəʊt əʊ stæt ‖ 'foʊţ ə- **~ed, ~ted** ɪd əd **~ing, ~ting** ɪŋ **~s** s
photostatic ˌfəʊt əʊ 'stæt ɪk ◂ ‖ ˌfoʊţ ə 'stæţ ɪk ◂ **~ally** ᵊl‿i
photosynthesis ˌfəʊt əʊ 'sɪnᵗθ əs ɪs -ɪs ɪs, §-əs ‖ ˌfoʊţ oʊ-
photosynthesis|e, photosynthesiz|e ˌfəʊt əʊ 'sɪnᵗθ ə saɪz -'·ɪ- ‖ ˌfoʊţ oʊ- **~ed** d **~es** ɪz əz **~ing** ɪŋ
photosynthetic ˌfəʊt əʊ sɪn 'θet ɪk ◂ ‖ ˌfoʊţ oʊ sɪn 'θeţ ɪk ◂ **~ally** ᵊl‿i
phototropic ˌfəʊt əʊ 'trɒp ɪk ◂ -'troʊp- ‖ ˌfoʊţ ə 'trɑːp ɪk ◂ -'troʊp- **~ally** ᵊl‿i
phototropism ˌfəʊt əʊ 'trəʊp ˌɪz əm fəʊ 'tɒtr ə ˌpɪz- ‖ foʊ 'tɑːtr ə ˌpɪz əm ˌfoʊţ oʊ 'troʊp ˌɪz-
phototypesett|er ˌfəʊt əʊ 'taɪp ˌset| ə '·ˌ·ˌ·· ‖ ˌfoʊţ oʊ 'taɪp seţ| ᵊr **~ers** əz ‖ ᵊrz **~ing** ɪŋ
photovoltaic ˌfəʊt əʊ vɒl 'teɪ ɪk ◂ ‖ ˌfoʊţ oʊ vɑːl- -voʊl'·-
phrasal 'freɪz ᵊl **~ly** i
ˌ**phrasal 'verb**
phrase freɪz *(= frays)* **phrased** freɪzd **phrases** 'freɪz ɪz -əz **phrasing/s** 'freɪz ɪŋ/z
'phrase ˌmarker
phrasebook 'freɪz bʊk §-buːk **~s** s
phraseological ˌfreɪz i‿ə 'lɒdʒ ɪk ᵊl ◂ ‖ -'lɑːdʒ- **~ly** ‿i
phraseolog|y ˌfreɪz i 'ɒl ədʒ |i ‖ -'ɑːl- **~ies** iz
phrase-structure 'freɪz ˌstrʌk tʃə ˌ·'· · ‖ -tʃᵊr
phratr|y 'freɪtr |i **~ies** iz
phreatic fri 'æt ɪk ‖ -'æţ-
phrenetic frə 'net ɪk frɪ-, fre- ‖ -'neţ ɪk **~al** ᵊl **~ally** ᵊl‿i

phrenic ˈfren ɪk
phrenological ˌfren ə ˈlɒdʒ ɪk ᵊl ◂ ‖ -ˈlɑːdʒ-
phrenolog|ist frə ˈnɒl ədʒ |ɪst frɪ-, fre-, §-əst ‖ -ˈnɑːl- **~ists** ɪsts §əsts **~y** i
Phrygi|a ˈfrɪdʒ i‿|ə **~an/s** ən/z
Phryne ˈfraɪn i
phthalein ˈθeɪl i‿ɪn ˈθæl-, ˈfθæl-, ən; ˈ·iːn ‖ ˈθæl i‿ən ˈθeɪl-, ˈ·iːn
phthalic ˈθæl ɪk ˈfθæl-, ˈθeɪl-
phthisis ˈθaɪs ɪs ˈtaɪs-, ˈfθaɪs-, §-əs
Phuket ˌpuː ˈket —*Thai* [ˈphuː ˀˈked]
phut, phutt fʌt
phwoar *BrE interjection* fwɔː —*or various non-speech vocalizations such as* [ɸuɔɑ]
phyco- *comb. form*
with stress-neutral suffix ¦faɪk əʊ ‖ -oʊ — **phycomycetous** ˌfaɪk əʊ maɪ ˈsiːt əs ◂ ‖ -oʊ maɪ ˈsiːt̬-
with stress-imposing suffix faɪ ˈkɒ+ ‖ -ˈkɑː+ — **phycology** faɪ ˈkɒl ədʒ i ‖ -ˈkɑːl-
Phyfe faɪf
phyla ˈfaɪl ə
phylacter|y fɪ ˈlækt ər |i **~ies** iz
phyletic faɪ ˈlet ɪk ‖ -ˈlet̬- **~ally** ᵊl i
Phyllida ˈfɪl ɪd ə -əd-
Phyllis ˈfɪl ɪs §-əs
phyllo ˈfiːl əʊ ‖ ˈfiːl oʊ
phyllo- *comb. form with stress-neutral suffix* ¦fɪl əʊ ‖ -ə — **phyllotaxis** ˌfɪl əʊ ˈtæks ɪs §-əs ‖ -ə-
Phyllosan *tdmk* ˈfɪl əʊ sæn ‖ -oʊ-
-phyllous ˈfɪl əs — **monophyllous** ˌmɒn əʊ ˈfɪl əs ◂ ‖ ˌmɑːn ə-
phylloxera fɪ ˈlɒks ər ə ˌfɪl ɒk ˈsɪər ə ‖ ˌfɪl ɑːk ˈsɪr ə fɪ ˈlɑːks ər ə
phylo- *comb. form*
with stress-neutral suffix ¦faɪl əʊ ‖ -oʊ — **phylogenetic** ˌfaɪl əʊ dʒə ˈnet ɪk ◂ -dʒɪˈ-- ‖ ˌfaɪl oʊ dʒə ˈnet̬ ɪk ◂
with stress-imposing suffix faɪ ˈlɒ+ ‖ -ˈlɑː+ — **phylogeny** faɪ ˈlɒdʒ ən i -ɪn- ‖ -ˈlɑːdʒ-
phylogen|y faɪ ˈlɒdʒ ən| i -ɪn- ‖ -ˈlɑːdʒ- **~ies** iz
phyl|um ˈfaɪl |əm **~a** ə
physalis faɪ ˈseɪl ɪs §-əs; ˈfaɪs əl-
Phys. Ed. ˌfɪz ˈed
physiatrist ˌfɪz i ˈætr ɪst §-əst
physic ˈfɪz ɪk **~ked** t **~king** ɪŋ **~s** s
physical ˈfɪz ɪk ᵊl **~ly** ‿i **~s** z
ˌphysical ˌeduˈcation; **ˌphysical ˈjerks**; **ˌphysical ˈtraining**
physicality ˌfɪz ɪ ˈkæl ət i ˌ·ə- ‖ -ət̬ i
physician fɪ ˈzɪʃ ᵊn fə- **~s** z
physicist ˈfɪz ɪs ɪst -əs-, §-əst **~s** s
physics ˈfɪz ɪks
physio ˈfɪz i əʊ ‖ -oʊ **~s** z
physio- *comb. form*
with stress-neutral suffix ¦fɪz i əʊ ‖ -oʊ -ə — **physiocrat** ˈfɪz i əʊ kræt ‖ -i oʊ- i‿ə-
with stress-imposing suffix ˌfɪz i ˈɒ+ ‖ -ˈɑː+ — **physiography** ˌfɪz i ˈɒg rəf i ‖ -ˈɑːg-
physiognomic ˌfɪz i‿ə ˈnɒm ɪk ◂ ‖ -ˈnɑːm- **~ally** ᵊl‿i
physiognom|y ˌfɪz i ˈɒn əm |i -ˈɒg nəm- ‖ -ˈɑːg nəm |i -ˈɑːn əm- **~ies** iz **~ist/s** ɪst/s §-əst/s
physiological ˌfɪz i‿ə ˈlɒdʒ ɪk ᵊl ◂ ‖ -ˈlɑːdʒ- **~ly** i
physiologist ˌfɪz i ˈɒl ədʒ ɪst §-əst ‖ -ˈɑːl- **~s** s
physiology ˌfɪz i ˈɒl ədʒ i ‖ -ˈɑːl-
physiotherapist ˌfɪz i‿əʊ ˈθer əp ɪst §-əst ‖ ˌ· ·oʊ- **~s** s
physiotherapy ˌfɪz i‿əʊ ˈθer əp i ‖ ˌ· ·oʊ-
physique fɪ ˈziːk fə- **~s** s
physostigmine ˌfaɪs əʊ ˈstɪg miːn ‖ -ə-
-phyte faɪt — **epiphyte** ˈep i faɪt
Phythian ˈfɪð i‿ən
phyto- *comb. form*
with stress-neutral suffix ¦faɪt əʊ ‖ ¦faɪt̬ oʊ — **phytopathology** ˌfaɪt əʊ pə ˈθɒl ədʒ i -pæˈ-- ‖ ˌfaɪt̬ oʊ pə ˈθɑːl-
with stress-imposing suffix faɪ ˈtɒ+ ‖ -ˈtɑː+ — **phytography** faɪ ˈtɒg rəf i ‖ -ˈtɑːg-
pi paɪ **pis** paɪz
Piacenza ˌpiːˌə ˈtʃents ə —*It* [pja ˈtʃen tsa]
Piaf ˈpiː æf ‖ piː ˈɑːf —*Fr* [pjaf]
piaff|e pi ˈæf **~ed** t **~ing** ɪŋ **~s** s
piaffer pi ˈæf ə ‖ -ᵊr **~s** z
Piaget pi ˈæʒ eɪ -ˈɑːʒ- ‖ ˌpiː ə ˈʒeɪ -ɑː- —*Fr* [pja ʒɛ]
Piagetian ˌpiːˌə ˈʒet i‿ən ◂ ˌ·ɑː-; -ˈʒeɪ ən ‖ -ˈʒeɪ ən **~s** z
pia mater ˌpaɪˌə ˈmeɪt ə ˌpiːˌ ‖ -ˈmeɪt̬ ᵊr ˌpiː ə ˈmɑːt̬ ᵊr, ˈ· ·ˌ· ·
pianissimo ˌpiːˌə ˈnɪs ɪ məʊ ˌ·ɑː-, -ə · ‖ -moʊ **~s** z
pianist ˈpiːˌən ɪst ˈpjɑːn ɪst, pi ˈæn ɪst, §-əst ‖ pi ˈæn əst ˈpiː ən- **~s** s
piano *adv; adj; n '(passage played) softly'* ˈpjɑːn əʊ pi ˈɑːn əʊ ‖ pi ˈɑːn oʊ **~s** z
piano *n 'instrument'* pi ˈæn əʊ -ˈɑːn-; ˈpjæn əʊ, ˈpjɑːn- ‖ -oʊ **~s** z
piˌano acˈcordion; **piˌano duˈet**; **piˈano ˌwire**
pianoforte pi ˌæn əʊ ˈfɔːt i -ˌɑːn-, -eɪ; -ˈfɔːt; ˌpjæn əʊˈ--, ˌpjɑːn- ‖ -oʊ ˈfɔːrt eɪ -ˈfoʊrt-, -i; -ˈ·ə fɔːrt, -foʊrt **~s** z
pianola, P~ *tdmk* ˌpiːˌə ˈnəʊl ə -æ-; pɪəˈ· · ‖ -ˈnoʊl- **~s** z
piassava ˌpiːˌə ˈsɑːv ə
piaster, piastre pi ˈæst ə -ˈɑːst- ‖ -ᵊr **~s** z
piazza pi ˈæts ə -ˈɑːts-, -ˈædz- ‖ -ˈɑːz ə -ˈæz- (*) —*It* [ˈpjat tsa] **~s** z
pibroch ˈpiːb rɒk -rɒx, -rɒʃ ‖ -rɑːk —*ScG* piobaireachd [ˈpiːb rɔxk] **~s** s
pic pɪk **pics** pɪks
pica ˈpaɪk ə **~s** z
picador ˈpɪk ə dɔː ‖ -dɔːr **~s** z
Picard ˈpɪk ɑːd ‖ piː ˈkɑːrd —*Fr* [pi kaːʁ]
Picardy ˈpɪk əd i ‖ -ᵊrd i —*Fr* Picardie [pi kaʁ di]
picaresque ˌpɪk ə ˈresk ◂
picaroon ˌpɪk ə ˈruːn **~s** z
Picasso pɪ ˈkæs əʊ -ˈkɑːs- ‖ -ˈkɑːs oʊ —*Sp* [pi ˈka so]
picayune ˌpɪk ə ˈjuːn ◂ -eɪ-, -i-, -i ˈuːn **~s** z

Phrasal verbs

1 Like other PHRASEs, a **phrasal verb** (= a verb consisting of two words, a verb word and an adverbial **particle**) is typically pronounced with late stress. So the particle has greater stress than the verb word itself.

ˌlook ˈdown
ˌtalk ˈover
Don't ˌlook ˈdown!
We must ˌtalk things ˈover.

2 A **prepositional verb** (= a verb consisting of a verb word and a prepositional particle), on the other hand, is in most cases pronounced with early stress. So the verb word has greater stress than the preposition.

ˈlook at
ˈtalk to
What are you ˈlooking at?
I ˌwant to ˈtalk to you.

3 If the preposition of a prepositional verb is **stranded** (= has no following noun or pronoun), it is pronounced in its strong form, even though unstressed.

ˌWhat are you ˈlooking [æt]**?**
compare **ˌLook** [ət] **ˈthat!**

4 Exceptionally, if the two parts of a phrasal verb are **separated** by a **noun** (not a pronoun), the main stress goes on the noun, not on the particle.

ˌpick ˈup
It'll be ˌpicked ˈup.
ˌPick it ˈup!
but **ˌPick your ˈbooks up!**
ˌtake ˈoff
The ˌplane ˌtook ˈoff.
but **She ˌtook her ˈshoes off.**

5 Some phrasal verbs have two particles, one adverbial and one prepositional. The first is stressed, the second unstressed.

He ˌlooked ˈdown on her.
(How do you) **ˌput ˈup with it?**
(I want) **to ˌfind ˈout about it.**

Piccadilly ˌpɪk ə ˈdɪl i ◂
 ˌPiccaˌdilly ˈCircus
piccalilli ˌpɪk ə ˈlɪl i ˈ· · · ·
piccaninn|y ˌpɪk ə ˈnɪn |i ˈ· · · · **~ies** iz
piccolo ˈpɪk ə ləʊ ‖ -loʊ **~s** z
pice paɪs
pichiciago ˌpɪtʃ i si ˈeɪg əʊ ˌ·ə-, -ˈɑːg- ‖ -oʊ **~s** z
pichiciego ˌpɪtʃ i si ˈeɪg əʊ ˌ·ə- ‖ -oʊ **~s** z
pick, Pick pɪk **picked** pɪkt **picking** ˈpɪk ɪŋ **picks** pɪks
pickaback ˈpɪk ə bæk

pickan... —*see* **piccan...**
pick-and-mix ˌpɪk ən ˈmɪks →-əm-
pickax, pickax|e ˈpɪk æks **~ed** t **~es** ɪz əz **~ing** ɪŋ
picker ˈpɪk ə ‖ -ᵊr **~s** z
pickerel ˈpɪk ᵊr‿əl **~s** z
Pickering ˈpɪk ər‿ɪŋ
picker-up ˌpɪk ər ˈʌp ‖ -ᵊr-
pick|et ˈpɪk |ɪt §-ət ‖ -|ət **~eted** ɪt ɪd §ət-, -əd ‖ ət̬ əd **~eting** ɪt ɪŋ §ət- ‖ ət̬ ɪŋ **~ets** ɪts §əts ‖ əts
ˈpicket line
Pickett ˈpɪk ɪt §-ət
Pickford ˈpɪk fəd ‖ -fᵊrd
pickings ˈpɪk ɪŋz
pickl|e ˈpɪk ᵊl **~ed** d **~es** z **~ing** ‿ɪŋ
Pickles ˈpɪk ᵊlz
picklock ˈpɪk lɒk ‖ -lɑːk **~s** s
pick-me-up ˈpɪk mi ʌp **~s** s
pickpocket ˈpɪk ˌpɒk ɪt §-ət ‖ -ˌpɑːk ət **~s** s
Pickthorne ˈpɪk θɔːn ‖ -θɔːrn
pick-up ˈpɪk ʌp **~s** s
Pickup *family name* ˈpɪk ʌp
Pickwick ˈpɪk wɪk
ˌPickwick ˈPapers ‖ ˈ. . ˌ. .
Pickwickian ₍ˌ₎pɪk ˈwɪk i‿ən
pick|y ˈpɪk |i **~ier** i‿ə ‖ i‿ᵊr **~iest** i‿ɪst i‿əst **~iness** i nəs i nɪs
picnic ˈpɪk nɪk **~ked** t **~king** ɪŋ **~s** s
picnicker ˈpɪk nɪk ə ‖ -ᵊr **~s** z
pico- ˈpiːk əʊ ˈpaɪk- ‖ -oʊ — **picofarad** ˈpiːk əʊ ˌfær əd ˈpaɪk-, -æd ‖ -oʊ- -ˌfer-
picot ˈpiːk əʊ pɪ ˈkəʊ ‖ -oʊ piː ˈkoʊ —*Fr* [pi ko]
picotee ˌpɪk ə ˈtiː **~s** z
picrate ˈpɪk reɪt **~s** s
picric ˈpɪk rɪk
Pict pɪkt **Picts** pɪkts
Pictish ˈpɪkt ɪʃ
pictogram ˈpɪkt əʊ græm ‖ -ə- **~s** z
pictograph ˈpɪkt əʊ grɑːf -græf ‖ -ə græf **~s** s
pictographic ˌpɪkt əʊ ˈgræf ɪk ◂ ‖ -ə- **~ally** ᵊl‿i
pictography pɪk ˈtɒg rəf i ‖ -ˈtɑːg-
Picton ˈpɪkt ən
Pictor ˈpɪkt ə ‖ -ᵊr
pictorial pɪk ˈtɔːr i‿əl ‖ -ˈtoʊr- **~ly** i
Pictoris pɪk ˈtɔːr ɪs §-əs ‖ -ˈtoʊr-
pic|ture ˈpɪk |tʃə -ʃə; ⚠ˈpɪ|tʃ ə ‖ ˈpɪk |tʃᵊr **~tured** tʃəd ʃəd ‖ tʃᵊrd **~tures** tʃəz ʃəz ‖ tʃᵊrz **~turing** tʃər ɪŋ ʃər‿ɪŋ
ˈpicture book; **ˈpicture frame**; **ˌpicture ˈpostcard**; **ˈpicture rail**
picture-perfect ˌpɪk tʃə ˈpɜːf ɪkt ◂ -ʃə-, -ekt, §-əkt ‖ -tʃᵊr ˈpɜːf-
picturesque ˌpɪk tʃə ˈresk ◂ -ʃə- **~ly** li **~ness** nəs nɪs
piddl|e ˈpɪd ᵊl **~ed** d **~es** z **~ing** ‿ɪŋ
piddock ˈpɪd ək **~s** s
Pidgeon ˈpɪdʒ ən
pidgin, P~ ˈpɪdʒ ɪn -ən **~s** z
ˌPidgin ˈEnglish
pidginis... —*see* **pidginiz...**
pidginization ˌpɪdʒ ɪn aɪ ˈzeɪʃ ᵊn ˌ-ən-, -ɪˈ-- ‖ -ən ə-
pidginize ˈpɪdʒ ɪ naɪz -ə-
pie paɪ **pies** paɪz
ˈpie chart
piebald ˈpaɪ bɔːld ‖ -bɑːld **~s** z
piece piːs *(= peace) —but in Fr phrases also* pi ˈes, pɪəs —*Fr* pièce [pjɛs] **pieced** piːst **pieces** ˈpiːs ɪz -əz **piecing** ˈpiːs ɪŋ —*see also phrases with this word*
ˌpiece of ˈcake; **ˌpieces of ˈeight**; **ˌpiece of ˈwork**; **ˈpiece rate**
piece de resistance, pièce de résistance pi ˌes də re ˈzɪst ɒ̃s -rɪˈ--, -rəˈ--, -riːˈ--; ˌpɪəs· ·ˈ·-; -ənᵗs; -ˌrez i ˈstɒ̃s ‖ pi ˌes də rɪ ˌziː ˈstɑːnᵗs —*Fr* [pjɛs də re zis tɑ̃ːs, pjɛz-]
piecemeal ˈpiːs miːᵊl
piecework ˈpiːs wɜːk ‖ -wɜːk
piecrust ˈpaɪ krʌst **~s** s
pied paɪd
ˌPied ˈPiper
pied-a-terre, pied-à-terre pi ˌeɪd ɑː ˈteə ˌpiː ed-, -əˈ· ‖ -ˈteᵊr —*Fr* [pje ta tɛːʁ] **pieds-~** pi ˌeɪd -ˌeɪdz; ˌpiː ed, ˌpiː edz —*Fr as in sing.*
Piedmont, p~ ˈpiːd mɒnt ‖ -mɑːnt
Piedmontese ˌpiːd mən ˈtiːz ◂ -mɒn- ‖ -mɑːn- -ˈtiːs
pie-eyed ˌpaɪ ˈaɪd ◂
pie|man ˈpaɪ| mən **~men** mən men
pier pɪə ‖ pɪᵊr *(= peer)* **piers** pɪəz ‖ pɪᵊrz
ˈpier glass
pierce, P~ pɪəs ‖ pɪᵊrs **pierced** pɪəst ‖ pɪᵊrst **pierces** ˈpɪəs ɪz -əz ‖ ˈpɪrs əz **piercing/ly** ˈpɪəs ɪŋ /li ‖ ˈpɪrs ɪŋ /li
Piercy ˈpɪəs i ‖ ˈpɪrs i
Pierian paɪ ˈɪər i‿ən pi-, -ˈer- ‖ -ˈɪr-
pieris ˈpaɪ‿ər ɪs paɪ ˈɪər-, §-əs
Pierre *place in SD* pɪə ‖ pɪᵊr
Pierre *personal name* pi ˈeə ˈpiː eə ‖ -ˈeᵊr —*Fr* [pjɛːʁ]
pierrot, P~ ˈpɪər əʊ ‖ ˈpiː ə roʊ ˌ· ·ˈ· —*Fr* [pjɛ ʁo] **~s** z
Piers pɪəz ‖ pɪᵊrz
pie-shaped ˈpaɪ ʃeɪpt
Piesporter ˈpiːz pɔːt ə ‖ -pɔːrt̬ ᵊr —*Ger* [ˈpiːs pɔʁt ɐ]
pieta, pietà ˌpiː e ˈtɑː -eɪ-, ˈ· · · ‖ -eɪ- —*It* [pje ˈta]
Pietermaritzburg ˌpiːt ə ˈmær ɪts bɜːg §-ˈəts- ‖ ˌpiːt̬ ᵊr ˈmær əts bɜːg -ˈmer-
pietism, P~ ˈpaɪ‿ə ˌtɪz əm -ɪ-
pietist, P~ ˈpaɪ‿ət ɪst -əst ‖ -ət̬- **~s** s
pietistic ˌpaɪ‿ə ˈtɪst ɪk ◂
piet|y ˈpaɪ‿ət |i -ɪt- ‖ -ət̬ |i **~ies** iz
piezo- *comb. form*
with stress-neutral suffix |piːz əʊ paɪ |iːz əʊ, pi |ets əʊ, |paɪ ɪ zəʊ ‖ pi |eɪz oʊ -|eɪts- — **piezochemistry** ˌpiːz əʊ ˈkem ɪst ri paɪ ˌiːz əʊˈ--, pi ˌets-, ˌpaɪ ɪ zəʊ-, -ˈəst- ‖ pi ˌeɪz oʊ- -ˌeɪts-
with stress-imposing suffix ˌpiː‿ə ˈzɒ + ˌpaɪ-, -ɪ-

‖ ˌpiː ə ˈzɑː+ ˌpaɪ-, -eɪ- — **piezometry** ˌpiː‿ə ˈzɒm ətr i ˌpaɪ-, ˌ·ɪ-, -ɪtr i ‖ -ˈzɑːm- ˌ·eɪ-
piezoelectric ˌpiːz əʊ ɪ ˈlek trɪk ◂ ˌpiːts-; paɪ ˌiːz əʊ ɪ'-, pi ˌets-, ˌpaɪ ɪ zəʊ ɪ'◂ ‖ pi ˌeɪz oʊ-ˌeɪts-
ˌpiezoeˌlectric ˈcrystal ‖ **piˌezo-**
Pifco *tdmk* ˈpɪf kəʊ ‖ -koʊ
piffl|e ˈpɪf ᵊl **~ed** d **~es** z **~ing** ‿ɪŋ
pig pɪg **pigged** pɪgd **pigging** ˈpɪg ɪŋ **pigs** pɪgz
ˈpig ˌiron; **ˈpig ˌLatin**
pigeon ˈpɪdʒ ən -ɪn **~s** z
pigeon-chested ˌpɪdʒ ən ˈtʃest ɪd ◂ -ɪn-, -əd ‖ ˈ·ˌ·ˌ·
pigeonhol|e ˈpɪdʒ ən həʊl -ɪn-, →-hɒʊl ‖ -hoʊl **~ed** d **~es** z **~ing** ɪŋ
pigeon-toed ˈpɪdʒ ən təʊd ˌ· ·ˈ· ‖ -toʊd
pigger|y ˈpɪg ər |i **~ies** iz
piggi... —*see* **piggy**
piggish ˈpɪg ɪʃ **~ly** li **~ness** nəs nɪs
Piggott ˈpɪg ət
pigg|y ˈpɪg |i **~ier** i‿ə ‖ i‿ᵊr **~ies** iz **~iest** i ɪst i‿əst
piggyback ˈpɪg i bæk **~ed** t **~ing** ɪŋ **~s** s
piggybank ˈpɪg i bæŋk **~s** s
pigheaded ˌpɪg ˈhed ɪd ◂ -əd **~ly** li **~ness** nəs nɪs
piglet ˈpɪg lət -lɪt **~s** s
pigmeat ˈpɪg miːt
pig|ment *v* pɪg ˈ|ment ˈpɪg |mənt **~mented** ment ɪd mənt-, -əd ‖ menţ əd mənţ- **~menting** ment ɪŋ mənt- ‖ menţ ɪŋ mənţ- **~ments** ments
pigment *n* ˈpɪg mənt **~s** s
pigmentation ˌpɪg men ˈteɪʃ ᵊn -mən- **~s** z
pig|my, Pig|my ˈpɪg |mi **~mies** miz
pignut ˈpɪg nʌt **~s** s
Pigott ˈpɪg ət
pigpen ˈpɪg pen **~s** z
pigskin ˈpɪg skɪn
pigsticking ˈpɪg ˌstɪk ɪŋ
pig|sty ˈpɪg |staɪ **~sties** staɪz
pigswill ˈpɪg swɪl
pigtail ˈpɪg teɪᵊl **~ed** d **~s** z
pigwash ˈpɪg wɒʃ ‖ -wɔːʃ -wɑːʃ
pigweed ˈpɪg wiːd
pika ˈpaɪk ə ˈpiːk- **~s** z
pike, Pike paɪk **piked** paɪkt **pikes, Pike's** paɪks **piking** ˈpaɪk ɪŋ
ˌPike's ˈPeak
pikelet ˈpaɪk lət -lɪt **~s** s
pike|man ˈpaɪk |mən **~men** mən men
pikeperch ˈpaɪk pɜːtʃ ‖ -pɜ˞ːtʃ **~es** ɪz əz
piker ˈpaɪk ə ‖ -ᵊr **~s** z
pikestaff ˈpaɪk stɑːf §-stæf ‖ -stæf **~s** s
pikey ˈpaɪk i **~s** z
pilaf, pilaff ˈpiːl æf ˈpɪl- ‖ pɪ ˈlɑːf ˈpiːl ɑːf **~s** s
pilaster pɪ ˈlæst ə pə- ‖ -ᵊr ˈpaɪl æst- **~ed** d **~s** z
Pilate ˈpaɪl ət
Pilates pɪ ˈlɑːt iːz pə-
Pilatus pɪ ˈlɑːt əs pə- —*Ger* [pi ˈlaː tʊs]
pilau ˈpiːl aʊ ˈpɪl-; pɪ ˈlaʊ, pə- ‖ pɪ ˈloʊ -ˈlɔː, -ˈlɑː, -ˈlaʊ **~s** z
pilchard ˈpɪltʃ əd ‖ -ᵊrd **~s** z
pile paɪᵊl **piled** paɪᵊld **piles** paɪᵊlz **piling** ˈpaɪᵊl ɪŋ
pilea ˈpɪl i‿ə ˈpaɪl- **~s** z
pileated ˈpaɪl i eɪt ɪd ˈpɪl-, -əd ‖ ˈpɪl i eɪţ- ˈpaɪl-
pile-driver ˈpaɪᵊl ˌdraɪv ə ‖ -ᵊr **~s** z
pile|um ˈpaɪl i‿|əm **~a** ə
pileup ˈpaɪᵊl ʌp **~s** s
pile|us ˈpaɪl i‿|əs **~i** aɪ iː
pilfer ˈpɪlf ə ‖ -ᵊr **~ed** d **pilfering** ˈpɪlf ər‿ɪŋ **~s** z
pilferage ˈpɪlf ər‿ɪdʒ
pilferer ˈpɪlf ər ə ‖ -ᵊr ər **~s** z
pilgrim, P~ ˈpɪl grɪm -grəm **~s, ~'s** z
ˌPilgrim ˈFathers
pilgrimag|e ˈpɪl grɪm ɪdʒ -grəm- **~es** ɪz əz
Pilipino ˌpɪl ɪ ˈpiːn əʊ -ə- ‖ -oʊ
Pilkington ˈpɪlk ɪŋ tən
pill pɪl **pilled** pɪld **pilling** ˈpɪl ɪŋ **pills** pɪlz
pillag|e ˈpɪl ɪdʒ **~ed** d **~es** ɪz əz **~ing** ɪŋ
pillager ˈpɪl ɪdʒ ə ‖ -ᵊr **~s** z
pillar ˈpɪl ə ‖ -ᵊr **~ed** d **~s** z
ˈpillar box; **ˌpillar box ˈred◂**
pillbox ˈpɪl bɒks ‖ -bɑːks **~es** ɪz əz
Pilley ˈpɪl i
Pilling ˈpɪl ɪŋ
pillion ˈpɪl jən ˈpɪl i‿ən **~s** z
pilliwinks ˈpɪl ɪ wɪŋks §-ə-
pillock ˈpɪl ək **~s** s
pillor|y ˈpɪl ər |i **~ied** id **~ies** iz **~ying** i ɪŋ
pillow ˈpɪl əʊ ‖ -oʊ **~ed** d **~ing** ɪŋ **~s** z
ˈpillow slip; **ˈpillow talk**
pillowcas|e ˈpɪl əʊ keɪs ‖ -ə- -oʊ- **~es** ɪz əz
Pillsbury ˈpɪlz bər‿i ‖ -ˌber i
pillwort ˈpɪl wɜːt §-wɔːt ‖ -wɜ˞ːt -wɔːrt
pilocarpine ˌpaɪl əʊ ˈkɑːp iːn -aɪn, -ɪn ‖ -oʊ ˈkɑːrp-
pilonidal ˌpaɪl əʊ ˈnaɪd ᵊl ◂ ‖ -ə-
pil|ot ˈpaɪl |ət **~oted** ət ɪd -əd ‖ əţ əd **~oting** ət ɪŋ ‖ əţ ɪŋ **~ots** əts
ˈpilot ˌburner; **ˈpilot lamp**; **ˈpilot light**; **ˈpilot ˌofficer**
pilotage ˈpaɪl ət ɪdʒ ‖ -əţ-
Pilsen ˈpɪlz ən ˈpɪls- —*Ger* [ˈpɪl zᵊn], *Czech* Plzeň [ˈpᵊl zeɲ]
pilsener, pilsner, P~ ˈpɪlz nə ˈpɪls-, ˈ·ən ə ‖ -nᵊr **~s** z
Pilsudski pɪl ˈsʊd ski —*Polish* Piłsudski [piw ˈsut ski]
Piltdown ˈpɪlt daʊn
Pilton ˈpɪlt ən
pilule ˈpɪl juːl **~s** z
Pima ˈpiːm ə **~s** z
Piman ˈpiːm ən
pimento pɪ ˈment əʊ pə- ‖ -ˈmenţ oʊ **~s** z
pimiento ˌpɪm i ˈent əʊ pɪm ˈjent-; pɪ ˈment-, pə- ‖ pəm ˈjenţ oʊ pə ˈmenţ- **~s** z
Pimlico ˈpɪm lɪ kəʊ -lə- ‖ -koʊ
Pimm pɪm **Pimm's** pɪmz

pimp pɪmp **pimped** pɪmp*t* **pimping** 'pɪmp ɪŋ **pimps** pɪmp*s*
pimpernel 'pɪmp ə nel -nᵊl ‖ -ᵊr- **~s** z
pimple 'pɪmp ᵊl **~d** d **~s** z
pimp|ly 'pɪmp |li **~liness** li nəs -nɪs
pimpmobile 'pɪmp məʊ ˌbiːl ‖ -mə- -moʊ- **~s** z
pin, PIN pɪn **pinned** pɪnd **pinning** 'pɪn ɪŋ **pins** pɪnz
'pin ˌmoney; **'PIN ˌnumber**; **ˌpins and 'needles**
pina colada, piña colada ˌpiːn ə kəʊ 'lɑːd ə ˌ-jə- ‖ -jə kə- -ə kə- —*Sp* [ˌpi ɲa ko 'la ða] **~s** z
pinafore 'pɪn ə fɔː ‖ -fɔːr -foʊr **~s** z
pinata, piñata piːn 'jɑːt ə pɪn- ‖ -'jɑːt̬ ə —*Sp* [pi 'ɲa ta] **~s** z
Pinatubo ˌpɪn ə 'tuːb əʊ ‖ ˌpiːn ə 'tuːb oʊ
pinball 'pɪn bɔːl →'pɪm- ‖ -bɑːl **~s** z
pince-nez *sing.* ˌpænᵗs 'neɪ ˌpɪnᵗs-, -'nez —*Fr* [pɛ̃s ne] **~** *pl* z
pincer 'pɪnᵗs ə ‖ -ᵊr **~s** z
'pincer ˌmovement
pincerlike 'pɪnᵗs ə laɪk ‖ -ᵊr-
pinch pɪn*t*ʃ **pinched** pɪn*t*ʃt **pinches** 'pɪn*t*ʃ ɪz -əz **pinching** 'pɪn*t*ʃ ɪŋ
pinchbeck, P~ 'pɪn*t*ʃ bek
Pincher 'pɪn*t*ʃ ə ‖ -ᵊr
pinch-|hit ˌpɪn*t*ʃ |'hɪt **~hits** 'hɪts **~hitter/s** 'hɪt ə/z ‖ 'hɪt̬ ᵊr/z **~hitting** 'hɪt ɪŋ ‖ 'hɪt̬ ɪŋ
pinchpenn|y 'pɪn*t*ʃ ˌpen |i **~ies** iz
Pinckney 'pɪŋk ni
Pincus 'pɪŋk əs
pincushion 'pɪn ˌkʊʃ ᵊn →'pɪŋ- **~s** z
Pindar 'pɪnd ə -ɑː ‖ -ᵊr -ɑːr
Pindaric (ˌ)pɪn 'dær ɪk ‖ -'der-
pindown 'pɪn daʊn
Pindus 'pɪnd əs
pine, Pine paɪn **pined** paɪnd **pines** paɪnz **pining** 'paɪn ɪŋ
'pine cone; **'pine ˌkernel**; **'pine ˌmarten**; **'pine ˌneedle**
pineal 'pɪn i‿əl (ˌ)paɪ 'niː‿əl
'pineal gland
pineapple 'paɪn æp ᵊl -ˌ· · **~s** z
'pineapple juice
pinene 'paɪn iːn
Pinero pɪ 'nɪər əʊ pə-, -'neər- ‖ -'nɪr oʊ -'ner-
pinetree 'paɪn triː **~s** z
pinet|um paɪ 'niːt |əm ‖ -'niːt̬ |əm **~a** ə
pinewood, P~ 'paɪn wʊd **~s** z
piney 'paɪn i
pinfall 'pɪn fɔːl ‖ -fɑːl **~s** z
Pinfold 'pɪn fəʊld →-fɒʊld ‖ -foʊld
ping pɪŋ **pinged** pɪŋd **pinging** 'pɪŋ ɪŋ **pings** pɪŋz
pinger 'pɪŋ ə ‖ -ᵊr **~s** z
pingo 'pɪŋ gəʊ ‖ -goʊ **~s** z
ping-pong, Ping-Pong *tdmk* 'pɪŋ pɒŋ ‖ -pɑːŋ -pɔːŋ
Pingtung ˌpɪŋ 'tʌŋ —*Chi* Píngdōng [^{2}pʰiŋ ^{1}tʊŋ]
pinguid 'pɪŋ gwɪd §-gwəd
pinhead 'pɪn hed **~s** z
pinhole 'pɪn həʊl →-hɒʊl ‖ -hoʊl **~s** z
pinion 'pɪn jən **~ed** d **~ing** ɪŋ **~s** z
pink pɪŋk **pinked** pɪŋ*k*t **pinker** 'pɪŋk ə ‖ -ᵊr **pinkest** 'pɪŋk ɪst §-əst **pinking** 'pɪŋk ɪŋ **pinks** pɪŋ*k*s
ˌpink 'elephant; **ˌpink 'gin**; **'pinking ˌscissors**; **'pinking shears**
pink-collar ˌpɪŋk 'kɒl ə ◂ ‖ -'kɑːl ᵊr ◂
Pinkerton 'pɪŋk ət ən ‖ -ᵊrt ᵊn
pinkeye 'pɪŋk aɪ
pinkie 'pɪŋk i **~s** z
pinkish 'pɪŋk ɪʃ
pinkness 'pɪŋk nəs -nɪs
pinko 'pɪŋk əʊ ‖ -oʊ **~es, ~s** z
pink|y 'pɪŋk |i **~ies** iz
pinn... —*see* **pin**
pinn|a 'pɪn |ə **~ae** iː **~as** əz
pinnac|e 'pɪn əs -ɪs **~es** ɪz əz
pinnacl|e 'pɪn ək ᵊl -ɪk- **~ed** d **~ing** ‿ɪŋ **~es** z
pinnate 'pɪn eɪt -ət, -ɪt **~ly** li
pinnatifid pɪ 'næt ɪ fɪd §-ə- ‖ -'næt̬-
pinner, P~ 'pɪn ə ‖ -ᵊr
Pinney 'pɪn i
Pinnock 'pɪn ək
pinn|y 'pɪn |i **~ies** iz
Pinocchio pɪ 'nəʊk i‿əʊ pə-, -'nɒk- ‖ -'noʊk i oʊ —*It* [pi 'nɔk kjo]
Pinochet 'piːn əʊ ʃeɪ -tʃeɪ ‖ ˌpiːn oʊ 'tʃet —*Sp* [pi no 'tʃet]
pinochle, pinocle 'piː ˌnʌk ᵊl -ˌnɒk-
pinocytosis ˌpɪn əʊ saɪ 'təʊs ɪs §-əs ‖ -ə saɪ 'toʊs-
pinole pɪ 'nəʊl i pə- ‖ -'noʊl i
Pinot 'piːn əʊ ‖ -oʊ —*Fr* [pi no]
pin|point 'pɪn |pɔɪnt →'pɪm- **~pointed** pɔɪnt ɪd -əd ‖ pɔɪnt̬ əd **~pointing** pɔɪnt ɪŋ ‖ pɔɪnt̬ ɪŋ **~points** pɔɪn*t*s
pinprick 'pɪn prɪk →'pɪm- **~ed** t **~ing** ɪŋ **~s** s
pinstripe 'pɪn straɪp **~d** t **~s** s
ˌpinstripe 'suit
pint paɪnt **pints** paɪn*t*s
pinta *'pint (of milk)'* 'paɪnt ə ‖ 'paɪnt̬ ə **~s** z
pinta *'tropical disease'*, **P~** 'pɪnt ə 'piːnt- ‖ 'pɪnt̬ ə 'pɪnt ɑː —*Sp* ['pin ta]
pintable 'pɪn ˌteɪb ᵊl **~s** z
pintado pɪn 'tɑːd əʊ ‖ -oʊ
pintail 'pɪn teᵊl **~s** z
Pinter 'pɪnt ə ‖ 'pɪnt̬ ᵊr
Pinteresque ˌpɪnt ər 'esk ◂ ‖ ˌpɪnt̬ ə 'resk ◂
Pinterish 'pɪnt ər ɪʃ ‖ 'pɪnt̬-
pintle 'pɪnt ᵊl ‖ 'pɪnt̬ ᵊl **~s** z
pinto 'pɪnt əʊ ‖ 'pɪnt oʊ **~s** z
'pinto bean
pint-size 'paɪnt saɪz **~d** d
pinup 'pɪn ʌp **~s** s
pinwheel 'pɪn wiːᵊl -hwiːᵊl ‖ -*h*wiːᵊl **~s** z
pinworm 'pɪn wɜːm ‖ -wɝːm **~s** z
pinxit 'pɪŋks ɪt §-ət
Pinxton 'pɪŋ*k*st ən
piny 'paɪn i
pinyin, P~ ˌpɪn 'jɪn ◂ —*Chi* pīnyīn [^{1}pʰin ^{1}jɪn]

pinyon, piñon pɪn ˈjɒn ‖ -ˈjoʊn -ˈjɑːn; ˈ· · —*Sp* piñón [pi ˈɲon]
piolet ˈpiː‿ə leɪ ‖ ˌpiː ə ˈleɪ **~s** z
pion ˈpaɪ ɒn -ən ‖ -ɑːn **~s** z
pioneer, P~ ˌpaɪ‿ə ˈnɪə ◂ ‖ -ˈnɪᵊr **~ed** d
pioneering ˌpaɪ‿ə ˈnɪər ɪŋ ◂ ‖ -ˈnɪr ɪŋ ◂ **~s** z
ˌpioˌneering ˈwork
pious ˈpaɪ‿əs **~ly** li **~ness** nəs nɪs
pip, Pip pɪp **pipped** pɪpt **pipping** ˈpɪp ɪŋ **pips** pɪps
pipal ˈpiːp ᵊl **~s** z
pipe paɪp **piped** paɪpt **pipes** paɪps **piping** ˈpaɪp ɪŋ
ˈpipe ˌcleaner; **ˌpiped ˈmusic**; **ˈpipe dream**; **ˈpipe ˌorgan**; **ˈpipe rack**; **ˌpiping ˈhot◂**
pipeclay ˈpaɪp kleɪ
pipefish ˈpaɪp fɪʃ **~es** ɪz əz
pipeful ˈpaɪp fʊl **~s** z
pipelin|e ˈpaɪp laɪn **~ed** d **~es** z **~ing** ɪŋ
piper, Piper ˈpaɪp ə ‖ -ᵊr **~s** z
piperaceous ˌpɪp ə ˈreɪʃ əs ˌpaɪp-
piperade ˌpɪp ə ˈrɑːd ˌpiːp- **~s** z
piperazine pɪ ˈper ə ziːn paɪ-, -zɪn
piperidine pɪ ˈper ɪ diːn paɪ-, -ə-, -dɪn
pipette pɪ ˈpet ‖ paɪ- **~s** s
pipework ˈpaɪp wɜːk ‖ -wɜ˞ːk
pipewort ˈpaɪp wɜːt -wɔːt ‖ -wɜ˞ːt -wɔːrt
Pipex *tdmk* ˈpaɪp eks
piping ˈpaɪp ɪŋ
pipistrelle ˌpɪp ɪ ˈstrel -ə-, ˈ· · · **~s** z
pipit ˈpɪp ɪt §-ət **~s** s
pipkin ˈpɪp kɪn §-kən **~s** z
pipp... —*see* **pip**
Pippa ˈpɪp ə
pippin ˈpɪp ɪn §-ən **~s** z
pipsqueak ˈpɪp skwiːk **~s** s
piquancy ˈpiːk ənᵗs i
piquant ˈpiːk ənt -ɑːnt **~ly** li
pique piːk *(= peak)* **piqued** piːkt **piques** piːks **piquing** ˈpiːk ɪŋ
piqué ˈpiːk eɪ ‖ piː ˈkeɪ —*Fr* [pi ke]
piquet *'card game'* pɪ ˈket -ˈkeɪ
Piquet ˈpiːk eɪ
pirac|y ˈpaɪᵊr əs |i ˈpɪr- **~ies** iz
Piraeus ₍ˌ₎paɪᵊ ˈriː‿əs pɪ ˈreɪ əs, pə- —*ModGk* Peiraiás [pi rɛ ˈas]
Piran ˈpɪr ən
Pirandello ˌpɪr ən ˈdel əʊ ‖ -oʊ —*It* [pi ran ˈdɛl lo]
piranha, piraña pə ˈrɑːn ə pɪ-, -jə ‖ -ˈræn- **~s** z
piˈranha fish
pir|ate ˈpaɪᵊr |ət -ɪt **~ated** ət ɪd ɪt-, -əd ‖ əṭ əd **~ates** əts ɪts **~ating** ət ɪŋ ɪt- ‖ əṭ ɪŋ
piratical ₍ˌ₎paɪᵊ ˈræt ɪk ᵊl pɪ-, pə- ‖ -ˈræṭ- **~ly** ‿i
Pirbright ˈpɜː braɪt ‖ ˈpɜ˞ː-
Pirelli *tdmk* pə ˈrel i pɪ- —*It* [pi ˈrɛl li]
Pirie ˈpɪr i
Pirithous, Pirithoüs paɪᵊ ˈrɪθ əʊ əs ‖ -oʊ əs
pirog, pirogue pɪ ˈrəʊg pə- ‖ -ˈroʊg ˈpiː roʊg **~s** z
piroshki pɪ ˈrɒʃ ki pə-; ˌpɪr əʃ ˈkiː ‖ -ˈrɔːʃ- -ˈrɑːʃ-, -ˈrʌʃ- —*Russ* [pʲi rʌ ˈʃkʲi]
pirou|ette ˌpɪr u |ˈet **~etted** ˈet ɪd -əd ‖ ˈeṭ əd **~ettes** ˈets **~etting** ˈet ɪŋ ‖ ˈeṭ ɪŋ
pirozhki —*see* **piroshki**
Pisa ˈpiːz ə —*It* [ˈpiː sa]
pis aller ˌpiːz ˈæl eɪ ‖ -æ ˈleɪ —*Fr* [pi za le]
Pisan ˈpiːz ᵊn **~s** z
piscatorial ˌpɪsk ə ˈtɔːr i‿əl ◂ ‖ -ˈtoʊr- **~ly** ‿i
piscatory ˈpɪsk ət‿ər i ‖ -ə tɔːr i -toʊr i
Piscean ˈpaɪs i‿ən ˈpɪsk-, ˈpɪs-; paɪ ˈsiː‿ **~s** z
Pisces ˈpaɪs iːz ˈpɪsk-, ˈpɪs-
pisci- *comb. form*
with stress-neutral suffix ˌpɪs ɪ
— **pisciculture** ˈpɪs ɪ ˌkʌltʃ ə ‖ -ᵊr
with stress-imposing suffix pɪ ˈsɪ + §pə-
— **piscivorous** pɪ ˈsɪv ər əs §pə-
piscin|a pɪ ˈsiːn |ə §pə-, -ˈʃiːn-, ˈsaɪn- **~ae** iː **~as** əz
piscine ˈpɪs aɪn ˈpɪsk-, ˈpaɪs-, -iːn **~s** z
Pisgah ˈpɪz gɑː -gə
pish pɪʃ
Pisidia paɪ ˈsɪd i‿ə
Pisistratus paɪ ˈsɪs trət əs ‖ -trəṭ-
piss pɪs **pissed** pɪst **pisses** ˈpɪs ɪz -əz **pissing** ˈpɪs ɪŋ
pissant ˈpɪs ænt **~ing** ɪŋ **~s** s
Pissarro pɪ ˈsɑːr əʊ ‖ -oʊ —*Fr* [pi sa ʁo]
pisser ˈpɪs ə ‖ -ᵊr **~s** z
pisshead ˈpɪs hed **~s** z
pissoir ˈpɪs wɑː ‖ piː ˈswɑːr —*Fr* [pi swaːʁ] **~s** z
piss-poor ˌpɪs ˈpɔː ◂ -ˈpʊə ◂ ‖ -ˈpʊᵊr ◂ -ˈpɔːr ◂, -ˈpoʊr ◂
piss-take ˈpɪs teɪk **~s** s
piss-up ˈpɪs ʌp **~s** s
pissy ˈpɪs i
pistachio pɪ ˈstɑːʃ i əʊ pə-, -ˈstæʃ-, -ˈstætʃ- ‖ -ˈstæʃ i oʊ -ˈstɑːʃ- **~s** z
piste piːst **pistes** piːsts
pistil ˈpɪst ɪl -ᵊl **~s** z
pistol ˈpɪst ᵊl **~s** z
ˈpistol grip
pistole pɪ ˈstəʊl ‖ -ˈstoʊl **~s** z
pistol-whip ˈpɪst ᵊl wɪp -hwɪp **~ped** t **~ping** ɪŋ **~s** s
piston ˈpɪst ən **~s** z
ˈpiston ring; **ˈpiston rod**
pit pɪt **pits** pɪts **pitted** ˈpɪt ɪd -əd ‖ ˈpɪṭ əd **pitting** ˈpɪt ɪŋ ‖ ˈpɪṭ ɪŋ
ˈpit bull, ˌpit bull ˈterrier; **ˈpit ˌpony**; **ˈpit stop**
pita ˈpɪt ə ˈpiːt- ‖ ˈpiːṭ ə
pit-a-pat ˌpɪt ə ˈpæt ˈ· · · ‖ ˈpɪṭ ə pæt -ɪ-
Pitcairn ˈpɪt keən ·ˈ· ‖ -kern —*as a family name, usually* ·ˈ·.
pitch pɪtʃ **pitched** pɪtʃt **pitches** ˈpɪtʃ ɪz -əz **pitching** ˈpɪtʃ ɪŋ
ˈpitch pine; **ˈpitch pipe**
pitch-and-putt ˌpɪtʃ ən ˈpʌt -ənd-, →əm-
pitch-and-toss ˌpɪtʃ ən ˈtɒs -ənd-, -ˈtɔːs ‖ -ˈtɔːs -ˈtɑːs
pitch-black ˌpɪtʃ ˈblæk ◂
pitchblende ˈpɪtʃ blend
pitch-dark ˌpɪtʃ ˈdɑːk ◂ ‖ -ˈdɑːrk

P

pitcher ˈpɪtʃ ə ‖ -ᵊr **~s** z
ˈpitcher plant
pitchfork ˈpɪtʃ fɔːk ‖ -fɔːrk **~s** s
pitch|man ˈpɪtʃ| mən -mæn **~men** mən men
pitchout ˈpɪtʃ aʊt **~s** s
pitch|y ˈpɪtʃ |i **~ier** i‿ə ‖ i‿ᵊr **~iest** i‿ɪst i‿əst **~iness** i nəs -nɪs
piteous ˈpɪt i‿əs **~ly** li **~ness** nəs nɪs
pitfall ˈpɪt fɔːl ‖ -fɑːl **~s** z
pith pɪθ **pithed** pɪθt **pithing** ˈpɪθ ɪŋ **piths** pɪθs
ˌpith ˈhelmet ‖ ˈ·ˌ··
pithead ˈpɪt hed **~s** z
pithecanthropus, P~ ˌpɪθ i ˈkænᵗθ rəp əs -kæn ˈθrəʊp- ‖ -kæn ˈθroʊp-
pith|y ˈpɪθ |i **~ier** i‿ə ‖ i‿ᵊr **~iest** i‿ɪst i‿əst **~ily** ɪ li əl i **~iness** i nəs i nɪs
pitiab|le ˈpɪt i‿əb |ᵊl ‖ ˈpɪţ- **~leness** ᵊl nəs -nɪs **~ly** li
pitie... —*see* **pity**
pitiful ˈpɪt ɪ fᵊl -ə-, -fʊl ‖ ˈpɪţ- **~ly** ‿i **~ness** nəs nɪs
pitiless ˈpɪt ɪ ləs -ə-, -lɪs; -ᵊl əs, -ɪs ‖ ˈpɪţ- **~ly** li **~ness** nəs nɪs
Pitjantjatjara ˌpɪtʃ ən tʃə ˈtʃær ə
Pitlochry pɪt ˈlɒx ri -ˈlɒk- ‖ -ˈlɑːk-
pit|man, P~ ˈpɪt |mən **~men** mən men
Pitney ˈpɪt ni
piton ˈpiːt ɒn -ɒ̃ ‖ -ɑːn —*Fr* [pi tɔ̃] **~s** z
pitot, Pitot ˈpiːt əʊ ‖ -oʊ **~s** z
ˈPitot tube
Pitsea ˈpɪt siː
Pitt pɪt
pitta *'kind of bread'* ˈpɪt ə ˈpiːt- ‖ ˈpɪţ ə
ˈpitta bread
pitta *'kind of bird'* ˈpɪt ə ‖ ˈpɪţ ə **~s** z
pittanc|e ˈpɪt ᵊnᵗs **~es** ɪz əz
Pittenweem ˌpɪt ᵊn ˈwiːm
pitter-patter ˈpɪt ə ˌpæt ə ˌ·ˈ·· ‖ ˈpɪţ ᵊr ˌpæţ ᵊr -i-
pittosporum pɪ ˈtɒsp ər əm ‖ -ˈtɑːsp-
Pittsburg, Pittsburgh ˈpɪts bɜːg ‖ -bɜ˞ːg
pituitar|y pɪ ˈtjuː‿ɪ‿tər |i pə-, →-ˈtʃuː‿, ‿ə‿ ‖ -ˈtuː ə ter |i -ˈtjuː- **~ies** iz
piˈtuitary gland
pituri ˈpɪtʃ ər i
pity ˈpɪt i ‖ ˈpɪţ i **pitied** ˈpɪt id ‖ ˈpɪţ id **pities** ˈpɪt iz ‖ ˈpɪţ iz **pitying/ly** ˈpɪt i‿ɪŋ /li ‖ ˈpɪţ i-
pityriasis ˌpɪt ɪ ˈraɪ‿əs ɪs ˌ·ə-, §-əs ‖ ˌpɪţ-
Pius ˈpaɪ‿əs
piv|ot ˈpɪv |ət **~oted** ət ɪd -əd ‖ əţ əd **~oting** ət ɪŋ ‖ əţ ɪŋ **~ots** əts
pivotal ˈpɪv ət ᵊl ‖ -əţ ᵊl **~ly** ‿i
pix pɪks *(= picks)*
pixel ˈpɪks ᵊl -el **~s** z
pix|elate ˈpɪks| ə leɪt →-ᵊl eɪt **~elated** ə leɪt ɪd -əd ‖ ᵊl eɪţ əd **~elates** ə leɪts →ᵊl eɪts **~elating** ə leɪt ɪŋ ‖ ᵊl eɪţ ɪŋ
pixelation ˌpɪks ə ˈleɪʃ ᵊn →-ᵊl ˈeɪʃ-
pixie ˈpɪks i **~s** z
pixilated ˈpɪks ɪ leɪt ɪd ˈ·ə- ‖ -leɪţ əd
pix|y ˈpɪks |i **~ies** iz
Pizarro pɪ ˈzɑːr əʊ ‖ -oʊ —*Sp* [pi ˈθa rro, -ˈsa-]
Piz Buin *tdmk* ˌpɪts ˈbuːɪn
pizza ˈpiːts ə **~s** z
ˈPizza Hut *tdmk*
pizzazz pə ˈzæz pɪ-
pizzeria ˌpiːts ə ˈriː‿ə ˌpɪts- **~s** z
Pizzey *(i)* ˈpɪts i, *(ii)* ˈpɪz i
pizzicato ˌpɪts ɪ ˈkɑːt əʊ -ə- ‖ -ˈkɑːţ oʊ **~s** z
pizzle ˈpɪz ᵊl **~s** z
pj's, PJ's ˈpiː dʒeɪz
PL/1 ˌpiː el ˈwʌn §-ˈwɒn
placab|le ˈplæk əb |ᵊl **~ly** li
placard *v* ˈplæk ɑːd ‖ -ɑːrd -ᵊrd; plə ˈkɑːrd, plæ- **~ed** ɪd əd **~ing** ɪŋ **~s** z
placard *n* ˈplæk ɑːd ‖ -ɑːrd -ᵊrd **~s** z
pla|cate plə ˈ|keɪt ‖ ˈpleɪ|k eɪt *(*)* **~cated** keɪt ɪd -əd ‖ keɪţ əd **~cates** keɪts **~cating** keɪt ɪŋ ‖ keɪţ ɪŋ
placatory plə ˈkeɪt ər i pleɪ-; ˈplæk ət‿ər i ‖ ˈpleɪk ə tɔːr i ˈplæk-, -toʊr i *(*)*
place pleɪs **placed** pleɪst **places** ˈpleɪs ɪz -əz **placing/s** ˈpleɪs ɪŋ/z
ˈplace card; **ˈplace mat**; **ˈplace name**; **ˈplace ˌsetting**
placebo plə ˈsiːb əʊ plæ- ‖ -oʊ **~s** z
plaˈcebo efˌfect
placekick ˈpleɪs kɪk **~ed** t **~er/s** ə/z ‖ ᵊr/z **~ing** ɪŋ **~s** s
place|man ˈpleɪs |mən **~men** mən
placement ˈpleɪs mənt **~s** s
pla|centa plə |ˈsent ə ‖ -|ˈsenţ ə **~centae** ˈsent iː **~cental** ˈsent ᵊl ‖ ˈsenţ ᵊl **~centas** ˈsent əz ‖ ˈsenţ əz
placer ˈpleɪs ə ‖ -ᵊr ˈplæs-
Placerville *place in CA* ˈplæs ə vɪl ‖ -ᵊr-
placet ˈpleɪs et -ɪt **~s** s
placid ˈplæs ɪd §-əd **~ly** li **~ness** nəs nɪs
placidity plə ˈsɪd ət i plæ-, -ɪt- ‖ -əţ i
placket ˈplæk ɪt §-ət **~s** s
plagal ˈpleɪg ᵊl
plage *'beach'* plɑːʒ **plages** ˈplɑːʒ ɪz -əz —*Fr* [plaːʒ]
plage *'bright region on the sun'* plɑːʒ pleɪdʒ **plages** ˈplɑːʒ ɪz ˈpleɪdʒ-, -əz
plagiaris... —*see* **plagiariz...**
plagiarism ˈpleɪdʒ ə ˌrɪz əm -i‿ə- **~s** z
plagiarist ˈpleɪdʒ ər ɪst -i‿ər-, §-əst **~s** s
plagiaristic ˌpleɪdʒ ə ˈrɪst ɪk ◂ -i‿ə-
plagiariz|e ˈpleɪdʒ ə raɪz -i‿ə- **~ed** d **~es** ɪz əz **~ing** ɪŋ
plagioclas|e ˈpleɪdʒ i‿ə kleɪz -kleɪs **~es** ɪz əz
plague pleɪg **plagued** pleɪgd **plagues** pleɪgz **plaguing** ˈpleɪg ɪŋ
plagu|ey, plagu|y ˈpleɪg |i **~ily** əl i ɪ li
plaice pleɪs *(= place)*
plaid plæd *(!)* **plaids** plædz
Plaid Cymru ˌplaɪd ˈkʌm ri -ˈkʊm-, -ˈkuːm- —*Welsh* [ˌplaid ˈkəm ri, -ri]
plain pleɪn *(= plane)* **plainer** ˈpleɪn ə ‖ -ᵊr **plainest** ˈpleɪn ɪst -əst
ˌplain ˈchocolate; **ˌplain ˈflour**; **ˌplain ˈsailing**

plainchant ˈpleɪn tʃɑːnt §-tʃænt ‖ -tʃænt
plain-clothes ˌpleɪn ˈkləʊðz ◂ ˌpleɪŋ-, -kləʊz ‖ -ˈkloʊz -ˈkloʊðz
plain|ly ˈpleɪn |li **~ness** nəs nɪs
plains|man ˈpleɪnz |mən **~men** mən men
plainsong ˈpleɪn sɒŋ ‖ -sɔːŋ -sɑːŋ
plainspoken ˌpleɪn ˈspəʊk ən ◂ ‖ -ˈspoʊk ən **~ness** nəs nɪs
plains|woman ˈpleɪnz |ˌwʊm ən **~women** ˌwɪm ɪn -ən
plaint pleɪnt **plaints** pleɪnts
plaintiff ˈpleɪnt ɪf §-əf ‖ ˈpleɪnţ əf **~s** s
plaintive ˈpleɪnt ɪv ‖ ˈpleɪnţ ɪv **~ly** li **~ness** nəs nɪs
Plaistow *(i)* ˈplɑːst əʊ ˈplæst- ‖ -oʊ, *(ii)* ˈpleɪst əʊ ‖ -oʊ —*The places in Greater London are (i). The family name may be either (i) or (ii).*
plait plæt ‖ pleɪt plæt *(!)* **plaited** ˈplæt ɪd -əd ‖ ˈpleɪţ əd ˈplæţ- **plaiting** ˈplæt ɪŋ ‖ ˈpleɪţ ɪŋ ˈplæţ- **plaits** plæts ‖ pleɪts plæts
plan plæn **planned** plænd **planning** ˈplæn ɪŋ **plans** plænz
ˈplanning perˌmission
planar ˈpleɪn ə ‖ -ᵊr *(= plainer)*
planarian plə ˈneər i‿ən ‖ -ˈner- -ˈnær- **~s** z
planchet ˈplɑːntʃ ɪt §ˈplæntʃ-, §-ət ‖ ˈplæntʃ ət **~s** s
planchette plɑːn ˈʃet plɒ̃-, plæn- ‖ plæn- —*Fr* [plɑ̃ ʃɛt] **~s** s
Planck plæŋk ‖ plɑːŋk —*Ger* [plaŋk]
plane pleɪn **planned** pleɪnd **planes** pleɪnz **planing** ˈpleɪn ɪŋ
ˈplane tree
planeload ˈpleɪn ləʊd ‖ -loʊd **~s** z
planer ˈpleɪn ə ‖ ᵊr **~s** z
planet ˈplæn ɪt §-ət **~s** s
planetari|um ˌplæn ə ˈteər i‿|əm ˌ·ɪ- ‖ -ˈter- -ˈtær- **~a** ə **~ums** əmz
planetary ˈplæn əţ‿ər i ˈ·ɪt‿ ‖ -ə ter i
planetesimal ˌplæn ɪ ˈtes ɪm ᵊl ◂ ˌ·ə-, -ˈtez-, -əm ᵊl
planetoid ˈplæn ə tɔɪd -ɪ- **~s** z
plangency ˈplændʒ ənᵗs i
plangent ˈplændʒ ənt **~ly** li
plani... —*see* **plane**
planigale ˈplæn ɪ geɪᵊl -ə- **~s** z
planimeter plæ ˈnɪm ɪt ə plə-, pleɪ- -ət- ‖ -əţ ᵊr **~s** z
planimetric ˌplæn ɪ ˈmetr ɪk ◂ -ə- **~al/ly** ᵊl ‿i
planimetry plæ ˈnɪm ətr i plə-, pleɪ-, -ɪtr-
plank plæŋk **planked** plæŋkt **planking** ˈplæŋk ɪŋ **planks** plæŋks
plankton ˈplæŋkt ən -ɒn ‖ ɑːn
planktonic plæŋk ˈtɒn ɪk ‖ -ˈtɑːn ɪk
plann... —*see* **plan**
planner ˈplæn ə ‖ -ᵊr **~s** z
plano-concave ˌpleɪn əʊ ˈkɒn keɪv ◂ →-ˈkɒŋ-, ˌ· · ·ˈ· ‖ -oʊ ˈkɑːn-
plano-convex ˌpleɪn əʊ ˈkɒn veks ◂ ˌ· · ·ˈ· ‖ -oʊ ˈkɑːn-

plant, Plant plɑːnt §plænt ‖ plænt **planted** ˈplɑːnt ɪd §ˈplænt-, -əd ‖ ˈplænţ əd **planting/s** ˈplɑːnt ɪŋ/z §ˈplænt- ‖ ˈplænţ ɪŋ/z
Plantagenet plæn ˈtædʒ ən‿ət -ˈ·ɪn-, -ɪt, -et **~s** s
plantain ˈplænt ɪn ˈplɑːnt-, -ən ‖ -ᵊn **~s** z
plantar ˈplænt ə -ɑː ‖ ˈplænţ ᵊr ˈplænt ɑːr
plantation plɑːn ˈteɪʃ ᵊn plæn- ‖ plæn- **~s** z
planter, P~ ˈplɑːnt ə §ˈplænt- ‖ ˈplænţ ᵊr **~s** s
plantigrade ˈplænt ɪ greɪd ˈplɑːnt-, §-ə- ‖ ˈplænţ ə- **~s** z
Plantin ˈplænt ɪn ˈplɑːnt-, -ən ‖ plɑːn ˈtæn
plantocrac|y ₍ₗ₎plɑːn ˈtɒkr əs |i §₍ₗ₎plæn- ‖ plæn ˈtɑːk- **~ies** iz

PLAQUE

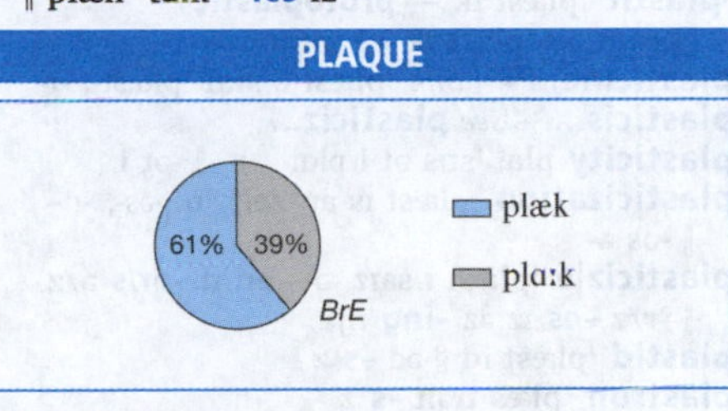

plaque plæk plɑːk, pleɪk — *Preference poll, BrE:* plæk *61%,* plɑːk *39%. Some people distinguish between a* plæk *on a wall and* plɑːk *or* pleɪk *on their teeth. In AmE always* plæk. **plaques** plæks plɑːks, pleɪks
plash plæʃ **plashed** plæʃt **plashes** ˈplæʃ ɪz -əz **plashing** ˈplæʃ ɪŋ
plashy ˈplæʃ i
-plasia ˈpleɪz i‿ə ‖ ˈpleɪʒ i‿ə ˈpleɪʒ ə — **hypoplasia** ˌhaɪp əʊ ˈpleɪz i‿ə ‖ -oʊ ˈpleɪʒ- -ˈ·ə
-plasm ˌplæz əm — **protoplasm** ˈprəʊt əʊ ˌplæz əm ‖ ˈproʊţ ə-
plasma ˈplæz mə **~s** z
plasmapheresis ˌplæz mə ˈfer əs ɪs -ˈfɪər-, §-əs
plasmid ˈplæz mɪd §-məd **~s** z
plasmo- *comb. form*
with stress-neutral suffix ˈplæz məʊ ‖ -mə — **plasmosome** ˈplæz məʊ səʊm ‖ -mə soʊm
with stress-imposing suffix plæz ˈmɒ+ ‖ -ˈmɑː+ — **plasmolysis** plæz ˈmɒl əs ɪs -ɪs ɪs, §-əs ‖ -ˈmɑːl-
plasmodi|um plæz ˈməʊd i‿|əm ‖ -ˈmoʊd- **~a** ə **~al** əl
Plassey ˈplæs i ‖ ˈplɑːs-
-plast plæst — **chloroplast** ˈklɔːr əʊ plæst ‖ -ə- ˈkloʊr-
plast|er ˈplɑːst |ə §ˈplæst- ‖ ˈplæst |ᵊr **~ered** əd ‖ ᵊrd **~ering** ər‿ɪŋ **~ers** əz ‖ ᵊrz
ˌplaster ˈcast, ˈ· · ·; **ˌplaster of ˈParis**
plasterboard ˈplɑːst ə bɔːd §ˈplæst- ‖ ˈplæst ᵊr bɔːrd -boʊrd
plasterer ˈplɑːst ər‿ə §ˈplæst- ‖ ˈplæst ᵊr ər **~s** z
plastic ˈplæst ɪk ˈplɑːst- — *Preference poll, BrE:* ˈplæst- *91% (English southerners 94%),* ˈplɑːst- *9% (English southerners 6%). In AmE always* ˈplæst-. **~s** s *See chart on p. 618.*

P

PLASTIC

91% 'plæst-
9% 'plɑːst-
BrE

ˌplastic 'art; ˌplastic 'bullet; ˌplastic ex'plosive; ˌplastic 'surgeon; ˌplastic 'surgery
-plastic 'plæst ɪk — **protoplastic** ˌprəʊt əʊ 'plast ɪk ◂ ‖ ˌproʊţ ə-
plasticine, P~ *tdmk* 'plæst ə siːn 'plɑːst-, -ɪ-
plasticis... —*see* **plasticiz...**
plasticity plæ 'stɪs ət i plɑː-, -ɪt- ‖ -əţ i
plasticization ˌplæst ɪs aɪ 'zeɪʃ ᵊn ˌ·əs-, -ɪ'-- ‖ -əs ə-
plasticiz|e 'plæst ɪ saɪz -ə- **~ed** d **~er/s** ə/z ‖ ᵊr/z **~es** ɪz əz **~ing** ɪŋ
plastid 'plæst ɪd §-əd **~s** z
plastron 'plæs trən **~s** z
-plasty ˌplæst i — **rhinoplasty** 'raɪn əʊ ˌplæst i ‖ -oʊ-
plat plæt **plats** plæts **platted** 'plæt ɪd -əd ‖ 'plæţ əd **platting** 'plæt ɪŋ ‖ ' plæţ ɪŋ
Plata 'plɑːt ə ‖ 'plɑːţ ə —*Sp* ['pla ta]
Plataea plə 'tiːˌə plæ-
plat du jour ˌplɑː duː 'ʒʊə -djuː-, -də- ‖ -də 'ʒʊᵊr —*Fr* [pla dy ʒuːʁ] **plats du jour** *same pronunciation*
plate, Plate pleɪt **plated** 'pleɪt ɪd -əd ‖ 'pleɪţ əd **plates** pleɪts **plating** 'pleɪt ɪŋ ‖ 'pleɪţ ɪŋ
ˌplate 'glass◂; 'plate rack; ˌplate tec'tonics
plateau 'plæt əʊ plæ 'təʊ, plə- ‖ plæ 'toʊ **~s, ~x** z
plateful 'pleɪt fʊl **~s** z
plate-glass ˌpleɪt 'glɑːs ◂ §-'glæs ‖ -'glæs ◂
ˌplate-glass 'window
platelayer 'pleɪt ˌleɪ ə ‖ -ᵊr **~s** z
platelet 'pleɪt lət -lɪt **~s** s
platen 'plæt ᵊn **~s** z
plater, P~ 'pleɪt ə ‖ 'pleɪţ ᵊr **~s** z
platform 'plæt fɔːm ‖ -fɔːrm **~s** z
Plath plæθ
Platignum *tdmk* plæ 'tɪg nəm plə-
platino- *comb. form*
with stress-neutral suffix ¦plæt ɪn əʊ -ən- ‖ -ən oʊ — **platinocyanic** ˌplæt ɪn əʊ saɪ 'æn ɪk ◂ ˌ·ən- ‖ ˌ·ən oʊ-
platinum 'plæt ɪn əm -ᵊnˌ ‖ -ᵊnˌəm
ˌplatinum 'blonde
platitude 'plæt ɪ tjuːd -ə-, →-tʃuːd ‖ 'plæţ ə tuːd -tjuːd **~s** z
platitudinis|e, platitudiniz|e ˌplæt ɪ 'tjuːd ɪ naɪz ˌ·ə-, →-'tʃuːd-, -ᵊn aɪz ‖ ˌplæţ ə 'tuːd ᵊn aɪz -'tjuːd- **~ed** d **~es** ɪz əz **~ing** ɪŋ
platitudinous ˌplæt ɪ 'tjuːd ɪn əs ◂ ˌ·ə-, →-'tʃuːd-, -ənˌəs ‖ ˌplæţ ə 'tuːd ᵊnˌəs ◂ **~ly** li
Plato 'pleɪt əʊ ‖ 'pleɪţ oʊ
platonic, P~ plə 'tɒn ɪk ‖ -'tɑːn ɪk **~ally** ᵊlˌi
Platonism 'pleɪt ə ˌnɪz əm -ᵊn ˌɪz- ‖ 'pleɪt ᵊn ˌɪz əm
Platonist 'pleɪt ən ɪst §-əst ‖ -ᵊn- **~s** s
platoon plə 'tuːn **~s** z
Platt plæt
Plattdeutsch 'plæt dɔɪtʃ ‖ 'plɑːt- —*Ger* ['plat dɔytʃ]
Platte plæt
platter 'plæt ə ‖ 'plæţ ᵊr **~s** z
Platting 'plæt ɪŋ ‖ 'plæţ ɪŋ
plat|y *'kind of fish'* 'plæt |i ‖ 'plæţ |i **~ies, ~ys** iz
platyhelminth ˌplæt i 'helm ɪnᵗθ ‖ ˌplæţ i- **~s** s
platykurtic ˌplæt i 'kɜːt ɪk ◂ ‖ ˌplæţ i 'kɜːţ ɪk ◂
platypus 'plæt ɪp əs -əp-; -ɪ pʊs ‖ 'plæţ- **~es** ɪz əz
platyrrhine 'plæt ɪ raɪn -ə- ‖ 'plæţ-
plaudit 'plɔːd ɪt §-ət ‖ 'plɑːd- **~s** s
plausibility ˌplɔːz ə 'bɪl ət i ˌ·ɪ-, -ɪt i ‖ -əţ i ˌplɑːz-
plausib|le 'plɔːz əb |ᵊl -ɪb- ‖ 'plɑːz- **~leness** ᵊl nəs -nɪs **~ly** li
Plautus 'plɔːt əs ‖ 'plɔːţ əs 'plɑːţ-
Plaxtol 'plækst ᵊl
play pleɪ **played** pleɪd **playing** 'pleɪ ɪŋ **plays** pleɪz
'play dough; 'playing card; 'playing field
playa *'player'* 'pleɪ ə **~s** z
playa *'beach'* 'plaɪˌə —*Sp* ['pla ja] **~s** z
playable 'pleɪ əb ᵊl
play-act 'pleɪ ækt **~ed** ɪd əd **~ing** ɪŋ **~or/s** ə/z ‖ ᵊr/z **~s** s
play-action 'pleɪ ˌæk ʃᵊn
playback 'pleɪ bæk **~s** s
playbill 'pleɪ bɪl **~s** z
playbook 'pleɪ bʊk §-buːk **~s** s
playboy 'pleɪ bɔɪ **~s** z
play-by-play ˌpleɪ baɪ 'pleɪ ◂
Play-Doh *tdmk* 'pleɪ dəʊ ‖ -doʊ
played-out ˌpleɪd 'aʊt ◂
player, P~ 'pleɪ ə ‖ -ᵊr **~s, ~'s** z
ˌplayer pi'ano
Playfair 'pleɪ feə ‖ -fer -fær
playfellow 'pleɪ ˌfel əʊ ‖ -oʊ **~s** z
Playford 'pleɪ fəd ‖ -fᵊrd
playful 'pleɪf ᵊl 'pleɪ fʊl **~ly** ˌi **~ness** nəs nɪs
playgoer 'pleɪ ˌgəʊ ə ‖ -ˌgoʊ ᵊr **~s** z
playground 'pleɪ graʊnd **~s** z
playgroup 'pleɪ gruːp **~s** s
play|house 'pleɪ |haʊs **~houses** haʊz ɪz -əz
playlet 'pleɪ lət -lɪt **~s** s
playlist 'pleɪ lɪst **~s** s
playmaker 'pleɪ ˌmeɪk ə ‖ -ᵊr **~s** z
playmate 'pleɪ meɪt **~s** s
play-off 'pleɪ ɒf -ɔːf ‖ -ɔːf -ɑːf **~s** s
playpen 'pleɪ pen **~s** z
playroom 'pleɪ ruːm -rʊm **~s** z

P

playschool 'pleɪ skuːl **~s** z
PlayStation *tdmk* 'pleɪ ˌsteɪʃ ᵊn
playsuit 'pleɪ suːt -sjuːt **~s** s
Playtex *tdmk* pleɪ teks
plaything 'pleɪ θɪŋ **~s** z
playtime 'pleɪ taɪm **~s** z
playwright 'pleɪ raɪt **~s** s
play-writing 'pleɪ ˌraɪt ɪŋ ‖ -ˌraɪţ-
plaza, Plaza 'plɑːz ə ‖ 'plæz- —*Sp* ['pla θa, -sa] **~s** z
plc ˌpiː el 'siː
plea pliː **pleas** pliːz *(= please)*
'plea ˌbargaining
pleach pliːtʃ **pleached** pliːtʃt **pleaches** 'pliːtʃ ɪz -əz **pleaching** 'pliːtʃ ɪŋ
plead pliːd **pleaded** 'pliːd ɪd -əd **pleading** 'pliːd ɪŋ **pleads** pliːdz **pled** pled
pleader 'pliːd ə ‖ -ᵊr **~s** z
pleading 'pliːd ɪŋ **~ly** li **~s** z
pleasanc|e, P~ 'plez ᵊnᵗs **~es** ɪz əz
pleas|ant 'plez| ᵊnt **~anter** ᵊnt ə ‖ ᵊnţ ᵊr **~antest** ᵊnt ɪst -əst ‖ ᵊnţ əst
pleasant|ly 'plez ᵊnt| li **~ness** nəs nɪs
pleasantr|y 'plez ᵊntr |i **~ies** iz
please pliːz **pleased** pliːzd **pleases** 'pliːz ɪz -əz **pleasing** 'pliːz ɪŋ
Pleasence 'plez ᵊnᵗs
pleaser 'pliːz ə ‖ -ᵊr **~s** z
pleasing 'pliːz ɪŋ **~ly** li
pleasurab|le 'pleʒ ər‿əb |ᵊl **~leness** ᵊl nəs -nɪs **~ly** li
pleas|ure 'pleʒ |ə ‖ -|ᵊr 'pleɪʒ- **~ured** əd ‖ ᵊrd **~ures** əz ‖ ᵊrz **~uring** ər‿ɪŋ
'pleasure boat; **'pleasure trip**
pleat pliːt **pleated** 'pliːt ɪd -əd ‖ 'pliːţ əd **pleating** 'pliːt ɪŋ ‖ 'pliːţ ɪŋ **pleats** pliːts
pleather 'pleð ə ‖ -ᵊr
pleb pleb **plebs** plebz
plebby 'pleb i
plebe pliːb **plebes** pliːbz
plebeian plə 'biː‿ən plɪ- **~s** z
plebiscite 'pleb ɪ saɪt -ə-; -ɪs ɪt, -əs-, -§ət **~s** s
plebs plebz
plec|tron 'plek |trən ‖ -|trɑːn **~tra** trə **~trum/s** trəm/z
pled pled
pledge pledʒ **pledged** pledʒd **pledges** 'pledʒ ɪz -əz **pledging** 'pledʒ ɪŋ
pledgee ˌpledʒ 'iː **~s** z
pledger,P~ 'pledʒ ə ‖ ᵊr **~s** z
pledget 'pledʒ ɪt §-ət **~s** s
pledgor ˌpledʒ 'ɔː ‖ -'ɔːr **~s** z
-plegia 'pliːdʒ ə 'pliːdʒ i‿ə — **paraplegia** ˌpær ə 'pliːdʒ ə -'‿i‿ə ‖ ˌper-
-plegic 'pliːdʒ ɪk — **quadriplegic** ˌkwɒdr ɪ 'pliːdʒ ɪk ◂ -ə- ‖ ˌkwɑːdr-
Pleiad, p~ 'plaɪ‿əd ‖ 'pliː əd 'pleɪ-, -æd **~s** z —*Fr* Pléiade [ple jad]
Pleiades 'plaɪ‿ə diːz ‖ 'pliː- 'pleɪ-
plein-air ˌpleɪn 'eə ◂ ‖ -'eᵊr ◂ -'æᵊr —*Fr* [plɛ nɛːʁ]
pleistocene, P~ 'plaɪst əʊ siːn ‖ -ə-
plenar|y 'pliːn ər |i 'plen- **~ies** iz **~ily** əl ɪ i li
plenipotentiar|y ˌplen ɪ pə 'tenᵗʃ ər‿|i ◂ ,·ə-, -pəʊ'·-, -'·i‿ər |i ‖ -'tenᵗʃ i er |i **~ies** iz
plenitude 'plen ɪ tjuːd -ə-, →-tʃuːd ‖ -ə tuːd -tjuːd **~s** z
plenteous 'plent i‿əs ‖ 'plenţ- **~ly** li **~ness** nəs nɪs
plentiful 'plent ɪf ᵊl -əf-, -ʊl ‖ 'plenţ- **~ly** ‿i **~ness** nəs nɪs
plenty 'plent i ‖ 'plenţ i —*A casual-speech form* 'plen i *is also heard in BrE*
plenum 'pliːn əm 'plen-, 'pleɪn- **~s** z
pleonasm 'pliː‿ə ˌnæz əm **~s** z
pleonastic ˌpliː‿ə 'næst ɪk ◂ **~ally** ᵊl‿i
plesiosaur 'pliːs i‿ə sɔː 'pliːz- ‖ 'pliːz i‿ə sɔːr **~s** z
plesiosaur|us ˌpliːs i‿ə 'sɔːr |əs ‖ ˌpliːz- **~i** aɪ
Plessey 'ples i
plethora 'pleθ ər ə ple 'θɔːr ə, plə-, plɪ-
plethoric ple 'θɒr ɪk plə-, plɪ- ‖ -'θɔːr ɪk -'θɑːr- **~ally** ᵊl‿i
plethysmograph plə 'θɪz məʊ grɑːf plɪ-, ple-, -'θɪs-, -græf ‖ -ə græf **~s** s
pleur|a 'plʊər |ə 'plɔːr- ‖ 'plʊr |ə **~ae** iː **~al** əl *(= plural)*
pleurisy 'plʊər əs i 'plɔːr-, -ɪs- ‖ 'plʊr-
pleuritic plʊᵊ 'rɪt ɪk ‖ -'rɪţ ɪk
pleuropneumonia ˌplʊər əʊ nju 'məʊn i‿ə §nu- ‖ ˌplʊr oʊ nu 'moʊn- nju- **~like** laɪk
Plexiglas, p~, plexiglass *tdmk* 'pleks i glɑːs §-glæs ‖ -glæs
plexor 'pleks ə ‖ -ᵊr **~s** z
plexus 'pleks əs **~es** ɪz əz
Pleydell *(i)* 'pled ᵊl, *(ii)* pleɪ 'del
pliability ˌplaɪ‿ə 'bɪl ət i -ɪt i ‖ -əţ i
pliab|le 'plaɪ‿əb |ᵊl **~leness** ᵊl nəs -nɪs **~ly** li
pliancy 'plaɪ‿ənᵗs i
pliant 'plaɪ‿ənt **~ly** li **~ness** nəs nɪs
plica 'plaɪk ə **plicae** 'plaɪs iː 'plaɪk-
plié 'pliː eɪ ‖ pliː 'eɪ —*Fr* [pli e] **~s** z
plie... —*see* **ply**
pliers 'plaɪ‿əz ‖ 'plaɪ‿ᵊrz
plight plaɪt **plighted** 'plaɪt ɪd -əd ‖ 'plaɪţ əd **plighting** 'plaɪt ɪŋ ‖ 'plaɪţ ɪŋ **plights** plaɪts
plimsole, plimsoll, P~ 'plɪmᵖs ᵊl 'plɪm səʊl ‖ -soʊl **~s** z
'Plimsoll line, 'Plimsoll mark
pling plɪŋ **plings** plɪŋz
plink plɪŋk **plinked** plɪŋkt **plinking** 'plɪŋk ɪŋ **plinks** plɪŋks
Plinlimmon plɪn 'lɪm ən
plinth plɪnᵗθ **plinths** plɪnᵗθs
Pliny 'plɪn i
pliocene, P~ 'plaɪ əʊ siːn ‖ -ə-
plip plɪp
plisse, plissé 'pliːs eɪ 'plɪs- ‖ plɪ 'seɪ
PLO ˌpiː el 'əʊ ‖ -'oʊ
plod plɒd ‖ plɑːd **plodded** 'plɒd ɪd -əd ‖ 'plɑːd əd **plodding** 'plɒd ɪŋ ‖ 'plɑːd ɪŋ **plods** plɒdz ‖ plɑːdz
plodder 'plɒd ə ‖ 'plɑːd ᵊr **~s** z
Ploesti, Ploiesti plɔɪ eʃt i —*Romanian* Ploieşti [plo 'jeʃtʲ]

P

Plomer *family name (i)* ˈpləʊm ə ‖ ˈploʊm ᵊr, *(ii)* ˈpluːm ə ‖ -ᵊr *—The writer William P~ inherited the pronunciation (i), but chose to change it to (ii).*
Plomley ˈplʌm li
plonk plɒŋk ‖ plɑːŋk **plonked** plɒŋkt **plonking/ly** ˈplɒŋk ɪŋ /li ‖ ˈplɑːŋk ɪŋ /li **plonks** plɒŋks ‖ plɑːŋks
plonker ˈplɒŋk ə ‖ ˈplɑːŋk ᵊr **~s** z
plop plɒp ‖ plɑːp **plopped** plɒpt ‖ plɑːpt **plopping** ˈplɒp ɪŋ ‖ ˈplɑːp ɪŋ **plops** plɒps ‖ plɑːps
plosion ˈpləʊʒ ᵊn ‖ ˈploʊʒ ᵊn **~s** z
plosive ˈpləʊs ɪv ˈpləʊz- ‖ ˈploʊs- ˈploʊz- **~s** z
plot plɒt ‖ plɑːt **plots** plɒts ‖ plɑːts **plotted** ˈplɒt ɪd -əd ‖ ˈplɑːţ əd **plotting** ˈplɒt ɪŋ ‖ ˈplɑːţ ɪŋ
Plotinus pləʊ ˈtaɪn əs plɒ- ‖ ploʊ-
plotless ˈplɒt ləs -lɪs ‖ ˈplɑːt-
plotter ˈplɒt ə ‖ ˈplɑːţ ᵊr **~s** z
plough, Plough plaʊ **ploughed** plaʊd **ploughing** ˈplaʊ‿ɪŋ **ploughs** plaʊz
ploughboy ˈplaʊ bɔɪ **~s** z
ploughland ˈplaʊ lænd
plough|man ˈplaʊ |mən **~men** mən men ˌ**ploughman's ˈlunch**
ploughshare ˈplaʊ ʃeə ‖ -ʃer -ʃær **~s** z
Plouviez ˈpluːv i eɪ
Plovdiv ˈplɒv dɪv ‖ ˈplɑːv- ˈploʊv- *—Bulgarian* [ˈplov dif]
plover ˈplʌv ə ‖ -ᵊr ˈploʊv- **~s** z
plow, Plow plaʊ **plowed** plaʊd **plowing** ˈplaʊ‿ɪŋ **plows** plaʊz
plowboy ˈplaʊ bɔɪ **~s** z
Plowden ˈplaʊd ᵊn
plowland ˈplaʊ lænd
plow|man ˈplaʊ |mən **~men** mən men
Plowright ˈplaʊ raɪt
plowshare ˈplaʊ ʃeə ‖ -ʃer -ʃær **~s** z
ploy plɔɪ **ploys** plɔɪz
pluck plʌk **plucked** plʌkt **plucking** ˈplʌk ɪŋ **plucks** plʌks
pluck|y ˈplʌk |i **~ier** i‿ə ‖ i‿ᵊr **~iest** i‿ɪst i‿əst **~ily** ɪ li əl i **~iness** i nəs i nɪs
plug plʌg **plugged** plʌgd **plugging** ˈplʌg ɪŋ **plugs** plʌgz
plug-and-play ˌplʌg ən ˈpleɪ ◂ →-əm-
plug-compatible ˌplʌg kəm ˈpæt əb ᵊl ◂ §ˌkɒm-, -ɪb ᵊl ‖ -ˈpæţ- **~s** z
plughole ˈplʌg həʊl →-hɒʊl ‖ -hoʊl **~s** z
plug-in ˈplʌg ɪn **~s** z
plug-ug|ly ˈplʌg ˌʌg |li **~lies** liz
plum plʌm **plums** plʌmz ˈ**plum cake**; ˌ**plum ˈduff**; ˌ**plum ˈpudding**; ˈ**plum tree**
plumag|e ˈpluːm ɪdʒ **~es** ɪz əz
plumb plʌm *(= plum)* **plumbed** plʌmd **plumbing** ˈplʌm ɪŋ **plumbs** plʌmz ˈ**plumb line**
plumbago plʌm ˈbeɪg əʊ ‖ -oʊ **~s** z
plumber ˈplʌm ə ‖ -ᵊr **~s** z ˌ**plumber's ˈfriend**, ˌ**plumber's ˈhelper**
plumbic ˈplʌm bɪk
plumbing ˈplʌm ɪŋ
plumbous ˈplʌm bəs
plumbum ˈplʌm bəm ˈplʊm-
plume pluːm **plumed** pluːmd **plumes** pluːmz **pluming** ˈpluːm ɪŋ
Plummer ˈplʌm ə ‖ -ᵊr
plumm|et ˈplʌm |ɪt §-ət ‖ -|ət **~eted** ɪt ɪd §ət-, -əd ‖ əţ əd **~eting** ɪt ɪŋ §ət- ‖ əţ ɪŋ **~ets** ɪts §əts ‖ əts
plumm|y ˈplʌm |i **~ier** i‿ə ‖ i‿ᵊr **~iest** i‿ɪst i‿əst **~iness** i nəs i nɪs
plumose ˈpluːm əʊs pluː ˈməʊs ‖ ˈpluːm oʊs pluː ˈmoʊs
plump plʌmp **plumped** plʌmpt **plumper** ˈplʌmp ə ‖ -ᵊr **plumpest** ˈplʌmp ɪst -əst **plumping** ˈplʌmp ɪŋ **plumply** ˈplʌmp li **plumpness** ˈplʌmp nəs -nɪs **plumps** plʌmps
Plumpton ˈplʌmpt ən
Plumptre, Plumtre ˈplʌmp triː
Plumstead ˈplʌmᵖst ɪd -ed
plumule ˈpluːm juːl **~s** z
plunder ˈplʌnd ə ‖ -ᵊr **~ed** d **plundering** ˈplʌnd‿ər ɪŋ **~s** z
plunderer ˈplʌnd‿ər ə ‖ -ər **~s** z
plunderous ˈplʌnd ər əs
plunge plʌndʒ **plunged** plʌndʒd **plunges** ˈplʌndʒ ɪz -əz **plunging** ˈplʌndʒ ɪŋ
plunger ˈplʌndʒ ə ‖ -ᵊr **~s** z
plunk plʌŋk **plunked** plʌŋkt **plunking** ˈplʌŋk ɪŋ **plunks** plʌŋks
Plunket, Plunkett ˈplʌŋk ɪt §-ət
pluperfect ˌpluː ˈpɜːf ɪkt ◂ -ekt, §-əkt ‖ -ˈpɝːf- ˈ.ˌ.. **~s** s
plural ˈplʊər əl ˈplɔːr- ‖ ˈplʊr əl **~s** z
pluralis... *—see* **pluraliz...**
pluralism ˈplʊər ə ˌlɪz əm ˈplɔːr-, -ᵊl ˌɪz- ‖ ˈplʊr-
pluralist ˈplʊər əl ɪst ˈplɔːr-, §-əst ‖ ˈplʊr- **~s** s
pluralistic ˌplʊər ə ˈlɪst ɪk ◂ ˌplɔːr- ‖ ˌplʊr- **~ally** ᵊl‿i
pluralit|y pluᵊ ˈræl ət |i ˌplʊə-, ˌplɔː-, -ɪt- ‖ -əţ |i **~ies** iz
pluralization ˌplʊər əl aɪ ˈzeɪʃ ᵊn ˌplɔːr-, -ɪˈ-- ‖ ˌplʊr əl ə-
pluraliz|e ˈplʊər ə laɪz ˈplɔːr- ‖ ˈplʊr- **~ed** d **~es** ɪz əz **~ing** ɪŋ
pluri- ¦plʊər i ¦plɔːr i ‖ ¦plʊr i — **plurisyllable** ˌplʊər i ˈsɪl əb ᵊl ˌplɔːr- ‖ ˌplʊr-
plus plʌs **pluses, plusses** ˈplʌs ɪz -əz ˌ**plus ˈfours**; ˈ**plus sign**
plus ça change ˌpluː sɑː ˈʃɒnʒ ‖ -ˈʃɑːnʒ *—Fr* [ply sa ʃɑ̃ːʒ]
plush plʌʃ
plush|y ˈplʌʃ |i **~ier** i‿ə ‖ i‿ᵊr **~iest** i‿ɪst i‿əst **~ily** ɪ li əl i **~iness** i nəs i nɪs
Plutarch ˈpluːt ɑːk ‖ -ɑːrk
Pluto ˈpluːt əʊ ‖ ˈpluːţ oʊ
plutocrac|y pluː ˈtɒk rəs |i ‖ -ˈtɑːk- **~ies** iz
plutocrat ˈpluːt əʊ kræt ‖ ˈpluːţ ə- **~s** s
plutocratic ˌpluːt əʊ ˈkræt ɪk ◂ ‖ ˌpluːţ ə ˈkræţ ɪk ◂ **~ally** ᵊl‿i
pluton ˈpluːt ɒn ‖ -ɑːn **~s** z
Plutonian pluː ˈtəʊn i‿ən ‖ -ˈtoʊn-

Plosive releases

1 The English plosives (see ARTICULATION) are p, t, k, b, d, g and the GLOTTAL STOP. In a plosive air is compressed for a moment behind the articulators and prevented from escaping. This stage of a plosive is called the **hold**. The movements leading up to the hold are called the **approach**, and those leading from the hold are called the **release**.

2 With the alveolar plosives t and d, to describe how the sound fits in with the surrounding sounds we sometimes need to consider the SOFT PALATE and also the sides of the tongue, since it may be their movements that constitute the approach or release stage.

3 If n is followed by d, as in **handy** ˈhænd i, the change from the nasal to the plosive is made by movin the SOFT PALATE up (to cut off the air flow through the nose), while the tongue remains in contact with the alveolar ridge. This is **nasal approach**, and usually causes no difficulty to EFL learners.

4 Conversely, if d is followed by n, as in **midnight** ˈmɪd naɪt, the change from the plosive to the nasal is made by moving the soft palate down (to allow air flow through the nose). This is known as **nasal release**, and may be difficult for some learners.

It would not sound right to release the d in **midnight** by moving the tongue tip down (**oral release**) and then moving it back up for the n. Similarly in **submit** səb ˈmɪt the lips do not move as we go from b to m – the b is released nasally.

The same applies if one word ends in a plosive and the next begins with a nasal, as in **did nothing** ˌdɪd ˈnʌθɪŋ.

5 In a word such as **suddenly**, shown in this dictionary as ˈsʌd ᵊn li, the usual pronunciation has no ə, which means that the n immediately follows d, so that the d has nasal release: ˈsʌd n li. (In the less usual pronunciation ˈsʌd ən li the d would have ordinary oral release.)

6 Where t is followed by n, as in **fitness** ˈfɪt nəs, **button** ˈbʌt ᵊn, **quite nice** ˌkwaɪt ˈnaɪs, the t may be pronounced as an alveolar plosive with nasal release. Alternatively, it may be pronounced as a glottal stop.

7 If d is followed by l, as in **sadly** ˈsæd li, **good luck** ˌɡʊd ˈlʌk, **middle** ˈmɪd l, the change from the plosive to the lateral (see LIQUIDS) is made by moving the side rims of the tongue down while keeping the tongue tip in contact with the alveolar ridge. This is known as **lateral release**.

Plosive releases ▸

Plosive releases continued

8 If t is followed by l, as in **brightly** ˈbraɪt li, **quite lucky** ˌkwaɪt ˈlʌk i, the t may be pronounced as an alveolar plosive with lateral release, or as a glottal stop. But where the l is syllabic, as in the usual pronunciation of **little** ˈlɪt l ‖ ˈlɪţ l, it is more usual to have a laterally released alveolar t.

9 If one plosive is immediately followed by another, as in **acting** ˈækt ɪŋ, **rubbed** ˈrʌbd, the first plosive in most styles of English has **no audible release**, because its release is **masked** by the articulation of the second plosive.

10 In the case of a geminate plosive (see DOUBLE CONSONANT SOUNDS) as in **midday** ˌmɪd ˈdeɪ, the first d in this word has no release and the second d has no approach. Together they make a single long dː.

plutonic pluː ˈtɒn ɪk ‖ -ˈtɑːn ɪk
plutonium pluː ˈtəʊn i‿əm ‖ -ˈtoʊn-
pluvial ˈpluːv i‿əl **~s** z
pluviometer ˌpluːv i ˈɒm ɪt ə -ət ə ‖ -ˈɑːm əţ ᵊr **~s** z
pluvious ˈpluːv i‿əs
ply plaɪ **plied** plaɪd **plies** plaɪz **plying** ˈplaɪ ɪŋ
Plymouth ˈplɪm əθ
ˌ**Plymouth** ˈ**Brethren**; ˌ**Plymouth** ˈ**Rock**
Plynlimon plɪn ˈlɪm ən —*Welsh* Pumlimon [pim ˈlim on]
plywood ˈplaɪ wʊd **~s** z
PM, pm ˌpiː ˈem ◂
PMT ˌpiː em ˈtiː
p-n ˌpiː ˈen
pneumatic nju ˈmæt ɪk §nu- ‖ nu ˈmæţ ɪk nju-, nə- **~ally** ᵊl‿i **~s** s
pneuˌ**matic** ˈ**drill**
pneumatophore ˈnjuːm ət əʊ fɔː §ˈnuːm-; nju ˈmæt-, §nu- ‖ nu ˈmæţ ə fɔːr nju-, nə-, -foʊr; ˈnuːm əţ-,ˈnjuːm- **~s** z
pneumo- *comb. form*
with stress-neutral suffix ¦njuːm əʊ §¦nuːm- ‖ ¦nuːm ə ¦njuːm- — **pneumogastric** ˌnjuːm əʊ ˈɡæs trɪk ◂ §ˌnuːm- ‖ ˌnuːm ə- ˌnjuːm-
with stress-imposing suffix nju ˈmɒ+ ‖ nu ˈmɑː+ nju- — **pneumography** nju ˈmɒɡ rəf i ‖ nu ˈmɑːɡ- nju-
pneumococ|cus ˌnjuːm əʊ ˈkɒk| əs §ˌnuːm- ‖ ˌnuːm ə ˈkɑːk| əs **~ci** aɪ saɪ, iː, siː
pneumoconiosis ˌnjuːm əʊ ˌkəʊn i ˈəʊs ɪs §ˌnuːm-, §-əs ‖ ˌnuːm oʊ ˌkoʊn i ˈoʊs əs ˌnjuːm-
pneumocystis ˌnjuːm əʊ ˈsɪst ɪs §-əs ‖ ˌnuːm ə- ˌnjuːm-
ˌ**pneumo**ˌ**cystis ca**ˈ**rinii** kə ˈraɪn i aɪ kæ-, -ˈrɪn-
pneumonia nju ˈməʊn i‿ə §nu- ‖ nu ˈmoʊn- nju-, nə-
pneumonic nju ˈmɒn ɪk §nu- ‖ nu ˈmɑːn ɪk nju-, nə-
pneumothorax ˌnjuːm əʊ ˈθɔːr æks §ˌnuːm- ‖ ˌnuːm ə- -ˈθoʊr-
PNG ˌpiː en ˈdʒiː
Pnom Penh ˌpnɒm ˈpen ˌnɒm-, pə ˌnɒm ˈpen ‖ ˌpnɑːm- ˌnɑːm —*Khmer* [pʰnɔm ˈpiɲ]
Pnyx pnɪks nɪks
po pəʊ ‖ poʊ
Po *'polonium'* ˌpiː ˈəʊ ‖ -ˈoʊ
Po *name of river, name of Teletubby* pəʊ ‖ poʊ —*It* [pɔ]
PO ˌpiː ˈəʊ ◂ ‖ -ˈoʊ ◂ **~s, ~'s** z
poach pəʊtʃ ‖ poʊtʃ **poached** pəʊtʃt ‖ poʊtʃt **poaches** ˈpəʊtʃ ɪz -əz ‖ ˈpoʊtʃ əz **poaching** ˈpəʊtʃ ɪŋ ‖ ˈpoʊtʃ ɪŋ
poacher ˈpəʊtʃ ə ‖ ˈpoʊtʃ ᵊr **~s** z
Pobjoy ˈpɒb dʒɔɪ ‖ ˈpɑːb-
Pocahontas ˌpɒk ə ˈhɒnt əs -æs ‖ ˌpoʊk ə ˈhɑːnţ əs
pochard ˈpəʊtʃ əd ˈpɒtʃ- ‖ ˈpoʊtʃ ᵊrd **~s** z
pochette pɒ ˈʃet ‖ poʊ- **~s** s
pock pɒk ‖ pɑːk **pocked** pɒkt ‖ pɑːkt
pock|et ˈpɒk |ɪt §-ət ‖ ˈpɑːk |ət **~eted** ɪt ɪd §ət-, -əd ‖ əţ əd **~eting** ɪt ɪŋ §ət- ‖ əţ ɪŋ **~ets** ɪts §əts ‖ əts
ˈ**pocket** ˌ**money**
pocketable ˈpɒk ɪt əb ᵊl §ˈ·ət- ‖ ˈpɑːk əţ-
pocketbook ˈpɒk ɪt bʊk §-ət-, §-buːk ‖ ˈpɑːk- **~s** s
pocketful ˈpɒk ɪt fʊl §-ət- ‖ ˈpɑːk- **~s** z
pocket-handker|chief ˌpɒk ɪt ˈhæŋk ə |tʃɪf §ˌ-ət-, -tʃəf, -tʃiːf ‖ ˌpɑːk ət ˈhæŋk ᵊr- **~chiefs** tʃɪfs tʃəfs, tʃiːfs, tʃiːvz
pocket|knife ˈpɒk ɪt |naɪf §-ət- ‖ ˈpɑːk- **~knives** naɪvz
pocket-sized ˈpɒk ɪt saɪzd -ət- ‖ ˈpɑːk-
Pocklington ˈpɒk lɪŋ tən ‖ ˈpɑːk-
pockmark ˈpɒk mɑːk ‖ ˈpɑːk mɑːrk **~ed** t **~ing** ɪŋ **~s** s
poco ˈpəʊk əʊ ‖ ˈpoʊk oʊ —*It* [ˈpɔː ko]
Pocock ˈpəʊ kɒk ‖ ˈpoʊ kɑːk
pococurante ˌpəʊk əʊ kjuᵊ ˈrænt i ‖ ˌpoʊk oʊ ku ˈrænţ i -kʊˈ--, -ˈrɑːnţ- **~s** z

Pocono 'pəuk ə nəu ‖ 'pouk ə nou **~s** z
pod pɒd ‖ pɑːd **podded** 'pɒd ɪd -əd ‖ 'pɑːd əd **podding** 'pɒdɪŋ ‖ 'pɑːd ɪŋ **pods** pɒdz ‖ pɑːdz
-pod pɒd ‖ pɑːd — **arthropod** 'ɑːθ rəʊ pɒd ‖ 'ɑːrθ rə pɑːd
podagra pɒ 'dæg rə pəʊ-, 'pɒd əg- ‖ pə- 'pɑːd əg-
podcast 'pɒd kɑːst →'pɒg-, §-kæst ‖ 'pɑːd kæst **~ing** ɪŋ **~s** s
podd|y 'pɒd |i ‖ 'pɑːd |i **~ies** iz
Podge, podge pɒdʒ ‖ pɑːdʒ
Podgorica 'pɒd gɒr ɪts ə ‖ 'pɑːd gɔːr- —*Serbian* ['pod go ri tsa]
podg|y 'pɒdʒ |i ‖ 'pɑːdʒ |i **~ier** i‿ə ‖ i‿ər **~iest** i‿ɪst i‿əst **~ily** ɪ li əl i **~iness** i nəs i nɪs
Podhoretz pɒd 'hɒr ets ‖ pɑːd 'hɔːr- -'hɑːr-
podiatric ˌpəʊd i 'ætr ɪk ◂ ˌpɒd- ‖ ˌpoʊd-
podiatr|ist pəʊ 'daɪ‿ətr| ɪst §-əst ‖ pə- poʊ- **~ists** ɪsts §əsts **~y** i
podi|um 'pəʊd i‿|əm ‖ 'poʊd- **~a** ə **~ums** əmz
Podmore 'pɒd mɔː ‖ 'pɑːd mɔːr -moʊr
-podous *stress-imposing* pəd əs — **gastropodous** gæ 'strɒp əd əs ‖ -'strɑːp-
podsol 'pɒd sɒl ‖ 'pɑːd sɑːl -sɔːl **~s** z
Podunk 'pəʊ dʌŋk ‖ 'poʊ-
podzol 'pɒd zɒl ‖ 'pɑːd zɑːl -zɔːl **~s** z
Poe pəʊ ‖ poʊ

POEM

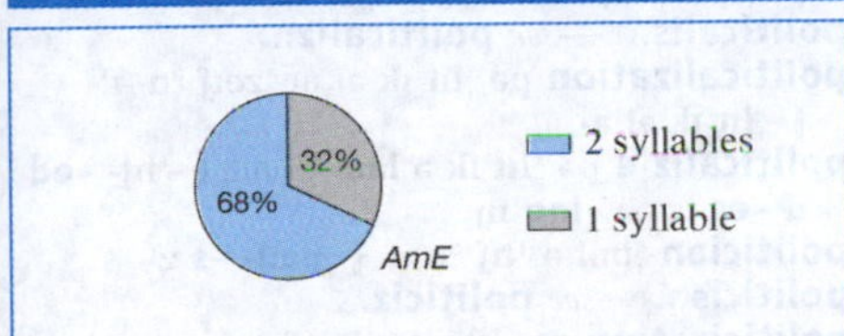

poem 'pəʊ ɪm -əm, -em; pəʊm ‖ 'poʊ əm poʊm **~s** z —*Preference poll, AmE: two syllables 68%, one syllable 32%.*
poes|y 'pəʊ əz |i -ɪz-, -ez- ‖ 'poʊ- -əs- **~ies** iz
poet 'pəʊ ɪt -ət, -et ‖ 'poʊ ət **~s** s
ˌ**poet 'laureate**
poetaster ˌpəʊ ɪ 'tæst ə -ə-, -e-, -'teɪst-, '· · · · ‖ 'poʊ ə tæst ər **~s** z
poetess ˌpəʊ ɪ 'tes -ə-, -e-; 'pəʊ ɪt ɪs, -ət-, -et-, -əs, -es ‖ 'poʊ əṭ əs **~es** ɪz əz
poetic pəʊ 'et ɪk ‖ poʊ 'eṭ ɪk **~al** əl **~ally** əl‿i **~s** s
poˌ**etic 'justice**; poˌ**etic 'licence**
poetry 'pəʊ ətr i -ɪtr- ‖ 'poʊ-
po-faced ˌpəʊ 'feɪst ◂ '· · ‖ ˌpoʊ-
pogey, pogie 'pəʊg i ‖ 'poʊg i **~s** z
pogge pɒg ‖ pɑːg **pogges** pɒgz ‖ pɑːgz
Poggenpohl *tdmk* 'pɒg ən pəʊl →-əm-, →-ŋ-, →-pɒʊl ‖ 'pɑːg ən poʊl —*Ger* ['pɔ gn̩ poːl]
pogo 'pəʊg əʊ ‖ 'poʊg oʊ
'**pogo stick**
pogrom 'pɒg rəm -rɒm ‖ 'poʊg rəm pə 'grɑːm, -'grʌm **~s** z
Pogue pəʊg ‖ poʊg **Pogues** pəʊgz ‖ poʊgz
pog|y 'pəʊg |i ‖ 'poʊg |i **~ies** iz

-poiesis pɔɪ 'iːs ɪs §-əs — **haemopoiesis** ˌhiːm əʊ pɔɪ 'iːs ɪs §-əs ‖ ˌ·ə-
-poietic pɔɪ 'et ɪk ‖ pɔɪ 'eṭ ɪk — **haemopoietic** ˌhiːm əʊ pɔɪ 'et ɪk ◂ ‖ -ə pɔɪ 'eṭ ɪk ◂
poignancy 'pɔɪn jən's i -ən's-
poignant 'pɔɪn jənt -ənt **~ly** li
poikilotherm 'pɔɪk ɪl əʊ θɜːm '·əl-; pɔɪ 'kɪl- ‖ -ə θɜːm -oʊ- **~s** z
poikilothermic ˌpɔɪk ɪl əʊ 'θɜːm ɪk ◂ ˌ·əl- ‖ -ə 'θɜːm ɪk ◂ -oʊ-
Poincaré 'pwæŋ kæ reɪ ˌ· ·'· ‖ ˌpwɑːŋ kɑː 'reɪ —*Fr* [pwɛ̃ ka ʁe]
poinciana ˌpɔɪn's i 'ɑːn ə -'æn- ‖ -'æn ə **~s** z
Poindexter 'pɔɪn ˌdekst ə ‖ -ər
poinsettia pɔɪn 'set i‿ə pɔɪnt- ‖ -'seṭ i‿ə ⚠-'seṭ ə **~s** z
point pɔɪnt **pointed** 'pɔɪnt ɪd -əd ‖ 'pɔɪnṭ əd **pointing** 'pɔɪnt ɪŋ ‖ 'pɔɪnṭ ɪŋ **points** pɔɪnts
'**point** ˌ**duty**; ˌ**point of 'order**; ˌ**point of 'view**
point-blank ˌpɔɪnt 'blæŋk ◂
ˌ**point-blank re'fusal**
point-by-point ˌpɔɪnt baɪ 'pɔɪnt ◂
pointe pwænt —*Fr* [pwɛ̃t]
Pointe-à-Pitre ˌpwænt ə 'piːtr -æ-, -ɑː-, -'piːtr ə —*Fr* [pwɛ̃ ta pitʁ]
pointed 'pɔɪnt ɪd -əd ‖ 'pɔɪnṭ əd **~ly** li **~ness** nəs nɪs
pointer 'pɔɪnt ə ‖ 'pɔɪnṭ ər **~s** z
pointillism 'pɔɪnt ɪ ˌlɪz əm 'pwænt-, -ə-, -ˌiː-, -ˌjɪz-; -əl ˌɪz- ‖ 'pɔɪnṭ əl ˌɪz əm 'pwænṭ- —*Fr* pointillisme [pwɛ̃ ti jism̥]
pointillist 'pɔɪnt ɪl ɪst 'pwænt-, -i-, -əl-, §-əst ‖ 'pɔɪnṭ əl- ˌpwæn tiː 'jiːst **~s** s —*Fr* pointilliste [pwɛ̃ ti jist]
pointless 'pɔɪnt ləs -lɪs **~ly** li **~ness** nəs nɪs
Pointon 'pɔɪnt ən ‖ -ən
points|man 'pɔɪnts |mən **~men** mən men
point-to-point ˌpɔɪnt tə 'pɔɪnt -tu-
pointy 'pɔɪnt i ‖ 'pɔɪnṭ i
pointy-headed ˌpɔɪnt i 'hed ɪd ◂ -əd ◂ ‖ ˌpɔɪnṭ-
Poirot 'pwɑːr əʊ ‖ pwɑː 'roʊ —*Fr* [pwa ʁo]
poise pɔɪz **poised** pɔɪzd **poises** 'pɔɪz ɪz -əz **poising** 'pɔɪz ɪŋ
poison 'pɔɪz ən **~ed** d **~ing** ‿ɪŋ **~s** z
ˌ**poison 'gas**, '· · ·; ˌ**poison 'ivy**
poisonous 'pɔɪz ən‿əs **~ly** li **~ness** nəs nɪs
poison-pen ˌpɔɪz ən 'pen →-əm-
ˌ**poison-'pen** ˌ**letter**
Poisson 'pwɑːs ɒn 'pwæs-, 'pwʌs-, -ɒ̃, -ən ‖ pwɑː 'soʊn -'sɔːn, -'sɑːn —*Fr* [pwa sɔ̃]
ˌ**Poisson** ˌ**distri'bution** ‖ ·ˌ· ˌ··'··
Poitier 'pwɒt i eɪ 'pwɑːt-, 'pɔɪt- ‖ 'pwɑːt- -jeɪ
Poitiers 'pwɑːt i eɪ 'pwɒt- ‖ ˌpwɑːṭ i 'eɪ —*Fr* [pwa tje]
poke pəʊk ‖ poʊk **poked** pəʊkt ‖ poʊkt **pokes** pəʊks ‖ poʊks **poking** 'pəʊk ɪŋ ‖ 'poʊk ɪŋ
Pokemon, Pokémon 'pəʊk ɪ mɒn 'pɒk-, -eɪ-, -e- ‖ 'poʊk ɪ mɑːn -eɪ- **~s** z —*Jp* [po ˌke moɴ]

P

poker 'pəʊk ə ‖ 'poʊk ᵊr **~s** z
'poker face
poker-faced 'pəʊk ə feɪst ˌ· ·'·◂ ‖ 'poʊk ᵊr-
pokerwork 'pəʊk ə wɜːk ‖ 'poʊk ᵊr wɜ·ːk
pokeweed 'pəʊk wiːd ‖ 'poʊk-
pok|ey, pok|ie, pokly 'pəʊk |i ‖ 'poʊk |i **~eys** iz **~ier** i‿ə ‖ i‿ᵊr **~ies** iz **~iest** i‿ɪst i‿əst **~ily** ɪ li əl i **~iness** i nəs i nɪs
pol pɒl ‖ pɑːl **pols** pɒlz ‖ pɑːlz
ˌPol 'Pot
Polabian pəʊ 'leɪb i‿ən -'lɑːb- ‖ poʊ-
Polack, Polak 'pəʊl æk -ək ‖ 'poʊl- **~s** s
Poland 'pəʊl ənd ‖ 'poʊl-
Polanski pə 'lænᵗsk i pɒ- ‖ poʊ-
polar 'pəʊl ə ‖ 'poʊl ᵊr
ˌpolar 'bear ‖ '· · ·
Polari pəʊ 'lɑːr i ‖ pə-
polarimeter ˌpəʊl ə 'rɪm ɪt ə -ət ə ‖ ˌpoʊl ə 'rɪm əṭ ᵊr **~s** z
Polaris pəʊ 'lɑːr ɪs -'lær-, -'leər-, §-əs ‖ pə 'lær əs poʊ-, -'ler-, -'lɑːr-
polaris... —see **polariz...**
polariscope pəʊ 'lær ɪ skəʊp -'·ə- ‖ poʊ 'lær ə skoʊp pə-, -'ler- **~s** s
polarit|y pəʊ 'lær ət |i -ɪt- ‖ poʊ 'lær əṭ |i pə-, -'ler- **~ies** iz
polarization ˌpəʊl ər aɪ 'zeɪʃ ᵊn -ɪ'·- ‖ ˌpoʊl ər ə- **~s** z
polariz|e 'pəʊl ə raɪz ‖ 'poʊl- **~ed** d **~es** ɪz əz **~ing** ɪŋ
Polaroid *tdmk* 'pəʊl ə rɔɪd ‖ 'poʊl- **~s** z
polder 'pəʊld ə →'pɒʊld-, 'pɒld- ‖ 'poʊld ᵊr **~s** z
Poldhu ₍ˌ₎pɒl 'djuː →-'dʒuː ‖ ₍ˌ₎pɑːl 'duː -'djuː
pole pəʊl →pɒʊl ‖ poʊl **poled** pəʊld →pɒʊld ‖ poʊld **poles** pəʊlz →pɒʊlz ‖ poʊlz **poling** 'pəʊl ɪŋ →'pɒʊl- ‖ 'poʊl ɪŋ
'pole poˌsition; 'pole star; 'pole vault
Pole *surname (i)* pəʊl →pɒʊl ‖ poʊl, *(ii)* puːl
Pole *'Polish person'* pəʊl →pɒʊl ‖ poʊl **Poles** pəʊlz →pɒʊlz ‖ 'poʊlz
poleax, poleax|e 'pəʊl æks →'pɒʊl- ‖ 'poʊl- **~ed** t **~es** ɪz əz **~ing** ɪŋ
polecat 'pəʊl kæt →'pɒʊl- ‖ 'poʊl- **~s** s
Polegate 'pəʊl geɪt →'pɒʊl- ‖ 'poʊl-
polemarch 'pɒl ɪ mɑːk -ə- ‖ 'pɑːl ə mɑːrk **~s** s
polemic pə 'lem ɪk pəʊ-, pɒ- **~al** ᵊl **~ally** ᵊl‿i **~s** s
polemicist pə 'lem ɪs ɪst -əs-, §-əst **~s** s
polenta pəʊ 'lent ə ‖ poʊ 'lenṭ ə pə-, -'lent ɑː
Polesden 'pəʊlz dən →'pɒʊlz- ‖ 'poʊlz-
ˌPolesden 'Lacey
Polesworth 'pəʊlz wəθ →'pɒʊlz-, -wɜːθ ‖ 'poʊlz wᵊrθ
pole-vault 'pəʊl vɔːlt →'pɒʊl-, -vɒlt ‖ 'poʊl- -vɑːlt **~ed** ɪd əd **~er/s** ə/z ‖ ᵊr/z **~ing** ɪŋ **~s** s
Poliakoff ˌpɒl i 'ɑːk ɒf ‖ ˌpɑːl i 'ɑːk ɔːf -ɑːf
polic|e pə 'liːs pʊ-; pliːs; §'pəʊl iːs **~ed** t **~es** ɪz əz **~ing** ɪŋ
poˌlice 'constable◂; po'lice dog; po'lice force; po'lice ˌofficer; po'lice state; po'lice ˌstation
police|man pə 'liːs |mən pʊ-; 'pliːs |mən; §'pəʊl iːs- **~men** mən men **~woman** ˌwʊm ən **~women** ˌwɪm ɪn §-ən
polic|y 'pɒl əs |i -ɪs- ‖ 'pɑːl- **~ies** iz
policyholder 'pɒl əs i ˌhəʊld ə '·ɪs-, →-ˌhɒʊld- ‖ 'pɑːl əs i ˌhoʊld ᵊr **~s** z
polimerism pə 'lɪm ə ˌrɪz əm pɒ-; 'pɒl ɪm-, '·əm- ‖ 'pɑːl əm-
polio 'pəʊl i əʊ ‖ 'poʊl i oʊ
poliomyelitis ˌpəʊl i‿əʊ ˌmaɪ‿ə 'laɪt ɪs -ɪ'·-, §-əs ‖ ˌpoʊl i oʊ ˌmaɪ ə 'laɪṭ əs
polis 'pɒl ɪs §-əs ‖ 'pɑːl əs 'poʊl-
-polis *stress-imposing* pəl ɪs §-əs — **Annapolis** ə 'næp əl ɪs §-əs
Polisario ˌpɒl ɪ 'sɑːr i əʊ ˌ·ə- ‖ ˌpoʊl ə 'sɑːr i oʊ ˌpɑːl-
poli sci ˌpɒl i 'saɪ ‖ ˌpɑːl-
polish *v, n* 'pɒl ɪʃ ‖ 'pɑːl ɪʃ **~ed** t **~er/s** ə/z ‖ ᵊr/z **~es** ɪz əz **~ing** ɪŋ
Polish *adj* 'pəʊl ɪʃ ‖ 'poʊl ɪʃ
politburo, P~ 'pɒl ɪt ˌbjʊər əʊ pə 'liːt-, pə 'lɪt-, -ˌbjɔːr-, -'· ·bjuᵊ ˌrəʊ ‖ 'pɑːl ət ˌbjʊr oʊ
po|lite pə |'laɪt **~litely** 'laɪt li **~liteness** 'laɪt nəs nɪs **~liter** 'laɪt ə ‖ 'laɪṭ ᵊr **~litest** 'laɪt ɪst -əst ‖ 'laɪṭ əst
politesse ˌpɒl ɪ 'tes -ə- ‖ ˌpɑːl-
politic 'pɒl ə tɪk -ɪ- ‖ 'pɑːl- **~ly** li **~s** s
political pə 'lɪt ɪk ᵊl ‖ -'lɪṭ- **~ly** ‿i
poˌlitical a'sylum; poˌlitical ge'ography; poˌlitical 'prisoner; poˌlitical 'science
politicalis... —see **politicaliz...**
politicalization pə ˌlɪt ɪk əl aɪ 'zeɪʃ ᵊn -ɪ'·- ‖ -ˌlɪṭ ɪk əl ə-
politicaliz|e pə 'lɪt ɪk ə laɪz -ᵊl aɪz ‖ -'lɪṭ- **~ed** d **~es** ɪz əz **~ing** ɪŋ
politician ˌpɒl ə 'tɪʃ ᵊn -ɪ- ‖ ˌpɑːl- **~s** z
politicis...—see **politiciz...**
politicization pə ˌlɪt ɪ saɪ 'zeɪʃ ᵊn -ˌ·ə-, -sɪ'·- ‖ -ˌlɪṭ əs ə-
politiciz|e pə 'lɪt ɪ saɪz -ə- ‖ -'lɪṭ- **~ed** d **~es** ɪz əz **~ing** ɪŋ
politick|ing 'pɒl ə tɪk| ɪŋ '·ɪ- ‖ 'pɑːl- **~ed** t
politico pə 'lɪt ɪ kəʊ ‖ -'lɪṭ ɪ koʊ **~s** z
politico- *comb. form* pə ¦lɪt ɪ kəʊ ‖ -¦lɪṭ ɪ koʊ — **politicoeconomic** pə ˌlɪt ɪk əʊ ˌiːk ə 'nɒm ɪk -ˌek- ‖ pə ˌlɪṭ ɪ koʊ ˌek ə 'nɑːm ɪk
politics 'pɒl ə tɪks -ɪ- ‖ 'pɑːl-
polit|y 'pɒl ət |i -ɪt- ‖ 'pɑːl əṭ |i **~ies** iz
Polk pəʊk ‖ poʊk
polk|a 'pɒlk |ə 'pəʊlk- ‖ 'poʊlk |ə 'poʊk- —*In* polka dot, *AmE usually* 'poʊk ə **~aed** əd **~aing** əʳ ɪŋ ‖ ə ɪŋ **~as** əz
'polka dot
Polkinghorn, Polkinghorne 'pɒlk ɪŋ hɔːn ‖ 'pɑːlk ɪŋ hɔːrn
poll *n, v* pəʊl →pɒʊl, §pɒl ‖ poʊl —*but in the obsolete senses 'parrot', 'student taking pass degree' was* pɒl ‖ pɑːl **polled** pəʊld →pɒʊld ‖ poʊld **polling** 'pəʊl ɪŋ →'pɒʊl- ‖ 'poʊl ɪŋ **polls** pəʊlz →pɒʊlz ‖ poʊlz
'polling booth; 'polling day; 'polling ˌstation; 'poll tax

Poll *name* pɒl ‖ pɑːl
pollack ˈpɒl ək ‖ ˈpɑːl- **~s** s
pollan ˈpɒl ən ‖ ˈpɑːl- **~s** z
pollard ˈpɒl əd -ɑːd ‖ ˈpɑːl ᵊrd **~ed** ɪd əd **~ing** ɪŋ **~s** z
Pollard ˈpɒl ɑːd -əd ‖ˈpɑːl ɑːrd -ᵊrd
pollen, P~ ˈpɒl ən ‖ ˈpɑːl-
 ˈpollen count
polli|nate ˈpɒl ə |neɪt -ɪ- ‖ ˈpɑːl- **~nated** neɪt ɪd -əd ‖ neɪţ əd **~nates** neɪts **~nating** neɪt ɪŋ ‖ neɪţ ɪŋ
pollination ˌpɒl ə ˈneɪʃ ᵊn -ɪ- ‖ ˌpɑːl- **~s** z
Pollit, Pollitt ˈpɒl ɪt -ət ‖ ˈpɑːl-
polliwog ˈpɒl i wɒg ‖ˈpɑːl i wɑːg -wɔːg **~s** z
Pollock, p~, Pollok ˈpɒl ək ‖ ˈpɑːl- **~s** s
Pollokshields ˌpɒl ək ˈʃiːᵊldz ‖ ˌpɑːl-
pollster ˈpəʊl stə →ˈpɒʊl-, §ˈpɒl- ‖ ˈpoʊl stᵊr **~s** z
pollutant pə ˈluːt ᵊnt -ˈljuːt- **~s** s
pol|lute pə |ˈluːt -ˈljuːt **~luted** ˈluːt ɪd ˈljuːt-, -əd ‖ ˈluːţ əd **~lutes** ˈluːts ˈljuːts **~luting** ˈluːt ɪŋ ˈljuːt- ‖ˈluːţ ɪŋ
polluter pə ˈluːt ə -ˈljuːt- ‖ -ˈluːţ ᵊr **~s** z
pollution pə ˈluːʃ ᵊn -ˈljuːʃ- **~s** z
Pollux ˈpɒl əks ‖ ˈpɑːl-
Polly ˈpɒl i ‖ ˈpɑːl i
Pollyanna ˌpɒl i ˈæn ə ‖ ˌpɑːl- **~s, ~'s** z
Pollyanna|ish ˌpɒl i ˈæn əʳ ɪʃ ◂ ‖ ˌpɑːl i ˈæn ə| ɪʃ ◂ **~ism** ˌɪz əm
Polmont ˈpəʊl mɒnt →ˈpɒʊl- ‖ ˈpoʊl mɑːnt —*but in Scotland, locally* -mənt
polo, Polo ˈpəʊl əʊ ‖ ˈpoʊl oʊ
 ˈpolo neck
polonais|e ˌpɒl ə ˈneɪz ‖ ˌpɑːl- ˌpoʊl- **~es** ɪz əz
polonium pə ˈləʊn i‿əm ‖ -ˈloʊn-
Polonius pə ˈləʊn i‿əs ‖ -ˈloʊn-
polony pə ˈləʊn i ‖ -ˈloʊn i
Polperro pɒl ˈper əʊ ‖ pɑːl ˈper oʊ
Polson ˈpəʊl sən →ˈpɒʊl- ‖ ˈpoʊl-
poltergeist ˈpɒlt ə gaɪst ˈpəʊlt-, ⚠-dʒaɪst ‖ ˈpoʊlt ᵊr- **~s** s
poltroon pɒl ˈtruːn ‖ pɑːl- **~s** z
poltroonery pɒl ˈtruːn ər i ‖ pɑːl-
Polwarth ˈpɒl wəθ ‖ ˈpɑːl wᵊrθ
poly ˈpɒl i ‖ ˈpɑːl i **~s** z
 ˈpoly bag
poly- *comb. form*
 with stress-neutral suffix ¦pɒl i ‖ ¦pɑːl i —*but in certain more familiar words, before a consonant, also* ¦pɒl ə ‖ ¦pɑːl ə — **polygenesis** ˌpɒl i ˈdʒen əs ɪs -ɪs ɪs, §-əs ‖ ˌpɑːl-
 with stress-imposing suffix pə ˈlɪ+ pɒ- — **polyphagous** pə ˈlɪf əg əs pɒ-
polyamide ˌpɒl i ˈæm aɪd -ɪd, §-əd ‖ ˌpɑːl- **~s** z
polyamory ˌpɒl i ˈæm ər i ‖ ˌpɑːl-
polyandrous ˌpɒl i ˈændr əs ◂ ‖ ˌpɑːl-
polyandry ˌpɒl i ˈændr i ˈ· ·ˌ· · ‖ ˌpɑːl-
polyanth|a ˌpɒl i ˈænᵗθ |ə ‖ ˌpɑːl- **~as** əz **~us/es** əs /ɪz -əz
Polybius pə ˈlɪb i‿əs pɒ-
polycarbonate ˌpɒl i ˈkɑːb ə neɪt -nət, -nɪt ‖ ˌpɑːl i ˈkɑːrb- **~s** s
Polycarp ˈpɒl i kɑːp ‖ ˈpɑːl i kɑːrp
Polycell *tdmk* ˈpɒl i sel ‖ ˈpɑːl-
polychaete ˈpɒl i kiːt ‖ ˈpɑːl- **~s** s
polychlorinated ˌpɒl i ˈklɔːr ɪ neɪt ɪd ◂ -ˈ·ə-, -əd ‖ ˌpɑːl i ˈklɔːr ə neɪţ əd ◂ -ˈkloʊr-
polychrom|e ˈpɒl i krəʊm ‖ ˈpɑːl i kroʊm **~y** i
polyclinic ˌpɒl i ˈklɪn ɪk ˈ· ·ˌ· · ‖ ˌpɑːl-
polycotton ˌpɒl i ˈkɒt ᵊn ◂ ‖ ˌpɑːl i ˈkɑːt ᵊn ◂
Polycrates pə ˈlɪk rə tiːz pɒ-
polydactyl ˌpɒl i ˈdækt ɪl ◂ -ᵊl ‖ ˌpɑːl-
polyester ˌpɒl i ˈest ə ◂ ˈ· ·ˌ· · ‖ ˈpɑːl i ˌest ᵊr **~s** z
polyethylene ˌpɒl i ˈeθ ə liːn ◂ -ˈ·ɪ-, -ᵊl iːn ‖ ˌpɑːl-
Polyfilla *tdmk* ˈpɒl i ˌfɪl ə ‖ˈpɑːl-
polygamist pə ˈlɪg əm ɪst pɒ-, §-əst **~s** s
polygamous pə ˈlɪg əm əs pɒ- **~ly** li
polygamy pə ˈlɪg əm i pɒ-
polygene ˈpɒl i dʒiːn ‖ ˈpɑːl- **~s** z
polygenic ˌpɒl i ˈdʒen ɪk ◂ ‖ ˌpɑːl-
polyglot ˈpɒl i glɒt ‖ ˈpɑːl i glɑːt **~s** s
polygon ˈpɒl ɪg ən -əg-; -i gɒn ‖ ˈpɑːl i gɑːn **~s** z
polygonal pə ˈlɪg ən ᵊl pɒ- **~ly** i
polygonum pə ˈlɪg ən əm pɒ-
polygraph ˈpɒl i grɑːf -græf ‖ ˈpɑːl i græf **~s** s
Polygrip *tdmk* ˈpɒl i grɪp ‖ ˈpɑːl-
polygynous pə ˈlɪdʒ ən əs pɒ-, -ɪn-
polygyny pə ˈlɪdʒ ən i pɒ-, -ɪn-
polyhedr|on ˌpɒl i ˈhiːdr |ən -ˈhedr- ‖ ˌpɑːl- **~a** ə **~al** əl **~ons** ənz
Polyhymnia ˌpɒl i ˈhɪm ni‿ə ‖ ˌpɑːl-
polylectal ˌpɒl i ˈlekt ᵊl ◂ ‖ ˌpɑːl-
polymath ˈpɒl i mæθ ‖ ˈpɑːl- **~s** s
polymer ˈpɒl ɪm ə -əm- ‖ ˈpɑːl əm ᵊr **~s** z
polymeras|e ˈpɒl ɪm ə reɪz ˈ·əm-; pə ˈlɪm-, -reɪs ‖ ˈpɑːl əm-
polymeric ˌpɒl ɪ ˈmer ɪk ◂ ‖ ˌpɑːl ə-
polymeris... —*see* **polymeriz...**
polymerization ˌpɒl ɪm ər aɪ ˈzeɪʃ ᵊn ˌ·əm-, -ɪˈ--; pə ˌlɪm- ‖ ˌpɑːl əm ər ə- pə ˌlɪm-
polymeriz|e ˈpɒl ɪm ə raɪz ˈ·əm-; pə ˈlɪm- ‖ ˈpɑːl- **~ed** d **~es** ɪz əz **~ing** ɪŋ
polymerous pə ˈlɪm ər əs pɒ-
polymorph|ic ˌpɒl i ˈmɔːf |ɪk ◂ ‖ ˌpɑːl i ˈmɔːrf |ɪk ◂ **~ism** ˌɪz əm **~ous** əs ◂

POLYNESIA

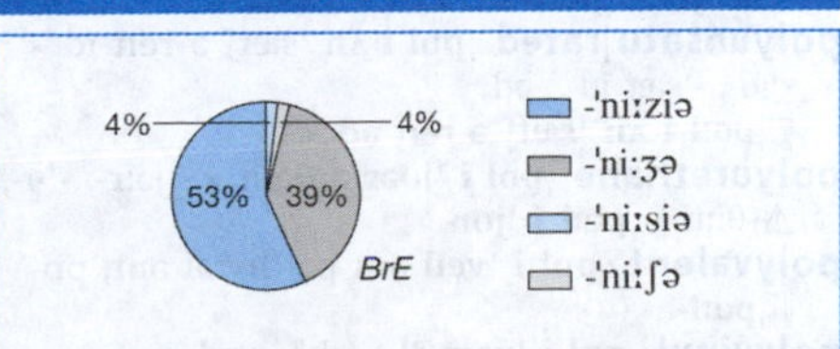

Polynesia ˌpɒl ɪ ˈniːz i‿ə ˌ·ə-, -ˈniːʒ ə, -ˈniːs i‿ə, -ˈniːʃ ə ‖ ˌpɑːl ə ˈniːʒ ə -ˈniːʃ- — *Preference poll, BrE:* -ˈniːziə *53%,* -ˈniːʒə *39%,* -ˈniːsiə *4%,* -ˈniːʃə *4%.*

Polynesian ˌpɒl ɪ ˈniːz i‿ən ˌ-ə-, -ˈniːʒ ən, -ˈniːs i‿ən, -ˈniːʃ ən ‖ ˌpɑːl ə ˈniːʒ ən -ˈniːʃ- **~s** z
Polynices ˌpɒl i ˈnaɪs iːz ‖ ˌpɑːl-
polynomial ˌpɒl i ˈnəʊm i‿əl ◂ ‖ ˌpɑːl ə ˈnoʊm- **~s** z
polyp ˈpɒl ɪp -əp ‖ ˈpɑːl əp **~s** s
polypeptide ˌpɒl i ˈpept aɪd ‖ ˌpɑːl- **~s** z
Polyphemus ˌpɒl ɪ ˈfiːm əs -ə- ‖ ˌpɑːl-
polyphonic ˌpɒl i ˈfɒn ɪk ◂ ‖ ˌpɑːl i ˈfɑːn ɪk ◂ **~ally** əl‿i
polyphon|y pə ˈlɪf ən |i pɒ- **~ies** iz
polypi ˈpɒl ɪ paɪ -ə- ‖ ˈpɑːl-
polyploid ˈpɒl i plɔɪd ‖ ˈpɑːl- **~s** z
polypod ˈpɒl i pɒd ‖ ˈpɑːl i pɑːd **~s** z
polypod|y ˈpɒl i pəʊd |i ‖ ˈpɑːl ə poʊd |i **~ies** iz
polypous ˈpɒl ɪp əs -əp- ‖ ˈpɑːl-
polypropylene ˌpɒl i ˈprəʊp ə liːn ◂ -ˈ-ɪ- ‖ ˌpɑːl i ˈproʊp-
polypus ˈpɒl ɪp əs -əp- ‖ ˈpɑːl- **~es** ɪz əz
polysaccharide ˌpɒl i ˈsæk ə raɪd ˌpɑːl- **~s** z
polysemous pə ˈlɪs ɪm əs pɒ-, -əm-; ˌpɒl i ˈsiːm əs ‖ ˌpɑːl i ˈsiːm əs **~ly** li
polysemy pə ˈlɪs ɪm i pɒ-, -əm-; ˈpɒl i ˌsiːm i, ˌ· ·ˈ· · ‖ ˌpɑːl i ˈsiːm i
polysorbate ˌpɒl i ˈsɔːb eɪt ◂ ‖ ˌpɑːl i ˈsɔːrb eɪt
polystyrene ˌpɒl i ˈstaɪər iːn ◂ ‖ ˌpɑːl-
polysyllabic ˌpɒl i sɪ ˈlæb ɪk ◂ -səˈ-- ‖ ˌpɑːl- **~ally** əl‿i
polysyllable ˈpɒl i ˌsɪl əb əl ˌ· ·ˈ· · · ‖ ˈpɑːl- **~s** z
polysyndeton ˌpɒl i ˈsɪnd ət ən -ˈ-ɪt- ‖ ˌpɑːl i ˈsɪnd ə tɑːn
polysynthetic ˌpɒl i sɪn ˈθet ɪk ◂ ‖ ˌpɑːl i sɪn ˈθeṭ ɪk ◂
polysystemic ˌpɒl i sɪ ˈstiːm ɪk ◂ -səˈ--, -ˈstem- ‖ ˌpɑːl-
polytechnic ˌpɒl i ˈtek nɪk -ə- ‖ ˌpɑːl- **~s** s
polytetrafluoroethylene ˌpɒl i ˌtetr ə ˌfluər əʊ ˈeθ ə liːn -ˌflɔːr- ‖ ˌpɑːl i ˌtetr ə ˌflʊr oʊ-
polytheism ˈpɒl i θi ˌɪz əm ˈ· ·ˌθiː ɪz əm ‖ ˈpɑːl-
polytheist ˈpɒl i θi ɪst ˈ· ·ˌθiː ɪst, §-əst ‖ ˈpɑːl- **~s** s
polytheistic ˌpɒl i θi ˈɪst ɪk ◂ ‖ ˌpɑːl- **~ally** əl‿i
polythene ˈpɒl ɪ θiːn -ə- ‖ ˈpɑːl-
polyunsaturate ˌpɒl i ʌn ˈsætʃ ə reɪt -ʊ-, -ˈsæt jʊ- ‖ ˌpɑːl- **~s** s
polyunsatu|rated ˌpɒl i ʌn ˈsætʃ ə reɪt ɪd ◂ -ˈ-ʊ-, -ˈsæt jʊ-, -əd ‖ ˌpɑːl i ʌn ˈsætʃ ə reɪṭ əd ◂
polyurethane ˌpɒl i ˈjʊər ə θeɪn ◂ -ˈjɔːr-, -ˈ-ɪ-, ⚠-θiːn ‖ ˌpɑːl i ˈjʊr-
polyvalent ˌpɒl i ˈveɪl ənt pə ˈlɪv əl ənt, pɒ- ‖ ˌpɑːl-
polyvinyl ˌpɒl i ˈvaɪn əl ◂ -ɪl ‖ ˌpɑːl-
Polyxena pə ˈlɪks ən ə pɒ-, -ɪn-
Polzeath pɒl ˈzeθ -ˈziːθ ‖ poʊl-
pom, Pom pɒm ‖ pɑːm **poms, Poms** pɒmz ‖ pɑːmz
poma, Poma ˈpɒm ə ˈpəʊm ə ‖ ˈpɑːm ə ˈpoʊm ə
pomace ˈpʌm ɪs ˈpɒm-, §-əs ‖ ˈpɑːm-
pomad|e pəʊ ˈmeɪd pɒ-, -ˈmɑːd ‖ poʊ- pɑː- **~ed** ɪd əd **~es** z **~ing** ɪŋ
Pomagne *tdmk* pəʊ ˈmeɪn ‖ poʊ-
pomander pəʊ ˈmænd ə ‖ ˈpoʊm ænd ər poʊ ˈmænd ər **~s** z
pome pəʊm ‖ poʊm **pomes** pəʊmz ‖ poʊmz
pomegranate ˈpɒm ɪ græn ət ˈ-ə-, -ɪt ‖ ˈpɑːm-ˈgræn ət, ˈpʌm- **~s** s
pomelo ˈpɒm ə ləʊ -ɪ-; pə ˈmel əʊ ‖ ˈpɑːm ə loʊ **~s** z
Pomerani|a ˌpɒm ə ˈreɪn i‿|ə ‖ ˌpɑːm- **~an/s** ən/z
Pomeroy *(i)* ˈpɒm ə rɔɪ ‖ ˈpɑːm-, *(ii)* ˈpəʊm- ‖ ˈpoʊm-
pomfret *'kind of fish'* ˈpɒm frət -frɪt ‖ ˈpɑːm-
Pomfret, p~ ˈpɒm frət ˈpʌm-, -fret ‖ ˈpɑːm-
ˈ**Pomfret cake**
pomiferous pɒ ˈmɪf ər əs pəṭ- ‖ poʊ-
pommel *n* ˈpɒm əl ˈpʌm- ‖ ˈpʌm əl ˈpɑːm- **~s** z
pommel *v* ˈpʌm əl ˈpɒm- **~ed, ~led** d **~ing, ~ling** ɪŋ **~s** z
pomm|ie, pomm|y, Pommy ˈpɒm |i ‖ ˈpɑːm |i **~ies** iz
Pomo ˈpəʊm əʊ ‖ ˈpoʊm oʊ **~s** z
Pomona, p~ pəʊ ˈməʊn ə ‖ pə ˈmoʊn ə
pomp pɒmp ‖ pɑːmp **pomps** pɒm*p*s ‖ pɑːm*p*s
pompadour, P~ ˈpɒmp ə dʊə -dɔː ‖ ˈpɑːmp ə dɔːr -doʊr, -dʊr —*Fr* [pɔ̃ pa duːʁ] **~s** z
pompano, P~ ˈpɒmp ə nəʊ ˈpʌmp- ˈpɑːmp ə noʊ **~s** z
ˌ**Pompano ˈBeach**
Pompeian, Pompeiian pɒm ˈpeɪ ən -ˈpiː ‖ pɑːm- **~s** z
Pompeii pɒm ˈpeɪ i -iː; pɒm ˈpeɪ ‖ pɑːm-
Pompey ˈpɒmp i ‖ ˈpɑːmp i
Pomphrey ˈpɒmᵖf ri ‖ ˈpɑːmᵖf-
Pompidou ˈpɒmp ɪ duː -ə- ‖ ˈpɑːmp- —*Fr* [pɔ̃ pi du]
pompom ˈpɒm pɒm ‖ ˈpɑːm pɑːm **~s** z
pompon ˈpɒm pɒn ‖ ˈpɑːm pɑːn —*Fr* [pɔ̃ pɔ̃] **~s** z
pomposit|y pɒm ˈpɒs ət |i -ɪt- ‖ pɑːm ˈpɑːs əṭ |i **~ies** iz
pompous ˈpɒmp əs ‖ ˈpɑːmp əs **~ly** li **~ness** nəs nɪs
'pon pɒn ‖ pɑːn
ponce pɒnᵗs ‖ pɑːnᵗs **ponced** pɒnᵗst ‖ pɑːnᵗst **ponces** ˈpɒnᵗs ɪz -əz ‖ ˈpɑːnᵗs əz **poncing** ˈpɒnᵗs ɪŋ ‖ ˈpɑːnᵗs ɪŋ
Ponce *Spanish name; place in PR* ˈpɒnᵗs eɪ pɒnᵗs ‖ ˈpɔːnᵗs eɪ ˈpɑːnᵗs-, ˈpoʊnᵗs- —*AmSp* [ˈpon se]
poncey ˈpɒnᵗs i ‖ ˈpɑːnᵗs i
poncho ˈpɒntʃ əʊ ‖ ˈpɑːntʃ oʊ —*Sp* [ˈpon tʃo] **~s** z
poncy ˈpɒnᵗs i ‖ ˈpɑːnᵗs i
pond, Pond pɒnd ‖ pɑːnd **ponds** pɒndz ‖ pɑːndz

P

pond|er ˈpɒnd |ə ‖ ˈpɑːnd |ᵊr **~ered** əd ‖ ᵊrd **~ering/s** ͜ər ɪŋ/z **~ers** əz ‖ ᵊrz
ponderosa ˌpɒnd ə ˈrəʊz ə -ˈrəʊs- ‖ ˌpɑːnd ə ˈroʊs ə -ˈroʊz- **~s** z
ponderous ˈpɒnd ͜ər əs ‖ ˈpɑːnd ͜ **~ly** li **~ness** nəs nɪs
Ponders ˈpɒnd əz ‖ ˈpɑːnd ᵊrz
Pondicherry ˌpɒnd ɪ ˈtʃer i §-ə-, -ˈʃer- ‖ ˌpɑːnd-
Pondo ˈpɒnd əʊ ‖ ˈpɑːnd oʊ **~land** lænd **~s** z
pondweed ˈpɒnd wiːd ‖ ˈpɑːnd-
pone pəʊn ‖ poʊn *—but in the sense 'player to right of dealer', also* ˈpəʊn i ‖ ˈpoʊn i **~s** z
pong pɒŋ ‖ pɑːŋ pɔːŋ **ponged** pɒŋd ‖ pɑːŋd pɔːŋd **ponging** ˈpɒŋ ɪŋ ‖ ˈpɑːŋ ɪŋ ˈpɔːŋ- **pongs** pɒŋz ‖ pɑːŋz pɔːŋz
pongee (ˌ)pɒn ˈdʒiː ˈ· ‖ (ˌ)pɑːn-
pongid ˈpɒndʒ ɪd §-əd ‖ ˈpɑːndʒ- **~s** z
pongo ˈpɒŋ gəʊ ‖ ˈpɑːŋ goʊ **~s** z
pongy ˈpɒŋ i ‖ ˈpɑːŋ i ˈpɔːŋ-
poniard ˈpɒn jəd -jɑːd ‖ ˈpɑːn jᵊrd **~ed** ɪd əd **~ing** ɪŋ **~s** z
ponie... *—see* **pony**
pons pɒnz ‖ pɑːnz **pontes** ˈpɒnt iːz ‖ ˈpɑːnt iːz
ˌ**pons** ˌ**asiˈnorum** ˌæs ɪ ˈnɔːr əm -ə-, -ʊm ‖ -ˈnoʊr-
Ponson ˈpɒnᵗs ən ‖ ˈpɑːnᵗs-
Ponsonby ˈpɒnᵗs ən bi →-əm- ‖ ˈpɑːnᵗs-
Pont pɒnt ‖ pɑːnt
Pontardawe ˌpɒnt ə ˈdaʊ ͜i -eɪ ‖ ˌpɑːnt̬ ᵊr- *—Welsh* [ˌpɔnt ar ˈdau e]
Pontardulais ˌpɒnt ə ˈdɪl əs -ˈdʌl-, -aɪs ‖ ˌpɑːnt̬ ᵊr- *—Welsh* Pontarddulais [ˌpɔnt ar ˈði laɪs]
Pontchartrain ˈpɒntʃ ə treɪn ˌ· ·ˈ· ‖ ˈpɑːntʃ ᵊr-
Pontefract ˈpɒnt ɪ frækt -ə- ‖ ˈpɑːnt̬- *—locally formerly also* ˈpʌmᵖf rət, ˈpɒmᵖf-, -rɪt
Ponteland ˌpɒnt ˈiːl ənd ‖ ˌpɑːnt-
pontes ˈpɒnt iːz ‖ ˈpɑːnt iːz
Pontfaen, Pont-faen (ˌ)pɒnt ˈvaɪn ‖ (ˌ)pɑːnt-
Ponti ˈpɒnt i ‖ ˈpɑːnt̬ i
Pontiac ˈpɒnt i æk ‖ ˈpɑːnt̬- **~s** s
Pontic ˈpɒnt ɪk ‖ ˈpɑːnt̬ ɪk
pontifex, P~ ˈpɒnt ɪ feks -ə- ‖ ˈpɑːnt̬ ə- **pontifices, P~** pɒn ˈtɪf ə siːz -ɪ- ‖ pɑːn-
pontiff ˈpɒnt ɪf ‖ ˈpɑːnt̬ əf **~s** s
pontifical pɒn ˈtɪf ɪk ᵊl ‖ pɑːn- **~ally** ᵊl ͜i **~s** z
pontifi|cate *v* pɒn ˈtɪf ɪ |keɪt -ə- ‖ pɑːn- **~cated** keɪt ɪd -əd ‖ keɪt̬ əd **~cates** keɪts **~cating** keɪt ɪŋ ‖ keɪt̬ ɪŋ
pontificate *n* pɒn ˈtɪf ɪk ət -ək ət, -ɪt; -ɪ keɪt, -ə keɪt ‖ pɑːn- **~s** s
pontification pɒn ˌtɪf ɪ ˈkeɪʃ ᵊn ˌpɒnt ɪf-, -ə- ‖ pɑːn- **~s** z
Pontin ˈpɒnt ɪn §-ən ‖ ˈpɑːnt ᵊn **~'s** z
Pontine, p~ ˈpɒnt aɪn ‖ ˈpɑːnt-
ˌ**Pontine** ˈ**Marshes**
Ponting ˈpɒnt ɪŋ ‖ ˈpɑːnt̬-
Pontius ˈpɒnt i ͜əs ˈpɒntʃ-, ˈpɒntʃ əs ‖ ˈpɑːntʃ əs
ˌ**Pontius** ˈ**Pilate**
Pont l'Évêque ˌpɒ̃ leɪ ˈvek ‖ ˌpɑːn- ˌpɑːnt- *—Fr* [pɔ̃ le vɛk]
Pontllan-fraith ˌpɒnt læn ˈvraɪθ -θlæn- ‖ ˌpɑːnt- *—Welsh* [pɔnt ɬan ˈvraiθ]
Ponton ˈpɒnt ən ‖ ˈpɑːnt ᵊn
pontoon (ˌ)pɒn ˈtuːn ‖ (ˌ)pɑːn- **~s** z
Pontop ˈpɒnt ɒp ‖ ˈpɑːnt ɑːp
ˌ**Pontop** ˈ**Pike**
Pontus ˈpɒnt əs ‖ ˈpɑːnt̬-
Pont-y-clun ˌpɒnt ə ˈkliːn -i- ‖ ˌpɑːnt- *—Welsh* [ˌpɔnt ə ˈkliːn]
Pontypool ˌpɒnt ə ˈpuːl -i-, ˈ· · · ‖ ˌpɑːnt̬- *—Welsh* [ˌpɔnt ə ˈpuːl]
Pontypridd ˌpɒnt ə ˈpriːð ˌ-i-, -ˈprɪd, ˈ· · · ‖ ˌpɑːnt̬- *—Welsh* [ˌpɔnt ə ˈpriːð]
pon|y ˈpəʊn |i ‖ ˈpoʊn |i **~ies** iz
ˌ**pony exˈpress**
ponytail ˈpəʊn i teɪᵊl ‖ ˈpoʊn- **~s** z
pony-trekk|ing ˈpəʊn i ˌtrek| ɪŋ ‖ ˈpoʊn- **~er/s** ə/z ‖ ᵊr/z
Ponzi ˈpɒnz i ‖ ˈpɑːnz i
ˈ**Ponzi scheme**
poo puː **pooed** puːd **pooing** ˈpuː ɪŋ **poos** puːz
pooch puːtʃ **pooches** ˈpuːtʃ ɪz -əz
poodle ˈpuːd ᵊl **~s** z
poof pʊf puːf **~s** s
poofter ˈpʊft ə ˈpuːft- ‖ -ᵊr **~s** z
poofy ˈpʊf i ˈpuːf-
pooh, Pooh puː
Pooh-Bah ˌpuː ˈbɑː
pooh-pooh ˌpuː ˈpuː **~ed** d **~ing** ɪŋ **~s** z
Poohsticks ˈpuː stɪks
Pook puːk
pool puːl **pooled** puːld **pooling** ˈpuːl ɪŋ **pools** puːlz
Poole puːl
Poolewe pʊl ˈjuː (ˌ)puːl-
Pooley ˈpuːl i
poolroom ˈpuːl ruːm -rʊm **~s** z
poolside ˈpuːl saɪd
poon puːn **poons** puːnz
Poona ˈpuːn ə
poontang ˈpuːn tæŋ
poop puːp **pooped** puːpt **pooping** ˈpuːp ɪŋ **poops** puːps
ˈ**poop deck**
pooper ˈpuːp ə ‖ -ᵊr **~s** z
pooper-scooper ˈpuːp ə ˌskuːp ə ‖ -ᵊr ˌskuːp ᵊr **~s** z
poo-poo ˈpuː puː
poop-scoop ˈpuːp skuːp **~ed** d **~ing** ɪŋ **~s** s
poopy ˈpuːp i
poor pɔː pʊə ‖ pʊᵊr pɔːr, poʊr *— Preference poll, BrE: pɔː 74%, pʊə 26% (born before 1942: 41%). See chart on p. 628.* **poorer** ˈpɔːr ə ˈpʊər- ‖ ˈpʊr ᵊr ˈpɔːr-, ˈpoʊr- **poorest** ˈpɔːr ɪst ˈpʊər-, -əst ‖ ˈpʊr əst ˈpɔːr-, ˈpoʊr-
ˈ**poor box**; ˈ**poor law**; ˌ**poor reˈlation**; ˌ**poor ˈwhite**
Poore pʊə pɔː ‖ pʊᵊr pɔːr, poʊr
poor|house ˈpɔː |haʊs ˈpʊə- ‖ ˈpʊr- ˈpɔːr-, ˈpoʊr- **~houses** haʊz ɪz -əz

P

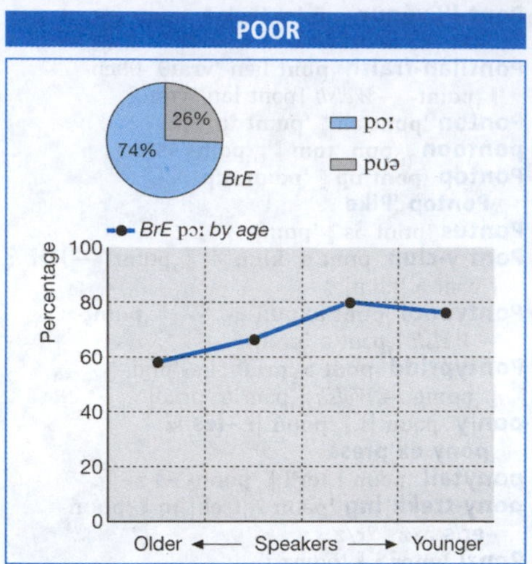

poorly *adv* ˈpɔː li ˈpʊə- ‖ ˈpʊr li ˈpɔːr-, ˈpoʊr-
ˌpoorly ˈoff◂
poorly *adj* ˈpɔːl i ˈpʊəl i ‖ ˈpʊrl i ˈpɔːrl-, ˈpoʊrl-
poorness ˈpɔː nəs ˈpʊə-, -nɪs ‖ ˈpʊr- ˈpɔːr-, ˈpoʊr-
poor-spirited ˌpɔː ˈspɪr ɪt ɪd ◂ ˌpʊə-, §-ət-, -əd ‖ ˌpʊr ˈspɪr əṭ əd ◂ ˌpɔːr-, ˌpoʊr-
Pooter ˈpuːt ə ‖ ˈpuːṭ ər
Pooterish ˈpuːt ər ɪʃ ‖ ˈpuːṭ-
pootl|e ˈpuːt əl ‖ ˈpuːṭ əl **~ed** d **~es** z **~ing** ˌɪŋ
poove puːv **pooves** puːvz
pop, Pop pɒp ‖ pɑːp **popped** pɒpt ‖ pɑːpt **popping** ˈpɒp ɪŋ ‖ ˈpɑːp ɪŋ **pops** pɒps ‖ pɑːps
ˈpop art, ˌ. ˈ.◂; **ˈpop ˌconcert**; **ˈpop group**; **ˈpop ˌmusic**; **ˈpopping crease**
popadam, popadom, popadum ˈpɒp əd əm ‖ ˈpɑːp- **~s** z
popcorn ˈpɒp kɔːn ‖ ˈpɑːp kɔːrn
pop-down ˈpɒp daʊn ‖ ˈ pɑːp-
pope, Pope pəʊp ‖ poʊp **popes, Pope's** pəʊps ‖ poʊps
ˌPope's ˈnose
popemobile ˈpəʊp məʊ ˌbiːəl ‖ ˈpoʊp mə- **~s** z
popery ˈpəʊp ər i ‖ ˈpoʊp-
Popeye ˈpɒp aɪ ‖ ˈpɑːp-
pop-eyed ˌpɒp ˈaɪd ◂ ˈ. . ‖ ˈpɑːp aɪd
popgun ˈpɒp ɡʌn ‖ ˈpɑːp- **~s** z
Popham ˈpɒp əm ‖ ˈpɑːp-
popinjay ˈpɒp ɪn dʒeɪ §-ən- ‖ ˈpɑːp- **~s** z
popish ˈpəʊp ɪʃ ‖ ˈpoʊp- **~ly** li **~ness** nəs nɪs
poplar, P~ ˈpɒp lə ‖ ˈpɑːp lər **~s** z
poplin ˈpɒp lɪn §-lən ‖ ˈpɑːp- **~s** z
popliteal ˌpɒp lɪ ˈtiːˌəl ◂ -lə-; pɒ ˈplɪt iˌəl ‖ ˌpɑːp-
Popocatepetl ˌpɒp əʊ kæt ə ˈpet əl -ɪˈ-; ˌ. ˈ. . . . ‖ ˌpoʊp ə kæṭ ə ˈpeṭ əl ˌpɑːp- —*Sp* Popacatépetl [po po ka ˈte petl]
popover ˈpɒp ˌəʊv ə ‖ ˈpɑːp ˌoʊv ər **~s** z
popp... —*see* **pop**
poppa, Poppa ˈpɒp ə ‖ ˈpɑːp ə **~s, ~'s** z
poppadom, poppadum ˈpɒp əd əm ‖ ˈpɑːp- **~s** z
Poppaea pɒ ˈpiːˌə ‖ pɑː-
popper, P~ ˈpɒp ə ‖ ˈpɑːp ər **~s** z
Popperian pɒ ˈpɪər iˌən ‖ pɑː ˈpɪr-
poppet ˈpɒp ɪt §-ət ‖ ˈpɑːp- **~s** s
poppi... —*see* **pop, poppy**
poppl|e ˈpɒp əl ‖ ˈpɑːp əl **~ed** d **~es** z **~ing** ˌɪŋ
Poppleton ˈpɒp əl tən ‖ ˈpɑːp-
Popplewell ˈpɒp əl wel ‖ ˈpɑːp-
popp|y, Poppy ˈpɒp |i ‖ ˈpɑːp |i **~ies** iz
ˈPoppy Day
poppycock ˈpɒp i kɒk ‖ ˈpɑːp i kɑːk
poppyseed ˈpɒp i siːd ‖ ˈpɑːp-
popshop ˈpɒp ʃɒp ‖ ˈpɑːp ʃɑːp **~s** s
popsicle, P~ *tdmk* ˈpɒps ɪk əl ‖ ˈpɑːps- **~s** z
pops|ie, pops|y ˈpɒps |i ‖ ˈpɑːps |i **~ies** iz
populace ˈpɒp jʊl əs -jəl-, -ɪs ‖ ˈpɑːp jəl əs
popular ˈpɒp jʊl ə -jəl- ‖ ˈpɑːp jəl ər
popularis... —*see* **populariz...**
popularity ˌpɒp ju ˈlær ət i ˌjə-, -ɪt i ‖ ˌpɑːp jə ˈlær əṭ i -ˈler-
popularization ˌpɒp jʊl ər aɪ ˈzeɪʃ ən ˌjəl-, -ɪˈ-- ‖ ˌpɑːp jəl ər ə- **~s** z
populariz|e ˈpɒp jʊl ə raɪz ˈ·jəl- ‖ ˈpɑːp jəl- **~ed** d **~es** ɪz əz **~ing** ɪŋ
popularly ˈpɒp jʊl ə li ˈ·jəl- ‖ ˈpɑːp jəl ər li
popu|late ˈpɒp ju |leɪt -jə- ‖ ˈpɑːp jə- **~lated** leɪt ɪd -əd ‖ leɪṭ əd **~lates** leɪts **~lating** leɪt ɪŋ ‖ leɪṭ ɪŋ
population ˌpɒp ju ˈleɪʃ ən -jə- ‖ ˌpɑːp jə- **~s** z
ˌpopuˈlation exˌplosion
populism, P~ ˈpɒp ju ˌlɪz əm -jə- ‖ ˈpɑːp jə-
populist, P~ ˈpɒp jʊl ɪst -jəl-, §-əst ‖ ˈpɑːp jəl- **~s** s
populous ˈpɒp jʊl əs -jəl- ‖ ˈpɑːp jəl əs **~ly** li **~ness** nəs nɪs
pop-under ˈpɒp ˌʌnd ə ‖ ˈpɑːp ˌʌnd ər **~s** z
pop-up ˈpɒp ʌp ‖ ˈpɑːp ʌp **~s** s
porbeagle ˈpɔː ˌbiːɡ əl ‖ ˈpɔːr- **~s** z
porcelain ˈpɔːs əl ˌɪn ən, -eɪn ‖ ˈpɔːrs- ˈpoʊrs- **~s** z
porch pɔːtʃ ‖ pɔːrtʃ poʊrtʃ **porches** ˈpɔːtʃ ɪz -əz ‖ ˈpɔːrtʃ əz ˈpoʊrtʃ-
Porchester ˈpɔːtʃ ɪst ə -əst-, §-est- ‖ ˈpɔːr ˌtʃest ər
porcine ˈpɔːs aɪn ‖ ˈpɔːrs-
porcin|o pɔː ˈtʃiːn| əʊ ‖ pɔːr ˈtʃiːn| oʊ **~i** iː —*It* [por ˈtʃiː no]
porcupine ˈpɔːk ju paɪn -jə- ‖ ˈpɔːrk jə- **~s** z
pore pɔː ‖ pɔːr poʊr **pored** pɔːd ‖ pɔːrd poʊrd **pores** pɔːz ‖ pɔːrz poʊrz **poring** ˈpɔːr ɪŋ ‖ ˈpoʊr-
porg|y, Porg|y ˈpɔːɡ |i ‖ ˈpɔːrɡ |i **~ies, ~y's** iz
pork pɔːk ‖ pɔːrk poʊrk
ˈpork ˌbarrel; **ˌpork ˈchop** ‖ ˈ. .; **ˌpork ˈpie**
porker ˈpɔːk ə ‖ ˈpɔːrk ər ˈpoʊrk- **~s** z
pork|ie, Pork|ie, porkly, Porkly ˈpɔːk |i ‖ ˈpɔːrk |i ˈpoʊrk- **~ies, ~y's** iz **~iness** i nəs i nɪs
pork-pie *hat* ˈpɔːk paɪ ‖ ˈpɔːrk- **~s** z
Porlock ˈpɔː lɒk ‖ ˈpɔːr lɑːk

porn pɔːn ‖ pɔːrn
porno ˈpɔːn əʊ ‖ ˈpɔːrn oʊ
pornographer pɔː ˈnɒg rəf ə pə- ‖ pɔːr ˈnɑːg rəf ᵊr **~s** z
pornographic ˌpɔːn ə ˈgræf ɪk ◂ ‖ ˌpɔːrn- **~ally** ᵊl‿i
pornography pɔː ˈnɒg rəf i pə- ‖ pɔːr ˈnɑːg-
poromeric ˌpɔːr əʊ ˈmer ɪk ◂ ˌpɒr- ‖ -ə- ˌpoʊr-
porosit|y pɔː ˈrɒs ət |i -ɪt- ‖ pə ˈrɑːs əţ |i pɔː-, poʊ- **~ies** iz
porous ˈpɔːr əs ‖ ˈpoʊr- **~ly** li **~ness** nəs nɪs
porphyria pɔː ˈfɪr i‿ə -ˈfaɪᵊr- ‖ pɔːr-
porphyrin ˈpɔːf ər ɪn -ɪr-, §-ən ‖ ˈpɔːrf- **~s** z
porphyr|y ˈpɔːf ər |i -ɪr- ‖ ˈpɔːrf- **~ies** iz
porpois|e ˈpɔːp əs ‖ ˈpɔːrp- —*occasionally also a spelling pronunciation* ˈpɔː pɔɪs, -pɔɪz ‖ ˈpɔːr- **~es** ɪz əz
porridge ˈpɒr ɪdʒ ‖ ˈpɔːr- ˈpɑːr-
porringer ˈpɒr ɪndʒ ə -əndʒ- ‖ ˈpɔːr əndʒ ᵊr ˈpɑːr- **~s** z
Porsche *tdmk* pɔːʃ ˈpɔːʃ ə ‖ pɔːrʃ ˈpɔːrʃ ə, -i —*Ger* [ˈpɔʁ ʃə] **Porsches** ˈpɔːʃ ɪz -əz ‖ ˈpɔːrʃ əz -iz
Porsena ˈpɔːs ən ə -ɪn- ‖ ˈpɔːrs-
Porson ˈpɔːs ᵊn ‖ ˈpɔːrs-
port pɔːt ‖ pɔːrt poʊrt **ported** ˈpɔːt ɪd -əd ‖ ˈpɔːrţ əd ˈpoʊrţ- **porting** ˈpɔːt ɪŋ ‖ ˈpɔːrţ ɪŋ ˈpoʊrţ- **ports** pɔːts ‖ pɔːrts poʊrts —*see also phrases with this word*
ˌ**Port E'lizabeth**; (ˌ)**Port 'Harcourt**; (ˌ)**Port 'Hedland**; (ˌ)**Port 'Jackson**; (ˌ)**Port 'Lincoln**; (ˌ)**Port 'Moresby**; ˌ**port of 'call**; ˌ**port of 'entry**; ˌ**Port of 'Spain**; (ˌ)**Port 'Stanley**
portability ˌpɔːt ə ˈbɪl ət i -ɪt i ‖ ˌpɔːrţ ə ˈbɪl əţ i ˌpoʊrţ-
portable ˈpɔːt əb ᵊl ‖ ˈpɔːrţ- ˈpoʊrţ- **~ness** nəs nɪs **~s** z
Portacrib *tdmk* ˈpɔːt ə krɪb ‖ ˈpɔːrţ- ˈpoʊrţ-
Portadown ˌpɔːt ə ˈdaʊn ‖ ˌpɔːrţ- ˌpoʊrţ-
portage ˈpɔːt ɪdʒ ˌpɔː ˈtɑːʒ ‖ ˈpɔːrţ ɪdʒ ˈpoʊrţ-; pɔːr ˈtɑːʒ
Portage ˈpɔːt ɪdʒ ‖ ˈpɔːrţ ɪdʒ ˈpoʊrţ-
ˌ**Portage la 'Prairie**
Portakabin *tdmk* ˈpɔːt ə ˌkæb ɪn §-ən ‖ ˈpɔːrţ- ˈpoʊrţ- **~s** z
portal, P~ ˈpɔːt ᵊl ‖ ˈpɔːrţ ᵊl ˈpoʊrţ- **~s** z
Portaloo, p~ *tdmk* ˈpɔːt ə luː ‖ ˈpɔːrţ- **~s** z
portament|o ˌpɔːt ə ˈment |əʊ ‖ ˌpɔːrţ ə ˈmenţ |oʊ ˌpoʊrţ- **~i** iː
porta-pott|y, Porta Pott|y *tdmk* ˈpɔːt ə ˌpɒt| i ‖ ˈpɔːrţ ə ˌpɑːţ| i **~ies** iz
Port Askaig (ˌ)pɔːt ˈæsk eɪg ‖ (ˌ)pɔːrţ- (ˌ)poʊrţ-
portative ˈpɔːt ət ɪv ‖ ˈpɔːrţ əţ ɪv ˈpoʊrţ-
Port-au-Prince ˌpɔːt əʊ ˈprɪnᵗs ‖ ˌpɔːrţ oʊ ˌpoʊrţ- —*Fr* [pɔ ʁo pʁɛ̃s]
Portbury ˈpɔːt bər‿i ‖ ˈpɔːrt ˌber i ˈpoʊrt-
portcullis pɔːt ˈkʌl ɪs -əs ‖ pɔːrt- poʊrt- **~es** ɪz əz
porte, P~ pɔːt ‖ pɔːrt poʊrt
porte-cochere, porte-cochère ˌpɔːt kɒ ˈʃeə ‖ ˌpɔːrt koʊ ˈʃeᵊr ˌpoʊrt- **~s** z
portend pɔː ˈtend ‖ pɔːr- poʊr- **~ed** ɪd əd **~ing** ɪŋ **~s** z
portent ˈpɔːt ent ‖ ˈpɔːrt ˈpoʊrt- **~s** s
portentous pɔː ˈtent əs ⚠-ˈtenᵗʃ- ‖ pɔːr ˈtenţ əs poʊr- **~ly** li **~ness** nəs nɪs
Porteous ˈpɔːt i‿əs ‖ ˈpɔːrţ-
porter, P~ ˈpɔːt ə ‖ ˈpɔːrţ ᵊr ˈpoʊrţ- **~s** z
porterage ˈpɔːt ər ɪdʒ ‖ ˈpɔːrţ- ˈpoʊrţ-
porterhouse ˈpɔːt ə haʊs ‖ ˈpɔːrţ ᵊr- ˈpoʊrţ-
ˌ**porterhouse 'steak**
Porteus ˈpɔːt i‿əs ‖ ˈpɔːrţ-
Port Eynon (ˌ)pɔːt ˈaɪn ən ‖ (ˌ)pɔːrţ- (ˌ)poʊrţ-
portfolio ˌpɔːt ˈfəʊl i‿əʊ ‖ ˌpɔːrt ˈfoʊl i oʊ ˌpoʊrt- **~s** z
Porth pɔːθ ‖ pɔːrθ —*see also phrases with this word*
Porthcawl (ˌ)pɔːθ ˈkɔːl -ˈkaʊl ‖ (ˌ)pɔːrθ- -ˈkɑːl
Porth Dinllaen ˌpɔːθ dɪn ˈθlaɪn ‖ ˌpɔːrθ- —*Welsh* [ˌpɔrθ din ˈɬain, -ˈɬiːn]
Porthleven (ˌ)pɔːθ ˈlev ᵊn ‖ (ˌ)pɔːrθ-
Porthmadog (ˌ)pɔːθ ˈmæd ɒg ‖ (ˌ)pɔːrθ ˈmæd ɔːg -ɑːg —*Welsh* [pɔrθ ˈma dɔg]
porthole ˈpɔːt həʊl →-hɒʊl ‖ ˈpɔːrt hoʊl ˈpoʊrt- **~s** z
Portia ˈpɔːʃ ə ˈpɔːʃ i‿ə ‖ ˈpɔːrʃ ə ˈpoʊrʃ-
portico ˈpɔːt ɪ kəʊ ‖ ˈpɔːrţ ɪ koʊ ˈpoʊrţ- **~s** z
portiere, portière ˌpɔːt i ˈeə ‖ ˌpɔːrţ i ˈeᵊr ˌpoʊrţ-; pɔːr ˈtɪᵊr, poʊr- —*Fr* [pɔʁ tjɛːʁ] **~s** z
Portillo pɔː ˈtɪl əʊ ‖ pɔːr ˈtɪl oʊ
portion ˈpɔːʃ ᵊn ‖ ˈpɔːrʃ ᵊn ˈpoʊrʃ- **~ed** d **~ing** ɪŋ **~less** ləs lɪs **~s** z
Portishead ˈpɔːt ɪs hed §-əs- ‖ ˈpɔːrţ- ˈpoʊrţ-
Portland, p~ ˈpɔːt lənd ‖ ˈpɔːrt- ˈpoʊrt-
ˌ**Portland ce'ment**; ˌ**Portland 'stone**
Portlaoise ˌpɔːt ˈliːʃ ə ‖ ˌpɔːrt- ˌpoʊrt-
port|ly ˈpɔːt |li ‖ ˈpɔːrt- ˈpoʊrt- **~liness** li nəs -nɪs
Portmadoc ˌpɔːt ˈmæd ək ‖ ˌpɔːrt- ˌpoʊrt-
Portman ˈpɔːt mən ‖ ˈpɔːrt- ˈpoʊrt-
portmanteau (ˌ)pɔːt ˈmænt əʊ ‖ pɔːrt ˈmænt oʊ poʊrt- **~s, ~x** z
(ˌ)**port'manteau word**
Portmeirion (ˌ)pɔːt ˈmer i‿ən ‖ (ˌ)pɔːrt- (ˌ)poʊrt-
Portnoy ˈpɔːt nɔɪ ‖ ˈpɔːrt- ˈpoʊrt-
Porto ˈpɔːt əʊ ‖ ˈpɔːrţ oʊ ˈpoʊrţ-
Porto Alegre ˌpɔːt əʊ ə ˈleg ri ˌ-u- ‖ ˌpɔːrţ u- -rə —*Port* Pôrto Alegre [por tu ɐ ˈlɛ gri]
Portobello ˌpɔːt əʊ ˈbel əʊ ◂ ‖ ˌpɔːrţ ə ˈbel oʊ ◂ ˌpoʊrţ-
Portofino ˌpɔːt əʊ ˈfiːn əʊ ‖ ˌpɔːrţ ə ˈfiːn oʊ —*It* [pɔr to ˈfiː no]
Porton ˈpɔːt ᵊn ‖ ˈpɔːrt ᵊn
Porto Ric|o ˌpɔːt əʊ ˈriːk |əʊ ‖ ˌpɔːrţ ə ˈriːk |oʊ ˌpoʊrţ- **~an/s** ən/z
portrait ˈpɔːtr ət -ɪt, -eɪt ‖ ˈpɔːrtr ət ˈpoʊrtr- **~s** s
portraitist ˈpɔːtr ət ɪst -ɪt-, -eɪt-, §-əst ‖ ˈpɔːrtr əţ əst ˈpoʊrtr- **~s** s
portraiture ˈpɔːtr ɪtʃ ə -ətʃ-; -ɪ tjʊə, -ə- ‖ ˈpɔːrtr ə tʃʊr ˈpoʊrtr-, -ətʃ ᵊr
portray pɔː ˈtreɪ ‖ pɔːr- poʊr-, pᵊr- **~ed** d **~ing** ɪŋ **~s** z
portrayal pɔː ˈtreɪ‿əl ‖ pɔːr- pᵊr- **~s** z

P

portrayer pɔː ˈtreɪ ə ‖ pɔːr ˈtreɪ ᵊr pᵊr- **~s** z
Portreath pɔː ˈtriːθ ‖ pɔːr-
Portree pɔː ˈtriː ‖ pɔːr-
Portrush $_{(1)}$pɔːt ˈrʌʃ ‖ $_{(1)}$pɔːrt- $_{(1)}$pourt-
Port Said ˌpɔːt ˈsaɪd -ˈsɑː iːd ‖ ˌpɔːrt- ˌpourt-
Port Salut ˌpɔː sæ ˈluː -sə- ‖ ˌpɔːr- ˌpour- —*Fr* [pɔʁ sa ly]
Portscatho $_{(1)}$pɔːt ˈskæθ əʊ ‖ $_{(1)}$pɔːrt ˈskæθ oʊ $_{(1)}$pourt-
Portsea ˈpɔːts i ˈpɔːt siː ‖ ˈpɔːrt siː ˈpourt-
Portslade ˌpɔːt ˈsleɪd ◂ ‖ ˌpɔːrt- ˌpourt-
Portsmouth ˈpɔːts məθ ‖ ˈpɔːrts- ˈpourts-
Port Talbot $_{(1)}$pɔːt ˈtɔːlb ət pɔː-, pə-, -ˈtælb-, -ˈtɒlb- ‖ $_{(1)}$pɔːrt- $_{(1)}$pourt-, -ˈtɑːlb-
portugaise ˌpɔːtʃ u ˈgeɪz ◂ ‖ ˌpɔːrtʃ- ˌpourtʃ- —*Fr* [pɔʁ ty gɛːz]
Portugal ˈpɔːtʃ ʊg ᵊl -əg-; ˈpɔːt jʊg- ‖ ˈpɔːrtʃ əg ᵊl ˈpourtʃ-
Portuguese ˌpɔːtʃ u ˈgiːz ◂ -ə-; ˌpɔːt ju- ‖ ˌpɔːrtʃ- ˌpourtʃ-, -ˈgiːs, ˈ· · ·
ˌPortuˌguese ˈfood; **ˌPortuguese ˌman-of-ˈwar**
pose pəʊz ‖ poʊz **posed** pəʊzd ‖ poʊzd **poses** ˈpəʊz ɪz -əz ‖ ˈpoʊz əz **posing** ˈpəʊz ɪŋ ‖ ˈpoʊz ɪŋ
Poseidon pə ˈsaɪd ᵊn pɒ- ‖ poʊ-
poser ˈpəʊz ə ‖ ˈpoʊz ᵊr **~s** z
poseur $_{(1)}$pəʊ ˈzɜː ‖ poʊ ˈzɜː **~s** z
posey ˈpəʊz i ‖ ˈpoʊz i
posh pɒʃ ‖ pɑːʃ —*In BrE there is also a jocular form* pəʊʃ **poshly** ˈpɒʃ li ‖ ˈpɑːʃ- **poshness** ˈpɒʃ nəs -nɪs ‖ ˈpɑːʃ-
pos|it ˈpɒz |ɪt §-ət ‖ ˈpɑːz |ət **~ited** ɪt ɪd §ət-, -əd ‖ əţ əd **~iting** ɪt ɪŋ §ət- ‖ əţ ɪŋ **~its** ɪts §əts ‖ əts
position pə ˈzɪʃ ᵊn **~ed** d **~ing** ˌɪŋ **~s** z
positional pə ˈzɪʃ ᵊnˌəl **~ly** i
positive ˈpɒz ət ɪv -ɪt-; ˈpɒz tɪv ‖ ˈpɑːz əţ ɪv ˈpɑːz tɪv **~ly** li —*but as an interj in AmE, sometimes* ˌpɑːz ə ˈtɪv li **~ness** nəs nɪs **~s** z
ˌpositive diˌscrimiˈnation; **ˌpositive ˈpole**
positivism ˈpɒz ət ɪv ˌɪz əm ˈ·ɪt- ‖ ˈpɑːz əţ-
positivist ˈpɒz ət ɪv ɪst ˈ·ɪt-, §-əst ‖ ˈpɑːz əţ- **~s** s
positron ˈpɒz ɪ trɒn -ə- ‖ ˈpɑːz ə trɑːn **~s** z
positronium ˌpɒz ɪ ˈtrəʊn i‿əm ˌ·ə- ‖ ˌpɑːz ə ˈtroʊn- **~s** z
Posner ˈpɒz nə ‖ ˈpɑːz nᵊr
posological ˌpɒs ə ˈlɒdʒ ɪk ᵊl ◂ ‖ ˌpɑːs ə ˈlɑːdʒ- **~ly** ˌi
posology pəʊ ˈsɒl ədʒ i ‖ pə ˈsɑːl- poʊ-
poss. pɒs ‖ pɑːs
posse ˈpɒs i ‖ ˈpɑːs i **~s** z
possess pə ˈzes **~ed** t **~es** ɪz əz **~ing** ɪŋ
possession pə ˈzeʃ ᵊn **~s** z
possessive pə ˈzes ɪv **~ly** li **~ness** nəs nɪs **~s** z
posˌsessive ˈpronoun
possessor pə ˈzes ə ‖ -ᵊr **~s** z
possessory pə ˈzes ər i
posset ˈpɒs ɪt §-ət ‖ ˈpɑːs ət **~s** s
possibilit|y ˌpɒs ə ˈbɪl ət |i ˌ·ɪ-, -ɪt i ‖ ˌpɑːs ə ˈbɪl əţ |i **~ies** iz
possible ˈpɒs əb ᵊl -ɪb- ‖ ˈpɑːs- **~s** z
possibly ˈpɒs əb li -ɪb- ‖ ˈpɑːs-
possum, P~ ˈpɒs əm ‖ ˈpɑːs- **~s** z
post, Post pəʊst ‖ poʊst **posted** ˈpəʊst ɪd -əd ‖ ˈpoʊst əd **posting** ˈpəʊst ɪŋ ‖ ˈpoʊst ɪŋ **posts** pəʊsts ‖ poʊsts
ˈpost exˌchange; **ˈpost horn**; **ˈpost house**; **ˈpost ˌoffice**; **ˈpost office box**
post- ¦pəʊst ‖ ¦poʊst —*if the following sound is a consonant (not* h*), the* t *can optionally be elided* — **post-Victorian** ˌpəʊst vɪk ˈtɔːr i‿ən ◂ ‖ ˌpoʊst- -ˈtour-
Posta ˈpɒst ə ‖ ˈpoʊst ə
postag|e ˈpəʊst ɪdʒ ‖ ˈpoʊst- **~es** ɪz əz
ˈpostage stamp
postal, P~ ˈpəʊst ᵊl ‖ ˈpoʊst- **~ly** i
ˌpostal ˈorder, ˈ· · ˌ· ·
postbag ˈpəʊ*s*t bæg ‖ ˈpoʊ*s*t- **~s** z
post-bellum ˌpəʊ*s*t ˈbel əm ◂ ‖ ˌpoʊ*s*t-
postbox ˈpəʊ*s*t bɒks ‖ ˈpoʊ*s*t bɑːks **~es** ɪz əz
postcard ˈpəʊ*s*t kɑːd ‖ ˈpoʊ*s*t kɑːrd **~s** z
post-chais|e ˈpəʊ*s*t ʃeɪz ‖ ˈpoʊ*s*t- **~es** ɪz əz
postcode ˈpəʊ*s*t kəʊd ‖ ˈpoʊ*s*t koʊd **~s** z
postconsonantal ˌpəʊ*s*t ˌkɒnᵗs ə ˈnænt ᵊl ◂ ‖ ˌpoʊ*s*t ˌkɑːnᵗs ə ˈnænţ ᵊl ◂ **~ly** i
post|date ˌpəʊ*s*t |ˈdeɪt ◂ ‖ ˌpoʊ*s*t- **~dated** ˈdeɪt ɪd -əd ‖ ˈdeɪţ əd **~dates** ˈdeɪts **~dating** ˈdeɪt ɪŋ ‖ ˈdeɪţ ɪŋ
postdoc ˌpəʊ*s*t ˈdɒk ‖ ˌpoʊ*s*t ˈdɑːk ˈ· · **~s** s
postdoctoral ˌpəʊ*s*t ˈdɒkt ər əl ◂ →-ˈdɒk trəl ‖ ˌpoʊ*s*t ˈdɑːkt-
poster, P~ ˈpəʊst ə ‖ ˈpoʊst ᵊr **~s** z
ˈposter ˌcolour; **ˈposter paint**
poste restante ˌpəʊst ˈrest ɒnt ‖ ˌpoʊst re ˈstɑːnt —*Fr* [pɔst ʁɛs tɑ̃ːt]
posterior pɒ ˈstɪər i‿ə ‖ pɑː ˈstɪr i‿ᵊr poʊ- **~ly** li **~s** z
posteriority pɒ ˌstɪər i ˈɒr ət i ˌpɒst ɪər-, -ɪt i ‖ pɑː ˌstɪr i ˈɔːr əţ i -ˈɑːr-
posterity pɒ ˈster ət i -ɪt- ‖ pɑː ˈster əţ i
postern ˈpɒst ən ˈpəʊst- ‖ ˈpoʊst ᵊrn ˈpɑːst- **~s** z
postfix ˈpəʊ*s*t fɪks ‖ ˈpoʊ*s*t-
post-free ˌpəʊ*s*t ˈfriː ◂ ‖ ˌpoʊ*s*t-
postgame ˌpəʊ*s*t ˈgeɪm ◂ ‖ ˌpoʊ*s*t-
Postgate ˈpəʊ*s*t geɪt ‖ ˈpoʊ*s*t-
postglacial ˌpəʊ*s*t ˈgleɪs i‿əl ◂ -ˈgleɪʃ i‿əl, -ˈgleɪʃ ᵊl ‖ ˌpoʊ*s*t ˈgleɪʃ ᵊl ◂
postgrad ˈpəʊ*s*t græd ˌ·ˈ· ‖ ˈpoʊ*s*t- **~s** z
postgraduate $_{(1)}$pəʊ*s*t ˈgræd ju‿ət -ˈgrædʒ u‿, ɪt ‖ $_{(1)}$poʊ*s*t ˈgrædʒ u‿ət **~s** s
posthaste ˌpəʊst ˈheɪst ‖ ˌpoʊst-
post hoc ˌpəʊst ˈhɒk -ˈhəʊk ‖ ˌpoʊst ˈhɑːk
posthumous ˈpɒst jʊm əs -jəm-; ˈpɒs tʃʊm-, -tʃəm- ‖ ˈpɑːs tʃəm əs -tʃʊm- **~ly** li **~ness** nəs nɪs
posthypnotic ˌpəʊst hɪp ˈnɒt ɪk ◂ -ɪp- ‖ ˌpoʊst hɪp ˈnɑːţ ɪk ◂
postich|e pɒ ˈstiːʃ ‖ pɔː- pɑː- **~es** ɪz əz
postie ˈpəʊst i ‖ ˈpoʊst i **~s** z
postilion, postillion pɒ ˈstɪl i‿ən pə- ‖ poʊ ˈstɪl jən pə- **~s** z
postimpressionism ˌpəʊst ɪm ˈpreʃ ᵊn ˌɪz əm -ə ˌnɪz- ‖ ˌpoʊst-

postimpressionist ˌpəust ɪm ˈpreʃ ᵊn‿ɪst ◂ əst ‖ ˌpoust- **~s** s
postindustrial ˌpəust ɪn ˈdʌs tri‿əl ◂ ‖ ˌpoust-
posting ˈpəust ɪŋ ‖ ˈpoust ɪŋ **~s** z
Post-it *tdmk* ˈpəust ɪt §-ət ‖ ˈpoust- **~s** s
Postlethwaite ˈpɒs ᵊl θweɪt ‖ ˈpɑːs-
postlude ˈpəust luːd -ljuːd ‖ ˈpoust- **~s** z
post|man ˈpəust |mən ‖ ˈpoust- **~men** mən
ˌpostman's ˈknock
postmark *n, v* ˈpəust mɑːk ‖ ˈpoust mɑːrk **~ed** t **~ing** ɪŋ **~s** s
postmaster ˈpəust ˌmɑːst ə §-ˌmæst- ‖ ˈpoust ˌmæst ᵊr **~s** z
ˌPostˌmaster ˈGeneral
postmen ˈpəust mən ‖ ˈpoust-
postmenopausal ˌpəust men ə ˈpɔːzᵊl ◂ ‖ ˌpoust- -ˈpɑːz-ᵊl
post meridiem ˌpəust mə ˈrɪd i‿əm -em ‖ ˌpoust-
postmistress ˈpəust ˌmɪs trəs -trɪs ‖ ˈpoust- **~es** ɪz əz
post-modern ˌpəust ˈmɒd ᵊn ‖ ˌpoust ˈmɑːd ᵊrn **~ism** ˌɪz əm **~ist/s** ɪst/s § əst/s
postmortem ˌpəust ˈmɔːt əm -em, ˈ·ˌ· · ‖ ˌpoust ˈmɔːrt̬ əm **~s** z
postnasal ˌpəustˈneɪz ᵊl ◂ ‖ ˌpoust-
postnatal ˌpəust ˈneɪt ᵊl ◂ ‖ ˌpoust ˈneɪt̬ ᵊl ◂ **~ly** i
post-op ˌpəust ˈɒp ◂ ‖ ˌpoust ˈɑːp ◂
postoperative ˌpəust ˈɒp ər‿ət ɪv ◂ -ə reɪt- ‖ ˌpoust ˈɑːp ər‿ət̬ ɪv ◂ **~ly** li
postpaid ˌpəust ˈpeɪd ◂ ‖ ˌpoust-
post-partum ˌpəust ˈpɑːt əm ◂ ‖ ˌpoust ˈpɑːrt̬ əm ◂
postpon|e ₍ˌ₎pəust ˈpəun ◂ pəs- ‖ ₍ˌ₎poust ˈpoun **~ed** d **~es** z **~ing** ɪŋ
postpos|e ˌpəust ˈpəuz ◂ ˈ· · ‖ ˌpoust ˈpouz ◂ ˈ· · **~ed** d **~es** ɪz əz **~ing** ɪŋ
postposition ˌpəust pə ˈzɪʃ ᵊn ‖ ˌpoust- **~al** ‿əl **~s** z
postpositive ˌpəust ˈpɒz ət ɪv -ɪt- ‖ ˌpoust ˈpɑːz ət̬ ɪv **~ly** li **~s** z
postprandial ˌpəust ˈprænd i‿əl ◂ ‖ ˌpoust-
postproduction ˌpəust prə ˈdʌk ʃᵊn ◂ ‖ ˌpoust-
postscript, P~ ˈpəust skrɪpt ‖ ˈpoust- **~s** s
postseason ˌpəustˈsiːz ᵊn ◂ ‖ ˌpoust-
postsecondary ˌpəust ˈsek ᵊnd‿ər i ◂ -ən der i ‖ ˌpoust ˈsek ən der i ◂
poststructural ˌpəust ˈstrʌk tʃᵊr‿əl ◂ ˈ·ʃᵊr_ ‖ ˌpoust- **~ism** ˌɪz əm **~ist/s** ɪst/s əst/s
posttest ˈpəust test ‖ ˈpoust- **~ed** ɪd əd **~ing** ɪŋ **~s** s
post-traumatic ˌpəust trɔː ˈmæt ɪk ◂ -trau-, -trə- ‖ ˌpoust trɔː ˈmæt̬ ɪk ◂ trə-
postulant ˈpɒs tjul ənt →-tʃul- ‖ ˈpɑːs tʃəl- **~s** s
postulate *n* ˈpɒs tjul ət →-tʃul-, -ɪt; -tju leɪt, →-tʃu- ‖ ˈpɑːs tʃəl ət -tʃə leɪt **~s** s
postu|late *v* ˈpɒs tju |leɪt -tʃu- ‖ ˈpɑːs tʃə- **~lated** leɪt ɪd -əd ‖ leɪt̬ əd **~lates** leɪts **~lating** leɪt ɪŋ ‖ leɪt̬ ɪŋ
postulation ˌpɒs tju ˈleɪʃ ᵊn →-tʃu- ‖ ˌpɑːs tʃə- **~s** z
Postum *tdmk* ˈpɒst əm ˈpəust- ‖ ˈpɑːst-
postural ˈpɒs tʃər əl -tjur- ‖ ˈpɑːs-
posture ˈpɒs tʃə -tjuə ‖ ˈpɑːs tʃᵊr **~d** d
posturing ˈpɒs tʃər ɪŋ -tjuər- ‖ ˈpɑːs- **~s** z
postviral ˌpəust ˈvaɪᵊr əl ◂ ‖ ˌpoust-
postvocalic ˌpəust vəu ˈkæl ɪk ◂ ‖ ˌpoust və- **~ally** ᵊl‿i
postwar ˌpəust ˈwɔː ◂ ‖ ˌpoust ˈwɔːr ◂
pos|y, Pos|y ˈpəuz |i ‖ ˈpouz |i **~ies, ~y's** iz
pot pɒt ‖ pɑːt **pots** pɒts ‖ pɑːts **potted** ˈpɒt ɪd -əd ‖ ˈpɑːt̬ əd **potting** ˈpɒt ɪŋ ‖ ˈpɑːt̬ ɪŋ
ˈpot plant; **ˈpotting shed**
potability ˌpəut ə ˈbɪl ət i -ɪt i ‖ ˌpout̬ ə ˈbɪl ət̬ i
potable ˈpəut əb ᵊl ‖ ˈpout̬- **~ness** nəs nɪs
potage pɒ ˈtɑːʒ pəu-; ˈpɒt ɑːʒ, ˈpəut- ‖ pou- —*Fr* [pɔ taːʒ]
potash ˈpɒt æʃ ‖ ˈpɑːt̬-
potassic pə ˈtæs ɪk
potassium pə ˈtæs i‿əm
poˌtassium ˈcyanide
potation pəu ˈteɪʃ ᵊn ‖ pou- **~s** z
potato pə ˈteɪt əu ⚠bə- ‖ pə ˈteɪt̬ ou pət̬ ˈeɪt̬-, -ə **~es** z
poˈtato ˌbeetle; **poˈtato cake**; **poˈtato chip**; **poˌtato ˈcrisp**; **poˈtato ˌpeeler**
potatory ˈpəut ət‿ər i ‖ ˈpout̬ ə tɔːr i -tour i
pot-au-feu ˌpɒt əu ˈfɜː ‖ ˌpɑːt̬ ou ˈfʌ —*Fr* [pɔ to fø]
Potawatomi ˌpɒt ə ˈwɒt əm i ‖ ˌpɑːt̬ ə ˈwɑːt̬- **~s** z
potbell|ied ˌpɒt ˈbel |id ◂ ˈ·ˌ· ‖ ˈpɑːt ˌbel |id **~y** i
potboiler ˈpɒt ˌbɔɪl ə ‖ ˈpɑːt ˌbɔɪl ᵊr **~s** z
potbound ˈpɒt baund ‖ ˈpɑːt-
potch pɒtʃ ‖ pɑːtʃ
poteen pə ˈtʃiːn pɒ-, pəu-, -ˈtiːn ‖ pou-
Potemkin pə ˈtemᵖ kɪn §-kən ‖ pou- —*Russ* [pʌ ˈtʲɔm kʲɪn]
Poˌtemkin ˈvillage
potenc|y ˈpəut ᵊnᵗs |i ‖ ˈpout- **~ies** iz
potent ˈpəut ᵊnt ‖ ˈpout- **~ly** li **~ness** nəs nɪs
potentate ˈpəut ᵊn teɪt ‖ ˈpout- **~s** s
potential pə ˈtenᵗʃ ᵊl pəu- **~ly** i **~s** z
potentialit|y pə ˌtenᵗʃ i ˈæl ət |i pəu-, -ɪt i ‖ -ət̬ |i **~ies** iz
potenti|ate pəu ˈtenᵗʃ i |eɪt ‖ pə- **~ated** eɪt ɪd -əd ‖ eɪt̬ əd **~ates** eɪts **~ating** eɪt ɪŋ ‖ eɪt̬ ɪŋ
potentiation pəu ˌtenᵗʃ i ˈeɪʃ ᵊn ‖ pə- **~s** z
potentilla ˌpəut ᵊn ˈtɪl ə ‖ ˌpout- **~s** z
potentiometer pə ˌtenᵗʃ i ˈɒm ɪt ə pəu-, -ət ə ‖ -ˈɑːm ət̬ ᵊr **~s** z
potful ˈpɒt ful ‖ ˈpɑːt- **~s** z
pothead ˈpɒt hed ‖ ˈpɑːt- **~s** z
potheen pə ˈtʃiːn pɒ-, pəu-, -ˈtiːn, -ˈθiːn ‖ pou-
poth|er ˈpɒð |ə ‖ ˈpɑːð |ᵊr **~ered** əd ‖ ᵊrd **~ering** ər‿ɪŋ **~ers** əz ‖ ᵊrz
potherb ˈpɒt hɜːb ‖ pɑːt̬ ɜːb **~s** z
potholder ˈpɒt ˌhəuld ə →ˌhɒuld- ‖ ˈpɑːt ˌhould ᵊr **~s** z

P

pothol|e ˈpɒt həʊl →-hɒʊl ‖ ˈpɑːt hoʊl **~ed** d **~er/s** ə/z ‖ ᵊr/z **~es** z **~ing** ɪŋ
pothook ˈpɒt hʊk §-huːk ‖ ˈpɑːt- **~s** s
pot|house ˈpɒt |haʊs ‖ ˈpɑːt- **~houses** haʊz ɪz -əz
pothunt|er ˈpɒt ˌhʌnt |ə ‖ ˈpɑːt ˌhʌnt̬ |ᵊr **~ers** əz ‖ ᵊrz **~ing** ɪŋ
potich|e pɒ ˈtiːʃ ‖ poʊ- —*Fr* [pɔ tiʃ] **~es** ɪz əz
Potidae|a ˌpɒt ɪ ˈdiː‿|ə -ə- ‖ ˌpɑːt̬- **~an/s** ən/z
potion ˈpəʊʃ ᵊn ‖ ˈpoʊʃ ᵊn **~s** z
Potiphar ˈpɒt ɪf ə -əf-; -ɪ fɑː, -ə- ‖ ˈpɑːt̬ əf ᵊr
potlatch ˈpɒt lætʃ ‖ ˈpɑːt- **~es** ɪz əz
potluck ˌpɒt ˈlʌk ‖ ˌpɑːt-
pot|man ˈpɒt |mən ‖ ˈpɑːt- **~men** mən men
Potomac pə ˈtəʊm æk -ək ‖ -ˈtoʊm ək -ɪk
potoroo ˌpəʊt ə ˈruː ˌpɒt- ‖ ˌpoʊt̬- **~s** z
Potosi *(i)* pə ˈtəʊs i ‖ -ˈtoʊs i *(ii)* ˌpɒt əʊ ˈsiː ‖ ˌpoʊt̬ ə- —*Places in the US are (i); in Bolivia, (ii)* —*Sp* Potosí [po to ˈsi]
potpourri ˌpəʊ pʊ ˈriː -ˈpʊr i, -ˈpʊər i ‖ ˌpoʊ- —*Fr* [po pu ʁi]
pot-roast ˈpɒt rəʊst ‖ ˈpɑːt roʊst **~ed** ɪd əd **~ing** ɪŋ **~s** s
Potsdam ˈpɒts dæm ‖ ˈpɑːts- —*Ger* [ˈpɔts dam]
potsherd ˈpɒt ʃɜːd ‖ ˈpɑːt ʃɜːd **~s** z
potshot ˈpɒt ʃɒt ‖ ˈpɑːt ʃɑːt **~s** s
Pott pɒt ‖ pɑːt
pott... —*see* **pot**
pottage ˈpɒt ɪdʒ ‖ ˈpɑːt̬-
potter, P~ ˈpɒt ə ‖ ˈpɑːt̬ ᵊr **~ed** d **pottering** ˈpɒt‿ər ɪŋ ‖ ˈpɑːt̬ ər ɪŋ **~s, ~'s** z **ˌpotter's ˈwheel**
Potteries ˈpɒt ər iz ‖ ˈpɑːt̬-
Potterton ˈpɒt ət ən ‖ ˈpɑːt̬ ᵊrt ᵊn
potter|y ˈpɒt‿ər |i ‖ ˈpɑːt̬ ər |i **~ies** iz
Pottinger ˈpɒt ɪndʒ ə -əndʒ- ‖ ˈpɑːt ᵊndʒ ᵊr
potto ˈpɒt əʊ ‖ ˈpɑːt oʊ **~s** z
Potts pɒts ‖ pɑːts
pott|y ˈpɒt |i ‖ ˈpɑːt̬ |i **~ier** i‿ə ‖ i‿ᵊr **~ies** iz **~iest** i‿ɪst i‿əst **~iness** i nəs i nɪs
potty-train ˈpɒt i treɪn ‖ ˈpɑːt̬- **~ed** d **~ing** ɪŋ **~s** z
pouch paʊtʃ **pouched** paʊtʃt **pouches** ˈpaʊtʃ ɪz -əz **pouching** ˈpaʊtʃ ɪŋ
pouf, pouffe *derogatory slang 'homosexual'* pʊf puːf **poufs, pouffes** pʊfs puːfs, puːvz
pouf, pouffe *'seat', 'hairstyle', 'padding'* puːf **poufs, pouffes** puːfs
Poughill *(i)* ˈpɒf ɪl -ᵊl ‖ ˈpɑːf-, *(ii)* pʌf-, *(iii)* ˈpaʊ-
Poughkeepsie pə ˈkɪps i *(!)*
Pouilly-Fumé ˌpuː ji ˈfuːm eɪ ‖ pu ˌjiː fu ˈmeɪ —*Fr* [pu ji fy me]
Poujad|ism ˌpuː ˈʒɑːd |ˌɪz əm ˈ· ·ˌ· · **~ist/s** ɪst/s əst/s
Poulenc ˈpuːl æŋk —*Fr* [pu lɛ̃k]
Poulsen, Poulson ˈpəʊl sən →ˈpɒʊl- ‖ ˈpoʊl-
poult *'chick'* pəʊlt →pɒʊlt ‖ poʊlt **poults** pəʊlts →pɒʊlts ‖ poʊlts
poult *'fabric'* puːlt pʊlt **poults** puːlts pʊlts
Poulteney ˈpəʊlt ni →ˈpɒʊlt- ‖ ˈpoʊlt-
Poulter ˈpəʊlt ə →ˈpɒʊlt- ‖ ˈpoʊlt ᵊr
poulterer ˈpəʊlt‿ər ə →ˈpɒʊlt‿ ‖ ˈpoʊlt ᵊr ər **~s** z
poultic|e ˈpəʊlt ɪs →ˈpɒʊlt-, -əs ‖ ˈpoʊlt əs **~ed** t **~es** ɪz əz **~ing** ɪŋ
Poultney ˈpəʊlt ni →ˈpɒʊlt- ‖ ˈpoʊlt-
Poulton ˈpəʊlt ən →ˈpɒʊlt- ‖ ˈpoʊlt-
Poulton-le-Fylde ˌpəʊlt ən lə ˈfaɪᵊld →ˌpɒʊlt-, -li- ‖ ˌpoʊlt-
poultry ˈpəʊltr i →ˈpɒʊltr- ‖ ˈpoʊltr i
poultry|man ˈpəʊltr i |mən →ˈpɒʊltr- ‖ ˈpoʊltr- **~men** mən men
pounce paʊnᵗs **pounced** paʊnᵗst **pounces** ˈpaʊnᵗs ɪz -əz **pouncing** ˈpaʊnᵗs ɪŋ
pound, Pound paʊnd **pounded** ˈpaʊnd ɪd -əd **pounding/s** ˈpaʊnd ɪŋ/z **pounds, Pound's** paʊndz **ˈpound cake**; **ˌpound ˈsterling**
poundag|e ˈpaʊnd ɪdʒ **~es** ɪz əz
-pounder ˈpaʊnd ə ‖ -ᵊr — **two-pounder** ˌtuː ˈpaʊnd ə ‖ -ᵊr
Pountney ˈpaʊnt ni
Poupart *(i)* ˈpuːp ɑːt ‖ puː ˈpɑːrt, *(ii)* ˈpəʊp- ‖ poʊ ˈpɑːrt
pour pɔː ‖ pɔːr poʊr *(= pore)* **poured** pɔːd ‖ pɔːrd poʊrd **pouring** ˈpɔːr ɪŋ ‖ ˈpoʊr- **pours** pɔːz ‖ pɔːrz poʊrz
pourboire pʊə ˈbwɑː ˈ· · ‖ pʊr ˈbwɑːr **~s** z —*Fr* [puʁ bwaːʁ]
pourer ˈpɔːr ə ‖ ˈpɔːr ᵊr ˈpoʊr- **~s** z
pous|sette puː |ˈset **~setted** ˈset ɪd -əd ‖ ˈset̬ əd **~settes** ˈsets **~setting** ˈset ɪŋ ‖ ˈset̬ ɪŋ
poussin, P~ ˈpuːs æn -ɪn, §-ᵊn ‖ puː ˈsæn —*Fr* [pu sɛ̃] **~s, ~'s** z
pout paʊt **pouted** ˈpaʊt ɪd -əd ‖ ˈpaʊt̬ əd **pouting** ˈpaʊt ɪŋ ‖ ˈpaʊt̬ ɪŋ **pouts** paʊts
pouter ˈpaʊt ə ‖ ˈpaʊt̬ ᵊr **~s** z
poutine ˌpuː ˈtiːn
poverty ˈpɒv ət i ‖ ˈpɑːv ᵊrt̬ i **ˈpoverty trap**
poverty-stricken ˈpɒv ət i ˌstrɪk ən ‖ ˈpɑːv ᵊrt̬-
Povey *(i)* ˈpəʊv i ‖ ˈpoʊv i, *(ii)* pə ˈveɪ
pow *interj* paʊ
POW ˌpiː əʊ ˈdʌb ᵊl juː ‖ ˌoʊ- -ə jə **~s, ~'s** z
powder ˈpaʊd ə ‖ -ᵊr **~ed** d **powdering** ˈpaʊd‿ər ɪŋ **~s** z **ˌpowder ˈblue◂**; **ˈpowder keg**; **ˈpowder puff**; **ˈpowder room**
Powderham ˈpaʊd‿ər əm
powdery ˈpaʊd‿ər i
Powell *(i)* ˈpaʊ‿əl paʊl, *(ii)* ˈpəʊ əl ‖ ˈpoʊ- —*The writer* Anthony P~ *is (ii).*
power, Power ˈpaʊ‿ə ‖ ˈpaʊ‿ᵊr **powered** ˈpaʊ‿əd ‖ ˈpaʊ‿ᵊrd **powering** ˈpaʊ‿ər ɪŋ ‖ ˈpaʊ‿ᵊr ɪŋ **powers** ˈpaʊ‿əz ‖ ˈpaʊ‿ᵊrz **ˈpower base**; **ˈpower ˌbroker**; **ˈpower cut**; **ˈpower dive**; **ˈpower drill**; **ˌpower of atˈtorney**; **ˈpower pack**; **ˈpower plant**; **ˈpower play**; **ˈpower point**; **ˌpower ˈpolitics**; **ˈpower ˌstation**; **ˌpower ˈsteering**; **ˈpower ˌstructure**
power-assisted ˌpaʊ‿ər ə ˈsɪst ɪd ◂ ‖ ˌpaʊ‿ər-

powerboat ˈpaʊ‿ə bəʊt ‖ ˈpaʊ‿ᵊr boʊt **~s** s
powered ˈpaʊ‿əd ‖ ˈpaʊ‿ᵊrd — **low-powered** ˌləʊ ˈpaʊ‿əd ◂ ‖ ˌloʊ ˈpaʊ‿ᵊrd ◂
powerful ˈpaʊ‿əf ᵊl ə fʊl ‖ ˈpaʊ‿ᵊrf ᵊl ᵊr fʊl **~ly** ‿i **~ness** nəs nɪs
power|house ˈpaʊ‿ə |haʊs ‖ ˈpaʊ‿ᵊr- **~houses** haʊz ɪz -əz
powerless ˈpaʊ‿ə ləs -lɪs ‖ ˈpaʊ‿ᵊr- **~ly** li **~ness** nəs nɪs
Powerpoint ˈpaʊ‿ə pɔɪnt ‖ ˈpaʊ‿ᵊr-
Powerscourt *(i)* ˈpaʊ‿əz kɔːt ‖ˈpaʊ‿ᵊrz kɔːrt -koʊrt, *(ii)* ˈpɔːz· ‖ ˈpɔːrz·
power-sharing ˈpaʊ‿ə ˌʃeər ɪŋ ‖ ˈpaʊ‿ᵊr-
Powhatan ˈpaʊ‿ə tæn ˌ· ·ˈ·; ˈpaʊ hæt ᵊn
Powis *(i)* ˈpaʊ ɪs §-əs, *(ii)* ˈpəʊ- ‖ ˈpoʊ-
Pownall ˈpaʊn ᵊl
powwow *n, v* ˈpaʊ waʊ **~ed** d **~ing** ɪŋ **~s** z
Powys *(i)* ˈpəʊ ɪs §-əs ‖ ˈpoʊ-, *(ii)* ˈpaʊ- —*Welsh* [ˈpə wis, ˈpo-] —*The Welsh county is (ii), but the family name is usually (i).*
pox pɒks ‖ pɑːks **poxes** ˈpɒks ɪz -əz ‖ ˈpɑːks əz
poxy ˈpɒks i ‖ ˈpɑːks i
Poynings ˈpɔɪn ɪŋz
Poynting ˈpɔɪnt ɪŋ ‖ ˈpɔɪnţ-
Pozidriv *tdmk* ˈpɒz ɪ draɪv -ə- ‖ ˈpɑːz-
Poznan, Poznań ˈpɒz næn ˌ·ˈ· ‖ ˈpoʊz nɑːn —*Polish* [ˈpɔ znaɲ]
P-plate ˈpiː pleɪt **~s** s
PPS ˌpiː pi ˈes
PR ˌpiː ˈɑː
Praa preɪ
practicability ˌpræktɪk ə ˈbɪl ət i -ɪt i ‖ -əţ i
practicab|le ˈprækt ɪk əb |ᵊl **~ly** li
practical ˈprækt ɪk ᵊl **~s** z
ˌ**practical** ˈ**joke**
practicalit|y ˌprækt ɪ ˈkæl ət |i ˌ·ə-, -ɪt i ‖ -əţ |i **~ies** iz
practically ˈprækt ɪk li -ɪk ᵊl‿i
practic|e, practis|e ˈprækt ɪs §-əs **~ed** t **~es** ɪz əz **~ing** ɪŋ
practicum ˈprækt ɪk əm
practitioner præk ˈtɪʃ ᵊn‿ə ‖ ər **~s** z
Prada ˈprɑːd ə
Prader-Willi ˌprɑːd ə ˈvɪl i -ˈwɪl i ‖ -ᵊr-
Pradesh prə ˈdeɪʃ -ˈdeʃ —*Hindi* [prə ɖeːʃ]
Prado ˈprɑːd əʊ ‖ -oʊ —*Sp* [ˈpra ðo]
praecox ˈpriː kɒks ˈpraɪ- ‖ -kɑːks
Praed preɪd
praedial ˈpriːd i‿əl
praelector ₍ₗ₎praɪ ˈlekt ə ₍ₗ₎priː-, -ɔː ‖ -ᵊr **~s** z
praemunire ˌpraɪ mju ˈnɪər i ˌpriː-, -mjə-, -ˈnaɪᵊr- ‖ -ˈnɪr
prae|nomen ˌpriː |ˈnəʊm en ˌpraɪ- ‖ -|ˈnoʊm ən **~nomina** ˈnɒm ɪn ə ˈnəʊm-, -ən- ‖ ˈnoʊm-
praepostor pri ˈpɒst ə ‖ -ˈpɑːst ᵊr **~s** z
praesidi|um prɪ ˈsɪd i‿|əm prə-, praɪ-, -ˈzɪd- **~a** ə
praetor ˈpriːt ə -ɔː ‖ ˈpriːţ ᵊr **~s** z
praetorian pri ˈtɔːr i‿ən praɪ- ‖ -ˈtoʊr- **~s** z
pragmatic præg ˈmæt ɪk ‖ -ˈmæţ ɪk **~ally** ᵊl‿i **~s** s

pragmatism ˈpræg mə ˌtɪz əm
pragmatist ˈpræg mət ɪst §-əst ‖ -məţ- **~s** s
Prague prɑːg
Praia ˈpraɪ ə —*Port* [ˈpra ja]
prairie ˈpreər i ‖ ˈprer i **~s** z
ˈ**prairie dog**; ˌ**prairie** ˈ**rose**
praise preɪz *(= prays)* **praised** preɪzd **praises** ˈpreɪz ɪz -əz **praising** ˈpreɪz ɪŋ
praiser ˈpreɪz ə ‖ ᵊr **~s** z
praiseworth|y ˈpreɪz ˌwɜːð |i ‖ -ˌwɜːð |i **~ily** ɪ li əl i **~iness** i nəs i nɪs
Prakrit ˈprɑːk rɪt **~s** s
praline ˈprɑːl iːn ‖ ˈpreɪl- ˈprɑːl- **~s** z
pram *'boat'* prɑːm præm **prams** prɑːmz præmz
pram *'baby carriage'* præm **prams** præmz
prana ˈprɑːn ə
prance prɑːnᵗs §prænᵗs ‖ prænᵗs **pranced** prɑːnᵗst §prænᵗst ‖ prænᵗst **prancer/s** ˈprɑːnᵗs ə/z §ˈprænᵗs- ‖ ˈprænᵗs ᵊr/z **prances** ˈprɑːnᵗs ɪz §ˈprænᵗs-, -əz ‖ ˈprænᵗs əz **prancing** ˈprɑːnᵗs ɪŋ §ˈprænᵗs- ‖ ˈprænᵗs ɪŋ
prancer ˈprɑːnᵗs ə §ˈprænᵗs ə ‖ ˈprænᵗs ᵊr **~s** z
prandial ˈprænd i‿əl **~ly** i
prang præŋ **pranged** præŋd **pranging** ˈpræŋ ɪŋ **prangs** præŋz
Prangnell ˈpræŋ nᵊl
prank præŋk **pranks** præŋks
prank|ish ˈpræŋk| ɪʃ **~some** səm
prankster ˈpræŋkst ə ‖ -ᵊr **~s** z
p'raps præps —*see* **perhaps**
prase preɪz
praseodymium ˌpreɪz i‿əʊ ˈdɪm i‿əm ‖ -oʊˈ-- ˌpreɪs-
prat præt **prats** præts
Pratchett ˈprætʃ ɪt §-ət
prate preɪt **prated** ˈpreɪt ɪd -əd ‖ ˈpreɪţ əd **prates** preɪts **prating** ˈpreɪt ɪŋ ‖ ˈpreɪţ ɪŋ
prater ˈpreɪt ə ‖ ˈpreɪţ ᵊr **~s** z
pratfall ˈpræt fɔːl ‖ -fɑːl **~s** z
pratincole ˈpræt ɪŋ kəʊl ˈpreɪt-, →-kɒʊl ‖ ˈpræt ᵊn koʊl **~s** z
pratique ˈpræt iːk -ɪk; præ ˈtiːk ‖ præ ˈtiːk
Pratt præt
prattl|e ˈpræt ᵊl ‖ ˈpræţ ᵊl **~ed** d **~er/s** ‿ə/z ‖ ‿ᵊrz **~es** z **~ing** ‿ɪŋ
Pravda ˈprɑːv də —*Russ* [ˈprav də]
prawn prɔːn ‖ prɑːn **prawns** prɔːnz ‖ prɑːnz
ˌ**prawn** ˈ**cocktail**; ˌ**prawn** ˈ**cracker**
praxis ˈpræks ɪs §-əs
Praxiteles præk ˈsɪt ə liːz -ɪ-; -ᵊl iːz ‖ -ˈsɪţ ᵊl iːz
pray preɪ **prayed** preɪd **praying** ˈpreɪ ɪŋ **prays** preɪz *(= praise)*
ˌ**praying** ˈ**mantis**
prayer *'one that prays'* ˈpreɪ ə ‖ -ᵊr **~s** z
prayer *'act / words of praying'* preə ‖ preᵊr præᵊr **~s** z
ˈ**prayer book**; ˈ**prayer** ˌ**meeting**; ˈ**prayer mat**; ˈ**prayer rug**; ˈ**prayer wheel**
prayerful ˈpreə fʊl ‖ ˈprer- ˈprær- **~ly** i **~ness** nəs nɪs
pre- ¦priː, pri, prə, ¦pre —*Compare* re- . *As a productive prefix meaning 'before' (sometimes spelt with a hyphen),* ¦priː (preadapt

ˌpriː‿ə ˈdæpt, pre-sleep ˌpriː ˈsliːp◂). *Otherwise, with a vaguer meaning,* pri, prə *before a consonant sound* (prepare pri ˈpeə prə- ‖ -ˈpeᵊr)*; but if stressed through the operation of a stressing rule usually* ¦pre+ (preparation ˌprep ə ˈreɪʃ ᵊn).

preach priːtʃ **preached** priːtʃt **preaches** ˈpriːtʃ ɪz -əz **preaching** ˈpriːtʃ ɪŋ

preacher, P~ ˈpriːtʃ ə ‖ -ᵊr **~s** z

preachi|fy ˈpriːtʃ ɪ |faɪ §-ə- **~fied** faɪd **~fies** faɪz **~fying** faɪ ɪŋ

preach|y ˈpriːtʃ |i **~ier** i‿ə ‖ i‿ᵊr **~iest** i‿ɪst ‿əst **~iness** i nəs -nɪs

preadamic ˌpriː‿ə ˈdæm ɪk ◂

preadamite ˌpriː ˈæd ə maɪt ◂ **~s** s

preamble pri ˈæm bᵊl ˈpriː ˌæm- **~s** z

pre-amp ˈpriː æmp **~s** s

preamplification ˌpriː ˌæmp lɪf ɪ ˈkeɪʃ ᵊn .ˌ. . .ˈ. ., -ləf .ˈ- -, §-ə'..

preampli|fy ₍ˌ₎priː ˈæmp lɪ |faɪ -lə- **~fied** faɪd **~fier/s** faɪ‿ə/z ‖ faɪ‿ᵊr/z **~fies** faɪz **~fying** faɪ ɪŋ

prearrang|e ˌpriː‿ə ˈreɪndʒ ◂ **~ed** d **~ement** mənt **~es** ɪz əz **~ing** ɪŋ

prebend ˈpreb ənd **~s** z

prebendar|y ˈpreb ənd‿ᵊr |i ‖ -ən der |i **~ies** iz

prebuttal ˌpriː ˈbʌt ᵊl pri- ‖ -ˈbʌţ- **~s** z

precambrian, Pre-Cambrian ₍ˌ₎priː ˈkæm bri‿ən

precancerous ˌpriː ˈkænᵗs ər‿əs

precarious pri ˈkeər i‿əs prə- ‖ -ˈker- -ˈkær- **~ly** li **~ness** nəs nɪs

precast ˌpriː ˈkɑːst ◂ §-ˈkæst ‖ -ˈkæst ◂ ˈ. **~ing** ɪŋ **~s** s

precatory ˈprek ət‿ər i ‖ -ə tɔːr i -toʊr i

precaution pri ˈkɔːʃ ᵊn prə- ‖ -ˈkɑːʃ- **~s** z

precautionary pri ˈkɔːʃ ᵊn ər‿i -ᵊn‿ər i ‖ -ə ner i -ˈkɑːʃ-

preced|e pri ˈsiːd prə- **~ed** ɪd əd **~es** z **~ing** ɪŋ

precedence ˈpres ɪd ənᵗs ˈpriːs-, -əd-; ˌpri ˈsiːd ᵊnᵗs, prə-

precedent *adj* pri ˈsiːd ᵊnt ˈpres ɪd ənt, ˈpriːs-, -əd- **~ly** li

precedent *n* ˈpres ɪd ənt ˈpriːs-, -əd- **~s** s

precedented ˈpres ɪ dent ɪd ˈpriːs-, ˈ.ə-, -dənt ., -əd ‖ -denţ əd

precedential ˌpres ɪ ˈdenᵗʃ ᵊl ◂ ˌpriːs-, -ə-

precentor pri ˈsent ə prə- ‖ -ˈsenţ ᵊr **~s** z

precept ˈpriː sept **~s** s

preceptor pri ˈsept ə prə- ‖ -ᵊr ˈpriː sept ᵊr **~s** z

precess pri ˈses prə- **~ed** t **~es** ɪz əz **~ing** ɪŋ

precession pri ˈseʃ ᵊn prə- **~s** z

precessional pri ˈseʃ ᵊn‿əl prə-

precinct ˈpriː sɪŋkt **~s** s

preciosity ˌpreʃ i ˈɒs ət i ˌpres-, -ɪt i ‖ -ˈɑːs əţ i

precious ˈpreʃ əs **~ly** li **~ness** nəs nɪs ˌprecious ˈmetal; ˌprecious ˈstone

precipic|e ˈpres əp ɪs -ɪp-, §-əs **~es** ɪz əz

precipitant pri ˈsɪp ɪt ənt prə-, -ət- **~s** s

precipi|tate *v* pri ˈsɪp ɪ |teɪt prə-, -ə- **~tated** teɪt ɪd -əd ‖ teɪţ əd **~tates** teɪts **~tating** teɪt ɪŋ ‖ teɪţ ɪŋ

precipitate *n, adj* pri ˈsɪp ɪt ət prə-, -ət-, -ɪt; -ɪ teɪt, -ə- ‖ -əţ ət -ə teɪt **~ly** li **~ness** nəs nɪs **~s** s

precipitation pri ˌsɪp ɪ ˈteɪʃ ᵊn prə-, -ə- **~s** z

precipitous pri ˈsɪp ɪt əs prə-, -ət- ‖ -əţ əs **~ly** li **~ness** nəs nɪs

precis, précis *n sing., v* ˈpreɪs iː ‖ preɪ ˈsiː (*) ~ *n pl* z **~ed** d **~es** z **~ing** ɪŋ

precise pri ˈsaɪs prə- **~ly** li **~ness** nəs nɪs

precision pri ˈsɪʒ ᵊn prə- **~ist/s** ɪst/s §əst/s ‖ əst/s

precision-made pri ˌsɪʒ ᵊn ˈmeɪd ◂ prə-, →-ᵊm-

preclassical ˌpriː ˈklæs ɪk ᵊl ◂

preclinical ˌpriː ˈklɪn ɪk ᵊl ◂

preclud|e pri ˈkluːd prə- **~ed** ɪd əd **~es** z **~ing** ɪŋ

preclusion pri ˈkluːʒ ᵊn prə-

preclusive pri ˈkluːs ɪv prə- ‖ -ˈkluːz- **~ly** li

precocial pri ˈkəʊʃ ᵊl prə- ‖ -ˈkoʊʃ-

precocious pri ˈkəʊʃ əs prə- ‖ -ˈkoʊʃ əs **~ly** li **~ness** nəs nɪs

precocity pri ˈkɒs ət i prə-, -ɪt- ‖ -ˈkɑːs əţ i

precognition ˌpriː kɒg ˈnɪʃ ᵊn ‖ -kɑːg-

pre-colonial ˌpriː kə ˈləʊn i‿əl ◂ ‖ -ˈloʊn-

pre-Columbian ˌpriː kə ˈlʌm bi‿ən ◂ ˌpre-Coˌlumbian ˈpottery

precompos|e ˌpriː kəm ˈpəʊz §-kɒm- ‖ -ˈpoʊz **~ed** d ◂ **~es** ɪz əz **~ing** ɪŋ

preconceiv|e ˌpriː kən ˈsiːv ◂ §-kɒn- **~ed** d **~es** z **~ing** ɪŋ ˌpreconˌceived iˈdeas

preconception ˌpriː kən ˈsep ʃᵊn §-kɒn- **~s** z

precon|cert ˌpriː kən |ˈsɜːt §-kɒn- ‖ -|ˈsɝːt **~certed** ˈsɜːt ɪd -əd ‖ ˈsɝːţ əd **~certing** ˈsɜːt ɪŋ ‖ ˈsɝːţ ɪŋ **~certs** ˈsɜːts ‖ ˈsɝːts

precondition ˌpriː kən ˈdɪʃ ᵊn §-kɒn- **~s** z

preconis|e, preconiz|e ˈpriːk ə naɪz **~ed** d **~es** ɪz əz **~ing** ɪŋ

preconsonantal ˌpriː ˌkɒnᵗs ə ˈnænt ᵊl ◂ ‖ -ˌkɑːnᵗs ə ˈnænţ ᵊl ◂ -ˈnenţ- **~ly** i

precook ˌpriː ˈkʊk §-ˈkuːk **~ed** t **~ing** ɪŋ **~s** s

precursive pri ˈkɜːs ɪv prə- ‖ -ˈkɝːs ɪv **~ly** li

precursor pri ˈkɜːs ə prə- ‖ -ˈkɝːs ᵊr **~s** z

precursor|y pri ˈkɜːs ər |i prə- ‖ -ˈkɝːs- **~ily** əl i ɪ li

predaceous, predacious pri ˈdeɪʃ əs prə- **~ness** nəs nɪs

pre|date *'antedate'* ₍ˌ₎priː |ˈdeɪt **~dated** ˈdeɪt ɪd -əd ‖ ˈdeɪţ əd **~dates** ˈdeɪts **~dating** ˈdeɪt ɪŋ ‖ ˈdeɪţ ɪŋ

pre|date *'prey on'* pri |ˈdeɪt prə- **~dated** ˈdeɪt ɪd -əd ‖ ˈdeɪţ əd **~dates** ˈdeɪts **~dating** ˈdeɪt ɪŋ ‖ ˈdeɪţ ɪŋ

predation pri ˈdeɪʃ ᵊn prə- **~s** z

predator ˈpred ət ə -ɪt- ‖ -əţ ᵊr -ə tɔːr **~s** z

predator|y ˈpred ət‿ər |i ‖ -ə tɔːr |i -toʊr i **~ily** əl i ɪ li **~iness** i nəs i nɪs

predawn ˌpriː ˈdɔːn ◂ ‖ -ˈdɑːn ◂

P

predeceas|e ˌpriː dɪ ˈsiːs -də- **~ed** t **~es** ɪz əz **~ing** ɪŋ

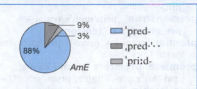

PREDECESSOR

9%
3%
88%
ˈpred-
ˌpred·ˈ· ·
ˈpriːd-
AmE

predecessor ˈpriːd ɪ ses ə ˈ·ə-, ˌ·ˈ· · ‖ ˈpred ə ses ᵊr ˌ· ·ˈ· ·; ˈpriːd- — *Preference poll, AmE:* ˈpred- *88%,* ˌpred·ˈ· · *9%,* ˈpriːd- *3%.* **~s** z

predefin|e ˌpriː dɪ ˈfaɪn -də- §-diː- **~ed** d ◂ **~ed** z **~ing** ɪŋ

predestinate *adj* ₍ᵢ₎priː ˈdest ɪn ət prɪ-, -ən-, -ɪt; -ɪ neɪt, -ə- **~ly** li

predesti|nate *v* ₍ᵢ₎priː ˈdest ɪ |neɪt prɪ-, -ə- **~nated** neɪt ɪd -əd ‖ neɪţ əd **~nates** neɪts **~nating** neɪt ɪŋ ‖ neɪţ ɪŋ

predestination priː ˌdest ɪ ˈneɪʃ ᵊn prɪ-, ˌpriː ˌ·ˈ·-, -əˈ·-

predestin|e ₍ᵢ₎priː ˈdest ɪn prɪ-, -ən **~ed** d **~es** z **~ing** ɪŋ

predetermination ˌpriː dɪ ˌtɜːm ɪ ˈneɪʃ ᵊn ˌ·də-, -ˌ·ə- ‖ -ˌtɜːm-

predetermin|e ˌpriː di ˈtɜːm ɪn ◂ -də-, -ən ‖ -ˈtɜːm ən **~ed** d **~es** z **~ing** ɪŋ

predeterminer ˌpriː di ˈtɜːm ɪn ə ˌ·də-, -ən ə ‖ -ˈtɜːm ən ᵊr **~s** z

predial ˈpriːd i ə̆l

predicability ˌpred ɪk ə ˈbɪl ət i -ɪt i ‖ -əţ i

predicable ˈpred ɪk əb ᵊl **~ness** nəs nɪs **~s** z

predicament pri ˈdɪk ə mənt prə- —*but in the sense 'logical category', also* ˈpred ɪk- **~s** s

predi|cate *v* ˈpred ɪ |keɪt **~cated** keɪt ɪd -əd ‖ keɪţ əd **~cates** keɪts **~cating** keɪt ɪŋ ‖ keɪţ ɪŋ

predicate *n* ˈpred ɪk ət ˈpriːd-, -ɪt; -ɪ keɪt **~s** s

predication ˌpred ɪ ˈkeɪʃ ᵊn -ə- **~s** z

predicative pri ˈdɪk ət ɪv prə- ‖ -əţ ɪv ˈpred ɪk-; ˈpred ɪ keɪţ ɪv **~ly** li **~ness** nəs nɪs **~s** z

predicator ˈpred ɪ keɪt ə ˈ·ə- ‖ -keɪţ ᵊr **~s** z

predict pri ˈdɪkt prə- **~ed** ɪd əd **~ing** ɪŋ **~s** s

predictability pri ˌdɪkt ə ˈbɪl ət i prə-, -ɪt i ‖ -əţ i

predictab|le pri ˈdɪkt əb |ᵊl prə- **~ly** li

prediction pri ˈdɪk ʃᵊn prə- **~s** z

predictive pri ˈdɪkt ɪv prə- **~ly** li **~ness** nəs nɪs

predictor pri ˈdɪkt ə prə- ‖ -ᵊr **~s** z

predigest ˌpriː daɪ ˈdʒest -dɪ-, -də- **~ed** ɪd əd **~ing** ɪŋ **~s** s

predilection ˌpriːd ɪ ˈlek ʃᵊn -ə-, -ᵊl ˈek-; ⚠-ˈlɪk- ‖ ˌpred ᵊl ˈek ʃᵊn ˌpriːd- **~s** z

predispos|e ˌpriː dɪ ˈspəʊz -də- ‖ -ˈspoʊz **~ed** d **~es** ɪz əz **~ing** ɪŋ

predisposition ˌpriː ˌdɪsp ə ˈzɪʃ ᵊn **~s** z

prednisolone pred ˈnɪs ə ləʊn ‖ -loʊn

prednisone ˈpred nɪ səʊn -nə-, -zəʊn ‖ -soʊn -zoʊn

predominanc|e pri ˈdɒm ɪn ənᵗs prə-, -ən- ‖ -ˈdɑːm- **~y** i

predominant pri ˈdɒm ɪn ənt prə-, -ən- ‖ -ˈdɑːm- **~ly** li

predomi|nate pri ˈdɒm ɪ |neɪt prə-, -ə- ‖ -ˈdɑːm- **~nated** neɪt ɪd -əd ‖ neɪţ əd **~nates** neɪts **~nating** neɪt ɪŋ ‖ neɪţ ɪŋ

Preece priːs

pre-echo ˌpriː ˈek əʊ ‖ -oʊ **~es** z

pre-eclampsia ˌpriː ɪ ˈklæmps i ə̆ ˌ·e-, ˌ·ə-

Preedy ˈpriːd i

preemie ˈpriːm i **~s** z

preeminence pri ˈem ɪn ənᵗs ˌpriː-, -ən-

preeminent pri ˈem ɪn ənt ˌpriː-, -ən- **~ly** li

preempt pri ˈempt ˌpriː- **~ed** ɪd əd **~ing** ɪŋ **~s** s

preemption pri ˈemp ʃᵊn ˌpriː- **~s** z

preemptive pri ˈempt ɪv ˌpriː- **~ly** li

preemptor pri ˈempt ə ˌpriː-, -ɔː ‖ -ᵊr **~s** z

preen, Preen priːn **preened** priːnd **preening** ˈpriːn ɪŋ **preens** priːnz

preexilian ˌpriː ɪg ˈzɪl i ə̆n ◂ ˌ·eg-, ˌ·əg-, ˌ·ɪk-, ˌ·ek-, ˌ·ək-

pre-exilic ˌpriː ɪg ˈzɪl ɪk ◂ eg-, əg-, ɪk-, ek-, ək-

preexist ˌpriː ɪg ˈzɪst -eg-, -əg-, -ɪk-, -ek-, -ək- **~ed** ɪd əd **~ing** ɪŋ **~s** s

preexistenc|e ˌpriː ɪg ˈzɪst ənᵗs -eg-, -əg-, -ɪk-, -ek-, -ək- **~es** ɪz əz

preexistent ˌpriː ɪg ˈzɪst ənt ◂ -eg-, -əg-, -ɪk-, -ek-, -ək- **~ly** li

prefab ˈpriː fæb **~s** z

prefabri|cate ˌpriː ˈfæb rɪ |keɪt -rə- **~cated** keɪt ɪd -əd ‖ keɪţ əd **~cates** keɪts **~cating** keɪt ɪŋ ‖ keɪţ ɪŋ

prefabrication ˌpriː ˌfæb rɪ ˈkeɪʃ ᵊn ˌ· ˌ· ·ˈ·-, -rə- **~s** z

prefac|e *n, v* ˈpref əs -ɪs **~ed** t **~es** ɪz əz **~ing** ɪŋ

prefator|y ˈpref ət ə̆r |i ‖ -ə tɔːr |i -toʊr i **~ily** əl i ɪ li

prefect ˈpriː fekt **~s** s

prefectorial ˌpriː fek ˈtɔːr i ə̆l ◂ ‖ -ˈtoʊr-

prefectural pri ˈfek tʃər əl ₍ᵢ₎-tjʊr-; ˈpriː fek-

prefecture ˈpriː fek tʃə -tʃʊə; -fekt jʊə ‖ -tʃᵊr **~s** z

prefer pri ˈfɜː prə- ‖ -ˈfɜː **~red** d **preferring** pri ˈfɜːr ɪŋ prə- ‖ -ˈfɜː ɪŋ **~s** z
preˌferred ˈstock

preferability ˌpref ᵊr ə̆ ˈbɪl ət i ⚠pri ˌfɜːr ə-, prə- ‖ -əţ i ⚠pri ˌfɜː ə-

preferab|le ˈpref ᵊr ə̆b |ᵊl ⚠pri ˈfɜːr əb |ᵊl, prə- ‖ ⚠pri ˈfɜː- **~leness** ᵊl nəs -nɪs **~ly** li

preferenc|e ˈpref ᵊr ə̆nᵗs **~es** ɪz əz
ˈpreference shares

preferential ˌpref ə ˈrenᵗʃ ᵊl ◂ **~ly** i

preferment pri ˈfɜː mənt prə- ‖ -ˈfɜː- **~s** s

prefiguration ˌpriː ˌfɪg ə ˈreɪʃ ᵊn -juᵊ- ‖ -jə- **~s** z

prefigure ₍ᵢ₎priː ˈfɪg ə ‖ -jᵊr *(*)* **~d** d **~s** z
prefiguring ₍ᵢ₎priː ˈfɪg ər ɪŋ ‖ -jər ɪŋ **~ment** mənt

prefix *n* ˈpriː fɪks **~es** ɪz əz

P

prefix *v* ˈpriː fɪks ₍ₗ₎priː ˈfɪks **~ed** t **~es** ɪz əz **~ing** ɪŋ
prefixal ₍ₗ₎priː ˈfɪks ᵊl ˈpriː fɪks- **~ly** i
preflight ˌpriː ˈflaɪt ◂
preformation ˌpriː fɔː ˈmeɪʃᵊn ‖ -fɔːr-
prefrontal ₍ₗ₎priː ˈfrʌnt ᵊl ‖ -ˈfrʌnţ ᵊl
pregame ˌpriː ˈɡeɪm ◂
preggers ˈpreɡ əz ‖ -ᵊrz
pregnanc|y ˈpreɡ nənᵗs |i **~ies** iz
pregnant ˈpreɡ nənt **~ly** li
prehead ˈpriː hed **~s** z
pre|heat ˌpriː |ˈhiːt ◂ **~heated** ˈhiːt ɪd -əd ‖ ˈhiːţ əd **~heating** ˈhiːt ɪŋ ‖ ˈhiːţ ɪŋ **~heats** ˈhiːts
ˌpreˌheated ˈoven
prehensile pri ˈhenᵗs aɪᵊl prə- ‖ -ᵊl *(*)*
prehistoric ˌpriː hɪ ˈstɒr ɪk ◂ -ɪ- ‖ -ˈstɔːr ɪk -ˈstɑːr- **~ally** ᵊl‿i
prehistory ˌpriː ˈhɪs tri -tər i
pre-ignition ˌpriː ɪɡ ˈnɪʃᵊn
prejudg|e ˌpriː ˈdʒʌdʒ **~ed** d **~ement, ~ment** mənt **~es** ɪz əz **~ing** ɪŋ
prejudic|e ˈpredʒ u dɪs -ə-, §-dəs, §-daɪs ‖ -əd əs **~ed** t **~es** ɪz əz **~ing** ɪŋ
prejudicial ˌpredʒ u ˈdɪʃ ᵊl ◂ -ə- ‖ -ə- **~ly** i
prelac|y ˈprel əs |i **~ies** iz
prelapsarian ˌpriː læp ˈseər i‿ən ◂ ‖ -ˈser- **~s** z
prelate ˈprel ət -ɪt **~s** s
prelim ˈpriː lɪm prɪ ˈlɪm, prə- **~s** z
preliminar|y pri ˈlɪm ɪn ᵊr‿|i prə-, -ᵊn‿ər |i; §-ɪ ner |i, §-ə ner i ‖ -ə ner |i **~ies** iz **~ily** əl i ɪ li
prelingual ˌpriː ˈlɪŋ ɡwəl ◂ ˌ·ˈlɪŋ ɡju‿əl ◂ **~ly** i
preliterate ₍ₗ₎priː ˈlɪt‿ər ət ◂ -ɪt ‖ -ˈlɪţ ər- →-ˈlɪtr·
pre-loved ˌpriː ˈlʌvd ◂
prelude ˈprel juːd ‖ ˈpreɪl-, -uːd; ˈpriː luːd **~s** z
prelusive pri ˈluːs ɪv -ˈljuːs- ‖ -ˈluːz- **~ly** li
Prem prem
premarital ₍ₗ₎priː ˈmær ɪt ᵊl -ət- ‖ -əţ ᵊl -ˈmer- **~ly** i

PREMATURE

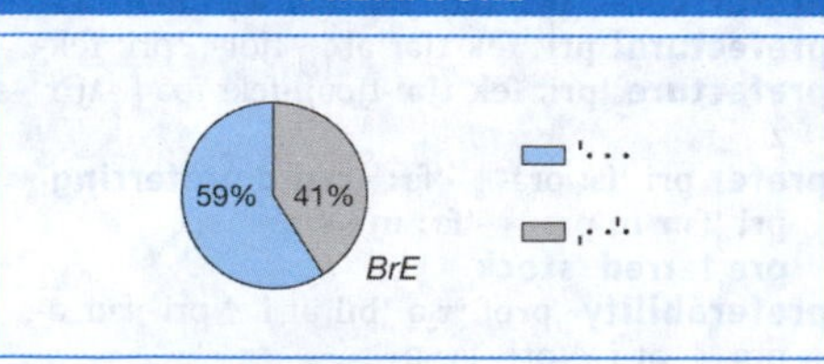

premature ˈprem ətʃ ə ˈpriːm-; -ə tjʊə, -tʃʊə, -tjɔː, -tʃɔː; ˌ·ə ˈtʃʊə, -ˈtʃɔː, -ˈtjʊə, -ˈtjɔː ‖ ˌpriːm ə ˈtʊᵊr ◂ -ˈtʃʊᵊr, -ˈtjʊᵊr; ˈ· · · — *Preference poll, BrE:* ˈ· · · *59%,* ˌ· ·ˈ· *41%. (*)* **~ly** li **~ness** nəs nɪs
prematurity ˌprem ə ˈtʃʊər ət i ˌpriːm-, -ˈtjʊər-, -ˈtjɔːr-, -ˈtʃɔːr-, -ɪt i ‖ ˌpriːm ə ˈtʊr əţ i -ˈtʃʊr-, -ˈtjʊr-
premed ₍ₗ₎priː ˈmed **~s** z
premedical ₍ₗ₎priː ˈmed ɪk ᵊl
premedication ˌpriː ˌmed ɪ ˈkeɪʃ ᵊn ·ˌ· ·ˈ·- **~s** z
premedi|tate ₍ₗ₎priː ˈmed ɪ |teɪt pri-, prə-, -ə- **~tated** teɪt ɪd -əd ‖ teɪţ əd **~tates** teɪts **~tating** teɪt ɪŋ ‖ teɪţ ɪŋ
premeditation pri ˌmed ɪ ˈteɪʃ ᵊn prə-, -ə-; ˌpriːˌ· ·ˈ·-, -əˈ·-
premenstrual ˌpriː ˈmenᵗs tru‿əl ◂
ˌpreˌmenstrual ˈtension
premier ˈprem i‿ə ˈpriːm- ‖ pri ˈmɪᵊr -ˈmjɪᵊr; ˈpriːm i‿ᵊr *(*)* **~s** z
premiere, première ˈprem i eə -i‿ə, ˌ· ·ˈeə ‖ pri ˈmɪᵊr pre-, -ˈmjɪᵊr; prɪm ˈjeᵊr *(*)* **~s** z
premiership ˈprem i‿ə ʃɪp ˈpriːm- ‖ pri ˈmɪᵊr ʃɪp -ˈmjɪᵊr-; ˈpriːm i‿ᵊr-
Preminger ˈprem ɪndʒ ə ‖ -ᵊr
premis|e *v* ˈprem ɪs §-əs; prɪ ˈmaɪz, prə- **~ed** t **~es** ɪz əz **~ing** ɪŋ
prem|ise *n* ˈprem| ɪs §-əs **~ises** ɪs ɪz əs-, -əz; ɪ siːz, ə-
premiss ˈprem ɪs §-əs **~es** ɪz əz
premium ˈpriːm i‿əm **~s** z
ˈpremium bond, ˈ· · · ·
premodification ˌpriː ˌmɒd ɪf ɪ ˈkeɪʃ ᵊn -ˌ·əf-, §-əˈ· · ‖ -ˌmɑːd-
premodi|fy ˌpriː ˈmɒd ɪ |faɪ -ə- ‖ -ˈmɑːd- **~fied** faɪd **~fier/s** faɪ‿ə/z ‖ faɪ‿ᵊr/z **~fies** faɪz **~fying** faɪ ɪŋ
premolar ₍ₗ₎priː ˈməʊl ə ‖ -ˈmoʊl ᵊr **~s** z
premonition ˌprem ə ˈnɪʃ ᵊn ˌpriːm- **~s** z
premonitor|y pri ˈmɒn ɪt‿ər |i prə-, ˌpriː-, -ˈət‿ ‖ -ˈmɑːn ə tɔːr |i -toʊr i **~ily** əl i ɪ li
prenatal ˌpriː ˈneɪt ᵊl ◂ ‖ -ˈneɪţ ᵊl ◂ **~ly** i
Prendergast ˈprend ə ɡɑːst -ɡæst ‖ -ᵊr ɡæst
prentice, P~, Prentis, Prentiss ˈprent ɪs §-əs ‖ ˈprenţ əs
prenuptial ˌpriː ˈnʌp ʃᵊl ◂ -tʃəl; ⚠-ˈnʌp ʃu‿əl, ⚠-tʃu‿əl **~ly** i **~s** z — *The nonstandard pronunciations are reflected in a nonstandard spelling* prenuptual
preoccupation pri ˌɒk ju ˈpeɪʃ ᵊn ˌpriːˌ· ·ˈ·-, -jəˈ·- ‖ -ˌɑːk jə- **~s** z
preoccu|py pri ˈɒk ju |paɪ ˌpriː-, -jə- ‖ -ˈɑːk jə- **~pied** paɪd **~pies** paɪz **~pying** paɪ ɪŋ
pre-op ˌpriː ˈɒp ◂ ‖ -ˈɑːp ◂
preoperative ˌpriː ˈɒp ər‿ət ɪv ◂ ‖ -ˈɑːp ər‿əţ ɪv **~ly** li
preordain ˌpriː ɔː ˈdeɪn ‖ -ɔːr- **~ed** d **~ing** ɪŋ **~s** z
preordination ₍ₗ₎priː ˌɔːd ɪ ˈneɪʃ ᵊn -əˈ·-, -ᵊn ˈeɪʃ- ‖ -ˌɔːrd ᵊn ˈeɪʃ ᵊn **~s** z
pre-owned ˌpriː ˈəʊnd ◂ ‖ -ˈoʊnd ◂
prep prep **prepped** prept **prepping** ˈprep ɪŋ
preps preps
ˈprep school
prepack ˌpriː ˈpæk ◂ **~ed** t **~ing** ɪŋ **~s** s
prepackag|e ˌpriː ˈpæk ɪdʒ ◂ **~ed** d **~es** ɪz əz **~ing** ɪŋ
prepaid ˌpriː ˈpeɪd ◂
preparation ˌprep ə ˈreɪʃ ᵊn **~s** z
preparative pri ˈpær ət ɪv prə- ‖ -əţ ɪv -ˈper- **~ly** li **~s** z
preparator|y pri ˈpær ət‿ər |i prə- ‖ -ə tɔːr |i -ˈper-, -toʊr i; ˈprep ər‿ə- **~ily** əl i ɪ li
preˈparatory school

prepare pri ˈpeə prə- ‖ -ˈpeᵊr -ˈpæᵊr **~d** d
preparing pri ˈpeər ɪŋ prə- ‖ -ˈper ɪŋ -ˈpær- **~s** z
preparedness pri ˈpeər ɪd nəs prə-, -əd-, -nɪs; -ˈpeəd nəs, -nɪs ‖ -ˈper əd- -ˈpær-; -ˈperd nəs, -ˈpærd-
pre|pay ˌpriː |ˈpeɪ ◂ **~paid** ˈpeɪd ◂ **~paying** ˈpeɪ ɪŋ **~payment** ˈpeɪ mənt **~pays** ˈpeɪz
prepense pri ˈpenᵗs ˌpriː-, prə- **~ly** li
preponderanc|e pri ˈpɒnd ər ənᵗs prə- ‖ -ˈpɑːnd‿ **~y** i
preponderant pri ˈpɒnd ər ənt prə- ‖ -ˈpɑːnd‿ **~ly** li
preponde|rate pri ˈpɒnd ə |reɪt prə- ‖ -ˈpɑːnd- **~rated** reɪt ɪd -əd ‖ reɪṭ əd **~rates** reɪts **~rating** reɪt ɪŋ ‖ reɪṭ ɪŋ
prepos|e ˌpriː ˈpəʊz ◂ ‖ -ˈpoʊz ◂ **~ed** d **~es** ɪz əz **~ing** ɪŋ
preposition ˌprep ə ˈzɪʃ ᵊn **~s** z
prepositional ˌprep ə ˈzɪʃ ᵊn‿əl ◂ **~ly** i **~s** z
ˌ**prepoˌsitional ˈphrase**
prepositive ₍ˌ₎priː ˈpɒz ət ɪv -ɪt- ‖ -ˈpɑːz əṭ ɪv **~ly** li **~s** z
prepossess ˌpriː pə ˈzes **~ed** t **~es** ɪz əz **~ing** ɪŋ
prepossessing|ly ˌpriː pə ˈzes ɪŋ |li **~ness** nəs nɪs
prepossession ˌpriː pə ˈzeʃ ᵊn **~s** z
preposterous pri ˈpɒst ər‿əs prə-, §priː- ‖ -ˈpɑːst- **~ly** li **~ness** nəs nɪs
prepotency ₍ˌ₎priː ˈpəʊt ᵊnᵗs i ‖ -ˈpoʊt-
prepotent ₍ˌ₎priː ˈpəʊt ᵊnt ‖ -ˈpoʊt- **~ly** li
prepp|ie, prepp|y ˈprep |i **~ier** i‿ə ‖ i‿ᵊr **~ies** iz **~iest** i‿ɪst ‿əst
preprint ˈpriː prɪnt **~s** s
preproduction ˌpriː prə ˈdʌk ʃᵊn
preprogrammed ˌpriː ˈprəʊ græmd ◂ §-grəmd ◂ ‖ -ˈproʊ-
prepubescent ˌpriː pju ˈbes ᵊnt ◂
prepuc|e ˈpriːp juːs **~es** ɪz əz
prequel ˈpriː kwəl **~s** z
Pre-Raphaelite ₍ˌ₎priː ˈræf ə laɪt ₍ˌ₎·ˈ·i‿ə ·, ₍ˌ₎·ˈ·eɪ ə · ‖ ₍ˌ₎·ˈreɪf- **~s** s
prerecord ˌpriː rɪ ˈkɔːd ◂ -rə-, §-riː- ‖ -ˈkɔːrd **~ed** ɪd əd **~ing** ɪŋ **~s** z
preregist|er ˌpriː ˈredʒ ɪst| ə -əst|- ‖ -ᵊr **~ered** əd ‖ ᵊrd **~ering** ər‿ɪŋ **~ers** əz ‖ ᵊrz
prerequisite ₍ˌ₎priː ˈrek wəz ɪt -wɪz-, §-ət **~s** s
prerogative pri ˈrɒg ət ɪv prə- ‖ -ˈrɑːg əṭ ɪv **~s** z
pres|a ˈpres| ə -ɑː ‖ ˈpreɪs| ə **~as** əz ɑːz **~e** eɪ —*It* [ˈpreː sa]
presag|e *v, n* ˈpres ɪdʒ -ɑːʒ; pri ˈseɪdʒ **~ed** d **~es** ɪz əz **~ing** ɪŋ
presbyopia ˌprez bi ˈəʊp i‿ə ˌpres-, ˌ·baɪ- ‖ -ˈoʊp-
presbyopic ˌprez bi ˈɒp ɪk ◂ ˌpres-, -baɪ- ‖ -ˈɑːp ɪk ◂
presbyter ˈprez bɪt ə ˈpres-, -bət- ‖ -bəṭ ᵊr **~s** z
Presbyterian, p~ ˌprez bɪ ˈtɪər i‿ən ◂ ˌpres-, ˌ·bə- ‖ -ˈtɪr- **~ism** ˌɪz əm **~s** z
presbyter|y ˈprez bɪt‿ər |i ˈpres-, ˈ·bət‿; §-bɪ ter i, §-bə · · ‖ -bə ter |i **~ies** iz

Prescelly, Prescely prɪ ˈsel i prə-, pre- —*Welsh* Preseli [pre ˈsɛ li]
preschool *adj* ˌpriː ˈskuːl ◂
ˌ**preschool ˈplaygroup**
preschool *n* ˈpriː skuːl **~er/s** ə/z ‖ ᵊr/z **~s** z
prescience ˈpres i‿ənᵗs ˈpreʃ- ‖ ˈpreʃ ᵊnᵗs ˈpriːʃ-, -i‿ənᵗs
prescient ˈpres i‿ənt ˈpreʃ- ‖ ˈpreʃ ᵊnt ˈpriːʃ-, -i‿ənt **~ly** li
prescientific ˌpriː ˌsaɪ‿ən ˈtɪf ɪk ◂
prescind pri ˈsɪnd prə- **~ed** ɪd əd **~ing** ɪŋ **~s** z
Prescot, Prescott ˈpresk ət -ɒt ‖ -ɑːt
prescrib|e pri ˈskraɪb prə- **~ed** d **~er/s** ə/z ‖ ᵊr/z **~es** z **~ing** ɪŋ
prescript *n* ˈpriː skrɪpt **~s** s
prescript *adj* pri ˈskrɪpt prə-; ˈpriː skrɪpt
prescription pri ˈskrɪp ʃᵊn prə- **~s** z
preˈscription charge; **preˈscription drug**
prescriptive pri ˈskrɪpt ɪv prə- **~ly** li **~ness** nəs nɪs
preˌscriptive ˈright
prescriptiv|ism pri ˈskrɪpt ɪv |ˌɪz əm prə- **~ist/s** ɪst/s §əst/s ‖ əst/s
preseason ˌpriː ˈsiːz ᵊn ◂ **~s** z
presenc|e ˈprez ᵊnᵗs **~es** ɪz əz
ˌ**presence of ˈmind**
present *adj; n 'gift'; n 'time now'* ˈprez ᵊnt **~ly** li **~s** s
ˌ**present ˈparticiple**; ˌ**present ˈperfect**; ˌ**present ˈtense**
pre|sent *v; n 'military stance'* pri |ˈzent prə- **~sented** ˈzent ɪd -əd ‖ ˈzenṭ əd **~senting** ˈzent ɪŋ ‖ ˈzenṭ ɪŋ **~sents** ˈzents
presentab|le pri ˈzent əb |ᵊl prə- ‖ -ˈzenṭ- **~leness** ᵊl nəs -nɪs **~ly** li
presentation ˌprez ᵊn ˈteɪʃ ᵊn ˌpriːz-, -en- **~s** z
ˌ**presenˈtation ˌcopy**
presentational ˌprez ᵊn ˈteɪʃ ən‿ᵊl ◂ ˌpriːz-, ˌ·en-
present-day ˌprez ᵊnt ˈdeɪ ◂
presenteeism ˌprez ᵊn ˈtiː ˌɪz əm
presentencing ˌpriː ˈsent ənᵗs ɪŋ ◂ ‖ -ᵊnᵗs-
presenter pri ˈzent ə prə- ‖ -ˈzenṭ ᵊr **~s** z
presentient pri ˈsenᵗʃ ᵊnt prə-, -ˈzenᵗʃ- -ˈ·i‿ənt, -ˈsent i‿ənt
presentiment pri ˈzent ɪ mənt prə-, -ˈsent-, -ə- ‖ -ˈzenṭ- **~s** s
presently ˈprez ᵊnt li
presentment pri ˈzent mənt prə-
preservable pri ˈzɜːv əb ᵊl prə- ‖ -ˈzɜːv-
preservation ˌprez ə ˈveɪʃ ᵊn ‖ -ᵊr- **~ist/s** ‿ɪst/s §‿əst/s **~s** z
ˌ**preserˈvation ˌorder**
preservative pri ˈzɜːv ət ɪv prə- ‖ -ˈzɜːv əṭ ɪv **~s** z
preserv|e pri ˈzɜːv prə- ‖ -ˈzɜːv **~ed** d **~er/s** ə/z ‖ ᵊr/z **~es** z **~ing** ɪŋ
pre|set ˌpriː |ˈset ◂ **~sets** ˈsets **~setting** ˈset ɪŋ ‖ ˈseṭ ɪŋ
Preshaw ˈpreʃ ɔː ‖ -ɑː
preshrunk ˌpriː ˈʃrʌŋk ◂
ˌ**preshrunk ˈjeans**
presid|e pri ˈzaɪd prə- **~ed** ɪd əd **~es** z **~ing** ɪŋ

P

presidenc|y 'prez ɪd ən^{t}s |i '·əd- ‖ -ə den^{t}s |i **~ies** iz

president, P~ 'prez ɪd ənt -əd- ‖ -ə dent **~s** s

president-elect ˌprez ɪd ənt ɪ 'lekt ˌ·əd-, -ə'· ‖ ˌ· ·ənt̬- ˌ·ə dent̬-

presidential ˌprez ɪ 'den^{t}ʃ ^{ə}l ◂ -ə- **~ly** i

presidio prɪ 'sɪd i əʊ prə-, -'zɪd- ‖ -oʊ -'si:d- —*Sp* [pre 'si ðjo] **~s** z

presidi|um prɪ 'sɪd i‿|əm prə-, pri:-, -'zɪd- **~a** ə

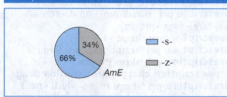

PRESLEY

34% 66% -s- -z- *AmE*

Presley 'pres li 'prez- — *Preference poll, AmE:* 'pres- *66%,* 'prez- *34%.*

pre-Socratic, Presocratic ˌpri: səʊ 'kræt ɪk ◂ ‖ -sə 'kræt̬- -soʊ- **~s** s

press, Press pres **pressed** prest **presses** 'pres ɪz -əz **pressing** 'pres ɪŋ **'press ˌagency**; **'press ˌagent**; **'press ˌbaron**; **'press box**; **'press ˌconference**; **'press ˌcutting**; **'press ˌgallery**; **'press ˌofficer**; **'press reˌlease**; **'press run**; **'press ˌsecretary**

pressgang 'pres gæŋ **~ed** d **~ing** ɪŋ **~s** z

pressie 'prez i **~s** z

pressing 'pres ɪŋ **~ly** li **~s** z

press|man 'pres |mæn -mən **~men** men -mən

pressmark 'pres mɑ:k ‖ -mɑ:rk **~s** s

pressroom 'pres ru:m -rʊm **~s** z

press-stud 'pres stʌd 'prest ʌd **~s** z

press-up 'pres ʌp **~s** s

pressure 'preʃ ə ‖ -^{ə}r **~d** d **pressuring** 'preʃ ər‿ɪŋ **~s** z **'pressure ˌcooker**; **'pressure gauge**; **'pressure group**; **'pressure point**

pressuris... —*see* **pressuriz...**

pressurization ˌpreʃ ər aɪ 'zeɪʃ ^{ə}n -ɪ'-- ‖ -ə'-- **~s** z

pressuriz|e 'preʃ ə raɪz **~ed** d **~es** ɪz əz **~ing** ɪŋ

Prestatyn pre 'stæt ɪn prɪ-, -^{ə}n ‖ -^{ə}n —*Welsh* [pre 'sdat ɨn, -ɪn]

Prestbury 'prest bər‿i

Prestcold *tdmk* 'prest kəʊld →-kɒʊld ‖ -koʊld

Presteigne $_{(ı)}$pre 'sti:n

Prestel *tdmk* 'pres tel

Prester 'prest ə ‖ -^{ə}r

prestidigitation ˌprest ɪ dɪdʒ ɪ 'teɪʃ ^{ə}n ˌ·ə-, -ə'-- **~s** z

prestidigitator ˌprest ɪ 'dɪdʒ ɪ teɪt ə ˌ·ə-, -'·ə- ‖ -teɪt̬ ^{ə}r **~s** z

prestige $_{(ı)}$pre 'sti:ʒ -'sti:dʒ

Prestige *family name* 'prest ɪdʒ

PRESTIGIOUS

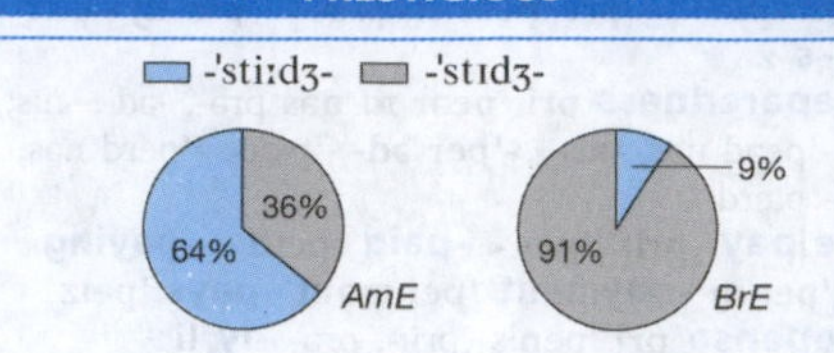

prestigious pre 'stɪdʒ əs prɪ-, prə-, -'sti:dʒ-, -'·i‿əs — *Preference polls, AmE:* -'sti:dʒ- *64%,* -'stɪdʒ- *36%; BrE:* -'stɪdʒ- *91%,* -'sti:dʒ- *9%.* **~ly** li **~ness** nəs nɪs

prestissimo pre 'stɪs ɪ məʊ -ə- ‖ -moʊ **~s** z

presto, P~ 'prest əʊ ‖ -oʊ **~s** z

Preston 'prest ən

Prestonpans ˌprest ən 'pænz →-əm-

prestressed ˌpri: 'strest ◂ **ˌprestressed 'concrete**

Prestwich 'prest wɪtʃ

Prestwick 'prest wɪk

presumably prɪ 'zju:m əb li prə-, -'zu:m-, §-'ʒu:m- ‖ -'zu:m-

PRESUME

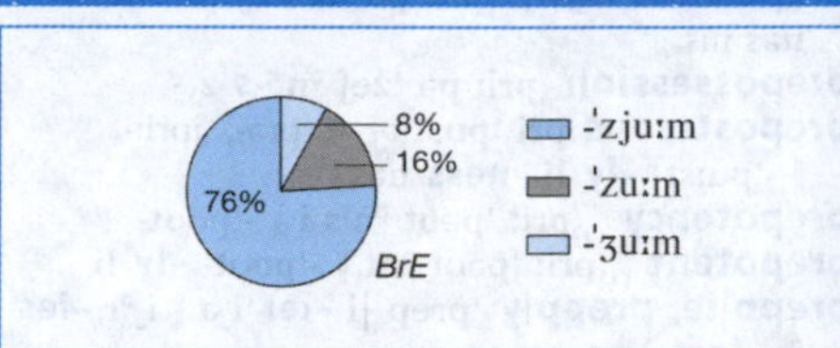

presum|e prɪ 'zju:m prə-, -'zu:m, §-'ʒu:m ‖ -'zu:m — *Preference poll, BrE:* -'zju:m *76%,* -'zu:m *16%,* -'ʒu:m *8%.* **~ed** d **~es** z **~ing** ɪŋ

presumedly prɪ 'zju:m ɪd li prə-, -'zu:m-, -'ʒu:m-, -əd- ‖ -'zum əd li -'zu:md li

presumption prɪ 'zʌm*p* ʃ^{ə}n prə- **~s** z

presumptive prɪ 'zʌm*p*t ɪv prə- **~ly** li

presumptuous prɪ 'zʌm*p* tʃu‿əs prə-, -tju‿əs, -ʃu‿əs; -'zʌm*p* tʃəs, -ʃəs **~ly** li **~ness** nəs nɪs

presuppos|e ˌpri: sə 'pəʊz ‖ -'poʊz **~ed** d **~es** ɪz əz **~ing** ɪŋ

presupposition ˌpri: ˌsʌp ə 'zɪʃ ^{ə}n **~s** z

Pret a Manger *tdmk* ˌpret ə 'mɒ̃ʒ eɪ -æ- ‖ ˌpret ɑ: mɑ: 'ʒeɪ —*Fr* prêt-à-manger [pʁɛ ta mɑ̃ ʒe]

prêt-à-porter ˌpret ɑ: 'pɔ:t eɪ ◂ ‖ -pɔ:r 'teɪ —*Fr* [pʁɛ ta pɔʁ te]

pretax ˌpri: 'tæks ◂ **ˌpretax 'profits**

preteen ˌpri: 'ti:n ◂ **~s** z

pretenc|e prɪ 'ten^{t}s prə- ‖ 'pri: ten^{t}s *(*)* **~es** ɪz əz

pretend prɪ 'tend prə- **~ed** ɪd əd **~ing** ɪŋ **~s** z

pretender prɪ 'tend ə prə- ‖ -^{ə}r **~s** z

pretens|e prɪ 'ten^{t}s prə- ‖ 'pri: ten^{t}s *(*)* **~es** ɪz əz

pretension prɪ 'ten^{t}ʃ ^{ə}n prə- **~s** z

pretentious prɪ 'ten^{t}ʃ əs prə- **~ly** li **~ness** nəs nɪs

P

preterit, preterite ˈpret ər ɪt -ət ‖ ˈpreṭ ər ət **~s** s
preterm ˌpriː ˈtɜːm ◂ ‖ -ˈtɜːm◂
pretermission ˌpriːt ə ˈmɪʃ ən ‖ ˌpriːṭ ər-
preter|mit ˌpriːt ə |ˈmɪt ‖ ˌpriːṭ ər- **~mits** ˈmɪts **~mitted** ˈmɪt ɪd -əd ‖ ˈmɪṭ əd **~mitting** ˈmɪt ɪŋ ‖ ˈmɪṭ ɪŋ
preternatural ˌpriːt ə ˈnætʃ ər əl ◂ ‖ ˌpriːṭ ər- **~ism** ˌɪz əm **~ly** i **~ness** nəs nɪs
pretest ˈpriː test **~s** s
pretext ˈpriː tekst **~s** s
pretonic ˌpriː ˈtɒn ɪk ◂ ‖ -ˈtɑːn ɪk ◂ **~ally** əl i
pretor ˈpriːt ə -ɔː ‖ ˈpriːṭ ər **~s** z
Pretori|a pri ˈtɔːr i |ə prə- ‖ -ˈtour- **~us** əs
pretorian pri ˈtɔːr i ən praɪ- ‖ -ˈtour- **~s** z
pretrial ˌpriː ˈtraɪ əl ◂ ‖ -ˈtraɪ əl ◂
pretti... —*see* **pretty**
prettification ˌprɪt ɪf ɪ ˈkeɪʃ ən ˌ-əf-, §-əˈ-- ‖ ˌprɪṭ- **~s** z
pretti|fy ˈprɪt ɪ |faɪ §-ə- ‖ ˈprɪṭ- **~fied** faɪd **~fier/s** faɪ ə/z ‖ faɪ ər/z **~fies** faɪz **~fying** faɪ ɪŋ
prett|y ˈprɪt |i ‖ ˈprɪṭ |i *(!) —In AmE there are also casual forms* ˈpɜːṭ i, ˈprʊṭ i **~ied** id **~ier** i ə ‖ i ər **~ies** iz **~iest** i ɪst i əst **~ily** ɪ li əl i **~iness** i nəs i nɪs **~ying** i ɪŋ
ˌ**pretty** ˈ**good**; **a** ˌ**pretty** ˈ**penny**
pretty-pretty ˈprɪt i ˌprɪt i ‖ ˈprɪṭ i ˌprɪṭ i
pretzel ˈprets əl **~s** z
prevail pri ˈveɪəl prə- **~ed** d **~ing/ly** ɪŋ /li **~s** z
prevalenc|e ˈprev əl ənts **~es** ɪz əz
prevalent ˈprev əl ənt **~ly** li
prevari|cate pri ˈvær ɪ |keɪt prə-, -ə- ‖ -ˈver- **~cated** keɪt ɪd -əd ‖ keɪṭ əd **~cates** keɪts **~cating** keɪt ɪŋ ‖ keɪṭ ɪŋ
prevarication pri ˌvær ɪ ˈkeɪʃ ən prə-, -əˈ-- ‖ -ˌver- **~s** z
prevaricator pri ˈvær ɪ keɪt ə prə-, -ˈ-ə- ‖ -keɪṭ ər -ˈver- **~s** z
prevenient pri ˈviːn i ənt prə- **~ly** li
pre|vent pri |ˈvent prə- *—but in the obsolete sense 'go before',* ˌpriː- **~vented** ˈvent ɪd -əd ‖ ˈvenṭ əd **~venting** ˈvent ɪŋ ‖ ˈvenṭ ɪŋ **~vents** ˈvents
preventability, preventibility pri ˌvent ə ˈbɪl ət i prə- ‖ -ˌvenṭ ə ˈbɪl əṭ i
preventab|le, preventib|le pri ˈvent əb |əl prə- ‖ -ˈvenṭ- **~ly** li
preventative pri ˈvent ət ɪv prə- ‖ -ˈvenṭ əṭ ɪv **~ly** li **~ness** nəs nɪs **~s** z
preventer pri ˈvent ə prə- ‖ -ˈvenṭ ər **~s** z
prevention pri ˈventʃ ən prə-
preventive pri ˈvent ɪv prə- ‖ -ˈvenṭ ɪv **~ly** li **~ness** nəs nɪs **~s** z
preverbal ˌpriː ˈvɜːb əl ◂ ‖ -ˈvɜːb əl ◂
preview ˈpriː vjuː **~ed** d **~ing** ɪŋ **~s** z
Previn ˈprev ɪn §-ən
previous ˈpriːv i əs **~ly** li **~ness** nəs nɪs
prevision ˌpriː ˈvɪʒ ən prɪ-, prə-
prevocalic ˌpriː vəʊ ˈkæl ɪk ◂ ‖ -voʊ- -və- **~ally** əl i
prewar ˌpriː ˈwɔː ◂ ‖ -ˈwɔːr ◂
ˌ**prewar** ˈ**prices**
prewash ˌpriː ˈwɒʃ ◂ ‖ -ˈwɑːʃ ◂ -ˈwɔːʃ ◂
Prewett ˈpruː ɪt §-ət
prey preɪ *(= pray)* **preyed** preɪd **preying** ˈpreɪ ɪŋ **preys** preɪz
preyer ˈpreɪ ə ‖ -ər **~s** z
prezzie ˈprez i **~s** z
Priam ˈpraɪ əm -æm
priapic praɪ ˈæp ɪk -ˈeɪp-
priapism ˈpraɪ ə ˌpɪz əm
Priapus praɪ ˈeɪp əs ˈpraɪ əp əs
Pribilof ˈprɪb ɪ lɒf -ə-, -ləf ‖ -lɑːf -lɔːf
price, Price praɪs **priced** praɪst **prices, Price's** ˈpraɪs ɪz -əz **pricing/s** ˈpraɪs ɪŋ/z
ˈ**price con**ˌ**trol**; ˈ**price list**; ˈ**price tag**; ˈ**price war**
price-cutting ˈpraɪs ˌkʌt ɪŋ ‖ -ˌkʌṭ-
priceless ˈpraɪs ləs -lɪs **~ly** li **~ness** nəs nɪs
price-sensitive ˌpraɪs ˈsents ət ɪv ◂ -ɪt- ‖ -əṭ-
PricewaterhouseCoopers ˌpraɪs ˌwɔːt ə haʊs ˈkuːp əz ‖ -ˌwɔːṭ ər haʊs ˈkuːp ərz -ˌwɑːṭ-
pric|ey, pric|y ˈpraɪs |i **~ier** i ə ‖ i ər **~iest** i ɪst i əst **~ily** ɪ li əl i **~iness** i nəs i nɪs
Prichard ˈprɪtʃ əd ‖ -ərd
prick prɪk **pricked** prɪkt **pricking/s** ˈprɪk ɪŋ/z **pricks** prɪks
pricker ˈprɪk ə ‖ -ər **~s** z
pricket ˈprɪk ɪt §-ət **~s** s
prickl|e ˈprɪk əl **~ed** d **~es** z **~ing** ɪŋ
prick|ly ˈprɪk |li -əl |i **~lier** li ə ‖ li ər **~iest** li ɪst li əst **~iness** li nəs -nɪs
ˌ**prickly** ˈ**heat**; ˌ**prickly** ˈ**pear**
pricy ˈpraɪs i —*see* **pricey**
pride, Pride praɪd **prided** ˈpraɪd ɪd -əd **prides, Pride's** praɪdz **priding** ˈpraɪd ɪŋ
Prideaux ˈprɪd əʊ ‖ -oʊ
prideful ˈpraɪd fəl **~ly** i **~ness** nəs nɪs
prie... —*see* **pry**
prie-dieu ˌpriː ˈdjɜː ˈ-- ‖ -ˈdjʊ **~s, ~x** z *—or as sing.* —*Fr* [pʁi djø]
priest priːst **priests** priːsts
priestcraft ˈpriːst krɑːft §-kræft ‖ -kræft
priestess ˌpriːst ˈes ◂ ˈpriːst es, -ɪs, -əs ‖ ˈpriːst əs **~es** ɪz əz
priesthood ˈpriːst hʊd
Priestland ˈpriːst lənd
Priestley ˈpriːst li
priest|ly ˈpriːst |li **~lier** li ə ‖ li ər **~liest** li ɪst li əst **~liness** li nəs li nɪs
priest-ridden ˈpriːst ˌrɪd ən
prig prɪg **prigs** prɪgz
priggery ˈprɪg ər i
priggish ˈprɪg ɪʃ **~ly** li **~ness** nəs nɪs
prim prɪm **primmer** ˈprɪm ə ‖ -ər **primmest** ˈprɪm ɪst -əst
prima ballerina ˌpriːm ə ˌbæl ə ˈriːn ə **~s** z
primac|y ˈpraɪm əs |i **~ies** iz
prima donna ˌpriːm ə ˈdɒn ə ‖ ˌprɪm ə ˈdɑːn ə ˌpriːm- **~s** z
primaeval praɪ ˈmiːv əl **~ly** i
prima facie ˌpraɪm ə ˈfeɪʃ i ◂ -ˈfeɪs-, -iː, -ˈ-i iː, §-ˈfeɪʃ ə
primal ˈpraɪm əl

P

primaquine 'praɪm ə kwiːn

PRIMARILY

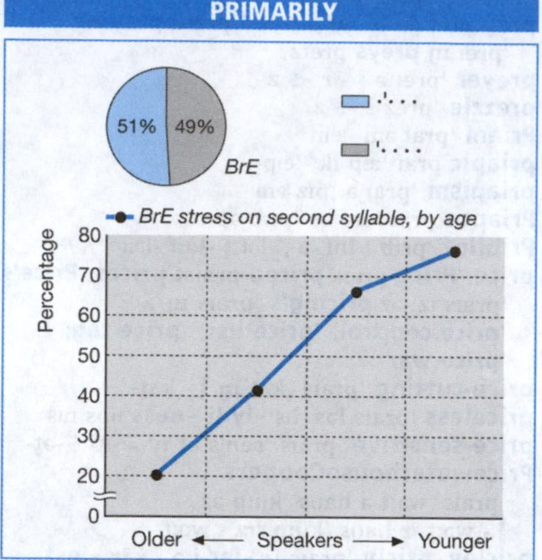

primarily praɪ 'mer əl i -'meər-, -'mær-, ɪ li; 'praɪm ər‿əl i ‖ 'praɪm er- — *Preference poll, BrE:* '· · · · *49%,* ·'· · · *51%.*

Primark *tdmk* 'praɪ mɑːk ‖ -mɑːrk

primar|y 'praɪm ər |i ‖ -er |i -ər i **~ies** iz
ˌ**primary 'accent**; ˌ**primary 'colour**; '**primary school**; ˌ**primary 'stress**

primate *'higher mammal'* 'praɪm eɪt **primates** 'praɪm eɪts praɪ 'meɪt iːz

primate *'archbishop'* 'praɪm ət -ɪt, -eɪt **~s** s **~ship/s** ʃɪp/s

primatolog|ist ˌpraɪm ə 'tɒl ədʒ |ɪst §-əst ‖ -'tɑːl- **~ists** ɪsts §əsts **~y** i

prime, Prime praɪm —*in the phrase* prime minister *also* ₍ˌ₎praɪ **primed** praɪmd **primes** praɪmz **priming/s** 'praɪm ɪŋ/z
ˌ**prime 'cost**; ˌ**prime me'ridian**; ˌ**prime 'minister**; ˌ**prime 'mover**; ˌ**prime 'number**; '**prime rate**, ˌ· '·; '**prime time**, ˌ· '·

primer *'paint'; 'explosive'* 'praɪm ə ‖ -ər **~s** z

primer *'introductory book'* 'praɪm ə ‖ 'prɪm ər (*) **~s** z

primeval praɪ 'miːv əl **~ly** i

primigrav|ida ˌpraɪm ɪ 'græv |ɪd ə ˌpriːm-, ˌ·ə-, -'·əd- **~idae** ɪ diː ə- **~idas** ɪd əz əd-

priming 'praɪm ɪŋ **~s** z

primip|ara praɪ 'mɪp |ər ə **~arae** ə riː **~aras** ər əz **~arous** ər əs

primitive 'prɪm ət ɪv -ɪt- ‖ -əṱ ɪv **~ly** li **~ness** nəs nɪs **~s** z

primitiv|ism 'prɪm ət ɪv| ˌɪz əm '·ɪt- ‖ '·əṱ- **~ist/s** ɪst/s §əst/s

primly 'prɪm li

primm... —*see* **prim**

primness 'prɪm nəs -nɪs

primo 'priːm əʊ ‖ -oʊ **~s** z

primogenitor ˌpraɪm əʊ 'dʒen ɪt ə ˌpriːm-, -ət ə ‖ -oʊ 'dʒen əṱ ər **~s** z

primogeniture ˌpraɪm əʊ 'dʒen ɪtʃ ə ˌpriːm-, -ətʃ ə, -ɪt jʊə ‖ -oʊ 'dʒen ətʃ ər -ə tʃʊr

primordial praɪ 'mɔːd i‿əl ‖ -'mɔːrd- **~ly** i **~s** z

primp prɪmp **primped** prɪmpt **primping** 'prɪmp ɪŋ **primps** prɪmps

primros|e, P~ 'prɪm rəʊz ‖ -roʊz **~es** ɪz əz
ˌ**primrose 'path**; ˌ**primrose 'yellow**◂

primula, P~ 'prɪm jʊl ə -jəl- ‖ -jəl ə **~s** z

primum mobile ˌpraɪm əm 'məʊb ɪl i ˌpriːm-, ˌ·ʊm-, -əl i; -ɪ leɪ, -ə · ‖ -'moʊb-

primus, P~ *tdmk* 'praɪm əs **~es** ɪz əz
ˌ**primus ˌinter 'pares** ˌɪnt ə 'pɑːr iːz -'pær-, -ɪz ‖ -ˌɪnṱ ər 'pær iːz -'per-; '**primus stove**

prince, P~ prɪnᵗs **princes, Prince's** 'prɪnᵗs ɪz -əz
₍ˌ₎**Prince 'Charming**; ˌ**prince 'consort**; ₍ˌ₎**Prince 'Edward ˌIsland** ‖ ·ˌ·· '··; ˌ**Prince of 'Wales**; ˌ**prince 'regent**

princedom 'prɪnᵗs dəm **~s** z

princeling 'prɪnᵗs lɪŋ **~s** z

prince|ly 'prɪnᵗs |li **~lier** li‿ə ‖ li‿ər **~liest** li‿ɪst ‿əst **~liness** li nəs -nɪs

Princes Risborough ˌprɪnᵗs ɪz 'rɪz bər‿ə ˌ·əz- ‖ -ˌbɜː oʊ

PRINCESS

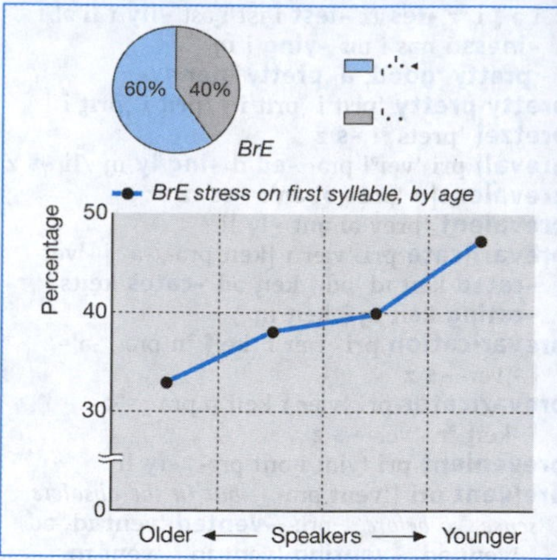

princess, P~ ˌprɪn 'ses◂ prɪn-; 'prɪnᵗs es ‖ 'prɪnᵗs əs 'prɪn ses **~es** ɪz əz — *Preference poll, BrE:* ˌ·'·◂ *60%,* '· · *40%. The streets named* Princess St *in Manchester and Huddersfield, in the north of England, are often pronounced locally as if spelt* Prince's Street.
ˌ**Princess 'Di**; ˌ**princess 'royal**

Princeton 'prɪnᵗs tən

Princetown 'prɪnᵗs taʊn

principal 'prɪnᵗs əp əl -ɪp- *(= principle)* **~s** z
ˌ**principal 'boy**; ˌ**principal 'parts**

principalit|y, P~ ˌprɪnᵗs ə 'pæl ət |i ˌ·ɪ-, -ɪt |i ‖ -əṱ |i **~ies** iz

principally 'prɪnᵗs əp əl‿i '·ɪp-

principalship 'prɪnᵗs əp əl ʃɪp '·ɪp- **~s** s

Principe, Príncipe 'prɪnᵗs ɪ peɪ -ə-; -ɪp i, -əp i, -ə —*Port* ['prĩ si pə]

Principia prɪn 'sɪp i‿ə

principi|um prɪn 'sɪp i‿əm prɪŋ 'kɪp- **~a** ə

principle 'prɪnᵗs əp ᵊl -ɪp- **~d** d **~s** z
Pring prɪŋ
Pringle 'prɪŋ gᵊl **~s** z
prink prɪŋk **prinked** prɪŋkt **prinking** 'prɪŋk ɪŋ **prinks** prɪŋks
Prinknash 'prɪn ɪdʒ *(!)*
Prinn prɪn
Prinnie, Prinny 'prɪn i
Prinsep 'prɪnᵗs ep
print prɪnt **printed** 'prɪnt ɪd -əd ‖ 'prɪnţ əd **printing/s** 'prɪnt ɪŋ/z ‖ 'prɪnţ ɪŋ/z **prints** prɪnts
ˌ**printed 'circuit**; '**printed ˌmatter**; '**printing ink**; '**printing maˌchine**; '**printing press**; '**print run**; '**print shop**
printable 'prɪnt əb ᵊl ‖ 'prɪnţ-
Printator *tdmk* ₍ᵢ₎prɪn 'teɪt ə ‖ -'teɪţ ᵊr **~s** z
printed-paper ˌprɪnt ɪd 'peɪp ə ◂ -əd-, -→-ɪb- ‖ ˌprɪnţ əd 'peɪp ᵊr ◂
printer 'prɪnt ə ‖ 'prɪnţ ᵊr **~s** z
printer|y 'prɪnt ər |i ‖ 'prɪnţ- **~ies** iz
printhead 'prɪnt hed **~s** z
printmak|er 'prɪnt ˌmeɪk ə ‖ -ᵊr **~ers** əz ‖ ᵊrz **~ing** ɪŋ
printout 'prɪnt aʊt ‖ 'prɪnţ- **~s** s
print-through 'prɪnt θruː
printwheel 'prɪnt wiːᵊl -hwiːᵊl ‖ -*h*wiːᵊl **~s** z
prion *bird* 'praɪ ɒn ‖ -ɑːn **~s** z
prion *infectious particle* 'priː ɒn 'praɪ- ‖ -ɑːn **~s** z
prior, Prior 'praɪ‿ə ‖ 'praɪ‿ᵊr **~s** z
prioress ˌpraɪ‿ə 'res 'praɪ‿ər es, -əs, -ɪs ‖ 'praɪ ər əs **~es** ɪz əz
priori... —*see* **priory**
prioritisation, prioritization praɪ ˌɒr ɪ taɪ 'zeɪʃ ᵊn -ˌə-, -tɪ'--, -tə'-- ‖ -ˌɔːr əţ ə- -ˌɑːr-
prioritis|e, prioritiz|e praɪ 'ɒr ɪ taɪz -ə- ‖ -'ɔːr- -'ɑːr- **~ed** d **~es** ɪz əz **~ing** ɪŋ
priorit|y praɪ 'ɒr ət |i -ɪt- ‖ -'ɔːr əţ |i -'ɑːr- **~ies** iz
prior|y, P~ 'praɪ‿ər |i **~ies** iz
Priscian 'prɪʃ i‿ən 'prɪʃ ᵊn
Priscilla prɪ 'sɪl ə prə-
prise praɪz *(= prize)* **prised** praɪzd **prises** 'praɪz ɪz -əz **prising** 'praɪz ɪŋ
prism 'prɪz əm **~s** z
prismatic ₍ᵢ₎prɪz 'mæt ɪk ‖ -'mæţ ɪk **~ally** ᵊl‿i
prison 'prɪz ᵊn **~s** z
'**prison camp**; ˌ**prison 'visitor**
prisoner 'prɪz ᵊn‿ə ‖ ‿ər **~s** z
ˌ**prisoner of 'war**
priss|y 'prɪs |i **~ier** i‿ə ‖ i‿ᵊr **~iest** i‿ɪst i‿əst **~ily** ɪ li əl i **~iness** i nəs i nɪs
Pristina prɪ 'stiːn ə -'ʃtiːn-; 'prɪʃt ɪn ə, 'priːʃt- —*Serbian* Priština ['priː ʃti na]
pristine 'prɪst iːn -aɪn; prɪ 'stiːn
Pritchard 'prɪtʃ əd -ɑːd ‖ -ᵊrd -ɑːrd
Pritchett 'prɪtʃ ɪt -ət
prithee 'prɪð i -iː
Pritt prɪt
Prius *tdmk* 'praɪ‿əs 'priː‿ ‖ 'priː əs

PRIVACY

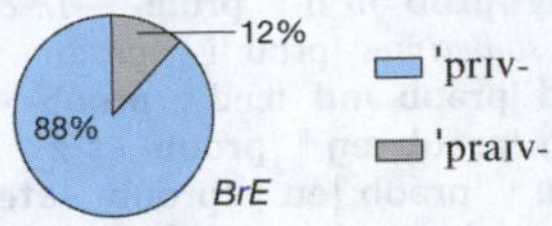

privacy 'prɪv əs i 'praɪv- ‖ 'praɪv- — *Preference poll, BrE:* 'prɪv- *88%,* 'praɪv- *12%.*
private 'praɪv ət -ɪt **~ly** li **~ness** nəs nɪs **~s** s
ˌ**private de'tective**; ˌ**private 'enterprise**; ˌ**private 'eye**; ˌ**private in'vestigator**; ˌ**private 'member('s bill)**; ˌ**private 'parts**; ˌ**private 'school**; ˌ**private 'sector** ◂; ˌ**private 'soldier**
privateer ˌpraɪv ə 'tɪə -ɪ- ‖ -'tɪᵊr **~s** z
privation praɪ 'veɪʃ ᵊn **~s** z
privatis... —*see* **privatiz...**
privative 'prɪv ət ɪv praɪ 'veɪt ɪv ‖ -əţ ɪv **~ly** li
privatization ˌpraɪv ət aɪ 'zeɪʃ ᵊn ˌ-ɪt-, -ɪ'-- ‖ -əţ ə- **~s** z
privatiz|e 'praɪv ə taɪz -ɪ- **~ed** d **~es** ɪz əz **~ing** ɪŋ
privet 'prɪv ɪt §-ət **~s** s
privi... —*see* **privy**
privileg|e 'prɪv əl‿ɪdʒ -ɪl- **~ed** d **~es** ɪz əz
privit|y 'prɪv ət |i -ɪt- ‖ -əţ |i **~ies** iz
priv|y 'prɪv |i **~ier** i‿ə ‖ i‿ᵊr **~ies** iz **~iest** i‿ɪst i‿əst **~ily** ɪ li əl i
ˌ**Privy 'Council**; ˌ**Privy 'Purse**; ˌ**Privy 'Seal**
prix fixe ˌpriː 'fiks '·fiks —*Fr* [pʁi fiks]
prize praɪz **prized** praɪzd **prizes** 'praɪz ɪz -əz **prizing** 'praɪz ɪŋ
ˌ**prize 'cattle**; '**prize day**; '**prize ˌmoney**; '**prize ring**
prize|fight 'praɪz |faɪt **~fighter/s** faɪt ə/z ‖ faɪţ ᵊr/z **~fighting** faɪt ɪŋ ‖ faɪţ ɪŋ
prize-giving 'praɪz ˌɡɪv ɪŋ **~s** z
prize|man 'praɪz |mən **~men** mən men
prizewinn|er 'praɪz ˌwɪn ə ‖ -ᵊr **~ers** əz ‖ ᵊrz **~ing** ɪŋ
pro prəʊ ‖ proʊ **pros** prəʊz ‖ proʊz
pro- ¦prəʊ, prə, prəʊ, ¦prɒ ‖ ¦proʊ, prə, ¦prɑː —*As a productive prefix meaning 'in favour of' (sometimes spelt with a hyphen),* ¦prəʊ ‖ ¦proʊ (pro-French ˌprəʊ 'frentʃ ◂ | ˌproʊ-). *Otherwise, with a vaguer meaning,* prə *(before a consonant sound only:* proclaim prə 'kleɪm*), or in less familiar words and slower speech* prəʊ ‖ proʊ*, but if stressed through the operation of a stressing rule usually* ¦prɒ+ ‖ ¦prɑː (proclamation ˌprɒk lə 'meɪʃ ᵊn ‖ ˌprɑːk-). *See individual entries.*
PRO *initials* ˌpiː ɑːr 'əʊ ‖ -ɑːr 'oʊ **~s, ~'s** z
PRO *grammatical term* prəʊ ‖ proʊ
proa 'prəʊ ə ‖ 'proʊ ə **~s** z
proactive ₍ᵢ₎prəʊ 'ækt ɪv ‖ ₍ᵢ₎proʊ-
pro-am ˌprəʊ 'æm ◂ ‖ ₍ᵢ₎proʊ-
probabilistic ˌprɒb əb ə 'lɪst ɪk ◂ ˌ·ɪ- ‖ ˌprɑːb- **~ally** ᵊl‿i

P

probabilit|y ˌprɒb ə ˈbɪl ət |i -ɪt i ‖ ˌprɑːb ə ˈbɪl əţ |i **~ies** iz
probable ˈprɒb əb ᵊl ‖ ˈprɑːb- **~s** z
probably ˈprɒb əb li ‖ ˈprɑːb- *—In casual speech sometimes* ˈprɒb li ‖ ˈprɑːb-
proband ˈprəʊb ænd -ænd ‖ ˈproʊb- **~s** z
probang ˈprəʊb æŋ ‖ ˈproʊb- **~s** z
prob|ate *v* ˈprəʊb |eɪt ‖ ˈproʊb- **~ated** eɪt ɪd -əd ‖ eɪţ əd **~ates** eɪts **~ating** eɪt ɪŋ ‖ eɪţ ɪŋ
probate *n* ˈprəʊb eɪt -ət, -ɪt ‖ ˈproʊb-
probation prə ˈbeɪʃ ᵊn prəʊ- ‖ proʊ- **~s** z
proˈbation ofˌficer
probationary prə ˈbeɪʃ ᵊn‿ər i prəʊ-, -ən ᵊr‿i ‖ proʊ ˈbeɪʃ ə ner i
probationer prə ˈbeɪʃ ᵊn‿ə prəʊ- ‖ proʊ ˈbeɪʃ ᵊn‿ər **~s** z
probative ˈprəʊb ət ɪv ‖ ˈproʊb əţ ɪv
probe prəʊb ‖ proʊb **probed** prəʊbd ‖ proʊbd **probes** prəʊbz ‖ proʊbz **probing** ˈprəʊb ɪŋ ‖ ˈproʊb ɪŋ
Probert *(i)* ˈprəʊb ət ‖ ˈproʊb ᵊrt, *(ii)* ˈprɒb- ‖ ˈprɑːb-
probing ˈprəʊb ɪŋ ‖ ˈproʊb ɪŋ **~ly** li **~s** z
probiotic ˌprəʊ baɪ ˈɒt ɪk ◂ ‖ ˌproʊ baɪ ˈɑːţ ɪk ◂ **~s** s
probity ˈprəʊb ət i -ɪt- ‖ ˈproʊb əţ i
problem ˈprɒb ləm -lɪm, -lem ‖ ˈprɑːb- *—In very casual speech also* -ᵊm **~s** z
ˈproblem child
problematic ˌprɒb lə ˈmæt ɪk ◂ -lɪ- ‖ ˌprɑːb lə ˈmæţ ɪk ◂ **~al** ᵊl ◂ **~ally** ᵊl‿i
problem-solution ˌprɒb ləm sə ˈluːʃ ᵊn -lɪm-, -lem -, -ˈljuːʃ- ‖ ˌprɑːb-
problem-solving ˈprɒb ləm ˌsɒlv ɪŋ -lɪm-, -lem-, §-ˌsəʊlv- ‖ ˈprɑːb ləm ˌsɑːlv ɪŋ
pro bono ˌprəʊ ˈbəʊn əʊ ‖ ˌproʊ ˈboʊn oʊ
proboscis prəʊ ˈbɒs ɪs -ˈbɒsk-, -ˈbəʊs-, §-əs ‖ prə ˈbɑːs əs -ˈbɑːsk- **~es** ɪz əz
Probyn ˈprəʊb ɪn §-ən ‖ ˈproʊb-
procaine ˈprəʊ keɪn -ˈ- ‖ ˈproʊ-
procathedral ˌprəʊ kə ˈθiːdr əl ‖ ˌproʊ- **~s** z
Procea *tdmk* ˈprəʊs i‿ə prəʊ ˈsiː‿ə ‖ ˈproʊs-
procedural prəʊ ˈsiːdʒ ᵊr‿əl -ˈsiːd jʊr əl ‖ prə- **~ly** i
procedure prəʊ ˈsiːdʒ ə -ˈsiːd jə ‖ prə ˈsiːdʒ ᵊr **~s** z
proceed *v* prə ˈsiːd prəʊ- ‖ proʊ- **~ed** ɪd əd **~ing/s** ɪŋ/z **~s** z
proceeds *n* ˈprəʊs iːdz ‖ ˈproʊs-
pro-celebrity ˌprəʊ sɪ ˈleb rət i ◂ ˌ-sɪ-, -rɪt i ‖ ˌproʊ sə ˈleb rəţ i ◂

PROCESS

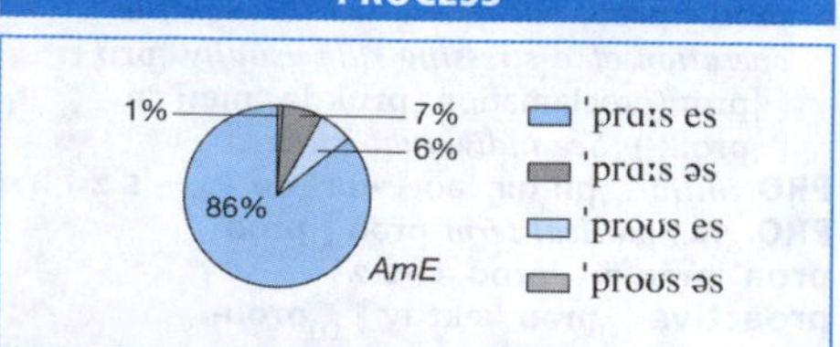

process *n; v 'treat, submit to a ~'* ˈprəʊs es ˈprɒs-, -ɪs, §-əs ‖ ˈprɑːs es ˈproʊs-, -əs *— Preference poll, AmE:* ˈprɑːs es *86%;* ˈprɑːs əs *7%;* ˈproʊs es *6%,* ˈproʊs əs *1%.* **~ed** t **~es** ɪz əz ‖ iːz **~ing** ɪŋ
ˌprocessed ˈcheese
process *v 'walk in procession'* prəʊ ˈses ‖ prə- **~ed** t **~es** ɪz əz **~ing** ɪŋ
procession prə ˈseʃ ᵊn **~s** z
processional prə ˈseʃ ᵊn‿əl **~ly** i **~s** z
processor ˈprəʊs es ə ˈprɒs-, -ɪs-, §-əs- ‖ ˈprɑːs es ᵊr **~s** z
pro-choice ˌprəʊ ˈtʃɔɪs ◂ ‖ ˌproʊ-
Procktor ˈprɒkt ə ‖ ˈprɑːkt ᵊr
proclaim prə ˈkleɪm prəʊ- ‖ proʊ- **~ed** d **~er/s** ə/z ‖ ᵊr/z **~ing** ɪŋ **~s** z
proclamation ˌprɒk lə ˈmeɪʃ ᵊn ‖ ˌprɑːk- **~s** z
proclamatory prəʊ ˈklæm ət‿ər i ‖ proʊ ˈklæm ə tɔːr i -toʊr i
proclitic ₍ˌ₎prəʊ ˈklɪt ɪk ‖ ₍ˌ₎proʊ ˈklɪţ ɪk **~s** s
proclivit|y prəʊ ˈklɪv ət |i -ɪt- ‖ proʊ ˈklɪv əţ |i **~ies** iz
Procne ˈprɒk ni ‖ ˈprɑːk-
proconsul ˌprəʊ ˈkɒnᵗs ᵊl ‖ ˌproʊ ˈkɑːnᵗs ᵊl **~s** z
proconsular ˌprəʊ ˈkɒnᵗs jʊl ə -jəl- ‖ ˌproʊ ˈkɑːnᵗs ᵊl‿ər
proconsulate ˌprəʊ ˈkɒnᵗs jʊl ət -jəl-, -ɪt ‖ ˌproʊ ˈkɑːnᵗs əl‿ət **~s** s
proconsulship ˌprəʊ ˈkɒnᵗs ᵊl ʃɪp ‖ ˌproʊ ˈkɑːnᵗs- **~s** s
procrasti|nate prəʊ ˈkræst ɪ |neɪt -ə- ‖ prə- proʊ-, pə- **~nated** neɪt ɪd -əd ‖ neɪţ əd **~nates** neɪts **~nating** neɪt ɪŋ ‖ neɪţ ɪŋ
procrastination prəʊ ˌkræst ɪ ˈneɪʃ ᵊn ˈprəʊ-, -ə- ‖ prə- proʊ-, pə- **~s** z
procrastinator prəʊ ˈkræst ɪ neɪt ə -ˈ-ə- ‖ prə ˈkræst ə neɪţ ᵊr proʊ-, pə- **~s** z
procre|ate ˈprəʊk ri |eɪt ˌ-ˈ- ‖ ˈproʊk- **~ated** eɪt ɪd -əd ‖ eɪţ əd **~ates** eɪts **~ating** eɪt ɪŋ ‖ eɪţ ɪŋ
procreation ˌprəʊk ri ˈeɪʃ ᵊn ‖ ˌproʊk-
procreative ˈprəʊk ri eɪt ɪv ˈprɒk-, ri‿ət-; ˌ- ˈeɪt- ‖ ˈproʊk ri eɪţ ɪv
Procrust|ean prəʊ ˈkrʌst |i‿ən ‖ proʊ- prə-, pə- **~es** iːz
Procter ˈprɒkt ə ‖ ˈprɑːkt ᵊr
proctitis prɒk ˈtaɪt ɪs §-əs ‖ prɑːk ˈtaɪţ əs
procto- *comb. form with stress-neutral suffix* ¦prɒkt əʊ ‖ ¦prɑːkt ə — **proctotome** ˈprɒkt əʊ təʊm ‖ ˈprɑːkt ə toʊm *with stress-imposing suffix* prɒk ˈtɒ+ ‖ prɑːk ˈtɑː+ — **proctology** prɒk ˈtɒl ədʒ i ‖ prɑːk ˈtɑːl-
proctor, P~ ˈprɒkt ə ‖ ˈprɑːkt ᵊr **~s** z
proctorial prɒk ˈtɔːr i‿əl ‖ prɑːk- -ˈtoʊr-
proctoscope ˈprɒkt ə skəʊp ‖ ˈprɑːkt ə skoʊp **~s** s
procumbent prəʊ ˈkʌm bənt ‖ proʊ-
procurable prə ˈkjʊər əb ᵊl prəʊ-, -ˈkjɔːr- ‖ -ˈkjʊr- proʊ-
procuration ˌprɒk juᵊ ˈreɪʃ ᵊn -jə- ‖ ˌprɑːk jə- **~s** z

procurator ˈprɒk juᵊ reɪt ə ˈ·jə- ‖ ˈprɑːk jə reɪţ ᵊr **~s** z
ˌprocurator ˈfiscal
procure prə ˈkjʊə prəʊ-, -ˈkjɔː ‖ -ˈkjʊᵊr proʊ- **~d** d **~ment/s** mənt/s **~s** z **procuring** prə ˈkjʊər ɪŋ prəʊ-, -ˈkjɔːr- ‖ -ˈkjʊr ɪŋ proʊ-
procurer prə ˈkjʊər ə prəʊ-, -ˈkjɔːr- ‖ -ˈkjʊr ᵊr proʊ- **~s** z
procuress prə ˈkjʊər es prəʊ-, -ˈkjɔːr-, -ɪs, -əs; ˈprɒk jʊr-, -jər- ‖ -ˈkjʊr əs proʊ- **~es** ɪz əz
Procyon ˈprəʊs i ͜ ən ‖ ˈproʊs i ɑːn
prod, Prod prɒd ‖ prɑːd **prodded** ˈprɒd ɪd -əd ‖ ˈprɑːd əd **prodding** ˈprɒd ɪŋ ‖ ˈprɑːd ɪŋ **prods, Prods** prɒdz ‖ prɑːdz
Prodd|ie, Prodd|y ˈprɒd| i ‖ ˈprɑːd| i **~ies** iz
Prodi ˈprəʊd i ‖ ˈproʊd i —*It* [ˈprɔː di]
prodigal ˈprɒd ɪg ᵊl ‖ ˈprɑːd- **~ly** ͜ i **~s** z
ˌprodigal ˈson
prodigalit|y ˌprɒd ɪ ˈgæl ət |i ˌ·ə-, -ɪt i ‖ ˌprɑːd ə ˈgæl əţ |i **~ies** iz
prodigious prə ˈdɪdʒ əs **~ly** li **~ness** nəs nɪs
prodig|y ˈprɒd ədʒ |i -ɪdʒ-; ⚠ˈprɒdʒ əd i ‖ ˈprɑːd- **~ies** iz
prodromal ₍ˌ₎prəʊ ˈdrəʊm ᵊl ‖ ₍ˌ₎proʊ ˈdroʊm ᵊl
prodrome ˈprəʊ drəʊm ‖ ˈproʊ droʊm **~s** z
produc|e *v* prə ˈdjuːs §-ˈduːs, →-ˈdʒuːs ‖ -ˈduːs -ˈdjuːs **~ed** t **~es** ɪz əz **~ing** ɪŋ
produce *n* ˈprɒd juːs ˈprɒdʒ uːs ‖ ˈproʊ duːs -djuːs; ˈprɑːd uːs, -juːs *(*)*
producer prə ˈdjuːs ə §-ˈduːs-, →ˈdʒuːs- ‖ -ˈduːs ᵊr **~s** z
producible prə ˈdjuːs əb ᵊl §-ˈduːs-, →ˈdʒuːs- ‖ -ˈduːs- -ˈdjuːs-
product ˈprɒd ʌkt -əkt ‖ ˈprɑːd- **~s** s
ˈproduct line
production prə ˈdʌk ʃᵊn **~s** z
proˈduction line
productive prə ˈdʌkt ɪv **~ly** li **~ness** nəs nɪs
productivity ˌprɒd ʌk ˈtɪv ət i ˌprəʊd-, ˌ·ək-, -ɪt i ‖ ˌproʊ dʌk ˈtɪv əţ i proʊ ˌdʌk ˈtɪv-, prə-; ˌprɑːd ək ˈtɪv-
proem ˈprəʊ em ‖ ˈproʊ- **~s** z
prof prɒf ‖ prɑːf **profs** prɒfs ‖ prɑːfs
Prof. prɒf ‖ prɑːf —*or see* Professor
profanation ˌprɒf ə ˈneɪʃ ᵊn ‖ ˌprɑːf-
profan|e *v, adj* prə ˈfeɪn prəʊ- ‖ proʊ- **~ed** d **~ely** li **~er/s** ə/z ‖ ᵊr/z **~eness** nəs nɪs **~es** z **~ing** ɪŋ
profanit|y prə ˈfæn ət |i prəʊ-, -ɪt- ‖ -əţ i proʊ- **~ies** iz
profess prə ˈfes prəʊ- ‖ proʊ- **~ed** t **~es** ɪz əz **~ing** ɪŋ
professedly prə ˈfes ɪd li prəʊ-, -əd- ‖ proʊ-
profession prə ˈfeʃ ᵊn **~s** z
professional prə ˈfeʃ ᵊn ͜ əl **~ism** ˌɪz əm **~ly** i
professor prə ˈfes ə ‖ -ᵊr **~s** z
professorate prə ˈfes ər ət -ɪt **~s** s
professorial ˌprɒf ə ˈsɔːr i ͜ əl ˌ·ɪ-, ˌ·e- ‖ ˌproʊf- ˌprɑːf-, -ˈsoʊr- **~ly** i
professoriate ˌprɒf ə ˈsɔːr i ͜ ət ˌ·ɪ-, ˌ·e-, ɪt, -eɪt ‖ ˌproʊf- ˌprɑːf-
professorship prə ˈfes ə ʃɪp ‖ -ᵊr- **~s** s

proff|er ˈprɒf |ə ‖ ˈprɑːf |ᵊr **~ered** əd ‖ ᵊrd **~ering** ər ͜ ɪŋ **~ers** əz ‖ ᵊrz
proficienc|y prə ˈfɪʃ ᵊnᵗs |i **~ies** iz
proficient prə ˈfɪʃ ᵊnt **~ly** li
profil|e ˈprəʊf aɪᵊl ‖ ˈproʊf- —*formerly also* -iːᵊl **~ed** d **~es** z **~ing** ɪŋ
prof|it ˈprɒf |ɪt §-ət ‖ ˈprɑːf |ət **~ited** ɪt ɪd §ət-, -əd ‖ əţ əd **~iting** ɪt ɪŋ §ət- ‖ əţ ɪŋ **~its** ɪts §əts ‖ əts
ˈprofit ˌmargin; **ˈprofit ˌsharing**
profitability ˌprɒf ɪt ə ˈbɪl ət i ˌ·ət-, -ɪt i ‖ ˌprɑːf əţ ə ˈbɪl əţ i
profitab|le ˈprɒf ɪt əb |ᵊl ˈ·ət- ‖ ˈprɑːf əţ- **~ly** li
profi|teer ˌprɒf ɪ |ˈtɪə -ə- ‖ ˌprɑːf ə |ˈtɪᵊr **~teered** ˈtɪəd ‖ ˈtɪᵊrd **~teering** ˈtɪər ɪŋ ‖ ˈtɪr ɪŋ **~teers** ˈtɪəz ‖ ˈtɪᵊrz
profiterole prə ˈfɪt ə rəʊl prɒ-, -ˈfiːt-, →-rɒʊl; ˈprɒf ɪt-, ˌ·ˌ·ˈ·ˈ· ‖ -ˈfɪţ ə roʊl **~s** z
profitless ˈprɒf ɪt ləs §-ət-, -lɪs ‖ ˈprɑːf-
profit-making ˈprɒf ɪt ˌmeɪk ɪŋ -ət- ‖ ˈprɑːf-
profit-taking ˈprɒf ɪt ˌteɪk ɪŋ -ət- ‖ ˈprɑːf-
profligacy ˈprɒf lɪg əs i ˈ·ləg- ‖ˈprɑːf-
profligate ˈprɒf lɪg ət -ləg-, -ɪt ‖ ˈprɑːf- **~ly** li **~ness** nəs nɪs
pro-form ˈprəʊ fɔːm ‖ ˈproʊ fɔːrm
pro forma ₍ˌ₎prəʊ ˈfɔːm ə ◂ ‖ ₍ˌ₎proʊ ˈfɔːrm ə
profound prə ˈfaʊnd prəʊ- ‖ proʊ- **~er** ə ‖ ᵊr **~est** ɪst əst **~ly** li **~ness** nəs nɪs
Profumo prə ˈfjuːm əʊ prəʊ- ‖ -oʊ
profundit|y prə ˈfʌnd ət |i prəʊ-, -ɪt- ‖ -əţ |i **~ies** iz
profuse prə ˈfjuːs prəʊ- ‖ proʊ- **~ly** li **~ness** nəs nɪs
profusion prə ˈfjuːʒ ᵊn prəʊ- ‖ proʊ- **~s** z
prog prɒg ‖ prɑːg **progs** prɒgz ‖ prɑːgz
progenitor prəʊ ˈdʒen ɪt ə §-ət- ‖ proʊ ˈdʒen əţ ᵊr prə- **~s** z
progen|y ˈprɒdʒ ən |i ˈprəʊdʒ-, -ɪn- ‖ ˈprɑːdʒ- **~ies** iz
progesterone prəʊ ˈdʒest ə rəʊn ‖ proʊ ˈdʒest ə roʊn
progestogen prəʊ ˈdʒest ədʒ ən -ɪn, -ə dʒen ‖ proʊ- **~s** z
proglott|id prəʊ ˈglɒt |ɪd §-əd ‖ proʊ ˈglɑːţ |əd **~ids** ɪdz §ədz ‖ ədz **~is** ɪs §əs
prognathic prɒg ˈnæθ ɪk ‖ prɑːg-
prognathism ˈprɒg nə ˌθɪz əm ‖ ˈprɑːg-
prognathous ˈprɒg nəθ əs prɒg ˈneɪθ- ‖ ˈprɑːg nəθ əs prɑːg ˈneɪθ-
prognos|is prɒg ˈnəʊs |ɪs §-əs ‖ prɑːg ˈnoʊs |əs **~es** iːz
prognostic prɒg ˈnɒst ɪk ‖ prɑːg ˈnɑːst ɪk **~s** s
prognosti|cate prɒg ˈnɒst ɪ |keɪt §-ə- ‖ prɑːg ˈnɑːst- **~cated** keɪt ɪd -əd ‖ keɪţ əd **~cates** keɪts **~cating** keɪt ɪŋ ‖ keɪţ ɪŋ
prognostication prɒg ˌnɒst ɪ ˈkeɪʃ ᵊn prəg-, ˌprɒg· ·ˈ·-, §-əˈ- ‖ prɑːg ˌnɑːst- **~s** z
prognosticator prɒg ˈnɒst ɪ keɪt ə §-ˈ·ə- ‖ prɑːg ˈnɑːst ə keɪţ ᵊr **~s** z
program ˈprəʊ græm §-grəm ‖ ˈproʊ- **~ed, ~med** d **~ing, ~ming** ɪŋ **~s** z

P

ˌprogrammed 'course; ˌprogrammed in'struction; ˌprogrammed 'learning; 'programme ˌmusic
programmable prəʊ 'græm əb ᵊl 'prəʊ græm- ‖ 'proʊ græm- ·'· · ·
programmatic ˌprəʊg rə 'mæt ɪk ◂ ‖ ˌproʊg rə 'mæţ ɪk ◂ **~ally** ᵊl ˌi
programm|e 'prəʊ græm §-grəm ‖ 'proʊ- **~ed** d **~es** z **~ing** ɪŋ
programmer 'prəʊ græm ə §-grəm- ‖ 'proʊ græm ᵊr -grəm- **~s** z
progress *n* 'prəʊ gres 'prɒg res ‖ 'prɑːg rəs -res
'progress ˌchaser; 'progress reˌport
progress *v* prəʊ 'gres '· · ‖ prə- **~ed** t **~es** ɪz əz **~ing** ɪŋ
progression prəʊ 'greʃ ᵊn ‖ prə- **~al** ˌəl **~s** z
progressive prəʊ 'gres ɪv ‖ prə- **~ly** li **~ness** nəs nɪs **~s** z
progressivism prəʊ 'gres ɪv ˌɪz əm ‖ prə-
prohib|it prəʊ 'hɪb |ɪt §-ət ‖ proʊ 'hɪb ət prə- **~ited** ɪt ɪd §ət-, -əd ‖ əţ əd **~iting** ɪt ɪŋ §ət- ‖ əţ ɪŋ **~its** ɪts §əts ‖ əts
prohibition ˌprəʊ ɪ 'bɪʃ ᵊn -hɪ-, -ə-, §-hə- ‖ ˌproʊ ə- **~ism** ˌɪz əm **~ist/s** ɪst/s §əst/s ‖ əst/s **~s** z
prohibitive prəʊ 'hɪb ɪt ɪv -ət- ‖ proʊ 'hɪb əţ ɪv prə- **~ly** li
prohibitory prəʊ 'hɪb ɪt ˌər i -'·ət ˌ ‖ proʊ 'hɪb ə tɔːr i prə-, -toʊr i

PROJECT

16% 84% -D- -əʊ- BrE

project *n* 'prɒdʒ ekt -ɪkt; 'prəʊ dʒekt ‖ 'prɑːdʒ- — *Preference poll, BrE:* ɒ *84%,* əʊ *16%.* **~s** s
project *v* prə 'dʒekt prəʊ-, prɒ- **~ed** ɪd əd **~ing** ɪŋ **~s** s
projectile prəʊ 'dʒekt aɪᵊl 'prɒdʒ ekt-, -ɪkt- ‖ prə 'dʒekt ᵊl **~s** z
projection prə 'dʒek ʃᵊn prəʊ-, prɒ- **~s** z
projectionist prə 'dʒek ʃᵊn ˌɪst prəʊ-, prɒ-, §ˌəst **~s** s
projective prəʊ 'dʒekt ɪv ‖ prə- **~ly** li
projector prə 'dʒekt ə prəʊ-, prɒ- ‖ -ᵊr **~s** z
prokaryote ₍ˌ₎prəʊ 'kær i əʊt -ɒt ‖ ₍ˌ₎proʊ 'kær i oʊt -'ker- **~s** s
prokaryotic prəʊ ˌkær i 'ɒt ɪk ˌ·ˌ· ·'·- ‖ proʊ ˌkær i 'ɑːţ ɪk ◂
Prokofiev prə 'kɒf i ef ‖ -'kɔːf i ˌəf -'koʊf-, -ef —*Russ* [prʌ 'kɔfʲ jɪf]
prolactin prəʊ 'lækt ɪn §-ən ‖ proʊ-
prolaps|e *n* 'prəʊ læps prəʊ 'læps ‖ proʊ 'læps '· · **~es** ɪz əz
prolaps|e *v* prəʊ 'læps 'prəʊ læps ‖ proʊ- **~ed** t **~es** ɪz əz **~ing** ɪŋ
prolate 'prəʊl eɪt prəʊ 'leɪt ‖ 'proʊl- **~ly** li **~ness** nəs nɪs
prolative prəʊ 'leɪt ɪv 'prəʊl ət- ‖ proʊ 'leɪţ ɪv
prole prəʊl →prɒʊl ‖ proʊl **proles** prəʊlz →prɒʊlz ‖ proʊlz
proleg 'prəʊ leg ‖ 'proʊ- **~s** z
prolegom|enon ˌprəʊl ə 'gɒm |ɪn ən ˌ·ɪ-,ˌ·e-, -ən ən; -|ɪ nɒn, -ə · ‖ ˌproʊl ɪ 'gɑːm |ə nɑːn **~ena** ɪn ə ən-
prolepsis prəʊ 'liːps ɪs -'leps-, §-əs ‖ proʊ 'leps əs
proleptic prəʊ 'lept ɪk ‖ proʊ- **~ally** ᵊl ˌi
proletarian ˌprəʊl ə 'teər i ˌən ◂ ˌ·ɪ-, ˌ·e- ‖ ˌproʊl ə 'ter- -'tær- **~s** z
proletariat ˌprəʊl ə 'teər i ˌət ˌ·ɪ-, ˌ·e-, -æt ‖ ˌproʊl ə 'ter- -'tær- **~s** s
pro-life ₍ˌ₎prəʊ 'laɪf ‖ ₍ˌ₎proʊ- **~r/s** ə/z ‖ ᵊr/z
prolife|rate prəʊ 'lɪf ə |reɪt ‖ prə- **~rated** reɪt ɪd -əd ‖ reɪţ əd **~rates** reɪts **~rating** reɪt ɪŋ ‖ reɪţ ɪŋ
proliferation prəʊ ˌlɪf ə 'reɪʃ ᵊn ‖ prə- **~s** z
prolific prəʊ 'lɪf ɪk ‖ prə- **~acy** əs i **~ally** ᵊl ˌi **~ness** nəs nɪs
prolix 'prəʊ lɪks ₍ˌ₎·'· ‖ proʊ 'lɪks '· · **~ly** li
prolixity prəʊ 'lɪks ət i -ɪt i ‖ proʊ 'lɪks əţ i
prolocutor prəʊ 'lɒk jʊt ə -jət- ‖ proʊ 'lɑːk jəţ ᵊr **~s** z
prolog, PROLOG, prologue 'prəʊ lɒg ‖ 'proʊ lɔːg -lɑːg **~s** z
prolong prəʊ 'lɒŋ ‖ prə 'lɔːŋ -'lɑːŋ **~ed** d **~ing** ɪŋ **~s** z
prolongation ˌprəʊ lɒŋ 'geɪʃ ᵊn ‖ ˌproʊ lɔːŋ- -lɑːŋ-; prəˌ·'· · **~s** z
prom, PROM prɒm ‖ prɑːm **proms, PROMs** prɒmz ‖ prɑːmz
promenad|e ˌprɒm ə 'nɑːd◂ -ɪ-, '· · · ‖ ˌprɑːm ə 'neɪd◂ -'nɑːd *(*) —but in square dancing,* -'neɪd◂ *even in BrE* **~ed** ɪd əd **~er/s** ə/z ‖ ᵊr/z **~es** z **~ing** ɪŋ
ˌpromenade 'concert, ˌ· ·'· ˌ· ·; ˌpromeˌnade deck
Promethean prəʊ 'miːθ i ˌən ‖ prə- **~s** z
Prometheus prəʊ 'miːθ juːs -'miːθ i ˌəs ‖ prə-
promethium prəʊ 'miːθ i ˌəm ‖ prə-
prominenc|e 'prɒm ɪn ənᵗs -ən- ‖ 'prɑːm- **~es** ɪz əz **~y** i
prominent 'prɒm ɪn ənt -ən- ‖ 'prɑːm- **~ly** li
promiscuit|y ˌprɒm ɪ 'skjuː ˌət |i ˌ·ə-, ɪt i ‖ ˌprɑːm ə 'skjuː əţ |i ˌproʊm- **~ies** iz
promiscuous prə 'mɪsk ju ˌəs prɒ- ‖ proʊ- **~ly** li **~ness** nəs nɪs
promis|e *v, n* 'prɒm ɪs §-əs ‖ 'prɑːm əs **~ed** t **~es** ɪz əz **~ing/ly** ɪŋ /li
ˌPromised 'Land ‖ '· · ·
promisee ˌprɒm ɪ 'siː §-ə- ‖ ˌprɑːm- **~s** z
promisor ˌprɒm ɪ 'sɔː '· · · ‖ ˌprɑːm ə 'sɔːr **~s** z
promissory 'prɒm ɪs ər ˌi prəʊ 'mɪs- ‖ 'prɑːm ə sɔːr i -soʊr i, -⚠ser i
prommer 'prɒm ə ‖ 'prɑːm ᵊr **~s** z
promo 'prəʊm əʊ ‖ 'proʊm oʊ **~s** z
promontor|y 'prɒm ənt ˌər |i ‖ 'prɑːm ən tɔːr |i -toʊr i **~ies** iz

pro|mote prə |ˈməʊt ‖ -|ˈmoʊt **~moted** ˈməʊt ɪd -əd ‖ ˈmoʊţ əd **~motes** ˈməʊts ‖ ˈmoʊts **~moting** ˈməʊt ɪŋ ‖ ˈmoʊţ ɪŋ
promoter prə ˈməʊt ə ‖ -ˈmoʊţ ᵊr **~s** z
promotion prə ˈməʊʃ ᵊn ‖ -ˈmoʊʃ ᵊn **~s** z
promotional prə ˈməʊʃ ᵊn‿əl ‖ -ˈmoʊʃ- **~ly** i
prompt prɒmpt ‖ prɑːmpt **prompted** ˈprɒmpt ɪd -əd ‖ ˈprɑːmpt əd **prompter/s** ˈprɒmpt ə/z ‖ ˈprɑːmpt ᵊr/z **promptest** ˈprɒmpt ɪst -əst ‖ ˈprɑːmpt əst **prompting/s** ˈprɒmpt ɪŋ/z ‖ ˈprɑːmpt- **prompts** prɒmpts ‖ prɑːmpts
promptitude ˈprɒmpt ɪ tjuːd -ə-, →-tʃuːd ‖ ˈprɑːmpt ə tuːd -tjuːd
prompt|ly ˈprɒmpt |li ‖ ˈprɑːmpt- **~ness** nəs nɪs
promul|gate ˈprɒm ᵊl |geɪt ‖ ˈprɑːm- proʊ ˈmʌl|g eɪt **~gated** geɪt ɪd -əd ‖ geɪţ əd **~gates** geɪts **~gating** geɪt ɪŋ ‖ geɪţ ɪŋ
promulgation ˌprɒm ᵊl ˈgeɪʃ ᵊn ‖ ˌprɑːm- ˌproʊm- **~s** z
promulgator ˈprɒm ᵊl geɪt ə ‖ ˈprɑːm ᵊl geɪţ ᵊr ˈproʊm- **~s** z
pronate prəʊ ˈneɪt ˈprəʊn eɪt ‖ ˈproʊn eɪt **pronated** prəʊ ˈneɪt ɪd -əd; ˈprəʊn eɪt- ‖ ˈproʊn eɪţ əd **pronates** prəʊ ˈneɪts ˈprəʊn eɪts ‖ ˈproʊn eɪts **pronating** prəʊ ˈneɪt ɪŋ ˈprəʊn eɪt- ‖ ˈproʊn eɪţ ɪŋ
pronation prəʊ ˈneɪʃ ᵊn ‖ proʊ-
pronator prəʊ ˈneɪt ə ‖ ˈproʊn eɪţ ᵊr **~s** z
-prone prəʊn ‖ proʊn — **accident-prone** ˈæks ɪd ənt prəʊn ˈ-əd- ‖ -proʊn
prone prəʊn ‖ proʊn
prone|ly ˈprəʊn |li ‖ ˈproʊn- **~ness** nəs nɪs
prong prɒŋ ‖ prɔːŋ prɑːŋ **pronged** prɒŋd ‖ prɔːŋd prɑːŋd **pronging** ˈprɒŋ ɪŋ ‖ ˈprɔːŋ ɪŋ ˈprɑːŋ- **prongs** prɒŋz ‖ prɔːŋz prɑːŋz
-pronged ˈprɒŋd ‖ ˈprɔːŋd ˈprɑːŋd — **three-pronged** ˌθriː ˈprɒŋd ◂ ‖ -ˈprɔːŋd ◂ -ˈprɑːŋd
pronghorn ˈprɒŋ hɔːn ‖ ˈprɔːŋ hɔːrn ˈprɑːŋ- **~s** z
pronominal prəʊ ˈnɒm ɪn ᵊl -ᵊn‿əl ‖ proʊ ˈnɑːm ᵊn‿əl **~s** z
pronominalis... —*see* **pronominaliz...**
pronominalization prəʊ ˌnɒm ɪn ᵊl aɪ ˈzeɪʃ ᵊn -ˌᵊn‿, -ɪˈ-- ‖ proʊ ˌnɑːm ᵊn‿əl ə- **~s** z
pronominaliz|e prəʊ ˈnɒm ɪn ə laɪz -ˈᵊn‿, -ᵊl aɪz ‖ proʊ ˈnɑːm- **~ed** d **~es** ɪz əz **~ing** ɪŋ
pronominally prəʊ ˈnɒm ɪn ᵊl i -ᵊn‿əl- ‖ proʊ ˈnɑːm ᵊn‿əl i
pronoun ˈprəʊ naʊn ‖ ˈproʊ- **~s** z
pronounc|e prə ˈnaʊnᵗs **~ed** t **~es** ɪz əz **~ing** ɪŋ
pronounceable prə ˈnaʊnᵗs əb ᵊl
pronouncedly prə ˈnaʊnᵗs ɪd li -əd-
pronouncement prə ˈnaʊnᵗs mənt **~s** s
pronto ˈprɒnt əʊ ‖ ˈprɑːnt oʊ
pronunciamento prə ˌnʌnᵗs i‿ə ˈment əʊ -ˌnʌnᵗʃ- ‖ proʊ ˌnʌnᵗs i‿ə ˈmenţ oʊ **~s** z
pronunciation prə ˌnʌnᵗs i ˈeɪʃ ᵊn ⚠-ˌnaʊnᵗs- **~s** z
proof pruːf §prʊf **proofs** pruːfs §prʊfs ˌ**proof ˈspirit** ‖ ˈ. ˌ. .
-proof pruːf §prʊf — **mothproof** ˈmɒθ pruːf §-prʊf ‖ ˈmɔːθ- ˈmɑːθ-
proof|read *pres* ˈpruːf |riːd §ˈprʊf- **~read** *past & pp* red **~reader/s** riːd ə/z ‖ riːd ᵊr/z **~reading** riːd ɪŋ **~reads** riːdz
Proops pruːps
prop prɒp ‖ prɑːp **propped** prɒpt ‖ prɑːpt **propping** ˈprɒp ɪŋ ‖ ˈprɑːp ɪŋ **props** prɒps ‖ prɑːps
ˈ**prop shaft**
propaedeutic ˌprəʊ piː ˈdjuːt ɪk ◂ §-ˈduːt-, →-ˈdʒuːt- ‖ ˌproʊ pɪ ˈduːţ ɪk ◂ -ˈdjuːţ- **~al** ᵊl **~s** s
propaganda ˌprɒp ə ˈgænd ə ‖ ˌprɑːp-
propagandis... —*see* **propagandiz...**
propagandist ˌprɒp ə ˈgænd ɪst §-əst ‖ ˌprɑːp- **~s** s
propagandiz|e ˌprɒp ə ˈgænd aɪz ‖ ˌprɑːp- **~ed** d **~es** ɪz əz **~ing** ɪŋ
propa|gate ˈprɒp ə |geɪt ‖ ˈprɑːp- **~gated** geɪt ɪd -əd ‖ geɪţ əd **~gates** geɪts **~gating** geɪt ɪŋ ‖ geɪţ ɪŋ
propagation ˌprɒp ə ˈgeɪʃ ᵊn ‖ ˌprɑːp- **~s** z
propagative ˈprɒp ə geɪt ɪv ‖ ˈprɑːp ə geɪţ ɪv **~ly** li
propagator ˈprɒp ə geɪt ə ‖ ˈprɑːp ə geɪţ ᵊr **~s** z
propane ˈprəʊp eɪn ‖ ˈproʊp-
proparoxytone ˌprəʊ pə ˈrɒks ɪ təʊn ◂ ˌpæ-, -ˈ-ə- ‖ ˌproʊ pæ ˈrɑːks ɪ toʊn ◂ -pə- **~s** z
propel prə ˈpel **~led** d **~ling** ɪŋ **~s** z
proˈ**pelling ˌpencil** . ˌ. ˈ. .
propellant, propellent prə ˈpel ənt **~s** s
propeller prə ˈpel ə ‖ -ᵊr **~s** z
proˈ**peller shaft**
propene ˈprəʊp iːn ‖ ˈproʊp-
propensit|y prəʊ ˈpenᵗs ət |i -ɪt- ‖ prə ˈpenᵗs əţ |i **~ies** iz
proper ˈprɒp ə ‖ ˈprɑːp ᵊr
ˌ**proper ˈfraction**; ˌ**proper ˈname**; ˌ**proper ˈnoun**
properly ˈprɒp əl i ‖ ˈprɑːp ᵊr li —*In RP there is also a casual form* ˈprɒp li
Propertius prəʊ ˈpɜːʃ əs -ˈpɜːʃ i‿əs ‖ proʊ ˈpɜːʃ əs
propert|y ˈprɒp ət |i ‖ ˈprɑːp ᵊrţ |i **~ied** id **~ies** iz
ˈ**property boom**
prophase ˈprəʊ feɪz ‖ ˈproʊ-
prophec|y *n* ˈprɒf əs |i -ɪs- ‖ ˈprɑːf- **~ies** iz
prophe|sy *v* ˈprɒf ə |saɪ -ɪ- ‖ ˈprɑːf- **~sied** saɪd **~sies** saɪz **~sying** saɪ ɪŋ
prophet, P~ ˈprɒf ɪt §-ət ‖ ˈprɑːf ət *(= profit)* **~s** s
prophetess ˌprɒf ɪ ˈtes -ə-, ˈ· · ·; ˈprɒf ɪt ɪs, -ət-, -əs ‖ ˈprɑːf əţ əs **~es** ɪz əz
prophethood ˈprɒf ɪt hʊd §-ət- ‖ ˈprɑːf ət-
prophetic prəʊ ˈfet ɪk ‖ prə ˈfeţ ɪk **~al** ᵊl **~ally** ᵊl‿i

P

prophylactic ˌprɒf ə ˈlækt ɪk ◂ -ɪ- ‖ ˌprouf-, ˌprɑːf- **~ally** ᵊl‿i **~s** s

prophylaxis ˌprɒf ə ˈlæks ɪs -ɪ-, §-əs ‖ ˌprouf-, ˌprɑːf-

propinquity prəʊ ˈpɪŋk wət i -wɪt- ‖ prə ˈpɪŋk wət̬ i

propionate ˈprəʊp i‿ə neɪt ‖ ˈproup-

propionic ˌprəʊp i ˈɒn ɪk ◂ ‖ ˌproup i ˈɑːn ɪk ◂

propiti|ate prəʊ ˈpɪʃ i |eɪt ‖ prou- **~ated** eɪt ɪd -əd ‖ eɪt̬ əd **~ates** eɪts **~ating** eɪt ɪŋ ‖ eɪt̬ ɪŋ

propitiation prəʊ ˌpɪʃ i ˈeɪʃ ᵊn ‖ prou- **~s** z

propitiator prəʊ ˈpɪʃ i eɪt ə ‖ prou ˈpɪʃ i eɪt̬ ᵊr **~s** z

propitiator|y prəʊ ˈpɪʃ i‿ə tər |i -eɪt ər |i, ·ˌ· ·ˈeɪt ər |i ‖ prou ˈpɪʃ i‿ə tɔːr |i -tour i **~ies** iz

propitious prə ˈpɪʃ əs **~ly** li **~ness** nəs nɪs

propjet ˈprɒp dʒet ‖ ˈprɑːp- **~s** s

propolis ˈprɒp əl ɪs §-əs ‖ ˈprɑːp-

proponent prə ˈpəʊn ənt ‖ -ˈpoun- **~s** s

Propontis prəʊ ˈpɒnt ɪs §-əs ‖ prə ˈpɑːnt̬ əs

proportion prə ˈpɔːʃ ᵊn ‖ -ˈpɔːrʃ ᵊn pə-, -ˈpourʃ- **~ed** d **~ing** ‿ɪŋ **~s** z

proportionab|le prə ˈpɔːʃ ᵊn‿əb |ᵊl ‖ -ˈpɔːrʃ- pə-, -ˈpourʃ- **~leness** ᵊl nəs -nɪs **~ly** li

proportional prə ˈpɔːʃ ᵊn‿əl ‖ -ˈpɔːrʃ- pə-, -ˈpourʃ- **~s** z

proˌportional ˌrepresenˈtation

proportionality prə ˌpɔːʃ ə ˈnæl ət i -ɪt i ‖ -ˌpɔːrʃ ə ˈnæl ət̬ i pə-, -ˌpourʃ-

proportionally prə ˈpɔːʃ ᵊn‿əl i ‖ -ˈpɔːrʃ- pə-, -ˈpourʃ-

proportionate *adj* prə ˈpɔːʃ ᵊn‿ət -ɪt ‖ -ˈpɔːrʃ- pə-, -ˈpourʃ- **~ly** li **~ness** nəs nɪs

proposal prə ˈpəʊz ᵊl ‖ -ˈpouz ᵊl **~s** z

propos|e prə ˈpəʊz ‖ -ˈpouz **~ed** d **~er/s** ə/z ‖ -ᵊr/z **~es** ɪz əz **~ing** ɪŋ

proposition ˌprɒp ə ˈzɪʃ ᵊn ‖ ˌprɑːp- **~ed** d **~ing** ‿ɪŋ **~s** z

propositional ˌprɒp ə ˈzɪʃ ᵊn‿əl ◂ ‖ ˌprɑːp- **~ly** i

propound prə ˈpaʊnd **~ed** ɪd əd **~ing** ɪŋ **~s** z

proppy ˈprɒp i ‖ ˈprɑːp i

propranolol prəʊ ˈpræn ə lɒl ‖ prou ˈpræn ə lɑːl -lɔːl, -loul

proprietar|y prə ˈpraɪ‿ət‿ər |i ‖ -ə ter |i **~ies** iz **~ily** əl i -ɪ li

proprietor prə ˈpraɪ‿ət ə ‖ ət̬ ᵊr **~s** z **~ship** ʃɪp

proprietorial prə ˌpraɪ‿ə ˈtɔːr i‿əl ‖ prou-, -ˈtour- **~ly** i

proprietress prə ˈpraɪ‿ətr əs -ɪs, -es **~es** ɪz əz

propriet|y prə ˈpraɪ‿ət |i -ɪt- ‖ -ət̬ |i **~ies** iz

proprioception ˌprəʊp ri‿ə ˈsep ʃᵊn ˌprɒp-, -əʊˈ·- ‖ ˌproup ri ou-

proprioceptive ˌprəʊp ri‿ə ˈsept ɪv ◂ ˌprɒp-, -əʊˈ·- ‖ ˌproup ri ou- **~ly** li

proprioceptor ˌprəʊp ri‿ə ˈsept ə ˌprɒp-, -əʊˈ·- ‖ ˌproup ri ou ˈsept ᵊr **~s** z

proptosis prɒp ˈtəʊs ɪs §-əs ‖ prɑːp ˈtous-

propulsion prə ˈpʌlʃ ᵊn

propulsive prə ˈpʌls ɪv

propyl ˈprəʊp ɪl -əl, -aɪᵊl ‖ ˈproup-

propylae|um ˌprɒp ɪ ˈliː‿|əm ˌprəʊp-, -ə- ‖ ˌprɑːp- ˌproup- **~a** ə

propylene ˈprəʊp liːn -ə- ‖ ˈproup-

pro rata (ˌ)prəʊ ˈrɑːt ə -ˈreɪt- ‖ (ˌ)prou ˈreɪt̬ ə -ˈrɑːt̬-, -ˈræt̬-

pro|rate ˌprəʊ |ˈreɪt ‖ (ˌ)prou- **~rated** ˈreɪt ɪd -əd ‖ ˈreɪt̬ əd **~rates** ˈreɪts **~rating** ˈreɪt ɪŋ ‖ ˈreɪt̬ ɪŋ

prorogation ˌprəʊ rəʊ ˈgeɪʃ ᵊn ˌprɒr ə- ‖ ˌprou rə- ˌprɔːr ə- **~s** z

prorogu|e prəʊ ˈrəʊg ‖ prou ˈroug prə- **~ed** d **~es** z **~ing** ɪŋ

prosaic prəʊ ˈzeɪ ɪk ‖ prou- **~ally** ᵊl‿i **~ness** nəs nɪs

pros and cons ˌprəʊz ᵊn ˈkɒnz -ᵊnd-, →ᵊŋ- ‖ ˌprouz ᵊn ˈkɑːnz

prosceni|um prəʊ ˈsiːn i‿|əm ‖ prou- **~a** ə **~ums** əmz

prosciutto prəʊ ˈʃuːt əʊ ‖ prou ˈʃuːt ou —*It* [pro ˈʃut to]

proscrib|e prəʊ ˈskraɪb ‖ prou- **~ed** d **~es** z **~ing** ɪŋ

proscription prəʊ ˈskrɪp ʃᵊn ‖ prou- **~s** z

proscriptive prəʊ ˈskrɪpt ɪv ‖ prou- **~ly** li **~ness** nəs nɪs

prose prəʊz ‖ prouz **prosed** prəʊzd ‖ prouzd **proses** ˈprəʊz ɪz -əz ‖ ˈprouz əz **prosing** ˈprəʊz ɪŋ ‖ ˈprouz ɪŋ

prose|cute ˈprɒs ɪ |kjuːt -ə- ‖ ˈprɑːs- **~cuted** kjuːt ɪd -əd ‖ kjuːt̬ əd **~cutes** kjuːts **~cuting** kjuːt ɪŋ ‖ kjuːt̬ ɪŋ

prosecution ˌprɒs ɪ ˈkjuːʃ ᵊn -ə- ‖ ˌprɑːs- **~s** z

prosecutor ˈprɒs ɪ kjuːt ə ˈ·ə- ‖ ˈprɑːs ɪ kjuːt̬ ᵊr **~s** z

prosecutorial ˌprɒs ɪ kjuː ˈtɔːr i əl ◂ -ə- ‖ ˌprɑːs- -ˈtour-

proselyte ˈprɒs ə laɪt -ɪ- ‖ ˈprɑːs- **~s** s

proselytis... —*see* **proselytiz...**

proselytism ˈprɒs əl ə ˌtɪz əm ˈ·ɪl-, -ɪ,- ‖ ˈprɑːs- ˈ·ə laɪ-

proselytiz|e ˈprɒs əl ə taɪz ˈ·ɪl-, -ɪ · ‖ ˈprɑːs- **~ed** d **~es** ɪz əz **~ing** ɪŋ

Proserpina prə ˈsɜːp ɪn ə prɒ-, prəʊ-, §-ən- ‖ prə ˈsɜːp- prou-

Proserpine ˈprɒs ə paɪn ‖ ˈprɑːs ᵊr-

prosimian prəʊ ˈsɪm i‿ən ‖ prou- **~s** z

prosodic prə ˈsɒd ɪk prəʊ-, -ˈzɒd- ‖ -ˈsɑːd ɪk **~ally** ᵊl‿i

prosodist ˈprɒs əd ɪst ˈprɒz-, ˈprəʊz-, §-əst ‖ ˈprɑːs- **~s** s

prosod|y ˈprɒs əd |i ˈprɒz-, ˈprəʊz- ‖ ˈprɑːs- **~ies** iz

prosopopeia, prosopopoeia ˌprɒs əʊp əʊ ˈpiː‿ə prəʊ ˌsəʊp- ‖ ˌprɑːs əp ə- prou ˌsoup ə-, ˌprous oup ə-

prospect *n* ˈprɒsp ekt ‖ ˈprɑːsp- **~s** s

prospect *v* prə ˈspekt prɒ-; ˈprɒsp ekt ‖ ˈprɑːsp ekt *(*)* **~ed** ɪd əd **~ing** ɪŋ **~s** s

prospective prə ˈspekt ɪv prɒ- ‖ prɑː- **~ly** li

prospector prə ˈspekt ə prɒ-; ˈprɒsp ekt ə ‖ ˈprɑːsp ekt ᵊr *(*)* **~s** z

prospectus prə ˈspekt əs prɒ- ‖ prɑː- **~es** ɪz əz

prosp|er ˈprɒsp |ə ‖ ˈprɑːsp |ᵊr **~ered** əd ‖ ᵊrd **~ering** ər‿ɪŋ **~ers** əz ‖ ᵊrz
prosperit|y prɒ ˈsper ət |i prə-, -ɪt i ‖ prɑː ˈsper əţ |i **~ies** iz
Prospero ˈprɒsp ə rəʊ ‖ ˈprɑːsp ə roʊ
prosperous ˈprɒsp ər‿əs ‖ ˈprɑːsp- **~ly** li **~ness** nəs nɪs
Prosser ˈprɒs ə ‖ ˈprɑːs ᵊr
Prost prɒst prəʊst ‖ proʊst
prostaglandin ˌprɒst ə ˈglænd ɪn §-ən ‖ ˌprɑːst- **~s** z
prostate ˈprɒst eɪt ‖ ˈprɑːst- **~s** s
ˈprostate gland
prostatectom|y ˌprɒst ə ˈtekt əm |i ‖ ˌprɑːst- **~ies** iz
prostatic prɒ ˈstæt ɪk prə- ‖ prɑː ˈstæţ ɪk
prosthes|is ₍ₗ₎prɒs ˈθiːs |ɪs prəs-, §-əs; ˈprɒs θəs-, -θɪs- ‖ prɑːs- **~es** iːz
prosthetic ₍ₗ₎prɒs ˈθet ɪk prəs- ‖ prɑːs ˈθeţ ɪk **~ally** ᵊl‿i **~s** s
prosthodont|ics ˌprɒs θəʊ ˈdɒnt| ɪks ‖ ˌprɑːs θə ˈdɑːnţ| ɪks **~ist/s** ɪst/s §əst/s
prosti|tute *v, n* ˈprɒst ɪ |tjuːt -ə-, →-tʃuːt ‖ ˈprɑːst ə |tuːt -tjuːt **~tuted** tjuːt ɪd →tʃuːt-, -əd ‖ tuːţ əd tjuːţ- **~tutes** tjuːts →tʃuːts ‖ tuːts tjuːts **~tuting** tjuːt ɪŋ →tʃuːt- ‖ tuːţ ɪŋ tjuːţ-
prostitution ˌprɒst ɪ ˈtjuːʃ ᵊn -ə-, →-ˈtʃuːʃ- ‖ ˌprɑːst ə ˈtuːʃ ᵊn -ˈtjuːʃ-
pro|strate *v* prɒ ˈ|streɪt prə- ‖ ˈprɑː|s treɪt *(*)* **~strated** streɪt ɪd -əd ‖ streɪţ əd **~strates** streɪts **~strating** streɪt ɪŋ ‖ streɪţ ɪŋ
prostrate *adj* ˈprɒs treɪt prɒ ˈstreɪt, prə- ‖ ˈprɑːs-
prostration prɒ ˈstreɪʃ ᵊn prə- ‖ prɑː- **~s** z
prostyle ˈprəʊ staɪᵊl ‖ ˈproʊ-
pros|y ˈprəʊz |i ‖ ˈproʊz |i **~ier** i‿ə ‖ i‿ᵊr **~iest** i‿ɪst i‿əst **~ily** ɪ li əl i **~iness** i nəs i nɪs
prot- *comb. form before vowel* prəʊt ‖ proʊt — **protoxide** prəʊ ˈtɒks aɪd ‖ proʊ ˈtɑːks-
protactinium ˌprəʊt æk ˈtɪn i‿əm ‖ ˌproʊţ-
protagonist prəʊ ˈtæg ən ɪst §-əst ‖ proʊ- **~s** s
Protagoras prəʊ ˈtæg ə ræs -ər əs ‖ proʊ-
protanopia ˌprəʊt ə ˈnəʊp i‿ə -ᵊn ˈəʊp- ‖ ˌproʊt ᵊn ˈoʊp-
protanopic ˌprəʊt ə ˈnɒp ɪk ◂ -ᵊn ˈɒp- ‖ ˌproʊt ᵊn ˈɑːp ɪk ◂
prot|asis ˈprɒt |əs ɪs §-əs ‖ ˈprɑːţ- **~ases** ə siːz
protea ˈprəʊt i‿ə ‖ ˈproʊţ i‿ə **~s** z
protean prəʊ ˈtiː‿ən ˈprəʊt i‿ən ‖ ˈproʊţ i‿ən proʊ ˈtiː ən
proteas|e ˈprəʊt i eɪz -eɪs ‖ ˈproʊţ- **~es** ɪz əz
protect prə ˈtekt prəʊ- ‖ proʊ- **~ed** ɪd əd **~ing** ɪŋ **~s** s
protecting|ly prə ˈtekt ɪŋ| li prəʊ- ‖ proʊ- **~ness** nəs nɪs
protection prə ˈtek ʃᵊn prəʊ- ‖ proʊ- **~ism** ˌɪz əm **~ist/s** ɪst/s §əst/s ‖ əst/s
proˈtection ˌracket
protective prə ˈtekt ɪv prəʊ- ‖ proʊ- **~ly** li **~ness** nəs nɪs
proˌtective ˈcustody
protector, P~ prə ˈtekt ə prəʊ- ‖ -ᵊr proʊ- **~ship/s** ʃɪp/s **~s** z
protectorate, P~ prə ˈtekt ər‿ət prəʊ-, -ɪt ‖ proʊ- **~s** s
protectress prə ˈtek trəs prəʊ-, -trɪs ‖ proʊ- **~es** ɪz əz
protege, protégé, protegee, protégée ˈprɒt ə ʒeɪ ˈprəʊt-, -ɪ- ‖ ˈproʊţ‿ˌʒeɪ —*Fr* [pʁɔ te ʒe] **~s** z
protein ˈprəʊt iːn ˈprəʊt i‿ɪn ‖ ˈproʊt- **~s** z
pro tem ₍ₗ₎prəʊ ˈtem ‖ ₍ₗ₎proʊ-
proterozoic, P~ ˌprəʊt‿ər əʊ ˈzəʊ ɪk ◂ ˌprɒt‿ ‖ ˌprɑːţ ər ə ˈzoʊ ɪk ◂ ˌproʊţ-
protest *v* prə ˈtest prəʊ-, ˈprəʊt est ‖ ˈproʊt est **~ed** ɪd əd **~ing/ly** ɪŋ /li **~s** s
protest *n* ˈprəʊt est ‖ ˈproʊt est **~s** s
protestant, P~ ˈprɒt ɪst ənt -əst- ‖ ˈprɑːţ- **~s** s
protestantism, P~ ˈprɒt ɪst ənt ˌɪz əm ˈ-əst- ‖ ˈprɑːţ əst ənţ-
protestation ˌprɒt ɪ ˈsteɪʃ ᵊn ˌprəʊt-, -ə-, -e- ‖ ˌprɑːţ ə- ˌproʊţ ə-, ˌproʊt e- **~s** z

PROTESTER

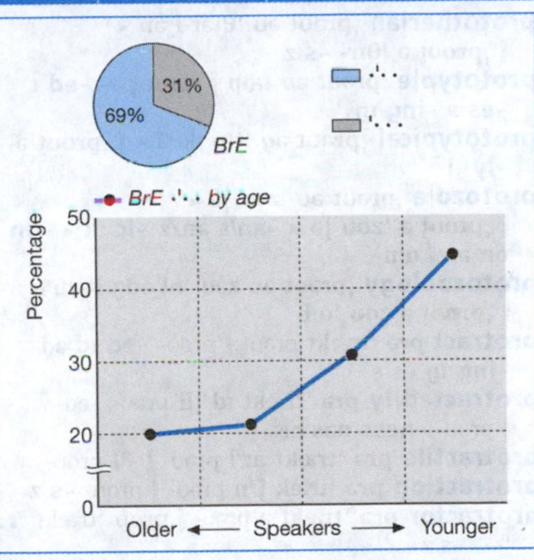

protester prə ˈtest ə prəʊ-; ˈprəʊt est ə ‖ ˈproʊt est ᵊr prə ˈtest- — *Preference poll, BrE: ·ˈ·· 69%, ˈ··· 31% (born since 1982: 45%).* **~s** z
Proteus ˈprəʊt juːs ˈprəʊt i‿əs ‖ ˈproʊţ i‿əs ˈproʊt juːs
prothalami|on ˌprəʊ θə ˈleɪm i‿|ən ‖ ˌproʊ- -|ɑːn **~a** ə **~um** əm
Prothero, Protheroe ˈprɒð ə rəʊ ‖ ˈprɑːð ə roʊ
proth|esis ˈprɒθ |əs ɪs -ɪs-, §-əs ‖ ˈprɑːθ- **~eses** ə siːz ɪ-
prothetic prəʊ ˈθet ɪk ‖ prə ˈθeţ ɪk prɑː- **~ally** ᵊl‿i
prothonotar|y ˌprəʊθ əʊ ˈnəʊt ər| i prəʊ ˈθɒn ət‿ər| i ‖ proʊ ˈθɑːn ə ter| i ˌproʊθ oʊ ˈnoʊţ ər| i **~ies** iz
protist ˈprəʊt ɪst §-əst ‖ ˈproʊţ- **~s** s
protist|a prəʊ ˈtɪst |ə ‖ proʊ- **~an/s** ən/z **~ic** ɪk
protium ˈprəʊt i‿əm ‖ ˈproʊţ- ˈproʊʃ-
proto- *comb. form*
with stress-neutral suffix ˌprəʊt əʊ

‖ ¦proʊt̬ oʊ — **Proto-Norse** ˌprəʊt əʊ ˈnɔːs ◂ ‖ ˌproʊt̬ oʊ ˈnɔːrs ◂
with stress-imposing suffix prəʊ ˈtɒ+ ‖ proʊ ˈtɑː+ — **protogynous** prəʊ ˈtɒdʒ ɪn əs -ən- ‖ proʊ ˈtɑːdʒ-
protoceratops ˌprəʊt əʊ ˈser ə tɒps ‖ ˌproʊt̬ oʊ ˈser ə tɑːps
protocol ˈprəʊt əʊ kɒl ‖ ˈproʊt̬ ə kɑːl -kɔːl, -koʊl **~s** z
Proto-Indo-European ˌprəʊt əʊ ˌɪnd əʊ jʊər ə ˈpiː‿ən -jɔːr əˈ-- ‖ ˌproʊt̬ oʊ ˌɪnd oʊ jʊr-
protolanguag|e ˈprəʊt əʊ ˌlæŋ gwɪdʒ -wɪdʒ, ˌ·ˈ·· ‖ ˈproʊt̬ oʊ- **~es** ɪz əz
proton, P~ ˈprəʊt ɒn ‖ ˈproʊt ɑːn **~s** z
protonotar|y ˌprəʊt əʊ ˈnəʊt ər| i prəʊ ˈtɒn ət‿ər| i ‖ proʊ ˈtɑːn ə ter| i ˌproʊt oʊ ˈnoʊt̬ ər| i **~ies** iz
protoplasm ˈprəʊt əʊ ˌplæz əm ‖ ˈproʊt̬ ə-
protoplast ˈprəʊt əʊ plæst -plɑːst ‖ ˈproʊt̬ ə- **~s** s
prototherian ˌprəʊt əʊ ˈθɪər i‿ən ◂ ‖ ˌproʊt̬ ə ˈθɪr- **~s** z
prototyp|e ˈprəʊt əʊ taɪp ‖ ˈproʊt̬ ə- **~ed** t **~es** s **~ing** ɪŋ
prototypical ˌprəʊt əʊ ˈtɪp ɪk əl ◂ ‖ ˌproʊt̬ ə- **~ly** ‿i
protozo|a ˌprəʊt əʊ ˈzəʊ |ə ◂ ‖ ˌproʊt̬ ə ˈzoʊ |ə ◂ **~an/s** ən/z **~ic** ɪk ◂ **~on** ɒn ən ‖ ɑːn
protozoology ˌprəʊt əʊ zəʊ ˈɒl ədʒ i -zuˈ-- ‖ ˌproʊt̬ ə zoʊ ˈɑːl-
protract prə ˈtrækt prəʊ- ‖ proʊ- **~ed** ɪd əd **~ing** ɪŋ **~s** s
protracted|ly prə ˈtrækt ɪd |li prəʊ-, -əd- ‖ proʊ- **~ness** nəs nɪs
protractile prə ˈtrækt aɪəl prəʊ- ‖ -əl proʊ-
protraction prə ˈtræk ʃən prəʊ- ‖ proʊ- **~s** z
protractor prə ˈtrækt ə prəʊ- ‖ proʊ ˈtrækt ər ˈ··· **~s** z
protrud|e prə ˈtruːd prəʊ- ‖ proʊ- **~ed** ɪd əd **~ing** ɪŋ **~es** z
protrusion prə ˈtruːʒ ən prəʊ- ‖ proʊ- **~s** z
protrusive prə ˈtruːs ɪv prəʊ-, §-ˈtruːz- ‖ proʊ- **~ly** li **~ness** nəs nɪs
protuberanc|e prə ˈtjuːb ər‿ənts prəʊ-, →-ˈtʃuːb-, ⚠-ˈtruːb- ‖ -ˈtuːb- -ˈtjuːb- **~es** ɪz əz
protuberant prə ˈtjuːb ər‿ənt prəʊ-, →-ˈtʃuːb-, ⚠-ˈtruːb- ‖ -ˈtuːb- -ˈtjuːb- **~ly** li
Protus ˈprəʊt əs ‖ ˈproʊt̬ əs
proud, Proud praʊd **prouder** ˈpraʊd ə ‖ -ər **proudest** ˈpraʊd ɪst -əst
Proudfoot ˈpraʊd fʊt
Proudhon ˈpruːd ɒn ‖ pruː ˈdɔːn -ˈdɑːn, -ˈdoʊn —*Fr* [pʁu dɔ̃]
Proudie ˈpraʊd i
proudly ˈpraʊd li
Proulx pruː
Proust pruːst —*Fr* [pʁust]
Proustian ˈpruːst i‿ən **~s** z
proustite ˈpruːst aɪt
Prout praʊt
provab|le ˈpruːv əb |əl **~ly** li
Provan ˈprɒv ən ˈprəʊv- ‖ ˈprɑːv-
prove pruːv *(!)* **proved** pruːvd **proven** ˈpruːv ən ˈprəʊv- **proves** pruːvz **proving** ˈpruːv ɪŋ
ˈproving ground
proven ˈpruːv ən ˈprəʊv-
provenance ˈprɒv ən ənts -ɪn- ‖ ˈprɑːv- -ə nɑːnts
Provencal, Provençal, Provencale, Provençale ˌprɒv ɒn ˈsɑːl ◂ -ɒ̃-, -ən- ‖ ˌprɑːv ɑːn- ˌproʊv- —*Fr* [pʁɔ vɑ̃ sal]
Provence prɒ ˈvɒ̃s prə- ‖ prə ˈvɑːnts proʊ- —*Fr* [pʁɔ vɑ̃ːs]
provender ˈprɒv ɪnd ə -ənd- ‖ ˈprɑːv ənd ər
provenience prə ˈviːn i‿ənts prəʊ- ‖ proʊ-
proverb, P~ ˈprɒv ɜːb ‖ ˈprɑːv ɜːb —*but as a grammatical term, 'kind of pro-form',* ˈprəʊ vɜːb ‖ ˈproʊ vɜːb **~s** z
proverbial prə ˈvɜːb i‿əl prɒ-, prəʊ- ‖ -ˈvɜːb- **~ly** i
provid|e prə ˈvaɪd prəʊ- **~ed** ɪd əd **~ing** ɪŋ **~es** z
providence, P~ ˈprɒv ɪd ənts -əd- ‖ ˈprɑːv- -ə dents
provident ˈprɒv ɪd ənt -əd- ‖ ˈprɑːv- **~ly** li
providential ˌprɒv ɪ ˈdentʃ əl ◂ -ə- ‖ ˌprɑːv- **~ly** i
provider prə ˈvaɪd ə §prəʊ- ‖ -ər **~s** z
provinc|e, P~ ˈprɒv ɪnts §-ənts ‖ ˈprɑːv- **~es** ɪz əz
Provincetown ˈprɒv ɪnts taʊn §-ənts- ‖ ˈprɑːv-
provincial prə ˈvɪntʃ əl **~ism** ˌɪz əm **~s** z
provinciality prə ˌvɪntʃ i ˈæl ət i -ɪt i ‖ -ət̬ i
provision prə ˈvɪʒ ən prəʊ- **~ed** d **~ing** ‿ɪŋ **~s** z
provisional, P~ prə ˈvɪʒ ən‿əl prəʊ- **~ism** ˌɪz əm **~ly** i **~s** z
proviso prə ˈvaɪz əʊ prəʊ- ‖ -oʊ **~s, ~es** z
provisor prə ˈvaɪz ə prəʊ- ‖ -ər **~s** z
provisory prə ˈvaɪz ər‿i
Provo, p~ ˈprəʊv əʊ ‖ ˈproʊv oʊ **~s** z
provocation ˌprɒv ə ˈkeɪʃ ən -əʊ- ‖ ˌprɑːv- **~s** z
provocative prə ˈvɒk ət ɪv prəʊ- ‖ -ˈvɑːk ət̬ ɪv **~ly** li **~ness** nəs nɪs
provok|e prə ˈvəʊk prəʊ- ‖ -ˈvoʊk **~ed** t **~es** s **~ing/ly** ɪŋ /li
provolone ˌprəʊv ə ˈləʊn i ‖ ˌproʊv ə ˈloʊn i —*It* [pro vo ˈloː ne]
provost ˈprɒv əst ˈprəʊv-, -ɒst ‖ ˈproʊv oʊst ˈprɑːv əst **~s** s **~ship/s** ʃɪp/s —*but in p~ marshal and other military senses,* prə ˈvəʊ ‖ ˈproʊv oʊ, *with a corresponding plural* **~s** z
proˌvost ˈmarshal ‖ ˌ·· ˈ··
prow praʊ **prows** praʊz
prowess ˈpraʊ es ˈprəʊ-, -ɪs, -əs, ·ˈes ‖ ˈpraʊ əs
prowl praʊl **prowled** praʊld **prowling** ˈpraʊl ɪŋ **prowls** praʊlz
ˈprowl car
prowler ˈpraʊl ə ‖ -ər **~s** z
Prowse *(i)* praʊs, *(ii)* praʊz
prox, prox. prɒks ‖ prɑːks

proxemic prɒk ˈsiːm ɪk ‖ prɑːk- **~s** s
proxie... —*see* **proxy**
Proxima ˈprɒks ɪm ə -əm- ‖ ˈprɑːks-
proximal ˈprɒks ɪm ᵊl -əm- ‖ ˈprɑːks- **~ly** i
proximate ˈprɒks ɪm ət -əm-, -ɪt ‖ˈprɑːks- **~ly** li
proxime accessit ˌprɒks ɪm i æk ˈses ɪt ˌ· ·eɪ-, -ək'·-, -ə ˈkes-, §-ət ‖ ˌprɑːks- **~s** s
proximit|y prɒk ˈsɪm ət |i -ɪt- ‖ prɑːk ˈsɪm əţ |i **~ies** iz
proximo ˈprɒks ɪ məʊ -ə- ‖ ˈprɑːks ə moʊ
prox|y ˈprɒks |i ‖ ˈprɑːks |i **~ies** iz
Prozac *tdmk* ˈprəʊz æk ‖ ˈproʊz-
Pru pruː
prude pruːd **prudes** pruːdz
prudence, P~ ˈpruːd ᵊnᵗs
prudent ˈpruːd ᵊnt **~ly** li
prudential, P~ pru ˈdenᵗʃ ᵊl **~ly** i
pruder|y ˈpruːd ər |i **~ies** iz
Prudhoe *(i)* ˈprʌd əʊ -həʊ ‖ -oʊ, *(ii)* ˈpruːd- —*The place in Northumberland is (i), locally* §ˈprʊd-; *but* P~ Bay *in AK is (ii).*
ˌ**Prudhoe ˈBay**
Prud'hon pruː ˈdɒ̃ ‖ -ˈdɑːn —*Fr* [pʁy dɔ̃]
prudish ˈpruːd ɪʃ **~ly** li **~ness** nəs nɪs
Prue pruː
Prufrock ˈpruː frɒk ‖ -frɑːk
prune pruːn **pruned** pruːnd **prunes** pruːnz
pruning ˈpruːn ɪŋ
ˈ**pruning hook**; ˈ**pruning knife**
Prunella, p~ pru ˈnel ə
prunus, P~ ˈpruːn əs **~es** ɪz əz
prurienc|e ˈprʊər iˌənᵗs ‖ ˈprʊr- **~y** i
prurient ˈprʊər iˌənt ‖ ˈprʊr- **~ly** li
pruriginous pruᵊ ˈrɪdʒ ɪn əs -ən-
prurigo pruᵊ ˈraɪg əʊ ‖ -oʊ
pruritus pruᵊ ˈraɪt əs ‖ -ˈraɪţ əs
pruˌ**ritus ˈani** ˈeɪn aɪ
prusik, P~ ˈprʌs ɪk **~ed** t **~ing** ɪŋ **~s** s
Prussi|a ˈprʌʃ |ə **~an/s** ᵊn/z
ˌ**Prussian ˈblue**◂
prussic ˈprʌs ɪk
ˌ**prussic ˈacid**
pry, Pry praɪ **pried** praɪd *(= pride)* **pries** praɪz *(= prize)* **prying/ly** ˈpraɪ ɪŋ /li
Pryce praɪs
Prynne prɪn
Pryor ˈpraɪˌə ‖ ˈpraɪˌᵊr
prytaneum ˌprɪt ə ˈniːˌəm -ᵊn ˈiːˌ ‖ -ᵊn ˈiː əm
Przewalski prəʒ ɪ ˈvæl ski -ə'·; ˌpɜːʒ·'·; ʃə'··; -ˈwɔːl-, -ˈwɒl- ‖ ʃə ˈvɑːl ski prɪz-, -ˈwɑːl- —*Russ* [prʒɨ ˈvalʲ skʲɪj] **~'s** z
Przeˌ**walski's ˈhorse**
PS, P.S. ˌpiː ˈes **~'s** ɪz əz
ps... *Note: words spelt with* ps... *are occasionally pronounced with initial* **ps**, *as written, rather than with the usual plain* **s** *sound. Thus* psalm *is occasionally pronounced* **psɑːm**. *This is not shown in individual entries.*
psalm sɑːm §sɑːlm, §sɒlm **psalms** sɑːmz §sɑːlmz, §sɒlmz
psalmist ˈsɑːm ɪst §ˈsɑːlm-, §ˈsɒlm-, §-əst **~s** s
psalmodic sæl ˈmɒd ɪk sɑː- ‖ -ˈmɑːd-
psalmod|y ˈsɑːm əd |i ˈsælm-, §ˈsɑːlm-, §ˈsɒlm- **~ies** iz
psalter, P~ ˈsɔːlt ə ˈsɒlt- ‖ -ᵊr ˈsɑːlt- **~s** z
psalteri|um sɔːl ˈtɪər iˌəm sɒl- ‖ -ˈtɪr- sɑːl- **~a** ə
psalter|y ˈsɔːlt ər |i ˈsɒlt- ‖ ˈsɑːlt- **~ies** iz
psephological ˌsiːf ə ˈlɒdʒ ɪk ᵊl ◂ ˌsef- ‖ -ˈlɑːdʒ- **~ly** ˌi
psephologist si ˈfɒl ədʒ ɪst sə-, se-, §-əst ‖ -ˈfɑːl- **~s** s
psephology si ˈfɒl ədʒ i sə-, se- ‖ -ˈfɑːl-
pseud sjuːd suːd ‖ suːd **pseuds** sjuːdz suːdz ‖ suːdz
pseudepigrapha ˌsjuːd ɪ ˈpɪg rəf ə ˌsuːd-, ˌ·ə-, ˌ·e- ‖ˌsuːd-
pseudo ˈsjuːd əʊ ˈsuːd- ‖ ˈsuːd oʊ
pseudo- *comb. form*
with stress-neutral suffix ¦sjuːd əʊ ¦suːd- ‖ ¦suːd oʊ — **pseudo-Marxist** ˌsjuːd əʊ ˈmɑːks ɪst ◂ ˌsuːd-, §-əst ‖ ˌsuːd oʊ ˈmɑːrks əst ◂
pseudomonas ˌsjuːd əʊ ˈməʊn əs ˌsuːd-; sjuː ˈdɒm ən əs, su- ‖ ˌsuːd ə ˈmoʊn əs suː ˈdɑːm ən əs
pseudonym ˈsjuːd ə nɪm ˈsuːd-, ᵊn ɪm ‖ ˈsuːd ᵊn ɪm **~s** z
pseudonymous sjuː ˈdɒn ɪm əs suː-, -əm- ‖ suː ˈdɑːn- **~ly** li
pseudopod ˈsjuːd əʊ pɒd ˈsuːd- ‖ ˈsuːd ə pɑːd **~s** z
pseudopodi|um ˌsjuːd əʊ ˈpəʊd iˌəm ˌsuːd- ‖ˌsuːd oʊ ˈpoʊd- -ə- **~a** ə
pseudy ˈsjuːd i ˈsuːd- ‖ ˈsuːd i
pshaw pɸə, pɸ, pʃɔː ‖ ʃɔː ʃɑː —*now obsolete: the spelling may have represented a bilabial affricate with 'lip voice' (a 'raspberry', a 'Bronx cheer').*
psi psaɪ saɪ **psis** psaɪz saɪz
psilocybin ˌsaɪl əʊ ˈsaɪb ɪn ˌsɪl-, §-ən ‖ ˌ-ə-
Psion *tdmk* ˈsaɪ ɒn ‖ -ɑːn
psittacine ˈsɪt ə saɪn -sɪn ‖ ˈsɪţ ə-
psittacosis ˌsɪt ə ˈkəʊs ɪs §-əs ‖ ˌsɪţ ə ˈkoʊs əs
psoas ˈsəʊ æs -əs ‖ ˈsoʊ-
psoriasis sə ˈraɪˌəs ɪs sɒ-, sɔː-, §-əs ‖ soʊ-
psoriatic ˌsɔːr i ˈæt ɪk ◂ sɔː ˈraɪˌət ɪk ‖ -ˈæţ ɪk ◂ ˌsoʊr-
psst ps, pst
psych, psyche *v* saɪk **psyched** saɪkt **psyches** *v* , **psychs** saɪks **psyching** ˈsaɪk ɪŋ
psyche *n*, **P~** ˈsaɪk i -iː **~s** z
psychedelia ˌsaɪk ə ˈdiːl iˌə ˌ·ɪ-
psychedelic ˌsaɪk ə ˈdel ɪk ◂ -ɪ- **~ally** ᵊlˌi
psychiatric ˌsaɪk i ˈætr ɪk ◂ -aɪ- **~al** ᵊl **~ally** ᵊlˌi
psychiatrist saɪ ˈkaɪˌətr ɪst sɪ-, sə-, §-əst **~s** s
psychiatry saɪ ˈkaɪˌətr i sɪ-, sə-
psychic ˈsaɪk ɪk **~al** ᵊl **~ally** ᵊlˌi **~s** s
psycho ˈsaɪk əʊ ‖ -oʊ **~s** z
psycho- *comb. form*
with stress-neutral suffix ¦saɪk əʊ ‖ -oʊ — **psychosocial** ˌsaɪk əʊ ˈsəʊʃ ᵊl ◂ ‖ -oʊ ˈsoʊʃ ᵊl ◂

P

with stress-imposing suffix saɪ ˈkɒ+ ‖ -ˈkɑː+ — **psychometry** saɪ ˈkɒm ətr i -ɪtr- ‖ -ˈkɑːm-
psychoacoustic ˌsaɪk əʊ ə ˈkuːst ɪk ◂ ‖ ˌ·oʊ- **~al** ᵊl **~ally** ᵊl‿i **~s** s
psychoactive ˌsaɪk əʊ ˈækt ɪv ◂ ‖ -oʊ-
psychoanalys|e ˌsaɪk əʊ ˈæn ə laɪz -ᵊl aɪz ‖ -oʊ ˈæn ᵊl aɪz **~ed** d **~es** ɪz əz **~ing** ɪŋ
psychoanalysis ˌsaɪk əʊ ə ˈnæl əs ɪs -ɪs ɪs §-əs ‖ ˌ·oʊ-
psychoanalyst ˌsaɪk əʊ ˈæn əl ɪst §-əst ‖ ˌ·oʊ- **~s** s
psychoanalytic ˌsaɪk əʊ ˌæn ə ˈlɪt ɪk ◂ -ᵊl ˈɪt- ‖ -oʊ ˌæn ᵊl ˈɪţ ɪk ◂ **~al** ᵊl **~ally** ᵊl‿i
psychoanalyz|e ˌsaɪk əʊ ˈæn ə laɪz -ᵊl aɪz ‖ -oʊ ˈæn ᵊl aɪz **~ed** d **~es** ɪz əz **~ing** ɪŋ
psychobabble ˈsaɪk əʊ ˌbæb ᵊl ‖ -oʊ-
psychobiology ˌsaɪk əʊ baɪ ˈɒl ədʒ i ‖ -oʊ baɪ ˈɑːl-
psychochemical ˌsaɪk əʊ ˈkem ɪk ᵊl ◂ ‖ ˌ·oʊ- **~s** z
psychodrama ˈsaɪk əʊ ˌdrɑːm ə ‖ -ə- -ˌdræm- **~s** z
psychognosis saɪ ˈkɒg nəs ɪs §-əs ‖ -ˈkɑːg-
psychokinesis ˌsaɪk əʊ kaɪ ˈniːs ɪs -kɪˈ--, §-kəˈ-- ‖ ˌ·oʊ-
psychokinetic ˌsaɪk əʊ kaɪ ˈnet ɪk ◂ -kɪˈ--, §-kəˈ-- ‖ -oʊ kaɪ ˈneţ ɪk ◂
psycholinguist ˌsaɪk əʊ ˈlɪŋ gwɪst §-gwəst ‖ -oʊ- **~s** s
psycholinguistic ˌsaɪk əʊ lɪŋ ˈgwɪst ɪk ◂ ‖ ˌ·oʊ- **~ally** ᵊl‿i **~s** s
psychological ˌsaɪk ə ˈlɒdʒ ɪk ᵊl ◂ ‖ -ˈlɑːdʒ- **~ly** i
ˌpsychoˌlogical ˈwarfare
psychologism saɪ ˈkɒl ə ˌdʒɪz əm ‖ -ˈkɑːl-
psychologist saɪ ˈkɒl ədʒ ɪst §-əst ‖ -ˈkɑːl-
psycholog|y saɪ ˈkɒl ədʒ |i ‖ -ˈkɑːl- **~ies** iz
psychometric ˌsaɪk əʊ ˈmetr ɪk ◂ ‖ -ə- **~ally** ᵊl‿i **~s** s
psychometry saɪ ˈkɒm ətr i -ɪtr- ‖ -ˈkɑːm-
psychopath ˈsaɪk əʊ pæθ ‖ -ə- **~s** s
psychopathic ˌsaɪk əʊ ˈpæθ ɪk ◂ ‖ -ə- **~ally** ᵊl‿i
psychopathological ˌsaɪk əʊ ˌpæθ ə ˈlɒdʒ ɪk ᵊl ‖ -oʊ ˌpæθ ə ˈlɑːdʒ-
psychopathology ˌsaɪk əʊ pə ˈθɒl ədʒ i -pæˈ-- ‖ -oʊ pə ˈθɑːl-
psychophysical ˌsaɪk əʊ ˈfɪz ɪk ᵊl ◂ ‖ ˌ·oʊ- **~ly** ‿i
psychoses saɪ ˈkəʊs iːz ‖ -ˈkoʊs-
psychosexual ˌsaɪk əʊ ˈseks ju‿əl ◂ -ˈsekʃ u‿, -ˈsekʃ ᵊl ‖ -oʊ ˈsekʃ u‿əl ◂ -ˈ·ᵊl **~ly** i
psychos|is saɪ ˈkəʊs |ɪs §-əs ‖ -ˈkoʊs- **~es** iːz
psychosocial ˌsaɪk əʊ ˈsəʊʃ ᵊl ◂ ‖ -oʊ ˈsoʊʃ- **~ly** -i
psychosomatic ˌsaɪk əʊ səʊ ˈmæt ɪk ◂ ‖ -ə sə ˈmæţ ɪk ◂ **~ally** ᵊl‿i
psychotherapeutic ˌsaɪk əʊ ˌθer ə ˈpjuːt ɪk ‖ -oʊ ˌθer ə ˈpjuːţ ɪk **~ally** ᵊl‿i **~s** s
psychotherapist ˌsaɪk əʊ ˈθer əp ɪst §-əst ‖ ˌ·oʊ- **~s** s
psychotherapy ˌsaɪk əʊ ˈθer əp i ‖ ˌ·oʊ-
psychotic saɪ ˈkɒt ɪk ‖ -ˈkɑːţ ɪk **~ally** ᵊl‿i **~s** s
psychotropic ˌsaɪk əʊ ˈtrɒp ɪk ◂ -ˈtrəʊp- ‖ -ə ˈtroʊp ɪk ◂ **~ally** ᵊl‿i **~s** s
psychrometer saɪ ˈkrɒm ɪt ə -ət- ‖ -ˈkrɑːm əţ ᵊr **~s** z
psyllid ˈsɪl ɪd §-əd **~s** z
psy ops ˈsaɪ ɒps ‖ -ɑːps
PTA ˌpiː tiː ˈeɪ
Ptah tɑː ptɑː; pə ˈtɑː
ptarmigan ˈtɑːm ɪg ən -əg- ‖ ˈtɑːrm- **~s** z
pteridology ˌter ɪ ˈdɒl ədʒ i ˌ·ə- ‖ -ˈdɑːl-
pteridophyte ˈter ɪd ə faɪt ˈ·əd-; tə ˈrɪd- **~s** s
pterodactyl ˌter əʊ ˈdækt ɪl -ᵊl ‖ -ə- **~s** z
pterosaur ˈter ə sɔː ‖ -sɔːr **~s** z
-pterous *stress-imposing* ptər əs — **dipterous** ˈdɪpt ər əs
pterygium tə ˈrɪdʒ i‿əm
pterygoid ˈter ɪ gɔɪd -ə-
PTFE ˌpiː tiː ef ˈiː
PTO, pto ˌpiː tiː ˈəʊ ‖ -ˈoʊ
Ptolemaeus ˌtɒl ə ˈmiː‿əs -ɪ-, -ˈmeɪ- ‖ ˌtɑːl-
Ptolemaic ˌtɒl ə ˈmeɪ ɪk ◂ -ɪ- ‖ ˌtɑːl-
Ptolemy ˈtɒl əm i -ɪm- ‖ ˈtɑːl-
ptomain, ptomaine ˈtəʊm eɪn təʊ ˈmeɪn ‖ ˈtoʊm- **~s** z
ptosed təʊzd ‖ toʊzd
ptosis ˈtəʊs ɪs §-əs ‖ ˈtoʊs-
ptotic ˈtəʊt ɪk ˈtɒt- ‖ ˈtoʊţ-
Pty —*see* **proprietary** prə ˈpraɪ‿ət‿ər |i ‖ -ə ter |i
ptyalin ˈtaɪ‿əl ɪn §-ən
p-type ˈpiː taɪp
pub pʌb **pubbed** pʌbd **pubbing** ˈpʌb ɪŋ **pubs** pʌbz
pub-crawl ˈpʌb krɔːl ‖ -krɑːl **~ed** d **~er/s** ə/z ‖ ᵊr/z **~ing** ɪŋ **~s** z
pube pjuːb **pubes** pjuːbz
pubertal ˈpjuːb ət ᵊl ‖ -ᵊrţ ᵊl
puberty ˈpjuːb ət i ‖ -ᵊrţ i
pubes *plural of* pubis ˈpjuːb iːz
pubes *'groin; pubic hair'* ˈpjuːb iːz —*but as a colloquial word, taken as a plural, usually* pjuːbz
pubescence pju ˈbes ᵊnᵗs
pubescent pju ˈbes ᵊnt
pubic ˈpjuːb ɪk
pub|is ˈpjuːb |ɪs §-əs **~es** iːz
public ˈpʌb lɪk
ˌpublic ˈbar; **ˌpublic ˈcompany**; **ˌpublic conˈvenience**; **ˌpublic ˈenemy**;; **ˌpublic ˈgallery**; **ˌpublic ˈhouse**; **ˌPublic ˈLending Right**; **ˌpublic ˈlibrary**; **ˌpublic ˈnuisance**; **ˌpublic ˈownership**; **ˌpublic oˈpinion**; **ˌpublic ˈprosecutor**; **ˌpublic reˈlations**; **ˌpublic ˈspirit**; **ˌpublic ˈspeaking**; **ˌpublic ˈschool, ˈ· · ·**; **ˌpublic ˈworks**
public-address ˌpʌb lɪk ə ˈdres
ˌpublic-adˈdress ˌsystem
publican ˈpʌb lɪk ən **~s** z
publication ˌpʌb lɪ ˈkeɪʃ ᵊn -lə- **~s** z
publicis|e ˈpʌb lɪ saɪz -lə- **~ed** d **~es** ɪz əz **~ing** ɪŋ
publicist ˈpʌb lɪs ɪst -ləs, §-əst **~s** s

publicity pʌb ˈlɪs ət i pəb-, -ɪt- ‖ -əţ i
publiciz|e ˈpʌb lɪ saɪz -lə- **~ed** d **~es** ɪz əz **~ing** ɪŋ
public|ly ˈpʌb lɪk |li **~ness** nəs nɪs
public-minded ˌpʌb lɪk ˈmaɪnd ɪd ◂ -əd ◂
public-spirited ˌpʌb lɪk ˈspɪr ɪt ɪd ◂ -ət ɪd, -əd ‖ -əţ əd ◂ **~ness** nəs nɪs
publish ˈpʌb lɪʃ **~ed** t **~es** ɪz əz **~ing** ɪŋ
ˈpublishing house
publishable ˈpʌb lɪʃ əb ᵊl
publisher ˈpʌb lɪʃ ə ‖ -ᵊr **~s** z
Publius ˈpʌb li‿əs
Puccini pu ˈtʃiːn i —*It* [put ˈtʃiː ni]
puccoon pə ˈkuːn pʌ- **~s** z
puce pjuːs
puck, Puck pʌk **pucks, Puck ˈs** pʌks
pucker ˈpʌk ə ‖ -ᵊr **~ed** d **puckering** ˈpʌk ər‿ɪŋ **~s** z
Puckeridge ˈpʌk ər‿ɪdʒ
puckish ˈpʌk ɪʃ **~ly** li **~ness** nəs nɪs
pud pʊd **puds** pʊdz
pudding ˈpʊd ɪŋ —*There is also a non-standard form* ⚠ˈpʊd ᵊn, *sometimes written* pudden **~s** z
puddl|e ˈpʌd ᵊl **~ed** d **~es** z **~ing** ‿ɪŋ
Puddletown ˈpʌd ᵊl taʊn
puddock ˈpʌd ək **~s** s
pudend|um pju ˈdend |əm **~a** ə
pudg|y ˈpʌdʒ |i **~ier** i‿ə ‖ i‿ᵊr **~iest** i‿ɪst i‿əst **~ily** ɪ li əl i **~iness** i nəs i nɪs
Pudsey ˈpʌd si ˈpʌdz i
pudu ˈpuːd uː **~s** z
pueblo, P~ ˈpweb ləʊ pu ˈeb ləʊ ‖ -loʊ —*Sp* [ˈpwe βlo] **~s** z
puerile ˈpjʊər aɪᵊl ˈpjɔːr-; ˈpjuː‿ə raɪᵊl ‖ ˈpjʊr ᵊl -aɪl **~ly** li **~ness** nəs nɪs
puerilit|y pjuᵊ ˈrɪl ət |i ₍ₗ₎pjʊə-, ₍ₗ₎pjɔː-, ˌpjuː‿ə-, -ɪt i ‖ -əţ i **~ies** iz
puerperal pju ˈɜːp ᵊr‿əl ‖ -ˈɜːp-
puerperium ˌpjuː‿ə ˈpɪər i‿əm ‖ -ᵊr ˈpɪr-
Puerto ˈpwɜːt əʊ ˈpweət- ‖ ˈpwerţ oʊ —*Sp* [ˈpwer to] —*see also phrases with this word*
Puerto Rican ˌpwɜːt əʊ ˈriːk |ən ◂ ˌpweət-, ˌpɔːt- ‖ ˌpwerţ ə- ˌpɔːrţ-, ˌpoʊrţ- **~s** z
Puerto Rico ˌpwɜːt əʊ ˈriːk əʊ ˌpweət-, ˌpɔːt- ‖ ˌpwerţ ə- ˌpɔːrţ-, ˌpoʊrţ- —*Sp* [pwer to ˈrri ko]
Puerto Vallarta ˌpwɜːt əʊ vaɪ ˈɑːt ə ˌpweət-, -və ˈlɑːt ə ‖ ˌpwerţ ə vɑː ˈjɑːrţ ə —*Sp* [ˌpwer to βa ˈjar ta, -ˈʎar-]
puff pʌf **puffed** pʌft **puffing** ˈpʌf ɪŋ **puffs** pʌfs
puffa ˈpʌf ə
ˈpuffa ˌjacket
puffball ˈpʌf bɔːl ‖ -bɑːl **~s** z
puffer ˈpʌf ə ‖ -ᵊr **~s** z
puffery ˈpʌf ər i
puffi... —*see* **puffy**
puffin ˈpʌf ɪn §-ᵊn **~s** z
puffin|ry ˈpʌf ɪn |ri §-ᵊn- **~ries** riz
puff-puff ˈpʌf pʌf **~s** s
puff|y ˈpʌf |i **~ier** i‿ə ‖ i‿ᵊr **~iest** i‿ɪst i‿əst **~iness** i nəs i nɪs

puftaloon ˌpʌft ə ˈluːn **~s** z
pug pʌg **pugged** pʌgd **pugging** ˈpʌg ɪŋ **pugs** pʌgz
Puget ˈpjuːdʒ ɪt §-ət
puggaree ˈpʌg ər‿i **~s** z
puggree ˈpʌg ri **~s** z —*Hindi* [pə gɽiː]
Pugh, Pughe pjuː
pugilism ˈpjuːdʒ ɪ ˌlɪz əm -ə-
pugilist ˈpjuːdʒ ɪl ɪst -əl-, §-əst **~s** s
pugilistic ˌpjuːdʒ ɪ ˈlɪst ɪk ◂ -ə- **~ally** ᵊl‿i
Pugin ˈpjuːdʒ ɪn §-ən
pug-mill ˈpʌg mɪl **~s** z
pugnacious pʌg ˈneɪʃ əs **~ly** li **~ness** nəs nɪs
pugnacity pʌg ˈnæs ət i -ɪt- ‖ -əţ i
pug-nose ˌpʌg ˈnəʊz ˈ· · ‖ ˈpʌg noʊz **~d** d ◂
Pugwash ˈpʌg wɒʃ ‖ -wɔːʃ -wɑːʃ
puisne ˈpjuːn i
puissance ˈpwiːs ɒ̃s -ɒnᵗs, -ᵊnᵗs, -ænᵗs ‖ ˈpjuː əs ənᵗs —*In poetic usage also* ˈpjuː‿ɪs ᵊnᵗs, -əs-; pju ˈɪs-; ˈpwɪs ᵊnᵗs
puissant ˈpwiːs ɒnt ˈpjuː‿ɪs ᵊnt, -əs-; pju ˈɪs-; ˈpwɪs ᵊnt ‖ ˈpjuː əs ənt **~ly** li
puja ˈpuːdʒ ə -ɑː **~s** z —*Hindi* [puː dʒaː]
puke pjuːk **puked** pjuːkt **pukes** pjuːks **puking** ˈpjuːk ɪŋ
pukeko ˈpʊk ə kəʊ ‖ -koʊ **~s** z
pukey, puky ˈpjuːk i
pukka ˈpʌk ə
pula ˈpuːl ə ˈpjuːl- ˈpʊl-
Pulaski pə ˈlæsk i pju-, pʊ-
Pulborough ˈpʊl bər‿ə ‖ -ˌbɜː oʊ
pulchritude ˈpʌlk rɪ tjuːd -rə-, →-tʃuːd ‖ -tuːd -tjuːd
pulchritudinous ˌpʌlk rɪ ˈtjuːd ɪn əs ◂ -rə-, →-ˈtʃuːd-, -ən‿əs ‖ -ˈtuːd ən‿əs ◂ -ˈtjuːd-
pule pjuːl **puled** pjuːld **pules** pjuːlz **puling/ly** ˈpjuːl ɪŋ /li
Pulham ˈpʊl əm
puli ˈpjuːl i ˈpʊl-, ˈpuːl- **~s** z
Pulitzer ˈpʊl ɪts ə ˈpjuːl-, §-əts- ‖ -ᵊr
pull pʊl **pulled** pʊld **pulling** ˈpʊl ɪŋ **pulls** pʊlz
pullback ˈpʊl bæk **~s** s
pull-down ˈpʊl daʊn
Pullen ˈpʊl ɪn -ən
pullet ˈpʊl ɪt -ət **~s** s
pulley ˈpʊl i **~s** z
pull-in ˈpʊl ɪn **~s** z
Pullman, p~ ˈpʊl mən **~s** z
pull-on ˈpʊl ɒn ‖ -ɑːn -ɔːn
pullorum pʊ ˈlɔːr əm pə- ‖ -ˈloʊr-
pull-out ˈpʊl aʊt **~s** s
pullover ˈpʊl ˌəʊv ə ‖ -ˌoʊv ᵊr **~s** z
pullthrough ˈpʊl θruː **~s** z
pullu|late ˈpʌl ju |leɪt -jə- ‖ -jə- **~lated** leɪt ɪd -əd ‖ leɪţ əd **~lates** leɪts **~lating** leɪt ɪŋ ‖ leɪţ ɪŋ
pullulation ˌpʌl ju ˈleɪʃ ᵊn -jə- ‖ -jə- **~s** z
Pullum ˈpʊl əm
pull-up ˈpʊl ʌp **~s** s
Pulman ˈpʊl mən
pulmonary ˈpʌl mən ər‿i ˈpʊl- ‖ -mə ner i

P

pulmonic pʌl ˈmɒn ɪk pʊl- ‖ -ˈmɑːn ɪk **~ally** əl‿i
pulp pʌlp **pulped** pʌlpt **pulping** ˈpʌlp ɪŋ **pulps** pʌlps
pulpit ˈpʊlp ɪt §ˈpʌlp-, §-ət **~s** s
pulpwood ˈpʌlp wʊd
pulp|y ˈpʌlp |i **~ier** i‿ə ‖ i‿ər **~iest** i‿ɪst i‿əst **~iness** i nəs i nɪs
pulque ˈpʊlk i ˈpuːlk-, -eɪ —*Sp* [ˈpul ke]
pulsar ˈpʌls ɑː ‖ -ɑːr **~s** z
pulsate pʌl ˈseɪt ‖ ˈpʌls eɪt **pulsated** pʌl ˈseɪt ɪd -əd ‖ ˈpʌls eɪţ əd **pulsates** pʌl ˈseɪts ‖ ˈpʌls eɪts **pulsating** pʌl ˈseɪt ɪŋ ‖ ˈpʌls eɪţ ɪŋ
pulsatile ˈpʌls ə taɪəl ‖ -əţ əl
pulsation pʌl ˈseɪʃ ən **~s** z
pulsative ˈpʌls ət ɪv ‖ -əţ-
pulsator pʌl ˈseɪt ə ‖ ˈpʌls eɪţ ər **~s** z
pulsatory pʌl ˈseɪt ər i ˈpʌls ət‿ər i ‖ ˈpʌls ə tɔːr i -toʊr i
pulse pʌls **pulsed** pʌlst **pulses** ˈpʌls ɪz -əz **pulsing** ˈpʌls ɪŋ
pulsimeter pʌl ˈsɪm ɪt ə -ət- ‖ -əţ ər **~s** z
Pulteney *(i)* ˈpʌlt ən‿i *(ii)* ˈpəʊlt- →ˈpɒʊlt- ‖ ˈpoʊlt-
pulu ˈpuːl uː
pulveris... —*see* **pulveriz...**
pulverization ˌpʌlv ər‿aɪ ˈzeɪʃ ən ˌpʊlv-,-ɪˈ-- ‖ -ər‿ə-
pulveriz|e ˈpʌlv ə raɪz ˈpʊlv- **~ed** d **~es** ɪz əz **~ing** ɪŋ
pulverulent pʌl ˈver ʊl ənt -jʊl-, -əl-
pulvinar pʌl ˈvaɪn ə ‖ -ər **~s** z
pulvi|nate ˈpʌlv ɪ |neɪt -ə- **~nated** neɪt ɪd -əd ‖ neɪţ əd **~nately** neɪt li
puma ˈpjuːm ə ‖ ˈpuːm- **~s** z
pumice ˈpʌm ɪs §-əs
pumice stone ˈpʌm ɪs stəʊn -ɪ-, §-əs- ‖ -stoʊn **~s** z
pummel ˈpʌm əl **~ed, ~led** d **~ing, ~ling** ɪŋ **~s** z
pump pʌmp **pumped** pʌmpt **pumping** ˈpʌmp ɪŋ **pumps** pʌmps
ˈpump room
pumpernickel ˈpʌmp ə ˌnɪk əl ˈpʊmp- ‖ -ər- —*Ger* [ˈpʊm pɐ nɪk əl]
Pumphrey ˈpʌmpf ri
pumpkin ˈpʌmp kɪn §-kən ‖ ⚠ˈpʌŋk ən **~s** z
pun pʌn **punned** pʌnd **punning/ly** ˈpʌn ɪŋ /li **puns** pʌnz
punch, Punch pʌntʃ **punched** pʌntʃt **punches, Punch's** ˈpʌntʃ ɪz -əz **punching** ˈpʌntʃ ɪŋ
ˈpunch ball; **ˈpunch bowl**; **ˈpunch card**; **ˌpunched ˈcard**; **ˈpunching bag**; **ˈpunch line**
Punch-and-Judy ˌpʌntʃ ən ˈdʒuːd i -ənd-
ˌPunch-and-ˈJudy show
punchbag ˈpʌntʃ bæg **~s** z
punch-drunk ˈpʌntʃ drʌŋk ˌ·ˈ·
puncheon ˈpʌntʃ ən **~s** z
puncher ˈpʌntʃ ə ‖ -ər **~s** z
Punchinello, p~ ˌpʌntʃ ɪ ˈnel əʊ -ə- ‖ -oʊ **~s, ~es** z
punchline ˈpʌntʃ laɪn **~s** z
punch-up ˈpʌntʃ ʌp **~s** s
punch|y ˈpʌntʃ |i **~ier** i‿ə ‖ i‿ər **~iest** i‿ɪst i‿əst **~ily** ɪ li əl i **~iness** i nəs i nɪs
punctate *adj* ˈpʌŋkt eɪt
punctilio pʌŋk ˈtɪl i əʊ ‖ -oʊ **~s** z
punctilious pʌŋk ˈtɪl i‿əs **~ly** li **~ness** nəs nɪs
punctual ˈpʌŋk tʃu‿əl -tju‿əl
punctuality ˌpʌŋk tʃu ˈæl ət i ˌ-tju-, -ɪt i ‖ -əţ i
punctually ˈpʌŋk tʃu‿əl i -tju‿əl-
punctu|ate ˈpʌŋk tʃu |eɪt -tju- **~ated** eɪt ɪd -əd ‖ eɪţ əd **~ates** eɪts **~ating** eɪt ɪŋ ‖ eɪţ ɪŋ
punctuation ˌpʌŋk tʃu ˈeɪʃ ən -tju- **~s** z
ˌpunctuˈation mark

PUNCTURE

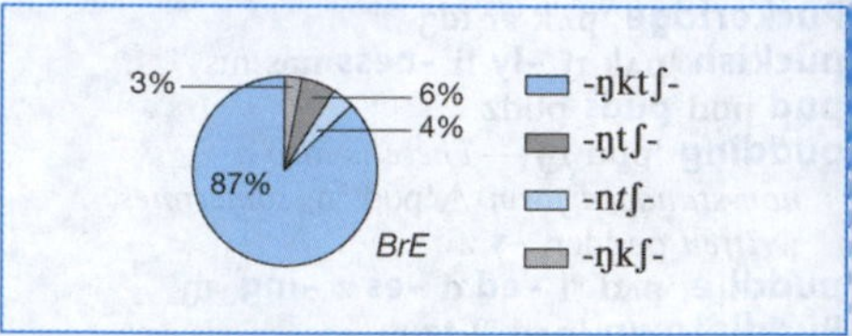

puncture ˈpʌŋk tʃə -ʃə; §ˈpʌntʃ ə ‖ -tʃər — *Preference poll, BrE:* -ŋktʃ- *87%,* -ŋtʃ- *6%,* -ntʃ- *4%,* -ŋkʃ- *3%.* **~d** d **puncturing** ˈpʌŋk tʃər ɪŋ -ʃər‿ɪŋ **~s** z
pundit ˈpʌnd ɪt §-ət **~s** s
Pune ˈpuːn ə
pungency ˈpʌndʒ əntˢ i
pungent ˈpʌndʒ ənt **~ly** li
puni... —*see* **puny**
Punic ˈpjuːn ɪk
punish ˈpʌn ɪʃ **~ed** t **~er/s** ə/z ‖ -ər/z **~es** ɪz əz **~ing/ly** ɪŋ /li
punishable ˈpʌn ɪʃ əb əl
punishment ˈpʌn ɪʃ mənt **~s** s
punitive ˈpjuːn ət ɪv -ɪt- ‖ -əţ ɪv **~ly** li **~ness** nəs nɪs
Punjab pʌn ˈdʒɑːb pʊn-, ˈ· · —*There is no etymological justification for the* pʊn *forms.*
Punjabi pʌn ˈdʒɑːb i pʊn-, -iː **~s** z
punji ˈpʌndʒ i **~s** z
punk pʌŋk **punks** pʌŋks
ˌpunk ˈrock; **ˌpunk ˈrocker**
punka, punkah ˈpʌŋk ə **~s** z
punkin *non-standard form of* pumpkin ˈpʌŋk ɪn -ən **~s** z
punk|y ˈpʌŋk |i **~ier** i‿ə ‖ i‿ər **~iest** i‿ɪst i‿əst **~iness** i nəs i nɪs
punnet ˈpʌn ɪt §-ət **~s** s
punster ˈpʌn stə ‖ -stər **~s** z
punt *'boat'; 'kick'; 'gamble'; 'hollow at base of bottle'* pʌnt **punted** ˈpʌntɪd -əd ‖ ˈpʌnţ əd **punting** ˈpʌntɪŋ ‖ ˈpʌnţ ɪŋ **punts** pʌnts
punt *'Irish pound'* pʊnt **punts** pʊnts
punter ˈpʌnt ə ‖ ˈpʌnţ ər **~s** z
punt|y ˈpʌnt |i ‖ ˈpʌnţ |i **~ies** iz
pun|y ˈpjuːn |i **~ier** i‿ə ‖ i‿ər **~iest** i‿ɪst i‿əst **~ily** ɪ li əl i **~iness** i nəs i nɪs

pup pʌp **pupped** pʌpt **pupping** ˈpʌp ɪŋ **pups** pʌps
pup|a ˈpjuːp |ə **~ae** iː **~al** ᵊl **~as** əz
pup|ate pjuː ˈp|eɪt ‖ ˈpjuːp |eɪt **~ated** eɪt ɪd -əd ‖ eɪţ əd **~ates** eɪts **~ating** eɪt ɪŋ ‖ eɪţ ɪŋ
pupation pjuː ˈpeɪʃ ᵊn
pupil ˈpjuːp ᵊl -ɪl **~s** z
pupilage, pupillage ˈpjuːp əl ɪdʒ -ɪl-
pupillary ˈpjuːp əl ər i ˈ·ɪl- ‖ -ə ler i
puppadum ˈpʌp ə dʌm **~s** z
puppet ˈpʌp ɪt §-ət **~s** s
puppeteer ˌpʌp ɪ ˈtɪə -ə- ‖ -ˈtɪᵊr **~s** z
puppetry ˈpʌp ɪtr i -ətr-
Puppis ˈpʌp ɪs
pupp|y ˈpʌp |i **~ies** iz
ˈpuppy dog; **ˈpuppy fat**; **ˈpuppy love**
Purbeck ˈpɜː bek ‖ ˈpɜ˞ː-
purblind ˈpɜː blaɪnd ‖ ˈpɜ˞ː- **~ly** li **~ness** nəs nɪs
Purcell *(i)* ˈpɜːs ᵊl ‖ ˈpɜ˞ːs ᵊl, *(ii)* pɜː ˈsel ‖ pɜ˞ː- *—The composer was (i).*
purchasable ˈpɜːtʃ əs əb ᵊl ˈ·ɪs- ‖ ˈpɜ˞ːtʃ-
purchas|e, P~ ˈpɜːtʃ əs -ɪs ‖ ˈpɜ˞ːtʃ əs **~ed** t **~er/s** ə/z ‖ ·ᵊr/z **~es** ɪz əz **~ing** ɪŋ
ˈpurchase tax; **ˈpurchasing ˌpower**
purda, purdah ˈpɜːd ə -ɑː ‖ ˈpɜ˞ːd ə *—Hindi-Urdu* [pər ḍaː]
Purdie ˈpɜːd i ‖ ˈpɜ˞ːd i
Purdon ˈpɜːd ᵊn ‖ ˈpɜ˞ːd ᵊn
Purdue ˈpɜːd juː ‖ pᵊr ˈduː
Purdy ˈpɜːd i ‖ ˈpɜ˞ːd i
pure pjʊə pjɔː ‖ pjʊᵊr pjɜ˞ː **purer** ˈpjʊər ə ˈpjɔːr- ‖ ˈpjʊr ᵊr ˈpjɜ˞ː- **purest** ˈpjʊər ɪst ˈpjɔːr-, -əst ‖ ˈpjʊr əst ˈpjɜ˞ː-
pureblood ˈpjʊə blʌd ˈpjɔː- ‖ ˈpjʊr- ˈpjɜ˞ː-
pureblooded ˌpjʊə ˈblʌd ɪd ◂ ˌpjɔː-, -əd ‖ ˌpjʊr- ˌpjɜ˞ː-
purebred ˈpjʊə bred ˈpjɔː- ‖ ˈpjʊr- ˈpjɜ˞ː- **~s** z
puree, purée ˈpjʊər eɪ ˈpjɔːr- ‖ pju ˈreɪ -ˈriː **~s** z
pure|ly ˈpjʊə| li ˈpjɔː|- ‖ ˈpjʊr|- ˈpjɜ˞ː|- **~ness** nəs nɪs
purfl|e ˈpɜːf ᵊl ‖ ˈpɜ˞ːf ᵊl **~ed** d **~es** z **~ing/s** ˌɪŋ/z
Purfleet ˈpɜː fliːt ‖ ˈpɜ˞ː-
purgation pɜː ˈgeɪʃ ᵊn ‖ pɜ˞ː-
purgative ˈpɜːg ət ɪv ⚠ˈpɜːdʒ- ‖ ˈpɜ˞ːg əţ ɪv **~s** z
purgatorial ˌpɜːg ə ˈtɔːr iˌəl ◂ ‖ ˌpɜ˞ːg- -ˈtoʊr-
purgator|y, P~ ˈpɜːg ətr |i ‖ ˈpɜ˞ːg ə tɔːr |i -toʊr i **~ies** iz
purge pɜːdʒ ‖ pɜ˞ːdʒ **purged** pɜːdʒd ‖ pɜ˞ːdʒd **purges** ˈpɜːdʒ ɪz -əz ‖ ˈpɜ˞ːdʒ əz **purging** ˈpɜːdʒ ɪŋ ‖ ˈpɜ˞ːdʒ ɪŋ
purification ˌpjʊər ɪf ɪ ˈkeɪʃ ᵊn ˌpjɔːr-, ˌ·əf-, §-əˈ·- ‖ ˌpjʊr- ˌpjɜ˞ː- **~s** z
purificator ˈpjʊər ɪf ɪ keɪt ə ˈpjɔːr-, ˈ·əf-, §-ə ·· ‖ ˈpjʊr əf ə keɪţ ᵊr ˈpjɜ˞ː- **~s** z
purificatory ˌpjʊər ɪf ɪ ˈkeɪt ər i ˌpjɔːr-, ˌ·əf-, §ˌ· ə-, ˈ· · · · -, ˈ· ·fɪk ət ər i ‖ pju ˈrɪf ɪk ə tɔːr i pjə-, -toʊr i; ˈpjʊr əf ək-, ˈpjɜ˞ː-
puri|fy ˈpjʊər ɪ |faɪ ˈpjɔːr-, -ə ‖ ˈpjʊr- ˈpjɜ˞ː- **~fied** faɪd **~fier/s** faɪˌə/z ‖ faɪˌᵊr/z **~fies** faɪz **~fying** faɪ ɪŋ
Purim ˈpʊər ɪm ˈpjʊər-, pʊᵊ ˈriːm ‖ ˈpʊr-
Purina *tdmk* pjə ˈriːn ə pjuᵊ-
purine ˈpjʊər iːn ˈpjɔːr-, -aɪn ‖ ˈpjʊr-
purism ˈpjʊər ˌɪz əm ˈpjɔːr- ‖ ˈpjʊr-
purist ˈpjʊər ɪst ˈpjɔːr-, §-əst ‖ ˈpjʊr əst **~s** s
puristic pjuᵊ ˈrɪst ɪk pjɔː- **~al** ᵊl **~ally** ᵊlˌi
Puritan ˈpjʊər ɪt ən ˈpjɔːr-, -ət- ‖ ˈpjʊr ət ᵊn **~s** z
puritanical ˌpjʊər ɪ ˈtæn ɪk ᵊl ◂ ˌpjɔːr-, ˌ·ə- ‖ ˌpjʊr- **~ly** ˌi **~ness** nəs nɪs
Puritanism ˈpjʊər ɪt ən ˌɪz əm ˈpjɔːr-, ˈ·ət- ‖ ˈpjʊr ət ᵊn-
purity ˈpjʊər ət i ˈpjɔːr-, -ɪt- ‖ ˈpjʊr əţ i
purl pɜːl ‖ pɜ˞ːl *(= pearl)* **purled** pɜːld ‖ pɜ˞ːld **purling** ˈpɜːl ɪŋ ‖ ˈpɜ˞ːl ɪŋ **purls** pɜːlz ‖ pɜ˞ːlz
purler ˈpɜːl ə ‖ ˈpɜ˞ːl ᵊr **~s** z
Purley ˈpɜːl i ‖ ˈpɜ˞ːl i
purlieu ˈpɜːl juː §-luː ‖ ˈpɜ˞ːl uː -juː **~s** z
purlin, purline ˈpɜːl ɪn §-ən ‖ ˈpɜ˞ːl- **~s** z
purloin pɜː ˈlɔɪn ˈ· · ‖ pɜ˞ː- **~ed** d **~ing** ɪŋ **~s** z
Purnell pɜː ˈnel ‖ pɜ˞ː-
purpl|e ˈpɜːp ᵊl ‖ ˈpɜ˞ːp ᵊl **~ed** d **~es** z **~ing** ˌɪŋ
ˌpurple ˈheart, ˌPurple ˈHeart; **ˌpurple ˈpassage**; **ˌpurple ˈpatch**
purplish ˈpɜːp ᵊlˌɪʃ ‖ ˈpɜ˞ːp-
purport *n* ˈpɜː pɔːt ˈpɜːp ət ‖ ˈpɜ˞ː pɔːrt -poʊrt **~s** s
purport *v* pə ˈpɔːt pɜː-; ˈpɜːp ət, -ɔːt ‖ pᵊr ˈpɔːrt -ˈpoʊrt **purported** pə ˈpɔːt ɪd pɜː-, -əd; ˈpɜːp ət-, -ɔːt- ‖ pᵊr ˈpɔːrţ əd -ˈpoʊrţ- **purporting** pə ˈpɔːt ɪŋ pɜː-; ˈpɜːp ət-, -ɔːt- ‖ pᵊr ˈpɔːrţ ɪŋ ˈpoʊrţ- **~s** s
purpos|e *n, v* ˈpɜːp əs ‖ ˈpɜ˞ːp əs **~ed** t **~es** ɪz əz **~ing** ɪŋ
purpose-built ˌpɜːp əs ˈbɪlt ◂ ‖ ˌpɜ˞ːp-
purposeful ˈpɜːp əs fᵊl -fʊl ‖ ˈpɜ˞ːp- **~ly** ˌi **~ness** nəs nɪs
purposeless ˈpɜːpəs ləs -lɪs ‖ ˈpɜ˞ːp- **~ly** li **~ness** nəs nɪs
purposely ˈpɜːp əs li ‖ ˈpɜ˞ːp-
purposive ˈpɜːp əs ɪv ‖ ˈpɜ˞ːp- pᵊr ˈpoʊs- **~ly** li **~ness** nəs nɪs
purpura ˈpɜːp jʊr ə -jər- ‖ ˈpɜ˞ːp jər ə -ər ə
purr pɜː ‖ pɜ˞ː **purred** pɜːd ‖ pɜ˞ːd **purring** ˈpɜːr ɪŋ ‖ ˈpɜ˞ː ɪŋ **purrs** pɜːz ‖ pɜ˞ːz
purse pɜːs ‖ pɜ˞ːs **pursed** pɜːst ‖ pɜ˞ːst **purses** ˈpɜːs ɪz -əz ‖ ˈpɜ˞ːs əz **pursing** ˈpɜːs ɪŋ ‖ ˈpɜ˞ːs ɪŋ
ˈpurse strings
purser ˈpɜːs ə ‖ ˈpɜ˞ːs ᵊr **~s** z
purse-snatch|er ˈpɜːs ˌsnætʃ |ə ‖ ˈpɜ˞ːs ˌsnætʃ |ᵊr **~ers** əz ‖ ᵊrz **~ing** ɪŋ
purslane ˈpɜːs lən -lɪn, -leɪn ‖ ˈpɜ˞ːs- **~s** z
pursuance pə ˈsjuːˌən*t*s -ˈsuːˌ ‖ pᵊr ˈsuː-
pursuant pə ˈsjuːˌənt -ˈsuːˌ ‖ pᵊr ˈsuː- **~ly** li
pur|sue pə |ˈsjuː -ˈsuː ‖ pᵊr |ˈsuː **~sued** ˈsjuːd ˈsuːd ‖ ˈsuːd **~sues** ˈsjuːz ˈsuːz ‖ ˈsuːz **~suing** ˈsjuːˌɪŋ ˈsuːˌ ‖ ˈsuː ɪŋ
pursuer pə ˈsjuːˌə -ˈsuːˌ ‖ pᵊr ˈsuːˌᵊr **~s** z
pursuit pə ˈsjuːt -ˈsuːt ‖ pᵊr ˈsuːt **~s** s

pursuivant ˈpɜːs ɪv ənt -əv-, -wɪv- ‖ ˈpɜːs- **~s** s
purty *non-standard form of* pretty ˈpɜːt i ‖ ˈpɜːţ i
purulenc|e ˈpjʊər ʊl ənᵗs -jʊl-, -əl- ‖ ˈpjʊr əl- -jəl- **~y** i
purulent ˈpjʊər ʊl ənᵗs -jʊl-, -əl- ‖ ˈpjʊr əl- -jəl- **~ly** li
Purves ˈpɜːv ɪs §-əs ‖ ˈpɜːv əs
purvey pə ˈveɪ pɜː- ‖ pᵊr ˈveɪ ˈpɜːv eɪ **~ed** d **~ing** ɪŋ **~s** z
purveyance pə ˈveɪ ənᵗs pɜː- ‖ pᵊr-
purveyor pə ˈveɪ ə pɜː- ‖ pᵊr ˈveɪ ᵊr **~s** z
purview ˈpɜː vjuː ‖ ˈpɜː- **~s** z
Purvis ˈpɜːv ɪs §-əs ‖ ˈpɜːv əs
pus pʌs
Pusan ˌpuː ˈsæn ‖ -ˈsɑːn —*Korean* [pu san]
Pusey ˈpjuːz i
Puseyite ˈpjuːz i aɪt **~s** s
push pʊʃ **pushed** pʊʃt **pushes** ˈpʊʃ ɪz -əz **pushing** ˈpʊʃ ɪŋ
ˈpush ˌbutton
pushbike ˈpʊʃ baɪk **~s** s
push-button ˈpʊʃ ˌbʌt ᵊn
pushcart ˈpʊʃ kɑːt ‖ -kɑːrt **~s** s
push-chain ˈpʊʃ tʃeɪn **~s** z
pushchair ˈpʊʃ tʃeə ‖ -tʃer **~s** z
pushdown ˈpʊʃ daʊn
pusher ˈpʊʃ ə ‖ -ᵊr **~s** z
pushful ˈpʊʃ fᵊl -fʊl **-ly** ͜i **~ness** nəs nɪs
Pushkin ˈpʊʃ kɪn —*Russ* [ˈpuʃ kʲɪn]
pushover ˈpʊʃ ˌəʊv ə ‖ -ˌoʊv ᵊr **~s** z
pushpin ˈpʊʃ pɪn **~s** z
push-pull ˌpʊʃ ˈpʊl ◂
pushrod ˈpʊʃ rɒd ‖ -rɑːd **~s** z
push-|start ˈpʊʃ |stɑːt ˌ·ˈ· ‖ -|stɑːrt **~started** stɑːtɪd -əd ‖ stɑːrţ əd **~starting** stɑːt ɪŋ ‖ stɑːrţ ɪŋ **~starts** stɑːts ‖ stɑːrts
Push|to ˈpʌʃ| təʊ ‖ -toʊ **~tu** tuː
push-up ˈpʊʃ ʌp **~s** s
push|y ˈpʊʃ |i **~ier** i ͜ə ‖ i ͜ᵊr **~iest** i ͜ɪst i ͜əst **~ily** ɪ li əl i **~iness** i nəs i nɪs
pusillanimity ˌpjuːs ɪl ə ˈnɪm ət i ˌpjuːz-, ˌ·əl-, -æˈ·-, -ɪt i ‖ -əţ i
pusillanimous ˌpjuːs ɪ ˈlæn ɪm əs ◂ ˌpjuːz-, ˌ·ə-, -əm əs **~ly** li
puss pʊs **pusses** ˈpʊs ɪz -əz
ˈpuss moth
puss|y *n* ˈpʊs |i **~ies** iz
ˌpussy ˈwillow
pussy *adj, 'purulent'* ˈpʌs i
pussycat ˈpʊs i kæt **~s** s
pussy|foot ˈpʊs i |fʊt **~footed** fʊt ɪd -əd ‖ fʊţ əd **~footer/s** fʊt ə/z ‖ fʊţ ᵊr/z **~footing** fʊtɪŋ ‖ fʊţ ɪŋ **~foots** fʊts
pustular ˈpʌst jʊl ə -jəl-; →ˈpʌs tʃʊl ə, -tʃəl- ‖ ˈpʌs tʃəl ᵊr
pustule ˈpʌst juːl →ˈpʌs tʃuːl ‖ ˈpʌs tʃuːl **~s** z
put pʊt **puts** pʊts **putting** ˈpʊt ɪŋ
putative ˈpjuːt ət ɪv ‖ ˈpjuːţ əţ ɪv **~ly** li
put-down ˈpʊt daʊn **~s** z
Putin ˈpuːt ɪn -ᵊn —*Russ* [ˈpu tʲɪn]
Putnam ˈpʌt nəm
Putney ˈpʌt ni
put-off ˈpʊt ɒf -ɔːf ‖ ˈpʊţ ɔːf -ɑːf **~s** s
put-on ˈpʊt ɒn ‖ ˈpʊţ ɑːn -ɔːn **~s** z
putonghua ˌpuː tɒŋ ˈhwɑː ‖ -tɔːŋ- -tɑːŋ- —*Chinese* pǔtōnghuà [³pʰu ¹tʰʊŋ ⁴xwa]
put-|put ˈpʌt |pʌt ˌ·ˈ·. **~puts** pʌts **~putted** pʌt ɪd -əd ‖ pʌţ əd **~putting** pʌt ɪŋ ‖ pʌţ ɪŋ
putrefaction ˌpjuːtr ɪ ˈfæk ʃᵊn -ə-
putrefactive ˌpjuːtr ɪ ˈfækt ɪv ◂ -ə-
putre|fy ˈpjuːtr ɪ |faɪ -ə- **~fied** faɪd **~fies** faɪz **~fying** faɪ ɪŋ
putresc|ence pjuː ˈtres |ᵊnᵗs **~ent** ᵊnt
putrid ˈpjuːtr ɪd §-əd
putridity pjuː ˈtrɪd ət i -ɪt- ‖ -əţ i
putrid|ly ˈpjuːtr ɪd |li §-əd- **~ness** nəs nɪs
putsch pʊtʃ **putsches** ˈpʊtʃ ɪz -əz
putt pʌt **putted** ˈpʌt ɪd -əd ‖ ˈpʌţ əd **putting** ˈpʌt ɪŋ ‖ ˈpʌţ ɪŋ **putts** pʌts
puttanesca ˌpʊt ə ˈnesk ə →-ᵊn ˈesk- ‖ ˌpuː tɑː ˈnesk ɑː —*It* [put ta ˈne ska]
puttee ˈpʌt i -iː, pʌ ˈtiː ‖ pʌ ˈtiː **~s** z
Puttenham ˈpʌt ᵊn͜əm
putter *v; n 'golfer, golf club'* ˈpʌt ə ‖ ˈpʌţ ᵊr **~s** z
putter *n 'one that puts'* ˈpʊt ə ‖ ˈpʊţ ᵊr **~s** z
putti *plural of* putto ˈpʊt i -iː ‖ ˈpuːt iː
puttie... —*see* **putty**
putting *pres part of* **putt** ˈpʌt ɪŋ ‖ ˈpʌţ ɪŋ
ˈputting green
putting *pres ptcp of* **put** ˈpʊt ɪŋ ‖ ˈpʊţ ɪŋ
Puttnam ˈpʌt nəm
putto ˈpʊt əʊ ‖ ˈpuːt oʊ **putti** ˈpʊt i -iː ‖ ˈpuːt iː
putt|y ˈpʌt |i ‖ ˈpʌţ |i **~ied** id **~ies** iz **~ying** i ɪŋ
put-up ˈpʊt ʌp ‖ ˈpʊţ ʌp
put-upon ˈpʊt ə ˌpɒn ‖ ˈpʊţ ə ˌpɑːn -ˌpɔːn
Put-U-Up *tdmk* ˈpʊt ju ʌp →ˈpʊtʃ u- ‖ ˈpʊtʃ u-
putz pʌts pʊts **putzes** ˈpʌts ɪz ˈpʊts-, -əz
Puy-de-Dôme ˌpwiː də ˈdəʊm ‖ -ˈdoʊm —*Fr* [pɥi͜ də doːm]
puzzl|e ˈpʌz ᵊl **~ed** d **~es** z **~ing/ly** ͜ɪŋ /li
puzzlement ˈpʌz ᵊl mənt
puzzler ˈpʌz ᵊl͜ə ‖ ᵊr **~s** z
PVC ˌpiː viː ˈsiː ◂
Pwllheli pə ˈθel i pʊ-, -ˈɬel-, pʊθ ˈlel i —*Welsh* [puːɬ ˈhe li, pʊɬ-]
PX ˌpiː ˈeks **~s** ɪz əz
pyaemia paɪ ˈiːm i͜ə
Pybus ˈpaɪb əs
Pydna ˈpɪd nə
Pye paɪ
Pyecombe ˈpaɪ kuːm
pye-dog ˈpaɪ dɒg ‖ -dɔːg -dɑːg **~s** z
pyelo- *comb. form*
with stress-neutral suffix ˈpaɪ͜ə ləʊ ‖ ˈpaɪ ə loʊ — **pyelogram** ˈpaɪ͜ə ləʊ græm ‖ ˈpaɪ ə loʊ-
with stress-imposing suffix ˌpaɪ͜ə ˈlɒ+ ‖ -ˈlɑː+ — **pyelography** ˌpaɪ͜ə ˈlɒg rəf i ‖ -ˈlɑːg-
pyemia paɪ ˈiːm i͜ə
pygmaean pɪg ˈmiː͜ən
Pygmalion pɪg ˈmeɪl i͜ən

pygmean pɪɡ ˈmiː‿ən
pygmy, Pygmy ˈpɪɡ mi **pygmies, P~** ˈpɪɡ miz
pyjama pə ˈdʒɑːm ə pɪ-, ⚠bə- ‖ -ˈdʒæm- **~s** z
Pyke paɪk
pyknic ˈpɪk nɪk *(= picnic)*
pylon ˈpaɪl ən -ɒn ‖ -ɑːn **~s** z
pyloric paɪ ˈlɒr ɪk -ˈlɔːr- ‖ -ˈlɔːr ɪk -ˈloʊr-
pylor|us paɪ ˈlɔːr |əs ‖ -ˈloʊr- **~i** aɪ iː
Pylos ˈpaɪl ɒs ‖ -ɑːs
Pym, Pymm pɪm
Pynchon ˈpɪntʃ ən
pyo- *comb. form*
with stress-neutral suffix ¦paɪ əʊ ‖ -ə
— **pyogenic** ˌpaɪ əʊ ˈdʒen ɪk ◂ -ˈdʒiːn- ‖ -ə-
with stress-imposing suffix paɪ ˈɒ+ ‖ -ˈɑː+
— **pyogenous** paɪ ˈɒdʒ ən əs ‖ -ˈɑːdʒ-
pyoid ˈpaɪ ɔɪd
Pyongyang ˌpjɒŋ ˈjæŋ ‖ ˌpjʌŋ ˈjɑːŋ ˌpjɑːŋ- —*Korean* [pʰjɔŋ jaŋ]
pyorrhea, pyorrhoea ˌpaɪ‿ə ˈrɪə §-ˈriː‿ə ‖ ˌpaɪ ə ˈriː ə
pyosis paɪ ˈəʊs ɪs §-əs ‖ -ˈoʊs əs
pyracantha ˌparᵊr ə ˈkæntθ ə **~s** z
Pyrah ˈparᵊr ə
pyramid ˈpɪr ə mɪd **~ed** ɪd əd **~ing** ɪŋ **~s** z
ˈpyramid ˌselling ˌ· · · ˈ· ·
pyramidal pɪ ˈræm ɪd ᵊl pə-, §-əd ᵊl; ˈpɪr ə mɪd ᵊl, ˌ· ·ˈ· · ◂ **~ly** i
Pyramus ˈpɪr əm əs
pyran ˈparᵊr æn parᵊ ˈræn
pyrargyrite parᵊ ˈrɑːdʒ ə raɪt -ɪ- ‖ -ˈrɑːrdʒ-
pyre ˈpaɪ‿ə ‖ ˈpaɪ‿ᵊr **pyres** ˈpaɪ‿əz ‖ ˈpaɪ‿ᵊrz
pyrene ˈparᵊr iːn —*but in the sense 'nutlet', also* parᵊ ˈriːn **~s** z
Pyrene paɪ ˈriːn i
Pyrenean ˌpɪr ə ˈniː‿ən ◂ -ɪ- **~s** z
Pyrenees ˌpɪr ə ˈniːz -ɪ- ‖ ˈpɪr ə niːz *(*)*
pyrethrin parᵊ ˈriːθ rɪn §-rən ‖ -ˈreθ-
pyrethrum parᵊ ˈriːθ rəm ‖ -ˈreθ-
pyretic parᵊ ˈret ɪk ‖ -ˈreţ ɪk
Pyrex *tdmk* ˈparᵊr eks
pyrexia parᵊ ˈreks i‿ə
Pyrford ˈpɜː fəd ‖ ˈpɜː fᵊrd
pyridine ˈpɪr ɪ diːn -ə-
pyriform ˈpɪr ɪ fɔːm ˈparᵊr-, -ə- ‖ -fɔːrm
pyrimidine parᵊ ˈrɪm ɪ diːn -ə- ‖ pə-
pyrite ˈparᵊr aɪt
pyrites parᵊ ˈraɪt iːz pɪ-, pə-; ˈparᵊr aɪts ‖ pə ˈraɪţ iz
pyritic parᵊ ˈrɪt ɪk pɪ-, pə- ‖ -ˈrɪţ ɪk
pyro- *comb. form*
with stress-neutral suffix ¦parᵊr əʊ ‖ -ə
— **pyrophosphate** ˌparᵊr əʊ ˈfɒs feɪt ‖ -ə ˈfɑːs-
with stress-imposing suffix parᵊ ˈrɒ+ ‖ -ˈrɑː+
— **pyrolysis** parᵊ ˈrɒl əs ɪs -ɪs-, §-əs ‖ -ˈrɑːl-
pyroclastic ˌparᵊr əʊ ˈklæst ɪk ◂ ‖ -ə-
ˌpyroˌclastic ˈflow
pyrogall|ic ˌparᵊr əʊ ˈɡæl| ɪk ◂ ‖ -ə- **~ol** ɒl ‖ ɔːl -ɑːl, -oʊl
pyromania ˌparᵊr əʊ ˈmeɪn i‿ə ‖ ˌ·ə-
pyromaniac ˌparᵊr əʊ ˈmeɪn i æk ‖ ˌ·ə- **~s** s
pyrosis parᵊ ˈrəʊs ɪs §-əs ‖ -ˈroʊs əs
pyrotechnic ˌparᵊr əʊ ˈtek nɪk ◂ ‖ -ə- **~al** ᵊl **~ally** ᵊl‿i **~s** s
pyroxene parᵊ ˈrɒks iːn ‖ -ˈrɑːks- pə-
Pyrrha ˈpɪr ə
Pyrrhic, p~ ˈpɪr ɪk **~s** s
Pyrrho ˈpɪr əʊ ‖ -oʊ
Pyrrhus ˈpɪr əs
pyrrole ˈpɪr əʊl →-ɒʊl; pɪ ˈrəʊl, §pə- ‖ ˈpɪr oʊl
pyruvic parᵊ ˈruːv ɪk
Pytchley ˈpaɪtʃ li
Pythagoras paɪ ˈθæɡ ər əs -ə ræs ‖ pə- pɪ-
Pythagorean paɪ ˌθæɡ ə ˈriː‿ən ◂ ˌpaɪ θæɡ əˈ·- ‖ pə- pɪ- **~ism** ˌɪz əm **~s** z
Pytheas ˈpɪθ i‿əs -æs
Pythia ˈpɪθ i‿ə
Pythian ˈpɪθ i‿ən
Pythias ˈpɪθ i æs -i‿əs
python, P~ ˈpaɪθ ᵊn ‖ -ɑːn -ᵊn **~s** z
Pythonesque ˌpaɪθ ə ˈnesk ◂
pythoness ˈpaɪθ ə nes -ən ɪs, -ən əs ‖ -ən əs ˈpɪθ- **~es** ɪz əz
pythonic paɪ ˈθɒn ɪk pɪ- ‖ -ˈθɑːn-
pyuria paɪ ˈjʊər i‿ə ‖ -ˈjʊr-
pyx pɪks *(= picks)* **pyxes** ˈpɪks ɪz -əz
pyxie ˈpɪks i **~s** z

P

Qq

q Spelling-to-sound

1 Except in occasional words from foreign languages, the letter **q** is always followed by **u**. Where the spelling is the resultant digraph **qu**, the pronunciation is regularly
kw as in **quite** kwaɪt or
k as in **picturesque** ˌpɪk tʃə ˈresk.

2 The pronunciation is generally kw. Examples: **queen** kwiːn, **squeak** skwiːk, **equal** ˈiːk wəl, **liquid** ˈlɪk wɪd.

3 However, in the case of **que** at the end of a word, and in a minority of other words, the pronunciation is k. Examples: **clique** kliːk, **cheque** tʃek (AmE spelling: **check**), **queue** kjuː, **liquor** ˈlɪk ə ‖ ˈlɪk ᵊr.

4 Where the spelling is **cqu**, the pronunciation is again either kw as in **acquaint** ə ˈkweɪnt or k as in **lacquer** ˈlæk ə ‖ ˈlæk ᵊr.

Q, q kjuː **Q's, q's, Qs, qs** kjuːz —*Communications code name:* Quebec
'Q ˌfever
Qaddafi, Qadhafi gə ˈdɑːf i -ˈdæf- —*Arabic* [ɣað ˈðaː fi]
Qaeda —*see* **Al-Qaeda**
Qantas *tdmk* ˈkwɒnt əs -æs ‖ ˈkwɑːnt-
qat kɑːt —*Arabic* [qaːt]
Qatar ˈkæt ɑː ˈgæt-, ˈkʌt-, ˈgʌt-; gæ ˈtɑː, kæ-, kə- ‖ ˈkɑːt ɑːr kə ˈtɑːr —*Arabic* [ˈqɑ tˤɑr]
Qatari kæ ˈtɑːr i gæ-, kə- **~s** z
QC, Q.C. ˌkjuː ˈsiː **~s, ~'s** z
QE2 ˌkjuː iː ˈtuː
QED, q.e.d. ˌkjuː iː ˈdiː
qi tʃiː —*Chi* qì [⁴tɕʰi]
qibla, qiblah ˈkɪb lə ‖ —*Arabic* [ˈqib lah]
Qin *dynasty* tʃɪn —*Chinese* Qín [²tɕʰɪn]
Qinetiq *tdmk* kɪ ˈnet ɪk ‖ -ˈneţ-
Qing *dynasty* tʃɪŋ —*Chinese* Qīng [¹tɕʰɪŋ]
Qingdao ˌtʃɪŋ ˈdaʊ —*Chinese* Qīngdǎo [¹tɕʰɪŋ ³tɑu]
Qinghai ˌtʃɪŋ ˈhaɪ —*Chinese* Qīnghǎi [¹tɕʰɪŋ ³xai]
Qom kʊm kɒm, xʊm —*Persian* [ɢom]
qoph kɒf kɔːf, kʊf, kəʊf ‖ kɔːf kɑːf, koʊf
Q-rating ˈkjuː ˌreɪt ɪŋ ‖ -ˌreɪţ ɪŋ
qt, q.t. ˌkjuː ˈtiː
Q-Tip *tdmk* ˈkjuː tɪp **~s** s
qua kweɪ kwɑː
Quaalude *tdmk* ˈkweɪ luːd **~s** z
quack kwæk **quacked** kwækt **quacking** ˈkwæk ɪŋ **quacks** kwæks
quackery ˈkwæk ər i
quad kwɒd ‖ kwɑːd **quads** kwɒdz ‖ kwɑːdz
Quadragesim|a ˌkwɒdr ə ˈdʒes ɪm |ə -əm ə ‖ ˌkwɑːdr- **~al** ᵊl
quadrangle ˈkwɒdr æŋ gᵊl ‖ ˈkwɑːdr- **~s** z
quadrangular kwɒ ˈdræŋ gjʊl ə -gjəl- ‖ kwɑː ˈdræŋ gjəl ᵊr
quadrant ˈkwɒdr ənt ‖ ˈkwɑːdr- **~s** s
quadrantal kwɒ ˈdrænt ᵊl ‖ kwɑː ˈdrænţ ᵊl
quadraphonic ˌkwɒdr ə ˈfɒn ɪk ◂ ‖ ˌkwɑːdr ə ˈfɑːn ɪk ◂ **~ally** ᵊl‿i **~s** s
quadraphony kwɒ ˈdrɒf ən i -ˈdræf-; ˈkwɒdr ə fɒn i ‖ kwɑː ˈdrɑːf- ˈkwɑːdr ə fɑːn i
quadrasonic ˌkwɒdr ə ˈsɒn ɪk ◂ ‖ ˌkwɑːdr ə ˈsɑːn ɪk ◂ **~ally** ᵊl‿i **~s** s
quadrat ˈkwɒdr ət -æt ‖ ˈkwɑːdr- **~s** s
quadr|ate *v* kwɒ ˈdr|eɪt ‖ ˈkwɑːdr |eɪt **~ated** eɪt ɪd -əd ‖ eɪţ əd **~ates** eɪts **~ating** eɪt ɪŋ ‖ eɪţ ɪŋ
quadrate *n, adj* ˈkwɒdr eɪt -ət, -ɪt ‖ ˈkwɑːdr- **~s** s
quadratic kwɒ ˈdræt ɪk ‖ kwɑː ˈdræţ ɪk **~s** s
quaˌdratic e'quation
quadrature ˈkwɒdr ətʃ ə -ɪtʃ-; -ət jʊə, -ɪt- ‖ ˈkwɑːdr ətʃ ᵊr -ə tʃʊr, -ə tʊr **~s** z
quadrenni|al kwɒ ˈdren i‿|əl ‖ kwɑː- **~a** ə **~ally** əl‿i **~um** əm

quadri- *comb. form*
with stress-neutral suffix ˈkwɒdr ɪ -ə ‖ ˈkwɑːdr ə — **quadrilingual** ˌkwɒdr ɪ ˈlɪŋ gwəl ◂ -ə-, §-ˈlɪŋ gju‿əl ‖ ˌkwɑːdr ə-
with stress-imposing suffix kwɒ ˈdrɪ+ ‖ kwɑː- — **quadripara** kwɒ ˈdrɪp ər ə ‖ kwɑː-

quadric ˈkwɒdr ɪk ‖ ˈkwɑːdr ɪk

quadriceps ˈkwɒdr ɪ seps -ə- ‖ ˈkwɑːdr- **~es** ɪz əz

quadriga kwɒ ˈdriːg ə kwə-, -ˈdraɪg- ‖ kwɑː- **~s** z

quadrilateral ˌkwɒdr ɪ ˈlæt‿ᵊr əl ◂ ˌ·ə- ‖ ˌkwɑːdr ə ˈlæţ ər əl ◂ →-ˈlætr əl **~s** z

quadrilingual ˌkwɒdr ɪ ˈlɪŋ gwəl ◂ -ə- ‖ ˌkwɑːdr- **~ly** i **~s** z

quadrille kwə ˈdrɪl kwɒ- ‖ kwɑː- **~s** z

quadrillion kwɒ ˈdrɪl jən -i‿ən ‖ kwɑː ˈdrɪl jən **~s** z

quadrinomial ˌkwɒdr ɪ ˈnəʊm i‿əl ◂ ˌ·ə- ‖ ˌkwɑːdr ə ˈnoʊm- **~s** z

quadripartite ˌkwɒdr ɪ ˈpɑːt aɪt ◂ -ə- ‖ ˌkwɑːdr ə ˈpɑːrt aɪt ◂

quadriplegia ˌkwɒdr ɪ ˈpliːdʒ i‿ə ˌ·ə-, -ˈpliːdʒ ə ‖ ˌkwɑːdr-

quadriplegic ˌkwɒdr ɪ ˈpliːdʒ ɪk ◂ ˌ·ə- ‖ ˌkwɑːdr- **~s** s

quadrivium kwɒ ˈdrɪv i‿əm ‖ kwɑː-

quadroon kwɒ ˈdruːn ‖ kwɑː- **~s** z

quadrophonic ˌkwɒdr ə ˈfɒn ɪk ◂ ‖ ˌkwɑːdr ə ˈfɑːn ɪk ◂ **~ally** ᵊl‿i **~s** s

quadrophony kwɒ ˈdrɒf ən i ˈkwɒdr ə fɒn i ‖ kwɑː ˈdrɑːf- ˈkwɑːdr ə fɑːn i

quadrumanous kwɒ ˈdruːm ən əs ‖ kwɑː-

quadruped ˈkwɒdr u ped -ə- ‖ ˈkwɑːdr ə- **~s** z

quadrupl|e ˈkwɒdr ʊp ᵊl -əp-; kwɒ ˈdruːp- ‖ kwɑː ˈdruːp ᵊl -ˈdrʌp-; ˈkwɑːdr əp- **~ed** d **~es** z **~ing** ‿ɪŋ

quadruplet ˈkwɒdr ʊp lət -əp-, -lɪt, -let; kwɒ ˈdruːp-, §-ˈdrʌp- ‖ kwɑː ˈdruːp- -ˈdrʌp-; ˈkwɑːdr əp- **~s** s

quadruplex ˈkwɒdr u pleks -ə-; kwɒ ˈdruːp leks ‖ ˈkwɑːdr ə pleks kwɑː ˈdruːp leks

quadruplicate *adj* kwɒ ˈdruːp lɪk ət -lək ət, -ɪt; -lɪ keɪt, -lə- ‖ kwɑː- **~s** s

quadrupli|cate *v* kwɒ ˈdruːp lɪ |keɪt -lə- ‖ kwɑː- **~cated** keɪt ɪd -əd ‖ keɪţ əd **~cates** keɪts **~cating** keɪt ɪŋ ‖ keɪţ ɪŋ

quadruply ˈkwɒdr ʊp li -əp-; kwɒ ˈdruːp- ‖ kwɑː ˈdruːp li -ˈdrʌp-; ˈkwɑːdr əp-

quaestor ˈkwiːst ə ˈkwaɪst-, -ɔː ‖ ˈkwest ᵊr ˈkwiːst- **~s** z

quaff kwɒf kwɑːf ‖ kwɑːf kwæf **quaffed** kwɒft kwɑːft ‖ kwɑːft kwæft **quaffing** ˈkwɒf ɪŋ ˈkwɑːf- ‖ ˈkwɑːf ɪŋ ˈkwæf- **quaffs** kwɒfs kwɑːfs ‖ kwɑːfs kwæfs

quaffer ˈkwɒf ə ˈkwɑːf- ‖ ˈkwɑːf ᵊr ˈkwæf- **~s** z

quag kwæg kwɒg ‖ kwɑːg **quags** kwægz kwɒgz ‖ kwɑːgz

quagga ˈkwæg ə ˈkwɒg- ‖ ˈkwɑːg- **~s** z

quagg|y ˈkwæg |i ˈkwɒg- ‖ ˈkwɑːg- **~ier** i‿ə ‖ i‿ᵊr **~iest** i‿ɪst i‿əst **~iness** i nəs i nɪs

Quaglino's *tdmk* kwæg ˈliːn əʊz ‖ kwɑːg ˈliːn oʊz

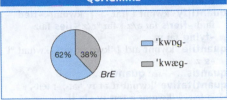

QUAGMIRE

62% 38%
BrE
ˈkwɒg-
ˈkwæg-

quagmire ˈkwɒg maɪ‿ə ˈkwæg- ‖ ˈkwæg maɪ‿ᵊr ˈkwɑːg- — *Preference poll, BrE:* ˈkwɒg- *62%,* ˈkwæg- *38%.* **~s** z

quahog ˈkwɑː hɒg ‖ ˈkwɔː hɔːg ˈkwɑː-, ˈkwoʊ-, ˈkoʊ-, -hɑːg **~s** z

Quaid kweɪd

Quai d'Orsay ˌkeɪ ˈdɔːs eɪ ‖ -dɔːr ˈseɪ —*Fr* [ke dɔʁ sɛ]

quail, Quail kweɪᵊl **quailed** kweɪᵊld **quailing** ˈkweɪᵊl ɪŋ **quails** kweɪᵊlz

Quain kweɪn

quaint kweɪnt **quainter** ˈkweɪnt ə ‖ ˈkweɪnţ ᵊr **quaintest** ˈkweɪnt ɪst -əst ‖ ˈkweɪnţ-

quaint|ly ˈkweɪnt |li **~ness** nəs nɪs

quake kweɪk **quaked** kweɪkt **quakes** kweɪks **quaking** ˈkweɪk ɪŋ

quake-proof ˈkweɪk pruːf §-prʊf **~ed** t **~ing** ɪŋ **~s** s

Quaker ˈkweɪk ə ‖ -ᵊr **~ly** li **~s** z

Quakerism ˈkweɪk ər ˌɪz əm

quak|y ˈkweɪk |i **~ier** i‿ə ‖ i‿ᵊr **~iest** i‿ɪst i‿əst **~ily** ɪ li əl i **~iness** i nəs i nɪs

Qualcast *tdmk* ˈkwɒl kɑːst -§kæst ‖ ˈkwɑːl kæst

Qualcomm *tdmk* ˈkwɒl kɒm ‖ ˈkwɑːl kɑːm

qualia ˈkweɪl i‿ə

qualification ˌkwɒl ɪf ɪ ˈkeɪʃ ᵊn ˌ·əf-, §-əˈ·- ‖ ˌkwɑːl- **~s** z

qualificative ˈkwɒl ɪf ɪk ət ɪv ˈ·əf-; -ɪ keɪt ɪv, -ə ·-; ˌ·ɪ ˈkeɪt ɪv◂, -əˈ· · ‖ ˈkwɑːl əf ə keɪţ ɪv

qualificatory ˌkwɒl ɪf ɪ ˈkeɪt ər‿i ˌ·əf-, §-əˈ·- ‖ ˈkwɑːl əf ɪk ə tɔːri ˈ·ɪf-, -toʊr i

quali|fy ˈkwɒl ɪ |faɪ -ə- ‖ ˈkwɑːl- **~fied** faɪd **~fier/s** faɪ‿ə/z ‖ faɪ‿ᵊr/z **~fies** faɪz **~fying** faɪ ɪŋ

qualitative ˈkwɒl ɪt ət ɪv ˈ·ət-; -ɪ teɪt-, -ə teɪt- ‖ ˈkwɑːl ə teɪţ ɪv **~ly** li

qualit|y ˈkwɒl ət |i -ɪt- ‖ ˈkwɑːl əţ |i **~ies** iz

qualm kwɑːm kwɔːm, §kwɑːlm ‖ kwɔːm, kwɑːlm **qualms** kwɑːmz kwɔːmz, §kwɑːlmz ‖ kwɔːmz, kwɑːlmz

qualmish ˈkwɑːm ɪʃ ˈkwɔːm-, §ˈkwɑːlm- ‖ ˈkwɔːm-, ˈkwɑːlm- **~ly** li **~ness** nəs nɪs

quandar|y ˈkwɒnd‿ər |i ‖ ˈkwɑːnd‿ **~ies** iz

quandong ˈkwɒnd ɒŋ ‖ ˈkwɑːnd ɑːŋ **~s** z

quango ˈkwæŋ gəʊ ‖ -goʊ **~s** z

Quant, quant kwɒnt ‖ kwɑːnt

quant|a ˈkwɒnt |ə ‖ ˈkwɑːnţ |ə **~al** ᵊl

Quantel *tdmk* ˌkwɒn ˈtel ˈ· · ‖ ˌkwɑːn-

quantic ˈkwɒnt ɪk ‖ ˈkwɑːnţ ɪk

quantifiable ˈkwɒnt ɪ faɪ‿əb əl ˈ-ə-, ˌ·ˈ·ˈ· · · ‖ ˈkwɑːnt̬-

quantification ˌkwɒnt ɪf ɪ ˈkeɪʃ ən ˌ·əf-, §- ‖ ˌkwɑːnt̬-

quanti|fy ˈkwɒnt ɪ |faɪ -ə- ‖ ˈkwɑːnt̬- **~fied** faɪd **~fier/s** faɪ‿ə/z ‖ faɪ‿ər/z **~fies** faɪz **~fying** faɪ ɪŋ

quantile ˈkwɒnt aɪəl ‖ ˈkwɑːnt aɪəl ˈkwɑːnt̬ əl **~s** z

quantis... —*see* **quantiz...**

quantitative ˈkwɒnt ɪt ət ɪv ˈ-ət-; -ɪ teɪt-, -ə teɪt- ‖ ˈkwɑːnt̬ ə teɪt̬ ɪv **~ly** li

quantit|y ˈkwɒnt ət |i -ɪt- ‖ˈkwɑːnt̬ ət̬ |i **~ies** iz

ˈquantity surˌveyor, ˌ· · · ·ˈ·

quantization ˌkwɒnt aɪ ˈzeɪʃ ən -ɪ- ‖ ˌkwɑːnt̬ ə-

quantiz|e ˈkwɒnt aɪz ‖ ˈkwɑːnt- **~ed** d **~es** ɪz əz **~ing** ɪŋ

Quantock ˈkwɒnt ək -ɒk ‖ ˈkwɑːnt ɑːk **~s** s

quant|um ˈkwɒnt |əm ‖ ˈkwɑːnt̬ |əm **~a** ə **ˌquantum ˈjump**; **ˌquantum ˈleap**; **ˌquantum meˈchanics**; **ˈquantum ˌtheory**

quarantin|e ˈkwɒr ən tiːn ‖ ˈkwɔːr- ˈkwɑːr- **~ed** d **~es** z **~ing** ɪŋ

quark *'soft cheese'* kwɑːk ‖ kwɑːrk —*Ger* [kvaʁk]

quark *'elementary particle'* kwɑːk kwɔːk ‖ kwɑːrk kwɔːrk **quarks** kwɑːks kwɔːks ‖ kwɑːrks kwɔːrks

QuarkXPress ˌkwɑːk ɪk ˈspres -ek-, -ək- ‖ ˌkwɑːrk- ˌkwɔːrk-

Quarles kwɔːlz kɔːlz ‖ kwɔːrlz

Quarndon ˈkwɔːn dən ˈkɔːn- ‖ ˈkwɔːrn-

quarrel ˈkwɒr əl ‖ ˈkwɑːr əl ˈkwɔːr- **~ed, ~led** d **~ing, ~ling** ɪŋ **~s** z

quarreler, quarreller ˈkwɒr əl ə ‖ ˈkwɑːr əl ər ˈkwɔːr- **~s** z

quarrelsome ˈkwɒr əl səm ‖ ˈkwɑːr- ˈkwɔːr- **~ly** li **~ness** nəs nɪs

quarr|y, Q~ ˈkwɒr |i ‖ ˈkwɑːr |i ˈkwɔːr- **~ied** id **~ies** iz **~ying** i ɪŋ

quarry|man ˈkwɒr i mən -mæn ‖ ˈkwɑːr- ˈkwɔːr- **~men** mən men

quart *'two pints'* kwɔːt kɔːt ‖ kwɔːrt **quarts** kwɔːts kɔːts ‖ kwɔːrts

quart *in fencing; at cards* kɑːt ‖ kɑːrt

quartan ˈkwɔːt ən ˈkɔːt- ‖ ˈkwɔːrt ən **~s** z

quarte kɑːt ‖ kɑːrt —*Fr* [kaʁt]

QUARTER

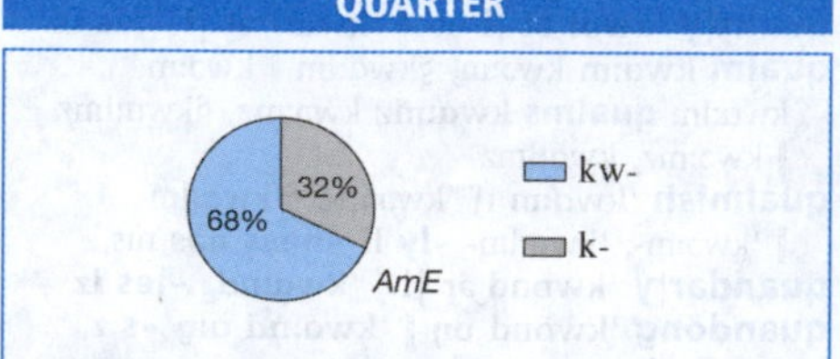

quart|er ˈkwɔːt |ə ˈkɔːt- ‖ ˈkwɔːrt̬ |ər ˈkɔːrt̬- —*AmE also occasionally dissimilated to* ˈkwɔːt̬ ər, ˈkɔːt̬ ər, *and similarly in compounds.* — *Preference poll, AmE:* kw- *68%,* k- *32%.* **~ered** əd ‖ ərd **~ering/s** ər ɪŋ/z **~ers** əz ‖ ərz **ˈquarter day**; **ˈquarter note**; **ˈquarter ˌsessions**

quarterback ˈkwɔːt ə bæk ˈkɔːt- ‖ ˈkwɔːrt̬ ər- ˈkɔːrt̬- **~s** s

quarterdeck ˈkwɔːt ə dek ˈkɔːt- ‖ ˈkwɔːrt̬ ər- **~s** s

quarterfinal ˌkwɔːt ə ˈfaɪn əl ˌkɔːt- ‖ ˌkwɔːrt̬ ər- **~ist/s** ɪst/s §əst/s **~s** z

quarterlight ˈkwɔːt ə laɪt ˈkɔːt-, -əl aɪt ‖ ˈkwɔːrt̬ ər- **~s** s

quarter|ly ˈkwɔːt ə|l i ˈkɔːt- ‖ ˈkwɔːrt̬ ər |li **~lies** liz

Quartermaine ˈkwɔːt ə meɪn ˈkɔːt- ‖ ˈkwɔːrt̬ ər-

quartermaster ˈkwɔːt ə ˌmɑːst ə ˈkɔːt-, §-ˌmæst- ‖ ˈkwɔːrt̬ ər ˌmæst ər **~s** z **ˌquarterˌmaster ˈgeneral**; **ˌquarterˌmaster ˈsergeant**

quartern ˈkwɔːt ən ˈkɔːt- ‖ ˈkwɔːrt̬ ərn **~s** z

quarter|staff ˈkwɔːt ə |stɑːf ˈkɔːt-, §-stæf ‖ ˈkwɔːrt̬ ər |stæf **~staves** steɪvz -stɑːvz

quartet, quartette ⁽ˌ⁾kwɔː ˈtet ⁽ˌ⁾kɔː- ‖ ⁽ˌ⁾kwɔːr- **~s** s

quartic ˈkwɔːt ɪk ˈkɔːt- ‖ ˈkwɔːrt̬ ɪk **~s** s

quartile ˈkwɔːt aɪəl ˈkɔːt- ‖ ˈkwɔːrt aɪəl ˈkwɔːrt̬ əl **~s** z

quarto ˈkwɔːt əʊ ˈkɔːt- ‖ ˈkwɔːrt̬ oʊ **~s** z

quartz kwɔːts kɔːts ‖ kwɔːrts *(= quarts)*

quartzite ˈkwɔːts aɪt ˈkɔːts- ‖ ˈkwɔːrts-

quasar ˈkweɪz ɑː ˈkweɪs- ‖ -ɑːr **~s** z

quash kwɒʃ ‖ kwɑːʃ **quashed** kwɒʃt ‖ kwɑːʃt **quashes** ˈkwɒʃ ɪz -əz ‖ ˈkwɑːʃ əz **quashing** ˈkwɒʃ ɪŋ ‖ ˈkwɑːʃ ɪŋ

Quashi, Quashie ˈkwɒʃ i ˈkwɑːʃ- ‖ ˈkwɑːʃ i

quasi ˈkweɪz aɪ ˈkweɪs-, ˈkwɑːz-, ˈkwæz-, -i

quasi- ¦kweɪz aɪ ¦kweɪs-, ¦kwɑːz-, ¦kwæz-, -i — **quasi-judicial** ˌkweɪz aɪ dʒu ˈdɪʃ əl ◂ ˌkweɪs-, ˌkwɑːz-, ˌkwæz-, ˌ·i-

Quasimodo ˌkwɑːz ɪ ˈməʊd əʊ ˌkwɒz-, ˌkwæz- ‖ -ˈmoʊd oʊ —*Formerly* ˌkweɪs aɪ-. *The Italian poet was* kwa ˈziː mo do, kwa zi ˈmɔː do.

quassia ˈkwɒʃ ə ˈkwɒʃ i‿ə ‖ ˈkwɑːʃ ə

quatercentenary ˌkwæt ə sen ˈtiːn ər i ˌkwɒt-, ˌkweɪt-, -ˈten- ‖ ˌkwɑːt̬ ər sen ˈten ər i -ˈsent ən er i

Quatermain ˈkwɔːt ə meɪn ˈkɔːt- ‖ ˈkwɑːt̬ ər-

Quatermass ˈkweɪt ə mæs ‖ ˈkweɪt̬ ər-

quaternar|y, Q~ kwə ˈtɜːn ər |i kwɒ- ‖ ˈkwɑːt̬ ər ner |i kwə ˈtɜːn ər |i **~ies** iz

quaternion kwə ˈtɜːn i‿ən kwɒ- ‖ kwə ˈtɜːn- kwɑː- **~s** z

quatrain ˈkwɒtr eɪn -ən ‖ ˈkwɑːtr- **~s** z

quatrefoil ˈkætr ə fɔɪəl ‖ ˈkæt̬ ər- **~s** z

Quattro ˈkwɒtr əʊ ˈkwætr- ‖ ˈkwɑːtr oʊ

quattrocento ˌkwætr əʊ ˈtʃent əʊ ˌkwɒtr- ‖ ˌkwɑːtr oʊ ˈtʃent oʊ —*It* [kwat tro ˈtʃɛn to]

quaver ˈkweɪv ə ‖ -ər **~ed** d **quavering/ly** ˈkweɪv ər‿ɪŋ /li **~s** z

quay, Quay kiː ‖ keɪ, kweɪ *(in BrE, and in AmE mostly, = key)* —*but as a family name, usually* kweɪ **quays** kiːz ‖ keɪz, kweɪz
quayage 'kiː ɪdʒ ‖ 'keɪ-, 'kweɪ-
Quayle kweɪᵊl
quayside 'kiː saɪd ‖ 'keɪ-, 'kweɪ-
quean kwiːn *(= queen)* **queans** kwiːnz
Queanbeyan 'kwiːn biˌən →'kwiːm-
queas|y 'kwiːz |i **~ier** iˌə ‖ iˌᵊr **~iest** iˌɪst iˌəst **~ily** ɪ li əl i **~iness** i nəs i nɪs
Quebec, Québec kwɪ 'bek kwə-, kə- —*Fr* [ke bɛk]
Quebecer, Quebecker kwɪ 'bek ə kwə-, kə- ‖ -ᵊr **~s** z
Quebecois, Québécois, q~ ˌkeɪb e 'kwɑː ◂ ˌkeb-, -ɪ-, -ə- —*Fr* [ke be kwa]
quebracho keɪ 'brɑːtʃ əʊ kɪ- ‖ -oʊ —*Sp* [ke 'βra tʃo] **~s** z
Quechua 'ketʃ uˌə ‖ '·wɑː **~s** z
queen, Queen kwiːn **queened** kwiːnd **queening** 'kwiːn ɪŋ **queens** kwiːnz
₍ᵢ₎**Queen 'Anne**; **'queen cake**; ˌ**queen 'consort**; ˌ**Queen E'lizabeth**; ˌ**queen 'mother**; ˌ**Queen's 'Bench**, ˌ**Queen's 'Bench Diˌvision**; ˌ**Queen's 'Council**; ˌ**Queen's 'English**; ˌ**queen's 'evidence**
Queenborough 'kwiːn bərˌə ‖ -ˌbɜː oʊ
queendom 'kwiːn dəm
Queenie 'kwiːn i
queenlike 'kwiːn laɪk
queen|ly 'kwiːn |li **~liness** li nəs -nɪs
Queens kwiːnz
Queensberry 'kwiːnz bərˌi §-ˌber i ‖ -ˌber i
ˌ**Queensberry 'Rules** ‖ '· · ·
Queensferry 'kwiːnz ˌfer i
queen-size 'kwiːn saɪz
Queensland 'kwiːnz lənd -lænd —*In Australia usually* -lænd
Queenstown 'kwiːnz taʊn
Queensway 'kwiːnz weɪ
queer kwɪə ‖ kwɪᵊr **queerer** 'kwɪər ə ‖ 'kwɪr ᵊr **queerest** 'kwɪər ɪst -əst ‖ 'kwɪr əst
'Queer Street
queerish 'kwɪər ɪʃ ‖ 'kwɪr-
queer|ly 'kwɪə |li ‖ 'kwɪr- **~ness** nəs nɪs
quefrency 'kwiːf rənᵗs i
quel kel —*Fr* [kɛl]
quell kwel **quelled** kweld **quelling** 'kwel ɪŋ **quells** kwelz
Quellenforschung 'kwel ən ˌfɔːʃ ʊŋ ‖ -ˌfɔːrʃ- —*Ger* ['kvɛ lən ˌfɔʁ ʃʊŋ]
Quemoy kɪ 'mɔɪ ke- —*Chinese* Jīnmén [¹tɕɪn ²mən]
quench kwentʃ **quenched** kwentʃt **quenches** 'kwentʃ ɪz -əz **quenching** 'kwentʃ ɪŋ
quencher 'kwentʃ ə ‖ -ᵊr **~s** z
quenda 'kwend ə **~s** z
quenelle kə 'nel **~s** z
Quenington 'kwen ɪŋ tən
Quennell kwɪ 'nel kwə-; 'kwen ᵊl
Quentin 'kwent ɪn §-ən ‖ -ᵊn
quercitron 'kwɜː sɪtr ən ˌ·'· · ‖ 'kwɜː- **~s** z
queri... —*see* **query**

quern kwɜːn ‖ kwɜːn **querns** kwɜːnz ‖ kwɜːnz
querulous 'kwer ʊl əs -jʊl-, -əl- ‖ -əl əs **~ly** li **~ness** nəs nɪs
quer|y 'kwɪər |i ‖ 'kwɪr |i 'kwer- **~ied** id **~ies** iz **~ying** i ɪŋ
quesadilla ˌkeɪs ə 'diː ə **~s** z —*Sp* [ke sa 'ði ʎa, -ja]
quest kwest **quested** 'kwest ɪd -əd **questing** 'kwest ɪŋ **quests** kwests
Quested 'kwest ɪd -əd
question 'kwes tʃən →'kweʃ-, -tjən **~ed** d **~ing/ly** ɪŋ/ li **~s** z
'question mark; **'question ˌmaster**; **'question tag**; **'question time**; **'question word**
questionab|le 'kwes tʃən əb |ᵊl →'kweʃ-, '·tjən- **~leness** ᵊl nəs -nɪs **~ly** li
questioner 'kwes tʃən ə 'kweʃ-, -tjən- ‖ -ᵊr **~s** z

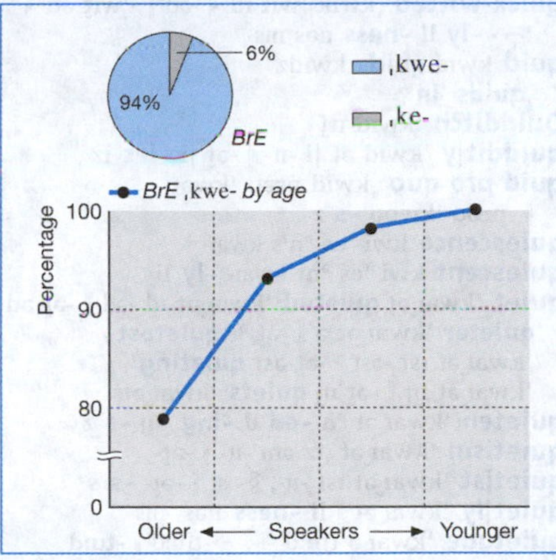

questionnaire ˌkwes tʃə 'neə ˌkes-, → ˌkweʃ-, ˌ·tiˌə', '· · · ‖ -'neᵊr -'næᵊr — *Preference poll, BrE:* 'kwe- *94% (born since 1973: 100%),* 'ke- *6%.* **~s** z
questor 'kwiːst ə 'kwaɪst-, -ɔː ‖ 'kwest ᵊr 'kwiːst- **~s** z
Quetta 'kwet ə ‖ 'kweṭ ə
quetzal 'kets ᵊl 'kwets-; ket 'sæl ‖ ket 'sɑːl -'sæl **~s** z
Quetzalcoatl ˌkets ᵊl kəʊ 'æt ᵊl ‖ ket 'sɑːl kwɑːṭ ᵊl ·'koʊ ˌɑːṭ ᵊl
queue kjuː *(! = cue)* **queued** kjuːd **queues** kjuːz **queuing** 'kjuːˌɪŋ
queue-jump 'kjuː dʒʌmp **~ed** t **~er/s** ə/z ‖ ᵊr/z **~ing** ɪŋ **~s** s
Quex kweks
Quezon 'keɪz ɒn 'keɪs- ‖ -ɑːn
ˌ**Quezon 'City**
Qufu ˌtʃuː 'fuː —*Chinese* Qūfù [¹tɕʰy ⁴fu]
quibbl|e 'kwɪb ᵊl **~ed** d **~er/s** ˌə/z ‖ ˌər/z **~es** z **~ing** ˌɪŋ
quiche kiːʃ **quiches** 'kiːʃ ɪz -əz

Q

quick, Quick kwɪk **quicker** 'kwɪk ə ‖ 'kwɪk ᵊr **quickest** 'kwɪk ɪst -əst

ˌ**quick 'march** ‖ '· ·

quick-and-dirty ˌkwɪk ən 'dɜːt i ◂ ‖ -'dɜːt i ◂

quick-change ˌkwɪk 'tʃeɪndʒ

quicken 'kwɪk ən **~ed** d **~ing** ‿ɪŋ **~s** z

quick-fire ˌkwɪk 'faɪ‿ə ◂ ‖ -'faɪ‿ᵊr

quick-|freeze ˌkwɪk |'friːz **~freezes** 'friːz ɪz -əz **~froze** 'frəʊz ‖ 'froʊz **~frozen** 'frəʊz ᵊn ◂ ‖ 'froʊz ᵊn ◂

quickie 'kwɪk i **~s** z

quicklime 'kwɪk laɪm

quickly, Q~ 'kwɪk li

quickness 'kwɪk nəs -nɪs

quicksand 'kwɪk sænd **~s** z

quickset 'kwɪk set

quicksilver 'kwɪk ˌsɪlv ə ‖ -ᵊr

quickstep 'kwɪk step **~s** s

quick-tempered ˌkwɪk 'temp əd ◂ ‖ -ᵊrd ◂ '·ˌ· ·

quickthorn 'kwɪk θɔːn ‖ -θɔːrn

quick-witted ˌkwɪk 'wɪt ɪd ◂ -əd ‖ -'wɪt̬ əd ◂ '·ˌ· · **~ly** li **~ness** nəs nɪs

quid kwɪd **quids** kwɪdz

ˌ**quids 'in**

Quidditch 'kwɪd ɪtʃ

quiddit|y 'kwɪd ət |i -ɪt- ‖ -ət̬ |i **~ies** iz

quid pro quo ˌkwɪd prəʊ 'kwəʊ ‖ -proʊ 'kwoʊ **~s** z

quiescence kwi 'es ᵊnᵗs kwaɪ-

quiescent kwi 'es ᵊnt kwaɪ- **~ly** li

quiet 'kwaɪ‿ət **quieted** 'kwaɪ‿ət ɪd -əd ‖ -ət̬ əd **quieter** 'kwaɪ‿ət ə ‖ -ət̬ ᵊr **quietest** 'kwaɪ‿ət ɪst -əst ‖ -ət̬ əst **quieting** 'kwaɪ‿ət ɪŋ ‖ -ət̬ ɪŋ **quiets** 'kwaɪ‿əts

quieten 'kwaɪ‿ət ᵊn **~ed** d **~ing** ‿ɪŋ **~s** z

quietism 'kwaɪ‿ət ˌɪz əm -ɪt- ‖ -ət̬-

quietist 'kwaɪ‿ət ɪst -ɪt-, §-əst ‖ -ət̬- **~s** s

quiet|ly 'kwaɪ‿ət ‖ li **~ness** nəs -nɪs

quietude 'kwaɪ‿ə tjuːd -ɪ-, →-tʃuːd ‖ -tuːd -tjuːd

quietus kwaɪ 'iːt əs kwi-, -'eɪt- ‖ -'iːt̬ əs **~es** ɪz əz

quiff kwɪf **quiffs** kwɪfs

Quiggin 'kwɪɡ ɪn §-ən

Quigley 'kwɪɡ li

quill kwɪl **quilled** kwɪld **quilling** 'kwɪl ɪŋ **quills** kwɪlz

Quiller-Couch ˌkwɪl ə 'kuːtʃ ‖ -ᵊr-

Quilliam 'kwɪl i‿əm

Quilp kwɪlp

quilt kwɪlt **quilted** 'kwɪlt ɪd -əd **quilting** 'kwɪlt ɪŋ **quilts** kwɪlts

Quilter, q~ 'kwɪlt ə ‖ -ᵊr

quim kwɪm **quims** kwɪmz

quin, Quin kwɪn **quins** kwɪnz

quinary 'kwaɪn ər i

Quinault *family name* 'kwɪn ᵊlt

quince kwɪnᵗs **quinces** 'kwɪnᵗs ɪz -əz

quincentenar|y ˌkwɪn sen 'tiːn ər |i ˌ·sᵊn-, -'ten- ‖ -'ten ər |i ˌ·'sent ᵊn er i **~ies** iz

quincentennial ˌkwɪn sen 'ten i‿əl ◂ ˌ·sᵊn- **~s** z

Quincey 'kwɪnᵗs i

quincuncial kwɪn 'kʌnᵗʃ ᵊl →kwɪŋ- **~ly** i

quincunx 'kwɪŋk ʌŋ*k*s **~es** ɪz əz

Quincy 'kwɪnᵗs i

quindecagon (ˌ)kwɪn 'dek əɡ ən ‖ -ə ɡɑːn **~s** z

quindecennial ˌkwɪn dɪ 'sen i‿əl ◂ ˌ·də-, ˌ·de- **~ly** i

Quindlen 'kwɪnd lɪn -lən

quinine kwɪ 'niːn kwə-; 'kwɪn iːn ‖ 'kwaɪn aɪn 'kwɪn- (*)

Quinion 'kwɪn i‿ən

Quink *tdmk* kwɪŋk

Quinlan 'kwɪn lən

Quinn kwɪn

quinoa ki 'nəʊ ə 'kiːn wɑː ‖ -'noʊ-

quinoline 'kwɪn ə liːn -lɪn, §-lən; -ᵊl iːn, -ɪn, §-ən ‖ -ᵊl iːn

quinone kwɪ 'nəʊn 'kwɪn əʊn ‖ -'noʊn 'kwaɪn oʊn

quinquagenarian ˌkwɪŋk wə dʒə 'neər i‿ən ◂ ˌ·wɪ-ˌ· ·dʒɪ- ‖ -'ner- -'nær- **~s** z

Quinquagesima ˌkwɪŋk wə 'dʒes ɪm ə ◂ ˌ·wɪ-, -əm ə

quinque- *comb. form*
with stress-neutral suffix |kwɪŋk wɪ §-wə — **quinquepartite** ˌkwɪŋk wɪ 'pɑːt aɪt ◂ §-wə- ‖ -'pɑːrt-

quinquenni|al kwɪŋ 'kwen i‿|əl kwɪn- **~a** ə **~ally** əl‿i **~um** əm

quinquevalent ˌkwɪŋk wɪ 'veɪl ənt ◂ §-wə-; kwɪn 'kwev əl-, →kwɪŋ-

quinsy 'kwɪnz i

quint kwɪnt kɪnt **quints** kwɪn*t*s kɪn*t*s

quintain 'kwɪnt ən -ɪn ‖ -ᵊn **~s** z

quintal 'kwɪnt ᵊl **~s** z

quintan 'kwɪnt ən ‖ -ᵊn **~s** z

quintessence kwɪn 'tes ᵊnᵗs

quintessential ˌkwɪnt ɪ 'senᵗʃ ᵊl ◂ -ə- ‖ ˌkwɪnt̬ ə- **~ly** i

quintet, quintette (ˌ)kwɪn 'tet **~s** s

quintic 'kwɪnt ɪk ‖ 'kwɪnt̬ ɪk

quintile 'kwɪnt aɪᵊl **~s** z

Quintilian kwɪn 'tɪl i‿ən

quintillion kwɪn 'tɪl jən -i‿ən **~s** z

Quintin 'kwɪnt ɪn §-ən ‖ -ᵊn

Quinton 'kwɪnt ən ‖ -ᵊn

quintupl|e 'kwɪnt jʊp ᵊl -əp-; kwɪn 'tjuːp- ‖ kwɪn 'tuːp ᵊl -'tjuːp-, -'tʌp-; 'kwɪnt̬ əp- **~ed** d **~es** z **~ing** ‿ɪŋ

quintuplet 'kwɪnt jʊp lət -əp-, -lɪt, -let; kwɪn 'tjuːp-, §-'tʌp- ‖ kwɪn 'tʌp lət -'tuːp-, -'tjuːp-; 'kwɪnt̬ əp- **~s** s

Quintus 'kwɪnt əs ‖ 'kwɪnt̬ əs

quinze kænz —*Fr* [kɛ̃ːz]

quip kwɪp **quipped** kwɪpt **quipping** 'kwɪp ɪŋ **quips** kwɪps

quipster 'kwɪps tə ‖ -tᵊr **~s** z

quipu 'kiːp uː 'kwɪp-

quire 'kwaɪ‿ə ‖ 'kwaɪ‿ᵊr *(= choir)* **quires** 'kwaɪ‿əz ‖ 'kwaɪ‿ᵊrz

Quirinal 'kwɪr ɪn ᵊl -ən-

Quirinus kwɪ 'raɪn əs kwə-

quirk kwɜːk ‖ kwɜ˞ːk **quirks** 'kwɜːks ‖ kwɜ˞ːks
Quirk, Quirke kwɜːk ‖ kwɜ˞ːk
quirk|y 'kwɜːk |i ‖ 'kwɜ˞ːk |i **~ier** i‿ə ‖ i‿ᵊr **~iest** i‿ɪst i‿əst **~ily** ɪ li əl i **~iness** i nəs i nɪs
quirt kwɜːt ‖ kwɜ˞ːt **quirts** kwɜːts ‖ kwɜ˞ːts
quisling 'kwɪz lɪŋ **~s** z
quit kwɪt **quits** kwɪts **quitted** 'kwɪt ɪd -əd ‖ 'kwɪţ əd **quitting** 'kwɪt ɪŋ ‖ 'kwɪţ ɪŋ
quitch kwɪtʃ
quite kwaɪt
Quito 'kiːt əʊ ‖ -oʊ —*Sp* ['ki to]
quitrent 'kwɪt rent
quits kwɪts
quittanc|e 'kwɪt ᵊnᵗs **~es** ɪz əz
quitter 'kwɪt ə ‖ 'kwɪţ ᵊr **~s** z
quittor 'kwɪt ə ‖ 'kwɪţ ᵊr
quiver 'kwɪv ə ‖ -ᵊr **~ed** d **quivering/ly** 'kwɪv ər‿ɪŋ /li **~s** z
quiverful 'kwɪv ə fʊl ‖ -ᵊr- **~s** z
qui vive ˌkiː 'viːv
Quix *tdmk* kwɪks
Quixote 'kwɪks ət -əʊt; kɪ 'həʊt i ‖ kiː 'hoʊţ i —*Sp* [ki 'xo te]
quixotic kwɪk 'sɒt ɪk ‖ -'sɑːţ ɪk **~al** ᵊl **~ally** ᵊl‿i
quixotism 'kwɪks ə ˌtɪz əm
quiz kwɪz **quizzed** kwɪzd **quizzes** 'kwɪz ɪz -əz **quizzing** 'kwɪz ɪŋ
quizmaster 'kwɪz ˌmɑːst ə §-ˌmæst- ‖ -ˌmæst ᵊr **~s** z
quizzical 'kwɪz ɪk ᵊl **~ly** ‿i
quo kwəʊ ‖ kwoʊ
ˌ**quo 'vadis** 'vɑːd ɪs 'wɑːd-, §-əs
quod kwɒd ‖ kwɑːd
quodlibet 'kwɒd lɪ bet -lə- ‖ 'kwɑːd- **~s** s

quoin kɔɪn kwɔɪn **quoined** kɔɪnd kwɔɪnd **quoining** 'kɔɪn ɪŋ 'kwɔɪn- **quoins** kɔɪnz kwɔɪnz
quoit kɔɪt kwɔɪt **quoits** kɔɪts kwɔɪts
quokka 'kwɒk ə ‖ 'kwɑːk ə **~s** z
quoll kwɒl ‖ kwɑːl **quolls** kwɒlz ‖ kwɑːlz
quondam 'kwɒnd æm -əm ‖ 'kwɑːnd-
Quonset *tdmk* 'kwɒnᵗs ɪt -ət, -et ‖ 'kwɑːnᵗs ət 'kwɑːnz-
'**Quonset hut**
quorate 'kwɔːr eɪt -ət, -ɪt ‖ 'kwoʊr-
Quorn kwɔːn ‖ kwɔːrn
quorum 'kwɔːr əm ‖ 'kwoʊr- **~s** z
Quosh *tdmk* 'kwɒʃ ‖ kwɑːʃ
quota 'kwəʊt ə §'kəʊt- ‖ 'kwoʊţ ə **~s** z
quotability ˌkwəʊt ə 'bɪl ət i §ˌkəʊt-, -ɪt i ‖ ˌkwoʊţ ə 'bɪl əţ i ˌkoʊţ-
quotab|le 'kwəʊt əb |ᵊl §'kəʊt- ‖ 'kwoʊţ- 'koʊţ- **~ly** li
quotation kwəʊ 'teɪʃ ᵊn kwə-, §kəʊ- ‖ kwoʊ- koʊ- **~s** z
quo'tation mark
quote kwəʊt §kəʊt ‖ kwoʊt koʊt **quoted** 'kwəʊt ɪd §'kəʊt- ‖ 'kwoʊţ əd 'koʊţ- **quotes** kwəʊts §kəʊts ‖ kwoʊts koʊts **quoting** 'kwəʊt ɪŋ §'kəʊt- ‖ 'kwoʊţ ɪŋ 'koʊţ-
quoth kwəʊθ §kəʊθ ‖ kwoʊθ
quotha 'kwəʊθ ə §'kəʊθ- ‖ 'kwoʊθ ə
quotidian kwəʊ 'tɪd i‿ən kwɒ-, §kəʊ- ‖ kwoʊ-
quotient 'kwəʊʃ ᵊnt §'kəʊʃ- ‖ 'kwoʊʃ ᵊnt **~s** s
Qur'an, Quran kɔː 'rɑːn kə-, kɒ-, -'ræn ‖ kə 'rɑːn -'ræn; kuᵊr 'ɑːn, -'æn —*Arabic* [qur 'ʔɑːn]
Quy kwaɪ
q.v. ˌkjuː 'viː
Qwaqwa 'kwɑːk wə
qwerty, QWERTY 'kwɜːt i ‖ 'kwɜ˞ːţ i 'kwerţ-

r Spelling-to-sound

1 Where the spelling is **r**, the pronunciation is regularly r as in **run** rʌn.

2 Where the spelling is double **rr**, the pronunciation is again regularly r as in **merry** ˈmer i.

3 When the spelling is **r** followed by a consonant letter or a silent **e**, or when **r** is at the end of a word, then the pronunciation differs in different varieties of English:

- In RP, the **r** is silent. The same applies to most varieties of English English, to Australian English, and to the other 'non-rhotic' accents. In connected speech, however, r may be pronounced at the end of a word if the next word begins with a vowel sound (see R-LIAISON).
- In GenAm, the pronunciation is r. The same applies to Scottish English, to Irish English, and to the other 'rhotic' accents. In GenAm, the r coalesces with a preceding ɜː vowel to give ɝː.
- Examples:

Examples:	RP	GenAm
farm	fɑːm	fɑːrm
more	mɔː	mɔːr
stir	stɜː	stɝː
murder	ˈmɜːd ə	ˈmɝːd ᵊr

4 In the middle or at the end of a word, **r** frequently affects the preceding vowel. Consequently **ar**, **er**, **ir**, **or**, **ur**, **yr** could be regarded as digraphs, and **air**, **are**, **ear**, **eer**, **eir**, **ere**, **eur**, **ier**, **ire**, **oar**, **oor**, **ore**, **our**, **ure** as trigraphs (see individual entries).

5 The sound r may also appear in non-rhotic accents in certain cases where no corresponding letter **r** is written, as when **thawing** is pronounced ˈθɔːr ɪŋ. This is known as 'intrusive r', see R-LIAISON. Note also the exceptional word **colonel** ˈkɜːn ᵊl ‖ ˈkɝːn ᵊl.

6 The exceptional word **iron** is pronounced as if written **iorn**, namely ˈaɪ‿ən ‖ ˈaɪ‿ᵊrn.

rh Spelling-to-sound

Where the spelling is the digraph **rh** or its doubled form **rrh**, the pronunciation is regularly the same as that of the letter **r**:

r as in **rhythm** ˈrɪð əm, **rhapsody** ˈræps əd i or

BrE silent, AmE r as in **catarrh** kə ˈtɑː ‖ kə ˈtɑːr.

R-liaison

1 In BrE (RP) and other **non-rhotic** accents, a word in isolation never ends in r. But in connected speech an r may be pronounced in some cases if the next word begins with a vowel sound.

2 This typically happens with a word that ends in one of the following vowels: ə, ɑː, ɔː, ɜː, ɪə, eə, ʊə.

far fɑː ‖ fɑːr In isolation, or before a consonant sound, this word is pronounced fɑː. But in a phrase such as **far away, far out** it is usually pronounced fɑːr.

near nɪə ‖ nɪ^{ə}r In isolation, the RP form is nɪə. But in a phrase such as **near enough** it is usually pronounced nɪər.

3 Usually, as in the cases just mentioned, the spelling includes **r**. The added r-sound is then known as **linking r**. It corresponds to a historical r, now lost before a consonant or pause. (In **rhotic** accents, such as GenAm, this r is still always present, and is therefore not 'linking'.)

4 In RP, however, as in other non-rhotic accents, the sound r is frequently added even if there is no letter **r** in the spelling. This **intrusive r** does not correspond to historical r, and there is no corresponding r in AmE.

comma ˈkɒm ə ‖ ˈkɑːm ə In isolation, the RP form is ˈkɒm ə. But in a phrase such as **put a comma in**, it is often pronounced ˈkɒm ər. (In GenAm it is always ˈkɑːm ə, whatever the environment.)

thaw θɔː ‖ θɒː In isolation, RP **thaw** is θɔː. In the phrase **thaw out**, intrusive r may be added, giving ˌθɔːr ˈaʊt. (In GenAm there is no r.)

5 In principle, this dictionary shows the CITATION pronunciation of words. Therefore it does not indicate places where r-liaison is likely across a word boundary. They can be inferred from the rules given above. However, it *does* show r-liaison within a word, both linking and intrusive. Linking r within a word, being obligatory, is shown in ordinary type; intrusive r, being optional (and disapproved of by some) is shown in raised type.

storing ˈstɔːr ɪŋ

thawing ˈθɔː^{r} ɪŋ

R, r ɑː ‖ ɑːr **R's, r's, Rs, rs** ɑːz ‖ ɑːrz —*Communications code name:* Romeo

RA ˌɑːr ˈeɪ ‖ ˌɑːr-

Ra rɑː

Raasay ˈrɑːs eɪ

Rab ræb

Raban ˈreɪb ən

Rabat rə ˈbɑːt rɑː-, -ˈbæt —*Arabic* [rɑ ˈbɑːtˁ], *Fr* [ʁa ba]

Rabaul rə ˈbaʊl

rabb|et ˈræb |ɪt §-ət ‖ -|ət **~eted** ɪt ɪd §ət-, -əd ‖ əţ əd **~eting** ɪt ɪŋ §ət- ‖ əţ ɪŋ **~ets** ɪts §əts ‖ əts

rabbi ˈræb aɪ **~s** z

Rabbie ˈræb i
rabbinate ˈræb ɪn ət §-ən-, -ɪt; -ɪ neɪt, -ə- **~s** s
rabbinic, R~ rə ˈbɪn ɪk ræ- **~al** ᵊl **~ally** ᵊl‿i
rabbinistic ˌræb ɪ ˈnɪst ɪk ◂ -ə-
rabb|it ˈræb |ɪt §-ət ‖ -|ət **~ited** ɪt ɪd §ət-, -əd ‖ əṭ əd **~iting** ɪt ɪŋ §ət- ‖ əṭ ɪŋ **~its** ɪts §əts ‖ əts
ˈrabbit hutch; **ˈrabbit punch**; **ˈrabbit ˌwarren**
rabbitfish ˈræb ɪt fɪʃ §-ət-
rabble ˈræb ᵊl **~s** z
rabble-rouser ˈræb ᵊl ˌraʊz ə ‖ -ᵊr **~s** z
rabble-rousing ˈræb ᵊl ˌraʊz ɪŋ
Rabelais ˈræb ə leɪ -ᵊl eɪ ‖ ˌ· ·ˈ· —*Fr* [ʁa blɛ]
Rabelaisian ˌræb ə ˈleɪz i‿ən ◂ -ˈleɪʒ ᵊn ‖ -ˈleɪʒ ᵊn ◂
rabid ˈræb ɪd ˈreɪb-, §-əd **~ly** li **~ness** nəs nɪs
rabidity rə ˈbɪd ət i -ɪt i ‖ -əṭ i
rabies ˈreɪb iːz -iz
rabietic ˌreɪb i ˈet ɪk ◂ ‖ -ˈeṭ ɪk ◂
Rabin ˈreɪb ɪn §-ən —*but as an Israeli name,* ræ ˈbiːn ‖ rɑː-
Rabindranath rə ˈbɪndr ə nɑːθ -nɑːt —*Hindi* [rə ʋɪn̪ d̪rə n̪aːtʰ], *Bengali* [ro bin̪ d̪ro natʰ]
Rabinowitz rə ˈbɪn ə wɪts ræ-, -vɪts
RAC ˌɑːr eɪ ˈsiː
Racal *tdmk* ˈreɪk ɔːl -ᵊl ‖ -ɑːl
raccoon rə ˈkuːn ræ- ‖ ræ- **~s** z
race reɪs **raced** reɪst **races** ˈreɪs ɪz -əz **racing** ˈreɪs ɪŋ
ˈrace card; **ˈrace ˌmeeting**; **ˌrace reˈlations**; **ˈrace ˌriot**
racecours|e ˈreɪs kɔːs ‖ -kɔːrs -koʊrs **~es** ɪz əz
racegoer ˈreɪs ˌgəʊ ə ‖ -ˌgoʊ ᵊr **~s** z
racehors|e ˈreɪs hɔːs ‖ -hɔːrs **~es** ɪz əz
raceme ˈræs iːm ˈreɪs-; ræ ˈsiːm, rə- ‖ reɪ ˈsiːm rə- **~s** z
racemic rə ˈsiːm ɪk ræ-, reɪ-, -ˈsem-
racer ˈreɪs ə ‖ -ᵊr **~s** z
racetrack ˈreɪs træk **~s** s **~s** z
raceway ˈreɪs weɪ
Rachael, Rachel ˈreɪtʃ əl —*but as a French name,* ræ ˈʃel —*Fr* [ʁa ʃɛl]
Rachelle rə ˈʃel ˈreɪtʃ əl
rachis ˈreɪk ɪs §-əs
rachitis rə ˈkaɪt ɪs ræ-, §-əs ‖ -ˈkaɪṭ əs
Rachman ˈræk mən
Rachmaninoff, Rachmaninov ræk ˈmæn ɪn ɒf ‖ rɑːk ˈmɑːn ə nɔːf -nɑːf —*Russ* [rʌx ˈma nʲɪ nəf]
Rachmanism, r~ ˈræk mən ˌɪz əm
racial ˈreɪʃ ᵊl ˈreɪʃ i‿əl, ˈreɪs i‿əl
racialism ˈreɪʃ ə ˌlɪz əm -ᵊl ˌɪz-; ˈreɪʃ i‿əl ˌɪz əm, ˈreɪs-
racialist ˈreɪʃ əl ɪst ˈreɪʃ i‿əl ɪst, ˈreɪs-, §-əst **~s** s
racially ˈreɪʃ ᵊl i ˈreɪʃ i‿əl i, ˈreɪs-
Racine *French writer* ræ ˈsiːn rə- —*Fr* [ʁa sin]
Racine *place in Wisconsin* rə ˈsiːn reɪ-
racism ˈreɪs ˌɪz əm
racist ˈreɪs ɪst ˈreɪʃ-, §-əst **~s** s
rack ræk **racked** rækt **racking** ˈræk ɪŋ **racks** ræks
rack-and-pinion ˌræk ən ˈpɪn jən →-əm-
rack|et ˈræk |ɪt §-ət ‖ -|ət **~eted** ɪt ɪd §ət-, -əd ‖ əṭ əd **~eting** ɪt ɪŋ §ət- ‖ əṭ ɪŋ **~ets** ɪts §əts ‖ əts
racketball ˈræk ɪt bɔːl §-ət- ‖ -bɑːl
racke|teer ˌræk ə |ˈtɪə -ɪ- ‖ -|ˈtɪᵊr **~teered** ˈtɪəd ‖ ˈtɪᵊrd **~teering** ˈtɪər ɪŋ ‖ ˈtɪr ɪŋ **~teers** ˈtɪəz ‖ ˈtɪᵊrz
rackety ˈræk ət i -ɪt- ‖ -əṭ i
Rackham ˈræk əm
rack-rail ˈræk reɪᵊl
rack-|rent ˈræk |rent **~ rented** rent ɪd -əd ‖ renṭ əd **~renter/s** rent ə/z ‖ renṭ ᵊr/z **~renting** rent ɪŋ ‖ renṭ ɪŋ **~rents** rents
raclette ræ ˈklet —*Fr* [ʁa klɛt]
raconteur ˌræk ɒn ˈtɜː ‖ -ɑːn ˈtɜ˞ː -ən- —*Fr* [ʁa kɔ̃ tœːʁ] **~s** z
racoon rə ˈkuːn ræ- ‖ ræ- **~s** z
racquet ˈræk ɪt §-ət **~s** s
racquetball ˈræk ɪt bɔːl -ət- ‖ -bɑːl
rac|y ˈreɪs |i **~ier** i‿ə ‖ i‿ᵊr **~iest** i‿ɪst i‿əst **~ily** ɪ li əl i **~iness** i nəs i nɪs
rad ræd **rads** rædz
RADA ˈrɑːd ə
radar ˈreɪd ɑː ‖ -ɑːr **~s** z
Radbourne ˈræd bɔːn →ˈræb- ‖ -bɔːrn -boʊrn
Radburn ˈræd bɜːn →ˈræb- ‖ -bɜ˞ːn
Radcliff, Radcliffe, Radclyffe ˈræd klɪf →ˈræg-
raddle ˈræd ᵊl **~d** d
Radetzky rə ˈdet ski ræ- ‖ rɑː- —*Ger* [ʁa ˈdɛts ki]
Radford ˈræd fəd ‖ -fᵊrd
radial ˈreɪd i‿əl **~ly** i **~s** z
ˌradial ˈtyre
radial-ply ˌreɪd i‿əl ˈplaɪ ◂ ˈ· · · ·
radian ˈreɪd i‿ən **~s** z
radiance ˈreɪd i‿ənᵗs
radiant ˈreɪd i‿ənt **~ly** li **~s** s
radi|ate ˈreɪd i |eɪt **~ated** eɪt ɪd -əd ‖ eɪṭ əd **~ates** eɪts **~ating** eɪt ɪŋ ‖ eɪṭ ɪŋ
radiation ˌreɪd i ˈeɪʃ ᵊn **~s** z
ˌradiˈation ˌsickness
radiator ˈreɪd i eɪt ə ‖ -eɪṭ ᵊr **~s** z
radical ˈræd ɪk ᵊl **~s** z
radicalis... —*see* **radicaliz...**
radicalism ˈræd ɪk ᵊl ˌɪz əm
radicaliz|e ˈræd ɪk ə laɪz **~ed** d **~es** ɪz əz **~ing** ɪŋ
radically ˈræd ɪk ᵊl i
radicand ˈræd ɪ kænd -ə- **~s** z
radicchio rə ˈdɪk i əʊ ræ-, -ˈdiːtʃ- ‖ rə ˈdiːk i‿oʊ rɑː- —*It* [ra ˈdik kjo]
Radice rə ˈdiːtʃ i -eɪ
radices ˈreɪd ɪ siːz ˈræd-, §-ə-
radicle ˈræd ɪk ᵊl *(= radical)* **~s** z
radii ˈreɪd i aɪ
radio ˈreɪd i əʊ ‖ -oʊ **~ed** d **~ing** ɪŋ **~s** z
ˌradio aˈlarm, ˈ· · · · ˌ·ˈ·; **ˌradio aˈstronomy,** ˈ· · · · ˌ·ˈ· · ·; **ˈradio ˌbeacon**; **ˈradio car**; **ˈradio ˌfrequency**; **ˌradio ˈtelescope**; **ˈradio wave**
radio- *comb. form*
with stress-neutral suffix ˈreɪd i əʊ ‖ -oʊ

— **radionuclide** ˌreɪd i əʊ ˈnjuːk laɪd §-ˈnuːk- ‖ -oʊ ˈnuːk- -ˈnjuːk-
with stress-imposing suffix ˌreɪd i ˈɒ+ ‖ -ˈɑː+
— **radioscopy** ˌreɪd i ˈɒsk əp i ‖ -ˈɑːsk-
radioactive ˌreɪd i‿əʊ ˈækt ɪv ◂ ‖ ˌ· ·oʊ- **~ly** li
ˌradio ˌactive deˈcay
radioactivity ˌreɪd i‿əʊ æk ˈtɪv ət i -ɪt i ‖ -oʊ æk ˈtɪv əţ i
radiocarbon ˌreɪd i əʊ ˈkɑːb ən ◂ ‖ -oʊ ˈkɑːrb ən ◂
ˌradioˌcarbon ˈdating
radio-cassette ˌreɪd i‿əʊ kə ˈset -kæˈ· ‖ -i oʊ-
radio-controlled ˌreɪd i‿əʊ kən ˈtrəʊld ◂ §-kɒnˈ·, →-ˈtrɒʊld ◂ ‖ -oʊ kən ˈtroʊld ◂
radiogram ˈreɪd i‿əʊ græm ‖ -i‿oʊ- **~s** z
radiograph ˈreɪd i‿əʊ grɑːf -græf ‖ -oʊ græf **~s** s
radiographer ˌreɪd i ˈɒg rəf ə ‖ -ˈɑːg rəf ər **~s** z
radiographic ˌreɪd ɪ‿əʊ ˈgræf ɪk ◂ ‖ -i‿ə- **~ally** əl‿i
radiography ˌreɪd i ˈɒg rəf i ‖ -ˈɑːg-
Radiohead ˈreɪd i‿əʊ hed ‖ -i oʊ-
radioisotope ˌreɪd i‿əʊ ˈaɪs əʊ təʊp ‖ -oʊ ˈaɪs ə toʊp **~s** s
radiolarian ˌreɪd i əʊ ˈleər i‿ən ‖ -oʊ ˈler- -ˈlær- **~s** z
radiolocation ˌreɪd i‿əʊ ləʊ ˈkeɪʃ ən ‖ -i‿oʊ loʊ-
radiological ˌreɪd i‿əʊ ˈlɒdʒ ɪk əl ◂ ‖ -ə ˈlɑːdʒ- **~ly** ‿i
radiologist ˌreɪd i ˈɒl ədʒ ɪst §-əst ‖ -ˈɑːl- **~s** s
radiology ˌreɪd i ˈɒl ədʒ i ‖ -ˈɑːl-
radionic ˌreɪd i ˈɒn ɪk ◂ ‖ -ˈɑːn- **~s** s
radiopag|e ˌreɪd i əʊ ˈpeɪdʒ ‖ -i oʊ- **~ed** d **~er/s** ə/z ‖ -ər/z **~es** ɪz əz **~ing** ɪŋ
radiopaque ˌreɪd i əʊ ˈpeɪk ◂ ‖ -i oʊ-
radiophonic ˌreɪd i‿əʊ ˈfɒn ɪk ◂ ‖ -oʊ ˈfɑːn ɪk ◂
radioscopy ˌreɪd i ˈɒsk əp i ‖ -ˈɑːsk-
radiosonde ˈreɪd i əʊ sɒnd ‖ -oʊ sɑːnd **~s** z
radiotherapist ˌreɪd i‿əʊ ˈθer əp ɪst §-əst ‖ ˌ· ·oʊ- **~s** s
radiotherapy ˌreɪd i‿əʊ ˈθer əp i ‖ ˌ· ·oʊ-
radish ˈræd ɪʃ **~es** ɪz əz
radium ˈreɪd i‿əm
radi|us ˈreɪd i‿|əs **~i** aɪ **~uses** əs ɪz -əz
radix ˈreɪd ɪks **radices** ˈreɪd ɪ siːz ˈræd-, §-ə- **radixes** ˈreɪd ɪks ɪz -əz
Radlett ˈræd lət -lɪt
Radley ˈræd li
Radnor ˈræd nə ‖ -nər -nɔːr **~shire** ʃə ʃɪə ‖ ʃər ʃɪr
radome ˈreɪd əʊm ‖ -oʊm **~s** z
radon ˈreɪd ɒn ‖ -ɑːn
Radovan ˈræd ə væn ‖ ˈrɑːd ə vɑːn —*Serbian* [ˈra do van]
Radox *tdmk* ˈreɪd ɒks ‖ -ɑːks
radula ˈræd jʊl ə §ˈrædʒ əl- ‖ ˈrædʒ əl ə **radulae** ˈræd ju liː §ˈrædʒ ə- ‖ ˈrædʒ ə liː
radwaste ˈræd weɪst
Rae reɪ
Raeburn ˈreɪ bɜːn ‖ -bɜːn
Rael-Brook *tdmk* ˌreɪəl ˈbrʊk
Raelene ˈreɪ liːn
RAF ˌɑːr eɪ ˈef —*also, informally,* ræf
Rafe reɪf
Rafferty, r~ ˈræf ət i ‖ -ərţ i
raffia ˈræf i‿ə
raffinose ˈræf ɪ nəʊz -ə-, -nəʊs ‖ -noʊs
raffish ˈræf ɪʃ **~ly** li **~ness** nəs nɪs
raffl|e ˈræf əl **~ed** d **~es** z **~ing** ‿ɪŋ
Raffles ˈræf əlz
rafflesia ræ ˈfliːz i‿ə -ˈfliːʒ- ‖ rə ˈfliːʒ ə ræ- **~s** z
Rafsanjani ˌræf sæn ˈdʒɑːn i -sɑːn- ‖ ˌrɑːf sən- ˌrʌf-, -sɑːn- —*Farsi* [ræf sæn dʒɑ ˈniː]
raft, Raft rɑːft §ræft ‖ ræft **rafted** rɑːft ɪd §ˈræft-, -əd ‖ ˈræft əd **rafting** ˈrɑːft ɪŋ §ˈræft- ‖ ˈræft ɪŋ **rafts** rɑːfts §ræfts ‖ ræfts
rafter ˈrɑːft ə §ˈræft- ‖ ˈræft ər **~s** z
rafts|man ˈrɑːfts |mən §ˈræfts- ‖ ˈræfts- **~men** mən -men
rag ræg **ragged** *past & pp* rægd **ragging** ˈrægɪŋ **rags** rægz
ˌrag ˈdoll ‖ ˈ· ·; **ˈrag trade**
raga ˈrɑːg ə rɑːg **~s** z
ragamuffin ˈræg ə ˌmʌf ɪn §-ən **~s** z
rag-and-bone |man ˌræg ən ˈbəʊn |mæn -ənd-, →-əm-, →-ˈbəʊm- ‖ -ˈboʊn- **~men** men
ragbag ˈræg bæg **~s** z
rage reɪdʒ **raged** reɪdʒd **rages** ˈreɪdʒ ɪz -əz **raging** ˈreɪdʒ ɪŋ
ragg... —*see* **rag**
ragga ˈræg ə
ragged *adj* ˈræg ɪd -əd **~ly** li **~ness** nəs nɪs
ˌragged ˈrobin
raggedy ˈræg əd i -ɪd-
raggle-taggle ˌræg əl ˈtæg əl ◂ ˈ· ˌ· ·
ragi... —*see* **rage**
raglan, R~ ˈræg lən **~s** z
Rag|man, r~ ˈræg |mən **~men** men mən
ragout ræ ˈguː ˈræg uː **~s** z
ragpicker ˈræg ˌpɪk ə ‖ -ər **~s** z
ragstone ˈræg stəʊn ‖ -stoʊn
rags-to-riches ˌrægz tə ˈrɪtʃ ɪz -əz
ragtag ˈræg tæg
ragtime ˈræg taɪm
ragtop ˈræg tɒp ‖ -tɑːp **~s** s
Ragu *tdmk* ræ ˈguː ˈræg uː
ragweed ˈræg wiːd
ragworm ˈræg wɜːm ‖ -wɜːm **~s** z
ragwort ˈræg wɜːt §-wɔːt ‖ -wɜːt -wɔːrt **~s** s
rah rɑː
rah-rah ˈrɑː rɑː ‖ ˈrɔː rɔː
Rahway *place in NJ* ˈrɔː weɪ ˈrɑː-
raid reɪd **raided** ˈreɪd ɪd -əd **raiding** ˈreɪd ɪŋ **raids** reɪdz
raider ˈreɪd ə ‖ -ər **~s** z
Raif reɪf
Raikes reɪks
rail reɪəl **railed** reɪəld **railing** ˈreɪəl ɪŋ **rails** reɪəlz
ˈrail ˌticket
railcar ˈreɪəl kɑː ‖ -kɑːr **~s** z

R

railcard ˈreɪəl kɑːd ‖ -kɑːrd **~s** z
railhead ˈreɪəl hed **~s** z
railing ˈreɪl ɪŋ **~s** z
railler|y ˈreɪl ər |i **~ies** iz
railroad ˈreɪəl rəʊd ‖ -roʊd **~ed** ɪd əd **~ing** ɪŋ **~s** z
Railton ˈreɪəlt ən
Railtrack *tdmk* ˈreɪəl træk
railway ˈreɪəl weɪ **~s** z
ˈrailway ˌstation; **ˈrailway train**
railway|man ˈreɪəl weɪ |mən -wi- **~men** mən men
raiment ˈreɪm ənt
rain reɪn **rained** reɪnd **raining** ˈreɪn ɪŋ **rains** reɪnz
ˈrain check; **ˈrain ˌforest**; **ˈrain gauge**
Raina *(i)* raɪ ˈiːn ə, *(ii)* ˈreɪn ə
rainbird ˈreɪn bɜːd ‖ -bɜːd **~s** z
rainbow, R~ ˈreɪn bəʊ →ˈreɪm- ‖ -boʊ **~s** z
raincoat ˈreɪn kəʊt →ˈreɪŋ- ‖ -koʊt **~s** s
raindrop ˈreɪn drɒp ‖ -drɑːp **~s** s
Raine reɪn
rainfall ˈreɪn fɔːl ‖ -fɑːl
Rainford ˈreɪn fəd ‖ -fərd
Rainhill ˌreɪn ˈhɪl
Rainier *Mount* ˈreɪn i‿ə rə ˈnɪə, reɪ- ‖ rə ˈnɪər reɪ-; ˈreɪn ɪr
Rainier *prince of Monaco* ˈreɪn i eɪ ‖ rə ˈnɪər reɪ-; ren ˈjeɪ —*Fr* [ʁɛ nje]
rainless ˈreɪn ləs -lɪs
rainmaker ˈreɪn ˌmeɪk ə →ˈreɪm- ‖ -ər **~s** z
rainproof ˈreɪn pruːf →ˈreɪm-, §-prʊf **~ed** t **~ing** ɪŋ **~s** s
rainstorm ˈreɪn stɔːm ‖ -stɔːrm **~s** z
rainwater ˈreɪn ˌwɔːt ə ‖ -ˌwɔːt̬ ər -ˌwɑːt̬-
rainwear ˈreɪn weə ‖ -wer -wær
rain|y ˈreɪn |i **~ier** i‿ə ‖ i‿ər **~iest** i‿ɪst i‿əst **~ily** ɪ li əl i **~iness** i nəs i nɪs
Raisa raɪ ˈiːs ə rɑː- ‖ rɑː- —*Russ* [rʌ ˈi sə]
raise reɪz **raised** reɪzd **raises** ˈreɪz ɪz -əz **raising** ˈreɪz ɪŋ
raiser ˈreɪz ə ‖ -ər **~s** z
raisin ˈreɪz ən **~s** z
Raison ˈreɪz ən
raison d'etre, raison d'être ˌreɪz ɒ̃ ˈdetr ə -ɒn- ‖ -oʊn- —*Fr* [ʁɛ zɔ̃ dɛtχ]
Raistrick ˈreɪs trɪk
raita ˈraɪt ə -ɑː
raj rɑːdʒ rɑːʒ —*There is no justification in Hindi for the pronunciation* rɑːʒ *often heard in English.* —*Hindi* [raːdʒ]
raja, rajah ˈrɑːdʒ ə **~s** z
Rajasthan ˌrɑːdʒ ə ˈstɑːn
Rajasthani ˌrɑːdʒ ə ˈstɑːn i ◂
Rajneesh ˌrɑːdʒ ˈniːʃ
Rajpoot, Rajput ˈrɑːdʒ pʊt **~s** s —*Hindi* [raːdʒ puːt̪]
Rajputana ˌrɑːdʒ pʊ ˈtɑːn ə
rake reɪk **raked** reɪkt **rakes** reɪks **raking** ˈreɪk ɪŋ
rake-off ˈreɪk ɒf ‖ -ɔːf -ɑːf **~s** s
raki ˈrɑːk i ˈræk-; rɑː ˈkiː
rakish ˈreɪk ɪʃ **~ly** li **~ness** nəs nɪs

R

rale, râle rɑːl ræl **rales, râles** rɑːlz rælz
Ralegh, Raleigh *(i)* ˈrɑːl i, *(ii)* ˈrɔːl i ‖ ˈrɑːl i, *(iii)* ˈræl i —*Sir Walter R~ was probably (ii), as is the place in NC; R~ bicycles are (ii) in AmE, (iii) in BrE.*
Ralf *(i)* rælf, *(ii)* reɪf
rallentando ˌræl ən ˈtænd əʊ -en- ‖ ˌrɑːl ən ˈtɑːnd oʊ *(*)* —*It* [ral len ˈtan do] **~s** z
rall|y ˈræl |i **~ied** id **~ies** iz **~ying** i‿ɪŋ
rallycross ˈræl i krɒs -krɔːs ‖ -krɔːs -krɑːs
Ralph *(i)* rælf, *(ii)* reɪf —*In AmE, (i).*
Ralston ˈrɔːlst ən ˈrɒlst- ‖ ˈrɑːlst-
ram, Ram, RAM ræm **rammed** ræmd **ramming** ˈræm ɪŋ **rams** ræmz
Rama ˈrɑːm ə
Ramachandra ˌrɑːm ə ˈtʃʌndr ə -ˈtʃændr-
ramada, R~ *tdmk* rə ˈmɑːd ə **~s** z
Ramadan ˌræm ə ˈdɑːn ˌrɑːm-, ˌrʌm-, -ˈdæn, ˈ...
Ramadge, Ramage ˈræm ɪdʒ
Ramakrishna ˌrɑːm ə ˈkrɪʃ nə
Raman ˈrɑːm ən
Ramayana rə ˈmaɪ‿ən ə -ˈmɑː jən- —*Hindi* [raː maː jəɳ]
Rambert ˈrɒm beə ˈrɒ̃- ‖ rɑːm ˈbeər
rambl|e ˈræm bəl **~ed** d **~es** z **~ing** ‿ɪŋ
rambler ˈræm blə ‖ -blər **~s** z
rambling *adj, n* ˈræm blɪŋ **~ly** li **~s** z
Rambo ˈræm bəʊ ‖ -boʊ
Ramboesque ˌræm bəʊ ˈesk ◂ ‖ -boʊ-
Rambouillet rɒm ˈbuː jeɪ ræm-, -leɪ; ˈ... ‖ ˌrɑːm bu ˈjeɪ ˌræm-, -ˈleɪ —*Fr* [ʁɑ̃ bu jɛ]
rambunctious ræm ˈbʌŋk ʃəs **~ly** li **~ness** nəs nɪs
rambutan ræm ˈbuːt ən ˌræm bu ˈtæn, -ˈtɑːn **~s** z
Rameau ˈrɑːm əʊ ˈræm- ‖ ræ ˈmoʊ rɑː- —*Fr* [ʁa mo]
ramekin ˈræm ɪ kɪn -ə-, ˈræm kɪn, §-kən **~s** z
Ramelson ˈræm əl sən
ramen ˈrɑːm en -ən —*Jp* [ˈraa meɴ]
Rameses ˈræm ɪ siːz -ə-
ramie ˈræm i ˈrɑːm-
ramification ˌræm ɪf ɪ ˈkeɪʃ ən ˌ-əf-, §-əˈ-- **~s** z
rami|fy ˈræm ɪ |faɪ -ə- **~fied** faɪd **~fies** faɪz **~fying** faɪ ɪŋ
Ramillies ˈræm ɪl iz -əl- —*Fr* [ʁa mi ji]
Ramirez, Ramírez rə ˈmɪər ez ‖ -ˈmɪr- —*Sp* [ra ˈmi reθ, -res]
ramjet ˈræm dʒet **~s** s
rammer ˈræm ə ‖ -ər **~s** z
rammish ˈræm ɪʃ **~ly** li **~ness** nəs nɪs
Ramon, Ramón rə ˈmɒn ræ- ‖ -ˈmoʊn —*Sp* [ra ˈmon]
Ramona rə ˈməʊn ə ræ- ‖ -ˈmoʊn ə
Ramos ˈrɑːm ɒs ‖ rɑː ˈmoʊs ˈreɪm oʊs —*Sp* [ˈra mos], *Port* [ˈrɐ muʃ, -mus]
ramose ˈreɪm əʊs -əʊz; ræ ˈməʊs ‖ -oʊs
ramp ræmp **ramped** ræmpt **ramping** ˈræmp ɪŋ **ramps** ræmps
rampag|e *n* ˈræmp eɪdʒ ræm ˈpeɪdʒ **~es** ɪz əz

rampag|e *v* ræm ˈpeɪdʒ ˈræmp eɪdʒ **~ed** d **~es** ɪz əz **~ing** ɪŋ
rampageous ræm ˈpeɪdʒ əs **~ly** li **~ness** nəs nɪs
rampant ˈræmp ənt **~ly** li
rampart ˈræmp ɑːt -ət ‖ -ɑːrt -ᵊrt **~s** s
rampion ˈræmp i‿ən **~s** z
Ramprakash ˈræm prə kæʃ
Rampton ˈræm*p*t ən
ram-raid ˈræm reɪd **~ed** ɪd əd **~er/s** ə/z ‖ ᵊr/z **~ing** ɪŋ **~s** z
ramrod ˈræm rɒd ‖ -rɑːd **~s** z
Ramsaran ˈrɑːmᵖs ər ən
Ramsay ˈræmz i
Ramsbotham ˈræmz ˌbɒθ əm -ˌbɒt- ‖ -ˌbɑːθ-
Ramsbottom ˈræmz ˌbɒt əm ‖ -ˌbɑːt̬-
Ramsden ˈræmz dən
Ramses ˈræm siːz
Ramsey ˈræmz i
Ramsgate ˈræmz geɪt -gɪt
ramshackle ˈræm ˌʃæk ᵊl
ramshorn ˈræmz hɔːn ‖ -hɔːrn
ramson ˈræmz ən ˈræmᵖs- **~s** z
ram|us ˈreɪm |əs **~i** aɪ
ran ræn
Ranby ˈræn bi →ˈræm-
Rance rænᵗs rɑːnᵗs ‖ rænᵗs
ranch rɑːn*t*ʃ §ræn*t*ʃ ‖ ræn*t*ʃ **ranched** rɑːn*t*ʃt §ræn*t*ʃt ‖ ræn*t*ʃt **ranches** ˈrɑːn*t*ʃ ɪz §ˈræn*t*ʃ-, -əz ‖ ˈræn*t*ʃ əz **ranching** ˈrɑːn*t*ʃ ɪŋ §ˈræn*t*ʃ- ‖ ˈræn*t*ʃ ɪŋ
ˈranch house
rancher ˈrɑːn*t*ʃ ə §ˈræn*t*ʃ- ‖ ˈræn*t*ʃ ᵊr **~s** z
ranchero rɑːn ˈtʃeər əʊ ræn- ‖ -ˈtʃer oʊ **~s** z
rancho, R~ ˈrɑːn*t*ʃ əʊ §ˈræn*t*ʃ- ‖ -oʊ **~s** z
rancid ˈrænᵗs ɪd §-əd **~ness** nəs nɪs
rancidity ræn ˈsɪd ət i -ɪt- ‖ -ət̬ i
rancor ˈræŋk ə ‖ -ᵊr
rancorous ˈræŋk ər əs **~ly** li **~ness** nəs nɪs
rancour ˈræŋk ə ‖ -ᵊr *(= ranker)*
rand, Rand rænd rɑːnt, rɒnt —*Afrikaans* [rɑnt]
Randal, Randall ˈrænd ᵊl
Randalstown ˈrænd ᵊlz taʊn
R and B, R & B ˌɑːr ən ˈbiː →-əm-, -ənd- ‖ ˌɑːr-
R and D, R & D ˌɑːr ən ˈdi -ənd- ‖ ˌɑːr-
randi... —*see* **randy**
Randolph ˈrænd ɒlf -ᵊlf ‖ -ɑːlf
random ˈrænd əm
randomis... —*see* **randomiz...**
randomization ˌrænd əm aɪ ˈzeɪʃ ᵊn -əm ɪ- ‖ -əm ə- **~s** z
randomiz|e ˈrænd ə maɪz §ˌ· ·ˈ· **~ed** d **~es** ɪz əz **~ing** ɪŋ
random|ly ˈrænd əm |li **~ness** nəs nɪs
R and R, R & R ˌɑːr ən*d* ˈɑː ‖ ˌɑːr ən*d* ˈɑːr
rand|y, Randy ˈrænd |i **~ier** i‿ə ‖ i‿ᵊr **~iest** i‿ɪst i‿əst **~ily** ɪ li əl i **~iness** i nəs i nɪs
ranee ˈrɑːn i (ˌ)rɑː ˈniː **~s** z
Ranelagh ˈræn ɪl ə -əl-, -i; -ə lɔː
Ranfurly ˈrænf əl i ræn ˈfɜːl i ‖ -ᵊrl i
rang ræŋ
range reɪndʒ **ranged** reɪn*d*ʒd **ranges** ˈreɪn*d*ʒ ɪz -əz **ranging** ˈreɪn*d*ʒ ɪŋ
ˈrange ˌfinder
ranger, R~ ˈreɪn*d*ʒ ə ‖ -ᵊr **~s** z
rangi... —*see* **range**
Rangoon (ˌ)ræŋ ˈguːn ‖ (ˌ)ræn-
rang|y ˈreɪn*d*ʒ |i **~ier** i‿ə ‖ i‿ᵊr **~iest** i‿ɪst i‿əst **~iness** i nəs i nɪs
rani ˈrɑːn i (ˌ)rɑː ˈniː **~s** z
ranitidine rə ˈnɪt ɪ diːn ræ-, -ə- ‖ -ˈnɪt̬-
Ranjit ˈrʌn dʒɪt ˈræn-
rank, Rank ræŋk —*but as a German name in AmE,* rɑːŋk **ranked** ræŋ*k*t **ranking** ˈræŋk ɪŋ **ranks** ræŋ*k*s
ˌrank and ˈfile
ranker ˈræŋk ə ‖ -ᵊr **~s** z
Rankin, Rankine ˈræŋk ɪn §-ən
rankl|e ˈræŋk ᵊl **~ed** d **~es** z **~ing** ɪŋ
rank|ly ˈræŋk| li **~ness** nəs nɪs
rankshift ˈræŋk ʃɪft **~ed** ɪd əd **~ing** ɪŋ **~s** s
Rannoch ˈræn ək -əx
ransack ˈræn sæk **~ed** t **~er/s** ə/z ‖ ᵊr/z **~ing** ɪŋ **~s** s
ransom ˈrænᵗs əm **~ed** d **~er/s** ə/z ‖ ᵊr/z **~ing** ɪŋ **~s** z
Ransom, Ransome ˈrænᵗs əm
rant rænt **ranted** ˈrænt ɪd -əd ‖ ˈrænt̬ əd **ranting/ly** ˈrænt ɪŋ /li ‖ ˈrænt̬- **rants** rænts
rantings ˈrænt ɪŋz ‖ ˈrænt̬-
Rantzen ˈræn*t*s ᵊn
Ranulph ˈræn ʌlf -ᵊlf
ranunc|ulus rə ˈnʌŋk |jʊl əs -jəl- ‖ -|jəl əs **~uli** ju laɪ jə- ‖ jə laɪ **~uluses** jʊl əs ɪz jəl-, -əz ‖ jəl əs əz
Raoul raʊ ˈuːl rɑː- ‖ rɑː- —*Fr* [ʁa ul]
rap ræp **rapped** ræpt **rapping** ˈræp ɪŋ **raps** ræps
rapacious rə ˈpeɪʃ əs **~ly** li **~ness** nəs nɪs
rapacity rə ˈpæs ət i -ɪt- ‖ -ət̬ i
Rapallo rə ˈpæl əʊ ‖ -ˈpɑːl oʊ —*It* [ra ˈpal lo]
rape reɪp **raped** reɪpt **rapes** reɪps **raping** ˈreɪp ɪŋ
ˈrape oil
Raper ˈreɪp ə ‖ -ᵊr
rapeseed ˈreɪp siːd
raphae ˈreɪf iː
Raphael ˈræf eɪ əl ˈræf eɪᵊl, ˈræf i‿əl —*These forms may be heard for the angel, the surname, and the artist (It* Raffaello [raf fa ˈɛl lo]*). The angel and surname, though not the artist, are further sometimes pronounced* ˈreɪf ᵊl, -jəl. *The artist is sometimes* ˈræf aɪ el ‖ ˌrɑːf aɪ ˈel.
raph|e ˈreɪf |i -iː **~ae** iː
rapid ˈræp ɪd §-əd **~ly** li **~ness** nəs nɪs **~s** z
ˌrapid ˈtransit
Rapidan ˌræp ɪ ˈdæn -ə-
rapid-fire ˌræp ɪd ˈfaɪ‿ə ◂ §-əd- ‖ ˌræp əd ˈfaɪ‿ᵊr ◂
rapidity rə ˈpɪd ət i ræ-, -ɪt- ‖ -ət̬ i
rapid-response ˌræp ɪd ri ˈspɒnᵗs ◂ ˌ·əd-, -rəˈ· ‖ -ˈspɑːnᵗs
rapier ˈreɪp i‿ə ‖ ᵊr **~s** z

R

rapine 'ræp aɪn -ɪn, §-ən
rapist 'reɪp ɪst §-əst **~s** s
Rapoport 'ræp əʊ pɔːt ‖ -ə pɔːrt
Rappahannock ˌræp ə 'hæn ək ◂
rapparee ˌræp ə 'riː **~s** z
rappel ræ 'pel rə- **~ed, ~led** d **~ing, ~ling** ɪŋ **~s** z
rapper 'ræp ə ‖ -ᵊr **~s** z
rapport ræ 'pɔː rə-; 'ræp ɔː ‖ -'pɔːr -'poʊr —*Fr* [ʁa pɔːʁ]
rapporteur ˌræp ɔː 'tɜː ‖ -ɔːr 'tɜː —*Fr* [ʁa pɔʁ tœːʁ] **~s** z
rapprochement ræ 'prɒʃ mɒ̃ rə-, -'prəʊʃ-, -mɒŋ ‖ ˌræp roʊʃ 'mɑːn —*Fr* [ʁa pʁɔʃ mɑ̃]
rapscallion ræp 'skæl i̯ən **~s** z
rapt ræpt
raptor 'ræpt ə -ɔː ‖ -ᵊr -ɔːr **~s** z
raptorial ræp 'tɔːr i̯əl ‖ -'toʊr-
rapture 'ræp tʃə ‖ -tʃᵊr **~s** z
rapturous 'ræp tʃər̮əs **~ly** li **~ness** nəs nɪs
Rapunzel rə 'pʌnz ᵊl
Raquel ræ 'kel rə- ‖ rɑː- —*Sp* [ra 'kel]
rara avis ˌreər əʳ 'eɪv ɪs ˌrɑːr əʳ 'æv-, -'ɑːv-, §-əs; -'ɑː wɪs ‖ ˌrer ə- ˌrær-
rare reə ‖ reᵊr ræᵊr **rarer** 'reər ə ‖ 'rer ᵊr 'rær- **rarest** 'reər ɪst -əst ‖ 'rer əst 'rær- **ˌrare 'earth, ˌrare 'earth ˌelement**
rarebit 'reə bɪt 'ræb ɪt, §-ət ‖ 'rer- 'rær-
rarefaction ˌreər ɪ 'fæk ʃᵊn -ə- ‖ ˌrer- ˌrær-
rare|fy 'reər ɪ |faɪ -ə- ‖ 'rer- 'rær- **~fied** faɪd **~fies** faɪz **~fying** faɪ ɪŋ
rarely 'reə li ‖ 'rer li 'rær-
rareness 'reə nəs -nɪs ‖ 'rer- 'rær-
rareripe 'reə raɪp ‖ 'rer- 'rær-
raring 'reər ɪŋ ‖ 'rer ɪŋ 'rær-
Raritan 'rær ɪt ən -ət- ‖ -ət ᵊn
rarit|y 'reər ət |i -ɪt- ‖ 'rer əṭ |i 'rær- **~ies** iz
Rarotonga ˌreər ə 'tɒŋ gə -'tɒŋ ə ‖ ˌrær ə 'tɑːŋ gə ˌrer-, ˌrɑːr-, -'tɔːŋ-
rasbora ræz 'bɔːr ə ‖ -'boʊr- **~s** z
rascal 'rɑːsk ᵊl §'ræsk- ‖ 'ræsk ᵊl **~s** z
rascalit|y rɑː 'skæl ət |i ræ-, -ɪt- ‖ ræ 'skæl əṭ |i **~ies** iz
rascally 'rɑːsk əl i §'ræsk- ‖ 'ræsk-
rash ræʃ **rasher** 'ræʃ ə ‖ -ᵊr **rashes** 'ræʃ ɪz -əz **rashest** 'ræʃ ɪst -əst
rasher 'ræʃ ə ‖ -ᵊr **~s** z
Rashid ræ 'ʃiːd ‖ rɑː-
rash|ly 'ræʃ |li **~ness** nəs nɪs
Rask ræsk —*Danish* [ʁasg]
Rasmus 'ræz məs
rasp rɑːsp §ræsp ‖ ræsp **rasped** rɑːspt §ræspt ‖ ræspt **rasping** 'rɑːsp ɪŋ §'ræsp- ‖ 'ræsp ɪŋ **rasps** rɑːsps §ræsps ‖ ræsps
raspberr|y, R~ 'rɑːz bər̮|i 'rɑːs-, §'ræz- ‖ 'ræz ˌber |i -bər̮|i *(*)* **~ies** iz
Rasputin ræ 'spjuːt ɪn -'spuː-, §-ᵊn ‖ -ᵊn —*Russ* [rʌ 'spu tʲin]
rasp|y 'rɑːsp| i §'ræsp| i ‖ 'ræsp| i **~ier** i̯ə ‖ i̯ᵊr **~iest** i̯ɪst i̯əst
Rasta 'ræst ə 'rʌst- ‖ 'rɑːst- **~s** z
Ras Tafari, Rastafari ˌræs tə 'fɑːr i —*in Jamaica also* -fə 'raɪ
Rastafarian, r~ ˌræst ə 'feər i̯ən ◂ ˌrʌst-, -'fɑːr- ‖ -'fer- **~ism** ˌɪz əm **~s** z
Rasta|man 'ræst ə| mæn 'rʌst- ‖ 'rɑːst- **~men** men
raster 'ræst ə ‖ -ᵊr **~s** z
rasteris|e, rasteriz|e 'ræst ə raɪz **~ed** d **~er/s** ə/z ‖ ᵊr/z **~es** ɪz əz **~ing** ɪŋ
Rastrick 'ræs trɪk
Rastus 'ræst əs
rat ræt **rats** ræts **ratted** 'ræt ɪd -əd ‖ 'ræṭ əd **ratting** 'rætɪŋ ‖ 'ræṭ ɪŋ **'rat race; 'rat run; 'rat trap**
rata *tree* 'rɑːt ə ‖ 'rɑːṭ ə **~s** z —*see also* **pro rata**
ratable 'reɪt əb ᵊl ‖ 'reɪṭ-
ratafia ˌræt ə 'fɪə -'fiː̯ə ‖ ˌræṭ ə 'fiː ə **~s** z
rataplan ˌræt ə 'plæn ‖ ˌræṭ- **~ned** d **~ning** ɪŋ **~s** z
rat-arsed 'ræt ɑːst ‖ -æst -ɑːrst
rat-a-tat ˌræt ə 'tæt '· · · ‖ ˌræṭ-
rat-a-tat-tat ˌræt ə ˌtæt 'tæt ‖ ˌræṭ-
ratatouille ˌræt ə 'twiː -æ-, -'tuː̯i ‖ ˌræṭ- —*Fr* [ʁa ta tuj]
ratbag 'ræt bæg **~s** z
rat-catcher 'ræt ˌkætʃ ə ‖ -ᵊr **~s** z
ratchet 'rætʃ ɪt §-ət **~s** s
Ratcliff, Ratcliffe 'ræt klɪf
rate reɪt **rated** 'reɪt ɪd -əd ‖ 'reɪṭ əd **rates** reɪts **rating** 'reɪt ɪŋ ‖ 'reɪṭ ɪŋ **ˌrate of ex'change**
rateable 'reɪt əb ᵊl ‖ 'reɪṭ- **ˌrateable 'value**
rate-cap 'reɪt kæp **~ped** t **~ping** ɪŋ **~s** s
ratel 'reɪt ᵊl 'rɑːt-, -el ‖ 'reɪṭ ᵊl 'rɑːṭ- **~s** z
ratepayer 'reɪt ˌpeɪ ə ‖ -ᵊr **~s** z
ratfink 'ræt fɪŋk **~s** s
Rathbone 'ræθ bəʊn ‖ -boʊn
rathe reɪð
rather 'rɑːð ə §'ræð- ‖ 'ræð ᵊr —*As a BrE interjection, 'certainly', also* ˌrɑː 'ðɜː
Rather *family name* 'ræð ə ‖ -ᵊr
Rathfarnham ræθ 'fɑːn əm ‖ -'fɑːrn-
Rathgar ræθ 'gɑː ‖ -'gɑːr
Rathlin 'ræθ lɪn §-lən
Rathmines ræθ 'maɪnz
ratification ˌræt ɪf ɪ 'keɪʃ ᵊn ˌ-əf-, §-ə'·- ‖ ˌræṭ- **~s** z
rati|fy 'ræt ɪ |faɪ -ə- ‖ 'ræṭ ə |faɪ **~fied** faɪd **~fier/s** faɪ̯ə/z ‖ faɪ̯ᵊr/z **~fies** faɪz **~fying** faɪ ɪŋ
rating 'reɪt ɪŋ ‖ 'reɪṭ ɪŋ **~s** z
ratio 'reɪʃ i̯əʊ ‖ oʊ 'reɪʃ oʊ **~s** z
ratioci|nate ˌræt i 'ɒs ɪ |neɪt ˌræʃ-, -'əʊs-, -ə neɪt, ᵊ|n eɪt ‖ ˌræʃ i 'ɑːs ᵊ|n eɪt ˌræṭ-, -'oʊs- **~nated** neɪt ɪd -əd ‖ neɪṭ əd **~nates** neɪts **~nating** neɪt ɪŋ ‖ neɪṭ ɪŋ
ratiocination ˌræt i ˌɒs ɪ 'neɪʃ ᵊn ˌræʃ-, -ˌəʊs-, -ə'·- ‖ ˌræʃ i ˌɑːs- ˌræṭ-, -ˌoʊs- **~s** z
ration 'ræʃ ᵊn ‖ 'reɪʃ- **~ed** d **~ing** ˌɪŋ **~s** z
rational 'ræʃ ᵊn̮əl
rationale ˌræʃ ə 'nɑːl -'næl; -'nɑːl eɪ ‖ -'næl **~s** z
rationalis... —*see* **rationaliz...**

R

rationalism ˈræʃ ən‿ə ˌlɪz əm -ən‿əl ˌɪz-
rationalist ˈræʃ ən‿əl ɪst §-əst **~s** s
rationalistic ˌræʃ ən‿ə ˈlɪst ɪk◂ **~ally** əl‿i
rationalit|y ˌræʃ ə ˈnæl ət |i -ɪt i ‖ -əţ |i **~ies** iz
rationalization ˌræʃ ən‿əl aɪ ˈzeɪʃ ən -əl ɪ- ‖ -əl ə- **~s** z
rationaliz|e ˈræʃ ən‿ə laɪz -ən‿əl aɪz **~ed** d **~es** ɪz əz **~ing** ɪŋ
rationally ˈræʃ ən‿əl i
Ratisbon ˈræt ɪz bɒn -ɪs-, -əz-, -əs- ‖ ˈræţ əs bɑːn
ratite ˈræt aɪt **~s** s
ratlin, ratline ˈræt lɪn §-lən **~s** z
Ratner ˈræt nə ‖ -nər
ratoon rə ˈtuːn ræ- **~ed** d **~ing** ɪŋ **~s** z
ratpack ˈræt pæk
Ratskeller ˈræts ˌkel ə ‖ ˈrɑːts ˌkel ər —*Ger* [ˈʁaːts ˌkɛl ɐ] **~s** z
ratt... —*see* **rat**
rat-tail ˈræt teɪəl **~s** z
rattan rə ˈtæn ræ- **~s** z
rat-tat ˌræt ˈtæt
rat-tat-tat ˌræt ə ˈtæt -æt- ‖ ˌræţ-
Rattenbury ˈræt ən bər‿i ‖ -ˌber i
ratter ˈræt ə ‖ ˈræţ ər **~s** z
Rattigan ˈræt ɪg ən -əg- ‖ ˈræţ-
rattl|e, R~ ˈræt əl ‖ ˈræţ əl **~ed** d **~es** z **~ing** ɪŋ
rattle-brained ˈræt əl breɪnd ‖ ˈræţ-
rattler ˈræt əl‿ə ‖ ˈræt lər ˈræţ əl ər **~s** z
rattlesnake ˈræt əl sneɪk ‖ ˈræţ- **~s** s
rattletrap ˈræt əl træp ‖ ˈræţ- **~s** s
rattling ˈræt əl‿ɪŋ ‖ ˈræt lɪŋ ˈræţ əl ɪŋ
rattly ˈræt əl‿i ‖ ˈræt li ˈræţ əl i
rattoon —*see* **ratoon**
rat-trap ˈræt træp **~s** s
Rattray ˈrætr i -eɪ
ratt|y ˈræt |i ‖ ˈræţ |i **~ier** i‿ə ‖ i‿ər **~iest** i‿ɪst i‿əst **~ily** ɪ li əl i **~iness** i nəs -nɪs
Ratzinger ˈræts ɪŋ ə ‖ -ər
raucous ˈrɔːk əs ‖ ˈrɑːk- **~ly** li **~ness** nəs nɪs
Raul raʊ ˈuːl rɑː- ‖ rɑː- —*Sp* [rra ˈul]
raunch rɔːntʃ ‖ rɑːntʃ
raunch|y ˈrɔːntʃ |i ‖ ˈrɑːntʃ- **~ier** i‿ə ‖ i‿ər **~iest** i‿ɪst i‿əst **~ily** ɪ li əl i **~iness** i nəs i nɪs
Raunds rɔːndz ‖ rɑːndz
Rauschenberg ˈraʊʃ ən bɜːg ‖ -bɜːg
rauwolfia rɔː ˈwʊlf i‿ə raʊ-, -ˈwɒlf- ‖ rɑː-
ravag|e ˈræv ɪdʒ **~ed** d **~es** ɪz əz **~ing** ɪŋ
rave reɪv **raved** reɪvd **raves** reɪvz **raving** ˈreɪv ɪŋ
ravel ˈræv əl **~ed, ~led** d **~ing, ~ling** ɪŋ **~s** z
Ravel ræ ˈvel rə- ‖ rɑː- —*Fr* [ʁa vɛl]
ravelin ˈræv lɪn §-lən **~s** z
raven *n, adj,* **Raven** ˈreɪv ən **~s** z
raven *v* ˈræv ən **~ed** d **~ing** ‿ɪŋ **~s** z
Ravenglass ˈreɪv ən glɑːs →-əŋ-, §-glæs ‖ -glæs
raven-haired ˌreɪv ən ˈheəd ◂ ‖ -ˈheərd ◂ -ˈhæərd
ravening ˈræv ən‿ɪŋ **~ly** li
Ravenna rə ˈven ə —*It* [ra ˈven na]
ravenous ˈræv ən‿əs **~ly** li **~ness** nəs nɪs
Ravensbourne ˈreɪv ənz bɔːn ‖ -bɔːrn -boʊrn
raver ˈreɪv ə ‖ -ər **~s** z
Raverat ˈrɑːv ə rɑː
rave-up ˈreɪv ʌp **~s** s
Ravilious rə ˈvɪl i‿əs
ravin ˈræv ɪn §-ən
ravine rə ˈviːn **~s** z
raving ˈreɪv ɪŋ **~ly** li **~s** z
ravioli ˌræv i ˈəʊl i ‖ -ˈoʊl i ˌrɑːv-
ravish ˈræv ɪʃ **~ed** t **~es** ɪz əz **~ing/ly** ɪŋ /li
raw rɔː ‖ rɑː **rawer** ˈrɔːr ə ‖ ˈrɔː ər ˈrɑː- **rawest** ˈrɔːr ɪst -əst ‖ ˈrɔː əst ˈrɑː-
ˌ**raw** ˈ**deal**; ˌ**raw ma**ˈ**terials**
Rawalpindi ˌrɔːl ˈpɪnd i ˌrɑː wəlˈ·- ‖ ˌrɑː wəlˈ·-
raw-boned ˌrɔː ˈbəʊnd ◂ ‖ -ˈboʊnd ◂ ˌrɑː-
Rawdon ˈrɔːd ən ‖ ˈrɑːd-
rawhide ˈrɔː haɪd ‖ ˈrɑː-
Rawle rɔːl ‖ rɑːl
Rawlings ˈrɔːl ɪŋz ‖ ˈrɑːl-
Rawlins ˈrɔːl ɪnz §-ənz ‖ ˈrɑːl-
Rawlinson ˈrɔːl ɪnts ən §-ənts- ‖ ˈrɑːl-
Rawlplug, r~ *tdmk* ˈrɔːl plʌg ‖ ˈrɑːl-
raw|ly ˈrɔː |li ‖ ˈrɑː- **~ness** nəs nɪs
Rawmarsh ˈrɔː mɑːʃ ‖ -mɑːrʃ ˈrɑː-
Rawson ˈrɔːs ən ‖ ˈrɑːs-
Rawsthorne ˈrɔːs θɔːn ‖ -θɔːrn ˈrɑːs-, ˈrɔːz-, ˈrɑːz-
Rawtenstall ˈrɒt ən stɔːl ˈrɔːt- ‖ ˈrɔːt- ˈrɑːt ən stɑːl
ray, Ray reɪ **rays** reɪz
Ray-Bans *tdmk* ˈreɪ bænz
Raybould ˈreɪ bəʊld →-bɒʊld ‖ -boʊld
Rayburn ˈreɪ bɜːn ‖ -bərn
Rayleen ˈreɪ liːn
Rayleigh ˈreɪl i
rayless ˈreɪ ləs -lɪs
Rayment ˈreɪm ənt
Raymond ˈreɪm ənd
Raynaud ˈreɪn əʊ ‖ reɪ ˈnoʊ —*Fr* [ʁɛ no]
Rayner ˈreɪn ə ‖ -ər
Raynes reɪnz
rayon ˈreɪ ɒn ‖ -ɑːn **~s** z
raze reɪz *(= raise)* **razed** reɪzd **razes** ˈreɪz ɪz -əz **razing** ˈreɪz ɪŋ
razoo rɑː ˈzuː rə-
razor ˈreɪz ə ‖ -ər **~ed** d **razoring** ˈreɪz ər ɪŋ **~s** z
ˈ**razor blade**; ˌ**razor** ˈ**edge**, ˌ**razor's** ˈ**edge**
razorback ˈreɪz ə bæk ‖ -ər- **~s** s
razorbill ˈreɪz ə bɪl ‖ -ər- **~s** z
razor-sharp ˌreɪz ə ˈʃɑːp ◂ ‖ -ər ˈʃɑːrp ◂
razorshell ˈreɪz ə ʃel ‖ -ər- **~s** z
razor-thin ˌreɪz ə ˈθɪn ◂ ‖ -ər-
razz ræz **razzed** ræzd **razzes** ˈræz ɪz -əz **razzing** ˈræz ɪŋ
razzamatazz ˌræz əm‿ə ˈtæz ˈ· · · ·
razzia ˈræz i‿ə **~s** z
razzle ˈræz əl
razzle-dazzle ˌræz əl ˈdæz əl ˈ· ·ˌ· ·
razzmatazz ˌræz mə ˈtæz ˈ· · ·
RC ˌɑː ˈsiː ‖ ˌɑːr-

r-colored, r-coloured 'ɑː ˌkʌl əd ‖ 'ɑːr ˌkʌl ᵊrd
Rd *—see* **Road**
're ə ‖ ᵊr → **they're, we're, you're**
re *note in music* reɪ
re *prep 'regarding'* riː reɪ
RE *'religious education'* ˌɑːr 'iː ‖ ˌɑːr-
re- ¦riː; ri, rə *—(i) As a productive prefix meaning 'again' (sometimes spelt with a hyphen),* ¦riː (refill *v* ˌriː 'fɪl, *n* 'riː fɪl). *Any words in* re- *not included below may be assumed to involve this productive prefix. (ii) Otherwise, with a vaguer meaning,* ri *before a vowel sound* (react ri 'ækt), *and* ri, rə *before a consonant* (return ri 'tɜːn, rə- ‖ -'tɝːn); *but if stressed through the operation of a stressing rule usually* ¦re+ (recommend ˌrek ə 'mend).
Rea *(i)* reɪ, *(ii)* riː
reach riːtʃ **reached** riːtʃt **reaches** 'riːtʃ ɪz -əz **reaching** 'riːtʃ ɪŋ
reachable 'riːtʃ əb ᵊl
reach-me-down 'riːtʃ mi daʊn **~s** z
reac|quaint ˌriː ə| 'kweɪnt **~quainted** 'kweɪnt ɪd -əd ‖ 'kweɪnt̬- **~quainting** 'kweɪnt ɪŋ ‖ 'kweɪnt̬ ɪŋ **~quaints** 'kweɪnts
react ri 'ækt **~ed** ɪd əd **~ing** ɪŋ **~s** s
reactance ri 'ækt ənᵗs
reactant ri 'ækt ənt **~s** s
reaction ri 'æk ʃᵊn **~s** z
re'action time
reactionar|y ri 'æk ʃᵊn ər‿|i -ʃᵊn‿ər |i ‖ -ʃə ner |i **~ies** iz
reacti|vate ri 'ækt ɪ |veɪt ˌriː-, -ə- **~vated** veɪt ɪd -əd ‖ veɪt̬ əd **~vates** veɪts **~vating** veɪt ɪŋ ‖ veɪt̬ ɪŋ
reactivation ri ˌækt ɪ 'veɪʃ ᵊn ˌriːˌ· ·'··, -ə'·· **~s** z
reactive ri 'ækt ɪv **~ly** li **~ness** nəs nɪs
reactor ri 'ækt ə ‖ -ᵊr **~s** z
read *v pres; n* riːd *(= reed)* **read** *v past, pp* red *(= red)* **reading** 'riːd ɪŋ **reads** riːdz
'reading ˌmatter; **'reading room**
Read riːd
readability ˌriːd ə 'bɪl ət i -ɪt i ‖ -ət̬ i
readab|le 'riːd əb |ᵊl **~ly** li
readdress ˌriː ə 'dres **~ed** t **~es** ɪz əz **~ing** ɪŋ
Reade riːd
reader, R~ 'riːd ə ‖ -ᵊr **~s** z
readership 'riːd ə ʃɪp ‖ -ᵊr- **~s** s
readi... *—see* **ready**
reading 'riːd ɪŋ **~s** z
Reading *name* 'red ɪŋ
readjust ˌriː ə 'dʒʌst **~ed** ɪd əd **~ing** ɪŋ **~ment/s** mənt/s **~s** s
Readman *(i)* 'red mən, *(ii)* 'riːd-
readmission ˌriː‿əd 'mɪʃ ᵊn →‿əb-, -æd- **~s** z
read|mit ˌriː‿əd |'mɪt →‿əb-, -æd- **~mits** 'mɪts **~mitted** 'mɪt ɪd -əd ‖ 'mɪt̬ əd **~mitting** 'mɪt ɪŋ ‖ 'mɪt̬ ɪŋ
readmittanc|e ˌriː‿əd 'mɪt ᵊnᵗs →‿əb-, -æd- **~es** ɪz əz
read-only ˌriːd 'əʊn li ◂ ‖ -'oʊn-
readout 'riːd aʊt **~s** s
readthrough 'riːd θruː **~s** z
read|y 'red |i **~ied** id **~ier** i‿ə ‖ i‿ᵊr **~ies** iz **~iest** i‿ɪst i‿əst **~ily** ɪ li ᵊl i **~iness** i nəs i nɪs **~ying** i ɪŋ
ˌready 'cash; **ˌready 'money**
ready-made ˌred i 'meɪd ◂ '· · · **~s** z
ready-mix ˌred i 'mɪks ◂ '· · · **~ed** t
ready-to-wear ˌred i tə 'weə ◂ -tu- ‖ -'weᵊr -'wæᵊr
reaffirm ˌriː‿ə 'fɜːm ‖ -'fɝːm **~ed** d **~ing** ɪŋ **~s** z
reaffirmation ˌriː ˌæf ə 'meɪʃ ᵊn ·ˌ· ·'·· ‖ -ᵊr'·· **~s** z
reafforest ˌriː‿ə 'fɒr ɪst -əst ‖ -'fɔːr əst -'fɑːr- **~ed** ɪd əd **~ing** ɪŋ **~s** s
reafforestation ˌriː‿ə ˌfɒr ɪ 'steɪʃ ᵊn -ˌ·ə- ‖ -ˌfɔːr- -ˌfɑːr- **~s** z
Reagan 'reɪg ən
Reaganomics ˌreɪg ə 'nɒm ɪks ‖ -'nɑːm-
reagent ri 'eɪdʒ ənt **~s** s

REAL

55% 45%
BrE
riːᵊl
rɪəl
BrE riːᵊl (same as reel) by age
Percentage
Older ← Speakers → Younger

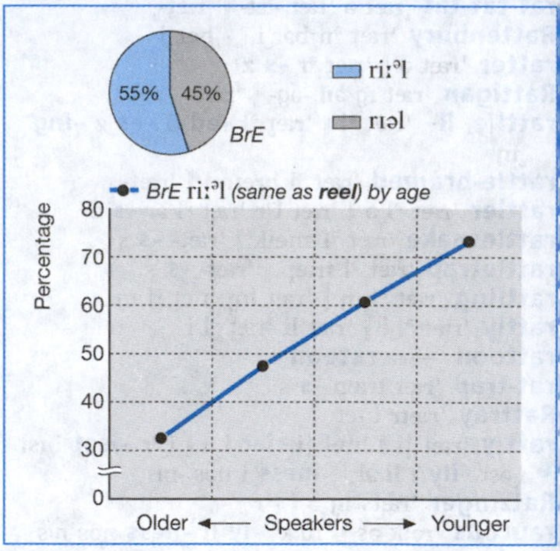

real *adj, adv, n 'reality'* rɪəl riːᵊl ‖ riːᵊl 'riː‿əl — *Preference poll, BrE:* riːᵊl (*i.e. same as* reel) *55%,* rɪəl *45%.*
'real eˌstate; **'real estate ˌagent**; **ˌreal 'property**
real *n 'coin',* **Real** *name of football team* ₍ˌ₎reɪ 'ɑːl 'reɪ‿əl *—Sp, Port* [ɾɾe 'al] **~s** z
realgar ri 'ælg ə -ɑː ‖ -ᵊr -ɑːr
realia reɪ 'ɑːl i‿ə ri 'eɪl-
realign ˌriː‿ə 'laɪn **~ed** d **~ing** ɪŋ **~ment/s** mənt/s **~s** z
realis... *—see* **realiz...**
realism 'rɪəl ˌɪz əm 'riːᵊl- ‖ 'riː ə ˌlɪz əm
realist 'rɪəl ɪst 'riːᵊl-, §-əst ‖ 'riː‿əl əst **~s** s
realistic ₍ˌ₎rɪə 'lɪst ɪk ◂ ˌriː ə- ‖ ˌriː ə 'lɪst ɪk ◂ **~ally** ᵊl‿i
realit|y ri 'æl ət |i -ɪt i ‖ -ət̬ |i **~ies** iz
realizable 'rɪəl aɪz əb ᵊl 'riːᵊl- ‖ 'riː ə laɪz əb ᵊl
realization ˌrɪəl aɪ 'zeɪʃ ᵊn ˌriːᵊl-, -ɪ'·· ‖ ˌriː əl ə 'zeɪʃ ᵊn **~s** z

R

ealiz|e ˈrɪəl aɪz ˈriːᵊl- ‖ ˈriː ə laɪz **~ed** d **~es** ɪz əz **~ing** ɪŋ
eal-life ˌrɪəl ˈlaɪf ◂ ˌriːᵊl- ‖ ˌriːᵊl-
eallo|cate ˌriː ˈæl əʊ |keɪt ‖ -ə |keɪt **~cated** keɪt ɪd -əd ‖ keɪţ əd **~cates** keɪts **~cating** keɪt ɪŋ ‖ keɪţ ɪŋ
eallocation ˌriː ˌæl əʊ ˈkeɪʃ ᵊn ‖ -ə-

REALLY

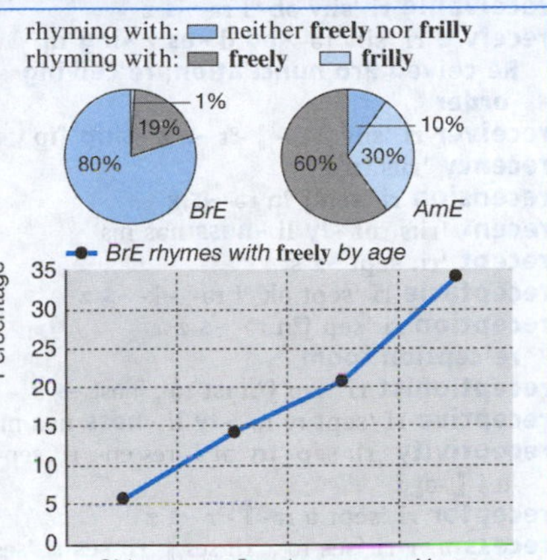

really ˈrɪəl i ˈriːᵊl i, ˈreəl i ‖ ˈriːl i ˈrɪl i, ˈriː əl i *— Preference polls, BrE: rhyming with neither* freely *nor* frilly *80%; rhyming with* freely *19%, rhyming with* frilly *1%; AmE: rhyming with* freely *60%, rhyming with* frilly *30%, rhyming with neither* freely *nor* frilly *10%.*
realm relm **realms** relmz
realpolitik reɪ ˈɑːl pɒl ɪ ˌtiːk -əˌ·, ·ˌ· · ·ˈ· ‖ -ˈ·poʊl- —*Ger* [ʁe ˈaːl po li ˌtiːk]
real-time ˌrɪəl ˈtaɪm ◂ ˌriːᵊl- ‖ ˌriːᵊl-
realtor, R~ *tdmk* ˈrɪəl tə ˈriːᵊl-, -tɔː ‖ ˈriːᵊlt ᵊr ⚠ˈriːl əţ ᵊr **~s** z
realty ˈrɪəl ti ˈriːᵊl- ‖ ˈriː‿əlt i
ream riːm **reamed** riːmd **reaming** ˈriːm ɪŋ **reams** riːmz
reamer ˈriːm ə ‖ -ᵊr **~s** z
reani|mate ₍ˌ₎riː ˈæn ɪ |meɪt -ə- **~mated** meɪt ɪd -əd ‖ meɪţ əd **~mates** meɪts **~mating** meɪt ɪŋ ‖ meɪţ ɪŋ
reap riːp **reaped** riːpt **reaping** ˈriːp ɪŋ **reaps** riːps
reaper ˈriːp ə ‖ -ᵊr **~s** z
reap|pear ˌriː‿ə |ˈpɪə ‖ -|ˈpɪᵊr **~peared** ˈpɪəd ‖ ˈpɪᵊrd **~pearing** ˈpɪər ɪŋ ‖ ˈpɪr ɪŋ **~pears** ˈpɪəz ‖ ˈpɪᵊrz
reappearanc|e ˌriː‿ə ˈpɪər ənᵗs ‖ -ˈpɪr- **~es** ɪz əz
reapplication ˌriː æp lɪ ˈkeɪʃ ᵊn ri ˌæp- **~s** z
reap|ply ˌriː‿ə |ˈplaɪ **~plied** ˈplaɪd **~plies** ˈplaɪz **~plying** ˈplaɪ ɪŋ
reap|point ˌriː‿ə |ˈpɔɪnt **~pointment/s** ˈpɔɪnt mənt/s **~pointed** ˈpɔɪnt ɪd -əd ‖ ˈpɔɪnţ əd **~pointing** ˈpɔɪnt ɪŋ ‖ ˈpɔɪnţ ɪŋ **~points** ˈpɔɪnts

reapportion ˌriː ə ˈpɔːʃ ᵊn ‖ -ˈpɔːrʃ- **~ment** mənt
reappraisal ˌriː‿ə ˈpreɪz ᵊl **~s** z
reapprais|e ˌriː‿ə ˈpreɪz **~ed** d **~es** ɪz əz **~ing** ɪŋ
rear rɪə ‖ rɪᵊr **reared** rɪəd ‖ rɪᵊrd **rearing** ˈrɪər ɪŋ ‖ ˈrɪr ɪŋ **rears** rɪəz ‖ rɪᵊrz **ˌrear ˈadmiral◂; ˌrear ˈend**
Rearden, Reardon ˈrɪəd ᵊn ‖ ˈrɪrd ᵊn
rear-end ˌrɪər ˈend ‖ ˌrɪr- **~ed** ɪd əd **~er/s** ə/z ‖ ᵊr/z **~ing** ɪŋ **~s** z
rearguard ˈrɪə gɑːd ‖ ˈrɪr gɑːrd **~s** z **ˌrearguard ˈaction**
rearm ri ˈɑːm ˌriː- ‖ -ˈɑːrm **~ed** d **~ing** ɪŋ **~s** z
rearmament ri ˈɑːm ə mənt ˌriː- ‖ -ˈɑːrm-
rearmost ˈrɪə məʊst ‖ ˈrɪr moʊst
rearrang|e ˌriː‿ə ˈreɪndʒ **~ed** d **~ement/s** mənt/s **~es** ɪz əz **~ing** ɪŋ
rearrest ˌriː ə ˈrest **~ed** ɪd əd **~ing** ɪŋ **~s** s
rearview ˈrɪə vjuː ‖ ˈrɪr- **ˌrearview ˈmirror**
rearward ˈrɪə wəd ‖ ˈrɪr wᵊrd **~s** z
reason, R~ ˈriːz ᵊn **~ed** d **~ing/s** ‿ɪŋ/z **~s** z
reasonab|le ˈriːz ᵊn‿əb |ᵊl **~ly** li **~ness** nəs nɪs
reasoner ˈriːz ᵊn‿ə ‖ ‿ər **~s** z
reasonless ˈriːz ᵊn ləs -lɪs **~ly** li **~ness** nəs nɪs
reassembl|e ˌriː‿ə ˈsem bᵊl **~ed** d **~es** z **~ing** ‿ɪŋ
reassembly ˌriː‿ə ˈsem bli
reas|sert ˌriː‿ə |ˈsɜːt -|ˈsɝːt **~serted** ˈsɜːt ɪd -əd ‖ ˈsɝːţ əd **~serting** ˈsɜːt ɪŋ ‖ ˈsɝːţ ɪŋ **~serts** ˈsɜːts ‖ ˈsɝːts
reassess ˌriː‿ə ˈses **~ed** t **~es** ɪz əz **~ing** ɪŋ **~ment/s** mənt/s
reassign ˌriː‿ə ˈsaɪn **~ed** d **~ing** ɪŋ **~s** z
reassuranc|e ˌriː‿ə ˈʃʊər ənᵗs -ˈʃɔːr- ‖ -ˈʃʊr- -ˈʃɝː- **~es** ɪz əz
reas|sure ˌriː‿ə |ˈʃɔː -ˈʃʊə; rɪəˈ· ‖ -|ˈʃʊᵊr -ˈʃɝː **~sured** ˈʃɔːd ˈʃʊəd ‖ ˈʃʊᵊrd ˈʃɝːd **~sures** ˈʃɔːz ˈʃʊəz ‖ ˈʃʊᵊrz ˈʃɝːz **~suring/ly** ˈʃɔːr ɪŋ /li ˈʃʊər- ‖ ˈʃʊr ɪŋ /li ˈʃɝː-
Reaumur, Réaumur ˈreɪ əʊ mjʊə ‖ ˌreɪ oʊ ˈmjʊᵊr —*Fr* [ʁe o myːʁ]
Reave riːv
reawaken ˌriː‿ə ˈweɪk ən **~ed** d **~ing** ‿ɪŋ **~s** z
Reay reɪ
reb, Reb reb **rebs, Rebs** rebz
rebarbative rɪ ˈbɑːb ət ɪv rə-, §riː- ‖ -ˈbɑːrb əţ ɪv
re|bate *v 'deduct'; 'form rebate in'* ri ˈ|beɪt rə-; ˈriː |beɪt **~bated** beɪt ɪd -əd ‖ beɪţ əd **~bates** beɪts **~bating** beɪt ɪŋ ‖ beɪţ ɪŋ
rebate *n 'deduction'* ˈriː beɪt ri ˈbeɪt, rə- **~s** s
rebate *n 'groove, joint'* ˈriː beɪt ˈræb ɪt, §-ət **~s** s
rebec, rebeck ˈriːb ek ˈreb- **~s** s
Rebecca, Rebekah ri ˈbek ə rə-
rebel *v* rɪ ˈbel rə-, §riː- **~led** d **~ling** ɪŋ **~s** z
rebel *n, adj* ˈreb ᵊl **~s** z
rebellion ri ˈbel jən rə-, -i‿ən **~s** z
rebellious ri ˈbel jəs rə-, -i‿əs **~ly** li **~ness** nəs nɪs

rebind ˌriː ˈbaɪnd **~ing** ɪŋ **~s** z **rebound** ˌriː ˈbaʊnd
rebirth ˌriː ˈbɜːθ ‖ -ˈbɜʳθ **~er/s** ə/z ‖ -ᵊr/z **~ing** ɪŋ **~s** s
reboot *n* ˈriː buːt ˌ·ˈ· **~s** s
re|boot *v* ˌriː |ˈbuːt **~booted** ˈbuːt ɪd -əd ‖ ˈbuːţ əd **~booting** ˈbuːt ɪŋ ‖ ˈbuːţ ɪŋ **~boots** ˈbuːts
rebore *v* ˌriː ˈbɔː ‖ -ˈbɔːr -ˈboʊr **~d** d **~s** z **reboring** ˌriː ˈbɔːr ɪŋ ‖ -ˈboʊr-
rebore *n* ˈriː bɔː ‖ -bɔːr -boʊr **~s** z
reborn ˌriː ˈbɔːn ‖ -ˈbɔːrn
rebound *n* ˈriː baʊnd **~s** z
rebound *v 'bounce back; have unexpected effect'* ri ˈbaʊnd rə- **~ed** ɪd əd **~ing** ɪŋ **~s** z
rebound *adj 'again subjected to binding'* ˌriː ˈbaʊnd ◂
rebozo rɪ ˈbəʊz əʊ rə- ‖ -ˈboʊz oʊ -ˈboʊs- —*AmSp* [re ˈβo so] **~s** z
rebrand ˌriː ˈbrænd **~ed** ɪd əd **~ing** ɪŋ **~s** z
rebuff *n* ri ˈbʌf rə-; ˈriː bʌf **~s** s
rebuff *v* ri ˈbʌf rə- **~ed** t **~ing** ɪŋ **~s** s
rebuild *n* ₍ˌ₎riː ˈbɪld ˈ· · **~s** z
rebuild *v* ₍ˌ₎riː ˈbɪld **~ing** ɪŋ **~s** z **rebuilt** ₍ˌ₎riː ˈbɪlt ◂
rebuk|e *v, n* ri ˈbjuːk rə- **~ed** t **~es** s **~ing** ɪŋ
rebus ˈriːb əs **~es** ɪz əz
re|but ri |ˈbʌt rə- **~buts** ˈbʌts **~butted** ˈbʌt ɪd -əd ‖ ˈbʌţ əd **~butting** ˈbʌtɪŋ ‖ ˈbʌţ ɪŋ
rebuttal ri ˈbʌt ᵊl rə- ‖ -ˈbʌţ ᵊl **~s** z
rebutter ri ˈbʌt ə rə- ‖ -ˈbʌţ ᵊr **~s** z
rec rek
recalcitranc|e ri ˈkæls ɪtr ənᵗs rə-, -ətr- **~y** i
recalcitrant ri ˈkæls ɪtr ənt rə-, -ətr- **~ly** li **~s** s
recalcu|late ˌriː ˈkælk ju| leɪt -jə|- ‖ -jə|- **~lated** leɪt ɪd -əd ‖ leɪţ əd **~lating** leɪt ɪŋ ‖ leɪţ ɪŋ
recall *v* ri ˈkɔːl rə- ‖ -ˈkɑːl **~ed** d **~ing** ɪŋ **~s** z
recall *n* ri ˈkɔːl rə-; ˈriː kɔːl ‖ -ˈkɑːl **~s** z
recallable ri ˈkɔːl əb ᵊl rə- ‖ -ˈkɑːl-
re|cant ri |ˈkænt rə- **~canted** ˈkænt ɪd -əd ‖ ˈkænţ əd **~canting** ˈkæntɪŋ ‖ ˈkænţ ɪŋ **~cants** ˈkæn*t*s
recantation ˌriː kæn ˈteɪʃ ᵊn **~s** z
recap *v 'retread'* ˌriː ˈkæp **~ped** t **~ping** ɪŋ **~s** s
recap *n 'retread'* ˈriː kæp **~s** s
recap *v 'recapitulate', n 'recapitulation'* ˈriː kæp ₍ˌ₎riː ˈkæp, rɪ-, rə- **~ped** t **~ping** ɪŋ **~s** s
recapitalisation, recapitalization ˌriː ˌkæp ɪt ᵊl aɪ ˈzeɪʃᵊn -ˈ·ət-, -ɪˈ· · ‖ -ˌkæp ɪţ ᵊl ə-
recapitalis|e, recapitaliz|e ˌriː ˈkæp ɪt ə laɪz -ˈ·ət-, -ᵊl aɪz ‖ -əţ ᵊl aɪz
recapitu|late ˌriː kə ˈpɪtʃ u |leɪt -ˈpɪt ju- ‖ -ˈpɪtʃ ə- **~lated** leɪt ɪd -əd ‖ leɪţ əd **~lates** leɪts **~lating** leɪt ɪŋ ‖ leɪţ ɪŋ
recapitulation ˌriː kə ˌpɪtʃ u ˈleɪʃ ᵊn -ˌpɪt ju- ‖ -ˌpɪtʃ ə- **~s** z
recapitulatory ˌriː kə ˈpɪtʃ ʊl ət‿ər i -ˈpɪt jʊl-; -pɪtʃ u ˈleɪt ər i, -pɪt ju- ‖ -əl ə tɔːr i -toʊr i
recap|ture ₍ˌ₎riː ˈkæp |tʃə -ʃə ‖ -|tʃᵊr **~tured** tʃəd ʃəd ‖ tʃᵊrd **~tures** tʃəz ʃəz ‖ tʃᵊrz **~turing** tʃər ɪŋ ʃər‿ɪŋ
recast ˌriː ˈkɑːst §-ˈkæst ‖ -ˈkæst **~ing** ɪŋ **~s** s
recce ˈrek i **~d, ~ed** d **~ing** ɪŋ **~s** z
reced|e ri ˈsiːd rə- **~ed** ɪd əd **~es** z **~ing** ɪŋ
re|ceipt ri |ˈsiːt rə- **~ceipted** ˈsiːt ɪd -əd ‖ ˈsiːţ əd **~ceipting** ˈsiːt ɪŋ ‖ ˈsiːţ ɪŋ **~ceipts** ˈsiːts
receivable ri ˈsiːv əb ᵊl rə- **~s** z
receiv|e ri ˈsiːv rə- **~ed** d **~es** z **~ing** ɪŋ **Reˌceived Proˌnunci'ation**; **re'ceiving ˌorder**
receiver ri ˈsiːv ə rə- ‖ -ᵊr **~s** z **~ship** ʃɪp
recency ˈriːs ᵊnᵗs i
recension ri ˈsenᵗʃ ᵊn rə- **~s** z
recent ˈriːs ᵊnt **~ly** li **~ness** nəs nɪs
recept ˈriː sept **~s** s
receptacle ri ˈsept ək ᵊl rə-, -ɪk- **~s** z
reception ri ˈsep ʃᵊn rə- **~s** z **re'ception room**
receptionist ri ˈsep ʃᵊn‿ɪst rə-, §‿əst **~s** s
receptive ri ˈsept ɪv rə- **~ly** li **~ness** nəs nɪs
receptivity ˌriː sep ˈtɪv ət i ˌres ep-, ri ˌsep-, -ɪt i ‖ -əţ i
receptor ri ˈsept ə rə- ‖ -ᵊr **~s** z
recess *n, v* ri ˈses rə-; ˈriː ses ‖ ˈriː ses ri ˈses —*Some speakers may distinguish the verb* ·ˈ· *from the noun* ˈ· · **~ed** t **~es** ɪz əz **~ing** ɪŋ
recession ri ˈseʃ ᵊn rə- **~s** z
recessional ri ˈseʃ ᵊn‿əl rə- **~s** z
recessive ri ˈses ɪv rə- **~ly** li **~ness** nəs nɪs **~s** z
Rechabite ˈrek ə baɪt **~s** s
recharg|e *n* ˈriː tʃɑːdʒ ‖ -tʃɑːrdʒ **~es** ɪz əz
recharg|e *v* ˌriː ˈtʃɑːdʒ ‖ -ˈtʃɑːrdʒ **~ed** d **~er/s** ə/z ‖ ᵊr/z **~es** ɪz əz **~ing** ɪŋ
recherche, recherché rə ˈʃeəʃ eɪ ‖ -ˌʃer ˈʃeɪ —*Fr* [ʁə ʃɛʁ ʃe]
re-chip ˌriː ˈtʃɪp **~ped** t **~ping** ɪŋ **~s** s
recidivism ri ˈsɪd ɪ ˌvɪz əm rə-, ˈ·ə-
recidivist ri ˈsɪd ɪv ɪst rə-, -əv-, §-əst **~s** s
Recife rə ˈsiːf i re-, -ə —*BrPort* [re ˈsi fi, xe-]
recipe ˈres əp i -ɪp- *(!)* **~s** z
recipient ri ˈsɪp i‿ənt rə- **~s** s
reciprocal ri ˈsɪp rək ᵊl rə- **~ly** i **~s** z
reciprocality ri ˌsɪp rə ˈkæl ət i rə- ‖ -əţ i
recipro|cate ri ˈsɪp rə |keɪt rə- **~cated** keɪt ɪd -əd ‖ keɪţ əd **~cates** keɪts **~cating** keɪt ɪŋ ‖ keɪţ ɪŋ
reciprocation ri ˌsɪp rə ˈkeɪʃ ᵊn rə- **~s** z
reciprocit|y ˌres ɪ ˈprɒs ət |i ˌ·ə-, -ɪt i ‖ -ˈprɑːs əţ |i **~ies** iz
recision ri ˈsɪʒ ᵊn rə- **~s** z
recital ri ˈsaɪt ᵊl rə- ‖ -ˈsaɪţ ᵊl **~ist/s** ɪst/s §əst/s ‖ əst/s **~s** z
recitation ˌres ɪ ˈteɪʃ ᵊn -ə- **~s** z
recitative *n* ˌres ɪt ə ˈtiːv ˌ·ət- ‖ -əţ ə- **~s** z
re|cite ri |ˈsaɪt rə- **~cited** ˈsaɪt ɪd -əd ‖ ˈsaɪţ əd **~cites** ˈsaɪts **~citing** ˈsaɪt ɪŋ ‖ ˈsaɪţ ɪŋ
reciter ri ˈsaɪt ə rə- ‖ -ˈsaɪţ rᵊ **~s** z
reck rek **recked** rekt **recking** ˈrek ɪŋ **recks** reks

R

eckless 'rek ləs -lɪs **~ly** li **~ness** nəs nɪs
eckon 'rek ən **~ed** d **~ing/s** ˬɪŋ/z **~s** z
eckoner 'rek ən ə ‖ -ən ər **~s** z
eclaim *n* ri 'kleɪm rə-, ˌriː-; 'riː kleɪm **~s** z
eclaim *v* ri 'kleɪm rə-, ˌriː- **~able** əb əl **~ed** d **~ing** ɪŋ **~s** z
eclamation ˌrek lə 'meɪʃ ən **~s** z
eclassi|fy ˌriː 'klæs ɪ| faɪ -ə- **~fied** faɪd **~fies** faɪz **~fying** faɪ ɪŋ
eclin|e ri 'klaɪn rə- **~ed** d **~er/s** ə/z ‖ ər/z **~es** z **~ing** ɪŋ
eclus|e ri 'kluːs rə-; 'rek luːs ‖ 'rek luːs ri 'kluːs **~es** ɪz əz
eclusive ri 'kluːs ɪv rə-, §-'kluːz- **~ly** li **~ness** nəs nɪs
ecognis... —*see* **recogniz...**
ecognition ˌrek əg 'nɪʃ ən ⚠-ə- **~s** z
ecognizability ˌrek əg ˌnaɪz ə 'bɪl ət i ⚠ˌ-ə-, -ɪt i ‖ -ət̬ i
ecognizab|le 'rek əg naɪz əb |əl ⚠'-ə-, ˌ· ·'·- **~ly** li
recognizanc|e ri 'kɒg nɪz ənᵗs rə-, -'kɒn ɪz- ‖ -'kɑːg nɪz ənᵗs -'kɑːn ɪz- **~es** ɪz əz
recogniz|e 'rek əg naɪz ⚠-ə naɪz; §ˌ· ·'· **~ed** d **~es** ɪz əz **~ing** ɪŋ
recoil *n* 'riː kɔɪəl ri 'kɔɪəl, rə- **~s** z
recoil *v* ri 'kɔɪəl rə- **~ed** d **~ing** ɪŋ **~s** z
recoilless ri 'kɔɪəl ləs rə-, -lɪs ‖ 'riː·
recollect ˌrek ə 'lekt **~ed** ɪd əd **~ing** ɪŋ **~s** s
recollection ˌrek ə 'lek ʃən **~s** z
recombinant (ˌ)riː 'kɒm bɪn ənt rɪ-, rə-, -'·bən- ‖ -'kɑːm- **~s** s
recombination ˌriː ˌkɒm bɪ 'neɪʃ ən ·ˌ·'·, -bə'·- ‖ -ˌkɑːm- **~s** z
recombin|e ˌriː kəm 'baɪn §-kɒm- **~ed** d **~es** z **~ing** ɪŋ
recommenc|e ˌriː kə 'menᵗs **~ed** t **~ement** mənt **~es** ɪz əz **~ing** ɪŋ
recommend ˌrek ə 'mend **~ed** ɪd əd **~ing** ɪŋ **~s** z
recommendation ˌrek ə men 'deɪʃ ən -mən'-- **~s** z
recompens|e *v, n* 'rek əm penᵗs **~ed** t **~es** ɪz əz **~ing** ɪŋ
recon 'riː kɒn ‖ -kɑːn
reconcilab|le 'rek ən saɪəl əb |əl →'-ŋ-, ˌ·ˌ'·· **~leness** əl nəs -nɪs **~ly** li
reconcil|e 'rek ən saɪəl →-ŋ-, ˌ·'· **~ed** d **~er/s** ə/z ‖ ər/z **~es** z **~ing** ɪŋ
reconciliation ˌrek ən sɪl i 'eɪʃ ən →ˌ-ŋ- **~s** z
reconciliatory ˌrek ən 'sɪl i ət ər i →ˌ-ŋ-, §ˌ· ·-'eɪt ər i ‖ ə tɔːr i -toʊr i
recondite 'rek ən daɪt →-ŋ-; ri 'kɒnd aɪt, rə- ‖ ri 'kɑːnd aɪt **~ly** li **~ness** nəs nɪs
recondition ˌriː kən 'dɪʃ ən §-kɒn- **~ed** d **~ing** ɪŋ **~s** z
reconnaissance ri 'kɒn ɪs ənᵗs rə-, -əs- ‖ -'kɑːn əz ənᵗs -əs-
reconnect ˌriː kə 'nekt **~ed** ɪd əd **~ing** ɪŋ **~s** s
recon|noiter, recon|noitre ˌrek ə |'nɔɪt ə ‖ ˌriːk ə |'nɔɪt̬ ər ˌrek- *(*)* **~noitered, ~noitred** 'nɔɪt əd ‖ 'nɔɪt̬ ərd **~noitering, ~noitring** 'nɔɪt ər ɪŋ ‖ 'nɔɪt̬ ər ɪŋ →'nɔɪtr ɪŋ **~noiters, ~noitres** 'nɔɪt əz ‖ 'nɔɪt̬ ərz
reconqu|er ˌriː 'kɒŋk| ə ‖ -'kɑːŋk| ər **~ered** əd ‖ ərd **~ering** ər ɪŋ **~ers** əz ‖ ərz
reconquest ˌriː 'kɒŋk west ‖ -'kɑːn kwest →-'kɑːŋ-, -kwəst **~s** s
reconsid|er ˌriː kən 'sɪd |ə §-kɒn- ‖ -|ər **~ered** əd ‖ ərd **~ering** ər ɪŋ **~ers** əz ‖ ərz
reconsideration ˌriː kən ˌsɪd ə 'reɪʃ ən §-kɒn-
reconsti|tute ˌriː 'kɒnᵗst ɪ |tjuːt -ə-, →-tʃuːt ‖ -'kɑːnᵗst ə |tuːt -tjuːt **~tuted** tjuːt ɪd →tʃuːt-, -əd ‖ tuːt̬ əd tjuːt̬- **~tutes** tjuːts →tʃuːts ‖ tuːts tjuːts **~tuting** tjuːt ɪŋ →tʃuːt- ‖ tuːt̬ ɪŋ tjuːt̬-
reconstitution ˌriː ˌkɒnᵗst ɪ 'tjuːʃ ən -ˌ·ə-, →-'tʃuːʃ- ‖ -ˌkɑːnᵗst ə 'tuːʃ ən -'tjuːʃ- **~s** z
reconstruct ˌriː kən 'strʌkt §-kɒn- **~ed** ɪd əd **~ing** ɪŋ **~s** s
reconstruction ˌriː kən 'strʌk ʃən §-kɒn- **~s** z
reconstructive ˌriː kən 'strʌkt ɪv ◂ §-kɒn-
reconven|e ˌriː kən 'viːn §-kɒn- **~ed** d **~es** z **~ing** ɪŋ
record *v* ri 'kɔːd rə- ‖ -'kɔːrd **~ed** ɪd əd **~ing/s** ɪŋ/z **~s** z
reˌcorded de'livery; **re'cording ˌstudio**
record *n, adj* 'rek ɔːd -əd ‖ -ərd **~s** z
'record ˌlibrary; **'record ˌplayer**
record-break|er 'rek ɔːd ˌbreɪk |ə §-əd-, →'·ɔːb- ‖ -ərd ˌbreɪk |ər **~ers** əz ‖ ərz **~ing** ɪŋ
recorder ri 'kɔːd ə rə- ‖ -'kɔːrd ər **~s** z **~ship** ʃɪp
record-holder 'rek ɔːd ˌhəʊld ə §-əd-, →-ˌhɒʊld- ‖ -ərd ˌhoʊld ər **~s** z
recordist ri 'kɔːd ɪst rə-, §-əst ‖ -'kɔːrd- **~s** s
record-keeping 'rek ɔːd ˌkiːp ɪŋ §-əd- ‖ -ərd-
re|count *v 'tell'* ri |'kaʊnt rə- **~counted** 'kaʊnt ɪd -əd ‖ 'kaʊnt̬ əd **~counting** 'kaʊnt ɪŋ ‖ 'kaʊnt̬ ɪŋ **~counts** 'kaʊnts
re|count *v 'count again'* ˌriː |'kaʊnt **~counted** 'kaʊnt ɪd -əd ‖ 'kaʊnt̬ əd **~counting** 'kaʊnt ɪŋ ‖ 'kaʊnt̬ ɪŋ **~counts** 'kaʊnts
recount *n* 'riː kaʊnt ˌ·'· **~s** s
recoup ri 'kuːp rə- **~ed** t **~ing** ɪŋ **~ment** mənt **~s** s
recourse ri 'kɔːs rə- ‖ 'riː kɔːrs -koʊrs; ri '·, rə- *(*)*
recov|er *'regain; find again; get better'* ri 'kʌv |ə rə- ‖ -|ər **~ered** əd ‖ ərd **~ering** ər ɪŋ **~ers** əz ‖ ərz
recov|er *'cover again'* ˌriː 'kʌv |ə ‖ -|ər **~ered** əd ‖ ərd **~ering** ər ɪŋ **~ers** əz ‖ ərz
recoverability ri ˌkʌv ər ə 'bɪl ət i rə-, -ɪt i ‖ -ət̬ i
recoverable ri 'kʌv ər əb əl rə-
recover|y ri 'kʌv ər |i rə- **~ies** iz
re'covery room
recreant 'rek ri ənt **~s** s
recre|ate *'create anew'* ˌriː kri |'eɪt **~ated** 'eɪt ɪd -əd ‖ 'eɪt̬ əd **~ates** 'eɪts **~ating** 'eɪt ɪŋ ‖ 'eɪt̬ ɪŋ
recreation *'creating anew'* ˌriː kri 'eɪʃ ən
recreation *'amusement'* ˌrek ri 'eɪʃ ən **~s** z
ˌrecre'ation ground; **ˌrecre'ation room**

R

recreational ˌrek ri ˈeɪʃ ᵊn‿əl

recrimi|nate ri ˈkrɪm ɪ |neɪt rə-, -ə- **~nated** neɪt ɪd -əd ‖ neɪţ əd **~nates** neɪts **~nating** neɪt ɪŋ ‖ neɪţ ɪŋ

recrimination ri ˌkrɪm ɪ ˈneɪʃ ᵊn rə-, -ə- **~s** z

recriminatory ri ˈkrɪm ɪn ət‿ər i rə-, -ˈ·ən‿; ·ˌ·ˈneɪt ər i ◂, -ə'·- ‖ -ən‿ə tɔːr i -tour i

recrudesc|e ˌriː kruː ˈdes ˌrek ruː- **~ed** t **~es** ɪz əz **~ing** ɪŋ

recrudescenc|e ˌriː kruː ˈdes ᵊnᵗs ˌrek ruː- **~es** ɪz əz

recrudescent ˌriː kruː ˈdes ᵊnt ◂ ˌrek ruː-

re|cruit *v, n* ri |ˈkruːt rə- **~cruited** ˈkruːt ɪd -əd ‖ ˈkruːţ əd **~cruiting** ˈkruːt ɪŋ ‖ ˈkruːţ ɪŋ **~cruits** ˈkruːts

recruiter ri ˈkruːt ə rə- ‖ -ˈkruːţ ᵊr **~s** z

recruitment ri ˈkruːt mənt rə-

rectal ˈrekt ᵊl **~ly** i

rectangle ˈrek tæŋ gᵊl **~s** z

rectangular rek ˈtæŋ gjʊl ə -gjəl- ‖ -gjəl ᵊr **~ly** li

rectifiable ˈrekt ɪ faɪ‿əb ᵊl ˌ·ə-, ˌ·ˈ·ˈ·

rectification ˌrekt ɪf ɪ ˈkeɪʃ ᵊn ˌ·əf-, §-əˈ·- **~s** z

recti|fy ˈrekt ɪ |faɪ -ə- **~fied** faɪd **~fier/s** faɪ‿ə/z ‖ faɪ‿ᵊr/z **~fies** faɪz **~fying** faɪ ɪŋ

rectilinear ˌrekt ɪ ˈlɪn i‿ə ◂ §ˌ·ə- ‖ ᵊr **~ly** li

rectitude ˈrekt ɪ tjuːd -ə-, →-tʃuːd ‖ -tuːd -tjuːd

recto ˈrekt əʊ ‖ -oʊ **~s** z

rector ˈrekt ə ‖ -ᵊr **~s** z **~ship/s** ʃɪp/s

rectorial rek ˈtɔːr i‿əl ‖ -ˈtour-

rector|y ˈrekt ər‿|i **~ies** iz

rectrix ˈrek trɪks **rectrices** ˈrek trɪ siːz -trə-; rek ˈtraɪs iːz

rectum ˈrekt əm **~s** z

Reculver ri ˈkʌlv ə rə- ‖ -ᵊr

recumbent ri ˈkʌm bənt rə- **~ly** li

recupe|rate ri ˈkjuːp ə |reɪt rə-, -ˈkuːp- **~rated** reɪt ɪd -əd ‖ reɪţ əd **~rates** reɪts **~rating** reɪt ɪŋ ‖ reɪţ ɪŋ

recuperation ri ˌkjuːp ə ˈreɪʃ ᵊn rə-, -ˌkuːp-

recuperative ri ˈkjuːp ər‿ət ɪv rə-, -ˈkuːp-, -ə reɪt- ‖ -ə reɪţ ɪv -ər‿əţ ɪv

recur ri ˈkɜː rə- ‖ -ˈkɜː **~red** d **recurring** ri ˈkɜːr ɪŋ rə- ‖ -ˈkɜː ɪŋ **~s** z

recurrenc|e ri ˈkʌr ənᵗs rə-, §-ˈkɜːr- ‖ -ˈkɜː ənᵗs **~es** ɪz əz

recurrent ri ˈkʌr ənt rə-, §-ˈkɜːr- ‖ -ˈkɜː ənt **~ly** li

recursion ri ˈkɜːʃ ᵊn rə-, §-ˈkɜːʒ- ‖ -ˈkɜːʒ ᵊn **~s** z

recursive ri ˈkɜːs ɪv rə- ‖ -ˈkɜːs ɪv **~ly** li **~ness** nəs nɪs

recurved ˌriː ˈkɜːvd ri-, rə- ‖ -ˈkɜːvd

recusancy ˈrek jʊz ənᵗs i ri ˈkjuːz-, rə- ‖ -jəz-

recusant ˈrek jʊz ənt ri ˈkjuːz-, rə- ‖ -jəz- **~s** s

recus|e ri ˈkjuːz rə- **~ed** d **~es** ɪz əz **~ing** ɪŋ

recyclable ˌriː ˈsaɪk ᵊl‿əb ᵊl ◂

recycl|e ˌriː ˈsaɪk ᵊl **~ed** d **~es** z **~ing** ‿ɪŋ

red, Red red **redder** ˈred ə ‖ -ᵊr **reddest** ˈred ɪst -əst **reds, Reds** redz ₍ˌ₎**red ˈadmiral**; ˌ**red aˈlert**; ˌ**red ˈblood cell**; ˌ**red ˈcarpet**; ˌ**Red ˈCrescent**; ˌ**Red ˈCross**; ˌ**red ˈdeer**; ˌ**red ˈdwarf**; ₍ˌ₎**Red ˈEnsign**; ˌ**red ˈflag**; ˌ**red ˈgiant**; ˌ**red ˈherring**; ˌ**Red ˈIndian**; ˌ**red ˈlight**; ˌ**red ˈmeat**; ˌ**red ˈpepper**; ˌ**Red ˈSea**; ˌ**red ˈsetter**; ˌ**red ˈtape**

redact ri ˈdækt rə- **~ed** ɪd əd **~ing** ɪŋ **~s** s

redaction ri ˈdæk ʃᵊn rə- **~s** z

redan ri ˈdæn rə- **~s** z

redback ˈred bæk →ˈreb- **~s** s

red-blooded ˌred ˈblʌd ɪd ◂ →ˌreb-, -əd **~ness** nəs nɪs

Redbourn, Redbourne ˈred bɔːn →ˈreb- ‖ -bɔːrn -bourn

redbreast ˈred brest →ˈreb- **~s** s

redbrick ˈred brɪk →ˈreb-, ˌ·ˈ· **~s** s

Redbridge ˈred brɪdʒ →ˈreb-

redbud ˈred bʌd →ˈreb- **~s** z

redcap ˈred kæp →ˈreg- **~s** s

Redcar ˈred kɑː →ˈreg- ‖ -kɑːr

Redcliffe ˈred klɪf →ˈreg-

redcoat ˈred kəʊt →ˈreg- ‖ -koʊt **~s** s

redcurrant ˌred ˈkʌr ənt ◂ →ˌreg-, ˈ·ˌ·· ‖ -ˈkɜː ənt **~s** s

Reddaway ˈred ə weɪ

redden ˈred ᵊn **~ed** d **~ing** ‿ɪŋ **~s** z

Redding ˈred ɪŋ

reddish, R~ ˈred ɪʃ **~ness** nəs nɪs

Redditch ˈred ɪtʃ

redeco|rate ₍ˌ₎riː ˈdek ə |reɪt **~rated** reɪt ɪd -əd ‖ reɪţ əd **~rates** reɪts **~rating** reɪt ɪŋ ‖ reɪţ ɪŋ

redecoration ₍ˌ₎riː ˌdek ə ˈreɪʃ ᵊn **~s** z

redeem ri ˈdiːm rə- **~ed** d **~ing** ɪŋ **~s** z

redeemable ri ˈdiːm əb ᵊl rə-

redeemer, R~ ri ˈdiːm ə rə- ‖ -ᵊr **~s** z

redefin|e ˌriː di ˈfaɪn -də- **~ed** d **~es** z **~ing** ɪŋ

redemption ri ˈdem*p* ʃᵊn rə-- **~s** z

redemptive ri ˈdem*p*t ɪv rə- **~ly** li

Redemptorist ri ˈdem*p*t ər‿ɪst rə-, §‿əst **~s** s

redeploy ˌriː di ˈplɔɪ -də- **~ed** d **~ing** ɪŋ **~ment** mənt **~s** z

Redesdale ˈriːdz deɪᵊl

redevelop ˌriː di ˈvel əp -də- **~ed** t **~ing** ɪŋ **~ment/s** mənt/s **~s** s

redeye ˈred aɪ **~s** z

red-faced ˌred ˈfeɪst ◂

red-facedly ˌred ˈfeɪs ɪd li -əd-; -ˈfeɪst li

Redfearn, Redfern ˈred fɜːn ‖ -fɜːn

redfin ˈred fɪn **~s** z

Redford ˈred fəd ‖ -fᵊrd

Redgrave ˈred greɪv →ˈreg-

red-handed ˌred ˈhænd ɪd ◂ -əd **~ly** li

redhead, R~ ˈred hed **~s** z

Redheugh *(i)* ˈred hjuːf, *(ii)* -juːf, *(iii)* -jəf

Redhill ˌred ˈhɪl

red-hot ˌred ˈhɒt ◂ ‖ -ˈhɑːt ◂ ˌ**red-hot ˈpoker**

redi|a ˈriːd i‿|ə **~ae** iː

redial ˌriː ˈdaɪ‿əl ◂ **~ed, ~led** d **~ing, ~ling** ɪŋ **~s** z

redid ˌriː ˈdɪd

Rediffusion *tdmk* ˌriː dɪ ˈfjuːʒ ᵊn -də-

redirect ˌriː də ˈrekt -dɪ-, -daɪᵊ- **~ed** ɪd əd **~ing** ɪŋ **~s** s

edirection ˌriː də ˈrek ʃən -dɪ-, -darə-
edistribute ˌriː dɪ ˈstrɪb juːt -də-; ˌriː ˈdɪs trɪ bjuːt, -trə- ‖ -jət **redistributed** ˌriː dɪ ˈstrɪb jʊt ɪd ˌ·də-, -əd; -ˈdɪs trɪ bjuːt-, -ˈ·trə- ‖ -jəţ əd **redistributes** ˌriː dɪ ˈstrɪb juːts -də-; -ˈdɪs trɪ bjuːts, -trə- **redistributing** ˌriː dɪ ˈstrɪb jʊt ɪŋ ˌ·də-; -ˈdɪs trɪ bjuːt- ‖ -jəţ ɪŋ
edistribution ˌriː ˌdɪs trɪ ˈbjuːʃ ən -trə- **~s** z
edivivus ˌred ɪ ˈvaɪv əs -ə-, -ˈviːv-
ed-letter ˌred ˈlet ə ‖ -ˈleţ ər ◂
ˌred-ˈletter day
ed-light ˌred ˈlaɪt
ˌred-ˈlight ˌdistrict
ed-lin|e ˈred laɪn **~ed** d **~es** z **~ing** ɪŋ
edly ˈred li
Redman ˈred mən →ˈreb-
Redmond ˈred mənd →ˈreb-
redneck ˈred nek **~s** s
redness ˈred nəs -nɪs **~es** ɪz əz
redo ˌriː ˈduː **redid** ˌriː ˈdɪd **redoes** ˌriː ˈdʌz **redoing** ˌriː ˈduːˌɪŋ **redone** ˌriː ˈdʌn
redolenc|e ˈred əl ənts -əʊl- **~y** i
redolent ˈred əl ənt -əʊl-; →-əl ənt **~ly** li
redoubl|e ˌriː ˈdʌb əl ri-, rə- **~ed** d **~es** z **~ing** ˌɪŋ
redoubt ri ˈdaʊt rə- **~s** s
redoubtab|le ri ˈdaʊt əb |əl rə- ‖ -ˈdaʊţ- **~ly** li
redound ri ˈdaʊnd rə- **~ed** ɪd əd **~ing** ɪŋ **~s** z
redox ˈriːd ɒks ˈred- ‖ -ɑːks
Redpath ˈred pɑːθ →ˈreb-, §-pæθ ‖ -pæθ
redpoll ˈred pəʊl →ˈreb-, →-pɒʊl, -pɒl ‖ -poʊl **~s** z
redraft *n* ˈriː drɑːft §-dræft ‖ -dræft **~s** s
redraft *v* ˌriː ˈdrɑːft §-ˈdræft ‖ -ˈdræft **~ed** ɪd əd **~ing** ɪŋ **~s** s
re|draw ˌriː ˈdrɔː ‖ -ˈdrɑː **~drawing** ˈdrɔːr ɪŋ ‖ ˈdrɔː ɪŋ ˈdrɑː- **~drawn** ˈdrɔːn ‖ ˈdrɑːn **~draws** ˈdrɔːz ˈdrɑːz **~drew** ˈdruː
redress *n 'satisfaction'* ri ˈdres rə-; ˈriː dres
redress *v 'put right'* ri ˈdres rə- **~ed** t **~es** ɪz əz **~ing** ɪŋ
Redruth ˌred ˈruːθ ˈ· ·
redshank ˈred ʃæŋk **~s** s
redshirt ˈred ʃɜːt ‖ -ʃɜːt **~s** s
redskin ˈred skɪn **~s** z
redstart ˈred stɑːt ‖ -stɑːrt **~s** s
red-top ˈred tɒp ‖ -tɑːp **~s** s
reduc|e ri ˈdjuːs rə-, →-ˈdʒuːs ‖ -ˈduːs -ˈdjuːs **~ed** t **~es** ɪz əz **~ing** ɪŋ
reˌduced ˈcircumstances
reducer ri ˈdjuːs ə rə-, →-ˈdʒuːs- ‖ -ˈduːs ər -ˈdjuːs- **~s** z
reducibility ri ˌdjuːs ə ˈbɪl ət i rə-, →-ˌdʒuːs-, -ɪt i ‖ rɪ ˌduːs ə ˈbɪl əţ i -ˌdjuːs-
reducib|le ri ˈdjuːs əb |əl rə-, →-ˈdʒuːs-, -ɪb- ‖ -ˈduːs- -ˈdjuːs- **~ly** li
reductase ri ˈdʌkt eɪz rə-, -eɪs
reductio ad absurdum ri ˌdʌkt i əʊ ˌæd əb ˈsɜːd əm rə-, -ˌdʌkʃ-, -æbˈ·- ‖ -oʊ ˌæd əb ˈsɜːd əm
reduction ri ˈdʌk ʃən rə- **~ism** ˌɪz əm **~ist/s** ɪst/s §əst/s ‖ əst/s **~s** z
reductive ri ˈdʌkt ɪv rə-
redundanc|y ri ˈdʌnd ənts |i rə- **~ies** iz
redundant ri ˈdʌnd ənt rə- **~ly** li
redupli|cate ri ˈdjuːp lɪ |keɪt rə-, ˌriː-, →-ˈdʒuːp-, -lə- ‖ -ˈduːp- -ˈdjuːp- **~cated** keɪt ɪd -əd ‖ keɪţ əd **~cates** keɪts **~cating** keɪt ɪŋ ‖ keɪţ ɪŋ
reduplication ri ˌdjuːp lɪ ˈkeɪʃ ən rə-, →-ˌdʒuːp-, ˌriː ˌ· ˈ· ·, -lə- ‖ -ˌduːp- -ˌdjuːp- **~s** z
reduplicative ri ˈdjuːp lɪk ət ɪv rə-, →-ˈdʒuːp-, -lək· ·; -lɪ keɪt ɪv, -lə· · ‖ ri ˈduːp lə keɪţ ɪv -ˈdjuːp-
redux ˈriː dʌks ri ˈdʌks
Redvers ˈred vəz ‖ -vərz
redwing, R~ ˈred wɪŋ **~s** z
redwood, R~ ˈred wʊd **~s** z
Ree riː
Rée reɪ
reebok, R~ *tdmk* ˈriː bɒk -bʌk ‖ -bɑːk **~s** s
Reece riːs
reecho ri ˈek əʊ ˌriː- ‖ -oʊ **~ed** d **~es** z **~ing** ɪŋ
reed, Reed riːd **reeded** ˈriːd ɪd -əd **reeding/s** ˈriːd ɪŋ/z **reeds** riːdz
ˈreed ˌorgan
re-ed|it ˌriː ˈed| ɪt §-ət **~ited** ɪt ɪd §-ət-, -əd ‖ -əţ- **~iting** ɪt ɪŋ §ət- ‖ -əţ- **~its** ɪts §əts
reedling ˈriːd lɪŋ **~s** z
reedu|cate ˌriː ˈed ju |keɪt -ˈedʒ u-, §-ˈedʒ ə- ‖ -ˈedʒ ə- **~cated** keɪt ɪd -əd ‖ keɪţ əd **~cates** keɪts **~cating** keɪt ɪŋ ‖ keɪţ ɪŋ
reeducation ˌriː ˌed ju ˈkeɪʃ ən -ˌedʒ u-, §-ˌedʒ ə- ‖ -ˌedʒ ə- ˌ· ˈ· ·
reed|y ˈriːd |i **~ier** i ə ‖ i ər **~iest** i ɪst i əst **~iness** i nəs i nɪs
reef riːf **reefed** riːft **reefing** ˈriːf ɪŋ **reefs** riːfs
ˈreef knot
reefer ˈriːf ə ‖ -ər **~s** z
ˈreefer ˌjacket
reek riːk **reeked** riːkt **reeking** ˈriːk ɪŋ **reeks** riːks
Reekie ˈriːk i
reel riːəl **reeled** riːəld **reeling** ˈriːəl ɪŋ **reels** riːəlz
reelect ˌriː ɪ ˈlekt -ə- **~ed** ɪd əd **~ing** ɪŋ **~s** s
reelection ˌriː ɪ ˈlek ʃən -ə- **~s** z
reel-to-reel ˌriːəl tə ˈriːəl ◂
re-emergence ˌriː i ˈmɜːdʒ ənts ˌ·ə- ‖ -ˈmɜːdʒ-
re-enact ˌriː ɪn ˈækt -en-, -ən **~ed** ɪd əd **~ing** ɪŋ **~ment/s** mənt/s **~s** s
reengi|neer ˌriː ˌendʒ ɪ| ˈnɪə §-ˌɪndʒ-, -ə|- ‖ -ˈnɪər **~neered** ˈnɪəd ‖ ˈnɪərd **~neering** ˈnɪər ɪŋ ‖ ˈnɪr ɪŋ **~neers** ˈnɪəz ‖ ˈnɪərz
reenter, re-enter ri ˈent ə ˌriː- ‖ -ˈenţ ər **~ed** d **reentering, re-entering** ri ˈent ər ɪŋ ˌriː- ‖ -ˈenţ ər ɪŋ →-ˈentr ɪŋ
reentrant, re-entrant ri ˈentr ənt **~s** s
reentr|y, re-entr|y ri ˈentr |i ˌriː- **~ies** iz
Reepham ˈriːf əm
Rees, Reese riːs *(!)*
reestablish ˌriː ɪ ˈstæb lɪʃ -ə- **~ed** t **~es** ɪz əz **~ing** ɪŋ **~ment** mənt
re-evalu|ate ˌriː i ˈvæl ju eɪt ˌ·ə- **~ated** eɪt ɪd -əd ‖ eɪţ əd **~ates** eɪts **~ating** eɪt ɪŋ ‖ eɪţ ɪŋ

reeve, Reeve riːv **reeved** riːvd **reeves** riːvz **reeving** 'riːv ɪŋ **rove** rəʊv ‖ roʊv
Reeves riːvz
reexamination ˌriː ɪg ˌzæm ɪ 'neɪʃ ᵊn ˌ-eg-, ˌ-əg-, ˌ-ɪk-, ˌ-ek-, ˌ-ək-, ˌ-ə'·- **~s** z
reexamin|e ˌriː ɪg 'zæm ɪn -eg-, -əg-, -ɪk-, -ek-, -ək-, §-ən **~ed** d **~es** z **~ing** ɪŋ
ref ref **refs** refs
refac|e ₍ˌ₎riː 'feɪs **~ed** t **~es** ɪz əz **~ing** ɪŋ
refashion ₍ˌ₎riː 'fæʃ ᵊn **~ed** d **~ing** ɪŋ **~s** z
refector|y ri 'fekt ər|i rə-; 'ref ɪkt-, 'ref əkt- **~ies** iz
refer ri 'fɜː rə- ‖ -'fɜː **~red** d **referring** ri 'fɜːr ɪŋ rə- ‖ -'fɜː ɪŋ **~s** z
referable ri 'fɜːr əb ᵊl rə-; 'ref ər əb ᵊl ‖ -'fɜː-
referee ˌref ə 'riː **~d** d **~ing** ɪŋ **~s** z
referenc|e 'ref ᵊr ən'ts **~ed** t **~es** ɪz əz **~ing** ɪŋ **'reference book**; **'reference ˌlibrary**
referend|um ˌref ə 'rend |əm **~a** ə **~ums** əmz
referent 'ref ᵊr ənt **~s** s
referential ˌref ə 'rentʃ ᵊl ◂ **~ly** i
referrab... —*see* **referab...**
referral ri 'fɜːr əl rə- ‖ -'fɜː əl **~s** z
reffo 'ref əʊ ‖ -oʊ **~s** z
refill *v* ˌriː 'fɪl **~ed** d **~ing** ɪŋ **~s** z
refill *n* 'riː fɪl ˌ·'· **~s** z
refinement ri 'faɪn mənt rə-, →-'faɪm- **~s** s
refiner|y ri 'faɪn ər |i rə- **~ies** iz
refinish ˌriː 'fɪn ɪʃ **~ed** t **~es** ɪz əz **~ing** ɪŋ
re|fit *v* ˌriː |'fɪt **~fits** 'fɪts **~fitted** 'fɪt ɪd -əd ‖ 'fɪţ əd **~fitting** 'fɪt ɪŋ ‖ 'fɪţ ɪŋ
refit *n* 'riː fɪt ˌ·'· **~s** s
re|flate ₍ˌ₎riː |'fleɪt **~flated** 'fleɪt ɪd -əd ‖ 'fleɪţ əd **~flates** 'fleɪts **~flating** 'fleɪt ɪŋ ‖ 'fleɪţ ɪŋ
reflation ₍ˌ₎riː 'fleɪʃ ᵊn **~s** z
reflationary ₍ˌ₎riː 'fleɪʃ ᵊn ər i -ᵊn ər i ‖ -ə ner i
reflect ri 'flekt rə- **~ed** ɪd əd **~ing** ɪŋ **~s** s **re'flecting ˌtelescope**
reflection ri 'flek ʃᵊn rə- **~s** z
reflective ri 'flekt ɪv rə- **~ly** li **~ness** nəs nɪs
reflectivit|y ˌriː flek 'tɪv ət |i ri ˌ·'· · ·, rə-; -ɪt i ‖ -əţ |i **~ies** iz
reflector ri 'flekt ə rə- ‖ -ᵊr **~s** z
reflet rə 'fleɪ rɪ- **~s** z —*Fr* [ʁə flɛ]
reflex *n, adj* 'riː fleks **~es** ɪz əz
reflex *v* ri 'fleks rə-, ˌriː-, 'riː fleks **~ed** t **~es** ɪz əz **~ing** ɪŋ
reflexion ri 'flek ʃᵊn rə- **~s** z
reflexive ri 'fleks ɪv rə- **~ly** li **~ness** nəs nɪs **~s** z
reˌflexive 'pronoun
reflexivis... —*see* **reflexiviz...**
reflexivity ˌriː flek 'sɪv ət i ri ˌ·'· · ·, rə- -ɪt i ‖ -əţ i
reflexivization ri ˌfleks ɪv aɪ 'zeɪʃ ᵊn rə-, -ˌəv-, -ɪ'·- ‖ -ə'·- **~s** z
reflexiviz|e ri 'fleks ɪ vaɪz rə-, -ə- **~ed** d **~es** ɪz əz **~ing** ɪŋ
reflexology ˌriː flek 'sɒl ədʒ i ‖ -'sɑːl-
re|float ˌriː |'fləʊt ‖ -|'floʊt **~floated** 'fləʊt ɪd -əd ‖ 'floʊţ əd **~floating** 'fləʊt ɪŋ ‖ 'floʊţ ɪŋ **~floats** 'fləʊts ‖ 'floʊts
refluent 'ref lu ənt
reflux *n* 'riː flʌks **~es** ɪz əz
reforest ₍ˌ₎riː 'fɒr ɪst -əst ‖ -'fɔːr əst -'fɑːr- **~ed** ɪd əd **~ing** ɪŋ **~s** s
reforestation riː ˌfɒr ɪ 'steɪʃ ᵊn ˌ·ˌ·'· ·, -ə'·- ‖ -ˌfɔːr- -ˌfɑːr- **~s** z
reform *v 'improve, rectify'*; *n* ri 'fɔːm rə- ‖ -'fɔːrm **~ed** d **~ing** ɪŋ **~s** z
reform, re-form *v 'form again'* ˌriː 'fɔːm ‖ -'fɔːrm **~ed** d **~ing** ɪŋ **~s** z
reform|at ˌriː 'fɔːm |æt ‖ -'fɔːrm- **~ats** æts **~atted** æt ɪd -əd ‖ æţ əd **~atting** æt ɪŋ ‖ æţ ɪŋ
reformation, R~ ˌref ə 'meɪʃ ᵊn ˌɔː- ‖ -ᵊr- **~s** z
reformative ri 'fɔːm ət ɪv rə- ‖ -'fɔːrm əţ ɪv
reformator|y ri 'fɔːm ət ər |i rə- ‖ -'fɔːrm ə tɔːr |i -toʊr i **~ies** iz
reformism ri 'fɔːm ˌɪz əm rə- ‖ -'fɔːrm-
reformist ri 'fɔːm ɪst rə-, §-əst ‖ -'fɔːrm- **~s** s
reformu|late ˌriː 'fɔːm ju leɪt -jə- ‖ -'fɔːrm jə- **~lated** leɪt ɪd -əd ‖ leɪţ əd **~lates** leɪts **~lating** leɪt ɪŋ ‖ leɪţ ɪŋ
refract ri 'frækt rə- **~ed** ɪd əd **~ing** ɪŋ **~s** s **re'fracting ˌtelescope**
refraction ri 'fræk ʃᵊn rə- **~s** z
refractive ri 'frækt ɪv rə- **~ly** li **~ness** nəs nɪs **reˌfractive 'index**
refractivity ˌriː fræk 'tɪv ət i ri ˌ·'· · ·, rə-, -ɪt i ‖ -əţ i
refractometer ˌriː fræk 'tɒm ɪt ə ri ˌ·'· · ·, rə-, -ət ə ‖ -'tɑːm əţ ᵊr **~s** z
refractor ri 'frækt ə rə- ‖ -ᵊr **~s** z
refractor|y ri 'frækt ᵊr |i rə- **~ies** iz **~ily** əl i ɪ li **~iness** i nəs i nɪs
refrain *v, n* ri 'freɪn rə- **~ed** d **~ing** ɪŋ **~s** z
re|freeze ˌriː| 'friːz **~freezes** 'friːz ɪz -əz **~froze** 'frəʊz ‖ 'froʊz **~frozen** 'frəʊz ᵊn ‖ 'froʊz ᵊn
refresh ri 'freʃ rə- **~ed** t **~er/s** ə/z ‖ ᵊr/z **~es** ɪz əz **~ing/ly** ɪŋ /li **re'fresher course**
refreshment ri 'freʃ mənt rə- **~s** s
refried ˌriː 'fraɪd ◂
refrigerant ri 'frɪdʒ ᵊr ənt rə- **~s** s
refrige|rate ri 'frɪdʒ ə |reɪt rə- **~rated** reɪt ɪd -əd ‖ reɪţ əd **~rates** reɪts **~rating** reɪt ɪŋ ‖ reɪţ ɪŋ
refrigeration ri ˌfrɪdʒ ə 'reɪʃ ᵊn rə-
refrigerator ri 'frɪdʒ ə reɪt ə rə- ‖ -reɪţ ᵊr **~s** z **reˌfrigerator-'freezer**, ·'· · · ·ˌ· ·
reft reft
refuel ˌriː 'fjuː əl ˌ·'fjuːl **~ed, ~led** d **~ing, ~ling** ɪŋ **~s** z
refug|e 'ref juːdʒ -juːʒ **~es** ɪz əz
refugee ˌref ju 'dʒiː **~s** z
refulgence ri 'fʌldʒ ən's rə-, -'fʊldʒ-
refulgent ri 'fʌldʒ ənt rə-, -'fʊldʒ- **~ly** li
refund *v* ri 'fʌnd rə-, ˌriː-, 'riː fʌnd **~ed** ɪd əd **~ing** ɪŋ **~s** z
refund *n* 'riː fʌnd **~s** z

R

efundable ri 'fʌnd əb ᵊl rə-, ˌriː-
efurbish ˌriː 'fɜːb ɪʃ ‖ rɪ-, -'fɜːb ɪʃ **~ed** t **~es** ɪz əz **~ing** ɪŋ **~ment/s** mənt/s
efusal ri 'fjuːz ᵊl rə- **~s** z
efus|e *v* ri 'fjuːz rə- **~ed** d **~es** ɪz əz **~ing** ɪŋ
efuse *n* 'ref juːs *(!)*
'refuse dump
efusenik ri 'fjuːz nɪk rə- **~s** s
efutable ri 'fjuːt əb ᵊl rə-; 'ref jʊt- ‖ ri 'fjuːţ-
efutation ˌref ju 'teɪʃ ᵊn **~s** z
e|fute ri |'fjuːt rə- **~futed** 'fjuːt ɪd -əd ‖ 'fjuːţ əd **~futes** 'fjuːts **~futing** 'fjuːt ɪŋ ‖ 'fjuːţ ɪŋ
Reg redʒ *(!)* **Reg's** 'redʒ ɪz -əz
-reg *BrE stress-neutral suffix relating to age of cars* redʒ **S-reg** 'es redʒ
regain ri 'geɪn rə-, ˌriː- **~ed** d **~ing** ɪŋ **~s** z
regal 'riːg ᵊl
regal|e ri 'geɪᵊl rə- **~ed** d **~es** z **~ing** ɪŋ
regalia ri 'geɪl i‿ə rə- ‖ -'-jə
regalit|y riː 'gæl ət |i ri-, -ɪt- ‖ -əţ |i **~ies** iz
regally 'riːg ᵊl i
Regan 'riːg ən
regard *v, n* ri 'gɑːd rə- ‖ -'gɑːrd **~ed** ɪd əd **~ing** ɪŋ **~s** z
regardful ri 'gɑːd fᵊl rə-, -fʊl ‖ -'gɑːrd- **~ly** ‿i **~ness** nəs nɪs
regardless ri 'gɑːd ləs rə-, -lɪs ‖ -'gɑːrd- **~ly** li **~ness** nəs nɪs
regatta ri 'gæt ə rə- ‖ -'gæţ ə -'gɑːţ- **~s** z
regenc|y, R~ 'riːdʒ ənᵗs |i **~ies** iz
regenerate *adj* ri 'dʒen ər‿ət rə-, ˌriː-, -ɪt, -ə reɪt **~ness** nəs nɪs
regene|rate *v* ri 'dʒen ə |reɪt rə-, ˌriː- **~rated** reɪt ɪd -əd ‖ reɪţ əd **~rates** reɪts **~rating** reɪt ɪŋ ‖ reɪţ ɪŋ
regeneration ri ˌdʒen ə 'reɪʃ ᵊn rə-, ˌriː ˌ· ·'·· **~s** z
regenerative ri 'dʒen ər‿ət ɪv rə-, ˌriː-, -ə reɪt ɪv ‖ -ər‿əţ ɪv -ə reɪţ ɪv **~ly** li
Regensburg 'reɪg ənz bɜːg -bʊəg ‖ -bɜːg —*Ger* ['ʁeːg ᵊns bʊʁk]
regent, R~ 'riːdʒ ənt **~s, ~'s** s **~ship/s** ʃɪp/s
ˌRegent's 'Park; **'Regent Street**
Reger 'reɪg ə ‖ -ᵊr
reggae 'reg eɪ
Reggie 'redʒ i
Reggio 'redʒ i əʊ ‖ -oʊ —*It* ['red dʒo]
regicide 'redʒ ɪ saɪd -ə- **~s** z
regime, régime reɪ 'ʒiːm re-, rɪ-, rə-, §-'dʒiːm; 'reɪʒ iːm ‖ rə- —*Fr* [ʁe ʒim] **~s** z
regimen 'redʒ ɪm ən -əm-; -ɪ men, -ə- **~s** z
regi|ment *v* 'redʒ ɪ |ment -ə-, ˌ· ·'|· —*See note at* -ment **~mented** ment ɪd -əd ‖ menţ əd **~menting** ment ɪŋ ‖ menţ ɪŋ **~ments** ments
regiment *n* 'redʒ ɪ mənt -ə- **~s** s
regimental ˌredʒ ɪ 'ment ᵊl ◂ -ə- ‖ -'menţ ᵊl ◂ **~ly** i **~s** z
regimentation ˌredʒ ɪ men 'teɪʃ ᵊn ˌ·ə-, -mən'·-
Regina rɪ 'dʒaɪn ə rə-, §riː- —*but as a personal name, sometimes* -'dʒiːn-
Reginald 'redʒ ɪn ᵊld -ᵊn‿əld

region 'riːdʒ ən **~s** z
regional 'riːdʒ ᵊn‿əl
regionalism 'riːdʒ ən‿ə ˌlɪz əm
regionality ˌriːdʒ ə 'næl ət i -ɪt i ‖ -əţ i
regionally 'riːdʒ ᵊn‿əl i
Regis 'riːdʒ ɪs §-əs
register 'redʒ ɪst ə -əst- ‖ -ᵊr **~ed** d
registering 'redʒ ɪst ər‿ɪŋ '·əst- **~s** z
ˌRegistered ˌGeneral 'Nurse; **ˌRegistered 'Nurse**; **ˌregistered 'mail**; **ˌregistered 'post**; **'register ˌoffice**
registrable 'redʒ ɪs trəb ᵊl '·əs-
registrant 'redʒ ɪs trənt -əs- **~s** s
registrar ˌredʒ ɪ 'strɑː -ə-, '· · · ‖ 'redʒ ə strɑːr **~s** z
registrar|y 'redʒ ɪs trər |i '·əs- ‖ -trer |i **~ies** iz
registration ˌredʒ ɪ 'streɪʃ ᵊn -ə- **~s** z
ˌregi'stration ˌdocument; **ˌregi'stration ˌnumber**
regis|try 'redʒ ɪs |tri -əs- **~tries** triz
'registry ˌoffice
Regius 'riːdʒ i‿əs 'riːdʒ əs
reglet 'reg lət -lɪt **~s** s
regnal 'reg nᵊl
regnant 'reg nənt
rego *'registration'* 'redʒ əʊ ‖ -oʊ
regress *v* ri 'gres rə-, ˌriː- **~ed** t **~es** ɪz əz **~ing** ɪŋ
regress *n* 'riː gres
regression ri 'greʃ ᵊn rə-, ˌriː- **~s** z
re'gression aˌnalysis
regressive ri 'gres ɪv rə-, ˌriː- **~ly** li **~ness** nəs nɪs
re|gret *v, n* ri |'gret rə- **~grets** 'grets **~gretted** 'gret ɪd -əd ‖ 'greţ əd **~gretting** 'gret ɪŋ ‖ 'greţ ɪŋ
regretful ri 'gret fᵊl rə-, -fʊl **~ly** ‿i **~ness** nəs nɪs
regrett... —*see* **regret...**
regrettab|le ri 'gret əb |ᵊl rə- ‖ -'greţ- **~ly** li
regroup ˌriː 'gruːp **~ed** t **~ing** ɪŋ **~s** s
regs *'regulations'* regz
regular 'reg jʊl ə -jəl-, ⚠-əl‿ə ‖ -jəl ᵊr **~s** z
regularis... —*see* **regulariz...**
regularit|y ˌreg ju 'lær ət |i ˌ·jə-, ⚠ˌ·ə-, -ɪt i ‖ -jə 'lær əţ |i -'ler- **~ies** iz
regularization ˌreg jʊl ər aɪ 'zeɪʃ ᵊn ˌ·jəl-, ⚠ˌ·əl‿, -ɪ'·- ‖ -jəl ər ə- **~s** z
regulariz|e 'reg jʊl ə raɪz '·jəl-, ⚠ˌ·əl ‖ '·jəl- **~ed** d **~es** ɪz əz **~ing** ɪŋ
regularly 'reg jʊl ə li '·jəl-, ⚠'·əl‿əl i ‖ -jəl ᵊr li
regu|late 'reg ju |leɪt -jə-, §-ə- ‖ -jə- **~lated** leɪt ɪd -əd ‖ leɪţ əd **~lates** leɪts **~lating** leɪt ɪŋ ‖ leɪţ ɪŋ
regulation ˌreg ju 'leɪʃ ᵊn -jə-, ⚠-ə- ‖ -jə- **~s** z
regulative 'reg jʊl ət ɪv '·jəl-; -ju leɪt ɪv ‖ -jə leɪţ ɪv -jəl ət-
regulator 'reg ju leɪt ə '·jə-, ⚠'·ə- ‖ -jə leɪţ ᵊr **~s** z

R

REGULATORY

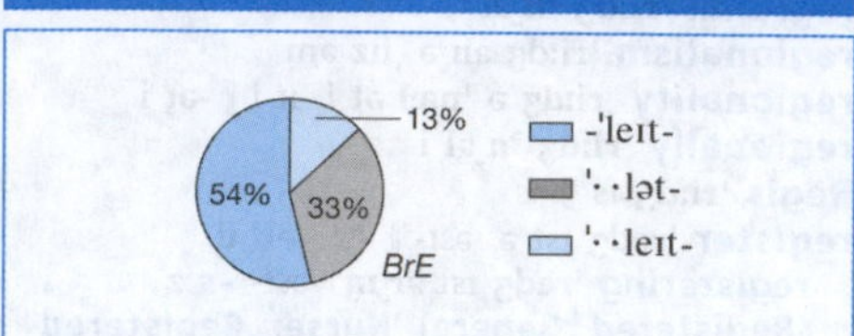

regulatory ˌreg ju 'leɪt ər i ˌ·jə-, ⚠·ə-, '· · · · · ·, '· ·lət ər i ‖ 'reg jəl ə tɔːr i -tour i — *Preference poll, BrE:* -'leɪt- *54%,* '· ·lət- *33%,* '· ·leɪt · · *13%.*
regulo 'reg ju ləʊ -jə-, ⚠-ə- ‖ -jə loʊ
regulus, R~ 'reg jʊl əs -jəl-, §-əl- ‖ -jəl-
regurgi|tate ri 'gɜːdʒ ɪ |teɪt rə-, ˌriː-, -ə- ‖ -'gɜ˞ːdʒ- **~tated** teɪt ɪd -əd ‖ teɪţ əd **~tates** teɪts **~tating** teɪt ɪŋ ‖ teɪţ ɪŋ
regurgitation ri ˌgɜːdʒ ɪ 'teɪʃ ən rə-, ˌriː,· ·'· ·, -ə'-- ‖ -ˌgɜ˞ːdʒ- **~s** z
rehab 'riː hæb
rehabili|tate ˌriː‿ə 'bɪl ɪ |teɪt ˌ·hə-, -'·ə- **~tated** teɪt ɪd -əd ‖ teɪţ əd **~tates** teɪts **~tating** teɪt ɪŋ ‖ teɪţ ɪŋ
rehabilitation ˌriː‿ə ˌbɪl ɪ 'teɪʃ ən ˌ·hə-, -ə'-- **~s** z
rehash *n* 'riː hæʃ ˌ·'· **~es** ɪz əz
rehash *v* ˌ(ˌ)riː 'hæʃ **~ed** t **~es** ɪz əz **~ing** ɪŋ
re|hear ˌriː |'hɪə ‖ -|'hɪər **~heard** 'hɜːd ‖ 'hɜ˞ːd **~hearing** 'hɪər ɪŋ ‖ 'hɪr ɪŋ **~hears** 'hɪəz ‖ 'hɪərz
rehearsal ri 'hɜːs əl rə- ‖ -'hɜ˞ːs əl **~s** z
rehears|e ri 'hɜːs rə- ‖ -'hɜ˞ːs **~ed** t **~es** ɪz əz **~ing** ɪŋ
reheat *n* 'riː hiːt **~s** s
re|heat *v* ˌriː |'hiːt **~heated** 'hiːt ɪd -əd ‖ 'hiːţ əd **~heating** 'hiːt ɪŋ ‖ 'hiːţ ɪŋ **~heats** 'hiːts
Rehnquist 'ren kwɪst →'reŋ-
Rehoboam, r~ ˌriː‿ə 'bəʊ əm -hə- ‖ -'boʊ əm **~s** z
rehous|e ˌriː 'haʊz **~ed** d **~es** ɪz əz **~ing** ɪŋ
re|hydrate ˌriː| haɪ 'dreɪt ‖ -'haɪdr eɪt **~hydrated** haɪ 'dreɪt ɪd əd ‖ 'haɪdr eɪţ əd **~hydrates** haɪ 'dreɪts ‖ 'haɪdr eɪts **~hydrating** haɪ 'dreɪt ɪŋ ‖ 'haɪdr eɪţ ɪŋ
rehydration ˌriː haɪ 'dreɪʃ ən
Reich raɪk raɪx, raɪʃ —*Ger* [ʁaiç]
Reichstag 'raɪks tɑːg 'raɪxs, 'raɪʃ- —*Ger* ['ʁaiçs taːk]
Reid riːd
reification ˌreɪ ɪf ɪ 'keɪʃ ən ˌriː-, ˌ·əf-, §-ə'--
rei|fy 'reɪ ɪ |faɪ 'riː-, -ə- **~fied** faɪd **~fies** faɪz **~fying** faɪ ɪŋ
Reigate 'raɪ geɪt -gɪt
reign reɪn *(= rain)* **reigned** reɪnd **reigning** 'reɪn ɪŋ **reigns** reɪnz
ˌreign of 'terror
reiki 'reɪk i —*Jp* ['ree ki]
Reilly 'raɪl i
reimburs|e ˌriː ɪm 'bɜːs -əm- ‖ -'bɜ˞ːs **~ed** t **~ement/s** mənt/s **~es** ɪz əz **~ing** ɪŋ
Reims riːmz —*Fr* [ʁɛ̃ːs]
rein reɪn *(= rain)* **reined** reɪnd **reining** 'reɪn ɪŋ **reins** reɪnz
reincarn|ate *v* ˌriː ɪn 'kɑːn |eɪt →-ɪŋ-; ˌ·'· · ·; -kɑː 'n|eɪt ‖ -'kɑːrn |eɪt **~ated** eɪt ɪd -əd ‖ eɪţ əd **~ates** eɪts **~ating** eɪt ɪŋ ‖ eɪţ ɪŋ
reincarnate *adj* ˌriː ɪn 'kɑːn ət ◂ →-ɪŋ-, -ɪt, -eɪt ‖ -'kɑːrn ət
reincarnation ˌriː ˌɪn kɑː 'neɪʃ ən →ˌɪŋ- ‖ -kɑːr'-- **~s** z
reindeer 'reɪn dɪə ‖ -dɪr
reinforc|e ˌriː ɪn 'fɔːs §-ən- ‖ -'fɔːrs -'foʊrs **~ed** t **~ement/s** mənt/s **~es** ɪz əz **~ing** ɪŋ
ˌreinforced 'concrete
Reinhardt, Reinhart 'raɪn hɑːt ‖ -hɑːrt
reinstal, reinstal|l ˌriː ɪn 'stɔːl ‖ -'stɑːl **~led** d **~ling** ɪŋ **~s** z
rein|state ˌriː ɪn |'steɪt **~stated** 'steɪt ɪd -əd ‖ 'steɪţ əd **~statement** 'steɪt mənt **~states** 'steɪts **~stating** 'steɪt ɪŋ ‖ 'steɪţ ɪŋ
reinsurance ˌriː ɪn 'ʃʊər ənts -'ʃɔːr- ‖ -'ʃʊr ənts -'ʃɜː-
reinsure ˌriː ɪn 'ʃʊə -'ʃɔː ‖ -'ʃʊər -'ʃɜː **~d** d
reinsuring ˌriː ɪn 'ʃʊər ɪŋ -'ʃɔːr- ‖ -'ʃʊr ɪŋ -'ʃɜː- **~s** z
reinterp|ret ˌriː ɪn 'tɜːp |rɪt -rət ‖ -'tɜ˞ːp |rət **~reted** rɪt ɪd rət əd ‖ rəţ əd **~reting** rɪt ɪŋ rət ɪŋ ‖ rəţ ɪŋ **~rets** rɪts rəts ‖ rəts
reinterpretation ˌriː ɪn ˌtɜːp rɪ 'teɪʃ ən -rə'-- ‖ -ˌtɜ˞ːp- **~s** z
reintroduc|e ˌriː ɪntr ə 'djuːs →-'dʒuːs, §-'duːs ‖ -'duːs -'djuːs **~ed** t **~es** ɪz əz **~ing** ɪŋ
reintroduction ˌriː ɪntrə 'dʌk ʃən **~s** z
rein|vent ˌriː ɪn| 'vent **~vented** 'vent ɪd -əd ‖ 'venţ ɪŋ **~venting** 'vent ɪŋ ‖ 'venţ ɪŋ **~vents** 'vents
reinvest ˌriː ɪn 'vest **~ed** ɪd əd **~ing** ɪŋ **~s** s
reinvigo|rate ˌriː ɪn 'vɪg ə |reɪt **~rated** reɪt ɪd -əd ‖ reɪţ əd **~rates** reɪts **~rating** reɪt ɪŋ ‖ reɪţ ɪŋ
reinvigoration ˌriː ɪn ˌvɪg ə 'reɪʃ ən
reissu|e *v, n* ˌriː 'ɪʃ uː -'ɪs juː, -'ɪʃ juː **~ed** d **~es** z **~ing** ɪŋ
reite|rate ri 'ɪt ə |reɪt ˌriː ‖ -'ɪţ- **~rated** reɪt ɪd -əd ‖ reɪţ əd **~rates** reɪts **~rating** reɪt ɪŋ ‖ reɪţ ɪŋ
reiteration ri ˌɪt ə 'reɪʃ ən ˌriː,· ·'· · ‖ -ˌɪţ- **~s** z
Reith riːθ
reject *v* ri 'dʒekt rə- **~ed** ɪd əd **~ing** ɪŋ **~s** s
reject *n* 'riː dʒekt **~s** s
rejection ri 'dʒek ʃən rə- **~s** z
rejig ˌriː 'dʒɪg **~ged** d **~ger/s** ə/z ‖ ər/z **~ging** ɪŋ **~s** z
rejoic|e ri 'dʒɔɪs rə- **~ed** t **~es** ɪz əz **~ing/ly** ɪŋ /li
rejoin *'join again'*, **re-join** ˌriː 'dʒɔɪn **~ed** d **~ing** ɪŋ **~s** z
rejoin *'reply'* ri 'dʒɔɪn rə- **~ed** d **~ing** ɪŋ **~s** z
rejoinder ri 'dʒɔɪnd ə rə- ‖ -ər **~s** z
rejuve|nate ri 'dʒuːv ə |neɪt rə-, -ɪ- **~nated** neɪt ɪd -əd ‖ neɪţ əd **~nates** neɪts **~nating** neɪt ɪŋ ‖ neɪţ ɪŋ

rejuvenation ri ˌdʒuːv ə ˈneɪʃ ən rə-, ˌriː,·-·ˈ··, -ɪˈ-- **~s** z
rejuvenesc|ence ˌriː ˌdʒuːv ə ˈnes |ənts riˌ·-·ˈ-·, rə-, -ɪˈ-- **~ent** ənt
rekindl|e (ˌ)riː ˈkɪnd əl **~ed** d **~es** z **~ing** ˌɪŋ
relaid ˌriː ˈleɪd ◂
relaps|e *v* ri ˈlæps rə- **~ed** t **~es** ɪz əz **~ing** ɪŋ
relaps|e *n* ri ˈlæps rə-; ˈriː læps **~es** ɪz əz
re|late, R~ ri |ˈleɪt rə- **~lated** ˈleɪt ɪd -əd ‖ ˈleɪţ əd **~lates** ˈleɪts **~lating** ˈleɪt ɪŋ ‖ ˈleɪţ ɪŋ
related ri ˈleɪt ɪd -əd ‖ -ˈleɪţ əd **~ness** nəs nɪs
relation ri ˈleɪʃ ən rə- **~s** z
relational ri ˈleɪʃ ən‿əl rə-
relationship ri ˈleɪʃ ən ʃɪp rə- **~s** s
relatival ˌrel ə ˈtaɪv əl ◂
relative ˈrel ət ɪv ‖-əţ ɪv **~ly** li **~ness** nəs nɪs **~s** z
ˌ**relative** ˈ**clause**; ˌ**relative** ˈ**pronoun**
relativis... —*see* **relativiz...**
relativism ˈrel ət ɪv ˌɪz əm ‖ ˈrel əţ-
relativistic ˌrel ət ɪv ˈɪst ɪk ◂ -əvˈ-- ‖ ˌrel əţ- **~ally** əl‿i
relativity, R~ ˌrel ə ˈtɪv ət i -ɪt i ‖ -əţ i
relativization ˌrel ət ɪv aɪ ˈzeɪʃ ən -ɪˈ-- ‖ ˌrel əţ ɪv ə- **~s** z
relativiz|e ˈrel ət ɪv aɪz ‖ ˈrel əţ- **~ed** d **~es** ɪz əz **~ing** ɪŋ
relator ri ˈleɪt ə rə- ‖ -ˈleɪţ ər **~s** z
relaunch *n* ˈriː lɔːntʃ ‖ -lɑːntʃ **~es** ɪz əz
relaunch *v* ˌriː ˈlɔːntʃ ‖ -ˈlɑːntʃ **~ed** t **~es** ɪz əz **~ing** ɪŋ
relax ri ˈlæks rə- **~ed** t **~es** ɪz əz **~ing** ɪŋ
relaxant ri ˈlæks ənt rə- **~s** s
relaxation ˌriː læk ˈseɪʃ ən ˌrel ək- **~s** z
re|lay *v 'lay again'* ˌriː |ˈleɪ **~laid** ˈleɪd **~laying** ˈleɪ ɪŋ **~lays** ˈleɪz
relay *n* ˈriː leɪ **~s** z
ˈ**relay race**; ˈ**relay** ˌ**station**
relay *v 'send by relay'* ˈriː leɪ ri ˈleɪ, rə- **~ed** d **~ing** ɪŋ **~s** z
releas|e *v, n* ri ˈliːs rə- **~ed** t **~es** ɪz əz **~ing** ɪŋ
rele|gate ˈrel ɪ |geɪt -ə- **~gated** geɪt ɪd -əd ‖ geɪţ əd **~gates** geɪts **~gating** geɪt ɪŋ ‖ geɪţ ɪŋ
relegation ˌrel ɪ ˈgeɪʃ ən -ə- **~s** z
re|lent ri |ˈlent rə- **~lented** ˈlent ɪd -əd ‖ ˈlenţ əd **~lenting** ˈlent ɪŋ ‖ ˈlenţ ɪŋ **~lents** ˈlents
relentless ri ˈlent ləs rə-, -lɪs **~ly** li **~ness** nəs nɪs
relevanc|e ˈrel əv ənts -ɪv-; ⚠ˈrev əl- **~y** i
relevant ˈrel əv ənt -ɪv-; ⚠ˈrev əl- **~ly** li
reliability ri ˌlaɪ‿ə ˈbɪl ət i rə-, -ɪt i ‖ -əţ i
reliab|le ri ˈlaɪ‿əb |əl rə- **~ly** li
reliance ri ˈlaɪ‿ənts rə-
reliant ri ˈlaɪ‿ənt rə- **~ly** li
relic ˈrel ɪk **~s** s
relict ˈrel ɪkt **~s** s
relie... —*see* **rely**
relief ri ˈliːf rə- **~s** s
reˈ**lief map**; **re**ˈ**lief road**
reliev|e ri ˈliːv rə- **~ed** d **~es** z **~ing** ɪŋ
reliever ri ˈliːv ə rə- ‖ -ər **~s** z
relievo ri ˈliːv əʊ rə-; ˌrel i ˈeɪv əʊ ‖ -oʊ **~s** z
religion ri ˈlɪdʒ ən rə- **~s** z
religiose ri ˈlɪdʒ i əʊs rə-, -əʊz ‖ -oʊs
religiosity ri ˌlɪdʒ i ˈɒs ət i rə-, -ɪt i; ˌrel ɪ ˈdʒɒs· ·, ˌ·ə- ‖ -ˈɑːs əţ i
religious ri ˈlɪdʒ əs rə- **~ly** li **~ness** nəs nɪs
relin|e ˌriː ˈlaɪn **~ed** d **~es** z **~ing** ɪŋ
relinquish ri ˈlɪŋk wɪʃ rə- **~ed** t **~es** ɪz əz **~ing** ɪŋ **~ment** mənt
reliquar|y ˈrel ɪk wər |i ˈ·ək- ‖ -ə kwer |i **~ies** iz
relish *n, v* ˈrel ɪʃ **~ed** t **~es** ɪz əz **~ing** ɪŋ
reliv|e ˌriː ˈlɪv **~ed** d **~es** z **~ing** ɪŋ
reload ˌriː ˈləʊd ‖ -ˈloʊd **~ed** ɪd əd **~ing** ɪŋ **~s** z
reloc|ate ˌriː ləʊ ˈk|eɪt ‖ ˌriː ˈloʊk |eɪt -loʊ ˈk|eɪt **~ated** eɪt ɪd -əd ‖ eɪţ əd **~ates** eɪts **~ating** eɪt ɪŋ ‖ eɪţ ɪŋ
relocation ˌriː ləʊ ˈkeɪʃ ən ‖ -loʊ- **~s** z
reluctance ri ˈlʌkt ənts rə-
reluctant ri ˈlʌkt ənt rə- **~ly** li
reluctivity ˌrel ʌk ˈtɪv ət i ˌriː lʌk-, ri ˌlʌk-, rə ˌlʌk-, -ɪt i ‖ -əţ i
re|ly ri |ˈlaɪ rə- **~lied** ˈlaɪd **~lies** ˈlaɪz **~lying** ˈlaɪ ɪŋ
rem rem
REM rem ˌɑːr iː ˈem ‖ ˌɑːr iː ˈem
remade ˌriː ˈmeɪd
remain ri ˈmeɪn rə- **~ed** d **~ing** ɪŋ **~s** z
remaind|er *n, v* ri ˈmeɪnd |ə rə- ‖ -|ər **~ered** əd ‖ ərd **~ering** ər‿ɪŋ **~ers** əz ‖ ərz
remake *n* ˈriː meɪk **~s** s
re|make *v* ˌriː |ˈmeɪk **~made** ˈmeɪd **~makes** ˈmeɪks **~making** ˈmeɪk ɪŋ
remand ri ˈmɑːnd rə-, §-ˈmænd ‖ -ˈmænd **~ed** ɪd əd **~ing** ɪŋ **~s** z
remanence ˈrem ən ənts
remark ri ˈmɑːk rə- ‖ -ˈmɑːrk **~ed** t **~ing** ɪŋ **~s** s
remarkab|le ri ˈmɑːk əb |əl rə- ‖ -ˈmɑːrk- **~ly** li
remarque, R~ ri ˈmɑːk rə- ‖ -ˈmɑːrk
remarriag|e ˌriː ˈmær ɪdʒ ‖ -ˈmer- **~es** ɪz əz
remarr|y ˌriː ˈmær |i ‖ -ˈmer- **~ied** id **~ies** iz **~ying** i ɪŋ
remaster ˌriː ˈmɑːst ə §-ˈmæst- ‖ -ˈmæst ər **~ed** d **~ing** ɪŋ **~s** z
rematch *n* ˈriː mætʃ **~es** ɪz əz
Rembrandt ˈrem brænt -brənt —*Dutch* [ˈrɛm brɑnt] **~s, ~'s** s
REME ˈriːm i
remediab|le ri ˈmiːd i‿əb |əl rə- **~leness** əl nəs -nɪs **~ly** li
remedial ri ˈmiːd i‿əl rə- **~ly** i
remediation ri ˌmiːd i ˈeɪʃ ən rə-
remed|y ˈrem əd |i -ɪd- **~ied** id **~ies** iz **~ying** i ɪŋ
remem|ber ri ˈmem |bə rə- ‖ -|bər **~bered** bəd ‖ bərd **~bering** bər‿ɪŋ **~bers** bəz ‖ bərz

remembranc|e ri ˈmem brənᵗs rə- ⚠-ˈmem bᵊr ənᵗs **~er/s** ə/z ‖ -ᵊr/z **~es** ɪz əz
Reˈmembrance Day; **Reˌmembrance ˈSunday**

Remick ˈrem ɪk

remilitaris... —*see* **remilitariz...**

remilitarization ˌriː ˌmɪl ɪt ər aɪ ˈzeɪʃ ᵊn -ˌ-ət-, -ˌ· · · ·ˈ· ·, -ɪˈ·- ‖ -əṭ ər ə-

remilitariz|e ₍ˌ₎riː ˈmɪl ɪt ə raɪz -ˈ-ət- ‖ -əṭ ə raɪz **~ed** d **~es** ɪz əz **~ing** ɪŋ

remind ri ˈmaɪnd rə- **~ed** ɪd əd **~ing** ɪŋ **~s** z

reminder ri ˈmaɪnd ə rə- ‖ -ᵊr **~s** z

Remington ˈrem ɪŋ tən

reminisc|e ˌrem ɪ ˈnɪs -ə- **~ed** t **~es** ɪz əz **~ing** ɪŋ

reminiscenc|e ˌrem ɪ ˈnɪs ᵊnᵗs -ə- **~es** ɪz əz

reminiscent ˌrem ɪ ˈnɪs ᵊnt ◂ -ə- **~ly** li

remiss ri ˈmɪs rə- **~ness** nəs nɪs

remission ri ˈmɪʃ ᵊn rə- **~s** z

re|mit *v* ri |ˈmɪt rə- **~mits** ˈmɪts **~mitted** ˈmɪt ɪd -əd ‖ ˈmɪṭ əd **~mitting** ˈmɪt ɪŋ ‖ ˈmɪṭ ɪŋ

remit *n* ˈriː mɪt ri ˈmɪt, rə- **~s** s

remittanc|e ri ˈmɪt ᵊnᵗs rə- **~es** ɪz əz

remittee ri ˌmɪt ˈiː rə- **~s** z

remittent ri ˈmɪt ᵊnt rə- **~ly** li

remitter ri ˈmɪt ə rə- ‖ -ˈmɪṭ ᵊr **~s** z

remix *n* ˈriː mɪks **~es** ɪz əz

remnant, R~ ˈrem nənt **~s** s

remodel ₍ˌ₎riː ˈmɒd ᵊl ‖ -ˈmɑːd ᵊl **~ed, ~led** d **~ing, ~ling** ɪŋ **~s** z

remold *v* ˌriː ˈməʊld →-ˈmɒʊld ‖ -ˈmoʊld **~ed** ɪd əd **~ing** ɪŋ **~s** z

remold *n* ˈriː məʊld →-mɒʊld ‖ -moʊld **~s** z

remonstranc|e ri ˈmɒn ᵗs trənᵗs rə- ‖ -ˈmɑːnᵗs- **~es** ɪz əz

remonstrant, R~ ri ˈmɒnᵗs trənt rə- ‖ -ˈmɑːnᵗs- **~s** s

remons|trate ˈrem ən s|treɪt ri ˈmɒn-, rə- ‖ ri ˈmɑːnᵗs |treɪt **~trated** treɪt ɪd -əd ‖ treɪṭ əd **~trates** treɪts **~trating** treɪt ɪŋ ‖ treɪṭ ɪŋ

remonstration ˌrem ən ˈstreɪʃ ᵊn ‖ ri ˌmɑːn- **~s** z

remonstrative ri ˈmɒnᵗs trət ɪv rə- ‖ -ˈmɑːnᵗs trəṭ ɪv

remontant ri ˈmɒnt ənt rə- ‖ -ˈmɑːnt ᵊnt **~s** s

remora ˈrem ər ə ri ˈmɔːr ə, rə- **~s** z

remorse ri ˈmɔːs rə- ‖ -ˈmɔːrs

remorseful ri ˈmɔːs fᵊl rə-, -fʊl ‖ -ˈmɔːrs- **~ly** ˌi **~ness** nəs nɪs

remorseless ri ˈmɔːs ləs rə-, -lɪs ‖ -ˈmɔːrs- **~ly** li **~ness** nəs nɪs

remortgag|e ˌriː ˈmɔːg ɪdʒ ‖ -ˈmɔːrg- **~ed** d **~es** ɪz əz **~ing** ɪŋ

re|mote ri |ˈməʊt rə- ‖ -|ˈmoʊt **~moter** ˈməʊt ə ‖ ˈmoʊṭ ᵊr **~motest** ˈməʊtɪst -əst ‖ ˈmoʊṭ əst
reˌmote conˈtrol

remote-controlled ri ˌməʊt kən ˈtrəʊld ◂ rə-, §-kɒn- ‖ -ˌmoʊt kən ˈtroʊld ◂

remote|ly ri ˈməʊt |li rə- ‖ -ˈmoʊt- **~ness** nəs nɪs

remoulade, rémoulade ˌrem ə ˈleɪd -u-, -ˈlɑːd ‖ ˌreɪm ə ˈlɑːd -u- **~s** z

remould *v* ˌriː ˈməʊld →-ˈmɒʊld ‖ -ˈmoʊld **~ed** ɪd əd **~ing** ɪŋ **~s** z

remould *n* ˈriː məʊld →-mɒʊld ‖ -moʊld **~s** z

re|mount *v* ˌriː |ˈmaʊnt **~mounted** ˈmaʊnt ɪd -əd ‖ ˈmaʊnṭ əd **~mounting** ˈmaʊnt ɪŋ ‖ ˈmaʊnṭ ɪŋ **~mounts** ˈmaʊnts

remount *n* ˈriː maʊnt ˌ·ˈ· **~s** s

removability ri ˌmuːv ə ˈbɪl ət i rə- ‖ -əṭ i

removab|le ri ˈmuːv əb |ᵊl rə- **~leness** ᵊl nəs -nɪs **~ly** li

removal ri ˈmuːv ᵊl rə- **~s** z
reˈmoval van

remov|e ri ˈmuːv rə- **~ed** d **~es** z **~ing** ɪŋ

-remover ri ˌmuːv ə rə- ‖ -ᵊr — **stain-remover** ˈsteɪn ri ˌmuːv ə -rə- ‖ -ᵊr

remover ri ˈmuːv ə rə- ‖ -ᵊr **~s** z

Remploy *tdmk* ˈrem plɔɪ

remune|rate ri ˈmjuːn ə |reɪt rə- **~rated** reɪt ɪd -əd ‖ reɪṭ əd **~rates** reɪts **~rating** reɪt ɪŋ ‖ reɪṭ ɪŋ

remuneration ri ˌmjuːn ə ˈreɪʃ ᵊn rə- ⚠-ˈnjuːm- **~s** z

remunerative ri ˈmjuːn ər ət ɪv rə-, ⚠-ˈnjuːm-, -ə reɪt- ‖ -ər ̮əṭ ɪv -ə reɪṭ- **~ly** li **~ness** nəs nɪs

Remus ˈriːm əs

Remy, Rémy ˈreɪm i ‖ reɪ ˈmiː —*Fr* [ʁə mi, ʁe-]

renaissanc|e, R~ ri ˈneɪs ᵊnᵗs rə-, -ɒ̃s; ˌren eɪ ˈsɒ̃s ‖ ˌren ə ˈsɑːnᵗs -ˈzɑːnᵗs, ˈ· · · *(*)* —*Fr* [ʁə nɛ sɑ̃ːs] **~es** ɪz əz

renal ˈriːn ᵊl

renam|e ₍ˌ₎riː ˈneɪm **~ed** d **~es** z **~ing** ɪŋ

renascenc|e ri ˈnæs ᵊnᵗs rə-, -ˈneɪs- **~es** ɪz əz

renascent ri ˈnæs ᵊnt rə-, -ˈneɪs-

Renata ri ˈnɑːt ə rə- ‖ -ˈnɑːṭ ə

Renault ˈren əʊ ‖ rə ˈnɔːlt -ˈnɑːlt, -ˈnoʊ *(*)* —*Fr* [ʁə no] **~s** z

rend rend **rending** ˈrend ɪŋ **rends** rendz **rent** rent

Rendall, Rendell ˈrend ᵊl

render ˈrend ə ‖ -ᵊr **~ed** d **rendering/s** ˈrend ər ɪŋ/z **~s** z

rendezvous *v, n sing.* ˈrɒnd ɪ vuː -ə-, -eɪ- ‖ ˈrɑːnd eɪ- —*Fr* [ʁɑ̃ de vu] **~** *n pl; v 3rd sing.* z **~ed** d **~ing** ɪŋ

rendition ren ˈdɪʃ ᵊn **~s** z

rendzina rend ˈziːn ə **~s** z

Rene, René *man's name(i)* ˈren eɪ ˈrən-, -i, *(ii)* rə ˈneɪ —*in AmE (ii)*

Renee, Renée *woman's name(i)* ˈren eɪ ˈrən-, *(ii)* rə ˈneɪ, *(iii)* ˈriːn i —*in AmE (ii)*

Rene *woman's name, short for* **Irene** ˈriːn i

renegade ˈren ɪ geɪd -ə- **~s** z

reneg|e, renegu|e ri ˈniːg rə-, -ˈneɪg, -ˈneg ‖ -ˈnɪg -ˈneg, -ˈniːg **~ed** d **~es** z **~ing** ɪŋ

renegotiable ˌriː nɪ ˈgəʊʃ i ̮əb ᵊl ·nə-, ˈgəʊʃ əb ᵊl ‖ -ˈgoʊʃ- -ˈgoʊʃəb ᵊl

renegoti|ate ˌriː nɪ ˈɡəʊʃ i eɪt ˌ·nə- ‖ -ˈɡoʊʃ- **~ated** eɪt ɪd -əd **~ates** eɪts **~ating** eɪt ɪŋ ‖ eɪţ ɪŋ
renew ri ˈnjuː rə-, ˌriː-, §-ˈnuː ‖ -ˈnuː -ˈnjuː **~ed** d **~ing** ɪŋ **~s** z
renewability ri ˌnjuː‿ə ˈbɪl ət i rə-, §-ˈnuː‿, -ɪt i ‖ -ˌnuː ə ˈbɪl əţ i -ˌnjuː-
renewable ri ˈnjuː‿əb ᵊl rə-, ˌriː-, §-ˈnuː‿ ‖ -ˈnuː əb ᵊl -ˈnjuː- **~s** z
renewal ri ˈnjuː‿əl rə-, ˌriː-, -ˈnjuːl, §-ˈnuː‿, §-ˈnuːl ‖ -ˈnuː əl -ˈnjuː- **~s** z
renewer ri ˈnjuː‿ə rə-, §-ˈnuː‿ ‖ -ˈnuː‿ᵊr -ˈnjuː‿ **~s** z
Renfrew ˈren fruː
reniform ˈren ɪ fɔːm ˈriːn-, -ə- ‖ -fɔːrm
renin ˈriːn ɪn §-ən
Renishaw ˈren ɪ ʃɔː §-ə- ‖ -ʃɑː
renminbi ˌren mɪn ˈbiː →ˌrem-, →-mɪm —*Chi* rénmínbì [²ʐən ²mɪn ⁴pi]
Rennell ˈren ᵊl ‖ rə ˈnel
Rennes ren —*Fr* [ʁɛn]
rennet ˈren ɪt §-ət
Rennie ˈren i **~s** *tdmk* z
rennin ˈren ɪn §-ən
Reno ˈriːn əʊ ‖ -oʊ
Renoir ˈren wɑː ˈrən-; rə ˈnwɑː ‖ rən ˈwɑːr ˈren· —*Fr* [ʁə nwaːʁ] **~s, ~'s** z
renounc|e ri ˈnaʊnᵗs rə- **~ed** t **~es** ɪz əz **~ing** ɪŋ **~ement** mənt
reno|vate ˈren əʊ |veɪt ‖ -ə- **~vated** veɪt ɪd -əd ‖ veɪţ əd **~vates** veɪts **~vating** veɪt ɪŋ ‖ veɪţ ɪŋ
renovation ˌren əʊ ˈveɪʃ ᵊn ‖ -ə- **~s** z
renown ri ˈnaʊn rə- **~ed** d
Renshaw ˈren ʃɔː ‖ -ʃɑː
Rensselaer ˌrenᵗs ə ˈlɪə ‖ -ˈlɪᵊr
rent rent **rented** ˈrent ɪd -əd ‖ ˈrenţ əd **renting** ˈrent ɪŋ ‖ ˈrenţ ɪŋ **rents** rents
ˈrent boy; **ˈrent strike**
rentable ˈrent əb ᵊl ‖ ˈrenţ-
rent-a-car ˈrent ə kɑː ‖ ˈrenţ ə kɑːr
rent-a-crowd ˈrent ə kraʊd ‖ ˈrenţ-
rental ˈrent ᵊl ‖ ˈrenţ ᵊl **~s** z
rent-a-mob ˈrent ə mɒb ‖ ˈrenţ ə mɑːb
rent-a-quote ˈrent ə kwəʊt ‖ ˈrenţ ə kwoʊt
renter ˈrent ə ‖ ˈrenţ ᵊr **~s** z
rent-free ˌrent ˈfriː ◂
rentier ˈrɒnt i eɪ ˈrɑːnt- ‖ rɑːn ˈtjeɪ —*Fr* [ʁɑ̃ tje] **~s** z
Rentokil *tdmk* ˈrent əʊ kɪl ‖ ˈrenţ ə-
Renton ˈrent ən ‖ -ᵊn
renumber ˌriː ˈnʌm bə ‖ -bᵊr **~ed** d **renumbering/s** ˌriː ˈnʌm bər‿ɪŋ/z **~s** z
renunciation ri ˌnʌnᵗs i ˈeɪʃ ᵊn rə- **~s** z
Renwick *(i)* ˈren ɪk, *(ii)* -wɪk
reop|en ri ˈəʊp |ən ˌriː- ‖ -ˈoʊp |ən **~ened** ənd →md **~ening** ən‿ɪŋ **~ens** ənz →mz
reorder ˌriː ˈɔːd ə ‖ -ˈɔːrd ᵊr **~ed** d **reordering** ˌriː ˈɔːd ər‿ɪŋ **~s** z
reorganis... —*see* **reorganiz...**
reorganization ri ˌɔːɡ ən aɪ ˈzeɪʃ ᵊn ˌriː ˌ· · ·ˈ· ·, -ɪˈ·- ‖ -ˌɔːrɡ ən‿ə- **~s** z
reorganiz|e ri ˈɔːɡ ə naɪz ˌriː- ‖ -ˈɔːrɡ- **~ed** d **~es** ɪz əz **~ing** ɪŋ
rep rep **reps** reps
repackag|e ˌriː ˈpæk ɪdʒ **~ed** d **~es** ɪz əz **~ing** ɪŋ
repaid ri ˈpeɪd rə-, ₍ˌ₎riː-
re|paint ˌriː| ˈpeɪnt **~painted** ˈpeɪnt ɪd -əd ‖ ˈpeɪnţ əd **~painting** ˈpeɪnt ɪŋ ‖ ˈpeɪnţ ɪŋ **~paints** ˈpeɪnts
repair ri ˈpeə rə- ‖ -ˈpeᵊr -ˈpæᵊr **~ed** d **repairing** ri ˈpeər ɪŋ rə- ‖ -ˈper ɪŋ -ˈpær- **~s** z
repairable ri ˈpeər əb ᵊl rə- ‖ -ˈper- -ˈpær-
repairer ri ˈpeər ə rə- ‖ -ˈper ᵊr -ˈpær- **~s** z
repair|man ri ˈpeə |mæn rə-, -mən ‖ -ˈper- -ˈpær- **~men** men mən
reparab|le ˈrep ər‿əb |ᵊl **~ly** li
reparation ˌrep ə ˈreɪʃ ᵊn **~s** z
reparative ri ˈpær ət ɪv rə-; ˈrep ᵊr‿ ‖ -əţ ɪv -ˈper-
repartee ˌrep ɑː ˈtiː ‖ -ɑːr ˈteɪ -ᵊr-, -ˈtiː
repast ri ˈpɑːst rə-, §-ˈpæst; ˈriː pɑːst, §-pæst ‖ -ˈpæst **~s** s
repatri|ate ˌriː ˈpætr i |eɪt ri- ‖ -ˈpeɪtr- *(*)* **~ated** eɪt ɪd -əd ‖ eɪţ əd **~ates** eɪts **~ating** eɪt ɪŋ ‖ eɪţ ɪŋ
repatriation ˌriː ˌpætr i ˈeɪʃ ᵊn ri ˌ· ·ˈ· ·, rə- ‖ riː ˌpeɪtr- ˌ· ·ˈ· · **~s** z
re|pay ri |ˈpeɪ rə- **~paid** ˈpeɪd **~paying** ˈpeɪ ɪŋ **~pays** ˈpeɪz
repayable ri ˈpeɪ əb ᵊl rə-, ˌriː-
repayment ri ˈpeɪ mənt rə- **~s** s
repeal *v, n* ri ˈpiːᵊl rə- **~ed** d **~ing** ɪŋ **~s** z
re|peat *v, n* ri |ˈpiːt rə- **~peated/ly** ˈpiːt ɪd /li -əd /li ‖ ˈpiːţ əd /li **~peating** ˈpiːt ɪŋ ‖ ˈpiːţ ɪŋ **~peats** ˈpiːts
repeatable ri ˈpiːt əb ᵊl rə- ‖ -ˈpiːţ-
repeater ri ˈpiːt ə rə- ‖ -ˈpiːţ ᵊr **~s** z
repechage, repêchage ˈrep ə ʃɑːʒ -ɪ-, ˌ· ·ˈ· —*Fr* [ʁə pɛ ʃaːʒ]
repel ri ˈpel rə- **~led** d **~ling** ɪŋ **~s** z
repellant, repellent ri ˈpel ənt rə- **~s** s
repellor ri ˈpel ə rə- ‖ -ᵊr **~s** z
re|pent ri |ˈpent rə- **~pented** ˈpent ɪd -əd ‖ ˈpenţ əd **~penting** ˈpent ɪŋ ‖ ˈpenţ ɪŋ **~pents** ˈpents
repentanc|e ri ˈpent ənᵗs rə- ‖ -ᵊnᵗs **~es** ɪz əz
repentant ri ˈpent ənt rə- ‖ -ᵊnt **~ly** li
repercussion ˌriːp ə ˈkʌʃ ᵊn ‖ -ᵊr- ˌrep- **~s** z
repertoire ˈrep ə twɑː ‖ -ᵊr twɑːr -ə- **~s** z
repertor|y ˈrep ət‿ər |i ‖ -ᵊr tɔːr |i ˈ·ə-, -toʊr i **~ies** iz
ˈrepertory ˌcompany
repetend ˈrep ɪ tend -ə-, ˌ· ·ˈ· **~s** z
repetiteur, répétiteur ri ˌpet ɪ ˈtɜː rə-, -ˌ·ə-; ˌrep ə tiː ˈ· ‖ ˌreɪ peɪt ɪ ˈtɜː ˌ·pet- —*Fr* [ʁe pe ti tœːʁ] **~s** z
repetition ˌrep ə ˈtɪʃ ᵊn -ɪ- **~s** z
repetitious ˌrep ə ˈtɪʃ əs ◂ -ɪ- **~ly** li **~ness** nəs nɪs
repetitive ri ˈpet ət ɪv rə-, -ɪt- ‖ -ˈpeţ əţ ɪv **~ly** li **~ness** nəs nɪs
rephras|e ˌriː ˈfreɪz **~ed** d **~es** ɪz əz **~ing** ɪŋ
repin|e ri ˈpaɪn rə- **~ed** d **~es** z **~ing** ɪŋ

R

replac|e ri ˈpleɪs rə-, ˌriː- **~ed** t **~es** ɪz əz **~ing** ɪŋ
replaceable ri ˈpleɪs əb ᵊl rə-, ˌriː-
replacement ri ˈpleɪs mənt rə-, ˌriː- **~s** s
replay *v* ˌriː ˈpleɪ **~ed** d **~ing** ɪŋ **~s** z
replay *n* ˈriː pleɪ **~s** z
replenish ri ˈplen ɪʃ rə- **~ed** t **~es** ɪz əz **~ing** ɪŋ **~ment/s** mənt/s
replete ri ˈpliːt rə- **~ness** nəs nɪs
repletion ri ˈpliːʃ ᵊn rə-
replevin ri ˈplev ɪn rə- §-ᵊn
replev|y ri ˈplev |i rə- **~ied** id **~ies** iz **~ying** i ɪŋ
replica ˈrep lɪk ə **~s** z
replicability ˌrep lɪk ə ˈbɪl ət i -ɪt i ‖ -əţ i
replicable ˈrep lɪk əb ᵊl
repli|cate *v* ˈrep lɪ |keɪt -lə- **~cated** keɪt ɪd -əd ‖ keɪţ əd **~cates** keɪts **~cating** keɪt ɪŋ ‖ keɪţ ɪŋ
replication ˌrep lɪ ˈkeɪʃ ᵊn -lə- **~s** z
re|ply ri |ˈplaɪ rə- **~plied** ˈplaɪd **~plies** ˈplaɪz **~plying** ˈplaɪ ɪŋ
reply-paid ri ˌplaɪ ˈpeɪd ◂ rə-
repo ˈriː pəʊ ‖ -poʊ **~s** z
répondez s'il vous plaît ri ˌpɒnd eɪ ˌsiː vuː ˈpleɪ rə-, reɪ-, -ˌsɪl- ‖ -ˌpɔːnd- -ˌpɑːnd- —*Fr* [ʁe pɔ̃ de sil vu plɛ]
re|port *v, n* ri |ˈpɔːt rə- ‖ -|ˈpɔːrt -ˈpoʊrt **~ported/ly** ˈpɔːt ɪd /li -əd- ‖ ˈpɔːrţ- ˈpoʊrţ- **~porting** ˈpɔːt ɪŋ ‖ ˈpɔːrţ ɪŋ ˈpoʊrţ- **~ports** ˈpɔːts ‖ ˈpɔːrts ˈpoʊrts
reˌported ˈspeech
reportage ˌrep ɔː ˈtɑːʒ ri ˈpɔːt ɪdʒ, rə- ‖ ri ˈpɔːrţ ɪdʒ -ˈpoʊrţ-; ˌrep ɔːr ˈtɑːʒ, -ᵊr-
reporter ri ˈpɔːt ə rə- ‖ -ˈpɔːrţ ᵊr -ˈpoʊrţ- **~s** z
reportorial ˌrep ɔː ˈtɔːr i‿əl ◂ ˌriːp-, ˌ-ə- ‖ ˌrep ᵊr- -ˈtoʊr- **~ly** i
repos|e *v, n* ri ˈpəʊz rə- ‖ -ˈpoʊz **~ed** d **~es** ɪz əz **~ing** ɪŋ
reposeful ri ˈpəʊz fᵊl rə-, -fʊl ‖ -ˈpoʊz- **~ly** i **~ness** nəs nɪs
reposition ˌriː pə ˈzɪʃ ᵊn **~ed** d **~ing** ‿ɪŋ **~s** z
repositor|y ri ˈpɒz ɪt‿ər |i rə-, -ˈ-ət‿ ‖ -ˈpɑːz ə tɔːr |i -toʊr i **~ies** iz
repossess ˌriː pə ˈzes **~ed** t **~es** ɪz əz **~ing** ɪŋ
repossession ˌriː pə ˈzeʃ ᵊn **~s** z
repousse, repoussé rə ˈpuːs eɪ ri- ‖ -ˌpuː ˈseɪ —*Fr* [ʁə pu se]
repp rep
reprehend ˌrep ri ˈhend -rə- **~ed** ɪd əd **~ing** ɪŋ **~s** z
reprehensibility ˌrep ri ˌhenᵗs ə ˈbɪl ət i ˌ-rə-, -ˌ-ɪ-, -ɪt i ‖ -əţ i
reprehensib|le ˌrep ri ˈhenᵗs əb |ᵊl ◂ ˌ-rə-, -ɪb ᵊl **~ly** li
reprehension ˌrep ri ˈhenᵗʃ ᵊn -rə-
re-pre|sent ˌriː pri |ˈzent -prə- **~sented** ˈzent ɪd -əd ‖ ˈzenţ əd **~senting** ˈzent ɪŋ ‖ ˈzenţ ɪŋ **~sents** ˈzents
repre|sent ˌrep ri |ˈzent -rə- **~sented** ˈzent ɪd -əd ‖ ˈzenţ əd **~senting** ˈzent ɪŋ ‖ ˈzenţ ɪŋ **~sents** ˈzents
representation ˌrep ri zen ˈteɪʃ ᵊn ˌ-rə-, -zən'-- **~s** z
representational ˌrep ri zen ˈteɪʃ ᵊn‿əl ◂ ˌ-rə-, -zən'-- **~ism** ˌɪz əm
representative ˌrep ri ˈzent ət ɪv ◂ ˌ-rə- ‖ -ˈzenţ əţ ɪv ◂ **~ly** li **~ness** nəs nɪs **~s** z
repress ri ˈpres rə- **~ed** t **~es** ɪz əz **~ing** ɪŋ
repression ri ˈpreʃ ᵊn rə- **~s** z
repressive ri ˈpres ɪv rə- **~ly** li **~ness** nəs nɪs
repressor ri ˈpres ə rə- ‖ -ᵊr **~s** z
repriev|e ri ˈpriːv rə- **~ed** d **~es** z **~ing** ɪŋ
reprimand *v* ˈrep ri mɑːnd -rə-, ˌ- -ˈ- ‖ -mænd **~ed** ɪd əd **~ing** ɪŋ **~s** z
reprimand *n* ˈrep ri mɑːnd -rə- ‖ -mænd **~s** z
reprint *n* ˈriː prɪnt ˌ-ˈ- **~s** s
re|print *v* ˌriː |ˈprɪnt **~printed** ˈprɪnt ɪd -əd ‖ ˈprɪnţ əd **~printing** ˈprɪnt ɪŋ ‖ ˈprɪnţ ɪŋ **~prints** ˈprɪnts
reprisal ri ˈpraɪz ᵊl rə- **~s** z
repris|e ri ˈpriːz rə-, -ˈpraɪz **~ed** d **~es** ɪz əz **~ing** ɪŋ
repro ˈriː prəʊ ‖ -proʊ **~s** z
reproach *n, v* ri ˈprəʊtʃ rə- ‖ -ˈproʊtʃ **~ed** t **~es** ɪz əz **~ing** ɪŋ
reproachful ri ˈprəʊtʃ fᵊl rə-, -fʊl ‖ -ˈproʊtʃ- **~ly** i **~ness** nəs nɪs
repro|bate ˈrep rəʊ |beɪt ‖ -rə- **~bated** beɪt ɪd -əd ‖ beɪţ əd **~bates** beɪts **~bating** beɪt ɪŋ ‖ beɪţ ɪŋ
reprobation ˌrep rəʊ ˈbeɪʃ ᵊn ‖ -rə-
reprocess ˌriː ˈprəʊs es -ˈprɒs-, -ɪs, §-əs ‖ -ˈprɑːs- **~ed** t **~es** ɪz əz **~ing** ɪŋ
reproduc|e ˌriːp rə ˈdjuːs ˌrep-, →-ˈdʒuːs ‖ -ˈduːs -ˈdjuːs **~ed** t **~er/s** ə/z ‖ ᵊr/z **~es** ɪz əz **~ing** ɪŋ
reproducible ˌriːp rə ˈdjuːs əb ᵊl ◂ ˌrep-, →-ˈdʒuːs-, -ɪb ᵊl ‖ -ˈduːs- -ˈdjuːs-
reproduction ˌriːp rə ˈdʌk ʃᵊn ˌrep- **~s** z
reproductive ˌriːp rə ˈdʌkt ɪv ◂ ˌrep- **~ly** li **~ness** nəs nɪs
reprographer rɪ ˈprɒg rəf ə riː- ‖ -ˈprɑːg rəf ᵊr **~s** z
reprographic ˌriːp rə ˈgræf ɪk ◂ ˌrep- **~ally** ᵊl‿i **~s** s
reprography rɪ ˈprɒg rəf i riː- ‖ -ˈprɑːg-
reproof *v, 'proof again'* ˌriː ˈpruːf §-ˈprʊf **~ed** t **~ing** ɪŋ **~s** s
reproof *n, 'rebuke'* ri ˈpruːf rə-, §-ˈprʊf **~s** s
reprov|e ri ˈpruːv rə- **~ed** d **~es** z **~ing/ly** ɪŋ /li
reptile ˈrept aɪᵊl ‖ -ᵊl -aɪᵊl **~s** z
reptilian rep ˈtɪl i‿ən **~s** z
Repton ˈrept ən
republic, R~ ri ˈpʌb lɪk rə- **~s** s
republican, R~ ri ˈpʌb lɪk ən rə- **~s** z
republicanism, R~ ri ˈpʌb lɪk ən ˌɪz əm rə-
repudi|ate ri ˈpjuːd i |eɪt rə- **~ated** eɪt ɪd -əd ‖ eɪţ əd **~ates** eɪts **~ating** eɪt ɪŋ ‖ eɪţ ɪŋ **~ator/s** eɪt ə/z ‖ eɪţ ᵊr/z
repudiation ri ˌpjuːd i ˈeɪʃ ᵊn rə- **~s** z
repugnance ri ˈpʌg nənᵗs rə-
repugnant ri ˈpʌg nənt rə- **~ly** li

repuls|e *v, n* ri ˈpʌls rə- **~ed** t **~es** ɪz əz **~ing** ɪŋ
repulsion ri ˈpʌlʃ ən rə- **~s** z
repulsive ri ˈpʌls ɪv rə- **~ly** li **~ness** nəs nɪs
repurpos|e ˌriː ˈpɜːp əs ‖ -ˈpɜːp- **~ed** t **~es** ɪz əz **~ing** ɪŋ
reputability ˌrep jʊt ə ˈbɪl ət i §ˌ·jət-, -ɪt i ‖ -jəţ ə ˈbɪl əţ i
reputab|le ˈrep jʊt əb |əl §ˈ·jət-; §ri ˈpjuːt-, §rə- ‖ ˈrep jəţ- **~ly** li
reputation ˌrep ju ˈteɪʃ ən §-jə- ‖ -jə- **~s** z
repute ri ˈpjuːt rə-
reputed ri ˈpjuːt ɪd rə-, -əd ‖ -ˈpjuːţ əd **~ly** li
request ri ˈkwest rə- **~ed** ɪd əd **~ing** ɪŋ **~s** s
reˈquest stop
requiem ˈrek wi‿əm -em **~s** z
ˌrequiem ˈmass
requiescat ˌrek wi ˈesk æt ‖ ˌreɪk-, -ɑːt
require ri ˈkwaɪ‿ə rə- ‖ -ˈkwaɪ‿ər **~d** d **~ment/s** mənt/s **~s** z **requiring** ri ˈkwaɪ‿ər ɪŋ rə- ‖ -ˈkwaɪ‿ər ɪŋ
requisite ˈrek wɪz ɪt -wəz-, §-ət **~s** s
requisition ˌrek wɪ ˈzɪʃ ən -wə- **~ed** d **~ing** ‿ɪŋ **~s** z
requital ri ˈkwaɪt əl rə- ‖ -ˈkwaɪţ əl **~s** z
re|quite ri |ˈkwaɪt rə- **~quited** ˈkwaɪt ɪd -əd ‖ ˈkwaɪţ əd **~quites** ˈkwaɪts **~quiting** ˈkwaɪt ɪŋ ‖ ˈkwaɪţ ɪŋ
reran ₍ₗ₎riː ˈræn
re|read *pres* ˌriː ˈriːd **~read** *past, pp* ˈred **~reading/s** ˈriːd ɪŋ/z **~reads** ˈriːdz
reredos ˈrɪə dɒs ‖ ˈrɪr dɑːs ˈrer ə dɑːs **~es** ɪz əz
rereleas|e *n* ˈriː ri liːs -rə-, ˌ· ·ˈ· **~es** ɪz əz
rereleas|e *v* ˌriː ri ˈliːs ◂ -rə- **~ed** t **~es** ɪz əz **~ing** ɪŋ
re|route ˌriː| ˈruːt -ˈraʊt —*see note at* route. **~routed** ˈruːt ɪd -əd ‖ ˈruːţ əd ˈraʊţ- **~routeing, ~routing** ˈruːt ɪŋ ‖ ˈruːţ ɪŋ ˈraʊţ- **~routes** ˈruːts ˈraʊts
rerun *n* ˈriː rʌn **~s** z
re|run *v* ₍ₗ₎riː |ˈrʌn **~ran** ˈræn **~running** ˈrʌn ɪŋ **~runs** ˈrʌnz
res reɪz reɪs, riːz ‖ reɪs riːz —*see also phrases with this word*
resale ˈriː seɪəl ˌ·ˈ· **~s** z
reschedul|e ˌriː ˈʃed juːl -ˈʃedʒ uːl, -ˈsked juːl, -ˈskedʒ uːl ‖ -ˈskedʒ ʊl -uːl, -əl **~ed** d **~es** z **~ing** ɪŋ
rescind ri ˈsɪnd rə- **~ed** ɪd əd **~ing** ɪŋ **~s** z
rescission ri ˈsɪʒ ən rə- **~s** z
rescript ˈriː skrɪpt **~s** s
resc|ue ˈresk |juː **~ued** juːd **~ues** juːz **~uing** juː‿ɪŋ
rescuer ˈresk juː‿ə ‖ ‿ər **~s** z
research *v, n* ri ˈsɜːtʃ rə-, §-ˈzɜːtʃ; ˈriː sɜːtʃ ‖ ri ˈsɝːtʃ ˈriː sɝːtʃ —*the* -ˈsɜːtʃ ‖ -ˈsɝːtʃ *form appears still to predominate in universities, although* ˈriː sɜːtʃ ‖ -sɝːtʃ *has increasingly displaced it in general usage both in Britain and in America. Some speakers may distinguish between the verb* ·ˈ· *and the noun* ˈ· ·. —*Preferences polls, BrE:* ·ˈ· *80%*

RESEARCH

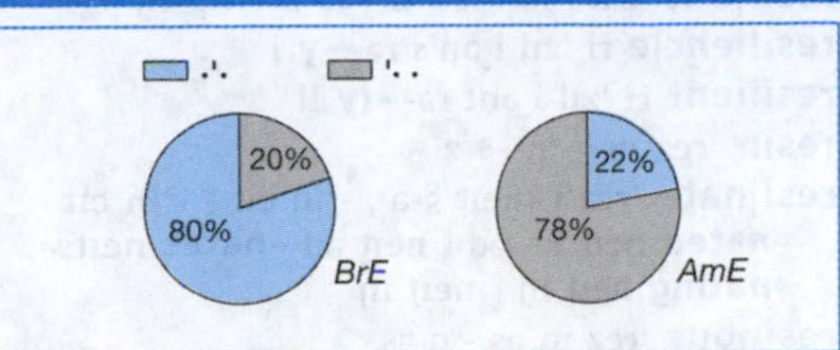

(university teachers: 95%), ˈ· · *20%; AmE, n:* ˈ· · *78%,* ·ˈ· *22%.* **~ed** t **~es** ɪz əz **~ing** ɪŋ
researcher ri ˈsɜːtʃ ə rə-, §-ˈzɜːtʃ-; ˈriː sɜːtʃ ə ‖ ri ˈsɝːtʃ ər ˈriː sɝːtʃ ər **~s** z
resect ri ˈsekt rə- **~ed** ɪd əd **~ing** ɪŋ **~s** s
resection ri ˈsek ʃən rə- **~s** z
reseda ˈres ɪd ə -əd-; rɪ ˈsiːd ə, rə- ‖ rɪ ˈsiːd ə ˈreɪz ə dɑː
reseed ˌriː ˈsiːd **~ed** ɪd əd **~ing** ɪŋ **~s** z
reselect ˌriː sə ˈlekt -sɪ- **~ed** ɪd əd **~ing** ɪŋ **~s** s
reselection ˌriː sə ˈlek ʃən -sɪ- **~s** z
resemblanc|e ri ˈzem blənts rə- **~es** ɪz əz
resembl|e ri ˈzem bəl rə- **~ed** d **~es** z **~ing** ‿ɪŋ
re|sent ri |ˈzent rə- **~sented** ˈzent ɪd -əd ‖ ˈzenţ əd **~senting** ˈzent ɪŋ ‖ ˈzenţ ɪŋ **~sents** ˈzents
resentful ri ˈzent fəl rə-, -fʊl **~ly** ‿i **~ness** nəs nɪs
resentment ri ˈzent mənt rə- **~s** s
reserpine ˈres ə piːn -pɪn; ri ˈsɜːp iːn, rə-, -ɪn, §-ən ‖ ˈres ər- ri ˈsɜːp iːn
reservation ˌrez ə ˈveɪʃ ən ‖ -ər- **~s** z
reserv|e *v, n* ri ˈzɜːv rə- ‖ -ˈzɝːv **~ed** d **~es** z **~ing** ɪŋ
reservedly ri ˈzɜːv ɪd li rə-, -əd- ‖ -ˈzɝːv-
reservist ri ˈzɜːv ɪst rə-, §-əst ‖ -ˈzɝːv- **~s** s
reservoir ˈrez əv wɑː §-ə vɔː ‖ -ərv wɑːr -əv-, -wɔːr, -ɔːr **~s** z
re|set ˌriː |ˈset **~sets** ˈsets **~setting/s** ˈset ɪŋ/z ‖ ˈseţ ɪŋ/z
resettl|e ₍ₗ₎riː ˈset əl ‖ -ˈseţ əl **~ed** d **~es** z **~ing** ‿ɪŋ
resettlement ₍ₗ₎riː ˈset əl mənt
res gestae ˌreɪz ˈgest aɪ ˌreɪs-, ˌriːz- -ˈdʒest-, -iː ‖ ˌreɪs- ˌriːz-
reshuffle *n* ˈriː ˌʃʌf əl ˌ·ˈ· · **~s** z
reshuffl|e *v* ₍ₗ₎riː ˈʃʌf əl **~ed** d **~es** z **~ing** ‿ɪŋ
resid|e ri ˈzaɪd rə- **~ed** ɪd əd **~es** z **~ing** ɪŋ
residenc|e ˈrez ɪd ənts -əd- ‖ -ə dents **~es** ɪz əz **~ies** iz **~y** i
resident ˈrez ɪd ənt -əd- ‖ -ə dent **~s** s
residential ˌrez ɪ ˈdentʃ əl ◂ -ə- **~ly** i
residentiar|y ˌrez ɪ ˈdentʃ ər |i ˌ·ə-, -ˈ·i ər |i ‖ -ˈ·i er |i **~ies** iz
residual ri ˈzɪd ju‿əl rə-, -ˈzɪdʒ u‿əl ‖ -ˈzɪdʒ u‿əl -ˈzɪdʒ əl **~ly** i **~s** z
residuary ri ˈzɪd ju‿ər i rə-, -ˈzɪd jʊr i; -ˈzɪdʒ uər i ‖ -ˈzɪdʒ u er i
residue ˈrez ɪ djuː -ə-, →-dʒuː ‖ -duː -djuː **~s** z
residu|um ri ˈzɪd ju‿|əm rə-, -ˈzɪdʒ u‿ ‖ -ˈzɪdʒ u‿|əm **~a** ə
resign ri ˈzaɪn rə- **~ed** d **~ing** ɪŋ **~s** z
resignation ˌrez ɪg ˈneɪʃ ən **~s** z

R

resignedly ri ˈzaɪn ɪd li rə-, -əd-
resil|e ri ˈzaɪᵊl rə- **~ed** d **~es** z **~ing** ɪŋ
resilienc|e ri ˈzɪl i‿ənᵗs rə- **~y** i
resilient ri ˈzɪl i‿ənt rə- **~ly** li
resin ˈrez ɪn §-ᵊn **~s** z
resi|nate ˈrez ɪ |neɪt §-ə-, -ᵊ|n eɪt ‖ -ᵊ|n eɪt **~nated** neɪt ɪd -əd ‖ neɪṭ əd **~nates** neɪts **~nating** neɪt ɪŋ ‖ neɪṭ ɪŋ
resinous ˈrez ɪn əs -ᵊn‿əs
res ipsa loquitur ˌreɪz ˌɪps ə ˈlɒk wɪt ə ˌreɪs-, ˌriːz-, -ˌ·ɑː-, §-wət ·, -ʊə ‖ ˌreɪs ˌɪps ə ˈloʊk wəṭ ᵊr ˌriːz-
resist ri ˈzɪst rə- **~ed** ɪd əd **~ing** ɪŋ **~s** s
resistanc|e ri ˈzɪst ənᵗs rə- **~es** ɪz əz
resistant ri ˈzɪst ənt rə- **~ly** li
resistib|le ri ˈzɪst əb |ᵊl rə-, -ɪb- **~ly** li
resistive ri ˈzɪst ɪv rə- **~ly** li
resistivity ˌriːz ɪ ˈstɪv ət i ˌrez-, §ˌ·ə-, -ɪt ·; ri ˌzɪ ˈstɪv-, rə- ‖ -əṭ i
resistor ri ˈzɪst ə rə- ‖ -ᵊr **~s** z
resit *n* ˈriː sɪt **~s** s
re|sit *v* ˌriː |ˈsɪt **~sat** ˈsæt **~sits** ˈsɪts **~sitting** ˈsɪt ɪŋ ‖ ˈsɪṭ ɪŋ
Resnais rə ˈneɪ re- —*Fr* [ʁɛ nɛ]
resol|e ˌriː ˈsəʊl →-ˈsɒʊl ‖ -ˈsoʊl **~ed** d **~es** z **~ing** ɪŋ
resoluble ri ˈzɒl jʊb ᵊl rə- ‖ -ˈzɑːl jəb ᵊl -ˈsɑːl- **~ness** nəs nɪs
resolute ˈrez ə luːt -ljuːt **~ly** li **~ness** nəs nɪs
resolution ˌrez ə ˈluːʃ ᵊn -ˈljuːʃ- **~s** z
resolvability ri ˌzɒlv ə ˈbɪl ət i rə-, -ˌzəʊlv-, -ɪt i ‖ -ˌzɑːlv ə ˈbɪl əṭ i
resolvable ri ˈzɒlv əb ᵊl rə-, -ˈzəʊlv- ‖ rɪ ˈzɑːlv- **~ness** nəs nɪs
resolv|e ri ˈzɒlv rə- §-ˈzəʊlv ‖ -ˈzɑːlv **~ed** d **~es** z **~ing** ɪŋ
Resolven ri ˈzɒlv ən ‖ -ˈzɑːlv-
resolvent ri ˈzɒlv ᵊnt rə-, §-ˈzəʊlv- ‖ -ˈzɑːlv- **~s** s
resonanc|e ˈrez ᵊn‿ənᵗs **~es** ɪz əz
resonant ˈrez ᵊn‿ənt **~ly** li **~s** s
reso|nate ˈrez ə |neɪt **~nated** neɪt ɪd -əd ‖ neɪṭ əd **~nates** neɪts **~nating** neɪt ɪŋ ‖ neɪṭ ɪŋ
resonation ˌrez ə ˈneɪʃ ᵊn
resonator ˈrez ə neɪt ə ‖ -neɪṭ ᵊr **~s** z
resorb ri ˈsɔːb rə-, ˌriː-, -ˈzɔːb ‖ -ˈsɔːrb -ˈzɔːrb **~ed** d **~ing** ɪŋ **~s** z
resorcinol ri ˈzɔːs ɪ nɒl rə-, re-, -ə- ‖ -ˈzɔːrs ᵊn ɔːl -ɑːl
resorption ri ˈsɔːp ʃᵊn rə-, ˌriː-, -ˈzɔːp- ‖ -ˈsɔːrp- -ˈzɔːrp-
resorptive ri ˈsɔːpt ɪv rə-, ˌriː-, -ˈzɔːpt- ‖ -ˈsɔːrpt- -ˈzɔːrpt-
re|sort *v, n* ri |ˈzɔːt rə- ‖ -|ˈzɔːrt **~sorted** ˈzɔːt ɪd -əd ‖ ˈzɔːrṭ əd **~sorting** ˈzɔːtɪŋ ‖ ˈzɔːrṭ ɪŋ **~sorts** ˈzɔːts ‖ ˈzɔːrts
resound ri ˈzaʊnd rə- **~ed** ɪd əd **~ing/ly** ɪŋ /li **~s** z

RESOURCE

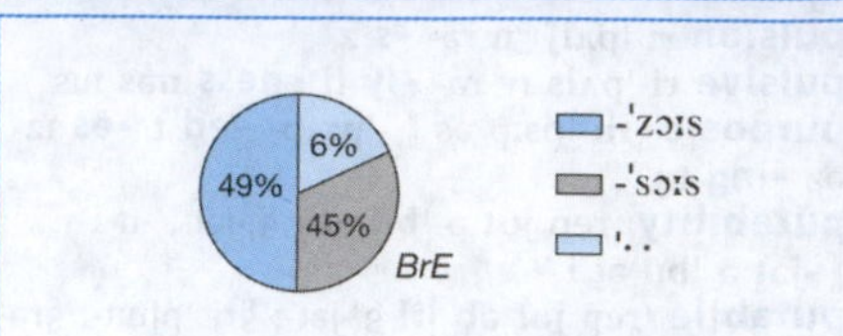

resourc|e ri ˈzɔːs rə-, -ˈsɔːs; ˈriː sɔːs, -zɔːs ‖ ˈriː sɔːrs -soʊrs — *Preference poll, BrE:* -ˈzɔːs *49%,* -ˈsɔːs *45%,* ˈ· · *6%.* **~ed** t **~es** ɪz əz **~ing** ɪŋ
resourceful ri ˈzɔːs fᵊl rə-, -ˈsɔːs-, -fʊl ‖ rɪ ˈsɔːrs- -ˈsoʊrs-, -ˈzɔːrs-, -ˈzoʊrs- **~ly** ‿i **~ness** nəs nɪs
respect *v, n* ri ˈspekt rə- **~ed** ɪd əd **~ing** ɪŋ **~s** s
respectability ri ˌspekt ə ˈbɪl ət i rə-, -ɪt i ‖ -əṭ i
respectab|le ri ˈspekt əb |ᵊl rə- **~leness** ᵊl nəs -nɪs **~ly** li
respecter ri ˈspekt ə rə- ‖ -ᵊr **~s** z
respectful ri ˈspekt fᵊl rə-, -fʊl **~ly** ‿i **~ness** nəs nɪs
respective ri ˈspekt ɪv rə- **~ly** li **~ness** nəs nɪs
Respighi re ˈspiːg i ri-, rə- —*It* [re ˈspiː gi]
respiration ˌresp ə ˈreɪʃ ᵊn -ɪ-
respirator ˈresp ə reɪt ə ‖ -reɪṭ ᵊr **~s** z

RESPIRATORY

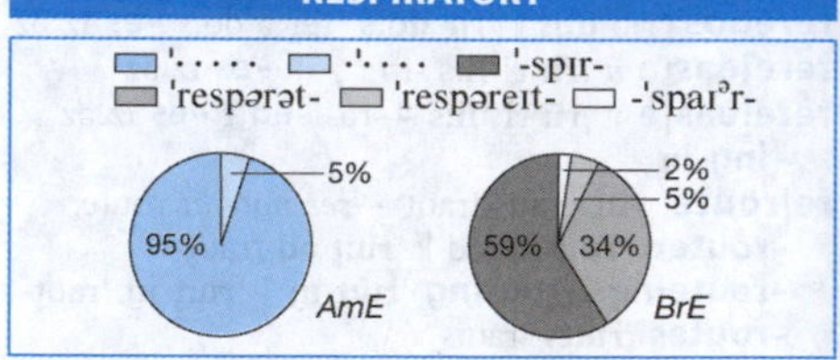

respiratory ri ˈspɪr ət‿ər i rə-, re-, -ˈspaɪᵊr-; ˈresp ər‿ət‿; ˈresp ə reɪt ər i, ·ˈ· · · · ‖ ˈresp ər‿ə tɔːr i ri ˈspaɪr ə-, -toʊr i — *Preference polls, AmE:* ˈ· · · · · *95%,* ·ˈ· · · · *5%; BrE:* -ˈspɪr- *59%,* ˈrespərət- *34%,* ˈrespəreɪt- *5%,* -ˈspaɪᵊr- *2%.*
respire ri ˈspaɪ‿ə rə- ‖ -ˈspaɪ‿ᵊr **~d** d **~s** z **respiring** ri ˈspaɪ‿ər ɪŋ rə- ‖ -ˈspaɪ‿ᵊr ɪŋ
respite ˈresp aɪt -ɪt, §-ət ‖ -ət ri ˈspaɪt **~s** s
resplendenc|e ri ˈsplend ənᵗs rə- **~y** i
resplendent ri ˈsplend ənt rə- **~ly** li
respond ri ˈspɒnd rə- ‖ -ˈspɑːnd **~ed** ɪd əd **~ing** ɪŋ **~s** z
respondent ri ˈspɒnd ənt rə- ‖ -ˈspɑːnd- **~s** s
respons|e ri ˈspɒnᵗs rə- ‖ -ˈspɑːnᵗs **~es** ɪz əz
responsibilit|y ri ˌspɒnᵗs ə ˈbɪl ət |i rə-, -ˌ·ɪ-, -ɪt i ‖ -ˌspɑːnᵗs ə ˈbɪl əṭ |i **~ies** iz
responsib|le ri ˈspɒnᵗs əb |ᵊl rə-, -ɪb- ‖ ri ˈspɑːnᵗs- **~ly** li
responsive ri ˈspɒnᵗs ɪv rə- ‖ -ˈspɑːnᵗs ɪv **~ly** li **~ness** nəs nɪs
responsor|y ri ˈspɒnᵗs ər |i rə- ‖ ri ˈspɑːnᵗs- **~ies** iz

respray *n* ˈriː spreɪ **~s** z
respray *v* ˌriː ˈspreɪ **~ed** d **~ing** ɪŋ **~s** z
rest rest **rested** ˈrest ɪd -əd **resting** ˈrest ɪŋ **rests** rests
ˈrest cure; **ˈrest home**; **ˈresting place**; **ˈrest ˌperiod**; **ˈrest room**
restag|e ˌriː ˈsteɪdʒ **~ed** d **~es** ɪz əz **~ing** ɪŋ
re|state ˌriː |ˈsteɪt **~stated** ˈsteɪt ɪd -əd ‖ ˈsteɪţ əd **~statement/s** ˈsteɪt mənt/s **~states** ˈsteɪts **~stating** ˈsteɪt ɪŋ ‖ ˈsteɪţ ɪŋ

RESTAURANT

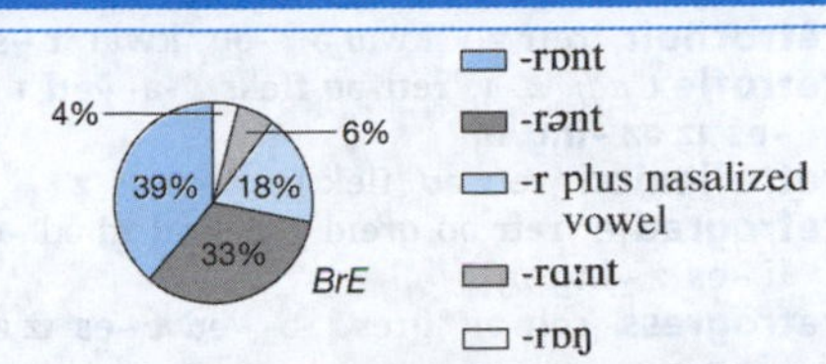

restau|rant ˈrest ə |rɒnt -rɑːnt, -rɒŋ, -rɒ̃, -rɑ̃ː, -rɔ̃ː; -ə|r ənt; ˈres t|rɒnt, -t|rɑːnt, -t|rɒ̃, -t|rənt ‖ ˈrest ə|r ənt -ə |rɑːnt; ˈres t|rənt, -t|rɑːnt — *Preference poll, BrE:* -rɒnt *39% (born since 1973: 72%),* -rənt *33%,* -r *plus nasalized vowel 18%,* -rɑːnt *6%,* -rɒŋ *4%.* **~rants** rɒnts rɑːnts, rɒŋz, rɒ̃z, rɑ̃ːz, rɔ̃ːz, rənts ‖ rənts rɑːnts
ˈrestaurant car
restaurateur ˌrest ər‿ə ˈtɜː -ɒr ə-, -ɔːr ə-, ⚠-ə rɒn- ‖ -ˈtɜː -ˈtʊᵊr —*Fr* [ʁɛs tɔ ʁa tœːʁ] **~s** z
restful ˈrest fᵊl -fʊl **~ly** i **~ness** nəs nɪs
restharrow ˈrest ˌhær əʊ ‖ -oʊ ˌher-
restitution ˌrest ɪ ˈtjuːʃ ᵊn -ə-, →-tʃuːʃ- ‖ -ˈtuːʃ ᵊn -ˈtjuːʃ- **~s** z
restive ˈrest ɪv **~ly** li **~ness** nəs nɪs
restless ˈrest ləs -lɪs **~ly** li **~ness** nəs nɪs
restock ˌriː ˈstɒk ‖ -ˈstɑːk **~ed** t **~ing** ɪŋ **~s** s
Reston ˈrest ən
restoration, R~ ˌrest ə ˈreɪʃ ᵊn **~s** z
restorative ri ˈstɔːr ət ɪv rə-, -ˈstɒr-; ˈrest ə reɪt- ‖ -əţ ɪv -ˈstoʊr- **~s** z
restore ri ˈstɔː rə- ‖ -ˈstɔːr -ˈstoʊr **~d** d **~s** z **restoring** ri ˈstɔːr ɪŋ rə- ‖ -ˈstoʊr-
restorer ri ˈstɔːr ə rə- ‖ -ᵊr -ˈstoʊr- **~s** z
restrain ri ˈstreɪn rə- **~ed** d **~er/s** ə/z ‖ -ᵊr/z **~ing** ɪŋ **~s** z
restraint rɪ ˈstreɪnt rə- **~s** s
restrict ri ˈstrɪkt rə- **~ed** ɪd əd **~ing** ɪŋ **~s** s
restriction ri ˈstrɪk ʃᵊn rə- **~s** z
restrictive ri ˈstrɪkt ɪv rə- **~ly** li **~ness** nəs nɪs
reˌstrictive ˈpractice
restructure ˌriː ˈstrʌk tʃə -ʃə ‖ -tʃᵊr **~d** d **~s** z **restructuring** ˌriː ˈstrʌk tʃər ɪŋ -ʃər‿ɪŋ
result *v, n* ri ˈzʌlt rə- **~ed** ɪd əd **~ing** ɪŋ **~s** s
resultant ri ˈzʌlt ənt rə- ‖ -ᵊnt **~s** s
resultative ri ˈzʌlt ət ɪv rə- ‖ -əţ ɪv **~s** z
resum|e *v* ri ˈzjuːm rə-, -ˈzuːm, §-ˈʒuːm ‖ -ˈzuːm **~ed** d **~es** z **~ing** ɪŋ
resume *n,* **résumé, resumé** ˈrez ju meɪ ˈreɪz-, -u-; rɪ ˈzjuːm eɪ, rə-, §riː-, -ˈzuːm- ‖ ˈrez ə meɪ ˈreɪz-, -u-, ˌ·ˈ· **~s** z
resumption ri ˈzʌmp ʃᵊn rə- **~s** z
resumptive ri ˈzʌmpt ɪv rə **~ly** li **~s** z
resurfac|e ˌriː ˈsɜːf ɪs -əs ‖ -ˈsɜːf əs **~ed** t **~es** ɪz əz **~ing** ɪŋ
resurg|e ri ˈsɜːdʒ rə- ‖ -ˈsɜːdʒ **~ed** d **~es** ɪz əz **~ing** ɪŋ
resurgenc|e ri ˈsɜːdʒ ənts rə- ‖ ri ˈsɜːdʒ- **~es** ɪz əz
resurgent ri ˈsɜːdʒ ənt rə- ‖ ri ˈsɜːdʒ-
resurrect ˌrez ə ˈrekt **~ed** ɪd əd **~ing** ɪŋ **~s** s
resurrection, R~ ˌrez ə ˈrek ʃᵊn **~s** z
resusci|tate ri ˈsʌs ɪ |teɪt rə-, ə- **~tated** teɪt ɪd -əd ‖ teɪţ əd **~tates** teɪts **~tating** teɪt ɪŋ ‖ teɪţ ɪŋ
resuscitation ri ˌsʌs ɪ ˈteɪʃ ᵊn rə-, ˌriː ˌ· ·ˈ· ·, -əˈ-- **~s** z
ret ret **rets** rets **retted** ˈret ɪd -əd ‖ ˈreţ əd **retting** ˈret ɪŋ ‖ ˈreţ ɪŋ
retable *n* ri ˈteɪb ᵊl rə-; ˈriː ˌ· · **~s** z
retail *n, adj* ˈriː teɪᵊl
ˌretail ˈprice ˌindex
retail *v 'sell'* ˈriː teɪᵊl ₍ₗ₎ˈ· **~ed** d **~ing** ɪŋ **~s** z
retail *v 'pass on, relate'* ri ˈteɪᵊl rə- **~ed** d **~ing** ɪŋ **~s** z
retailer ˈriː teɪᵊl ə ‖ -ᵊr **~s** z
retain ri ˈteɪn rə- **~ed** d **~ing** ɪŋ **~s** z
retainer ri ˈteɪn ə rə- ‖ -ᵊr **~s** z
retake *n* ˈriː teɪk **~s** s
re|take *v* ₍ₗ₎riː |ˈteɪk **~taken** ˈteɪk ən **~takes** ˈteɪks **~taking** ˈteɪk ɪŋ **~took** ˈtʊk §ˈtuːk
retali|ate ri ˈtæl i |eɪt rə- **~ated** eɪt ɪd -əd ‖ eɪţ əd **~ates** eɪts **~ating** eɪt ɪŋ ‖ eɪţ ɪŋ
retaliation ri ˌtæl i ˈeɪʃ ᵊn rə- **~s** z
retaliatory ri ˈtæl i ə‿tər i rə-; -eɪt ər i, ·ˌ· ·ˈeɪt- ‖ -ə tɔːr i -toʊr i
Retallack ri ˈtæl ək rə-
retard *v; n 'slowdown'* ri ˈtɑːd rə- ‖ -ˈtɑːrd **~ed** ɪd əd **~ing** ɪŋ **~s** z
retard *n 'mentally retarded person'* ˈriː tɑːd ‖ -tɑːrd **~s** z
retardant ri ˈtɑːd ᵊnt rə- ‖ rɪ ˈtɑːrd- **~s** s
retardate ri ˈtɑːd eɪt rə- ‖ -ˈtɑːrd- **~s** s
retardation ˌriː tɑː ˈdeɪʃ ᵊn ‖ -tɑːr- ri ˌ·ˈ· · **~s** z
retch retʃ riːtʃ **retched** retʃt riːtʃt **retches** ˈretʃ ɪz ˈriːtʃ-, -əz **retching** ˈretʃ ɪŋ ˈriːtʃ-
rete ˈriːt i ‖ ˈriːţ i ˈreɪţ **retia** ˈriːt i‿ə ˈriːʃ- ‖ ˈriːţ i‿ə ˈreɪţ-
re|tell ˌriː |ˈtel **~telling** ˈtel ɪŋ **~tells** ˈtelz **~told** ˈtəʊld →ˈtɒʊld ‖ ˈtoʊld
retention ri ˈtenʃ ᵊn rə- **~s** z
reˈtention fee
retentive ri ˈtent ɪv rə- ‖ -ˈtenţ ɪv **~ly** li **~ness** nəs nɪs
Retford ˈret fəd ‖ -fᵊrd
rethink *n* ˈriː θɪŋk ˌ·ˈ· **~s** s
re|think *v* ˌriː |ˈθɪŋk **~thinking** ˈθɪŋk ɪŋ **~thinks** ˈθɪŋks **~thought** ˈθɔːt ‖ ˈθɑːt
retiari|us ˌret i ˈeər i‿əs ˌriːt-, ˌriːʃ-, -ˈɑːr- ‖ ˌreţ i ˈer- **~i** aɪ iː
reticence ˈret ɪs ənts -əs- ‖ ˈreţ əs-
reticent ˈret ɪs ənt -əs- ‖ ˈreţ əs- **~ly** li
reticle ˈret ɪk ᵊl ‖ ˈreţ- **~s** z
reticular ri ˈtɪk jʊl ə rə-, -jəl- ‖ -jəl ᵊr

R

reticu|late *v* ri ˈtɪk ju |leɪt rə-, -jə- ‖ -jə- **~lated** leɪt ɪd -əd ‖ leɪţ əd **~lates** leɪts **~lating** leɪt ɪŋ ‖ leɪţ ɪŋ
reticulate *adj* ri ˈtɪk jʊl ət rə-, -jəl-, -ɪt
reticulation ri ˌtɪk ju ˈleɪʃ ən rə-, -jə- ‖ -jə- **~s** z
reticule ˈret ɪ kjuːl -ə- ‖ ˈreţ- **~s** z
reticul|um, R~ rɪ ˈtɪk jʊl |əm rə-, -jəl- ‖ -jəl- **~a** ə
ret|ina ˈret |ɪn ə §-ən‿ə ‖ -|ən‿ə **~inae** ɪ niː §ən iː ‖ -ən iː **~inas** ɪn əz ən‿əz ‖ ən‿əz
retinal ˈret ɪn əl §-ən‿əl ‖ ˈret ən‿əl
retinitis ˌret ɪ ˈnaɪt ɪs -ə-, -ən ˈaɪt-, §-əs ‖ ˌret ən ˈaɪţ əs
ˌretiˌnitis ˌpigmenˈtosa ˌpɪg men ˈtəʊs ə -ˈtəʊz- ‖ -ˈtoʊs ə
retino- *comb. form*
with stress-neutral suffix ¦ret ɪn əʊ -ən- ‖ ¦ret ən ə — **retinoscope** ˈret ɪn əʊ skəʊp ‖ -ən ə skoʊp
with stress-imposing suffix ˌret ɪ ˈnɒ+ -ə- ‖ ˌret ən ˈɑː+ — **retinopathy** ˌret ɪ ˈnɒp əθ i ˌ·ə- ‖ ˌret ən ˈɑːp-
retinol ˈret ɪ nɒl -ə- ‖ ˈret ən ɔːl -ɑːl, -oʊl
retinue ˈret ɪ njuː §-ə-; §-ən juː, -uː ‖ ˈret ən uː -juː **~s** z
retire ri ˈtaɪ‿ə rə- ‖ -ˈtaɪ‿ər **~d** d **~s** z
retiring/ly ri ˈtaɪ‿ər ɪŋ /li ‖ -ˈtaɪ‿ər ɪŋ /li
retiree ri ˌtaɪ‿ə ˈriː rə-, ˌriː-; ·ˈ· · ‖ ri ˌtaɪə ˈriː **~s** z
retirement ri ˈtaɪ‿ə mənt rə- ‖ -ˈtaɪ‿ər mənt **~s** s
reˈtirement age; **reˈtirement ˌpension**
re|tort *v, n* ri |ˈtɔːt rə- ‖ -|ˈtɔːrt **~torted** ˈtɔːt ɪd -əd ‖ ˈtɔːrţ əd **~torting** ˈtɔːt ɪŋ ‖ ˈtɔːrţ ɪŋ **~torts** ˈtɔːts ‖ ˈtɔːrts
retortion ri ˈtɔːʃ ən rə- ‖ -ˈtɔːrʃ-
retouch *v* ˌriː ˈtʌtʃ **~ed** t **~es** ɪz əz **~ing** ɪŋ
retouch *n* ˈriː tʌtʃ ˌ·ˈ· **~es** ɪz əz
retrac|e ri ˈtreɪs rə-, ˌriː- **~ed** t **~es** ɪz əz **~ing** ɪŋ
retract ri ˈtrækt rə- **~ed** ɪd əd **~ing** ɪŋ **~s** s
retractable, retractible ri ˈtrækt əb əl rə-
retractile ri ˈtrækt aɪəl rə- ‖ -əl
retraction ri ˈtræk ʃən rə- **~s** z
retractor ri ˈtrækt ə rə- ‖ -ər **~s** z
retread *n* ˈriː tred **~s** z
retread *v* ˌriː ˈtred **~ed** ɪd əd **~ing** ɪŋ **~s** z
retrod ˌriː ˈtrɒd ‖ -ˈtrɑːd **retrodden** ˌriː ˈtrɒd ən ‖ -ˈtrɑːd ən
re|treat *v, n* ri |ˈtriːt rə- **~treated** ˈtriːt ɪd -əd ‖ ˈtriːţ əd **~treating** ˈtriːt ɪŋ ‖ ˈtriːţ ɪŋ **~treats** ˈtriːts
retrench ri ˈtrentʃ rə- **~ed** t **~es** ɪz əz **~ing** ɪŋ **~ment/s** mənt/s
retri... —*see* **retry**
retrial ˌriː ˈtraɪ‿əl ˈ·ˌ· · ‖ -ˈtraɪ‿əl ˈ·ˌ· · **~s** z
retribution ˌretr ɪ ˈbjuːʃ ən -ə-
retributive ri ˈtrɪb jʊt ɪv rə-, -jət-; §ˈretr ɪ bjuːt-, ˈ·ə- ‖ -jəţ ɪv **~ly** li
retributory ri ˈtrɪb jʊt‿ər i rə-, -jət‿ ‖ -jə tɔːr i -toʊr-
retrievability ri ˌtriːv ə ˈbɪl ət i rə-, -ɪt i ‖ -əţ i
retrievable ri ˈtriːv əb əl rə-
retrieval ri ˈtriːv əl rə- **~s** z
retriev|e ri ˈtriːv rə- **~ed** d **~es** z **~ing** ɪŋ
retriever ri ˈtriːv ə rə- ‖ -ər **~s** z
retro ˈretr əʊ ‖ -oʊ
retro- ¦retr əʊ ‖ -oʊ —*formerly also* ¦riːtr- — **retrobronchial** ˌretr əʊ ˈbrɒŋk i‿əl ◂ ‖ -oʊ ˈbrɑːŋk-
retroactive ˌretr əʊ ˈækt ɪv ◂ ‖ -oʊ- **~ly** li
retroced|e ˌretr əʊ ˈsiːd ‖ -oʊ- **~ed** ɪd əd **~es** z **~ing** ɪŋ
retrocession ˌretr əʊ ˈseʃ ən ‖ -oʊ-
retrochoir ˈretr əʊ ˌkwaɪ‿ə ‖ -oʊ ˌkwaɪ‿ər **~s** z
retroflex *adj, n, v* ˈretr əʊ fleks ‖ -ə- **~ed** t **~es** ɪz əz **~ing** ɪŋ
retroflexion ˌretr əʊ ˈflek ʃən ‖ -ə- **~s** z
retrograd|e ˈretr əʊ greɪd ‖ -ə- **~ed** ɪd əd **~ely** li **~es** z **~ing** ɪŋ
retrogress ˌretr əʊ ˈgres ‖ -ə- **~ed** t **~es** ɪz əz **~ing** ɪŋ
retrogression ˌretr əʊ ˈgreʃ ən ‖ -ə- **~s** z
retrogressive ˌretr əʊ ˈgres ɪv ◂ ‖ -ə- **~ly** li
retrorocket ˈretr əʊ ˌrɒk ɪt §-ət ‖ -oʊ ˌrɑːk ət **~s** s
retrospect ˈretr əʊ spekt ‖ -ə-
retrospection ˌretr əʊ ˈspek ʃən ‖ -ə-
retrospective ˌretr əʊ ˈspekt ɪv ◂ ‖ -ə- **~ly** li **~ness** nəs nɪs **~s** z
ˌretroˌspective ˌexhiˈbition
retrousse, retroussé rə ˈtruːs eɪ ri- ‖ rə ˌtruː ˈseɪ ˌretr u- (*) —*Fr* [ʁə tʁu se]
retroversion ˌretr əʊ ˈvɜːʃ ən -ˈvɜːʒ- ‖ -oʊ ˈvɜːʒ ən **~s** z
Retrovir *tdmk* ˈretr əʊ vɪə ‖ -oʊ vɪr
retrovirus ˈretr əʊ ˌvaɪər əs ˌ·ˈ·· ‖ -ə- **~es** ɪz əz
re|try ˌriː |ˈtraɪ **~tried** ˈtraɪd **~tries** ˈtraɪz **~trying** ˈtraɪ ɪŋ
retsina ret ˈsiːn ə ˈrets ɪn ə, -ən- —*ModGk* [rɛ ˈtsi na] **~s** z
Rett ret
return *v, n* ri ˈtɜːn rə- ‖ -ˈtɜːn **~ed** d **~ing** ɪŋ **~s** z
reˈturning ˌofficer
returnable ri ˈtɜːn əb əl rə- ‖ -ˈtɜːn- **~s** z
returnee ri ˌtɜː ˈniː rə-, -ˈtɜːn iː ‖ rɪ ˌtɜː ˈniː **~s** z
returner ri ˈtɜːn ə rə- ‖ -tɜːn ər **~s** z
retuse ri ˈtjuːs rə-, §-ˈtuːs, →-ˈtʃuːs ‖ -ˈtuːs -ˈtjuːs **~ness** nəs nɪs
Reuben ˈruːb ən -ɪn
reunification ˌriː ˌjuːn ɪf ɪ ˈkeɪʃ ən ·ˌ· · ·ˈ· ·, -əf ·ˈ·-, §-əˈ·- **~s** z
reuni|fy (ˌ)riː ˈjuːn ɪ |faɪ -ə- **~fied** faɪd **~fies** faɪz **~fying** faɪ ɪŋ
reunion (ˌ)riː ˈjuːn i‿ən ‖ -ˈjuːn jən **~s** z
Reunion, Réunion *island* (ˌ)riː ˈjuːn i‿ən ‖ -ˈjuːn jən —*Fr* [ʁe y njɔ̃]
reu|nite ˌriː ju |ˈnaɪt **~nited** ˈnaɪt ɪd -əd ‖ ˈnaɪţ əd **~nites** ˈnaɪts **~niting** ˈnaɪt ɪŋ ‖ ˈnaɪţ ɪŋ
reusable (ˌ)riː ˈjuːz əb əl ◂
reuse *n* ˌriː ˈjuːs

reus|e *v* ˌriː ˈjuːz **~ed** d **~es** ɪz əz **~ing** ɪŋ
Reuter ˈrɔɪt ə ‖ ˈrɔɪţ ər **~s** z
rev rev **revs** revz **revved** revd **revving** ˈrev ɪŋ
ˈrev ˌcounter
Rev rev *or as* Reverend
revaluation ˌriː ˌvæl ju ˈeɪʃ ən ·ˌ· ·ˈ· · **~s** z
reval|ue (ˌ)riː ˈvæl |juː **~ued** juːd **~ues** juːz **~uing** ju‿ɪŋ
revamp *v* (ˌ)riː ˈvæmp **~ed** t **~ing** ɪŋ **~s** s
revamp *n* ˈriː væmp ˌ·ˈ· **~s** s
revanch|ism ri ˈvæntʃ |ˌɪz əm rə, -ˈvɑːntʃ-, -ˈvɒ̃ʃ- **~ist/s** ɪst/s §əst/s ‖ əst/s
Revd —*see* **Reverend**
reveal *v, n* ri ˈviːəl rə- **~ed** d **~ing/ly** ɪŋ /li **~s** z
reveille ri ˈvæl i rə-, -ˈvel- ‖ ˈrev əl i *(*)* **~s** z
revel *v, n* ˈrev əl **~ed, ~led** d **~ing, ~ling** ɪŋ **~s** z
revelation, R~ ˌrev ə ˈleɪʃ ən **~s** z
revelatory ˌrev ə ˈleɪt ər i ˈrev əl‿ət‿ər i ‖ ˈrev əl‿ə tɔːr i ri ˈvel ə-
reveler, reveller ˈrev əl ə ‖ -əl‿ər **~s** z
Revell ˈrev əl
revel|ry ˈrev əl |ri **~ries** riz
Revelstoke ˈrev əl stəʊk ‖ -stoʊk
reven|ant ˈrev ən |ənt -ɪn-; -ə n|ænt, -n|ɑ̃ː **~ants** ənts ænts, ɑ̃ːz
reveng|e *v, n* ri ˈvendʒ rə- **~ed** d **~es** ɪz əz **~ing** ɪŋ
revengeful ri ˈvendʒ fəl rə- **~ly** ‿i **~ness** nəs nɪs
revenue ˈrev ə njuː -ɪ-, §-nuː ‖ -nuː —*formerly also* ri ˈven juː, rə- **~s** z
reverb ˈriː vɜːb ri ˈvɜːb, rə- ‖ ˈriː vɜ˞ːb ri ˈvɜ˞ːb **~s** z
reverberant ri ˈvɜːb ər‿ənt rə- ‖ -ˈvɜ˞ːb- **~ly** li
reverbe|rate ri ˈvɜːb ə |reɪt rə- ‖ -ˈvɜ˞ːb- **~rated** reɪt ɪd -əd ‖ reɪţ əd **~rates** reɪts **~rating** reɪt ɪŋ ‖ reɪţ ɪŋ
reverberation ri ˌvɜːb ə ˈreɪʃ ən rə- ‖ -ˌvɜ˞ːb- **~s** z
reverberator|y ri ˈvɜːb ər‿ət‿ər |i rə-, -reɪt ər |i ‖ ri ˈvɜ˞ːb ər‿ə tɔːr |i -toʊr i; ⚠·ˈ·ə · · **~ies** iz
revere, R~ ri ˈvɪə rə- ‖ -ˈvɪər **~d** d **~s** z
revering ri ˈvɪər ɪŋ rə- ‖ -ˈvɪr ɪŋ
reverenc|e ˈrev ər‿ənts **~ed** t **~es** ɪz əz **~ing** ɪŋ
rever|end, R~ ˈrev ər‿|ənd ⚠‿ənt **~ends** əndz ⚠ənts
ˌReverend ˈMother
reverent ˈrev ər‿ənt **~ly** li
reverential ˌrev ə ˈrentʃ əl ◂ **~ly** i
reverie ˈrev ər i **~s** z
revers *sing.* ri ˈvɪə rə-, -ˈveə ‖ -ˈvɪər -ˈveər *(!)* **~** *pl* z
reversal ri ˈvɜːs əl rə- ‖ -ˈvɜ˞ːs əl **~s** z
revers|e *adj, n, v* ri ˈvɜːs rə- ‖ -ˈvɜ˞ːs **~ed** t **~ely** li **~es** ɪz əz **~ing** ɪŋ
reˌverse diˌscrimiˈnation; **reˈversing light**
reversi ri ˈvɜːs i rə- ‖ -ˈvɜ˞ːs i
reversibility ri ˌvɜːs ə ˈbɪl ət i rə-, -ˌɪ-, -ɪt i ‖ -ˌvɜ˞ːs ə ˈbɪl əţ i
reversib|le ri ˈvɜːs əb |əl rə-, -ɪb- ‖ -ˈvɜ˞ːs- **~leness** əl nəs -nɪs **~ly** li
reversion ri ˈvɜːʃ ən rə-, -ˈvɜːʒ ‖ -ˈvɜ˞ːʒ ən -ˈvɜ˞ːʃ- **~s** z
reversionary ri ˈvɜːʃ ən‿ər i rə-, -ˈvɜːʒ-, -ən ər‿i ‖ ri ˈvɜ˞ːʒ ə ner i -ˈvɜ˞ːʃ-
re|vert ri |ˈvɜːt rə- ‖ -|ˈvɜ˞ːt **~verted** ˈvɜːt ɪd -əd ‖ ˈvɜ˞ːţ əd **~verting** ˈvɜːt ɪŋ ‖ ˈvɜ˞ːţ ɪŋ **~verts** ˈvɜːts ‖ ˈvɜ˞ːts
re|vet ri |ˈvet rə- **~vets** ˈvets **~vetted** ˈvet ɪd -əd ‖ ˈveţ əd **~vetting** ˈvet ɪŋ ‖ ˈveţ ɪŋ
revetment ri ˈvet mənt rə- **~s** s
Revie ˈriːv i
review *n, v* ri ˈvjuː rə- **~ed** d **~ing** ɪŋ **~s** z
reviewer ri ˈvjuː‿ə rə- ‖ ər **~s** z
revil|e ri ˈvaɪəl rə- **~ed** d **~er/s** ə/z -ər/z **~es** z **~ing** ɪŋ
Revill ˈrev əl -ɪl
revis|e ri ˈvaɪz rə- **~ed** d **~er/s** ə/z ‖ -ər/z **~es** ɪz əz **~ing** ɪŋ
Reˌvised ˈVersion
revision ri ˈvɪʒ ən rə- **~s** z
revisionism ri ˈvɪʒ ən ˌɪz əm rə-
revisionist ri ˈvɪʒ ən‿ɪst rə-, §-əst **~s** s
revis|it ˌriː ˈvɪz |ɪt §-ət ‖ -|ət **~ited** ɪt ɪd §ət-, -əd ‖ əţ əd **~iting** ɪt ɪŋ §ət- ‖ əţ ɪŋ **~its** ɪts §əts ‖ əts
revitalis... —*see* **revitaliz...**
revitalization ˌriː ˌvaɪt əl aɪ ˈzeɪʃ ən ·ˌ· · ·ˈ· · ‖ riː ˌvaɪţ əl ə ˈzeɪʃ ən ·ˌ· · ·ˈ· ·
revitaliz|e (ˌ)riː ˈvaɪt ə laɪz -əl aɪz ‖ -ˈvaɪţ əl aɪz **~ed** d **~es** ɪz əz **~ing** ɪŋ
revival ri ˈvaɪv əl rə- **~s** z
revivalism ri ˈvaɪv əl ˌɪz əm rə-
revivalist ri ˈvaɪv əl ɪst rə-, §-əst **~s** s
reviv|e ri ˈvaɪv rə- **~ed** d **~es** z **~ing** ɪŋ
revivi|fy (ˌ)riː ˈvɪv ɪ |faɪ ri-, ə- **~fied** faɪd **~fies** faɪz **~fying** faɪ ɪŋ
reviviscence ˌrev ɪ ˈvɪs ənts -ə-
Revlon *tdmk* ˈrev lɒn ‖ -lɑːn
revocab|le ˈrev ək əb |əl rɪ ˈvəʊk-, rə-, §riː- ‖ rɪ ˈvoʊk- **~leness** əl nəs -nɪs **~ly** li
revocation ˌrev əʊ ˈkeɪʃ ən ‖ -ə- **~s** z
revok|e ri ˈvəʊk rə- ‖ -ˈvoʊk **~ed** t **~es** s **~ing** ɪŋ
revolt *v, n* ri ˈvəʊlt rə-, →-ˈvɒʊlt ‖ -ˈvoʊlt **~ed** ɪd əd **~ing/ly** ɪŋ /li **~s** s
revolution ˌrev ə ˈluːʃ ən -ˈljuːʃ- **~s** z
revolutionar|y ˌrev ə ˈluːʃ ən ər‿|i ◂ -ˈljuːʃ-, -ən‿ər |i ‖ -ə ner |i **~ies** iz
revolutionis|e, revolutioniz|e ˌrev ə ˈluːʃ ə naɪz -ˈljuːʃ- **~ed** d **~es** ɪz əz **~ing** ɪŋ
revolv|e ri ˈvɒlv rə-, §-ˈvəʊlv ‖ -ˈvɑːlv **~ed** d **~es** z **~ing** ɪŋ
reˌvolving ˈcredit; **reˌvolving ˈdoor**
revolver ri ˈvɒlv ə rə-, §-ˈvəʊlv- ‖ -ˈvɑːlv ər **~s** z
revue ri ˈvjuː rə- *(= review)* **~s** z
revulsion ri ˈvʌlʃ ən rə- **~s** z
Rew ruː
reward *n, v* ri ˈwɔːd rə- ‖ -ˈwɔːrd **~ed** ɪd əd **~ing/ly** ɪŋ /li **~s** z
rewind *v* (ˌ)riː ˈwaɪnd **~ing** ɪŋ **~s** z **rewound** (ˌ)riː ˈwaʊnd

R

rewind *n* 'riː waɪnd ˌ(ˌ)'· **~s** z
rewire ˌriː 'waɪ‿ə ‖ -'waɪ‿ᵊr **~d** d **~s** z
rewiring/s ˌriː 'waɪ‿ər ɪŋ/z ‖ -'waɪ‿ᵊr ɪŋ/z
reword ˌriː 'wɜːd ‖ -'wɜːd **~ed** ɪd əd **~ing/s** ɪŋ/z **~s** z
rework ˌriː 'wɜːk ‖ -'wɜːk **~ed** t **~ing/s** ɪŋ/z **~s** s
re|write *v* ˌriː |'raɪt **~writes** 'raɪts **~written** 'rɪt ᵊn ◂ **~wrote** 'rəʊt ‖ 'roʊt
rewrite *n* 'riː raɪt ˌ·'· **~s** s
Rex, rex reks **Rex's** 'reks ɪz -əz
rexine, R~ *tdmk* 'reks iːn
Rey reɪ
Reye raɪ reɪ **Reye's** raɪz reɪz
'Reye's ˌsyndrome
Reyes raɪz reɪz
Reykjavik 'reɪk jə vɪk 'rek-, 'raɪk-, -viːk —*Icelandic* Reykjavík ['reːi ca viːk]
Reynard, r~ 'ren ɑːd 'reɪn-, -əd ‖ -ɑːrd -ᵊrd
Reynold 'ren ᵊld
Reynolds 'ren ᵊldz
Rh ˌɑːr 'eɪtʃ ◂ §ˌɑː 'heɪtʃ ‖ ˌɑːr 'eɪtʃ ◂ —*or as* 'Rhesus
ˌR'h factor; **ˌRh 'negative**; **ˌRh 'positive**
rhabdo- *comb. form* ¦ræbd əʊ ‖ -oʊ
rhabdovirus 'ræbd əʊ ˌvaɪᵊr əs ‖ -oʊ-
Rhadamanth|us ˌræd ə 'mænᵗθ |əs **~ine** aɪn ◂ ‖ ᵊn ◂ aɪn ◂ **~ys** ɪs §əs
Rhaet|ia 'riːʃ |ə -'i‿ə **~an/s** ᵊn/z i‿ən/z
Rhaetic 'riːt ɪk ‖ 'riːţ ɪk
Rhaeto-Romance ˌriːt əʊ rəʊ 'mænᵗs ◂ ‖ ˌriːţ oʊ roʊ-
Rhaeto-Romanic ˌriːt əʊ rəʊ 'mæn ɪk ◂ ‖ ˌriːţ oʊ roʊ-
rhapsodic ræp 'sɒd ɪk ‖ -'sɑːd ɪk **~ally** ᵊl‿i
rhapsodis|e, rhapsodiz|e 'ræps ə daɪz **~ed** d **~es** ɪz əz **~ing** ɪŋ
rhapsod|y 'ræps əd |i **~ies** iz
rhatan|y 'ræt ən |i ‖ 'ræt ᵊn |i **~ies** iz
Rhayader 'raɪ‿əd ə ‖ ᵊr
rhea, Rhea rɪə 'riː‿ə ‖ 'riː ə **rheas, Rhea's** rɪəz 'riː‿əz ‖ 'riː əz
rhebok 'riː bɒk ‖ -bɑːk **~s** s
Rhee riː
Rhees riːs
Rheidol 'raɪd ɒl ‖ -ɑːl -ɔːl, -oʊl —*Welsh* ['hrəi dol]
Rheims riːmz —*French* Reims [ʁɛ̃ːs]
rhematic riː 'mæt ɪk ‖ -'mæţ-
rheme riːm *(= ream)* **rhemes** riːmz
Rhenish 'ren ɪʃ 'riːn-
rhenium 'riːn i‿əm
rheo- *comb. form*
with stress-neutral suffix ¦riː‿ə -əʊ ‖ -oʊ
— **rheoscope** 'riː‿ə skəʊp -əʊ- ‖ -skoʊp
with stress-imposing suffix ri 'ɒ+ ‖ ri 'ɑː+
— **rheology** ri 'ɒl ədʒ i ‖ ri 'ɑːl-
rheostat 'riː‿ə stæt -əʊ- **~s** s
rhesus, R~ 'riːs əs
'Rhesus ˌfactor; **'rhesus ˌmonkey**; **ˌRhesus 'negative**
Rhet... —*see* **Rhaet...**
rhetoric 'ret ə rɪk ‖ 'reţ- *(!)*
rhetorical ri 'tɒr ɪk ᵊl rə- ‖ ri 'tɔːr- -'tɑːr- **~ly** i
rheˌtorical 'question
rhetorician ˌret ə 'rɪʃ ᵊn ‖ ˌreţ- **~s** z
Rhett ret
rheum ruːm
rheumatic ru 'mæt ɪk ‖ -'mæţ ɪk **~s** s
rheuˌmatic 'fever
rheumaticky ru 'mæt ɪk i ‖ -'mæţ-
rheumatism 'ruːm ə tɪz əm
rheumatoid 'ruːm ə tɔɪd
rheumatological ˌruːm ət ə 'lɒdʒ ɪk ᵊl ◂ ‖ -əţ ə 'lɑːdʒ- **~ly** i
rheumatologist ˌruːm ə 'tɒl ədʒ ɪst §-əst ‖ -'tɑːl- **~s** s
rheumatology ˌruːm ə 'tɒl ədʒ i ‖ -'tɑːl-
rheumy 'ruːm i
Rhian 'riː‿ən —*Welsh* ['hriː an]
Rhiannon ri 'æn ən —*Welsh* [hri 'an on]
Rhianydd ri 'æn ɪð —*Welsh* [hri 'a nið, nɨð]
Rhine raɪn —*Ger* Rhein [ʁain]
Rhineland 'raɪn lænd -lənd —*Ger* Rheinland ['ʁain lant]
rhinestone 'raɪn stəʊn ‖ -stoʊn **~s** z
rhinitis raɪ 'naɪt ɪs §-əs ‖ -'naɪţ əs
Rhinns rɪnz
rhino 'raɪn əʊ ‖ -oʊ **~s** z
rhino- *comb. form*
with stress-neutral suffix ¦raɪn əʊ ‖ -oʊ
— **rhinoplasty** 'raɪn əʊ ˌplæst i ‖ -oʊ-
with stress-imposing suffix raɪ 'nɒ+ ‖ -'nɑː+
— **rhinologist** raɪ 'nɒl ədʒ ɪst §-əst ‖ -'nɑːl-
rhinoceros raɪ 'nɒs ər‿əs ‖ -'nɑːs- **~es** ɪz əz
Rhinog 'riːn ɒg 'rɪn- ‖ -ɑːg —*Welsh* ['hriː nog]
Rhiwbina ru 'baɪn ə —*Welsh* [hrɪu 'bəi na]
rhizo- *comb. form*
with stress-neutral suffix ¦raɪz əʊ ‖ -oʊ —
rhizocarpous ˌraɪz əʊ 'kɑːp əs ◂ ‖ -oʊ 'kɑːrp-
with stress-imposing suffix raɪ 'zɒ+ ‖ -'zɑː+
— **rhizotomy** raɪ 'zɒt əm i ‖ -'zɑːţ-
rhizome 'raɪz əʊm ‖ -oʊm **~s** z
rho rəʊ ‖ roʊ *(= roe)* **rhos** rəʊz ‖ roʊz
Rhoda 'rəʊd ə ‖ 'roʊd ə
rhodamine 'rəʊd ə miːn ‖ 'roʊd-
Rhode Island 'rəʊd ˌaɪl ənd ˌ·'· · ‖ roʊd 'aɪl ənd ˌ·- **~er/s** ə/z ‖ ᵊr/z
ˌRhode ˌIsland 'Red ‖ · ˌ· · '·
Rhodes rəʊdz ‖ roʊdz
ˌRhodes 'scholar, '· ˌ· ·
Rhodesi|a rəʊ 'diːʃ |ə -'diːʒ-, -i‿ə; -'diːs |i‿ə, -'diːz- ‖ roʊ 'diːʒ |ə **~an/s** ᵊn/z i‿ən/z
Rhodian 'rəʊd i‿ən ‖ 'roʊd- **~s** z
rhodium 'rəʊd i‿əm ‖ 'roʊd-
rhododendron ˌrəʊd ə 'dendr ən -ɪ- ‖ ˌroʊd- **~s** z
rhodolite 'rɒd ə laɪt 'rəʊd-, -ᵊl aɪt ‖ 'roʊd ᵊl aɪt **~s** s
Rhodope 'rɒd əp i rɒ 'dəʊp i, rəʊ- ‖ 'rɑːd-
rhodopsin rəʊ 'dɒps ɪn §-ən ‖ roʊ 'dɑːps ən
rhodora rəʊ 'dɔːr ə ‖ roʊ- -'doʊr- **~s** z
Rhodri 'rɒdr i ‖ 'rɑːdr i —*Welsh* ['hrod ri]

rhomb rɒm rɒmb ‖ rɑːm rɑːmb **rhombs** rɒmz rɒmbz ‖ rɑːmz rɑːmbz
rhombohedr|on ˌrɒm bəʊ 'hiːdr |ən -'hedr- ‖ ˌrɑːm boʊ- -bə- **~a** ə **~ons** ənz
rhomboid 'rɒm bɔɪd ‖ 'rɑːm- **~s** z
rhom|bus 'rɒm |bəs ‖ 'rɑːm- **~bi** baɪ **~buses** bəs ɪz -əz
Rhona 'rəʊn ə ‖ 'roʊn ə
rhonch|us 'rɒŋk |əs ‖ 'rɑːŋk- **~i** aɪ
Rhonda 'rɒnd ə ‖ 'rɑːnd ə
Rhondda 'rɒnd ə 'rɒn ðə ‖ 'rɑːnd ə —*Welsh* ['hron ða]
ˌRhondda 'Valley
Rhone, Rhône rəʊn ‖ roʊn —*French* [ʁoːn]
Rhonwen 'rɒn wɪn -wən, -wen ‖ 'rɑːn- —*Welsh* ['hron wen]
Rhoose ruːs
Rhos rəʊs ‖ roʊs —*Welsh* [hroːs]
Rhosllanerchrugog ˌrəʊs ˌlæn ə 'kriːg ɒg ‖ ˌroʊs ˌlæn ər 'kriːg ɑːg —*Welsh* [ˌhroːs ˌɬa nerχ 'ri gog, -'ri-]
Rhosneigr ˌrəʊs 'naɪg ə ‖ ˌroʊs 'naɪg ər —*Welsh* [ˌhroːs 'nəigr, -'nəi gir]
Rhossili rɒ 'sɪl i ‖ rɑː-
rhotacis... —*see* **rhotaciz...**
rhotacism 'rəʊt ə ˌsɪz əm ‖ 'roʊţ- **~s** z
rhotacization ˌrəʊt əs aɪ 'zeɪʃ ən -ɪ'-- ‖ ˌroʊţ əs ə- **~s** z
rhotaciz|e 'rəʊt ə saɪz ‖ 'roʊţ- **~ed** d **~es** ɪz əz **~ing** ɪŋ
rhotic 'rəʊt ɪk ‖ 'roʊţ ɪk **~s** s
rhoticity rəʊ 'tɪs ət i -ɪt- ‖ roʊ 'tɪs əţ i
rhubarb 'ruːb ɑːb ‖ -ɑːrb
Rhuddlan 'rɪð lən 'rʌd-, -læn —*Welsh* ['hrið lan, 'hrið-]
Rhum rʌm
rhumb rʌm *(= rum)* **rhumbs** rʌmz
Rhyd-ddu ˌriːd 'ðiː —*Welsh* [ˌhriːd 'ðiː, ˌhriːd 'ðiː]
Rhydderch 'rʌð ək -əx ‖ -ərk —*Welsh* ['hrə ðerχ]
Rhydding 'rɪd ɪŋ
Rhyl rɪl —*Welsh* [hril, hrɪl]
rhyme raɪm *(= rime)* **rhymed** raɪmd **rhymes** raɪmz **rhyming** 'raɪm ɪŋ
'rhyming slang ˌ.. '.
rhymer 'raɪm ə ‖ -ər **~s** z
rhymester 'raɪmᵖst ə ‖ -ər **~s** z
Rhymney 'rʌm ni
rhyolite 'raɪ‿ə laɪt **~s** s
rhyolitic ˌraɪ‿ə 'lɪt ɪk ◂ ‖ -'lɪţ ɪk ◂
Rhys *(i)* riːs; *(ii)* raɪs —*Welsh* [hriːs, hriːs] —*The writer Jean Rhys is (i).*
rhythm 'rɪð əm **~s** z
ˌrhythm and 'blues; **'rhythm ˌmethod**; **'rhythm ˌsection**
rhythmic 'rɪð mɪk **~ally** əl‿i
ria 'riː‿ə **~s** z
rial ri 'ɑːl 'riː ɑːl ‖ -'ɔːl —*but as an obsolete English coin,* 'raɪ‿əl **~s** z
Rialto ri 'ælt əʊ ‖ -oʊ —*It* [ri 'al to]
rib rɪb **ribbed** rɪbd **ribbing** 'rɪb ɪŋ **ribs** rɪbz
'rib cage
ribald 'rɪb əld 'raɪb-, -ɔːld ‖ -ɔːld, -ɑːld **~ly** li **~s** z
ribaldr|y 'rɪb əldr |i 'raɪb-, -ɔːldr- **~ies** iz
riband 'rɪb ənd **~s** z
Ribbentrop 'rɪb ən trɒp →-m- ‖ -trɑːp —*Ger* ['ʁɪb n tʁɔp]
Ribble 'rɪb əl
ribb|on 'rɪb |ən **~oned** ənd →md **~oning** ən‿ɪŋ **~ons** ənz →mz
ˌribbon de'velopment
Ribena *tdmk* raɪ 'biːn ə
riboflavin, riboflavine ˌraɪb əʊ 'fleɪv ɪn -iːn, §-ən ‖ -oʊ- '. ·ˌ· ·
ribonucleic ˌraɪb əʊ nju 'kliː‿ɪk ◂ §-nu'·-, -'kleɪ- ‖ -oʊ nu- -nju'·-
ribosomal ˌraɪb əʊ 'səʊm əl ◂ ‖ -ə 'soʊm əl ◂
ribosome 'raɪb əʊ səʊm ‖ -ə soʊm -zoʊm **~s** z
Rib|ston 'rɪb stən **~stone** stəʊn ‖ stoʊn
ribwort 'rɪb wɜːt -wɔːt ‖ -wɜːt **~s** s
Ricard|o rɪ 'kɑːd |əʊ ‖ -'kɑːrd |oʊ **~ian** i‿ən
Riccarton 'rɪk ət ən ‖ -ərt ən
Ricci 'riːtʃ i —*It* ['rit tʃi]
rice, Rice raɪs **riced** raɪst **rices** 'raɪs ɪz -əz **ricing** 'raɪs ɪŋ
'rice bowl; **ˌRice 'Krispies** *tdmk*; **'rice ˌpaddy**; **'rice ˌpaper**; **ˌrice 'pudding**
Rice-a-Roni *tdmk* ˌraɪs ə 'rəʊn i ‖ -'roʊn i
ricer 'raɪs ə ‖ -ər **~s** z
rich, Rich rɪtʃ **richer** 'rɪtʃ ə ‖ -ər **richest** 'rɪtʃ ɪst -əst
Richard 'rɪtʃ əd ‖ -ərd
Richards 'rɪtʃ ədz ‖ -ərdz
Richardson 'rɪtʃ əd sən ‖ -ərd-
Richelieu 'riːʃ ljɜː 'rɪʃ-, -ljuː, '·ə · ‖ 'rɪʃ luː 'riːʃ-, -ljuː, ˌ· '·; '·ə-, ˌ·ə'· —*Fr* [ʁi ʃə ljø]
riches, R~ 'rɪtʃ ɪz -əz
Richey, Richie 'rɪtʃ i
Richfield 'rɪtʃ fiːəld
Richland 'rɪtʃ lənd
richly 'rɪtʃ li
Richmal 'rɪtʃ məl
Richmond 'rɪtʃ mənd
ˌRichmond 'Hill; **ˌRichmond-u₍ₜ₎pon-'Thames**; **ˌRichmond, Vir'ginia**; **ˌRichmond, 'Yorks**
richness 'rɪtʃ nəs -nɪs
Richter 'rɪkt ə 'rɪxt- ‖ -ər —*Ger* ['ʁɪç tɐ], *Russ* ['rʲix tʲɪr] —*Charles R~, the seismologist, was an American; it is therefore appropriate for the* Richter scale *he devised to be pronounced in an English way, with* [k]. *Nevertheless, in BrE it is often said with* [x].
Richthofen 'rɪxt əʊf ən 'rɪkt- ‖ 'rɪkt oʊf ən —*Ger* ['ʁɪçt hoːf n]
ricin 'raɪs ɪn 'rɪs-, §-ən
ricinoleate ˌraɪs ɪ 'nəʊl i eɪt ˌrɪs-, ˌ·ə- ‖ -'noʊl-
ricinoleic ˌrɪs ɪn əʊ 'liː ɪk ◂ ˌraɪs-, ˌ·ən-, -'leɪ-; -'əʊl i ɪk ‖ -ən oʊ-
rick, Rick rɪk **ricked** rɪkt **ricking** 'rɪk ɪŋ **ricks** rɪks
Rickard 'rɪk ɑːd ‖ -ɑːrd
Rickards 'rɪk ɑːdz ‖ -ɑːrdz
Rickenbacker 'rɪk ən bæk ə ‖ -ər

R

rickets ˈrɪk ɪts §-əts
Rickett ˈrɪk ɪt §-ət
Ricketts ˈrɪk ɪts §-əts
rickettsi|a rɪ ˈkets i‿ə **~ae** iː **~al** əl **~as** əz
rickety ˈrɪk ət i -ɪt- ‖ -ət̬ i
Rickey, r~, Ricki, Rickie ˈrɪk i
Rickmansworth ˈrɪk mənz wɜːθ -wəθ ‖ -wɜːθ
Rickover ˈrɪk əʊv ə ‖ -oʊv ᵊr
rickrack ˈrɪk ræk
Ricks rɪks
ricksha, rickshaw ˈrɪk ʃɔː ‖ -ʃɑː **~s** z
Ricky ˈrɪk i
Rico ˈriːk əʊ ‖ -oʊ
rico|chet ˈrɪk ə |ʃeɪ -ʃet, ˌ· · ˈ|· **~cheted, ~chetted** ʃeɪd ʃet ɪd, -əd **~cheting, ~chetting** ʃeɪ ɪŋ ʃet ɪŋ **~chets** ʃeɪz ʃets —*The -tt- spellings are used, if at all, only by the minority, if it still exists, who pronounce* -ʃet, -ˈʃet. *It is very possible that both this spelling and this pronunciation are now obsolete.*
Ricoh *tdmk* ˈriːk əʊ ‖ -oʊ —*Jp* [ɾi ˌkoo]
ricotta rɪ ˈkɒt ə rə- ‖ -ˈkɔːt̬ ə -ˈkɑːt̬- —*It* [ri ˈkɔt ta]
rictus ˈrɪkt əs **~es** ɪz əz
rid rɪd **ridded** ˈrɪd ɪd -əd **ridding** ˈrɪd ɪŋ **rids** rɪdz
riddance ˈrɪd ᵊnᵗs
Riddell *(i)* ˈrɪd ᵊl *(ii)* rɪ ˈdel rə-
ridden ˈrɪd ᵊn
-ridden ˌrɪd ᵊn — **damp-ridden** ˈdæmp ˌrɪd ᵊn
Ridding ˈrɪd ɪŋ
riddl|e, R~ ˈrɪd ᵊl **~ed** d **~es** z **~ing** ‿ɪŋ
ride raɪd **ridden** ˈrɪd ᵊn **rides** raɪdz **riding** ˈraɪd ɪŋ **rode** rəʊd ‖ roʊd
Rideout ˈraɪd aʊt
rider, Rider ˈraɪd ə ‖ -ᵊr **~s** z
riderless ˈraɪd ə ləs -lɪs; -ᵊl əs, -ɪs ‖ -ᵊr-
ridge, Ridge rɪdʒ **ridged** rɪdʒd **ridges** ˈrɪdʒ ɪz -əz **ridging** ˈrɪdʒ ɪŋ
ridgel ˈrɪdʒ ᵊl **~s** z
ridgeling ˈrɪdʒ lɪŋ **~s** z
ridgepole ˈrɪdʒ pəʊl →-pɒʊl ‖ -poʊl **~s** z
ridgeway, R~, Ridgway ˈrɪdʒ weɪ **~s** z
ridicul|e *n, v* ˈrɪd ɪ kjuːl -ə- **~ed** d **~es** z **~ing** ɪŋ
ridiculous rɪ ˈdɪk jʊl əs rə-, -jəl- ‖ -jəl- **~ly** li **~ness** nəs nɪs
riding, R~ ˈraɪd ɪŋ **~s** z
Ridley ˈrɪd li
Ridout *(i)* ˈraɪd aʊt *(ii)* ˈrɪd aʊt
Ridpath ˈrɪd pɑːθ →ˈrɪb-, §-pæθ ‖ -pæθ
Riefenstahl ˈriːf ᵊn ʃtɑːl -stɑːl —*Ger* [ˈʁiːf n ʃtaːl]
Riegger ˈriːg ə ‖ -ᵊr
Riemann ˈriː mən ‖ -mɑːn —*Ger* [ˈʁiː man]
riesling, R~ ˈriːz lɪŋ ˈriːs- —*Ger* [ˈʁiːs lɪŋ] **~s** z
Rieu ri ˈuː ˈriː uː
Rievaulx ˈriːv əʊ -əʊz; ˈrɪv əz ‖ -oʊ
rife raɪf **rifer** ˈraɪf ə ‖ -ᵊr **rifest** ˈraɪf ɪst -əst
riff, Riff rɪf **riffs** rɪfs
riffl|e ˈrɪf ᵊl **~ed** d **~es** z **~ing** ‿ɪŋ
riffraff ˈrɪf ræf
Rifkind ˈrɪf kɪnd

rifl|e ˈraɪf ᵊl **~ed** d **~es** z **~ing** ‿ɪŋ **ˈrifle range**
rifle|man ˈraɪf ᵊl |mən -mæn **~men** mən men
rift rɪft **rifted** ˈrɪft ɪd -əd **rifting** ˈrɪft ɪŋ **rifts** rɪfts **ˈrift ˌvalley,** ˌ· ˈ· ·
rig rɪg **rigged** rɪgd **rigging/s** ˈrɪg ɪŋ/z **rigs** rɪgz
Riga ˈriːg ə —*formerly also* ˈraɪg ə —*Latvian* Rīga [ˈriː ga]
rigadoon ˌrɪg ə ˈduːn **~s** z
rigamarole ˈrɪg əm ə rəʊl →-rɒʊl ‖ -roʊl **~s** z
rigatoni ˌrɪg ə ˈtəʊn i ‖ -ˈtoʊn i
Rigby ˈrɪg bi
Rigel ˈraɪg ᵊl ˈraɪdʒ-
Rigg rɪg
rigg... —*see* **rig**
rigger ˈrɪg ə ‖ -ᵊr **~s** z
right raɪt *(= rite, write)* **righted** ˈraɪt ɪd -əd ‖ ˈraɪt̬ əd **righter** ˈraɪt ə ‖ ˈraɪt̬ ᵊr **rightest** ˈraɪt ɪst -əst ‖ ˈraɪt̬ əst **righting** ˈraɪt ɪŋ ‖ ˈraɪt̬ ɪŋ **rights** raɪts **ˈright ˌangle,** ˌ· ˈ· ·; **ˌright aˈway**; **ˌright of ˈway**; **ˈrights ˌissue**; **ˌright ˈtriangle**; **ˌright ˈwhale**; **ˌright ˈwing** ◂
right-about ˈraɪt ə ˌbaʊt ‖ ˈraɪt̬-
right-angled ˈraɪt ˌæŋ gᵊld ˌ· ˈ· · ‖ ˈraɪt̬-
right-branching ˈraɪt ˌbrɑːntʃ ɪŋ §-ˌbræntʃ-, ˌ· ˈ· · ‖ -ˌbræntʃ ɪŋ
right-click ˌraɪt ˈklɪk **~ed** t **~ing** ɪŋ **~s** s
righteous ˈraɪtʃ əs ˈraɪt i‿əs **~ly** li **~ness** nəs nɪs
rightful ˈraɪt fᵊl -fʊl **~ly** i **~ness** nəs nɪs
right-hand ˌraɪt ˈhænd ◂ ‖ ˈ· · **ˌright-hand ˈbend**; **ˌright-hand ˈman**
right-handed ˌraɪt ˈhænd ɪd ◂ -əd **~ly** li **~ness** nəs nɪs
right-hander ˌraɪt ˈhænd ə ‖ -ᵊr **~s** z
rightism ˈraɪt ˌɪz əm ‖ ˈraɪt̬-
rightist ˈraɪt ɪst §-əst ‖ ˈraɪt̬ əst **~s** s
rightly ˈraɪt li
right-minded ˌraɪt ˈmaɪnd ɪd ◂ -əd **~ly** li **~ness** nəs nɪs
rightness ˈraɪt nəs -nɪs
righto ˌraɪt ˈəʊ ‖ ˌraɪt̬ ˈoʊ
right-of-centre, right-of-center ˌraɪt əv ˈsent ə ◂ ‖ ˌraɪt̬ əv ˈsent̬ ᵊr ◂
right-on ˌraɪt ˈɒn ◂ ‖ ˌraɪt̬ ˈɑːn ◂
right-size *v* ˈraɪt saɪz **~ing** ɪŋ
right-thinking ˈraɪt ˌθɪŋk ɪŋ ˌ· ˈ· ·
right-to-die ˌraɪt tə ˈdaɪ
right-to-lif|e ˌraɪt tə ˈlaɪf **~er/s** ə/z ‖ ᵊr/z
right-to-work ˌraɪt tə ˈwɜːk ‖ -ˈwɜːk
rightward ˈraɪt wəd ‖ -wᵊrd **~s** z
right-wing ˌraɪt ˈwɪŋ ◂ **~er/s** ə/z ‖ ᵊr/z
righty ˈraɪt i ‖ ˈraɪt̬ i
righty-ho ˌraɪt i ˈhəʊ ‖ ˌraɪt̬ i ˈhoʊ
rigid ˈrɪdʒ ɪd §-əd
rigidit|y rɪ ˈdʒɪd ət |i rə-, -ɪt- ‖ -ət̬ |i **~ies** iz
rigid|ly ˈrɪdʒ ɪd |li §-əd- **~ness** nəs nɪs
Rigil ˈraɪdʒ ᵊl -ɪl
rigmarole ˈrɪg mə rəʊl →-rɒʊl ‖ -roʊl **~s** z

R

Rigoletto ˌrɪg ə ˈlet əʊ ‖ -ˈleţ oʊ —*It* [ri go ˈlet to]
rigor ˈrɪg ə ‖ -ər —*but as a medical term, also* ˈraɪg ɔː ‖ -ɔːr **~s** z
rigor mortis ˈmɔːt ɪs §-əs ‖ ˈmɔːrţ əs ˌ**rigor ˈmortis**
rigorous ˈrɪg ər‿əs **~ly** li **~ness** nəs nɪs
rigour ˈrɪg ə ‖ -ər **~s** z
rig-out ˈrɪg aʊt **~s** s
Rigsby ˈrɪgz bi
Rig-Veda ˌrɪg ˈveɪd ə
Rihanna ri ˈæn ə ‖ -ˈɑːn-
Riis riːs
Rijeka ri ˈek ə -ˈeɪk- —*Croatian* [rri ˈˈɛ ka]
Rikers ˈraɪk əz ‖ -ərz
Rikki ˈrɪk i
Rikki-Tiki-Tavi ˌrɪk i tɪk i ˈtɑːv i -ˈteɪv- ‖ -ˈtæv-
rile raɪəl **riled** raɪəld **riles** raɪəlz **riling** ˈraɪəl ɪŋ
Riley ˈraɪl i
riliev|o ˌrɪl i ˈeɪv |əʊ ‖ rɪl ˈjeɪv |oʊ —*It* [ri ˈljɛː vo] **~i** iː
Rilke ˈrɪlk ə —*Ger* [ˈʁɪl kə]
rill rɪl **rills** rɪlz
rillettes ˌ(ˌ)riː ˈet —*Fr* [ʁi jɛt]
rim rɪm **rimmed** rɪmd **rimming** ˈrɪm ɪŋ **rims** rɪmz
Rimbaud ˈræm bəʊ ‖ ræm ˈboʊ —*Fr* [ʁɛ̃ bo]
Rimbault *English family name* ˈrɪm bəʊlt →-bɒʊlt ‖ -boʊlt
rime raɪm **rimed** raɪmd **rimes** raɪmz **riming** ˈraɪm ɪŋ —*see also phrases with this word*
rime riche ˌriːm ˈriːʃ **rimes riches** *same pronunciation*
rimester ˈraɪmpst ə ‖ -ər **~s** z
Rimington ˈrɪm ɪŋ tən
Rimini ˈrɪm ən i -ɪn- —*It* [ˈriː mi ni]
rimless ˈrɪm ləs -lɪs
-rimmed ˈrɪmd — **plastic-rimmed** ˌplæst ɪk ˈrɪmd ◂ ˌplɑːst-
Rimmer ˈrɪm ə ‖-ər
Rimmington ˈrɪm ɪŋ tən
Rimsky-Korsakov ˌrɪmp ski ˈkɔːs ə kɒf -kɒv ‖ -ˈkɔːrs ə kɔːf -kɑːf —*Russ* [ˌrʲim skʲij ˈkor sə kəf]
Rinaldo rɪ ˈnæld əʊ rə- ‖ -ˈnɑːld oʊ -ˈnæld-
rind raɪnd **rinds** raɪndz
rinderpest ˈrɪnd ə pest ‖ -ər-
rindless ˈraɪnd ləs -lɪs
ring, Ring rɪŋ **rang** ræŋ **ringed** rɪŋd **ringing** ˈrɪŋ ɪŋ **rings** rɪŋz **rung** rʌŋ ˈ**ring ˌbinder**, ˈ· ˌ··; ˈ**ring ˌfinger**; ˈ**ring main**; ˈ**ring road**; ˈ**ring ˌspanner**
ringbark ˈrɪŋ bɑːk ‖ -bɑːrk **~ed** t **~ing** ɪŋ **~s** s
ringbolt ˈrɪŋ bəʊlt →-bɒʊlt ‖ -boʊlt **~s** s
ringer, R~ ˈrɪŋ ə ‖ -ər **~s** z
ring-fenc|e ˌrɪŋ ˈfents **~ed** t ◂ **~es** ɪz əz **~ing** ɪŋ
ringgit ˈrɪŋ gɪt §-gət **~s** s
ringhals ˈrɪŋ hæls -hɑːls
ringleader ˈrɪŋ ˌliːd ə ‖ -ər **~s** z
ringlet ˈrɪŋ lət -lɪt **ringleted** ˈrɪŋ lət ɪd -lɪt-, -əd ‖ -ləţ əd **~s** s
ringmaster ˈrɪŋ ˌmɑːst ə §-ˌmæst- ‖ -ˌmæst ər **~s** z
ringneck ˈrɪŋ nek **~s** s
ring-pull ˈrɪŋ pʊl **~s** z
ringside ˈrɪŋ saɪd
ring-tailed ˈrɪŋ teɪəld
ringtone ˈrɪŋ təʊn ‖ -toʊn **~s** z
Ringway ˈrɪŋ weɪ
Ringwood ˈrɪŋ wʊd
ringworm ˈrɪŋ wɜːm ‖ -wɜːm
rink rɪŋk **rinks** rɪŋks
rinkhals ˈrɪŋk hæls -hɑːls
rinky-dink ˈrɪŋk i dɪŋk
rinse rɪnts **rinsed** rɪntst **rinses** ˈrɪnts ɪz -əz **rinsing** ˈrɪnts ɪŋ
Rintoul rɪn ˈtuːl ˈ· ·
Rio ˈriː əʊ ‖ -oʊ —*Sp* [ˈrri o], *Port* [ˈrri u, ˈxi u] ˌ**Rio de Jaˈneiro** də ʒə ˈnɪər əʊ deɪ-, di-, -dʒəˈ-, -ˈneər- ‖ deɪ ʒə ˈner oʊ -ˈnɪr- —*Port* [ˌxiu di ʒe ˈnei ru]; ˌ**RioˈGrande** grænd ˈgrænd i —*Sp* [ˈgran de]; ˌ**Rio ˈTinto** ˈtɪnt əʊ ‖ -oʊ —*Sp* [ˈtin to]
Rioja ri ˈɒk ə -ˈɒx-, -ˈəʊk-, -ˈəʊx- ‖ -ˈoʊ hɑː —*Sp* [ˈrjo xa]
Riordan ˈrɪəd ən ‖ ˈrɪrd ən
riot ˈraɪ‿ət **rioted** ˈraɪ‿ət ɪd -əd ‖ -əţ əd **rioting** ˈraɪ‿ət ɪŋ ‖ -əţ ɪŋ **riots** ˈraɪ‿əts ˈ**riot act**
rioter ˈraɪ‿ət ə ‖ -əţ ər **~s** z
riotous ˈraɪ‿ət əs ‖ -əţ əs **~ly** li **~ness** nəs nɪs
rip, Rip rɪp **ripped** rɪpt **ripping** ˈrɪp ɪŋ **rips** rɪps ˌ**Rip Van ˈWinkle**
RIP ˌɑːr aɪ ˈpiː ‖ ˌɑːr-
riparian raɪ ˈpeər i‿ən rɪ- ‖ -ˈper- **~s** z
ripcord ˈrɪp kɔːd ‖ -kɔːrd **~s** z
ripe raɪp **riper** ˈraɪp ə ‖ -ər **ripest** ˈraɪp ɪst -əst
ripely ˈraɪp li
ripen ˈraɪp ən **~ed** d **~ing** ‿ɪŋ **~s** z
ripeness ˈraɪp nəs -nɪs
ripieno ˌrɪp i ˈeɪn əʊ ‖ -oʊ —*It* [ri ˈpjɛː no] **~s** z
Ripley ˈrɪp li
Ripman ˈrɪp mən
rip-off ˈrɪp ɒf -ɔːf ‖ -ɔːf -ɑːf **~s** s
Ripon ˈrɪp ən
ripost, ripost|e *n, v* rɪ ˈpɒst -ˈpəʊst ‖ -ˈpoʊst **~ed** ɪd əd **~ing** ɪŋ **~es, ~s** s
ripp... —*see* **rip**
ripper ˈrɪp ə ‖ -ər **~s** z
ripping ˈrɪp ɪŋ **~ly** li
rippl|e ˈrɪp əl **~ed** d **~es** z **~ing/ly** ‿ɪŋ /li
ripplet ˈrɪp lət -lɪt **~s** s
Rippon ˈrɪp ən
riprap ˈrɪp ræp **~ped** t **~ping** ɪŋ **~s** s
rip-roaring ˌrɪp ˈrɔːr ɪŋ ◂ ‖ -ˈroʊr-
ripsaw ˈrɪp sɔː ‖ -sɑː **~s** z
ripsnort|er ˈrɪp snɔːt ə ‖ -snɔːrţ ər **~ers** əz ‖ ərz **~ing/ly** ɪŋ /li
riptide ˈrɪp taɪd **~s** z
ripuarian, R~ ˌrɪp ju ˈeər i‿ən ◂ ‖ -ˈer- **~s** z
Risborough, Risboro' ˈrɪz bər‿ə ‖ -ˌbɜː oʊ

R

RISC, risc rɪsk
Risca 'rɪsk ə
Risdon 'rɪz dən
rise raɪz **risen** 'rɪz ᵊn *(!)* **rises** 'raɪz ɪz -əz **rising** 'raɪz ɪŋ **rose** rəʊz ‖ roʊz
riser 'raɪz ə ‖ -ᵊr **~s** z
risibility ˌrɪz ə 'bɪl ət i ˌraɪz-, ˌ·ɪ-, -ɪt i ‖ -əţ i
risib|le 'rɪz əb |ᵊl 'raɪz-, -ɪb- **~ly** li
rising 'raɪz ɪŋ **~s** z
ˌrising 'damp
risk rɪsk **risked** rɪskt **risking** 'rɪsk ɪŋ **risks** rɪsks
risk-tak|ing 'rɪsk ˌteɪk |ɪŋ **~er/s** ə/z ‖ ᵊr/z
risk|y 'rɪsk |i **~ier** i‿ə ‖ i‿ᵊr **~iest** i‿ɪst i‿əst **~ily** ɪ li əl i **~iness** i nəs i nɪs
Risley 'rɪz li
Risorgimento rɪ ˌsɔːdʒ ɪ 'ment əʊ rə-, riː-, -ˌ·ə- ‖ rɪ ˌsɔːrdʒ ɪ 'ment oʊ -ˌzɔːrdʒ-; ˌriː· ·'· · —*It* [ri sor dʒi 'men to]
risotto rɪ 'zɒt əʊ -'sɒt- ‖ -'sɔːt oʊ -'sɑːţ-, -'zɑːţ- —*It* [ri 'sɔt to] **~s** z
risque, risqué 'rɪsk eɪ ‖ rɪ 'skeɪ —*Fr* [ʁis ke]
Riss rɪs
rissole 'rɪs əʊl →-ɒʊl ‖ -oʊl rɪ 'soʊl **~s** z
Rita 'riːt ə ‖ 'riːţ ə
Ritalin *tdmk* 'rɪt ᵊl ɪn ‖ 'rɪţ-
ritardando ˌrɪt ɑː 'dænd əʊ ‖ ˌriː tɑːr 'dɑːnd oʊ rɪ ˌtɑːr- **~s** z
Ritchie 'rɪtʃ i
rite raɪt —*but as a French word,* riːt —*Fr* [ʁit] **rites** raɪts
ritenuto ˌrɪt ə 'njuːt əʊ -'nuːt- ‖ ˌriːt ə 'nuːt oʊ
ritornell|o ˌrɪt ə 'nel |əʊ -ɔː-; -ᵊn 'el- ‖ ˌrɪţ ᵊr 'nel |oʊ **~i** iː **~os** əʊz ‖ oʊz
Ritson 'rɪts ən
ritual 'rɪtʃ u‿əl 'rɪt ju‿əl ‖ 'rɪtʃ ᵊl **~s** z
ritualis... —*see* **ritualiz...**
ritualism 'rɪtʃ u‿əl ˌɪz əm 'rɪt ju‿ ‖ 'rɪtʃ əl ˌ· ·
ritualist 'rɪtʃ u‿əl ɪst 'rɪt ju‿, §-əst ‖ 'rɪtʃ əl· **~s** s
ritualistic ˌrɪtʃ u‿ə 'lɪst ɪk ◂ ˌrɪt ju-, ˌrɪtʃ u 'lɪst- ‖ ˌrɪtʃ ə 'lɪst- **~ally** ᵊl‿i
ritualization ˌrɪtʃ u‿əl aɪ 'zeɪʃ ᵊn ˌrɪt ju‿, -ɪ'·- ‖ -ə'·- ˌ·əl·'· ·
ritualiz|e 'rɪtʃ u‿ə laɪz 'rɪt ju‿, 'rɪtʃ u· ‖ 'rɪtʃ ə laɪz **~ed** d **~es** ɪz əz **~ing** ɪŋ
ritually 'rɪtʃ u‿əl i 'rɪt ju‿ ‖ 'rɪtʃ əl i
Ritz rɪts
ritz|y 'rɪts |i **~ier** i‿ə ‖ i‿ᵊr **~iest** i‿ɪst i‿əst **~ily** ɪ li əl i **~iness** i nəs i nɪs
rival 'raɪv ᵊl **~ed, ~led** d **~ing, ~ling** ɪŋ **~s** z
rival|ry 'raɪv ᵊl |ri **~ries** riz
rive raɪv **rived** raɪvd **riven** 'rɪv ᵊn *(!)* **rives** raɪvz **riving** 'raɪv ɪŋ
Rivelin 'rɪv ᵊl‿ɪn
riven 'rɪv ᵊn
river, River 'rɪv ə ‖ -ᵊr **~s** z
'river ˌbasin; 'river ˌblindness
Rivera rɪ 'veər ə ‖ -'ver ə —*Sp* [rri 'βe ra]
riverbank 'rɪv ə bæŋk ‖ -ᵊr- **~s** s
riverbed 'rɪv ə bed ‖ -ᵊr- **~s** z
riverboat 'rɪv ə bəʊt ‖ -ᵊr boʊt **~s** s
riverfront 'rɪv ə frʌnt ‖ -ᵊr- **~s** s
Riverina ˌrɪv ə 'riːn ə
riverine 'rɪv ə raɪn -riːn, -rɪn
Rivers 'rɪv əz ‖ -ᵊrz
riverside, R~ 'rɪv ə saɪd ‖ -ᵊr-
riv|et 'rɪv |ɪt §-ət ‖ -|ət **~eted** ɪt ɪd §ət-, -əd ‖ əţ əd **~eting** ɪt ɪŋ §ət- ‖ əţ ɪŋ **~ets** ɪts §əts ‖ əts
riveter 'rɪv ɪt ə -ət- ‖ -əţ ᵊr **~s** z
Rivett rɪ 'vet
riviera, R~ ˌrɪv i 'eər ə ‖ -'er ə **~s** z
Rivington 'rɪv ɪŋ tən
rivulet 'rɪv jʊl ət -ɪt, -ju let ‖ -jəl- **~s** s
Rix rɪks
Riyadh 'riː æd -ɑːd, ·'· ‖ riː 'jɑːd —*Arabic* [ri 'jɑːðˤ]
riyal ri 'ɑːl -'jɑːl, -'æl, '· · **~s** z
Rizla *tdmk* 'rɪz lə
RN ˌɑːr 'en
RNA ˌɑːr en 'eɪ
Roaccutane *tdmk* rəʊ 'æk ju teɪn ‖ roʊ 'æk jə-
roach, Roach rəʊtʃ ‖ roʊtʃ **roaches, Roach's** 'rəʊtʃ ɪz -əz ‖ 'roʊtʃ əz
road rəʊd ‖ roʊd **roads** rəʊdz ‖ roʊdz
'road hog; 'road ˌmanager; 'road ˌmender; 'road ˌroller; 'road sense; 'road tax; 'road test; 'road works
roadbed 'rəʊd bed →'rəʊb- ‖ 'roʊd-
roadblock 'rəʊd blɒk →'rəʊb- ‖ 'roʊd blɑːk **~s** s
roadbook 'rəʊd bʊk →'rəʊb-, §-buːk ‖ 'roʊd- **~s** s
roadholding 'rəʊd ˌhəʊld ɪŋ →-ˌhɒʊld- ‖ 'roʊd ˌhoʊld ɪŋ
road|house 'rəʊd |haʊs ‖ 'roʊd- **~houses** haʊz ɪz -əz
roadie 'rəʊd i ‖ 'roʊd i **~s** z
roadkill 'rəʊd kɪl →'rəʊg- ‖ 'roʊd-
road|man 'rəʊd |mən →'rəʊb-, -mæn ‖ 'roʊd- **~men** mən men
roadrunner 'rəʊd ˌrʌn ə ‖ 'roʊd ˌrʌn ᵊr **~s** z
roadshow 'rəʊd ʃəʊ ‖ 'roʊd ʃoʊ **~s** z
roadside 'rəʊd saɪd ‖ 'roʊd- **~s** z
roadstead 'rəʊd sted ‖ 'roʊd- **~s** z
roadster 'rəʊd stə ‖ 'roʊd stᵊr **~s** z
road-test 'rəʊd test ‖ 'roʊd- **~ed** ɪd əd **~ing** ɪŋ **~s** s
roadway 'rəʊd weɪ ‖ 'roʊd- **~s** z
roadwork 'rəʊd wɜːk ‖ 'roʊd wɝːk **~s** s
roadworth|y 'rəʊd ˌwɜːð |i ‖ 'roʊd ˌwɝːð |i **~iness** i nəs i nɪs
Roald 'rəʊ əld ‖ 'roʊ- —*Norw* ['rru al]
roam rəʊm ‖ roʊm **roamed** rəʊmd ‖ roʊmd **roaming** 'rəʊm ɪŋ ‖ 'roʊm ɪŋ **roams** rəʊmz ‖ roʊmz
roamer 'rəʊm ə ‖ 'roʊm ᵊr **~s** z
roan rəʊn ‖ roʊn
Roanoke 'rəʊ ə nəʊk 'rəʊn əʊk ‖ 'roʊ ə noʊk 'roʊn oʊk
roar rɔː ‖ rɔːr roʊr **roared** rɔːd ‖ rɔːrd roʊrd **roaring** 'rɔːr ɪŋ ‖ 'roʊr- **roars** rɔːz ‖ rɔːrz roʊrz
ˌroaring 'forties
roarer 'rɔːr ə ‖ -ᵊr 'roʊr- **~s** z

roast rəust ‖ roust **roasted** 'rəust ɪd -əd ‖ 'roust əd **roasting/s** 'rəust ɪŋ/z ‖ 'roust ɪŋ/z **roasts** rəusts ‖ rousts
roaster 'rəust ə ‖ 'roust ᵊr **~s** z
Roatan, Roatán ˌrəu ə 'tæn ‖ ˌrou ə 'tɑːn —*Sp* [ro a 'tan]
Roath rəuθ ‖ rouθ
rob, Rob rɒb ‖ rɑːb **robbed** rɒbd ‖ rɑːbd **robbing** 'rɒb ɪŋ ‖ 'rɑːb ɪŋ **robs** rɒbz ‖ rɑːbz **ˌRob 'Roy**
robalo rəu 'bɑːl əu ‖ rou 'bɑːl ou **~s** z
Robb rɒb ‖ rɑːb
robb... —*see* **rob**
Robbe-Grillet ˌrɒb griː 'eɪ ‖ ˌroub- ˌrɑːb- —*Fr* [ʁɔb gʁi jɛ]
Robben 'rɒb ɪn -ən ‖ 'rɑːb ən
robber 'rɒb ə ‖ 'rɑːb ᵊr **~s** z **ˌrobber 'baron,** '· · ˌ· ·
robber|y 'rɒb ər |i ‖ 'rɑːb- **~ies** iz
Robbialac *tdmk* 'rɒb i̯ə læk ‖ 'rɑːb-
Robbie 'rɒb i ‖ 'rɑːb i
Robbin 'rɒb ɪn §-ən ‖ 'rɑːb ən
Robbins 'rɒb ɪnz §-ənz ‖ 'rɑːb ənz
robe, Robe rəub ‖ roub **robed** rəubd ‖ roubd **robes** rəubz ‖ roubz **robing** 'rəub ɪŋ ‖ 'roub ɪŋ
Robens 'rəub ɪnz -ənz ‖ 'roub ənz
Robert 'rɒb ət ‖ 'rɑːb ᵊrt
Roberta rə 'bɜːt ə rɒ-, rəu- ‖ rə 'bɜ̃ːţ ə rou-
Roberto rə 'bɜːt əu rɒ-, rəu- ‖ rə 'bɜ̃ːţ ou rou- —*It* [ro 'bɛr to], *Sp* [rro 'βer to]
Roberts 'rɒb əts ‖ 'rɑːb ᵊrts
Robertson 'rɒb ət sən ‖ 'rɑːb ᵊrt-
Robeson 'rəub sən ‖ 'roub-
Robespierre 'rəubz pɪə 'rəubz pi̯eə ‖ 'roubz pɪr 'roubz pi er —*Fr* [ʁɔ bɛs pjɛːʁ]
Robey 'rəub i ‖ 'roub i
robin, Robin 'rɒb ɪn §-ən ‖ 'rɑːb ən **~s** z **ˌRobin 'Hood** ‖ '· ·
Robina rɒ 'biːn ə rəu- ‖ rə 'biːn ə
robinia, R~ rə 'bɪn i̯ə rɒ-, rəu- **~s** z
Robinne 'rɒb ɪn §-ən ‖ 'rɑːb ən
Robins *(i)* 'rɒb ɪnz §-ənz ‖ 'rɑːb ənz, *(ii)* 'rəub- ‖ 'roub-
Robinson 'rɒb ɪn sən §-ən- ‖ 'rɑːb- **ˌRobinson 'Crusoe**
Robitussin *tdmk* ˌrəub i 'tʌs ɪn -ᵊn ‖ ˌroub-
roble 'rəub leɪ ‖ 'roub- **~s** z
robocop 'rəub əu kɒp ‖ 'roub ou kɑːp **~s** s
robot 'rəub ɒt -ət ‖ 'roub ɑːt -ət **~s** s
robotic rəʊ 'bɒt ɪk ‖ rou 'bɑːţ ɪk **~s** s
Robson 'rɒb sən ‖ 'rɑːb-
robust rəʊ 'bʌst 'rəu bʌst ‖ rou 'bʌst '· · **~ly** li **~ness** nəs nɪs
robusta rəʊ 'bʌst ə ‖ rou- **~s** z
Roby 'rəub i ‖ 'roub i
Robyn 'rɒb ɪn §-ən ‖ 'rɑːb ən
roc rɒk ‖ rɑːk *(= rock)*
rocaille rɒ 'kaɪ rəʊ- ‖ rou- rɑː- —*Fr* [ʁɔ kaj]
rocambole 'rɒk əm bəul →-bɒul ‖ 'rɑːk əm boul
Rocco 'rɒk əʊ ‖ 'rɑːk ou —*It* ['rɔk ko]
Rocester 'rəust ə ‖ 'roust ᵊr
Rochdale 'rɒtʃ deɪᵊl ‖ 'rɑːtʃ-
Roche *(i)* rəutʃ ‖ routʃ, *(ii)* rəuʃ ‖ rouʃ, *(iii)* rɒʃ ‖ rɑːʃ
Rochelle rɒ 'ʃel rə- ‖ rou-
roche moutonnée ˌrɒʃ mu 'tɒn eɪ -ˌmuːt ɒ 'neɪ ‖ ˌrɔːʃ ˌmuːt ᵊn 'eɪ ˌrouʃ- **roches moutonnées** *same pronunciation, or* -z
Rochester 'rɒtʃ ɪst ə -əst- ‖ 'rɑːtʃ est ᵊr -əst-
rochet 'rɒtʃ ɪt -ət ‖ 'rɑːtʃ ət **~s** s
Rochford 'rɒtʃ fəd ‖ 'rɑːtʃ fᵊrd
rock, Rock rɒk ‖ rɑːk **rocked** rɒkt ‖ rɑːkt **rocking** 'rɒk ɪŋ ‖ 'rɑːk ɪŋ **rocks** rɒks ‖ rɑːks **ˌrock 'bottom** ◂; **'rock cake**; **'rock dash**; **'rock dove**; **'rock ˌgarden**; **'rock ˌhopper**; **'rocking chair**; **'rocking horse**; **'rock ˌmusic**; **'rock muˌsician**; **'rock plant**; **'rock ˌsalmon**; **'rock salt**
rockabilly 'rɒk ə ˌbɪl i ‖ 'rɑːk-
rockbound 'rɒk baund ‖ 'rɑːk-
rock-climb|er 'rɒk ˌklaɪm |ə ‖ 'rɑːk ˌklaɪm |ᵊr **~ers** əz ‖ ᵊrz **~ing** ɪŋ
rock-crystal 'rɒk ˌkrɪst ᵊl ‖ 'rɑːk-
Rockefeller 'rɒk ə ˌfel ə -ɪ- ‖ 'rɑːk ə ˌfel ᵊr **'Rockefeller ˌCenter** ‖ ˌ· · · ˌ· ·
rocker 'rɒk ə ‖ 'rɑːk ᵊr **~s** z
rocker|y 'rɒk ər |i ‖ 'rɑːk- **~ies** iz
rock|et 'rɒk |ɪt §-ət ‖ 'rɑːk |ət **~eted** ɪt ɪd §ət-, -əd ‖ əţ əd **~eting** ɪt ɪŋ §ət- ‖ əţ ɪŋ **~ets** ɪts §əts ‖ əts **'rocket ˌengine**; **'rocket ˌlauncher**; **'rocket range**
rocketry 'rɒk ɪt ri §-ət- ‖ 'rɑːk-
Rockettes rɒ 'kets ‖ rɑː-
rockfall 'rɒk fɔːl ‖ 'rɑːk- -fɑːl **~s** z
rockfish 'rɒk fɪʃ ‖ 'rɑːk- **~es** ɪz əz
Rockford 'rɒk fəd ‖ 'rɑːk fᵊrd
Rockhampton rɒk 'hæmp tən ‖ rɑːk-
rock-hard ˌrɒk 'hɑːd ◂ ‖ ˌrɑːk 'hɑːrd ◂
Rockies 'rɒk iz ‖ 'rɑːk iz
Rockingham 'rɒk ɪŋ əm ‖ 'rɑːk-
Rockley 'rɒk li ‖ 'rɑːk li
rockling 'rɒk lɪŋ ‖ 'rɑːk-
Rockne 'rɒk ni ‖ 'rɑːk-
rock 'n' roll, rock'n'roll ˌrɒk ən 'rəul →-ŋ-, →-'rɒul ‖ ˌrɑːk ən 'roul **~er/s** ə/z ‖ ᵊr/z
rockros|e 'rɒk rəuz ‖ 'rɑːk rouz **~es** ɪz əz
rock-solid ˌrɒk 'sɒl ɪd ◂ §-əd ‖ ˌrɑːk 'sɑːl-
rock-steady ˌrɒk 'sted i ◂ ‖ ˌrɑːk-
Rockwell 'rɒk wəl -wel ‖ 'rɑːk-
rock-wool 'rɒk wʊl ‖ 'rɑːk-
rock|y, Rock|y 'rɒk |i ‖ 'rɑːk |i **~ier** i̯ə ‖ i̯ᵊr **~ies, ~y's** iz **~iest** i̯ɪst i̯əst **~iness** i nəs i nɪs **ˌRocky ˌMountain 'goat**; **ˌRocky 'Mountains**
rococo rə 'kəuk əu rəu- ‖ -'kouk ou ˌrouk ə 'kou
rod rɒd ‖ rɑːd **rods** rɒdz ‖ rɑːdz
Rod, Rodd rɒd ‖ rɑːd
Roddick 'rɒd ɪk ‖ 'rɑːd ɪk
Roddy 'rɒd i ‖ 'rɑːd i
rode rəud ‖ roud *(= road)*
rodent 'rəud ᵊnt ‖ 'roud ᵊnt **~s** s **ˌrodent 'ulcer**

R

rodeo rəʊ ˈdeɪ əʊ ˈrəʊd i- ‖ roʊ ˈdeɪ oʊ ˈroʊd i- **~s** z
Roderic, Roderick ˈrɒd‿ər ɪk ‖ ˈrɑːd-
Rodger ˈrɒdʒ ə ‖ ˈrɑːdʒ ᵊr
Rodgers ˈrɒdʒ əz ‖ ˈrɑːdʒ ᵊrz
Rodin ˈrəʊd æn -æ̃ ‖ roʊ ˈdæn —*Fr* [ʁɔ dæ̃]
Roding ˈrəʊd ɪŋ ‖ ˈroʊd ɪŋ —*Locally also* ˈruːð-, ˈruːd-
Rodman ˈrɒd mən ‖ ˈrɑːd-
Rodney ˈrɒd ni ‖ ˈrɑːd ni
rodomontad|e ˌrɒd ə mɒn ˈtɑːd ˌrəʊd-, -ˈteɪd ‖ ˌrɑːd ə mɑːn ˈteɪd ˌroʊd-, -əm ən-, -ˈtɑːd **~ed** ɪd əd **~es** z **~ing** ɪŋ
Rodrigues, Rodriguez *(i)* rɒ ˈdriːgz ‖ rɑː-, *(ii)* rɒ ˈdriːg ez ‖ rɑː- —*Port* [ʀru ˈðri ɣɪʃ, xo ˈdri gis], *Span* [rro ˈðri ɣeθ, -ɣes] —*In AmE usually (ii).*
Rodway ˈrɒd weɪ ‖ ˈrɑːd-
roe, Roe rəʊ ‖ roʊ **roes** rəʊz ‖ roʊz *(= rose)* ˈ**roe deer**
Roebling ˈrəʊb lɪŋ ‖ ˈroʊb-
roebuck, R~ ˈrəʊ bʌk ‖ ˈroʊ- **~s** s
Roedean ˈrəʊ diːn ‖ ˈroʊ-
Roeg rəʊg ‖ roʊg
Roehampton ₍ˌ₎rəʊ ˈhæmp tən ˈ· · · ‖ roʊ-
roentgen, R~ ˈrɒnt gən ˈrʌnt-, ˈrɜːnt-, -jən ‖ ˈrent gən ˈrʌnt-, ˈrʊnt-, -dʒən —*Ger* [ˈʁœnt gᵊn] **~s** z
roentgenium ˌrɒnt ˈdʒiːn i‿əm ˌrəʊnt-, ˌrʌnt-, -ˈgiːn- ‖ ˌroʊnt- rent-
Roethke ˈret ki ˈrɜːθ- ‖ ˈreθ-, -kə
Roff, Roffe rɒf ‖ rɔːf rɑːf
Roffey ˈrɒf i ‖ ˈrɔːf i ˈrɑːf-
rogan josh ˌrəʊg ən ˈdʒəʊʃ -ˈdʒɒʃ ‖ ˌroʊg ən ˈdʒoʊʃ
rogation, R~ rəʊ ˈgeɪʃ ᵊn ‖ roʊ- **Roˈgation Days**
Roger, roger ˈrɒdʒ ə ‖ ˈrɑːdʒ ᵊr **~ed** d **rogering** ˈrɒdʒ ər ɪŋ **~s** z
Rogers ˈrɒdʒ əz ‖ ˈrɑːdʒ ᵊrz
Roget ˈrɒʒ eɪ ˈrəʊʒ- ‖ roʊ ˈʒeɪ ˈ· · **~'s** z
rogue rəʊg ‖ roʊg **rogued** rəʊgd ‖ roʊgd **rogues** rəʊgz ‖ roʊgz **roguing** ˈrəʊg ɪŋ ‖ ˈroʊg ɪŋ
ˌrogues' ˈgallery
roguer|y ˈrəʊg ər |i ‖ ˈroʊg- **~ies** iz
roguish ˈrəʊg ɪʃ ‖ ˈroʊg- **~ly** li **~ness** nəs nɪs
Rohan ˈrəʊ ən ‖ ˈroʊ-
Rohypnol *tdmk* rəʊ ˈhɪp nɒl ‖ roʊ ˈhɪp nɔːl -nɑːl
roil rɔɪᵊl **roiled** rɔɪᵊld **roiling** ˈrɔɪᵊl ɪŋ **roils** rɔɪᵊlz
Roisin, Roisín rʌ ˈʃiːn rɒ-
roister ˈrɔɪst ə ‖ -ᵊr **~ed** d **roistering** ˈrɔɪst ər‿ɪŋ **~s** z
roisterer ˈrɔɪst ər‿ə ‖ ‿ᵊr **~s** z
Rokeby ˈrəʊk bi ‖ ˈroʊk-
Roker ˈrəʊk ə ‖ ˈroʊk ᵊr
Rolaids *tdmk* ˈrəʊl eɪdz →ˈrɒʊl- ‖ ˈroʊl-
Roland ˈrəʊl ənd ‖ ˈroʊl-
role, rôle rəʊl →rɒʊl ‖ roʊl *(= roll)* **roles, rôles** rəʊlz →rɒʊlz ‖ roʊlz
ˈrole ˌmodel; **ˈrole play, ˈrole ˌplaying**

role-play ˈrəʊl pleɪ →ˈrɒʊl- ‖ ˈroʊl- **~ed** d **~ing** ɪŋ **~s** z
Rolex *tdmk* ˈrəʊl eks ‖ ˈroʊl- **~es** ɪz əz
Rolf, rolf rɒlf ‖ rɑːlf rɔːlf **rolfed** rɒlft ‖ rɑːlft rɔːlft **rolfing** ˈrɒlf ɪŋ ‖ ˈrɑːlf ɪŋ ˈrɔːlf- **rolfs, Rolf's** rɒlfs ‖ rɑːlfs rɔːlfs
Rolfe *(i)* rəʊf ‖ roʊf, *(ii)* rɒlf ‖ rɑːlf rɔːlf
roll rəʊl →rɒʊl ‖ roʊl **rolled** rəʊld →rɒʊld ‖ roʊld **rolling** ˈrəʊl ɪŋ →ˈrɒʊl- ‖ ˈroʊl ɪŋ
ˈroll bar; **ˈroll call**; **ˌrolled ˈgold ◂**; **ˈrolling mill**; **ˈrolling pin**; **ˈrolling stock**; **ˌrolling ˈstone, ˌRolling ˈStones**; **ˌroll of ˈhonour**
rollaway ˈrəʊl ə ˌweɪ →ˈrɒʊl- ‖ ˈroʊl- **~s** z
rollback ˈrəʊl bæk →ˈrɒʊl- ‖ ˈroʊl- **~s** s
Rollei *tdmk* ˈrəʊl aɪ ‖ ˈroʊl- —*Ger* [ˈʁɔl ai]
roller ˈrəʊl ə →ˈrɒʊl- ‖ ˈroʊl ᵊr **~s** z
ˈroller ˌbearing; **ˈroller blind**; **ˈroller ˌcoaster**; **ˈRoller ˌDerby, ˌ· ·ˈ· ·** *tdmk*; **ˈroller skate**; **ˈroller ˌtowel**
Rollerblad|e *tdmk, r~* ˈrəʊl ə bleɪd →ˈrɒʊl- ‖ ˈroʊl ᵊr- **~ed** ɪd əd **~er/s** ə/z ‖ -ᵊr/z **~es** z **~ing** ɪŋ
roller-|skate ˈrəʊl ə |skeɪt →ˈrɒʊl- ‖ ˈroʊl ᵊr- **~skated** skeɪt ɪd -əd ‖ skeɪţ əd **~skater/s** skeɪt ə/z ‖ skeɪţ ᵊr/z **~skates** skeɪts **~skating** skeɪt ɪŋ ‖ skeɪţ ɪŋ
Rolleston ˈrəʊlst ən →ˈrɒʊlst- ‖ ˈroʊlst-
rollick ˈrɒl ɪk ‖ ˈrɑːl ɪk **~ed** t **~ing/ly** ɪŋ /li **~s** s
Rollins ˈrɒl ɪnz §-ənz ‖ ˈrɑːl-
rollmop ˈrəʊl mɒp →ˈrɒʊl- ‖ ˈroʊl mɑːp **~s** s
rollneck ˈrəʊl nek →ˈrɒʊl- ‖ ˈroʊl- **~s** s
Rollo ˈrɒl əʊ ‖ ˈrɑːl oʊ
roll-on ˈrəʊl ɒn →ˈrɒʊl- ‖ ˈroʊl ɑːn -ɔːn **~s** z
ˌroll-on ˌroll-ˈoff ◂ ˌrəʊl ˈɒf ◂ →ˌrɒʊl-, -ˈɔːf ‖ ˌroʊl ˈɔːf ◂ -ˈɑːf; **ˌroll-on ˌroll-off ˈcar ˌferry**
roll-out ˈrəʊl aʊt →ˈrɒʊl- ‖ ˈroʊl- **~s** s
rollover ˈrəʊl ˌəʊv ə →ˈrɒʊl- ‖ ˈroʊl ˌoʊv ᵊr
Rolls rəʊlz →rɒʊlz ‖ roʊlz **~es** ɪz əz
Rolls-Royc|e *tdmk* ˌrəʊlz ˈrɔɪs →ˌrɒʊlz- ‖ ˌroʊlz- **~es** ɪz əz
rolltop ˈrəʊl tɒp →ˈrɒʊl- ‖ ˈroʊl tɑːp **~s** s
rollup ˈrəʊl ʌp →ˈrɒʊl- ‖ ˈroʊl- **~s** s
Rolo *tdmk* ˈrəʊl əʊ →ˈrɒʊl- ‖ ˈroʊl oʊ **~s** z
Rolodex *tdmk* ˈrəʊl ə deks →ˈrɒʊl- ‖ ˈroʊl-
Rolph rɒlf ‖ rɑːlf
Rolston ˈrəʊlst ən →ˈrɒʊlst- ‖ ˈroʊlst-
Rolt rəʊlt →rɒʊlt ‖ roʊlt
roly-pol|y ˌrəʊl i ˈpəʊl |i ◂ →ˌrɒʊl i ˈpɒʊl i ‖ ˌroʊl i ˈpoʊl |i ◂ **~ies** iz
ˌroly-ˌpoly ˈpudding
ROM *'computer memory'* rɒm ‖ rɑːm
Rom *'gypsy'* rɒm rəʊm ‖ roʊm
Roma *city; people and language* ˈrəʊm ə ‖ ˈroʊm ə —*It* [ˈroːm a]
Romagna rəʊ ˈmɑːn jə ‖ roʊ- —*It* [ro ˈmaɲ ɲa]
Romaic rəʊ ˈmeɪ ɪk ‖ roʊ-
Romaine, r~ rəʊ ˈmeɪn ‖ roʊ-
roˌmaine ˈlettuce

Roman, roman ˈrəʊm ən ‖ ˈroʊm ən —*but as a French word,* rəʊ ˈmɒ̃ ‖ roʊ ˈmɑːn —*Fr* [ʁɔ mɑ̃] *(see phrases)* **~s** z
ˌ**Roman ˈalphabet**; ˌ**Roman ˈcandle**; ˌ**Roman ˈCatholic**; ˌ**Roman Caˈtholiˌcism**; ˌ**Roman ˈEmpire**; ˌ**Roman ˈlaw**; ˌ**Roman ˈnose**; ˌ**Roman ˈnumeral**

roman à clef rəʊ ˌmɒ̃ ɑː ˈkleɪ -ˌmɑːn- ‖ roʊ ˌmɑːn- **romans à clef** *same pronunciation* —*Fr* [ʁɔ mɑ̃ a kle]

romanc|e, R~ rəʊ ˈmænᵗs ˈrəʊm ænᵗs ‖ roʊ ˈmænᵗs ˈroʊm ænᵗs **~ed** t **~er/s** ə/z ‖ ᵊr/z **~es** ɪz əz **~ing** ɪŋ

Romanes *family name* rəʊ ˈmɑːn ɪz -ɪs, -es ‖ roʊ-

Romanes *language* ˈrɒm ə nes -ən ɪs, §-əs ‖ ˈrɑːm-

Romanesque ˌrəʊm ə ˈnesk ◂ ‖ ˌroʊm-

roman fleuve rəʊ ˌmɒ̃ ˈflɜːv ‖ roʊ ˌmɑːn ˈflʌv **romans fleuve** *same pronunciation* —*Fr* [ʁɔ mɑ̃ flœːv]

Romani|a ru ˈmeɪn i‿ə rəʊ- ‖ roʊ- **~an/s** ən/z

romanic, R~ rəʊ ˈmæn ɪk ‖ roʊ-

romanis... —*see* **romaniz...**

Romanism ˈrəʊm ən ˌɪz əm ‖ ˈroʊm-

Romanist ˈrəʊm ən ɪst §-əst ‖ ˈroʊm- **~s** s

romanization ˌrəʊm ən aɪ ˈzeɪʃ ᵊn -ɪˈ-- ‖ ˌroʊm ən ə- **~s** z

romaniz|e ˈrəʊm ə naɪz ‖ ˈroʊm- **~ed** d **~er/s** ə/z ‖ ᵊr/z **~es** ɪz əz **~ing** ɪŋ

Romano, r~ rəʊ ˈmɑːn əʊ ‖ roʊ ˈmɑːn oʊ

Romano- rəʊ ¦mɑːn əʊ -¦mæn- ‖ rə ¦mɑːn oʊ — **Romano-British** rəʊ ˌmɑːn əʊ ˈbrɪt ɪʃ ◂ -ˌmæn- ‖ rə ˌmɑːn oʊ ˈbrɪţ ɪʃ ◂

Roma|nov ˈrəʊm ə |nɒf -nɒv ‖ ˈroʊm ə |nɔːf -nɑːf —*Russ* [rʌ ˈma nəf] **~novs** nɒfs nɒvz ‖ nɔːfs nɑːfs

Romansch, Romansh rəʊ ˈmænᵗʃ ru- ‖ roʊ- -ˈmɑːnᵗʃ

romantic rəʊ ˈmænt ɪk ‖ roʊ ˈmænţ ɪk rə- **~ally** ᵊl‿i **~s** s

romanticis... —*see* **romanticiz...**

romanticism rəʊ ˈmænt ɪ ˌsɪz əm -ə- ‖ roʊ ˈmænţ ə- rə-

romanticist rəʊ ˈmænt ɪs ɪst -əs-, §-əst ‖ roʊ ˈmænţ- rə-

romanticization rəʊ ˌmænt ɪs aɪ ˈzeɪʃ ᵊn -ˌ-əs-, -ɪˈ-- ‖ roʊ ˌmænţ əs ə-

romanticiz|e rəʊ ˈmænt ɪ saɪz -ə- ‖ roʊ ˈmænţ ə- rə- **~ed** d **~es** ɪz əz **~ing** ɪŋ

Roman|y ˈrɒm ən |i ˈrəʊm- ‖ ˈrɑːm- ˈroʊm- **~ies** iz

Rombauer ˈrɒm baʊ‿ə ‖ ˈrɑːm baʊ‿ᵊr

Romberg ˈrɒm bɜːg ‖ ˈrɑːm bɝːg

rom com ˈrɒm kɒm ‖ ˈrɑːm kɑːm **~s** z

Rome rəʊm ‖ roʊm —*Formerly also* ruːm **Rome's** rəʊmz ‖ roʊmz —*It* Roma [ˈroː ma]

Romeo ˈrəʊm i‿əʊ ‖ ˈroʊm i‿oʊ **~s, ~'s** z

romer ˈrəʊm ə ‖ ˈroʊm ᵊr **~s** z

Romero rəʊ ˈmeər əʊ ‖ roʊ ˈmer oʊ rə- —*Sp* [rro ˈme ro]

Romford ˈrɒm fəd ˈrʌm- ‖ ˈrɑːm fᵊrd

romic, Romic ˈrəʊm ɪk ‖ ˈroʊm-

Romiley, Romilly ˈrɒm əl i -ɪl- ‖ ˈrɑːm-

Romish ˈrəʊm ɪʃ ‖ ˈroʊm ɪʃ

Rommel ˈrɒm ᵊl ‖ ˈrɑːm ᵊl ˈrʌm- —*Ger* [ˈʁɔm ᵊl]

Romney ˈrɒm ni ˈrʌm- ‖ ˈrɑːm-

romneya ˈrɒm ni‿ə ‖ ˈrɑːm- **~s** z

romp rɒmp ‖ rɑːmp **romped** rɒmpt ‖ rɑːmpt **romping** ˈrɒmp ɪŋ ‖ ˈrɑːmp ɪŋ **romps** rɒmps ‖ rɑːmps

romper ˈrɒmp ə ‖ ˈrɑːmp ᵊr **~s** z
ˈ**romper suit**

Romsey ˈrɒm zi ˈrʌm- ‖ ˈrɑːm zi

Romulus ˈrɒm jʊl əs ‖ ˈrɑːm jəl əs

Ron rɒn ‖ rɑːn

Rona ˈrəʊn ə ‖ ˈroʊn ə

Ronald ˈrɒn ᵊld ‖ ˈrɑːn ᵊld

Ronaldinho ˌrɒn ᵊl ˈdiːn jəʊ ‖ ˌrɑːn ᵊl ˈdiːn oʊ —*BrPort* [ʁɔ nal ˈdʒi ɲu]

Ronaldo rɒ ˈnæld əʊ rə- ‖ roʊ ˈnɑːld oʊ —*BrPort* [ʁɔ ˈnal du]

Ronaldsay ˈrɒn ᵊld seɪ -ʃeɪ ‖ ˈrɑːn-

Ronaldsway ˈrɒn ᵊldz weɪ ‖ ˈrɑːn-

Ronan ˈrəʊn ən ‖ ˈroʊn-

rondavel ˈrɒnd ə vel rɒn ˈdɑːv ᵊl ‖ ˈrɑːnd- **~s** z

rondeau ˈrɒnd əʊ ‖ ˈrɑːnd oʊ rɑːn ˈdoʊ **~s, ~x** z —*or as sing.*

rondel ˈrɒnd ᵊl ‖ ˈrɑːnd ᵊl rɑːn ˈdel **~s** z

rondo ˈrɒnd əʊ ‖ ˈrɑːnd oʊ rɑːn ˈdoʊ **~s** z

roneo, R~ *tdmk* ˈrəʊn i‿əʊ ‖ ˈroʊn i‿oʊ **~ed** d **~ing** ɪŋ **~s** z

Ronnie ˈrɒn i ‖ ˈrɑːn i

Ronsard ˈrɒn sɑː ‖ roʊn ˈsɑːr —*Fr* [ʁɔ̃ saːʁ]

Ronson ˈrɒnᵗs ən ‖ ˈrɑːnᵗs ən

Ronstadt ˈrɒn stæt ‖ ˈrɑːn-

röntgen, R~ ˈrɒnt gən ˈrʌnt-, ˈrɜːnt-, -jən ‖ ˈrent gən ˈrʌnt-, ˈrʊnt-, -dʒən —*Ger* [ˈʁœnt gᵊn] **~s** z

Ronuk *tdmk* ˈrɒn ək ˈrəʊn-, -ʌk ‖ ˈrɑːn-

roo, Roo ruː **roos** ruːz

rood ruːd *(= rude)* **roods** ruːdz
ˈ**rood loft**; ˈ**rood screen**

roof ruːf rʊf **roofed** ruːft rʊft, ruːvd **roofing** ˈruːf ɪŋ ˈrʊf-, ˈruːv- **roofs** ruːfs ruːvz, rʊfs
ˈ**roof ˌgarden**; ˈ**roof rack**

roofer ˈruːf ə ˈrʊf- ‖ -ᵊr **~s** z

roofies ˈruːf iz

roofless ˈruːf ləs ˈrʊf-, -lɪs

rooftop ˈruːf tɒp ˈrʊf- ‖ -tɑːp **~s** s

rooftree ˈruːf triː ˈrʊf- **~s** z

rooibos ˈrɔɪ bɒs ‖ -bɔːs -bɑːs

rooinek ˈrɔɪ nek **~s** s

rook rʊk §ruːk **rooked** rʊkt §ruːkt **rooking** ˈrʊk ɪŋ §ˈruːk- **rooks** rʊks §ruːks

Rook, Rooke rʊk §ruːk

rooker|y ˈrʊk ər |i §ˈruːk- **~ies** iz

rook|ie, rook|y ˈrʊk |i **~ies** iz

ROOM

ruːm 81% / rʊm 19% — BrE

ruːm 93% / rʊm 7% — AmE

room ruːm rʊm — *Preference polls, BrE:* ruːm *81%,* rʊm *19%; AmE:* ruːm *93%,* rʊm *7%. Some who say* ruːm *for this word on its own nevertheless say* rʊm *in compounds: see* bedroom. **roomed** ruːmd rʊmd **rooming** ˈruːm ɪŋ ˈrʊm- **rooms** ruːmz rʊmz **ˈrooming house**; **ˈroom ˌservice**

Room, Roome ruːm

-roomed ˈruːmd ˈrʊmd — **three-roomed** ˌθriː ˈruːmd ◂ -ˈrʊmd

roomer ˈruːm ə ˈrʊm- ‖ -ᵊr **~s** z

roomette ˌruːm ˈet ˌrʊm- **~s** s

roomful ˈruːm fʊl ˈrʊm- **~s** z

roomie ˈruːm i ˈrʊm i **~s** z

roommate ˈruːm meɪt ˈrʊm- **~s** s

room|y ˈruːm |i ˈrʊm- **~ier** i‿ə ‖ i‿ᵊr **~iest** i‿ɪst i‿əst **~ily** ɪ li əl i **~iness** i nəs i nɪs

Rooney ˈruːn i

Roope ruːp

Roosevelt ˈrəʊz ə velt ˈrəʊs-, -vᵊlt; ˈruːs- ‖ ˈroʊz- **~s, ~'s** s

roost ruːst **roosted** ˈruːst ɪd -əd **roosting** ˈruːst ɪŋ **roosts** ruːsts

rooster ˈruːst ə ‖ -ᵊr **~s** z

root, Root ruːt §rʊt **rooted** ˈruːt ɪd §ˈrʊt-, -əd ‖ ˈruːţ əd ˈrʊţ- **rooting** ˈruːt ɪŋ §ˈrʊt- ‖ ˈruːţ ɪŋ ˈrʊţ- **roots** ruːts §rʊts **ˈroot beer,** ˌ· ˈ·; **ˈroot caˌnal**; **ˌroot ˌmean ˈsquare**; **ˈroot crop**; **ˈroot ˌvegetable,** ˌ· ˈ· · ·

Rootes ruːts

rootl|e ˈruːt ᵊl ‖ ˈruːţ ᵊl **~ed** d **~es** z **~ing** ɪŋ

rootless ˈruːt ləs §ˈrʊt-, -lɪs **~ness** nəs nɪs

rootlet ˈruːt lət §ˈrʊt-, -lɪt **~s** s

rootstock ˈruːt stɒk §ˈrʊt- ‖ -stɑːk **~s** s

rootsy ˈruːts i

rope rəʊp ‖ roʊp **roped** rəʊpt ‖ roʊpt **ropes** rəʊps ‖ roʊps **roping** ˈrəʊp ɪŋ ‖ ˈroʊp ɪŋ **ˌrope ˈladder,** ˈ· ˌ· ·

ropedancer ˈrəʊp ˌdɑːnᵗs ə -ˌdænᵗs- ‖ ˈroʊp ˌdænᵗs ᵊr **~s** z

Roper ˈrəʊp ə ‖ ˈroʊp ᵊr

ropewalk ˈrəʊp wɔːk ‖ ˈroʊp- -wɑːk **~ed** t **~ing** ɪŋ **~s** s

ropewalker ˈrəʊp ˌwɔːk ə ‖ ˈroʊp ˌwɔːk ᵊr -ˌwɑːk- **~s** z

ropeway ˈrəʊp weɪ ‖ ˈroʊp- **~s** z

rop|ey, rop|y ˈrəʊp |i ‖ ˈroʊp |i **~ier** i‿ə ‖ i‿ᵊr **~iest** i‿ɪst i‿əst **~ily** ɪ li əl i **~iness** i nəs i nɪs

Roquefort, r~ ˈrɒk fɔː ‖ ˈroʊk fᵊrt —*Fr* [ʁɔk fɔːʁ]

roquet ˈrəʊk i -eɪ ‖ roʊ ˈkeɪ **~ed** d **~ing** ɪŋ **~s** z

roquette rɒ ˈket ‖ roʊ- —*Fr* [ʁɔ kɛt]

Rorke rɔːk ‖ rɔːrk roʊrk

ro-ro ˈrəʊ rəʊ ‖ ˈroʊ roʊ **~s, ~'s** z

rorqual ˈrɔːk wəl -ᵊl ‖ ˈrɔːrk- **~s** z

Rorschach ˈrɔː ʃɑːk -ʃæk ‖ ˈrɔːr- ˈroʊr- —*Ger* [ˈʁɔʁ ʃax] **ˈRorschach test**

rort rɔːt ‖ rɔːrt **rorts** rɔːts ‖ rɔːrts

Rory ˈrɔːr i ‖ ˈroʊr-

Ros *short for* **Rosalind** *etc* rɒz ‖ rɑːz

Ros *family name* rɒs ‖ rɔːs rɑːs

Rosa ˈrəʊz ə ‖ ˈroʊz ə

rosacea rəʊ ˈzeɪʃ ə -i‿ə ‖ roʊ-

rosaceous rəʊ ˈzeɪʃ əs ‖ roʊ-

Rosaleen *(i)* ˈrɒz ə liːn ‖ ˈrɑːz-, *(ii)* ˈrəʊz- ‖ ˈroʊz-

Rosalie *(i)* ˈrɒz ə li ‖ ˈrɑːz-, *(ii)* ˈrəʊz- ‖ ˈroʊz-

Rosalind ˈrɒz ə lɪnd ‖ ˈrɑːz-

Rosaline ˈrɒz ə lɪn -liːn, -laɪn ‖ ˈrɑːz-

Rosamond, Rosamund ˈrɒz ə mənd ‖ ˈrɑːz- ˈroʊz-

rosaniline rəʊ ˈzæn ə liːn -laɪn; -ᵊl iːn, -aɪn; -əl ɪn, §-ən ‖ roʊ ˈzæn ᵊl ən -aɪn

Rosanna rəʊ ˈzæn ə ‖ roʊ-

Rosanne rəʊ ˈzæn ‖ roʊ-

Rosario rəʊ ˈzɑːr i əʊ -ˈsɑːr- ‖ roʊ ˈsɑːr i oʊ -ˈzɑːr- —*Sp* [rro ˈsa rjo]

rosari|um rəʊ ˈzeər i‿|əm ‖ roʊ ˈzer- -ˈzær- **~a** ə **~ums** əmz

rosar|y ˈrəʊz ər |i ‖ ˈroʊz- **~ies** iz

Roscoe, r~ ˈrɒsk əʊ ‖ ˈrɑːsk oʊ **~s, ~'s** z

Roscommon rɒs ˈkɒm ən ‖ rɑːs ˈkɑːm ən

rose, Rose rəʊz ‖ roʊz **roses** ˈrəʊz ɪz -əz ‖ ˈroʊz əz **ˈrose ˌgarden**; **ˌrose ˈwindow,** ˈ· ˌ· ·

rosé ˈrəʊz eɪ rəʊ ˈzeɪ ‖ roʊ ˈzeɪ **~s** z

Roseanne *(i)* rəʊ ˈzæn ‖ roʊ-, *(ii)* ˌrəʊz i ˈæn ‖ ˌroʊz-

roseate ˈrəʊz i‿ət -ɪt, -eɪt ‖ ˈroʊz- **~ly** li

Roseau rəʊ ˈzəʊ ‖ roʊ ˈzoʊ

rosebay ˌrəʊz ˈbeɪ ˈ· · ‖ ˈroʊz beɪ **~s** z

Roseberry, Rosebery ˈrəʊz bər‿i ‖ ˈroʊz ˌber i

rosebud ˈrəʊz bʌd ‖ ˈroʊz- **~s** z

rose-colored, rose-coloured ˈrəʊz ˌkʌl əd ‖ ˈroʊz ˌkʌl ᵊrd

Rosecrans ˈrəʊz kræntˢ ˈrəʊz ə kræntˢ ‖ ˈroʊz-

Rosedale ˈrəʊz deɪᵊl ‖ ˈroʊz-

rose hip, rosehip ˈrəʊz hɪp ‖ ˈroʊz- **~s** s

rosella rəʊ ˈzel ə ‖ roʊ- **~s** z

roselle, R~ rəʊ ˈzel ‖ roʊ- **~s, ~'s** z

Rosemarie ˌrəʊz mə ˈriː ‖ ˌroʊz- ˈ· · ·

rosemar|y, R~ ˈrəʊz mər‿|i ‖ ˈroʊz ˌmer |i **~ies** iz

Rosen ˈrəʊz ᵊn ‖ ˈroʊz ᵊn

Rosenberg ˈrəʊz ᵊn bɜːg ‖ ˈroʊz ᵊn bɜːg **~s** z

Rosencrantz ˈrəʊz ᵊn krænts ‖ ˈroʊz-

Rosenthal *(i)* ˈrəʊz ᵊn θɔːl ‖ ˈroʊz- -θɑːl, *(ii)* -tɑːl

roseola rəʊ ˈziː‿əl ə ˌrəʊz i ˈəʊl ə ‖ roʊ ˈziː əl ə ˌroʊz i ˈoʊl ə **~s** z

roseroot ˈrəʊz ruːt §-rʊt ‖ ˈroʊz-

rose-tinted ˈrəʊz ˌtɪnt ɪd -əd ‖ ˈroʊz ˌtɪnţ əd

Rosetta rəʊ ˈzet ə ‖ roʊ ˈzeţ ə
 Roˌsetta ˈstone ‖ ·ˌ· · ·
rosette rəʊ ˈzet ‖ roʊ- ~s s
Rosewall ˈrəʊz wɔːl ‖ ˈroʊz- -wɑːl
Rosewarne ˈrəʊz wɔːn ‖ ˈroʊz wɔːrn
rosewater ˈrəʊz ˌwɔːt ə ‖ ˈroʊz ˌwɔːţ ᵊr -ˌwɑːţ-
rosewood ˈrəʊz wʊd ‖ ˈroʊz-
Rosheen rɒ ˈʃiːn ‖ roʊ-
Rosh Hashana, Rosh Hashanah ˌrɒʃ hə ˈʃɑːn ə -hæ- ‖ ˌroʊʃ hɑː ˈʃɔːn ə ˌrɔːʃ-, ˌrɑːʃ-, -hə-, -ˈʃɑːn-, -ˈʃoʊn-
Rosicrucian ˌrəʊz i ˈkruːʃ ᵊn ˌrɒz-, -ˈkruːʃ i‿ən ‖ ˌroʊz ə- ~s z
Rosie ˈrəʊz i ‖ ˈroʊz i
rosin ˈrɒz ɪn §-ᵊn ‖ ˈrɑːz- ~ed d ~ing ɪŋ ~s z
Rosinante ˌrɒz ɪ ˈnænt i -ə- ‖ ˌrɑːz- —*Sp* [rro si ˈnan te]
Roskilde ˈrɒsk ɪld ə ‖ ˈrɑːsk- ˈroʊsk- —*Danish* [ˈʁɔs ki lə]
Roslea rɒs ˈleɪ ‖ rɔːs- rɑːs-
Roslin, Roslyn ˈrɒz lɪn §-lən ‖ ˈrɑːz-
ROSPA, RoSPA ˈrɒsp ə ‖ ˈrɑːsp ə
Ross rɒs ‖ rɔːs rɑːs
 ˌRoss ˈSea
Rossall ˈrɒs ᵊl ‖ ˈrɔːs- ˈrɑːs-
Rossendale ˈrɒs ᵊn deɪᵊl ‖ ˈrɔːs- ˈrɑːs-
Rossetti *(i)* rə ˈzet i rɒ- ‖ roʊ ˈzeţ i, *(ii)* -ˈset i ‖ -ˈseţ i
Rossini rɒ ˈsiːn i rə- ‖ roʊ- —*It* [ros ˈsiː ni]
Rossiter ˈrɒs ɪt ə -ət- ‖ ˈrɔːs əţ ᵊr ˈrɑːs-
Rosslare ˌrɒs ˈleə ˈ· · ‖ ˌrɔːs ˈleᵊr ˌrɑːs-, -ˈlæᵊr
Rosslyn ˈrɒs lɪn §-lən ‖ ˈrɔːs- ˈrɑːs-
Ross-on-Wye ˌrɒs ɒn ˈwaɪ ‖ ˌrɔːs ɑːn- ˌrɑːs-, -ɔːn-
Rostand rɒ ˈstɒ̃ ‖ roʊ ˈstɑːnd —*Fr* [ʁɔs tɑ̃]
roster ˈrɒst ə ‖ ˈrɑːst ᵊr ~ed d **rostering** ˈrɒst ər‿ɪŋ ‖ ˈrɑːst ər‿ɪŋ ~s z
Rostock ˈrɒst ɒk ‖ ˈrɑːst ɑːk —*Ger* [ˈʁɔs tɔk]
Rostov ˈrɒst ɒv -ɒf ‖ ˈrɑːst ɑːv -ɑːf —*Russ* [rʌs ˈtɔf]
 Rostov-on-ˈDon
ros|tra ˈrɒs |trə ‖ ˈrɑːs- ~tral trəl ~trate treɪt
Rostrevor rɒs ˈtrev ə ‖ rɑːs ˈtrev ᵊr
Rostropovich ˌrɒs trə ˈpəʊv ɪtʃ ‖ ˌrɑːs trə ˈpoʊv ɪtʃ —*Russ* [rəs trʌ ˈpɔ vʲɪtʃ]
ros|trum ˈrɒs |trəm ‖ ˈrɑːs- ~tra trə ~trums trəmz
Roswell ˈrɒz wel ‖ ˈrɑːz-
ros|y ˈrəʊz |i ‖ ˈroʊz |i ~ier i‿ə ‖ i‿ᵊr ~iest i‿ɪst i‿əst ~ily ɪ li əl i ~iness i nəs i nɪs
Rosyth rə ˈsaɪθ rɒ-
rot rɒt ‖ rɑːt **rots** rɒts ‖ rɑːts **rotted** ˈrɒt ɪd -əd ‖ ˈrɑːţ əd **rotting** ˈrɒt ɪŋ ‖ ˈrɑːţ ɪŋ
rota, Rota ˈrəʊt ə ‖ ˈroʊţ ə ~s z
Rotarian rəʊ ˈteər i‿ən ‖ roʊ ˈter- ~s z
rotar|y, R~ ˈrəʊt ər |i ‖ ˈroʊţ- ~ies iz
 ˈRotary Club; ˌrotary ˈtiller
rotatab|le rəʊ ˈteɪt əb |ᵊl ‖ ˈroʊt eɪţ- ~ly li
rotate rəʊ ˈteɪt ‖ ˈroʊt eɪt **rotated** rəʊ ˈteɪt ɪd -əd ‖ ˈroʊt eɪţ əd **rotates** rəʊ ˈteɪts ‖ ˈroʊt eɪts **rotating** rəʊ ˈteɪt ɪŋ ‖ ˈroʊt eɪţ ɪŋ
rotation rəʊ ˈteɪʃ ᵊn ‖ roʊ- ~al ᵊl ◂ ~s z
rotative rəʊ ˈteɪt ɪv ˈrəʊt ət- ‖ ˈroʊţ əţ ɪv ~ly li
rotator rəʊ ˈteɪt ə ‖ ˈroʊt eɪţ ᵊr ~s z
rotatory rəʊ ˈteɪt ər i ˈrəʊt ət‿ər i ‖ ˈroʊţ ə tɔːr i -toʊr i *(*)*
Rotavator —*see* **Rotovator**
rotavirus ˈrəʊt ə ˌvaɪᵊr əs ‖ ˈroʊţ- ~es ɪz əz
rote rəʊt ‖ roʊt *(= wrote)*
rotenone ˈrəʊt ə nəʊn -ɪ-, -ᵊn əʊn ‖ ˈroʊt ᵊn oʊn
rotgut ˈrɒt gʌt ‖ ˈrɑːt-
Roth *(i)* rɒθ ‖ rɔːθ rɑːθ, *(ii)* rəʊθ ‖ roʊθ
Rothamsted ˈrɒθ əm sted ‖ ˈrɑːθ-
Rothay ˈrɒθ eɪ ‖ ˈrɑːθ-
Rothbury ˈrɒθ bər‿i ‖ ˈrɑːθ-
Rothenstein ˈrəʊθ ᵊn staɪn ˈrəʊt-, ˈrɒθ- ‖ ˈrɑːθ-
Rother ˈrɒð ə ‖ ˈrɑːð ᵊr
Rotherfield ˈrɒð ə fiːᵊld ‖ ˈrɑːð ᵊr-
Rotherham ˈrɒð ər‿əm ‖ ˈrɑːð-
Rotherhithe ˈrɒð ə haɪð ‖ ˈrɑːð ᵊr-
Rothermere ˈrɒð ə mɪə ‖ ˈrɑːð ᵊr mɪr
Rothersthorpe ˈrɒð əz θɔːp ‖ ˈrɑːð ᵊrz θɔːrp —*In Northants, locally also* θrəp
Rotherwick ˈrɒð ə wɪk ‖ ˈrɑːð ᵊr- —*formerly also* -ər ɪk
Rothes ˈrɒθ ɪz -ɪs, §-əz, §-əs ‖ ˈrɑːθ-
Rothesay ˈrɒθ si -seɪ ‖ ˈrɑːθ-
Rothko ˈrɒθ kəʊ ‖ ˈrɑːθ koʊ
Rothman ˈrɒθ mən ‖ ˈrɔːθ- ˈrɑːθ-
Rothschild ˈrɒθs tʃaɪᵊld ˈrɒθ- ‖ ˈrɔːθs- ˈrɑːθs-, ˈrɔːθ-, ˈrɑːθ- ~s, ~'s z
Rothwell ˈrɒθ wel -wəl ‖ ˈrɑːθ- —*In Northants, locally also* ˈrəʊ əl
roti ˈrəʊt i ‖ ˈroʊţ i ~s z —*Hindi* [roː ʈi]
rotifer ˈrəʊt ɪf ə §-əf- ‖ ˈroʊţ əf ᵊr ~s z
rotifer|a rəʊ ˈtɪf ər‿|ə ‖ roʊ- ~al ᵊl ~ous əs
rotisserie rəʊ ˈtɪs ər i -ˈtiːs- ‖ roʊ- ~s z
roto ˈrəʊt əʊ ‖ ˈroʊţ oʊ ~s z
Rotodyne ˈrəʊt əʊ daɪn ‖ ˈroʊţ ə-
rotogravure ˌrəʊt əʊ grə ˈvjʊə ‖ ˌroʊţ ə grə ˈvjʊᵊr
rotor ˈrəʊt ə ‖ ˈroʊţ ᵊr ~s z
Roto-rooter *tdmk* ˈrəʊt əʊ ˌruːt ə ‖ ˈroʊţ oʊ ˌruːţ ᵊr
Rotorua ˌrəʊt ə ˈruː‿ə ‖ ˌroʊţ-
rototill ˈrəʊt ə tɪl ‖ ˈroʊţ- ~ed d ~ing ɪŋ ~s z
rototiller, R~ *tdmk* ˈrəʊt ə ˌtɪl ə ‖ ˈroʊţ ə ˌtɪl ᵊr ~s z
roto|vate ˈrəʊt ə |veɪt ‖ ˈroʊţ- ~vated veɪt ɪd -əd ‖ veɪţ əd ~vates veɪts ~vating veɪt ɪŋ ‖ veɪţ ɪŋ
rotovator, R~ *tdmk* ˈrəʊt ə veɪt ə ‖ ˈroʊţ ə veɪţ ᵊr ~s z
rotten ˈrɒt ᵊn ‖ ˈrɑːt ᵊn ~er ə ‖ ᵊr ~est ɪst əst ~ly li ~ness nəs nɪs
 ˌrotten ˈborough
rottenstone ˈrɒt ᵊn stəʊn ‖ ˈrɑːt ᵊn stoʊn
rotter ˈrɒt ə ‖ ˈrɑːţ ᵊr ~s z
Rotterdam ˈrɒt ə dæm ˌ· ˈ· ‖ ˈrɑːţ ᵊr- —*Dutch* [rɔt ər ˈdɑm]
Rottingdean ˈrɒt ɪŋ diːn ‖ ˈrɑːţ- —*locally also* ˌ· ˈ·

Rottweiler, r~ ˈrɒt waɪl ə -vaɪl- ‖ ˈrɑːt waɪl ᵊr **~s** z
rotund rəʊ ˈtʌnd ˈrəʊt ʌnd ‖ roʊ ˈtʌnd ˈroʊt ʌnd
rotunda, R~ rəʊ ˈtʌnd ə ‖ roʊ- **~s** z
rotundity rəʊ ˈtʌnd ət i -ɪt- ‖ roʊ ˈtʌnd əṭ i
rotund|ly rəʊ ˈtʌnd |li ˈrəʊt ʌnd- ‖ roʊ ˈtʌnd- ˈroʊt ʌnd- **~ness** nəs nɪs
rouble ˈruːb ᵊl **~s** z
roué ˈruː eɪ ‖ ru ˈeɪ **~s** z
Rouen ˈruː ɒ̃ ‖ ru ˈɑːn —*Fr* [ʁwɑ̃]
rouge ruːʒ **rouged** ruːʒd **rouges** ˈruːʒ ɪz -əz **rouging** ˈruːʒ ɪŋ —*Fr* [ʁuʒ] **ˌrouge et ˈnoir** eɪ ˈnwɑː ‖ˈnwɑːr —*Fr* [e nwaːʁ]
rough rʌf *(= ruff)* **roughed** rʌft **rougher** ˈrʌf ə ‖ -ᵊr **roughest** ˈrʌf ɪst -əst **roughing** ˈrʌf ɪŋ **roughs** rʌfs **ˌrough ˈdiamond**; **ˌrough ˈpaper**; **ˈrough stuff**; **ˌrough ˈtrade**
Rough rʌf —*but* Rough Tor *in Cornwall is* raʊ
roughage ˈrʌf ɪdʒ
rough-and-ready ˌrʌf ᵊn ˈred i ◂ ᵊnd-
rough-and-tumble ˌrʌf ᵊn ˈtʌm bᵊl -ᵊnd-
roughcast ˈrʌf kɑːst §-kæst ‖ -kæst **~ing** ɪŋ **~s** s
rough-|dry ˈrʌf |draɪ ˌ·ˈ· **~dried** draɪd **~dries** draɪz **~drying** draɪ ɪŋ
roughen ˈrʌf ᵊn **~ed** d **~ing** ˌɪŋ **~s** z
rough-|hew ˌrʌf |ˈhjuː **~hewed** ˈhjuːd **~hewing** ˈhjuː ɪŋ **~hewn** ˈhjuːn ◂ **~hews** ˈhjuːz
roughhouse *n* ˈrʌf haʊs
roughish ˈrʌf ɪʃ **~ness** nəs nɪs
roughly ˈrʌf li
roughneck ˈrʌf nek **~s** s
roughness ˈrʌf nəs -nɪs **~es** ɪz əz
roughrider ˌrʌf ˈraɪd ə ˈ·ˌ·· ‖ -ᵊr **~s** z
roughshod ˈrʌf ʃɒd ‖ -ʃɑːd
Roughton *(i)* ˈraʊt ᵊn, *(ii)* ˈruːt ᵊn
roulade ru ˈlɑːd **~s** z
rouleau ˈruːl əʊ ‖ ru ˈloʊ **~s, ~x** z
rou|lette ru |ˈlet **~letted** ˈlet ɪd -əd ‖ ˈleṭ əd **~lettes** ˈlets **~letting** ˈlet ɪŋ ‖ ˈleṭ ɪŋ
Roumani|a ru ˈmeɪn i_|ə **~an/s** ən/z
round raʊnd **rounded** ˈraʊnd ɪd -əd **rounder** ˈraʊnd ə ‖ -ᵊr **roundest** ˈraʊnd ɪst -əst **rounding** ˈraʊnd ɪŋ **rounds** raʊndz **ˌround ˈbracket**; **ˌround ˈrobin**; **ˌRound ˈTable**; **ˌround ˈtrip**
roundabout *n, adj, prep* ˈraʊnd ə ˌbaʊt **~s** s
round-arm ˈraʊnd ɑːm ‖ -ɑːrm
rounded ˈraʊnd ɪd -əd **~ly** li **~ness** nəs nɪs
roundel ˈraʊnd ᵊl **~s** z
roundelay ˈraʊnd ə leɪ -ɪ-, -ᵊl eɪ **~s** z
rounders ˈraʊnd əz ‖ -ᵊrz
round-eyed ˌraʊnd ˈaɪd ◂
roundhand ˈraʊnd hænd
Roundhay ˈraʊnd eɪ -i —*There is also a spelling pronunciation* -heɪ.
Roundhead ˈraʊnd hed **~s** z
round|house ˈraʊnd |haʊs **~houses** haʊz ɪz -əz
roundish ˈraʊnd ɪʃ **~ness** nəs nɪs
round|ly ˈraʊnd |li **~ness** nəs nɪs
round-shouldered ˌraʊnd ˈʃəʊld əd ◂ →-ˈʃɒʊld- ‖ -ˈʃoʊld ᵊrd ◂
rounds|man ˈraʊndz |mən **~men** mən -men
round-table ˌraʊnd ˈteɪb ᵊl ◂ **ˌround-ˌtable diˈscussions**
round-the-clock ˌraʊnd ðə ˈklɒk ◂ ‖ -ˈklɑːk ◂
round-trip ˌraʊnd ˈtrɪp ◂ **ˌround-trip ˈticket**
roundup ˈraʊnd ʌp **~s** s
roundwood, R~ ˈraʊnd wʊd
roundworm ˈraʊnd wɜːm ‖ -wɜːm **~s** z
Rountree ˈraʊn triː
roup *bird disease* ruːp
Rourke rɔːk ‖ rɔːrk roʊrk
Rous raʊs
rouse raʊz **roused** raʊzd **rouses** ˈraʊz ɪz -əz **rousing/ly** ˈraʊz ɪŋ /li
Rouse raʊs
Rousseau ˈruːs əʊ ‖ ruː ˈsoʊ —*Fr* [ʁu so]
Roussillon ˌruːs iː ˈɒ̃ -ˈjɒ̃ ‖ -ˈjoʊn —*Fr* [ʁu si jɔ̃]
roust raʊst **rousted** ˈraʊst ɪd -əd **rousting** ˈraʊst ɪŋ **rousts** raʊsts
roustabout ˈraʊst ə ˌbaʊt **~s** s
rout, Rout raʊt **routed** ˈraʊt ɪd -əd ‖ ˈraʊṭ əd **routing** ˈraʊt ɪŋ ‖ ˈraʊṭ ɪŋ **routs** raʊts

ROUTE

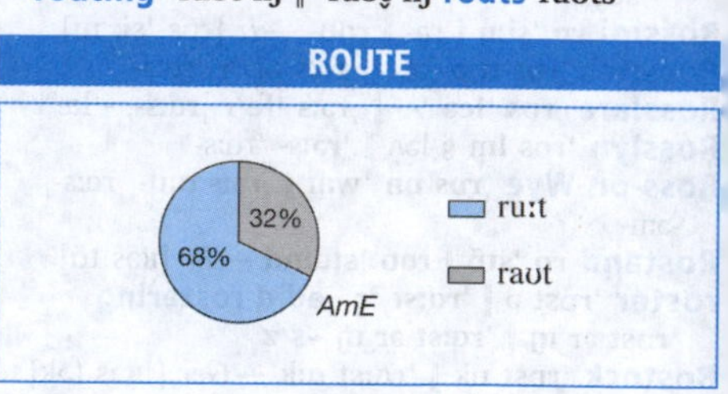

route ruːt raʊt —*in BrE the form* raʊt *is confined to army usage, but in AmE it is more widespread. — Preference poll, AmE:* ruːt *68%,* raʊt *32%.* **routed** ˈruːt ɪd -əd ‖ ˈruːṭ əd ˈraʊṭ- **routeing/s, routing/s** ˈruːt ɪŋ/z ‖ ˈruːṭ ɪŋ/z ˈraʊṭ- **routes** ruːts raʊts **ˈroute march**
router *'tool for hollowing'* ˈraʊt ə ‖ ˈraʊṭ ᵊr **~s** z
router *'computer networking device'* ˈruːt ə ‖ ˈruːṭ ᵊr ˈraʊṭ- **~s** z
Routh raʊθ
routine ˌruː ˈtiːn ◂ ru- **~ly** li **~s** z
Routledge ˈraʊt lɪdʒ ˈrʌt-, -ledʒ
roux *sing.* ruː *(= rue)* **roux** *pl* ruːz *or as sing.*
rove, Rove rəʊv ‖ roʊv **roved** rəʊvd ‖ roʊvd **roves** rəʊvz ‖ roʊvz **roving** ˈrəʊv ɪŋ ‖ ˈroʊv ɪŋ **ˌroving comˈmission**; **ˌroving ˈeye**
rover, Rover ˈrəʊv ə ‖ ˈroʊv ᵊr **~s, ~'s** z
row *'quarrel'* raʊ **rowed** raʊd **rowing** ˈraʊ_ɪŋ **rows** raʊz *(= rouse)*
row *v 'use oars', n 'line', 'trip in rowing boat',* **Row** *name of thoroughfare* rəʊ ‖ roʊ *(= roe)*

rowed rəʊd ‖ roʊd *(= road)* **rowing** ˈrəʊ ɪŋ ‖ ˈroʊ ɪŋ **rows** rəʊz ‖ roʊz *(= rose)*
ˈrow house; **ˈrowing boat**; **ˈrowing maˌchine**
Rowallan rəʊ ˈæl ən ‖ roʊ-
rowan, Rowan ˈrəʊ ən ˈraʊ‿ən ‖ ˈroʊ ən **~s** z
ˈrowan tree
rowanberr|y ˈrəʊ ən ˌber |i ˈraʊ‿ən-, →-əm- ‖ ˈroʊ- **~ies** iz
Rowant ˈraʊ‿ənt
rowboat ˈrəʊ bəʊt ‖ ˈroʊ boʊt **~s** s
Rowbotham, Rowbottom ˈrəʊ ˌbɒt əm ‖ ˈroʊ ˌbɑːṭ əm
rowd|y ˈraʊd |i **~ier** i‿ə ‖ i‿ᵊr **~ies** iz **~iest** i‿ɪst i‿əst **~ily** ɪ li əl i **~iness** i nəs i nɪs **~yism** i ˌɪz əm
Rowe rəʊ ‖ roʊ
rowel ˈraʊ‿əl raʊl ‖ ˈraʊ‿əl **~ed, ~led** d **~ing, ~ling** ɪŋ **~s** z
Rowena rəʊ ˈiːn ə ‖ roʊ-
Rowenta *tdmk* rəʊ ˈent ə ‖ roʊ ˈenṭ ə
rower ˈrəʊ ə ‖ ˈroʊ ᵊr **~s** z
Rowland ˈrəʊl ənd ‖ ˈroʊl-
Rowlands ˈrəʊl əndz ‖ ˈroʊl-
Rowlandson ˈrəʊl ənd sən ‖ ˈroʊl-
Rowley ˈrəʊl i ‖ ˈroʊl i —*but* R~ Regis *in WMids is* ˈraʊl i
Rowling ˈrəʊl ɪŋ →ˈrɒʊl- ‖ ˈroʊl ɪŋ —*This is appropriate for J. K. Rowling, author of the Harry Potter series.*
rowlock ˈrɒl ək ˈrʌl- ‖ ˈrɑːl-—*Also, but not among sailors,* ˈrəʊ lɒk ‖ ˈroʊ lɑːk **~s** s
Rowney *(i)* ˈraʊn i, *(ii)* ˈrəʊn i ‖ ˈroʊn i
Rowntree ˈraʊn triː
ˌRowntree ˈMackintosh *tdmk*
Rowridge ˈraʊ rɪdʒ
Rowse raʊs
Rowsley ˈrəʊz li ‖ ˈroʊz-
Rowton ˈraʊt ᵊn
Roxana rɒk ˈsɑːn ə ‖ rɑːk ˈsæn ə
Roxanna rɒk ˈsæn ə ‖ rɑːk-
Roxanne, r~ rɒk ˈsæn ‖ rɑːk-
Roxburgh ˈrɒks bər‿ə ‖ ˈrɑːks ˌbɜː oʊ
Roxy ˈrɒks i ‖ ˈrɑːks i
Roy rɔɪ
royal ˈrɔɪ‿əl **~s** z
ˌroyal ˈblue ◂; **ˌroyal ˈflush**; **ˌRoyal ˈHighness**; **ˌroyal preˈrogative**
royale, R~ rɔɪ ˈɑːl -ˈæl ‖ -ˈæl
royalism ˈrɔɪ‿əl ˌɪz əm
royalist ˈrɔɪ‿əl ɪst §-əst **~s** s
royally ˈrɔɪ‿əl i
royalty ˈrɔɪ‿əl ti
Royce rɔɪs
Royden, Roydon ˈrɔɪd ᵊn
Royle rɔɪᵊl
Royston ˈrɔɪst ən
Royton ˈrɔɪt ᵊn
Roz rɒz ‖ rɑːz
rozzer ˈrɒz ə ‖ ˈrɑːz ᵊr **~s** z
RP ˌɑː ˈpiː ‖ ˌɑːr-
rpm ˌɑː piː ˈem ‖ ˌɑːr-

-rrhagia ˈreɪdʒ i‿ə ˈreɪdʒ ə ‖ ˈreɪdʒ ə ˈreɪʒ ə — **menorrhagia** ˌmen ə ˈreɪdʒ i‿ə ˌ·ˈ·ə ‖ -ˈreɪdʒ ə -ˈreɪʒ-
-rrhaphy *stress-imposing* rəf i — **colporrhaphy** kɒl ˈpɒr əf i ‖ kɑːl ˈpɔːr- -ˈpɑːr-
-rrhea, -rrhoea ˈrɪə ˈriː‿ə ‖ ˈriː ə — **blenorrhea, blennorrhoea** ˌblen ə ˈrɪə -ˈriː‿ə ‖ -ˈriː ə
RSJ ˌɑːr es ˈdʒeɪ **~s** z
RSVP ˌɑːr es viː ˈpiː
Ruabon ru ˈæb ən —*Welsh* [riu ˈa bon]
Ruanda ru ˈænd ə ‖ -ˈɑːnd ə
Ruane ru ˈeɪn
Ruaridh ˈrʊər i ˈrɔːr- ‖ ˈrʊr i
rub rʌb **rubbed** rʌbd **rubbing/s** ˈrʌb ɪŋ/z **rubs** rʌbz
rub-a-dub ˈrʌb ə dʌb
rub-a-dub-dub ˌrʌb ə dʌb ˈdʌb
rubaiyat, rubáiyát, R~ ˈruː baɪ æt -jæt, -ɑːt, -jɑːt, ·ˈ· · ‖ -jɑːt
rubato ru ˈbɑːt əʊ ‖ -oʊ **~s** z
rubb... —*see* **rub**
rubber ˈrʌb ə ‖ ˈrʌb ᵊr **~s** z
ˌrubber ˈband; **ˈrubber boot**; **ˌrubber ˈdinghy**; **ˈrubber plant**; **ˌrubber ˈstamp**; **ˈrubber tree**
rubberis|e, rubberiz|e ˈrʌb ə raɪz **~ed** d **~es** ɪz əz **~ing** ɪŋ
rubberneck ˈrʌb ə nek ‖ -ᵊr- **~ed** t **~er/s** ə/z ‖ ᵊr/z **~ing** ɪŋ **~s** s
rubber-stamp ˌrʌb ə ˈstæmp ‖ ᵊr- **~ed** t **~ing** ɪŋ **~s** s
rubbery ˈrʌb ər i
rubbish ˈrʌb ɪʃ **~ed** t **~es** ɪz əz **~ing** ɪŋ
ˈrubbish bin
rubbishy ˈrʌb ɪʃ i
rubble ˈrʌb ᵊl
Rubbra ˈrʌb rə
rubdown ˈrʌb daʊn **~s** z
rube, Rube ruːb **rubes, Rube's** ruːbz
rubella ru ˈbel ə
Ruben ˈruːb ɪn -ən
Rubens ˈruːb ɪnz -ənz —*Dutch* [ˈryː bəns]
rubeola ru ˈbiː‿əl ə ˌruːb i ˈəʊl ə ‖ ˌruːb i ˈoʊl ə
Rubery ˈruːb ər i
rubesc|ence ru ˈbes |ᵊnᵗs **~ent** ᵊnt
Rubicon ˈruːb ɪk ən -ɪ kɒn, §-ə- ‖ -ɪ kɑːn
rubicund ˈruːb ɪk ənd §-ək-, -ɪ kʌnd, §-ə-
rubicundity ˌruːb ɪ ˈkʌnd ət i §-ə-, -ɪt i ‖ -əṭ i
rubidium ru ˈbɪd i‿əm
rubie... —*see* **ruby**
Rubik ˈruːb ɪk **~'s** s
Rubin ˈruːb ɪn §-ən
Rubinstein ˈruːb ɪn staɪn -ən-
ruble ˈruːb ᵊl **~s** z
rubric ˈruːb rɪk **~s** s
ruby, Ruby ˈruːb i **rubies** ˈruːb iz
RUC ˌɑː juː ˈsiː ‖ ˌɑːr-
ruche ruːʃ **ruched** ruːʃt **ruches** ˈruːʃ ɪz -əz
ruching ˈruːʃ ɪŋ
ruck rʌk **rucked** rʌkt **rucking** ˈrʌk ɪŋ **rucks** rʌks
ruckle ˈrʌk ᵊl **~s** z

R

rucksack 'rʌk sæk 'rʊk- **~s** s
ruckus 'rʌk əs **~es** ɪz əz
rucola 'ru:k əl ə
ruction 'rʌk ʃᵊn **~s** z
rudbeckia rʌd 'bek i‿ə →rʌb-, ˌru:d- **~s** z
Rudd, rudd rʌd **rudds** rʌdz
rudder 'rʌd ə ‖ -ᵊr **~ed** d **~s** z
rudderless 'rʌd ə ləs -lɪs, -ᵊl əs ‖ -ᵊr-
Ruddigore 'rʌd ɪ gɔ: ‖ -gɔ:r
ruddl|e 'rʌd ᵊl **~ed** d **~es** z **~ing** ‿ɪŋ
Ruddock, r~ 'rʌd ək **~s** s
rudd|y 'rʌd |i **~ier** i‿ə ‖ i‿ᵊr **~iest** i‿ɪst i‿əst **~ily** ɪ li əl i **~iness** i nəs i nɪs
rude ru:d **rudely** 'ru:d li **rudeness** 'ru:d nəs -nɪs **ruder** 'ru:d ə ‖ -ᵊr **rudest** 'ru:d ɪst -əst
Rudge rʌdʒ
Rudgwick 'rʌdʒ wɪk -ɪk
Rudi 'ru:d i
rudiment 'ru:d ɪ mənt -ə- **~s** s
rudi|mentary ˌru:d ɪ |'ment‿ər i ◂ ˌ·ə- **~mentarily** 'ment‿ər əl i -ɪ li; men 'ter əl i **~mentariness** 'ment‿ər i nəs -nɪs
Rudolf, Rudolph 'ru:d ɒlf ‖ -ɑ:lf
Rudy 'ru:d i
Rudyard 'rʌd jəd -jɑ:d; 'rʌdʒ əd ‖ -jᵊrd -jɑ:rd
rue ru: **rued** ru:d *(= rude)* **rues** ru:z **ruing** 'ru:‿ɪŋ
rueful 'ru: fᵊl -fʊl **~ly** ‿i **~ness** nəs nɪs
ruff, Ruff rʌf **ruffed** rʌft **ruffing** 'rʌf ɪŋ **ruffs** rʌfs
ruffian 'rʌf i‿ən **~ism** ‿ɪz əm **~ly** li **~s** z
ruffl|e 'rʌf ᵊl **~ed** d **~es** z **~ing** ‿ɪŋ
Rufflette *tdmk* ˌrʌf 'let ˌrʌf ᵊl 'et
Rufford 'rʌf əd ‖ -ᵊrd
rufous 'ru:f əs
Rufus 'ru:f əs
rug rʌg **rugs** rʌgz
Rugbeian rʌg 'bi:‿ən **~s** z
rugby, Rugby 'rʌg bi **ˌrugby 'football**; **ˌRugby 'League**; **ˌRugby 'Union**
Rugeley 'ru:dʒ li 'ru:ʒ-
rugged 'rʌg ɪd §-əd **~ly** li **~ness** nəs nɪs
rugger 'rʌg ə ‖ -ᵊr **'rugger ball**; **'rugger ˌplayer**
rugose 'ru:g əʊs -əʊz; ru 'gəʊs ‖ 'ru:g oʊs **~ly** li
rugosity ru: 'gɒs ət i -ɪt- ‖ -'gɑ:s əţ i
rugrat 'rʌg ræt **~s** s
Ruhr rʊə ‖ rʊᵊr —*Ger* [ʁu:ɐ]
ruin 'ru:‿ɪn §‿ən **~ed** d **~ing** ɪŋ **~s** z
ruination ˌru:‿ɪ 'neɪʃ ᵊn §‿ə-
ruinous 'ru:‿ɪn əs §‿ən- **~ly** li **~ness** nəs nɪs
Ruisdael 'raɪz dɑ:l 'ri:z-, -deɪᵊl —*Dutch* ['rœyz da:l]
Ruislip 'raɪs lɪp
rule, Rule ru:l **ruled** ru:ld **rules** ru:lz **ruling** 'ru:l ɪŋ **ˌrule of 'thumb**
rulebook 'ru:l bʊk §-bu:k **~s** s
ruler 'ru:l ə ‖ -ᵊr **~s** z
ruling 'ru:l ɪŋ **~s** z **ˌruling 'class**
rum rʌm **rummer** 'rʌm ə ‖ -ᵊr **rummest** 'rʌm ɪst -əst **rums** rʌmz
Rumani|a ru 'meɪn i‿|ə **~an/s** ən/z
rumba 'rʌm bə 'rʊm- ‖ 'ru:m- **~ed** d **rumbaing** 'rʌm bəʳ ɪŋ 'rʊm- ‖ -bə ɪŋ 'ru:m- **~s** z
Rumbelow 'rʌm bə ləʊ ‖ -loʊ
rumbl|e 'rʌm bᵊl **~ed** d **~es** z **~ing** ‿ɪŋ
rumbling 'rʌm blɪŋ **~ly** li **~s** z
Rumbold 'rʌm bəʊld →-bɒʊld ‖ -boʊld
rumbustious rʌm 'bʌs tʃəs -'bʌs ti‿əs, ⚠-'bʌs tʃu‿əs **~ly** li **~ness** nəs nɪs
Rumelia ru 'mi:l i‿ə
rum|en 'ru:m |en -ɪn, -ən **~ens** enz ɪnz, ənz **~ina** ɪn ə ən ə
Rumford 'rʌm fəd ‖ -fᵊrd
ruminant 'ru:m ɪn ənt -ən- **~s** s
rumi|nate 'ru:m ɪ |neɪt -ə- **~nated** neɪt ɪd -əd ‖ neɪţ əd **~nates** neɪts **~nating/ly** neɪt ɪŋ /li ‖ neɪţ ɪŋ /li
rumination ˌru:m ɪ 'neɪʃ ᵊn -ə- **~s** z
ruminative 'ru:m ɪ nət ɪv '·ə-, -neɪt ɪv ‖ -ə neɪţ ɪv **~ly** li
rumly 'rʌm li
rummag|e 'rʌm ɪdʒ **~ed** d **~er/s** ə/z ‖ ᵊr/z **~es** ɪz əz **~ing** ɪŋ **'rummage sale**
rummer 'rʌm ə ‖ -ᵊr **~s** z
rumm|y 'rʌm |i **~ier** i‿ə ‖ i‿ᵊr **~ies** iz **~iest** i‿ɪst ‿əst
rumness 'rʌm nəs -nɪs
rumor, rumour 'ru:m ə ‖ -ᵊr **~ed** d **rumoring, rumouring** 'ru:m ər ɪŋ **~s** z
rumormonger, rumourmonger 'ru:m ə ˌmʌŋ gə §-ˌmɒŋ- ‖ -ᵊr ˌmʌŋ gᵊr -ˌmɑ:ŋ- **~s** z
rump rʌmp **rumps** rʌm*ps* **ˌrump 'steak**
Rumpelstiltskin ˌrʌmp ᵊl 'stɪlt skɪn
rumpl|e 'rʌmp ᵊl **~ed** d **~es** z **~ing** ‿ɪŋ
Rumpole 'rʌmp əʊl →-ɒʊl ‖ -oʊl
rumpus 'rʌmp əs **~es** ɪz əz **'rumpus room**
Rumsfeld 'rʌmz feld -felt
run rʌn **ran** ræn **running** 'rʌn ɪŋ **runs** rʌnz
runabout 'rʌn ə ˌbaʊt **~s** s
runagate 'rʌn ə geɪt **~s** s
run-around 'rʌn ə ˌraʊnd
runaway 'rʌn ə ˌweɪ **~s** z
runcible 'rʌnᵗs əb ᵊl -ɪb-
Runcie 'rʌnᵗs i
Runciman 'rʌnᵗs ɪ mən
runcinate 'rʌnᵗs ɪn ət -ᵊn-, -ɪt; -ɪ neɪt, -ə-
Runcorn 'rʌn kɔ:n →'rʌŋ- ‖ -kɔ:rn
Rundall, Rundell, Rundle 'rʌnd ᵊl
run-down *adj* ˌrʌn 'daʊn ◂
rundown *n* 'rʌn daʊn **~s** z
rune ru:n **runes** ru:nz
rung rʌŋ **rungs** rʌŋz
runic 'ru:n ɪk
run-in *n* 'rʌn ɪn **~s** z
runnel 'rʌn ᵊl **~s** z
runner 'rʌn ə ‖ -ᵊr **~s** z **'runner bean**, ˌ· · '·

runn|er-up ˌrʌn |ər ˈʌp ‖ -|ər ˈʌp **~ers-up** əz ˈʌp ‖ ᵊrz ˈʌp
running ˈrʌn ɪŋ
ˈrunning board; **ˌrunning ˈjump**; **ˈrunning light**; **ˈrunning mate**; **ˌrunning ˈwater**
runn|y ˈrʌn |i **~ier** i‿ə ‖ i‿ᵊr **~iest** i‿ɪst i‿əst **~iness** i nəs -nɪs
Runnymede ˈrʌn i miːd
runoff, run-off ˈrʌn ɒf -ɔːf ‖ -ɔːf -ɑːf **~s** s
run-of-the-mill ˌrʌn əv ðə ˈmɪl ◂ -ə ðə-
run-on ˈrʌn ɒn ‖ -ɑːn -ɔːn **~s** z
run-out ˈrʌn aʊt **~s** s
runt rʌnt **runts** rʌnts
run-through ˈrʌn θruː **~s** z
runtish ˈrʌnt ɪʃ ‖ ˈrʌnt̬ ɪʃ
runt|y ˈrʌnt |i ‖ ˈrʌnt̬ |i **~iness** i nəs i nɪs
run-up ˈrʌn ʌp **~s** s
runway ˈrʌn weɪ **~s** z
Runyon ˈrʌn jən
rupee ˌruː ˈpiː ru- ‖ ˈruːp iː ru ˈpiː **~s** z
Rupert ˈruːp ət ‖ -ᵊrt
rupiah ru ˈpiː‿ə **~s** z
rupture ˈrʌp tʃə -ʃə ‖ -tʃᵊr **~d** d **~s** z **rupturing** ˈrʌp tʃər ɪŋ -ʃər‿ɪŋ
rural ˈrʊər əl ‖ ˈrʊr əl
ˌrural ˈdean
rurality ruᵊ ˈræl ət i -ɪt- ‖ -ət̬ i
rurally ˈrʊər əl i ‖ ˈrʊr əl i
ruridecanal ˌrʊər ɪ dɪ ˈkeɪn ᵊl ◂ ˌ·ə-, -dəˈ·- ‖ ˌrʊr-
Ruritani|a ˌrʊər ɪ ˈteɪn i‿|ə ˌ·ə- ‖ ˌrʊr- **~an/s** ən/z
ruse ruːz ‖ ruːs ruːz **ruses** ˈruːz ɪz -əz ‖ ˈruːs- ˈruːz-
rusé ˈruːz eɪ ‖ ruː ˈzeɪ *—Fr* [ʁy ze]
Rusedski ru ˈzet ski -ˈsed-, -ˈset-
rush, Rush rʌʃ **rushed** rʌʃt **rushes** ˈrʌʃ ɪz -əz **rushing/ly** ˈrʌʃ ɪŋ /li
ˈrush hour
Rushdie ˈrʊʃ di *—This is reportedly the writer* Salman R~'s *preference, though he is often referred to as* ˈrʌʃ di
rusher ˈrʌʃ ə ‖ -ᵊr **~s** z
rushlight ˈrʌʃ laɪt **~s** s
Rushmere ˈrʌʃ mɪə ‖ -mɪr
Rushmore ˈrʌʃ mɔː ‖ -mɔːr -moʊr
Rusholme ˈrʌʃ həʊm -əm ‖ -hoʊm
Rushton ˈrʌʃt ən
Rushworth ˈrʌʃ wɜːθ ‖ -wɜːθ
rush|y ˈrʌʃ |i **~ier** i‿ə ‖ i‿ᵊr **~iest** i‿ɪst i‿əst **~iness** i nəs i nɪs
rusk, Rusk rʌsk **rusks** rʌsks
Ruskin ˈrʌsk ɪn §-ən
Rusper ˈrʌsp ə ‖ -ᵊr
Russ rʌs
russe ruːs
Russel, Russell ˈrʌs ᵊl
russet ˈrʌs ɪt §-ət **~s** s
Russia ˈrʌʃ ə **~s, ~'s** z
Russian ˈrʌʃ ᵊn **~s** z
ˌRussian rouˈlette
Russianis... *—see* **Russianiz...**

Russianization, r~ ˌrʌʃ ən aɪ ˈzeɪʃ ᵊn -ɪˈ·- ‖ -əˈ·-
Russianiz|e, r~ ˈrʌʃ ə naɪz -ᵊn aɪz **~ed** d **~er/s** ə/z ‖ ᵊr/z **~es** ɪz əz **~ing** ɪŋ
Russianness ˈrʌʃ ᵊn nəs -nɪs
Russification ˌrʌs ɪf ɪ ˈkeɪʃ ᵊn ˌ·əf-, §-əˈ·-
Russi|fy ˈrʌs ɪ |faɪ -ə- **~fied** faɪd **~fies** faɪz **~fying** faɪ ɪŋ
Russk|i, Russk|y ˈrʌsk i **~ies** iz
Russo- ¦rʌs əʊ ‖ -oʊ — **Russo-Japanese** ˌrʌs əʊ ˌdʒæp ə ˈniːz ‖ ˌrʌs oʊ-
rust, Rust rʌst **rusted** ˈrʌst ɪd -əd **rusting** ˈrʌst ɪŋ **rusts** rʌsts
ˈrust belt
rustbucket ˈrʌst ˌbʌkɪt §-ət **~s** s
rustic ˈrʌst ɪk **~s** s
rusti|cate ˈrʌst ɪ |keɪt §-ə- **~cated** keɪt ɪd -əd ‖ keɪt̬ əd **~cates** keɪts **~cating** keɪt ɪŋ ‖ keɪt̬ ɪŋ
rustication ˌrʌst ɪ ˈkeɪʃ ᵊn §-ə- **~s** z
rusticity rʌ ˈstɪs ət i -ɪt i ‖ -ət̬ i
rustl|e ˈrʌs ᵊl **~ed** d **~es** z **~ing** ‿ɪŋ
rustler ˈrʌs lə ˈrʌs ᵊl‿ə ‖ -lᵊr **~s** z
rustless ˈrʌst ləs -lɪs
rustling ˈrʌs ᵊl‿ɪŋ **~ly** li
Ruston ˈrʌst ən
rustproof ˈrʌst pruːf §-prʊf **~ed** t **~ing** ɪŋ **~s** s
rust|y, Rusty ˈrʌst |i **~ier** i‿ə ‖ i‿ᵊr **~iest** i‿ɪst i‿əst **~ily** ɪ li əl i **~iness** i nəs i nɪs
Ruswarp ˈrʌs əp ‖ -ᵊrp
rut rʌt **ruts** rʌts **rutted** ˈrʌt ɪd -əd ‖ ˈrʌt̬ əd **rutting** ˈrʌt ɪŋ ‖ ˈrʌt̬ ɪŋ
rutabaga ˌruːt ə ˈbeɪg ə ˌrʊt-, ˈ· ·ˌ· · ‖ ˌruːt̬- **~s** z
Rutgers ˈrʌt gəz ‖ -gᵊrz
Ruth, ruth ruːθ
Rutheni|a ru ˈθiːn i‿|ə **~an/s** ən/z
ruthenic ru ˈθen ɪk -ˈθiːn-
ruthenium ru ˈθiːn i‿əm
Rutherford, r~ ˈrʌð ə fəd ‖ -ᵊr fᵊrd **~s, ~'s** z
rutherfordium ˌrʌð ə ˈfɔːd i‿əm ‖ ˌ·ᵊr ˈfɔːrd- -ˈfoʊrd-
Rutherglen ˈrʌð ə glen ‖ -ᵊr- *—locally* -glən
Ruthie ˈruːθ i
Ruthin ˈrɪθ ɪn *—also, from those unfamiliar with the name, a spelling pronunciation* ˈruːθ-. *—Welsh* Rhuthun [ˈhrɨ θɨn, ˈhri θin]
ruthless ˈruːθ ləs -lɪs **~ly** li **~ness** nəs nɪs
Ruthven *(i)* ˈrɪv ᵊn, *(ii)* ˈruːθ v ən, *(iii)* ˈrʌθ vən *—The place in Tayside, and the Baron, are (i); the place in Grampian and the loch are (iii).*
rutilant ˈruːt ɪl ənt -əl- ‖ ˈruːt̬ ᵊl-
rutile ˈruːt aɪᵊl ‖ -iːᵊl -aɪᵊl
Rutland ˈrʌt lənd
Rutledge ˈrʌt lɪdʒ
rutt... *—see* **rut, rutty**
Rutter ˈrʌt ə ‖ ˈrʌt̬ ᵊr
ruttish ˈrʌt ɪʃ ‖ ˈrʌt̬ ɪʃ **~ly** li **~ness** nəs nɪs
rutt|y ˈrʌt |i ‖ ˈrʌt̬ |i **~ier** i‿ə ‖ i‿ᵊr **~iest** i‿ɪst ‿əst **~iness** i nəs -nɪs
Ruud ruːd *—Dutch* [ʁyːt]
Ruwenzori ˌruː‿ən ˈzɔːr i -en- ‖ -ˈzoʊr-

R

Ruysdael 'raɪz dɑːl 'riːz-, -deɪᵊl —*Dutch* ['rœyz daːl]
Ruyter 'raɪt ə ‖ 'raɪţ ᵊr —*Dutch* ['rœy tər]
Rwand|a ru 'ænd |ə -'ɒnd- ‖ -'ɑːnd- **~an/s** ən/z
-ry +ri — **heraldry** 'her əldr i
Ryan 'raɪ‿ən
Ryanair *tdmk* 'raɪ‿ən eə ˌ·-'· ‖ -eᵊr
Rycroft 'raɪ krɒft ‖ -krɔːft -krɑːft
Rydal 'raɪd ᵊl
Ryde raɪd
Ryder 'raɪd ə ‖ -ᵊr
rye, Rye raɪ **ryes** raɪz
rye-grass 'raɪ grɑːs §-græs ‖ -græs **~es** ɪz əz
Ryeland, Ryland 'raɪ lənd
Rylands 'raɪ ləndz
Ryle raɪᵊl
Ryman 'raɪm ən
ryot 'raɪ‿ət *(= riot)* **~s** s
Ryton 'raɪt ᵊn
Ryukyu ri 'uː kjuː —*Jp* [ɾjɯˌɯ 'kjɯɯ] **~s** z
Ryvita *tdmk* ₍ˌ₎raɪ 'viːt ə ‖ -'viːţ ə
Rzeszów 'ʒeʃ uːv —*Polish* ['ʒɛ ʃuf]

R

Ss

s Spelling-to-sound

1 Where the spelling is **s**, the pronunciation is regularly
s as in **sense** senˈs ('voiceless S') or
z as in **rises** ˈraɪz ɪz ('voiced S').
Less frequently, it is
ʒ as in **pleasure** ˈpleʒ ə ‖ ˈpleʒ ᵊr.
s may also form part of the digraphs **sh** or **si**, and of **sc** or **sch** (see under **c**).

2 At the beginning of a word, the pronunciation is regularly s as in **say** seɪ, **sleep** sliːp, **stand** stænd. (In this position, with spelling **s**, the pronunciation is never z.) This also applies in compounds, for example **insight** ˈɪn saɪt.
Exceptionally, the pronunciation is ʃ at the beginning of the words **sure** ʃɔː ʃʊə ‖ ʃʊᵊr ʃɜː and **sugar** ˈʃʊɡ ə ‖ ˈʃʊɡ ᵊr and their derivatives (for example: **assurance**, **sugary**).

3 In the middle of a word, it is necessary to take account of the letters on either side of the **s**.

- Where **s** is between a vowel letter and a consonant letter, the pronunciation is usually s if the following consonant sound is voiceless, z if it is voiced. Thus:
  s in **taste** teɪst
  z in **wisdom** ˈwɪz dəm.
  Before silent **t**, however, the pronunciation is s as in **listen** ˈlɪs ᵊn.
- Where **s** is between two vowel letters, the pronunciation may be either
  s as in **basin** ˈbeɪs ᵊn, **crisis** ˈkraɪs ɪs or
  z as in **poison** ˈpɔɪz ᵊn, **easy** ˈiːz i.
  There is no rule: each word must be considered separately.
  Where the spelling is **s** between a vowel and **ion**, **ual**, **ure**, the pronunciation is mostly ʒ as in **explosion** ɪk ˈspləʊʒ ᵊn ‖ ɪk ˈsploʊʒ ᵊn (silent **i**), **usual** ˈjuːʒ ᵊl, **pleasure** ˈpleʒ ə ‖ ˈpleʒ ᵊr.
  Where the spelling is **s** between a vowel and **ia**, **ian**, speakers vary: some use ʃ, some use ʒ as in **Asia** ˈeɪʃ ə or ˈeɪʒ ə (silent **i**).
- Where **s** follows a consonant letter, the pronunciation is usually s in **ls**, **ns**, **rs** or if the preceding sound is voiceless, but z otherwise. Thus:
  s in **consider** kən ˈsɪd ə ‖ -ᵊr, **cursor** ˈkɜːs ə ‖ ˈkɜːs ᵊr, **gipsy** ˈdʒɪps i
  z in **clumsy** ˈklʌmz i, **observe** əb ˈzɜːv ‖ əb ˈzɜːv.
  Compare **insist** ɪn ˈsɪst and **resist** ri ˈzɪst. However, in some words both pronunciations are in use, for example

absorb -ˈsɔːb ‖ -ˈsɔːrb or -ˈzɔːb ‖ -ˈzɔːrb, **translate** -ns- or -nz-.

Where the spelling has **s** between **l**, **n**, **r** and **ion**, **ial**, **ure**, the pronunciation is correspondingly ʃ (with **i** silent) as in **expulsion** ɪk ˈspʌlʃ ən, **tension** ˈtenᵗʃ ən, **controversial** ˌkɒntr ə ˈvɜːʃ əl ‖ ˌkɑːntr ə ˈvɜːʃ əl. However, in **-ersion**, **-ersia(n)** AmE has ʒ as in **Persian** ˈpɜːʃ ən ‖ ˈpɜːʒ ən.

4 Where the spelling has **s** at the end of a word, or before silent **e** at the end of a word, the pronunciation may be either

s as in **gas** gæs, **loose** luːs, **case** keɪs or

z as in **has** hæz, **choose** tʃuːz, **phrase** freɪz.

For **s** in **lse**, **nse**, **rse**, the pronunciation is usually

s as in **else** els, **immense** ɪ ˈmenᵗs, **horse** hɔːs ‖ hɔːrs.

Beyond this, there is no rule: each word must be considered separately. Sometimes there is a distinction between related parts of speech that are spelled identically, as with **use** (juːs noun, juːz verb) and **close** (kləʊs ‖ kloʊs adjective, kləʊz ‖ kloʊz verb). (But there are also cases with no such distinction as in **promise** and **base**, always with s.) There is a BrE–AmE difference in the word **erase** ɪ ˈreɪz ‖ ɪ ˈreɪs.

5 The inflectional endings **-s**, **-es** are discussed in their alphabetic places.

6 Where the spelling has double **ss**, the pronunciation is regularly

s as in **lesson** ˈles ən, **kiss** kɪs.

Exceptionally, it is

z, notably in the words **dessert** dɪ ˈzɜːt ‖ dɪ ˈzɜːt, **possess** pə ˈzes, **scissors** ˈsɪz əz ‖ ˈsɪz ərz and their derivatives.

In **ssion**, **ssia**, **ssian**, **ssure**, it is

ʃ as in **mission** ˈmɪʃ ən, **pressure** ˈpreʃ ə ‖ ˈpreʃ ər.

7 **s** is silent in various words, including **island** ˈaɪl ənd and several words of French origin, among them **corps** kɔː ‖ kɔːr, **aisle** aɪl, **debris** ˈdeb riː ‖ də ˈbriː, **précis** ˈpreɪs iː ‖ preɪ ˈsiː, **viscount** ˈvaɪ kaʊnt, **Grosvenor** ˈgrəʊv nə ‖ ˈgroʊv nər, **Illinois** -ˈnɔɪ.

8 The sound s is also often written **c**, **sc** before **e**, **i**, **y**.

S

sh Spelling-to-sound

1 Where the spelling is the digraph **sh**, the pronunciation is regularly ʃ as in **sheep** ʃiːp, **fish** fɪʃ.

2 **sh** is not a digraph in words such as **mishap** ˈmɪs hæp. The spelling of certain proper names has been reinterpreted in pronunciation so as to make **sh** a digraph: **Lewisham** was once **Lewis** plus **ham**, but is now ˈluː‿ɪʃ əm.

3 ʃ is also written in a number of other ways, including those represented in the examples **ocean**, **machine**, **precious**, **sugar**, **conscience**, **compulsion**, **pressure**, **mission**, **creation**.

S, s es **S's, s's, Ss** 'es ɪz -əz —*Communications code name:* Sierra
ˌS'I ˌunit; **ˌS(ˌ)V'O ˌlanguage**

-s, -es *pl ending; 3rd sing. present ending,* **-'s** *possessive sing. ending;* **-s', -es'** *possessive pl ending* **s, z, ɪz** əz —*There are three regular pronunciations: After a sibilant (***s, z, ʃ, ʒ, tʃ, dʒ***), the pronunciation is* **ɪz** *or, less commonly in BrE but usually in AmE,* **əz**, *as* faces **'feɪs ɪz** -əz, Mitch's **'mɪtʃ ɪz** -əz. *(In singing, exceptionally, a strong-vowelled variant ez is usual if the spelling is es, as* **'feɪs ez.***) Otherwise, after a voiced consonant (***b, d, g, v, ð, m, n, ŋ, l,** *AmE* **r***) or a vowel sound, the pronunciation is* **z**, *as* names, name's **neɪmz**; *after a voiceless consonant (***p, t, k, f, θ***), the pronunciation is* **s**, *as* cats, cat's **kæts**.
—Certain nouns whose last sound is a voiceless fricative switch it to a voiced fricative before the plural and plural possessive endings. The ending naturally then takes the form **z**. *The change is shown in spelling in the case of* **f —v** *(*wife **waɪf** — wives, wives' **waɪvz***), but not for* **θ —ð, s —z** *(*mouth **maʊθ** — mouths, mouths' **maʊðz***). In the possessive sing. and with the contracted forms of* is *and* has, *there is no such change (*wife's **waɪfs**, mouth's **maʊθs***).*
—With proper names ending in a sibilant, usage varies. Usually, the possessive is pronounced regularly, though the spelling may vary: Jones' , Jones's **'dʒəʊnz ɪz** ‖ **'dʒoʊnz əz**. *Less commonly, the possessive ending is unpronounced (***dʒəʊnz** ‖ **dʒoʊnz***); the corresponding spelling is then* Jones'.

-'s *contracted form of* **is** **s, z, ɪz** —*The rules are identical to those for the 3rd sing. present ending (except that it is not usually used after a sibilant and that there is no strong-vowelled variant):* the boy's asleep **ðə ˌbɔɪz ə 'sliːp**

-'s *contracted form of* **has** **s, z, əz** —*The rules are identical to those for the 3rd sing. present ending:* the boy's begun **ðə ˌbɔɪz bɪ 'gʌn** *—except that on the rare occasions when it is used after a sibilant the pronunciation is* **əz:** the bus's arrived **ðə ˌbʌs əz ə 'raɪvd**

s.a.e. ˌes eɪ 'iː

Saab *tdmk* **sɑːb Saabs sɑːbz**

saag sɑːg

Saami 'sɑːm i

Saar sɑː ‖ sɑːr —*Ger* [zaːɐ]

Saarbrücken ˌsɑː 'brʊk ən '· · · ‖ ˌsɑːr- '· · · —*Ger* [zaːɐ 'bʁʏk ᵊn]

Saarland 'sɑː lænd ‖ 'sɑːr- —*Ger* ['zaːɐ lant]

Saatchi 'sɑːtʃ i

Saba *ancient kingdom in Arabia* 'seɪb ə 'sɑːb ə

Saba *island in the Caribbean* 'seɪb ə —*though some reference books wrongly claim it is* 'sɑːb ə *or* 'sæb ə

sabadilla ˌsæb ə 'dɪl ə

Sabaean sə 'biː‿ən **~s** z

Sabah *territory in Malaysia* 'sɑːb ə -ɑː

Sabaoth 'sæb eɪ ɒθ -i-; sæ 'beɪ ɒθ, sə-, -əθ ‖ -ɑːθ -ɔːθ

Sabatier sə 'bæt i eɪ ‖ ˌsɑːb ɑː 'tjeɪ —*Fr* [sa ba tje]

Sabatini ˌsæb ə 'tiːn i

sabbatarian, S~ ˌsæb ə 'teər i‿ən ◂ ‖ -'ter- **~s** z

Sabbath 'sæb əθ **~s** s

sabbatical, S~ sə 'bæt ɪk ᵊl ‖ -'bæṭ- **~s** z
sabˌbatical 'year

Sabean sə 'biː‿ən **~s** z

Sabellian sə 'bel i‿ən **~s** z

Sabena *tdmk* sə 'biːn ə sæ- —*Fr* [sa be na]

saber... —*see* **sabre...**

Sabian 'seɪb i‿ən **~s** z

sabin 'seɪb ɪn §-ən **~s** z

Sabin *(i)* 'seɪb ɪn §-ən, *(ii)* 'sæb-

Sabina sə 'biːn ə

Sabine *family name(i)* 'sæb aɪn, *(ii)* 'seɪb aɪn -ɪn, §-ən —*Usually (i) in Britain, (ii) in US*

Sabine *ancient people and language* 'sæb aɪn ‖ 'seɪb- **~s** z

Sabine *river, lake and pass in the US* sə 'biːn

sabir, Sabir sə 'bɪə sæ- ‖ -'bɪᵊr

sable 'seɪb ᵊl **~s** z

sabot 'sæb əʊ ‖ -oʊ sæ 'boʊ, sə- —*Fr* [sa bo] **~s** z

sabotag|e *n, v* 'sæb ə tɑːʒ -tɑːdʒ **~ed** d **~es** ɪz əz **~ing** ɪŋ

saboteur ˌsæb ə 'tɜː '· · · ‖ -'tɜː -'tʊᵊr **~s** z

sabra, Sabra 'sɑːb rə **~s** z

sab|re, sab|er 'seɪb |ə ‖ -|ᵊr **~red, ~ered** əd ‖ ᵊrd **~res, ~ers** əz ‖ ᵊrz **~ring, ~ering** ər‿ɪŋ

sabre-rattling, saber-rattling 'seɪb ə ˌræt ᵊl‿ɪŋ ‖ -ᵊr ˌræṭ-

sabretach|e 'sæb ə tæʃ -tɑːʃ **~es** ɪz əz

sabre-toothed, saber-toothed ˌseɪb ə 'tuːθt ◂ §-'tʊθt ‖ ᵊr-
ˌsabre-toothed 'tiger

Sabrina sə 'briːn ə -'braɪn-

sac sæk *(= sack)* **sacs** sæks

Sacajawea ˌsæk ədʒ ə 'wiː‿ə

saccade sæ 'kɑːd sə-, -'keɪd **~s** z

saccharide 'sæk ə raɪd **~s** z

S

saccharin, saccharine *n* ˈsæk ər‿ɪn §-ər‿ən, -ə riːn **~s** z
saccharine *adj* ˈsæk ə riːn -raɪn, -ər‿ɪn, §-ər‿ən **~ly** li
Sacco ˈsæk əʊ ‖ -oʊ
saccule ˈsæk juːl **~s** z
sacerdotal ˌsæs ə ˈdəʊt əl ◂ ˌsæk- ‖ -ər ˈdoʊṭ əl ◂ **~ly** i
Sacha ˈsæʃ ə
sachem ˈseɪtʃ əm
sachet ˈsæʃ eɪ ‖ sæ ˈʃeɪ *(*)* **~s** z
Sacheverell sə ˈʃev ər‿əl
Sachs sæks *—but as a German name,* zæks ‖ zɑːks *—Ger* [zaks]
sack sæk **sacked** sækt **sacking** ˈsæk ɪŋ **sacks** sæks
ˈsack race
sackbut ˈsæk bʌt **~s** s
sackcloth ˈsæk klɒθ -klɔːθ ‖ -klɔːθ -klɑːθ
Sacker ˈsæk ə ‖ -ər
sackful ˈsæk fʊl **~s** z **sacksful** ˈsæks fʊl
sacking ˈsæk ɪŋ **~s** z
sackload ˈsæk ləʊd **~s** z
Sacks sæks
Sackville ˈsæk vɪl -vəl
ˌSackville-ˈWest
sacral ˈseɪk rəl ˈsæk- *—Some speakers (esp. AmE) distinguish between* ˈseɪk- *'holy' and* ˈsæk- *'of the sacrum'.*
sacrament, S~ ˈsæk rə mənt **~s** s
sacramental ˌsæk rə ˈment əl ◂ ‖ -ˈmenṭ əl ◂ **~ly** i
Sacramento ˌsæk rə ˈment əʊ ‖ -ˈmenṭ oʊ
sacred ˈseɪk rɪd -rəd **~ly** li **~ness** nəs nɪs
ˌsacred ˈcow; **Sacred ˈHeart**
sacrific|e *n, v* ˈsæk rɪ faɪs -rə- **~ed** t **~es** ɪz əz **~ing** ɪŋ
sacrificial ˌsæk rɪ ˈfɪʃ əl ◂ -rə- **~ly** i
sacrilege ˈsæk rəl ɪdʒ -rɪl-
sacrilegious ˌsæk rə ˈlɪdʒ əs ◂ -rɪ- **~ly** li **~ness** nəs nɪs
sacring ˈseɪk rɪŋ
sacristan ˈsæk rɪst ən -rəst- **~s** z
sacrist|y ˈsæk rɪst |i -rəst- **~ies** iz
sacroiliac ˌseɪk rəʊ ˈɪl i æk ˌsæk- ‖ ˌ·roʊ-
sacrosanct ˈsæk rəʊ sæŋ*k*t ‖ -roʊ- **~ness** nəs nɪs
sacrosanctity ˌsæk rəʊ ˈsæŋ*k*t ət i -ɪt i ‖ -roʊ ˈsæŋ*k*t əṭ i
sac|rum ˈseɪk |rəm ˈsæk- ‖ ˈsæk- ˈseɪk- **~ra** rə
sad sæd **sadder** ˈsæd ə ‖ -ər **saddest** ˈsæd ɪst -əst
Sadat sə ˈdæt ‖ -ˈdɑːt sɑː- *—Arabic* [saː daːt]
Saddam sə ˈdæm ₍ˌ₎sæ-, -ˈdɑːm, ˈsæd əm *—Arabic* [sɑdˤ ˈdˤɑm]
sadden ˈsæd ən **~ed** d **~ing/ly** ɪŋ /li **~s** z
saddl|e ˈsæd əl **~ed** d **~es** z **~ing** ‿ɪŋ
ˈsaddle soap; **ˈsaddle stitch**
saddleback ˈsæd əl bæk **~s** s
saddlebag ˈsæd əl bæg **~s** z
saddlecloth ˈsæd əl klɒθ -klɔːθ ‖ -klɔːθ -klɑːθ
saddler, S~ ˈsæd lə ‖ -lər **~s** z
saddlery ˈsæd lər i
saddle-sore ˈsæd əl sɔː ‖ -sɔːr -soʊr
saddo ˈsæd əʊ ‖ -oʊ **~s** z
Sadducee ˈsæd ju siː ‖ ˈsædʒ ə siː ˈsæd jə- **~s** z
Sade *French writer* sɑːd *—Fr* [sad]
Sade *singer* ˈʃɑː deɪ
sadhu ˈsɑːd uː **~s** z
Sadie ˈseɪd i
ˌSadie ˈHawkins Day
sadiron ˈsæd ˌaɪ‿ən ‖ -ˌaɪ‿ərn **~s** z
sadism ˈseɪd ˌɪz əm ‖ ˈsæd-
sadist ˈseɪd ɪst §-əst ‖ ˈsæd- **~s** s
sadistic sə ˈdɪst ɪk **~ally** əl‿i
Sadleir, Sadler ˈsæd lə ‖ -lər
ˌSadler's ˈWells
sad|ly ˈsæd |li **~ness** nəs nɪs
sadomasochism ˌseɪd əʊ ˈmæs ə ˌkɪz əm -ˈmæz- ‖ ·oʊ- ˌsæd-
sadomasochistic ˌseɪd əʊ ˌmæs ə ˈkɪst ɪk -ˌmæz- ‖ ·oʊ- ˌsæd-
safari sə ˈfɑːr i **~s** z
saˈfari park; **saˈfari suit**
safe seɪf **safer** ˈseɪf ə ‖ -ər **safes** seɪfs **safest** ˈseɪf ɪst -əst
ˌsafe ˈhouse; **ˈsafe ˌperiod**; **ˌsafe ˈsex**
safebreaker ˈseɪf ˌbreɪk ə ‖ -ər **~s** z
safe-conduct ˌseɪf ˈkɒn dʌkt -dəkt ‖ -ˈkɑːn- **~s** s
safe-cracker ˈseɪf ˌkræk ə ‖ -ər **~s** z
safe-deposit ˈseɪf di ˌpɒz ɪt -də-, §-ət, ˌ·ˈ·· ‖ -ˌpɑːz ət **~s** s
ˈsafe-deˌposit box
safeguard ˈseɪf gɑːd ‖ -gɑːrd **~ed** ɪd əd **~ing** ɪŋ **~s** z
safekeeping ˌseɪf ˈkiːp ɪŋ
safely ˈseɪf li
safe|ty ˈseɪf |ti §ˈseɪf ə|t i **~ties** tiz
ˈsafety belt; **ˈsafety catch**; **ˈsafety ˌcurtain**; **ˈsafety-deˌposit ˌbox**; **ˈsafety glass**; **ˈsafety ˌhelmet**; **ˈsafety ˌisland**; **ˈsafety lamp**; **ˈsafety match**; **ˈsafety net**; **ˈsafety pin**; **ˈsafety ˌrazor**; **ˈsafety valve**
safety-first ˌseɪf ti ˈfɜːst ◂ ‖ -ˈfɜːst ◂
Safeway *tdmk* ˈseɪf weɪ **~'s** z
Saffa ˈsæf ə **~s** z
safflower ˈsæf laʊ‿ə ‖ -laʊ‿ər
saffron, S~ ˈsæf rən
Safire ˈsæf aɪ‿ə ‖ ˈsæf aɪ‿ər
sag sæg **sagged** sægd **sagging** ˈsæg ɪŋ **sags** sægz
saga ˈsɑːg ə **~s** z
sagacious sə ˈgeɪʃ əs **~ly** li **~ness** nəs nɪs
sagacity sə ˈgæs ət i -ɪt- ‖ -əṭ i
sagamore ˈsæg ə mɔː ‖ -mɔːr -moʊr **~s** z
Sagan *British/American family name* ˈseɪg ən *—but the French name is* [sa gɑ̃]
Sagar ˈseɪg ə ‖ -ər
sage seɪdʒ **sager** ˈseɪdʒ ə ‖ -ər **sages** ˈseɪdʒ ɪz -əz **sagest** ˈseɪdʒ ɪst -əst
ˌsage ˈgreen◂
sagebrush ˈseɪdʒ brʌʃ
sagely ˈseɪdʒ li
Sager ˈseɪg ə ‖ -ər

saggar, sagger ˈsæɡ ə ‖ -ᵊr **~s** z
sagg|y ˈsæɡ |i **~ier** i‿ə ‖ i‿ᵊr **~iest** i‿ɪst i‿əst **~iness** i nəs i nɪs
Saginaw ˈsæɡ ɪ nɔː -ə- ‖ -nɑː
sagitta, S~ sə ˈdʒɪt ə -ˈɡɪt- ‖ -ˈdʒɪţ ə
sagittal ˈsædʒ ɪt ᵊl §-ət-; sə ˈdʒɪt ᵊl ‖ -əţ ᵊl **~ly** i
Sagittari|us ˌsædʒ ɪ ˈteər i‿|əs ˌ·ə- ‖ -ˈter- **~an/s** ən/z
sago ˈseɪɡ əʊ ‖ -oʊ
saguaro sə ˈɡwɑːr əʊ -ˈwɑːr- ‖ -oʊ -ə **~s** z
Saguenay ˌsæɡ ə ˈneɪ ◂
Sahaptin sɑː ˈhæpt ɪn sə-, §-ən **~s** z
Sahar|a sə ˈhɑːr |ə ‖ -ˈhær |ə -ˈher-, -ˈhɑːr- **~an** ən
Sahel sə ˈhel sɑː-
sahib sɑːb ˈsɑː hɪb, -ɪb, -iːb **~s** z
said sed §seɪd *(!)*
Said *place* saɪd sɑː ˈiːd —*Arabic* [sɑ ʕiːd]
saiga ˈsaɪɡ ə
Saigon ˌsaɪ ˈɡɒn ‖ -ˈɡɑːn
sail seɪᵊl **sailed** seɪᵊld **sailing/s** ˈseɪᵊl ɪŋ/z **sails** seɪᵊlz
ˈsailing boat; **ˈsailing ship**
sailboard ˈseɪᵊl bɔːd ‖ -bɔːrd -boʊrd **~ing** ɪŋ **~s** z
sailboat ˈseɪᵊl bəʊt ‖ -boʊt **~s** s
sailcloth ˈseɪᵊl klɒθ -klɔːθ ‖ -klɔːθ -klɑːθ
sailfish ˈseɪᵊl fɪʃ
sailor ˈseɪl ə ˈseɪᵊl- ‖ -ᵊr **~s** z
ˈsailor suit
sailplane ˈseɪᵊl pleɪn **~s** z
sainfoin ˈsæn fɔɪn ˈseɪn-
Sainsbury ˈseɪnz bər‿i ‖ -ˌber i **~'s** z
saint, Saint *strong form* seɪnt, *weak form* sᵊnt —*but in French names* sæ̃ —*Fr* [sæ̃]. —*For the common noun and family name, only the strong form is used. For the title before a name the weak form is usual in BrE but not in AmE.* **sainted** ˈseɪnt ɪd -əd ‖ ˈseɪnţ əd **saints, Saints** seɪnts —*For names beginning* Saint —*see under* **St-**
ˈsaint's day
Saint-Etienne, Saint-Étienne ˌsænt et i ˈen ˌ·eɪ- —*Fr* [sæ̃ te tjɛn]
sainthood ˈseɪnt hʊd
Saint John *place in New Brunswick* seɪnt ˈdʒɒn ‖ -ˈdʒɑːn
saint|ly ˈseɪnt |li **~lier** li‿ə ‖ li‿ᵊr **~liest** li‿ɪst ‿əst **~liness** li nəs -nɪs
saintpaulia sᵊnt ˈpɔːl i‿ə →sᵊm-, ˌseɪnt- ‖ ˌseɪnt- -ˈpɑːl- **~s** z
Saint-Saens, Saint-Saëns ˌsæ̃ ˈsɒ̃s -ˈsɒ̃ ‖ ˌsæn ˈsɑːn -ˈsɑːns —*Fr* [sæ̃ sɑ̃ːs]
Saintsbury ˈseɪnts bər‿i ‖ -ˌber i
Saipan ˌsaɪ ˈpæn
Saisho *tdmk* ˈseɪʃ əʊ ‖ -oʊ
saith seθ seɪθ; ˈseɪ ɪθ, -əθ
saithe seɪθ seɪð
sake *'advantage, purpose'* seɪk **sakes** seɪks
for ˌgoodness ˈsake, · ˈ· · ·
sake *'alcoholic drink'* ˈsɑːk i -eɪ —*Jp* [sa ˌke]
saker ˈseɪk ə ‖ -ᵊr **~s** z

Sakhalin ˈsæk ə liːn ˈsɑːk-, -lɪn, ˌ· ·ˈ· —*Russ* [sə xʌ ˈlʲin]
Sakharov ˈsæk ə rɒf -rɒv ‖ ˈsɑːk ə rɔːf ˈsæk-, -rɑːf —*Russ* [ˈsa xə rəf, sʌ ˈxa rəf] —*The physicist* Andrei S~ *was* [ˈsa xə rəf]
saki, Saki ˈsɑːk i **~s** z
Saks sæks
sal, Sal sæl
ˌsal amˈmoniac
salaam sə ˈlɑːm sæ- **~ed** d **~ing** ɪŋ **~s** z
salable ˈseɪl əb ᵊl
salacious sə ˈleɪʃ əs **~ly** li **~ness** nəs nɪs
salacity sə ˈlæs ət i -ɪt- ‖ -əţ i
salad ˈsæl əd **~s** z
ˈsalad bar; **ˈsalad cream**; **ˈsalad days**; **ˌsalad ˈdressing,** ‖ ˈ· · ˌ· ·; **ˈsalad oil**
Saladin ˈsæl əd ɪn §-ən
Salaman ˈsæl ə mæn -mən
Salamanca ˌsæl ə ˈmæŋk ə —*Sp* [sa la ˈmaŋ ka]
salamander ˈsæl ə mænd ə ‖ -ᵊr **~s** z
salami sə ˈlɑːm i **~s** z
Salamis ˈsæl əm ɪs §-əs
salariat sə ˈleər i æt -i‿ət ‖ -ˈlær- -ˈler-
salar|y ˈsæl ər |i **~ied** id **~ies** iz **~yman** i mæn **~ymen** i men
Salazar ˌsæl ə ˈzɑː ‖ -ˈzɑːr —*Port* [sɐ lɐ ˈzar]
salbutamol sæl ˈbjuːt ə mɒl ‖ -ˈbjuːţ ə mɔːl -mɑːl, -moʊl
salchow ˈsælk əʊ ˈsɔːlk-, ˈsɒlk- ‖ -oʊ **~s** z
Salcombe ˈsɔːlk əm ˈsɒlk- ‖ ˈsɑːlk-
sale, Sale seɪᵊl *(= sail)* **sales** seɪᵊlz
ˈsales pitch; **ˈsales repreˌsentative**; **ˈsales reˌsistance**; **ˈsales slip**; **ˈsales staff**; **ˈsales talk**; **ˈsales tax**
saleable ˈseɪl əb ᵊl
Salem ˈseɪl əm -em
Salerno sə ˈlɜːn əʊ -ˈleən- ‖ -ˈlern oʊ -ˈlɜːn- —*It* [sa ˈlɛr no]
saleroom ˈseɪᵊl ruːm -rʊm **~s** z
salesclerk ˈseɪᵊlz klɑːk ‖ -klɜːk **~s** s
salesgirl ˈseɪᵊlz ɡɜːl ‖ -ɡɜːl **~s** z
Salesian sə ˈliːz i‿ən -ˈliːʒ- ‖ sə ˈliːʒ ᵊn -ˈliːʃ- **~s** z
saleslad|y ˈseɪᵊlz ˌleɪd |i **~ies** iz
sales|man ˈseɪᵊlz |mən **~manship** mən ʃɪp **~men** mən men **~people** ˌpiːp ᵊl **~person/s** ˌpɜːs ᵊn/z ‖ ˌpɜːs ᵊn/z
salesroom ˈseɪᵊlz ruːm -rʊm **~s** z
sales|woman ˈseɪᵊlz |ˌwʊm ən **~women** ˌwɪm ɪn §-ən
Salford ˈsɔːl fəd ˈsɒl- ‖ -fᵊrd ˈsɑːl- —*A spelling pronunciation* ˈsæl- *is sometimes heard.*
Salfords ˈsæl fədz ˈsɔːl-, ˈsɒl- ‖ -fᵊrdz
Salian ˈseɪl i‿ən **~s** z
Salic, salic ˈsæl ɪk ˈseɪl-
salicylate sə ˈlɪs ɪ leɪt -ə-, -ᵊl eɪt **~s** s
salicylic ˌsæl ɪ ˈsɪl ɪk ◂ -ə-
salienc|e ˈseɪl i‿ənᵗs **~y** i
salient ˈseɪl i‿ənt **~ly** li **~ness** nəs nɪs **~s** s
Salieri ˌsæl i ˈeər i ‖ sæl ˈjer i sæl- —*It* [sa ˈljɛː ri]
saliferous sə ˈlɪf ər‿əs sæ-

S

sali|fy ˈsæl ɪ |faɪ §-ə- **~fied** faɪd **~fies** faɪz **~fying** faɪ ɪŋ

Salina *place in KS* sə ˈlaɪn ə

Salinas *place in CA* sə ˈliːn əs

saline ˈseɪl aɪn -iːn ‖ -iːn -aɪn

Saline *place in Fife* ˈsæl ɪn §-ən

Saline *place in MI* sə ˈliːn

Salinger ˈsæl ɪndʒ ə §-əndʒ- ‖ -ᵊr

salinity sə ˈlɪn ət i sæ-, -ɪt- ‖ -əţ i

salinometer ˌsæl ɪ ˈnɒm ɪt ə ˌ·ə-, -ət ə ‖ -ˈnɑːm əţ ᵊr **~s** z

Salisbury ˈsɔːlz bər‿i ˈsɒlz- ‖ ˈsɑːlz-, -ˌber i *(!)*
ˌSalisbury ˈPlain

Salish ˈseɪl ɪʃ **~an** ən

saliva sə ˈlaɪv ə

salivary ˈsæl ɪv ər‿i ˈ·əv-; sə ˈlaɪv ər i ‖ ˈsæl ə ver i

sali|vate ˈsæl ɪ |veɪt -ə- **~vated** veɪt ɪd -əd ‖ veɪţ əd **~vates** veɪts **~vating** veɪt ɪŋ ‖ veɪţ ɪŋ

salivation ˌsæl ɪ ˈveɪʃ ᵊn -ə-

Salk sɔːlk sɔːk ‖ sɑːlk, sɔːk, sɑːk

Salkeld ˈsɔːlk ᵊld ˈsɒlk- ‖ ˈsɑːlk-—*locally also* ˈsæf ᵊld

sallet ˈsæl ɪt -ət **~s** s

Sallis ˈsæl ɪs §-əs

sallow ˈsæl əʊ ‖ -oʊ **~ed** d **~ing** ɪŋ **~ly** li **~ness** nəs nɪs **~s** z **~y** i

Sallust ˈsæl əst

sall|y, Sall|y ˈsæl |i **~ied** id **~ies, ~y's** iz **~ying** i‿ɪŋ

Sally-Ann, Sally-Anne ˌsæl i ˈæn

salmagundi ˌsælm ə ˈgʌnd i **~s** z

salmanazar, S~ ˌsælm ə ˈneɪz ə -ˈnæz- ‖ -ᵊr **~s** z

salmi, salmis ˈsælm i -iː

salmon, S~ ˈsæm ən **~s** z
ˌsalmon ˈpink◂; ˈsalmon trout

Salmond ˈsæm ənd

salmonell|a ˌsælm ə ˈnel |ə ˌsæm- **~ae** iː **~as** əz

Salome sə ˈləʊm i -eɪ ‖ -ˈloʊm-

salon ˈsæl ɒn -ɒ̃, §-ɒŋ ‖ sə ˈlɑːn ˈsæl ɑːn **~s** z

Salonica, Salonika sə ˈlɒn ɪk ə, ˌsæl ə ˈnaɪk ə, -ˈniːk- ‖ sə ˈlɑːn- —*Gk* Thessaloniki [θɛ sa lɔ ˈni ci]

saloon sə ˈluːn **~s** z
saˈloon bar

Salop ˈsæl əp -ɒp

salopettes ˌsæl ə ˈpets

Salopian sə ˈləʊp i‿ən ‖ -ˈloʊp- **~s** z

salpingectom|y ˌsælp ɪn ˈdʒekt əm |i **~ies** iz

salpingitis ˌsælp ɪn ˈdʒaɪt ɪs §-əs ‖ -ˈdʒaɪţ əs

salpingo- *comb. form*
with stress-neutral suffix sæl ˈpɪŋ gəʊ ‖ -gə — **salpingogram** sæl ˈpɪŋ gəʊ græm ‖ -ə græm
with stress-imposing suffix ˌsælp ɪŋ ˈgɒ+ ‖ -ˈgɑː+ — **salpingoscopy** ˌsælp ɪŋ ˈgɒsk əp i ‖ -ˈgɑːsk-

salsa ˈsæls ə ‖ ˈsɑːls ə ˈsɔːls- —*Sp* [ˈsal sa]

salsify ˈsæls əf i ˈsɔːls-, ˈsɒls-, -ɪf-; -ə faɪ, -ɪ-

SALT

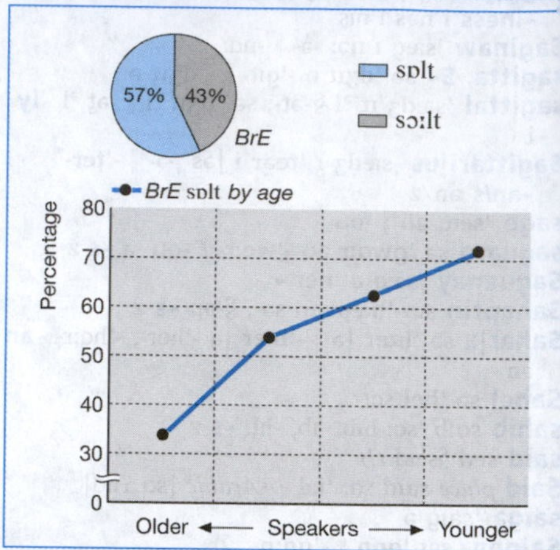

sɒlt
sɔːlt
57%
43%
BrE
BrE sɒlt *by age*
Percentage
80
70
60
50
40
30
0
Older ← Speakers → Younger

salt, Salt, SALT sɔːlt sɒlt ‖ sɑːlt — *Preference poll, BrE:* sɔːlt *43%,* sɒlt *57%.* **salted** ˈsɔːlt ɪd ˈsɒlt-, -əd ‖ ˈsɔːlt əd ˈsɑːlt- **salting** ˈsɔːlt ɪŋ ˈsɒlt- ‖ ˈsɑːlt- **salts** sɔːlts sɒlts ‖ sɑːlts
ˈsalt dome; ˌSalt Lake ˈCity; ˈsalt marsh; ˈsalt ˌshaker

Saltaire ₍ˌ₎sɔːlt ˈeə ₍ˌ₎sɒlt- ‖ -ˈeᵊr ₍ˌ₎sɑːlt-, -ˈæᵊr

salt-and-pepper ˌsɔːlt ən ˈpep ə ˌsɒlt-, →-əm- ‖ -ᵊr ˌsɑːlt

saltant ˈsælt ənt ˈsɔːlt-, ˈsɒlt- ‖ ˈsɔːlt-, ˈsɑːlt-

saltarell|o ˌsælt ə ˈrel |əʊ ˌsɔːlt-, ˌsɒlt- ‖ -|oʊ ˌsɑːlt- **~i** iː

Saltash ˈsɔːlt æʃ ˈsɒlt- ‖ ˈsɔːlt- ˈsɑːlt-

saltation sæl ˈteɪʃ ᵊn sɔːl-, sɒl- ‖ sɔːl-, sɑːl- **~s** z

saltbox, salt-box ˈsɔːlt bɒks ˈsɒlt- ‖ -bɑːks ˈsɑːlt- **~es** ɪz əz

Saltburn ˈsɔːlt bɜːn ˈsɒlt- ‖ -bɝːn ˈsɑːlt-

saltbush ˈsɔːlt bʊʃ ˈsɒlt- ‖ ˈsɑːlt-

saltcellar ˈsɔːlt ˌsel ə ˈsɒlt- ‖ -ᵊr ˈsɑːlt- **~s** z

Saltcoats ˈsɔːlt kəʊts ˈsɒlt- ‖ -koʊts ˈsɑːlt-

Salter, s~ ˈsɔːlt ə ˈsɒlt- ‖ -ᵊr ˈsɑːlt- **~s, ~'s** z

Salterton ˈsɔːlt ət ən ˈsɒlt- ‖ -ᵊrt ᵊn ˈsɑːlt-

saltfish ˈsɔːlt fɪʃ ˈsɒlt- ‖ ˈsɑːlt-

Salthouse ˈsɔːlt haʊs ˈsɒlt- ‖ ˈsɑːlt-

saltimbocca ˌsælt ɪm ˈbɒk ə ˌsɔːlt-, ˌsɒlt- ‖ ˌsɑːlt ɪm ˈboʊk ə ˌsɔːlt-, ˌsɑːlt-, -ˈbɑːk- —*It* [sal tim ˈbok ka] **~s** z

saltine sɔːl ˈtiːn sɒl- ‖ sɑːl- **~s** z

saltire ˈsɔːlt aɪ‿ə ˈsɒlt- ‖ -aɪ‿ᵊr ˈsɑːlt- **~s** z

Saltley ˈsɔːlt li ˈsɒlt- ‖ ˈsɑːlt-

saltlick ˈsɔːlt lɪk ˈsɒlt- ‖ ˈsɑːlt- **~s** s

Saltmarsh ˈsɔːlt mɑːʃ ˈsɒlt- ‖ -mɑːrʃ ˈsɑːlt-

Salton ˈsɔːlt ən ˈsɒlt- ‖ ˈsɑːlt-
ˌSalton ˈSea

Saltoun ˈsɔːlt ən ˈsælt-, ˈsɒlt- ‖ ˈsɑːlt-

saltpan ˈsɔːlt pæn ˈsɒlt- ‖ ˈsɑːlt- **~s** z

saltpeter, saltpetre ˌsɔːlt ˈpiːt ə ˌsɒlt-, ˈ·ˌ·· ‖ -ˈpiːţ ᵊr ˌsɑːlt-

saltwater ˈsɔːlt ˌwɔːt ə ˈsɒlt- ‖ -ˌwɔːţ ᵊr ˈsɑːlt-, -ˌwɑːţ-

saltworks ˈsɔːlt wɜːks ˈsɒlt- ‖ -wɝːks ˈsɑːlt-

saltwort ˈsɔːlt wɜːt ˈsɒlt-, §-wɔːt ‖ -wɜːt ˈsɑːlt-, -wɔːrt **~s** s

salt|y ˈsɔːlt |i ˈsɒlt- ‖ ˈsɑːlt- **~ier** i‿ə ‖ i‿ᵊr **~iest** i‿ɪst i‿əst **~ily** ɪ li əl i **~iness** i nəs i nɪs

salubrious sə ˈluːb ri‿əs -ˈljuːb- **~ly** li **~ness** nəs nɪs

salubrity sə ˈluːb rət i -ˈljuːb-, -rɪt- ‖ -rəţ i

Saluki, s~ sə ˈluːk i **~s** z

salutar|y ˈsæl jʊt‿ər |i ‖ -jə ter |i **~iness** i nəs i nɪs

salutation ˌsæl ju ˈteɪʃ ᵊn ‖ -jə- **~s** z

salutatorian sə ˌluːt ə ˈtɔːr i‿ən -ˌljuːt- ‖ -ˌluːţ- **~s** z

sa|lute sə |ˈluːt -ˈljuːt **~luted** ˈluːt ɪd ˈljuːt-, -əd ‖ ˈluːţ əd **~lutes** ˈluːts ˈljuːts **~luting** ˈluːt ɪŋ ˈljuːt- ‖ ˈluːţ ɪŋ

Salvador ˈsælv ə dɔː ˌ· ·ˈ· ‖ -dɔːr —*Sp* [sal βa ˈðor]

Salvadorean, Salvadorian ˌsælv ə ˈdɔːr i‿ən ◂ **~s** z

salvag|e ˈsælv ɪdʒ **~ed** d **~es** ɪz əz **~ing** ɪŋ

salvageable ˈsælv ɪdʒ əb ᵊl

salvarsan ˈsælv ə sæn -əs ən ‖ -ᵊr-

salvation sæl ˈveɪʃ ᵊn ˌsæl- **~s** z

Salˌvation ˈArmy, ˌ·ˌ· · ˈ··

salvationist, S~ sæl ˈveɪʃ ᵊn‿ɪst §‿əst **~s** z

salve *n, v 'soothe'* sælv sɑːv ‖ sæv (*) **salved** sælvd sɑːvd ‖ sævd **salves** sælvz sɑːvz ‖ sævz **salving** ˈsælv ɪŋ ˈsɑːv- ‖ ˈsæv ɪŋ

salve *v 'salvage'* sælv **salved** sælvd **salves** sælvz **salving** ˈsælv ɪŋ

salve *Latin interj* ˈsælv eɪ -i; ˈsæl weɪ ‖ ˈsɑːl weɪ **~s** z

salver ˈsælv ə ‖ -ᵊr **~s** z

Salvesen, Salveson ˈsælv ɪs ən -əs-

salvia ˈsælv i‿ə **~s** z

salvo ˈsælv əʊ ‖ -oʊ **~s, ~es** z

sal volatile ˌsæl və ˈlæt əl i vɒ- ‖ -ˈlæţ ᵊl i

salwar sʌl ˈwɑː ‖ -ˈwɑːr **~s** z

Salyut sæl ˈjuːt sɒl- ‖ sɑːl- —*Russ* [sʌ ˈlʲut]

Salzburg ˈsælts bɜːg ˈsɔːlts-, ˈsɒlts- ‖ ˈsɔːlz bɜːg ˈsɑːlz- —*Ger* [ˈzalts bʊʁk]

Sam sæm

SAM sæm ˌes eɪ ˈem

Samantha sə ˈmænᵗθ ə

samara ˈsæm ər ə sə ˈmɑːr ə **~s** z

Samara sə ˈmɑːr ə —*Russ* [sʌ ˈma rə]

Samaranch ˈsæm ə ræn —*Catalan* [sə mə ˈrank]

Samaria sə ˈmeər i‿ə ‖ sə ˈmer- -ˈmær-

Samaritan sə ˈmær ɪt ən -ət- ‖ -ət ᵊn -ˈmer- **~s** z

samarium sə ˈmeər i‿əm ‖ sə ˈmer- -ˈmær-

Samarkand ˌsæm ɑː ˈkænd -ə-, ˈ· · · ‖ -ᵊr- —*Russ* [sə mʌr ˈkant]

samarskite ˈsæm ɑːsk aɪt -ə skaɪt; sə ˈmɑːsk aɪt ‖ ˈsæm ɑːrsk- sə ˈmɑːrsk-

sam|ba ˈsæm |bə ‖ ˈsɑːm- **~baed** bəd **~baing** bəʳ ɪŋ ‖ bə ɪŋ **~bas** bəz

sambal ˈsæm bᵊl —*Malay* [ˈsam bal]

sambar, sambur ˈsæm bə ˈsɑːm- ‖ -bᵊr **~s** z

sambo, Sambo ˈsæm bəʊ ‖ -boʊ **~s, ~'s** z

same seɪm

same-day ˌseɪm ˈdeɪ ◂

sameness ˈseɪm nəs nɪs

same-sex ˌseɪm ˈseks ◂

samey ˈseɪm i

Samhain saʊn ˈsɑː wɪn, ˈsaʊ‿ən —*Irish* [saunʲ]

Sami ˈsæm i ˈsɑːm i ‖ ˈsɑːm i

Samian ˈseɪm i‿ən **~s** z

samisen ˈsæm ɪ sen §-ə- **~s** z

samite ˈsæm aɪt ˈseɪm-

samizdat ˌsæm ɪz ˈdæt ˈ· · · ‖ ˈsɑːm iːz dɑːt —*Russ* [sə mʲɪ ˈzdat]

Samlesbury ˈsæmz bər‿i ˈsɑːmz- ‖ -ˌber i

Sammie, Sammy ˈsæm i

Samnite ˈsæm naɪt **~s** s

Samnium ˈsæm ni‿əm

Samo|a sə ˈməʊ |ə sɑː- ‖ -ˈmoʊ |ə **~an/s** ən/z

Samos ˈseɪm ɒs ˈsæm- ‖ -ɑːs ˈsæm oʊs —*ModGk* [ˈsa mɔs]

samosa sə ˈməʊs ə sæ-, -ˈməʊz- ‖ -ˈmoʊs ə **~s** z

Samothrace ˈsæm əʊ θreɪs ‖ -ə-

samovar ˈsæm ə vɑː ˌ· · ˈ· ‖ -vɑːr —*Russ* [sə mʌ ˈvar] **~s** z

Samoyed, Samoyede sə ˈmɔɪ ed -ɪd; ˌsæm ɔɪ ˈed, -ə ˈjed **~s** z

samp sæmp

sampan ˈsæm pæn **~s** z

Sampford ˈsæmp fəd ‖ -fᵊrd

samphire ˈsæmᵖf aɪ‿ə ‖ -aɪ‿ᵊr

sampl|e ˈsɑːmp ᵊl §ˈsæmp- ‖ ˈsæmp ᵊl **~ed** d **~es** z **~ing** ‿ɪŋ

sampler ˈsɑːmp lə §ˈsæmp- ‖ ˈsæmp lᵊr **~s** z

Sampras ˈsæmp rəs

Sampson ˈsæmps ən

Samson ˈsæmᵖs ən

Samsonite *tdmk* ˈsæmᵖs ən aɪt

Samsung *tdmk* ˈsæm sʌŋ —*Korean* [ˈsam sɒŋ]

Samuel ˈsæm ju‿əl

Samuels ˈsæm ju‿əlz

samurai ˈsæm uᵊ raɪ -ə-, -juᵊ- ‖ -ə- —*Jp* [sa ˌmɯ rai] **~s** z

San, san sæn —*but in foreign names, AmE* sɑːn —*It, Sp* [san]

San'a, Sanaa sə ˈnɑː sɑː-, ˈsɑːn ə —*Arabic* [sˤan ʕaːʔ]

San Andreas ˌsæn æn ˈdreɪ əs ◂

ˌSan AndˌreasˈFault

San Antonio ˌsæn æn ˈtəʊn i əʊ ‖ -ˈtoʊn i oʊ

sanatari|um ˌsæn ə ˈteər i‿|əm ‖ -ˈter- -ˈtær- **~a** ə **~ums** əmz

Sanatogen *tdmk* sə ˈnæt ədʒ ən -ə dʒen ‖ -ˈnæţ-

sanatori|um ˌsæn ə ˈtɔːr i‿|əm ‖ -ˈtoʊr- **~a** ə **~ums** əmz

San Bernardino ˌsæn ˌbɜːn ə ˈdiːn əʊ →ˌsæm- ‖ -ˌbɜːn ᵊr ˈdiːn oʊ -ˌ·ə-

ˌSan BernarˌdinoˈMountains

San Carlos ₍ˌ₎sæn ˈkɑːl ɒs →₍ˌ₎sæŋ-, -əs ‖ -ˈkɑːrl əs

Sancerre sɒ̃ ˈseə sæn- ‖ sɑːn ˈseᵊr —*Fr* [sɑ̃ sɛːʁ]

Sanchez ˈsæntʃ ez —*Sp* Sánchez [ˈsan tʃeθ, -tʃes]

S

Sancho 'sæntʃ əʊ ‖ 'sɑːntʃ oʊ —*Sp* ['san tʃo]
ˌ**Sancho 'Panza** 'pænz ə ‖ 'pɑːnz ə —*Sp* ['pan θa, -sa]
San Clemente ˌsæn klə 'ment i →ˌsæŋ-, -klɪ- ‖ -'menṭ i
sanctification ˌsæŋkt ɪf ɪ 'keɪʃ ᵊn ˌ-əf-, §-ə'--
sancti|fy 'sæŋkt ɪ |faɪ -ə- **~fied** faɪd **~fier/s** faɪ‿ə/z ‖ faɪ‿ᵊr/z **~fies** faɪz **~fying** faɪ ɪŋ
sanctimonious ˌsæŋkt ɪ 'məʊn i‿əs ◂ ˌ-ə- ‖ 'moʊn- **~ly** li **~ness** nəs nɪs
sanctimony 'sæŋkt ɪ mən i '-ə-, -məʊn i ‖ -moʊn i
sanction 'sæŋkʃ ᵊn **~ed** d **~ing** ‿ɪŋ **~s** z
sanctit|y 'sæŋkt ət |i -ɪt- ‖ -əṭ |i **~ies** iz
sanctuar|y, S~ 'sæŋktʃ u‿ər |i 'sæŋkt ju‿ ‖ -er |i **~ies** iz
sanct|um 'sæŋkt |əm **~a** ə **~ums** əmz
ˌ**sanctum 'sanctorum** sæŋk 'tɔːr əm
Sanctus 'sæŋkt əs -ʊs
'**Sanctus bell**
sand sænd **sanded** 'sænd ɪd -əd **sanding** 'sænd ɪŋ **sands** sændz
'**sand ˌdollar**; '**sand dune**; '**sand fly**; '**sand ˌmartin**; '**sand ˌtable**; '**sand trap**; '**sand yacht**
Sand *name of novelist* sɒ̃d ‖ sɑːnd —*Fr* [sɑ̃ːd]
sandal 'sænd ᵊl **~ed, ~led** d **~s** z
sandalwood 'sænd ᵊl wʊd **~s** z
sandarac, sandarach 'sænd ə ræk **~s** s
Sanday 'sænd eɪ -i
Sandbach 'sænd bætʃ →'sæm-
sandbag 'sænd bæg →'sæm- **~ged** d **~ger/s** ə/z ‖ -ᵊr/z **~ging** ɪŋ **~s** z
sandbank 'sænd bæŋk →'sæm- **~s** s
sandbar 'sænd bɑː →'sæm- ‖ -bɑːr **~s** z
sandblast 'sænd blɑːst →'sæm-, §-blæst ‖ -blæst **~ed** ɪd əd **~er/s** ə/z ‖ -ᵊr/z **~ing** ɪŋ **~s** s
sandboard 'sænd bɔːd →'sæm- ‖ -bɔːrd -boʊrd **~ing** ɪŋ **~s** z
sandbox 'sænd bɒks →'sæm- ‖ -bɑːks **~es** ɪz əz
'**sandbox tree**
sandboy 'sænd bɔɪ →'sæm- **~s** z
Sandburg 'sænd bɜːg ‖ -bɜːg
sandcastle 'sænd ˌkɑːs ᵊl →'sæŋ-, §-ˌkæs- ‖ -ˌkæs ᵊl **~s** z
Sandell *(i)* 'sænd ᵊl, *(ii)* sæn 'del
Sandeman 'sænd ɪ mən -ə-; 'sænd mən
sander 'sænd ə ‖ -ᵊr **~s** z
sanderling 'sænd ə lɪŋ -dᵊl ɪŋ ‖ -ᵊr- **~s** z
Sanders 'sɑːnd əz §'sænd- ‖ 'sænd ᵊrz
Sanderson 'sɑːnd əs ən §'sænd- ‖ 'sænd ᵊr sən
Sanderstead 'sɑːnd ə sted §'sænd-, -stɪd ‖ 'sænd ᵊr-
Sandes sændz
sand|fly 'sænd |flaɪ **~flies** flaɪz
Sandford 'sænd fəd -fɔːd ‖ -fᵊrd -fɔːrd, -foʊrd
Sandgate 'sænd geɪt →'sæŋ-, -gɪt
sandglass 'sænd glɑːs →'sæŋ-, §-glæs ‖ -glæs **~es** ɪz əz
sandhi 'sænd i 'sʌnd-, -hiː —*Hindi* [sən̪ d̪ʱi]
'**sandhi pheˌnomena**
Sandhurst 'sænd hɜːst ‖ -hɜːst
Sandiacre 'sænd i ˌeɪk ə ‖ -ᵊr
Sandie, S~ 'sænd i
San Diego ˌsæn di 'eɪg əʊ ‖ -oʊ
Sandinista ˌsænd ɪ 'niːst ə ◂ -ə- **~s** z
sandlot 'sænd lɒt ‖ -lɑːt
sandman 'sænd mæn →'sæm-
San Domingo ˌsæn də 'mɪŋ gəʊ ‖ -goʊ —*Sp* [san do 'miŋ go]
Sandor 'sænd ə ‖ -ᵊr —*but as a Hungarian name also* 'ʃɑːnd-, -ɔː ‖-ɔːr —*Hung* Sándor ['ʃaːn dor]
Sandown 'sænd aʊn
Sandoz *tdmk* 'sænd ɒz ‖ -ɑːz —*Fr* [sɑ̃ do]
sandpaper 'sænd ˌpeɪp ə →'sæm- ‖ -ᵊr **~ed** d
sandpapering 'sænd ˌpeɪp ər‿ɪŋ **~s** z
sandpiper 'sænd ˌpaɪp ə →'sæm- ‖ -ᵊr **~s** z
sandpit 'sænd pɪt →'sæm- **~s** s
Sandra 'sændr ə 'sɑːndr-
Sandringham 'sændr ɪŋ əm §-həm
Sands sændz
sandshoe 'sænd ʃuː **~s** z
sandstone 'sænd stəʊn ‖ -stoʊn **~s** z
sandstorm 'sænd stɔːm ‖ -stɔːrm **~s** z
Sandusky sæn 'dʌsk i sᵊn-

SANDWICH

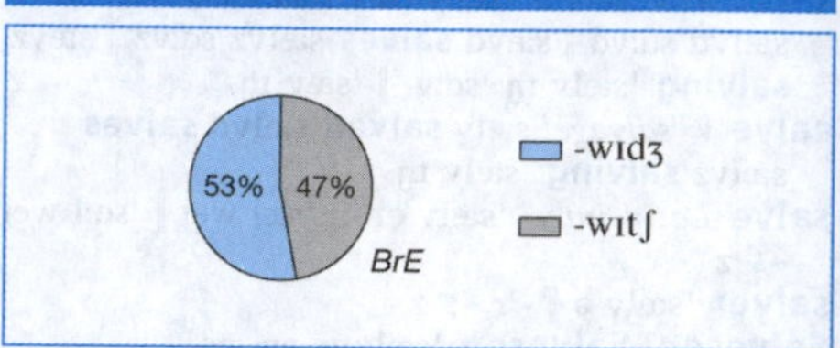

sandwich, S~ 'sæn wɪdʒ 'sænd-, 'sæm-, -wɪtʃ — *Preference poll, BrE:* -wɪdʒ *53%,* -wɪtʃ *47%.*
sandwiched 'sæn wɪdʒd 'sænd-, 'sæm-, -wɪtʃt **~es** ɪz əz **~ing** ɪŋ
'**sandwich board**; '**sandwich course**; '**sandwich man**
sandworm 'sænd wɜːm ‖ -wɜːm **~s** z
sandwort 'sænd wɜːt §-wɔːt ‖ -wɜːt **~s** s
sand|y, Sand|y 'sænd |i **~ier** i‿ə ‖ i‿ᵊr **~iest** i‿ɪst i‿əst **~iness** i nəs i nɪs **S~y's** iz
ˌ**Sandy 'Hook**
sandyacht 'sænd jɒt ‖ -jɑːt **~s** s
Sandys sændz
sane seɪn **saner** 'seɪn ə ‖ -ᵊr **sanest** 'seɪn ɪst -əst
sane|ly 'seɪn |li **~ness** nəs nɪs
San Fernando ˌsæn fə 'nænd əʊ ‖ -fᵊr 'nænd oʊ
Sanford 'sæn fəd ‖ -fᵊrd
Sanforis|e, Sanforiz|e *tdmk* 'sæn fə raɪz **~ed** d **~es** ɪz əz **~ing** ɪŋ
San Francisco ˌsæn frən 'sɪsk əʊ -fræn- ‖ -oʊ
ˌ**San FranˌCisco 'Bay**
San Gabriel sæn 'geɪb ri‿əl →sæŋ-
sangaree ˌsæŋ gə 'riː
Sanger 'sæŋ ə ‖ -ᵊr
sangfroid ˌsɒŋ 'frwɑː ˌsæŋ-, ˌsɑːŋ- ‖ ˌsɑːŋ- —*Fr* [sɑ̃ fʁwa]

Sango ˈsæŋ gəʊ ˈsɑːŋ- ‖ ˈsɑːŋ goʊ

Sangre de Cristo ˌsæŋ gri də ˈkrɪst əʊ ◂ ‖ -oʊ ◂

sangria sæn ˈgriː‿ə →sæŋ-; ˈsæŋ gri‿ə —*Sp* san g ría [saŋ ˈgri a]

Sangster ˈsæŋᵏst ə ‖ -ᵊr

sanguinary ˈsæŋ gwɪn ər‿i ˈ·gwən- ‖ -gwə ner i

sanguine ˈsæŋ gwɪn §-gwən **~ly** li **~ness** nəs nɪs

sanguineous sæŋ ˈgwɪn i‿əs sæn-

sanguinity sæŋ ˈgwɪn ət i sæn-, -ɪt- ‖ -əţ i

Sanhedrin ˈsæn ə drɪn -ɪ-, §-ədr ən; sæn ˈhedr ɪn, -ˈhiːdr-, §-ən ‖ sæn ˈhedr ən

sanicle ˈsæn ɪk ᵊl **~s** z

sanitarily ˈsæn ət‿ər əl i ˈ·ɪt‿, -ɪ li; ˌsæn ə ˈter-, ˌ·ɪ- ‖ ˌsæn ə ˈter-

sanitari|um ˌsæn ə ˈteər i‿|əm ˌ·ɪ- ‖ -ˈter-, -ˈtær- **~a** ə **~ums** əmz

sanitary ˈsæn ət‿ər i ˌ·ɪt‿ ‖ -ə ter i
 ˌsanitary ˈnapkin; ˈsanitary ˌtowel

sanitation ˌsæn ɪ ˈteɪʃ ᵊn -ə-
 ˌsaniˈtation ˌworker

sanitis|e, sanitiz|e ˈsæn ɪ taɪz -ə- **~ed** d **~es** ɪz əz **~ing** ɪŋ

sanitori|um ˌsæn ə ˈtɔːr i‿|əm ˌ·ɪ- ‖ -ˈtoʊr- **~a** ə **~ums** əmz

sanity ˈsæn ət i -ɪt- ‖ -əţ i

San Jacinto *(i)* ˌsæn dʒə ˈsɪnt əʊ ‖ -ˈsɪnţ oʊ -ˈsiːnt-, *(ii)* -hə- —*in TX (i), in CA (ii)*

San Joaquin *river and valley in CA* ˌsæn wɑː ˈkiːn ‖ -wɔː-

San Jose *place in CA*, **San José** *place in Costa Rica* ˌsæn həʊ ˈzeɪ -əʊ- ‖ -ə ˈzeɪ -hoʊ-, -oʊ-, -ˈseɪ —*Sp* [saŋ xo ˈse]

San Juan ˌsæn ˈwɑːn -ˈhwɑːn
 ˌSan ˌJuan Capiˈstrano ˌkæp ɪ ˈstrɑːn əʊ -ə- ‖ -oʊ

sank sæŋk

Sankey ˈsæŋk i

San Leandro ˌsæn li ˈændr əʊ ‖ -oʊ

San Luis Obispo ˌsæn ˌluː‿ɪs ə ˈbɪsp əʊ ·ˌ·‿ əs ə-, i ə- ‖ -oʊ -ˈbiːsp-

San Marcos sæn ˈmɑːk əs →sæm- ‖ -ˈmɑːrk əs

San Marino ˌsæn mə ˈriːn əʊ →ˌsæm- ‖ -oʊ

San Mateo ˌsæn mə ˈteɪ əʊ ‖ -oʊ

San Miguel ˌsæn mɪ ˈgel →ˌsæm- —*Sp* [sam mi ˈgel]

San Pedro *(i)* sæn ˈpedr əʊ →sæm- ‖ -oʊ, *(ii)* sæn ˈpiːdr əʊ →sæm- ‖ -oʊ —*The suburb of Los Angeles CA, and the river in AZ, are usually (i); all other places are (ii).* —*Sp* [sam ˈpe ðro]

San Quentin sæn ˈkwent ɪn →sæŋ-, §-ən ‖ -ᵊn

Sanquhar ˈsæŋk ə ‖ -ᵊr

San Rafael *place in CA* ˌsæn rə ˈfel

San Remo ₍ˌ₎sæn ˈreɪm əʊ -ˈriːm- ‖ -oʊ —*It* [san ˈrɛː mo]

sans sænz —*Fr* [sɑ̃]

San Salvador ₍ˌ₎sæn ˈsælv ə dɔː ‖ -dɔːr

sans-culotte ˌsænz kju ˈlɒt -ku- ‖ -ˈlɑːt —*Fr* [sɑ̃ ky lɔt] **~s** s

San Sebastian, San Sebastián ˌsæn sə ˈbæst i‿ən ˌ·sɪ- ‖ -ˈbæs tʃən —*Sp* [san se βas ˈtjan]

sansei ˈsæn seɪ ‖ ˈsɑːn- —*Jp* [ˈsaɴ see]

sanserif ˌsæn ˈser ɪf ˌsænz-, -əf

sansevieria ˌsæn sɪ ˈvɪər i‿ə ˌ·sə- ‖ -ˈvɪr- **~s** z

Sanskrit ˈsænᵗs krɪt -krət

Sanskritic sæn ˈskrɪt ɪk ‖ -ˈskrɪţ ɪk

Sansom ˈsænᵗs əm

Sanson ˈsænᵗs ᵊn

sans serif, sanserif ˌsæn ˈser ɪf ˌsænz-, -əf

Santa ˈsænt ə ˈsɑːnt- ‖ ˈsænţ ə —*and in AmE, but only for saints' names treated as Italian or Spanish (not for place names in the US, not for Santa Claus), also* ˈsɑːnt ə —*It, Sp* [ˈsan ta] **~s, 's** z

Santa Ana ˌsænt əʳ ˈæn ə ‖ ˌsænţ ə-

Santa Barbara ˌsænt ə ˈbɑːb ər‿ə ‖ ˌsænţ ə ˈbɑːrb-

Santa Catalina ˌsænt ə ˌkæt ə ˈliːn ə → -ᵊl ˈiːn ə ‖ ˌsænţ ə ˌkæţ-

Santa Claus ˈsænt ə klɔːz ˈsɑːnt-, ˌ· ·ˈ· ‖ ˈsænţ- -ɪ-, -klɑːz

Santa Cruz *place in CA* ˌsænt ə ˈkruːz ‖ ˈsænţ ə kruːz ˌ· · ˈ· —*locally usually* ˈ· · ·

Santa Fe, Santa Fé ˌsænt ə ˈfeɪ ˈ· · · ‖ ˈsænţ ə feɪ ˌ· · ˈ·

Santali sʌn ˈtɑːl i sᵊn-, sæn-

Santa Maria ˌsænt ə mə ˈriː‿ə ‖ ˌsænţ- —*Sp* [san ta ma ˈri a]

Santa Monica ˌsænt ə ˈmɒn ɪk ə §-ək ə ‖ ˌsænţ ə ˈmɑːn-

Santander ˌsænt ən ˈdeə ˌsæn tæn-, ⚠sæn ˈtænd ə ‖ ˌsɑːn tɑːn ˈdeᵊr —*Sp* [san tan ˈdeɾ]

Santa Rosa ˌsænt ə ˈrəʊz ə ‖ ˌsænţ ə ˈroʊz ə

Santayana ˌsænt ə ˈjɑːn ə -aɪ ˈɑːn- ‖ ˌsænţ i ˈæn ə -ˈɑːn ə

Santee ₍ˌ₎sæn ˈtiː ˈ· ·

Santer ˈsænt ə ‖ ˈsænţ ᵊr —*Fr* [sɑ̃ tɛːʁ]

santeria, S~ ˌsænt ə ˈriː‿ə ‖ ˌsænţ- ˌsɑːnţ- —*Sp* santeria [san te ˈri a]

Santiago ˌsænt i ˈɑːg əʊ ‖ ˌsænţ i ˈɑːg oʊ ˌsɑːnţ- —*Sp* [san ˈtja ɣo]

Santo, santo ˈsænt əʊ ‖ ˈsænţ oʊ ˈsɑːnt- —*It, Sp* [ˈsan to] **~s** z

Santo Domingo ˌsænt əʊ də ˈmɪŋ gəʊ ‖ ˌsænţ ə də ˈmɪŋ goʊ —*Sp* [san to ðo ˈmiŋ go]

santolina ˌsænt ə ˈliːn ə -ᵊl ˈiːn- ‖ ˌsænţ ᵊl ˈiːn ə

santonica sæn ˈtɒn ɪk ə ‖ -ˈtɑːn-

santonin ˈsænt ən ɪn §-ən

Santorini ˌsænt ə ˈriːn i ‖ ˌsæn tə-

Santos ˈsænt ɒs ‖ ˈsænţ əs —*Port* [ˈsɐn tuʃ, -tus]

Sanyo *tdmk* ˈsæn jəʊ ‖ -joʊ —*Jp* [sa ˌɴ joo, sa ˌĩ-]

Saoirse ˈseəʃ ə ‖ ˈserʃ ə —*Irish* [ˈseːrʲ ʃə]

Saône səʊn ‖ soʊn —*Fr* [soːn]

São Paulo saʊm ˈpaʊl əʊ saʊ-, -u ‖ -oʊ —*Port* [sɐ̃ʊm ˈpaulu]

São Tomé ˌsaʊn tə ˈmeɪ ˌsaʊ- —*Port* [sɐ̃un tu ˈmɛ]
sap sæp **sapped** sæpt **sapping** ˈsæp ɪŋ **saps** sæps
sapele, S~ sə ˈpiːl i
saphen|a sə ˈfiːn |ə **~ae** iː
saphenous sə ˈfiːn əs ˈsæf ɪn əs, -ən-
sapid ˈsæp ɪd §-əd
sapience ˈseɪp i‿ənts ˈsæp-
sapiens ˈsæp i enz ˈseɪp-
sapient ˈseɪp i‿ənt ˈsæp- **~ly** li
Sapir sə ˈpɪə ˈseɪ pɪə ‖ sə ˈpɪər
sapling ˈsæp lɪŋ **~s** z
sapodilla ˌsæp ə ˈdɪl ə **~s** z
saponaceous ˌsæp ə ˈneɪʃ əs ◂ **~ness** nəs nɪs
saponification sə ˌpɒn ɪf ɪ ˈkeɪʃ ən -ˌ·əf-, §-ə'·- ‖ sə ˌpɑːn-
saponi|fy sə ˈpɒn ɪ |faɪ -ə- ‖ sə ˈpɑːn- **~fied** faɪd **~fier/s** faɪ‿ə/z ‖ faɪ‿ər/z **~fies** faɪz **~fying** faɪ ɪŋ
saponin ˈsæp ən ɪn §-ən **~s** z
sapp... —*see* **sap**
sapper ˈsæp ə ‖ -ər **~s** z
sapphic, S~ ˈsæf ɪk **~s** s
Sapphira sə ˈfaɪər ə sæ-
sapphire ˈsæf aɪ‿ə ‖ ˈsæf aɪ‿ər **~s** z
sapphism ˈsæf ˌɪz əm
Sappho ˈsæf əʊ ‖ -oʊ
Sapporo sə ˈpɔːr əʊ sæ- ‖ -oʊ —*Jp* [sap ˌpo ɾo]
sapp|y ˈsæp |i **~ier** i‿ə ‖ i‿ər **~iest** i‿ɪst i‿əst **~ily** ɪ li əl i **~iness** i nəs i nɪs
sapro- *comb. form*
with stress-neutral suffix ˈsæp rəʊ ‖ -rə — **saprophyte** ˈsæp rəʊ faɪt ‖ -rə-
with stress-imposing suffix sæ ˈprɒ+ ‖ sæ ˈprɑː+ — **saprophagous** sæ ˈprɒf əg əs ‖ sæ ˈprɑːf-
saprobe ˈsæp rəʊb ‖ -roʊb **~s** z
sapwood ˈsæp wʊd
Sara *(i)* ˈsɑːr ə, *(ii)* ˈseər ə ‖ ˈser ə ˈsær-
saraband, sarabande ˈsær ə bænd ‖ ˈser- **~s** z
Saracen ˈsær əs ən ‖ ˈser- **~s** z
Saracenic ˌsær ə ˈsen ɪk ◂ ‖ ˌser-
Saragossa ˌsær ə ˈgɒs ə ‖ -ˈgɑːs ə ˌser- —*Sp* Zaragoza [θa ɾa ˈɣo θa]
Sarah ˈseər ə ‖ ˈser ə ˈsær-
Sarah-Jane ˌseər ə ˈdʒeɪn ‖ ˌser- ˌsær-
Sarajevo ˌsær ə ˈjeɪv əʊ ‖ -oʊ ˌser- —*SCr* [sa ɾa ˈjɛ vɔ]
saran, Saran sə ˈræn
Saranac ˈsær ə næk ‖ ˈser-
Sarandon sə ˈrænd ən
Sarasota ˌsær ə ˈsəʊt ə ‖ -ˈsoʊţ ə ˌser-
Saratoga ˌsær ə ˈtəʊg ə ‖ -ˈtoʊg ə ˌser- **ˌSaraˌtoga ˈSprings**
Saratov sə ˈrɑːt ɒv ‖ -ɑːv —*Russ* [sʌ ˈra təf]
Sarawak sə ˈrɑː wək -wə, -wæk; ˈsær ə- ‖ -wɑːk
sarcasm ˈsɑːk ˌæz əm ‖ ˈsɑːrk-
sarcastic sɑː ˈkæst ɪk ‖ sɑːr- **~ally** əl‿i
sarcenet ˈsɑːs nət -nɪt -net ‖ ˈsɑːrs-
sarco- *comb. form*
with stress-neutral suffix ˈsɑːk əʊ ‖ ˈsɑːrk ə — **sarcocele** ˈsɑːk əʊ siːəl ‖ ˈsɑːrk ə-
with stress-imposing suffix sɑː ˈkɒ+ ‖ sɑːr ˈkɑː+ — **sarcolysis** sɑː ˈkɒl əs ɪs -ɪs-, §-əs ‖ sɑːr ˈkɑːl-
sarcoma sɑː ˈkəʊm ə ‖ sɑːr ˈkoʊm ə **~s** z
sarcoph|agus sɑː ˈkɒf |əg əs ‖ sɑːr ˈkɑːf- **~agi** ə gaɪ -dʒaɪ
sard sɑːd ‖ sɑːrd **sards** sɑːdz ‖ sɑːrdz
Sardanapalus ˌsɑːd ə ˈnæp əl əs ˌsɑːd ən ˈæp-; ˌsɑːd ən ə ˈpɑːl əs ‖ ˌsɑːrd ən ˈæp-
sardine *fish* ˌsɑː ˈdiːn ◂ ‖ ˌsɑːr- **~s** z **ˌsardine ˈsandwich**
sardine *gemstone* ˈsɑːd aɪn ‖ ˈsɑːrd- **~s** z
Sardini|a sɑː ˈdɪn i‿|ə ‖ sɑːr- **~an/s** ən/z
Sardis ˈsɑːd ɪs §-əs ‖ ˈsɑːrd-
sardius ˈsɑːd i‿əs ‖ ˈsɑːrd- **~es** ɪz əz
sardonic sɑː ˈdɒn ɪk ‖ sɑːr ˈdɑːn ɪk **~ally** əl‿i
sardonyx ˈsɑːd ə nɪks ən ɪks; ˌsɑː ˈdɒn ɪks ‖ sɑːr ˈdɑːn ɪks ˈsɑːrd ən- **~es** ɪz əz
saree ˈsɑːr i —*Hindi* [ˈsaː ɽi] **~s** z
Sargant ˈsɑːdʒ ənt ‖ ˈsɑːrdʒ-
sargasso, S~ sɑː ˈgæs əʊ ‖ sɑːr ˈgæs oʊ **~s** z **Sarˌgasso ˈSea**
sarge sɑːdʒ ‖ sɑːrdʒ
Sargeant, Sargent ˈsɑːdʒ ənt ‖ ˈsɑːrdʒ-
Sargon ˈsɑːg ɒn ‖ ˈsɑːrg ɑːn
sari ˈsɑːr i —*Hindi* [ˈsaː ɽi] **~s** z
Sarille *tdmk* sə ˈrɪl
sarin ˈsɑːr ɪn ˈsær-, §-ən
Sark, sark sɑːk ‖ sɑːrk **Sark's, sarks** sɑːks ‖ sɑːrks
sarking ˈsɑːk ɪŋ ‖ ˈsɑːrk ɪŋ
Sarkozy sɑː ˈkəʊz i ‖ ˌsɑːrk oʊ ˈziː —*Fr* [saʁ ko zi]
sark|y ˈsɑːk |i ‖ ˈsɑːrk |i **~ier** i‿ə ‖ i‿ər **~iest** i‿ɪst i‿əst **~ily** ɪ li əl i **~iness** i nəs i nɪs
Sarmatia sɑː ˈmeɪʃ ə -ˈmeɪʃ i‿ə ‖ sɑːr-
Sarmatian sɑː ˈmeɪʃ ən -ˈmeɪʃ i‿ən ‖ sɑːr- **~s** z
Sarnia ˈsɑːn i‿ə ‖ ˈsɑːrn i‿ə
sarnie *'sandwich'* ˈsɑːn i ‖ — **~s** z
sarong sə ˈrɒŋ ‖ -ˈrɔːŋ -ˈrɑːŋ **~s** z
Saronic, s~ sə ˈrɒn ɪk ‖ -ˈrɑːn ɪk
saros ˈseər ɒs ˈseɪ rɒs ‖ ˈser ɑːs ˈsær- **~es** ɪz əz
Saro-Wiwa ˌsær əʊ ˈwiː wə ˌsɑːr- ‖ ˌsɑːr oʊ- ˌsær-
Saroyan sə ˈrɔɪ ən
Sarpedon sɑː ˈpiːd ən -ɒn ‖ sɑːr- -ɑːn
sarracenia ˌsær ə ˈsiːn i‿ə -ˈsen- ‖ ˌser- **~s** z
Sarre sɑː ‖ sɑːr
Sars, SARS sɑːz ‖ sɑːrz
sarsaparilla ˌsɑːsp ə ˈrɪl ə ◂ ˌsɑːs əp ə ˈrɪl ə ‖ ˌsæsp- ˌsɑːrsp-, -ˈrel-
sarsen ˈsɑːs ən ‖ ˈsɑːrs ən **~s** z
sarsenet ˈsɑːs nət -nɪt, -net ‖ ˈsɑːrs-
Sarson ˈsɑːs ən ‖ ˈsɑːrs ən
sartor, S~ ˈsɑːt ə -ɔː ‖ ˈsɑːrţ ər
sartorial sɑː ˈtɔːr i‿əl ‖ sɑːr- -ˈtoʊr- **~ly** i
sartorius sɑː ˈtɔːr i‿əs ‖ sɑːr- -ˈtoʊr-
Sartre sɑːtr ˈsɑːtr ə ‖ ˈsɑːrtr ə —*Fr* [saʁtχ]
Sarum ˈseər əm ‖ ˈser əm ˈsær-
SAS ˌes eɪ ˈes

S

sash sæʃ **sashed** sæʃt **sashes** 'sæʃ ɪz -əz **sashing** 'sæʃ ɪŋ
'**sash cord**; ˌ**sash 'window**, 'ˌ'·
Sasha 'sæʃ ə ‖ 'sɑːʃ ə
sashay 'sæʃ eɪ sæ 'ʃeɪ ‖ sæ 'ʃeɪ **~ed** d **~ing** ɪŋ **~s** z
sashimi sæ 'ʃiːm i sə- ‖ sɑː- —*Jp* [sa ˌɕi 'mi]
Saskatchewan sæ 'skætʃ ə wən sə-, -ɪ-, -wɒn ‖ -wɑːn
Saskatoon, s~ ˌsæsk ə 'tuːn
Saskia 'sæsk i‿ə
Sasquatch, s~ 'sæsk wætʃ -wɒtʃ ‖ -wɑːtʃ
sass sæs **sassed** sæst **sasses** 'sæs ɪz -əz **sassing** 'sæs ɪŋ
sassab|y 'sæs əb |i **~ies** iz
sassafras 'sæs ə fræs **~es** ɪz əz
Sassanid 'sæs ən ɪd §-əd **~s** z
Sassanidae sə 'sæn ɪ diː -ə-
Sasse sæs
Sassenach 'sæs ə næk -næx; -ən ək, -ən əx —*ScG and Ir* ['sa sə nəx] **~s** s
Sassoon sə 'suːn sæ-
sass|y 'sæs |i **~ier** i‿ə ‖ i‿ᵊr **~iest** i‿ɪst i‿əst **~ily** ɪ li əl i **~iness** i nəs i nɪs
sat sæt
Satan 'seɪt ᵊn —*formerly also* 'sæt-
satanic sə 'tæn ɪk **~al** ᵊl **~ally** ᵊl‿i
Satanism 'seɪt ᵊn ˌɪz əm
Satanist 'seɪt ᵊn ɪst §-əst **~s** s
satay 'sæt eɪ 'sɑːt- ‖ 'sɑːt-
satchel 'sætʃ əl **~s** z
sate seɪt **sated** 'seɪt ɪd -əd ‖ 'seɪţ əd **sates** seɪts **sating** 'seɪt ɪŋ ‖ 'seɪţ ɪŋ
saté 'sæt eɪ 'sɑːt- ‖ 'sɑːt-
sateen sə 'tiːn sæ- **~s** z
satellite 'sæt ə laɪt -ɪ-, →-ᵊl aɪt ‖ 'sæţ ᵊl aɪt **~s** s
satem 'sɑːt əm 'sæt-, 'seɪt-, -em ‖ 'sɑːţ əm
satiab|le 'seɪʃ əb |ᵊl 'seɪʃ i‿əb |ᵊl **~leness** ᵊl nəs -nɪs **~ly** li
sati|ate *v* 'seɪʃ i |eɪt **~ated** eɪt ɪd -əd ‖ eɪţ əd **~ates** eɪts **~ating** eɪt ɪŋ ‖ eɪţ ɪŋ
satiation ˌseɪʃ i 'eɪʃ ᵊn
Satie 'sæt i 'sɑːt i ‖ sæ 'tiː sɑː- —*Fr* [sa ti]
satiety sə 'taɪ‿ət i 'seɪʃ i‿, -ɪt i ‖ -əţ i
satin 'sæt ɪn §-ᵊn ‖ -ᵊn **~s** z
satinet, satinette ˌsæt ɪ 'net §-ə-, -ᵊn 'et ‖ -ᵊn 'et
satinwood 'sæt ɪn wʊd §-ᵊn- ‖ -ᵊn-
satiny 'sæt ɪn i §-ᵊn- ‖ -ᵊn i
satire 'sæt aɪ‿ə ‖ 'sæt aɪ‿ᵊr **~s** z
satiric sə 'tɪr ɪk **~al** ᵊl **~ally** ᵊl‿i **~alness** ᵊl nəs -nɪs
satiris... —*see* **satiriz...**
satirist 'sæt ər ɪst -ɪr-, §-əst ‖ 'sæţ- **~s** s
satirization ˌsæt ər aɪ 'zeɪʃ ᵊn ˌ·ɪr-, -ɪ'·- ‖ ˌsæţ ər ə-
satiriz|e 'sæt ə raɪz -ɪ- ‖ 'sæţ- **~ed** d **~es** ɪz əz **~ing** ɪŋ
satisfaction ˌsæt ɪs 'fæk ʃᵊn -əs- ‖ ˌsæţ- **~s** z
satisfactor|y ˌsæt ɪs 'fækt ər‿|i ◂ ˌ·əs- ‖ ˌsæţ- **~ily** əl i ɪ li **~iness** i nəs i nɪs
satis|fy 'sæt ɪs |faɪ -əs- ‖ 'sæţ- **~fied** faɪd **~fier/s** faɪ‿ə/z ‖ faɪ‿ᵊr/z **~fies** faɪz **~fying/ly** faɪ ɪŋ /li
sat-nav 'sæt næv
satori sə 'tɔːr i —*Jp* [sa ˌto ɾi]
satphone 'sæt fəʊn ‖ -foʊn **~s** z
satrap 'sætr æp -əp ‖ 'seɪtr- **~s** s
satrap|y 'sætr əp |i ‖ 'seɪtr- **~ies** iz
satsuma, S~ sæt 'suːm ə 'sæts əm ə, -u mɑː —*Jp* ['sa tsɯ ma] **~s** z
Satterthwaite 'sæt ə θweɪt ‖ 'sæţ ᵊr-
satu|rate 'sætʃ ə |reɪt -ʊ-; 'sæt jʊ- **~rated** reɪt ɪd -əd ‖ reɪţ əd **~rates** reɪts **~rating** reɪt ɪŋ ‖ reɪţ ɪŋ
saturation ˌsætʃ ə 'reɪʃ ᵊn -ʊ-; ˌsæt jʊ-
ˌ**satu'ration point**
Saturday 'sæt ə deɪ -di; ⚠'sæt di ‖ 'sæţ ᵊr- —*See note at* -day **~s** z
ˌ**Saturday 'night**
Saturn 'sæt ɜːn -ᵊn ‖ 'sæţ ᵊrn **~'s** z
saturnalia, S~ ˌsæt ə 'neɪl i‿ə ˌ·ɜː- ‖ ˌsæţ ᵊr-
Saturnian, s~ sæ 'tɜːn i‿ən sə- ‖ -'tɜːn-
saturnine 'sæt ə naɪn ‖ 'sæţ ᵊr-
satyagraha, S~ sʌt 'jɑːg rə hə 'sʌt jəg rə hə, -jə grɑː hə, -hɑː —*Hindi* [sə tjə grəh]
satyr 'sæt ə ‖ 'seɪţ ᵊr 'sæţ- **~s** z
satyriasis ˌsæt ə 'raɪ‿əs ɪs ˌ·ɪ-, §-əs ‖ ˌseɪţ- ˌsæţ-
satyric sə 'tɪr ɪk ‖ seɪ-
sauce sɔːs ‖ sɑːs **sauced** sɔːst ‖ sɑːst **sauces** 'sɔːs ɪz -əz ‖ 'sɑːs- **saucing** 'sɔːs ɪŋ ‖ 'sɑːs-
saucepan 'sɔːs pən §'sɒs-, §-pæn ‖ -pæn 'sɑːs- **~s** z
saucer 'sɔːs ə ‖ -ᵊr 'sɑːs- **~s** z
Sauchiehall ˌsɒk i 'hɔːl ˌsɔːk-, ˌsɒx-, ˌsɔːx- ‖ ˌsɑːk i 'hɔːl ˌsɔːk-, -'hɑːl
Saucony *tdmk* sɔː 'kəʊn i ‖ -'koʊn i sɑː-
sauc|y 'sɔːs |i ‖ 'sɑːs- **~ier** i‿ə ‖ i‿ᵊr **~iest** i‿ɪst i‿əst **~ily** ɪ li əl i **~iness** i nəs i nɪs
Saud saʊd sɑː 'uːd —*Arabic* [sa 'ʕuːd]
Saudi 'saʊd i 'sɔːd-; sɑː 'uːd i ‖ 'sɔːd-, 'sɑːd- —*Arabic* [sa 'ʕuː diː] **~s** z
ˌ**Saudi A'rabia**
sauerbraten 'saʊ‿ə brɑːt ᵊn ‖ 'saʊ‿ᵊr- —*Ger* ['zaʊ ɐ ˌbʁaː tn]
sauerkraut 'saʊ‿ə kraʊt ‖ 'saʊ‿ᵊr- —*Ger* ['zaʊ ɐ kʁaʊt]
sauger 'sɔːg ə ‖ -ᵊr 'sɑːg- **~s** z
Saughall 'sɔːk ᵊl ‖ 'sɑːk-
Saughton 'sɒxt ən ‖ 'sɔːkt ən 'sɑːkt-
Saugus 'sɔːg əs ‖ 'sɑːg-
Sauk sɔːk ‖ sɑːk **Sauks** sɔːks ‖ sɑːks
Saul sɔːl ‖ sɑːl
Sault Sainte Marie, Sault Ste Marie ˌsuː ˌseɪnt mə 'riː
sauna 'sɔːn ə 'saʊn- ‖ 'sɑːn-, 'saʊn- —*Finnish* ['sau nɑ] **~s** z
Saunders *(i)* 'sɔːnd əz ‖ -ᵊrz, *(ii)* 'sɑːnd-
Saundersfoot 'sɔːnd əz fʊt ‖ -ᵊrz- 'sɑːnd-
Saunderson *(i)* 'sɔːnd əs ən ‖ -ᵊrs-, *(ii)* 'sɑːnd-
saunter 'sɔːnt ə ‖ 'sɔːnţ ᵊr 'sɑːnţ- **~ed** d **sauntering** 'sɔːnt‿ər ɪŋ ‖ 'sɔːnţ ər ɪŋ 'sɑːnţ- **~s** z
Saunton 'sɔːnt ən ‖ 'sɑːnt-

-saur sɔː ‖ sɔːr — **stegosaur** ˈsteg ə sɔː ‖ -sɔːr
saurian ˈsɔːr i‿ən **~s** z
sauropod ˈsɔːr əʊ pɒd ‖ -ə pɑːd **~s** z
-saurus ˈsɔːr əs — **stegosaurus** ˌsteg ə ˈsɔːr əs
sausag|e ˈsɒs ɪdʒ ‖ ˈsɔːs ɪdʒ ˈsɑːs- *(!)* **~es** ɪz əz **ˈsausage dog**; **ˈsausage meat**; **ˌsausage ˈroll**
Saussure səʊ ˈsjʊə -ˈsʊə ‖ soʊ ˈsʊᵊr -ˈsjʊᵊr —*Fr* [so syːʁ]
Saussurean, Saussurian səʊ ˈsjʊər i‿ən -ˈsʊər- ‖ soʊ ˈsʊr- -ˈsjʊr- **~s** z
saute, sauté ˈsəʊt eɪ ˈsɔːt-, -i ‖ soʊ ˈteɪ sɔː-, sɑː- **~d, ~ed** d **~ing** ɪŋ **~s** z
Sauterne, Sauternes səʊ ˈtɜːn -ˈteən ‖ soʊ ˈtɜːn -ˈteᵊrn —*Fr* Sauternes [so tɛʁn]
sauve qui peut ˌsəʊv kiː ˈpɜː ‖ ˌsoʊv kiː ˈpʊ —*Fr* [sov ki pø]
Sauvignon ˈsəʊv iːn jɒn -ɪn-, -jɒ̃, ˌ· ·ˈ· ‖ ˌsoʊv iːn ˈjoʊn —*Fr* [so vi njɔ̃]
savag|e, S~ ˈsæv ɪdʒ **~ed** d **~ely** li **~eness** nəs nɪs **~es** ɪz əz **~ing** ɪŋ
savager|y ˈsæv ɪdʒ ər‿i **~ies** iz
savanna, savannah, S~ sə ˈvæn ə **~s** z
savant ˈsæv ᵊnt ‖ sə ˈvɑːnt sæ- *(*)* —*Fr* [sa vɑ̃] **~s** s
savarin, S~ ˈsæv ə ræ̃ -rɪn; -ər ən —*Fr* [sa va ʁɛ̃] **~s** z
save seɪv **saved** seɪvd **saves** seɪvz **saving** ˈseɪv ɪŋ **ˌsaving ˈgrace**
saveloy ˈsæv ə lɔɪ -ɪ-, ˌ· ·ˈ· **~s** z
saver ˈseɪv ə ‖ -ᵊr **~s** z
Savernake ˈsæv ə næk ‖ -ᵊr- —*There is also a spelling pronunciation* ⚠-neɪk.
Savile, Savill ˈsæv ᵊl -ɪl
savings ˈseɪv ɪŋz **ˈsavings acˌcount**; **ˌsavings and ˈloan, ˌsavings and ˈloan associˌation**; **ˈsavings bank**
savior, saviour, S~ ˈseɪv jə ‖ -jᵊr **~s** z
Savlon *tdmk* ˈsæv lɒn ‖ -lɑːn
savoir-faire ˌsæv wɑː ˈfeə ˌsʌv- ‖ -wɑːr ˈfeᵊr -ˈfæᵊr —*Fr* [sa vwaʁ fɛːʁ]
savoir-vivre ˌsæv wɑː ˈviːv rə ˌsʌv- ‖ -wɑːr- —*Fr* [sa vwaʁ viːvʁ]
Savonarola ˌsæv ən‿ə ˈrəʊl ə ‖ -ˈroʊl ə —*It* [sa vo na ˈrɔː la]
savor, savour ˈseɪv ə ‖ -ᵊr **~ed** d **savoring, savouring** ˈseɪv ər‿ɪŋ **~s** z
savor|y, savour|y, Savory ˈseɪv ər‿i **~ies** iz
Savoy, savoy sə ˈvɔɪ **~s, ~'s** z
Savoyard sə ˈvɔɪ ɑːd ˌsæv ɔɪ ˈɑːd ‖ ˌsæv ɔɪ ˈɑːrd **~s** z
savv|y ˈsæv |i **~ied** id **~ies** iz **~ying** i‿ɪŋ
saw sɔː ‖ sɑː **sawed** sɔːd ‖ sɑːd **sawing** ˈsɔːʳ ɪŋ ‖ ˈsɔː ɪŋ ˈsɑː- **sawn** sɔːn ‖ sɑːn **saws** sɔːz ‖ sɑːz **ˈsaw atˌtachment**
Saward ˈseɪ wəd ‖ -wᵊrd
Sawatch sə ˈwɒtʃ ‖ -ˈwɑːtʃ
sawbones ˈsɔː bəʊnz ‖ -boʊnz ˈsɑː-
Sawbridgeworth ˈsɔː brɪdʒ wɜːθ -wəθ ‖ -wɜːθ ˈsɑː- —*Formerly locally also* ˈsæps wəθ
sawbuck ˈsɔː bʌk ‖ ˈsɑː- **~s** s
sawdust ˈsɔː dʌst ‖ ˈsɑː-
sawed-off ˌsɔːd ˈɒf ◂ -ˈɔːf ‖ -ˈɔːf ◂ ˌsɑːd ˈɑːf◂ **ˌsawed-off ˈshotgun**
sawfish ˈsɔː fɪʃ ‖ ˈsɑː-
saw|fly ˈsɔː |flaɪ ‖ ˈsɑː- **~flies** flaɪz
sawhors|e ˈsɔː hɔːs ‖ -hɔːrs ˈsɑː- **~es** ɪz əz
sawmill ˈsɔː mɪl ‖ ˈsɑː- **~s** z
sawn sɔːn ‖ sɑːn
sawn-off ˌsɔːn ˈɒf ◂ -ˈɔːf ‖ -ˈɔːf ◂ ˌsɑːn ˈɑːf◂ **ˌsawn-off ˈshotgun**
sawpit ˈsɔː pɪt ‖ ˈsɑː- **~s** s
Sawston ˈsɔːst ən ‖ ˈsɑːst-
sawtooth ˈsɔː tuːθ §-tʊθ ‖ ˈsɑː- **~ed** t
Sawtry ˈsɔːtr i ‖ ˈsɑːtr-
saw-wort ˈsɔː wɜːt -wɔːt ‖ -wɜːt ˈsɑː-, -wɔːrt
sawyer, S~ ˈsɔː jə ‖ -jᵊr ˈsɑː-; ˈsɔɪ‿ᵊr **~s** z
sax sæks **saxes** ˈsæks ɪz -əz
Saxa *tdmk* ˈsæks ə
Saxby ˈsæks bi
saxe, Saxe sæks **ˌsaxe ˈblue◂**
Saxe-Coburg-Gotha ˌsæks ˌkəʊ bɜːg ˈgəʊθ ə -ˈgəʊt- ‖ -ˌkoʊ bɜːg ˈgoʊθ ə
saxhorn ˈsæks hɔːn ‖ -hɔːrn **~s** z
saxifrag|e ˈsæks ɪ freɪdʒ -ə-, -frɪdʒ, -freɪʒ **~es** ɪz əz
Saxin *tdmk* ˈsæks ɪn §-ən
Saxmundham sæks ˈmʌnd əm
Saxo ˈsæks əʊ ‖ -oʊ **ˌSaxo Gramˈmaticus** grə ˈmæt ɪk əs ‖ -ˈmæṭ-
Saxon ˈsæks ᵊn **~s** z
Saxone *tdmk* ˌsæk ˈsəʊn ‖ -ˈsoʊn
Saxony, s~ ˈsæks ən i
saxophone ˈsæks ə fəʊn ‖ -foʊn **~s** z
saxophonist sæk ˈsɒf ən ɪst ˈsæks ə fəʊn-, §-əst ‖ ˈsæks ə foʊn əst
Saxton ˈsækst ən

SAYS

16%
84%
sez
seɪz
BrE

say seɪ **said** sed *(!)* **saying/s** ˈseɪ ɪŋ/z **says** sez §seɪz — *Preference poll, BrE:* sez *84%,* seɪz *16%.*
Saybolt ˈseɪ bəʊlt →-bɒʊlt ‖ -boʊlt
Sayce seɪs
Sayer, s~ ˈseɪ ə ‖ -ᵊr
Sayers ˈseɪ əz ‖ -ᵊrz
Sayle seᵊl
says sez §seɪz *(!)*
say-so ˈseɪ səʊ ‖ -soʊ **~s** z
sazarac, sazerac, S~ *tdmk* ˈsæz ə ræk **~s** s
S-bend ˈes bend **~s** z

scab skæb **scabbed** skæbd **scabbing** 'skæb ɪŋ **scabs** skæbz
scabbard 'skæb əd ‖ -ᵊrd **~s** z
scabb|y 'skæb |i **~ier** i‿ə ‖ i‿ᵊr **~iest** i‿ɪst i‿əst **~ily** ɪ li əl i **~iness** i nəs i nɪs
scabies 'skeɪb i:z 'skeɪb i‿i:z
scabious 'skeɪb i‿əs **~es** ɪz əz
scabrous 'skeɪb rəs 'skæb- ‖ 'skæb- **~ly** li **~ness** nəs nɪs
scad skæd **scads** skædz
Scafell ˌskɔ: 'fel ◂ ˌskɑ:- ˌ**Scafell 'Pike**
scaffold 'skæf əʊld →-ɒʊld, -ᵊld ‖ -ᵊld -oʊld **~ed** ɪd əd **~er/s** ə/z ‖ -ᵊr/z **~ing** ɪŋ **~s** z
scag skæg
scagliola skæl 'jəʊl ə ‖ -'joʊl ə —*It* [skaʎ 'ʎɔ: la]
scala, Scala 'skɑ:l ə —*In anatomy, also* 'skeɪl ə
scalability ˌskeɪᵊl ə 'bɪl ət i -ɪt i ‖ -əţ i
scalable 'skeɪlᵊl əb ᵊl
scalar 'skeɪl ə -ɑ: ‖ -ᵊr -ɑ:r **~s** z
scalawag 'skæl ə wæg -i- **~s** z
scald skɔ:ld §skɒld ‖ skɑ:ld **scalded** 'skɔ:ld ɪd §'skɒld-, -əd ‖ 'skɑ:ld- **scalding/s** 'skɔ:ld ɪŋ/z §'skɒld- ‖ 'skɑ:ld- **scalds** skɔ:ldz §skɒldz ‖ skɑ:ldz
scale skeɪᵊl **scaled** skeɪᵊld **scales** skeɪᵊlz **scaling** 'skeɪᵊl ɪŋ
scalene 'skeɪl i:n ˌskeɪ 'li:n ◂
scalen|us skeɪ 'li:n |əs skə- **~i** aɪ
scaler 'skeɪl ə ‖ -ᵊr **~s** z
Scalextric *tdmk* ˌskeɪ 'leks trɪk
Scaliger 'skæl ɪdʒ ə -§ədʒ- ‖ -ᵊr
scallion 'skæl i‿ən ‖ 'skæl jən **~s** z

SCALLOP

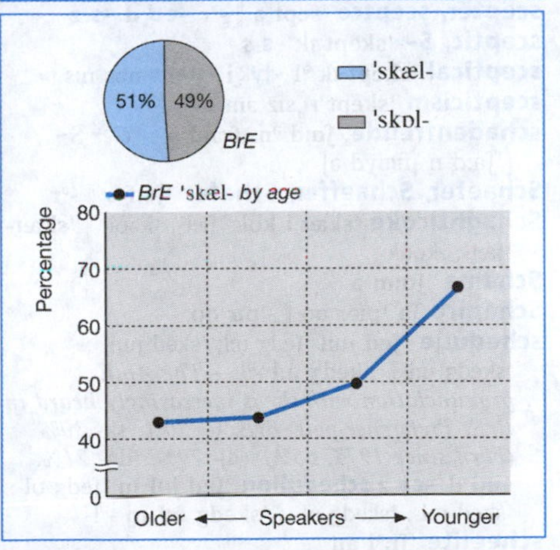

scallop 'skɒl əp 'skæl- ‖ 'skæl əp 'skɑ:l- — *Preference poll, BrE:* 'skɒl- *49%,* 'skæl- *51%.* **~ed** t **~ing** ɪŋ **~s** s
scall|y 'skæl| i **~ies** iz
scallywag 'skæl i wæg **~s** z
scaloppin|e ˌskæl ə 'pi:n |i ‖ ˌskɑ:l- **~i** i: i

scalp skælp **scalped** skælpt **scalping** 'skælp ɪŋ **scalps** skælps
Scalpay 'skælp eɪ -i
scalpel 'skælp ᵊl **~s** z
scalper 'skælp ə ‖ -ᵊr **~s** z
scal|y 'skeɪl |i **~ier** i‿ə ‖ i‿ᵊr **~iest** i‿ɪst i‿əst **~iness** i nəs i nɪs
scam skæm **scammed** skæmd **scamming** 'skæm ɪŋ **scams** skæmz
Scammell 'skæm ᵊl
scammer 'skæm ə ‖ -ᵊr **~s** z
scammon|y 'skæm ən |i **~ies** iz
scamp skæmp **scamped** skæmpt **scamping** 'skæmp ɪŋ **scamps** skæmps
scamper 'skæmp ə ‖ -ᵊr **~ed** d **scampering/s** 'skæmp ər‿ɪŋ/z **~s** z
scampi 'skæmp i
scampish 'skæmp ɪʃ **~ly** li **~ness** nəs nɪs
scan skæn **scanned** skænd **scanning** 'skæn ɪŋ **scans** skænz
scandal 'skænd ᵊl **~s** z
scandalis|e, scandaliz|e 'skænd ᵊl aɪz -ə laɪz **~ed** d **~es** ɪz əz **~ing** ɪŋ
scandalmonger 'skænd ᵊl ˌmʌŋ gə -ˌmɒŋ- ‖ -gᵊr -ˌmɑ:ŋ- **~s** z
scandalous 'skænd ᵊl əs **~ly** li **~ness** nəs nɪs
scandent 'skænd ənt
Scanderbeg 'skænd ə beg ‖ -ᵊr-
Scandi|a, s~ 'skænd i‿|ə **~an** ən
Scandic 'skænd ɪk
Scandinavi|a ˌskænd ɪ 'neɪv i‿|ə ˌ-ə- **~an/s** ən/z
scandium 'skænd i‿əm
Scania *tdmk* 'skæn i‿ə
Scanlan, Scanlon 'skæn lən
scann... —*see* **scan**
scanner 'skæn ə ‖ -ᵊr **~s** z
scansion 'skænᵗʃ ᵊn **~s** z
scansorial skæn 'sɔ:r i‿əl ‖ -'soʊr-
scant skænt **scanter** 'skænt ə ‖ 'skænţ ᵊr **scantest** 'skænt ɪst -əst ‖ 'skænţ əst
scanti... —*see* **scanty**
scantling 'skænt lɪŋ **~s** z
scant|ly 'skænt |li **~ness** nəs nɪs
scant|y 'skænt |i ‖ 'skænţ |i **~ier** i‿ə ‖ i‿ᵊr **~ies** iz **~iest** i‿ɪst i‿əst **~ily** ɪ li əl i **~iness** i nəs i nɪs
Scapa 'skɑ:p ə 'skæp- ˌ**Scapa 'Flow**
-scape skeɪp — **seascape** 'si: skeɪp
scape|goat 'skeɪp |gəʊt ‖ -|goʊt **~goated** gəʊt ɪd -əd ‖ goʊţ əd **~goating** gəʊt ɪŋ ‖ goʊţ ɪŋ **~goats** gəʊts ‖ goʊts
scapegrac|e 'skeɪp greɪs **~es** ɪz əz
scaphoid 'skæf ɔɪd **~s** z
scapolite 'skæp əʊ laɪt ‖ -ə-
scap|ula 'skæp |jʊl ə §-jəl- ‖ -|jəl ə **~ulae** ju li: jə- ‖ jə li: **~ulas** jʊl əz jəl- ‖ jəl əz
scapular 'skæp jʊl ə §-jəl- ‖ -jəl ᵊr **~s** z
scar skɑ: ‖ skɑ:r **scarred** skɑ:d ‖ skɑ:rd **scarring** 'skɑ:r ɪŋ **scars** skɑ:z ‖ skɑ:rz **'scar ˌtissue**
scarab 'skær əb ‖ 'sker- **~s** z

S

scarabae|us ˌskær ə ˈbiː‿|əs ‖ ˌsker- **~i** aɪ

Scaramouch, Scaramouche ˈskær ə muːtʃ -muːʃ, -maʊtʃ ‖ ˈsker-

Scarboro', Scarborough ˈskɑː bᵊr‿ə ‖ ˈskɑːr ˌbɝː oʊ

Scarbrough ˈskɑː brə ‖ ˈskɑːr- -broʊ

scarce skeəs ‖ skeᵊrs skæᵊrs **scarcer** ˈskeəs ə ‖ ˈskeᵊrs ᵊr ˈskæᵊrs- **scarcest** ˈskeəs ɪst -əst ‖ ˈskeᵊrs əst ˈskæᵊrs-

scarce|ly ˈskeəs |li ‖ ˈskeᵊrs |li ˈskæᵊrs- **~ness** nəs nɪs

scarcit|y ˈskeəs ət |i -ɪt- ‖ ˈskers əţ |i ˈskærs- **~ies** iz

scare skeə ‖ skeᵊr skæᵊr **scared** skeəd ‖ skeᵊrd skæᵊrd **scares** skeəz ‖ skeᵊrz skæᵊrz **scaring** ˈskeər ɪŋ ‖ ˈsker ɪŋ ˈskær-

scarecrow ˈskeə krəʊ ‖ ˈsker kroʊ ˈskær- **~s** z

scaredy-cat, scaredy cat ˈskeəd i kæt ‖ ˈskerd- ˈskærd- **~s** s

scaremonger ˈskeə ˌmʌŋ gə -ˌmɒŋ- ‖ ˈsker ˌmʌŋ gᵊr ˈskær-, -ˌmɑːŋ- **~s** z

scaremongering ˈskeə ˌmʌŋ gər‿ɪŋ -ˌmɒŋ- ‖ -ˌmɑːŋ-

scarer ˈskeər ə ‖ ˈsker ᵊr **~s** z

scar|ey ˈskeər |i ‖ ˈsker |i ˈskær- **~ier** i‿ə ‖ i‿ᵊr **~iest** i‿ɪst i‿əst **~ily** əl i ɪ li **~iness** i nəs i nɪs

scarf skɑːf ‖ skɑːrf **scarfed** skɑːft ‖ skɑːrft **scarfing** ˈskɑːf ɪŋ ‖ ˈskɑːrf ɪŋ **scarfs** skɑːfs ‖ skɑːrfs **scarves** skɑːvz ‖ skɑːrvz

Scarface ˈskɑː feɪs ˈskɑːr-

Scarfe skɑːf ‖ skɑːrf

Scargill ˈskɑː gɪl ˈskɑːg ᵊl ‖ ˈskɑːr-

scari... —*see* **scary**

scarification ˌskær ɪf ɪ ˈkeɪʃ ᵊn ˌskeər-, ˌ·əf-, §-ə'·- ‖ ˌsker- **~s** z

scarificator ˈskær ɪf ɪ keɪt ə ˈskeər-, ˈ·əf-, §ˈ· ·ə- ‖ -keɪţ ᵊr ˈsker- **~s** z

scari|fy ˈskær ɪ |faɪ ˈskeər-, -ə- ‖ ˈsker- **~fied** faɪd **~fier/s** faɪ‿ə/z ‖ faɪ‿ᵊr/z **~fies** faɪz **~fying** faɪ ɪŋ

Scarisbrick ˈskeəz brɪk ‖ ˈskerz- ˈskærz-

scarlatina ˌskɑːl ə ˈtiːn ə ‖ ˌskɑːrl-

Scarlatti skɑː ˈlæt i ‖ skɑːr ˈlɑːţ i —*It* [skar ˈlat ti]

scarlet ˈskɑːl ət -ɪt ‖ ˈskɑːrl- ˌ**scarlet** ˈ**fever**; ˌ**scarlet** ˈ**pimpernel**; ˌ**scarlet** ˈ**runner**; ˌ**scarlet** ˈ**woman**

Scarlett ˈskɑːl ət -ɪt ‖ ˈskɑːrl-

Scarman ˈskɑː mən ‖ ˈskɑːr-

scarp skɑːp ‖ skɑːrp **scarped** skɑːpt ‖ skɑːrpt **scarping** ˈskɑːp ɪŋ ‖ ˈskɑːrp ɪŋ **scarps** skɑːps ‖ skɑːrps

scarper ˈskɑːp ə ‖ ˈskɑːrp ᵊr **~ed** d **scarpering** ˈskɑːp ər‿ɪŋ ‖ ˈskɑːrp- **~s** z

scarr... —*see* **scar**

SCART skɑːt skɑːrt

scarves skɑːvz ‖ skɑːrvz

scar|y ˈskeər |i ‖ ˈsker |i ˈskær- **~ier** i‿ə ‖ i‿ᵊr **~iest** i‿ɪst i‿əst **~ily** əl i ɪ li **~iness** i nəs i nɪs

Scase skeɪs

scat skæt **scats** skæts **scatted** ˈskæt ɪd -əd ‖ ˈskæţ əd **scatting** ˈskæt ɪŋ ‖ ˈskæţ ɪŋ

scathing ˈskeɪð ɪŋ **~ly** li

scatological ˌskæt ə ˈlɒdʒ ɪk ᵊl ◂ -ᵊl ˈɒdʒ- ‖ ˌskæţ ᵊl ˈɑːdʒ- **~ly** ˌi

scatology skæ ˈtɒl ədʒ i ‖ -ˈtɑːl-

scatter ˈskæt ə ‖ ˈskæţ ᵊr **~ed** d **scattering** ˈskæt‿ər ɪŋ ‖ ˈskæţ ər ɪŋ **~s** z ˈ**scatter** ˌ**cushion**; ˈ**scatter** ˌ**diagram**

scatterbrain ˈskæt ə breɪn ‖ ˈskæţ ᵊr- **~ed** d **~s** z

Scattergood ˈskæt ə gʊd ‖ ˈskæţ ᵊr-

scatter-gun ˈskæt ə gʌn ‖ ˈskæţ ᵊr- **~s** z

scattershot ˈskæt ə ʃɒt ‖ ˈskæţ ᵊr ʃɑːt

scatt|y ˈskæt |i ‖ ˈskæţ |i **~ier** i‿ə ‖ i‿ᵊr **~iest** i‿ɪst i‿əst **~ily** ɪ li əl i **~iness** i nəs i nɪs

scaup skɔːp ‖ skɑːp **scaups** skɔːps ‖ skɑːps

scaveng|e ˈskæv ɪn*d*ʒ -ᵊn*d*ʒ **~ed** d **~es** ɪz əz **~ing** ɪŋ

scavenger ˈskæv ɪn*d*ʒ ə -ᵊn*d*ʒ- ‖ -ᵊr **~s** z

scena ˈʃeɪn ə ‖ -ɑː —*It* [ˈʃɛː na]

scenario sə ˈnɑːr i‿əʊ sɪ-, se-, -ˈneər- ‖ sə ˈnær i oʊ -ˈner-, -ˈnɑːr- **~s** z

scenarist ˈsiːn ər ɪst sə ˈnɑːr-, sɪ-, se-, §-əst ‖ sə ˈnær əst -ˈner-, -ˈnɑːr-

scene siːn *(= seen)* **scenes** siːnz

scenery ˈsiːn ər i

sceneshifter ˈsiːn ʃɪft ə ‖ -ᵊr **~s** z

scenic ˈsiːn ɪk ˈsen- **~ally** ᵊl‿i

scenographer siː ˈnɒg rəf ə ‖ -ˈnɑːg rəf ᵊr **~s** z

scenographic ˌsiːn əʊ ˈgræf ɪk ◂ ‖ -ə- **~ally** ᵊl‿i

scenography siː ˈnɒg rəf i ‖ -ˈnɑːg-

scent sent *(= cent, sent)* **scented** ˈsent ɪd -əd ‖ ˈsenţ əd **scenting** ˈsent ɪŋ ‖ ˈsenţ ɪŋ **scents** sen*t*s ˈ**scent mark**

scentless ˈsent ləs -lɪs

scepter, sceptre ˈsept ə ‖ -ᵊr **~ed** d **~s** z

sceptic, S~ ˈskept ɪk **~s** s

sceptical ˈskept ɪk ᵊl **~ly** ‿i **~ness** nəs nɪs

scepticism ˈskept ɪ ˌsɪz əm -ə-

schadenfreude ˈʃɑːd ᵊn ˌfrɔɪd ə —*Ger* S~ [ˈʃaːd n ˌfʁɔyd ə]

Schaefer, Schaeffer, Schafer ˈʃeɪf ə ‖ -ᵊr

Schaghticoke ˈskæt i kʊk ˈʃæt-, -kəʊk ‖ ˈskæţ- ˈʃæţ-, -koʊk

Schama ˈʃɑːm ə

Schapiro ʃə ˈpɪər əʊ ‖ -ˈpɪr oʊ

schedul|e ˈʃed juːl ˈʃedʒ uːl; ˈsked juːl, ˈskedʒ uːl ‖ ˈskedʒ uːl -ᵊl —*The AmE pronunciation with sk- is increasingly heard in BrE. Preference poll, BrE:* ʃ- *70%,* sk- *30% (born since 1973, 65%);* -dj- *79%,* -dʒ- *21%.* **~ed** d **~es** z **scheduling** ˈʃed jʊl ɪŋ ˈʃedʒ ʊl-; ˈsked jʊl-, ˈskedʒ ʊl- ‖ ˈskedʒ uːl ɪŋ -ᵊl-

scheelite ˈʃiːᵊl aɪt

Scheherazade ʃə ˌher ə ˈzɑːd ə ʃɪ-, -ˌhɪər-, -ˈzɑːd

Scheldt ʃelt skelt —*Dutch* Schelde [ˈsxɛl də]

Schelling ˈʃel ɪŋ —*Ger* [ˈʃɛl ɪŋ]

schema ˈskiːm ə **~s** z **schemata** ˈskiːm ət ə skiː ˈmɑːt ə ‖ ˈskiːm əţ ə skiː ˈmɑːţ ə —*The*

SCHEDULE

ʃ- sk- -dj- -dʒ-
30% 70% BrE
21% 79% BrE
BrE sk- by age
Percentage 80 70 60 50 40 30 20 10 0
Older ← Speakers → Younger

classically correct plural form, with initial stress, is being displaced by a new form with penultimate stress.

schematic skiː ˈmæt ɪk skɪ- ‖ -ˈmæţ ɪk **~ally** əl‿i **~s** s
schematis... —*see* **schematiz...**
schematism ˈskiːm ə ˌtɪz əm **~s** z
schematization ˌskiːm ət aɪ ˈzeɪʃ ən -ɪˈ-- ‖ -əţ ə- **~s** z
schematiz|e ˈskiːm ə taɪz **~ed** d **~es** z **~ing** ɪŋ
scheme skiːm **schemed** skiːmd **schemes** skiːmz **scheming** ˈskiːm ɪŋ
schemer ˈskiːm ə ‖ -ər **~s** z
Schenectady skɪ ˈnekt əd i skə-
Schengen ˈʃeŋ ən —*Ger* [ˈʃɛŋ ən]
Schering ˈʃɪər ɪŋ ‖ ˈʃɪr- —*Ger* [ˈʃeːr ɪŋ]
scherzando skeət ˈsænd əʊ skɜːt- ‖ skert ˈsɑːnd oʊ —*It* [sker ˈtsan do] **~s** z
scherz|o ˈskeəts |əʊ ˈskɜːt- ‖ ˈskerts |oʊ —*It* [ˈsker tso] **~i** iː **~os** əʊz |oʊz
Scheveningen ˈskeɪv ən‿ɪŋ ən —*Dutch* [ˈsxeː və nɪŋ ən]
Schiaparelli ˌskæp ə ˈrel i ˌʃæp- ‖ ˌskjɑːp- —*It* [skja pa ˈrɛl li]
Schick ʃɪk
Schiedam ˈskiː dæm ˌ·ˈ·, skɪ- —*Dutch* [sxi ˈdɑm]
Schiffer ˈʃɪf ə ‖ -ər —*Ger* [ˈʃɪf ɐ]
Schiller, S~ ˈʃɪl ə ‖ -ər —*Ger* [ˈʃɪl ɐ]
schilling ˈʃɪl ɪŋ **~s** z
Schindler ˈʃɪnd lə ‖ -lər —*Ger* [ˈʃɪnd lɐ]
Schiphol ˈskɪp ɒl ‖ -oʊl —*Dutch* [sxɪp ˈhɔl, ˈ· ·]
schipperke ˈʃɪp ək i ˈskɪp- ‖ -ərk i **~s** z
schism ˈskɪz əm ˈsɪz- —*The traditional* ˈsɪz- *is being displaced, except perhaps among the clergy, by* ˈskɪz-. *Preference poll, BrE:* ˈskɪz- *71%,* ˈsɪz- *29%.* **~s** z
schismatic skɪz ˈmæt ɪk sɪz- ‖ -ˈmæţ ɪk **~ally** əl‿i **~s** s
schist ʃɪst **schists** ʃɪsts
schistosome ˈʃɪst ə səʊm ‖ -soʊm -zoʊm **~s** z

SCHISM

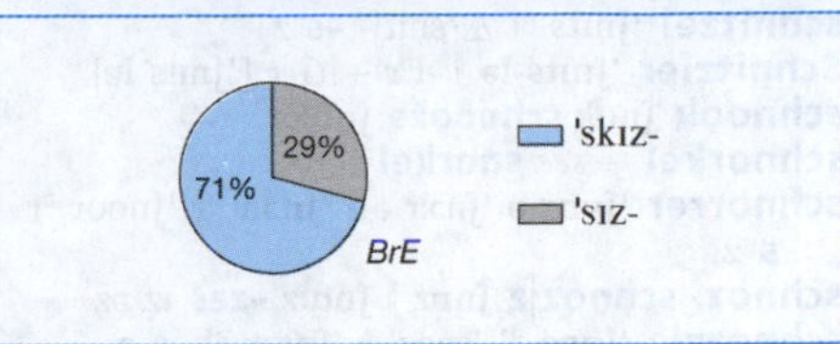

schistosomiasis ˌʃɪst ə səʊ ˈmaɪ‿əs ɪs §-əs ‖ -ə soʊ-
schizandra skɪt ˈsændr ə
schizanthus, S~ skɪt ˈsæn*t*θ əs skɪ ˈzæn*t*θ- **~es** ɪz əz
schizo ˈskɪts əʊ ‖ -oʊ **~s** z
schizo- *comb. form*
with stress-neutral suffix ˈskɪts əʊ ˈskɪz-, ˈskaɪz- — **schizocarp** ˈskɪts əʊ kɑːp ˈskɪz-, ˈskaɪz- ‖ -ə kɑːrp
with stress-imposing suffix skɪt ˈsɒ+ skɪ ˈzɒ+, skaɪ- ‖ -ˈsɑː+ — **schizogony** skɪt ˈsɒg ən i skɪ ˈzɒg-, skaɪ- ‖ skɪ ˈzɑːg- skɪt ˈsɑːg-
schizoid ˈskɪts ɔɪd ˈskɪdz- **~s** z
schizont ˈskɪts ɒnt ˈskaɪz-, ˈskɪz- ‖ -ɑːnt **~s** s
schizophrenia ˌskɪts əʊ ˈfriːn i‿ə ‖ ˌ-ə- -ˈfren-
~s z
schizophrenic ˌskɪts əʊ ˈfren ɪk ◂ -ˈfriːn- ‖ -ə- **~ally** əl‿i **~s** s
Schlegel ˈʃleɪg əl —*Ger* [ˈʃleː gəl]
Schleicher ˈʃlaɪk ə ˈʃlaɪx- ‖ -ər —*Ger* [ˈʃlai çɐ]
schlemiel ʃlə ˈmiːəl **~s** z
schlep, schlepp ʃlep **schlepped** ʃlept **schlepping** ˈʃlep ɪŋ **schleps, schlepps** ʃleps
Schlesinger ˈʃles ɪndʒ ə ˈsles-, -əndʒ- ‖ -ər
Schleswig ˈʃlez vɪg ˈʃles-, -wɪg —*Ger* [ˈʃleːs vɪç]
Schleswig-Holstein ˌʃlez vɪg ˈhɒl staɪn ˌʃles-, -wɪg-, -ˈhəʊl- ‖ -ˈhoʊl- —*Ger* [ˌʃleːs vɪç ˈhɔl ʃtain]
Schliemann ˈʃliː mən -mæn —*Ger* [ˈʃliː man]
schlieren ˈʃlɪər ən ‖ ˈʃlɪr ən
Schlitz ʃlɪts
schlock ʃlɒk ‖ ʃlɑːk
schlock|y ˈʃlɒk |i ‖ ˈʃlɑːk |i **~ier** i‿ə ‖ i‿ər **~iest** i‿ɪst i‿əst
schlong ʃlɒŋ ‖ ʃlɑːŋ ʃlɔːŋ **schlongs** ʃlɒŋz ‖ ʃlɑːŋz ʃlɔːŋz
schmaltz, schmalz ʃmɔːlts ʃmɒlts, ʃmælts ‖ ʃmɑːlts ʃmɔːlts
schmaltzy, schmalzy ˈʃmɔːlts i ˈʃmɒlts-, ˈʃmælts- ‖ ˈʃmɑːlts i ˈʃmɔːlts-
Schmeichel ˈsmaɪk əl —*Danish* [ˈsmɑɪ ɡ̊l]
Schmidt ʃmɪt
schmo, schmoe ʃməʊ ‖ ʃmoʊ **schmoes** ʃməʊz ‖ ʃmoʊz
schmooze ʃmuːz **schmoozed** ʃmuːzd **schmoozes** ˈʃmuːz ɪz -əz **schmoozing** ˈʃmuːz ɪŋ
schmuck ʃmʌk **schmucks** ʃmʌks
Schnabel ˈʃnɑːb əl
schnapps, schnaps ʃnæps
schnauzer ˈʃnaʊts ə ‖ -ər ˈʃnaʊz- **~s** z

S

Schneider, s~ 'ʃnaɪd ə ‖ -ᵊr —*Ger* ['ʃnai dɐ] **~s** z

schnitzel 'ʃnɪts ᵊl ⚠'snɪtʃ- **~s** z

Schnitzler 'ʃnɪts lə ‖ -lᵊr —*Ger* ['ʃnɪts lɐ]

schnook ʃnʊk **schnooks** ʃnʊks

schnorkel —*see* **snorkel**

schnorrer 'ʃnɒr ə 'ʃnɔːr ə ‖ 'ʃnɔːr ᵊr 'ʃnoʊr ᵊr **~s** z

schnoz, schnoz|z ʃnɒz ‖ ʃnɑːz **~zes** ɪz əz

schnozzle 'ʃnɒz ᵊl 'snɒz- ‖ 'ʃnɑːz ᵊl **~s** z

Schoenberg, Schönberg 'ʃɜːn bɜːg ‖ 'ʃoʊn bɜ˞ːg 'ʃɜ˞ːn- —*Ger* ['ʃøːn bɛʁk]

Schofield 'skəʊ fiːᵊld ‖ 'skoʊ-

schola cantorum ˌskəʊl ə kæn 'tɔːr əm ‖ ˌskoʊl- -'toʊr-

scholar 'skɒl ə ‖ 'skɑːl ᵊr **~s** z

scholar|ly 'skɒl ə |li ‖ 'skɑːl ᵊr |li **~liness** li nəs -nɪs

scholarship 'skɒl ə ʃɪp ‖ 'skɑːl ᵊr- **'scholarship boy**

scholastic skə 'læst ɪk skɒ- **~ally** ᵊl‿i **~s** s

scholasticism skə 'læst ɪ ˌsɪz əm skɒ-, -'ə-

Scholefield 'skəʊl fiːᵊld →'skɒʊl- ‖ 'skoʊl-

Scholes skəʊlz →skɒʊlz ‖ skoʊlz

Scholey 'skəʊl i ‖ 'skoʊl i

Scholfield *(i)* 'skəʊ fiːᵊld ‖ 'skoʊ-, *(ii)* 'skəʊl- →'skɒʊl- ‖ 'skoʊl-

scholiast 'skəʊl i æst əst ‖ 'skoʊl- **~s** s

scholi|um 'skəʊl i‿|əm ‖ 'skoʊl- **~a** ə **~ums** əmz

Scholl *(i)* ʃɒl ‖ ʃɑːl ʃɔːl, *(ii)* ʃəʊl →ʃɒʊl ‖ ʃoʊl

Schonberg, Schönberg 'ʃɜːn bɜːg -beəg ‖ 'ʃoʊn bɜ˞ːg 'ʃɜ˞ːn- —*Ger* ['ʃøːn bɛʁk]

Schonfield 'skɒn fiːᵊld ‖ 'skɑːn-

school skuːl **schooled** skuːld **schooling** 'skuːl ɪŋ **schools** skuːlz **'school board**; **ˌschool 'tie**; **ˌschool 'uniform**; **ˌschool 'year**

schoolboy 'skuːl bɔɪ **~s** z

school|child 'skuːl |tʃaɪᵊld **~children** ˌtʃɪldr ən ˌtʃʊldr-

schoolday 'skuːl deɪ **~s** z

schoolfellow 'skuːl ˌfel əʊ ‖ -oʊ **~s** z

schoolgirl 'skuːl gɜːl ‖ -gɜ˞ːl **~s** z

school|house 'skuːl |haʊs **~houses** ˌhaʊz ɪz -əz

schoolkid 'skuːl kɪd **~s** z

school-leaver ˌskuːl 'liːv ə '·ˌ·· ‖ -ᵊr **~s** z

school-leaving ˌskuːl 'liːv ɪŋ '·ˌ··

school|man 'skuːl |mæn -mən **~men** men mən

schoolmarm 'skuːl mɑːm ‖ -mɑːrm **~ish** ɪʃ **~s** z

schoolmast|er 'skuːl ˌmɑːst |ə §-ˌmæst- ‖ -ˌmæst |ᵊr **~ering** ər ɪŋ **~ers** əz ‖ ᵊrz

schoolmate 'skuːl meɪt **~s** s

schoolmen 'skuːl men -mən

schoolmistress 'skuːl ˌmɪs trəs -trɪs **~es** ɪz əz

schoolmistressy 'skuːl ˌmɪs trəs i -trɪs-

schoolroom 'skuːl ruːm -rʊm **~s** z

schoolteacher 'skuːl ˌtiːtʃ ə ‖ -ᵊr **~s** z

schoolteaching 'skuːl ˌtiːtʃ ɪŋ

schoolwork 'skuːl wɜːk ‖ -wɜ˞ːk

schoolyard 'skuːl jɑːd ‖ -jɑːrd **~s** z

schooner 'skuːn ə ‖ -ᵊr **~s** z

Schopenhauer 'ʃəʊp ən haʊ‿ə 'ʃɒp- ‖ 'ʃoʊp ən haʊ‿ᵊr —*Ger* ['ʃoːp n haʊ ɐ]

schorl ʃɔːl ‖ ʃɔːrl

schottisch|e ʃɒ 'tiːʃ ‖ 'ʃɑːţ ɪʃ **~es** ɪz əz

Schottky 'ʃɒt ki ‖ 'ʃɑːt ki

Schreiber 'ʃraɪb ə ‖ -ᵊr

Schreiner 'ʃraɪn ə ‖ -ᵊr

Schroder 'ʃrəʊd ə ‖ 'ʃroʊd ᵊr

Schröder 'ʃrɜːd ə ‖ 'ʃroʊd ᵊr 'ʃreɪd- —*Ger* ['ʃʁøː dɐ]

Schrodinger, Schrödinger 'ʃrɜːd ɪŋ ə ‖ 'ʃroʊd ɪŋ ᵊr 'ʃreɪd- —*Ger* ['ʃʁøː dɪŋ ɐ]

Schroeder 'ʃrɜːd ə ‖ 'ʃroʊd ᵊr 'ʃreɪd- —*Ger* ['ʃʁøː dɐ]

schtick ʃtɪk

schtuck ʃtʊk

schtum, schtoom ʃtʊm

schtup ʃtʊp **schtupped** ʃtʊpt **schtupping** 'ʃtʊp ɪŋ **schtups** ʃtʊps

Schubert 'ʃuːb ət -ɜːt ‖ -ᵊrt —*Ger* ['ʃuː bɐt]

Schultz, Schulz ʃʊlts

Schumacher 'ʃuː ˌmæk ə ‖ -ᵊr -ˌmɑːk- —*Ger* ['ʃuː ˌmax ɐ]

Schuman 'ʃuːm ən —*Fr* [ʃu man]

Schumann 'ʃuːm ən -æn, -ɑːn ‖ -ɑːn —*Ger* ['ʃuː man]

schuss ʃʊs ʃuːs, ʃuːʃ —*Ger* [ʃʊs] **schussed** ʃʊst ʃuːst, ʃuːʃt **schusses** 'ʃʊs ɪz 'ʃuːs-, 'ʃuːʃ-, -əz **schussing** 'ʃʊs ɪŋ 'ʃuːs-, 'ʃuːʃ-

Schuyler 'skaɪl ə ‖ -ᵊr

Schuylerville 'skaɪl ə vɪl ‖ -ᵊr-

Schuylkill *river in PA* 'skuːl kɪl 'skuːk ᵊl

schwa ʃwɑː ʃvɑː **schwas** ʃwɑːz ʃvɑːz

Schwab ʃwɑːb

Schwann ʃwɒn ʃvæn ‖ ʃwɑːn ʃvɑːn —*Ger* [ʃvan]

Schwartz ʃwɔːts ‖ ʃwɔːrts —*but as a German name,* ʃvɑːts ‖ ʃvɑːrts —*Ger* [ʃvaʁts]

Schwartzenegger 'ʃwɔːts ə neg ə ‖ 'ʃwɔːrts ə neg ᵊr —*Ger* ['ʃvaʁts ᵊn ɛg ɐ]

Schwartzschild 'ʃwɔːts ʃɪld →'ʃwɔːtʃ-; -tʃaɪᵊld ‖ 'ʃwɔːrts- —*Ger* ['ʃvaʁts ʃɪlt]

Schwarzkopf 'ʃvɑːts kɒpf 'ʃwɑːts-, 'ʃwɔːts- ‖ 'ʃwɔːrts kɑːpf 'ʃvɑːrts- —*Ger* ['ʃvaʁts kɔpf]

Schwarzwald 'ʃvɑːts væld 'ʃwɑːts-, -wæld ‖ 'ʃvɑːrts vɑːld —*Ger* ['ʃvaʁts valt]

Schweitzer 'ʃwaɪts ə 'ʃvaɪts- ‖ -ᵊr —*Ger* ['ʃvai tsɐ]

Schweppes *tdmk* ʃweps

sciatic saɪ 'æt ɪk ‖ -'æţ ɪk

sciatica saɪ 'æt ɪk ə ‖ -'æţ-

Scicon *tdmk* 'saɪ kɒn ‖ -kɑːn

science 'saɪ‿ənᵗs **sciences** 'saɪ‿ənᵗs ɪz -əz **ˌscience 'fiction**; **'science park**

scientific ˌsaɪ‿ən 'tɪf ɪk ◂ **~ally** ᵊl‿i **ˌscienˌtific 'method**

scientism 'saɪ‿ən ˌtɪz əm

scientist 'saɪ‿ənt ɪst §-əst ‖ 'saɪ ənţ əst **~s** s

scientologist, S~ ˌsaɪ‿ən 'tɒl ədʒ ɪst §-əst ‖ -'tɑːl- **~s** s

Scientology *tdmk* ˌsaɪ‿ən 'tɒl ədʒ i ‖ -'tɑːl-

sci-fi ˌsaɪ 'faɪ◂

scilicet 'sɪl ɪ set 'saɪl-, -ə-; 'skiːl ɪ ket
scilla, S~ 'sɪl ə **~s** z
Scillies 'sɪl iz
Scillonian sɪ 'ləʊn i ən sə- ‖ -'loʊn- **~s** z
Scill|y 'sɪl |i **~ies** iz
scimitar 'sɪm ɪt ə -ət-; -ɪ tɑː, -ə- ‖ -əṭ ᵊr -ə tɑːr **~s** z
scintilla sɪn 'tɪl ə **~s** z
scintill|ate 'sɪnt ɪ l|eɪt -ə-, -ᵊl |eɪt ‖ 'sɪnṭ ᵊl |eɪt **~ated** eɪt ɪd -əd ‖ eɪṭ əd **~ates** eɪts **~ating** eɪt ɪŋ ‖ eɪṭ ɪŋ
scintillation ˌsɪnt ɪ 'leɪʃ ᵊn -ə-, -ᵊl 'eɪʃ- ‖ ˌsɪnṭ ᵊl 'eɪʃ ᵊn **~s** z
scintillator 'sɪnt ɪ leɪt ə ˈ·ə-, -ᵊl eɪt ə ‖ 'sɪnṭ ᵊl eɪṭ ᵊr **~s** z
scintillometer ˌsɪnt ɪ 'lɒm ɪt ə ˌ·ə-, -ᵊl 'ɒm-, -ət ə ‖ ˌsɪnṭ ᵊl 'ɑːm əṭ ᵊr **~s** z
sciolism 'saɪ ə ˌlɪz əm -əʊ-
sciolist 'saɪ əl ɪst -əʊl-, §-əst **~s** s
sciolistic ˌsaɪ ə 'lɪst ɪk ◂ -əʊ-
scion 'saɪ ən **~s** z
Scioto *river in OH* saɪ 'əʊt əʊ ‖ -'oʊṭ ə -'oʊṭ oʊ
Scipio 'skɪp i əʊ 'sɪp- ‖ -oʊ
scire facias ˌsaɪᵊr i 'feɪʃ i æs -əs
scirocco, S~ sɪ 'rɒk əʊ sə-, ʃɪ- ‖ -'rɑːk oʊ —*It* [ʃi 'rɔk ko] **~s** z
scirrh|us 'sɪr |əs 'skɪr- **~i** aɪ **~ous** əs **~uses** əs ɪz -əz
scission 'sɪʒ ᵊn 'sɪʃ- **~s** z
scissor 'sɪz ə ‖ -ᵊr *(!)* **~ed** d **scissoring** 'sɪz ər ɪŋ **~s** z
scissors-and-paste ˌsɪz əz ən 'peɪst →-əm'--, -ənd'-- ‖ ˌsɪz ᵊrz- ˌscissors-and-'paste job
Scituate 'sɪtʃ u eɪt
sclaff sklæf **sclaffed** sklæft **sclaffing** 'sklæf ɪŋ **sclaffs** sklæfs
sclera 'sklɪər ə ‖ 'sklɪr ə 'skler-
sclero- *comb. form*
with stress-neutral suffix ¦sklɪər əʊ ¦skler- ‖ ¦sklɪr ə ¦skler- — **scleroderma** ˌsklɪər əʊ 'dɜːm ə ˌskler- ‖ ˌsklɪr ə 'dɝːm ə ˌskler-
with stress-imposing suffix sklə 'rɒ+ sklɪ-, sklɪə-, skle- ‖ sklə 'rɑː+ sklɪ- — **sclerotomy** sklə 'rɒt əm i sklɪ-, sklɪə-, skle- ‖ -'rɑːṭ-
sclerom|a sklə 'rəʊm |ə sklɪ-, sklɪə-, skle- ‖ -'roʊm |ə **~as** əz **~ata** ət ə ‖ əṭ ə
scleros|is sklə 'rəʊs |ɪs sklɪ-, sklɪə-, skle-, §-əs ‖ -'roʊs |əs **~es** iːz
sclerotic sklə 'rɒt ɪk sklɪ-, sklɪə-, skle- ‖ -'rɑːṭ ɪk
sclerous 'sklɪər əs 'skler- ‖ 'sklɪr əs 'skler-
Scobell ₍ˌ₎skəʊ 'bel ‖ 'skoʊ bel
Scobie, Scoby 'skəʊb i ‖ 'skoʊb i
scoff skɒf ‖ skɑːf skɔːf **scoffed** skɒft ‖ skɑːft skɔːft **scoffing/ly** 'skɒf ɪŋ /li ‖ 'skɑːf- 'skɔːf- **scoffs** skɒfs ‖ skɑːfs skɔːfs
scoffer 'skɒf ə ‖ 'skɑːf ᵊr 'skɔːf- **~s** z
scofflaw 'skɒf lɔː ‖ 'skɑːf- -lɑː **~s** z
Scofield 'skəʊ fiːᵊld ‖ 'skoʊ-
scold skəʊld →skɒʊld ‖ skoʊld **scolded** 'skəʊld ɪd →'skɒʊld-, -əd ‖ 'skoʊld əd
scolding/s 'skəʊld ɪŋ/z →'skɒʊld- ‖ 'skoʊld ɪŋ/z **scolds** skəʊldz →skɒʊldz ‖ skoʊldz
scoliosis ˌskɒl i 'əʊs ɪs ˌskəʊl-, §-əs ‖ ˌskoʊl i 'oʊs əs ˌskɑːl-
scoliotic ˌskɒl i 'ɒt ɪk ◂ ˌskəʊl- ‖ ˌskoʊl i 'ɑːṭ ɪk ◂ ˌskɑːl-
scollop 'skɒl əp ‖ 'skɑːl əp **~ed** t **~ing** ɪŋ **~s** s
scombroid 'skɒm brɔɪd ‖ 'skɑːm- **~s** z
sconce skɒnᵗs ‖ skɑːnᵗs **sconced** skɒnᵗst ‖ skɑːnᵗst **sconces** 'skɒnᵗs ɪz -əz ‖ 'skɑːnᵗs əz **sconcing** 'skɒnᵗs ɪŋ ‖ 'skɑːnᵗs ɪŋ

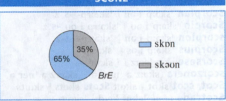

SCONE

	BrE
skɒn	65%
skəʊn	35%

scone skɒn skəʊn ‖ skoʊn skɑːn — *Preference poll, BrE:* skɒn *65%,* skəʊn *35%.* **scones** skɒnz skəʊnz ‖ skoʊnz skɑːnz
Scone *place in Tayside* skuːn
Scooby-doo ˌskuːb i 'duː
scoop skuːp **scooped** skuːpt **scooping** 'skuːp ɪŋ **scoops** skuːps
scooper 'skuːp ə ‖ -ᵊr **~s** z
scoot skuːt **scooted** 'skuːt ɪd -əd ‖ 'skuːṭ əd **scooting** 'skuːt ɪŋ ‖ 'skuːṭ ɪŋ **scoots** skuːts
scoot|er 'skuːt |ə ‖ 'skuːṭ |ᵊr **~ered** əd ‖ ᵊrd **~ering** ər ɪŋ **~ers** əz ‖ ᵊrz
-scope skəʊp ‖ skoʊp — **microscope** 'maɪk rə skəʊp ‖ -skoʊp
scope skəʊp ‖ skoʊp **scopes** skəʊps ‖ skoʊps **scoping** 'skəʊp ɪŋ ‖ 'skoʊp ɪŋ
Scopes skəʊps ‖ skoʊps
-scopic 'skɒp ɪk ‖ 'skɑːp ɪk — **microscopic** ˌmaɪk rəʊ 'skɒp ɪk ◂ ‖ -rə 'skɑːp ɪk
scopolamine skəʊ 'pɒl ə miːn -mɪn, §-mən ‖ skə 'pɑːl- skoʊ-; ˌskoʊp ə 'læm ən
scopoline 'skəʊp ə liːn -lɪn, §-lən ‖ 'skoʊp-
scops skɒps ‖ skɑːps
Scopus 'skəʊp əs ‖ 'skoʊp əs
-scopy *stress-imposing* +skəp i — **microscopy** maɪ 'krɒsk əp i ‖ -'krɑːsk-
scorbutic skɔː 'bjuːt ɪk ‖ skɔːr 'bjuːṭ ɪk **~ally** ᵊl i
scorch skɔːtʃ ‖ skɔːrtʃ **scorched** skɔːtʃt ‖ skɔːrtʃt **scorches** 'skɔːtʃ ɪz -əz ‖ 'skɔːrtʃ əz **scorching/ly** 'skɔːtʃ ɪŋ /li ‖ 'skɔːrtʃ ɪŋ /li ˌscorched 'earth, ˌscorched 'earth ˌpolicy
scorcher 'skɔːtʃ ə ‖ 'skɔːrtʃ ᵊr **~s** z
score skɔː ‖ skɔːr skoʊr **scored** skɔːd ‖ skɔːrd skoʊrd **scores** skɔːz ‖ skɔːrz skoʊrz **scoring** 'skɔːr ɪŋ ‖ 'skoʊr- 'score draw
scoreboard 'skɔː bɔːd ‖ 'skɔːr bɔːrd 'skoʊr boʊrd **~s** z
scorebook 'skɔː bʊk §-buːk ‖ 'skɔːr- 'skoʊr- **~s** s

scorecard ˈskɔː kɑːd ‖ ˈskɔːr kɑːrd ˈskoʊr- **~s** z
scorekeeper ˈskɔː ˌkiːp ə ‖ ˈskɔːr ˌkiːp ᵊr ˈskoʊr- **~s** z
scoreless ˈskɔː ləs -lɪs ‖ ˈskɔːr- ˈskoʊr-
scoreline ˈskɔː laɪn ‖ ˈskɔːr- **~s** z
scorer ˈskɔːr ə ‖ -ᵊr ˈskoʊr- **~s** z
scoresheet ˈskɔː ʃiːt ‖ ˈskɔːr- ˈskoʊr- **~s** s
scoria ˈskɔːr i‿ə skə ˈriː‿ə ‖ ˈskoʊr-
scoriaceous ˌskɔːr i ˈeɪʃ əs ◂ ‖ ˌskoʊr-
scorn skɔːn ‖ skɔːrn **scorned** skɔːnd ‖ skɔːrnd **scorning** ˈskɔːn ɪŋ ‖ ˈskɔːrn ɪŋ **scorns** skɔːnz ‖ skɔːrnz
scornful ˈskɔːn fᵊl -fʊl ‖ ˈskɔːrn- **~ly** i **~ness** nəs nɪs
Scorpian ˈskɔːp i‿ən ‖ ˈskɔːrp- **~s** z
Scorpio ˈskɔːp i‿əʊ ‖ ˈskɔːrp i oʊ **~s** z
scorpion ˈskɔːp i‿ən ‖ ˈskɔːrp- **~s** z
Scorpius ˈskɔːp i‿əs ‖ ˈskɔːrp-
Scorsese skɔː ˈseɪz i ‖ skɔːr-
scorzonera ˌskɔːz ə ˈnɪər ə ‖ ˌskɔːrz ə ˈner ə
Scot, scot skɒt ‖ skɑːt **Scots** skɒts ‖ skɑːts
Scotcade *tdmk* ˈskɒt keɪd ‖ ˈskɑːt-
Scotch, s~ skɒtʃ ‖ skɑːtʃ **scotched** skɒtʃt ‖ skɑːtʃt **scotches** ˈskɒtʃ ɪz -əz ‖ ˈskɑːtʃ əz **scotching** ˈskɒtʃ ɪŋ ‖ ˈskɑːtʃ ɪŋ **ˌScotch ˈbroth**; **ˌScotch ˈegg**; **ˌScotch ˈmist**; **ˌScotch ˈpancake**; **ˌScotch ˈtape** *tdmk*, ˈ·· ; **ˌScotch ˈwhisky**
Scotchgard *tdmk* ˈskɒtʃ gɑːd ‖ ˈskɑːtʃ gɑːrd
Scotch-Irish ˌskɒtʃ ˈaɪᵊr ɪʃ ◂ ‖ ˌskɑːtʃ-
Scotch|man ˈskɒtʃ |mən ‖ ˈskɑːtʃ- **~men** mən **~woman** ˌwʊm ən **~women** ˌwɪm ɪn §-ən
scoter ˈskəʊt ə ‖ ˈskoʊt̬ ᵊr **~s** z
scot-free ˌskɒt ˈfriː ‖ ˌskɑːt-
Scotia, s~ ˈskəʊʃ ə ‖ ˈskoʊʃ ə
Scotland ˈskɒt lənd ‖ ˈskɑːt- **ˌScotland ˈYard**
scotoma skɒ ˈtəʊm ə skəʊ- ‖ skə ˈtoʊm ə skoʊ- **~s** z
Scots skɒts ‖ skɑːts **ˌScots ˈpine**
Scots|man ˈskɒts |mən ‖ ˈskɑːts- **~men** mən
Scotstoun ˈskɒts tən ‖ ˈskɑːts-
Scots|woman ˈskɒts |ˌwʊm ən ‖ ˈskɑːts- **~women** ˌwɪm ɪn §-ən
Scott skɒt ‖ skɑːt
Scotticism ˈskɒt ɪ ˌsɪz əm -ə- ‖ ˈskɑːt̬ ə- **~s** z
Scottie, s~ ˈskɒt i ‖ ˈskɑːt̬ i **~s** z
Scottish ˈskɒt ɪʃ ‖ ˈskɑːt̬ ɪʃ **~ness** nəs nɪs **ˌScottish ˈGaelic**; **ˌScottish ˈterrier**
Scottsdale ˈskɒts deɪᵊl ‖ ˈskɑːts-
Scott|y. s~ ˈskɒt |i ‖ ˈskɑːt̬ |i **~ies, ~y's** iz
Scotus ˈskəʊt əs ‖ ˈskoʊt̬ əs
scoundrel ˈskaʊndr əl **~s** z
scoundrelly ˈskaʊndr əl i
scour ˈskaʊ‿ə ‖ skaʊ‿ᵊr **scoured** ˈskaʊ‿əd ‖ skaʊ‿ᵊrd **scouring** ˈskaʊ‿ər ɪŋ ‖ ˈskaʊ‿ᵊr ɪŋ **scours** ˈskaʊ‿əz ‖ skaʊ‿ᵊrz
scourer ˈskaʊ‿ər ə ‖ ˈskaʊ‿ᵊr ᵊr **~s** z
scourge skɜːdʒ ‖ skɝːdʒ **scourged** skɜːdʒd ‖ skɝːdʒd **scourges** ˈskɜːdʒ ɪz -əz ‖ ˈskɝːdʒ əz **scourging** ˈskɜːdʒ ɪŋ ‖ ˈskɝːdʒ ɪŋ

Scouse, s~ skaʊs
Scouser ˈskaʊs ə ‖ -ᵊr **~s** z
scout, Scout skaʊt **scouted** ˈskaʊt ɪd -əd ‖ ˈskaʊt̬ əd **scouting** ˈskaʊt ɪŋ ‖ skaʊt̬ ɪŋ **scouts** skaʊts
scouter, S~ ˈskaʊt ə ‖ ˈskaʊt̬ ᵊr **~s** z
scoutmaster ˈskaʊt ˌmɑːst ə §-ˌmæst- ‖ -ˌmæst ᵊr **~s** z
scow skaʊ **scows** skaʊz
scowl skaʊl **scowled** skaʊld **scowler/s** ˈskaʊl ə/z ‖ -ᵊr/z **scowling/ly** ˈskaʊl ɪŋ /li **scowls** skaʊlz
scrabbl|e, S~ *tdmk* ˈskræb ᵊl **~ed** d **~es** z **~ing** ‿ɪŋ
scrabbl|y ˈskræb ᵊl‿|i **~ier** i‿ə ‖ i‿ᵊr **~iest** i‿ɪst i‿əst
scrag skræg **scragged** skrægd **scragging** ˈskræg ɪŋ **scrags** skrægz **ˌscrag ˈend**
scraggl|y ˈskræg ᵊl‿|i **~ier** i‿ə ‖ i‿ᵊr **~iest** i‿ɪst i‿əst **~iness** i nəs i nɪs
scragg|y ˈskræg |i **~ier** i‿ə ‖ i‿ᵊr **~iest** i‿ɪst i‿əst **~ily** ɪ li əl i **~iness** i nəs i nɪs
scram skræm **scrammed** skræmd **scramming** ˈskræm ɪŋ **scrams** skræmz
scrambl|e ˈskræm bᵊl **~ed** d **~es** z **~ing** ‿ɪŋ **ˌscrambled ˈegg**
scrambler ˈskræm blə ‖ -blᵊr **~s** z
scramjet ˈskræm dʒet **~s** s
scran skræn
Scranton ˈskrænt ən ‖ -ᵊn
scrap skræp **scrapped** skræpt **scrapping** ˈskræp ɪŋ **scraps** skræps **ˈscrap heap**; **ˈscrap ˌiron**; **ˈscrap ˌpaper**, ˌ·ˈ··
scrapbook ˈskræp bʊk §-buːk **~s** s
scrape skreɪp **scraped** skreɪpt **scrapes** skreɪps **scraping/s** ˈskreɪp ɪŋ/z
scrapeover ˈskreɪp ˌəʊv ə ‖ -ˌoʊv ᵊr **~s** z
scraper ˈskreɪp ə ‖ -ᵊr **~s** z
scraperboard ˈskreɪp ə bɔːd ‖ -ᵊr bɔːrd -boʊrd **~s** z
scrapheap ˈskræp hiːp **~s** s
scrapie ˈskreɪp i
scraping ˈskreɪp ɪŋ **~s** z
scrapp... —*see* **scrap**
scrapple ˈskræp ᵊl
scrapp|y ˈskræp |i **~ier** i‿ə ‖ i‿ᵊr **~iest** i‿ɪst i‿əst **~ily** ɪ li əl i **~iness** i nəs i nɪs
scratch skrætʃ **scratched** skrætʃt **scratches** ˈskrætʃ ɪz -əz **scratching/s** ˈskrætʃ ɪŋ/z **ˈscratch ˌpaper**; **ˈscratch sheet**; **ˈscratch test**
scratch-and-sniff ˌskrætʃ ən ˈsnɪf ◂
scratchcard ˈskrætʃ kɑːd ‖ -kɑːrd **~s** z
scratcher ˈskrætʃ ə ‖ -ᵊr **~s** z
scratchmaster ˈskrætʃ ˌmɑːst ə §-ˌmæst- ‖ -ˌmæst ᵊr **~s** z
scratchpad ˈskrætʃ pæd **~s** z
Scratchwood ˈskrætʃ wʊd
scratch|y ˈskrætʃ |i **~ier** i‿ə ‖ i‿ᵊr **~iest** i‿ɪst i‿əst **~ily** ɪ li əl i **~iness** i nəs i nɪs

scrawl skrɔːl ‖ skrɑːl **scrawled** skrɔːld ‖ skrɑːld **scrawling** 'skrɔːl ɪŋ ‖ 'skrɑːl- **scrawls** skrɔːlz ‖ skrɑːlz
scrawler 'skrɔːl ə ‖ -ᵊr 'skrɑːl- **~s** z
scrawl|y 'skrɔːl |i ‖ 'skrɑːl- **~ier** i‿ə ‖ i‿ᵊr **~iest** i‿ɪst i‿əst **~iness** i nəs i nɪs
scrawn|y 'skrɔːn |i ‖ 'skrɑːn- **~ier** i‿ə ‖ i‿ᵊr **~iest** i‿ɪst i‿əst **~ily** ɪ li əl i **~iness** i nəs i nɪs
scream skriːm **screamed** skriːmd **screaming/ly** 'skriːm ɪŋ /li **screams** skriːmz
screamer 'skriːm ə ‖ -ᵊr **~s** z
scree skriː **screes** skriːz
screech skriːtʃ **screeched** skriːtʃt **screeches** 'skriːtʃ ɪz -əz **screeching** 'skriːtʃ ɪŋ **'screech owl**
screecher 'skriːtʃ ə ‖ -ᵊr **~s** z
screech|y 'skriːtʃ| i **~ier** i‿ə ‖ i‿ᵊr **~iest** i ɪst i əst
screed skriːd **screeds** skriːdz
screen skriːn **screened** skriːnd **screening/s** 'skriːn ɪŋ/z **screens** skriːnz **'screen ˌprinting**; **'screen ˌsaver**; **'screen test**
screengrab 'skriːn græb →'skriːŋ- **~s** z
screenplay 'skriːn pleɪ →'skriːm- **~s** z
screenshot 'skriːn ʃɒt ‖ -ʃɑːt **~s** s
screenwrit|er 'skriːn ˌraɪt |ə ‖ -ˌraɪţ |ᵊr **~ers** əz ‖ ᵊrz **~ing** ɪŋ
screw skruː **screwed** skruːd **screwing** 'skruː‿ɪŋ **screws** skruːz **'screw cap**; **'screw jack**; **'screw pine**; **'screw thread**; **'screw top** *n* ˌ·'·
screwball 'skruː bɔːl ‖ -bɑːl **~s** z
screwdriver 'skruː ˌdraɪv ə ‖ -ᵊr **~s** z
screw-top *adj* ˌskruː 'tɒp ◂ '· · ‖ -'tɑːp◂ **ˌscrew-top 'jar**
screw-up 'skruː ʌp **~s** s
screwworm 'skruː wɜːm ‖ -wɜ˞ːm **~s** z
screw|y 'skruː‿|i **~ier** i‿ə ‖ i‿ᵊr **~iest** i‿ɪst i‿əst
Scriabin skri 'æb ɪn §-ən; 'skrɪəb ɪn ‖ -'ɑːb ən —*Russ* ['skrʲæ bʲin]
scribal 'skraɪb ᵊl
scribbl|e 'skrɪb ᵊl **~ed** d **~es** z **~ing/s** ‿ɪŋ/z
scribbler 'skrɪb ᵊl‿ə ‖ ər **~s** z
scribe skraɪb **scribed** skraɪbd **scribes** skraɪbz **scribing** 'skraɪb ɪŋ
scriber 'skraɪb ə ‖ -ᵊr **~s** z
Scribner 'skrɪb nə ‖ -nᵊr
scrim skrɪm **scrims** skrɪmz
Scrimgeour, Scrimger 'skrɪm dʒə ‖ -dʒᵊr
scrimmag|e 'skrɪm ɪdʒ **~ed** d **~es** ɪz əz **~ing** ɪŋ
scrimp skrɪmp **scrimped** skrɪmpt **scrimping** 'skrɪmp ɪŋ **scrimps** skrɪmps
scrimshank 'skrɪm ʃæŋk **~ed** t **~er/s** ə/z ‖ ᵊr/z **~ing** ɪŋ **~s** s
scrimshaw 'skrɪm ʃɔː ‖ -ʃɑː **~ed** d **scrimshawing** 'skrɪm ʃɔːr ɪŋ ‖ -ʃɔː ɪŋ -ʃɑː- **~s** z
scrip skrɪp **scrips** skrɪps **'scrip ˌissue**
Scripps skrɪps
scripsit 'skrɪps ɪt §-ət
script skrɪpt **scripted** 'skrɪpt ɪd -əd **scripting** 'skrɪpt ɪŋ **scripts** skrɪpts
scriptori|um skrɪp 'tɔːr i‿|əm ‖ -'toʊr- **~a** ə **~ums** əmz
scriptural 'skrɪp tʃᵊr əl -ʃᵊr‿ **~ly** i
scripture, S~ 'skrɪp tʃə -ʃə ‖ -tʃᵊr **~s** z
scriptwriter 'skrɪpt ˌraɪt ə ‖ -ˌraɪţ ᵊr **~s** z
scrivener, S~ 'skrɪv ᵊn‿ə ‖ ər **~s** z
scrod skrɒd ‖ skrɑːd **scrods** skrɒdz ‖ skrɑːdz
scrofula 'skrɒf jʊl ə §-jəl- ‖ 'skrɑːf jəl ə 'skrɔːf-
scrofulous 'skrɒf jʊl əs §-jəl- ‖ 'skrɑːf jəl əs 'skrɔːf- **~ly** li **~ness** nəs nɪs
scroggin 'skrɒg ɪn -ən ‖ 'skrɑːg ən
scroll skrəʊl →skrɒʊl ‖ skroʊl **scrolled** skrəʊld →skrɒʊld ‖ skroʊld **scrolling** 'skrəʊl ɪŋ →'skrɒʊl- ‖ 'skroʊl ɪŋ **scrolls** skrəʊlz →skrɒʊlz ‖ skroʊlz
scrollwork 'skrəʊl wɜːk →'skrɒʊl- ‖ 'skroʊl wɜ˞ːk
Scrooby 'skruːb i
Scrooge, s~ skruːdʒ **Scrooges, s~** 'skruːdʒ ɪz -əz
scrot|um 'skrəʊt |əm ‖ 'skroʊţ |əm **~a** ə **~al** ᵊl **~ums** əmz
scrounge skraʊndʒ **scrounged** skraʊndʒd **scrounges** 'skraʊndʒ ɪz -əz **scrounging** 'skraʊndʒ ɪŋ
scrounger 'skraʊndʒ ə ‖ -ᵊr **~s** z
scrub skrʌb **scrubbed** skrʌbd **scrubbing** 'skrʌb ɪŋ **scrubs** skrʌbz **'scrubbing brush, 'scrub brush**
scrubber 'skrʌb ə ‖ -ᵊr **~s** z
scrubb|y 'skrʌb |i **~ier** i‿ə ‖ i‿ᵊr **~iest** i‿ɪst i‿əst **~iness** i nəs i nɪs
scrubland 'skrʌb lənd -lænd ‖ -lænd
scruff skrʌf **scruffs** skrʌfs
scruff|y 'skrʌf |i **~ier** i‿ə ‖ i‿ᵊr **~iest** i‿ɪst i‿əst **~ily** ɪ li əl i **~iness** i nəs i nɪs
scrum skrʌm **scrummed** skrʌmd **scrumming** 'skrʌm ɪŋ **scrums** skrʌmz
scrumcap 'skrʌm kæp **~s** s
scrum|half ˌskrʌm |'hɑːf §-'hæf ‖ -|'hæf **~halves** 'hɑːvz §'hævz ‖ 'hævz
scrummag|e 'skrʌm ɪdʒ **~ed** d **~es** ɪz əz **~ing** ɪŋ
scrump skrʌmp **scrumped** skrʌmpt **scrumping** 'skrʌmp ɪŋ **scrumps** skrʌmps
scrumptious 'skrʌmp ʃəs **~ly** li **~ness** nəs nɪs
scrumpy 'skrʌmp i
scrunch skrʌntʃ **scrunched** skrʌntʃt **scrunches** 'skrʌntʃ ɪz -əz **scrunching** 'skrʌntʃ ɪŋ
scrunch|ie, scrunch|y 'skrʌntʃ| i **~ies** iz
scrupl|e 'skruːp ᵊl **~ed** d **~es** z **~ing** ‿ɪŋ
scrupulosit|y ˌskruːp ju 'lɒs ət| i ·jə- ‖ -jə 'lɑːs əţ| i **~ies** iz
scrupulous 'skruːp jʊl əs -jəl- ‖ -jəl əs **~ly** li **~ness** nəs nɪs
scrutable 'skruːt əb ᵊl ‖ 'skruːţ-
scrutator skru 'teɪt ə ‖ -'teɪţ ᵊr **~s** z
scrutineer ˌskruːt ɪ 'nɪə -ə-, -ᵊn 'ɪə ‖ ˌskruːt ᵊn 'ɪᵊr **~s** z

S

scrutinis|e, scrutiniz|e ˈskruːt ɪ naɪz -ə-, -ən aɪz ‖ -ən aɪz **~ed** d **~es** ɪz əz **~ing** ɪŋ
scrutin|y ˈskruːt ɪn |i -ən‿i ‖ -ən‿|i **~ies** iz
Scruton ˈskruːt ən
scry skraɪ **scried** skraɪd **scries** skraɪz **scrying** ˈskraɪ ɪŋ
Scrymgeour ˈskrɪm dʒə ‖ -dʒər
SCSI ˈskʌz i
scuba ˈskuːb ə
ˈscuba ˌdiving
scud skʌd **scudded** ˈskʌd ɪd -əd **scudding** ˈskʌd ɪŋ **scuds** skʌdz
Scudamore ˈskjuːd ə mɔː ˈskuːd- ‖ -mɔːr -moʊr
scuff skʌf **scuffed** skʌft **scuffing** ˈskʌf ɪŋ **scuffs** skʌfs
scuffl|e ˈskʌf əl **~ed** d **~es** z **~ing** ‿ɪŋ
scuffmark ˈskʌf mɑːk ‖ -mɑːrk **~s** s
scull skʌl *(= skull)* **sculled** skʌld **sculling** ˈskʌl ɪŋ **sculls** skʌlz
sculler ˈskʌl ə ‖ -ər **~s** z
sculler|y ˈskʌl ər‿|i **~ies** iz
Sculley ˈskʌl i
Scullin ˈskʌl ɪn §-ən
scullion ˈskʌl i‿ən ‖ ˈskʌl jən **~s** z
Scully ˈskʌl i
sculpsit ˈskʌlps ɪt §-ət
sculpt skʌlpt **sculpted** ˈskʌlpt ɪd -əd **sculpting** ˈskʌlpt ɪŋ **sculpts** skʌlpts
sculptor ˈskʌlpt ə ‖ -ər **~s** z
sculptress ˈskʌlp trəs -trɪs, -tres **~es** ɪz əz
sculptural ˈskʌlp tʃər‿əl -ʃər‿ **~ly** i
sculp|ture ˈskʌlp |tʃə -ʃə ‖ -|tʃər **~tured** tʃəd ʃəd ‖ tʃərd **~tures** tʃəz ʃəz ‖ tʃərz **~turing** tʃər ɪŋ ʃər‿ɪŋ
sculpturesque ˌskʌlp tʃə ˈresk ◂ -ʃə- **~ly** li **~ness** nəs nɪs
scum skʌm **scummed** skʌmd **scumming** ˈskʌm ɪŋ **scums** skʌmz
scumbag ˈskʌm bæg **~s** z
scumbl|e ˈskʌm bəl **~ed** d **~es** z **~ing** ‿ɪŋ
scummy ˈskʌm i
scuncheon ˈskʌntʃ ən **~s** z
scunge skʌndʒ
scung|y ˈskʌndʒ| i **~ier** i‿ə ‖ i‿ər **~ies** iz **~iest** i‿ɪst ‿əst
scunner ˈskʌn ə ‖ -ər **~ed** d **scunnering** ˈskʌn ər‿ɪŋ **~s** z
Scunthorpe ˈskʌn θɔːp ‖ -θɔːrp
scup skʌp
scupper ˈskʌp ə ‖ -ər **~ed** d **scuppering** ˈskʌp ər‿ɪŋ **~s** z
Scuppernong, s~ ˈskʌp ə nɒŋ ‖ -ər nɑːŋ -nɔːŋ **~s** z
scurf skɜːf ‖ skɜːf
scurf|y ˈskɜːf |i ‖ ˈskɜːf |i **~iness** i nəs i nɪs
scurri... —*see* **scurry**
scurrilit|y skə ˈrɪl ət |i skʌ-, -ɪt- ‖ -əţ |i **~ies** iz
scurrilous ˈskʌr əl əs -ɪl- ‖ ˈskɜː- **~ly** li **~ness** nəs nɪs
scurr|y ˈskʌr |i ‖ ˈskɜː |i **~ied** id **~ies** iz **~ying** i‿ɪŋ
S-curve ˈes kɜːv ‖ -kɜːv **~s** z

scurv|y ˈskɜːv |i ‖ ˈskɜːv |i **~ier** i‿ə ‖ i‿ər **~iest** i‿ɪst i‿əst **~ily** ɪ li əl i **~iness** i nəs i nɪs
ˈscuse skjuːz
scut skʌt **scuts** skʌts
scuta —*see* **scutum**
Scutari ˈskuːt ər i sku ˈtɑːr i ‖ ˈskuːţ ər i —*It* [ˈskuː ta ri]
scutch skʌtʃ **scutched** skʌtʃt **scutches** ˈskʌtʃ ɪz -əz **scutching** ˈskʌtʃ ɪŋ
scutcheon ˈskʌtʃ ən **~s** z
scute skjuːt skuːt **scutes** skjuːts skuːts
scutell|um skju ˈtel |əm sku- **~a** ə
scutt|er ˈskʌt| ə ‖ ˈskʌţ| ər **~ered** əd ‖ -ərd **~ering** ər ɪŋ ‖ ər ɪŋ **~ers** əz ‖ -ərz
scuttl|e ˈskʌt əl ‖ ˈskʌţ əl **~ed** d **~es** z **~ing** ‿ɪŋ
scuttlebutt ˈskʌt əl bʌt ‖ ˈskʌţ- **~s** s
scut|um, S~ ˈskjuːt |əm ˈskuːt- ‖ ˈskjuːţ |əm ˈskuːţ- **~a** ə
scuzz skʌz
scuzz|y ˈskʌz |i **~ier** i‿ə ‖ i‿ər **~iest** i‿ɪst i‿əst
Scylla ˈsɪl ə
scythe saɪð §saɪθ **scythed** saɪðd §saɪθt **scythes** saɪðz §saɪθs **scything** ˈsaɪð ɪŋ §ˈsaɪθ-
Scythi|a ˈsɪð i‿|ə ˈsɪθ- ‖ ˈsɪθ- **~an/s** ən/z
SDI ˌes diː ˈaɪ
SDLP ˌes di el ˈpiː
SDP ˌes diː ˈpiː
se *in Latin expressions* seɪ siː, *in French expressions* sə —*see also phrases with this word*
SE ˌes ˈiː ◂ —*see* southeast, southeastern
sea siː *(= see)* **seas** siːz
ˈsea aˌnemone; **ˈsea breeze, ˌ·ˈ·**; **ˈsea ˌcaptain**; **ˈsea change**; **ˈsea cow**; **ˈsea dog**; **ˌsea ˈgreen◂**; **ˌsea ˌisland ˈcotton**; **ˈsea king**; **ˈsea legs**; **ˈsea ˌlevel**; **ˈsea ˌlion**; **ˈsea mile**; **ˈsea mist**; **ˈsea ˌpower**; **ˈSea Scout**; **ˈsea ˌserpent**; **ˈsea slug**; **ˈsea ˌurchin**
seabed ˈsiː bed
Seabee ˈsiː biː **~s** z
seabird ˈsiː bɜːd ‖ -bɜːd **~s** z
seaboard ˈsiː bɔːd ‖ -bɔːrd -boʊrd
Seaborg ˈsiː bɔːg ‖ -bɔːrg
seaborne ˈsiː bɔːn ‖ -bɔːrn -boʊrn
seacoast ˈsiː kəʊst ‖ -koʊst **~s** s
seafarer ˈsiː ˌfeər ə ‖ -ˌfer ər -ˌfær- **~s** z
seafaring ˈsiː ˌfeər ɪŋ ‖ -ˌfer ɪŋ -ˌfær-
seafood ˈsiː fuːd
Seaford *(i)* ˈsiːf əd ‖ -ərd, *(ii)* ˌsiː ˈfɔːd ‖ -ˈfɔːrd -ˈfoʊrd —*Both (i) and (ii) are used for the place in East Sussex; the place in Long Island, NY is (i)*
Seaforth ˈsiː fɔːθ ‖ -fɔːrθ -foʊrθ
seafront ˈsiː frʌnt **~s** s
Seaga si ˈɑːg ə
Seagal ˈsiːg əl
seagirt ˈsiː gɜːt ‖ -gɜːt
seagoing ˈsiː ˌgəʊ ɪŋ ‖ -ˌgoʊ ɪŋ
sea-green ˌsiː ˈgriːn ◂
seagull ˈsiː gʌl **~s** z
seahors|e ˈsiː hɔːs ‖ -hɔːrs **~es** ɪz əz
seakale ˈsiː keɪəl

seal, Seal siːᵊl **sealed** siːᵊld **sealing** 'siːᵊl ɪŋ **seals** siːᵊlz
'sealing wax
sealant 'siːᵊl ənt **~s** s
Seale siːᵊl
sealer 'siːᵊl ə ‖ -ᵊr **~s** z
Sealey 'siːl i
sealift 'siː lɪft **~s** s
Sealink *tdmk* 'siː lɪŋk
sealskin 'siːᵊl skɪn
Sealyham 'siːl i‿əm ‖ -hæm **~s** z
seam siːm *(= seem)* **seamed** siːmd **seaming** 'siːm ɪŋ **seams** siːmz
sea|man, S~ 'siː |mən **~men** mən men
seaman|like 'siː mən |laɪk **~ship** ʃɪp
Seamas 'ʃeɪm əs
seamen 'siː mən -men
seamer, S~ 'siːm ə ‖ -ᵊr **~s** z
seamless 'siːm ləs -lɪs **~ly** li **~ness** nəs nɪs
seamstress 'semᵖs trəs 'siːmᵖs-, -trɪs ‖ 'siːmᵖs- **~es** ɪz əz
Seamus 'ʃeɪm əs
seam|y 'siːm |i **~ier** i‿ə ‖ i‿ᵊr **~iest** i‿ɪst i‿əst **~iness** i nəs i nɪs
Sean ʃɔːn ‖ ʃɑːn *—Irish* Seán [ʃɑːn]
Seanad 'ʃæn əd -əð *—Irish* ['ʃa nəd]
seanc|e, séanc|e 'seɪ ɒ̃s -ɑːnᵗs, -ɒnᵗs ‖ -ɑːnᵗs *—Fr* [se ɑ̃ːs] **~es** ɪz əz
seaplane 'siː pleɪn **~s** z
seaport 'siː pɔːt ‖ -pɔːrt -poʊrt **~s** s
sear sɪə ‖ sɪᵊr **seared** sɪəd ‖ sɪᵊrd **searing/ly** 'sɪər ɪŋ /li ‖ 'sɪr ɪŋ /li **sears** sɪəz ‖ sɪᵊrz
search sɜːtʃ ‖ sɜ˞ːtʃ **searched** sɜːtʃt ‖ sɜ˞ːtʃt **searches** 'sɜːtʃ ɪz -əz ‖ 'sɜ˞ːtʃ əz **searching/ly** 'sɜːtʃ ɪŋ /li ‖ 'sɜ˞ːtʃ ɪŋ /li
'search,party; **'search,warrant**
searcher 'sɜːtʃ ə ‖ 'sɜ˞ːtʃ ᵊr **~s** z
searchlight 'sɜːtʃ laɪt ‖ 'sɜ˞ːtʃ- **~s** s
Searcy *(i)* 'sɪəs i ‖ 'sɪrs i, *(ii)* 'sɜːs i ‖ 'sɜ˞ːs i *—The place in AL is (ii)*
Searle sɜːl ‖ sɜ˞ːl
Sears sɪəz ‖ sɪᵊrz
Seascale 'siː skeɪᵊl
seascape 'siː skeɪp **~s** s
seashell 'siː ʃel **~s** z
seashore 'siː ʃɔː ‖ -ʃɔːr -ʃoʊr **~s** z
seasick 'siː sɪk
seasickness 'siː sɪk nəs -ˌsɪk-, -nɪs
seaside 'siː saɪd ,·'·
season 'siːz ᵊn **~ed** d **~ing** ‿ɪŋ **~s** z
'season,ticket ‖ ,· · '· ·
seasonab|le 'siːz ᵊn‿əb |ᵊl **~ly** li
seasonal 'siːz ᵊn‿əl **~ly** i
seasonality ˌsiːz ə 'næl ət i -ɪt i ‖ -əţ i
seasoning 'siːz ᵊn‿ɪŋ **~s** z
seat siːt **seated** 'siːt ɪd -əd ‖ 'siːţ əd **seating** 'siːt ɪŋ ‖ 'siːţ ɪŋ **seats** siːts
'seat belt
SEAT *tdmk* 'seɪ æt -ət ‖ -ɑːt
-seater 'siːt ə ‖ 'siːţ ᵊr — **three-seater** ˌθriː 'siːt ə ◂ ‖ -'siːţ ᵊr ◂
Seathwaite 'siː θweɪt
seating 'siːt ɪŋ ‖ 'siːţ ɪŋ **~s** z
seatmate 'siːt meɪt **~s** s
SEATO 'siːt əʊ ‖ -oʊ
seat-of-the-pants ˌsiːt əv ðə 'pænts ‖ ˌsiːţ-
Seaton 'siːt ᵊn
Seattle si 'æt ᵊl ‖ -'æţ ᵊl
seawall ˌsiː 'wɔːl '· · ‖ -wɑːl **~s** z
seaward 'siː wəd ‖ -wᵊrd **~s** z
seawater 'siː ˌwɔːt ə ‖ -ˌwɔːţ ᵊr -ˌwɑːţ-
seaway 'siː weɪ **~s** z
seaweed 'siː wiːd
seaworth|y 'siː ˌwɜːð |i ‖ -ˌwɜ˞ːð |i **~iness** i nəs i nɪs
Seb seb
sebaceous sə 'beɪʃ əs sɪ-
Sebastian sə 'bæst i‿ən sɪ- ‖ sə 'bæs tʃən
Sebastopol sə 'bæst ə pɒl sɪ-, -pᵊl ‖ -poʊl *—Russ* Sevastopol [sʲi vʌ 'sto pəlʲ]
Sebba 'seb ə
seborrhea, seborrhoea ˌseb ə 'riː‿ə
Sebring 'siːb rɪŋ
sebum 'siːb əm
sec sek
SECAM 'siː kæm
secant 'siːk ənt 'sek- ‖ -ænt **~s** s
secateurs sek ət əz -ə tɜːz, ˌsek ə 'tɜːz ‖ ˌsek ə 'tɜ˞ːz
Secaucus sɪ 'kɔːk əs sə- ‖ -'kɑːk-
secco 'sek əʊ ‖ -oʊ *—It* ['sek ko] **~s** z
Seccotine *tdmk* 'sek ə tiːn
seced|e sɪ 'siːd sə- **~ed** ɪd əd **~es** z **~ing** ɪŋ
secession sɪ 'seʃ ᵊn sə- **~ism** ˌɪz əm **~ist/s** ɪst/s §əst/s ‖ əst/s **~s** z
sech *'hyperbolic secant'* seʃ setʃ, ʃek *—or as* sec h
Secker 'sek ə ‖ -ᵊr
seclud|e sɪ 'kluːd sə- **~ed** ɪd əd **~es** z **~ing** ɪŋ
secluded|ly sɪ 'kluːd ɪd |li -əd- **~ness** nəs nɪs
seclusion sɪ 'kluːʒ ᵊn sə-
seclusive sɪ 'kluːs ɪv sə-, §-'kluːz- **~ly** li **~ness** nəs nɪs
Secombe 'siːk əm
second *adj; n; number; adv; determiner; v 'support'* 'sek ənd ⚠-ənt **~ed** ɪd əd **~ing** ɪŋ **~s** z
ˌsecond 'best◂; **ˌsecond 'childhood**; **ˌsecond 'class**; **ˌSecond 'Coming**; **ˌsecond 'cousin**; **'second hand** *(on a clock)*; **at ˌsecond 'hand** *'indirectly'*; **ˌsecond 'helping**; **ˌsecond lieu'tenant◂**; **ˌsecond 'mortgage**; **ˌsecond 'nature**; **ˌsecond 'person◂**, **ˌsecond ˌperson 'plural**; **ˌsecond 'sight**; **ˌsecond 'thoughts**; **ˌsecond 'wind**; **ˌSecond ˌWorld 'War**
second *v 'move to special duty'* sɪ 'kɒnd sə- ‖ -'kɑːnd **~ed** ɪd əd **~ing** ɪŋ **~s** z
secondarily 'sek ənd‿ər əl i ˌ-ən 'der əl i, '· · · · · ‖ ˌsek ən 'der əl i '· · · · ·
secondar|y 'sek ənd‿ər |i §-ən der- ‖ -ən der |i **~ies** iz **~iness** i nəs i nɪs
ˌsecondary 'modern; **ˌsecondary 'accent**, **ˌsecondary'stress**

S

second-class ˌsek ənd ˈklɑːs ◂ →-ŋ-, §-ˈklæs ‖ -ˈklæs ◂

ˌ**second-class ˈcitizen**

second-degree ˌsek ənd dɪ ˈgriː ◂ →ˌ·ŋ-, -dəˈ-, §-diːˈ·

ˌ**second-deˌgree ˈburn**

seconder ˈsek ənd ə ‖ -ᵊr **~s** z

second-generation ˌsek ənd ˌdʒen ə ˈreɪʃ ᵊn ◂ →ˌ·ŋ-

ˌ**second-geneˌration Auˈstralian**

second-guess ˌsek ənd ˈges →-ŋ- **~ed** t **~er/s** ə/z ‖ ᵊr/z **~es** ɪz əz **~ing** ɪŋ

secondhand, second-hand *adj* ˌsek ənd ˈhænd ◂

ˌ**second-hand ˈfurniture**

second-in-command ˌsek ənd ɪn kə ˈmɑːnd →-ɪŋ-ˈ, §-ˈmænd ‖ -ˈmænd **~s** z

secondly ˈsek ənd li

secondment sɪ ˈkɒnd mənt sə- ‖ -ˈkɑːnd- **~s** s

second|o se ˈkɒnd |əʊ sɪ-, sə- ‖ sɪ ˈkoʊnd |oʊ -ˈkɑːnd- **~i** iː

second-rate ˌsek ənd ˈreɪt ◂ →-ŋ- **~ness** nəs nɪs

ˌ**second-rate perˈformance**

second-rater ˌsek ənd ˈreɪt ə ‖ -ˈreɪt̬ ᵊr **~s** z

second-string ˌsek ənd ˈstrɪŋ ◂ →-ŋ-

secrecy ˈsiːk rəs i -rɪs-

secret ˈsiːk rət -rɪt **~s** s

ˌ**secret ˈagent**; ˌ**secret poˈlice**; ˌ**secret ˈservice**

secretaire ˌsek rə ˈteə -rɪ- ‖ -ˈteᵊr **~s** z

secretarial ˌsek rə ˈteər i‿əl ◂ ˌ·rɪ- ‖ -ˈter-

secretariat ˌsek rə ˈteər i‿ət ˌ·rɪ-, -æt ‖ -ˈter- **~s** s

secretar|y ˈsek rət‿ər |i ˈ·rɪt‿, ⚠ˈ·jʊt‿, ⚠ˈ·ət‿; -rə ter |i, -rɪ · ·, ⚠-ju · ·, ⚠-ə · · ‖ -rə ter |i ⚠-ə· · **~ies** iz

secretary-general ˌsek rət‿ər i ˈdʒen ᵊr‿əl ˌ·rɪt‿, ⚠ˌ·jʊt‿, ⚠ˌ·ət‿, ˌ·rə ter i-, ˌ·rɪ-, ⚠ˌ·ju-, ⚠ˌ·ə- ‖ ˌ·rə ter-

secrete sɪ ˈkriːt sə- **secreted** sɪ ˈkriːt ɪd sə-, -əd; ⚠ˈsiːk rət-, ⚠-rɪt- ‖ -ˈkriːt̬ əd **secretes** sɪ ˈkriːts sə- **secreting** sɪ ˈkriːt ɪŋ sə-; ⚠ˈsiːk rət ɪŋ, ⚠-rɪt- ‖ -ˈkriːt̬ ɪŋ

secretion sɪ ˈkriːʃ ᵊn sə- **~s** z

secretive ˈsiːk rət ɪv -rɪt-; sɪ ˈkriːt ɪv, sə- ‖ ˈsiːk rət̬ ɪv sɪ ˈkriːt̬ ɪv **~ly** li **~ness** nəs nɪs

secretly ˈsiːk rət li -rɪt-

secretor|y sɪ ˈkriːt‿ər |i sə- **~ies** iz

sect sekt **sects** sekts

sectarian sek ˈteər i‿ən ‖ -ˈter- **~ism** ˌɪz əm **~s** z

sectar|y ˈsekt ər |i **~ies** iz

section ˈsek ʃᵊn **~ed** d **~ing** ‿ɪŋ **~s** z

sectional ˈsek ʃᵊn‿əl **~ly** i

sectionalis... —*see* **sectionaliz...**

sectionalism ˈsek ʃᵊn‿əl ˌɪz əm

sectionalization ˌsek ʃᵊn‿əl aɪ ˈzeɪʃ ᵊn -ɪˈ- ‖ -əˈ-

sectionaliz|e ˈsek ʃᵊn‿ə laɪz **~ed** d **~es** ɪz əz **~ing** ɪŋ

sector ˈsekt ə ‖ -ᵊr **~s** z

sectoral ˈsekt ər əl

secular ˈsek jʊl ə -jəl- ‖ -jəl ᵊr **~ly** li **~s** z

secularis... —*see* **seculariz...**

secularism ˈsek jʊl ə ˌrɪz əm -jəl ə- ‖ -jəl ə-

secularist ˈsek jʊl ər ɪst -jəl ər-, §-əst ‖ -jəl ər-

secularity ˌsek ju ˈlær ət i ˌ·jə-, -ɪt i ‖ -jə ˈlær ət̬ i -ˈler-

secularization ˌsek jʊl ər aɪ ˈzeɪʃ ᵊn ˌ·jəl-, -ɪˈ- ‖ -jəl ər ə-

seculariz|e ˈsek jʊl ə raɪz -jəl ə- ‖ -jəl ə- **~ed** d **~es** ɪz əz **~ing** ɪŋ

secure sɪ ˈkjʊə sə-, -ˈkjɔː ‖ -ˈkjʊᵊr **~d** d **~s** z

securing sɪ ˈkjʊər ɪŋ sə-, -ˈkjɔːr- ‖ -ˈkjʊr ɪŋ

securely sɪ ˈkjʊə li sə-, -ˈkjɔː- ‖ -ˈkjʊᵊr li

Securicor *tdmk* sɪ ˈkjʊər ɪ kɔː sə-, -ˈkjɔːr-, -ə- ‖ -ˈkjʊr ə kɔːr

securitis... —*see* **securitiz...**

securitization sɪ ˌkjʊər ɪt aɪ ˈzeɪʃ ᵊn sə-, -ˌkjɔːr-, ˌ·ət-, -ɪˈ- ‖ ˌkjʊr ət̬ ə-

securitiz|e sɪ ˈkjʊər ɪ taɪz sə-, -ˈkjɔːr-, -ə- ‖ -ˈkjʊr ə taɪz **~ed** d **~es** ɪz əz **~ing** ɪŋ

securit|y sɪ ˈkjʊər ət |i sə-, -ˈkjɔːr-, -ɪt i ‖ -ˈkjʊr ət̬ |i **~ies** iz

seˈcurity ˌblanket; **seˈcurity ˌclearance**; **Seˈcurity ˌCouncil**; **seˈcurity risk**

Sedaka sə ˈdɑːk ə sɪ-

sedan, Sedan sɪ ˈdæn sə- —*Fr* [sə dɑ̃] **~s** z

seˌdan ˈchair ‖ ˈ·ˌ·

sedate *adj, v* sɪ ˈdeɪt sə- **sedated** sɪ ˈdeɪt ɪd sə-, -əd ‖ -ˈdeɪt̬ əd **~ly** li **~ness** nəs nɪs **~s** s

sedating sɪ ˈdeɪt ɪŋ sə- ‖ -ˈdeɪt̬ ɪŋ

sedation sɪ ˈdeɪʃ ᵊn sə- **~s** z

sedative ˈsed ət ɪv ‖ -ət̬ ɪv **~s** z

Sedbergh ˈsed bə →ˈseb-, -bɜːg, ˈsed bər‿ə ‖ -bɜːg

Seddon ˈsed ᵊn

sedentarily ˈsed ᵊnt‿ər əl i ˈsed ᵊn ter əl i, -ɪ li, ˌ· ·ˈ· · ·; §sɪ ˈdent‿, sə- ‖ ˌsed ᵊn ˈter əl i

sedentar|y ˈsed ᵊnt‿ər |i §-ᵊn ter |i; §sɪ ˈdent ər |i, §sə- ‖ -ᵊn ter |i **~iness** i nəs i nɪs

Seder ˈseɪd ə ‖ -ᵊr

sedge sedʒ **sedges** ˈsedʒ ɪz -əz

Sedgefield ˈsedʒ fiːᵊld

Sedgemoor ˈsedʒ mɔː -mʊə ‖ -mʊr

Sedgewick, Sedgwick ˈsedʒ wɪk

sedgy ˈsedʒ i

sedilia sɪ ˈdɪl i‿ə -ˈdiːl-, -ˈdaɪl-

sediment ˈsed ɪ mənt -ə- **~s** s

sedimentary ˌsed ɪ ˈment‿ər i ◂ ˌ·ə-

sedimentation ˌsed ɪ men ˈteɪʃ ᵊn ˌ·ə-, -mənˈ-

sedition sɪ ˈdɪʃ ᵊn sə-

seditious sɪ ˈdɪʃ əs sə- **~ly** li **~ness** nəs nɪs

Sedlescombe ˈsed ᵊlz kəm

Sedley ˈsed li

seduc|e sɪ ˈdjuːs sə-, →-ˈdʒuːs ‖ -ˈduːs -ˈdjuːs **~ed** t **~er/s** ə/z ‖ ᵊr/z **~es** ɪz əz **~ing** ɪŋ

seduction sɪ ˈdʌk ʃᵊn sə- **~s** z

seductive sɪ ˈdʌkt ɪv sə- **~ly** li **~ness** nəs nɪs

seductress sɪ ˈdʌk trəs sə-, -trɪs **~es** ɪz əz

sedulity sɪ ˈdjuːl ət i sə-, →-ˈdʒuːl-, -ɪt- ‖ -ˈduːl ət̬ i -ˈdjuːl-

sedulous ˈsed jʊl əs §-jəl-; ˈsedʒ ʊl- ‖ ˈsedʒ əl əs **~ly** li **~ness** nəs nɪs

sedum 'siːd əm **~s** z
see siː **saw** sɔː ‖ sɑː **seeing** 'siː ɪŋ **seen** siːn **sees** siːz
ˌ**Seeing 'Eye dog**
Seear 'siː‿ə ‖ ᵊr
Seebeck 'siː bek —*Ger* ['zeː bɛk]
'Seebeck efˌfect
seed, Seed siːd **seeded** 'siːd ɪd -əd **seeding** 'siːd ɪŋ **seeds** siːdz
seedbed 'siːd bed →'siːb- **~s** z
seedcake 'siːd keɪk →'siːg- **~s** s
seedcorn 'siːd kɔːn →'siːg- ‖ -kɔːrn
seed-eater 'siːd ˌiːt ə ‖ -ˌiːţ ᵊr **~s** z
seeder 'siːd ə ‖ -ᵊr **~s** z
seedless 'siːd ləs -lɪs
seedling 'siːd lɪŋ **~s** z
seeds|man 'siːdz |mən **~men** mən men
seedtime 'siːd taɪm **~s** z
seed|y 'siːd |i **~ier** i‿ə ‖ i‿ᵊr **~iest** i‿ɪst i‿əst **~ily** ɪ li əl i **~iness** i nəs i nɪs
Seeger 'siːg ə ‖ -ᵊr
seek siːk **seeking** 'siːk ɪŋ **seeks** siːks **sought** sɔːt ‖ sɑːt
seeker 'siːk ə ‖ -ᵊr **~s** z
Seeley, Seely 'siːl i
seem siːm **seemed** siːmd **seeming/ly** 'siːm ɪŋ /li **seems** siːmz
seem|ly 'siːm |li **~lier** li‿ə ‖ li‿ᵊr **~liest** li‿ɪst li‿əst **~liness** li nəs li nɪs
seen siːn
seep siːp **seeped** siːpt **seeping** 'siːp ɪŋ **seeps** siːps
seepag|e 'siːp ɪdʒ **~es** ɪz əz
seer sɪə 'siː‿ə ‖ sɪᵊr 'siː ᵊr **seers** sɪəz 'siː‿əz ‖ sɪᵊrz 'siː ᵊrz
seersucker 'sɪə ˌsʌk ə ‖ 'sɪr ˌsʌk ᵊr
seesaw 'siː sɔː ‖ -sɑː **~ed** d **seesawing** 'siː sɔːʳ ɪŋ ‖ -sɔː ɪŋ -sɑː- **~s** z
seethe siːð **seethed** siːðd **seethes** siːðz **seething** 'siːð ɪŋ
see-through 'siː θruː
Seferis se 'feər ɪs sɪ-, sə-, §-əs —*Greek* [sɛ 'fɛ ris]
Sefton 'seft ən
Sega *tdmk* 'siːg ə 'seɪg ə
Segal 'siːg ᵊl
Seggie 'seg i
segment *n* 'seg mənt **~s** s
seg|ment *v* ₍ₗ₎seg '|ment sɪg-, səg- ‖ '. . **~mented** ment ɪd -əd ‖ menţ əd **~menting** ment ɪŋ ‖ menţ ɪŋ **~ments** ments
segmental seg 'ment ᵊl sɪg-, səg- ‖ -'menţ- **~ly** i **~s** z
segmentation ˌseg men 'teɪʃ ᵊn -mən- **~s** z
segno 'seg nəʊ 'sen jəʊ, 'seɪn- ‖ 'seɪn joʊ —*It* ['seɲ ɲo]
sego 'siːg əʊ ‖ -oʊ **~s** z
ˌ**sego 'lily**
Ségolène ˌseg əʊ 'leɪn ‖ ˌseɪg oʊ- —*Fr* [se go lɛn]
Segovia sɪ 'gəʊv i‿ə sə-, se- ‖ -'goʊv- —*Sp* [se 'ɣo βja]
Segrave 'siː greɪv
segre|gate 'seg rɪ |geɪt -rə- **~gated** geɪt ɪd -əd ‖ geɪţ əd **~gates** geɪts **~gating** geɪt ɪŋ ‖ geɪţ ɪŋ
segregation ˌseg rɪ 'geɪʃ ᵊn -rə- **~ist/s** ɪst/s §əst/s ‖ əst/s
segue 'seg weɪ 'seɪg-, -wi —*It* ['seː gwe] **~d** d **~ing** ɪŋ **~s** z
seguidilla ˌseg i 'diːl jə -'diː- —*Sp* [se ɣi 'ði ʎa, -ja] **~s** z
sei seɪ *(= say)*
'sei whale
seiche seɪʃ **seiches** 'seɪʃ ɪz -əz
Seidlitz 'sed lɪts §-ləts
Seifert 'siːf ət ‖ -ᵊrt
seigneur sen 'jɜː seɪn-; 'seɪn jə ‖ seɪn 'jɜː siːn- —*Fr* [sɛ ɲœːʁ] **~s** z
seigneurial sen 'jɜːr i‿əl seɪn- ‖ seɪn 'jɜː- -'jʊr-
seignior 'seɪn jə ‖ -jɔːr -'. **~s** z
seigniorage 'seɪn jər ɪdʒ
seigniorial ₍ₗ₎seɪn 'jɔːr i‿əl ‖ -'joʊr-
seignior|y 'seɪn jər |i **~ies** iz
Seiko *tdmk* 'seɪk əʊ 'siːk- ‖ -oʊ —*Jp* [se ˌi koo, se ˌe-]
seine, Seine seɪn —*Fr* [sɛn] **seined** seɪnd **seines** seɪnz **seining** 'seɪn ɪŋ
'seine net
Seinfeld 'saɪn feld
Seiriol 'saɪᵊr i ɒl əl ‖ -ɑːl -ɔːl —*Welsh* ['səir jol]
seise siːz *(= seize, sees, seas)* **seised** siːzd
seisin 'siːz ɪn §-ᵊn
seismic 'saɪz mɪk **~ally** ᵊl‿i
seismicity ₍ₗ₎saɪz 'mɪs ət i -ɪt i ‖ -əţ i
seismograph 'saɪz mə grɑːf -græf ‖ -græf **~s** s
seismographic ˌsaɪz mə 'græf ɪk ◂ **~ally** ᵊl‿i
seismography saɪz 'mɒg rəf i ‖ -'mɑːg-
seismologist saɪz 'mɒl ədʒ ɪst §-əst ‖ -'mɑːl- **~s** s
seismology saɪz 'mɒl ədʒ i ‖ -'mɑːl-
seismometer ₍ₗ₎saɪz 'mɒm ɪt ə -ət ə ‖ -'mɑːm əţ ᵊr **~s** z
seitan 'seɪ tæn ‖ -tɑːn
seize siːz *(= sees, seas)* **seized** siːzd **seizes** 'siːz ɪz -əz **seizing** 'siːz ɪŋ
seizure 'siːʒ ə 'siːz jə ‖ -ᵊr **~s** z
sejant 'siːdʒ ənt
Sejanus sɪ 'dʒeɪn əs sə-
selah, Selah 'siːl ə -ɑː
Selangor sə 'læŋ ə sɪ-, -ɔː ‖ -ᵊr -'lɑːŋ-, -ɔːr -gɔːr
Selassie sə 'læs i sɪ- ‖ -'lɑːs i
Selborne, Selbourne 'sel bɔːn ‖ -bɔːrn -boʊrn
Selby 'sel bi
Selden 'seld ən
seldom 'seld əm
select sə 'lekt sɪ- **~ed** ɪd əd **~ing** ɪŋ **~ness** nəs nɪs **~s** z
seˌlect com'mittee
selectee sə ˌlek 'tiː sɪ- **~s** z
selection sə 'lek ʃᵊn sɪ- **~s** z
selective sə 'lekt ɪv sɪ- **~ly** li **~ness** nəs nɪs
selectivity sə ˌlek 'tɪv ət i sɪ-, ˌsɪl ek-, ˌsiːl ek-, ˌsel ek-, -ɪt i ‖ -əţ i
selector sə 'lekt ə sɪ- ‖ -ᵊr **~s** z

S

Selena sə ˈliːn ə sɪ-
Selene sə ˈliːn i sɪ-
selenic sə ˈliːn ɪk sɪ-, -ˈlen-
selenite ˈsel ə naɪt -ɪ-
selenium sə ˈliːn i‿əm
seleno- *comb. form*
with stress-neutral suffix sə ¦liːn əʊ sɪ- ‖ -oʊ -ə
— **selenographic** sə ˌliːn əʊ ˈgræf ɪk ◂
‖ -oʊ- -ə-
with stress-imposing suffix ˌsiːl ə ˈnɒ+ -ɪ-
‖ ˌsel ə ˈnɑː+ — **selenology**
ˌsiːl ə ˈnɒl ədʒ i -ɪ- ‖ ˌsel ə ˈnɑːl-
Seles ˈsel ez -əs —*Serbian* Seleš [ˈsɛ lɛʃ]
Seleucia sə ˈluːs i‿ə sɪ-, -ˈluːʃ-, -ˈljuːs-, -ˈljuːʃ-
Seleucid sə ˈluːs ɪd sɪ-, -ˈljuːs-, §-əd **~s** z
Seleucus sə ˈluːk əs sɪ-, -ˈljuːk-
self, Self self **selves** selvz
self- ¦self —*Words with this prefix normally have late stress.* — **self-abasement**
ˌself ə ˈbeɪs mənt
self-abnegation ˌself ˌæb nɪ ˈgeɪʃ ən -neˈ··, -nəˈ··
self-absorbed ˌself əb ˈsɔːbd ◂ -æb-, -ˈzɔːbd
‖ -ˈsɔːrbd ◂ -ˈzɔːrbd
self-abuse *n* ˌself ə ˈbjuːs
self-access ˌself ˈæk ses
self-acting ˌself ˈækt ɪŋ ◂
self-actualization, self-actualisation
ˌself ˌæk tʃu‿ə laɪ ˈzeɪʃ ən -tju‿, ‿əl ɪ- ‖ ‿əl ə-
self-addressed ˌself ə ˈdrest ◂
self-adhesive ˌself əd ˈhiːs ɪv ◂ §-æd-
self-administered ˌself əd ˈmɪn ɪst əd §ˌæd-, -əst- ‖ -ərd
self-aggrandizement ˌself ə ˈgrænd ɪz mənt -əz·, -aɪz ·
self-aggrandizing ˌself ə ˈgrænd aɪz ɪŋ ◂
self-appointed ˌself ə ˈpɔɪnt ɪd ◂ -əd
‖ -ˈpɔɪnţ əd ◂
self-assembly ˌself ə ˈsem bli
self-assertion ˌself ə ˈsɜːʃ ən ‖ -ˈsɜːʃ ən
self-assertive ˌself ə ˈsɜːt ɪv ‖ -ˈsɜːţ ɪv **~ly** li **~ness** nəs nɪs
self-assessment ˌself ə ˈses mənt **~s** s
self-assurance ˌself ə ˈʃɔːr ənts -ˈʃʊər-
‖ -ˈʃʊr ənts -ˈʃɜː-
self-assured ˌself ə ˈʃɔːd ◂ -ˈʃʊəd ‖ -ˈʃʊərd -ˈʃɜːd
self-awareness ˌself ə ˈweə nəs -nɪs ‖ -ˈwer- -ˈwær-
self-build ˌself ˈbɪld ◂
self-catering ˌself ˈkeɪt‿ər ɪŋ ‖ -ˈkeɪţ-
self-centered, self-centred ˌself ˈsent əd
‖ -ˈsenţ ərd **~ly** li **~ness** nəs nɪs
self-certification ˌself ˌsɜːt ɪf ɪ ˈkeɪʃ ən -əf·ˈ· ·, -əˈ· · ‖ -ˌsɜːţ-
self-command ˌself kə ˈmɑːnd §-ˈmænd
‖ -ˈmænd
self-concept ˌself ˈkɒn sept ‖ -ˈkɑːn- **~s** s
self-confessed ˌself kən ˈfest ◂ §-kɒn-
ˌ**self-conˌfessed ˈliar**
self-confid|ence ˌself ˈkɒn fɪd |ənts §-fəd-
‖ -ˈkɑːn- **~ent/ly** ənt /li

self-congratulation
ˌself kən ˌgrætʃ u ˈleɪʃ ən →ˌ·kəŋ-, §→ˌ·kɒŋ-, -ˌgræt juˈ· · ‖ -ˌgrætʃ ə- -ˌgrædʒ ə-
self-congratulatory
ˌself kən ˌgrætʃ u ˈleɪt ər i ◂ →ˌ·kəŋ-, §ˌ·kɒn-, -ˌ·ə-, -ˌgræt ju-; ˌ· ·ˈ·. ·lət‿ər i
‖ ˌself kən ˈgrætʃ əl‿ə tɔːr i -ˈgrædʒ-, -toʊr i
self-conscious ˌself ˈkɒntʃ əs ◂ ‖ -ˈkɑːntʃ əs **~ly** li **~ness** nəs nɪs
self-contained ˌself kən ˈteɪnd ◂ §-kɒn-
self-contradictory ˌself ˌkɒntr ə ˈdɪkt ər‿i
‖ -ˌkɑːntr-
self-control ˌself kən ˈtrəʊl §-kɒn-, →-ˈtrɒʊl
‖ -ˈtroʊl **~led** d
self-correcting ˌself kə ˈrekt ɪŋ ◂
self-critical ˌself ˈkrɪt ɪk əl ‖ -ˈkrɪţ-
self-criticism ˌself ˈkrɪt ɪ ˌsɪz əm -ə- ‖ -ˈkrɪţ-
self-deception ˌself di ˈsep ʃən -də-
self-defeating ˌself di ˈfiːt ɪŋ ◂ -də-
‖ -ˈfiːţ ɪŋ ◂
self-defence, self-defense ˌself di ˈfents -də-
self-denial ˌself di ˈnaɪ‿əl -də- **~s** z
self-deprecating ˌself ˈdep rə keɪt ɪŋ ◂
‖ -keɪţ ɪŋ ◂
self-described ˌself di ˈskraɪbd ◂ -də-
self-destruct ˌself di ˈstrʌkt -də- **~ed** ɪd əd **~ing** ɪŋ **~s** s
self-destruction ˌself di ˈstrʌk ʃən -də-
self-destructive ˌself di ˈstrʌkt ɪv ◂ -də- **~ly** li **~ness** nəs nɪs
self-determination ˌself di ˌtɜːm ɪ ˈneɪʃ ən ˌ·də-, -əˈ·- ‖ -ˌtɜːm-
self-directed ˌself də ˈrekt ɪd ◂ -di-, -daɪə-
self-discipline ˌself ˈdɪs ə plɪn -ɪ-, §ˌ·dɪ ˈsɪp lɪn **~d** d ◂
self-|doubt ˌself |ˈdaʊt **~doubting** ˈdaʊt ɪŋ
‖ ˈdaʊţ ɪŋ
self-drive ˌself ˈdraɪv ◂
self-educated ˌself ˈed ju keɪt ɪd ◂ -ˈedʒ u-, §-ˈedʒ ə- ‖ -ˈedʒ ə keɪţ əd ◂
self-effac|ement ˌself ɪ ˈfeɪs |mənt -ə- **~ing** ɪŋ ◂
self-em|ployed ˌself ɪm |ˈplɔɪd ◂ §-əm- **~ployment** ˈplɔɪ mənt
self-esteem ˌself ɪ ˈstiːm §-ə-
self-evident ˌself ˈev ɪd ənt ◂ -əd-, §-ə dent **~ly** li
self-examination ˌself ɪg ˌzæm ɪ ˈneɪʃ ən ·eg-, ˌ·əg-, ˌ·ɪk-, ·ek-, ˌ·ək-, -əˈ·-
self-explanatory ˌself ɪk ˈsplæn ət‿ər i ◂ ˌ·ek-, ˌ·ək- ‖ -ə tɔːr i -toʊr i
self-expression ˌself ɪk ˈspreʃ ən -ek-, -ək-
self-fulfilling ˌself fʊl ˈfɪl ɪŋ ◂
ˌ**self-fulˌfilling ˈprophecy**
self-governing ˌself ˈgʌv ən‿ɪŋ ◂ ‖ -ərn ɪŋ ◂
self-government ˌself ˈgʌv ən mənt →-əm- ‖ -ərn-
self-hatred ˌself ˈheɪtr ɪd -əd
selfheal ˈself hiːəl **~s** z
self-help ˌself ˈhelp
selfhood ˈself hʊd
self-imag|e ˌself ˈɪm ɪdʒ **~es** ɪz əz

self-import|ance ˌself ɪm ˈpɔːt |ᵊnᵗs ‖ -ˈpɔːrt |ᵊnᵗs **~ant/ly** ᵊnt /li
self-imposed ˌself ɪm ˈpəʊzd ◂ ‖ -ˈpoʊzd ◂
ˌself-imˌposed ˈtask
self-improvement ˌself ɪm ˈpruːv mənt
self-induced ˌself ɪn ˈdjuːst ◂ →-ˈdʒuːst, §-ˈduːst ‖ -ˈduːst ◂ -ˈdjuːst
self-indulg|ence ˌself ɪn ˈdʌldʒ |ənᵗs **~ent/ly** ənt /li
self-inflicted ˌself ɪn ˈflɪkt ɪd ◂ -əd
self-interest ˌself ˈɪntr əst -ɪst, -est; ˈɪnt ə rest ‖ ˈɪnṱ ə rest **~ed** ɪd əd
selfish ˈself ɪʃ **~ly** li **~ness** nəs nɪs
self-knowledge ˌself ˈnɒl ɪdʒ ‖ -ˈnɑːl-
selfless ˈself ləs -lɪs **~ly** li **~ness** nəs nɪs
self-locking ˌself ˈlɒk ɪŋ ◂ ‖ -ˈlɑːk ɪŋ ◂
self-made ˌself ˈmeɪd ◂
ˌself-made ˈman
self-opinionated ˌself ə ˈpɪn jə neɪt ɪd ◂ §ˌəʊ-, -əd ‖ -neɪṱ-
self-perpetuating ˌself pə ˈpetʃ u eɪt ɪŋ ◂ -ˈpet ju- ‖ -pᵊr ˈpetʃ u eɪṱ ɪŋ ◂
self-pity ˌself ˈpɪt i ‖ -ˈpɪṱ i **~ing/ly** ɪŋ /li
self-possessed ˌself pə ˈzest ◂ **~ly** li
self-possession ˌself pə ˈzeʃ ᵊn
self-preservation ˌself ˌprez ə ˈveɪʃ ᵊn ‖ -ᵊr-
self-proclaimed ˌself prəʊˈkleɪmd ◂
self-raising ˌself ˈreɪz ɪŋ
ˌself-ˈraising flour, ˌ·ˌ·· ˈ··
self-regulating ˌself ˈreg ju leɪt ɪŋ ◂ -ˈ·jə- ‖ -jə leɪṱ ɪŋ ◂
self-regulation ˌself ˌreg ju ˈleɪʃ ᵊn -jə-
self-regulatory ˌself ˌreg ju ˈleɪt ər i -jəˈ--, -ˈ· · · · ·, ˈ· ·lət ər i ‖ -ˈreg jəl ə tɔːr i -toʊr i
self-reli|ance ˌself ri ˈlaɪ |ənᵗs -rə- **~ant/ly** ənt /li
self-respect ˌself ri ˈspekt -rə- **~ing** ɪŋ ◂
self-restraint ˌself ri ˈstreɪnt -rə-
Selfridg|e ˈself rɪdʒ **~es** ɪz əz
self-righteous ˌself ˈraɪtʃ əs ◂ -ˈraɪt i əs **~ly** li **~ness** nəs nɪs
self-rising ˌself ˈraɪz ɪŋ ◂
self-rule ˌself ˈruːl
self-sacrific|e ˌself ˈsæk rɪ faɪs -rə- **~ing** ɪŋ
selfsame ˈself seɪm ˌˈ·
self-satisfied ˌself ˈsæt ɪs faɪd ◂ -əs- ‖ -ˈsæṱ əs-
self-seek|er ˌself ˈsiːk |ə ‖ -|ᵊr **~ers** əz ‖ ᵊrz **~ing** ɪŋ ◂
self-service ˌself ˈsɜːv ɪs ◂ §-əs ‖ -ˈsɜːv əs ◂
self-serving ˌself ˈsɜːv ɪŋ ◂ ‖ -ˈsɜːv-
self-starter ˌself ˈstɑːt ə ‖ -ˈstɑːrṱ ᵊr **~s** z
self-styled ˌself ˈstaɪᵊld ◂
self-suffici|ency ˌself sə ˈfɪʃ |ᵊnᵗs i **~ent/ly** ᵊnt /li
self-supporting ˌself sə ˈpɔːt ɪŋ ‖ -ˈpɔːrṱ ɪŋ -ˈpoʊrṱ-
self-sustaining ˌself sə ˈsteɪn ɪŋ ◂
self-taught ˌself ˈtɔːt ◂ ‖ -ˈtɑːt ◂
self-titled ˌself ˈtaɪt ᵊld ◂ ‖ -ˈtaɪṱ-
self-will ˌself ˈwɪl **~ed** d ◂
self-winding ˌself ˈwaɪnd ɪŋ ◂
self-worth ˌself ˈwɜːθ ‖ -wɜːθ
Selhurst ˈsel hɜːst ‖ -hɜːst
Seligman, Seligmann ˈsel ɪg mən
Selina sə ˈliːn ə sɪ-
Seljuk ˌsel ˈdʒuːk ˈ··
Selkirk ˈsel kɜːk ‖ -kɜːk
sell sel **selling** ˈselɪŋ **sells** selz **sold** səʊld →sɒʊld ‖ soʊld
ˈselling point
Sellafield ˈsel ə fiːᵊld
Sellar ˈsel ə ‖ -ᵊr
Sellars ˈsel əz ‖ -ᵊrz
sell-by date ˈsel baɪ deɪt
seller ˈsel ə ‖ -ᵊr **~s** z
ˌseller's ˈmarket
Sellers ˈsel əz ‖ -ᵊrz
Sellick ˈsel ɪk
Sellinge ˈsel ɪndʒ
sell-off ˈsel ɒf -ɔːf ‖ -ɔːf -ɑːf
sellotap|e, S~ *tdmk* ˈsel əʊ teɪp ‖ -ə- **~ed** t **~es** s **~ing** ɪŋ
sell-out ˈsel aʊt **~s** s
Selly ˈsel i
Selma ˈselm ə
Selous sə ˈluː
Selsey ˈsels i
seltzer, S~ ˈselts ə ‖ -ᵊr **~s** z
selvag|e, selvedg|e ˈselv ɪdʒ **~es** ɪz əz
selves selvz
Selwyn ˈsel wɪn
Selznick ˈselz nɪk
semanteme sə ˈmænt iːm sɪ- **~s** z
semantic sə ˈmænt ɪk sɪ- ‖ -ˈmænṱ ɪk **~ally** ᵊl i **~s** s
semantician sə ˌmæn ˈtɪʃ ᵊn sɪ- **~s** z
semanticist sə ˈmænt əs ɪst sɪ-, -ɪs-, §-əst ‖ -ˈmænṱ- **~s** s
semaphore ˈsem ə fɔː ‖ -fɔːr -foʊr **~d** d **~s** z
semaphoring ˈsem ə fɔːr ɪŋ ‖ -foʊr ɪŋ
semaphoric ˌsem ə ˈfɒr ɪk ◂ ‖ -ˈfɔːr ɪk ◂ -ˈfɑːr- **~ally** ᵊl i
semasiology sə ˌmeɪz i ˈɒl ədʒ i sɪ-, -ˌmeɪs- ‖ -ˈɑːl-
sematic sə ˈmæt ɪk sɪ- ‖ -ˈmæṱ ɪk
semblanc|e ˈsem blənᵗs **~es** ɪz əz
semeio... —*see* **semio...**
Semele ˈsem əl i -ɪl-; -ə leɪ, -ɪ-
sememe ˈsiːm iːm **~s** z
semen ˈsiːm ən -en (*= seamen*)
Semer Water ˈsem ə ˌwɔːt ə ‖ -ᵊr ˌwɔːṱ ᵊr -ˌwɑːṱ-
semester sə ˈmest ə sɪ- ‖ -ᵊr **~s** z
semi ˈsem i ‖ -aɪ **~s** z
semi- ¦sem i ‖ -aɪ —*Words with this prefix mostly have late stress; certain exceptions are found in the list below. — Preference poll, AmE: -i 60%, -aɪ 40%. See chart on p. 728.* — **semiblind** ˌsem i ˈblaɪnd ◂ ‖ -aɪ-
semiannual ˌsem i ˈæn ju əl ◂ ‖ ˌsem aɪ- **~ly** i
semi-arid ˌsem i ˈær ɪd ◂ §-əd ‖ -aɪ-, -ˈer-
semi-autobiographical ˌsem i ˌɔːt əʊbaɪ ə ˈgræf ɪk ᵊl ◂ ‖ -ˌɔːṱ ə- ˌsem aɪ-, -ˌɑːṱ ə-

S

SEMI-

semiautomatic ˌsem i ˌɔːt ə ˈmæt ɪk ◂ ‖ -ˌɔːt̬ ə ˈmæt̬ ɪk ◂, ˌaɪ- **~ally** əl_i
semibreve ˈsem i briːv ‖ -aɪ-, -brev **~s** z
semicircle ˈsem i ˌsɜːk əl ‖ -ˌsɝːk əl **~s** z
semicircular ˌsem i ˈsɜːk jʊl ə ◂ -jəl ə ‖ -ˈsɝːk jəl ər ◂
semicolon ˌsem i ˈkəʊl ən -ɒn, ˈ· ˌ· ˌ· ‖ ˈsem i ˌkoʊl ən **~s** z
semiconduct|ing ˌsem i kən ˈdʌkt |ɪŋ §-kɒn'·· ‖ ˌaɪ- **~or/s** ə/z ‖ -ər/z
semiconscious ˌsem i ˈkɒntʃ əs ◂ ‖ -ˈkɑːntʃ- -aɪ-
semiconsonant ˌsem i ˈkɒntsən ənt ˈ· ˌ· ˌ· ‖ -ˈkɑːnts- ˌsem aɪ- **~s** s
semiconsonantal ˌsem i ˌkɒnts ə ˈnænt əl ◂ ‖ -ˌkɑːnts ə ˈnænt̬ əl ◂ ˌsem aɪ-
semidarkness ˌsem i ˈdɑːk nəs -nɪs ‖ -ˈdɑːrk- -aɪ-
semidetached ˌsem i di ˈtætʃt ◂ -i də- ‖ ˌsem aɪ-
ˌsemideˌtached ˈbungalow
semifinal ˌsem i ˈfaɪn əl ◂ ‖ -aɪ- **~s** z
semifinalist ˌsem i ˈfaɪn əl ɪst §-əst ‖ ˌaɪ- **~s** s
semigloss ˈsem i glɒs ‖ -glɔːs aɪ-, -glɑːs
semillon, S~ ˈsem i õ ˈseɪm- ‖ ˌ· i ˈjoʊn —*Fr* Sémillon [se mi jõ]
seminal ˈsem ɪn əl ˈsiːm-, -ən- **~ly** i
seminar ˈsem ɪ nɑː -ə- ‖ -nɑːr **~s** z
seminarian ˌsem ɪ ˈneər i_ən ˌ·ə- ‖ -ˈner- **~s** z
seminarist ˈsem ɪn ər ɪst ˈ·ən-, §-əst **~s** s
seminar|y ˈsem ɪn ər_|i ˈ·ən- ‖ -ə ner |i **~ies** iz
Seminole ˈsem ɪ nəʊl -ə-, →-nɒʊl ‖ -noʊl **~s** z
seminomadic ˌsem i nəʊ ˈmæd ɪk ◂ ‖ -noʊˈ· · ˌaɪ-
semiolog|ist ˌsem i ˈɒl ədʒ |ɪst ˌsiːm-, §-əst ‖ -ˈɑːl- **~ists** ɪsts §əsts **~y** i
semiology ˌsem i ˈɒl ədʒ i ˌsiːm- ‖ -ˈɑːl- ˌaɪ-
semiotic ˌsem i ˈɒt ɪk ◂ ˌsiːm- ‖ -ˈɑːt̬ ɪk ◂ -aɪ- **~s** s
semiotician ˌsem i_ə ˈtɪʃ ən ˌsiːm- **~s** z
Semipalatinsk ˌsem i pə ˈlæt ɪnsk ‖ -ˈlɑːt- —*Russ* [sʲɪ mʲi pə ˈła tʲinsk]
semipermeable ˌsem i ˈpɜːm i_əb əl ◂ ‖ -ˈpɝːm- ˌsem aɪ-
semiprecious ˌsem i ˈpreʃ əs ◂ -aɪ-
semiprivate ˌsem i ˈpraɪv ət ◂ -ɪt ‖ -aɪ-
semiprofessional ˌsem i prə ˈfeʃ ən_əl ◂ ˌaɪ- **~s** z
semiquaver ˈsem i ˌkweɪv ə ‖ -ər **~s** z
Semiramide ˌsem i ˈrɑːm ɪd i -əd i; -ɪ deɪ
Semiramis sə ˈmɪr ə mɪs sɪ-, se-, §-əm əs
semi-retired ˌsem i ri ˈtaɪ_əd ◂ -rəˈ· · ‖ -ˈtaɪ_ərd ◂ ˌsem aɪ-
semiskilled ˌsem ɪ ˈskɪld ◂ ‖ -aɪ-
semi-skimmed ˌsem i ˈskɪmd ◂ ‖ -aɪ-
semisweet ˌsem i ˈswiːt ◂ ‖ -aɪ-
Semite ˈsiːm aɪt ˈsem- ‖ ˈsem aɪt **~s** s
Semitic sə ˈmɪt ɪk sɪ- ‖ -ˈmɪt̬ ɪk **~s** s
semitone ˈsem i təʊn ‖ -toʊn -aɪ- **~s** z
semitrailer ˈsem i ˌtreɪl ə ‖ ˈsem aɪ ˌtreɪl ər -i- **~s** z
semitropical ˌsem i ˈtrɒp ɪk əl ◂ ‖ -ˈtrɑːp- ˌaɪ-
semivocalic ˌsem i vəʊ ˈkæl ɪk ◂ ‖ -voʊˈ--
semivowel ˈsem i ˌvaʊ_əl ˈ· ·vaʊl **~s** z
semiweek|ly ˌsem i ˈwiːk |li ◂ ‖ -aɪ- **~lies** liz
semolina ˌsem ə ˈliːn ə
ˌsemoˌlina ˈpudding
Semper, s~ ˈsemp ə ‖ -ər
sempiternal ˌsemp ɪ ˈtɜːn əl ◂ -ə- ‖ -ˈtɝːn əl ◂ **~ly** i
Semple ˈsemp əl
semplice ˈsemp lɪtʃ i -lɪ tʃeɪ —*It* [ˈsem pli tʃe]
sempre ˈsemp ri -reɪ —*It* [ˈsɛm pre]
sempstress ˈsempˢ trəs -trɪs **~es** ɪz əz
Semtex *tdmk* ˈsem teks
sen *unit of currency* sen
Sen., sen. —*see* **senator, senior**
SEN ˌes iː ˈen **~s** z
senary ˈsiːn ər i ˈsen-
senate, S~ ˈsen ət -ɪt **~s** s
senator, S~ ˈsen ət ə ‖ -ət̬ ər —*In AmE, as a title also* ˈsent ər **~s** z
senatorial ˌsen ə ˈtɔːr i_əl ◂ ‖ -ˈtoʊr- **~ly** i
send, Send send **sending** ˈsend ɪŋ **sends** sendz **sent** sent
Sendai ˈsend aɪ —*Jp* [ˈsen dai]
Sendak ˈsend æk
sender ˈsend ə ‖ -ər **~s** z
send-off ˈsend ɒf -ɔːf ‖ -ɔːf -ɑːf **~s** s
send-up ˈsend ʌp **~s** s
Senec|a ˈsen ɪk |ə -ək- **~an** ən **~as** əz
ˌSeneca ˈFalls; **ˌSeneca ˈLake**
Senedd ˈsen eð -ɪð, -əð
Senegal ˌsen ɪ ˈgɔːl -ə-, -ˈgɑːl
Senegalese ˌsen ɪg ə ˈliːz ◂ -ɔːˈ·
Senegambia ˌsen ɪ ˈgæm bi_ə ˌ·ə-
senescence sɪ ˈnes ənts sə-
senescent sɪ ˈnes ənt sə-
seneschal ˈsen ɪʃ əl -əʃ-; -ɪ ʃɑːl, -ə- **~s** z
Senghenydd seŋ ˈhen ɪð
Senhor, s~ sen ˈjɔː ‖ seɪn ˈjɔːr —*Port* [sɪ ˈɲoɾ]
Senhora, s~ sen ˈjɔːr ə ‖ seɪn- -ˈjoʊr- —*Port* [sɪ ˈɲo ɾɐ]
Senhorita, s~ ˌsen jɔː ˈriːt ə -jə- ‖ ˌseɪn jə ˈriːt̬ ə —*Port* [sɪ ɲo ˈɾi tɐ] **~s** z
senile ˈsiːn aɪəl ‖ ˈsen-, -əl **~ly** li
senility sə ˈnɪl ət i sɪ-, -ɪt- ‖ -ət̬ i
senior, S~ ˈsiːn i_ə ‖ ˈsiːn jər **~s** z
ˌsenior ˈcitizen
seniorit|y ˌsiːn i ˈɒr ət |i -ɪt i ‖ siːn ˈjɔːr ət̬ |i -ˈjɑːr- **~ies** iz
Senlac ˈsen læk
senna, Senna ˈsen ə
Sennacherib se ˈnæk ər ɪb sə-, sɪ-, §-əb
sennet ˈsen ɪt §-ət **~s** s
Sennett ˈsen ɪt §-ət

sennight, se'nnight ˈsen aɪt **~s** s

Senor, Señor, s~ sen ˈjɔː ‖ seɪn ˈjɔːr —*Sp* [se ˈɲor]

Senora, Señora, s~ sen ˈjɔːr ə ‖ seɪn- -ˈjour- —*Sp* [se ˈɲo ra]

Senorita, Señorita, s~ ˌsen jɔː ˈriːt ə -jə- ‖ ˌseɪn jə ˈriːţ ə —*Sp* [se ɲo ˈri ta] **~s** z

sensate ˈsen^{t}s eɪt -ət, -ɪt

sensation sen ˈseɪʃ ^{ə}n s^{ə}n- **~s** z

sensational sen ˈseɪʃ ^{ə}n‿əl s^{ə}n- **~ly** i

sensationalis|e, sensationaliz|e sen ˈseɪʃ ^{ə}n‿ə laɪz s^{ə}n- **~ed** d **~es** ɪz əz **~ing** ɪŋ

sensational|ism sen ˈseɪʃ ^{ə}n‿əl |ˌɪz əm s^{ə}n- **~ist/s** ɪst/s §əst/s ‖ əst/s

sense sen^{t}s **sensed** sen^{t}st **senses** ˈsen^{t}s ɪz -əz **sensing** ˈsen^{t}s ɪŋ

ˈ**sense organ**

senseless ˈsen^{t}s ləs -lɪs **~ly** li **~ness** nəs nɪs

sensibilit|y ˌsen^{t}s ə ˈbɪl ət |i ˌ·ɪ-, -ɪt i ‖ -əţ |i **~ies** iz

sensib|le ˈsen^{t}s əb |^{ə}l -ɪb- **~leness** ^{ə}l nəs -nɪs **~ly** li

Sensimetrics *tdmk* ˌsen^{t}s ɪ ˈmetr ɪks -ə-

sensitis... —*see* **sensitiz...**

sensitive ˈsen^{t}s ət ɪv -ɪt- ‖ -əţ ɪv **~ly** li **~ness** nəs nɪs **~s** z

sensitivit|y ˌsen^{t}s ə ˈtɪv ət |i ˌ·ɪ-, -ɪt i ‖ -əţ |i **~ies** iz

sensitization ˌsen^{t}s ət aɪ ˈzeɪʃ ^{ə}n ˌ·ɪt-, ɪˈ-- ‖ -əţ ə- **~s** z

sensitiz|e ˈsen^{t}s ə taɪz -ɪ- **~ed** d **~es** ɪz əz **~ing** ɪŋ

Sensodyne *tdmk* ˈsen^{t}s əʊ daɪn ‖ -ə-

sensor ˈsen^{t}s ə ‖ -^{ə}r *(= censor)* **~s** z

sensorimotor ˌsen^{t}s ər‿i ˈməʊt ə ◂ ‖ -ˈmoʊţ ^{ə}r

sensory ˈsen^{t}s ər‿i

sensual ˈsen^{t}s ju‿əl ˈsen^{t}ʃ u‿əl ‖ ˈsen^{t}ʃ u‿əl ˈsen^{t}ʃ əl **~ism** ˌɪz əm **~ist/s** ɪst/s §əst/s ‖ əst/s **~ly** i

sensualit|y ˌsen^{t}s ju ˈæl ət |i ˌsen^{t}ʃ u-, -ɪt i ‖ ˌsen^{t}ʃ u ˈæl əţ |i **~ies** iz

sensuous ˈsen^{t}s ju‿əs ˈsen^{t}ʃ u‿əs ‖ ˈsen^{t}ʃ u‿əs **~ly** li **~ness** nəs nɪs

sent sent

Sentamu ˈsent ə muː

sentenc|e ˈsent ən^{t}s ‖ -^{ə}n^{t}s **~ed** t **~es** ɪz əz **~ing** ɪŋ

ˈ**sentence** ˌ**structure**

sentential sen ˈten^{t}ʃ ^{ə}l **~ly** i

sententious sen ˈten^{t}ʃ əs **~ly** li **~ness** nəs nɪs

sentience ˈsen^{t}ʃ ^{ə}n^{t}s ˈsen^{t}ʃ i‿ən^{t}s; ˈsent i‿ən^{t}s ‖ ˈsenţ i‿ən^{t}s

sentient ˈsen^{t}ʃ ^{ə}nt ˈsen^{t}ʃ i‿ənt; ˈsent i‿ənt ‖ ˈsenţ i‿ənt **~ly** li **~s** s

sentiment ˈsent ɪ mənt -ə- ‖ ˈsenţ ə- **~s** s

sentimental ˌsent ɪ ˈment ^{ə}l ◂ -ə- ‖ ˌsenţ ə ˈmenţ ^{ə}l ◂

sentimentalis... —*see* **sentimentaliz...**

sentimentalism ˌsent ɪ ˈment ə ˌlɪz əm ˌ·ə-, -^{ə}l ˌɪz- ‖ ˌsenţ ə ˈmenţ ^{ə}l ˌɪz əm

sentimentalist ˌsent ɪ ˈment ^{ə}l ɪst ˌ·ə- ‖ ˌsenţ ə ˈmenţ- **~s** s

sentimentality ˌsent ɪ men ˈtæl ət i ˌ·ə-, -mənˈ--, -ɪt i ‖ ˌsenţ ə men ˈtæl əţ i -mənˈ--

sentimentalization ˌsent ɪ ˌment əl aɪ ˈzeɪʃ ^{ə}n ˌ·ə- ‖ ˌsenţ ə ˌmenţ ^{ə}l ə-

sentimentaliz|e ˌsent ɪ ˈment ə laɪz ˌ·ə-, -^{ə}l aɪz ‖ ˌsenţ ə ˈmenţ ^{ə}l aɪz **~ed** d **~es** ɪz əz **~ing** ɪŋ

sentimentally ˌsent ɪ ˈment ^{ə}l i ˌ·ə- ‖ ˌsenţ ə ˈmenţ ^{ə}l i

sentinel ˈsent ɪn ^{ə}l -ən- ‖ ˈsent ^{ə}n‿əl **~s** z

sentr|y ˈsentr |i **~ies** iz

ˈ**sentry box**

sentry-go ˈsentr i gəʊ ‖ -goʊ

senza ˈsen*t*s ə -ɑː —*It* [ˈsent tsa]

Seonaid ʃə ˈneɪd —*ScG* [ˈʃo nidʒ]

Seoul səʊl→sɒʊl ‖ soʊl —*Korean* [ˈsə ul]

sepal ˈsep ^{ə}l ˈsiːp- **~s** z

-sepalous ˈsep əl əs — **polysepalous** ˌpɒl i ˈsep əl əs ◂ ‖ ˌpɑːl-

-sepaly ˈsep əl i — **polysepaly** ˌpɒl i ˈsep əl i ‖ ˌpɑːl-

separability ˌsep ər‿ə ˈbɪl ət i -ɪt i ‖ -əţ i

separab|le ˈsep ər‿əb |^{ə}l **~ly** li

separate *adj, n* ˈsep ^{ə}r‿ət ɪt **~ly** li **~ness** nəs nɪs **~s** s

sepa|rate *v* ˈsep ə |reɪt **~rated** reɪt ɪd -əd ‖ reɪţ əd **~rates** reɪts **~rating** reɪt ɪŋ ‖ reɪţ ɪŋ

separation ˌsep ə ˈreɪʃ ^{ə}n **~s** z

separatism, S~ ˈsep ^{ə}r‿ət ˌɪz əm ɪt ˌ-- ‖ əţ ˌ--

separatist, S~ ˈsep ^{ə}r‿ət ɪst ɪt ɪst, §-əst ‖ əţ əst **~s** s

separative ˈsep ^{ə}r‿ət ɪv ‖ əţ ɪv -ə reɪţ ɪv

separator ˈsep ə reɪt ə ‖ -reɪţ ^{ə}r **~s** z

Sephard|i sɪ ˈfɑːd |i sə-, se- ‖ -ˈfɑːrd |i **~ic** ɪk **~im** ɪm §əm ‖ əm

sepia ˈsiːp i‿ə **~s** z

sepiolite ˈsiːp i‿ə laɪt

sepoy ˈsiːp ɔɪ **~s** z

sepsis ˈseps ɪs §-əs

sept sept **septs** septs

September sep ˈtem bə sɪp-, səp- ‖ -b^{ə}r **~s** z

septennial sep ˈten i‿əl **~ly** i

septet, septette (ˌ)sep ˈtet **~s** s

septic ˈsept ɪk

ˌ**septic** ˈ**tank** ˈ· · ·

septicaemia, septicemia ˌsept ɪ ˈsiːm i‿ə §ˌ·ə-

Septimus ˈsept ɪm əs -əm-

septuagenarian ˌsept ju‿ə dʒə ˈneər i‿ən ◂ ˌsep tʃu‿, -dʒɪˈ-- ‖ ˌsep tʃu‿ə dʒə ˈner- ˌsept u‿, ˌsept ju‿ **~s** z

Septuagesima ˌsept ju‿ə ˈdʒes ɪm ə ˌsep tʃu‿, -əm ə ‖ ˌsep tʃu‿ ˌsept u‿ ˌsept ju‿

Septuagint ˈsept ju‿ə dʒɪnt ˈsep tʃu‿ ‖ -u‿ə- ˈsep tʃu‿, ˈsept ju‿

sept|um ˈsept |əm **~a** ə

sepulcher ˈsep ^{ə}lk ə ‖ -^{ə}r **~s** z

sepulchral sə ˈpʌlk rəl sɪ-, se- **~ly** i

sepulchre ˈsep ^{ə}lk ə ‖ -^{ə}r **~s** z

sepulture ˈsep ^{ə}ltʃ ə -^{ə}l tjʊə ‖ -^{ə}ltʃ ^{ə}r -^{ə}l tʃʊr

Sepulveda sə ˈpʌlv əd ə -ˈpʊlv- —*Also, inappropriately,* ˌsep ^{ə}l ˈveɪd ə

sequel 'siːk wəl **~s** z

sequel|a sɪ 'kwiːl |ə sə-, se-, -'kwel- **~ae** iː

sequenc|e 'siːk wənᵗs **~ed** t **~er/s** ə/z ‖ ᵊr/z **~es** ɪz əz **~ing** ɪŋ

sequent 'siːk wənt **~s** s

sequential sɪ 'kwentʃ ᵊl sə- **~ly** i

sequester sɪ 'kwest ə sə- ‖ -ᵊr **~ed** d **sequestering** sɪ 'kwest ər‿ɪŋ **~s** z

sequestrant 'siːk wəs trənt 'sek-, -wɪs-, -wes-; sɪ 'kwes-, sə- **~s** s

seque|strate 'siːk wə |streɪt 'sek-, -wɪ-, -we-; sɪ 'kwe|s treɪt, sə- **~strated** streɪt ɪd -əd ‖ streɪṭ əd **~strates** streɪts **~strating** streɪt ɪŋ ‖ streɪṭ ɪŋ

sequestration ˌsiːk wə 'streɪʃ ᵊn ˌsek-, -wɪ-, -we- **~s** z

seques|trum sɪ 'kwes trəm sə- **~tra** trə

sequin 'siːk wɪn §-wən **~ed, ~ned** d **~s** z

sequoia, S~, Sequoya, Sequoyah sɪ 'kwɔɪ ə sə-, se- **~s** z

sera 'sɪər ə ‖ 'sɪr ə

seraglio sə 'rɑːl i‿əʊ sɪ-, se- ‖ -'ræl joʊ -'rɑːl- **~s** z

serape sə 'rɑːp i sɪ-, se-, -'ræp-, -eɪ **~s** z

ser|aph 'ser |əf **~aphim** ə fɪm **~aphs** əfs

seraphic sə 'ræf ɪk sɪ-, se- **~ally** ᵊl‿i

seraphim 'ser ə fɪm

Seraphina ˌser ə 'fiːn ə

Serapis 'ser əp ɪs §-əs ‖ sə 'reɪp-

Serb sɜːb ‖ sɜ˞ːb **Serbs** sɜːbz ‖ sɜ˞ːbz

Serbi|a 'sɜːb i‿|ə ‖ 'sɜ˞ːb- **~an/s** ən/z

Serbo-Croat ˌsɜːb əʊ 'krəʊ æt ◂ ‖ ˌsɜ˞ːb oʊ 'kroʊ æt ◂

Serbo-Croatian ˌsɜːb əʊ krəʊ 'eɪʃ ᵊn ◂ ‖ ˌsɜ˞ːb oʊ kroʊ 'eɪʃ ᵊn ◂

sere sɪə ‖ sɪᵊr *(= sear)*

Serena sə 'riːn ə sɪ-, se-, -'reɪn-

serenad|e ˌser ə 'neɪd -ɪ-, '· · · **~ed** ɪd əd **~es** z **~ing** ɪŋ

serendipitous ˌser ən 'dɪp ət əs ˌ·en-, -ɪt əs ‖ -əṭ əs **~ly** li

serendipity ˌser ən 'dɪp ət i ˌ·en-, -ɪt i ‖ -əṭ i

serene sə 'riːn sɪ- **~ly** li **~ness** nəs nɪs

Serengeti ˌser ən 'get i →-əŋ-, -ɪn-, →-ɪŋ- ‖ -'geṭ i

serenit|y sə 'ren ət |i sɪ-, -ɪt- ‖ -əṭ |i **~ies** iz

serf sɜːf ‖ sɜ˞ːf *(= surf)* **serfs** sɜːfs ‖ sɜ˞ːfs

serf|dom 'sɜːf |dəm ‖ 'sɜ˞ːf- **~hood** hʊd

serge sɜːdʒ ‖ sɜ˞ːdʒ

Serge sɜːdʒ ‖ sɜ˞ːdʒ —*Fr* [sɛʁʒ]

sergeant 'sɑːdʒ ənt ‖ 'sɑːrdʒ ənt **~s** s ˌ**sergeant 'major**

sergeant|-at-arms ˌsɑːdʒ ənt| ət 'ɑːmz ‖ ˌsɑːrdʒ ənṭ| əṭ 'ɑːrmz **sergeants~** ˌ·ənts

Sergei 'seə geɪ 'sɜːg-, ˌ·'· ‖ ser 'geɪ —*Russ* [ˈsʲɪr gʲej]

Sergio 'sɜːdʒ i əʊ ‖ 'sɜ˞ːdʒ i oʊ —*It* ['sɛr dʒo]

serial 'sɪər i‿əl ‖ 'sɪr- **~s** z **'serial ˌnumber**; ˌ**serial mo'nogamy**; **'serial rights**

serialis... —*see* **serializ...**

serialization ˌsɪər i‿əl aɪ 'zeɪʃ ᵊn -ɪ'·- ‖ ˌsɪr i‿əl ə- **~s** z

serializ|e 'sɪər i‿ə laɪz ‖ 'sɪr- **~ed** d **~es** ɪz əz **~ing** ɪŋ

serially 'sɪər i‿əl i ‖ 'sɪr-

seriatim ˌsɪər i 'eɪt ɪm ˌser-, -'ɑːt-, §-əm ‖ ˌsɪr ɪ 'eɪṭ əm -'æṭ-

sericulture 'sɪər ɪ ˌkʌltʃ ə 'ser-, §-ə- ‖ 'ser ə ˌkʌltʃ ᵊr

seriema ˌser i 'iːm ə **~s** z

series *sing., pl* 'sɪər iːz -ɪz ‖ 'sɪr iːz —*Some BrE speakers pronounce the sing. with* -ɪz, *the pl with* -iːz

serif 'ser ɪf -əf **~s** s

serin 'ser ɪn §-ən **~s** z

Seringapatam sə ˌrɪŋ gə pə 'tɑːm sɪ-, -'tæm

seriocomic ˌsɪər i əʊ 'kɒm ɪk ◂ ‖ ˌsɪr i oʊ 'kɑːm ɪk ◂ **~ally** ᵊl‿i

serious 'sɪər i‿əs ‖ 'sɪr- **~ly** li **~ness** nəs nɪs

serjeant 'sɑːdʒ ənt ‖ 'sɑːrdʒ ənt **~s** s

serjeant|-at-arms ˌsɑːdʒ ənt| ət 'ɑːmz ‖ ˌsɑːrdʒ ənṭ| əṭ 'ɑːrmz **serjeants~** ˌ·ənts

Serle sɜːl ‖ sɜ˞ːl

sermon 'sɜːm ən ‖ 'sɜ˞ːm ən **~s** z

sermonette ˌsɜːm ə 'net ‖ ˌsɜ˞ːm- **~s** s

sermonis|e, sermoniz|e 'sɜːm ə naɪz ‖ 'sɜ˞ːm- **~ed** d **~er/s** ə/z ‖ ᵊr/z **~es** ɪz əz **~ing** ɪŋ

serocon|vert ˌsɪər əʊ kən |'vɜːt §-kɒn'· ‖ ˌsɪr oʊ kən |'vɜ˞ːt **~verted** 'vɜːt ɪd -əd ‖ 'vɜ˞ːṭ əd **~verting** 'vɜːt ɪŋ ‖ 'vɜ˞ːṭ ɪŋ **~verts** 'vɜːts ‖ 'vɜ˞ːts

serological ˌsɪər ə 'lɒdʒ ɪk ᵊl ◂ ‖ ˌsɪr ə 'lɑːdʒ- **~ly** ‿i

serology sɪ 'rɒl ədʒ i sɪə- ‖ -'rɑːl-

seronegative ˌsɪər əʊ 'neg ət ɪv ◂ ‖ ˌsɪr oʊ 'neg əṭ ɪv ◂

seropositive ˌsɪər əʊ 'pɒz ət ɪv ◂ -ɪt ɪv ‖ ˌsɪr oʊ 'pɑːz əṭ ɪv ◂

seropositivity ˌsɪər əʊ ˌpɒz ə 'tɪv ət i -ɪ'·-, -ɪt i ‖ ˌsɪr oʊ ˌpɑːz ə 'tɪv əṭ i

Serota sə 'rəʊt ə sɪ- ‖ -'roʊṭ ə

serotine 'ser əʊ taɪn ‖ -ə- -tɪn **~s** z

serotonin ˌsɪər əʊ 'təʊn ɪn ˌser-, §-ən ‖ ˌsɪr ə 'toʊn ən ˌser-

serous 'sɪər əs ‖ 'sɪr əs

serow 'ser əʊ ‖ -oʊ sə 'roʊ **~s** z

Seroxat *tdmk* sə 'rɒks æt sɪ- ‖ -'rɑːks-

Serpell 'sɜːp ᵊl ‖ 'sɜ˞ːp ᵊl

Serpens 'sɜːp enz -ənz ‖ 'sɜ˞ːp-

serpent 'sɜːp ənt →-mt ‖ 'sɜ˞ːp- **~s** s

serpentine, S~ 'sɜːp ən taɪn →-m- ‖ 'sɜ˞ːp ən tiːn -taɪn

SERPS sɜːps ‖ sɜ˞ːps

Serra 'ser ə —*Sp* ['se rra]

serrated sə 'reɪt ɪd sɪ-, se-, -əd ‖ -'reɪṭ əd

serration sə 'reɪʃ ᵊn sɪ-, se- **~s** z

serried 'ser id

ser|um 'sɪər |əm ‖ 'sɪr |əm **~a** ə **~ums** əmz

serval 'sɜːv ᵊl ‖ 'sɜ˞ːv ᵊl **~s** z

servant 'sɜːv ᵊnt ‖ 'sɜ˞ːv ᵊnt **~s** s

serve sɜːv ‖ sɜ˞ːv **served** sɜːvd ‖ sɜ˞ːvd **serves** sɜːvz ‖ sɜ˞ːvz **serving** 'sɜːv ɪŋ ‖ 'sɜ˞ːv ɪŋ

server 'sɜːv ə ‖ 'sɜ˞ːv ᵊr **~s** z

server|y 'sɜːv ər |i ‖ 'sɜ˞ːv- **~ies** iz

S

servic|e, S~ 'sɜːv ɪs §-əs ‖ 'sɜ˞ːv əs **~ed** t **~es** ɪz əz **~ing** ɪŋ
'service charge; **'service flat**; **'service road**; **'service ˌstation**
serviceability ˌsɜːv ɪs ə 'bɪl ət i §ˌ·əs-, -ɪt i ‖ ˌsɜ˞ːv əs ə 'bɪl əţ i
serviceab|le 'sɜːv ɪs əb |əl §'·əs- ‖ 'sɜ˞ːv əs- **~leness** əl nəs -nɪs **~ly** li
serviceberr|y 'sɜːv ɪs ˌber |i -əs- ‖ 'sɜ˞ːv əs- **~ies** iz
service|man 'sɜːv ɪs |mən §-əs- ‖ 'sɜ˞ːv əs- -mæn **~men** mən men **~woman** ˌwʊm ən **~women** ˌwɪm ɪn §-ən
serviette ˌsɜːv i 'et ‖ ˌsɜ˞ːv- **~s** s
servile 'sɜːv aɪəl ‖ 'sɜ˞ːv əl -aɪəl **~ly** li **~ness** nəs nɪs
servility sɜː 'vɪl ət i -ɪt- ‖ sɜ˞ː 'vɪl əţ i
serving 'sɜːv ɪŋ ‖ 'sɜ˞ːv ɪŋ **~s** z
'serving spoon
Servis *tdmk* 'sɜːv ɪs §-əs ‖ 'sɜ˞ːv-
Servite 'sɜːv aɪt ‖ 'sɜ˞ːv- **~s** s
servitor 'sɜːv ɪt ə -ət- ‖ 'sɜ˞ːv əţ ər **~s** z
servitude 'sɜːv ɪ tjuːd -ə-, →-tʃuːd ‖ 'sɜ˞ːv ə tuːd -tjuːd
servo 'sɜːv əʊ ‖ 'sɜ˞ːv oʊ **~s** z
servomechanism 'sɜːv əʊ ˌmek ə nɪz əm ‖ 'sɜ˞ːv oʊ- **~s** z
servomotor 'sɜːv əʊ ˌməʊt ə ‖ 'sɜ˞ːv oʊ ˌmoʊţ ər **~s** z
sesame 'ses əm i
'sesame seeds
Sesotho sɪ 'suːt uː sə-, se-
sesqui- ¦sesk wi — **sesquioxide** ˌsesk wi 'ɒks aɪd ‖ -'ɑːks-
sesquicentennial ˌsesk wi sen 'ten i‿əl **~s** z
sesquipedalian ˌsesk wi pɪ 'deɪl i‿ən ◂ ˌ·wə-, -pə'--, -pe'-- **~s** z
sessile 'ses aɪəl -əl, -ɪl
session 'seʃ ən **~s** z
sessional 'seʃ ən‿əl **~ly** i **~s** z
Sessions 'seʃ ənz
sest|erce 'sest |ɜːs ‖ -|ɜ˞ːs **~erces** ɜːs ɪz əs-, -əz; ə siːz ‖ ɜ˞ːs əz
sesterti|um se 'stɜːt i‿|əm -'stɜːʃ- ‖ -'stɜ˞ːʃ- -stɜ˞ːʃ |əm **~a** ə
sestet ₍ˌ₎ses 'tet **~s** s
set set **sets** sets **setting** 'set ɪŋ ‖ 'seţ ɪŋ
ˌset 'book; **ˌset 'piece**; **ˌset 'point**; **'set ˌtheory**
seta 'siːt ə ‖ 'siːţ ə **setae** 'siːt iː -eɪ, -aɪ
setaceous sɪ 'teɪʃ əs sə-, siː-
Setanta se 'tænt ə si-, sə-
setaside 'set ə ˌsaɪd ‖ 'seţ-
setback 'set bæk **~s** s
set-down 'set daʊn
se-tenant sə 'ten ənt sɪ-, siː- ‖ ˌset ən 'ɑːn —*Fr* [sə tə nɑ̃]
Seth seθ —*but as an Indian name,* seɪt
Seton, s~ 'siːt ən
setscrew 'set skruː **~s** z
setsquare 'set skweə ‖ -skwer -skwær **~s** z
sett set **setts** sets
settee se 'tiː sə- **~s** z
setter, S~ 'set ə ‖ 'seţ ər **~s** z
setting 'set ɪŋ ‖ 'seţ ɪŋ **~s** z
settl|e 'set əl ‖ 'seţ əl **~ed** d **~es** z **~ing** ‿ɪŋ
settlement 'set əl mənt **~s** s
settler 'set əl‿ə ‖ 'seţ əl‿ər **~s** z
set-to 'set tuː ˌ·'· **~s** z
set-top 'set tɒp ‖ -tɑːp
Setubal, Setúbal sə 'tuːb əl se-, -æl —*Port* [sə 'tu βɛl]
set-up, setup 'set ʌp ‖ 'seţ ʌp **~s** s
Seumas 'ʃuːm əs —*ScG* ['ʃu məs]
Seurat 'sɜːr ɑː ‖ sʊ 'rɑː —*Fr* [sœ ʁa]
Seuss sjuːs suːs ‖ suːs
Sevastopol sə 'væst ə pɒl sɪ-, -pəl ‖ -poʊl —*Russ* Sevastopol [sʲɪ vʌ 'sto pəlʲ]
seven 'sev ən —*In casual speech also* →'seb m *(not before a vowel sound)* **~s** z
sevenfold 'sev ən fəʊld →'seb m-, →fɒʊld ‖ -foʊld
sevenish 'sev ən ɪʃ
Sevenoaks 'sev ən əʊks ‖ -oʊks
seventeen ˌsev ən 'tiːn ◂ —*In casual speech also* →ˌseb m- **~s** z **~th/s** θ/s
seventh 'sev əntθ —*Casually also* →'seb mᵖθ **~s** s
ˌseventh 'heaven
Seventh-Day ˌsev əntθ 'deɪ ◂
seventh-inning ˌsev ntθ 'ɪn ɪŋ ◂
seventieth 'sev ənt i‿əθ ɪθ ‖ 'sev ənţ- —*Casually also* →'seb mᵖt i‿əθ **~s** s
sevent|y 'sev ənt |i ‖ -ənţ |i —*Casually also* →'seb mᵖt |i **~ies** iz
seventy-eight ˌsev ənt i 'eɪt ◂ ‖ ˌsev ənţ- —*Casually also* →ˌseb mᵖt- **~s** s
Seven-Up, 7-Up *tdmk* ˌsev ən 'ʌp **~s** s
seven-year ˌsev ən 'jɪə ◂ -'jɜː ‖ -'jɪər ◂ —*Casually also* →ˌseb m-
ˌseven-year 'itch
sever 'sev ə ‖ -ər **~ed** d **severing** 'sev ər‿ɪŋ **~s** z
several 'sev rəl 'sev ər‿əl **~ly** i
severanc|e 'sev ər‿ənts **~es** ɪz əz
'severance pay
severe sɪ 'vɪə sə- ‖ -'vɪər **severer** sɪ 'vɪər ə sə- ‖ -'vɪr ər **severest** sɪ 'vɪər ɪst sə-, -əst ‖ -'vɪr əst **~ly** li **~ness** nəs nɪs
severed 'sev əd ‖ -ərd
severit|y sɪ 'ver ət |i sə-, -ɪt i ‖ -əţ |i **~ies** iz
Severn 'sev ən ‖ -ərn
Severus sɪ 'vɪər əs sə- ‖ -'vɪr əs
seviche sɪ 'viːtʃ eɪ sə-, seɪ-, -i —*AmSp* [se 'vi tʃe]
Seville sə 'vɪl sɪ-, se- —*Sp* Sevilla [se 'βi ʎa, -ja] —*but usually* 'sev əl, -ɪl *in the expression*
ˌSeville 'orange
Sevres, Sèvres 'seɪv rə 'sev- ‖ 'sev rə —*Fr* [sɛːvʁ]
sew səʊ ‖ soʊ *(= so)* **sewed** səʊd ‖ soʊd **sewing** 'səʊ ɪŋ ‖ 'soʊ ɪŋ **sews** səʊz ‖ soʊz
'sewing maˌchine
sewage 'suː‿ɪdʒ 'sjuː‿
'sewage farm

S

Seward *(i)* 'siː wəd ‖ -wᵊrd, *(ii)* 'sjuː‿əd 'suː‿ ‖ 'suː‿ᵊrd
Sewell 'sjuː‿əl 'suː‿; 'sjuːl, 'suːl ‖ 'suː‿əl
sewer *'drain'; 'servant'* 'suː‿ə 'sjuː‿ ‖ ᵊr **~s** z
sewer *'one that sews'* 'səʊ ə ‖ 'soʊ ᵊr **~s** z
sewerage 'suː‿ər ɪdʒ 'sjuː‿
sewn səʊn ‖ soʊn
sex seks **sexed** sekst *(= sext)* **sexes** 'seks ɪz -əz **sexing** 'seks ɪŋ
'sex ap,peal; **'sex ,hormone**; **'sex ,object**; **'sex ,organ**
sexagenarian ˌseks ə dʒə 'neər i‿ən ◂ -dʒɪ'--, -dʒe'-- ‖ -'ner- **~s** z
Sexagesima ˌseks ə 'dʒes ɪm ə -əm ə
-sexed 'sekst — **highly-sexed** ˌhaɪ li 'sekst ◂
sexi... *—see* **sexy**
sexism 'seks ˌɪz əm
sexist 'seks ɪst §-əst **~s** s
sexless 'seks ləs -lɪs **~ly** li **~ness** nəs nɪs
sex-linked ˌseks 'lɪŋkt ◂ '· ·
sexological ˌseks ə 'lɒdʒ ɪk ᵊl ◂ ‖ -'lɑːdʒ-
sexologist sek 'sɒl ədʒ ɪst §-əst ‖ -'sɑːl- **~s** s
sexology sek 'sɒl ədʒ i ‖ -'sɑːl-
sexploitation ˌseks plɔɪ 'teɪʃ ᵊn
sexpot 'seks pɒt ‖ -pɑːt **~s** s
sex-starved 'seks stɑːvd ˌ·'· ‖ -stɑːrvd
sext, Sext sekst
Sextans 'sekst ənz
sextant 'sekst ənt **~s** s
sextet ₍ˌ₎seks 'tet **~s** s
sextile 'sekst aɪᵊl
sextodecimo ˌsekst əʊ 'des ɪ məʊ -ə· ‖ -oʊ 'des ə moʊ
sexton, S~ 'sekst ən **~s** z
sextupl|e 'sekst jʊp ᵊl -jəp-; sek 'stjuːp- ‖ sek 'stuːp ᵊl -'stʊp-, -'stʌp-; 'sekst əp- **~ed** d **~es** z **~ing** ‿ɪŋ
sextuplet 'seks tjʊp lət seks 'tjuːp-, §-'tʌp-, -lɪt, -let ‖ sek 'stʌp- -'stuːp-, -'stjuːp-; 'sekst əp- **~s** s
sexual 'sek ʃu‿əl 'seks ju‿əl, 'sek ʃᵊl **~ly** i
,sexual 'intercourse
sexualit|y ˌsek ʃu 'æl ət |i ˌseks ju-, -ɪt i ‖ -əţ |i **~ies** iz
sexualization, sexualisation ˌsek ʃu‿əl aɪ 'zeɪʃ ᵊn ˌseks ju‿, -ɪ'· · ‖ -ə'· ·
sexualiz|e, sexualis|e 'sek ʃu‿ə laɪz 'seks ju‿ **~ed** d **~es** ɪz əz **~ing** ɪŋ
Sexwale se 'kwɑːl eɪ *—Venda* [se 'xwaː le]
sex|y 'seks |i **~ier** i‿ə ‖ i‿ᵊr **~iest** i‿ɪst i‿əst **~ily** ɪ li əl i **~iness** i nəs i nɪs
Seychelles ₍ˌ₎seɪ 'ʃelz -'ʃel, '· ·
Seychellois ˌseɪ ʃel 'wɑː ◂
Seyfert 'saɪf ət 'siːf- ‖ -ᵊrt
Seymour *(i)* 'siː mɔː ‖ -mɔːr -moʊr, *(ii)* 'siːm ə ‖ -ᵊr, *(iii)* 'seɪm ə ‖ -ᵊr
sez *non-standard spelling of* says sez
SF ˌes 'ef
sforzand|o ₍ˌ₎sfɔːt 'sænd |əʊ ‖ ₍ˌ₎sfɔːrt 'sɑːnd |oʊ -'sænd- **~i** iː
sgian-dhu ˌskiː‿ən 'duː ˌskiːn'·
SGML ˌes dʒiː em 'el
sgraffit|o skræ 'fiːt| əʊ ‖ -oʊ *—It* [zgraf 'fiː to] **~i** iː i
Sgurr skʊə ‖ skʊᵊr *—ScG* [skur]
sh, shh, ssh ʃ
Shaanxi ˌʃɑːn 'ʃiː *—Chi* Shǎnxī [³ʂan ¹ɕi]
Shabbat ʃə 'bæt -'bɑːt ‖ -'bɑːt 'ʃɑːb əs
shabb|y 'ʃæb |i **~ier** i‿ə ‖ i‿ᵊr **~iest** i‿ɪst i‿əst **~ily** ɪ li əl i **~iness** i nəs i nɪs
shack ʃæk **shacked** ʃækt **shacking** 'ʃæk ɪŋ **shacks** ʃæks
shackl|e 'ʃæk ᵊl **~ed** d **~es** z **~ing** ɪŋ
Shackleton 'ʃæk ᵊl tən **~s, ~'s** z
shad ʃæd **shads** ʃædz
Shadbolt 'ʃæd bəʊlt →'ʃæb-, →-bɒʊlt ‖ -boʊlt
shadbush 'ʃæd bʊʃ **~es** ɪz əz
shaddock, S~ 'ʃæd ək **~s** s
shade ʃeɪd **shaded** 'ʃeɪd ɪd -əd **shades** ʃeɪdz **shading/s** 'ʃeɪd ɪŋ/z
shadoof ʃə 'duːf ʃæ- **~s** s
shadow 'ʃæd əʊ ‖ -oʊ **~ed** d **~ing** ɪŋ **~s** z
,shadow 'cabinet; **'shadow play**
shadowbox 'ʃæd əʊ bɒks ‖ -oʊ bɑːks **~ed** t **~es** ɪz əz **~ing** ɪŋ
shadow|y 'ʃæd əʊ |i ‖ -oʊ |i **~ier** i‿ə ‖ i‿ᵊr **~iest** i‿ɪst i‿əst **~iness** i nəs i nɪs
Shadrach 'ʃædr æk 'ʃeɪdr-, -ɑːx
Shadwell 'ʃæd wel -wəl
shad|y 'ʃeɪd |i **~ier** i‿ə ‖ i‿ᵊr **~iest** i‿ɪst i‿əst **~ily** ɪ li əl i **~iness** i nəs i nɪs
SHAEF ʃeɪf
Shaeffer 'ʃeɪf ə ‖ -ᵊr
Shafaye ʃə 'feɪ
Shaffer 'ʃæf ə ‖ -ᵊr
shaft ʃɑːft §ʃæft ‖ ʃæft **shafted** 'ʃɑːft ɪd §'ʃæft-, -əd ‖ 'ʃæft əd **shafting/s** 'ʃɑːft ɪŋ/z §'ʃæft- ‖ 'ʃæft ɪŋ/z **shafts** ʃɑːfts §ʃæfts ‖ ʃæfts
Shaftesbury 'ʃɑːfts bər‿i §'ʃæfts- ‖ 'ʃæfts ˌber i
Shafto, Shaftoe 'ʃɑːft əʊ §'ʃæft- ‖ 'ʃæft oʊ
shag ʃæg **shagged** ʃægd **shagging** 'ʃæg ɪŋ **shags** ʃægz
,shagged 'out
shagbark 'ʃæg bɑːk ‖ -bɑːrk **~s** s
shagger 'ʃæg ə ‖ -ᵊr **~s** z
shagg|y 'ʃæg |i **~ier** i‿ə ‖ i‿ᵊr **~iest** i‿ɪst i‿əst **~ily** ɪ li əl i **~iness** i nəs i nɪs
shaggy-dog ˌʃæg i 'dɒg ‖ -'dɔːg -'dɑːg
,shaggy-'dog ,story
shagreen ʃə 'griːn ʃæ-
shah, Shah ʃɑː **shahs** ʃɑːz
shaheed, shahid ʃə 'hiːd ʃæ- *—Arabic* [ʃa 'hiːd]
Shairp *(i)* ʃɑːp ‖ ʃɑːrp, *(ii)* ʃeəp ‖ ʃeᵊrp
Shaka 'ʃɑːk ə 'ʃɑːg-
shake ʃeɪk **shaken** 'ʃeɪk ən **shakes** ʃeɪks **shaking/s** 'ʃeɪk ɪŋ/z **shook** ʃʊk §ʃuːk
shakedown 'ʃeɪk daʊn **~s** z
shaken 'ʃeɪk ən
shake-out, shakeout 'ʃeɪk aʊt **~s** s
shaker, S~ 'ʃeɪk ə ‖ -ᵊr **~s** z
Shakerley 'ʃæk ə li ‖ -ᵊr-
Shakeshaft 'ʃeɪk ʃɑːft §-ʃæft ‖ -ʃæft
Shakespear, Shakespeare 'ʃeɪk spɪə ‖ -spɪr
Shakespearean ₍ˌ₎ʃeɪk 'spɪər i‿ən ‖ -'spɪr- **~s** z

Shakespeareana ₍ˌ₎ʃeɪk ˌspɪər i 'ɑːn ə ‖ -ˌspɪr i 'æn ə -'ɑːn-, -'eɪn-
Shakespearian ₍ˌ₎ʃeɪk 'spɪər iˌən ‖ -'spɪr- **~s** z
Shakespeariana ₍ˌ₎ʃeɪk ˌspɪər i 'ɑːn ə ‖ -ˌspɪr i 'æn ə -'ɑːn-, -'eɪn-
shake-up 'ʃeɪk ʌp **~s** s
shako 'ʃæk əʊ 'ʃeɪk-, 'ʃɑːk- ‖ -oʊ **~s** z
shak|y 'ʃeɪk |i **~ier** iˌə ‖ iˌ^{ə}r **~iest** iˌɪst iˌəst **~ily** ɪ li əl i **~iness** i nəs i nɪs
Shalden, Shaldon 'ʃɔːld ən 'ʃɒld- ‖ 'ʃɑːld-
shale ʃer^{ə}l **shales** ʃer^{ə}lz
Shalford 'ʃæl fəd ‖ -f^{ə}rd
shall *strong form* ʃæl, *weak form* ʃ^{ə}l *—There are also weak forms* ʃə, ʃ, *used only before a following word beginning with a consonant.*
shallop 'ʃæl əp **~s** s
shallot ʃə 'lɒt ‖ -'lɑːt 'ʃæl ət **~s** s
shallow 'ʃæl əʊ ‖ -oʊ **~ed** d **~er** ə ‖ ^{ə}r **~est** ɪst əst **~ing** ɪŋ **~ly** li **~ness** nəs nɪs **~s** z
shalom ʃæ 'lɒm ʃə-, -'ləʊm ‖ ʃɑː 'loʊm ʃə-
shaˌlom a'leichem ə 'leɪx əm
shalt *strong form* ʃælt, *weak form* ʃ^{ə}lt
shalwar ʃʌl 'wɑː ‖ -'wɑːr **~s** z
shalˌwar ka'meez
sham ʃæm **shammed** ʃæmd **shamming** 'ʃæm ɪŋ **shams** ʃæmz
shaman 'ʃæm ən 'ʃeɪm-, 'ʃɑːm- ‖ 'ʃɑːm ən 'ʃeɪm-, 'ʃæm- **~ism** ˌɪz əm **~s** z
shamanistic ˌʃæm ə 'nɪst ɪk ◂ ˌʃɑːm-, ˌʃeɪm- ‖ ˌʃɑːm- ˌʃeɪm-, ˌʃæm-
shamateur 'ʃæm ət ə -ə tʃʊə, -tʃə, -tjʊə; ˌʃæm ə 'tɜː ◂ ‖ 'ʃæm ə tʃʊr -əṭ ^{ə}r, -ə tjʊr **~s** z
shamateurism 'ʃæm ət ər ˌɪz əm -ətʃ ər-, -ə tɜːr-, -ə tʃʊər-, -ə tjʊər- ‖ 'ʃæm ə tʃʊr- -əṭ ^{ə}r-, -ə tjʊr-
shambl|e 'ʃæm b^{ə}l **~ed** d **~es** z **~ing** ˌɪŋ
shambolic ʃæm 'bɒl ɪk ‖ -'bɑːl ɪk **~ally** ^{ə}l ˌi
shame ʃeɪm **shamed** ʃeɪmd **shames** ʃeɪmz **shaming** 'ʃeɪm ɪŋ
shamefaced ˌʃeɪm 'feɪst ◂
shamefaced|ly ˌʃeɪm 'feɪst |li -'feɪs ɪd |li, -əd- **~ness** nəs nɪs
shameful 'ʃeɪm f^{ə}l -fʊl **~ly** ˌi **~ness** nəs nɪs
shameless 'ʃeɪm ləs -lɪs **~ly** li **~ness** nəs nɪs
shaming 'ʃeɪm ɪŋ **~ly** li
shamisen 'ʃæm ɪ sen ‖ 'ʃɑːm- *—Jp* [ɕa ˌmi seɴ] **~s** z
shamm... *—see* **sham**
shamm|y 'ʃæm |i **~ies** iz
shampoo ₍ˌ₎ʃæm 'puː **~ed** d **~ing** ɪŋ **~s** z
shamrock 'ʃæm rɒk ‖ -rɑːk **~s** s
shamus 'ʃɑːm əs 'ʃeɪm- **~es** ɪz əz
Shan ʃɑːn *—for the people and language, also* ʃæn **Shans** ʃɑːnz ʃænz
Shandong ˌʃæn 'dɒŋ ‖ ˌʃɑːn 'dɔːŋ *—Chi* Shāndōng [^{1}ʂan ^{1}tʊŋ]
shand|y 'ʃænd |i **~ies** iz
shandygaff 'ʃænd i gæf **~s** s
Shane ʃeɪn
Shang *dynasty* ʃæŋ ‖ ʃɑːŋ *—Chi* Shāng [^{1}ʂaŋ]
Shangaan ʃæŋ 'gɑːn **~s** z
Shanghai, s~ ˌʃæŋ 'haɪ ' · *—Chi* Shànghǎi [^{4}ʂaŋ ^{3}xai] **~ed** d **~ing** ɪŋ **~s** z
Shango 'ʃæŋ gəʊ ‖ -goʊ
Shangri-La ˌʃæŋ gri 'lɑː
Shanita ʃə 'niːt ə ‖ -'niːṭ ə
shank ʃæŋk **shanks** ʃæŋks
ˌshank's'mare
Shankill 'ʃæŋk ɪl -^{ə}l
Shanklin 'ʃæŋk lɪn §-lən
Shankly 'ʃæŋk li
Shanks ʃæŋks
shanks's 'ʃæŋks ɪz -əz
ˌshanks's 'pony
Shannon 'ʃæn ən
shan't ʃɑːnt ‖ ʃænt
Shantou ˌʃæn 'təʊ ‖ ˌʃɑːn 'toʊ *—Chi* Shàntóu [^{4}ʂan ^{2}tʰou]
shantung, S~ ʃæn 'tʌŋ *—Chi* Shāndōng [^{1}ʂan ^{1}tʊŋ]
shant|y 'ʃænt |i ‖ 'ʃænṭ |i **~ies** iz
shanty-town 'ʃænt i taʊn ‖ 'ʃænṭ- **~s** z
Shanxi ˌʃæn 'ʃiː *—Chi* Shānxī [^{1}ʂan ^{1}ɕi]
Shap ʃæp
shape ʃeɪp **shaped** ʃeɪpt **shapes** ʃeɪps **shaping** 'ʃeɪp ɪŋ
SHAPE ʃeɪp
-shaped ʃeɪpt — **pear-shaped** 'peə ʃeɪpt ‖ 'per-
shapeless 'ʃeɪp ləs **~ly** li **~ness** nəs nɪs
shape|ly 'ʃeɪp |li **~lier** li ə ‖ li ^{ə}r **~liest** li ɪst əst **~liness** li nəs -nɪs
Shapiro ʃə 'pɪər əʊ ‖ -'pɪr oʊ
shard ʃɑːd ‖ ʃɑːrd **shards** ʃɑːdz ‖ ʃɑːrdz
share ʃeə ‖ ʃe^{ə}r ʃæ^{ə}r **shared** ʃeəd ‖ ʃe^{ə}rd ʃæ^{ə}rd **shares** ʃeəz ‖ ʃe^{ə}rz ʃæ^{ə}rz **sharing** 'ʃeər ɪŋ ‖ 'ʃer ɪŋ 'ʃær-
'share cerˌtificate
sharecropper 'ʃeə krɒp ə ‖ 'ʃer krɑːp ^{ə}r 'ʃær- **~s** z
shareholder 'ʃeə ˌhəʊld ə →ˌhɒʊld- ‖ 'ʃer ˌhoʊld ^{ə}r 'ʃær- **~s** z
shareholding 'ʃeə ˌhəʊld ɪŋ →ˌhɒʊld- ‖ 'ʃer ˌhoʊld ɪŋ **~s** z
share-out 'ʃeər aʊt ‖ 'ʃer aʊt 'ʃær- **~s** s
shareware 'ʃeə weə ‖ 'ʃer wer 'ʃær wær
sharia, shari'ah ʃə 'riːˌə ʃɑː- *—Ar* [ʃa 'riː ʕa]
Sharif, s~ ʃə 'riːf ʃɑː-, ʃæ-
Sharjah 'ʃɑːdʒ ɑː 'ʃɑːʒ-, -ə ‖ 'ʃɑːrdʒ-
shark ʃɑːk ‖ ʃɑːrk **sharks** ʃɑːks ‖ ʃɑːrks
sharkskin 'ʃɑːk skɪn ‖ 'ʃɑːrk-
Sharman 'ʃɑːm ən ‖ 'ʃɑːrm-
Sharm el-Sheikh ˌʃɑːm el 'ʃeɪk -^{ə}l- ‖ ˌʃɑːrm- *—Arabic* [ˌʃarm aʃ 'ʃeix]
Sharon *personal name* 'ʃær ən ‖ 'ʃer-
Sharon *Israeli politician* ʃə 'rɒn -'rəʊn ‖ -'roʊn
Sharon *place name; (rose of ~)* 'ʃeər ən 'ʃɑːr-, 'ʃær-, -ɒn ‖ 'ʃær ən 'ʃer-
'Sharon fruit
sharp ʃɑːp ‖ ʃɑːrp **sharped** ʃɑːpt ‖ ʃɑːrpt **sharper** 'ʃɑːp ə ‖ 'ʃɑːrp ^{ə}r **sharpest** 'ʃɑːp ɪst -əst ‖ 'ʃɑːrp əst **sharping** 'ʃɑːp ɪŋ ‖ 'ʃɑːrp ɪŋ **sharps** ʃɑːps ‖ ʃɑːrps
'sharp end; **ˌsharp 'practice**
Sharp, Sharpe ʃɑːp ‖ ʃɑːrp
sharp-eared ˌʃɑːp 'ɪəd ◂ ‖ ˌʃɑːrp 'ɪ^{ə}rd ◂

shar pei ˌʃɑː ˈpeɪ ‖ ˌʃɑːr- **~s** z —*Chi* shā pí [^{1}ʂa ^{2}pʰi]
sharpen ˈʃɑːp ən ‖ ˈʃɑːrp ən **~ed** d **~ing** ˌɪŋ **~s** z
sharpener ˈʃɑːp nə ˈʃɑːp ən‿ə ‖ ˈʃɑːrp ᵊn‿ər
sharper ˈʃɑːp ə ‖ ˈʃɑːrp ᵊr **~s** z
Sharpeville ˈʃɑːp vɪl ‖ ˈʃɑːrp-
sharp-eyed ˌʃɑːp ˈaɪd ◂ ‖ ˌʃɑːrp-
sharpie ˈʃɑːp i ‖ ˈʃɑːrp i **~s** z
sharpish ˈʃɑːp ɪʃ ‖ ˈʃɑːrp ɪʃ **~ly** li
Sharples ˈʃɑːp ᵊlz ‖ ˈʃɑːrp ᵊlz
sharp|ly ˈʃɑːp |li ‖ ˈʃɑːrp |li **~ness** nəs nɪs
Sharpness ˌʃɑːp ˈnes ‖ ˌʃɑːrp-
sharp-set ˌʃɑːp ˈset ◂ ‖ ˌʃɑːrp-
sharpshooter ˈʃɑːp ˌʃuːt ə ‖ ˈʃɑːrp ˌʃuːṭ ᵊr **~s** z
sharp-sighted ˌʃɑːp ˈsaɪt ɪd ◂ -əd ‖ ˌʃɑːrp ˈsaɪṭ əd ◂
sharp-tongued ˌʃɑːp ˈtʌŋd ◂ ‖ ˌʃɑːrp-
sharp-witted ˌʃɑːp ˈwɪt ɪd ◂ -əd ‖ ˌʃɑːrp ˈwɪṭ əd ◂
Sharwood ˈʃɑː wʊd ‖ ˈʃɑːr-
shashlik ˈʃæʃ lɪk ˈʃɑːʃ- ‖ ˈʃɑːʃ- ˌ'ˌ **~s** s
Shasta ˈʃæst ə
 ˌShasta ˈdaisy
shat ʃæt
Shatner ˈʃæt nə ‖ -nᵊr
shatter ˈʃæt ə ‖ ˈʃæṭ ᵊr **~ed** d **shattering/ly** ˈʃæt‿ər ɪŋ /li ‖ ˈʃæṭ ər ɪŋ /li **~s** z
shatterproof ˈʃæt ə pruːf §-prʊf ‖ ˈʃæṭ ᵊr-
Shaughnessy ˈʃɔːn əs i ‖ ˈʃɑːn-
Shaun ʃɔːn ‖ ʃɑːn
shave ʃeɪv **shaved** ʃeɪvd **shaves** ʃeɪvz
 shaving ˈʃeɪv ɪŋ
 ˈshaving cream; **ˈshaving foam**
shaveling ˈʃeɪv lɪŋ **~s** z
shaven ˈʃeɪv ᵊn
shaver ˈʃeɪv ə ‖ -ᵊr **~s** z
Shavian ˈʃeɪv i‿ən **~s** z
shaving ˈʃeɪv ɪŋ **~s** z
Shaw, shaw ʃɔː ‖ ʃɑː
Shawcross ˈʃɔː krɒs -krɔːs ‖ -krɔːs ˈʃɑː krɑːs
shawl ʃɔːl ‖ ʃɑːl **shawls** ʃɔːlz ‖ ʃɑːlz
shawm ʃɔːm ‖ ʃɑːm **shawms** ʃɔːmz ‖ ʃɑːmz
Shawn ʃɔːn ‖ ʃɑːn
Shawnee ˌʃɔː ˈniː ‖ ₍ˌ₎ʃɑː- **~s** z
shay ʃeɪ **shays** ʃeɪz
Shayler ˈʃeɪl ə ‖ -ᵊr
s/he ˌʃiː ɔː ˈhiː ‖ ᵊr-
she *strong form* ʃiː, *weak form* ʃi
she- ˈʃiː — **she-cat** ˈʃiː kæt
shea *tree* ʃiː ˈʃiː‿ə
 ˈshea nut
Shea *name* ʃeɪ
sheaf ʃiːf **sheaves** ʃiːvz
Sheaffer ˈʃeɪf ə ‖ -ᵊr
shear ʃɪə ‖ ʃɪᵊr *(= sheer)* **sheared** ʃɪəd ‖ ʃɪᵊrd
 shearing ˈʃɪər ɪŋ ‖ ˈʃɪr ɪŋ **shears** ʃɪəz ‖ ʃɪᵊrz
 shorn ʃɔːn ‖ ʃɔːrn ʃoʊrn
Sheard *(i)* ʃeəd ‖ ʃeᵊrd, *(ii)* ʃɪəd ‖ ʃɪᵊrd, *(iii)* ʃɜːd ‖ ʃɜːd
shearer, S~ ˈʃɪər ə ‖ ˈʃɪr ᵊr **~s** z
shearling ˈʃɪə lɪŋ ‖ ˈʃɪr- **~s** z
Shearman ˈʃɪə mən ‖ ˈʃɪr-
shears ʃɪəz ‖ ʃɪᵊrz
shearwater ˈʃɪə ˌwɔːt ə ‖ ˈʃɪr ˌwɔːṭ ᵊr -ˌwɑːṭ- **~s** z
sheath *n* ʃiːθ **sheaths** ʃiːðz ʃiːθs
 ˈsheath knife
sheathe *v* ʃiːð **sheathed** ʃiːðd **sheathes** ʃiːðz
 sheathing ˈʃiːð ɪŋ
sheave ʃiːv **sheaved** ʃiːvd **sheaves** ʃiːvz
 sheaving ˈʃiːv ɪŋ
Sheba ˈʃiːb ə
shebang ʃɪ ˈbæŋ ʃə-
she-bear ˈʃiː beə ‖ -ber **~s** z
shebeen ʃɪ ˈbiːn ʃə- **~s** z
Sheboygan ʃɪ ˈbɔɪg ən ʃə-
shed ʃed **shedding** ˈʃed ɪŋ **sheds** ʃedz
she'd *strong form* ʃiːd, *occasional weak form* ʃid
she-devil ˈʃiː ˌdev ᵊl -ɪl **~s** z
shedload ˈʃed ləʊd ‖ -loʊd **~s** z
Sheehan ˈʃiː hən
Sheelagh ˈʃiːl ə
sheen, Sheen ʃiːn
Sheena, Sheenagh, Sheenah ˈʃiːn ə
Sheene ʃiːn
sheep ʃiːp **sheep's** ʃiːps
 ˈsheep's eyes; **ˈsheep tick**
sheepdip ˈʃiːp dɪp **~s** s
sheepdog ˈʃiːp dɒg ‖ -dɔːg -dɑːg **~s** z
sheepfold ˈʃiːp fəʊld →-fɒʊld ‖ -foʊld **~s** z
sheepish ˈʃiːp ɪʃ **~ly** li **~ness** nəs nɪs
sheepmeat ˈʃiːp miːt
sheep-pen ˈʃiːp pen **~s** z
sheepsbit ˈʃiːps bɪt **~s** s
sheepshank ˈʃiːp ʃæŋk **~s** s
sheepskin ˈʃiːp skɪn **~s** z
sheer ʃɪə ‖ ʃɪᵊr **sheered** ʃɪəd ‖ ʃɪᵊrd **sheerer** ˈʃɪər ə ‖ ˈʃɪr ᵊr **sheerest** ˈʃɪər ɪst -əst ‖ ˈʃɪr əst
 sheering ˈʃɪər ɪŋ ‖ ˈʃɪr ɪŋ **sheers** ʃɪəz ‖ ʃɪᵊrz
Sheerness ˌʃɪə ˈnes ◂ ‖ ˌʃɪr-
sheesh ʃiːʃ
sheesha ˈʃiːʃ ə —*Arabic* [ˈʃiː ʃah]
sheet ʃiːt **sheeting** ˈʃiːt ɪŋ ‖ ˈʃiːṭ ɪŋ **sheets** ʃiːts
 ˈsheet ˌanchor; **ˈsheet ˌfeeder**; **ˈ. ˌ. ˌsheet ˈlightning**, **ˈ. ˌ.** ; **ˌsheet ˈmusic**, **ˈ. ˌ.**
Sheetrock *tdmk* ˈʃiːt rɒk ‖ -rɑːk
Sheffer ˈʃef ə ‖ -ᵊr
Sheffield ˈʃef iːᵊld
 ˌSheffield ˈplate
Shefford ˈʃef əd ‖ -ᵊrd
Sheherazade ʃə ˌher ə ˈzɑːd ə ʃɪ-, -ˌhɪər-, -ə ˈzɑːd ‖ -ˌhɪr-
sheikh, sheik, S~ ʃeɪk ʃiːk **sheikhs, sheiks** ʃeɪks ʃiːks
sheikhdom, sheikdom ˈʃeɪk dəm ˈʃiːk- **~s** z
Sheila, s~ ˈʃiːl ə **~s, ~'s** z
shekel ˈʃek ᵊl **~s** z
Shelagh ˈʃiːl ə
Shelburne ˈʃel bən -bɜːn ‖ -bɜːn
Shelby ˈʃel bi
Sheldon ˈʃeld ən
Sheldonian ʃel ˈdəʊn i‿ən ‖ -ˈdoʊn-
sheldrake, S~ ˈʃel dreɪk **~s** s
shelduck ˈʃel dʌk **~s** s

shelf ʃelf **shelves** ʃelvz
'shelf life
Shelford 'ʃel fəd ‖ -fᵊrd
shell, Shell ʃel **shelled** ʃeld **shelling** 'ʃel ɪŋ **shells, Shell's** ʃelz
she'll *strong form* ʃiːᵊl, *occasional weak form* ʃil
shellac ʃə 'læk ʃe-; 'ʃel æk **~ked** t **~king** ɪŋ **~s** s
shellback 'ʃel bæk **~s** s
Shelley 'ʃel i
shellfire 'ʃel ˌfaɪ‿ə ‖ -ˌfaɪ‿ᵊr
shellfish 'ʃel fɪʃ **~es** ɪz əz
shell-like 'ʃel laɪk
Shell-Mex *tdmk* ˌʃel 'meks
shellshock 'ʃel ʃɒk ‖ -ʃɑːk **~ed** t
Shelta 'ʃelt ə
shelter 'ʃelt ə ‖ -ᵊr **~ed** d **sheltering** 'ʃelt‿ər ɪŋ **~s** z
shelt|ie, shelt|y 'ʃelt |i **~ies** iz
Shelton 'ʃelt ən
shelve ʃelv **shelved** ʃelvd **shelves** ʃelvz **shelving** 'ʃelv ɪŋ
Shem ʃem
shemozzle ʃɪ 'mɒz ᵊl ʃə- ‖ -'mɑːz-
Shena 'ʃiːn ə
Shenandoah ˌʃen ən 'dəʊ ə ◂ ‖ -'doʊ ə ◂
ˌShenanˌdoah 'Valley
shenanigan ʃɪ 'næn ɪg ən ʃə-, §-əg- **~s** z
Shenfield 'ʃen fiːᵊld
Shenyang ˌʃen 'jæŋ ˌʃʌn- ‖ -'jɑːŋ *—Chi* Shěnyáng [³ʂən ²jɑŋ]
Shenzhen ˌʃen 'dʒen ˌʃʌn 'dʒʌn *—Chi* Shēnzhèn [¹ʂən ⁴ʈʂən]
Sheol, She'ol 'ʃiː ɒl -əʊl ‖ -oʊl -'·
Shepard 'ʃep əd ‖ -ᵊrd
shepherd, S~ 'ʃep əd ‖ -ᵊrd **~ed** ɪd əd **~ing** ɪŋ **~s** z
ˌshepherd's 'pie
shepherdess ˌʃep ə 'des '· · ·, -dɪs ‖ 'ʃep ᵊrd əs **~es** ɪz əz
shepherd's-purse ˌʃep ədz 'pɜːs ‖ -ᵊrdz 'pɜːs
Sheppard 'ʃep əd ‖ -ᵊrd
ˌSheppard's cor'rection
Sheppey 'ʃep i
Shepreth 'ʃep rəθ
Shepshed 'ʃep ʃed
Shepton 'ʃept ən
ˌShepton 'Mallet
Sher *(i)* ʃɜː ‖ ʃɜː, *(ii)* ʃeə ‖ ʃeᵊr
Sheraton 'ʃer ət ən ‖ -ᵊn **~s** z
sherbert, sherbet 'ʃɜːb ət ‖ 'ʃɜːb- -ᵊrt **~s** s
Sherborne, Sherbourne 'ʃɜː bən -bɔːn ‖ 'ʃɜː bɔːrn
Sherbrooke 'ʃɜː brʊk ‖ 'ʃɜː-
sherd ʃɜːd ‖ ʃɜːd **sherds** ʃɜːdz ‖ ʃɜːdz
Shere ʃɪə ‖ ʃɪᵊr
Sheree, Sheri 'ʃer i
sheria ʃə 'riː‿ə
Sheridan 'ʃer ɪd ən -əd- ‖ -ᵊn
sheriff 'ʃer ɪf -əf **~s** s
Sheringham 'ʃer ɪŋ əm
Sherlaw 'ʃɜː lɔː ‖ 'ʃɜː- -lɑː
Sherley 'ʃɜːl i ‖ 'ʃɜːl i
Sherlock 'ʃɜː lɒk ‖ 'ʃɜː lɑːk
ˌSherlock 'Holmes
Sherlockian ʃɜː 'lɒk i‿ən ‖ ʃɜː 'lɑːk- **~s** z
Sherman 'ʃɜː mən ‖ 'ʃɜː mən
Sherpa, s~ 'ʃɜːp ə ‖ 'ʃɜːp ə **~s** z
Sherratt 'ʃer ət
Sherree, Sherri 'ʃer i
Sherrin 'ʃer ɪn §-ən
Sherrington 'ʃer ɪŋ tən
sherr|y, S~ 'ʃer |i **~ies** iz
Sherwin ʃɜː wɪn -wən ‖ 'ʃɜː-
Sherwood 'ʃɜː wʊd ‖ 'ʃɜː-
ˌSherwood 'Forest
Sheryl 'ʃer ɪl -əl
she's *strong form* ʃiːz, *occasional weak form* ʃiz
Shetland 'ʃet lənd **~s** z
ˌShetland 'pony
Shetlander 'ʃet lənd ə ‖ -ᵊr **~s** z
Shettleston 'ʃet ᵊls tən ‖ 'ʃeṭ-
Shevardnadze ˌʃev əd 'nɑːd zeɪ -zi ‖ -ᵊrd-
Shevington 'ʃev ɪŋ tən
Shevon, Shevonne ʃə 'vɒn ʃɪ- ‖ -'vɑːn
Shew ʃuː
shew... *—see* **show...**
shewbread 'ʃəʊ bred ‖ 'ʃoʊ-
Shewell 'ʃuː‿əl ʃuːl
she-|wolf 'ʃiː wʊlf **~wolves** wʊlvz
shh *interjection* ʃ
Shia, Shi'a, Shi'a, Shiah 'ʃiː ə
shiatsu ʃi 'æts uː -'ɑːts- ‖ -'ɑːts- *—Jp* [ɕi ˌa tsɯ]
shibboleth 'ʃɪb ə leθ -əl əθ, -əl ɪθ **~s** s
shicker 'ʃɪk ə ‖ -ᵊr **~ed** d
shie... *—see* **shy**
shield, Shield ʃiːᵊld **shielded** 'ʃiːᵊld ɪd -əd **shielding** 'ʃiːᵊld ɪŋ **shields** 'ʃiːᵊldz
Shields ʃiːldz
shieling 'ʃiːl ɪŋ **~s** z
shift ʃɪft **shifted** 'ʃɪft ɪd -əd **shifting** 'ʃɪft ɪŋ **shifts** ʃɪfts
'shift key; **'shift stick**; **'shift ˌworker**; **'shift ˌworking**
shifter 'ʃɪft ə ‖ -ᵊr **~s** z
shiftless 'ʃɪft ləs -lɪs **~ly** li **~ness** nəs nɪs
shiftwork 'ʃɪft wɜːk ‖ -wɜːk **~er/s** ə/z ‖ ᵊr/z
shift|y 'ʃɪft |i **~ier** i‿ə ‖ i‿ᵊr **~iest** i‿ɪst i‿əst **~ily** ɪ li əl i **~iness** i nəs i nɪs
shigell|a ʃɪ 'gel |ə **~ae** iː **~as** əz
shigellosis ˌʃɪg ə 'ləʊs ɪs -e-, §-əs ‖ -'loʊs əs
shih-tzu, shih tzu, shi tzu, S~ ˌʃiːt 'zuː ˌʃɪt-, -'suː *—Chi* shīzi [¹ʂɨ˧dzɯ] **~s** z
Shiism 'ʃiː ˌɪz əm
shiitake ʃɪ 'tɑːk eɪ ˌʃiː‿ɪ'· ·, -i *—Jp* ['ɕii ta ke]
Shiite, Shi'ite, Shi'ite 'ʃiː aɪt **~s** s
Shijiazhuang ˌʃiː dʒiː‿ə dʒu 'æŋ ‖ -'ɑːŋ *—Chi* Shíjiāzhuāng [²ʂɨ˧ ¹tɕja ¹ʈʂwɑŋ]
shikaree, shikari ʃɪ 'kɑːr i ʃə-, -'kær- **~s** z
Shikoku 'ʃiːk əʊ kuː ‖ -oʊ- *—Jp* [ɕi̥ 'ko kɯ]
shiksa, shikse 'ʃɪks ə **~s** z
shill ʃɪl **shilled** ʃɪld **shilling** 'ʃɪl ɪŋ **shills** ʃɪlz
shillelagh ʃɪ 'leɪl ə ʃə-, -i **~s** z
Shillibeer 'ʃɪl ɪ bɪə -ə- ‖ -bɪr
shilling, S~ 'ʃɪl ɪŋ **~s** z

S

Shillong ʃɪ ˈlɒŋ ‖ -ˈlɔːŋ -ˈlɑːŋ
Shilluk ʃɪ ˈlʊk ‖ -ˈluːk **~s** s
shilly-shall|y ˈʃɪl i ˌʃæl |i **~ied** id **~ies** iz **~ying** i‿ɪŋ
Shiloh ˈʃaɪl əʊ ‖ -oʊ
Shilton ˈʃɪlt ən
shim ʃɪm **shimmed** ʃɪmd **shimming** ˈʃɪm ɪŋ **shims** ʃɪmz
shimmer ˈʃɪm ə ‖ -ᵊr **~ed** d **shimmering** ˈʃɪm ər‿ɪŋ **~s** z
shimm|y ˈʃɪm |i **~ied** id **~ies** iz **~ying** i‿ɪŋ
shin ʃɪn **shinned** ʃɪnd **shinning** ˈʃɪn ɪŋ **shins** ʃɪnz
shinbone ˈʃɪn bəʊn →ˈʃɪm- ‖ -boʊn **~s** z
shindig ˈʃɪn dɪg **~s** z
shind|y ˈʃɪnd |i **~ies** iz
shine ʃaɪn **shined** ʃaɪnd **shines** ʃaɪnz **shining** ˈʃaɪn ɪŋ **shone** ʃɒn ‖ ʃoʊn *(*)*
shiner ˈʃaɪn ə ‖ -ᵊr **~s** z
shingl|e ˈʃɪŋ gᵊl **~ed** d **~es** z **~ing** ‿ɪŋ
shingly ˈʃɪŋ gli
shining ˈʃaɪn ɪŋ **~ly** li
shinn|y ˈʃɪn |i **~ied** id **~ies** iz **~ying** i‿ɪŋ
Shinto ˈʃɪnt əʊ ‖ -oʊ —*Jp* [ˈɕin to] **~ism** ˌɪz əm **~ist/s** ɪst/s §əst/s ‖ əst/s
shinty ˈʃɪnt i ‖ ˈʃɪnţ i
Shinwell ˈʃɪn wel -wəl
shin|y ˈʃaɪn |i **~ier** i‿ə ‖ i‿ᵊr **~iest** i‿ɪst i‿əst **~ily** ɪ li əl i **~iness** i nəs i nɪs
-ship ʃɪp — **workmanship** ˈwɜːk mən ʃɪp ‖ ˈwɜ˞ːk-
ship ʃɪp **shipped** ʃɪpt **shipping** ˈʃɪp ɪŋ **ships** ʃɪps
ˈship ˌbiscuit; **ˈship caˌnal**; **ˌship's ˈchandler**
shipboard ˈʃɪp bɔːd ‖ -bɔːrd -boʊrd
shipbroker ˈʃɪp ˌbrəʊk ə ‖ -ˌbroʊk ᵊr **~s** z
shipbuild|er ˈʃɪp ˌbɪld |ə ‖ -|ᵊr **~ers** əz ᵊrz **~ing** ɪŋ
Shiplake ˈʃɪp leɪk
Shipley ˈʃɪp li
shipload ˈʃɪp ləʊd ‖ -loʊd **~s** z
Shipman ˈʃɪp mən
shipmate ˈʃɪp meɪt **~s** s
shipment ˈʃɪp mənt **~s** s
shipowner ˈʃɪp ˌəʊn ə ‖ -ˌoʊn ᵊr **~s** z
Shippam ˈʃɪp əm
shipper ˈʃɪp ə ‖ -ᵊr **~s** z
shipping ˈʃɪp ɪŋ
ˈshipping ˌforecast; **ˈshipping lane**
shipshape ˈʃɪp ʃeɪp
Shipston ˈʃɪpst ən
Shipton ˈʃɪpt ən
ship-to-shore ˌʃɪp tə ˈʃɔː -tu- ‖ -ˈʃɔːr -ˈʃoʊr
shipway ˈʃɪp weɪ **~s** z
shipworm ˈʃɪp wɜːm ‖ -wɜ˞ːm **~s** z
shipwreck ˈʃɪp rek **~ed** t **~ing** ɪŋ **~s** s
shipwright ˈʃɪp raɪt **~s** s
shipyard ˈʃɪp jɑːd ‖ -jɑːrd **~s** z
Shiraz, s~ ʃɪ ˈræz ʃɪə-, ˈrɑːz ‖ -ˈrɑːz
-shire ʃə ʃɪə ‖ ʃᵊr ʃɪr— **Lincolnshire** ˈlɪŋk ən ʃə -ʃɪə ‖ -ʃᵊr -ʃɪr
shire ˈʃaɪ‿ə ‖ ˈʃaɪ‿ᵊr **shires** ˈʃaɪ‿əz ‖ ˈʃaɪ‿ᵊrz
ˈshire ˌcounties; **ˈshire horse**
Shire, Shiré *river and region in Malawi* ˈʃɪər eɪ -ə ‖ ˈʃɪr-
shirk ʃɜːk ‖ ʃɜ˞ːk **shirked** ʃɜːkt ‖ ʃɜ˞ːkt **shirking** ˈʃɜːk ɪŋ ‖ ˈʃɜ˞ːk ɪŋ **shirks** ʃɜːks ‖ ʃɜ˞ːks
shirker ˈʃɜːk ə ‖ ˈʃɜ˞ːk ᵊr **~s** z
Shirley ˈʃɜːl i ‖ ˈʃɜ˞ːl i
shirr ʃɜː ‖ ʃɜ˞ː **shirred** ʃɜːd ‖ ʃɜ˞ːd **shirring** ˈʃɜːr ɪŋ ‖ ˈʃɜ˞ː ɪŋ **shirrs** ʃɜːz ‖ ʃɜ˞ːz
shirt, Shirt ʃɜːt ‖ ʃɜ˞ːt **shirts** ʃɜːts ‖ ʃɜ˞ːts
shirtdress ˈʃɜːt dres ‖ ˈʃɜ˞ːt- **~es** ɪz əz
shirtfront ˈʃɜːt frʌnt ‖ ˈʃɜ˞ːt- **~s** s
shirting ˈʃɜːt ɪŋ ‖ ˈʃɜ˞ːţ ɪŋ **~s** z
shirtsleeve ˈʃɜːt sliːv ‖ ˈʃɜ˞ːt- **~d** d **~s** z
shirttail ˈʃɜːt teɪᵊl ‖ ˈʃɜ˞ːt- **~s** z
shirtwaist ˈʃɜːt weɪst ˌ·ˈ· ‖ ˈʃɜ˞ːt- **~er/s** ə/z ‖ ᵊr/z **~s** s
shirt|y ˈʃɜːt |i ‖ ˈʃɜ˞ːţ |i **~ier** i‿ə ‖ i‿ᵊr **~iest** i‿ɪst i‿əst **~iness** i nəs i nɪs
shish kebab ˌʃɪʃ kə ˈbæb ˌʃiːʃ-, -kɪ-, ˈ· · · ‖ ˈʃɪʃ kə bɑːb **~s** z
shit ʃɪt **shat** ʃæt **shits** ʃɪts **shitted** ˈʃɪt ɪd -əd ‖ ˈʃɪţ əd **shitting** ˈʃɪt ɪŋ ‖ ˈʃɪţ ɪŋ
shitake, shitaki ʃɪ ˈtɑːk i ˌʃiː‿ɪˈ· ·, -eɪ —*Jp* [ˈɕii ta ke]
shitbag ˈʃɪt bæg **~s** z
shite ʃaɪt
shitfaced ˈʃɪt feɪst
shithead ˈʃɪt hed **~s** z
shithole ˈʃɪt həʊl →-hɒʊl ‖ -hoʊl **~s** z
shit-hot ˌʃɪt ˈhɒt ◂ ‖ -ˈhɑːt ◂
shithouse ˈʃɪt haʊs
shitless ˈʃɪt ləs -lɪs
shit-scared ˌʃɪt ˈskeəd ◂ ‖ -ˈskeᵊrd ◂
Shittim, s~ ˈʃɪt ɪm §-əm ‖ ˈʃɪţ əm
shitt|y ˈʃɪt |i ‖ ˈʃɪţ |i **~ier** i‿ə ‖ i‿ᵊr **~iest** i‿ɪst i‿əst **~ily** ɪ li əl i **~iness** i nəs i nɪs
shitzu ˌʃiːt ˈzuː ˌʃɪt-, -ˈsuː —*Chi* shīzi [1ʂɨ˩dzɯ] **~s** z
shiv ʃɪv **shivs** ʃɪvz
Shiva ˈʃiːv ə ˈʃɪv- —*Hindi* [ʃɪʋ]
shivaree ˌʃɪv ə ˈriː ˈ· · · **~s** z
shiver ˈʃɪv ə ‖ -ᵊr **~ed** d **shivering/ly** ˈʃɪv ər‿ɪŋ /li **~s** z
shivery ˈʃɪv ər‿i
shl... *—see* **schl...**
Shloer *tdmk* ʃlɜː ‖ ʃlɜ˞ː
shmuck ʃmʌk **shmucks** ʃmʌks
shmutter, schmatte ˈʃmʌt ə ‖ ˈʃmɑːţ ə
Shoah ˈʃəʊ ɑː ‖ ˈʃoʊ-
shoal ʃəʊl →ʃɒʊl ‖ ʃoʊl **shoaled** ʃəʊld →ʃɒʊld ‖ ʃoʊld **shoaling** ˈʃəʊl ɪŋ →ˈʃɒʊl- ‖ ˈʃoʊl ɪŋ **shoals** ʃəʊlz →ʃɒʊlz ‖ ʃoʊlz
shoat ʃəʊt ‖ ʃoʊt **shoats** ʃəʊts ‖ ʃoʊts
shock ʃɒk ‖ ʃɑːk **shocked** ʃɒkt ‖ ʃɑːkt **shocking/ly** ˈʃɒk ɪŋ /li ‖ ˈʃɑːk ɪŋ /li **shocks** ʃɒks ‖ ʃɑːks
ˈshock abˌsorber; **ˌshocking ˈpink◂**; **ˈshock ˌtreatment**; **ˈshock troops**; **ˈshock wave**
shocker ˈʃɒk ə ‖ ˈʃɑːk ᵊr **~s** z
Shockey ˈʃɒk i ‖ ˈʃɑːk i

S

shockheaded ˌʃɒk ˈhed ɪd ◂ -əd ‖ ʃɑːk-
shockproof ˈʃɒk pruːf §-prʊf ‖ ˈʃɑːk-
shod ʃɒd ‖ ʃɑːd
shodd|y ˈʃɒd |i ‖ ˈʃɑːd |i **~ier** i‿ə ‖ i‿ər **~ies** iz **~iest** i‿ɪst i‿əst **~ily** ɪ li əl i **~iness** i nəs i nɪs
shoe ʃuː *(= shoo)* **shod** ʃɒd ‖ ʃɑːd **shoed** ʃuːd **shoeing** ˈʃuː ɪŋ **shoes** ʃuːz
shoebill ˈʃuː bɪl **~s** z
shoeblack ˈʃuː blæk **~s** s
shoebox ˈʃuː bɒks ‖ -bɑːks **~es** ɪz əz
Shoeburyness ˌʃuː bər‿i ˈnes
shoehorn ˈʃuː hɔːn ‖ -hɔːrn **~ed** d **~ing** ɪŋ **~s** z
shoelace ˈʃuː leɪs **~es** ɪz əz
shoeless ˈʃuː ləs -lɪs
shoemaker, S~ ˈʃuː ˌmeɪk ə ‖ -ər **~s** z
shoeshine ˈʃuː ʃaɪn
shoestring ˈʃuː strɪŋ **~s** z
shoetree ˈʃuː triː **~s** z
shogun ˈʃəʊ gʌn -guːn, -gən ‖ ˈʃoʊ- —*Jp* [ɕoˌo ŋɯɴ, -gɯɴ] **~s** z
shogunate ˈʃəʊ gə neɪt -guː-, -gʌ-; -gən ət, -ɪt ‖ ˈʃoʊ- **~s** z
Sholokhov ˈʃɒl ə kɒf ‖ ˈʃɔːl ə kɔːf ˈʃɑːl ə kɑːf —*Russian* [ˈʃo lə xəf]
Sholto ˈʃɒlt əʊ ‖ ˈʃɑːlt oʊ
Shona *Zimbabwean language and people* ˈʃɒn ə ˈʃəʊn- ‖ ˈʃoʊn ə **~s** z
Shona *personal name* ˈʃəʊn ə ‖ ˈʃoʊn ə
shone ʃɒn ‖ ʃoʊn *(*)*
shonk|y ˈʃɒŋk| i ‖ ˈʃɑːŋk| i **~ier** i‿ə ‖ i‿ər **~iest** i‿ɪst ‿əst
shoo ʃuː **shooed** ʃuːd **shooing** ˈʃuː ɪŋ **shoos** ʃuːz
shoofly ˈʃuː flaɪ
ˌ**shoofly ˈpie** ‖ ˈ· · ·
shoo-in ˈʃuː ɪn **~s** z
shook ʃʊk §ʃuːk
shoot ʃuːt **shooting/s** ˈʃuːt ɪŋ/z ‖ ˈʃuːţ ɪŋ/z **shoots** ʃuːts **shot** ʃɒt ‖ ʃɑːt
ˈ**shooting box**; ˈ**shooting brake**; ˈ**shooting ˌgallery**; ˈ**shooting match**; ˌ**shooting ˈstar**; ˈ**shooting stick**
shoot-'em-up ˈʃuːt əm ʌp ‖ ˈʃuːţ- **~s** s
-shooter ʃuːt ə ‖ ʃuːţ ər — **duck-shooter** ˈdʌk ˌʃuːt ə ‖ -ˌʃuːţ ər
shooter, S~ ˈʃuːt ə ‖ ˈʃuːţ ər **~s** z
shoot-out ˈʃuːt aʊt ‖ ˈʃuːţ- **~s** s
shop ʃɒp ‖ ʃɑːp **shopped** ʃɒpt ‖ ʃɑːpt **shopping** ˈʃɒp ɪŋ ‖ ˈʃɑːp ɪŋ **shops** ʃɒps ‖ ʃɑːps
ˈ**shop asˌsistant**; ˌ**shop ˈfloor**, ˈ· ·; ˈ**shopping ˌbasket**; ˈ**shopping ˌcentre**; ˈ**shopping mall**; ˌ**shop ˈsteward** ‖ ˈ· ˌ· ·; ˌ**shop ˈwindow**
shopaholic ˌʃɒp ə ˈhɒl ɪk ‖ ˌʃɑːp ə ˈhɔːl ɪk -ˈhɑːl- **~s** s
shop-bought ˈʃɒp bɔːt ‖ ˈʃɑːp- -bɑːt
shopfitt|er ˈʃɒp ˌfɪt| ə ‖ ˈʃɑːp ˌfɪţ| ər **~ers** əz ‖ -ərz **~ing** ɪŋ
shopfront ˈʃɒp frʌnt ‖ ˈʃɑːp- **~s** s
shophar ˈʃəʊf ɑː ‖ ˈʃoʊf ɑːr -ər **~s** z
shopkeeper ˈʃɒp ˌkiːp ə ‖ ˈʃɑːp ˌkiːp ər **~s** z
shoplift ˈʃɒp lɪft ‖ ˈʃɑːp- **~ed** ɪd əd **~er/s** ə/z ‖ ər/z **~ing** ɪŋ **~s** s
shopp... —*see* **shop**
shoppe ʃɒp ‖ ʃɑːp —*jocularly also* ˈʃɒp i ‖ ˈʃɑːp i
shopper ˈʃɒp ə ‖ ˈʃɑːp ər **~s** z
shopsoiled ˈʃɒp sɔɪəld ‖ ˈʃɑːp-
shopwalker ˈʃɒp ˌwɔːk ə ‖ ˈʃɑːp ˌwɔːk ər -ˌwɑːk- **~s** z
shopworn ˈʃɒp wɔːn ‖ ˈʃɑːp wɔːrn -woʊrn
shore, Shore ʃɔː ‖ ʃɔːr ʃoʊr **shored** ʃɔːd ‖ ʃɔːrd ʃoʊrd **shores** ʃɔːz ‖ ʃɔːrz ʃoʊrz **shoring** ˈʃɔːr ɪŋ ‖ ˈʃoʊr-
ˈ**shore leave**
Shoreditch ˈʃɔː dɪtʃ ‖ ˈʃɔːr- ˈʃoʊr-
Shoreham ˈʃɔːr əm ‖ ˈʃoʊr-
shoreline ˈʃɔː laɪn ‖ ˈʃɔːr- ˈʃoʊr- **~s** z
shorn ʃɔːn ‖ ʃɔːrn ʃoʊrn
short, Short ʃɔːt ‖ ʃɔːrt **shorted** ˈʃɔːt ɪd -əd ‖ ˈʃɔːrţ əd **shorter** ˈʃɔːt ə ‖ ˈʃɔːrţ ər **shortest** ˈʃɔːt ɪst -əst ‖ ˈʃɔːrţ əst **shorting** ˈʃɔːt ɪŋ ‖ ˈʃɔːrţ ɪŋ **shorts** ʃɔːts ‖ ʃɔːrts
ˌ**short ˌback and ˈsides**; ˌ**short ˈcircuit**; ˈ**short cut**, ˌ· ˈ· — *Preference poll, BrE:* ˈ· · *59%,* ˌ· ˈ· *41%*; ˈ**short list**; ˌ**short ˈshrift**; ˌ**short ˈstory**; ˌ**short ˈterm**; ˌ**short ˈtime**; ˌ**short ˈwave**
shortag|e ˈʃɔːt ɪdʒ ‖ ˈʃɔːrţ- **~es** ɪz əz
shortbread ˈʃɔːt bred ‖ ˈʃɔːrt- **~s** z
shortcake ˈʃɔːt keɪk ‖ ˈʃɔːrt- **~s** s
short-chang|e ˌʃɔːt ˈtʃeɪndʒ ‖ ˌʃɔːrt- **~ed** d **~es** ɪz əz **~ing** ɪŋ
short-circu|it ˌʃɔːt ˈsɜːk |ɪt §-ət ‖ ˌʃɔːrt ˈsɜːk |ət **~ited** ɪt ɪd §ət-, -əd ‖ əţ əd **~iting** ɪt ɪŋ §ət- ‖ əţ ɪŋ **~its** ɪts §əts ‖ əts
shortcoming ˈʃɔːt ˌkʌm ɪŋ ˌ·ˈ· ‖ ˈʃɔːrt- **~s** z
shortcrust ˈʃɔːt krʌst ‖ ˈʃɔːrt-

SHORT CUT

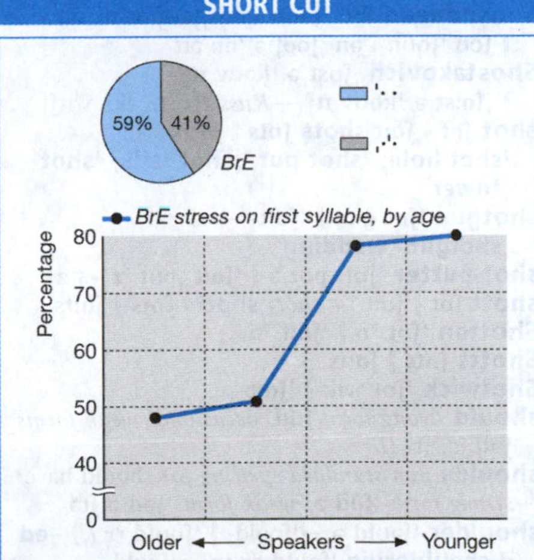

shortcut ˈʃɔːt kʌt ˌ·ˈ· ‖ ˈʃɔːrt- **~s** s
short-dated ˌʃɔːt ˈdeɪt ɪd ◂ -əd ‖ ˌʃɔːrt ˈdeɪţ əd ◂
short-day ˈʃɔːt deɪ ‖ ˈʃɔːrt-
short-eared ˌʃɔːt ˈɪəd ◂ ‖ ˈʃɔːrţ ɪrd

S

shorten 'ʃɔːt ən ‖ 'ʃɔːrt ən **~ed** d **~ing** ɪŋ **~s** z
Shorter 'ʃɔːt ə ‖ 'ʃɔːrṭ ər
shortfall 'ʃɔːt fɔːl ‖ 'ʃɔːrt- -fɑːl **~s** z
shorthand 'ʃɔːt hænd ‖ 'ʃɔːrt-
 ˌshorthand 'typist
shorthanded ˌʃɔːt 'hænd ɪd ◂ -əd ‖ ˌʃɔːrt-
short-haul 'ʃɔːt hɔːl ˌ·'· ‖ 'ʃɔːrt- -hɑːl
shorthold 'ʃɔːt həʊld →-hɒʊld ‖ 'ʃɔːrt hoʊld **~s** z
shorthorn, S~ 'ʃɔːt hɔːn ‖ 'ʃɔːrt hɔːrn **~s** z
shortie 'ʃɔːt i ‖ 'ʃɔːrṭ i **~s** z
shortish 'ʃɔːt ɪʃ ‖ 'ʃɔːrṭ ɪʃ
Shortland 'ʃɔːt lənd ‖ 'ʃɔːrt-
short-list 'ʃɔːt lɪst ‖ 'ʃɔːrt- **~ed** ɪd əd **~ing** ɪŋ **~s** s
short-lived ˌʃɔːt 'lɪvd ◂ ‖ ˌʃɔːrt 'laɪvd ◂ -'lɪvd
short|ly 'ʃɔːt |li ‖ 'ʃɔːrt |li **~ness** nəs nɪs
Shorto 'ʃɔːt əʊ ‖ 'ʃɔːrṭ oʊ
short-order 'ʃɔːt ˌɔːd ə ˌ·'· · ‖ 'ʃɔːrṭ ˌɔːrd ər
short-range ˌʃɔːt 'reɪndʒ ◂ ‖ ˌʃɔːrt-
short-|sheet 'ʃɔːt |ʃiːt ‖ 'ʃɔːrt- **~sheeted** ʃiːt ɪd -əd ‖ ʃiːṭ əd **~sheeting** ʃiːt ɪŋ ‖ ʃiːṭ ɪŋ **~sheets** ʃiːts
shortsighted ˌʃɔːt 'saɪt ɪd ◂ -əd ‖ ˌʃɔːrt 'saɪṭ əd ◂ **~ly** li **~ness** nəs nɪs
short-sleeved ˌʃɔːt 'sliːvd ◂ ‖ ˌʃɔːrt-
short-staffed ˌʃɔːt 'stɑːft ◂ §-'stæft ‖ ˌʃɔːrt 'stæft ◂
short-stay ˌʃɔːt 'steɪ ◂ ‖ ˌʃɔːrt-
shortstop 'ʃɔːt stɒp ‖ 'ʃɔːrt stɑːp **~s** s
short-tempered ˌʃɔːt 'temp əd ◂ ‖ ˌʃɔːrt 'temp ərd ◂
short-term ˌʃɔːt 'tɜːm ◂ ‖ ˌʃɔːrt 'tɜːm ◂ **~ism** ˌɪz əm
shortwave ˌʃɔːt 'weɪv ◂ '·· ‖ ˌʃɔːrt-
short-winded ˌʃɔːt 'wɪnd ɪd ◂ -əd ‖ ˌʃɔːrt-
short|y 'ʃɔːt |i ‖ 'ʃɔːrṭ |i **~ies** iz
Shoshone ʃəʊ 'ʃəʊn i ‖ ʃoʊ 'ʃoʊn i ʃə- **~s** z
Shoshonean ʃəʊ 'ʃəʊn i‿ən ˌʃəʊʃ ə 'niː‿ən ‖ ʃoʊ 'ʃoʊn i‿ən ˌʃoʊʃ ə 'niː ən
Shostakovich ˌʃɒst ə 'kəʊv ɪtʃ ‖ ˌʃɑːst ə 'koʊv ɪtʃ —*Russ* [ʃɨ stʌ 'kɔ vʲɪtʃ]
shot ʃɒt ‖ ʃɑːt **shots** ʃɒts ‖ ʃɑːts
 'shot hole; **'shot put**; **ˌshot 'silk**; **'shot ˌtower**
shotgun 'ʃɒt gʌn ‖ 'ʃɑːt- **~s** z
 ˌshotgun 'wedding
shot-putter 'ʃɒt ˌpʊt ə ‖ 'ʃɑːt ˌpʊṭ ər **~s** z
shott ʃɒt ‖ ʃɑːt *(= shot)* **shotts** ʃɒts ‖ ʃɑːts
Shotton 'ʃɒt ən ‖ 'ʃɑːt ən
Shotts ʃɒts ‖ ʃɑːts
Shotwick 'ʃɒt wɪk ‖ 'ʃɑːt-
should *strong form* ʃʊd, *occasional weak forms* ʃəd ʃd, ʃt *(!)*
shoulda *non-standard spelling for* should have*: strong form* 'ʃʊd ə, *weak forms* ʃəd ə ʃtə
shoulder 'ʃəʊld ə →'ʃɒʊld- ‖ 'ʃoʊld ər *(!)* **~ed** d **shouldering** 'ʃəʊld‿ər ɪŋ →'ʃɒʊld‿ ‖ 'ʃoʊld‿ər ɪŋ **~s** z
 'shoulder bag; **'shoulder blade**; **'shoulder strap**
shoulder-high ˌʃəʊld ə 'haɪ◂ →ˌʃɒʊld- ‖ ˌʃoʊld ər-
shoulder-length 'ʃəʊld ə leŋkθ →'ʃɒʊld-, -lentθ ‖ 'ʃoʊld ər-
shouldn't 'ʃʊd ənt
shouldst *strong form* ʃʊdst ʃʊtst, *occasional weak form* ʃədst ʃətst
should've *strong form* 'ʃʊd əv, *occasional weak form* ʃtəv
shout ʃaʊt **shouted** 'ʃaʊt ɪd -əd ‖ 'ʃaʊṭ əd **shouting** 'ʃaʊt ɪŋ ‖ 'ʃaʊṭ ɪŋ **shouts** ʃaʊts
shove ʃʌv **shoved** ʃʌvd **shoves** ʃʌvz **shoving** 'ʃʌv ɪŋ
shove-halfpenny, shove-ha'penny ˌʃʌv 'heɪp ni
shovel 'ʃʌv əl **~ed, ~led** d **~ing, ~ling** ɪŋ **~s** z
shovelboard 'ʃʌv əl bɔːd ‖ -bɔːrd -boʊrd
shoveler, shoveller 'ʃʌv əl‿ə ‖ ər **~s** z
shovelful 'ʃʌv əl fʊl **~s** z
shovelware 'ʃʌv əl weə ‖ -wer -wær
show ʃəʊ ‖ ʃoʊ **showed** ʃəʊd ‖ ʃoʊd **showing** 'ʃəʊ ɪŋ ‖ 'ʃoʊ ɪŋ **shown** ʃəʊn ‖ ʃoʊn **shows** ʃəʊz ‖ ʃoʊz
 'show ˌbusiness; **'show ˌjumper**; **'show ˌjumping**; **ˌshow of 'hands**; **'show ˌtrial**
showband 'ʃəʊ bænd ‖ 'ʃoʊ- **~s** z
showbiz 'ʃəʊ bɪz ‖ 'ʃoʊ-
showboat 'ʃəʊ bəʊt ‖ 'ʃoʊ boʊt **~s** s
showcas|e 'ʃəʊ keɪs ‖ 'ʃoʊ- **~es** ɪz əz
showdown 'ʃəʊ daʊn ‖ 'ʃoʊ- **~s** z
shower *'one that shows'* 'ʃəʊ ə ‖ 'ʃoʊ ər **~s** z
shower *v; n 'sudden rain; ~ bath; etc.'* 'ʃaʊ‿ə ‖ 'ʃaʊ‿ər **~ed** d **showering** 'ʃaʊ‿ər ɪŋ ‖ 'ʃaʊ‿ər ɪŋ **~s** z
 'shower bath; **'shower gel**
showerproof 'ʃaʊ‿ə pruːf -§prʊf ‖ 'ʃaʊ‿ər pruːf **~ed** t **~ing** ɪŋ **~s** s
showery 'ʃaʊ‿ər i ‖ 'ʃaʊ‿ər i
showgirl 'ʃəʊ gɜːl ‖ 'ʃoʊ gɜːl **~s** z
showground 'ʃəʊ graʊnd ‖ 'ʃoʊ- **~s** z
showi... —*see* **showy**
show|man 'ʃəʊ |mən ‖ 'ʃoʊ- **~manship** mən ʃɪp **~men** mən men
shown ʃəʊn §'ʃəʊ ən ‖ ʃoʊn
show-off 'ʃəʊ ɒf -ɔːf ‖ 'ʃoʊ ɔːf -ɑːf **~s** s
showpiec|e 'ʃəʊ piːs ‖ 'ʃoʊ- **~es** ɪz əz
showplac|e 'ʃəʊ pleɪs ‖ 'ʃoʊ- **~es** ɪz əz
showroom 'ʃəʊ ruːm -rʊm ‖ 'ʃoʊ- **~s** z
show-stopper 'ʃəʊ ˌstɒp ə ‖ 'ʃoʊ ˌstɑːp ər **~s** z
show-stopping 'ʃəʊ ˌstɒp ɪŋ ‖ 'ʃoʊ ˌstɑːp ɪŋ
showtime 'ʃəʊ taɪm ‖ 'ʃoʊ-
show|y 'ʃəʊ |i ‖ 'ʃoʊ |i **~ier** i‿ə ‖ i‿ər **~iest** i‿ɪst i‿əst **~ily** ɪ li əl i **~iness** i nəs i nɪs
shoyu 'ʃɔɪ uː —*Jp* [ɕo‚o jɯ]
shrank ʃræŋk
shrapnel, S~ 'ʃræp nəl
shred ʃred **shredded** 'ʃred ɪd -əd **shredding** 'ʃred ɪŋ **shreds** ʃredz
shredder 'ʃred ə ‖ -ər **~s** z
Shreveport 'ʃriːv pɔːt ‖ -pɔːrt -poʊrt
shrew ʃruː **shrews** ʃruːz
 'shrew mole

Short vowel, long vowel

IN SPELLING

1 To each vowel letter in English spelling there correspond two vowel sounds, the vowel letter then traditionally being known as 'short' or 'long' respectively (see **a, e, i, o, u**). (There are also other possibilities that have no traditional names.) The following guidelines are to help you decide whether the short or long pronunciation is likely to be appropriate.

2 A single vowel letter generally counts as **short**

- in a word of one syllable, ending in a consonant (**back, red, tip, rod, cut, hymn**)
- in a stressed penultimate syllable, where the vowel is followed by two or more consonant letters (**battle, jelly, middle, doctor, system**).

3 A single vowel letter generally counts as **long**

- before one consonant letter plus silent **e** (**take, complete, time, rope, rude, type**). However, there are several exceptions, including **have, give, one, come, love**.
- in a word of one syllable, where the vowel is not followed by a consonant (**me, hi, go, flu, try**).
- in a stressed penultimate syllable, where the vowel is followed by only one consonant letter, or by a vowel letter (**potato, thesis, item, over, tribunal, asylum; chaos, neon, triumph, heroic, ruin, dying**).

4 There are many cases not covered by these guidelines. Furthermore, the guidelines have exceptions. That is why you need a pronunciation dictionary.

IN PHONETICS

5 The English vowels can also be divided into short and long on the basis of their pronunciation. Other things being equal, a long vowel has greater duration than a short vowel. However, vowel duration is strongly influenced by the phonetic environment. In general, the difference between short and long vowels is less noticeable in AmE than in BrE.

6 The **short** vowels are ɪ, e, æ, ɒ, ʊ, ʌ, together with the WEAK vowels ə, i, u. Of these, æ is a special case: it is not similar in quality to any long vowel, and many speakers lengthen it (particularly before certain consonants, notably b and d).

7 The **long** vowels are iː, uː, ɑː, ɔː, together with BrE ɜː and AmE ɝː. In the phonetic transcription system used in this dictionary, long vowels are always written with the length mark ː, in accordance with the PHONEME principle; but long vowels may in certain environments be phonetically quite short (see CLIPPING).

8 The duration of **diphthongs** is like that of long vowels.

Short vowel, long vowel ▸

Short vowel, long vowel continued

9 With one exception, the 'short' vowels of spelling correspond to phonetically short vowels. The exception is AmE ɑː, which is phonetically long, yet is associated with the traditional 'short O'. (The corresponding BrE ɒ is phonetically short.) The 'long vowels' of spelling correspond to three phonetic diphthongs (eɪ, aɪ, əʊ‖oʊ), one long vowel (iː), and one sequence of semivowel plus long vowel (juː).

shrewd ʃruːd **shrewder** 'ʃruːd ə ‖ -ᵊr **shrewdest** 'ʃruːd ɪst -əst **shrewdly** 'ʃruːd li **shrewdness** 'ʃruːd nəs -nɪs
shrewish 'ʃruː ɪʃ **~ly** li **~ness** nəs nɪs
Shrewsbury *(i)* 'ʃrəʊz bər͵i ‖ 'ʃroʊz ˌber i, *(ii)* 'ʃruːz- *—The place in England is usually (i), though locally also (ii). The places in the US are (ii).*
shriek ʃriːk **shrieked** ʃriːkt **shrieking/ly** 'ʃriːk ɪŋ /li **shrieks** ʃriːks
shrift ʃrɪft
shrike ʃraɪk **shrikes** ʃraɪks
shrill ʃrɪl **shrilled** ʃrɪld **shriller** 'ʃrɪl ə ‖ -ᵊr **shrillest** 'ʃrɪl ɪst -əst **shrilling** 'ʃrɪl ɪŋ **shrills** ʃrɪlz
shrillness 'ʃrɪl nəs -nɪs
shrilly *adv* 'ʃrɪl li -i
shrimp ʃrɪmp **shrimped** ʃrɪmpt **shrimping** 'ʃrɪmp ɪŋ **shrimps** ʃrɪmps
shrimper 'ʃrɪmp ə ‖ -ᵊr **~s** z
Shrimpton 'ʃrɪmpt ən
shrine ʃraɪn **shrines** ʃraɪnz
Shriner 'ʃraɪn ə ‖ -ᵊr **~s** z
shrink ʃrɪŋk **shrank** ʃræŋk **shrinking/ly** 'ʃrɪŋk ɪŋ /li **shrinks** ʃrɪŋks **shrunk** ʃrʌŋk **shrunken** 'ʃrʌŋk ən **ˌshrinking 'violet**
shrinkag|e 'ʃrɪŋk ɪdʒ **~es** ɪz əz
shrink-wrap 'ʃrɪŋk ræp ˌ·'· **~ped** t **~ping** ɪŋ **~s** s
shrive ʃraɪv **shrived** ʃraɪvd **shriven** 'ʃrɪv ᵊn *(!)* **shrives** ʃraɪvz **shriving** 'ʃraɪv ɪŋ **shrove** ʃrəʊv ‖ ʃroʊv
shrivel 'ʃrɪv ᵊl **~ed, ~led** d **~ing, ~ling** ɪŋ **~s** z
shriven 'ʃrɪv ᵊn
Shrivenham 'ʃrɪv ᵊn͵əm
Shriver 'ʃraɪv ə ‖ -ᵊr
shroff ʃrɒf ‖ ʃrɑːf **shroffed** ʃrɒft ‖ ʃrɑːft **shroffing** 'ʃrɒf ɪŋ ‖ 'ʃrɑːf ɪŋ **shroffs** ʃrɒfs ‖ ʃrɑːfs
'shroom ʃruːm ʃrʊm **'shrooms** ʃruːmz ʃrʊmz
Shropshire 'ʃrɒp ʃə -ʃɪə ‖ 'ʃrɑːp ʃᵊr -ʃɪr
shroud ʃraʊd **shrouded** 'ʃraʊd ɪd -əd **shrouding** 'ʃraʊd ɪŋ **shrouds** ʃraʊdz
shroud-waving 'ʃraʊd ˌweɪv ɪŋ
shrove, S~ ʃrəʊv ‖ ʃroʊv **ˌShrove 'Tuesday**
Shrovetide 'ʃrəʊv taɪd ‖ 'ʃroʊv-
shrub ʃrʌb **shrubs** ʃrʌbz
shrubber|y 'ʃrʌb ər |i **~ies** iz
shrubb|y 'ʃrʌb |i **~ier** i͵ə ‖ i͵ᵊr **~iest** i͵ɪst i͵əst **~iness** i nəs i nɪs
shrug ʃrʌg **shrugged** ʃrʌgd **shrugging** 'ʃrʌg ɪŋ **shrugs** ʃrʌgz
shrunk ʃrʌŋk
shrunken 'ʃrʌŋk ən
shtetl 'ʃtet ᵊl 'ʃteɪt- **~s** z
shtick ʃtɪk **shticks** ʃtɪks
shtook, shtuck ʃtʊk
shtum ʃtʊm
shtup ʃtʊp **shtupped** ʃtʊpt **shtupping** 'ʃtʊp ɪŋ **shtups** ʃtʊps
shubunkin ʃu 'bʌŋk ɪn §-ən **~s** z
shuck ʃʌk **shucked** ʃʌkt **shucking** 'ʃʌk ɪŋ **shucks** ʃʌks
Shuckburgh 'ʃʌk bər͵ə ‖ 'ʃʌk bɜːg
shudder 'ʃʌd ə ‖ -ᵊr **~ed** d **shuddering/ly** 'ʃʌd͵ər ɪŋ /li **~s** z
shuffl|e 'ʃʌf ᵊl **~ed** d **~es** z **~ing** ˌɪŋ
shuffleboard 'ʃʌf ᵊl bɔːd ‖ -bɔːrd -bourd
Shufflebottom 'ʃʌf ᵊl ˌbɒt əm ‖ -ˌbɑːţ əm
shuffler 'ʃʌf ᵊl͵ə ‖ ͵ᵊr **~s** z
Shufflewick 'ʃʌf ᵊl wɪk
shufti, shufty 'ʃʊft i **shuftis** 'ʃʊft iz
Shughie 'ʃuː͵i
shul ʃuːl ʃʊl **shuln** ʃuːln ʃʊln
Shula 'ʃuːl ə
Shulamite 'ʃuːl ə maɪt **~s** s
Shulman 'ʃuːl mən
shun ʃʌn **shunned** ʃʌnd **shunning** 'ʃʌn ɪŋ **shuns** ʃʌnz
'shun *military command: 'attention'* ʃʌn
shunt ʃʌnt **shunted** 'ʃʌntɪd -əd ‖ 'ʃʌnţ əd **shunting** 'ʃʌnt ɪŋ ‖ 'ʃʌnţ ɪŋ **shunts** ʃʌnts **'shunting ˌengine**
shush ʃʊʃ ʃʌʃ **shushed** ʃʊʃt ʃʌʃt **shushes** 'ʃʊʃ ɪz 'ʃʌʃ-, -əz **shushing** 'ʃʊʃ ɪŋ 'ʃʌʃ-
Shuster 'ʃʊst ə 'ʃuːst- ‖ -ᵊr
Shuswap 'ʃʊs wɒp 'ʃʊʃ- ‖ -wɑːp
shut ʃʌt **shuts** ʃʌts **shutting** 'ʃʌt ɪŋ ‖ 'ʃʌţ ɪŋ
shutdown 'ʃʌt daʊn **~s** z
Shute ʃuːt
Shuter 'ʃuːt ə ‖ 'ʃuːţ ᵊr
shut-eye 'ʃʌt aɪ ‖ 'ʃʌţ aɪ
shut-in *n* 'ʃʌt ɪn ‖ 'ʃʌţ- **~s** z
shut-in *adj* ˌʃʌt 'ɪn ◂ ‖ ˌʃʌţ-
shutoff *n* 'ʃʌt ɒf -ɔːf ‖ 'ʃʌţ ɔːf -ɑːf **~s** s
shutout *n* 'ʃʌt aʊt ‖ 'ʃʌţ- **~s** s
shutter 'ʃʌt ə ‖ 'ʃʌţ ᵊr **~ed** d **shuttering** 'ʃʌt͵ər ɪŋ ‖ 'ʃʌţ ər ɪŋ **~s** z

shutterbug ˈʃʌt ə bʌg ‖ -ərˑ- **~s** z
shuttl|e ˈʃʌt ᵊl ‖ ˈʃʌţ ᵊl **~ed** d **~es** z **~ing** ˌɪŋ
ˈshuttle diˌplomacy
shuttlecock ˈʃʌt ᵊl kɒk ‖ ˈʃʌţ ᵊl kɑːk **~s** s
Shuttleworth ˈʃʌt ᵊl wɜːθ -wəθ ‖ ˈʃʌţ ᵊl wɜːθ
Shuy ʃaɪ
shwa ʃwɑː ʃvɑː **shwas** ʃwɑːz ʃvɑːz
-shy ʃaɪ — **work-shy** ˈwɜːk ʃaɪ ‖ ˈwɜːk-
shy ʃaɪ **shied** ʃaɪd **shier, shyer** ˈʃaɪ‿ə ‖ ˈʃaɪ‿ər **shies** ʃaɪz **shiest, shyest** ˈʃaɪ ɪst -əst **shying** ˈʃaɪ ɪŋ
Shylock ˈʃaɪ lɒk ‖ -lɑːk
shy|ly ˈʃaɪ |li **~ness** nəs nɪs
shyster ˈʃaɪst ə ‖ -ər **~s** z
si siː
SI ˌes ˈaɪ
sial ˈsaɪ‿əl
sialagogue, sialogogue saɪ ˈæl ə gɒg ˈsaɪ‿əl- ‖ -gɑːg **~s** z
Siam ˌsaɪ ˈæm ˈ··
siamang ˈsiː‿ə mæŋ ˈsaɪ‿ **~s** z
Siamese ˌsaɪ‿ə ˈmiːz ◂ ‖ -ˈmiːs
ˌSiamese ˈcat; **ˌSiamese ˈtwin**
Sian, Siân ʃɑːn
sib sɪb **sibs** sɪbz
Sibelius sɪ ˈbeɪl i‿əs sə- —*Swed, Finnish* [si ˈbeː li us]
Siberi|a saɪ ˈbɪər i‿|ə ‖ -ˈbɪr- **~an/s** ən/z
sibilanc|e ˈsɪb ɪl ənᵗs -əl- **~y** i
sibilant ˈsɪb ɪl ənt -əl- **~ly** li **~s** s
sibi|late ˈsɪb ɪ |leɪt -ə- **~lated** leɪt ɪd -əd ‖ leɪţ əd **~lates** leɪts **~lating** leɪt ɪŋ ‖ leɪţ ɪŋ
sibilation ˌsɪb ɪ ˈleɪʃ ᵊn -ə- **~s** z
Sibley ˈsɪb li
sibling ˈsɪb lɪŋ **~s** z
sibyl, Sibyl ˈsɪb ɪl -ᵊl **~s, ~'s** z
sibylline, S~ ˈsɪb ɪ laɪn -ə-; sɪ ˈbɪl aɪn, sə- ‖ -liːn
sic sɪk siːk —*see also phrases with this word* **sicced** sɪkt **siccing** ˈsɪk ɪŋ **sics** sɪks
siccative ˈsɪk ət ɪv ‖ -əţ- **~s** z
Sichuan ˌsɪtʃ ˈwɑːn —*Chi* Sìchuān [⁴sɯ ¹tʂʰwan]
Sicilian sɪ ˈsɪl i‿ən sə- **~s** z
Sicil|y ˈsɪs əl |i -ɪl- **~ies** iz
sick sɪk **sicker** ˈsɪk ə ‖ ˈsɪk ər **sickest** ˈsɪk ɪst -əst
ˈsick call; **ˌsick ˈheadache**; **ˈsick leave**; **ˈsick paˌrade**; **ˈsick pay**
sickbag ˈsɪk bæg **~s** z
sickbay ˈsɪk beɪ **~s** z
sickbed ˈsɪk bed **~s** z
sicken ˈsɪk ən **~ed** d **~ing/ly** ˌɪŋ /li **~s** z
Sickert ˈsɪk ət ‖ -ərt
sickie ˈsɪk i **~s** z
sickl|e ˈsɪk ᵊl **~ed** d **~es** z **~ing** ˌɪŋ
sickle-cell ˈsɪk ᵊl sel
ˌsickle-cell aˈnaemia
sick|ly ˈsɪk |li **~lier** li‿ə ‖ li‿ər **~liest** li‿ɪst li‿əst **~liness** li nəs li nɪs
sickness ˈsɪk nəs -nɪs **~es** ɪz əz
ˈsickness ˌbenefit
sicko ˈsɪk əʊ ‖ -oʊ **~s** z
sickout ˈsɪk aʊt **~s** s
sickroom ˈsɪk ruːm -rʊm **~s** z
sic transit gloria mundi ˌsɪk ˈtrænz ɪt ˌglɔːr i‿ə ˈmʊnd i ˌsiːk-, -ˈtrænᵗs-, -ˈtrɑːnz-, -ˈtrɑːnᵗs-, §-ˈət-, -ɑː'--, -iː ‖ -ˌgloʊr-
Sid sɪd
Sidcup ˈsɪd kʌp →ˈsɪg-, -kəp
Siddall ˈsɪd ɔːl ‖ -ɑːl
Siddeley ˈsɪd ᵊl i
Siddhartha sɪ ˈdɑːt ə ‖ -ˈdɑːrţ ə
Siddons ˈsɪd ᵊnz
side saɪd **sided** ˈsaɪd ɪd -əd **sides** saɪdz **siding** ˈsaɪd ɪŋ
ˈside dish; **ˈside efˌfect**; **ˈside ˌissue**; **ˈside ˌorder**; **ˈside street**
sidearm ˈsaɪd ɑːm ‖ -ɑːrm **~s** z
sideband ˈsaɪd bænd →ˈsaɪb-
sidebar ˈsaɪd bɑː →ˈsaɪb ‖ -bɑːr **~s** z
sideboard ˈsaɪd bɔːd →ˈsaɪb- ‖ -bɔːrd -boʊrd **~s** z
Sidebotham, Sidebottom ˈsaɪd ˌbɒt əm →ˈsaɪb- ‖ -ˌbɑːţ əm —*Some bearers of these names insist on fanciful pronunciations such as* ˈsiːd-, -ˌbəʊθ əm ‖ -ˌboʊθ-, *or even* ˌsɪd ɪ bə ˈtɑːm, -ˈtəʊm ‖ -ˈtoʊm
sideburn ˈsaɪd bɜːn →ˈsaɪb- ‖ -bɜːn **~s** z
sidecar ˈsaɪd kɑː →ˈsaɪg- ‖ -kɑːr **~s** z
-sided ˈsaɪd ɪd -əd — **many-sided** ˌmen i ˈsaɪd ɪd ◂ -əd
sidekick ˈsaɪd kɪk →ˈsaɪg- **~s** s
sidelight ˈsaɪd laɪt **~s** s
sidelin|e ˈsaɪd laɪn **~ed** d **~es** z **~ing** ɪŋ
sidelong ˈsaɪd lɒŋ ‖ -lɔːŋ -lɑːŋ
side|man ˈsaɪd |mən →ˈsaɪb-, -mæn **~men** men mən
side-on ˌsaɪd ˈɒn ◂ ‖ -ˈɑːn -ˈɔːn
sidereal saɪ ˈdɪər i‿əl sɪ- ‖ -ˈdɪr-
siderite ˈsaɪd ə raɪt ˈsɪd- ‖ ˈsɪd-
siderostat ˈsɪd‿ər əʊ stæt **~s** s
sidesaddle ˈsaɪd ˌsæd ᵊl **~s** z
sideshow ˈsaɪd ʃəʊ ‖ -ʃoʊ **~s** z
sideslip ˈsaɪd slɪp **~ped** t **~ping** ɪŋ **~s** s
sides|man ˈsaɪdz |mən **~men** mən men
sidesplitting ˈsaɪd ˌsplɪt ɪŋ ‖ -ˌsplɪţ ɪŋ **~ly** li
sidestep ˈsaɪd step **~ped** t **~ping** ɪŋ **~s** s
sidestroke ˈsaɪd strəʊk ‖ -stroʊk
sideswip|e ˈsaɪd swaɪp **~ed** t **~es** s **~ing** ɪŋ
sidetrack ˈsaɪd træk **~ed** t **~ing** ɪŋ **~s** s
side-view ˈsaɪd vjuː
sidewalk ˈsaɪd wɔːk ‖ -wɑːk **~s** s
ˈsidewalk ˌartist
sidewall ˈsaɪd wɔːl ‖ -wɑːl **~s** z
sideward ˈsaɪd wəd ‖ -wᵊrd **~s** z
sideways ˈsaɪd weɪz
side-wheeler ˈsaɪd wiːᵊl ə -hwiːᵊl- ‖ -ər
sidewinder ˈsaɪd ˌwaɪnd ə ‖ -ər **~s** z
Sidgwick ˈsɪdʒ wɪk
siding ˈsaɪd ɪŋ **~s** z
sidl|e ˈsaɪd ᵊl **~ed** d **~es** z **~ing** ˌɪŋ
Sidmouth ˈsɪd məθ →ˈsɪb-
Sidney ˈsɪd ni
Sidon ˈsaɪd ᵊn
Sidonian saɪ ˈdəʊn i‿ən ‖ -ˈdoʊn- **~s** z

S

Sidonie sɪ ˈdəʊn i ‖ -ˈdoʊn i
SIDS sɪdz
Sieff siːf
siege siːdʒ siːʒ **sieges** ˈsiːdʒ ɪz ˈsiːʒ-, -əz
Siegel ˈsiːg ᵊl
Siegfried ˈsiːg friːd —*Ger* [ˈziːk fʁiːt]
Sieg Heil ˌsiːg ˈhaɪᵊl —*Ger* [ˌziːk ˈhail]
Sieglinde siː ˈglɪnd ə sɪ- —*Ger* [ziːk ˈlɪn də]
Siemens, s~ ˈsiːm ənz —*Ger* [ˈziː məns, -mɛns]
Siena si ˈen ə —*It* [ˈsjɛː na]
Sienese ˌsiː e ˈniːz ◂ -ə- ‖ -ˈniːs
sienna si ˈen ə
sierra, S~ si ˈer ə -ˈeər-; ˈsɪər ə —*Sp* [ˈsje rra] **~s** z —*see also phrases with this word*
Siˌerra Neˈvada
Sierra Leone si ˌer ə li ˈəʊn -ˌeər-, -ˈəʊn i; ˌsɪər· ·ˈ· ‖ -ˈoʊn -ˈoʊn i
Sierra Leonean, Sierra Leonian si ˌer ə li ˈəʊn i‿ən ◂ -ˌeər-; ˌsɪər· ·ˈ·- ‖ -ˈoʊn- **s** z
Sierra Madre si ˌer ə ˈmɑːdr eɪ -ˌeər-, -i —*Sp* [ˈmað re]
siesta si ˈest ə **~s** z
sieve sɪv *(!)* **sieved** sɪvd **sieves** sɪvz **sieving** ˈsɪv ɪŋ
sievert, S~ ˈsiːv ət ‖ -ᵊrt **~s** s
sift sɪft **sifted** ˈsɪft ɪd -əd **sifting/s** ˈsɪft ɪŋ/z **sifts** sɪfts
Sifta *tdmk* ˈsɪft ə
sifter ˈsɪft ə ‖ -ᵊr **~s** z
Sigal ˈsiːg ᵊl
sigh saɪ **sighed** saɪd *(= side)* **sighing** ˈsaɪ ɪŋ **sighs** saɪz *(= size)*
sight saɪt *(= site, cite)* **sighted** ˈsaɪt ɪd -əd ‖ ˈsaɪţ əd **sighting** ˈsaɪt ɪŋ ‖ ˈsaɪţ ɪŋ **sights** saɪts
-sighted ˈsaɪt ɪd -əd ‖ ˈsaɪţ əd — **far-sighted** ˌfɑː ˈsaɪt ɪd ◂ -əd ‖ ˌfɑːr ˈsaɪţ əd ◂
sightless ˈsaɪt ləs -lɪs **~ly** li **~ness** nəs nɪs
sightline ˈsaɪt laɪn **~s** z
sight|ly ˈsaɪt |li **~lier** li‿ə ‖ li‿ᵊr **~liest** li‿ɪst li‿əst
sight-|read *pres* ˈsaɪt |riːd **~read** *past & pp* red **~reader/s** riːd ə/z ‖ -ᵊr/z **~reading** riːd ɪŋ **~reads** riːdz
sightscreen ˈsaɪt skriːn **~s** z
sightseeing ˈsaɪt ˌsiː ɪŋ
sightseer ˈsaɪt ˌsiː‿ə ‖ ᵊr **~s** z
sigint, SIGINT ˈsɪg ɪnt
Sigismond, Sigismund ˈsɪg ɪs mənd ˈsɪdʒ-, -ɪz-
sig|lum ˈsɪg |ləm **~la** lə
sigma ˈsɪg mə **~s** z
sigmatic sɪg ˈmæt ɪk ‖ -ˈmæţ ɪk
sigmoid ˈsɪg mɔɪd
Sigmund ˈsɪg mənd —*Ger* [ˈziːk mʊnt]
sign saɪn *(= sine)* **signed** saɪnd **signing** ˈsaɪn ɪŋ **signs** saɪnz
ˈsign ˌlanguage
signage ˈsaɪn ɪdʒ
signal ˈsɪg nᵊl **~ed, ~led** d **~ing, ~ling** ɪŋ **~s** z
ˈsignal box; **ˈsignal ˌtower**
signaler ˈsɪg nəl ə ‖ -ᵊr **~s** z
signalis|e, signaliz|e ˈsɪg nə laɪz -nᵊl aɪz **~ed** d **~es** ɪz əz **~ing** ɪŋ
signaller ˈsɪg nəl ə ‖ -ᵊr **~s** z
signally ˈsɪg nəl i
signal|man ˈsɪg nᵊl |mən -mæn **~men** mən men
signalment ˈsɪg nᵊl mənt **~s** s
signal-to-noise ˌsɪg nᵊl tə ˈnɔɪz
ˌsignal-to-ˈnoise ˌratio
signator|y ˈsɪg nət‿ər |i ‖ -nə tɔːr |i -toʊr i **~ies** iz
signature ˈsɪg nətʃ ə -nɪtʃ- ‖ -ᵊr -nə tʃʊr **~s** z
ˈsignature tune
signboard ˈsaɪn bɔːd →ˈsaɪm- ‖ -bɔːrd -boʊrd **~s** z
signer ˈsaɪn ə ‖ -ᵊr **~s** z
signet ˈsɪg nɪt -nət **~s** s
ˈsignet ring
significance sɪg ˈnɪf ɪk ənᵗs -ək-
significant sɪg ˈnɪf ɪk ənt -ək- **~ly** li
signification ˌsɪg nɪf ɪ ˈkeɪʃ ᵊn ˌ-nəf-, §-ə'·- **~s** z
significative sɪg ˈnɪf ɪk ət ɪv -ˈ-ək-; -ɪ keɪt-, -ə keɪt- ‖ -ə keɪţ ɪv **~ly** li **~ness** nəs nɪs
signi|fy ˈsɪg nɪ |faɪ -nə- **~fied** faɪd **~fier/s** faɪ‿ə/z ‖ faɪ‿ᵊr/z **~fies** faɪz **~fying** faɪ ɪŋ
Signor, S~ ˈsiːn jɔː ·ˈ· ‖ -jɔːr —*It* [siɲ ˈɲor]
Signora, s~ siːn ˈjɔːr ə —*It* [siɲ ˈɲoː ra]
Signorina, s~ ˌsiːn jɔː ˈriːn ə ◂ -jə- —*It* [siɲ ɲo ˈriː na]
signpost ˈsaɪn pəʊst →ˈsaɪm- ‖ -poʊst **~ed** ɪd əd **~ing** ɪŋ **~s** s
signwrit|er ˈsaɪn ˌraɪt| ə ‖ -ˌraɪţ| ᵊr **~ers** əz ‖ -ᵊrz **~ing** ɪŋ
Sigourney sɪ ˈgɔːn i -ˈgʊən- ‖ -ˈgʊrn i
Sigurd ˈsɪg ʊəd ˈsiːg-, -ɜːd ‖ -ᵊrd
Sihanouk ˈsiː‿ə nuːk
sika ˈsiːk ə **~s** z
sike, Sike saɪk **sikes, Sikes** saɪks
Sikh siːk sɪk —*Hindi* [sɪkʰ] **Sikhs** siːks sɪks
Sikhism ˈsiːk ˌɪz əm ˈsɪk-
Sikkim ˈsɪk ɪm sɪ ˈkɪm
Sikkimese ˌsɪk ɪ ˈmiːz ◂ ‖ -ˈmiːs ◂
Sikorsky sɪ ˈkɔːsk i ‖ -ˈkɔːrsk-
silage ˈsaɪl ɪdʒ
silane ˈsɪl eɪn ˈsaɪl-
Silas ˈsaɪl əs
Silbury ˈsɪl bər‿i ‖ -ˌber i
ˌSilbury ˈHill
Silchester ˈsɪltʃ ɪst ə -əst-; ˈsɪl tʃest ə ‖ -ᵊr
Silcox ˈsɪl kɒks ‖ -kɑːks
sild sɪld **silds** sɪldz
sildenafil sɪl ˈden ə fɪl
Sile, Síle *personal name* ˈʃiːl ə
Sileby ˈsaɪᵊl bi
silenc|e ˈsaɪl ənᵗs **~ed** t **~es** ɪz əz **~ing** ɪŋ
silencer ˈsaɪl ənᵗs ə ‖ -ᵊr **~s** z
silent ˈsaɪl ənt **~ly** li **~ness** nəs nɪs
ˌsilent ˈpartner
Silenus saɪ ˈliːn əs sɪ-, -ˈleɪn-
Silesia, s~ saɪ ˈliːz i‿ə sɪ-, -ˈliːs-; -ˈliːʒ ə, -ˈliːʃ- ‖ saɪ ˈliːʒ ə sɪ-, -ˈliːʃ-

S

Silesian saɪ ˈliːz i‿ən sɪ-, -ˈliːs-; -ˈliːʒ ən, -ˈliːʃ- ‖ saɪ ˈliːʒ ən sɪ-, -ˈliːʃ- **~s** z
silex ˈsaɪl eks
silhou|ette ˌsɪl u ˈ|et -ju-, ˌ· · ˈ· **~etted** et ɪd -əd ‖ eţ əd **~ettes** ets **~etting** et ɪŋ ‖ eţ ɪŋ
silica ˈsɪl ɪk ə
silicate ˈsɪl ɪ keɪt -ə-; -ɪk ət, -ɪt **~s** s
silicic sɪ ˈlɪs ɪk sə-
silicon ˈsɪl ɪk ən -ək-; -ɪ kɒn, -ə-, ⚠-kəʊn ‖ -ɪ kɑːn
ˌ**silicon ˈchip**; ˌ**Silicon ˈValley**
silicone ˈsɪl ɪ kəʊn -ə- ‖ -koʊn **~s** z
silicosis ˌsɪl ɪ ˈkəʊs ɪs -ə-, §-əs ‖ -ˈkoʊs əs
silicotic ˌsɪl ɪ ˈkɒt ɪk ◂ -ə- ‖ -ˈkɑːţ- **~s** s
silk, Silk sɪlk **silks** sɪlks
silken ˈsɪlk ən
silki... —*see* **silky**
Silkin ˈsɪlk ɪn §-ən
silkscreen ˈsɪlk skriːn **~ing** ɪŋ
silkworm ˈsɪlk wɜːm ‖ -wɜːm **~s** z
silk|y ˈsɪlk |i **~ier** i‿ə ‖ iər **~iest** i‿ɪst i‿əst **~ily** ɪ li əl i **~iness** i nəs i nɪs
sill sɪl **sills** sɪlz
sillabub ˈsɪl ə bʌb **~s** z
Sillars ˈsɪl əz ‖ -ərz
Sillery ˈsɪl ər i
silli... —*see* **silly**
sillimanite ˈsɪl ɪm ə naɪt ˈ-əm-
Sillito, Sillitoe ˈsɪl ɪ təʊ -ə- ‖ -toʊ
Silloth ˈsɪl əθ
Sills sɪlz
sill|y ˈsɪl |i **~ier** i‿ə ‖ i‿ər **~ies** iz **~iest** i‿ɪst i‿əst **~iness** i nəs i nɪs
ˌ**silly ˈbilly,** ˈ· · ˌ· ·; ˈ**silly ˌseason**
silo ˈsaɪl əʊ ‖ -oʊ **~s** z
Siloam saɪ ˈləʊ əm sɪ-, -æm ‖ -ˈloʊ-
siloxane sɪ ˈlɒks eɪn saɪ-, sə- ‖ -ˈlɑːks-
Silsoe ˈsɪls əʊ ‖ -oʊ
silt sɪlt **silted** ˈsɪlt ɪd -əd **silting** ˈsɪlt ɪŋ **silts** sɪlts
siltation sɪl ˈteɪʃ ən
silty ˈsɪlt i
Silures saɪ ˈlʊər iːz sɪ-, -ˈljʊər-, -ˈljɔːr- ‖ ˈsɪl jər-
Silurian saɪ ˈlʊər i‿ən sɪ-, -ˈljʊər-, -ˈljɔːr- ‖ -ˈlʊr-
Silva ˈsɪlv ə
silvan ˈsɪlv ən
Silvanus sɪl ˈveɪn əs
silver, S~ ˈsɪlv ə ‖ -ər **~ed** d **silvering** ˈsɪlv ər‿ɪŋ **~s** z
ˌ**silver ˈbirch**; ˈ**silver foil,** ˌ· ˈ·; ˌ**silver ˈjubilee,** ˌ· · ˌ· ˈ·; ˌ**silver ˈmedal**; ˌ**silver ˈnitrate**; ˌ**silver ˈpaper**; ˌ**silver ˈplate**◂; ˌ**silver ˈwedding,** ˌ**silver ˈwedding anniˌversary**
silverfish ˈsɪlv ə fɪʃ ‖ -ər- **~es** ɪz əz
silveri... —*see* **silvery**
Silverman ˈsɪlv ə mən ‖ -ər-
Silvers ˈsɪlv əz ‖ -ərz
silverside ˈsɪlv ə saɪd ‖ -ər- **~s** z
silversmith ˈsɪlv ə smɪθ ‖ -ər- **~ing** ɪŋ **~s** s
Silverstone ˈsɪlv ə stəʊn ‖ -ər stoʊn
silver-tongued ˌsɪlv ə ˈtʌŋd◂ §-ˈtɒŋd ‖ -ər-
Silvertown ˈsɪlv ə taʊn ‖ -ər-
silverware ˈsɪlv ə weə ‖ -ər wer -wær
silverweed ˈsɪlv ə wiːd ‖ -ər-
silver-Y ˌsɪlv ə ˈwaɪ ‖ -ər-
ˌ**silver-ˈY moth**
silver|y ˈsɪlv ər‿|i **~iness** i nəs i nɪs
Silvester sɪl ˈvest ə ‖ -ər
Silvia ˈsɪlv i‿ə
silviculture ˈsɪlv ɪ ˌkʌltʃ ə §-ə- ‖ -ər
Silvie ˈsɪlv i
Silvikrin *tdmk* ˈsɪlv ɪ krɪn -ə-
s'il vous plait, s'il vous plaît ˌsiː vuː ˈpleɪ ˌsiːəl- —*Fr* [sil vu plɛ]
Sim, sim sɪm
sima ˈsaɪm ə
simazine ˈsaɪm ə ziːn
simba, Simba ˈsɪm bə
Simca *tdmk* ˈsɪm kə **~s** z
Simcox ˈsɪm kɒks ‖ -kɑːks
Simenon ˈsiːm ə nɒ̃ ˈsɪm-, -nɒn ‖ ˌsiːm ə ˈnɔːn -ˈnoʊn, -ˈnɑːn —*Fr* [sim nɔ̃]
Simeon ˈsɪm i‿ən
Simes saɪmz
Simey ˈsaɪm i
Simi sɪ ˈmiː ˈsiːm i
simian ˈsɪm i‿ən **~s** z
similar ˈsɪm əl‿ə -ɪl ə ‖ -əl‿ər
similarit|y ˌsɪm ə ˈlær ət |i ˌ·ɪ-, -ɪt |i ‖ -əţ |i -ˈler- **~ies** iz
similarly ˈsɪm əl‿ə li -ɪl ə li ‖ -əl‿ər li
simile ˈsɪm əl i -ɪl- **~s** z
similitude sɪ ˈmɪl ɪ tjuːd sə-, -ə-, →-tʃuːd ‖ -ə tuːd -tjuːd **~s** z
Simla ˈsɪm lə
Simm sɪm
simmer ˈsɪm ə ‖ -ər **~ed** d **simmering** ˈsɪm ər‿ɪŋ **~s** z
Simmonds ˈsɪm əndz
Simmons ˈsɪm ənz
Simms sɪmz
simnel, S~ ˈsɪm nəl
Simon ˈsaɪm ən —*but as a French name,* siː ˈmɒ̃ ‖ -ˈmoʊn —*Fr* [si mɔ̃]
ˌ**Simon ˈsays**
Simonds *(i)* ˈsɪm əndz, *(ii)* ˈsaɪm əndz
Simone sɪ ˈməʊn sə- ‖ -ˈmoʊn
simoniacal ˌsaɪm ə ˈnaɪ‿ək əl ◂
Simonides saɪ ˈmɒn ɪ diːz -ə- ‖ -ˈmɑːn-
simon-pure ˌsaɪm ən ˈpjʊə ◂ -ˈpjɔː ‖ -ˈpjʊər ◂
Simons ˈsaɪm ənz
Simonsbath ˈsɪm ənz bɑːθ §-bæθ ‖ -bæθ
Simonstown ˈsaɪm ənz taʊn
simony ˈsaɪm ən i ˈsɪm-
simoom sɪ ˈmuːm §sə- **~s** z
simpatico sɪm ˈpæt ɪ kəʊ -ˈpɑːt- ‖ -ˈpɑːţ ɪ koʊ -ˈpæţ- —*It* [sim ˈpaː ti ko]
simper ˈsɪmp ə ‖ -ər **~ed** d **simpering/ly** ˈsɪmp ər‿ɪŋ /li **~s** z
Simpkin ˈsɪm*p* kɪn
Simpkins ˈsɪm*p* kɪnz
Simpkinson ˈsɪm*p* kɪn sən
simple ˈsɪmp əl **simpler** ˈsɪmp lə ‖ -lər **simples** ˈsɪmp əlz **simplest** ˈsɪmp lɪst -ləst

S

ˌsimple 'fracture; ˌsimple 'interest; ˌsimple 'life; ˌsimple ma'chine; ˌsimple 'time

simple-hearted ˌsɪmp əl 'hɑːt ɪd ◂ -əd ‖ -'hɑːrţ əd ◂

simple-minded ˌsɪmp əl 'maɪnd ɪd ◂ -əd **~ly** li **~ness** nəs nɪs

simpleness 'sɪmp əl nəs -nɪs

simpleton 'sɪmp əl tən **~s** z

simplex 'sɪm pleks

simplicit|y sɪm 'plɪs ət |i -ɪt- ‖ -əţ |i **~ies** iz

simplification ˌsɪmp lɪf ɪ 'keɪʃ ən ˌ·ləf-, §-ə'·- **~s** z

simpli|fy 'sɪmp lɪ |faɪ -lə- **~fied** faɪd **~fier/s** faɪ‿ə/z ‖ faɪ‿ər/z **~fies** faɪz **~fying** faɪ ɪŋ

simplistic sɪm 'plɪst ɪk **~ally** əl‿i

Simplon 'sæm plɒn 'sɪm- ‖-plɑːn —*Fr* [sɛ̃ plɔ̃]

simply 'sɪmp li

Simpson 'sɪm*p*s ən **~s** z

ˌSimpson 'Desert

Sims sɪmz

Simson 'sɪmᵖ sən

simulac|rum ˌsɪm ju 'leɪk |rəm §-jə-, -'læk- ‖ ˌsɪm jə- **~ra** rə

simu|late 'sɪm ju |leɪt -jə- ‖-jə- **~lated** leɪt ɪd -əd ‖ leɪţ əd **~lates** leɪts **~lating** leɪt ɪŋ ‖ leɪţ ɪŋ

simulation ˌsɪm ju 'leɪʃ ən -jə- ‖ -jə- **~s** z

simulator 'sɪm ju leɪt ə '-jə- ‖ -jə leɪţ ər **~s** z

simulcast 'sɪm əl kɑːst §-kæst ‖ 'saɪm əl kæst (*) **~ed** ɪd əd **~ing** ɪŋ **~s** s

simultaneity ˌsɪm əl tə 'neɪ ət i -'niː‿, -ɪt i ‖ ˌsaɪm əl tə 'niː əţ i (*)

SIMULTANEOUS

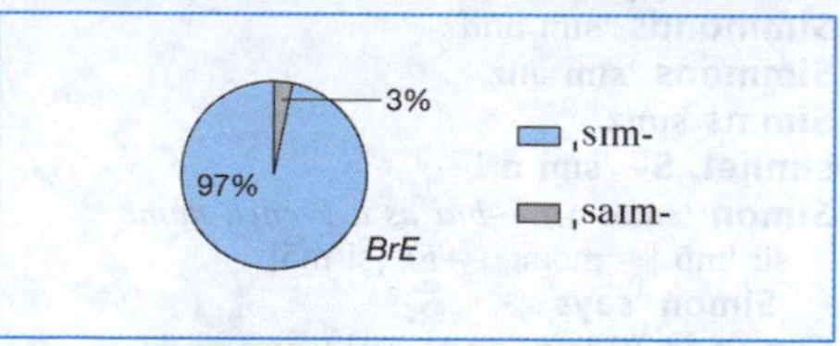

simultaneous ˌsɪm əl 'teɪn i‿əs ◂ ‖ ˌsaɪm- (*) — *Preference poll, BrE:* ˌsɪm- *97%,* ˌsaɪm- *3%.* **~ly** li **~ness** nəs nɪs

simvastatin ˌsɪm və 'stæt ɪn §-ən ‖ -ən

sin *'do wrong'* sɪn **sinned** sɪnd **sinning** 'sɪn ɪŋ **sins** sɪnz

sin *in trigonometry* saɪn

Sinai 'saɪn aɪ 'saɪn i‿aɪ, 'saɪn eɪ aɪ

Sinatra sɪ 'nɑːtr ə sə-

Sinbad 'sɪn bæd →'sɪm-

sin-bin 'sɪn bɪn →'sɪm- **~s** z

since sɪnᵗs

sin|cere sɪn |'sɪə sən- ‖ -|'sɪər **~cerely** 'sɪə li ‖ 'sɪr li **~cerer** 'sɪər ə ‖ 'sɪr ər **~cerest** 'sɪər ɪst -əst ‖ 'sɪr əst

sincerity sɪn 'ser ət i sən-, -ɪt i ‖ -əţ i

Sinclair *(i)* 'sɪn kleə →'sɪŋ-, §-klə ‖ -kler -klær, *(ii)* sɪn 'kleə →sɪŋ- ‖ -'kleər -'klæər

Sind, Sindh sɪnd —*Hindi* [sɪn̪d̪ʱ]

Sindbad 'sɪnd bæd

Sinden 'sɪnd ən

Sindhi 'sɪnd i -hi —*Hindi* [sɪn̪ d̪ʱi] **~s** z

Sindy *tdmk* 'sɪnd i

sine *prep, Latin* 'sɪn i 'saɪn-, 'siːn-, -eɪ —*see also phrases with this word*

sine *n, in trigonometry* saɪn **sines** saɪnz

'sine wave

Sinead, Sinéad ʃɪ 'neɪd -'neəd

sinecure 'sɪn ɪ kjʊə 'saɪn-, -§ə-, -kjɔː **~s** z

sine die ˌsaɪn i 'daɪ iː -i; ˌsɪn i 'diː eɪ, -eɪ-; ⚠ˌsaɪn i 'daɪ

sine qua non ˌsɪn i ˌkwɑː 'nɒn ˌsiːn-, -eɪ-, -'nəʊn; ˌsaɪn i ˌkweɪ- ‖ -'nɑːn -'noʊn

sinew 'sɪn juː **~s** z

sinewy 'sɪn juː‿i

sinfonia, S~ ˌsɪn fə 'nɪə sɪn 'fəʊn i‿ə ‖ ˌsɪn fə 'niː ə -foʊ- **~s** z

sinfonietta ˌsɪn fəʊn i 'et ə ˌ·fən-, ˌ·fɒn-; ˌ· ·'jet ə ‖ ˌsɪn fən 'jeţ ə -foʊn- **~s** z

sinful 'sɪn fəl -fʊl **~ly** i **~ness** nəs nɪs

sing sɪŋ **sang** sæŋ **singing** 'sɪŋ ɪŋ **sings** sɪŋz **sung** sʌŋ

'Sing Sing

singable 'sɪŋ əb əl

singalong 'sɪŋ ə lɒŋ ‖ -lɔːŋ -lɑːŋ **~s** z

Singapore ˌsɪŋ ə 'pɔː ◂ -gə-, '· · · ‖ 'sɪŋ gə pɔːr -ə-, -poʊr

Singaporean ˌsɪŋ ə 'pɔːr i‿ən ◂ -gə-, -pɔː 'riː‿ən ‖ -'poʊr- **~s** z

singe sɪndʒ **singed** sɪn*d*ʒd **singeing** 'sɪn*d*ʒ ɪŋ **singes** 'sɪn*d*ʒ ɪz -əz

singer, S~ 'sɪŋ ə ‖ -ər **~s** z

singer-songwriter ˌsɪŋ ə 'sɒŋ ˌraɪt ə ‖ ˌsɪŋ ər 'sɔːŋ ˌraɪţər -'sɑːŋ- **~s** z

Singh sɪŋ

Singhala 'sɪŋ həl ə

Singhalese ˌsɪŋ ə 'liːz ◂ -hə-, -gə- ‖ -gə- -'liːs

singing 'sɪŋ ɪŋ

singl|e 'sɪŋ gəl **~ed** d **~es** z **~ing** ‿ɪŋ

ˌsingle 'file; ˌsingle 'parent

single-action ˌsɪŋ gəl 'æk ʃən ◂

single-breasted ˌsɪŋ gəl 'brest ɪd ◂ -əd

single-decker ˌsɪŋ gəl 'dek ə ◂ ‖ -ər **~s** z

single-family ˌsɪŋ gəl 'fæm li ◂ -'fæm əl i, -ɪl i

single-handed ˌsɪŋ gəl 'hænd ɪd ◂ -əd **~ly** li **~ness** nəs nɪs

single-lens ˌsɪŋ gəl 'lenz ◂

ˌsingle-lens 'reflex (ˌcamera)

single-minded ˌsɪŋ gəl 'maɪnd ɪd ◂ -əd **~ly** li **~ness** nəs nɪs

singleness 'sɪŋ gəl nəs -nɪs

single-sex ˌsɪŋ gəl 'seks ◂

single-spac|ed ˌsɪŋ gəl 'speɪs|t ◂ **~ing** ɪŋ

singlestick 'sɪŋ gəl stɪk **~s** s

singlet 'sɪŋ glət -glɪt **~s** s

singleton, S~ 'sɪŋ gəl tən **~s** z

single-track ˌsɪŋ gəl 'træk ◂

single-user ˌsɪŋ gəl 'juːz ə ◂ ‖ -ər

singly 'sɪŋ gli

singsong 'sɪŋ sɒŋ ‖ -sɔːŋ -sɑːŋ **~s** z

singular 'sɪŋ gjʊl ə -gjəl- ‖-gjəl ər **~ly** li **~ness** nəs nɪs **~s** z

singularit|y ˌsɪŋ gju ˈlær ət |i ˌ·gjə-, -ɪt i ‖ -gjə ˈlær əṱ |i -ˈler- **~ies** iz
singulary ˈsɪŋ gjʊl ər i ‖ -gjə ler i
sinh ʃaɪn sɪnᵗʃ, ˌsaɪn ˈeɪtʃ ‖ sɪnᵗʃ
Sinhala ˈsɪn həl ə ˈsɪŋ-
Sinhalese ˌsɪn hə ˈliːz ◂ ˌsɪŋ-, -ə- ‖ -ˈliːs
sinister ˈsɪn ɪst ə §-əst- ‖ -ᵊr **~ly** li **~ness** nəs nɪs
sinistral ˈsɪn ɪs trəl -əs- **~ly** i **~s** z
sinistrorse ˈsɪn ɪ strɔːs -ə-, ˌ· ·ˈ· ‖ -strɔːrs **~ly** li
Sinitic saɪ ˈnɪt ɪk sɪ- ‖ -ˈnɪṱ-
Sinitta sɪ ˈniːt ə sə- ‖ -ˈniːṱ-
sink sɪŋk **sank** sæŋk **sinking** ˈsɪŋk ɪŋ **sinks** sɪŋks **sunk** sʌŋk **sunken** ˈsʌŋk ən **ˈsinking ˌfeeling**; **ˈsinking fund**
sinkable ˈsɪŋk əb ᵊl
sinker ˈsɪŋk ə ‖ -ᵊr **~s** z
sinkhole ˈsɪŋk həʊl →-hɒʊl ‖ -hoʊl **~s** z
sinless ˈsɪn ləs -lɪs **~ly** li **~ness** nəs nɪs
Sinnatt ˈsɪn ət
sinner ˈsɪn ə ‖ -ᵊr **~s** z
Sinn Fein ˌʃɪn ˈfeɪn —*Ir* Sinn Féin [ˌʃiːŋʲ ˈheːnʲ] **~er/s** ə/z ‖ -ᵊr/z
Sinnott ˈsɪn ət
Sino- ¦saɪn əʊ ‖ -oʊ — **Sino-Japanese** ˌsaɪn əʊ ˌdʒæp ə ˈniːz ‖ ˌ·oʊ- -ˈniːs
sinological ˌsaɪn əʊ ˈlɒdʒ ɪk ᵊl ◂ ˌsɪn- ‖ -ə ˈlɑːdʒ-
sinologist saɪ ˈnɒl ədʒ ɪst sɪ-, §sə-, §-əst ‖ -ˈnɑːl- **~s** s
sinologue ˈsaɪn əʊ lɒg ˈsɪn-, -ᵊl ɒg ‖ -ᵊl ɔːg -ɑːg **~s** z
sinology saɪ ˈnɒl ədʒ i sɪ-, §sə- ‖ -ˈnɑːl-
Sino-Tibetan ˌsaɪn əʊ tɪ ˈbet ᵊn ◂ ˌsɪn-, -tə'- ‖ ˌ·oʊ-
sinsemilla ˌsɪnᵗs ə ˈmɪl ə -ɪ-, -ˈmiːl-, -ˈmiː-, -jə
sinter ˈsɪnt ə ‖ ˈsɪnṱ ᵊr **~ed** d **sintering** ˈsɪnt ər ɪŋ ‖ ˈsɪnṱ- **~s** z
sinuosit|y ˌsɪn ju ˈɒs ət |i -ɪt i ‖ -ˈɑːs əṱ |i **~ies** iz
sinuous ˈsɪn ju‿əs **~ly** li **~ness** nəs nɪs
sinus ˈsaɪn əs **~es** ɪz əz
sinusitis ˌsaɪn ə ˈsaɪt ɪs §-əs ‖ -ˈsaɪṱ əs
sinusoid ˈsaɪn ə sɔɪd **~s** z
sinusoidal ˌsaɪn ə ˈsɔɪd ᵊl ◂ **~ly** i
Siobhan, Siobhán ʃə ˈvɔːn ʃɪ- ‖ -ˈvɑːn
Sion *'Zion'* ˈsaɪ‿ən ˈzaɪ‿
Sion, Siôn *male personal name, Welsh* ʃɔːn ‖ ʃɑːn
Sion *place in Switzerland* si ˈɒ̃ ‖ -ˈɔːn -ˈɑːn, -ˈoʊn —*Fr* [sjɔ̃]
Siouan ˈsuː‿ən
Sioux *sing.* suː **Sioux** *pl* suːz suː
Siouxsie ˈsuːz i
sip sɪp **sipped** sɪpt **sipping** ˈsɪp ɪŋ **sips** sɪps
siphon ˈsaɪf ᵊn **~ed** d **~ing** ‿ɪŋ **~s** z
siphonic saɪ ˈfɒn ɪk ‖ -ˈfɑːn-
siphonophore saɪ ˈfɒn ə fɔː ˈsɪf ən ə- ‖ -ˈfɑːn ə fɔːr -foʊr **~s** z
Siple ˈsaɪp ᵊl
Siqueiros sɪ ˈkeər ɒs ‖ -ˈkeɪ roʊs —*Sp* [si ˈkei ɾos]

sir, Sir *strong form* sɜː ‖ sɜ˞ː, *weak form* sə ‖ sᵊr —*The weak form is customary in BrE whenever this word is used with a name, as* Sir John; Sir Peter Smith. *Otherwise the strong form is usual:* yes, sir. *In AmE the weak form is little used.* **sirs** sɜːz ‖ sɜ˞ːz —*There is no weak form of the plural.*
sirdar, S~ ˈsɜːd ɑː sɜː ˈdɑː ‖ ˈsɜ˞ːd ɑːr **~s** z
sire ˈsaɪ‿ə ‖ ˈsaɪ‿ᵊr **sired** ˈsaɪ‿əd ‖ ˈsaɪ‿ᵊrd **sires** ˈsaɪ‿əz ‖ ˈsaɪ‿ᵊrz **siring** ˈsaɪ‿ər ɪŋ ‖ ˈsaɪ‿ᵊr ɪŋ
siree ˌsɜː ˈriː sə ˈriː ‖ sə ˈriː ˌsɜ˞ː ˈiː
siren ˈsaɪᵊr ən -ɪn **~s** z
sirenian saɪᵊ ˈriːn i‿ən **~s** z
Sirhowy sɜː ˈhaʊ‿i ‖ sɜ˞ː-
Sirius ˈsɪr i‿əs ˈsaɪᵊr-
sirloin ˈsɜː lɔɪn ‖ ˈsɜ˞ː- **~s** z **ˌsirloin ˈsteak**
sirocco sɪ ˈrɒk əʊ sə- ‖ -ˈrɑːk oʊ **~s** z
Siros ˈsɪər ɒs ‖ ˈsɪr ɑːs —*Gk* [ˈsi ɾos]
sirrah ˈsɪr ə
sirree ˌsɜː ˈriː sə- ‖ sə ˈriː ˌsɜ˞ː ˈiː
sis sɪs
sisal ˈsaɪs ᵊl ˈsaɪz-
siskin ˈsɪsk ɪn §-ən **~s** z
Sisley ˈsɪz li
Sissie ˈsɪs i
sissified ˈsɪs ɪ faɪd -ə-
Sissinghurst ˈsɪs ɪŋ hɜːst ‖ -hɜ˞ːst
Sisson ˈsɪs ᵊn
Sissons ˈsɪs ᵊnz
siss|y ˈsɪs |i **~ies** iz
sister, S~ ˈsɪst ə ‖ -ᵊr **~s** z
sisterhood ˈsɪst ə hʊd ‖ -ᵊr- **~s** z
sister-|in-law ˈsɪst ər‿ɪn ˌlɔː ˈsɪs tə-, §‿ən‿ˌ· ‖ -ᵊr- -ˌlɑː **sisters-~** ˈsɪst əz ‖ ˈsɪst ᵊrz
sist|erly ˈsɪst |ə li -|ᵊl i ‖ -|ᵊr li **~erliness** ə li nəs ᵊl i-, -nɪs ‖ ᵊr li nəs
Sistine ˈsɪst iːn -aɪn
sis|trum ˈsɪs |trəm **~tra** trə **~troid** trɔɪd **~trums** trəmz
siSwati sɪ ˈswɑːt i
Sisyphean ˌsɪs ɪ ˈfiː‿ən ◂ -ə-
Sisyphus ˈsɪs ɪf əs -əf-
sit sɪt **sat** sæt **sits** sɪts **sitting** ˈsɪt ɪŋ ‖ ˈsɪṱ ɪŋ
sitar sɪ ˈtɑː ˈsɪt ɑː ‖ sɪ ˈtɑːr —*Hindi* [sɪ t̪aːr] **~s** z
sitcom ˈsɪt kɒm ‖ -kɑːm **~s** z
sit-down ˈsɪt daʊn
site saɪt *(= sight, cite)* **sited** ˈsaɪt ɪd -əd ‖ ˈsaɪṱ əd **sites** saɪts **siting** ˈsaɪt ɪŋ ‖ ˈsaɪṱ ɪŋ
site-specific ˌsaɪt spə ˈsɪf ɪk ◂ -spɪ-
sit-in ˈsɪt ɪn ‖ ˈsɪṱ ɪn **~s** z
Sitka, sitka ˈsɪt kə
sitrep ˈsɪt rep **~s** s
sitter ˈsɪt ə ‖ ˈsɪṱ ᵊr **~s** z
sitting ˈsɪt ɪŋ ‖ ˈsɪṱ ɪŋ **~s** z **ˌSitting ˈBull**; **ˌsitting ˈduck**; **ˈsitting room**; **ˌsitting ˈtarget**; **ˌsitting ˈtenant**
Sittingbourne ˈsɪt ɪŋ bɔːn ‖ ˈsɪṱ ɪŋ bɔːrn -boʊrn
situ|ate *v* ˈsɪtʃ u |eɪt ˈsɪt ju-, §ˈsɪt u- **~ated** eɪt ɪd -əd ‖ eɪṱ əd **~ates** eɪts **~ating** eɪt ɪŋ ‖ eɪṱ ɪŋ

S

situate *adj* 'sɪtʃ u eɪt 'sɪt ju-, §'sɪt u-, -ət, -ɪt

SITUATION

1% 35% 64%
-tj- -tʃ- -t-
BrE

BrE -tʃ- by age
Percentage
50 40 30 20 10 0
Older ← Speakers → Younger

situation ˌsɪtʃ u 'eɪʃ ᵊn ˌsɪt ju-, §ˌsɪt u- — *Preference poll, BrE* tʃ *35%,* tj *64%,* t *1%.* **~al** ᵊl **~ally** ᵊl‿i **~s** z
ˌsituˌation 'comedy, ˌ.·'. . . ·; **ˌsitu'ation room**
sit-up 'sɪt ʌp ‖ 'sɪţ ʌp **~s** s
sit-upon 'sɪt ə ˌpɒn ‖ 'sɪţ ə ˌpɑːn **~s** z
Sitwell 'sɪt wəl -wel **~s** z
sitz sɪts *(= sits)*
'sitz bath
Siva 'ʃiːv ə 'ʃɪv-, 'siːv-, 'sɪv- —*Hindi* [ʃɪʋ]
Siwash, s~ 'saɪ wɒʃ -wɑːʃ -wɔːʃ
six sɪks **sixes** 'sɪks ɪz -əz
ˌSix 'Counties; **ˌSix ˌDay 'War**
sixer 'sɪks ə ‖ -ᵊr **~s** z
six-figure sɪks 'fɪg ə ‖ -jᵊr
sixfold 'sɪks fəʊld →-fɒʊld ‖ -foʊld
six-footer ˌsɪks 'fʊt ə ‖ -'fʊţ ᵊr **~s** z
sixgun 'sɪks gʌn **~s** z
sixish 'sɪks ɪʃ
six-pack 'sɪks pæk **~s** s
sixpenc|e 'sɪks pənᵗs **~es** ɪz əz
sixpenny 'sɪks pən i
six-shooter 'sɪks ˌʃuːt ə →'sɪkʃ-, ˌ.'. · ‖ -ˌʃuːţ ᵊr **~s** z
sixte sɪkst
sixteen ˌsɪks 'tiːn ◂ **~s** z
sixteenmo, 16mo ˌsɪks 'tiːn məʊ →'tiːm- ‖ -moʊ
sixteenth ˌsɪks 'tiːnᵗθ ◂ **~ly** li **~s** s
ˌsix'teenth note
sixth sɪksθ sɪkstθ, ⚠sɪkθ **sixths** sɪksθs sɪkstθs, ⚠sɪkθs —*but in casual speech both sing. and pl are sometimes* sɪks *or* sɪkst
'sixth form; **ˌsixth 'sense**
sixties 'sɪkst iz
sixtieth 'sɪkst i‿əθ ɪθ **~s** s
Sixtus 'sɪkst əs
sixt|y 'sɪkst |i **~ies** iz

sixty-four ˌsɪkst i 'fɔː ◂ ‖ -'fɔːr ◂ -'foʊr
ˌsixty-four ˌthousand ˌdollar 'question, -'. ˌ. ˌ. .
sixty-fourth ˌsɪkst i 'fɔːθ ◂ ‖ -'fɔːrθ ◂ -'foʊrθ **~s** s
sixty-nine ˌsɪkst i 'naɪn ◂
sizab|le 'saɪz əb |ᵊl **~leness** ᵊl nəs -nɪs **~ly** li
sizar 'saɪz ə ‖ -ᵊr **~s** z
size saɪz **sized** saɪzd **sizes** 'saɪz ɪz -əz **sizing** 'saɪz ɪŋ
sizeab|le 'saɪz əb |ᵊl **~leness** ᵊl nəs -nɪs **~ly** li
-sized 'saɪzd saɪzd — **medium-sized** ˌmiːd i‿əm 'saɪzd ◂
Sizer, Sizergh 'saɪz ə ‖ -ᵊr
Sizewell 'saɪz wəl -wel
sizzl|e 'sɪz ᵊl **~ed** d **~es** z **~ing/ly** ‿ɪŋ /li
sizzler 'sɪz ᵊl‿ə ‖ ər **~s** z
sjambok 'ʃæm bɒk -bʌk ‖ ʃæm 'bɑːk -'bʌk —*Afrikaans* ['ʃam bok] **~s** s
ska skɑː
skag skæg
Skagerrak 'skæg ə ræk —*Danish* ['sgaː ɣə ʁak, 'sga-]
Skagway 'skæg weɪ
skank skæŋk
skanky 'skæŋk i
Skara Brae ˌskær ə 'breɪ ‖ ˌsker-
skat skæt ‖ skɑːt skæt —*Ger* [skaːt]
skate skeɪt **skated** 'skeɪt ɪd -əd ‖ 'skeɪţ əd **skates** skeɪts **skating** 'skeɪt ɪŋ ‖ 'skeɪţ ɪŋ
skateboard 'skeɪt bɔːd ‖ -bɔːrd -boʊrd **~er/s** ə/z ‖ ᵊr/z **~ing** ɪŋ **~s** z
skater 'skeɪt ə ‖ 'skeɪţ ᵊr **~s** z
skatole 'skæt əʊl →-ɒʊl ‖ -oʊl
skean skiːn 'skiː‿ən **skeans** skiːnz 'skiː‿ənz
ˌskean 'dhu duː
Skeat skiːt
skedaddl|e skɪ 'dæd ᵊl skə- **~ed** d **~es** z **~ing** ‿ɪŋ
skeet skiːt
'skeet ˌshooting
skeeter 'skiːt ə ‖ 'skiːţᵊr **~s** z
skeeve skiːv **skeeved** skiːvd **skeeves** skiːvz **skeeving** 'skiːv ɪŋ
Skeffington 'skef ɪŋ tən
skeg skeg **skegs** skegz
Skegness ˌskeg 'nes ◂
skein skeɪn **skeins** skeɪnz
skeletal 'skel ɪt ᵊl -ət-; skɪ 'liːt-, skə- ‖ 'skel əţ ᵊl skə 'liːţ ᵊl **~ly** i
skeleton 'skel ɪt ən -ət-, ⚠-ɪnt- ‖ -ᵊn **~s** z
'skeleton key
Skelmersdale 'skelm əz deɪᵊl ‖ -ᵊrz- —*locally also* 'skem-
Skelton 'skelt ən
skep skep **skeps** skeps
skeptic, S~ 'skept ɪk **~s** s
skeptical 'skept ɪk ᵊl **~ly** ‿i **~ness** nəs nɪs
skepticism 'skept ɪ ˌsɪz əm -ə-
Skerritt 'sker ɪt §-ət
skerr|y 'sker |i **~ies** iz
sketch sketʃ **sketched** sketʃt **sketches** 'sketʃ ɪz -əz **sketching** 'sketʃ ɪŋ

S

sketchbook 'sketʃ bʊk §-bu:k
sketchi... *—see* **sketchy**
Sketchley 'sketʃ li
sketchpad 'sketʃ pæd **~s** z
sketch|y 'sketʃ |i **~ier** i‿ə ‖ i‿ᵊr **~iest** i‿ɪst i‿əst **~ily** ɪ li əl i **~iness** i nəs i nɪs
skew skju: **skewed** skju:d **skewing** 'skju: ɪŋ **skews** skju:z
skewbald 'skju: bɔ:ld ‖ -bɑ:ld **~s** z
Skewen 'skju:‿ɪn §‿ən
skewer 'skju:‿ə ‖ ‿ᵊr **~ed** d **skewering** 'skju:‿ər ɪŋ **~s** z
skewness 'skju: nəs -nɪs
skew-whiff ˌskju: 'wɪf ◂ -'hwɪf
ski ski: *—In 1935 BBC announcers were recommended to say* ʃi:. *Yet this form is now entirely obsolete.* **skied** ski:d **skiing** 'ski: ɪŋ **skis** ski:z
'ski jump; **'ski ˌjumping**; **'ski lift**; **'ski plane**; **'ski pole**; **'ski stick**
skibob 'ski: bɒb ‖ -bɑ:b **~ber/s** ə/z ‖ ᵊr/z **~bing** ɪŋ **~s** z
skid skɪd **skidded** 'skɪd ɪd -əd **skidding** 'skɪd ɪŋ **skids** skɪdz
ˌskid 'row
Skiddaw 'skɪd ɔ: ‖ -ɑ:
skiddoo skɪ 'du: **~ed** d **~ing** ɪŋ **~s** z
skidlid 'skɪd lɪd **~s** z
Skidmore 'skɪd mɔ: ‖ -mɔ:r
skidoo skɪ 'du: **~ed** d **~ing** ɪŋ **~s** z
skidpan 'skɪd pæn →'skɪb- **~s** z
skidproof 'skɪd pru:f §-prʊf
skied *past of* **sky** skaɪd
skied *past of* **ski** ski:d
skier 'ski:‿ə ‖ ᵊr **~s** z
skies skaɪz
skiff skɪf **skiffs** skɪfs
skiffle 'skɪf ᵊl
skijoring 'ski: ˌdʒɔ:r ɪŋ ˌ·'·· ‖ ˌdʒoʊr-
skilful 'skɪl fᵊl -fʊl **~ly** ‿i **~ness** nəs nɪs
skill skɪl **skilled** skɪld **skills** skɪlz
skillet 'skɪl ɪt -ət **~s** s
skillful 'skɪl fᵊl -fʊl **~ly** ‿i **~ness** nəs nɪs
skilly 'skɪl i
skim skɪm **skimmed** skɪmd **skimming/s** 'skɪm ɪŋ/z **skims** skɪmz
ˌskimmed 'milk, **ˌskim 'milk**
skimmer 'skɪm ə ‖ -ᵊr **~s** z
skimmia 'skɪm i‿ə **~s** z
skimp skɪmp **skimped** skɪmpt **skimping** 'skɪmp ɪŋ **skimps** skɪmps
skimp|y 'skɪmp |i **~ier** i‿ə ‖ i‿ᵊr **~iest** i‿ɪst i‿əst **~ily** ɪ li əl i **~iness** i nəs i nɪs
skin skɪn **skinned** skɪnd **skinning** 'skɪn ɪŋ **skins** skɪnz
'skin ˌdiver; **'skin ˌdiving**; **'skin flick**; **'skin graft**
skincare 'skɪn keə →'skɪŋ- ‖ -ker
skin-deep ˌskɪn 'di:p ◂
skin-|dive 'skɪn |daɪv **~dived** daɪvd **~dives** daɪvz **~diving** daɪv ɪŋ **~dove** dəʊv ‖ doʊv
skinflint 'skɪn flɪnt **~s** s
skinful 'skɪn fʊl **~s** z
skinhead 'skɪn hed **~s** z
skink skɪŋk **skinks** skɪŋks
skinless 'skɪn ləs -lɪs
skinlike 'skɪn laɪk
skinn... *—see* **skin**
-skinned 'skɪnd — **thick-skinned** ˌθɪk 'skɪnd ◂
Skinner, S~ 'skɪn ə ‖ -ᵊr **~s, ~'s** z
Skinnerian skɪ 'nɪər i‿ən ‖ -'nɪr- -'ner- **~s** z
skinn|y 'skɪn |i **~ier** i‿ə ‖ i‿ᵊr **~iest** i‿ɪst i‿əst **~iness** i nəs i nɪs
skinny-dip 'skɪn i dɪp **~ped** t **~per/s** ə/z ‖ ᵊr/z **~ping** ɪŋ **~s** s
skint skɪnt
skin-tight ˌskɪn 'taɪt ◂
skip skɪp **skipped** skɪpt **skipping** 'skɪp ɪŋ **skips** skɪps
skipjack 'skɪp dʒæk **~s** s
skipper 'skɪp ə ‖ -ᵊr **~ed** d **skippering** 'skɪp ər‿ɪŋ **~s** z
skipping-rope 'skɪp ɪŋ rəʊp ‖ -roʊp **~s** s
Skippy 'skɪp i
Skipton 'skɪp tən
skirl skɜ:l ‖ skɜ˞:l **skirled** skɜ:ld ‖ skɜ˞:ld **skirling** 'skɜ:l ɪŋ ‖ 'skɜ˞:l ɪŋ **skirls** skɜ:lz ‖ skɜ˞:lz
skirmish 'skɜ:m ɪʃ ‖ 'skɜ˞:m- **~ed** t **~er/s** ə/z ‖ -ᵊr/z **~es** ɪz əz **~ing** ɪŋ
skirret 'skɪr ɪt -ət
skirt skɜ:t ‖ skɜ˞:t **skirted** 'skɜ:t ɪd -əd ‖ 'skɜ˞:ţ əd **skirting/s** 'skɜ:t ɪŋ/z ‖ 'skɜ˞:ţ ɪŋ/z **skirts** skɜ:ts ‖ skɜ˞:ts
'skirting board
skis ski:z
skit skɪt **skits** skɪts
skite skaɪt **skited** 'skaɪt ɪd -əd ‖ 'skaɪţ- **skites** skaɪts **skiting** 'skaɪt ɪŋ ‖ 'skaɪţ-
skitter 'skɪt ə ‖ 'skɪţ ᵊr **~ed** d **skittering** 'skɪt‿ər ɪŋ ‖ 'skɪţ ər ɪŋ **~s** z
skittish 'skɪt ɪʃ ‖ 'skɪţ ɪʃ **~ly** li **~ness** nəs nɪs
skittl|e 'skɪt ᵊl ‖ 'skɪţ ᵊl **~ed** d **~es** z **~ing** ‿ɪŋ
skive skaɪv **skived** skaɪvd **skives** skaɪvz **skiving** 'skaɪv ɪŋ
skiver 'skaɪv ə ‖ -ᵊr **~s** z
skivv|y 'skɪv |i **~ied** id **~ies** iz **~ying** i‿ɪŋ
skiwear 'ski: weə ‖ -wer -wær
skoal skəʊl →skɒʊl ‖ skoʊl
Skoda, Škoda *tdmk* 'skəʊd ə 'ʃkəʊd- ‖ 'skoʊd ə *—Czech* ['ʃko da] **~s** z
Skokholm 'skɒk həʊm 'skəʊk əm ‖ 'skɑ:k hoʊm
Skokie 'skəʊk i ‖ 'skoʊk i
skol, Skol *tdmk* skɒl skəʊl ‖ skoʊl
Skomer 'skəʊm ə ‖ 'skoʊm ᵊr
Skopje 'skɒp ji -jeɪ ‖ 'skɑ:p- 'skɔ:p-, skoʊp- *—Macedonian* ['skɔp jɛ], *Serbian* Skoplje ['skɔp lʲɛ]
Skrine *(i)* skri:n, *(ii)* skraɪn
skua 'skju:‿ə **~s** z
Skues skju:z
skulduggery skʌl 'dʌg ər i
skulk skʌlk **skulked** skʌlkt **skulking** 'skʌlk ɪŋ **skulks** skʌlks

S

skull skʌl **skulls** skʌlz
skullcap ˈskʌl kæp **~s** s
skullduggery skʌl ˈdʌg ər i
skunk skʌŋk **skunks** skʌŋ*k*s
ˈ**skunk** ˌ**cabbage**
skunkworks ˈskʌŋk wɜːks ‖ -wɜːks
sky skaɪ **skied** skaɪd **skies** skaɪz **skying** ˈskaɪ ɪŋ
sky-blue ˌskaɪ ˈbluː ◂
skycap ˈskaɪ kæp **~s** s
skydiv|er/s ˈskaɪ ˌdaɪv |ə/z ‖ -|ᵊr/z **~ing** ɪŋ
Skye skaɪ
sky-high ˌskaɪ ˈhaɪ ◂
skyhook ˈskaɪ hʊk **~s** s
skyjack ˈskaɪ dʒæk **~ed** t **~er/s** ə/z ‖ ᵊr/z **~ing** ɪŋ **~s** s
Skylab ˈskaɪ læb
skylark ˈskaɪ lɑːk ‖ -lɑːrk **~ed** t **~ing** ɪŋ **~s** s
skylight ˈskaɪ laɪt **~s** s
skyline ˈskaɪ laɪn
Skype skaɪp
skyrock|et ˈskaɪ ˌrɒk |ɪt §-ət ‖ -ˌrɑːk |ət **~eted** ɪt ɪd §ət-, -əd ‖ əṭ əd **~eting** ɪt ɪŋ §ət- ‖ əṭ ɪŋ **~ets** ɪts §əts ‖ əts
skyscape ˈskaɪ skeɪp **~s** s
skyscraper ˈskaɪ ˌskreɪp ə ‖ -ᵊr **~s** z
Skywalker ˈskaɪ ˌwɔːk ə ‖ -ᵊr -ˌwɑːk-
skyward ˈskaɪ wəd ‖ -wᵊrd **~s** z
skywriting ˈskaɪ ˌraɪt ɪŋ ‖ -ˌraɪṭ ɪŋ
slab slæb **slabbed** slæbd **slabbing** ˈslæb ɪŋ **slabs** slæbz
ˈ**slab cake**
Slabbert ˈslæb ət ‖ -ᵊrt
slack, Slack slæk **slacked** slækt **slacker** ˈslæk ə ‖ -ᵊr **slackest** ˈslæk ɪst -əst **slacking** ˈslæk ɪŋ **slacks** slæks
slacken ˈslæk ən **~ed** d **~ing** ˌɪŋ **~s** z
slacker ˈslæk ə ‖ -ᵊr **~s** z
slack-jawed ˌslæk ˈdʒɔːd ◂ ‖ -ˈdʒɑːd ◂
slack|ly ˈslæk |li **~ness** nəs nɪs
Slade sleɪd
slag slæg **slagged** slægd **slagging** ˈslæg ɪŋ **slags** slægz
slagg|y ˈslæg| i **~ier** i‿ə ‖ i‿ᵊr **~iest** i‿ɪst i‿əst
slagheap ˈslæg hiːp **~s** s
slain sleɪn
slainte, slàinte ˈslɑːntʃ ə ˈslɑːndʒ ə, ˈslɑːn jə —*ScG* [ˈsɫaː ɲə]
ˌ**slàinte** ˈ**mhath** vaː —*ScG* [va]
Slaithwaite ˈslæθ weɪt —*locally also* ˈslaʊ ɪt
slake sleɪk **slaked** sleɪkt **slakes** sleɪks **slaking** ˈsleɪk ɪŋ
slalom ˈslɑːl əm **~s** z
slam slæm **slammed** slæmd **slamming** ˈslæm ɪŋ **slams** slæmz
slam-bang ˌslæm ˈbæŋ
slammer ˈslæm ə ‖ -ᵊr **~s** z
slander ˈslɑːnd ə §ˈslænd- ‖ ˈslænd ᵊr **~ed** d **slandering** ˈslɑːnd‿ər ɪŋ §ˈslænd‿ ‖ ˈslænd‿ər ɪŋ **~s** z
slanderer ˈslɑːnd‿ər ə §ˈslænd‿ ‖ ˈslænd‿ər ᵊr **~s** z
slanderous ˈslɑːnd‿ər əs §ˈslænd‿ ‖ ˈslænd‿ər əs **~ly** li **~ness** nəs nɪs
slang slæŋ **slanged** slæŋd **slanging** ˈslæŋ ɪŋ **slangs** slæŋz
ˈ**slanging match**
slang|y ˈslæŋ |i **~ily** ɪ li əl i **~iness** i nəs i nɪs
slant slɑːnt §slænt ‖ slænt **slanted** ˈslɑːnt ɪd §ˈslænt-, -əd ‖ ˈslænṭ əd **slanting/ly** ˈslɑːnt ɪŋ /li §ˈslænt- ‖ ˈslænṭ ɪŋ /li **slants** slɑːn*t*s §slæn*t*s ‖ slæn*t*s
slant|ways ˈslɑːnt weɪz §ˈslænt- ‖ ˈslænt- **~wise** waɪz
slap slæp **slapped** slæpt **slapping** ˈslæp ɪŋ **slaps** slæps
slap-bang ˌslæp ˈbæŋ
slapdash ˈslæp dæʃ ˌˈ·
slaphapp|y ˈslæp ˌhæp |i ˌ·ˈ·· **~ier** i‿ə ‖ i‿ᵊr **~iest** i‿ɪst i‿əst
slaphead ˈslæp hed **~s** z
slapjack ˈslæp dʒæk **~s** s
slapper ˈslæp ə ‖ -ᵊr **~s** z
slapstick ˈslæp stɪk **~s** s
slap-up ˈslæp ʌp ˌ·ˈ·
slash slæʃ **slashed** slæʃt **slashes** ˈslæʃ ɪz -əz **slashing** ˈslæʃ ɪŋ
ˈ**slash mark**
slash-and-burn ˌslæʃ ᵊn ˈbɜːn →ᵊm- ‖ -ˈbɜːn
slasher ˈslæʃ ə ‖ -ᵊr **~s** z
slat slæt **slats** slæts **slatted** ˈslæt ɪd -əd ‖ ˈslæṭ əd **slatting** ˈslæt ɪŋ ‖ ˈslæṭ ɪŋ
slate sleɪt **slated** ˈsleɪt ɪd -əd ‖ ˈsleɪṭ əd **slates** sleɪts **slating** ˈsleɪt ɪŋ ‖ ˈsleɪṭ ɪŋ
slater, S~ ˈsleɪt ə ‖ ˈsleɪṭ ᵊr **~s** z
slather ˈslæð ə ‖ -ᵊr **~ed** d **slathering** ˈslæð ər‿ɪŋ **~s** z
slattern ˈslæt ᵊn -ɜːn ‖ ˈslæṭ ᵊrn **~liness** li nəs -nɪs **~ly** li **~s** z
Slattery ˈslæt ər i ‖ ˈslæṭ-
slaty ˈsleɪt i ‖ ˈsleɪṭ i
slaughter, S~ ˈslɔːt ə ‖ ˈslɔːṭ ᵊr ˈslɑːṭ- **~ed** d **slaughtering** ˈslɔːt‿ər ɪŋ ‖ ˈslɔːṭ ər ɪŋ ˈslɑːṭ- **~s** z
slaughterer ˈslɔːt ər ə ‖ ˈslɔːṭ ᵊr ər ˈslɑːṭ- **~s** z
slaughter|house ˈslɔːt ə |haʊs ‖ ˈslɔːṭ ᵊr- ˈslɑːṭ- **~houses** ˌhaʊz ɪz -əz
Slav slɑːv ‖ slæv **Slavs** slɑːvz ‖ slævz
slave sleɪv **slaved** sleɪvd **slaves** sleɪvz **slaving** ˈsleɪv ɪŋ
ˈ**slave** ˌ**driver**; ˌ**slave** ˈ**labour**; ˈ**slave trade**; ˈ**slave** ˌ**traffic**
slaver *v 'drool'; n 'saliva'* ˈslæv ə ˈsleɪv- ‖ ˈslæv ᵊr ˈsleɪv-, ˈslɑːv- **~ed** d **slavering** ˈslæv ər‿ɪŋ ˈsleɪv- ‖ ˈsleɪv-, ˈslɑːv- **~s** z
slaver *n 'one dealing in slaves'* ˈsleɪv ə ‖ -ᵊr **~s** z
slavery ˈsleɪv ər‿i
slavey ˈsleɪv i **~s** z
Slavic ˈslɑːv ɪk ˈslæv-
slavish ˈsleɪv ɪʃ **~ly** li **~ness** nəs nɪs
Slavo- ¦slɑːv əʊ ¦slæv- ‖ -oʊ — **Slavophile** ˈslɑːv əʊ faɪᵊl ˈslæv-, -fɪl ‖ -oʊ-
Slavonia slə ˈvəʊn i‿ə ‖ -ˈvoʊn-
Slavonic slə ˈvɒn ɪk slæ- ‖ -ˈvɑːn ɪk

slaw slɔː ‖ slɑː
slay sleɪ **slain** sleɪn **slayed** sleɪd **slaying** 'sleɪ ɪŋ **slays** sleɪz **slew** sluː
slayer 'sleɪ ə ‖ -ᵊr **~s** z
Slazenger *tdmk* 'slæz ɪndʒ ə -əndʒ- ‖ -ᵊr
Sleaford 'sliː fəd ‖ -fᵊrd
sleaze sliːz
sleaze|bag/s 'sliːz| bæg/z **~ball/s** bɔːl/z ‖ bɑːl/z
sleaz|y 'sliːz |i **~ier** i‿ə ‖ i‿ᵊr **~iest** i‿ɪst i‿əst **~ily** ɪ li əl i **~iness** i nəs i nɪs
sled sled **sledded** 'sled ɪd -əd **sledding** 'sled ɪŋ **sleds** sledz
sledge sledʒ **sledged** sledʒd **sledges** 'sledʒ ɪz -əz **sledging** 'sledʒ ɪŋ
sledgehammer 'sledʒ ˌhæm ə ‖ -ᵊr **~s** z
sleek sliːk **sleeked** sliːkt **sleeker** 'sliːk ə ‖ -ᵊr **sleekest** 'sliːk ɪst -əst **sleeking** 'sliːk ɪŋ **sleeks** sliːks
sleek|ly 'sliːk |li **~ness** nəs nɪs
sleep sliːp **sleeping** 'sliːp ɪŋ **sleeps** sliːps **slept** slept
'sleeping bag; **'sleeping car**; **'sleeping draught**; **ˌsleeping 'partner** *'inactive business partner'*; **'sleeping pill**; **ˌsleeping po'liceman**; **'sleeping ˌsickness**
Sleepeezee *tdmk* ˌsliːp 'iːz i
sleeper 'sliːp ə ‖ -ᵊr **~s** z
sleepi... —*see* **sleepy**
sleepless 'sliːp ləs -lɪs **~ly** li **~ness** nəs nɪs
sleepover 'sliːp ˌəʊv ə ‖ -ˌoʊv ᵊr **~s** z
sleepwalk 'sliːp wɔːk ‖ -wɑːk **~ed** t **~er/s** ə/z ‖ ᵊr/z **~ing** ɪŋ **~s** s
sleepwear 'sliːp weə ‖ -wer -wær
sleep|y 'sliːp |i **~ier** i‿ə ‖ i‿ᵊr **~iest** i‿ɪst i‿əst **~ily** ɪ li əl i **~iness** i nəs i nɪs
sleepyhead 'sliːp i hed **~s** z
sleet sliːt **sleeted** 'sliːt ɪd -əd ‖ 'sliːţ əd **sleeting** 'sliːt ɪŋ ‖ 'sliːţ ɪŋ **sleets** sliːts
sleety 'sliːt i ‖ 'sliːţ i
sleeve sliːv **sleeved** sliːvd **sleeves** sliːvz **sleeving** 'sliːv ɪŋ
-sleeved 'sliːvd — **short-sleeved** ˌʃɔːt 'sliːvd ◂ ‖ ˌʃɔːrt-
sleeveless 'sliːv ləs -lɪs
sleigh sleɪ *(= slay)* **sleighed** sleɪd **sleighing** 'sleɪ ɪŋ **sleighs** sleɪz
sleighbell 'sleɪ bel **~s** z
sleight slaɪt *(= slight)*
slend|er 'slend |ə ‖ -|ᵊr **~erer** ər ə ‖ ᵊr ər **~erest** ər ɪst -əst
slenderis|e, slenderiz|e 'slend ə raɪz **~ed** d **~es** ɪz əz **~ing** ɪŋ
slender|ly 'slend ə |li ‖ -ᵊr- **~ness** nəs nɪs
slept slept
Slessor 'sles ə ‖ -ᵊr
sleuth sluːθ sljuːθ **sleuthed** sluːθt sljuːθt **sleuthing** 'sluːθ ɪŋ 'sljuːθ- **sleuths** sluːθs sljuːθs
sleuthhound 'sluːθ haʊnd 'sljuːθ- **~s** z
slew sluː sljuː **slewed** sluːd sljuːd **slewing** 'sluː ɪŋ 'sljuː- **slews** sluːz sljuːz

slice slaɪs **sliced** slaɪst **slices** 'slaɪs ɪz -əz **slicing** 'slaɪs ɪŋ
ˌsliced 'bread
slice-of-life ˌslaɪs əv 'laɪf
slicer 'slaɪs ə ‖ -ᵊr **~s** z
slick slɪk **slicked** slɪkt **slicker** 'slɪk ə ‖ 'slɪk ᵊr **slickest** 'slɪk ɪst -əst **slicking** 'slɪk ɪŋ **slicks** slɪks
slickenside 'slɪk ən saɪd →-ŋ- **~s** z
slicker 'slɪk ə ‖ -ᵊr **~s** z
slick|ly 'slɪk |li **~ness** nəs nɪs
slide slaɪd **slid** slɪd **slides** slaɪdz **sliding** 'slaɪd ɪŋ
'slide rule; **'slide valve**; **ˌsliding 'door**; **ˌsliding 'scale**
slider 'slaɪd ə ‖ -ᵊr **~s** z
Slieve sliːv
slight slaɪt **slighted** 'slaɪt ɪd -əd ‖ 'slaɪţ əd **slighter** 'slaɪt ə ‖ 'slaɪţ ᵊr **slightest** 'slaɪt ɪst -əst ‖ 'slaɪţ əst **slighting/ly** 'slaɪt ɪŋ /li ‖ 'slaɪţ ɪŋ /li **slights** slaɪts
slightly 'slaɪt li
Sligo 'slaɪg əʊ ‖ -oʊ
slily 'slaɪ li
slim, Slim slɪm **slimmed** slɪmd **slimmer** 'slɪm ə ‖ -ᵊr **slimmest** 'slɪm ɪst -əst **slimming** 'slɪm ɪŋ **slims** slɪmz
Slimbridge 'slɪm brɪdʒ
Slimcea *tdmk* 'slɪm si‿ə
slime slaɪm **slimed** slaɪmd **slimes** slaɪmz **sliming** 'slaɪm ɪŋ
slimeball 'slaɪm bɔːl ‖ -bɑːl **~s** z
slimi... —*see* **slimy**
slimline 'slɪm laɪn
slim|ly 'slɪm |li **~ness** nəs nɪs
slimm... —*see* **slim**
slimmed-down ˌslɪm*d* 'daʊn ◂
slimmer 'slɪm ə ‖ -ᵊr **~s** z
slim|y 'slaɪm |i **~ier** i‿ə ‖ i‿ᵊr **~iest** i‿ɪst i‿əst **~ily** ɪ li əl i **~iness** i nəs i nɪs
sling slɪŋ **slinging** 'slɪŋ ɪŋ **slings** slɪŋz **slung** slʌŋ
slingback 'slɪŋ bæk **~s** s
slinger 'slɪŋ ə ‖ -ᵊr **~s** z
slingshot 'slɪŋ ʃɒt ‖ -ʃɑːt **~s** s
slink slɪŋk **slinking** 'slɪŋk ɪŋ **slinks** slɪŋ*k*s **slunk** slʌŋk
slink|y 'slɪŋk |i **~ier** i‿ə ‖ i‿ᵊr **~iest** i‿ɪst i‿əst **~ily** ɪ li əl i **~iness** i nəs i nɪs
slip slɪp **slipped** slɪpt **slipping** 'slɪp ɪŋ **slips** slɪps
ˌslipped 'disc; **'slip road**
slipcas|e 'slɪp keɪs **~es** ɪz əz
slipcover 'slɪp ˌkʌv ə ‖ -ᵊr **~s** z
slipknot 'slɪp nɒt ‖ -nɑːt **~s** s
slip-on 'slɪp ɒn ‖ -ɑːn -ɔːn **~s** z
slipover 'slɪp ˌəʊv ə ‖ -ˌoʊv ᵊr **~s** z
slipp... —*see* **slip**
slippag|e 'slɪp ɪdʒ **~es** ɪz əz
slipper 'slɪp ə ‖ -ᵊr **~s** z
slipper|y 'slɪp ər‿|i **~ier** i‿ə ‖ i‿ᵊr **~iest** i‿ɪst i‿əst **~ily** əl i ɪ li **~iness** i nəs i nɪs

S

slipp|y ˈslɪp |i **~ier** i‿ə ‖ i‿ᵊr **~iest** i‿ɪst i‿əst **~iness** i nəs i nɪs
slipshod ˈslɪp ʃɒd ‖ -ʃɑːd
slipstitch ˈslɪp stɪtʃ **~ed** t **~es** ɪz əz **~ing** ɪŋ
slipstream ˈslɪp striːm **~s** z
slip-up ˈslɪp ʌp **~s** s
slipway ˈslɪp weɪ **~s** z
slit slɪt **slits** slɪts **slitting** ˈslɪt ɪŋ ‖ ˈslɪţ ɪŋ
slither ˈslɪð ə ‖ -ᵊr **~ed** d **slithering** ˈslɪð ər‿ɪŋ **~s** z
slithery ˈslɪð ər‿i
sliver ˈslɪv ə ‖ -ᵊr —*but in some rare technical senses* ˈslaɪv- **~ed** d **slivering** ˈslɪv ər‿ɪŋ **~s** z
slivovitz ˈslɪv ə vɪts ˈsliːv-
Sliwa ˈsliː wə
Sloan, Sloane sləʊn ‖ sloʊn **Sloanes, Sloan's** sləʊnz ‖ sloʊnz
ˌSloane ˈRanger; ˌSloane ˈSquare
slob slɒb ‖ slɑːb **slobs** slɒbz ‖ slɑːbz
slobber ˈslɒb ə ‖ ˈslɑːb ᵊr **~ed** d **slobbering** ˈslɒb ər‿ɪŋ ‖ ˈslɑːb- **~s** z
slobberer ˈslɒb ər ə ‖ ˈslɑːb ᵊr ər **~s** z
slobber|y ˈslɒb ər |i ‖ ˈslɑːb- **~iness** i nəs i nɪs
slobbish ˈslɒb ɪʃ ‖ ˈslɑːb-
Slocombe, Slocum ˈsləʊk əm ‖ ˈsloʊk-
sloe sləʊ ‖ sloʊ *(= slow)* **sloes** sləʊz ‖ sloʊz
sloe-eyed ˌsləʊ ˈaɪd ◂ ˈ· · ‖ ˌsloʊ-
slog slɒg ‖ slɑːg **slogged** slɒgd ‖ slɑːgd **slogging** ˈslɒg ɪŋ ‖ ˈslɑːg ɪŋ **slogs** slɒgz ‖ slɑːgz
slogan ˈsləʊg ən ‖ ˈsloʊg ən **~s** z
sloganeer ˌsləʊg ə ˈnɪə ‖ ˌsloʊg ə ˈnɪᵊr **~ed** d **sloganeering** ˌsləʊg ə ˈnɪər ɪŋ ‖ ˌsloʊg ə ˈnɪr ɪŋ **~s** z
slogger ˈslɒg ə ‖ ˈslɑːg ᵊr **~s** z
Sloman ˈsləʊ mən ‖ ˈsloʊ-
slo-mo ˌsləʊ ˈməʊ ‖ ˌsloʊ ˈmoʊ
sloop sluːp **sloops** sluːps
slop slɒp ‖ slɑːp **slopped** slɒpt ‖ slɑːpt **slopping** ˈslɒp ɪŋ ‖ ˈslɑːp ɪŋ **slops** slɒps ‖ slɑːps
slope sləʊp ‖ sloʊp **sloped** sləʊpt ‖ sloʊpt **slopes** sləʊps ‖ sloʊps **sloping/ly** ˈsləʊp ɪŋ /li ‖ ˈsloʊp ɪŋ /li
slopp|y ˈslɒp |i ‖ ˈslɑːp |i **~ier** i‿ə ‖ i‿ᵊr **~iest** i‿ɪst i‿əst **~ily** ɪ li əl i **~iness** i nəs i nɪs
slosh slɒʃ ‖ slɑːʃ **sloshed** slɒʃt ‖ slɑːʃt **sloshes** ˈslɒʃ ɪz -əz ‖ ˈslɑːʃ əz **sloshing** ˈslɒʃ ɪŋ ‖ ˈslɑːʃ ɪŋ
slosh|y ˈslɒʃ |i ‖ ˈslɑːʃ |i **~ier** i‿ə ‖ i‿ᵊr **~iest** i‿ɪst i‿əst **~ily** ɪ li əl i **~iness** i nəs i nɪs
slot slɒt ‖ slɑːt **slots** slɒts ‖ slɑːts **slotted** ˈslɒt ɪd -əd ‖ ˈslɑːţ əd **slotting** ˈslɒt ɪŋ ‖ ˈslɑːţ ɪŋ
ˈslot maˌchine
sloth sləʊθ §slɒθ ‖ slɔːθ slɑːθ, sloʊθ **sloths** sləʊθs §slɒθs ‖ slɔːθs slɑːθs, sloʊθs
slothful ˈsləʊθ fᵊl ˈslɒθ-, -fʊl ‖ ˈslɔːθ- ˈslɑːθ-, ˈsloʊθ- **~ly** ‿i **~ness** nəs nɪs
slouch slaʊtʃ **slouched** slaʊtʃt **slouches** ˈslaʊtʃ ɪz -əz **slouching/ly** ˈslaʊtʃ ɪŋ /li
ˌslouch ˈhat
slouch|y ˈslaʊtʃ |i **~ily** ɪ li əl i **~iness** i nəs i nɪs
slough *v; n 'cast-off skin'* slʌf **sloughed** slʌft **sloughing** ˈslʌf ɪŋ **sloughs** slʌfs
slough *n 'mud, marsh, swamp'* slaʊ ‖ sluː slaʊ *(*) —Some Americans make a distinction between* sluː *in the literal sense and* slaʊ *in the figurative* (**ˌslough of deˈspond**). **sloughs** slaʊz ‖ sluːz slaʊz
Slough *place in Berks (formerly Bucks)* slaʊ
Slovak ˈsləʊv æk -ɑːk ‖ ˈsloʊv- **~s** s
Slovakia sləʊ ˈvæk i‿ə -ˈvɑːk- ‖ sloʊ-
sloven ˈslʌv ᵊn **~s** z
Slovene ˈsləʊv iːn sləʊ ˈviːn ‖ ˈsloʊv- **~s** z
Sloveni|a sləʊ ˈviːn i‿|ə ‖ sloʊ- **~an/s** ən/z
sloven|ly ˈslʌv ᵊn |li **~liness** li nəs -nɪs
Slovo ˈsləʊv əʊ ‖ ˈsloʊv oʊ
slow sləʊ ‖ sloʊ **slowed** sləʊd ‖ sloʊd **slower** ˈsləʊ ə ‖ ˈsloʊ ᵊr **slowest** ˈsləʊ ɪst -əst ‖ ˈsloʊ əst **slowing** ˈsləʊ ɪŋ ‖ ˈsloʊ ɪŋ **slows** sləʊz ‖ sloʊz
ˌslow ˈmotion
slowcoach ˈsləʊ kəʊtʃ ‖ ˈsloʊ koʊtʃ **~es** ɪz əz
slowdown ˈsləʊ daʊn ‖ ˈsloʊ- **~s** z
slowly ˈsləʊ li ‖ ˈsloʊ li
slow-motion ˌsləʊ ˈməʊʃ ᵊn ‖ ˌsloʊ ˈmoʊʃ ᵊn ◂
slow-moving ˌsləʊ ˈmuːv ɪŋ ◂ ‖ ˌsloʊ-
slowness ˈsləʊ nəs -nɪs ‖ ˈsloʊ nəs
slowpitch ˈsləʊ pɪtʃ ‖ ˈsloʊ-
slowpoke ˈsləʊ pəʊk ‖ ˈsloʊ poʊk **~s** s
slow-witted ˌsləʊ ˈwɪt ɪd ◂ -əd ‖ ˌsloʊ ˈwɪţ əd ◂
slowworm ˈsləʊ wɜːm ‖ ˈsloʊ wɜːm **~s** z
slub slʌb **slubbed** slʌbd **slubbing** ˈslʌb ɪŋ **slubs** slʌbz
sludge slʌdʒ
sludgy ˈslʌdʒ i
slue sluː **slued** sluːd **slues** sluːz **sluing** ˈsluː ɪŋ
slug slʌg **slugged** slʌgd **slugging** ˈslʌg ɪŋ **slugs** slʌgz
slugfest ˈslʌg fest **~s** s
sluggard ˈslʌg əd ‖ -ᵊrd **~ly** li **~s** z
slugger ˈslʌg ə ‖ -ᵊr **~s** z
sluggish ˈslʌg ɪʃ **~ly** li **~ness** nəs nɪs
sluice sluːs **sluiced** sluːst **sluices** ˈsluːs ɪz -əz **sluicing** ˈsluːs ɪŋ
sluicegate ˈsluːs geɪt **~s** s
sluiceway ˈsluːs weɪ **~s** z
slum slʌm **slummed** slʌmd **slumming** ˈslʌm ɪŋ **slums** slʌmz
ˈslum ˌclearance; ˈslum ˌdweller
slumber ˈslʌm bə ‖ -bᵊr **~ed** d **slumbering** ˈslʌm bər‿ɪŋ **~s** z
slumberer ˈslʌm bər‿ə ‖ -bᵊr ər **~s** z
slumberland, S~ *tdmk* ˈslʌm bə lænd ‖ -bᵊr-
slumberous ˈslʌm bər‿əs **~ly** li **~ness** nəs nɪs
slumberwear ˈslʌm bə weə ‖ -bᵊr wer
slumbrous ˈslʌm brəs **~ly** li **~ness** nəs nɪs
slumlord ˈslʌm lɔːd ‖ -lɔːrd **~s** z
slumm|y ˈslʌm |i **~ier** i‿ə ‖ i‿ᵊr **~iest** i‿ɪst i‿əst **~iness** i nəs i nɪs

slump slʌmp **slumped** slʌmpt **slumping** ˈslʌmp ɪŋ **slumps** slʌmps
slung slʌŋ
slunk slʌŋk
slur slɜː ‖ slɝː **slurred** slɜːd ‖ slɝːd **slurring** ˈslɜːr ɪŋ ‖ ˈslɝː ɪŋ **slurs** slɜːz ‖ slɝːz
slurp slɜːp ‖ slɝːp **slurped** slɜːpt ‖ slɝːpt **slurping** ˈslɜːp ɪŋ ‖ ˈslɝːp ɪŋ **slurps** slɜːps ‖ slɝːps
slurr... —*see* **slur**
slurr|y ˈslʌr |i ‖ ˈslɝː |i **~ies** iz
slush slʌʃ **slushed** slʌʃt **slushes** ˈslʌʃ ɪz -əz **slushing** ˈslʌʃ ɪŋ
ˈslush fund
slush|y ˈslʌʃ |i **~ier** i‿ə ‖ i‿ᵊr **~iest** i‿ɪst i‿əst **~ily** ɪ li əl i **~iness** i nəs i nɪs
slut slʌt **sluts** slʌts
sluttish ˈslʌt ɪʃ ‖ ˈslʌţ ɪʃ **~ly** li **~ness** nəs nɪs
slutty ˈslʌt i ‖ ˈslʌţ i
sly, Sly slaɪ **slier, slyer** ˈslaɪ‿ə ‖ ˈslaɪ‿ᵊr **sliest, slyest** ˈslaɪ ɪst -əst
sly|ly ˈslaɪ |li **~ness** nəs nɪs
slype slaɪp **slypes** slaɪps
smack smæk **smacked** smækt **smacking/s** ˈsmæk ɪŋ/z **smacks** smæks
smack-dab ˌsmæk ˈdæb
smacker ˈsmæk ə ‖ -ᵊr **~s** z
smackeroo ˌsmæk ə ˈruː **~s** z
Smail, Smale smeɪᵊl
Smails, Smales smeɪᵊlz
small smɔːl ‖ smɑːl **smaller** ˈsmɔːl ə ‖ -ᵊr ˈsmɑːl- **smallest** ˈsmɔːl ɪst -əst ‖ ˈsmɑːl- **smalls** smɔːlz ‖ smɑːlz
ˈsmall ad; **ˈsmall arms** ‖ ˌ· ˈ·; **ˌsmall ˈbeer**; **ˌsmall ˈcapital**; **ˌsmall ˈchange**; **ˌsmall ˈfortune**; **ˈsmall fry**; **ˈsmall hours**; **ˌsmall inˈtestine**; **ˌsmall ˈprint,** ˈ· ·; **ˌsmall ˈscreen,** ˈ· ·; **ˈsmall talk**
small-boned ˌsmɔːl ˈbəʊnd ◂ ‖ -ˈboʊnd ◂ ˌsmɑːl-
small-calibre, small-caliber ˌsmɔːl ˈkæl ɪb ə ◂ ‖ -ᵊr ◂ ˌsmɑːl-
Smalley ˈsmɔːl i ‖ ˈsmɑːl-
smallholder ˈsmɔːl ˌhəʊld ə →-ˌhɒʊld- ‖ -ˌhoʊld ᵊr ˈsmɑːl- **~s** z
smallholding ˈsmɔːl ˌhəʊld ɪŋ →-ˌhɒʊld- ‖ -ˌhoʊld ɪŋ ˈsmɑːl- **~s** z
smallish ˈsmɔːl ɪʃ ‖ ˈsmɑːl-
small-minded ˌsmɔːl ˈmaɪnd ɪd ◂ -əd ‖ ˌsmɑːl- **~ly** li **~ness** nəs nɪs
smallness ˈsmɔːl nəs -nɪs ‖ ˈsmɑːl-
Smallpiece ˈsmɔːl piːs ‖ ˈsmɑːl-
smallpox ˈsmɔːl pɒks ‖ -pɑːks ˈsmɑːl-
small-scale ˌsmɔːl ˈskeɪᵊl ◂ ‖ ˌsmɑːl-
small-tim|e ˌsmɔːl ˈtaɪm ◂ ‖ ˌsmɑːl- **~er/s** ə/z ‖ ᵊr/z
ˌsmall-time ˈgangsters
small-town ˌsmɔːl ˈtaʊn ◂ ‖ ˌsmɑːl-
Smallwood ˈsmɔːl wʊd ‖ ˈsmɑːl-
smalt smɔːlt smɒlt ‖ smɑːlt
smaltite ˈsmɔːlt aɪt ˈsmɒlt- ‖ ˈsmɑːlt-
Smarden ˈsmɑːd ᵊn -en ‖ ˈsmɑːrd ᵊn
smarm smɑːm ‖ smɑːrm **smarmed** smɑːmd ‖ smɑːrmd **smarming** ˈsmɑːm ɪŋ ‖ ˈsmɑːrm ɪŋ **smarms** smɑːmz ‖ smɑːrmz
smarm|y ˈsmɑːm |i ‖ ˈsmɑːrm |i **~ier** i‿ə ‖ i‿ᵊr **~iest** i‿ɪst i‿əst
smart, Smart smɑːt ‖ smɑːrt **smarted** ˈsmɑːt ɪd -əd ‖ ˈsmɑːrţ əd **smarter** ˈsmɑːt ə ‖ ˈsmɑːrţ ᵊr **smartest** ˈsmɑːt ɪst -əst ‖ ˈsmɑːrţ əst **smarting** ˈsmɑːt ɪŋ ‖ ˈsmɑːrţ ɪŋ **smarts** smɑːts ‖ smɑːrts —*see also phrases with this word*
ˈsmart card
smart aleck ˈsmɑːt ˌæl ɪk -ek, ˌ·ˈ· · ‖ ˈsmɑːrţ- -ˌel- **~s** s
smart-alecky ˈsmɑːt ˌæl ɪk i ◂ -ek i, -ək i, ˌ·ˈ· · · ‖ ˈsmɑːrţ- -ˌel-
smart-arse, smart-ass ˈsmɑːt ɑːs -æs ‖ ˈsmɑːrţ æs
smarten ˈsmɑːt ᵊn ‖ ˈsmɑːrt ᵊn **~ed** d **~ing** ‿ɪŋ **~s** z
Smartie *tdmk* ˈsmɑːt i ‖ ˈsmɑːrţ i **~s** z
smartish ˈsmɑːt ɪʃ ‖ ˈsmɑːrţ ɪʃ
smart|ly ˈsmɑːt |li ‖ ˈsmɑːrt |li **~ness** nəs nɪs
smart-mouthed ˌsmɑːt ˈmaʊðd ◂ -ˈmaʊθt ◂ ‖ ˌsmɑːrt-
smartphone ˈsmɑːt fəʊn ‖ ˈsmɑːrt foʊn **~s** z
smart|y ˈsmɑːt |i ‖ ˈsmɑːrţ |i **~ies** iz
smarty-pants ˈsmɑːt i pænts ‖ ˈsmɑːrţ-
smash smæʃ **smashed** smæʃt **smashes** ˈsmæʃ ɪz -əz **smashing** ˈsmæʃ ɪŋ
smash-and-grab ˌsmæʃ ᵊnd ˈgræb →-ᵊŋ-
ˌsmash-and-ˈgrab raid
smasher ˈsmæʃ ə ‖ -ᵊr **~s** z
smash-up ˈsmæʃ ʌp **~s** s
smatana ˈsmæt ən ə ‖ -ᵊn ə
smattering ˈsmæt‿ər ɪŋ ‖ ˈsmæţ ər ɪŋ **~s** z
smear smɪə ‖ smɪᵊr **smeared** smɪəd ‖ smɪᵊrd **smearing** ˈsmɪər ɪŋ ‖ ˈsmɪr ɪŋ **smears** smɪəz ‖ smɪᵊrz
ˈsmear test
smeary ˈsmɪər i ‖ ˈsmɪr i
Smeaton ˈsmiːt ᵊn
smectic ˈsmekt ɪk **~s** s
Smedley ˈsmed li
Smee smiː
smegma ˈsmeg mə
smell smel **smelled** smeld **smelling** ˈsmel ɪŋ **smells** smelz **smelt** smelt
ˈsmelling salts
Smellie ˈsmel i
smell|y ˈsmel |i **~ier** i‿ə ‖ i‿ᵊr **~iest** i‿ɪst i‿əst **~iness** i nəs i nɪs
smelt smelt **smelted** ˈsmelt ɪd -əd **smelting** ˈsmelt ɪŋ **smelts** smelts
smelter ˈsmelt ə ‖ -ᵊr **~s** z
Smetana ˈsmet ən ə ‖ -ᵊn ə —*Czech* [ˈsme ta na]
Smethurst ˈsmeθ ɜːst -hɜːst ‖ -hɝːst
Smethwick ˈsmeð ɪk
smew smjuː **smews** smjuːz
smidgen, smidgin ˈsmɪdʒ ən -ɪn **~s** z
Smike smaɪk
smilax ˈsmaɪl æks

smile smaɪᵊl **smiled** smaɪᵊld **smiles** smaɪᵊlz **smiling/ly** 'smaɪl ɪŋ /li
Smiles smaɪᵊlz
smiley 'smaɪl i **~s** z
Smiley, Smily 'smaɪl i
Smillie 'smaɪl i
smirch smɜːtʃ ‖ smɜˑːtʃ **smirched** smɜːtʃt ‖ smɜˑːtʃt **smirches** 'smɜːtʃ ɪz -əz ‖ 'smɜˑːtʃ əz **smirching** 'smɜːtʃ ɪŋ ‖ 'smɜˑːtʃ ɪŋ
smirk smɜːk ‖ smɜˑːk **smirked** smɜːkt ‖ smɜˑːkt **smirking/ly** 'smɜːk ɪŋ /li ‖ 'smɜˑːk- **smirks** smɜːks ‖ smɜˑːks
Smirke smɜːk ‖ smɜˑːk
Smirnoff *tdmk* 'smɜːn ɒf ‖ 'smɜˑːn ɔːf 'smɪr-, -nɑːf —*Russ* [smʲɪr 'nɔf]
smite smaɪt **smit** smɪt **smites** smaɪts **smiting** 'smaɪt ɪŋ ‖ 'smaɪţ ɪŋ **smitten** 'smɪt ᵊn **smote** sməʊt ‖ smoʊt
smith, Smith smɪθ **smiths, Smith's** smɪθs
smithereens ˌsmɪð ə 'riːnz
Smithers 'smɪð əz ‖ -ᵊrz
Smithfield 'smɪθ fiːᵊld
Smithson 'smɪθ sən
Smithsonian smɪθ 'səʊn iˌən ‖ -'soʊn-
smithsonite 'smɪθ sə naɪt
smith|y 'smɪð |i 'smɪθ- **~ies** iz
smitten 'smɪt ᵊn
smock smɒk ‖ smɑːk **smocked** smɒkt ‖ smɑːkt **smocking** 'smɒk ɪŋ ‖ 'smɑːk ɪŋ **smocks** smɒks ‖ smɑːks
smog smɒg ‖ smɑːg smɔːg **smogs** smɒgz ‖ smɑːgz smɔːgz
smogg|y 'smɒg |i ‖ 'smɑːg |i 'smɔːg- **~ier** iˌə ‖ iˌᵊr **~iest** iˌɪst iˌəst
smoke sməʊk ‖ smoʊk **smoked** sməʊkt ‖ smoʊkt **smokes** sməʊks ‖ smoʊks **smoking** 'sməʊk ɪŋ ‖ 'smoʊk ɪŋ
'smoking ˌjacket; **'smoking comˌpartment**
smoke-filled 'sməʊk fɪld ‖ 'smoʊk-
smoke-free ˌsməʊk 'friː ◂ ‖ ˌsmoʊk-
smokeless 'sməʊk ləs -lɪs ‖ 'smoʊk-
smoker, S~ 'sməʊk ə ‖ 'smoʊk ᵊr **~s** z
smokescreen 'sməʊk skriːn ‖ 'smoʊk- **~s** z
smokestack 'sməʊk stæk ‖ 'smoʊk- **~s** s
'smokestack ˌindustry
Smokey 'sməʊk i ‖ 'smoʊk i
smoko 'sməʊk əʊ ‖ 'smoʊk oʊ **~s** z
smok|y 'sməʊk |i ‖ 'smoʊk |i **~ier** iˌə ‖ iˌᵊr **~iest** iˌɪst iˌəst **~ily** ɪ li əl i **~iness** i nəs i nɪs
smold|er 'sməʊld |ə →'smɒʊld- ‖ 'smoʊld |ᵊr **~ered** əd ‖ ᵊrd **~ering** ˌər ɪŋ **~ers** əz ‖ ᵊrz
Smolensk smɒ 'lenᵗsk smə- ‖ smoʊ- —*Russ* [smʌ 'lʲensk]
Smollett 'smɒl ɪt §-ət ‖ 'smɑːl-
smolt sməʊlt →smɒʊlt ‖ smoʊlt **smolts** sməʊlts →smɒʊlts ‖ smoʊlts
smooch smuːtʃ **smooched** smuːtʃt **smooches** 'smuːtʃ ɪz -əz **smooching** 'smuːtʃ ɪŋ
smoochy 'smuːtʃ i
smooth smuːð **smoothed** smuːðd **smoother** 'smuːð ə ‖ -ᵊr **smoothes** smuːðz **smoothest** 'smuːð ɪst -əst **smoothing** 'smuːð ɪŋ
smoothbore 'smuːð bɔː ‖ -bɔːr -boʊr **~s** z
smoothe smuːð **smoothed** smuːðd **smoothes** smuːðz **smoothing** 'smuːð ɪŋ
smoothie 'smuːð i **~s** z
smooth|ly 'smuːð |li **~ness** nəs nɪs
smooth-talking ˌsmuːð 'tɔːk ɪŋ ◂ ‖ -'tɑːk-
smooth|y 'smuːð |i **~ies** iz
smorgasbord 'smɔːg əs bɔːd 'smɜːg-, -əz- ‖ 'smɔːrg əs bɔːrd -boʊrd —*Swedish* smörgåsbord ['smør gɔs bu†]
smote sməʊt ‖ smoʊt
smother 'smʌð ə ‖ -ᵊr **~ed** d **smothering** 'smʌð ərˌɪŋ **~s** z
smould|er 'sməʊld |ə →'smɒʊld- ‖ 'smoʊld |ᵊr **~ered** əd ‖ ᵊrd **~ering** ˌər ɪŋ **~ers** əz ‖ ᵊrz
smudge smʌdʒ **smudged** smʌdʒd **smudges** 'smʌdʒ ɪz -əz **smudging** 'smʌdʒ ɪŋ
smudgepot 'smʌdʒ pɒt ‖ -pɑːt **~s** s
smudg|y 'smʌdʒ |i **~ily** ɪ li əl i **~iness** i nəs i nɪs
smug smʌg **smugger** 'smʌg ə ‖ -ᵊr **smuggest** 'smʌg ɪst -əst
smuggl|e 'smʌg ᵊl **~ed** d **~er/s** ˌə/z ‖ ər/z **~es** z **~ing** ˌɪŋ
smug|ly 'smʌg |li **~ness** nəs nɪs
smurf smɜːf ‖ smɜˑːf **smurfs** smɜːfs ‖ smɜˑːfs
smut smʌt **smuts, Smuts** smʌts
smutt|y 'smʌt |i ‖ 'smʌţ |i **~ier** iˌə ‖ iˌᵊr **~iest** iˌɪst iˌəst **~ily** ɪ li əl i **~iness** i nəs i nɪs
Smyrna 'smɜːn ə ‖ 'smɜˑːn ə —*Turkish* İzmir ['iz mir]
Smyth *(i)* smɪθ, *(ii)* smaɪθ, *(iii)* smaɪð
Smythe *(i)* smaɪð, *(ii)* smaɪθ
snack snæk **snacked** snækt **snacking** 'snæk ɪŋ **snacks** snæks
'snack bar
Snaefell ˌsneɪ 'fel
snaffl|e 'snæf ᵊl **~ed** d **~es** z **~ing** ˌɪŋ
'snaffle bit
snafu snæ 'fuː **~ed** d **~ing** ɪŋ **~s** z
snag snæg **snagged** snægd **snagging** 'snæg ɪŋ **snags** snægz
Snagge snæg
snaggletooth 'snæg ᵊl tuːθ §-tʊθ **~ed** t
snail sneɪᵊl **snails** sneɪᵊlz
'snail's pace
Snaith sneɪθ
snake, Snake sneɪk **snaked** sneɪkt **snakes** sneɪks **snaking** 'sneɪk ɪŋ
'snake ˌcharmer; **ˌsnakes and 'ladders**
snakebite 'sneɪk baɪt **~s** s
snakeroot 'sneɪk ruːt ‖ -rʊt **~s** s
snakeskin 'sneɪk skɪn **~s** z
snak|y 'sneɪk |i **~ier** iˌə ‖ iˌᵊr **~iest** iˌɪst iˌəst **~ily** ɪ li əl i **~iness** i nəs i nɪs
snap snæp **snapped** snæpt **snapping** 'snæp ɪŋ **snaps** snæps
'snap ˌfastener
snapdragon 'snæp ˌdræg ən **~s** z
Snape sneɪp
snap-on 'snæp ɒn ‖ -ɑːn -ɔːn
snapper 'snæp ə ‖ -ᵊr **~s** z
snappish 'snæp ɪʃ **~ly** li **~ness** nəs nɪs
Snapple *tdmk* 'snæp ᵊl

snapp|y ˈsnæp |i **~ier** i‿ə ‖ i‿ᵊr **~iest** i‿ɪst i‿əst **~ily** ɪ li əl i **~iness** i nəs i nɪs
snapshot ˈsnæp ʃɒt ‖ -ʃɑːt **~s** s
snare sneə ‖ sneᵊr **snared** sneəd ‖ sneᵊrd **snares** sneəz ‖ sneᵊrz **snaring** ˈsneər ɪŋ ‖ ˈsner ɪŋ
ˈsnare drum
snarf snɑːf ‖ snɑːrf **snarfed** snɑːft ‖ snɑːrft **snarfing** ˈsnɑːf ɪŋ ‖ ˈsnɑːrf ɪŋ **snarfs** snɑːfs ‖ snɑːrfs
snark snɑːk ‖ snɑːrk **snarks** snɑːks ‖ snɑːrks
snarky ˈsnɑːk i ‖ ˈsnɑːrk i
snarl snɑːl ‖ snɑːrl **snarled** snɑːld ‖ snɑːrld **snarling/ly** ˈsnɑːl ɪŋ /li ‖ ˈsnɑːrl ɪŋ /li **snarls** snɑːlz ‖ snɑːrlz
snarl-up ˈsnɑːl ʌp ‖ ˈsnɑːrl- **~s** z
snatch snætʃ **snatched** snætʃt **snatches** ˈsnætʃ ɪz -əz **snatching** ˈsnætʃ ɪŋ
snatcher ˈsnætʃ ə ‖ -ᵊr **~s** z
snazz|y ˈsnæz |i **~ier** i‿ə ‖ i‿ᵊr **~iest** i‿ɪst i‿əst **~ily** ɪ li əl i **~iness** i nəs i nɪs
Snead sniːd
sneak sniːk **sneaked** sniːkt **sneaking** ˈsniːk ɪŋ **sneaks** sniːks **snuck** snʌk
ˌsneak ˈpreview; **ˈsneak thief**
sneaker ˈsniːk ə ‖ -ᵊr **~s** z
sneaking ˈsniːk ɪŋ **~ly** li **~ness** nəs nɪs
sneak|y ˈsniːk |i **~ier** i‿ə ‖ i‿ᵊr **~iest** i‿ɪst i‿əst **~ily** ɪ li əl i **~iness** i nəs i nɪs
sneer snɪə ‖ snɪᵊr **sneered** snɪəd ‖ snɪᵊrd **sneering/ly** ˈsnɪər ɪŋ /li ‖ ˈsnɪr ɪŋ /li **sneers** snɪəz ‖ snɪᵊrz
sneeze sniːz **sneezed** sniːzd **sneezes** ˈsniːz ɪz -əz **sneezing** ˈsniːz ɪŋ
sneezeweed ˈsniːz wiːd **~s** z
sneezewort ˈsniːz wɜːt -wɔːt ‖ -wɜːt -wɔːrt **~s** s
Sneezum ˈsniːz əm
Sneinton ˈsnent ən ‖ -ᵊn
Snelgrove, Snellgrove ˈsnel grəʊv ‖ -groʊv
snell, Snell snel
Snetterton ˈsnet ət ən ‖ ˈsneṭ ᵊrt ᵊn
Sneyd sniːd
snib snɪb **snibbed** snɪbd **snibbing** ˈsnɪb ɪŋ **snibs** snɪbz
snick snɪk **snicked** snɪkt **snicking** ˈsnɪk ɪŋ **snicks** snɪks
snicker ˈsnɪk ə ‖ -ᵊr **~ed** d **snickering/ly** ˈsnɪk ər‿ɪŋ /li **~s** z
Snickers *tdmk* ˈsnɪk əz ‖ -ᵊrz
snickersnee ˌsnɪk ə ˈsniː ˈ. . . ‖ -ᵊr- **~s** z
snicket ˈsnɪk ɪt §-ət **~s** s
snide snaɪd **snider** ˈsnaɪd ə ‖ -ᵊr **snidest** ˈsnaɪd ɪst -əst
snide|ly ˈsnaɪd |li **~ness** nəs nɪs
sniff snɪf **sniffed** snɪft **sniffing** ˈsnɪf ɪŋ **sniffs** snɪfs
sniffer ˈsnɪf ə ‖ -ᵊr **~s** z
ˈsniffer dog
sniffl|e ˈsnɪf ᵊl **~ed** d **~es** z **~ing** ‿ɪŋ
sniff|y ˈsnɪf |i **~ier** i‿ə ‖ i‿ᵊr **~iest** i‿ɪst i‿əst **~ily** ɪ li əl i **~iness** i nəs i nɪs
snifter ˈsnɪft ə ‖ -ᵊr **~s** z
snigger ˈsnɪg ə ‖ -ᵊr **~ed** d **sniggering/ly** ˈsnɪg ər‿ɪŋ /li **~s** z
snip snɪp **snipped** snɪpt **snipping** ˈsnɪp ɪŋ **snips** snɪps
snipe snaɪp **sniped** snaɪpt **snipes** snaɪps **sniping** ˈsnaɪp ɪŋ
sniper ˈsnaɪp ə ‖ -ᵊr **~s** z
snipper ˈsnɪp ə ‖ -ᵊr **~s** z
snippet ˈsnɪp ɪt §-ət **~s** s
snippy ˈsnɪp i
snit snɪt **snits** snɪts
snitch snɪtʃ **snitched** snɪtʃt **snitches** ˈsnɪtʃ ɪz -əz **snitching** ˈsnɪtʃ ɪŋ
snivel ˈsnɪv ᵊl **~ed, ~led** d **~er/s, ~ler/s** ə/z ‖ ᵊr/z **~ing, ~ling** ɪŋ **~s** z
snob snɒb ‖ snɑːb **snobs** snɒbz ‖ snɑːbz
snobbery ˈsnɒb ər i ‖ ˈsnɑːb-
snobbish ˈsnɒb ɪʃ ‖ ˈsnɑːb- **~ly** li **~ness** nəs nɪs
snobbism ˈsnɒb ˌɪz əm ‖ ˈsnɑːb-
snobb|y ˈsnɒb |i ‖ ˈsnɑːb |i **~ier** i‿ə ‖ i‿ᵊr **~iest** i‿ɪst i‿əst **~ily** ɪ li əl i **~iness** i nəs i nɪs
SNOBOL ˈsnəʊb ɒl ‖ ˈsnoʊb ɔːl -ɑːl
Sno-Cat *tdmk* ˈsnəʊ kæt ‖ ˈsnoʊ- **~s** s
Snodgrass ˈsnɒd grɑːs §-græs ‖ ˈsnɑːd græs
Snodland ˈsnɒd lənd ‖ ˈsnɑːd-
snoek snuːk snʊk *(= snook)*
snog snɒg ‖ snɑːg **snogged** snɒgd ‖ snɑːgd **snogging** ˈsnɒg ɪŋ ‖ ˈsnɑːg ɪŋ **snogs** snɒgz ‖ snɑːgz
snood snuːd snʊd **snoods** snuːdz snʊdz
snook *'gesture of defiance'* snuːk snʊk ‖ snʊk snuːk **snooks** snuːks snʊks ‖ snʊks snuːks
snook *fish* snuːk snʊk
snooker ˈsnuːk ə ‖ ˈsnʊk ᵊr *(*)* **~ed** d **snookering** ˈsnuːk ər‿ɪŋ ‖ ˈsnʊk ər‿ɪŋ **~s** z
snoop snuːp **snooped** snuːpt **snooping** ˈsnuːp ɪŋ **snoops** snuːps
snooper ˈsnuːp ə ‖ -ᵊr **~s** z
Snoopy, snoop|y ˈsnuːp |i **~ier** i‿ə ‖ i‿ᵊr **~iest** i‿ɪst i‿əst
snoot snuːt **snoots** snuːts
snoot|y ˈsnuːt |i ‖ ˈsnuːṭ |i **~ier** i‿ə ‖ i‿ᵊr **~iest** i‿ɪst i‿əst **~ily** ɪ li əl i **~iness** i nəs i nɪs
snooze snuːz **snoozed** snuːzd **snoozes** ˈsnuːz ɪz -əz **snoozing** ˈsnuːz ɪŋ
snore snɔː ‖ snɔːr snoʊr **snored** snɔːd ‖ snɔːrd snoʊrd **snores** snɔːz ‖ snɔːrz snoʊrz **snoring** ˈsnɔːr ɪŋ ‖ ˈsnoʊr-
snorer ˈsnɔːr ə ‖ -ᵊr ˈsnoʊr- **~s** z
snorkel ˈsnɔːk ᵊl ‖ ˈsnɔːrk ᵊl **~ed, ~led** d **~ing, ~ling** ɪŋ **~s** z
snort snɔːt ‖ snɔːrt **snorted** ˈsnɔːt ɪd -əd ‖ ˈsnɔːrṭ əd **snorting** ˈsnɔːt ɪŋ ‖ ˈsnɔːrṭ ɪŋ **snorts** snɔːts ‖ snɔːrts
snorter ˈsnɔːt ə ‖ ˈsnɔːrṭ ᵊr
snot snɒt ‖ snɑːt
snott|y ˈsnɒt |i ‖ ˈsnɑːṭ |i **~ier** i‿ə ‖ i‿ᵊr **~iest** i‿ɪst i‿əst **~ily** ɪ li əl i **~iness** i nəs i nɪs
snotty-nosed ˌsnɒt i ˈnəʊzd ◂ ‖ ˌsnɑːṭ i ˈnoʊzd
snout snaʊt **snouts** snaʊts

snow, Snow snəʊ ‖ snoʊ **snowed** snəʊd ‖ snoʊd **snowing** 'snəʊ ɪŋ ‖ 'snoʊ ɪŋ **snows** snəʊz ‖ snoʊz
'snow ˌblindness; **ˌSnow 'White**
snowball, S~ 'snəʊ bɔːl ‖ 'snoʊ- -bɑːl **~ed** d **~ing** ɪŋ **~s** z
snowberr|y 'snəʊ bər‿|i '·ˌber |i ‖ 'snoʊ ˌber |i **~ies** iz
snowbird 'snəʊ bɜːd ‖ 'snoʊ bɜːd **~s** z
snow-blind 'snəʊ blaɪnd ‖ 'snoʊ-
snowblower 'snəʊ ˌbləʊ ə ‖ 'snoʊ ˌbloʊ ᵊr **~s** z
snowbound 'snəʊ baʊnd ‖ 'snoʊ-
snow-capped 'snəʊ kæpt ‖ 'snoʊ-
ˌsnow-capped 'peaks
Snowcem *tdmk* 'snəʊ sem ‖ 'snoʊ-
snow-clad 'snəʊ klæd ‖ 'snoʊ-
Snowden, Snowdon 'snəʊd ᵊn ‖ 'snoʊd ᵊn
Snowdonia snəʊ 'dəʊn i‿ə ‖ snoʊ 'doʊn-
Snowdown 'snəʊ daʊn ‖ 'snoʊ-
snowdrift 'snəʊ drɪft ‖ 'snoʊ- **~s** s
snowdrop 'snəʊ drɒp ‖ 'snoʊ drɑːp **~s** s
snowfall 'snəʊ fɔːl ‖ 'snoʊ- -fɑːl **~s** z
snowfield 'snəʊ fiːᵊld ‖ 'snoʊ- **~s** z
snowflake 'snəʊ fleɪk ‖ 'snoʊ- **~s** s
snowline 'snəʊ laɪn ‖ 'snoʊ- **~s** z
snow|man 'snəʊ |mæn ‖ 'snoʊ- **~men** men
snowmobile 'snəʊ məˌbiːᵊl -moʊ- ‖ 'snoʊ- -moʊ- **~s** z
snowplough, snowplow 'snəʊ plaʊ ‖ 'snoʊ- **~s** z
snowshoe 'snəʊ ʃuː ‖ 'snoʊ- **~s** z
snowstorm 'snəʊ stɔːm ‖ 'snoʊ stɔːrm **~s** z
snow-white ˌsnəʊ 'waɪt ◂ -'hwaɪt ‖ ˌsnoʊ '*h*waɪt ◂
snow|y, Snowy 'snəʊ |i ‖ 'snoʊ |i **~ier** i‿ə ‖ i‿ᵊr **~iest** i‿ɪst i‿əst **~ily** ɪ li əl i **~iness** i nəs i nɪs
ˌSnowy 'Mountains
SNP ˌes en 'piː →-em-
snr, Snr —*see* **senior**
snub snʌb **snubbed** snʌbd **snubbing** 'snʌb ɪŋ **snubs** snʌbz
snubb|y 'snʌb |i **~ier** i‿ə ‖ i‿ᵊr **~iest** i‿ɪst i‿əst **~iness** i nəs i nɪs
snub-nosed ˌsnʌb 'nəʊzd ◂ '·· ‖ -'noʊzd ◂
snuck snʌk
snuff snʌf **snuffed** snʌft **snuffing** 'snʌf ɪŋ **snuffs** snʌfs
snuffbox 'snʌf bɒks ‖ -bɑːks **~es** ɪz əz
snuffer 'snʌf ə ‖ -ᵊr **~s** z
snuffl|e 'snʌf ᵊl **~ed** d **~er/s** ‿ə/z ‖ ər/z **~es** z **~ing** ‿ɪŋ
snug, Snug snʌg **snugger** 'snʌg ə ‖ -ᵊr **snuggest** 'snʌg ɪst -əst
snugger|y 'snʌg ər |i **~ies** iz
snuggl|e 'snʌg ᵊl **~ed** d **~es** z **~ing** ‿ɪŋ
snug|ly 'snʌg |li **~ness** nəs nɪs
so səʊ ‖ soʊ —*There is an occasional weak form* sə
soak səʊk ‖ soʊk **soaked** səʊkt ‖ soʊkt **soaking** 'səʊk ɪŋ ‖ 'soʊk ɪŋ **soaks** səʊks ‖ soʊks
soakage 'səʊk ɪdʒ ‖ 'soʊk-
soakaway 'səʊk ə ˌweɪ ‖ 'soʊk- **~s** z
Soames səʊmz ‖ soʊmz
so-and-so 'səʊ ən səʊ -ənd- ‖ 'soʊ ən soʊ **~s** z
Soane səʊn ‖ soʊn
soap səʊp ‖ soʊp **soaped** səʊpt ‖ soʊpt **soaping** 'səʊp ɪŋ ‖ 'soʊp ɪŋ **soaps** səʊps ‖ soʊps
'soap ˌbubble; **'soap ˌopera**
soapberr|y 'səʊp ˌber |i ‖ 'soʊp- **~ies** iz
soapbox 'səʊp bɒks ‖ 'soʊp bɑːks **~es** ɪz əz
soapflakes 'səʊp fleɪks ‖ 'soʊp-
soapi... —*see* **soapy**
soapstone 'səʊp stəʊn ‖ 'soʊp stoʊn
soapsuds 'səʊp sʌdz ‖ 'soʊp-
soapwort 'səʊp wɜːt §-wɔːt ‖ 'soʊp wɜːt -wɔːrt **~s** s
soap|y 'səʊp |i ‖ 'soʊp |i **~ier** i‿ə ‖ i‿ᵊr **~iest** i‿ɪst i‿əst **~ily** ɪ li əl i **~iness** i nəs i nɪs
soar sɔː ‖ sɔːr soʊr *(= sore)* **soared** sɔːd ‖ sɔːrd soʊrd **soaring/ly** 'sɔːr ɪŋ /li ‖ 'soʊr- **soars** sɔːz ‖ sɔːrz soʊrz
Soar *river* sɔː ‖ sɔːr soʊr
Soar *place in Wales* 'səʊ ɑː ‖ 'soʊ ɑːr
soaraway 'sɔːr ə ˌweɪ ‖ 'soʊr-
Soares 'swɑːr eʃ —*Port* [swarʃ, 'swariʃ]
SOAS 'səʊ æs -æz; ˌes əʊ eɪ 'es ‖ 'soʊ-
Soave 'swɑːv eɪ —*It* [so 'aː ve]
Soay 'səʊ eɪ -ə ‖ 'soʊ-
sob sɒb ‖ sɑːb **sobbed** sɒbd ‖ sɑːbd **sobbing** 'sɒb ɪŋ ‖ 'sɑːb ɪŋ **sobs** sɒbz ‖ sɑːbz
'sob ˌstory
sobeit səʊ 'biː ɪt ‖ soʊ-
Sobell 'səʊ bel ‖ 'soʊ-
sober 'səʊb ə ‖ 'soʊb ᵊr **sobered** 'səʊb əd ‖ 'soʊb -ᵊrd **soberer** 'səʊb ər‿ə ‖ 'soʊb ᵊr‿ər **soberest** 'səʊb ər‿ɪst əst ‖ 'soʊb- **sobering/ly** 'səʊb ər ɪŋ /li ‖ 'soʊb- **~ly** li **~ness** nəs nɪs
Sobers 'səʊb əz ‖ 'soʊb ᵊrz
Sobranie *tdmk* səʊ 'brɑːn i ‖ soʊ-
sobriety səʊ 'braɪ‿ət i ɪt i ‖ soʊ 'braɪ əṭ i
sobriquet 'səʊb rɪ keɪ -rə- ‖ 'soʊb- ˌ·'· **~s** z
soca 'səʊk ə ‖ 'soʊk ə
socage 'sɒk ɪdʒ ‖ 'sɑːk-
so-called ˌsəʊ 'kɔːld ◂ ‖ ˌsoʊ- -'kɑːld ◂
soccer 'sɒk ə ‖ 'sɑːk ᵊr
sociability ˌsəʊʃ ə 'bɪl ət i -ɪt i ‖ ˌsoʊʃ ə 'bɪl əṭ i
sociab|le 'səʊʃ əb |ᵊl ‖ 'soʊʃ- **~leness** ᵊl nəs -nɪs **~ly** li
social 'səʊʃ ᵊl ‖ 'soʊʃ ᵊl **~s** z
ˌsocial ˌanthro'pology; **ˌsocial 'climber**; **ˌSocial 'Democrat**; **'social diˌsease**; **ˌsocial 'distance**; **ˌSocial 'Register** *tdmk*; **ˌsocial 'science**; **ˌsocial se'curity**; **ˌsocial 'services**; **'social ˌstudies**; **'social work**
socialis... —*see* **socializ...**
socialism 'səʊʃ ə ˌlɪz əm -ᵊl ˌɪz- ‖ 'soʊʃ-
socialist 'səʊʃ əl ɪst §-əst ‖ 'soʊʃ- **~s** s
socialistic ˌsəʊʃ ə 'lɪst ɪk ◂ ‖ˌsoʊʃ- **~ally** ᵊl‿i
socialite 'səʊʃ ə laɪt ‖ 'soʊʃ- **~s** s

socialization ˌsəʊʃ əl aɪ ˈzeɪʃ ᵊn -ɪ'-- ‖ ˌsoʊʃ əl ə-
socializ|e ˈsəʊʃ ə laɪz ‖ ˈsoʊʃ- **~ed** d **~es** ɪz əz **~ing** ɪŋ
ˌsocialized ˈmedicine
socially ˈsəʊʃ əl i ‖ ˈsoʊʃ-
societal sə ˈsaɪ‿ət ᵊl ‖ -əţ ᵊl **~ly** i
societ|y sə ˈsaɪ‿ət |i ‖ -əţ |i **~ies** iz
Socinian səʊ ˈsɪn i‿ən ‖ soʊ- sə- **~s** z
Socinus səʊ ˈsaɪn əs ‖ soʊ- sə-
socio- *comb. form*
with stress-neutral suffix |səʊʃ i‿əʊ |səʊs- ‖ |soʊs i‿oʊ — **sociobiology** ˌsəʊʃ i‿əʊ baɪ ˈɒl ədʒ i ˌsəʊs- ‖ ˌsoʊs i‿oʊ baɪ ˈɑːl-
with stress-imposing suffix ˌsəʊs i ˈɒ+ ˌsəʊʃ- ‖ ˌsoʊs i ˈɑː+ — **sociometry** ˌsəʊs i ˈɒm ətr i ˌsəʊʃ-, -ɪtr i ‖ ˌsoʊs i ˈɑːm-
sociocultural ˌsəʊʃ i‿əʊ ˈkʌltʃ ᵊr‿əl ◂ ˌsəʊs- ‖ ˌsoʊs i‿oʊ-
socioeconomic ˌsəʊʃ i‿əʊ ˌiːk ə ˈnɒm ɪk ˌsəʊs-, -ˌek- ‖ ˌsoʊs i‿oʊ ˌek ə ˈnɑːm ɪk -ˌiːk- **~ally** ᵊl‿i
sociolect ˈsəʊʃ i‿əʊ lekt ˈsəʊs- ‖ ˈsoʊs i‿oʊ- **~s** s
sociolectal ˌsəʊʃ i‿əʊ ˈlekt ᵊl ◂ ˌsəʊs- ‖ ˌsoʊs i‿oʊ-
sociolinguist ˌsəʊʃ i‿əʊ ˈlɪŋ gwɪst ˌsəʊs- ‖ ˌsoʊs i‿oʊ- **~s** s
sociolinguistic ˌsəʊʃ i‿əʊ lɪŋ ˈgwɪst ɪk ◂ ˌsəʊs- ‖ ˌsoʊs i‿oʊ- **~ally** ᵊl‿i **~s** s
sociological ˌsəʊʃ i‿ə ˈlɒdʒ ɪk ᵊl ◂ ˌsəʊs- ‖ ˌsoʊs i‿ə ˈlɑːdʒ- **~ly** ‿i
sociologist ˌsəʊʃ i ˈɒl ədʒ ɪst ˌsəʊs-, §-əst ‖ ˌsoʊs i ˈɑːl- **~s** s
sociology ˌsəʊʃ i ˈɒl ədʒ i ˌsəʊs- ‖ ˌsoʊs i ˈɑːl-
sociopath ˈsəʊʃ i‿əʊ pæθ ˈsəʊs- ‖ ˈsoʊs i‿oʊ- **~s** s
sociopolitical ˌsəʊʃ i‿əʊ pə ˈlɪt ɪk ᵊl ◂ ˌsəʊs- ‖ ˌsoʊs i‿oʊ pə ˈlɪţ-
sock sɒk ‖ sɑːk **socked** sɒkt ‖ sɑːkt **socking** ˈsɒk ɪŋ ‖ ˈsɑːk ɪŋ **socks** sɒks ‖ sɑːks
sockdolager, sockdologer ˌsɒk ˈdɒl ədʒ ə ‖ sɑːk ˈdɑːl ɪdʒ ᵊr **~s** z
sock|et ˈsɒk |ɪt §-ət ‖ ˈsɑːk |ət **~eted** ɪt ɪd §ət-, -əd ‖ əţ əd **~eting** ɪt ɪŋ §ət- ‖ əţ ɪŋ **~ets** ɪts §əts ‖ əts
sockeye ˈsɒk aɪ ‖ ˈsɑːk aɪ **~s** z
Socotra səʊ ˈkəʊtr ə sɒ- ‖ soʊ ˈkoʊtr ə sə-
Socrates ˈsɒk rə tiːz ‖ ˈsɑːk-
Socratic sɒ ˈkræt ɪk səʊ- ‖ sə ˈkræţ ɪk soʊ- **~ally** ᵊl‿i
sod sɒd ‖ sɑːd **sods** sɒdz ‖ sɑːdz
ˌsod's ˈlaw, ˈ·.
soda ˈsəʊd ə ‖ ˈsoʊd ə **~s** z
ˈsoda bread; **ˈsoda ˌfountain**; **ˈsoda ˌwater**
sodality səʊ ˈdæl ət |i -ɪt- ‖ soʊ ˈdæl əţ |i **~ies** iz
sodden ˈsɒd ᵊn ‖ ˈsɑːd ᵊn **~ed** d **~ing** ‿ɪŋ **~ly** li **~ness** nəs nɪs **~s** z
sodding ˈsɒd ɪŋ ‖ ˈsɑːd ɪŋ
Soddy ˈsɒd i ‖ ˈsɑːd i
sodium ˈsəʊd i‿əm ‖ ˈsoʊd-
ˌsodium ˈchloride
Sodom ˈsɒd əm ‖ ˈsɑːd əm
sodomis|e ˈsɒd ə maɪz ‖ ˈsɑːd- **~ed** d **~es** ɪz əz **~ing** ɪŋ
sodomite ˈsɒd ə maɪt ‖ ˈsɑːd- **~s** s
sodomiz|e ˈsɒd ə maɪz ‖ ˈsɑːd- **~ed** d **~es** ɪz əz **~ing** ɪŋ
sodomy ˈsɒd əm i ‖ ˈsɑːd-
Sodor ˈsəʊd ə ‖ ˈsoʊd ᵊr
soever səʊ ˈev ə ‖ soʊ ˈev ᵊr
sofa ˈsəʊf ə ‖ ˈsoʊf ə **~s** z
sofabed ˈsəʊf ə bed ‖ ˈsoʊf- **~s** z
Sofer ˈsəʊf ə ‖ ˈsoʊf ᵊr
soffit ˈsɒf ɪt §-ət ‖ ˈsɑːf ət **~s** s
Sofia ˈsəʊf i‿ə ˈsɒf-; səʊ ˈfiː‿ə, -ˈfaɪ‿ə ‖ ˈsoʊf i‿ə —*Bulgarian* [ˈso fi ja]
soft sɒft sɔːft ‖ sɔːft sɑːft **softer** ˈsɒft ə ˈsɔːft- ‖ ˈsɔːft ᵊr ˈsɑːft- **softest** ˈsɒft ɪst ˈsɔːft-, -əst ‖ ˈsɔːft əst ˈsɑːft-
ˌsoft ˈfruit; **ˌsoft ˈfurnishings**; **ˌsoft ˈlanding**; **ˌsoft ˈoption**; **ˌsoft ˈpalate**; **ˌsoft ˈsell**; **ˌsoft ˈsoap**; **ˈsoft spot**; **ˌsoft ˈtouch**
softball ˈsɒft bɔːl ˈsɔːft- ‖ ˈsɔːft- ˈsɑːft bɑːl **~s** z
soft-boiled ˌsɒft ˈbɔɪᵊld ◂ ˌsɔːft- ‖ ˌsɔːft- ˌsɑːft-
ˌsoft-boiled ˈeggs
soft-centered, soft-centred ˌsɒft ˈsent əd ◂ ˌsɔːft- ‖ ˌsɔːft ˈsenţ ᵊrd ◂ ˌsɑːft-
soft-core ˌsɒft ˈkɔː ◂ ˌsɔːft- ‖ ˌsɔːft ˈkɔːr ◂ ˌsɑːft-, -ˈkoʊr
ˌsoft-core ˈporn
soft-cover ˌsɒft ˈkʌv ə ˌsɔːft- ‖ ˌsɔːft ˈkʌv ᵊr ◂ ˌsɑːft-
soften ˈsɒf ᵊn ˈsɔːf- ‖ ˈsɔːf ᵊn ˈsɑːf- **~ed** d **~ing** ‿ɪŋ **~s** z
softener ˈsɒf ᵊn‿ə ˈsɔːf- ‖ ˈsɔːf ᵊn‿ər ˈsɑːf- **~s** z
softhearted ˌsɒft ˈhɑːt ɪd ◂ ˌsɔːft-, §-əd ‖ ˌsɔːft ˈhɑːrţ əd ◂ ˌsɑːft- **~ness** nəs nɪs
softie ˈsɒft i ˈsɔːft- ‖ ˈsɔːft i ˈsɑːft- **~s** z
softish ˈsɒft ɪʃ ˈsɔːft- ‖ ˈsɔːft- ˈsɑːft-
soft|ly ˈsɒft |li ˈsɔːft- ‖ ˈsɔːft |li ˈsɑːft- **~ness** nəs nɪs
softly-softly ˌsɒft li ˈsɒft li ˌsɔːft li ˈsɔːft- ‖ ˌsɔːft li ˈsɔːft li ˌsɑːft li ˈsɑːft-
softly-spoken ˌsɒft li ˈspəʊk ən ◂ ˌsɔːft- ‖ ˌsɔːft li ˈspoʊk ən ◂ ˌsɑːft-
soft-pedal ˌsɒft ˈped ᵊl ˌsɔːft- ‖ ˌsɔːft- ˌsɑːft- **~ed, ~led** d **~ing, ~ling** ‿ɪŋ **~s** z
soft-shoe ˈsɒft ʃuː ˈsɔːft- ‖ ˈsɔːft- ˈsɑːft-
soft-soap ˌsɒft ˈsəʊp ˌsɔːft- ‖ ˌsɔːft ˈsoʊp ˌsɑːft- **~ed** t **~ing** ɪŋ **~s** s
soft-spoken ˌsɒft ˈspəʊk ən ◂ ˌsɔːft- ‖ ˌsɔːft ˈspoʊk ən ◂ ˌsɑːft-
soft-top ˈsɒft tɒp ˈsɔːft- ‖ ˈsɔːft- ˈsɑːft-
software ˈsɒft weə ˈsɔːft- ‖ ˈsɔːft wer ˈsɑːft-, -wær
ˈsoftware house
softwood ˈsɒft wʊd ˈsɔːft- ‖ ˈsɔːft- ˈsɑːft- **~s** z
soft|y ˈsɒft |i ˈsɔːft- ‖ ˈsɔːft |i ˈsɑːft- **~ies** iz
SOGAT ˈsəʊ gæt ‖ ˈsoʊ-
Sogdian ˈsɒgd i‿ən ‖ ˈsɑːgd- **~s** z
Sogdiana ˌsɒgd i ˈɑːn ə -ˈeɪn ə ‖ ˌsɑːgd i ˈæn ə

sogg|y 'sɒg |i ‖ 'sɑːg |i 'sɔːg- **~ier** i‿ə ‖ i‿ᵊr **~iest** i‿ɪst i‿əst **~ily** ɪ li əl i **~iness** i nəs i nɪs

soh səʊ ‖ soʊ *(= so)*

Soham 'səʊ əm ‖ 'soʊ-

Soho, SoHo 'səʊ həʊ ˌ·'· ‖ 'soʊ hoʊ **ˌSoho 'Square**

soi-disant ˌswɑː 'diːz ɒ̃ ◂ -diː 'zɒ̃ ‖ -diː 'zɑːn ◂ —*Fr* [swa di zɑ̃]

soigne, soigné, soignee, soignée 'swɑːn jeɪ ·'· ‖ swɑːn 'jeɪ —*Fr* [swan je]

soil sɔɪᵊl **soiled** sɔɪᵊld **soiling** 'sɔɪᵊl ɪŋ **soils** sɔɪᵊlz

soilpipe 'sɔɪᵊl paɪp **~s** s

soiree, soirée 'swɑːr eɪ ‖ swɑː 'reɪ —*Fr* [swa ʁe] **~s** z

soixante-neuf ˌswæs ɒnt 'nɜːf ˌswʌs- ‖ ˌswɑːs ɑːnt 'nʌf -'nʌf —*Fr* [swa sɑ̃t nœf]

sojourn 'sɒdʒ ən 'sʌdʒ-, -ɜːn ‖ soʊ 'dʒɜːn '· · *(*)—Some speakers of AmE make a stress difference between the noun '· · and the verb ·'·* **~ed** d **~ing** ɪŋ **~s** z

sojourner 'sɒdʒ ən ə 'sʌdʒ-, -ɜːn- ‖ soʊ 'dʒɜːn ᵊr '· · · **~s** z

soke səʊk ‖ soʊk *(= soak)*

Sokoto 'səʊk ə təʊ ‖ 'soʊk oʊ toʊ

sol, Sol sɒl ‖ sɑːl sɔːl *—but as the name of a coin, in AmE also* soʊl **sols** sɒlz ‖ sɑːlz

sola 'səʊl ə ‖ 'soʊl ə **ˌsola 'topi**

solac|e 'sɒl əs -ɪs ‖ 'sɑːl əs **~ed** t **~es** ɪz əz **~ing** ɪŋ

solan 'səʊl ən ‖ 'soʊl ən **~s** z

Solana sə 'lɑːn ə sɒ-, səʊ- ‖ soʊ- —*Sp* [so 'la na]

solanaceous ˌsɒl ə 'neɪʃ əs ◂ ˌsəʊl- ‖ ˌsoʊl-

solanum səʊ 'leɪn əm ‖ sə-

solar, Solar 'səʊl ə §-ɑː ‖ 'soʊl ᵊr **ˌsolar 'cell**; **ˌsolar 'panel**; **ˌsolar 'plexus**; **'solar ˌsystem**; **ˌsolar 'wind**; **ˌsolar 'year**

solari|um sə 'leər i‿|əm səʊ- ‖ -'lær- soʊ-, -'ler- **~a** ə **~ums** əmz

solati|um səʊ 'leɪʃ i‿|əm -'leɪʃ |əm ‖ soʊ- **~a** ə **~ums** əmz

sold səʊld →sɒʊld ‖ soʊld *(= soled)*

sold|er 'sɒld |ə 'səʊld-, §'sɒd-, §'sɔːd- ‖ 'sɑːd |ᵊr *(*)* **~ered** əd ‖ ᵊrd **~ering** ‿ər ɪŋ **~ers** əz ‖ ᵊrz **'soldering ˌiron**

soldier 'səʊldʒ ə →'sɒʊldʒ- ‖ 'soʊldʒ ᵊr *—There is also an occasional spelling pronunciation* 'səʊld i‿ə ‖ 'soʊld i‿ᵊr **~ed** d **soldiering** 'səʊldʒ ər‿ɪŋ →'sɒʊldʒ- ‖ 'soʊldʒ ər‿ɪŋ **~s** z **ˌsoldier of 'fortune**

soldierlike 'səʊldʒ ə laɪk →'sɒʊldʒ- ‖ 'soʊldʒ ᵊr-

soldierly 'səʊldʒ ə li →'sɒʊldʒ- ‖ 'soʊldʒ ᵊr-

soldier|y 'səʊldʒ ər |i →'sɒʊldʒ- ‖ 'soʊldʒ- **~ies** iz

sole səʊl →sɒʊl ‖ soʊl **soled** səʊld sɒʊld ‖ soʊld **soles** səʊlz →sɒʊlz ‖ soʊlz **soling** 'səʊl ɪŋ →'sɒʊl- ‖ 'soʊl ɪŋ

solecism 'sɒl ɪ ˌsɪz əm 'səʊl-, -ə- ‖ 'sɑːl- 'soʊl- **~s** z

Soledad 'sɒl ɪ dæd -ə- ‖ 'sɑːl- —*Sp* [so le 'ðað]

solely 'səʊl li →'sɒʊl- ‖ 'soʊl li

solemn 'sɒl əm ‖ sɑːl əm **~ly** li **~ness** nəs nɪs

solemnis... *—see* **solemniz...**

solemnit|y sə 'lem nət |i sɒ-, -nɪt i ‖ -nəţ |i **~ies** iz

solemnization ˌsɒl əm naɪ 'zeɪʃ ᵊn -nɪ'- ‖ ˌsɑːl əm nə- **~s** z

solemniz|e 'sɒl əm naɪz ‖ 'sɑːl- **~ed** d **~es** ɪz əz **~ing** ɪŋ

solenoid 'sɒl ə nɔɪd 'səʊl-, -ɪ- ‖ 'soʊl- 'sɑːl- **~s** z

Solent 'səʊl ənt ‖ 'soʊl-

solera sə 'leər ə -'lɪər- ‖ -'ler- -'lær- —*Sp* [so 'le ɾa]

Soley 'səʊl i ‖ 'soʊl i

sol-fa ˌsɒl 'fɑː §ˌsəʊl- ‖ ˌsoʊl-

solfatara ˌsɒlf ə 'tɑːr ə ‖ ˌsoʊlf- **~s** z

solfegg|io sɒl 'fedʒ |i əʊ -'fedʒ |əʊ ‖ sɑːl 'fedʒ |oʊ **~i** iː

solferino, S~ ˌsɒlf ə 'riːn əʊ ‖ ˌsɑːlf ə 'riːn oʊ

solic|it sə 'lɪs |ɪt §səʊ-, §-ət ‖ -|əţ **~ited** ɪt ɪd §ət-, -əd ‖ əţ əd **~iting** ɪt ɪŋ §ət- ‖ əţ ɪŋ **~its** ɪts §əts ‖ əts

solicitation sə ˌlɪs ɪ 'teɪʃ ᵊn §səʊ-, -ˌ·ə- **~s** z

solicitor sə 'lɪs ɪt ə §səʊ-, -ət- ‖ -əţ ᵊr **~s** z **Soˌlicitor 'General**

solicitous sə 'lɪs ɪt əs §səʊ-, -ət- ‖ -əţ əs **~ly** li **~ness** nəs nɪs

solicitude sə 'lɪs ɪ tjuːd §səʊ-, -ə-, →-tʃuːd ‖ -tuːd -tjuːd

solid 'sɒl ɪd §-əd ‖ 'sɑːl əd **~s** z

solidago ˌsɒl ɪ 'deɪg əʊ -ə- ‖ ˌsɑːl ə 'deɪg oʊ

solidarity ˌsɒl ɪ 'dær ət i ˌ·ə-, -ɪt i ‖ ˌsɑːl ə 'dær əţ i -'der-

solidi 'sɒl ɪ daɪ -ə-, -diː ‖ 'sɑːl-

solidification sə ˌlɪd ɪf ɪ 'keɪʃ ᵊn sɒ-, -ˌ·əf-, §-ə'·-

solidify sə 'lɪd ɪ faɪ sɒ-, -'·ə-

solidity sə 'lɪd ət i sɒ-, -ɪt i ‖ -əţ i

solid|ly 'sɒl ɪd |li §-əd- ‖ 'sɑːl əd- **~ness** nəs nɪs

solid-state ˌsɒl ɪd 'steɪt ◂ §-əd- ‖ ˌsɑːl əd-

sol|idus 'sɒl |ɪd əs -əd- ‖ 'sɑːl |əd əs **~idi** ɪ daɪ -ə-, -diː

Solignum *tdmk* səʊ 'lɪg nəm ‖ soʊ-

Solihull ˌsəʊl i 'hʌl ˌsɒl- ‖ ˌsoʊl-

soliloquis|e, soliloquiz|e sə 'lɪl ə kwaɪz səʊ-, sɒ- **~ed** d **~es** ɪz əz **~ing** ɪŋ

soliloq|uy sə 'lɪl ək |wi səʊ-, sɒ- **~uies** wiz

solipsism 'sɒl ɪp ˌsɪz əm 'səʊl-, -əp- ‖ 'sɑːl əp-

solipsist 'sɒl ɪp sɪst 'səʊl-, -əp-, §-səst ‖ 'sɑːl əp səst **~s** s

solipsistic ˌsɒl ɪp 'sɪst ɪk ◂ ˌsəʊl-, -əp- ‖ ˌsɑːl əp- **~ally** ᵊl‿i

solitaire ˌsɒl ɪ 'teə -ə-, '· · · ‖ 'sɑːl ə ter -tær **~s** z

solitarily 'sɒl ə‿tər əl i '·ɪ-, -ɪ li; ˌ· · ·'teər ə- ‖ ˌsɑːl ə 'ter əl i

solitar|y 'sɒl ə̤tər |i '·ɪ̤ ‖ 'sɑːl ə ter |i **~ies** iz **~iness** i nəs i nɪs
ˌsolitary conˈfinement
solitude 'sɒl ə tjuːd -ɪ-, →-tʃuːd ‖ 'sɑːl ə tuːd -tjuːd **~s** z
solleret ˌsɒl ə 'ret ‖ ˌsɑːl- **~s** s
solo 'səʊl əʊ ‖ 'soʊl oʊ **~s** z
soloist 'səʊl əʊ ɪst §-əst ‖ 'soʊl oʊ- **~s** s
Solomon 'sɒl əm ən ‖ 'sɑːl-
Solomons 'sɒl əm ənz ‖ 'sɑːl-
Solon 'səʊl ɒn -ən ‖ 'soʊl ən -ɑːn
solstic|e 'sɒlst ɪs -əs ‖ 'sɑːlst əs 'soʊlst- **~es** ɪz əz
Solti 'ʃɒlt i ‖ 'ʃoʊlt i —*Hung* ['ʃol ti]
solubility ˌsɒl ju 'bɪl ət i ˌ·jə- -ɪt i ‖ ˌsɑːl jə 'bɪl əṭ i
solub|le 'sɒl jʊb |əl -jəb- ‖ 'sɑːl jəb |əl **~leness** əl nəs -nɪs **~ly** li
solus 'səʊl əs ‖ 'soʊl əs
solute 'sɒl juːt sɒ 'luːt, -ljuːt ‖ 'sɑːl- **~s** s
solution sə 'luːʃ ən -'ljuːʃ- **~s** z
Solutrean sə 'luːtr i̯ən
solvability ˌsɒlv ə 'bɪl ət i -ɪt i ‖ ˌsɑːlv ə 'bɪl əṭ i
solvable 'sɒlv əb əl ‖ 'sɑːlv-
solv|ate *v* sɒl 'v|eɪt 'sɒlv |eɪt ‖ 'sɑːlv |eɪt **~ated** eɪt ɪd -əd ‖ eɪṭ əd **~ates** eɪts **~ating** eɪt ɪŋ ‖ eɪṭ ɪŋ
solvate *n* 'sɒlv eɪt ‖ 'sɑːlv- **~s** s
solvation sɒl 'veɪʃ ən ‖ sɑːl-
Solvay 'sɒlv eɪ ‖ 'sɑːlv- —*Fr* [sɔl vɛ]
'Solvay ˌprocess
solve sɒlv §səʊlv ‖ sɑːlv **solved** sɒlvd §səʊlvd ‖ sɑːlvd **solves** sɒlvz §səʊlvz ‖ sɑːlvz **solving** 'sɒlv ɪŋ §'səʊlv- ‖ 'sɑːlv ɪŋ
solvency 'sɒlv ənts i §'səʊlv- ‖ 'sɑːlv-
solvent 'sɒlv ənt §'səʊlv- ‖ 'sɑːlv- **~s** s
'solvent aˌbuse
solver 'sɒlv ə §'səʊlv- ‖ 'sɑːlv ər **~s** z
Solway 'sɒl weɪ ‖ 'sɑːl-
ˌSolway 'Firth
Solzhenitsyn ˌsɒl ʒə 'nɪts ɪn -ʒɪ-, -'niːts-, §-ən ‖ ˌsoʊl- —*Russ* [səɫ ʒɨ 'nʲi tsɨn]
soma 'səʊm ə ‖ 'soʊm ə
Somali, s~ sə 'mɑːl i səʊ- ‖ soʊ- **~s** z
Somali|a sə 'mɑːl i̯|ə səʊ- ‖ soʊ- **~an/s** ən/z **~land** lænd
somatic səʊ 'mæt ɪk ‖ soʊ 'mæṭ ɪk sə-
somato- *comb. form*
with stress-neutral suffix ¦səʊm ət ə ¦səʊm ə təʊ; səʊ ¦mæt ə ‖ ¦soʊm əṭ ə sə 'mæṭ ə — **somatoplasm** 'səʊm ət əʊ ˌplæz əm səʊ 'mæt ə- ‖ sə 'mæṭ ə- 'soʊm əṭ ə-
with stress-imposing suffix ˌsəʊm ə 'tɒ+ ‖ ˌsoʊm ə 'tɑː+ — **somatology** ˌsəʊm ə 'tɒl ədʒ i ‖ ˌsoʊm ə 'tɑːl-
somatotype 'səʊm ət əʊ taɪp səʊ 'mæt- ‖ sə 'mæṭ ə- 'soʊm əṭ ə- **~s** s
somber, sombre 'sɒm bə ‖ 'sɑːm bər **~ly** li **~ness** nəs nɪs
sombrero sɒm 'breər əʊ ‖ sɑːm 'brer oʊ səm- **~s** z

some *strong form* sʌm, *weak form* səm —*In stranded (exposed) position only the strong form is used:* I've found some. aɪv 'faʊnd sʌm. *Otherwise the weak form is usual if the word is unstressed:* I've found some coins aɪv ˌfaʊnd səm 'kɔɪnz
-some səm— **burdensome** 'bɜːd ən səm ‖ 'bɜ˞ːd- — **eightsome** 'eɪt səm —*With this pronunciation,* -some *forms adjectives or collective numerals: compare the following.*
-some *in biology, 'body'* səʊm ‖ soʊm zoʊm — **chromosome** 'krəʊm ə səʊm ‖ 'kroʊm ə soʊm -zoʊm —*This* -some *is used with combining forms and means 'body': compare the preceding.*
somebody 'sʌm bəd i -ˌbɒd- ‖ -ˌbɑːd- —*There is also a casual form* 'sʌm di
someday 'sʌm deɪ
somehow 'sʌm haʊ —*There is also a casual form* 'sʌm aʊ
someone 'sʌm wʌn §-wɒn
ˌsomeone 'clever; **ˌsomeone 'else**
someplace 'sʌm pleɪs —*Compare the phrase* ˌsome 'place
Somerfield 'sʌm ə fiːəld ‖ -ər-
Somerleyton 'sʌm ə ˌleɪt ən ‖ -ər-
Somers 'sʌm əz ‖ -ərz
somersault 'sʌm ə sɔːlt -sɒlt ‖ -ər- -sɑːlt **~ed** ɪd əd **~ing** ɪŋ **~s** s
Somerset 'sʌm ə set -sɪt ‖ -ər-
Somerton 'sʌm ət ən ‖ -ərt ən
Somerville 'sʌm ə vɪl ‖ -ər-
something 'sʌm θɪŋ ⚠-θɪŋk; 'sʌmpθ ɪŋ, →'sʌntθ-, ⚠-ɪŋk ‖ →'sʌmp m —*There are casual forms* 'sʌm hɪŋ, 'sʌm ɪŋ
ˌsomething 'else
sometime 'sʌm taɪm *(NB not ·'·)*—*Compare the phrase* some 'time səm 'taɪm, *as in* I ˌneed some ˌtime to 'think
sometimes 'sʌm taɪmz *(NB not ·'·)*
someway 'sʌm weɪ
somewhat 'sʌm wɒt -hwɒt, §-ət ‖ wʌt -hwʌt, -wɑːt, -hwɑːt, -wət, -hwət
somewhere 'sʌm weə -hweə ‖ -wer -hwer, -wær, -hwær **~s** z
ˌsomewhere 'else
somite 'səʊm aɪt ‖ 'soʊm- **~s** s
Somme sɒm ‖ sɑːm sʌm —*Fr* [sɔm]
sommelier sɒ 'mel i̯ə sʌ-, -eɪ; ˌsʌm əl 'jeɪ, ˌsɒm-, '· · · ‖ ˌsʌm əl 'jeɪ —*Fr* [sɔ mə lje] **~s** z
somnambulant sɒm 'næm bjʊl ənt -bjəl ənt ‖ sɑːm 'næm bjəl ənt **~s** s
somnambu|late sɒm 'næm bju |leɪt -bjə leɪt ‖ sɑːm 'nɑːm bjə- **~lated** leɪt ɪd -əd ‖ leɪṭ əd **~lates** leɪts **~lating** leɪt ɪŋ ‖ leɪṭ ɪŋ
somnambulation sɒm ˌnæm bju 'leɪʃ ən ˌ· ·'·-, -bjə'·- ‖ sɑːm ˌnæm bjə-
somnambulism sɒm 'næm bju ˌlɪz əm -'·bjə- ‖ sɑːm 'næm bjə-
somnambulist sɒm 'næm bjʊl ɪst -'·bjəl-, §-əst ‖ sɑːm 'næm bjəl əst **~s** s
somniferous sɒm 'nɪf ər əs ‖ sɑːm-
somnolence 'sɒm nəl ənts ‖ 'sɑːm-

S

somnolent ˈsɒm nəl ənt ‖ ˈsɑːm- **~ly** li
Somoza sə ˈməʊz ə ‖ -ˈmoʊz- -ˈmoʊs- — *AmSp* [so ˈmo sa]
Sompting ˈsɒmpt ɪŋ ˈsʌmpt- ‖ ˈsɑːmpt-
son *'male child'*, **Son** sʌn *(= sun)* **sons** sʌnz
son *French word, 'sound'*, sɒn ‖ sɔːn soʊn —*Fr* [sɔ̃] —*see also phrases with this word*
sonagram ˈsəʊn ə græm ˈsɒn- ‖ ˈsoʊn- ˈsɑːn- **~s** z
sonagraph, S~ *tdmk* ˈsəʊn ə grɑːf ˈsɒn-, -græf ‖ ˈsoʊn ə græf ˈsɑːn- **~s** s
sonant ˈsəʊn ənt ˈsɒn- ‖ ˈsoʊn- **~s** s
sonar ˈsəʊn ɑː ‖ ˈsoʊn ɑːr **~s** z
sonata sə ˈnɑːt ə ‖ -ˈnɑːt̬- **~s** z
sonatina ˌsɒn ə ˈtiːn ə ‖ ˌsɑːn- **~s** z
sonde sɒnd ‖ sɑːnd **sondes** sɒndz ‖ sɑːndz
Sondheim ˈsɒnd haɪm ‖ ˈsɑːnd-
sone səʊn ‖ soʊn **sones** səʊnz ‖ soʊnz
son et lumiere, son et lumière ˌsɒn eɪ ˈluːm i eə ˌ· ·ˌ· ·ˈ· ‖ ˌsɑːn eɪ luːm ˈjeᵊr ˌsoʊn- —*Fr* [sɔ̃ ɛ ly mjɛːʁ]
song sɒŋ ‖ sɔːŋ sɑːŋ **songs** sɒŋz ‖ sɔːŋz sɑːŋz **ˌsong and ˈdance**; **ˈsong thrush**
songbird ˈsɒŋ bɜːd ‖ ˈsɔːŋ bɜːd ˈsɑːŋ- **~s** z
songbook ˈsɒŋ bʊk §-buːk ‖ ˈsɔːŋ- ˈsɑːŋ- **~s** s
Songhai ⁽ˌ⁾sɒŋ ˈgaɪ ‖ ⁽ˌ⁾sɔːŋ- ⁽ˌ⁾sɑːŋ- **~s** z
songster ˈsɒŋ stə ˈsɒŋᵏst ə ‖ ˈsɔːŋᵏst ᵊr ˈsɑːŋᵏst- **~s** z
songstress ˈsɒŋ strəs -strɪs, -stres ‖ ˈsɔːŋᵏs trəs ˈsɑːŋᵏs- **~es** ɪz əz
songwriter ˈsɒŋ ˌraɪt ə ‖ ˈsɔːŋ ˌraɪt̬ ᵊr ˈsɑːŋ- **~s** z
Sonia ˈsɒn i͜ə ˈsəʊn- ‖ ˈsoʊn jə
sonic, Sonic ˈsɒn ɪk ‖ ˈsɑːn ɪk **~s** s **ˌsonic ˈboom**
son-in-law ˈsʌn ɪn ˌlɔː §-ən- ‖ -ˌlɑː **sons-in-law** ˈsʌnz ɪn ˌlɔː §-ən- ‖ -ˌlɑː
Sonja ˈsɒn jə ˈsəʊn- ‖ ˈsoʊn-
sonnet ˈsɒn ɪt -ət ‖ ˈsɑːn ət **~s** s
sonneteer ˌsɒn ɪ ˈtɪə -ə- ‖ ˌsɑːn ə ˈtɪᵊr **~s** z
Sonning ˈsɒn ɪŋ ˈsʌn- ‖ ˈsɑːn-
sonn|y, Sonn|y ˈsʌn |i *(= sunny)* **~ies, ~y's** iz
son-of-a-bitch ˌsʌn əv ə ˈbɪtʃ **~es** ɪz əz **sons-of-bitches** ˌsʌnz əv ˈbɪtʃ ɪz -əz
son-of-a-gun ˌsʌn əv ə ˈgʌn **sons-of-guns** ˌsʌnz əv ˈgʌnz
sonogram ˈsəʊn ə græm ˈsɒn- ‖ ˈsoʊn- ˈsɑːn- **~s** z
sonograph ˈsəʊn ə grɑːf ˈsɒn-, -græf ‖ ˈsoʊn ə græf ˈsɑːn- **~s** s
Sonoma sə ˈnəʊm ə ‖ -ˈnoʊm-
sonometer səʊ ˈnɒm ɪt ə sɒ-, -ət ə ‖ soʊ ˈnɑːm ət̬ ᵊr sə- **~s** z
Sonor|a sə ˈnɔːr |ə ‖ -ˈnoʊr- **~an** ən
sonorant ˈsɒn ər ənt ˈsəʊn- ‖ ˈsoʊn- ˈsɑːn-; sə ˈnɔːr-, soʊ-, -ˈnoʊr- **~s** s
sonority sə ˈnɒr ət i səʊ-, -ɪt i ‖ sə ˈnɔːr ət̬ i sə ˈnɑːr-
sonorous ˈsɒn ər əs sə ˈnɔːr- ‖ sə ˈnɔːr əs -ˈnoʊr-; ˈsɑːn ər- **~ly** li
sons-... —*see* **son-...**
sonsy, sonsie ˈsɒnᵗs i ‖ ˈsɑːnᵗs i
Sontag ˈsɒn tæg ‖ ˈsɑːn-
Sony *tdmk* ˈsəʊn i ˈsɒn- ‖ ˈsoʊn i —*Jp* [ˈso ɲii]
Sonya ˈsɒn jə ‖ ˈsoʊn-
soon suːn §sʊn **sooner** ˈsuːn ə §ˈsʊn- ‖ -ᵊr **soonest** ˈsuːn ɪst §ˈsʊn-, -əst

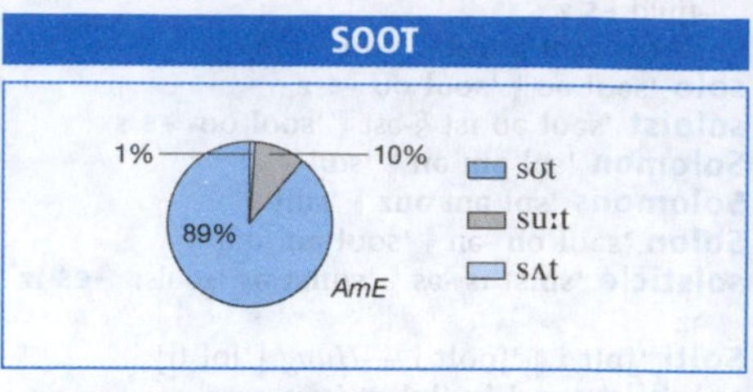

soot sʊt ‖ suːt, sʌt — *Preference poll, AmE:* sʊt *89%,* suːt *10%,* sʌt *1%.*
sooth suːθ
soothe suːð **soothed** suːðd **soothes** suːðz **soothing** ˈsuːð ɪŋ
soother ˈsuːð ə ‖ -ᵊr **~s** z
soothing ˈsuːð ɪŋ **~ly** li **~ness** nəs nɪs
soothsay|er ˈsuːθ ˌseɪ ə ‖ -ᵊr **~ers** əz ‖ ᵊrz **~ing** ɪŋ
soot|y, Sooty ˈsʊt |i ‖ ˈsʊt̬ |i ˈsuːt-, ˈsʌt̬- **~ier** i͜ə ‖ i͜ ᵊr **~iest** i͜ ɪst i͜ əst **~iness** i nəs i nɪs
sop sɒp ‖ sɑːp **sopped** sɒpt ‖ sɑːpt **sopping** ˈsɒp ɪŋ ‖ ˈsɑːp ɪŋ **sops** sɒps ‖ sɑːps
Soper ˈsəʊp ə ‖ ˈsoʊp ᵊr
Sophia səʊ ˈfaɪ͜ə -ˈfiː͜ə ‖ soʊ ˈfiː ə sə-
Sophie ˈsəʊf i ‖ ˈsoʊf i
sophism ˈsɒf ˌɪz əm ‖ ˈsɑːf-
sophist ˈsɒf ɪst §-əst ‖ ˈsɑːf əst **~s** s
sophister ˈsɒf ɪst ə §-əst- ‖ ˈsɑːf əst ᵊr **~s** z
sophistic sə ˈfɪst ɪk sɒ- ‖ sɑː- **~al** ᵊl **~ally** ᵊl͜ i
sophisti|cate *v* sə ˈfɪst ɪ |keɪt §-ə keɪt **~cated** keɪt ɪd -əd ‖ keɪt̬ əd **~cates** keɪts **~cating** keɪt ɪŋ ‖ keɪt̬ ɪŋ
sophisticate *n* sə ˈfɪst ɪ keɪt §-ə-; -ɪk ət, §-ək-, -ɪt **~s** s
sophistication sə ˌfɪst ɪ ˈkeɪʃ ᵊn §-ə-
sophis|try ˈsɒf ɪs |tri -əs- ‖ ˈsɑːf- **~tries** triz
Sophoclean ˌsɒf ə ˈkliː͜ən ‖ ˌsɑːf-
Sophocles ˈsɒf ə kliːz ‖ ˈsɑːf-
sophomore ˈsɒf ə mɔː ‖ ˈsɑːf ə mɔːr -moʊr; ˈsɑːf mɔːr, -moʊr **~s** z
sophomoric ˌsɒf ə ˈmɒr ɪk ◂ ‖ ˌsɑːf-
Sophronia səʊ ˈfrəʊn i͜ə ‖ sə ˈfroʊn-
-sophy *stress-imposing* səf i — **philosophy** fɪ ˈlɒs əf i ‖ -ˈlɑːs-
Sophy ˈsəʊf i ‖ ˈsoʊf i
soporific ˌsɒp ə ˈrɪf ɪk ◂ ˌsəʊp- ‖ ˌsɑːp- ˌsoʊp- **~s** s
sopping ˈsɒp ɪŋ ‖ ˈsɑːp ɪŋ **ˌsopping ˈwet◂**
sopp|y ˈsɒp |i ‖ ˈsɑːp |i **~ier** i͜ə ‖ i͜ᵊr **~iest** i͜ ɪst i͜ əst **~ily** ɪ li əl i **~iness** i nəs i nɪs
sopranino ˌsɒp rə ˈniːn əʊ ‖ ˌsoʊp rə ˈniːn oʊ **~s** z
sopran|o sə ˈprɑːn |əʊ ‖ -ˈpræn |oʊ -ˈprɑːn- **~i** -iː **~os** əʊz ‖ oʊz
Sopwith ˈsɒp wɪθ ‖ ˈsɑːp-
Soraya sə ˈraɪ͜ə

sorb, Sorb sɔːb ‖ sɔːrb **sorbs, Sorbs** sɔːbz ‖ sɔːrbz
sorbet 'sɔːb eɪ -ət, -ɪt ‖ 'sɔːrb ət sɔːr 'beɪ **sorbets** 'sɔːb eɪz -əts, -ɪts ‖ 'sɔːrb əts sɔːr 'beɪz
Sorbian 'sɔːb i‿ən ‖ 'sɔːrb- **~s** z
sorbic 'sɔːb ɪk ‖ 'sɔːrb-
sorbitol 'sɔːb ɪ tɒl -ə- ‖ 'sɔːrb ə tɔːl -tɑːl, -toʊl
sorbo, Sorbo *tdmk* 'sɔːb əʊ ‖ 'sɔːrb oʊ
Sorbonne ₍ₗ₎sɔː 'bɒn ‖ sɔːr 'bʌn -'bɑːn —*Fr* [sɔʁ bɔn]
sorbose 'sɔːb əʊz -əʊs ‖ 'sɔːrb oʊs
sorcerer 'sɔːs ər‿ə ‖ 'sɔːrs ᵊr‿ər **~s** z
sorceress 'sɔːs ə res -ər‿əs, ɪs, ˌsɔːs ə 'res ‖ 'sɔːrs ᵊr‿əs **~es** ɪz əz
sorcer|y 'sɔːs ər‿|i ‖ 'sɔːrs- **~ies** iz
sordid 'sɔːd ɪd §-əd ‖ 'sɔːrd əd **~ly** li **~ness** nəs nɪs
sordin|o sɔː 'diːn| əʊ ‖ sɔːr 'diːn| oʊ **~i** iː
sore sɔː ‖ sɔːr soʊr *(= soar)* **sorer** 'sɔːr ə ‖ 'sɔːr ᵊr 'soʊr- **sores** sɔːz ‖ sɔːrz soʊrz **sorest** 'sɔːr ɪst -əst ‖ 'soʊr-
ˌ**sore 'throat**
sorehead 'sɔː hed ‖ 'sɔːr- 'soʊr- **~s** z
sore|ly 'sɔː |li ‖ 'sɔːr- 'soʊr- **~ness** nəs nɪs
Sorensen 'sɒr ən sən ‖ 'sɔːr- 'sɑːr-
sorghum 'sɔːg əm ‖ 'sɔːrg əm
sorites sɒ 'raɪt iːz sə- ‖ soʊ-
Soroptimist, s~ sə 'rɒpt ɪm ɪst -əm-, §-əst ‖ -'rɑːpt- **~s** s
sororit|y sə 'rɒr ət |i sɒ-, -ɪt i ‖ -'rɔːr əţ |i -'rɑːr- **~ies** iz
Soros 'sɔːr ɒs 'sɒr-, 'ʃɒr-, -ɒʃ, -əs, -əʃ ‖ -ɑːs -oʊs
soros|is sə 'rəʊs| ɪs §-əs ‖ -'roʊs|- **~es** iːz
sorrel 'sɒr əl ‖ 'sɔːr əl 'sɑːr- **~s** z
Sorrel, Sorrell *(i)* 'sɒr əl ‖ 'sɔːr əl 'sɑːr-, *(ii)* sə 'rel
Sorrento sə 'rent əʊ ‖ -oʊ —*It* [sor 'rɛn to]
sorri|ly 'sɒr |əl i -ɪ li ‖ 'sɔːr- 'sɑːr- **~iness** i nəs i nɪs
sorrow 'sɒr əʊ ‖ 'sɔːr oʊ 'sɑːr- **~ed** d **~ing/ly** ɪŋ /li **~s** z
sorrowful 'sɒr əʊ fᵊl -fʊl ‖ 'sɔːr ə- 'sɑːr-, -oʊ- **~ly** ‿i **~ness** nəs nɪs

SORRY

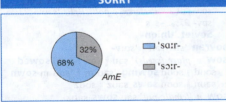

32%
68%
'sɑːr-
'sɔːr-
AmE

sorr|y 'sɒr |i ‖ 'sɑːr |i 'sɔːr- — *Preference poll, AmE:* 'sɑːr- *68%,* 'sɔːr- *32%.* **~ier** i‿ə ‖ i‿ᵊr **~iest** i‿ɪst i‿əst
sort sɔːt ‖ sɔːrt **sorted** 'sɔːt ɪd -əd ‖ 'sɔːrţ əd **sorting** 'sɔːt ɪŋ ‖ 'sɔːrţ ɪŋ **sorts** sɔːts ‖ sɔːrts
sorta 'sɔːt ə ‖ 'sɔːrţ ə
sortal 'sɔːt ᵊl ‖ 'sɔːrţ ᵊl **~s** z
sorter 'sɔːt ə ‖ 'sɔːrţ ᵊr **~s** z
sortie 'sɔːt i -iː ‖ 'sɔːrţ i sɔːr 'tiː **~s** z
sortilege 'sɔːt ɪl ɪdʒ -əl- ‖ 'sɔːrţ ᵊl-
sort-out 'sɔːt aʊt ‖ 'sɔːrţ- **~s** s
sorus 'sɔːr əs ‖ 'soʊr-
SOS ˌes əʊ 'es ‖ -oʊ- **~s, ~'s** ɪz əz
Soskice 'sɒsk ɪs §-əs ‖ 'sɑːsk-
so-so 'səʊ səʊ ‖ 'soʊ soʊ
sostenut|o ˌsɒst ə 'nuːt |əʊ -ɪ-, -'njuːt- ‖ ˌsɑːst ə 'nuːt |oʊ ˌsoʊst- **~i** iː **~os** əʊz ‖ oʊz
sot sɒt ‖ sɑːt **sots** sɒts ‖ sɑːts
soteriology səʊ ˌtɪər i 'ɒl ədʒ i sɒ- ‖ soʊ ˌtɪr i 'ɑːl-
Sotheby 'sʌð ə bi **~'s** z
Sothic 'səʊθ ɪk 'sɒθ- ‖ 'soʊθ ɪk 'sɑːθ-
Sotho 'suːt uː 'səʊt əʊ ‖ 'soʊt oʊ **~s** z
sottish 'sɒt ɪʃ ‖ 'sɑːţ ɪʃ **~ly** li **~ness** nəs nɪs
sotto voce ˌsɒt əʊ 'vəʊtʃ i ‖ ˌsɑːţ oʊ 'voʊtʃ i —*It* [ˌsot to 'voː tʃe]
sou suː **sous** suːz
soubise su 'biːz
soubrette su 'bret **~s** s
soubriquet 'suːb rɪ keɪ -rə-, ˌ·ˈ·
souchong ˌsuː 'tʃɒŋ ◂ -'ʃɒŋ ‖ -'tʃɑːŋ ˌsoʊ-, -'ʃɑːŋ, '· ·
souffle *'egg dish',* **soufflé** 'suːf leɪ ‖ su 'fleɪ **~s** z
souffle *'blowing sound'* 'suːf ᵊl **~s** z
Soufriere, Soufrière su 'frɪə 'suːf ri eə ‖ -'frɪᵊr
sough *'sigh, murmur'* saʊ sʌf **soughed** saʊd sʌft **soughing** 'saʊ ɪŋ 'sʌf- **soughs** saʊz sʌfs
sought sɔːt ‖ sɑːt
sought-after 'sɔːt ˌɑːft ə §-ˌæft- ‖ 'sɔːţ ˌæft ᵊr 'sɑːţ-
souk suːk **souks** suːks
soul, Soul səʊl →sɒʊl ‖ soʊl *(= sole)* **souls** səʊlz →sɒʊlz ‖ soʊlz
'soul ˌbrother; **'soul mate**; **'soul ˌmusic**; **'soul ˌsister**
Soulbury 'səʊl bər‿i →'sɒʊl- ‖ 'soʊl ˌber i
Soulby 'səʊl bi →'sɒʊl- ‖ 'soʊl bi
soul-destroying 'səʊl dɪ ˌstrɔɪ ɪŋ də-, §-diː- ‖ 'soʊl-
soulful 'səʊl fᵊl →'sɒʊl-, -fʊl ‖ 'soʊl- **~ly** ‿i **~ness** nəs nɪs
soulless 'səʊl ləs →'sɒʊl-, -lɪs ‖ 'soʊl- **~ly** li **~ness** nəs nɪs
soul-searching 'səʊl ˌsɜːtʃ ɪŋ →'sɒʊl- ‖ 'soʊl ˌsɝːtʃ ɪŋ
sound saʊnd **sounded** 'saʊnd ɪd -əd **sounding/s** 'saʊnd ɪŋ/z **sounds** saʊndz
'sound ˌbarrier; **'sound bite**; **'sounding board**; **'sound ˌsystem**; **'sound wave**
soundboard 'saʊnd bɔːd →'saʊm- ‖ -bɔːrd -boʊrd **~s** z
soundless 'saʊnd ləs -lɪs **~ly** li
soundly 'saʊnd li
soundness 'saʊnd nəs -nɪs
soundproof 'saʊnd pruːf →'saʊm-, §-prʊf **~ed** t **~ing** ɪŋ **~s** s
soundsmith 'saʊnd smɪθ **~s** s
soundstage 'saʊnd steɪdʒ **~s** ɪz əz
soundtrack 'saʊnd træk **~s** s
Souness 'suːn əs -ɪs

S

soup suːp **soups** suːps
ˈsoup ˌkitchen; **ˈsoup spoon**
soupcon, soupçon ˈsuːps ɒn -õ ‖ -ɑːn suːp ˈsoʊn —*Fr* [sup sɔ̃] **~s** z
souped-up ˌsuːpt ˈʌp ◂
soupy ˈsuːp i **soupier** ˈsuːp i‿ə ‖ ᵊr **soupiest** ˈsuːp i‿ɪst əst
sour ˈsaʊ‿ə ‖ ˈsaʊ‿ᵊr **soured** ˈsaʊ‿əd ‖ ˈsaʊ‿ᵊrd **sourer** ˈsaʊ‿ər ə ‖ ˈsaʊ‿ᵊr ᵊr **sourest** ˈsaʊ‿ər ɪst -əst ‖ ˈsaʊ‿ᵊr əst **souring** ˈsaʊ‿ər ɪŋ ‖ ˈsaʊ‿ᵊr ɪŋ **sours** ˈsaʊ‿əz ‖ ˈsaʊ‿ᵊrz
ˌsour ˈcream; **ˌsour ˈgrapes**
source sɔːs ‖ sɔːrs soʊrs **sourced** sɔːst ‖ sɔːrst soʊrst **sources** ˈsɔːs ɪz -əz ‖ ˈsɔːrs əz ˈsoʊrs- **sourcing** ˈsɔːs ɪŋ ‖ ˈsɔːrs ɪŋ ˈsoʊrs-
sourceless ˈsɔːs ləs -lɪs ‖ ˈsɔːrs- ˈsoʊrs-
sourdine (ı)sʊə ˈdiːn ‖ sʊr- **~s** z
sourdough ˈsaʊ‿ə dəʊ ‖ ˈsaʊ‿ᵊr doʊ **~s** z
sour-faced ˌsaʊ‿ə ˈfeɪst ◂ ˈ· · ‖ ˌsaʊᵊr-
sour|ly ˈsaʊ‿ə |li ‖ ˈsaʊ‿ᵊr |li **~ness** nəs nɪs
sourpuss ˈsaʊ‿ə pʊs ‖ ˈsaʊ‿ᵊr pʊs **~es** ɪz əz
soursop ˈsaʊ‿ə sɒp ‖ ˈsaʊ‿ᵊr sɑːp **~s** s
Sousa ˈsuːz ə
sousaphone ˈsuːz ə fəʊn ‖ -foʊn **~s** z
sous-chef ˈsuː ʃef **~s** s
souse saʊs **soused** saʊst **souses** ˈsaʊs ɪz -əz **sousing** ˈsaʊs ɪŋ
Sousse suːs
soutach|e su ˈtæʃ **~es** ɪz əz
soutane su ˈtɑːn -ˈtæn **~s** z
Soutar, Souter ˈsuːt ə ‖ ˈsuːt̬ ᵊr
south, South saʊθ
(ı)South ˈAfrica; **ˌSouth Aˈmerica**; **ˌSouth Auˈstralia**; **ˌSouth ˌCaroˈlina**; **ˌSouth Daˈkota**; **ˌSouth Glaˈmorgan**; **ˌSouth ˈPole**; **ˌSouth Sea ˈBubble**; **ˌSouth ˈYorkshire**
Southall *family name* ˈsʌð ɔːl -ᵊl ‖ -ɑːl
Southall *place in London* ˈsaʊθ ɔːl ˈsaʊð- ‖ -ɑːl
Southam ˈsaʊð əm
Southampton (ı)saʊθ ˈhæmpt ən saʊ ˈθæmpt-, sə-; sə ˈðæmpt-
Southborough ˈsaʊθ bər‿ə ‖ -ˌbɜː oʊ
southbound ˈsaʊθ baʊnd
Southcott ˈsaʊθ kɒt -kət ‖ -kɑːt
Southdown ˈsaʊθ daʊn
southeast, S~ ˌsaʊθ ˈiːst ◂
ˌSoutheast ˈAsia
southeaster ˌsaʊθ ˈiːst ə ‖ -ᵊr **~s** z
southeaster|ly (ı)saʊθ ˈiːst ə |li -ᵊ|l i ‖ -ᵊr |li **~lies** liz
southeastern (ı)saʊθ ˈiːst ən ‖ -ᵊrn
southeastward (ı)saʊθ ˈiːst wəd ‖ -wᵊrd **~s** z
Southend ˌsaʊθ ˈend
ˌSouthend-on-ˈSea
souther|ly ˈsʌð ə |li ‖ -ᵊr- *(!)* **~lies** liz
southern, S~ ˈsʌð ᵊn ‖ -ᵊrn *(!)*
ˌSouthern ˈCross; **ˌsouthern ˈlights**
Southerndown ˈsʌð ᵊn daʊn ‖ -ᵊrn-
southerner, S~ ˈsʌð ᵊn‿ə ‖ -ᵊrn‿ər -ᵊn‿ **~s** z
southernmost ˈsʌð ᵊn məʊst →-ᵊm- ‖ -ᵊrn moʊst
southernwood ˈsʌð ᵊn wʊd ‖ -ᵊrn-
Southey *(i)* ˈsaʊð i, *(ii)* ˈsʌð i
Southgate ˈsaʊθ geɪt -gɪt
southing ˈsaʊð ɪŋ ˈsaʊθ- **~s** z
southland ˈsaʊθ lænd
southpaw ˈsaʊθ pɔː ‖ -pɑː **~s** z
Southport ˈsaʊθ pɔːt ‖ -pɔːrt -poʊrt
Southron, S~ ˈsʌð rən **~s** z
Southsea ˈsaʊθ siː
southward ˈsaʊθ wəd ‖ -wᵊrd —*also naut* ˈsʌð əd ‖ -ᵊrd **~s** z
Southwark ˈsʌð ək ‖ -ᵊrk *(!)*
Southwell *(i)* ˈsʌð ᵊl, *(ii)* ˈsaʊθ wəl
southwest, S~ ˌsaʊθ ˈwest ◂ —*also naut* (ı)saʊ-
southwester (ı)saʊθ ˈwest ə ‖ -ᵊr —*also naut* (ı)saʊ- **~s** z
southwester|ly (ı)saʊθ ˈwest ə |li -ᵊ|l i ‖ -ᵊr |li —*also naut* (ı)saʊ- **~lies** liz
southwestern, S~ (ı)saʊθ ˈwest ən ‖ -ᵊrn —*also naut* (ı)saʊ-
southwestward (ı)saʊθ ˈwest wəd ‖ -wᵊrd —*also naut* (ı)saʊ- **~s** z
Southwick ˈsaʊθ wɪk —*But the places in Northants and Hants are sometimes* ˈsʌð ɪk
Southwold ˈsaʊθ wəʊld →-wɒʊld ‖ -woʊld
Souttar, Soutter ˈsuːt ə ‖ ˈsuːt̬ ᵊr
souvenir ˌsuːv ə ˈnɪə ◂ ˈ· · · ‖ -ˈnɪᵊr **~s** z
souvlaki su ˈvlɑːk i —*ModGk* [su ˈvla ci] **~a** ‿ə **~s** z
sou'wester saʊ ˈwest ə ‖ -ᵊr **~s** z
sovereign ˈsɒv rɪn -rən ‖ ˈsɑːv rən ˈsɑːv ᵊr ən **~s** z
sovereign|ty ˈsɒv rən |ti -rɪn- ‖ ˈsɑːv- ˈsɑːv ᵊr ən |ti **~ties** tiz

SOVIET

27% ˈsəʊv- 73% ˈsɒv- BrE

(Chart legend: ˈsəʊv- 73%; ˈsɒv- 27%; BrE)

soviet, S~ ˈsəʊv i‿ət ˈsɒv-, -et ‖ ˈsoʊv i et ˈsɑːv-, ət — *Preference poll, BrE:* ˈsəʊv- *73%,* ˈsɒv- *27%.* **~s** s
ˌSoviet ˈUnion
sovran ˈsɒv rən ‖ ˈsɑːv-
sow *v 'place (seeds)'* səʊ ‖ soʊ *(= so)* **sowed** səʊd ‖ soʊd **sowing** ˈsəʊ ɪŋ ‖ ˈsoʊ ɪŋ **sown** səʊn ‖ soʊn **sows** səʊz ‖ soʊz
sow *n 'female pig'* saʊ **sows** saʊz
sowbread ˈsaʊ bred
sower ˈsəʊ ə ‖ ˈsoʊ ᵊr **~s** z
Sowerbutts ˈsaʊ‿ə bʌts ‖ ˈsaʊ‿ᵊr bʌts
Sowerby *(i)* ˈsaʊ‿ə bi ‖ ˈsaʊ‿ᵊr-, *(ii)* ˈsəʊ ə bi ‖ ˈsoʊ ᵊr-
Soweto sə ˈwet əʊ -ˈweɪt- ‖ -oʊ —*Xhosa/Zulu* [sɔ ˈweː tɔ]
sown səʊn ‖ soʊn
sox sɒks ‖ sɑːks *(= socks)*

soy sɔɪ
ˌ**soy 'sauce,** '·.·
soya 'sɔɪ ə
'**soya bean**
soybean 'sɔɪ biːn **~s** z
Soyinka sɔɪ 'ɪŋk ə
Soyuz sɔɪ 'uːz —*Russ* [sʌ 'jus]
sozzled 'sɒz ᵊld ‖ 'sɑːz-
spa, Spa spɑː **spas** spɑːz
space speɪs **spaced** speɪst **spaces** 'speɪs ɪz -əz
spacing 'speɪs ɪŋ
'**space ˌcapsule**; ˌ**spaced 'out◂**; '**space flight**; '**space ˌheater**; '**space probe**; '**space ˌshuttle**; '**space ˌstation**
space-age 'speɪs eɪdʒ
space-bar 'speɪs bɑː ‖ -bɑːr **~s** z
spacecraft 'speɪs krɑːft §-kræft ‖ -kræft **~s** s
Spacek 'speɪs ek
spacelab 'speɪs læb **~s** z
space|man 'speɪs |mæn -mən **~men** men -mən
spacer 'speɪs ə ‖ -ᵊr **~s** z
spaceship 'speɪs ʃɪp →'speɪʃ- **~s** s
spacesuit 'speɪs suːt -sjuːt **~s** s
space-time ˌspeɪs 'taɪm
spacewalk 'speɪs wɔːk ‖ -wɑːk
space|woman 'speɪs |ˌwʊm ən **~women** ˌwɪm ɪn -ən
spac|ey 'speɪs i **~ier** i‿ə ‖ i‿ᵊr **~iest** i‿ɪst ‿əst
spacing 'speɪs ɪŋ **~s** z
spacious 'speɪʃ əs **~ly** li **~ness** nəs nɪs
spackle 'spæk ᵊl
spade speɪd **spades** speɪdz
spadeful 'speɪd fʊl **~s** z
spadework 'speɪd wɜːk ‖ -wɜːk
spadix 'speɪd ɪks **spadices** 'speɪd ɪ siːz -ə-
spag bol ˌspæg 'bɒl ‖ -'bɑːl
spaghetti spə 'get i ‖ -'geţ-
spahi 'spɑː hiː **~s** z
Spain speɪn
spake speɪk
Spalding 'spɔːld ɪŋ ‖ 'spɑːld-
spall spɔːl ‖ spɑːl **spalled** spɔːld ‖ spɑːld
spalling 'spɔːl ɪŋ ‖ 'spɑːl- **spalls** spɔːlz ‖ spɑːlz
spallation spɔː 'leɪʃ ᵊn ‖ spɑː- **~s** z
spalpeen spæl 'piːn 'spælp iːn **~s** z
spam, Spam *tdmk* spæm **spammed** spæmd
spamming 'spæm ɪŋ **spams** spæmz
spamblocking 'spæm ˌblɒk ɪŋ ‖ -blɑːk-
spamdexing 'spæm deks ɪŋ
spammer 'spæm ə ‖ -ᵊr **~s** z
span spæn **spanned** spænd **spanning** 'spæn ɪŋ **spans** spænz
Spandau 'spænd aʊ —*Ger* ['ʃpan dau]
spandex 'spænd eks
spandrel 'spændr əl **~s** z
spangl|e 'spæŋ gᵊl **~ed** d **~es** z **~ing** ‿ɪŋ
Spanglish 'spæŋ glɪʃ
Spaniard 'spæn jəd ‖ -jᵊrd **~s** z
spaniel 'spæn jəl **~s** z
Spanier 'spæn jeɪ -jə ‖ -jᵊr
Spanish 'spæn ɪʃ
ˌ**Spanish 'Main**; ˌ**Spanish 'onion**
Spanish-American ˌspæn ɪʃ ə 'mer ɪk ən ◂ **~s** z
spank spæŋk **spanked** spæŋ*k*t **spanking/s** 'spæŋk ɪŋ/z **spanks** spæŋks
spanker 'spæŋk ə ‖ -ᵊr **~s** z
spanner 'spæn ə ‖ -ᵊr **~s** z
spar spɑː ‖ spɑːr **sparred** spɑːd ‖ spɑːrd
sparring 'spɑːr ɪŋ **spars** spɑːz ‖ spɑːrz
'**sparring ˌpartner**
sparaxis spə 'ræks ɪs §-əs
spare speə ‖ speᵊr spæᵊr **spared** speəd ‖ speᵊrd spæᵊrd **spares** speəz ‖ speᵊrz spæᵊrz
sparing 'speər ɪŋ ‖ 'sper ɪŋ 'spær-
ˌ**spare 'part**; ˌ**spare-part 'surgery**; ˌ**spare 'tyre**
sparerib 'speə rɪb ˌ·'· ‖ 'sper- 'spær-, -əb **~s** z
sparing|ly 'speər ɪŋ |li ‖ 'sper- 'spær- **~ness** nəs nɪs
spark spɑːk ‖ spɑːrk **sparked** spɑːkt ‖ spɑːrkt
sparking 'spɑːk ɪŋ ‖ 'spɑːrk ɪŋ **sparks** spɑːks ‖ spɑːrks
'**sparking plug,** '**spark plug**
Spark, Sparke spɑːk ‖ spɑːrk **Sparkes** spɑːks ‖ spɑːrks
sparkl|e 'spɑːk ᵊl ‖ 'spɑːrk ᵊl **~ed** d **~es** z **~ing** ‿ɪŋ
sparkler 'spɑːk lə ‖ 'spɑːrk lᵊr **~s** z
Sparklet *tdmk* 'spɑːk lət -lɪt ‖ 'spɑːrk- **~s** s
sparkling *adj* 'spɑːk lɪŋ ‖ 'spɑːrk- **~ly** li
spark|y 'spɑːk| i ‖ 'spɑːrk| i **~ier** i‿ə ‖ i‿ᵊr **~iest** i‿ɪst i‿əst **~iness** i nəs i nɪs
sparr... —*see* **spar**
sparrow, S~ 'spær əʊ ‖ -oʊ 'sper- **~s** z
sparrowhawk 'spær əʊ hɔːk ‖ -oʊ- 'sper-, -hɑːk **~s** s
sparse spɑːs ‖ spɑːrs **sparser** 'spɑːs ə ‖ 'spɑːrs ᵊr **sparsest** 'spɑːs ɪst -əst ‖ 'spɑːrs-
sparse|ly 'spɑːs |li ‖ 'spɑːrs |li **~ness** nəs nɪs
sparsity 'spɑːs ət i -ɪt- ‖ 'spɑːrs əţ i
Spart spɑːt ‖ spɑːrt
Sparta 'spɑːt ə ‖ 'spɑːrţ ə
Spartacist 'spɑːt əs ɪst §-əst ‖ 'spɑːrţ- **~s** s
Spartacus 'spɑːt ək əs ‖ 'spɑːrţ-
spartan, S~ 'spɑːt ᵊn ‖ 'spɑːrt ᵊn **~s** z
Spartist 'spɑːt ɪst §-əst ‖ 'spɑːrţ- **~s** s
spasm 'spæz əm **~s** z
spasmodic spæz 'mɒd ɪk ‖ -'mɑːd- **~ally** ᵊl‿i
spastic 'spæst ɪk **~ally** ᵊl‿i **~s** s
spasticity spæ 'stɪs ət i -ɪt i ‖ -əţ i
spat spæt **spats** spæts
spatchcock 'spætʃ kɒk ‖ -kɑːk **~ed** t **~ing** ɪŋ **~s** s
spate speɪt **spates** speɪts
spathe speɪð **spathes** speɪðz
spathic 'spæθ ɪk
spatial 'speɪʃ ᵊl 'speɪʃ i‿əl **~ly** i
spatiotemporal ˌspeɪʃ i‿əʊ 'temp ᵊr‿əl ◂ ‖ -i‿oʊ- **~ly** i
Spätlese 'ʃpeɪt ˌleɪz ə —*Ger* ['ʃpɛːt leːz ə, 'ʃpeːt-]
spatter 'spæt ə ‖ 'spæţ ᵊr **~ed** d **spattering** 'spæt‿ər ɪŋ ‖ 'spæţ ər ɪŋ **~s** z
spatterdash 'spæt ə dæʃ ‖ 'spæţ ᵊr- **~es** ɪz əz

spatterdock ˈspæt ə dɒk ‖ ˈspæṭ ᵊr dɑːk **~s** s
spatula ˈspæt jʊl ə §ˈspætʃ əl ə ‖ ˈspætʃ əl‿ə **~s** z
spavin ˈspæv ɪn -ᵊn **~ed** d
spawn spɔːn ‖ spɑːn **spawned** spɔːnd ‖ spɑːnd **spawning** ˈspɔːn ɪŋ ‖ ˈspɑːn- **spawns** spɔːnz ‖ spɑːnz
spay speɪ **spayed** speɪd *(= spade)* **spaying** ˈspeɪ ɪŋ **spays** speɪz
SPE ˌes pi ˈiː
Speaight speɪt
speak spiːk **speaking** ˈspiːk ɪŋ **speaks** spiːks **spoke** spəʊk ‖ spoʊk **spoken** ˈspəʊk ən ‖ ˈspoʊk ən
ˌ**speaking ˈclock**; ˈ**speaking tube**
-speak spiːk — **doublespeak** ˈdʌb ᵊl spiːk
speakeas|y ˈspiːk ˌiːz |i **~ies** iz
speaker, S~ ˈspiːk ə ‖ -ᵊr **~s** z
ˌ**Speaker's ˈCorner**
speakerphone ˈspiːk ə fəʊn ‖ -ᵊr foʊn **~s** z
speakership ˈspiːk ə ʃɪp ‖ -ᵊr-
-speaking ˌspiːk ɪŋ — **English-speaking** ˈɪŋ glɪʃ ˌspiːk ɪŋ
Spean ˈspiː‿ən
spear spɪə ‖ spɪᵊr **speared** spɪəd ‖ spɪᵊrd **spearing** ˈspɪər ɪŋ ‖ ˈspɪr ɪŋ **spears** spɪəz ‖ spɪᵊrz
spearhead ˈspɪə hed ‖ ˈspɪr- **~ed** ɪd əd **~ing** ɪŋ **~s** z
spear|man, S~ ˈspɪə |mən ‖ ˈspɪr- **~men** mən men
spearmint ˈspɪə mɪnt ‖ ˈspɪr-
Spears spɪəz ‖ spɪᵊrz
spearwort ˈspɪə wɜːt §-wɔːt ‖ ˈspɪr wɜːt -wɔːrt **~s** s
spec spek *(= speck)* **specs** speks
special ˈspeʃ ᵊl **~s** z
ˈ**Special Branch**; ˌ**special deˈlivery**; ˌ**special ˈdrawing rights**; ˌ**special ˈlicence**; ˌ**special ˈpleading**; ˈ**special school**
specialis... —*see* **specializ...**
specialism ˈspeʃ ᵊl ˌɪz əm -ə ˌlɪz- **~s** z
specialist ˈspeʃ ᵊl ɪst §-əst **~s** s
specialit|y ˌspeʃ i ˈæl ət |i -ɪt i ‖ -əṭ |i **~ies** iz
specialization ˌspeʃ əl‿aɪ ˈzeɪʃ ᵊn -əl‿ɪ- ‖ -əl‿ə- **~s** z
specializ|e ˈspeʃ ə laɪz -ᵊl aɪz **~ed** d **~es** ɪz əz **~ing** ɪŋ
specially ˈspeʃ ᵊl‿i
special|ty ˈspeʃ ᵊl |ti **~ties** tiz
speciation ˌspiːs i ˈeɪʃ ᵊn ˌspiːʃ-
specie ˈspiːʃ i -iː
species ˈspiːʃ iːz ˈspiːs-, -ɪz —*Some speakers pronounce the sing. with* -ɪz, *the pl with* -iːz
speciesism ˈspiːʃ iːz ˌɪz əm ˈspiːs-, ˈ·ɪz-
specifiable ˈspes ə faɪ‿əb ᵊl ˈ·ɪ-, ˌ·ˈ··-
specific spə ˈsɪf ɪk spɪ- **~ally** ᵊl‿i **~s** s
speˌ**cific ˈgravity**
specification ˌspes əf ɪ ˈkeɪʃ ᵊn ˌ·ɪf-, §-əˈ-- **~s** z
specificity ˌspes ə ˈfɪs ət i ˌ·ɪ-, -ɪt i ‖ -əṭ i
speci|fy ˈspes ə |faɪ -ɪ- **~fied** faɪd **~fier/s** faɪ‿ə/z ‖ faɪ‿ᵊr/z **~fies** faɪz **~fying** faɪ ɪŋ
specimen ˈspes ə mɪn -ɪ-, -mən **~s** z
specious ˈspiːʃ əs **~ly** li **~ness** nəs nɪs
speck spek **specked** spekt **specks** speks
speckl|e ˈspek ᵊl **~ed** d **~es** z **~ing** ‿ɪŋ
speckless ˈspek ləs -lɪs **~ly** li **~ness** nəs nɪs
specs speks
spectacle ˈspekt ək ᵊl -ɪk- **~d** d **~s** z
spectacular spek ˈtæk jʊl ə -jəl ə ‖ -jəl ᵊr **~ly** li **~s** z
spect|ate spek ˈt|eɪt ˈspekt |eɪt ‖ ˈspekt |eɪt **~ated** eɪt ɪd -əd ‖ eɪṭ əd **~ates** eɪts **~ating** eɪt ɪŋ ‖ eɪṭ ɪŋ

SPECTATOR

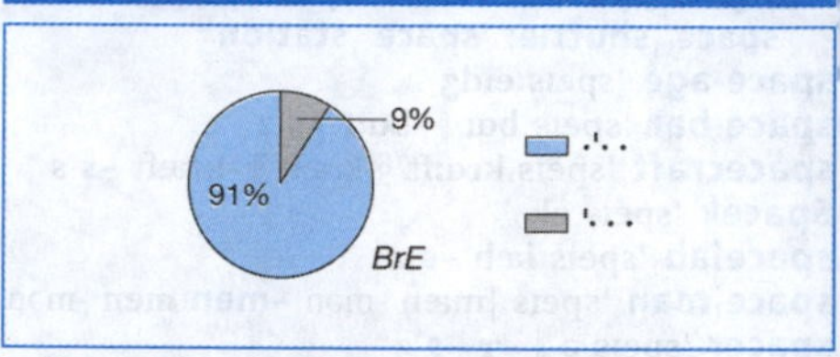

spectator, S~ spek ˈteɪt ə ˈspekt eɪt ə ‖ ˈspekt eɪṭ ᵊr — *Preference poll, BrE:* ·ˈ·· *91%,* ˈ··· *9%.* **~s z**
specter ˈspekt ə ‖ -ᵊr **~s** z
Spector ˈspekt ə ‖ -ᵊr
spectra ˈspek trə
spectral ˈspek trəl **~ly** i
spectre ˈspekt ə ‖ -ᵊr **~s** z
spectro- *comb. form*
with stress-neutral suffix ¦spek trəʊ ‖ ¦spek troʊ — **spectrophotometer** ˌspek trəʊ fəʊ ˈtɒm ɪt ə -ət ə ‖ -troʊ fə ˈtɑːm əṭ ᵊr
with stress-imposing suffix spek ˈtrɒ+ ‖ spek ˈtrɑː+ — **spectrometer** spek ˈtrɒm ɪt ə -ət ə ‖ -ˈtrɑːm əṭ ᵊr
spectrogram ˈspek trəʊ græm ‖ -trə- **~s** z
spectrograph ˈspek trəʊ grɑːf -græf ‖ -trə græf **~s** s
spectrographic ˌspek trəʊ ˈgræf ɪk ◂ ‖ -trə- **~ally** ᵊl‿i
spectrography spek ˈtrɒg rəf i ‖ -ˈtrɑːg-
spectroscape ˈspek trəʊ skeɪp ‖ -trə- **~s** s
spectroscope ˈspek trə skəʊp ‖ -trə skoʊp **~s** s
spectroscopic ˌspek trə ˈskɒp ɪk ◂ ‖ -ˈskɑːp- **~ally** ᵊl‿i
spectroscopy spek ˈtrɒsk əp i ‖ -ˈtrɑːsk-
spec|trum ˈspek |trəm **~tra** trə
specu|late ˈspek ju |leɪt -jə- ‖ -jə- **~lated** leɪt ɪd -əd ‖ leɪṭ əd **~lates** leɪts **~lating** leɪt ɪŋ ‖ leɪṭ ɪŋ
speculation ˌspek ju ˈleɪʃ ᵊn -jə- ‖ -jə- **~s** z
speculative ˈspek jʊl ət ɪv ˈ·jəl-; -ju leɪt-, -jə leɪt- ‖ -jə leɪṭ- -jə ləṭ- **~ly** li **~ness** nəs nɪs
speculator ˈspek ju leɪt ə ˈ·jə- ‖ -jə leɪṭ ᵊr **~s** z
specul|um ˈspek jʊl |əm -jəl- ‖ -jəl- **~a** ə **~ums** əmz
sped sped
speech spiːtʃ **speeches** ˈspiːtʃ ɪz -əz
ˈ**speech comˌmunity**; ˈ**speech day**; ˈ**speech deˌfect**, ·ˈ·ˌ·; ˌ**speech paˈthology**;

Spelling pronunciation

1 A **spelling pronunciation** of a word is a pronunciation that, unlike the traditional pronunciation, corresponds closely to the spelling.

2 Examples of spelling pronunciations often heard from native speakers of English include **ate** eɪt (rathen than et), **envelope** ˈen və ləʊp ‖ -loʊp (rather than ˈɒn- ‖ ˈɑːn-), and **synod** ˈsɪn ɒd ‖ -ɑːd (rather than -əd – compare **method**). People whose first encounter with the word **awry** is as a written form sometimes fail to recognize its analysis as prefix **a-** plus stem **wry**, and infer a spelling pronunciation ˈɔːr i rather than the proper ə ˈraɪ.

3 Learners of EFL should avoid using spelling pronunciations that native speakers do not use. Do not, for example, use a strong vowel ɔː in the second syllable of **effort** ˈef ət ‖ -ᵊrt, **information** ˌɪnf ə ˈmeɪʃ ᵊn ‖ -ᵊr-, **Oxford** ˈɒks fəd ‖ ˈɑːks fᵊrd. Do not use ɑː in the first and last syllables of **particular** pə ˈtɪk jʊl ə ‖ pᵊr ˈtɪk jəl ᵊr. Do not pronounce a b in **climb** klaɪm or **debt** det.

4 British place-names are especially difficult. Spelling pronunciations of **Gloucester, Southwark** and **Harwich** sound absurd and would possibly not be understood.

ˌ**speech ˈsynthesis**, ˈ· ˌ· · ·; ˌ**speech ˈsynthesizer**, ˈ· ˌ· · · ·; ˈ**speech ˌtherapist**, ˌ· ˈ· · ·; ˌ**speech ˈtherapy**, ˌ· ˈ· · ·

speechification ˌspiːtʃ ɪf ɪ ˈkeɪʃ ᵊn §ˌ·əf-, §-əˈ·-

speechi|fy ˈspiːtʃ ɪ |faɪ §-ə- **~fied** faɪd **~fier/s** faɪ ə/z ‖ faɪ ᵊr/z **~fies** faɪz **~fying** faɪ ɪŋ

speechless ˈspiːtʃ ləs -lɪs **~ly** li **~ness** nəs nɪs

speechwriter ˈspiːtʃ ˌraɪt ə ‖ -ˌraɪṭ ᵊr **~s** z

speed spiːd **sped** sped **speeded** ˈspiːd ɪd -əd **speeding** ˈspiːd ɪŋ **speeds** spiːdz ˈ**speed ˌlimit**; ˈ**speed ˌmerchant**; ˈ**speed trap**

speedball ˈspiːd bɔːl ‖ -bɑːl **~s** z

speedboat ˈspiːd bəʊt →ˈspiːb- ‖ -boʊt **~s** s

speedo ˈspiːd əʊ ‖ -oʊ **~s** z

speedometer spɪ ˈdɒm ɪt ə ⁽ˌ⁾spiːd ˈɒm-, -ət ə ‖ -ˈdɑːm əṭ ᵊr **~s** z

speedster ˈspiːd stə ‖ -stᵊr **~s** z

speed-up ˈspiːd ʌp **~s** s

speedway ˈspiːd weɪ **~s** z

speedwell ˈspiːd wel **~s** z

Speedwriting *tdmk* ˈspiːd ˌraɪt ɪŋ ‖ -ˌraɪṭ-

speed|y ˈspiːd |i **~ier** i ə ‖ i ᵊr **~iest** i ɪst i əst **~ily** ɪ li əl i **~iness** i nəs i nɪs

Speenhamland ˈspiːn əm lænd

Speight speɪt

Speir spɪə ‖ spɪᵊr

speiss spaɪs (= *spice*)

Speke spiːk

spelae... —*see* **spele...**

speleological ˌspiːl i ə ˈlɒdʒ ɪk ᵊl ◂ ˌspel- ‖ -ˈlɑːdʒ- **~ly** i

speleologist ˌspiːl i ˈɒl ədʒ ɪst ˌspel-, §-əst ‖ -ˈɑːl- **~s** s

speleology ˌspiːl i ˈɒl ədʒ i ˌspel- ‖ -ˈɑːl-

spell spel **spelled** speld **spelling/s** ˈspel ɪŋ/z **spells** spelz **spelt** spelt ˈ**spelling bee**; ˈ**spelling pronunciˌation**, ˌ· · ˌ· · ˈ· ·

spellbind ˈspel baɪnd **~er/s** ə/z ‖ ᵊr/z **~ing** ɪŋ **~s** z **spellbound** ˈspel baʊnd

spellcheck ˈspel tʃek **~ed** t **~er/s** ə/z ‖ -ᵊr/z **~ing** ɪŋ **~s** s

speller, S~ ˈspel ə ‖ -ᵊr **~s** z

Spellman ˈspel mən

spelt spelt

spelter ˈspelt ə ‖ -ᵊr

spelunk spɪ ˈlʌŋk spə-, spiː- **~ed** t **~er/s** ə/z ‖ ᵊr/z **~ing** ɪŋ **~s** s

Spen spen

Spenborough ˈspen bər ə →ˈspem- ‖ -ˌbɜː oʊ

Spence spenᵗs

Spencer, s~ ˈspenᵗs ə ‖ -ᵊr **~s** z

Spencerian spen ˈsɪər i ən ‖ -ˈsɪr- **~s** z

spend spend **spending** ˈspend ɪŋ **spends** spendz **spent** spent

spendaholic ˌspend ə ˈhɒl ɪk ◂ ‖ -ˈhɔːl- -ˈhɑːl- **~s** s

spender, S~ ˈspend ə ‖ -ᵊr **~s** z

spending money ˈ**spending ˌmoney**

spendthrift ˈspend θrɪft **~s** s

Spengler ˈspeŋ lə -glə ‖ -glᵊr —*Ger* [ˈʃpɛŋ lɐ]

S

Spennymoor 'spen i mɔː -mʊə ‖ -mɔːr -moʊr, -mʊr
Spens spenz
Spenser 'spenᵗs ə ‖ -ᵊr
Spenserian spen 'sɪər i‿ən ‖ -'sɪr- -'ser-
spent spent
-sperm spɜːm ‖ spɝːm — **gymnosperm** 'dʒɪm nəʊ spɜːm ‖ -nə spɝːm
sperm spɜːm ‖ spɝːm **sperms** spɜːmz ‖ spɝːmz **'sperm bank**; **'sperm count**; **'sperm oil**; **'sperm whale**
spermaceti ˌspɜːm ə 'set i -'siːt i ‖ ˌspɝːm ə 'set̬ i -'siːt̬ i
spermatic spɜː 'mæt ɪk ‖ spɝː 'mæt̬ ɪk
spermato- *comb. form*
with stress-neutral suffix ¦spɜːm ət əʊ spɜː ¦mæt- ‖ spɝː ¦mæt̬ ə — **spermatocyte** 'spɜːm ət əʊ saɪt spɜː 'mæt- ‖ spɝː 'mæt̬ ə-
with stress-imposing suffix ˌspɜːm ə 'tɒ+ ‖ ˌspɝːm ə 'tɑː+ — **spermatolysis** ˌspɜːm ə 'tɒl əs ɪs -ɪs ɪs, §-əs ‖ ˌspɝːm ə 'tɑːl-
spermatozo|on ˌspɜːm ət ə 'zəʊ |ɒn -ən ‖ ˌspɝːm ət̬ ə 'zoʊ |ən spɜː ˌmæt̬-, -ɑːn **~a** ə **~al** əl **~an** ən **~ic** ɪk
spermicidal ˌspɜːm ɪ 'saɪd ᵊl ◂ ˌ-ə- ‖ ˌspɝːm-
spermicide 'spɜːm ɪ saɪd -ə saɪd ‖ 'spɝːm- **~s** z
Sperry 'sper i
spew spjuː **spewed** spjuːd **spewing** 'spjuː ɪŋ **spews** spjuːz
Spey speɪ
sphagnum 'sfæg nəm
sphalerite 'sfæl ə raɪt 'sfeɪl-
sphene sfiːn
sphenoid 'sfiːn ɔɪd **~s** z
sphere sfɪə ‖ sfɪᵊr **spheres** sfɪəz ‖ sfɪᵊrz
-sphere sfɪə ‖ sfɪr — **biosphere** 'baɪ əʊ sfɪə ‖ -ə sfɪr
-spheric 'sfer ɪk 'sfɪər ɪk ‖ 'sfɪr ɪk — **biospheric** ˌbaɪ əʊ 'sfer ɪk ◂ -'sfɪər ɪk ‖ -ə- -'sfɪr ɪk
spherical 'sfer ɪk ᵊl ‖ 'sfɪr- **~ly** ‿i **~ness** nəs nɪs
spheroid 'sfɪər ɔɪd ‖ 'sfɪr- 'sfer- **~s** z
spheroidal sfɪə 'rɔɪd ᵊl ‖ sfɪ- sfe- **~ly** i
sphincter 'sfɪŋkt ə ‖ -ᵊr **~s** z
sphinx, S~ sfɪŋks **sphinxes, Sphinx's** 'sfɪŋks ɪz -əz
sphragistic sfrə 'dʒɪst ɪk **~s** s
sphygmo- *comb. form*
with stress-neutral suffix ¦sfɪg məʊ ‖ -mə — **sphygmogram** 'sfɪg məʊ græm ‖ -mə-
with stress-imposing suffix sfɪg 'mɒ+ ‖ -'mɑː+ — **sphygmography** sfɪg 'mɒg rəf i ‖ -'mɑːg-
sphygmomanometer ˌsfɪg məʊ mə 'nɒm ɪt ə -ət ə; ⚠ˌsfɪg mə 'nɒm- ‖ -moʊ mə 'nɑːm ət̬ ᵊr **~s** z
spic spɪk **spics** spɪks
spica, Spica 'spaɪk ə 'spiːk-
spic-and-span ˌspɪk ən 'spæn ◂ →-ŋ-
spiccato spɪ 'kɑːt əʊ ‖ -'kɑːt̬ oʊ —*It* [spik 'kaː to]
spice spaɪs **spiced** spaɪst **spices** 'spaɪs ɪz -əz **spicing** 'spaɪs ɪŋ
spicebush 'spaɪs bʊʃ **~es** ɪz əz
spick-and-span ˌspɪk ən 'spæn ◂ →-ŋ-
spicule 'spɪk juːl 'spaɪk- **~s** z
spic|y 'spaɪs |i **~ier** i‿ə ‖ i‿ᵊr **~iest** i‿ɪst i‿əst **~ily** ɪ li əl i **~iness** i nəs i nɪs
spider 'spaɪd ə ‖ -ᵊr **~s** z
'spider plant
spider|man, S~ 'spaɪd ə |mæn ‖ -ᵊr- **~men** men
spiderweb 'spaɪd ə web ‖ -ᵊr- **~s** z
spiderwort 'spaɪd ə wɜːt -wɔːt ‖ -ᵊr wɝːt **~s** s
spidery 'spaɪd ər i
spie... —*see* **spy**
spiegeleisen 'spiːg ᵊl aɪz ᵊn
Spiegl 'spiːg ᵊl
spiel ʃpiːᵊl spiːᵊl **spiels** ʃpiːᵊlz spiːᵊlz
Spielberg 'spiːl bɜːg ‖ -bɝːg
Spier *(i)* spɪə ‖ spɪᵊr, *(ii)* 'spaɪ‿ə ‖ 'spaɪ‿ᵊr
spiff spɪf **spiffed** spɪft **spiffing** 'spɪf ɪŋ **spiffs** spɪfs
spiffli|cate 'spɪf lɪ |keɪt -lə- **~cated** keɪt ɪd -əd ‖ keɪt̬ əd **~cates** keɪts **~cating** keɪt ɪŋ ‖ keɪt̬ ɪŋ
spiff|y 'spɪf |i **~ier** i‿ə ‖ i‿ᵊr **~iest** i‿ɪst i‿əst **~ily** ɪ li əl i **~iness** i nəs i nɪs
spignel 'spɪg nᵊl
spigot 'spɪg ət **~s** s
spik spɪk **spiks** spɪks
spike spaɪk **spiked** spaɪkt **spikes** spaɪks **spiking** 'spaɪk ɪŋ
spikelet 'spaɪk lət -lɪt **~s** s
spikenard 'spaɪk nɑːd 'spaɪk ə nɑːd ‖ -nɑːrd
spik|y 'spaɪk |i **~ier** i‿ə ‖ i‿ᵊr **~iest** i‿ɪst i‿əst **~ily** ɪ li əl i **~iness** i nəs i nɪs
spile spaɪᵊl **spiled** spaɪᵊld **spiles** spaɪᵊlz **spiling** 'spaɪᵊl ɪŋ
spill spɪl **spilled** spɪld **spilling** 'spɪl ɪŋ **spills** spɪlz **spilt** spɪlt
spillag|e 'spɪl ɪdʒ **~es** ɪz əz
Spillane spɪ 'leɪn §spə-
Spiller 'spɪl ə ‖ -ᵊr
spillikin 'spɪl ɪk ɪn §-ək-, §-ən **~s** z
spillover 'spɪl ˌəʊv ə ‖ -ˌoʊv ᵊr **~s** z
spillway 'spɪl weɪ **~s** z
Spilsbury 'spɪlz bər‿i ‖ -ˌber i
spilt spɪlt
spin spɪn **span** spæn **spinning** 'spɪn ɪŋ **spins** spɪnz **spun** spʌn
ˌ**spin 'bowler**; '**spin** ˌ**doctor**
spina bifida ˌspaɪn ə 'bɪf ɪd ə -'baɪf-, -əd ə
spinach 'spɪn ɪdʒ -ɪtʃ ‖ -ɪtʃ
spinal 'spaɪn ᵊl **~ly** i
ˌ**spinal 'cord** ‖ '· · ·
spindle 'spɪnd ᵊl **~s** z
spindleberry 'spɪnd ᵊl ˌber i
spindleshanks 'spɪnd ᵊl ʃæŋks
spindling 'spɪnd lɪŋ
spind|ly 'spɪnd |li **~lier** li‿ə ‖ li‿ᵊr **~liest** li‿ɪst li‿əst
spindrift 'spɪn drɪft
spin-|dry ˌspɪn '|draɪ '· · **~dried** draɪd **~dries** draɪz **~drying** draɪ ɪŋ

spin-dryer ˌspɪn ˈdraɪ‿ə ˈ· · · ‖ -ˈdraɪ‿ər **~s** z
spine spaɪn **spined** spaɪnd **spines** spaɪnz
spine-chiller ˈspaɪn ˌtʃɪl ə ‖ -ər **~s** z
spine-chilling ˈspaɪn ˌtʃɪl ɪŋ
spinel spɪ ˈnel §spə-
spineless ˈspaɪn ləs -lɪs **~ly** li **~ness** nəs nɪs
spinet spɪ ˈnet §spə-; ˈspɪn et, -ɪt, §-ət ‖ ˈspɪn ət **~s** s
spine-tingling ˈspaɪn ˌtɪŋ gəl ɪŋ
spinifex ˈspɪn ɪ feks -ə-
Spink spɪŋk
spinnaker ˈspɪn ək ə -ɪk- ‖ -ər **~s** z
spinner ˈspɪn ə ‖ -ər **~s** z
spinneret ˈspɪn ə ret ˌ· ·ˈ· **~s** s
spinney ˈspɪn i **~s** z
spinning ˈspɪn ɪŋ
ˌspinning ˈjenny, ˈ· · ˌ· ·; **ˈspinning wheel**
spin-off ˈspɪn ɒf -ɔːf ‖ -ɔːf -ɑːf **~s** s
spinose ˈspaɪn əʊs spaɪ ˈnəʊs ‖ **-ous**
spinous ˈspaɪn əs
Spinoza spɪ ˈnəʊz ə §spə- ‖ -ˈnoʊz- —*Dutch* [spi ˈnoː zaː]
spinster ˈspɪn*t*st ə ‖ -ər **~hood** hʊd **~s** z
spinsterish ˈspɪn*t*st ər ɪʃ **~ness** nəs nɪs
spintharisc ope spɪn ˈθær ɪ skəʊp -ə- ‖ -skoʊp -ˈθer- **~s** s
spinule ˈspaɪn juːl ˈspɪn- **~s** z
spin|y ˈspaɪn |i **~ier** i‿ə ‖ i‿ər **~iest** i‿ɪst i‿əst **~iness** i nəs i nɪs
Spion Kop ˌspaɪ ən ˈkɒp →‿əŋ- ‖ -ˈkɑːp
spiracle ˈspaɪər ək əl ˈspɪr-, -ɪk- **~s** z
spiraea spaɪə ˈrɪə -ˈriː‿ə
spiral ˈspaɪər əl **~ed, ~led** d **~ing, ~ling** ɪŋ **~s** z
spiral-bound ˈspaɪər əl baʊnd
spirant ˈspaɪər ənt **~s** s
spirantisation, spirantization ˌspaɪər ənt aɪ ˈzeɪʃ ən -ɪˈ·- ‖ -əˈ·- **~s** z
spire ˈspaɪ‿ə ‖ ˈspaɪ‿ər **spires** ˈspaɪ‿əz ‖ ˈspaɪ‿ərz
spirea spaɪə ˈrɪə -ˈriː‿ə
Spirella *tdmk* spaɪə ˈrel ə
spirill|um spaɪə ˈrɪl| əm **~a** ə
spir|it, S~ ˈspɪr |ɪt -ət ‖ -|ət **~ited** ɪt ɪd -ət-, -əd ‖ əṱ əd **~iting** ɪt ɪŋ ət- ‖ əṱ ɪŋ **~its** ɪts əts ‖ əts
ˈspirit ˌlevel
-spirited ˈspɪr ɪt ɪd -ət-, -əd ‖ -əṱ əd — **public-spirited** ˌpʌb lɪk ˈspɪr ɪt ɪd ◂ -ət-, -əd ‖ -əṱ əd
spirited|ly ˈspɪr ɪt ɪd |li ˈ·ət-, -əd · ‖ -əṱ əd |li **~ness** nəs nɪs
spiritism ˈspɪr ɪt ˌɪz əm -ət- ‖ -əṱ-
spiritist ˈspɪr ɪt ɪst -ət-, §-əst ‖ -əṱ- **~s** s
spiritless ˈspɪr ɪt ləs -ət-, -lɪs **~ly** li **~ness** nəs nɪs
spiritous ˈspɪr ɪt əs -ət- ‖ -əṱ-
spiritual ˈspɪr ɪtʃ u‿əl ˈ·ətʃ-; -ɪt ju‿, -ət ju‿ ‖ ˈspɪr ɪtʃ əl **~s** z
spiritualis... —*see* **spiritualiz...**
spiritualism ˈspɪr ɪtʃ u ˌlɪz əm ˈ·ətʃ-, ˈ· ·ə-; ˈ·‥‿əˌ· ·, ˈ·ɪt ju‿, ˈ·ət-
spiritualist ˈspɪr ɪtʃ ʊl ɪst ˈ·ətʃ-, -əl ·, §-əst; ˈ· ·u‿əl ·, ˈ·ɪt ju‿, ˈ·ət- **~s** s
spiritualistic ˌspɪr ɪtʃ u ˈlɪst ɪk ◂ ˌ·ətʃ-, ˌ· ·ə-, ˌ· · ·‿əˈ· ·, ˌ·ɪt ju‿, ˌ·ət-
spiritualit|y ˌspɪr ɪtʃ u ˈæl ət |i -ətʃ u-, -ɪt ju-, -ət ju-, -ɪt i ‖ -əṱ |i **~ies** iz
spiritualization ˌspɪr ɪtʃ ʊl aɪ ˈzeɪʃ ən ˈ·ətʃ-, -ɪˈ·-; ˌ·u‿əl ˈ·, ˌ·ɪt ju‿, ˌ·ət- ‖ -əˈ·-
spiritualiz|e ˈspɪr ɪtʃ u laɪz -ətʃ u-; ˈ·ɪtʃ u‿ə ·, ˈ·ɪt ju‿, ˈ·ət- **~ed** d **~es** ɪz əz **~ing** ɪŋ
spiritually ˈspɪr ɪtʃ ʊl i ˈ·ətʃ-; ˈ· ·u‿əl i; ˈ·ɪt ju‿əl i, -ət ju‿
spirituous ˈspɪr ɪtʃ u‿əs -ətʃ u‿, -ɪt ju‿, -ət ju‿ **~ness** nəs nɪs
spiritus ˈspɪr ɪt əs -ət- ‖ -əṱ-
spirochaete ˈspaɪər əʊ kiːt ‖ -ə- **~s** s
spirograph ˈspaɪər əʊ grɑːf -græf ‖ -ə græf **~s** s
spirogyra ˌspaɪər əʊ ˈdʒaɪər ə ‖ -ə-
spirt spɜːt ‖ spɜːt **spirted** ˈspɜːt ɪd -əd ‖ ˈspɜːṱ əd **spirting** ˈspɜːt ɪŋ ‖ ˈspɜːṱ ɪŋ **spirts** spɜːts ‖ spɜːts
spirula ˈspaɪər ʊl ə -əl ə ‖ -jəl ə
spit spɪt **spat** spæt **spits** spɪts **spitted** ˈspɪt ɪd -əd ‖ ˈspɪṱ əd **spitting** ˈspɪt ɪŋ ‖ ˈspɪṱ ɪŋ
ˌspit and ˈpolish; ˌspitting ˈimage
Spital ˈspɪt əl ‖ ˈspɪṱ əl
Spitalfields ˈspɪt əl fiːəldz ‖ ˈspɪṱ-
spitball ˈspɪt bɔːl ‖ -bɑːl **~s** z
spite spaɪt **spited** ˈspaɪt ɪd -əd ‖ ˈspaɪṱ əd **spites** spaɪts **spiting** ˈspaɪt ɪŋ ‖ ˈspaɪṱ ɪŋ
spiteful ˈspaɪt fəl -fʊl **~ly** i **~ness** nəs nɪs
spitfire, S~ ˈspɪt ˌfaɪ‿ə ‖ -ˌfaɪ‿ər **~s** z
Spithead ˌspɪt ˈhed ◂
Spitsbergen ˈspɪts ˌbɜːg ən ˌ·ˈ· · ‖ -ˌbɜːg-
spitt... —*see* **spit**
Spittal ˈspɪt əl ‖ ˈspɪṱ əl
spittle ˈspɪt əl ‖ ˈspɪṱ əl
spittoon spɪ ˈtuːn §spə- **~s** z
spitz, Spitz spɪts —*Ger* [ʃpɪts] **spitzes** ˈspɪts ɪz -əz
spiv spɪv **spivs** spɪvz
spivvy ˈspɪv i
splanchnic ˈsplæŋk nɪk
splash splæʃ **splashed** splæʃt **splashes** ˈsplæʃ ɪz -əz **splashing** ˈsplæʃ ɪŋ
ˈsplash guard
splashback ˈsplæʃ bæk **~s** s
splashdown ˈsplæʃ daʊn **~s** z
splash|y ˈsplæʃ |i **~ier** i‿ə ‖ i‿ər **~iest** i‿ɪst i‿əst **~ily** ɪ li əl i **~iness** i nəs i nɪs
splat splæt **splats** splæts
splatter ˈsplæt ə ‖ ˈsplæṱ ər **~ed** d **splattering** ˈsplæt‿ər ɪŋ ‖ ˈsplæṱ ər ɪŋ
splay spleɪ **splayed** spleɪd **splaying** ˈspleɪ ɪŋ **splays** spleɪz
splay|foot ˈspleɪ |fʊt **~feet** fiːt
splayfooted ˌspleɪ ˈfʊt ɪd ◂ -əd ‖ -ˈfʊṱ- **~ly** li **~ness** nəs nɪs
spleen spliːn
spleenwort ˈspliːn wɜːt §-wɔːt ‖ -wɜːt -wɔːrt
Splenda *tdmk* ˈsplend ə
splendid ˈsplend ɪd -əd **~ly** li **~ness** nəs nɪs
splendiferous (ˌ)splen ˈdɪf ər əs **~ly** li **~ness** nəs nɪs

splendor, splendour 'splend ə ‖ -ᵊr **~s** z
splendrous 'splendr əs **~ly** li
splenetic splə 'net ɪk splɪ- ‖ -'neṭ ɪk **~ally** ᵊl̮ i
splenic 'splen ɪk 'spli:n-
spleno- *comb. form*
with stress-neutral suffix ¦spli:n əʊ ‖ -oʊ
— **splenomegaly** ˌspli:n əʊ 'meg əl i ‖ ˌoʊ-
with stress-imposing suffix spli: 'nɒ+
‖ -'nɑ:+ — **splenography** spli: 'nɒg rəf i
‖ -'nɑ:g-
splice splaɪs **spliced** splaɪst **splices** 'splaɪs ɪz
-əz **splicing** 'splaɪs ɪŋ
splicer 'splaɪs ə ‖ -ᵊr **~s** z
spliff splɪf **spliffs** splɪfs
spline splaɪn **splined** splaɪnd **splines** splaɪnz
splining 'splaɪn ɪŋ
splint splɪnt **splinted** 'splɪnt ɪd -əd
‖ 'splɪnṭ əd **splinting** 'splɪnt ɪŋ ‖ 'splɪnṭ ɪŋ
splints splɪnts
splinter 'splɪnt ə ‖ 'splɪnṭ ᵊr **~ed** d
splintering 'splɪnt‿ər ɪŋ ‖ 'splɪnṭ ər ɪŋ **~s** z
'splinter group
splintery 'splɪnt ər i
split, Split splɪt **splits** splɪts **splitting**
'splɪt ɪŋ ‖ 'splɪṭ ɪŋ
ˌsplit 'end; **ˌsplit in'finitive**; **ˌsplit 'pea**;
ˌsplit ˌperso'nality; **ˌsplit 'ring**; **ˌsplit
'second**
split-level ˌsplɪt 'lev ᵊl ◂
split-second ˌsplɪt 'sek ənd ◂ ⚠-ənt
split-up 'splɪt ʌp ‖ 'splɪṭ ʌp **~s** s
splodge splɒdʒ ‖ splɑ:dʒ **splodges** 'splɒdʒ ɪz
-əz ‖ 'splɑ:dʒ əz
splodg|y 'splɒdʒ |i ‖ 'splɑ:dʒ |i **~ier** i‿ə ‖ i‿ᵊr
~iest i‿ɪst i‿əst **~iness** i nəs i nɪs
splosh splɒʃ ‖ splɑ:ʃ **sploshed** splɒʃt ‖ splɑ:ʃt
sploshes 'splɒʃ ɪz -əz ‖ 'splɑ:ʃ əz **sploshing**
'splɒʃ ɪŋ ‖ 'splɑ:ʃ ɪŋ
splotch splɒtʃ ‖ splɑ:tʃ **splotched** splɒtʃt
‖ splɑ:tʃt **splotches** 'splɒtʃ ɪz -əz ‖ 'splɑ:tʃ əz
splotch|y 'splɒtʃ |i ‖ 'splɑ:tʃ |i **~ier** i‿ə ‖ i‿ᵊr
~iest i‿ɪst i‿əst **~iness** i nəs i nɪs
Splott splɒt ‖ splɑ:t
splurge splɜ:dʒ ‖ splɜ˞:dʒ **splurged** splɜ:dʒd
‖ splɜ˞:dʒd **splurges** 'splɜ:dʒ ɪz -əz
‖ 'splɜ˞:dʒ əz **splurging** 'splɜ:dʒ ɪŋ
‖ 'splɜ˞:dʒ ɪŋ
splutter 'splʌt ə ‖ 'splʌṭ ᵊr **~ed** d **spluttering**
'splʌt‿ər ɪŋ ‖ 'splʌṭ ər ɪŋ **~s** z
Spock spɒk ‖ spɑ:k
Spode, spode spəʊd ‖ spoʊd
spodumene 'spɒd ju mi:n §'spɒdʒ ə-
‖ 'spɑ:dʒ ə-
Spofforth 'spɒf əθ -ɔ:θ ‖ 'spɑ:f ᵊrθ
Spohr spɔ: ‖ spɔ:r spoʊr —*Ger* [ʃpo:ɐ]
spoil spɔɪᵊl **spoiled** spɔɪᵊld **spoiling** 'spɔɪᵊl ɪŋ
spoils spɔɪᵊlz **spoilt** spɔɪᵊlt
spoilage 'spɔɪᵊl ɪdʒ
spoiler 'spɔɪᵊl ə ‖ -ᵊr **~s** z
spoilsport 'spɔɪᵊl spɔ:t ‖ -spɔ:rt -spoʊrt **~s** s
spoilt spɔɪᵊlt
Spokane spəʊ 'kæn ‖ spoʊ- *(!)*
spoke spəʊk ‖ spoʊk **spokes** spəʊks ‖ spoʊks
-spoken 'spəʊk ən ‖ -'spoʊk ən —
nicely-spoken ˌnaɪs li 'spəʊk ən ◂ ‖ -'spoʊk-
spoken 'spəʊk ən ‖ 'spoʊk ən
spoken-word ˌspəʊk ən 'wɜ:d ◂ ‖ -'wɜ˞:d ◂
spokeshave 'spəʊk ʃeɪv ‖ 'spoʊk- **~s** z
spokes|man 'spəʊks |mən ‖ 'spoʊks- **~men**
mən men **~people** ˌpi:p ᵊl **~person/s**
ˌpɜ:s ᵊn/z ‖ ˌpɜ˞:s ᵊn/z **~woman** ˌwʊm ən
~women ˌwɪm ɪn -ən
spoliation ˌspəʊl i 'eɪʃ ᵊn ‖ ˌspoʊl-
spondaic spɒn 'deɪ ɪk ‖ spɑ:n-
spondee 'spɒnd i: ‖ 'spɑ:nd i: **~s** z
Spondon 'spɒnd ən ‖ 'spɑ:nd ən
spondulicks, spondulix spɒn 'du:l ɪks
-'dju:l-, →-'dʒu:l- ‖ spɑ:n 'du:l-
spondylitis ˌspɒnd ɪ 'laɪt ɪs -ə-, §-əs
‖ ˌspɑ:nd ə 'laɪṭ əs
Spong spɒŋ ‖ spɑ:ŋ
sponge spʌndʒ **sponged** spʌndʒd **sponges**
'spʌndʒ ɪz -əz **sponging** 'spʌndʒ ɪŋ
'sponge bag; **'sponge cake**; **ˌsponge
'pudding**; **ˌsponge 'rubber**
sponger 'spʌndʒ ə ‖ -ᵊr **~s** z
spongiform 'spʌndʒ ɪ fɔ:m ‖ -fɔ:rm
spong|y 'spʌndʒ |i **~ier** i‿ə ‖ i‿ᵊr **~iest** i‿ɪst
i‿əst **~iness** i nəs i nɪs
sponsion 'spɒnᵗʃ ᵊn ‖ 'spɑ:nᵗʃ ᵊn
sponson 'spɒnᵗs ᵊn ‖ 'spɑ:nᵗs ᵊn **~s** z
sponsor 'spɒnᵗs ə ‖ 'spɑ:nᵗs ᵊr **~ed** d
sponsoring 'spɒnᵗs ər‿ɪŋ ‖ 'spɑ:nᵗs ər ɪŋ **~s**
z **~ship** ʃɪp
spontaneity ˌspɒnt ə 'neɪ ət i -'ni:‿, -ɪt i
‖ ˌspɑ:nt ᵊn 'i: əṭ i -'eɪ-
spontaneous ₍ˌ₎spɒn 'teɪn i‿əs spən- ‖ spɑ:n-
~ly li **~ness** nəs nɪs
Spontex *tdmk* 'spɒnt eks ‖ 'spɑ:nt-
spoof spu:f **spoofed** spu:ft **spoofing** 'spu:f ɪŋ
spoofs spu:fs
spook spu:k **spooked** spu:kt **spooking**
'spu:k ɪŋ **spooks** spu:ks
spook|y 'spu:k |i **~ier** i‿ə ‖ i‿ᵊr **~iest** i‿ɪst i‿əst
~ily ɪ li əl i **~iness** i nəs i nɪs
spool spu:l **spooled** spu:ld **spooling** 'spu:l ɪŋ
spools spu:lz
spoon spu:n **spooned** spu:nd **spooning**
'spu:n ɪŋ **spoons** spu:nz
spoonbill 'spu:n bɪl →'spu:m- **~s** z
Spooner 'spu:n ə ‖ -ᵊr
spoonerism 'spu:n ə ˌrɪz əm **~s** z
spoon|feed 'spu:n |fi:d **~fed** fed **~feeding**
fi:d ɪŋ **~feeds** fi:dz
spoonful 'spu:n fʊl **~s** z **spoonsful**
'spu:nz fʊl
spoor spʊə spɔ: ‖ spʊᵊr spɔ:r, spoʊr **spoors**
spʊəz spɔ:z ‖ spʊᵊrz spɔ:rz, spoʊrz
Sporades 'spɒr ə di:z spə 'rɑ:d i:z ‖ 'spɔ:r-
sporadic spə 'ræd ɪk spɒ- **~ally** ᵊl̮ i
sporangi|um spə 'rændʒ i‿|əm **~a** ə
spore spɔ: ‖ spɔ:r spoʊr **spores** spɔ:z ‖ spɔ:rz
spoʊrz
spork spɔ:k ‖ spɔ:rk **sporks** spɔ:ks ‖ spɔ:rks

S

sporo- *comb. form*
with stress-neutral suffix ¦spɔːr əʊ ¦spɒr- ‖ ¦spɔːr ə ¦spour- — **sporocyst** 'spɔːr əʊ sɪst 'spɒr- ‖ -ə- 'spour-
sporogeny spɔː 'rɒdʒ ən i spə- ‖ spə 'rɑːdʒ-
sporogony spɔː 'rɒg ən i spə-, -'rɒdʒ- ‖ spə 'rɑːg-
sporran 'spɒr ən ‖ 'spɔːr ən 'spɑːr- **~s** z
sport spɔːt ‖ spɔːrt spourt **sported** 'spɔːt ɪd -əd ‖ 'spɔːrṭ əd 'spourṭ- **sporting/ly** 'spɔːt ɪŋ /li ‖ 'spɔːrṭ ɪŋ /li 'spourṭ- **sports** spɔːts ‖ spɔːrts spourts
'sports car; **'sports day**; **'sports ˌjacket**
sport-fishing 'spɔːt ˌfɪʃ ɪŋ ‖ 'spɔːrt-
sporti... —*see* **sporty**
sportive 'spɔːt ɪv ‖ 'spɔːrṭ ɪv 'spourṭ- **~ly** li **~ness** nəs nɪs
sportscast 'spɔːts kɑːst §-kæst ‖ 'spɔːrts kæst 'spourts- **~er/s** ə/z ‖ -ᵊr/z **~ing** ɪŋ
sports|man 'spɔːts |mən ‖ 'spɔːrts- 'spourts- **~manlike** mən laɪk **~manship** mən ʃɪp **~men** mən **~person** ˌpɜːs ᵊn ‖ ˌpɜʴs ᵊn **~people** ˌpiːp ᵊl
sportswear 'spɔːts weə ‖ 'spɔːrts wer 'spourts-, -wær
sports|woman 'spɔːts |ˌwʊm ən ‖ 'spɔːrts- 'spourts- **~women** ˌwɪm ɪn -ən
sport-utility ˌspɔːt ju 'tɪl ət i -ɪt i ‖ ˌspɔːrt ju 'tɪl əṭ i ˌspourt-
sport|y 'spɔːt |i ‖ 'spɔːrṭ |i 'spourṭ- **~ier** i‿ə ‖ i‿ᵊr **~iest** i‿ɪst i‿əst **~ily** ɪ li əl i **~iness** i nəs i nɪs
sporule 'spɒr uːl -juːl ‖ 'spɔːr juːl 'spour- **~s** z
s'pose *nonstandard version of* suppose spəʊz ‖ spouz **s'posing** 'spəʊz ɪŋ ‖ 'spouz ɪŋ
spot spɒt ‖ spɑːt **spots** spɒts ‖ spɑːts **spotted** 'spɒt ɪd -əd ‖ 'spɑːṭ əd **spotting** 'spɒt ɪŋ ‖ 'spɑːṭ ɪŋ
ˌspot 'check ‖ '. .; **ˌspotted 'dick**
spot-check ˌspɒt 'tʃek '. . ‖ 'spɑːt tʃek **~ed** t **~ing** ɪŋ **~s** s
spotless 'spɒt ləs -lɪs ‖ 'spɑːt- **~ly** li **~ness** nəs nɪs
spot|light 'spɒt |laɪt ‖ 'spɑːt- **~lighted** laɪt ɪd -əd ‖ laɪṭ əd **~lighting** laɪt ɪŋ ‖ laɪṭ ɪŋ **~lights** laɪts **~lit** lɪt
spot-on ˌspɒt 'ɒn ◂ ‖ ˌspɑːṭ 'ɑːn -'ɔːn
Spotsylvania ˌspɒt sɪl 'veɪn i‿ə ˌ·sᵊl- ‖ ˌspɑːt-
spott... —*see* **spot**
spotter 'spɒt ə ‖ 'spɑːṭ ᵊr **~s** z
'spotter plane
Spottiswoode *(i)* 'spɒts wʊd ‖ 'spɑːts-; *(ii)* 'spɒt ɪs wʊd -ɪz-, -əs- ‖ 'spɑːṭ-
spott|y 'spɒt |i ‖ 'spɑːṭ |i **~ier** i‿ə ‖ i‿ᵊr **~iest** i‿ɪst i‿əst **~ily** ɪ li əl i **~iness** i nəs i nɪs
spot-weld 'spɒt weld ‖ 'spɑːt- **~ed** ɪd əd **~ing** ɪŋ **~s** z
spousal 'spaʊz ᵊl 'spaʊs ᵊl
spouse spaʊs spaʊz **spouses** 'spaʊs ɪz 'spaʊz-, -əz
spout spaʊt **spouted** 'spaʊt ɪd -əd ‖ 'spaʊṭ əd **spouting** 'spaʊt ɪŋ ‖ 'spaʊṭ ɪŋ **spouts** spaʊts
sprachgefuhl, sprachgefühl, S~ 'ʃprɑːx gə ˌfjuːl 'ʃprɑːk-, -fuːl ‖ 'sprɑːk- —*Ger* ['ʃpʁaːx gə ˌfyːl]
sprag spræg **spragged** sprægd **spragging** 'spræg ɪŋ **sprags** sprægz
Spragge spræg
Sprague spreɪg
sprain spreɪn **sprained** spreɪnd **spraining** 'spreɪn ɪŋ **sprains** spreɪnz
spraint spreɪnt **spraints** spreɪnts
sprang spræŋ
sprat spræt **sprats** spræts
Sprat|ly 'spræt| li **~lies, ~lys** liz
Spratt spræt
sprawl sprɔːl ‖ sprɑːl **sprawled** sprɔːld ‖ sprɑːld **sprawling/ly** 'sprɔːl ɪŋ /li ‖ 'sprɑːl- **sprawls** sprɔːlz ‖ sprɑːlz
spray spreɪ **sprayed** spreɪd **spraying** 'spreɪ ɪŋ **sprays** spreɪz
'spray gun
spraycan 'spreɪ kæn **~s** z
sprayer 'spreɪ ə ‖ -ᵊr **~s** z
spray-on 'spreɪ ɒn ‖ -ɑːn ◂ -ɔːn
ˌspray-on de'odorant
spread spred **spreading** 'spred ɪŋ **spreads** spredz
spreadable 'spred əb ᵊl
spread-eagl|e ₍ˌ₎spred 'iːg ᵊl ‖ 'spred ˌiːg ᵊl *(*)* **~ed** d **~es** z **~ing** ‿ɪŋ
spreader 'spred ə ‖ -ᵊr **~s** z
spreadsheet 'spred ʃiːt **~s** s
sprechgesang, S~ 'ʃprex gə ˌzæŋ 'ʃprek-, -ˌzʌŋ ‖ 'sprek- —*Ger* ['ʃpʁɛç gə ˌzaŋ]
sprechstimme, S~ 'ʃprex ˌʃtɪm ə 'ʃprek- ‖ 'sprek ˌstɪm ə —*Ger* ['ʃpʁɛç ˌʃtɪm ə]
spree spriː **sprees** spriːz
sprig sprɪg **sprigged** sprɪgd **sprigging** 'sprɪg ɪŋ **sprigs** sprɪgz
Sprigg sprɪg
spright|ly 'spraɪt |li **~lier** li‿ə ‖ li‿ᵊr **~liest** li‿ɪst li‿əst **~liness** li nəs -nɪs
spring, S~ sprɪŋ **sprang** spræŋ **springing** 'sprɪŋ ɪŋ **springs** sprɪŋz **sprung** sprʌŋ
ˌspring 'balance; **ˌspring 'chicken**; **ˌspring 'fever**; **ˌspring 'onion**; **ˌspring 'roll**; **ˌspring 'tide**
springboard 'sprɪŋ bɔːd ‖ -bɔːrd -bourd **~s** z
springbok, S~ 'sprɪŋ bɒk ‖ -bɑːk **~s** s
Springburn 'sprɪŋ bɜːn ‖ -bɜʴn
spring-clean *v* ˌsprɪŋ 'kliːn ◂ **~ed** d **~ing** ɪŋ **~s** z
spring-clean *n* 'sprɪŋ kliːn ˌ.'. **~s** z
springe sprɪndʒ **springes** 'sprɪndʒ ɪz -əz
springer, S~ 'sprɪŋ ə ‖ -ᵊr **~s** z
Springfield 'sprɪŋ fiːᵊld
springlike 'sprɪŋ laɪk
spring-loaded ˌsprɪŋ 'ləʊd ɪd ◂ -əd ‖ -'loud-
Springs sprɪŋz
Springsteen 'sprɪŋ stiːn
springtail 'sprɪŋ teɪᵊl **~s** z
springtime 'sprɪŋ taɪm
spring|y 'sprɪŋ |i **~ier** i‿ə ‖ i‿ᵊr **~iest** i‿ɪst i‿əst **~ily** ɪ li əl i **~iness** i nəs i nɪs

S

sprinkl|e ˈsprɪŋk ᵊl **~ed** d **~es** z **~ing** ˌɪŋ

sprinkler ˈsprɪŋk lə ˈsprɪŋk ᵊlˌə ‖ -lᵊr **~s** z

sprinkling *n* ˈsprɪŋk lɪŋ **~s** z

sprint sprɪnt **sprinted** ˈsprɪnt ɪd -əd ‖ ˈsprɪnt̬ əd **sprinting** ˈsprɪnt ɪŋ ‖ ˈsprɪnt̬ ɪŋ **sprints** sprɪnts

sprinter ˈsprɪnt ə ‖ ˈsprɪnt̬ ᵊr **~s** z

sprit sprɪt **sprits** sprɪts

sprite spraɪt **sprites** spraɪts

spritsail ˈsprɪt sᵊl -seɪᵊl **~s** z

spritz sprɪts ʃprɪts **spritzed** sprɪtst ʃprɪtst **spritzes** ˈsprɪts ɪz ˈʃprɪts-, -əz **spritzing** ˈsprɪts ɪŋ ˈʃprɪts-

spritzer ˈsprɪts ə ˈʃprɪts- ‖ -ᵊr **~s** z

Sproat sprəʊt ‖ sproʊt

sprocket ˈsprɒk ɪt §-ət ‖ ˈsprɑːk ət **~s** s

sprog sprɒg ‖ sprɑːg **sprogs** sprɒgz ‖ sprɑːgz

Sprot, Sprott sprɒt ‖ sprɑːt

Sproughton ˈsprɔːt ᵊn ‖ ˈsprɑːt-

Sproule *(i)* sprəʊl ‖ sproʊl, *(ii)* spruːl

sprout spraʊt **sprouted** ˈspraʊt ɪd -əd ‖ ˈspraʊt̬ əd **sprouting** ˈspraʊt ɪŋ ‖ ˈspraʊt̬ ɪŋ **sprouts** spraʊts

spruce spruːs **spruced** spruːst **sprucer** ˈspruːs ə ‖ ˈspruːs ᵊr **spruces** ˈspruːs ɪz -əz **sprucest** ˈspruːs ɪst -əst **sprucing** ˈspruːs ɪŋ

spruce|ly ˈspruːs |li **~ness** nəs nɪs

sprue spruː **sprues** spruːz

spruik spruːk **spruiked** spruːkt **spruiker/s** ˈspruːk ə/z ‖ -ᵊr/z **spruiking** ˈspruːk ɪŋ **spruiks** spruːks

sprung sprʌŋ

spry, Spry spraɪ **spryer** ˈspraɪˌə ‖ ˈspraɪˌᵊr **spryest** ˈspraɪ ɪst -əst **spryly** ˈspraɪ li **spryness** ˈspraɪ nəs -nɪs

spud spʌd **spuds** spʌdz

spumante spu ˈmænt i ‖ -ˈmɑːnt eɪ —*It* [spu ˈman te]

spume spjuːm **spumed** spjuːmd **spumes** spjuːmz **spuming** ˈspjuːm ɪŋ

spun spʌn

spunk spʌŋk

spunk|y ˈspʌŋk |i **~ier** iˌə ‖ iˌᵊr **~iest** iˌɪst iˌəst **~ily** ɪ li əl i **~iness** i nəs i nɪs

spur spɜː ‖ spɝː **spurred** spɜːd ‖ spɝːd **spurring** ˈspɜːr ɪŋ ‖ ˈspɝː ɪŋ **spurs** spɜːz ‖ spɝːz

spurge spɜːdʒ ‖ spɝːdʒ **spurges** ˈspɜːdʒ ɪz -əz ‖ ˈspɝːdʒ əz

Spurgeon ˈspɜːdʒ ən ‖ ˈspɝːdʒ ən

spurious ˈspjʊər iˌəs ˈspjɔːr- ‖ ˈspjʊr- **~ly** li **~ness** nəs nɪs

Spurling ˈspɜːl ɪŋ ‖ ˈspɝːl ɪŋ

spurn, Spurn spɜːn ‖ spɝːn **spurned** spɜːnd ‖ spɝːnd **spurning** ˈspɜːn ɪŋ ‖ ˈspɝːn ɪŋ **spurns** spɜːnz ‖ spɝːnz ˌ**Spurn ˈHead**

spur-of-the-moment ˌspɜːr əv ðə ˈməʊm ənt ◂ -ə ðə- ‖ ˌspɝː əv ðə ˈmoʊm-

Spurrell ˈspʌr əl ‖ ˈspɝːˌəl

spurrey ˈspʌr i ‖ ˈspɝː i **~s** z

Spurrier, s~ ˈspʌr iˌə ‖ ˈspɝː iˌᵊr **~s** z

spurr|y ˈspʌr |i ‖ ˈspɝː |i **~ies** iz

spurt spɜːt ‖ spɝːt **spurted** ˈspɜːt ɪd -əd ‖ ˈspɝːt̬ əd **spurting** ˈspɜːt ɪŋ ‖ ˈspɝːt̬ ɪŋ **spurts** spɜːts ‖ spɝːts

sputnik ˈspʊt nɪk ˈspʌt- ‖ ˈspuːt- **~s** s

sputter ˈspʌt ə ‖ ˈspʌt̬ ᵊr **~ed** d **sputtering** ˈspʌtˌər ɪŋ ‖ ˈspʌt̬ ər ɪŋ **~s** z

sputum ˈspjuːt əm ‖ ˈspjuːt̬ əm

Spuyten Duyvil ˌspaɪt ᵊn ˈdaɪv ᵊl ◂ ˌ**Spuyten ˌDuyvil ˈCreek**

spy spaɪ **spied** spaɪd **spies** spaɪz **spying** ˈspaɪ ɪŋ

spycatcher ˈspaɪ ˌkætʃ ə ‖ -ᵊr **~s** z

spyglass ˈspaɪ glɑːs §-glæs ‖ -glæs **~es** ɪz əz

spyhole ˈspaɪ həʊl →-hɒʊl ‖ -hoʊl **~s** z

spymaster ˈspaɪ ˌmɑːst ə §-ˌmæst- ‖ -ˌmæst ᵊr **~s** z

spyware ˈspaɪ weə ‖ -wer -wær

sq —*see* **square**

Sqezy *tdmk* ˈskwiːz i

squab skwɒb ‖ skwɑːb **squabs** skwɒbz ‖ skwɑːbz

squabbl|e ˈskwɒb ᵊl ‖ ˈskwɑːb ᵊl **~ed** d **~er/s** ˌə/z ‖ ər/z **~es** z **~ing** ˌɪŋ

squacco ˈskwæk əʊ ‖ ˈskwɑːk oʊ **~s** z

squad skwɒd ‖ skwɑːd **squads** skwɒdz ‖ skwɑːdz ˈ**squad car**

squadd|ie, squadd|y ˈskwɒd |i ‖ ˈskwɑːd |i **~ies** iz

squadron ˈskwɒdr ən ‖ ˈskwɑːdr ən **~s** z ˌ**squadron ˈleader◂**, ˈ· · ˌ· ·

squalid ˈskwɒl ɪd §-əd ‖ ˈskwɑːl əd ˈskwɔːl- **~ly** li **~ness** nəs nɪs

squalidity skwɒ ˈlɪd ət i -ɪt- ‖ skwɑː ˈlɪd ət̬ i skwɔː-

squall skwɔːl ‖ skwɑːl **squalled** skwɔːld ‖ skwɑːld **squalling** ˈskwɔːl ɪŋ ‖ ˈskwɑːl- **squalls** skwɔːlz ‖ skwɑːlz

squally ˈskwɔːl i ‖ ˈskwɑːl-

squalor ˈskwɒl ə ‖ ˈskwɑːl ᵊr ˈskwɔːl-

squam|a ˈskweɪm |ə ˈskwɑːm- **~ae** iː

Squamish ˈskwɑːm ɪʃ ‖ ˈskwɔːm- **~es** ɪz əz

squamous ˈskweɪm əs **~ly** li **~ness** nəs nɪs

squander ˈskwɒnd ə ‖ ˈskwɑːnd ᵊr **~ed** d **squandering** ˈskwɒndˌər ɪŋ ‖ ˈskwɑːnd ər ɪŋ **~s** z

squanderer ˈskwɒndˌər ə ‖ ˈskwɑːnd ᵊr ər **~s** z

Squanto ˈskwɒnt əʊ ‖ ˈskwɑːnt oʊ

square skweə ‖ skweᵊr skwæᵊr **squared** skweəd ‖ skweᵊrd skwæᵊrd **squares** skweəz ‖ skweᵊrz skwæᵊrz **squaring** ˈskweər ɪŋ ‖ ˈskwer ɪŋ ˈskwær- ˌ**square ˈbracket**; ˈ**square dance**; ˈ**square knot**; ˌ**square ˈleg**, ˌ**square leg ˈumpire**; ˌ**square ˈmeal**; ˌ**square ˈone**; ˌ**square ˈroot**

square-bashing ˈskweə ˌbæʃ ɪŋ ‖ ˈskwer- ˈskwær-

square-danc|e ˈskweə dɑːnᵗs §-dænᵗs ‖ ˈskwer dænᵗs ˈskwær- **~er/s** ə/z ‖ ᵊr/z **~ing** ɪŋ

squarely ˈskweə li ‖ ˈskwer li ˈskwær-

squareness ˈskweə nəs -nɪs ‖ ˈskwer- ˈskwær-
square-rigged ˌskweə ˈrɪgd ◂ ‖ ˌskwer- ˌskwær-
squarish ˈskweər ɪʃ ‖ ˈskwer ɪʃ ˈskwær-
squash skwɒʃ ‖ skwɑːʃ skwɔːʃ **squashed** skwɒʃt ‖ skwɑːʃt skwɔːʃt **squashes** ˈskwɒʃ ɪz -əz ‖ ˈskwɑːʃ əz ˈskwɔːʃ- **squashing** ˈskwɒʃ ɪŋ ‖ ˈskwɑːʃ ɪŋ ˈskwɔːʃ-
squash|y ˈskwɒʃ |i ‖ ˈskwɑːʃ |i ˈskwɔːʃ- **~ier** i‿ə ‖ i‿ᵊr **~iest** i‿ɪst i‿əst **~ily** ɪ li əl i **~iness** i nəs i nɪs
squat skwɒt ‖ skwɑːt **squats** skwɒts ‖ skwɑːts **squatted** ˈskwɒt ɪd -əd ‖ ˈskwɑːţ əd **squatting** ˈskwɒt ɪŋ ‖ ˈskwɑːţ ɪŋ
squatter ˈskwɒt ə ‖ ˈskwɑːţ ᵊr **~s** z
squaw skwɔː ‖ skwɑː **squaws** skwɔːz ‖ skwɑːz
squawk skwɔːk skɔːk ‖ skwɑːk **squawked** skwɔːkt skɔːkt ‖ skwɑːkt **squawking** ˈskwɔːk ɪŋ ˈskɔːk- ‖ ˈskwɑːk- **squawks** skwɔːks skɔːks ‖ skwɑːks
squeak skwiːk **squeaked** skwiːkt **squeaking** ˈskwiːk ɪŋ **squeaks** skwiːks
squeaker ˈskwiːk ə ‖ -ᵊr **~s** z
squeak|y ˈskwiːk |i **~ier** i‿ə ‖ i‿ᵊr **~iest** i‿ɪst i‿əst **~ily** ɪ li əl i **~iness** i nəs i nɪs
squeaky-clean ˌskwiːk i ˈkliːn ◂
squeal skwiːᵊl **squealed** skwiːᵊld **squealing** ˈskwiːᵊl ɪŋ **squeals** skwiːᵊlz
squealer ˈskwiːᵊl ə ‖ -ᵊr **~s** z
squeamish ˈskwiːm ɪʃ **~ly** li **~ness** nəs nɪs
squeegee ˈskwiː dʒiː ˌ·ˈ· **~d** d **~ing** ɪŋ **~s** z
Squeers skwɪəz ‖ skwɪᵊrz
squeeze skwiːz **squeezed** skwiːzd **squeezes** ˈskwiːz ɪz -əz **squeezing** ˈskwiːz ɪŋ
squeezebox ˈskwiːz bɒks ‖ -bɑːks **~es** ɪz əz
squeezer ˈskwiːz ə ‖ -ᵊr **~s** z
squelch skweltʃ **squelched** skweltʃt **squelches** ˈskweltʃ ɪz -əz **squelching/ly** ˈskweltʃ ɪŋ /li
squelchy ˈskweltʃ i
squib skwɪb **squibs** skwɪbz
squid skwɪd **squids** skwɪdz
squidg|y ˈskwɪdʒ| i **~ier** i‿ə ‖ i‿ᵊr **~iest** i‿ɪst ‿əst **~ily** ɪ li əl i **~iness** i nəs i nɪs
squiff|y ˈskwɪf| i **~ier** i‿ə ‖ i‿ᵊr **~iest** i‿ɪst ‿əst **~ily** ɪ li əl i **~iness** i nəs i nɪs
squiggl|e ˈskwɪg ᵊl **~ed** d **~es** z **~ing** ɪŋ
squiggly ˈskwɪg ᵊl‿i
squill skwɪl **squills** skwɪlz
squillion ˈskwɪl jən **~s** z
squinch skwɪntʃ **squinched** skwɪntʃt **squinches** ˈskwɪntʃ ɪz -əz **squinching** ˈskwɪntʃ ɪŋ
squint skwɪnt **squinted** ˈskwɪnt ɪd -əd ‖ ˈskwɪnţ əd **squinting** ˈskwɪnt ɪŋ ‖ ˈskwɪnţ ɪŋ **squints** skwɪnts
squinty ˈskwɪnt i ‖ ˈskwɪnţ i
squirarch|y, squirearch|y ˈskwaɪ‿ər ɑːk |i ‖ ˈskwaɪ‿ᵊr ɑːrk |i **~ies** iz
squire, Squire ˈskwaɪ‿ə ‖ ˈskwaɪ‿ᵊr **squired** ˈskwaɪ‿əd ‖ ˈskwaɪ‿ᵊrd **squires** ˈskwaɪ‿əz ‖ ˈskwaɪ‿ᵊrz **squiring** ˈskwaɪ‿ər ɪŋ ‖ ˈskwaɪ‿ᵊr ɪŋ
Squires ˈskwaɪ‿əz ‖ ˈskwaɪ‿ᵊrz
squirm skwɜːm ‖ skwɜ˞ːm **squirmed** skwɜːmd ‖ skwɜ˞ːmd **squirming** ˈskwɜːm ɪŋ ‖ ˈskwɜ˞ːm ɪŋ **squirms** skwɜːmz ‖ skwɜ˞ːmz
squirm|y ˈskwɜːm| i ‖ ˈskwɜ˞ːm| i **~ier** i‿ə ‖ i‿ᵊr **~iest** i‿ɪst ‿əst **~ily** ɪ li əl i **~iness** i nəs i nɪs
squirrel ˈskwɪr əl ‖ ˈskwɜ˞ː‿əl *(*)* **~ed, ~led** d **~ing, ~ling** ɪŋ **~s** z
squirrelly, squirrely ˈskwɪr əl i ‖ ˈskwɜ˞ː‿əl i
squirt skwɜːt ‖ skwɜ˞ːt **squirted** ˈskwɜːt ɪd -əd ‖ ˈskwɜ˞ːţ əd **squirting** ˈskwɜːt ɪŋ ‖ ˈskwɜ˞ːţ ɪŋ **squirts** skwɜːts ‖ skwɜ˞ːts
squish skwɪʃ **squished** skwɪʃt **squishes** ˈskwɪʃ ɪz -əz **squishing** ˈskwɪʃ ɪŋ
squish|y ˈskwɪʃ |i **~ier** i‿ə ‖ i‿ᵊr **~iest** i‿ɪst i‿əst **~ily** ɪ li əl i **~iness** i nəs i nɪs
squit skwɪt **squits** skwɪts
squitters ˈskwɪt əz ‖ ˈskwɪţ ᵊrz
Sr *—see* **Senior; Señor**
Sranan ˈsrɑːn ən
Srebrenica ˌsreb rə ˈniːts ə
Sri, sri sriː ʃriː *—see also phrases with this word*
Sri Lank|a srɪ ˈlæŋk |ə ʃrɪ-, ˌsriː-, ˌʃriː- ‖ -ˈlɑːŋk |ə **~an/s** ən/z
Srinagar srɪ ˈnʌg ə ˈsrɪn ə gɑː ‖ -ᵊr ˈsrɪn ə gɑːr *—Hindi* [sɪ riː nə gər]
SS ˌes ˈes ◂ ˌ**SS ˈKittiwake**
ssh ʃ
-st *archaic and liturgial second person sing. ending* st — **didst** ˈdɪdst *—see* **-est**
St, St. *'Street'* striːt *—In names of thoroughfares, unstressed:* ˈOxford St
St, St. *'Saint'* sənt sən ‖ seɪnt *—In RP the strong form* seɪnt *is not customary when* St *is prefixed to a name; and of the two weak forms listed* sən *tends to be restricted to cases where the following name begins with a consonant. In GenAm there is no weak form. In French names* St *may be pronounced* sæn, sæ̃ *—Fr* [sɛ̃]. *—Proper names beginning* St *are listed in this dictionary alphabetically as* St-, *not as* Saint-.
St ˈAnthony; **St ˈLawrence, St ˌLawrence ˈSeaway**
Staaten *Australian river* ˈstæt ᵊn
stab stæb **stabbed** stæbd **stabbing** ˈstæb ɪŋ **stabs** stæbz
Stabat Mater ˌstɑːb æt ˈmɑːt ə ˌstæb-, -ət- ‖ -ɑːt ˈmɑːţ ᵊr
stabb... *—see* **stab**
stabber ˈstæb ə ‖ -ᵊr **~s** z
St Abb's sənt ˈæbz §sən- ‖ seɪnţ ˈæbz
stabilis... *—see* **stabiliz...**
stability stə ˈbɪl ət i -ɪt i ‖ -əţ i
stabilization ˌsteɪb əl aɪ ˈzeɪʃ ᵊn ˌ·ɪl-, -ɪˈ- ‖ -əˈ- **~s** z
stabiliz|e ˈsteɪb ə laɪz -ɪ-; -ᵊl aɪz **~ed** d **~es** ɪz əz **~ing** ɪŋ
stabilizer ˈsteɪb ə laɪz ə ˈ-ɪ-; -ᵊl aɪz- ‖ -ᵊr **~s** z

S

stabl|e 'steɪb ᵊl **~ed** d **~er** ˌə ‖ ər **~es** z **~est** ˌɪst əst **~ing** ˌɪŋ
'stable boy; **ˌstable 'door**
stable|man 'steɪb ᵊl |mæn **~men** men
stablemate 'steɪb ᵊl meɪt **~s** s
stablish 'stæb lɪʃ **~ed** t **~es** ɪz əz **~ing** ɪŋ
staccato stə 'kɑːt əʊ stæ- ‖ -oʊ **~s** z
Stacey, Stacie 'steɪs i
stack stæk **stacked** stækt **stacking** 'stæk ɪŋ **stacks** stæks
Stackhouse 'stæk haʊs
Stacpoole 'stæk puːl
stacte 'stækt i -iː
Stacy 'steɪs i
stade steɪd **stades** steɪdz
stadia 'steɪd i ə
stadiometer ˌsteɪd i 'ɒm ɪt ə -ət ə ‖ -'ɑːm əṭ ᵊr **~s** z
stadi|um 'steɪd i |əm **~a** ə **~ums** əmz
staff stɑːf §stæf ‖ stæf **staffed** stɑːft §stæft ‖ stæft **staffing** 'stɑːf ɪŋ §'stæf- ‖ 'stæf ɪŋ **staffs** stɑːfs §stæfs ‖ stæfs
'staff college; **'staff nurse**; **'staff ˌofficer**; **'staff ˌsergeant**
Staffa 'stæf ə
staffer 'stɑːf ə ‖ 'stæf ᵊr **~s** z
Stafford 'stæf əd ‖ -ᵊrd **~shire** ʃə ʃɪə ‖ ʃᵊr ʃɪr
Staffs, Staffs. stæfs
stag stæg **stagged** stægd **stagging** 'stæg ɪŋ **stags** stægz
'stag ˌbeetle; **'stag ˌparty**
stage steɪdʒ **staged** steɪdʒd **stages** 'steɪdʒ ɪz -əz **staging** 'steɪdʒ ɪŋ
'stage diˌrection; **ˌstage 'door◂**; **ˌstage door 'Johnny**; **'stage efˌfect**; **'stage fright**; **ˌstage 'manager** ‖ '. ˌ. . ; **'stage name**; **ˌstage 'whisper** ‖ '. ˌ. .; **'staging post**
stagecoach 'steɪdʒ kəʊtʃ ‖ -koʊtʃ **~es** ɪz əz
stagecraft 'steɪdʒ krɑːft §-kræft ‖ -kræft
stagehand 'steɪdʒ hænd **~s** z
stage-manag|e ˌsteɪdʒ 'mæn ɪdʒ '.ˌ. . ‖ 'steɪdʒ ˌmæn ɪdʒ **~ed** d **~es** ɪz əz **~ing** ɪŋ
stager 'steɪdʒ ə ‖ -ᵊr **~s** z
stagestruck 'steɪdʒ strʌk
stag|ey 'steɪdʒ |i **~ier** i ə ‖ i ᵊr **~iest** i ɪst i əst **~ily** ɪ li əl i **~iness** i nəs i nɪs
stagflation ˌstæg 'fleɪʃ ᵊn
Stagg stæg
stagger 'stæg ə ‖ -ᵊr **~ed** d **staggering/ly** 'stæg ər ɪŋ /li **~s** z
staghorn 'stæg hɔːn ‖ -hɔːrn
staghound 'stæg haʊnd **~s** z
staging 'steɪdʒ ɪŋ **~s** z
Stagira stə 'dʒaɪᵊr ə 'stædʒ ɪr ə, -ər ə
Stagirite 'stædʒ ɪ raɪt -ə- **~s** s
stagnancy 'stæg nənᵗs i
stagnant 'stæg nənt **~ly** li
stag|nate ₍ₗ₎stæg '|neɪt '. . ‖ 'stæg |neɪt **~nated** neɪt ɪd -əd ‖ neɪṭ əd **~nates** neɪts **~nating** neɪt ɪŋ ‖ neɪṭ ɪŋ
stagnation ₍ₗ₎stæg 'neɪʃ ᵊn
St Agnes sənt 'æg nɪs §sən-, -nəs ‖ seɪnṭ-
stag|y 'steɪdʒ |i **~ier** i ə ‖ i ᵊr **~iest** i ɪst i əst **~ily** ɪ li əl i **~iness** i nəs i nɪs
staid steɪd *(= stayed)* **staidly** 'steɪd li **staidness** 'steɪd nəs nɪs
stain steɪn **stained** steɪnd **staining** 'steɪn ɪŋ **stains** steɪnz
ˌstained 'glass◂, **ˌstained glass 'window**
Stainby 'steɪn bi →'steɪm-
stainer, S~ 'steɪn ə ‖ -ᵊr
Staines steɪnz
Stainforth 'steɪn fɔːθ -fəθ ‖ -fɔːrθ -foʊrθ
stainless 'steɪn ləs -lɪs **~ly** li **~ness** nəs nɪs
ˌstainless 'steel◂, **ˌstainless steel 'cutlery**
Stainton 'steɪnt ən ‖ -ᵊn
stair steə ‖ steᵊr stæᵊr **stairs** steəz ‖ steᵊrz stæᵊrz
'stair rod
staircas|e 'steə keɪs ‖ 'ster- 'stær- **~es** ɪz əz
stairway 'steə weɪ ‖ 'ster- 'stær- **~s** z
stairwell 'steə wel ‖ 'ster- 'stær- **~s** z
staithe steɪð **staithes, S~** steɪðz
stake steɪk **staked** steɪkt **stakes** steɪks **staking** 'steɪk ɪŋ
stakeholder 'steɪk ˌhəʊld ə →-ˌhɒʊld- ‖ -ˌhoʊld ᵊr **~s** z
stakeout 'steɪk aʊt **~s** s
stakhanovism stə 'kæn ə ˌvɪz əm stæ-, -'kɑːn- ‖ -'kɑːn-
stakhanovite stə 'kæn ə vaɪt stæ-, -'kɑːn- ‖ -'kɑːn- **~s** s
stalactite 'stæl ək taɪt ‖ stə 'lækt aɪt *(*)* **~s** s
Stalag 'stæl æg -əg ‖ 'stɑːl ɑːg 'stæl əg —*Ger* ['ʃta lak]
stalagmite 'stæl əg maɪt ‖ stə 'læg- *(*)* **~s** s
St Albans sənt 'ɔːlb ənz §sən-, -'ɒlb- ‖ seɪnṭ- -'ɑːlb-
St Aldate's sənt 'ɔːld əts -'ɒld-, -ɪts, -eɪts ‖ seɪnṭ-'ɑːld-
stale steɪᵊl **staler** 'steɪᵊl ə ‖ -ᵊr **stalest** 'steɪᵊl ɪst -əst **stalely** 'steɪᵊl li
stale|mate 'steɪᵊl |meɪt **~mated** meɪt ɪd -əd ‖ meɪṭ əd **~mates** meɪts **~mating** meɪt ɪŋ ‖ meɪṭ ɪŋ
staleness 'steɪᵊl nəs -nɪs
Stalin 'stɑːl ɪn 'stæl-, §-ən ‖ -iːn —*Russ* ['sta lʲɪn]
Stalingrad 'stɑːl ɪn græd 'stæl-, →-ɪŋ-, §-ən- —*Russ* [stə lʲɪn 'grat]
Stalinism 'stɑːl ɪ ˌnɪz əm 'stæl-, -ə-
Stalinist 'stɑːl ɪn ɪst 'stæl-, -ən-, §-əst **~s** s
stalk stɔːk ‖ stɑːk **stalked** stɔːkt ‖ stɑːkt **stalking** 'stɔːk ɪŋ ‖ 'stɑːk- **stalks** stɔːks ‖ stɑːks
stalker, S~ 'stɔːk ə ‖ -ᵊr 'stɑːk- **~s** z
stalking-hors|e 'stɔːk ɪŋ hɔːs ‖ -hɔːrs 'stɑːk- **~es** ɪz əz
Stalky, s~ 'stɔːk i ‖ 'stɑːk-
stall stɔːl ‖ stɑːl **stalled** stɔːld ‖ stɑːld **stalling** 'stɔːl ɪŋ ‖ 'stɑːl- **stalls** stɔːlz ‖ stɑːlz
stallage 'stɔːl ɪdʒ
stallholder 'stɔːl ˌhəʊld ə →-ˌhɒʊld- ‖ -ˌhoʊld ᵊr 'stɑːl- **~s** z
stallion 'stæl jən **~s** z

Stallone stə ˈləʊn stæ- ‖ -ˈloʊn
Stallybrass ˈstæl i brɑːs §-bræs ‖ -bræs
stalwart ˈstɔːl wət ˈstɒl- ‖ -wᵊrt ˈstɑːl- **~ly** li **~ness** nəs nɪs **~s** s
Stalybridge ˈsteɪl i brɪdʒ ˌ· ·ˈ·
Stamboul, Stambul ₍ₗ₎stæm ˈbuːl
stamen ˈsteɪm en -ən **~s** z
Stamford ˈstæmᵖf əd ‖ -ᵊrd
stamina ˈstæm ɪn ə -ən-
stammer ˈstæm ə ‖ -ᵊr **~ed** d **stammering/ly** ˈstæm ər‿ɪŋ /li **~s** z
stamp, Stamp stæmp **stamped** stæm*p*t **stamping** ˈstæmp ɪŋ **stamps** stæm*p*s ˈ**stamp colˌlection**; ˈ**stamp ˌduty**; ˈ**stamping ground**
stamped|e ₍ₗ₎stæm ˈpiːd **~ed** ɪd əd **~es** z **~ing** ɪŋ
stamper ˈstæmp ə ‖ -ᵊr **~s** z
Stan stæn
Stanbury ˈstæn bər‿i →ˈstæm- ‖ -ˌber i
stance stænᵗs stɑːnᵗs **stances** ˈstænᵗs ɪz ˈstɑːnᵗs-, -əz
stanch stɑːn*t*ʃ §stæn*t*ʃ ‖ stɔːn*t*ʃ **stanched** stɑːn*t*ʃt §stæn*t*ʃt ‖ stɔːn*t*ʃt **stanching** ˈstɑːn*t*ʃ ɪŋ §ˈstæn*t*ʃ- ‖ ˈstɔːn*t*ʃ- **stanches** ˈstɑːn*t*ʃ ɪz §ˈstæn*t*ʃ-, -əz ‖ ˈstɔːn*t*ʃ-
stanchion ˈstɑːn*t*ʃ ən ˈstæn*t*ʃ- ‖ ˈstæn*t*ʃ ən **~s** z
Stancliffe ˈstæn klɪf →ˈstæŋ-
stand stænd **standing** ˈstænd ɪŋ **stands** stændz **stood** stʊd ˌ**standing** ˈ**order**; ˌ**standing oˈvation**; ˈ**standing room**
stand-alone ˈstænd ə ˌləʊn ˌ· ·ˈ· ‖ -ˌloʊn
standard ˈstænd əd ‖ -ᵊrd **~s** z ˌ**standard ˌdeviˈation**; ˈ**standard lamp**; ˌ**standard of ˈliving**; ˌ**standard ˈtime**
standard-bearer ˈstænd əd ˌbeər ə →-əb- ‖ -ᵊrd ˌber ᵊr -ˌbær- **~s** z
standardis... —*see* **standardiz...**
standard-issue ˌstænd əd ˈɪʃ uː ◂ -ˈɪs juː, -ˈɪʃ juː ‖ -ᵊrd ˈɪʃ uː ◂
standardization ˌstænd əd aɪ ˈzeɪʃ ᵊn -ɪˈ·- ‖ -ᵊrd ə- **~s** z
standardiz|e ˈstænd ə daɪz ‖ -ᵊr- **~ed** d **~es** ɪz əz **~ing** ɪŋ
standby ˈstæn*d* baɪ →ˈstæm*b*- **~s** z
Standedge ˈstæn edʒ ˈstænd-
standee stæn ˈdiː **~s** z
Standen ˈstænd ən
stand-in ˈstænd ɪn **~s** z
Standish ˈstænd ɪʃ
standoff ˈstænd ɒf -ɔːf ‖ -ɔːf -ɑːf **~s** s ˌ**standoff ˈhalf**, ˈ· · ·
standoffish ˌstænd ˈɒf ɪʃ -ˈɔːf- ‖ -ˈɔːf- -ˈɑːf- **~ly** li **~ness** nəs nɪs
standout ˈstænd aʊt **~s** s
standpipe ˈstæn*d* paɪp →ˈstæm*b*- **~s** s
standpoint ˈstæn*d* pɔɪnt →ˈstæm*b*- **~s** s
St Andrews sənt ˈændr uːz §sən- ‖ seɪnṭ- —*locally* sɪn ˈtændr-
standstill ˈstæn*d* stɪl **~s** z
stand-up ˈstænd ʌp
Stanfield ˈstæn fiːᵊld
Stanford ˈstæn fəd ‖ -fᵊrd
Stanford-Binet ˌstæn fəd ˈbiːn eɪ ˌ· ·bɪ ˈneɪ ‖ ˌ·fᵊrd bɪ ˈneɪ ˌ**Stanford-Biˈnet test**
Stanford-le-Hope ˌstæn fəd li ˈhəʊp ‖ -fᵊrd lə ˈhoʊp
stang stæŋ
Stanhope, s~ ˈstæn əp -həʊp ‖ -hoʊp **~s, ~'s** s
Stanislas ˈstæn ɪs ləs -əs-; -ɪ slæs, -ə-, -slɑːs
Stanislaus ˈstæn ɪ slaʊs -ə-, -slɔːs ‖ -slɔːs -slɑːs
Stanislavski, Stanislavsky ˌstæn ɪ ˈslæv ski -ə- ‖ -ˈslɑːv ski —*Russ* [stə nʲɪ ˈsłaf skʲɪj]
stank stæŋk
Stanley ˈstæn li ˌ**Stanley ˈFalls**; ˈ**Stanley knife**
Stanmore ˈstæn mɔː →ˈstæm- ‖ -mɔːr -moʊr
Stannard ˈstæn əd ‖ -ᵊrd
stannar|y ˈstæn ər |i **~ies** iz
St Anne's sənt ˈænz §sən- ‖ seɪnṭ-
stannic ˈstæn ɪk
stannous ˈstæn əs
Stansfield ˈstænz fiːᵊld ˈstænᵗs-
Stansgate ˈstænz geɪt
Stansted ˈstæn sted ˈstænᵗst ɪd, -əd
St Anthony sənt ˈænt ən i §sən- ‖ seɪnṭ ˈænt ᵊn i -ˈænᵗθ ən i
Stanton ˈstænt ən ‖ -ᵊn
Stanway ˈstæn weɪ
Stanwell ˈstæn wel -wəl
Stanwick, Stanwyck *(i)* ˈstæn ɪk, *(ii)* -wɪk
stanza ˈstænz ə **~s** z
stanzaic stæn ˈzeɪ ɪk
stapelia stə ˈpiːl i‿ə ‖ -ˈpiːl jə
stapes ˈsteɪp iːz
staph stæf
staphylo- *comb. form*
with stress-neutral suffix ˈstæf ɪl əʊ -ᵊl- ‖ -ə -oʊ — **staphyloplasty** ˈstæf ɪl əʊ ˌplæst i ˈ·ᵊl- ‖ -əˌ·-, -oʊˌ·-
with stress-imposing suffix ˌstæf ɪ ˈlɒ+ -ə- ‖ -ˈlɑː+ — **staphylorrhaphy** ˌstæf ɪ ˈlɒr əf i ˌ·ə- ‖ -ˈlɑːr- -ˈlɔːr-
staphylo|coccus ˌstæf ɪl əʊ |ˈkɒk əs ˌ·ᵊl- ‖ -ə |ˈkɑːk əs -oʊˈ·- **~coccal** ˈkɒk ᵊl ◂ ‖ -ˈkɑːk ᵊl ◂ **~cocci** ˈkɒks aɪ ˈkɒk-, ˈkɒs-, -iː ‖ ˈkɑːks aɪ ˈkɑːk-, -iː
stapl|e ˈsteɪp ᵊl **~ed** d **~es** z **~ing** ‿ɪŋ
Stapleford ˈsteɪp ᵊl fəd ‖ -fᵊrd —*but the place in Leics is* ˈstæp-
Staplehurst ˈsteɪp ᵊl hɜːst ‖ -hɜːst
stapler ˈsteɪp lə ‖ -lᵊr **~s** z
Stapleton ˈsteɪp ᵊl tən
star stɑː ‖ stɑːr **starred** stɑːd ‖ stɑːrd **starring** ˈstɑːr ɪŋ **stars** stɑːz ‖ stɑːrz ˌ**star ˈchamber** ‖ ˈ· ˌ·; ˌ**Stars and ˈStripes**; ˈ**star sign**; ˈ**star wars**
star-apple ˌstɑːr ˈæp ᵊl ˈ·ˌ·· ‖ ˈstɑːr ˌæp ᵊl **~s** z
starboard ˈstɑː bəd -bɔːd ‖ ˈstɑːr bᵊrd
Starbuck ˈstɑː bʌk ‖ ˈstɑːr- **~s, ~'s** s
starburst ˈstɑː bɜːst ‖ ˈstɑːr bɜːst **~s** s
starch stɑːtʃ ‖ stɑːrtʃ **starched** stɑːtʃt ‖ stɑːrtʃt **starches** ˈstɑːtʃ ɪz -əz ‖ ˈstɑːrtʃ əz **starching** ˈstɑːtʃ ɪŋ ‖ ˈstɑːrtʃ ɪŋ

S

starch-reduced ˌstɑːtʃ ri ˈdjuːst ◂ -rə-, →-ˈdʒuːst, ˈ·ˌ· ‖ ˌstɑːrtʃ ri ˈduːst ◂ -ˈdjuːst
ˌstarch-reˌduced ˈcrispbread
starch|y ˈstɑːtʃ |i ‖ ˈstɑːrtʃ |i **~ier** i‿ə ‖ i‿ər **~iest** i‿ɪst i‿əst **~ily** ɪ li əl i **~iness** i nəs i nɪs
star-crossed ˈstɑː krɒst -krɔːst, ˌ·ˈ· ‖ ˈstɑːr krɒst -krɑːst
stardom ˈstɑː dəm ‖ ˈstɑːr-
stardom ˈstɑː dəm ‖ ˈstɑːr-
stardust ˈstɑː dʌst ‖ ˈstɑːr-
stare steə ‖ steər stæər **stared** steəd ‖ steərd stæərd **stares** steəz ‖ steərz stæərz **staring** ˈsteər ɪŋ ‖ ˈster ɪŋ ˈstær-
starfish ˈstɑː fɪʃ ‖ ˈstɑːr- **~es** ɪz əz
starfruit ˈstɑː fruːt ‖ ˈstɑːr-
stargazer ˈstɑː ˌɡeɪz ə ‖ ˈstɑːr ˌɡeɪz ər **~s** z
stargazing ˈstɑː ˌɡeɪz ɪŋ ‖ ˈstɑːr-
staring ˈsteər ɪŋ ‖ ˈster ɪŋ ˈstær- **~ly** li
stark, Stark stɑːk ‖ stɑːrk **starker** ˈstɑːk ə ‖ ˈstɑːrk ər **starkest** ˈstɑːk ɪst -əst ‖ ˈstɑːrk əst
starkers ˈstɑːk əz ‖ ˈstɑːrk ərz
Starkey, Starkie ˈstɑːk i ‖ ˈstɑːrk i
starkly ˈstɑːk li ‖ ˈstɑːrk li
stark-naked ˌstɑːk ˈneɪk ɪd ◂ -əd ‖ ˌstɑːrk-
starkness ˈstɑːk nəs -nɪs ‖ ˈstɑːrk-
starless ˈstɑː ləs -lɪs ‖ ˈstɑːr-
starlet ˈstɑː lət -lɪt ‖ ˈstɑːr- **~s** s
starlight ˈstɑː laɪt ‖ ˈstɑːr-
starling, S~ ˈstɑːl ɪŋ ‖ ˈstɑːrl- **~s** z
starlit ˈstɑː lɪt ‖ ˈstɑːr-
Starr stɑː ‖ stɑːr
starr... —*see* **star**
starr|y ˈstɑːr |i **~ier** i‿ə ‖ i‿ər **~iest** i‿ɪst i‿əst **~iness** i nəs i nɪs
starry-eyed ˌstɑːr i ˈaɪd ◂
starship ˈstɑː ʃɪp ‖ ˈstɑːr- **~s** s
Starsky ˈstɑː ski ˈstɑːsk i ‖ ˈstɑːr ski
star-spangled ˈstɑː ˌspæŋ ɡəld ˌ·ˈ·· ‖ ˌstɑːr ˈspæŋ ɡəld ◂
ˌStar-ˌSpangled ˈBanner
starstruck ˈstɑː strʌk ‖ ˈstɑːr-
star-studded ˈstɑː ˌstʌd ɪd -əd, ˌ·ˈ·· ‖ ˈstɑːr-
star-studded ˈstɑː ˌstʌd ɪd -əd ‖ ˈstɑːr-
start, Start stɑːt ‖ stɑːrt **started** ˈstɑːt ɪd -əd ‖ ˈstɑːrţ əd **starting** ˈstɑːt ɪŋ ‖ ˈstɑːrţ ɪŋ **starts** stɑːts ‖ stɑːrts
ˈstarting block; **ˈstarting gate**; **ˈstarting ˌpistol**; **ˈstarting price**
starter ˈstɑːt ə ‖ ˈstɑːrţ ər **~s** z
Startin ˈstɑːt ɪn §-ən ‖ ˈstɑːrt ən
startl|e ˈstɑːt əl ‖ ˈstɑːrţ əl **~ed** d **~es** z **~ing/ly** ‿ɪŋ /li
Start-rite *tdmk* ˈstɑːt raɪt ‖ ˈstɑːrt-
start-up ˈstɑːt ʌp ‖ ˈstɑːrţ ʌp **~s** s
starvation ₍ˌ₎stɑː ˈveɪʃ ən ‖ ₍ˌ₎stɑːr-
starˈvation ˌwages, ·ˌ· · ˈ·
starve stɑːv ‖ stɑːrv **starved** stɑːvd ‖ stɑːrvd **starves** stɑːvz ‖ stɑːrvz **starving** ˈstɑːv ɪŋ ‖ ˈstɑːrv ɪŋ
starveling ˈstɑːv lɪŋ ‖ ˈstɑːrv- **~s** z
starwort ˈstɑː wɜːt §-wɔːt ‖ ˈstɑːr wɜːt -wɔːrt **~s** s

St Asaph sənt ˈæs əf §sən- ‖ seɪnţ-
stash stæʃ **stashed** stæʃt **stashes** ˈstæʃ ɪz -əz **stashing** ˈstæʃ ɪŋ
Stasi ˈstɑːz i —*Ger* [ˈʃtaː zi]
stas|is ˈsteɪs |ɪs ˈstæs-, §-əs **~es** iːz
Stassen ˈstæs ən
-stat stæt — **thermostat** ˈθɜːm əʊ stæt ‖ ˈθɜːm ə-
state, State steɪt **stated** ˈsteɪt ɪd -əd ‖ ˈsteɪţ əd **states, States** steɪts **stating** ˈsteɪt ɪŋ ‖ ˈsteɪţ ɪŋ
ˈState Deˌpartment; **ˌstate's ˈevidence**
statecraft ˈsteɪt krɑːft §-kræft ‖ -kræft
statehood ˈsteɪt hʊd
state|house, S~ ˈsteɪt |haʊs **~houses** haʊz ɪz -əz
stateless ˈsteɪt ləs -lɪs **~ness** nəs nɪs
state|ly ˈsteɪt |li **~lier** li‿ə ‖ li‿ər **~iest** li‿ɪst əst **~iness** li nəs -nɪs
ˌstately ˈhome
statement ˈsteɪt mənt **~ed** ɪd əd **~ing** ɪŋ **~s** s
Staten ˈstæt ən
ˌStaten ˈIsland
state-of-the-art ˌsteɪt əv ði ˈɑːt ◂ ˌ·ə- ‖ ˌsteɪţ əv ði ˈɑːrt ◂
stater ˈsteɪt ə ‖ ˈsteɪţ ər **~s** z
stateroom ˈsteɪt ruːm -rʊm **~s** z
stateside ˈsteɪt saɪd
states|man ˈsteɪts |mən **~men** mən
statesman|like ˈsteɪts mən |laɪk **~ship** ʃɪp
states|woman ˈsteɪts ˌwʊm ən **~women** ˌwɪm ɪn §-ən
statewide ˌsteɪt ˈwaɪd ◂
Statham *(i)* ˈsteɪθ əm, *(ii)* ˈsteɪð əm
St Athan sənt ˈæθ ən §sən- ‖ seɪnţ-
static ˈstæt ɪk ‖ ˈstæţ ɪk **~ally** əl‿i **~s** s
statice ˈstæt ɪs i -əs i; ˈstæt ɪs, §-əs ‖ ˈstæţ əs i ˈstæţ əs
statin ˈstæt ɪn §-ən ‖ -ən **~s** z
station ˈsteɪʃ ən **~ed** d **~ing** ‿ɪŋ **~s** z
ˈstation break; **ˈstation house**; **ˌstations of the ˈCross**; **ˈstation ˌwagon**
stationary ˈsteɪʃ ən ər‿i -ən‿ər i ‖ -ə ner i
stationer ˈsteɪʃ ən‿ə ‖ ər **~s** z
stationery ˈsteɪʃ ən ər‿i -ən‿ər i ‖ -ə ner i *(= stationary)*
stationmaster ˈsteɪʃ ən ˌmɑːst ə §-ˌmæst- ‖ -ˌmæst ər **~s** z
statism ˈsteɪt ˌɪz əm ‖ ˈsteɪţ-
statist *'advocate of state power'* ˈsteɪt ɪst §-əst ‖ ˈsteɪţ əst **~s** s
statist *'statistician'* ˈstæt ɪst -əst ‖ ˈstæţ əst **~s** s
statistic stə ˈtɪst ɪk **~s** s
statistical stə ˈtɪst ɪk əl **~ly** i
statistician ˌstæt ɪ ˈstɪʃ ən -ə- ‖ ˌstæţ- **~s** z
Statius ˈsteɪʃ i‿əs ˈsteɪt-
stative ˈsteɪt ɪv ‖ ˈsteɪţ- **~s** z
stato- *comb. form* *with stress-neutral suffix* ˌstæt əʊ ‖ ˌstæţ ə — **statolith** ˈstæt əʊ lɪθ ‖ ˈstæţ ə- -əl ɪθ

with stress-imposing suffix stæ 'tɒ+ ‖ -'tɑː+ — **statometer** stæ 'tɒm ɪt ə -ət ə ‖ -'tɑːm əṭ ᵊr
Staton 'steɪt ᵊn
stator 'steɪt ə ‖ 'steɪṭ ᵊr **~s** z
stats *'statistics'* stæts
statuar|y 'stætʃ u‿ər |i 'stæt ju‿ ‖ -er |i **~ies** iz
statue 'stætʃ uː 'stæt juː **~s** z
statuesque ˌstætʃ u 'esk ◂ ˌstæt ju- **~ly** li
statuette ˌstætʃ u 'et ˌstæt ju- **~s** s
stature 'stætʃ ə ‖ -ᵊr **~s** z
status 'steɪt əs 'stæt- ‖ 'steɪṭ əs 'stæṭ- **~es** ɪz əz
ˌstatus 'quo
statute 'stætʃ uːt 'stæt juːt **~s** s
'statute book; **'statute law**
statutor|y 'stætʃ ʊt‿ər |i '-uːt‿; 'stæt jʊt‿, '-juːt‿; §stə 'tjuːt ər |i ‖ 'stætʃ ə tɔːr |i '-u-, -toʊr i **~ily** əl i -ɪ li
St Aubyn sənt 'ɔːb ɪn §sən-, §-ən ‖ seɪnṭ-'ɑːb-
Staughton 'stɔːt ᵊn ‖ 'stɑːt-
St Augustine sənt ɔː 'gʌst ɪn §sən-, ˌseɪnt-, §-ən ‖ ˌseɪnṭ ɔː- ˌɑː-
staunch *adj* stɔːntʃ ‖ stɑːntʃ —*in RP formerly also* stɑːntʃ **stauncher** 'stɔːntʃ ə ‖ -ᵊr 'stɑːntʃ- **staunchest** 'stɔːntʃ ɪst -əst ‖ 'stɑːntʃ-
staunch *v* stɔːntʃ stɑːntʃ, §stæntʃ **staunched** stɔːntʃt stɑːntʃt, §stæntʃt **staunches** 'stɔːntʃ ɪz 'stɑːntʃ-, §'stæntʃ-, -əz **staunching** 'stɔːntʃ ɪŋ 'stɑːntʃ-, §'stæntʃ-
staunch|ly 'stɔːntʃ |li ‖ 'stɑːntʃ- **~ness** nəs nɪs
Staunton *(i)* 'stɔːnt ən ‖ 'stɑːnt-, *(ii)* 'stænt ən ‖ -ᵊn —*The English family name is (i), as is the place in IL; the place in VA is (ii)*
staurolite 'stɔːr ə laɪt **~s** s
stauroscope 'stɔːr ə skəʊp ‖ -skoʊp **~s** s
stauroscopic ˌstɔːr ə 'skɒp ɪk ◂ ‖ -'skɑːp- **~ally** ᵊl i
St Austell sənt 'ɔːst ᵊl §sən-, -'ɒst-, -'ɔːs- ‖ seɪnṭ-'ɑːst-
Stavanger stə 'væŋ ə ‖ stɑː 'vɑːŋ ᵊr —*Norw* [sta 'vaŋ ər]
stave steɪv **staved** steɪvd **staves** steɪvz **staving** 'steɪv ɪŋ **stove** stəʊv ‖ stoʊv
Staveley 'steɪv li
Staverton 'stæv ət ən ‖ -ᵊrt ᵊn
staves *pl of* **staff** steɪvz
stavesacre 'steɪvz ˌeɪk ə ‖ -ᵊr **~s** z
Stawell stɔːl ‖ stɑːl
stay steɪ **stayed** steɪd *(= staid)* **staying** 'steɪ ɪŋ **stays** steɪz
'staying ˌpower
stay-at-home 'steɪ ət ˌhəʊm ‖ -ˌhoʊm **~s** z
stayer 'steɪ ə ‖ -ᵊr **~s** z
Stayman 'steɪ mən
staysail 'steɪ sᵊl -seɪᵊl **~s** z
St Barts sənt 'bɑːts ‖ seɪnt 'bɑːrts
St Bernard sənt 'bɜːn əd →səm- ‖ ˌseɪnt bᵊr 'nɑːrd —*Fr* [sɛ̃ bɛʁ naːʁ] **~s** z
St ˌBernard 'Pass ‖ **ˌSt Berˌnard 'Pass**
St Briavels sənt 'brev ᵊlz →sᵊm- ‖ seɪnt-
St Christopher sənt 'krɪst əf ə →səŋ- ‖ seɪnt 'krɪst əf ᵊr
St Clair sənt 'kleə →sᵊŋ- ‖ seɪnt 'kleᵊr -'klæᵊr —*but as a family name also* 'sɪŋ kleə, 'sɪn- ‖ -kler, -klær
St Cloud sæŋ 'kluː —*Fr* [sɛ̃ klu] —*but the place in MN is* seɪnt 'klaʊd
St Croix sənt 'krɔɪ ‖ seɪnt-
STD ˌes tiː 'diː
St David's sənt 'deɪv ɪdz §-ədz ‖ seɪnt-
St 'David's day
St Denis sənt 'den ɪs §-əs ‖ seɪnt- —*but for the places in Paris and Réunion* ˌsæn də 'niː, —*Fr* [sɛ̃d ni]
St Dogmaels sənt 'dɒg mᵊlz ‖ seɪnt 'dɔːg- -'dɑːg-
St Donat's sənt 'dɒn əts ‖ seɪnt 'dɑːn-
stead sted
Stead *(i)* sted, *(ii)* stiːd
steadfast 'sted fɑːst -fəst, §-fæst ‖ -fæst **~ly** li **~ness** nəs nɪs
steading 'sted ɪŋ **~s** z
Steadman 'sted mən →'steb-
stead|y 'sted |i **~ier** i‿ə ‖ i‿ᵊr **~iest** i‿ɪst i‿əst **~ily** ɪ li əl i **~iness** i nəs i nɪs
ˌsteady 'state, ˌsteady 'state ˌtheory
steak steɪk *(= stake)* **steaks** steɪks
ˌsteak tar'tare
steak|house 'steɪk |haʊs **~houses** haʊz ɪz -əz
steal stiːᵊl *(= steel)* **stealing** 'stiːᵊl ɪŋ **steals** stiːᵊlz **stole** stəʊl →stɒʊl ‖ stoʊl **stolen** 'stəʊl ən →'stɒʊl- ‖ 'stoʊl ən
stealer 'stiːᵊl ə ‖ -ᵊr **~s** z
stealth stelθ
stealth|y 'stelθ |i **~ier** i‿ə ‖ i‿ᵊr **~iest** i‿ɪst i‿əst **~ily** ɪ li əl i **~iness** i nəs i nɪs
steam stiːm **steamed** stiːmd **steaming** 'stiːm ɪŋ **steams** stiːmz
'steam ˌiron; **'steam ˌshovel**
steamboat 'stiːm bəʊt ‖ -boʊt **~s** s
steamed-up ˌstiːmd 'ʌp ◂
steam-engine 'stiːm ˌendʒ ɪn §-ˌɪndʒ-, -ən **~s** z
steamer 'stiːm ə ‖ -ᵊr **~s** z
steamroll 'stiːm ˌrəʊl →-ˌrɒʊl ‖ -ˌroʊl **~ed** d **~ing** ɪŋ **~s** z
steamroll|er 'stiːm ˌrəʊl |ə →-ˌrɒʊl- ‖ -ˌroʊl |ᵊr **~ered** əd ‖ ᵊrd **~ering** ər ɪŋ **~ers** əz ‖ ᵊrz
steamship 'stiːm ʃɪp **~s** s
steam|y 'stiːm |i **~ier** i‿ə ‖ i‿ᵊr **~iest** i‿ɪst i‿əst **~ily** ɪ li əl i **~iness** i nəs i nɪs
stearate 'stɪər eɪt ‖ 'stiː ə reɪt 'stɪr eɪt **~s** s
stearic sti 'ær ɪk ‖ -'er-; 'stɪr ɪk
stearin 'stɪər ɪn §-ən ‖ 'stiː ər ən 'stɪr ən
Stearn, Stearne stɜːn ‖ stɜːn
stearoptene ˌstɪə 'rɒpt iːn ‖ ˌstiː ə 'rɑːpt-
steatite 'stiː‿ə taɪt
steatolysis ˌstiː‿ə 'tɒl əs ɪs -ɪs ɪs, §-əs ‖ -'tɑːl-
steatopygia ˌstiː‿ət əʊ 'paɪdʒ i‿ə -'pɪdʒ- ‖ sti ˌæṭ ə- ˌstiː əṭ ə-
steatopygous ˌstiː‿ət əʊ 'paɪg əs ◂ ˌstiː‿ə 'tɒp ɪg əs, §-əg əs ‖ sti ˌæṭ ə- ˌstiː əṭ ə-; ˌstiː ə 'tɑːp əg əs

S

steatorrhea, steatorrhoea ˌstiː ət ə ˈriː ə ‖ sti ˌæṭ ə- ˌstiː əṭ ə-
Stebbing ˈsteb ɪŋ
Stechford ˈstetʃ fəd ‖ -fᵊrd
stedfast ˈsted fɑːst -fəst, §-fæst ‖ -fæst **~ly** li **~ness** nəs nɪs
Stedman ˈsted mən →ˈsteb-
St Edmunds sənt ˈed məndz §sən-, →-ˈeb- ‖ seɪnṭ-
steed, Steed stiːd **steeds, Steed's** stiːdz
steel stiːᵊl **steeled** stiːᵊld **steeling** ˈstiːᵊl ɪŋ **steels** stiːᵊlz
ˈsteel band; **ˌsteel ˈwool**
Steel, Steele stiːᵊl
steel-grey, steel-gray ˌstiːᵊl ˈgreɪ ◂
steeli... —*see* **steely**
steelmak|er ˈstiːᵊl ˌmeɪk ə ‖ -ᵊr **~ers** əz ‖ ᵊrz **~ing** ɪŋ
steelworker ˈstiːᵊl ˌwɜːk ə ‖ -ˌwɜːk ᵊr **~s** z
steelworks ˈstiːᵊl wɜːks ‖ -wɜːks
steel|y ˈstiːᵊl |i **~ier** i ə ‖ i ᵊr **~iest** i ɪst i əst **~iness** i nəs i nɪs
steelyard ˈstiːᵊl jɑːd ˈstɪl-, -jəd ‖ ˈstiːᵊl jɑːrd ˈstɪl jᵊrd **~s** z
steely-eyed ˌstiːᵊl i ˈaɪd ◂
Steen stiːn —*but as a Dutch name,* steɪn *Dutch* [steːn]
steenbok ˈstiːn bɒk →ˈstiːm-, ˈsteɪn-, ˈstɪən-, -bʌk ‖ -bɑːk **~s** s
steep stiːp **steeper** ˈstiːp ə ‖ -ᵊr **steepest** ˈstiːp ɪst -əst
steepen ˈstiːp ən **~ed** d **~ing** ɪŋ **~s** z
steeple ˈstiːp ᵊl **~s** z
steeplechas|e ˈstiːp ᵊl tʃeɪs **~er/s** ə/z ‖ -ᵊr/z **~es** ɪz əz **~ing** ɪŋ
steeplejack ˈstiːp ᵊl dʒæk **~s** s
steep|ly ˈstiːp |li **~ness** nəs nɪs
steer stɪə ‖ stɪᵊr **steered** stɪəd ‖ stɪᵊrd **steering** ˈstɪər ɪŋ ‖ ˈstɪr ɪŋ **steers** stɪəz ‖ stɪᵊrz
ˈsteering comˌmittee; **ˈsteering wheel**
steerage ˈstɪər ɪdʒ ‖ ˈstɪr- **~way** weɪ
steers|man ˈstɪəz |mən ‖ ˈstɪrz- **~men** mən men
Stefan ˈstef ᵊn -æn
Stefanie ˈstef ən i
Steffens ˈstef ᵊnz
stegodon ˈsteg ə dɒn ‖ -dɑːn **~s** z
stegosaur ˈsteg ə sɔː ‖ -sɔːr **~s** z
stegosaurus ˌsteg ə ˈsɔːr əs **~es** ɪz əz
Steiff ʃtaɪf
Steiger ˈstaɪg ə ‖ -ᵊr
stein staɪn —*Ger* [ʃtain] **steins** staɪnz
Stein *(i)* staɪn, *(ii)* stiːn —*but as a German name,* ʃtaɪn —*Ger* [ʃtain]
Steinbeck ˈstaɪn bek →ˈstaɪm-
Steinberg ˈstaɪn bɜːg →ˈstaɪm- ‖ -bɜːg
steinbock, steinbok ˈstaɪn bɒk →ˈstaɪm-, -bʌk ‖ -bɑːk **~s** s
Steine *place in Brighton, Sx* stiːn
Steinem ˈstaɪn əm
Steiner ˈstaɪn ə ‖ -ᵊr —*Ger* [ˈʃtai nɐ]
Steinway *tdmk* ˈstaɪn weɪ **~s** z

S

stel|a ˈstiːl |ə **~ae** iː
Stelazine *tdmk* ˈstel ə ziːn
stele *(i)* ˈstiːl i -iː *(ii)* stiːᵊl —*in archaeology usually (i), in botany usually (ii)* **steles** *(i)* ˈstiːl iz -iːz *(ii)* stiːᵊlz
Stella ˈstel ə
stellar ˈstel ə ‖ -ᵊr
stellate *adj* ˈstel eɪt -ət, -ɪt
Stellenbosch ˈstel ən bɒs →-əm-, -bɒʃ ‖ -bɑːs -bɑːʃ
Steller ˈstel ə ‖ -ᵊr **~'s** z
ˌSteller's ˈjay
St Elmo sənt ˈelm əʊ §sən- ‖ seɪnṭ ˈelm oʊ **~'s** z
St ˌElmo's ˈfire
stem stem **stemmed** stemd **stemming** ˈstem ɪŋ **stems** stemz
stemm|a ˈstem| ə **~ata** ət ə ‖ əṭ ə
-stemmed ˈstemd — **long-stemmed** ˌlɒŋ ˈstemd ◂ ‖ ˌlɔːŋ- ˌlɑːŋ-
stemware ˈstem weə ‖ -wer -wær
Sten sten
ˈSten gun
stench stentʃ **stenches** ˈstentʃ ɪz -əz
stencil ˈstenᵗs ᵊl -ɪl **~ed, ~led** d **~ing, ~ling** ɪŋ **~s** z
Stendhal ˈstɒnd ɑːl ‖ sten ˈdɑːl —*Fr* [stɛ̃ dal], *though popularly believed in Britain to be* [stɒ̃-]
Stenhousemuir ˌsten haʊs ˈmjʊə -əs-, -ˈmjɔː ‖ -ˈmjʊᵊr
steno ˈsten əʊ ‖ -oʊ **~s** z
steno- *comb. form*
with stress-neutral suffix ¦sten əʊ ‖ -ə — **stenothermal** ˌsten əʊ ˈθɜːm ᵊl ◂ ‖ -ə ˈθɜːm-
with stress-imposing suffix ste ˈnɒ+ stə- ‖ -nɑː+ — **stenophagous** ste ˈnɒf əg əs stə- ‖ -ˈnɑːf-
stenograph ˈsten ə grɑːf -græf ‖ -græf **~ed** t **~ing** ɪŋ **~s** s
stenographer stə ˈnɒg rəf ə ste- ‖ -ˈnɑːg rəf ᵊr **~s** z
stenographic ˌsten ə ˈgræf ɪk ◂ **~ally** ᵊl i
stenography stə ˈnɒg rəf i ste- ‖ -ˈnɑːg-
stenos|is ste ˈnəʊs |ɪs stɪ-, stə-, §-əs ‖ -ˈnoʊs- **~es** iːz
stenotype, S~ *tdmk* ˈsten əʊ taɪp ‖ -ə- **~s** s
stenotypist ˈsten əʊ taɪp ɪst §-əst ‖ ˈ-ə- **~s** s
stenotypy ˈsten əʊ taɪp i ‖ ˈ-ə-
stent stent **stented** ˈstent ɪd -əd ‖ ˈstenṭ əd **stenting** ˈstent ɪŋ ‖ ˈstenṭ ɪŋ **stents** stents
Stentor, s~ ˈstent ɔː -ə ‖ ˈstent ɔːr ˈstenṭ ᵊr **~s** z
stentorian sten ˈtɔːr i ən ‖ -ˈtoʊr-
step step **stepped** stept **stepping** ˈstep ɪŋ **steps** steps
step- ¦step —*Compounds of* step- *not listed below mostly have late stress, thus* ˌstepˈgrandson
stepbrother ˈstep ˌbrʌð ə ‖ -ᵊr **~s** z
step-by-step ˌstep baɪ ˈstep ◂
step|child ˈstep |tʃaɪᵊld **~children** ˌtʃɪldr ən

stepdaughter ˈstep ˌdɔːt ə ‖ -ˌdɔːṭ ᵊr -ˌdɑːṭ- **~s** z
step-down ˈstep daʊn **~s** z
stepfather ˈstep ˌfɑːð ə ‖ -ᵊr **~s** z
Stepford ˈstep fəd ‖ -fᵊrd
Stephanie ˈstef ən i
stephanotis ˌstef ə ˈnəʊt ɪs §-əs ‖ -ˈnoʊṭ əs
Stephen ˈstiːv ᵊn
Stephens ˈstiːv ᵊnz
Stephenson ˈstiːv ᵊn sən
step-in ˈstep ɪn **~s** z
Stepinac ˈstep ɪ næts -ə- —*Croatian* [stɛ ˈpiː nats]
stepladder ˈstep ˌlæd ə ‖ -ᵊr **~s** z
stepmother ˈstep ˌmʌð ə ‖ -ᵊr **~s** z
Stepney ˈstep ni
ˌ**Stepney ˈGreen**
stepparent ˈstep ˌpeər ənt ‖ -ˌper- -ˌpær- **~s** s
steppe step *(= step)* **steppes** steps
stepped-up ˌstept ˈʌp ◂
stepper ˈstep ə ‖ -ᵊr **~s** z
stepping-stone ˈstep ɪŋ stəʊn ‖ -stoʊn **~s** z
stepsister ˈstep ˌsɪst ə ‖ -ᵊr **~s** z
stepson ˈstep sʌn **~s** z
Steptoe ˈstep təʊ ‖ -toʊ
step-up ˈstep ʌp **~s** s
stepwise ˈstep waɪz
-ster *stress-neutral* stə ‖ stᵊr — **songster** ˈsɒŋᵏst ə ˈsɒŋ stə ‖ ˈsɔːŋᵏst ᵊr ˈsɑːŋᵏst-; ˈsɔːŋ stᵊr, ˈsɑːŋ-
Steradent *tdmk* ˈster ə dent
steradian stə ˈreɪd i‿ən **~s** z
stercoraceous ˌstɜːk ə ˈreɪʃ əs ◂ ‖ ˌstɜ˞ːk-

STEREO

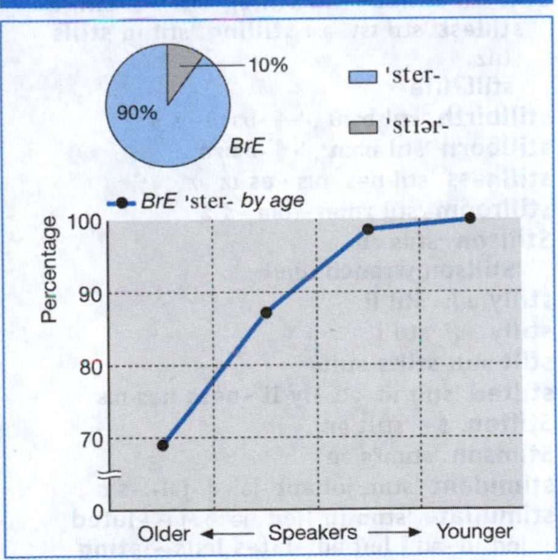

stereo ˈster i əʊ ˈstɪər- ‖ ˈster i oʊ ˈstɪr- —*Preference poll, BrE:* ˈster- *90%,* ˈstɪər- *10%.* **~s** z
stereo- *comb. form*
with stress-neutral suffix ¦ster i əʊ ¦stɪər- ‖ ¦ster i oʊ ¦stɪr- — **stereoisomer** ˌster i əʊ ˈaɪs əʊm ə ˌstɪər- ‖ ˌster i oʊ ˈaɪs əm ᵊr ˌstɪr-
with stress-imposing suffix ˌster i ˈɒ+ ˌstɪər- ‖ ˌster i ˈɑː+ ˌstɪr- — **stereography** ˌster i ˈɒg rəf i ˌstɪər- ‖ ˌster i ˈɑːg- ˌstɪr-
stereobate ˈster i əʊ beɪt ˈstɪər- ‖ ˈster i oʊ- **~s** s
stereophonic ˌster i‿ə ˈfɒn ɪk ◂ ˌstɪər-, -i əʊ- ‖ ˌster i‿ə ˈfɑːn ɪk ◂ ˌstɪr- **~ally** ᵊl‿i **S~s** s
stereoscope ˈster i‿ə skəʊp ˈstɪər-, -i əʊ- ‖ ˈster i‿ə skoʊp ˈstɪr- **~s** s
stereoscopic ˌster i‿ə ˈskɒp ɪk ◂ ˌstɪər-, -i əʊ- ‖ ˌster i‿ə ˈskɑːp ɪk ◂ ˌstɪr- **~ally** ᵊl‿i
stereotyp|e ˈster i‿ə taɪp ˈstɪər- ‖ ˈstɪr- **~ed** t **~er/s** ə/z ‖ ᵊr/z **~es** s **~ing** ɪŋ
stereotypical ˌster i‿ə ˈtɪp ɪk ᵊl ◂ ˌstɪər-, -i əʊ- ‖ ˌstɪr- **~ly** ‿i
stereotypy ˈster i‿ə taɪp i ˈstɪər- ‖ ˈstɪr-
Stergene *tdmk* ˈstɜːdʒ iːn ‖ ˈstɜ˞ːdʒ-
steric ˈster ɪk ˈstɪər- ‖ ˈstɪr-
sterilant ˈster əl ənt -ɪl- **~s** s
sterile ˈster aɪᵊl ‖ ˈster əl *(*)* **~ly** li **~ness** nəs nɪs
sterilis... —*see* **steriliz...**
sterility stə ˈrɪl ət i ste-, -ɪt i ‖ -əṭ i
sterilization ˌster əl aɪ ˈzeɪʃ ᵊn ˌ·ɪl-, -ɪˈ-- ‖ -əˈ-- **~s** z
steriliz|e ˈster ə laɪz -ɪ- **~ed** d **~er/s** ə/z ‖ ᵊr/z **~es** ɪz əz **~ing** ɪŋ
sterling, S~ ˈstɜːl ɪŋ ‖ ˈstɜ˞ːl ɪŋ
stern stɜːn ‖ stɜ˞ːn **sterner** ˈstɜːn ə ‖ ˈstɜ˞ːn ᵊr **sternest** ˈstɜːn ɪst -əst ‖ ˈstɜ˞ːn əst
Stern stɜːn ‖ stɜ˞ːn —*but as a German name,* ʃteən ‖ ʃtern —*Ger* [ʃtɛʁn]
sterna ˈstɜːn ə ‖ ˈstɜ˞ːn ə
Sterne stɜːn ‖ stɜ˞ːn
sternly ˈstɜːn li ‖ ˈstɜ˞ːn li
sternmost ˈstɜːn məʊst →ˈstɜːm- ‖ ˈstɜ˞ːn moʊst
sternness ˈstɜːn nəs -nɪs ‖ ˈstɜ˞ːn-
sternpost ˈstɜːn pəʊst →ˈstɜːm- ‖ ˈstɜ˞ːn poʊst **~s** s
stern|um ˈstɜːn |əm ‖ ˈstɜ˞ːn |əm **~a** ə
sternutation ˌstɜːn ju ˈteɪʃ ᵊn ‖ ˌstɜ˞ːn jə- **~s** z
sternutator|y ˌstɜːn ju ˈteɪt ər |i stɜː ˈnjuːt ət‿ər |i ‖ stᵊr ˈnuːṭ ə tɔːr |i -ˈnjuːṭ-, -toʊr i **~ies** iz
steroid ˈstɪər ɔɪd ˈster- ‖ ˈstɪr- **~s** z
sterol ˈstɪər ɒl ˈster- ‖ ˈstɪr ɔːl -ɑːl, -oʊl **~s** z
stertor ˈstɜːt ə ‖ ˈstɜ˞ːṭ ᵊr
stertorous ˈstɜːt ər əs ‖ ˈstɜ˞ːṭ- **~ly** li **~ness** nəs nɪs
stet stet **stets** stets **stetted** ˈstet ɪd -əd ‖ ˈsteṭ əd **stetting** ˈstet ɪŋ ‖ ˈsteṭ ɪŋ
stethoscope ˈsteθ ə skəʊp ‖ -skoʊp **~s** s
stethoscopic ˌsteθ ə ˈskɒp ɪk ◂ ‖ -ˈskɑːp- **~ally** ᵊl‿i
stethoscopy ste ˈθɒsk əp i ‖ -ˈθɑːsk-
stetson, S~ ˈstets ən **~s** z
Steuart ˈstjuː‿ət →ˈstʃuː‿ ‖ ˈstuː‿ᵊrt ˈstjuː‿
Steuben ˈstjuːb ən →ˈstʃuːb- ‖ ˈstuːb ən ˈstjuːb-; stu ˈben, stju-
Stevas ˈstiːv əs -æs
Steve stiːv
stevedore ˈstiːv ə dɔː -ɪ- ‖ -dɔːr -doʊr **~d** d **~s** z **stevedoring** ˈstiːv ə dɔːr ɪŋ ˈ·ɪ- ‖ -doʊr ɪŋ

S

Steven ˈstiːv ən
Stevenage ˈstiːv ən ɪdʒ
Stevens ˈstiːv ənz
Stevenson ˈstiːv ən sən
Steventon ˈstiːv ən tən
Stevie ˈstiːv i
stew stjuː →stʃuː ‖ stuː stjuː **stewed** stjuːd →stʃuːd ‖ stuːd stjuːd **stewing** ˈstjuː‿ɪŋ →ˈstʃuː‿ ‖ ˈstuː ɪŋ ˈstjuː- **stews** stjuːz →stʃuːz ‖ stuːz stjuːz
steward, S~ ˈstjuː‿əd →ˈstʃuː‿ ‖ ˈstuː‿ərd ˈstjuː‿ **~ed** ɪd əd **~ing** ɪŋ **~s** z
stewardess ˌstjuː‿ə ˈdes →ˌstʃuː‿, ˈ· · ·, ə dɪs, §‿ə dəs ‖ ˈstuː‿ərd əs **~es** ɪz əz
stewardship ˈstjuː‿əd ʃɪp →ˈstʃuː‿ ‖ ˈstuː‿ərd ʃɪp ˈstjuː‿ **~s** s
Stewart ˈstjuː‿ət →ˈstʃuː‿ ‖ ˈstuː‿ərt ˈstjuː‿
stewpan ˈstjuː pæn →ˈstʃuː- ‖ ˈstuː- ˈstjuː- **~s** z
Steyn *family name* staɪn
Steyne *place name* stiːn
Steyning ˈsten ɪŋ
St Fagan's sənt ˈfæg ənz ‖ seɪnt-
St George sənt ˈdʒɔːdʒ ‖ seɪnt ˈdʒɔːrdʒ **~'s** ɪz əz
St ˌGeorge's ˈChannel
St Gotthard sənt ˈgɒt əd -ɑːd ‖ seɪnt ˈgɑːṭ ərd —*Ger* [zaŋkt ˈgɔt haʁt]
St Helena *name of saint* sənt ˈhel ən ə §sən-, -ɪn ə; -hɪ ˈliːn ə, -hə'-- ‖ seɪnt-
St Helena *island* ˌsent *hɪ* ˈliːn ə sənt-, *-hə-*, -ˈleɪn ə
St. Helena *place in CA* ˌseɪnt *hɪ* ˈliːn ə sənt-, *-hə-* ‖ ˌseɪnṭ ɪ- ˌseɪnt hɪ-
St Helens sənt ˈhel ənz -ɪnz ‖ seɪnt-
St Helier sənt ˈhel i‿ə ‖ seɪnt ˈhel jər
sthenic ˈsθen ɪk
stibine ˈstɪb aɪn ‖ -iːn
stibnite ˈstɪb naɪt
Stich ʃtiːk —*Ger* [ʃtɪç]
stichometry stɪ ˈkɒm ətr i §stə-, -ɪtr i ‖ -ˈkɑːm-
stichomythia ˌstɪk əʊ ˈmɪθ i‿ə ‖ ˌ·ə-
stick stɪk **sticking** ˈstɪk ɪŋ **sticks** stɪks **stuck** stʌk
ˈsticking ˌplaster; **ˈsticking point**; **ˈstick ˌinsect**; **ˈstick shift**
stickball ˈstɪk bɔːl ‖ -bɑːl
sticker ˈstɪk ə ‖ -ər **~s** z
stick-in-the-mud ˈstɪk ɪn ðə ˌmʌd §ˈ·ən- ‖ ˈstɪk ən- **~s** z
stickleback ˈstɪk əl bæk **~s** s
Sticklepath ˈstɪk əl pɑːθ §-pæθ ‖ -pæθ
stickler ˈstɪk lə ‖ -lər **~s** z
stick-on ˈstɪk ɒn ‖ -ɑːn -ɔːn
stickpin ˈstɪk pɪn **~s** z
stick-to-it-iveness ˌstɪk ˈtuː ɪt ɪv nəs -nɪs ‖ -ˈtuː əṭ-
stickum ˈstɪk əm **~s** z
stick-up ˈstɪk ʌp **~s** s
stick|y ˈstɪk |i **~ier** i‿ə ‖ i‿ər **~iest** i‿ɪst i‿əst **~ily** ɪ li əl i **~iness** i nəs i nɪs
ˌsticky ˈend; **ˌsticky ˈwicket**
stie... —*see* **sty**
stiff stɪf **stiffer** ˈstɪf ə ‖ -ər **stiffest** ˈstɪf ɪst -əst
ˌstiff ˌupper ˈlip
stiff-arm ˈstɪf ɑːm ‖ -ɑːrm **~ed** d **~ing** ɪŋ **~s** z
stiffen ˈstɪf ən **~ed** d **~ing** ‿ɪŋ **~s** z
stiffener ˈstɪf ən‿ə ‖ ər **~s** z
stiffie ˈstɪf i **~s** z
Stiffkey ˈstɪf kiː —*formerly also* ˈstjuːk i, ˈstuːk i
stiffly ˈstɪf li
stiff-necked ˌstɪf ˈnekt ◂
stiffness ˈstɪf nəs -nɪs **~es** ɪz əz
stiff|y ˈstɪf |i **~ies** iz
stifl|e ˈstaɪf əl **~ed** d **~es** z **~ing/ly** ‿ɪŋ /li
stigma ˈstɪg mə **~s** z **stigmata** ˈstɪg mət ə stɪg ˈmɑːt ə ‖ stɪg ˈmɑːṭ ə ˈstɪg məṭ ə
stigmatic stɪg ˈmæt ɪk ‖ -ˈmæṭ- **~s** s
stigmatis... —*see* **stigmatiz...**
stigmatization ˌstɪg mət aɪ ˈzeɪʃ ən -ɪ'-- ‖ -məṭ ə- **~s** z
stigmatiz|e ˈstɪg mə taɪz **~ed** d **~es** ɪz əz **~ing** ɪŋ
stilb stɪlb
stilbene ˈstɪlb iːn
stilbestrol stɪl ˈbiːs trɒl -ˈbes-, -trəl ‖ -ˈbes trɔːl -trɑːl, -troʊl
stilbite ˈstɪlb aɪt
stilboestrol stɪl ˈbiːs trɒl -ˈbes-, -trəl ‖ -ˈbes trɔːl -trɑːl, -troʊl
stile staɪəl *(= style)* **stiles** staɪəlz
Stiles staɪəlz
stiletto stɪ ˈlet əʊ stə- ‖ -ˈleṭ oʊ **~s** z
stiˌletto ˈheel
Stilgoe ˈstɪlg əʊ ‖ -oʊ
Stilicho ˈstɪl ɪ kəʊ ‖ -koʊ
still stɪl **stilled** stɪld **stiller** ˈstɪl ə ‖ ˈstɪl ər **stillest** ˈstɪl ɪst -əst **stilling** ˈstɪl ɪŋ **stills** stɪlz
ˌstill ˈlife
stillbirth ˈstɪl bɜːθ ˌ·ˈ· ‖ -bɜ˞ːθ **~s** s
stillborn ˈstɪl bɔːn ˌ·ˈ· ‖ -bɔːrn
stillness ˈstɪl nəs -nɪs **~es** ɪz əz
stillroom ˈstɪl ruːm -rʊm **~s** z
Stillson ˈstɪls ən
ˈStillson wrench *tdmk*
stilly *adv* ˈstɪl li
stilly *adj* ˈstɪl i
stilt stɪlt **stilts** stɪlts
stilted ˈstɪlt ɪd -əd **~ly** li **~ness** nəs nɪs
Stilton, s~ ˈstɪlt ən
Stimson ˈstɪmps ən
stimulant ˈstɪm jʊl ənt -jəl- ‖ -jəl- **~s** s
stimu|late ˈstɪm ju |leɪt -jə- ‖ -jə- **~lated** leɪt ɪd -əd ‖ leɪṭ əd **~lates** leɪts **~lating** leɪt ɪŋ ‖ leɪṭ ɪŋ
stimulation ˌstɪm ju ˈleɪʃ ən -jə- ‖ -jə- **~s** z
stimulative ˈstɪm jʊl ət ɪv -ju leɪt ɪv ‖ -jə leɪṭ ɪv
stimulator ˈstɪm ju leɪt ə ˈ·jə- ‖ -jə leɪṭ ər **~s** z
stim|ulus ˈstɪm |jʊl əs -jəl əs ‖ -|jəl əs **~uli** ju laɪ jə-, -liː ‖ jə-
stimy ˈstaɪm i **stimied** ˈstaɪm id **stimies** ˈstaɪm iz **stimying** ˈstaɪm i ɪŋ

sting stɪŋ **stinging** ˈstɪŋ ɪŋ **stings** stɪŋz **stung** stʌŋ
ˈstinging ˌnettle
stinger ˈstɪŋ ə ‖ -ᵊr **~s** z
stingi... —*see* **stingy**
stingo ˈstɪŋ gəʊ ‖ -goʊ
stingray ˈstɪŋ reɪ **~s** z
sting|y *'ungenerous'* ˈstɪndʒ |i **~ier** i‿ə ‖ i‿ᵊr **~iest** i‿ɪst i‿əst **~ily** ɪ li əl i **~iness** i nəs i nɪs
stingy *'having a sting'* ˈstɪŋ i
stink stɪŋk **stank** stæŋk **stinking/ly** ˈstɪŋk ɪŋ /li **stinks** stɪŋks **stunk** stʌŋk
stink-bomb ˈstɪŋk bɒm ‖ -bɑːm **~s** z
stinker ˈstɪŋk ə ‖ -ᵊr **~s** z
stinkhorn ˈstɪŋk hɔːn ‖ -hɔːrn **~s** z
stinkpot ˈstɪŋk pɒt ‖ -pɑːt **~s** s
stint stɪnt **stinted** ˈstɪnt ɪd -əd ‖ ˈstɪnṱ əd **stinting** ˈstɪnt ɪŋ ‖ ˈstɪnṱ ɪŋ **stints** stɪnts
stipe staɪp **stipes** staɪps
stipend ˈstaɪp end -ənd **~s** z
stipendiar|y staɪ ˈpend i‿ər |i stɪ-, ⚠-ˈpend‿ər |i ‖ -i er |i **~ies** iz
stiˌpendiary ˈmagistrate
stipes *sing.* ˈstaɪp iːz
stippl|e ˈstɪp ᵊl **~ed** d **~es** z **~ing** ‿ɪŋ
stipu|late *v* ˈstɪp ju |leɪt -jə- ‖ -jə- **~lated** leɪt ɪd -əd ‖ leɪṱ əd **~lates** leɪts **~lating** leɪt ɪŋ ‖ leɪṱ ɪŋ
stipulation ˌstɪp ju ˈleɪʃ ᵊn -jə- ‖ -jə- **~s** z
stipulatory ˈstɪp jʊl ət‿ər i ˌstɪp ju ˈleɪt ər i ‖ ˈstɪp jəl ə tɔːr i -toʊr i
stipule ˈstɪp juːl **~s** z
stir stɜː ‖ stɜ˞ː **stirred** stɜːd ‖ stɜ˞ːd **stirring/ly** ˈstɜːr ɪŋ /li ‖ ˈstɜ˞ː- **stirs** stɜːz ‖ stɜ˞ːz
stir-crazy ˌstɜː ˈkreɪz i ‖ ˌstɜ˞ː-
stir-|fry ˌstɜː |ˈfraɪ ‖ ˌstɜ˞ː- **~fried** ˈfraɪd ◂ **~fries** ˈfraɪz **~frying** ˈfraɪ ɪŋ
Stirling ˈstɜːl ɪŋ ‖ ˈstɜ˞ːl ɪŋ
stirps stɜːps ‖ stɜ˞ːps **stirpes** ˈstɜːp iːz ‖ ˈstɜ˞ːp iːz
stirr... —*see* **stir**
stirrer ˈstɜːr ə ‖ ˈstɜ˞ː ᵊr **~s** z
stirrup ˈstɪr əp ‖ ˈstɜ˞ː əp ˈstɪr- *(*)* **~s** s
ˈstirrup cup; **ˈstirrup pump**
stitch stɪtʃ **stitched** stɪtʃt **stitches** ˈstɪtʃ ɪz -əz **stitching** ˈstɪtʃ ɪŋ
stitchery ˈstɪtʃ ər i
stitchwort ˈstɪtʃ wɜːt §-wɔːt ‖ -wɜ˞ːt -wɔːrt **~s** s
St Ivel *tdmk* sənt ˈaɪv ᵊl §sən- ‖ seɪnṱ-
St Ives sənt ˈaɪvz §sən- ‖ seɪnṱ-
Stivichall ˈstaɪtʃ ᵊl -ɔːl *(!)*
St James sənt ˈdʒeɪmz ‖ seɪnt- **St James's** sənt ˈdʒeɪmz ɪz -əz; sənt ˈdʒeɪmz ‖ seɪnt-
St John sənt ˈdʒɒn ‖ seɪnt ˈdʒɑːn —*but as a surname also* ˈsɪndʒ ən
St John's sənt ˈdʒɒnz ‖ seɪnt ˈdʒɑːnz
St ˈJohn's wort ˌ·ˈ·
St Kilda sənt ˈkɪld ə →sᵊŋ- ‖ seɪnt-
St Kitts sənt ˈkɪts →sᵊŋ- ‖ seɪnt-
St Kitts-Nevis sənt ˌkɪts ˈniːv ɪs →sᵊŋ-, §-əs ‖ seɪnt-
St Laurent ˌsæn lɒ ˈrɒ̃ -lɔː-, -lə-, -ˈrɑːnt ‖ -loʊ ˈrɑːn -lɔː-, -lɑː- —*Fr* [sɛ̃ lɔ ʁɑ̃]
St Leger sənt ˈledʒ ə ‖ seɪnt ˈledʒ ᵊr —*but as a surname also* ˈsel ɪndʒ ə, -əndʒ- ‖ -ᵊr
St Louis sənt ˈluː‿ɪs i, §‿əs ‖ seɪnt-
St Lucia sənt ˈluːʃ ə -ˈluːʃ i‿ə, ˈluːs- ‖ seɪnt-
St Malo sæ̃ ˈmɑːl əʊ sæn-, sᵊnt- ‖ ˌsæn mɑː ˈloʊ —*Fr* [sɛ̃ ma lo]
St Mary Axe sənt ˌmeər i ˈæks ‖ seɪnt ˌmer i- -ˌmær- —*formerly* ˌsɪm ər i ˈæks
St Moritz ˌsæn mə ˈrɪts →sæm-; sənt ˈmɒr ɪts ‖ -moʊ- —*Ger* Sankt Moritz [zaŋkt ˈmoː ʁɪts, -mo ˈʁɪts]
St Neots sənt ˈniː‿əts -ˈniːts ‖ seɪnt-
stoa ˈstəʊ ə ‖ ˈstoʊ ə **~s** z
stoat stəʊt ‖ stoʊt **stoats** stəʊts ‖ stoʊts
Stobart ˈstəʊb ɑːt ‖ ˈstoʊb ɑːrt
Stobie ˈstəʊb i ‖ ˈstoʊb i
stochastic stə ˈkæst ɪk stɒ- ‖ stoʊ- **~ally** ᵊl‿i
stock, Stock stɒk ‖ stɑːk **stocked** stɒkt ‖ stɑːkt **stocking** ˈstɒk ɪŋ ‖ ˈstɑːk ɪŋ **stocks** stɒks ‖ stɑːks
ˈstock cerˌtificate; **ˈstock cube**; **ˈstock exˌchange**; **ˈstock ˌmarket**
stockad|e stɒ ˈkeɪd ‖ stɑː- **~ed** ɪd əd **~es** z **~ing** ɪŋ
stockbreed|er ˈstɒk ˌbriːd ə ‖ ˈstɑːk ˌbriːd ᵊr **~ers** əz ‖ ᵊrz **~ing** ɪŋ
Stockbridge ˈstɒk brɪdʒ ‖ ˈstɑːk-
stockbroker ˈstɒk ˌbrəʊk ə ‖ ˈstɑːk ˌbroʊk ᵊr **~s** z
ˈstockbroker belt
stockbrokerage ˈstɒk ˌbrəʊk ər ɪdʒ ‖ ˈstɑːk ˌbroʊk ər‿ɪdʒ
stockbroking ˈstɒk ˌbrəʊk ɪŋ ‖ ˈstɑːk ˌbroʊk ɪŋ
stockcar ˈstɒk kɑː ‖ ˈstɑːk kɑːr **~s** z
Stockdale ˈstɒk deɪᵊl ‖ ˈstɑːk-
stockfish ˈstɒk fɪʃ ‖ ˈstɑːk-
Stockhausen ˈʃtɒk ˌhaʊz ᵊn ˈstɒk- ‖ ˈʃtɑːk- —*Ger* [ˈʃtɔk haʊ zᵊn]
stockhold|er ˈstɒk ˌhəʊld ə →-ˌhɒʊld- ‖ ˈstɑːk ˌhoʊld ᵊr **~ers** əz ‖ ᵊrz **~ing** ɪŋ
Stockholm ˈstɒk həʊm §-həʊlm ‖ ˈstɑːk hoʊm -hoʊlm —*Swed* [ˈstɔk hɔlm]
stockinet, stockinette ˌstɒk ɪ ˈnet -ə- ‖ ˌstɑːk-
stocking ˈstɒk ɪŋ ‖ ˈstɑːk ɪŋ **~ed** d **~s** z
stocking-filler ˈstɒk ɪŋ ˌfɪl ə ‖ ˈstɑːk ɪŋ ˌfɪl ᵊr **~s** z
stock-in-trade ˌstɒk ɪn ˈtreɪd §-ən- ‖ ˌstɑːk ən- ˈ·ˌ·
stockist ˈstɒk ɪst §-əst ‖ ˈstɑːk əst **~s** s
stockjobber ˈstɒk ˌdʒɒb ə ‖ ˈstɑːk ˌdʒɑːb ᵊr **~s** z
Stockley ˈstɒk li ‖ ˈstɑːk li
stock|man ˈstɒk |mən -mæn ‖ ˈstɑːk- **~men** mən men
stockpil|e ˈstɒk paɪᵊl ‖ ˈstɑːk- **~ed** d **~es** z **~ing** ɪŋ
Stockport ˈstɒk pɔːt ‖ ˈstɑːk pɔːrt -poʊrt
stockpot ˈstɒk pɒt ‖ ˈstɑːk pɑːt **~s** s
stockroom ˈstɒk ruːm -rʊm ‖ ˈstɑːk- **~s** z
Stocks stɒks ‖ stɑːks
Stocksbridge ˈstɒks brɪdʒ ‖ ˈstɑːks-

stock-still ˌstɒk ˈstɪl ◂ ‖ ˌstɑːk-

stocktaking ˈstɒk ˌteɪk ɪŋ ‖ ˈstɑːk-

Stockton ˈstɒkt ən ‖ ˈstɑːkt ən

Stockton-on-Tees ˌstɒkt ən ɒn ˈtiːz ‖ ˌstɑːkt ən ɑːn- -ɔːn-

Stockwell ˈstɒk wel -wəl ‖ ˈstɑːk-

Stockwood ˈstɒk wʊd ‖ ˈstɑːk-

stock|y ˈstɒk |i ‖ ˈstɑːk |i **~ier** i‿ə ‖ i‿ᵊr **~iest** i‿ɪst i‿əst **~ily** ɪ li əl i **~iness** i nəs i nɪs

stockyard ˈstɒk jɑːd ‖ ˈstɑːk jɑːrd **~s** z

Stoddard ˈstɒd əd ‖ ˈstɑːd ᵊrd

Stoddart ˈstɒd ət ‖ ˈstɑːd ᵊrt

stodge stɒdʒ ‖ stɑːdʒ **stodged** stɒdʒd ‖ stɑːdʒd **stodges** ˈstɒdʒ ɪz -əz ‖ ˈstɑːdʒ əz **stodging** ˈstɒdʒ ɪŋ ‖ ˈstɑːdʒ ɪŋ

stodg|y ˈstɒdʒ |i ‖ ˈstɑːdʒ |i **~ier** i‿ə ‖ i‿ᵊr **~iest** i‿ɪst i‿əst **~ily** ɪ li əl i **~iness** i nəs i nɪs

stoep stuːp stʊp **stoeps** stuːps stʊps

stog|ey, stog|ie, stogy ˈstəʊg |i ‖ ˈstoʊg |i **~ies** iz

Stogumber stə ˈgʌm bə stəʊ-; ˈstɒg əm- ‖ -bᵊr

Stogursey stə ˈgɜːz i stəʊ- ‖ -ˈgɝːz i

stoic, Stoic ˈstəʊ ɪk ‖ ˈstoʊ ɪk **~s** s

stoical ˈstəʊ ɪk ᵊl ‖ ˈstoʊ- **~ly** ‿i

stoichiometric ˌstɔɪk i‿ə ˈmetr ɪk ◂ -əʊˈ-- ‖ -oʊˈ-- **~ally** ᵊl‿i

stoichiometry ˌstɔɪk i ˈɒm ətr i -ɪtr i ‖ -ˈɑːm-

stoicism ˈstəʊ ɪ ˌsɪz əm -ə- ‖ ˈstoʊ ə-

stoke, Stoke stəʊk ‖ stoʊk **stoked** stəʊkt ‖ stoʊkt **stokes** stəʊks ‖ stoʊks **stoking** ˈstəʊk ɪŋ ‖ ˈstoʊk ɪŋ ˌ**Stoke ˈd'Abernon** ˈdæb ən ən ˈdɑːb- ‖ -ᵊrn-; ˌ**Stoke ˈMandeville**; ˌ**Stoke ˈPoges** ˈpəʊdʒ ɪz -əz ‖ ˈpoʊdʒ əz

stokehold ˈstəʊk həʊld →-hɒʊld ‖ ˈstoʊk hoʊld **~s** z

stokehole ˈstəʊk həʊl →-hɒʊl ‖ ˈstoʊk hoʊl **~s** z

Stoke-on-Trent ˌstəʊk ɒn ˈtrent ◂ ‖ ˌstoʊk ɑːn- -ɔːn-

stoker ˈstəʊk ə ‖ ˈstoʊk ᵊr **~s** z

Stokes stəʊks ‖ stoʊks **Stokes'** stəʊks ˈstəʊks ɪz, -əz ‖ stoʊks ˈstoʊks əz

Stokowski stə ˈkɒf ski -ˈkɒv- ‖ -ˈkɔːf- -ˈkɑːf-; -ˈkaʊsk i

STOL, stol stɒl ˈest ɒl ‖ stɑːl stɔːl; ˈest ɔːl, -ɑːl

St Olaves sənt ˈɒl əvz §sən-, -ɪvz ‖ seɪnṭ ˈɑːl-

stole stəʊl →stɒʊl ‖ stoʊl **stoles** stəʊlz →stɒʊlz ‖ stoʊlz

stolen ˈstəʊl ən →ˈstɒʊl- ‖ ˈstoʊl ən

stolid ˈstɒl ɪd §-əd ‖ ˈstɑːl əd **~ly** li **~ness** nəs nɪs

stolidity stə ˈlɪd ət i stɒ-, -ɪt i ‖ -əṭ i stɑː-

Stoll *(i)* stɒl ‖ stɑːl stɔːl, *(ii)* stəʊl →stɒʊl ‖ stoʊl

stollen ˈstɒl ən ‖ ˈstoʊl ən ˈstɔːl-, ˈstɑːl-, ˈstʌl- —*Ger* [ˈʃtɔl ən] **~s** z

stolon ˈstəʊl ɒn -ən ‖ ˈstoʊl ən -ɑːn **~s** z

Stolport, STOLport ˈstɒl pɔːt ‖ ˈstɔːl pɔːrt ˈstɑːl-, -poʊrt **~s** s

stoma ˈstəʊm ə ‖ ˈstoʊm ə **~s** z **stomata** ˈstəʊm ət ə ˈstɒm-; stəʊ ˈmɑːt ə ‖ ˈstoʊm əṭ ə ˈstɑːm-; stoʊ ˈmɑːṭ ə

stomach ˈstʌm ək §-ɪk **~ed** t **~s** s **~ing** ɪŋ ˈ**stomach pump**

stomachache ˈstʌm ək eɪk §-ɪk- **~s** s

stomach-churning ˈstʌm ək ˌtʃɜːn ɪŋ §-ɪk- ‖ -ˌtʃɝːn-

stomacher ˈstʌm ək ə §-ɪk- ‖ -ᵊr —*formerly* -ətʃ-, -ədʒ- **~s** z

stomachful ˈstʌm ək fʊl §-ɪk- **~s** z

stomachic stə ˈmæk ɪk stəʊ-; ˈstʌm ək-

stomata ˈstəʊm ət ə ˈstɒm-; stəʊ ˈmɑːt ə ‖ ˈstoʊm əṭ ə ˈstɑːm-; stoʊ ˈmɑːṭ ə

stomatitis ˌstəʊm ə ˈtaɪt ɪs ˌstɒm-, §-əs ‖ ˌstoʊm ə ˈtaɪṭ əs ˌstɑːm-

stomato- *comb. form* *with stress-neutral suffix* ¦stəʊm ət ə ¦stɒm- ‖ ¦stoʊm əṭ ə stoʊ ¦mæṭ ə — **stomatoplasty** ˈstəʊm ət ə ˌplæst i ˈstɒm- ‖ ˈstoʊm əṭ- stoʊ ˈmæṭ- *with stress-imposing suffix* ˌstəʊm ə ˈtɒ+ ˌstɒm- ‖ ˌstoʊm ə ˈtɑː+ ˌstɑːm- — **stomatology** ˌstəʊm ə ˈtɒl ədʒ i ˌstɒm- ‖ ˌstoʊm ə ˈtɑːl- ˌstɑːm-

-stome stəʊm ‖ stoʊm — **cyclostome** ˈsaɪk ləʊ stəʊm ‖ -lə stoʊm

-stomous *stress-imposing* stəm əs — **monostomous** mɒ ˈnɒst əm əs mə- ‖ mɑː ˈnɑːst-

stomp stɒmp ‖ stɑːmp **stomped** stɒmpt ‖ stɑːmpt **stomping** ˈstɒmp ɪŋ ‖ ˈstɑːmp ɪŋ **stomps** stɒmps ‖ stɑːmps

-stomy *stress-imposing* stəm i — **colostomy** kə ˈlɒst əm i ‖ -ˈlɑːst-

stone, Stone stəʊn ‖ stoʊn **stoned** stəʊnd ‖ stoʊnd **stones** stəʊnz ‖ stoʊnz **stoning** ˈstəʊn ɪŋ ‖ ˈstoʊn ɪŋ ˈ**Stone Age**; ˈ**stone fruit**; ˈ**stone ˌmarten**; ˈ**stone's throw**

stone-blind ˌstəʊn ˈblaɪnd ◂ →ˌstəʊm- ‖ ˌstoʊn-

stonebreaker ˈstəʊn ˌbreɪk ə →ˈstəʊm- ‖ ˈstoʊn ˌbreɪk ᵊr **~s** z

Stonebridge ˈstəʊn brɪdʒ →ˈstəʊm- ‖ ˈstoʊn-

stonechat ˈstəʊn tʃæt ‖ ˈstoʊn- **~s** s

stone-cold ˌstəʊn ˈkəʊld ◂ →ˈstəʊŋ-, →-kɒʊld ‖ ˌstoʊn ˈkoʊld ◂

stonecrop ˈstəʊn krɒp →ˈstəʊŋ- ‖ ˈstoʊn krɑːp **~s** s

stonecutter ˈstəʊn ˌkʌt ə →ˈstəʊŋ- ‖ ˈstoʊn ˌkʌṭ ᵊr **~s** z

stone-dead ˌstəʊn ˈded ◂ ‖ ˌstoʊn-

stone-deaf ˌstəʊn ˈdef ◂ ‖ ˌstoʊn-

stone-faced ˌstəʊn ˈfeɪst ◂ ˈ·· ‖ ˈstoʊn feɪst

stonefish ˈstəʊn fɪʃ ‖ ˈstoʊn- **~es** ɪz əz

stone-ground ˈstəʊn graʊnd →ˈstəʊŋ-, ˌ·ˈ· ‖ ˈstoʊn-

Stonehaven ˌstəʊn ˈheɪv ᵊn ‖ ˌstoʊn- —*There is also a local pronunciation* ˌsteɪn ˈhaɪ.

Stonehenge ˌstəʊn ˈhendʒ ◂ ‖ ˈstoʊn hendʒ

Stonehouse ˈstəʊn haʊs ‖ ˈstoʊn-

Stoneleigh ˌstəʊn ˈliː ‖ ˌstoʊn-

stoneless ˈstəʊn ləs -lɪs ‖ ˈstoʊn-

stonemason ˈstəʊn ˌmeɪs ᵊn →ˈstəʊm- ‖ ˈstoʊn- **~s** z

stonewall, S~ ˌstəun ˈwɔːl ◂ ˈ· · ‖ ˈstoun wɔːl -wɑːl **~ed** d **~er/s** ə/z ‖ -ᵊr/z **~ing** ɪŋ **~s** z
stoneware ˈstəun weə ‖ ˈstoun wer -wær
stonewashed ˈstəun wɒʃt ˌ·ˈ· ‖ˈstoun wɔːʃt -wɑːʃt
stonework ˈstəun wɜːk ‖ ˈstoun wɜ˞ːk
stonk stɒŋk ‖ stɑːŋk **stonked** stɒŋkt ‖ stɑːŋkt **stonking** ˈstɒŋk ɪŋ ‖ ˈstɑːŋk ɪŋ **stonks** stɒŋks ‖ stɑːŋks
stonker ˈstɒŋk ə ‖ ˈstɑːŋk ᵊr **~ed** d **~s** z
stonking ˈstɒŋk ɪŋ ‖ ˈstɑːŋk ɪŋ **~ly** li
Stonor *(i)* ˈstəun ə ‖ ˈstoun ᵊr, *(ii)* ˈstɒn ə ‖ ˈstɑːn ᵊr
ston|y ˈstəun |i ‖ ˈstoun |i **~ier** i‿ə ‖ i‿ᵊr **~iest** i‿ɪst i‿əst **~ily** ɪ li əl i **~iness** i nəs i nɪs **ˌstony ˈbroke**; **ˈStony Brook** *NY*; **ˌStony ˈPoint**
stood stʊd
Stoodley ˈstuːd li
stooge stuːdʒ **stooged** stuːdʒd **stooges** ˈstuːdʒ ɪz -əz **stooging** ˈstuːdʒ ɪŋ
stook stuːk stʊk **stooks** stuːks stʊks
stool stuːl **stools** stuːlz
stoolie ˈstuːl i **~s** z
stoolpigeon ˈstuːl ˌpɪdʒ ən -ɪn **~s** z
stoop stuːp **stooped** stuːpt **stooping** ˈstuːp ɪŋ **stoops** stuːps
stop stɒp ‖ stɑːp **stopped** stɒpt ‖ stɑːpt **stopping** ˈstɒp ɪŋ ‖ ˈstɑːp ɪŋ **stops** stɒps ‖ stɑːps **ˌstop ˈpress**◂
stop-and-go ˌstɒp ən ˈgəu →-ᵊŋ- ‖ ˌstɑːp ən ˈgou
stopcock ˈstɒp kɒk ‖ ˈstɑːp kɑːk **~s** s
stope stəup ‖ stoup **stoped** stəupt ‖ stoupt **stopes** stəups ‖ stoups **stoping** ˈstəup ɪŋ ‖ ˈstoup ɪŋ
Stopes stəups ‖ stoups
Stopford ˈstɒp fəd ‖ ˈstɑːp fᵊrd
stopgap ˈstɒp gæp ‖ ˈstɑːp- **~s** s
stop-go ˌstɒp ˈgəu ◂ ‖ ˌstɑːp ˈgou ◂
stoplight ˈstɒp laɪt ‖ ˈstɑːp- **~s** s
stoploss, stop-loss ˈstɒp lɒs -lɔːs ‖ ˈstɑːp lɔːs -lɑːs
stopoff ˈstɒp ɒf -ɔːf ‖ ˈstɑːp ɔːf -ɑːf **~s** s
stopover ˈstɒp ˌəuv ə ‖ ˈstɑːp ˌouv ᵊr **~s** z
stoppable ˈstɒp əb ᵊl ‖ ˈstɑːp-
stoppag|e ˈstɒp ɪdʒ ‖ ˈstɑːp- **~es** ɪz əz
Stoppard ˈstɒp ɑːd -əd ‖ ˈstɑːp ɑːrd -ᵊrd
stopper ˈstɒp ə ‖ ˈstɑːp ᵊr **~ed** d **stoppering** ˈstɒp ər ɪŋ ‖ ˈstɑːp ər ɪŋ **~s** z
stopwatch ˈstɒp wɒtʃ ‖ ˈstɑːp wɑːtʃ **~es** ɪz əz
storage ˈstɔːr ɪdʒ ‖ ˈstour- **ˈstorage deˌvice**; **ˈstorage ˌheater**
storax ˈstɔːr æks ‖ ˈstour-
store stɔː ‖ stɔːr stour **stored** stɔːd ‖ stɔːrd stourd **stores** stɔːz ‖ stɔːrz stourz **storing** ˈstɔːr ɪŋ ‖ ˈstour- **ˈstore deˌtective**
storefront ˈstɔː frʌnt ‖ ˈstɔːr- ˈstour- **~s** s
store|house ˈstɔː |haus ‖ ˈstɔːr- ˈstour- **~houses** hauz ɪz -əz
storekeeper ˈstɔː ˌkiːp ə ‖ ˈstɔːr ˌkiːp ᵊr ˈstour- **~s** z
storeroom ˈstɔː ruːm -rʊm ‖ ˈstɔːr- ˈstour- **~s** z
storey, S~ ˈstɔːr i ‖ ˈstour i *(= story)* **~s** z
-storeyed, -storied ˈstɔːr id ‖ ˈstour id — **three-storeyed, three-storied** ˌθriː ˈstɔːr id ◂ ‖ -ˈstour-
stori... —*see* **story**
stori|ate ˈstɔːr i| eɪt ‖ ˈstour- **~ated** eɪt ɪd -əd ‖ -eɪţ əd **~ates** eɪts **~ating** eɪt ɪŋ ‖ eɪţ ɪŋ
storiation ˌstɔːr i ˈeɪʃ ᵊn ˌstour-
stork, Stork stɔːk ‖ stɔːrk **storks** stɔːks ‖ stɔːrks
storksbill ˈstɔːks bɪl ‖ ˈstɔːrks- **~s** z
storm, Storm stɔːm ‖ stɔːrm **stormed** stɔːmd ‖ stɔːrmd **storming** ˈstɔːm ɪŋ ‖ ˈstɔːrm ɪŋ **storms** stɔːmz ‖ stɔːrmz **ˈstorm cloud**; **ˈstorm cone**; **ˈstorm ˌpetrel**; **ˈstorm ˌtrooper**
stormbound ˈstɔːm baund ‖ ˈstɔːrm-
Stormont ˈstɔː mənt -mɒnt ‖ ˈstɔːr- -mɑːnt
stormproof ˈstɔːm pruːf §-prʊf ‖ ˈstɔːrm- **~ed** t **~ing** ɪŋ **~s** s
storm|y ˈstɔːm |i ‖ ˈstɔːrm |i **~ier** i‿ə ‖ i‿ᵊr **~iest** i‿ɪst i‿əst **~ily** ɪ li əl i **~iness** i nəs i nɪs **ˌstormy ˈpetrel**
Stornoway ˈstɔːn ə weɪ ‖ ˈstɔːrn-
Storr stɔː ‖ stɔːr
Storrington ˈstɒr ɪŋ tən ‖ ˈstɔːr- ˈstɑːr-
Storrs stɔːz ‖ stɔːrz
Stortford ˈstɔːt fəd ˈstɔː- ‖ ˈstɔːrt fᵊrd
Storthing, Storting ˈstɔː tɪŋ ‖ ˈstɔːr-
story ˈstɔːr i ‖ ˈstour- **storied** ˈstɔːr id ‖ ˈstour- **stories** ˈstɔːr iz ‖ ˈstour- **ˈstory line**
storyboard ˈstɔːr i bɔːd ‖ -bɔːrd ˈstour i bourd **~s** z
storybook ˈstɔːr i bʊk §-buːk ‖ ˈstour- **~s** s
storytell|er ˈstɔːr i ˌtel ə ‖ -ᵊr ˈstour- **~ers** əz ‖ ᵊrz **~ing** ɪŋ
Storyville ˈstɔːr i vɪl ‖ ˈstour-
stoss stɒs ʃtɒs ‖ stous stɑːs, stɔːs —*Ger* [ʃtoːs]
St Osyth sənt ˈəuz ɪθ §sən-, -ˈəus- ‖ seɪnţ ˈouz əθ
stot stɒt ‖ stɑːt **stots** stɒts ‖ stɑːts **stotted** ˈstɒt ɪd -əd ‖ ˈstɑːţ əd **stotting** ˈstɒt ɪŋ ‖ ˈstɑːţ ɪŋ
stotious ˈstəuʃ əs ‖ ˈstouʃ əs
Stott stɒt ‖ stɑːt
Stouffer ˈstəuf ə ‖ ˈstouf ᵊr *(!)*
Stoughton *(i)* ˈstəut ᵊn ‖ ˈstout ᵊn, *(ii)* ˈstaut ᵊn, *(iii)* ˈstɔːt ᵊn ‖ ˈstɑːt- —*For the publishers* Hodder & ~, *(i) is appropriate, although (ii) is probably more often heard.*
stoup stuːp *(= stoop)* **stoups** stuːps
Stour *(i)* stuə ‖ stuᵊr, *(ii)* ˈstau‿ə ‖ ˈstau‿ᵊr, *(iii)* ˈstəu ə ‖ ˈstou ᵊr —*The river in Suffolk and Essex is (i), as, usually, is that in Kent. That in Warwickshire is (ii) or (iii). Others are mostly (ii).*
Stourbridge ˈstau‿ə brɪdʒ ˈstəu ə- ‖ ˈstau‿ᵊr-
Stourhead *(i)* ˌstɔː ˈhed ‖ ˌstɔːr- ˌstour-, *(ii)* ˌstau‿ə ˈhed ‖ ˌstau‿ᵊr-

S

Stourmouth ˈstaʊ‿ə maʊθ ˈstʊə maʊθ ‖ ˈstaʊ‿ᵊr-
Stourport ˈstaʊ‿ə pɔːt ˈstʊə pɔːt ‖ ˈstaʊ‿ᵊr pɔːrt -poʊrt
Stourton *(i)* ˈstɜːt ᵊn ‖ ˈstɜːt ᵊn, *(ii)* ˈstɔːt ᵊn ‖ ˈstɔːrt ᵊn ˈstoʊrt-
stoush staʊʃ **stoushed** staʊʃt **stoushes** ˈstaʊʃ ɪz -əz **stoushing** ˈstaʊʃ ɪŋ
stout, Stout staʊt **stouter** ˈstaʊt ə ‖ ˈstaʊt̬ ᵊr **stoutest** ˈstaʊt ɪst -əst ‖ ˈstaʊt̬ əst
stouthearted ˌstaʊt ˈhɑːt ɪd ◂ -əd ‖ -ˈhɑːrt̬- **~ly** li **~ness** nəs nɪs
stoutish ˈstaʊt ɪʃ ‖ ˈstaʊt̬ ɪʃ
stout|ly ˈstaʊt |li **~ness** nəs nɪs
stove stəʊv ‖ stoʊv **stoves** stəʊvz ‖ stoʊvz
stovepipe ˈstəʊv paɪp ‖ ˈstoʊv- **~s** s
ˌstovepipe ˈhat
stover ˈstəʊv ə ‖ ˈstoʊv ᵊr
stow, Stow stəʊ ‖ stoʊ **stowed** stəʊd ‖ stoʊd **stowing** ˈstəʊ ɪŋ ‖ ˈstoʊ ɪŋ **stows** stəʊz ‖ stoʊz
stowage ˈstəʊ ɪdʒ ‖ ˈstoʊ-
stowaway ˈstəʊ ə ˌweɪ ‖ ˈstoʊ- **~s** z
Stowe stəʊ ‖ stoʊ
Stowell ˈstəʊ əl ‖ ˈstoʊ əl
Stowey ˈstəʊ i ‖ ˈstoʊ i
Stowmarket ˈstəʊ ˌmɑːk ɪt §-ət ‖ ˈstoʊ ˌmɑːrk ət
Stow-on-the-Wold ˌstəʊ ɒn ðə ˈwəʊld →-ˈwɒʊld ‖ ˌstoʊ ɑːn ðə ˈwoʊld -ɔːn-
St Pancras s*ə*nt ˈpæŋk rəs →səm- ‖ seɪnt-
St Paul s*ə*nt ˈpɔːl ‖ seɪnt- -ˈpɑːl **~'s** z
St Peter s*ə*nt ˈpiːt ə ‖ seɪnt ˈpiːt̬ ᵊr **~'s** z
St ˌPeter ˈPort
St Petersburg s*ə*nt ˈpiːt əz bɜːg ‖ seɪnt ˈpiːt̬ ᵊrz bɜːg —*Russ* Sankt Peterburg [ˌsankt pʲɪ tʲɪr ˈburk]
Strabane strə ˈbæn
strabismus strə ˈbɪz məs stræ-
Strabo ˈstreɪb əʊ ‖ -oʊ
Strabolgi strə ˈbəʊg i ‖ -ˈboʊg i
Strachan *(i)* ˈstrɔːn ‖ strɑːn, *(ii)* ˈstræk ən ˈstræx-
Strachey ˈstreɪtʃ i ˈstræx-
Strad stræd **Strads** strædz
Strada *tdmk* ˈstrɑːd ə **~s** z
Stradbroke ˈstræd brʊk →ˈstræb-, -brəʊk ‖ -broʊk
straddl|e ˈstræd ᵊl **~ed** d **~es** z **~ing** ˌɪŋ
Stradey ˈstræd i
Stradivari ˌstræd ɪ ˈvɑːr i -ə- ‖ ˌstrɑːd-
Stradivari|us ˌstræd ɪ ˈveər i‿əs ˌ-ə-, -ˈvɑːr- ‖ -ˈver- -ˈvær- **~i** aɪ
Stradling ˈstræd lɪŋ
strafe strɑːf streɪf ‖ streɪf **strafed** strɑːft streɪft ‖ streɪft **strafes** strɑːfs streɪfs ‖ streɪfs **strafing/s** ˈstrɑːf ɪŋ/z ˈstreɪf- ‖ ˈstreɪf ɪŋ/z
Strafford ˈstræf əd ‖ -ᵊrd
straggl|e ˈstræg ᵊl **~ed** d **~er/s** ˌə/z ‖ ˌər/z **~es** z **~ing** ˌɪŋ
straggl|y ˈstræg ᵊl‿i **~ier** i‿ə ‖ i‿ᵊr **~iest** i‿ɪst i‿əst

straight streɪt *(= strait)* **straighter** ˈstreɪt ə ‖ ˈstreɪt̬ ᵊr **straightest** ˈstreɪt ɪst -əst ‖ ˈstreɪt̬ əst **straights** streɪts
ˌstraight and ˈnarrow; **ˌstraight ˈfight**; **ˈstraight man**
straight-arm ˈstreɪt ɑːm ‖ ˈstreɪt̬ ɑːrm **~ed** d **~ing** ɪŋ **~s** z
straightaway ˌstreɪt ə ˈweɪ ‖ ˌstreɪt̬-
straightedg|e ˈstreɪt edʒ ‖ ˈstreɪt̬- **~ed** d **~es** ɪz əz
straighten ˈstreɪt ᵊn **~ed** d **~er/s** ˌə/z ‖ ˌər/z **~ing** ˌɪŋ **~s** z
straight-faced ˌstreɪt ˈfeɪst ◂
straightforward ˌstreɪt ˈfɔː wəd ◂ ‖ -ˈfɔːr wᵊrd ◂ **~ly** li **~ness** nəs nɪs
straightjacket ˈstreɪt ˌdʒæk ɪt §-ət **~s** s
straight-laced ˌstreɪt ˈleɪst ◂
straight-out ˌstreɪt ˈaʊt ◂ ‖ ˌstreɪt̬-
ˌstraight-out ˈanswer
straight-to-video ˌstreɪt tə ˈvɪd i əʊ ◂ ‖ -oʊ
straightway ˈstreɪt weɪ ˌ-ˈ-
strain streɪn **strained** streɪnd **straining** ˈstreɪn ɪŋ **strains** streɪnz
ˈstrain gauge
strainer ˈstreɪn ə ‖ -ᵊr **~s** z
strait streɪt **straits** streɪts
straitened ˈstreɪt ᵊnd
straitjacket ˈstreɪt ˌdʒæk ɪt §-ət **~s** s
straitlaced ˌstreɪt ˈleɪst ◂
strake streɪk **strakes** streɪks
Straker ˈstreɪk ə ‖ -ᵊr
stramonium strə ˈməʊn i‿əm ‖ -ˈmoʊn-
strand, Strand strænd **stranded** ˈstrænd ɪd -əd **stranding** ˈstrænd ɪŋ **strands** strændz
Strang stræŋ
strange, Strange streɪn*d*ʒ **stranger** ˈstreɪn*d*ʒ ə ‖ -ᵊr **strangest** ˈstreɪn*d*ʒ ɪst -əst
strange|ly ˈstreɪn*d*ʒ |li **~ness** nəs nɪs
stranger ˈstreɪn*d*ʒ ə ‖ -ᵊr **~s** z
Strangeways ˈstreɪn*d*ʒ weɪz
Strangford ˈstræŋ fəd ‖ -fᵊrd
strangl|e ˈstræŋ gᵊl **~ed** d **~es** z **~ing** ˌɪŋ
stranglehold ˈstræŋ gᵊl həʊld →-hɒʊld ‖ -hoʊld **~s** z
strangler ˈstræŋ glə ‖ -glᵊr **~s** z
strangu|late ˈstræŋ gju |leɪt -gjə- ‖ -gjə- **~lated** leɪt ɪd -əd ‖ leɪt̬ əd **~lates** leɪts **~lating** leɪt ɪŋ ‖ leɪt̬ ɪŋ
strangulation ˌstræŋ gju ˈleɪʃ ᵊn -gjə- ‖ -gjə- **~s** z
strangury ˈstræŋ gjər i -gjuᵊr-
Stranraer ₍ˌ₎stræn ˈrɑː strən- ‖ -ˈrɑːr
strap stræp **strapped** stræpt **strapping** ˈstræp ɪŋ **straps** stræps
straphanger ˈstræp ˌhæŋ ə ‖ -ᵊr **~s** z
straphanging ˈstræp ˌhæŋ ɪŋ
strapless ˈstræp ləs -lɪs
strapline ˈstræp laɪn **~s** z
strapper ˈstræp ə ‖ -ᵊr **~s** z
strappy ˈstræp i
Strasberg ˈstræs bɜːg ‖ -bɜːg

Strasbourg, Strassburg ˈstræz bɜːg ˈstræs-, -bʊəg, -bɔːg ‖ ˈstrɑːs bɜːg ˈstrɑːz-, -bʊrg —*Fr* [stʁaz buːʁ], *Ger* Straßburg [ˈʃtʁaːs bʊʁk]
strass stræs
strata ˈstrɑːt ə ˈstreɪt- ‖ ˈstreɪţ ə ˈstræţ- **~s** z
stratagem ˈstræt ədʒ əm -ɪdʒ-; -ə dʒem, -ɪ- ‖ ˈstræţ- **~s** z
stratal ˈstrɑːt ᵊl ˈstreɪt- ‖ ˈstrɑːţ ᵊl
strategic strə ˈtiːdʒ ɪk **~al** ᵊl **~ally** ᵊl‿i
strategist ˈstræt ədʒ ɪst -ɪdʒ-, §-əst ‖ ˈstræţ- **~s** s
strateg|y ˈstræt ədʒ |i -ɪdʒ- ‖ ˈstræţ- **~ies** iz
Stratford ˈstræt fəd ‖ -fᵊrd
Stratford-atte-Bowe ˌstræt fəd ˌæt i ˈbəʊ -əˈ· ‖ -fᵊrd ˌæţ i ˈboʊ
Stratford-on-Avon ˌstræt fəd ɒn ˈeɪv ᵊn ‖ -fᵊrd ɑːn ˈeɪv ɑːn -ɔːnˈ·-
Stratford-upon-Avon ˌstræt fəd ə ˌpɒn ˈeɪv ᵊn ‖ -fᵊrd ə ˌpɑːn ˈeɪv ɑːn -ˌpɔːn-
strath, Strath stræθ strɑːθ **straths** stræθs
Strath- stræθ strəθ —*For many speakers,* stræθ *functions as the strong form of this prefix, used in unfamiliar names or careful style, and* strəθ *as the weak form, appropriate for familiar names and casual style. This applies in the entries that follow.*
Strathaven *place in Strathclyde* ˈstreɪv ᵊn *(!)*
Strathclyde ₍ˌ₎stræθ ˈklaɪd strəθ-
Strathcona stræθ ˈkəʊn ə strəθ- ‖ -ˈkoʊn ə
Strathearn stræθ ˈɜːn strəθ- ‖ -ˈɜːn
Stratheden stræθ ˈiːd ᵊn strəθ-
Strathleven stræθ ˈliːv ᵊn strəθ-
Strathmore stræθ ˈmɔː strəθ- ‖ -ˈmɔːr -ˈmoʊr
Strathpeffer stræθ ˈpef ə strəθ- ‖ -ᵊr
strathspey, S~ stræθ ˈspeɪ strəθ- ‖ ˈ· · **~s** z
Strathtay stræθ ˈteɪ strəθ-
stratification ˌstræt ɪf ɪ ˈkeɪʃ ᵊn ˌ·əf-, §-əˈ·- ‖ ˌstræţ- **~al** ‿əl **~ally** əl‿i **~s** z
stratiform ˈstræt ɪ fɔːm -ə- ‖ ˈstræţ ə fɔːrm
strati|fy ˈstræt ɪ |faɪ -ə- ‖ ˈstræţ- **~fied** faɪd **~fies** faɪz **~fying** faɪ ɪŋ
stratigraphic ˌstræt ɪ ˈgræf ɪk ◂ §-ə- ‖ ˌstræţ- **~ally** ᵊl‿i
stratigraphy strə ˈtɪg rəf i
stratocum|ulus ˌstreɪt əʊ ˈkjuːm |jʊl əs ˌstræt-, -jəl əs ‖ ˌstreɪţ oʊ ˈkjuːm |jəl əs ˌstræţ- **~uli** ju laɪ jə laɪ ‖ jə laɪ
stratopause ˈstræt əʊ pɔːz ‖ ˈstræţ ə- -pɑːz
stratosphere ˈstræt ə sfɪə -əʊ- ‖ ˈstræţ ə sfɪr
stratospheric ˌstræt ə ˈsfer ɪk -əʊ- ‖ ˌstræţ- -ˈsfɪr-
Stratton ˈstræt ᵊn
strat|um ˈstrɑːt |əm ˈstreɪt- ‖ ˈstreɪţ |əm ˈstræţ- **~a** ə
stratus ˈstreɪt əs ‖ ˈstreɪţ əs ˈstræţ-
Strauli ˈstrɔːl i ‖ ˈstrɑːl-
Strauss straʊs —*Ger* [ʃtʁaus]
Stravinsky strə ˈvɪnᵗ ski —*Russ* [stra ˈvʲin skʲij]
straw strɔː ‖ strɑː **straws** strɔːz ‖ strɑːz
 ˌstraw ˈman; **ˌstraw ˈpoll** ‖ ˈ· ·; **ˌstraw ˈvote** ‖ ˈ· ·
strawberr|y, S~ ˈstrɔː bər‿|i ‖ ˈstrɔː ˌber |i -bər‿|i **~ies** iz
 ˌstrawberry ˈblonde; **ˈstrawberry mark**
strawboard ˈstrɔː bɔːd ‖ -bɔːrd ˈstrɑː-, -boʊrd
straw-colored, straw-coloured ˈstrɔː ˌkʌl əd ‖ -ᵊrd ˈstrɑː-
Strawson ˈstrɔːs ᵊn ‖ ˈstrɑːs-
strawweight ˈstrɔː weɪt ‖ ˈstrɑː-
strawy ˈstrɔːʳ i ‖ ˈstrɔː i ˈstrɑː i
stray streɪ **strayed** streɪd **straying** ˈstreɪ ɪŋ **strays** streɪz
streak striːk **streaked** striːkt **streaking** ˈstriːk ɪŋ **streaks** striːks
streaker ˈstriːk ə ‖ -ᵊr **~s** z
streak|y ˈstriːk |i **~ier** i‿ə ‖ i‿ᵊr **~iest** i‿ɪst i‿əst **~ily** ɪ li əl i **~iness** i nəs i nɪs
stream striːm **streamed** striːmd **streaming** ˈstriːm ɪŋ **streams** striːmz
streamer ˈstriːm ə ‖ -ᵊr **~s** z
streamlet ˈstriːm lət -lɪt **~s** s
streamlin|e ˈstriːm laɪn **~ed** d **~es** z **~ing** ɪŋ
Streatfeild, Streatfield ˈstret fiːᵊld
Streatham ˈstret əm ‖ ˈstreţ əm
Streatley *place in Berks* ˈstriːt li
Streep striːp
street, Street striːt **streets** striːts —*Unlike all other words referring to thoroughfares,* street *is usually not accented in names:* ˈOxford Street, ˈRegent Street *(compare* ˌOxford ˈRoad, ˌRegent ˈCrescent*)*
 ˌstreet ˌcrediˈbility; **ˈstreet light**; **ˈstreet smarts**; **ˈstreet ˌvalue**
streetcar ˈstriːt kɑː ‖ -kɑːr **~s** z
street-cred ˌstriːt ˈkred
Streeter ˈstriːt ə ‖ ˈstriːţ ᵊr
street-smart ˈstriːt smɑːt ‖ -smɑːrt
streetwalker ˈstriːt ˌwɔːk ə ‖ -ᵊr -ˌwɑːk- **~s** z
streetwise ˈstriːt waɪz
Streisand ˈstraɪ sænd -zænd, -sənd
strelitzia stre ˈlɪts i‿ə strə- **~s** z

STRENGTH

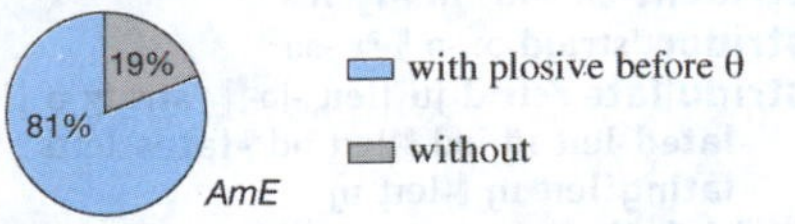

[Pie chart, AmE: with plosive before θ 81%; without 19%]

strength streŋᵏθ §strenᵗθ — *Preference poll, AmE: with plosive before θ 81%, without 19%.*
 strengths streŋᵏθs §strenᵗθs
strengthen ˈstreŋᵏθ ᵊn §ˈstrenᵗθ- **~ed** d **~er/s** ‿ə/z ‖ ‿ᵊr/z **~ing** ‿ɪŋ **~s** z
strenuous ˈstren ju‿əs **~ly** li **~ness** nəs nɪs
strep strep
strepto|coccal ˌstrept ə |ˈkɒk ᵊl ◂ ‖ -|ˈkɑːk ᵊl ◂ **~cocci** ˈkɒks aɪ ˈkɒk-, ˈkɒs-, -iː ‖ ˈkɑːks aɪ ˈkɑːk-, -iː **~coccus** ˈkɒk əs ‖ ˈkɑːk əs
streptomycin ˌstrept ə ˈmaɪs ɪn §-ᵊn

streptothricin, streptothrysin ˌstrept ə ˈθraɪs ɪn -əʊ-, -ˈθrɪs-, §-ən

-stress strəs strɪs, stres — **songstress** ˈsɒŋks trəs -trɪs, -tres; ˈsɒŋ strəs, -strɪs, -stres ‖ ˈsɔːŋks trəs ˈsɑːŋks-; ˈsɔːŋ strəs, ˈsɑːŋ-

stress stres **stressed** strest **stresses** ˈstres ɪz -əz **stressing** ˈstres ɪŋ
ˈstress mark

stressful ˈstres fəl -fʊl **~ly** ˌi **~ness** nəs nɪs

stress-related ˈstres ri leɪt ɪd -rə· ·, -əd ‖ -leɪţ·

stretch stretʃ **stretched** stretʃt **stretches** ˈstretʃ ɪz -əz **stretching** ˈstretʃ ɪŋ

stretchable ˈstretʃ əb əl

stretch|er ˈstretʃ| ə ‖ -ər **~ered** əd ‖ ərd **~ering** ər ɪŋ **~ers** əz ‖ ərz
ˈstretcher ˌparty

stretcher-bearer ˈstretʃ ə ˌbeər ə ‖ -ər ˌber ər -ˌbær- **~s** z

stretchmark ˈstretʃ mɑːk ‖ -mɑːrk **~s** s

stretchy ˈstretʃ i

Stretford ˈstret fəd ‖ -fərd

stretto ˈstret əʊ ‖ ˈstreţ oʊ —*It* [ˈstret to] **~s** z

Stretton ˈstret ən

Strevens ˈstrev ənz

strew struː **strewed** struːd **strewing** ˈstruː ɪŋ **strewn** struːn §ˈstruː‿ən **strews** struːz

strewth struːθ

stria ˈstraɪ‿ə **striae** ˈstraɪ iː

striated straɪ ˈeɪt ɪd -əd ‖ ˈstraɪ eɪţ əd *(*)*

striation straɪ ˈeɪʃ ən **~s** z

Strick, strick strɪk

stricken ˈstrɪk ən

Strickland ˈstrɪk lənd

strickl|e ˈstrɪk əl **~ed** d **~es** z **~ing** ‿ɪŋ

strict strɪkt **stricter** ˈstrɪkt ə ‖ -ər **strictest** ˈstrɪkt ɪst -əst

strict|ly ˈstrɪk*t* |li **~ness** nəs nɪs

stricture ˈstrɪk tʃə ‖ -tʃər **~s** z

stride, Stride straɪd **stridden** ˈstrɪd ən **strides** straɪdz **striding** ˈstraɪd ɪŋ **strode** strəʊd ‖ stroʊd

stridency ˈstraɪd ənts i

strident ˈstraɪd ənt **~ly** li

stridor ˈstraɪd ɔː -ə ‖ ər -ɔːr

stridu|late ˈstrɪd ju |leɪt -jə- ‖ ˈstrɪdʒ ə |leɪt **~lated** leɪt ɪd -əd ‖ leɪţ əd **~lates** leɪts **~lating** leɪt ɪŋ ‖ leɪţ ɪŋ

stridulation ˌstrɪd ju ˈleɪʃ ən -jə- ‖ ˌstrɪdʒ ə- **~s** z

strife straɪf

strigil ˈstrɪdʒ ɪl -əl **~s** z

strike straɪk **strikes** straɪks **striking** ˈstraɪk ɪŋ **struck** strʌk
ˈstrike pay

strikebound ˈstraɪk baʊnd

strikebreaker ˈstraɪk ˌbreɪk ə ‖ -ər **~s** z

strikebreaking ˈstraɪk ˌbreɪk ɪŋ

strikeout ˈstraɪk aʊt **~s** s

striker ˈstraɪk ə ‖ -ər **~s** z

striking ˈstraɪk ɪŋ **~ly** li **~ness** nəs nɪs
ˈstriking ˌdistance

strim strɪm **strimmed** strɪmd **strimming** ˈstrɪm ɪŋ **strims** strɪmz

strimmer, S~ *tdmk* ˈstrɪm ə ‖ -ər **~s** z

Strindberg ˈstrɪnd bɜːg →ˈstrɪmb- ‖ -bɜːg —*Swed* [ˈstrind bærj]

Strine straɪn

string strɪŋ **stringing** ˈstrɪŋ ɪŋ **strings** strɪŋz **strung** strʌŋ
ˌstring ˈbean, ˈ· ·; **ˌstringed ˈinstrument**

stringency ˈstrɪndʒ ənts i

stringent ˈstrɪndʒ ənt **~ly** li

stringer, S~ ˈstrɪŋ ə ‖ -ər **~s** z

Stringfellow ˈstrɪŋ ˌfel əʊ ‖ -oʊ

string|y ˈstrɪŋ |i **~ier** i‿ə ‖ i‿ər **~iest** i‿ɪst i‿əst **~ily** ɪ li əl i **~iness** i nəs i nɪs

strip strɪp **stripped** strɪpt **stripping** ˈstrɪp ɪŋ **strips** strɪps
ˌstrip carˈtoon; **ˈstrip club**; **ˈstrip ˌlighting**; **ˈstrip ˌmining**; **ˌstrip ˈpoker**

stripe straɪp **striped** straɪpt **stripes** straɪps **striping** ˈstraɪp ɪŋ

stripling ˈstrɪp lɪŋ **~s** z

stripp... —*see* **strip**

strippagram ˈstrɪp ə græm **~s** z

stripped-down ˌstrɪpt ˈdaʊn ◂

stripper ˈstrɪp ə ‖ -ər **~s** z

stripperama ˌstrɪp ə ˈrɑːm ə **~s** z

strippogram ˈstrɪp ə græm **~s** z

strip-search ˌstrɪp ˈsɜːtʃ ˈ· · ‖ ˈstrɪp sɜːtʃ **~ed** t **~es** ɪz əz **~ing** ɪŋ

striptease ˈstrɪp tiːz ˌ·ˈ·

strip|y ˈstraɪp |i **~ier** i‿ə ‖ i‿ər **~iest** i‿ɪst i‿əst **~iness** i nəs i nɪs

strive straɪv **striven** ˈstrɪv ən *(!)* **strives** straɪvz **striving/s** ˈstraɪv ɪŋ/z **strove** strəʊv ‖ stroʊv

striver ˈstraɪv ə ‖ -ər **~s** z

strobe strəʊb ‖ stroʊb **strobes** strəʊbz ‖ stroʊbz
ˈstrobe light

stroboscope ˈstrəʊb ə skəʊp ‖ ˈstroʊb ə skoʊp **~s** s

stroboscopic ˌstrəʊb ə ˈskɒp ɪk ◂ ˌstrɒb- ‖ ˌstroʊb ə ˈskɑːp ɪk ◂ **~ally** əl i

strode, Strode strəʊd ‖ stroʊd

stroganoff ˈstrɒg ə nɒf ‖ ˈstroʊg ə nɔːf ˈstrɔːg-, ˈstrɑːg-, -nɑːf

stroke strəʊk ‖ stroʊk **stroked** strəʊkt ‖ stroʊkt **strokes** strəʊks ‖ stroʊks **stroking** ˈstrəʊk ɪŋ ‖ ˈstroʊk ɪŋ

stroll strəʊl →strɒʊl ‖ stroʊl **strolled** strəʊld →strɒʊld ‖ stroʊld **strolling** ˈstrəʊl ɪŋ →ˈstrɒʊl- ‖ ˈstroʊl ɪŋ **strolls** strəʊlz →strɒʊlz ‖ stroʊlz

stroller ˈstrəʊl ə →ˈstrɒʊl- ‖ ˈstroʊl ər **~s** z

strom|a ˈstrəʊm |ə ‖ ˈstroʊm |ə **~ata** ət ə ‖ əţ ə

stromatolite strəʊ ˈmæt ə laɪt -əl aɪt ‖ stroʊ ˈmæţ əl aɪt **~s** s

Stromboli ˈstrɒm bəl i ‖ ˈstrɑːm- —*It* [ˈstrom bo li]

Stromness ˈstrɒm nes ˈstrʌm- ‖ ˈstrɑːm-

Stress

1 A **stressed** syllable is one that carries a **rhythmic beat**. It is marked by greater loudness than unstressed syllables, and often by pitch-prominence, or greater duration, or more clearly defined vowel qualities.

2 An **accent** is the placement of intonational pitch-prominence (= higher or lower pitch than the surroundings) on a word. Speakers choose to accent certain words (or to de-accent others) because of the particular meaning they wish to convey in a particular situation. Accents can be located only on stressed syllables. Thus to accent the word **collapse** kə ˈlæps the pitch-prominence goes on the syllable læps, but in **tumble** ˈtʌm bᵊl on the syllable tʌm.

3 The stresses marked in the *Longman Pronunciation Dictionary* (LPD) are **lexical** (= potential) stresses. Whether they are realized as accents depends on intonation.

4 LPD recognizes two levels of stress:

primary stress (ˈ)	When a word is said in isolation, this is where the nuclear tone (= sentence accent) goes. A word or phrase has only one primary stress.
secondary stress (ˌ)	In a word or phrase that potentially has more than one stress, this symbol marks the place of a stress other than the primary one. If this syllable is **before** the primary stress, it may also bear an accent. See STRESS SHIFT.

5 We regard as unstressed the STRONG-vowelled syllables at the end of words such as **hesitate** ˈhez ɪ teɪt, **acorn** ˈeɪk ɔːn.

6 If the primary stress is located on the third or later syllable of a word, then there must also be a secondary stress on one or other of the first two syllables. Thus **ˌorganiˈzation** has the same stress pattern as **ˌExeter ˈstation**; **asˌsociˈation** has the same stress pattern as **aˌnother ˈnation.**

strong, Strong strɒŋ ‖ strɔːŋ strɑːŋ **stronger** ˈstrɒŋ gə ‖ ˈstrɔːŋ gᵊr ˈstrɑːŋ- **strongest** ˈstrɒŋ gɪst -gəst ‖ ˈstrɔːŋ gəst ˈ strɑːŋ-
ˌstrong ˈlanguage

strongarm ˈstrɒŋ ɑːm ‖ ˈstrɔːŋ ɑːrm ˈstrɑːŋ-

strongbox ˈstrɒŋ bɒks ‖ ˈstrɔːŋ bɑːks ˈstrɑːŋ- **~es** ɪz əz

stronghold ˈstrɒŋ həʊld ‖ ˈstrɔːŋ hoʊld ˈstrɑːŋ- **~s** z

strongly ˈstrɒŋ li ‖ ˈstrɔːŋ li ˈstrɑːŋ-

strong|man ˈstrɒŋ |mæn ‖ ˈstrɔːŋ- ˈstrɑːŋ- **~men** men

strong-minded ˌstrɒŋ ˈmaɪnd ɪd ◂ -əd ‖ ˌstrɔːŋ- ˌstrɑːŋ- **~ly** li **~ness** nəs nɪs

strongpoint, strong point ˈstrɒŋ pɔɪnt ‖ ˈstrɔːŋ- ˈstrɑːŋ- **~s** s

strongroom ˈstrɒŋ ruːm -rʊm ‖ ˈstrɔːŋ- ˈstrɑːŋ- **~s** z

strong-willed ˌstrɒŋ ˈwɪld ◂ ‖ ˌstrɔːŋ- ˌstrɑːŋ-

Stronsay ˈstrɒnz eɪ ‖ ˈstrɑːnz eɪ

strontia ˈstrɒnt i̯ə ˈstrɒnᵗʃ- ‖ ˈstrɑːnᵗʃ i̯ə ˈstrɑːnt̬-

Strontian *place in Highland* ₍ˌ₎strɒn ˈtiː ən ‖ ₍ˌ₎strɑːn-

strontium ˈstrɒnt i̯əm ˈstrɒnᵗʃ- ‖ ˈstrɑːnᵗʃ i̯əm ˈstrɑːnt̬-
ˌstrontium ˈ90

Strood struːd

strop strɒp ‖ strɑːp **stropped** strɒpt ‖ strɑːpt **stropping** ˈstrɒp ɪŋ ‖ ˈstrɑːp ɪŋ **strops** strɒps ‖ strɑːps

S

Stress shift

1 Some words seem to change their stress pattern in connected speech. Although in isolation we say **fundamental** with the primary stress on ment and **Japanese** with the primary stress on niːz, in connected speech these words often have a different pattern. For example, there might be greater stress on fʌnd than on ment, or greater stress on dʒæp than on niːz. This phenomenon is known as **stress shift**.

2 A phrase usually receives late stress (see COMPOUNDS AND PHRASES). The placing of primary stress on the last element of the phrase means that the basic stress of the first element is weakened: combining ˈ**weekly** and ˈ**lessons** gives the phrase ˌ**weekly** ˈ**lessons**. So you might expect that ˌ**fundaˈmental** plus **miˈstake** would give **fundaˌmental miˈstake**, and that ˌ**Japaˈnese** plus ˈ**language** would give **Japaˌnese** ˈ**language**.

But these stress patterns are unbalanced. To balance them, native speakers of English usually switch round the stress levels in the first element, and say ˌ**fundamental miˈstake**, ˌ**Japanese** ˈ**language**.

The same thing happens in a phrase such as ˌ**very** ˈ**lazy** plus ˈ**people**. Stress shift produces ˌ**very lazy** ˈ**people**.

3 In principle, stress shift can apply to any word that has a secondary stress before its primary stress. In practice, though, it is most likely to apply to those which are regularly followed in a phrase by a more strongly stressed word: most adjectives, but only certain nouns. As a helpful reminder, in this dictionary the symbol ◂ is attached to the words in which stress shift is most likely.

4 Conversely, the decision whether or not to mark a secondary stress sometimes depends on whether or not stress shift can occur. In some cases usage is divided, and then this dictionary writes the secondary stress mark in parentheses: **antique** is written ₍ˌ₎æn ˈtiːk because in a phrase such as **an antique chair** some speakers stress-shift, saying **an** ˌ**antique** ˈ**chair**, but others do not, saying **an anˌtique** ˈ**chair**.

strophanth|in strəʊ 'fæn^{t}θ |ɪn strɒ-, §-^{ə}n ‖ stroʊ- **~us** əs
strophe 'strəʊf i 'strɒf-, -iː ‖ 'stroʊf i **~s** z
strophic 'strɒf ɪk 'strəʊf- ‖ 'stroʊf ɪk 'strɑːf-
stropp|y 'strɒp |i ‖ 'strɑːp |i **~ier** i̮ə ‖ i̮^{ə}r **~iest** i̮ɪst i̮əst **~ily** ɪ li əl i **~iness** i nəs i nɪs
Stroud, stroud straʊd
Stroudley 'straʊd li
strove strəʊv ‖ stroʊv
Strowger 'straʊdʒ ə ‖ -^{ə}r
struck strʌk
structural 'strʌk tʃ^{ə}r̮əl -ʃ^{ə}r̮ **~ly** i
structuralism 'strʌk tʃ^{ə}r̮ə ˌlɪz əm '·ʃ^{ə}r̮, əl ˌɪz-
structuralist 'strʌk tʃ^{ə}r̮əl ɪst '·ʃ^{ə}r̮, §-əst **~s** s
structure 'strʌk tʃə -ʃə ‖ -tʃ^{ə}r **~d** d **~s** z **structuring** 'strʌk tʃ^{ə}r̮ɪŋ -ʃ^{ə}r̮
strudel 'struːd ^{ə}l —*Ger* ['ʃtʁuː d^{ə}l] **~s** z
struggl|e 'strʌg ^{ə}l **~ed** d **~er/s** ̮ə/z ‖ ̮ər/z **~es** z **~ing/ly** ̮ɪŋ /li
strum strʌm **strummed** strʌmd **strumming** 'strʌm ɪŋ **strums** strʌmz
struma, S~ 'struːm ə **~s** z
Strumble 'strʌm b^{ə}l
strumpet 'strʌmp ɪt §-ət **~s** s
strung strʌŋ
strung-out ˌstrʌŋ 'aʊt ◂
strung-up ˌstrʌŋ 'ʌp ◂
strut strʌt **struts** strʌts **strutted** 'strʌt ɪd -əd ‖ 'strʌt̬ əd **strutting/ly** 'strʌt ɪŋ /li ‖ 'strʌt̬ ɪŋ /li
struth struːθ
Struthers 'strʌð əz ‖ -^{ə}rz
Strutt strʌt

Struwwelpeter ˌstruː əl ˈpiːt ə ˈ· ·ˌ· ·; ˌstruːlˈ· ·, ˈ·ˌ· · ‖ -ˈpiːt̬ ər —*Ger* [ˈʃtʁʊv əl ˌpeː tɐ]
strychnine ˈstrɪk niːn -nɪn, -naɪn, §-nən ‖ -naɪn -nən, -niːn
Strymon ˈstraɪm ən
Strzelecki *Australian name* strez ˈlek i —*Polish* [st-ʃe ˈlets ki]
St Thomas sənt ˈtɒm əs ‖ seɪnt ˈtɑːm əs
St Tropez ˌsæn trəʊ ˈpeɪ ‖ -troʊ- —*Fr* Saint-Tropez [sɛ̃ tʁo pe]
Stu stjuː →stʃuː ‖ stuː stjuː
Stuart ˈstjuːˌət →ˈstʃuː ‖ ˈstuːˌərt ˈstjuː
stub stʌb **stubbed** stʌbd **stubbing** ˈstʌb ɪŋ **stubs** stʌbz
stubble ˈstʌb əl
stubbly ˈstʌb əl i
stubborn ˈstʌb ən ‖ -ərn **~ly** li **~ness** nəs nɪs
Stubbs stʌbz
stubb|y ˈstʌb |i **~ier** iˌə ‖ iˌər **~ies** iz **~iest** iˌɪst iˌəst **~ily** ɪ li əl i **~iness** i nəs i nɪs
stucco ˈstʌk əʊ ‖ -oʊ **~ed** d **~es, ~s** z **~ing** ɪŋ
stuck stʌk
stuck-up ˌstʌk ˈʌp ◂
stud stʌd **studded** ˈstʌd ɪd -əd **studding** ˈstʌd ɪŋ **studs** stʌdz
ˌ**stud ˈpoker**
studbook ˈstʌd bʊk →ˈstʌb-, §-buːk **~s** s
studdingsail ˈstʌd ɪŋ seɪəl —*also naut* ˈstʌnˈs əl **~s** z
Studebaker ˈstuːd ə beɪk ə ˈstjuːd-, ˈ·ɪ- ‖ -ər **~s** z

STUDENT

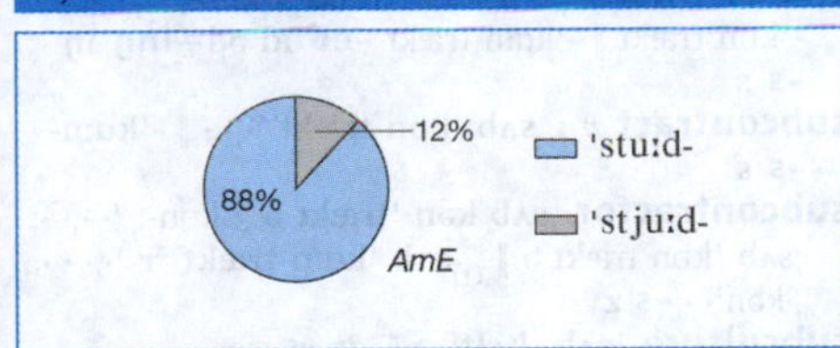

student ˈstjuːd ənt →ˈstʃuːd-, §ˈstuːd- ‖ ˈstuːd ənt ˈstjuːd- — *Preference poll, AmE:* ˈstuːd- *88%*, ˈstjuːd- *12%*. **~s** s **~ship/s** ʃɪp/s
ˌ**students' ˈunion**
studied ˈstʌd id **~ly** li **~ness** nəs nɪs
studio ˈstjuːd iˌəʊ →ˈstʃuːd-, §ˈstuːd- ‖ ˈstuːd i oʊ ˈstjuːd- **~s** z
ˈ**studio couch**
studious ˈstjuːd iˌəs →ˈstʃuːd-, ˈstuːd- ‖ ˈstuːd- ˈstjuːd- **~ly** li **~ness** nəs nɪs
Studland ˈstʌd lənd
Studley ˈstʌd li
study ˈstʌd i **studied** ˈstʌd id **studies** ˈstʌd iz **studying** ˈstʌd i ɪŋ
stuff stʌf **stuffed** stʌft **stuffing/s** ˈstʌf ɪŋ/z **stuffs** stʌfs
ˌ**stuffed ˈshirt**, ˈ· ·
stuffed-up ˌstʌft ˈʌp ◂
stuff|y ˈstʌf |i **~ier** iˌə ‖ iˌər **~iest** iˌɪst iˌəst **~ily** ɪ li əl i **~iness** i nəs i nɪs
Stuka ˈstuːk ə **~s** z —*Ger* [ˈʃtuː ka, ˈʃtʊ-]
stultification ˌstʌlt ɪf ɪ ˈkeɪʃ ən ˌ·əf-, §-əˈ-
stulti|fy ˈstʌlt ɪ |faɪ -ə- **~fied** faɪd **~fies** faɪz **~fying/ly** faɪ ɪŋ /li
stum, stumm *'silent'* ʃtʊm
stum *'grape juice'* stʌm
stumbl|e ˈstʌm bəl **~ed** d **~es** z **stumbling/ly** ˈstʌm blɪŋ /li
ˈ**stumbling block**
stumblebum ˈstʌm bəl bʌm **~s** z
stumbler ˈstʌm blə ‖ -blər **~s** z
stumer ˈstjuːm ə →ˈstʃuːm- ‖ ˈstuːm ər ˈstjuːm- **~s** z
stumm ʃtʊm
stump stʌmp **stumped** stʌmpt **stumping** ˈstʌmp ɪŋ **stumps** stʌmps
stumpage ˈstʌmp ɪdʒ
stump|y ˈstʌmp |i **~ier** iˌə ‖ iˌər **~iest** iˌɪst iˌəst **~iness** i nəs i nɪs
stun stʌn **stunned** stʌnd **stunning/ly** ˈstʌn ɪŋ /li **stuns** stʌnz
ˈ**stun gun**
stung stʌŋ
stunk stʌŋk
stunn... —*see* **stun**
stunner ˈstʌn ə ‖ -ər **~s** z
stunsail, stuns'l ˈstʌn səl **~s** z
stunt stʌnt **stunted** ˈstʌnt ɪd -əd ‖ ˈstʌnt̬ əd **stunting** ˈstʌnt ɪŋ ‖ ˈstʌnt̬ ɪŋ **stunts** stʌnts
ˈ**stunt man**, ˈ**stunt** ˌ**woman**
stupa ˈstuːp ə **~s** z
stupe stjuːp ‖ stuːp stjuːp **stupes** stjuːps ‖ stuːps stjuːps
stupefaction ˌstjuːp ɪ ˈfæk ʃən ˌstjʊp-, §ˌstuːp-, →ˌstʃuːp-, ˌ-ə- ‖ ˌstuːp- ˌstjuːp-
stupe|fy ˈstjuːp ɪ |faɪ ˈstjʊp-, §ˈstuːp-, →ˈstʃuːp-, -ə- ‖ ˈstuːp- ˈstjuːp- **~fied** faɪd **~fier/s** faɪˌə/z ‖ faɪˌər/z **~fies** faɪz **~fying** faɪ ɪŋ
stupendous stju ˈpend əs →stʃu-, §stu- ‖ stu- stju- **~ly** li **~ness** nəs nɪs
stupid ˈstjuːp ɪd ˈstjʊp-, §ˈstuːp-, →ˈstʃuːp-, §-əd ‖ ˈstuːp əd ˈstjuːp- **~er** ə ‖ ər **~est** ɪst əst
stupidit|y stju ˈpɪd ət |i →stʃu-, §stu-, -ɪt i ‖ stu ˈpɪd ət̬ |i stju- **~ies** iz
stupid|ly ˈstjuːp ɪd |li ˈstjʊp-, §ˈstuːp-, →ˈstʃuːp-, §-əd- ‖ ˈstuːp əd |li ˈstjuːp- **~ness** nəs nɪs
stupor ˈstjuːp ə →ˈstʃuːp-, §ˈstuːp- ‖ ˈstuːp ər ˈstjuːp- **~s** z
sturd|y ˈstɜːd |i ‖ ˈstɝːd |i **~ier** iˌə ‖ iˌər **~iest** iˌɪst iˌəst **~ily** ɪ li əl i **~iness** i nəs i nɪs
Sturge stɜːdʒ ‖ stɝːdʒ
sturgeon, S~ ˈstɜːdʒ ən ‖ ˈstɝːdʒ ən **~s** z
Sturmer ˈstɜːm ə ‖ ˈstɝːm ər
Sturminster ˈstɜː ˌmɪnˈst ə ‖ ˈstɝː ˌmɪnˈst ər
Sturm und Drang ˌʃtʊəm ʊnt ˈdræŋ ‖ ˌʃtʊrm ʊnt ˈdrɑːŋ —*Ger* [ˌʃtʊʁm ʊnt ˈdʁaŋ]
Sturridge ˈstʌr ɪdʒ ‖ ˈstɝː ɪdʒ
Sturrock ˈstʌr ək ‖ ˈstɝː ək
Sturt stɜːt ‖ stɝːt
Sturtevant, Sturtivant ˈstɜːt ɪv ənt -əv- ‖ ˈstɝːt̬-
Sturton ˈstɜːt ən ‖ ˈstɝːt ən
Stuttaford ˈstʌt ə fəd ‖ ˈstʌt̬ ə fərd

S

Stuttard 'stʌt əd ‖ 'stʌţ ᵊrd
stutter 'stʌt ə ‖ 'stʌţ ᵊr **~ed** d **stuttering** 'stʌt‿ər ɪŋ ‖ 'stʌţ ər ɪŋ **~s** z
stutterer 'stʌt‿ər ə ‖ 'stʌţ ᵊr ər →'stʌtr ᵊr **~s** z
Stuttgart 'ʃtʊt gɑːt ‖ -gɑːrt 'ʃtuːt- —*Ger* ['ʃtʊt gaʁt]
Stuyvesant 'staɪv əs ənt -ɪs-
St Vincent sənt 'vɪnᵗs ənt ‖ seɪnt-
St Vitus sənt 'vaɪt əs ‖ seɪnt 'vaɪţ əs **St Vitus', St Vitus's** sənt 'vaɪt əs ɪz -əz; -'·əs ‖ seɪnt 'vaɪţ əs əz -'·əs
St ˌVitus' 'dance
St Weonards sənt 'wen ədz ‖ seɪnt 'wen ᵊrdz
sty staɪ **sties** staɪz
Styal 'staɪ‿əl staɪᵊl
stye staɪ *(= sty)* **styes** staɪz
Stygian, s~ 'stɪdʒ i‿ən
style staɪᵊl **styled** staɪᵊld **styles** staɪᵊlz **styling** 'staɪᵊl ɪŋ
-style staɪᵊl — **peristyle** 'per ɪ staɪᵊl -ə-, -i-
Styles staɪᵊlz
stylet 'staɪl ət 'staɪᵊl-, -ɪt **~s** s
stylis... —*see* **styliz...**
stylish 'staɪl ɪʃ 'staɪᵊl- **~ly** li **~ness** nəs nɪs
stylist 'staɪl ɪst 'staɪᵊl-, -əst **~s** s
stylistic staɪ 'lɪst ɪk **~ally** ᵊl‿i **~s** s
stylite 'staɪl aɪt 'staɪᵊl- **~s** s
Stylites staɪ 'laɪt iːz
stylization ˌstaɪl aɪ 'zeɪʃ ᵊn ˌstaɪᵊl-, -ɪ- ‖ -ə- **~s** z
styliz|e 'staɪl aɪz 'staɪᵊl- **~ed** d **~es** ɪz əz **~ing** ɪŋ
stylo 'staɪl əʊ ‖ -oʊ **~s** z
stylo- *comb. form*
with stress-neutral suffix ¦staɪl əʊ ‖ -oʊ — **stylohyoid** ˌstaɪl əʊ 'haɪ ɔɪd ◂ ‖ -oʊ-
with stress-imposing suffix staɪ 'lɒ+ ‖ -'lɑː+ — **stylography** staɪ 'lɒg rəf i ‖ -'lɑːg-
stylobate 'staɪl ə beɪt -əʊ- ‖ -oʊ- **~s** s
stylograph 'staɪl əʊ grɑːf -græf ‖ -ə græf **~s** s
styloid 'staɪl ɔɪd
stylus 'staɪl əs **~es** ɪz əz
stymie, stymy 'staɪm i **stymied** 'staɪm id **stymies** 'staɪm iz **stymieing, stymying** 'staɪm i ɪŋ
styptic 'stɪpt ɪk **~s** s
styrax 'staɪᵊr æks
styrene 'staɪᵊr iːn
Styri|a 'stɪr i‿|ə **~an/s** ən/z
styrofoam, S~ *tdmk* 'staɪᵊr ə fəʊm ‖ -foʊm
Styx stɪks
Su suː
suasion 'sweɪʒ ᵊn
suave swɑːv —*Formerly also* sweɪv
suave|ly 'swɑːv |li 'sweɪv- **~ness** nəs nɪs
suavity 'swɑːv ət i 'sweɪv-, -ɪt i ‖ -əţ i
sub sʌb —*but as a Latin word also* sʊb **subbed** sʌbd **subbing** 'sʌb ɪŋ **subs** sʌbz —*see also phrases with this word*
sub- səb, ¦sʌb —*As a productive prefix,* ¦sʌb ('subcomˌmittee, ˌ·ˌ·'· ·)*; as a fossilized prefix, usually* səb, §sʌb *if the following syllable is stressed* (sub'stantial), ¦sʌb *if not* ('substance).
subacute ˌsʌb ə 'kjuːt ◂ **~ly** li
subalpine ˌsʌb 'ælp aɪn ◂
subaltern 'sʌb ᵊlt ən ‖ sə 'bɔːlt ᵊrn -'bɑːlt- *(*)* **~s** z
subaqua, sub-aqua ˌsʌb 'æk wə ‖ -'ɑːk-
subarachnoid ˌsʌb ə 'ræk nɔɪd ◂
subarctic ˌsʌb 'ɑːkt ɪk ◂ ‖ -'ɑːrkt- -'ɑːrţ-
subarea 'sʌb ˌeər i‿ə ‖ -ˌer-,ˌær-
Subaru *tdmk* 'suːb ə ruː ˌ· ·'· —*Jp* ['sɯ ba ɾɯ] **~s** z
subassem|bly 'sʌb ə ˌsem |bli ˌ· ·'· · **~blies** bliz
subatomic ˌsʌb ə 'tɒm ɪk ◂ ‖ -'tɑːm- ˌ**subaˌtomic 'particles**
subb... —*see* **sub**
subbuteo, S~ *tdmk* sə 'buːt i əʊ sʌ-, -'bjuːt- ‖ -'buːţ i oʊ
subcategory 'sʌb ˌkæt ɪg ər‿i -əg· · ‖ -ˌkæţ ə gɔːr i -goʊr i
subclass 'sʌb klɑːs §-klæs ‖ -klæs **~ed** t **~es** ɪz əz **~ing** ɪŋ
subclinical ˌsʌb 'klɪn ɪk ᵊl ◂
subcommittee 'sʌb kə ˌmɪt i ˌ· ·'· · ‖ -ˌmɪţ- **~s** z
subcompact ˌsʌb kəm 'pækt ◂ §-kɒm-; -'kɒm pækt ‖ ₍ˌ₎sʌb 'kɑːm pækt **~s** s
subconscious ₍ˌ₎sʌb 'kɒnᵗʃ əs ‖ -'kɑːnᵗʃ- **~ly** li **~ness** nəs nɪs
subcontinent ˌsʌb 'kɒnt ɪn ənt -ən-, 'ˌ· · · ‖ -'kɑːnt ᵊn‿ənt **~s** s
subcontinental ˌsʌb ˌkɒnt ɪ 'nent ᵊl -ə- ‖ -ˌkɑːnt ᵊn 'enţ ᵊl
subcontract *v* ˌsʌb kən 'trækt §-kɒn-, -'kɒn trækt ‖ -'kɑːn trækt **~ed** ɪd əd **~ing** ɪŋ **~s** s
subcontract *n* ₍ˌ₎sʌb 'kɒn trækt 'ˌ· · ‖ -'kɑːn- **~s** s
subcontractor ˌsʌb kən 'trækt ə §-kɒn-, '· ·ˌ· ·; ˌsʌb 'kɒn trækt ə ‖ ₍ˌ₎sʌb 'kɑːn trækt ᵊr '·ˌ· · ·, ˌkən'· · **~s** z
subculture 'sʌb ˌkʌltʃ ə ‖ -ᵊr **~s** z
subcutaneous ˌsʌb kju 'teɪn i‿əs ◂ **~ly** li
subdirector|y 'sʌb daɪᵊˌrekt ər‿|i -'də-, '·dɪ- ‖ '·də- **~ies** iz
subdivid|e ˌsʌb dɪ 'vaɪd -də-, §-diː-; '· · · **~ed** ɪd əd **~es** z **~ing** ɪŋ
subdivision 'sʌb dɪ ˌvɪʒ ᵊn -də-, ˌ· ·'· · —*The stressing* ˌ· ·'· · *is mostly restricted to the sense 'act of subdividing'; a portion resulting from this act is a* '· ·ˌ· · **~s** z
subdominant ˌsʌb 'dɒm ɪn ənt -ən‿ ‖ -'dɑːm- **~s** s
subduct səb 'dʌkt ₍ˌ₎sʌb- **~ed** ɪd əd **~ing** ɪŋ **~s** s
subduction səb 'dʌk ʃᵊn ₍ˌ₎sʌb- **~s** z
sub'duction zone
subdu|e səb 'djuː §sʌb-, →'dʒuː ‖ -'duː -'djuː **~ed** d **~es** z **~ing** ɪŋ
subdural ₍ˌ₎sʌb 'djʊər əl →-'dʒʊər-, -'djɔːr- ‖ -'dʊr- -'djʊr-
subed|it ˌsʌb 'ed |ɪt §-ət, 'ˌ· · ‖ -|ət **~ited** ɪt ɪd §ət-, -əd ‖ əţ əd **~iting** ɪt ɪŋ §ət- ‖ əţ ɪŋ **~its** ɪts §əts ‖ əts

subeditor ˌsʌb ˈed ɪt ə §-ət ə, ˈ·ˌ· · · ‖ -əṱ ᵊr **~s** z

subfamil|y ˈsʌb ˌfæm əl‿|i -ɪl |i **~ies** iz

subfreezing ˌsʌb ˈfriːz ɪŋ ◂

subfusc ˈsʌb fʌsk ˌ·ˈ·

subglottal ˌsʌb ˈglɒt ᵊl ◂ ‖ -ˈglɑːṱ-

subgroup ˈsʌb gruːp **~s** s

subharmonic ˌsʌb hɑː ˈmɒn ɪk ‖ -hɑːr ˈmɑːn- **~s** s

subhead ˈsʌb hed ˌ·ˈ· **~ing/s** ɪŋ/z **~s** z

subhuman ˌsʌb ˈhjuːm ən §-ˈjuːm-

Subic ˈsuːb ɪk

subjacency (ˌ)sʌb ˈdʒeɪs ᵊnᵗs i

subjacent (ˌ)sʌb ˈdʒeɪs ᵊnt **~ly** li

subject *v* səb ˈdʒekt sʌb-; ˈsʌb dʒekt, -dʒɪkt **~ed** ɪd əd **~ing** ɪŋ **~s** s

subject *n, adj* ˈsʌb dʒekt -dʒɪkt **~s** s
ˈsubject ˌmatter

subjection səb ˈdʒek ʃᵊn sʌb-

subjectival ˌsʌb dʒɪk ˈtaɪv ᵊl ◂ -dʒek-

subjectiv|e səb ˈdʒekt ɪv (ˌ)sʌb- **~ely** li **~eness** nəs nɪs **~ism** ˌɪz əm **~ist/s** ɪst/s §əst/s

subjectivity ˌsʌb dʒek ˈtɪv ət i -ɪt i ‖ -əṱ i

subject-raising ˈsʌb dʒek*t* ˌreɪz ɪŋ -dʒɪk*t*-

subjoin ˌsʌb ˈdʒɔɪn **~ed** d **~ing** ɪŋ **~s** z

sub judice ˌsʌb ˈdʒuːd əs i ˌsʊb-, -ˈjuːd-, -ɪs i; -ə seɪ, -ɪ-, -keɪ

subju|gate ˈsʌb dʒu |geɪt -dʒə- ‖ -dʒə- **~gated** geɪt ɪd -əd ‖ geɪṱ əd **~gates** geɪts **~gating** geɪt ɪŋ ‖ geɪṱ ɪŋ

subjugation ˌsʌb dʒu ˈgeɪʃ ᵊn -dʒə- ‖ -dʒə-

subjugator ˈsʌb dʒu geɪt ə ˈ·dʒə- ‖ -dʒə geɪṱ ᵊr **~s** z

subjunct ˈsʌb dʒʌŋ*k*t **~s** s

subjunctive səb ˈdʒʌŋ*k*t ɪv §sʌb- **~ly** li **~s** z

subleas|e *v* ˌsʌb ˈliːs ˈ· · **~ed** t **~es** ɪz əz **~ing** ɪŋ

subleas|e *n* ˈsʌb liːs ˌ·ˈ· **~es** ɪz əz

sub|let ˌsʌb |ˈlet **~lets** ˈlets **~letting** ˈlet ɪŋ ‖ ˈleṱ ɪŋ

sublieutenant ˌsʌb lef ˈten ənt -ləf- ‖ -lu- **~s** s

subli|mate *v* ˈsʌb lɪ |meɪt -lə- **~mated** meɪt ɪd -əd ‖ meɪṱ əd **~mates** meɪts **~mating** meɪt ɪŋ ‖ meɪṱ ɪŋ

sublimate *n* ˈsʌb lɪm ət -ləm-, -ɪt; -lɪ meɪt, -lə- **~s** s

sublimation ˌsʌb lɪ ˈmeɪʃ ᵊn -lə-

sublim|e sə ˈblaɪm **~ed** d **~ely** li **~eness** nəs nɪs **~es** z **~ing** ɪŋ

subliminal ˌsʌb ˈlɪm ɪn ᵊl sə ˈblɪm-, -ən- **~ly** i

sublimity sə ˈblɪm ət i -ɪt i ‖ -əṱ i

sublingual ˌsʌb ˈlɪŋ gwəl◂

sublunary (ˌ)sʌb ˈluːn ər i ‖ ˈsʌb lu ner i

submachine gun ˌsʌb mə ˈʃiːn gʌn →-ˈʃiːŋ- **~s** z

submarin|e *n, adj* ˈsʌb mə riːn ˌ·ˈ· — *Preference polls, BrE:* ˈ· · · *42%,* ˌ·ˈ· *58%; AmE:* ˈ· · · *61%,* ˌ·ˈ· *39%.* **~ing** ɪŋ **~es** z

submariner (ˌ)sʌb ˈmær ɪn ə -ən- ‖ ˈsʌb mə riːn ᵊr ˌ· ·ˈ· · *(*)* **~s** z

submediant (ˌ)sʌb ˈmiːd i‿ənt **~s** s

submerg|e səb ˈmɜːdʒ sʌb- ‖ -ˈmɝːdʒ **~ed** d **~es** ɪz əz **~ing** ɪŋ

SUBMARINE

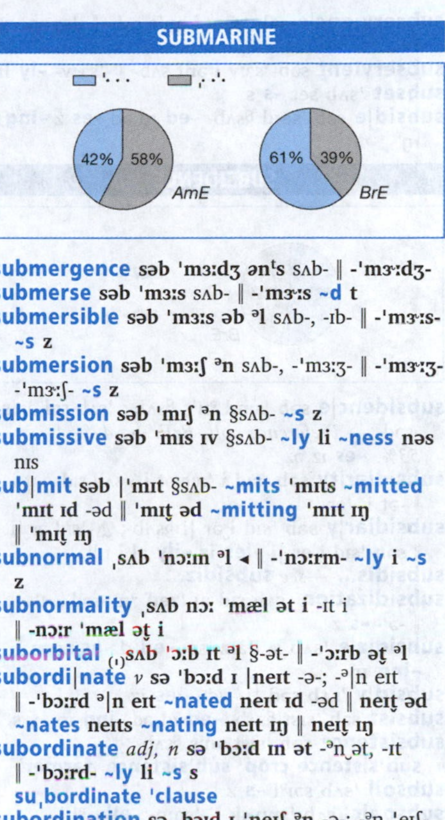

submergence səb ˈmɜːdʒ ənᵗs sʌb- ‖ -ˈmɝːdʒ-

submerse səb ˈmɜːs sʌb- ‖ -ˈmɝːs **~d** t

submersible səb ˈmɜːs əb ᵊl sʌb-, -ɪb- ‖ -ˈmɝːs- **~s** z

submersion səb ˈmɜːʃ ᵊn sʌb-, -ˈmɜːʒ- ‖ -ˈmɝːʒ- -ˈmɝːʃ- **~s** z

submission səb ˈmɪʃ ᵊn §sʌb- **~s** z

submissive səb ˈmɪs ɪv §sʌb- **~ly** li **~ness** nəs nɪs

sub|mit səb |ˈmɪt §sʌb- **~mits** ˈmɪts **~mitted** ˈmɪt ɪd -əd ‖ ˈmɪṱ əd **~mitting** ˈmɪt ɪŋ ‖ ˈmɪṱ ɪŋ

subnormal ˌsʌb ˈnɔːm ᵊl ◂ ‖ -ˈnɔːrm- **~ly** i **~s** z

subnormality ˌsʌb nɔː ˈmæl ət i -ɪt i ‖ -nɔːr ˈmæl əṱ i

suborbital (ˌ)sʌb ˈɔːb ɪt ᵊl §-ət- ‖ -ˈɔːrb əṱ ᵊl

subordi|nate *v* sə ˈbɔːd ɪ |neɪt -ə-; -ᵊ|n eɪt ‖ -ˈbɔːrd ᵊ|n eɪt **~nated** neɪt ɪd -əd ‖ neɪṱ əd **~nates** neɪts **~nating** neɪt ɪŋ ‖ neɪṱ ɪŋ

subordinate *adj, n* sə ˈbɔːd ɪn ət -ᵊn‿ət, -ɪt ‖ -ˈbɔːrd- **~ly** li **~s** z
suˌbordinate ˈclause

subordination sə ˌbɔːd ɪ ˈneɪʃ ᵊn -ə-; -ᵊn ˈeɪʃ- ‖ ˌbɔːrd ᵊn ˈeɪʃ ᵊn

subordinative sə ˈbɔːd ɪn ət ɪv -ˈ·ᵊn- ‖ -ˈbɔːrd ᵊn eɪṱ ɪv

suborn sə ˈbɔːn sʌ- ‖ -ˈbɔːrn **~ed** d **~ing** ɪŋ **~s** z

subornation ˌsʌb ɔː ˈneɪʃ ᵊn ‖ -ɔːr- -ᵊr-

Subotica ˈsuːb ɒ tiːts ə ‖ ˈ·oʊ- —*Serbian* [ˈsu bɔ ti tsa]

subpar ˌsʌb ˈpɑː◂ ‖ -ˈpɑːr ◂

subpen|a sə ˈpiːn |ə səb-, ˌsʌb- **~aed** əd **~aing** əʳ ɪŋ ‖ ə ɪŋ **~as** əz

subplot ˈsʌb plɒt ‖ -plɑːt **~s** s

subpoen|a sə ˈpiːn |ə səb-, ˌsʌb- **~aed** əd **~aing** əʳ ɪŋ ‖ ə ɪŋ **~as** əz

sub-post offic|e ˌsʌb ˈpəʊst ˌɒf ɪs §-əs ‖ -ˈpoʊst ˌɔːf əs -ˌɑːf- **~es** ɪz əz

sub rosa ˌsʌb ˈrəʊz ə ‖ -ˈroʊz ə

subroutine ˈsʌb ru ˌtiːn **~s** z

subscrib|e səb ˈskraɪb §sʌb- **~ed** d **~er/s** ə/z ‖ ᵊr/z **~es** z **~ing** ɪŋ

subscript ˈsʌb skrɪpt **~ed** ɪd əd **~s** s

subscription səb ˈskrɪp ʃᵊn §sʌb- **~s** z

subsection ˈsʌb ˌsek ʃᵊn **~s** z

subsequenc|e *'sequence that is subordinate'* ˈsʌb ˌsiːk wənᵗs **~es** ɪz əz

subsequence *'being subsequent'* ˈsʌb sɪk wənᵗs -sək-

subsequent ˈsʌb sɪk wənt -sək- **~ly** li

S

subservienc|e səb ˈsɜːv i‿ənᵗs sʌb- ‖ -ˈsɜːv- **~y** i
subservient səb ˈsɜːv i‿ənt sʌb- ‖ -ˈsɜːv- **~ly** li
subset ˈsʌb set **~s** s
subsid|e səb ˈsaɪd §sʌb- **~ed** ɪd əd **~es** z **~ing** ɪŋ

SUBSIDENCE

53% 47%
ˈ· ·
·ˈ·
BrE

subsidenc|e səb ˈsaɪd ᵊnᵗs §sʌb-; ˈsʌb sɪd ənᵗs, -səd- — *Preference poll, BrE:* ·ˈ· · *47%,* ˈ· · · *53%.* **~es** ɪz əz
subsidiarity səb ˌsɪd i ˈær ət i, ˌsʌb sɪd-, -ɪt i ‖ -əţ i -ˈer-
subsidiar|y səb ˈsɪd i‿ər |i §sʌb-; ⚠-ˈsɪd ər‿|i ‖ səb ˈsɪd i er |i **~ies** iz **~ily** əl i ɪ li
subsidis... —*see* **subsidiz...**
subsidization ˌsʌb sɪd aɪ ˈzeɪʃ ᵊn ˌ·səd-, -ɪˈ-- ‖ -əˈ· **~s** z
subsidiz|e ˈsʌb sɪ daɪz -sə- **~ed** d **~es** ɪz əz **~ing** ɪŋ
subsid|y ˈsʌb səd |i -sɪd- **~ies** iz
subsist səb ˈsɪst §sʌb- **~ed** ɪd əd **~ing** ɪŋ **~s** s
subsistence səb ˈsɪst ənᵗs §sʌb-
subˈsistence crop; **subˈsistence ˌfarmer**
subsoil ˈsʌb sɔɪᵊl **~s** z
subsonic ˌsʌb ˈsɒn ɪk ‖ -ˈsɑːn- **~ally** ᵊl‿i
subspecies ˈsʌb ˌspiːʃ iːz -ˌspiːs-, -ɪz —*see note at* species
substanc|e ˈsʌb stənᵗs **~es** ɪz əz
substandard ˌsʌb ˈstænd əd ◂ ‖ -ᵊrd ◂

SUBSTANTIAL

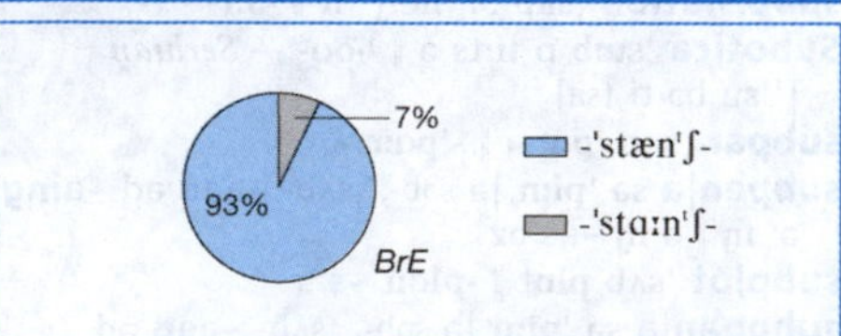

substantial səb ˈstænᵗʃ ᵊl §sʌb-, -ˈstɑːnᵗʃ- — *Preference poll, BrE:* -ˈstænᵗʃ- *93% (English southerners 90%),* -ˈstɑːnᵗʃ- *7%. In AmE always* -ˈstænᵗʃ-. **~ly** i
substanti|ate səb ˈstænᵗʃ i |eɪt §sʌb-, -ˈstɑːnᵗʃ-, -ˈstænᵗs- **~ated** eɪt ɪd -əd ‖ eɪţ əd **~ates** eɪts **~ating** eɪt ɪŋ ‖ eɪţ ɪŋ
substantiation səb ˌstænᵗʃ i ˈeɪʃ ᵊn §sʌb-, -ˌstɑːnᵗʃ-, -ˌstænᵗs-
substantival ˌsʌb stən ˈtaɪv ᵊl ◂
substantive *adj* səb ˈstænt ɪv §sʌb-; ˈsʌb stənt- ‖ ˈsʌb stənt ɪv **~ly** li **~ness** nəs nɪs
substantive *n* ˈsʌb stənt ɪv səb ˈstænt ɪv, §sʌb- **~s** z
substation ˈsʌb ˌsteɪʃ ᵊn **~s** z
substitutability ˌsʌb stɪ tjuːt ə ˈbɪl ət i ˌ·stə-, →ˌ· ·tʃuːt-, -ɪt i ‖ -tuːţ ə ˈbɪl əţ i -tjuːţ·ˈ--
substitutable ˈsʌb stɪ tjuːt əb ᵊl ˈ·stə-, →-tʃuːt · ·, ˌ· ·ˈ· · · ‖ -tuːţ əb ᵊl -tjuːţ-
substi|tute *v, n* ˈsʌb stɪ |tjuːt -stə-, →-tʃuːt ‖ -|tuːt -tjuːt **~tuted** tjuːt ɪd →tʃuːt-, -əd ‖ tuːţ əd tjuːţ- **~tutes** tjuːts →tʃuːts ‖ tuːts tjuːts **~tuting** tjuːt ɪŋ →tʃuːt- ‖ tuːţ ɪŋ tjuːţ-
substitution ˌsʌb stɪ ˈtjuːʃ ᵊn -stə-, →-ˈtʃuːʃ- ‖ -ˈtuːʃ- -ˈtjuːʃ- **~s** z
substitutive ˈsʌb stɪ tjuːt ɪv ˈ·stə-, →tʃuːt · ‖ -tuːţ ɪv -tjuːţ·
substrate ˈsʌb streɪt **~s** s
substrat|um ˈsʌb ˌstrɑːt |əm -ˌstreɪt-, ˌ·ˈ· · ‖ -ˌstreɪţ |əm -ˌstræţ- **~a** ə
substructure ˈsʌb ˌstrʌk tʃə -ʃə ‖ -tʃᵊr **~s** z
subsum|e səb ˈsjuːm §sʌb-, -ˈsuːm ‖ -ˈsuːm **~ed** d **~es** z **~ing** ɪŋ
subsystem ˈsʌb ˌsɪst əm -ɪm
subteen ˌsʌb ˈtiːn ◂
subtenanc|y ˌsʌb ˈten ənᵗs |i ˈ·ˌ· · **~ies** iz
subtenant ˌsʌb ˈten ənt ˈ·ˌ· · **~s** s
subtend səb ˈtend §sʌb- **~ed** ɪd əd **~ing** ɪŋ **~s** z
subterfug|e ˈsʌb tə fjuːdʒ -fjuːʒ ‖ -tᵊr- **~es** ɪz əz
subterranean ˌsʌb tə ˈreɪn i‿ən ◂ **~ly** li
subtext ˈsʌb tekst **~s** s
subtitl|e ˈsʌb ˌtaɪt ᵊl ‖ -ˌtaɪţ ᵊl **~ed** d **~es** z **~ing** ɪŋ
subtle ˈsʌt ᵊl ‖ ˈsʌţ ᵊl *(!)* **~ness** nəs nɪs **~er** ‿ə ‖ ər **~est** ‿ɪst əst
subtle|ty ˈsʌt ᵊl |ti ‖ ˈsʌţ- **~ties** tiz
subtly ˈsʌt ᵊl‿i ‖ ˈsʌţ ᵊl i →ˈsʌt li
subtonic ˌsʌb ˈtɒn ɪk ◂ ‖ -ˈtɑːn- **~s** s
subtopi|a sʌb ˈtəʊp i‿|ə ‖ -ˈtoʊp- **~an** ən
subtotal ˈsʌb ˌtəʊt ᵊl ˌ·ˈ· · ‖ -ˌtoʊţ ᵊl **~ed, ~led** d **~ing, ~ling** ɪŋ **~s** z
subtract səb ˈtrækt §sʌb- **~ed** ɪd əd **~ing** ɪŋ **~s** s
subtraction səb ˈtræk ʃᵊn §sʌb- **~s** z
subtractive səb ˈtrækt ɪv §sʌb- **~ly** li
subtrahend ˈsʌb trə hend **~s** z
subtropic ˌsʌb ˈtrɒp ɪk ‖ -ˈtrɑːp- **~al** ᵊl ◂ **~s** s
subtype ˈsʌb taɪp **~s** s
suburb ˈsʌb ɜːb §-əb ‖ -ɜːb **~s** z
suburban sə ˈbɜːb ən ‖ -ˈbɝːb-
suburbanite sə ˈbɜːb ə naɪt ‖ -ˈbɝːb- **~s** s
suburbia sə ˈbɜːb i‿ə ‖ -ˈbɝːb-
subvariet|y ˈsʌb və ˌraɪ‿ət |i ‿ɪt |i ‖ -ˌraɪ əţ |i **~ies** iz
subvention səb ˈvenᵗʃ ᵊn sʌb- **~s** z
subversion səb ˈvɜːʃ ᵊn sʌb-, §-ˈvɜːʒ- ‖ -ˈvɝːʒ ᵊn -ˈvɝːʃ-
subversive səb ˈvɜːs ɪv sʌb-, §-ˈvɜːz- ‖ -ˈvɝːs- **~ly** li **~ness** nəs nɪs **~s** z
sub|vert səb |ˈvɜːt sʌb- ‖ -|ˈvɝːt **~verted** ˈvɜːt ɪd -əd ‖ ˈvɝːţ əd **~verting** ˈvɜːt ɪŋ ‖ ˈvɝːţ ɪŋ **~verts** ˈvɜːts ‖ ˈvɝːts
subway ˈsʌb weɪ **~s** z
Suby ˈsuːb i
subzero ˌsʌb ˈzɪər əʊ ◂ ‖ -ˈzɪr oʊ ◂
ˌsubˌzero ˈtemperatures

succeed sək ˈsiːd §sʌk- **~ed** ɪd əd **~ing** ɪŋ **~s** z
succes, succès ˌsʊk ˈseɪ ◂ sək- —*Fr* [syk sɛ]
ˌsuccès de scanˈdale, sucˌcès- də skɒn ˈdɑːl ‖ -skɑːn ˈ· —*Fr* [də skɑ̃ dal]; **ˌsuccès dʼeˈstime, sucˌcès** - de ˈstiːm —*Fr* [dɛs tim]; **ˌsuccès ˈfou, sucˌcès-** fuː —*Fr* [fu]
success sək ˈses §sʌk- **~es** ɪz əz
sucˈcess ˌstory
successful sək ˈses fᵊl §sʌk-, -fʊl **~ly** ˌi
succession sək ˈseʃ ᵊn §sʌk- **~al** ˌəl **~ally** ˌəl i **~s** z
successive sək ˈses ɪv §sʌk- **~ly** li **~ness** nəs nɪs
successor sək ˈses ə §sʌk- ‖ -ᵊr **~s** z
succinate ˈsʌks ɪ neɪt -ə-
succinct sək ˈsɪŋkt sʌk-, sə- **~ly** li **~ness** nəs nɪs
succinic sʌk ˈsɪn ɪk sək-
succ|or ˈsʌk| ə ‖ -ᵊr *(= sucker)* **~ored** əd ‖ ᵊrd **~oring** ər ɪŋ **~ors** əz ‖ -ᵊrz
succory ˈsʌk ər i
succotash ˈsʌk ə tæʃ
Succoth ˈsʊk əs ˈsʌk-; su ˈkɒt ‖ su ˈkoʊs
succ|our ˈsʌk| ə ‖ -ᵊr *(= sucker)* **~oured** əd ‖ ᵊrd **~ouring** ər ɪŋ **~ours** əz ‖ -ᵊrz
succ|uba ˈsʌk |jʊb ə -jəb- ‖ -|jəb ə **~ubae** ju biː jə-, -baɪ ‖ jə- **~ubi** ju baɪ jə-, -biː ‖ jə- **~ubus** jʊb əs jəb- ‖ jəb-
succulence ˈsʌk jʊl ənᵗs -jəl- ‖ -jəl-
succulent ˈsʌk jʊl ənt -jəl- ‖ -jəl- **~ly** li
succumb sə ˈkʌm **~ed** d **~ing** ɪŋ **~s** z
such *strong form* sʌtʃ, *occasional weak form* sətʃ
ˈsuch and ˌsuch
Suchard *tdmk* ˈsuːʃ ɑːd -ɑː ‖ su ˈʃɑːrd —*Fr* [sy ʃaːʁ]
Suchet ˈsuːʃ eɪ
suchlike ˈsʌtʃ laɪk
suck sʌk **sucked** sʌkt **sucking** ˈsʌk ɪŋ **sucks** sʌks
ˈsucking pig
sucker ˈsʌk ə ‖ -ᵊr **~s** z
suckl|e ˈsʌk ᵊl **~ed** d **~es** z **~ing** ˌɪŋ
suckling *n,* **S~** ˈsʌk lɪŋ **~s** z
sucky ˈsʌk i
sucre, Sucre ˈsuːk reɪ —*Sp* [ˈsuk re] **~s** z
sucrose ˈsuːk rəʊs ˈsjuːk-, -rəʊz ‖ -roʊs
suction ˈsʌk ʃᵊn **~ed** d **~ing** ˌɪŋ **~s** z
ˈsuction pump
Sudan su ˈdɑːn -ˈdæn ‖ -ˈdæn
Sudanese ˌsuːd ə ˈniːz ◂ ˌsʊd-, ᵊn ˈiːz ◂ ‖ ˌsuːd ᵊn ˈiːz ◂ -ˈiːs ◂
Sudanic su ˈdæn ɪk
sudari|um su ˈdeər iˌ|əm sju- ‖ -ˈder- -ˈdær- **~a** ə
sudatori|um ˌsuːd ə ˈtɔːr iˌ|əm ˌsjuːd- ‖ -ˈtoʊr- **~a** ə
sudator|y ˈsuːd ət̬ ər |i ˈsjuːd- ‖ ˈsuːd ə tɔːr |i -toʊr i **~ies** iz
Sudbury ˈsʌd bərˌi →ˈsʌb- ‖ -ˌber i
Suddaby ˈsʌd əb i

sudden ˈsʌd ᵊn **~ly** li **~ness** nəs nɪs
ˌsudden ˈdeath
Sudeten su ˈdeɪt ᵊn **~land** lænd
sudoku, su doku su ˈdəʊk uː -ˈdɒk-; ˈsuːd ə kuː ‖ -ˈdoʊk- —*Jp* [sɯˌɯ do kɯ]
sudorific ˌsuːd ə ˈrɪf ɪk ◂ ˌsjuːd-, -ɒ-, -ɔː- **~s** s
suds sʌdz
sudsy ˈsʌdz i
sue sjuː suː ‖ suː **sued** sjuːd suːd ‖ suːd **sues** sjuːz suːz ‖ suːz **suing** ˈsjuːˌɪŋ ˈsuːˌ ‖ ˈsuː ɪŋ
Sue suː
suede, suède sweɪd *(= swayed)*
ˌsuede ˈshoes
suet ˈsuːˌɪt ˈsjuːˌ, §-ət
ˌsuet ˈpudding
Suetonius ˌsuːˌɪ ˈtəʊn i əs ˌsjuːˌ, əˈ-, swiːˈ- ‖ -ˈtoʊn-
Suez ˈsuːˌɪz ˈsjuːˌ ‖ ˌsuː ˈez ˈsuː ez *(*)*
ˌSuez Caˈnal
suffer ˈsʌf ə ‖ -ᵊr **~ed** d **suffering** ˈsʌf ər ˌɪŋ **~s** z
sufferab|le ˈsʌf ər ˌəb |ᵊl **~ly** li
sufferance ˈsʌf ᵊr ˌənᵗs
sufferer ˈsʌf ᵊr ˌə ‖ ər **~s** z
suffic|e sə ˈfaɪs **~ed** t **~es** ɪz əz **~ing** ɪŋ
sufficiency sə ˈfɪʃ ᵊnᵗs i
sufficient sə ˈfɪʃ ᵊnt **~ly** li
suffix *n* ˈsʌf ɪks **~es** ɪz əz
suffix *v* ˈsʌf ɪks sə ˈfɪks, sʌ- **~ed** t **~es** ɪz əz **~ing** ɪŋ
suffixal ˈsʌf ɪks ᵊl sə ˈfɪks ᵊl, sʌ-
suffixation ˌsʌf ɪk ˈseɪʃ ᵊn
suffo|cate ˈsʌf ə |keɪt **~cated** keɪt ɪd -əd ‖ keɪt̬ əd **~cates** keɪts **~cating/ly** keɪt ɪŋ /li ‖ keɪt̬ ɪŋ /li
suffocation ˌsʌf ə ˈkeɪʃ ᵊn
Suffolk ˈsʌf ək
suffragan ˈsʌf rəg ən ⚠-rədʒ- **~s** z
suffrag|e ˈsʌf rɪdʒ **~es** ɪz əz
suffragette ˌsʌf rə ˈdʒet -rɪ- **~s** s
suffragist ˈsʌf rədʒ ɪst -rɪdʒ-, §-əst **~s** s
suffus|e sə ˈfjuːz sʌ- **~ed** d **~es** ɪz əz **~ing** ɪŋ
suffusion sə ˈfjuːʒ ᵊn sʌ- **~s** z
Sufi ˈsuːf i **~s** z
Sufism ˈsuːf ˌɪz əm
Sugababes ˈʃʊg ə beɪbz
sugar ˈʃʊg ə ‖ -ᵊr *(!)* **~ed** d **sugaring** ˈʃʊg ər ˌɪŋ **~s** z
ˌsugar ˈbeet, ˈ· · ·; **ˈsugar bowl**; **ˈsugar ˌdaddy**
sugarcane ˈʃʊg ə keɪn ‖ -ᵊr-
sugarcoated ˌʃʊg ə ˈkəʊt ɪd ◂ -əd ‖ -ᵊr ˈkoʊt̬ əd ◂
sugar-free ˌʃʊg ə ˈfriː ◂ ‖ -ᵊr-
sugariness ˈʃʊg ər ˌi nəs -nɪs
sugarless ˈʃʊg ə ləs -lɪs ‖ -ᵊr-
sugarloaf ˈʃʊg ə ləʊf ‖ -ᵊr loʊf
sugarplum ˈʃʊg ə plʌm ‖ -ᵊr- **~s** z
sugary ˈʃʊg ər i
Sugden ˈsʌg dən

S

SUGGEST

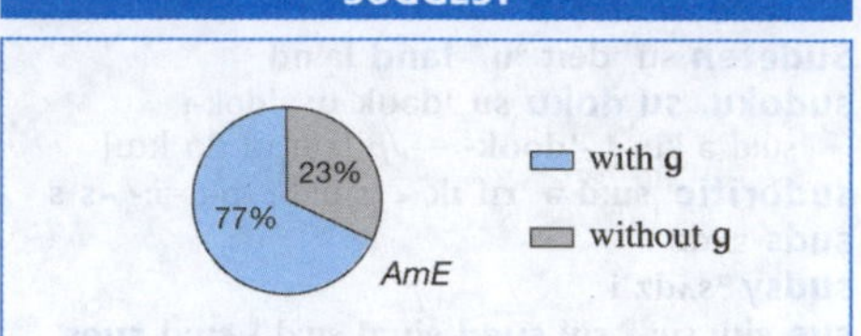

suggest sə ˈdʒest ‖ səg ˈdʒest sə- — *Preference poll, AmE: with* g *77%, without* g *23%.* **~ed** ɪd əd **~ing** ɪŋ **~s** s
suggestibility sə ˌdʒest ə ˈbɪl ət i -ˌ·ɪ-, -ɪt i ‖ səg ˌdʒest ə ˈbɪl ət̬ i
suggestible sə ˈdʒest əb ᵊl -ɪb- ‖ səg-
suggestion sə ˈdʒes tʃən →-ˈdʒeʃ- ‖ səg- **~s** z
suggestive sə ˈdʒest ɪv ‖ səg- **~ly** li **~ness** nəs nɪs
Sugrew, Sugrue ˈsuː gruː
Suharto su ˈhɑːt əʊ ‖ -ˈhɑːrt̬ oʊ
sui ˈsuː aɪ ˈsjuː-, -iː
ˌsui ˈgeneris ˈdʒen ər ɪs ˈgen-; **ˌsui ˈjuris** ˈdʒʊər ɪs ˈjʊər-
Sui *dynasty* sweɪ ˈsuː i —*Chi* Suí [²swei]
suicidal ˌsuː ɪ ˈsaɪd ᵊl ◂ ˌsjuː‿, ə- **~ly** i
suicide ˈsuː‿ɪ saɪd ˈsjuː‿, ə- **~s** z
suint swɪnt ˈsuː‿ɪnt, ˈsjuː‿

SUIT

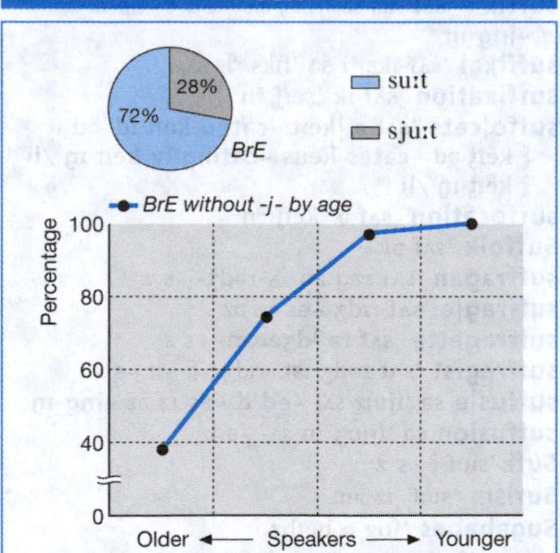

suit suːt sjuːt — *Preference poll, BrE:* suːt *72%,* sjuːt *28%. In AmE always* suːt. **suited** ˈsuːt ɪd ˈsjuːt-, -əd ‖ ˈsuːt̬ əd **suiting/s** ˈsuːt ɪŋ/z ˈsjuːt- ‖ ˈsuːt̬ ɪŋ/z **suits** suːts sjuːts ‖ suːts
suitability ˌsuːt ə ˈbɪl ət i ˌsjuːt-, -ɪt i ‖ ˌsuːt̬ ə ˈbɪl ət̬ i
suitab|le ˈsuːt əb |ᵊl ˈsjuːt- ‖ ˈsuːt̬- **~leness** ᵊl nəs -nɪs **~ly** li
suitcas|e ˈsuːt keɪs ˈsjuːt- **~es** ɪz əz
suite swiːt *(= sweet) —but in AmE sometimes* suːt *in the sense 'suite of furniture'* **suites** swiːts
suitor ˈsuːt ə ˈsjuːt- ‖ ˈsuːt̬ ᵊr **~s** z
Sukey, Sukie ˈsuːk i
sukiyaki ˌsuːk i ˈjɑːk i ˌsʊk- —*Jp* [sɯ̥ ˌki ja ki]
Sukkot, Sukkoth su ˈkəʊt ˈsʊk əs, ˈsʌk-, -ət ‖ ˈsʊk oʊt -oʊs, -əs
Sulawesi ˌsuːl ə ˈweɪs i
sulcal ˈsʌlk ᵊl **~ly** i
sulcalis... —*see* **sulcaliz...**
sulcalization ˌsʌlk ə laɪ ˈzeɪʃ ᵊn -lɪˈ· · ‖ ˌ·ᵊl ə
sulcaliz|e ˈsʌlk ə laɪz **~ed** d **~es** ɪz əz **~ing** ɪŋ
sulcate *adj* ˈsʌlk eɪt
sulcus ˈsʌlk əs **sulci** ˈsʌls aɪ ˈsʌlk-, -iː
Suleiman ˌsʊl i ˈmɑːn ˌsuːl-, -eɪ-, ˈ· · ·
sulfa ˈsʌlf ə
ˈsulfa drug
sulfadiazine ˌsʌlf ə ˈdaɪ‿ə ziːn
sulfaguanidine ˌsʌlf ə ˈgwɑːn ɪ diːn -ˈ·ə-
sulfamic sʌl ˈfæm ɪk
sulfanilamide ˌsʌlf ə ˈnɪl ə maɪd
sulfate ˈsʌlf eɪt **~s** s
sulfathiazole ˌsʌlf ə ˈθaɪ‿ə zəʊl →-zɒʊl ‖ -zoʊl
sulfide ˈsʌlf aɪd **~s** z
sulfite ˈsʌlf aɪt **~s** s
sulfonamide sʌl ˈfɒn ə maɪd ‖ -ˈfɑːn- -ˈfoʊn-
sulfo|nate ˈsʌlf ə |neɪt **~nated** neɪt ɪd -əd ‖ neɪt̬ əd **~nates** neɪts **~nating** neɪt ɪŋ ‖ neɪt̬ ɪŋ
sulfone ˈsʌlf əʊn ‖ -oʊn **~s** z
sulfonic sʌl ˈfɒn ɪk ‖ -ˈfɑːn- -ˈfoʊn-
sulfur ˈsʌlf ə ‖ -ᵊr
sulfureous sʌl ˈfjʊər i‿əs -ˈfjɔːr- ‖ -ˈfjʊr-
sulfu|ret ˈsʌlf juᵊ |ret -jə-, -ə-, ˌ·ˈ·. ‖ -ə- **~reted, ~retted** ret ɪd -əd ‖ ret̬ əd **~reting, ~retting** ret ɪŋ ‖ ret̬ ɪŋ **~rets** rets
sulfuric sʌl ˈfjʊər ɪk -ˈfjɔːr- ‖ -ˈfjʊr-
sulˌfuric ˈacid
sulfurous ˈsʌlf ər əs -jʊr- **~ly** li **~ness** nəs nɪs
Sulgrave ˈsʌl greɪv
sulk sʌlk **sulked** sʌlkt **sulking** ˈsʌlk ɪŋ **sulks** sʌlks
sulk|y ˈsʌlk |i **~ier** i‿ə ‖ i‿ᵊr **~iest** i‿ɪst i‿əst **~ily** ɪ li əl i **~iness** i nəs i nɪs
Sulla ˈsʌl ə ˈsʊl-
sullage ˈsʌl ɪdʒ
sullen ˈsʌl ən **~ly** li **~ness** nəs nɪs
sulli... —*see* **sully**
Sullivan ˈsʌl ɪv ən -əv-
Sullom Voe ˌsuːl əm ˈvəʊ ˌsʌl- ‖ -ˈvoʊ
sully, Sully ˈsʌl i **sullied** ˈsʌl id **sullies** ˈsʌl iz **sullying** ˈsʌl i ɪŋ
sulpha ˈsʌlf ə
ˈsulpha drug
sulphadiazine ˌsʌlf ə ˈdaɪ‿ə ziːn
sulphaguanidine ˌsʌlf ə ˈgwɑːn ɪ diːn -ˈ·ə-
sulphamic sʌl ˈfæm ɪk
sulphanilamide ˌsʌlf ə ˈnɪl ə maɪd
sulphate ˈsʌlf eɪt **~s** s
sulphathiazole ˌsʌlf ə ˈθaɪ‿ə zəʊl →-zɒʊl ‖ -zoʊl
sulphide ˈsʌlf aɪd **~s** z
sulphite ˈsʌlf aɪt **~s** s
sulphonamide sʌl ˈfɒn ə maɪd ‖ -ˈfɑːn- -ˈfoʊn-

sulpho|nate 'sʌlf ə |neɪt **~nated** neɪt ɪd -əd ‖ neɪţ əd **~nates** neɪts **~nating** neɪt ɪŋ ‖ neɪţ ɪŋ
sulphone 'sʌlf əʊn ‖ -oʊn **~s** z
sulphonic sʌl 'fɒn ɪk ‖ -'fɑːn- -'foʊn-
sulphur 'sʌlf ə ‖ -ᵊr
sulphureous sʌl 'fjʊər i‿əs -'fjɔːr- ‖ -'fjʊr-
sulphu|ret 'sʌlf juᵊ |ret -jə-, -ə-; ˌ· ·'· ‖ -ə- **~reted, ~retted** ret ɪd -əd ‖ reţ əd **~reting, ~retting** ret ɪŋ ‖ reţ ɪŋ **~rets** rets
sulphuric sʌl 'fjʊər ɪk -'fjɔːr- ‖ -'fjʊr-
sulˌphuric 'acid
sulphurous 'sʌlf ər əs -jʊr- **~ly** li **~ness** nəs nɪs
sultan 'sʌlt ən ‖ -ᵊn **~s** z
sultana sʌl 'tɑːn ə səl- ‖ -'tæn- **~s** z
sultanate 'sʌlt ən ət -ɪt; -ə neɪt, -ᵊn eɪt ‖ -ᵊn eɪt **~s** s
sultr|y 'sʌltr |i **~ier** i‿ə ‖ i‿ᵊr **~iest** i‿ɪst i‿əst **~ily** əl i ɪ li **~iness** i nəs i nɪs
Sulu 'suːl uː
Sulwen 'siːᵊl wen -wən —*Welsh* ['sɪl wen, 'sil-]
Sulwyn 'siːᵊl wɪn —*Welsh* ['sɪl win, 'sil-]
sum sʌm **summed** sʌmd **summing** 'sʌm ɪŋ **sums** sʌmz
ˌsum 'total
sumac, sumach 'ʃuːm æk 'suːm-, 'sjuːm- **~s** s
Sumatr|a su 'mɑːtr |ə sju-, sə- **~an/s** ən/z
Sumburgh 'sʌm bər‿ə
Sumer 'suːm ə ‖ -ᵊr
Sumerian su 'mɪər i‿ən sju-, sə-, -'meər- ‖ -'mer- -'mɪr- **~s** z
Sumitomo ˌsuːm i 'təʊm əʊ ‖ -'toʊm oʊ —*Jp* [sɯ ˌmi to mo]
summa 'sʌm ə 'sʊm-, -ɑː
ˌsumma cum 'laude
summarily 'sʌm ᵊr‿əl i ‿ɪl-; sə 'mer- ‖ sə 'mer əl i
summaris|e, summariz|e 'sʌm ə raɪz **~ed** d **~es** ɪz əz **~ing** ɪŋ
summar|y 'sʌm ər |i **~ies** iz
summat 'sʌm ət —*Since this is mainly a North of England dialect word, in practice it is more usually* 'sʊm-
summation sʌ 'meɪʃ ᵊn sə- **~s** z
summer 'sʌm ə ‖ -ᵊr **~s** z
'summer school
Summer 'sʌm ə ‖ -ᵊr **~s** z
Summerfield 'sʌm ə fiːᵊld ‖ -ᵊr-
Summerhayes 'sʌm ə heɪz ‖ -ᵊr-
Summerhill 'sʌm ə hɪl ‖ -ᵊr-
summer|house 'sʌm ə |haʊs ‖ -ᵊr- **~houses** haʊz ɪz -əz
summeriness 'sʌm ər i nəs -nɪs
Summers 'sʌm əz ‖ -ᵊrz
Summerscale 'sʌm ə skerᵊl ‖ -ᵊr-
Summerskill 'sʌm ə skɪl ‖ -ᵊr-
summertime 'sʌm ə taɪm ‖ -ᵊr-
summery 'sʌm ər i
summing-up ˌsʌm ɪŋ 'ʌp **summings-up** ˌsʌm ɪŋz 'ʌp
summit 'sʌm ɪt §-ət **~s** s
'summit ˌconference
summiteer ˌsʌm ɪ 'tɪə -ə- ‖ -'tɪᵊr **~s** z
summitry 'sʌm ɪtr i §-ətr-
summon 'sʌm ən **~ed** d **~ing** ɪŋ **~s** z
summons 'sʌm ənz **~ed** d **~es** ɪz əz **~ing** ɪŋ
summum bonum ˌsʌm əm 'bəʊn əm ˌsʊm-, -ʊm-, -'bɒn-, -ʊm ‖ -'boʊn-
Sumner 'sʌm nə ‖ -nᵊr
sumo 'suːm əʊ ‖ -oʊ —*Jp* [sɯ ˌmoo]
sump sʌmp **sumps** sʌmps
sumptuary 'sʌmp tʃu‿ər i -tju‿ər- ‖ -er i
sumptuous 'sʌmp tʃu‿əs -tju‿ **~ly** li **~ness** nəs nɪs
Sumter 'sʌmᵖt ə ‖ -ᵊr
sun sʌn **sunned** sʌnd **sunning** 'sʌn ɪŋ **suns** sʌnz
'sun god; **'sun lounge**; **'sun parlor**; **'sun porch**; **'sun ˌvisor**
sunbaked 'sʌn beɪkt →'sʌm-
sunbath|e 'sʌn beɪð →'sʌm- **~ed** d **~er/s** ə/z ‖ ᵊr/z **~es** z **~ing** ɪŋ
sunbeam, S~ 'sʌn biːm →'sʌm- **~s** z
sunbed 'sʌn bed →'sʌm- **~s** z
sunbelt, S~ 'sʌn belt →'sʌm-
sunbird 'sʌn bɜːd →'sʌm- ‖ -bɜːd **~s** z
sunblind 'sʌn blaɪnd →'sʌm- **~s** z
sunblock 'sʌn blɒk →'sʌm- ‖ -blɑːk **~s** s
sunbonnet 'sʌn ˌbɒn ɪt →'sʌm-, §-ət ‖ -ˌbɑːn ət **~s** s
sunburn 'sʌn bɜːn →'sʌm- ‖ -bɜːn **~ed** d
sunburnt 'sʌn bɜːnt →'sʌm- ‖ -bɜːnt
sunburst 'sʌn bɜːst →'sʌm- ‖ -bɜːst **~s** s
Sunbury 'sʌn bər‿i →'sʌm- ‖ -ˌber i
Sunda 'sʌnd ə 'sʊnd-, 'suːnd-
sundae 'sʌnd eɪ -i **~s** z
Sundanese ˌsʌnd ə 'niːz ◂ ˌsʊnd-, ˌsuːnd- ‖ -'niːs ◂
Sunday 'sʌn deɪ 'sʌnd i —*see note at* -day **~s** z
ˌSunday 'best; **'Sunday school**
sundeck 'sʌn dek **~s** s
sunder 'sʌnd ə ‖ -ᵊr **~ed** d **sundering** 'sʌnd‿ər ɪŋ **~s** z
Sunderland 'sʌnd ə lənd →-ᵊl ənd ‖ -ᵊr-
sundew 'sʌn djuː →-dʒuː ‖ -duː -djuː **~s** z
sundial 'sʌn ˌdaɪ‿əl **~s** z
sundown 'sʌn daʊn **~s** z
sundowner 'sʌn daʊn ə ‖ -ᵊr **~s** z
sundrenched 'sʌn drentʃt
sundress 'sʌn dres **~es** ɪz əz
Sundridge 'sʌndr ɪdʒ
sun-dried 'sʌn draɪd ˌ·'· ◂
sundr|y 'sʌndr| i **~ies** iz
sunfish 'sʌn fɪʃ **~es** ɪz əz
sunflower 'sʌn ˌflaʊ‿ə ‖ -ˌflaʊ‿ᵊr **~s** z
sung sʌŋ
sunglasses 'sʌn ˌglɑːs ɪz →'sʌŋ-, §-ˌglæs-, -əz ‖ -ˌglæs əz
sunhat 'sʌn hæt **~s** s
sunk sʌŋk
sunken 'sʌŋk ən
sunkissed, Sunkist *tdmk* 'sʌn kɪst →'sʌŋ-
sunlamp 'sʌn læmp **~s** s

S

sunless ˈsʌn ləs -lɪs **~ly** li **~ness** nəs nɪs
sunlight, S~ ˈsʌn laɪt
sunlit ˈsʌn lɪt
sunlounger ˈsʌn ˌlaʊndʒ ə ‖ -ᵊr **~s** z
Sunna ˈsʊn ə ˈsʌn-
Sunni ˈsʊn i ˈsʌn- **~s** z
Sunningdale ˈsʌn ɪŋ deɪᵊl
Sunnite ˈsʊn aɪt ˈsʌn- **~s** s
sunn|y, Sunn|y ˈsʌn |i **~ier** i‿ə ‖ i‿ᵊr **~iest** i‿ɪst i‿əst **~ily** ɪ li əl i **~iness** i nəs i nɪs
Sunnyside ˈsʌn i saɪd
sunny-side up ˌsʌn i saɪd ˈʌp
sunray ˈsʌn reɪ **~s** z
sunris|e ˈsʌn raɪz **~es** ɪz əz
ˈsunrise ˌindustry
sunroof ˈsʌn ruːf -rʊf **~s** s
sunroom ˈsʌn ruːm -rʊm **~s** z
sunscreen ˈsʌn skriːn **~s** z
sunseeker ˈsʌn ˌsiːk ə ‖ -ᵊr **~s** z
sunset ˈsʌn set **~s** s
sunshade ˈsʌn ʃeɪd **~s** z
sunshine ˈsʌn ʃaɪn
sunspot ˈsʌn spɒt ‖ -spɑːt **~s** s
sunstroke ˈsʌn strəʊk ‖ -stroʊk
suntan ˈsʌn tæn **~ned** d **~ning** ɪŋ **~s** z
Suntory *tdmk* ˈsʌn tɔːr i ·ˈ· · —*Jp* [ˈsan to ɾii]
suntrap ˈsʌn træp **~s** s
sun-up ˈsʌn ʌp **~s** s
Sun Yatsen ˌsʌn jæt ˈsen ‖ -jɑːt- —*Chi* Sūn Zhōngshān [¹swən ¹ʈʂʊŋ ¹ʂan]
sup sʌp **supped** sʌpt **supping** ˈsʌp ɪŋ **sups** sʌps
supe suːp **supes** suːps
super ˈsuːp ə ˈsjuːp- ‖ -ᵊr **~s** z
super- ¦suːp ə ¦sjuːp ə ‖ -ᵊr — **superpower** ˈsuːp ə ˌpaʊ‿ə ˈsjuːp- ‖ ˈsuːp ᵊr ˌpaʊ‿ᵊr
superabundance ˌsuːp ər‿ə ˈbʌnd ənᵗs ˌsjuːp-, -ə ə-
superabundant ˌsuːp ər‿ə ˈbʌnd ənt ◂ ˌsjuːp-, -ə ə- **~ly** li
superannu|ate ˌsuːp ər ˈæn ju |eɪt ˌsjuːp- ‖ ˌ·ər- **~ated** eɪt ɪd -əd ‖ eɪţ əd **~ates** eɪts **~ating** eɪt ɪŋ ‖ eɪţ ɪŋ
superannuation ˌsuːp ər ˌæn ju ˈeɪʃ ᵊn ˌsjuːp- ‖ ˌ·ər- **~s** z
superb su ˈpɜːb sju-, sə- ‖ -ˈpɜːb **~ly** li **~ness** nəs nɪs
Superbowl ˈsuːp ə bəʊl ˈsjuːp-, →-bɒʊl ‖ -ᵊr boʊl
superbug ˈsuːp ə bʌg ˈsjuːp ‖ -rᵊ- **~s** z
supercargo ˌsuːp ə ˈkɑːg əʊ ˌsjuːp-, ˈ· ·ˌ· · ‖ -ᵊr ˈkɑːrg oʊ **~s** z
supercharg|e ˈsuːp ə tʃɑːdʒ ˈsjuːp-, ˌ· ·ˈ· ‖ -ᵊr tʃɑːrdʒ **~ed** d **~es** ɪz əz **~ing** ɪŋ
supercharger ˈsuːp ə ˌtʃɑːdʒ ə ˈsjuːp-, ˌ· ·ˈ· · ‖ -ᵊr ˌtʃɑːrdʒ ᵊr **~s** z
supercilious ˌsuːp ə ˈsɪl i‿əs ◂ ˌsjuːp- ‖ ˌ·ᵊr- **~ly** li **~ness** nəs nɪs
supercomputer ˈsuːp ə kəm ˌpjuːt ə ˈsjuːp-, §-ə kɒm- ‖ ˈsuːp ᵊr kəm ˌpjuːţ ᵊr **~s** z
superconduction ˌsuːp ə kən ˈdʌk ʃᵊn ˌsjuːp-, §-kɒn'-- ‖ ˌ·ᵊr-
superconductive ˌsuːp ə kən ˈdʌkt ɪv ◂ ˌsjuːp-, §-ə kɒn- ‖ ˌsuːp ᵊr-
superconductivity ˌsuːp ə ˌkɒn dʌk ˈtɪv ət i ˌsjuːp-, -ɪt i ‖ -ᵊr ˌkɑːn dʌk ˈtɪv əţ i
superconductor ˌsuːp ə kən ˈdʌkt ə ˌsjuːp-, §-kɒn'· ‖ -ᵊr kən ˈdʌkt ᵊr **~s** z
supercool ˌsuːp ə ˈkuːl ◂ ˌsjuːp-, ˈ· · · ‖ -ᵊr- **~ed** d **~ing** ɪŋ **~s** z
Superdrug *tdmk* ˈsuːp ə drʌg ˈsjuːp- ‖ -rᵊ-
superduper ˌsuːp ə ˈduːp ə ◂ ˌsjuːp- ‖ -ᵊr ˈduːp ᵊr
superego ˌsuːp ər ˈiːg əʊ ˌsjuːp-, -ə-, -ˈeg- ‖ -ˈiːg oʊ **~s** z
superelevation ˌsuːp ər ˌel ɪ ˈveɪʃ ᵊn ˌ·ə-, -əˈ-
supererogation ˌsuːp ər er ə ˈgeɪʃ ᵊn ˌsjuːp-, ˌ·ə-
supererogatory ˌsuːp ər er ə ˈgeɪt ər i ˌsjuːp-, ˌ· ·ɪˈrɒg ət· · ‖ -ˈrɑːg ə tɔːr i -toʊr i
superficial ˌsuːp ə ˈfɪʃ ᵊl ◂ ˌsjuːp- ‖ -ᵊr- **~ly** i **~ness** nəs nɪs
superficiality ˌsuːp ə ˌfɪʃ i ˈæl ət i ˌsjuːp-, -ɪt i ‖ -ᵊr ˌfɪʃ i ˈæl əţ i
superficies ˌsuːp ə ˈfɪʃ iːz ˌsjuːp-, -ˈfɪʃ i iːz ‖ -ᵊr-
superfine ˈsuːp ə faɪn ˈsjuːp-, ˌ· ·ˈ· ‖ -ᵊr- **~ness** nəs nɪs
superfix ˈsuːp ə fɪks ˈsjuːp- ‖ -ᵊr- **~es** ɪz əz
superfluid ˈsuːp ə ˌfluː‿ɪd ˈsjuːp-, §‿əd ‖ -ᵊr- **~s** z
superfluidity ˌsuːp ə flu ˈɪd ət i ˌsjuːp-, -ɪt i ‖ -ᵊr flu ˈɪd əţ i
superfluit|y ˌsuːp ə ˈfluː‿ət |i ˌsjuːp-, ɪt i ‖ -ᵊr ˈfluː əţ |i **~ies** iz
superfluous su ˈpɜːf lu‿əs sju- ‖ -ˈpɜːf- *(!)* **~ly** li **~ness** nəs nɪs
Superfund ˈsuːp ə fʌnd ˈsjuːp- ‖ -ᵊr-
super-G ˈsuːp ə dʒiː ˈsjuːp- ‖ -ᵊr-
supergiant ˈsuːp ə ˌdʒaɪ‿ənt ˈsjuːp- ‖ -ᵊr- **~s** s
superglue, Super Glue *tdmk* ˈsuːp ə gluː ˈsjuːp- ‖ -ᵊr-
supergrass ˈsuːp ə grɑːs ˈsjuːp-, §-græs ‖ -ᵊr græs **~es** ɪz əz
superhero ˈsuːp ə ˌhɪər əʊ ˈsjuːp-, ˌ· ·ˈ· · ‖ -ᵊr ˌhɪr oʊ -ˌhiː roʊ **~es** z
superhet ˈsuːp ə het ˈsjuːp- ‖ -ᵊr- **~s** s
superhighway ˌsuːp ə ˈhaɪ weɪ ˌsjuːp-, ˈ· ·ˌ· · ‖ -ᵊr- **~s** z
superhuman ˌsuːp ə ˈhjuːm ən ◂ ˌsjuːp-, §-ˈjuːm- ‖ -ᵊr-
ˌsuperˌhuman ˈefforts
superimpos|e ˌsuːp ər‿ɪm ˈpəʊz ˌsjuːp-, ˌ·ə- ‖ -ˈpoʊz **~ed** d **~es** ɪz əz **~ing** ɪŋ
superimposition ˌsuːp ər ˌɪmp ə ˈzɪʃ ᵊn ˌsjuːp-, ˌ·ə-
superintend ˌsuːp ər‿ɪn ˈtend ˌsjuːp-, ˌ·ə-, §‿ənˈ· **~ed** ɪd əd **~ency** ənᵗs i **~ing** ɪŋ **~s** z
superintendent ˌsuːp ər‿ɪn ˈtend ənt ˌsjuːp-, ˌ·ə-, §‿ənˈ-- **~s** s
superior, S~ su ˈpɪər i‿ə sju- ‖ su ˈpɪr i‿ᵊr sə- **~ly** li **~s** z
superiority su ˌpɪər i ˈɒr ət i sju-, -ɪt i ‖ su ˌpɪr i ˈɔːr əţ i sə-, -ˈɑːr-
suˌperiˈority ˌcomplex

superlative su ˈpɜːl ət ɪv sju- ‖ sʊ ˈpɝːl əṭ ɪv **~ly** li **~ness** nəs nɪs **~s** z
supermall ˈsuːp ə mɔːl ˈsjuːp-, -mæl ‖ -ᵊr- -mɑːl **~s** z
super|man, S~ ˈsuːp ə |mæn ˈsjuːp- ‖ -ᵊr- **~men** men
supermarket ˈsuːp ə ˌmɑːk ɪt ˈsjuːp-, §-ət ‖ -ᵊr ˌmɑːrk ət **~s** s
supermen ˈsuːp ə men ˈsjuːp- ‖ -ᵊr-
supermodel ˈsuːp ə ˌmɒd ᵊl ˈsjuːp- ‖ -ᵊr ˌmɑːd ᵊl **~s** z
supermom ˈsuːp ə mɒm ˈsjuːp- ‖ -r mɑːm
supernal su ˈpɜːn ᵊl sju- ‖ -ˈpɝːn- **~ly** i
supernatural ˌsuːp ə ˈnætʃ ᵊr‿əl ◂ ˌsjuːp- ‖ ˌ·ᵊr- **~ly** i **~ness** nəs nɪs
supernormal ˌsuːp ə ˈnɔːm ᵊl ◂ ˌsjuːp- ‖ -ᵊr ˈnɔːrm- **~ly** i
supernov|a ˌsuːp ə ˈnəʊv |ə ˌsjuːp- ‖ -ᵊr ˈnoʊv- **~ae** iː **~as** əz
supernumerar|y ˌsuːp ə ˈnjuːm ᵊr‿ər |i ◂ ˌsjuːp-, ⚠-ˈ·ər |i ‖ ˌsuːp ᵊr ˈnuːm ə rer |i ◂ -ˈnjuːm-, ⚠-ˈ·ər |i **~ies** iz
superordinate *adj, n* ˌsuːp ər ˈɔːd ᵊn‿ət ◂ ˌsjuːp-, ɪt, -ɪn ət, -ɪn ɪt; -ə neɪt, -ᵊn eɪt, -ɪ neɪt ‖ -ᵊr ˈɔːrd- **~s** s
superphosphate ˌsuːp ə ˈfɒs feɪt ˌsjuːp- ‖ -ᵊr ˈfɑːs- **~s** s
superpower ˈsuːp ə ˌpaʊ‿ə ˈsjuːp-, ˌ· ·ˈ· · ‖ -ᵊr ˌpaʊ‿ᵊr **~s** z
supersatu|rate ˌsuːp ə ˈsætʃ ə |reɪt ˌsjuːp-, -ˈsætʃ u-, -ˈsæt ju- ‖ ˌ·ᵊr- **~rated** reɪt ɪd -əd ‖ reɪṭ əd **~rates** reɪts **~rating** reɪt ɪŋ ‖ reɪṭ ɪŋ
superscript ˈsuːp ə skrɪpt ˈsjuːp- ‖ -ᵊr- **~s** s
superscription ˌsuːp ə ˈskrɪp ʃᵊn ˌsjuːp- ‖ -ᵊr- **~s** z
supersed|e ˌsuːp ə ˈsiːd ˌsjuːp- ‖ -ᵊr- **~ed** ɪd əd **~es** z **~ing** ɪŋ
supersession ˌsuːp ə ˈseʃ ᵊn ˌsjuːp- ‖ -ᵊr- **~s** z
superset ˈsuːp ə set ˈsjuːp- ‖ -ᵊr- **~s** s
supersiz|e ˈsuːp ə saɪz ˈsjuːp- ‖ -ᵊr- **~ed** d **~es** ɪz əz **~ing** ɪŋ
supersonic ˌsuːp ə ˈsɒn ɪk ◂ ˌsjuːp- ‖ -ᵊr ˈsɑːn- **~ally** ᵊl‿i **~s** s
superstar ˈsuːp ə stɑː ˈsjuːp- ‖ -ᵊr stɑːr **~dom** dəm **~s** z
superstate ˈsuːp ə steɪt ˈsjuːp- ‖ -ᵊr- **~s** s
superstition ˌsuːp ə ˈstɪʃ ᵊn ˌsjuːp- ‖ -ᵊr- **~s** z
superstitious ˌsuːp ə ˈstɪʃ əs ◂ ˌsjuːp- ‖ -ᵊr- **~ly** li **~ness** nəs nɪs
superstore ˈsuːp ə stɔː ˈsjuːp- ‖ -ᵊr stɔːr -stoʊr **~s** z
superstrate ˈsuːp ə streɪt ˈsjuːp- ‖ -ᵊr- **~s** s
superstring ˈsuːp ə strɪŋ ˈsjuːp- ‖ -ᵊr- **~s** z
superstructure ˈsuːp ə ˌstrʌk tʃə ˈsjuːp-, -ʃə ‖ -ᵊr ˌstrʌk tʃᵊr **~s** z
supertanker ˈsuːp ə ˌtæŋk ə ˈsjuːp- ‖ -ᵊr ˌtæŋk ᵊr **~s** z
supertax ˈsuːp ə tæks ˈsjuːp- ‖ -ᵊr-
supertonic ˌsuːp ə ˈtɒn ɪk ◂ ˌsjuːp-, ˈ· ·ˌ· · ‖ -ᵊr ˈtɑːn- **~s** s
superven|e ˌsuːp ə ˈviːn ˌsjuːp- ‖ -ᵊr- **~ed** d **~es** z **~ing** ɪŋ
supervis|e ˈsuːp ə vaɪz ˈsjuːp ‖ -ᵊr- **~ed** d **~es** ɪz əz **~ing** ɪŋ
supervisee ˌsuːp ə vaɪ ˈziː ˌsjuːp- ‖ ˌ·ᵊr- **~s** z
supervision ˌsuːp ə ˈvɪʒ ᵊn ˌsjuːp- ‖ -ᵊr- **~s** z
supervisor ˈsuːp ə vaɪz ə ˈsjuːp- ‖ -ᵊr vaɪz ᵊr **~s** z
supervisory ˌsuːp ə ˈvaɪz ər i ◂ ˌsjuːp-, -ˈvɪz-; ˈ· · · · · ‖ ˌ·ᵊr-
super|woman ˈsuːp ə |ˌwʊm ən ˈsjuːp- ‖ -ᵊr- **~women** ˌwɪm ɪn §-ən
supi|nate ˈsuːp ɪ |neɪt ˈsjuːp-, -ə- **~nated** neɪt ɪd -əd ‖ neɪṭ əd **~nates** neɪts **~nating** neɪt ɪŋ ‖ neɪṭ ɪŋ
supination ˌsuːp ɪ ˈneɪʃ ᵊn ˌsjuːp-, -ə-
supinator ˈsuːp ɪ neɪt ə ˈsjuːp-, ˈ-ə- ‖ -neɪṭ ᵊr **~s** z
supine *grammatical term* ˈsuːp aɪn ˈsjuːp- **~s** z
supine *'lying on the back'; 'lazy'* ˈsuːp aɪn ˈsjuːp-; ˌsuː ˈpaɪn, ˌsjuː- **~ly** li **~ness** nəs nɪs
Suppé ˈsuːp eɪ ‖ su ˈpeɪ —*Ger* [zʊ ˈpeː]
supper ˈsʌp ə ‖ -ᵊr **~s** z
suppertime ˈsʌp ə taɪm ‖ -ᵊr- **~s** z
sup|plant sə |ˈplɑːnt §-ˈplænt ‖ -|ˈplænt **~planted** ˈplɑːnt ɪd §ˈplænt-, -əd ‖ ˈplænṭ əd **~planting** ˈplɑːnt ɪŋ §ˈplænt- ‖ ˈplænṭ ɪŋ **~plants** ˈplɑːnts §ˈplænts ‖ ˈplænts
supple, S~ ˈsʌp ᵊl **~ly** li **~ness** nəs nɪs
supplejack ˈsʌp ᵊl dʒæk
supplement *n* ˈsʌp lɪ mənt -lə- **~s** s
supple|ment *v* ˈsʌp lɪ |ment -lə-, ˌ· ·ˈ· —*see note at* -ment **~mented** ment ɪd -əd ‖ menṭ əd **~menting** ment ɪŋ ‖ menṭ ɪŋ **~ments** ments
supplemental ˌsʌp lɪ ˈment ᵊl ◂ -lə- ‖ -ˈmenṭ ᵊl **~ly** i
supplementar|y ˌsʌp lɪ ˈment‿ər |i ◂ ˌ·lə- ‖ -ˈmenṭ ər |i -ˈmentr |i **~ies** iz
ˌsuppleˌmentary ˈbenefit
supplementation ˌsʌp lɪ men ˈteɪʃ ᵊn ˌ·lə-, -mən'-
suppletion sə ˈpliːʃ ᵊn
suppletive sə ˈpliːt ɪv ˈsʌp lət ɪv, -lɪt- ‖ sə ˈpliːṭ ɪv ˈsʌp ləṭ ɪv **~s** z
suppliant ˈsʌp li‿ənt **~ly** li **~s** s
supplicant ˈsʌp lɪk ənt -lək- **~s** s
suppli|cate ˈsʌp lɪ |keɪt -lə- **~cated** keɪt ɪd -əd ‖ keɪṭ əd **~cates** keɪts **~cating** keɪt ɪŋ ‖ keɪṭ ɪŋ
supplication ˌsʌp lɪ ˈkeɪʃ ᵊn -lə- **~s** z
supplicatory ˌsʌp lɪ ˈkeɪt‿ər i ◂ ˈ· · ·-; ˈsʌp lɪk ət‿ər i ‖ ˈsʌp lɪk ə tɔːr i -toʊr i *(*)*
supplier sə ˈplaɪ‿ə ‖ -ˈplaɪ‿ᵊr **~s** z
sup|ply *v, n* sə |ˈplaɪ **~plied** ˈplaɪd **~plies** ˈplaɪz **~plying** ˈplaɪ ɪŋ
supˌply and deˈmand; **supˈply ˌteacher**
supply *adv of* **supple** ˈsʌp ᵊl li -ᵊl‿i
supply-sid|e sə ˈplaɪ saɪd **~er/s** ə/z ‖ ᵊr/z
sup|port *v, n* sə |ˈpɔːt ‖ -|ˈpɔːrt -ˈpoʊrt **~ported** ˈpɔːt ɪd -əd ‖ ˈpɔːrṭ əd ˈpoʊrṭ- **~porting** ˈpɔːt ɪŋ ‖ ˈpɔːrṭ ɪŋ ˈpoʊrṭ- **~ports** ˈpɔːts ‖ ˈpɔːrts ˈpoʊrts
supˌporting ˈpart; **supˌporting ˈprogramme**; **supˌporting ˈrole**

supportab|le sə ˈpɔːt əb |əl ‖ -ˈpɔːrţ- -ˈpourţ- **~ly** li
supporter sə ˈpɔːt ə ‖ -ˈpɔːrţ ər -ˈpourţ- **~s** z
supˈporters' club
supportive sə ˈpɔːt ɪv ‖ -ˈpɔːrţ- -ˈpourţ- **~ly** li **~ness** nəs nɪs
suppos|e sə ˈpəuz ‖ -ˈpouz *—but the phrase* I suppose *is often* aɪ ˈspəuz ‖ -ˈspouz **~es** ɪz əz **~ing** ɪŋ
supposed *in* (be) supposed to *'ought to'* sə ˈpəust →ˈspəust; səˈpəuzd ‖ -ˈpouzd
supposed *past and pp of* **suppose** sə ˈpəuzd ‖ -ˈpouzd
supposed *adj* sə ˈpəuzd -ˈpəuz ɪd, -əd ‖ -ˈpouzd -ˈpouz əd
supposedly sə ˈpəuz ɪd li -əd- ‖ -ˈpouz-
supposition ˌsʌp ə ˈzɪʃ ən **~s** z
suppositional ˌsʌp ə ˈzɪʃ ən‿əl **~ly** i
suppositious ˌsʌp ə ˈzɪʃ əs ◂
supposititious sə ˌpɒz ɪ ˈtɪʃ əs ◂ -ə- ‖ -ˌpɑːz- **~ly** li **~ness** nəs nɪs
suppositive sə ˈpɒz ət ɪv -ɪt- ‖ -ˈpɑːz əţ- **~ly** li **~s** z
suppositor|y sə ˈpɒz ɪt‿ər |i -ˈət‿ ‖ sə ˈpɑːz ə tɔːr |i -tour i **~ies** iz
suppress sə ˈpres **~ed** t **~es** ɪz əz **~ing** ɪŋ
suppressant sə ˈpres ənt **~s** s
suppression sə ˈpreʃ ən **~s** z
suppressive sə ˈpres ɪv **~ly** li
suppressor sə ˈpres ə ‖ -ər **~s** z
suppu|rate ˈsʌp juə |reɪt -jə- ‖ -jə- **~rated** reɪt ɪd -əd ‖ reɪţ əd **~rates** reɪts **~rating** reɪt ɪŋ ‖ reɪţ ɪŋ
suppuration ˌsʌp juə ˈreɪʃ ən -jə- -jə-
suppurative ˈsʌp jʊr ət ɪv ˈ·jər-; -ju reɪt ɪv, -jə · · ‖ ˈsʌp jər əţ ɪv -jə reɪţ-; ˈsʌp rəţ ɪv **~s** z
supra ˈsuːp rə ˈsjuːp-, -rɑː
supra- ¦suːp rə ¦sjuːp— **suprarenal** ˌsuːp rə ˈriːn əl ◂ ˌsjuːp-
supraglottal ˌsuːp rə ˈglɒt əl ◂ ˌsjuːp- ‖ -ˈglɑːţ-
ˌsupraˌglottal ˈtract
supralapsarian ˌsuːp rə læp ˈseər i‿ən ◂ ˌsjuːp- ‖ -ˈser- -ˈsær- **~ism** ˌɪz əm
supranational ˌsuːp rə ˈnæʃ ən‿əl ◂ ˌsjuːp-
suprasegmental ˌsuːp rə seg ˈment əl ◂ ˌsjuːp- ‖ -ˈmenţ- **~s** z
supremacist su ˈprem əs ɪst sju-, §-əst **~s** s
supremac|y su ˈprem əs |i sju- **~ies** iz
supreme *French word, cooking term,* **suprême** su ˈpriːm sju-, -ˈprem, -ˈpreɪm *—Fr* [sy pʁɛm]
supreme *'highest', 'greatest', 'ultimate'* su ˈpriːm sju-, ˌsuː-, ˌsjuː- **~ly** li **~ness** nəs nɪs **S~s** z
SuˌpremeˈBeing; **SuˌpremeˈCourt**
supremo su ˈpriːm əu sju- ‖ -ou **~s** z
sur- ¦sɜː ‖ ¦sɜ˞ː *but in certain words* sə ‖ sər —**surrejoinder** ˌsɜː rɪ ˈdʒɔɪnd ə -rə-, §-riː- ‖ ˌsɜ˞ː rɪ ˈdʒɔɪnd ər
sura ˈsuər ə ‖ ˈsur ə **~s** z
Surabaya ˌsuər ə ˈbaɪ‿ə ‖ ˌsur ə ˈbɑː jə
surah ˈsuər ə ‖ ˈsur ə **~s** z
sural ˈsjuər əl ˈsuər- ‖ ˈsur əl
Surbiton ˈsɜːb ɪt ən §-ət- ‖ ˈsɜ˞ːb ət ən

surceas|e (ˌ)sɜː ˈsiːs ˈ· · ‖ (ˌ)sɜ˞ː- **~ed** t **~es** ɪz əz **~ing** ɪŋ
surcharg|e *n, v* ˈsɜː tʃɑːdʒ (ˌ)sɜː ˈtʃɑːdʒ ‖ ˈsɜ˞ː tʃɑːrdʒ **~ed** d **~es** ɪz əz **~ing** ɪŋ
surcingle ˈsɜː ˌsɪŋ gəl ‖ ˈsɜ˞ː- **~s** z
surcoat ˈsɜː kəut ‖ ˈsɜ˞ː kout **~s** s
surd sɜːd ‖ sɜ˞ːd **surds** sɜːdz ‖ sɜ˞ːdz

SURE

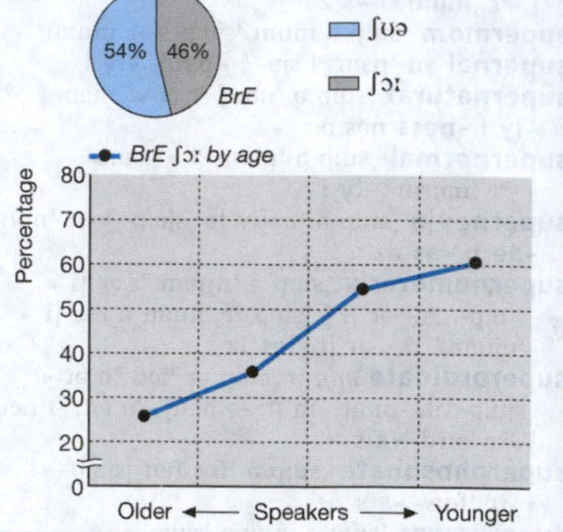

sure ʃɔː ʃuə ‖ ʃuər ʃɜ˞ː *— Preference poll, BrE:* ʃɔː *46% (born since 1973: 60%),* ʃuə *54%.*
surer ˈʃɔːr ə ˈʃuər ə ‖ ˈʃur ər ˈʃɜ˞ː- **surest** ˈʃɔːr ɪst ˈʃuər-, -əst ‖ ˈʃur əst ˈʃɜ˞ː-
ˌsure ˈthing
surefire ˈʃɔː ˌfaɪ‿ə ˈʃuə- ‖ ˈʃur ˌfaɪ‿ər ˈʃɜ˞ː-
surefooted ˌʃɔː ˈfut ɪd ◂ ˌʃuə-, -əd ‖ ˌʃur ˈfuţ əd ◂ ˌʃɜ˞ː-, ˈ·ˌ· · **~ness** nəs nɪs
sure|ly ˈʃɔː |li ˈʃuə- ‖ ˈʃur |li ˈʃɜ˞ː- **~ness** nəs nɪs
suret|y ˈʃɔːr ət |i ˈʃuər-, ɪt- ‖ ˈʃur əţ |i ˈʃɜ˞ː-; ˈʃurţ |i, ˈʃɜ˞ːţ i *—in RP formerly also* ˈʃuət |i **~ies** iz **~yship/s** i ʃɪp/s
surf sɜːf ‖ sɜ˞ːf **surfed** sɜːft ‖ sɜ˞ːft **surfing** ˈsɜːf ɪŋ ‖ ˈsɜ˞ːf ɪŋ **surfs** sɜːfs ‖ sɜ˞ːfs
surfac|e *n, v, adj* ˈsɜːf ɪs -əs ‖ ˈsɜ˞ːf əs **~ed** t **~es** ɪz əz **~ing** ɪŋ
ˈsurface mail; **ˈsurface noise**; **ˈsurface ˌstructure**; **ˌsurface ˈtension**
surface-to-air ˌsɜːf ɪs tu ˈeə ◂ ˌ·əs- ‖ ˌsɜ˞ːf əs tə ˈeər ◂ -ˈæər
surface-to-surface ˌsɜːf ɪs tə ˈsɜːf ɪs ◂ -əs tə-, -əs ‖ ˌsɜ˞ːf əs tə ˈsɜ˞ːf əs ◂
surfactant sɜː ˈfækt ənt sə-; ˈsɜː fækt ənt ‖ sɜ˞ː- **~s** s
surfboard ˈsɜːf bɔːd ‖ ˈsɜ˞ːf bɔːrd -bourd **~er/s** ə/z ‖ ər/z **~ing** ɪŋ **~s** z
surfboat ˈsɜːf bəut ‖ ˈsɜ˞ːf bout **~s** s
surf|eit *n, v* ˈsɜːf |ɪt -ət, -iːt ‖ ˈsɜ˞ːf |ət **~eited** ɪt ɪd ət-, iːt-, -əd ‖ əţ əd **~eiting** ɪt ɪŋ ət-, iːt- ‖ əţ ɪŋ **~eits** ɪts əts, iːts ‖ əts
surfer ˈsɜːf ə ‖ ˈsɜ˞ːf ər **~s** z
surfie ˈsɜːf i ‖ ˈsɜ˞ːf i **~s** z
surfing ˈsɜːf ɪŋ ‖ ˈsɜ˞ːf ɪŋ
surfrid|ing ˈsɜːf ˌraɪd |ɪŋ ‖ ˈsɜ˞ːf- **~er/s** ə/z ‖ ər/z

S

surge sɜːdʒ ‖ sɜ˞ːdʒ **surged** sɜːdʒd ‖ sɜ˞ːdʒd **surges** 'sɜːdʒ ɪz -əz ‖ 'sɜ˞ːdʒ əz **surging** 'sɜːdʒ ɪŋ ‖ 'sɜ˞ːdʒ ɪŋ
surgeon 'sɜːdʒ ən ‖ 'sɜ˞ːdʒ ən **~s** z
surger|y 'sɜːdʒ ər‿i ‖ 'sɜ˞ːdʒ- **~ies** iz
surgical 'sɜːdʒ ɪk ᵊl ‖ 'sɜ˞ːdʒ- **~ly** ‿i
ˌsurgical 'spirit
suricate 'sʊər ɪ keɪt 'sjʊər-, -ə- ‖ 'sʊr- **~s** s
surimi su 'riːm i —*Jp* [sɯ ˌri 'mi]
Surinam, Suriname ˌsʊər ɪ 'næm ˌsjʊər-, -ə-; '· · · ‖ 'sʊr ə nɑːm -næm —*Dutch* [sy ri 'naː mə]
Surinamese ˌsʊər ɪ næ 'miːz ◂ ˌsjʊər-, ˌ-ə-, -nə'- ‖ ˌsʊr ə nə 'miːz ◂ -'miːs
surly 'sɜːl i ‖ 'sɜ˞ːl i **surlier** 'sɜːl i‿ə ‖ 'sɜ˞ːl i‿ᵊr **surliest** 'sɜːl i‿ɪst əst ‖ 'sɜ˞ːl- **surlily** 'sɜːl ɪl i -əl- ‖ 'sɜ˞ːl- **surliness** 'sɜːl i nəs -nɪs ‖ 'sɜ˞ːl-
surmis|e *v, n* sə 'maɪz sɜː-; 'sɜː maɪz ‖ sᵊr- **~ed** d **~es** ɪz əz **~ing** ɪŋ
sur|mount sə |'maʊnt sɜː- ‖ sᵊr- **~mounted** 'maʊnt ɪd -əd ‖ 'maʊnt̬ əd **~mounting** 'maʊnt ɪŋ ‖ 'maʊnt̬ ɪŋ **~mounts** 'maʊnts
surname 'sɜː neɪm ‖ 'sɜ˞ː- **~d** d **~s** z
surpass sə 'pɑːs sɜː-, §-'pæs ‖ sᵊr 'pæs **~ed** t **~es** ɪz əz **~ing/ly** ɪŋ /li
surplic|e 'sɜːp ləs -lɪs ‖ 'sɜ˞ːp- **~ed** t **~es** ɪz əz
surplus 'sɜːp ləs ‖ 'sɜ˞ː plʌs 'sɜ˞ːp ləs **~es** ɪz əz
surpris|e sə 'praɪz ‖ sᵊr- sə- **~ed** d **~es** ɪz əz **~ing/ly** ɪŋ /li
sur'prise ˌparty
surreal sə 'rɪəl -'riːᵊl ‖ -'riːᵊl **~ly** i
surrealism sə 'rɪəl ˌɪz əm -'riːᵊl- ‖ sə 'riː ə ˌlɪz əm
surrealist sə 'rɪəl ɪst -'riːᵊl-, §-əst ‖ sə 'riː əl əst **~s** s
surrealistic sə ˌrɪə 'lɪst ɪk ◂ sjʊ-, -ˌriː ə '- ‖ sə ˌriː ə 'lɪst ɪk ◂ **~ally** ᵊl‿i
surrebutter ˌsʌr i 'bʌt ə -ə- ‖ ˌsɜ˞ː ri 'bʌt̬ ᵊr -ɪ- **~s** z
surrejoinder ˌsʌr i 'dʒɔɪnd ə -ə- ‖ ˌsɜ˞ː ri 'dʒɔɪnd ᵊr -ɪ- **~s** z
surrender sə 'rend ə ‖ -ᵊr **~ed** d **surrendering** sə 'rend‿ər ɪŋ **~s** z
sur'render ˌvalue
surreptitious ˌsʌr əp 'tɪʃ əs ◂ -ɪp-, -ep- ‖ ˌsɜ˞ː- **~ly** li **~ness** nəs nɪs
Surrey, s~ 'sʌr i ‖ 'sɜ˞ː i **~s** z
Surridge 'sʌr ɪdʒ ‖ 'sɜ˞ː-
surrogacy 'sʌr əg əs i ‖ 'sɜ˞ː-
surrogate *n, adj* 'sʌr əg ət -ɪt, -ə geɪt ‖ 'sɜ˞ː- **~s** s **~ship** ʃɪp
surround sə 'raʊnd **~ed** ɪd əd **~ing/s** ɪŋ/z **~s** z
surround-sound sə 'raʊnd saʊnd
sursum corda ˌsɜːs əm 'kɔːd ə -ʊm- ‖ ˌsʊrs əm 'kɔːrd ə -'koʊrd-, -ɑː
surtax 'sɜː tæks ‖ 'sɜ˞ː- **~ed** t **~es** ɪz əz **~ing** ɪŋ
Surtees 'sɜː tiːz ‖ 'sɜ˞ː-
surtitle 'sɜː ˌtaɪt ᵊl ‖ 'sɜ˞ː ˌtaɪt̬ ᵊl **~ed** d **~ing** ‿ɪŋ **~s** z
Surtsey 'sɜːts i -eɪ ‖ 'sɜ˞ːts i —*Icelandic* ['syr̥ts ei]
surveil sə 'veɪᵊl **~led** d **~ling** ɪŋ **~s** z
surveillance sə 'veɪl ənᵗs sɜː- ‖ sᵊr- -jənᵗs; -'veɪ-
survey *n* 'sɜːv eɪ ˌ·'·, sə 'veɪ ‖ 'sɜ˞ːv eɪ sᵊr 'veɪ **~s** z
survey *v* sə 'veɪ sɜː-; 'sɜːv eɪ ‖ sᵊr- **~ed** d **~ing** ɪŋ **~s** z
surveyor sə 'veɪ ə ‖ sᵊr 'veɪ ᵊr **~s** z
survivability sə ˌvaɪv ə 'bɪl ət i -ɪt i ‖ sᵊr ˌvaɪv ə 'bɪl ət̬ i
survivable sə 'vaɪv əb ᵊl ‖ sᵊr-
survival sə 'vaɪv ᵊl ‖ sᵊr- **~s** z
sur'vival kit; **surˌvival of the 'fittest**; **sur'vival ˌvalue**
survivalist sə 'vaɪv ᵊl ɪst §-əst ‖ sᵊr- **~s** s
surviv|e sə 'vaɪv ‖ sᵊr- **~ed** d **~es** z **~ing** ɪŋ
survivor sə 'vaɪv ə ‖ sᵊr 'vaɪv ᵊr **~s** z **~ship** ʃɪp
sus sʌs **sussed** sʌst **susses** 'sʌs ɪz -əz **sussing** 'sʌs ɪŋ
Susa 'suːz ə 'suːs-
Susan 'suːz ᵊn
Susann su 'zæn
Susanna, Susannah su 'zæn ə
susceptance sə 'sept ənᵗs
susceptibilit|y sə ˌsept ə 'bɪl ət |i -ˌ·ɪ-, -ɪt i ‖ -ət̬ |i **~ies** iz
susceptib|le sə 'sept əb |ᵊl -ɪb- **~leness** ᵊl nəs -nɪs **~ly** li
susceptive sə 'sept ɪv **~ness** nəs nɪs
susceptivity ˌsʌs ep 'tɪv ət i -ɪt i ‖ -ət̬ i
sushi 'suːʃ i 'sʊʃ-, -iː —*Jp* [sɯ̥ 'ɕi]
Susie 'suːz i
suslik 'sʊs lɪk 'sʌs-, 'suːs- **~s** s
suspect *v* sə 'spekt **~ed** ɪd əd **~ing** ɪŋ **~s** s
suspect *n, adj* 'sʌsp ekt **~s** s
suspend sə 'spend **~ed** ɪd əd **~ing** ɪŋ **~s** z
suˌspended 'sentence
suspender sə 'spend ə ‖ -ᵊr **~s** z
su'spender belt
suspense sə 'spenᵗs **~ful** fᵊl fʊl
suspension sə 'spenᵗʃ ᵊn **~s** z
su'spension bridge
suspensive sə 'spenᵗs ɪv **~ly** li **~ness** nəs nɪs
suspensor|y sə 'spenᵗs ər‿|i **~ies** iz
suspicion sə 'spɪʃ ᵊn **~s** z
suspicious sə 'spɪʃ əs **~ly** li **~ness** nəs nɪs
Susquehann|a ˌsʌsk wɪ 'hæn |ə -wə- **~ock** ək
suss sʌs **sussed** sʌst **susses** 'sʌs ɪz -əz **sussing** 'sʌs ɪŋ
Sussex 'sʌs ɪks §-əks
Susskind 'sʊs kɪnd 'sʌs-
sustain sə 'steɪn **~ed** d **~ing** ɪŋ **~s** z
sustainability sə ˌsteɪn ə 'bɪl ət i -ɪt i ‖ -ət̬ i
sustainable sə 'steɪn əb ᵊl
sustainer sə 'steɪn ə ‖ -ᵊr **~s** z
sustainment sə 'steɪn mənt →-'steɪm-
sustenance 'sʌst ən‿ənᵗs -ɪn-
sustentation ˌsʌst en 'teɪʃ ᵊn -ən-
sustention sə 'stenᵗʃ ᵊn
Sustrans 'sʌs trænz -trɑːnz, -trænᵗs, -trɑːnᵗs ‖ -trænᵗs -trænz
Sutch sʌtʃ
Sutcliff, Sutcliffe 'sʌt klɪf

S

Sutherland ˈsʌð ə lənd ‖ -ᵊr-
Sutlej ˈsʌt lɪdʒ -ledʒ
sutler ˈsʌt lə ‖ -lᵊr **~s** z
sutra, Sutra ˈsuːtr ə **~s** z
Sutro ˈsuːtr əʊ ‖ -oʊ
suttee ˈsʌt iː sʌ ˈtiː *—Hindi* [sə t̪iː] **~s** z
Sutter ˈsʌt ə ‖ ˈsʌţ ᵊr *—but the 19th-century German-born owner of* ˌSutter's ˈMill, *CA, (Ger* Suter [ˈzuː tɐ]*) is sometimes referred to as* ˈsuːt ə ‖ ˈsuːţ ᵊr
Sutton ˈsʌt ᵊn
ˌSutton ˈColdfield ˈkəʊld fiːᵊld →ˈkɒʊld-;
ˌSutton ˈHoo
Suttor ˈsʌt ə ‖ ˈsʌţ ᵊr
suture ˈsuːtʃ ə ‖ ˈsuːtʃ ᵊr *—There are also very careful or precious variants* ˈsjuːt jʊə, ˈsuːt-, -jə ‖ -jʊr, -jᵊr **~d** d **~s** z **suturing** ˈsuːtʃ ər ɪŋ
SUV ˌes juː ˈviː **~s** z
Suva ˈsuːv ə
Suwannee sə ˈwɒn i su- ‖ -ˈwɑːn- -ˈwɔːn-
Suzanna, Suzannah su ˈzæn ə
Suzanne su ˈzæn
suzerain ˈsuːz ə reɪn ˈsjuːz-, -ᵊr‿ən **~s** z
suzerain|ty ˈsuːz ə reɪn |ti ˈsjuːz-, -ᵊr‿ən |ti **~ties** tiz
Suzette su ˈzet
Suzhou ˌsuː ˈdʒəʊ ‖ -ˈdʒoʊ *—Chi* Sūzhōu [¹su ¹ţsou]
Suzie ˈsuːz i
Suzman *(i)* ˈsʊz mən, *(ii)* ˈsuːz mən
Suzuki *tdmk* sə ˈzuːk i su- *—Jp* [sɯ ˌdzɯ ki] **~s** z
Suzy ˈsuːz i
Svalbard ˈsvæl bɑːd ˈsvɑːl-, -bɑː ‖ ˈsvɑːl bɑːrd -bɑːr *—Norw* [ˈsvɑːl bar]
svarabhakti ˌsfʌr ə ˈbʌkt i ˌsfɑːr-; ˌsfær ə ˈbækt i *—Hindi* [sʋər bək t̪i]
svelte sfelt svelt **svelter** ˈsfelt ə ˈsvelt- ‖ -ᵊr **sveltest** ˈsfelt ɪst ˈsvelt-, -əst
Svengali, s~ sfen ˈɡɑːl i sven-, →sfeŋ-
Sverdlovsk ˌsfeəd ˈlɒfsk -ˈlɒvsk; ·ˈ· ‖ ˌsferd ˈlɔːfsk -lɑːfsk *—Russ* [svʲɪr ˈdłɔfsk]
swab swɒb ‖ swɑːb **swabbed** swɒbd ‖ swɑːbd **swabbing** ˈswɒb ɪŋ ‖ ˈswɑːb ɪŋ **swabs** swɒbz ‖ swɑːbz
swabber ˈswɒb ə ‖ ˈswɑːb ᵊr **~s** z
Swabi|a ˈsweɪb i‿|ə **~an/s** ən/z
Swaby ˈsweɪb i
swaddie ˈswɒd i ‖ ˈswɑːd i **~s** z
swaddl|e ˈswɒd ᵊl ‖ ˈswɑːd ᵊl **~ed** d **~es** z **~ing** ‿ɪŋ
ˈswaddling clothes
swadd|y ˈswɒd |i ‖ ˈswɑːd |i **~ies** iz
Swadlincote ˈswɒd lɪn kəʊt →-lɪŋ-, §-lən- ‖ ˈswɑːd lən koʊt
Swaffer ˈswɒf ə ‖ ˈswɑːf ᵊr
Swaffham ˈswɒf əm ‖ ˈswɑːf-
Swaffield ˈswɒf iːᵊld ‖ ˈswɑːf-
swag swæɡ
swage sweɪdʒ **swaged** sweɪdʒd **swages** ˈsweɪdʒ ɪz -əz **swaging** ˈsweɪdʒ ɪŋ
Swaggart ˈswæɡ ət ‖ -ᵊrt
swagger ˈswæɡ ə ‖ -ᵊr **~ed** d **swaggering/ly** ˈswæɡ ər‿ɪŋ /li **~s** z
ˈswagger stick
swaggerer ˈswæɡ ər ə ‖ -ᵊr ər **~s** z
swag|man ˈswæɡ |mæn -mən **~men** men mən *—in Australia,* -mən
Swahili swə ˈhiːl i swɑː- **~s** z
swain, Swain sweɪn **swains, Swain's** sweɪnz
Swainson ˈsweɪn sən
Swalcliffe ˈsweɪ klɪf
Swale, swale sweɪᵊl **swales** sweɪᵊlz
Swaledale ˈsweɪᵊl deɪᵊl
Swales sweɪᵊlz
swallow, S~ ˈswɒl əʊ ‖ ˈswɑːl oʊ **~ed** d **~er/s** ə/z ‖ ᵊr/z **~ing** ɪŋ **~s** z
ˈswallow dive
swallowtail ˈswɒl əʊ teɪᵊl ‖ ˈswɑːl oʊ- -ə- **~ed** d **~s** z
swam swæm
swami, Swami ˈswɑːm i *—Hindi* [sʋaː mi] **~s** z
swamp swɒmp ‖ swɑːmp swɔːmp **swamped** swɒm*p*t ‖ swɑːm*p*t swɔːm*p*t **swamping** ˈswɒmp ɪŋ ‖ ˈswɑːmp ɪŋ ˈswɔːmp- **swamps** ˈswɒm*p*s ‖ swɑːm*p*s swɔːm*p*s
swamper ˈswɒmp ə ‖ ˈswɑːmp ᵊr ˈswɔːmp- **~s** z
swampland ˈswɒmp lænd ‖ ˈswɑːmp- ˈswɔːmp- **~s** z
swamp|y, S~ ˈswɒmp |i ‖ ˈswɑːmp |i ˈswɔːmp |i **~ier** i‿ə ‖ i‿ᵊr **~iest** i‿ɪst i‿əst **~iness** i nəs i nɪs
swan, Swan swɒn ‖ swɑːn **swanned** swɒnd ‖ swɑːnd **swanning** ˈswɒn ɪŋ ‖ ˈswɑːn ɪŋ **swans** swɒnz ‖ swɑːnz
ˈswan dive
Swanage ˈswɒn ɪdʒ ‖ ˈswɑːn-
Swanee ˈswɒn i ‖ ˈswɑːn i ˈswɔːn i
swank swæŋk **swanked** swæŋ*k*t **swanking** ˈswæŋk ɪŋ **swanks** swæŋ*k*s
swank|y ˈswæŋk |i **~ier** i‿ə ‖ i‿ᵊr **~iest** i‿ɪst i‿əst **~ily** ɪ li əl i **~iness** i nəs i nɪs
Swanley ˈswɒn li ‖ ˈswɑːn-
Swann swɒn ‖ swɑːn
swanner|y ˈswɒn ər |i ‖ ˈswɑːn- **~ies** iz
Swanscombe ˈswɒnz kəm ‖ ˈswɑːnz-
swansdown, swan's-down ˈswɒnz daʊn ‖ ˈswɑːnz-
Swansea *place in Wales* ˈswɒnz i ‖ ˈswɑːn siː ˈswɑːnz i
Swanson ˈswɒnᵗs ən ‖ ˈswɑːnᵗs ən
swansong ˈswɒn sɒŋ ‖ ˈswɑːn sɔːŋ -sɑːŋ **~s** z
Swanton ˈswɒnt ən ‖ ˈswɑːnt ᵊn
swan-upp|ing ˌswɒn ˈʌp |ɪŋ ˈ·ˌ·· ‖ ˌswɑːn- **~er/s** ə/z ‖ ᵊr/z
Swanwick ˈswɒn ɪk ‖ ˈswɑːn-
swap swɒp ‖ swɑːp **swapped** swɒpt ‖ swɑːpt **swapping** ˈswɒp ɪŋ ‖ ˈswɑːp ɪŋ **swaps** swɒps ‖ swɑːps
ˈswap meet
SWAPO ˈswɑːp əʊ ˈswɒp- ‖ -oʊ
Swarbrick ˈswɔː brɪk ‖ ˈswɔːr-

sward swɔːd ‖ swɔːrd **swards** swɔːdz ‖ swɔːrdz
sware sweə ‖ sweᵊr swæᵊr
swarf swɔːf swɑːf ‖ swɔːrf
Swarfega *tdmk* swɔː ˈfiːg ə swɑː- ‖ swɔːr-
Swarkeston, Swarkestone ˈswɔːkst ən ‖ ˈswɔːrkst-
swarm swɔːm ‖ swɔːrm **swarmed** swɔːmd ‖ swɔːrmd **swarming** ˈswɔːm ɪŋ ‖ ˈswɔːrm ɪŋ **swarms** swɔːmz ‖ swɔːrmz
Swarofski *tdmk* swə ˈrɒf ski ‖ -ˈrɑːf- -ˈrɔːf-
swart, Swart swɔːt ‖ swɔːrt
swarth|y ˈswɔːð |i ‖ ˈswɔːrð |i **~ier** i‿ə ‖ i‿ᵊr **~iest** i‿ɪst i‿əst **~ily** ɪ li əl i **~iness** i nəs i nɪs
swash swɒʃ ‖ swɑːʃ swɔːʃ **swashed** swɒʃt ‖ swɑːʃt swɔːʃt **swashes** ˈswɒʃ ɪz -əz ‖ ˈswɑːʃ əz ˈswɔːʃ- **swashing** ˈswɒʃ ɪŋ ‖ ˈswɑːʃ ɪŋ ˈswɔːʃ-
swashbuckl|er ˈswɒʃ ˌbʌk ᵊl‿|ə ‖ ˈswɑːʃ ˌbʌk ᵊl‿|ər ˈswɔːʃ- **~ers** əz ‖ ᵊrz **~ing** ɪŋ
swastika ˈswɒst ɪk ə ‖ ˈswɑːst- **~s** z
swat, Swat, SWAT swɒt ‖ swɑːt *(= swot)* **swats** swɒts ‖ swɑːts **swatted** ˈswɒt ɪd -əd ‖ ˈswɑːṭ əd **swatting** ˈswɒt ɪŋ ‖ ˈswɑːṭ ɪŋ
swatch, Swatch *tdmk* swɒtʃ ‖ swɑːtʃ **swatches** ˈswɒtʃ ɪz -əz ‖ ˈswɑːtʃ əz
swath swɒθ swɔːθ ‖ swɑːθ swɔːθ **swaths** swɒθs swɔːθs, swɔːðz ‖ swɑːθs swɔːθs
swathe sweɪð **swathed** sweɪðd **swathes** sweɪðz **swathing** ˈsweɪð ɪŋ
Swatow ˌswɑː ˈtaʊ —*Chi* Shàntóu [⁴ʂan ²tʰou]
swatter ˈswɒt ə ‖ ˈswɑːṭ ᵊr **~s** z
Swavesey ˈsweɪvz i ˈsweɪv əz i
sway, Sway sweɪ **swayed** sweɪd **swaying/ly** ˈsweɪ ɪŋ /li **sways** sweɪz
swayback ˈsweɪ bæk **~ed** t
Swayze ˈsweɪz i
Swazi ˈswɑːz i **~s** z
Swaziland ˈswɑːz i lænd
swear sweə ‖ sweᵊr **swearing** ˈsweər ɪŋ ‖ ˈswer ɪŋ **swears** sweəz ‖ sweᵊrz **swore** swɔː ‖ swɔːr swoʊr
swearer ˈsweər ə ‖ ˈswer ᵊr **~s** z
swearing-in ˌsweər ɪŋ ˈɪn ‖ ˌswer-
swearword ˈsweə wɜːd ‖ ˈswer wɜːd **~s** z
sweat swet **sweated** ˈswet ɪd -əd ‖ ˈsweṭ əd **sweating** ˈswet ɪŋ ‖ ˈsweṭ ɪŋ **sweats** swets **ˈsweat gland**
sweatband ˈswet bænd **~s** z
sweater ˈswet ə ‖ ˈsweṭ ᵊr **~s** z
sweatpants ˈswet pænts
sweatshirt ˈswet ʃɜːt ‖ -ʃɜ˞ːt **~s** s
sweatshop ˈswet ʃɒp ‖ -ʃɑːp **~s** s
sweatsuit ˈswet suːt -sjuːt **~s** s
sweat|y ˈswet |i ‖ ˈsweṭ |i **~ier** i‿ə ‖ i‿ᵊr **~iest** i‿ɪst i‿əst **~ily** ɪ li əl i **~iness** i nəs i nɪs
Swede, swede swiːd **Swedes, swedes** swiːdz
Sweden ˈswiːd ᵊn
Swedenborg ˈswiːd ᵊn bɔːg ‖ -bɔːrg —*Swedish* [ˈsveː dən bɔrj]
Swedenborgian ˌswiːd ᵊn ˈbɔːdʒ i‿ən ◂ -ˈbɔːg- ‖ -ˈbɔːrdʒ- -ˈbɔːrg- **~s** z
Swedish ˈswiːd ɪʃ
Sweeney ˈswiːn i **ˌSweeney ˈTodd**
sweeny ˈswiːn i
sweep swiːp **sweeping** ˈswiːp ɪŋ **sweeps** swiːps **swept** swept
sweeper ˈswiːp ə ‖ -ᵊr **~s** z
sweeping ˈswiːp ɪŋ **~ly** li **~s** z
sweepstake ˈswiːp steɪk **~s** s
sweet, Sweet swiːt **sweeter** ˈswiːt ə ‖ ˈswiːṭ ᵊr **sweetest** ˈswiːt ɪst -əst ‖ ˈswiːṭ əst **ˌsweet ˈgum**; **ˌsweet ˈnothings**; **ˌsweet ˈpea** ‖ ˈ· ·; **ˌsweet ˈpea**; **ˌsweet poˈtato** ‖ ˈ· ·ˌ· ·; **ˈsweet talk**; **ˌsweet ˈtooth** ‖ ˈ· ·; **ˌsweet ˈwilliam**
sweet-and-sour ˌswiːt ᵊn ˈsaʊ‿ə ◂ -ᵊnd- ‖ -ˈsaʊ‿ᵊr
sweetbread ˈswiːt bred **~s** z
sweetbriar, sweetbrier ˈswiːt ˌbraɪ‿ə ‖ -ˌbraɪ‿ᵊr **~s** z
sweetcorn ˈswiːt kɔːn ‖ -kɔːrn
sweeten ˈswiːt ᵊn **~ed** d **~er/s** ‿ə/z ‖ ᵊr/z **~ing** ‿ɪŋ **~s** z
Sweetex *tdmk* ˈswiːt eks
sweetheart ˈswiːt hɑːt ‖ -hɑːrt **~s** s
sweetie ˈswiːt i ‖ ˈswiːṭ i **~s** z
sweeting, S~ ˈswiːt ɪŋ ‖ ˈswiːṭ ɪŋ
sweetish ˈswiːt ɪʃ ‖ ˈswiːṭ ɪʃ
sweetlip ˈswiːt lɪp **~s** s
sweetly ˈswiːt li
sweetmeal ˈswiːt miːᵊl
sweetmeat ˈswiːt miːt **~s** s
sweetness ˈswiːt nəs -nɪs
sweetshop ˈswiːt ʃɒp ‖ -ʃɑːp **~s** s
sweetsop ˈswiːt sɒp ‖ -sɑːp **~s** s
sweet-talk ˈswiːt tɔːk ,ˌˈ ‖ -tɑːk **~ed** t **~ing** ɪŋ **~s** s
sweet-tempered ˌswiːt ˈtemp əd ◂ ‖ -ᵊrd ◂
swell swel **swelled** sweld **swelling/s** ˈswel ɪŋ/z **swells** swelz **swollen** ˈswəʊl ən ‖ ˈswoʊl ən
swelter ˈswelt ə ‖ -ᵊr **~ed** d **sweltering/ly** ˈswelt‿ər ɪŋ /li **~s** z
swept swept
swept-back ˌswept ˈbæk ◂ ˈ· ·
swept-wing ˌswept ˈwɪŋ ◂
swerve swɜːv ‖ swɜ˞ːv **swerved** swɜːvd ‖ swɜ˞ːvd **swerves** swɜːvz ‖ swɜ˞ːvz **swerving** ˈswɜːv ɪŋ ‖ ˈswɜ˞ːv ɪŋ
Swetenham, Swettenham ˈswet ᵊn‿əm
swift, Swift swɪft **swifter** ˈswɪft ə ‖ -ᵊr **swiftest** ˈswɪft ɪst -əst **swifts** swɪfts
swiftlet ˈswɪft lət -lɪt **~s** s
swift|ly ˈswɪft |li **~ness** nəs nɪs
swig swɪg **swigged** swɪgd **swigging** ˈswɪg ɪŋ **swigs** swɪgz
swill swɪl **swilled** swɪld **swilling** ˈswɪl ɪŋ **swills** swɪlz
swim swɪm **swam** swæm **swimming** ˈswɪm ɪŋ **swims** swɪmz **swum** swʌm **ˈswimming bath**; **ˈswimming ˌcostume**; **ˈswimming pool**; **ˈswimming trunks**
swimathon ˈswɪm ə θɒn ‖ -θɑːn **~s** z

S

swimmer ˈswɪm ə ‖ -ᵊr **~s** z
swimmeret ˈswɪm ə ret ˌ· ·ˈ· **~s** s
swimmingly ˈswɪm ɪŋ li
swimsuit ˈswɪm suːt -sjuːt **~s** s
swimwear ˈswɪm weə ‖ -wer -wær
Swinbourne ˈswɪn bɔːn →ˈswɪm- ‖ -bɔːrn -boʊrn
Swinburn, Swinburne ˈswɪn bɜːn →ˈswɪm- ‖ -bɝːn
Swindells *(i)* ˈswɪnd ᵊlz, *(ii)* ₍ı₎swɪn ˈdelz
swindl|e ˈswɪnd ᵊl **~ed** d **~er/s** ‿ə/z ‖ ᵊr/z **~es** z **~ing** ‿ɪŋ
Swindon ˈswɪnd ən
swine swaɪn
ˈswine ˌfever
swineherd ˈswaɪn hɜːd ‖ -hɝːd **~s** z
Swiney *(i)* ˈswaɪn i, *(ii)* ˈswɪn i
swing swɪŋ **swinging** ˈswɪŋ ɪŋ **swings** swɪŋz **swung** swʌŋ
ˌswing ˈdoor
swingeing ˈswɪndʒ ɪŋ **~ly** li
swinger ˈswɪŋ ə ‖ -ᵊr **~s** z
swingl|e ˈswɪŋ gᵊl **~ed** d **~es** z **~ing** ‿ɪŋ
Swingler ˈswɪŋ glə ‖ -glᵊr
swingletree ˈswɪŋ gᵊl triː **~s** z
swingometer ₍ı₎swɪŋ ˈɒm ɪt ə -ət ə ‖ -ˈɑːm əṱ ᵊr **~s** z
swing-wing ˌswɪŋ ˈwɪŋ ◂
swinish ˈswaɪn ɪʃ **~ly** li **~ness** nəs nɪs
Swinley ˈswɪn li
Swinnerton ˈswɪn ət ən ‖ -ᵊrt ᵊn
Swinton ˈswɪnt ən ‖ -ᵊn
swipe swaɪp **swiped** swaɪpt **swipes** swaɪps **swiping** ˈswaɪp ɪŋ
Swire ˈswaɪ‿ə ‖ ˈswaɪ‿ᵊr
swirl swɜːl ‖ swɝːl **swirled** swɜːld ‖ swɝːld **swirling** ˈswɜːl ɪŋ ‖ ˈswɝːl ɪŋ **swirls** swɜːlz ‖ swɝːlz
swish swɪʃ **swished** swɪʃt **swishes** ˈswɪʃ ɪz -əz **swishing** ˈswɪʃ ɪŋ
swish|y ˈswɪʃ |i **~ier** i‿ə ‖ i‿ᵊr **~iest** i‿ɪst i‿əst **~ily** ɪ li əl i **~iness** i nəs i nɪs
Swiss swɪs
ˌSwiss ˈchard; **ˌSwiss ˈcheese**; **ˌswiss ˈroll**, ˈ· ·
Swissair *tdmk* ˈswɪs eə ˌ·ˈ· ‖ -er -ær
switch swɪtʃ **switched** swɪtʃt **switches** ˈswɪtʃ ɪz -əz **switching** ˈswɪtʃ ɪŋ
switchable ˈswɪtʃ əb ᵊl
switchback ˈswɪtʃ bæk **~s** s
switchblade ˈswɪtʃ bleɪd **~s** z
switchboard ˈswɪtʃ bɔːd ‖ -bɔːrd -boʊrd **~s** z
switched-on ˌswɪtʃt ˈɒn ◂ ‖ -ˈɑːn ◂ -ˈɔːn
switchgear ˈswɪtʃ gɪə ‖ -gɪr
switch-|hit ˌswɪtʃ |ˈhɪt **~hits** ˈhɪts **~hitter/s** ˈhɪt ə/z ‖ ˈhɪṱ ᵊr/z **~hitting** ˈhɪt ɪŋ ‖ ˈhɪṱ ɪŋ
switch|man ˈswɪtʃ |mən **~men** mən men
switchover ˈswɪtʃ ˌəʊv ə ‖ -ˌoʊv ᵊr **~s** z
Swithin, Swithun ˈswɪð ᵊn ˈswɪθ-, -ɪn **~'s** z
Switzerland ˈswɪts ə lənd -ᵊl‿ənd ‖ -ᵊr-
swive swaɪv **swived** swaɪvd **swives** swaɪvz **swiving** ˈswaɪv ɪŋ

swivel ˈswɪv ᵊl **~ed, ~led** d **~ing, ~ling** ‿ɪŋ **~s** z
swiz, swizz swɪz
swizzle ˈswɪz ᵊl
ˈswizzle stick
swob —*see* **swab**
swollen ˈswəʊl ən →ˈswɒʊl- ‖ ˈswoʊl-
ˌswollen ˈhead
swollen-headed ˌswəʊl ən ˈhed ɪd ◂ →ˌswɒʊl-, -əd ‖ ˌswoʊl- **~ly** li **~ness** nəs nɪs
swoon swuːn **swooned** swuːnd **swooning** ˈswuːn ɪŋ **swoons** swuːnz
swoop swuːp **swooped** swuːpt **swooping** ˈswuːp ɪŋ **swoops** swuːps
swoosh swuːʃ swʊʃ **swooshed** swuːʃt swʊʃt **swooshes** ˈswuːʃ ɪz ˈswʊʃ-, -əz **swooshing** ˈswuːʃ ɪŋ ˈswʊʃ-
a ˈswooshing noise
swop swɒp ‖ swɑːp **swopped** swɒpt ‖ swɑːpt **swopping** ˈswɒp ɪŋ ‖ ˈswɑːp ɪŋ **swops** swɒps ‖ swɑːps
sword sɔːd ‖ sɔːrd soʊrd *(!)* **swords** sɔːdz ‖ sɔːrdz soʊrdz
ˈsword dance, ˈsword ˌdancer; **ˌsword of ˈDamocles**
swordbearer ˈsɔːd ˌbeər ə →ˈsɔːb- ‖ ˈsɔːrd ˌber ᵊr ˈsoʊrd- **~s** z
swordfish ˈsɔːd fɪʃ ‖ ˈsɔːrd- ˈsoʊrd- **~es** ɪz əz
swordplay ˈsɔːd pleɪ →ˈsɔːb- ‖ ˈsɔːrd- ˈsoʊrd- **~er/s** ə/z ‖ ᵊr/z
swords|man ˈsɔːdz |mən ‖ ˈsɔːrdz- ˈsoʊrdz- **~manship** mən ʃɪp **~men** mən
swordstick ˈsɔːd stɪk ‖ ˈsɔːrd- ˈsoʊrd- **~s** s
sword-swallower ˈsɔːd ˌswɒl əʊ ə ‖ ˈsɔːrd ˌswɑːl oʊ ᵊr ˈsoʊrd- **~s** z
swore swɔː ‖ swɔːr swoʊr
sworn swɔːn ‖ swɔːrn swoʊrn
swot swɒt ‖ swɑːt **swots** swɒts ‖ swɑːts **swotted** ˈswɒt ɪd -əd ‖ ˈswɑːṱ əd **swotting** ˈswɒt ɪŋ ‖ ˈswɑːṱ ɪŋ
swum swʌm
swung swʌŋ
ˌswung ˈdash
Swyer, Swyre ˈswaɪ‿ə ‖ ˈswaɪ‿ᵊr
Syal ˈsaɪ‿əl
Sybaris ˈsɪb ər ɪs §-əs; sɪ ˈbɑːr-
sybarite ˈsɪb ə raɪt **~s** s
sybaritic ˌsɪb ə ˈrɪt ɪk ◂ ‖ -ˈrɪṱ- **~ally** ᵊl‿i
Sybil ˈsɪb ᵊl -ɪl
sycamore ˈsɪk ə mɔː ‖ -mɔːr -moʊr **~s** z
syce saɪs **syces** ˈsaɪs ɪz -əz
sycophanc|y ˈsɪk əf ənᵗs |i ˈsaɪk-, -ə fænᵗs |i ‖ ˈsɪk ə fænᵗs |i **~ies** iz
sycophant ˈsɪk əf ənt ˈsaɪk-, -ə fænt ‖ -ə fænt əf ənt **~s** s
sycophantic ˌsɪk əʊ ˈfænt ɪk ◂ ˌsaɪk- ‖ -ə ˈfænṱ- **~ally** ᵊl‿i
Sydenham ˈsɪd ᵊn‿əm
Sydney ˈsɪd ni
Sydneysider ˈsɪd ni saɪd ə ‖ -ᵊr **~s** z
syenite ˈsaɪ‿ə naɪt
Sykes saɪks
Sylheti sɪl ˈhet i sɪ ˈlet i **~s** z

Syllabic consonants

1 Most syllables contain an obvious vowel sound. Sometimes, though, a syllable consists phonetically only of a consonant or consonants. If so, this consonant (or one of them) is a nasal (usually n) or a liquid (l or, especially in AmE, r). For example, in the usual pronunciation of **suddenly** ˈsʌd n li, the second syllable consists of n alone. Such a consonant is a **syllabic consonant**.

2 Instead of a syllabic consonant it is always possible to pronounce a vowel ə plus an ordinary (non-syllabic) consonant. Thus it is possible, though not usual, to say ˈsʌd ən li rather than ˈsʌd n li.

3 Likely syllabic consonants are shown in the *Longman Pronunciation Dictionary* (LPD) with the symbol ᵊ, thus **suddenly** ˈsʌd ᵊn li. LPD's regular principle is that a raised symbol indicates a sound whose inclusion LPD does not recommend (see OPTIONAL SOUNDS). Hence this notation implies that LPD prefers bare n in the second syllable. Since there is then no proper vowel in this syllable, the n must be syllabic.

4 Similarly, in **middle** ˈmɪd ᵊl LPD recommends a pronunciation with syllabic l, thus ˈmɪd l. In **father** ˈfɑːð ə ‖ ˈfɑːð ᵊr LPD recommends for AmE a pronunciation with syllabic r, thus ˈfɑːð r.

5 The IPA provides a special diacritic ˌ to show syllabicity. If syllabification is not shown in a transcription, then syllabic consonants need to be shown explicitly, thus n̩. For the syllabic r of AmE, the special symbol ɚ is sometimes used. Because LPD uses spaces to show syllabification, it does not need these conventions. Any nasal or liquid in a syllable in which there is other vowel must automatically be syllabic.

6 Syllabic consonants are also sometimes used where LPD shows italic ə plus a nasal or liquid, thus **distant** ˈdɪst ənt. Although there is a possible pronunciation ˈdɪst nt, LPD recommends ˈdɪst ənt. (In some varieties of English or styles of speech, a syllabic consonant may in fact arise from almost any sequence of ə and a nasal or liquid.)

7 When followed by a weak vowel, a syllabic consonant may lose its syllabic quality, becoming a plain non-syllabic consonant: see COMPRESSION. For example, **threatening** ˈθret ᵊn‿ɪŋ may be pronounced with three syllables, including syllabic n, thus ˈθret.n.ɪŋ; or compressed into two syllables, with plain n, thus ˈθret.nɪŋ.

syllabar|y ˈsɪl əb ər‿|i ‖ -ə ber |i **~ies** iz

syllabi ˈsɪl ə baɪ -biː

syllabic sɪ ˈlæb ɪk sə- **~ally** ᵊl‿i **~s** s
  sylˌlabic ˈconsonant

syllabi|cate sɪ ˈlæb ɪ |keɪt sə-, §-ə- **~cated** keɪt ɪd -əd ‖ keɪţ əd **~cates** keɪts **~cating** keɪt ɪŋ ‖ keɪţ ɪŋ

syllabication sɪ ˌlæb ɪ ˈkeɪʃ ᵊn sə-, -ə- **~s** z

syllabicity ˌsɪl ə ˈbɪs ət i -ɪt i ‖ -əţ i

syllabification sɪ ˌlæb ɪf ɪ ˈkeɪʃ ᵊn sə-, -ˌ·əf-, §-əˈ·- **~s** z

syllabi|fy sɪ ˈlæb ɪ |faɪ sə-, -ə- **~fied** faɪd **~fies** faɪz **~fying** faɪ ɪŋ

syllable ˈsɪl əb ᵊl **~s** z
  ˈsyllable ˌboundary; **ˈsyllable ˌstructure**

syllabub ˈsɪl ə bʌb **~s** z

syll|abus ˈsɪl |əb əs **~abi** ə baɪ -biː **~abuses** əb əs ɪz -əz

S

sylleps|is sɪ ˈleps |ɪs sə-, -ˈliːps-, §-əs **~es** iːz

syllogism ˈsɪl ə ˌdʒɪz əm **~s** z

syllogistic ˌsɪl ə ˈdʒɪst ɪk ◂ **~ally** ᵊl‿i

sylph sɪlf **sylphs** sɪlfs

Sylphides sɪl ˈfiːd —*Fr* [sil fid]

sylphlike ˈsɪlf laɪk

sylvan ˈsɪlv ən **~s** z

sylvatic sɪl ˈvæt ɪk sᵊl- ‖ -ˈvæţ-

Sylvester sɪl ˈvest ə sᵊl- ‖ -ᵊr

Sylvia ˈsɪlv i‿ə

sym- sɪm, ¦sɪm — **sympatric** sɪm ˈpætr ɪk

Sym sɪm

symbiont ˈsɪm baɪ ɒnt -bi- ‖ -ɑːnt **~s** s

symbiosis ˌsɪm baɪ ˈəʊs ɪs -bi-, §-əs ‖ -ˈoʊs-

symbiotic ˌsɪm baɪ ˈɒt ɪk ◂ -bi- ‖ -ˈɑːţ- **~ally** ᵊl‿i

symbol ˈsɪm bᵊl **~s** z

symbolic sɪm ˈbɒl ɪk ‖ -ˈbɑːl- **~al** ᵊl **~ally** ᵊl‿i **~alness** ᵊl nəs -nɪs

symbolis... —*see* **symboliz...**

symbolism ˈsɪm bə ˌlɪz əm -bʊ- **~s** z

symbolist ˈsɪm bəl ɪst -bʊl-, §-əst **~s** s

symbolization ˌsɪm bəl aɪ ˈzeɪʃ ᵊn ˌ·bʊl-, -ɪˈ·- ‖ -əˈ·- **~s** z

symboliz|e ˈsɪm bə laɪz -bʊ- **~ed** d **~es** ɪz əz **~ing** ɪŋ

symbology sɪm ˈbɒl ədʒ i ‖ -ˈbɑːl-

Syme saɪm

Symington *(i)* ˈsaɪm ɪŋ tən, *(ii)* ˈsɪm-

symmetric sɪ ˈmetr ɪk sə-

symmetrical sɪ ˈmetr ɪk ᵊl sə- **~ly** ‿i

symmetr|y ˈsɪm ətr |i -ɪtr- **~ies** iz

Symon ˈsaɪm ən

Symonds *(i)* ˈsɪm əndz, *(ii)* ˈsaɪm əndz
ˌSymonds ˈYat ˌsɪm əndz ˈjæt

Symons *(i)* ˈsɪm ənz, *(ii)* ˈsaɪm ənz

sympathectom|y ˌsɪmp ə ˈθekt əm |i **~ies** iz

sympathetic ˌsɪmp ə ˈθet ɪk ◂ ‖ -ˈθeţ- **~ally** ᵊl‿i
ˌsympaˌthetic ˈmagic

sympathis|e, sympathiz|e ˈsɪmp ə θaɪz **~ed** d **~er/s** ə/z ‖ ᵊr/z **~es** ɪz əz **~ing** ɪŋ

sympath|y ˈsɪmp əθ |i **~ies** iz

symphonic sɪm ˈfɒn ɪk ‖ -ˈfɑːn-

symphonist ˈsɪmᵖf ən ɪst §-əst **~s** s

symphon|y ˈsɪmᵖf ən |i **~ies** iz
ˈsymphony ˌorchestra

symph|ysis ˈsɪmᵖf |ɪs ɪs -əs-, §-əs **~yses** ɪ siːz -ə-

symposia sɪm ˈpəʊz i‿ə ‖ -ˈpoʊz-

symposiac sɪm ˈpəʊz i æk ‖ -ˈpoʊz-

symposiarch sɪm ˈpəʊz i ɑːk ‖ -ˈpoʊz i ɑːrk **~s** s

symposiast sɪm ˈpəʊz i æst ‖ -ˈpoʊz- **~s** s

symposi|um sɪm ˈpəʊz i‿|əm ‖ -ˈpoʊz- **~a** ə

symptom ˈsɪm*pt* əm **~s** z

symptomatic ˌsɪm*pt* ə ˈmæt ɪk ◂ ‖ -ˈmæţ- **~ally** ᵊl‿i

syn- sɪn, ¦sɪn — **synonym** ˈsɪn ə nɪm

synaer|esis sɪ ˈnɪər |əs ɪs sə-, -ɪs-, §-əs ‖ -ˈnɪr- **~eses** ə siːz -ɪ-

synaesthesia ˌsɪn iːs ˈθiːz i‿ə, ·ɪs-, §ˌ·əs-, -ˈθiːʒ ə ‖ ˌsɪn əs ˈθiːʒ ə -ˈ·i‿ə

synagogue ˈsɪn ə gɒg ‖ -gɑːg **~s** z

synalepha, synaloepha ˌsɪn ə ˈliːf ə -ˈlef- **~s** z

synaps|e ˈsaɪn æps ˈsɪn-; sɪ ˈnæps ‖ ˈsɪn æps sə ˈnæps **~es** ɪz əz

synaps|is sɪ ˈnæps| ɪs **~es** iːz

synaptic sɪ ˈnæpt ɪk **~ally** ᵊl‿i

synarthros|is ˌsɪn ɑː ˈθrəʊs |ɪs §-əs ‖ -ɑːr ˈθroʊs- **~es** iːz

synax|is sɪ ˈnæks |ɪs sə-, §-əs **~es** iːz

sync, synch sɪŋk *(= sink)*

synchro ˈsɪŋk rəʊ ‖ -roʊ **~s** z

synchroflash ˈsɪŋk rəʊ flæʃ ‖ -roʊ- **~es** ɪz əz

synchromesh ˈsɪŋk rəʊ meʃ ‖ -roʊ- **~es** ɪz əz

synchronic sɪn ˈkrɒn ɪk →sɪŋ- ‖ -ˈkrɑːn- **~ally** ᵊl‿i

synchronicity ˌsɪŋ krə ˈnɪs ət i ˌsɪn-, ˌ·krɒ-, -ɪt i ‖ -əţ i ˌ·krɑː-

synchronis... —*see* **synchroniz...**

synchronism ˈsɪŋk rə ˌnɪz əm

synchronistic ˌsɪŋk rə ˈnɪst ɪk ◂ **~ally** ᵊl‿i

synchronization ˌsɪŋk rən aɪ ˈzeɪʃ ᵊn -ɪˈ·- **~s** z

synchroniz|e ˈsɪŋk rə naɪz **~ed** d **~es** ɪz əz **~ing** ɪŋ

synchronous ˈsɪŋk rən əs **~ly** li **~ness** nəs nɪs

synchron|y ˈsɪŋk rən |i **~ies** iz

synchrotron ˈsɪŋk rəʊ trɒn ‖ -rə trɑːn **~s** z

synclinal ₍ˌ₎sɪŋ ˈklaɪn ᵊl ₍ˌ₎sɪn- **~ly** i

syncline ˈsɪŋ klaɪn ‖ ˈsɪn- **~s** z

synco|pate ˈsɪŋk ə |peɪt **~pated** peɪt ɪd -əd ‖ peɪţ əd **~pates** peɪts **~pating** peɪt ɪŋ ‖ peɪţ ɪŋ

syncopation ˌsɪŋk ə ˈpeɪʃ ᵊn **~s** z

syncope ˈsɪŋk əp i **~s** z

syncretic ₍ˌ₎sɪŋ ˈkret ɪk ₍ˌ₎sɪn- ‖ -ˈkreţ-

syncretism ˈsɪŋk rə ˌtɪz əm -rɪ- **~s** z

syncretistic ˌsɪŋk rə ˈtɪst ɪk ◂ -rɪ-

syncretiz|e ˈsɪŋk rə taɪz -rɪ- **~ed** d **~es** ɪz əz **~ing** ɪŋ

syndactyl sɪn ˈdækt ɪl -ᵊl, -aɪᵊl **~y** i

syndesis ˈsɪnd ɪs ɪs -əs-, §-əs; sɪn ˈdiːs-

syndesmosis ˌsɪn dez ˈməʊs ɪs -des-, §-əs ‖ -ˈmoʊs əs

syndetic sɪn ˈdet ɪk ‖ -ˈdeţ-

syndic ˈsɪnd ɪk **~s** s

syndicalism ˈsɪnd ɪk ə ˌlɪz əm -ᵊl ˌɪz-

syndicalist ˈsɪnd ɪk əl ɪst §-əst **~s** s

syndi|cate *v* ˈsɪnd ɪ |keɪt -ə- **~cated** keɪt ɪd -əd ‖ keɪţ əd **~cates** keɪts **~cating** keɪt ɪŋ ‖ keɪţ ɪŋ

syndicate *n* ˈsɪnd ɪk ət -ək-, -ɪt; -ɪ keɪt, -ə- **~s** s

syndication ˌsɪnd ɪ ˈkeɪʃ ᵊn -ə- **~s** z

syndiotactic ˌsɪn daɪ‿ə ˈtækt ɪk ◂ -di‿ə-

Syndonia sɪn ˈdəʊn i‿ə ‖ -ˈdoʊn-

syndrome ˈsɪn drəʊm -drəm ‖ -droʊm —*Formerly also* -drəʊm i **~s** z

syndyotactic ˌsɪn daɪ‿ə ˈtækt ɪk ◂ -di‿ə-

syne saɪn zaɪn

synecdoche sɪ ˈnek dək i **~s** z

synecious sɪ ˈniːʃ əs

syner|esis sɪ ˈnɪər |əs ɪs sə-, -ɪs-, §-əs ‖ -ˈner- -ˈnɪr- **~eses** ə siːz -ɪ-

synergic sɪ ˈnɜːdʒ ɪk sə- ‖ -ˈnɜːdʒ-

Syllables

1 In phonetics, a **syllable** is a group of sounds that are pronounced together. Every English word consists of one or more complete syllables.

glad consists of one syllable: glæd

coming consists of two syllables: ˈkʌm and ɪŋ

So does **valley**: ˈvæl and i

tobacco consists of three syllables: tə, ˈbæk, and əʊ or oʊ.

Each syllable contains exactly one vowel. This vowel may be preceded or followed by one or more consonants. The vowel itself may be a short vowel, a long vowel, or a diphthong; or, if it is the weak vowel ə, it may be combined with a nasal or liquid to give a SYLLABIC CONSONANT.

2 **Phonetic** (spoken) syllables must not be confused with **orthographic** (written) syllables. An orthographic syllable is a group of letters in spelling. When a word is split across two lines of writing, it should be broken at an orthographic syllable boundary. (Word processors do this automatically with a **hyphenation** program.) In some cases an orthographic boundary may not correspond exactly to a phonetic syllable boundary. For example, in the word **happen** the spelling includes two **p**s, and the orthographic syllabification is **hap.pen**. But the pronunciation has only a single p, and the syllables are ˈhæp and ᵊn.

3 This Dictionary shows the syllabification of words by putting spaces between successive syllables. See SYLLABIFICATION.

synergism ˈsɪn ə ˌdʒɪz əm -ɜː-; sɪ ˈnɜːdʒ ˌɪz əm, sə- ‖ -ᵊr- **~s** z
synergist ˈsɪn ədʒ ɪst -ɜːdʒ-, §-əst; sɪ ˈnɜːdʒ-, sə- ‖ -ᵊrdʒ- **~s** s
synergistic ˌsɪn ə ˈdʒɪst ɪk ◂ -ɜː- ‖ -ᵊr- **~ally** ᵊl‿i
synerg|y ˈsɪn ədʒ |i ˈsaɪn-, -ɜːdʒ- ‖ -ᵊrdʒ- **~ies** iz
synesis ˈsɪn ɪs ɪs -əs-, §-əs
synesthesia ˌsɪn iːs ˈθiːz i‿ə ˌ·ɪs-, §ˌ·əs-, -ˈθiːʒ ə ‖ ˌsɪn əs ˈθiːʒ ə -ˈ·i‿ə
Synge sɪŋ
synizes|is ˌsɪn ɪ ˈziːs |ɪs -ə-, §-əs **~es** iːz
synod ˈsɪn əd -ɒd ‖ -ɑːd **~s** z
synodal ˈsɪn əd ᵊl -ɒd- ‖ -ɑːd-
synodic sɪ ˈnɒd ɪk sə- ‖ -ˈnɑːd- **~al** ᵊl
synoecious sɪ ˈniːʃ əs
synonym ˈsɪn ə nɪm **~s** z
synonymous sɪ ˈnɒn əm əs sə-, -ɪm- ‖ -ˈnɑːn- **~ly** li
synonym|y sɪ ˈnɒn əm |i sə-, -ɪm- ‖ -ˈnɑːn- **~ies** iz
synops|is sɪ ˈnɒps |ɪs sə-, §-əs ‖ -ˈnɑːps- **~es** iːz
synoptic sɪ ˈnɒpt ɪk sə- ‖ -ˈnɑːpt- **~ally** ᵊl‿i
  syˌnoptic ˈgospels
synovi|a saɪ ˈnəʊv i‿|ə sɪ-, sə- ‖ -ˈnoʊv- **~al** əl
synovitis ˌsaɪn əʊ ˈvaɪt ɪs ˌsɪn-, §-əs ‖ -ə ˈvaɪt̬ əs
syntactic sɪn ˈtækt ɪk **~al** ᵊl **~ally** ᵊl‿i **~s** s
syntagm ˈsɪn tæm **~s** z
syntag|ma sɪn ˈtæg |mə **~mata** mət ə ‖ mət̬ ə
syntagmatic ˌsɪnt æg ˈmæt ɪk ◂ ‖ -ˈmæt̬- **~ally** ᵊl‿i
syntax ˈsɪnt æks **~es** ɪz əz
synth sɪnᵗθ **synths** sɪnᵗθs
synth|esis ˈsɪnᵗθ |əs ɪs -ɪs-, §-əs **~eses** ə siːz ɪ-
  ˌsynthesis-by-ˈrule
synthesis|e, synthesiz|e ˈsɪnᵗθ ə saɪz -ɪ- **~ed** d **~er/s** ə/z ‖ ᵊr/z **~es** ɪz əz **~ing** ɪŋ
synthespian sɪn ˈθesp i‿ən **~s** z
synthetic sɪn ˈθet ɪk ‖ -ˈθet̬- **~al** ᵊl **~ally** ᵊl‿i **~s** s
Syon ˈsaɪ‿ən
syphilis ˈsɪf əl ɪs -ɪl-, §-əs
syphilitic ˌsɪf ə ˈlɪt ɪk ◂ -ɪ- ‖ -ˈlɪt̬- **~s** s
syphon ˈsaɪf ᵊn **~ed** d **~ing** ‿ɪŋ **~s** z
Syracusan ˌsaɪᵊr ə ˈkjuːz ᵊn ◂ ˌsɪr- **~s** z
Syracuse *place in NY* ˈsɪr ə kjuːs -kjuːz

Syracuse *place in Sicily* 'sarᵊr ə kju:z 'sɪr-
Syrah 'sɪər ə ‖ sɪ 'rɑ:
Syria 'sɪr i‿ə
Syriac 'sɪr i æk
Syrian 'sɪr i‿ən **~s** z
syringa sɪ 'rɪŋ gə sə- **~s** z
syring|e *n, v* sɪ 'rɪndʒ sə-; 'sɪr ɪndʒ **~ed** d **~es** ɪz əz **~ing** ɪŋ
syrinx, S~ 'sɪr ɪŋks **~es** ɪz əz
syrphid 'sɜ:f ɪd §-əd ‖ 'sɜ˞:f- 'sɪrf- **~s** z
Syrtis 'sɜ:t ɪs §-əs ‖ 'sɜ˞:ţ əs

SYRUP

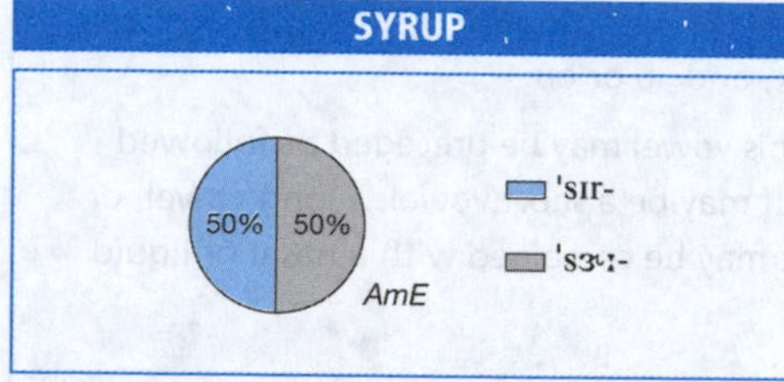

syrup 'sɪr əp ‖ 'sɜ˞:- — *Preference poll, AmE:* 'sɪr- *50%*, 'sɜ˞:- *50%.* **~s** s
syrupy 'sɪr əp i ‖ 'sɜ˞:-
sysadmin 'sɪs ˌæd mɪn 'sɪs əd ˌmɪn **~s** z
sysop 'sɪs ɒp ‖ -ɑ:p **~s** s
systaltic sɪ 'stælt ɪk sə-
system 'sɪst əm -ɪm **~s** z
 'systems ˌanalyst, ˌ· · '· · ·
systematic ˌsɪst ə 'mæt ɪk ◂ -ɪ- ‖ -'mæţ- **~al** ᵊl **~ally** ᵊl‿i **~s** s
systematis... —*see* **systematiz...**
systematist 'sɪst əm ət ɪst sɪ 'stem-, sə-, §-əst ‖ -əţ əst **~s** s
systematization ˌsɪst əm ət aɪ 'zeɪʃ ᵊn ˌ·ɪm-, -ɪ'·-; sɪ ˌstem-, sə- ‖ -əm əţ ə- **~s** z
systematiz|e 'sɪst əm ə taɪz sɪ 'stem-, sə-, -'sti:m- **~ed** d **~es** ɪz əz **~ing** ɪŋ
systemic sɪ 'sti:m ɪk -'stem- ‖ -'stem- **~ally** ᵊl‿i **~s** s
systole 'sɪst əl i 'sɪst əʊl
systolic sɪ 'stɒl ɪk ‖ -'stɑ:l-
Syston 'saɪst ən
syzyg|y 'sɪz ədʒ |i -ɪdʒ- **~ies** iz
Szczecin 'ʃtʃetʃ i:n —*Polish* ['ʃtʃe tɕin], *German* Stettin [ʃtɛ 'ti:n]
Szechuan, Szechwan ˌsetʃ 'wɑ:n ˌseɪtʃ- —*Chi* Sìchuān [⁴sɯ ¹tsʰwan]
Szeged 'seg ed —*Hung* ['sɛ gɛd]
Szerelmy sə 'relm i
Szold zəʊld →zɒʊld ‖ zoʊld

S

Tt

t Spelling-to-sound

1 Where the spelling is **t**, the pronunciation is regularly
t as in **tent** tent.
Less frequently, it is regularly
tʃ as in **nature** ˈneɪtʃ ə ‖ ˈneɪtʃ ᵊr or
ʃ as in **nation** ˈneɪʃ ᵊn.
t may also be part of the digraph **th**.

2 In AmE, t has the variant t̬ in certain positions (see T-VOICING). This is shown explicitly in this dictionary's transcriptions, for example **atom** ˈæt əm ‖ ˈæt̬ əm.

3 Where the spelling is double **tt**, the pronunciation is again t as in **button** ˈbʌt ᵊn, **better** ˈbet ə ‖ ˈbet̬ ᵊr.

4 The pronunciation is tʃ in most words ending **-ture**, for example **departure** di ˈpɑːtʃ ə ‖ dɪ ˈpɑːrtʃ ᵊr, **picture** ˈpɪk tʃə ‖ ˈpɪk tʃᵊr. Historically, this pronunciation came about through yod coalescence (see ASSIMILATION). More generally, the pronunciation is usually tʃ wherever the spelling is **t** followed by weak **u** as in **actual** ˈæk tʃu‿əl, **situated** ˈsɪtʃ u eɪt ɪd ‖ -eɪt̬ əd. In some words of this type, however, there is an older or more careful pronunciation with tj, and this is regularly the case where the **u** is strong as in **attitude** ˈæt ɪ tjuːd ‖ ˈæt̬ ə tuːd. In this latter type, AmE prefers plain t.
In BrE, the pronunciation is also tʃ wherever conservative RP would have tj as in **Tuesday** ˈtjuːz- or ˈtʃuːz-, **tune** tjuːn or tʃuːn.

5 Where **t** at the end of a stressed syllable is followed by **i** plus a vowel within a word, the pronunciation is regularly ʃ as in **partial** ˈpɑːʃ ᵊl ‖ ˈpɑːrʃ ᵊl, **action** ˈæk ʃᵊn, **superstitious** ˌsuːp ə ˈstɪʃ əs ‖ -ᵊr-. When the following vowel is weak as in the examples just given, the **t** is silent; but when it is strong, the pronunciation is i as in **initiate** ɪ ˈnɪʃ i eɪt. Sometimes there is an alternative possibility with s, particularly if the word already contains a ʃ as in **negotiation** -ˌɡəʊʃ- ‖ -ˌɡoʊʃ- or -ˌɡəʊs- ‖ -ˌɡoʊs-.

6 **t** is usually silent in two groups of words:

- in **-sten**, **-stle** as in **listen** ˈlɪs ᵊn, **thistle** ˈθɪs ᵊl; also in **Christmas** ˈkrɪs məs, **soften** ˈsɒf ᵊn ‖ ˈsɔːf ᵊn and sometimes in **often** ˈɒf ᵊn or ˈɒft ən ‖ ˈɔːf ᵊn or ˈɔːft ən
- at the end of words recently borrowed from French as in **chalet** ˈʃæl eɪ ‖ ʃæ ˈleɪ.

The sound t is often elided (see ELISION), giving further silent **ts** in words such as **postman**.

th Spelling-to-sound

1 Where the spelling is the digraph **th**, the pronunciation is regularly
θ as in **thick** θɪk or
ð as in **mother** ˈmʌð ə ‖ ˈmʌð ᵊr.
Exceptionally, it is also
t as in **Thomas** ˈtɒm əs ‖ ˈtɑːm əs.

2 At the beginning of a word, the pronunciation is θ or ð depending on the grammatical class to which the word belongs. In the definite article and other determiners, and in pronouns, conjunctions and pronominal adverbs, it is ð as in **this** ðɪs, **they** ðeɪ, **though** ðəʊ ‖ ðoʊ, **thus** ðʌs. Otherwise it is θ as in **three** θriː, **thing** θɪŋ, **thread** θred.

3 In the middle of a word (provided that **th** is not at the end of a stem), the pronunciation is generally
θ in words of Greek or Latin origin as in **method** ˈmeθ əd, **author** ˈɔːθ-, **ether** ˈiːθ-
ð in words of Germanic origin as in **father** ˈfɑːð-, **together** -ˈgeð-, **heathen** -ˈhiːð-.

4 At the end of a word or stem the pronunciation is usually
θ as in **breath** breθ, **truth** truːθ but
ð in **smooth** smuːð and one or two other words.
In **with**, RP prefers ð, GenAm θ.
Before silent **e**, and in inflected forms of the stems concerned, the pronunciation is regularly
ð as in **breathe** briːð, **soothing** ˈsuːð ɪŋ (from **soothe**).

5 Several stems switch from θ to ð on adding the plural ending (**mouth** maʊθ, **mouths** maʊðz), on adding **-ern** or **-erly** (**northern** ˈnɔːð- , **southerly** ˈsʌð-), or on converting from noun to verb (to **mouth** maʊð).

6 The pronunciation is t in **thyme** taɪm and certain proper names, including **Chatham** ˈtʃæt əm, **Streatham** ˈstret əm ‖ ˈstreţ əm, **Thames** temz, **Thomas** ˈtɒm əs ‖ ˈtɑːm əs. In some cases, however, t has been or is being displaced by θ because of the influence of the spelling.

7 **th** is sometimes silent in **asthma**, **clothes**, **isthmus**. It is not a digraph in **hothouse**, **apartheid**.

T, t tiː *(= tea, tee)* **t's, Ts, T's** tiːz
—*Communications code name:* Tango
'T cell
't t —*see* 'tain't, 'tis, 'twas, 'twere, 'twill, 'twould

ta *'thank you'* tɑː
Taaffe tæf
Taal *'Afrikaans'* tɑːl
Taal *volcano in Philippines* tɑː ˈɑːl

T-voicing

1 For most Americans and Canadians the phoneme t is sometimes pronounced as a voiced sound. Where this is the usual AmE pronunciation it is shown in this dictionary by the symbol ţ.

2 Phonetically, ţ is a voiced alveolar tap (flap). It sounds like a quick English d, and also like the r of some languages. For many Americans, it is actually identical with their d in the same environment, so that AmE **shutter** ˈʃʌţ ᵊr may sound just the same as **shudder** ˈʃʌd ᵊr.

3 Learners of English as a foreign language who take AmE as their model are encouraged to use ţ where appropriate.

4 After n, AmE ţ can optionally be ELIDED. Accordingly, it is shown in this dictionary in italics, as *ţ*. Thus AmE **winter** ˈwɪnţ ᵊr can sound exactly the same as **winner** ˈwɪn ᵊr. Some Americans, though, consider this pronunciation incorrect.

5 In connected speech, t at the *end of a word* may change to ţ if *both* the following conditions apply:

- the sound before the t is a vowel sound or r
- the next word begins with a vowel sound and follows without a pause.

Thus in AmE **right** raɪt may be pronounced raɪţ in the phrases **right away** ˌraɪţ ə ˈweɪ, **right out** ˌraɪţ ˈaʊt. But in **right now** ˌraɪt ˈnaʊ no ţ is possible; nor in **left over** ˌleft ˈoʊv ᵊr.

6 Under the same conditions, if the sound before a t at the end of a word is n, the t may change to ţ (and therefore possibly disappear): **paint** peɪnt, but **paint it** ˈpeɪnţ ɪt. Again, some people consider this incorrect.

tab tæb **tabbed** tæbd **tabbing** ˈtæb ɪŋ **tabs** tæbz
tabard ˈtæb ɑːd -əd ‖ -ᵊrd **~s** z
tabasco, T~ *tdmk* tə ˈbæsk əʊ ‖ -oʊ
  taˌbasco ˈsauce
Tabatha ˈtæb əθ ə
tabbouleh tə ˈbuːl ə -i, -eɪ
tabb|y ˈtæb |i **~ies** iz
tabernacle ˈtæb ə næk ᵊl ‖ ˈ·ᵊr- **~s** z
Taberner *(i)* ˈtæb ən ə ‖ -ᵊrn ᵊr; *(ii)* tə ˈbɜːn ə ‖ -ˈbɜːn ᵊr
tabes ˈteɪb iːz
  ˌtabes dorˈsalis dɔː ˈseɪl ɪs -ˈsɑːl-, §-əs ‖ dɔːr ˈseɪl- -ˈsæl-
Tabitha ˈtæb ɪθ ə -əθ-
tabla ˈtæb lə ‖ ˈtɑːb- —*Hindi* [ţəb laː] **~s** z
tablature ˈtæb lətʃ ə -lɪtʃ-; -lə tjʊə, -lɪ- ‖ -lə tʃʊr -lətʃ ᵊr **~s** z
table ˈteɪb ᵊl —*see also phrases with this word*
  tabled ˈteɪb ᵊld **tables** ˈteɪb ᵊlz **tabling** ˈteɪb ᵊl‿ɪŋ
  ˈtable ˌlinen; **ˈtable ˌmanners**; **ˈtable talk**; **ˈtable ˌtennis**; **ˈtable wine**
tableau ˈtæb ləʊ tæ ˈbləʊ ‖ tæ ˈbloʊ ˈtæb loʊ **~s, ~x** z —*or as sing.*
table|cloth ˈteɪb ᵊl |klɒθ -klɔːθ ‖ -|klɔːθ -klɑːθ **~cloths** klɒθs klɒðz, klɔːðz, klɔːθs ‖ klɔːðz klɔːθs, klɑːðz, klɑːθs
table d'hote, table d'hôte ˌtɑːb ᵊl ˈdəʊt ‖ -ˈdoʊt ˌtæb- —*Fr* [ta blə dot]
tableland ˈteɪb ᵊl lænd **~s** z
tablemat ˈteɪb ᵊl mæt **~s** s
tablespoon ˈteɪb ᵊl spuːn **~s** z
tablespoonful ˈteɪb ᵊl spuːn fʊl **~s** z
  tablespoonsful ˈteɪb ᵊl spuːnz fʊl
tablet ˈtæb lət -lɪt **~s** s
tabletop ˈteɪb ᵊl tɒp ‖ -tɑːp **~s** s
tableware ˈteɪb ᵊl weə ‖ -wer -wær
tabloid ˈtæb lɔɪd **~s** z
taboo tə ˈbuː ₍ₜ₎tæ- **~ed** d **~ing** ɪŋ **~s** z
tabor ˈteɪb ə -ɔː ‖ -ᵊr **~s** z

T

Tabor 'teɪb ɔː -ə ‖ -ᵊr
tabouleh, tabouli tə 'buːl i -ə, -eɪ
tabular 'tæb jʊl ə -jəl- ‖ -jəl ᵊr **~ly** li
tabula rasa ˌtæb jʊl ə 'rɑːz ə ˌ·jəl-, -'rɑːs ə ‖ -jəl ə-
tabu|late 'tæb ju |leɪt -jə- ‖ -jə- **~lated** leɪt ɪd -əd ‖ leɪt̬ əd **~lates** leɪts **~lating** leɪt ɪŋ ‖ leɪt̬ ɪŋ
tabulation ˌtæb ju 'leɪʃ ᵊn -jə- ‖ -jə- **~s** z
tabulator 'tæb ju leɪt ə '·jə- ‖ -jə leɪt̬ ᵊr **~s** z
tacamahac 'tæk əm ə hæk **~s** s
tache *'moustache'* tæʃ tɑːʃ **taches** 'tæʃ ɪz 'tɑːʃ- -əz
tachism 'tæʃ ˌɪz əm —*Fr* tachisme [ta ʃism̥]
tachistoscope tə 'kɪst ə skəʊp ‖ -skoʊp **~s** s
tachistoscopic tə ˌkɪst ə 'skɒp ɪk ◂ ‖ -'skɑːp- **~ally** ᵊl i
tachograph 'tæk ə grɑːf -græf ‖ -græf **~s** s
tachometer tæ 'kɒm ɪt ə -ət ə ‖ -'kɑːm ət̬ ᵊr **~s** z
tachycardia ˌtæk i 'kɑːd i ə ‖ -'kɑːrd-
tachymeter tæ 'kɪm ɪt ə -ət ə ‖ -ət̬ ᵊr **~s** z
tacit 'tæs ɪt §-ət **~ly** li **~ness** nəs nɪs
taciturn 'tæs ɪ tɜːn -ə- ‖ -tɜːn **~ly** li
taciturnity ˌtæs ɪ 'tɜːn ət i ˌ·ə-, -ɪt i ‖ -'tɜːn ət̬ i
Tacitus 'tæs ɪt əs -ət- ‖ -ət̬ əs
tack tæk **tacked** tækt *(= tact)* **tacking** 'tæk ɪŋ **tacks** tæks *(= tax)*
tacki... —*see* **tacky**
tackl|e 'tæk ᵊl —*but as a nautical term, often* 'teɪk ᵊl **~ed** d **~es** z **~ing** ɪŋ
tack|y 'tæk |i **~ier** i ə ‖ i ᵊr **~iest** i ɪst i əst **~ily** ɪ li əl i **~iness** i nəs i nɪs
taco 'tæk əʊ 'tɑːk- ‖ 'tɑːk oʊ **~s** z
Tacolneston 'tæk ᵊl stən *(!)*
Tacoma tə 'kəʊm ə ‖ -'koʊm-
Taconic tə 'kɒn ɪk ‖ -kɑːn-
taconite 'tæk ə naɪt
tact tækt
tactful 'tækt fᵊl -fʊl **~ly** i **~ness** nəs nɪs
tactic 'tækt ɪk **~s** s
-tactic 'tækt ɪk — **morphotactic** ˌmɔːf əʊ 'tækt ɪk ◂ ‖ ˌmɔːrf ə-
tactical 'tækt ɪk ᵊl **~ly** i
tactician tæk 'tɪʃ ᵊn **~s** z
tactile 'tækt aɪᵊl ‖ 'tækt ᵊl -aɪᵊl
tactless 'tækt ləs -lɪs **~ly** li **~ness** nəs nɪs
tactual 'tæk tʃu əl 'tækt ju əl **~ly** i
tad, Tad tæd **tads, Tad's** tædz
ta-da, ta-dah tə 'dɑː
Tadcaster 'tæd ˌkæst ə -kəst-, -ˌkɑːst- ‖ -ˌkæst ᵊr
Tadema 'tæd ɪm ə -əm-
Tadhg taɪg teɪg
Tadley 'tæd li
tadpol|e 'tæd pəʊl →'tæb-, →-pɒʊl ‖ -poʊl **~es** z **~ing** ɪŋ
Tadzhik tɑː 'dʒiːk 'tɑːdʒ ɪk **~s** s
Tadzhikistan tɑː ˌdʒiːk ɪ 'stɑːn -ˌdʒɪk-, -ə-, -'stæn ‖ ·'· . .
Tae Bo ˌtaɪ 'bəʊ ‖ -'boʊ
Taegu ˌteɪ 'guː —*Korean* ['d̥ɛ gu]
tae kwon do, taekwondo ˌtaɪ kwɒn 'dəʊ ˌteɪ-, -'kwɒn dəʊ ‖ ˌtaɪ kwɑːn 'doʊ —*Korean* [tʰɛ gwɒn do]
tael teɪᵊl *(= tail, tale)* **taels** teɪᵊlz
ta'en teɪn
taeni|a 'tiːn i |ə **~ae** iː
Taff tæf
taffeta 'tæf ɪt ə -ət- ‖ -ət̬ ə **~s** z
taffia, T~ 'tæf i ə
taffrail 'tæf reɪᵊl -rəl, -rɪl **~s** z
taff|y, Taff|y 'tæf |i **~ies** iz
tafia 'tæf i ə
Taft tæft tɑːft
tag tæg **tagged** tægd **tagging** 'tæg ɪŋ **tags** tægz
'**tag** ˌ**wrestling**
Tagalog tə 'gɑːl ɒg -'gæl-, -əg ‖ -əg -ɔːg, -ɑːg **~s** z
tagalong 'tæg ə 'lɒŋ ◂ ‖ -'lɔːŋ ◂ -'lɑːŋ ◂ **~s** z
Tagamet *tdmk* 'tæg ə met **~s** s
tagetes tæ 'dʒiːt iːz
tagg... —*see* **tag**
Taggart 'tæg ət ‖ -ᵊrt
tagliatelle ˌtæl jə 'tel i ˌtæg li ə 'tel i ‖ ˌtɑːl-
tagmeme 'tæg miːm **~s** z
tagmemic tæg 'miːm ɪk **~s** s
Tagore tə 'gɔː ‖ -'gɔːr —*Bengali* [tʰa kur]
tagua 'tɑːg wə
Tagus 'teɪg əs
tahini tə 'hiːn i tɑː-
Tahiti tə 'hiːt i tɑː- ‖ -'hiːt̬ i
Tahitian tə 'hiːʃ ᵊn tɑː-, -'hiːt i ən **~s** z
Tahoe 'tɑː həʊ ‖ -hoʊ
tahr tɑː ‖ tɑːr *(= tar)* **tahrs** tɑːz ‖ tɑːrz
Tai taɪ
tai chi, t'ai chi ˌtaɪ 'tʃiː ◂ -'dʒiː —*Chi* tàijí [⁴tʰai ²tɕi]
ˌ**t'ai chi 'ch'uan** tʃu 'æn ‖ -'ɑːn —*Chi* quán [²tɕʰyɛn]
Taichung, T'ai-chung ˌtaɪ 'tʃʊŋ —*Chi* Táizhōng [²tʰai ¹tʂʊŋ]
taig, Taig teɪg **taigs, Taigs** teɪgz
taiga 'taɪg ə -ɑː —*Russ* [tʌj 'ga]
taikonaut 'taɪk əʊ nɔːt ‖ -nɑːt **~s** s
tail teɪᵊl **tailed** teɪᵊld **tailing/s** 'teɪᵊl ɪŋ/z **tails** teɪᵊlz
ˌ**tail 'end**; '**tail pipe**
tailback 'teɪᵊl bæk **~s** s
tailboard 'teɪᵊl bɔːd ‖ -bɔːrd -boʊrd **~s** z
tailbone 'teɪᵊl bəʊn ‖ -boʊn **~s** z
tailcoat ˌteɪᵊl 'kəʊt '·· ‖ -'koʊt **~s** s
-tailed 'teɪᵊld — **long-tailed** ˌlɒŋ 'teɪᵊld ◂ ‖ ˌlɔːŋ- ˌlɑːŋ-
tail-end ˌteɪᵊl 'end **~er/s** ə/z ‖ ᵊr/z **~s** z
tail|gate 'teɪᵊl |geɪt **~gated** geɪt ɪd -əd ‖ geɪt̬ əd **~gater/s** geɪt ə/z ‖ geɪt̬ ᵊr/z **~gates** geɪts **~gating** geɪt ɪŋ ‖ geɪt̬ ɪŋ
tailless 'teɪᵊl ləs -lɪs **~ness** nəs nɪs
taillight 'teɪᵊl laɪt **~s** s
tailor 'teɪl ə ‖ -ᵊr **~ed** d **tailoring** 'teɪl ər ɪŋ **~s** z
tailor-made ˌteɪl ə 'meɪd ◂ ‖ -ᵊr-
tailpiec|e 'teɪᵊl piːs **~es** ɪz əz

tailpipe ˈteɪᵊl paɪp **~s** s
tailplane ˈteɪ ᵊl pleɪn **~s** z
tailrac|e ˈteɪᵊl reɪs **~es** ɪz əz
tailskid ˈteɪᵊl skɪd **~s** z
tailspin ˈteɪᵊl spɪn **~s** z
tailwind ˈteɪᵊl wɪnd **~s** z
Tain, tain teɪn
Taine teɪn —*Fr* [tɛn]
Taino ˈtaɪn əʊ taɪ ˈiːn-, tɑː ˈiːn- ‖ -oʊ **~s** z
taint teɪnt **tainted** ˈteɪnt ɪd -əd ‖ ˈteɪnṭ əd **tainting** ˈteɪnt ɪŋ ‖ ˈteɪnṭ ɪŋ **taints** teɪnts
'taint, 'tain't teɪnt
taipan ˈtaɪp æn **~s** z
Taipei, T'aipei ˌtaɪ ˈpeɪ —*Chi* Táiběi [^{2}tʰai ^{3}pei]
Taiping ˌtaɪ ˈpɪŋ —*Chi* Taìpíng [^{4}tʰai ^{2}pʰɪŋ]
Taishan ˌtaɪ ˈʃæn ‖ -ˈʃɑːn —*Chi* Tàishān [^{4}tʰai ^{1}ʂan]
Tait teɪt
Taittinger ˌteɪt æn ˈʒeɪ ˈ· · ·, -ɪŋ ə —*Fr* [tɛ tæ̃ ʒe]
Taiwan, T'aiwan ˌtaɪ ˈwɑːn -ˈwɒn, -ˈwæn —*Chi* Táiwān [^{2}tʰai ^{1}wan]
Taiwanese ˌtaɪ wə ˈniːz ◂ -wɑː- ‖ -ˈniːs
Taizé ˈteɪz eɪ ˈtez- ‖ teɪ ˈzeɪ te- —*Fr* [tɛ ze]
Tajik tɑː ˈdʒiːk ˈtɑːdʒ ɪk **~s** s
Tajikistan tɑː ˌdʒiːk ɪ ˈstɑːn -ˌdʒɪk-, -ə-, -ˈstæn ‖ -ˈ· · ·
tajine tə ˈʒiːn tɑː-, -ˈdʒiːn **~s** z
Taj Mahal ˌtɑːdʒ mə ˈhɑːl ˌtɑːʒ- —*Hindi* [t̪aːdʒ mə həl]
takahe ˈtɑːk ə hiː -ɑː- **~s** z
take teɪk ⚠tek **taken** ˈteɪk ən ⚠ˈtek- **takes** teɪks ⚠teks **taking** ˈteɪk ɪŋ ⚠ˈtek- **took** tʊk §tuːk
takeaway ˈteɪk ə ˌweɪ **~s** z
takedown ˈteɪk daʊn **~s** z
take-home pay ˈteɪk həʊm peɪ ˌ· · ˈ·, ˌ·ˈ· · ‖ -hoʊm-
take-it-or-leave-it ˌteɪk ɪt ɔː ˈliːv ɪt -ᵊˈ-, §ˌ·ət-, -ət ‖ ˌteɪk əṭ ᵊr ˈliːv ət
taken ˈteɪk ən
takeoff ˈteɪk ɒf -ɔːf ‖ -ɔːf -ɑːf **~s** s
takeout ˈteɪk aʊt **~s** s
takeover ˈteɪk ˌəʊv ə ‖ -ˌoʊv ᵊr **~s** z
taker ˈteɪk ə ‖ -ᵊr **~s** z
take-up, takeup ˈteɪk ʌp
takin ˈtɑːk iːn **~s** z
taking ˈteɪk ɪŋ **~ly** li **~ness** nəs nɪs **~s** z
Talacre *place in Clwyd* tæ ˈlæk reɪ —*Welsh* [ta ˈlak re]
talapoin ˈtæl ə pɔɪn **~s** z
Talbot, t~ *(i)* ˈtɔːlb ət ˈtɒlb- ‖ ˈtɑːlb-, *(ii)* ˈtælb ət —*In BrE usually (i), in AmE usually (ii).* **~s, ~'s** s
talc tælk **talced, talcked** tælkt **talcing, talcking** ˈtælk ɪŋ **talcs** tælks
Talcott ˈtɔːlk ət ˈtɒlk-, ˈtælk-, -ɒt ‖ ˈtɔːl kɑːt ˈtɑːl-, ˈtæl-
talcum ˈtælk əm
ˈtalcum ˌpowder
tale teɪᵊl *(= tail)* **tales** teɪᵊlz
talebear|er ˈteɪᵊl ˌbeər |ə ‖ -ˌber |ᵊr -ˌbær- **~ers** əz ‖ ᵊrz **~ing** ɪŋ
talent ˈtæl ənt **talented** ˈtæl ənt ɪd əd ‖ -ənṭ əd **~s** s
ˈtalent scout; **ˈtalent ˌspotter**
talentless ˈtæl ənt ləs -lɪs
tales *'group summoned for jury service'* ˈteɪl iːz **~man** mən mæn **~men** mən men
tales *pl of* **tale** teɪᵊlz
taleteller ˈteɪᵊl ˌtel ə ‖ -ᵊr **~s** z
Talfan ˈtælv ən —*Welsh* [ˈtal van]
Talgarth ˈtæl gɑːθ ‖ -gɑːrθ
tali —*see* **talus**
Taliban ˈtæl ɪ bæn ˈtɑːl-, -ə-, -bɑːn, ˌ··ˈ· ‖ ˈtɑːl ə bɑːn ˈtæl-
Taliesin ˌtæl i ˈes ɪn ˌtæl ˈjes ɪn, §-ᵊn —*Welsh* [tal ˈjes in]
talipes ˈtæl ɪ piːz -ə-
talipot ˈtæl ɪ pɒt -ə- ‖ -pɑːt **~s** s
talisman ˈtæl ɪz mən -əz-, -ɪs-, -əs- ‖ -əs- -əz- **~s** z
talismanic ˌtæl ɪz ˈmæn ɪk ◂ -əz-, -ɪs-, -əs- ‖ -əs- -əz-
Talitha ˈtæl ɪθ ə -əθ-
talk tɔːk ‖ tɑːk **talked** tɔːkt ‖ tɑːkt **talking** ˈtɔːk ɪŋ ‖ ˈtɑːk- **talks** tɔːks ‖ tɑːks
ˌtalking ˈhead; **ˈtalking point**; **ˈtalking shop**; **ˈtalk show**
talkathon ˈtɔːk ə θɒn ‖ -θɑːn ˈtɑːk- **~s** z
talkative ˈtɔːk ət ɪv ‖ -əṭ ɪv ˈtɑːk- **~ly** li **~ness** nəs nɪs
talkback ˈtɔːk bæk ‖ ˈtɑːk- **~s** s
talker ˈtɔːk ə ‖ -ᵊr ˈtɑːk- **~s** z
talkie ˈtɔːk i ‖ ˈtɑːk- **~s** z
talking-to ˈtɔːk ɪŋ tuː -tu ‖ ˈtɑːk- **~s** z
talktime ˈtɔːk taɪm ‖ ˈtɑːk-
talky ˈtɔːk i ‖ ˈtɑːk i
tall tɔːl ‖ tɑːl **taller** ˈtɔːl ə ‖ -ᵊr ˈtɑːl- **tallest** ˈtɔːl ɪst -əst ‖ ˈtɑːl-
ˌtall ˈstory
tallage ˈtæl ɪdʒ
Tallaght ˈtæl ə
Tallahassee ˌtæl ə ˈhæs i
tallboy ˈtɔːl bɔɪ ‖ ˈtɑːl- **~s** z
Talleyrand ˈtæl i rænd —*Fr* [ta lɛ ʁɑ̃]
Tallin, Tallinn ˈtæl ɪn tæ ˈlɪn, -ˈliːn ‖ ˈtɑːl ɪn —*Estonian* [ˈtal lin]
Tallis ˈtæl ɪs §-əs
tallish ˈtɔːl ɪʃ ‖ ˈtɑːl-
tallith ˈtæl ɪθ ˈtɑːl-, -ɪs —*Hebrew* [ta ˈliːt]
tallness ˈtɔːl nəs -nɪs ‖ ˈtɑːl-
tallow ˈtæl əʊ ‖ -oʊ
tallowy ˈtæl əʊ i ‖ -oʊ-
Tallulah tə ˈluːl ə
tally ˈtæl i **tallied** ˈtæl id **tallies** ˈtæl iz **tallying** ˈtæl i ɪŋ
tallyho ˌtæl i ˈhəʊ ‖ -ˈhoʊ
tally|man ˈtæl i |mən **~men** mən men
Talmud ˈtæl mʊd -məd, -mʌd ‖ ˈtɑːl-
talmudic tæl ˈmʊd ɪk -ˈmjuːd-, -ˈmʌd- ‖ tɑːl- **~al** ᵊl
talon ˈtæl ən **~ed** d **~s** z
talus *'anklebone'* ˈteɪl əs **tali** ˈteɪl aɪ

talus *'slope'* 'teɪl əs 'tæl- **~es** ɪz əz
Talybont, Tal-y-bont ˌtæl i 'bɒnt -ə- ‖ -'bɑːnt —*Welsh* [tal ə 'bɔnt] —*see note at* -y-
Tal-y-llyn ˌtæl i 'lɪn -ə-, -'θlɪn —*Welsh* [tal ə 'ɬin, -'ɬɪn] —*see note at* -y-
Tam, tam tæm —*see also phrases with this word* **tams, Tam's** tæmz
tamable 'teɪm əb ᵊl
tamagotchi ˌtæm ə 'gɒtʃ i ‖ ˌtɑːm ə 'goʊtʃ i -'gɑːtʃ i — Jp [ta 'ma got tɕi]
tamale tə 'mɑːl i -eɪ **~s** z
tamandua ˌtæm ən 'duː͜ ə ‖ tə 'mænd u͜ ə ˌ·ˌ·'ɑː **~s** z
Tamar 'teɪm ɑː -ə ‖ -ᵊr —*the river in Devon and Cornwall is locally* -ə, §-ᵊr
Tamara *(i)* tə 'mɑːr ə -'mær-, *(ii)* 'tæm ər ə
tamarack 'tæm ə ræk **~s** s
tamarillo ˌtæm ə 'rɪl əʊ ‖ -oʊ **~s** z
tamarin 'tæm ər ɪn §-ən; -ə ræn **~s** z
tamarind 'tæm ər ɪnd §-ənd **~s** z
tamarisk 'tæm ər ɪsk §-əsk **~s** s
tamber 'tæm bə ‖ -bᵊr **~s** z
tambour 'tæm bʊə -bɔː ‖ -bʊr ·'· **~s** z
tamboura tæm 'bʊər ə -'bɔːr- ‖ -'bʊr- **~s** z
tambourin 'tæm bər ɪn **~s** z
tambourine ˌtæm bə 'riːn **~s** z
Tamburlaine 'tæm bə leɪn ‖ -bᵊr-
tame, Tame teɪm **tamed** teɪmd **tamer** 'teɪm ə ‖ -ᵊr **tames** teɪmz **tamest** 'teɪm ɪst -əst **taming** 'teɪm ɪŋ
tameable 'teɪm əb ᵊl
tame|ly 'teɪm |li **~ness** nəs nɪs
tamer 'teɪm ə ‖ -ᵊr **~s** z
Tamerlane 'tæm ə leɪn ‖ -ᵊr-
Tameside 'teɪm saɪd
Tamiflu *tdmk* 'tæm ɪ fluː -ə-
Tamika 'tæm ɪk ə
Tamil 'tæm ᵊl -ɪl ‖ 'tɑːm- **~s** z
ˌTamil 'Nadu 'nɑːd uː
Tamla Motown ˌtæm lə 'məʊ taʊn ‖ -'moʊ-
Tammany 'tæm ən i
Tammie, Tammy, t~ 'tæm i
Tam O'Shanter, tam-o'-shanter ˌtæm ə 'ʃænt ə ‖ -'ʃænṭ ᵊr **~s, ~'s** z
tamoxifen tə 'mɒks ɪ fen tæ-, -ə- ‖ -'mɑːks əf ən
tamp tæmp **tamped** tæmpt **tamping** 'tæmp ɪŋ **tamps** tæmps
Tampa 'tæmp ə
Tampax *tdmk* 'tæmp æks
tamper 'tæmp ə ‖ -ᵊr **~ed** d **tampering** 'tæmp ər͜ ɪŋ **~s** z
Tampere 'tæmp ə reɪ ‖ 'tɑːmp- —*Finnish* ['tɑm pe re]
tamper-evident ˌtæmp ər 'ev ɪd ənt ◂ -əd·, §-ɪ dent, §-ə dent ‖ ˌ·ᵊr-
tamper-proof 'tæmp ə pruːf §-prʊf ‖ -ᵊr-
tamper-resistant ˌtæmp ə ri 'zɪst ənt ◂ -ə rə- ‖ ˌtæmp ᵊr-
Tampico tæm 'piːk əʊ ‖ -oʊ tɑːm- —*Sp* [tam 'pi ko]
tampion 'tæmp i͜ ən **~s** z
tampon 'tæmp ɒn -ən ‖ -ɑːn **~s** z
tamponade ˌtæmp ə 'neɪd **~s** z
Tamsin, Tamsyn *(i)* 'tæm sɪn, *(ii)* -zɪn
Tamworth, t~ 'tæm wɜːθ -wəθ, §-əθ ‖ -wɜːθ **~s, ~'s** s
tan tæn **tanned** tænd **tanning** 'tæn ɪŋ **tans** tænz
tana, Tana 'tɑːn ə
tanager 'tæn ədʒ ə -ɪdʒ- ‖ -ᵊr **~s** z
Tanagra 'tæn əg rə
Tánaiste 'tɔːn əʃ tʃə 'tɑːn-, -ɪʃ- —*Irish* ['t̪ʰɑː nˠəɕ tʲə]
Tanami 'tæn ə maɪ
Tancock 'tæn kɒk →'tæŋ- ‖ -kɑːk
Tancred 'tæŋk rɪd -red, §-rəd
tandem 'tænd əm **~s** z
tandoor 'tænd ʊə -ɔː; tæn 'dʊə, -'dɔː ‖ tɑːn 'dʊᵊr **~s** z
tandoori, tanduri tæn 'dʊər i tʌn-, -'dɔːr- ‖ tɑːn 'dʊr- -'dɜː-
Tandy 'tænd i
Taney 'tɔːn i ‖ 'tɑːn- *(!)*
tang tæŋ **tangs** tæŋz
Tang, T'ang *dynasty* tæŋ tʌŋ ‖ tɑːŋ —*Chi* Táng [²tʰɑŋ]
tanga, Tanga 'tæŋ gə **~s** z
Tanganyika ˌtæŋ gən 'jiːk ə ˌ·gæn-
tangelo 'tændʒ ə ləʊ ‖ -loʊ **~s** z
tangent 'tændʒ ənt **~s** s
tangential tæn 'dʒenᵗ ʃᵊl **~ly** i
tangerine, T~ ˌtændʒ ə 'riːn '· · · **~s** z
tangibility ˌtændʒ ə 'bɪl ət i ˌ·ɪ-, -ɪt i ‖ -əṭ i
tangib|le 'tændʒ əb |ᵊl -ɪb- **~ly** li
Tangier ₍ₗ₎tæn 'dʒɪə ‖ -'dʒɪᵊr
Tangiers ₍ₗ₎tæn 'dʒɪəz ‖ -'dʒɪᵊrz
tangl|e 'tæŋ gᵊl **~ed** d **~es** z **~ing** ͜ ɪŋ
Tanglewood 'tæŋ gᵊl wʊd
tangly 'tæŋ gli
Tangmere 'tæŋ mɪə ‖ -mɪr
tango 'tæŋ gəʊ ‖ -goʊ **~ed** d **~ing** ɪŋ **~s** z
tangram 'tæn græm →'tæŋ- **~s** z
Tangshan ˌtæŋ 'ʃæn ‖ ˌtɑːŋ 'ʃɑːn —*Chi* Tángshān [²tʰɑŋ ¹ʂan]
Tanguy 'tæŋ gi ‖ tɑːn 'giː —*Fr* [tɑ̃ gi]
tangy 'tæŋ i
Tangye 'tæŋ gi
tanh θæn tænᵗʃ, ˌtæn 'eɪtʃ
Tania 'tɑːn i͜ ə ‖ 'tɑːn jə
tank tæŋk **tanked** tæŋkt **tanking** 'tæŋk ɪŋ **tanks** tæŋks
ˌtanked 'up; **'tank ˌengine**; **'tank top**
tanka 'tæŋk ə 'tɑːŋk- ‖ 'tɑːŋk ə —*Jp* ['taŋ ka] **~s** z
tankage 'tæŋk ɪdʒ
tankard 'tæŋk əd ‖ -ᵊrd **~s** z
tanker 'tæŋk ə ‖ -ᵊr **~s** z
tankful 'tæŋk fʊl **~s** z
tann... —*see* **tan**
tannate 'tæn eɪt
tanner, T~ 'tæn ə ‖ -ᵊr **~s** z
tanner|y 'tæn ər |i **~ies** iz
Tannhauser, Tannhäuser 'tæn ˌhɔɪz ə -ˌhaʊz- ‖ 'tɑːn ˌhɔɪz ᵊr —*Ger* ['tan hɔʏ zɐ]
tannic 'tæn ɪk

tannin ˈtæn ɪn §-ən **~s** z
tannoy, T~ *tdmk* ˈtæn ɔɪ **~s** z
Tanoan tə ˈnəʊ ən ˈtɑːn əʊ- ‖ tə ˈnoʊ ən ˈtɑːn oʊ-
Tanqueray ˈtæŋk ər i -ə reɪ
Tansey ˈtænz i
tans|y, Tansy ˈtænz |i **~ies** iz
tantalic tæn ˈtæl ɪk
tantalis|e, tantaliz|e ˈtænt ə laɪz -ᵊl aɪz ‖ ˈtænṭ ᵊl aɪz **~ed** d **~es** ɪz əz **~ing** ɪŋ
tantalous ˈtænt əl əs ‖ ˈtænṭ-
tantalum ˈtænt əl əm ‖ ˈtænṭ-
tantalus, T~ ˈtænt əl əs ‖ ˈtænṭ-
tantamount ˈtænt ə maʊnt ‖ ˈtænṭ-
tantara ˌtænt ə ˈrɑː ˈtænt ər ə, tæn ˈtɑːr ə ‖ tæn ˈtær ə
tantiv|y tæn ˈtɪv |i **~ies** iz
Tantr|a, t~ ˈtæntr| ə ˈtʌntr| ə ‖ ˈtʌntr| ə ˈtɑːntr| ə, ˈtæntr| ə **~ic** ɪk **~ism** ɪz əm
tantrum ˈtæntr əm **~s** z
Tanya ˈtɑːn jə ˈtæn-, -i‿ə
Tanzani|a ˌtæn zə ˈniː‿|ə tæn ˈzeɪn i‿|ə **~an/s** ən/z
Tao taʊ daʊ —*Chi* Dào [^{4}tɐu]
ˌTao Te ˈChing teɪ ˈtʃɪŋ də ˈdʒɪŋ —*Chi* Dào dé jīng [^{4}tɐu ^{2}tɤ ^{1}tɕɪŋ]
Tao Chi ˌtaʊ ˈtʃiː
Taoiseach ˈtiːʃ ɒk -ək, -əx —*Ir* [ˈṱiː ʃax, -ʃa, -ʃəx]
Taoism ˈtaʊ ˌɪz əm ˈdaʊ-; ˈteɪ əʊ ˌ· ·, ˈtɑː-
Taoist ˈtaʊ ɪst ˈdaʊ-, §-əst; ˈteɪ əʊ-, ˈtɑː- **~s** s
Taos taʊs
tap tæp **tapped** tæpt **tapping** ˈtæp ɪŋ **taps** tæps
ˈtap dance; **ˈtap ˌdancer**; **tap ˌdancing**
tapa ˈtɑːp ə
tapas ˈtæp æs -əs ‖ ˈtɑːp- —*Sp* [ˈta pas]
tape teɪp **taped** teɪpt **tapes** teɪps **taping** ˈteɪp ɪŋ
ˈtape deck; **ˈtape ˌmeasure**; **ˈtape reˌcorder**
tapenade, tapénade ˌtæp ə ˈnɑːd ‖ ˌtɑːp- **~s** z —*Fr* [ta pe nad]
taper ˈteɪp ə ‖ -ᵊr **~ed** d **tapering/ly** ˈteɪp ər‿ɪŋ /li **~s** z
tape-record ˈteɪp ri ˌkɔːd -rə- ‖ -kɔːrd **~ed** ɪd əd **~er/s** ə/z ‖ -ᵊr/z **~ing** ɪŋ **~s** z
tapes|try ˈtæp ɪs |tri -əs- **~tries** triz
tapeworm ˈteɪp wɜːm ‖ -wɜːm **~s** z
tapioca ˌtæp i ˈəʊk ə ‖ -ˈoʊk ə
tapir ˈteɪp ə -ɪə ‖ -ᵊr **~s** z
tapis ˈtæp i -iː ‖ tæ ˈpiː —*Fr* [ta pi]
Taplin ˈtæp lɪn §-lən
Taplow ˈtæp ləʊ ‖ -loʊ
Tapp tæp
tapp... —*see* **tap**
tapper ˈtæp ə ‖ -ᵊr **~s** z
tappet ˈtæp ɪt §-ət **~s** s
taproom ˈtæp ruːm -rʊm **~s** z
taproot ˈtæp ruːt **~s** s
Tapscott ˈtæps kɒt ‖ -kɑːt
Tapsell ˈtæps ᵊl
tapster ˈtæpst ə ‖ -ᵊr **~s** z
taqueria ˌtæk ə ˈriː ə **~s** z
tar tɑː ‖ tɑːr **tarred** tɑːd ‖ tɑːrd **tarring** ˈtɑːr ɪŋ **tars** tɑːz ‖ tɑːrz
Tara ˈtɑːr ə ˈtær ə ‖ ˈtær ə ˈter ə, ˈtɑːr ə
ta-ra tə ˈrɑː
taradiddle ˈtær ə dɪd ᵊl ‖ ˈter-, ˌ·ˈ·· **~s** z
Tarahumara ˌtær ə hu ˈmɑːr ə ◂
taramasalata, taramosalata ˌtær əm ə sə ˈlɑːt ə tə ˌrɑːm-, tə ˈræm- ‖ ˈtɑːr əm ə sə ˌlɑːṭ ə ˌ· · · ·ˈ· · —*ModGk* [ta ra mɔ sa ˈla ta]
Taranaki ˌtær ə ˈnæk i
tarantella ˌtær ən ˈtel ə **~s** z
Tarantino ˌtær ən ˈtiːn əʊ ‖ -oʊ ˌter-
Taranto tə ˈrænt əʊ ‖ -oʊ -ˈrɑːnt-; ˈtɑːr ənt- —*It* [ˈtaː ran to]
tarantula tə ˈrænt jʊl ə -jəl ə; -ˈræntʃ əl- ‖ -ˈræntʃ əl‿ə -ˈrænṭ ᵊl ə **~s** z
Tarawa ˈtær ə wə
taraxacum, T~ tə ˈræks ək əm
Tarbert ˈtɑːb ət ‖ ˈtɑːrb ᵊrt
Tarbet ˈtɑːb ɪt -ət ‖ ˈtɑːrb ət
tarboosh ˌtɑː ˈbuːʃ ‖ tɑːr- ˈ· · **~es** ɪz əz
Tarbuck ˈtɑː bʌk ‖ ˈtɑːr-
tardigrade ˈtɑːd ɪ greɪd §-ə- ‖ ˈtɑːrd- **~s** z
Tardis ˈtɑːd ɪs §-əs ‖ ˈtɑːrd-
tard|y ˈtɑːd |i ‖ ˈtɑːrd |i **~ier** i‿ə ‖ i‿ᵊr **~iest** i‿ɪst i‿əst **~ily** ɪ li əl i **~iness** i nəs i nɪs
tare teə ‖ teᵊr tæᵊr **tares** teəz ‖ teᵊrz tæᵊrz
Tarentum tə ˈrent əm
targ|et ˈtɑːg |ɪt §-ət ‖ ˈtɑːrg |ət **~eted** ɪt ɪd §ət-, -əd ‖ əṭ əd **~eting** ɪt ɪŋ §ət- ‖ əṭ ɪŋ **~ets** ɪts §əts ‖ əts
ˈtarget ˌlanguage
tariff ˈtær ɪf §-əf ‖ ˈter- **~s** s
Tariq ˈtær ɪk ˈtɑːr-
Tarka ˈtɑːk ə ‖ ˈtɑːrk ə
Tarkington ˈtɑːk ɪŋ tən ‖ ˈtɑːrk-
Tarleton ˈtɑːl tən ‖ ˈtɑːrl-
tarmac, T~ *tdmk* ˈtɑː mæk ‖ ˈtɑːr- **~ked** t **~king** ɪŋ **~s** s
tarmacadam ˌtɑː mə ˈkæd əm ‖ ˌtɑːr-
tarn, Tarn tɑːn ‖ tɑːrn **tarns** tɑːnz ‖ tɑːrnz
tarnation tɑː ˈneɪʃ ᵊn ‖ tɑːr-
tarnish ˈtɑːn ɪʃ ‖ ˈtɑːrn ɪʃ **~ed** t **~es** ɪz əz **~ing** ɪŋ
taro ˈtɑːr əʊ ‖ -oʊ ˈtær-, ˈter- **~s** z
taroc, tarok ˈtær ək -ɒk ‖ -ɑːk ˈter- **~s** s
tarot ˈtær əʊ ‖ -oʊ ˈter- **~s** z
tarp tɑːp ‖ tɑːrp **tarps** tɑːps ‖ tɑːrps
tarpaper ˈtɑː ˌpeɪp ə ‖ ˈtɑːr ˌpeɪp ᵊr
tarpaulin ⁽ˌ⁾tɑː ˈpɔːl ɪn §-ən ‖ tɑːr- -ˈpɑːl-; ˈtɑːrp əl- **~s** z
Tarpeian tɑː ˈpiː‿ən ‖ tɑːr-
tarpon ˈtɑːp ɒn -ən ‖ ˈtɑːrp ɑːn -ən **~s** z
Tarporley ˈtɑːp əl‿i ‖ ˈtɑːrp ᵊr li
Tarquin ˈtɑːk wɪn §-wən ‖ ˈtɑːrk-
Tarquinius tɑː ˈkwɪn i‿əs ‖ tɑːr-
Tarr tɑː ‖ tɑːr
tarr... —*see* **tar**
tarradiddle ˈtær ə dɪd ᵊl ‖ ˈter-, ˌ·ˈ·· **~s** z
tarragon ˈtær əg ən ‖ ˈter-

T

Tarragona ˌtær ə ˈɡəʊn ə ‖ -ˈɡoʊn- ˌter-, ˌtɑːr- —*Sp* [ta rra ˈɣo na]
Tarrant ˈtær ənt ‖ ˈter-
Tarring *place in West Sussex; family name* ˈtær ɪŋ ‖ ˈter-
tarr|y *v 'delay'* ˈtær |i ‖ ˈter- **~ied** id **~ies** iz **~ying** i ɪŋ
tarry *adj 'tar-covered, tar-like'* ˈtɑːr i
Tarrytown ˈtær i taʊn ‖ ˈter-
tarsal ˈtɑːs ᵊl ‖ ˈtɑːrs ᵊl **~s** z
Tarshish ˈtɑːʃ ɪʃ ‖ ˈtɑːrʃ ɪʃ
tarsier ˈtɑːs i‿ə ‖ ˈtɑːrs i‿ᵊr -eɪ **~s** z
tars|us, T~ ˈtɑːs |əs ‖ ˈtɑːrs- **~i** aɪ
tart tɑːt ‖ tɑːrt **tarted** ˈtɑːt ɪd -əd ‖ ˈtɑːrt̬ əd **tarting** ˈtɑːt ɪŋ ‖ ˈtɑːrt̬ ɪŋ **tarts** tɑːts ‖ tɑːrts
tartan ˈtɑːt ᵊn ‖ ˈtɑːrt ᵊn **~s** z
tartar, T~ ˈtɑːt ə -ɑː ‖ ˈtɑːrt̬ ᵊr **~s** z **ˌtartar ˈsauce**, ˈ..
tartare tɑː ˈtɑː ⚠-ˈteə ‖ tɑːr ˈtɑːr
Tartarean tɑː ˈteər i‿ən ‖ tɑːr ˈter- -ˈter-
tartaric tɑː ˈtær ɪk ‖ tɑːr- -ˈter- **tarˌtaric ˈacid**
Tartarus ˈtɑːt ər əs ‖ ˈtɑːrt̬-
Tartary ˈtɑːt ər i ‖ ˈtɑːrt̬-
tartlet ˈtɑːt lət -lɪt ‖ ˈtɑːrt- **~s** s
tart|ly ˈtɑːt |li ‖ ˈtɑːrt |li **~ness** nəs nɪs
tartrate ˈtɑːtr eɪt ‖ ˈtɑːrtr- **~s** s
tartrazine ˈtɑːtr ə ziːn ‖ ˈtɑːrtr-
Tartuffe ₍ˌ₎tɑː ˈtuːf -ˈtʊf ‖ ₍ˌ₎tɑːr- —*Fr* [taʁ tyf]
tart|y ˈtɑːt| i ‖ ˈtɑːrt̬| i **~ier** i‿ə ‖ i‿ᵊr **~iest** i‿ɪst i‿əst **~ily** ɪ li əl i **~iness** i nəs i nɪs
Tarvin ˈtɑːv ɪn §-ᵊn ‖ ˈtɑːrv ᵊn
Tarzan ˈtɑːz ᵊn -æn ‖ ˈtɑːrz-
taser ˈteɪz ə ‖ -ᵊr **~s** z
Tasha ˈtæʃ ə ‖ ˈtɑːʃ ə
Tashkent ˌtæʃ ˈkent ‖ ˌtɑːʃ- —*Russ* [taʃ ˈkʲent]
task tɑːsk §tæsk ‖ tæsk **tasked** tɑːskt §tæskt ‖ tæskt **tasking** ˈtɑːsk ɪŋ §ˈtæsk- ‖ ˈtæsk ɪŋ **tasks** tɑːsks §tæsks ‖ tæsks **ˈtask force**
taskbar ˈtɑːsk bɑː ‖ ˈtæsk bɑːr **~s** z
Tasker ˈtæsk ə ‖ -ᵊr
taskmaster ˈtɑːsk ˌmɑːst ə §ˈtæsk ˌmæst ə ‖ ˈtæsk ˌmæst ᵊr **~s** z
taskmistress ˈtɑːsk ˌmɪs trəs §ˈtæsk-, -trɪs ‖ ˈtæsk- **~es** ɪz əz

Tasman ˈtæz mən
Tasmani|a tæz ˈmeɪn i‿|ə **~an/s** ən/z
Tass tæs ‖ tɑːs
tassel ˈtæs ᵊl **~ed, ~led** d **~s** z
tassie *'cup'* ˈtæs i **~s** z
Tassie *'Tasmanian'* ˈtæz i **~s** z
Tasso ˈtæs əʊ ‖ ˈtɑːs oʊ ˈtæs- —*It* [ˈtas so]
taste teɪst **tasted** ˈteɪst ɪd -əd **tastes** teɪsts **tasting** ˈteɪst ɪŋ **ˈtaste bud**
tasteful ˈteɪst fᵊl -fʊl **~ly** ‿i **~ness** nəs nɪs
tasteless ˈteɪst ləs -lɪs **~ly** li **~ness** nəs nɪs
taster ˈteɪst ə ‖ -ᵊr **~s** z
tast|y ˈteɪst |i **~ier** i‿ə ‖ i‿ᵊr **~iest** i‿ɪst i‿əst **~ily** ɪ li əl i **~iness** i nəs i nɪs
tat tæt **tats** tæts **tatted** ˈtæt ɪd -əd ‖ ˈtæt̬ əd **tatting** ˈtæt ɪŋ ‖ ˈtæt̬ ɪŋ

tata, ta-ta ₍ˌ₎tæ ˈtɑː tə-
tatami tə ˈtɑːm i tɑː-, tæ- —*Jp* [ta ˌta mi] **~s** z
Tatar ˈtɑːt ə ‖ ˈtɑːt̬ ᵊr **~s** z
Tatchell ˈtætʃ əl
Tate teɪt
tater ˈteɪt ə ‖ ˈteɪt̬ ᵊr **~s** z
Tatham *(i)* ˈtæt əm ‖ ˈtæt̬ əm, *(ii)* ˈteɪθ əm, *(iii)* ˈteɪð əm
Tati tæ ˈtiː tɑː- ‖ tɑː- —*Fr* [ta ti]
Tatiana ˌtæt i ˈɑːn ə ‖ tɑːt ˈjɑːn ə
tatie ˈteɪt i ‖ ˈteɪt̬ i **~s** z
Tatler *tdmk* ˈtæt lə ‖ -lᵊr
Tatra ˈtɑːtr ə ˈtætr ə
tatter ˈtæt ə ‖ ˈtæt̬ ᵊr **~ed** d **~s** z
tatterdemalion ˌtæt ə dɪ ˈmeɪl i‿ən -dəˈ-, -ˈmæl- ‖ ˌtæt̬ ᵊr-
Tattersall, t~ ˈtæt ə sɔːl -sᵊl ‖ ˈtæt̬ ᵊr- -sɑːl **~s, ~'s** z
tattie ˈtæt i ‖ ˈtæt̬ i **~s** z
tattl|e ˈtæt ᵊl ‖ ˈtæt̬ ᵊl **~ed** d **~es** z **~ing/ly** ‿ɪŋ /li
tattler ˈtæt ᵊl‿ə ‖ ˈtæt̬ ᵊl‿ər **~s** z
tattletale ˈtæt ᵊl teɪᵊl **~s** z
Tatton ˈtæt ᵊn
tattoo tæ ˈtuː tə- **~ed** d **~ing** ɪŋ **~s** z
tattooist tæ ˈtuː ɪst tə-, §-əst **~s** s
tatt|y ˈtæt |i ‖ ˈtæt̬ |i **~ier** i‿ə ‖ i‿ᵊr **~iest** i‿ɪst i‿əst **~ily** ɪ li əl i **~iness** i nəs i nɪs
Tatum ˈteɪt əm ‖ ˈteɪt̬ əm
Tatung *tdmk* ˈtɑː tʊŋ
tau tɔː taʊ ‖ taʊ tɔː, tɑː
taught tɔːt ‖ tɑːt *(= taut)*
taunt tɔːnt ‖ tɑːnt **taunted** ˈtɔːnt ɪd -əd ‖ ˈtɔːnt̬ əd ˈtɑːnt̬- **taunting/ly** ˈtɔːnt ɪŋ /li ‖ ˈtɔːnt̬- ˈtɑːnt̬- **taunts** tɔːnts ‖ tɑːnts
Taunton ˈtɔːnt ən ‖ ˈtɔːnt ᵊn ˈtɑːnt- —*in Somerset, locally also* tɑːnt-
Taunus ˈtɔːn əs ˈtaʊn- ‖ ˈtaʊn- —*Ger* [ˈtaʊ nʊs]
taupe təʊp ‖ toʊp *(= tope)*
Taurean, t~ ˈtɔːr i‿ən tɔː ˈriː‿ən **~s** z
taurine *n '$C_2H_7NO_3S$'* ˈtɔːr iːn -ɪn
taurine *adj 'bovine'* ˈtɔːr aɪn
Taurus ˈtɔːr əs
taut tɔːt ‖ tɑːt **tauter** ˈtɔːt ə ‖ ˈtɔːt̬ ᵊr ˈtɑːt̬- **tautest** ˈtɔːt ɪst -əst ‖ ˈtɔːt̬ əst ˈtɑːt̬-
tauten ˈtɔːt ᵊn ‖ ˈtɑːt- **~ed** d **~ing** ‿ɪŋ **~s** z
taut|ly ˈtɔːt |li ‖ ˈtɑːt- **~ness** nəs nɪs
tauto- *comb. form*
with plain suffix ¦tɔːt əʊ ‖ ¦tɔːt̬ ə ¦tɑːt̬- — **tautomeric** ˌtɔːt ə ˈmer ɪk ◂ ‖ ˌtɔːt̬- ˌtɑːt̬-
with stress-imposing suffix tɔː ˈtɒ+ ‖ tɔː ˈtɑː+ tɑː- — **tautomerism** tɔː ˈtɒm ər ˌɪz əm ‖ -ˈtɑːm- tɑː-
tautological ˌtɔːt ə ˈlɒdʒ ɪk ᵊl ◂ ‖ ˌtɔːt̬ ə ˈlɑːdʒ- ˌtɑːt̬- **~ly** ‿i
tautologous tɔː ˈtɒl əɡ əs ⚠-ədʒ əs ‖ -ˈtɑːl- tɑː-
tautolog|y tɔː ˈtɒl ədʒ |i ‖ -ˈtɑːl- tɑː- **~ies** iz
tautomer ˈtɔːt əm ə ‖ ˈtɔːt̬ əm ᵊr ˈtɑːt̬- **~s** z
tautonym ˈtɔːt ə nɪm -ᵊn ɪm ‖ ˈtɔːt ᵊn ɪm ˈtɑːt- **~s** z
tautosyllabic ˌtɔːt əʊ sɪ ˈlæb ɪk ◂ -səˈ- ‖ ˌtɔːt̬ oʊ- ˌtɑːt̬-

Tavare, Tavaré 'tæv ə reɪ
Tavener 'tæv ən ə ‖ -ər
tavern 'tæv ən ‖ -ərn **~s** z
taverna tə 'vɜːn ə tæ- ‖ -'vɜːn- —*ModGk* [ta 'vɛr na] **~s** z
Taverne tə 'vɜːn ‖ -'vɜːn
Taverner 'tæv ən ə ‖ -ərn ər
Tavistock 'tæv ɪ stɒk -ə- ‖ -stɑːk
Tavy 'teɪv i
taw tɔː ‖ tɑː **tawed** tɔːd ‖ tɑːd **tawing** 'tɔːr ɪŋ ‖ 'tɔː ɪŋ 'tɑː- **taws** tɔːz ‖ tɑːz
tawdr|y 'tɔːdr |i ‖ 'tɑːdr- **~ier** i‿ə ‖ i‿ər **~iest** i‿ɪst i‿əst **~ily** əl i ɪ li **~iness** i nəs i nɪs
Tawe *river* 'taʊ‿i -eɪ —*Welsh* ['ta we]
Tawney 'tɔːn i ‖ 'tɑːn-
tawn|y 'tɔːn |i ‖ 'tɑːn- **~ier** i‿ə ‖ i‿ər **~iest** i‿ɪst i‿əst **~iness** i nəs i nɪs
tawse tɔːz ‖ tɑːz
tax tæks **taxed** tækst **taxes** 'tæks ɪz -əz **taxing/ly** 'tæks ɪŋ /li
'tax e,vasion; **'tax ,exile**; **'tax ,haven**; **'tax re,turn**; **'tax ,shelter**; **'tax year**
taxa 'tæks ə
taxability ,tæks ə 'bɪl ət i -ɪt i ‖ -əţ i
taxable 'tæks əb əl **~ness** nəs nɪs
taxation tæk 'seɪʃ ən **~s** z
tax-deductible ,tæks di 'dʌkt əb əl ◂ ,·də-, -ɪb əl; '·,··,···
tax-deferred ,tæks di 'fɜːd ◂ -də- ‖ -'fɜːd ◂
taxeme 'tæks iːm **~s** z
taxemic tæk 'siːm ɪk **~s** s
tax-exempt ,tæks ɪg 'zempt ◂ -eg-, -əg-, -ɪk-, -ek-, -ək-
tax-free ,tæks 'friː ◂
taxi 'tæks i **~ed** d **~ing** ɪŋ **~es, ~s** z
'taxi ,driver; **'taxi rank**; **'taxi stand**
taxicab 'tæks i kæb **~s** z
taxiderm|al ,tæks ɪ 'dɜːm| əl ◂ -ə- ‖ -'dɜːm- **~ic** ɪk
taxidermist 'tæks ɪ dɜːm ɪst '·ə-, §-əst, ,··'··; tæk 'sɪd əm- ‖'tæks ə dɜːm əst **~s** s
taxidermy 'tæks ɪ dɜːm i '·ə- ‖-dɜːm i
taximeter 'tæks i ,miːt ə ‖ -,miːţ ər **~s** z
taxis *sing. n,* **Taxis** 'tæks ɪs §-əs
taxis *pl of* **taxi** 'tæks iz
-taxis 'tæks ɪs §-əs — **thermotaxis** ,θɜːm əʊ 'tæks ɪs §-əs ‖ ,θɜːm ə-
taxiway 'tæks i weɪ **~s** z
tax|man 'tæks |mæn **~men** men
taxon 'tæks ɒn ‖ -ɑːn **~s** z **taxa** 'tæks ə
taxonomic ,tæks ə 'nɒm ɪk ◂ ‖ -'nɑːm- **~al** əl **~ally** əl‿i
,taxo,nomic pho'nemics
taxonomist tæk 'sɒn əm ɪst §-əst ‖ -'sɑːn- **~s** s
taxonom|y tæk 'sɒn əm |i ‖ -'sɑːn- **~ies** iz
taxpayer 'tæks ,peɪ ə ‖ -ər **~s** z
taxying 'tæks i ɪŋ
Tay teɪ
tayberr|y 'teɪ bər‿i -,ber |i ‖ -,ber |i **~ies** iz
Tayler, Taylor 'teɪl ə ‖ -ər
Taylorian teɪ 'lɔːr i‿ən
Taylour 'teɪl ə ‖ -ər
Tayport 'teɪ pɔːt ‖ -pɔːrt -poʊrt
tayra 'taɪər ə **~s** z
Tay-Sachs ,teɪ 'sæks
,Tay 'Sachs di,sease
Tayside 'teɪ saɪd
Taz tæz
TB ,tiː 'biː
T-ball 'tiː bɔːl ‖ -bɑːl
T-bar 'tiː bɑː ‖ -bɑːr **~s** z
Tbilisi tə 'bliːs i tə bɪ 'liːs i, -bə-
T-bill 'tiː bɪl **~s** z
T-bond 'tiː bɒnd ‖ -bɑːnd **~s** z
T-bone 'tiː bəʊn ‖ -boʊn **~s** z
T-cell 'tiː sel **~s** z
Tchaikovsky tʃaɪ 'kɒf ski ‖ -'kɔːf- -'kɑːf- —*Russ* [tʃɪj 'kɔf skʲɪj]
TCP *tdmk* ,tiː siː 'piː
te tiː —*see also phrases with this word*
tea tiː *(= tee)* **teas** tiːz *(= tease)*
'tea break; **'tea ,caddy**; **'tea chest**; **'tea cloth**; **'tea ,cosy**; **'tea ,party**; **'tea ,service**; **'tea ,towel**; **'tea ,trolley**; **'tea ,wagon**
teabag 'tiː bæg **~s** z
teabread 'tiː bred
teacake 'tiː keɪk **~s** s
teach, Teach tiːtʃ **taught** tɔːt ‖ tɑːt **teaches** 'tiːtʃ ɪz -əz **teaching/s** 'tiːtʃ ɪŋ/z
'teaching ,practice; **'teaching ,hospital**
teachability ,tiːtʃ ə 'bɪl ət i -ɪt i ‖ -əţ i
teachable 'tiːtʃ əb əl
teacher, T~ 'tiːtʃ ə ‖ -ər **~s** z
,teacher 'training ,college
teach-in 'tiːtʃ ɪn **~s** z
teacup 'tiːk ʌp 'tiː kʌp **~s** s
teacupful 'tiːk ʌp fʊl 'tiː kʌp- **~s** z **teacupsful** 'tiːk ʌps fʊl 'tiː kʌps-
teagarden, T~ 'tiː ,gɑːd ən ‖ -,gɑːrd- **~s** z
Teague tiːg
tea|house 'tiː |haʊs **~houses** haʊz ɪz -əz
teak tiːk
teakettle 'tiː ,ket əl ‖ -,keţ- **~s** z
teal, Teal tiːəl **teals** tiːəlz
tea|leaf 'tiː |liːf **~leaves** liːvz
team tiːm *(= teem)* **teamed** tiːmd **teaming** 'tiːm ɪŋ **teams** tiːmz
,team 'spirit
tea-maker 'tiː ,meɪk ə ‖ -ər **~s** z
team-mate 'tiːm meɪt **~s** s
teamster 'tiːmpst ə ‖ -ər **~s** z
teamwork 'tiːm wɜːk ‖ -wɜːk
Tean tiːn
teapot 'tiːp ɒt 'tiː pɒt ‖ 'tiː pɑːt **~s** s
teapoy 'tiːp ɔɪ **~s** z
tear *'rip', 'rush'* teə ‖ teər tæər *(= tare)* **tearing** 'teər ɪŋ ‖ 'ter ɪŋ 'tær- **tears** teəz ‖ teərz tæərz **tore** tɔː ‖ tɔːr toʊr **torn** tɔːn ‖ tɔːrn toʊrn
tear *'liquid from the eye'* tɪə ‖ tɪər **tears** tɪəz ‖ tɪərz
'tear duct; **'tear gas**
tearaway 'teər ə ,weɪ ‖ 'ter- 'tær- **~s** z
teardrop 'tɪə drɒp ‖ 'tɪr drɑːp **~s** s
tearful 'tɪəf əl ‖ 'tɪrf əl **~ly** ‿i **~ness** nəs nɪs

T

teargas ˈtɪə gæs ‖ ˈtɪr- **~sed** t **~ses** ɪz əz **~sing** ɪŋ
tearing ˈteər ɪŋ ‖ ˈter ɪŋ ˈtær-
tearjerker ˈtɪə ˌdʒɜːk ə ‖ ˈtɪr ˌdʒɜːk ᵊr **~s** z
Tearlach ˈtʃɑːl əx -ək ‖ ˈtʃɑːrl ək —*ScG* [ˈtʲaːr ləx]
tearless *'unweeping'* ˈtɪə ləs -lɪs ‖ ˈtɪr- **~ly** li **~ness** nəs nɪs
tearoff ˈteər ɒf -ɔːf ‖ ˈter ɔːf ˈtær-, -ɑːf
tearoom ˈtiː ruːm -rʊm **~s** z
tearstained ˈtɪə steɪnd ‖ ˈtɪr-
teary ˈtɪər i ‖ ˈtɪr i
Teasdale ˈtiːz deɪᵊl
tease tiːz **teased** tiːzd **teases** ˈtiːz ɪz -əz **teasing/ly** ˈtiːz ɪŋ /li
teasel ˈtiːz ᵊl **~ed, ~led** d **~ing, ~ling** ɪŋ **~s** z
teaser ˈtiːz ə ‖ -ᵊr **~s** z
teashop ˈtiː ʃɒp ‖ -ʃɑːp **~s** s
Teasmade *tdmk* ˈtiːz meɪd
teaspoon ˈtiːsp uːn ˈtiː spuːn **~s** z
teaspoonful ˈtiːsp uːn fʊl ˈtiː spuːn- **~s** z **teaspoonsful** ˈtiːsp uːnz fʊl ˈtiː spuːnz-
teat tiːt **teats** tiːts
teatime ˈtiːt aɪm ˈtiː taɪm
tea-tree ˈtiː triː **~s** z
tea-urn ˈtiː ɜːn ‖ -ɜːn **~s** z
teazel, teazle ˈtiːz ᵊl **teazeled, teazelled, teazled** ˈtiːz ᵊld **teazeling, teazelling, teazling** ˈtiːz ᵊl ɪŋ **teazels, teazles** ˈtiːz ᵊlz
Tebay *place in Cumbria* ˈtiːb eɪ —*but locally* -i
Tebbit, Tebbitt ˈteb ɪt §-ət
tec tek **tecs** teks
tech tek
techie ˈtek i **~s** z
technetium tek ˈniːʃ i‿əm -ˈniːs-; -ˈniːʃ əm
technical ˈtek nɪk ᵊl
 ˈtechnical ˌcollege; **ˌtechnical ˈknockout**
technicalit|y ˌtek nɪ ˈkæl ət |i ˌ·nə-, -ɪt i ‖ -əṭ |i **~ies** iz
technically ˈtek nɪk ᵊl‿i
technician tek ˈnɪʃ ᵊn **~s** z
Technicolor *tdmk,* **t~, technicolour** ˈtek nɪ ˌkʌl ə -nə- ‖ -ᵊr
technics, T~ ˈtek nɪks
technique ₍ₗ₎tek ˈniːk **~s** s
techno ˈtek nəʊ ‖ -noʊ
techno- *comb. form*
 with stress-neutral suffix ¦tek nəʊ ‖ -noʊ — **technophobia** ˌtek nəʊ ˈfəʊb i‿ə ‖ -noʊ ˈfoʊb-
 with stress-imposing suffix tek ˈnɒ+ ‖ -ˈnɑː+ — **technography** tek ˈnɒg rəf i ‖ -ˈnɑːg-
technocrac|y tek ˈnɒk rəs |i ‖ -ˈnɑːk- **~ies** iz
technocrat ˈtek nə kræt **~s** s
technocratic ˌtek nə ˈkræt ɪk ◂ ‖ -ˈkræṭ- **~ally** ᵊl‿i
techno-geek ˈtek nəʊ giːk ‖ -noʊ- **~s** s
technological ˌtek nə ˈlɒdʒ ɪk ᵊl ◂ ‖ -ˈlɑːdʒ- **~ly** ‿i
technologist tek ˈnɒl ədʒ ɪst §-əst ‖ -ˈnɑːl- **~s** s
technolog|y tek ˈnɒl ədʒ |i ‖ -ˈnɑːl- **~ies** iz
technophobe ˈtek nəʊ fəʊb ‖ -noʊ foʊb **~s** z
tech|y *'technical enthusiast'* ˈtek| i **~ies** iz
Teck tek
tectonic tek ˈtɒn ɪk ‖ -ˈtɑːn- **~s** s
Tecumseh tɪ ˈkʌmᵖs ə tə-, -i
Tecwyn ˈtek wɪn
ted, Ted ted **tedded** ˈted ɪd -əd **tedding** ˈted ɪŋ **teds** tedz
Tedder, t~ ˈted ə ‖ -ᵊr **~s** z
Teddie ˈted i
Teddington ˈted ɪŋ tən
tedd|y, Tedd|y ˈted |i **~ies, ~y's** iz
 ˈteddy bear; **ˈteddy boy**
Te Deum ˌtiː ˈdiː‿əm ˌteɪ ˈdeɪ-, -ʊm **~s** z
tedious ˈtiːd i‿əs §ˈtiːdʒ əs **~ly** li **~ness** nəs nɪs
tedium ˈtiːd i‿əm
tee tiː **teed** tiːd **teeing** ˈtiː ɪŋ **tees** tiːz
 ˈtee shirt
tee-ball ˈtiː bɔːl ‖ -bɑːl
teehee ˌtiː ˈhiː
teem tiːm **teemed** tiːmd **teeming** ˈtiːm ɪŋ **teems** tiːmz
teen tiːn **teens** tiːnz
Teena ˈtiːn ə
teenage ˈtiːn eɪdʒ **~d** d
teenager ˈtiːn eɪdʒ ə ‖ -ᵊr **~s** z
teens|y ˈtiːnz |i **~ier** i‿ə ‖ i‿ᵊr **~iest** i‿ɪst i‿əst
 ˌteensy ˈweensy◂
teen|y ˈtiːn |i **~ier** i‿ə ‖ i‿ᵊr **~iest** i‿ɪst i‿əst
 ˌteeny ˈweeny◂
teenybopper ˈtiːn i ˌbɒp ə ‖ -ˌbɑːp ᵊr **~s** z
teepee ˈtiːp iː **~s** z
Tees tiːz
Teesdale ˈtiːz deɪᵊl
Teesside ˈtiː saɪd ˈtiːz-
teeter ˈtiːt ə ‖ ˈtiːṭ ᵊr **~ed** d **teetering** ˈtiːt ər ɪŋ ‖ ˈtiːṭ ər ɪŋ **~s** z
teeterboard ˈtiːt ə bɔːd ‖ ˈtiːṭ ᵊr bɔːrd -boʊrd **~s** z
teeter-totter ˈtiːt ə ˌtɒt ə ‖ ˈtiːṭ ᵊr ˌtɑːṭ ᵊr **~s** z
teeth tiːθ
teethe tiːð **teethed** tiːðd **teethes** tiːðz **teething** ˈtiːð ɪŋ
 ˈteething ring; **ˈteething troubles**
teetotal ˌtiː ˈtəʊt ᵊl ◂ ‖ -ˈtoʊṭ ᵊl ◂ ˈ·ˌ··
teetotaler, teetotaller ₍ₗ₎tiː ˈtəʊt ᵊl‿ə ‖ -ˈtoʊṭ ᵊl ər **~s** z
tef, t'ef, teff tef
TEFL ˈtef ᵊl
Teflon *tdmk,* **t~** ˈtef lɒn ‖ -lɑːn
teg teg **tegs** tegz
Tegucigalpa te ˌguːs ɪ ˈgælp ə -ə- ‖ -ˈgɑːlp-, -ɑː —*AmSp* [te ɣu si ˈɣal pa]
tegument ˈteg ju mənt ‖ -jə- **~s** s
Tehachapi tə ˈhætʃ əp i tɪ-
Teheran, Tehran ˌteə ˈrɑːn -ˈræn; ˌte hə ˈ· ‖ ˌte ˈrɑːn -ˈræn; ˌteɪ ə ˈ·
Teifi ˈtaɪv i —*Welsh* [ˈtəi vi]
Teign tiːn tɪn
Teignmouth ˈtɪn məθ ˈtiːn-, →ˈtɪm-
Teilhard de Chardin ˌteɪ ɑː də ˈʃɑːd æn ·ˌ· --, ·ˌjɑː-, -ˌʃɑː ˈdæ̃ ‖ teɪ ˌjɑːr də ʃɑːr ˈdæn —*Fr* [tɛ jaʁ də ʃaʁ dæ̃]
Te Kanawa ti ˈkɑːn ə wə tə-

tektite 'tekt aɪt **~s** s
telamon, T~ 'tel əm ən -ə mɒn ‖ -ə mɑːn **~s** z
Tel Aviv ˌtel ə 'viːv -'vɪv
telco 'tel kəʊ ‖ -koʊ **~s** z
tele 'tel i
tele- *comb form*
with stress-neutral suffix ¦tel ɪ -ə *—but when an independent prefix* ¦tel i ‖ ¦tel ə —
telephone 'tel ɪ fəʊn -ə- ‖ -ə foʊn
with stress-imposing suffix tə 'le+ tɪ-, te-
— **telescopy** tə 'lesk əp i tɪ-, te-
telecast *v, n* 'tel i kɑːst -ə-, §-kæst ‖ -ə kæst **~ed** ɪd əd **~ing** ɪŋ **~s** s
telecom, T~ 'tel i kɒm -ə- ‖ -ə kɑːm **~s** z
telecommunication ˌtel i kə ˌmjuːn ɪ 'keɪʃ ᵊn ˌ·ə-, -ˌ·ə- ‖ ˌtel ə- **~s** z
telecom|mute ˌtel i kə |'mjuːt ‖ 'tel ə-|ˌ· **~muted** 'mjuːt ɪd -əd ‖ -ˌmjuːţ əd **~muter/s** 'mjuːt ə/z ‖ ˌmjuːţ ᵊr/z **~mutes** 'mjuːts ‖ˌmjuːts **~muting** 'mjuːt ɪŋ ‖ ˌmjuːţ ɪŋ
teleconferenc|e 'tel i ˌkɒn fᵊr ən'ts ˌ·ˈ· · · ‖ -ə ˌkɑːn- **~es** ɪz əz **~ing** ɪŋ
teledu *'stinking badger'* 'tel ɪ duː -ə- *—but the Welsh word for 'television', also spelt like this, is* [te 'le di, -dɨ] **~s** z
telegenic ˌtel i 'dʒen ɪk ◂ ‖ ˌtel ə-
Telegonus tɪ 'leg ən əs tə-
telegony tɪ 'leg ən i tə-
telegram 'tel ɪ græm -ə- **~s** z
telegraph *n, v* 'tel ɪ grɑːf -ə-, -græf ‖-ə græf **~ed** t **~ing** ɪŋ **~s** s
'telegraph pole; **'telegraph post**
telegrapher tə 'leg rəf ə tɪ-, te- ‖ ᵊr **~s** z
telegraphese ˌtel ɪ grɑːf 'iːz ˌ·ə-, -græf'·, -grəf'· ‖ -ə græf 'iːz -'iːs
telegraphic ˌtel ɪ 'græf ɪk ◂ -ə- **~ally** ᵊl‿i
telegraphist tə 'leg rəf ɪst tɪ-, te-, §-əst **~s** s
telegraphy tə 'leg rəf i tɪ-, te-
telekinesis ˌtel ɪ kaɪ 'niːs ɪs ˌ·ə-, -kɪ'--, §-kə'--, §-əs
Telemachus tə 'lem ək əs tɪ-, te-
Telemann 'teɪl ə mæn 'tel- ‖ -mɑːn *—Ger* ['teː lə man]
telemark, T~ 'tel i mɑːk -ə- ‖ -ə mɑːrk **~s** s
telemarketing 'tel i ˌmɑːk ɪt ɪŋ '·ə-, §-ət ɪŋ, ˌ··'· · · ‖ -ə ˌmɑːrk əţ ɪŋ
Telemessag|e *tdmk,* **t~** 'tel i ˌmes ɪdʒ ‖ -ə- **~es** ɪz əz
telemeter tə 'lem ɪt ə tɪ-, te-, §-ət ə; 'tel ɪ ˌmiːt ə, -ə- ‖ tə 'lem əţ ᵊr 'tel ə ˌmiːţ ᵊr **~ed** d **~s** z
telemetry tə 'lem ətr i tɪ-, te-, -ɪtr i
teleological ˌtiːl i‿ə 'lɒdʒ ɪk ᵊl ◂ ˌtel- ‖ -'lɑːdʒ- **~ly** ‿i
teleologist ˌtiːl i 'ɒl ədʒ ɪst ˌtel-, §-əst ‖ -'ɑːl- **~s** s
teleolog|y ˌtiːl i 'ɒl ədʒ |i ˌtel- ‖ -'ɑːl- **~ies** iz
teleost 'tiːl i ɒst 'tel- ‖ -ɑːst **~s** s
telepathic ˌtel ɪ 'pæθ ɪk ◂ -ə- **~ally** ᵊl‿i
telepathist tə 'lep əθ ɪst tɪ-, te-, §-əst **~s** s
telepathy tə 'lep əθ i tɪ-, te-
telepherique, téléphérique ˌtel ɪ fə 'riːk ˌ·ə-, ˌ·eɪ-, -fe'· *—Fr* [te le fe ʁik] **~s** s
telephon|e *n, v* 'tel ɪ fəʊn -ə- ‖ -ə foʊn **~ed** d **~es** z **~ing** ɪŋ
'telephone book; **'telephone booth**; **'telephone box**; **'telephone diˌrectory**; **'telephone exˌchange**; **'telephone ˌkiosk**; **'telephone ˌnumber**
telephonic ˌtel ɪ 'fɒn ɪk ◂ -ə- ‖ -ə 'fɑːn- **~ally** ᵊl‿i
telephonist tə 'lef ən ɪst tɪ-, te-, §-əst ‖ 'tel ə foʊn- **~s** s
telephony tə 'lef ən i tɪ-, te-
telephoto, Telephoto *tdmk* ˌtel i 'fəʊt əʊ ◂ -ə- ‖ -ə 'foʊt oʊ ◂ **~s** z
ˌteleˌphoto 'lens
telephotograph ˌtel i 'fəʊt ə grɑːf ˌ·ə-, -græf ‖ ˌtel ə 'foʊţ ə græf **~s** s
telephotographic ˌtel i ˌfəʊt ə 'græf ɪk ˌ·ə- ‖ -ə ˌfoʊţ ə- **~ally** ᵊl‿i
telephotography ˌtel i fə 'tɒg rəf i ˌ·ə- ‖ -ə fə 'tɑːg-
teleplay 'tel i pleɪ -ə- **~s** z
telepoint 'tel i pɔɪnt ‖ -ə- **~s** s
tele|port 'tel i |pɔːt -ə- ‖ -ə |pɔːrt -poʊrt **~ported** pɔːt ɪd -əd ‖ pɔːrţ əd poʊrţ əd **~porting** pɔːt ɪŋ ‖ pɔːrţ ɪŋ poʊrţ ɪŋ **~ports** pɔːts ‖ pɔːrts poʊrts
teleprinter 'tel i ˌprɪnt ə -ə- ‖ -ə ˌprɪnţ ᵊr **~s** z
teleprompter, TelePrompTer *tdmk* 'tel i ˌprɒmpt ə -ə- ‖ -ə ˌprɑːmpt ᵊr **~s** z
Teleri tə 'ler i tɪ- *—Welsh* [te 'le ri]
telesales 'tel i seɪᵊlz ‖ -ə-
telescop|e *n, v* 'tel ɪ skəʊp -ə- ‖ -ə skoʊp **~ed** t **~es** s **~ing** ɪŋ
telescopic ˌtel ɪ 'skɒp ɪk ◂ -ə- ‖ -ə 'skɑːp- **~ally** ᵊl‿i
telescopist tɪ 'lesk əp ɪst tə-, te-, §-əst **~s** s
telescopy tɪ 'lesk əp i tə-, te-
teleselling 'tel i ˌsel ɪŋ -ə-, ˌ··'· · ‖ -ə-
teleshopping 'tel i ˌʃɒp ɪŋ ‖ -ə ˌʃɑːp-
teletex, T~ *tdmk* 'tel i teks -ə-
teletext 'tel i tekst -ə-
telethon 'tel ə θɒn -ɪ- ‖ -θɑːn **~s** z
Teletubb|y 'tel i ˌtʌb| i -ə- **~ies** iz
teletyp|e, T~ *tdmk* 'tel i taɪp -ə- ‖ -ə- **~ed** t **~es** s **~ing** ɪŋ
teletypewriter ˌtel i 'taɪp ˌraɪţ ᵊr ˌtel ə-
televangelism ˌtel i 'vændʒ ə ˌlɪz əm ˌtel ə-, -'vændʒ i- ‖ ˌtel ə-
televangelist ˌtel i 'vændʒ əl ɪst ˌtel ə-, -ɪl-, §-əst ‖ ˌtelə- **~s** s
teleview|er 'tel i vjuː‿ə ‖ -ə ˌvjuː‿ᵊr **~ers** əz ‖ ᵊrz **~ing** ɪŋ
televis|e 'tel ɪ vaɪz -ə- ‖ -ə- **~ed** d **~es** ɪz əz **~ing** ɪŋ
television 'tel ɪ ˌvɪʒ ᵊn -ə-, ˌ··'· · ‖ -ə- **~s** z
'television set, ˌ··'· ·
televisual ˌtel ɪ 'vɪʒ u‿əl ◂ ˌ·ə-, -'vɪz ju‿əl ‖ -ə 'vɪʒ ᵊl **~ly** i
telework|er 'tel i ˌwɜːk| ə ‖ -ə ˌwɜ˞ːk ᵊr **~ers** əz ‖ ᵊrz **~ing** ɪŋ
telex *n, v* 'tel eks **~ed** t **~es** ɪz əz **~ing** ɪŋ
telfer, T~ 'telf ə ‖ -ᵊr **~s** z
Telford 'telf əd ‖ -ᵊrd

T

telic 'tel ɪk 'tiːl-

tell, Tell tel **telling/ly** 'tel ɪŋ /li **tells** telz **told** təʊld →tɒʊld ‖ toʊld

teller, T~ 'tel ə ‖ -ᵊr **~s** z

telling-off ˌtel ɪŋ 'ɒf -'ɔːf ‖ -'ɔːf -'ɑːf **tellings-off** ˌtel ɪŋz 'ɒf -'ɔːf ‖ -'ɔːf -'ɑːf

telltale 'tel teɪᵊl **~s** z

tellurian te 'lʊər i‿ən tɪ-, tə-, -'ljʊər- ‖ -'lʊr- **~s** z

telluric te 'lʊər ɪk tɪ-, tə-, -'ljʊər- ‖ -'lʊr-

telluride, T~ 'tel juᵊ raɪd ‖ -jə-

tellurium te 'lʊər i‿əm tɪ-, tə-, -'ljʊər- ‖ -'lʊr-

telly 'tel i **tellies** 'tel iz

tel|net 'tel| net **~nets** nets **~netted** net ɪd -əd ‖ neţ əd **~netting** net ɪŋ ‖ neţ ɪŋ

telomerase 'tiːl ə mɪər eɪz 'tel- ‖ 'tel əm ə reɪz

telomere 'tiːl əʊ mɪə 'tel- ‖ 'tel ə mɪr **~s** z

telophase 'tiːl ə feɪz

telpher 'telf ə ‖ -ᵊr **~s** z

telpherage 'telf ər ɪdʒ

Telscombe 'tels kəm

telson 'tels ᵊn **~s** z

Telstar *tdmk* 'tel stɑː ‖ -stɑːr

Telstra 'tel strə

Telugu 'tel ə guː -u- **~s** z

temazepam tɪ 'mæz ɪ pæm te-, tə-, -'meɪz-, -ə-

temblor ˌtem 'blɔː '· ·, '·blə ‖ -'blɔːr -'bloʊr, '· ·, '·blᵊr **~s** z

temerarious ˌtem ə 'reər i‿əs ◂ ‖ -'rer- -'rær-

temerity tə 'mer ət i tɪ-, te-, -ɪt i ‖ -əţ i

Temne 'tem ni

temp temp **temped** tem*p*t **temping** 'temp ɪŋ **temps** tem*p*s

tempe, tempeh 'temp eɪ

Tempe 'temp i

temper 'temp ə ‖ -ᵊr **~ed** d **tempering** 'temp ər‿ɪŋ **~s** z

tempera 'temp ər ə

temperament 'temp ᵊr‿ə mənt **~s** s

temperamental ˌtemp ᵊr‿ə 'ment ᵊl ◂ ‖ -'menţ ᵊl ◂ **~ly** i

temperance 'temp ᵊr‿ənᵗs

temperate 'temp ər‿ət ɪt **~ly** li **~ness** nəs nɪs

temperature 'temp ᵊr‿ətʃ ə ‿ɪtʃ ə ‖ ‿ətʃ ᵊr ‿ə tʃʊr **~s** z

-tempered 'temp əd ‖ -ᵊrd — **even-tempered** ˌiːv ᵊn 'temp əd ◂ ‖ -ᵊrd ◂

Temperley 'temp ə li ‖ -ᵊr-

Temperton 'temp ət ən ‖ -ᵊrt ᵊn

tempest 'temp ɪst -əst **~s** s

tempestuous tem 'pes tʃu‿əs təm-, →-'peʃ-; -'pest ju‿əs **~ly** li **~ness** nəs nɪs

tempi 'temp iː

Templar 'temp lə ‖ -lᵊr **~s** z

template 'tem pleɪt 'temp lət, -lɪt **~s** s

temple, T~ 'temp ᵊl **~s** z

templet 'temp lət -lɪt **~s** s

Templeton 'temp ᵊl tən

temp|o 'temp |əʊ ‖ -|oʊ **~i** iː **~os** əʊz ‖ oʊz

temporal 'temp ᵊr‿əl **~ly** i

temporalit|y ˌtemp ə 'ræl ət |i -ɪt i ‖ -əţ |i **~ies** iz

temporarily 'temp ᵊr‿ər əl i -ɪ li; ˌtemp ə 'rer-, -'reər-; ⚠ 'temp rəl i ‖ ˌtemp ə 'rer-

temporar|y 'temp ᵊr‿ər |i §-ə reər i ‖ -ə rer |i —*in casual speech also* 'temp r|i **~ies** iz **~iness** i nəs i nɪs

temporis|e, temporiz|e 'temp ə raɪz **~ed** d **~es** ɪz əz **~ing** ɪŋ

tempt tem*p*t **tempted** 'tem*p*t ɪd -əd **tempting/ly** 'tem*p*t ɪŋ /li **tempts** tem*p*ts

temptation tem*p* 'teɪʃ ᵊn **~s** z

tempter 'tem*p*t ə ‖ -ᵊr **~s** z

temptress 'temp trəs -trɪs **~es** ɪz əz

tempura tem 'pʊər ə 'temp ər ə ‖ tem 'pʊr ə -'pɜː —*Jp* [teˌm pɯ ra]

tempus fugit ˌtemp əs 'fjuːdʒ ɪt -'fjuːg-, -'fuːg-, §-ət

ten ten **tens** tenz

tenability ˌten ə 'bɪl ət i ˌtiːn-, -ɪt i ‖ -əţ i

tenab|le 'ten əb |ᵊl 'tiːn- **~leness** ᵊl nəs -nɪs **~ly** li

tenac|e 'ten eɪs -əs, -ɪs; te 'neɪs **~es** ɪz əz

tenacious tɪ 'neɪʃ əs tə-, te- **~ly** li **~ness** nəs nɪs

tenacity tɪ 'næs ət i tə-, te-, -ɪt i ‖ -əţ i

Tenafly 'ten ə flaɪ

tenanc|y 'ten ənᵗs |i **~ies** iz

tenant 'ten ənt **~s** s

ˌtenant 'farmer

tenantr|y 'ten əntr |i **~ies** iz

Tenbury 'ten bər‿i →'tem-

Tenby 'ten bi →'tem-

tench, Tench ten*t*ʃ **tenches** 'ten*t*ʃ ɪz -əz

tend tend **tended** 'tend ɪd -əd **tending** 'tend ɪŋ **tends** tendz

tendenc|y 'tend ənᵗs |i **~ies** iz

tendentious ten 'denᵗʃ əs **~ly** li **~ness** nəs nɪs

tender 'tend ə ‖ -ᵊr **tendered** 'tend əd ‖ -ᵊrd **tenderer/s** 'tend ər‿ə/z ‖ -ᵊr‿ər/z **tenderest** 'tend ər‿ɪst əst **tendering** 'tend‿ər ɪŋ **tenders** 'tend əz ‖ -ᵊrz

tender|foot 'tend ə |fʊt ‖ -ᵊr- **~feet** fiːt

tenderhearted ˌtend ə 'hɑːt ɪd ◂ -əd ‖ 'tend ᵊr ˌhɑːrţ əd **~ly** li **~ness** nəs nɪs

tenderis|e, tenderiz|e 'tend ə raɪz **~ed** d **~er/s** ə/z ‖ -ᵊr/z **~es** ɪz əz **~ing** ɪŋ

tenderloin 'tend ə lɔɪn ‖ -ᵊr-

tenderly 'tend ə li -ᵊl i ‖ -ᵊr li

tenderness 'tend ə nəs -nɪs ‖ -ᵊr- **~es** ɪz əz

tendinitis ˌtend ɪ 'naɪt ɪs -ə-, §-əs ‖ -ə 'naɪţ əs

tendon 'tend ən **~s** z

tendonitis ˌtend ə 'naɪt ɪs §-əs ‖ -'naɪţ əs

tendril 'tendr əl -ɪl **~s** z

tenebrae, T~ 'ten ə breɪ -ɪ-, -briː, -braɪ

tenebrous 'ten əb rəs -ɪ-

Tenedos 'ten ɪ dɒs -ə- ‖ -dɑːs -doʊs

tenement 'ten ə mənt -ɪ- **~s** s

Tenerife, Teneriffe ˌten ə 'riːf —*Sp* [te ne 'ri fe]

tenesmus tɪ 'nez məs tə-

tenet 'ten ɪt 'tiːn-, -et, §-ət **~s** s

tenfold 'ten fəʊld →-fɒʊld ‖ -foʊld

ten-gallon hat ˌten ˌgæl ən 'hæt →ˌteŋ- **~s** s

tenia 'tiːn i‿ə

Teniers 'ten ɪəz ‖ -jᵊrz —*Dutch* [tə 'niːrs]

Tenison 'ten ɪs ən -əs-

Tenko 'teŋk əʊ ‖ -oʊ

Tennant 'ten ənt

tenner 'ten ə ‖ -ᵊr **~s** z

Tennessean, Tennesseean ˌten ə 'siː‿ən ◂ -ɪ- **~s** z

Tennessee ˌten ə 'siː ◂ -ɪ- —*locally also* '·əs i, -ɪs i

Tenniel 'ten i‿əl

tennies 'ten iz

tennis 'ten ɪs §-əs
'tennis ball; **ˌtennis 'elbow**; **'tennis match**; **'tennis ˌplayer**; **'tennis ˌracquet**

Tennison, Tennyson 'ten ɪs ən -əs-

Tennysonian ˌten ɪ 'səʊn i‿ən ˌ·ə- ‖ -'soʊn jən **~s** z

tenon 'ten ən **~s** z
'tenon saw

tenor 'ten ə ‖ -ᵊr *(= tenner)* **~s** z

tenpin 'ten pɪn →'tem- **~s** z
ˌtenpin 'bowling

tenrec 'ten rek **~s** s

tense tenᵗs **tensed** tenᵗst **tensely** 'tenᵗs li **tenseness** 'tenᵗs nəs -nɪs **tenser** 'tenᵗs ə ‖ -ᵊr **tenses** 'tenᵗs ɪz -əz **tensest** 'tenᵗs ɪst -əst **tensing** 'tenᵗs ɪŋ
ˌtensed 'up

tensile 'tenᵗs aɪᵊl ‖ -ᵊl *(*)*

tensility ten 'sɪl ət i -ɪt i ‖ -əţ i

tension 'tenᵗʃ ᵊn **~ed** d **~ing** ɪŋ **~s** z

tensity 'tenᵗs ət i -ɪt i ‖ -əţ i

tensor 'tenᵗs ə -ɔː ‖ -ᵊr -ɔːr **~s** z

ten-speed 'ten spiːd **~s** z

tent tent **tented** 'tent ɪd -əd ‖ 'tenţ əd **tenting** 'tent ɪŋ ‖ 'tenţ ɪŋ **tents** tents

tentacle 'tent ək ᵊl -ɪk- ‖ 'tenţ- **~d** d **~s** z

tentacular ten 'tæk jʊl ə -jəl- ‖ -jəl ᵊr

tentative 'tent ət ɪv ‖ 'tenţ əţ ɪv **~ly** li **~ness** nəs nɪs

Tenterden 'tent ə dən ‖ 'tenţ ᵊr-

tenterhook 'tent ə hʊk ⚠'tend-, §-huːk ‖ 'tenţ ᵊr- **~s** s

tenth tenᵗθ **tenthly** 'tenᵗθ li **tenths** tenᵗθs →tenᵗs

tenu|is 'ten ju‿ɪs §‿əs **~es** iːz eɪz

tenuity te 'njuː‿ət i tə-, tɪ-, ɪt i ‖ -'nuː əţ i -'njuː-

tenuous 'ten ju‿əs **~ly** li **~ness** nəs nɪs

tenure 'ten jə -jʊə ‖ -jᵊr **~d** d **~s** z

tenure-track 'ten jə træk -jʊə- ‖ -jᵊr-

Tenzing 'tenz ɪŋ

teosinte ˌteɪ əʊ 'sɪnt i ‖ -oʊ 'sɪnţ i

tepal 'tep ᵊl 'tiːp- **~s** z

tepee 'tiːp iː **~s** z

tephra 'tef rə

tephrite 'tef raɪt

tepid 'tep ɪd §-əd **~ly** li **~ness** nəs nɪs

tepidity te 'pɪd ət i -ɪt i ‖ -əţ i

teppanyaki ˌtep ən 'jæk i →-m- ‖ -'jɑːk i —*Jp* [tep ˌpan ja ki]

tequila tɪ 'kiːl ə tə-, te- ‖ teɪ-

tera- ¦ter ə — **terahertz** 'ter ə hɜːts ‖ -hɝːts

terabyte 'ter ə baɪt **~s** s

teraflop 'ter ə flɒp ‖ -flɑːp **~s** s

teraph 'ter əf **teraphim** 'ter ə fɪm

teratogenic ˌter ət əʊ 'dʒen ɪk ◂ ‖ -əţ ə-

teratology ˌter ə 'tɒl ədʒ i ‖ -'tɑːl-

teratoma ˌter ə 'təʊm ə ‖ -'toʊm ə **~s** z

terbium 'tɜːb i‿əm ‖ 'tɝːb-

terce tɜːs ‖ tɝːs *(= terse)*

tercel 'tɜːs ᵊl ‖ 'tɝːs ᵊl **~s** z

Tercel 'tɜːs el ‖ tᵊr 'sel **~s** z

tercentenar|y ˌtɜː sen 'tiːn ər |i ˌ·sᵊn-, -'ten- ‖ ˌtɝː sen 'ten ər |i ˌ·'sent ᵊn er i **~ies** iz

tercentennial ˌtɜː sen 'ten i‿əl ◂ ˌ·sᵊn- ‖ ˌtɝː- **~s** z

tercet 'tɜːs ɪt -et, §-ət; (ˌ)tɜː 'set ‖ 'tɝːs ət **~s** s

terebene 'ter ə biːn -ɪ-

terebinth 'ter ə bɪnᵗθ -ɪ- **~s** s

teredo tə 'riːd əʊ tɪ-, te-, -'reɪd- ‖ -oʊ **~s** z

Terence 'ter ənᵗs

Teresa *(i)* tə 'riːz ə tɪ-, te-, *(ii)* -'reɪz-, *(iii)* -'riːs-, *(iv)* -'reɪs- —*(iii) and (iv) are AmE, but not usually BrE*

Terese *(i)* tə 'riːz tɪ-, te-, -'riːs, *(ii)* -'reɪz

Terfel 'tɜːv ᵊl 'teəv- ‖ 'tɝːv- —*Welsh* ['ter vel]

tergivers|ate 'tɜːdʒ ɪ vɜːs |eɪt -və s|eɪt ‖ tɝː 'dʒɪv ᵊr s|eɪt -'gɪv-; ˌtɜːdʒ ə 'vɝːs |eɪt *(*)* **~ated** eɪt ɪd -əd ‖ eɪţ əd **~ates** eɪts **~ating** eɪt ɪŋ ‖ eɪţ ɪŋ

tergiversation ˌtɜːdʒ ɪ vɜː 'seɪʃ ᵊn §ˌ·ə-, -və'·- ‖ tɝː ˌdʒɪv ᵊr- -ˌgɪv-; ˌtɝːdʒ ə vɝː- **~s** z

teriyaki ˌter i 'æk i ‖ -'jɑːk i —*Jp* [te ˌri ja ki]

Terkel 'tɜːk ᵊl ‖ 'tɝːk ᵊl

term tɜːm ‖ tɝːm **termed** tɜːmd ‖ tɝːmd **terming** 'tɜːm ɪŋ ‖ 'tɝːm ɪŋ **terms** tɜːmz ‖ tɝːmz
ˌterms of 'reference

termagant 'tɜːm əg ənt ‖ 'tɝːm- **~s** s

terminable 'tɜːm ɪn əb ᵊl -ən‿əb- ‖ 'tɝːm- **~ness** nəs nɪs

terminal 'tɜːm ɪn ᵊl -ən- ‖ 'tɝːm ᵊn‿əl **~ly** i **~s** z
ˌTerminal 'Four

termi|nate 'tɜːm ɪ |neɪt -ə- ‖ 'tɝːm- **~nated** neɪt ɪd -əd ‖ neɪţ əd **~nates** neɪts **~nating** neɪt ɪŋ ‖ neɪţ ɪŋ

termination ˌtɜːm ɪ 'neɪʃ ᵊn -ə- ‖ ˌtɝːm- **~s** z

terminative 'tɜːm ɪn ət ɪv -ən-; -ɪ neɪt ɪv, -ə· · ‖ 'tɝːm ə neɪţ ɪv **~ly** li

terminator 'tɜːm ɪ neɪt ə '·ə- ‖ 'tɝːm ə neɪţ ᵊr **~s** z

termini 'tɜːm ɪ naɪ -ə- ‖ 'tɝːm-

terminological ˌtɜːm ɪn ə 'lɒdʒ ɪk ᵊl ◂ ˌ·ən-, -ᵊl 'ɒdʒ- ‖ ˌtɝːm ən ᵊl 'ɑːdʒ- **~ly** ‿i

terminolog|y ˌtɜːm ɪ 'nɒl ədʒ |i ˌ·ə- ‖ ˌtɝːm ə 'nɑːl- **~ies** iz

term|inus 'tɜːm |ɪn əs -ən- ‖ 'tɝːm- **~ini** ɪ naɪ ə-
ˌterminus ad 'quem æd 'kwem ‖ ɑːd-;
ˌterminus a 'quo ɑː 'kwəʊ ‖ ɑː 'kwoʊ

termite 'tɜːm aɪt ‖ 'tɝːm- **~s** s

termly 'tɜːm li ‖ 'tɝːm-

termtime 'tɜːm taɪm ‖ 'tɝːm-

tern tɜːn ‖ tɜ˞ːn *(= turn)* **terns** tɜːnz ‖ tɜ˞ːnz
ternar|y 'tɜːn ər |i ‖ 'tɜ˞ːn- **~ies** iz
terpene 'tɜːp iːn ‖ 'tɜ˞ːp- **~s** z
terpsichorean, T~ ˌtɜːps ɪk ə 'riːˌən ◂ -ɒ'--; ˌ·ɪ 'kɔːr iˌən ‖ ˌtɜ˞ːps-
Terpsichore tɜːp 'sɪk ər i ‖ tɜ˞ːp-
terra, Terra 'ter ə
ˌterra 'cotta 'kɒt ə ‖ 'kɑːţ ə; **ˌterra 'firma** 'fɜːm ə ‖ 'fɜ˞ːm ə; **ˌterra in'cognita** ɪn 'kɒg nɪt ə →ɪŋ-; ˌɪŋ kɒg 'niːt ə ‖ ˌɪn kɑːg 'niːţ ə ɪn 'kɑːg nəţ ə; **ˌterra 'nullius** 'nʊl iˌəs
terrac|e 'ter əs -ɪs **~ed** t **~es** ɪz əz **~ing** ɪŋ
terracotta ˌter ə 'kɒt ə ◂ ‖ -'kɑːţ ə
terrain tə 'reɪn te-, tɪ-; 'ter eɪn
terramycin, T~ *tdmk* ˌter ə 'maɪs ɪn §-ən
terrapin 'ter ə pɪn §-əp ən
terrari|um tə 'reər iˌ|əm te-, tɪ- ‖ -'rer- -'rær- **~a** ə **~ums** əmz
terrazzo te 'ræts əʊ tə-, tɪ- ‖ -'ræz oʊ -'rɑːts-
Terre Haute ˌter ə 'həʊt ‖ -'hoʊt -'hʌt
Terrence 'ter ənts
terrene 'ter iːn te 'riːn
terrestrial tə 'res triˌəl tɪ-, te- **~ly** i **~s** z
terret 'ter ɪt -ət **~s** s
Terri 'ter i
terrible 'ter əb əl -ɪb- **~ness** nəs nɪs
terribly 'ter əb li -ɪb-
terrier 'ter iˌə ‖ ər **~s** z
terrific tə'rɪf ɪk —*casually also* 'trɪf ɪk **~ally** əl i
terri|fy 'ter ə |faɪ -ɪ- **~fied** faɪd **~fies** faɪz **~fying/ly** faɪ ɪŋ /li
terrine te 'riːn tə-; 'ter iːn **~s** z
territorial ˌter ə 'tɔːr iˌəl ◂ ˌ·ɪ- ‖ -'toʊr- **~ly** i **~s** z
ˌTerriˌtorial 'Army; **ˌterriˌtorial 'waters**
territoriality ˌter ə ˌtɔːr i 'æl ət i ˌ·ɪ-, -ɪt i ‖ -əţ i -ˌtoʊr-
territor|y 'ter əˌtər |i '·ɪ- ‖ -tɔːr |i -toʊr i *(*)* **~ies** iz
terror 'ter ə ‖ -ər **~s** z
terroris... —*see* **terroriz...**
terrorism 'ter ər ˌɪz əm
terrorist 'ter ər ɪst §-əst **~s** s
terroriz|e 'ter ə raɪz **~ed** d **~es** ɪz əz **~ing** ɪŋ
terror-stricken 'ter ə ˌstrɪk ən ‖ -ər-
terror-struck 'ter ə strʌk ‖ -ər-
terry, Terry 'ter i
terrycloth 'ter i klɒθ -klɔːθ ‖ -klɔːθ -klɑːθ
terse tɜːs ‖ tɜ˞ːs **tersely** 'tɜːs li ‖ 'tɜ˞ːs li
terseness 'tɜːs nəs -nɪs ‖ 'tɜ˞ːs nəs **terser** 'tɜːs ə ‖ 'tɜ˞ːs ər **tersest** 'tɜːs ɪst -əst ‖ 'tɜ˞ːs əst
tertian 'tɜːʃ ən 'tɜːʃ iˌən ‖ 'tɜ˞ːʃ ən
tertiar|y, T~ 'tɜːʃ ər |i -iˌər- ‖ 'tɜ˞ːʃ i er |i '·ər |i **~ies** iz
ˌtertiary ˌedu'cation; **ˌtertiary 'stress**
tertium quid ˌtɜːʃ iˌəm 'kwɪd ˌtɜːt- ‖ ˌtɜ˞ːʃ- ˌtɜ˞ːţ-
Tertius 'tɜːʃ iˌəs ‖ 'tɜ˞ːʃ-
Tertullian tɜː 'tʌl iˌən tə- ‖ tər-
terylene, T~ *tdmk* 'ter ə liːn -ɪ-
terza rima ˌteəts ə 'riːm ə ˌtɜːts- ‖ ˌterts- —*It* [ˌter tsa 'riː ma]
Tesco *tdmk* 'tesk əʊ ‖ -oʊ
TESL 'tes əl
Tesla, tesla 'tes lə **~s** z
TESOL 'tiːs ɒl ‖ -ɑːl 'tes əl
Tess tes
Tessa, TESSA 'tes ə
tessel|late 'tes ə |leɪt -ɪ- **~lated** leɪt ɪd -əd ‖ leɪţ əd **~lates** leɪts **~lating** leɪt ɪŋ ‖ leɪţ ɪŋ
tessellation ˌtes ə 'leɪʃ ən -ɪ- **~s** z
tesser|a 'tes ər| ə **~ae** iː
tesseract 'tes ə rækt **~s** s
Tessie 'tes i
tessitura ˌtes ɪ 'tʊər ə -ə-, -'tjʊər ə ‖ -'tʊr ə —*It* [tes si 'tuː ra]
test, Test test **tested** 'test ɪd -əd **testing** 'test ɪŋ **tests** tests
'test ban; **'test card**; **'test case**; **'testing ground**; **'test match**; **'test ˌpaper**; **'test ˌpilot**; **'test tube**
testability ˌtest ə 'bɪl ət i -ɪt i ‖ -əţ i
testable 'test əb əl
testament 'test ə mənt **~s** s
testamentary ˌtest ə 'ment ər i ◂ ‖ -'menţ ər i →-'mentr i
testamur te 'steɪm ə ‖ -ər **~s** z
testate 'test eɪt -ət, -ɪt
testator te 'steɪt ə ‖ 'test eɪţ ər te 'steɪţ ər **~s** z
testatr|ix te 'steɪtr |ɪks ‖ 'test eɪtr- **~ices** ɪ siːz -ə-
test-bed 'test bed
test-|drive 'test |draɪv **~driven** drɪv ən **~drives** draɪvz **~driving** draɪv ɪŋ **~drove** drəʊv ‖ droʊv
tester, T~ 'test ə ‖ -ər **~s** z
testes 'test iːz
test-|fly 'test|flaɪ **~flew** fluː **~flies** flaɪz **~flown** fləʊn §ˌfləʊ ən ‖ floʊn
testicle 'test ɪk əl **~s** z
testicular te 'stɪk jʊl ə -jəl- ‖ -jəl ər
testi|fy 'test ɪ |faɪ -ə- **~fied** faɪd **~fier/s** faɪˌə/z ‖ faɪˌər/z **~fies** faɪz **~fying** faɪ ɪŋ
testimonial ˌtest ɪ 'məʊn iˌəl ◂ ˌ·ə- ‖ -'moʊn- **~s** z
testimon|y 'test ɪ mən |i '·ə- ‖ -ə moʊn |i *(*)* **~ies** iz
test|is 'test |ɪs §-əs **~es** iːz
testosterone te 'stɒst ə rəʊn ‖ -'stɑːst ə roʊn
test-tube 'test tjuːb →-tʃuːb ‖ -tuːb -tjuːb **~s** z
ˌtest-tube 'baby
testud|o te 'stjuːd |əʊ →-'stʃuːd- ‖ -'stuːd |oʊ -'stjuːd- **~ines** ɪ niːz ə-, -neɪz **~os** əʊz ‖ oʊz
test|y 'test |i **~ier** iˌə ‖ iˌər **~iest** iˌɪst iˌəst **~ily** ɪ li əl i **~iness** i nəs i nɪs
Tet tet
tetanic te 'tæn ɪk tɪ-, tə-
tetanus 'tet ənˌəs
tetany 'tet ən i
Tetbury 'tet bərˌi ‖ -ˌber i
tetch|y 'tetʃ |i **~ier** iˌə ‖ iˌər **~iest** iˌɪst iˌəst **~ily** ɪ li əl i **~iness** i nəs i nɪs

tete-a-tete, tête-à-tête ˌteɪt ə ˈteɪt ˌtet-, ɑː-, -ˈtet ‖ ˌteɪt̬ ə ˈteɪt ˌtet̬ ə ˈtet; ˈ· · · —*Fr* [tɛ ta tɛt] **~s** s
tete-beche, tête-bêche ˌteɪt ˈbeʃ ˌtet-, -ˈbeɪʃ —*Fr* [tɛd bɛʃ]
tether ˈteð ə ‖ -ər **~ed** d **tethering** ˈteð ər ɪŋ **~s** z
tetherball ˈteð ə bɔːl ‖ -ər- -bɑːl
Tethys ˈtiːθ ɪs ˈteθ-, §-əs
Tetley ˈtet li
Teton ˈtiːt ən -ɒn ‖ -ɑːn -ən **~s** z
tetra ˈtetr ə **~s** z
tetra- *comb form*
with stress-neutral suffix |tetr ə — **tetrachloride** ˌtetr ə ˈklɔːr aɪd ‖ -ˈklour-
with stress-imposing suffix te ˈtræ+ — **tetramerous** te ˈtræm ər əs
tetrabrik ˈtetr ə brɪk **~s** s
tetrachord ˈtetr ə kɔːd ‖ -kɔːrd **~s** z
tetracycline ˌtetr ə ˈsaɪk liːn -lɪn, -laɪn
tetrad ˈtetr æd **~s** z
tetraethyl ˌtetr ə ˈiːθ aɪəl -ˈeθ ɪl, -əl ‖ -əl
tetragrammaton, T~ ˌtetr ə ˈgræm ət ən -ə tɒn ‖ -ə tɑːn
tetrahedr|on ˌtetr ə ˈhiːdr |ən -ˈhedr- **~a** ə **~al** əl **~ons** ənz
tetralog|y te ˈtræl ədʒ |i ‖ -ˈtrɑːl- **~ies** iz
tetrameter te ˈtræm ɪt ə -ət ə ‖ -ət̬ ər **~s** z
tetrapod ˈtetr ə pɒd ‖ -pɑːd **~s** z
tetrarch ˈtetr ɑːk ‖ -ɑːrk **~s** s
tetravalent ˌtetr ə ˈveɪl ənt
tetrode ˈtetr əʊd ‖ -oud **~s** z
Tettenhall ˈtet ən hɔːl ‖ -hɑːl
tetter ˈtet ə ‖ ˈtet̬ ər
Teucer ˈtjuːs ə →ˈtʃuːs- ‖ ˈtuːs ər ˈtjuːs-
Teucrian ˈtjuːk ri ən →ˈtʃuːk- ‖ ˈtuːk- ˈtjuːk- **~s** z
Teuton ˈtjuːt ən →ˈtʃuːt- ‖ ˈtuːt ən ˈtjuːt- **~s** z
Teutonic tju ˈtɒn ɪk →tʃu- ‖ tu ˈtɑːn ɪk tju-
Teversham ˈtev əʃ əm ‖ -ərʃ-
Teviot ˈtiːv i ət ˈtev-
Tew tjuː →tʃuː ‖ tuː tjuː
Tewa ˈteɪ wə ˈtiː- **~s** z
Tewkesbury ˈtjuːks bər i →ˈtʃuːks- ‖ ˈtuːks ˌber i ˈtjuːks- —*but locally* -bər i *in MA, just as in Gloucs.*
Tex teks
TeX *software* tek — *although its author Knuth insists on* tex
Texaco *tdmk* ˈteks ə kəʊ ‖ -koʊ -ɪ-
Texan ˈteks ən **~s** z
Texas ˈteks əs ‖ -əz
ˌTexas ˈRanger
Texel ˈteks əl
Tex-Mex ˌteks ˈmeks ◂
text tekst **texted** ˈtekst ɪd -əd; tekst **texting** ˈtekst ɪŋ ˈteks- **texts** teksts
text-based ˈtekst beɪst ˌ·ˈ·◂
textbook ˈtekst bʊk §-buːk **~s** s
textile ˈtekst aɪəl ‖ -əl **~s** z
textual ˈteks tʃu əl ˈtekst ju **~ly** i
textuality ˌteks tju ˈæl ət i -tʃuˈ--, -ɪt i ‖ ˌteks tʃu ˈæl ət̬ i
textural ˈteks tʃər əl
texture ˈteks tʃə ‖ -tʃər **~d** d **texturing** ˈteks tʃər ɪŋ **~s** z
ˌtextured ˌvegetable ˈprotein
-textured ˈteks tʃəd ‖ -tʃərd — **even-textured** ˌiːv ən ˈteks tʃəd ◂ ‖ -tʃərd
Tey teɪ
-th θ — **fourth** fɔːθ ‖ fɔːrθ fourθ
Thabo ˈtɑːb əʊ ‖ -oʊ —*Xhosa* [ˈtʰɑː ɓo]
Thackeray ˈθæk ər i -ə reɪ
Thad θæd
Thaddeus ˈθæd i əs θæ ˈdiː əs
Thai taɪ **Thais** taɪz
Thailand ˈtaɪ lænd -lənd
Thais, Thaïs *personal name* ˈθeɪ ɪs §-əs
Thais *pl of* **Thai** taɪz
thal|amus ˈθæl |əm əs **~ami** ə maɪ -miː
thalassaemia, thalassemia ˌθæl ə ˈsiːm i ə
thalassic θə ˈlæs ɪk
thalassotherapy θə ˌlæs əʊ ˈθer əp i θæ- ‖ ·ˌ·ə-
thaler ˈtɑːl ə ‖ -ər **~s** z
Thales ˈθeɪl iːz
Thalia θə ˈlaɪ ə ˈθeɪl i ə, ˈθæl-
thalidomide θə ˈlɪd ə maɪd
thallium ˈθæl i əm
thall|us ˈθæl |əs **~i** aɪ **~uses** əs ɪz -əz
Thame teɪm *(!)*
Thames *(i)* temz *(!), (ii)* θeɪmz —*The rivers in England, Canada and NZ are (i), the one in CT usually (ii).*
than *strong form* ðæn, *weak form* ðən
Thanatos ˈθæn ə tɒs ‖ -tɑːs
thane θeɪn **thanes** θeɪnz
thaneship ˈθeɪn ʃɪp **~s** s
Thanet ˈθæn ɪt -ət
thang θæŋ
thank θæŋk **thanked** θæŋkt **thanking** ˈθæŋk ɪŋ **thanks** θæŋks
thank you ˈθæŋk ju —*There are also casual forms such as* ˈhæŋk ju, ˈŋk ju
thankful ˈθæŋk fəl -fʊl **~ly** i **~ness** nəs nɪs
thankless ˈθæŋk ləs -lɪs **~ly** li **~ness** nəs nɪs

THANKSGIVING

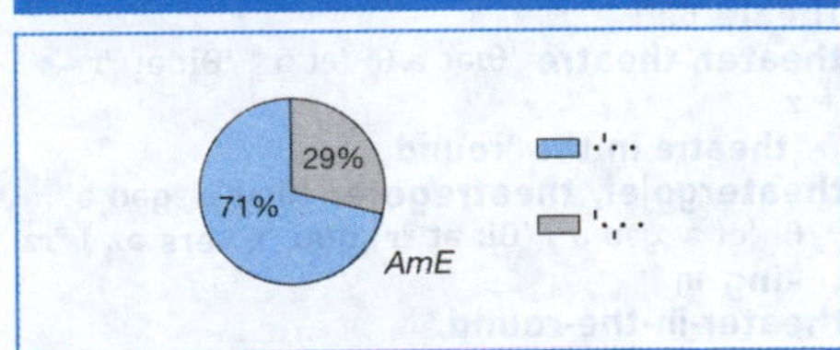

thanksgiving, T~ ˈθæŋks ˌgɪv ɪŋ ˌ·ˈ·· ‖ θæŋks ˈgɪv ɪŋ ˈ·ˌ·· — *Preference poll, AmE:* ˌ·ˈ·· *71%,* ˈ·ˌ·· *29%.* **~s** z
Thanksˈgiving Day
thankyou *n, adj* ˈθæŋk ju **~s** z
Thapsus ˈθæps əs
Tharp θɑːp ‖ θɑːrp
that *determiner (demonstrative adj), demonstrative pronoun, and adverb* ðæt

—*There is no weak form for* that *in this sense:* that (ðæt) man, stop that, not that bad.
that *complementizer (conjunction and relative pronoun): strong form* **ðæt**, *weak form* **ðət** —*Normally, the weak form is used:* say that (ðət) she's right, the one that I chose .
thataway ˈðæt ə weɪ ‖ ˈðæt̬-
thatch θætʃ **thatched** θætʃt **thatches** ˈθætʃ ɪz -əz **thatching** ˈθætʃ ɪŋ
Thatcham ˈθætʃ əm
thatcher, T~ ˈθætʃ ə ‖ -ᵊr **~s** z
Thatcherism ˈθætʃ ər ˌɪz əm
Thatcherite ˈθætʃ ə raɪt **~s** s
that'll *strong form* ˈðæt ᵊl ‖ ˈðæt̬ ᵊl, *weak form* ðət ᵊl ‖ ðət̬ ᵊl —*see entries at* that: I think that'll (ðæt ᵊl) please you, a thing that'll (ðət ᵊl) please you
that's *strong form* **ðæts**, *weak form* **ðəts** —*see entries at* that: I think that's (**ðæts**) right, a thing that's (**ðəts**) wrong
thaumatology ˌθɔːm ə ˈtɒl ədʒ i ‖ -ˈtɑːl- ˌθɑːm-
thaumaturg|e ˈθɔːm ə tɜːdʒ ‖ -tɜːdʒ ˈθɑːm- **~es** ɪz əz
thaumaturgic ˌθɔːm ə ˈtɜːdʒ ɪk ◂ ‖ -ˈtɜːdʒ- ˌθɑːm- **~al** ᵊl
thaumaturgy ˈθɔːm ə tɜːdʒ i ‖ -tɜːdʒ i ˈθɑːm-
thaw, Thaw θɔː ‖ θɑː **thawed** θɔːd ‖ θɑːd **thawing** ˈθɔːʳ ɪŋ ‖ ˈθɔː ɪŋ ˈθɑː- **thaws** θɔːz ‖ θɑːz
Thawpit *tdmk* ˈθɔːp ɪt §-ət ‖ ˈθɑːp-
Thayer ˈθeɪ ə θeə ‖ ˈθeɪ ᵊr θeᵊr, θæᵊr
the *strong form* **ðiː**, *weak forms* **ði, ðə** —*The EFL learner is advised to use* **ðə** *before a consonant sound* (the boy, the house), **ði** *before a vowel sound* (the egg, the hour). *Native speakers, however, sometimes ignore this distribution, in particular by using* **ðə** *before a vowel (which in turn is usually reinforced by a preceding* **ʔ**), *or by using* **ðiː** *in any environment, though especially before a hesitation pause. Furthermore, some speakers use stressed* **ðə** *as a strong form, rather than the usual* **ðiː**.
Thea ˈθiː‿ə
Theale θiːᵊl
theater, theatre ˈθɪət ə θi ˈet ə ‖ ˈθiː ət̬ ᵊr **~s** z
ˌtheatre in the ˈround
theatergo|er, theatrego|er ˈθɪət ə ˌɡəʊ ə θi ˈet ə ˌɡəʊ ə ‖ ˈθiː ət̬ ᵊr ˌɡoʊ ᵊr **~ers** əz ‖ ᵊrz **~ing** ɪŋ
theater-in-the-round, theatre-in-the-round ˈθɪət ər ɪn ðə ˈraʊnd θi ˌet ər- ‖ ˌθiː ət̬ ᵊr-
theaterland, theatreland ˈθɪət ə lænd θi ˈet ə lænd ‖ ˈθiː ət̬ ᵊr lænd
theatrical θi ˈætr ɪk ᵊl §-ˈetr- **~ly** ‿i **~ness** nəs nɪs **~s** z
theatricality θi ˌætr ɪ ˈkæl ət i §-ˌetr-, -ˌ-ə-, -ɪt i ‖ -ət̬ i
theatrics θi ˈætr ɪks §-ˈetr-
Thebaid ˈθiːb eɪ ɪd -i-, §-əd
Theban ˈθiːb ən **~s** z
Thebes θiːbz
theca ˈθiːk ə **thecae** ˈθiːs iː ˈθiːk-
thecodont ˈθiːk əʊ dɒnt ‖ -ə dɑːnt **~s** s
thee *strong form* ðiː, *weak form* ði
theft θeft **thefts** θefts
thegn θeɪn *(= thane)* **thegns** θeɪnz
their ðeə §ˈðeɪ ə ‖ ðeᵊr ðæᵊr —*In GenAm there is also a weak form* **ðᵊr**. *In RP there is either no weak form, or just an occasional weak form* **ðər** *used only before a following vowel.*
theirs ðeəz §ˈðeɪ əz ‖ ðeᵊrz ðæᵊrz
theism ˈθiː ˌɪz əm
theist ˈθiː ɪst §-əst **~s** s
theistic θi ˈɪst ɪk **~al** ᵊl **~ally** ᵊl‿i
Thelma ˈθelm ə
Thelwall ˈθel wɔːl ‖ -wɑːl
Thelwell ˈθel wəl -wel
them *strong form* **ðem**, *weak form* **ðəm**
thematic θɪ ˈmæt ɪk θiː- ‖ -ˈmæt̬ ɪk **~ally** ᵊl‿i
theme θiːm **themes** θiːmz
ˈtheme park; **ˈtheme song**; **ˈtheme tune**
Themis ˈθem ɪs ˈθiːm-, §-əs
Themistocles θə ˈmɪst ə kliːz θɪ-, θe-
themself ðəm ˈself
themselves ðəm ˈselvz —*occasionally also, with contrastive stress,* ˈðem selvz
then ðen
thenar ˈθiːn ə -ɑː ‖ -ᵊr -ɑːr **~s** z
thence ðenᵗs ‖ θenᵗs
thenceforth ˌðenᵗs ˈfɔːθ ‖ -ˈfɔːrθ ˌθenᵗs-, -ˈfoʊrθ
thenceforward ˌðenᵗs ˈfɔː wəd ‖ -ˈfɔːr wᵊrd ˌθenᵗs-, -ˈfoʊr- **~s** z
theo- *comb. form*
with stress-neutral suffix ¦θiː əʊ ‖ -ə — **theocentric** ˌθiː əʊ ˈsentr ɪk ◂ ‖ -ə-
with stress-imposing suffix θi ˈɒ+ ‖ -ˈɑː+ — **theophagy** θi ˈɒf ədʒ i ‖ -ˈɑːf-
Theo ˈθiː‿əʊ ‖ -oʊ
Theobald ˈθiː‿ə bɔːld ‖ -bɑːld —*Formerly also* ˈtɪb ᵊld **~s** z
theobromine ˌθiː əʊ ˈbrəʊm iːn -ɪn ‖ -ə ˈbroʊm-
theocrac|y θi ˈɒk rəs |i ‖ -ˈɑːk- **~ies** iz
theocrat ˈθiː‿ə kræt **~s** s
theocratic ˌθiː‿ə ˈkræt ɪk ◂ ‖ -ə ˈkræt̬- **~ally** ᵊl‿i
Theocritus θi ˈɒk rɪt əs -rət- ‖ -ˈɑːk-
theodic|y θi ˈɒd əs |i -ɪs- ‖ -ˈɑːd- **~ies** iz
theodolite θi ˈɒd ə laɪt -ᵊl aɪt ‖ -ˈɑːd ᵊl aɪt **~s** s
Theodora ˌθiː‿ə ˈdɔːr ə ‖ -ˈdoʊr-
Theodorakis ˌθiː‿ə dɔː ˈrɑːk ɪs -də'--, §-əs —*ModGk* [θɛ ɔ ðɔ ˈra cis]
Theodore ˈθiː‿ə dɔː ‖ -dɔːr -doʊr
Theodoric θi ˈɒd ər ɪk ‖ -ˈɑːd-
Theodosi|us ˌθiː‿ə ˈdəʊs i‿|əs ‖ -ˈdoʊʃ- **~an** ən
theogon|y θi ˈɒɡ ən |i ‖ -ˈɑːɡ- **~ies** iz
theologian ˌθiː‿ə ˈləʊdʒ i‿ən -ˈ-ən ‖ -ˈloʊdʒ- **~s** z
theological ˌθiː‿ə ˈlɒdʒ ɪk ᵊl ◂ ‖ -ˈlɑːdʒ- **~ly** ‿i
theolog|y θi ˈɒl ədʒ |i ‖ -ˈɑːl- **~ies** iz

theomachy θi ˈɒm ək i ‖ -ˈɑːm-
theomancy ˈθiː əʊ ˌmæn*t*s i ‖ -oʊ-
theophan|y θi ˈɒf ən |i ‖ -ˈɑːf- **~ies** iz
Theophilus θi ˈɒf ɪl əs -əl- ‖ -ˈɑːf-
Theophrastus ˌθiː‿ə ˈfræst əs
theophylline ˌθiː‿ə ˈfɪl iːn -ɪn, -aɪn; θi ˈɒf ɪ liːn, -ə-, -lɪn, -laɪn
theorbo θi ˈɔːb əʊ ‖ -ˈɔːrb oʊ **~s** z
theorem ˈθɪər əm §ˈθiː ər əm ‖ ˈθiː ər əm ˈθɪr əm **~s** z
theoretic ˌθɪə ˈret ɪk ◂ §ˌθiː əˈ-- ‖ ˌθiː ə ˈreţ ɪk ◂ θɪˈ-- **~al** ᵊl **~ally** ᵊl‿i **~s** s
theoretician ˌθɪər ə ˈtɪʃ ᵊn -e-, -ɪ- ‖ ˌθiː ər ə ˈtɪʃ ᵊn ˌθɪr əˈ· · **~s** z
theorie... —*see* **theory**
theoris... —*see* **theoriz...**
theorist ˈθɪər ɪst §ˈθiː ər-, §-əst ‖ ˈθiː ər əst ˈθɪr əst **~s** s
theoriz|e ˈθɪər aɪz §ˈθiː ə raɪz ‖ ˈθiː ə raɪz **~ed** d **~es** ɪz əz **~ing** ɪŋ
theor|y ˈθɪər |i ˈθiː ər |i ‖ ˈθiː ər |i ˈθɪr |i **~ies** iz
theosophical ˌθiː‿ə ˈsɒf ɪk ᵊl ◂ ‖ -ˈsɑːf- **~ly** ˌi
theosophist θi ˈɒs əf ɪst §-əst ‖ -ˈɑːs- **~s** s
theosoph|y θi ˈɒs əf |i ‖ -ˈɑːs- **~ies** iz
Thera ˈθɪər ə ‖ ˈθɪr ə —*ModGk* [ˈθi ra]
therapeutic ˌθer ə ˈpjuːt ɪk ◂ ‖ -ˈpjuːţ ɪk ◂ **~ally** ᵊl‿i **~s** s
therapie... —*see* **therapy**
therapist ˈθer əp ɪst §-əst **~s** s
therapsid θə ˈræps ɪd θɪ-, θe-, §-əd **~s** z
therap|y ˈθer əp |i **~ies** iz
Theravada ˌθer ə ˈvɑːd ə
there *existential pronoun (adv): strong form* ðeə ‖ ðer ðær, *weak form* ðə ‖ ðᵊr —*Some speakers hardly use the weak form, even though the word is never stressed; others hardly use the strong form*
there *adv of place; interj* ðeə ‖ ðeᵊr ðæᵊr
thereabout ˌðeər ə ˈbaʊt ˈ· ·ˌ· ‖ ˌðer- ˌðær-
thereabouts ˌðeər ə ˈbaʊts ˈ· ·ˌ· ‖ ðer- ˌðær-
thereafter ₍ˌ₎ðeər ˈɑːft ə §-ˈæft- ‖ ₍ˌ₎ðer ˈæft ᵊr ₍ˌ₎ðær-
thereat ˌðeər ˈæt ‖ ˌðer-
thereby ˌðeə ˈbaɪ ˈ· · ‖ ˌðer- ˌðær-
there'd *strong form* ðeəd ‖ ðerd ðærd, *weak form* ðəd ‖ ðᵊrd —*See note at* there
therefor ˌðeə ˈfɔː ‖ ˌðer ˈfɔːr ˌðær-
therefore ˈðeə fɔː §-fə ‖ ˈðer fɔːr ˈðær-, -foʊr
therefrom ˌðeə ˈfrɒm ‖ ˌðer ˈfrʌm -ˈfrɑːm
therein ˌðeər ˈɪn ‖ ˌðer- ˌðær-
thereinafter ˌðeər ɪn ˈɑːft ə §-ˈæft- ‖ ˌðer ɪn ˈæft ᵊr ˌðær-
there'll *strong form* ðeəl ðeər əl ‖ ðerl ðærl, ðer əl, ðær əl, *weak form* ðəl ðər əl ‖ ðᵊrl ðᵊr əl —*See note at* there
theremin, thérémin, T~ ˈθer əm ɪn §-ən **~s** z
thereof ˌðeər ˈɒv ‖ ˌðer ˈʌv ˌðær-, -ˈɑːv
thereon ˌðeər ˈɒn ‖ ˌðer ˈɑːn ˌðær-, -ˈɔːn
there's *strong form* ðeəz ‖ ðerz ðærz, *weak form* ðəz ‖ ðᵊrz —*See note at* there
Theresa tə ˈriːz ə tɪ-, -ˈreɪz- ‖ -ˈriːs- *(!)*
Therese, Thérèse tə ˈreɪz —*Fr* [te ʁɛːz]

thereto ˌðeə ˈtuː ‖ ˌðer- ˌðær-
theretofore ˌðeə tu ˈfɔː ‖ ˈðerţ ə fɔːr -foʊr
thereunder ˌðeər ˈʌnd ə ‖ ðer ˈʌnd ᵊr ðær-
thereupon ˌðeər ə ˈpɒn ˈ· ·ˌ· ‖ ˌðer ə ˈpɑːn ˌðær-, -ˈpɔːn
there've *strong form* ðeəv ‖ ðerv ðærv, *weak form* ðəv ðər əv ‖ ðᵊrv ðər əv —*See note at* there
therewith ˌðeə ˈwɪð -ˈwɪθ ‖ ˌðer- ˌðær-
therewithal ˈðeə wɪð ɔːl -wɪθ-, ˌ· ·ˈ· ‖ ˈðer- ˈðær-, -ɑːl
therm θɜːm ‖ θɜ˞ːm **therms** θɜːmz ‖ θɜ˞ːmz
thermal ˈθɜːm ᵊl ‖ ˈθɜ˞ːm ᵊl **~ly** i **~s** z
thermic ˈθɜːm ɪk ‖ ˈθɜ˞ːm ɪk
Thermidor ˈθɜːm ɪ dɔː §-ə- ‖ ˈθɜ˞ːm ə dɔːr —*Fr* [tɛʁ mi dɔːʁ]
thermion ˈθɜːm i‿ən ‖ ˈθɜ˞ːm- -ɑːn **~s** z
thermionic ˌθɜːm i ˈɒn ɪk ◂ ‖ ˌθɜ˞ːm i ˈɑːn ɪk ◂ **~s** s
ˌthermiˌonic ˈvalve
thermistor θɜː ˈmɪst ə ˈθɜːm ɪst ə ‖ θɜ˞ː ˈmɪst ᵊr ˈθɜ˞ːm ɪst- **~s** z
thermite ˈθɜːm aɪt ‖ ˈθɜ˞ːm-
thermo- *comb. form*
with stress-neutral suffix ¦θɜːm əʊ ‖ ¦θɜ˞ːm ə — **thermographic** ˌθɜːm əʊ ˈgræf ɪk ◂ ‖ ˌθɜ˞ːm ə-
with stress-imposing suffix θɜː ˈmɒ+ ‖ θɜ˞ː ˈmɑː+ — **thermography** θɜː ˈmɒg rəf i ‖ θɜ˞ː ˈmɑːg-
thermocouple ˈθɜːm əʊ ˌkʌp ᵊl ‖ ˈθɜ˞ːm ə- **~s** z
thermodynamic ˌθɜːm əʊ daɪ ˈnæm ɪk ◂ ‖ ˌθɜ˞ːm oʊ- **~ally** ᵊl‿i **~s** s
thermoelectric ˌθɜːm əʊ ɪ ˈlek trɪk ◂ -əˈ-- ‖ ˌθɜ˞ːm oʊ- **~ally** ᵊl‿i
thermometer θə ˈmɒm ɪt ə -ət- ‖ θᵊr ˈmɑːm əţ ᵊr **~s** z
thermonuclear ˌθɜːm əʊ ˈnjuːk li‿ə ◂ §-ˈnuːk- ‖ ˌθɜ˞ːm oʊ ˈnuːk li‿ᵊr -ˈnjuːk-, ⚠-jəl ᵊr
thermoplastic ˌθɜːm əʊ ˈplæst ɪk ◂ -ˈplɑːst- ‖ ˌθɜ˞ːm ə- **~s** s
Thermopylae θə ˈmɒp əl i θɜː-, -ɪl-, -iː ‖ θᵊr ˈmɑːp-
thermos, T~ *tdmk* ˈθɜːm əs -ɒs ‖ ˈθɜ˞ːm əs **~es** ɪz əz
ˈthermos flask
thermosetting ˈθɜːm əʊ ˌset ɪŋ ˌ· ·ˈ· · ‖ ˈθɜ˞ːm oʊ ˌseţ ɪŋ
thermostat ˈθɜːm əʊ stæt ‖ ˈθɜ˞ːm ə- **~s** s
thermostatic ˌθɜːm əʊ ˈstæt ɪk ◂ ‖ ˌθɜ˞ːm ə ˈstæţ ɪk ◂ **~ally** ᵊl‿i
-thermy ˌθɜːm i ‖ ˌθɜ˞ːm i — **diathermy** ˈdaɪ‿ə ˌθɜːm i ‖ -ˌθɜ˞ːm i
theropod ˈθer ə pɒd ‖ -pɑːd **~s** z
Theroux θə ˈruː
Thersites θɜː ˈsaɪt iːz ‖ θᵊr-
thesaur|us θɪ ˈsɔːr |əs θə- **~i** aɪ **~uses** əs ɪz -əz
these ðiːz
theses ˈθiːs iːz
Theseus ˈθiːs juːs ˈθiːs i‿əs ‖ ˈθiːs i‿əs ˈθiːs uːs
Thesiger ˈθes ɪdʒ ə ‖ -ᵊr

thesis 'θiːs ɪs §-əs *—but as a metrical term, sometimes* 'θes- **theses** 'θiːs iːz

THESPIAN

20% 80% AmE
-sp-
-zb-

thespian, T~ 'θesp i‿ən ‖ 'θez bi‿ən — *Preference poll, AmE:* -sp- *80%,* -zb- *20%.* **~s** z

Thespis 'θesp ɪs §-əs

Thessalian θe 'seɪl i‿ən θɪ-, θə- **~s** z

Thessalonian ˌθes ə 'ləʊn i‿ən ◂ ‖ -'loʊn- **~s** z

Thessalonica ˌθes ə 'lɒn ɪk ə §-ək ə ‖ -'lɑːn- *—ModGk* Thessaloniki [θɛ sa lɔ 'ni ci]

Thessaly 'θes əl i

theta 'θiːt ə ‖ 'θeɪṭ ə 'θiːṭ- **~s** z

Thetford 'θet fəd ‖ -fᵊrd

thetic 'θet ɪk ‖ 'θeṭ ɪk

Thetis *(i)* 'θet ɪs §-əs ‖ 'θeṭ-, *(ii)* 'θiːt ɪs -əs ‖ 'θiːṭ- *—The Greek sea goddess is usually (i), the personal name (ii)*

thew θjuː ‖ θuː θjuː **thews** θjuːz ‖ θuːz θjuːz

they ðeɪ

they'd ðeɪd

Theydon Bois ˌθeɪd ᵊn 'bɔɪz

they'd've ðeɪd əv

they'll ðeɪᵊl ðeəl

they're ðeə §'ðeɪ ə ‖ ðer *(= there) —In GenAm there is also a weak form* **ð**ᵊ**r**. *There is no RP weak form.*

they've ðeɪv

thiamin, thiamine 'θaɪ‿ə miːn -mɪn; §-ə mən

thiazine 'θaɪ‿ə ziːn -zaɪn

thiazole 'θaɪ‿ə zəʊl →-zɒʊl ‖ -zoʊl

thick θɪk **thicker** 'θɪk ə ‖ -ᵊr **thickest** 'θɪk ɪst -əst

thicken 'θɪk ən **~ed** d **~ing** ‿ɪŋ **~s** z

thickener 'θɪk ən‿ə ‖ -ᵊn‿ər **~s** z

thicket 'θɪk ɪt §-ət **~s** s

thickhead 'θɪk hed **~s** z

thickheaded ˌθɪk 'hed ɪd ◂ -əd ‖ 'ˌ· · **~ly** li **~ness** nəs nɪs

thickie 'θɪk i **~s** z

thickish 'θɪk ɪʃ

thickly 'θɪk li

thickness 'θɪk nəs -nɪs **~es** ɪz əz

thickset ˌθɪk 'set ◂ ‖ '· ·

thick-skinned ˌθɪk 'skɪnd ◂ ‖ '· ·

thick-witted ˌθɪk 'wɪt ɪd ◂ -əd ‖ -'wɪṭ əd ◂ 'ˌ· · **~ly** li **~ness** nəs nɪs

thief θiːf **thief's** θiːfs **thieves** θiːvz

Thierry ti 'er i ‖ ˌtiː ə 'riː *—Fr* [tjɛ ʁi]

thieve θiːv **thieved** θiːvd **thieves** θiːvz **thieving** 'θiːv ɪŋ

thievery 'θiːv ər i

thievish 'θiːv ɪʃ **~ly** li **~ness** nəs nɪs

thigh θaɪ **thighs** θaɪz

thighbone 'θaɪ bəʊn ‖ -boʊn **~s** z

thigmo- *comb. form*
with stress-neutral suffix ¦θɪg məʊ ‖ -mə — **thigmotaxis** ˌθɪg məʊ 'tæks ɪs §-əs ‖ -mə-
with stress-imposing suffix θɪg 'mɒ+ ‖ -'mɑː+ — **thigmotropism** θɪg 'mɒtr ə ˌpɪz əm ‖ -'mɑːtr-, *also* ˌθɪg məʊ'trəʊp ˌɪz ᵊm ‖ -mə 'troʊp-

thill θɪl **thills** θɪlz

thimble 'θɪm bᵊl **~s** z

thimbleful 'θɪm bᵊl fʊl **~s** z

thimblerig 'θɪm bᵊl rɪg **~ged** d **~ging** ɪŋ **~s** z

thimerosal θaɪ 'mer ə sæl

Thimphu, Thimbu 'tɪmp uː

thin θɪn **thinned** θɪnd **thinner** 'θɪn ə ‖ -ᵊr **thinnest** 'θɪn ɪst -əst **thinning** 'θɪn ɪŋ **thins** θɪnz
thin 'air

thine ðaɪn

thing θɪŋ **things** θɪŋz

thingama... *—see* **thingummy...**

thingie 'θɪŋ i **~s** z

thinguma... *—see* **thingummy...**

thingumm|y 'θɪŋ əm |i **~ies** iz

thingummybob 'θɪŋ əm i bɒb -ə bɒb ‖ -ə bɑːb **~s** z

thingummyjig 'θɪŋ əm i dʒɪg -ə dʒɪg **~s** z

thing|y 'θɪŋ |i **~ies** iz

think θɪŋk **thinking** 'θɪŋk ɪŋ **thinks** θɪŋ*k*s **thought** θɔːt ‖ θɑːt
'think piece; **'think tank**

thinkable 'θɪŋk əb ᵊl

thinker 'θɪŋk ə ‖ -ᵊr **~s** z

thinly 'θɪn li

thinn... *—see* **thin**

thinner 'θɪn ə ‖ -ᵊr **~s** z

thinness 'θɪn nəs -nɪs

thin-skinned ˌθɪn 'skɪnd ◂ ‖ '· ·

thio 'θaɪ əʊ ‖ -oʊ

thio- *comb. form*
with stress-neutral suffix ¦θaɪ əʊ ‖ -ə — **thiosulfate, thiosulphate** ˌθaɪ əʊ 'sʌlf eɪt ‖ -ə-

thiokol, T~ *tdmk* 'θaɪ‿ə kɒl ‖ -kɑːl -kɔːl, koʊl

thiol 'θaɪ ɒl ‖ -ɑːl -ɔːl, -oʊl **~s** z

thionate 'θaɪ‿ə neɪt

thiouracil ˌθaɪ əʊ 'jʊər ə sɪl ‖ -oʊ 'jʊr-

third θɜːd ‖ θɜ˞ːd **thirds** θɜːdz ‖ θɜ˞ːdz
ˌthird de'gree; **ˌthird 'party**; **ˌthird 'person**; **ˌthird 'reading**; **ˌThird 'World**◂

third-class ˌθɜːd 'klɑːs ◂ →ˌθɜːg-, §-'klæs ‖ ˌθɜ˞ːd 'klæs ◂

third-degree ˌθɜːd dɪ 'griː ◂ -də-, §-diː- ‖ ˌθɜ˞ːd-
ˌthird-deˌgree 'burns

thirdhand ˌθɜːd 'hænd ◂ ‖ ˌθɜ˞ːd-

thirdly 'θɜːd li ‖ 'θɜ˞ːd li

third-rate ˌθɜːd 'reɪt ◂ ‖ ˌθɜ˞ːd-

Thirkell 'θɜːk ᵊl ‖ 'θɜ˞ːk ᵊl

Thirlmere 'θɜːl mɪə ‖ 'θɜ˞ːl mɪr

Thirsk θɜːsk ‖ θɜ˞ːsk

thirst θɜːst ‖ θɜ˞ːst **thirsted** 'θɜːst ɪd -əd ‖ 'θɜ˞ːst əd **thirsting** 'θɜːst ɪŋ ‖ 'θɜ˞ːst ɪŋ **thirsts** θɜːsts ‖ θɜ˞ːsts

thirst-quenching 'θɜːst ˌkwentʃ ɪŋ ‖ 'θɜ˞ːst-

thirst|y 'θɜːst |i ‖ 'θɜ˞ːst |i **~ier** i‿ə ‖ i‿ᵊr **~iest** i‿ɪst i‿əst **~ily** ɪ li əl i **~iness** i nəs i nɪs

thirteen ˌθɜː 'tiːn ◂ §ˌθɜːt- ‖ ˌθɜ˞ː- ˌθɜːt- **~s** z

thirteenth ˌθɜː 'tiːnᵗθ ◂ §ˌθɜːt- ‖ ˌθɜ˞ː- ˌθɜːt- **~s** s

thirtieth 'θɜːt i‿əθ §-ti-, -ɪθ ‖ 'θɜ˞ːţ i əθ **~s** s

thirt|y 'θɜːt |i §'θɜːt t|i ‖ 'θɜ˞ːţ |i **~ies** iz

ˌ**Thirty** ₍ˌ₎**Years' 'War**

thirtyfold 'θɜːt i fəʊld →-fɒʊld ‖ 'θɜ˞ːţ i foʊld

thirty-nine ˌθɜːt i 'naɪn ◂ §-ti- ‖ ˌθɜ˞ːţ- **~s** z

ˌ**Thirty-nine 'Articles**

thirty-something 'θɜːt i ˌsʌm θɪŋ §-ti-; ˌ· ·'· · ‖ 'θɜ˞ːţi-

this ðɪs —*In BrE some speakers use a weak form* ðəs *in the expressions* ~ afternoon, ~ evening, ~ morning. *In AmE, this weak form is used more widely.* **these** ðiːz

Thisbe 'θɪz bi

thistle 'θɪs ᵊl **~s** z

thistledown 'θɪs ᵊl daʊn

Thistlethwaite 'θɪs ᵊl θweɪt

thistly 'θɪs ᵊl‿i

thither 'ðɪð ə §'θɪð- ‖ 'θɪð ᵊr 'ðɪð- **~ward/s** wəd/z ‖ wᵊrd/z

thixotropic ˌθɪks ə 'trɒp ɪk ◂ ‖ -'trɑːp-

thixotropy θɪk 'sɒtr əp i ‖ -'sɑːtr-

tho, tho' ðəʊ §θəʊ ‖ ðoʊ

Thoday 'θəʊd eɪ ‖ 'θoʊd eɪ

Thody 'θəʊd i ‖ 'θoʊd i

thole θəʊl →θɒʊl ‖ θoʊl **tholes** θəʊlz →θɒʊlz ‖ θoʊlz

tholepin 'θəʊl pɪn →'θɒʊl- ‖ 'θoʊl- **~s** z

Thom tɒm ‖ tɑːm

Thomas 'tɒm əs ‖ 'tɑːm əs *(!)*

Thomasena, Thomasina ˌtɒm ə 'siːn ə ‖ ˌtɑːm-

Thomism 'təʊm ˌɪz əm ‖ 'toʊm-

Thompson 'tɒm*p*s ən ‖ 'tɑːm*p*s ən

Thomson 'tɒmᵖs ən ‖ 'tɑːmᵖs ən

thon ðɒn ‖ ðɑːn

-thon θɒn ‖ θɑːn — **singathon** 'sɪŋ ə θɒn ‖ -θɑːn —*See note at* -on.

thong θɒŋ ‖ θɔːŋ θɑːŋ **thongs** θɒŋz ‖ θɔːŋz θɑːŋz

Thor θɔː ‖ θɔːr

Thora 'θɔːr ə

thoraces 'θɔːr ə siːz θɔː 'reɪs iːz ‖ 'θoʊr-

thoracic θɔː 'ræs ɪk θɒ-, θə- ‖ θə-

thoraco- *comb. form*
with stress-neutral suffix |θɔːr ə kəʊ θɔː |ræk əʊ ‖ -koʊ |θoʊr- — **thoracoplasty** 'θɔːr ə kəʊ ˌplæst i θɔː 'ræk- ‖ -koʊ,- 'θoʊr-
with stress-imposing suffix ˌθɔːr ə 'kɒ+ ‖ -'kɑː+ ˌθoʊr- — **thoracotomy** ˌθɔːr ə 'kɒt əm i ‖ -'kɑːţ- ˌθoʊr-

thorax 'θɔːr æks ‖ 'θoʊr- **thoraces** 'θɔːr ə siːz θɔː 'reɪs iːz ‖ 'θoʊr- **~es** ɪz əz

Thorazine *tdmk* 'θɔːr ə ziːn ‖ 'θoʊr-

Thorburn 'θɔː bɜːn ‖ 'θɔːr bɜ˞ːn

Thoreau 'θɔːr əʊ θɔː 'rəʊ, θə- ‖ θə 'roʊ θɔː-; 'θɔːr oʊ

thorite 'θɔːr aɪt ‖ 'θoʊr-

thorium 'θɔːr i‿əm ‖ 'θoʊr-

Thorley 'θɔːl i ‖ 'θɔːrl i

thorn, Thorn θɔːn ‖ θɔːrn **thorns** θɔːnz ‖ θɔːrnz

'thorn ˌapple

Thornaby 'θɔːn əb i ‖ 'θɔːrn-

thornbill 'θɔːn bɪl →'θɔːm- ‖ 'θɔːrn- **~s** z

Thorndike 'θɔːn daɪk ‖ 'θɔːrn-

Thorne θɔːn ‖ θɔːrn

Thorner 'θɔːn ə ‖ 'θɔːrn ᵊr

Thorneycroft 'θɔːn i krɒft ‖ 'θɔːrn i krɔːft -krɑːft

Thornham 'θɔːn əm ‖ 'θɔːrn-

Thornhill 'θɔːn hɪl ‖ 'θɔːrn-

thornless 'θɔːn ləs -lɪs ‖ 'θɔːrn-

Thornley 'θɔːn li ‖ 'θɔːrn-

Thornton 'θɔːn tən ‖ 'θɔːrn tᵊn

thorn|y 'θɔːn |i ‖ 'θɔːrn |i **~ier** i‿ə ‖ i‿ᵊr **~iest** i‿ɪst i‿əst **~iness** i nəs i nɪs

Thorogood 'θʌr ə gʊd ‖ 'θɜː-

Thorold 'θɒr ᵊld 'θʌr-, -əʊld ‖ 'θɔːr ᵊld 'θɑːr-

thoron 'θɔːr ɒn ‖ -ɑːn 'θoʊr-

thorough 'θʌr ə ‖ 'θɜ˞ː oʊ *(*)*

thoroughbred 'θʌr ə bred ‖ 'θɜ˞ː oʊ- -ə- **~s** z

thoroughfare 'θʌr ə feə ‖ 'θɜ˞ː oʊ fer -ə-, -fær **~s** z

thoroughgoing ˌθʌr ə 'gəʊ ɪŋ ◂ ‖ ˌθɜ˞ː oʊ 'goʊ ɪŋ ◂ -ə-

thorough|ly 'θʌr ə |li ‖ 'θɜ˞ː oʊ |li **~ness** nəs nɪs

Thorp, Thorpe θɔːp ‖ θɔːrp

Thorpeness ˌθɔːp 'nes ˌθɔːrp-

those ðəʊz ‖ ðoʊz

Thoth θəʊθ təʊt, θɒθ ‖ θoʊθ toʊt

thou *pronoun* ðaʊ —*In dialectal speech there may also be a weak form such as* ðə.

thou *'thousand', 'thousandth'* θaʊ **thous** θaʊz

though ðəʊ §θəʊ ‖ ðoʊ

thought θɔːt ‖ θɑːt **thoughts** θɔːts ‖ θɑːts

thoughtful 'θɔːt fᵊl -fʊl ‖ 'θɑːt- **~ly** ˌi **~ness** nəs nɪs

thoughtless 'θɔːt ləs -lɪs ‖ 'θɑːt- **~ly** li **~ness** nəs nɪs

thought-out ˌθɔːt 'aʊt ◂ ‖ ˌθɔːţ- ˌθɑːţ-

thought-provoking 'θɔːt prə ˌvəʊk ɪŋ ‖ -ˌvoʊk-

thought-reader 'θɔːt ˌriːd ə ‖ -ᵊr 'θɑːt- **~s** z

Thouless 'θaʊ les

thousand 'θaʊz ᵊnd **~s** z

ˌ**Thousand 'Islands**; ˌ**Thousand ˌIsland 'dressing**

thousandfold 'θaʊz ᵊnd fəʊld →-fɒʊld ‖ -foʊld

thousandth 'θaʊz ᵊnᵗθ -ᵊndθ **~s** s

Thrace θreɪs

Thracian 'θreɪʃ ᵊn 'θreɪʃ i‿ən **~s** z

Thraco-Phrygian ˌθreɪk əʊ 'frɪdʒ i‿ən ◂ ‖ ˌ·oʊ-

thraldom 'θrɔːl dəm ‖ 'θrɑːl-

Thrale θreɪᵊl

thrall θrɔːl ‖ θrɑːl

thralldom ˈθrɔːl dəm ‖ ˈθrɑːl-
thrang θræŋ
thrash θræʃ **thrashed** θræʃt **thrashes** ˈθræʃ ɪz -əz **thrashing** ˈθræʃ ɪŋ
thrasher ˈθræʃ ə ‖ -ᵊr **~s** z
thread θred **threaded** ˈθred ɪd -əd **threading** ˈθred ɪŋ **threads** θredz
threadbare ˈθred beə →ˈθreb- ‖ -ber -bær **~ness** nəs nɪs
threadlike ˈθred laɪk
Threadneedle ˌθred ˈniːd ᵊl ˈ·ˌ· ·
threadworm ˈθred wɜːm ‖ -wɝːm **~s** z
threat θret **threats** θrets
threaten ˈθret ᵊn **~ed** d **~ing/ly** ‿ɪŋ /li **~s** z
three θriː **threes** θriːz
ˌthree 'R's
three-cornered ˌθriː ˈkɔːn əd ◂ ‖ -ˈkɔːrn ᵊrd ◂
three-D, 3-D ˌθriː ˈdiː ◂
three-day ˌθriː ˈdeɪ ◂
ˌthree-day 'week
three-decker ˌθriː ˈdek ə ◂ ‖ -ᵊr **~s** z
three-dimensional ˌθriː daɪ ˈmenᵗʃ ᵊn‿əl ◂ ˌ·dɪ-, ˌ·də-
threefold ˈθriː fəʊld →-fɒʊld, ˌ·ˈ· ‖ -foʊld
three-halfpence ˌθriː ˈheɪp ənᵗs →-mᵖs
threeish ˈθriː ɪʃ
three-legged ˌθriː ˈleg ɪd ◂ -əd; ˌ·ˈlegd
ˌthree-'legged race
three-line ˌθriː ˈlaɪn ◂
ˌthree-line 'whip
three-peat ˈθriː piːt
threepence *n '3d'* ˈθrep ənᵗs ˈθrʌp-, ˈθrɪp-, ˈθrʊp-, →-mᵖs *—but meaning '3p', in modern currency, usually* three pence ˌθriː ˈpenᵗs
threepenny *adj '3d'* ˈθrep ən‿i ˈθrʌp-, ˈθrɪp-, ˈθrʊp- *—but meaning '3p', in modern currency, usually* three-penny ˌθriː ˈpen i ◂
ˌthreepenny 'bit
three-piece ˌθriː ˈpiːs ◂
ˌthree-piece 'suite
three-ply ˈθriː plaɪ ˌ·ˈ·
three-point ˌθriː ˈpɔɪnt ◂
ˌthree-point 'turn
three-pointer ˌθriː ˈpɔɪnt ə ‖ -ˈpɔɪnţ ᵊr **~s** z
three-quarter ˌθriː ˈkwɔːt ə ◂ -ˈkɔːt- ‖ -ˈkwɔːrţ ᵊr ◂ **~s** z
three-ring ˌθriː ˈrɪŋ ◂
ˌthree-ring 'circus
threescore ˌθriː ˈskɔː ◂ ‖ -ˈskɔːr ◂ -ˈskoʊr
threesome ˈθriː səm **~s** z
three-star ˌθriː ˈstɑː ◂ ‖ -ˈstɑːr ◂
ˌthree-star ho'tel
three-way ˌθriː ˈweɪ ◂
three-wheeler ˌθriː ˈwiːᵊl ə -ˈhwiːᵊl- ‖ -ˈ*h*wiːᵊl ᵊr **~s** z
Threlfall ˈθrel fɔːl ‖ -fɑːl
Threlkeld ˈθrel keld
threnod|y ˈθren əd |i ˈθriːn- **~ies** iz
thresh θreʃ **threshed** θreʃt **threshes** ˈθreʃ ɪz -əz **threshing** ˈθreʃ ɪŋ
thresher, T~ ˈθreʃ ə ‖ -ᵊr **~s** z
threshold ˈθreʃ həʊld -əʊld, →-hɒʊld ‖ -oʊld -hoʊld **~s** z
threw θruː *(= through)*
Thribb θrɪb
thrice θraɪs
thrift θrɪft **thrifts** θrɪfts
thriftless ˈθrɪft ləs -lɪs **~ly** li **~ness** nəs nɪs
thrift|y ˈθrɪft |i **~ier** i‿ə ‖ i‿ᵊr **~iest** i‿ɪst i‿əst **~ily** ɪ li əl i **~iness** i nəs i nɪs
thrill θrɪl **thrilled** θrɪld **thrilling/ly** ˈθrɪl ɪŋ /li **thrills** θrɪlz
thriller ˈθrɪl ə ‖ -ᵊr **~s** z
thrill-seeker ˈθrɪl ˌsiːk ə ‖ -ᵊr **~s** z
Thring θrɪŋ
thrips θrɪps
thrive θraɪv **thrived** θraɪvd **thriven** ˈθrɪv ᵊn *(!)* **thrives** θraɪvz **thriving/ly** ˈθraɪv ɪŋ /li
throve θrəʊv ‖ θroʊv
thro, thro' θruː
throat θrəʊt ‖ θroʊt **throats** θrəʊts ‖ θroʊts
throaty ˈθrəʊt |i ‖ ˈθroʊţ |i **~ier** i‿ə ‖ i‿ᵊr **~iest** i‿ɪst i‿əst **~ily** ɪ li əl i **~iness** i nəs i nɪs
throb θrɒb ‖ θrɑːb **throbbed** θrɒbd ‖ θrɑːbd **throbbing/ly** ˈθrɒb ɪŋ /li ‖ ˈθrɑːb ɪŋ /li **throbs** θrɒbz ‖ θrɑːbz
throes θrəʊz ‖ θroʊz *(= throws)*
Throgmorton ₍ˈ₎θrɒg ˈmɔːt ᵊn ˈ· · · ‖ θrɑːg ˈmɔːrt ᵊn
thrombi ˈθrɒm baɪ ‖ ˈθrɑːm-
thrombin ˈθrɒm bɪn §-bən ‖ ˈθrɑːm-
thrombo- *comb. form with stress-neutral suffix* ¦θrɒm bəʊ ‖ ¦θrɑːm boʊ — **thromboplastic** ˌθrɒm bəʊ ˈplæst ɪk ◂ ‖ ˌθrɑːm boʊ- *with stress-imposing suffix* θrɒm ˈbɒ+ ‖ θrɑːm ˈbɑː+ — **thrombolysis** θrɒm ˈbɒl əs ɪs -ɪs-, §-əs ‖ θrɑːm ˈbɑːl-
thrombolysis ˌθrɒm bəʊ ˈlaɪs ɪs θrɒm ˈbɒl əs ɪs, §-əs ‖ ˌθrɑːm boʊ ˈlaɪs əs θrɑːm ˈbɑːl əs əs
thrombos|e ˈθrɒm bəʊz -bəʊs, ·ˈ· ‖ -boʊz -boʊs **~ed** d **~es** ɪz əz **~ing** ɪŋ
thrombos|is θrɒm ˈbəʊs |ɪs §-əs ‖ θrɑːm ˈboʊs |əs **~es** iːz
thrombotic θrɒm ˈbɒt ɪk ‖ θrɑːm ˈbɑːţ ɪk
throm|bus ˈθrɒm |bəs ‖ ˈθrɑːm |bəs **~bi** baɪ
throne θrəʊn ‖ θroʊn **throned** θrəʊnd ‖ θroʊnd **thrones** θrəʊnz ‖ θroʊnz **throning** ˈθrəʊn ɪŋ ‖ ˈθroʊn ɪŋ
throng θrɒŋ ‖ θrɔːŋ θrɑːŋ **thronged** θrɒŋd ‖ θrɔːŋd θrɑːŋd **thronging** ˈθrɒŋ ɪŋ ‖ ˈθrɔːŋ ɪŋ ˈθrɑːŋ- **throngs** θrɒŋz ‖ θrɔːŋz θrɑːŋz
throstle ˈθrɒs ᵊl ‖ ˈθrɑːs ᵊl **~s** z
throttl|e ˈθrɒt ᵊl ‖ ˈθrɑːţ ᵊl **~ed** d **~es** z **~ing** ‿ɪŋ
through θruː
throughout θru ˈaʊt
throughput ˈθruː pʊt
throughway ˈθruː weɪ **~s** z
throve θrəʊv ‖ θroʊv
throw θrəʊ ‖ θroʊ **threw** θruː **throwing** ˈθrəʊ ɪŋ ‖ ˈθroʊ ɪŋ **thrown** θrəʊn §ˈθrəʊ ən ‖ θroʊn **throws** θrəʊz ‖ θroʊz
throwaway ˈθrəʊ ə ˌweɪ ‖ ˈθroʊ- **~s** z

throwback 'θrəʊ bæk ‖ 'θroʊ- **~s** s
throwdown 'θrəʊ daʊn ‖ 'θroʊ- **~s** z
thrower, T~ 'θrəʊ ə ‖ 'θroʊ ᵊr **~s** z
throw-in 'θrəʊ ɪn ‖ 'θroʊ- **~s** z
thrown θrəʊn §'θrəʊ ən ‖ 'θroʊn *(usually = throne)*
thru θru:
thrum θrʌm **thrummed** θrʌmd **thrumming** 'θrʌm ɪŋ **thrums** θrʌmz
thrush θrʌʃ **thrushes** 'θrʌʃ ɪz -əz
thrust θrʌst **thrusting/ly** 'θrʌst ɪŋ /li **thrusts** θrʌsts
thruster 'θrʌst ə ‖ -ᵊr **~s** z
thruway 'θru: weɪ **~s** z
Thucydidean θju ˌsɪd ə 'di:ˌən ◂ -ɪ- ‖ θu-
Thucydides θju 'sɪd ə di:z -ɪ- ‖ θu-
thud θʌd **thudded** 'θʌd ɪd -əd **thudding** 'θʌd ɪŋ **thuds** θʌdz
thug θʌg **thugs** θʌgz
thuggery 'θʌg ər i
thuggish 'θʌg ɪʃ **~ly** li **~ness** nəs nɪs
thuja 'θju:dʒ ə 'θu:dʒ-; 'θju: jə, 'θu:- ‖ 'θu:dʒ ə **~s** z
Thule θju:l 'θju:l i, 'θu:l-, -i: ‖ 'θu:l i —*but the base in Greenland is* 'tu:l i
thulium 'θju:l iˌəm 'θu:l- ‖ 'θu:l-
thumb θʌm **thumbed** θʌmd **thumbing** 'θʌm ɪŋ **thumbs** θʌmz
ˌ**thumbs 'down**; ˌ**thumbs 'up**
thumbnail 'θʌm neɪᵊl **~s** z
thumbprint 'θʌm prɪnt **~s** s
thumbscrew 'θʌm skru: **~s** z
thumbtack 'θʌm tæk **~ed** t **~ing** ɪŋ **~s** s
thummim 'θʌm ɪm 'θʊm-, 'tʊm-
thump θʌmp **thumped** θʌmpt **thumping/ly** 'θʌmp ɪŋ /li **thumps** θʌmps
thumper 'θʌmp ə ‖ -ᵊr **~s** z
thunbergia θʌn 'bɜ:dʒ iˌə θʊn-, ·'·ə ‖ -'bɜ˞:dʒ- **~s** z
thunder 'θʌnd ə ‖ -ᵊr **~ed** d **thundering/ly** 'θʌndˌər ɪŋ /li **~s** z
ˌ**Thunder 'Bay**
thunderbird, T~ 'θʌnd ə bɜ:d ‖ -ᵊr bɜ˞:d **~s** z
thunderbolt 'θʌnd ə bəʊlt →-bɒʊlt ‖ -ᵊr boʊlt **~s** s
thunderclap 'θʌnd ə klæp ‖ -ᵊr- **~s** s
thundercloud 'θʌnd ə klaʊd ‖ -ᵊr- **~s** z
thunderer 'θʌndˌər ə ‖ ᵊr ər
thunder|fly 'θʌnd ə| flaɪ ‖ -ᵊr|- **~flies** flaɪz
thunderhead 'θʌnd ə hed ‖ -ᵊr- **~z** z
thunderous 'θʌndˌər əs **~ly** li
thundershower 'θʌnd ə ˌʃaʊˌə ‖ 'θʌnd ᵊr ʃaʊˌᵊr **~s** z
thunderstorm 'θʌnd ə stɔ:m ‖ -ᵊr stɔ:rm **~s** z
thunderstruck 'θʌnd ə strʌk ‖ -ᵊr-
thundery 'θʌn dərˌi
thunk θʌŋk
Thurber 'θɜ:b ə ‖ 'θɜ˞:b ᵊr
Thurgarton 'θɜ:g ət ən ‖ 'θɜ˞:g ᵊrt ᵊn
Thurgood 'θɜ: gʊd ‖ 'θɜ˞:-
thurible 'θjʊər ɪb ᵊl -əb- ‖ 'θʊr- 'θɜ:- **~s** z
thurifer 'θjʊər ɪf ə -əf- ‖ 'θʊr əf ᵊr 'θɜ:- **~s** z

Thuringi|a θjuᵊ 'rɪndʒ iˌ|ə tuᵊ-, -'rɪŋ gi ˌ; ·'·|ə ‖ θu- **~an/s** ən/z
Thurleigh *place in Bedfordshire* ˌθɜ: 'laɪ ‖ ˌθɜ˞:-
Thurlestone 'θɜ:l stən ‖ 'θɜ˞:l-
Thurloe, Thurlow 'θɜ:l əʊ ‖ 'θɜ˞:l oʊ
Thurman 'θɜ:m ən ‖ 'θɜ˞:m-
Thurmond 'θɜ:m ənd ‖ 'θɜ˞:m-
Thurrock 'θʌr ək ‖ 'θɜ˞: ək
Thursday 'θɜ:z deɪ -di ‖ 'θɜ˞:z-—*See note at* -day **~s** z
Thurso 'θɜ:s əʊ ‖ 'θɜ˞:s oʊ
Thurston 'θɜ:st ən ‖ 'θɜ˞:st ən
thus ðʌs **thusly** 'ðʌs li
thwack θwæk **thwacked** θwækt **thwacking** 'θwæk ɪŋ **thwacks** θwæks
Thwaite θweɪt **Thwaites** θweɪts
thwart θwɔ:t ‖ θwɔ:rt **thwarted** 'θwɔ:t ɪd -əd ‖ 'θwɔ:rţ əd **thwarting** 'θwɔ:t ɪŋ ‖ 'θwɔ:rţ ɪŋ **thwarts** θwɔ:ts ‖ θwɔ:rts
thy ðaɪ
Thyestean θaɪ 'est iˌən
Thyestes θaɪ 'est i:z
thylacine 'θaɪl ə si:n -saɪn **~s** z
thyme taɪm *(! = time)*
-thymia 'θaɪm iˌə — **cyclothymia** ˌsaɪk ləʊ 'θaɪm iˌə ‖ ˌ·lə-
thymidine 'θaɪm ɪ di:n -ə-
thymine 'θaɪm i:n
thymol 'θaɪm ɒl ‖ -oʊl -ɔ:l, -ɑ:l
thymus 'θaɪm əs **~es** ɪz əz
Thynne θɪn
thyratron 'θaɪᵊr ə trɒn ‖ -trɑ:n **~s** z
thyristor θaɪᵊ 'rɪst ə ‖ -ᵊr **~s** z
thyro- *comb. form*
with stress-neutral suffix ˌθaɪᵊr əʊ ‖ -oʊ — **thyrohyoid** ˌθaɪᵊr əʊ 'haɪ ɔɪd ◂ ‖ -oʊ-
with stress-imposing suffix θaɪᵊ 'rɒ+ ‖ -'rɑ:+ — **thyropathy** ˌθaɪᵊ 'rɒp əθ i ‖ -'rɑ:p-
thyroid 'θaɪᵊr ɔɪd **~s** z
thyroxine θaɪᵊ 'rɒks i:n -ɪn, §-ᵊn ‖ -'rɑ:ks-
thyrs|us 'θɜ:s |əs ‖ 'θɜ˞:s |əs **~i** aɪ
thyself ðaɪ 'self
Thyssen 'ti:s ᵊn —*Ger* ['tʏs ᵊn]
ti *'musical note'; 'Cordyline tree'* ti: **tis** ti:z
TI ˌti: 'aɪ
Tia Maria *tdmk* ˌti:ˌə mə 'ri:ˌə **~s** z
Tiananmen ti ˌæn ən 'men ◂ ˌti:ˌən·'·, -'mɪn ‖ -ˌɑ:n-, ˌæn-; 'tjen əm ən —*Chi* Tiān'ānmén [¹tʰjæn ¹an ²mən]
Tiˌananmen **'Square**
Tianjin ti ˌæn 'dʒɪn -ˌen- ‖ -ˌɑ:n- —*Chi* Tiānjīn [¹tʰjæn ¹tɕɪn]
tiara ti 'ɑ:r ə ‖ -'ær ə -'er-, -'ɑ:r- **~s** z
Tibbenham 'tɪb ənˌəm
Tibbett 'tɪb ɪt §-ət
Tibbitts 'tɪb ɪts §-əts
Tibbles 'tɪb ᵊlz
Tibbs tɪbz
Tibenham 'tɪb ənˌəm
Tiber 'taɪb ə ‖ -ᵊr
Tiberias taɪ 'bɪər i æs -əs ‖ -'bɪr-
Tiberius taɪ 'bɪər iˌəs ‖ -'bɪr-
Tibet tɪ 'bet §tə- —*Chi* Xīzàng [¹ɕi ⁴tsɑŋ]

Tibetan tɪ 'bet ən §tə- **~s** z
Tibeto-Burman tɪ ˌbet əʊ 'bɜːm ən ◂ §tə- ‖ tə ˌbeṭ oʊ 'bɜ·ːm ən ◂
tibi|a 'tɪb i‿|ə **~ae** iː **~as** əz
Tibullus tɪ 'bʌl əs §tə-, -'bʊl-
tic tɪk *(= tick)* **tics** tɪks
ˌtic ˌdoulou'reux ˌduːl ə 'rɜː ‖ -'ruː —*Fr* [tik du lu ʁø]
tice taɪs **tices** 'taɪs ɪz -əz
Ticehurst 'taɪs hɜːst ‖ -hɜ·ːst
Tichborne 'tɪtʃ bɔːn ‖ -bɔːrn -bourn
Ticino tɪ 'tʃiːn əʊ ‖ -oʊ —*It* [ti 'tʃiː no]
tick tɪk **ticked** tɪkt **ticking** 'tɪk ɪŋ **ticks** tɪks
ˌticking'off *n*
ticker 'tɪk ə ‖ -ər **~s** z
ticker-tape 'tɪk ə teɪp ‖ -ər-
tick|et 'tɪk |ɪt §-ət ‖ -|ət **~eted** ɪt ɪd §ət-, -əd ‖ əṭ əd **~eting** ɪt ɪŋ §ət- ‖ əṭ ɪŋ **~ets** ɪts §əts ‖ əts
'ticket ˌagency; **'ticket colˌlector**; **'ticket ˌoffice**; **'ticket tout**
tickety-boo ˌtɪk ət i 'buː ˌ·ɪt- ‖ -əṭ i-
ticking 'tɪk ɪŋ
tickl|e 'tɪk əl **~ed** d **~es** z **~ing** ɪŋ
tickler 'tɪk əl‿ə ‖ ər **~s** z
ticklish 'tɪk əl‿ɪʃ **~ly** li **~ness** nəs nɪs
tick-over 'tɪk ˌəʊv ə ‖ -ˌoʊv ər
ticktack 'tɪk tæk
tick-tack-toe, tic-tac-toe ˌtɪk tæk 'təʊ ‖ -'toʊ
ticktock 'tɪk tɒk ˌ·'· ‖ -tɑːk **~ed** t **~ing** ɪŋ **~s** s
ticky-tacky 'tɪk i ˌtæk i
Ticonderoga ˌtaɪ kɒnd ə 'rəʊg ə ˌ·ˌ· ·'· · ‖ ˌtaɪ kɑːnd ə 'roʊg ə
tidal 'taɪd əl
ˌtidal 'wave, '· · ·
tidbit 'tɪd bɪt →'tɪb- **~s** s
tiddledywink 'tɪd əld i wɪŋk **~s** s
tiddler 'tɪd əl‿ə ‖ ər **~s** z
Tiddles 'tɪd əlz
tiddley, tiddly 'tɪd əl‿i
tiddleywink, tiddlywink 'tɪd əl‿i wɪŋk **~s** s
tide taɪd **tided** 'taɪd ɪd -əd **tides** taɪdz **tiding** 'taɪd ɪŋ
'tide ˌtable
tideland 'taɪd lænd **~s** z
tidemark 'taɪd mɑːk →'taɪb- ‖ -mɑːrk **~s** s
Tidenham 'tɪd ən əm
Tideswell 'taɪds wel —*Locally also* 'tɪdz əl
tidewater 'taɪd ˌwɔːt ə ‖ -ˌwɔːṭ ər -ˌwɑːṭ-
tideway 'taɪd weɪ
tidi... —*see* **tidy**
tidily 'taɪd ɪ li -əl i
tidiness 'taɪd i nəs -nɪs
tidings 'taɪd ɪŋz
Tidmarsh 'tɪd mɑːʃ →'tɪb- ‖ -mɑːrʃ
tidy, Tidy 'taɪd i **tidied** 'taɪd id **tidier** 'taɪd i‿ə ‖ ər **tidies** 'taɪd iz **tidiest** 'taɪd i‿ɪst əst **tidying** 'taɪd i‿ɪŋ
tie taɪ **tied** taɪd **ties** taɪz **tying** 'taɪ ɪŋ
'tie clip; **ˌtied 'cottage**; **ˌtied 'house**
tiebreak 'taɪ breɪk **~s** s
tiebreaker 'taɪ ˌbreɪk ə ‖ -ər **~s** z
tie-dye 'taɪ daɪ **~d** d **~s** z **~ing** ɪŋ
tie-in 'taɪ ɪn **~s** z
tie-on 'taɪ ɒn ‖ -ɑːn -ɔːn **~s** z
tiepin 'taɪ pɪn **~s** z
Tiepolo ti 'ep ə ləʊ ‖ -loʊ —*It* ['tjɛː po lo]
tier *'one that ties'* 'taɪ‿ə ‖ 'taɪ‿ər **tiers** 'taɪ‿əz ‖ 'taɪ‿ərz
tier *'rank, row'* tɪə ‖ tɪər *(= tear 'eye-water')*
tiered tɪəd ‖ tɪərd **tiering** 'tɪər ɪŋ ‖ 'tɪr ɪŋ
tiers tɪəz ‖ tɪərz
tierce tɪəs ‖ tɪərs —*but in cards also* tɜːs ‖ tɜːs
tiercel 'tɪəs əl 'tɜːs- ‖ 'tɪrs əl **~s** z
Tierney 'tɪən i ‖ 'tɪrn i
tierra ti 'eər ə -'er-; 'tɪər ə ‖ ti 'er ə—*Sp* ['tje rra]
tiˌerra ˌcali'ente ˌkæl i 'ent eɪ ‖ ˌkɑːl-;
Tiˌerra del 'Fuego del 'fweɪg əʊ ‖ -oʊ —*Sp* [ðel 'fwe ɣo]; **tiˌerra 'fria** 'friːə —*Sp* ['fri a]; **tiˌerra he'lada** he 'lɑːd ə —*Sp* [e 'la ða]; **tiˌerra tem'plada** tem 'plɑːd ə —*Sp* [tem 'pla ða]
tie-up 'taɪ ʌp **~s** s
tiff tɪf **tiffs** tɪfs
Tiffan|y, t~ 'tɪf ən |i **~ies, y's** iz
tiffin, T~ 'tɪf ɪn §-ən **~s** z
Tiflis 'tɪf lɪs §-ləs
tig tɪg
Tigellinus ˌtɪdʒ ə 'laɪn əs
tiger 'taɪg ə ‖ -ər **~s** z
'tiger cat; **tiger ˌlily**; **'tiger moth**; **'tiger shark**
tigerish 'taɪg ər ɪʃ **~ly** li
Tigger 'tɪg ə ‖ -ər
Tiggy-Winkle 'tɪg i ˌwɪŋk əl ˌ·'· ·
Tighe taɪ
tight taɪt **tighter** 'taɪt ə ‖ 'taɪṭ ər **tightest** 'taɪt ɪst -əst ‖ 'taɪṭ əst **tights** taɪts
tighten 'taɪt ən **~ed** d **~ing** ‿ɪŋ **~s** z
tightfisted ˌtaɪt 'fɪst ɪd ◂ -əd
tight-fitting ˌtaɪt 'fɪt ɪŋ ◂ ‖ -'fɪṭ ɪŋ ◂
tightie whities ˌtaɪt i 'waɪt iz -'hwaɪt- ‖ ˌtaɪṭ i 'hwaɪṭ iz
tightknit ˌtaɪt 'nɪt ◂ ‖ '· ·
tight-lipped ˌtaɪt 'lɪpt ◂ ‖ '· ·
tight|ly 'taɪt |li **~ness** nəs nɪs
tightrope 'taɪt rəʊp ‖ -roʊp **~s** s
'tightrope ˌwalker
tightwad 'taɪt wɒd ‖ -wɑːd **~s** z
Tiglath-pileser ˌtɪg læθ paɪ 'liːz ə -pɪ'--, -pə'-- ‖ -ər
tiglic 'tɪg lɪk
Tignes tiːn —*Fr* [tiɲ]
tigon 'taɪg ən **~s** z
Tigray, Tigre, Tigré 'tɪg reɪ ‖ tiː 'greɪ
tigress 'taɪg rəs -rɪs, -res **~es** ɪz əz
Tigrinya tɪ 'griːn jə -'griːn-
Tigris 'taɪg rɪs -rəs
Tijuana ti 'wɑːn ə ˌtiː‿ə 'wɑːn-, 'hwɑːn- ‖ ˌtiː ə 'wɑːn ə —*Sp* [ti 'xwa na]
tike taɪk **tikes** taɪks
tiki 'tiːk i **~s** z
tikka 'tiːk ə 'tɪk-
ˌtikka ma'sala mə 'sɑːl ə
Tikrit tɪ 'kriːt —*Arabic* [tɪ 'kriːt]

T

tll *'sesame'* tɪl
'til tɪl *see also* till
tilak 'tɪl æk **~s** s
tilapia tɪ 'læp i‿ə tə-, -'leɪp- ‖ -'lɑːp- **~s** z
Tilbury, t~ 'tɪl bər‿i ‖ -ˌber i
tilde 'tɪld ə -i, -eɪ; tɪld **~s** z
Tilden 'tɪld ən
tile taɪəl **tiled** taɪəld **tiles** taɪəlz **tiling** 'taɪl ɪŋ
Tilehurst 'taɪəl hɜːst ‖ -hɜːst
till tɪl *Note: for the prep and conj (not for the noun and verb) there is also an occasional weak form* təl **tilled** tɪld **tilling** 'tɪl ɪŋ **tills** tɪlz
tillage 'tɪl ɪdʒ
Tillamook 'tɪl ə mʊk
tiller, T~ 'tɪl ə ‖ -ər **~s** z
Tilley 'tɪl i
 'Tilley lamp
Tillicoultry ˌtɪl ɪ 'kuːtr i -ə-
Tillie, Tilly 'tɪl i
Tilsit, t~ 'tɪls ɪt 'tɪlz-, §-ət —*Ger* ['tɪl zɪt]
tilt tɪlt **tilted** 'tɪlt ɪd -əd **tilting** 'tɪlt ɪŋ **tilts** tɪlts
tilth tɪlθ
Tilton 'tɪlt ən
Tim tɪm
timbale 'tɪm bəl tæm 'bɑːl, tɪm- —*Fr* [tɛ̃ bal] **~s** z
timber 'tɪm bə ‖ -bər **~ed** d **timbering** 'tɪm bər ɪŋ **~s** z
Timberlake 'tɪm bə leɪk ‖ -bər-
timberland, T~ 'tɪm bə lænd ‖ -bər-
timberline 'tɪm bə laɪn ‖ -bər-
timberyard 'tɪm bə jɑːd ‖ -bər jɑːrd **~s** z
timbre 'tæm bə 'tɪm- ‖ -bər —*Fr* [tɛ̃ːbʁ] **~s** z
timbrel 'tɪm brəl **~s** z
Timbuctoo, Timbuktu ˌtɪm bʌk 'tuː -bək-
time taɪm **timed** taɪmd **times** taɪmz **timing** 'taɪm ɪŋ
 ˌtime and a 'half; **ˌtime-and-'motion ˌstudy**; **'time bomb**; **'time ˌcapsule**; **'time clock**; **'time exˌposure**; **'time fuse**; **ˌtime ˌimme'morial**; **'time lag**; **'time ˌlimit**; **'time lock**; **'time maˌchine**; **ˌtime 'off**; **'time sheet**; **'time ˌsignal**; **'time ˌsignature**; **'time span**; **'time switch**; **'time ˌtrial**; **'time warp**; **'time zone**
time-consuming 'taɪm kən ˌsjuːm ɪŋ §-kɒn-, -ˌsuːm- ‖ -ˌsuːm-
time-honored, time-honoured 'taɪm ˌɒn əd ‖ -ˌɑːn ərd
timekeep|er 'taɪm ˌkiːp ə ‖ -ər **~ers** əz ‖ ərz **~ing** ɪŋ
time-lapse 'taɪm læps
timeless 'taɪm ləs -lɪs **~ly** li **~ness** nəs nɪs
timeline 'taɪm laɪn **~s** z
time|ly 'taɪm |li **~lier** li‿ə ‖ li‿ər **~liest** li‿ɪst li‿əst **~liness** li nəs -nɪs
timeous 'taɪm əs **~ly** li
timeout, time-out, time out ˌtaɪm 'aʊt
timepiec|e 'taɪm piːs **~es** ɪz əz
time-poor ˌtaɪm 'pɔː ◂ -'pʊə ◂ ‖ -'pʊər ◂ -'pɔːr ◂, -'poʊr ◂
timer 'taɪm ə ‖ -ər **~s** z
Times taɪmz
 ˌTimes 'Roman
timesav|ing 'taɪm ˌseɪv |ɪŋ **~er/s** ə/z ‖ ər/z
timescale 'taɪm skeɪəl **~s** z
timeserver 'taɪm ˌsɜːv ə ‖ -ˌsɜːv ər **~s** z
timeserving 'taɪm ˌsɜːv ɪŋ ‖ -ˌsɜːv-
timeshare 'taɪm ʃeə ‖ -ʃer -ʃær **~s** z
time-sharing 'taɪm ˌʃeər ɪŋ ‖ -ˌʃer ɪŋ -ˌʃær-
time-shift 'taɪm ʃɪft **~ed** ɪd əd **~ing** ɪŋ **~s** s
timetabl|e 'taɪm ˌteɪb əl **~ed** d **~es** z **~ing** ‿ɪŋ
timework 'taɪm wɜːk ‖ -wɜːk **~er/s** ə/z ‖ ər/z
timeworn 'taɪm wɔːn ‖ -wɔːrn -woʊrn
Timex *tdmk* 'taɪm eks
timid 'tɪm ɪd §-əd **~ly** li **~ness** nəs nɪs
timidity tɪ 'mɪd ət i -ɪt i ‖ -əṭ i
timing 'taɪm ɪŋ **~s** z
 'timing chain
Timisoara ˌtɪm i 'ʃwɑːr ə ˌtiːm- —*Romanian* Timişoara [ti mi 'ʃo̯a ra]
Timmie, Timmy 'tɪm i
Timon 'taɪm ən -ɒn
Timor 'tiːm ɔː 'taɪm- ‖ -ɔːr
Timorese ˌtɪm ə 'riːz◂ ‖ -'riːs◂
timorous 'tɪm ər‿əs **~ly** li **~ness** nəs nɪs
Timotei *tdmk* 'tɪm ə teɪ
Timothy, t~ 'tɪm əθ i
timpani 'tɪmp ən i -ə niː
timpanist 'tɪm pən ɪst §-əst **~s** s
Timpson 'tɪm*p*s ən
tin tɪn **tinned** tɪnd **tinning** 'tɪn ɪŋ **tins** tɪnz
 ˌtin 'can; **ˌtin 'god**; **ˌtin 'hat**; **'tin ˌopener**; **ˌtin pan 'alley**; **ˌtin 'whistle**
Tina 'tiːn ə
Tinbergen 'tɪn ˌbɜːg ən →'tɪm- ‖ -ˌbɜːg- —*Dutch* ['tɪn bɛr xə]
tinctorial tɪŋ*k* 'tɔːr i‿əl ‖ -'toʊr-
tincture 'tɪŋ*k* tʃə -ʃə ‖ -tʃər **~d** d **tincturing** 'tɪŋ*k* tʃər ɪŋ -ʃər ɪŋ **~s** z
Tindal 'tɪnd əl
Tindale 'tɪnd əl -eɪəl
Tindall 'tɪnd əl -ɔːl
Tindell 'tɪnd əl 'tɪn del
tinder 'tɪnd ə ‖ -ər
tinderbox 'tɪnd ə bɒks ‖ -ər bɑːks **~es** ɪz əz
tinder-dry ˌtɪnd ə 'draɪ ◂ ‖ -ər-
tine taɪn **tines** taɪnz
tinea 'tɪn i‿ə
tinfoil 'tɪn fɔɪəl
ting, Ting *tdmk* tɪŋ **tinged** tɪŋd **tinging** 'tɪŋ ɪŋ **tings** tɪŋz
tingaling ˌtɪŋ ə 'lɪŋ **~s** z
tinge tɪndʒ **tinged** tɪndʒd **tinges** 'tɪndʒ ɪz -əz **tingeing, tinging** 'tɪndʒ ɪŋ
tinged *past & pp of* **ting** tɪŋd
tinged *past & pp of* **tinge** tɪndʒd
Tingewick 'tɪndʒ wɪk
tingl|e, T~ 'tɪŋ gəl **~ed** d **~es** z **~ing** ‿ɪŋ **~y** ‿i
tingly 'tɪŋ gli 'tɪŋ gəl‿i **tinglier** 'tɪŋ gli‿ə ‖ ‿ər **tingliest** 'tɪŋ gli‿ɪst ‿əst
Tingwall 'tɪŋ wəl
tinhorn 'tɪn hɔːn ‖ -hɔːrn **~s** z
tini... —*see* **tiny**

tinker, T~ ˈtɪŋk ə ‖ -ᵊr **~ed** d **tinkering** ˈtɪŋk ər‿ɪŋ **~s** z

Tinkerbell ˈtɪŋk ə bel ‖ -ᵊr-

Tinkertoy *tdmk* ˈtɪŋk ə tɔɪ ‖ -ᵊr-

tinkl|e ˈtɪŋk ᵊl **~ed** d **~es** z **~ing** ‿ɪŋ

Tinky-Winky ˌtɪŋk i ˈwɪŋk i

tinn... —*see* **tin**

Tinney ˈtɪn i

TINNITUS

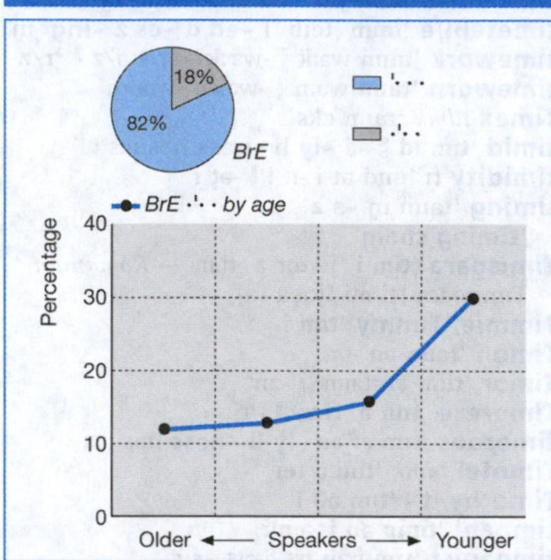

tinnitus ˈtɪn ɪt əs -ət-; tɪ ˈnaɪt əs, tə- ‖ -əţ- — *Preference poll, BrE:* ˈtɪn- *82%,* -ˈnaɪt- *18% (born since 1981, 30%).*

tinny ˈtɪn i **tinnier** ˈtɪn i‿ə ‖ ᵊr **tinnies** ˈtɪn iz **tinniest** ˈtɪn i‿ɪst əst **tinnily** ˈtɪn ɪ li -əl i **tinniness** ˈtɪn i nəs -nɪs

tinplate ˈtɪn pleɪt →ˈtɪm-

tinpot, tin-pot ˈtɪn pɒt →ˈtɪm- ‖ -pɑːt

tinsel ˈtɪnᵗs ᵊl **~ed, ~led** d **~ing, ~ling** ‿ɪŋ **~s** z

tinselly ˈtɪnᵗs ᵊl i

Tinseltown ˈtɪnᵗs ᵊl taʊn

Tinsley ˈtɪnz li

tinsmith ˈtɪn smɪθ **~s** s

tint tɪnt **tinted** ˈtɪnt ɪd -əd ‖ ˈtɪnţ əd **tinting** ˈtɪnt ɪŋ ‖ ˈtɪnţ ɪŋ **tints** tɪnts

tintack ˈtɪn tæk **~s** s

Tintagel tɪn ˈtædʒ əl

tinter ˈtɪnt ə ‖ ˈtɪnţ ᵊr **~s** z

Tintern ˈtɪnt ən ‖ -ᵊrn

T-intersection ˈtiː ˌɪnt ə sek ʃᵊn ‖ -ˌɪnţ ᵊr- **~s** z

Tintin ˈtɪn tɪn

tintinnabulation ˌtɪn tɪ ˌnæb jʊ ˈleɪʃ ᵊn ˌ·tə- ‖ -ˌ·jə- **~s** z

Tintoretto ˌtɪnt ə ˈret əʊ ‖ ˌtɪn tə ˈreţ oʊ —*It* [tin to ˈret to] **~s** z

tiny ˈtaɪn i **tinier** ˈtaɪn i‿ə ‖ ᵊr **tiniest** ˈtaɪn i‿ɪst əst

-tion *stress-imposing* ʃᵊn — **solution** sə ˈluːʃ ᵊn -ˈljuːʃ-

Tio Pepe *tdmk* ˌtiː əʊ ˈpep eɪ -i ‖ -oʊ-

-tious *stress-imposing* ʃəs — **fictitious** fɪk ˈtɪʃ əs

tip tɪp **tipped** tɪpt **tipping** ˈtɪp ɪŋ **tips** tɪps

tip-and-run ˌtɪp ən ˈrʌn →-m-

tipcat ˈtɪp kæt

tipi ˈtiːp i **~s** z

tip-off ˈtɪp ɒf -ɔːf ‖ -ɔːf -ɑːf **~s** s

Tippecanoe ˌtɪp i kə ˈnuː ˌ·ə-

tipper ˈtɪp ə ‖ -ᵊr **~s** z
 ˈtipper truck

Tipperary ˌtɪp ə ˈreər i ‖ -ˈrer i -ˈrær i

tippet, T~, Tippett ˈtɪp ɪt §-ət **~s** s

Tippex, Tipp-Ex *tdmk* ˈtɪp eks **~ed** t **~es** ɪz əz **~ing** ɪŋ

tippl|e ˈtɪp ᵊl **~ed** d **~es** z **~ing** ‿ɪŋ

tippler ˈtɪp ᵊl‿ə ‖ ər **~s** z

tippytoes ˈtɪp i təʊz ‖ -toʊz

tipstaff ˈtɪp stɑːf §-stæf ‖ -stæf **~s** s **tipstaves** ˈtɪp steɪvz

tipster ˈtɪp stə ‖ -stᵊr **~s** z

tips|y ˈtɪps |i **~ier** i‿ə ‖ i‿ᵊr **~iest** i‿ɪst i‿əst **~ily** ɪ li əl i **~iness** i nəs i nɪs

tiptoe ˈtɪp təʊ ‖ -toʊ **~d** d **~ing** ɪŋ **~s** z

Tipton ˈtɪpt ən

tip-top ˌtɪp ˈtɒp ◂ ‖ -ˈtɑːp ◂

Tiptree ˈtɪp triː

tip-up ˈtɪp ʌp

tirade (ˌ)taɪᵊ ˈreɪd tə-, tɪ- ‖ ˈtaɪᵊr eɪd **~s** z

tiramisu ˌtɪr əm i ˈsuː ‖ -ə ˈmiː suː —*It* tiramisù [ti ra mi ˈsu]

Tirana tɪ ˈrɑːn ə —*Albanian* Tiranë [ti ˈra nə]

tire ˈtaɪ‿ə ‖ ˈtaɪ‿ᵊr **tired** ˈtaɪ‿əd ‖ ˈtaɪ‿ᵊrd **tires** ˈtaɪ‿əz ‖ ˈtaɪ‿ᵊrz **tiring** ˈtaɪ‿ər ɪŋ ‖ ˈtaɪ‿ᵊr ɪŋ

tired ˈtaɪ‿əd ‖ ˈtaɪ‿ᵊrd **~ly** li **~ness** nəs nɪs

Tiree (ˌ)taɪᵊ ˈriː

tireless ˈtaɪ‿ə ləs -lɪs ‖ ˈtaɪ‿ᵊr ləs **~ly** li **~ness** nəs nɪs

Tiresias taɪᵊ ˈriːs i æs -ˈres-, -əs

tiresome ˈtaɪ‿ə səm ‖ ˈtaɪ‿ᵊr səm **~ly** li **~ness** nəs nɪs

tiro ˈtaɪᵊr əʊ ‖ -oʊ **~s** z

Tirol tɪ ˈrəʊl tə-, →-ˈrɒʊl; ˈtɪr əl, -əʊl ‖ -ˈroʊl —*Ger* [ti ˈʁoːl]

Tirolean ˌtɪr əʊ ˈliː‿ən ◂ tɪ ˈrəʊl i‿ən, tə- ‖ -ə- **~s** z

Tirolese ˌtɪr əʊ ˈliːz ◂ ‖ -ə-ˈliːs ◂

Tirpitz ˈtɜːp ɪts §-əts ‖ ˈtɜːp- —*Ger* [ˈtɪʁ pɪts]

'tis tɪz

tisane tɪ ˈzæn tiː- ‖ -ˈzɑːn **~s** z

Tiscali *tdmk* ˈtɪsk əl i

Tishbite ˈtɪʃ baɪt **~s** s

Tisiphone taɪ ˈsɪf ən i tɪ-

Tissot ˈtiːs əʊ ‖ tiː ˈsoʊ —*Fr* [ti so] **~s** z

tissue ˈtɪʃ uː ˈtɪs juː, ˈtɪʃ juː **~s** z
 ˈtissue ˌculture; **ˈtissue ˌpaper**

tit tɪt **tits** tɪts
 ˌtit for ˈtat

titan, Titan ˈtaɪt ᵊn **~s** z

titanate ˈtaɪt ə neɪt -ᵊn eɪt ‖ -ᵊn eɪt

Titania, t~ tɪ ˈtɑːn i‿ə taɪ-, -ˈteɪn- ‖ -ˈteɪn-

titanic, T~ taɪ ˈtæn ɪk **~ally** ᵊl‿i

titanium taɪ ˈteɪn i‿əm tɪ-

titbit ˈtɪt bɪt **~s** s

titch tɪtʃ **titches** ˈtɪtʃ ɪz -əz

Titchmarsh ˈtɪtʃ mɑːʃ ‖ -mɑːrʃ

titch|y ˈtɪtʃ |i **~ier** i‿ə ‖ i‿ᵊr **~iest** i‿ɪst i‿əst **~iness** i nəs i nɪs

titer 'tiːt ə 'taɪt- ‖ 'taɪţ ər 'tiːţ ər **~s** z

titfer 'tɪt fə ‖ -fər **~s** z

tithe taɪð **tithed** taɪðd **tithes** taɪðz **tithing/s** 'taɪð ɪŋ/z

Tithonus tɪ 'θəʊn əs taɪ- ‖ -'θoʊn-

titi *monkey* tɪ 'tiː 'tiː tiː **~s** z

titi *tree* 'tiː tiː 'taɪ taɪ **~s** z

Titian, t~ 'tɪʃ ən 'tɪʃ i‿ən **~s** z

Titicaca ˌtɪt ɪ 'kɑːk ə -'kɑː kɑː ‖ ˌtɪţ- —*Sp* [ti ti 'ka ka]

titill|ate 'tɪt ɪ l|eɪt -ə-, -əl |eɪt ‖ 'tɪţ əl |eɪt **~ated** eɪt ɪd -əd ‖ eɪţ əd **~ates** eɪts **~ating** eɪt ɪŋ ‖ eɪţ ɪŋ

titillation ˌtɪt ɪ 'leɪʃ ən -ə-, ˌtɪt əl 'eɪʃ- ‖ ˌtɪţ əl 'eɪʃ ən **~s** z

titi|vate 'tɪt ɪ |veɪt -ə- ‖ 'tɪţ- **~vated** veɪt ɪd -əd ‖ veɪţ əd **~vates** veɪts **~vating** veɪt ɪŋ ‖ veɪţ ɪŋ

titivation ˌtɪt ɪ 'veɪʃ ən -ə- ‖ ˌtɪţ- **~s** z

titlark 'tɪt lɑːk ‖ -lɑːrk **~s** s

titl|e 'taɪt əl ‖ 'taɪţ əl **~ed** d **~es** z **~ing** ‿ɪŋ **'title deed**, ˌ· · '·; **'title page**; **'title role**, ˌ· · '·

titleholder 'taɪt əl ˌhəʊld ə →-ˌhɒʊld- ‖ 'taɪţ əl ˌhoʊld ər **~s** z

titlist, Titleist *tdmk* 'taɪt əl ɪst §-əst ‖ 'taɪţ- **~s** s

Titmarsh 'tɪt mɑːʃ ‖ -mɑːrʃ

tit|mouse 'tɪt |maʊs **~mice** maɪs

Titmus 'tɪt məs

Tito 'tiːt əʊ ‖ 'tiːţ oʊ **~ism** ˌɪz əm

titrant 'taɪtr ənt **~s** s

titr|ate taɪ 'tr|eɪt tɪ-; 'taɪtr |eɪt ‖ 'taɪtr |eɪt **~ated** eɪt ɪd -əd ‖ eɪţ əd **~ates** eɪts **~ating** eɪt ɪŋ ‖ eɪţ ɪŋ

titration taɪ 'treɪʃ ən tɪ- **~s** z

titre 'tiːt ə 'taɪt- ‖ 'taɪţ ər 'tiːţ ər **~s** z

Tittensor 'tɪt ən sə -sɔː ‖ -sər -sɔːr

titter 'tɪt ə ‖ 'tɪţ ər **~ed** d **tittering** 'tɪt ər ɪŋ ‖ 'tɪţ ər ɪŋ **~s** z

tittiv... —*see* **titiv...**

tittle 'tɪt əl ‖ 'tɪţ əl **~s** z

tittle-tattl|e *n, v* 'tɪt əl ˌtæt əl ˌ· '· · ‖ 'tɪţ əl ˌtæţ əl **~ed** d **~es** z **~ing** ‿ɪŋ

tittup 'tɪt əp ‖ 'tɪţ əp **~ed, ~ped** t **~ing, ~ping** ɪŋ **~s** s

titt|y 'tɪt |i ‖ 'tɪţ |i **~ies** iz

titubation ˌtɪt ju 'beɪʃ ən §ˌtɪtʃ ə- ‖ ˌtɪtʃ ə-

titular 'tɪtʃ ʊl ə §-əl-; 'tɪt jʊl ə, -jəl- ‖ 'tɪtʃ əl‿ər **~ly** li **~s** z

titular|y 'tɪtʃ ʊl ər |i §'·əl-; 'tɪt jʊl-, '·jəl- ‖ 'tɪtʃ ə ler |i **~ies** iz

Titus 'taɪt əs ‖ 'taɪţ əs

Tiv tɪv

Tiverton 'tɪv ət ən ‖ -ərt ən

TiVo *tdmk* 'tiː vəʊ ‖ -voʊ

Tivoli 'tɪv əl i —*It* ['tiː vo li]

Tivy 'taɪv i

Tiwa 'tiː wə **~s** z

tiz, tizz tɪz

Tizard *(i)* 'tɪz ɑːd ‖ -ɑːrd, *(ii)* -əd ‖ -ərd

Tizer *tdmk* 'taɪz ə ‖ -ər

tizzwazz, tizzwoz 'tɪz wɒz ‖ -wɑːz

tizz|y 'tɪz |i **~ies** iz

T-junction 'tiː ˌdʒʌŋk ʃən **~s** z

TLC ˌtiː el 'siː

Tlingit 'tlɪŋ gɪt -kɪt, §-gət **~s** s

T-lymphocyte 'tiː ˌlɪmpf ə saɪt **~s** s

tmesis 'tmiːs ɪs 'miːs-, §-əs; tə 'miːs-

TNT ˌtiː en 'tiː

to *strong form* **tuː**, *weak forms* **tu, tə** —*The BrE-oriented EFL learner is advised to use* **tə** *before a consonant sound,* **tu** *before a vowel sound. Native speakers, however, sometimes ignore this distribution, in particular by using* **tə** *before a vowel (usually reinforced by a preceding* **ʔ** *— see HARD ATTACK) or, in very formal speech, by using* **tu** *even before a consonant. In AmE the weak form* **tə** *is used before both consonants and vowels. In* got to, ought to, used to, want to, *one* **t** *may be elided.*

toad təʊd ‖ toʊd **toads** təʊdz ‖ toʊdz

toadflax 'təʊd flæks ‖ 'toʊd- **~es** ɪz əz

toad-in-the-hole ˌtəʊd ɪn ðə 'həʊl ˌ·ən-, →-'hɒʊl ‖ ˌtoʊd ən ðə 'hoʊl

toadstool 'təʊd stuːl ‖ 'toʊd- **~s** z

toad|y 'təʊd |i ‖ 'toʊd |i **~ied** id **~ies** iz **~ying** i ɪŋ

to-and-fro ˌtuː‿ən 'frəʊ ‖ -'froʊ

toast təʊst ‖ toʊst **toasted** 'təʊst ɪd -əd ‖ 'toʊst əd **toasting** 'təʊst ɪŋ ‖ 'toʊst ɪŋ **toasts** təʊsts ‖ toʊsts **'toasting fork**; **'toast rack**

toaster 'təʊst ə ‖ 'toʊst ər **~s** z

toastie 'təʊst i ‖ 'toʊst i **~s** z

toastmaster 'təʊst ˌmɑːst ə §-ˌmæst- ‖ 'toʊst ˌmæst ər **~s** z

toastmistress 'təʊst ˌmɪs trəs -trɪs ‖ 'toʊst- **~es** ɪz əz

toast|y 'təʊst |i ‖ 'toʊst |i **~ier** i‿ə ‖ i‿ər **~iest** i‿ɪst i‿əst

tobacco tə 'bæk əʊ ‖ -oʊ **~es, ~s** z

tobacconist tə 'bæk ən ɪst §-əst **~s** s

Tobago tə 'beɪg əʊ ‖ -oʊ

Tobagonian ˌtəʊb ə 'gəʊn i‿ən ‖ ˌtoʊb ə 'goʊn- **~s** z

-to-be tə 'biː tu- — **mother-to-be** ˌmʌð ə tə 'biː -tu'· ‖ ˌ·ər-

Tobermory ˌtəʊb ə 'mɔːr i ‖ ˌtoʊb ər-

Tobey 'təʊb i ‖ 'toʊb i

ToBI 'təʊb i ‖ 'toʊb i

Tobias tə 'baɪ‿əs

Tobin 'təʊb ɪn §-ən ‖ 'toʊb-

Tobit 'təʊb ɪt §-ət ‖ 'toʊb-

Toblerone *tdmk* ˌtəʊb lə 'rəʊn '· · · ‖ ˌtoʊb lə 'roʊn

toboggan tə 'bɒg ən ‖ -'bɑːg- **~ed** d **~er/s** ə/z ‖ ər/z **~ing** ɪŋ **~ist/s** ɪst/s §əst/s ‖ əst/s **~s** z

Tobruk tə 'brʊk

Tob|y, tob|y 'təʊb |i ‖ 'toʊb |i **~ies, ~y's** iz **'toby jug**

toccata tə 'kɑːt ə tɒ- ‖ -'kɑːţ ə —*It* [tok 'kaː ta] **~s** z

Toc H ˌtɒk 'eɪtʃ §-'heɪtʃ ‖ ˌtɑːk-

Tocharian tɒ 'kɑːr i‿ən tə-, -'keər- ‖ toʊ 'ker i‿ən -'kær- **~s** z

tocopherol tɒ 'kɒf ə rɒl tə- ‖ toʊ 'kɑːf ə rɔːl -rɑːl, -roʊl
Tocqueville 'tɒk vɪl 'təʊk- ‖ 'toʊk- —*Fr* [tɔk vil]
tocsin 'tɒks ɪn §-ən ‖ 'tɑːks ən *(= toxin)* **~s** z
tod, Tod tɒd ‖ tɑːd
today tə 'deɪ tu- **~'s** z
Todd tɒd ‖ tɑːd
toddl|e 'tɒd ᵊl ‖ 'tɑːd ᵊl **~ed** d **~es** z **~ing** ‿ɪŋ
toddler 'tɒd ᵊl‿ə ‖ 'tɑːd ᵊl‿ər **~s** z
todd|y 'tɒd |i ‖ 'tɑːd |i **~ies** iz
todger 'tɒdʒ ə ‖ 'tɑːdʒ ᵊr **~s** z
Todhunter 'tɒd ˌhʌnt ə ‖ 'tɑːd ˌhʌnt̬ ᵊr
to-die-for tə 'daɪ fɔː ‖ -fɔːr -fᵊr
Todman 'tɒd mən →'tɒb- ‖ 'tɑːd-
Todmorden 'tɒd məd ən -mɔːd- ‖ 'tɑːd mɔːrd ᵊn
to-do tə 'duː tu- **~s** z
tody 'təʊd |i ‖ 'toʊd |i **~ies** iz
toe təʊ ‖ toʊ **toed** təʊd ‖ toʊd **toeing** 'təʊ ɪŋ ‖ 'toʊ ɪŋ **toes** təʊz ‖ toʊz
'toe cap
toe-curling 'təʊ ˌkɜːl ɪŋ ‖ 'toʊ ˌkɜːl ɪŋ
TOEFL *tdmk* 'təʊf ᵊl ‖ 'toʊf ᵊl
toehold 'təʊ həʊld →-hɒʊld ‖ 'toʊ hoʊld **~s** z
TOEIC *tdmk* 'təʊ ɪk ‖ 'toʊ ɪk
toe-in 'təʊ ɪn ‖ 'toʊ- **~s** z
toenail 'təʊ neɪᵊl ‖ 'toʊ- **~s** z
toerag 'təʊ ræg ‖ 'toʊ- **~s** z
toe-to-toe ˌtəʊ tə 'təʊ ‖ ˌtoʊ tə 'toʊ
toff tɒf ‖ tɑːf **toffs** tɒfs ‖ tɑːfs
toffee 'tɒf i ‖ 'tɑːf i 'tɔːf- **~s** z
'toffee ˌapple, ˌ· · '· ·
toffee-nosed 'tɒf i nəʊzd ˌ· · '· ‖ ˌtɑːf i 'noʊzd ◂ ˌtɔːf-
toff|y 'tɒf |i ‖ 'tɑːf |i 'tɔːf- **~ies** iz
Toft, toft tɒft ‖ tɑːft tɔːft
Tofts tɒfts ‖ tɑːfts tɔːfts
tofu 'təʊf uː ‖ 'toʊf uː —*Jp* [to‿o ɸɯ]
tog tɒg ‖ tɑːg tɔːg **togs** tɒgz ‖ tɑːgz tɔːgz
toga 'təʊg ə ‖ 'toʊg ə **~ed** d **~s** z
together tə 'geð ə tu- ‖ -ᵊr **~ness** nəs nɪs
togethering tə 'geð ər‿ɪŋ
toggl|e 'tɒg ᵊl ‖ 'tɑːg ᵊl **~ed** d **~es** z **~ing** ‿ɪŋ
Togo 'təʊg əʊ ‖ 'toʊg oʊ **~land** lænd
Togolese ˌtəʊg əʊ 'liːz ◂ ‖ ˌtoʊg ə- -oʊ-, -'liːs
Tóibín təʊ 'biːn ‖ toʊ- —*Irish* [t̪oː 'bʲiːnʲ]
toil tɔɪᵊl **toiled** tɔɪᵊld **toiling** 'tɔɪᵊl ɪŋ **toils** tɔɪᵊlz
toile twɑːl
toiler 'tɔɪᵊl ə ‖ -ᵊr **~s** z
toil|et 'tɔɪl |ət -ɪt ‖ -|ət **~eted** ɪt ɪd §ət-, -əd ‖ ət̬ əd **~eting** ɪt ɪŋ §ət- ‖ ət̬ ɪŋ **~ets** ɪts §əts ‖ əts
'toilet ˌpaper; **'toilet roll**; **'toilet ˌtraining**; **'toilet ˌwater**
toiletr|y 'tɔɪl ətr |i -ɪtr- **~ies** iz
toilette twɑː 'let —*Fr* [twa lɛt]
toilet-trained 'tɔɪl ət treɪnd -ɪt-
toilsome 'tɔɪᵊl səm **~ly** li **~ness** nəs nɪs
toilworn 'tɔɪᵊl wɔːn ‖ -wɔːrn -woʊrn

to-ing and fro-ing ˌtuː‿ɪŋ ən 'frəʊ ɪŋ ‖ -'froʊ ɪŋ **to-ings and fro-ings** ˌtuː‿ɪŋz ən 'frəʊ ɪŋz ‖ -'froʊ ɪŋz
tokamak 'təʊk ə mæk 'tɒk- ‖ 'toʊk- 'tɑːk- **~s** s
Tokay, tokay təʊ 'keɪ tɒ-, -'kaɪ, '· · ‖ toʊ- —*Hung* ['to kɒj] **~s** z
toke təʊk ‖ toʊk **tokes** təʊks ‖ toʊks
Tokelau 'təʊk ə laʊ 'tɒk- ‖ 'toʊk-
token 'təʊk ən ‖ 'toʊk ən **~ed** d **~ing** ‿ɪŋ **~ism** ˌɪz əm **~s** z
Tokharian tɒ 'kɑːr i‿ən tə-, -'keər- ‖ toʊ 'ker i‿ən -'kær- **~s** z
Toklas 'tɒk ləs 'təʊk- ‖ 'toʊk-
Tok Pisin ˌtɒk 'pɪz ɪn §-ᵊn ‖ ˌtɑːk- ˌtɔːk-
Tokyo 'təʊk i‿əʊ ‖ 'toʊk i‿oʊ —*Jp* [to‿o kjoo]
tola 'təʊl ə ‖ 'toʊl ə **~s** z
tolbutamide tɒl 'bjuːt ə maɪd ‖ tɑːl 'bjuːt̬-
told təʊld →tɒʊld ‖ toʊld
tole təʊl →tɒʊl ‖ toʊl —*Fr* tôle [toːl]
Toledo *(i)* tə 'liːd əʊ ‖ -oʊ, *(ii)* tɒ 'leɪd əʊ tə- ‖ toʊ 'leɪd oʊ —*The place in OH is (i), as is the trade name for a car. The place in Spain is usually (ii) in BrE.* —*Sp* [to 'le ðo]
tolerab|le 'tɒl ər‿əb |ᵊl ‖ 'tɑːl- **~leness** ᵊl nəs -nɪs **~ly** li
toleranc|e 'tɒl ər ənᵗs -ᵊr‿ənᵗs ‖ 'tɑːl- **~es** ɪz əz
tolerant 'tɒl ər ənt -ᵊr‿ənt ‖ 'tɑːl- **~ly** li
tole|rate 'tɒl ə |reɪt ‖ 'tɑːl- **~rated** reɪt ɪd -əd ‖ reɪt̬ əd **~rates** reɪts **~rating** reɪt ɪŋ ‖ reɪt̬ ɪŋ
toleration ˌtɒl ə 'reɪʃ ᵊn ‖ ˌtɑːl-
Tolkien 'tɒl kiːn ‖ 'toʊl- 'tɑːl-
toll təʊl →tɒʊl, §tɒl ‖ toʊl **tolled** təʊld →tɒʊld, §tɒld ‖ toʊld *(usually = told)* **tolling** 'təʊl ɪŋ →'tɒʊl-, §'tɒl- ‖ 'toʊl ɪŋ **tolls** təʊlz →tɒʊlz, §tɒlz ‖ toʊlz
'toll bridge
toll|booth 'təʊl |buːð →'tɒʊl-, 'tɒl-, -buːθ ‖ 'toʊl |buːθ **~booths** buːðz buːθs ‖ buːθs
Tollemache 'tɒl mæʃ -mɑːʃ ‖ 'tɑːl-
Tolleshunt 'təʊlz hʌnt →'tɒʊlz- ‖ 'toʊlz-
ˌTolleshunt 'd'Arcy 'dɑːs i ‖ 'dɑːrs i
toll-free ˌtəʊl 'friː ◂ →ˌtɒʊl- ‖ ˌtoʊl-
tollgate 'təʊl geɪt →'tɒʊl-, §'tɒl- ‖ 'toʊl- **~s** s
toll|house 'təʊl |haʊs →'tɒʊl-, §'tɒl- ‖ 'toʊl- **~houses** haʊz ɪz -əz
tollway 'təʊl weɪ →'tɒʊl- ‖ 'toʊl- **~s** z
Tolman 'təʊl mən →'tɒʊl- ‖ 'toʊl-
Tolpuddle 'tɒl ˌpʌd ᵊl ‖ 'tɑːl- —*locally also* ˌpɪd-
Tolstoy 'tɒl stɔɪ ‖ 'toʊl- 'tɑːl-, ˌ·'· —*Russ* [tʌɫ 'stɔj]
Toltec 'tɒl tek ‖ 'toʊl- 'tɑːl-
tolu tɒ 'luː təʊ-, -'ljuː ‖ tɑː 'luː tɔː-, tə-
toluene 'tɒl ju iːn ‖ 'tɑːl-
toluic tɒ 'ljuː ɪk təʊ-, -'luː- ‖ tə 'luː ɪk
Tolworth 'tɒl wəθ 'təʊl-, -wɜːθ ‖ 'tɑːl wɜːθ
Tom, tom tɒm ‖ tɑːm **toms, Tom's** tɒmz ‖ tɑːmz
ˌTom 'Collins; **ˌTom, ˌDick, and 'Harry**; **ˌTom 'Thumb**
tomahawk 'tɒm ə hɔːk ‖ 'tɑːm- -hɑːk **~s** s
Tomalin 'tɒm əl ɪn §-ən ‖ 'tɑːm-
tomato tə 'mɑːt əʊ ‖ tə 'meɪt̬ oʊ *(*)* **~es** z

tomb tuːm *(!)* **tombs** tuːmz
tombac 'tɒm bæk ‖ 'tɑːm-
tombola tɒm 'bəʊl ə 'tɒm bəl ə ‖ tɑːm 'boʊl ə
tomboy 'tɒm bɔɪ ‖ 'tɑːm- **~s** z
Tombs tuːmz
tombstone, T~ 'tuːm stəʊn ‖ -stoʊn **~s** z
tomcat 'tɒm kæt ‖ 'tɑːm- **~s** s
tome təʊm ‖ toʊm **tomes** təʊmz ‖ toʊmz
-tome təʊm ‖ toʊm — **microtome** 'maɪk rəʊ təʊm ‖ -rə toʊm
tomentose tə 'ment əʊs -əʊz; 'təʊm ən təʊs ‖ toʊ 'ment oʊs 'toʊm ən toʊs
tomfool ˌtɒm 'fuːl ◂ ‖ ˌtɑːm-
tomfooler|y ₍ˌ₎tɒm 'fuːl ər |i ‖ ˌtɑːm- **~ies** iz
-tomical 'tɒm ɪk ᵊl ‖ 'tɑːm- — **anatomical** ˌæn ə 'tɒm ɪk ᵊl ◂ ‖ -'tɑːm-
Tomintoul ˌtɒm ɪn 'taʊl -ən- ‖ ˌtɑːm-
Tomkins 'tɒmᵖ kɪnz ‖ 'tɑːmᵖ-
Tomlin 'tɒm lɪn §-lən ‖ 'tɑːm-
Tomlinson 'tɒm lɪn sən §-lən- ‖ 'tɑːm-
Tommie, Tommy, tommie, tommy 'tɒm i ‖ 'tɑːm i **tommies, Tommy's** 'tɒm iz ‖ 'tɑːm iz
'tommy gun
tommyrot 'tɒm i rɒt ‖ 'tɑːm i rɑːt
tomogram 'təʊm ə græm 'tɒm- ‖ 'toʊm- **~s** z
tomography təʊ 'mɒg rəf i ‖ toʊ 'mɑːg-

TOMORROW

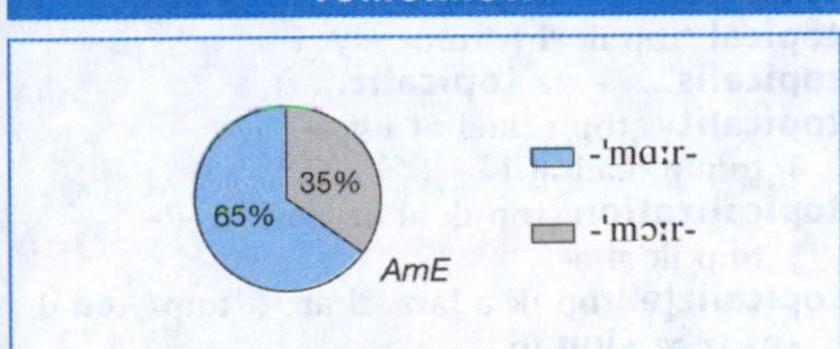

tomorrow tə 'mɒr əʊ tu- ‖ tə 'mɑːr oʊ -'mɔːr- —*In* ~ morning, ~ night *also* -ə, -u, *in* ~ afternoon, ~ evening *also* -u — *Preference poll, AmE:* -'mɑːr- *65%,* -'mɔːr- *35%.* **~s, ~'s** z
toˌmorrow ˌafter'noon; toˌmorrow 'evening; toˌmorrow 'morning; toˌmorrow 'night
Tompion 'tɒmp i ən ‖ 'tɑːmp-
Tomp|kin 'tɒmp| kɪn ‖ 'tɑːmp|- **~kins** kɪnz **~kinson** kɪn sən
Toms tɒmz ‖ tɑːmz
Tomsk tɒmᵖsk ‖ tɔːmᵖsk tɑːmᵖsk —*Russ* [tɔmsk]
tomtit 'tɒm tɪt ,'. ‖ 'tɑːm- **~s** s
tom-tom 'tɒm tɒm ‖ 'tɑːm tɑːm **~s** z
-tomy *stress-imposing* təm i — **anatomy** ə 'næt əm i ‖ -'næṭ-
ton *French word 'style'* tõ ‖ tɔːn toʊn —*Fr* [tɔ̃]
ton *'unit of weight, displacement, or speed'* tʌn *(= tun)* **tons** tʌnz
tonal 'təʊn ᵊl ‖ 'toʊn ᵊl **~ly** i
tonalit|y təʊ 'næl ət |i -ɪt i ‖ toʊ 'næl əṭ |i **~ies** iz
Tonbridge 'tʌn brɪdʒ →'tʌm-
Ton-du *place in MidGlam* ˌtɒn 'diː ‖ ˌtɔːn-
tone, Tone təʊn ‖ toʊn **toned** təʊnd ‖ toʊnd **tones** təʊnz ‖ toʊnz **toning** 'təʊn ɪŋ ‖ 'toʊn ɪŋ
'tone ˌlanguage; 'tone ˌpoem
tone-deaf ˌtəʊn 'def ◂ ‖ 'toʊn def **~ness** nəs nɪs
toneless 'təʊn ləs -lɪs ‖ 'toʊn- **~ly** li **~ness** nəs nɪs
tonematic ˌtəʊn ɪ 'mæt ɪk ◂ -iː-, -ə- ‖ ˌtoʊn ə 'mæṭ ɪk ◂
toneme 'təʊn iːm ‖ 'toʊn- **~s** z
tonemic təʊ 'niːm ɪk ‖ toʊ- **~ally** ᵊl i **~s** s
toner 'təʊn ə ‖ 'toʊn ᵊr **~s** z
tonetic təʊ 'net ɪk ‖ toʊ 'neṭ ɪk **~ally** ᵊl i **~s** s
ton|ey 'təʊn| i ‖ 'toʊn| i **~ier** i ə ‖ i ᵊr **~iest** i ɪst i əst
Tonfanau tɒn 'væn aɪ ‖ tɑːn- —*Welsh* [ton 'va nai, -nai, -ne, -na]
tong, Tong tɒŋ ‖ tɑːŋ tɔːŋ **tongs** tɒŋz ‖ tɑːŋz tɔːŋz
tonga 'tɒŋ gə ‖ 'tɑːŋ- **~s** z
Tonga *African people and language* 'tɒŋ gə ‖ 'tɑːŋ-
Tonga *place in Polynesia* 'tɒŋ ə -gə ‖ 'tɑːŋ-
Tongan 'tɒŋ ən -gən ‖ 'tɑːŋ- **~s** z
Tonge *surname(i)* tɒŋ ‖ tɑːŋ, *(ii)* tɒndʒ ‖ tɑːndʒ, *(iii)* tʌŋ
Tonge *placename* tɒŋ ‖ tɑːŋ
tongs tɒŋz ‖ tɑːŋz tɔːŋz
tongue, T~ tʌŋ §tɒŋ **tongued** tʌŋd **tongues** tʌŋz **tonguing** 'tʌŋ ɪŋ
'tongue ˌtwister
tongue-in-cheek ˌtʌŋ ɪn 'tʃiːk ◂ §ˌtɒŋ-
tongue-lashing 'tʌŋ ˌlæʃ ɪŋ §'tɒŋ-
tongue-tied 'tʌŋ taɪd §'tɒŋ-
Toni 'təʊn i ‖ 'toʊn i
Tonia 'təʊn i ə ‖ 'toʊn jə
Tonibell *tdmk* 'təʊn i bel ‖ 'toʊn-
tonic 'tɒn ɪk ‖ 'tɑːn ɪk **~s** s
ˌtonic ˌsol-'fa; 'tonic ˌwater
tonicit|y təʊ 'nɪs ət |i tɒ-, -ɪt i ‖ toʊ 'nɪs əṭ |i **~ies** iz
tonight tə 'naɪt tu- **~'s** s
tonite *'tonight'* tə 'naɪt
tonite *n 'explosive'* 'təʊn aɪt ‖ 'toʊn-
tonka, Tonka 'tɒŋk ə ‖ 'tɑːŋk ə
'tonka bean
Tonkin *part of Vietnam* ˌtɒn 'kɪn →ˌtɒŋ- ‖ ˌtɑːn- →ˌtɑːŋ-
Tonkin *family name* 'tɒŋk ɪn §-ən ‖ 'tɑːŋk-
Tonks tɒŋks ‖ tɑːŋks
tonnag|e 'tʌn ɪdʒ **~es** ɪz əz
tonne tʌn tɒn **tonnes** tʌnz tɒnz
tonneau 'tɒn əʊ ‖ tə 'noʊ 'tɑːn oʊ **~s, ~x** z
tonogenesis ˌtəʊn əʊ 'dʒen əs ɪs -ɪs ɪs, §-əs ‖ ˌtoʊn oʊ-
tonology təʊ 'nɒl ədʒ i ‖ toʊ 'nɑːl-
tonsil 'tɒnᵗs ᵊl -ɪl ‖ 'tɑːnᵗs ᵊl **~s** z
tonsillectom|y ˌtɒnᵗs ə 'lekt əm |i ˌ-ɪ- ‖ ˌtɑːnᵗs- **~ies** iz
tonsillitis ˌtɒnᵗs ə 'laɪt ɪs -ɪ-, §-əs ‖ ˌtɑːnᵗs ə 'laɪṭ əs
tonsorial tɒn 'sɔːr i əl ‖ tɑːn- -'soʊr-

T

tonsure 'tɒnᵗʃ ə 'tɒnᵗs juə ‖ 'tɑːnᵗʃ ᵊr **~d** d **tonsuring** 'tɒnᵗʃ ər ɪŋ 'tɒnᵗs juər ɪŋ ‖ 'tɑːnᵗʃ ər ɪŋ **~s** z
tontine 'tɒnt aɪn -iːn; ˌtɒn 'tiːn ‖ 'tɑːnt iːn tɑːn 'tiːn **~s** z
Tonto 'tɒnt əʊ ‖ 'tɑːnţ oʊ
ton-up ˌtʌn 'ʌp ◂
tonus 'təʊn əs ‖ 'toʊn-
ton|y 'təʊn| i ‖ 'toʊn| i **~ier** i‿ə ‖ i‿ᵊr **~iest** i‿ɪst i‿əst
Tony 'təʊn i ‖ 'toʊn i **Tonies, Tony's** 'təʊn iz ‖ 'toʊn iz
Tonypandy ˌtɒn ə 'pænd i ˌtəʊn-, -i- ‖ ˌtɑːn- —*Welsh* [tɔn ə 'pan di]
Tonyrefail ˌtɒn i 'rev aɪᵊl ‖ ˌtɑːn- —*Welsh* [tɔn ər 'e vail]
too tuː —*NB this word has no weak form*
toodle-oo ˌtuːd ᵊl 'uː
toodle-pip ˌtuːd ᵊl 'pɪp
Toogood 'tuː gʊd
took tʊk §tuːk
Took, Tooke tʊk §tuːk
tool tuːl **tooled** tuːld **tooling** 'tuːl ɪŋ **tools** tuːlz
toolbar 'tuːl bɑː ‖ -bɑːr **~s** z
toolbox 'tuːl bɒks ‖ -bɑːks **~es** ɪz əz
Tooley 'tuːl i
tool-maker 'tuːl ˌmeɪk ə ‖ -ᵊr **~s** z
toolshed 'tuːl ʃed **~s** z
toon tuːn **toons** tuːnz
toonie 'tuːn i **~s** z
toot *'toilet'; 'paper bag'* tʊt **toots** tʊts
toot *'sound (horn)'; 'spree'* tuːt **tooted** 'tuːt ɪd -əd ‖ 'tuːţ əd **tooting** 'tuːt ɪŋ ‖ 'tuːţ ɪŋ **toots** tuːts
Tootal *tdmk* 'tuːt ᵊl ‖ 'tuːţ ᵊl
tooth, Tooth tuːθ §tʊθ **teeth** tiːθ **toothed** tuːθt tuːðd, §tʊθt **toothing** 'tuːθ ɪŋ §'tʊθ- **tooths** tuːθs §tʊθs
'tooth ˌpowder
toothache 'tuːθ eɪk §'tʊθ- **~s** s
toothbrush 'tuːθ brʌʃ §'tʊθ- **~es** ɪz əz
toothcomb 'tuːθ kəʊm §'tʊθ- ‖ -koʊm **~s** z
toothed *adj* tuːθt tuːðd, §tʊθt ‖ 'tuːθ əd
Toothill 'tuːt hɪl
toothless 'tuːθ ləs §'tʊθ-, -lɪs **~ly** li **~ness** nəs nɪs
toothmug 'tuːθ mʌg §'tʊθ- **~s** z
toothpaste 'tuːθ peɪst §'tʊθ- **~s** s
toothpick 'tuːθ pɪk §'tʊθ- **~s** s
toothsome 'tuːθ səm §'tʊθ- **~ly** li **~ness** nəs nɪs
toothwort 'tuːθ wɜːt §'tʊθ-, §-wɔːt ‖ -wɜːt -wɔːrt **~s** s
tooth|y 'tuːθ |i §'tʊθ- **~ier** i‿ə ‖ i‿ᵊr **~iest** i‿ɪst i‿əst **~ily** ɪ li əl i **~iness** i nəs i nɪs
Tooting 'tuːt ɪŋ ‖ 'tuːţ ɪŋ
tootl|e 'tuːt ᵊl ‖ 'tuːţ ᵊl **~ed** d **~es** z **~ing** ‿ɪŋ
toots tuːts tʊts
toots|ie, toots|y 'tʊts |i 'tuːts- **~ies** iz
Toowoomba tə 'wʊm bə tu-

top tɒp ‖ tɑːp **topped** tɒpt ‖ tɑːpt **topping** 'tɒp ɪŋ ‖ 'tɑːp ɪŋ **tops** tɒps ‖ tɑːps
ˌtop 'brass; **ˌtop 'dog**; **ˌtop 'drawer**; **ˌtop 'hat**
Topa Inca 'təʊp əʳ ˌɪŋk ə ‖ 'toʊp-
topaz 'təʊp æz ‖ 'toʊp- **~es** ɪz əz
top-class ˌtɒp 'klɑːs ◂ §-'klæs ◂ ‖ ˌtɑːp 'klæs ◂
Topcliff, Topcliffe 'tɒp klɪf ‖ 'tɑːp-
topcoat 'tɒp kəʊt ‖ 'tɑːp koʊt **~s** s
top-down ˌtɒp 'daʊn ◂ ‖ ˌtɑːp-
top-dress ˌtɒp 'dres '· · ‖ 'tɑːp dres **~ed** t **~es** ɪz əz **~ing/s** ɪŋ/z
tope, Tope təʊp ‖ toʊp **toped** təʊpt ‖ toʊpt **topes** təʊps ‖ toʊps **toping** 'təʊp ɪŋ ‖ 'toʊp ɪŋ
topee 'təʊp iː -i ‖ 'toʊp iː toʊ 'piː **~s** z
Topeka təʊ 'piːk ə ‖ tə-
top-end 'tɒp end ‖ 'tɑːp-
top-flight ˌtɒp 'flaɪt ◂ ‖ ˌtɑːp-
topgallant tɒp 'gæl ənt tə- ‖ ˌtɑːp- —*naut* tə-
top-grossing 'tɒp ˌgrəʊs ɪŋ ‖ 'tɑːp ˌgroʊs ɪŋ
Topham 'tɒp əm ‖ 'tɑːp-
top-heav|y ˌtɒp 'hev |i ◂ ‖ 'tɑːp ˌhev |i **~iness** i nəs i nɪs
Tophet 'təʊf et ‖ 'toʊf-
toph|us 'təʊf |əs ‖ 'toʊf- **~i** aɪ
topi 'təʊp iː -i ‖ 'toʊp iː toʊ 'piː **~s** z
topiar|y 'təʊp i‿ər |i ‖ 'toʊp i er |i **~ies** iz
topic 'tɒp ɪk ‖ 'tɑːp ɪk **~s** s
topical 'tɒp ɪk ᵊl ‖ 'tɑːp- **~ly** ‿i
topicalis... —*see* **topicaliz...**
topicality ˌtɒp ɪ 'kæl ət i §ˌ·ə-, -ɪt i ‖ ˌtɑːp ə 'kæl əţ i
topicalization ˌtɒp ɪk əl aɪ 'zeɪʃ ᵊn -ɪ'-- ‖ ˌtɑːp ɪk əl ə-
topicaliz|e 'tɒp ɪk ə laɪz -ᵊl aɪz ‖ 'tɑːp- **~ed** d **~es** ɪz əz **~ing** ɪŋ
topknot 'tɒp nɒt ‖ 'tɑːp nɑːt **~s** s
Toplady 'tɒp ˌleɪd i ‖ 'tɑːp-
topless 'tɒp ləs -lɪs ‖ 'tɑːp-
top-level ˌtɒp 'lev ᵊl ◂ ‖ ˌtɑːp-
topmast 'tɒp mɑːst -məst, §-mæst ‖ 'tɑːp mæst
topmost 'tɒp məʊst ‖ 'tɑːp moʊst
topnotch ˌtɒp 'nɒtʃ ◂ ‖ ˌtɑːp 'nɑːtʃ ◂
topo 'tɒp əʊ ‖ 'tɑːp oʊ **~s** z
topo- *comb. form*
with stress-neutral suffix ¦tɒp ə ‖ ¦tɑːp ə — **toponymic** ˌtɒp ə 'nɪm ɪk ◂ ‖ ˌtɑːp-
with stress-imposing suffix tə 'pɒ+ tɒ- ‖ tə 'pɑː+ — **toponymy** tə 'pɒn əm i tɒ-, -ɪm i ‖ -'pɑːn-
top-of-the-line ˌtɒp əv ðə 'laɪn ◂ ‖ ˌtɑːp-
top-of-the-range ˌtɒp əv ðə 'reɪndʒ ◂ ‖ ˌtɑːp-
topographer tə 'pɒg rəf ə tɒ- ‖ tə 'pɑːg rəf ᵊr **~s** z
topographical ˌtɒp ə 'græf ɪk ᵊl ◂ ‖ ˌtɑːp- **~ly** ‿i
topograph|y tə 'pɒg rəf |i tɒ- ‖ -'pɑːg- **~ies** iz
topological ˌtɒp ə 'lɒdʒ ɪk ᵊl ◂ ‖ ˌtɑːp ə 'lɑːdʒ- **~ly** ‿i
topologist tə 'pɒl ədʒ ɪst tɒ-, §-əst ‖ -'pɑːl- **~s** s
topolog|y tə 'pɒl ədʒ |i tɒ- ‖ -'pɑːl- **~ies** iz

Topolsky tə 'pɒl ski ‖ -'pɑːl-
toponym 'tɒp ə nɪm ‖ 'tɑːp- **~s** z
toponymy tə 'pɒn əm i tɒ-, -ɪm i ‖ -'pɑːn-
top|os 'tɒp |ɒs ‖ 'toʊp |ɑːs **~oi** ɔɪ
topper, T~ 'tɒp ə ‖ 'tɑːp ᵊr **~s** z
topping, T~ 'tɒp ɪŋ ‖ 'tɑːp ɪŋ **~s** z
topping-out ˌtɒp ɪŋ 'aʊt ‖ ˌtɑːp-
toppl|e 'tɒp ᵊl ‖ 'tɑːp ᵊl **~ed** d **~es** z **~ing** ˌɪŋ
top-quality ˌtɒp 'kwɒl ət i ◂ -ɪt i ◂ ‖ ˌtɑːp 'kwɑːl əţ i ◂
top-|ranked ˌtɒp |'ræŋkt ◂ ‖ ˌtɑːp- **~ranking** 'ræŋk ɪŋ ◂
top-rated ˌtɒp 'reɪt ɪd ◂ -əd ◂ ‖ ˌtɑːp 'reɪţ əd ◂
topsail 'tɒp seɪᵊl -sᵊl ‖ 'tɑːp- —*naut* -sᵊl **~s** z
top-secret ˌtɒp 'siːk rət ◂ -rɪt ‖ ˌtɑːp-
Topsham 'tɒps əm 'tɒpʃ- ‖ 'tɑːps-
Topshop 'tɒp ʃɒp ‖ 'tɑːp ʃɑːp
topside 'tɒp saɪd ‖ 'tɑːp-
Topsider *tdmk* 'tɒp saɪd ə ‖ 'tɑːp saɪd ᵊr **~s** z
topsoil 'tɒp sɔɪᵊl ‖ 'tɑːp- **~s** z
topspin 'tɒp spɪn ‖ 'tɑːp-
topspinner 'tɒp spɪn ə ‖ -ᵊr **~s** z
Topsy 'tɒps i ‖ 'tɑːps i
topsy-turv|y ˌtɒps i 'tɜːv |i ◂ ‖ ˌtɑːps i 'tɜːv |i ◂ **~idom** i dəm **~iness** i nəs i nɪs
top-up *n* 'tɒp ʌp ‖ 'tɑːp- **~s** s
toque təʊk ‖ toʊk *(= toke)* **toques** təʊks ‖ toʊks
tor tɔː ‖ tɔːr **tors** tɔːz ‖ tɔːrz
Torah 'tɔːr ə 'təʊ rə; tɔː 'rɑː ‖ 'toʊr- —*Hebrew* [tɔ 'ra]
Torbay ˌtɔː 'beɪ ◂ ‖ ˌtɔːr-
torch tɔːtʃ ‖ tɔːrtʃ **torched** tɔːtʃt ‖ tɔːrtʃt **torches** 'tɔːtʃ ɪz -əz ‖ 'tɔːrtʃ əz **torching** 'tɔːtʃ ɪŋ ‖ 'tɔːrtʃ ɪŋ
torch-bearer 'tɔːtʃ ˌbeər ə ‖ 'tɔːrtʃ ˌber ᵊr -ˌbær- **~s** z
torchlight 'tɔːtʃ laɪt ‖ 'tɔːrtʃ-
Torcross ˌtɔː 'krɒs -'krɔːs ‖ ˌtɔːr 'krɔːs -'krɑːs
Tordoff 'tɔːd ɒf ‖ 'tɔːrd ɑːf
tore tɔː ‖ tɔːr toʊr
toreador 'tɒr i‿ə dɔː ‖ 'tɔːr i‿ə dɔːr **~s** z
torero tɒ 'reər əʊ tə- ‖ tə 'rer oʊ **~s** z
Torfaen ˌtɔː 'vaɪn ‖ ˌtɔːr- —*Welsh* [tor 'vain, -'vaɨn]
tori 'tɔːr aɪ ‖ 'toʊr-
toric 'tɒr ɪk 'tɔːr- ‖ 'tɔːr ɪk 'tɑːr-, 'toʊr-
Torie... —*see* **Tory**
torii 'tɔːr i iː ‖ 'toʊr- —*Jp* [to ˌrii]
Torino tə 'riːn əʊ ‖ -oʊ —*It* [to 'riː no]
torment *n* 'tɔː ment ‖ 'tɔːr- **~s** s
tor|ment *v* ₍ₗ₎tɔː |'ment ‖ ₍ₗ₎tɔːr |'ment '· · **~mented/ly** 'ment ɪd /li -əd ‖ 'menţ- **~menting/ly** 'ment ɪŋ /li ‖ 'menţ- **~ments** 'ments
tormentil 'tɔːm ən tɪl ‖ 'tɔːrm- **~s** z
tormentor ₍ₗ₎tɔː 'ment ə ‖ ₍ₗ₎tɔːr 'menţ ᵊr '· · · **~s** z
torn tɔːn ‖ tɔːrn toʊrn
tornado tɔː 'neɪd əʊ ‖ tɔːr 'neɪd oʊ **~es, ~s** z
toroid 'tɔːr ɔɪd ‖ 'toʊr- **~s** z
toroidal tɔː 'rɔɪd ᵊl ‖ toʊ-
Toronto tə 'rɒnt əʊ ‖ -'rɑːnţ oʊ
torpedo tɔː 'piːd əʊ ‖ tɔːr 'piːd oʊ **~es** z
tor'pedo boat
Torpenhow 'tɔːp ən haʊ ‖ 'tɔːrp- —*locally also* trɪ 'pen ə, trə-
torpid 'tɔːp ɪd §-əd ‖ 'tɔːrp əd **~ly** li **~ness** nəs nɪs **~s** z
torpidity tɔː 'pɪd ət i -ɪt i ‖ tɔːr 'pɪd əţ i
Torpoint ˌtɔː 'pɔɪnt ‖ ˌtɔːr-
torpor 'tɔːp ə ‖ 'tɔːrp ᵊr
Torquay ˌtɔː 'kiː ◂ ‖ ˌtɔːr-
torque tɔːk ‖ tɔːrk **torques** tɔːks ‖ tɔːrks
Torquemada ˌtɔːk wɪ 'mɑːd ə -ɪ-, -wə- ‖ ˌtɔːrk ə- —*Sp* [tor ke 'ma ða]
Torquil 'tɔːk wɪl -wəl ‖ 'tɔːrk-
torr tɔː ‖ tɔːr **torrs** tɔːz ‖ tɔːrz
Torrance 'tɒr ənᵗs ‖ 'tɔːr- 'tɑːr-
torrefaction ˌtɒr ɪ 'fæk ʃᵊn -ə- ‖ ˌtɔːr- ˌtɑːr-
torre|fy 'tɒr ɪ |faɪ -ə- ‖ 'tɔːr- 'tɑːr- **~fied** faɪd **~fies** faɪz **~fying** faɪ ɪŋ
Torremolinos ˌtɒr ɪm ə 'liːn ɒs ˌ-əm- ‖ ˌtɔːr əm ə 'liːn oʊs —*Sp* [to rre mo 'li nos]
Torrens 'tɒr ənz ‖ 'tɔːr ənz 'tɑːr-
torrent 'tɒr ənt ‖ 'tɔːr ənt 'tɑːr- **~s** s
torrential tə 'renʃ ᵊl tɒ- ‖ tɔː- tə- **~ly** i
Torres 'tɒr ɪs 'tɔːr-, -ɪz, §-əs ‖ 'tɔːr əs
Torrey 'tɒr i ‖ 'tɔːr i 'tɑːr-
torrid 'tɒr ɪd §-əd ‖ 'tɔːr əd 'tɑːr- **~ly** li **~ness** nəs nɪs
Torrington 'tɒr ɪŋ tən ‖ 'tɔːr- 'tɑːr-
Tórshavn 'tɔːs haʊn ‖ 'tɔːrs- —*Faroese* ['tɔuʂ haun]
torsion 'tɔːʃ ᵊn ‖ 'tɔːrʃ ᵊn **~al** əl
torso 'tɔːs əʊ ‖ 'tɔːrs oʊ **~s** z
tort tɔːt ‖ tɔːrt **torts** tɔːts ‖ tɔːrts
torte tɔːt ‖ tɔːrt —*Ger* T~ ['tɔʁ tə]
Tortelier tɔː 'tel i eɪ ‖ ˌtɔːrt el 'jeɪ —*Fr* [tɔʁ tə lje]
tortellini ˌtɔːt ə 'liːn i -ᵊl 'iːn- ‖ ˌtɔːrţ ᵊl 'iːn i —*It* [tor tel 'liː ni]
tort-feasor ˌtɔːt 'fiːz ə ‖ ˌtɔːrt 'fiːz ᵊr **~s** z
torticollis ˌtɔːt ɪ 'kɒl ɪs §-ə-, §-əs ‖ ˌtɔːrţ ə 'kɑːl əs
tortilla tɔː 'tiː ə -jə; -'tɪl ə ‖ tɔːr- —*Sp* [tor 'ti ʎa, -ja] **~s** z
tortious 'tɔːʃ əs ‖ 'tɔːrʃ əs **~ly** li
tortois|e 'tɔːt əs §'tɔː tɔɪs, §-tɔɪz ‖ 'tɔːrţ əs **~es** ɪz əz
tortoiseshell 'tɔːt əs ʃel →-əʃ-, -ə- ‖ 'tɔːrţ-
Tortola tɔː 'təʊl ə ‖ tɔːr 'toʊl ə
Tortuga tɔː 'tuːg ə ‖ tɔːr-
tortuosit|y ˌtɔːtʃ u 'ɒs ət |i ˌtɔːt ju-, -ɪt i ‖ ˌtɔːrtʃ u 'ɑːs əţ |i **~ies** iz
tortuous 'tɔːtʃ u‿əs 'tɔːt ju‿əs ‖ 'tɔːrtʃ u‿əs **~ly** li **~ness** nəs nɪs
torture *v, n* 'tɔːtʃ ə ‖ 'tɔːrtʃ ᵊr **~d** d **torturing** 'tɔːtʃ ər‿ɪŋ ‖ 'tɔːrtʃ ər‿ɪŋ **~s** z
torturer 'tɔːtʃ ər‿ə ‖ 'tɔːrtʃ ᵊr‿ər **~s** z
torturous 'tɔːtʃ ər‿əs ‖ 'tɔːrtʃ- **~ly** li
Torun 'tɔːr uːn 'tɒr- —*Polish* Toruń ['tɔ ruɲ]
tor|us 'tɔːr |əs ‖ 'toʊr- **~i** aɪ
Torvalds 'tɔːv ælts -ældz ‖ 'tɔːrv- —*Swed* ['tuːɹ valḑs]

Torvill ˈtɔː vɪl ‖ ˈtɔːr-

Tor|y ˈtɔːr |i ‖ ˈtour- **~ies** iz **~yism** i ˌɪz əm

Tosa, tosa ˈtəuz ə ˈtəus ə ‖ ˈtous ə **~s** z —*Jp* [ˈto sa]

Toscanini ˌtɒsk ə ˈniːn i ‖ ˌtɑːsk- —*It* [to ska ˈniː ni]

tosh, Tosh tɒʃ ‖ tɑːʃ

Toshack ˈtɒʃ æk ‖ ˈtɑːʃ-

Toshiba *tdmk* tɒ ˈʃiːb ə tə- ‖ tə- tou- —*Jp* [toˌo çi ba]

toss tɒs tɔːs ‖ tɔːs tɑːs **tossed** tɒst tɔːst ‖ tɔːst tɑːst **tosses** ˈtɒs ɪz ˈtɔːs-, -əz ‖ ˈtɔːs əz ˈtɑːs- **tossing** ˈtɒs ɪŋ ˈtɔːs- ‖ ˈtɔːs ɪŋ ˈtɑːs-

tosser ˈtɒs ə ‖ ˈtɔːs ᵊr ˈtɑːs- **~s** z

tosspot ˈtɒs pɒt ‖ ˈtɔːs pɑːt ˈtɑːs- **~s** s

toss-up ˈtɒs ʌp ˈtɔːs- ‖ ˈtɔːs- ˈtɑːs- **~s** s

tostada tɒ ˈstɑːd ə ‖ tou- —*AmSp* [toh ˈta ða] **~s** z

tot tɒt ‖ tɑːt **tots** tɒts ‖ tɑːts **totted** ˈtɒt ɪd -əd ‖ ˈtɑːţ əd **totting** ˈtɒt ɪŋ ‖ ˈtɑːţ ɪŋ

total ˈtəut ᵊl ‖ ˈtouţ ᵊl **~ed, ~led** d **~ing, ~ling** ɪŋ **~s** z

totalis... —*see* **totaliz...**

totalitarian təu ˌtæl ɪ ˈteər i‿ən ◂ ˌtəu tæl-, -əˈ-- ‖ tou ˌtæl ə ˈter- ˌtou tæl- **~ism** ˌɪz əm

totalit|y təu ˈtæl ət |i -ɪt i ‖ tou ˈtæl əţ |i **~ies** iz

totalizator ˈtəut əl aɪ zeɪt ə -ɪ· · ‖ ˈtouţ ᵊl ə zeɪţ ᵊr **~s** z

totaliz|e ˈtəut ə laɪz -ᵊl aɪz ‖ ˈtouţ ᵊl aɪz **~ed** d **~er/s** ə/z ‖ ᵊr/z **~es** ɪz əz **~ing** ɪŋ

totally ˈtəut əl i ‖ ˈtouţ ᵊl i

totaquine ˈtəut ə kwiːn ‖ ˈtouţ-

tote təut ‖ tout **toted** ˈtəut ɪd -əd ‖ ˈtouţ əd **totes** təuts ‖ touts **toting** ˈtəut ɪŋ ‖ ˈtouţ ɪŋ **ˈtote bag**

totem ˈtəut əm ‖ ˈtouţ- **~ism** ˌɪz əm **~s** z **ˈtotem pole**

totemic təu ˈtem ɪk ‖ tou-

tother, t'other ˈtʌð ə ‖ -ᵊr

Tothill ˈtɒt hɪl -ɪl ‖ ˈtɑːt-

Totley ˈtɒt li ‖ ˈtɑːt-

Totnes ˈtɒt nɪs -nəs ‖ ˈtɑːt-

toto ˈtəut əu ‖ ˈtout ou

Totpak *tdmk* ˈtɒt pæk ‖ ˈtɑːt- **~s** s

tott... —*see* **tot**

Tottenham ˈtɒt ᵊn‿əm ‖ ˈtɑːt- **ˌTottenham ˌCourt ˈRoad**; **ˌTottenham ˈHotspur**

totter ˈtɒt ə ‖ ˈtɑːţ ᵊr **~ed** d **tottering/ly** ˈtɒt ər ɪŋ /li ‖ ˈtɑːţ ər ɪŋ /li **~s** z

Totteridge ˈtɒt ər ɪdʒ ‖ ˈtɑːţ-

tottery ˈtɒt ər i ‖ ˈtɑːţ-

tott|ie, tott|y ˈtɒt |i ‖ ˈtɑːţ |i **~ies** iz

Totton ˈtɒt ᵊn ‖ ˈtɑːt ᵊn

toucan ˈtuːk ən -æn, -ɑːn ‖ -æn -ɑːn; tuː ˈkɑːn **~s** z

touch tʌtʃ *(!)* **touched** tʌtʃt **touches** ˈtʌtʃ ɪz -əz **touching/ly** ˈtʌtʃ ɪŋ /li **ˈtouch judge**

Touch *family name* tautʃ

Touch *place in Fife* tuːx

touch-and-go ˌtʌtʃ ən ˈgəu ◂ →-əŋ- ‖ -ˈgou

touchdown ˈtʌtʃ daun **~s** z

touche, touché ˈtuːʃ eɪ ‖ tuː ˈʃeɪ

Touche tuːʃ

touchi... —*see* **touchy**

touchline ˈtʌtʃ laɪn **~s** z

touch-me-not ˈtʌtʃ mi nɒt ‖ -nɑːt **~s** s

touchpad ˈtʌtʃ pæd **~s** z

touchpaper ˈtʌtʃ ˌpeɪp ə ‖ -ᵊr

touchstone ˈtʌtʃ stəun ‖ -stoun **~s** z

touch-tone, Touch-Tone *tdmk* ˈtʌtʃ təun ‖ -toun

touch-typ|e ˈtʌtʃ taɪp **~ed** t **~es** s **~ing** ɪŋ **~ist/s** ɪst/s §əst/s

touch-up *n* ˈtʌtʃ ʌp **~s** s

touchwood ˈtʌtʃ wud

touch|y ˈtʌtʃ |i **~ier** i‿ə ‖ i‿ᵊr **~iest** i‿ɪst i‿əst **~ily** ɪ li əl i **~iness** i nəs i nɪs

touchy-feel|ie, ~y ˌtʌtʃ i ˈfiːᵊl i ◂ **~ies** iz

tough tʌf *(!) (= tuff)* **tougher** ˈtʌf ə ‖ -ᵊr **toughest** ˈtʌf ɪst -əst **ˌtough ˈluck**

Tough *place in Grampian* tuːx ‖ tuːk

Tough *family name (i)* tʌf, *(ii)* tuːx ‖ tuːk

toughen ˈtʌf ᵊn **~ed** d **~ing** ‿ɪŋ **~s** z

toughie ˈtʌf i **~s** z

toughly ˈtʌf li

tough-minded ˌtʌf ˈmaɪnd ɪd ◂ -əd **~ly** li **~ness** nəs nɪs

toughness ˈtʌf nəs -nɪs

Toulon (ˌ)tuː ˈlɒ̃ ‖ -ˈlɔːn -ˈlɑːn —*Fr* [tu lɔ̃]

Toulouse (ˌ)tuː ˈluːz tə- —*Fr* [tu luːz]

Toulouse-Lautrec ˌtuː luːz ləu ˈtrek ·ˌ··ˈ·, tə- ‖ tuː ˌluːz lə ˈtrek —*Fr* [tu luz lo tʁɛk]

toupee, toupée ˈtuːp eɪ ˌtuː ˈpeɪ ‖ tuː ˈpeɪ —*Fr* toupet [tu pe] **~s** z

tour tuə tɔː ‖ tuᵊr **toured** tuəd tɔːd ‖ tuᵊrd **touring** ˈtuər ɪŋ ˈtɔːr- ‖ ˈtur ɪŋ **tours** tuəz tɔːz ‖ tuᵊrz **ˌtour de ˈforce** —*Fr* [tuʁ də fɔʁs]; **ˌTour de ˈFrance** —*Fr* [tuʁ də fʁɑ̃ːs]; **ˈtour ˌoperator**

tourer ˈtuər ə ˈtɔːr- ‖ ˈtur ᵊr **~s** z

Tourette tuᵊ ˈret **~'s** s

tourism ˈtuər ˌɪz əm ˈtɔːr- ‖ ˈtur-

tourist ˈtuər ɪst ˈtɔːr-, §-əst ‖ ˈtur əst **~s** s **ˈtourist class**

touristic (ˌ)tuə ˈrɪst ɪk (ˌ)tɔː- ‖ tu- **~ally** ᵊl‿i

touristy ˈtuər ɪst i ˈtɔːr-, -əst- ‖ ˈtur-

tourmaline ˈtuəm ə liːn ˈtɜːm-, -lɪn ‖ ˈturm-

tournament ˈtuən ə mənt ˈtɔːn-, ˈtɜːn- ‖ ˈturn- ˈtɔːrn-, ˈtɜːn- **~s** s

tournedos *sing.* ˈtuən ə dəu ˈtɔːn-, ˈtɜːn- ‖ ˌturn ə ˈdou **~** *pl* z

tourney ˈtuən i ˈtɔːn-, ˈtɜːn- ‖ ˈturn i ˈtɔːrn-, ˈtɜːn- **~ed** d **~ing** ɪŋ **~s** z

tourniquet ˈtɔːn ɪ keɪ ˈtuən-, ˈtɜːn-, -ə- ‖ ˈtɜːn ək ət ˈturn-, -ɪk- (*) **~s** z ‖ s

Tours *place in France* tuə tuəz, tɔːz ‖ tuᵊr —*Fr* [tuːʁ]

Tours *English family name* tuəz tɔːz ‖ tuᵊrz

tourtière ˌtɔːt i ˈeə ‖ ˌturt i ˈeᵊr **~s** z

tousl|e ˈtauz ᵊl **~ed** d **~es** z **~ing** ‿ɪŋ

tout *adj, adv, in French expressions* tuːt —*but before consonants* tuː

ˌtout 'court ˌtuː 'kʊə -'kɔː ‖ -'kʊᵊr —*Fr* [tu kuːʁ]; **ˌtout en'semble** ˌtuːt ɒn 'sɒm bᵊl ‖ -ɑːn 'sɑːm- —*Fr* [tu tɑ̃ sɑ̃ːbl]
tout *v, n* taʊt **touted** 'taʊt ɪd -əd ‖ 'taʊṭ əd **touting** 'taʊt ɪŋ ‖ 'taʊṭ ɪŋ **touts** taʊts
Tovell 'təʊv ᵊl ‖ 'toʊv-
Tovey *(i)* 'təʊv i ‖ 'toʊv i, *(ii)* 'tʌv i
tow təʊ §taʊ ‖ toʊ *(usually = toe)* **towed** təʊd §taʊd ‖ toʊd *(usually = toad)* **towing** 'təʊ ɪŋ §'taʊ- ‖ 'toʊ ɪŋ **tows** təʊz §taʊz ‖ toʊz
'tow truck
towage 'təʊ ɪdʒ ‖ 'toʊ-
toward *prep* tə 'wɔːd tu-; tɔːd ‖ tɔːrd toʊrd; tə 'wɔːrd, twɔːrd, twoʊrd
toward *adj* 'təʊ əd tɔːd ‖ tɔːrd toʊrd **~liness** li nəs -nɪs **~ly** li **~ness** nəs nɪs
towards tə 'wɔːdz tu-; tɔːdz ‖ tɔːrdz toʊrdz; tə 'wɔːrdz, twɔːrdz, twoʊrdz
towaway 'təʊ ə ˌweɪ ‖ 'toʊ-
towbar 'təʊ bɑː ‖ 'toʊ bɑːr **~s** z
towboat 'təʊ bəʊt ‖ 'toʊ boʊt **~s** s
Towcester 'təʊst ə ‖ 'toʊst ᵊr
towel 'taʊ‿əl taʊl ‖ 'taʊ‿əl **toweled, towelled** 'taʊ‿əld taʊld ‖ 'taʊ‿əld **toweling, towelling** 'taʊ‿əl ɪŋ 'taʊl ɪŋ ‖ 'taʊ‿əl ɪŋ **towels** 'taʊəlz taʊlz ‖ 'taʊ‿əlz
towelette ˌtaʊ ə 'let ˌtaʊ 'let **~s** s
tower, Tower 'taʊ‿ə ‖ 'taʊ‿ᵊr **~ed** d **towering** 'taʊ‿ər ɪŋ ‖ 'taʊ‿ᵊr ɪŋ **~s** z
'tower block; **ˌTower 'Bridge◂**, **ˌTower ˌBridge 'Road**; **ˌTower 'Hamlets**; **ˌtower of 'strength**
Towers 'taʊ‿əz ‖ 'taʊ‿ᵊrz
tow-haired ˌtəʊ 'heəd ◂ ‖ ˌtoʊ 'heᵊrd ◂ -'hæᵊrd
towhead 'təʊ hed ‖ 'toʊ- **~ed** ɪd əd **~s** z
Tow Law ˌtaʊ 'lɔː ‖ -'lɑː
towline 'təʊ laɪn §'taʊ- ‖ 'toʊ- **~s** z
town taʊn **towns** taʊnz
ˌtown 'clerk; **ˌtown 'crier**; **ˌtown 'hall**; **'town house**; **ˌtown 'planning**
Towne taʊn
Townes taʊnz
townie 'taʊn i **~s** z
Townley 'taʊn li
townscape 'taʊn skeɪp **~s** s
Townsend 'taʊnz end
townsfolk 'taʊnz fəʊk ‖ -foʊk
Townshend 'taʊnz end
township 'taʊn ʃɪp **~s** s
towns|man 'taʊnz |mən **~men** mən men **~people** ˌpiːp ᵊl
Townsville 'taʊnz vɪl -vᵊl
towns|woman 'taʊnz |ˌwʊm ən **~women** ˌwɪm ɪn §-ən
tow|path 'təʊ |pɑːθ §'taʊ-, §-pæθ ‖ 'toʊ |pæθ **~paths** pɑːðz §pæðz, §pɑːθs, §pæθs ‖ pæðz pæθs
towrope 'təʊ rəʊp §'taʊ- ‖ 'toʊ roʊp **~s** s
Towy 'taʊ i —*Welsh* ['tə wi, 'to-]
Towyn 'taʊ ɪn 'təʊ- —*Welsh* ['tə win, 'to-, -wɨn]
toxaemia, toxemia tɒk 'siːm i‿ə ‖ tɑːk-
toxic 'tɒks ɪk ‖ 'tɑːks ɪk **~ally** ᵊl‿i
ˌtoxic 'shock ˌsyndrome
toxicit|y tɒk 'sɪs ət |i -ɪt i ‖ tɑːk 'sɪs əṭ |i **~ies** iz
toxicological ˌtɒks ɪk əʊ 'lɒdʒ ɪk ᵊl ◂ ‖ ˌtɑːks ɪk ə 'lɑːdʒ- **~ly** ‿i
toxicologist ˌtɒks ɪ 'kɒl ədʒ ɪst ˌ·ə-, §-əst ‖ ˌtɑːks ɪ 'kɑːl- **~s** s
toxicology ˌtɒks ɪ 'kɒl ədʒ i ˌ·ə- ‖ ˌtɑːks ɪ 'kɑːl-
toxin 'tɒks ɪn §-ən ‖ 'tɑːks ən **~s** z
toxocariasis ˌtɒks əʊ kə 'raɪ‿əs ɪs §-əs ‖ ˌtɑːks ə-
toxoid 'tɒks ɔɪd ‖ 'tɑːks- **~s** z
toxophilite tɒk 'sɒf ə laɪt -ɪ- ‖ tɑːk 'sɑːf- **~s** s
toxoplasmosis ˌtɒks əʊ plæz 'məʊs ɪs -əs ‖ ˌtɑːks ə plæz 'moʊs əs ˌ·oʊ-
Toxteth 'tɒkst əθ -ɪθ, -eθ ‖ 'tɑːkst-
toy tɔɪ **toyed** tɔɪd **toying** 'tɔɪ ɪŋ **toys** tɔɪz
'toy ˌfactory *where toys are made*, **ˌtoy 'factory** *for a child to play with*; **ˌtoy 'gun**; **ˌtoy 'poodle**; **ˌtoy 'soldier**
Toya, Toyah 'tɔɪ ə
toyboy 'tɔɪ bɔɪ **~s** z
Toye tɔɪ
toymaker 'tɔɪ ˌmeɪk ə ‖ -ᵊr **~s** z
Toynbee 'tɔɪn bi →'tɔɪm-, -biː
Toyota *tdmk* tɔɪ 'əʊt ə ‖ -'oʊṭ ə **~s** z —*Jp* ['to jo ta]
toyshop 'tɔɪ ʃɒp ‖ -ʃɑːp **~s** s
Toys "R" Us *tdmk* ˌtɔɪz ᵊr 'ʌs
Tozer 'təʊz ə ‖ 'toʊz ᵊr
T'Pau tə 'paʊ
Trabant *tdmk* 'træb ænt -ənt —*Ger* [tʁa 'bant]
trace treɪs **traced** treɪst **traces** 'treɪs ɪz -əz **tracing** 'treɪs ɪŋ
'trace ˌelement
traceable 'treɪs əb ᵊl
tracer 'treɪs ə ‖ -ᵊr **~s** z
tracer|y 'treɪs ər‿|i **~ies** iz
Tracey 'treɪs i
trache|a trə 'kiː‿|ə 'treɪk i‿|ə ‖ 'treɪk i‿|ə **~ae** iː **~al** əl **~as** əz
tracheitis ˌtreɪk i 'aɪt ɪs ˌtræk-, §-əs ‖ -'aɪṭ əs
tracheo- *comb. form*
with stress-neutral suffix ¦treɪk i əʊ ¦træk- ‖ -oʊ — **tracheocele** 'treɪk i əʊ siːᵊl 'træk- ‖ -i oʊ-
with stress-imposing suffix ˌtreɪk i 'ɒ+ ˌtræk- ‖ -'ɑː+ — **tracheostomy** ˌtreɪk i 'ɒst əm i ˌtræk- ‖ -'ɑːst-
tracheotom|y ˌtræk i 'ɒt əm |i ˌtreɪk- ‖ ˌtreɪk i 'ɑːṭ- **~ies** iz
trachoma trə 'kəʊm ə ‖ -'koʊm-
tracing 'treɪs ɪŋ **~s** z
'tracing ˌpaper
track træk **tracked** trækt *(= tract)* **tracking** 'træk ɪŋ **tracks** træks
'track eˌvent; **'tracking ˌstation**; **'track ˌrecord**; **'track rod**
trackage 'træk ɪdʒ
trackball 'træk bɔːl ‖ -bɑːl **~s** z
tracker 'træk ə ‖ -ᵊr **~s** z

T

tracklay|er ˈtræk ˌleɪ |ə ‖ -|ᵊr **~ers** əz ‖ ᵊrz **~ing** ɪŋ
trackless ˈtræk ləs -lɪs
track|suit ˈtræk |suːt -sjuːt **~suited** suːt ɪd sjuːt-, -əd ‖ suːţ əd **~suits** suːts sjuːts
tract trækt **tracts** trækts
tractability ˌtrækt ə ˈbɪl ət i -ɪt i ‖ -əţ i
tractab|le ˈtrækt əb |ᵊl **~leness** ᵊl nəs -nɪs **~ly** li
Tractarian træk ˈteər i‿ən ‖ -ˈter- **~s** z
tractate ˈtrækt eɪt **~s** s
tractile ˈtrækt aɪᵊl ‖ -ᵊl -aɪᵊl
traction ˈtræk ʃᵊn
ˈtraction ˌengine
tractive ˈtrækt ɪv
tractor ˈtrækt ə ‖ -ᵊr **~s** z
tractorfeed ˈtrækt ə fiːd ‖ -ᵊr-
tractor-trailer ˈtrækt ə ˌtreɪl ə ‖ -ᵊr ˌtreɪl ᵊr **~s** z
Tracy ˈtreɪs i
trad træd
trade treɪd **traded** ˈtreɪd ɪd -əd **trades** treɪdz **trading** ˈtreɪd ɪŋ
ˈtrade gap; **ˈtrade name**; **ˈtrade price**; **ˈtrade route**; **ˌtrade ˈsecret**; **ˌTrades ˌUnion ˈCongress**; **₍ˌ₎trade ˈunion**; **ˈtrade wind**; **ˈtrading eˌstate**; **ˈtrading post**; **ˈtrading stamp**; **ˌtrade(s) ˈunion** ‖ ˈ. ˌ.
trade-in ˈtreɪd ɪn **~s** z
trademark ˈtreɪd mɑːk →ˈtreɪb- ‖ -mɑːrk **~ed** t **~ing** ɪŋ **~s** s
trade-off ˈtreɪd ɒf -ɔːf ‖ -ɔːf -ɑːf **~s** s
trader ˈtreɪd ə ‖ -ᵊr **~s** z
Tradescant trə ˈdesk ənt
tradescantia ˌtræd ɪ ˈskænt i‿ə ˌtreɪd-, ˌ-e-, ˌ-ə-, -ˈskænᵗʃ- ‖ -ˈskænᵗʃ- **~s** z
trades|man ˈtreɪdz |mən **~men** mən men **~people** ˌpiːp ᵊl
tradition trə ˈdɪʃ ᵊn **~s** z
traditional trə ˈdɪʃ ᵊn‿əl **~ism** ˌɪz əm **~ist/s** ɪst/s §əst/s ‖ əst/s **~ly** i
traduc|e trə ˈdjuːs →-ˈdʒuːs ‖ -ˈduːs -ˈdjuːs **~ed** t **~es** ɪz əz **~ing** ɪŋ
Trafalgar trə ˈfælg ə ‖ -ᵊr ˈfɑːlg- —*But the pronunciation* ˌtræf ᵊl ˈgɑː ◂ ‖ -ˈgɑːr ◂ *was formerly used for the viscountcy and is still sometimes used for* T~ House *—near Salisbury. —Sp* [tra fal ˈɣar]
traffic ˈtræf ɪk **~ked** t **~king** ɪŋ **~s** s
ˈtraffic ˌcircle; **ˈtraffic ˌisland**; **ˈtraffic jam**; **ˈtraffic light**; **ˈtraffic ˌsignal**; **ˈtraffic ˌwarden**
trafficator ˈtræf ɪ keɪt ə §ˈ·ə- ‖ -keɪţ ᵊr **~s** z
trafficker ˈtræf ɪk ə ‖ -ᵊr **~s** z
Trafford ˈtræf əd ‖ -ᵊrd
tragacanth ˈtræg ə kænᵗθ ˈtrædʒ-
tragedian trə ˈdʒiːd i‿ən **~s** z
tragedienne trə ˌdʒiːd i ˈen **~s** z
traged|y ˈtrædʒ əd |i -ɪd i **~ies** iz
Trager ˈtreɪg ə ‖ -ᵊr
tragic ˈtrædʒ ɪk **~ally** ᵊl‿i
tragicomed|y ˌtrædʒ i ˈkɒm əd |i ‖ -ˈkɑːm- **~ies** iz

tragicomic ˌtrædʒ i ˈkɒm ɪk ◂ ‖ -ˈkɑːm- **~ally** ᵊl‿i
tragopan ˈtræg ə pæn **~s** z
tragus ˈtreɪg əs **tragi** ˈtreɪdʒ aɪ ˈtreɪg-
Traherne trə ˈhɜːn ‖ -ˈhɝːn
trail treɪᵊl **trailed** treɪᵊld **trailing** ˈtreɪᵊl ɪŋ **trails** treɪᵊlz
ˈtrail bike; **ˌtrailing ˈedge**, ˈ. .
trailblaz|er ˈtreɪᵊl ˌbleɪz |ə ‖ -|ᵊr **~ers** əz ‖ ᵊrz **~ing** ɪŋ
trailer ˈtreɪl ə ‖ -ᵊr **~s** z
ˈtrailer camp; **ˈtrailer park**
trailhead ˈtreɪᵊl hed **~s** z
Traill treɪᵊl
train, Train treɪn **trained** treɪnd **training** ˈtreɪn ɪŋ **trains** treɪnz
ˈtraining ˌcollege; **ˈtraining course**; **ˈtrain set**
trainbearer ˈtreɪn ˌbeər ə →ˈtreɪm- ‖ -ˌber ᵊr -ˌbær- **~s** z
trainee ˌtreɪ ˈniː **~s** z **~ship/s** ʃɪp/s
trainer ˈtreɪn ə ‖ -ᵊr **~s** z
trainload ˈtreɪn ləʊd ‖ -loʊd **~s** z
train|man ˈtreɪn |mən →ˈtreɪm- **~men** mən men
train-spott|er ˈtreɪn spɒt| ə ‖ -spɑːţ| ᵊr **~ers** əz ‖ ᵊrz **~ing** ɪŋ
traipse treɪps **traipsed** treɪpst **traipses** ˈtreɪps ɪz -əz **traipsing** ˈtreɪps ɪŋ
trait treɪ treɪt ‖ treɪt **traits** treɪz treɪts ‖ treɪts
traitor ˈtreɪt ə ‖ ˈtreɪţ ᵊr **~s** z
traitorous ˈtreɪt ər‿əs ‖ ˈtreɪţ ər əs →ˈtreɪtr əs **~ly** li **~ness** nəs nɪs
Trajan ˈtreɪdʒ ən
trajector|y trə ˈdʒek tər‿|i ˈtrædʒ ɪk-, ˈ-ək- **~ies** iz
tra-la trɑː ˈlɑː trə-
tra-la-la ˌtrɑːl ɑː ˈlɑː -ə-
Tralee trə ˈliː
tram træm **trams** træmz
tramcar ˈtræm kɑː ‖ -kɑːr **~s** z
tramline ˈtræm laɪn **~s** z
trammel ˈtræm ᵊl **~ed, ~led** d **~ing, ~ling** ɪŋ **~s** z
tramontane trə ˈmɒnt eɪn ‖ -ˈmɑːnt- **~s** z
tramp træmp **tramped** træm*p*t **tramping** ˈtræmp ɪŋ **tramps** træm*p*s
trampl|e ˈtræmp ᵊl **~ed** d **~es** z **~ing** ‿ɪŋ
trampolin|e ˈtræmp ə liːn -lɪn, ˌ· ·ˈ· **~ed** d **~es** z **~ing** ɪŋ
tramway ˈtræm weɪ **~s** z
trance trɑːnᵗs §trænᵗs ‖ trænᵗs **trances** ˈtrɑːnᵗs ɪz §ˈtrænᵗs-, -əz ‖ ˈtrænᵗs əz
tranche trɑːnᵗʃ trɔːnᵗʃ, trænᵗʃ **tranches** ˈtrɑːnᵗʃ ɪz ˈtrɔːnᵗʃ-, ˈtrænᵗʃ-, -əz
trank træŋk **tranks** træŋ*k*s
Tranmere ˈtræn mɪə →ˈtræm- ‖ -mɪr
trann|ie, ~y ˈtræn |i **~ies** iz
tranquil ˈtræŋk wɪl -wəl **~ly** li
tranquility, tranquillity træŋ ˈkwɪl ət i -ɪt i ‖ træn ˈkwɪl əţ i →træŋ-

tranquiliz|e, tranquillis|e, tranquillizle 'træŋk wə laɪz -wɪ- **~ed** d **~er/s** ə/z ‖ -^{ə}r/z **~es** ɪz əz **~ing** ɪŋ

trans- træn^{t}s trænz, trɑːn^{t}s, trɑːnz *—For EFL learners, the form* **træns** *is acceptable in all contexts in all kinds of English. Actual usage preferences are fairly complex. —In the choice between* **s** *and* **z** *forms we can distinguish various phonetic contexts according to the sound with which the stem begins, as follows. (1) Before a voiceless sound* (trans'form), **s** *is usual. (2) Before* **l** (trans'late) *and before an unstressed vowel sound* ('transit), **s** *is usual though a minority use* **z**. *(3) Before other consonants* (trans'gress, trans'mit), *and before a stressed vowel sound* (trans'act), *the tendency is for BrE to prefer* **z**, *but AmE to prefer* **s**. *This also applies in any word where the prefix is felt as separate* (ˌtransˌconti'nental). *—For the vowel, RP prefers* **æ**, *although a substantial minority use* **ɑː**, *and some words have variants with* **ə**; *AmE always has* **æ**. *—Before a stem beginning with* **s** *the final consonant sound is often lost* (trans + scribe *giving* transcribe **træn 'skraɪb**).

transact træn 'zækt trɑːn-, trən-, -'sækt; ˌtræn^{t}s 'ækt ‖ -'sækt -'zækt **~ed** ɪd əd **~ing** ɪŋ **~s** s

transactinide ˌtræn^{t}s 'ækt ɪ naɪd ˌtrɑːn^{t}s-, ˌtrænz-, §-ə- **~s** z

transaction træn 'zæk ʃ^{ə}n trɑːn-, trən-, -'sæk-; ˌtræn^{t}s 'æk- ‖ -'sæk- -'zæk- **~al** ˌəl **~s** z

transalpine $_{(1)}$trænz 'ælp aɪn $_{(1)}$trɑːnz-, $_{(1)}$træn^{t}s- ‖ $_{(1)}$træn^{t}s-$_{(1)}$trænz-, -ən **~s** z

transatlantic ˌtrænz ət 'lænt ɪk ◂ ˌtrɑːnz-, §ˌtræn^{t}s-, -æt- ‖ ˌtræn^{t}s ət 'lænţ ɪk ◂ ˌtrænz-

Transcarpathian ˌtrænz kɑː 'peɪθ iˌən ◂ ˌtrɑːnz-, ˌtræn^{t}s- ‖ ˌtræn^{t}s kɑːr-

Transcaucasia ˌtrænz kɔː 'keɪz iˌə ˌtrɑːnz-, ˌtræn^{t}s-, -'keɪʒ ə ‖ ˌtræn^{t}s kɔː 'keɪʒ ə -kɑː-, -'keɪʃ ə

transceiver træn 'siːv ə trɑːn- ‖ -^{ə}r **~s** z

transcend træn 'send trɑːn- **~ed** ɪd əd **~ing** ɪŋ **~s** z

transcendenc|e træn 'send ən^{t}s trɑːn- **~y** i

transcendent træn 'send ənt trɑːn- **~ly** li

transcendental ˌtræn^{t}s en 'dent ^{ə}l ◂ ˌtrɑːn^{t}s-, -^{ə}n- ‖ -'denţ ^{ə}l ◂ **~ism** ˌɪz əm **~ly** i

ˌtranscenˌdental ˌmedi'tation

transcontinental ˌtrænz ˌkɒnt ɪ 'nent ^{ə}l ˌtrɑːnz-, ˌtræn^{t}s-, ə- ‖ ˌtræn^{t}s ˌkɑːnt ^{ə}n 'enţ ^{ə}l

transcrib|e $_{(1)}$træn 'skraɪb $_{(1)}$trɑːn-; $_{(1)}$træn^{t}s 'kraɪb **~ed** d **~er/s** ə/z ‖ ^{ə}r/z **~es** z **~ing** ɪŋ

transcript 'træn^{t}s krɪpt 'trɑːn^{t}s- **~s** s

transcriptase $_{(1)}$træn 'skrɪpt eɪz $_{(1)}$trɑːn-, -eɪs; $_{(1)}$træn^{t}s 'krɪpt-

transcription $_{(1)}$træn 'skrɪp ʃ^{ə}n $_{(1)}$trɑːn-; $_{(1)}$træn^{t}s 'krɪp- **~al** ˌəl **~ally** ˌəl i **~s** z

transducer $_{(1)}$trænz 'djuːs ə $_{(1)}$trɑːnz-, $_{(1)}$træn^{t}s-, $_{(1)}$trɑːn^{t}s-, →-'dʒuːs- ‖ $_{(1)}$træn^{t}s 'duːs ^{ə}r -'djuːs- **~s** z

transept 'træn^{t}s ept 'trɑːn^{t}s- **~s** s

transeunt 'træn^{t}s iˌənt 'trɑːn^{t}s-

transexual træn 'sek ʃuˌəl trɑːn-, trænz-, trɑːnz-, ˌtræn^{t}s-, ˌtrɑːn^{t}s-, -'seks juˌəl, -'sek ʃ^{ə}l ‖ træn^{t}s- **~ism** ˌɪz əm **~s** z

trans|fer *v* træn^{t}s |'fɜː trɑːn^{t}s-, trən^{t}s-, '· · ‖ træn^{t}s |'fɜ˞ː '· · **~ferred** 'fɜːd ‖ 'fɜ˞ːd **~ferring** 'fɜːr ɪŋ ‖ 'fɜ˞ː ɪŋ **~fers** 'fɜːz ‖ 'fɜ˞ːz

transfer *n* 'træn^{t}s fɜː 'trɑːn^{t}s- ‖ -fɜ˞ː **~s** z

'transfer fee

transferability træn^{t}s ˌfɜːr ə 'bɪl ət i trɑːn^{t}s-, ˌ· ·-, ˌ·fərˌə-, -ɪt i ‖ -ˌfɜ˞ː ə 'bɪl əţ i

TRANSFERABLE

18% -'fɜːr-
82% '· · · ·
BrE

transferable træn^{t}s 'fɜːr əb ^{ə}l trɑːn^{t}s-, ˌ·-, trən^{t}s-; 'træn^{t}s fərˌəb ^{ə}l, 'trɑːn^{t}s- ‖ -'fɜ˞ː- — *Preference poll, BrE:* -'fɜːr- *82%*, '· · · · *18%*.

transferal, transferral træn^{t}s 'fɜːr əl trɑːn^{t}s-, trən^{t}s- ‖ træn^{t}s 'fɜ˞ː əl **~s** z

transferas|e 'træn^{t}s fə reɪz 'trɑːn^{t}s-, -reɪs **~es** ɪz əz

transferee ˌtræn^{t}s fɜːr 'iː -fər- ‖ -fɜ˞ː- **~s** z

transferenc|e 'træn^{t}s f^{ə}r ən^{t}s 'trɑːn^{t}s-; $_{(1)}$træn^{t}s 'fɜːr ən^{t}s, $_{(1)}$trɑːn^{t}s-, trən^{t}s- ‖ træn^{t}s 'fɜ˞ː ən^{t}s '·f^{ə}r · **~es** ɪz əz

transferor, transferrer træn^{t}s 'fɜːr ə 'trɑːn^{t}s- ‖ -'fɜ˞ː ^{ə}r **~s** z

transfiguration, T~ ˌtræn^{t}s ˌfɪɡ ə 'reɪʃ ^{ə}n ˌtrɑːn^{t}s-, ·ˌ·'·, -jə-, -ju^{ə}- ‖ -jə- **~s** z

transfigure træn^{t}s 'fɪɡ ə trɑːn^{t}s- ‖ -j^{ə}r *(*)* **~d** d **~s** z **transfiguring** træn^{t}s 'fɪɡ ər ɪŋ trɑːn^{t}s- ‖ -jər ɪŋ

transfinite træn^{t}s 'faɪn aɪt trɑːn^{t}s-

transfix træn^{t}s 'fɪks trɑːn^{t}s- **~ed** t **~es** ɪz əz **~ing** ɪŋ

transform *n* 'træn^{t}s fɔːm 'trɑːn^{t}s- ‖ -fɔːrm **~s** z

transform *v* træn^{t}s 'fɔːm trɑːn^{t}s-, trən^{t}s-; 'træn^{t}s fɔːm, 'trɑːn^{t}s- ‖ -'fɔːrm **~ed** d **~ing** ɪŋ **~s** z

transformable træn^{t}s 'fɔːm əb ^{ə}l trɑːn^{t}s-, trən^{t}s- ‖ -'fɔːrm-

transformation ˌtræn^{t}s fə 'meɪʃ ^{ə}n ˌtrɑːn^{t}s-, -fɔː- ‖ -f^{ə}r- -fɔːr- **~al** ˌəl ◂ **~ally** ^{ə}lˌi **~s** z

ˌtransforˌmational 'grammar

transformer træn^{t}s 'fɔːm ə trɑːn^{t}s-, trən^{t}s- ‖ -'fɔːrm ^{ə}r '· · · **~s** z

transfus|e træn^{t}s 'fjuːz trɑːn^{t}s-, trən^{t}s- **~ed** d **~es** ɪz əz **~ing** ɪŋ

transfusion træn^{t}s 'fjuːʒ ^{ə}n trɑːn^{t}s-, §trən^{t}s- **~s** z

transgender ˌtrænz 'dʒend ə ˌtrɑːnz-, ˌtræn^{t}s-, ˌtrɑːn^{t}s- ‖ ˌtræn^{t}s 'dʒend^{ə}r ˌtrænz-

transgenic ˌtrænz 'dʒen ɪk ◂ ˌtrɑːnz-, ˌtræn^{t}s-, ˌtrɑːn^{t}s- ‖ ˌtræn^{t}s- ˌtrænz-

T

transgress trænz ˈgres trɑːnz-, trænᵗs-, trɑːnᵗs-, trənz- ‖ trænᵗs- trænz- **~ed** t **~es** ɪz əz **~ing** ɪŋ
transgression trænz ˈgreʃ ᵊn trɑːnz-, trænᵗs-, trɑːnᵗs-, §trənz- ‖ trænᵗs- trænz- **~s** z
transgressor trænz ˈgres ə trɑːnz-, trænᵗs-, trɑːnᵗs-, §trənz- ‖ trænᵗs ˈgres ᵊr trænz- **~s** z
tranship trænᵗs ˈʃɪp trɑːnᵗs-, →trænᵗʃ-, →trɑːnᵗʃ-, træn-, trɑːn-, trænz-, trɑːnz-, §trənᵗs-, →§trənᵗʃ-, §trən-, §trənz- ‖ trænᵗs- →trænᵗʃ- **~ped** t **~ping** ɪŋ **~s** s
transhumance trænᵗs ˈhjuːm ənᵗs trɑːnᵗs-, §-ˈjuːm-
transienc|e ˈtrænz i‿ənᵗs ˈtrɑːnz-, ˈtrænᵗs-, ˈtrɑːnᵗs- ‖ ˈtrænᵗʃ ənᵗs, ˈtrænʒ- **~y** i
transient ˈtrænz i‿ənt ˈtrɑːnz-, ˈtrænᵗs-, ˈtrɑːnᵗs- ‖ ˈtrænᵗʃ ənt, ˈtrænʒ- **~ly** li **~ness** nəs nɪs

TRANSISTOR

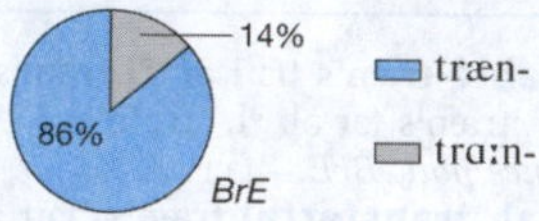

transistor træn ˈzɪst ə trɑːn-, §trən-, -ˈsɪst- ‖ -ᵊr — *Preference poll, BrE:* træn- *86% (English southerners 84%),* trɑːn- *14% (English southerners 16%);* -ˈzɪst- *63%,* -ˈsɪst- *37%.* **~s** z
tranˌsistor ˈradio
transistoris|e, transistoriz|e træn ˈzɪst ə raɪz trɑːn-, §trən-, -ˈsɪst- **~ed** d **~es** ɪz əz **~ing** ɪŋ
trans|it ˈtrænᵗs |ɪt ˈtrɑːnᵗs-, ˈtrænz-, ˈtrɑːnz-, §-ət ‖ ˈtrænᵗs |ət ˈtrænz- **~ited** ɪt ɪd §ət-, -əd ‖ əṭ əd **~iting** ɪt ɪŋ §ət- ‖ əṭ ɪŋ **~its** ɪts §əts əts
ˈtransit lounge; **ˈtransit ˌpassengers**; **ˈtransit ˌvisa**

TRANSITION

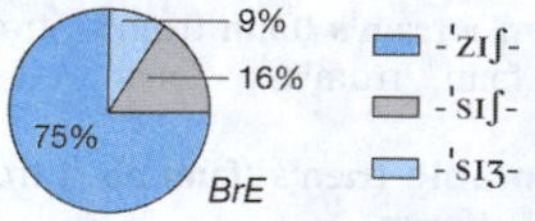

transition træn ˈzɪʃ ᵊn trɑːn-, trən-, -ˈsɪʃ-, -ˈsɪʒ- — *Preference poll, BrE:* -ˈzɪʃ- *75%,* -ˈsɪʃ- *16%,* -ˈsɪʒ- *9%.* **~al** ‿əl **~ally** ‿əl i **~s** z
transitive ˈtrænᵗs ət ɪv ˈtrɑːnᵗs-, ˈtrænz-, ˈtrɑːnz-, -ɪt ɪv ‖ ˈtrænᵗs əṭ ɪv ˈtrænz- **~ly** li **~ness** nəs nɪs **~s** z
transitivity ˌtrænᵗs ə ˈtɪv ət i ˌtrɑːnᵗs-, ˌtrænz-, ˌtrɑːnz-, ˌ·ɪ-, -ɪt i ‖ -əṭ i
transitor|y ˈtrænᵗs ət‿ᵊr |i ˈtrɑːnᵗs-, ˈtrænz-, ˈtrɑːnz-, ·ɪt‿ ‖ ˈtrænᵗs ə tɔːr |i ˈtrænz-, -toʊr i (*) **~ily** əl i ɪ li **~iness** i nəs i nɪs
Transkei ˌtrænᵗs ˈkaɪ ˌtrɑːnᵗs-, ˌtrænz-, ˌtrɑːnz-

translatable trænᵗs ˈleɪt əb ᵊl trɑːnᵗs-, trænz-, trɑːnz-, trənᵗs-, trənz ‖ ˈtræns leɪṭ əb ᵊl ˈtrænz-, ˌ·ˈ--

TRANSLATE

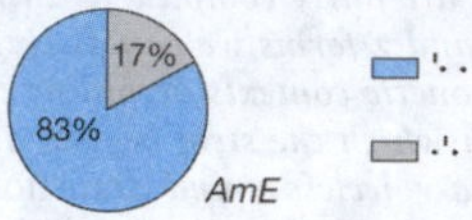

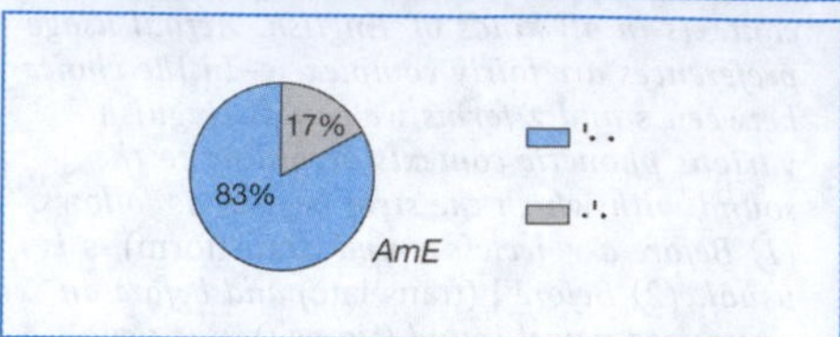

trans|late trænᵗs |ˈleɪt trɑːnᵗs-, trænz-, trɑːnz-, trənᵗs-, trənz- ‖ ˈtrænᵗs |leɪt ˈtrænz-, ·ˈ· — *Preference poll, AmE:* ˈ·· *83%,* ·ˈ· *17%.* **~lated** ˈleɪt ɪd -əd ‖ leɪṭ əd **~lates** ˈleɪts ‖ leɪts **~lating** ˈleɪt ɪŋ ‖ leɪṭ ɪŋ
translation trænᵗs ˈleɪʃ ᵊn trɑːnᵗs-, trænz-, trɑːnz-, trənᵗs-, trənz- ‖ trænz- **~al** ‿əl **~s** z
translator trænᵗs ˈleɪt ə trɑːnᵗs-, trænz-, trɑːnz-, trənᵗs-, trənz- ‖ trænᵗs ˈleɪṭ ᵊr trænz-, ˈ·· **~s** z
translite|rate trænᵗs ˈlɪt ə |reɪt trɑːnᵗs-, trænz-, trɑːnz-, ˌ·ˈ-, trənᵗs-, trənz- ‖ trænᵗs ˈlɪṭ- trænz- **~rated** reɪt ɪd -əd ‖ reɪṭ əd **~rates** reɪts **~rating** reɪt ɪŋ ‖ reɪṭ ɪŋ
transliteration trænᵗs ˌlɪt ə ˈreɪʃ ᵊn trɑːnᵗs-, trænz-, trɑːnz-, ˌ·ˌ··-, trənz- ‖ trænᵗs ˌlɪṭ- trænz-, ˌ·ˌ··- **~s** z
translo|cate ˈtrænᵗs ləʊ| keɪt ˈtrɑːnᵗs-, ˈtrænz-, ˈtrɑːnz-, ˌ·ˈ· ‖ ˈtrænz loʊ|- ˈtrænᵗs-, ˌ·ˈ·· **~cated** keɪt ɪd -əd ‖ keɪṭ əd **~cates** keɪts **~cating** keɪt ɪŋ ‖ keɪṭ ɪŋ
translocation ˌtrænᵗs ləʊ ˈkeɪʃ ᵊn ˌtrɑːnᵗs-, ˌtrænz-, ˌtrɑːnz- ‖ ˌtrænz loʊ- ˌtrænᵗs-
translucenc|e trænᵗs ˈluːs ᵊnᵗs trɑːnᵗs-, trænz-, trɑːnz-, -ˈljuːs- **~y** i
translucent trænᵗs ˈluːs ᵊnt trɑːnᵗs-, trænz-, trɑːnz-, -ˈljuːs- **~ly** li
transmig|rate ˌtrænz maɪ ˈg|reɪt ˌtrɑːnz-, ˌtrænᵗs-, ˌtrɑːnᵗs- ‖ ˌtrænᵗs ˈmaɪg |reɪt ˌtrænz-, ˌ·ˈ·· (*) **~rated** reɪt ɪd -əd ‖ reɪṭ əd **~rates** reɪts **~rating** reɪt ɪŋ ‖ reɪṭ ɪŋ
transmigration ˌtrænz maɪ ˈgreɪʃ ᵊn ˌtrɑːnz-, ˌtrænᵗs-, ˌtrɑːnᵗs- ‖ ˌtrænᵗs-ˌtrænz- **~s** z
transmissibility trænz ˌmɪs ə ˈbɪl ət i trɑːnz-, trænᵗs-, trɑːnᵗs-, ˌ·ˌ··-, -ɪˈ·-, -ɪt i ‖ trænᵗs ˌmɪs ə ˈbɪl əṭ i trænz-, ˌ·ˌ··-
transmissible trænz ˈmɪs əb ᵊl trɑːnz-, trænᵗs-, trɑːnᵗs-, -ɪb ᵊl ‖ trænᵗs- trænz-
transmission trænz ˈmɪʃ ᵊn trɑːnz-, trænᵗs-, trɑːnᵗs- ‖ trænᵗs- trænz- **~s** z
transmissive trænz ˈmɪs ɪv trɑːnz-, trænᵗs-, trɑːnᵗs- ‖ trænᵗs- trænz-
transmissivity ˌtrænz mɪ ˈsɪv ət i ˌtrɑːnz-, ˌtrænᵗs-, ˌtrɑːnᵗs-, -ɪt i ‖ ˌtrænᵗs mɪ ˈsɪv əṭ i ˌtrænz-
trans|mit trænz |ˈmɪt trɑːnz-, trænᵗs-, trɑːnᵗs- ‖ trænᵗs- trænz- **~mits** ˈmɪts **~mitted** ˈmɪt ɪd -əd ‖ ˈmɪṭ əd **~mitting** ˈmɪt ɪŋ ‖ ˈmɪṭ ɪŋ
transmittal trænz ˈmɪt ᵊl trɑːnz-, trænᵗs-, trɑːnᵗs- ‖ trænᵗs ˈmɪṭ ᵊl trænz- **~s** z

transmittanc|e trænz ˈmɪt ^{ə}n^{t}s trɑːnz-, træn^{t}s-, trɑːn^{t}s- ‖ træn^{t}s- trænz- **~y** i

transmitter trænz ˈmɪt ə trɑːnz-, træn^{t}s-, trɑːn^{t}s- ‖ træn^{t}s ˈmɪţ ^{ə}r trænz-, ˈ· · · **~s** z

transmogrification trænz ˌmɒg rɪf ɪ ˈkeɪʃ ^{ə}n trɑːnz-, træn^{t}s-, trɑːn^{t}s-, ˌ·ˌ·-·, -rəf ·ˈ--, §-əˈ-- ‖ træn^{t}s ˌmɑːg rəf ə- trænz-, ˌ·ˌ·-- **~s** z

transmogri|fy trænz ˈmɒg rɪ |faɪ trɑːnz-, træn^{t}s-, trɑːn^{t}s-, ˌ·--, -rə faɪ ‖ træn^{t}s ˈmɑːg rə- trænz-, ˌ·-- **~fied** faɪd **~fies** faɪz **~fying** faɪ ɪŋ

transmutation ˌtrænz mju ˈteɪʃ ^{ə}n ˌtrɑːnz-, ˌtræn^{t}s-, ˌtrɑːn^{t}s- ‖ ˌtræn^{t}s- ˌtrænz- **~s** z

trans|mute trænz |ˈmjuːt trɑːnz-, træn^{t}s-, trɑːn^{t}s- ‖ træn^{t}s- trænz- **~muted** ˈmjuːt ɪd -əd ‖ ˈmjuːţ əd **~mutes** ˈmjuːts **~muting** ˈmjuːt ɪŋ ‖ ˈmjuːţ ɪŋ

transnational ˌtrænz ˈnæʃ ^{ə}n‿əl ◂ ˌtrɑːnz-, ˌtræn^{t}s-, ˌtrɑːn^{t}s- ‖ ˌtræn^{t}s- ˌtrænz- **~s** z

transoceanic ˌtrænz ˌəʊʃ i ˈæn ɪk ˌtrɑːnz-, ˌtræn^{t}s-, ˌtrɑːn^{t}s-, -ˌəʊs- ‖ ˌtræn^{t}s ˌoʊʃ- ˌtrænz-

transom ˈtræn^{t}s əm **~ed** d **~s** z

transparenc|y træn^{t}s ˈpær ənt$^{}$s |i trɑːn^{t}s-, trænz-, trɑːnz-, ˌ·-, trɒn^{t}s-, trɒnz-, -ˈpeər- ‖ -ˈper- **~ies** iz

transparent træn^{t}s ˈpær ənt trɑːn^{t}s-, trænz-, trɑːnz-, ˌ·-, trɒn^{t}s-, trɒnz-, -ˈpeər- ‖ -ˈper- **~ly** li **~ness** nəs nɪs

transpiration ˌtræn^{t}s pə ˈreɪʃ ^{ə}n ˌtrɑːn^{t}s-, -pɪ-

tran|spire træn |ˈspaɪ‿ə trɑːn-, træn-, trɑːn-, §trɒn- ‖ -|ˈspaɪ‿^{ə}r **~spired** ˈspaɪ‿əd ‖ ˈspaɪ‿^{ə}rd **~spires** ˈspaɪ‿əz ‖ ˈspaɪ‿^{ə}rz **~spiring** ˈspaɪ‿ər ɪŋ ‖ ˈspaɪ‿ər ɪŋ

trans|plant *v* ˌtræn^{t}s |ˈplɑːnt ˌtrɑːn^{t}s-, §-ˈplænt ‖ ˌtræn^{t}s |ˈplænt **~planted** ˈplɑːnt ɪd §ˈplænt-, -əd ‖ ˈplænţ əd **~planting** ˈplɑːnt ɪŋ §ˈplænt- ‖ ˈplænţ ɪŋ **~plants** ˈplɑːnts §ˈplænts ‖ ˈplænts

transplant *n* ˈtræn^{t}s plɑːnt ˈtrɑːn^{t}s-, §-plænt ‖ ˈtræn^{t}s plænt **~s** s

transplantation ˌtræn^{t}s plɑːn ˈteɪʃ ^{ə}n ˌtrɑːn^{t}s-, -plæn- ‖ ˌtræn^{t}s plæn- **~s** z

transpolar ˌtrænz ˈpəʊl ə ◂ ˌtrɑːnz-, ˌtræn^{t}s-, ˌtrɑːn^{t}s- ‖ ˌtræn^{t}s ˈpoʊl ^{ə}r ◂

transponder træn ˈspɒnd ə trɑːn- ‖ træn ˈspɑːnd ^{ə}r træn^{t}s ˈpɑːnd- **~s** z

transpontine ˌtrænz ˈpɒnt aɪn ◂ ˌtrɑːnz-, ˌtræn^{t}s-, ˌtrɑːn^{t}s- ‖ ˌtræn^{t}s ˈpɑːnt-

trans|port *v* træn^{t}s |ˈpɔːt trɑːn^{t}s- ‖ træn^{t}s |ˈpɔːrt -ˈpoʊrt, ˈ· · **~ported** ˈpɔːt ɪd -əd ‖ ˈpɔːrţ əd ˈpoʊrţ- **~porting** ˈpɔːt ɪŋ ‖ ˈpɔːrţ ɪŋ ˈpoʊrţ- **~ports** ˈpɔːts ‖ ˈpɔːrts ˈpoʊrts

transport *n* ˈtræn^{t}s pɔːt ˈtrɑːn^{t}s- ‖ ˈtræn^{t}s pɔːrt -poʊrt **~s** z

ˈtransport ˌcafe

transportable træn^{t}s ˈpɔːt əb ^{ə}l trɑːn^{t}s- ‖ træn^{t}s ˈpɔːrţ- -ˈpoʊrţ-

transportation ˌtræn^{t}s pɔː ˈteɪʃ ^{ə}n ˌtrɑːn^{t}s-, -pə- ‖ ˌtræn^{t}s p^{ə}r-

transporter træn^{t}s ˈpɔːt ə trɑːn^{t}s- ‖ træn^{t}s ˈpɔːrţ ^{ə}r -ˈpoʊrţ-, ˈ· · · **~s** z

transˈporter bridge

transpos|e træn^{t}s ˈpəʊz trɑːn^{t}s- ‖ træn^{t}s ˈpoʊz **~al** ^{ə}l **~ed** d **~es** ɪz əz **~ing** ɪŋ

transposition ˌtræn^{t}s pə ˈzɪʃ ^{ə}n ˌtrɑːn^{t}s- **~s** z

transposon træn^{t}s ˈpəʊz ɒn trɑːn^{t}s- ‖ træn^{t}s ˈpoʊz ɑːn **~s** z

transputer træn^{t}s ˈpjuːt ə trɑːn^{t}s-, trænz-, trɑːnz- ‖ træn^{t}s ˈpjuːţ ^{ə}r **~s** z

transsexual træn ˈsek ʃu‿əl trɑːn-, trænz-, trɑːnz-, ˌtræn^{t}s-, ˌtrɑːn^{t}s-, -ˈseks ju‿əl, -ˈsek ʃ^{ə}l ‖ træn^{t}s- **~ism** ˌɪz əm **~s** z

transship træn^{t}s ˈʃɪp trɑːn^{t}s-, →træn^{t}ʃ-, →trɑːn^{t}ʃ-, træn-, trɑːn-, trænz-, trɑːnz-, §trɒn^{t}s-, →§trɒn^{t}ʃ-, §trɒn-, §trɒnz- ‖ træn^{t}s- →træn^{t}ʃ- **~ment/s** mənt/s **~ped** t **~ping** ɪŋ **~s** s

Trans-Siberian ˌtrænz saɪ ˈbɪər i‿ən ◂ ˌtrɑːnz- ‖ ˌtræn^{t}s saɪ ˈbɪr-

transubstanti|ate ˌtræn^{t}s əb ˈstæn^{t}ʃ i |eɪt ˌtrɑːn^{t}s-, §ˌ·ʌb-, -ˈstɑːn^{t}ʃ-, -ˈstæn^{t}s- **~ated** eɪt ɪd -əd ‖ eɪţ əd **~ates** eɪts **~ating** eɪt ɪŋ ‖ eɪţ ɪŋ

transubstantiation ˌtræn^{t}s əb ˌstæn^{t}ʃ i ˈeɪʃ ^{ə}n ˌtrɑːn^{t}s-, §ˌ·ʌb-, -ˌstɑːn^{t}ʃ-, -ˌstæn^{t}s-

transudate ˈtræn^{t}s ju deɪt ˈtrɑːn^{t}s-, ˈtrænz-, ˈtrɑːnz-, -u- ‖ ˈtræn^{t}ʃ ə- **~s** s

transudation ˌtræn^{t}s ju ˈdeɪʃ ^{ə}n ˌtrɑːn^{t}s-, trænz-, ˌtrɑːnz-, -u- ‖ ˌtræn^{t}ʃ ə- **~s** z

transud|e træn ˈsjuːd trɑːn-, -ˈsuːd, -ˈzjuːd, -ˈzuːd ‖ -ˈsuːd **~ed** ɪd əd **~es** z **~ing** ɪŋ

transuranic ˌtrænz ju^{ə} ˈræn ɪk ◂ ˌtrɑːnz-, ˌtræn^{t}s-, ˌtrænz- ‖ ˌtræn^{t}s- ˌtrænz-, →ˌtræn^{t}ʃ-, →ˌtrænʒ-, -ə-

Transvaal ˈtrænz vɑːl ˈtrɑːnz-, ˈtræn^{t}s-, ˈtrɑːn^{t}s-, ˌ·ˈ· ‖ ˌtræn^{t}s ˈvɑːl ˌtrænz- —*locally also* ˌ·ˈfɑːl **~er/s** ə/z ‖ -^{ə}r/z

transvers|e $_{(,)}$trænz ˈvɜːs $_{(,)}$trɑːnz-, $_{(,)}$træn^{t}s-, $_{(,)}$trɑːn^{t}s-, ˈ· · ‖ $_{(,)}$træn^{t}s ˈvɜ˞ːs $_{(,)}$trænz-, ˈ· · **~al** ^{ə}l **~ally** ^{ə}l‿i **~ely** li

transvestism trænz ˈvest ˌɪz əm trɑːnz-, træn^{t}s-, trɑːn^{t}s- ‖ træn^{t}s- trænz-

transvestite trænz ˈvest aɪt trɑːnz-, træn^{t}s-, trɑːn^{t}s- ‖ træn^{t}s- trænz- **~s** s

Transworld *tdmk* ˌtrænz ˈwɜːld ◂ ˌtrɑːnz-, ˌtræn^{t}s-, ˌtrɑːn^{t}s- ‖ ˌtræn^{t}s ˈwɜ˞ːld ◂ ˌtrænz-

Transylvani|a ˌtræn^{t}s ɪl ˈveɪn i‿|ə ˌtrɑːn^{t}s-, ˌ·^{ə}l- **~an/s** ən/z

Trant trænt

Tranter ˈtrænt ə ‖ ˈtrænţ ^{ə}r

trap træp **trapped** træpt **trapping** ˈtræp ɪŋ **traps** træps

trapdoor ˌtræp ˈdɔː ˈ· · ‖ -ˈdɔːr -ˈdoʊr **~s** z

trapes treɪps **trapesed** treɪpst **trapeses** ˈtreɪps ɪz -əz **trapesing** ˈtreɪps ɪŋ

trapez|e trə ˈpiːz ‖ træ- **~es** ɪz əz

traˈpeze ˌartist

trapezi|um trə ˈpiːz i‿|əm **~a** ə **~i** aɪ **~ums** əmz **~us/es** əs /ɪz -əz

trapezoid ˈtræp ɪ zɔɪd -ə- **~s** z

Trapp træp

trapp... —*see* **trap**

trapper ˈtræp ə ‖ -^{ə}r **~s** z

trappings ˈtræp ɪŋz

T

Trappist ˈtræp ɪst §-əst **~s** s
trapshooting ˈtræp ˌʃuːt ɪŋ ‖ -ˌʃuːţ-
trash træʃ **trashed** træʃt **trashes** ˈtræʃ ɪz -əz **trashing** ˈtræʃ ɪŋ
trashcan ˈtræʃ kæn **~s** z
trash|man ˈtræʃ |mæn -mən **~men** men mən
trash|y ˈtræʃ |i **~ier** i‿ə ‖ i‿ᵊr **~iest** i‿ɪst i‿əst **~ily** ɪ li əl i **~iness** i nəs i nɪs
Trasimene ˈtræz ɪ miːn -ə-
trass træs
trattoria ˌtræt ə ˈriː‿ə ‖ ˌtrɑːţ- —*It* trattoria [trat to ˈriː a] **~s** z
traum|a ˈtrɔːm |ə ˈtraʊm- ‖ ˈtraʊm |ə ˈtrɔːm-, ˈtrɑːm- **~as** əz **~ata** ət ə ‖ əţ ə
traumatic trɔː ˈmæt ɪk traʊ- ‖ trə ˈmæţ ɪk traʊ-, trɔː-, trɑː- **~ally** ᵊl‿i
traumatis... —*see* **traumatiz...**
traumatism ˈtrɔːm ə ˌtɪz əm ˈtraʊm- ‖ ˈtraʊm- ˈtrɔːm-, ˈtrɑːm- **~s** z
traumatization ˌtrɔːm ət aɪ ˈzeɪʃ ᵊn ˌtraʊm-, -ɪ'-- ‖ ˌtraʊm əţ ə- ˌtrɔːm-, ˌtrɑːm-
traumatiz|e ˈtrɔːm ə taɪz ˈtraʊm- ‖ ˈtraʊm- ˈtrɔːm-, ˈtrɑːm- **~ed** d **~es** ɪz əz **~ing** ɪŋ
travail ˈtræv eɪᵊl trə ˈveɪᵊl **~ed** d **~ing** ɪŋ **~s** z
Travancore ˌtræv ᵊn ˈkɔː →-ᵊŋ- ‖ ˈtræv ᵊn kɔːr -koʊr
travel ˈtræv ᵊl **~ed, ~led** d **~ing, ~ling** ɪŋ **~s** z **ˈtravel ˌagency**; **ˈtravel ˌagent**; **ˈtravel((l)ing) exˌpenses**; **ˌtravel(l)ing ˈsalesman**
travelator ˈtræv ə leɪt ə -ᵊl eɪt- ‖ -ᵊl eɪţ ᵊr **~s** z
Travelcard ˈtræv ᵊl kɑːd ‖ -kɑːrd **~s** z
traveler, traveller ˈtræv ᵊl‿ə ‖ ər **~s** z **ˌtraveller's ˈcheque** ‖ **ˈtraveler's check**
Travelodge *tdmk* ˈtræv ə lɒdʒ ‖ -lɑːdʒ
travelog, travelogue ˈtræv ə lɒg ‖ -lɔːg -lɑːg **~s** z
travelsick ˈtræv ᵊl sɪk **~ness** nəs nɪs
Travers ˈtræv əz ‖ -ᵊrz
travers|e *n* ˈtræv ɜːs -əs; trə ˈvɜːs, træ- ‖ ˈtræv ɝːs trə ˈvɝːs, træ- **~es** ɪz əz
travers|e *v* trə ˈvɜːs træ-, ˈtræv ɜːs, -əs ‖ trə ˈvɝːs træ-, ˈtræv ᵊrs **~ed** t **~es** ɪz əz **~ing** ɪŋ
travertine ˈtræv ət ɪn §-ən; -ə tiːn ‖ -ᵊr tiːn
travest|y ˈtræv əst |i -ɪst i **~ies** iz
Traviata ˌtræv i ˈɑːt ə ‖ ˌtrɑːv- —*It* [tra vi ˈaː ta, tra ˈvjaː ta]
Travis ˈtræv ɪs §-əs
travois *sing.* trə ˈvɔɪ ˈtræv ɔɪ **~** *pl* z
travolator ˈtræv ə leɪt ə -ᵊl eɪt- ‖ ᵊl eɪţ ᵊr **~s** z
Travolta trə ˈvɒlt ə -ˈvəʊlt- ‖ -ˈvoʊlt ə
trawl trɔːl ‖ trɑːl **trawled** trɔːld ‖ trɑːld **trawling** ˈtrɔːl ɪŋ ‖ ˈtrɑːl- **trawls** trɔːlz ‖ trɑːlz **ˈtrawl line**
trawler ˈtrɔːl ə ‖ -ᵊr ˈtrɑːl- **~man** mən **~men** mən men **~s** z
Trawsfynydd ˌtraʊs ˈvʌn ɪð ˌtrɔːz-, -ˈfɪn-, -ɪd —*Welsh* [traus ˈvə nið, -nið]
tray treɪ **trays** treɪz
Treacher ˈtriːtʃ ə ‖ -ᵊr
treacherous ˈtretʃ ər‿əs **~ly** li **~ness** nəs nɪs
treacher|y ˈtretʃ ər |i **~ies** iz
treacle ˈtriːk ᵊl **~s** z
treacly ˈtriːk ᵊl i
tread tred **treading** ˈtred ɪŋ **treads** tredz **trod** trɒd ‖ trɑːd **trodden** ˈtrɒd ᵊn ‖ ˈtrɑːd ᵊn
treadle ˈtred ᵊl **~s** z
treadmill ˈtred mɪl →ˈtreb- **~s** z
treason ˈtriːz ᵊn **~s** z
treasonab|le ˈtriːz ᵊn‿əb |ᵊl **~leness** ᵊl nəs -nɪs **~ly** li
treasonous ˈtriːz ᵊn‿əs **~ly** li
treas|ure ˈtreʒ |ə ‖ -|ᵊr ˈtreɪʒ- **~ured** əd ‖ ᵊrd **~ures** əz ‖ ᵊrz **~uring** ər‿ɪŋ **ˈtreasure hunt**; **ˈtreasure trove**
treasure-house ˈtreʒ ə haʊs ‖ -ᵊr-
treasurer ˈtreʒ ər‿ə ‖ ‿ᵊr ˈtreɪʒ- **~ship/s** ʃɪp/s **~s** z
treasur|y, T~ ˈtreʒ ər‿|i ‖ ˈtreɪʒ- **~ies** iz **ˈtreasury bill**; **ˈtreasury note**
treat triːt **treated** ˈtriːt ɪd -əd ‖ ˈtriːţ əd **treating** ˈtriːt ɪŋ ‖ ˈtriːţ ɪŋ **treats** triːts
treatable ˈtriːt əb ᵊl ‖ ˈtriːţ-
treatis|e ˈtriːt ɪz -ɪs, §-əz, §-əs ‖ ˈtriːţ əs **~es** ɪz əz
treatment ˈtriːt mənt **~s** s
treat|y ˈtriːt |i ‖ ˈtriːţ |i **~ies** iz **ˈtreaty port**
Trebizond ˈtreb ɪ zɒnd -ə- ‖ -ə zɑːnd
treble ˈtreb ᵊl **~d** d **~s** z **trebling** ˈtreb ᵊl‿ɪŋ **ˌtreble ˈchance**; **ˌtreble ˈclef**
Treblinka tre ˈblɪŋk ə trə-
Trebor *tdmk* ˈtriː bɔː ‖ -bɔːr
trebuchet ˈtreb ju ʃet ə-, -ʃeɪ, ˌ· ·ˈ·
Tredegar trɪ ˈdiːg ə trə- ‖ -ᵊr
tree, Tree triː **treed** triːd **treeing** ˈtriː ɪŋ **trees** triːz **ˈtree ˌdiagram**; **ˈtree fern**; **ˈtree frog**; **ˈtree ˌsurgeon**
treecreeper ˈtriː ˌkriːp ə ‖ -ᵊr **~s** z
tree|house ˈtriː |haʊs **~houses** haʊz ɪz -əz
tree-hugg|er ˈtriː ˌhʌg |ə ‖ -|ᵊr **~ers** əz ‖ ᵊrz **~ing** ɪŋ
treeless ˈtriː ləs -lɪs
treeline ˈtriː laɪn **~d** d
treen triːn
treetop ˈtriː tɒp ‖ -tɑːp **~s** s
treetrunk ˈtriː trʌŋk **~s** s
Trefdraeth ˈtrev draɪθ
Trefeglwys trɪv ˈeg lu‿ɪs
Trefgarne ˈtref gɑːn ‖ -gɑːrn
trefoil ˈtref ɔɪᵊl ˈtriː fɔɪᵊl **~ed** d **~s** z
Trefor ˈtrev ə ‖ -ᵊr —*Welsh* [ˈtre vor]
Trefusis trɪ ˈfjuːs ɪs trə-, §-əs
Tregaron trɪ ˈgær ən trə- ‖ -ˈger-
Treharris trɪ ˈhær ɪs trə-, §-əs ‖ -ˈher-
Trehearne, Treherne trɪ ˈhɜːn trə- ‖ -ˈhɝːn
trek trek **trekked** trekt **trekking** ˈtrek ɪŋ **treks** treks
trekker ˈtrek ə ‖ -ᵊr **~s** z
trekkie, T~ ˈtrek i **~s** z
Trelawney trə ˈlɔːn i trɪ- ‖ -ˈlɑːn-
trellis ˈtrel ɪs §-əs **~ed** t **~es** ɪz əz **~ing** ɪŋ **~work** wɜːk ‖ wɝːk

T

Tremain trɪ 'meɪn trə-
trematode 'trem ə təʊd 'triːm- ‖ -toʊd **~s** z
tremble 'trem bᵊl **~d** d **~s** z **trembling/ly** 'trem blɪŋ /li
trembler 'trem blə ‖ -blᵊr **~s** z
trem|bly 'trem| bli **~blier** bli‿ə ‖ bli‿ᵊr **~bliest** bli‿ɪst ‿əst
tremendous trə 'mend əs trɪ-, ⚠-'mendʒ- **~ly** li **~ness** nəs nɪs
Tremlett 'trem lət -lɪt
tremolo 'trem ə ləʊ ‖ -loʊ **~s** z
tremor 'trem ə ‖ -ᵊr *—as a medical term, also* 'triːm- **~s** z
tremulant 'trem jʊl ənt -jəl- ‖ -jəl-
tremulous 'trem jʊl əs -jəl- ‖ -jəl- **~ly** li **~ness** nəs nɪs
trench, T~ trentʃ **trenched** trentʃt **trenches** 'trentʃ ɪz -əz **trenching** 'trentʃ ɪŋ
'trench coat
trenchancy 'trentʃ ənᵗs i
trenchant 'trentʃ ənt **~ly** li
Trenchard 'trentʃ ɑːd -əd ‖ -ɑːrd -ᵊrd
trencher 'trentʃ ə ‖ -ᵊr **~s** z
trencher|man 'trentʃ ə |mən ‖ -ᵊr- **~men** mən men
trend trend **trended** 'trend ɪd -əd **trending** 'trend ɪŋ **trends** trendz
trendsett|ing 'trend ˌset |ɪŋ ‖ -ˌseţ |ɪŋ **~er/s** ə/z ‖ ᵊr/z
trend-spott|er 'trend ˌspɒt |ə ‖ -ˌspɑːţ |ᵊr **~ers** əz ‖ ᵊrz **~ing** ɪŋ
trend|y 'trend |i **~ier** i‿ə ‖ i‿ᵊr **~iest** i‿ɪst i‿əst **~ily** ɪ li əl i **~iness** i nəs i nɪs
Trengganu treŋ 'gɑːn uː
Trent trent
Trentham 'trent əm
Trenton 'trent ən ‖ -ᵊn
Treorchy tri 'ɔːk i ‖ -'ɔːrk i
trepan trɪ 'pæn trə- **~ned** d **~ning** ɪŋ **~s** z
trepang trɪ 'pæŋ trə-; 'triː pæŋ **~s** z
trephination ˌtref ɪ 'neɪʃ ᵊn §-ə- **~s** z
trephin|e trɪ 'fiːn trə-, tre-, -'faɪn **~ed** d **~es** z **~ing** ɪŋ
trepidation ˌtrep ɪ 'deɪʃ ᵊn §-ə-
treponem|a ˌtrep ə 'niːm |ə **~ata** ət ə ‖ əţ ə
Tresco 'tresk əʊ ‖ -oʊ
Trescothick trɪ 'skɒθ ɪk trə- ‖ -'skɑːθ-
Tresillian trɪ 'sɪl i‿ən trə-
trespass 'tresp əs §'tres pɑːs, §-pæs ‖ 'tres pæs **~ed** t **~er/s** ə/z ‖ ᵊr/z **~es** ɪz əz **~ing** ɪŋ
tress tres **tresses** 'tres ɪz -əz
trestle 'tres ᵊl **~s** z
Tretchikoff 'tretʃ ɪ kɒf ‖ -kɔːf -kɑːf
Trethowan trɪ 'θaʊ‿ən trə-, -'θəʊ-
trevall|y trɪ 'væl| i trə- **~ies** iz
Trevelyan *(i)* trɪ 'vɪl jən trə-, *(ii)* -'vel- *—In Cornwall, (i).*
Trevethick trɪ 'veθ ɪk trə-
Trevino trə 'viːn əʊ trɪ- ‖ -oʊ
Trevithick 'trev ɪθ ɪk -əθ-; trə 'vɪθ ɪk
Trevor 'trev ə ‖ -ᵊr
trews truːz
trey treɪ *(= tray)* **treys** treɪz

tri- *as a productive prefix* ¦traɪ *— but in certain established words* ¦trɪ *(see entries)* **— trichromatic** ˌtraɪ krəʊ 'mæt ɪk ◂ ‖ -kroʊ 'mæţ-
triable 'traɪ‿əb ᵊl
triad, Triad 'traɪ æd 'traɪ‿əd **~s** z
triage 'triː ɑːʒ 'traɪ-, -ɪdʒ ‖ tri 'ɑːʒ
trial 'traɪ‿əl ‖ 'traɪ‿əl **~ed, ~led** d **~ing, ~ling** ɪŋ **~s** z
'trial court; ˌ**trial 'run**
triangle 'traɪ æŋ gᵊl **~s** z
triangular traɪ 'æŋ gjʊl ə -gjəl- ‖ -gjəl ᵊr **~ly** li
triangularity traɪ ˌæŋ gju 'lær ət i ˌ·,·-,-gjə-, -ɪt i ‖ -gjə 'lær əţ i -'ler-
triangu|late traɪ 'æŋ gju |leɪt -gjə- ‖ -gjə- **~lated** leɪt ɪd -əd ‖ leɪţ əd **~lates** leɪts **~lating** leɪt ɪŋ ‖ leɪţ ɪŋ
triangulation traɪ ˌæŋ gju 'leɪʃ ᵊn ˌ·,·-, -gjə- ‖ -gjə- **~s** z
triassic, T~ traɪ 'æs ɪk
triathlete ⁽ˌ⁾traɪ 'æθ liːt **~s** s
triathlon ⁽ˌ⁾traɪ 'æθ lən -lɒn ‖ -lɑːn
tribade 'trɪb əd **~s** z
tribadism 'trɪb əd ˌɪz əm
tribal 'traɪb ᵊl **~ly** i **~s** z
tribalism 'traɪb ə ˌlɪz əm -ᵊl ˌɪz-
tribalistic ˌtraɪb ə 'lɪst ɪk ◂
tribe traɪb **tribes** traɪbz
Tribeca traɪ 'bek ə
tribes|man 'traɪbz |mən **~men** mən men **~people** ˌpiːp ᵊl **~woman** ˌwʊm ən **~women** ˌwɪm ɪn §-ən
tribo- *comb. form*
with stress-neutral suffix ¦traɪb əʊ ¦trɪb- ‖ -oʊ **— triboluminescent** ˌtraɪb əʊ ˌluːm ɪ 'nes ᵊnt ˌtrɪb-, -ˌljuːm-, -ə'-- ‖ ˌ·oʊ-
with stress-imposing suffix traɪ 'bɒ+ trɪ- ‖ -'bɑː+ **— tribology** traɪ 'bɒl ədʒ i trɪ- ‖ -'bɑːl-
tribrach 'trɪb ræk 'traɪ bræk **~s** s
tribulation ˌtrɪb ju 'leɪʃ ᵊn -jə- ‖ -jə- **~s** z
tribunal traɪ 'bjuːn ᵊl trɪ- **~s** z
tribune 'trɪb juːn ‖ trɪ 'bjuːn **~s** z
tributar|y 'trɪb jʊt‿ər |i ‖ -jə ter |i **~ies** iz
tribute 'trɪb juːt ‖ -jət **~s** s
trice traɪs
Tricel *tdmk* 'traɪ sel
triceps 'traɪs eps
triceratops ⁽ˌ⁾traɪ 'ser ə tɒps ‖ -tɑːps
trichin|a trɪ 'kaɪn |ə trə- **~ae** iː **~as** əz
trichinosis ˌtrɪk ɪ 'nəʊs ɪs -ə-, §-əs ‖ -'noʊs-
trichloroethylene ˌtraɪ ˌklɔːr əʊ 'eθ ə liːn -ˌklɒr-, -ɪ liːn, -ᵊl iːn ‖ -oʊ'-- ˌkloʊr-
trichological ˌtrɪk ə 'lɒdʒ ɪk ᵊl ◂ ‖ -'lɑːdʒ- **~ly** ˌi
trichologist trɪ 'kɒl ədʒ ɪst §-əst ‖ -'kɑːl- **~s** s
trichology trɪ 'kɒl ədʒ i ‖ -'kɑːl-
trichomoniasis ˌtrɪk əʊ məʊ 'naɪ‿əs ɪs -mə'--, §-əs ‖ ˌtrɪk əm ə-
trichotom|y ˌtraɪ 'kɒt əm |i ‖ -'kɑːţ- **~ies** iz
Tricia 'trɪʃ ə ‖ 'triːʃ-

T

tri-city ˌtraɪ ˈsɪt i ◂ ˈ·ˌ· · ‖ -ˈsɪţ-
Tricity *tdmk* ˈtrɪs ət i -ɪt i ‖ -əţ i
trick trɪk **tricked** trɪkt **tricking** ˈtrɪk ɪŋ **tricks** trɪks
ˌ**trick or ˈtreat**
tricker|y ˈtrɪk ər |i **~ies** iz
trickl|e ˈtrɪk ᵊl **~ed** d **~es** z **~ing** ˌɪŋ
trickle-down ˈtrɪk ᵊl daʊn
trick-or-treating ˌtrɪk ɔː ˈtriːt ɪŋ ‖ ˌtrɪk ᵊr ˈtriːţ ɪŋ
trickster ˈtrɪk stə ‖ -stᵊr **~s** z
tricksy ˈtrɪks i
trick|y ˈtrɪk |i **~ier** iˌə ‖ iˌᵊr **~iest** iˌɪst iˌəst **~ily** ɪ li əl i **~iness** i nəs i nɪs
triclini|um trɪ ˈklɪn iˌ|əm trə-, -ˈklaɪn- **~a** ə
tricolor, tricolour ˈtrɪk əl ə ˈtraɪ ˌkʌl ə ‖ ˈtraɪ ˌkʌl ᵊr **~s** z
tricorn ˈtraɪ kɔːn ‖ -kɔːrn **~s** z
tricot ˈtrɪk əʊ ˈtriːk- ‖ ˈtriːk oʊ **~s** z
tricuspid ₍ˌ₎traɪ ˈkʌsp ɪd §-əd **~s** z
tricycl|e ˈtraɪs ɪk ᵊl -ək- **~ed** d **~es** z **~ing** ˌɪŋ
trident, T~ ˈtraɪd ᵊnt **~s** s
Tridentine traɪ ˈdent aɪn trɪ-, trə-, -iːn, -ɪn
tried traɪd
triennial traɪ ˈen iˌəl **~ly** i
trienni|um traɪ ˈen iˌ|əm **~a** ə **~ums** əmz
trier ˈtraɪˌə ‖ ˈtraɪˌᵊr **~s** z
Trier *place in Germany* trɪə ‖ trɪᵊr —*Ger* [tʁiːɐ]
trierarch ˈtraɪˌə rɑːk ‖ -rɑːrk **~s** s
tries traɪz
Trieste tri ˈest —*It* [tri ˈɛs te]
triffid ˈtrɪf ɪd §-əd **~s** z
trifid ˈtraɪf ɪd §-əd
trifl|e ˈtraɪf ᵊl **~ed** d **~es** z **~ing** ˌɪŋ
trifler ˈtraɪf lə ‖ -lᵊr **~s** z
trifling *adj* ˈtraɪf lɪŋ **~ly** li **~ness** nəs nɪs
trifocal ˌtraɪ ˈfəʊk ᵊl ‖ ˌtraɪ ˈfoʊk ᵊl **~s** z
trifori|um traɪ ˈfɔːr iˌ|əm ‖ -ˈfoʊr- **~a** ə
trig, Trig trɪg
trigeminal ₍ˌ₎traɪ ˈdʒem ɪn ᵊl -ən ᵊl
trigger, T~ ˈtrɪg ə ‖ -ᵊr **~ed** d **triggering** ˈtrɪg ər ɪŋ **~s** z
trigger-happy ˈtrɪg ə ˌhæp i ‖ -ᵊr-
triglyceride traɪ ˈglɪs ə raɪd **~s** z
triglyph ˈtrɪg lɪf ˈtraɪ glɪf **~s** s
trigonal ˈtrɪg ən ᵊl **~ly** i
trigonometric ˌtrɪg ən ə ˈmetr ɪk ◂ **~al** ᵊl **~ally** ᵊl ˌi
ˌ**trigonoˌmetric ˈfunction**
trigonometry ˌtrɪg ə ˈnɒm ətr i -ɪtr i ‖ -ˈnɑːm-
trigraph ˈtraɪ grɑːf -græf ‖ -græf **~s** s
trijet ˈtraɪ dʒet **~s** s
trike traɪk **trikes** traɪks
trilateral ˌtraɪ ˈlæt ər əl ◂ ‖ -ˈlæţ ər əl →ˈlætr əl **~ly** i
trilb|y, T~ ˈtrɪlb |i **~ies** iz
ˌ**trilby ˈhat**
trilingual ˌtraɪ ˈlɪŋ gwəl ◂ -gju əl **~ly** i **~s** z
triliteral ˌtraɪ ˈlɪt ər əl ◂ ‖ -ˈlɪţ ər əl →-ˈlɪtr əl **~s** z
trill trɪl **trilled** trɪld **trilling** ˈtrɪl ɪŋ **trills** trɪlz
Trilling ˈtrɪl ɪŋ
trillion ˈtrɪl jən ˈ·iˌən **~s** z
trillionth ˈtrɪl jənᵗθ ˈ·iˌənᵗθ **~s** s
trillium ˈtrɪl iˌəm
trilobite ˈtraɪl əʊ baɪt ‖ -ə- **~s** s
trilog|y ˈtrɪl ədʒ |i **~ies** iz
trim, Trim trɪm **trimmed** trɪmd **trimming/s** ˈtrɪm ɪŋ/z **trims** trɪmz
trimaran ˈtraɪm ə ræn ˌ· · ˈ· **~s** z
Trimble ˈtrɪm bᵊl
trimester traɪ ˈmest ə trɪ- ‖ -ᵊr ˈ· · · **~s** z
trimeter ˈtrɪm ɪt ə -ət- ‖ -əţ ᵊr **~s** z
trimly ˈtrɪm li
trimm... —*see* **trim**
trimmer ˈtrɪm ə ‖ -ᵊr **~s** z
trimness ˈtrɪm nəs -nɪs
Trina ˈtriːn ə
Trincomalee ˌtrɪŋk əʊ mə ˈliː ‖ -ə mə-
Trinculo ˈtrɪŋk ju ləʊ -jə- ‖ -jə loʊ
Trinder ˈtrɪnd ə ‖ -ᵊr
trine traɪn **trines** traɪnz
Tring trɪŋ
Trinidad ˈtrɪn ɪ dæd -ə-, ˌ· · ˈ·
Trinidadian ˌtrɪn ɪ ˈdæd iˌən ◂ ˌ·ə-, -ˈdeɪd- **~s** z
trinitarian, T~ ˌtrɪn ə ˈteər iˌən ◂ ˌ·ɪ- ‖ -ˈter- **~ism** ˌɪz əm **~s** z
trinitrotoluene ˌtraɪ ˌnaɪtr əʊ ˈtɒl ju iːn · ˌ· ‖ -oʊ ˈtɑːl-
trinity, T~ ˈtrɪn ət i -ɪt i ‖ -əţ i
ˌ**Trinity ˈCollege, ˌTrinity ˌCollege ˈCambridge**; ˌ**Trinity ˈHouse**; ˌ**Trinity ˈSunday**
trinket ˈtrɪŋk ɪt §-ət **~s** s
Trinn|ie, Trinn|y ˈtrɪn i **~ies** iz
trinomial traɪ ˈnəʊm iˌəl ‖ -ˈnoʊm- **~s** z
trio ˈtriː əʊ ‖ -oʊ **~s** z
triode ˈtraɪ əʊd ‖ -oʊd **~s** z
triolet ˈtriːˌə let ˈtraɪˌ, -əʊ-, -lət, -lɪt **~s** s
trioxide ₍ˌ₎traɪ ˈɒks aɪd ‖ -ˈɑːks- **~s** z
trip trɪp **tripped** trɪpt **tripping/ly** ˈtrɪp ɪŋ /li **trips** trɪps
tripartite ₍ˌ₎traɪ ˈpɑːt aɪt ‖ -ˈpɑːrt-
tripe traɪp **tripes** traɪps
triphammer ˈtrɪp ˌhæm ə ‖ -ᵊr **~s** z
triphthong ˈtrɪf θɒŋ ˈtrɪp- ‖ -θɔːŋ -θɑːŋ **~s** z
triphthongal ˌtrɪf ˈθɒŋ gᵊl ◂ ˌtrɪp- ‖ -ˈθɔːŋ- -ˈθɑːŋ- **~ly** i
tripl|e ˈtrɪp ᵊl **~ed** d **~es** z **~ing** ˌɪŋ
ˌ**Triple Alˈliance**; ˈ**triple jump,** ˌ· · ˈ·
triplet ˈtrɪp lət -lɪt **~s** s
triplex, T~ *tdmk* ˈtrɪp leks
triplicate *adj, n* ˈtrɪp lɪk ət -lək-, -ɪt
tripli|cate *v* ˈtrɪp lɪ |keɪt -lə- **~cated** keɪt ɪd -əd ‖ keɪţ əd **~cates** keɪts **~cating** keɪt ɪŋ ‖ keɪţ ɪŋ
triploid ˈtrɪp lɔɪd **~s** z
tripod ˈtraɪ pɒd ‖ -pɑːd **~s** z
Tripoli, t~ ˈtrɪp əl i
Tripolis ˈtrɪp əl ɪs §-əs
Tripolitania ˌtrɪp əl ɪ ˈteɪn iˌə -əˈ-
tripos ˈtraɪp ɒs ‖ -ɑːs **~es** ɪz əz
Tripp trɪp
tripp... —*see* **trip**
tripper ˈtrɪp ə ‖ -ᵊr **~s** z

triptan 'trɪpt æn
triptane 'trɪpt eɪn
Triptolemus trɪp 'tɒl ɪm əs -əm- ‖ -'tɑːl-
triptych 'trɪpt ɪk **~s** s
triptyque trɪp 'tiːk **~s** s
Tripura 'trɪp ʊr ə -ər-
tripwire 'trɪp ˌwaɪ ə ‖ -ˌwaɪ ər **~s** z
trireme 'traɪə riːm **~s** z
trisect (ˌ)traɪ 'sekt **~ed** ɪd əd **~ing** ɪŋ **~s** s
Trish trɪʃ
Trisha 'trɪʃ ə
trishaw 'traɪ ʃɔː ‖ -ʃɑː **~s** z
triskaidekaphobia ˌtrɪs kaɪ ˌdek ə 'fəʊb i ə ˌ·ˌ·· ‖ -'foʊb-
triskeli|on trɪ 'skel i |ɒn (ˌ)traɪ-, ən ‖ -|ɑːn **~a** ə
trismus 'trɪz məs
trisomy 'trɪs əm i 'traɪ səʊm i ‖ 'traɪ soʊm i
Tristan 'trɪst ən
ˌ**Tristan da 'Cunha** də 'kuːn ə -jə
Tri-Star *tdmk* 'traɪ stɑː ‖ -stɑːr **~s** z
tristate 'traɪ steɪt
Tristram 'trɪs trəm
trisyllabic ˌtraɪ sɪ 'læb ɪk ◂ -sə- **~ally** əl i
trisyllable ˌtraɪ 'sɪl əb əl 'ˌ·ˌ·· **~s** z
trite traɪt **triter** 'traɪt ə ‖ 'traɪṭ ər **tritest** 'traɪt ɪst -əst ‖ 'traɪṭ əst
trite|ly 'traɪt |li **~ness** nəs nɪs
triticale ˌtrɪt ɪ 'keɪl i -ə- ‖ ˌtrɪṭ ə-
tritium 'trɪt i əm ‖ 'trɪṭ- 'trɪʃ-
triton *'nucleus of a tritium atom'* 'traɪt ɒn -ən ‖ -ɑːn
Triton *'sea god', 'mollusc', 'satellite of Neptune'*, **t~** 'traɪt ən -ɒn ‖ -ɑːn
tritone 'traɪ təʊn ‖ -toʊn **~s** z
triumph *n, v,* **T~** 'traɪ ʌmpf 'traɪ əmpf **~ed** t **~ing** ɪŋ **~s** s
triumphal traɪ 'ʌmpf əl **~ism** ˌɪz əm
triumphant traɪ 'ʌmpf ənt **~ly** li
triumvir traɪ 'ʌm və tri-, 'traɪ əm-, -vɜː ‖ -vər **~s** z
triumvirate traɪ 'ʌm vər ət tri-, -vɪr-, -ɪt **~s** s
triune 'traɪ juːn
trivalent (ˌ)traɪ 'veɪl ənt 'trɪv əl-
Trivandrum trɪ 'vændr əm
trivet 'trɪv ɪt §-ət **~s** s
trivia 'trɪv i ə
trivial 'trɪv i əl **~ly** i
trivialis... —*see* **trivializ...**
trivialit|y ˌtrɪv i 'æl ət |i -ɪt i ‖ -əṭ |i **~ies** iz
trivialization ˌtrɪv i əl aɪ 'zeɪʃ ən -ɪ'-- ‖ -ə'--
trivializ|e 'trɪv i ə laɪz **~ed** d **~es** ɪz əz **~ing** ɪŋ
trivium 'trɪv i əm
triweek|ly (ˌ)traɪ 'wiːk |li **~ies** iz
Trixie 'trɪks i
Troad 'trəʊ æd ‖ 'troʊ-
Troas 'trəʊ æs ‖ 'troʊ-
Trobriand 'trəʊb ri ənd -ænd ‖ 'troʊb-
Trocadero ˌtrɒk ə 'dɪər əʊ ‖ ˌtrɑːk ə 'der oʊ
trocar 'trəʊk ɑː ‖ 'troʊk ɑːr **~s** z
trochaic trəʊ 'keɪ ɪk ‖ troʊ- **~s** s
trochanter trəʊ 'kænt ə ‖ troʊ 'kænṭ ər **~s** z
troche trəʊʃ 'trəʊk iː ‖ 'troʊk iː **troches** 'trəʊʃ ɪz -əz; 'trəʊk iːz ‖ 'troʊk iːz
trochee 'trəʊk iː -i ‖ 'troʊk- **~s** z
trochle|a 'trɒk li ə ‖ 'trɑːk- **~ae** iː
trochlear 'trɒk li ə ‖ 'trɑːk li ər
trochoid 'trəʊk ɔɪd 'trɒk- ‖ 'troʊk- 'trɑːk- **~s** z
trod trɒd ‖ trɑːd
trodden 'trɒd ən ‖ 'trɑːd ən
trog trɒg ‖ trɑːg trɔːg
troglodyte 'trɒg lə daɪt ‖ 'trɑːg- **~s** s
troglodytes *sing. 'wren'* ˌtrɒg lə 'daɪt iːz trɒ 'glɒd ə tiːz, -ɪ- ‖ ˌtrɑːg-
troglodytic ˌtrɒg lə 'dɪt ɪk ◂ ‖ ˌtrɑːg lə 'dɪṭ ɪk ◂
trogon, T~ 'trəʊg ɒn ‖ 'troʊg ɑːn **~s** z
troika 'trɔɪk ə 'trəʊ ɪk ə **~s** z
troilism 'trɔɪ ˌlɪz əm
Troilus 'trɔɪl əs 'trəʊ ɪl əs, §-əl- ‖ 'troʊ əl-
Trojan 'trəʊdʒ ən ‖ 'troʊdʒ ən **~s** z
ˌ**Trojan 'horse**; ˌ**Trojan 'War**
troll trɒl trəʊl ‖ troʊl —*In BrE both pronunciations shown appear to be in use for all the various meanings (both n and v) of the word.* **trolled** trɒld trəʊld ‖ troʊld **trolling** 'trɒl ɪŋ 'trəʊl- ‖ 'troʊl ɪŋ **trolls** trɒlz trəʊlz ‖ troʊlz
trolley 'trɒl i ‖ 'trɑːl i **~s** z
trolleybus 'trɒl i bʌs ‖ 'trɑːl- **~es** ɪz əz
trollop 'trɒl əp ‖ 'trɑːl əp **~s** s
Trollope 'trɒl əp ‖ 'trɑːl əp
trombone trɒm 'bəʊn ‖ trɑːm 'boʊn '·· **~s** z
trombonist trɒm 'bəʊn ɪst §-əst ‖ trɑːm 'boʊn- '··· **~s** s
tromp trɒmp ‖ trɑːmp **tromped** trɒmpt ‖ trɑːmpt **tromping** 'trɒmp ɪŋ ‖ 'trɑːmp ɪŋ **tromps** trɒmps ‖ trɑːmps
trompe l'oeil ˌtrɒmp 'lɔɪ -'ləʊ i, -'lɜː jə ‖ ˌtrɔːmp- ˌtrɑːmp-, -'leɪ —*Fr* [tʁɔ̃p lœj]
Tromsø 'trɒm səʊ ‖ 'trɑːm soʊ —*Norw* [ˈˈtrʊm sø]
Trondheim 'trɒnd haɪm 'trɒn- ‖ 'trɑːn heɪm —*Norw* ['trɔn hɛim]
Troon truːn
troop truːp **trooped** truːpt **trooping** 'truːp ɪŋ **troops** truːps
'**troop** ˌ**carrier**
trooper 'truːp ə ‖ -ər **~s** z
troopship 'truːp ʃɪp **~s** s
trope trəʊp ‖ troʊp **tropes** trəʊps ‖ troʊps
-trope trəʊp ‖ troʊp — **heliotrope** 'hiːl i ə trəʊp ‖ -troʊp
trophic 'trɒf ɪk ‖ 'troʊf ɪk 'trɑːf- **~ally** əl i
-trophic 'trɒf ɪk ‖ 'troʊf ɪk 'trɑːf- — **hypertrophic** ˌhaɪp ə 'trɒf ɪk ◂ ‖ -ər 'troʊf- -'trɑːf-
tropho- *comb. form*
with stress-neutral suffix ¦trɒf əʊ ‖ ¦troʊf ə ¦trɑːf ə — **trophoplasm** 'trɒf əʊ ˌplæz əm ‖ 'troʊf ə- 'trɑːf-
with stress-imposing suffix trəʊ 'fɒ+ trɒ- ‖ troʊ 'fɑː+ — **trophology** trəʊ 'fɒl ədʒ i trɒ- ‖ troʊ 'fɑːl-
troph|y 'trəʊf |i ‖ 'troʊf |i **~ies** iz

T

-trophy *stress-imposing* trəf i — **hypertrophy** haɪ ˈpɜːtr əf i ‖ -ˈpɝːtr-
tropic ˈtrɒp ɪk ‖ ˈtrɑːp ɪk **~s** s
-tropic ˈtrɒp ɪk ‖ ˈtroʊp ɪk — **heliotropic** ˌhiːl i‿əʊ ˈtrɒp ɪk ◂ ‖ ə ˈtroʊp-
tropical ˈtrɒp ɪk ^{ə}l ‖ ˈtrɑːp- **~ly** ‿i
ˌtropical ˈstorm
tropicalis|e, tropicaliz|e ˈtrɒp ɪk ə laɪz -^{ə}l aɪz ‖ ˈtrɑːp- **~ed** d **~es** ɪz əz **~ing** ɪŋ
tropism ˈtrəʊp ˌɪz əm ‖ ˈtroʊp- **~s** z
-tropism trə ˌpɪz əm ˈtrəʊp ˌɪz əm, ˌ·· ·
—*Usage varies as to whether this suffix is stress-imposing or stress-neutral.* — **heliotropism** ˌhiːl i ˈɒtr ə ˌpɪz əm əʊ ˈtrəʊp ˌɪz əm, ˈ· · ·ˌ· · · ‖ -ˈɑːtr ə ˌpɪz əm ə ˈtroʊp ˌɪz əm
tropo- *comb. form*
with stress-neutral suffix ¦trɒp əʊ ‖ ¦troʊp ə ˈtrɑːp- — **tropophyte** ˈtrɒp əʊ faɪt ‖ ˈtroʊp ə- ˈtrɑːp-
with stress-imposing suffix trɒ ˈpɒ+ trə- ‖ troʊ ˈpɑː+ — **tropophilous** trɒ ˈpɒf ɪl əs trə-, -əl əs ‖ troʊ ˈpɑːf-
tropopause ˈtrɒp ə pɔːz ‖ ˈtroʊp- ˈtrɑːp-, -pɑːz
troposphere ˈtrɒp ə sfɪə ‖ ˈtroʊp ə sfɪr ˈtrɑːp-
-tropous *stress-imposing* trəp əs — **heterotropous** ˌhet ə ˈrɒtr əp əs ◂ ‖ ˌhet̬ ə ˈrɑːtr-
troppo ˈtrɒp əʊ ‖ ˈtrɑːp oʊ —*It* [ˈtrɔp po]
Trossachs ˈtrɒs əks -æks, -əxs ‖ ˈtrɑːs-
trot, Trot trɒt ‖ trɑːt **trots** trɒts ‖ trɑːts **trotted** ˈtrɒt ɪd -əd ‖ ˈtrɑːt̬ əd **trotting** ˈtrɒt ɪŋ ‖ ˈtrɑːt̬ ɪŋ
troth trəʊθ trɒθ ‖ trɔːθ trɑːθ, troʊθ
Trotsky ˈtrɒt ski ‖ ˈtrɑːt- **~ism** ˌɪz əm
Trotskyist ˈtrɒt ski ɪst §-əst ‖ ˈtrɑːt- **~s** s
Trotskyite ˈtrɒt ski aɪt ‖ ˈtrɑːt- **~s** s
Trott trɒt ‖ trɑːt
trott... —*see* **trot**
trotter, T~ ˈtrɒt ə ‖ ˈtrɑːt̬ ^{ə}r **~s** z
Trottiscliffe ˈtrɒz li ‖ ˈtrɑːz- *(!)*
troubadour ˈtruːb ə dʊə -dɔː ‖ -dɔːr -doʊr, -dʊr **~s** z
troubl|e ˈtrʌb ^{ə}l *(!)* **~ed** d **~es** z **~ing** ɪŋ
ˈtrouble spot
trouble-free ˌtrʌb ^{ə}l ˈfriː ◂
troublemak|er ˈtrʌb ^{ə}l ˌmeɪk| ə ‖ -^{ə}r **~ers** əz ‖ ^{ə}rz **~ing** ɪŋ
troubleshoot ˈtrʌb ^{ə}l ʃuːt **~s** s
troubleshoot|er ˈtrʌb ^{ə}l ˌʃuːt| ə ‖ -ˌʃuːt̬| -^{ə}r **~ers** əz ‖ ^{ə}rz **~ing** ɪŋ
troublesome ˈtrʌb ^{ə}l səm **~ly** li **~ness** nəs nɪs
troublous ˈtrʌb ləs
Troubridge ˈtruː brɪdʒ
trough trɒf trɔːf ‖ trɔːf trɑːf **troughs** trɒfs trɔːfs ‖ trɔːfs trɑːfs
Troughton ˈtraʊt ^{ə}n
trounce traʊn^{t}s **trounced** traʊn^{t}st **trounces** ˈtraʊn^{t}s ɪz -əz **trouncing** ˈtraʊn^{t}s ɪŋ
troupe truːp *(= troop)* **troupes** truːps
trouper ˈtruːp ə ‖ -^{ə}r **~s** z
troupial ˈtruːp i‿əl **~s** z
trouser ˈtraʊz ə ‖ -^{ə}r **~ed** d
ˈtrouser press; ˈtrouser suit
trousers ˈtraʊz əz ⚠-ɪz ‖ -^{ə}rz
trousseau ˈtruːs əʊ truː ˈsəʊ ‖ truː ˈsoʊ ˈtruːs oʊ **~s, ~x** z
trout traʊt **trouts** traʊts
Troutbeck ˈtraʊt bek
trove trəʊv ‖ troʊv
trow trəʊ traʊ ‖ troʊ
Trowbridge ˈtrəʊ brɪdʒ ‖ ˈtroʊ-
trowel ˈtraʊ‿əl traʊl ‖ ˈtraʊ‿əl **troweled, trowelled** ˈtraʊ‿əld traʊld ‖ ˈtraʊ‿əld **troweling, trowelling** ˈtraʊ‿əl ɪŋ ˈtraʊl ɪŋ ‖ ˈtraʊ‿əl ɪŋ **trowels** ˈtraʊ‿əlz traʊlz ‖ ˈtraʊ‿əlz
Trowell *(i)* ˈtraʊ‿əl traʊl ‖ ˈtraʊ‿əl, *(ii)* ˈtrəʊ əl ‖ ˈtroʊ‿əl
Troy, troy trɔɪ
ˈtroy weight
truanc|y ˈtruː‿ən^{t}s |i **~ies** iz
tru|ant ˈtruː‿|ənt **~anted** ənt ɪd -əd ‖ ənt̬ əd **~anting** ənt ɪŋ ‖ ənt̬ ɪŋ **~ants** ənts
Trubenised, Trubenized *tdmk* ˈtruːb ə naɪzd
Trubetzkoy ˌtruːb ets ˈkɔɪ -ɪts-, -əts- —*Russ* [tru bʲɪts ˈkɔj]
Trubner, Trübner ˈtruːb nə ‖ -n^{ə}r —*Ger* [ˈtʁyːb nɐ]
Trubshaw ˈtrʌb ʃɔː ‖ -ʃɑː
truce truːs **truces** ˈtruːs ɪz -əz
trucial, T~ ˈtruːʃ ^{ə}l ˈtruːs i‿əl
truck trʌk **trucked** trʌkt **trucking** ˈtrʌk ɪŋ **trucks** trʌks
ˈtruck farm; ˈtruck stop
truckage ˈtrʌk ɪdʒ
Truckee ˈtrʌk i
trucker ˈtrʌk ə ‖ -^{ə}r **~s** z
truckl|e ˈtrʌk ^{ə}l **~ed** d **~es** z **~ing** ‿ɪŋ
truckload ˈtrʌk ləʊd ‖ -loʊd **~s** z
truculence ˈtrʌk jʊl ən^{t}s -jəl- ‖ -jəl-
truculent ˈtrʌk jʊl ənt -jəl- ‖ -jəl- **~ly** li
Trudeau ˈtruːd əʊ ‖ truː ˈdoʊ —*Fr* [tʁy do]
trudge trʌdʒ **trudged** trʌdʒd **trudges** ˈtrʌdʒ ɪz -əz **trudging** ˈtrʌdʒ ɪŋ
Trudgen, t~ ˈtrʌdʒ ən
Trudgill ˈtrʌd gɪl →ˈtrʌg-, §-g^{ə}l
Trudi, Trudy ˈtruːd i
true truː **trued** truːd **trueing, truing** ˈtruː‿ɪŋ **truer** ˈtruː‿ə ‖ ^{ə}r **trues** truːz **truest** ˈtruː‿ɪst əst
ˌtrue ˈnorth
true-blue ˌtruː ˈbluː ◂ **~s** z
trueborn ˌtruː ˈbɔːn ◂ ‖ -ˈbɔːrn ◂
true-breeding ˈtruː ˌbriːd ɪŋ
true-false ˌtruː ˈfɔːls ◂ -ˈfɒls ◂ ‖ -ˈfɑːls ◂
truehearted ˌtruː ˈhɑːt ɪd ◂ -əd ‖ -ˈhɑːrt̬ əd ◂ ˈ. . .
true-life ˌtruː ˈlaɪf ◂
truelove, T~ ˈtruː lʌv **~s** z
Trueman ˈtruːm ən
trueness ˈtruː nəs -nɪs
true-to-life ˌtruː tə ˈlaɪf ◂ ‖ -t̬ə-
TrueType *tdmk* ˈtruː taɪp
Truffaut ˈtruːf əʊ ˈtruːf- ‖ tru ˈfoʊ —*Fr* [tʁy fo]

truffle 'trʌf ᵊl **~s** z
trug trʌg **trugs** trʌgz
truism 'tru: ˌɪz əm **~s** z
Trujillo tru 'hi: jəʊ -'hi:l- ‖ -joʊ —*Sp* [tru 'xi ʎo, -jo]
Truk trʌk trʊk
truly 'tru: li
Truman 'tru:m ən
Trumbull 'trʌm bᵊl
trump, Trump trʌmp **trumped** trʌmpt **trumping** 'trʌmp ɪŋ **trumps** trʌmps **'trump card**
trumped-up ˌtrʌmpt 'ʌp ◂ **ˌtrumped-up 'charges**
trumper|y 'trʌmp ər |i **~ies** iz
trump|et 'trʌmp |ɪt §-ət ‖ -|ət **~eted** ɪt ɪd §ət-, -əd ‖ əṭ əd **~eting** ɪt ɪŋ §ət- ‖ əṭ ɪŋ **~ets** ɪts §əts ‖ əts
trumpeter 'trʌmp ɪt ə §-ət- ‖ -əṭ ᵊr **~s** z
trun|cate trʌŋ '|keɪt 'trʌŋ|k eɪt ‖ 'trʌŋ|k eɪt 'trʌn |keɪt **~cated** keɪt ɪd -əd ‖ keɪṭ əd **~cates** keɪts **~cating** keɪt ɪŋ ‖ keɪṭ ɪŋ
truncation trʌŋ 'keɪʃ ᵊn **~s** z
truncheon 'trʌntʃ ən 'trʌndʒ- **~ed** d **~ing** ɪŋ **~s** z
trundl|e 'trʌnd ᵊl **~ed** d **~es** z **~ing** ˌɪŋ
trunk trʌŋk **trunks** trʌŋks **'trunk call**; **'trunk road**; **'trunk route**
trunnel 'trʌn ᵊl **~s** z
trunnion 'trʌn i‿ən ‖ 'trʌn jən **~ed** d **~s** z
Truro 'trʊər əʊ ‖ 'trʊr oʊ
Truscott 'trʌsk ət -ɒt ‖ -ɑ:t
truss trʌs **trussed** trʌst *(= trust)* **trusses** 'trʌs ɪz -əz **trussing** 'trʌs ɪŋ
trust trʌst **trusted** 'trʌst ɪd -əd **trusting** 'trʌst ɪŋ **trusts** trʌsts **'trust fund**; **'trust ˌterritory**
trustee ˌtrʌ 'sti: ◂ **~s** z
trusteeship ˌtrʌ 'sti: ʃɪp **~s** s
trustful 'trʌst fᵊl -fʊl **~ly** i
Trusthouse 'trʌst haʊs
trusting 'trʌst ɪŋ **~ly** li
trustworth|y 'trʌst ˌwɜ:ð |i ‖ -ˌwɝ:ð |i **~ily** ɪ li əl i **~iness** i nəs i nɪs
trust|y 'trʌst |i **~ier** i‿ə ‖ i‿ᵊr **~ies** iz **~iest** i‿ɪst i‿əst **~ily** ɪ li əl i **~iness** i nəs i nɪs
truth tru:θ **truths** tru:ðz tru:θs **'truth drug**; **'truth ˌtable**
truthful 'tru:θ fᵊl -fʊl **~ly** ‿i **~ness** nəs nɪs
try traɪ **tried** traɪd **tries** traɪz **trying** 'traɪ ɪŋ —*see note at* trying
Tryfan 'trɪv ᵊn 'trɪf-, 'trʌv- —*Welsh* ['trə van]
trying 'traɪ ɪŋ **~ly** li **~ness** nəs nɪs —*As a close-knit expression,* trying to *has casual weak forms* 'traɪ‿ənt ə 'traɪ‿ən ə ‖ 'traɪ ənṭ ə *(or with final* u *for* ə *before a following vowel sound).*
try-on 'traɪ ɒn ‖ -ɑ:n -ɔ:n **~s** z
Tryon 'traɪ‿ən
try-out 'traɪ aʊt **~s** s
trypanosome 'trɪp ən ə səʊm trɪ 'pæn- ‖ -soʊm **~s** z
trypanosomiasis ˌtrɪp ən əʊ səʊ 'maɪ‿əs ɪs trɪ ˌpæn-, §-əs ‖ -ə sə'--
trypsin 'trɪps ɪn §-ᵊn
tryptophan 'trɪpt əʊ fæn ‖ -ə-
tryst trɪst traɪst **trysted** 'trɪst ɪd 'traɪst-, -əd **trysting** 'trɪst ɪŋ 'traɪst- **trysts** trɪsts traɪsts
tsar zɑ: tsɑ: ‖ zɑ:r tsɑ:r **tsars** zɑ:z tsɑ:z ‖ zɑ:rz tsɑ:rz
tsarevich, tsarevitch 'zɑ:r ə vɪtʃ 'tsɑ:r- **~es** ɪz əz
tsarina zɑ: 'ri:n ə tsɑ:- **~s** z
tsar|ism 'zɑ:r ˌɪz əm 'tsɑ:r- **~ist/s** ɪst/s §əst/s
TSB *tdmk* ˌti: es 'bi:
tsetse 'tets i 'tsets i, 'sets i **'tsetse fly**
Tshiluba tʃi: 'lu:b ə
T-shirt, t-shirt 'ti: ʃɜ:t ‖ -ʃɝ:t **~s** s
Tshwane 'tʃwɑ:n eɪ
Tsimshian 'sɪm ʃi æn 'tʃɪm-, -ʃi‿ən **~s** z
Tsing Tao ˌtʃɪŋ 'daʊ —*Chi* Qīngdǎo [¹tɕʰiŋ ³tɑu]
tsk | —*This is a conventional spelling for the alveolar CLICK.*
tsotsi 'tsɒts i ‖ 'tsɑ:ts i **~s** z
T-square 'ti: skweə ‖ -skwer -skwær **~s** z
tsunami tsu 'nɑ:m i su-, -'næm- —*Jp* [tsɯ ˌna mi] **~s** z
tsutsugamushi ˌtsu:ts əg ə 'mu:ʃ i ˌtsʊts-, ˌsu:ts-, ˌ-u:g-, ˌ-ʊg-, -'mʊʃ i —*Jp* [tsɯ̥ ˌtsɯ 'ŋa mɯ ɕi, -'ga-] **ˌtsutsuga'mushi diˌsease**
Tswana 'tswɑ:n ə 'swɑ:n- **~s** z
Tuamotu ˌtu:‿ə 'məʊt u: ‖ -'moʊt-
Tuareg 'twɑ:r eg **~s** z
tuatara ˌtu:‿ə 'tɑ:r ə **~s** z
tub tʌb **tubbed** tʌbd **tubbing** 'tʌb ɪŋ **tubs** tʌbz
tuba 'tju:b ə →'tʃu:b- ‖ 'tu:b ə 'tju:b- **~s** z
tubal 'tju:b ᵊl →'tʃu:b- ‖ 'tu:b ᵊl 'tju:b-
tubb|y 'tʌb |i **~ier** i‿ə ‖ i‿ᵊr **~iest** i‿ɪst i‿əst **~iness** i nəs i nɪs

TUBE

9%
91%
tu:b
tju:b
AmE

tube tju:b →tʃu:b ‖ tu:b tju:b — *Preference poll, AmE:* tu:b *91%,* tju:b *9%.* **tubed** tju:bd →tʃu:bd ‖ tu:bd tju:bd **tubes** tju:bz →tʃu:bz ‖ tu:bz tju:bz **tubing** 'tju:b ɪŋ →'tʃu:b- ‖ 'tu:b ɪŋ 'tju:b-
tubeless 'tju:b ləs →'tʃu:b-, -lɪs ‖ 'tu:b- 'tju:b-
tuber 'tju:b ə →'tʃu:b- ‖ 'tu:b ᵊr 'tju:b- **~s** z
tubercle 'tju:b ək ᵊl →'tʃu:b- ‖ 'tu:b ᵊrk ᵊl 'tjub- **~s** z
tubercular tju 'bɜ:k jʊl ə tə-, tu-, →tʃu-, -jəl- ‖ tu 'bɝ:k jəl ᵊr tju-, tə-

tuberculin tju ˈbɜːk jʊl ɪn tə-, tu-, →tʃu-, -jəl-, §-ən ‖ tu ˈbɝːk jəl ən tju-, tə-
tuberculosis tju ˌbɜːk ju ˈləʊs ɪs tə-, tu-, →tʃu-, -jə-, §-əs ‖ tu ˌbɝːk jə ˈloʊs əs tju-, tə-
tuberculous tju ˈbɜːk jʊl əs tə-, tu-, →tʃu-, -jəl- ‖ tu ˈbɝːk jəl əs tju-, tə-
tuberos|e *n* ˈtjuːb ə rəʊz →ˈtʃuːb-, ˌ·ˈ· ‖ ˈtuːb ə roʊz ˈtjuːb- —*Also, by folk etymology,* ⚠ˈtjuːb rəʊz →ˈtʃuːb- ‖ ⚠ˈtuːb roʊz, ˈtjuːb- **~es** ɪz əz
tuberose *adj* ˈtjuːb ə rəʊs →ˈtʃuːb- ‖ ˈtuːb ə roʊs, ˈtjuːb-
tuberosit|y ˌtjuːb ə ˈrɒs ət |i →ˌtʃuːb-, -ɪt i ‖ ˌtuːb ə ˈrɑːs əṱ |i ˌtjuːb- **~ies** iz
tuberous ˈtjuːb ər əs →ˈtʃuːb- ‖ ˈtuːb- ˈtjuːb-
tubful ˈtʌb fʊl **~s** z
tubifex ˈtjuːb ɪ feks →ˈtʃuːb-, §-ə- ‖ ˈtuːb- ˈtjuːb- **~es** ɪz əz
tubiform ˈtjuːb ɪ fɔːm →ˈtʃuːb-, §-ə- ‖ ˈtuːb ə fɔːrm ˈtjuːb-
tubing ˈtjuːb ɪŋ →ˈtʃuːb- ‖ ˈtuːb ɪŋ ˈtjuːb-
Tubingen ˈtjuːb ɪŋ ən ˈtuːb-, →ˈtʃuːb- ‖ ˈtuːb- —*Ger* Tübingen [ˈtyː bɪŋ ən]
Tubman ˈtʌb mən
tub-thump|ing ˈtʌb ˌθʌmp |ɪŋ **~er/s** ə/z ‖ ᵊr/z
tubular ˈtjuːb jʊl ə →ˈtʃuːb-, -jəl- ‖ ˈtuːb jəl ᵊr ˈtjuːb-
tubule ˈtjuːb juːl →ˈtʃuːb- ‖ ˈtuːb- ˈtjuːb- **~s** z
TUC ˌtiː juː ˈsiː
tuck, Tuck tʌk **tucked** tʌkt **tucking** ˈtʌk ɪŋ **tucks** tʌks
ˈtuck box; **ˈtuck shop**
tuckahoe ˈtʌk ə həʊ ‖ -hoʊ **~s** z
tucker, T~ ˈtʌk ə ‖ -ᵊr **~ed** d **~s** z
tuckerbag ˈtʌk ə bæg ‖ -ᵊr- **~s** z
tuckeroo ˌtʌk ə ˈruː **~s** z
tuck-in ˈtʌk ɪn
Tucson ˈtuː sɒn ˌ·ˈ· ‖ -sɑːn *(!)*
-tude tjuːd →tʃuːd ‖ tuːd tjuːd — **amplitude** ˈæmp lɪ tjuːd -lə-, →-tʃuːd ‖ -tuːd -tjuːd
Tudor ˈtjuːd ə →ˈtʃuːd- ‖ ˈtuːd ᵊr ˈtjuːd- **~s** z
Tudur ˈtɪd ɪə ‖ -ɪr —*Welsh* [ˈti dir, ˈti dɨr]
Tue tjuː →tʃuː ‖ tuː tjuː
Tuesday ˈtjuːz deɪ →ˈtʃuːz-, -di ‖ ˈtuːz- ˈtjuːz- —*see note at* -day **~s** z
tufa ˈtjuːf ə →ˈtʃuːf-, ˈtuːf- ‖ ˈtuːf ə ˈtjuːf-
tufaceous tju ˈfeɪʃ əs →tʃu-, tu- ‖ tu- tju-
tuff tʌf
tuffet ˈtʌf ɪt §-ət **~s** s
Tuffnell, Tufnell ˈtʌf nᵊl
ˌTufnell ˈPark
tuft tʌft **tufted** ˈtʌft ɪd -əd **tufting** ˈtʌft ɪŋ **tufts** tʌfts
Tufts tʌfts
tuft|y ˈtʌft |i **~ier** i‿ə ‖ i‿ᵊr **~iest** i‿ɪst i‿əst **~iness** i nəs i nɪs
tug tʌg **tugged** tʌgd **tugging** ˈtʌg ɪŋ **tugs** tʌgz
tugboat ˈtʌg bəʊt ‖ -boʊt **~s** s
Tugendhat ˈtuːg ən hɑːt
tugg... —*see* **tug**
tug-of-love ˌtʌg əv ˈlʌv ◂
tug-of-war ˌtʌg əv ˈwɔː -ə- ‖ -ˈwɔːr
tugrik ˈtuːg rɪk **~s** s
Tuileries ˈtwiːl ər i -iz —*Fr* [tɥil ʁi]
Tuite *(i)* tjuːt →tʃuːt ‖ tuːt tjuːt, *(ii)* ˈtjuː‿ɪt →ˈtʃuː‿, §-ət ‖ ˈtuː ət ˈtjuː-
tuition tju ˈɪʃ ᵊn →tʃu- ‖ tu- tju-
Tuitt ˈtjuː‿ɪt →ˈtʃuː‿, §-ət ‖ ˈtuː ət ˈtjuː-
Tuke tjuːk →tʃuːk ‖ tuːk tjuːk
tuk-tuk ˈtʊk tʊk **~s** s
tularaemia, tularemia ˌtuːl ə ˈriːm i‿ə ˌtjuːl-
Tulare tu ˈleər i -ˈleə ‖ tu ˈler i -ˈlær-; -ˈleᵊr, -ˈlæᵊr
Tule, tule ˈtuːl i **~s** z
tulip ˈtjuːl ɪp →ˈtʃuːl-, §-əp ‖ ˈtuːl əp ˈtjuːl- **~s** s
ˈtulip tree
Tull tʌl
Tullamarine ˌtʌl ə mə ˈriːn
tulle tjuːl →tʃuːl ‖ tuːl —*Fr* [tyl] **tulles** tjuːlz →tʃuːlz ‖ tuːlz
Tulloch ˈtʌl ək -əx
Tully ˈtʌl i
Tulsa ˈtʌls ə
Tulse tʌls
ˌTulse ˈHill
tum tʌm **tums** tʌmz
tumbl|e ˈtʌm bᵊl **~ed** d **~es** z **~ing** ˌɪŋ
tumbledown ˈtʌm bᵊl daʊn
tumble-drier, tumble-dryer ˌtʌm bᵊl ˈdraɪ‿ə ˈ·ˌ·ˌ·· ‖ -ˈdraɪ‿ᵊr **~s** z
tumble-|dry ˌtʌm bᵊl |ˈdraɪ ˈ·ˌ·ˌ· **~dried** ˈdraɪd **~dries** ˈdraɪz **~drying** ˈdraɪ ɪŋ
tumbler ˈtʌm blə ‖ -blᵊr **~ful/s** fʊl/z **~s** z
tumbleweed ˈtʌm bᵊl wiːd **~s** z
tumbrel, tumbril ˈtʌm brəl -brɪl **~s** z
tumefacient ˌtjuːm ɪ ˈfeɪʃ i ənt ◂ →ˌtʃuːm-, §ˌ-ə-, -ˈfeɪs-, -ˈfeɪʃ ᵊnt ‖ ˌtuːm- ˌtjuːm-
tumefaction ˌtjuːm ɪ ˈfæk ʃᵊn →ˌtʃuːm-, §-ə- ‖ ˌtuːm- ˌtjuːm-
tume|fy ˈtjuːm ɪ |faɪ →ˈtʃuːm-, -ə- ‖ ˈtuːm- ˈtjuːm- **~fied** faɪd **~fies** faɪz **~fying** faɪ ɪŋ
tumescence tju ˈmes ᵊnᵗs →tʃu- ‖ tu- tju-
tumescent tju ˈmes ᵊnt →tʃu- ‖ tu- tju-
tumid ˈtjuːm ɪd →ˈtʃuːm-, §-əd ‖ ˈtuːm əd ˈtjuːm- **~ly** li **~ness** nəs nɪs
tumidity tju ˈmɪd ət i →tʃu-, -ɪt- ‖ tu ˈmɪd əṱ i tju-
Tummel ˈtʌm ᵊl
tumm|y ˈtʌm |i **~ies** iz
tumor, tumour ˈtjuːm ə →ˈtʃuːm- ‖ ˈtuːm ᵊr ˈtjuːm- **~s** z
tump tʌmp **tumps** tʌmps
tumuli ˈtjuːm ju laɪ →ˈtʃuːm-, -jə- ‖ ˈtuːm jə laɪ ˈtjuːm-
tumult ˈtjuːm ʌlt →ˈtʃuːm-, -ᵊlt ‖ ˈtuːm- ˈtjuːm- **~s** s
tumultuous tju ˈmʌltʃ u‿əs →tʃu-, -ˈmʌlt ju‿ ‖ tu- tju- **~ly** li **~ness** nəs nɪs
tum|ulus ˈtjuːm |jʊl əs →ˈtʃuːm-, -jəl- ‖ ˈtuːm |jəl əs ˈtjuːm- **~uli** ju laɪ jə- ‖ jə laɪ
tun tʌn **tuns** tʌnz
tuna ˈtjuːn ə ˈtuːn-, →ˈtʃuːn- ‖ ˈtuːn ə ˈtjuːn- **~s** z
ˈtuna fish; **ˌtuna ˈsalad**

Tunbridge 'tʌn brɪdʒ →'tʌm-
ˌTunbridge 'Wells
tundish 'tʌn dɪʃ **~es** ɪz əz
tundra 'tʌndr ə

TUNE

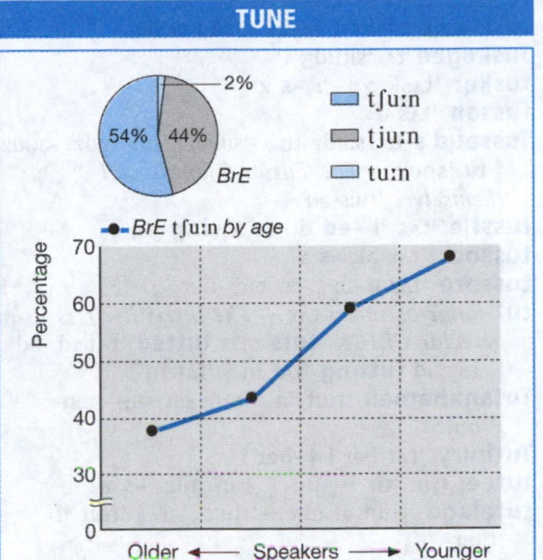

tune tjuːn →tʃuːn ‖ tuːn tjuːn — *Preference poll, BrE:* tʃuːn *54% (born since 1981, 68%),* tjuːn *44%,* tuːn *2%.* **tuned** tjuːnd →tʃuːnd ‖ tuːnd tjuːnd **tunes** tjuːnz →tʃuːnz ‖ tuːnz tjuːnz **tuning** 'tjuːn ɪŋ →'tʃuːn- ‖ 'tuːn ɪŋ 'tjuːn- **'tuning fork**; **'tuning peg**
tuneful 'tjuːn fᵊl →'tʃuːn-, -fʊl ‖ 'tuːn- 'tjuːn- **~ly** i **~ness** nəs nɪs
tuneless 'tjuːn ləs →'tʃuːn-, -lɪs ‖ 'tuːn- tjuːn- **~ly** li **~ness** nəs nɪs
tuner 'tjuːn ə →'tʃuːn- ‖ 'tuːn ᵊr 'tjuːn- **~s** z
tunesmith 'tjuːn smɪθ →'tʃuːn- ‖ 'tuːn 'tjuːn- **~s** s
tune-up 'tjuːn ʌp →'tʃuːn- ‖ 'tuːn- 'tjuːn- **~s** s
tung tʌŋ
Tung Chee Hwa ˌtʊŋ ˌtʃiː 'hwɑː —*Chi* Dǒng Jiànhuá [³tʊŋ ⁴tɕian ²xua], *Cantonese* [²toŋ ³kiːn ⁴waː]
tungsten 'tʌŋᵏst ən
Tungus 'tʊŋ gʊs tʊŋ 'guːz **~es** ɪz əz
Tungusic tʊŋ 'gʊs ɪk -'guːz-
tunic 'tjuːn ɪk →'tʃuːn- ‖ 'tuːn ɪk 'tjuːn- **~s** s
tunicate 'tjuːn ɪk ət →'tʃuːn-, §-ək-, -ɪt; -ɪ keɪt, -ə- ‖ 'tuːn- 'tjuːn- **~s** s
tunicle 'tjuːn ɪk ᵊl →'tʃuːn-, §-ək- ‖ 'tuːn- 'tjuːn- **~s** z
Tunis 'tjuːn ɪs →'tʃuːn-, §-əs ‖ 'tuːn əs 'tjuːn-
Tunisi|a tju 'nɪz i ə →tʃu-, -'nɪs- ‖ tu 'niːʒ |ə tju-, -'niːʃ-, -'nɪʒ-, -'nɪʃ- *(*)* **~an/s** ən/z ‖ ᵊn/z
tunnel 'tʌn ᵊl **~ed, ~led** d **~ing, ~ling** ɪŋ **~s** z
ˌtunnel 'vision, '. . ˌ. .
tunneler, tunneller 'tʌn ᵊl ə ‖ -ᵊr **~s** z
Tunney 'tʌn i
Tunnicliff, Tunnicliffe 'tʌn i klɪf
tunn|y 'tʌn |i **~ies** iz
Tunstall 'tʌnᵗst ᵊl 'tʌn stɔːl
Tuohey, Tuohy 'tuː i -hi
Tuolumne tu 'ɒl əm i -ni ‖ -'ɑːl-

tup tʌp **tupped** tʌpt **tupping** 'tʌp ɪŋ **tups** tʌps
Tupamaro ˌtuːp ə 'mɑːr əʊ ‖ -oʊ **~s** z —*Sp* [tu pa 'ma ro, -s]
tupelo, T~ 'tjuːp ə ləʊ →'tʃuːp- ‖ 'tuːp ə loʊ 'tjuːp- **~s** z
Tupi tu 'piː 'tuːp i **~s** z
-tuple tjuːp ᵊl tjʊp ᵊl, tʌp ᵊl, →tʃuːp-, →tʃʊp-; '• • ‖ tuːp ᵊl tjuːp ᵊl, tʌp ᵊl *usually unstressed*
tuppenc|e 'tʌp ənᵗs →-mᵖs **~es** ɪz əz
tuppenny 'tʌp ən i
ˌtuppenny 'ha'penny◂
Tupper 'tʌp ə ‖ -ᵊr
Tupperware *tdmk* 'tʌp ə weə ‖ -ᵊr wer -wær
tuque tuːk **tuques** tuːks
tu quoque ˌtuː 'kwɒk wi -'kwəʊk-, -weɪ ‖ -'kwoʊk-
Turandot 'tjʊər ən dɒt 'tʊər-, →'tʃʊər-, -dəʊ ‖ 'tʊr ən dɑːt -doʊ —*It* [tu ran 'dɔt]
Turanian tjuᵊ 'reɪn i ən →tʃuᵊ- ‖ tu- tju- **~s** z
turban 'tɜːb ən ‖ 'tɝːb ən **~ed** d **~s** z
turbar|y 'tɜːb ər |i ‖ 'tɝːb- **~ies** iz
turbid 'tɜːb ɪd §-əd ‖ 'tɝːb- **~ly** li **~ness** nəs nɪs
turbidity tɜː 'bɪd ət i -ɪt- ‖ tɝː 'bɪd əṭ i
turbinate 'tɜːb ɪn ət -ən-, -ɪt; -ɪ neɪt, -ə- ‖ 'tɝːb-
turbine 'tɜːb aɪn -ɪn, §-ən ‖ 'tɝːb- **~s** z
turbo 'tɜːb əʊ ‖ 'tɝːb oʊ **~s** z
turbo- ¦tɜːb əʊ ‖ ¦tɝːb oʊ — **turboelectric** ˌtɜːb əʊ ɪ 'lek trɪk ◂ -ə'-- ‖ ˌtɝːb oʊ-
turbocharg|e 'tɜːb əʊ tʃɑːdʒ ‖ 'tɝːb oʊ tʃɑːrdʒ **~ed** d **~er/s** ə/z ‖ ᵊr/z **~es** ɪz əz **~ing** ɪŋ
turbofan 'tɜːb əʊ fæn ˌ'·'· ‖ 'tɝːb oʊ- **~s** z
turbojet 'tɜːb əʊ dʒet ‖ 'tɝːb oʊ- **~s** s
turboprop 'tɜːb əʊ prɒp ‖ 'tɝːb oʊ prɑːp **~s** s
turbot 'tɜːb ət ‖ 'tɝːb ət **~s** s
turbulenc|e 'tɜːb jʊl ənᵗs -jəl- ‖ 'tɝːb jəl- **~y** i
turbulent 'tɜːb jʊl ənt -jəl- ‖ 'tɝːb jəl- **~ly** li
Turco- ¦tɜːk əʊ ‖ ¦tɝːk oʊ — **Turco-Greek** ˌtɜːk əʊ 'griːk ◂ ‖ ˌtɝːk oʊ-
turd tɜːd ‖ tɝːd **turds** tɜːdz ‖ tɝːdz
tureen tjuᵊ 'riːn ˌtjʊə-, tuᵊ-, →tʃuᵊ, §→ˌtʃʊə-, tjə-, tə- ‖ tə- tju-, tu- **~s** z
turf tɜːf ‖ tɝːf **turfed** tɜːft ‖ tɝːft **turfing** 'tɜːf ɪŋ ‖ 'tɝːf ɪŋ **turfs** tɜːfs ‖ tɝːfs **turves** tɜːvz ‖ tɝːvz
'turf acˌcountant
Turgenev tʊə 'geɪn jev tɜː-, -'gen- ‖ tʊr- tɝː- —*Russ* [tur 'gʲe nʲɪf]
turgid 'tɜːdʒ ɪd §-əd ‖ 'tɝːdʒ- **~ly** li **~ness** nəs nɪs
turgidity tɜː 'dʒɪd ət i -ɪt- ‖ tɝː 'dʒɪd əṭ i
turgor 'tɜːg ə ‖ 'tɝːg ᵊr
Turin ˌtjʊə 'rɪn tjuᵊ-; 'tʊər ɪn ‖ tu 'rɪn 'tʊr ən, 'tjʊr-, 'tɝː-
the ˌTurin 'shroud
Turing 'tjʊər ɪŋ →'tʃʊər- ‖ 'tʊr ɪŋ 'tjʊr-, 'tɝː-
'Turing maˌchine
Turk tɜːk ‖ tɝːk **Turks** tɜːks ‖ tɝːks
ˌTurks and 'Caicos 'keɪk ɒs ‖ -oʊs
Turkestan ˌtɜːk ɪ 'stɑːn -ə-, -'stæn ‖ ˌtɝːk-
Turkey, t~ 'tɜːk i ‖ 'tɝːk i **~s** z

T

turkeycock 'tɜːk i kɒk ‖ 'tɜːk i kɑːk **~s** s
Turkic 'tɜːk ɪk ‖ 'tɜ˞ːk-
Turkish 'tɜːk ɪʃ ‖ 'tɜ˞ːk-
ˌTurkish 'bath; **ˌTurkish de'light**
Turkmen 'tɜːk men -mən ‖ 'tɜ˞ːk-
Turkmeni|a tɜːk 'miːn i|‿ə ‖ tɜ˞ːk- **~an/s** ‿ən/z
Turkmenistan ˌtɜːk men ɪ 'stɑːn ·ˌ·-, -ə-, -'stæn ‖ˌtɜ˞ːk-
Turkoman 'tɜːk əm ən -ə mæn, -ə mɑːn ‖ 'tɜ˞ːk- **~s** z
Turku 'tʊək uː ‖ 'tʊrk uː —*Finnish* ['tur ku]
Turl, Turle tɜːl ‖ tɜ˞ːl
turmeric 'tɜːm ər ɪk ‖ 'tɜ˞ːm-
turmoil 'tɜːm ɔɪ^əl ‖ 'tɜ˞ːm-
turn tɜːn ‖ tɜ˞ːn **turned** tɜːnd ‖ tɜ˞ːnd **turning** 'tɜːn ɪŋ ‖ 'tɜ˞ːn ɪŋ **turns** tɜːnz ‖ tɜ˞ːnz
'turning ˌcircle; **'turning point**
turnabout 'tɜːn ə ˌbaʊt ‖ 'tɜ˞ːn- **~s** s
turnaround 'tɜːn ə ˌraʊnd ‖ 'tɜ˞ːn- **~s** z
Turnberry 'tɜːn bər‿i →'tɜːm- ‖ 'tɜ˞ːn ˌber i
turnbuckle 'tɜːn ˌbʌk ^əl →'tɜːm- ‖ 'tɜ˞ːn- **~s** z
Turnbull 'tɜːn bʊl →'tɜːm- ‖ 'tɜ˞ːn-
turncoat 'tɜːn kəʊt →'tɜːŋ- ‖ 'tɜ˞ːn koʊt **~s** s
turncock 'tɜːn kɒk →'tɜːŋ- ‖ 'tɜ˞ːn kɑːk **~s** s
turndown 'tɜːn daʊn ‖ 'tɜ˞ːn-
turner, T~ 'tɜːn ə ‖ 'tɜ˞ːn ^ər **~s** z
turner|y 'tɜːn ər |i ‖ 'tɜ˞ːn- **~ies** iz
Turnham 'tɜːn əm ‖ 'tɜ˞ːn-
Turnhouse 'tɜːn haʊs ‖ 'tɜ˞ːn-
turning 'tɜːn ɪŋ ‖ tɜ˞ːn ɪŋ **~s** z
'turning point
turnip 'tɜːn ɪp §-əp ‖ 'tɜ˞ːn əp **~s** s
turnkey 'tɜːn kiː →'tɜːŋ- ‖ 'tɜ˞ːn- **~s** z
turn-off 'tɜːn ɒf -ɔːf ‖ 'tɜ˞ːn ɔːf -ɑːf **~s** s
turn-of-the-century ˌtɜːn əv ðə 'sentʃ ər‿i ◂ ‖ˌtɜ˞ːn-
turn-on 'tɜːn ɒn ‖ 'tɜ˞ːn ɑːn -ɔːn **~s** z
turnout 'tɜːn aʊt ‖ 'tɜ˞ːn- **~s** s
turnover 'tɜːn ˌəʊv ə ‖ 'tɜ˞ːn ˌoʊv ^ər **~s** z
turnpike 'tɜːn paɪk →'tɜːm- ‖ 'tɜ˞ːn- **~s** s
turnround 'tɜːn raʊnd ‖ 'tɜ˞ːn- **~s** z
turnstile 'tɜːn staɪ^əl ‖ 'tɜ˞ːn- **~s** z
turnstone 'tɜːn stəʊn ‖ 'tɜ˞ːn stoʊn **~s** z
turntable 'tɜːn ˌteɪb ^əl ‖ 'tɜ˞ːn- **~s** z
turntablist 'tɜːn ˌteɪb ^əl‿ɪst §‿əst ‖ 'tɜ˞ːn- **~s** s
turn-up 'tɜːn ʌp ‖ 'tɜ˞ːn- **~s** s
turpentine 'tɜːp ən taɪn →-m-, -ɪn- ‖ 'tɜ˞ːp-
Turpin 'tɜːp ɪn §-ən ‖ 'tɜ˞ːp ən
turpitude 'tɜːp ɪ tjuːd -ə-, →-tʃuːd ‖ 'tɜ˞ːp ə tuːd -tjuːd
turps tɜːps ‖ tɜ˞ːps
turquoise 'tɜːk wɔɪz -wɑːz ‖ 'tɜ˞ːk- -ɔɪz
turr|et 'tʌr |ɪt -ət ‖ 'tɜ˞ː |ət **~eted** ɪt ɪd §ət-, -əd ‖ əṱ əd **~ets** ɪts §əts ‖ əts
Turriff 'tʌr ɪf -əf ‖ 'tɜ˞ː əf
turtle 'tɜːt ^əl ‖ 'tɜ˞ːṱ ^əl **~s** z
turtledove 'tɜːt ^əl dʌv ‖ 'tɜ˞ːṱ- **~s** z
turtleneck 'tɜːt ^əl nek ‖ 'tɜ˞ːṱ- **~s** s
Turton 'tɜːt ^ən ‖ 'tɜ˞ːt ^ən
turves tɜːvz ‖ tɜ˞ːvz
Turvey 'tɜːv i ‖ 'tɜ˞ːv i
Tuscan 'tʌsk ən **~s** z
Tuscany 'tʌsk ən i
Tuscarora ˌtʌsk ə 'rɔːr ə ‖ -'roʊr-
tush *interj; n 'tusk'* tʌʃ
tush *n 'buttocks'* tʊʃ **tushes** 'tʊʃ ɪz -əz
tushery 'tʌʃ ər i
tushie 'tʊʃ i **~s** z
tusk tʌsk **tusked** tʌskt **tusks** tʌsks
Tuskegee tʌ 'skiːdʒ i
tusker 'tʌsk ə ‖ -^ər **~s** z
tussah 'tʌs ə
Tussaud's tə 'sɔːdz tu-, -'səʊdz; 'tuːs ɔːdz, -əʊdz ‖ tu 'soʊz —*The Tussaud family call themselves* 'tuːs əʊ
tussl|e 'tʌs ^əl **~ed** d **~es** z **~ing** ‿ɪŋ
tussock 'tʌs ək **~s** s
tussore 'tʌs ə -ɔː ‖ -^ər -ɔːr, -oʊr
tut *name of interj* tʌt —*The interj itself is* ǀ, *an alveolar CLICK.* **tuts** tʌts **tutted** 'tʌt ɪd -əd ‖ 'tʌṱ əd **tutting** 'tʌt ɪŋ ‖ 'tʌṱ ɪŋ
Tutankhamen ˌtuːt ^ən 'kɑːm en -əŋ-, -æŋ- ‖ -ɑːŋ-
Tutbury 'tʌt bər‿i ‖ -ber i
tutee ˌtjuː 'tiː →ˌtʃuː- ‖ ˌtuː- ˌtjuː- **~s** z
tutelage 'tjuːt əl ɪdʒ →'tʃuːt-, -ɪl- ‖ 'tuːṱ ^əl- 'tjuːṱ-
tutelar 'tjuːt əl ə →'tʃuːt-, -ɪl- ‖ 'tuːṱ ^əl ər 'tjuːṱ-, -ɑːr
tutelary 'tjuːt əl ər i →'tʃuːt-, '·ɪl- ‖ 'tuːṱ ^əl er i 'tjuːṱ-
Tutin 'tjuːt ɪn →'tʃuːt-, §-^ən ‖ 'tuːt ^ən 'tjuːt-
tutor 'tjuːt ə →'tʃuːt- ‖ 'tuːṱ ^ər 'tjuːṱ- **~ed** d **tutoring** 'tjuːt ər ɪŋ →'tʃuːt- ‖ 'tuːṱ- 'tjuːṱ- **~s** z
tutorage 'tjuːt ər ɪdʒ →'tʃuːt- ‖ 'tuːṱ- 'tjuːṱ-
tutorial tju 'tɔːr i‿əl →tʃu- ‖ tu- -'toʊr- **~s** z
tutorship 'tjuːt ə ʃɪp →'tʃuːt- ‖ 'tuːṱ ^ər- 'tjuːṱ- **~s** s
tutsan 'tʌts ^ən
Tutsi 'tʊts i 'tuːts-
tutti 'tʊt i 'tuːt-, -iː —*It* ['tut ti] **~s** z
tutti-frutti ˌtuːt i 'fruːt i ‖ ˌtuːṱ i 'fruːṱ i **~s** z
Tuttle 'tʌt ^əl ‖ 'tʌṱ ^əl
tut-|tut *name of interj; v* ˌtʌt |'tʌt —*The interj itself is* ǀ ǀ, *a repeated alveolar CLICK.* **~tuts** 'tʌts **~tutted** 'tʌt ɪd -əd ‖ 'tʌṱ əd **~tutting** 'tʌt ɪŋ ‖ 'tʌṱ ɪŋ
tutty 'tʌt i ‖ 'tʌṱ i
tutu, Tutu 'tuːt uː **~s** z
Tuva 'tuːv ə —*Russ* [tu 'va]
Tuvalu tu 'vɑːl uː ˌtuːv ə 'luː **~an/s** ən/z
tu-whit tu-whoo tə ˌwɪt tə 'wuː tu ˌwɪt tu-, -ˌhwɪt-, -'hwuː
tux tʌks **tuxes** 'tʌks ɪz -əz
tuxedo, T~ tʌk 'siːd əʊ ‖ -oʊ **~s** z
Tuxford 'tʌks fəd ‖ -f^ərd
Tuzla 'tʊz lə 'tuːz- ‖ 'tuːz- —*S-Cr* ['tuz la]
TV ˌtiː 'viː ◂ **TVs, TV's** ˌtiː 'viːz
ˌTV 'dinner; **ˌT'V ˌprogram(me)**
Twaddell *(i)* 'twɒd ^əl ‖ 'twɑːd ^əl, *(ii)* twɒ 'del ‖ twɑː-
twaddle 'twɒd ^əl ‖ 'twɑːd ^əl
twain, Twain tweɪn
twang twæŋ **twanged** twæŋd **twanging** 'twæŋ ɪŋ **twangs** twæŋz

Twankey, Twanky ˈtwæŋk i
'twas *strong form* twɒz ‖ twʌz twɑːz, *weak form* twəz
twat twɒt twæt ‖ twɑːt **twats** twɒts twæts ‖ twɑːts
twayblade ˈtweɪ bleɪd **~s** z
tweak twiːk **tweaked** twiːkt **tweaking** ˈtwiːk ɪŋ **tweaks** twiːks
twee twiː **tweer** ˈtwiː ə ‖ -ᵊr **tweest** ˈtwiː ɪst -əst
tweed, Tweed twiːd **tweeds** twiːdz
Tweeddale ˈtwiːd deɪᵊl
Tweedie ˈtwiːd i
Tweedledee ˌtwiːd ᵊl ˈdiː
Tweedledum ˌtwiːd ᵊl ˈdʌm
Tweedsmuir ˈtwiːdz mjʊə -mjɔː ‖ -mjʊr
tweed|y ˈtwiːd |i **~ier** i‿ə ‖ i‿ᵊr **~iest** i‿ɪst i‿əst **~iness** i nəs i nɪs
'tween, tween twiːn **tweening** ˈtwiːn ɪŋ
tween|y ˈtwiːn |i **~ies** iz
tweet twiːt **tweeted** ˈtwiːt ɪd -əd ‖ ˈtwiːţ əd **tweeting** ˈtwiːt ɪŋ ‖ ˈtwiːţ ɪŋ **tweets** twiːts
tweeter ˈtwiːt ə ‖ ˈtwiːţ ᵊr **~s** z
tweeze twiːz **tweezed** twiːzd **tweezes** ˈtwiːz ɪz -əz **tweezing** ˈtwiːz ɪŋ
tweezer ˈtwiːz ə ‖ -ᵊr **~s** z
twelfth twelfθ twelθ **twelfthly** ˈtwelfθ li ˈtwelθ- **twelfths** twelfθs twelθs
ˌTwelfth ˈNight ‖ ˈ· ·
twelve twelv **twelves** twelvz
twelvemonth ˈtwelv mʌnθ **~s** s
twelve-tone ˌtwelv ˈtəʊn ◂ ˈ· · ‖ -ˈtoʊn ◂
twelvish ˈtwelv ɪʃ
twentieth ˈtwent i‿əθ ˈtwen-, ɪθ ‖ ˈtwenţ- **~s** s
twent|y ˈtwent |i ˈtwen i ‖ ˈtwenţ |i **~ies** iz
twenty-first ˌtwent i ˈfɜːst ◂ ˌtwen- ‖ ˌtwenţ i ˈfɜːst ◂ **~s** s
twentyfold ˈtwent i fəʊld ˈtwen-, →-fɒʊld ‖ ˈtwenţ i foʊld
twenty-four ˌtwent i ˈfɔː ◂ ˌtwen- ‖ ˌtwenţ i ˈfɔːr ◂ -ˈfoʊr
ˌtwenty-four ˈseven
twenty-one ˌtwent i ˈwʌn ◂ ˌtwen- ‖ ˌtwenţ- **~s** z
twentysomething ˈtwent i ˌsʌm θɪŋ ˈtwen i- ‖ ˈtwenţ i- **~s** z
twenty-twenty ˌtwent i ˈtwent i ◂ ˌtwen i ˈtwen i ◂ ‖ ˌtwenţ i ˈtwenţ i ◂
ˌtwenty-ˌtwenty ˈvision
twenty-two ˌtwent i ˈtuː ◂ ˌtwen i- ‖ ˌtwenţi-
'twere *strong form* twɜː tweə ‖ twɜː, *weak form* twə ‖ twᵊr
twerp twɜːp ‖ twɜːp **twerps** twɜːps ‖ twɜːps
Twi twiː —*Twi* [tɕɥi]
twice twaɪs
twice-told ˌtwaɪs ˈtəʊld ◂ →-ˈtɒʊld ‖ -ˈtoʊld ◂
Twickenham ˈtwɪk ən‿əm
Twickers ˈtwɪk əz ‖ -ᵊrz
twiddl|e ˈtwɪd ᵊl **~ed** d **~er/s** ‿ə/z ‖ ‿ᵊr/z **~es** z **~ier** ‿i ə ‖ ‿i ᵊr **~iest** ‿i ɪst -əst **~ing** ‿ɪŋ **~y** ‿i
twig twɪg **twigged** twɪgd **twigging** ˈtwɪg ɪŋ **twigs** twɪgz
Twigg twɪg
twigg|y, T~ ˈtwɪg |i **~ier** i‿ə ‖ i‿ᵊr **~iest** i‿ɪst i‿əst
twilight ˈtwaɪ laɪt
twilit ˈtwaɪ lɪt
'twill twɪl —*sometimes with a weak form* twəl
twill twɪl **twilled** twɪld **twilling** ˈtwɪl ɪŋ **twills** twɪlz
twin twɪn **twinned** twɪnd **twinning** ˈtwɪn ɪŋ **twins** twɪnz
ˌtwin ˈbed; **ˈtwin set**
twin-bedded ˌtwɪn ˈbed ɪd ◂ -əd
twine twaɪn **twined** twaɪnd **twines** twaɪnz **twining** ˈtwaɪn ɪŋ
twin-engine ˌtwɪn ˈendʒ ɪn ◂ §-ˈɪndʒ-, -ən **~d** d
twinge twɪndʒ **twinged** twɪndʒd **twinges** ˈtwɪndʒ ɪz -əz **twingeing, twinging** ˈtwɪndʒ ɪŋ
Twining ˈtwaɪn ɪŋ
twink twɪŋk **twinks** twɪŋks
Twinkie *tdmk* ˈtwɪŋk i **~s** z
twinkl|e ˈtwɪŋk ᵊl **~ed** d **~es** z **~ing** ‿ɪŋ
twinkling *n* ˈtwɪŋk lɪŋ ˈtwɪŋk ᵊl‿ɪŋ **~s** z
Twinn twɪn
twinset ˈtwɪn set **~s** s
twin-size ˈtwɪn saɪz **~d** d
twin-tub ˌtwɪn ˈtʌb ◂ ˈ· ·
twirl twɜːl ‖ twɜːl **twirled** twɜːld ‖ twɜːld **twirling** ˈtwɜːl ɪŋ ‖ ˈtwɜːl ɪŋ **twirls** twɜːlz ‖ twɜːlz
twirp twɜːp ‖ twɜːp **twirps** twɜːps ‖ twɜːps
Twisleton ˈtwɪs ᵊl tən
twist twɪst **twisted** ˈtwɪst ɪd -əd **twisting** ˈtwɪst ɪŋ **twists** twɪsts
ˈtwist grip
twister ˈtwɪst ə ‖ -ᵊr **~s** z
twist|y ˈtwɪst| i **~ier** i‿ə ‖ i‿ᵊr **~iest** i‿ɪst ‿əst
twit twɪt **twits** twɪts **twitted** ˈtwɪt ɪd -əd ‖ ˈtwɪţ əd **twitting** ˈtwɪt ɪŋ ‖ ˈtwɪţ ɪŋ
twitch twɪtʃ **twitched** twɪtʃt **twitches** ˈtwɪtʃ ɪz -əz **twitching/s** ˈtwɪtʃ ɪŋ/z
twitcher ˈtwɪtʃ ə ‖ -ᵊr **~s** z
Twitchett ˈtwɪtʃ ɪt §-ət
twitch|y ˈtwɪtʃ |i **~ier** i‿ə ‖ i‿ᵊr **~iest** i‿ɪst i‿əst **~iness** i nəs i nɪs
twite twaɪt **twites** twaɪts
twitter ˈtwɪt ə ‖ ˈtwɪţ ᵊr **~ed** d **twittering/ly** ˈtwɪt‿ər ɪŋ /li ‖ ˈtwɪţ ər ɪŋ /li **~s** z
twittery ˈtwɪt ər i ‖ ˈtwɪţ-
twixt, 'twixt twɪkst
twizzler, T~ ˈtwɪz ᵊl‿ə ‖ ‿ᵊr **~s** z
two tuː *(= too)* **twos** tuːz
ˌtwo ˈbits
two-bit ˈtuː bɪt
two-by-four ˌtuː bə ˈfɔː -bi-, -baɪ- ‖ -ˈfɔːr -ˈfoʊr
twoc twɒk ‖ twɑːk **twocking** ˈtwɒk ɪŋ ‖ ˈtwɑːk-
two-dimensional ˌtuː daɪ ˈmenᵗʃ ᵊn‿əl ◂ ˌ·dɪ-, ˌ·də- **~ly** i
two-edged ˌtuː ˈedʒd ◂

T

two|faced ˌtuː |ˈfeɪst ◂ **~facedly** ˈfeɪs ɪd li -əd-; ˈfeɪst li **~facedness** ˈfeɪs ɪd nəs -əd-, -nɪs; ˈfeɪst nəs, -nɪs
twofer ˈtuːf ə ‖ -ᵊr **~s** z
two-fisted ˌtuː ˈfɪst ɪd ◂ -əd
twofold ˈtuː fəʊld →-fɒʊld ‖ -foʊld
two-four ˌtuː ˈfɔː ‖ -ˈfɔːr -ˈfoʊr **~s** z
two-handed ˌtuː ˈhænd ɪd ◂ -əd **~ly** li **~ness** nəs nɪs
Twohy ˈtuː‿i
two-ish ˈtuː ɪʃ
two-legged ˌtuː ˈleg ɪd ◂ -əd; -ˈlegd ◂
two-man ˌtuː ˈmæn ◂
Twomey ˈtuːm i
two-minute ˌtuː ˈmɪn ɪt ◂ §-ət
ˌ**two-minute ˈsilence**
two-one ˌtuː ˈwʌn §-wɒn **~s** z
twoonie ˈtuːn i **~s** z
two-party ˌtuː ˈpɑːt i ◂ ‖ -ˈpɑːrṭ i ◂
ˌ**two-party aˈgreement**
twopenc|e *n '2d'* ˈtʌp ənᵗs →-mᵖs *—but meaning '2p', in modern currency, usually* two pence ˌtuː ˈpenᵗs **~es** ɪz əz
twopenn|y *adj '2d', and in figurative senses* ˈtʌp ən‿|i *—but meaning '2p', in modern currency, usually* two-penny ˌtuː ˈpen |i ◂ **~ies** iz
twopenny-halfpenny ˌtʌp ən‿i ˈheɪp ən‿i ◂
two-person ˌtuː ˈpɜːs ᵊn ◂ ‖ -ˈpɜːs-
ˌ**two-person ˈhousehold**
two-piece ˈtuː piːs
two-ply ˈtuː plaɪ
two-seater ˌtuː ˈsiːt ə ‖ -ˈsiːṭ ᵊr **~s** z
two-sided ˌtuː ˈsaɪd ɪd ◂ -əd **~ness** nəs nɪs
twosome ˈtuː səm **~s** z
two-star ˈtuː stɑː ˌ·ˈ· ‖ -stɑːr
two-step ˈtuː step **~s** s
two-stroke ˈtuː strəʊk ‖ -stroʊk **~s** s
two-tim|e ˈtuː taɪm **~ed** d **~es** z **~ing** ɪŋ
two-tone ˈtuː təʊn ‖ -toʊn
two-two, 2:2 ˌtuː ˈtuː ◂ **~s** z
'twould twʊd
two-way ˌtuː ˈweɪ ◂
ˌ**two-way ˈradio**
Twyford ˈtwaɪ fəd ‖ -fᵊrd
Ty taɪ *—but in Welsh place names,* tiː *—Welsh* Tŷ [tiː, tiː]
ˌ**Ty ˈCoch** ˌtiː ˈkəʊk -ˈkəʊx ‖ -ˈkoʊk *—Welsh* [ˌtiː ˈkoːχ, ˌtiː-]
-ty ti — **sixty** ˈsɪkst i *—The pronunciation* taɪ *is occasionally used in order to avoid the danger of confusion resulting from the near-homophony of* -ty *and* -teen, *thus* ˈsɪks taɪ
Tybalt ˈtɪb ᵊlt
Tyburn ˈtaɪ bən -bɜːn ‖ -bᵊrn
Tyche ˈtaɪk i
Tycho ˈtaɪk əʊ ‖ -oʊ *—Danish* [ˈty go]
tycoon ₍ₗ₎taɪ ˈkuːn **~s** z
Tye taɪ
tying ˈtaɪ ɪŋ
tyke taɪk **tykes** taɪks
Tyldesley ˈtɪldz li
Tylenol *tdmk* ˈtaɪl ə nɒl ‖ -nɔːl -nɑːl, -noʊl
Tyler ˈtaɪl ə ‖ -ᵊr
tympan ˈtɪmp ən **~s** z
tympana ˈtɪmp ən ə
tympani ˈtɪmp ən i
tympanic tɪm ˈpæn ɪk
tympanist ˈtɪmp ən ɪst §-əst **~s** s
tympan|um ˈtɪmp ən |əm **~a** ə **~ums** əmz **~y** i
Tynan ˈtaɪn ən
Tyndale ˈtɪnd ᵊl ˈtɪn deɪᵊl
Tyndall ˈtɪnd ᵊl
Tyndrum ₍ₗ₎taɪn ˈdrʌm
Tyne taɪn
ˌ**Tyne and ˈWear** ˈwɪə ‖ ˈwɪᵊr
Tynemouth ˈtaɪn maʊθ →ˈtaɪm-, ˈtɪn-, -məθ
Tynesid|e ˈtaɪn saɪd **~er/s** ə/z ‖ ᵊr/z
Tynwald ˈtɪn wəld ˈtaɪn-
-type taɪp — **prototype** ˈprəʊt əʊ taɪp ‖ ˈproʊṭ ə-
type taɪp **typed** taɪpt **types** taɪps **typing** ˈtaɪp ɪŋ
typebar ˈtaɪp bɑː ‖ -bɑːr **~s** z
typecast ˈtaɪp kɑːst §-kæst ‖ -kæst **~ing** ɪŋ **~s** s
typefac|e ˈtaɪp feɪs **~es** ɪz əz
typescript ˈtaɪp skrɪpt **~s** s
type|set ˈtaɪp |set **~sets** sets **~setting** set ɪŋ ‖ seṭ ɪŋ
typesetter ˈtaɪp ˌset ə ‖ -ˌseṭ ᵊr **~s** z
typewriter ˈtaɪp ˌraɪt ə ‖ -ˌraɪṭ ᵊr **~s** z
typewriting ˈtaɪp ˌraɪt ɪŋ ‖ -ˌraɪṭ-
typewritten ˈtaɪp ˌrɪt ᵊn
Typhoeus taɪ ˈfiː‿əs -ˈfəʊ juːs
typhoid ˈtaɪf ɔɪd
ˌ**typhoid ˈfever**
Typhon ˈtaɪf ᵊn -əʊn, -ɒn ‖ -ɑːn
typhonic taɪ ˈfɒn ɪk ‖ -ˈfɑːn-
Typhoo *tdmk* ₍ₗ₎taɪ ˈfuː
typhoon ₍ₗ₎taɪ ˈfuːn **~s** z
typhus ˈtaɪf əs
-typic ˈtɪp ɪk — **autotypic** ˌɔːt əʊ ˈtɪp ɪk ◂ ‖ ˌɔːṭ ə- ˌɑːṭ-
typical ˈtɪp ɪk ᵊl **~ness** nəs nɪs
typicality ˌtɪp ɪ ˈkæl ət i ˌ-ə-, -ɪt i ‖ -əṭ i
typically ˈtɪp ɪk ᵊl‿i
typi|fy ˈtɪp ɪ |faɪ -ə- **~fied** faɪd **~fier/s** faɪ‿ə/z ‖ faɪ‿ᵊr/z **~fies** faɪz **~fying** faɪ ɪŋ
typing ˈtaɪp ɪŋ
ˈ**typing pool**
typist ˈtaɪp ɪst §-əst **~s** s
typo ˈtaɪp əʊ ‖ -oʊ **~s** z
typographer taɪ ˈpɒg rəf ə ‖ -ˈpɑːgr əf ᵊr **~s** z
typographic ˌtaɪp ə ˈgræf ɪk ◂ **~al** ᵊl **~ally** ᵊl‿i
typograph|y taɪ ˈpɒg rəf |i ‖ -ˈpɑːg- **~ies** iz
typological ˌtaɪp ə ˈlɒdʒ ɪk ᵊl ◂ ‖ -ˈlɑːdʒ- **~ly** ‿i
typolog|y taɪ ˈpɒl ədʒ |i ‖ -ˈpɑːl- **~ies** iz
-typy ˌtaɪp i *—sometimes treated as stress-imposing,* tɪp i, təp i — **autotypy** ˈɔːt əʊ ˌtaɪp i ɔː ˈtɒt ɪp i, -əp i ‖ ˈɔːṭ oʊ ˌtaɪp i ˈɑːṭ-; ɔː ˈtɑːṭ əp i, ɑː-
Tyr tɪə tjʊə ‖ tɪᵊr
tyramine ˈtarᵊr ə miːn ˈtɪr-

tyrannical tɪ 'ræn ɪk ᵊl tə-, taɪᵊ- **~ly** ˌi **~ness** nəs nɪs
tyrannicide tɪ 'ræn ɪ saɪd tə-, taɪᵊ-, -ə- **~s** z
tyrannis|e, tyranniz|e 'tɪr ə naɪz **~ed** d **~es** ɪz əz **~ing** ɪŋ
tyrannosaur tɪ 'ræn ə sɔː tə-, taɪᵊ- ‖ -sɔːr **~s** z
tyrannosaurus tɪ ˌræn ə 'sɔːr əs ◂ tə-, taɪᵊ- **~es** ɪz əz
Tyˌrannoˌsaurus 'rex
tyrannous 'tɪr ən əs **~ly** li
tyrann|y 'tɪr ən |i **~ies** iz
tyrant 'taɪᵊr ənt **~s** s
tyre, Tyre 'taɪ͜ə ‖ 'taɪ͜ᵊr *(= tire)* **tyres** 'taɪ͜əz ‖ 'taɪ͜ᵊrz
Tyrian 'tɪr i͜ən
Tyrie 'tɪr i
tyro 'taɪᵊr əʊ ‖ -oʊ **~s** z
Tyrol tɪ 'rəʊl tə-, →-'rɒʊl; 'tɪr əl, -əʊl ‖ -'roʊl —*Ger* Tirol [ti 'ʁoːl]
Tyrolean ˌtɪr əʊ 'liː͜ən ◂ tɪ 'rəʊl i͜ən, tə- ‖ -ə- **~s** z
Tyrolese ˌtɪr əʊ 'liːz ◂ ‖ -ə- -'liːs ◂
Tyrolienne tɪ ˌrəʊl i 'en tə-, ˌtɪr əʊl- ‖ -ˌroʊl- **~s** z
Tyrone *county in N.Ireland* tɪ 'rəʊn tə- ‖ -'roʊn
Tyrone *personal name* 'taɪᵊr əʊn ˌtaɪᵊ 'rəʊn, tɪ-, tə- ‖ -oʊn
tyrosine 'taɪᵊr əʊ siːn 'tɪr-, -sɪn ‖ -ə-
tyrothricin ˌtaɪᵊr əʊ 'θraɪs ɪn §-ᵊn ‖ -ə-
Tyrozets *tdmk* 'taɪᵊr ə zets 'tɪr-
Tyrrell 'tɪr əl
Tyrrhenian tɪ 'riːn i͜ən tə-
Tyson 'taɪs ᵊn
Tyte taɪt
Tywyn 'taʊ ɪn —*Welsh* ['tə win, -wɨn]
Tyzack *(i)* 'taɪz æk -ək, *(ii)* 'tɪz-
tzar zɑː tsɑː ‖ zɑːr tsɑːr **tzars** zɑːz tsɑːz ‖ zɑːrz tsɑːrz
tzarina zɑː 'riːn ə tsɑː- **~s** z
tzar|ism 'zɑːr ˌɪz əm 'tsɑːr- **~ist/s** ɪst/s §əst/s
tzatziki tæt 'siːk i tsæt- ‖ tɑːt- —*ModGk* [dza 'dzi ci]
tzetze 'tets i 'tsets i, 'sets i

T

Uu

u Spelling-to-sound

1 Where the spelling is **u**, the pronunciation differs according to whether the vowel is short or long, followed or not by **r**, and strong or weak.

2 The 'strong' pronunciation is regularly
ʌ as in **cup** kʌp ('short U') or
juː as in **music** ˈmjuːz ɪk ('long U').

3 Less frequently, it is
ʊ as in **push** pʊʃ (especially before **sh**, **l**).

4 Where the spelling is **ur**, the 'strong' pronunciation is
ɜː ‖ ɜ˞ː as in **turn** tɜːn ‖ tɜ˞ːn or
jʊə ‖ jʊ as in **pure** pjʊə ‖ pjʊr (in BrE ʊə is often replaced by ɔː, thus pjɔː)
or, indeed, there may be the regular 'short' pronunciation
ʌ ‖ ɜ˞ː as in **hurry** ˈhʌr i ‖ ˈhɜ˞ː i (in most AmE, the ʌ and r coalesce into ɜ˞ː).

5 In the case of expected juː, jʊə, jʊ, the j drops out as follows:

- after the consonant sounds tʃ, dʒ, ʃ, r, j, as in **jury** ˈdʒʊər i ‖ ˈdʒʊr i **rude** ruːd
- sometimes in BrE, and always in AmE, after l, θ, s, z, as in **assume** ə ˈs(j)uːm ‖ ə ˈsuːm
- usually in AmE, but not in BrE, after t, d, n as in **tune** tjuːn ‖ tuːn (see also ASSIMILATION for the BrE possibility of tʃuːn).

6 Note the exceptional words **busy** ˈbɪz i, **business** ˈbɪz nəs, **bury** ˈber i.

7 The 'weak' pronunciation is
jʊ ‖ jə as in **stimulus** ˈstɪm jʊl əs ‖ ˈstɪm jəl əs (but in BrE at the end of a syllable the vowel may be tenser, and in this dictionary is written as ju, thus **stimulate** ˈstɪm ju leɪt ‖ ˈstɪm jə leɪt)
ə as in **album** ˈælb əm, **Arthur** ˈɑːθ ə ‖ ˈɑːrθ ᵊr or
jə as in **failure** ˈfeɪl jə ‖ ˈfeɪl jᵊr.
In the ending **-ure** the vowel is usually weak. Note also **minute** (noun) ˈmɪn ɪt ‖ ˈmɪn ət, **lettuce** ˈlet ɪs ‖ ˈleţ əs, where the BrE vowel sound is ɪ rather than ə.

8 **u** also forms part of the digraphs **au, eu, ou, ue, ui, uy**.

ue Spelling-to-sound

1 Where the spelling is the digraph **ue**, the pronunciation is regularly
juː as in **cue** kjuː or
uː as in **blue** bluː.
(For the dropping of j, see **u** 5 above.)

2 **ue** is not a digraph in **duet**, **cruel**, **pursuer**.

ui Spelling-to-sound

1 Where the spelling is the digraph **ui**, the pronunciation is regularly
juː as in **nuisance** ˈnjuːs ᵊnᵗs (AmE usually ˈnuːs-) or
uː as in **fruit** fruːt.
(For the dropping of j, see **u** 5 above.)

2 Less frequently, the pronunciation is
ɪ as in **build** bɪld or
aɪ as in **guide** gaɪd, also
ɪ ‖ ə as in **biscuit** ˈbɪsk ɪt ‖ ˈbɪsk ət (when weak).

3 Note the exceptional case **suite** swiːt.

4 **ui** is not a digraph in **fluid**, **tuition**, nor in **quick**, **quite** (where the digraph **qu** is followed by **i**).

uy Spelling-to-sound

In the rare cases where the spelling is the digraph **uy**, the pronunciation is regularly
aɪ as in **buy** baɪ.

U, u juː *(= you)* **U's, u's, Us** juːz —*Communications code name:* Uniform
UAE ˌjuː ei ˈiː
UART ˈjuː ɑːt ‖ -ɑːrt
UB40 ˌjuː ˌbiː ˈfɔːt i ‖ -ˈfɔːrţ i
U-bend ˈjuː bend **~s** z
ubermensch, übermensch ˈuːb ə menᵗʃ ˈjuːb- ‖ -ᵊr- —*Ger Ü~* [ˈyː bɐ mɛnᵗʃ]
ubiquitous ju ˈbɪk wɪt əs -wət- ‖ -wəţ əs **~ly** li **~ness** nəs nɪs
ubiquity ju ˈbɪk wət i -wɪt- ‖ -wəţ i
U-boat ˈjuː bəʊt ‖ -boʊt **~s** s
Ubu Roi ˌuːb uː ˈrwɑː
UC ˌjuː ˈsiː
UCAS ˈjuːk æs
ˈUCAS form
Uccello uː ˈtʃel əʊ ‖ -oʊ —*It* [ut ˈtʃɛl lo]
Uckfield ˈʌk fiːᵊld
UCL ˌjuː siː ˈel
UCLA ˌjuː siː el ˈeɪ
UDA ˌjuː diː ˈeɪ
Udall *(i)* ˈjuːd ᵊl -ɔːl, -æl ‖ ˈjuːd ɔːl -ɑːl, *(ii)* ju ˈdæl -ˈdɔːl ‖ -ˈdɔːl, -ˈdɑːl
udder ˈʌd ə ‖ -ᵊr **~s** z
UDI ˌjuː diː ˈaɪ
Udimore ˈjuːd ɪ mɔː ˈʌd-, -ə- ‖ -mɔːr -moʊr
Udmurt ˈʊd mʊət ·ˈ· ‖ -mʊrt **~s** s
UDR ˌjuː diː ˈɑː ‖ -ˈɑːr
UEFA ju ˈeɪf ə -ˈiːf-; ˈjuːf ə

UFC ˌjuː ef ˈsiː
Uffizi ju ˈfɪts i u-, -ˈfiːts- —*It* [uf ˈfit tsi]
UFO ˌjuː ef ˈəʊ ˈjuːf əʊ ‖ ˌjuː ef ˈoʊ ˈjuːf oʊ **~s** z
ufolog|y ˌjuː ˈfɒl ədʒ| i ‖ -ˈfɑːl- **~ist/s** ɪst/s
Ugand|a ju ˈgænd |ə ‖ u ˈgɑːnd |ə **~an/s** ən/z
Ugaritic ˌuːg ə ˈrɪt ɪk ◂ ˌjuːg- ‖ -ˈrɪţ-
UGC ˌjuː dʒiː ˈsiː
ugh ʊx ʌg, jʌx, ɯə, uː —*and various other non-speech exclamations typically involving a vowel in the range* [ɯ, u, ʌ, ɜ] *and sometimes a consonant such as* [x, ɸ, h]
ugli ˈʌg li **~s** z
uglification ˌʌg lɪf ɪ ˈkeɪʃ ən ˌ·ləf-, §-əˈ·-
ugli|fy ˈʌg lɪ |faɪ -lə- **~fied** faɪd **~fies** faɪz **~fying** faɪ ɪŋ
ugly ˈʌg li **uglier** ˈʌg li‿ə ‖ ər **ugliest** ˈʌg li‿ɪst əst **ugliness** ˈʌg li nəs -nɪs
ˌugly ˈduckling
Ugrian ˈjuːg ri‿ən ˈuːg- **~s** z
Ugric ˈjuːg rɪk ˈuːg-
U-Haul *tdmk* ˈjuː hɔːl ‖ -hɑːl
UHF ˌjuː eɪtʃ ˈef §-heɪtʃ-
uh huh, uh-huh *'yes'* ˈʌ̃ hʌ̃ ˈə̃ hə̃, ˈm m̥m, ˈn n̥n; ·ˈ· ‖ ˈ· ˈ· —*usually with a low-rise tone*
uhlan ˈuːl ɑːn ˈjuːl-, -ən; u ˈlɑːn, ju- **~s** z
uh oh *said when you have made a mistake or something bad has happened* ˈʔʌʔ əʊ -ɜː ‖ ˈʔʌʔ oʊ ·ˈ· —*usually with the first syllable on a high level tone, the second on a mid or low-rising tone*
UHT ˌjuː eɪtʃ ˈtiː ◂ §-heɪtʃ-
Uhu *tdmk* ˈjuː huː ˈuː-
uh uh, uh-uh *'no'* ˈʔʌ̃ʔ ʌ̃ ˈʔə̃ʔ ə̃, ˈʔmʔ m —*always with a falling tone*
Ui ˈuː‿i
U-ie *'U-turn'* ˈjuː i **~s** z
Uig ˈuː ɪg ˈjuː-
Uighur, Uigur ˈwiːg ə ˌuː i ˈgʊə ◂ ‖ -r -ʊr; ˌuː i ˈgʊər ◂ —*Uighur* [ʔʊɪ ˈʁʊː] **~s** z
Uinta ju ˈɪnt ə ‖ -ˈɪnţ ə
Uist ˈjuː ɪst
Uitenhage ˈjuːt ən heɪg
UK ˌjuː ˈkeɪ ◂
ukas|e ju ˈkeɪz -ˈkeɪs **~es** ɪz əz
ukelele ˌjuːk ə ˈleɪl i **~s** z
Ukiah *place in CA* ju ˈkaɪ‿ə
UKIP, Ukip ˈjuːk ɪp
Ukraine ju ˈkreɪn
Ukrainian ju ˈkreɪn i‿ən **~s** z
Ukridge ˈjuːk rɪdʒ
ukulele ˌjuːk ə ˈleɪl i **~s** z
Ulaanbaatar, Ulan Bator ˌuːl ɑːn ˈbɑːt ɔː u ˌlɑːn ˈ· · ‖ -ɔːr
-ular *stress-imposing* jʊl ə jəl ə ‖ jəl ər — **mandibular** mæn ˈdɪb jʊl ə -jəl- ‖ -jəl ər
ulcer ˈʌls ə ‖ -ər **~s** z
ulce|rate ˈʌls ə |reɪt **~rated** reɪt ɪd -əd ‖ reɪţ əd **~rates** reɪts **~rating** reɪt ɪŋ ‖ reɪţ ɪŋ
ulceration ˌʌls ə ˈreɪʃ ən **~s** z
ulcerative ˈʌls ər‿ət ɪv -ə reɪt- ‖ -ə reɪţ- -ər‿əţ-
ulcerous ˈʌls ər‿əs **~ly** li
Uldall ˈʊl dɔːl
-ule juːl — **globule** ˈglɒb juːl ‖ ˈglɑːb-
ulema ˈuːl ɪm ə -əm-; -ɪ mɑː, -ə-, ˌ· ·ˈ· **~s** z
-ulence *stress-imposing* jʊl ənts jəl- ‖ jəl- — **opulence** ˈɒp jʊl ənts -jəl- ‖ ˈɑːp jəl ənts
-ulent *stress-imposing* jʊl ənt jəl- ‖ jəl- — **corpulent** ˈkɔːp jʊl ənt -jəl- ‖ ˈkɔːrp jəl ənt
Ulfilas ˈʊlf ɪ læs -ə-; -ɪl əs, -əl-
Ulick ˈjuːl ɪk
ullage ˈʌl ɪdʒ
Ullapool ˈʌl ə puːl
Ullman, Ullmann ˈʊl mən
Ullswater ˈʌlz ˌwɔːt ə ‖ -ˌwɔːţ ər -ˌwɑːţ-
Ulm ʊlm
ulna ˈʌln ə **ulnae** ˈʌln iː **ulnas** ˈʌln əz
ulnar ˈʌln ə ‖ -ər -ɑːr
ulpan ˈʊlp æn -ɑːn
Ulpian ˈʌlp i‿ən
Ulrich ˈʊl rɪk -rɪx —*Ger* [ˈʔʊl ʁɪç]
Ulrika ʊl ˈriːk ə
Ulster, u~ ˈʌlst ə ‖ -ər **~s, ~'s** z
Ulster|man ˈʌlst ə |mən ‖ -ər- **~men** mən men **~woman** ˌwʊm ən **~women** ˌwɪm ɪn §-ən
ult, ult. ʌlt
ulterior ʌl ˈtɪər i‿ə ‖ -ˈtɪr i‿ər **~ly** li
ultima ˈʌlt ɪm ə -əm-
ultimate ˈʌlt ɪm ət -əm-, -ɪt **~ly** li **~ness** nəs nɪs
ultimat|um ˌʌlt ɪ ˈmeɪt |əm -ə- ‖ -ˈmeɪţ |əm -ˈmɑːţ- **~a** ə **~ums** əmz
ultimo ˈʌlt ɪ məʊ -ə- ‖ -moʊ
ultra ˈʌltr ə ˈʊltr-, -ɑː **~s** z
ˌultra ˈvires ˈvaɪər iːz ˈvɪər-, -eɪz
ultra- ¦ʌltr ə — **ultramodern** ˌʌltr ə ˈmɒd ən ◂ ‖ -ˈmɑːd ərn ◂
ultrahigh ˌʌltr ə ˈhaɪ ◂
ˌultrahigh ˈfrequency
ultralight ˌʌltr ə ˈlaɪt ◂
ultramarine ˌʌltr ə mə ˈriːn ◂
ultra-modern ˌʌltr ə ˈmɒd ən ◂ ‖ -ˈmɑːd ərn ◂
ultramontane ˌʌltr ə ˈmɒnt eɪn ◂ -mɒn ˈteɪn ‖ -ˈmɑːnt eɪn ◂ -mɑːn ˈteɪn
ultranationalist ˌʌltr ə ˈnæʃ ən‿əl ɪst ◂ §-əst **~s** s
ultrasonic ˌʌltr ə ˈsɒn ɪk ◂ ‖ -ˈsɑːn- **~ally** əl‿i **~s** s
ultrasound ˈʌltr ə saʊnd ˌ· ·ˈ·
ultraviolet ˌʌltr ə ˈvaɪ‿əl ət ◂ -ɪt
ULU ˈjuːl uː
ulu|late ˈjuːl ju |leɪt ˈʌl-, -jə- ‖ -jə- **~lated** leɪt ɪd -əd ‖ leɪţ əd **~lates** leɪts **~lating** leɪt ɪŋ ‖ leɪţ ɪŋ
ululation ˌjuːl ju ˈleɪʃ ən ˌʌl-, -jə- ‖ -jə- **~s** z
Uluru ˌuːl ə ˈruː ◂
ˌUluru ˌNational ˈPark
Ulverston, Ulverstone ˈʌlv əst ən ‖ -ərst-
Ulysses ju ˈlɪs iːz ˈjuːl ɪ siːz, -ə-
um *hesitation noise* ʌm əm, ɜːm, ə̃ —*usually with a level tone*
umami u ˈmɑːm i —*Jp* [ɯ ˌma mi]
Umatilla ˌjuːm ə ˈtɪl ə
umbel ˈʌm bəl **~s** z
umbellifer ʌm ˈbel ɪf ə -əf- ‖ -ər **~s** z
umbelliferae ˌʌm bə ˈlɪf ə riː ˌ·be-
umbelliferous ˌʌm bə ˈlɪf ər‿əs ◂ ˌ·be-

umber ˈʌm bə ‖ -bᵊr **~s** z
Umberto ʊm ˈbeət əʊ -ˈbɜːt- ‖ -ˈbert oʊ —*It* [um ˈbɛr to]
umbilical ʌm ˈbɪl ɪk ᵊl -ək-; ˌʌm bɪ ˈlaɪk ᵊl ◂, -bə-
umbilicus ʌm ˈbɪl ɪk əs -ək-; ˌʌm bɪ ˈlaɪk əs, -bə- **umbilici** ʌm ˈbɪl ə saɪ -ɪ-; ˌʌm bɪ ˈlaɪs aɪ, -bə-
umble ˈʌm bᵊl **~s** z
umbo ˈʌm bəʊ ‖ -boʊ **umbones** ʌm ˈbəʊn iːz ‖ -ˈboʊn- **umbos** ˈʌm bəʊz ‖ -boʊz
um|bra ˈʌm |brə **~brae** briː **~bras** brəz
umbrage ˈʌm brɪdʒ

UMBRELLA

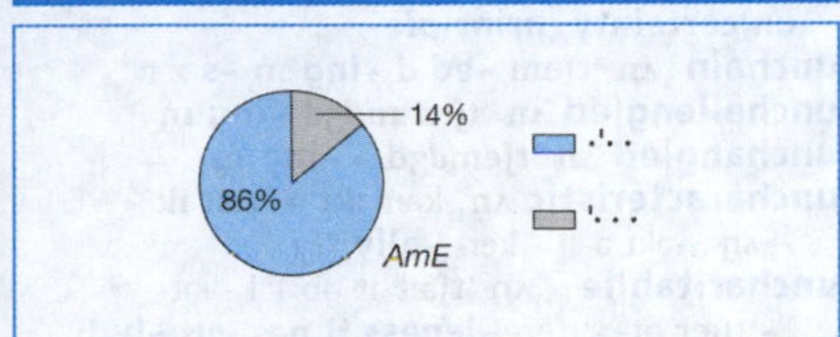

umbrella ʌm ˈbrel ə ‖ ˈ· · · —*Preference poll, AmE:* ·ˈ· · *86%,* ˈ· · · *14%.* **~s** z
Umbria ˈʌm bri‿ə
Umbrian ˈʌm bri‿ən **~s** z
Umbriel ˈʌm bri‿əl
Umbro *tdmk* ˈʌm brəʊ ‖ -broʊ
umiak ˈuːm i æk **~s** s
UMIST ˈjuːm ɪst
um|laut ˈʊm |laʊt **~lauted** laʊt ɪd -əd ‖ laʊţ əd **~lauting** laʊt ɪŋ ‖ laʊţ ɪŋ **~lauts** laʊts
umma, ummah ˈʊm ə —*Arabic* [ˈʔum mah]
ump ʌmp **umps** ʌmps
umpire ˈʌmp aɪ‿ə ‖ -aɪ‿ᵊr **~d** d **~s** z **umpiring** ˈʌmp aɪ‿ər ɪŋ ‖ ˈʌmp aɪ‿ər ɪŋ
umpteen ˌʌmp ˈtiːn ◂
umpteenth ˌʌmp ˈtiːnᵗθ ◂
'un *nonstandard weak form of* **one** ən, ᵊn — **a big 'un** ə ˈbɪg ən
un- ʌn, ˌʌn —*This prefix may lexically be stressed or unstressed. It is unstressed particularly where it is not a true prefix* (unˈwieldy); *it is stressed particularly (a) where the initial syllable of the stem does not bear the primary stress* (ˌunaˈshamed), *and (b) in verbs* (ˌunˈcoil). *In some words usage is divided or uncertain* (₍ˌ₎unˈbearable).
UN ˌjuː ˈen ◂
ˌUN ˈtroops
Una ˈjuːn ə
unabashed ˌʌn ə ˈbæʃt ◂
unabated ˌʌn ə ˈbeɪt ɪd ◂ -əd ‖ -ˈbeɪţ əd ◂
unable ʌn ˈeɪb ᵊl ˌ·ˈ··
unabridged ˌʌn ə ˈbrɪdʒd ◂
unaccented ˌʌn ək ˈsent ɪd ◂ -æk-, -əd ‖ ˌʌn æk ˈsenţ əd ◂
unacceptability ˌʌn ək ˌsept ə ˈbɪl ət i ˌ·æk-, ˌ·ɪk-, -ɪt i ‖ -əţ i
unacceptab|le ˌʌn ək ˈsept əb |ᵊl ◂ ˌ·ɪk- **~ly** li
unaccompanied ˌʌn ə ˈkʌmp ən‿id ◂
ˌunacˌcompanied ˈchildren
unaccountab|le ˌʌn ə ˈkaʊnt əb |ᵊl ◂ ‖ -ˈkaʊnţ- **~ly** li
unaccounted-for ˌʌn ə ˈkaʊnt ɪd fɔː ◂ -əd· ‖ -ˈkaʊnţ əd fɔːr ◂
unaccusative ˌʌn ə ˈkjuːz ət ɪv ◂ ‖ -əţ ɪv **~s** z
unaccusativity ˌʌn ə ˌkjuːz ə ˈtɪv ət i -ɪt i ‖ -əţ i
unaccustomed ˌʌn ə ˈkʌst əmd ◂
ˌunacˌcustomed ˈduty
unacknowledged ˌʌn ək ˈnɒl ɪdʒd ◂ -æk-, -ɪk- ‖ -ˈnɑːl-
unadopted ˌʌn ə ˈdɒpt ɪd ◂ -əd ‖ -ˈdɑːpt-
unadorned ˌʌn ə ˈdɔːnd ◂ ‖ -ˈdɔːrnd ◂
unadulterated ˌʌn ə ˈdʌlt ə reɪt ɪd ◂ -əd ‖ -reɪţ əd
unadvised ˌʌn əd ˈvaɪzd ◂ §-æd-
unaffected ˌʌn ə ˈfekt ɪd ◂ -əd
unafraid ˌʌn ə ˈfreɪd ◂
unaided ₍ˌ₎ʌn ˈeɪd ɪd -əd
unalienable ₍ˌ₎ʌn ˈeɪl i‿ən əb ᵊl
unaligned ˌʌn ə ˈlaɪnd ◂
unalloyed ˌʌn ə ˈlɔɪd ◂
unalterab|le ʌn ˈɔːlt‿ər əb| ᵊl ˌʌn-, -ˈɒlt‿ ‖ -ˈɑːlt‿ **~ly** li
unambiguous ˌʌn æm ˈbɪg ju‿əs ◂
un-American ˌʌn ə ˈmer ɪk ən ◂ -ək ən
unanalysable, unanalyzable ʌn ˈæn ə laɪz əb ᵊl →-ˈæn ᵊl aɪz-; ˌ·ˌ··ˈ···
unanimity ˌjuːn ə ˈnɪm ət i ˌ·æ-, -ɪt ‖ -əţ i
unanimous ju ˈnæn ɪm əs -əm əs **~ly** li **~ness** nəs nɪs
unannounced ˌʌn ə ˈnaʊnᵗst ◂
unanswerable ₍ˌ₎ʌn ˈɑːnᵗs ər‿əb ᵊl §-ˈænᵗs- ‖ -ˈænᵗs-
unanswered ˌʌn ˈɑːnᵗs əd ◂ §-ˈænᵗs- ‖ -ˈænᵗs ᵊrd ◂
ˌunanswered ˈquestions
unapologetic ˌʌn ə ˌpɒl ə ˈdʒet ɪk ◂ ‖ -ˌpɑːl ə ˈdʒeţ ɪk ◂
unappealing ˌʌn ə ˈpiːᵊl ɪŋ
unappetizing, unappetising ₍ˌ₎ʌn ˈæp ɪ taɪz ɪŋ -ə taɪz-
unapproachable ˌʌn ə ˈprəʊtʃ əb ᵊl ◂ ‖ -ˈproʊtʃ-
unappropriated ˌʌn ə ˈprəʊp ri eɪt ɪd ◂ -əd ‖ -ˈproʊp ri eɪţ əd ◂
unarguab|le ʌn ˈɑːg ju‿əb |ᵊl ‖ -ˈɑːrg- **~ly** li
unarmed ˌʌn ˈɑːmd ◂ ‖ -ˈɑːrmd ◂
ˌunarmed ˈcombat
unary ˈjuːn ər i
unashamed ˌʌn ə ˈʃeɪmd ◂
unashamed|ly ˌʌn ə ˈʃeɪm ɪd |li -ˈəd-; -ˈʃeɪmd |li **~ness** nəs nɪs
unasked ˌʌn ˈɑːskt ◂ §-ˈæskt ‖ -ˈæskt ◂
unaspirated ₍ˌ₎ ʌn ˈæsp ə reɪt ɪd ◂ -ˈ·ɪ-, -əd ‖ -reɪţ əd
unassailable ˌʌn ə ˈseɪl əb ᵊl ◂
unassisted ˌʌn ə ˈsɪst ɪd ◂ -əd
unassuming ˌʌn ə ˈsjuːm ɪŋ ◂ -ˈsuːm-, §-ˈʃuːm- ‖ -ˈsuːm- **~ly** li **~ness** nəs nɪs
unattached ˌʌn ə ˈtætʃt ◂

U

unattainable ˌʌn ə ˈteɪn əb ᵊl
unattended ˌʌn ə ˈtend ɪd ◂ -əd
unattractive ˌʌn ə ˈtrækt ɪv ◂ **~ly** li
unauthorized, unauthorised ʌn ˈɔːθ ə raɪzd ‖ -ˈɑːθ-
unavailable ˌʌn ə ˈveɪl əb ᵊl ◂
unavailing ˌʌn ə ˈveɪl ɪŋ ◂
unavoidab|le ˌʌn ə ˈvɔɪd əb |ᵊl ◂ **~leness** ᵊl nəs -nɪs **~ly** li
unaware ˌʌn ə ˈweə ‖ -ˈweᵊr -ˈwæᵊr **~s** z
unbalanc|e ˌʌn ˈbæl ənᵗs →ˌʌm- **~ed** t **~es** ɪz əz **~ing** ɪŋ
unbar ˌʌn ˈbɑː ◂ →ˌʌm- ‖ -ˈbɑːr ◂ **~red** d
unbarring ˌʌn ˈbɑːr ɪŋ →ˌʌm- **~s** z
unbearab|le (ı)ʌn ˈbeər əb |ᵊl →(ı)ʌm- ‖ -ˈber- -ˈbær- **~leness** ᵊl nəs -nɪs **~ly** li
unbeatab|le (ı)ʌn ˈbiːt əb |ᵊl →(ı)ʌm- ‖ -ˈbiːt̬- **~ly** li
unbeaten (ı)ʌn ˈbiːt ᵊn
unbecoming ˌʌn bi ˈkʌm ɪŋ ◂ →ˌʌm-, -bə- **~ly** li **~ness** nəs nɪs
unbeknown ˌʌn bi ˈnəʊn ◂ →ˌʌm-, -bə- ‖ -ˈnoʊn ◂
unbeknownst ˌʌn bi ˈnəʊnᵗst →ˌʌm-, -bə- ‖ -ˈnoʊnᵗst
unbelief ˌʌn bi ˈliːf →ˌʌm-, -bə-
unbelievab|le ˌʌn bi ˈliːv əb |ᵊl ◂ →ˌʌm-, ˌbə- **~leness** ᵊl nəs -nɪs **~ly** li
unbeliever ˌʌn bi ˈliːv ə →ˌʌm-, -bə- ‖ -ᵊr **~s** z
unbelieving ˌʌn bi ˈliːv ɪŋ ◂ →ˌʌm-, -bə- **~ly** li
unbend ˌʌn ˈbend →ˌʌm- **~ing** ɪŋ **~s** z **unbent** ˌʌn ˈbent ◂ →ˌʌm-
unbending *adj 'inflexible'* ʌn ˈbend ɪŋ →ʌm- **~ly** li **~ness** nəs nɪs
unbent ˌʌn ˈbent ◂ →ˌʌm-
unbiased, unbiassed (ı)ʌn ˈbaɪ‿əst →(ı)ʌm- **~ly** li **~ness** nəs nɪs
unbidden ˌʌn ˈbɪd ᵊn →ˌʌm-
unbind ˌʌn ˈbaɪnd →ˌʌm- **~ing** ɪŋ **unbound** ˌʌn ˈbaʊnd ◂
unblemished ʌn ˈblem ɪʃt →ʌm, ˌ-
unblinking ˌʌn ˈblɪŋk ɪŋ →ˌʌm- **~ly** li
unblock ˌʌn ˈblɒk ◂ →ˌʌm- ‖ -ˈblɑːk ◂ **~ed** t **~ing** ɪŋ **~s** s
unblushing ˌʌn ˈblʌʃ ɪŋ ◂ →ˌʌm- **~ly** li
unbolt ˌʌn ˈbəʊlt ◂ →ˌʌm-, →-ˈbɒʊlt ‖ -ˈboʊlt ◂ **~ed** ɪd əd **~ing** ɪŋ **~s** s
unborn ˌʌn ˈbɔːn ◂ →ˌʌm- ‖ -ˈbɔːrn ◂
unbosom ˌʌn ˈbʊz əm →ˌʌm-, §-ˈbuːz- **~ed** d **~ing** ɪŋ **~s** z
unbound ˌʌn ˈbaʊnd ◂ →ˌʌm-
unbounded (ı)ʌn ˈbaʊnd ɪd -əd **~ly** li **~ness** nəs nɪs
unbowed ˌʌn ˈbaʊd ◂ →ˌʌm-
unbreakable ʌn ˈbreɪk əb ᵊl →ʌm-
unbridgeable ʌn ˈbrɪdʒ əb ᵊl →ʌm-
unbridled (ı)ʌn ˈbraɪd ᵊld →(ı)ʌm-
unbroken (ı)ʌn ˈbrəʊk ən →(ı)ʌm- ‖ -ˈbroʊk- **~ly** li **~ness** nəs nɪs
unbuckl|e ˌʌn ˈbʌk ᵊl →ˌʌm- **~ed** d **~es** z **~ing** ‿ɪŋ
unburden ˌʌn ˈbɜːd ᵊn →ˌʌm- ‖ -ˈbɜʳːd- **~ed** d **~ing** ‿ɪŋ **~s** z
unbutton ˌʌn ˈbʌt ᵊn ◂ →ˌʌm- **~ed** d **~ing** ‿ɪŋ **~s** z
uncalled-for (ı)ʌn ˈkɔːld fɔː →(ı)ʌŋ- ‖ -fɔːr -ˈkɑːld-
uncann|y ʌn ˈkæn |i →ʌŋ- **~ily** ɪ li əl i **~iness** i nəs i nɪs
uncap ˌʌn ˈkæp →ˌʌŋ- **~ped** t ◂ **~ping** ɪŋ **~s** s
uncared-for (ı)ʌn ˈkeəd fɔː →(ı)ʌŋ- ‖ -ˈkerd fɔːr -ˈkærd-
unceasing ʌn ˈsiːs ɪŋ ˌ- **~ly** li **~ness** nəs nɪs
unceremonious ˌʌn ˌser ɪ ˈməʊn i‿əs -ˌ-ə- ‖ -ˈmoʊn- **~ly** li **~ness** nəs nɪs
uncertain ʌn ˈsɜːt ᵊn ˌ--, -ɪn ‖ -ˈsɜʳːt ᵊn **~ly** li
uncertain|ty ʌn ˈsɜːt ᵊn |ti -ɪn- ‖ -ˈsɜʳːt- **~ties** tiz
unˈcertainty ˌprinciple
unchain ˌʌn ˈtʃeɪn **~ed** d **~ing** ɪŋ **~s** z
unchalleng|ed ʌn ˈtʃæl ɪndʒd **~ing** ɪŋ
unchang|ed ʌn ˈtʃeɪndʒd ◂ **~ing** ɪŋ
uncharacteristic ʌn ˌkær ɪkt ə ˈrɪst ɪk ◂ →ʌŋ-, -əkt ə- ‖ -ˌker- **~ally** ᵊl‿i
uncharitab|le (ı)ʌn ˈtʃær ɪt əb |ᵊl -ˈ-ət- ‖ -ˈtʃær ət̬- -ˈtʃer- **~leness** ᵊl nəs -nɪs **~ly** li
uncharted ˌʌn ˈtʃɑːt ɪd ◂ -əd ‖ -ˈtʃɑːrt̬ əd ◂
unchecked ˌʌn ˈtʃekt ◂
unchristian (ı)ʌn ˈkrɪs tʃən →(ı)ʌŋ-, -ˈkrɪst i‿ən **~ly** li
unci ˈʌnᵗs aɪ
uncial ˈʌnᵗs i‿əl ˈʌnᵗʃ-; ˈʌnᵗʃ ᵊl ‖ ˈʌnᵗʃ ᵊl -i‿əl **~s** z
unciform ˈʌnᵗs ɪ fɔːm -ə- ‖ -fɔːrm
uncinate ˈʌnᵗs ɪn ət -ən-, -ɪt; -ɪ neɪt, -ə-
uncircumcised ˌʌn ˈsɜːk əm saɪzd ◂ ‖ -ˈsɜʳːk-
uncircumcision ˌʌn ˌsɜːk əm ˈsɪʒ ᵊn ‖ -ˌsɜʳːk-
uncivilised, uncivilized (ı)ʌn ˈsɪv ə laɪzd -ɪ-, -ᵊl aɪzd
unclad ˌʌn ˈklæd ◂ →ˌʌŋ-
unclaimed ˌʌn ˈkleɪmd ◂ →ˌʌŋ-
ˌunclaimed ˈbaggage
unclasp ˌʌn ˈklɑːsp →ˌʌŋ-, §-ˈklæsp ‖ -ˈklæsp **~ed** t **~ing** ɪŋ **~s** s
unclassified ˌʌn ˈklæs ɪ faɪd ◂ →ˌʌŋ-, -ə-
uncle ˈʌŋk ᵊl **~s** z
ˌUncle ˈSam; ˌUncle ˈTom
unclean ˌʌn ˈkliːn ◂ →ˌʌŋ- **~er** ə ‖ ᵊr **~est** ɪst əst **~ly** li **~ness** nəs nɪs
unclean|ly *adj* ˌʌn ˈklen |li →ˌʌŋ- **~liness** li nəs -nɪs
unclear ˌʌn ˈklɪə ◂ →ˌʌŋ- ‖ -ˈklɪᵊr ◂ **~ly** li
unclench ˌʌn ˈklentʃ ◂ →ˌʌŋ- **~ed** t **~es** ɪz əz **~ing** ɪŋ
unclog ˌʌn ˈklɒg ◂ →ˌʌŋ- ‖ -ˈklɑːg ◂ **~ged** d **~ging** ɪŋ **~s** z
unclothed ʌn ˈkləʊðd →ʌŋ- ‖ -ˈkloʊðd
unclouded (ı)ʌn ˈklaʊd ɪd ◂ →(ı)ʌŋ-, -əd
uncluttered ˌʌn ˈklʌt əd ◂ →ˌʌŋ- ‖ -ˈklʌt̬ ᵊrd ◂
unco ˈʌŋk ə -əʊ ‖ -oʊ
uncoil ˌʌn ˈkɔɪᵊl ◂ →ˌʌŋ- **~ed** d **~ing** ɪŋ **~s** z
uncolored, uncoloured ˌʌn ˈkʌl əd ◂ →ˌʌŋ- ‖ -ᵊrd ◂
uncomfortab|le ʌn ˈkʌmᵖft əb |ᵊl →ʌŋ-, -ˈkʌmᵖf ət əb |ᵊl ‖ -ᵊrb |ᵊl; -ˈkʌmᵖf ət̬ əb |ᵊl, -ˈ-ᵊrt̬- **~leness** ᵊl nəs-nɪs **~ly** li

uncommitted ˌʌn kə ˈmɪt ɪd ◂ →ˌʌŋ-, -əd ‖ -mɪţ əd ◂
uncommon ʌn ˈkɒm ən →ʌŋ-, ˌ·- ‖ -ˈkɑːm- **~ly** li **~ness** nəs nɪs
uncommunicative ˌʌn kə ˈmjuːn ɪk ət ɪv ◂ →ˌʌŋ-, §-ˈ·ək-, -eɪt ɪv ‖ -ə keɪţ ɪv -ək əţ- **~ly** li **~ness** nəs nɪs
uncompetitive ˌʌn kəm ˈpet ət ɪv ◂ →ˌʌŋ-, §ˌ·kɒm-, -ˈ·ɪt- ‖ -ˈpeţ əţ- **~ness** nəs nɪs
uncomplaining ˌʌn kəm ˈpleɪn ɪŋ ◂ →ˌʌŋ-, §-kɒm- **~ly** li
uncomplicated ₍ˌ₎ʌn ˈkɒmp lɪ keɪt ɪd →₍ˌ₎ʌŋ-, -lə·-, -əd ‖ ʌn ˈkɑːmp lə keɪţ əd
uncomprehending ˌʌn ˌkɒmp ri ˈhend ɪŋ ◂ →ˌʌŋ-, -rə-
uncompromising ʌn ˈkɒmp rə maɪz ɪŋ →ʌŋ- ‖ -ˈkɑːmp- **~ly** li **~ness** nəs nɪs
unconcern ˌʌn kən ˈsɜːn →ˌʌŋ-, §-kɒn- ‖ -ˈsɜ˞ːn **~ed** d
unconcerned|ly ˌʌn kən ˈsɜːn ɪd |li -ˈ·əd-; -ˈsɜːnd |li ‖ -ˈsɜ˞ːn- **~ness** nəs nɪs
unconditional ˌʌn kən ˈdɪʃ ən‿əl ◂→ˌʌŋ-, §ˌ·kɒn- **~ly** i
unconfirmed ˌʌn kən ˈfɜːmd ◂ →ˌʌŋ-, §-kɒn- ‖ -ˈfɜ˞ːmd ◂
ˌunconfirmed reˈports
unconnected ˌʌn kə ˈnekt ɪd →ˌʌŋ-, -əd **~ly** li **~ness** nəs nɪs
unconquerab|le ʌn ˈkɒŋk ər‿əb| əl →ʌŋ- ‖ -ˈkɑːŋk- **~ly** li
unconscionab|le ʌn ˈkɒnᵗʃ ən‿əb |əl →ʌŋ- ‖ -ˈkɑːnᵗʃ- **~leness** əl nəs -nɪs **~ly** li
unconscious ʌn ˈkɒnᵗʃ əs →ʌŋ-, ˌ·- ‖ -ˈkɑːnᵗʃ- **~ly** li **~ness** nəs nɪs
unconsidered ˌʌn kən ˈsɪd əd ◂ →ˌʌŋ-, §-kɒn- ‖ -ərd ◂
ˌunconˌsidered ˈtrifles
unconstitutional ˌʌn ˌkɒnᵗst ɪ ˈtjuːʃ ən‿əl →ˌʌŋ-, -ˌ·ə-, →-ˈtʃuːʃ- ‖ -ˌkɑːnᵗst ə ˈtuːʃ- -ˈtjuːʃ- **~ly** i
uncontested ˌʌn kən ˈtest ɪd ◂ →ˌʌŋ-, §-kɒn-, -əd
uncontrollab|le ˌʌn kən ˈtrəʊl əb| əl ◂ →ˌʌŋ-, §ˌ·kɒn-, →-ˈtrɒʊl- ‖ -ˈtroʊl- **~ly** li
uncontrolled ˌʌn kən ˈtrəʊld ◂ →ˌʌŋ-, §-kɒn-, ˈtrɒʊld ◂ ‖ -ˈtroʊld ◂
ˌuncontrolled inˈflation
unconventional ˌʌn kən ˈvenᵗʃ ən‿əl ◂ →ˌʌŋ-, §ˌ·kɒn- **~ly** i
unconvinced ˌʌn kən ˈvɪnᵗst →ˌʌŋ-
unconvincing ˌʌn kən ˈvɪnᵗs ɪŋ →ˌʌŋ- **~ly** li
uncooked ˌʌn ˈkʊkt ◂ →ˌʌŋ-, § ˈkuːkt
ˌuncooked ˈfood
uncool ˌʌn ˈkuːl ◂ →ˌʌŋ-
uncooperative ˌʌn kəʊ ˈɒp ər‿ət ɪv ◂ →ˌʌŋ-, -ˈɒp ə reɪt ɪv ◂ ‖ ˌʌn koʊ ˈɑːp ər‿əţ ɪv ◂ -ə reɪţ ɪv ◂
uncoordinated ˌʌn kəʊ ˈɔːd ɪ neɪt ɪd ◂ →ˌʌŋ-, -ən eɪt-, -əd ‖ ˌʌn koʊ ˈɔːrd ən eɪţ əd ◂
uncork ˌʌn ˈkɔːk ◂ →ˌʌŋ- ‖ -ˈkɔːrk ◂ **~ed** t **~ing** ɪŋ **~s** s
uncorroborated ˌʌn kə ˈrɒb ə reɪt ɪd ◂ →ˌʌŋ-, -əd ◂ ‖ -ˈrɑːb ə reɪţ əd ◂
uncount ˈʌn kaʊnt →ˈʌŋ-
uncountable ˌʌn ˈkaʊnt əb əl ◂ →ˌʌŋ- ‖ -ˈkaʊnţ-
uncounted ₍ˌ₎ʌn ˈkaʊnt ɪd →₍ˌ₎ʌŋ-, -əd ‖ -ˈkaʊnţ əd
uncoupl|e ˌʌn ˈkʌp əl →ˌʌŋ- **~ed** d **~es** z **~ing** ɪŋ
uncouth ʌn ˈkuːθ →ʌŋ-, ˌ·- **~ly** li **~ness** nəs nɪs
uncover ʌn ˈkʌv ə →ʌŋ-, ˌ·- ‖ -ər **~ed** d
uncovering ʌn ˈkʌv ər‿ɪŋ →ʌŋ-, ˌ·- **~s** z
uncritical ₍ˌ₎ʌn ˈkrɪt ɪk əl →₍ˌ₎ʌŋ- ‖ -ˈkrɪţ- **~ly** i
uncrowned ˌʌn ˈkraʊnd ◂ →ˌʌŋ-
ˌuncrowned ˈking
uncrushable ₍ˌ₎ʌn ˈkrʌʃ əb əl
unction ˈʌŋk ʃən
unctuous ˈʌŋk tʃu‿əs -tju‿əs **~ly** li **~ness** nəs nɪs
uncurl ˌʌn ˈkɜːl ◂ →ˌʌŋ- ‖ -ˈkɜ˞ːl ◂ **~ed** d **~ing** ɪŋ **~s** z
uncus ˈʌŋk əs **unci** ˈʌnᵗs aɪ
uncut ˌʌn ˈkʌt ◂ →ˌʌŋ-
undamaged ₍ˌ₎ʌn ˈdæm ɪdʒd
undamped ˌʌn ˈdæmpt ◂
undated ˌʌn ˈdeɪt ɪd ◂ -əd ‖ -ˈdeɪţ-
undaunted ₍ˌ₎ʌn ˈdɔːnt ɪd -əd ‖ -ˈdɔːnţ əd -ˈdɑːnţ- **~ly** li **~ness** nəs nɪs
undecagon ʌn ˈdek əg ən -ə gɒn ‖ -ə gɑːn **~s** z
undeceiv|e ˌʌn di ˈsiːv -də- **~ed** d **~es** z **~ing** ɪŋ
undecided ˌʌn di ˈsaɪd ɪd ◂ -də-, -əd **~ly** li **~ness** nəs nɪs
undeclared ˌʌn di ˈkleəd ◂ -də- ‖ -ˈkleərd ◂ -ˈklæərd
undefined ˌʌn di ˈfaɪnd ◂ -də-
undemocratic ˌʌn ˌdem ə ˈkræt ɪk ◂ ‖ -ˈkræţ- **~ally** əl‿i
undemonstrative ˌʌn di ˈmɒnᵗs trət ɪv ◂ ˌ·də- ‖ -ˈmɑːnᵗs trəţ- **~ly** li **~ness** nəs nɪs
undeniab|le ˌʌn dɪ ˈnaɪ‿əb |əl ◂ ˌ·də- **~ly** li
undenominational ˌʌn di ˌnɒm ɪ ˈneɪʃ ən‿əl ˌ·də-, -ˌ·ə- ‖ -ˌnɑːm- **~ly** i
under ˈʌnd ə ‖ -ər
under- ¦ʌnd ə ‖ -ər —*but before a vowel sound* ¦ʌnd ər ‖ -ər
underachiev|e ˌʌnd ər ə ˈtʃiːv ‖ ˌ·ər- **~ed** d **~er/s** ə/z ‖ ər/z **~es** z **~ing** ɪŋ
underact ˌʌnd ər ˈækt ‖ -ər- **~ed** ɪd əd **~ing** ɪŋ **~s** s
underage ˌʌnd ər ˈeɪdʒ ‖ -ər-
ˌunderage ˈdrinking
underarm ˈʌnd ər ɑːm ‖ -ər ɑːrm
underbell|y ˈʌnd ə ˌbel |i ‖ -ər- **~ies** iz
underbid ˌʌnd ə ˈbɪd ‖ -ər- **~ding** ɪŋ **~s** z
underbrush ˈʌnd ə brʌʃ ‖ -ər-
undercapitalis|e, undercapitaliz|e ˌʌnd ə ˈkæp ɪt ə laɪz §-ˈ·ət-, -əl aɪz ‖ -ər ˈkæp əţ- **~ed** d **~es** ɪz əz **~ing** ɪŋ
undercarriag|e ˈʌnd ə ˌkær ɪdʒ ‖ -ər- -ˌker- **~es** ɪz əz
undercart ˈʌnd ə kɑːt ‖ ər kɑːrt **~s** s

undercharg|e *n* ˈʌnd ə tʃɑːdʒ ˌ· ·ˈ· ‖ -ᵊr tʃɑːrdʒ **~es** ɪz əz
undercharg|e *v* ˌʌnd ə ˈtʃɑːdʒ ‖ -ᵊr ˈtʃɑːrdʒ **~ed** d **~es** ɪz əz **~ing** ɪŋ
underclass ˈʌnd ə klɑːs §-klæs ‖ -ᵊr klæs **~es** ɪz əz
underclass|man ˌʌnd ə ˈklɑːs mən §-ˈklæs- ‖ -ᵊr ˈklæs- **~men** mən
underclothes ˈʌnd ə kləʊðz -kləʊz ‖ -ᵊr kloʊz -kloʊðz
underclothing ˈʌnd ə ˌkləʊð ɪŋ ‖ -ᵊr ˌkloʊð-
undercoat ˈʌnd ə kəʊt ‖ -ᵊr koʊt **~s** s
undercook ˌʌnd ə ˈkʊk §-ˈkuːk ‖ -ᵊr- **~ed** t ◂ **~ing** ɪŋ **~s** s
under|count *v* ˌʌnd ə |ˈkaʊnt ‖ -ᵊr- **~counted** ˈkaʊnt ɪd -əd ‖ ˈkaʊnţ əd **~counting** ˈkaʊnt ɪŋ ‖ ˈkaʊnţ ɪŋ **~counts** ˈkaʊnts
undercount *n* ˈʌnd ə kaʊnt ‖ -ᵊr- **~s** s
undercover ˌʌnd ə ˈkʌv ə ◂ ˈ· ·ˌ· · ‖ -ᵊr ˈkʌv ᵊr ◂
undercroft ˈʌnd ə krɒft ‖ -ᵊr krɔːft -krɑːft **~s** s
undercurrent ˈʌnd ə ˌkʌr ənt ‖ -ᵊr ˌkɜː- **~s** s
under|cut *v* ˌʌnd ə |ˈkʌt ‖ -ᵊr- **~cuts** ˈkʌts **~cutting** ˈkʌt ɪŋ ‖ ˈkʌţ ɪŋ
undercut *n* ˈʌnd ə kʌt ‖ -ᵊr- **~s** s
underdevelop ˌʌnd ə dɪ ˈvel əp -dəˈ-, §-diːˈ- ‖ ˌ·ᵊr- **~ed** t **~ing** ɪŋ **~ment** mənt **~s** s
ˌunderdeˌveloped ˈcountries
underdog ˈʌnd ə dɒg ‖ -ᵊr dɔːg -dɑːg **~s** z
underdone ˌʌnd ə ˈdʌn ◂ ‖ -ᵊr-
ˌunderdone ˈmeat
underdressed ˌʌnd ə ˈdrest ‖ -ᵊr-
underemployed ˌʌnd ər ɪm ˈplɔɪd ◂ -əmˈ- ‖ ˌ·ər-
underemployment ˌʌnd ər ɪm ˈplɔɪ mənt -əmˈ·- ‖ ˌ·ər-
underestimate *n* ˌʌnd ər ˈest ɪm ət -əm ət, -ɪt; -ɪ meɪt, -ə meɪt ‖ ˌ·ər- **~s** s
underesti|mate *v* ˌʌnd ər ˈest ɪ |meɪt -ə· ‖ ˌ·ər- **~mated** meɪt ɪd -əd ‖ meɪţ əd **~mates** meɪts **~mating** meɪt ɪŋ ‖ meɪţ ɪŋ
underexpos|e ˌʌnd ər ɪk ˈspəʊz -əkˈ·, -ekˈ· ‖ -ər ɪk ˈspoʊz **~ed** d **~es** ɪz əz **~ing** ɪŋ
underexposure ˌʌnd ər ɪk ˈspəʊʒ ə -əkˈ·-, -ekˈ·- ‖ -ər ɪk ˈspoʊʒ ᵊr **~s** z
under|feed ˌʌnd ə |ˈfiːd ‖ -ᵊr- **~fed** ˈfed ◂ **~feeding** ˈfiːd ɪŋ **~feeds** ˈfiːdz
underfelt ˈʌnd ə felt ‖ -ᵊr- **~s** s
underfloor ˌʌnd ə ˈflɔː ◂ ‖ -ᵊr ˈflɔːr ◂ -ˈfloʊr
ˌunderfloor ˈheating
underfoot ˌʌnd ə ˈfʊt ‖ -ᵊr-
underfund ˌʌnd ə ˈfʌnd ‖ -ᵊr- **~ed** ɪd əd **~ing** ɪŋ **~s** z
undergarment ˈʌnd ə ˌgɑːm ənt ‖ -ᵊr ˌgɑːrm- **~s** s
under|go ˌʌnd ə |ˈgəʊ ‖ -ᵊr |ˈgoʊ **~goes** ˈgəʊz ‖ ˈgoʊz **~gone** ˈgɒn §ˈgɑːn ‖ ˈgɔːn ˈgɑːn **~went** ˈwent
undergrad ˈʌnd ə græd ˌ· ·ˈ· ‖ -ᵊr- **~s** z
undergraduate ˌʌnd ə ˈgrædʒ u‿ət ◂ -ˈgræd ju‿ət, ɪt, -eɪt ‖ ˌ·ᵊr- **~s** s
underground *n,* **U~** ˈʌnd ə graʊnd ‖ -ᵊr- **~s** z
underground *adj, adv* ˌʌnd ə ˈgraʊnd ◂ ˈ· · · ‖ -ᵊr-
ˌunderground ˈpassages
undergrowth ˈʌnd ə grəʊθ ‖ -ᵊr groʊθ
underhand ˌʌnd ə ˈhænd ◂ ˈ· · · ‖ -ᵊr-
underhanded ˌʌnd ə ˈhænd ɪd ◂ -əd ‖ -ᵊr- **~ly** li **~ness** nəs nɪs
Underhill ˈʌnd ə hɪl ‖ -ᵊr-
underhung ˌʌnd ə ˈhʌŋ ◂ ‖ -ᵊr-
underinsure ˌʌnd ər ɪn ˈʃʊə -ˈʃɔː ‖ -ər ɪn ˈʃʊᵊr -ˈʃɜː **~d** d
underlaid ˌʌnd ə ˈleɪd ‖ -ᵊr-
underlain ˌʌnd ə ˈleɪn ‖ -ᵊr-
underlay *n* ˈʌnd ə leɪ ‖ -ᵊr- **~s** z
under|lie ˌʌnd ə |ˈlaɪ ‖ -ᵊr- **~lay** ˈleɪ **~lies** ˈlaɪz **~lying/ly** ˈlaɪ ɪŋ /li
ˌunderˌlying ˈform
underline *n* ˈʌnd ə laɪn ˌ· ·ˈ· ‖ -ᵊr- **~s** z
underlin|e *v* ˌʌnd ə ˈlaɪn ˈ· · · ‖ -ᵊr- **~ed** d **~es** z **~ing** ɪŋ
underling ˈʌnd ə lɪŋ ‖ -ᵊr- **~s** z
underlying ˌʌnd ə ˈlaɪ ɪŋ ◂ ‖ ˌ·ᵊr- **~ly** li
undermanned ˌʌnd ə ˈmænd ◂ ‖ -ᵊr-
undermentioned ˌʌnd ə ˈmenᵗʃ ᵊnd ◂ ‖ -ᵊr-
undermin|e ˌʌnd ə ˈmaɪn ‖ -ᵊr- **~ed** d **~es** z **~ing** ɪŋ
underneath ˌʌnd ə ˈniːθ ◂ ‖ -ᵊr-
undernourish ˌʌnd ə ˈnʌr ɪʃ ‖ -ᵊr ˈnɜː- **~ed** t **~es** ɪz əz **~ing** ɪŋ
underpaid ˌʌnd ə ˈpeɪd ◂ ‖ -ᵊr-
underpants ˈʌnd ə pænts ‖ -ᵊr-
underpass ˈʌnd ə pɑːs §-pæs ‖ -ᵊr pæs **~es** ɪz əz
under|pay ˌʌnd ə |ˈpeɪ ‖ -ᵊr- **~paid** ˈpeɪd **~paying** ˈpeɪ ɪŋ **~payment/s** ˈpeɪ mənt/s **~pays** ˈpeɪz
underperform ˌʌnd ə pə ˈfɔːm ‖ -ᵊr pᵊr ˈfɔːrm ◂ **~ed** d **~ing** ɪŋ **~s** z
underpin ˌʌnd ə ˈpɪn ‖ -ᵊr- **~ned** d **~ning** ɪŋ **~s** z
underpinning *n* ˌʌnd ə ˈpɪn ɪŋ ˈ· ·ˌ· · ‖ -ᵊr- **~s** z
underplay *v* ˌʌnd ə ˈpleɪ ‖ -ᵊr- **~ed** d **~ing** ɪŋ **~s** z
underpowered ˌʌnd ə ˈpaʊ‿əd ◂ ‖ -r ˈpaʊ‿ᵊrd ◂
underpric|e *v* ˌʌnd ə ˈpraɪs ‖ -ᵊr- **~ed** t **~es** ɪz əz **~ing** ɪŋ
underprivileged ˌʌnd ə ˈprɪv əl ɪdʒd ◂ -ɪl ɪdʒd ‖ ˌ·ᵊr-
underproof ˌʌnd ə ˈpruːf ‖ -ᵊr-
under|quote ˌʌnd ə |ˈkwəʊt ‖ -ᵊr |ˈkwoʊt **~quoted** ˈkwəʊt ɪd -əd ‖ ˈkwoʊţ əd **~quotes** ˈkwəʊts ‖ ˈkwoʊts **~quoting** ˈkwəʊt ɪŋ ‖ ˈkwoʊţ ɪŋ
under|rate ˌʌnd ə |ˈreɪt ‖ -ᵊr- **~rated** ˈreɪt ɪd -əd ‖ ˈreɪţ əd **~rates** ˈreɪts **~rating** ˈreɪt ɪŋ ‖ ˈreɪţ ɪŋ
underrepresented ˌʌnd ə ˌrep ri ˈzent ɪd ◂ -rə ˈzent-, -əd ‖ ˌʌnd ᵊr rep rə ˈzenţ əd ◂
underresourced ˌʌnd ə ri ˈzɔːst ◂ -ə rə- ‖ ˌʌnd ᵊr rə ˈzɔːrst ◂
under|run ˌʌnd ə |ˈrʌn ‖ -ᵊr- **~ran** ˈræn **~running** ˈrʌn ɪŋ **~runs** ˈrʌnz

underscore *v* ˌʌnd ə ˈskɔː ˈ· · · ‖ ˈʌnd ᵊr skɔːr -skoʊr **~d** d **~s** z **underscoring** ˌʌnd ə ˈskɔːr ɪŋ ˈ· · · · ‖ ˈʌnd ᵊr skɔːr ɪŋ -skoʊr ɪŋ
underscore *n* ˈʌnd ə skɔː ‖ -ᵊr skɔːr -skoʊr **~s** z
undersea ˌʌnd ə ˈsiː ◂ ˈ· · · ‖ -ᵊr-
underseal *n, v* ˈʌnd ə siːᵊl ‖ -ᵊr- **~ed** d **~ing** ɪŋ **~s** z
undersecretar|y ˌʌnd ə ˈsek rət‿ər |i -ˈ·rɪt‿, ⚠-ˈ·jʊt‿, ⚠-ˈ·ət‿; -ˈsek rə ter |i, ˈ·rɪ-, ⚠-ˈ·ju-, ⚠-ˈ·ə- ‖ ˌʌnd ᵊr ˈsek rə ter |i **~ies** iz
under|sell ˌʌnd ə |ˈsel ‖ -ᵊr- **~selling** ˈsel ɪŋ **~sells** ˈselz **~sold** ˈsəʊld →ˈsɒʊld ‖ ˈsoʊld
underserved ˌʌnd ə ˈsɜːvd ◂ ‖ ˌʌnd ᵊr ˈsɜːvd ◂
undersexed ˌʌnd ə ˈsekst ◂ ‖ -ᵊr-
Undershaft ˈʌnd ə ʃɑːft §-ʃæft ‖ -ᵊr ʃæft
undershirt ˈʌnd ə ʃɜːt ‖ -ᵊr ʃɜːt **~s** s
undershoot *n* ˈʌnd ə ʃuːt ‖ -ᵊr-
under|shoot *v* ˌʌnd ə ˈ|ʃuːt ˈ· · · ‖ -ᵊr- **~shooting** ʃuːt ɪŋ ‖ ʃuːt̬ ɪŋ **~shoots** ʃuːts **~shot** ʃɒt ‖ ʃɑːt
undershorts ˈʌnd ə ʃɔːts ‖ -ᵊr ʃɔːrts
underside ˈʌnd ə saɪd ‖ -ᵊr-
undersigned ˌʌnd ə ˈsaɪnd ◂ ˈ· · · ‖ -ᵊr-
undersize ˌʌnd ə ˈsaɪz ◂ ‖ -ᵊr- **~d** d
underslung ˌʌnd ə ˈslʌŋ ◂ ‖ -ᵊr-
undersold ˌʌnd ə ˈsəʊld →-ˈsɒʊld ‖ -ᵊr ˈsoʊld
under|spend ˌʌnd ə |ˈspend ‖ -ᵊr- **~spending** ˈspend ɪŋ **~spends** ˈspendz **~spent** ˈspent
understaffed ˌʌnd ə ˈstɑːft §-ˈstæft ‖ -ᵊr ˈstæft
understand ˌʌnd ə ˈstænd ‖ -ᵊr- **~ing** ɪŋ **~s** z **understood** ˌʌnd ə ˈstʊd ‖ -ᵊr-
understandab|le ˌʌnd ə ˈstænd əb |ᵊl |ˌ·ᵊr- **~ly** li
understanding ˌʌnd ə ˈstænd ɪŋ ‖ -ᵊr- **~ly** li **~s** z
under|state ˌʌnd ə |ˈsteɪt ‖ -ᵊr- **~stated** ˈsteɪt ɪd -əd ‖ ˈsteɪt̬ əd **~states** ˈsteɪts **~stating** ˈsteɪt ɪŋ ‖ ˈsteɪt̬ ɪŋ
understatement ˌʌnd ə ˈsteɪt mənt ˈ· ·‚ · ‖ ᵊr-
understeer *v* ˌʌnd ə ˈstɪə ˈ· · · ‖ -ᵊr ˈstɪᵊr **~ed** d **understeering** ˌʌnd ə ˈstɪər ɪŋ ‖ -ᵊr ˈstɪr ɪŋ **~s** z
understeer *n* ˈʌnd ə stɪə ‖ ᵊr stɪr
understood ˌʌnd ə ˈstʊd ‖ -ᵊr-
understorey, understory ˈʌnd ə ˌstɔːr i ‖ -ᵊr- -ˌstoʊr i
understrapper ˈʌnd ə ˌstræp ə ‖ -ᵊr ˌstræp ᵊr **~s** z
understud|y *v, n* ˈʌnd ə ˌstʌd |i ‖ -ᵊr- **~ied** id **~ies** iz **~ying** i‿ɪŋ
undersubscribed ˌʌnd ə səb ˈskraɪbd ◂ §-ə sʌb- ‖ -ᵊr-
under|take ˌʌnd ə |ˈteɪk ‖ -ᵊr- **~taken** ˈteɪk ən **~takes** ˈteɪks **~taking** ˈteɪk ɪŋ **~took** ˈtʊk §ˈtuːk
undertaker *'funeral director'* ˈʌnd ə teɪk ə ‖ -ᵊr teɪk ᵊr **~s** z
undertaking *n 'task'; 'promise'* ˌʌnd ə ˈteɪk ɪŋ ˈ· · · · ‖ -ᵊr- **~s** z
undertaking *n 'funeral direction'* ˈʌnd ə teɪk ɪŋ ‖ -ᵊr-
under-the-counter ˌʌnd ə ðə ˈkaʊnt ə ◂ ‖ -ᵊr ðə ˈkaʊnt̬ ᵊr ◂
undertone ˈʌnd ə təʊn ‖ -ᵊr toʊn **~s** z
undertook ˌʌnd ə ˈtʊk §-ˈtuːk ‖ -ᵊr-
undertow ˈʌnd ə təʊ ‖ -ᵊr toʊ **~s** z
underused ˌʌnd ə ˈjuːzd ◂ ‖ -ᵊr-
underutilization, underutilisation ˌʌnd ə ˌjuːt ɪl aɪ ˈzeɪʃ ᵊn -ˌ·əl-, -ɪˈ· · ‖ ˌʌnd ᵊr ˌjuːt ᵊl ə-
underutilized, underutilised ˌʌnd ə ˈjuːt ɪ laɪzd ◂ -ᵊl aɪzd ◂ ‖ ˌʌnd ᵊr ˈjuːt ᵊl aɪzd ◂
undervalu|e ˌʌnd ə ˈvæl juː ‖ -ᵊr- **~ed** d **~es** z **~ing** ‿ɪŋ
underwater ˌʌnd ə ˈwɔːt ə ◂ ‖ -ᵊr ˈwɔːt̬ ᵊr ◂ -ˈwɑːt̬-
underway ˌʌnd ə ˈweɪ ‖ -ᵊr-
underwear ˈʌnd ə weə ‖ -ᵊr wer -wær
underweight ˌʌnd ə ˈweɪt ◂ ‖ -ᵊr-
underwent ˌʌnd ə ˈwent ‖ -ᵊr-
underwhelm ˌʌnd ə ˈwelm -ˈhwelm ‖ -ᵊr- **~ed** d **~ing** ɪŋ **~s** z
underwing ˈʌnd ə wɪŋ ‖ -ᵊr- **~s** z
underwire ˈʌnd ə ˌwaɪ‿ə ‖ -ᵊr ˌwaɪ‿ᵊr
Underwood, u~ ˈʌnd ə wʊd ‖ -ᵊr-
underworld, U~ ˈʌnd ə wɜːld ‖ -ᵊr wɜːld **~s** z
under|write ˌʌnd ə |ˈraɪt ˈ· · · ‖ -ᵊr- **~writes** ˈraɪts **~written** ˈrɪt ᵊn **~wrote** ˈrəʊt ‖ ˈroʊt
underwriter ˈʌnd ə raɪt ə ‖ -ᵊr raɪt̬ ᵊr **~s** z
undeserv|ed ˌʌn di ˈzɜːv|d ◂ -də- ‖ -ˈzɜːv|d ◂ **~edly** ɪd li əd li **~ing** ɪŋ
undesirability ˌʌn di ˌzaɪ‿ər ə ˈbɪl ət i ˌ·də-, -ɪt i ‖ -ˌzaɪ‿ər ə ˈbɪl ət̬ i
undesirable ˌʌn di ˈzaɪ‿ər əb ᵊl ◂ ˌ·də- ‖ -ˈzaɪ‿ər- **~s** z
undetect|able ˌʌn di ˈtekt |əb ᵊl ◂ **~ed** ɪd əd
undetermined ˌʌn di ˈtɜːm ɪnd ◂ -də-, -ənd ‖ -ˈtɜːm-
undeterred ˌʌn di ˈtɜːd ◂ -də- ‖ -tɜːd ◂
undeveloped ˌʌn di ˈvel əpt ◂ ˌ·də-
undeviating ˌ(ˌ)ʌn ˈdiːv i eɪt ɪŋ ‖ -eɪt̬ ɪŋ **~ly** li
undid ˌ(ˌ)ʌn ˈdɪd
undies ˈʌnd iz
undifferentiated ˌʌn ˌdɪf ə ˈrentʃ i eɪt ɪd ◂ -əd ‖ -eɪt̬-
undignified ʌn ˈdɪg nɪ faɪd -nə-
undiluted ˌʌn daɪ ˈluːt ɪd ◂ -dɪ-, §-də-, -ˈljuːt-, -əd ‖ -ˈluːt̬ əd ◂
undiminished ˌʌn dɪ ˈmɪn ɪʃt ◂ -də-
Undine, u~ ˈʌnd iːn ʌn ˈdiːn, ʊn- **~s** z
undischarged ˌʌn dɪs ˈtʃɑːdʒd ◂ ‖ -ˈtʃɑːrdʒd ◂ ˌundischarged ˈbankrupt
undisciplined ʌn ˈdɪs əp lɪnd -ɪp-, -lənd
undisclosed ˌʌn dɪs ˈkləʊzd ◂ -dəs- ‖ -ˈkloʊzd ◂ an ˌundisclosed ˈsum
undiscriminating ˌʌn dɪ ˈskrɪm ɪ neɪt ɪŋ ˌ·də-, -ə · · ‖ -neɪt̬ ɪŋ
undisguised ˌʌn dɪs ˈgaɪzd ◂ -dɪz-, -dəs-
undismayed ˌʌn dɪs ˈmeɪd ◂ -dɪz-
undisputed ˌʌn dɪ ˈspjuːt ɪd ◂ -də-, -əd ‖ -ˈspjuːt̬-

U

undistinguished ˌʌn dɪ ˈstɪŋ gwɪʃt ◂ ˌ·də-, -wɪʃt
undisturbed ˌʌn dɪ ˈstɜːbd ◂ -də- ‖ -ˈstɝːbd◂
undivided ˌʌn dɪ ˈvaɪd ɪd ˌ·də-, -əd
un|do ₍ˌ₎ʌn |ˈduː **~did** ˈdɪd **~does** ˈdʌz **~doing** ˈduː‿ɪŋ **~done** ˈdʌn
undocumented ʌn ˈdɒk ju ment ɪd -ˈ·jə-, -əd ‖ ʌn ˈdɑːk jə menṭ əd
undomesticated ˌʌn də ˈmest ɪ keɪt ɪd ◂ -ˈ·ə-, -əd ‖ -keɪṭ əd ◂
undone ₍ˌ₎ʌn ˈdʌn
undoubted ʌn ˈdaʊt ɪd -əd ‖ -ˈdaʊṭ əd **~ly** li
undreamed-of ʌn ˈdriːmd ɒv ˌʌn-, -ˈdrempt-, -əv ‖ -ʌv -ɑːv
undreamt-of ʌn ˈdrempt ɒv ˌʌn-, -əv ‖ -ʌv -ɑːv
undress *v, n* ʌn ˈdres ˌʌn- **~ed** t **~es** ɪz əz **~ing** ɪŋ
undue ˌʌn ˈdjuː◂ →-ˈdʒuː ‖ -ˈduː ◂ -ˈdjuː
undulant ˈʌnd jʊl ənt ˈʌndʒ ʊl- ‖ ˈʌndʒ əl- ˈʌnd jəl-, -əl-
undu|late ˈʌnd ju |leɪt ˈʌndʒ u- ‖ ˈʌndʒ ə- ˈʌnd jə-, -ə- **~lated** leɪt ɪd -əd ‖ leɪṭ əd **~lates** leɪts **~lating** leɪt ɪŋ ‖ leɪṭ ɪŋ
undulation ˌʌnd ju ˈleɪʃ ən ˌʌndʒ u- ‖ ˌʌndʒ ə- ˌʌnd jə-, -ə- **~s** z
undulatory ˈʌnd jʊl ət‿ər i ˈʌndʒ ʊl-; ˌʌnd ju ˈleɪt ər i, ˌʌndʒ u- ‖ ˈʌndʒ əl ə tɔːr i ˈʌnd jəl-, -əl-, -toʊr i
unduly ₍ˌ₎ʌn ˈdjuː li →-ˈdʒuː- ‖ -ˈduː- ˈdjuː-
undying ₍ˌ₎ʌn ˈdaɪ ɪŋ **~ly** li
unearned ˌʌn ˈɜːnd ◂ ‖ -ˈɝːnd ◂
ˌunearned ˈincome
unearth ₍ˌ₎ʌn ˈɜːθ ‖ -ˈɝːθ **~ed** t **~ing** ɪŋ **~s** s
unearth|ly ʌn ˈɜːθ |li ‖ -ˈɝːθ- **~lier** li‿ə ‖ li‿ər **~liest** li‿ɪst əst **~liness** li nəs nɪs
unease ʌn ˈiːz ˌʌn-
uneas|y ʌn ˈiːz |i ˌʌn- **~ier** i‿ə ‖ i‿ər **~iest** i‿ɪst i‿əst **~ily** ɪ li əl i **~iness** i nəs i nɪs
uneatable ʌn ˈiːt əb əl ‖ -ˈiːṭ-
uneaten ˌʌn ˈiːt ən
uneconomic ˌʌn ˌiːk ə ˈnɒm ɪk ◂ -ˌek- ‖ -ˈnɑːm- **~al** əl **~ally** əl‿i
unedifying ʌn ˈed ɪ faɪ ɪŋ -ˈ·ə- **~ly** li
uneducated ₍ˌ₎ʌn ˈed ju keɪt ɪd -ˈedʒ u-, -əd ‖ -ˈedʒ ə keɪṭ əd
unelected ˌʌn ɪ ˈlekt ɪd ◂ -ə-, -əd
unemotional ˌʌn ɪ ˈməʊʃ ən‿əl ˌ·ə- ‖ -ˈmoʊʃ- **~ly** i
unemployable ˌʌn ɪm ˈplɔɪ əb əl ◂ ˌ·em-, ˌ·əm- **~s** z
unemployed ˌʌn ɪm ˈplɔɪd ◂ -em-, -əm-
unemployment ˌʌn ɪm ˈplɔɪ mənt -em-, -əm-
ˌunemˈployment ˌbenefit
unencumbered ˌʌn ɪn ˈkʌm bəd ◂ →-ɪŋ-, -ən- ‖ -bərd ◂
unending ʌn ˈend ɪŋ ˌ·- **~ly** li
unendurable ˌʌn ɪn ˈdjʊər əb əl ˌ·en-, ˌ·ən-, →-ˈdʒʊər-, -ˈdjɔːr-, →-ˈdʒɔːr- ‖ -ˈdʊr- -ˈdjʊr-
unenlightened ˌʌn ɪn ˈlaɪt ənd ◂ -en-, -ən-
unenthusiastic ˌʌn ɪn ˌθjuːz i ˈæst ɪk ˌ·ən-, -ˈθuːz- ‖ -ˈθuːz-
unenviab|le ₍ˌ₎ʌn ˈen vi‿əb |əl **~ly** li
unequal ₍ˌ₎ʌn ˈiːk wəl **~ed, ~led** d **~ly** i **~s** z
unequivocal ˌʌn ɪ ˈkwɪv ək əl ◂ ˌ·ə- **~ly** ‿i
unerring ₍ˌ₎ʌn ˈɜːr ɪŋ §-ˈer- ‖ -ˈer- -ˈɝː- **~ly** li
Unesco, UNESCO ju ˈnesk əʊ ‖ -oʊ
unethical ʌn ˈeθ ɪk əl **~ly** ‿i
uneven ₍ˌ₎ʌn ˈiːv ən **~ly** li **~ness** nəs nɪs
uneventful ˌʌn ɪ ˈvent fəl ◂ -ə-, -fʊl **~ly** i **~ness** nəs nɪs
unexampled ˌʌn ɪg ˈzɑːmp əld ◂ -eg-, -əg-, -ɪk-, -ek-, -ək-, §-ˈzæmp- ‖ -ˈzæmp-
unexceptionab|le ˌʌn ɪk ˈsep ʃən‿əb |əl ◂ ˌ·ek-, ˌ·ək- **~leness** əl nəs -nɪs **~ly** li
unexceptional ˌʌn ɪk ˈsep ʃən‿əl ˌ·ek-, ˌ·ək- **~ly** i
unexciting ˌʌn ɪk ˈsaɪt ɪŋ ◂ -ek-, -ək- ‖ -ˈsaɪṭ-
unexcused ˌʌn ɪk ˈskjuːzd ◂ -ek-, -ək-
unexpected ˌʌn ɪk ˈspekt ɪd ◂ -ek-, -ək-, -əd **~ly** li **~ness** nəs nɪs
unexplained ˌʌn ɪk ˈspleɪnd ◂ -ek-, -ək-
unexploded ˌʌn ɪk ˈspləʊd ɪd ◂ -ek-, -ək-, -əd ‖ -ˈsploʊd-
an ˌunexploded ˈbomb
unexplored ˌʌn ɪk ˈsplɔːd ◂ -ek-, -ək- ‖ -ˈsplɔːrd ◂ -ˈsploʊrd ◂
unexpurgated ₍ˌ₎ʌn ˈeks pə geɪt ɪd -ˈpɜː-, -əd ‖ -pər geɪṭ əd
unfailing ʌn ˈfeɪl ɪŋ **~ly** li
unfair ˌʌn ˈfeə ◂ ‖ -ˈfeər ◂ -ˈfæər **~ly** li **~ness** nəs nɪs
unfaithful ₍ˌ₎ʌn ˈfeɪθ fəl -fʊl **~ly** i **~ness** nəs nɪs
unfaltering ₍ˌ₎ʌn ˈfɔːlt‿ər ɪŋ ˈfɒlt- ‖ -ˈfɑːlt‿ **~ly** li
unfamiliar ˌʌn fə ˈmɪl i‿ə ‖ -ˈmɪl jər **~ly** li
unfamiliarity ˌʌn fə ˌmɪl i ˈær ət i -ɪt i ‖ -ˌ·ˈjær əṭ i -ˈjer-; -ˌ·i ˈær-, -ˌ·i ˈer-
unfashionable ʌn ˈfæʃ ən‿əb əl
unfasten ₍ˌ₎ʌn ˈfɑːs ən §-ˈfæs- ‖ -ˈfæs- **~ed** d **~ing** ‿ɪŋ **~s** z
unfathomab|le ʌn ˈfæð əm‿əb |əl **~leness** əl nəs -nɪs **~ly** li
unfathomed ₍ˌ₎ʌn ˈfæð əmd
unfavorab|le, unfavourab|le ₍ˌ₎ʌn ˈfeɪv ər‿əb |əl **~leness** əl nəs -nɪs **~ly** li
unfazed ˌʌn ˈfeɪzd
unfeasib|le ʌn ˈfiːz əb |əl **~ly** li
unfeeling ʌn ˈfiːl ɪŋ **~ly** li **~ness** nəs nɪs
unfettered ˌʌn ˈfet əd ◂ ‖ -ˈfeṭ ərd ◂
unfilled ˌʌn ˈfɪld ◂
unfinished ˌʌn ˈfɪn ɪʃt ◂
un|fit *v, adj* ₍ˌ₎ʌn |ˈfɪt **~fitly** ˈfɪt li **~fitness** ˈfɪt nəs -nɪs **~fits** ˈfɪts **~fitted** ˈfɪt ɪd -əd ‖ ˈfɪṭ əd **~fitting/ly** ˈfɪt ɪŋ /li ‖ ˈfɪṭ ɪŋ /li
unflagging ₍ˌ₎ʌn ˈflæg ɪŋ **~ly** li
unflappab|le ₍ˌ₎ʌn ˈflæp əb |əl **~ly** li
unflattering ʌn ˈflæt ər‿ɪŋ ‖ -ˈflæṭ ər-
unflinching ₍ˌ₎ʌn ˈflɪntʃ ɪŋ **~ly** li
unfocused, unfocussed ˌʌn ˈfəʊk əst ◂ ‖ -ˈfoʊk-
unfold ʌn ˈfəʊld ˌʌn-, →-ˈfɒʊld ‖ -ˈfoʊld **~ed** ɪd əd **~ing** ɪŋ **~s** z
unforced ˌʌn ˈfɔːst ◂ -ˈfɔːrst ◂ ‖ -ˈfoʊrst ◂
unforeseeable ˌʌn fɔː ˈsiː əb əl ◂ ‖ ˌ·fɔːr- ˌ·foʊr-

unforeseen ˌʌn fɔː ˈsiːn ◂ -fə- ‖ -fɔːr- -foʊr-, -fᵊr-
ˌunforeseen ˈcircumstances
unforgettab|le ˌʌn fə ˈget əb |ᵊl ◂ ‖ -fᵊr ˈgeṭ- **~ly** li
unforgiv|able ˌʌn fə ˈgɪv| əb ᵊl ˌʌn fɔː- ‖ ʌn fᵊr- **~ably** əb li **~ing** ɪŋ
unformed ˌʌn ˈfɔːmd ◂ ‖ -ˈfɔːrmd ◂
unforthcoming ˌʌn fɔːθ ˈkʌm ɪŋ ◂ ‖ -fɔːrθ-
unfortunate ʌn ˈfɔːtʃ ən‿ət -ɪt ‖ -ˈfɔːrtʃ- **~ly** li **~s** s
unfounded ₍ₗ₎ʌn ˈfaʊnd ɪd -əd
unfrequented ˌʌn frɪ ˈkwent ɪd ◂ -frə-, -əd ‖ -ˈkwenṭ əd ◂
ˌunfreˌquented ˈbyways
unfriend|ly ₍ₗ₎ʌn ˈfrend |li **~liness** li nəs -nɪs
unfrock ˌʌn ˈfrɒk ‖ -ˈfrɑːk **~ed** t **~ing** ɪŋ **~s** s
unfulfilled ˌʌn fʊl ˈfɪld ◂
unfunded ˌʌn ˈfʌnd ɪd ◂ -əd
unfunny ˌʌn ˈfʌn i ◂
unfurl ˌʌn ˈfɜːl ‖ -ˈfɜːl **~ed** d **~ing** ɪŋ **~s** z
unfurnished ˌʌn ˈfɜːn ɪʃt ◂ ‖ -ˈfɜːn-
ungain|ly ₍ₗ₎ʌn ˈgeɪn |li →₍ₗ₎ʌŋ- **~liness** li nəs -nɪs
Ungava ʌŋ ˈgɑːv ə -ˈgeɪv-
ungenerous ₍ₗ₎ʌn ˈdʒen ər‿əs **~ly** li
ungetatable ˌʌn get ˈæt əb ᵊl ◂ →ˌʌŋ- ‖ -geṭ ˈæṭ-
unglued ʌn ˈgluːd →ʌŋ-
ungod|ly ʌn ˈgɒd |li →ʌŋ-, ˌʌn- ‖ -ˈgɑːd- **~liness** li nəs -nɪs
Ungoed *(i)* ˈɪŋ gɔɪd, *(ii)* ˈʌŋ gɔɪd
ungovernab|le ₍ₗ₎ʌn ˈgʌv ən‿əb |ᵊl →₍ₗ₎ʌŋ- ‖ -ᵊrn əb- **~leness** ᵊl nəs -nɪs **~ly** li
ungracious ₍ₗ₎ʌn ˈgreɪʃ əs→₍ₗ₎ʌŋ- **~ly** li **~ness** nəs nɪs
ungrammatical ˌʌn grə ˈmæt ɪk ᵊl ◂ →ˌʌŋ- ‖ -ˈmæṭ- **~ly** ‿i
ungrammaticality ˌʌn grə ˌmæt ɪ ˈkæl ət i →ˌʌŋ-, §-ˌ·ə-, -ɪt i ‖ -ˌmæṭ ə ˈkæl əṭ i
ungrateful ʌn ˈgreɪt fᵊl →ʌŋ-, ˌʌn-, -fʊl **~ly** ‿i **~ness** nəs nɪs
ungrudging ₍ₗ₎ʌn ˈgrʌdʒ ɪŋ →₍ₗ₎ʌŋ- **~ly** li
unguarded ₍ₗ₎ʌn ˈgɑːd ɪd →₍ₗ₎ʌŋ-, -əd ‖ -ˈgɑːrd- **~ly** li **~ness** nəs nɪs
unguent ˈʌŋ gwənt ˈʌŋ gju‿ənt, ⚠ˈʌndʒ ənt **~s** s
un|gula ˈʌŋ |gjʊl ə -gjəl- ‖ -|gjəl ə **~gulae** gju liː gjə- ‖ gjə liː
ungulate ˈʌŋ gju leɪt -gjʊl ət, -gjəl-, -ɪt ‖ -gjə- **~s** s
unhallowed ₍ₗ₎ʌn ˈhæl əʊd ‖ -oʊd
unhand ˌʌn ˈhænd **~ed** ɪd əd **~ing** ɪŋ **~s** z
unhapp|y ʌn ˈhæp |i ˌʌn- **~ily** ɪ li əl i **~iness** i nəs i nɪs
unharmed ʌn ˈhɑːmd ‖ -ˈhɑːrmd
unhealth|y ʌn ˈhelθ |i ˌʌn- **~ily** ɪ li əl i **~iness** i nəs i nɪs
unheard ₍ₗ₎ʌn ˈhɜːd ‖ ˈhɜːd
unheard-of ₍ₗ₎ʌn ˈhɜːd ɒv -əv ‖ -ˈhɜːd ʌv -ɑːv
unhelpful ʌn ˈhelp fᵊl -fʊl **~ly** ‿i **~ness** nəs nɪs
unheralded ʌn ˈher ᵊld ɪd -əd
unhesitating ʌn ˈhez ɪ teɪt ɪŋ -ˈ·ə- ‖ -teɪṭ ɪŋ **~ly** li
unhing|e ₍ₗ₎ʌn ˈhɪndʒ **~ed** d **~es** ɪz əz **~ing** ɪŋ
unhip ˌʌn ˈhɪp
unhitch ˌʌn ˈhɪtʃ **~ed** t **~es** ɪz əz **~ing** ɪŋ
unhol|y ₍ₗ₎ʌn ˈhəʊl |i ‖ -ˈhoʊl |i **~iness** i nəs i nɪs
unˌholy alˈliance
unhook ₍ₗ₎ʌn ˈhʊk §-ˈhuːk **~ed** t **~ing** ɪŋ **~s** s
unhoped-for ₍ₗ₎ʌn ˈhəʊpt fɔː ‖ -ˈhoʊpt fɔːr
unhors|e ₍ₗ₎ʌn ˈhɔːs ‖ -ˈhɔːrs **~ed** t **~es** ɪz əz **~ing** ɪŋ
unhurried ˌʌn ˈhʌr id ◂ ‖ -ˈhɜː-
unhurt ʌn ˈhɜːt ‖ -ˈhɜːt
unhygienic ˌʌn haɪ ˈdʒiːn ɪk ◂
uni ˈjuːn i **unis** ˈjuːn iz
uni- |juːn i *—but in certain established words* |juːn ɪ, -ə — **unilingual** ˌjuːn i ˈlɪŋ gwəl ◂
Uniat ˈjuːn i æt
Uniate ˈjuːn i‿ət ‿ɪt, -eɪt
unicameral ˌjuːn i ˈkæm ᵊr‿əl ◂
UNICEF ˈjuːn i sef -ə-
unicellular ˌjuːn i ˈsel jʊl ə ◂ -jəl ə ‖ -jəl ᵊr
Unichem *tdmk* ˈjuːn i kem
Unicode ˈjuːn i kəʊd ‖ -koʊd
unicorn ˈjuːn ɪ kɔːn -ə- ‖ -kɔːrn **~s** z
unicycle ˈjuːn i ˌsaɪk ᵊl **~s** z
unidentified ˌʌn aɪ ˈdent ɪ faɪd ◂ -ˈ·ə- ‖ -ˈdenṭ-
unification ˌjuːn ɪf ɪ ˈkeɪʃ ᵊn ˌ·əf-, §-əˈ-- **~s** z
unifie... *—see* **unify**
uniform ˈjuːn ɪ fɔːm -ə- ‖ -fɔːrm *—The adj is occasionally stressed* ˌ·ˈ· **~ed** d **~ly** li **~ness** nəs nɪs **~s** z
uniformity ˌjuːn ɪ ˈfɔːm ət i ˌ·ə-, -ɪt i ‖ -ˈfɔːrm əṭ i
uni|fy ˈjuːn ɪ |faɪ -ə- **~fied** faɪd **~fier/s** faɪ‿ə/z ‖ faɪ‿ᵊr/z **~fies** faɪz **~fying** faɪ ɪŋ
Unigate *tdmk* ˈjuːn i geɪt
unilateral ˌjuːn i ˈlæt‿ᵊr əl ◂ ˌ·ə- ‖ -ˈlæṭ ər əl -ˈlætr əl **~ism** ˌɪz əm **~ist/s** ɪst/s §əst/s ‖ əst/s **~ly** i
Unilever *tdmk* ˈjuːn i ˌliːv ə -ə- ‖ -ᵊr
unimagin|able ˌʌn ɪ ˈmædʒ ɪn |əb ᵊl ◂ -ˈmædʒ ən‿ **~ably** əb li **~ative** ət ɪv ◂ ‖ əṭ ɪv ◂
unimagined ˌʌn ɪ ˈmædʒ ɪnd ◂ -ənd ◂
unimpaired ˌʌn ɪm ˈpeəd ◂ ‖ -ˈpeᵊrd ◂ -ˈpæᵊrd ◂
unimpeachab|le ˌʌn ɪm ˈpiːtʃ əb |ᵊl ◂ **~ly** li
unimpeded ˌʌn ɪm ˈpiːd ɪd ◂ -əd
unimportant ˌʌn ɪm ˈpɔːt ᵊnt ◂ ‖ -ˈpɔːrt-
unimpressed ˌʌn ɪm ˈprest ◂
unimpressive ˌʌn ɪm ˈpres ɪv ◂
unimproved ˌʌn ɪm ˈpruːvd ◂
unincorporated ˌʌn ɪn ˈkɔːp ə reɪt ɪd ◂ →ˌʌn ɪŋ- ‖ -ˈkɔːrp ə reɪṭ əd ◂
uninformed ˌʌn ɪn ˈfɔːmd ◂ ‖ -ˈfɔːrmd ◂
uninhabit|able ˌʌn ɪn ˈhæb ɪt |əb ᵊl §-ˈ·ət- ‖ -ˈ·əṭ- **~ed** ɪd əd
uninhibited ˌʌn ɪn ˈhæb ɪt ɪd ◂ §-ət ɪd, -əd ‖ -əṭ əd ◂ **~ly** li **~ness** nəs nɪs
uninitiated ˌʌn ɪ ˈnɪʃ i eɪt ɪd -əd ‖ -eɪṭ əd

uninspired ˌʌn ɪn ˈspaɪ‿əd ◂ ‖ -ˈspaɪ‿ᵊrd ◂
uninspiring ˌʌn ɪn ˈspaɪ‿ər ɪŋ ‖ -ˈspaɪ‿ᵊr- **~ly** li
uninstall ˌʌn ɪn ˈstɔːl ◂ ‖ -ˈstɑːl ◂ **~ed** d **~ing** ɪŋ **~s** z
uninsured ˌʌn ɪn ˈʃʊəd ◂ -ˈʃɔːd ◂ ‖ -ˈʃʊᵊrd ◂ -ˈʃɜːd ◂
unintelligib|le ˌʌn ɪn ˈtel ɪdʒ əb |ᵊl ◂ **~ly** li
unintended ˌʌn ɪn ˈtend ɪd ◂ -əd
unintentional ˌʌn ɪn ˈtenᵗʃ ᵊn‿əl ◂ **~ly** i
uninterested ⁽ˌ⁾ʌn ˈɪntr əst ɪd -ɪst-, -əd; -ˈɪnt ə rest- ‖ -ˈɪnţ ə rest-, -ər əst- **~ly** li **~ness** nəs nɪs
uninterrupted ˌʌn ˌɪnt ə ˈrʌpt ɪd -əd ‖ -ˌɪnţ ə- **~ly** li **~ness** nəs nɪs
uninvit|ed ˌʌn ɪn ˈvaɪt |ɪd ◂ -əd ‖ -ˈvaɪţ- **~ing** ɪŋ
union ˈjuːn i‿ən ‖ ˈjuːn jən **~s** z
ˈunion card; **ˈUnion flag, ˌ· · ˈ·**; **ˌUnion ˈJack** ‖ ˈ· · ·
unionis... —*see* **unioniz...**
Unionism ˈjuːn i‿ə ˌnɪz əm ən ˌɪz- ‖ ˈjuːn jə ˌnɪz əm
unionist, U~ ˈjuːn i‿ən ɪst §-əst ‖ ˈjuːn jən əst **~s** s
unionization ˌjuːn i‿ən aɪ ˈzeɪʃ ᵊn -ɪˈ-- ‖ ˌjuːn jən ə ˈzeɪʃ ᵊn
unioniz|e ˈjuːn i‿ə naɪz ‖ ˈjuːn jə naɪz **~ed** d **~es** ɪz əz **~ing** ɪŋ
Unipart *tdmk* ˈjuːn i pɑːt ‖ -pɑːrt
unique ju ˈniːk ˌjuː- **~ly** li **~ness** nəs nɪs
Uniroyal *tdmk* ˈjuːn i ˌrɔɪ‿əl
unisex ˈjuːn i seks -ə-
unisexual ˌjuːn i ˈsek ʃu‿əl ◂ -ˈseks ju‿əl, -ˈsek ʃᵊl **~ly** i
unison ˈjuːn ɪs ən -ɪz-, -əs-, -əz-
unit ˈjuːn ɪt §-ət **~s** s
ˌunit ˈtrust
UNITA ju ˈniːt ə ‖ -ˈniːţ ə
unitard ˈjuːn ɪ tɑːd -ə- ‖ -tɑːrd **~s** z
Unitarian, u~ ˌjuːn ɪ ˈteər i‿ən ◂ ˌ·ə- ‖ -ˈter- -ˈtær- **~s** z
unitary ˈjuːn ɪt‿ər i ˈ·ət‿ ‖ -ə ter i
Unitas *tdmk* ˈjuːn ɪ tæs -ə-
u|nite ju |ˈnaɪt ˌjuː- **~nited** ˈnaɪt ɪd -əd ‖ ˈnaɪţ əd **~nites** ˈnaɪts **~niting** ˈnaɪt ɪŋ ‖ ˈnaɪţ ɪŋ
Uˌnited ˌArab ˈEmirates; **Uˌnited ˈKingdom**; **Uˌnited ˈNations, Uˌnited ˈNations Associˌation**; **Uˌnited Reˈformed Church**; **Uˌnited ˈStates◂, Uˌnited ˌStates of Aˈmerica**
unit-linked ˌjuːn ɪt ˈlɪŋkt ◂ §-ət-
unit|y, Unity ˈjuːn ət |i -ɪt- ‖ -əţ |i **~ies** iz
Univac *tdmk* ˈjuːn ɪ væk -ə-
univalve ˈjuːn i vælv **~s** z
univariate ˌjuːn i ˈveər i‿ət ◂ ɪt ‖ -ˈver- -ˈvær-
universal ˌjuːn ɪ ˈvɜːs ᵊl ◂ ˌ·ə- ‖ -ˈvɝːs- **~s** z
ˌuniˌversal ˈjoint; **ˌuniˌversal ˈlanguage**
universalism, U~ ˌjuːn ɪ ˈvɜːs ə ˌlɪz əm ˌ·ə-, -ᵊl ˌɪz- ‖ -ˈvɝːs-
universalist, U~ ˌjuːn ɪ ˈvɜːs əl ɪst ˌ·ə-, §-əst ‖ -ˈvɝːs- **~s** s
universality ˌjuːn ɪ vɜː ˈsæl ət i ˌ·ə-, -ɪt i ‖ -vɝː ˈsæl əţ i
universal|ly ˌjuːn ɪ ˈvɜːs ᵊl |i ˌ·ə- ‖ -ˈvɝːs- **~ness** nəs nɪs
univers|e ˈjuːn ɪ vɜːs -ə- ‖ -vɝːs **~es** ɪz əz
universit|y ˌjuːn ɪ ˈvɜːs ət |i ˌ·ə-, -ɪt i ‖ -ˈvɝːs əţ |i **~ies** iz
Unix, UNIX *tdmk* ˈjuːn ɪks
unjust ˌʌn ˈdʒʌst ◂ **~ly** li **~ness** nəs nɪs
unjustifiab|le ˌʌn ˌdʒʌst ɪ ˈfaɪ əb |ᵊl -əˈ--, ⁽ˌ⁾ˈ· · · · · **~ly** li
unjustified ʌn ˈdʒʌst ɪ faɪd ˌʌn-, -ə- **~ly** li
unkempt ˌʌn ˈkempt ◂ →ˌʌŋ- **~ly** li **~ness** nəs nɪs
unkind ˌʌn ˈkaɪnd ◂ →ˌʌŋ-, ʌn- **~er** ə ‖ ᵊr **~est** ɪst əst **~ly** li **~ness** nəs nɪs
unkind|ly ⁽ˌ⁾ʌn ˈkaɪnd |li →⁽ˌ⁾ʌŋ- **~lier** li‿ə ‖ li‿ᵊr **~liest** li‿ɪst li‿əst **~liness** li nəs -nɪs
un|knit ˌʌn |ˈnɪt **~knits** ˈnɪts **~knitted** ˈnɪt ɪd -əd ‖ ˈnɪţ əd **~knitting** ˈnɪt ɪŋ ‖ ˈnɪţ ɪŋ
un|knot ˌʌn |ˈnɒt ‖ -|ˈnɑːt **~knots** ˈnɒts ‖ ˈnɑːts **~knotted** ˈnɒt ɪd -əd ‖ ˈnɑːţ əd **~knotting** ˈnɒt ɪŋ ‖ ˈnɑːţ ɪŋ
unknowab|le ⁽ˌ⁾ʌn ˈnəʊ əb |ᵊl ‖ -ˈnoʊ- **~leness** ᵊl nəs -nɪs **~les** ᵊlz **~ly** li
unknowing ⁽ˌ⁾ʌn ˈnəʊ ɪŋ ‖ -ˈnoʊ- **~ly** li
unknown ˌʌn ˈnəʊn ◂ ‖ -ˈnoʊn ◂ **~ness** nəs nɪs **~s** z
ˌunknown ˈquantity; **ˌUnknown ˈSoldier**
unlac|e ˌʌn ˈleɪs **~ed** t **~es** ɪz əz **~ing** ɪŋ
unlawful ⁽ˌ⁾ʌn ˈlɔː fᵊl -fʊl ‖ -ˈlɑː- **~ly** ‿i **~ness** nəs nɪs
unleaded ⁽ˌ⁾ʌn ˈled ɪd ◂ -əd
unlearn ˌʌn ˈlɜːn ‖ -ˈlɝːn **~ed** d **~ing** ɪŋ **~s** z
unleash ⁽ˌ⁾ʌn ˈliːʃ **~ed** t **~es** ɪz əz **~ing** ɪŋ
unleavened ⁽ˌ⁾ʌn ˈlev ᵊnd ◂
unless ən ˈles ʌn- —*occasionally also, for emphasis,* ˌʌn-
unlettered ˌʌn ˈlet əd ◂ ‖ -ˈleţ ᵊrd ◂
unlicensed ⁽ˌ⁾ʌn ˈlaɪs ᵊnᵗst
unlike ˌʌn ˈlaɪk ◂ **~ness** nəs nɪs
unlike|ly ʌn ˈlaɪk |li ˌʌn- **~liness** li nəs -nɪs
unlimited ʌn ˈlɪm ɪt ɪd ˌ·-, §-ət ɪd, -əd ‖ -əţ əd **~ly** li **~ness** nəs nɪs
unlisted ʌn ˈlɪst ɪd ˌ·-, -əd
unlit ˌʌn ˈlɪt ◂
unload ⁽ˌ⁾ʌn ˈləʊd ‖ -ˈloʊd **~ed** ɪd əd **~ing** ɪŋ **~s** z
unlock ⁽ˌ⁾ʌn ˈlɒk ‖ -ˈlɑːk **~ed** t **~ing** ɪŋ **~s** s
unlooked-for ⁽ˌ⁾ʌn ˈlʊkt fɔː ‖ -fɔːr
unloos|e ⁽ˌ⁾ʌn ˈluːs **~ed** t **~es** ɪz əz **~ing** ɪŋ
unloosen ⁽ˌ⁾ʌn ˈluːs ᵊn **~ed** d **~ing** ‿ɪŋ **~s** z
unlovab|le ʌn ˈlʌv əb |ᵊl **~ly** li
unloved ˌʌn ˈlʌvd ◂
unloving ˌʌn ˈlʌv ɪŋ ◂
unluck|y ⁽ˌ⁾ʌn ˈlʌk |i **~ier** i‿ə ‖ i‿ᵊr **~iest** i‿ɪst i‿əst **~ily** ɪ li əl i **~iness** i nəs i nɪs
unmade ˌʌn ˈmeɪd ◂ →ˌʌm-
unman ˌʌn ˈmæn →ˌʌm- **~ned** d **~ing** ɪŋ **~s** z
unmanageab|le ʌn ˈmæn ɪdʒ əb |ᵊl →ʌm- **~ly** li
unman|ly ˌʌn ˈmæn |li →ˌʌm- **~lier** li‿ə ‖ li‿ᵊr **~liest** li‿ɪst əst **~liness** li nəs -nɪs

unmanner|ly ʌn ˈmæn ə |li →ʌm- ‖ -ᵊr-
~liness li nəs -nɪs
unmarked ˌʌn ˈmɑːkt ◂ →ˌʌm- ‖ -ˈmɑːrkt ◂
ˌunmarked ˈcar
unmarried ˌʌn ˈmær id ◂ →ˌʌm- ‖ -ˈmer- **~s** z
unmask ˌʌn ˈmɑːsk →ˌʌm-, §-ˈmæsk ‖ -ˈmæsk
~ed t **~ing** ɪŋ **~s** s
unmatched ˌʌn ˈmætʃt ◂ →ˌʌm-
unmeasured ₍ₗ₎ʌn ˈmeʒ əd →₍ₗ₎ʌm- ‖ -ᵊrd
-ˈmeɪʒ-
unmediated ˌʌn ˈmiːd i eɪt ɪd →ˌʌm-, -əd
‖ -eɪt̬-
unmentionab|le ʌn ˈmenᵗʃ ᵊn‿əb |ᵊl →ʌm-
~leness ᵊl nəs -nɪs **~les** ᵊlz **~ly** li
unmerciful ʌn ˈmɜːs ɪ fᵊl ˌ·ˈ·-, -ə-, -fʊl ‖ ˈmɜ˞ːs-
~ly ‿i **~ness** nəs nɪs
unmet ˌʌn ˈmet ◂ →ˌʌm-
unmindful ₍ₗ₎ʌn ˈmaɪnd fᵊl →₍ₗ₎ʌm-, -fʊl **~ly** i
~ness nəs nɪs
unmissable ʌn ˈmɪs əb ᵊl →ʌm-
unmistakab|le, unmistakeab|le
ˌʌn mɪ ˈsteɪk əb |ᵊl ◂ →ˌʌm-, ˌ·mə- **~leness**
ᵊl nəs -nɪs **~ly** li
unmitigated ʌn ˈmɪt ɪ geɪt ɪd →ʌm-, §-ˈ·ə-, -əd
‖ -ˈmɪt̬ ə geɪt̬ əd **~ly** li
unmixed ˌʌn ˈmɪkst ◂ →ˌʌm-
unmolested ˌʌn mə ˈlest ɪd ◂ →ˌʌm-, -məʊ-,
-əd
unmoved ₍ₗ₎ʌn ˈmuːvd →₍ₗ₎ʌm-
unnamed ˌʌn ˈneɪmd ◂
unnatural ₍ₗ₎ʌn ˈnætʃ ᵊr‿əl **~ly** i **~ness** nəs nɪs
unnecessarily ʌn ˈnes əs ᵊr‿əl i, ˌʌn-, -ˈ·ɪs-, ɪ li;
ˌʌn ˌnes ə ˈser əl i, ʌn,ˌ·-, -ɪˈ·-, -ɪ li
‖ ˌʌn ˌnes ə ˈser əl i
unnecessar|y ʌn ˈnes əs ər‿|i ˌʌn-, -ˈ·ɪs-;
-ə ser i, ˈ·ɪ- ‖ -ə ser |i **~iness** i nəs i nɪs
unneeded ʌn ˈniːd ɪd -əd
unnerv|e ˌʌn ˈnɜːv ‖ -ˈnɜ˞ːv **~ed** d **~es** z **~ing**
ɪŋ
unnoticed ʌn ˈnəʊt ɪst §-əst ‖ -ˈnoʊt̬-
unnumbered ˌʌn ˈnʌm bəd ◂ ‖ -bᵊrd
UNO ˈjuːn əʊ ‖ -oʊ
Uno *tdmk, car model* ˈuːn əʊ ˈjuːn- ‖ -oʊ
unobserved ˌʌn əb ˈzɜːvd ‖ -ˈzɜ˞ːvd
unobstructed ˌʌn əb ˈstrʌkt ɪd ◂ §-ɒb-, -əd
unobtainable ˌʌn əb ˈteɪn əb ᵊl §ˌ·ɒb-
unobtrusive ˌʌn əb ˈtruːs ɪv ◂ -ɒb-, §-ˈtruːz-
~ly li **~ness** nəs nɪs
unoccupied ₍ₗ₎ʌn ˈɒk ju paɪd ‖ -ˈɑːk jə-
unofficial ˌʌn ə ˈfɪʃ ᵊl ◂ §-əʊ- **~ly** i
unopened ʌn ˈəʊp ənd ‖ -ˈoʊp-
unopposed ˌʌn ə ˈpəʊzd ◂ ‖ -ˈpoʊzd ◂
unorganized, unorganised ʌn ˈɔːg ə naɪzd
‖ -ˈɔːrg-
unorthodox ʌn ˈɔːθ ə dɒks ˌʌn-
‖ -ˈɔːrθ ə dɑːks **~ly** li
unorthodox|y ʌn ˈɔːθ ə dɒks |i ˌʌn-
‖ -ˈɔːrθ ə dɑːks |i **~ies** iz
unpack ˌʌn ˈpæk →ˌʌm- **~ed** t **~ing** ɪŋ **~s** s
unpaid ˌʌn ˈpeɪd ◂ →ˌʌm-
ˌunpaid ˈbills
unpalatable ʌn ˈpæl ət əb ᵊl →ʌm-, ˌ·ˈ·- ‖ -ˈ·ət̬-
unparalleled ₍ₗ₎ʌn ˈpær ə leld -əl əld ‖ -ˈper-

unpardonab|le ʌn ˈpɑːd ᵊn‿əb |ᵊl →ʌm-
‖ -ˈpɑːrd- **~ly** li
unparliamentary ˌʌn ˌpɑːl ə ˈment‿ər i
→ˌʌm-, ˌ·ɪ-, -ˌ·i‿ə'·- ‖ ˌpɑːrl ə ˈment̬-
unpatriotic ˌʌn ˌpætr i ˈɒt ɪk ◂ →ˌʌm-, ˌpeɪtr-
‖ -ˌpeɪtr i ˈɑːt̬ ɪk ◂
unpaved ˌʌn ˈpeɪvd ◂ →ˌʌm-
unpeeled ˌʌn ˈpiːᵊld ◂ →ˌʌm-
unpeg ˌʌn ˈpeg →ˌʌm- **~ged** d **~ging** ɪŋ **~s** z
unperson ˌʌn ˈpɜːs ᵊn →ˌʌm-, ˈ·ˌ·· ‖ -ˈpɜ˞ːs- **~s**
z
unperturbed ˌʌn pə ˈtɜːbd ◂ →ˌʌm-
‖ -pᵊr ˈtɜ˞ːbd ◂
unpick ˌʌn ˈpɪk →ˌʌm- **~ed** t **~ing** ɪŋ **~s** s
unplaced ˌʌn ˈpleɪst ◂ →ˌʌm-
unplanned ˌʌn ˈplænd ◂ →ˌʌm-
unplayable ₍ₗ₎ʌn ˈpleɪ əb ᵊl →₍ₗ₎ʌm-
unpleasant ʌn ˈplez ᵊnt →ʌm- **~ly** li
unpleasantness ʌn ˈplez ᵊnt nəs →ʌm-, -nɪs
~es ɪz əz
unplug ˌʌn ˈplʌg →ˌʌm- **~ged** d **~ging** ɪŋ **~s** z
unplumbed ˌʌn ˈplʌmd ◂ →ˌʌm-
ˌunplumbed ˈdepths
unpolished ʌn ˈpɒl ɪʃt ‖ -ˈpɑːl-
unpopular ₍ₗ₎ʌn ˈpɒp jʊl ə →₍ₗ₎ʌm-, -jəl ə
‖ -ˈpɑːp jəl ᵊr **~ly** li
unpopularity ˌʌn ˌpɒp ju ˈlær ət i →ˌʌm-,
-ˌ·jə-, -ɪt i ‖ -ˌpɑːp jə ˈlær ət̬ i -ˈler-
unpracticed, unpractised ₍ₗ₎ʌn ˈprækt ɪst
→₍ₗ₎ʌm-, §-əst
unprecedented ʌn ˈpres ɪ dent ɪd →ʌm-, ˌ·ˈ·-,
-ˈpriːs-, -ˈ·ə-, -ɪd ənt-, -əd ənt-, -əd; ˌ·ˌ·ˈdent·,
ˌ·ˌ·- ‖ -ˈpres ə dent̬ əd **~ly** li
unpredictability ˌʌn pri ˌdɪkt ə ˈbɪl ət i
→ˌʌm-, ˌ·prə-, -ɪt i ‖ -ət̬ i
unpredictab|le ˌʌn pri ˈdɪkt əb |ᵊl ◂ →ˌʌm-,
ˌ·prə- **~leness** ᵊl nəs -nɪs **~ly** li
unprejudiced ₍ₗ₎ʌn ˈpredʒ ʊd ɪst →₍ₗ₎ʌm-,
-ˈ·əd-, §-əst, §-aɪst ‖ -əd əst
unpremeditated ˌʌn priː ˈmed ɪ teɪt ɪd ◂
→ˌʌm-, ˌ·prɪ-, -əd ‖ -teɪt̬ əd ◂
unprepared ˌʌn pri ˈpeəd ◂ →ˌʌm-, -prə-
‖ -ˈpeᵊrd ◂ -ˈpæᵊrd
unprepared|ly ˌʌn pri ˈpeər ɪd |li →ˌʌm-,
ˌ·prə-, -əd · ‖ -ˈper əd |li -ˈpær- **~ness** nəs nɪs
unprepossessing ˌʌn ˌpriː pə ˈzes ɪŋ →ˌʌm-;
ˌ·ˌ·-; ₍ₗ₎· ˌ·ˌ·· **~ly** li
unpretentious ˌʌn pri ˈtenᵗʃ əs ◂ →ˌʌm-, -prə-
~ly li **~ness** nəs nɪs
unprincipled ₍ₗ₎ʌn ˈprɪnᵗs əp ᵊld →₍ₗ₎ʌm-, -ɪp-
unprintable ₍ₗ₎ʌn ˈprɪnt əb ᵊl →₍ₗ₎ʌm-
‖ -ˈprɪnt̬-
unproductive ˌʌn prə ˈdʌkt ɪv ◂ →ˌʌm- **~ly** li
unprofessional ˌʌn prə ˈfeʃ ᵊn‿əl ◂ →ˌʌm- **~ly**
i
Unprofor ˈʌn prə fɔː →ˈʌm- ‖ -fɔːr
unprompted ₍ₗ₎ʌn ˈprɒmpt ɪd →₍ₗ₎ʌm-, -əd
‖ -ˈprɑːmpt əd
unpronounceable ˌʌn prə ˈnaʊnᵗs əb ᵊl
→ˌʌm-
unproven ˌʌn ˈpruːv ᵊn ◂ →ˌʌm-, -ˈprəʊv-
unprovoked ˌʌn prə ˈvəʊkt ◂ →ˌʌm-
‖ -ˈvoʊkt ◂

unpublished ˌʌn ˈpʌb lɪʃt ◂ →ˌʌm-
unpunctual ˌʌn ˈpʌŋk tʃu‿əl →ˌʌm-, -tju‿əl **~ly** i
unpunctuality ˌʌn ˌpʌŋk tʃu ˈæl ət i -ˌ·tju-, -ɪt i ‖ -əţ i
unpunished (ˌ)ʌn ˈpʌn ɪʃt (ˌ)ʌm-
unputdownable ˌʌn pʊt ˈdaʊn əb əl →ˌʌm-
unqualified *'lacking qualifications'* ˌʌn ˈkwɒl ɪ faɪd ◂→ˌʌŋ-, -ə- ‖-ˈkwɑːl-
unqualified *'downright, not limited'* ʌn ˈkwɒl ɪ faɪd →ʌŋ-, -ə- ‖ -ˈkwɑːl-
unquenchable ʌn ˈkwentʃ əb əl
unquestionab|le (ˌ)ʌn ˈkwes tʃən‿əb |əl →(ˌ)ʌŋ-, →-ˈkweʃ-, -ˈ·tjən- **~leness** əl nəs -nɪs **~ly** li
unquestioned (ˌ)ʌn ˈkwes tʃənd →(ˌ)ʌŋ-, →-ˈkweʃ-, -tjənd
unquestioning (ˌ)ʌn ˈkwes tʃən ɪŋ →(ˌ)ʌŋ-, →ˈkweʃ-, -tjən- **~ly** li
unquiet ˌʌn ˈkwaɪ‿ət ◂ →ˌʌŋ- **~ly** li **~ness** nəs nɪs
unquote ˌʌn ˈkwəʊt →ˌʌŋ-, -ˈkəʊt ‖ ˈʌn kwoʊt
unrated ˌʌn ˈreɪt ɪd -əd ‖ -ˈreɪţ-
unravel (ˌ)ʌn ˈræv əl **~ed, ~led** d **~ing, ~ling** ɪŋ **~s** z
unread ˌʌn ˈred ◂
unreadab|le (ˌ)ʌn ˈriːd əb |əl **~leness** əl nəs -nɪs **~ly** li
unread|y ˌʌn ˈred |i **~ily** ɪ li əl i **~iness** i nəs i nɪs
unreal (ˌ)ʌn ˈrɪəl -ˈriːəl ‖ -ˈriː‿əl
unrealistic ˌʌn rɪə ˈlɪst ɪk ‖ ˌʌn ˌriː ə ˈlɪst ɪk **~ally** əl‿i
unreality ˌʌn ri ˈæl ət i -ɪt i ‖ -əţ i
unrealized, unrealised ˌʌn ˈrɪəl aɪzd ◂ ‖ ˌʌn ˈriː ə laɪzd ◂
unreasonab|le (ˌ)ʌn ˈriːz ən‿əb |əl **~leness** əl nəs -nɪs **~ly** li
unreasoning (ˌ)ʌn ˈriːz ən‿ɪŋ **~ly** li
unrecognizab|le, unrecognisab|le ˌʌn ˈrek əg naɪz əb |əl ˈ·ə-; ˌ·ˌ·ˈ·· **~ly** li
unrecognized, unrecognised ˌʌn ˈrek əg naɪzd ◂ -ə-
unreconstructed ˌʌn ˌriː kən ˈstrʌkt ɪd ◂ §-kɒn-, -əd
unrecorded ˌʌn ri ˈkɔːd ɪd ◂ ˌʌn rə-, -əd ‖ -ˈkɔːrd-
unrecoverable ˌʌn ri ˈkʌv ər‿əb əl ˌʌn rə-
unreel ˌʌn ˈriːəl ◂ **~ed** d **~ing** ɪŋ **~s** z
unrefined ˌʌn ri ˈfaɪnd ◂ -rə-
unregenerate ˌʌn ri ˈdʒen ər‿ət ˌ·rə-, ɪt, -ə reɪt **~ly** li
unregistered ˌʌn ˈredʒ ɪst əd ◂ §-əst ‖ -ərd ◂
unregulated ˌʌn ˈreg ju leɪt ɪd -əd ‖ -jə leɪţ əd
unrelated ˌʌn ri ˈleɪt ɪd -rə-, -əd ‖ -ˈleɪţ-
unrelenting ˌʌn ri ˈlent ɪŋ ◂ -rə- ‖ -ˈlenţ ɪŋ ◂ **~ly** li **~ness** nəs nɪs
unreliability ˌʌn ri ˌlaɪ‿ə ˈbɪl ət i ˌ·rə-, -ɪt i ‖ -əţ i
unreliab|le ˌʌn ri ˈlaɪ‿əb |əl ◂ ˌ·rə- **~leness** əl nəs -nɪs **~ly** li
unrelieved ˌʌn ri ˈliːvd ◂ -rə-
ˌ**unrelieved 'boredom**
unremarkable ˌʌn ri ˈmɑːk əb əl ◂ ˌʌn rə- ‖ -ˈmɑːrk-
unremitting ˌʌn ri ˈmɪt ɪŋ ◂ -rə- ‖ -ˈmɪţ ɪŋ ◂ **~ly** li **~ness** nəs nɪs
ˌ**unremitting 'efforts**
unrepeatable ˌʌn ri ˈpiːt əb əl ◂ ˌʌn rə- ‖ -ˈpiːţ-
unrepentant ˌʌn ri ˈpent ənt -rə- ‖ -ˈpenţ-
unreported ˌʌn ri ˈpɔːt ɪd ◂ -rə-, -əd ‖ -ˈpɔːrţ-
unrepresentative ˌʌn ˌrep ri ˈzent ət ɪv ◂ -ˌrep rə- ‖ -ˈzenţ əţ ɪv ◂
unrequited ˌʌn ri ˈkwaɪt ɪd ◂ -rə-, -əd ‖ -ˈkwaɪţ əd ◂
ˌ**unrequited 'love**
unre|served ˌʌn ri |ˈzɜːvd ◂ -rə- ‖ -|ˈzɜːvd **~servedly** ˈzɜːv ɪd li -əd- ‖ ˈzɜ˞ːv-
unresisting ˌʌn ri ˈzɪst ɪŋ -rə- **~ly** li
unresolved ˌʌn ri ˈzɒlvd ◂ -rə-, §-ˈzəʊlvd, §→-ˈzɒʊlvd ‖ -ˈzɑːlvd
unresponsive ˌʌn ri ˈspɒnts ɪv ◂ -rə- ‖ -ˈspɑːnts-
unrest (ˌ)ʌn ˈrest
unrestrained ˌʌn ri ˈstreɪnd ◂ -rə-
unrestrainedly ˌʌn ri ˈstreɪn ɪd li ˌ·rə-, -əd li
unrestricted ˌʌn ri ˈstrɪkt ɪd ◂ -rə-, -əd
ˌ**unrestricted 'access**
unrewarded ˌʌn ri ˈwɔːd ɪd ◂ -rə-, -əd ‖ -ˈwɔːrd-
unrip (ˌ)ʌn ˈrɪp **~ped** t **~ping** ɪŋ **~s** s
unripe ˌʌn ˈraɪp ◂ **~ness** nəs nɪs
unrivaled, unrivalled ʌn ˈraɪv əld ˌʌn-
unroll (ˌ)ʌn ˈrəʊl →-ˈrɒʊl ‖ -ˈroʊl **~ed** d **~ing** ɪŋ **~s** z
unround ˌʌn ˈraʊnd ◂ **~ed** ɪd əd **~ing** ɪŋ **~s** z
unruffled (ˌ)ʌn ˈrʌf əld
unrul|y ʌn ˈruːl |i **~iness** i nəs i nɪs
UNRWA ˈʌn rə
unsaddl|e (ˌ)ʌn ˈsæd əl **~ed** d **~es** z **~ing** ‿ɪŋ
unsafe (ˌ)ʌn ˈseɪf **~ly** li **~ness** nəs nɪs
unsaid (ˌ)ʌn ˈsed
unsanitary ˌʌn ˈsæn ɪt‿ər i -ət‿ ‖ -ə ter i
unsatisfactory ˌʌn ˌsæt ɪs ˈfækt ər‿i ◂ -ə- ‖ -ˌsæţ-
unsatisfied ˌʌn ˈsæt ɪs faɪd -əs- ‖ -ˈsæţ-
unsaturated (ˌ)ʌn ˈsætʃ ə reɪt ɪd -ˈ·ʊ, -əd; -ˈsæt jʊ- ‖ -reɪţ əd
unsavor|y, unsavour|y (ˌ)ʌn ˈseɪv ər‿|i **~iness** i nəs i nɪs
un|say ˌʌn |ˈseɪ —*but as contrasted with* say, ˈ. . **~said** ˈsed **~saying** ˈseɪ ɪŋ **~says** ˈsez ˈseɪz
unscathed (ˌ)ʌn ˈskeɪðd
unscheduled ˌʌn ˈʃed juːld ◂ -ˈsked- ‖ -ˈskedʒ uːld ◂ -əld
unschooled ˌʌn ˈskuːld
unscientific ˌʌn ˌsaɪ‿ən ˈtɪf ɪk **~ally** əl‿i
Unscom, UNSCOM ˈʌn skɒm ‖ -skɑːm
unscrambl|e (ˌ)ʌn ˈskræm bəl **~ed** d **~es** z **~ing** ‿ɪŋ
unscrew ˌʌn ˈskruː **~ed** d **~ing** ɪŋ **~s** z
unscripted ˌʌn ˈskrɪpt ɪd ◂ ʌn-, -əd

unscrupulous ʌn ˈskruːp jʊl əs ˌʌn-, -jəl- ‖ -jəl əs **~ly** li **~ness** nəs nɪs
unseal ˌʌn ˈsiːᵊl **~ed** d **~ing** ɪŋ **~s** z
unseasonab|le ʌn ˈsiːz ᵊn‿əb |ᵊl ˌʌn- **~leness** ᵊl nəs -nɪs **~ly** li
un|seat ˌʌn |ˈsiːt **~seated** ˈsiːt ɪd -əd ‖ ˈsiːţ əd **~seating** ˈsiːt ɪŋ ‖ ˈsiːţ ɪŋ **~seats** ˈsiːts
unsecured ˌʌn sɪ ˈkjʊəd ◂ -sə-, §-siː-, -ˈkjɔːd ‖ -ˈkjʊᵊrd ◂
ˌunsecured ˈloan
unseeded ˌʌn ˈsiːd ɪd -əd
unseeing ˌʌn ˈsiː‿ɪŋ ◂
unseem|ly ʌn ˈsiːm |li **~liness** li nəs -nɪs
unseen ˌʌn ˈsiːn ◂ **~s** z
unselfish (ˌ)ʌn ˈself ɪʃ **~ly** li **~ness** nəs nɪs
Unser ˈʌnz ə ‖ -ᵊr
unserviceab|le (ˌ)ʌn ˈsɜːv ɪs əb |ᵊl §-ˈəs- ‖ -ˈsɜːv əs- **~leness** ᵊl nəs -nɪs **~ly** li
unsettl|e (ˌ)ʌn ˈset ᵊl ‖ -ˈseţ ᵊl **~ed** d **~es** z **~ing** ‿ɪŋ
unsettled *adj* ˌʌn ˈset ᵊld ◂ ‖ -ˈseţ ᵊld ◂ **~ness** nəs nɪs
unsex (ˌ)ʌn ˈseks **~ed** t **~es** ɪz əz **~ing** ɪŋ
unshakab|le, unshakeab|le ʌn ˈʃeɪk əb |ᵊl **~leness** ᵊl nəs -nɪs **~ly** li
unshaken ʌn ˈʃeɪk ən
unshaven ˌʌn ˈʃeɪv ᵊn ◂
unsheath|e (ˌ)ʌn ˈʃiːð **~ed** d **~es** z **~ing** ɪŋ
unshockable ˌʌn ˈʃɒk əb ᵊl ◂ ‖ -ˈʃɑːk-
unshod ˌʌn ˈʃɒd ◂ ‖ -ˈʃɑːd ◂
unsight|ly ʌn ˈsaɪt |li **~liness** li nəs -nɪs
unsigned ˌʌn ˈsaɪnd ◂
unsinkable ʌn ˈsɪŋk əb ᵊl
unskilled ˌʌn ˈskɪld ◂
unsmiling ˌʌn ˈsmaɪᵊl ɪŋ ◂
unsociab|le (ˌ)ʌn ˈsəʊʃ əb |ᵊl ‖ -ˈsoʊʃ- **~leness** ᵊl nəs -nɪs **~ly** li
unsocial ˌʌn ˈsəʊʃ ᵊl ◂ ‖ -ˈsoʊʃ- **~ly** i
ˌunˌsocial ˈhours
unsold ˌʌn ˈsəʊld ◂ →-ˈsɒʊld ‖ -ˈsoʊld ◂
unsolicited ˌʌn sə ˈlɪs ɪt ɪd ◂ §-ət-, -əd ‖ -əţ əd ◂
unsolved ˌʌn ˈsɒlvd ◂ §-ˈsəʊlvd ◂, §→ˈsɒʊlvd ◂ ‖ -ˈsɑːlvd ◂
unsophisticated ˌʌn sə ˈfɪst ɪ keɪt ɪd ◂ §-ˈ·ə-, -əd ‖ -ə keɪţ əd ◂
unsound ˌʌn ˈsaʊnd
unsparing ʌn ˈspeər ɪŋ ‖ -ˈsper ɪŋ -ˈspær- **~ly** li **~ness** nəs nɪs
unspeakab|le ʌn ˈspiːk əb |ᵊl **~leness** ᵊl nəs -nɪs **~ly** li
unspecified ʌn ˈspes ɪ faɪd -ə-
unspoiled ˌʌn ˈspɔɪᵊld ◂ -ˈspɔɪᵊlt
unspoilt ˌʌn ˈspɔɪᵊlt ◂
unspoken (ˌ)ʌn ˈspəʊk ən ‖ -ˈspoʊk ən
unsporting ˌʌn ˈspɔːt ɪŋ ‖ -ˈspɔːrţ- -ˈspoʊrţ-
unsportsmanlike ʌn ˈspɔːts mən laɪk ‖ -ˈspɔːrts- -ˈspoʊrts-
unspotted ˌʌn ˈspɒt ɪd ◂ -əd ‖ -ˈspɑːţ əd ◂ **~ness** nəs nɪs
Unst ʌnᵗst
unstab|le (ˌ)ʌn ˈsteɪb |ᵊl **~leness** ᵊl nəs -nɪs **~ly** li
unstated ˌʌn ˈsteɪt ɪd ◂ -əd ‖ -ˈsteɪţ-
unstead|y (ˌ)ʌn ˈsted |i **~ied** id **~ier** i‿ə ‖ i‿ᵊr **~ies** iz **~iest** i‿ɪst i‿əst **~ily** ɪ li ᵊl i **~iness** i nəs i nɪs **~ying** i ɪŋ
unstick ˌʌn ˈstɪk **~ing** ɪŋ **~s** s **unstuck** ˌʌn ˈstʌk
unstinted ʌn ˈstɪnt ɪd -əd ‖ -ˈstɪnţ əd
unstinting ʌn ˈstɪnt ɪŋ ‖ -ˈstɪnţ ɪŋ **~ly** li
unstop ˌʌn ˈstɒp ‖ -ˈstɑːp **~ped** t **~ping** ɪŋ **~s** s
unstoppab|le ʌn ˈstɒp əb |ᵊl ˌʌn- ‖ -ˈstɑːp- **~leness** ᵊl nəs -nɪs **~ly** li
unstreamed ˌʌn ˈstriːmd ◂
unstressed ˌʌn ˈstrest ◂
ˌunstressed ˈsyllables
unstructured (ˌ)ʌn ˈstrʌk tʃəd -ʃəd ‖ -tʃᵊrd **~ly** li **~ness** nəs nɪs
unstrung ˌʌn ˈstrʌŋ
unstuck ˌʌn ˈstʌk ◂
unstudied ˌʌn ˈstʌd id ◂
unsubscrib|e ˌʌn səb ˈskraɪb §-sʌb- **~ed** d **~es** z **~ing** ɪŋ
unsubstantiated ˌʌn səb ˈstænᵗʃ i eɪt ɪd ◂ §ˌ·sʌb-, -əd ‖ -eɪţ-
unsubtle ˌʌn ˈsʌt ᵊl ‖ -ˈsʌţ ᵊl
unsuccessful ˌʌn sək ˈses fᵊl ◂ §-sʌk-, -fʊl **~ly** ‿i **~ness** nəs nɪs
unsuitab|le (ˌ)ʌn ˈsuːt əb |ᵊl -ˈsjuːt- ‖ -ˈsuːţ- **~leness** ᵊl nəs -nɪs **~ly** li
unsuited ʌn ˈsuːt ɪd -ˈsjuːt-, -əd ‖ -ˈsuːţ-
unsullied ˌʌn ˈsʌl id
unsung ˌʌn ˈsʌŋ ◂
ˌunsung ˈhero
unsupervised ˌʌn ˈsuːp ə vaɪzd -ˈsjuːp- ‖ -ᵊr vaɪzd
unsupported ˌʌn sə ˈpɔːt ɪd ◂ -əd ‖ -ˈpɔːrţ əd ◂ -ˈpoʊrţ-
unsure ˌʌn ˈʃʊə ◂ -ˈʃɔː ‖ -ˈʃʊᵊr ◂ -ˈʃɜː **~ly** li **~ness** nəs nɪs
unsurpassed ˌʌn sə ˈpɑːst ◂ §ˈpæst ‖ -sᵊr ˈpæst ◂
unsurprising ˌʌn sə ˈpraɪz ɪŋ ◂ ‖ -sᵊr- -sə- **~ly** li
unsuspected ˌʌn sə ˈspekt ɪd ◂ -əd **~ly** li
unsuspecting ˌʌn sə ˈspekt ɪŋ ◂ **~ly** li
unsustainable ˌʌn sə ˈsteɪn əb ᵊl ◂
unswayed ˌʌn ˈsweɪd
unsweetened ˌʌn ˈswiːt ᵊnd ◂
unswerving ʌn ˈswɜːv ɪŋ ˌʌn- ‖ -ˈswɜːv ɪŋ **~ly** li
Unsworth ˈʌnz wɜːθ -wəθ ‖ -wɜːθ
unsympathetic ˌʌn ˌsɪmp ə ˈθet ɪk ◂ ‖ -ˈθeţ- **~ally** ᵊl‿i
unsystematic ˌʌn ˌsɪst ə ˈmæt ɪk -ɪ- ‖ -ˈmæţ ɪk **~ally** ᵊl‿i
untainted ˌʌn ˈteɪnt ɪd -əd ‖ -ˈteɪnţ-
untalented (ˌ)ʌn ˈtæl ənt ɪd -əd ‖ -ənţ əd
untamable, untameable ˌʌn ˈteɪm əb ᵊl ◂
untamed ˌʌn ˈteɪmd ◂
untangl|e (ˌ)ʌn ˈtæŋ gᵊl **~ed** d **~es** z **~ing** ‿ɪŋ
untapped ˌʌn ˈtæpt ◂
untarnished (ˌ)ʌn ˈtɑːn ɪʃt ‖ -ˈtɑːrn ɪʃt
untaught ˌʌn ˈtɔːt ◂ ‖ -ˈtɑːt

untenable ʌn 'ten əb əl ˌʌn-, -'tiːn-
untested ˌʌn 'test ɪd ◂ -əd
Unthank 'ʌn θæŋk
unthinkab|le ʌn 'θɪŋk əb |əl **~leness** əl nəs -nɪs **~ly** li
unthinking (ˌ)ʌn 'θɪŋk ɪŋ **~ly** li **~ness** nəs nɪs
unthought-of ʌn 'θɔːt ɒv -əv ‖ -'θɔːt̬ ʌv -'θɑːt̬-, -əv
unthought-out ˌʌn θɔːt 'aʊt ◂ ‖ θɔːt̬- -θɑːt̬-
untid|y (ˌ)ʌn 'taɪd |i **~ied** id **~ier** i‿ə ‖ i‿ər **~ies** iz **~iest** i‿ɪst i‿əst **~ily** ɪ li əl i **~iness** i nəs i nɪs **~ying** i‿ɪŋ
untie ˌʌn 'taɪ **~d** d **~s** z **untying** ʌn 'taɪ ɪŋ
until ən 'tɪl (ˌ)ʌn- —*also occasionally, in STRESS SHIFT environments* (ˌuntil 'now), 'ʌn təl
untime|ly (ˌ)ʌn 'taɪm |li **~liness** li nəs -nɪs
untinged ˌʌn 'tɪndʒd
untiring ʌn 'taɪ‿ər ɪŋ ‖ -'taɪ‿ər ɪŋ **~ly** li
untitled ʌn 'taɪt əld ‖ -'taɪt̬-
unto 'ʌn tu —*also, esp before a consonant,* -tə
untold ˌʌn 'təʊld ◂ ʌn-, →-'tɒʊld ‖ -'toʊld ◂
ˌuntold 'suffering
untouchability ˌʌn ˌtʌtʃ ə 'bɪl ət i -ɪt i ‖ -ət̬ i
untouchable (ˌ)ʌn 'tʌtʃ əb əl **~s** z
untouched (ˌ)ʌn 'tʌtʃt
untoward ˌʌn tə 'wɔːd ◂ -tu-; ˌʌn 'təʊ əd ‖ ʌn 'tɔːrd -'toʊrd *(*)* **~ly** li **~ness** nəs nɪs
untrained ˌʌn 'treɪnd ◂
untrammeled, untrammelled (ˌ)ʌn 'træm əld
untreated ˌʌn 'triːt ɪd ◂ -əd ‖ -'triːt̬-
untried ˌʌn 'traɪd ◂
untrue (ˌ)ʌn 'truː
untrustworthy ˌʌn 'trʌst ˌwɜːð i ‖ -ˌwɜ˞ːð i
un|truth (ˌ)ʌn |'truːθ '·· **~truths** 'truːðz 'truːθs
untruthful (ˌ)ʌn 'truːθ fəl -fʊl **~ly** ‿i **~ness** nəs nɪs
untuck ˌʌn 'tʌk **~ed** t **~ing** ɪŋ **~s** s
unturned ʌn 'tɜːnd ‖ -'tɜ˞ːnd
untutored ˌʌn 'tjuːt əd ◂ →-'tʃuːt- ‖ -'tuːt̬ ərd ◂ -'tjuːt̬-
untypical ʌn 'tɪp ɪk əl **~ly** ‿i
unusable ʌn 'juːz əb əl
unused *'not made use of'* ˌʌn 'juːzd ◂
unused *'unaccustomed'* (ˌ)ʌn 'juːst
unusual ʌn 'juːʒ u‿əl ˌʌn-, -ju‿əl; -'juːʒ əl
unusually ʌn 'juːʒ u‿əl i ˌʌn-, -'ju‿; -'juːʒ əl i
unutterab|le ʌn 'ʌt‿ər əb |əl ‖ -'ʌt̬ ər- **~leness** əl nəs -nɪs **~ly** li
unvarnished ˌʌn 'vɑːn ɪʃt ◂ ʌn- ‖ -'vɑːrn ɪʃt ◂
unveil ˌʌn 'veɪəl **~ed** d **~ing** ɪŋ **~s** z
unversed (ˌ)ʌn 'vɜːst ‖ -'vɜ˞ːst
unvoic|e ˌʌn 'vɔɪs ◂ **~ed** t **~es** ɪz əz **~ing** ɪŋ
unwaged ˌʌn 'weɪdʒd ◂
unwanted ˌʌn 'wɒnt ɪd ◂ §-'wʌnt-, -əd ‖ -'wɑːnt̬- -'wɔːnt̬-, ˌ'wʌnt̬-
unwarrantab|le ʌn 'wɒr ənt əb |əl ‖ -'wɔːr ənt̬- -'wɑːr- **~ly** li
unwarranted ʌn 'wɒr ənt ɪd -əd ‖ -'wɔːr ənt̬ əd -'wɑːr-
unwar|y (ˌ)ʌn 'weər |i ‖ -'wer |i -'wær- **~ily** əl i ɪ li **~iness** i nəs i nɪs
unwashed ˌʌn 'wɒʃt ◂ ‖ -'wɔːʃt -'wɑːʃt
unwavering ʌn 'weɪv ər‿ɪŋ **~ly** li
unwed ˌʌn 'wed ◂
unwelcom|e ʌn 'welk əm ˌʌn- **~ing** ɪŋ
unwell (ˌ)ʌn 'wel
unwholesome (ˌ)ʌn 'həʊl səm →-'hɒʊl- ‖ -'hoʊl- **~ly** li **~ness** nəs nɪs
unwield|y ʌn 'wiːəld |i **~ily** ɪ li əl i **~iness** i nəs i nɪs
unwilling (ˌ)ʌn 'wɪl ɪŋ **~ness** nəs nɪs
unwillingly ʌn 'wɪl ɪŋ li
Unwin 'ʌn wɪn
unwind ˌʌn 'waɪnd **~ing** ɪŋ **~s** z **unwound** ˌʌn 'waʊnd
unwise ˌʌn 'waɪz ◂ **~ly** li
unwished-for (ˌ)ʌn 'wɪʃt fɔː ‖ -fɔːr
unwitting (ˌ)ʌn 'wɪt ɪŋ ‖ -'wɪt̬ ɪŋ **~ly** li
unwonted ʌn 'wəʊnt ɪd -əd ‖ -'wɔːnt̬ əd -'wɑːnt̬-, -'woʊnt̬-, -'wʌnt̬- *(*)* **~ly** li **~ness** nəs nɪs
unworkable (ˌ)ʌn 'wɜːk əb əl ‖ -'wɜ˞ːk-
unworld|ly (ˌ)ʌn 'wɜːld |li ‖ -'wɜ˞ːld- **~liness** li nəs -nɪs
unworried ʌn 'wʌr id ‖ -'wɜː id
unworth|y (ˌ)ʌn 'wɜːð |i ‖ -'wɜ˞ːð |i **~ily** ɪ li əl i **~iness** i nəs i nɪs
unwound ˌʌn 'waʊnd
unwrap ˌʌn 'ræp ◂ **~ped** t **~ping** ɪŋ **~s** s
unwritten ˌʌn 'rɪt ən ◂
ˌunˌwritten 'law
unyielding ˌʌn 'jiːəld ɪŋ
unyok|e ˌʌn 'jəʊk ʌn- ‖ -'joʊk **~ed** t **~es** s **~ing** ɪŋ
Unzen 'ʊn zen —*Jp* ['ɯn dzeɴ]
unzip ˌʌn 'zɪp **~ped** t **~ping** ɪŋ **~s** s
up ʌp **upped** ʌpt **upping** 'ʌp ɪŋ **ups** ʌps
ˌups and 'downs
up- ˌʌp — **upgrowth** 'ʌp grəʊθ ‖ -groʊθ
up-and-com|ing ˌʌp ən 'kʌm |ɪŋ ◂ -ənd-, →-m-, →-əŋ- **~er/s** ə/z ‖ ər/z
up-and-down ˌʌp ən 'daʊn -ənd-, →-m-
up-and-up ˌʌp ən 'ʌp -ənd-
Upanishad u 'pʌn ɪʃ əd ju-, -'pæn-, -əʃ-; -ɪ ʃæd ‖ u 'pɑːn ɪ ʃɑːd **~s** z
upas 'juːp əs **~es** ɪz əz
upbeat 'ʌp biːt **~s** s
upbraid ʌp 'breɪd **~ed** ɪd əd **~ing** ɪŋ **~s** z
upbringing 'ʌp brɪŋ ɪŋ
upcast 'ʌp kɑːst §-kæst ‖ -kæst **~s** s
upchuck 'ʌp tʃʌk **~ed** t **~ing** ɪŋ **~s** s
upcoming 'ʌp ˌkʌm ɪŋ ˌ·'··
up-country ˌʌp 'kʌntr i ◂
up|date *v* ˌʌp |'deɪt **~dated** 'deɪt ɪd -əd ‖ 'deɪt̬ əd **~dates** 'deɪts **~dating** 'deɪt ɪŋ ‖ 'deɪt̬ ɪŋ
update *n* 'ʌp deɪt ˌ·'· **~s** s
Updike 'ʌp daɪk
updraft, updraught 'ʌp drɑːft §-dræft ‖ -dræft **~s** s
upend ʌp 'end **~ed** ɪd əd **~ing** ɪŋ **~s** z
upfront ˌʌp 'frʌnt **~ness** nəs nɪs
upgrad|e *v* ˌʌp 'greɪd '·· **~ed** ɪd əd **~ing** ɪŋ **~es** z

upgrade *n* 'ʌp greɪd ˌ·'· **~s** z
upheaval ʌp 'hiːv ᵊl **~s** z
upheld ʌp 'held
uphill ˌʌp 'hɪl ◂
ˌ**uphill 'struggle**
uphold ʌp 'həʊld →-'hɒʊld ‖ -'hoʊld **upheld** ʌp 'held **~er/s** ə/z ‖ ᵊr/z **~ing** ɪŋ **~s** z
upholst|er ʌp 'həʊlst |ə əp-, →-'hɒʊlst- ‖ ʌp 'hoʊlst |ᵊr ə 'poʊlst- **~ered** əd ‖ ᵊrd **~ering** ər‿ɪŋ **~ers** əz ‖ ᵊrz
upholsterer ʌp 'həʊlst ər‿ə əp-, →-'hɒʊlst- ‖ ʌp 'hoʊlst ᵊr‿ər ə 'poʊlst- **~s** z
upholster|y ʌp 'həʊlst ər‿|i əp-,→-'hɒʊlst- ‖ ʌp 'hoʊlst- ə 'poʊlst- **~ies** iz
UPI ˌjuː piː 'aɪ
Upjohn 'ʌp dʒɒn ‖ -dʒɑːn
upkeep 'ʌp kiːp
upland 'ʌp lənd -lænd **~s** z
uplift *v* ₍ˌ₎ʌp 'lɪft '· · **~ed** ɪd əd **~ing** ɪŋ **~s** s
uplift *n* 'ʌp lɪft **~s** s
uplighter 'ʌp ˌlaɪt ə ‖ -ˌlaɪţ ᵊr **~s** z
upload ˌʌp 'ləʊd ◂ ‖ -'loʊd ◂ **~ed** ɪd əd **~ing** ɪŋ **~s** z
up-market ˌʌp 'mɑːk ɪt ◂ §-ət ‖ -'mɑːrk ət ◂
Upminster 'ʌp mɪnˈst ə ‖ -ᵊr
upmost 'ʌp məʊst ‖ -moʊst
upon ə 'pɒn ‖ ə 'pɑːn -'pɔːn —*There is also an occasional weak form* əp ən
upper 'ʌp ə ‖ -ᵊr **~s** z
ˌ**upper 'case**◂; ˌ**Upper 'Chamber**; ˌ**upper 'class**◂; ˌ**upper 'crust**◂; ˌ**upper 'hand**; ˌ**Upper 'House**
upper-class ˌʌp ə 'klɑːs ◂ §-'klæs ‖ -ᵊr 'klæs ◂ **~man** mən **~men** mən **~woman** ˌwʊm ən **~women** ˌwɪm ɪn §-mən
an ˌ**upper-class 'accent**
uppercut 'ʌp ə kʌt ‖ -ᵊr- **~s** s
uppermost 'ʌp ə məʊst ‖ -ᵊr moʊst
Uppingham 'ʌp ɪŋ əm
uppish 'ʌp ɪʃ **~ly** li **~ness** nəs nɪs
uppity 'ʌp ət i -ɪt- ‖ -əţ i
Uppsala ʊp 'sɑːl ə ʌp-, '· · · —*Swedish* [''ʊp sɑː la]
upraised ˌʌp 'reɪzd ◂
up|rate *v* ₍ˌ₎ʌp |'reɪt **~rated** 'reɪt ɪd -əd ‖ 'reɪţ əd **~rates** 'reɪts **~rating** 'reɪt ɪŋ ‖ 'reɪţ ɪŋ
Uprichard ʌp 'rɪtʃ əd ju-, -ɑːd ‖ -ᵊrd
upright 'ʌp raɪt ˌ·'· **~ly** li **~ness** nəs nɪs **~s** s
uprising 'ʌp ˌraɪz ɪŋ ˌ·'· · **~s** z
upriver ˌʌp 'rɪv ə ◂ ‖ -ᵊr ◂
uproar 'ʌp rɔː ‖ -rɔːr -roʊr **~s** z
uproarious ʌp 'rɔːr i‿əs ‖ -'roʊr- **~ly** li **~ness** nəs nɪs
up|root ₍ˌ₎ʌp |'ruːt '· · ‖ -'rʊt **~rooted** 'ruːt ɪd -əd ‖ 'ruːţ əd 'rʊţ- **~rooting** 'ruːt ɪŋ ‖ 'ruːţ ɪŋ 'rʊţ- **~roots** 'ruːts ‖ 'rʊts
uprush 'ʌp rʌʃ **~es** ɪz əz
UPS ˌjuː piː 'es
upsadaisy ˌʌps ə 'deɪz i
upscale ˌʌp 'skeɪᵊl ◂
upset *n* 'ʌp set ·'· **~s** s
upset *adj* ˌʌp 'set ◂
ˌ**upset 'stomach**
up|set *v* ʌp |'set **~sets** 'sets **~setting** 'set ɪŋ ‖ 'seţ ɪŋ
Upshire 'ʌp ˌʃaɪ‿ə 'ʌp ʃə ‖ -ˌʃaɪ‿ᵊr 'ʌp ʃᵊr
upshot 'ʌp ʃɒt ‖ -ʃɑːt
upside 'ʌp saɪd **~s** z
upside down, upside-down ˌʌp saɪd 'daʊn -saɪ-
upsilon juːp 'saɪl ən uːp-, ʊp-, -ɒn; 'juːps ɪl ən, 'ʌps-, -ɒn ‖ 'uːps ə lɑːn 'juːps-, 'ʌps-, -əl ən (*) **~s** z
upsiz|e ˌʌp 'saɪz **~ed** d **~es** ɪz əz **~ing** ɪŋ
upskilling 'ʌp ˌskɪl ɪŋ
upstag|e ˌʌp 'steɪdʒ **~ed** d **~es** ɪz əz **~ing** ɪŋ
upstairs ˌʌp 'steəz ◂ ‖ -'steᵊrz -'stæᵊrz
upstanding ˌʌp 'stænd ɪŋ ◂ ʌp- **~ness** nəs nɪs
upstart 'ʌp stɑːt ‖ -stɑːrt **~s** s
upstate ˌʌp 'steɪt ◂
upstream ˌʌp 'striːm ◂
upstretched ˌʌp 'stretʃt ◂
upstroke 'ʌp strəʊk ‖ -stroʊk **~s** s
upsurg|e *n* 'ʌp sɜːdʒ ‖ -sɜːdʒ **~es** ɪz əz
upswept ˌʌp 'swept◂ '· ·
upswing *n* 'ʌp swɪŋ **~s** z
upsy-daisy ˌʌps i 'deɪz i
uptake *n* 'ʌp teɪk **~s** s
up-tempo ˌʌp 'temp əʊ ◂ ‖ -oʊ
upthrust *n* 'ʌp θrʌst **~s** s
uptick 'ʌp tɪk **~s** s
uptight 'ʌp taɪt ˌ·'· **~ness** nəs nɪs
uptime 'ʌp taɪm
up-to-date ˌʌp tə 'deɪt ◂ **~ness** nəs nɪs
Upton 'ʌpt ən
up-to-the-minute ˌʌp tə ðə 'mɪn ɪt ◂ §-ət
uptown ˌʌp 'taʊn ◂
an ˌ**uptown 'bus**
uptrend 'ʌp trend **~s** z
upturn *n* 'ʌp tɜːn ‖ -tɜːn **~s** z
upturned ˌʌp 'tɜːnd ◂ ‖ -'tɜːnd ◂
ˌ**upturned 'cars**
upward, U~ 'ʌp wəd ‖ -wᵊrd **~ly** li
upwardly-mobile ˌʌp wəd li 'məʊb aɪᵊl ◂ ‖ -wᵊrd li 'moʊb ᵊl ◂ -iːᵊl, -aɪᵊl
upwards 'ʌp wədz ‖ -wᵊrdz
upwind ˌʌp 'wɪnd ◂
Ur *ancient city* ɜː ʊə ‖ ɜː ʊᵊr
ur- *'primeval'* |ʊə |ɜː ‖ |ʊr —*Ger* [ʔuːɐ]
— **Ursprache** 'ʊə ˌʃprɑːx ə 'ɜː- ‖ 'ʊr ʃprɑːk ə 'ɜː- *Ger* ['ʔuːɐ ʃpʁaː xə]

uracil 'jʊər ə sɪl
uraemia juᵊ 'riːm i‿ə
Ural 'jʊər əl 'jɔːr- ‖ 'jʊr əl —*Russ* [u 'rɑɫ] **~s** z
Ural-Altaic ˌjʊər əl æl 'teɪ ɪk ◂ ˌjɔːr- ‖ ˌjʊr-
Uralian juᵊ 'reɪl i‿ən
Uralic juᵊ 'ræl ɪk
Urani|a juᵊ 'reɪn i‿|ə **~an/s** ən/z
uranic juᵊ 'ræn ɪk
uranium juᵊ 'reɪn i‿əm
uˌ**ranium 023'5**
uranographic ˌjʊər ən əʊ 'græf ɪk ◂ ˌjɔːr- ‖ ˌjʊr ən ə-

uranography ˌjʊər ə ˈnɒg rəf i ˌjɔːr- ‖ ˌjʊr ə ˈnɑːg-
uranous ˈjʊər ən əs ˈjɔːr- ‖ ˈjʊr-
Uranus ˈjʊər ən əs ˈjɔːr-; juᵊ ˈreɪn- ‖ ˈjʊr-
urban, Urban ˈɜːb ən ‖ ˈɜ˞ːb ən
Urbana ɜː ˈbæn ə -ˈbɑːn- ‖ ɜ˞ː-
urbane ɜː ˈbeɪn ‖ ɜ˞ː- **~ly** li **~ness** nəs nɪs
urbanis... *—see* **urbaniz...**
urbanite ˈɜːb ə naɪt ‖ ˈɜ˞ːb- **~s** s
urbanit|y ɜː ˈbæn ət |i -ɪt- ‖ ɜ˞ː ˈbæn əţ |i **~ies** iz
urbanization ˌɜːb ən aɪ ˈzeɪʃ ᵊn -ɪˈ-- ‖ ˌɜ˞ːb ən ə-
urbaniz|e ˈɜːb ə naɪz ‖ ˈɜ˞ːb- **~ed** d **~es** ɪz əz **~ing** ɪŋ
urbi et orbi ˌɜːb i et ˈɔːb i ˌʊəb- ‖ ˌɜ˞ːb i et ˈɔːrb i
urchin ˈɜːtʃ ɪn §-ən ‖ ˈɜ˞ːtʃ ən **~s** z
Urdd Gobaith Cymru ˌɪəð ˌgɒb aɪθ ˈkʌm ri -ˌgəʊb- ‖ ˌɪrð ˌgoʊb- *—Welsh* [ˌirð ˌgo baɪθ ˈkəm ri, ˌirð-, -ri]
Urdu ˈʊəd uː ˈɜːd- ‖ ˈʊrd uː *—Hindi-Urdu* [ʊr ḍuː]
Ure jʊə ‖ jʊᵊr
-ure jə jʊə ‖ jᵊr jʊr *—The* j *normally coalesces with a preceding* t, d, s, z, *to give* tʃ, dʒ, ʃ, ʒ *repectively —* **closure** ˈkləʊʒ ə ‖ ˈkloʊʒ ᵊr
urea juᵊ ˈriːˌə ˈjʊər iˌə, ˈjɔːr-
ureide ˈjʊər i aɪd ˈjɔːr- ‖ ˈjʊr- **~s** z
uremia juᵊ ˈriːm iˌə
Uren juᵊ ˈren
ureter juᵊ ˈriːt ə ˈjʊər ɪt ə, -ət- ‖ ˈjʊr əţ ᵊr ju ˈriːţ ᵊr **~s** z
urethane ˈjʊər ə θeɪn ˈjɔːr-, -ɪ-, ⚠-θiːn ‖ ˈjʊr-
ureth|ra juᵊ ˈriːθ |rə **~rae** riː **~ras** rəz
urethritis ˌjʊər ə ˈθraɪt ɪs ˌjɔːr-, -ɪ-, §-əs ‖ ˌjʊr ə ˈθraɪţ əs
Urey ˈjʊər i ‖ ˈjʊr i
urge ɜːdʒ ‖ ɜ˞ːdʒ **urged** ɜːdʒd ‖ ɜ˞ːdʒd **urges** ˈɜːdʒ ɪz -əz ‖ ˈɜ˞ːdʒ əz **urging/s** ˈɜːdʒ ɪŋ/z ‖ ˈɜ˞ːdʒ ɪŋ/z
urgency ˈɜːdʒ ənᵗs i ‖ ˈɜ˞ːdʒ-
urgent ˈɜːdʒ ənt ‖ ˈɜ˞ːdʒ- **~ly** li
urgh ɜːg ɜːx ‖ jʌk *—or various non-speech sounds, including* ɯː
-urgy ɜːdʒ i ‖ ɜ˞ːdʒ i— **thaumaturgy** ˈθɔːm ə tɜːdʒ i ‖ -tɜ˞ːdʒ i ˈθɑːm- *—but see also* **metallurgy**
-uria ˈjʊər iˌə ˈjɔːr- ‖ ˈjʊr iˌə — **polyuria** ˌpɒl i ˈjʊər iˌə -ˈjɔːr- ‖ ˌpɑːl i ˈjʊr iˌə
Uriah juᵊ ˈraɪˌə
uric ˈjʊər ɪk ˈjɔːr- ‖ ˈjʊr ɪk
uridine ˈjʊər ɪ diːn -ə-, -daɪn ‖ ˈjʊr-
uridylic ˌjʊər ɪ ˈdɪl ɪk ◂ ˌjɔːr-, -ə- ‖ ˌjʊr-
Uriel ˈjʊər iˌəl ˈjɔːr- ‖ ˈjʊr-
urim, Urim ˈjʊər ɪm ˈjɔːr-, §-əm ‖ ˈjʊr əm
urinal juᵊ ˈraɪn ᵊl ˈjʊər ɪn ᵊl, ˈjɔːr-, -ən- ‖ ˈjʊr ən ᵊl **~s** z
urinalysis ˌjʊər ɪ ˈnæl əs ɪs ˌjɔːr-, ˌ·ə-, -ɪs ·, §-əs ‖ ˌjʊr-
urinary ˈjʊər ɪn ər̮i ˈjɔːr-, ˈ·ən- ‖ ˈjʊr ə ner i
uri|nate ˈjʊər ɪ |neɪt ˈjɔːr-, -ə- ‖ ˈjʊr ə- **~nated** neɪt ɪd -əd ‖ neɪţ əd **~nates** neɪts **~nating** neɪt ɪŋ ‖ neɪţ ɪŋ
urination ˌjʊər ɪ ˈneɪʃ ᵊn ˌjɔːr-, -ə- ‖ ˌjʊr ə- **~s** z
urine ˈjʊər ɪn ˈjɔːr-, §-ən, §-aɪn ‖ ˈjʊr ən
URL ˌjuː ɑːr ˈel ‖ -ɑːr-
Urmston ˈɜːmᵖst ən ‖ ˈɜ˞ːmᵖst-
urn ɜːn ‖ ɜ˞ːn *(= earn)* **urns** ɜːnz ‖ ɜ˞ːnz
uro- *comb. form*
with stress-neutral suffix ¦jʊər əʊ ¦jɔːr- ‖ ¦jʊr oʊ — **urogenital** ˌjʊər əʊ ˈdʒen ɪt ᵊl ◂ ˌjɔːr-, -ət ᵊl ‖ ˌjʊr oʊ ˈdʒen əţ ᵊl ◂
with stress-imposing suffix juᵊ ˈrɒ+ ‖-ˈrɑː+ — **uroscopy** juᵊ ˈrɒsk əp i ‖ -ˈrɑːsk-
urologist juᵊ ˈrɒl ədʒ ɪst §-əst ‖ jə ˈrɑːl- **~s** s
urology juᵊ ˈrɒl ədʒ i ‖ -ˈrɑːl-
Urquhart ˈɜːk ət ‖ ˈɜ˞ːk ᵊrt
Ursa ˈɜːs ə ‖ ˈɜ˞ːs ə
ˌUrsa ˈMajor
ursine ˈɜːs aɪn ‖ ˈɜ˞ːs-
Ursula ˈɜːs jʊl ə -jəl- ‖ ˈɜ˞ːs əl ə
Ursuline ˈɜːs ju laɪn ˈɜːʃ-, -jə-, -lɪn ‖ ˈɜ˞ːs əl ən -ə laɪn, -ə liːn **~s** z
urticaria ˌɜːt ɪ ˈkeər iˌə §ˌ·ə- ‖ ˌɜ˞ːţ ə ˈker iˌə -ˈkær-
Uruguay ˈjʊər ə gwaɪ ˈʊər-, ˈʊr-, ˈjɔːr-, -ʊ-, ˌ· ·ˈ· ‖ ˈjʊr- ˈʊr-, -gweɪ—*Sp* [u ru ˈɣwai]
Uruguayan ˌjʊər ə ˈgwaɪ ən ◂ ˌʊər-, ˌʊr-, ˌjɔːr-, -ʊ- ‖ ˌjʊr- ˈgweɪ- **~s** z
Urumqi, Ürümqi ˌʊr ʊm ˈtʃiː ˌjʊr- *—Chi* Wūlǔmùqí [[1]wu [3]lu [4]mu [2]tɕʰi]
urus ˈjʊər əs ˈjɔːr- ‖ ˈjʊr əs **~es** ɪz əz
Urwin ˈɜː wɪn ‖ ˈɜ˞ː-
us *strong form* ʌs §ʌz, *weak form* əs §əz *—see also* **'s**
US ˌjuː ˈes ◂
ˌUS ˈNavy
USA ˌjuː es ˈeɪ
usab|le ˈjuːz əb |ᵊl **~leness** ᵊl nəs -nɪs **~ly** li
USAF ˌjuː es eɪ ˈef
usag|e ˈjuːs ɪdʒ ˈjuːz- *—Preference poll, BrE:* ˈjuːs- *72%,* ˈjuːz- *28%.* **~es** ɪz əz
usanc|e ˈjuːz ᵊnᵗs **~es** ɪz əz
USB ˌjuː es ˈbiː
Usborne ˈʌz bɔːn ‖ -bɔːrn -boʊrn
USCIS ˈʌsk ɪs
USDAW ˈʌs dɔː ˈʌz- ‖ -dɑː
use *v* juːz *(= yews)* **used** juːzd **uses** ˈjuːz ɪz -əz **using** ˈjuːz ɪŋ *—See also* **used to**
use *n* juːs **uses** ˈjuːs ɪz -əz
use-by ˈjuːz baɪ
ˌpast its ˈuse-by date
used *'was/were accustomed' (expressing a former fact or state)* **: used to** *final or before a vowel* ˈjuːst tu, *before a cons* ˈjuːst tə
used *adj 'accustomed'* juːst
used *'made use of'* juːzd
usedn't ˈjuːs ᵊnt ˈjuːst-
useful ˈjuːs fᵊl -fʊl **~ly** ˌi **~ness** nəs nɪs
useless ˈjuːs ləs -lɪs **~ly** li **~ness** nəs nɪs
Usenet ˈjuːz net
usen't ˈjuːs ᵊnt

U

USAGE

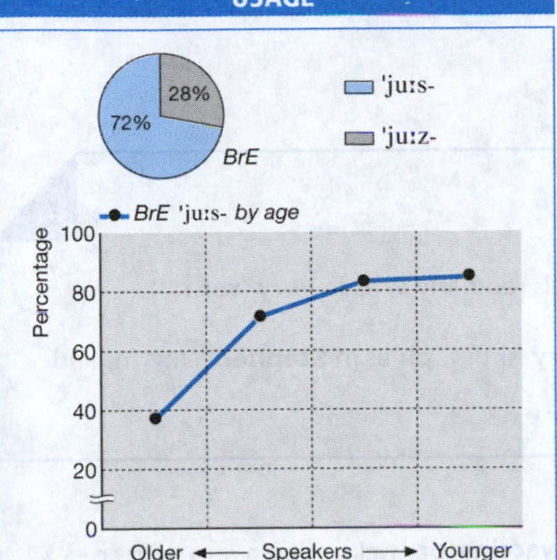

user 'juːz ə ‖ -ᵊr **~s** z
user-defined ˌjuːz ə di 'faɪnd ◂ -də'. ‖ ˌ·ᵊr-
user-friend|ly ˌjuːz ə 'frend |li ◂ ‖ -ᵊr- **~liness** li nəs -nɪs
userid 'juːz ər aɪ ˌdiː **~s** z
username 'juːz ə neɪm ‖ -ᵊr- **~s** z
Ushant 'ʌʃ ᵊnt
usher, Usher 'ʌʃ ə ‖ -ᵊr **~ed** d **ushering** 'ʌʃ ər‿ɪŋ **~s** z
usherette ˌʌʃ ə 'ret **~s** s
Usk ʌsk
USN ˌjuːes 'en
USP ˌjuː es 'piː
usquebaugh 'ʌsk wɪ bɔː -wə- ‖ -bɑː
Ussher 'ʌʃ ə ‖ -ᵊr
USSR ˌjuː es es 'ɑː ‖ -'ɑːr
Ustinov 'juːst ɪ nɒf 'uːst-, -ə-, -nɒv ‖ -nɔːf -nɑːf —*Russ* [u 'sʲtʲi nəf]
usual 'juːʒ u‿əl -ju‿; 'juːʒ ᵊl **~ness** nəs nɪs
usually 'juːʒ u‿əl i '·ju‿; 'juːʒ ᵊl‿i
usufruct 'juːs ju frʌkt 'juːz- ‖ -ə-
usurer 'juːʒ ər‿ə ‖ -ᵊr ər **~s** z
usurious ju 'zjʊər i‿əs -'ʒʊər-, -'zjɔːr- ‖ -'ʒʊr- -'zʊr- **~ly** li **~ness** nəs nɪs
usurp ju 'zɜːp -'sɜːp ‖ ju 'sɜːp -'zɜːp **~ed** t **~ing** ɪŋ **~s** s
usurpation ˌjuːz ɜː 'peɪʃ ᵊn ˌjuːs- ‖ ˌjuːs ᵊr- ˌjuːz- **~s** z
usur|y 'juːʒ ər‿|i -ʊər-, -jʊər-, -ʊr- **~ies** iz
ut ʊt ʌt, uːt
Utah 'juːt ɑː -ɔː ‖ -ɑː
Utahan, Utahn 'juːt ɑːn -ɔːn ‖ -ɔːn -ɑːn **~s** z
Ute juːt 'juːt i **Utes** juːts 'juːt iz
utensil ju 'tenᵗs ᵊl -ɪl **~s** z
uterine 'juːt ə raɪn -rɪn, -rən ‖ 'juːţ-
ut|erus 'juːt|‿ər əs ‖ 'juːţ|- **~eri** ə raɪ
Uther 'juːθ ə ‖ -ᵊr
ˌ**Uther Pen'dragon**
Utica 'juːt ɪk ə ‖ 'juːţ-
utilis... —*see* **utiliz...**
utilitarian ju ˌtɪl ɪ 'teər i‿ən ◂ ˌjuːt ɪl-, -ə'-- ‖ -'ter- **~ism** ˌɪz əm **~s** z
utilit|y ju 'tɪl ət |i -ɪt- ‖ -əţ |i **~ies** iz
u'tility room
utilizable 'juːt ɪ laɪz əb ᵊl '·ə-, '·ᵊl aɪz-, ˌ· ·'-- ‖ 'juːţ ᵊl aɪz-
utilization ˌjuːt ɪl aɪ 'zeɪʃ ᵊn ˌ·əl-, -ɪ'-- ‖ ˌjuːţ ᵊl ə- **~s** z
utiliz|e 'juːt ɪ laɪz -ə-, -ᵊl aɪz ‖ 'juːţ ᵊl aɪz **~ed** d **~es** ɪz əz **~ing** ɪŋ
utmost 'ʌt məʊst -məst ‖ -moʊst
Uto-Aztecan ˌjuːt əʊ 'æz tek ən ◂ -·'·· ‖ ˌjuːţ oʊ- **~s** z
utopi|a, U~ ju 'təʊp i‿|ə ‖ -'toʊp- **~an/s** ən/z **~anism** ən ˌɪz əm **~as** əz
Utrecht 'juːtr ekt -ext; ˌjuː 'trekt, -'trext —*Dutch* ['yː trɛxt]
utricle 'juːtr ɪk ᵊl **~s** z
Utrillo ju 'trɪl əʊ ‖ -oʊ —*Fr* [y tʁi jo] **~s** z
Utsira uːt 'sɪər ə ‖ -'sɪr ə —*Norw* [''ʉːt siː ɾa]
Uttar Pradesh ˌʊt ə prə 'deʃ -'deɪʃ ‖ ˌʊţ ᵊr- —*Hindi* [ʊt̪ t̪ər prə d̪eːʃ]
utter 'ʌt ə ‖ 'ʌţ ᵊr **uttered** 'ʌt əd ‖ 'ʌţ ᵊrd **uttering** 'ʌt‿ər ɪŋ ‖ 'ʌţ ər ɪŋ **utters** 'ʌt əz ‖ 'ʌţ ᵊrz
utteranc|e 'ʌt‿ᵊr ənᵗs ‖ 'ʌţ ər ənᵗs **~es** ɪz əz
utterly 'ʌt ə li -ᵊl i ‖ 'ʌţ ᵊr li
uttermost 'ʌt ə məʊst ‖ 'ʌţ ᵊr moʊst
Uttoxeter ju 'tɒks ɪt ə ʌ-, -ət-; 'ʌks ɪt ə, -ət- ‖ ju 'tɑːks əţ ᵊr
U-turn 'juː tɜːn ·'· ‖ -tɜːn **~s** z
uencod|e ˌjuː juː ɪn 'kəʊd ◂ -en'·, -ən'· ‖ -'koʊd ◂ **~ed** ɪd əd **~es** z **~ing** ɪŋ
UV ˌjuː 'viː
UVA ˌjuː viː 'eɪ
UVB ˌjuː viː 'biː
uvea 'juːv i‿ə
UVF ˌjuː viː 'ef
uv|ula 'juːv |jʊl ə -jəl- ‖ -jəl ə **~ulae** ju liː jə- ‖ jə liː **~ulas** jʊl əz jəl- ‖ jəl əz
uvular 'juːv jʊl ə -jəl- ‖ -jəl ᵊr **~s** z
uvularis... —*see* **uvulariz...**
uvularity ˌjuːv ju 'lær ət i ˌ·jə-, -ɪt i ‖ -jə 'lær əţ i -'ler-
uvularization ˌjuːv jʊl ər aɪ 'zeɪʃ ᵊn ˌ·jəl-, -ɪ'-- ‖ ˌ·jəl ər ə-
uvulariz|e 'juːv jʊl ə raɪz '·jəl- ‖ '·jəl- **~ed** d **~es** ɪz əz **~ing** ɪŋ
UWIST 'juː wɪst
Uxbridge 'ʌks brɪdʒ
uxorial ʌk 'sɔːr i‿əl ‖ -'soʊr-; ʌg 'zɔːr-, -'zoʊr-
uxoricide ʌk 'sɔːr ɪ saɪd §-ə- ‖ -'soʊr-; ʌg 'zɔːr-, -'zoʊr- **~s** z
uxorious ʌk 'sɔːr i‿əs ‖ -'soʊr-; ʌg 'zɔːr-, -'zoʊr- **~ly** li **~ness** nəs nɪs
Uzbek 'ʊz bek 'ʌz- **~s** s
Uzbekistan ˌʊz bek ɪ 'stɑːn ˌʌz-, -ə'-, -'stæn ‖ ʊz 'bek ə stæn -ɪ stæn
Uzi *tdmk* 'uːz i

Vv

v Spelling-to-sound

1 Where the spelling is **v**, the pronunciation is regularly v, as in **very** ˈver i.

2 v is also occasionally written **vv** as in **skivvy** ˈskɪv i, **ph** as in **Stephen** ˈstiːv ^{ə}n, and **f** in the single word **of** ɒv, əv ‖ ʌv, ɑːv, əv.

V, v viː **V's, v's, Vs** viːz —*Communications code name:* Victor **ˌV and ˈA**; **ˌV'O ˌlanguage**; **ˌV'U ˌmeter**

v *'versus'* ˈvɜːs əs viː ‖ ˈvɜːs-

V-1 ˌviː ˈwʌn §-ˈwɒn **~s** z

V-2 ˌviː ˈtuː **~s** z

Vaal vɑːl

vac væk **vacs** væks

vacanc|y ˈveɪk ən^{t}s |i →-ŋ^{t}s- **~ies** iz

vacant ˈveɪk ənt →-ŋt **~ly** li **~ness** nəs nɪs

vacate və ˈkeɪt veɪ- ‖ ˈveɪk eɪt *(*)* **vacated** və ˈkeɪt ɪd veɪ-, -əd ‖ ˈveɪk eɪţ əd **vacates** və ˈkeɪts veɪ- ‖ ˈveɪk eɪts **vacating** və ˈkeɪt ɪŋ veɪ- ‖ ˈveɪk eɪţ ɪŋ

VACATION

veɪ- və-

9% 91% AmE

61% 39% BrE

BrE veɪ- by age

Percentage

100 80 60 40 20 0

Older ⟵ Speakers ⟶ Younger

vacation veɪ ˈkeɪʃ ^{ə}n və- — *Preference polls, AmE:* veɪ- *91%,* və- *9%; BrE:* veɪ- *61%,* və- *39%.* **~er/s** ‿ə/z ‖ ‿^{ə}r/z **~ist/s** ‿ɪst/s §‿əst/s ‖ ‿əst/s **~s** z

vacci|nate ˈvæks ɪ |neɪt -ə- **~nated** neɪt ɪd -əd ‖ neɪţ əd **~nates** neɪts **~nating** neɪt ɪŋ ‖ neɪţ ɪŋ

vaccination ˌvæks ɪ ˈneɪʃ ^{ə}n -ə- **~s** z

vaccinator ˈvæks ɪ neɪt ə -ə- ‖ -neɪţ ^{ə}r **~s** z

vaccine ˈvæks iːn -ɪn ‖ væk ˈsiːn *(*)* **~s** z

vaccinia væk ˈsɪn i‿ə

Vachel, Vachell *(i)* ˈveɪtʃ ^{ə}l, *(ii)* ˈvætʃ ^{ə}l

Vacher ˈvæʃ ə ‖ -^{ə}r

vacherin ˈvæʃ ə ræ̃ -ɪn **~s** z —*Fr* [vaʃ ræ̃]

vacil|late ˈvæs ɪ |leɪt -ə- **~lated** leɪt ɪd -əd ‖ leɪţ əd **~lates** leɪts **~lating** leɪt ɪŋ ‖ leɪţ ɪŋ

vacillation ˌvæs ɪ ˈleɪʃ ^{ə}n -ə- **~s** z

Vaclav, Václav ˈvɑːt slɑːv ˈvæt-, -slæv, -slɑːf, -slæf —*also, by those unfamiliar with the name,* ˈvɑːk-, ˈvæk- —*Czech* [ˈvaːts laf]

vactor, VActor *tdmk* ˈvækt ə ‖ -^{ə}r **~s** z

vacua ˈvæk ju‿ə

vacuit|y væ ˈkjuː‿ət |i və-, ɪt i ‖ -əţ |i **~ies** iz

vacuole ˈvæk ju əʊl →-ɒʊl ‖ -oʊl **~s** z

vacuous ˈvæk ju‿əs **~ly** li **~ness** nəs nɪs

vacuum ˈvæk ju‿əm ˈvæk jʊm, -juːm **~s** z **ˈvacuum ˌcleaner**; **ˈvacuum flask**; **ˈvacuum pump**

vacuum-packed ˌvæk ju‿əm ˈpækt ◂ ˌjʊm'-, ˌjuːm'-, '. . . **ˌvacuum-packed ˈcheese**

vade mecum ˌvɑːd i ˈmeɪ kəm ˌwɑːd-, ˌ·eɪ-, -kʊm; ˌveɪd i ˈmiː-, -kʌm **~s** z

Vaduz vɑː ˈduːts —*Ger* [fa ˈdʊts, va ˈduːts]

vagabond ˈvæg ə bɒnd ‖ -bɑːnd **~s** z

vagabondage ˈvæg ə bɒnd ɪdʒ ‖ -bɑːnd ɪdʒ

vagal ˈveɪg ^{ə}l

vagar|y ˈveɪg ər |i ‖ və ˈger |i, -ˈgær- —*in BrE formerly also* və ˈgeər |i **~ies** iz

vagin|a və ˈdʒaɪn |ə **~ae** iː **~as** əz

vaginal və ˈdʒaɪn ^{ə}l ˈvædʒ ɪn ^{ə}l, -ən- ‖ ˈvædʒ ən ^{ə}l **~ly** i

vaginismus ˌvædʒ ɪ ˈnɪz məs -ə-, -ˈnɪs-

vagotom|y veɪ ˈgɒt əm |i və-, væ- ‖ -ˈgɑːţ- **~ies** iz

vagrancy ˈveɪg rən^{t}s i

vagrant ˈveɪg rənt **~s** s

vague veɪg **vaguely** ˈveɪg li **vagueness** ˈveɪg nəs -nɪs **vaguer** ˈveɪg ə ‖ -^{ə}r **vaguest** ˈveɪg ɪst -əst

vagus ˈveɪg əs **vagi** ˈveɪdʒ aɪ ˈveɪg-

Vail, vail veɪᵊl *(= veil)* **vailed** veɪᵊld **vailing** 'veɪᵊl ɪŋ **vails** veɪᵊlz
vain veɪn **vainer** 'veɪn ə ‖ -ᵊr **vainest** 'veɪn ɪst -əst
vainglorious ₍ₗ₎veɪn 'glɔːr i_əs ‖ -'gloʊr- **~ly** li **~ness** nəs nɪs
vainglor|y ₍ₗ₎veɪn 'glɔːr |i ‖ -'gloʊr-; '.̦ . . **~ies** iz
vain|ly 'veɪn |li **~ness** nəs nɪs
Vaizey 'veɪz i
Val væl
valanc|e 'væl ənᵗs **~ed** t **~es** ɪz əz
Valda 'væld ə
Valdemar 'væld ə mɑː -ɪ- ‖ 'vɑːld ə mɑːr 'væld-
Valderma *tdmk* væl 'dɜːm ə ‖ -'dɝːm-
Valderrama ˌvæl də 'rɑːm ə ‖ ˌvɑːl- —*Sp* [bal de 'rra ma]
Valdez *place in AK* væl 'diːz
Val d'Isère ˌvæl di 'zeə ‖ -'zeᵊr —*Fr* [val di zɛːʁ]
vale *Latin interj, n 'farewell'* 'vɑːl eɪ 'væl-, 'veɪl-, -i
vale *n 'valley'* veɪᵊl **vales** veɪᵊlz
valediction ˌvæl ɪ 'dɪk ʃᵊn -ə- **~s** z
valedictorian ˌvæl ɪ dɪk 'tɔːr i_ən ˌ·ə- ‖ -'toʊr- **~s** z
valedictor|y ˌvæl ɪ 'dɪk tər_|i ◂ ˌ·ə- **~ies** iz
valenc|e 'veɪl ənᵗs **~es** ɪz əz
Valencia *place in Spain* və 'lenᵗʃ i_ə -'lenᵗs-, -'lenᵗʃ ə —*Sp* [ba 'len θja]
Valenciennes ˌvæl ənᵗs i 'en ˌ·ɒ̃s-; və ˌlenᵗs- ‖ -'enz —*Fr* [va lɑ̃ sjɛn]
valenc|y 'veɪl ənᵗs |i **~ies** iz
Valency *river; family name* və 'lenᵗs i
Valentia *island in Ireland* və 'lenᵗʃ i_ə -'lenᵗʃ ə
valentine, V~ 'væl ən taɪn -tɪn **~s** z
Valentinian ˌvæl ən 'tɪn i_ən
Valentino ˌvæl ən 'tiːn əʊ ‖ -oʊ
Valera və 'lɪər ə -'leər- ‖ 'ler- -'lɪr-
valerian, V~ və 'lɪər i_ən -'leər- ‖ -'lɪr- **~s** z
valeric və 'lɪər ɪk -'leər-, -'ler- ‖ -'lɪr- -'ler-
Valerie 'væl ər_i
Valéry ˌvæl ə 'riː -eə-, '. . . ‖ ˌvɑːl-, -e- —*Fr* [va le ʁi]
valet 'væl ɪt -ət, -eɪ ‖ væ 'leɪ —*The traditional form with* t *is rivalled by an imitated French form in* -eɪ. **valeted** 'væl ɪt ɪd -ət-, -əd; 'væl eɪd ‖ 'væl əţ əd væ 'leɪd **valeting** 'væl ɪt ɪŋ -ət-, -eɪ- ‖ 'væl əţ ɪŋ væ 'leɪ ɪŋ **valets** 'væl ɪts -əts, -eɪz ‖ væ 'leɪz
valetudinarian ˌvæl ɪ ˌtjuːd ɪ 'neər i_ən ˌ·ə-, →-ˌtʃuːd-, -ə'--, -ᵊn 'eər- ‖ -ˌtuːd ᵊn 'er- -ˌtjuːd- **~s** z
valetudinary ˌvæl ɪ 'tjuːd ɪn ər_i ◂ ˌ·ə-, →-'tʃuːd-, -'·ən- ‖ -'tuːd ᵊn er i -'tjuːd-
valgus 'vælg əs **~es** ɪz əz
Valhalla væl 'hæl ə ‖ vɑːl 'hɑːl ə
valiant 'væl i_ənt ‖ 'væl jənt **~ly** li **~ness** nəs nɪs
valid 'væl ɪd §-əd **~ly** li **~ness** nəs nɪs
vali|date 'væl ɪ |deɪt -ə- **~dated** deɪt ɪd -əd ‖ deɪţ əd **~dates** deɪts **~dating** deɪt ɪŋ ‖ deɪţ ɪŋ
validation ˌvæl ɪ 'deɪʃ ᵊn -ə- **~s** z
validit|y və 'lɪd ət |i væ-, -ɪt i ‖ -əţ |i **~ies** iz
valis|e və 'liːz væ-, -'liːs ‖ -'liːs **~es** ɪz əz
valium, V~ *tdmk* 'væl i_əm **~s** z
Valkyrie 'vælk ər i -ɪr-, -ɪər-; væl 'kɪr i, -'kɪər-, -'kaɪᵊr- ‖ væl 'kɪr i 'vælk ər i **~s** z
Valladolid ˌvæl ə dəʊ 'lɪd ‖ -doʊ· —*Sp* [ba ʎa ðo 'lið, -ja-]
Vallance, Vallans 'væl ənᵗs
Valle Crucis ˌvæl i 'kruːs ɪs
Vallee 'væl i
Vallejo *place in CA* və 'leɪ əʊ væ-, -həʊ ‖ -oʊ -hoʊ
Valletta və 'let ə
valley, V~ 'væl i **~s** z
Vallins 'væl ɪnz §-ənz
vallum 'væl əm
Valois 'væl wɑː ‖ væl 'wɑː —*Fr* [va lwa] —*but the place in NY is* və 'lɔɪs
valor, Valor *tdmk* 'væl ə ‖ -ᵊr
valoris... —*see* **valoriz...**
valorization ˌvæl ər aɪ 'zeɪʃ ᵊn -ɪ'- ‖ -ə'--
valoriz|e 'væl ə raɪz **~ed** d **~es** ɪz əz **~ing** ɪŋ
valorous 'væl ər əs **~ly** li **~ness** nəs nɪs
valour 'væl ə ‖ -ᵊr
Valparaiso *place in IN* ˌvæl pə 'reɪz əʊ ‖ -oʊ
Valparaiso *place in Chile* ˌvæl pə 'raɪz əʊ -'reɪz- ‖ -oʊ —*Sp* Valparaíso [bal pa ra 'i so]
Valpeda *tdmk* væl 'piːd ə
Valpolicella, v~ ˌvæl pɒl ɪ 'tʃel ə ‖ ˌvɑːl poʊl- —*It* [val po li 'tʃɛl la]
valse vɑːls væls, vɔːls **valses** 'vɑːls ɪz 'væls-, 'vɔːls-, -əz
valuable 'væl jʊb ᵊl -ju_əb ᵊl ‖ -jəb- **~ness** nəs nɪs **~s** z
valuation ˌvæl ju 'eɪʃ ᵊn **~s** z
value 'væl juː -ju **~d** d **~s** z **valuing** 'væl juː_ɪŋ **'value ˌjudgment**
value-added ˌvæl juː 'æd ɪd ◂ -əd
ˌvalue-'added tax, ˌ. . . '. .
valueless 'væl ju ləs -lɪs
valuer 'væl ju_ə ‖ ᵊr **~s** z
Valujet *tdmk* 'væl ju dʒet
valvate 'vælv eɪt
valve vælv **valved** vælvd **valves** vælvz
Valvoline *tdmk* 'vælv ə liːn
valvular 'vælv jʊl ə -jəl- ‖ -jəl ᵊr
vamoos|e və 'muːs væ- **~ed** t **~es** ɪz əz **~ing** ɪŋ
vamp væmp **vamped** væmpt **vamping** 'væmp ɪŋ **vamps** væmps
vampire 'væmp aɪ_ə ‖ -aɪ_ᵊr **~s** z **'vampire bat**
vampirism 'væmp aɪ_ər ˌɪz əm ‖ -aɪ_ᵊr-
vampish 'væmp ɪʃ **~ness** nəs nɪs
van, Van væn **vans** vænz
vanadate 'væn ə deɪt **~s** s
vanadic və 'næd ɪk -'neɪd-
vanadinite və 'næd ɪ naɪt -'neɪd-, -ə-, -ᵊn aɪt
vanadium və 'neɪd i_əm

vanadous 'væn əd əs və 'neɪd-
Van Allen væn 'æl ən
Vananchal və 'nɑːntʃ əl
Vanbrugh 'væn brə →'væm- ‖ væn 'bruː
Van Buren væn 'bjʊər ən ‖ -'bjʊr- -'bjɜː-
Vance vænᵗs vɑːnᵗs
Van Cleef væn 'kliːf
vancomycin ˌvæŋk əʊ 'maɪs ɪn -ᵊn ‖ -ə maɪs ᵊn
Vancouver væn 'kuːv ə →væŋ- ‖ -ᵊr
vandal, V~ 'vænd ᵊl **~s** z
Vandalia væn 'deɪl i‿ə ‖ -'deɪl jə
vandalis... —*see* **vandaliz...**
vandalism 'vænd ə ˌlɪz əm -ᵊl ˌɪz-
vandaliz|e 'vænd ə laɪz -ᵊl aɪz **~ed** d **~es** ɪz əz **~ing** ɪŋ
Van de Graaff ˌvæn də 'grɑːf ◂ -'græf ‖ -'græf
ˌVan de ˌGraaff 'generator
Vandenberg, Van den Bergh 'vænd ən bɜːg →-əm- ‖ -bɝːg
Vanden Plas ˌvænd ən 'plæs →-əm-, -'plɑːs
Vanderbilt 'vænd ə bɪlt ‖ -ᵊr-
Vanderbyl 'vænd ə baɪᵊl ‖ -ᵊr-
van der Post ˌvæn də 'pɒst ‖ -dᵊr 'pɑːst
Van der Waals ˌvæn də 'wɑːlz ◂ ‖ -dᵊr- -'wɔːlz —*Dutch* [vɑn dər 'waːls]
ˌVan der ˌWaals 'forces
Van Diemen ₍ˌ₎væn 'diːm ən
Van Dyck, Vandyke, v~ ₍ˌ₎væn 'daɪk
vane, Vane veɪn *(= vain)* **vanes** veɪnz
Vanessa və 'nes ə
Van Eyck væn 'aɪk
vang væŋ **vangs** væŋz
Van Gogh væn 'gɒf →væŋ-, -'gɒx ‖ -'goʊ —*Dutch* [vɑn 'xɔx]
vanguard 'væn gɑːd →'væŋ- ‖ -gɑːrd **~s** z
vanilla və 'nɪl ə ‖ -'nel- **~s** z
vanillin və 'nɪl ɪn §-ən; 'væn əl-, -ɪl-
vanish 'væn ɪʃ **~ed** t **~es** ɪz əz **~ing/ly** ɪŋ /li
'vanishing point
vanitory, V~ *tdmk* 'væn ət‿ər i 'ɪt‿ ‖ -ə tɔːr i -toʊr i
vanit|y 'væn ət |i -ɪt- ‖ -əţ |i **~ies** iz
Van Nuys væ 'naɪz væn-
vanquish 'væŋk wɪʃ ‖ 'væn kwɪʃ **~ed** t **~es** ɪz əz **~ing** ɪŋ
Vansittart væn 'sɪt ət ‖ -'sɪţ ᵊrt
van Straubenzee ˌvæn strɔː 'benz i ‖ -strɑː-
vantage 'vɑːnt ɪdʒ §'vænt- ‖ 'vænţ ɪdʒ
vantagepoint 'vɑːnt ɪdʒ pɔɪnt §'vænt- ‖ 'vænţ- **~s** s

Vanuatu ˌvæn u 'ɑːt uː -'æt-; ˌvæn ə 'wɑːt uː; '. . . . ‖ ˌvɑːn-
Van Winkle væn 'wɪŋk ᵊl
Van Wyck væn 'waɪk ‖ -'wɪk
Van ˌWyck Ex'pressway
Vanya 'vɑːn jə 'væn-
Vanzetti væn 'zet i ‖ -'zeţ i
vapid 'væp ɪd §-əd **~ly** li **~ness** nəs nɪs
vapidity væ 'pɪd ət i və-, -ɪt- ‖ -əţ i
vapor... —*see* **vapour...**
vaporett|o ˌvæp ə 'ret |əʊ ‖ -'reţ |oʊ **~i** iː **~os** əʊz ‖ oʊz —*It* [va po 'ret to, -ti]
vaporis... —*see* **vaporiz...**
vaporization ˌveɪp ər aɪ 'zeɪʃ ᵊn -ɪ'-- ‖ -ə'--
vaporiz|e 'veɪp ə raɪz **~ed** d **~er/s** ə/z ‖ ᵊr/z **~es** ɪz əz **~ing** ɪŋ
vaporous 'veɪp ər əs **~ly** li **~ness** nəs nɪs
vapour 'veɪp ə ‖ -ᵊr **~ed** d **vapouring/s** 'veɪp ər ɪŋ/z **~s** z
'vapour trail
vapourer 'veɪp ər ə ‖ -ᵊr ər **~s** z
vapourware 'veɪp ə weə ‖ -ᵊr weᵊr -ᵊr wæᵊr
vapoury 'veɪp ər i
Varah 'vɑːr ə
Varangian və 'rændʒ i‿ən **~s** z
Varden 'vɑːd ᵊn ‖ 'vɑːrd ᵊn
varec 'vær ek -ɪk
Varèse və 'rez
varia 'veər i‿ə ‖ 'ver- 'vær-
variability ˌveər i‿ə 'bɪl ət i -ɪt i ‖ ˌver i‿ə 'bɪl əţ i ˌvær-
variab|le 'veər i‿əb |ᵊl ‖ 'ver- 'vær- **~les** ᵊlz **~ly** li
varianc|e 'veər i‿ənᵗs ‖ 'ver- 'vær- **~es** ɪz əz
variant 'veər i‿ənt ‖ 'ver- 'vær- **~s** s
variate 'veər i‿ət ɪt, -eɪt ‖ 'ver- 'vær- **~s** s
variation ˌveər i 'eɪʃ ᵊn ‖ ˌver- ˌvær- **~s** z
variational ˌveər i 'eɪʃ ᵊn‿əl ◂ ‖ ˌver- ˌvær- **~ly** i
variationist ˌveər i 'eɪʃ ᵊn‿ɪst §‿əst ‖ ˌver- ˌvær- **~s** s
varicella ˌvær i 'sel ə ‖ ˌver-
varices 'vær ɪ siːz 'veər-, ˌə- ‖ 'ver-
varicocele 'vær ɪ kəʊ siːᵊl '.ə- ‖ -ə koʊ siːᵊl 'ver- **~s** z
varicolored, varicoloured 'veər i ˌkʌl əd ‖ 'ver i ˌkʌl ᵊrd 'vær-
varicose 'vær ɪ kəʊs -ə-, -kəʊz, -kəs ‖ -ə koʊs 'ver-
ˌvaricose 'veins
varicosit|y ˌvær ɪ 'kɒs ət |i ˌ.ə-, -ɪt i ‖ -ə 'kɑːs əţ |i ˌver- **~ies** iz
varicotom|y ˌvær ɪ 'kɒt əm |i ˌ.ə- ‖ -ə 'kɑːţ- ˌver- **~ies** iz
varied 'veər id ‖ 'ver id 'vær- **~ly** li
variegated 'veər i‿ə geɪt ɪd '.i‿ɪ . ., -əd; '.ɪ geɪt ., '.ə- ‖ 'ver ɪ geɪţ əd 'vær-, '.i‿ə .
variegation ˌveər i‿ə 'geɪʃ ᵊn ˌ.i‿ɪ'. .; ˌ.ɪ'. ., ˌ.ə'. . ‖ ˌver i 'geɪʃ ᵊn ˌvær-, ˌ.i‿ə'. .
varietal və 'raɪ‿ət ᵊl ɪt- ‖ -əţ ᵊl **~ly** i
variet|y və 'raɪ‿ət |i ɪt- ‖ -'raɪ əţ |i **~ies** iz
va'riety show; va'riety store
varifocal 'veər i fəʊk ᵊl ˌ.'. . ‖ 'ver i foʊk ᵊl ˌ.'. . **~s** z
variform 'veər ɪ fɔːm -ə- ‖ 'ver i fɔːrm 'vær-
Varig *tdmk* 'vær ɪg ‖ 'ver-
variola və 'raɪ‿əl ə ‖ ˌver i 'oʊl ə
variolate 'veər i‿ə leɪt ‖ 'ver- 'vær-
variolite 'veər i‿ə laɪt ‖ 'ver- 'vær-
variometer ˌveər i 'ɒm ɪt ə -ət ə ‖ ˌver i 'ɑːm əţ ᵊr ˌvær- **~s** z
variorum ˌveər i 'ɔːr əm ˌvær- ‖ ˌver- ˌvær-, -'oʊr-
various 'veər i‿əs ‖ 'ver i‿əs 'vær- **~ly** li **~ness** nəs nɪs

variphone ˈveər i fəʊn ‖ ˈver i foʊn ˈvær- **~s** z
Varityper *tdmk* ˈveər i taɪp ə ‖ ˈver i taɪp ᵊr ˈvær- **~s** z
varix ˈveər ɪks ‖ ˈver- ˈvær- **varices** ˈvær ɪ siːz ˈveər-, -ə- ‖ ˈver-
varlet ˈvɑːl ət -ɪt ‖ ˈvɑːrl ət **~s** s
Varley ˈvɑːl i ‖ ˈvɑːrl i
varmint ˈvɑːm ɪnt -ənt ‖ ˈvɑːrm- **~s** s
Varney ˈvɑːn i ‖ ˈvɑːrn i
varnish ˈvɑːn ɪʃ ‖ ˈvɑːrn ɪʃ **~ed** t **~es** ɪz əz **~ing** ɪŋ
Varro ˈvær əʊ ‖ -oʊ ˈver-
varroa və ˈrəʊ ə ˈvær əʊ ə ‖ -ˈroʊ-
varsit|y ˈvɑːs ət |i -ɪt- ‖ ˈvɑːrs əṭ |i **~ies** iz
Varteg ˈvɑːt eg ‖ ˈvɑːrt-
varus ˈveər əs ‖ ˈver əs ˈvær- **~es** ɪz əz
varve vɑːv ‖ vɑːrv **varves** vɑːvz ‖ vɑːrvz
var|y ˈveər |i ‖ ˈver |i ˈvær- **~ied** id **~ies** iz **~ying** i ɪŋ
vas væs vɑːs **vasa** ˈveɪz ə ˈvɑːz-, ˈveɪs-, ˈvɑːs-
ˌ**vas** ˈ**deferens** ˈdef ə renz
Vasco da Gama ˌvæsk əʊ də ˈgɑːm ə ‖ ˌvɑːsk oʊ- -ˈgæm- —*Port* [ˌvaʃ ku ðɐ ˈɣɐ mɐ]
vascul|um ˈvæsk jʊl |əm -jəl- ‖ -jəl |əm **~a** ə **~ar** ə ‖ ᵊr
vase vɑːz ‖ veɪs veɪz *(*)—in BrE formerly also* vɔːz **vases** ˈvɑːz ɪz -əz ‖ ˈveɪs əz ˈveɪz-
vasectom|y və ˈsekt əm |i væ- **~ies** iz
vaseline, V~ *tdmk* ˈvæs ə liːn ˈvæz-, -ɪ-, -ᵊl iːn, ˌ..ˈ.
Vashti ˈvæʃt aɪ
vasoconstriction ˌveɪz əʊ kən ˈstrɪk ʃᵊn §-kɒnˈ-- ‖ ˌ.oʊ-
vasoconstrictor ˌveɪz əʊ kən ˈstrɪkt ə §-kɒnˈ-- ‖ -oʊ kən ˈstrɪkt ᵊr **~s** z
vasodilator ˌveɪz əʊ daɪ ˈleɪt ə ‖ -oʊ daɪ ˈleɪṭ ᵊr -dəˈ--; -ˈdaɪl eɪṭ ᵊr **~s** z
vasomotor ˌveɪz əʊ ˈməʊt ə ◂ ‖ -oʊ ˈmoʊṭ ᵊr ˌvæs-, -ə-
vasopressin ˌveɪz əʊ ˈpres ɪn §-ᵊn ‖ -oʊ- ˌvæs-
vassal, V~ ˈvæs ᵊl **~s** z
vassalage ˈvæs ᵊl ɪdʒ
Vassar ˈvæs ə ‖ -ᵊr
vast vɑːst §væst ‖ væst **vaster** ˈvɑːst ə §ˈvæst- ‖ ˈvæst ᵊr **vastest** ˈvɑːst ɪst §ˈvæst-, -əst ‖ ˈvæst əst
vast|ly ˈvɑːst |li §ˈvæst- ‖ ˈvæst |li **~ness/es** nəs ɪz nɪs-, -əz
vat væt **vats** væts
VAT ˌviː eɪ ˈtiː væt —*But as an informal verb, always* væt **VAT'd** ˈvæt ɪd -əd ‖ ˈvæṭ əd **VAT'ing** ˈvæt ɪŋ ‖ ˈvæṭ ɪŋ **VAT's** væts
VATable ˈvæt əb ᵊl ‖ ˈvæṭ-
Vatersay ˈvæt ə seɪ ‖ ˈvæṭ ᵊr-
Vathek ˈvɑːθ ek ˈvæθ-
vatic ˈvæt ɪk ‖ ˈvæṭ ɪk
Vatican ˈvæt ɪk ən ‖ ˈvæṭ-
ˌ**Vatican** ˈ**City**
vatici|nate væ ˈtɪs ɪ |neɪt -ə-, -ᵊ|n eɪt ‖ -ᵊ|n eɪt **~nated** neɪt ɪd -əd ‖ neɪṭ əd **~nates** neɪts **~nating** neɪt ɪŋ ‖ neɪṭ ɪŋ
vaticination ˌvæt ɪs ɪ ˈneɪʃ ᵊn ˌ.əs-; væ ˌtɪs-, və- ‖ və ˌtɪs- ˌvæṭ əs- **~s** z
VAT|man ˈvæt mæn **~men** men
Vaucluse vəʊ ˈkluːz ‖ voʊ- —*Fr* [vo klyːz]
vaudeville ˈvɔːd ə vɪl ˈvəʊd-; ˈ-vɪl, -vᵊl ‖ ˈvɑːd-
Vaughan, Vaughn vɔːn ‖ vɑːn
ˌ**Vaughan** ˈ**Williams**
vault vɔːlt vɒlt ‖ vɑːlt **vaulted** ˈvɔːlt ɪd ˈvɒlt-, -əd ‖ ˈvɑːlt- **vaulting** ˈvɔːlt ɪŋ ˈvɒlt- ‖ ˈvɑːlt- **vaults** vɔːlts vɒlts ‖ vɑːlts
ˈ**vaulting horse**
vaunt vɔːnt ‖ vɑːnt **vaunted** ˈvɔːnt ɪd -əd ‖ ˈvɔːnṭ əd ˈvɑːnṭ- **vaunting/ly** ˈvɔːnt ɪŋ /li ‖ ˈvɔːnṭ ɪŋ /li ˈvɑːnṭ- **vaunts** vɔːnts ‖ vɑːnts
Vaux *(i)* vɔːks ‖ vɑːks, *(ii)* vəʊ ‖ voʊ, *(iii)* vɒks ‖ vɑːks
Vauxhall ˈvɒks ɔːl -hɔːl; ˌvɒk ˈsɔːl, ˌvɒks ˈhɔːl ‖ ˈvɑːks- ˈvɔːks-, -ɑːl, -hɔːl, -hɑːl
vavasor, vavasour, V~ ˈvæv ə sɔː -sʊə; -əs ə ‖ -sɔːr -soʊr **~s** z
Vavasseur ˌvæv ə ˈsɜː ‖ -ˈsɜː
va-va-voom ˌvæv ə ˈvuːm ˌvɑː vɑː-
VAX *tdmk* væks
Vaz væz
VC ˌviː ˈsiː **~s, ~'s** z
V-chip ˈviː tʃɪp **~s** s
vCJD ˌviː siː dʒeɪ ˈdiː
VCR ˌviː siː ˈɑː ‖ -ˈɑːr **~s, ~'s** z
VD ˌviː ˈdiː
VDT ˌviː diː ˈtiː **~s** z
VDU, vdu ˌviː diː ˈjuː **~s** z
've əv *—but after a pronoun ending in a vowel sound,* v — some've done it ˌsʌm əv ˈdʌn ɪt, they've tried ðeɪv ˈtraɪd
veal, Veal viːᵊl
Veblen ˈveb lən
Vectis ˈvekt ɪs §-əs
vector ˈvekt ə ‖ -ᵊr **~ed** d **vectoring** ˈvekt ər ɪŋ **~s** z
vectorial vek ˈtɔːr i‿əl ‖ -ˈtoʊr-
Vectra *tdmk* ˈvek trə
Veda ˈveɪd ə ˈviːd- **~s** z
Vedanta vɪ ˈdɑːnt ə ve-, veɪ-, və-, -ˈdænt- —*Hindi* [veː d̪ɑːn̪ʈ]
Vedda ˈved ə **~s** z
vedette vɪ ˈdet və- **~s** s
Vedic ˈveɪd ɪk ˈviːd-
veejay ˈviː dʒeɪ **~s** z
veep viːp **veeps** viːps
veer vɪə ‖ vɪᵊr **veered** vɪəd ‖ vɪᵊrd **veering** ˈvɪər ɪŋ ‖ ˈvɪr ɪŋ **veers** vɪəz ‖ vɪᵊrz
veg vedʒ
Vega *name of star* ˈviːg ə ˈveɪg-
Vega *Spanish name* ˈveɪg ə —*Sp* [ˈbe ɣa]
vegan ˈviːg ən **~ism** ˌɪz əm **~s** z
Veganin *tdmk* ˈvedʒ ən ɪn §-ən
Vegas ˈveɪg əs
vegeburger ˈvedʒ i ˌbɜːg ə ‖ -bɜːg ᵊr **~s** z
vegemite, V~ *tdmk* ˈvedʒ ə maɪt -ɪ-
vegetable ˈvedʒ təb ᵊl ˈvedʒ ət əb ᵊl, ˈ·ɪt- ‖ ˈ·əṭ əb ᵊl **~s** z
ˈ**vegetable knife**; ˌ**vegetable** ˈ**marrow**
vegetal ˈvedʒ ɪt ᵊl -ət- ‖ -əṭ ᵊl

V

vegetarian ˌvedʒ ə ˈteər i‿ən ◂ ˌ·ɪ- ‖ -ˈter- -ˈtær- **~ism** ˌɪz əm **~s** s
vege|tate ˈvedʒ ə |teɪt -ɪ- **~tated** teɪt ɪd -əd ‖ teɪţ əd **~tates** teɪts **~tating** teɪt ɪŋ ‖ teɪţ ɪŋ
vegetation ˌvedʒ ə ˈteɪʃ ən -ɪ-
vegetative ˈvedʒ ət ət ɪv -ˈ·ɪt-; -ə teɪt-, -ɪ teɪt- ‖ -ə teɪţ ɪv **~ly** li **~ness** nəs nɪs
veggie, veggy, vegie ˈvedʒ i **~s** z
veggieburger ˈvedʒ i ˌbɜːg ə ‖ -bɜːg ər **~s** z
vehemence ˈviːˌəm ənts ˈveɪ-, ˌɪm-, -həm-, -hɪm-
vehement ˈviːˌəm ənt ˈveɪ-, ˌɪm-, -həm-, -hɪm- **~ly** li

VEHICLE

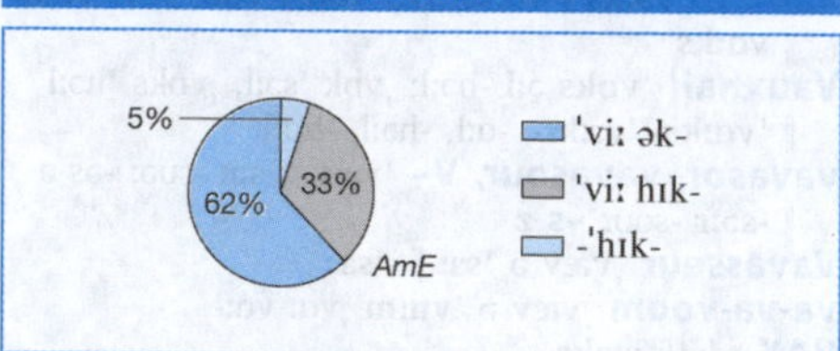

vehicle ˈviːˌɪk əl ˌək-, §-hɪk- ‖ ˈviː ək əl -hɪk-, ·ˈhɪk· — *Preference poll, AmE:* ˈviː ək- *62%,* ˈviː hɪk- *33%;* -ˈhɪk- *5%.* **~s** z
vehicular vɪ ˈhɪk jʊl ə və-, viː-, -jəl- ‖ viː ˈhɪk jəl ər
veil veɪəl *(= vale)* **veiled** veɪəld **veiling** ˈveɪəl ɪŋ **veils** veɪlz
vein veɪn *(= vain)* **veined** veɪnd **veining** ˈveɪn ɪŋ **veins** veɪnz
vela, Vela ˈviːl ə
velar ˈviːl ə ‖ -ər **~s** z
velaric viː ˈlær ɪk vɪ- ‖ -ˈler-
velaris... —*see* **velariz...**
velarity viː ˈlær ət i vɪ-, -ɪt- ‖ -əţ i -ˈler-
velarization ˌviːl ər aɪ ˈzeɪʃ ən -ɪˈ·- ‖ -əˈ-
velariz|e ˈviːl ə raɪz **~ed** d **~es** ɪz əz **~ing** ɪŋ
Velasquez, Velázquez vɪ ˈlæsk wɪz və-, ve-, -ɪz, -wez, -wɪθ ‖ və ˈlɑːsk eɪs -ˈlæsk-, -əs —*Sp* [be ˈlas keθ, -ˈlaθ-]
Velcro *tdmk,* **v~** ˈvel krəʊ ‖ -kroʊ **~ed** d
veld, veldt velt felt
veleta və ˈliːt ə vɪ- ‖ -ˈliːţ ə **~s** z
Velia ˈviːl i‿ə
velic ˈviːl ɪk
Velindre ve ˈlɪn dreɪ -ˈlɪndr ə
velleit|y ve ˈliːˌət |i və-, -ɪt- ‖ -əţ |i **~ies** iz
vellum ˈvel əm
Velma ˈvelm ə
velocipede və ˈlɒs ə piːd vɪ-, -ɪ- ‖ -ˈlɑːs- **~s** z
velociraptor vəˌlɒs ɪ ˈræpt ə vɪ-, -ə-; ·ˈ· · · · ‖ -ˌlɑːs ə ˈræpt ər ·ˈ· · · · **~s** z
velocit|y və ˈlɒs ət |i vɪ-, -ɪt- ‖ -ˈlɑːs əţ |i **~ies** iz
velodrome ˈvel ə drəʊm ˈviːl- ‖ -droʊm **~s** z
velour, velours və ˈlʊə ve- ‖ -ˈlʊər
veloute, velouté və ˈluːt eɪ ve- ‖ vəˌluː ˈteɪ
velum ˈviːl əm **vela** ˈviːl ə
Velux *tdmk* ˈviː lʌks
Velveeta *tdmk* vel ˈviːt ə ‖ -ˈviːţ ə
velvet ˈvelv ɪt §-ət **~s** s
velveteen ˌvelv ə ˈtiːn -ɪ-, ˈ· · · **~s** z
velvety ˈvelv ət i -ɪt- ‖ -əţ i
vena ˈviːn ə **venae** ˈviːn iː
ˌ**vena** ˈ**cava** ˈkeɪv ə
Venable ˈven əb əl
Venables ˈven əb əlz
venal ˈviːn əl **~ly** i
venality viː ˈnæl ət i vɪ-, -ɪt- ‖ -əţ i
vend vend **vended** ˈvend ɪd -əd **vending** ˈvend ɪŋ **vends** vendz
ˈ**vending ma**ˌ**chine**
Venda ˈvend ə
vendace ˈvend ɪs -əs, -eɪs
vendee ˌven ˈdiː **~s** z
vender ˈvend ə ‖ -ər **~s** z
vendetta ven ˈdet ə ‖ -ˈdeţ ə **~s** z
vendor ˈvend ə ‖ -ər —*for contrast also* -ɔː ‖ -ɔːr, *or* ˌven ˈdɔː ‖ -ˈdɔːr **~s** z
veneer və ˈnɪə vɪ- ‖ -ˈnɪər **~ed** d **veneering** və ˈnɪər ɪŋ vɪ- ‖ -ˈnɪr ɪŋ **~s** z
venerab|le ˈven ərˌəb |əl **~leness** əl nəs -nɪs **~ly** li
vene|rate ˈven ə |reɪt **~rated** reɪt ɪd -əd ‖ reɪţ əd **~rates** reɪts **~rating** reɪt ɪŋ ‖ reɪţ ɪŋ
veneration ˌven ə ˈreɪʃ ən
venerator ˈven ə reɪt ə ‖ -reɪţ ər **~s** z
venereal və ˈnɪər i‿əl vɪ- ‖ -ˈnɪr-
veˌ**nereal di'sease**, ·ˈ· · · ·ˌ·
venereologist və ˌnɪər i ˈɒl ədʒ ɪst vɪ-, §-əst ‖ -ˌnɪr i ˈɑːl- **~s** s
venereology və ˌnɪər i ˈɒl ədʒ i vɪ- ‖ -ˌnɪr i ˈɑːl-
venery ˈven ər i ˈviːn-
Veness və ˈnes vɪ-
Venetia və ˈniːʃ ə vɪ-, -ˈniːʃ i‿ə
Venetian, v~ və ˈniːʃ ən vɪ-, -ˈniːʃ i‿ən **~s** z
veˌ**netian** ˈ**blind**
Venetic və ˈnet ɪk vɪ-, ve- ‖ -ˈneţ ɪk
Venezuel|a ˌven ə ˈzweɪl |ə -ɪ-, -e- —*AmSp* [be ne ˈswe la] **~an/s** ən/z
vengeance ˈvendʒ ənts
vengeful ˈvendʒ fəl -fʊl **~ly** i **~ness** nəs nɪs
veni, vidi, vici ˌveɪn iː ˌviːd iː ˈviːk iː -ˈviːtʃ i; ˌweɪn i ˌwiːd i ˈwiːk i
venial ˈviːn i‿əl **~ly** i **~ness** nəs nɪs
veniality ˌviːn i ˈæl ət i -ɪt i ‖ -əţ i
Venice ˈven ɪs §-əs
venison ˈven ɪs ən -əs-, -ɪz-, -əz-; ˈvenz ən
Venite və ˈnaɪt i vɪ-, ve-, -ˈniːt eɪ ‖ -ˈnaɪţ i -ˈniːt eɪ
Venn ven
Venner ˈven ə ‖ -ər
venom ˈven əm
venomous ˈven əm əs **~ly** li **~ness** nəs nɪs
Veno's *tdmk* ˈviːn əʊz ‖ -oʊz
venous ˈviːn əs **~ly** li
vent vent **vented** ˈvent ɪd -əd ‖ ˈvenţ əd **venting** ˈvent ɪŋ ‖ ˈvenţ ɪŋ **vents** ven*t*s
Vent-Axia *tdmk* ˌvent ˈæks i‿ə
Venter ˈvent ə ‖ ˈvenţ ər
venti|late ˈvent ɪ |leɪt -ə-, -əl eɪt ‖ ˈvenţ əl eɪt **~lated** leɪt ɪd -əd ‖ leɪţ əd **~lates** leɪts **~lating** leɪt ɪŋ ‖ leɪţ ɪŋ

ventilation ˌvent ɪ ˈleɪʃ ᵊn -ə-, -ᵊl ˈeɪʃ- ‖ ˌvenţ ᵊl ˈeɪʃ ᵊn
ventilator ˈvent ɪ leɪt ə -ə-, -ᵊl eɪt- ‖ ˈvenţ ᵊl eɪţ ᵊr **~s** z
Ventnor ˈvent nə ‖ -nᵊr
Ventolin *tdmk* ˈvent əʊ lɪn -ᵊl ɪn, §-ən ‖ ˈvenţ ᵊl ən
ventral ˈventr əl **~ly** i
ventricle ˈventr ɪk ᵊl **~s** z
ventricular ven ˈtrɪk jʊl ə vən-, -jəl- ‖ -jəl ᵊr
ventriloquial ˌventr ɪ ˈləʊk wi‿əl ◂ ˌ-ə- ‖ -ˈloʊk-
ventriloquism ven ˈtrɪl ə ˌkwɪz əm
ventriloquist ven ˈtrɪl ək wɪst §-wəst **~s** s
ventriloquy ven ˈtrɪl ək wi
Ventris ˈventr ɪs §-əs
Ventura ven ˈtjʊər ə →-ˈtʃʊər ə ‖ -ˈtʊr ə -ˈtjʊr ə
venture, V~ ˈventʃ ə ‖ -ᵊr **~d** d **~s** z
venturing ˈventʃ ər‿ɪŋ
ˈ**venture** ˌ**capital**
venturer ˈventʃ ər ə ‖ -ᵊr‿ər **~s** z
venturesome ˈventʃ ə səm ‖ -ᵊr- **~ly** li **~ness** nəs nɪs
Venturi, v~ ven ˈtjʊər i →-ˈtʃʊər i ‖ -ˈtʊr i **~s** z
ven'turi tube
venturous ˈventʃ ər‿əs **~ly** li **~ness** nəs nɪs
venue ˈven juː **~s** z
venule ˈven juːl ˈviːn- **~s** z
Venus ˈviːn əs **~es, ~'s** ɪz əz
ˌ**Venus('s) 'flytrap**
Venusian və ˈnjuːz i‿ən vɪ-, -ˈnjuːs- ‖ -ˈnuːʒ ᵊn -ˈnuːʃ-, -ˈnjuːʒ-, -ˈnjuːʃ-, -ˈ·i‿ən **~s** z
Vera ˈvɪər ə ‖ ˈvɪr ə
veracious və ˈreɪʃ əs vɪ-, ve- **~ly** li **~ness** nəs nɪs
veracit|y və ˈræs ət |i vɪ-, ve-, -ɪt- ‖ -əţ |i **~ies** iz
Veracruz, Vera Cruz ˌvɪər ə ˈkruːz ˌver-, ˌveər- ‖ ˌver- —*AmSp* [ˌbe ra ˈkrus]
veranda, verandah və ˈrænd ə **~ed** d **~s** z
verb vɜːb ‖ vɜ˞ːb **verbs** vɜːbz ‖ vɜ˞ːbz
verbal ˈvɜːb ᵊl ‖ ˈvɜ˞ːb ᵊl **~ed, ~led** d **~ing, ~ling** ɪŋ **~ly** i **~s** z
ˌ**verbal 'noun**
verbalis... —*see* **verbaliz...**
verbalism ˈvɜːb ə ˌlɪz əm -ᵊl ˌɪz- ‖ ˈvɜ˞ːb-
verbalization ˌvɜːb əl aɪ ˈzeɪʃ ᵊn -ɪ'-- ‖ ˌvɜ˞ːb əl ə- **~s** z
verbaliz|e ˈvɜːb ə laɪz -ᵊl aɪz ‖ ˈvɜ˞ːb- **~ed** d **~es** ɪz əz **~ing** ɪŋ
verbatim vɜː ˈbeɪt ɪm -ˈbɑːt-, §-əm ‖ vɜ˞ː ˈbeɪţ əm -ɪm
verbena vɜː ˈbiːn ə və- ‖ vɜ˞ː-
verbiage ˈvɜːb i‿ɪdʒ ‖ ˈvɜ˞ːb-
verbose vɜː ˈbəʊs ‖ vɜ˞ː ˈboʊs **~ly** li **~ness** nəs nɪs
verbosity vɜː ˈbɒs ət i -ɪt- ‖ vɜ˞ː ˈbɑːs əţ i
verboten fə ˈbəʊt ᵊn və- ‖ fᵊr ˈboʊt ᵊn vᵊr- —*Ger* [fɛɐ ˈboː tᵊn]
Vercingetorix ˌvɜːs ɪn ˈdʒet ə rɪks ˌᵊn-, -ˈget- ‖ ˌvɜ˞ːs ᵊn ˈdʒeţ- -ˈgeţ-

verd vɜːd ‖ vɜ˞ːd
verdancy ˈvɜːd ᵊnᵗs i ‖ ˈvɜ˞ːd-
verdant ˈvɜːd ᵊnt ‖ ˈvɜ˞ːd- **~ly** li
Verde *(i)* vɜːd veəd ‖ vɜ˞ːd, *(ii)* ˈvɜːd i ˈveəd i ‖ ˈvɜ˞ːd i ˈverd i— Cape Verde *and its islands are (i), or an imitation of the Portuguese form; the river in AZ is (ii).* —*Port* [ˈver də]
Verdean ˈvɜːd i‿ən ˈveəd- ‖ ˈvɜ˞ːd- **~s** z
verderer ˈvɜːd ər ə ‖ ˈvɜ˞ːd ᵊr ər **~s** z
Verdi ˈveəd i ‖ ˈverd i —*It* [ˈver di]
verdict ˈvɜːd ɪkt ‖ ˈvɜ˞ːd- **~s** s
verdigris ˈvɜːd ɪ griː -ə-, -griːs, -grɪs ‖ ˈvɜ˞ːd ə grɪs -griːs
Verdun vɜː ˈdʌn ‖ vɜ˞ː- —*Fr* [vɛʁ dœ̃, -dæ̃]
verdure ˈvɜːdʒ ə ˈvɜːd jə, -jʊə ‖ ˈvɜ˞ːdʒ ᵊr *(usually = verger)*
Vere vɪə ‖ vɪᵊr
verge vɜːdʒ ‖ vɜ˞ːdʒ **verged** vɜːdʒd ‖ vɜ˞ːdʒd **verges** ˈvɜːdʒ ɪz -əz ‖ ˈvɜ˞ːdʒ əz **verging** ˈvɜːdʒ ɪŋ ‖ ˈvɜ˞ːdʒ ɪŋ
verger ˈvɜːdʒ ə ‖ ˈvɜ˞ːdʒ ᵊr **~s** z
Vergil ˈvɜːdʒ ɪl -əl ‖ ˈvɜ˞ːdʒ əl
Vergilian vɜː ˈdʒɪl i‿ən və- ‖ vɜ˞ː-
veridical və ˈrɪd ɪk ᵊl ve-, vɪ- **~ly** ˌi
veridicality və ˌrɪd ɪ ˈkæl ət i ve-, vɪ-, §-ˌə-, -ɪt i ‖ -əţ i
veriest ˈver i‿ɪst əst
verifiab|le ˈver ɪ faɪ‿əb |ᵊl ˈ·ə-, ˌ··ˈ·· **~ly** li
verification ˌver ɪf ɪ ˈkeɪʃ ᵊn ˌəf-, §-əˈ-- **~s** z
veri|fy ˈver ɪ |faɪ -ə- **~fied** faɪd **~fier/s** faɪ‿ə/z ‖ faɪ‿ᵊr/z **~fies** faɪz **~fying** faɪ ɪŋ
verily ˈver əl i -ɪl i
verisimilitude ˌver ɪ sɪ ˈmɪl ɪ tjuːd ˌ·ə-, ˌ·i-, -səˈ--, -ˈ·ə-, →-tʃuːd ‖ -tuːd -tjuːd
verismo ve ˈrɪz məʊ və-, -ˈriːz- ‖ -moʊ —*It* [ve ˈriz mo]
veritab|le ˈver ɪt əb |ᵊl ˈ·ət- ‖ ˈ·əţ- **~leness** ᵊl nəs -nɪs **~ly** li
verit|y, V~ ˈver ət |i -ɪt- ‖ -əţ |i **~ies** iz
Verizon *tdmk* və ˈraɪz ᵊn
verjuice ˈvɜː dʒuːs ‖ ˈvɜ˞ː-
verkrampte fə ˈkræmpt ə ‖ fᵊr- —*Afrikaans* [fər ˈkram tə] **~s** z
Verlaine və ˈleɪn veə- ‖ vᵊr- ver- —*Fr* [vɛʁ lɛn]
verligte fə ˈlɪxt ə ‖ fᵊr ˈlɪkt ə —*Afrikaans* [fər ˈləx tə] **~s** z
Vermeer və ˈmɪə vɜː-, -ˈmeə ‖ vᵊr ˈmɪᵊr —*Dutch* [vər ˈmeːr] **~s** z
vermeil ˈvɜːm eɪᵊl -ɪl, §-ᵊl ‖ ˈvɜ˞ːm-
vermicelli ˌvɜːm ɪ ˈtʃel i -ə-, -ˈsel- ‖ ˌvɜ˞ːm-
vermicide ˈvɜːm ɪ saɪd -ə- ‖ ˈvɜ˞ːm- **~s** z
vermiculate vɜː ˈmɪk ju leɪt və-, -jə- ‖ vɜ˞ː ˈmɪk jə-
vermiculite vɜː ˈmɪk ju laɪt və-, -jə- ‖ vɜ˞ː ˈmɪk jə-
vermiform ˈvɜːm ɪ fɔːm §-ə- ‖ ˈvɜ˞ːm ə fɔːrm
ˌ**vermiform ap'pendix**
vermifug|e ˈvɜːm ɪ fjuːdʒ §-ə- ‖ ˈvɜ˞ːm- **~es** ɪz əz
vermilion və ˈmɪl i‿ən vɜː- ‖ vᵊr ˈmɪl jən **~ed** d **~s** z
vermin ˈvɜːm ɪn §-ən ‖ ˈvɜ˞ːm ən

verminous ˈvɜːm ɪn əs §-ən- ‖ ˈvɜ˞ːm ən əs **~ly** li **~ness** nəs nɪs

Vermont və ˈmɒnt vɜː- ‖ vᵊr ˈmɑːnt

Vermonter və ˈmɒnt ə vɜː- ‖ vᵊr ˈmɑːnt̬ ᵊr **~s** z

vermouth ˈvɜːm əθ -uːθ; və ˈmuːθ, vɜː- ‖ vᵊr ˈmuːθ **~s** s

Verna ˈvɜːn ə ‖ ˈvɜ˞ːn ə

vernacular və ˈnæk jʊl ə -jəl- ‖ vᵊr ˈnæk jəl ᵊr və- **~ly** li **~s** z

vernal ˈvɜːn ᵊl ‖ ˈvɜ˞ːn ᵊl **~ly** i

ˌvernal ˈequinox

vernalis... —*see* **vernaliz...**

vernalization ˌvɜːn əl aɪ ˈzeɪʃ ᵊn -ɪˈ-- ‖ ˌvɜ˞ːn ᵊl ə-

vernaliz|e ˈvɜːn ə laɪz -ᵊl aɪz ‖ ˈvɜ˞ːn ᵊl aɪz **~ed** d **~es** ɪz əz **~ing** ɪŋ

Verne vɜːn veən ‖ vɜ˞ːn —*Fr* [vɛʁn]

Verner ˈvɜːn ə ˈveən- ‖ ˈvɜ˞ːn ᵊr —*Danish* [ˈvɛʁʔ nɒ] **~'s** z

ˈVerner's law

Verney ˈvɜːn i ‖ ˈvɜ˞ːn i

vernier ˈvɜːn i‿ə ‖ ˈvɜ˞ːn i‿ᵊr **~s** z

vernissag|e ˌvɜːn ɪ ˈsɑːʒ ‖ ˌvɜ˞ːn- **~es** ɪz əz

Vernon ˈvɜːn ən ‖ ˈvɜ˞ːn ən

Verona və ˈrəʊn ə ve-, vɪ- ‖ -ˈroʊn- —*It* [ve ˈroː na]

veronal, V~ *tdmk* ˈver ən ᵊl **~s** z

Veronese ˌver əʊ ˈneɪz i ‖ -ə- -ˈneɪs- —*It* [ve ro ˈneː se]

veronica, V~ və ˈrɒn ɪk ə ve-, vɪ- ‖ -ˈrɑːn- **~s, ~'s** z

Verrazano ˌver ə ˈzɑːn əʊ ‖ -oʊ —*It* [ver rat ˈtsaː no]

ˌVerraˌzano ˈNarrows

ver|ruca və |ˈruːk ə ve-, vɪ- **~rucae** ˈruːs iː ˈruːk-, -aɪ **~rucas** ˈruːk əz

versa ˈvɜːs ə ‖ ˈvɜ˞ːs ə

Versace və ˈsɑːtʃ i vɜː- ‖ vᵊr-

Versailles veə ˈsaɪ vɜː- ‖ ver- —*Fr* [vɛʁ saj]

versant ˈvɜːs ᵊnt ‖ ˈvɜ˞ːs- **~s** s

versatile ˈvɜːs ə taɪᵊl ‖ ˈvɜ˞ːs ət̬ ᵊl *(*)* **~ly** li **~ness** nəs nɪs

versatility ˌvɜːs ə ˈtɪl ət i -ɪt- ‖ ˌvɜ˞ːs ə ˈtɪl ət̬ i

verse vɜːs ‖ vɜ˞ːs **versed** vɜːst ‖ vɜ˞ːst **verses** ˈvɜːs ɪz -əz ‖ ˈvɜ˞ːs əz

versicle ˈvɜːs ɪk ᵊl ‖ ˈvɜ˞ːs- **~s** z

versification ˌvɜːs ɪf ɪ ˈkeɪʃ ᵊn ˌ-əf-, §-əˈ- ‖ ˌvɜ˞ːs- **~s** z

versi|fy ˈvɜːs ɪ |faɪ -ə- ‖ ˈvɜ˞ːs- **~fied** faɪd **~fier/s** faɪ‿ə/z ‖ faɪ‿ᵊr/z **~fies** faɪz **~fying** faɪ ɪŋ

version ˈvɜːʃ ᵊn ˈvɜːʒ- ‖ ˈvɜ˞ːʒ ᵊn ˈvɜ˞ːʃ- **~s** z

verso ˈvɜːs əʊ ‖ ˈvɜ˞ːs oʊ **~s** z

versus ˈvɜːs əs ‖ ˈvɜ˞ːs əs

vert vɜːt ‖ vɜ˞ːt

vert|ebra ˈvɜːt |ɪb rə -əb- ‖ ˈvɜ˞ːt̬- **~ebrae** ɪ breɪ ə-, -briː **~ebras** ɪb rəz əb-

vertebral ˈvɜːt ɪb rəl -əb- ‖ ˈvɜ˞ːt̬- vɜː ˈtiːb-

Vertebrata, v~ ˌvɜːt ɪ ˈbrɑːt ə -ə-, -ˈbreɪt- ‖ ˌvɜ˞ːt̬ ə ˈbrɑːt̬ ə -ˈbreɪt̬-

vertebrate ˈvɜːt ɪb rət -əb-, -rɪt; -ɪ breɪt, -ə- ‖ ˈvɜ˞ːt̬- **~s** s

vertex ˈvɜːt eks ‖ ˈvɜ˞ːt- **vertices** ˈvɜːt ɪ siːz -ə- ‖ ˈvɜ˞ːt̬-

vertical ˈvɜːt ɪk ᵊl ‖ ˈvɜ˞ːt̬- **~ly** ‿i **~s** z

verticality ˌvɜːt ɪ ˈkæl ət i ˌ-ə-, -ɪt i ‖ ˌvɜ˞ːt̬ ə ˈkæl ət̬ i

vertices ˈvɜːt ɪ siːz -ə- ‖ ˈvɜ˞ːt̬-

vertiginous vɜː ˈtɪdʒ ɪn əs -ən əs ‖ vɜ˞ː- **~ly** li **~ness** nəs nɪs

vertigo ˈvɜːt ɪ gəʊ -ə- ‖ ˈvɜ˞ːt̬ ɪ goʊ **~s** z

Verulam ˈver ʊl əm -jʊl- ‖ -jəl-

Verulamium ˌver u ˈleɪm i‿əm ˌ-ju- ‖ ˌ-jə-

vervain ˈvɜːv eɪn ‖ ˈvɜ˞ːv-

verve vɜːv ‖ vɜ˞ːv

vervet ˈvɜːv ɪt §-ət ‖ ˈvɜ˞ːv ət **~s** s

Verwoerd fə ˈvʊət feə- ‖ fᵊr ˈvʊᵊrt —*Afrikaans* [fər ˈvuːrt]

very ˈver i —*Some speakers use a casual weak form* vər i **veriest** ˈver i‿ɪst əst

ˌvery ˌhigh ˈfrequency

Very ˈvɪər i ˈver- ‖ ˈver i ˈvɪr-

ˈVery light

Veryan ˈver i‿ən

Vesalius və ˈseɪl i‿əs vɪ-

Vesey ˈviːz i

vesic|a ˈves ɪk |ə vɪ ˈsaɪk |ə, və- **~al** ᵊl **~ant/s** ənt/s **~as** əz

vesicle ˈves ɪk ᵊl ˈviːs- **~s** z

vesicular və ˈsɪk jʊl ə ve-, vɪ-, -jəl ə ‖ -jəl ᵊr **~ly** li

Vespa *tdmk* ˈvesp ə **~s** z

Vespasian ve ˈspeɪʒ ᵊn -ˈ-i‿ən; -ˈspeɪz i‿ən

vesper, V~ ˈvesp ə ‖ -ᵊr **~s** z

vespertine ˈvesp ə taɪn -tiːn ‖ -ᵊr- —*Björk's album V~ is usually* -tiːn

vespine ˈvesp aɪn

Vespucci ve ˈspuːtʃ i —*It* [ve ˈsput tʃi]

vessel ˈves ᵊl **~s** z

vest vest **vested** ˈvest ɪd -əd **vesting** ˈvest ɪŋ **vests** vests

ˌvested ˈinterest

Vesta, vesta ˈvest ə **~s, ~'s** z

vestal ˈvest ᵊl **~s** z

ˌvestal ˈvirgin

vestibular ve ˈstɪb jʊl ə -jəl- ‖ -jəl ᵊr

vestibule ˈvest ɪ bjuːl -ə- **~s** z

vestig|e ˈvest ɪdʒ **~es** ɪz əz

vestigial ves ˈtɪdʒ i‿əl -ˈtɪdʒ əl **~ly** i

vestment ˈvest mənt **~s** s

vest-pocket ˌvest ˈpɒk ɪt ◂ §-ət ‖ -ˈpɑːk-

ves|try ˈves |tri **~tries** triz

vestry|man ˈves tri |mən **~men** mən men

vesture ˈves tʃə ‖ -tʃᵊr **~d** d **~s** z

Vesuvianite və ˈsuːv i‿ə naɪt vɪ-, -ˈsjuːv-

Vesuvius və ˈsuːv i‿əs vɪ-, -ˈsjuːv-

vet vet **vets** vets **vetted** ˈvet ɪd -əd ‖ ˈvet̬ əd **vetting** ˈvet ɪŋ ‖ ˈvet̬ ɪŋ

vetch vetʃ **vetches** ˈvetʃ ɪz -əz

vetchling ˈvetʃ lɪŋ **~s** z

veteran ˈvet‿ər ən ‖ ˈvet̬ ər ən →ˈvetr ən **~s** z

ˈVeterans Day

veterinarian ˌvet‿ər ɪ ˈneər i‿ən -əˈ--; ˌvet ə ˈneər i‿ən ‖ ˌvet̬ ər ə ˈner i‿ən →ˌvetr ə ˈner- **~s** z

veterinar|y ˈvet‿ᵊr ən ər‿|i -ɪn ər‿i; ˈvet ɪn ər‿|i, ˈvet ᵊn ər‿|i ‖ ˈveţ ər ə ner |i →ˈvetr ə ner |i, ˈvet ᵊn er |i **~ies** ɪz
ˌ**veterinary ˈsurgeon**
vetiver ˈvet ɪv ə ‖ -ᵊr
veto ˈviːt əʊ ‖ ˈviːţ oʊ ˈviːt- **~ed** d **~es** z **~ing** ɪŋ
Vettriano ˌvetr i ˈɑːn əɪ ‖ -oʊ
Veuve vɜːv ‖ vʌv —*Fr* [vœːv]
ˌ**~ Clicquot** *tdmk* ˈkliːk əʊ ‖ kliː ˈkoʊ —*Fr* [kli ko]
vex veks **vexed** vekst **vexes** ˈveks ɪz -əz **vexing** ˈveks ɪŋ
vexation vek ˈseɪʃ ᵊn **~s** z
vexatious vek ˈseɪʃ əs **~ly** li **~ness** nəs nɪs
vexillology ˌveks ɪ ˈlɒl ədʒ i ˌ-ə- ‖ -ˈlɑːl-
V-formation ˈviː fɔː ˌmeɪʃ ᵊn ‖ -fɔːr-
VH1 ˌviː eɪtʃ ˈwʌn
VHF ˌviː eɪtʃ ˈef §-heɪtʃ-
VHS *tdmk* ˌviː eɪtʃ ˈes §-heɪtʃ-
Vi vaɪ

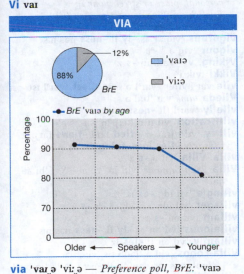

VIA

12%
88%
ˈvaɪə
ˈviːə
BrE
BrE ˈvaɪə by age
Percentage
100
90
80
70
0
Older ← Speakers → Younger

via ˈvaɪ‿ə ˈviː‿ə — *Preference poll, BrE:* ˈvaɪə *88% (born before 1942, 92%),* ˈviːə *12%. —see also phrases with this word*
viability ˌvaɪ‿ə ˈbɪl ət i -ɪt i ‖ -əţ i
viab|le ˈvaɪ‿əb |ᵊl **~ly** li
Viacom *tdmk* ˈvaɪ‿ə kɒm ‖ -kɑːm
Via Dolorosa, via d~ ˌviː‿ə ˌdɒl ə ˈrəʊs ə ‖ -ˌdɑːl ə ˈroʊs- -ˌdoʊl-
viaduct ˈvaɪ‿ə dʌkt **~s** s
Viagra *tdmk* vaɪ ˈæg rə vi- ‖ -ˈɑːg-
vial ˈvaɪ‿əl ‖ ˈvaɪ‿ᵊl **~s** z
via media ˌvaɪ‿ə ˈmiːd i‿ə ˌviː‿ə ˈmeɪd-
viand ˈvaɪ‿ənd ˈviː‿ **~s** z
viatic|al vaɪ ˈæt ɪk |ᵊl vi- ‖ -ˈæţ- **~a** ə **~um/s** əm/z
vibe vaɪb **vibes** vaɪbz
vibist ˈvaɪb ɪst §-əst **~s** s
vibraharp ˈvaɪb rə hɑːp ‖ -hɑːrp **~s** s
Vibram *tdmk* ˈvaɪb rəm
vibrancy ˈvaɪb rənᵗs i
vibrant ˈvaɪb rənt **~ly** li **~s** s
vibraphone ˈvaɪb rə fəʊn ‖ -foʊn **~s** z
vib|rate vaɪ ˈb|reɪt ‖ ˈvaɪb |reɪt *(*)* **~rated** reɪt ɪd -əd ‖ reɪţ əd **~rates** reɪts **~rating** reɪt ɪŋ ‖ reɪţ ɪŋ
vibratile ˈvaɪb rə taɪᵊl ‖ -rəţ ᵊl
vibration vaɪ ˈbreɪʃ ᵊn **~s** z
vibrational vaɪ ˈbreɪʃ ᵊn‿əl
vibrationless vaɪ ˈbreɪʃ ᵊn ləs -lɪs
vibrative vaɪ ˈbreɪt ɪv ˈvaɪb rət- ‖ ˈvaɪb rəţ ɪv
vibrato vɪ ˈbrɑːt əʊ §və-, vaɪ-, viː- ‖ -oʊ **~s** z
vibrator vaɪ ˈbreɪt ə ‖ ˈvaɪb reɪţ ᵊr *(*)* **~s** z
vibratory vaɪ ˈbreɪt ər i ˈvaɪb rət‿ər i ‖ ˈvaɪb rə tɔːr i -toʊr i *(*)*
vibrio ˈvɪb ri əʊ ‖ -oʊ **~s** z
vibriss|a vaɪ ˈbrɪs |ə **~ae** iː
vibro- ¦vaɪb rəʊ ‖ -roʊ — **vibromassage** ˈvaɪb rəʊ ˌmæs ɑːʒ ˌ·ˈ· · ‖ -roʊ mə ˌsɑːʒ ˌ· ·ˈ·
viburnum vaɪ ˈbɜːn əm ‖ -ˈbɜːn- **~s** z
Vic vɪk
vicar ˈvɪk ə ‖ -ᵊr **~s** z
vicarag|e ˈvɪk ər‿ɪdʒ **~es** ɪz əz
vicarial vɪ ˈkeər i‿əl və-, vaɪ- ‖ -ˈker- -ˈkær-
vicarious vɪ ˈkeər i‿əs və-, vaɪ- ‖ -ˈker- -ˈkær- **~ly** li **~ness** nəs nɪs
vice *n* vaɪs **vices** ˈvaɪs ɪz -əz
ˈ**vice squad**
vice *prep, Latin* ˈvaɪs i -ə; vaɪs, ˈviːs eɪ
ˌ**vice ˈversa** ˈvɜːs ə ‖ ˈvɜːs ə
vice- ¦vaɪs — **vice-presidency** ˌvaɪs ˈprez ɪd ənᵗs i -ˈ·əd- ‖ -ə denᵗs i
vice-chair ˌvaɪs ˈtʃeə ‖ -ˈtʃeᵊr -ˈtʃæᵊr **~man** mən **~men** mən **~person/s** ˌpɜːs ᵊn/z ‖ ˌpɜːs ᵊn/z **~woman** ˌwʊm ən **~women** ˌwɪm ɪn §-ən
vice-chancellor ˌvaɪs ˈtʃɑːnᵗs əl‿ə §-ˈtʃænᵗs- ‖ -ˈtʃænᵗs ᵊl‿ər **~ship** ʃɪp **~s** z
vicegerant ˌvaɪs ˈdʒer ənt -ˈdʒɪər- ‖ -ˈdʒɪr- **~s** s
vicelike ˈvaɪs laɪk
viceregal ˌvaɪs ˈriːg ᵊl◂ **~ly** i
vicereine ˌvaɪs ˈreɪn ˈ· · **~s** z
viceroy ˈvaɪs rɔɪ **~s** z
Vichy ˈviːʃ i ˈvɪʃ- —*Fr* [vi ʃi]
ˈ**Vichy ˌwater**
Vichyite ˈviːʃ i aɪt ˈvɪʃ- **~s** s
vichyssoise ˌviːʃ i ˈswɑːz ˌvɪʃ- —*Fr* [vi ʃi swaːz]
vicinal ˈvɪs ɪn ᵊl -ən‿ᵊl
vicinit|y və ˈsɪn ət |i vɪ-, -ɪt- ‖ -əţ |i **~ies** iz
vicious ˈvɪʃ əs **~ly** li **~ness** nəs nɪs
ˌ**vicious ˈcircle**
vicissitude vaɪ ˈsɪs ə tjuːd və-, vɪ-, →-tʃuːd ‖ və ˈsɪs ə tuːd vaɪ-, -tjuːd **~s** z
Vick vɪk
Vickers ˈvɪk əz ‖ -ᵊrz
Vickery ˈvɪk ər i
Vicki, Vickie ˈvɪk i
Vicksburg ˈvɪks bɜːg ‖ -bɜːg
Vicky ˈvɪk i
victim ˈvɪkt ɪm §-əm **~hood** hʊd **~s** z
victimis... —*see* **victimiz...**
victimization ˌvɪkt ɪm aɪ ˈzeɪʃ ᵊn ˌ-əm-, -ɪˈ·- ‖ -əˈ·- **~s** z

V

victimiz|e 'vɪkt ɪ maɪz -ə- ‖ -ə- **~ed** d **~es** ɪz əz **~ing** ɪŋ
victimless 'vɪkt ɪm ləs §-əm-, -lɪs
victor, V~ 'vɪkt ə ‖ -ᵊr **~s** z
ˌvictor lu'dorum lu 'dɔːr əm
Victoria, v~ vɪk 'tɔːr i‿ə ‖ -'toʊr- *—but the London railway terminus is sometimes double-stressed,* ˌ·'·· ◂ **~s, ~'s** z
Vicˌtoria 'Cross; **Vicˌtoria 'Falls**; **vicˌtoria 'plum**; **Vicˌtoria 'Station,** ˌ·ˌ··
Victorian vɪk 'tɔːr i‿ən ‖ -'toʊr- **~ism** ˌɪz əm **~s** z
Victoriana vɪk ˌtɔːr i 'ɑːn ə ˌ· · ·'· · ‖ -ˌtoʊr-, -'æn-
victorious vɪk 'tɔːr i‿əs ‖ -'toʊr- **~ly** li **~ness** nəs nɪs
victor|y 'vɪkt ər |i →'vɪk tr|i **~ies** iz
Victory-V *tdmk* ˌvɪk tri 'viː
Victrola *tdmk* vɪk 'trəʊl ə ‖ -'troʊl ə
victual 'vɪt ᵊl *(!)* **~s** z
victualer, victualler 'vɪt ᵊl‿ə ‖ ər *—Also sometimes a spelling pronunciation* 'vɪk tʃu‿əl ə ‖ -ᵊr **~s** z
vicuna, vicuña vɪ 'kjuːn ə və-, vaɪ-, -'kuːn-, -jə *—Sp* [bi 'ku ɲa] **~s** z
Vidal *(i)* vɪ 'dɑːl və-, ˌviː-, -'dæl, *(ii)* 'vaɪd ᵊl *—The writer* Gore Vidal *is (i).*
vide 'vaɪd i 'vɪd-, 'viːd-, -eɪ
videlicet vɪ 'diːl ɪ set və-, vaɪ-, -'deɪl-, -'del-, -ə-, -ket
video 'vɪd i əʊ ‖ -oʊ **~ed** d **~ing** ɪŋ **~s** z
'video ˌcamera; **'video game**; **'video link**; **'video reˌcorder**
videocard 'vɪd i əʊ kɑːd ‖ -oʊ kɑːrd **~s** z
videocassette ˌvɪd i əʊ kə 'set '· · · ·ˌ· ‖ ˌi oʊ-
ˌvideo cas'sette reˌcorder
videoconferenc|e 'vɪd i əʊ ˌkɒn fər‿ənᵗs ‖ '·· oʊ ˌkɑːn- **~ing** ɪŋ
videodisc 'vɪd i əʊ dɪsk ‖ -oʊ dɪsk **~s** s
videofit 'vɪd i əʊ fɪt ‖ -oʊ- **~s** s
videographer ˌvɪd i 'ɒg rəf ə ‖ -'ɑːg rəf ᵊr **~s** z
videophone, V~ *tdmk* 'vɪd i əʊ fəʊn ‖ -oʊ foʊn **~s** z
videotap|e 'vɪd i əʊ teɪp ‖ -oʊ teɪp **~ed** t **~es** s **~ing** ɪŋ
'videotape reˌcorder
videotex 'vɪd i əʊ teks ‖ -oʊ teks
videotext 'vɪd i əʊ tekst ‖ -oʊ tekst
vidicon 'vɪd i kɒn ‖ -kɑːn **~s** z
Vidler 'vɪd lə ‖ -lᵊr
vie vaɪ **vied** vaɪd **vies** vaɪz **vying** 'vaɪ ɪŋ
Vienna vi 'en ə
Viennese ˌviː‿ə 'niːz ◂ ‖ -'niːs ◂
Vientiane vi ˌent i 'ɑːn *—Fr* [vjɛn tjan]
Vietcong, Viet Cong ˌviː et 'kɒŋ ◂ -ɪt-, vi‿ˌet- ‖ -'kɑːŋ -'kɔːŋ
Vietminh, Viet Minh ˌviː et 'mɪn ◂ -ɪt-, vi‿ˌet-
Vietnam, Viet Nam ˌviː et 'næm ◂ -ɪt-, vi‿ˌet-, -'nɑːm ‖ -'nɑːm
Vietnamese vi ˌet nə 'miːz ◂ ˌviː et-, viː ɪt- ‖ -'miːs ◂
view vjuː **viewed** vjuːd **viewing** 'vjuː ɪŋ **views** vjuːz
viewdata, V~ 'vjuː ˌdeɪt ə -ˌdɑːt- ‖ -ˌdeɪţ ə -ˌdæţ-, -ˌdɑːţ-
viewer 'vjuː‿ə ‖ ᵊr **~ship** ʃɪp **~s** z
viewfinder 'vjuː ˌfaɪnd ə ‖ -ᵊr **~s** z
Viewgraph *tdmk* 'vjuː grɑːf -græf ‖ -græf **~s** s
viewpoint 'vjuː pɔɪnt **~s** s
Vigar 'vaɪg ə -ɑː ‖ -ᵊr -ɑːr
vigesimal vaɪ 'dʒes ɪm ᵊl -əm-
vigil 'vɪdʒ ɪl -əl **~s** z
vigilance 'vɪdʒ əl ənᵗs -ɪl-
'vigilance comˌmittee
vigilant 'vɪdʒ əl ənt -ɪl- **~ly** li
vigilante ˌvɪdʒ ɪ 'lænt i -ə- ‖ -'lænţ i -'lɑːnţ- **~s** z
vigilantism ˌvɪdʒ ɪ 'lænt ˌɪz əm ‖ -'lænţ- -ə-
vignette vɪn 'jet viːn- *—Fr* [vi ɲɛt] **~s** s
Vigo *(i)* 'viːg əʊ ‖ -oʊ, *(ii)* 'vaɪg- *—Sp* ['bi ɣo] *—For the place in Spain, usually (i); as a personal, place or street name in English-speaking countries, often (ii).*
vigor 'vɪg ə ‖ -ᵊr
vigorous 'vɪg ər‿əs **~ly** li **~ness** nəs nɪs
vigour 'vɪg ə ‖ -ᵊr
Viking, v~ 'vaɪk ɪŋ **~s** z
Vikki 'vɪk i
vile vaɪᵊl **viler** 'vaɪᵊl ə ‖ -ᵊr **vilest** 'vaɪᵊl ɪst -əst
Vileda *tdmk* vaɪ 'liːd ə
vile|ly 'vaɪᵊl |li **~ness** nəs nɪs
vilification ˌvɪl ɪf ɪ 'keɪʃ ᵊn ˌ-əf-, §-ə'-
vili|fy 'vɪl ɪ |faɪ -ə- **~fied** faɪd **~fier/s** faɪ‿ə/z ‖ faɪ‿ᵊr/z **~fies** faɪz **~fying** faɪ ɪŋ
villa, Villa 'vɪl ə **~s** z
Villa *Spanish name* 'viːl jə 'viː ə *—Sp* ['bi ʎa, -ja]
villag|e 'vɪl ɪdʒ **~es** ɪz əz
villager 'vɪl ɪdʒ ə §-ədʒ- ‖ -ᵊr **~s** z
villain 'vɪl ən **~s** z
villainous 'vɪl ən əs **~ly** li **~ness** nəs nɪs
villain|y 'vɪl ən |i **~ies** iz
Villa-Lobos ˌviːl ə 'ləʊb ɒs ˌviː-, -jə- ‖ -'loʊb oʊs -əs, -oʊʃ *—BrPort* [ˌvi la 'lo bus]
villanella ˌvɪl ə 'nel ə **~s** z
villanelle ˌvɪl ə 'nel **~s** z
Villanovan ˌvɪl ə 'nəʊv ᵊn ◂ ‖ -'noʊv-
-ville vɪl — **dullsville** 'dʌlz vɪl
villein 'vɪl eɪn -ɪn, -ən **~s** z
villeinage, villenage 'vɪl ən ɪdʒ -eɪn-, -ɪn-
Villeneuve 'viːᵊl nɜːv ‖ ˌviːᵊl 'nuːv *—Fr* [vil nœːv]
villi 'vɪl aɪ
Villiers *(i)* 'vɪl əz ‖ -ᵊrz, *(ii)* 'vɪl i‿əz ‖ ‿ᵊrz
Villon 'viː õ 'vɪl ən ‖ -ɑːn -oʊn *—Fr* [vi jɔ̃, -lɔ̃]
villosit|y vɪ 'lɒs ət |i -ɪt- ‖ vɪ 'lɑːs əţ |i **~ies** iz
villous 'vɪl əs **~ly** li
vill|us 'vɪl| əs **~i** aɪ iː
Vilnius, Vilnyus 'vɪl ni‿əs -ʊs
vim, Vim *tdmk* vɪm
Vimto *tdmk* 'vɪm təʊ ‖ -toʊ
vin væ̃ væn *—Fr* [væ̃]
ˌvin 'blanc blɒ̃ blɒŋ ‖ blɑːn *—Fr* [blɑ̃]
vinaceous vaɪ 'neɪʃ əs vɪ-, §və-

Viña del Mar ˌviːn jə del ˈmɑː ‖ -ˈmɑːr —*AmSp* [ˌbi ɲa ðel ˈmaɾ]
vinaigrette ˌvɪn eɪ ˈgret -ɪ-, -ə- **~s** s
vinca ˈvɪŋk ə **~s** z
Vince vɪnᵗs
Vincennes *(i)* væn ˈsen væ̃- —*Fr* [væ̃ sɛn]; *(ii)* vɪn ˈsenz —*In France, (i); in Indiana, (ii).*
Vincent ˈvɪnᵗs ənt
Vincentian vɪn ˈsenᵗʃ ən **~s** z
Vinci ˈvɪntʃ i —*It* [ˈvin tʃi]
vinculum ˈvɪŋk jʊl əm -jəl- ‖ -jəl-
vindaloo ˌvɪnd ə ˈluː **~s** z
vindi|cate ˈvɪnd ɪ |keɪt §-ə- **~cated** keɪt ɪd -əd ‖ keɪţ əd **~cates** keɪts **~cating** keɪt ɪŋ ‖ keɪţ ɪŋ
vindication ˌvɪnd ɪ ˈkeɪʃ ən §-ə-
vindictive vɪn ˈdɪkt ɪv **~ly** li **~ness** nəs nɪs
Vindolanda ˌvɪnd əʊ ˈlænd ə ‖ -oʊ- -ˈlɑːnd ə
vin du pays ˌvæn du peɪ ˈiː ˌvæ̃-, ˌ-dju- —*Fr* [væ̃ dy pe i]
vine, Vine vaɪn **vines** vaɪnz
vinegar ˈvɪn ɪg ə §-əg- ‖ -ᵊr **~s** z
vinegary ˈvɪn ɪg ər‿i §ˈ·əg-
Vineland ˈvaɪn lənd
Viner ˈvaɪn ə ‖ -ᵊr
viner|y ˈvaɪn ər |i **~ies** iz
vineyard ˈvɪn jəd -jɑːd ‖ -jᵊrd **~s** z
vingt-et-un ˌvænt eɪ ˈɜː ˌvæ̃t-, -ˈɜːn ‖ -ˈʊn -ˈʌn —*Fr* [væ̃ te œ̃, -æ̃]
vinho verde ˌviːn əʊ ˈvɜːd i ‖ -oʊ ˈvɜ˞ːd i —*Port* [ˌvi ɲu ˈver di]
vinic ˈvaɪn ɪk ˈvɪn-
viniculture ˈvɪn i ˌkʌltʃ ə ˈvaɪn-, §ˈ·ə- ‖ -ᵊr
Vinland ˈvɪn lənd -lænd
Vinnie ˈvɪn i
vino ˈviːn əʊ ‖ -oʊ
vin ordinaire ˌvæn ˌɔːd ɪ ˈneə ə- ‖ -ˌɔːrd ən ˈeᵊr —*Fr* [væ̃ nɔʁ di nɛːʁ]
vinosity vaɪ ˈnɒs ət i vɪ-, §və-, -ɪt- ‖ -ˈnɑːs əţ i
vinous ˈvaɪn əs
vin rouge ˌvæn ˈruːʒ ˌvæ̃- —*Fr* [væ̃ ʁuʒ]
Vinson ˈvɪnᵗs ən
vintag|e ˈvɪnt ɪdʒ ‖ ˈvɪnţ ɪdʒ **~es** ɪz əz
ˌ**vintage 'car**; ˌ**vintage 'year**
vintner ˈvɪnt nə ‖ -nᵊr **~s** z
vinyl ˈvaɪn ᵊl -ɪl **~s** z
ˌ**vinyl 'chloride**
vinylidene vaɪ ˈnɪl ɪ diːn -ə-
viol ˈvaɪ‿əl ‖ ˈvaɪ‿ᵊl -oʊl **~s** z
viola *'kind of flower'*, **Viola** *personal name* ˈvaɪ‿əl ə ˈviː‿, -əʊl ə; vi ˈəʊl ə, vaɪ- ‖ vaɪ ˈoʊl ə vi-; ˈvaɪ əl ə **~s, ~'s** z
viola *'musical instrument'* vi ˈəʊl ə vaɪ-; ˈviː‿əl ə ‖ vi ˈoʊl ə **~s** z
viˌ**ola da 'gamba** də ˈgæm bə ‖ -ˈgɑːm-;
viˌ**ola d'a'more** dæ ˈmɔːr i -eɪ ‖ dɑː ˈmɔːr eɪ
vio|late ˈvaɪ‿ə |leɪt **~lated** leɪt ɪd -əd ‖ leɪţ əd **~lates** leɪts **~lating** leɪt ɪŋ ‖ leɪţ ɪŋ
violation ˌvaɪ‿ə ˈleɪʃ ən **~s** z
violator ˈvaɪ‿ə leɪt ə ‖ -leɪţ ᵊr **~s** z
violence ˈvaɪ‿əl ənᵗs §ˈvaɪl ənᵗs
violent ˈvaɪ‿əl ənt ˈ§vaɪl ənt **~ly** li
violet, V~ ˈvaɪ‿əl ət -ɪt; §ˈvaɪl ət, -ɪt **~s** s
violin ˌvaɪ‿ə ˈlɪn ˈ· · · **~s** z
violinist ˌvaɪ‿ə ˈlɪn ɪst §-əst, ˈ· · · · **~s** s
violist *'viola player'* vi ˈəʊl ɪst §-əst ‖ -ˈoʊl- **~s** s
violist *'viol player'* ˈvaɪ‿əl ɪst §-əst **~s** s
violoncellist ˌvaɪ‿əl ən ˈtʃel ɪst §-əst **~s** s
violoncello ˌvaɪ‿əl ən ˈtʃel əʊ ‖ -oʊ **~s** z
violone ˈvaɪ‿ə ləʊn ˈviː‿; ˌviː‿ə ˈləʊn eɪ ‖ ˌviː ə ˈloʊn eɪ **~s** z
Vioxx *tdmk* ˈvaɪ ɒks ‖ -ɑːks
VIP ˌviː aɪ ˈpiː **~s, ~'s** z
viper ˈvaɪp ə ‖ -ᵊr **~s** z
viperine ˈvaɪp ə raɪn
viperish ˈvaɪp ər ɪʃ
viperous ˈvaɪp ər‿əs
virago və ˈrɑːg əʊ vɪ- ‖ -oʊ **~es, ~s** z
viral ˈvaɪᵊr əl
vire ˈvaɪ‿ə vɪə ‖ ˈvaɪ‿ᵊr vɪᵊr **vired** ˈvaɪ‿əd vɪəd ‖ ˈvaɪ‿ᵊrd vɪᵊrd **vires** ˈvaɪ‿əz vɪəz ‖ ˈvaɪ‿ᵊrz vɪᵊrz **viring** ˈvaɪ‿ər ɪŋ ˈvɪər ɪŋ ‖ ˈvaɪ‿ər ɪŋ ˈvɪr ɪŋ
virement ˈvaɪ‿ə mənt ˈvɪə mɒ̃ ‖ ˈvaɪ‿ᵊr mənt vɪr ˈmɑːn —*Fr* [viʁ mɑ̃]
vireo ˈvɪr i əʊ ‖ -oʊ **~s** z
vires *Latin, 'powers'* ˈvaɪᵊr iːz
vires *3 sing of vire* ˈvaɪ‿əz vɪəz ‖ ˈvaɪ‿ᵊrz vɪᵊrz
Virgil ˈvɜːdʒ ɪl -əl ‖ ˈvɜ˞ːdʒ əl
Virgilian vɜː ˈdʒɪl i‿ən və- ‖ vɜ˞ː-
virgin, V~ ˈvɜːdʒ ɪn §-ən ‖ ˈvɜ˞ːdʒ ən **~s** z
ˌ**virgin 'birth**; ˈ**Virgin ˌIslands** ‖ ˌ· · ˈ· ·;
ˌ**Virgin 'Mary**; ˌ**Virgin 'Queen**
virginal ˈvɜːdʒ ɪn ᵊl -ən- ‖ ˈvɜ˞ːdʒ- **~s** z
Virginia, v~ və ˈdʒɪn i‿ə ‖ vᵊr ˈdʒɪn jə
Virˌginia 'Beach; **virˌginia 'creeper**;
Virˌginia 'reel
Virginian və ˈdʒɪn i‿ən ‖ vᵊr ˈdʒɪn jən **~s** z
virginity və ˈdʒɪn ət i vɜː-, -ɪt- ‖ vᵊr ˈdʒɪn əţ i
Virgo ˈvɜːg əʊ ‖ ˈvɜ˞ːg oʊ **~s** z
ˌ**virgo in'tacta** ɪn ˈtækt ə
Virgoan vɜː ˈgəʊ ən ‖ vɜ˞ː ˈgoʊ ən **~s** z
virgule ˈvɜːg juːl ‖ ˈvɜ˞ːg- **~s** z
viridescence ˌvɪr ɪ ˈdes ᵊnᵗs ˌ·ə-
viridescent ˌvɪr ɪ ˈdes ᵊnt ◂ ˌ·ə-
viridian və ˈrɪd i‿ən vɪ-
virile ˈvɪr aɪᵊl ‖ -ᵊl *(*)*
virility və ˈrɪl ət i vɪ-, -ɪt- ‖ -əţ i
virion ˈvaɪᵊr i‿ən ˈvɪr-, -ɒn ‖ -i ɑːn **~s** z
viroid ˈvaɪᵊr ɔɪd ˈvɪr-
Virol *tdmk* ˈvaɪᵊr ɒl ‖ -ɑːl -ɔːl, -oʊl
virologist vaɪᵊ ˈrɒl ədʒ ɪst §-əst ‖ -ˈrɑːl- **~s** s
virology vaɪᵊ ˈrɒl ədʒ i ‖ -ˈrɑːl-
virtu vɜː ˈtuː ‖ vɜ˞ː-
virtual ˈvɜːtʃ u‿əl ˈvɜːt ju‿ ‖ ˈvɜ˞ːtʃ u‿əl ˈ·əl **~ly** i
virtue ˈvɜːtʃ uː ˈvɜːt juː ‖ ˈvɜ˞ːtʃ uː **~s** z
virtuosic ˌvɜːtʃ u ˈɒs ɪk ◂ ˌvɜːt ju-, -ˈəʊs- ‖ ˌvɜ˞ːtʃ u ˈɑːs ɪk ◂
virtuosity ˌvɜːtʃ u ˈɒs ət i ˌvɜːt ju-, -ɪt i ‖ ˌvɜ˞ːtʃ u ˈɑːs əţ i
virtuoso ˌvɜːtʃ u ˈəʊs əʊ ◂ ˌvɜːt ju-, -ˈəʊz- ‖ ˌvɜ˞ːtʃ u ˈoʊs oʊ ◂ -ˈoʊz- **~s** z
virtuous ˈvɜːtʃ u‿əs ˈvɜːt ju‿ ‖ ˈvɜ˞ːtʃ- **~ly** li **~ness** nəs nɪs

virulenc|e ˈvɪr ʊl ənʼs -jʊl-, -jəl-, -əl- ‖ -əl- -jəl- **~y** i
virulent ˈvɪr ʊl ənt -jʊl-, -jəl-, -əl- ‖ -əl- -jəl- **~ly** li
virus ˈvaɪᵊr əs **~es** ɪz əz
vis vɪs

VISA

55% 45%
ˈviːz-
ˈviːs-
AmE

visa, Visa *tdmk* ˈviːz ə ‖ ˈviːs- — *Preference poll, AmE:* ˈviːz- *55%,* ˈviːs- *45%.* **~ed** d **visaing** ˈviːz əʳ ɪŋ ‖ ˈviːz ə ɪŋ ˈviːs- **~s** z
visag|e ˈvɪz ɪdʒ **~es** ɪz əz
-visaged ˈvɪz ɪdʒd — **grim-visaged** ˌɡrɪm ˈvɪz ɪdʒd ◂
visagist ˈvɪz ədʒ ɪst §-əst **~s** s
visagiste ˌviːz ɑː ˈʒiːst **~s** s
Visalia vaɪ ˈseɪl i‿ə vɪ-
vis-a-vis, vis-à-vis ˌviːz ə ˈviː ◂ ˌvɪz-, -ɑː-, -æ-
viscacha vɪ ˈskɑːtʃ ə -ˈskætʃ ə **~s** z
viscera ˈvɪs ər ə
visceral ˈvɪs ər əl
viscid ˈvɪs ɪd §-əd **~ly** li **~ness** nəs nɪs
Visconti vɪ ˈskɒnt i ‖ -ˈskɔːnt i -ˈskɑːnt- —*It* [vis ˈkon ti]
viscose ˈvɪsk əʊs -əʊz ‖ -oʊs -oʊz
viscosit|y vɪ ˈskɒs ət |i -ɪt- ‖ -ˈskɑːs əţ |i **~ies** iz
viscount ˈvaɪ kaʊnt **~s** s
viscount|cy ˈvaɪ kaʊnt |si **~sies** siz
viscountess ˌvaɪ kaʊn ˈtes ◂ ˈvaɪ kaʊnt ɪs, -əs ‖ ˈvaɪ kaʊnţ əs **~es** ɪz əz
viscous ˈvɪsk əs **~ly** li **~ness** nəs nɪs
vise vaɪs *(= vice)* **vises** ˈvaɪs ɪz -əz
Vise-Grips *tdmk* ˈvaɪs ɡrɪps
vise-like ˈvaɪs laɪk
Vishnu ˈvɪʃ nuː
visibilit|y ˌvɪz ə ˈbɪl ət |i ˌ-ɪ-, -ɪt i ‖ -əţ |i **~ies** iz
visib|le ˈvɪz əb |ᵊl -ɪb- **~les** ᵊlz **~ly** li
ˌvisible ˈspeech
VisiCalc *tdmk* ˈvɪz i kælk
Visigoth ˈvɪz i ɡɒθ ˈvɪs- ‖ -ɡɑːθ **~s** s
Visine *tdmk* vaɪ ˈziːn
vision ˈvɪʒ ᵊn **~s** z
visionar|y ˈvɪʒ ᵊn ər‿|i ‖ -ə ner |i **~ies** iz
vis|it ˈvɪz |ɪt §-ət ‖ -|ət **~ited** ɪt ɪd §ət-, -əd ‖ əţ əd **~iting** ɪt ɪŋ §ət- ‖ əţ ɪŋ **~its** ɪts §əts ‖ əts
ˈvisiting card; **ˌvisiting ˈfireman**; **ˌvisiting proˈfessor**
visitant ˈvɪz ɪt ənt §-ət- **~s** s
visitation ˌvɪz ɪ ˈteɪʃ ᵊn §-ə- **~s** z
visitor ˈvɪz ɪt ə §-ət- ‖ -əţ ᵊr **~s** z
ˈvisitors' book
visna ˈvɪz nə ˈvɪs-

visor ˈvaɪz ə ‖ -ᵊr **~s** z
vista ˈvɪst ə **~s** z
Vistula ˈvɪst jʊl ə ˈvɪs tʃəl ə ‖ ˈvɪs tʃʊl ə —*Polish* Wisła [ˈvis wa]
visual ˈvɪʒ u‿əl ˈvɪz ju‿, ˈvɪʒ ju‿ **~ly** i **~s** z
ˌvisual ˈaid; **ˌvisual diˈsplay ˌunit**
visualis... —*see* **visualiz...**
visualization ˌvɪʒ u‿əl aɪ ˈzeɪʃ ᵊn ˌvɪz ju‿, ˌvɪʒ ju‿, -ɪˈ-- ‖ -ə ˈzeɪʃ ᵊn ˌvɪʒ əl əˈ-- **~s** z
visualiz|e ˈvɪʒ u‿ə laɪz ˈvɪz ju‿, ˈvɪʒ ju‿ ‖ ˈvɪʒ ə laɪz **~ed** d **~es** ɪz əz **~ing** ɪŋ
vita ˈviːt ə ˈvaɪt- ‖ ˈviːţ ə ˈvaɪţ- **~s** z
Vitaglass *tdmk* ˈvaɪt ə ɡlɑːs ‖ ˈvaɪţ ə ɡlæs
vital ˈvaɪt ᵊl ‖ ˈvaɪţ ᵊl **~ly** i **~s** z
ˌvital caˈpacity; **ˌvital ˈsigns**; **ˌvital staˈtistics**
vitalis... —*see* **vitaliz...**
vitality vaɪ ˈtæl ət i -ɪt- ‖ -əţ i
vitaliz|e ˈvaɪt ə laɪz -ᵊl aɪz ‖ ˈvaɪţ- **~ed** d **~es** ɪz əz **~ing** ɪŋ
vitally ˈvaɪt ᵊl i ‖ ˈvaɪţ ᵊl i
vitamin ˈvɪt əm ɪn ˈvaɪt-, §-ən ‖ ˈvaɪţ- **~s** z
ˌvitamin ˈC
VitBe *tdmk* ˈvɪt bi
vitelline vɪ ˈtel aɪn -ɪn, §-ən
viti|ate ˈvɪʃ i |eɪt **~ated** eɪt ɪd -əd ‖ eɪţ əd **~ates** eɪts **~ating** eɪt ɪŋ ‖ eɪţ ɪŋ
vitiation ˌvɪʃ i ˈeɪʃ ᵊn
viticulture ˈvɪt i ˌkʌltʃ ə ˈvaɪt-, §ˈ·ə- ‖ ˈvɪţ ə ˌkʌltʃ ᵊr
Viti Levu ˌviːt i ˈlev uː
vitiligo ˌvɪt ɪ ˈlaɪɡ əʊ -ə-, -ᵊl ˈaɪɡ- ‖ ˌvɪţ ᵊl ˈaɪɡ oʊ
vitreous ˈvɪtr i‿əs **~ness** nəs nɪs
vitrifaction ˌvɪtr ɪ ˈfæk ʃᵊn -ə-
vitrification ˌvɪtr ɪf ɪ ˈkeɪʃ ᵊn ˌ·əf-, §-əˈ-
vitri|fy ˈvɪtr ɪ |faɪ -ə- **~fied** faɪd **~fies** faɪz **~fying** faɪ ɪŋ
vitriol ˈvɪtr i‿əl -ɒl
vitriolic ˌvɪtr i ˈɒl ɪk ◂ ‖ -ˈɑːl- **~ally** ᵊl‿i
vitro ˈviːtr əʊ ‖ -oʊ
Vitruvius vɪ ˈtruːv i‿əs və-
Vittel *tdmk* vɪ ˈtel
vittles ˈvɪt ᵊlz ‖ ˈvɪţ ᵊlz
vitupe|rate vaɪ ˈtjuːp ə |reɪt vɪ-, §və-, →-ˈtʃuːp- ‖ -ˈtuːp- -ˈtjuːp-
vituperation vaɪ ˌtjuːp ə ˈreɪʃ ᵊn vɪ-, §və-, →-ˌtʃuːp- ‖ -ˌtuːp- -ˌtjuːp-
vituperative vaɪ ˈtjuːp ər‿ət ɪv vɪ-, §və-, →-ˈtʃuːp-, -ə reɪt- ‖ -ˈtuːp ər‿əţ ɪv -ˈtjuːp-, -ə reɪţ-
Vitus ˈvaɪt əs ‖ ˈvaɪţ əs
viva *'long live'*, **Viva** *tdmk* ˈviːv ə **~s** z
viva *'oral examination'* ˈvaɪv ə **~ed** d **vivaing** ˈvaɪv əʳ ɪŋ ‖ ˈvaɪv ə ɪŋ **~s** z
vivace vɪ ˈvɑːtʃ i §və-, -eɪ
vivacious vɪ ˈveɪʃ əs §və-, vaɪ- **~ly** li **~ness** nəs nɪs
vivacity vɪ ˈvæs ət i §və-, -ɪt- ‖ -əţ i
Vivaldi vɪ ˈvæld i ‖ -ˈvɑːld- —*It* [vi ˈval di]
vivari|um vaɪ ˈveər i‿|əm vɪ-, §və- ‖ -ˈver- -ˈvær- **~a** ə **~ums** əmz
vivat ˈvaɪv æt ˈviːv- ‖ -ɑːt **~s** s

viva voce ˌvaɪv ə ˈvəʊtʃ i ˌviːv-, ˈvəʊs- ‖ -ˈvoʊtʃ- -ˈvoʊs-
vivax ˈvaɪv æks
Vivian ˈvɪv i‿ən
vivid ˈvɪv ɪd §-əd **~ly** li **~ness** nəs nɪs
Vivien ˈvɪv i‿ən
Vivienne *(i)* ˈvɪv i‿ən, *(ii)* ˌvɪv i ˈen
vivification ˌvɪv ɪf ɪ ˈkeɪʃ ən §ˌ·əf-, §-əˈ--
vivi|fy ˈvɪv ɪ |faɪ §-ə- **~fied** faɪd **~fier/s** faɪ‿ə/z ‖ faɪ‿ər/z **~fies** faɪz **~fying** faɪ ɪŋ
viviparous vɪ ˈvɪp ər əs vaɪ-, §və- **~ly** li
vivisect ˈvɪv ɪ sekt -ə-, ˌ·ˈ· **~ed** ɪd əd **~ing** ɪŋ **~s** s
vivisection ˌvɪv ɪ ˈsek ʃən §-ə-
vivisectionist ˌvɪv ɪ ˈsek ʃən‿ɪst §ˌ-ə-, §‿əst **~s** s
vixen ˈvɪks ən **~s** z
vixenish ˈvɪks ən ɪʃ
Viyella *tdmk* vaɪ ˈel ə
viz, viz. vɪz —*Usually read aloud as* namely ˈneɪm li
Viz —*name of publication* vɪz
vizier vɪ ˈzɪə §və-; ˈvɪz ɪə ‖ və ˈzɪər **~s** z
vizsla ˈvɪʒ lə —*Hung* [ˈviʒ lɒ] **~s** z
VJ ˌviː ˈdʒeɪ **~s** z
Vlach vlɑːk **Vlachs** vlɑːks
Vlad vlæd —*Romanian* [vlad]
Vladimir ˈvlæd ɪ mɪə -ə- ‖ -ə mɪr —*Russ* [vɫʌ ˈdʲi mʲɪr], *Czech* Vladimír [ˈvla dʲi miːr]
Vladivostok ˌvlæd ɪ ˈvɒst ɒk §-ə- ‖ -ˈvɑːst ɑːk —*Russ* [vɫə dʲi vʌ ˈstɔk]
VLSI ˌviː el es ˈaɪ
Vltava ˈvʊlt əv ə —*Czech* [ˈvl ta va]
V-neck ˈviː nek ˌ·ˈ· **~ed** t **~s** s
vocab ˈvəʊk æb ‖ ˈvoʊk-
vocabular|y vəʊ ˈkæb jʊl ər |i -ˈ·jəl-; §-ju ler i, §-ˈ·jə-, §-ˈ·ə- ‖ voʊ ˈkæb jə ler |i və- **~ies** iz
vocal ˈvəʊk əl ‖ ˈvoʊk əl **~ly** i **~s** z
ˌvocal ˈcords, ˈ· · · ‖ ˈ· · ·; **ˌvocal ˈfolds** ‖ ˈ· · ·
vocalic vəʊ ˈkæl ɪk ‖ voʊ- və-
vocalis... —*see* **vocaliz...**
vocalism ˈvəʊk ə ˌlɪz əm -əl ˌɪz- ‖ ˈvoʊk-
vocalist ˈvəʊk əl ɪst §-əst ‖ ˈvoʊk- **~s** s
vocalization ˌvəʊk əl aɪ ˈzeɪʃ ən -ɪˈ-- ‖ ˌvoʊk əl ə- **~s** z
vocaliz|e ˈvəʊk ə laɪz -əl aɪz ‖ ˈvoʊk- **~ed** d **~es** ɪz əz **~ing** ɪŋ
vocally ˈvəʊk əl i ‖ ˈvoʊk-
vocation vəʊ ˈkeɪʃ ən ‖ voʊ- **~s** z
vocational vəʊ ˈkeɪʃ ən‿əl ‖ voʊ- **~ly** i
vocative ˈvɒk ət ɪv ‖ ˈvɑːk əṱ ɪv **~s** z
Voce vəʊs ‖ voʊs
vocife|rate vəʊ ˈsɪf ə |reɪt ‖ voʊ- **~rated** reɪt ɪd -əd ‖ reɪṱ əd **~rates** reɪts **~rating** reɪt ɪŋ ‖ reɪṱ ɪŋ
vociferation vəʊ ˌsɪf ə ˈreɪʃ ən ‖ voʊ- **~s** z
vociferous vəʊ ˈsɪf ər‿əs ‖ voʊ- **~ly** li **~ness** nəs nɪs
vocoder ˌvəʊ ˈkəʊd ə ‖ ˌvoʊ ˈkoʊd ər **~s** z
vocoid ˈvəʊk ɔɪd ‖ ˈvoʊk- **~s** z
vocoidal vəʊ ˈkɔɪd əl ‖ voʊ-
Vodafone *tdmk* ˈvəʊd ə fəʊn ‖ ˈvoʊd ə foʊn **~s** z
vodka ˈvɒd kə ‖ ˈvɑːd kə **~s** z
voe, Voe vəʊ ‖ voʊ **voes** vəʊz ‖ voʊz
Vogt *(i)* vəʊkt ‖ voʊkt, *(ii)* vəʊt ‖ voʊt, *(iii)* vɒt ‖ vɑːt
vogue vəʊg ‖ voʊg **vogues** vəʊgz ‖ voʊgz
voguish ˈvəʊg ɪʃ ‖ ˈvoʊg- **~ness** nəs nɪs
Vogul ˈvəʊg ʊl -əl ‖ ˈvoʊg- **~s** z
voice vɔɪs **voiced** vɔɪst **voices** ˈvɔɪs ɪz -əz **voicing** ˈvɔɪs ɪŋ
ˈvoice box; **ˈvoice mail**
-voiced ˈvɔɪst — **gruff-voiced** ˌgrʌf ˈvɔɪst ◂
voiceless ˈvɔɪs ləs -lɪs **~ly** li **~ness** nəs nɪs
voice-over ˈvɔɪs ˌəʊv ə ˌ·ˈ· · ‖ -ˌoʊv ər **~s** z
voiceprint ˈvɔɪs prɪnt **~s** s
void vɔɪd **voided** ˈvɔɪd ɪd -əd **voiding** ˈvɔɪd ɪŋ **voids** vɔɪdz
voidable ˈvɔɪd əb əl **~ness** nəs nɪs
voidance ˈvɔɪd ənˈs
Voight, Voigt vɔɪt
voila, voilà vwæ ˈlɑː vwʌ-, vwɑː- ‖ vwɑː- —*Fr* [vwa la]
voile vɔɪəl vwɑːl —*Fr* [vwal]
VoIP vɔɪp
voix vwɑː *Fr* [vwa]
ˌvoix ceˈleste, ˌvoix céˈleste sɪ ˈlest sə- —*Fr* [se lɛst]
Vojvodina ˌvɔɪv ə ˈdiːn ə —*Serbian* [ˈˈvɔj vɔ di na]
vol, vol. vɒl ‖ vɑːl —*or as* volume
volant ˈvəʊl ənt ‖ ˈvoʊl-
Volapuk, Volapük ˈvɒl ə puːk ˈvəʊl-, -pʊk, ˌ·ˈ· ‖ ˈvoʊl- ˈvɑːl- —*Volapük* [vo la ˈpyk]
volatile ˈvɒl ə taɪəl ‖ ˈvɑːl əṱ əl *(*)* **~s** z —*but see also* **sal volatile**
volatilis... —*see* **volatiliz...**
volatility ˌvɒl ə ˈtɪl ət i -ɪt i ‖ ˌvɑːl ə ˈtɪl əṱ i
volatilization və ˌlæt ɪl aɪ ˈzeɪʃ ən vɒ-, vəʊ-, -ˌ·əl-, -ɪˈ·-; ˌvɒl ət- ‖ ˌvɑːl əṱ əl‿ə ˈzeɪʃ ən
volatiliz|e və ˈlæt ɪ laɪz vɒ-, vəʊ-, ˈvɒl ət-, -ə laɪz, -əl aɪz ‖ ˈvɑːl əṱ əl aɪz **~ed** d **~es** ɪz əz **~ing** ɪŋ
vol-au-vent ˈvɒl ə vɒ̃ ˈvəʊl-, -əʊ-, -vɒn, -vɒŋ, ˌ·ˈ· ‖ ˌvɔːl oʊ ˈvɑːn ˌvɑːl- —*Fr* [vɔ lo vɑ̃] **~s** z
volcanic vɒl ˈkæn ɪk ‖ vɑːl- **~ally** əl‿i
volcanism ˈvɒlk ə ˌnɪz əm ‖ ˈvɑːlk-
volcano vɒl ˈkeɪn əʊ ‖ vɑːl ˈkeɪn oʊ **~s** z
volcanological ˌvɒlk ən ə ˈlɒdʒ ɪk əl ◂ ‖ ˌvɑːlk ən ə ˈlɑːdʒ- **~ly** ‿i
volcanologist ˌvɒlk ə ˈnɒl ədʒ ɪst §-əst ‖ ˌvɑːlk ə ˈnɑːl- **~s** s
volcanology ˌvɒlk ə ˈnɒl ədʒ i ‖ ˌvɑːlk ə ˈnɑːl-
Voldemort ˈvɒl də mɔːt ˈvəʊl-, -mɔː ‖ ˈvoʊl də mɔːrt -mɔːr —*J.K. Rowling pronounces this name French-style, with no final* t*; the Harry Potter films, however, use one.*
vole vəʊl →vɒʊl ‖ voʊl **voles** vəʊlz →vɒʊlz ‖ voʊlz

volenti non fit injuria vəʊ ˌlent i ˌnəʊn fɪt ɪn ˈdʒʊər i̯ə vɒ-, -ˌnɒn-, -ˈjʊər- ‖ voʊ ˌlent i ˌnɑːn fɪt ɪn ˈdʒʊr i̯ə
Volga ˈvɒlg ə ‖ ˈvɑːlg ə —*Russ* [ˈvɔɫ gə]
Volgograd ˈvɒlg əʊ græd ‖ ˈvɑːlg ə- —*Russ* [vəɫ gʌ ˈgrat]
volitant ˈvɒl ɪt ənt -ət- ‖ ˈvɑːl ət ᵊnt
volition vəʊ ˈlɪʃ ᵊn ‖ voʊ- və-
volitional vəʊ ˈlɪʃ ᵊn̩əl ‖ voʊ- və- **~ly** i
volitive ˈvɒl ət ɪv -ɪt- ‖ ˈvɑːl əţ ɪv
Volk *family name(i)* vɒlk ‖ vɑːlk, *(ii)* vəʊlk →vɒʊlk ‖ voʊlk
Volk *German, 'people'* fɒlk vɒlk ‖ fɔːlk fɑːlk —*Ger* [fɔlk]
Volkswagen *tdmk* ˈvɒlks ˌwæg ən ˈvəʊks-, ˈfɒlks-, -ˌwɑːg-, -ˌvɑːg- ‖ ˈvoʊks- -ˌwɑːg- —*Ger* [ˈfɔlks ˌvaːg ən] **~s** z
volley ˈvɒl i ‖ ˈvɑːl i **~ed** d **~ing** ɪŋ **~s** z
volleyball ˈvɒl i bɔːl ‖ ˈvɑːl- -bɑːl
volplan|e ˈvɒl pleɪn ‖ ˈvɑːl- **~ed** d **~es** z **~ing** ɪŋ
Volpone vɒl ˈpəʊn i ‖ vɑːl ˈpoʊn i vɔːl-
Volsci ˈvɒls ki -aɪ, -iː ‖ ˈvɑːls-
Volscian ˈvɒls ki̯ən ‖ ˈvɑːls- **~s** z
Volstead ˈvɒl sted ‖ ˈvɑːl-
volt vəʊlt →vɒʊlt, vɒlt ‖ voʊlt **volts** vəʊlts →vɒʊlts, vɒlts ‖ voʊlts
volta *dance, piece of music, 'time, turn'* ˈvɒlt ə ‖ ˈvoʊlt ə ˈvɑːlt- —*It* [ˈvɔl ta] **~s** z
Volta *lake and river* ˈvɒlt ə ‖ ˈvoʊlt ə
Volta *physicist* ˈvəʊlt ə ˈvɒlt- ‖ ˈvoʊlt ə —*It* [ˈvɔl ta]
voltag|e ˈvəʊlt ɪdʒ →ˈvɒʊlt-, ˈvɒlt- ‖ ˈvoʊlt- **~es** ɪz əz
voltaic, V~ vɒl ˈteɪ ɪk vəʊl- ‖ vɑːl- voʊl-
Voltaire vɒl ˈteə vəʊl-, ˈ· · ‖ voʊl ˈteᵊr —*Fr* [vɔl tɛːʁ]
volte-fac|e ˌvɒlt ˈfɑːs -ˈfæs ‖ ˌvɔːlt ˈfɑːs ˌvɑːlt-, ˌvoʊlt- —*Fr* [vɔl tə fas] **~es** ɪz əz —*or as sing.*
voltmeter ˈvəʊlt ˌmiːt ə ˈvɒlt- ‖ ˈvoʊlt ˌmiːţ ᵊr **~s** z
volubility ˌvɒl ju ˈbɪl ət i ˌ·jə-, -ɪt i ‖ ˌvɑːl jə ˈbɪl əţ i
volub|le ˈvɒl jʊb |ᵊl §-jəb- ‖ ˈvɑːl jəb |ᵊl **~leness** ᵊl nəs -nɪs **~ly** li
volume ˈvɒl juːm -jʊm ‖ ˈvɑːl jəm -jʊm, -juːm **~s** z
volumetric ˌvɒl ju ˈmetr ɪk ◂ §-jə- ‖ ˌvɑːl jə- **~ally** ᵊl̩ i
voluminous və ˈluːm ɪn əs vɒ-, -ˈljuːm-, -ən- **~ly** li **~ness** nəs nɪs
voluntarily ˌvɒl ən ˈter əl i -ˈteər-, -ˈtær-, ɪ li; ˈvɒl ənt̮ər əl i, -ɪ li ‖ ˌvɑːl ən ˈter əl i -ˈtær-; ˈ· · · · · — *Preference poll, BrE:* -ˈter- *41%,* ˈvɒl- *32%,* -ˈteər- *15%,* -ˈtær- *12%.*
voluntarism ˈvɒl ənt ə ˌrɪz əm ‖ ˈvɑːl-
voluntar|y ˈvɒl ənt̮ər |i -ən ter- ‖ ˈvɑːl ən ter |i **~ies** iz **~iness** i nəs i nɪs
volunteer ˌvɒl ən ˈtɪə ‖ ˌvɑːl ən ˈtɪᵊr **~ed** d
volunteering ˌvɒl ən ˈtɪər ɪŋ ‖ ˌvɑːl ən ˈtɪr ɪŋ **~s** z

VOLUNTARILY

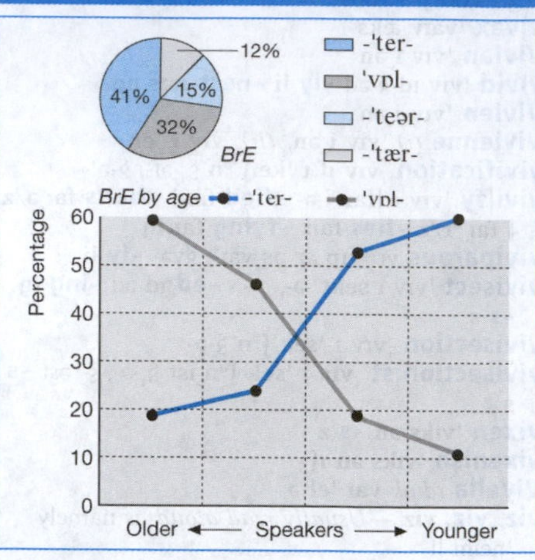

volunteerism ˌvɒl ən ˈtɪər ˌɪz əm ‖ ˌvɑːl ən ˈtɪr-
voluptuar|y və ˈlʌp tʃu̯ər |i -ˈlʌp tju̯, -ˈlʌp tʃər |i ‖ -tʃu er |i **~ies** iz
voluptuous və ˈlʌp tʃu̯əs -tju̯əs **~ly** li **~ness** nəs nɪs
volute və ˈluːt vɒ-, vəʊ-, -ˈljuːt **~s** s
voluted və ˈluːt ɪd vɒ-, vəʊ-, -ˈljuːt-, -əd ‖ -ˈluːţ əd
volution və ˈluːʃ ᵊn vɒ-, vəʊ-, -ˈljuːʃ-
volv|a ˈvɒlv |ə ‖ ˈvɑːlv |ə **~ae** iː
Volvic *tdmk* ˈvɒlv ɪk ‖ ˈvɑːlv- ˈvoʊlv-
Volvo *tdmk* ˈvɒlv əʊ ‖ ˈvɑːlv oʊ ˈvoʊlv- **~s** z
volvox ˈvɒlv ɒks ‖ ˈvɑːlv ɑːks
vomer ˈvəʊm ə ‖ ˈvoʊm ᵊr **~s** z
vom|it ˈvɒm |ɪt §-ət ‖ ˈvɑːm |ət **~ited** ɪt ɪd §ət-, -əd ‖ əţ əd **~iting** ɪt ɪŋ §ət- ‖ əţ ɪŋ **~its** ɪts §əts ‖ əts
vomitori|um ˌvɒm ɪ ˈtɔːr i̯|əm ˌ·ə- ‖ ˌvɑːm ə- -ˈtoʊr- **~a** ə **~ums** əmz
vomitor|y ˈvɒm ɪ̯tər |i ˈ·ə- ‖ ˈvɑːm ə tɔːr |i -toʊr i **~ies** iz
von, Von *in family names* vɒn fɒn ‖ vɑːn —*Ger* [fɔn]
Vonage ˈvɒn ɪdʒ ‖ ˈvɑːn ɪdʒ
Von Braun vɒn ˈbraʊn fɒn- ‖ vɔːn- vɑːn- —*Ger* [fɔn ˈbʁaʊn]
Vonnegut ˈvɒn ɪ gʌt -ə- ‖ ˈvɑːn- ˈvɔːn-
Vono *tdmk* ˈvəʊn əʊ ‖ ˈvoʊn oʊ
voodoo ˈvuːd uː **~ism** ˌɪz əm
Voortrekker ˈfʊə ˌtrek ə ˈvʊə-, ˈfɔː-, ˈvɔː- ‖ ˈfɔːr ˌtrek ᵊr ˈfoʊr- —*Afrikaans* [ˈfoːr ˌtrɛk ər] **~s** z
voracious və ˈreɪʃ əs vɒ- **~ly** li **~ness** nəs nɪs
voracity və ˈræs ət i vɒ-, -ɪt- ‖ -əţ i
Vorderman ˈvɔːd ə mən ‖ ˈvɔːrd ᵊr-
-vorous *stress-imposing* vər əs — **omnivorous** ɒm ˈnɪv ər əs ‖ ɑːm-
Vorsprung durch Technik ˌvɔː sprʌŋ ˌdɜːx ˈtex nɪk -tek ˈniːk ‖ ˌvɔːr sprʌŋ dɜːk ˈtek nɪk —*Ger* [ˌfoːɐ ʃpʁʊŋ dʊʁç ˈtɛç nɪk]

V

Voiced and voiceless

1 **Voiced** sounds are produced with the vocal folds vibrating – opening and closing rapidly, producing **voice**. **Voiceless** sounds are made with the vocal folds apart, allowing the air to pass freely between them.

2 The sounds p, t, k, tʃ, f, θ, s, ʃ, h are normally voiceless, while the remaining English sounds are classified as voiced.

3 There is a difficulty with this classification, since it refers to PHONEMES – yet in reality a given English phoneme may have both voiced and voiceless ALLOPHONEs. For example, in AmE the 'voiceless' phoneme t includes the voiced allophone ţ, which is so noticeable that this dictionary gives it a separate symbol (see T-VOICING).

4 Another difficulty arises with b, d, g, dʒ, v, ð, z, ʒ. It is only when they are between other voiced sounds that these consonants are reliably voiced. In other positions there is often little or no actual vibration of the vocal folds during their production. Hence they are sometimes classified as **lenis** rather than as voiced. The corresponding term for p, t, k, tʃ, f, θ, s, ʃ is **fortis**, rather than voiceless.

5 A **devoiced** lenis does not sound quite like a fortis. Quite apart from differences such as those described in the notes at ASPIRATION and CLIPPING, b, d, g etc. have less articulatory force than p, t, k etc. This may be due to the vocal folds, which in the case of a devoiced lenis sound probably remain in the narrowed 'whisper' configuration, distinct from their wide open configuration for a true voiceless (fortis) sound.

vortex 'vɔːt eks ‖ 'vɔːrt- **~es** ɪz əz **vortices** 'vɔːt ɪ siːz -ə- ‖ 'vɔːrţ-
vorticism 'vɔːt ɪ ˌsɪz əm -ə- ‖ 'vɔːrţ-
Vortigern 'vɔːt ɪ gɜːn -ɪg ən ‖ 'vɔːrţ ɪ gɝːn
Vosburgh 'vɒs bəˌrə ‖ 'vɑːs-
Vosene *tdmk* 'vəʊz iːn ‖ 'voʊz-
Vosges vəʊʒ ‖ voʊʒ —*Fr* [voːʒ]
Voss vɒs ‖ vɑːs vɔːs
Vostok 'vɒst ɒk ‖ 'vɑːst ɑːk —*Russ* [vʌ 'stɔk]
votaress 'vəʊt ə res -ər əs, -ər ɪs ‖ 'voʊţ ər əs **~es** ɪz əz
votar|y 'vəʊt ər |i ‖ 'voʊţ- **~ies** iz
vote vəʊt ‖ voʊt **voted** 'vəʊt ɪd -əd ‖ 'voʊţ əd **votes** vəʊts ‖ voʊts **voting** 'vəʊt ɪŋ ‖ 'voʊţ ɪŋ
ˌ**vote of 'thanks**; '**voting booth**; '**voting maˌchine**
vote-getter 'vəʊt ˌget ə ‖ 'voʊt ˌgeţ ᵊr **~s** z
voteless 'vəʊt ləs -lɪs ‖ 'voʊt-
voter 'vəʊt ə ‖ 'voʊţ ᵊr **~s** z
votive 'vəʊt ɪv ‖ 'voʊţ ɪv
Votyak 'vɒt jæk 'vəʊt-, '·i æk ‖ 'voʊt jɑːk -jæk
vouch vaʊtʃ **vouched** vaʊtʃt **vouches** 'vaʊtʃ ɪz -əz **vouching** 'vaʊtʃ ɪŋ
voucher 'vaʊtʃ ə ‖ -ᵊr **~s** z
vouchsaf|e ₍ˌ₎vaʊtʃ 'seɪf '· · **~ed** t **~es** s **~ing** ɪŋ
Vouvray 'vuːv reɪ ‖ vuː 'vreɪ —*Fr* [vu vʁɛ]
vow vaʊ **vowed** vaʊd **vowing** 'vaʊ ɪŋ **vows** vaʊz
vowel 'vaʊ̯ əl vaʊl ‖ 'vaʊ͜əl **voweled, vowelled** 'vaʊ͜əld vaʊld ‖ 'vaʊ͜əld **voweling, vowelling** 'vaʊ͜əl ɪŋ 'vaʊl ɪŋ ‖ 'vaʊ͜əl ɪŋ **vowels** 'vaʊəlz vaʊlz ‖ 'vaʊ͜əlz
vowelless 'vaʊ͜əl ləs 'vaʊl ləs; -lɪs ‖ 'vaʊ͜əl-
vowel-like 'vaʊ͜əl laɪk 'vaʊl laɪk ‖ 'vaʊ͜əl-
Vowles *(i)* vəʊlz →vɒʊlz ‖ voʊlz, *(ii)* vaʊᵊlz
vox vɒks ‖ vɑːks
ˌ**vox hu'mana** hju 'mɑːn ə; ˌ**vox 'pop**; ˌ**vox 'populi** 'pɒp ju laɪ -jə-, -liː ‖ 'pɑːp jə-
voyag|e 'vɔɪ ɪdʒ **~ed** d **~es** ɪz əz **~ing** ɪŋ
voyager, V~ 'vɔɪ ɪdʒ ə -ədʒ- ‖ -ᵊr **~s** z
voyeur ₍ˌ₎vwaɪ 'ɜː ₍ˌ₎vɔɪ-; ₍ˌ₎vwɑː 'jɜː; 'vɔɪ ə, 'vwɔɪ- ‖ vwɑː 'jɝː —*Fr* [vwa jœːʁ] **~s** z
voyeurism ₍ˌ₎vwaɪ 'ɜːr ˌɪz əm ₍ˌ₎vɔɪ-; ₍ˌ₎vwɑː 'jɜːr-; 'vɔɪ ər-, 'vwɔɪ- ‖ vwɑː 'jɝː-
voyeuristic ˌvwaɪ ɜː 'rɪst ɪk ◂ ˌvɔɪ-, ˌvwɔɪ-, -ə-; ˌvwɑː jɜː- ‖ ˌvwɑː jə- **~ally** ᵊl͜i
VP ˌviː 'piː **~s** z
VRML 'vɜːm ᵊl ‖ 'vɝːm ᵊl

vroom vruːm vrʊm
vs, vs. ˈvɜːs əs ‖ ˈvɜ˞ːs əs
V-shaped ˈviː ʃeɪpt
V-sign ˈviː saɪn **~s** z
VSO ˌviː es ˈəʊ ‖ -ˈoʊ
 ˌVSˈO ˌlanguage
VTOL ˈviː tɒl ˌviː tiː əʊ ˈel ‖ ˈviː tɔːl -tɑːl
VTR ˌviː tiː ˈɑː ‖ -ˈɑːr **~s, ~'s** z
vug, vugg, vugh vʌg **vuggs, vughs, vugs** vʌgz
Vuitton *tdmk* ˈvjuː ɪ tɒn -ɪt ᵊn, §-ət-; ˈvwiːt õ ‖ ˈvjuː ə tɑːn ˈvwiː tɑːn —*Fr* [vɥi tɔ̃]
Vukovar ˈvuːk ə vɑː ‖ -vɑːr —*Croatian* [vu ˈˈkɔ vaːr]
Vulcan ˈvʌlk ən
vulcanis... —*see* **vulcaniz...**
vulcanism ˈvʌlk ə ˌnɪz əm
vulcanite ˈvʌlk ə naɪt
vulcanization ˌvʌlk ən aɪ ˈzeɪʃ ᵊn -ɪˈ-- ‖ -əˈ--
vulcaniz|e ˈvʌlk ə naɪz **~ed** d **~es** ɪz əz **~ing** ɪŋ
vulcanological ˌvʌlk ən ə ˈlɒdʒ ɪk ᵊl ◂ ‖ -ˈlɑːdʒ- **~ly** ˌi
vulcanologist ˌvʌlk ə ˈnɒl ədʒ ɪst §-əst ‖ -ˈnɑːl- **~s** s
vulcanology ˌvʌlk ə ˈnɒl ədʒ i ‖ -ˈnɑːl-
vulgar ˈvʌlg ə ‖ -ᵊr **~ly** li **~ness** nəs nɪs
 ˌvulgar ˈfraction; **ˌVulgar ˈLatin**
vulgarian vʌl ˈgeər iˌən ‖ -ˈger- -ˈgær- **~s** z
vulgaris... —*see* **vulgariz...**
vulgarism ˈvʌlg ə ˌrɪz əm **~s** z
vulgarit|y vʌl ˈgær ət |i -ɪt- ‖ -əṭ |i -ˈger- **~ies** iz
vulgarization ˌvʌlg ər aɪ ˈzeɪʃ ᵊn -ɪˈ-- ‖ -əˈ--
vulgariz|e ˈvʌlg ə raɪz **~ed** d **~es** ɪz əz **~ing** ɪŋ
Vulgate ˈvʌlg eɪt -ət, -ɪt
Vulliamy ˈvʌl jəm i
vulnerability ˌvʌln ərˌə ˈbɪl ət i ˌvʌn-, -ɪt i ‖ -əṭ i
vulnerab|le ˈvʌln ərˌəb |ᵊl ˈvʌn- **~leness** ᵊl nəs -nɪs **~ly** li
vulnerary ˈvʌln ər ər i ‖ -ə rer i
Vulpecula vʌl ˈpek jʊl ə -jəl- ‖ -jəl ə
vulpine ˈvʌlp aɪn
vulture ˈvʌltʃ ə ‖ -ᵊr **~s** z
vulv|a ˈvʌlv |ə **~ae** iː **~as** əz
vulvitis vʌl ˈvaɪt ɪs §-əs ‖ -ˈvaɪṭ əs
vulvovaginitis ˌvʌlv əʊ ˌvædʒ ɪ ˈnaɪt ɪs -əˈ--, §-əs ‖ -oʊ ˌvædʒ ə ˈnaɪṭ əs
VW *tdmk* ˌviː ˈdʌb ᵊl juː -ju ‖ -jə
vying ˈvaɪ ɪŋ
Vyrnwy ˈvɜːn wi ˈvɜːn u i ‖ ˈvɜ˞ːn-
Vyvyan ˈvɪv iˌən

Ww

w Spelling-to-sound

1. Where the spelling is **w**,
   - either the pronunciation is w as in **swim** swɪm, **away** ə ˈweɪ or else
   - the **w** forms part of one of the digraphs **aw**, **ew**, **ow** (see under **a**, **e**, **o** respectively) as in **few** fjuː.
2. **w** is always silent in **wr** at the beginning of a word or stem as in **wreck** rek, **rewrite** (noun) ˈriː raɪt, also in the exceptionally spelled words **two** tuː, **answer** ˈɑːnˈs ə ‖ ˈænˈs ᵊr.
3. w is also regularly written **u** as in **persuade** pə ˈsweɪd ‖ pᵊr- and as part of the digraph **qu** as in **quite** kwaɪt.

wh Spelling-to-sound

1. Where the spelling is the digraph **wh**, the pronunciation in most cases is w, as in **white** waɪt. An alternative pronunciation, depending on regional, social and stylistic factors, is hw, thus hwaɪt. This h pronunciation is usual in Scottish and Irish English, and decreasingly so in AmE, but not otherwise. (Among those who pronounce simple w, the pronunciation with hw tends to be considered 'better', and so is used by some people in formal styles only.) Learners of EFL are recommended to use plain w.
2. Occasionally, the pronunciation is h as in **whole** həʊl ‖ hoʊl, **who** huː.

W, w ˈdʌb ᵊl juː -ju ‖ -jə *—in AmE sometimes reduced to* ˈdʌb jə **W's, w's, Ws** ˈdʌb ᵊl juːz *—Communications code name:* Whisky **ˌW'C**; **ˌw'h ˌquestion**; **ˌWˌH'O**; **ˌWˌP'C**

WAAC wæk

WAAF, Waaf wæf **Waafs** wæfs

Wabash ˈwɔː bæʃ ‖ ˈwɑː-

WAC, Wac wæk **Wacs** wæks

Wace weɪs

wack wæk

wacko ˈwæk əʊ ‖ -oʊ

wack|y ˈwæk |i **~ier** i‿ə ‖ i‿ᵊr **~iest** i‿ɪst i‿əst **~ily** ɪ li əl i **~iness** i nəs i nɪs

Waco ˈweɪk əʊ ‖ -oʊ

wad wɒd ‖ wɑːd **wadded** ˈwɒd ɪd -əd ‖ ˈwɑːd əd **wadding** ˈwɒd ɪŋ ‖ ˈwɑːd ɪŋ **wads** wɒdz ‖ wɑːdz

Waddell *(i)* ˈwɒd ᵊl ‖ ˈwɑːd ᵊl, *(ii)* wɒ ˈdel wə- ‖ wɑː-

Waddesdon ˈwɒdz dən ‖ ˈwɑːdz-

wadding ˈwɒd ɪŋ ‖ ˈwɑːd ɪŋ

Waddington ˈwɒd ɪŋ tən ‖ ˈwɑːd-

waddl|e ˈwɒd ᵊl ‖ ˈwɑːd ᵊl **~ed** d **~es** z **~ing** ‿ɪŋ

Waddon ˈwɒd ᵊn ‖ ˈwɑːd ᵊn

wadd|y ˈwɒd| i ‖ ˈwɑːd| i **~ies** iz

wade, Wade weɪd **waded** ˈweɪd ɪd -əd **wades** weɪdz **wading** ˈweɪd ɪŋ **'wading bird**; **'wading pool**

Wadebridge ˈweɪd brɪdʒ →ˈweɪb-

Wade-Giles ˌweɪd ˈdʒaɪᵊlz **ˌWade-'Giles ˌsystem**

wader ˈweɪd ə ‖ -ᵊr **~s** z

wadge, Wadge wɒdʒ ‖ wɑːdʒ **wadges** ˈwɒdʒ ɪz -əz ‖ ˈwɑːdʒ əz
Wadham ˈwɒd əm ‖ ˈwɑːd-
Wadhurst ˈwɒd hɜːst ‖ ˈwɑːd hɝːst
wadi ˈwɒd i ˈwɑːd i ‖ ˈwɑːd i **~s** z
wading —*see* **wade**
Wadsworth ˈwɒdz wəθ -wɜːθ ‖ ˈwɑːdz wᵊrθ
wad|y ˈwɒd |i ˈwɑːd- ‖ ˈwɑːd |i **~ies** iz
wafer ˈweɪf ə ‖ -ᵊr **~s** z
wafer-thin ˌweɪf ə ˈθɪn ◂ ‖ -ᵊr-
waffl|e ˈwɒf ᵊl ‖ ˈwɑːf ᵊl **~ed** d **~er/s** ə/z ‖ ᵊr/z **~es** z **~ing** ˌɪŋ
ˈwaffle ˌiron
waffler ˈwɒf ᵊl‿ə ‖ ˈwɑːf ᵊl‿ər **~s** z
waffly ˈwɒf ᵊl‿i ‖ ˈwɑːf ᵊl‿i
waft wɑːft wɒft, wɔːft, §wæft ‖ wæft **wafted** ˈwɑːft ɪd ˈwɒft-, ˈwɔːft-, §ˈwæft-, -əd ‖ ˈwæft- **wafting** ˈwɑːft ɪŋ ˈwɒft-, ˈwɔːft-, §ˈwæft- ‖ ˈwæft- **wafts** wɑːfts wɒfts, wɔːfts, §wæfts ‖ wæfts
wag wæg **wagged** wægd **wagging** ˈwæg ɪŋ **wags** wægz
wage weɪdʒ **waged** weɪdʒd **wages** ˈweɪdʒ ɪz -əz **waging** ˈweɪdʒ ɪŋ
ˈwage ˌearner; **ˈwage ˌpacket**; **ˈwage rate**; **ˈwage rise**; **ˈwage slave**
wager ˈweɪdʒ ə ‖ -ᵊr **~ed** d **wagering** ˈweɪdʒ ər‿ɪŋ **~s** z
Wagg wæg
wagga, Wagga ˈwɒg ə ‖ ˈwɑːg ə
Wagga Wagga ˈ· · ˌ· ·‖ˈ· · ˈ· ·
waggery ˈwæg ər i
waggish ˈwæg ɪʃ **~ly** li **~ness** nəs nɪs
waggl|e ˈwæg ᵊl **~ed** d **~es** z **~ing** ˌɪŋ
waggly ˈwæg ᵊl‿i
waggon ˈwæg ən **~s** z
waggoner ˈwæg ən ə ‖ -ᵊn ər **~s** z
waggonette ˌwæg ə ˈnet **~s** s
waggonload ˈwæg ən ləʊd ‖ -loʊd **~s** z
Waghorn ˈwæg hɔːn ‖ -hɔːrn
Wagnall ˈwæg nᵊl
Wagner *German name, composer* ˈvɑːg nə ‖ -nᵊr —*Ger* [ˈvaːg nɐ]
Wagner *English or American family name* ˈwæg nə ‖ -nᵊr
Wagnerian vɑːg ˈnɪər i‿ən ‖ -ˈnɪr- -ˈner- **~s** z
wagon ˈwæg ən **~s** z
ˈwagon train
wagoner ˈwæg ən ə ‖ -ᵊn ər **~s** z
wagonette ˌwæg ə ˈnet **~s** s
wagon-lit ˌvæg ɒn ˈliː -ɔ̃- ‖ ˌvɑːg ən- -ɔːn-, -oʊn- —*Fr* [va gɔ̃ li] **~s** *same as sing., less commonly* z
wagonload ˈwæg ən ləʊd ‖ -loʊd **~s** z
Wagstaff ˈwæg stɑːf §-stæf ‖ -stæf
wagtail ˈwæg teɪᵊl **~s** z
Wahabi, Wahhabi wə ˈhɑːb i wɑː-
wahoo wɑː ˈhuː ˈ· · **~s** z
wah-wah ˈwɑː wɑː **~s** z
waif weɪf **waifs** weɪfs
waif-like ˈweɪf laɪk
Waikato waɪ ˈkæt əʊ -ˈkɑːt- ‖ -ˈkɑːţ oʊ
Waikiki ˈwaɪk ɪ kiː ˌ· ·ˈ·
wail weɪᵊl **wailed** weɪᵊld **wailing** ˈweɪᵊl ɪŋ **wails** weɪᵊlz
wain weɪn **wains** weɪnz
Wain, Waine weɪn
Wainfleet ˈweɪn fliːt
wainscot ˈweɪn skət -skɒt ‖ -skɑːt, -skoʊt
wainscoted, wainscotted ˈweɪn skət ɪd -skɒt-, -əd ‖ -skəţ əd -skɑːţ-, -skoʊţ-
wainscoting, wainscotting ˈweɪn skət ɪŋ -skɒt- ‖ -skəţ ɪŋ -skɑːţ-, -skoʊţ- **~s** s
Wainwright, w~ ˈweɪn raɪt **~s** s
waist weɪst *(= waste)* **waisted** ˈweɪst ɪd -əd **waists** weɪsts
waistband ˈweɪst bænd **~s** z
waistcoat ˈweɪs kəʊt ˈweɪst-; ˈwesk ət, -ɪt ‖ ˈwesk ət ˈweɪst koʊt **~s** s
waist-deep ˌweɪst ˈdiːp ◂
waist-high ˌweɪst ˈhaɪ ◂
waistline ˈweɪst laɪn **~s** z
wait weɪt **waited** ˈweɪt ɪd -əd ‖ ˈweɪţ əd **waiting** ˈweɪt ɪŋ ‖ ˈweɪţ ɪŋ **waits** weɪts
ˈwaiting game; **ˈwaiting list**; **ˈwaiting room**
wait-and-see ˌweɪt ᵊn ˈsiː -ᵊnd-
Waitangi ⁽ˌ⁾waɪ ˈtæŋ i
Waite weɪt
waiter ˈweɪt ə ‖ ˈweɪţ ᵊr **~s** z
Waites weɪts
waitlist ˈweɪt lɪst **~ed** ɪd əd **~ing** ɪŋ **~s** s
wait|person ˈweɪt ˌpɜːs ᵊn ‖ -ˌpɝːs ᵊn **~people** ˌpiːp ᵊl
waitress ˈweɪtr əs -ɪs **~es** ɪz əz **~ing** ɪŋ
waitron ˈweɪtr ən **~s** z
Waitrose *tdmk* ˈweɪt rəʊz ‖ -roʊz
waitstaff ˈweɪt stɑːf §-stæf ‖ -stæf
waive weɪv *(= wave)* **waived** weɪvd **waives** weɪvz **waiving** ˈweɪv ɪŋ
waiver ˈweɪv ə ‖ -ᵊr *(= waver)* **~s** z
Wajda ˈvaɪd ə —*Polish* [ˈvai da]
wake, Wake weɪk **waked** weɪkt **wakes** weɪks **waking** ˈweɪk ɪŋ **woke** wəʊk ‖ woʊk **woken** ˈwəʊk ən ‖ ˈwoʊk ən
wakeboard ˈweɪk bɔːd ‖ -bɔːrd -boʊrd **~er/s** ə/z ‖ ᵊr/z **~ing** ɪŋ **~s** z
Wakefield ˈweɪk fiːᵊld
wakeful ˈweɪk fᵊl -fʊl **~ly** ˌi **~ness** nəs nɪs
Wakeham ˈweɪk əm
Wakehurst ˈweɪk hɜːst ‖ -hɝːst
Wakelin ˈweɪk lɪn §-lən
waken ˈweɪk ən **~ed** d **~ing** ˌɪŋ **~s** z
Wakering ˈweɪk ər ɪŋ
wake-robin ˈweɪk ˌrɒb ɪn §-ən ‖ -ˌrɑːb-
wake-up ˈweɪk ʌp
wakey ˈweɪk i
ˌwakey ˈwakey!
waking —*see* **wake**
Wakley *(i)* ˈwæk li, *(ii)* ˈweɪk li
Walachi|a wɒ ˈleɪk i‿|ə wə- ‖ wɑː- **~an/s** ən/z
Walberswick ˈwɔːlb əz wɪk ˈwɒlb- ‖ -ᵊrz- ˈwɑːlb-
Walbrook ˈwɔːl brʊk ˈwɒl- ‖ ˈwɑːl-
Walcot, Walcott ˈwɔːl kət ˈwɒl-, -kɒt ‖ ˈwɑːl-, -kɑːt

Waldegrave *(i)* ˈwɔːld greɪv ˈwɒld- ‖ ˈwɑːld-, *(ii)* ˈwɔːld ɪ greɪv ˈwɒld-, -ə- ‖ ˈwɑːld-
Waldemar ˈvæld ə mɑː ˈwɔːld-, -ɪ- ‖ ˈvɑːld ə mɑːr —*Ger* [ˈval də maʁ], *Swed* [-mar]
Walden ˈwɔːld ən ˈwɒld- ‖ ˈwɑːld-
Waldens|es wɔːl ˈdenᵗs |iːz wɒl- ‖ wɑːl- **~ian/s** i ə̯n/z
Waldheim ˈvɑːld haɪm ‖ ˈwɑːld- —*Ger* [ˈvalt haim]
Waldo ˈwɔːld əʊ ˈwɒld- ‖ -oʊ ˈwɑːld-
Waldorf ˈwɔːld ɔːf ˈwɒld- ‖ -ɔːrf ˈwɑːld-
ˌWaldorf ˈsalad
Waldron ˈwɔːldr ən ˈwɒldr- ‖ ˈwɑːldr-
Waldstein *(i)* ˈvæld staɪn ˈvɑːld-, ˈvɒld- ‖ vɑːld-, *(ii)* ˈwɔːld staɪn ˈwɒld- ‖ ˈwɑːld- —*For the Beethoven sonata, and as a German name, (i)* —*Ger* [ˈvalt ʃtain]; *as an American family name, (ii).*
wale weɪᵊl **wales** weɪᵊlz
Wales weɪᵊlz
Walesa, Wałęsa vɑː ˈwenᵗs ə və-, wə-, -ˈwenz-, -ˈlenᵗs- ‖ wɑː ˈlenᵗs ə —*Polish* [va ˈwew̃ sa]
Waley ˈweɪl i
Walford ˈwɔːl fəd ˈwɒl- ‖ -fᵊrd ˈwɑːl-
Walgreens *tdmk* ˈwɔːl griːnz ˈwɒl- ‖ ˈwɑːl-
Walham ˈwɒl əm ‖ ˈwɑːl-
Walian ˈweɪl i ə̯n
walk wɔːk ‖ wɑːk **walked** wɔːkt ‖ wɑːkt **walking** ˈwɔːk ɪŋ ‖ ˈwɑːk- **walks** wɔːks ‖ wɑːks
ˈwalking ˌpapers; **ˈwalking shoes**; **ˈwalking stick**; **ˈwalking tour**; **ˌwalk of ˈlife**
walkabout ˈwɔːk ə ˌbaʊt
walkathon ˈwɔːk ə θɒn ‖ ˈwɑːk- **~s** z
walkaway ˈwɔːk ə ˌweɪ ‖ ˈwɑːk- **~s** z
Walkden ˈwɔːk dən ‖ ˈwɑːk-
walker, W~ ˈwɔːk ə ‖ -ᵊr ˈwɑːk- **~s** z
walkies ˈwɔːk iz ‖ ˈwɑːk-
walkie-talkie ˌwɔːk i ˈtɔːk i ‖ ˌwɑːk i ˈtɑːk i **~s** z
walk-in ˈwɔːk ɪn ‖ ˈwɑːk- **~s** z
Walkman *tdmk,* **w~** ˈwɔːk mən ‖ ˈwɑːk- **~s** z
walk-on ˈwɔːk ɒn ‖ -ɑːn ˈwɑːk-, -ɔːn **~s** z
walkout ˈwɔːk aʊt ‖ ˈwɑːk- **~s** s
walkover ˈwɔːk ˌəʊv ə ‖ -ˌoʊv ᵊr ˈwɑːk- **~s** z
walk-through ˈwɔːk θruː ‖ ˈwɑːk- **~s** z
walk-up ˈwɔːk ʌp ‖ ˈwɑːk- **~s** s
walkway ˈwɔːk weɪ ‖ ˈwɑːk- **~s** z
walky-talk|y ˌwɔːk i ˈtɔːk| i ‖ ˌwɑːk i ˈtɑːk| i **~ies** iz
wall, Wall wɔːl ‖ wɑːl **walled** wɔːld ‖ wɑːld **walling** ˈwɔːl ɪŋ ‖ ˈwɑːl- **walls** wɔːlz ‖ wɑːlz
ˈwall ˌpainting; **ˈWall Street, ˌWall Street ˈJournal**
walla, Walla ˈwɒl ə ‖ ˈwɑːl ə
wallab|y ˈwɒl əb |i ‖ ˈwɑːl- **~ies** iz
Wallace ˈwɒl ɪs -əs ‖ ˈwɑːl əs ˈwɔːl-
Wallachi|a wɒ ˈleɪk i |ə wə- ‖ wɑː- **~an/s** ən/z
wallah ˈwɒl ə ‖ ˈwɑːl ə **~s** z
wallaroo, W~ ˌwɒl ə ˈruː ‖ ˌwɑːl- **~s** z
Wallasey ˈwɒl əs i ‖ ˈwɑːl-
wallboard ˈwɔːl bɔːd ‖ -bɔːrd ˈwɑːl-, -boʊrd **~s** z
wallchart ˈwɔːl tʃɑːt ‖ -tʃɑːrt ˈwɑːl- **~s** s
Waller *(i)* ˈwɒl ə ‖ ˈwɑːl ᵊr, *(ii)* ˈwɔːl ə ‖ -ᵊr ˈwɑːl-
Wallerawang wə ˈleər ə wæŋ ‖ -ˈler-
wallet ˈwɒl ɪt -ət ‖ ˈwɑːl ət **~s** s
walleye ˈwɔːl aɪ ‖ ˈwɑːl- **~s** z
wall-eyed ˈwɔːl aɪd ˌ·ˈ· ‖ ˈwɑːl-
wallflower ˈwɔːl ˌflaʊ ə ‖ ˌ ᵊr ˈwɑːl- **~s** z
wallie... —*see* **wally**
Walliker ˈwɒl ɪk ə -ək- ‖ ˈwɑːl ək ᵊr
Wallingford ˈwɒl ɪŋ fəd ‖ ˈwɑːl ɪŋ fᵊrd
Wallington ˈwɒl ɪŋ tən ‖ ˈwɑːl-
Wallis ˈwɒl ɪs §-əs ‖ ˈwɑːl əs ˈwɔːl-
wall-mounted ˈwɔːl ˌmaʊnt ɪd -əd ‖ -ˌmaʊnt̬- ˈwɑːl-
Wallonia wɒ ˈləʊn i ə wə- ‖ wɑː ˈloʊn-
Walloon wɒ ˈluːn wə- ‖ wɑː- **~s** z
wallop, W~ ˈwɒl əp ‖ ˈwɑːl əp **~ed** t **~ing/s** ɪŋ/z **~s** s
wallow ˈwɒl əʊ ‖ ˈwɑːl oʊ **~ed** d **~er/s** ə/z ‖ ᵊr/z **~ing** ɪŋ **~s** z
wallpaper ˈwɔːl ˌpeɪp ə ‖ -ᵊr ˈwɑːl- **~ed** d
wallpapering ˈwɔːl ˌpeɪp ər ɪŋ ‖ ˈwɑːl- **~s** z
Walls wɔːlz ‖ wɑːlz
Wallsend ˈwɔːlz end ‖ ˈwɑːlz-
wall-to-wall ˌwɔːl tə ˈwɔːl ◂ -tu- ‖ ˌwɑːl tə ˈwɑːl
ˌwall-to-wall ˈcarpeting
wallum ˈwɒl əm ‖ ˈwɑːl-
Wallwork ˈwɔːl wɜːk ˈwɒl- ‖ -wɜːk ˈwɑːl-
wall|y *n,* **Wally** ˈwɒl |i ‖ ˈwɑːl |i **~ies** iz
Wal-Mart *tdmk* ˈwɒl mɑːt ˈwɔːl- ‖ ˈwɔːl mɑːrt ˈwɑːl-, ˈwɔː-, ˈwɑː-
Walmer ˈwɔːlm ə ˈwɒlm- ‖ -ᵊr ˈwɑːlm-
Walmesley, Walmisley, Walmsley ˈwɔːmz li ‖ ˈwɑːmz-
Walmley ˈwɔːm li ‖ ˈwɑːm-
Walney ˈwɔːln i ˈwɒln- ‖ ˈwɑːln-
walnut ˈwɔːl nʌt ‖ ˈwɑːl- **~s** s
Walpamur *tdmk* ˈwɔːl pə mjʊə ˈwɒl-, -mɜː ‖ -mjʊr ˈwɑːl-
Walpole ˈwɔːl pəʊl ˈwɒl-, →-pɒʊl ‖ -poʊl ˈwɑːl-
Walpurgis væl ˈpʊəg ɪs vɑːl-, -ˈpɜːg-, §-əs ‖ vɑːl ˈpʊrg əs
walrus ˈwɔːl rəs ˈwɒl-, -rʌs ‖ ˈwɑːl- **~es** ɪz əz
ˌwalrus mouˈstache ‖ ˈ···
Walsall ˈwɔːl sɔːl ˈwɒl-, -sᵊl ‖ ˈwɑːl sɑːl —*locally also* ˈwɔːs ᵊl
Walsh wɔːlʃ wɒlʃ ‖ wɑːlʃ
Walsham ˈwɔːlʃ əm ˈwɒlʃ- ‖ ˈwɑːlʃ- —*locally also* ˈwɒls əm
Walsingham *(i)* ˈwɔːls ɪŋ əm ˈwɒls- ‖ ˈwɑːls-, *(ii)* ˈwɔːlz- ˈwɒlz- ‖ ˈwɑːlz- —*the personal name is (i), but the place in Nfk is (ii)*
Walt wɔːlt wɒlt ‖ wɑːlt
Walter ˈwɔːlt ə ˈwɒlt- ‖ -ᵊr ˈwɑːlt- —*but as a German name,* ˈvɑːlt ə ‖ -ᵊr —*Ger* [ˈval tɐ]
ˌWalter ˈMitty ˈmɪt i ‖ ˈmɪt̬ i
Walters ˈwɔːlt əz ˈwɒlt- ‖ -ᵊrz ˈwɑːlt-

Waltham ˈwɔːlθ əm ˈwɒlθ- ‖ ˈwɑːlθ- —*but* Great W~ *and* Little W~ *in Essex are traditionally* ˈwɔːlt-; W~ *in MA is locally* ˈwɔːl θæm
 ˌWaltham ˈForest
Walthamstow ˈwɔːlθ əm stəʊ ˈwɒlθ- ‖ -stoʊ ˈwɑːlθ- —*previously* ˈwɔːlt-, ˈwɒlt-
Walton ˈwɔːlt ən ˈwɒlt- ‖ ˈwɑːlt-
Walton-le-Dale ˌwɔːlt ən li ˈdeɪᵊl ˌwɒlt- ‖ ˌwɑːlt-
Walton-on-the-Naze ˌwɔːlt ən ˌɒn ðə ˈneɪz ˌwɒlt- ‖ -ˌɑːn- ˌwɑːlt-, -ˌɔːn-
waltz wɔːls wɒls, wɔːlts, wɒlts ‖ wɔːlts wɑːlts, wɔːls, wɑːls **waltzed** wɔːlst wɒlst, wɔːltst, wɒltst ‖ wɔːltst wɑːltst, wɔːlst, wɑːlst **waltzes** ˈwɔːls ɪz ˈwɒls-, ˈwɔːlts-, ˈwɒlts-, -əz ‖ ˈwɔːlts əz ˈwɑːlts-, ˈwɔːls-, ˈwɑːls- **waltzing** ˈwɔːls ɪŋ ˈwɒls-, ˈwɔːlts-, wɒlts- ‖ ˈwɔːlts ɪŋ ˈwɑːlts-, ˈwɔːls-, ˈwɑːls-
waltzer ˈwɔːls ə ˈwɒls-, ˈwɔːlts-, ˈwɒlts- ‖ ˈwɔːlts ᵊr ˈwɑːlts-, ˈwɔːls-, ˈwɑːls- **~s** z
Walvis Bay ˌwɔːlv ɪs ˈbeɪ §-əs- ‖ ˌwɑːlv-
Walworth ˈwɔːl wəθ ˈwɒl-, -wɜːθ ‖ -wᵊrθ ˈwɑːl-
Wampanoag ˌwɒmp ə ˈnəʊ æg ‖ ˌwɑːmp ə ˈnoʊ ɑːg
wampum ˈwɒmp əm ‖ ˈwɑːmp-
wan *'pale'* wɒn ‖ wɑːn **wanner** ˈwɒn ə ‖ ˈwɑːn ᵊr **wannest** ˈwɒn ɪst -əst ‖ ˈwɑːn əst
WAN, wan *'wide area network'* wæn
Wanadoo *tdmk* ˈwɒn ə duː ‖ ˈwɑːn-
Wanamaker ˈwɒn ə meɪk ə ‖ ˈwɑːn ə meɪk ᵊr
Wanchai ˌwɒn ˈtʃaɪ ‖ ˌwɑːn- —*Cantonese* [^{1}waːn ^{2}tsɐj]
wand wɒnd ‖ wɑːnd **wands** wɒndz ‖ wɑːndz
Wanda ˈwɒnd ə ‖ ˈwɑːnd ə
wander ˈwɒnd ə ‖ ˈwɑːnd ᵊr **~ed** d
 wandering/s ˈwɒnd‿ər ɪŋ/z ‖ ˈwɑːnd‿ər ɪŋ/z **~s** z
 ˌWandering ˈJew
wanderer ˈwɒnd‿ər ə ‖ ˈwɑːnd‿ər ər **~s** z
wanderlust ˈwɒnd ə lʌst ‖ ˈwɑːnd ᵊr- —*Ger* W~ [ˈvan dɐ lʊst]
Wandle ˈwɒnd ᵊl ‖ ˈwɑːnd ᵊl
Wandsworth ˈwɒndz wəθ -wɜːθ ‖ ˈwɑːndz wᵊrθ -wɜːθ
wane weɪn **waned** weɪnd **wanes** weɪnz
 waning ˈweɪn ɪŋ
Wang *tdmk* wæŋ ‖ wɑːŋ
Wanganui ˌwɒŋ ə ˈnuː i -gə- ‖ ˌwɑːŋ-
Wangaratta ˌwæŋ gə ˈræt ə ‖ -ˈræţ-
wangl|e ˈwæŋ gᵊl **~ed** d **~es** z **~ing** ‿ɪŋ
wanigan ˈwɒn ɪg ən ‖ ˈwɑːn- **~s** z

wank wæŋk **wanked** wæŋkt **wanking** ˈwæŋk ɪŋ **wanks** wæŋks
Wankel, w~ ˈwæŋk ᵊl ‖ ˈwɑːŋk ᵊl —*Ger* [ˈvaŋ kᵊl]
wanker ˈwæŋk ə ‖ -ᵊr **~s** z
wanly ˈwɒn li ‖ ˈwɑːn li
wanna *casual form of* want to, want a ˈwɒn ə ‖ ˈwɑːn ə ˈwɔːn ə, ˈwʌn ə —*not standard in BrE; the RP equivalent is* ˈwɒnt ə. *Before a vowel sound, also* -u *rather than* -ə
wannabe, wannabee ˈwɒn əb i -ə biː ‖ ˈwɑːn- ˈwɔːn- **~s** z
wanne... —*see* **wan**
wanness ˈwɒn nəs -nɪs ‖ ˈwɑːn nəs
Wansbeck ˈwɒnz bek ‖ ˈwɑːnz-
Wanstead ˈwɒn stɪd -sted, §-stəd ‖ ˈwɑːn-
want wɒnt ‖ wɑːnt wɔːnt, wʌnt **wanted** ˈwɒnt ɪd -əd ‖ ˈwɑːnţ əd ˈwɔːnţ-, ˈwʌnţ-
 wanting ˈwɒnt ɪŋ ‖ ˈwɑːnţ ɪŋ ˈwɔːnţ-, ˈwʌnţ-
 wants wɒnts ‖ wɑːnts wɔːnts, wʌnts —*In the close-knit phrase* want to *before a verb, the consonants are often simplified to* ˈwɒnt ə, §ˈwɒn ə ‖ ˈwɑːn ə, ˈwɔːn ə, ˈwʌn ə —. *See also* **wanna.**
 ˈwant ad
Wantage, W~ ˈwɒnt ɪdʒ ‖ ˈwɑːnţ ɪdʒ ˈwɔːnţ-
Wantagh ˈwɒnt ɔː ‖ ˈwɑːnt- -ɑː
wanton ˈwɒnt ən ‖ ˈwɑːnt ᵊn **~ly** li **~ness** nəs nɪs **~s** z
WAP wæp
wapentake ˈwɒp ən teɪk ˈwæp- ‖ ˈwɑːp- **~s** s
wapiti ˈwɒp ət i -ɪt- ‖ ˈwɑːp əţ i **~s** z
Waple ˈweɪp ᵊl
Wapner ˈwɒp nə ‖ ˈwɑːp nᵊr
Wapping ˈwɒp ɪŋ ‖ ˈwɑːp ɪŋ
Wappingers Falls ˌwɒp ɪndʒ əz ˈfɔːlz ‖ ˌwɑːp əndʒ ᵊrz- ˈfɑːlz
war wɔː ‖ wɔːr **warred** wɔːd ‖ wɔːrd **warring** ˈwɔːr ɪŋ **wars** wɔːz ‖ wɔːrz
 ˈwar bride; **ˈwar clouds**; **ˈwar corre͵spondent**; **ˈwar crime**; **ˈwar cry**; **ˈwar dance**; **ˈwar game**; **ˌwar of ˈnerves**; **ˈwar paint**
waratah ˈwɒr ə tɑː ˌ·ˈ· ‖ ˈwɔːr- **~s** z
Warbeck ˈwɔː bek ‖ ˈwɔːr-
warbl|e ˈwɔːb ᵊl ‖ ˈwɔːrb ᵊl **~ed** d **~es** z **~ing** ‿ɪŋ
 ˈwarble fly
warbler ˈwɔːb lə ‖ ˈwɔːrb lᵊr **~s** z
Warboys ˈwɔː bɔɪz ‖ ˈwɔːr-
Warburg ˈwɔː bɜːg ‖ ˈwɔːr bɜːg
Warburton ˈwɔːb ət ən ˈwɔː ˌbɜːt ᵊn ‖ ˈwɔːr ˌbɜːt ᵊn
warchalking ˈwɔː ˌtʃɔːk ɪŋ ‖ ˈwɔːr- -ˌtʃɑːk-
ward, Ward wɔːd ‖ wɔːrd **warded** ˈwɔːd ɪd -əd ‖ ˈwɔːrd əd **warding** ˈwɔːd ɪŋ ‖ ˈwɔːrd ɪŋ
 wards wɔːdz ‖ wɔːrdz
-ward wəd ‖ wᵊrd — **heavenward** ˈhev ᵊn wəd ‖ -wᵊrd
Wardell wɔː ˈdel ‖ wɔːr-
warden, W~ ˈwɔːd ᵊn ‖ ˈwɔːrd ᵊn **~s** z **~ship** ʃɪp
warder ˈwɔːd ə ‖ ˈwɔːrd ᵊr **~s** z
Wardian ˈwɔːd i‿ən ‖ ˈwɔːrd-
Wardle ˈwɔːd ᵊl ‖ ˈwɔːrd ᵊl
Wardour ˈwɔːd ə ‖ ˈwɔːrd ᵊr
wardress ˈwɔːdr əs -ɪs, -es ‖ ˈwɔːrdr- **~es** ɪz əz
wardrobe ˈwɔːdr əʊb ‖ ˈwɔːrdr oʊb **~s** z
wardroom ˈwɔːd ruːm -rʊm ‖ ˈwɔːrd- **~s** z
-wards wədz ‖ wᵊrdz — **seawards** ˈsiː wədz ‖ -wᵊrdz
wardship ˈwɔːd ʃɪp ‖ ˈwɔːrd- **~s** s

ware, Ware weə ‖ weᵊr wæᵊr **wares** weəz ‖ weᵊrz wæᵊrz
-ware weə ‖ wer wær — **silverware** ˈsɪlv ə weə ‖ -ᵊr wer -wær
Wareham ˈweər əm ‖ ˈwer əm ˈwær-
ware|house *v* ˈweə |haʊz -haʊs ‖ ˈwer- ˈwær- **~housed** haʊzd haʊst **~houses** haʊz ɪz haʊs-, -əz **~housing** haʊz ɪŋ haʊs-
ware|house *n* ˈweə |haʊs ‖ ˈwer- ˈwær- **~houses** haʊz ɪz -əz
warehouse|man ˈweə haʊs |mən ‖ ˈwer- ˈwær- **~men** mən men
Wareing ˈweər ɪŋ ‖ ˈwer ɪŋ ˈwær-
warfare ˈwɔː feə ‖ ˈwɔːr fer -fær
warfarin ˈwɔːf ər ɪn §-ən ‖ ˈwɔːrf-
Wargrave ˈwɔː greɪv ‖ ˈwɔːr-
warhead ˈwɔː hed ‖ ˈwɔːr- **~s** z
Warhol ˈwɔː həʊl →-hɒʊl ‖ ˈwɔːr hoʊl
warhors|e ˈwɔː hɔːs ‖ ˈwɔːr hɔːrs **~es** ɪz əz
wari... —*see* **wary**
Waring ˈweər ɪŋ ‖ ˈwer ɪŋ ˈwær-
Warks —*see* **Warwickshire**
Warkworth ˈwɔːk wəθ -wɜːθ ‖ ˈwɔːrk wɜːθ ˈwɑːrk-
Warley ˈwɔːl i ‖ ˈwɔːrl i
warlike ˈwɔː laɪk ‖ ˈwɔːr-
Warlingham ˈwɔːl ɪŋ əm ‖ ˈwɔːrl-
warlock, W~ ˈwɔː lɒk ‖ ˈwɔːr lɑːk **~s** s
warlord ˈwɔː lɔːd ‖ ˈwɔːr lɔːrd **~ism** ˌɪz əm **~s** z
warm wɔːm ‖ wɔːrm **warmed** wɔːmd ‖ wɔːrmd **warmer** ˈwɔːm ə ‖ ˈwɔːrm ᵊr **warmest** ˈwɔːm ɪst -əst ‖ ˈwɔːrm əst **warming** ˈwɔːm ɪŋ ‖ ˈwɔːrm ɪŋ **warms** wɔːmz ‖ wɔːrmz
ˈwarming pan
warm-blooded ˌwɔːm ˈblʌd ɪd ◂ -əd ‖ ˌwɔːrm- **~ness** nəs nɪs
warm-down ˈwɔːm daʊn ‖ ˈwɔːrm- **~s** z
warmed-over ˌwɔːmd ˈəʊv ə ◂ ‖ ˌwɔːrmd ˈoʊv ᵊr ◂
warmed-up ˌwɔːmd ˈʌp ◂ ‖ ˌwɔːrmd-
warmer ˈwɔːm ə ‖ ˈwɔːrm ᵊr **~s** z
warm-hearted ˌwɔːm ˈhɑːt ɪd ◂ -əd ‖ ˌwɔːrm ˈhɑːrṭ əd ◂ **~ly** li **~ness** nəs nɪs
Warmington ˈwɔːm ɪŋ tən ‖ ˈwɔːrm-
Warminster ˈwɔː mɪnᵗst ə ‖ ˈwɔːr mɪnᵗst ᵊr
warmly ˈwɔːm li ‖ ˈwɔːrm li
warmness ˈwɔːm nəs -nɪs ‖ ˈwɔːrm-
warmonger ˈwɔː ˌmʌŋ gə ‖ ˈwɔːr ˌmʌŋ gᵊr -ˌmɑːŋ- **~s** z
warmongering ˈwɔː ˌmʌŋ gər ɪŋ ‖ ˈwɔːr- -ˌmɑːŋ-
warmth wɔːmᵖθ ‖ wɔːrmᵖθ
warm-up ˈwɔːm ʌp ‖ ˈwɔːrm- **~s** s
warn wɔːn ‖ wɔːrn **warned** wɔːnd ‖ wɔːrnd **warning/ly** ˈwɔːn ɪŋ /li ‖ ˈwɔːrn- **warns** wɔːnz ‖ wɔːrnz
Warne wɔːn ‖ wɔːrn
Warner ˈwɔːn ə ‖ ˈwɔːrn ᵊr
Warnham ˈwɔːn əm ‖ ˈwɔːrn-
warning ˈwɔːn ɪŋ ‖ ˈwɔːrn ɪŋ **~s** z
Warninglid ˈwɔːn ɪŋ lɪd ‖ ˈwɔːrn-
Warnock ˈwɔːn ɒk ‖ ˈwɔːrn ɑːk
warp wɔːp ‖ wɔːrp **warped** wɔːpt ‖ wɔːrpt **warping** ˈwɔːp ɪŋ ‖ ˈwɔːrp ɪŋ **warps** wɔːps ‖ wɔːrps
warpath ˈwɔː pɑːθ §-pæθ ‖ ˈwɔːr pæθ
warplane ˈwɔː pleɪn ‖ ˈwɔːr- **~s** z
Warr wɔː ‖ wɔːr
Warragamba ˌwɒr ə ˈgæm bə ‖ ˌwɔːr-
warr|ant ˈwɒr |ənt ‖ ˈwɔːr |ənt ˈwɑːr- **~anted** ənt ɪd -əd ‖ ənṭ əd **~anting** ənt ɪŋ ‖ ənṭ ɪŋ **~ants** ənts
ˈwarrant ˌofficer
warrantab|le ˈwɒr ənt əb| ᵊl ‖ ˈwɔːr- ˈwɑːr- **~ly** li
warrantee ˌwɒr ən ˈtiː ‖ ˌwɔːr- ˌwɑːr- **~s** z
warrantor ˈwɒr ən tɔː ˌ·ˈ· ‖ ˈwɔːr ən tɔːr ˈwɑːr-, ˌ··ˈ· **~s** z
warrant|y ˈwɒr ənt |i ‖ ˈwɔːr ənṭ |i ˈwɑːr- **~ies** iz
Warre wɔː ‖ wɔːr
warren, W~ ˈwɒr ən ‖ ˈwɔːr ən ˈwɑːr- —*formerly also* -ɪn **~s** z
Warrender ˈwɒr ənd ə -ɪnd- ‖ ˈwɔːr ənd ᵊr ˈwɑːr-
warrigal ˈwɒr ɪg ᵊl -əg- ‖ ˈwɔːr- ˈwɑːr- **~s** z
warring ˈwɔːr ɪŋ
Warrington ˈwɒr ɪŋ tən ‖ ˈwɔːr- ˈwɑːr-
warrior ˈwɒr i͜ə ‖ ˈwɔːr i͜ᵊr ˈwɑːr- **~s** z
Warriss ˈwɒr ɪs §-əs ‖ ˈwɔːr əs ˈwɑːr-
Warrumbungle ˌwɒr əm ˈbʌŋ gᵊl ‖ ˌwɔːr-
Warsaw ˈwɔː sɔː ‖ ˈwɔːr- -sɑː
ˌWarsaw ˈPact
warship ˈwɔː ʃɪp ‖ ˈwɔːr- **~s** s
Warsop ˈwɔː sɒp ‖ ˈwɔːr sɑːp
Warspite ˈwɔː spaɪt ‖ ˈwɔːr-
wart wɔːt ‖ wɔːrt **warts** wɔːts ‖ wɔːrts
Wartburg *tdmk* ˈwɔːt bɜːg ˈvɑːt- ‖ ˈwɔːrt bɜːg —*Ger* [ˈvaʁt bʊʁk]
warthog ˈwɔːt hɒg ‖ ˈwɔːrt hɔːg -hɑːg **~s** z
wartime ˈwɔː taɪm ‖ ˈwɔːr-
Warton ˈwɔːt ᵊn ‖ ˈwɔːrt ᵊn
war-torn ˈwɔː tɔːn ‖ ˈwɔːr tɔːrn -toʊrn
wart|y ˈwɔːt |i ‖ ˈwɔːrṭ |i **~ier** i͜ə ‖ i͜ᵊr **~iest** i͜ɪst i͜əst **~iness** i nəs i nɪs
war-wear|y ˈwɔː ˌwɪər| i ˌ·ˈ·· ‖ ˈwɔːr ˌwɪr| i **~iness** i nəs i nɪs
Warwick *(i)* ˈwɒr ɪk ‖ ˈwɔːr ɪk ˈwɑːr-, *(ii)* ˈwɔː wɪk ‖ ˈwɔːr- —*The English name and the places in Warks and Queensland are (i); the place in RI and the American name are usually (ii).*
Warwickshire ˈwɒr ɪk ʃə -ʃɪə ‖ ˈwɔːr ɪk ʃᵊr ˈwɑːr-, -ʃɪr
war|y ˈweər |i ‖ ˈwer |i ˈwær- **~ier** i͜ə ‖ i͜ᵊr **~iest** i͜ɪst i͜əst **~ily** əl i ɪ li **~iness** i nəs i nɪs
was *strong form* wɒz ‖ wʌz wɑːz, *weak form* wəz
wasabi ˈwɑːs ə biː -ɑː-; wə ˈsɑːb i —*Jp* [ˈɰa sa bi]
Wasatch ˈwɔː sætʃ ‖ ˈwɑː-
Wasdale ˈwɒs dᵊl -derᵊl ‖ ˈwɑːs-
wash, Wash wɒʃ ‖ wɑːʃ wɔːʃ —*There are also non-standard AmE forms* wɔːrʃ, wɑːrʃ **washed**

wɒʃt ‖ wɑːʃt wɔːʃt **washes** ˈwɒʃ ɪz -əz ‖ ˈwɑːʃ əz ˈwɔːʃ- **washing** ˈwɒʃ ɪŋ ‖ ˈwɑːʃ ɪŋ ˈwɔːʃ-
ˈwash ˌdrawing; **ˈwashing day**; **ˈwashing maˌchine**; **ˈwashing ˌpowder**
washable ˈwɒʃ əb əl ‖ ˈwɑːʃ- ˈwɔːʃ-
wash-and-wear ˌwɒʃ ən ˈweə ‖ ˌwɑːʃ ən ˈweər ˌwɔːʃ-
washbasin ˈwɒʃ ˌbeɪs ən ‖ ˈwɑːʃ- ˈwɔːʃ- **~s** z
washboard ˈwɒʃ bɔːd ‖ ˈwɑːʃ bɔːrd ˈwɔːʃ-, -bourd **~s** z
Washbourn, Washbourne ˈwɒʃ bɔːn ‖ ˈwɑːʃ bɔːrn ˈwɔːʃ-, -bourn
washbowl ˈwɒʃ bəʊl →-bɒʊl ‖ ˈwɑːʃ boʊl ˈwɔːʃ- **~s** z
Washbrook ˈwɒʃ brʊk ‖ ˈwɑːʃ- ˈwɔːʃ-
Washburn ˈwɒʃ bɜːn ‖ ˈwɑːʃ bɜ˞ːn ˈwɔːʃ-
wash|cloth ˈwɒʃ |klɒθ -klɔːθ ‖ ˈwɑːʃ |klɔːθ ˈwɔːʃ-, -klɑːθ **~cloths** klɒθs klɔːθs, klɒðz, klɔːðz ‖ klɔːðz klɑːðz, klɔːθs, klɑːθs
washday ˈwɒʃ deɪ ‖ ˈwɑːʃ- ˈwɔːʃ- **~s** z
washed-out ˌwɒʃt ˈaʊt ◂ ‖ ˌwɑːʃt- ˌwɔːʃt-
washed-up ˌwɒʃt ˈʌp ◂ ‖ ˌwɑːʃt- ˌwɔːʃt-
washer ˈwɒʃ ə ‖ ˈwɑːʃ ər ˈwɔːʃ- **~s** z
washer-dryer ˌwɒʃ ə ˈdraɪ‿ə ‖ ˌwɑːʃ ər ˈdraɪ‿ər ˌwɔːʃ- **~s** z
washer-up ˌwɒʃ ər ˈʌp ‖ ˌwɑːʃ ər ˈʌp ˌwɔːʃ- **washers-up** ˌwɒʃ əz ˈʌp ‖ ˌwɑːʃ ərz ˈʌp ˌwɔːʃ-
washer|woman ˈwɒʃ ə |ˌwʊm ən ‖ ˈwɑːʃ ər- ˈwɔːʃ- **~women** ˌwɪm ɪn -ən
washer|y ˈwɒʃ ər |i ‖ ˈwɑːʃ- ˈwɔːʃ- **~ies** iz
wash|house ˈwɒʃ |haʊs ‖ ˈwɑːʃ- ˈwɔːʃ- **~houses** haʊz ɪz -əz
Washington ˈwɒʃ ɪŋ tən ‖ ˈwɑːʃ- ˈwɔːʃ-
Washingtonian ˌwɒʃ ɪŋ ˈtəʊn i‿ən ◂ ‖ ˌwɑːʃ ɪŋ ˈtoʊn- ˌwɔːʃ- **~s** z
washing-up ˌwɒʃ ɪŋ ˈʌp ‖ ˌwɑːʃ- ˌwɔːʃ-
washleather ˈwɒʃ ˌleð ə ‖ ˈwɑːʃ ˌleð ər ˈwɔːʃ- **~s** z
washload ˈwɒʃ ləʊd ‖ ˈwɑːʃ loʊd ˈwɔːʃ- **~s** z
Washoe ˈwɒʃ əʊ ‖ ˈwɑːʃ oʊ
washout ˈwɒʃ aʊt ‖ ˈwɑːʃ- ˈwɔːʃ- **~s** s
washpot ˈwɒʃ pɒt ‖ ˈwɑːʃ pɑːt ˈwɔːʃ- **~s** s
washrag ˈwɒʃ ræg ‖ ˈwɑːʃ- ˈwɔːʃ- **~s** z
washroom ˈwɒʃ ruːm -rʊm ‖ ˈwɑːʃ- ˈwɔːʃ- **~s** z
washstand ˈwɒʃ stænd ‖ ˈwɑːʃ- ˈwɔːʃ- **~s** z
washtub ˈwɒʃ tʌb ‖ ˈwɑːʃ- ˈwɔːʃ- **~s** z
wash-up ˈwɒʃ ʌp ‖ ˈwɑːʃ- ˈwɔːʃ- **~s** s
wash-wipe ˌwɒʃ ˈwaɪp ‖ ˌwɑːʃ- ˌwɔːʃ-
wash|woman ˈwɒʃ |ˌwʊm ən ‖ ˈwɑːʃ- ˈwɔːʃ- **~women** ˌwɪm ɪn -ən
wash|y ˈwɒʃ |i ‖ ˈwɑːʃ |i ˈwɔːʃ- **~ier** i‿ə ‖ i‿ər **~iest** i‿ɪst i‿əst **~iness** i nəs i nɪs
wasn't ˈwɒz ənt ‖ ˈwʌz ənt ˈwɑːz-
wasp, WASP, Wasp wɒsp ‖ wɑːsp **wasps, WASPs, Wasps** wɒsps ‖ wɑːsps
waspish ˈwɒsp ɪʃ ‖ ˈwɑːsp ɪʃ **~ly** li **~ness** nəs nɪs
wasp-waisted ˌwɒsp ˈweɪst ɪd ◂ -əd, ˈ.ˌ.. ‖ ˈwɑːsp ˌweɪst əd
wasp|y, Wasp|y, WASP|y ˈwɒsp |i ‖ ˈwɑːsp |i **~ier** i‿ə ‖ i‿ər **~iest** i‿ɪst i‿əst **~ily** ɪ li əl i **~iness** i nəs i nɪs
wassail ˈwɒs eɪəl -əl ‖ ˈwɑːs- **~ed** d **~ing** ɪŋ **~s** z
Wassermann ˈwæs ə mən ˈvæs-, ˈvɑːs- ‖ ˈwɑːs ər- —*Ger* [ˈvas ɐ man]
ˈWassermann test
Wasson ˈwɒs ən ‖ ˈwɑːs ən
wassup wɒ ˈsʌp ‖ wə- wɑː-
wast *strong form* wɒst ‖ wɑːst, *weak form* wəst
wastag|e ˈweɪst ɪdʒ **~es** ɪz əz
Wastdale ˈwɒs dəl ˈwɒst-, -deɪəl ‖ ˈwɑːst-
waste weɪst *(= waist)* **wasted** ˈweɪst ɪd -əd **wastes** weɪsts **wasting** ˈweɪst ɪŋ
ˌwaste ˈpaper, ˈ.ˌ.. ; **ˌwaste ˈpaper ˌbasket**, ˈ. . ˌ. . ‖ ˈ. . ˌ. . ; **ˈwaste pipe**; **ˈwaste ˌproduct**
wastebasket ˈweɪst ˌbɑːsk ɪt §-ˌbæsk-, §-ət ‖ -ˌbæsk ət **~s** s
wasteful ˈweɪst fəl -fʊl **~ly** ‿i **~ness** nəs nɪs
wasteland ˈweɪst lænd -lənd **~s** z
wastepaper ˌweɪst ˈpeɪp ə ˈ.ˌ.. ‖ ˈweɪst ˌpeɪp ər
wastepipe ˈweɪst paɪp **~s** s
waster ˈweɪst ə ‖ -ər **~s** z
wastewater ˈweɪst ˌwɔːt ə ‖ -ˌwɔːt̬ ər -ˌwɑːt̬ ər
wastrel ˈweɪs trəl **~s** z
Wastwater ˈwɒst ˌwɔːt ə ‖ ˈwɑːst ˌwɔːt̬ ər -ˌwɑːt̬-
Wat, wat wɒt ‖ wɑːt
watch wɒtʃ ‖ wɑːtʃ wɔːtʃ **watched** wɒtʃt ‖ wɑːtʃt wɔːtʃt **watches** ˈwɒtʃ ɪz -əz ‖ ˈwɑːtʃ əz ˈwɔːtʃ- **watching** ˈwɒtʃ ɪŋ ‖ ˈwɑːtʃ ɪŋ ˈwɔːtʃ-
ˌwatching ˈbrief; **ˈwatch night**
watchable ˈwɒtʃ əb əl ‖ ˈwɑːtʃ- ˈwɔːtʃ-
watchband ˈwɒtʃ bænd ‖ ˈwɑːtʃ- ˈwɔːtʃ- **~s** z
watchcas|e ˈwɒtʃ keɪs ‖ ˈwɑːtʃ- ˈwɔːtʃ- **~es** ɪz əz
watchdog ˈwɒtʃ dɒg ‖ ˈwɑːtʃ dɔːg ˈwɔːtʃ-, -dɑːg **~s** z
watcher ˈwɒtʃ ə ‖ ˈwɑːtʃ ər ˈwɔːtʃ- **~s** z
Watchet ˈwɒtʃ ɪt §-ət ‖ ˈwɑːtʃ ət
watchful ˈwɒtʃ fəl -fʊl ‖ ˈwɑːtʃ- ˈwɔːtʃ- **~ly** ‿i **~ness** nəs nɪs
watchkeeper ˈwɒtʃ ˌkiːp ə ‖ ˈwɑːtʃ ˌkiːp ər ˈwɔːtʃ-
watchmaker ˈwɒtʃ ˌmeɪk ə ‖ ˈwɑːtʃ ˌmeɪk ər ˈwɔːtʃ- **~s** z
watch|man ˈwɒtʃ |mən ‖ ˈwɑːtʃ- ˈwɔːtʃ- **~men** mən men
watchnight ˈwɒtʃ naɪt ‖ ˈwɑːtʃ- ˈwɔːtʃ-
watchstrap ˈwɒtʃ stræp ‖ ˈwɑːtʃ- ˈwɔːtʃ- **~s** s
watchtower ˈwɒtʃ ˌtaʊ‿ə ‖ ˈwɑːtʃ ˌtaʊ‿ər ˈwɔːtʃ- **~s** z
watchword ˈwɒtʃ wɜːd ‖ ˈwɑːtʃ wɜ˞ːd ˈwɔːtʃ- **~s** z
Watendlath wɒ ˈtend ləθ ‖ wɑː-
water ˈwɔːt ə ‖ ˈwɔːt̬ ər ˈwɑːt̬- **~ed** d **watering** ˈwɔːt‿ər ɪŋ ‖ ˈwɔːt̬ ər ɪŋ ˈwɑːt̬- **~s** z
ˈwater bird; **ˈwater ˌbiscuit**; **ˈwater ˌbuffalo**; **ˈwater butt**; **ˈwater ˌcannon**;

ˌwater ˈchestnut ‖ ˈ· · ˌ· ·; ˈwater ˌcloset; ˈwater ˌcooler; ˌwatered ˈsilk; ˈwater ice; ˈwatering can; ˈwatering hole; ˈwatering place; ˈwater jump; ˈwater ˌlevel; ˈwater ˌlily; ˈwater main; ˈwater ˌmeadow; ˈwater pipe; ˈwater ˌpolo; ˈwater rat; ˈwater rate; ˈwater ˌsoftener; ˈwater supˌply; ˈwater ˌtable; ˈwater ˌtower; ˈwater ˌvapour; ˈwater vole

waterbed ˈwɔːt ə bed ‖ ˈwɔːt̬ ər- ˈwɑːt̬ ər **~s** z

waterborne ˈwɔːt ə bɔːn ‖ ˈwɔːt̬ ər bɔːrn ˈwɑːt̬-, -bourn

waterbuck ˈwɔːt ə bʌk ‖ ˈwɔːt̬ ər- ˈwɑːt̬-

Waterbury ˈwɔːt ə bər‿i ‖ ˈwɔːt̬ ər ˌber i ˈwɑːt̬-, -bər‿i

watercolor, watercolour ˈwɔːt ə ˌkʌl ə ‖ ˈwɔːt̬ ər ˌkʌl ər ˈwɑːt̬- **~s** z

watercolorist, watercolourist ˈwɔːt ə ˌkʌl ər ɪst §-əst ‖ ˈwɔːt̬ ər ˌkʌl ər ɪst ˈwɑːt̬- **~s** s

water-cool ˈwɔːt ə kuːl ‖ ˈwɔːt̬ ər- ˈwɑːt̬- **~ed** d **~ing** ɪŋ **~s** z

watercours|e ˈwɔːt ə kɔːs ‖ ˈwɔːt̬ ər kɔːrs ˈwɑːt̬-, -kours **~es** ɪz əz

watercraft ˈwɔːt ə krɑːft §-kræft ‖ ˈwɔːt̬ ər kræft ˈwɑːt̬- **~s** s

watercress ˈwɔːt ə kres ‖ ˈwɔːt̬ ər- ˈwɑːt̬-

watered-down ˌwɔːt əd ˈdaʊn ◂ ‖ ˌwɔːt̬ ərd- ˌwɑːt̬-

waterfall ˈwɔːt ə fɔːl ‖ ˈwɔːt̬ ər- ˈwɑːt̬-, -fɑːl **~s** z

Waterford ˈwɔːt ə fəd ‖ ˈwɔːt̬ ər fərd ˈwɑːt̬-

waterfowl ˈwɔːt ə faʊl ‖ ˈwɔːt̬ ər- ˈwɑːt̬- **~s** z

waterfront ˈwɔːt ə frʌnt ‖ ˈwɔːt̬ ər- ˈwɑːt̬- **~s** s

Watergate ˈwɔːt ə geɪt ‖ ˈwɔːt̬ ər- ˈwɑːt̬-

waterhole ˈwɔːt ə həʊl →-hɒʊl ‖ ˈwɔːt̬ ər hoʊl ˈwɑːt̬- **~s** z

Waterhouse ˈwɔːt ə haʊs ‖ ˈwɔːt̬ ər- ˈwɑːt̬-

wateriness ˈwɔːt‿ər i nəs -nɪs ‖ ˈwɔːt̬- ˈwɑːt̬-

waterless ˈwɔːt ə ləs -lɪs; -əl əs, -ɪs ‖ ˈwɔːt̬ ər ləs ˈwɑːt̬-

waterline ˈwɔːt ə laɪn -əl aɪn ‖ ˈwɔːt̬ ər laɪn ˈwɑːt̬- **~s** z

waterlog ˈwɔːt ə lɒg -əl ɒg ‖ ˈwɔːt̬ ər lɔːg ˈwɑːt̬-, -lɑːg **~ged** d **~ging** ɪŋ **~s** z

Waterloo ˌwɔːt ə ˈluː ◂ -əl ˈuː ‖ ˌwɔːt̬ ər ˈluː ˌwɑːt̬-, ˈ· · ·
ˌWaterloo ˈRoad; ˌWaterloo ˈStation

Waterlooville ˌwɔːt ə ˌluː ˈvɪl ‖ ˌwɔːt̬ ər- ˌwɑːt̬-

water|man, W~ ˈwɔːt ə |mən ‖ ˈwɔːt̬ ər- ˈwɑːt̬- **~men** mən men

watermark ˈwɔːt ə mɑːk ‖ ˈwɔːt̬ ər mɑːrk ˈwɑːt̬- **~ed** t **~ing** ɪŋ **~s** s

watermelon ˈwɔːt ə ˌmel ən ‖ ˈwɔːt̬ ər- ˈwɑːt̬- **~s** z

watermill ˈwɔːt ə mɪl ‖ ˈwɔːt̬ ər- ˈwɑːt̬- **~s** z

waterpower ˈwɔːt ə ˌpaʊ‿ə ‖ ˈwɔːt̬ ər ˌpaʊ‿ər ˈwɑːt̬-

waterproof ˈwɔːt ə pruːf §-prʊf ‖ ˈwɔːt̬ ər- ˈwɑːt̬- **~ed** t **~ing** ɪŋ **~s** s

water-repellent ˌwɔːt ə rɪ ˈpel ənt ◂ -rə'--, §-riː'--, ˈ· · ·ˌ· · ‖ ˈwɔːt̬ ər rɪ ˌpel ənt ˈwɑːt̬-

water-resistant ˌwɔːt ə rɪ ˈzɪst ənt ◂ -rə'--, §-riː'--, ˈ· · ·ˌ· · ‖ ˈwɔːt̬ ər rɪ ˌzɪst ənt ˈwɑːt̬-

Waters ˈwɔːt əz ‖ ˈwɔːt̬ ərz ˈwɑːt̬-

watershed ˈwɔːt ə ʃed ‖ ˈwɔːt̬ ər- ˈwɑːt̬- **~s** z

Watership ˈwɔːt ə ʃɪp ‖ ˈwɔːt̬ ər- ˈwɑːt̬-
ˌWatership ˈDown

waterside ˈwɔːt ə saɪd ‖ ˈwɔːt̬ ər- ˈwɑːt̬-

water-ski ˈwɔːt ə skiː ‖ ˈwɔːt̬ ər- ˈwɑːt̬- **~ed** d **~er/s** ə/z ‖ ər/z **~ing** ɪŋ **~s** z

water-soluble ˈwɔːt ə ˌsɒl jʊb əl -jəb əl ‖ ˈwɔːt̬ ər ˌsɑːl jəb əl ˈwɑːt̬-

Waterson ˈwɔːt əs ən ‖ ˈwɔːt̬ ərs ən ˈwɑːt̬-

waterspout ˈwɔːt ə spaʊt ‖ ˈwɔːt̬ ər- ˈwɑːt̬- **~s** s

Waterstone ˈwɔːt ə stəʊn ‖ ˈwɔːt̬ ər stoʊn ˈwɑːt̬-

watertight ˈwɔːt ə taɪt ‖ ˈwɔːt̬ ər- ˈwɑːt̬-

Waterton ˈwɔːt ət ən ‖ ˈwɔːt̬ ərt ən ˈwɑːt̬-

Watertown ˈwɔːt ə taʊn ‖ ˈwɔːt̬ ər- ˈwɑːt̬-

waterway ˈwɔːt ə weɪ ‖ ˈwɔːt̬ ər- ˈwɑːt̬- **~s** z

waterweed ˌwɔːt ə wiːd ‖ ˈwɔːt̬ ər- ˈwɑːt̬- **~s** z

waterwheel ˈwɔːt ə wiːəl -hwiːəl ‖ ˈwɔːt̬ ər- ˈwɑːt̬- **~s** z

waterwings ˈwɔːt ə wɪŋz ‖ ˈwɔːt̬ ər- ˈwɑːt̬-

waterworks ˈwɔːt ə wɜːks ‖ ˈwɔːt̬ ər wɜːks ˈwɑːt̬-

Waterworth ˈwɔːt ə wɜːθ -wəθ ‖ ˈwɔːt̬ ər wɜːθ ˈwɑːt̬-

watery ˈwɔːt ər i ‖ ˈwɔːt̬ ər i ˈwɑːt̬-

Wates weɪts

Watford ˈwɒt fəd ‖ ˈwɑːt fərd

Wath wɒθ ‖ wɑːθ

Watkin ˈwɒt kɪn ‖ ˈwɑːt-

Watkins ˈwɒt kɪnz ‖ ˈwɑːt-

Watkinson ˈwɒt kɪn sən ‖ ˈwɑːt-

Watling ˈwɒt lɪŋ ‖ ˈwɑːt-
ˈWatling Street

Watney ˈwɒt ni ‖ ˈwɑːt ni

WATS wɒts ‖ wɑːts

Watson ˈwɒts ən ‖ ˈwɑːts ən

watt, Watt wɒt ‖ wɑːt **watts** wɒts ‖ wɑːts

wattag|e ˈwɒt ɪdʒ ‖ ˈwɑːt̬ ɪdʒ **~es** ɪz əz

Watteau ˈwɒt əʊ ‖ wɑː ˈtoʊ —*Fr* [va to]

watt-hour ˌwɒt ˈaʊ‿ə ‖ ˌwɑːt̬ ˈaʊ‿ər **~s** z

wattle ˈwɒt əl ‖ ˈwɑːt̬ əl **~d** d **~s** z
ˌwattle and ˈdaub

wattlebird ˈwɒt əl bɜːd ‖ ˈwɑːt̬ əl bɜːd **~s** z

wattmeter ˈwɒt ˌmiːt ə ‖ ˈwɑːt ˌmiːt̬ ər **~s** z

Watts wɒts ‖ wɑːts

Watusi wə ˈtuːs i wɑː-, ˈtuːz-

Wauchope *(i)* ˈwɔːk əp ˈwɒx- ‖ ˈwɑːk-, *(ii)* ˈwɔː həʊp ‖ -hoʊp ˈwɑː-

Waugh *(i)* wɔː ‖ wɑː, *(ii)* wɒf wɑːf, wɒx ‖ wɑːf —*The writers* Evelyn Waugh *and* Auberon Waugh *were (i).*

Waunfawr ˈwaɪn vaʊ‿ə ‖ -vaʊ‿ər —*Welsh* [ˈwain vaur, ˈwain-]

WAV, wav wæv
ˈwav files

wave weɪv **waved** weɪvd **waves** weɪvz **waving** ˈweɪv ɪŋ
ˈwave band; ˈwave meˌchanics

waveform ˈweɪv fɔːm ‖ -fɔːrm **~s** z

waveguide 'weɪv gaɪd **~s** z
wavelength 'weɪv leŋᵏθ §-lenᵗθ **~s** s
wavelet 'weɪv lət -lɪt **~s** s
Wavell 'weɪv ᵊl
Waveney 'weɪv ən‿i
waver 'weɪv ə ‖ -ᵊr **~ed** d **wavering/ly** 'weɪv ər‿ɪŋ /li **~s** z
waverer 'weɪv ər‿ə ‖ -ᵊr‿ər **~s** z
Waverley 'weɪv ə li ‖ -ᵊr-
Wavertree 'weɪv ə triː ‖ -ᵊr-
waving 'weɪv ɪŋ
wav|y 'weɪv |i **~ier** i‿ə ‖ i‿ᵊr **~iest** i‿ɪst i‿əst **~ily** ɪ li əl i **~iness** i nəs i nɪs
Wawona wɔː 'wəʊn ə ‖ -'woʊn- wɑː-
wax, Wax wæks **waxed** wækst **waxes** 'wæks ɪz -əz **waxing** 'wæks ɪŋ
'waxed ˌpaper; **'wax ˌpaper**
waxbill 'wæks bɪl **~s** z
waxen 'wæks ᵊn
waxplant 'wæks plɑːnt §-plænt ‖ -plænt **~s** s
waxwing 'wæks wɪŋ **~s** z
waxwork 'wæks wɜːk ‖ -wɜːk **~s** s
wax|y 'wæks |i **~ier** i‿ə ‖ i‿ᵊr **~iest** i‿ɪst i‿əst **~iness** i nəs i nɪs
way, Way weɪ **ways** weɪz
ˌway 'in; **ˌway 'out**
waybill 'weɪ bɪl **~s** z
wayfarer 'weɪ ˌfeər ə ‖ -ˌfer ᵊr -ˌfær- **~s** z
wayfaring 'waɪ ˌfeər ɪŋ ‖ -ˌfer ɪŋ -ˌfær-
'wayfaring tree
waylaid ₍ˌ₎weɪ 'leɪd
Wayland 'weɪ lənd
waylay ₍ˌ₎weɪ 'leɪ **waylaid** ₍ˌ₎weɪ 'leɪd **~ing** ɪŋ **~s** z
wayleave 'weɪ liːv **~s** z
waymark 'weɪ mɑːk ‖ -mɑːrk **~ed** t **~ing** ɪŋ **~s** s
Wayne weɪn
Waynflete 'weɪn fliːt
way-out *adj* ˌweɪ 'aʊt ◂
ˌway-out 'fashions
-ways weɪz — **sideways** 'saɪd weɪz
wayside 'weɪ saɪd **~s** z
wayward 'weɪ wəd ‖ -wᵊrd **~ly** li **~ness** nəs nɪs
Waziristan wə ˌzɪər ɪ 'stɑːn -ə- ‖ -ˌzɪr-
wazoo wə 'zuː wɑː-
we *strong form* wiː, *weak form* wi
weak wiːk *(= week)* **weaker** 'wiːk ə ‖ -ᵊr **weakest** 'wiːk ɪst -əst
'weaker sex, ˌ· · '·
weaken 'wiːk ən **~ed** d **~ing** ‿ɪŋ **~s** z
weak-kneed ˌwiːk 'niːd ◂
weakling 'wiːk lɪŋ **~s** z
weakly 'wiːk li
weak-minded ˌwiːk 'maɪnd ɪd ◂ -əd **~ly** li **~ness** nəs nɪs
weakness 'wiːk nəs -nɪs **~es** ɪz əz
weak-willed ˌwiːk 'wɪld ◂
weal wiːᵊl **weals** wiːᵊlz
Weald, weald wiːᵊld
wealden, W~ 'wiːᵊld ən
Wealdstone 'wiːᵊl*d* stəʊn ‖ -stoʊn

wealth welθ
wealth|y 'welθ |i **~ier** i‿ə ‖ i‿ᵊr **~iest** i‿ɪst i‿əst **~ily** ɪ li əl i **~iness** i nəs i nɪs
wean wiːn **weaned** wiːnd **weaning** 'wiːn ɪŋ **weans** wiːnz
weaner 'wiːn ə ‖ -ᵊr **~s** z
weapon 'wep ən **~s** z
weaponry 'wep ən ri
wear weə ‖ weᵊr wæᵊr **wearing** 'weər ɪŋ ‖ 'wer ɪŋ 'wær- **wears** weəz ‖ weᵊrz wæᵊrz **wore** wɔː ‖ wɔːr woʊr **worn** wɔːn ‖ wɔːrn woʊrn
ˌwear and 'tear
Wear *river* wɪə ‖ wɪᵊr
wearability ˌweər ə 'bɪl ət i -ɪt i ‖ ˌwer ə 'bɪl əţ i ˌwær-
wearable 'weər əb ᵊl ‖ 'wer- 'wær-
Weardale 'wɪə deɪᵊl ‖ 'wɪr-
wearer 'weər ə ‖ 'wer ᵊr 'wær- **~s** z
weari... —*see* **weary**
wearisome 'wɪər i səm ‖ 'wɪr- **~ly** li **~ness** nəs nɪs
Wearmouth 'wɪə maʊθ -məθ ‖ 'wɪr-
wear|y 'wɪər |i ‖ 'wɪr |i **~ied** id **~ier** i‿ə ‖ i‿ᵊr **~ies** iz **~iest** i‿ɪst i‿əst **~ily** əl i ɪ li **~iness** i nəs i nɪs **~ying** i ɪŋ
weasel 'wiːz ᵊl **~ed** d **~ing** ‿ɪŋ **~s** z
weaselly 'wiːz ᵊl i
weather 'weð ə ‖ -ᵊr **~ed** d **weathering** 'weð ər ɪŋ **~s** z
'weather balˌloon; **'weather ˌforecast**; **'weather map**; **'weather ship**; **'weather ˌstation**; **'weather vane**
Weatherall 'weð ər ɔːl ‖ ɑːl
weather-beaten 'weð ə ˌbiːt ᵊn ‖ -ᵊr-
weatherboard 'weð ə bɔːd ‖ -ᵊr bɔːrd -boʊrd **~ing** ɪŋ **~s** z
weather-bound 'weð ə baʊnd ‖ -ᵊr-
weathercock 'weð ə kɒk ‖ -ᵊr kɑːk **~s** s
weatherglass 'weð ə glɑːs §-glæs ‖ -ᵊr glæs **~es** ɪz əz
Weatherhead 'weð ə hed ‖ -ᵊr-
weatherization ˌweð ər aɪ 'zeɪʃ ᵊn -ər ɪ- ‖ -ər ə-
weatheriz|e 'weð ə raɪz **~ed** d **~es** ɪz əz **~ing** ɪŋ
weather|man, W~ 'weð ə |mæn ‖ -ᵊr- **~men** men
weatherproof 'weð ə pruːf §-prʊf ‖ -ᵊr- **~ed** t **~ing** ɪŋ **~s** s
weathertight 'weð ə taɪt ‖ -ᵊr-
weave wiːv **weaved** wiːvd **weaves** wiːvz **weaving** 'wiːv ɪŋ **wove** wəʊv ‖ woʊv **woven** 'wəʊv ᵊn ‖ 'woʊv ᵊn
weaver, W~ 'wiːv ə ‖ -ᵊr **~s** z
weaverbird 'wiːv ə bɜːd ‖ -ᵊr bɜːd **~s** z
web web **webbed** webd **webbing** 'web ɪŋ **webs** webz
ˌweb 'offset; **'web page**
Webb web
Webber 'web ə ‖ -ᵊr
webbing 'web ɪŋ
webcam 'web kæm **~s** z

Weak forms

1 Many English function words (= articles, pronouns, prepositions, auxiliaries, modals, etc.) have more than one pronunciation. In particular, they have a **strong form**, containing a **strong** vowel, and a **weak form**, containing a **weak** vowel. An example is **at**, with the strong form æt and the weak form ət.

2 The weak form is generally used if the word is unstressed (as is usually the case with function words). The strong form is used only when the word is stressed, usually because it is accented (see STRESS).

Jim's ət **lunch. He'll be back** ət **one.**

We say 'ˈæt **home', not 'in home'.**

I'll invite ðəm **round.**

Tell me how they ˈwɜː ‖ ˈwɜ˞ː**.**

They wə ‖ wᵊr **delighted.**

3 Nevertheless, the strong form is used for unaccented function words in certain positions:

- usually, for a preposition when it is between a weak syllable and a pronoun, to help the rhythm:

  I'm ˈ**looking** æt ju. (Compare: **Don't** ˈ**look** ət mi.)

- always, when a function word is **stranded** (= left exposed by a syntactic operation involving the movement or deletion of the word on which it depends):

  Where does she ˈkʌm frɒm‖frʌm**? (...from X)**

  ˈaɪ kən **speak English better than** ˈjuː kæn**. (= than you can speak)**

  It was ˈeɪmd æt **but not achieved. (= they aimed at it)**

4 It is important for learners of English to use weak forms appropriately. Otherwise, listeners may think they are emphasizing a word where this is not really so. Equally, native speakers should not be misled into supposing that careful or declamatory speech demands strong forms throughout. One exception is the pronunciation style used for **singing**, where strong forms are often used. Even here, though, articles are usually weak.

webcast 'web kɑːst §-kæst ‖ -kæst **~ing** ɪŋ **~s** s

webding, W~ 'web dɪŋ **~s** z

weber *unit of magnetic flux* 'veɪb ə 'web- ‖ -ᵊr **~s** z

Weber *English family name (i)* 'web ə ‖ -ᵊr, *(ii)* 'wiːb ə ‖ -ᵊr, *(iii)* 'weɪb ə ‖ -ᵊr

Weber *German family name; composer, sociologist* 'veɪb ə ‖ -ᵊr —*Ger* ['veː bɐ]

Webern 'veɪb ɜːn -ən ‖ -ɜ˞ːn —*Ger* ['veː bɐn]

web|foot 'web |fʊt **~feet** fiːt

web-footed ˌweb 'fʊt ɪd ◂ -əd, '·ˌ· · ‖ -'fʊţ əd ◂

webhead 'web hed **~s** z

Webley 'web li

webliograph|y ˌweb li 'ɒg rəf |i ‖ -'ɑːg- **~ies** iz

weblog 'web lɒg ‖ -lɔːg -lɑːg **~s** z

webmaster 'web ˌmɑːst ə §-ˌmæst- ‖ -ˌmæst ᵊr **~s** z

webology we 'bɒl ədʒ i ‖ -'bɑːl-

Weak vowels

1 Among unstressed syllables it is useful to distinguish between those that nevertheless contain a strong vowel and those that have a weak vowel. This distinction has implications for syllabification, as shown in the *Longman Pronunciation Dictionary* (LPD), and for rhythm.

2 A stressed syllable (shown in words of more than one syllable by one of the marks ˈ and ˌ) must always contain a **strong** vowel (= any vowel or diphthong except ə, i, u). All the syllables in the following words, whether stressed or unstressed, are strong-vowelled: **red** red, **hope** həʊp ‖ hoʊp, **bedtime** ˈbed taɪm, **undone** ˌʌn ˈdʌn, **acorn** ˈeɪk ɔːn ‖ ˈeɪk ɔːrn, **butane** ˈbjuːt eɪn.

3 The vowels ə, i, u are always weak. The vowel ɪ, too, is weak in many cases, and also sometimes ʊ in BrE and oʊ in AmE. The unstressed syllables in the following words are all **weak**-vowelled: **allow** ə ˈlaʊ, **happy** ˈhæp i, **situation** ˌsɪtʃ u ˈeɪʃ ᵊn, **carelessness** ˈkeə ləs nəs -lɪs -nɪs ‖ ˈker-, **remember** ri ˈmem bə rə- ‖ rɪ ˈmem bᵊr, **uselessness** ˈjuːs ləs nəs, **annoying** ə ˈnɔɪ ɪŋ, **seductive** sɪ ˈdʌkt ɪv, **standard** ˈstænd əd ‖ ˈstænd ᵊrd, **stimulus** ˈstɪm jʊl əs ‖ ˈstɪm jəl əs. The weak vowel ə may be realized in the form of a SYLLABIC CONSONANT, as in **suddenly** ˈsʌd ᵊn li. If a diphthong is created through the COMPRESSION of weak syllables, it remains weak, as in **annual** ˈæn ju‿əl.

4 The distinction between weak ɪ and ə has the power of distinguishing words in RP. For example, **V. I. Lenin** is ˈlen ɪn, but **John Lennon** is ˈlen ən. The words **rabbit** ˈræb ɪt and **abbot** ˈæb ət do not rhyme. In certain other kinds of English, however, this distinction may be NEUTRALIZED, with ə used instead of weak ɪ in virtually all positions, or with the choice between ə and ɪ dependent upon the phonetic context. Accordingly, at **rabbit** LPD shows a secondary pronunciation ˈræb ət.

5 Even in RP and in other kinds of English that maintain the distinction between weak ɪ and ə, many words may be heard with either pronunciation, and this is shown in LPD. For example, **carelessness, civil, private** are nowadays more usually pronounced ˈkeə ləs nəs, ˈsɪv ᵊl, ˈpraɪv ət. A conservative minority say ˈkeə lɪs nɪs, ˈsɪv ɪl, ˈpraɪv ɪt, and these are given in LPD as secondary pronunciations.

website ˈweb saɪt **~s** s
Webster ˈweb stə ‖ -stᵊr **~'s** z
web-toed ˌweb ˈtəʊd ◂ ‖ -ˈtoʊd ◂
Wechsler ˈweks lə ‖ -lᵊr
wed wed **wedded** ˈwed ɪd -əd **wedding** ˈwed ɪŋ **weds** wedz
we'd *strong form* wiːd, *weak form* wid
Wed —*see* **Wednesday**
wedded ˈwed ɪd -əd
Weddell *(i)* ˈwed ᵊl, *(ii)* wɪ ˈdel wə- —*For the W~ Sea, (i)*
Wedderburn ˈwed ə bɜːn ‖ -ᵊr bɝːn
wedding ˈwed ɪŋ **~s** z
ˈwedding ˌbreakfast; **ˈwedding cake**; **ˈwedding day**; **ˈwedding march**; **ˈwedding ring**
wedel ˈveɪd ᵊl **~ed, ~led** d **~ing, ~ling** ‿ɪŋ **~s** z
wedeln ˈveɪd ᵊln **~ing** ɪŋ
wedge wedʒ **wedged** wedʒd **wedges** ˈwedʒ ɪz -əz **wedging** ˈwedʒ ɪŋ
Wedgewood, Wedgwood ˈwedʒ wʊd
wedlock ˈwed lɒk ‖ -lɑːk
Wedmore ˈwed mɔː →ˈweb- ‖ -mɔːr

Wednesbury ˈwenz bər‿i ‖ -ˌber i —*There is also a spelling pronunciation* ˈwed nɪz bər‿i, ˈwed nəz-; *locally also* ˈwedʒ bər‿i
Wednesday ˈwenz deɪ -di; ˈwed ᵊnz deɪ, -di —*see note at* -day **~s** z
Wednesfield ˈwenᵗs fiːᵊld —*There is also a spelling pronunciation* ˈwed nɪs fiːᵊld, -nəs-; *locally also* ˈwedʒ fiːᵊld
Weds —*see* **Wednesday** —*sometimes spoken as* wedz
wee wiː **weed** wiːd **weeing** ˈwiː ɪŋ **wees** wiːz
Weech wiːtʃ
weed wiːd **weeded** ˈwiːd ɪd -əd **weeding** ˈwiːd ɪŋ **weeds** wiːdz
weeder ˈwiːd ə ‖ -ᵊr **~s** z
weedi... —*see* **weedy**
weedkiller ˈwiːd ˌkɪl ə →ˈwiːg- ‖ -ᵊr **~s** z
Weedon ˈwiːd ᵊn
weed|y ˈwiːd |i **~ier** i‿ə ‖ i‿ᵊr **~iest** i‿ɪst i‿əst **~ily** ɪ li əl i **~iness** i nəs i nɪs
Weehawken wiː ˈhɔːk ən ‖ -ˈhɑːk-
Weejuns *tdmk* ˈwiːdʒ ənz
week wiːk **weeks** wiːks
weekday ˈwiːk deɪ **~s** z
weekend ˌwiːk ˈend ◂ ˈ· · ‖ ˈ· · **~ed** ɪd əd **~ing** ɪŋ **~s** z
weekender ˌwiːk ˈend ə ‖ ˈwiːk end ᵊr **~s** z
Weekes wiːks
Weekley ˈwiːk li
weeklong ˈwiːk lɒŋ ‖ -lɔːŋ -lɑːŋ
week|ly ˈwiːk |li **~lies** liz
weeknight ˈwiːk naɪt **~s** s
Weeks wiːks
ween wiːn
weenie ˈwiːn i **~s** z
weensy ˈwiːnz i
ween|y ˈwiːn |i **~ier** i‿ə ‖ i‿ᵊr **~ies** iz **~iest** i‿ɪst i‿əst
weenybopper ˈwiːn i ˌbɒp ə ‖ -ˌbɑːp ᵊr **~s** z
weep wiːp **weeping** ˈwiːp ɪŋ **weeps** wiːps **wept** wept
ˌweeping ˈwillow
weeper ˈwiːp ə ‖ -ᵊr **~s** z
weep|ie, weep|y ˈwiːp |i **~ier** i‿ə ‖ i‿ᵊr **~ies** iz **~iest** i‿ɪst i‿əst **~iness** i nəs i nɪs
Weetabix *tdmk* ˈwiːt ə bɪks ‖ ˈwiːţ- **~es** ɪz əz
weever ˈwiːv ə ‖ -ᵊr **~s** z
weevil ˈwiːv ᵊl -ɪl **~s** z
wee-wee ˈwiː wiː **~d** d **~ing** ɪŋ **~s** z
weft weft
Wehrmacht ˈveə mɑːxt -mɑːkt, -mæxt, -mækt ‖ ˈver mɑːkt *Ger* [ˈveːɐ maxt]
Weidenfeld ˈvaɪd ᵊn felt ˈwaɪd-
Weidman ˈwaɪd mən →ˈwaɪb-
weigela waɪ ˈdʒiːl ə wɪ-, wə-, -ˈdʒel-, -ˈgiːl-; ⚠ˈ·i‿ə; ˈwaɪg ɪl ə, -əl- **~s** z
weigh weɪ *(= way)* **weighed** weɪd *(= wade)* **weighing** ˈweɪ ɪŋ **weighs** weɪz
weighbridg|e ˈweɪ brɪdʒ **~es** ɪz əz
Weighell *(i)* wiːᵊl, *(ii)* ˈweɪ əl
weigh-in ˈweɪ ɪn
weight, W~ weɪt *(= wait)* **weighted** ˈweɪt ɪd -əd ‖ ˈweɪţ əd **weighting/s** ˈweɪt ɪŋ/z ‖ ˈweɪţ ɪŋ/z **weights** weɪts
weightless ˈweɪt ləs -lɪs **~ly** li **~ness** nəs nɪs
weightlift|ing ˈweɪt ˌlɪft |ɪŋ **~er/s** ə/z ‖ ᵊr/z
Weighton ˈwiːt ᵊn
weightwatch|er ˈweɪt ˌwɒtʃ| ə ‖ -ˌwɑːtʃ| ᵊr **~ers, Weightwatchers** *tdmk* əz ‖ ᵊrz **~ing** ɪŋ
weight|y ˈweɪt |i ‖ ˈweɪţ |i **~ier** i‿ə ‖ i‿ᵊr **~iest** i‿ɪst i‿əst **~ily** ɪ li əl i **~iness** i nəs i nɪs
Weil, Weill *(i)* vaɪᵊl, *(ii)* wiːᵊl —*Ger, Fr* [vail]
Weimar ˈvaɪm ɑː ‖ -ɑːr —*Ger* [ˈvai maʁ]
Weimaraner, W~ ˈvaɪm ə rɑːn ə ˈwaɪm-, ˌ·ˈ·· ‖ -ᵊr **~s** z
Weinberger ˈwaɪn bɜːg ə →ˈwaɪm- ‖ -bɜːg ᵊr
Weinstock ˈwaɪn stɒk ‖ -stɑːk
weir, Weir wɪə ‖ wɪᵊr **weirs** wɪəz ‖ wɪᵊrz
weird wɪəd ‖ wɪᵊrd **weirder** ˈwɪəd ə ‖ ˈwɪrd ᵊr **weirdest** ˈwɪəd ɪst -əst ‖ ˈwɪrd əst
weirdie ˈwɪəd i ‖ ˈwɪrd i **~s** z
weird|ly ˈwɪəd |li ‖ ˈwɪrd |li **~ness** nəs nɪs
weirdo ˈwɪəd əʊ ‖ ˈwɪrd oʊ **~es** z
Weismann ˈvaɪs mən ‖ -mɑːn —*Ger* [ˈvais man]
Weiss *(i)* vaɪs, *(ii)* weɪs —*Ger* [vais]
Weissmuller ˈwaɪs mʌl ə ˈvaɪs-, -mʊl- ‖ -ᵊr
Weizmann ˈvaɪts mən ‖ -mɑːn —*Ger* [ˈvaits man]
Welbeck ˈwel bek
Welbourne ˈwel bɔːn ‖ -bɔːrn -boʊrn
Welby ˈwel bi
welch weltʃ welʃ **welched** weltʃt welʃt **welches** ˈweltʃ ɪz ˈwelʃ-, -əs **welching** ˈweltʃ ɪŋ ˈwelʃ-
Welch *(i)* weltʃ, *(ii)* welʃ
welcom|e ˈwelk əm **~ed** d **~es** z **~ing** ɪŋ **~eness** nəs nɪs **~er/s** ə/z ‖ ᵊr/z
weld, Weld weld **welded** ˈweld ɪd -əd **welding** ˈweld ɪŋ **welds** weldz
welder ˈweld ə ‖ -ᵊr **~s** z
Weldon ˈweld ən
welfare, W~ ˈwel feə ‖ -fer -fær
ˌwelfare ˈstate ‖ ˈ· · ·
welfarism ˈwel feər ˌɪz əm ‖ -fer- -fær-
Welford ˈwel fəd ‖ -fᵊrd
welkin ˈwelk ɪn §-ən
well wel **welled** weld **welling** ˈwel ɪŋ **wells** welz —*When used as an interjection (but not otherwise) this word has an occasional weak form* wəl
we'll *strong form* wiːᵊl, *weak form* wil
well-acquainted ˌwel ə ˈkweɪnt ɪd -əd ‖ -ˈkweɪnţ-
well-adjusted ˌwel ə ˈdʒʌst ɪd ◂ -əd
well-advised ˌwel əd ˈvaɪzd ◂ §-æd-
Welland ˈwel ənd
well-appointed ˌwel ə ˈpɔɪnt ɪd ◂ -əd ‖ -ˈpɔɪnţ əd ◂
well-attended ˌwel ə ˈtend ɪd ◂ -əd
well-baby ˌwel ˈbeɪb i
well-balanced ˌwel ˈbæl ənᵗst ◂
well-behaved ˌwel bi ˈheɪvd ◂ -bə-
wellbeing ˌwel ˈbiː ɪŋ ˈ·ˌ· ·

Wellbeloved ˈwel bi lʌvd -bə-
wellborn ˌwel ˈbɔːn ◂ ‖ -ˈbɔːrn ◂
well-bred ˌwel ˈbred ◂
well-brought-up ˌwel ˌbrɔːt ˈʌp ◂ ‖ -ˌbrɔːt̬- -ˌbrɑːt̬-
well-built ˌwel ˈbɪlt ◂
well-chosen ˌwel ˈtʃəʊz ᵊn ◂ ‖ -ˈtʃoʊz-
Wellcome ˈwelk əm
well-connected ˌwel kə ˈnekt ɪd ◂ -əd
well-cooked ˌwel ˈkʊkt ◂ §-ˈkuːkt
well-defined ˌwel di ˈfaɪnd ◂ -də-
well-deserved ˌwel di ˈzɜːvd ◂ -də- ‖ -ˈzɜːvd ◂
well-developed ˌwel di ˈvel əpt -də-
well-disposed ˌwel dɪ ˈspəʊzd ◂ -də- ‖ -ˈspoʊzd ◂
well-documented ˌwel dɒk ju ment ɪd ◂ -jə- ◂, -əd ‖ -ˈdɑːk jə ment̬ əd ◂
well-done ˌwel ˈdʌn ◂
well-dressed ˌwel ˈdrest ◂
well-earned ˌwel ˈɜːnd ◂ ‖ -ˈɜːnd ◂
well-educated ˌwel ˈed ju keɪt ɪd ◂ -ˈedʒ u-, -ˈedʒ ə-, -əd ‖ -ˈedʒ ə keɪt̬ əd ◂
well-endowed ˌwel ɪn ˈdaʊd ◂ -en-, -ən-
Weller ˈwel ə ‖ -ᵊr
Welles welz
Wellesbourne ˈwelz bɔːn ‖ -bɔːrn -boʊrn
Wellesley ˈwelz li
well-established ˌwel ɪ ˈstæb lɪʃt ◂ -ə-
well-favoured ˌwel ˈfeɪv əd ◂ ‖ -ᵊrd ◂
well-fed ˌwel ˈfed ◂
well-formed ˌwel ˈfɔːmd ◂ ‖ -ˈfɔːrmd ◂
well-formedness ˌwel ˈfɔːm ɪd nəs -əd-, -nɪs ‖ -ˈfɔːrm-
well-found ˌwel ˈfaʊnd ◂
well-founded ˌwel ˈfaʊnd ɪd ◂ -əd
well-groomed ˌwel ˈgruːmd ◂ -ˈgrʊmd
well-grounded ˌwel ˈgraʊnd ɪd ◂ -əd
wellhead ˈwel hed **~s** z
well-heeled ˌwel ˈhiːᵊld ◂
well-hung ˌwel ˈhʌŋ ◂
wellie ˈwel i **~s** z
well-informed ˌwel ɪn ˈfɔːmd ◂ ‖ -ˈfɔːrmd ◂
Welling ˈwel ɪŋ
Wellingborough ˈwel ɪŋ bər ə ‖ -ˌbɜː oʊ
Wellington, w~ ˈwel ɪŋ tən *—but in New Zealand, locally usually* ˈwæl- **~s, ~'s** z
ˌwellington ˈboot
wellingtonia ˌwel ɪŋ ˈtəʊn i ə ‖ -ˈtoʊn- **~s** z
well-intentioned ˌwel ɪn ˈtentʃ ᵊnd ◂
well-kept ˌwel ˈkept ◂
well-knit ˌwel ˈnɪt ◂
well-known ˌwel ˈnəʊn ◂ ‖ -ˈnoʊn ◂
well-liked ˌwel ˈlaɪkt ◂
well-lined ˌwel ˈlaɪnd ◂
well-made ˌwel ˈmeɪd ◂
well-mannered ˌwel ˈmæn əd ◂ ‖ -ᵊrd ◂
well-meaning ˌwel ˈmiːn ɪŋ ◂
well-meant ˌwel ˈment ◂
wellness ˈwel nəs -nɪs
well-nigh ˌwel ˈnaɪ ◂
well-off ˌwel ˈɒf ◂ -ˈɔːf ‖ -ˈɑːf
well-oiled ˌwel ˈɔɪᵊld ◂
well-ordered ˌwel ˈɔːd əd ◂ ‖ -ˈɔːrd ᵊrd ◂
well-paid ˌwel ˈpeɪd ◂
well-planned ˌwel ˈplænd ◂
well-preserved ˌwel prɪ ˈzɜːvd ◂ -prə-, §-priː- ‖ -ˈzɜːvd ◂
well-proportioned ˌwel prə ˈpɔːʃ ᵊnd ◂ ‖ -ˈpɔːrʃ- -ˈpoʊrʃ-
well-qualified ˌwel ˈkwɒl ɪ faɪd ◂ -ə- ‖ -ˈkwɑːl-
well-read ˌwel ˈred ◂
well-rounded ˌwel ˈraʊnd ɪd ◂ -əd
well-run ˌwel ˈrʌn ◂
Wells welz
well-set ˌwel ˈset ◂
well-spoken ˌwel ˈspəʊk ən ◂ ‖ -ˈspoʊk-
wellspring ˈwel sprɪŋ **~s** z
well-stocked ˌwel ˈstɒkt ◂ ‖ -ˈstɑːkt ◂
well-suited ˌwel ˈsuːt ɪd ◂ -ˈsjuːt-, -əd ‖ -ˈsuːt̬-
well-tempered ˌwel ˈtemp əd ◂ ‖ -ᵊrd ◂
well-thought-of ˌwel ˈθɔːt ɒv ◂ -əv ‖ -ˈθɔːt̬ ʌv -ˈθɑːt̬-, -ɑːv
well-thought-out ˌwel θɔːt ˈaʊt ◂ ‖ -θɔːt̬- -θɑːt̬-
well-thumbed ˌwel ˈθʌmd ◂
well-timed ˌwel ˈtaɪmd ◂
well-to-do ˌwel tə ˈduː ◂ -tu-
well-travelled, well-traveled ˌwel ˈtræv ᵊld ◂
well-tried ˌwel ˈtraɪd ◂
well-turned ˌwel ˈtɜːnd ◂ ‖ -ˈtɜːnd ◂
well-turned-out ˌwel ˌtɜːnd ˈaʊt ◂ ‖ -ˌtɜːnd-
well-versed ˌwel ˈvɜːst ◂ ‖ -ˈvɜːst ◂
well-wisher ˈwel wɪʃ ə ˌ·ˈ·· ‖ -ᵊr **~s** z
well-woman ˌwel ˈwʊm ən
well-worn ˌwel ˈwɔːn ◂ ‖ -ˈwɔːrn ◂ -ˈwoʊrn
well|y ˈwel |i **~ies** iz
Welsh, welsh welʃ **welshed** welʃt **welshes** ˈwelʃ ɪz -əz **welshing** ˈwelʃ ɪŋ
ˌWelsh ˈrabbit, ˌWelsh ˈrarebit
welsher ˈwelʃ ə ‖ -ᵊr **~s** z
Welsh|man ˈwelʃ |mən **~men** mən men **~ness** nəs nɪs
Welshpool ˈwelʃ puːl ˌ·ˈ·
Welsh|woman ˈwelʃ |ˌwʊm ən **~women** ˌwɪm ɪn §-ən
welt welt **welted** ˈwelt ɪd -əd **welting** ˈwelt ɪŋ **welts** welts
weltanschauung ˈvelt æn ʃaʊ ʊŋ -ən-, ˌ·ˈ·ˈ·· ‖ -ɑːn- *—Ger* W~ [ˈvɛlt ˌan ʃau ʊŋ]
welter ˈwelt ə ‖ -ᵊr **~ed** d **weltering** ˈwelt ər ɪŋ **~s** z
welterweight ˈwelt ə weɪt ‖ -ᵊr- **~s** s
Welthorpe ˈwel θɔːp ‖ -θɔːrp
weltschmerz ˈvelt ʃmeəts ‖ -ʃmerts *—Ger* W~ [ˈvɛlt ʃmɛʁts]
Welty ˈwelt i
welwitschia wel ˈwɪtʃ i ə **~s** z
Welwyn ˈwel ɪn §-ən
Wem wem
Wembley ˈwem bli
Wemmick ˈwem ɪk
Wemyss wiːmz
wen wen **wens** wenz

W

Wenceslas, Wenceslaus ˈwenᵗs əs ləs -ɪs-, ⚠-ləs-, -læs ‖ -lɔːs, -lɑːs
wench wentʃ **wenched** wentʃt **wenches** ˈwentʃ ɪz -əz **wenching** ˈwentʃ ɪŋ
wend, Wend wend **wended** ˈwend ɪd -əd **wending** ˈwend ɪŋ **wends, Wends** wendz
Wendell ˈwend ᵊl
Wenden ˈwend ən
Wendish ˈwend ɪʃ
Wendon ˈwend ən
Wendover ˈwend əʊv ə ‖ -oʊv ᵊr
Wendy ˈwend i
ˈWendy house
Wenger ˈveŋ ə ‖ -ᵊr —*Fr* [vɛ̃ ɡɛːʁ]
Wenham ˈwen əm
Wenlock ˈwen lɒk ‖ -lɑːk
ˌWenlock ˈEdge
Wensley ˈwenz li ˈwenᵗs-
Wensleydale, w~ ˈwenz li deɪᵊl ˈwenᵗs-
Wensum ˈwenᵗs əm
went went
wentletrap ˈwent ᵊl træp **~s** s
Wentworth ˈwent wəθ -wɜːθ ‖ -wɜːθ
Wenvoe ˈwen vəʊ ‖ -voʊ
Weobley ˈweb li
wept wept

WERE

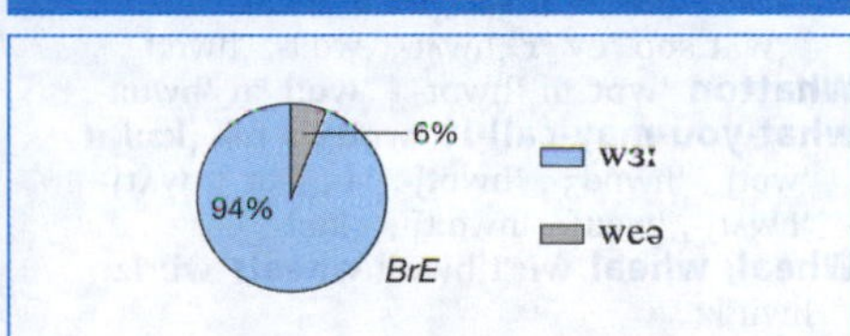

were *strong forms* wɜː weə ‖ wɜˑː, *weak form* wə ‖ wᵊr — *Preference poll (strong form), BrE:* wɜː *94%,* weə *6%.*
we're wɪə ‖ wɪᵊr *(= weir)*
weren't wɜːnt weənt ‖ wɜˑːnt
were|wolf ˈweə |wʊlf ˈwɪə-, ˈwɜː- ‖ ˈwer- ˈwɪr-, ˈwɜˑː- **~wolves** wʊlvz
Werner ˈwɜːn ə ‖ ˈwɜˑːn ᵊr —*Ger* [ˈvɛʁ nɐ]
Wernicke ˈveən ɪk ə ‖ ˈvern- -i —*Ger* [ˈvɛʁ nɪk ə]
ˈWernicke's ˌarea
wert *strong form* wɜːt ‖ wɜˑːt, *weak form* wət ‖ wᵊrt
Weser ˈveɪz ə ‖ -ᵊr —*Ger* [ˈveː zɐ]
Wesker ˈwesk ə ‖ -ᵊr
Wesley *(i)* ˈwes li, *(ii)* ˈwez li —*The founder of Methodism was actually (i), though often pronounced as (ii).* **~s, ~'s** z
Wesleyan ˈwez li‿ən ˈwes- **~s** z
Wessex ˈwes ɪks §-əks
Wesson ˈwes ᵊn
west, West west
ˌWest ˈBank; **ˌWest ˈCoast◂**; **ˈWest ˌCountry**, ˌ· ˈ· ·◂; **ˌWest ˈEnd◂**; **ˌWest Glaˈmorgan**; **₍ˌ₎West ˈIndian**, **₍ˌ₎West ˈIndies**; **ˌWest ˈMidlands**; **ˌWest Virˈginia**; **ˌWest ˈYorkshire**

westbound ˈwest baʊnd
Westbourne ˈwest bɔːn -bən ‖ -bɔːrn -boʊrn
Westbrook ˈwest brʊk
Westbury ˈwest bər‿i ‖ -ˌber i
Westbury-on-Trym ˌwest bər‿i ɒn ˈtrɪm ‖ -ɑːnˈ- -ɔːnˈ-
Westclox *tdmk* ˈwest klɒks ‖ -klɑːks
Westcott ˈwest kət
wester, W~ ˈwest ə ‖ -ᵊr **~ed** d **westering** ˈwest ər ɪŋ **~s** z
Westerham ˈwest ər əm →ˈwes trəm
wester|ly ˈwest ə |li -ᵊ|l i ‖ -ᵊr |li **~lies** liz
western, W~ ˈwest ən ‖ -ᵊrn **~s** z
ˌWestern Auˈstralia; **ˌWestern ˈIsles**
westerner, W~ ˈwest ən ə ‖ -ᵊrn ᵊr -ᵊn ər **~s** z
westernis... —*see* **westerniz...**
westernization ˌwest ən aɪ ˈzeɪʃ ᵊn -ɪˈ- ‖ -ᵊrn ə-
westerniz|e ˈwest ə naɪz ‖ -ᵊr- **~ed** d **~es** ɪz əz **~ing** ɪŋ
westernmost ˈwest ən məʊst →-əm- ‖ -ᵊrn moʊst
Westfield ˈwest fiːᵊld
Westgate ˈwest geɪt -gɪt, -gət
Westhoughton ˌwest ˈhɔːt ᵊn ‖ -ˈhɑːt-
Westin ˈwest ɪn §-ən
Westinghouse ˈwest ɪŋ haʊs
Westlake ˈwest leɪk
Westland *tdmk* ˈwest lənd **~'s** z
Westmeath ˌwest ˈmiːð
Westminster ˈwest mɪnᵗst ə ˌ·ˈ·· ; ⚠ˌ·ˈmɪn ɪst ə, ⚠-əst ə ‖ -ᵊr
ˌWestminster ˈAbbey
Westmoreland, Westmorland ˈwest mə lənd ‖ -mɔːr- -moʊr-
west-northwest ˌwest nɔːθ ˈwest ‖ -nɔːrθ- —*also naut* -nɔː- ‖ -nɔːr-
Westoby *(i)* ˈwest əb i, *(ii)* we ˈstəʊb i ‖ -ˈstoʊb-
Weston ˈwest ən
Westoning ˈwest ən ɪŋ
Weston-super-Mare ˌwest ən ˌsuːp ə ˈmeə -ˌsjuːp-; ˌ· ·ˈ· · · ‖ -ᵊr ˈmeᵊr -ˈmæᵊr
Westphali|a west ˈfeɪl i‿|ə **~an/s** ən/z
Westray ˈwes treɪ -tri
west-southwest ˌwest saʊθ ˈwest —*also naut* -saʊ-
westward ˈwest wəd ‖ -wᵊrd **~s** z
ˌWestward ˈHo!
Westwood ˈwest wʊd
wet wet **wets** wets **wetted** ˈwet ɪd -əd ‖ ˈweṭ əd **wetter** ˈwet ə ‖ ˈweṭ ᵊr **wettest** ˈwet ɪst -əst ‖ ˈweṭ əst **wetting** ˈwet ɪŋ ‖ ˈweṭ ɪŋ
ˌwet ˈblanket ‖ ˈ· ˌ· ·; **ˌwet ˈdream**; **ˈwet nurse**; **ˈwet suit**; **ˈwetting ˌagent**
wetback ˈwet bæk **~s** s
wether ˈweð ə ‖ -ᵊr *(= weather)* **~s** z
Wetherall ˈweð ər ɔːl -ᵊr‿əl ‖ -ɑːl
Wetherby ˈweð ə bi ‖ -ᵊr-
wetland ˈwet lænd -lənd **~s** z
wet-look ˈwet lʊk §-luːk
Wetmore ˈwet mɔː ‖ -mɔːr

wetness ˈwet nəs -nɪs
wett... —*see* **wet**
Wetton ˈwet ᵊn
Wetzel ˈwets ᵊl
we've *strong form* wiːv, *weak form* wiv
Wexford ˈweks fəd ‖ -fᵊrd
Wexler ˈweks lə ‖ -lᵊr
Wey weɪ
Weybridge ˈweɪ brɪdʒ
Weyman *(i)* ˈwaɪ mən, *(ii)* ˈweɪ mən
Weymouth ˈweɪ məθ
whack wæk hwæk **whacked** wækt hwækt **whacking/s** ˈwæk ɪŋ/z ˈhwæk- **whacks** wæks hwæks
ˌwhacked ˈout
whacko ˌwæk ˈəʊ ˌhwæk- ‖ -ˈoʊ
whacky ˈwæk i
whale weɪᵊl hweɪᵊl **whales** weɪᵊlz hweɪᵊlz
ˈwhale of a ˌtime
whaleboat ˈweɪᵊl bəʊt ˈhweɪᵊl- ‖ -boʊt **~s** s
whalebone ˈweɪᵊl bəʊn ˈhweɪᵊl- ‖ -boʊn
whaler ˈweɪᵊl ə ˈhweɪᵊl- ‖ -ᵊr **~s** z
Whaley ˈweɪl i ˈhweɪl-
whaling ˈweɪᵊl ɪŋ ˈhweɪᵊl-
Whalley *(i)* ˈwɒl i ˈhwɒl- ‖ ˈwɑːl i ˈhwɑːl i, *(ii)* ˈwɔːl i ˈhwɔːl i ‖ ˈwɔːl i ˈwɑːl i, ˈhwɔːl i, ˈhwɑːl i, *(iii)* ˈweɪl i ˈhweɪl- —*The place near Blackburn, Lancs., is (ii), but* W~ Range *in Manchester is (i).*
wham, Wham wæm hwæm **whammed** wæmd hwæmd **whamming** ˈwæm ɪŋ ˈhwæm- **whams** wæmz hwæmz
whammo ˈwæm əʊ ˈhwæm- ‖ -oʊ
whamm|y ˈwæm |i ˈhwæm- **~ies** iz
Whampoa ˌwæm ˈpəʊ ˌhwæm- ‖ ˌwɑːm ˈpoʊ ˌhwɑːm- —*Chi* Huángpǔ [²xuaŋ ³pʰu]
whang wæŋ hwæŋ **whanged** wæŋd hwæŋd **whanging** ˈwæŋ ɪŋ ˈhwæŋ- **whangs** wæŋz hwæŋz
whangee ˌwæŋ ˈiː ˌhwæŋ-, -ˈgiː ‖ ˌ*h*wæŋ- **~s** z
whare ˈwɒr i ˈhwɒr i ‖ ˈwɑːr i ˈhwɑːr i **~s** z
wharf wɔːf hwɔːf ‖ wɔːrf hwɔːrf **wharfs** wɔːfs hwɔːfs ‖ wɔːrfs hwɔːrfs **wharves** wɔːvz hwɔːvz ‖ wɔːrvz hwɔːrvz
wharfage ˈwɔːf ɪdʒ ˈhwɔːf- ‖ ˈwɔːrf- ˈhwɔːrf-
Wharfe wɔːf hwɔːf ‖ wɔːrf hwɔːrf
Wharfedale ˈwɔːf deɪᵊl ˈhwɔːf- ‖ ˈwɔːrf- ˈhwɔːrf-
wharfinger ˈwɔːf ɪn*d*ʒ ə ˈhwɔːf-, §-ən*d*ʒ- ‖ ˈwɔːrf ən*d*ʒ ᵊr ˈhwɔːrf- **~s** z
Wharton ˈwɔːt ᵊn ˈhwɔːt- ‖ ˈwɔːrt ᵊn ˈhwɔːrt-
wharve wɔːv hwɔːv ‖ wɔːrv hwɔːrv **wharves** wɔːvz hwɔːvz ‖ wɔːrvz hwɔːrvz
whassup wɒ ˈsʌp ‖ wə- wɑː-
what wɒt hwɒt ‖ wʌt wɑːt, hwʌt, hwɑːt —*Also, when followed by weak* do/does/did, *sometimes* wɒ ‖ wʌ, wɑː, hwʌ, hwɑː — *as* What do you do? ˌwɒd ə ju ˈduː ‖ ˌwʌd-
ˌwhat ˈfor
whatchamacallit ˈwɒtʃ əm ə ˌkɔːl ɪt §-ət ‖ ˈwʌtʃ- ˈwɑːtʃ-, ˈhwʌtʃ-, ˈhwɑːtʃ-, -ˌkɑːl-
what-d'you-call-it ˈwɒdʒ u ˌkɔːl ɪt ˈwɒdʒ ə-, ˈwɒt dʒu-, ˈwɒt dʒə-, §-ət ‖ ˈwʌdʒ- ˈwɑːdʒ-, ˈhwʌdʒ-, ˈhwɑːdʒ-, -ˌkɑːl-
whate'er wɒt ˈeə hwɒt- ‖ wʌţ ˈeᵊr hwʌţ-, wɑːţ-, hwɑːţ-
whatever wɒt ˈev ə hwɒt- ‖ wʌţ ˈev ᵊr hwʌţ-, wɑːţ-, hwɑːţ-
what-if ˈwɒt ɪf ˈhwɒt- ‖ ˈwʌţ- ˈhwʌţ-, ˈwɑːţ-, ˈhwɑːţ- **~s** s
Whatmore ˈwɒt mɔː ˈhwɒt- ‖ ˈwɑːt mɔːr ˈhwɑːt-
Whatmough ˈwɒt məʊ ˈhwɒt-, -mʌf ‖ ˈwɑːt moʊ ˈhwɑːt-
whatnot ˈwɒt nɒt ˈhwɒt- ‖ ˈwʌt nɑːt ˈhwʌt-, ˈwɑːt-, ˈhwɑːt- **~s** s
what's wɒts hwɒts ‖ wʌts hwʌts, wɑːts, hwɑːts
what's-her-name ˈwɒts ə neɪm ‖ ˈwʌts ᵊr- ˈhwʌts-, ˈwɑːts-, ˈhwɑːts-
what's-his-name ˈwɒts ɪz neɪm -əz- ‖ ˈwʌts- ˈhwʌts-, ˈwɑːts-, ˈhwɑːts-
whatsit, what's it ˈwɒts ɪt ˈhwɒts-, §-ət ‖ ˈwʌts ət ˈhwʌts-, ˈwɑːts-, ˈhwɑːts- **~s** s
whatsitsname, what's its name ˈwɒts ɪts neɪm ˈhwɒts-, §-əts- ‖ ˈwʌts- ˈhwʌts-, ˈwɑːts-, ˈhwɑːts-
whatsoe'er ˌwɒt səʊ ˈeə ˌhwɒt- ‖ ˌwʌt soʊ ˈeᵊr ˌhwʌt-, ˌwɑːt-, ˌhwɑːt-
whatsoever ˌwɒt səʊ ˈev ə ˌhwɒt- ‖ ˌwʌt soʊ ˈev ᵊr ˌhwʌt-, ˌwɑːt-, ˌhwɑːt-
Whatton ˈwɒt ᵊn ˈhwɒt- ‖ ˈwɑːt ᵊn ˈhwɑːt-
what-you-may-call-it ˈwɒdʒ ə mə ˌkɔːl ɪt ˈwɒtʃ-, ˈhwɒdʒ-, ˈhwɒtʃ-, ˈ·i-, §-ət ‖ ˈwʌtʃ- ˈhwʌtʃ-, ˈwɑːtʃ-, ˈhwɑːtʃ-, -ˌkɑːl-
Wheal, wheal wiːᵊl hwiːᵊl **wheals** wiːᵊlz hwiːᵊlz
wheat wiːt hwiːt
ˈwheat germ
Wheatcroft ˈwiːt krɒft ˈhwiːt- ‖ -krɔːft -krɑːft
wheatear ˈwiːt ɪə ˈhwiːt- ‖ ˈwiːţ ɪr ˈhwiːţ- **~s** z
wheaten ˈwiːt ᵊn ˈhwiːt-
Wheathampstead ˈwiːt əm*p* sted ˈhwiːt-, ˈwet-, ˈhwet- ‖ ˈwiːţ-
Wheaties *tdmk* ˈwiːt iz ˈhwiːt iz ‖ ˈwiːţ iz ˈhwiːţ iz
Wheatley ˈwiːt li ˈhwiːt-
wheatmeal ˈwiːt miːᵊl ˈhwiːt-
Wheatstone ˈwiːt stən ˈhwiːt-, -stəʊn ‖ ˈwiːt stoʊn ˈhwiːt-
whee wiː hwiː —*usually uttered on a prolonged high-fall tone*
wheedl|e ˈwiːd ᵊl ˈhwiːd- **~ed** d **~es** z **~ing/ly** ɪŋ/li
wheel wiːᵊl hwiːᵊl **wheeled** wiːᵊld hwiːᵊld **wheeling** ˈwiːᵊl ɪŋ ˈhwiːᵊl- **wheels** wiːᵊlz hwiːᵊlz
wheelbarrow ˈwiːᵊl ˌbær əʊ ˈhwiːᵊl- ‖ -ˌbær oʊ -ˌber oʊ **~s** z
wheelbas|e ˈwiːᵊl beɪs ˈhwiːᵊl- **~es** ɪz əz
wheelchair ˈwiːᵊl tʃeə ˈhwiːᵊl-; ˌ·ˈ· ‖ -tʃer -tʃær **~s** z
-wheeler ˈwiːᵊl ə ˈhwiːᵊl- ‖ -ᵊr — **three-wheeler** ˌθriː ˈwiːᵊl ə ˈhwiːᵊl ə ‖ -ᵊr
Wheeler, w~ ˈwiːl ə ˈhwiːl- ‖ -ᵊr **~s** z

W

wheeler-dealer ˌwiːl ə ˈdiːl ə ˌhwiːl- ‖ ˌwiːᵊl ᵊr ˈdiːl ᵊr ˌhwiːl- **~s** z
wheel|house ˈwiːᵊl |haʊs ˈhwiːᵊl- **~houses** haʊz ɪz -əz
wheelie ˈwiːᵊl i ˈhwiːᵊl- **~s** z
wheelwright ˈwiːᵊl raɪt ˈhwiːᵊl- **~s** s
Wheen wiːn hwiːn
wheeze wiːz hwiːz **wheezed** wiːzd hwiːzd **wheezes** ˈwiːz ɪz ˈhwiːz-, -əz **wheezing/ly** ˈwiːz ɪŋ /li ˈhwiːz-
wheez|y ˈwiːz |i ˈhwiːz- **~ier** i‿ə ‖ i‿ᵊr **~iest** i‿ɪst i‿əst **~ily** ɪ li əl i **~iness** i nəs i nɪs
Whelan ˈwiːl ən ˈhwiːl-
whelk welk hwelk —*An initial* hw *in the sense 'shellfish' is not supported by the etymology.* **whelks** welks hwelks
whelp welp hwelp **whelped** welpt hwelpt **whelping** ˈwelp ɪŋ ˈhwelp- **whelps** welps hwelps
when wen hwen —*There is also an occasional weak form* wən
whence wenᵗs hwenᵗs
whene'er wen ˈeə hwen-, wən- ‖ -ˈeᵊr
whenever wen ˈev ə hwen-, wən- ‖ - ᵊr
where weə hweər ‖ weᵊr hweᵊr, wæᵊr, hwæᵊr
whereabouts *n* ˈweər ə baʊts ˈhweər- ‖ ˈwer- ˈhwer-, ˈwær-, ˈhwær-
whereabouts *interrogative adv* ˌweər ə ˈbaʊts ◂ ˌhweər- ‖ ˈwer ə baʊts ˈhwer-, ˈwær-, ˈhwær-
whereas weər ˈæz hweər-, ˌ·ˈ·, wer- ‖ wer- hwer-, wær-, hwær-
whereat weər ˈæt hweər-, ˌ·ˈ·, wer- ‖ wer- hwer-, wær-, hwær-
whereby weə ˈbaɪ hweə-, ˌ·ˈ· ‖ wer- hwer-, wær-, hwær-
where'er weər ˈeə hweər-, ˌ·ˈ·, wer- ‖ wer ˈeᵊr hwer-, wær-, hwær-
wherefore ˈweə fɔː ˈhweə- ‖ ˈwer fɔːr ˈhwer-, ˈwær-, ˈhwær-, -foʊr **~s** z
wherein weər ˈɪn hweər-, ˌ·ˈ·, wer- ‖ wer- hwer-, wær-, hwær-
whereof weər ˈɒv hweər-, ˌ·ˈ·, wer- ‖ wer ˈʌv hwer-, wær-, hwær-, -ˈɑːv
whereon weər ˈɒn hweər-, ˌ·ˈ·, wer- ‖ wer ˈɑːn hwer-, wær-, hwær-, -ˈɔːn
where's weəz hweəz ‖ weᵊrz hweᵊrz, wæᵊrz, hwæᵊrz
wheresoever ˌweə səʊ ˈev ə ˌhweə- ‖ ˌwer soʊ ˈev ᵊr ˌhwer-, ˌwær-, ˌhwær-
whereto weə ˈtuː hweə- ‖ wer- hwer-, wær-, hwær-
whereunto weər ˈʌn tu hweər-, ˌ·ˈ·; ˌ·ˈ·ˈtuː ‖ wer-
whereupon ˌweər ə ˈpɒn ˌhweər-, ˈ··· ‖ ˌwer ə ˈpɑːn ˌhwer-, ˌwær-, ˌhwær-, -ˈpɔːn
wherever weər ˈev ə hweər-, ˌ·ˈ·· ‖ wer ˈev ᵊr hwer-, wær-, hwær-
wherewithal *n* ˈweə wɪð ɔːl ˈhweə-, §-wɪθ-, ˌ··ˈ· ‖ ˈwer- ˈhwer-, ˈwær-, ˈhwær-, -wɪθ-, -ɑːl
Whernside ˈwɜːn saɪd ˈhwɜːn- ‖ wɜːn- ˈhwɜːn-
wherr|y ˈwer |i ˈhwer- **~ies** iz

whet wet hwet **whets** wets hwets **whetted** ˈwet ɪd ˈhwet-, -əd ‖ weţ əd ˈhweţ- **whetting** ˈwet ɪŋ ˈhwet- ‖ ˈweţ ɪŋ ˈhweţ-
whether ˈweð ə ˈhweð- ‖ -ᵊr
whetstone, W~ ˈwet stəʊn ˈhwet- ‖ -stoʊn **~s** z
whew fjuː hwjuː —*and non-speech sounds such as* ʍ, ʍu, ɸ, pɸː, ɣu̥
Wheway ˈwiː weɪ ˈhwiː-
Whewell ˈhjuː‿əl hjuːl
whey weɪ hweɪ
wheyfaced ˈweɪ feɪst ˈhweɪ-
which wɪtʃ hwɪtʃ
Whicher ˈwɪtʃ ə ˈhwɪtʃ- ‖ -ᵊr
whichever wɪtʃ ˈev ə hwɪtʃ-, ˌ·ˈ·· ‖ - ᵊr
whicker, W~ ˈwɪk ə ˈhwɪk- ‖ -ᵊr **~ed** d **whickering** ˈwɪk ər ɪŋ ˈhwɪk- **~s** z
whiff wɪf hwɪf **whiffed** wɪft hwɪft **whiffing** ˈwɪf ɪŋ ˈhwɪf- **whiffs** wɪfs hwɪfs
Whiffen ˈwɪf ɪn ˈhwɪf-, §-ᵊn ‖ -ᵊn
whiffl|e ˈwɪf ᵊl ˈhwɪf- **~ed** d **~es** z **~ing** ˌɪŋ
whiffleball ˈwɪf ᵊl bɔːl ‖ -bɑːl
whiff|y ˈwɪf |i ˈhwɪf- **~ier** i‿ə ‖ i‿ᵊr **~iest** i‿ɪst i‿əst **~iness** i nəs i nɪs
Whig wɪg hwɪg **Whigs** wɪgz hwɪgz
Whigg|ery ˈwɪg| ər i **~ish** ɪʃ **~ism** ɪz əm
while waɪᵊl hwaɪᵊl **whiled** waɪᵊld hwaɪᵊld **whiles** waɪᵊlz hwaɪᵊlz **whiling** ˈwaɪᵊl ɪŋ ˈhwaɪᵊl-
whilst waɪᵊlst hwaɪᵊlst
whim wɪm hwɪm **whims** wɪmz hwɪmz
whimbrel ˈwɪm brəl ˈhwɪm- **~s** z
whimper ˈwɪmp ə ˈhwɪmp- ‖ -ᵊr **~ed** d **whimpering/ly** ˈwɪmp ər‿ɪŋ /li ˈhwɪmp- **~s** z
whimsey ˈwɪmz i ˈhwɪmz- **~s** z
whimsical ˈwɪmz ɪk ᵊl ˈhwɪmz- **~ly** ‿i
whimsicalit|y ˌwɪmz ɪ ˈkæl ət |i ˌhwɪmz-, §ˌ·ə-, -ɪt i ‖ -əţ |i **~ies** iz
whims|y ˈwɪmz |i ˈhwɪmz- **~ies** iz
whin wɪn hwɪn
whinchat ˈwɪn tʃæt ˈhwɪn- **~s** s
whine waɪn hwaɪn **whined** waɪnd hwaɪnd **whines** waɪnz hwaɪnz **whining/ly** ˈwaɪn ɪŋ /li ˈhwaɪn-
whiner ˈwaɪn ə ˈhwaɪn- ‖ -ᵊr **~s** z
whinge wɪndʒ hwɪndʒ **whinged** wɪndʒd hwɪndʒd **whinges** ˈwɪndʒ ɪz ˈhwɪndʒ-, -əz **whingeing, whinging** ˈwɪndʒ ɪŋ ˈhwɪndʒ-
whinger ˈwɪndʒ ə ˈhwɪndʒ- ‖ -ᵊr **~s** z
whinn|y ˈwɪn |i ˈhwɪn- **~ied** id **~ies** iz **~ying** i ɪŋ
whinstone ˈwɪn stəʊn ˈhwɪn- ‖ -stoʊn
whin|y ˈwaɪn |i ˈhwaɪn- **~ier** i‿ə ‖ i‿ᵊr **~iest** i ɪst -əst **~iness** i nəs -nɪs
whip wɪp hwɪp **whipped** wɪpt hwɪpt **whipping/s** ˈwɪp ɪŋ/z ˈhwɪp- **whips** wɪps hwɪps
'whip hand, ˌ· ˈ·; **'whipping boy**; **'whipping cream**
whipcord ˈwɪp kɔːd ˈhwɪp- ‖ -kɔːrd
whiplash ˈwɪp læʃ ˈhwɪp- **~es** ɪz əz
whipp... —*see* **whip**

whipp|er-in ˌwɪp |ər ˈɪn ˌhwɪp- **~ers-in** əz ˈɪn ‖ ᵊrz-
whippersnapper ˈwɪp ə ˌsnæp ə ˈhwɪp- ‖ ˈwɪp ᵊr ˌsnæp ᵊr ˈhwɪp- **~s** z
whippet ˈwɪp ɪt ˈhwɪp-, §-ət **~s** s
whippoorwill ˈwɪp ə wɪl ˈhwɪp-, -ʊə-, -pʊə-, ˌ·ˈ·ˌ· ‖ -ᵊr- **~s** z
whipp|y ˈwɪp |i ˈhwɪp- **~ier** i‿ə ‖ i‿ᵊr **~iest** i‿ɪst i‿əst
whip-round ˈwɪp raʊnd ˈhwɪp- **~s** z
whipsaw ˈwɪp sɔː ˈhwɪp- ‖ -sɑː **~s** z
Whipsnade ˈwɪp sneɪd ˈhwɪp-
whir wɜː hwɜː ‖ wɜ˞ː hwɜ˞ː **whirred** wɜːd hwɜːd ‖ wɜ˞ːd hwɜ˞ːd **whirring** ˈwɜːr ɪŋ ˈhwɜːr- ‖ ˈwɜ˞ː ɪŋ ˈhwɜ˞ː- **whirs** wɜːz hwɜːz ‖ wɜ˞ːz hwɜ˞ːz
whirl wɜːl hwɜːl ‖ wɜ˞ːl hwɜ˞ːl **whirled** wɜːld hwɜːld ‖ wɜ˞ːld hwɜ˞ːld **whirling** ˈwɜːl ɪŋ ˈhwɜːl- ‖ wɜ˞ːl ɪŋ hwɜ˞ːl- **whirls** wɜːlz hwɜːlz ‖ wɜ˞ːlz hwɜ˞ːlz
whirligig ˈwɜːl i gɪg ˈhwɜːl- ‖ ˈwɜ˞ːl- ˈhwɜ˞ːl- **~s** z
whirlpool ˈwɜːl puːl ˈhwɜːl- ‖ ˈwɜ˞ːl- ˈhwɜ˞ːl- **~s** z
whirlwind ˈwɜːl wɪnd ˈhwɜːl- ‖ ˈwɜ˞ːl- ˈhwɜ˞ːl- **~s** z
whirlybird ˈwɜːl i bɜːd ˈhwɜːl- ‖ ˈwɜ˞ːl i bɜ˞ːd ˈhwɜ˞ːl- **~s** z
whirr wɜː hwɜː ‖ wɜ˞ː hwɜ˞ː **whirred** wɜːd hwɜːd ‖ wɜ˞ːd hwɜ˞ːd **whirring** ˈwɜːr ɪŋ ˈhwɜːr- ‖ wɜ˞ː ɪŋ ˈhwɜ˞ː- **whirrs** wɜːz hwɜːz ‖ wɜ˞ːz hwɜ˞ːz
whisk wɪsk hwɪsk **whisked** wɪskt hwɪskt **whisking** ˈwɪsk ɪŋ ˈhwɪsk- **whisks** wɪsks hwɪsks
Whiskas *tdmk* ˈwɪsk əz ˈhwɪsk-
whisker ˈwɪsk ə ˈhwɪsk- ‖ -ᵊr **~ed** d **~s** z
whiskey ˈwɪsk i ˈhwɪsk- **~s** z
whisk|y ˈwɪsk |i ˈhwɪsk- **~ies** iz
whisper ˈwɪsp ə ˈhwɪsp- ‖ -ᵊr **~ed** d **whispering/s** ˈwɪsp ər‿ɪŋ/z ˈhwɪsp- **~s** z **ˈwhispering camˌpaign**
whisperer ˈwɪsp ər ə ˈhwɪsp- ‖ -ᵊr ər **~s** z
whist wɪst hwɪst **ˈwhist drive**
whistl|e ˈwɪs ᵊl ˈhwɪs- **~ed** d **~es** z **~ing** ‿ɪŋ **ˈwhistle stop**
whistle-blower ˈwɪs ᵊl ˌbləʊ ə ˈhwɪs- ‖ -ˌbloʊ ᵊr **~s** z
whistler, W~ ˈwɪs lə ˈhwɪs- ‖ -ᵊr **~s, ~'s** z
whistle-stop ˈwɪs ᵊl stɒp ˈhwɪs- ‖ -stɑːp **~ped** t **~ping** ɪŋ **~s** s **ˌwhistle-stop ˈtour**
whit, Whit wɪt hwɪt **ˌWhit ˈMonday**; **ˌWhit ˈSunday**
Whitaker ˈwɪt ək ə ˈhwɪt, -ɪk- ‖ ˈwɪţ ək ᵊr ˈhwɪţ-
Whitbread ˈwɪt bred ˈhwɪt-
Whitby ˈwɪt bi ˈhwɪt-
Whitchurch ˈwɪt tʃɜːtʃ ˈhwɪt- ‖ -tʃɜ˞ːtʃ —*in Wales usually* ˈwɪtʃ ɜːtʃ, -ətʃ
Whitcut, Whitcutt ˈwɪt kʌt ˈhwɪt-

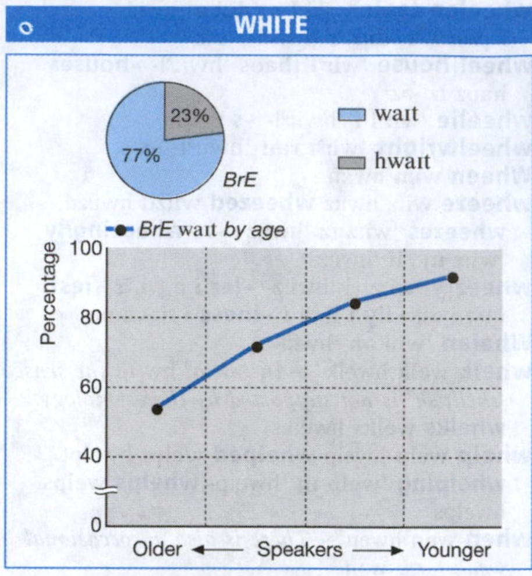

white, White waɪt hwaɪt — *Preference poll, BrE:* waɪt *77%,* hwaɪt *23%.* **whited** ˈwaɪt ɪd ˈhwaɪt-, -əd ‖ ˈwaɪţ əd ˈhwaɪţ- **whiter** ˈwaɪt ə ˈhwaɪt- ‖ ˈwaɪţ ᵊr ˈhwaɪţ- **whites** waɪts hwaɪts **whitest** ˈwaɪt ɪst -əst ‖ ˈwaɪţ əst ˈhwaɪţ- **whiting** ˈwaɪt ɪŋ ˈhwaɪt- ‖ ˈwaɪţ ɪŋ ˈhwaɪţ- **ˌwhite ˈant**; **ˌwhite ˈblood cell**; **ˌwhite ˈcorpuscle, - corˈpuscle**; **ˌwhited ˈsepulchre**; **ˌwhite ˈdwarf**; **ˌwhite ˈelephant**; **ˌwhite ˈflag**; **ˈwhite goods**; **ˌwhite ˈheat**; **ˈWhite House** —*This is the AmE stress pattern for the President's official residence. In BrE it is sometimes stressed* ˌ· ˈ·; **ˌwhite ˈknight**; **ˌwhite ˈlead led**; **ˌwhite ˈlie**; **ˌwhite ˈmagic**; **ˈwhite man**; **ˌwhite ˈmeat**; **ˌwhite ˈmetal**; **a ˌwhite ˈpaper**; **ˌwhite ˈpepper**; **ˈwhite ˌpeople**; **ˌwhite ˈsauce** ‖ ˈ· ·; **ˌwhite ˈslavery**; **ˌwhite ˈspirit**; **ˌwhite ˈtie**; **ˌwhite ˈtrash**; **ˌwhite ˈwater**; **ˌwhite ˈwedding**
whitebait ˈwaɪt beɪt ˈhwaɪt-
whitebeam ˈwaɪt biːm ˈhwaɪt- **~s** z
whiteboard ˈwaɪt bɔːd ˈhwaɪt- ‖ -bɔːrd -boʊrd
whitecap ˈwaɪt kæp ˈhwaɪt- **~s** s
Whitechapel ˈwaɪt ˌtʃæp ᵊl ˈhwaɪt-
white-collar ˌwaɪt ˈkɒl ə ◂ ˌhwaɪt- ‖ -ˈkɑːl ᵊr ◂
Whitefield *(i)* ˈwɪt fiːᵊld ˈhwɪt-, *(ii)* ˈwaɪt- ˈhwaɪt- —*The family name may be (i) or (ii); the Methodist evangelist was (i). The place in Manchester is (ii).*
whitefish ˈwaɪt fɪʃ ˈhwaɪt-
white|fly ˈwaɪt |flaɪ ˈhwaɪt- **~flies** flaɪz
Whitefriars ˈwaɪt ˌfraɪ‿əz ˈhwaɪt-, ˌ·ˈ·· ‖ -ˌfraɪ‿ᵊrz
Whitehall ˈwaɪt hɔːl ˈhwaɪt-, ˌ·ˈ· ‖ -hɑːl
Whitehaven ˈwaɪt ˌheɪv ᵊn ˈhwaɪt-
Whitehead ˈwaɪt hed ˈhwaɪt-
Whitehorn ˈwaɪt hɔːn ˈhwaɪt- ‖ -hɔːrn
Whitehorse ˈwaɪt hɔːs ˈhwaɪt- ‖ -hɔːrs
white-hot ˌwaɪt ˈhɒt ◂ ˌhwaɪt- ‖ -ˈhɑːt ◂
Whitehouse ˈwaɪt haʊs ˈhwaɪt-
white-knuckle ˌwaɪt ˈnʌk ᵊl ˌhwaɪt- **~d** d

Whitelaw 'waɪt lɔː 'hwaɪt- ‖ -lɑː
Whiteley 'waɪt li 'hwaɪt-
white-livered ˌwaɪt 'lɪv əd ◂ ˌhwaɪt- ‖ -ᵊrd ◂
whiten 'waɪt ᵊn 'hwaɪt- **~ed** d **~er/s** ə/z ‖ ˌər/z **~ing** ˌɪŋ **~s** z
whiteness 'waɪt nəs 'hwaɪt-, -nɪs **~es** ɪz əz
whiteout 'waɪt aʊt 'hwaɪt- ‖ 'waɪṭ aʊt 'hwaɪṭ- **~s** s
white-tailed ˌwaɪt 'teɪld ◂ ˌhwaɪt-
ˌ**white-tailed 'deer**
whitethorn 'waɪt θɔːn 'hwaɪt- ‖ -θɔːrn **~s** z
whitethroat 'waɪt θrəʊt 'hwaɪt- ‖ -θroʊt **~s** s
white-tie ˌwaɪt 'taɪ ◂ ˌhwaɪt-
whitewall 'waɪt wɔːl 'hwaɪt- ‖ -wɑːl
whitewash 'waɪt wɒʃ 'hwaɪt- ‖ -wɑːʃ -wɔːʃ **~ed** t **~es** ɪz əz **~ing** ɪŋ
whitewater, W~ 'waɪt ˌwɔːt ə 'hwaɪt- ‖ -ˌwɔːṭ ᵊr -ˌwɑːṭ-
whitewood 'waɪt wʊd 'hwaɪt-
whitey 'waɪt i 'hwaɪt- ‖ 'waɪṭ i 'hwaɪṭ i **~s** z
Whitfield 'wɪt fiːᵊld 'hwɪt-
Whitgift 'wɪt gɪft 'hwɪt-
whither 'wɪð ə 'hwɪð- ‖ -ᵊr
whithersoever ˌwɪð ə səʊ 'ev ə ˌhwɪð- ‖ -ᵊr soʊ 'ev ᵊr
Whithorn 'wɪt hɔːn 'hwɪt-
whiting, W~ 'waɪt ɪŋ 'hwaɪt- ‖ 'waɪṭ ɪŋ 'hwaɪṭ- **~s** z
whitish 'waɪt ɪʃ 'hwaɪt- ‖ 'waɪṭ ɪʃ 'hwaɪṭ- **~ness** nəs nɪs
Whitlam 'wɪt ləm 'hwɪt-
Whitley 'wɪt li 'hwɪt-
Whitlock 'wɪt lɒk 'hwɪt- ‖ -lɑːk
whitlow 'wɪt ləʊ 'hwɪt- ‖ -loʊ **~s** z
Whitman 'wɪt mən 'hwɪt-
Whitmore 'wɪt mɔː 'hwɪt- ‖ -mɔːr
Whitney 'wɪt ni 'hwɪt-
Whitstable 'wɪt stəb ᵊl 'hwɪt-
Whitsun 'wɪt sᵊn 'hwɪt- **~s** z
Whitsuntide 'wɪt sᵊn taɪd 'hwɪt- **~s** z
Whittaker 'wɪt ək ə 'hwɪt-, -ɪk- ‖ 'wɪṭ ək ᵊr 'hwɪṭ-
Whittall 'wɪt ᵊl 'hwɪt-, -ɔːl ‖ 'wɪṭ ᵊl 'hwɪṭ-
Whittier 'wɪt i ə 'hwɪt- ‖ 'wɪṭ i ᵊr 'hwɪṭ-
Whittington 'wɪt ɪŋ tən 'hwɪt- ‖ 'wɪṭ- 'hwɪṭ-
whittl|e, W~ 'wɪt ᵊl 'hwɪt- ‖ 'wɪṭ ᵊl 'hwɪṭ- **~ed** d **~es** z **~ing** ˌɪŋ
Whittle-le-Woods ˌwɪt ᵊl lə 'wʊdz ˌhwɪt-, -li'. ‖ ˌwɪṭ- ˌhwɪṭ-
Whittlesford 'wɪt ᵊlz fəd 'hwɪt- ‖ 'wɪṭ ᵊlz fᵊrd 'hwɪṭ-
Whitton 'wɪt ᵊn 'hwɪt-
Whitty 'wɪt i 'hwɪt i ‖ 'wɪṭ i 'hwɪṭ i
Whitworth 'wɪt wɜːθ 'hwɪt-, -wəθ ‖ -wɜːθ
whit|y 'waɪt |i 'hwaɪt- ‖ waɪṭ |i 'hwaɪṭ |i **~ies** iz
whiz, whizz wɪz hwɪz **whizzed** wɪzd hwɪzd **whizzes** 'wɪz ɪz 'hwɪz-, -əz **whizzing** 'wɪz ɪŋ 'hwɪz-
'whiz kid, 'whizz kid
whizbang, whizzbang 'wɪz bæŋ 'hwɪz- **~s** z

who *strong form* **huː**, *occasional weak forms* **hu, u** *—The weak forms are used, if at all, only for the relative (not the interrogative).*
Who *name of pop group* **huː**
whoa wəʊ hwəʊ, həʊ ‖ woʊ hwoʊ, hoʊ
Whoberley 'wəʊb ə li ‖ 'woʊb ᵊr-
who'd *strong form* **huːd**, *occasional weak forms* **hud, ud** *—The weak forms are used, if at all, only for the relative (not the interrogative).*
whodunit, whodunnit ˌhuː 'dʌn ɪt §-ət **~s** s
whoe'er hu 'eə ‖ -'eᵊr
whoever hu 'ev ə ‖ -ᵊr *—also* u- *when not clause-initial* **~'s** z
whole həʊl →hɒʊl, §huːl ‖ **hoʊl** *(= hole)*
wholes həʊlz →hɒʊlz, §huːlz ‖ **hoʊlz**
'whole note; ˌ**whole 'number** ‖ 'ˌ·
wholefood 'həʊl fuːd →'hɒʊl-, §'huːl- ‖ 'hoʊl- **~s** z
wholegrain 'həʊl greɪn →'hɒʊl-, §'huːl- ‖ 'hoʊl-
whole-hearted ˌhəʊl 'hɑːt ɪd ◂ →ˌhɒʊl-, §ˌhuːl-, -əd ‖ ˌhoʊl 'hɑːrṭ əd ◂ **~ly** li **~ness** nəs nɪs
wholemeal 'həʊl miːᵊl →'hɒʊl-, §'huːl- ‖ 'hoʊl-
wholeness 'həʊl nəs →'hɒʊl, §'huːl-, -nɪs ‖ 'hoʊl-
wholesale 'həʊl seɪᵊl →'hɒʊl-, §'huːl- ‖ 'hoʊl-
wholesaler 'həʊl seɪᵊl ə →'hɒʊl-, §'huːl- ‖ 'hoʊl seɪᵊl ᵊr **~s** z
wholesome 'həʊl səm →'hɒʊl-, §'huːl- ‖ 'hoʊl- **~ly** li **~ness** nəs nɪs
wholewheat 'həʊl wiːt →'hɒʊl-, §'huːl-, -hwiːt ‖ 'hoʊl ***hwiːt***
wholistic həʊ 'lɪst ɪk ‖ hoʊ- **~ally** ᵊl ˌi
who'll *strong form* **huːl**, *occasional weak forms* **hul, ul** *—The weak forms are used, if at all, only for the relative (not the interrogative).*
wholly 'həʊl li →'hɒʊl-; 'həʊl i, §'huːl- ‖ 'hoʊl li -i
whom *strong form* **huːm**, *occasional weak forms* **hum, um** *—The weak forms are used, if at all, only for the relative (not the interrogative).*
whomever huːm 'ev ə ‖ -ᵊr
whomp **wɒmp** hwɒmp ‖ **wɑːmp** hwɑːmp, wɔːmp, hwɔːmp **whomped** **wɒmpt** hwɒmpt ‖ **wɑːmpt** hwɑːmpt, hwɔːmpt wɔːmpt **whomping** 'wɒmp ɪŋ 'hwɒmp- ‖ 'wɑːmp- 'hwɑːmp-, 'wɔːmp-, 'hwɔːmp- **whomps** **wɒmps** hwɒmps ‖ **wɑːmps** hwɑːmps, wɔːmps, hwɔːmps
whomsoever ˌhuːm səʊ 'ev ə ‖ -soʊ 'ev ᵊr
whoop **wuːp** huːp, wʊp ‖ **huːp** hʊp, wʊp, wuːp, hwʊp, hwuːp **whooped** **wuːpt** huːpt, wʊpt ‖ **huːpt** hʊpt, wʊpt, wuːpt, hwʊpt, hwuːpt **whooping** 'wuːp ɪŋ 'huːp-, 'wʊp- ‖ 'huːp ɪŋ 'hʊp-, 'wʊp-, 'wuːp-, 'hwʊp-, 'hwuːp- **whoops** **wuːps** huːps, wʊps ‖ **huːps** hʊps, wʊps, wuːps, hwʊps, hwuːps
whoop-de-do ˌwuːp di 'duː ˌhwuːp- ‖ ˌwuːp- ˌhwuːp- **~s** z
whoopee *interj* wʊ 'piː hʊ-, ˌwuː- ‖ 'wʊp i 'hwʊp i; wʊ 'piː, hwʊ-, wuː-, hwuː-

whoopee *n,* **Whoopi** ˈwʊp iː ˈwuːp-, -i ‖ ˈwʊp i ˈhwʊp-, ˈwuːp-, ˈhwuːp-
whooping cough ˈhuːp ɪŋ kɒf §ˈwuːp-, -kɔːf ‖ ˈhuːp ɪŋ kɔːf ˈhʊp-, -kɑːf
whoops wʊps wuːps, hwʊps, hwuːps
whoops-a-daisy ˌwʊps ə ˈdeɪz i ˌhwʊps-; ˈ· ·ˌ·· ‖ ˌhwʊps-, ˌwuːps-, ˌhwuːps-
whoosh wʊʃ wuːʃ, hwʊʃ, hwuːʃ ‖ wuːʃ hwuːʃ, wʊʃ, hwʊʃ
whop wɒp hwɒp ‖ wɑːp hwɑːp **whopped** wɒpt hwɒpt ‖ wɑːpt hwɑːpt **whopping** ˈwɒp ɪŋ ˈhwɒp- ‖ ˈwɑːp- ˈhwɑːp- **whops** wɒps hwɒps ‖ wɑːps hwɑːps
whopper ˈwɒp ə ˈhwɒp- ‖ ˈwɑːp ᵊr ˈhwɑːp- **~s** z
whopping ˈwɒp ɪŋ ˈhwɒp- ‖ ˈ*h*wɑːp ɪŋ
whore hɔː ‖ hɔːr hoʊr, hʊᵊr *(= hoar)* **whored** hɔːd ‖ hɔːrd hoʊrd, hʊᵊrd *(= hoard)* **whores** hɔːz ‖ hɔːrz hoʊrz, hʊᵊrz **whoring** ˈhɔːr ɪŋ ‖ ˈhoʊr-, ˈhʊr-
who're ˈhuːˌə ‖ ᵊr
whoredom ˈhɔː dəm ‖ ˈhɔːr- ˈhoʊr-, ˈhʊr-
whore|house ˈhɔː |haʊs ‖ ˈhɔːr- ˈhoʊr-, ˈhʊr- **~houses** haʊz ɪz -əz
whoremaster ˈhɔː ˌmɑːst ə §-ˌmæst- ‖ ˈhɔːr ˌmæst ᵊr ˈhoʊr-, ˈhʊr- **~s** z
whoremonger ˈhɔː ˌmʌŋ ɡə §-ˌmɒŋ- ‖ ˈhɔːr ˌmʌŋ ɡᵊr ˈhoʊr-, ˈhʊr-, -ˌmɑːŋ- **~s** z
whoreson ˈhɔː sᵊn ‖ ˈhɔːr- ˈhoʊr-, ˈhʊr- **~s** z
Whorf wɔːf hwɔːf ‖ wɔːrf hwɔːrf
whorish ˈhɔːr ɪʃ ‖ ˈhoʊr-, ˈhʊr- **~ly** li **~ness** nəs nɪs
whorl wɜːl hwɜːl, wɔːl, hwɔːl ‖ wɜᵊl hwɜːl, wɔːrl, hwɔːl **whorled** wɜːld hwɜːld, wɔːld, hwɔːld ‖ wɜːld hwɜːld, wɔːrld, hwɔːrld **whorls** wɜːlz hwɜːlz, §wɔːlz, §hwɔːlz ‖ wɜᵊlz hwɜᵊlz, wɔːrlz, hwɔːrlz
whortleberr|y ˈwɜːt ᵊl ˌber |i ˈhwɜːt-, -bərˌi ‖ ˈwɜːṭ ᵊl ˌber |i ˈhwɜːṭ- **~ies** iz
who's *strong form* huːz, *occasional weak forms* huz, uz —*The weak forms are used, if at all, only for the relative (not the interrogative).*
whose *strong form* huːz, *occasional weak forms* huz, uz —*The weak forms are used, if at all, only for the relative (not the interrogative).*
whoso ˈhuː səʊ ‖ -soʊ
whosoever ˌhuː səʊ ˈev ə ◂ ‖ -soʊ ˈev ᵊr ◂
who've *strong form* huːv, *occasional weak forms* huv, uv —*The weak forms are used, if at all, only for the relative (not the interrogative).*
whump wʌmp hwʌmp **whumped** wʌm*p*t hwʌm*p*t **whumping** ˈwʌmp ɪŋ ˈhwʌmp- **whumps** wʌm*p*s hwʌm*p*s
whup wʌp hwʌp **whupped** wʌpt hwʌpt **whupping** ˈwʌp ɪŋ ˈhwʌp- **whups** wʌps hwʌps
why waɪ hwaɪ **whys** waɪz hwaɪz
Whyalla waɪ ˈæl ə hwaɪ-
Whyatt ˈwaɪˌət ˈhwaɪˌ
why'd waɪd waɪd
whydah, W~ ˈwɪd ə ˈhwɪd ə **~s** z
why'll ˈwaɪˌəl ˈhwaɪˌ
why're ˈwaɪˌə ˈhwaɪˌə ‖ ˈwaɪˌᵊr ˈhwaɪˌᵊr
why's waɪz hwaɪz
Whyte waɪt hwaɪt
Whyteleaf ˈwaɪt liːf ˈhwaɪt-
Whythorne ˈwaɪt hɔːn ˈhwaɪt- ‖ -hɔːrn
why've waɪv hwaɪv
Wibberley ˈwɪb ə li ‖ -ᵊr-
wibbly ˈwɪb ᵊl ˌi
Wibsey ˈwɪb si -zi —*The place in WYks is locally also* →ˈwɪp si
Wicca, wicca ˈwɪk ə
Wichita ˈwɪtʃ ɪ tɔː -ə- ‖ -tɑː
Wichnor ˈwɪtʃ nɔː -nə ‖ -nɔːr
wick, Wick wɪk **wicks** wɪks
wicked ˈwɪk ɪd §-əd **~er** ə ‖ ᵊr **~est** ɪst əst **~ly** li **~ness** nəs nɪs
Wicken ˈwɪk ən -ɪn **~s** z
wicker, W~ ˈwɪk ə ‖ -ᵊr
wickerwork ˈwɪk ə wɜːk ‖ -ᵊr wɜːk
wicket ˈwɪk ɪt §-ət **~s** s
ˈwicket gate; **ˈwicket ˌkeeper**
Wickham ˈwɪk əm
Wickins ˈwɪk ɪnz §-ənz
wickiup ˈwɪk i ʌp **~s** s
Wicklow ˈwɪk ləʊ ‖ -loʊ
Wicks wɪks
Widdecombe, Widdicombe ˈwɪd ɪ kəm -ə-
widdershins ˈwɪd ə ʃɪnz ‖ -ᵊr-
widdl|e ˈwɪd ᵊl **~ed** d **~es** z **~ing** ˌɪŋ
Widdowes, Widdows ˈwɪd əʊz ‖ -oʊz
Widdowson ˈwɪd əʊ sᵊn ‖ -oʊ-
wide waɪd **wider** ˈwaɪd ə ‖ -ᵊr **wides** waɪdz **widest** ˈwaɪd ɪst -əst
ˈwide boy
wide-angle ˌwaɪd ˈæŋ ɡᵊl ◂
wide-awake *adj* ˌwaɪd ə ˈweɪk ◂
wide-awake *n* ˈwaɪd əˌweɪk **~s** s
wide-bod|y ˈwaɪd ˌbɒd |i ˈwaɪb- ‖ -ˌbɑːd- **~ied** id **~ies** iz
Widecombe ˈwɪd ɪ kəm -ə-
wide-eyed ˌwaɪd ˈaɪd ◂
Wideford ˈwaɪd fəd ‖ -fᵊrd
widely ˈwaɪd li
Widemouth ˈwɪd məθ →ˈwɪb-
widen ˈwaɪd ᵊn **~ed** d **~ing** ˌɪŋ **~s** z
wideness ˈwaɪd nəs -nɪs
wide-open ˌwaɪd ˈəʊp ən ◂ ‖ -ˈoʊp-
Wideopen ˈwaɪd ˌəʊp ən ‖ -ˌoʊp-
wide-ranging ˌwaɪd ˈreɪndʒ ɪŋ ◂
wide-scale ˌwaɪd ˈskeɪᵊl ◂
wide-screen ˌwaɪd ˈskriːn ◂ ˈ··
widespread ˈwaɪd spred ˌ·ˈ·
widgeon ˈwɪdʒ ən -ɪn **~s** z
Widgery ˈwɪdʒ ər i
widget ˈwɪdʒ ɪt §-ət **~s** s
widish ˈwaɪd ɪʃ
Widlake ˈwɪd leɪk
Widmark ˈwɪd mɑːk →ˈwɪb- ‖ -mɑːrk
Widmerpool ˈwɪd mə puːl ‖ -mᵊr-
Widnes ˈwɪd nɪs -nəs
widow ˈwɪd əʊ ‖ -oʊ **~ed** d **~ing** ɪŋ **~s** z
widower ˈwɪd əʊ ə ‖ -oʊ ᵊr **~s** z
widowhood ˈwɪd əʊ hʊd ‖ -oʊ-

W

width wɪdθ wɪtθ **widths** wɪdθs wɪtθs
width|ways 'wɪdθ |weɪz 'wɪtθ- **~wise** waɪz
wield wiːəld **wielded** 'wiːəld ɪd -əd **wielding** 'wiːəld ɪŋ **wields** wiːəldz
wielder 'wiːəld ə ‖ -ər **~s** z
wiener, W~ 'wiːn ə ‖ -ər -i —*but as a German name,* 'viːn- —*Ger* W~ ['viː nɐ] **~s** z
Wiener schnitzel ˌviːn ə 'ʃnɪts əl ⚠-'snɪtʃ- ‖ 'viːn ər ˌ· · 'wiːn-, -ˌsnɪts- **~s** z
wienie 'wiːn i **~s** z
Wiesbaden 'viːs ˌbɑːd ən 'viːz- —*Ger* ['viːs baː dən]
Wiesenthal 'wiːz ən tɑːl 'viːz-, -θɔːl —*Ger* ['viː zn̩ taːl]
wife waɪf **wife's** waɪfs **wives** waɪvz **'wife ˌswapping**
wife|hood 'waɪf hʊd **~less** ləs -lɪs **~like** laɪk **~ly** li
Wiffle *tdmk* 'wɪf əl **'Wiffle ball**
Wi-Fi *tdmk* 'waɪ faɪ
wig wɪg **wigged** wɪgd **wigging/s** 'wɪg ɪŋ/z **wigs** wɪgz
Wigan 'wɪg ən §-ɪn
wigeon 'wɪdʒ ən -ɪn **~s** z
Wigg wɪg
wigg... —*see* **wig**
Wiggin 'wɪg ɪn §-ən
Wiggins 'wɪg ɪnz §-ənz
wiggl|e 'wɪg əl **~ed** d **~es** z **~ing** ˌɪŋ
Wigglesworth 'wɪg əlz wɜːθ -wəθ ‖ -wɜːθ
wiggly 'wɪg əl̩ i
Wight, wight waɪt
Wightman 'waɪt mən
Wightwick 'wɪt ɪk ‖ 'wɪţ-
Wigley 'wɪg li
Wigmore 'wɪg mɔː ‖ -mɔːr
Wigoder 'wɪg əd ə ‖ -ər
Wigram 'wɪg rəm
Wigston 'wɪg stən
Wigton 'wɪg tən
Wigtown 'wɪg taʊn -tən
wigwag 'wɪg wæg **~ged** d **~ging** ɪŋ **~s** z
wigwam 'wɪg wæm ‖ -wɑːm **~s** z
Wii *tdmk* wiː
Wii *tdmk* wiː
Wike waɪk
wiki 'wɪk i **~s** z
Wikipedia ˌwɪk i 'piːd iˌə
Wilberforce 'wɪlb ə fɔːs ‖ -ər fɔːrs -foʊrs
Wilbert 'wɪlb ət ‖ -ərt
Wilbraham 'wɪlb rə həm -hæm; 'wɪlb rəm
Wilbur 'wɪlb ə ‖ -ər
Wilby, Wilbye 'wɪl bi
wilco 'wɪl kəʊ ˌ·'· ‖ -koʊ
Wilcock 'wɪl kɒk ‖ -kɑːk
Wilcocks, Wilcox 'wɪl kɒks ‖ -kɑːks
Wilcoxon wɪl 'kɒks ən ‖ -'kɑːks-
wild, Wild waɪəld **wilder** 'waɪəld ə ‖ -ər **wildest** 'waɪəld ɪst -əst **wilds** waɪəldz **ˌwild boar**; **'wild ˌflower**; **ˌwild 'oats**; **ˌwild 'rice**; **ˌWild 'West**
Wildblood 'waɪə*l*d blʌd
wild|cat 'waɪə*l*d |kæt **~cats** kæts **~catted** kæt ɪd -əd ‖ kæţ əd **~catting** kæt ɪŋ ‖ kæţ ɪŋ **ˌwildcat 'strike**
wildcatter 'waɪə*l*d kæt ə ‖ -kæţ ər **~s** z
Wilde waɪəld
Wildean 'waɪəld iˌən
wildebeest 'wɪld ə biːst 'wɪld-, -ɪ-, -bɪəst **~s** s
Wildenstein 'wɪld ən staɪn —*Ger* ['vɪl dən ʃtain]
Wilder 'waɪəld ə ‖ -ər
wilderness, W~ 'wɪld ə nəs -nɪs ‖ -ər- **~es** ɪz əz
wild-eyed ˌwaɪəld 'aɪd ◂ '·
Wildfell 'waɪl*d* fel
wildfire 'waɪə*l*d ˌfaɪˌə ‖ -ˌfaɪˌər
wildfowl 'waɪə*l*d faʊl **~ed** d **~er/s** ə/z ‖ ər/z **~ing** ɪŋ **~s** z
wild-goose chase ˌwaɪə*l*d 'guːs tʃeɪs
Wilding, w~ 'waɪəld ɪŋ **~s** z
wildland 'waɪə*l*d lænd **~s** z
wildlife 'waɪə*l*d laɪf
wild|ly 'waɪə*l*d |li **~ness** nəs nɪs
wildwood 'waɪəld wʊd **~s** z
wile waɪəl **wiled** waɪəld *(= wild)* **wiles** waɪəlz **wiling** 'waɪəl ɪŋ
Wiley 'waɪl i
Wilf wɪlf
Wilford 'wɪl fəd ‖ -fərd
Wilfred, Wilfrid 'wɪlf rɪd §-rəd
wilful 'wɪl fəl -fʊl **~ly** ˌi **~ness** nəs nɪs
Wilhelmina ˌwɪl hel 'miːn ə -ə-
wili... —*see* **wily**
wiliness 'waɪl i nəs -nɪs
Wilkes wɪlks
Wilkes-Barre *place in PA* 'wɪlks ˌbær i -ˌber-, -ə
Wilkie 'wɪlk i
Wilkins 'wɪlk ɪnz §-ənz
Wilkinson 'wɪlk ɪn*t*s ən §-ən-
Wilks wɪlks
will *modal v: strong form* wɪl, *occasional weak forms* wəl, əl —*see also* **'ll**
will *v 'wish, intend', 'bequeath'; n* wɪl **willed** wɪld **willing** 'wɪl ɪŋ **wills** wɪlz
Will wɪl
Willa 'wɪl ə
Willamette wɪ 'læm ɪt wə-, §-ət
Willandra wɪ 'lændr ə
Willard 'wɪl ɑːd ‖ -ərd
Willcock 'wɪl kɒk ‖ -kɑːk
Willcocks, Willcox 'wɪl kɒks ‖ -kɑːks
-willed 'wɪld — **strong-willed** ˌstrɒŋ 'wɪld ◂ ‖ ˌstrɔːŋ- ˌstrɑːŋ-
Willenhall 'wɪl ən hɔːl ‖ -hɑːl
Willesden 'wɪlz dən
willet 'wɪl ɪt -ət **~s** s
Willey 'wɪl i
willful 'wɪl fəl -fʊl **~ly** ˌi **~ness** nəs nɪs
William 'wɪl jəm
Williams 'wɪl jəmz
Williamsburg 'wɪl jəmz bɜːg ‖ -bɜːg
Williamson 'wɪl jəm sən
Williamsport 'wɪl jəmz pɔːt ‖ -pɔːrt -poʊrt

Willie, W~ ˈwɪl i **~s** z

willing ˈwɪl ɪŋ **~ly** li **~ness** nəs nɪs

Willis ˈwɪl ɪs §-əs

williwaw ˈwɪl i wɔː ‖ -wɑː **~s** z

Willmott ˈwɪl mət -mɒt

Willock ˈwɪl ək

will-o'-the-wisp ˌwɪl ə ðə ˈwɪsp **~s** s

Willoughby ˈwɪl ə bi

willow ˈwɪl əʊ ‖ -oʊ **~s** z **ˈwillow ˌpattern**

willowherb ˈwɪl əʊ hɜːb ‖ -oʊ ɜ˞ːb **~s** z

willowy ˈwɪl əʊ i ‖ -oʊ-

willpower ˈwɪl ˌpaʊ‿ə ‖ -ˌpaʊ‿ᵊr

Wills wɪlz

Willy, will|y ˈwɪl |i **~ies** iz

willy-nilly ˌwɪl i ˈnɪl i

Wilma ˈwɪlm ə

Wilmcote ˈwɪlm kəʊt ‖ -koʊt

Wilmer ˈwɪlm ə ‖ -ᵊr

Wilmette wɪl ˈmet

Wilmington ˈwɪlm ɪŋ tən

Wilmot, Wilmott ˈwɪl mət -mɒt

Wilmslow ˈwɪlmz ləʊ ‖ -loʊ

Wilsher ˈwɪl ʃə ‖ -ʃᵊr

Wilson ˈwɪls ᵊn

Wilsonian wɪl ˈsəʊn i‿ən ‖ -ˈsoʊn-

wilt *'wither, droop'* wɪlt **wilted** ˈwɪlt ɪd -əd **wilting** ˈwɪlt ɪŋ **wilts** wɪlts

wilt *archaic and liturgical second person sing. form of will: strong form* wɪlt, *weak form* wəlt

Wilton ˈwɪlt ən **~s** z

Wilts wɪlts

Wiltshire ˈwɪlt ʃə -ʃɪə ‖ -ʃᵊr -ʃɪr

wil|y ˈwaɪl |i **~ier** i‿ə ‖ i‿ᵊr **~iest** i‿ɪst i‿əst

wimble ˈwɪm bᵊl **~s** z

Wimbledon ˈwɪm bᵊl dən

Wimborne, Wimbourne ˈwɪm bɔːn ‖ -bɔːrn -boʊrn

Wimbush ˈwɪm bʊʃ

wimin, wimmin ˈwɪm ɪn §-ən

Wimmera ˈwɪm ər ə

Wimoweh ˈwɪm ə weɪ

wimp wɪmp **wimps** wɪmps

Wimpey ˈwɪmp i

wimpish ˈwɪmp ɪʃ **~ly** li **~ness** nəs nɪs

wimple, W~ ˈwɪmp ᵊl **~s** z

Wimpole ˈwɪm pəʊl →-pɒʊl ‖ -poʊl

wimpy, Wimpy *tdmk* ˈwɪmp i **ˈWimpy bar**

Wimsey ˈwɪmz i

Wimshurst ˈwɪmz hɜːst ‖ -hɜ˞ːst

win wɪn **winning** ˈwɪn ɪŋ **wins** wɪnz **won** wʌn

Winalot *tdmk* ˈwɪn ə lɒt ‖ -lɑːt

Wincanton wɪn ˈkænt ən →wɪŋ- ‖ -ᵊn

Wincarnis *tdmk* wɪn ˈkɑːn ɪs →wɪŋ-, §-əs ‖ -ˈkɑːrn-

wince wɪnᵗs **winced** wɪnᵗst **winces** ˈwɪnᵗs ɪz -əz **wincing/ly** ˈwɪnᵗs ɪŋ /li

wincey ˈwɪnᵗs i **~s** z

winceyette ˌwɪnᵗs i ˈet

winch, Winch wɪntʃ **winched** wɪntʃt **winches** ˈwɪntʃ ɪz -əz **winching** ˈwɪntʃ ɪŋ

Winchelsea ˈwɪntʃ ᵊl siː

Winchester, w~ ˈwɪntʃ ɪst ə -əst-, §ˈwɪn ˌtʃest ə ‖ ˈwɪn ˌtʃest ᵊr **~s** z

Winchmore ˈwɪntʃ mɔː ‖ -mɔːr

wind *n 'breeze, moving air'* wɪnd **winds** wɪndz **ˈwind ˌinstrument**; **ˈwind gauge**; **ˈwind ˌtunnel**; **ˈwind ˌturbine**

wind *n 'bend'* waɪnd **winds** waɪndz

wind *v 'make breathless', 'give respite to', 'smell'* wɪnd **winded** ˈwɪnd ɪd -əd **winding** ˈwɪnd ɪŋ **winds** wɪndz

wind *v 'turn'; 'blow on horn'* waɪnd **winded** ˈwaɪnd ɪd -əd **winding/s** ˈwaɪnd ɪŋ/z **winds** waɪndz **wound** waʊnd

windag|e ˈwɪnd ɪdʒ **~es** ɪz əz

windbag ˈwɪn*d* bæg →ˈwɪm*b*- **~s** z

windblown ˈwɪn*d* bləʊn →ˈwɪm*b*- ‖ -bloʊn

wind-borne ˈwɪn*d* bɔːn →ˈwɪm*b*- ‖ -bɔːrn -boʊrn

windbreak ˈwɪn*d* breɪk →ˈwɪm*b*- **~s** s

windbreaker, W~ *tdmk* ˈwɪn*d* ˌbreɪk ə →ˈwɪm*b*- ‖ -ᵊr **~s** z

windburn ˈwɪn*d* bɜːn →ˈwɪm*b*- ‖ -bɜ˞ːn

windcheater ˈwɪn*d* ˌtʃiːt ə ‖ -ˌtʃiːt̬ ᵊr **~s** z

wind-chill ˈwɪn*d* tʃɪl

winder ˈwaɪnd ə ‖ -ᵊr **~s** z

Windermere ˈwɪnd ə mɪə ‖ -ᵊr mɪr

Windeyer ˈwɪnd i‿ə ‖ -‿ᵊr

windfall ˈwɪn*d* fɔːl ‖ -fɑːl **~s** z

windflower ˈwɪn*d* ˌflaʊ‿ə ‖ -ˌflaʊ‿ᵊr **~s** z

Windhoek ˈwɪnd hʊk ˈvɪnd-, ˈwɪnt-, ˈvɪnt-

windhover ˈwɪnd ˌhɒv ə -ˌhʌv- ‖ -ˌhʌv ᵊr -ˌhɑːv- **~s** z

windi... —*see* **windy**

Windies ˈwɪnd iz

winding *adj, n* ˈwaɪnd ɪŋ **~ly** li **~s** z **ˈwinding sheet**

winding-up ˌwaɪnd ɪŋ ˈʌp

windjammer ˈwɪn*d* ˌdʒæm ə ‖ -ᵊr **~s** z

windlass ˈwɪnd ləs **~es** ɪz əz

Windlesham ˈwɪnd ᵊl ʃəm

windless ˈwɪn*d* ləs -lɪs

windmill ˈwɪn*d* mɪl →ˈwɪm*b*- **~ed** d **~ing** ɪŋ **~s** z

Windolene *tdmk* ˈwɪnd əʊ liːn ‖ -oʊ-

window ˈwɪnd əʊ ‖ -oʊ **~ed** d **~ing** ɪŋ **~s** z **ˈwindow box**; **ˈwindow ˌdressing**; **ˈwindow seat**; **ˈwindow shade**

windowless ˈwɪnd əʊ ləs -lɪs ‖ -oʊ-

windowpane ˈwɪnd əʊ peɪn ‖ -oʊ- -ə- **~s** z

Windows *tdmk* ˈwɪnd əʊz ‖ -oʊz **ˌWindows ˌ9ˈ7**

window-shop ˈwɪnd əʊ ʃɒp ‖ -oʊ ʃɑːp -ə- **~ped** t **~ping** ɪŋ **~s** s

windowsill ˈwɪnd əʊ sɪl ‖ -oʊ- -ə- **~s** z

windpipe ˈwɪn*d* paɪp →ˈwɪm*b*- **~s** s

windproof ˈwɪn*d* pruːf §-prʊf

windrow ˈwɪnd rəʊ ‖ -roʊ **~s** z

Windrush ˈwɪnd rʌʃ

Windscale ˈwɪn*d* skeɪᵊl

windscreen ˈwɪnd skriːn **~s** z
ˈwindscreen ˌwiper
windshear ˈwɪnd ʃɪə ‖ -ʃɪr
windshield ˈwɪnd ʃiːəld **~s** z
ˈwindshield ˌwiper
windsock ˈwɪnd sɒk ‖ -sɑːk **~s** s
Windsor ˈwɪnz ə ˈwɪndz- ‖ -ər
ˌWindsor ˈCastle
windstorm ˈwɪnd stɔːm ‖ -ˌstɔːrm **~s** z
windsurf ˈwɪnd sɜːf ‖ -sɜːf **~ed** t **~er/s** ə/z ‖ ər/z **~ing** ɪŋ **~s** s
windswept ˈwɪnd swept
wind-up ˈwaɪnd ʌp **~s** s
Windus ˈwɪnd əs
windward, W~ ˈwɪnd wəd §ˈwɪn- ‖ -wərd **~s** z
wind-whipped ˈwɪnd wɪpt -hwɪpt ‖ -hwɪpt
wind|y ˈwɪnd |i **~ier** i‿ə ‖ i‿ər **~iest** i‿ɪst i‿əst **~ily** ɪ li əl i **~iness** i nəs i nɪs
wine waɪn **wined** waɪnd **wines** waɪnz **wining** ˈwaɪn ɪŋ
ˈwine bar; **ˈwine ˌbottle**
winebibber ˈwaɪn ˌbɪb ə →ˈwaɪm- ‖ -ər **~s** z
winebibbing ˈwaɪn ˌbɪb ɪŋ →ˈwaɪm- **~s** z
wineglass ˈwaɪn glɑːs →ˈwaɪŋ-, §-glæs ‖ -glæs **~es** ɪz əz
winegrow|er ˈwaɪn ˌgrəʊ| ə →ˈwaɪŋ- ‖ -ˌgroʊ| ər **~ers** əz ‖ ərz **~ing** ɪŋ
Winehouse ˈwaɪn haʊs
winemak|er ˈwaɪn ˌmeɪk| ə →ˈwaɪm- ‖ -ər **~ers** əz ‖ ərz **~ing** ɪŋ
winepress ˈwaɪn pres →ˈwaɪm- **~es** ɪz əz
winer|y ˈwaɪn ər |i **~ies** iz
wineskin ˈwaɪn skɪn **~s** z
Winfield ˈwɪn fiːəld
Winford ˈwɪn fəd ‖ -fərd
Winfred ˈwɪn frɪd §-frəd
Winfrey ˈwɪn fri
Winfrith ˈwɪn frɪθ §-frəθ
wing, Wing wɪŋ **winged** wɪŋd **winging** ˈwɪŋ ɪŋ **wings** wɪŋz
ˈwing comˌmander; **ˈwing nut**
Wingate ˈwɪn geɪt →ˈwɪŋ-, -gɪt, -gət
wingding ˈwɪŋ dɪŋ **~s** z
winge *'complain'* —*see* **whinge**
winged *adj 'having wings'; pp of* **wing** wɪŋd —*but formerly, and sometimes in verse still, also* ˈwɪŋ ɪd, -əd
winger ˈwɪŋ ə ‖ -ər **~s** z
-winger wɪŋ ə ‖ -ər — **left-winger** ˌleft ˈwɪŋ ə ‖ -ər
Wingfield ˈwɪŋ fiːəld
wingless ˈwɪŋ ləs -lɪs **~ness** nəs nɪs
winglet ˈwɪŋ lət -lɪt **~s** s
wingspan ˈwɪŋ spæn **~s** z
wingspread ˈwɪŋ spred **~s** z
wingtip ˈwɪŋ tɪp **~s** s
Winifred ˈwɪn ɪf rɪd -əf-, §-rəd
wink wɪŋk **winked** wɪŋkt **winking** ˈwɪŋk ɪŋ **winks** wɪŋks
winker ˈwɪŋk ə ‖ -ər **~s** z
winkl|e ˈwɪŋk əl **~ed** d **~es** z **~ing** ɪŋ
winkle-picker ˈwɪŋk əl ˌpɪk ə ‖ -ər **~s** z
winless ˈwɪn ləs -lɪs

Winn wɪn
Winnebago ˌwɪn ɪ ˈbeɪg əʊ -ə- ‖ -oʊ **~s** z
winner, W~ ˈwɪn ə ‖ -ər **~s** z
Winnie ˈwɪn i
Winnie-the-Pooh ˌwɪn i ðə ˈpuː
winning ˈwɪn ɪŋ **~est** ɪst əst **~ly** li **~ness** nəs nɪs **~s** z
ˈwinning post
Winnipeg ˈwɪn ɪ peg §-ə-
Winnipegosis ˌwɪn ɪ pɪ ˈgəʊs ɪs -§ˌə-, -pəˈ--, §-əs ‖ -ˈgoʊs əs
Winnipesaukee ˌwɪn ɪp ə ˈsɔːk i ˌ·əp- ‖ -ˈsɑːk-
winnow ˈwɪn əʊ ‖ -oʊ **~ed** d **~er/s** ə/z ‖ ər/z **~ing** ɪŋ **~s** z
wino ˈwaɪn əʊ ‖ -oʊ **~s** z
Winona wɪ ˈnəʊn ə wə- ‖ -ˈnoʊn ə
Winsford ˈwɪnz fəd ˈwɪnᵗs- ‖ -fərd
Winslade ˈwɪn sleɪd
Winslet ˈwɪnz lɪt -lət
Winslow ˈwɪnz ləʊ ‖ -loʊ
winsome, W~ ˈwɪnᵗs əm **~ly** li **~ness** nəs nɪs
Winstanley *(i)* ˈwɪnᵗst ən li, *(ii)* wɪn ˈstæn li —*The place in Greater Manchester is (i); the family name is usually (ii)*
Winston ˈwɪnᵗst ən
Winston-Salem ˌwɪnᵗst ən ˈseɪl əm
winter, W~ ˈwɪnt ə ‖ ˈwɪnṭ ər **~ed** d **wintering** ˈwɪnt‿ər ɪŋ ‖ ˈwɪnṭ ərɪŋ →ˈwɪntr ɪŋ **~s** z
ˌwinter ˈsports
Winterbotham, Winterbottom ˈwɪnt ə ˌbɒt əm ‖ ˈwɪnṭ ər ˌbɑːṭ əm
Winterbourn, Winterbourne, w~ ˈwɪnt ə bɔːn ‖ ˈwɪnṭ ər bɔːrn -bourn **~s** z
wintergreen ˈwɪnt ə griːn ‖ ˈwɪnṭ ər- **~s** z
winterization ˌwɪnt ər aɪ ˈzeɪʃ ən -ɪˈ-- ‖ ˌwɪnṭ ər ə-
winteriz|e ˈwɪnt ər aɪz ‖ ˈwɪnṭ ər- **~ed** d **~es** ɪz əz **~ing** ɪŋ
Winters ˈwɪnt əz ‖ ˈwɪnṭ ərz
Winterthur ˈwɪnt ə θɜː ‖ ˈwɪnṭ ər θɜː —*Ger* [ˈvɪn tɐ tuːɐ]
wintertime ˈwɪnt ə taɪm ‖ ˈwɪnṭ ər-
Winterton ˈwɪnt ət ən ‖ ˈwɪnṭ ərt ən
wintery ˈwɪnt ər‿i ‖ ˈwɪnṭ ər i —*see also* **wintry**
Winthrop ˈwɪn θrɒp ˈwɪnᵗθ rəp ‖ ˈwɪnᵗθ rəp
Winton ˈwɪnt ən ‖ -ən
Wintour ˈwɪnt ə ‖ ˈwɪnṭ ər
wintr|y ˈwɪntr |i **~ier** i‿ə ‖ i‿ər **~iest** i‿ɪst i‿əst **~ily** əl i ɪ li **~iness** i nəs i nɪs
Winwick ˈwɪn ɪk
win-win ˌwɪn ˈwɪn
wipe waɪp **wiped** waɪpt **wipes** waɪps **wiping** ˈwaɪp ɪŋ
ˌwiped ˈout
wipeout ˈwaɪp aʊt **~s** s
wiper ˈwaɪp ə ‖ -ər **~s** z
wire ˈwaɪ‿ə ‖ ˈwaɪ‿ər **~d** d **~s** z **wiring** ˈwaɪ‿ər ɪŋ ‖ ˈwaɪ‿ər ɪŋ
ˌwire ˈnetting; **ˌwire ˈwool**
wirecutters ˈwaɪ‿ə ˌkʌt əz ‖ ˈwaɪ‿ər ˌkʌṭ ərz

wire|draw 'waɪ͜ə |drɔː ‖ 'waɪ͜ᵊr- -drɑː **~drawing** drɔːʳ ɪŋ ‖ drɔː ɪŋ drɑː- **~drawn** drɔːn ‖ -drɑːn **~draws** drɔːz ‖ drɑːz **~drew** druː

wire-haired ˌwaɪ͜ə 'heəd ◂ ‖ 'waɪ͜ᵊr herd -hærd

wireless 'waɪ͜ə ləs -lɪs ‖ 'waɪ͜ᵊr- **~ed** d **~es** ɪz əz **~ing** ɪŋ

wirepuller 'waɪ͜ə ˌpʊl ə ‖ 'waɪ͜ᵊr ˌpʊl ᵊr **~s** z

wire-rimmed ˌwaɪ͜ə 'rɪmd ◂ ‖ ˌwaɪ͜ᵊr-

wiretap 'waɪ͜ə tæp ‖ 'waɪ͜ᵊr- **~s** s

wire-tapping 'waɪ͜ə ˌtæp ɪŋ ‖ 'waɪ͜ᵊr-

wireworm 'waɪ͜ə wɜːm ‖ 'waɪ͜ᵊr wɜːm **~s** z

wiri... *—see* **wiry**

wiring 'waɪ͜ər ɪŋ ‖ 'waɪ͜ər ɪŋ **~s** z

Wirksworth 'wɜːks wəθ -wɜːθ ‖ 'wɜːks wɜːθ

Wirral 'wɪr əl ‖ 'wɜː-

wir|y 'waɪ͜ər |i ‖ 'waɪ͜ər |i **~ier** i͜ə ‖ i͜ᵊr **~iest** i͜ɪst i͜əst **~ily** əl i ɪ li **~iness** i nəs i nɪs

Wisbech 'wɪz biːtʃ

Wisconsin wɪ 'skɒnᵗs ɪn §-ən ‖ -'skɑːnᵗs-

Wisconsinite wɪ 'skɒnᵗs ɪ naɪt §-ə- ‖ -'skɑːnᵗs- **~s** s

Wisden 'wɪz dən

wisdom, W~ 'wɪz dəm

'wisdom tooth

-wise waɪz — **timewise** 'taɪm waɪz

wise, Wise waɪz **wised** waɪzd **wiser** 'waɪz ə ‖ ᵊr **wises** 'waɪz ɪz -əz **wisest** 'waɪz ɪst -əst **wising** 'waɪz ɪŋ

'wise guy

wiseacre 'waɪz ˌeɪk ə ‖ -ᵊr **~s** z

wisecrack 'waɪz kræk **~ed** t **~ing** ɪŋ **~s** s

wisely 'waɪz li

Wiseman 'waɪz mən

wisent 'viːz ent 'wiːz-, -ᵊnt **~s** s

wish wɪʃ **wished** wɪʃt **wishes** 'wɪʃ ɪz -əz **wishing** 'wɪʃ ɪŋ

Wishart 'wɪʃ ət ‖ -ᵊrt

Wishaw 'wɪʃ ɔː ‖ -ɑː

wishbone 'wɪʃ bəʊn ‖ -boʊn **~s** z

wishful 'wɪʃ fᵊl -fʊl **~ly** i **~ness** nəs nɪs

ˌwishful 'thinking

wishing-well 'wɪʃ ɪŋ wel **~s** z

wishy-wash|y 'wɪʃ i ˌwɒʃ |i ˌ· ·'· · ‖ -ˌwɑːʃ |i -ˌwɔːʃ- **~iness** i nəs i nɪs

Wisley 'wɪz li

wisp wɪsp **wisps** wɪsps

Wispa *tdmk* 'wɪsp ə

wispy 'wɪsp i

wist wɪst

wistaria, wisteria wɪ 'stɪər i͜ə -'steər- ‖ -'stɪr- **~s** z

wistful 'wɪst fᵊl -fʊl **~ly** i **~ness** nəs nɪs

Wiston 'wɪst ən

Wistow 'wɪst əʊ ‖ -oʊ

Wistrich 'wɪs trɪtʃ

Wisty 'wɪst i

wit wɪt **wits** wɪts

witch wɪtʃ **witched** wɪtʃt **witches** 'wɪtʃ ɪz -əz **witching/ly** 'wɪtʃ ɪŋ /li

'witching ˌhour

witchcraft 'wɪtʃ krɑːft §-kræft ‖ -kræft

witchdoctor 'wɪtʃ ˌdɒkt ə ‖ -ˌdɑːkt ᵊr **~s** z

witcher|y 'wɪtʃ ər |i **~ies** iz

witchetty 'wɪtʃ ət i -ɪt- ‖ -əţ i

witch-hazel 'wɪtʃ ˌheɪz ᵊl **~s** z

witch-hunt 'wɪtʃ hʌnt **~s** s

witenagemot 'wɪt ᵊn͜ə gɪ ˌməʊt -gə,', ˌ· · · ·'. ‖ -gə ˌmoʊt

Wite-out *tdmk* 'waɪt aʊt ‖ 'waɪţ-

WITH

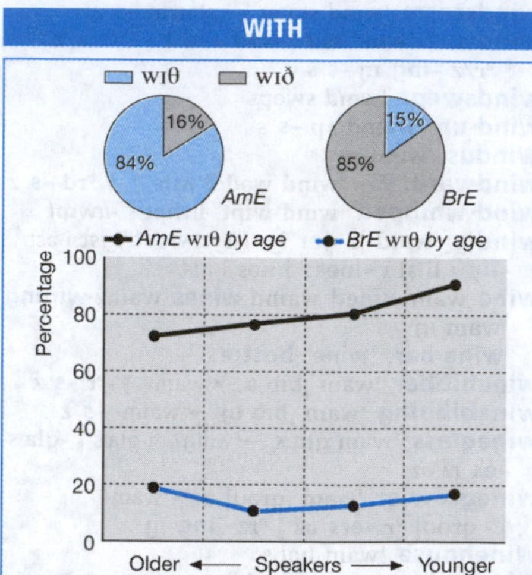

with wɪð §wɪθ ‖ wɪθ wɪð — *Preference polls, AmE:* wɪθ *84%,* wɪð *16%; BrE:* wɪð *85%,* wɪθ *15%. —In Britain,* wɪθ *is nevertheless frequent in Scotland (preferred by 82% of Scottish respondents). —In some varieties, including GenAm but not RP, there may also be a weak form* wəð, wəθ

withal wɪð 'ɔːl §wɪθ- ‖ -'ɑːl

Witham *river* 'wɪð əm

Witham *family name; place in Essex* 'wɪt əm ‖ 'wɪţ-

with|draw wɪð| 'drɔː wɪθ|- ‖-'drɑː **~drawing** 'drɔːʳ ɪŋ ‖ 'drɔː ɪŋ -'drɑː ɪŋ **~drawn** 'drɔːn ‖ 'drɑːn **~draws** 'drɔːz ‖ 'drɑːz **~drew** 'druː

withdrawal wɪð 'drɔːʳəl wɪθ-, -'drɔːl ‖ -'drɔː͜əl -'drɑː͜əl **~s** z

with'drawal ˌsymptoms

withdrawn wɪð 'drɔːn wɪθ- ‖ -'drɑːn

withdrew wɪð 'druː wɪθ-

withe wɪθ waɪð, wɪð **withes** wɪθs waɪðz, wɪðz

wither 'wɪð ə ‖ -ᵊr **~ed** d **withering/ly** 'wɪð ər͜ɪŋ /li **~s** z

Withernsea 'wɪð ᵊn si ‖ -ᵊrn-

Withers, w~ 'wɪð əz ‖ -ᵊrz

Witherspoon 'wɪð ə spuːn ‖ -ᵊr-

with|hold wɪð |'həʊld wɪθ-, →-'hɒʊld ‖ -|'hoʊld **~held** 'held **~holding** 'həʊld ɪŋ -→'hɒʊld- ‖ 'hoʊld ɪŋ **~holds** 'həʊldz →'hɒʊldz ‖ 'hoʊldz

with'holding tax

within wɪð 'ɪn §wɪθ-

Withington 'wɪð ɪŋ tən

with-it 'wɪð ɪt 'wɪθ-, §-ət ‖ 'wɪθ- 'wɪð-

without wɪð 'aʊt §wɪθ-

withstand wɪð ˈstænd wɪθ- **~ing** ɪŋ **~s** z
withstood wɪð ˈstʊd wɪθ-
with|y, Withy ˈwɪð |i §ˈwɪθ- **~ies** iz
Withycombe ˈwɪð i kəm
witless ˈwɪt ləs -lɪs **~ly** li **~ness** nəs nɪs
Witley ˈwɪt li
witness ˈwɪt nəs -nɪs **~ed** t **~es** ɪz əz **~ing** ɪŋ
ˈwitness box; **ˈwitness stand**
Witney ˈwɪt ni
-witted ˈwɪt ɪd -əd ‖ ˈwɪṭ əd — **slow-witted** ˌsləʊ ˈwɪt ɪd ◂ -əd ‖ ˌsloʊ ˈwɪṭ əd ◂
Wittenberg ˈwɪt ən bɜːg ‖ -bɜːg —*Ger* [ˈvɪt ən bɛʁk]
witter ˈwɪt ə ‖ ˈwɪṭ ər **~ed** d **wittering** ˈwɪt‿ər ɪŋ ‖ ˈwɪṭ ər ɪŋ **~s** z
Wittgenstein ˈvɪt gən ʃtaɪn -staɪn
witti... —*see* **witty**
witticism ˈwɪt ɪ ˌsɪz əm -ə- ‖ ˈwɪṭ ə- **~s** z
witting ˈwɪt ɪŋ ‖ ˈwɪṭ ɪŋ **~ly** li
Witton ˈwɪt ən
witt|y, Witty ˈwɪt |i ‖ ˈwɪṭ |i **~ier** i‿ə ‖ i ər **~iest** i‿ɪst i‿əst **~ily** ɪ li əl i **~iness** i nəs i nɪs
Witwatersrand wɪt ˈwɔːt əz rænd ˌ··-, -ˈwɑːt-, -rɑːnd, -rɒnt, -rɑːnt, ˌ·ˌ··ˈ·, ˈ· · · · ‖ ˈwɪt wɔːṭ ərz- ˈ·wɑːṭ- —*Afrikaans* [ˌvit ˌvat ərs ˈrant]
Wiveliscombe ˈwɪv ə lɪs kəm —*locally also* ˈwɪls kəm
Wivelsfield ˈwɪv əlz fiːəld
Wivenhoe ˈwɪv ən həʊ ‖ -hoʊ
wives waɪvz
Wix wɪks
wiz wɪz
wizard ˈwɪz əd ‖ -ərd **~s** z
wizardry ˈwɪz əd ri ‖ -ərd-
wizened ˈwɪz ənd
woad wəʊd ‖ woʊd
wobbl|e ˈwɒb əl ‖ ˈwɑːb əl **~ed** d **~es** z **~ing** ‿ɪŋ
wobb|ly, W~ ˈwɒb |li ‖ ˈwɑːb- **~lier** li‿ə ‖ li ər **~lies** liz **~liest** li‿ɪst əst
Wobegon ˈwəʊ bɪ gɒn -bə- ‖ ˈwoʊ bɪ gɔːn -gɑːn
Woburn ˈwəʊ bɜːn ˈwuː-, -bən ‖ ˈwoʊ bɜːn
Wodehouse ˈwʊd haʊs §-əs
Woden ˈwəʊd ən ‖ ˈwoʊd ən
wodge wɒdʒ ‖ wɑːdʒ **wodges** ˈwɒdʒ ɪz -əz ‖ ˈwɑːdʒ əz
woe wəʊ ‖ woʊ **woes** wəʊz ‖ woʊz
woebegone, Wobegon ˈwəʊ bi gɒn -bə- ‖ ˈwoʊ bi gɔːn -gɑːn
woeful ˈwəʊ fəl -fʊl ‖ ˈwoʊ- **~ly** ‿i **~ness** nəs nɪs
wog wɒg ‖ wɑːg wɔːg **wogs** wɒgz ‖ wɑːgz wɔːgz
Wogan ˈwəʊg ən ‖ ˈwoʊg ən
woggle ˈwɒg əl ‖ ˈwɑːg əl **~s** z
Wojtyla vɔɪ ˈtɪl ə —*Polish* Wojtyła [voj ˈtɨ wa]
wok wɒk ‖ wɑːk —*Cantonese* [⁶wɔːk] **woks** wɒks ‖ wɑːks
woke wəʊk ‖ woʊk
woken ˈwəʊk ən ‖ ˈwoʊk ən
Woking ˈwəʊk ɪŋ ‖ ˈwoʊk ɪŋ
Wokingham ˈwəʊk ɪŋ əm ‖ ˈwoʊk-
wold wəʊld →wɒʊld ‖ woʊld **wolds, Wolds** wəʊldz →wɒʊldz ‖ woʊldz
Woldingham ˈwəʊld ɪŋ əm →ˈwɒʊld- ‖ ˈwoʊld-
Woledge ˈwʊl ɪdʒ
wolf wʊlf **wolfed** wʊlft **wolfing** ˈwʊlf ɪŋ **wolfs** wʊlfs **wolves** wʊlvz
ˈwolf cub; **ˈwolf ˌwhistle**
Wolf wʊlf —*but as a German name, also* vɒlf ‖ vɔːlf, vɑːlf —*Ger* [vɔlf]
Wolfe wʊlf
Wolfenden ˈwʊlf ən dən
Wolff wʊlf —*Ger, Fr* [vɔlf]
Wolfgang ˈwʊlf gæŋ —*Ger* [ˈvɔlf gaŋ]
wolfhound ˈwʊlf haʊnd **~s** z
wolfish ˈwʊlf ɪʃ **~ly** li **~ness** nəs nɪs
Wolfit ˈwʊlf ɪt §-ət
wolflike ˈwʊlf laɪk
Wolford ˈwʊl fəd ‖ -fərd
Wolfowitz ˈwʊlf ə wɪts
wolfram ˈwʊlf rəm
wolframite ˈwʊlf rə maɪt
wolfsbane ˈwʊlfs beɪn
Wollaston ˈwʊl əst ən
wollastonite ˈwʊl əst ə naɪt
Wollongong ˈwʊl ən gɒŋ →-əŋ- ‖ -gɔːŋ -gɑːŋ
Wollstonecraft ˈwʊlst ən krɑːft §-kræft ‖ -kræft
Wolmer ˈwʊlm ə ‖ -ər
Wolof ˈwɒl ɒf ‖ ˈwoʊl ɑːf
Wolseley ˈwʊlz li
Wolsey ˈwʊlz i
Wolsingham ˈwʊlz ɪŋ əm ˈwɒls- ‖ ˈwɑːls-
Wolstenholme ˈwʊlst ən həʊm ‖ -hoʊm
Wolverhampton ˌwʊlv ə ˈhæmpt ən ˈ·ˌ·· ‖ -ər-
wolverine ˈwʊlv ə riːn **~s** z
Wolverton ˈwʊlv ət ən ‖ -ərt ən
wolves wʊlvz
woman ˈwʊm ən **woman's** ˈwʊm ənz **women** ˈwɪm ɪn §-ən **women's** ˈwɪm ɪnz §-ənz
ˌWomen's ˈInstutute; **ˌwomen's ˈlib**; **ˌwomen's ˌlibeˈration**; **ˈwomen's ˌmovement**; **ˈwomen's ˌstudies**
womanhood ˈwʊm ən hʊd
womanis... —*see* **womaniz...**
womanish ˈwʊm ən ɪʃ **~ly** li **~ness** nəs nɪs
womaniz|e ˈwʊm ə naɪz **~ed** d **~er/s** ə/z ‖ ər/z **~es** ɪz əz **~ing** ɪŋ
womankind ˈwʊm ən kaɪnd →-əŋ-, ˌ· ·ˈ·
woman|ly ˈwʊm ən |li **~liness** li nəs -nɪs
woman-to-woman ˌwʊm ən tə ˈwʊm ən ◂
womb wuːm *(!)* **wombs** wuːmz
wombat ˈwɒm bæt -bət ‖ ˈwɑːm- **~s** s
wombl|e, W~ ˈwɒm bəl ‖ ˈwɑːm- **~ed** d **~es** z **~ing** ‿ɪŋ
Wombourne ˈwɒm bɔːn ‖ ˈwɑːm bɔːrn -boʊrn
Wombwell ˈwʊm wel ˈwuːm-, ˈwɒm-, -wəl
women ˈwɪm ɪn §-ən
womenfolk ˈwɪm ɪn fəʊk -ən-, §-fəʊlk ‖ -foʊk
womyn ˈwɪm ɪn §-ən
won *Korean currency* wɒn ‖ wɑːn
won *past & pp of* **win** wʌn

wonder, W~ 'wʌnd ə ‖ -ᵊr **~ed** d **wondering/ly** 'wʌnd‿ər ɪŋ /li **~s** z
Wonderbra *tdmk* 'wʌnd ə brɑː ‖ -ᵊr-
Wonderbread, Wonder Bread *tdmk* 'wʌnd ə bred ‖ -ᵊr-
wonderful 'wʌnd ə fᵊl -fʊl ‖ -ᵊr- —*In casual AmE also* 'wʌn ᵊr- **~ly** ‿i **~ness** nəs nɪs
wonderland 'wʌnd ə lænd ‖ -ᵊr- **~s** z
wonderment 'wʌnd ə mənt ‖ -ᵊr-
wondrous 'wʌndr əs **~ly** li **~ness** nəs nɪs
Wonersh 'wɒn ɜːʃ ‖ 'wɑːn ɜːʃ
Wong wɒŋ ‖ wɑːŋ wɔːŋ —*Cantonese* [⁴wɔːŋ]
wonga 'wɒŋ gə ‖ 'wɑːŋ gə
wonga-wonga 'wɒŋ gə ˌwɒŋ gə ˌ· ˈ· · ‖ 'wɑːŋ gə ˌwɑːŋ gə
wonk wɒŋk ‖ wɑːŋk wɔːŋk **wonks** wɒŋks ‖ wɑːŋks wɔːŋks
wonk|y 'wɒŋk |i ‖ 'wɑːŋk |i **~ier** i‿ə ‖ i‿ᵊr **~iest** i‿ɪst i‿əst
wont wəʊnt wɒnt ‖ wɔːnt wɑːnt, woʊnt
won't wəʊnt ‖ woʊnt wʊnt —*Also, esp. before a consonant,* wəʊn ‖ woʊn. *This word has no weak form.*
wonted 'wəʊnt ɪd -əd ‖ 'wɔːnt̬ əd 'wɑːnt̬-, 'woʊnt̬-
wonton ˌwɒn 'tɒn ◂ 'ˌ· · ‖ 'wɑːn tɑːn **ˌwonton 'soup**
woo wuː **wooed** wuːd **wooing** 'wuː‿ɪŋ **woos** wuːz
Woo wuː —*Chi* Wú [²wu], *Cantonese* [⁴wuː]
wood, Wood wʊd **wooded** 'wʊd ɪd -əd **wooding** 'wʊd ɪŋ **woods** wʊdz **ˌwood 'alcohol**; **'wood pulp**
Woodall 'wʊd ɔːl ‖ -ɑːl
woodbine 'wʊd baɪn →'wʊb- **~s** z
woodblock 'wʊd blɒk →'wʊb- ‖ -blɑːk **~s** s
Woodbridge 'wʊd brɪdʒ →'wʊb-
Woodburn 'wʊd bɜːn →'wʊb- ‖ -bɝːn
Woodbury 'wʊd bər‿i →'wʊb- ‖ -ˌber i
woodcarv|er 'wʊd ˌkɑːv| ə →'wʊg- ‖ -ˌkɑːrv| ᵊr **~ers** əz ‖ ᵊrz **~ing/s** ɪŋ/z
woodchip 'wʊd tʃɪp
woodchuck 'wʊd tʃʌk **~s** s
woodcock, W~ 'wʊd kɒk →'wʊg- ‖ -kɑːk **~s** s
woodcraft 'wʊd krɑːft →'wʊg-, §-kræft ‖ -kræft **~s** s
woodcut 'wʊd kʌt →'wʊg- **~s** s
woodcutter 'wʊd ˌkʌt ə →'wʊg- ‖ -ˌkʌt̬ ᵊr **~s** z
wooded 'wʊd ɪd -əd
wooden 'wʊd ᵊn **~ly** li **~ness** nəs nɪs **ˌwooden 'spoon**
woodenheaded ˌwʊd ᵊn 'hed ɪd ◂ -əd
Woodford 'wʊd fəd ‖ -fᵊrd
Woodhall 'wʊd hɔːl ‖ -hɑːl
Woodhead 'wʊd hed
Woodhouse 'wʊd haʊs
woodland, W~ 'wʊd lənd -lænd **~s** z
woodlark 'wʊd lɑːk ‖ -lɑːrk **~s** s
Woodlesford 'wʊd ᵊlz fəd ‖ -fᵊrd
Woodley 'wʊd li
Woodliff 'wʊd lɪf
wood|louse 'wʊd |laʊs **~lice** laɪs

wood|man, W~ 'wʊd |mən →'wʊb- **~men** mən
woodnote 'wʊd nəʊt ‖ -noʊt **~s** s
Woodnutt 'wʊd nʌt
woodpecker 'wʊd ˌpek ə →'wʊb- ‖ -ᵊr **~s** z
woodpile 'wʊd paɪᵊl →'wʊb- **~s** z
Woodrow 'wʊd rəʊ ‖ -roʊ
woodruff, W~ 'wʊd rʌf **~s** s
Woods wʊdz
woodscrew 'wʊd skruː **~s** z
woodshed 'wʊd ʃed **~s** z
woodsia 'wʊdz i‿ə **~s** z
Woodside ˌwʊd 'saɪd '· ·
woods|man 'wʊdz |mən **~men** mən
Woodstock 'wʊd stɒk ‖ -stɑːk
woods|y 'wʊdz |i **~ier** i‿ə ‖ i‿ᵊr **~iest** i‿ɪst i‿əst
Woodward 'wʊd wəd ‖ -wᵊrd
woodwind 'wʊd wɪnd
woodwork 'wʊd wɜːk ‖ -wɝːk **~ing** ɪŋ
woodworm 'wʊd wɜːm ‖ -wɝːm
wood|y, Woody 'wʊd |i **~ier** i‿ə ‖ i‿ᵊr **~iest** i‿ɪst i‿əst **~iness** i nəs i nɪs
wooer 'wuː‿ə ‖ ᵊr **~s** z
woof *'dog's bark'* wʊf **woofs** wʊfs
woof *'threads'* wuːf ‖ wʊf wuːf **woofs** wuːfs ‖ wʊfs wuːfs
woofer 'wʊf ə 'wuːf- ‖ -ᵊr **~s** z
Woofferton 'wʊf ət ən ‖ -ᵊrt ᵊn
woofter 'wʊft ə ‖ -ᵊr **~s** z
Wookey 'wʊk i
wool, Wool wʊl **wools** wʊlz
Woolacombe 'wʊl ə kəm
Woolard 'wʊl ɑːd ‖ -ɑːrd
woolen 'wʊl ən **~s** z
Wooler 'wʊl ə ‖ -ᵊr
Woolf wʊlf
Woolford 'wʊl fəd ‖ -fᵊrd
woolgather|ing 'wʊl ˌgæð ər‿|ɪŋ ‖ -ᵊr‿|ɪŋ **~er/s** ‿ə/z ‖ ‿ər/z
Woolite *tdmk* 'wʊl aɪt
Woollard 'wʊl ɑːd ‖ -ɑːrd
Woollcott 'wʊl kət -kɒt ‖ -kɑːt
woollen 'wʊl ən **~s** z
Woolley 'wʊl i
Woolloomooloo ˌwʊl əm ə 'luː
wooll|y 'wʊl |i **~ier** i‿ə ‖ i‿ᵊr **~ies** iz **~iest** i‿ɪst i‿əst **~iness** i nəs i nɪs
woolly-headed ˌwʊl i 'hed ɪd ◂ -əd
Woolmer 'wʊlm ə ‖ -ᵊr
woolpack 'wʊl pæk **~s** s
woolsack 'wʊl sæk **~s** s
Woolton 'wʊlt ən
Woolwich 'wʊl ɪdʒ -ɪtʃ
Woolworth 'wʊl wəθ -wɜːθ ‖ -wɝːθ **~'s** s
Woomera, w~ 'wʊm ər ə 'wuːm- **~s** z
Woon wuːn
Woonsocket wuːn 'sɒk ɪt §-ət ‖ -'sɑːk-
Woore wɔː ‖ wɔːr woʊr
Woosnam 'wuːz nəm
Wooster 'wʊst ə 'wuːst- ‖ -ᵊr
Wootten, Wootton 'wʊt ᵊn
wooz|y 'wuːz |i 'wʊz- **~ier** i‿ə ‖ i‿ᵊr **~iest** i‿ɪst i‿əst **~ily** ɪ li əl i **~iness** i nəs i nɪs

wop wɒp ‖ wɑːp **wops** wɒps ‖ wɑːps
Worcester ˈwʊst ə ‖ -ər **~shire** ʃə ʃɪə ‖ ʃər ʃɪr
ˌWorcester(shire) ˈsauce ‖ ˈ· ·(·) ·
Worcestershire ˈwʊst ə ʃə -ʃɪə ‖ -ər ʃər -ʃɪr
Worcs —*see* **Worcestershire**
word, Word wɜːd ‖ wɜːd **worded** ˈwɜːd ɪd -əd ‖ ˈwɜːd əd **wording/s** ˈwɜːd ɪŋ/z ‖ ˈwɜːd ɪŋ/z **words** wɜːdz ‖ wɜːdz **ˈword ˌblindness**; **ˈword class**; **ˈword count**; **ˈword ˌorder**; **ˈword ˌprocessing**; **ˈword ˌprocessor**; **ˈword square**
wordag|e ˈwɜːd ɪdʒ ‖ ˈwɜːd- **~es** ɪz əz
wordbreak ˈwɜːd breɪk →ˈwɜːb- ‖ ˈwɜːd- **~s** s
wordless ˈwɜːd ləs -lɪs ‖ ˈwɜːd ləs **~ly** li **~ness** nəs nɪs
word-perfect, WordPerfect *tdmk* ˌwɜːd ˈpɜːf ɪkt ◂ →ˌwɜːb-, -ekt, §-əkt ‖ ˌwɜːd ˈpɜːf ɪkt ◂ **~ly** li
wordplay ˈwɜːd pleɪ →ˈwɜːb- ‖ ˈwɜːd-
wordsmith ˈwɜːd smɪθ ‖ ˈwɜːd- **~s** s
Wordstar, WordStar *tdmk* ˈwɜːd stɑː ‖ ˈwɜːd stɑːr
Wordsworth ˈwɜːdz wəθ -wɜːθ ‖ ˈwɜːdz wɜːθ **~'s** s
Wordsworthian ˌwɜːdz ˈwɜːð iˌən -ˈwɜːθ- ‖ ˌwɜːdz ˈwɜːθ- -ˈwɜːð- **~s** z
wordwrap ˈwɜːd ræp ‖ ˈwɜːd-
word|y ˈwɜːd |i ‖ ˈwɜːd |i **~ier** iˌə ‖ iˌər **~iest** iˌɪst iˌəst **~ily** ɪ li əl i **~iness** i nəs i nɪs
wore wɔː ‖ wɔːr woʊr
work wɜːk ‖ wɜːk **worked** wɜːkt ‖ wɜːkt **working/s** ˈwɜːk ɪŋ/z ‖ ˈwɜːk ɪŋ/z **works** wɜːks ‖ wɜːks **ˌworked ˈup**◂; **ˌworking ˈclass** ‖ ˈ· · ·; **ˌworking ˈday** ‖ ˈ· · ·; **ˌworking ˈknowledge**◂; **ˌworking ˈorder** ‖ ˈ· · ˌ· ·; **ˈworking ˌparty**; **ˌworking ˈweek** ‖ ˈ· · ·
-work wɜːk ‖ wɜːk — **spadework** ˈspeɪd wɜːk ‖ -wɜːk
workab|le ˈwɜːk əb |əl ‖ ˈwɜːk- **~leness** əl nəs -nɪs **~ly** li
workaday ˈwɜːk ə deɪ ‖ ˈwɜːk-
workaholic ˌwɜːk ə ˈhɒl ɪk ◂ ‖ ˌwɜːk ə ˈhɑːl ɪk ◂ -ˈhɔːl- **~s** s
workaround ˈwɜːk ə ˌraʊnd ‖ ˈwɜːk- **~s** z
workbag ˈwɜːk bæg ‖ ˈwɜːk- **~s** z
workbasket ˈwɜːk ˌbɑːsk ɪt §-ˌbæsk-, §-ət ‖ ˈwɜːk ˌbæsk ət **~s** s
workbench ˈwɜːk bentʃ ‖ ˈwɜːk- **~es** ɪz əz
workbook ˈwɜːk bʊk ‖ ˈwɜːk- **~s** s
workbox ˈwɜːk bɒks ‖ ˈwɜːk bɑːks **~es** ɪz əz
workday ˈwɜːk deɪ ‖ ˈwɜːk-
worker ˈwɜːk ə ‖ ˈwɜːk ər **~s** z
worker-priest ˌwɜːk ə ˈpriːst ‖ ˌwɜːk ər- **~s** s
workfare ˈwɜːk feə ‖ ˈwɜːk fer -fær
workflow ˈwɜːk fləʊ ‖ ˈwɜːk floʊ
workforce ˈwɜːk fɔːs ‖ ˈwɜːk fɔːrs -foʊrs
workhors|e ˈwɜːk hɔːs ‖ ˈwɜːk hɔːrs **~es** ɪz əz
work|house ˈwɜːk |haʊs ‖ ˈwɜːk- **~houses** haʊz ɪz -əz
work-in ˈwɜːk ɪn ‖ ˈwɜːk- **~s** z
working-class ˌwɜːk ɪŋ ˈklɑːs ◂ §-ˈklæs ‖ ˈwɜːk ɪŋ klæs
working-out ˌwɜːk ɪŋ ˈaʊt ‖ ˌwɜːk-
Workington ˈwɜːk ɪŋ tən ‖ ˈwɜːk-
workload ˈwɜːk ləʊd ‖ ˈwɜːk loʊd **~s** z
work|man, W~ ˈwɜːk |mən ‖ ˈwɜːk- **~manlike** mən laɪk **~manship** mən ʃɪp **~men** mən
workmate, W~ *tdmk* ˈwɜːk meɪt ‖ ˈwɜːk- **~s** s
workmen ˈwɜːk mən ‖ ˈwɜːk-
workout ˈwɜːk aʊt ‖ ˈwɜːk- **~s** s
workpeople ˈwɜːk ˌpiːp əl ‖ ˈwɜːk-
workplac|e ˈwɜːk pleɪs ‖ ˈwɜːk- **~es** ɪz əz
workroom ˈwɜːk ruːm -rʊm ‖ ˈwɜːk- **~s** z
work-sharing ˈwɜːk ˌʃeər ɪŋ ‖ ˈwɜːk ˌʃer ɪŋ -ˌʃær-
worksheet ˈwɜːk ʃiːt ‖ ˈwɜːk- **~s** s
workshop ˈwɜːk ʃɒp ‖ ˈwɜːk ʃɑːp **~s** s
workshy ˈwɜːk ʃaɪ ‖ ˈwɜːk-
Worksop ˈwɜːk sɒp ‖ ˈwɜːk sɑːp
workspace ˈwɜːk speɪs ‖ ˈwɜːk-
workstation ˈwɜːk ˌsteɪʃ ən ‖ ˈwɜːk- **~s** z
work-study ˈwɜːk ˌstʌd i ‖ ˈwɜːk-
worktable ˈwɜːk ˌteɪb əl ‖ ˈwɜːk- **~s** z
worktop ˈwɜːk tɒp ‖ ˈwɜːk tɑːp **~s** s
work-to-rule ˌwɜːk tə ˈruːl -tu- ‖ ˌwɜːk-
workup ˈwɜːk ʌp ‖ ˈwɜːk- **~s** s
workweek ˈwɜːk wiːk ‖ ˈwɜːk- **~s** s
world wɜːld ‖ wɜːld **worlds** wɜːldz ‖ wɜːldz **ˌWorld ˈBank**; **ˌWorld ˈCup**; **ˌWorld ˈHealth Organiˌzation**; **ˌworld ˈpower**; **ˌWorld ˈSeries**; **ˌworld ˈwar**; **ˌWorld ˌWar ˈTwo**; **ˌWorld Wide ˈWeb**
world-beater ˈwɜːl*d* ˌbiːt ə ‖ ˈwɜːl*d* ˌbiːt ər **~s** z
world-class ˌwɜːl*d* ˈklɑːs ◂ §-ˈklæs ‖ ˌwɜːl*d* ˈklæs ◂
world-famous ˌwɜːl*d* ˈfeɪm əs ◂ ‖ ˌwɜːl*d*- ˈ·ˌ· ·
worldling ˈwɜːld lɪŋ ‖ ˈwɜːld- **~s** z
world|ly ˈwɜːl*d* |li ‖ ˈwɜːl*d* |li **~lier** li ə ‖ li ər **~liest** li ɪst əst **~liness** li nəs -nɪs
worldly-wise ˌwɜːl*d* li ˈwaɪz ◂ ‖ ˌwɜːl*d*- ˈ· ·
worldshaking ˈwɜːld ˌʃeɪk ɪŋ ‖ ˈwɜːld-
worldview ˌwɜːld ˈvjuː ‖ ˌwɜːld- **~s** z
world-wear|y ˌwɜːld ˈwɪər |i ◂ ˈ· ˌ· · ‖ ˈwɜːld ˌwɪr |i **~ier** iˌə ‖ iˌər **~iest** iˌɪst iˌəst **~ily** əl i ɪ li **~iness** i nəs i nɪs
worldwide ˌwɜːl*d* ˈwaɪd ◂ ‖ ˌwɜːl*d*-
Worley ˈwɜːl i ‖ ˈwɜːl i
Worlingham ˈwɜːl ɪŋ əm ‖ ˈwɜːl-
worm wɜːm ‖ wɜːm **wormed** wɜːmd ‖ wɜːmd **worming** ˈwɜːm ɪŋ ‖ ˈwɜːm ɪŋ **worms** wɜːmz ‖ wɜːmz **ˈworm cast**; **ˈworm gear**
Wormald ˈwɜːm əld ‖ ˈwɜːm-
wormcast ˈwɜːm kɑːst §-kæst ‖ ˈwɜːm kæst **~s** s
worm-eaten ˈwɜːm ˌiːt ən ‖ ˈwɜːm-
wormhole ˈwɜːm həʊl →-hɒʊl ‖ ˈwɜːm hoʊl **~s** z
Wormold ˈwɜːm əʊld →-ɒʊld, -əld ‖ ˈwɜːm oʊld
Worms *place in Germany* vɔːmz wɜːmz ‖ wɜːmz —*Ger* [vɔʁms]
wormwood, W~ ˈwɜːm wʊd ‖ ˈwɜːm- **ˌWormwood ˈScrubs**

worm|y 'wɜːm |i ‖ 'wɜ˞ːm |i **~ier** i‿ə ‖ i‿ᵊr **~iest** i‿ɪst i‿əst **~iness** i nəs i nɪs
worn wɔːn ‖ wɔːrn woʊrn
worn-out ˌwɔːn 'aʊt ◂ ‖ ˌwɔːrn- ˌwoʊrn-
Worple 'wɔːp ᵊl ‖ 'wɔːrp ᵊl
Worplesdon 'wɔːp ᵊlz dən ‖ 'wɔːrp-
Worrall 'wɒr əl ‖ 'wɔːr- 'wɑːr-
worrie... —*see* **worry**
worriment 'wʌr i mənt ‖ 'wɜ˞ː- **~s** s
worrisome 'wʌr i səm ‖ 'wɜ˞ː- **~ly** li
worr|it 'wʌr |ɪt §-ət ‖ 'wɜ˞ː |ət **~ited** ɪt ɪd §ət-, -əd ‖ əţ əd **~iting** ɪt ɪŋ §ət- ‖ əţ ɪŋ **~its** ɪts §əts ‖ əts
worr|y 'wʌr |i ‖ 'wɜ˞ː |i **~ied/ly** id /li **~ier/s** i‿ə/z ‖ i‿ᵊr/z **~ies** iz **~ying/ly** i‿ɪŋ /li
'worry beads
worrywart 'wʌr i wɔːt ‖ 'wɜ˞ː i wɔːrt **~s** s
worse wɜːs ‖ wɜ˞ːs
worsen 'wɜːs ᵊn ‖ 'wɜ˞ːs ᵊn **~ed** d **~ing** ‿ɪŋ **~s** z
worship, W~ 'wɜːʃ ɪp §-əp ‖ 'wɜ˞ːʃ əp **~ed, ~ped** t **~ing, ~ping** ɪŋ **~s** s
worshiper, worshipper 'wɜːʃ ɪp ə §-əp- ‖ 'wɜ˞ːʃ əp ᵊr **~s** z
worshipful 'wɜːʃ ɪp fᵊl §-əp-, -fʊl ‖ 'wɜ˞ːʃ əp- **~ly** i **~ness** nəs nɪs
Worsley 'wɜːs li 'wɜːz- ‖ 'wɜ˞ːs-
Worsnip 'wɜːs nɪp §-nəp ‖ 'wɜ˞ːs-
worst wɜːst ‖ wɜ˞ːst **worsted** 'wɜːst ɪd -əd ‖ 'wɜ˞ːst əd **worsting** 'wɜːst ɪŋ ‖ 'wɜ˞ːst ɪŋ **worsts** wɜːsts ‖ wɜ˞ːsts
worst-case ˌwɜːst'keɪs ◂ ‖ ˌwɜ˞ːst- **ˌworst-case sce'nario**
worsted *'cloth'* 'wʊst ɪd -əd ‖ 'wɜːst əd
Worsthorne 'wɜːs θɔːn ‖ 'wɜ˞ːs θɔːrn
wort wɜːt §wɔːt ‖ wɜ˞ːt wɔːrt
worth wɜːθ ‖ wɜ˞ːθ
-worth wəθ wɜːθ ‖ wɜ˞ːθ — **poundsworth** 'paʊndz wəθ -wɜːθ ‖ -wɜ˞ːθ
Worth wɜːθ ‖ wɜ˞ːθ —*but as a French name* vɔːt ‖ vɔːrt —*Fr* [vɔʁt]
worthi... —*see* **worthy**
Worthing 'wɜːð ɪŋ ‖ 'wɜ˞ːð ɪŋ
Worthington 'wɜːð ɪŋ tən ‖ 'wɜ˞ːð-
worthless 'wɜːθ ləs -lɪs ‖ 'wɜ˞ːθ- **~ly** li **~ness** nəs nɪs
worthwhile ˌwɜːθ 'waɪᵊl ◂ -'hwaɪᵊl ‖ ˌwɜ˞ːθ '*h*waɪᵊl ◂
worth|y, W~ 'wɜːð |i ‖ 'wɜ˞ːð |i **~ier** i‿ə ‖ i‿ᵊr **~ies** iz **~iest** i‿ɪst i‿əst **~ily** ɪ li ə l i **~iness** i nəs i nɪs
-worthy ˌwɜːð i ‖ ˌwɜ˞ːð i — **blameworthy** 'bleɪm ˌwɜːð i ‖ -ˌwɜ˞ːð-
Wortley 'wɜːt li ‖ 'wɜ˞ːt-
Worzel 'wɜːz ᵊl ‖ 'wɜ˞ːz ᵊl
wot wɒt ‖ wɑːt
Wotan 'vəʊt ɑːn -æn ‖ 'voʊt- —*Ger* ['voː tan]
wotcha, wotcher 'wɒtʃ ə ‖ 'wɑːtʃ ə -ᵊr
Wotton 'wʊt ᵊn 'wɒt- ‖ 'wɑːt-
Wotton-under-Edge ˌwʊt ᵊn ˌʌnd ər 'edʒ ‖ -ər'· —*locally also* ˌ· ·'ʌndr ɪdʒ
would *strong form* wʊd *(= wood), occasional weak forms* wəd, əd —*see also* **'d**
would-be 'wʊd biː →'wʊb-, -bi
wouldn't 'wʊd ᵊnt §'wʊt ᵊnt
wouldst wʊdst wʊtst
would've 'wʊd əv
Woulfe wʊlf
wound *past & pp of* **wind** waʊnd
wound *'injure, injury'* wuːnd **wounded/ly** 'wuːnd ɪd /li -əd /li **wounding/ly** 'wuːnd ɪŋ /li **wounds** wuːndz
wound-up ˌwaʊnd 'ʌp ◂
woundwort 'wuːnd wɜːt §-wɔːt ‖ -wɜ˞ːt -wɔːrt **~s** s
wove wəʊv ‖ woʊv
woven 'wəʊv ᵊn ‖ 'woʊv ᵊn
wow waʊ **wowed** waʊd **wowing** 'waʊ ɪŋ **wows** waʊz
wowser 'waʊz ə ‖ -ᵊr **~s** z
Wozniak 'wɒz ni æk ‖ 'wɑːz- *Polish* Woźniak ['vɔʑ ɲak]
Wozzeck 'vɒts ek 'vɔːts- ‖ 'vɔːts- 'vɑːts-
WRAC ræk
wrack ræk *(= rack)* **wracked** rækt **wracking** 'ræk ɪŋ **wracks** ræks
Wragg, Wragge ræg
wraith, W~ reɪθ **wraiths** reɪθs
wraithlike 'reɪθ laɪk
Wrangel, Wrangell 'ræŋ gᵊl
wrangl|e 'ræŋ gᵊl **~ed** d **~es** z **~ing** ‿ɪŋ
wrangler, W~ *tdmk* 'ræŋ glə ‖ -glᵊr **~s** z
wrap ræp *(= rap)* **wrapped** ræpt **wrapping/s** 'ræp ɪŋ/z **wraps** ræps
wraparound 'ræp ə ˌraʊnd **~s** z
wrapper 'ræp ə ‖ -ᵊr *(= rapper)* **~s** z
wrapround 'ræp raʊnd **~s** z
wrap-up 'ræp ʌp **~s** s
wrasse ræs **wrasses** 'ræs ɪz -əz
wrath, Wrath rɒθ rɔːθ, §rɑːθ, §ræθ ‖ ræθ *(*)*
Wrathall 'rɒθ ᵊl ‖ 'ræθ ɔːl -ɑːl
wrathful 'rɒθ fᵊl 'rɔːθ-, §'rɑːθ-, §'ræθ-, -fʊl ‖ 'ræθ- **~ly** i **~ness** nəs nɪs
Wray reɪ
Wraysbury 'reɪz bər‿i ‖ -ber i
wreak riːk §rek *(= reek)* **wreaked** riːkt **wreaking** 'riːk ɪŋ **wreaks** riːks
wreath riːθ **wreaths** riːðz riːθs
wreathe riːð **wreathed** riːðd **wreathes** riːðz **wreathing** 'riːð ɪŋ
wreck rek *(= reck)* **wrecked** rekt **wrecking** 'rek ɪŋ **wrecks** reks *(= rex)*
wreckage 'rek ɪdʒ
wrecker 'rek ə ‖ -ᵊr **~s** z
Wrekin 'riːk ɪn §-ən
wren, Wren ren **wrens, Wrens, Wren's** renz
wrench, W~ rentʃ **wrenched** rentʃt **wrenches** 'rentʃ ɪz -əz **wrenching** 'rentʃ ɪŋ
Wrenn ren
wrest rest *(= rest)* **wrested** 'rest ɪd -əd **wresting** 'rest ɪŋ **wrests** rests
wrestl|e 'res ᵊl ‖ 'ræs- **~ed** d **~es** z **~ing** ‿ɪŋ
wrestler 'res lə '·ᵊl‿ə ‖ 'res lᵊr 'ræs- **~s** z
wretch retʃ **wretches** 'retʃ ɪz -əz
wretched 'retʃ ɪd -əd *(!)* **~ly** li **~ness** nəs nɪs
Wrexham 'reks əm

wrick rɪk *(= rick)* **wricked** rɪkt **wricking** 'rɪk ɪŋ **wricks** rɪks
wrie... —*see* **ry**
wriggl|e 'rɪg ᵊl **~ed** d **~er/s** ə/z ‖ ᵊr/z **~es** z **~ing** ɪŋ **~y** i
wright, Wright raɪt *(= right)* **wrights, Wright's** raɪts
Wrightington 'raɪt ɪŋ tən ‖ 'raɪţ-
Wrighton 'raɪt ᵊn
Wrigley 'rɪg li **~'s** z
wring rɪŋ *(= ring)* **wringing** 'rɪŋ ɪŋ **wrings** rɪŋz **wrung** rʌŋ
ˌwringing 'wet◂
wringer 'rɪŋ ə ‖ -ᵊr *(= ringer)* **~s** z
wrinkl|e 'rɪŋk ᵊl **~ed** d **~es** z **~ing** ɪŋ
wrink|ly 'rɪŋk |li **~lies** liz
Wriothesley 'raɪ‿əθs li
wrist rɪst **wrists** rɪsts
wristband 'rɪst bænd **~s** z
wristlet 'rɪst lət -lɪt **~s** s
wristwatch 'rɪst wɒtʃ ‖ -wɑːtʃ **~es** ɪz əz
wristy 'rɪst i
writ rɪt **writs** rɪts
writable, writeable 'raɪt əb ᵊl ‖ 'raɪţ-
write raɪt *(= right)* **writes** raɪts **writing** 'raɪt ɪŋ ‖ 'raɪţ ɪŋ **written** 'rɪt ᵊn **wrote** rəʊt ‖ roʊt
write-in 'raɪt ɪn ‖ 'raɪţ ɪn **~s** z
write-off 'raɪt ɒf -ɔːf ‖ 'raɪţ ɔːf -ɑːf **~s** s
write-protected ˌraɪt prə 'tekt ɪd ◂ -prəʊ-, -əd ‖ -proʊ-
writer 'raɪt ə ‖ 'raɪţ ᵊr **~s** z
ˌwriter's 'cramp ‖ '· · ·
write-up 'raɪt ʌp ‖ 'raɪţ ʌp **~s** s
writhe raɪð **writhed** raɪðd **writhes** raɪðz **writhing** 'raɪð ɪŋ
writing 'raɪt ɪŋ ‖ 'raɪţ ɪŋ **~s** z
'writing desk; **'writing ˌpaper**
written 'rɪt ᵊn
Wroclaw, Wrocław 'vrɒts lɑːv -læv ‖ 'vrɔːts lɑːf 'vrɑːts- —*Polish* ['vrɔts waf]
wrong rɒŋ ‖ rɔːŋ rɑːŋ **wronged** rɒŋd ‖ rɔːŋd rɑːŋd **wronger** 'rɒŋ ə ‖ 'rɔːŋ ᵊr 'rɑːŋ- **wrongest** 'rɒŋ ɪst -əst ‖ 'rɔːŋ- 'rɑːŋ- **wronging** 'rɒŋ ɪŋ ‖ 'rɔːŋ ɪŋ 'rɑːŋ- **wrongs** rɒŋz ‖ rɔːŋz rɑːŋz
wrongdoer 'rɒŋ ˌduː‿ə ˌ·'· · ‖ 'rɔːŋ ˌduː ᵊr 'rɑːŋ-; ˌ·'· · **~s** z
wrongdoing 'rɒŋ ˌduː‿ɪŋ ˌ·'· · ‖ 'rɔːŋ- 'rɑːŋ- **~s** z
wrong-|foot ˌrɒŋ |'fʊt ‖ ˌrɔːŋ- ˌrɑːŋ- **~footed** 'fʊt ɪd -əd ‖ 'fʊţ əd **~footing** 'fʊt ɪŋ ‖ 'fʊţ ɪŋ **~foots** fʊts
wrongful 'rɒŋ fᵊl -fʊl ‖ 'rɔːŋ- 'rɑːŋ- **~ly** i **~ness** nəs nɪs
wrongheaded ˌrɒŋ 'hed ɪd ◂ -əd ‖ ˌrɔːŋ- ˌrɑːŋ- **~ly** li **~ness** nəs nɪs
wrong|ly 'rɒŋ |li ‖ 'rɔːŋ |li 'rɑːŋ- **~ness** nəs nɪs
wrote rəʊt ‖ roʊt *(= rote)*
wroth rəʊθ rɒθ ‖ rɔːθ rɑːθ *(*)*
Wrotham *place in Kent* 'ruːt əm ‖ 'ruːţ-
Wrottesley 'rɒts li ‖ 'rɑːts-
wrought rɔːt ‖ rɑːt
ˌwrought 'iron◂
wrought-up ˌrɔːt 'ʌp ◂ ‖ ˌrɔːţ- ˌrɑːţ-
Wroxeter 'rɒks ɪt ə ‖ 'rɑːks əţ ᵊr
Wroxham 'rɒks əm ‖ 'rɑːks-
wrung rʌŋ *(= rung)*
wrung-out ˌrʌŋ 'aʊt ◂
wry raɪ *(= rye)* **wrier, wryer** 'raɪ ə ‖ 'raɪ ᵊr **wriest, wryest** 'raɪ ɪst -əst
wryly 'raɪ li
wryneck 'raɪ nek **~s** s
wryness 'raɪ nəs -nɪs
Wrythe raɪð
Wu wuː —*Chi* Wú [²wu], *Cantonese* [⁴wuː]
Wuhan ˌwuː 'hæn ‖ -'hɑːn —*Chi* Wǔhàn [³wu ⁴xan]
wulfenite 'wʊlf ə naɪt -ɪ-
Wulfrun 'wʊlf rən
Wulstan 'wʊlst ən
wunderkind 'wʌnd ə kɪnd 'vʊnd- ‖ -ᵊr- —*Ger* ['vʊn dɐ kɪnt] **~s** z
Wundt vʊnt
Wuppertal 'vʊp ə tɑːl 'wʊp- ‖ -ᵊr- —*Ger* ['vʊp ɐ taːl]
Wurlitzer 'wɜːl ɪts ə -əts- ‖ 'wɜːl əts ᵊr **~s** z
wurst wɜːst wʊəst, vʊəst ‖ wɜːst wʊrst, wʊst —*Ger* [vʊʁst]
Wurttemberg, Württemberg 'vɜːt əm bɜːg 'wɜːt- ‖ 'wɜːţ əm bɜːg —*Ger* ['vʏʁ təm bɛʁk]
Wurzburg, Würzburg 'vɜːts bɜːg 'wɜːts- ‖ 'wɜːts bɜːg —*Ger* ['vʏʁts bʊʁk]
wuss wʊs **wusses** 'wʊs ɪz -əz
wussy 'wʊs i **wussies** 'wʊs iz
wuthering, W~ 'wʌð ər ɪŋ
ˌWuthering 'Heights
Wuxi ˌwuː 'ʃiː —*Chi* Wúxī [²wu ¹ɕi]
Wyandot, wyandotte 'waɪ‿ən dɒt ‖ -dɑːt **~s** s
Wyatt 'waɪ‿ət
wych-elm 'wɪtʃ elm **~s** z
Wycherley 'wɪtʃ ə li ‖ -ᵊr-
wych-hazel 'wɪtʃ ˌheɪz ᵊl **~s** z
Wychwood 'wɪtʃ wʊd
Wyclif, Wycliffe 'wɪk lɪf
Wycliffite 'wɪk lɪ faɪt -lə- **~s** s
Wycombe 'wɪk əm
Wye, wye waɪ *(= Y)* **wyes, Wye's** waɪz *(= wise)*
Wyeth 'waɪ‿əθ
Wyke waɪk
Wykeham 'wɪk əm
Wykehamist 'wɪk əm ɪst §-əst **~s** s
Wyld, Wylde waɪᵊld
Wylfa 'wɪlv ə —*Welsh* ['uil va, 'wil-]
Wylie, Wyllie, Wylye 'waɪl i
Wyman 'waɪ mən
Wymondham *(i)* 'waɪm ənd əm, *(ii)* 'wɪnd əm, *(iii)* 'wɪm ənd əm —*The place in Leics is (i), that in Nfk (ii) or (iii).*
Wyn wɪn
wynd waɪnd **wynds** waɪndz
Wyndham 'wɪnd əm
Wynette wɪ 'net wə-

Wynford ˈwɪn fəd ‖ -fᵊrd
Wynn, Wynne wɪn
Wyoming waɪ ˈəʊm ɪŋ ‖ -ˈoʊm-
Wyomingite waɪ ˈəʊm ɪŋ aɪt ‖ -ˈoʊm- **~s** s
Wyre *district and river in England* ˈwaɪ͜ə ‖ ˈwaɪ͜ᵊr
Wyre *Welsh personal name* ˈwɪr ə
Wyrley ˈwɜːl i ‖ ˈwɜːl i
WYSIWYG, wysiwyg ˈwɪz i wɪɡ
Wystan ˈwɪst ən
Wytch wɪtʃ
Wythenshawe ˈwɪð ᵊn ʃɔː ‖ -ʃɑː
wyvern ˈwaɪv ᵊn -ɜːn ‖ -ᵊrn **~s** z

x Spelling-to-sound

1 Where the spelling is **x**, the pronunciation is regularly ks as in **six** sɪks. Less commonly, it is gz, and occasionally z or kʃ.

2 The pronunciation gz is found mainly in words beginning **ex-** before a stressed vowel, for example **exist** ɪg ˈzɪst. There is a variant pronunciation with kz. However, in words beginning **exce-**, **exci-**, the pronunciation is ks, with the **c** silent as in **exceed** ɪk ˈsiːd.

3 The pronunciation is regularly z at the beginning of a word as in **xerox** ˈzɪər ɒks ‖ ˈzɪr ɑːks. Note also **anxiety** æŋ ˈzaɪ‿ət i ‖ -əṭ i.

4 The pronunciation is kʃ in words ending **xious**, **xion**, **xure**, for example **crucifixion**, **anxious** ˈæŋk ʃəs. In **luxury** and its derivatives some speakers use kʃ, some gʒ.

5 ks is also regularly written
cks as in **kicks** kɪks
ks as in **thanks** θæŋks and
cc as in **accident** ˈæks ɪd ənt.

6 **x** is silent in certain names and other words borrowed from French as in **prix** priː.

X, x eks **X's, x's, Xs** ˈeks ɪz -əz —*Communications code name:* ˈX-ray
ˈX ˌchromosome
X-acto *tdmk* eks ˈækt əʊ ‖ -oʊ
Xan zæn
Xanadu ˈzæn ə duː ˈgzæn-, ˌ· ·ˈ· —*Chi* (Yuán)shàngdū [(²ɥɛn) ⁴ʂɑŋ ¹tu]
xanth- *comb. form before vowel*
with unstressed suffix ˈzænᵗθ ˈgzænᵗθ — **xanthene** ˈzænᵗθ iːn ˈgzænᵗθ-
with stressed suffix zæn θ+ gzæn θ+ — **xanthoma** zæn ˈθəʊm ə gzæn- ‖ -ˈθoʊm ə
Xanthe ˈzænᵗθ i ˈgzænᵗθ-
xanthelasma ˌzænᵗθ ɪ ˈlæz mə -ə-
xanthic ˈzænᵗθ ɪk
Xanthippe zæn ˈθɪp i gzæn-, -ˈtɪp-
xantho- *comb. form*
with stress-neutral suffix ¦zænᵗθ əʊ ¦gzænᵗθ əʊ ‖ -ə — **xanthochroic** ˌzænᵗθ əʊ ˈkrəʊ ɪk ◂ ˌgzænᵗθ- ‖ -ə ˈkroʊ-
with stress-imposing suffix zæn ˈθɒ+ gzæn ˈθɒ+ ‖ -ˈθɑː+ — **xanthochroism** zæn ˈθɒk rəʊ ˌɪz əm gzæn- ‖ -ˈθɑːk roʊ-
Xantia *tdmk* ˈzænt i‿ə
Xantippe zæn ˈtɪp i gzæn-
Xavier ˈzæv i‿ə ˈzeɪv- ‖ ᵊr —*Sp* [xa ˈβjer]
Xavierian zæ ˈvɪər i‿ən zeɪ- ‖ -ˈvɪr- **~s** z
x-axis ˈeks ˌæks ɪs §-əs
X-bar ˈeks bɑː ‖ -bɑːr
Xbox *tdmk* ˈeks bɒks ‖ -bɑːks **~es** ɪz əz
X-certificate ˈeks sə ˌtɪf ɪk ət -ɪt ‖ ˈeks sᵊr-
x-coordinate ˈeks kəʊ ˌɔːd ɪn ət -ᵊn‿ət, -ɪt ‖ -koʊ ˌɔːrd ᵊn‿ət -eɪt **~s** s
xebek ˈziːb ek ˈzeɪb- **~s** s
Xenia, xenia ˈziːn i‿ə ˈzen-
Xenical *tdmk* ˈzen ɪ kæl -ə-
Xenix *tdmk* ˈziːn ɪks
xeno- *comb. form*
with stress-neutral suffix ¦zen əʊ ¦ziːn əʊ ‖ -ə — **xenophile** ˈzen əʊ faɪᵊl ˈziːn- ‖ -ə-
with stress-imposing suffix ze ˈnɒ+ ziː-, zɪ- ‖ -ˈnɑː+ — **xenogamy** ze ˈnɒg əm i ziː-, zɪ- ‖ -ˈnɑːg-
xenon ˈziːn ɒn ˈzen-, ˈzen- ‖ ˈziːn ɑːn ˈzen-
Xenophanes ze ˈnɒf ə niːz zɪ-, zə- ‖ -ˈnɑːf-

xenophobe 'zen ə fəʊb 'ziːn- ‖ -foʊb **~s** z
xenophobia ˌzen ə 'fəʊb i͜ə ˌziːn- ‖ -'foʊb-
xenophobic ˌzen ə 'fəʊb ɪk ◂ ˌziːn- ‖ -'foʊb-
Xenophon 'zen əf ən -ə fɒn ‖ -ə fɑːn
xenotransplant 'zen əʊ ˌtrænᵗs plɑːnt 'ziːn-, -ˌtrɑːnᵗs-, §-plænt ‖ -oʊ ˌtrænᵗs plænt **~s** s
xer- *comb. form before vowel*
with unstressed suffix 'zɪər ‖ 'zɪr — **xerarch** 'zɪər ɑːk ‖ 'zɪr ɑːrk
with stressed suffix zɪə r+ zɪ r+, zə r+ ‖ zə r+ zɪ r+ — **xerosis** zɪə 'rəʊs ɪs zɪ-, zə- ‖ zə 'roʊs əs zɪ-
xeric 'zɪər ɪk ‖ 'zɪr ɪk
xero- *comb. form*
with stress-neutral suffix ¦zɪər əʊ ¦gzɪər əʊ ‖ ¦zɪr ə — **xeroderma** ˌzɪər əʊ 'dɜːm ə ˌgzɪər- ‖ ˌzɪr ə 'dɝːm ə
with stress-imposing suffix zɪə 'rɒ+ ze-, zɪ-, gzɪə-, gze-, §ziː- ‖ zə 'rɑː+ zɪ- — **xerophilous** zɪə 'rɒf ɪl əs ze-, zɪ-, gzɪə-, gze-, §ziː-, §-əl- ‖ zə 'rɑːf əl əs zɪ-
xerographic ˌzɪər ə 'græf ɪk ◂ ‖ ˌzɪr- **~ally** ᵊl͜ i
xerography zɪə 'rɒg rəf i ze-, zɪ-, §ziː- ‖ zə 'rɑːg- zɪ-
xerophthalmia ˌzɪər ɒf 'θælm i͜ə ˌ·ɒp- ‖ ˌzɪr ɑːf- ˌ·ɑːp-
xerophyte 'zɪər əʊ faɪt 'gzɪər- ‖ 'zɪr ə- **~s** s
xerox, Xerox *tdmk* 'zɪər ɒks ‖ 'zɪr ɑːks **~ed** t **~es** ɪz əz **~ing** ɪŋ
Xerxes 'zɜːks iːz ‖ 'zɝːks-
Xhosa 'kɔːs ə 'kəʊs-, 'kɔːz-, 'kəʊz- ‖ 'koʊs ə 'hoʊs- —*Xhosa* ['ǁʰɔː sa] **~s** z
xi *name of Greek letter* saɪ ksaɪ, zaɪ, gzaɪ ‖ zaɪ
xis, xi's saɪz ksaɪz, zaɪz, gzaɪz ‖ zaɪz
Xia *dynasty* ʃi 'ɑː —*Chi* Xià [⁴ɕja]
Xiamen ˌʃɑː 'mʌn ʃi ˌɑː- —*Chi* Xiàmén [⁴ɕja ²mən]
Xian, Xi'an ˌʃiː 'æn ‖ -'ɑːn —*Chi* Xī'ān [¹ɕi ¹an]
Ximenes 'zɪm ə niːz -ɪ- ‖ hɪ 'men ez —*Sp* [xi 'me nes]
xing, XING *in road signs* 'krɒs ɪŋ 'krɔːs- ‖ 'krɔːs ɪŋ 'krɑːs-
Xingu, Xingú ʃɪŋ 'guː ʃiːŋ-, '· · —*Port* [ʃiŋ 'gu]
Xinhua *News Agency* ˌʃɪn 'hwɑː —*Chi* Xīnhuá [¹ɕɪn ²xwa]
Xinjiang ˌʃɪn dʒi 'æŋ ‖ -'ɑːŋ —*Chi* Xīnjiāng [¹ɕɪn ¹tɕjaŋ]
xiphoid 'zɪf ɔɪd
Xmas 'krɪs məs 'eks-
XML ˌeks em 'el ◂
XP *Christian symbol, chi-ro* ˌkaɪ 'rəʊ ‖ -'roʊ
XP *computer operating system* ˌeks 'piː
X-rat|ed 'eks ˌreɪt ɪd -əd ‖ - -ˌreɪţ- **~ing** ɪŋ
x-ray, X-ray 'eks reɪ ˌ·'·◂ **~ed** d **~ing** ɪŋ **~s** z
Xsara *tdmk* 'zɑːr ə
xth eksθ
xyl- *comb. form before vowel*
with unstressed suffix zaɪl gzaɪl — **xylyl** 'zaɪl ɪl 'gzaɪl-, §-əl
with stressed suffix zaɪ 'l+ gzaɪ 'l+ — **xylamidine** zaɪ 'læm ɪ diːn gzaɪ-, §-ə-
xylem 'zaɪl əm -em
xylene 'zaɪl iːn 'gzaɪl-
xylidine 'zaɪl ɪ diːn -ə-
xylo- *comb. form*
with stress-neutral suffix ¦zaɪl əʊ ¦gzaɪl- ‖ -ə — **xylocarpous** ˌzaɪl əʊ 'kɑːp əs ◂ ˌgzaɪl- ‖ -ə 'kɑːrp-
with stress-imposing suffix zaɪ 'lɒ+ gzaɪ- ‖ -'lɑː+ — **xylography** zaɪ 'lɒg rəf i gzaɪ- ‖ -'lɑːg-
xylol 'zaɪl ɒl 'gzaɪl- ‖ -ɔːl -ɑːl, -oʊl
xylonite, X~ *tdmk* 'zaɪl ə naɪt 'gzaɪl-
xylophone 'zaɪl ə fəʊn 'zɪl-, 'gzaɪl- ‖ -foʊn **~s** z
xylophonist zaɪ 'lɒf ən ɪst 'zaɪl ə fəʊn-, §-əst ‖ 'zaɪl ə foʊn əst **~s** s
xylose 'zaɪl əʊz 'gzaɪl-, -əʊs ‖ -oʊs
xyster 'zɪst ə 'gzɪst- ‖ -ᵊr **~s** z

Y y

y Spelling-to-sound

1 At the beginning of a word or syllable, where the spelling is **y**, the pronunciation is j as in **yet** jet, **beyond** bi ˈjɒnd ‖ bɪ ˈjɑːnd.

2 Elsewhere, the same pronunciations correspond to **y** as to **i**, namely

ɪ ('short') as in **crystal** ˈkrist ᵊl

aɪ ('long') as in **type** taɪp

weak i as in **happy** ˈhæp i

or **y** may be part of one of the digraphs **ay, ey, oy, uy** (see under **a, e, o, u** respectively).

3 The sound j is also sometimes written **i**, as in **onion** ˈʌn jən.

It frequently arises through COMPRESSION of i with a following weak vowel as in **convenient** kən ˈviːn i‿ənt, → kən ˈviːn jənt. As part of the sequence juː (or one of its derivatives juə, jʊ, jɔː, ju, je) it is regularly written **eu, ew, u, ue**.

Y, y *name of letter* waɪ **Y's, y's, Ys** waɪz —*Communications code name:* Yoke
ˈY ˌchromosome
Y, y *in Welsh expressions* ə
-y i — **panicky** ˈpæn ɪk i
-y- *in Welsh place names* i ə —*Welsh* [ə]
yabber ˈjæb ə ‖ -ᵊr **~ed** d **yabbering** ˈjæb ər‿ɪŋ **~s** z
yabb|ie, yabb|y ˈjæb |i **~ies** iz
yacht jɒt ‖ jɑːt **yachted** ˈjɒt ɪd -əd ‖ ˈjɑːţ əd **yachting** ˈjɒt ɪŋ ‖ ˈjɑːţ ɪŋ **yachts** jɒts ‖ jɑːts
yachts|man ˈjɒts |mən ‖ ˈjɑːts- **~manship** mən ʃɪp **~men** mən **~woman** ˌwʊm ən **~women** ˌwɪm ɪn §-ən
yack jæk **yacked** jækt **yacking** ˈjæk ɪŋ **yacks** jæks
yackety-yak ˌjæk ət i ˈjæk ˌ·ɪt- ‖ ˌjæk əţ- **~ked** t **~king** ɪŋ **~s** s
yada yada, yadda yadda ˌjæd ə ˈjæd ə ‖ ˌjɑːd ə ˈjɑːd ə **yada ~, yadda ~** ˌjæd ə ‖ ˌjɑːd ə
yaffle ˈjæf ᵊl **~s** z
Yagi, yagi ˈjɑːg i ˈjæg- —*Jp* [ˈja ŋi, -gi, ·ˌ·] **~s** z
yah jɑː
yah-boo ˌjɑː ˈbuː ◂
ˌyah-boo ˈsucks
yahoo, Yahoo ⁽ˌ⁾jɑː ˈhuː jə-, ˈjɑː huː **~s** z
Yahveh ˈjɑː veɪ
Yahweh ˈjɑː weɪ
yak jæk **yaks** jæks
Yakima ˈjæk ɪ mɑː -ə- ‖ -mɔː -mɑː **~s** z
yakitori ˌjæk i ˈtɔːr i ‖ ˌjɑːk- ˌjæk- —*Jp* [ja ˌki̥ to ɾi]
yakka ˈjæk ə
Yakult *tdmk* ˈjæk ᵊlt
Yakut jə ˈkʊt jæ-, jɑː- ‖ -ˈkuːt **~s** s
Yakutsk jə ˈkʊtsk jæ-, jɑː- ‖ -ˈkuːtsk —*Russ* [jɪ ˈkutsk]
yakuza jə ˈkuːz ə ˈjæk u zɑː —*Jp* [ˈja kɯ dza]
Yalden ˈjɔːld ən ˈjɒld- ‖ ˈjɑːld-
Yale jeɪᵊl
y'all jɔːl ‖ jɑːl
Yalta ˈjælt ə ˈjɔːlt-, ˈjɒlt- ‖ ˈjɔːlt ə ˈjɑːlt- —*Russ* [ˈjał tə]
yam jæm **yams** jæmz
Yamaha *tdmk* ˈjæm ə hɑː -hə ‖ ˈjɑːm- **~s** z —*Jp* [ja ˌma ha]
Yamani jə ˈmɑːn i
yammer ˈjæm ə ‖ -ᵊr **~ed** d **yammering** ˈjæm ər ɪŋ **~s** z
Yamoussoukro ˌjæm u ˈsuːk rəʊ ‖ ˌjɑːm u ˈsuːk roʊ —*Fr* [ja mu su kʁo]
yang, Yang jæŋ ‖ jɑːŋ jæŋ
Yangon, Yangôn ˌjæŋ ˈgɒn ‖ ˌjɑːn ˈgoʊn

Yangtse, Yangtze 'jæŋᵏt si ‖ 'jɑːŋᵏt si —*Chi* Yángzǐ [²jɑŋ ³tsɯ]
ˌYangtse Ki'ang, -'Kiang ki 'æŋ kjæŋ ‖ -'ɑːŋ —*Chi* Jiāng [¹tɕjɑŋ]
Yangzhou ˌjæŋ 'dʒəʊ ‖ ˌjɑːŋ 'dʒoʊ —*Chi* Yángzhōu [²jɑŋ ¹tʂou]
yank, Yank jæŋk **yanked** jæŋkt **yanking** 'jæŋk ɪŋ **yanks, Yanks** jæŋks
Yankee 'jæŋk i **~dom** dəm **~ism/s** ˌɪz əm/z **~s** z
ˌYankee 'Doodle
Yaounde, Yaoundé jɑː 'ʊnd eɪ ‖ ˌjɑː ʊn 'deɪ —*Fr* [ja un de]
yap jæp **yapped** jæpt **yapping/ly** 'jæp ɪŋ /li **yaps** jæps
Yap *island* jæp jɑːp ‖ jɑːp
yapok jə 'pɒk ‖ -'pɑːk **~s** s
yapp, Yapp jæp
yapper 'jæp ə ‖ -ᵊr **~s** z
yappy 'jæp i
Yaqui 'jɑːk i **~s** z
Yarborough, y~ 'jɑː bər‿ə ‖'jɑːr ˌbɝː oʊ **~s** z
yard jɑːd ‖ jɑːrd **yards** jɑːdz ‖ jɑːrdz
yardag|e 'jɑːd ɪdʒ ‖ 'jɑːrd- **~es** ɪz əz
yardarm 'jɑːd ɑːm ‖ 'jɑːrd ɑːrm **~s** z
yardbird 'jɑːd bɜːd →'jɑːb- ‖ 'jɑːrd bɝːd **~s** z
yardie, Y~ 'jɑːd i ‖ 'jɑːrd i **~s** z
Yardley 'jɑːd li ‖ 'jɑːrd-
yardstick 'jɑːd stɪk ‖ 'jɑːrd- **~s** s
yardwork 'jɑːd wɜːk ‖ 'jɑːrd wɝːk
Yare, yare jeə ‖ jeᵊr jæᵊr, jɑːr
Yaren 'jɑːr en 'jær-, -ən
Yarm jɑːm ‖ jɑːrm
Yarmouth 'jɑː məθ ‖ 'jɑːr-
yarmulka, yarmulke 'jɑːm ʊlk ə 'jʌm-, -ᵊlk- ‖ 'jɑːrm- 'jɑːm-, -ək- **~s** z
yarn jɑːn ‖ jɑːrn **yarned** jɑːnd ‖ jɑːrnd **yarning** 'jɑːn ɪŋ ‖ 'jɑːrn ɪŋ **yarns** jɑːnz ‖ jɑːrnz
Yarra 'jær ə
Yarralumla ˌjær ə 'lʌm lə
yarrow, Y~ 'jær əʊ ‖ -oʊ 'jer- **~s** z
Yarwood 'jɑː wʊd ‖ 'jɑːr-
yashmak 'jæʃ mæk ‖ 'jɑːʃ mɑːk **~s** s
Yasmin, Yasmine 'jæs mɪn 'jæz-, 'jɑːs-
Yasser, Yassir 'jæs ə ‖ 'jɑːs ᵊr —*Arabic* ['jaː sir]
yataghan 'jæt əg ən ‖ 'jæţ ə gæn -əg ən **~s** z
Yates jeɪts
yatter 'jæt ə ‖ 'jæţ ᵊr **~ed** d **yattering** 'jæt‿ər ɪŋ ‖ 'jæţ ər ɪŋ **~s** z
Yaunde jɑː 'ʊnd eɪ ‖ ˌjɑː ʊn 'deɪ —*Fr* Yaoundé [ja un de]
Yavapai 'jæv ə paɪ ‖ 'jɑːv- -ɑː-
yaw jɔː ‖ jɑː **yawed** jɔːd ‖ jɑːd **yawing/s** 'jɔːʳ ɪŋ/z ‖ 'jɔː ɪŋz 'jɑː- **yaws** jɔːz ‖ jɑːz
yawl jɔːl ‖ jɑːl **yawls** jɔːlz ‖ jɑːlz
yawn jɔːn ‖ jɑːn **yawned** jɔːnd ‖ jɑːnd **yawning/ly** 'jɔːn ɪŋ /li ‖ 'jɑːn- **yawns** jɔːnz ‖ jɑːnz
yawp jɔːp ‖ jɑːp **yawped** jɔːpt ‖ jɑːpt **yawping** 'jɔːp ɪŋ ‖ 'jɑːp- **yawps** jɔːps ‖ jɑːps
yaws jɔːz ‖ jɑːz
y-axis 'waɪ ˌæks ɪs §-əs
yclept ɪ 'klept iː-
y-coordinate 'waɪ kəʊ ˌɔːd ɪn ət -ᵊn‿ət, -ɪt ‖ -koʊ ˌɔːrd ᵊn‿ət -eɪt **~s** s
ye *pronoun strong form* jiː, *weak form* ji
ye *'the'* jiː —*or see* **the**
yea jeɪ **yeas** jeɪz
Yeading 'jed ɪŋ
Yeadon *(i)* 'jiːd ᵊn, *(ii)* 'jeɪd ᵊn, *(iii)* 'jed ᵊn —*The place in WYks is (i), that in PA (ii). The family name may be any of the three.*
yeah jeə ‖ 'je ə

YEAR

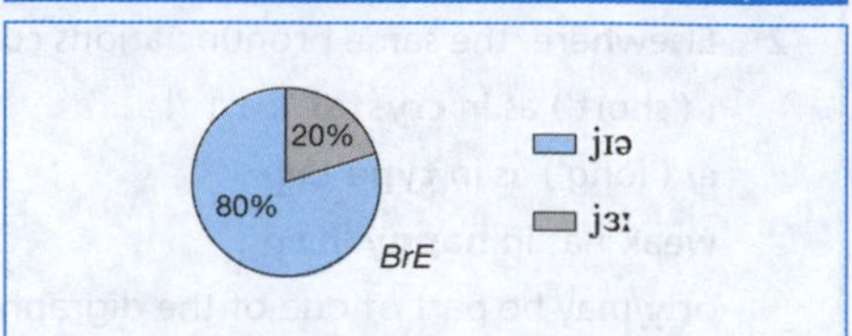

year jɪə jɜː ‖ jɪᵊr — *Preference poll, BrE:* jɪə *80%,* jɜː *20%.* **years** jɪəz jɜːz ‖ jɪᵊrz
ˌyear 'dot
yearbook 'jɪə bʊk 'jɜː- ‖ 'jɪr- **~s** s
year-end ˌjɪər'end ◂ ‖ ˌjɪr-
yearling 'jɪə lɪŋ 'jɜː- ‖ 'jɪr- **~s** z
yearlong ˌjɪə 'lɒŋ ◂ ˌjɜː- ‖ ˌjɪr 'lɔːŋ ◂ -'lɑːŋ
yearly 'jɪə li 'jɜː- ‖ 'jɪr li
yearn jɜːn ‖ jɝːn **yearned** jɜːnd ‖ jɝːnd **yearning** 'jɜːn ɪŋ ‖ 'jɝːn ɪŋ **yearns** jɜːnz ‖ jɝːnz
yearning 'jɜːn ɪŋ ‖ 'jɝːn ɪŋ **~ly** li **~s** z
year-round ˌjɪə 'raʊnd ◂ ˌjɜː- ‖ ˌjɪr-
yeast jiːst **yeasts** jiːsts
yeast|y 'jiːst |i **~ier** i‿ə ‖ i‿ᵊr **~iest** i‿ɪst i‿əst **~ily** ɪ li əl i **~iness** i nəs i nɪs
Yeates, Yeats jeɪts *(!)*
yecch, yech jex jek, jʌx, jʌk
Yehudi jɪ 'huːd i jə-, je-
yell, Yell jel **yelled** jeld **yelling** 'jel ɪŋ **yells** jelz
Yelland 'jel ənd
yellow 'jel əʊ ‖ -oʊ **~ed** d **~ing** ɪŋ **~s** z
ˌyellow 'fever; **ˌYellow 'Pages** ‖ '. . ˌ. .; **'yellow ˌrattle**; **ˌYellow 'Sea**
yellowhammer 'jel əʊ ˌhæm ə ‖ -oʊ ˌhæm ᵊr -ə- **~s** z
yellowish 'jel əʊ ɪʃ ‖ -oʊ-
Yellowknife 'jel əʊ naɪf ‖ -oʊ- -ə-
yellow|ly 'jel əʊ |li ‖ -oʊ- **~ness** nəs nɪs
Yellowstone 'jel əʊ stəʊn ‖ -oʊ stoʊn -ə-
yellowwood 'jel əʊ wʊd ‖ -oʊ- -ə- **~s** z
yellowy 'jel əʊ i ‖ -oʊ-
yelp jelp **yelped** jelpt **yelping** 'jelp ɪŋ **yelps** jelps
Yeltsin 'jelts ɪn -ᵊn —*Russ* ['jelʲ tsin]
Yelverton 'jelv ət ən ‖ -ᵊrt ᵊn
Yemen 'jem ən 'jeɪm-
Yemeni 'jem ən i 'jeɪm- **~s** z
yen *'Japanese currency'* jen —*Jp* ['eɴ]

Y

yen *'long(ing)'* jen **yenned** jend **yenning** ˈjen ɪŋ **yens** jenz
Yenisei, Yenisey ˌjen ɪ ˈseɪ -ə- —*Russ* [jɪ nʲɪ ˈsʲej]
Yeo jəʊ ‖ joʊ *(!)*
yeo|man ˈjəʊ |mən ‖ ˈjoʊ- **~manly** mən li **~manry** mən ri **~men** mən ˌ**yeoman 'service** ‖ ˈ· · ˌ· ·
Yeovil ˈjəʊ vɪl -vᵊl ‖ ˈjoʊ-
yep jep —*usually said with no audible release of the* p
yer *'weak vowel in Slavonic languages'* jɜː ‖ jɜ˞ː **yers** jɜːz ‖ jɜ˞ːz
yer *informal spelling of the weak form of 'your' or 'you're'* jə ‖ jᵊr
yer *informal spelling of the weak form of 'you' (BrE only)* jə ‖ —
yer *informal 'yes' (BrE only)* jeə jɜː ‖ —
Yerba Buena ˌjeəb ə ˈbweɪn ə ˌjɜːb- ‖ ˌjerb- ˌjɜ˞ːb-
Yerevan ˌjer ə ˈvæn -vɑːn, -ɪ-, ˈ· · · ‖ -ˈvɑːn —*Russ* [jɪ rʲɪ ˈvan]
Yerkes ˈjɜːk iːz ‖ ˈjɜ˞ːk-
yes jes —*Casual variants include* yah, yeah, yep, yup *(see).* **yeses** ˈjes ɪz -əz
yeshiva, yeshivah jə ˈʃiːv ə **~s** z
yes-|man ˈjes |mæn **~men** men
yes/no question ˌjes ˈnəʊ ˌkwes tʃən -ˌkweʃ- ‖ -ˈnoʊ- **~s** z
yessir ˈjes ɜː ‖ -ɜ˞ː
yesterday ˈjest əd i -ə deɪ; §ˌ· ·ˈdeɪ ‖ -ᵊrd i -ᵊr deɪ **~s, ~'s** z
yesteryear ˈjest ə jɪə -jɜː, ˌ· ·ˈ· ‖ -ᵊr jɪr
yet jet
Yetholm ˈjet əm ‖ ˈjeṭ-
yeti ˈjet i ‖ ˈjeṭ i **~s** z
Yevtushenko ˌjev tu ˈʃeŋk əʊ -tə- ‖ -oʊ —*Russ* [jɪf tu ˈʃeŋ kə]
yew juː *(= you, ewe, U)* **yews** juːz *(= use v.)*
Y-front *tdmk* ˈwaɪ frʌnt **~s** s
Ygdrasil, Yggdrasil ˈɪg drə sɪl
YHA ˌwaɪ eɪtʃ ˈeɪ §-heɪtʃ-
yid jɪd **yids** jɪdz
Yiddish ˈjɪd ɪʃ
yiddisher, Y~ ˈjɪd ɪʃ ə ‖ -ᵊr **~s** z
yield jiːᵊld **yielded** ˈjiːᵊld ɪd -əd **yielding/ly** ˈjiːᵊld ɪŋ /li **yields** jiːᵊldz
yikes jaɪks
yin, Yin jɪn
yip jɪp **yipped** jɪpt **yipping** ˈjɪp ɪŋ **yips** jɪps
yippee ₍ˌ₎jɪ ˈpiː ‖ ˈjɪp i
-yl ᵊl ɪl, aɪᵊl ‖ -iːᵊl —*in BrE there is an inconsistent preference for* aɪᵊl *in* butyl *but* ᵊl *in* methyl
ylang-ylang ˌiːl æŋ ˈiːl æŋ ˌiːl æŋ i ˈlæŋ; ⚠jə ˌlæŋ jə ˈlæŋ ‖ ˌiːl ɑːŋ ˈiːl ɑːŋ
YMCA ˌwaɪ em siː ˈeɪ
-yne aɪn — **alkyne** ˈælk aɪn
yngling ˈɪŋ lɪŋ **~s** z
Ynys ˈʌn ɪs ⚠ˈɪn- —*Welsh* [ˈə nis, -nis] ˌ**Ynys 'Mon,** ˌ**Ynys 'Môn** mɔːn —*Welsh* [moːn]
Ynys-ddu ˌʌn ɪs ˈdiː -ˈðiː —*Welsh* [ˌə nis ˈðiː]
Ynysybwl ˌʌn ɪs ə ˈbʊl —*Welsh* [ˌə nis ə ˈbʊl]
yo jəʊ ‖ joʊ
yob jɒb ‖ jɑːb **yobs** jɒbz ‖ jɑːbz
yobbish ˈjɒb ɪʃ ‖ ˈjɑːb- **~ly** li **~ness** nəs nɪs
yobbism ˈjɒb ˌɪz əm ‖ ˈjɑːb-
yobbo ˈjɒb əʊ ‖ ˈjɑːb oʊ **~s** z
yod jɒd ‖ jɑːd jɔːd, jʊd **yods** jɒdz ‖ jɑːdz jɔːdz, jʊdz
yodel ˈjəʊd ᵊl ‖ ˈjoʊd ᵊl **~ed, ~led** d **~ing, ~ling** ɪŋ **~s** z
yoga ˈjəʊg ə ‖ ˈjoʊg ə
yogh jɒg jəʊg ‖ joʊg joʊk, joʊx **yoghs** jɒgz jəʊgz ‖ joʊgz joʊks, joʊxs
yoghourt, yoghurt ˈjɒg ət -ʊət ‖ ˈjoʊg ᵊrt *(*)* **~s** s
yogi ˈjəʊg i ‖ ˈjoʊg i **~s** z
yogic ˈjəʊg ɪk ‖ ˈjoʊg-
yogurt ˈjɒg ət -ʊət ‖ ˈjoʊg ᵊrt *(*)* **~s** s
yo-heave-ho jəʊ ˌhiːv ˈhəʊ ‖ joʊ ˌhiːv ˈhoʊ
yohimbine jəʊ ˈhɪm biːn ‖ joʊ-
yo-ho ₍ˌ₎jəʊ ˈhəʊ ‖ ₍ˌ₎joʊ ˈhoʊ
yo-ho-ho ˌjəʊ ˌhəʊ ˈhəʊ ‖ ˌjoʊ ˌhoʊ ˈhoʊ
yoicks jɔɪks
yoke jəʊk ‖ joʊk **yoked** jəʊkt ‖ joʊkt **yokes** jəʊks ‖ joʊks **yoking** ˈjəʊk ɪŋ ‖ ˈjoʊk ɪŋ
yokel ˈjəʊk ᵊl ‖ ˈjoʊk ᵊl **~s** z
Yoknapatawpha ˌjɒk nə pə ˈtɔːf ə ‖ ˌjɑːk- -ˈtɑːf-
Yoko ˈjəʊk əʊ ‖ ˈjoʊk oʊ —*Jp* [ˈjoo ko]
Yokohama ˌjəʊk əʊ ˈhɑːm ə ‖ ˌjoʊk ə- —*Jp* [jo ˌko ha ma]
Yolanda jəʊ ˈlænd ə ‖ joʊ- -ˈlɑːnd-
yolk jəʊk ‖ joʊk joʊlk, jelk *(= yoke)* **yolks** jəʊks ‖ joʊks joʊlks, jelks
Yom Kippur ˌjɒm kɪ ˈpʊə ·ˈkɪp ə ‖ ˌjoʊm ˈkɪp ᵊr ˌjɔːm-, ˌjɑːm-, -kɪ ˈpʊᵊr
yomp jɒmp ‖ jɑːmp **yomped** jɒmpt ‖ jɑːmpt **yomping** ˈjɒmp ɪŋ ‖ ˈjɑːmp ɪŋ **yomps** jɒmps ‖ jɑːmps
yon jɒn ‖ jɑːn
yond jɒnd ‖ jɑːnd
yonder ˈjɒnd ə ‖ ˈjɑːnd ᵊr
Yonge jʌŋ
yoni ˈjəʊn i ‖ ˈjoʊn i **~s** z
Yonkers ˈjɒŋk əz ‖ ˈjɑːŋk ᵊrz
yonks jɒŋks ‖ jɑːŋks
yoof *non-standard variant of* youth juːf
yoo-hoo ˌjuː ˈhuː ˈ· · ‖ ˈjuː huː
YOP jɒp ‖ jɑːp
Yorba Linda ˌjɔːb ə ˈlɪnd ə ‖ ˌjɔːrb- —*Sp* [ˌjor βa ˈlin da]
yore, Yore jɔː ‖ jɔːr joʊr
Yorick ˈjɒr ɪk ‖ ˈjɔːr ɪk ˈjɑːr-
York, york, Yorke jɔːk ‖ jɔːrk **yorked** jɔːkt ‖ jɔːrkt **yorking** ˈjɔːk ɪŋ ‖ ˈjɔːrk ɪŋ **yorks, York's** jɔːks ‖ jɔːrks
yorker ˈjɔːk ə ‖ ˈjɔːrk ᵊr **~s** z
yorkie, Y~ *tdmk* ˈjɔːk i ‖ ˈjɔːrk i **~s** z
Yorkist ˈjɔːk ɪst §-əst ‖ ˈjɔːrk- **~s** s
Yorks. jɔːks ‖ jɔːrks

Yorkshire 'jɔːk ʃə -ʃɪə ‖ 'jɔːrk ʃᵊr -ʃɪr **~man** mən **~men** mən men **~s** z **~woman** ˌwʊm ən **~women** ˌwɪm ɪn §-ən
ˌYorkshire 'pudding; **ˌYorkshire 'terrier**
Yorktown 'jɔːk taʊn ‖ 'jɔːrk-
Yoruba 'jɒr ʊb ə ‖ 'jɔːr əb ə **~s** z
Yosemite jəʊ 'sem ət i -ɪt- ‖ joʊ 'sem əṭ i
Yossarian jɒ 'seər i ən -'sɑːr- ‖ joʊ 'ser- -'sɑːr-
Yost jəʊst ‖ joʊst
you *strong form* **juː**, *weak forms* **ju jə**, *before a vowel also* §j *—(1) Learners of BrE are advised not to use weak forms other than* **ju**; **jə** *is unusual in RP, while* **j** *is clearly non-RP. In GenAm, on the other hand, the weak form* **jə** *is acceptable. —(2) The initial* **j** *of this word readily coalesces with the final* **t** *or* **d** *of a preceding word to give* **tʃ** *or* **dʒ** *respectively:* don't you **'dəʊntʃ u** ‖ **'doʊntʃ ə**, did you **'dɪdʒ u** ‖ **-ə**
you-all ju 'ɔːl jɔːl ‖ jɔːl, ju 'ɑːl, jɑːl
you'd *strong form* **juːd**, *weak forms* **jud** jəd *—See note (1) at* you
Youel, Youell 'juː əl juːl
Youens 'juː ɪnz ənz
Youghal jɔːl ‖ jɑːl
you-know-what ˌjuː nəʊ 'wɒt -'hwɒt ‖ -noʊ 'wʌt -'wɑːt, -'hwʌt, -'hwɑːt
you-know-who ˌjuː nəʊ 'huː ‖ -noʊ-
you'll *strong forms* **juːl** juː əl, *weak forms* **jul** jəl *—See note (1) at* you
young, Young jʌŋ **younger** 'jʌŋ gə ‖ -gᵊr **youngest** 'jʌŋ gɪst -gəst
ˌyoung 'man; **ˌyoung 'woman**
Younger 'jʌŋ gə ‖ -gᵊr
Younghusband 'jʌŋ ˌhʌz bənd
youngish 'jʌŋ ɪʃ -gɪʃ
youngling 'jʌŋ lɪŋ **~s** z
youngster 'jʌŋᵏst ə ‖ -ᵊr **~s** z
Youngstown 'jʌŋz taʊn
your *strong forms* **jɔː** jʊə ‖ **jʊᵊr** jɔːr, joʊr, *weak form* **jə** ‖ **jᵊr** *—Learners of BrE are advised not to use the weak form* **jə**, *which is fairly unusual in RP.*
you're *strong forms* **jɔː** jʊə ‖ **jʊᵊr**, *weak form* **jə** ‖ **jᵊr** *—Learners of BrE are advised not to use the weak form* **jə**, *which is fairly unusual in RP. (= your)*

YOURS

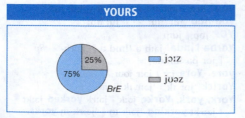

jɔːz 75%
jʊəz 25%
BrE

yours jɔːz jʊəz ‖ jʊᵊrz jɔːrz, joʊrz — *Preference poll, BrE:* jɔːz *75%,* jʊəz *25%.*
ˌyours 'truly
your|self jɔː |'self jʊə-, jə- ‖ jʊr- jɔːr-, jᵊr-, joʊr- **~selves** 'selvz
yous, youse *strong form* **juːz**, *weak forms* **jəz**, jɪz *—This second person pl pronoun, being non-standard, has no standard pronunciation.*

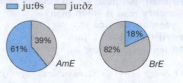

YOUTHS

juːθs 61%
juːðz 39%
AmE
juːθs 18%
juːðz 82%
BrE

youth juːθ **youths** juːðz juːθs ‖ **juːθs** juːðz *— Preference polls, AmE:* juːθs *61%,* juːðz *39%; BrE:* juːðz *82%,* juːθs *18%.* **youth's** **juːθs**
'youth club; **'youth ˌhostel**
youthful 'juːθ fᵊl -fʊl **~ly** i **~ness** nəs nɪs
YouTube 'juː tjuːb →-tʃuːb ‖ -tuːb -tjuːb
you've *strong form* **juːv**, *weak forms* **juv** jəv *—See note (1) at* you
yow jaʊ
yowl jaʊl **yowled** jaʊld **yowling** 'jaʊl ɪŋ **yowls** jaʊlz
yoyo, yo-yo, Yo-Yo *tdmk* 'jəʊ jəʊ ‖ 'joʊ joʊ **~s** z
Ypres 'iːp rə -rəz, -əz; iːp; 'waɪp əz *—Fr* [ipχ]
Yr, yr *in Welsh expressions* ər
Ystalyfera ˌʌst əl ə 'ver ə *—Welsh* [ˌəs dal ə 've ra]
Ystrad 'ʌs trəd *—Welsh* ['əs drad]
Ystradgynlais ˌʌs trəd 'gʌn laɪs -træd- *—Welsh* [ˌəs drad 'gən lais]
Ystwyth 'ʌst wɪθ *—Welsh* ['əs duiθ, -duɨθ]
Ythan 'aɪθ ᵊn
YTS ˌwaɪ tiː 'es
ytterbium ɪ 'tɜːb i əm ‖ -'tɝːb-
yttrium 'ɪtr i əm
Yu juː *—Cantonese* [⁴jyː]
yuan, Yuan ju 'æn -'ɑːn ‖ -'ɑːn *—Chi* yuán [²ɥæn]
Yucatan, Yucatán ˌjʊk ə 'tɑːn ˌjuːk-, -'tæn ‖ ˌjuːk ə 'tæn -'tɑːn *—Sp* [ju ka 'tan]
yucca 'jʌk ə 'juːk- **~s** z
yuck jʌk
yuck|y 'jʌk |i **~ier** i ə ‖ i ᵊr **~iest** i ɪst i əst
Yudkin 'juːd kɪn
Yue *(i)* ju 'eɪ *—Chi* Yuè [⁴ɥɛ]; *(ii)* juː, *Cantonese* [⁴jyː]
Yugoslav 'juːg əʊ slɑːv ˌ·'· ‖ ˌjuːg oʊ 'slɑːv ◂ -'slæv **~s** z
Yugoslavi|a ˌjuːg əʊ 'slɑːv i |ə ‖ ˌ·oʊ- **~an/s** ən/z
yuk jʌk **yukked** jʌkt **yukking** 'jʌk ɪŋ **yuks** jʌks
yukk|y 'jʌk |i **~ier** i ə ‖ i ᵊr **~iest** i ɪst i əst
Yukon 'juːk ɒn ‖ -ɑːn
yuks jʌks
Yul juːl
yule, Yule juːl
'yule log
yuletide, Y~ 'juːl taɪd
yum jʌm

Yuma ˈjuːm ə **~s** z
Yuman ˈjuːm ən
yumm|y ˈjʌm |i **~ier** i‿ə ‖ i‿ᵊr **~iest** i‿ɪst i‿əst
yum-yum, Yum-Yum ˌjʌm ˈjʌm
Yunnan ˌjuː ˈnæn ˌjʊn- ‖ -ˈnɑːn —*Chi* Yúnnán [²jʏn ²nan]
yup jʌp —*usually said with no audible release of the* p
Yupik ˈjuːp ɪk **~s** s
yuppie, Y~ ˈjʌp i **~s** z
yuppification ˌjʌp ɪf ɪ ˈkeɪʃ ᵊn ˌ·əf-, §-əˈ·-
yuppi|fy ˈjʌp ɪ |faɪ §-ə- **~fied** faɪd **~fies** faɪz **~fying** faɪ ɪŋ
yupp|y, Yupp|y ˈjʌp| i **~ies** iz
Yuri ˈjʊər i ‖ ˈjʊr i ˈjɜː- —*Russ* [ˈju rʲi]
Yurok ˈjʊər ɒk ‖ ˈjʊr ɑːk
yurt jʊət jɜːt ‖ jʊᵊrt **yurts** jʊəts jɜːts ‖ jʊᵊrts
Yussuf ˈjʊs ʊf -əf
Yves iːv —*Fr* [iːv]
Yvette ɪ ˈvet ₍ˌ₎iː-
Yvonne ɪ ˈvɒn ₍ˌ₎iː- ‖ -ˈvɑːn

Y

Zz

z Spelling-to-sound

1 Where the spelling is **z**, the pronunciation is regularly z as in **lazy** ˈleɪz i.

2 Where the spelling is double **zz**, the pronunciation is again z as in **dazzle** ˈdæz ᵊl.

3 Because of yod coalescence (see ASSIMILATION), the pronunciation is occasionally ʒ as in **seizure** ˈsiːʒ ə ‖ ˈsiːʒ ᵊr.

4 In certain words borrowed from foreign languages, spelling with **z**, **zz** or the foreign digraph **tz**, the pronunciation is ts as in **Nazi** ˈnɑːts i, **pizza** ˈpiːts ə, **quartz** kwɔːts ‖ kwɔːrts.

5 The sound z is also regularly written **s** as in **choose** tʃuːz.

Z, z zed ‖ ziː *(*)* **Z's, z's, Zs** zedz ‖ ziːz —*Communications code name:* Zulu
-z *alternative, non-standard, spelling of the plural ending -s.* **Bratz** *tdmk* bræts **boyz** bɔɪz *See* **-s**
zabaglione ˌzæb ᵊl ˈjəʊn i -æl-, -eɪ ‖ ˌzɑːb ᵊl ˈjoʊn i —*It* zabaione [dza ba ˈjoː ne] **~s** z
Zachariah ˌzæk ə ˈraɪ‿ə
Zachary ˈzæk ər i
Zadok ˈzeɪd ɒk ‖ -ɑːk
zaftig ˈzɑːft ɪɡ ˈzæft- —*Ger* saftig [ˈzaf tɪç]
Zagreb ˈzɑːɡ reb ˈzæɡ-, ˌzɑː ˈɡreb —*Croatian* [ˈza ɡrɛb]
Zaire, Zaïre, zaire ₍ˌ₎zaɪ ˈɪə zɑː- ‖ zɑː ˈɪᵊr ˈzɑː ɪr
Zairean, Zaïrean zaɪ ˈɪər i‿ən zɑː- ‖ zɑː ˈɪr- **~s** z
Zak zæk
Zambezi ₍ˌ₎zæm ˈbiːz i
Zambia ˈzæm bi‿ə
Zambian ˈzæm bi‿ən **~s** z
zambuck, Z~, Zam-Buk *tdmk* ˈzæm bʌk **~s** s
Zamenhof ˈzæm ən hɒf -en- ‖ ˈzɑːm ən hoʊf
Zander, z~ ˈzænd ə ‖ -ᵊr **~s** z
Zandra ˈzɑːndr ə ˈzændr-
Zane zeɪn
Zangwill ˈzæŋ wɪl -wəl, -ɡwɪl, -ɡwəl
Zantac *tdmk* ˈzænt æk
Zante ˈzænt i
ZANU ˈzɑːn uː ˈzæn-
Zanuck ˈzæn ək
zan|y ˈzeɪn |i **~ier** i‿ə ‖ i‿ᵊr **~ies** iz **~iest** i‿ɪst i‿əst **~ily** ɪ li əl i **~iness** i nəs i nɪs
Zanzibar ˈzænz ɪ bɑː -ə-, ˌ· ·ˈ· ‖ -bɑːr
Zanzibari ˌzænz ɪ ˈbɑːr i ◂ -ə- **~s** z
zap zæp **zapped** zæpt **zapping** ˈzæp ɪŋ **zaps** zæps
Zapata zə ˈpɑːt ə zæ- ‖ -ˈpɑːt̬- —*AmSp* [sa ˈpa ta]
Zapotec ˈzæp ə tek ˈzɑːp-, ˌ· ·ˈ·
zapp... —*see* **zap**
Zappa ˈzæp ə
zapper ˈzæp ə ‖ -ᵊr **~s** z
Zara ˈzɑːr ə
Zaragoza ˌsær ə ˈɡɒs ə ‖ ˌzær ə ˈɡoʊz ə —*Sp* [θa ɾa ˈɣo θa]
Zarathustra ˌzær ə ˈθuːs trə ‖ ˌzer-
Zaria ˈzɑːr i‿ə
Zarqawi zɑː ˈkɑː wi ‖ zɑːr- —*Arabic* [zar ˈqaː wiː]
Zatopek ˈzæt ə pek ‖ ˈzæt̬- —*Czech* Zátopek [ˈzaː to pek]
zax zæks **zaxes** ˈzæks ɪz -əz
z-axis ˈzed ˌæks ɪs §-əs ‖ ˈziː-
zeal, Zeal ziːᵊl
Zealand ˈziː lənd
zealot ˈzel ət **~s** s
zealotry ˈzel ət ri
zealous ˈzel əs **~ly** li **~ness** nəs nɪs
Zebedee ˈzeb ə diː -ɪ-
zebra ˈzeb rə ˈziːb- ‖ ˈziːb- — *Preference poll, BrE:* ˈzeb- *83%,* ˈziːb- *17%.* **~s** z **ˌzebra ˈcrossing**
zebu ˈziːb uː -juː **~s** z
Zebulon, Zebulun ˈzeb jʊl ən ze ˈbjuːl-, zə-
Zechariah ˌzek ə ˈraɪ‿ə
zed zed **zeds** zedz

ZEBRA

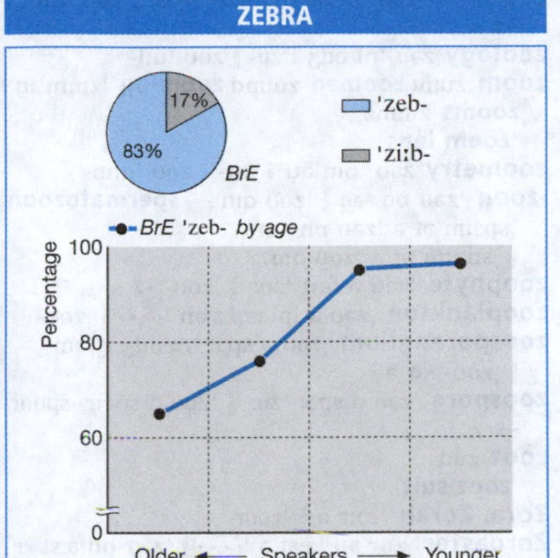

Zedekiah ˌzed ɪ ˈkaɪ ə -ə-
zedoary ˈzed əʊ ər i zə ˈdəʊ- ‖ -oʊ er i
zee ziː **zees** ziːz
Zeebrugge ˌzeɪ ˈbrʊɡ ə ˌziː-, ˈ·ˌ· ·, zɪ'· ·; ˈzeɪ bruːʒ —*Dutch* [ˈzeː ˌbrɪɣ ə]
Zeeland ˈziː lənd —*Dutch* [ˈzeː lɑnt]
Zeeman ˈziː mən —*Dutch* [ˈzeː mɑn]
Zeffirelli ˌzef ə ˈrel i -ɪ- —*It* [dzef fi ˈrɛl li]
Zeiss zaɪs —*Ger* [tsais]
zeitgeist ˈzaɪt ɡaɪst —*Ger* Z~ [ˈtsait ɡaist]
zek, Zek zek **zeks** zeks
Zelda ˈzeld ə
Zeldin ˈzeld ɪn §-ən
zelkova ˈzelk əv ə zel ˈkəʊv ə ‖ zel ˈkoʊv ə **~s** z
Zellweger ˈzel weɡ ə ‖ -ᵊr
Zelotes zɪ ˈləʊt iːz zə-, ze- ‖ -ˈloʊt-
Zen zen —*Jp* [ˈdzeɴ, dzeˌɴ]
 ˌZen ˈBuddhism
Zena ˈziːn ə
zenana ze ˈnɑːn ə zɪ-, zə- **~s** z
Zend zend
Zenda ˈzend ə
Zeneca *tdmk* ˈzen ɪk ə -ək-
Zener ˈziːn ə ˈzen- ‖ -ᵊr
 ˌZener ˈdiode
zenith ˈzen ɪθ ˈziːn-, §-əθ ‖ ˈziːn əθ **~s** s
zenithal ˈzen ɪθ ᵊl ˈziːn-, §-əθ- ‖ ˈziːn əθ ᵊl
Zennor ˈzen ə ‖ -ᵊr
Zeno ˈziːn əʊ ‖ -oʊ
Zenobia zɪ ˈnəʊb i ə zə-, ze- ‖ -ˈnoʊb-
zeolite ˈziː ə laɪt **~s** s
Zephaniah ˌzef ə ˈnaɪ ə
zephyr ˈzef ə ‖ -ᵊr **~s** z
Zephyrus ˈzef ər əs -ɪr-
zeppelin, Z~ ˈzep əl ɪn §-ən —*Ger* [ˈtsɛp ə liːn] **~s** z
Zermatt ˈzɜː mæt ‖ tser ˈmɑːt —*Ger* [tsɛʁ ˈmat]
zero ˈzɪər əʊ ˈzɪr- ‖ ˈzɪr oʊ ˈziː roʊ **~ed** d **~es, ~s** z **~ing** ɪŋ
 ˌzero ˈgravity; **ˈzero ˌhour**
zero-coupon ˌzɪər əʊ ˈkuːp ɒn ◂ ‖ ˌzɪr oʊ ˈkuːp ɑːn -ˈkjuːp-
zero-rated ˌzɪər əʊ ˈreɪt ɪd ◂ ˌzɪr-, -əd, ˈ· ·ˌ· · ‖ ˌzɪr oʊ ˈreɪţ əd ◂ ˌziː roʊ-
zero-sum ˌzɪər əʊ ˈsʌm ◂ ‖ ˌzɪr oʊ- ˈ· · ·
zeroth *ordinal numeral* ˈzɪər əʊθ ˈzɪr- ‖ ˈzɪr oʊθ ˈziː roʊθ
zest zest
zestful ˈzest fᵊl -fʊl **~ly** i
zest|y ˈzest |i **~ier** i ə ‖ i ᵊr **~iest** i ɪst i əst
zeta, Zeta ˈziːt ə ‖ ˈzeɪţ ə ˈziːţ- **~s** z
Zetec *tdmk* ˈziː tek
Zetland ˈzet lənd
Zetters ˈzet əz ‖ ˈzeţ ᵊrz
zeugma ˈzjuːɡ mə ˈzuːɡ- ‖ ˈzuːɡ- **~s** z
Zeus zjuːs zuːs; ˈziː əs ‖ zuːs
Zeuxis ˈzjuːks ɪs ˈzuːks-, §-əs ‖ ˈzuːks-
Zewe ˈziː wi
Zhang dʒæŋ ‖ dʒɑːŋ —*Chi* Zhāng [¹ʈʂɑŋ]
Zhejiang ˌdʒɜː dʒi ˈæŋ ‖ ˌdʒʌdʒ i ˈɑːŋ —*Chi* Zhèjiāng [⁴ʈʂɤ ¹tɕjɑŋ]
Zhirinovsky ˌʒɪr ɪ ˈnɒf ski -ə- ‖ -ˈnɑːf- —*Russ* [ʐɨ rʲi ˈnɔf skʲij]
Zhivago ʒɪ ˈvɑːɡ əʊ ʒə- ‖ -oʊ
Zhou *dynasty* dʒəʊ tʃəʊ ‖ dʒoʊ tʃoʊ —*Chi* Zhōu [¹ʈʂou]
 ˌZhou En'lai ˌtʃəʊ en ˈlaɪ -ən- ‖ ˌtʃoʊ- —*Chi* Zhōu Ēnlái [¹ʈʂou ¹ən ²lai]
Zhuhai ˌdʒuː ˈhaɪ —*Chi* Zhūhǎi [¹ʈʂu ³xai]
Zhukov ˈʒuːk ɒv -ɒf ‖ -ɔːf -ɑːf—*Russ* [ˈʒu kəf]
zibeline, zibelline ˈzɪb ə laɪn -ᵊl aɪn, -ɪn, §-ən ‖ -ə liːn
Zidane zɪ ˈdæn -ˈdɑːn —*Fr* [zi dan]
Ziegfeld ˈzɪɡ feld ˈziːɡ-, fiːᵊld
Ziegler ˈziːɡ lə ‖ -lᵊr —*Ger* [ˈtsiː ɡlɐ]
ziggurat ˈzɪɡ u ræt -ə- ‖ -ə- **~s** s
Ziggy ˈzɪɡ i
zigzag *n, v, adv* ˈzɪɡ zæɡ **~ged** d **~ging** ɪŋ **~s** z
zilch zɪltʃ
zillion ˈzɪl jən ˈ·i ən **~s** z
Zimbabwe zɪm ˈbɑːb wi -ˈbæb-, -weɪ
Zimbabwean zɪm ˈbɑːb wi ən -ˈbæb-, -weɪ- **~s** z
zimmer, Z~ *tdmk* ˈzɪm ə ‖ -ᵊr **~s** z
Zimmerman ˈzɪm ə mæn -mən ‖ -ᵊr-
zinc zɪŋk **zinced, zincked** zɪŋkt **zincing, zincking** ˈzɪŋk ɪŋ **zincs** zɪŋks
 ˌzinc ˈoxide
zincite ˈzɪŋk aɪt
zine ziːn **zines** ziːnz
zineb ˈzɪn eb ˈzaɪn-
Zinédine ˌzɪn eɪ ˈdiːn ˌziːn-, -i- —*Fr* [zi ne din]
zinfandel, Z~ ˈzɪn fən del ˌ· ·ˈ· **~s** z
zing zɪŋ **zinged** zɪŋd **zinging** ˈzɪŋ ɪŋ **zings** zɪŋz
zinger ˈzɪŋ ə ‖ -ᵊr **~s** z
zinjanthropus zɪn ˈdʒænᵗθ rəp əs ˌzɪndʒ æn ˈθrəʊp- ‖ ˌzɪndʒ æn ˈθroʊp-
zinkenite ˈzɪŋk ə naɪt
zinnia ˈzɪn i ə **~s** z

Z

Zinoviev zɪ ˈnəʊv i ev zə- ‖ -ˈnoʊv- —*Russ* [zʲɪ ˈno vʲɪf]
Zion ˈzaɪ‿ən
Zionism ˈzaɪ‿ə ˌnɪz əm
Zionist ˈzaɪ‿ən ɪst §-əst **~s** s
zip zɪp **zipped** zɪpt **zipping** ˈzɪp ɪŋ **zips** zɪps
ˈzip code; ˌzip ˈfastener
zip-lock, Ziploc *tdmk* ˈzɪp lɒk ‖ -lɑːk
zip-on ˈzɪp ɒn ‖ -ɑːn -ɔːn
zipper ˈzɪp ə ‖ -ᵊr **~ed** d **~s** z
Zippo *tdmk* ˈzɪp əʊ ‖ -oʊ
Zipporah ˈzɪp ər ə
zipp|y ˈzɪp |i **~ier** i‿ə ‖ i‿ᵊr **~iest** i‿ɪst i‿əst
zip-up ˈzɪp ʌp
zircon ˈzɜːk ɒn -ən ‖ ˈzɜ˞ːk ɑːn **~s** z
zirconia zɜː ˈkəʊn i‿ə ‖ zɜ˞ː ˈkoʊn-
zirconium zɜː ˈkəʊn i‿əm ‖ zɜ˞ː ˈkoʊn-
zit zɪt **zits** zɪts
zither ˈzɪð ə ‖ -ᵊr ˈzɪθ- **~s** z
zizz zɪz
zloty ˈzlɒt i ‖ ˈzlɔːṱ i ˈzlɑːṱ- —*Polish* [ˈzwɔ ti] **~s** z
-zoa ˈzəʊ ə ‖ ˈzoʊ ə — **spermatozoa** ˌspɜːm ət ə ˈzəʊ ə ‖ ˌspɜ˞ːm əṱ ə ˈzoʊ ə
Zocor *tdmk* ˈzəʊ kɔː ‖ -kɔːr
zodiac ˈzəʊd i æk ‖ ˈzoʊd-
zodiacal zəʊ ˈdaɪ‿ək ᵊl ‖ zoʊ-
Zoe, Zoë ˈzəʊ i ‖ ˈzoʊ i zoʊ
zoetrope ˈzəʊ i trəʊp ‖ ˈzoʊ i troʊp **~s** s
Zoff *tdmk* zɒf ‖ zɔːf zɑːf
Zoffany ˈzɒf ən i ‖ ˈzɑːf-
Zog zɒg ‖ zɔːg zɑːg —*Albanian* Zogu [ˈzo gu]
-zoic ˈzəʊ ɪk ‖ ˈzoʊ ɪk — **paleozoic** ˌpæl i əʊ ˈzəʊ ɪk ◂ ˌpeɪl- ‖ ˌpeɪl i‿ə ˈzoʊ ɪk ◂
zoisite ˈzɔɪs aɪt
Zola ˈzəʊl ə ‖ ˈzoʊl ə —*Fr* [zɔ la]
Zollner, Zöllner ˈzɒl nə ‖ ˈzɑːl nᵊr **~'s** z —*Ger* [ˈtsœl nɐ]
ˌZollner's ˈlines
Zomba ˈzɒm bə ‖ ˈzɑːm-
zombi, zombie ˈzɒm bi ‖ ˈzɑːm- **~s** z
zonal ˈzəʊn ᵊl ‖ ˈzoʊn ᵊl **~ly** i
zonation zəʊ ˈneɪʃ ᵊn ‖ zoʊ- **~s** z
zone zəʊn ‖ zoʊn **zoned** zəʊnd ‖ zoʊnd **zones** zəʊnz ‖ zoʊnz **zoning** ˈzəʊn ɪŋ ‖ ˈzoʊn ɪŋ
zonk zɒŋk ‖ zɑːŋk zɔːŋk **zonked** zɒŋ*k*t ‖ zɑːŋ*k*t zɔːŋ*k*t **zonking** ˈzɒŋk ɪŋ ‖ ˈzɑːŋk ɪŋ ˈzɔːŋk- **zonks** zɒŋ*k*s ‖ zɑːŋ*k*s zɔːŋ*k*s
Zonta ˈzɒnt ə ‖ ˈzɑːnṱ ə
Zontian ˈzɒnt i‿ən ‖ ˈzɑːnṱ i‿ən **~s** z
zonule ˈzɒn juːl ˈzəʊn- ‖ ˈzoʊn- **~s** z
zoo zuː **zoos** zuːz
zoo- *comb. form*
with stress-neutral suffix ¦zəʊ ə ˈzuː ə ‖ ¦zoʊ ə — **zoophile** ˈzəʊ ə faɪᵊl ‖ ˈzoʊ-
with stress-imposing suffix zəʊ ˈɒ+ zu ˈɒ+ ‖ zoʊ ˈɑː+ — **zoophilous** zəʊ ˈɒf ɪl əs zu-, -əl- ‖ zoʊ ˈɑːf-
zooid ˈzəʊ ɔɪd ‖ ˈzoʊ- **~s** z
zoo-keeper ˈzuː ˌkiːp ə ‖ -ᵊr **~s** z
zoological ˌzəʊ ə ˈlɒdʒ ɪk ᵊl ◂ ˌzuː‿ə-, zu ˈlɒdʒ- ‖ ˌzoʊ ə ˈlɑːdʒ- **~ly** ‿i
ˌzooˌlogical ˈgardens
zoologist zəʊ ˈɒl ədʒ ɪst zu-, §-əst ‖ zoʊ ˈɑːl- **~s** s
zoology zəʊ ˈɒl ədʒ i zu- ‖ zoʊ ˈɑːl-
zoom zuːm **zoomed** zuːmd **zooming** ˈzuːm ɪŋ **zooms** zuːmz
ˈzoom lens
zoometry zəʊ ˈɒm ətr i -ɪtr- ‖ zoʊ ˈɑːm-
-zoon ˈzəʊ ɒn -ən ‖ ˈzoʊ ɑːn — **spermatozoon** ˌspɜːm ət ə ˈzəʊ ɒn -ən ‖ ˌspɜ˞ːm əṱ ə ˈzoʊ ɑːn
zoophyte ˈzəʊ ə faɪt ˈzuː‿ ‖ ˈzoʊ- **~s** s
zooplankton ˌzəʊ ə ˈplæŋ*k*t ən ˈ· ·ˌ· · ‖ ˌzoʊ-
zoosporangi|um ˌzəʊ ə spɔː ˈrændʒ i‿|əm ‖ ˌzoʊ- **~a** ə
zoospore ˈzəʊ ə spɔː ˈzuː‿ ‖ ˈzoʊ ə spɔːr -spoʊr **~s** z
zoot zuːt
ˈzoot suit
Zora, Zorah ˈzɔːr ə ‖ ˈzoʊr-
Zoroaster ˌzɒr əʊ ˈæst ə ˈ· · · · ‖ ˈzɔːr oʊ æst ᵊr ˈzoʊr-
Zoroastrian ˌzɒr əʊ ˈæs tri‿ən ◂ ‖ ˌzɔːr oʊ-, ˌzoʊr- **~ism** ˌɪz əm **~s** z
Zorro ˈzɒr əʊ ‖ ˈzɔːr oʊ —*Sp* [ˈθo rro, ˈso-]
zoster ˈzɒst ə ‖ ˈzɑːst ᵊr
zouave, Z~ zu ˈɑːv ˈzuː ɑːv, zwɑːv **zouaves, Z~** zu ˈɑːvz ˈzuː ɑːvz, zwɑːvz
zounds zaʊndz zuːndz
Zovirax *tdmk* zəʊ ˈvaɪᵊr æks ‖ zoʊ-
Zsa Zsa ˈʒɑː ʒɑː
Zubes *tdmk* zuːbz zjuːbz
zucchetto zu ˈket əʊ ‖ -ˈkeṱ oʊ **~s** z
zucchini zu ˈkiːn i
Zuckerberg ˈzʌk ə bɜːg ‖ -ᵊr bɜ˞ːg
Zuckerman ˈzʊk ə mən ‖ -ᵊr- ˈzʌk-
Zugspitze ˈzʊg ˌʃpɪts ə —*Ger* [ˈtsuːk ˌʃpɪts ə]
zugzwang ˈzuːg zwæŋ —*Ger* [ˈtsuːk tsvaŋ]
Zuider Zee ˌzaɪd ə ˈziː ‖ -ᵊr- —*Dutch* [ˌzœy dər ˈzeː]
Zuleika zu ˈleɪk ə -ˈlaɪk-
Zulu ˈzuːl uː **~s** z
Zululand ˈzuːl uː lænd
Zuni, Zuñi ˈzuːn i -ji —*AmSp* [ˈsu ɲi] **~s** z
Zurich, Zürich ˈzʊər ɪk ˈzjʊər- ‖ ˈzʊr ɪk —*Ger* [ˈtsyː ʁɪç]
Zutphen ˈzʌt fən —*Dutch* [ˈzʏt fən]
Zuyder Zee ˌzaɪd ə ˈziː ‖ -ᵊr- —*Dutch* [ˌzœy dər ˈzeː]
Zwemmer ˈzwem ə ‖ -ᵊr
zwieback ˈzwiː bæk -bɑːk ‖ ˈzwaɪ- ˈswiː-, ˈswaɪ-, ˈzwiː **~s** s
Zwingli ˈzwɪŋ gli -li —*Ger* [ˈtsvɪŋ li]
Zwinglian ˈzwɪŋ gli‿ən -li‿ **~s** z
zwitterion ˈzwɪt ər ˌaɪ‿ən ˈtsvɪt-, -ɒn ‖ ˈzwɪṱ ə ˌraɪ‿ən -ɑːn **~s** z
zydeco ˈzaɪd ə kəʊ -ɪ- ‖ -koʊ
zyg- *comb. form before vowel*
with unstressed suffix ¦zaɪg — **zygote** ˈzaɪg əʊt ‖ -oʊt
with stressed suffix zaɪ g+ zɪ g+ — **zygosis** zaɪ ˈgəʊs ɪs zɪ-, §-əs ‖ -ˈgoʊs-
zygo- *comb. form*
with stress-neutral suffix ¦zaɪg əʊ ¦zɪg əʊ ‖ -ə

Z

zygospore 'zaɪg əʊ spɔː ' zɪg- ‖ -ə spɔːr spoʊr
with stress-imposing suffix zaɪ 'gɒ+ zɪ- ‖ -'gɑː+ — **zygopteran** zaɪ 'gɒpt ər ən zɪ- ‖ -'gɑːpt-
zygoma zaɪ 'gəʊm ə zɪ- ‖ -'goʊm ə **~s** z
zygomatic ˌzaɪg əʊ 'mæt ɪk ◂ ˌzɪg- ‖ -ə 'mæţ-
zygote 'zaɪg əʊt 'zɪg- ‖ -oʊt **~s** s
zygotic zaɪ 'gɒt ɪk zɪ- ‖ -'gɑːţ- **~ally** əl̮ i
zym- *comb. form before vowel*
with unstressed suffix ¦zaɪm — **zymurgy** 'zaɪm ɜːdʒ i ‖ -ɝːdʒ-
with stressed suffix zaɪ m+ — **zymoma** zaɪ 'məʊm ə ‖ -'moʊm-
zymase 'zaɪm eɪs -eɪz
zymo- *comb. form*
with stress-neutral suffix ¦zaɪm əʊ ‖ -ə — **zymolytic** ˌzaɪm əʊ 'lɪt ɪk ◂ ‖ -ə 'lɪţ-
with stress-imposing suffix zaɪ 'mɒ+ ‖ -'mɑː+ — **zymolysis** zaɪ 'mɒl əs ɪs -ɪs-, §-əs ‖ -'mɑːl-
zymosis zaɪ 'məʊs ɪs §-əs ‖ -'moʊs-
zymotic zaɪ 'mɒt ɪk ‖ -'mɑːţ ɪk **~ally** əl̮ i
Zyrian, Zyryan 'zɪr i̮ən **~s** z
zzz —*sometimes said aloud as* zː

Z

Typographical conventions, stress marks, other symbols

RP	*Gen Am*		
		raised	letters: sounds sometimes optionally inserted
•	•	^{ə}l	midd**le**, tot**al**
•	•	^{ə}n	sudd**en**ly, serv**an**t
	•	^{ə}r	fath**er**, stand**ar**d
•	•	m^{p}f	e**mph**asis
•	•	n^{t}s	fe**nce**
•	•	ŋ^{k}s	ga**ngs**ter
		italic	letters: sounds sometimes optionally omitted
•	•	*ə*	dist**a**nt
•		n*t*ʃ	lu**nch**
•	•	n*d*ʒ	hi**nge**
•		a*ɪ*	f**i**re
	•	n*ţ*	wi**nt**er

ˈ primary word stress (reˈMEMber)

ˌ secondary stress (ˌACaˈDEMic; ˈBUTter ˌFINgers)

¦ (in prefixes) stressed, but level undefined: primary (ˈ) or secondary (ˌ) as appropriate

◄ stress shift possible

‖ GenAm pronunciation follows

§ BrE non-RP

⚠ considered incorrect

\+ (in affixes) attracts consonant from next syllable

→ variant derived by automatic rule

‿ possible compression (two syllables become one) of adjacent syllables (ˈliːn i‿ənt) = *lenient*

syllable divisions are shown by spaces